Stanley Gibbons
Simplified Catalogue

Stamps of the World

Stanley Gibbons Simplified Catalogue

Stamps of the World 5

2012 Edition

Countries **New South Wales – Singapore**

Stanley Gibbons Ltd
London and Ringwood

By Appointment to
Her Majesty The Queen
Stanley Gibbons Limited
London
Philatelists

77th Edition
Published in Great Britain by
Stanley Gibbons Ltd
Publications Editorial, Sales Offices and Distribution Centre
7, Parkside, Christchurch Road,
Ringwood, Hampshire BH24 3SH
Telephone +44 (0) 1425 472363

British Library Cataloguing in
Publication Data.
A catalogue record for this book is available
from the British Library.

Volume 5
ISBN 10: 0-85259-837-8
ISBN 13: 978-0-85259-837-5

Published as Stanley Gibbons Simplified Catalogue from 1934 to 1970, renamed Stamps of the World in 1971, and produced in two (1982-88), three (1989-2001), four (2002-2005) five (2006-2010) and six from 2011 volumes as Stanley Gibbons Simplified Catalogue of Stamps of the World.

Item No. 2881– Set12

Printed and bound in Wales by Stephens & George

Contents – Volume 5

About Us

Our History
Edward Stanley Gibbons started trading postage stamps in his father's chemist shop in 1856. Since then we have been at the forefront of stamp collecting for over 150 years. We hold the Royal Warrant, offer unsurpassed expertise and quality and provide collectors with the peace of mind of a certificate of authenticity on all of our stamps. If you think of stamp collecting, you think of Stanley Gibbons and we are proud to uphold that tradition for you.

399 Strand
Our world famous stamp shop is a collector's paradise, with all of our latest catalogues, albums and accessories and, of course, our unrivalled stockholding of postage stamps.
www.stanleygibbons.com shop@stanleygibbons.com +44 (0)20 7836 8444

Specialist Stamp Sales
For the collector that appreciates the value of collecting the highest quality examples, Stanley Gibbons is the only choice. Our extensive range is unrivalled in terms of quality and quantity, with specialist stamps available from all over the world.
www.stanleygibbons.com/stamps shop@stanleygibbons.com +44 (0)20 7836 8444

Stanley Gibbons Auctions and Valuations
Sell your collection or individual rare items through our prestigious public auctions or our regular postal auctions and benefit from the excellent prices being realised at auction currently. We also provide an unparalleled valuation service.
www.stanleygibbons.com/auctions auctions@stanleygibbons.com +44 (0)20 7836 8444

Stanley Gibbons Publications
The world's first stamp catalogue was printed by Stanley Gibbons in 1865 and we haven't looked back since! Our catalogues are trusted worldwide as the industry standard and we print countless titles each year. We also publish consumer and trade magazines, Gibbons Stamp Monthly and Philatelic Exporter to bring you news, views and insights into all things philatelic. Never miss an issue by subscribing today and benefit from exclusive subscriber offers each month.
www.stanleygibbons.com/shop orders@stanleygibbons.com +44 (0)1425 472 363

Stanley Gibbons Investments
The Stanley Gibbons Investment Department offers a unique range of investment propositions that have consistently outperformed more traditional forms of investment, from capital protected products with unlimited upside to portfolios made up of the world's rarest stamps and autographs.
www.stanleygibbons.com/investment investment@stanleygibbons.com +44 (0)1481 708 270

Fraser's Autographs
Autographs, manuscripts and memorabilia from Henry VIII to current day. We have over 60,000 items in stock, including movie stars, musicians, sport stars, historical figures and royalty. Fraser's is the UK's market leading autograph dealer and has been dealing in high quality autographed material since 1978.
www.frasersautographs.com sales@frasersautographs.com +44 (0)20 7557 4404

stanleygibbons.com
Our website offers the complete philatelic service. Whether you are looking to buy stamps, invest, read news articles, browse our online stamp catalogue or find new issues, you are just one click away from anything you desire in the world of stamp collecting at stanleygibbons.com. Happy browsing!
www.stanleygibbons.com

Introduction

The ultimate reference work for all stamps issued around the world since the very first Penny Black of 1840, now with an improved layout.

Stamps of the World provides a comprehensive, illustrated, priced guide to postage stamps, and is the standard reference tool for every collector. It will help you to identify those elusive stamps, to value your collection, and to learn more about the background to issues. *Stamps of the World* was first published in 1934 and has been updated every year since 1950.

The helpful article 'Putting on a Good Show' provides expert advice on starting and developing a collection, then making the most of its presentation. Also included is a guide to stamp identification so that you can easily discover which country issued your stamp.

Re-designed to provide more colourful, clearer, and easy-to-navigate listings, these volumes continue to present you with a wealth of information to enhance your enjoyment of stamp collecting.

Features:

- Current values for every stamp in the world from the experts
- Easy-to-use simplified listings
- World-recognised Stanley Gibbons catalogue numbers
- A wealth of historical, geographical and currency information
- Indexing and cross-referencing throughout the volumes
- Worldwide miniature sheets listed and priced
- Thousands of new issues since the last edition

For this edition, prices have been thoroughly reviewed for Great Britain up to date, and all Commonwealth countries up to 1970, with further updates for Commonwealth countries which have appeared in our recently-published or forthcoming comprehensive catalogues under the titles *Cyprus, Gibraltar and Malta, Eastern Pacific and St Helena, Ascension and Tristan da Cunha*. Other countries with complete price updates from the following comprehensive catalogues are: *China, Germany, Portugal and Spain and United States of America*. New issues received from all other countries have been listed and priced. The first *Gibbons Stamp Monthly* Catalogue Supplement to this edition is September 2011.

Information for users

Scope of the Catalogue

Stamps of the World contains listings of postage stamps only. Apart from the ordinary definitive, commemorative and air-mail stamps of each country there are sections for the following, where appropriate. Noted below are the Prefixes used for each section (see Guide to Entries for further information):

- postage due stamps – Prefix in listing D
- parcel post or postcard stamps – Prefix P
- official stamps – Prefix O
- express and special delivery stamps - Prefix E
- frank stamps – Prefix F
- charity tax stamps – Prefix J
- newspaper and journal stamps – Prefix N
- printed matter stamps – Prefix
- registration stamps - Prefix R
- acknowledgement of receipt stamps – Prefix AR
- late fee and too late stamps – Prefix L
- military post stamps- Prefix M
- recorded message stamps – Prefix RM
- personal delivery stamps – Prefix P
- concessional letter post – Prefix CL
- concessional parcel post – Prefix CP
- pneumatic post stamps – Prefix PE
- publicity envelope stamps – Prefix B
- bulk mail stamps – Prefix BP
- telegraph used for postage – Prefix PT
- telegraph (Commonwealth Countries) – Prefix T
- obligatory tax – Prefix T
- Frama Labels and Royal Mail Postage Labels No Prefix-

As this is a simplified listing, the following are NOT included:
Fiscal or revenue stamps: stamps used solely in collecting taxes or fees for non-postal purposes. For example, stamps which pay a tax on a receipt, represent the stamp duty on a contract, or frank a customs document. Common inscriptions found include: Documentary, Proprietary, Inter. Revenue and Contract Note.
Local stamps: postage stamps whose validity and use are limited in area to a prescribed district, town or country, or on certain routes where there is no government postal service. They may be issued by private carriers and freight companies, municipal authorities or private individuals.
Local carriage labels and Private local issues: many labels exist ostensibly to cover the cost of ferrying mail from one of Great Britain's offshore islands to the nearest mainland post office. They are not recognised as valid for national or international mail. Examples: Calf of Man, Davaar, Herm, Lundy, Pabay, Stroma.
Telegraph stamps: stamps intended solely for the prepayment of telegraphic communication.
Bogus or "phantom" stamps: labels from mythical places or non-existent administrations. Examples in the classical period were Sedang, Counani, Clipperton Island and in modern times Thomond and Monte Bello Islands. Numerous labels have also appeared since the War from dissident groups as propaganda for their claims and without authority from the home governments. Common examples are the numerous issues for Nagaland.
Railway letter fee stamps: special stamps issued by railway companies for the conveyance of letters by rail. Example: Talyllyn Railway. Similar services are now offered by some bus companies and the labels they issue likewise do not qualify for inclusion in the catalogue.
Perfins ("perforated initials"): stamps perforated with the initials or emblems of firms as a security measure to prevent pilferage by office staff.
Labels: Slips of paper with an adhesive backing. Collectors tend to make a distinction between stamps, which have postal validity and anything else, which has not.

However, Frama Labels and Royal Mail Postage Labels are both classified as postage stamps and are therefore listed in this catalogue.
Cut-outs: Embossed or impressed stamps found on postal stationery, which are cut out if the stationery has been ruined and re-used as adhesives.

Further information on a wealth of terms is in *Philatelic Terms Illustrated*, published by Stanley Gibbons, details are listed under Stanley Gibbons Publications. There is also a priced listing of the postal fiscals of Great Britain in our *Commonwealth & British Empire Stamps 1840-1970* Catalogue and in Volume 1 of the *Great Britain Specialised Catalogue* (5th and later editions). Again, further details are listed under the Stanley Gibbons Publications section (see p.xii).

Organisation of the Catalogue

The catalogue lists countries in alphabetical order with country headers on each page and extra introductory information such as philatelic historical background at the beginning of each section. The Contents list provides a detailed guide to each volume, and the Index has full cross-referencing to locate each country in each volume.

Each country lists postage stamps in order of date of issue, from earliest to most recent, followed by separate sections for categories such as postage due stamps, express stamps, official stamps, and so on (see above for a complete listing).

"Appendix" Countries

Since 1968 Stanley Gibbons has listed in an appendix stamps which are judged to be in excess of true postal needs. The appendix also contains stamps which have not fulfilled all the normal conditions for full catalogue listing. Full catalogue listing requires a stamp to be:

- issued by a legitimate postal authority
- recognised by the government concerned
- adhesive
- valid for proper postal use in the class of service for which they are inscribed
- available to the general public at face value with no artificial restrictions being imposed on their distribution (with the exception of categories as postage dues and officials)

Only stamps issued from component parts of otherwise united territories which represent a genuine political, historical or postal division within the country concerned have a full catalogue listing. Any such issues which do not fulfil this stipulation will be recorded in the Catalogue Appendix only.

Stamps listed in the Appendix are constantly under review in light of newly acquired information about them. If we are satisfied that a stamp qualifies for proper listing in the body of the catalogue it will be moved in the next edition.

"Undesirable Issues"

The rules governing many competitive exhibitions are set by the Federation Internationale de Philatelie and stipulate a downgrading of marks for stamps classed as "undesirable issues".

This catalogue can be taken as a guide to status. All stamps in the main listings are acceptable. Stamps in the Appendix are considered, "undesirable issues" and should not be entered for competition.

Correspondence

We welcome information and suggestions but we must ask correspondents to include the cost of postage for the return of any materials, plus registration where appropriate. Letters and emails should be addressed to Michelle Briggs, 7 Parkside, Christchurch Road, Ringwood, Hampshire BH24 3SH, UK. mrbriggs@stanleygibbons.co.uk. Where information is solicited purely for the benefit of the enquirer we regret we are seldom able to reply.

Identification of Stamps

We regret we do not give opinion on the authenticity of stamps, nor do we identify stamps or number them by our Catalogue.

Thematic Collectors

Stanley Gibbons publishes a range of thematic catalogues (see page xxxix for details) and *Stamps of the World* is ideal to use with these titles, as it supplements those listings with extra information.

Type numbers

Type numbers (in bold) refer to illustrations, and are not the Stanley Gibbons Catalogue numbers.

A brief description of the stamp design subject is given below or beside the illustrations, or close by in the entry, where needed. Where a design is not illustrated, it is usually the same shape and size as a related design, unless otherwise indicated.

Watermarks

Watermarks are not covered in this catalogue. Stamps of the same issue with differing watermarks are not listed separately.

Perforations

Perforations – all stamps are perforated unless otherwise stated. No distinction is made between the various gauges of perforation but early stamp issues which exist both imperforate and perforated are usually listed separately. Where a heading states, "Imperf or perf"or "Perf. or rouletted" this does not necessarily mean that all values of the issue are found in both conditions

Se-tenant Pairs

Se-tenant Pairs – Many modern issues are printed in sheets containing different designs or face values. Such pairs, blocks, strips or sheets are described as being "*se-tenant*" and they are outside the scope of this catalogue, although reference to them may occur in instances where they form a composite design.

Miniature Sheets are now fully listed.

Guide to Entries

A Country of Issue

B Part Number – shows where to find more detailed listings in the Stanley Gibbons Comprehensive Catalogue. Part 6 refers to France and so on – see p. xli for further information on the breakdown of the Catalogue.

C Country Information – Brief geographical and historical details for the issuing country.

D Currency – Details of the currency, and dates of earliest use where applicable, on the face value of the stamps. Where a Colony has the same currency as the Mother Country, see the details given in that country.

E Year Date – When a set of definitive stamps has been issued over several years the Year Date given is for the earliest issue, commeorative sets are listed in chronological order. As stamps of the same design or issue are usually grouped together a list of King George VI stamps, for example, headed "1938" may include stamps issued from 1938 to the end of the reign.

F Stanley Gibbons Catalogue number – This is a unique number for each stamp to help the collector identify stamps in the listing. The Stanley Gibbons numbering system is universally recognized as definitive. The majority of listings are in chronological order, but where a definitive set of stamps has been re-issued with a new watermark, perforation change or imprint date, the cheapest example is given; in such cases catalogue numbers may not be in numerical order.

Where insufficient numbers have been left to provide for additional stamps to a listing, some stamps will have a suffix letter after the catalogue number. If numbers have been left for additions to a set and not used they will be left vacant.

The separate type numbers (in bold) refer to illustrations (see **M**).

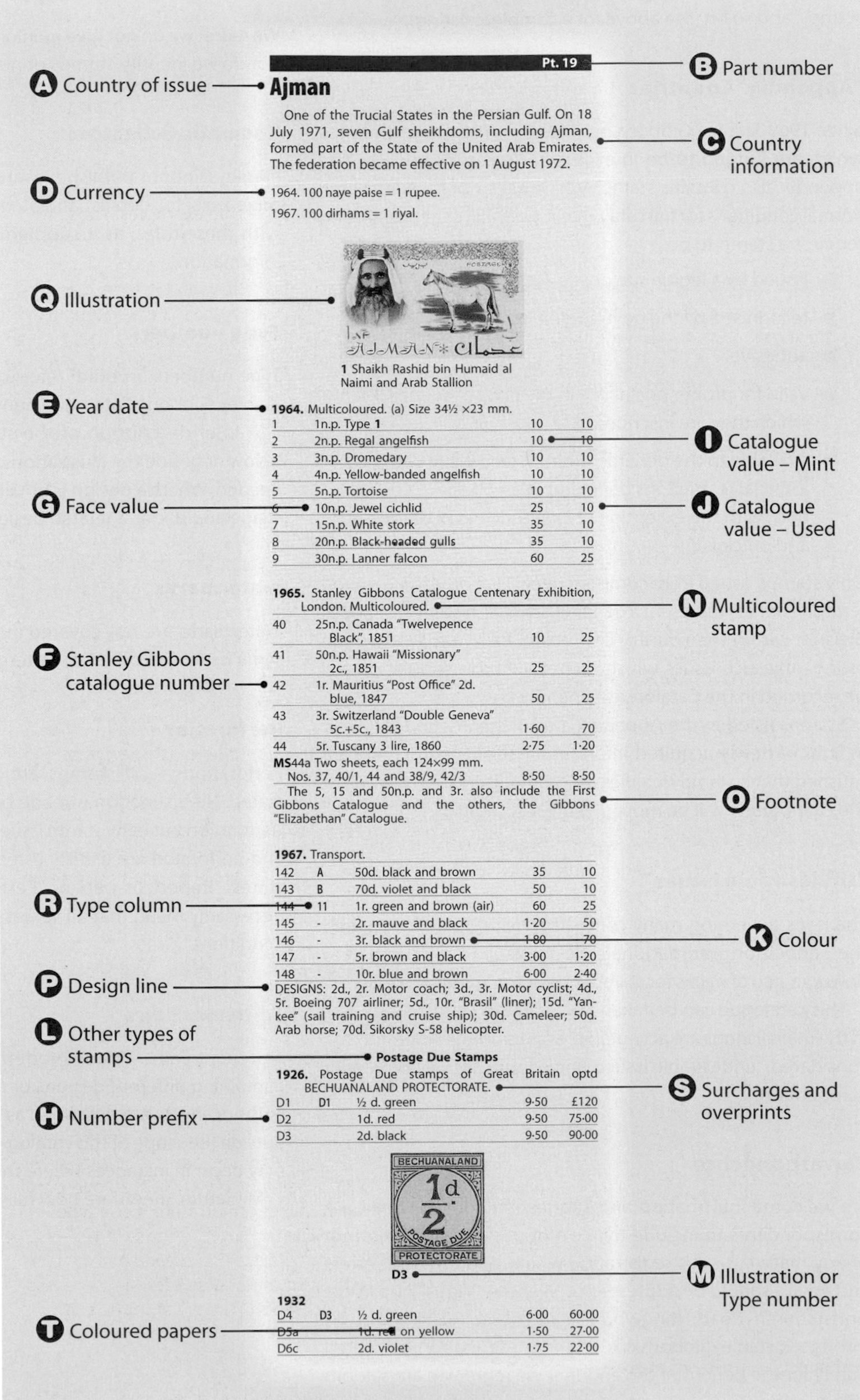

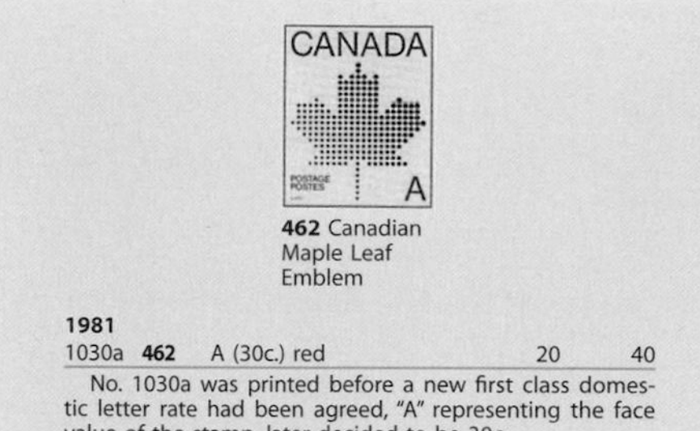

462 Canadian Maple Leaf Emblem

1981
1030a **462** A (30c.) red 20 40

No. 1030a was printed before a new first class domestic letter rate had been agreed, "A" representing the face value of the stamp, later decided to be 30c.

G Face value – This refers to the value of each stamp and is the price it was sold for at the Post Office when issued. Some modern stamps do not have their values in figures but instead shown as a letter, see for example the entry above for Canada 1030a/Illustration 462.

H Number Prefix – Stamps other than definitives and commemoratives have a prefix letter before the catalogue number. Such stamps may be found at the end of the normal listing for each country. (See Scope of the Catalogue p.viii for a list of other types of stamps covered, together with the list of the main abbreviations used in the Catalogue).

Other prefixes are also used in the Catalogue. Their use is explained in the text: some examples are A for airmail, E for East Germany or Express Delivery stamps.

I Catalogue Value – Mint/Unused. Prices quoted for pre-1945 stamps are for lightly hinged examples. Prices quoted of unused King Edward VIII to Queen Elizabeth II issues are for unmounted mint.

J Catalogue Value – Used. Prices generally refer to fine postally used examples. For certain issues they are for cancelled-to-order.

Prices

Prices are given in pence and pounds. Stamps worth £100 and over are shown in whole pounds:

Shown in Catalogue as	Explanation
10	10 pence
1.75	£1.75
15.00	£15
£150	£150
£2300	£2300

Prices assume stamps are in 'fine condition'; we may ask more for superb and less for those of lower quality. The minimum catalogue price quoted is 10p and is intended as a guide for catalogue users. The lowest price for individual stamps purchased from Stanley Gibbons is £1.

Prices quoted are for the cheapest variety of that particular stamp. Differences of watermark, perforation, or other details, outside the scope of this catalogue, often increase the value. Prices quoted for mint issues are for single examples. Those in *se-tenant* pairs, strips, blocks or sheets may be worth more. Where no prices are listed it is either because the stamps are not known to exist in that particular condition, or, more usually, because there is no reliable information on which to base their value.

All prices are subject to change without prior notice and we cannot guarantee to supply all stamps as priced. Prices quoted in advertisements are also subject to change without prior notice. Due to differing production schedules it is possible that new editions of Parts 2 to 22 will show revised prices which are not included in that year's Stamps of the World.

K Colour – Colour of stamp (if fewer than four colours, otherwise noted as "multicoloured"– see N below). Colour descriptions are simple in this catalogue, and only expanded to aid identification – see other more comprehensive Stanley Gibbons catalogues for more detailed colour descriptions (see p.xxxix).

Where stamps are printed in two or more colours, the central portion of the design is the first colour given, unless otherwise stated.

L Other Types of Stamps – See Scope of the Catalogue p.viii for a list of the types of stamps included.

M Illustration or Type Number – These numbers are used to help identify stamps, either in the listing, type column, design line or footnote, usually the first value in a set. These type numbers are in a bold type face – **123**; when bracketed (**123**) an overprint or a surcharge is indicated. Some type numbers include a lower-case letter – **123a**, this indicates they have been added to an existing set. New cross references are also normally shown in bold, as in the example below.

1990. Small Craft of Canada (2nd series). Early Work Boats. As T **563**. Multicoloured.

N Multicoloured – Nearly all modern stamps are multicoloured; this is indicated in the heading, with a description of the stamp given in the listing.

O Footnote – further information on background or key facts on issues

P Design line – Further details on design variations

Q Illustration – Generally, the first stamp in the set. Stamp illustrations are reduced to 75%, with overprints and surcharges shown actual size.

R Key Type – indicates a design type (see p. xii for further details) on which the stamp is based. These are the bold figures found below each illustration. The type numbers are also given in bold in the second column of figures alongside the stamp description to indicate the design of each stamp. Where an issue comprises stamps of similar design, the corresponding type number should be taken as indicating the general design. Where there are blanks in the type number column it means that the type of the corresponding stamp is that shown by the number in the type column of the same issue. A dash (–) in the type column means that the stamp is not illustrated. Where type numbers refer to stamps of another country, e.g. where stamps of one country are overprinted for use in another, this is always made clear in the text.

S Surcharges and Overprints – usually described in the headings. Any actual wordings are shown in bold type. Descriptions clarify words and figures used in the overprint. Stamps with the same overprints in different colours are not listed separately. Numbers in brackets after the descriptions are the catalogue numbers of the non-overprinted stamps. The words "inscribed" or "inscription" refer to the wording incorporated in the design of a stamp and not surcharges or overprints.

T Coloured Papers – stamps printed on coloured paper are shown – e.g. "brn on yell" indicates brown printed on yellow paper. No information on the texture of paper, e.g. laid or wove, is provided in this catalogue.

Key-Types

Standard designs frequently occuring on the stamps of the French, German, Portuguese and Spanish colonies are illustrated below together with the descriptive names and letters by which they are referred to in the lists to avoid repetition. Please see the Guide to Entries for further information.

French Group

A "Blanc" **B** "Mouchon" **C** "Merson" **D** "Tablet"

INTERNATIONAL COLONIAL EXHIBITION

E **F** " **G** **H**

I "Faidherbe" **J** "Palms" **K** "Balay" **L** "Natives" **M** "Figure"

German Group

N "Yacht" **O** "Yacht"

Spanish Group

X "Alfonso XII" **Y** "Baby" **Z** "Curly Head"

Portuguese Group

P "Crown"

Q "Embossed"

R "Figures"

S "Carlos"

T "Manoel"

U Ceres"

V "Newspaper"

W "Due"

Pt. 1

NEW SOUTH WALES

A S.E. state of the Australian Commonwealth, whose stamps it now uses.

12 pence = 1 shilling; 20 shillings = 1 pound.

1 Seal of the Colony

1850. Imperf.

11		1d. red	£4000	£325
25		2d. blue	£3500	£150
42		3d. green	£4750	£225

8

1851. Imperf.

47	**8**	1d. red	£1300	£140
83	**8**	1d. orange	£300	27·00
86	**8**	2d. blue	£190	12·00
87	**8**	3d. green	£350	38·00
76	**8**	6d. brown	£2250	£250
79	**8**	8d. yellow	£7000	£600

11

16

1854. Imperf.

109	**16**	1d. red	£225	24·00
112	**16**	2d. blue	£180	14·00
115	**16**	3d. green	£850	80·00
88	**11**	5d. green	£1100	£650
90	**11**	6d. grey	£850	35·00
96	**11**	6d. brown	£900	35·00
98	**11**	8d. orange	£11000	£1300
100	**11**	1s. red	£1600	70·00

For these stamps perforated, see No. 134 etc.

24

1860. Perf.

195	**16**	1d. red	80·00	32·00
134		2d. blue	£160	13·00
226e	**16**	3d. green	6·00	1·00
233d	**11**	5d. green	10·00	1·25
143	**11**	6d. brown	£450	55·00
165	**11**	6d. violet	90·00	4·75
236	**11**	8d. yellow	£160	19·00
170	**11**	1s. red	£130	8·00
297c	**24**	5s. purple	48·00	13·00

26

28

1862. Queen Victoria. Various frames.

223f	**26**	1d. red	7·50	1·00
225g	**28**	2d. blue	13·00	1·00
230c	-	4d. brown	60·00	2·75
234	-	6d. lilac	80·00	1·50
346a	-	10d. lilac	13·00	4·50
237	-	1s. black	£100	5·50

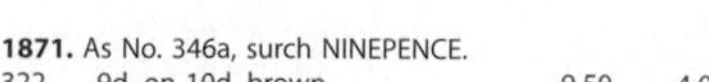

1871. As No. 346a, surch NINEPENCE.

322		9d. on 10d. brown	9·50	4·00

42

1885

238b	**42**	5s. green and lilac	£475	95·00
275	**42**	10s. red and violet	£190	50·00
242	**42**	£1 red and lilac	£5000	£3000

45 View of Sydney

46 Emu

52 Capt. Arthur Phillip, 1st Governor, and Lord Carrington, Governor in 1888

1888. Cent of New South Wales.

253	**45**	1d. mauve	9·50	1·00
254e	**46**	2d. blue	13·00	40
338	-	4d. brown	10·00	4·00
256	-	6d. red	30·00	4·25
297fb	-	6d. green	23·00	13·00
306	-	6d. yellow	14·00	6·00
257	-	8d. purple	25·00	7·00
347	-	1s. brown	27·00	1·75
263	-	5s. violet	£170	32·00
350b	**52**	20s. blue	£250	65·00

DESIGNS—As Type **45**: 4d. Capt. Cook; 6d. Queen Victoria and Arms; 8d. Superb lyrebird; 1s. Kangaroo. As Type **52**: 5s. Map of Australia.

55 Allegorical Figure of Australia

1890

265	**55**	2½d. blue	10·00	60

1891. Types as 1862, but new value and colours, surch in words.

266	**26**	½d. on 1d. grey	3·75	4·25
267a	-	7½d. on 6d. brown	5·00	3·00
268c	-	12½d. on 1s. red	12·00	14·00

58

62

63

64

66 Superb Lyrebird

67

1892

272	**58**	½d. grey	3·75	25
298	**58**	½d. green	2·50	1·00
300	**62**	1d. red	3·50	40
335	**63**	2d. blue	2·25	30
296b	**64**	2½d. violet	20·00	1·75
303	**64**	2½d. blue	6·00	70
352	**67**	9d. brown and blue	15·00	1·75
349b	**66**	2s.6d. green	35·00	22·00

60

1897. Diamond Jubilee and Hospital Charity.

280	**60**	1d. (1s.) green and brown	45·00	50·00
281	-	2½d. (2s.6d.) gold & blue	£200	£200

DESIGN—VERT: 2½d. Two female figures.

OFFICIAL STAMPS

1879. Various issues optd **O S.**

O20b	**26**	1d. red	9·00	1·40
O21c	**28**	2d. blue	8·50	1·00
O25c	**16**	3d. green	5·00	4·00
O26a	-	4d. brown (No. 230c)	13·00	3·75
O29b	**11**	5d. green	14·00	17·00
O31b	-	6d. lilac (No. 234)	20·00	6·00
O32	**11**	8d. orange	22·00	11·00
O11		9d. on 10d. (No. 322)	£550	£550
O18a	-	10d. lilac (No. 346a)	£250	£100
O33b	-	1s. black (No. 237)	26·00	8·00
O18	**24**	5s. purple	£300	85·00

B. Fiscal stamps of 1885.

O37	**24**	10s. red and violet	£3250	£1100
O38	**24**	£1 red and violet	£15000	£8500

C. Issue of 1888 (Nos. 253/350b)

O39b	1d. mauve	3·00	75
O40	2d. blue	4·50	40
O41	4d. brown	11·00	4·00
O42	6d. red	8·50	7·00
O43	8d. purple	21·00	12·00
O44	1s. brown	28·00	4·00
O49a	5s. violet	£250	90·00
O48	20s. blue	£2750	£850

D. Issues of 1890 and 1892.

O55	**26**	½d. on 1d. grey	60·00	65·00
O58b	**58**	½d. grey	6·50	11·00
O54	**55**	2½d. blue	11·00	10·00
O56	-	7½d. on 6d. (No. 283)	42·00	60·00
O57	-	12½d. on 1s. (No. 284c)	65·00	95·00

POSTAGE DUE STAMPS

D1

1891

D1	**D 1**	½d. green	9·00	5·50
D2b	**D 1**	1d. green	14·00	2·75
D3e	**D 1**	2d. green	20·00	3·00
D4	**D 1**	3d. green	48·00	8·50
D5b	**D 1**	4d. green	35·00	2·75
D6	**D 1**	6d. green	42·00	10·00
D7	**D 1**	8d. green	£100	24·00
D8	**D 1**	5s. green	£160	50·00
D9	**D 1**	10s. green	£350	65·00
D10b	**D 1**	20s. green	£350	£275

REGISTRATION STAMPS

15

1856

102	**15**	(6d.) red and blue (Imp)	£1200	£170
105	**15**	(6d.) orange and blue (Imp)	£1100	£200
119	**15**	(6d.) orange and blue (Perf)	£650	60·00
127	**15**	(6d.) red and blue (Perf)	£140	20·00

Pt. 1

NEW ZEALAND

A group of islands in the south Pacific Ocean. A Commonwealth Dominion.

1855. 12 pence = 1 shilling; 20 shillings = 1 pound.
1967. 100 cents = 1 dollar.

1

1855. Imperf.

34	**1**	1d. orange	£700	£275
35	**1**	1d. red	£450	£300
39	**1**	2d. blue	£650	85·00
40	**1**	3d. lilac	£600	£160
43	**1**	6d. brown	£1500	£100
45	**1**	1s. green	£1500	£350

1862. Perf.

110	**1**	1d. orange	£225	38·00
132	**1**	1d. brown	£225	45·00
114	**1**	2d. blue	£225	22·00
133	**1**	2d. orange	£170	29·00
117	**1**	3d. lilac	£150	35·00
119	**1**	4d. rose	£3250	£250
120	**1**	4d. yellow	£250	£110
122	**1**	6d. brown	£325	28·00
136	**1**	6d. blue	£200	55·00
125	**1**	1s. green	£300	£110

3

1873

151	**3**	½d. pink	14·00	2·00

5

6

7

8

9

10

11

1874. Inscr "POSTAGE".

180	**5**	1d. lilac	60·00	8·00
181	**6**	2d. red	60·00	7·00
154	**7**	3d. brown	£150	65·00
182	**8**	4d. purple	£180	55·00
183	**9**	6d. blue	£110	12·00
184	**10**	1s. green	£180	48·00
185	**11**	2s. red	£375	£300
186	**11**	5s. grey	£375	£300

13

16

19

1882. Inscr "POSTAGE & REVENUE".

227	**13**	½d. black	4·00	60
237	**10**	1d. red	4·75	10
238	**9**	2d. mauve	15·00	1·00
239	**16**	2½d. blue	50·00	3·75
240	**10**	3d. yellow	55·00	8·50
241a	**6**	4d. green	55·00	4·50
223	**19**	5d. black	60·00	24·00
243	**8**	6d. brown	70·00	5·50
244	**9**	8d. blue	75·00	55·00
245	**7**	1s. brown	95·00	7·00

23 Mount Cook or Aorangi

24 Lake Taupo and Mount Ruapehu

25 Pembroke Peak, Milford Sound

26 Lake Wakatipu and Mount Earnslaw

28 Sacred Huia Birds

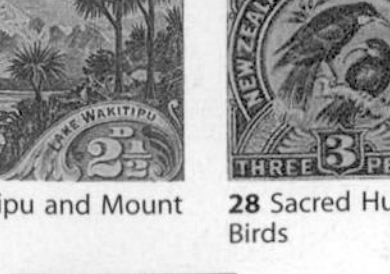

29 White Terrace, Rotomahana

30 Otira Gorge and Mount Ruapehu

31 Brown Kiwi

32 Maori War Canoe

33 Pink Terrace, Rotomahana

34 Kea and Kaka

35 Milford Sound

1898

246	**23**	½d. purple	8·50	1·50
302	**23**	½d. green	7·50	1·25
247	**24**	1d. blue and brown	6·00	60
248	**25**	2d. red	38·00	25
249	**26**	2½d. blue (A)*	11·00	42·00
320	**26**	2½d. blue (B)*	23·00	4·25
261	**28**	3d. brown	24·00	2·25
252	**29**	4d. red	16·00	19·00
263	**30**	5d. brown	35·00	4·50
254	**31**	6d. green	65·00	45·00
312	**31**	6d. red	38·00	7·50
325	**32**	8d. blue	38·00	11·00
326	**33**	9d. purple	32·00	8·00
268a	**34**	1s. orange	60·00	4·00
328	**35**	2s. green	£110	32·00
329b	-	5s. red	£200	£250

*Type A of 2½d. is inscr "WAKITIPU", Type B "WAKATIPU".

40 Commemorative of the New Zealand Contingent in the South African War

1900

274	**29**	1d. red	13·00	20
275b	**40**	1½d. brown	9·50	4·00
319	**25**	2d. purple	5·50	2·50
322d	**24**	4d. blue and brown	4·00	3·25

The 1d., 2d. and 4d. are smaller than the illustrations of their respective types.

42

1901

303	**42**	1d. red	3·00	10

44 Maori Canoe "Te Arawa"

1906. New Zealand Exhibition, Christchurch. Inscr "COMMEMORATIVE SERIES OF 1906".

370	**44**	½d. green	32·00	32·00
371	-	1d. red	16·00	16·00
372	-	3d. brown and blue	55·00	85·00
373	-	6d. red and green	£200	£275

DESIGNS: 1d. Maori art; 3d. Landing of Cook; 6d. Annexation of New Zealand.

50

1907

386	**50**	1d. red	23·00	2·75
383	**28**	3d. brown	45·00	15·00
376	**31**	6d. red	40·00	8·50
385	**34**	1s. orange	£110	24·00

These are smaller in size than the 1898 and 1901 issues. Type **50** also differs from Type **42** in the corner ornaments.

51 King Edward VII

53 Dominion

1909

387	**51**	½d. green	5·00	50
405	**53**	1d. red	1·75	10
388	**51**	2d. mauve	9·50	6·50
389	**51**	3d. brown	23·00	1·25
390a	**51**	4d. yellow	6·00	9·50
396	**51**	4d. orange	20·00	15·00
391	**51**	5d. brown	17·00	4·50
392	**51**	6d. red	40·00	1·50
393	**51**	8d. blue	11·00	3·00
394	**51**	1s. red	48·00	5·00

1913. Auckland Industrial Exhibition. Optd AUCKLAND EXHIBITION, 1913.

412	**51**	½d. green	20·00	55·00
413	**53**	1d. red	26·00	50·00
414	**51**	3d. brown	£130	£250
415	**51**	6d. red	£160	£300

62 King George V

1915

435	**62**	½d. green	1·50	20
416	**62**	1½d. grey	3·25	2·25
438	**62**	1½d. brown	2·25	20
417a	**62**	2d. violet	7·00	45·00
439	**62**	2d. yellow	2·25	20
419	**62**	2½d. blue	3·25	7·00
440	**62**	3d. brown	7·00	75
421	**62**	4d. yellow	4·25	55·00
422e	**62**	4d. violet	7·00	50
423	**62**	4½d. green	15·00	28·00
424	**62**	5d. blue	7·00	1·00
425	**62**	6d. red	9·00	50
426	**62**	7½d. brown	13·00	25·00
427a	**62**	8d. blue	8·50	50·00
428	**62**	8d. brown	26·00	1·50
429	**62**	9d. green	17·00	2·75
430c	**62**	1s. orange	14·00	50

1915. No. 446 optd WAR STAMP and stars.

452	½d. green	2·25	50

64 "Peace" and Lion

65 "Peace" and Lion

1920. Victory. Inscr "VICTORY" or dated "1914 1919" (6d.).

453	**64**	½d. green	3·00	2·50
454	**65**	1d. red	4·50	60
455	-	1½d. orange	3·00	50
456	-	3d. brown	12·00	14·00
457	-	6d. violet	14·00	17·00
458	-	1s. orange	23·00	50·00

DESIGNS—HORIZ (As Type **65**): 1½d. Maori chief. (As Type **64**): 3d. Lion; 1s. King George V. VERT (As Type **64**): 6d. "Peace" and "Progress".

1922. No. 453 surch 2d. 2d. TWOPENCE.

459	**64**	2d. on ½d. green	4·25	1·40

69 New Zealand

1923. Restoration of Penny Postage.

460	**69**	1d. red	3·25	60

70 Exhibition Buildings

1925. Dunedin Exhibition.

463	**70**	½d. green on green	3·00	14·00
464	**70**	1d. red on rose	4·25	6·00
465	**70**	4d. mauve on mauve	30·00	75·00

71

1926

468	**71**	1d. red	75	20
469	-	2s. blue	75·00	29·00
467	-	3s. mauve	£110	£200

The 2s. and 3s. are larger, 21×25 mm.

73 Nurse

1929. Anti-T.B. Fund.

544	**73**	1d.+1d. red	11·00	18·00

1930. Inscr "HELP PROMOTE HEALTH".

545	1d.+1d. red	20·00	42·00

74 Smiling Boy

1931. Health Stamps.

546	**74**	1d.+1d. red	75·00	75·00
547	**74**	2d.+1d. blue	75·00	60·00

75 New Zealand Lake Scenery

1931. Air.

548	**75**	3d. brown	22·00	15·00
549	**75**	4d. purple	22·00	22·00
550	**75**	7d. orange	22·00	9·00

1931. Air. Surch FIVE PENCE.

551	5d. on 3d. green	10·00	10·00

77 Hygeia Goddess of Health

1932. Health Stamp.

552	**77**	1d.+1d. red	21·00	29·00

78 The Path to Health

1933. Health Stamp.

553	**78**	1d.+1d. red	14·00	17·00

1934. Air. Optd TRANS-TASMAN AIR MAIL "FAITH IN AUSTRALIA".

554	**75**	7d. blue	35·00	45·00

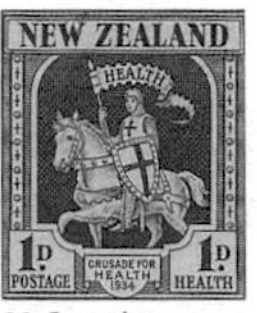

80 Crusader

1934. Health Stamp.

555	**80**	1d.+1d. red	11·00	17·00

81 Collared Grey Fantail

83 Maori Woman

85 Mt. Cook

86 Maori Girl

87 Mitre Peak

89 Harvesting

91 Maori Panel

93 Capt. Cook at Poverty Bay

1935

556	**81**	½d. green	2·50	1·50
578	-	1d. red	3·00	10
558a	**83**	1½d. brown	6·50	10·00
580	-	2d. orange	30	10
581c	**85**	2½d. brown and grey	1·00	5·50
561	**86**	3d. brown	12·00	3·75
583d	**87**	4d. black and brown	1·00	20
584c	-	5d. blue	2·00	2·25
585c	**89**	6d. red	1·25	20
586d	-	8d. brown	4·00	1·50
631	**91**	9d. red and black	3·75	4·75
588	-	1s. green	3·00	1·25
589e	**93**	2s. olive	5·50	1·50
590c	-	3s. chocolate and brown	4·00	3·25

DESIGNS—As Type **81**: 1d. Brown kiwi; 2d. Maori carved house; 1s. Parson bird. As Type **87**: 8d. Tuatara lizard. As Type **85**: 5d. Swordfish; 3s. Mt. Egmont.

95 Bell Block Aerodrome

1935. Air.

570	**95**	1d. red	1·00	70
571	**95**	3d. violet	5·00	3·00
572	**95**	6d. blue	9·50	3·00

96 King George V and Queen Mary

1935. Silver Jubilee.

573	**96**	½d. green	75	1·00
574	**96**	1d. red	1·00	80
575	**96**	6d. orange	20·00	32·00

97 "The Key to Health"

1935. Health Stamp.

576	**97**	1d.+1d. red	2·50	3·75

99 N.Z. Soldier at Anzac Cove

1936. Charity. 21st Anniv of "Anzac" Landing at Gallipoli.

591	**99**	½d.+½d. green	75	1·75
592	**99**	1d.+1d. red	75	1·40

100 Wool

1936. Congress of British Empire Chambers of Commerce, Wellington. Inscr as in T 100.

593	**100**	½d. green	30	30
594	-	1d. red (Butter)	30	20
595	-	2½d. blue (Sheep)	1·50	8·00
596	-	4d. violet (Apples)	1·25	5·50
597	-	6d. brown (Exports)	3·25	6·00

105 Health Camp

1936. Health Stamp.

598	**105**	1d.+1d. red	2·75	3·75

106 King George VI and Queen Elizabeth

1937. Coronation.

599	**106**	1d. red	30	10
600	**106**	2½d. blue	80	2·50
601	**106**	6d. orange	1·10	2·25

107 Rock climbing

1937. Health Stamp.

602	**107**	1d.+1d. red	3·25	3·75

108 King George VI

1938

603	**108**	½d. green	7·50	10
604	**108**	½d. brown	20	40
605	**108**	1d. red	5·00	10
606	**108**	1d. green	20	10
607	**108**	1½d. brown	26·00	3·25
608	**108**	1½d. red	20	80
680	**108**	2d. orange	30	10
609	**108**	3d. blue	20	10
681	**108**	4d. purple	80	1·00
682	**108**	5d. grey	1·00	1·00
683	**108**	6d. red	1·00	10
684	**108**	8d. violet	1·00	1·25
685	**108**	9d. brown	2·00	60
686b	-	1s. brown and red	50	80
687	-	1s.3d. brown and blue	2·25	1·25
688	-	2s. orange and green	5·00	2·50
689	-	3s. brown and grey	4·50	3·50

The shilling values are larger, 22×25½ mm, and "NEW ZEALAND" appears at the top.

109 Children playing

1938. Health Stamp.

610	**109**	1d.+1d. red	7·50	3·25

110 Beach Ball

1939. Health Stamps. Surch.

611	**110**	1d. on ½d.+½d. green	4·75	5·00
612	**110**	2d. on 1d.+1d. red	5·50	5·00

112 "Endeavour", Chart of N.Z. and Captain Cook

1940. Centenary of Proclamation of British Sovereignty. Inscr "CENTENNIAL OF NEW ZEALAND 1840 1940".

613	-	½d. green	40	10
614	**112**	1d. brown and red	3·75	10
615	-	1½d. blue and mauve	30	60
616	-	2d. green and brown	1·50	10
617	-	2½d. green and blue	2·00	1·00
618	-	3d. purple and red	3·75	1·25
619	-	4d. brown and red	13·00	1·50
620	-	5d. blue and brown	9·50	3·75
621	-	6d. green and violet	11·00	1·25
622	-	7d. black and red	1·75	4·00
623	-	8d. black and red	11·00	4·50
624	-	9d. green and orange	7·50	2·00
625	-	1s. green and deep green	13·00	3·75

DESIGNS—HORIZ (as T **112**): ½d. Arrival of the Maoris, 1350; 1½d. British Monarchs; 2d. Abel Tasman with "Heemskerk" and chart; 3d. Landing of immigrants, 1840; 4d. Road, rail, ocean and air transport; 6d. "Dunedin" and "frozen mutton" sea route to London; 7, 8d. Maori council; 9d. Gold mining methods, 1861 and 1940. (25×21 mm): 5d. H.M.S. "Britomart" at Akaroa, 1840. VERT (21×25 mm): 2½d. Treaty of Waitangi. (As T **112**): 1s. Giant kauri tree.

1940. Health Stamps.

626	**110**	1d.+½d. green	11·00	14·00
627	**110**	2d.+1d. orange	11·00	14·00

1941. Surch.

628	**108**	1d. on ½d. green	1·75	10
629	**108**	2d. on 1½d. brown	1·75	10

1941. Health Stamps. Optd 1941.

632	**110**	1d.+½d. green	50	2·25
633	**110**	2d.+1d. orange	50	2·25

125 Boy and Girl on Swing

1942. Health Stamps.

634	**125**	1d.+½d. green	30	1·25
635	**125**	2d.+1d. orange	30	1·25

126 Princess Margaret

1943. Health Stamps.

636	**126**	1d.+½d. green	20	1·50
637	-	2d.+1d. brown	20	25

DESIGN: 2d. Queen Elizabeth II as Princess.

1944. Surch TENPENCE between crosses.

662		10d. on 1½d. blue and mauve (No. 615)	15	30

129 Queen Elizabeth II as Princess and Princess Margaret

1944. Health Stamps.

663	**129**	1d.+½d. green	30	40
664	**129**	2d.+1d. blue	30	30

130 Peter Pan Statue, Kensington Gardens

1945. Health Stamps.

665	**130**	1d.+½d. green and buff	15	20
666	**130**	2d.+1d. red and buff	15	20

131 Lake Matheson

132 King George VI and Parliament House, Wellington

133 St. Paul's Cathedral

139 "St. George" (Wellington College War Memorial window)

1946. Peace Issue.

667	**131**	½d. green and brown	20	65
668	**132**	1d. green	10	10
669	**133**	1½d. red	10	50
670	-	2d. purple	15	10
671	-	3d. blue and grey	30	15
672	-	4d. green and orange	20	20
673	-	5d. green and blue	1·00	1·75
674	-	6d. brown and red	15	30
675	**139**	8d. black and red	15	30
676	-	9d. blue and black	15	30
677	-	1s. grey	1·00	40

DESIGNS—As Type **132**: 2d. The Royal Family. As Type **131**: 3d. R.N.Z.A.F. badge and airplanes; 4d. Army badge, tank and plough; 5d. Navy badge, H.M.N.Z.S. "Achilles" (cruiser) and "Dominion Monarch" (liner); 6d. N.Z. coat of arms, foundry and farm; 9d. Southern Alps and Franz Josef Glacier. As T **139**: 1s. National Memorial campanile.

142 Soldier helping Child over Stile

1946. Health Stamps.

678	**142**	1d.+½d. green and orange	15	15
679	**142**	2d.+1d. brown & orange	15	15

145 Statue of Eros

1947. Health Stamps.

690	**145**	1d.+½d. green	15	15
691	**145**	2d.+1d. red	15	15

146 Port Chalmers, 1848

1948. Centenary of Otago. Various designs inscr "CENTENNIAL OF OTAGO".

692	**146**	1d. blue and green	25	35
693	-	2d. green and brown	25	35
694	-	3d. purple	30	60
695	-	6d. black and red	30	60

DESIGNS—HORIZ: 2d. Cromwell, Otago; 6d. Otago University. VERT: 3d. First Church, Dune-din.

150 Boy sunbathing and Children playing

1948. Health Stamps.

696	**150**	1d.+½d. blue and green	15	20
697	**150**	2d.+1d. purple and red	15	20

151 Nurse and Child

1949. Health Stamps.

698	**151**	1d.+½d. green	25	20
699	**151**	2d.+1d. blue	25	20

1950. As Type F 6, but without value, surch 1½d. POSTAGE.

700	1½d. red	40	30

Type F **6** is illustrated next to Type **74**.

153 Queen Elizabeth II and Prince Charles

1950. Health Stamps.

701	**153**	1d.+½d. green	25	20
702	**153**	2d.+1d. purple	25	20

155 Cairn on Lyttleton Hills

1950. Centenary of Canterbury, N.Z.

703	-	1d. green and blue	60	85
704	**155**	2d. red and orange	60	85
705	-	3d. deep blue and blue	60	1·00
706	-	6d. brown and blue	75	1·00
707	-	1s. purple and blue	75	1·40

DESIGNS—VERT: 1d. Christchurch Cathedral; 3d. John Robert Godley. HORIZ: 6d. Canterbury University College; 1s. Aerial view of Timaru.

159 "Takapuna" class Yachts

1951. Health Stamps.

708	**159**	1½d.+½d. red and yellow	30	1·00
709	**159**	2d.+1d. green and yellow	30	25

160 Princess Anne

161 Prince Charles

1952. Health Stamps.

710	**160**	1½d.+½d. red	15	30
711	**161**	2d.+1d. brown	15	20

1952. Surch in figures.

712	**108**	1d. on ½d. orange	20	1·00
713	**108**	3d. on 1d. green	10	10

164 Queen Elizabeth II

165 Coronation State Coach

166 Westminster Abbey

1953. Coronation.

714	-	2d. blue	30	30
715	**164**	3d. brown	30	10
716	**165**	4d. red	1·40	2·50
717	**166**	8d. grey	1·00	1·60
718	-	1s.6d. purple and blue	2·25	3·25

DESIGNS—As Type **165**: 2d. Queen Elizabeth II and Buckingham Palace; 1s.6d. St. Edward's Crown and Royal Sceptre.

168 Girl Guides

169 Boy Scouts

1953. Health Stamps.

719	**168**	1½d.+½d. blue	15	10
720	**169**	2d.+1d. green	15	40

170 Queen Elizabeth II

171 Queen Elizabeth II and Duke of Edinburgh

1953. Royal Visit.

721	**170**	3d. purple	10	10
722	**171**	4d. blue	10	60

172

173

174 Queen Elizabeth II

1953. Small figures of value.

723	**172**	½d. black	15	30
724	**172**	1d. orange	15	10
725	**172**	1½d. brown	20	10
726	**172**	2d. green	20	10
727	**172**	3d. red	20	10
728	**172**	4d. blue	40	50
729	**172**	6d. purple	70	1·60
730	**172**	8d. red	60	60
731	**173**	9d. brown and green	60	60
732	**173**	1s. black and red	65	10
733	**173**	1s.6d. black and blue	1·50	60
733c	**173**	1s.9d. black and orange	4·00	1·50
733d	**174**	2s.6d. brown	15·00	8·00
734	**174**	3s. green	12·00	50
735	**174**	5s. red	26·00	4·50
736	**174**	10s. blue	50·00	19·00

175 Young Climber and Mts. Aspiring and Everest

1954. Health Stamps.

737	**175**	1½d.+½d. brown and violet	15	30
738	**175**	2d.+1d. brown and blue	15	30

176 Maori Mail-carrier

177 Queen Elizabeth II

1955. Centenary of First New Zealand Stamps. Inscr "1855–1955".

739	**176**	2d. brown and green	10	10
740	**177**	3d. red	10	10
741	-	4d. black and blue	60	1·00

DESIGN—HORIZ (As Type **176**): 4d. Douglas DC-3 airliner.

179 Children's Health Camps Federation Emblem

1955. Health Stamps.

742	**179**	1½d.+½d. brown and chestnut	10	60
743	**179**	2d.+1d. red and green	10	35
744	**179**	3d.+1d. brown and red	15	15

180

1955. As 1953 but larger figures of value and stars omitted from lower right corner.

745	**180**	1d. orange	50	10
746	**180**	1½d. brown	60	60
747	**180**	2d. green	40	10
748b	**180**	3d. red	30	10
749	**180**	4d. blue	1·00	80
750	**180**	6d. purple	8·00	20
751	**180**	8d. brown	4·50	6·00

181 "The Whalers of Foveaux Strait"

183 Takahe

1956. Southland Centennial.

752	**181**	2d. green	30	15
753	-	3d. brown	10	10
754	**183**	8d. violet and red	1·25	1·75

DESIGN—As Type **181**: 3d. Allegory of farming.

184 Children picking Apples

1956. Health Stamps.

755	**184**	1½d.+½d. brown	15	70
756	**184**	2d.+1d. green	15	55
757	**184**	3d.+1d. red	15	15

185 New Zealand Lamb and Map

1957. 75th Anniv of First Export of N.Z. Lamb.

758	**185**	4d. blue	50	1·00
759	-	8d. red	75	1·25

DESIGN—HORIZ: 8d. Lamb, sailing ship "Dunedin" and "Port Brisbane" (refrigerated freighter).

187 Sir Truby King

1957. 50th Anniv of Plunket Society.

760	**187**	3d. red	10	10

188 Life-savers in Action

1957. Health Stamps.

761	**188**	2d.+1d. black and green	15	70
762	-	3d.+1d. blue and red	15	10
MS762b		Two sheets, each 112×96 mm, with Nos. 761 and 762 in blocks of 6 (2×3) Per pair	9·00	25·00

DESIGN: 3d. Children on seashore.

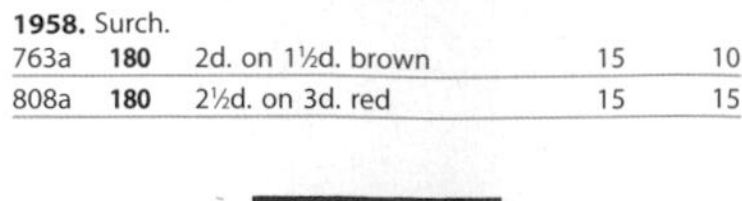

1958. Surch.

763a	**180**	2d. on 1½d. brown	15	10
808a	**180**	2½d. on 3d. red	15	15

192 Boys' Brigade Bugler

1958. Health Stamps.

764	-	2d.+1d. green	20	40
765	**192**	3d.+1d. blue	20	40
MS765a		Two sheets, each 104×124 mm, with Nos. 764/5 in blocks of 6 (3×2) Per pair	10·00	22·00

DESIGN: 2d. Girls' Life Brigade cadet.

193 Sir Charles Kingsford-Smith and Fokker F. IIa/3m Southern Cross

1958. 30th Anniv of 1st Air Crossing of Tasman Sea.

766	**193**	6d. blue	50	75

194 Seal of Nelson

1958. Centenary of City of Nelson.

767	**194**	3d. red	10	10

195 "Pania" Statue, Napier

196 Australian Gannets on Cape Kidnappers

1958. Centenary of Hawke's Bay Province.

768	**195**	2d. green	10	10
769	**196**	3d. blue	30	10
770	-	8d. brown	70	1·50

DESIGN—As Type **195**: 8d. Maori sheep-shearer.

197 "Kiwi", Jamboree Badge

1959. Pan-Pacific Scout Jamboree, Auckland.

771	**197**	3d. brown and red	30	10

198 Careening H.M.S. "Endeavour" at Ship Cove

1959. Centenary of Marlborough Province. Inscr as in T 198.

772	**198**	2d. green	30	10
773	-	3d. blue	30	10
774	-	8d. brown	1·25	2·25

DESIGNS: 3d. Shipping wool, Wairau Bar, 1857; 8d. Salt industry, Grassmere.

201 Red Cross Flag

1959. Red Cross Commemoration.

775	**201**	3d.+1d. red and blue	20	10

202 Grey Teal

1959. Health Stamps.

776	**202**	2d.+1d. yellow, olive and red	50	65
777	-	3d.+1d. black, pink and blue	50	65
MS777c		Two sheets, each 95×109 mm, with Nos. 776/7 in blocks of 6 (3×2) Per pair	9·00	26·00

DESIGN: 3d. New Zealand stilt.

207 Manuka (Tea Tree)

215 Timber Industry

219 Taniwha (Maori Rock Drawing)

1960

781	**207**	½d. green and red	10	10
782	-	1d. multicoloured	10	10
783	-	2d. multicoloured	10	10
784	-	2½d. multicoloured	1·00	10
785	-	3d. multicoloured	30	10
786	-	4d. multicoloured	40	10
787	-	5d. multicoloured	1·25	10
788	-	6d. lilac, green and turquoise	50	10
788d	-	7d. red, green and yellow	1·00	1·40
789	-	8d. multicoloured	40	10
790	-	9d. red and blue	40	10
791	**215**	1s. brown and green	30	10
792b	-	1s.3d. red, sepia and blue	2·00	25
793	-	1s.6d. olive and brown	75	10
794	-	1s.9d. brown	12·00	15
795	-	1s.9d. multicoloured	2·50	1·00
796	**219**	2s. black and buff	2·50	10
797	-	2s.6d. yellow and brown	1·50	1·00
798	-	3s. sepia	20·00	1·00
799	-	3s. bistre, blue and green	2·00	1·75
800	-	5s. myrtle	2·25	80
801	-	10s. blue	4·50	3·25
802	-	£1 mauve	10·00	8·00

DESIGNS—VERT (as Type **207**): 1d. Karaka; 2d. Kowhai Ngutu-kaka (Kaka Beak); 2½d. Titoki (plant); 3d. Kowhai; 4d. Puarangi (Hibiscus); 5d. Matua tikumu (Mountain daisy); 6d. Pikiarero (Clematis); 7d. Koromiko; 8d. Rata. (As T **215**): 1s.3d. Rainbow trout; 1s.6d. Tiki. (As T **219**): 5s. Sutherland Falls; £1 Potutu Geyser. HORIZ (as T **215**): 9d. National flag; 1s.9d. Aerial top- dressing. (As Type **219**): 2s.6d. Butter-making; 3s. Tongariro National Park and Chateau; 10s. Tasman Glacier.

225 Sacred Kingfisher

1960. Health Stamps.

803	**225**	2d.+1d. sepia and blue	50	75
804	-	3d.+1d. purple & orange	50	75
MS804b		Two sheets, each 95×107 mm, with Nos. 803/4 in blocks of 6 Per pair	26·00	38·00

DESIGN: 3d. New Zealand pigeon.

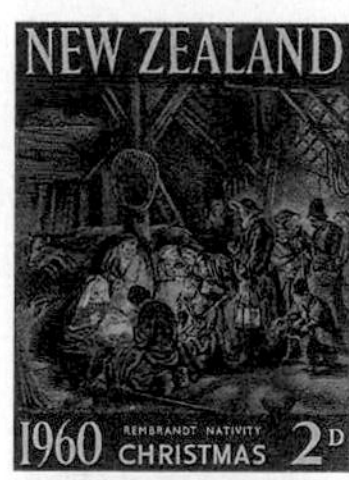

227 "The Adoration of the Shepherds" (Rembrandt)

1960. Christmas.

805	**227**	2d. red & brown on cream	15	10

228 Great Egret

1961. Health Stamps.

806	**228**	2d.+1d. black and purple	50	70
807	-	3d.+1d. sepia and green	50	70
MS807a		Two sheets, each 97×121 mm, with Nos. 806/7 in blocks of 6 (3×2) Per pair	26·00	32·00

DESIGN: 3d. New Zealand falcon.

232 "Adoration of the Magi" (Durer)

1961. Christmas.

809	**232**	2½d. multicoloured	10	10

233 Morse Key and Port Hills, Lyttleton

1962. Telegraph Centenary.

810	**233**	3d. sepia and green	10	10
811	-	8d. black and red	90	90

DESIGN: 8d. Modern teleprinter.

236 Tieke Saddleback

1962. Health Stamps.

812		2½d.+1d. multicoloured	50	70
813	**236**	3d.+1d. multicoloured	50	70
MS813b		Two sheets, each 96×101 mm, with Nos. 812/13 in blocks of 6 (3×2) Per pair	45·00	50·00

DESIGN: 2½d. Red-fronted parakeet.

237 "Madonna in Prayer" (Sassoferrato)

1962. Christmas.

814	**237**	2½d. multicoloured	10	10

238 Prince Andrew

1963. Health Stamps.

815b	**238**	2½d.+1d. blue	30	40
816	-	3d.+1d. red	30	10
MS816a		Two sheets, each 93×100 mm, with Nos. 815/16 in blocks of 6 (3×2) Per pair	25·00	40·00

DESIGN: 3d. Prince Andrew (different).

240 "The Holy Family" (Titian)

1963. Christmas.

817	**240**	2½d. multicoloured	10	10

241 Steam Locomotive "Pilgrim" (1863) and Class DG Diesel Locomotive

1963. Centenary of New Zealand Railway. Inscr as in T 241. Multicoloured.

818		3d. Type **241**	40	10
819		1s.9d. Diesel express and Mt. Ruapehu	1·50	1·25

243 "Commonwealth Cable"

1963. Opening of COMPAC (Trans-Pacific Telephone Cable).

820	**243**	8d. multicoloured	50	1·25

244 Road Map and Car Steering-wheel

1964. Road Safety Campaign.

821	**244**	3d. black, yellow and blue	30	10

245 Silver Gulls

1964. Health Stamps. Multicoloured.

822		2½d.+1d. Type **245**	40	50
823		3d.+1d. Little penguin	40	50
MS823b		Two sheets, each 171×84 mm, with Nos. 822/3 in blocks of 8 (4×2) Per pair	48·00	65·00

246 Rev. S. Marsden taking first Christian Service at Rangihoua Bay, 1814

1964. Christmas.

824	**246**	2½d. multicoloured	10	10

1964. Surch 7D POSTAGE.

825	**F6**	7d. on (-) red	50	1·50

248 Anzac Cove

1965. 50th Anniv of Gallipoli Landing.

826	**248**	4d. brown	10	10
827	-	5d. green and red	10	60

DESIGN: 5d. Anzac Cove and poppy.

249 I.T.U. Emblem and Symbols

1965. Centenary of I.T.U.

828	**249**	9d. blue and brown	55	35

250 Sir Winston Churchill

1965. Churchill Commemoration.

829 **250** 7d. black, grey and blue 30 50

251 Wellington Provincial Council Building

1965. Centenary of Government in Wellington.

830 **251** 4d. multicoloured 10 10

252 Kaka

1965. Health Stamps. Multicoloured.

831 3d.+1d. Type **252** 40 65

832 4d.+1d. Collared grey fantail 40 65

MS832c Two sheets, each 100×109 mm, with Nos. 831/2 in blocks of 6 (3×2) Per pair 38·00 48·00

254 I.C.Y. Emblem

1965. International Co-operation Year.

833 **254** 4d. red and olive 20 10

255 "The Two Trinities" (Murillo)

1965. Christmas.

834 **255** 3d. multicoloured 10 10

256 Arms of New Zealand

1965. 11th Commonwealth Parliamentary Conf. Multicoloured.

835 4d. Type **256** 25 20

836 9d. Parliament House, Wellington, and Badge 55 75

837 2s. Wellington from Mt. Victoria 3·25 5·00

259 "Progress" Arrowhead

1966. 4th National Scout Jamboree, Trentham.

838 **259** 4d. gold and green 15 10

260 New Zealand Bell Bird

1966. Health Stamps. Multicoloured.

839 3d.+1d. Type **260** 50 75

840 4d.+1d. Weka rail 50 75

MS841 Two sheets, each 107×91 mm. Nos. 839/40 in blocks of 6 (3×2) Per pair 22·00 50·00

262 "The Virgin with Child" (Maratta)

1966. Christmas.

842 **262** 3d. multicoloured 10 10

263 Queen Victoria and Queen Elizabeth II

1967. Centenary of New Zealand Post Office Savings Bank.

843 **263** 4d. black, gold and purple 10 10

844 - 9d. multicoloured 10 20

DESIGN: 9d. Half-sovereign of 1867 and commemorative dollar coin.

265 Manuka (Tea Tree)

1967. Decimal Currency. Designs as earlier issues, but with values inscr in decimal currency as T 265.

845	**265**	½c. blue, green and red	10	10
846	-	1c. mult (No. 782)	10	10
847	-	2c. mult (No. 783)	10	10
848	-	2½c. mult (No. 785)	10	10
849	-	3c. mult (No. 786)	10	10
850	-	4c. mult (No. 787)	30	10
851	-	5c. lilac, olive and green (No. 788)	50	60
852	-	6c. mult (No. 788d)	50	1·00
853	-	7c. mult (No. 789)	60	1·50
854	-	8c. red and blue (No. 790)	60	60
855	**215**	10c. brown and green	60	80
856	-	15c. green and brown (No. 793)	2·25	2·25
857	**219**	20c. black and buff	1·00	20
858	-	25c. yellow and brown (No. 797)	1·25	2·00
859	-	30c. yellow, green and blue (No. 799)	1·25	25
860	-	50c. green (No. 800)	1·75	50
861	-	$1 blue (No. 801)	9·00	1·00
862	-	$2 mauve (No. 802)	4·00	6·00
F219a	**F 6**	$4 violet	2·50	1·50
F220a	**F 6**	$6 green	3·00	3·25
F221a	**F 6**	$8 blue	3·00	4·50
F222a	**F 6**	$10 blue	3·00	3·75

For 15c. in different colours, see No. 874.

268 Running with Ball

1967. Health Stamps. Rugby Football.

867 **268** 2½c.+1c. multicoloured 15 15

868 - 3c.+1c. multicoloured 15 15

MS869 Two sheets. (a) 76×130 mm (867). (b) 130×76 mm (868). Containing blocks of six Per pair 23·00 40·00

DESIGN—HORIZ: 3c. Positioning for place-kick.

271 Brown Trout **273** Forest and Timber

1967

870		7c. multicoloured	1·00	1·00
871	**271**	7½c. multicoloured	50	70
872	-	8c. multicoloured	75	70
873	**273**	10c. multicoloured	50	10
874	-	15c. green, deep green and red (as No. 793)	1·00	1·00
875	-	18c. multicoloured	1·00	55
876	-	20c. multicoloured	1·00	20
877	-	25c. multicoloured	1·75	2·00
878	-	28c. multicoloured	60	10
879	-	$2 black, ochre and blue (as No. 802)	13·00	13·00

DESIGNS: 7c. "Kaitia" (trawler) and catch; 8c. Apples and orchard; 18c. Sheep and the "Woolmark"; 20c. Consignments of beef and herd of cattle; 25c. Dairy farm, Mt. Egmont and butter consignment. VERT: 28c. Fox Glacier, Westland National Park.

No. 871 was originally issued to commemorate the introduction of the brown trout into New Zealand.

No. 874 is slightly larger than No. 793, measuring 21×25 mm, and the inscr and numerals differ in size.

278 "The Adoration of the Shepherds" (Poussin)

1967. Christmas.

880 **278** 2½c. multicoloured 10 10

279 Mount Aspiring, Aurora Australis and Southern Cross

1967. Cent of Royal Society of New Zealand.

881 **279** 4c. multicoloured 25 20

882 - 8c. multicoloured 25 80

DESIGN: 8c. Sir James Hector (founder).

281 Open Bible

1968. Centenary of Maori Bible.

883 **281** 3c. multicoloured 10 10

282 Soldiers and Tank

1968. New Zealand Armed Forces. Multicoloured.

884 4c. Type **282** 25 15

885 10c. Airmen, Fairey Firefly and English Electric Canberra aircraft 40 60

886 28c. Sailors and H.M.N.Z.S. "Achilles", 1939, and H.M.N.Z.S. "Waikato", 1968 70 2·00

285 Boy breasting Tape and Olympic Rings

1968. Health Stamps. Multicoloured.

887 2½c.+1c. Type **285** 20 15

888 3c.+1c. Girl swimming and Olympic rings 20 15

MS889 Two sheets, each 145×95 mm. Nos. 887/8 in blocks of 6 Per pair 16·00 45·00

287 Placing Votes in Ballot Box

1968. 75th Anniv of Universal Suffrage in New Zealand.

890 **287** 3c. ochre, green and blue 10 10

288 Human Rights Emblem

1968. Human Rights Year.

891 **288** 10c. red, yellow and green 10 30

289 "Adoration of the Holy Child" (G. van Honthorst)

1968. Christmas.

892 **289** 2½c. multicoloured 10 10

290 I.L.O. Emblem

1969. 50th Anniv of Int Labour Organization.

893 **290** 7c. black and red 15 30

291 Supreme Court Building, Auckland

1969. Centenary of New Zealand Law Society.

894 **291** 3c. multicoloured 10 10

895 - 10c. multicoloured 20 45

896 - 18c. multicoloured 30 1·25

DESIGNS—VERT: 10c. Law Society's coat of arms; 18c. "Justice" (from Memorial Window in University of Canterbury, Christchurch).

295 Student being conferred with Degree

1969. Centenary of Otago University. Mult.

No.	Type	Description	Mint	Used
897		3c. Otago University (vert)	15	10
898		10c. Type **295**	30	25

296 Boys playing Cricket

1969. Health Stamps.

No.	Type	Description	Mint	Used
899	**296**	2½c.+1c. multicoloured	40	65
900	-	3c.+1c. multicoloured	40	65
901	-	4c.+1c. brown and ultramarine	40	2·00
MS902		Two sheets, each 144×84 mm. Nos. 899/900 in blocks of 6 Per pair	16·00	50·00

DESIGNS—HORIZ: 3c. Girls playing cricket. VERT: 4c. Dr. Elizabeth Gunn (founder of first Children's Health Camp).

299 Oldest existing House in New Zealand, and Old Stone Mission Store, Kerikeri

1969. Early European Settlement in New Zealand, and 150th Anniv of Kerikeri. Multicoloured.

No.	Type	Description	Mint	Used
903		4c. Type **299**	20	25
904		6c. View of Bay of Islands	30	1·75

301 "The Nativity" (Federico Fiori Barocci)

1969. Christmas.

No.	Type	Description	Mint	Used
905	**301**	2½c. multicoloured	10	10

302 Captain Cook, Transit of Venus and "Octant"

1969. Bicentenary of Captain Cook's Landing in New Zealand.

No.	Type	Description	Mint	Used
906	**302**	4c. black, red and blue	40	25
907	-	6c. green, brown and black	55	1·25
908	-	18c. brown, green and black	80	1·00
909	-	28c. red, black and blue	1·40	2·50
MS910		109×90 mm. Nos. 906/9	14·00	30·00

DESIGNS: 6c. Sir Joseph Banks (naturalist) and outline of H.M.S. "Endeavour"; 18c. Dr. Daniel Solander (botanist) and his plant; 28c. Queen Elizabeth II and Cook's chart, 1769.

306 Girl, Wheat Field and C.O.R.S.O. Emblem

1969. 25th Anniv of C.O.R.S.O. (Council of Organizations for Relief Services Overseas). Multicoloured.

No.	Type	Description	Mint	Used
911		7c. Type **306**	35	1·10
912		8c. Mother feeding her child, dairy herd and C.O.R.S.O. emblem (horiz)	35	1·25

308 "Cardigan Bay" (champion trotter)

1970. Return of "Cardigan Bay" to New Zealand.

No.	Type	Description	Mint	Used
913	**308**	10c. multicoloured	30	30

309 "Vanessa gonerilla" (butterfly)

310 Queen Elizabeth II and New Zealand Coat of Arms

1970

No.	Type	Description	Mint	Used
914	-	½c. multicoloured	10	20
915	**309**	1c. multicoloured	10	10
916	-	2c. multicoloured	10	10
917	-	2½c. multicoloured	30	20
918	-	3c. multicoloured	15	10
919	-	4c. multicoloured	15	10
920	-	5c. multicoloured	30	10
921	-	6c. black, green and red	30	1·00
922	-	7c. multicoloured	50	1·00
923	-	7½c. multicoloured	75	1·75
924	-	8c. multicoloured	50	1·00
925	**310**	10c. multicoloured	50	15
926	-	15c. black, flesh and brown	75	50
927	-	18c. green, brown & black	75	50
928	-	20c. black and brown	75	15
929	-	23c. multicoloured	60	30
930b	-	25c. multicoloured	50	75
931	-	30c. multicoloured	50	15
932	-	50c. multicoloured	50	20
933	-	$1 multicoloured	1·00	1·25
934	-	$2 multicoloured	2·50	1·75

DESIGNS—VERT (as T **309**): ½c. "Lycaena salustius" (butterfly); 2c. "Argyrophenga antipodum" (butterfly); 2½c. "Nyctemera annulata (moth); 3c. "Detunda egregia" (moth); 4c. Charagia virescens" (moth); 5c. Scarlet wrasse ("Scarlet parrot fish"); 6c. Big-bellied sea horses; 7c. Leather-jacket (fish); 7½c. Intermediate halfbeak ("Garfish"); 8c. John Dory (fish). (As T **310**): 18c. Maori club; 25c. Hauraki Gulf Maritime Park; 30c. Mt. Cook National Park. HORIZ (as T **310**): 15c. Maori fish hook; 20c. Maori tattoo pattern; 23c. Egmont National Park; 50c. Abel Tasman National Park; $1 Geothermal power; $2 Agricultural technology.

311 Geyser Restaurant

1970. World Fair, Osaka. Multicoloured.

No.	Type	Description	Mint	Used
935		7c. Type **311**	20	75
936		8c. New Zealand Pavilion	20	75
937		18c. Bush Walk	40	75

312 U.N. H.Q. Building

1970. 25th Anniv of United Nations.

No.	Type	Description	Mint	Used
938	**312**	3c. multicoloured	10	10
939	-	10c. red and yellow	20	20

DESIGN: 10c. Tractor on horizon.

313 Soccer

1970. Health Stamps. Multicoloured.

No.	Type	Description	Mint	Used
940		2½c.+1c. Netball (vert)	25	70
941		3c.+1c. Type **313**	25	70
MS942		Two sheets. (a) 102×125 mm (940). (b) 125×102 mm (941). Containing blocks of six Per pair	18·00	50·00

314 "The Virgin adoring the Child" (Correggio)

1970. Christmas.

No.	Type	Description	Mint	Used
943	**314**	2½c. multicoloured	10	10
944	-	3c. multicoloured	10	10
945	-	10c. black, orange & silver	30	75

DESIGNS—VERT: 3c. Stained glass window, Invercargill Presbyterian Church "The Holy Family". HORIZ: 10c. Tower of Roman Catholic Church, Seckburn.

316 Chatham Islands Lily

1970. Chatham Islands. Multicoloured.

No.	Type	Description	Mint	Used
946		1c. Type **316**	10	35
947		2c. Shy albatross	30	40

317 Country Women's Institute Emblem

1971. 50th Annivs of Country Women's Institutes and Rotary International in New Zealand. Multicoloured.

No.	Type	Description	Mint	Used
948		4c. Type **317**	10	10
949		10c. Rotary emblem and map of New Zealand	20	60

318 "Rainbow II" (yacht)

1971. One Ton Cup Racing Trophy. Mult.

No.	Type	Description	Mint	Used
950		5c. Type **318**	25	25
951		8c. One Ton Cup	25	1·50

319 Civic Arms of Palmerston North

1971. City Centenaries. Multicoloured.

No.	Type	Description	Mint	Used
952		3c. Type **319**	10	10
953		4c. Arms of Auckland	10	15
954		5c. Arms of Invercargill	15	1·10

320 Antarctica on Globe

1971. 10th Anniv of Antarctic Treaty.

No.	Type	Description	Mint	Used
955	**320**	6c. multicoloured	1·00	1·75

321 Child on Swing

1971. 25th Anniv of UNICEF.

No.	Type	Description	Mint	Used
956	**321**	7c. multicoloured	50	1·00

1971. No. 917 surch 4c.

No.	Type	Description	Mint	Used
957		4c. on 2½c. multicoloured	15	10

323 Satellite-tracking Aerial

1971. Opening of Satellite Earth Station.

No.	Type	Description	Mint	Used
958	**323**	8c. black, grey and red	50	1·50
959	-	10c. black, green and violet	50	1·00

DESIGN: 10c. Satellite.

324 Girls playing Hockey

1971. Health Stamps. Multicoloured.

No.	Type	Description	Mint	Used
960		3c.+1c. Type **324**	45	65
961		4c.+1c. Boys playing hockey	45	65
962		5c.+1c. Dental health	75	2·00
MS963		Two sheets, each 122×96 mm. Nos. 960/1 in blocks of six Per pair	19·00	45·00

325 "Madonna bending over the Crib" (Maratta)

1971. Christmas. Multicoloured.

No.	Type	Description	Mint	Used
964		3c. Type **325**	10	10
965		4c. "The Annunciation" (stained-glass window)	10	10
966		10c. "The Three Kings"	70	1·25

Nos. 965/6 are smaller, size 21½×38 mm.

326 "Tiffany" Rose

1971. 1st World Rose Convention, Hamilton. Mult.

No.	Type	Description	Mint	Used
967		2c. Type **326**	15	30
968		5c. "Peace"	35	35
969		8c. "Chrysler Imperial"	60	1·10

327 Lord Rutherford and Alpha Particles

1971. Birth Centenary of Lord Rutherford (scientist). Multicoloured.

No.	Type	Description	Mint	Used
970		1c. Type **327**	20	50
971		7c. Lord Rutherford and formula	55	1·75

328 Benz (1895)

1972. International Vintage Car Rally. Mult.

No.	Type	Description	Mint	Used
972		3c. Type **328**	20	10
973		4c. Oldsmobile (1904)	20	10
974		5c. Ford "Model T" (1914)	20	10
975		6c. Cadillac Service car (1915)	25	45
976		8c. Chrysler (1924)	40	2·00
977		10c. Austin "7" (1923)	40	1·50

329 Coat of Arms of Wanganui

1972. Anniversaries.

978	**329**	3c. multicoloured	15	10
979	-	4c. orange, brown & black	15	10
980	-	5c. multicoloured	25	10
981	-	8c. multicoloured	40	1·10
982	-	10c. multicoloured	40	1·10

DESIGNS AND EVENTS—VERT: 3c. Type **329** (centenary of Wanganui Council); 5c. De Havilland D.H.89 Dragon Rapide and Boeing 737 (25th anniv of National Airways Corp); 8c. French frigate and Maori palisade (bicentenary of landing by Marion du Fresne). HORIZ: 4c. Postal Union symbol (10th anniv of Asian–Oceanic Postal Union); 10c. Stone cairn (150th anniv of New Zealand Methodist Church).

330 Black Scree Cotula

1972. Alpine Plants. Multicoloured.

983	4c. Type **330**	30	10
984	6c. North Island edelweiss	40	40
985	8c. Haast's buttercup	60	85
986	10c. Brown Mountain daisy	70	1·25

331 Boy playing Tennis

1972. Health Stamps.

987	**331**	3c.+1c. grey and brown	30	50
988	-	4c.+1c. brown, grey and yellow	30	50
MS989		Two sheets, each 107×123 mm. Nos. 987/8 in blocks of six Per pair	18·00	40·00

DESIGN: No. 988, Girl playing tennis.

332 "Madonna with Child" (Murillo)

1972. Christmas. Multicoloured.

990	3c. Type **332**	10	10
991	5c. "The Last Supper" (stained-glass window, St. John's Church, Levin)	15	10
992	10c. Pohutukawa flower	35	70

333 Lake Waikaremoana

1972. Lake Scenes. Multicoloured.

993	6c. Type **333**	75	1·00
994	8c. Lake Hayes	85	1·00
995	18c. Lake Wakatipu	1·25	2·00
996	23c. Lake Rotomahana	1·40	2·25

334 Old Pollen Street

1973. Commemorations.

997	**334**	3c. multicoloured	10	10
998	-	4c. multicoloured	15	10
999	-	5c. multicoloured	15	15
1000	-	6c. multicoloured	50	50
1001	-	8c. grey, blue and gold	35	50
1002	-	10c. multicoloured	50	80

DESIGNS AND EVENTS: 3c. (centenary of Thames Borough); 4c. Coalmining and pasture (centenary of Westport Borough); 5c. Cloister (centenary of Canterbury University); 6c. Forest, birds and lake (50th anniv of Royal Forest and Bird Protection Society); 8c. Rowers (Success of N.Z. rowers in 1972 Olympics); 10c. Graph and people (25th anniv of E.C.A.F.E.).

335 Class W Locomotive

1973. New Zealand Steam Locomotives. Mult.

1003	3c. Type **335**	25	10
1004	4c. Class X	25	10
1005	5c. Class Ab	25	10
1006	10c. Class Ja No. 1274	1·00	1·40

336 "Maori Woman and Child"

1973. Paintings by Frances Hodgkins. Mult.

1027	5c. Type **336**	25	15
1028	8c. "Hilltop"	40	80
1029	10c. "Barn in Picardy"	40	65
1030	18c. "Self-portrait Still Life"	75	2·00

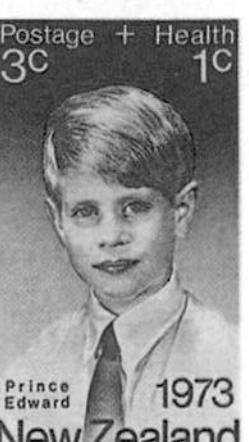

337 Prince Edward

1973. Health Stamps.

1031	**337**	3c.+1c. green & brown	30	50
1032	**337**	4c.+1c. red and brown	30	50
MS1033		Two sheets, each 96×121 mm, with Nos. 1031/2 in blocks of 6 (3×2) Per pair	16·00	40·00

338 "Tempi Madonna" (Raphael)

1973. Christmas. Multicoloured.

1034	3c. Type **338**	10	10
1035	5c. "Three Kings" (stained- glass window, St. Theresa's Church, Auckland)	10	10
1036	10c. Family entering church	25	50

339 Mitre Peak

1973. Mountain Scenery. Multicoloured.

1037	6c. Type **339**	45	80
1038	8c. Mt. Ngauruhoe	55	1·25
1039	18c. Mt. Sefton (horiz)	70	2·00
1040	23c. Burnett Range (horiz)	80	2·50

340 Hurdling

1974. 10th British Commonwealth Games, Christchurch.

1041	**340**	4c. multicoloured	10	10
1042	-	5c. black and violet	10	10
1043	-	10c. multicoloured	60	15
1044	-	18c. multicoloured	15	50
1045	-	23c. multicoloured	20	80

DESIGNS: 5c. Ball-player (4th Paraplegic Games, Dunedin); 10c. Cycling; 18c. Rifle-shooting; 23c. Bowls.

341 Queen Elizabeth II

1974. New Zealand Day. Sheet 131×74 mm, containing T 341 and similar horiz designs, size 37×20 mm. Multicoloured.

MS1046	4c.×5 Treaty House, Waitangi; Signing Waitangi Treaty; Type **341**; Parliament Buildings extensions; Children in class	70	2·50

342 "Spirit of Napier" Fountain

1974. Centenaries of Napier and U.P.U. Mult.

1047	4c. Type **342**	10	10
1048	5c. Clock Tower, Berne	20	30
1049	8c. U.P.U. Monument, Berne	55	1·60

343 Boeing Seaplane, 1919

1974. History of New Zealand Airmail Transport. Multicoloured.

1050	3c. Type **343**	25	10
1051	4c. Lockheed 10 Electra "Kauha", 1937	30	10
1052	5c. Bristol Type 170 Freighter Mk 31, 1958	30	30
1053	23c. Short S.30 modified "G" Class flying boat "Aotearoa", 1940	1·40	2·00

344 Children, Cat and Dog

1974. Health Stamps.

1054	**344**	3c.+1c. multicoloured	20	50
1055	-	4c.+1c. multicoloured	25	50
1056	-	5c.+1c. multicoloured	1·00	1·50
MS1057		145×123 mm. No. 1055 in block of ten	17·00	40·00

Nos. 1055/6 are similar to Type **344**, showing children with pets.

345 "The Adoration of the Magi" (Konrad Witz)

1974. Christmas. Multicoloured.

1058	3c. Type **345**	10	10
1059	5c. "The Angel Window" (stained glass window, Old St. Pauls Church, Wellington)	10	10
1060	10c. Madonna lily	30	90

346 Great Barrier Island

1974. Offshore Islands. Multicoloured.

1061	6c. Type **346**	25	40
1062	8c. Stewart Island	40	1·25
1063	18c. White Island	50	1·50
1064	23c. The Brothers	55	1·75

347 Crippled Child

1975. Anniversaries and Events. Multicoloured.

1065	3c. Type **347**	10	10
1066	5c. Farming family	10	10
1067	10c. I.W.Y. symbols	15	65
1068	18c. Medical School Building, Otago University	40	1·75

COMMEMORATIONS: 3c. 40th anniv of New Zealand Crippled Children Society; 5c. 50th anniv of Women's Division, Federated Farmers of New Zealand; 10c. International Women's Year; 18c. Centenary of Otago Medical School.

348 Scow "Lake Erie"

1975. Historic Sailing Ships.

1069	**348**	4c. black and red	30	10
1070	-	5c. black and blue	30	10
1071	-	8c. black and yellow	40	70
1072	-	10c. black and yellow	45	70
1073	-	18c. black and brown	75	2·25
1074	-	23c. black and lilac	85	2·25

SHIPS: 5c. Schooner "Herald"; 8c. Brigantine "New Zealander"; 10c. Topsail schooner "Jessie Kelly"; 18c. Barque "Tory"; 23c. Full-rigged clipper "Rangitiki".

349 Lake Sumner Forest Park

1975. Forest Park Scenes. Multicoloured.

1075	6c. Type **349**	30	60
1076	8c. North-west Nelson	40	1·00
1077	18c. Kaweka	65	1·75
1078	23c. Coromandel	90	1·75

350 Girl feeding Lamb

1975. Health Stamps. Multicoloured.

1079	3c.+1c. Type **350**	15	30
1080	4c.+1c. Boy with hen and chicks	15	30
1081	5c.+1c. Boy with duck and duckling	40	1·50
MS1082	123×146 mm. No. 1080×10	13·00	40·00

351 "Virgin and Child" (Zanobi Machiavelli)

1975. Christmas. Multicoloured.

1083	3c. Type **351**	10	10
1084	5c. "Cross in Landscape" (stained-glass window, Greendale Church) (horiz)	10	10
1085	10c. "I saw three ships" (carol) (horiz)	35	65

352 "Sterling Silver"

353 Queen Elizabeth II (photograph by W. Harrison)

353a Maripi (knife)

353b Rainbow Abalone or Paua

1975. (a) Garden Roses. Multicoloured.

1086	1c. Type **352**	10	10
1087	2c. "Lilli Marlene"	10	20
1088	3c. "Queen Elizabeth"	60	10
1089	4c. "Super Star"	10	60
1090	5c. "Diamond Jubilee"	10	10
1091a	6c. "Cresset"	40	1·00
1092a	7c. "Michele Meilland"	40	10
1093a	8c. "Josephine Bruce"	30	10
1094	9c. "Iceberg"	30	60

(b) Type 353.

1094ab	10c. multicoloured	30	10

(c) Maori Artefacts.

1095	**353a**	11c. brown, yellow & black	30	80
1096	-	12c. brown, yellow & black	30	50
1097	-	13c. brown, mauve & black	40	1·00
1098	-	14c. brown, yellow & black	30	20

DESIGNS: 12c. Putorino (flute); 13c. Wahaika (club); 14c. Kotiate (club).

(d) Sea Shells. Multicoloured.

1099	20c. Type **353b**	15	20
1100	30c. Toheroa clam	25	50
1101	40c. Old woman or coarse dosinia	30	45
1102	50c. New Zealand or spiny murex	40	45
1103	$1 New Zealand scallop	70	1·00
1104	$2 Circular saw	1·00	1·75

(e) Building. Multicoloured.

1105	$5 "Beehive" (section of Parliamentary Buildings, Wellington) (22×26 mm)	1·75	1·50

354 Family and League of Mothers Badge

1976. Anniversaries and Metrication. Mult.

1110	6c. Type **354**	10	10
1111	7c. Weight, temperature, linear measure and capacity	10	10
1112	8c. "William Bryon" (immigrant ship), mountain and New Plymouth	15	10
1113	10c. Two women shaking hands and Y.W.C.A. badge	15	60
1114	25c. Map of the world showing cable links	30	1·25

ANNIVERSARIES: 6c. 50th anniv of League of Mothers; 7c. Metrication; 8c. Centenary of New Plymouth; 10c. 50th anniv of New Zealand Y.W.C.A.; 25c. Link with International Telecommunications Network.

355 Gig

1976. Vintage Farm Transport. Multicoloured.

1115	6c. Type **355**	15	40
1116	7c. Thornycroft lorry	15	10
1117	8c. Scandi wagon	30	15
1118	9c. Traction engine	20	40
1119	10c. Wool wagon	20	40
1120	25c. Cart	65	2·25

356 Purakaunui Falls

1976. Waterfalls. Multicoloured.

1121	10c. Type **356**	25	10
1122	14c. Marakopa Falls	40	95
1123	15c. Bridal Veil Falls	45	1·10
1124	16c. Papakorito Falls	55	1·25

357 Boy and Pony

1976. Health Stamps. Multicoloured.

1125	7c.+1c. Type **357**	20	30
1126	8c.+1c. Girl and calf	20	30
1127	10c.+1c. Girls and bird	40	90
MS1128	96×121 mm. Nos. 1125/7×2	2·50	6·00

358 "Nativity" (Spanish carving)

1976. Christmas. Multicoloured.

1129	7c. Type **358**	15	10
1130	11c. "Resurrection" (stained-glass window, St. Joseph's Catholic Church, Grey Lynn) (horiz)	25	30
1131	18c. Angels (horiz)	40	1·00

359 Arms of Hamilton

1977. Anniversaries. Multicoloured.

1132	8c. Type **359**	15	35
1133	8c. Arms of Gisborne	15	35
1134	8c. Arms of Masterton	15	35
1135	10c. A.A. emblem	15	50
1136	10c. Arms of the Royal Australasian College of Surgeons	15	50

ANNIVERSARIES: No. 1132, Cent of Hamilton; 1133, Cent of Gisborne; 1134, Cent of Masterton; 1135, 75th anniv of Automobile Association in New Zealand; 1136, 50th anniv of R.A.C.S.

360 Queen Elizabeth II

1977. Silver Jubilee. Sheet 178×82 mm, containing T 360 and similar vert designs showing different portraits.

MS1137	8c.×5 multicoloured	65	1·60

361 Physical Education and Maori Culture

1977. Education. Multicoloured.

1138	8c. Type **361**	40	70
1139	8c. Geography, science and woodwork	40	70
1140	8c. Teaching the deaf, kindergarten and woodwork	40	70
1141	8c. Tertiary and language classes	40	70
1142	8c. Home science, correspondence school and teacher training	40	70

1977. Nos. 918/19 surch.

1143	7c. on 3c. "Detunda egregia" (moth)	40	70
1144	8c. on 4c. "Charagia virescens" (moth)	40	70

363 Karitane Beach

1977. Seascapes. Multicoloured.

1145	10c. Type **363**	15	10
1146	16c. Ocean Beach, Mount Maunganui	30	30
1147	18c. Piha Beach	30	30
1148	30c. Kaikoura Coast	35	40

364 Girl with Pigeon

1977. Health Stamps. Multicoloured.

1149	7c.+2c. Type **364**	20	50
1150	8c.+2c. Boy with frog	20	55
1151	10c.+2c. Girl with butterfly	40	1·00
MS1152	97×120 mm. Nos. 1149/51×2	1·40	6·50

Stamps from No. **MS**1152 are without white border and together form a composite design.

365 "The Holy Family" (Correggio)

1977. Christmas. Multicoloured.

1153	7c. Type **365**	15	10
1154	16c. "Madonna and Child" (stained-glass window, St. Michael's and All Angels, Dunedin) (vert)	25	25
1155	23c. "Partridge in a Pear Tree" (vert)	40	1·25

366 Merryweather Manual Pump, 1860

1977. Fire Fighting Appliances. Multicoloured.

1156	10c. Type **366**	15	10
1157	11c. 2-wheel hose, reel and ladder, 1880	15	25
1158	12c. Shand Mason steam fire engine, 1873	20	30
1159	23c. Chemical fire engine, 1888	30	90

367 Town Clock and Coat of Arms, Ashburton

1978. Centenaries.

1160	**367**	10c. multicoloured	15	25
1161	-	10c. multicoloured	15	25
1162	-	12c. red, yellow and black	15	15
1163	-	20c. multicoloured	20	30

DESIGNS—VERT: No. 1161, Mount Egmont (cent of Stratford); 1162, Early telephone (cent of telephone in New Zealand). HORIZ: No. 1163, Aerial view of Bay of Islands (cent of Bay of Islands County).

368 Students and Ivey Hall, Lincoln College

1978. Land Resources and Centenary of Lincoln College of Agriculture. Multicoloured.

1164	10c. Type **368**	15	10
1165	12c. Sheep grazing	15	30
1166	15c. Fertiliser ground spreading	15	30
1167	16c. Agricultural Field Days	15	40
1168	20c. Harvesting grain	20	40
1169	30c. Dairy farming	30	90

369

1978. Coil Stamps.

1170	**369**	1c. purple	10	65
1171	**369**	2c. orange	10	65
1172	**369**	5c. brown	10	65
1173	**369**	10c. blue	30	80

370 Maui Gas Drilling Platform

1978. Resources of the Sea. Multicoloured.

1174	12c. Type **370**	15	15
1175	15c. Trawler	15	20
1176	20c. Map of 200 mile fishing limit	20	30
1177	23c. Humpback whale and bottle-nosed dolphins	25	35
1178	35c. Kingfish, snapper, grouper and squid	40	60

371 First Health Charity Stamp

1978. Health Stamps.

1179	**371**	10c.+2c. black, red and gold	20	35
1180	-	12c.+2c. multicoloured	20	40
MS1181		97×124 mm. Nos. 1179/80×3	1·00	4·00

DESIGNS: 10c. Type **371** (50th anniv of Health Stamps); 12c. Heart Operation (National Heart Foundation).

372 "The Holy Family" (El Greco)

1978. Christmas. Multicoloured.

1182	7c. Type **372**	10	10
1183	16c. All Saint's Church, Howick (horiz)	25	35
1184	23c. Beach scene (horiz)	30	50

373 Sir Julius Vogel

1979. Statesmen. Designs each brown and drab.

1185	10c. Type **373**	25	50
1186	10c. Sir George Grey	25	50
1187	10c. Richard John Seddon	25	50

374 Riverlands Cottage, Blenheim

1979. Architecture (1st series).

1188	**374**	10c. black, light blue and blue	10	10
1189	-	12c. black, light green and green	15	25
1190	-	15c. black and grey	20	40
1191	-	20c. black, brown and sepia	25	40

DESIGNS: 12c. The Mission House, Waimate North; 15c. "The Elms", Tauranga; 20c. Provincial Council Buildings, Christchurch.

See also Nos. 1217/20 and 1262/5.

375 Whangaroa Harbour

1979. Small Harbours. Multicoloured.

1192	15c. Type **375**	15	10
1193	20c. Kawau Island	20	40
1194	23c. Akaroa Harbour (vert)	20	50
1195	35c. Picton Harbour (vert)	30	70

376 Children with Building Bricks

1979. International Year of the Child.

1196	**376**	10c. multicoloured	15	10

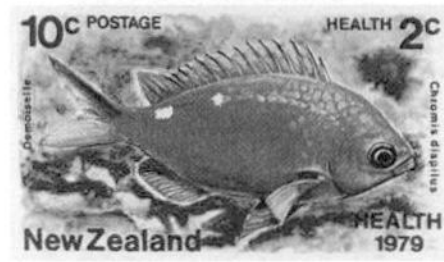

377 Two-spotted Chromis

1979. Health Stamps. Marine Life. Multicoloured.

1197	10c.+2c. Type **377**	20	50
1198	10c.+2c. Sea urchin	20	50
1199	12c.+2c. Red goatfish and underwater cameraman (vert)	20	50
MS1200	144×72 mm. Nos. 1197/9, each×2	1·00	2·75

1979. Nos. 1091a/3a and 1094ab surch.

1201	4c. on 8c. "Josephine Bruce"	10	50
1202	14c. on 10c. Type **353**	20	10
1203	17c. on 6c. "Cresset"	25	1·00
1203a	20c. on 7c. "Michele Meilland"	25	10

379 "Madonna and Child" (sculpture, Ghiberti)

1979. Christmas. Multicoloured.

1204	10c. Type **379**	15	10
1205	25c. Christ Church, Russell	30	50
1206	35c. Pohutukawa (tree)	40	70

380 Chamber, House of Representatives

1979. 25th Commonwealth Parliamentary Conf, Wellington. Multicoloured.

1207	14c. Type **380**	15	10
1208	20c. Mace and Black Rod	20	30
1209	30c. "Beehive" wall hanging	30	75

381 1855 1d. Stamp

1980. Anniversaries and Events.

1210	**381**	14c. black, red and yellow	20	30
1211	-	14c. black, blue & yellow	20	30
1212	-	14c. black, green & yellow	20	30
1213	-	17c. multicoloured	20	30
1214	-	25c. multicoloured	25	35
1215	-	30c. multicoloured	25	40
MS1216		146×96 mm. Nos. 1210/12 (as horiz strip) (sold at 52c.)	1·00	4·00

DESIGNS: No. 1211, 1855 2d. stamp; 1212, 1855 1s. stamp (125th anniv of New Zealand stamps); 1213, Geyser, wood-carving and building (Centenary of Rotorua (town)); 1214, "Earina autumnalis" and "Thelymitra venosa" (International Orchid Conference, Auckland); 1215, Ploughing and Golden Plough Trophy (World Ploughing Championships, Christchurch).

382 Ewelme Cottage, Parnell

1980. Architecture (2nd series). Multicoloured.

1217	14c. Type **382**	15	10
1218	17c. Broadgreen, Nelson	15	25
1219	25c. Courthouse, Oamaru	20	35
1220	30c. Government Buildings, Wellington	25	40

383 Auckland Harbour

1980. Large Harbours. Multicoloured.

1221	25c. Type **383**	20	20
1222	30c. Wellington Harbour	25	30
1223	35c. Lyttelton Harbour	25	35
1224	50c. Port Chalmers	30	1·10

384 Surf-fishing

1980. Health Stamps. Fishing. Multicoloured.

1225	14c.+2c. Type **384**	25	85
1226	14c.+2c. Wharf-fishing	25	85
1227	17c.+2c. Spear-fishing	25	55
MS1228	148×75 mm. Nos. 1225/7, each×2	1·25	3·25

385 "Madonna and Child with Cherubim" (sculpture, Andrea della Robbia)

1980. Christmas. Multicoloured.

1229	10c. Type **385**	15	10
1230	25c. St. Mary's Church, New Plymouth	25	25
1231	35c. Picnic scene	40	1·00

386 Te Heu Heu (chief)

1980. Maori Personalities. Multicoloured.

1232	15c. Type **386**	15	10
1233	25c. Te Hau (chief)	15	20
1234	35c. Te Puea (princess)	20	10
1235	45c. Ngata (politician)	30	30
1236	60c. Te Ata-O-Tu (warrior)	30	50

387 Lt. Col. the Hon. W. H. A. Feilding and Borough of Feilding Crest (cent)

1981. Commemorations.

1237	**387**	20c. multicoloured	20	20
1238	-	25c. orange and black	25	25

DESIGN AND COMMEMORATION: 25c. I.Y.D. emblem and cupped hands (International Year of the Disabled).

388 The Family at Play

1981. "Family Life". Multicoloured.

1239	20c. Type **388**	15	10
1240	25c. The family young and old	20	20
1241	30c. The family at home	20	35
1242	35c. The family at church	25	45

389 Kaiauai River

1981. River Scenes. Multicoloured.

1243	30c. Type **389**	20	25
1244	35c. Mangahao	20	30
1245	40c. Shotover (horiz)	25	40
1246	60c. Cleddau (horiz)	35	65

390 St. Paul's Cathedral

1981. Royal Wedding. Multicoloured.

1247	20c. Type **390**	30	30
1248	20c. Prince Charles and Lady Diana Spencer	30	30

391 Girl with Starfish

1981. Health Stamps. Children playing by the Sea. Multicoloured.

1249	20c.+2c. Type **391**	20	65
1250	20c.+2c. Boy fishing	20	65
1251	25c.+2c. Children exploring rock pool	20	35
MS1252	100×125 mm. Nos. 1249/51, each×2	1·00	3·00

Nos. 1249/50 were printed together, se-tenant, forming a composite design.

The stamps from No. **MS**1252 were printed together, se-tenant, in horizontal strips, each forming a composite design.

392 "Madonna suckling the Child" (painting, d'Oggiono)

1981. Christmas. Multicoloured.

1253	14c. Type **392**	15	10
1254	30c. St. John's Church, Wakefield	20	25
1255	40c. Golden tainui (flower)	35	35

393 Tauranga Mission House

1981. Commemorations. Multicoloured.

1256	20c. Type **393**	20	10
1257	20c. Water tower, Hawera	20	10
1258	25c. Cat	25	35
1259	30c. "Dunedin" (refrigerated sailing ship)	25	40
1260	35c. Scientific research equipment	25	45

COMMEMORATIONS: No. 1256, Centenary of Tauranga (town); 1257, Centenary of Hawera (town); 1258, Centenary of S.P.C.A. (Society for the Prevention of Cruelty to Animals in New Zealand); 1259, Centenary of frozen meat exports; 1260, International Year of Science.

394 Map of New Zealand

1982

1261	**394**	24c. green and blue	30	10

395 Alberton, Auckland

1982. Architecture (3rd series). Multicoloured.

1262	20c. Type **395**	15	15
1263	25c. Caccia Birch, Palmerston North	15	25
1264	30c. Railway station, Dunedin	40	30
1265	35c. Post Office, Ophir	25	40

396 Kaiteriteri Beach, Nelson (Summer)

1982. New Zealand Scenes. Multicoloured.

1266	35c. Type **396**	20	30
1267	40c. St. Omer Park, Queenstown (Autumn)	25	35
1268	45c. Mt. Ngauruhoe, Tongariro National Park (Winter)	25	40
1269	70c. Wairarapa farm (Spring)	40	60

397 Labrador

1982. Health Stamps. Dogs. Multicoloured.

1270	24c.+2c. Type **397**	65	1·00
1271	24c.+2c. Border collie	65	1·00
1272	30c.+2c. Cocker spaniel	65	1·00
MS1273	98×125 mm. Nos. 1270/2, each×2	3·25	6·50

398 "Madonna with Child and Two Angels" (painting by Piero di Cosimo)

1982. Christmas. Multicoloured.

1274	18c. Type **398**	15	10
1275	35c. Rangiatea Maori Church, Otaki	25	30
1276	45c. Surf life-saving	40	40

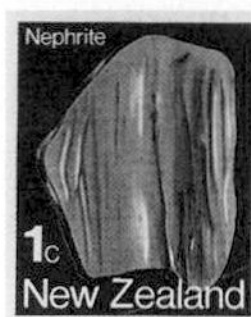

399 Nephrite

399a Grapes

399b Kokako

1982. (a) Minerals. Multicoloured.

1277	1c. Type **399**	10	10
1278	2c. Agate	10	10
1279	3c. Iron pyrites	10	10
1280	4c. Amethyst	15	10
1281	5c. Carnelian	15	10
1282	9c. Native sulphur	20	10

(b) Fruits. Multicoloured.

1283	10c. Type **399a**	50	10
1284	20c. Citrus fruit	35	10
1285	30c. Nectarines	30	10
1286	40c. Apples	35	10
1287	50c. Kiwifruit	40	10

(c) Native Birds. Multicoloured.

1288	30c. Kakapo	60	25
1289	40c. Mountain ("Blue") duck	60	35
1290	45c. New Zealand falcon	1·25	35
1291	60c. New Zealand teal	2·25	1·50
1292	$1 Type **399b**	1·00	30
1293	$2 Chatham Island robin	1·00	50
1294	$3 Stitchbird	1·25	1·40
1295	$4 Saddleback	1·50	2·00
1296	$5 Takahe	3·75	3·25
1297	$10 Little spotted kiwi	4·00	6·00

400 Old Arts Building, Auckland University

1983. Commemorations. Multicoloured.

1303	24c. Salvation Army Centenary logo	20	10
1304	30c. Type **400**	20	40
1305	35c. Stylized kangaroo and kiwi	20	40
1306	40c. Rainbow trout	25	55
1307	45c. Satellite over Earth	25	55

COMMEMORATIONS: 24c. Salvation Army centenary; 30c. Auckland University centenary; 35c. Closer Economic Relationship agreement with Australia; 40c. Centenary of introduction of rainbow trout into New Zealand; 45c. World Communications Year.

401 Queen Elizabeth II

1983. Commonwealth Day. Multicoloured.

1308	24c. Type **401**	20	10
1309	35c. Maori rock drawing	30	50
1310	40c. Woolmark and woolscouring symbols	30	80
1311	45c. Coat of arms	30	80

402 "Boats, Island Bay" (Rita Angus)

1983. Paintings by Rita Angus. Multicoloured.

1312	24c. Type **402**	20	10
1313	30c. "Central Otago Landscape"	25	45
1314	35c. "Wanaka Landscape"	30	50
1315	45c. "Tree"	35	70

403 Mt. Egmont

1983. Beautiful New Zealand. Multicoloured.

1316	35c. Type **403**	20	35
1317	40c. Cooks Bay	25	40
1318	45c. Lake Matheson (horiz)	25	45
1319	70c. Lake Alexandrina (horiz)	40	70

404 Tabby

1983. Health Stamps. Cats. Multicoloured.

1320	24c.+2c. Type **404**	35	75
1321	24c.+2c. Siamese	35	75
1322	30c.+2c. Persian	50	1·00
MS1323	100×126 mm. Nos. 1320/2, each×2	1·75	3·00

405 "The Family of the Holy Oak Tree" (Raphael)

1983. Christmas. Multicoloured.

1324	18c. Type **405**	15	10
1325	35c. St. Patrick's Church, Greymouth	30	45
1326	45c. "The Glory of Christmas"	35	80

406 Geology

1984. Antarctic Research. Multicoloured.

1327	24c. Type **406**	25	10
1328	40c. Biology	30	40
1329	58c. Glaciology	50	1·60
1330	70c. Meteorology	45	90
MS1331	126×110 mm. Nos. 1327/30	1·50	3·50

407 "Mountaineer", Lake Wakatipu

1984. New Zealand Ferry Boats. Multicoloured.

1332	24c. Type **407**	20	10
1333	40c. "Waikana", Otago	25	45
1334	58c. "Britannia", Waitemata	30	1·40
1335	70c. "Wakatere", Firth of Thames	45	85

408 Mount Hutt

1984. Ski-slope Scenery. Multicoloured.

1336	35c. Type **408**	20	25
1337	40c. Coronet Park	25	30
1338	45c. Turoa	25	30
1339	70c. Whakapapa	40	75

409 Hamilton's Frog

1984. Amphibians and Reptiles. Multicoloured.

1340	24c. Type **409**	20	30
1341	24c. Great Barrier skink	20	30
1342	30c. Harlequin gecko	20	35
1343	58c. Otago skink	30	70
1344	70c. Gold-striped gecko	40	75

410 Clydesdales ploughing

1984. Health Stamps. Horses. Multicoloured.

1345	24c.+2c. Type **410**	40	75
1346	24c.+2c. Shetland ponies	40	75
1347	30c.+2c. Thoroughbreds	40	75
MS1348	148×75 mm. Nos. 1345/7, each×2	1·75	3·25

411 "Adoration of the Shepherds" (Lorenzo di Credi)

1984. Christmas. Multicoloured.

1349	18c. Type **411**	15	10
1350	35c. Old St. Paul's, Wellington (vert)	20	30
1351	45c. "The Joy of Christmas" (vert)	30	70

412 Mounted Riflemen, South Africa, 1901

1984. New Zealand Military History. Mult.

1352	24c. Type **412**	20	10
1353	40c. Engineers, France, 1917	30	45
1354	58c. Tanks of 2nd N.Z. Divisional Cavalry, North Africa, 1942	40	1·50
1355	70c. Infantryman in jungle kit, and 25-pounder gun, Korea and South-East Asia, 1950–72	45	90
MS1356	122×106 mm. Nos. 1352/5	1·00	2·25

413 St. John Ambulance Badge

1985. Centenary of St. John Ambulance in New Zealand.

1357	**413**	24c. black, gold and red	20	15
1358	**413**	30c. black, silver and blue	25	45
1359	**413**	40c. black and grey	30	1·10

The colours of the badge depicted are those for Bailiffs and Dames Grand Cross (24c.), Knights and Dames of Grace (30c.) and Commanders, Officer Brothers and Sisters (40c.).

414 Nelson Horse Tram, 1862

1985. Vintage Trams. Multicoloured.

1360	24c. Type **414**	30	10
1361	30c. Graham's Town steam tram, 1871	35	60
1362	35c. Dunedin cable car, 1881	35	70
1363	40c. Auckland electric tram, 1902	35	70
1364	45c. Wellington electric tram, 1904	35	90
1365	58c. Christchurch electric tram, 1905	40	1·75

415 Shotover Bridge

1985. Bridges of New Zealand. Multicoloured.

1366	35c. Type **415**	35	60
1367	40c. Alexandra Bridge	35	60
1368	45c. South Rangitikei Railway Bridge (vert)	40	1·25
1369	70c. Twin Bridges (vert)	55	1·25

416 Queen Elizabeth II (from photo by Camera Press)

1985. Multicoloured, background colours given.

1370	**416**	25c. red	35	10
1371	**416**	35c. blue	65	10

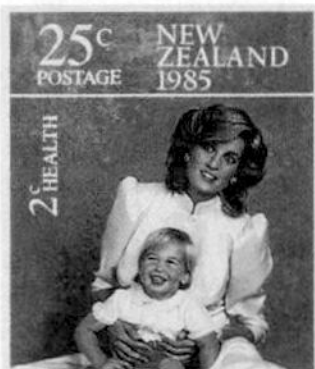

417 Princess of Wales and Prince William

1985. Health Stamps. Designs showing photographs by Lord Snowdon. Multicoloured.

1372	25c.+2c. Type **417**	90	1·25
1373	25c.+2c. Princess of Wales and Prince Henry	90	1·25
1374	35c.+2c. Prince and Princess of Wales with Princes William and Henry	90	1·25
MS1375	118×84 mm. Nos. 1372/4, each×2	4·25	6·00

418 The Holy Family in the Stable

1985. Christmas. Multicoloured.

1376	18c. Type **418**	20	10
1377	40c. The shepherds	45	85
1378	50c. The angels	45	1·00

419 H.M.N.Z.S. "Philomel" (1914–47)

1985. New Zealand Naval History. Multicoloured.

1379	25c. Type **419**	60	15
1380	45c. H.M.N.Z.S. "Achilles" (1936–46)	80	1·40
1381	60c. H.M.N.Z.S. "Rotoiti" (1949–65)	1·10	2·00
1382	75c. H.M.N.Z.S. "Canterbury" (from 1971)	1·40	2·25
MS1383	124×108 mm. Nos. 1379/82	3·50	5·25

420 Police Computer Operator

1986. Centenary of New Zealand Police. Designs showing historical aspects above modern police activities. Multicoloured.

1384	25c. Type **420**	35	55
1385	25c. Detective and mobile control room	35	55
1386	25c. Policewoman and badge	35	55
1387	25c. Forensic scientist, patrol car and policeman with child	35	55
1388	25c. Police College, Porirua, "Lady Elizabeth II" (patrol boat) and dog handler	35	55

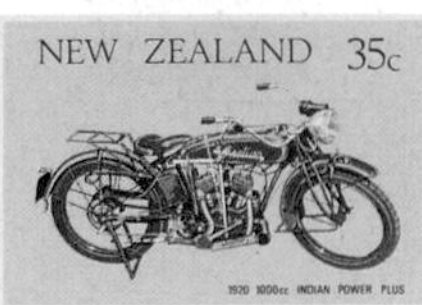

421 Indian "Power Plus" 1000cc Motor Cycle (1920)

1986. Vintage Motor Cycles. Multicoloured.

1389	35c. Type **421**	40	45
1390	45c. Norton "CS1" 500cc (1927)	45	65
1391	60c. B.S.A. "Sloper". 500cc (1930)	55	1·50
1392	75c. Triumph "Model H" 550cc (1915)	60	1·75

422 Tree of Life

1986. International Peace Year. Multicoloured.

1393	25c. Type **422**	30	30
1394	25c. Peace dove	30	30

423 Knights Point

1986. Coastal Scenery. Multicoloured.

1395	55c. Type **423**	55	55
1396	60c. Becks Bay	55	70
1397	65c. Doubtless Bay	60	1·00
1398	80c. Wainui Bay	75	1·00
MS1399	124×99 mm. No. 1398 (sold at $1.20)	1·00	1·25

424 "Football" (Kylie Epapara)

1986. Health Stamps. Children's Paintings (1st series). Multicoloured.

1400	30c.+3c. Type **424**	40	65
1401	30c.+3c. "Children at Play" (Philip Kata)	40	65
1402	45c.+3c. "Children Skipping" (Mia Flannery) (horiz)	50	65
MS1403	144×81 mm. Nos. 1400/2, each×2	2·25	2·75

See also Nos. 1433/5.

425 "A Partridge in a Pear Tree"

1986. Christmas. "The Twelve Days of Christmas" (carol). Multicoloured.

1404	25c. Type **425**	20	10
1405	55c. "Two turtle doves"	45	55
1406	65c. "Three French hens"	50	1·00

426 Conductor and Orchestra

1986. Music in New Zealand.

1407	**426**	30c. multicoloured	25	10
1408	-	60c. black, blue & orange	45	70
1409	-	80c. multicoloured	70	1·75
1410	-	$1 multicoloured	80	1·25

DESIGNS: 60c. Cornet and brass band; 80c. Piper and Highland pipe band; $1 Guitar and country music group.

427 Jetboating

1987. Tourism. Multicoloured.

1411	60c. Type **427**	50	50
1412	70c. Sightseeing flights	60	60
1413	80c. Camping	70	75
1414	85c. Windsurfing	70	85
1415	$1.05 Mountaineering	90	1·10
1416	$1.30 River rafting	1·10	1·40

428 Southern Cross Cup

1987. Yachting Events. Designs showing yachts. Multicoloured.

1417	40c. Type **428**	35	15
1418	80c. Admiral's Cup	50	80
1419	$1.05 Kenwood Cup	60	1·25
1420	$1.30 America's Cup	70	1·40

429 Hand writing Letter and Postal Transport

1987. New Zealand Post Ltd Vesting Day. Mult.

1421	40c. Type **429**	1·00	1·50
1422	40c. Posting letter, train and mailbox	1·00	1·50

430 Avro Type 626 and Wigram Airfield, 1937

1987. 50th Anniv of Royal New Zealand Air Force. Multicoloured.

1423	40c. Type **430**	65	15
1424	70c. Curtiss Kittyhawk I over World War II Pacific airstrip	90	1·75
1425	80c. Short S25 Sunderland flying boat and Pacific lagoon	1·00	1·75
1426	85c. Douglas A-4F Skyhawk and Mt. Ruapehu	1·10	1·60
MS1427	115×105 mm. Nos. 1423/6	5·00	6·00

431 Urewera National Park and Fern Leaf

1987. Centenary of National Parks Movement. Multicoloured.

1428	70c. Type **431**	50	55
1429	80c. Mt. Cook and buttercup	55	60
1430	85c. Fiordland and pineapple shrub	55	65
1431	$1.30 Tongariro and tussock	80	95
MS1432	123×99 mm. No. 1431 (sold at $1.70)	1·00	1·75

432 "Kite Flying" (Lauren Baldwin)

1987. Health Stamps. Children's Paintings (2nd series). Multicoloured.

1433	40c.+3c. Type **432**	80	1·50
1434	40c.+3c. "Swimming" (Ineke Schoneveld)	80	1·50
1435	60c.+3c. "Horse Riding" (Aaron Tylee) (vert)	1·25	1·50
MS1436	100×117 mm. Nos. 1433/5, each×2	5·00	7·00

433 "Hark the Herald Angels Sing"

1987. Christmas. Multicoloured.

1437	35c. Type **433**	30	10
1438	70c. "Away in a Manger"	65	70
1439	85c. "We Three Kings of Orient Are"	80	85

434 Knot ("Pona")

1987. Maori Fibre-work. Multicoloured.

1440		40c. Type **434**	25	10
1441		60c. Binding ("Herehere")	35	55
1442		80c. Plait ("Whiri")	45	1·25
1443		85c. Cloak weaving ("Korowai") with flax fibre ("Whitau")	50	1·40

435 "Geothermal"

1988. Centenary of Electricity. Each shows radiating concentric circles representing energy generation.

1444	**435**	40c. multicoloured	25	10
1445	-	60c. black, red and brown	35	45
1446	-	70c. multicoloured	40	75
1447	-	80c. multicoloured	40	65

DESIGNS: 60c. "Thermal"; 70c. "Gas"; 80c. "Hydro".

436 Queen Elizabeth II and 1882 Queen Victoria 1d. Stamp

1988. Centenary of Royal Philatelic Society of New Zealand. Multicoloured.

1448		40c. Type **436**	35	75
1449		40c. As Type **436**, but 1882 Queen Victoria 2d.	35	75
MS1450		107×160 mm. $1 "Queen Victoria" (Chalon) (vert)	3·00	3·50

437 "Mangopare"

1988. Maori Rafter Paintings. Multicoloured.

1451		40c. Type **437**	30	45
1452		40c. "Koru"	30	45
1453		40c. "Raupunga"	30	45
1454		60c. "Koiri"	45	75

438 "Good Luck"

1988. Greetings Stamps. Multicoloured.

1455		40c. Type **438**	85	1·00
1456		40c. "Keeping in touch"	85	1·00
1457		40c. "Happy birthday"	85	1·00
1458		40c. "Congratulations" (41×27 mm)	85	1·00
1459		40c. "Get well soon" (41×27 mm)	85	1·00

439 Paradise Shelduck

1988. Native Birds. Multicoloured.

1459a		5c. Sooty crake	15	50
1460		10c. Double-banded plover	15	40
1461		20c. Yellowhead	20	35
1462		30c. Grey-backed white-eye ("Silvereye")	30	30
1463		40c. Brown kiwi	35	40
1463b		45c. Rock wren	50	50
1464		50c. Sacred kingfisher	50	60
1465		60c. Spotted cormorant ("Spotted shag")	50	70
1466		70c. Type **439**	80	1·25
1467		80c. Victoria penguin ("Fiordland Crested Penguin")	1·00	1·25
1467a		80c. New Zealand falcon	1·00	1·50
1468		90c. New Zealand robin	1·25	1·50

The 40 and 45c. also exist self-adhesive.

440 Milford Track

1988. Scenic Walking Trails. Multicoloured.

1469		70c. Type **440**	35	60
1470		80c. Heaphy Track	40	75
1471		85c. Copland Track	40	80
1472		$1.30 Routeburn Track	60	1·25
MS1473		124×99 mm. No. 1472 (sold at $1.70)	1·50	1·50

441 Kiwi and Koala at Campfire

1988. Bicentenary of Australian Settlement.

1474	**441**	40c. multicoloured	40	50

A stamp in a similar design was also issued by Australia.

442 Swimming

1988. Health Stamps. Olympic Games, Seoul. Mult.

1475		40c.+3c. Type **442**	40	70
1476		60c.+3c. Athletics	60	1·10
1477		70c.+3c. Canoeing	70	1·10
1478		80c.+3c. Show-jumping	90	1·40
MS1479		120×90 mm. Nos. 1475/8	3·25	4·50

443 "O Come All Ye Faithful"

1988. Christmas. Carols. Designs showing illuminated verses. Multicoloured.

1480		35c. Type **443**	30	15
1481		70c. "Hark the Herald Angels Sing"	50	65
1482		80c. "Ding Dong Merrily on High"	50	90
1483		85c. "The First Nowell"	55	1·10

444 "Lake Pukaki" (John Gully)

1988. New Zealand Heritage (1st issue). "The Land". Designs showing 19th-century paintings. Multicoloured.

1484		40c. Type **444**	25	20
1485		60c. "On the Grass Plain below Lake Arthur" (William Fox)	35	45
1486		70c. "View of Auckland" (John Hoyte)	45	70
1487		80c. "Mt. Egmont from the Southward" (Charles Heaphy)	50	70
1488		$1.05 "Anakiwa, Queen Charlotte Sound" (John Kinder)	60	1·40
1489		$1.30 "White Terraces, Lake Rotomahana", (Charles Barraud)	70	1·60

See also Nos. 1505/10, 1524/9, 1541/6, 1548/53 and 1562/7.

445 Brown Kiwi

1988

1490	**445**	$1 green	2·00	3·50
1490b	**445**	$1 red	2·25	3·25
1490c	**445**	$1 blue	1·00	1·75
2090	**445**	$1 violet	1·00	1·00
2090a	**445**	$1.10 gold	1·00	1·75
2090b	**445**	£1.50 brown	1·10	1·25

See also Nos. **MS**1745, **MS**1786 and **MS**2342.

446 Humpback Whale and Calf

1988. Whales. Multicoloured.

1491		60c. Type **446**	80	85
1492		70c. Killer whales	90	1·10
1493		80c. Southern right whale	90	1·25
1494		85c. Blue whale	95	1·50
1495		$1.05 Southern bottlenose whale and calf	1·25	2·00
1496		$1.30 Sperm whale	1·40	2·25

Although inscribed "ROSS DEPENDENCY" Nos. 1491/6 were available from post offices throughout New Zealand.

447 Clover

1989. Wild Flowers. Multicoloured.

1497		40c. Type **447**	40	20
1498		60c. Lotus	50	65
1499		70c. Montbretia	60	1·25
1500		80c. Wild ginger	70	1·25

448 Katherine Mansfield

1989. New Zealand Authors. Multicoloured.

1501		40c. Type **448**	25	15
1502		60c. James K. Baxter	35	50
1503		70c. Bruce Mason	40	70
1504		80c. Ngaio Marsh	40	75

449 Moriori Man and Map of Chatham Islands

1989. New Zealand Heritage (2nd Issue). The People.

1505	**449**	40c. multicoloured	50	25
1506	-	60c. brown, grey and deep brown	75	75
1507	-	70c. green, grey and deep green	55	90
1508	-	80c. blue, grey and deep blue	1·25	90
1509	-	$1.05 grey, light grey and black	75	1·60
1510	-	$1.30 red, grey and brown	90	2·00

DESIGNS: 60c. Gold prospector; 70c. Settler ploughing; 80c. Whaling; $1.05, Missionary preaching to Maoris; $1.30, Maori village.

450 White Pine (Kahikatea)

1989. Native Trees. Multicoloured.

1511		80c. Type **450**	45	80
1512		85c. Red pine (Rimu)	45	85
1513		$1.05 Totara	60	1·10
1514		$1.30 Kauri	65	1·40
MS1515		102×125 mm. No. 1514 (sold at $1.80)	1·50	1·75

451 Duke and Duchess of York with Princess Beatrice

1989. Health Stamps. Multicoloured.

1516		40c.+3c. Type **451**	80	1·50
1517		40c.+3c. Duchess of York with Princess Beatrice	80	1·50
1518		80c.+3c. Princess Beatrice	1·40	1·75
MS1519		120×89 mm. Nos. 1516/18, each×2	5·50	7·50

452 One Tree Hill, Auckland through Bedroom Window

1989. Christmas. Designs showing Star of Bethlehem. Multicoloured.

1520		35c. Type **452**	30	15
1521		65c. Shepherd and dog in mountain valley	65	70
1522		80c. Star over harbour	75	1·10
1523		$1 Star over globe	1·00	1·40

453 Windsurfing

1989. New Zealand Heritage (3rd issue). The Sea. Multicoloured.

1524		40c. Type **453**	50	25
1525		60c. Fishes of many species	85	70
1526		65c. Striped marlin and game fishing launch	90	85
1527		80c. Rowing boat and yachts in harbour	1·00	90
1528		$1 Coastal scene	1·25	1·10
1529		$1.50 "Rotoiti" (container ship) and tug	1·90	2·25

454 Games Logo

1989. 14th Commonwealth Games, Auckland. Mult.

1530	40c. Type **454**	30	30
1531	40c. Goldie (games kiwi mascot)	30	30
1532	40c. Gymnastics	30	30
1533	50c. Weightlifting	35	35
1534	65c. Swimming	40	45
1535	80c. Cycling	80	70
1536	$1 Lawn bowling	70	90
1537	$1.80 Hurdling	1·25	1·75
MS1538	Two sheets, each 105×92 mm, with different margin designs. (a) Nos. 1530/1 (horiz pair). (b) Nos. 1530/1 (vert pair) Set of 2 sheets	5·00	5·50

455 Short S.30 modified "G" Class Flying Boat "Aotearoa" and Boeing 747-200

1990. 50th Anniv of Air New Zealand.

1539	**455**	80c. multicoloured	1·40	1·10

456 Chief Kawiti signing Treaty

1990. 150th Anniv of Treaty of Waitangi. Sheet 80×118 mm, containing T 456 and similar multicoloured design.

MS1540	40c. Type **456**; 40c. Chief Hone Heke (first signatory) and Lieut-Governor Hobson (horiz)	2·50	3·75

457 Maori Voyaging Canoe

1990. New Zealand Heritage (4th issue). The Ships. Multicoloured.

1541	40c. Type **457**	60	25
1542	50c. H.M.S. "Endeavour" (Cook), 1769	85	80
1543	60c. "Tory" (barque), 1839	95	1·00
1544	80c. "Crusader" (full-rigged immigrant ship), 1871	1·40	1·50
1545	$1 "Edwin Fox" (full-rigged immigrant ship), 1873	1·60	1·50
1546	$1.50 "Arawa" (steamer), 1884	2·00	3·00

458 *Thelymitra pulchella*

1990. "New Zealand 1990" International Stamp Exhibition, Auckland. Native Orchids. Sheet 179×80 mm, containing T 458 and similar vert designs. Multicoloured.

MS1547	40c. Type **458**; 40c. "Corybas macranthus"; 40c. "Dendrobium cunninghamii"; 40c. "Pterostylis banksii"; 80c. "Aporostylis bifolia" (sold at $4.90)	4·50	4·50

The stamps in No. **MS**1547 form a composite design.

459 Grace Neill (social reformer) and Maternity Hospital, Wellington

1990. New Zealand Heritage (5th issue). Famous New Zealanders. Multicoloured.

1548	40c. Type **459**	55	30
1549	50c. Jean Batten (pilot) and Percival P.3 Gull Six aircraft	65	85
1550	60c. Katherine Sheppard (suffragette) and 19th-century women	70	1·50
1551	80c. Richard Pearse (inventor) and early flying machine	90	1·50
1552	$1 Lt.-Gen. Sir Bernard Freyberg and tank	1·10	1·50
1553	$1.50 Peter Buck (politician) and Maori pattern	1·25	2·50

460 Akaroa

1990. 150th Anniv of European Settlements. Mult.

1554	80c. Type **460**	5·00	70
1555	$1 Wanganui	70	75
1556	$1.50 Wellington	1·10	2·25
1557	$1.80 Takapuna Beach, Auckland	1·25	2·25
MS1558	125×100 mm. No. 1557 (sold at $2.30)	3·50	3·50

461 Jack Lovelock (athlete) and Race

1990. Health Stamps. Sportsmen (1st series). Mult.

1559	40c.+5c. Type **461**	70	1·00
1560	80c.+5c. George Nepia (rugby player) and match	90	1·75
MS1561	115×96 mm. Nos. 1559/60, each×2	3·25	5·00

See also Nos. 1687/8.

462 Creation Legend of Rangi and Papa

1990. New Zealand Heritage (6th issue). The Maori. Multicoloured.

1562	40c. Type **462**	35	30
1563	50c. Pattern from Maori feather cloak	45	80
1564	60c. Maori women's choir	50	90
1565	80c. Maori facial tattoos	60	1·00
1566	$1 War canoe prow (detail)	70	1·25
1567	$1.50 Maori haka	1·10	2·75

463 Queen Victoria

1990. 150th Anniv of the Penny Black. Sheet 169×70 mm, containing T 463 and similar vert designs.

MS1568	40c.×6 blue (Type **463**, King Edward VII, King George V, King Edward VIII, King George VI, Queen Elizabeth II)	4·25	5·50

464 Angel

1990. Christmas.

1569	**464**	40c. purple, blue & brn	30	10
1570	-	$1 purple, green & brown	70	50
1571	-	$1.50 purple, red & brown	1·10	2·50
1572	-	$1.80 purple, red & brown	1·25	2·50

DESIGNS: $1 to $1.80, Different angels.

465 Antarctic Petrel

1990. Antarctic Birds. Multicoloured.

1573	40c. Type **465**	80	30
1574	50c. Wilson's storm petrel	90	75
1575	60c. Snow petrel	1·10	1·25
1576	80c. Southern fulmar	1·25	1·25
1577	$1 Bearded penguin ("Chinstrap Penguin")	1·40	1·25
1578	$1.50 Emperor penguin	1·60	3·50

Although inscribed "Ross Dependency" Nos. 1573/8 were available from post offices throughout New Zealand.

466 Coopworth Ewe and Lambs

1991. New Zealand Farming and Agriculture. Sheep Breeds. Multicoloured.

1579	40c. Type **466**	35	20
1580	60c. Perendale	45	60
1581	80c. Corriedale	60	70
1582	$1 Drysdale	75	75
1583	$1.50 South Suffolk	1·00	2·50
1584	$1.80 Romney	1·25	2·50

467 Moriori, Royal Albatross, Nikau Palm and Artefacts

1991. Bicentenary of Discovery of Chatham Islands. Multicoloured.

1585	40c. Type **467**	75	50
1586	80c. Carvings, H.M.S. "Chatham", Moriori house of 1870, and Tommy Solomon	1·50	2·25

468 Goal and Footballers

1991. Centenary of New Zealand Football Association. Multicoloured.

1587	80c. Type **468**	1·10	1·75
1588	80c. Five footballers and referee	1·10	1·75

Nos. 1587/8 were printed together, se-tenant, forming a composite design.

469 Tuatara on Rocks

1991. Endangered Species. The Tuatara. Mult.

1590	40c. Type **469**	40	60
1591	40c. Tuatara in crevice	40	60
1592	40c. Tuatara with foliage	40	60
1593	40c. Tuatara in dead leaves	40	60

470 Clown

1991. "Happy Birthday". Multicoloured.

1594	40c. Type **470**	75	85
1595	40c. Balloons	75	85
1596	40c. Party hat	75	85
1597	40c. Birthday present (41×27 mm)	75	85
1598	40c. Birthday cake (41×27 mm)	75	85
1599	45c. Type **470**	75	85
1600	45c. As No. 1595	75	85
1601	45c. As No. 1596	75	85
1602	45c. As No. 1597	75	85
1603	45c. As No. 1598	75	85

471 Cat at Window

1991. "Thinking of You". Multicoloured.

1604	40c. Type **471**	75	85
1605	40c. Cat playing with slippers	75	85
1606	40c. Cat with alarm clock	75	85
1607	40c. Cat in window (41×27 mm)	75	85
1608	40c. Cat at door (41×27 mm)	75	85
1609	45c. Type **471**	75	85
1610	45c. As No. 1605	75	85
1611	45c. As No. 1606	75	85
1612	45c. As No. 1607	75	85
1613	45c. As No. 1608	75	85

472 Punakaiki Rocks

1991. Scenic Landmarks. Multicoloured.

1614	40c. Type **472**	40	30
1615	50c. Moeraki Boulders	55	55
1616	80c. Organ Pipes	85	85
1617	$1 Castle Hill	95	95
1618	$1.50 Te Kaukau Point	1·50	1·60
1619	$1.80 Ahuriri River Clay Cliffs	1·75	1·90

473 Dolphins Underwater

1991. Health Stamps. Hector's Dolphin. Mult.

1620	45c.+5c. Type **473**	90	1·25
1621	80c.+5c. Dolphins leaping	1·25	2·00
MS1622	115×100 mm. Nos. 1620/1, each×2	5·00	6·50

474 Children's Rugby

1991. World Cup Rugby Championship. Mult.

1623	80c. Type **474**	75	1·00
1624	$1 Women's rugby	80	75
1625	$1.50 Senior rugby	1·50	2·75
1626	$1.80 "All Blacks" (national team)	1·75	2·75
MS1627	113×90 mm. No. 1626 (sold at $2.40)	3·25	5·00

475 "Three Shepherds"

1991. Christmas. Multicoloured.

1628	45c. Type **475**	55	80
1629	45c. Two Kings on camels	55	80
1630	45c. Mary and Baby Jesus	55	80
1631	45c. King with gift	55	80
1632	65c. Star of Bethlehem	70	80
1633	$1 Crown	85	95
1634	$1.50 Angel	1·40	2·25

476 "Dodonidia helmsii"

1991. Butterflies. Multicoloured.

1635	$1 Type **476**	1·00	60
1641	$2 "Zizina otis oxleyi"	2·50	1·75
1642	$3 "Vanessa itea"	3·25	3·00
1643	$4 "Lycaena salustius"	2·50	3·00
1644	$5 "Bassaris gonerilla"	4·75	4·50

479 Yacht "Kiwi Magic", 1987

1992. New Zealand Challenge for America's Cup. Multicoloured.

1655	45c. Type **479**	45	20
1656	80c. Yacht "New Zealand", 1988	80	70
1657	$1 Yacht "America", 1851	95	85
1658	$1.50 "America's Cup" Class yacht, 1992	1·60	1·60

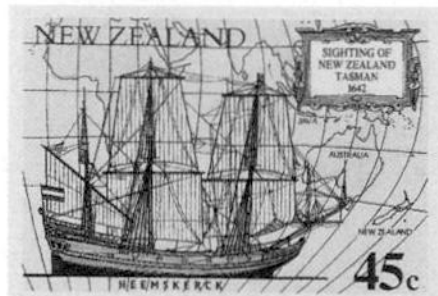

480 "Heemskerk"

1992. Great Voyages of Discovery. Mult.

1659	45c. Type **480**	55	25
1660	80c. "Zeehan"	90	1·10
1661	$1 "Santa Maria"	1·25	1·10
1662	$1.50 "Pinta" and "Nina"	1·50	2·50

Nos. 1659/60 commemorate the 350th anniv of Tasman's discovery of New Zealand and Nos. 1661/2 the 500th anniv of discovery of America by Columbus.

481 Sprinters

1992. Olympic Games, Barcelona (1st issue).

1663	**481** 45c. multicoloured	50	50

See also Nos. 1670/3.

482 Weddell Seal and Pup

1992. Antarctic Seals. Multicoloured.

1664	45c. Type **482**	70	30
1665	50c. Crabeater seals swimming	80	60
1666	65c. Leopard seal and Adelie penguins	1·00	1·50
1667	80c. Ross seal	1·25	1·25
1668	$1 Southern elephant seal and harem	1·40	1·25
1669	$1.80 Hooker's sea lion and pup	2·25	3·50

Although inscribed "ROSS DEPENDENCY" Nos. 1664/9 were available from post offices throughout New Zealand.

483 Cycling

1992. Olympic Games, Barcelona (2nd issue). Multicoloured.

1670	45c. Type **483**	65	35
1671	80c. Archery	90	70
1672	$1 Equestrian three-day eventing	1·00	85
1673	$1.50 Sailboarding	1·50	1·40
MS1674	125×100 mm. Nos. 1670/3	4·00	5·00

484 Ice Pinnacles, Franz Josef Glacier

1992. Glaciers. Multicoloured.

1675	45c. Type **484**	40	25
1676	50c. Tasman Glacier	50	45
1677	80c. Snowball Glacier, Marion Plateau	70	70
1678	$1 Brewster Glacier	85	85
1679	$1.50 Fox Glacier	1·40	1·60
1680	$1.80 Franz Josef Glacier	1·50	1·60

485 "Grand Finale" Camellia

1992. Camellias. Multicoloured.

1681	45c. Type **485**	60	25
1682	50c. "Showa-No-Sakae"	70	60
1683	80c. "Sugar Dream"	90	80
1684	$1 "Night Rider"	1·10	85
1685	$1.50 "E.G. Waterhouse"	1·50	2·75
1686	$1.80 "Dr. Clifford Parks"	1·75	3·00

1992. Health Stamps. Sportsmen (2nd series). As T 461. Multicoloured.

1687	45c.+5c. Anthony Wilding (tennis player) and match	1·00	1·25
1688	80c.+5c. Stewie Dempster (cricketer) and batsman	1·00	1·50
MS1689	115×96 mm. Nos. 1687/8, each×2	4·50	5·50

486 Tree and Hills

1992. Landscapes. Multicoloured.

1690	45c. Type **486**	60	65
1691	45c. River and hills	60	65
1692	45c. Hills and mountain	60	65
1693	45c. Glacier	60	65
1694	45c. Hills and waterfall	60	65
1695	45c. Tree and beach	60	65
1696	45c. Estuary and cliffs	60	65
1697	45c. Fjord	60	65
1698	45c. River delta	60	65
1699	45c. Ferns and beach	60	65

487 Reindeer over Houses

1992. Christmas. Multicoloured.

1700	45c. Type **487**	90	1·25
1701	45c. Santa Claus on sleigh over houses	90	1·25
1702	45c. Christmas tree in window	90	1·25
1703	45c. Christmas wreath and children at window	90	1·25
1704	65c. Candles and fireplace	1·10	90
1705	$1 Family going to church	1·40	1·00
1706	$1.50 Picnic under Pohutukawa tree	2·00	3·50

488 1920s Fashions

1992. New Zealand in the 1920s. Multicoloured.

1707	45c. Type **488**	50	20
1708	50c. Dr. Robert Jack and early radio announcer	55	65
1709	80c. "All Blacks" rugby player, 1924	85	1·00
1710	$1 Swaggie and dog	95	1·00
1711	$1.50 Ford "Model A" car and young couple	1·75	2·25
1712	$1.80 Amateur aviators and biplane	2·00	2·75

489 "Old Charley" Toby Jug

1993. Royal Doulton Ceramics Exhibition, New Zealand. Multicoloured.

1713	45c. Type **489**	50	20
1714	50c. "Bunnykins" nursery plate	55	60
1715	80c. "Maori Art" tea set	85	85
1716	$1 "Ophelia" handpainted plate	1·00	90
1717	$1.50 "St. George" figurine	1·60	2·50
1718	$1.80 "Lambeth" salt-glazed stoneware vase	1·90	2·50
MS1719	125×100 mm. No. 1718	1·60	2·50

490 Women's Fashions of the 1930s

1993. New Zealand in the 1930s. Multicoloured.

1720	45c. Type **490**	50	15
1721	50c. Unemployed protest march	55	60
1722	80c. "Phar Lap" (racehorse)	85	85
1723	$1 State housing project	85	75
1724	$1.50 Boys drinking free school milk	1·50	3·00
1725	$1.80 Cinema queue	1·60	2·75

491 Women signing Petition

1993. Centenary of Women's Suffrage. Mult.

1726	45c. Type **491**	40	10
1727	80c. Aircraft propeller and woman on tractor	75	75
1728	$1 Housewife with children	75	75
1729	$1.50 Modern women	1·25	2·25

492 Champagne Pool

1993. Thermal Wonders, Rotorua. Multicoloured.

1730	45c. Type **492**	60	20
1731	50c. Boiling mud	60	40
1732	80c. Emerald pool	85	70
1733	$1 Hakereteke Falls	95	80
1734	$1.50 Warbrick Terrace	1·50	1·75
1735	$1.80 Pohutu Geyser	1·60	1·75

See also No. **MS**1770.

493 Yellow-eyed Penguin, Hector's Dolphin and New Zealand Fur Seal

1993. Endangered Species Conservation. Mult.

1736	45c. Type **493**	85	1·25
1737	45c. Taiko (bird), Mount Cook lily and mountain duck ("Blue Duck")	85	1·25
1738	45c. Giant snail, rock wren and Hamilton's frog	85	1·25
1739	45c. Kaka (bird), New Zealand pigeon and giant weta	85	1·25
1740	45c. Tusked weta (23×28 mm)	85	1·25

494 Boy with Puppy

1993. Health Stamps. Children's Pets. Mult.

1741	45c.+5c. Type **494**	60	90
1742	80c.+5c. Girl with kitten	90	1·50
MS1743	115×96 mm. Nos. 1741/2, each×2	2·75	4·25

1993. "Taipei '93" Asian International Stamp Exhibition, Taiwan. (a) No. MS1743 optd TAIPEI '93 and emblem on sheet margin. Mult.

MS1744	Nos. 1741/2, each×2	17·00	20·00

(b) Sheet 125×100 mm, containing Nos. 1490/c.

MS1745	**445** $1 green, $1 blue, $1 red	5·00	5·00

495 Christmas Decorations (value at left)

1993. Christmas. Multicoloured.

1746	45c. Type **495**	60	85
1747	45c. Christmas decorations (value at right)	60	85
1748	45c. Sailboards, gifts and Christmas pudding (value at left)	60	85
1749	45c. Sailboards, gifts and Christmas pudding (value at right)	60	85

1750 $1 Sailboards, baubles and Christmas cracker 1·50 1·25
1751 $1.50 Sailboards, present and wreath 2·00 3·25

496 Rainbow Abalone or Paua

1993. Marine Life. Multicoloured.
1752 45c. Type **496** 1·00 1·00
1753 45c. Green mussels 1·00 1·00
1754 45c. Tarakihi 1·00 1·00
1755 45c. Salmon 1·00 1·00
1756 45c. Southern blue-finned tuna, yellow-finned tuna and kahawai 1·00 1·00
1757 45c. Rock lobster 1·00 1·00
1758 45c. Snapper 1·00 1·00
1759 45c. Grouper 1·00 1·00
1760 45c. Orange roughy 1·00 1·00
1761 45c. Squid, hoki and black oreo 1·00 1·00

497 Sauropod

1993. Prehistoric Animals. Multicoloured.
1762 45c. Type **497** 60 45
1763 45c. Carnosaur and sauropod (30×25 mm) 75 60
1764 80c. Pterosaur 1·10 85
1765 $1 Ankylosaur 1·25 95
1766 $1.20 Mauisaurus 1·50 2·50
1767 $1.50 Carnosaur 1·60 2·50
MS1768 125×100 mm. $1.50 No. 1767 2·00 2·00

1993. "Bangkok '93" International Stamp Exhibition, Thailand. (a) No. MS1768 optd BANGKOK '93 and emblem on sheet margin. Multicoloured.
MS1769 $1.50 No. 1767 1·60 2·00

(b) Sheet 115×100 mm, containing No. 1735.
MS1770 $1.80 multicoloured 2·75 3·75

498 Soldiers, National Flag and Pyramids

1993. New Zealand in the 1940s. Multicoloured.
1771 45c. Type **498** 80 25
1772 50c. Aerial crop spraying 85 60
1773 80c. Hydro-electric scheme 1·10 80
1774 $1 Marching majorettes 1·40 90
1775 $1.50 American troops 1·90 2·00
1776 $1.80 Crowd celebrating victory 2·00 2·25

499 Bungy Jumping

1994. Tourism. Multicoloured.
1777 45c. Type **499** 40 25
1778 45c. White water rafting (25×25 mm) 40 55
1779 80c. Trout fishing 60 70
1780 $1 Jet boating (horiz) 70 80
1781 $1.50 Tramping 1·10 2·00
1782 $1.80 Heli-skiing 1·50 2·00
See also No. **MS**1785.

500 "New Zealand Endeavour" (yacht)

1994. Round the World Yacht Race.
1783 **500** $1 multicoloured 1·40 1·75

501 Mt. Cook and New Zealand Symbols

1994
1784 **501** $20 blue and gold 13·00 14·00

1994. "Hong Kong '94" International Stamp Exhibition. Multicoloured.
MS1785 95×115 mm. $1.80 No. 1782 3·50 3·50
MS1786 100×125 mm. $1×3 As Nos. 1490/c 4·50 5·00

503 Rock and Roll Dancers

1994. New Zealand in the 1950s. Multicoloured.
1787 45c. Type **503** 45 25
1788 80c. Sir Edmund Hillary on Mt. Everest 75 75
1789 $1 Aunt Daisy (radio personality) 85 85
1790 $1.20 Queen Elizabeth II during 1953 royal visit 1·25 1·25
1791 $1.50 Children playing with Opo the dolphin 1·60 2·00
1792 $1.80 Auckland Harbour Bridge 1·90 2·00

504 Mt. Cook and Mt. Cook Lily ("Winter")

1994. The Four Seasons. Multicoloured.
1793 45c. Type **504** 40 25
1794 70c. Lake Hawea and Kowhai ("Spring") 55 55
1795 $1.50 Opononi Beach and Pohutukawa ("Summer") 1·10 1·25
1796 $1.80 Lake Pukaki and Puriri ("Autumn") 1·40 1·50

505 Rainbow Abalone or Paua Shell

1994. New Zealand Life. Multicoloured.
1797 45c. Type **505** (25×20 mm) 40 45
1798 45c. Pavlova dessert (35×20 mm) 40 45
1799 45c. Hokey pokey ice cream (25×20 mm) 40 45
1800 45c. Fish and chips (35×20 mm) 40 45
1801 45c. Jandals (30×20 mm) 40 45
1802 45c. Bush shirt (25×30½ mm) 40 45
1803 45c. Buzzy Bee (toy) (35×30½ mm) 40 45
1804 45c. Gumboots and black singlet (25×30½ mm) 40 45
1805 45c. Rugby boots and ball (35×30½ mm) 40 45
1806 45c. Kiwifruit (30×30½ mm) 40 45
See also Nos. 2318/27.

506 Maui pulls up Te Ika

1994. Maori Myths. Multicoloured.
1807 45c. Type **506** 40 20
1808 80c. Rona snatched up by Marama 65 60
1809 $1 Maui attacking Tuna 75 65
1810 $1.20 Tane separating Rangi and Papa 1·00 1·75
1811 $1.50 Matakauri slaying the Giant of Wakatipu 1·10 1·75
1812 $1.80 Panenehu showing crayfish to Tangaroa 1·40 1·75

507 1939 2d. on 1d.+1d. Health Stamp and Children playing with Ball

1994. Health Stamps. 75th Anniv of Children's Health Camps. Multicoloured.
1813 45c.+5c. Type **507** 50 80
1814 45c.+5c. 1949 1d.+½d. stamp and nurse holding child 50 80
1815 45c.+5c. 1969 4c.+1c. stamp and children reading 50 80
1816 80c.+5c. 1931 2d.+1d. stamp and child in cap 75 1·00
MS1817 130×90 mm. Nos. 1813/16 2·00 3·25

508 Astronaut on Moon (hologram)

1994. 25th Anniv of First Manned Moon Landing.
1818 **508** $1.50 multicoloured 2·25 2·50

509 "people reaching people"

1994. Self-adhesive.
1818ab **509** 40c. multicoloured 75 55
1819 **509** 45c. multicoloured 1·00 65

510 African Elephants

1994. Stamp Month. Wild Animals. Multicoloured.
1820 45c. Type **510** 90 1·00
1821 45c. White rhinoceros 80 1·00
1822 45c. Lions 90 1·00
1823 45c. Common zebras 90 1·00
1824 45c. Giraffe and calf 90 1·00
1825 45c. Siberian tiger 90 1·00
1826 45c. Hippopotamuses 90 1·00
1827 45c. Spider monkey 90 1·00
1828 45c. Giant panda 90 1·00
1829 45c. Polar bear and cub 90 1·00

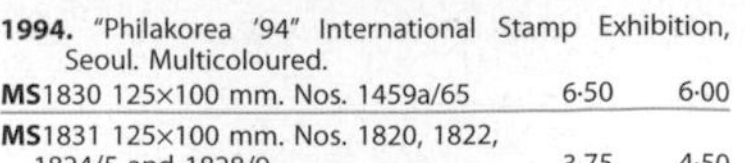
1994. "Philakorea '94" International Stamp Exhibition, Seoul. Multicoloured.
MS1830 125×100 mm. Nos. 1459a/65 6·50 6·00
MS1831 125×100 mm. Nos. 1820, 1822, 1824/5 and 1828/9 3·75 4·50

511 Children with Crib

1994. Christmas. Multicoloured.
1832 45c. Father Christmas and children (30×25 mm) 40 40
1833 45c. Type **511** 40 20
1834 70c. Man and toddler with crib 65 80
1835 80c. Three carol singers 70 85
1836 $1 Five carol singers 80 90
1837 $1.50 Children and candles 1·00 2·00
1838 $1.80 Parents with child 1·25 2·00
MS1839 125×100 mm. Nos. 1833/6 2·50 2·75

512 Batsman

1994. Centenary of New Zealand Cricket Council. (a) Horiz designs, each 30×25 mm. Multicoloured.
1840 45c. Bathers catching balls 75 80
1841 45c. Child on surf board at top 75 80
1842 45c. Young child with rubber ring at top 75 90
1843 45c. Man with beach ball at top 75 90
1844 45c. Woman with cricket bat at right 75 90
1845 45c. Boy in green cap with bat 75 90
1846 45c. Man in spotted shirt running 75 90
1847 45c. Woman in striped shorts with bat 75 90
1848 45c. Boy in wet suit with surf board at right 75 90
1849 45c. Sunbather with newspaper at right 75 80

(b) T 512 and similar vert designs. Multicoloured.
1850 45c. Type **512** 85 40
1851 80c. Bowler 1·50 80
1852 $1 Wicket keeper 1·75 1·00
1853 $1.80 Fielder 2·75 3·00

1995. "POST X '95" Postal History Exhibition, Auckland. Sheet 130×90 mm, containing No. 1297 and a reproduction of No. 557 optd "SPECIMEN".
MS1854 $10 multicoloured 18·00 18·00

513 Auckland

1995. New Zealand by Night. Multicoloured.
1855 45c. Type **513** 60 25
1856 80c. Wellington 90 65
1857 $1 Christchurch 1·25 85
1858 $1.20 Dunedin 1·40 1·40
1859 $1.50 Rotorua 1·50 1·60
1860 $1.80 Queenstown 1·75 1·60
See also No. **MS**1915.

514 The 15th Hole, Waitangi

1995. New Zealand Golf Courses. Multicoloured.

1861	45c. Type **514**	65	30
1862	80c. The 6th hole, New Plymouth	1·00	90
1863	$1.20 The 9th hole, Rotorua	1·50	2·50
1864	$1.80 The 5th hole, Queenstown	2·40	3·00

515 New Zealand Pigeon and Nest

1995. Environment. Multicoloured.

1865	45c. Type **515**	65	65
1866	45c. Planting sapling	65	65
1867	45c. Dolphins and whales	65	65
1868	45c. Thunderstorm	65	65
1869	45c. Backpackers	65	65
1870	45c. Animal pests	65	65
1871	45c. Noxious plants	65	65
1872	45c. Undersized fish and shellfish	65	65
1873	45c. Pollution from factories	65	65
1874	45c. Family at picnic site	65	65

516 Teacher with Guitar and Children

1995. Maori Language Year. Multicoloured.

1875	45c. Type **516**	40	20
1876	70c. Singing group	60	55
1877	80c. Mother and baby	65	60
1878	$1 Women performing traditional welcome	75	75
1879	$1.50 Grandfather reciting family genealogy	1·25	2·00
1880	$1.80 Tribal orator	1·50	2·00

517 Map of Australasia and Asia

1995. Meetings of Asian Development Bank Board of Governors and International Pacific Basin Economic Council, Auckland. Multicoloured.

1881	$1 Type **517**	1·25	1·00
1882	$1.50 Map of Australasia and Pacific	1·75	2·75

518 "Black Magic" (yacht)

1995. New Zealand's Victory in 1995 America's Cup.

1883	**518**	45c. multicoloured	55	55

519 Boy on Skateboard

1995. Health Stamps. Children's Sports. Mult.

1884	45c.+5c. Type **519**	75	1·25
1885	80c.+5c. Girl on bicyle	1·75	1·75
MS1886	130×90 mm. Nos. 1884/5, each×2	4·75	5·00

1995. "Stampex '95" National Stamp Exhibition, Wellington. No. MS1886 additionally inscr with "Stampex '95" and emblem on sheet margin. Mult.

MS1887	130×90 mm. Nos. 1884/5, each×2	5·50	6·50

520 Lion Red Cup and Players

1995. Centenary of Rugby League. Multicoloured.

1888	45c. Trans Tasman test match (30×25 mm)	50	60
1889	45c. Type **520**	50	20
1890	$1 Children's rugby and mascot	1·25	1·10
1891	$1.50 George Smith, Albert Baskerville and early match	2·00	2·50
1892	$1.80 Courtney Goodwill Trophy and match against Great Britain	2·25	2·50
MS1893	125×100 mm. No. 1892	3·00	3·00

521 Sheep and Lamb

1995. Farmyard Animals. Multicoloured.

1894	40c. Type **521**	75	75
1895	40c. Deer	75	75
1896	40c. Mare and foal	75	75
1897	40c. Cow with calf	75	75
1898	40c. Goats and kid	75	75
1899	40c. Common turkey	75	75
1900	40c. Ducks	75	75
1901	40c. Red junglefowl	75	75
1902	40c. Sow with piglets	75	75
1903	40c. Border collie	75	75
1904	45c. As Type **521**	75	75
1905	45c. As No. 1895	75	75
1906	45c. As No. 1896	75	75
1907	45c. As No. 1897	75	75
1908	45c. As No. 1898	75	75
1909	45c. As No. 1899	75	75
1910	45c. As No. 1900	75	75
1911	45c. As No. 1901	75	75
1912	45c. As No. 1902	75	75
1913	45c. As No. 1903	75	75

1995. "Singapore '95" International Stamp Exhibition. Multicoloured.

MS1914	170×70 mm. Nos. 1909/13	3·25	4·00
MS1915	148×210 mm. Nos. 1855/60	11·00	14·00

No. **MS**1915 also includes the "JAKARTA '95" logo.

522 Archangel Gabriel

1995. Christmas. Stained Glass Windows from St. Mary's Anglican Church, Merivale (Nos. 1916/18), The Lady Chapel of St. Luke's Anglican Church, Christchurch (Nos. 1919/22) or St. John the Evangelist Church, Cheviot (No. 1923). Multicoloured. (a) As T 522.

1916	40c. Type **522**	70	25
1917	45c. Type **522**	70	25
1918	70c. Virgin Mary	1·00	90
1919	80c. Shepherds	1·10	1·00
1920	$1 Virgin and Child	1·40	1·10
1921	$1.50 Two Wise Men	2·25	2·75
1922	$1.80 Wise Man kneeling	2·50	2·75

(b) Smaller design, 25×30 mm.

1923	40c. Angel with trumpet	60	50

523 Face and Nuclear Disarmament Symbol

1995. Nuclear Disarmament.

1924	**523**	$1 multicoloured	1·00	1·25

524 Mt. Cook

1995. New Zealand Scenery. Multicoloured.

1925	5c. Type **524**	10	10
1926	10c. Champagne Pool	10	10
1927	20c. Cape Reinga	15	20
1928	30c. Mackenzie Country	20	25
1929	40c. Mitre Peak (vert)	30	35
1930	50c. Mt. Ngauruhoe	35	40
1931	60c. Lake Wanaka (vert)	45	50
1932	70c. Giant kauri tree (vert)	50	55
1933	80c. Doubtful Sound (vert)	60	65
1934	90c. Waitomo Limestone Cave (vert)	65	70
1934a	90c. Rangitoto Island	1·50	70
1934b	$1 Taiaroa Head (27×22 mm)	1·00	80
1934c	$1.10 Kaikoura Coast (27×22 mm)	1·00	85
1934d	$1.30 Lake Camp, South Canterbury (27×22 mm)	3·25	1·25
1934e	$2 Great Barrier Island (27×22 mm)	1·50	1·60
1934f	$3 Cape Kidnappers (27×22 mm)	2·25	2·40
1935	$10 Mt. Ruapehu (38×32 mm)	7·50	7·75

For similar self-adhesive designs see Nos. 1983a/91b.

For miniature sheets containing some of these designs see Nos. **MS**1978, **MS**1998, **MS**2005, **MS**2328 and **MS**2401.

525 Dame Kiri te Kanawa (opera singer)

1995. Famous New Zealanders. Multicoloured.

1936	40c. Type **525**	1·00	40
1937	80c. Charles Upham, V.C. (war hero)	1·00	85
1938	$1 Barry Crump (author)	1·25	1·00
1939	$1.20 Sir Brian Barratt-Boyes (surgeon)	1·75	1·25
1940	$1.50 Dame Whina Cooper (Maori leader)	1·75	1·75
1941	$1.80 Sir Richard Hadlee (cricketer)	3·00	2·25

526 National Flags, Peace Dove and "50"

1995. 50th Anniv of United Nations.

1942	**526**	$1.80 multicoloured	2·75	2·50

527 Fern and Globe

1995. Commonwealth Heads of Government Meeting, Auckland. Multicoloured.

1943	40c. Type **527**	75	40
1944	$1.80 Fern and New Zealand flag	3·50	2·75

528 "Kiwi"

1996. Famous Racehorses. Multicoloured.

1945	40c. Type **528**	55	20
1946	80c. "Rough Habit"	85	90
1947	$1 "Blossom Lady"	1·00	85
1948	$1.20 "Il Vicolo"	1·40	1·60
1949	$1.50 "Horlicks"	1·50	2·00
1950	$1.80 "Bonecrusher"	2·00	2·50
MS1951	Seven sheets, each 162×110 mm. (a) No. 1945. (b) No. 1946. (c) No. 1947. (d) No. 1948. (e) No. 1949. (f) No. 1950. (g) Nos. 1945/50 Set of 7 sheets	16·00	19·00

529 Kete (basket)

1996. Maori Crafts. Multicoloured.

1952	40c. Type **529**	30	15
1953	80c. Head of Taiaha (spear)	60	50
1954	$1 Taniko (embroidery)	70	60
1955	$1.20 Pounamu (greenstone)	85	1·50
1956	$1.50 Hue (gourd)	1·10	2·25
1957	$1.80 Korowai (feather cloak)	1·25	2·25

See also No. **MS**2049.

530 Southern Black-backed Gulls

1996. Marine Life. Multicoloured. Self-adhesive or ordinary gum.

1968	40c. Type **530**	55	60
1969	40c. Children, sea cucumber and spiny starfish	55	60
1970	40c. Yacht, gull and common shrimps	55	60
1971	40c. Gaudy nudibranch	55	60
1972	40c. Large rock crab and clingfish	55	60
1973	40c. Snake skin chiton and red rock crab	55	60
1974	40c. Estuarine triplefin and cat's-eye shell	55	60
1975	40c. Cushion star and sea horses	55	60
1976	40c. Blue-eyed triplefin and Yaldwyn's triplefin	55	60
1977	40c. Common octopus	55	60

1996. "SOUTHPEX '96" Stamp Show, Invercargill. Sheet 100×215 mm, containing No. 1929×10.

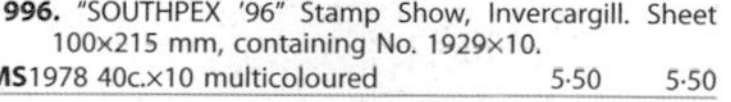

MS1978	40c.×10 multicoloured	5·50	5·50

531 Fire and Ambulance Services

1996. Rescue Services. Multicoloured.

1979	40c. Type **531**	50	40
1980	80c. Civil Defence	90	90
1981	$1 Air-sea rescue	1·10	1·10
1982	$1.50 Air ambulance and rescue helicopter	1·60	2·50
1983	$1.80 Mountain rescue and Red Cross	2·25	2·50

532 Mt. Egmont, Taranaki

1996. New Zealand Scenery. Self-adhesive. Mult.

1983a	10c. Champagne Pool	1·00	1·25
1984b	40c. Type **532**	35	40
1985	40c. Piercy Island, Bay of Islands	55	55

1986b 40c. Tory Channel, Marlborough Sounds 35 40
1987 40c. "Earnslaw" (ferry), Lake Wakatipu 55 55
1988b 40c. Lake Matheson 35 40
1989b 40c. Fox Glacier 35 40
1990 80c. Doubtful Sound (as No. 1933) 90 90
1990b 90c. Rangitoto Island (as No. 1934a) 90 90
1991 $1 Pohutukawa tree (33×22 mm) 1·00 1·00
1991b $1.10 Kaikoura Coast 1·00 1·25

533 Yellow-eyed Penguin

1996. Marine Wildlife. Multicoloured.
1992 40c. Type **533** 50 50
1993 80c. Royal albatross (horiz) 90 90
1994 $1 Great egret (horiz) 95 1·10
1995 $1.20 Flukes of sperm whale (horiz) 1·10 1·60
1996 $1.50 Fur seals 1·25 2·00
1997 $1.80 Bottlenose dolphin 1·50 2·00
See also Nos. **MS**1999 and **MS**2037.

1996. "CHINA '96" 9th International Stamp Exhibition, Peking. Multicoloured.
MS1998 180×80 mm. Nos. 1926/8 and 1930 1·75 2·00
MS1999 140×90 mm. Nos. 1994 and 1996 2·75 3·00
No. **MS**1999 also shows designs as Nos. 1992/3, 1995 and 1997, but without face values.

534 Baby in Car Seat

1996. Health Stamps. Child Safety. Multicoloured. Self-adhesive (2003) or ordinary (others) gum.
2000 40c.+5c. Type **534** 50 75
2001 80c.+5c. Child and adult on zebra crossing 90 1·50
2003 40c.+5c. Type **534** (21½×38 mm) 50 75
MS2002 130×90 mm. Nos. 2000/1, each×2 2·75 2·75
Stamps from No. **MS**2002 are slightly larger with "NEW ZEALAND" and the face values redrawn.

1996. "CAPEX '96" International Stamp Exhibition, Toronto. (a) No. MS2002 optd CAPEX '96 and emblem on sheet margin. Mult.
MS2004 Nos. 2000/1, each×2 3·25 2·75

(b) Sheet 180×80 mm, containing Nos. 1931/4.
MS2005 $3 multicoloured 3·25 3·25

535 Violin

1996. 50th Anniv of New Zealand Symphony Orchestra. Multicoloured.
2006 40c. Type **535** 40 40
2007 80c. French horn 1·00 1·75

536 Swimming

1996. Centennial Olympic Games, Atlanta. Mult.
2008 40c. Type **536** 50 25
2009 80c. Cycling 1·25 1·00
2010 $1 Running 1·00 1·00
2011 $1.50 Rowing 1·25 3·00
2012 $1.80 Dinghy racing 1·25 3·00
MS2013 120×80 mm. Nos. 2008/12 4·75 6·50

537 "Hinemoa"

1996. Centenary of New Zealand Cinema. Mult.
2014 40c. Type **537** 4·00 30
2015 80c. "Broken Barrier" 75 75
2016 $1.50 "Goodbye Pork Pie" 1·00 2·25
2017 $1.80 "Once Were Warriors" 1·10 2·25

538 Danyon Loader (swimmer) and Blyth Tait (horseman)

1996. New Zealand Olympic Gold Medal Winners, Atlanta.
2018 **538** 40c. multicoloured 50 50

539 Beehive Ballot Box

1996. New Zealand's First Mixed Member Proportional Representation Election.
2019 **539** 40c. black, red and yellow 50 50

540 King following Star

1996. Christmas. Multicoloured. (a) Size 35×35 mm.
2020 40c. Type **540** 40 20
2021 70c. Shepherd and Baby Jesus 65 70
2022 80c. Angel and shepherd 70 70
2023 $1 Mary, Joseph and Baby Jesus 80 90
2024 $1.50 Mary and Joseph with donkey 1·50 2·75
2025 $1.80 The Annunciation 50 2·50

(b) Size 30×24 mm. Self-adhesive.
2026 40c. Angels with trumpets 50 60
2027 40c. King with gift 50 50

541 Adzebill

1996. Extinct Birds. Multicoloured. (a) Size 40×28 mm.
2028 40c. Type **541** 60 40
2029 80c. South Island whekau ("Laughing Owl") 1·25 1·25
2030 $1 Piopio 1·25 1·10
2031 $1.20 Huia 1·50 1·75
2032 $1.50 Giant eagle 1·75 2·50
2033 $1.80 Giant moa 2·00 2·50
MS2034 105×92 mm. No. 2033 2·00 2·00

(b) Size 30×24 mm. Self-adhesive.
2035 40c. Stout-legged wren 60 50

1996. "TAIPEI '96" 10th Asian International Stamp Exhibition, Taiwan. (a) No. MS2034 overprinted with "TAIPEI '96" logo on sheet margin. Multicoloured.
MS2036 105×92 mm. No. 2033 2·75 2·75

(b) Sheet 140×90 mm, containing Nos. 1993 and 1997. Multicoloured.
MS2037 Nos. 1993 and 1997 2·75 2·75
No. **MS**2037 also shows designs as Nos. 1992 and 1994/6, but without face values.

542 Seymour Square, Blenheim

1996. Scenic Gardens. Multicoloured.
2038 40c. Type **542** 40 25
2039 80c. Pukekura Park, New Plymouth 75 75
2040 $1 Wintergarden, Auckland 85 85
2041 $1.50 Botanic Garden, Christchurch 1·40 2·50
2042 $1.80 Marine Parade Gardens, Napier 1·60 2·55

543 Holstein Friesian Cattle

1997. Cattle Breeds. Multicoloured.
2043 40c. Type **543** 75 25
2044 80c. Jersey 1·40 1·00
2045 $1 Simmental 1·60 1·00
2046 $1.20 Ayrshire 1·90 1·60
2047 $1.50 Angus 1·90 2·00
2048 $1.80 Hereford 2·25 2·00

1997. "HONG KONG '97" International Stamp Exhibition. Multicoloured.
MS2049 130×110 mm. Nos. 1952/3 and 1956 2·50 3·00
MS2050 101×134 mm. Nos. 2044/5 and 2047 2·75 3·50
No. **MS**2050 is also inscribed for the Chinese New Year ("Year of the Ox").

544 James Cook and Sextant

1997. Millennium Series (1st issue). Discoverers of New Zealand. Multicoloured.
2051 40c. Type **544** 80 45
2052 80c. Kupe and ocean-going canoe 1·00 90
2053 $1 Carved panel depicting Maui (vert) 1·25 1·00
2054 $1.20 Anchor and "St. Jean Baptiste" (Jean de Surville) (vert) 1·75 1·60
2055 $1.50 Dumont d'Urville, crab and "Lastrolabe" 2·00 2·00
2056 $1.80 Abel Tasman and illustration from journal 2·00 2·00
See also Nos. 2140/5, 2216/21, 2239/44, 2304/9 and 2310.

545 Rippon Vineyard, Central Otago

1997. New Zealand Vineyards. Multicoloured.
2057 40c. Type **545** 25 25
2058 80c. Te Mata Estate, Hawke's Bay 80 80
2059 $1 Cloudy Bay Vineyard, Marlborough 90 90
2060 $1.20 Pegasus Bay Vineyard, Waipara 1·10 1·75
2061 $1.50 Milton Vineyard, Gisborne 1·40 2·50
2062 $1.80 Goldwater Estate, Waiheke Island 1·60 2·50
MS2063 Seven sheets, each 150×110 mm. (a) No. 2057. (b) No. 2058. (c) No. 2059. (d) No. 2060. (e) No. 2061. (f) No. 2062. (g) Nos. 2057/62 Set of 7 sheets 13·00 15·00
See also No. **MS**2081.

546 Cottage Letterbox

1997. Curious Letterboxes. Multicoloured. Self-adhesive.
2064 40c. Type **546** 50 50
2065 40c. Owl letterbox 50 50
2066 40c. Blue whale letterbox 50 50
2067 40c. "Kilroy is Back" letterbox 50 50
2068 40c. Nesting box letterbox 50 50
2069 40c. Piper letterbox 50 50
2070 40c. Diver's helmet letterbox 50 50
2071 40c. Aircraft letterbox 50 50
2072 40c. Water tap letterbox 50 50
2073 40c. Indian palace letterbox 50 50

547 "The Promised Land", 1948 (Colin McCahon)

1997. Contemporary Paintings by Colin McCahon. Multicoloured.
2074 40c. Type **547** 40 20
2075 $1 "Six Days in Nelson and Canterbury", 1950 90 75
2076 $1.50 "Northland Panels" (detail), 1958 1·25 2·25
2077 $1.80 "Moby Dick is sighted off Muriwai Beach", 1972 1·50 2·25

548 Carrier Pigeon (based on 1899 "Pigeon-gram" local stamp)

1997. Centenary of Great Barrier Island Pigeon Post.
2078 **548** 40c. red 50 75
2079 **548** 80c. blue 90 1·50
See also Nos. **MS**2080 and **MS**2122.

1997. "Pacific '97" International Stamp Exhibition, San Francisco. Multicoloured.
MS2080 137×120 mm. Nos. 2078/9, each×2 2·50 2·50
MS2081 140×100 mm. Nos. 2057, 2059 and 2061 3·00 3·00
No. **MS**2080 is in a triangular format.

549 Rainbow Trout and Red Setter Fly

1997. Fly Fishing. Multicoloured.
2082 40c. Type **549** 40 35
2083 $1 Sea-run brown trout and grey ghost fly 1·00 90
2084 $1.50 Brook charr and twilight beauty fly 1·40 2·50
2085 $1.80 Brown trout and Hare and Cooper fly 1·60 2·50
See also No. **MS**2172.

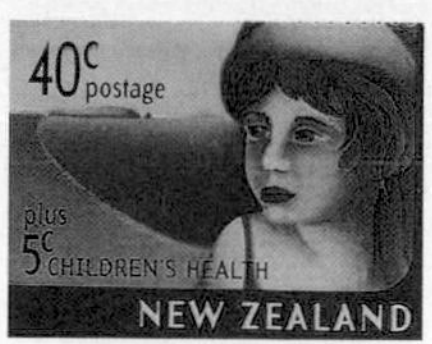

550 "Beach Scene" (Fern Petrie)

1997. Children's Health. Children's paintings. Mult. (a) Ordinary gum.

2086	40c.+5c. Type **550**	45	75
2087	80c.+5c. "Horse-riding on the Waterfront" (Georgia Dumergue)	80	1·25
MS2088	130×90 mm. Nos. 2086/7 and 40c.+5c. As No. 2089 (25×36 mm)	1·75	1·75

(b) Self-adhesive.

2089	40c.+5c. "Picking Fruit" (Anita Pitcher)	70	60

551 The "Overlander" at Paremata, Wellington

1997. Scenic Railway Services. Multicoloured.

2091	40c. Type **551**	50	35
2092	80c. The "Tranz Alpine" in the Southern Alps	90	80
2093	$1 The "Southener" at Canterbury	1·00	90
2094	$1.20 The "Coastal Pacific" on the Kaikoura Coast	1·40	2·00
2095	$1.50 The "Bay Express" at Central Hawke's Bay	1·60	2·25
2096	$1.80 The "Kaimai Express" at Tauranga Harbour	1·75	2·25

See also No. **MS**2173.

552 Samuel Marsden's "Active", Bay of Islands

1997. Christmas. Multicoloured. (a) Ordinary gum.

2097	40c. Type **552**	40	20
2098	70c. Revd. Marsden preaching	65	65
2099	80c. Marsden and Maori chiefs	75	75
2100	$1 Maori family	90	90
2101	$1.50 Handshake and cross	1·25	2·00
2102	$1.80 Pohutukawa (flower) and Rangihoua Bay	1·40	2·00

(b) Smaller design, 29×24 mm. Self-adhesive.

2103	40c. Memorial cross, Pohutukawa and Bay of Islands	40	40

553 Huhu Beetle

1997. Insects. Multicoloured. Self-adhesive.

2104	40c. Type **553**	50	50
2105	40c. Giant land snail	50	50
2106	40c. Giant weta	50	50
2107	40c. Giant dragonfly	50	50
2108	40c. Peripatus	50	50
2109	40c. Cicada	50	50
2110	40c. Puriri moth	50	50
2111	40c. Veined slug	50	50
2112	40c. Katipo	50	50
2113	40c. Flax weevil	50	50

554 "Rosa rugosa"

1997. New Zealand–China Joint Issue. Roses. Mult.

2114	40c. Type **554**	50	50
2115	40c. "Aotearoa"	50	50
MS2116	115×95 mm. 80c. Nos. 2114/15	1·00	1·00

555 Queen Elizabeth II and Prince Philip

1997. Golden Wedding of Queen Elizabeth and Prince Philip.

2117	**555**	40c. multicoloured	50	75

556 Cartoon Kiwi on Busy-bee

1997. New Zealand Cartoons. "Kiwis Taking on the World". Multicoloured.

2118	40c. Type **556**	60	25
2119	$1 "Let's have 'em for Breakfast"	1·10	80
2120	$1.50 Kiwi dinghy winning race	1·40	1·75
2121	$1.80 "CND" emblem cut in forest	1·75	1·75

1997. "Aupex '97" National Stamp Exhibtion, Auckland. Sheet 140×120 mm. Multicoloured.

MS2122	Nos. 2078/9, each×2	2·10	2·10

No. **MS**2122 is in a triangular format.

1997. International Stamp and Coin Exhibition 1997, Shanghai. Sheet as No. MS2116, but redrawn to include "Issued by New Zealand Post to commemorate the International Stamp and Coin Expo. Shanghai, China. 19–23 November 1997" inscr in English and Chinese with additional die-stamped gold frame and logo.

MS2123	115×95 mm. Nos. 2114/15	1·00	1·00

557 Modern Dancer

1998. Performing Arts. Multicoloured.

2124	40c. Type **557**	35	25
2125	80c. Trombone player	75	75
2126	$1 Opera singer	1·50	85
2127	$1.20 Actor	1·00	1·50
2128	$1.50 Singer	1·25	2·50
2129	$1.80 Ballet dancer	1·50	2·50
MS2130	Seven sheets, each 150×110 mm. (a) No. 2124. (b) No. 2125. (c) No. 2126. (d) No. 2127. (e) No. 2128. (f) No. 2129. (g) Nos. 2124/9 Set of 7 sheets	15·00	18·00

558 Museum of New Zealand

1998. Opening of Museum of New Zealand, Wellington. Multicoloured.

2131	40c. Type **558**	30	35
2132	$1.80 Museum, spotted cormorant and silver gull	1·40	1·40

559 Domestic Cat

1998. Cats. Multicoloured.

2133	40c. Type **559**	35	25
2134	80c. Burmese	70	70
2135	$1 Birman	75	75
2136	$1.20 British blue	80	1·40
2137	$1.50 Persian	1·00	2·25
2138	$1.80 Siamese	1·40	2·00

1998. Chinese New Year ("Year of the Tiger"). Multicoloured.

MS2139	100×135 mm. Nos. 2133, 2135 and 2138	2·50	3·00

560 Maoris and Canoe

1998. Millennium Series (2nd issue). Immigrants. Multicoloured.

2140	40c. Type **560**	35	15
2141	80c. 19th-century European settlers and immigrant ship	75	65
2142	$1 Gold miners and mine	1·00	80
2143	$1.20 Post 1945 European migrants and liner	1·25	1·10
2144	$1.50 Pacific islanders and church	1·40	1·75
2145	$1.80 Asian migrant and jumbo jet	1·60	1·60

561 "With Great Respect to the Mehmetcik" Statue, Gallipoli

1998. Joint Issue New Zealand–Turkey. Memorial Statues. Multicoloured.

2146	40c. Type **561**	40	35
2147	$1.80 "Mother with Children", National War Memorial, Wellington	1·25	1·40

562 Mother and Son Hugging

1998. "Stay in Touch" Greetings Stamps. Mult. Self-adhesive.

2148	40c. Type **562**	35	35
2149	40c. Couple on beach	35	35
2150	40c. Boys striking hands	35	35
2151	40c. Grandmother and grandson	35	35
2152	40c. Young boys in pool (horiz)	35	35
2153	40c. "I'LL MISS YOU ... PLEASE WRITE" (horiz)	35	35
2154	40c. Symbolic couple and clouds (horiz)	35	35
2155	40c. Young couple kissing (horiz)	35	35
2156	40c. Couple sat on sofa (horiz)	35	35
2157	40c. Maoris rubbing noses (horiz)	35	35

563 Mount Cook or Aorangi

1998. Centenary of 1898 Pictorial Stamps. Designs as T 23/26 and 28/35 with modern face values as T 563.

2158	**563**	40c. brown	40	50
2159	**24**	40c. blue and brown	40	50
2160	**25**	40c. brown	40	50
2161	**28**	40c. brown	40	50
2162	**29**	40c. red	40	50
2163	**31**	40c. green	40	50
2164	**32**	40c. blue	40	50
2165	**34**	40c. orange	40	50
2166	**26**	80c. blue (inscr "LAKE WAKITIPU") (35×23 mm)	75	75
2167	**26**	80c. blue (inscr "LAKE WAKATIPU") (35×23 mm)	75	75
2168	**30**	$1 brown (23×35 mm)	80	85
2169	**33**	$1.20 brown (35×23 mm)	85	1·60
2170	**35**	$1.50 green (35×23 mm)	1·00	1·75
2171	-	$1.80 red (as No. 329) (23×35 mm)	1·25	1·75

See also Nos. **MS**2188 and **MS**2214.

1998. "Israel '98" World Stamp Exhibition, Tel Aviv. Multicoloured.

MS2172	112×90 mm. Nos. 2082 and 2085	2·50	2·75
MS2173	125×100 mm. Nos. 2092/3 and 2095	4·00	4·00

564 "Wounded at Cassino"

1998. Paintings by Peter McIntyre. Multicoloured.

2174	40c. Type **564**	30	20
2175	$1 "The Cliffs of Rangitikei"	75	75
2176	$1.50 "Maori Children, King Country"	1·00	1·40
2177	$1.80 "The Anglican Church, Kakahi"	1·25	1·50

See also No. **MS**2215.

565 Girl wearing Lifejacket

1998. Children's Health. Water Safety. Mult. (a) Ordinary gum.

2178	40c.+5c. Type **565**	40	50
2179	80c.+5c. Boy learning to swim	60	75
MS2180	125×90 mm. Nos. 2178/9, each×2	2·00	2·00

(b) Smaller design, 25×37 mm. Self-adhesive.

2181	40c.+5c. Type **565**	30	50

566 Sunrise near Cambridge

1998. Scenic Skies. Multicoloured.

2182	40c. Type **566**	40	20
2183	80c. Clouds over Lake Wanaka	75	65
2184	$1 Sunset over Mount Maunganui	85	75
2185	$1.20 Rain clouds over South Bay, Kaikoura	1·00	1·10
2186	$1.50 Sunset near Statue of Wairaka, Whakatane Harbour	1·40	1·25
2187	$1.80 Cloud formation above Lindis Pass	1·60	1·75

See also No. **MS**2245.

1998. "TARAPEX '98" National Stamp Exhibition, New Plymouth.

MS2188	90×80 mm. Nos. 2166/7	1·60	1·75

567 Virgin Mary and Christ Child

1998. Christmas. Multicoloured. (a) Ordinary gum.

2189	40c. Type **567**	40	15
2190	70c. Shepherds approaching the stable	65	55
2191	80c. Virgin Mary, Joseph and Christ Child	75	65
2192	$1 Magi with gift of gold	90	80
2193	$1.50 Three magi	1·50	2·00
2194	$1.80 Angel and shepherds	1·60	2·00

(b) Smaller design, 24×29 mm. Self-adhesive.

2195	40c. Type **567**	35	30

568 Lemon and Mineral Water Bottle, Paeroa

1998. Town Icons. Multicoloured. Self-adhesive.

2196	40c. Type **568**	40	40
2197	40c. Carrot, Ohakune	40	40
2198	40c. Brown Trout, Gore (25×36 mm)	40	40
2199	40c. Crayfish, Kaikoura (25×36 mm)	40	40
2200	40c. Sheep-shearer, Te Kuiti (25×36 mm)	40	40
2201	40c. "Pania of the Reef" (Maori legend), Napier (25×36 mm)	40	40
2202	40c. Paua Shell, Riverton (24×29 mm)	40	40
2203	40c. Kiwifruit, Te Puke (24×29 mm)	40	40
2204	40c. Border Collie, Lake Tekapo (24×29 mm)	40	40
2205	40c. "Big Cow", Hawera (24×29 mm)	40	40

569 Moonfish

1998. International Year of the Ocean. Mult.

2206	40c. Type **569**	35	50
2207	40c. Mako shark	35	50
2208	40c. Yellowfin tuna	35	50
2209	40c. Giant squid	35	50
2210	80c. Striped marlin	60	70
2211	80c. Porcupine fish	60	70
2212	80c. Eagle ray	60	70
2213	80c. Sandager's wrasse	60	70

Nos. 2206/9 and 2210/13 respectively were printed together, se-tenant, forming composite designs.

See also Nos. **MS**2246 and **MS**2277.

1998. "Italia '98" International Philatelic Exhibition, Milan. Multicoloured.

MS2214	90×80 mm. Nos. 2167 and 2170	3·00	3·25
MS2215	112×90 mm. Nos. 2176/7	2·00	2·25

570 Wellington in 1841 and 1998

1998. Millennium Series (3rd issue). Urban Transformations. Multicoloured.

2216	40c. Type **570**	45	30
2217	80c. Auckland in 1852 and 1998	65	55
2218	$1 Christchurch in 1851 and 1998	75	70
2219	$1.20 Westport in 1919 and 1998	80	1·25
2220	$1.50 Tauranga in 1880 and 1998	1·00	1·75
2221	$1.80 Dunedin in 1862 and 1998	1·10	1·75

571 "Fuchsia excorticata"

1999. Flowering Trees of New Zealand. Mult.

2222	40c. Type **571**	30	20
2223	80c. "Solanum laciniatum"	50	55
2224	$1 "Sophora tetraptera"	60	70
2225	$1.20 "Carmichaelia stevensonii"	70	1·00
2226	$1.50 "Olearia angustfolia"	90	1·60
2227	$1.80 "Metrosideros umbellata"	1·10	1·60

See also No. **MS**2286.

572 Civic Theatre, Auckland

1999. Art Deco Architecture. Multicoloured.

2228	40c. Type **572**	50	20
2229	$1 Masonic Hotel, Napier	2·00	80
2230	$1.50 Medical and Dental Chambers, Hastings	1·00	1·60
2231	$1.80 Buller County Chambers, Westport	1·25	1·60

573 Labrador Puppy and Netherland Dwarf Rabbit

1999. Popular Pets. Multicoloured.

2232	40c. Type **573**	40	30
2233	80c. Netherland dwarf rabbit	80	55
2234	$1 Tabby kitten and Netherland dwarf rabbit	90	70
2235	$1.20 Lamb	1·25	1·25
2236	$1.50 Welsh pony	1·40	1·50
2237	$1.80 Two budgerigars	1·50	1·60
MS2238	100×135 mm. Nos. 2232/4	1·75	1·75

No. **MS**2238 also commemorates the Chinese New Year ("Year of the Rabbit").

See also No. **MS**2287.

574 Toy Fire Engine and Marbles

1999. Millennium Series (4th issue). Nostalgia. Multicoloured.

2239	40c. Type **574**	35	20
2240	80c. Commemorative tin of biscuits and cereal packet	50	50
2241	$1 Tram, tickets and railway crockery	70	70
2242	$1.20 Radio and "Woman's Weekly" magazine	80	1·25
2243	$1.50 Coins, postcards and stamps	90	1·60
2244	$1.80 Lawn mower and seed packets	1·10	1·60

1999. "Australia '99" World Stamp Exhibition, Melbourne. Multicoloured.

MS2245	130×70 mm. Nos. 2182 and 2187	1·90	1·90
MS2246	130×90 mm. Nos. 2206/7 and 2210/11	2·00	2·00

575 Hunter Building, Victoria University

1999. Centenary of Victoria University, Wellington.

2247	**575** 40c. multicoloured	30	30

576 Auckland Blues Player kicking Ball

1999. New Zealand U-Bix Rugby Super 12 Championship. Multicoloured. Ordinary or self-adhesive gum.

2248	40c. Type **576**	40	40
2249	40c. Auckland Blues player being tackled	40	40
2250	40c. Chiefs player being tackled	40	40
2251	40c. Chiefs lineout jump	40	40
2252	40c. Wellington Hurricanes player being tackled	40	40
2253	40c. Wellington Hurricanes player passing ball	40	40
2254	40c. Canterbury Crusaders lineout jump	40	40
2255	40c. Canterbury Crusaders player kicking ball	40	40
2256	40c. Otago Highlanders player diving for try	40	40
2257	40c. Otago Highlanders player running with ball	40	40

577 "The Lake, Tuai"

1999. Paintings by Doris Lusk. Multicoloured.

2268	40c. Type **577**	30	20
2269	$1 "The Pumping Station"	70	70
2270	$1.50 "Arcade Awning, St. Mark's Square, Venice (2)"	90	1·40
2271	$1.80 "Tuam St. II"	1·10	1·40

See also No. **MS**2276.

578 "A Lion in the Meadow" (Margaret Mahy)

1999. Children's Health. Children's Books. Mult. (a) Ordinary gum.

2272	40c.+5c. Type **578**	55	55
2273	80c.+5c. "Greedy Cat" (Joy Cowley)	70	70
MS2274	130×90 mm. 40c. + 5c. Type **578**; 40c. + 5c. As No. 2275 (37×25 mm); 80c. + 5c. No. 2273	1·40	1·40

(b) Smaller design, 37×25 mm. Self-adhesive.

2275	40c.+5c. "Hairy Maclary's Bone" (Lynley Dodd) (37×25 mm)	50	50

1999. "PhilexFrance '99" International Stamp Exhibiton, Paris. Multicoloured.

MS2276	112×90 mm. Nos. 2268 and 2271	1·75	1·75
MS2277	130×90 mm. Nos. 2208/9 and 2212/13	2·00	2·00

579 "APEC"

1999. 10th Asia-Pacific Economic Co-operation Meeting, New Zealand.

2278	**579** 40c. multicoloured	30	30

580 West Ruggedy Beach, Stewart Island

1999. Scenic Walks. Multicoloured.

2279	40c. Type **580**	30	20
2280	80c. Ice lake, Butler Valley, Westland	50	50
2281	$1 Tonga Bay, Abel Tasman National Park	65	65
2282	$1.20 East Matakitaki Valley, Nelson Lakes National Park	75	90
2283	$1.50 Great Barrier Island	90	1·40
2284	$1.80 Mt. Egmont, Taranaki	1·10	1·40
MS2285	Seven sheets, each 150×110 mm. (a) No. 2279. (b) No. 2280. (c) No. 2281. (d) No. 2282. (e) No. 2283. (f) No. 2284. (g) Nos. 2279/84 Set of 7 sheets	11·00	13·00

See also No. **MS**2295.

1999. "China '99" International Stamp Exhibition, Peking. Multicoloured.

MS2286	112×90 mm. Nos. 2222/3	1·00	1·00
MS2287	100×135 mm. Nos. 2232 and 2234	1·00	1·00

581 Baby Jesus with Animals

1999. Christmas. Multicoloured. (a) Ordinary gum.

2288	40c. Type **581**	25	15
2289	80c. Virgin Mary praying	55	55
2290	$1.10 Mary and Joseph on way to Bethlehem	70	75
2291	$1.20 Angel playing harp	75	80
2292	$1.50 Three shepherds	90	1·25
2293	$1.80 Three wise men with gifts	1·10	1·40

(b) Smaller design, 23×28 mm. Self-adhesive.

2294	40c. Type **581**	30	30

1999. "Palmpex '99" National Stamp Exhibition, Palmerston North. Sheet 130×90 mm, containing No. 2284. Multicoloured.

MS2295	$1.80, Mt. Egmont, Taranaki	1·40	1·40

582 "P" Class Dinghy

1999. Yachting. Multicoloured. (a) Size 28×39 mm. Ordinary gum.

2296	40c. Type **582**	35	15
2297	80c. Laser dinghy	55	55
2298	$1.10 18ft skiff	70	75
2299	$1.20 Hobie catamaran	75	80
2300	$1.50 Racing yacht	90	1·25
2301	$1.80 Cruising yacht	1·10	1·40
MS2302	125×100 mm. Nos. 2296/301	3·75	5·00

(b) Size 23×28 mm. Self-adhesive.

2303	40c. Optimist dinghy	30	30

583 Group of Victorian Women (female suffrage, 1893)

1999. Millenium Series (5th issue). New Zealand Achievements. Multicoloured.

2304	40c. Type **583**	30	15
2305	80c. Richard Pearse's aircraft (powered flight, 1903)	75	55
2306	$1.10 Lord Rutherford (splitting the atom, 1919)	80	85
2307	$1.20 Boat on lake (invention of jet boat, 1953)	80	90
2308	$1.50 Sir Edmund Hillary (conquest of Everest, 1953)	1·10	1·50
2309	$1.80 Protesters and warship (nuclear free zone, 1987)	1·10	1·60

584 Sunrise and World Map

2000. Millennium Series (6th issue).

2310	**584** 40c. multicoloured	65	30

585 Araiteuru (North Island sea guardian)

2000. Chinese New Year ("Year of the Dragon"). Maori Spirits and Guardians. Multicoloured.

2311	40c. Type **585**	30	15
2312	80c. Kurangaituku (giant bird woman)	50	40
2313	$1.10 Te Hoata and Te Pupu (volcanic taniwha sisters)	65	60
2314	$1.20 Patupaiarehe (mountain fairy tribe)	70	70
2315	$1.50 Te Ngarara-huarau (giant first lizard)	80	1·00
2316	$1.80 Tuhirangi (South Island sea guardian)	90	1·25
MS2317	125×90 mm. Nos. 2315/16	2·50	2·50

586 Chilly Bin (cool box)

2000. New Zealand Life (2nd series). Each including a cartoon kiwi. Multicoloured. Self-adhesive.

2318	40c. Type **586**	35	45
2319	40c. Pipis (seafood delicacy)	35	45
2320	40c. "Lilo"	35	45
2321	40c. Chocolate fish	35	45
2322	40c. Bach or Crib (holiday home)	35	45
2323	40c. Barbeque	35	45
2324	40c. Ug (fur-lined) boots	35	45
2325	40c. Anzac biscuits	35	45
2326	40c. Hot dog	35	45
2327	40c. Meat pie	35	45

2000. "The Stamp Show 2000" International Stamp Exhibition, London. Sheet 110×80 mm, containing Nos. 1934b and 1934e/f. Multicoloured.

MS2328	$1 Taiaroa Head; $2 Great Barrier Island; $3 Cape kidnappers	4·00	4·50

587 Volkswagen Beetle

2000. "On The Road". Motor Cars.

2329	**587** 40c. brown and black	35	30
2330	- 80c. blue and black	60	55
2331	- $1.10 brown and black	80	80
2332	- $1.20 green and black	85	85
2333	- $1.50 brown and black	1·10	1·25
2334	- $1.80 lilac and black	1·25	1·40

DESIGNS: 80c. Ford Zephyr Mk I; $1.10, Morris Mini Mk II; $1.20, Holden HQ Kingswood; $1.50, Honda Civic; $1.80, Toyota Corolla.

588 Lake Lyndon, Canterbury

2000. Scenic Reflections. Multicoloured.

2336	40c. Type **588**	50	30
2337	80c. Lion (cruising launch) on Lake Wakatipu	85	55
2338	$1.10 Eruption of Mount Ruapehu	1·00	80
2339	$1.20 Rainbow Mountain Scenic Reserve, Rotorua	1·00	85
2340	$1.50 Tairua Harbour, Coromandel Peninsula	1·10	1·60
2341	$1.80 Lake Alexandrina	1·25	1·60

See also No. **MS**2368.

2000. "EXPO 2000" World Stamp Exhibition, Anaheim, U.S.A. Sheet 132×78 mm, containing Nos. 1490, 1490b/c and 2090/a.

MS2342	$1 red; $1 blue; $1 violet; $1 green; $1.10 gold	3·25	4·00

589 Lady Elizabeth Bowes-Lyon and Glamis Castle, 1907

2000. Queen Elizabeth the Queen Mother's 100th Birthday. Multicoloured.

2343	40c. Type **589**	60	30
2344	$1.10 Fishing in New Zealand, 1966	1·10	70
2345	$1.80 Holding bunch of daisies, 1997	1·75	1·60
MS2346	115×60 mm. Nos. 2343/5	3·00	2·75

590 Rowing

2000. Olympic Games, Sydney, and other Sporting Events. Multicoloured.

2347	40c. Type **590**	35	30
2348	80c. Show jumping	65	55
2349	$1.10 Cycling	1·25	80
2350	$1.20 Triathlon	85	85
2351	$1.50 Bowling	1·10	1·25
2352	$1.80 Netball	1·10	1·40

Nos. 2351/2 omit the Olympic logo.

591 Virgin Mary and Baby Jesus

2000. Christmas. Multicoloured. (a) Ordinary gum.

2353	40c. Type **591**	35	15
2354	80c. Mary and Joseph on way to Bethlehem	60	40
2355	$1.10 Baby Jesus in manger	85	80
2356	$1.20 Archangel Gabriel	95	90
2357	$1.50 Shepherd with lamb	1·25	1·60
2358	$1.80 Three Wise Men	1·40	1·60

(b) Self-adhesive. Size 30×25 mm.

2359	40c. Type **591**	35	30

592 Geronimo (teddy bear)

2000. Children's Health. Teddy Bears and Dolls. Multicoloured. (a) Ordinary gum.

2360	40c.+5c. Type **592**	45	50
2361	80c.+5c. Antique French doll and wooden Schoenhut doll	70	80
2362	$1.10 Chad Valley bear	75	70
2363	$1.20 Poppy (doll)	80	80
2364	$1.50 Swanni (large bear) and Dear John (small bear)	90	1·25
2365	$1.80 Lia (doll) and bear	1·10	1·25
MS2366	100×60 mm. 40c. + 5c. Type **592**; 80c. + 5c. As No. 2361	1·00	1·00

(b) Self-adhesive. Size 29×24 mm.

2367	40c.+5c. Type **592**	35	40

2000. "CANPEX 2000" National Stamp Exhibition, Christchurch. Sheet 95×80 mm, containing Nos. 2336 and 2341. Multicoloured.

MS2368	40c. Type **588**; $1.80 Lake Alexandrina	1·60	1·75

593 Lesser Kestrel

2000. Threatened Birds. Multicoloured.

2369	40c. Type **593**	50	30
2370	40c. Yellow-fronted parakeet	50	30
2371	80c. New Zealand stilt ("Black Stilt")	70	55
2372	$1.10 Fernbird ("Stewart Island Fernbird")	75	70
2373	$1.20 Kakapo	90	1·00
2374	$1.50 Weka rail ("North Island Weka")	1·10	1·25
2375	$1.80 Brown kiwi ("Okarito Brown Kiwi")	1·25	1·25

Nos. 2369 and 2375 form a joint issue with France.
See also No. **MS**2393.

594 *Sonoma* (mail ship) at Quay

2001. Moving the Mail in the 20th Century.

2376	**594** 40c. purple and red	30	35
2377	- 40c. green	30	35
2378	- 40c. agate	30	35
2379	- 40c. blue	30	35
2380	- 40c. brown	30	35
2381	- 40c. purple	30	35
2382	- 40c. black and cinnamon	30	35
2383	- 40c. multicoloured	30	35
2384	- 40c. mauve	30	35
2385	- 40c. multicoloured	30	35

DESIGNS: No. 2377, Stagecoach crossing river; 2378, Early postal lorry; 2379, Paddle steamer on River Wanganui; 2380, Railway T.P.O.; 2381, Loading mail through nose door of aircraft; 2382, Postwoman with bicycle; 2383, Loading lorry by fork-lift truck; 2384, Aircraft at night; 2385, Computer mouse.
See also No. **MS**2424.

595 Green Turtle

2001. Chinese New Year ("Year of the Snake"). Marine Reptiles. Multicoloured.

2386	40c. Type **595**	55	20
2387	80c. Leathery turtle	80	55
2388	90c. Loggerhead turtle	80	60
2389	$1.30 Hawksbill turtle	1·25	1·10
2390	$1.50 Banded sea-snake	1·50	1·40
2391	$2 Yellow-bellied sea-snake	1·60	1·40
MS2392	125×90 mm. Nos. 2390/1	3·00	3·00

2001. "Hong Kong 2001" Stamp Exhibition. Sheet 100×80 mm, containing Nos. 2374/5. Multicoloured.

MS2393	$1.50, North Island weka; $1.80, Okarito brown kiwi	2·50	2·50

596 Camellia

2001. Garden Flowers. Multicoloured.

2394	40c. Type **596**	30	20
2395	80c. Siberian iris	60	55
2396	90c. Daffodil	65	60
2397	$1.30 Chrysanthemum	85	1·10
2398	$1.50 Sweet pea	90	1·25
2399	$2 Petunia	1·10	1·25
MS2400	95×125 mm. Nos. 2394/9	4·00	4·25

2001. Invercargill "Stamp Odyssey 2001" National Stamp Exhibition. Sheet 133×81 mm, containing Nos. 1934a/d. Multicoloured.

MS2401	90c. Rangitoto Island; $1 Taiaroa Head; $1.10, Kaikoura Coast; $1.30, Lake Camp, South Canterbury	2·75	3·00

597 Greenstone Amulet

2001. Art from Nature. Multicoloured.

2402	40c. Type **597**	30	30
2403	80c. Oamaru stone sculpture	55	55
2404	90c. Paua ornament	60	60
2405	$1.30 Kauri ornament	85	1·10
2406	$1.50 Flax basket	1·00	1·25
2407	$2 Silver-dipped fern frond	1·25	1·25

Nos. 2402/7 were each printed in sheets of 25 (5×5) in which the stamps were included in four different orientations so that four blocks of 4 in each sheet showed the complete work of art.

598 Douglas DC-3

2001. Aircraft. Multicoloured.

2408	40c. Type **598**	35	30
2409	80c. Fletcher FU24 Topdresser	65	55
2410	90c. De Havilland DH82A Tiger Moth	70	60
2411	$1.30 Fokker FVIIb/3m Southern Cross	90	1·10
2412	$1.50 De Havilland DH100 Vampire	1·00	1·25
2413	$2 Boeing & Westervelt seaplane	1·25	1·25

599 Parcel

2001. Greetings Stamps. Multicoloured.

2414	40c. Type **599**	35	45
2415	40c. Trumpet	35	45
2416	40c. Heart and ribbon	35	45
2417	40c. Balloons	35	45
2418	40c. Flower	35	45
2419	90c. Photo frame	65	80
2420	90c. Fountain pen and letter	65	80
2421	90c. Candles on cake	65	80
2422	90c. Star biscuits	65	80
2423	90c. Candle and flowers	65	80

2001. "Belgica 2001" International Stamp Exhibition, Brussels. Sheet 180×90 mm, containing Nos. 2376/85. Multicoloured.

MS2424	40c. × 10, Nos. 2376/85	4·00	4·50

600 Bungy Jumping, Queenstown

2001. Tourism Centenary. Multicoloured. (a) Size 38×32 mm. Ordinary gum.

2425	40c. Type **600**	25	15
2426	80c. Maori Canoe on Lake Rotoiti	45	50
2427	90c. Sightseeing from Mount Alfred	55	60
2428	$1.30 Fishing on Glenorchy river	75	80
2429	$1.50 Sea-kayaking in Abel Tasman National Park	85	1·10
2430	$2 Fiordland National Park	1·10	1·25

(b) Size 30×25 mm. Self-adhesive.

2431	40c. Type **600**	45	45
2432	90c. Sightseeing from Mount Alfred	80	85
2433	$1.50 Sea-kayaking in Abel Tasman National Park	1·25	1·40

2001. "Philanippon '01" International Stamp Exhibition, Tokyo. Sheet 90×82 mm, containing Nos. 2429/30. Multicoloured.

MS2434 $1.50 Sea-kayaking in Abel Tasman National Park; $2 Fiordland National Park	2·75	3·00

601 Family cycling

2001. Children's Health. Cycling. Multicoloured. (a) Size 39×29 mm. Ordinary gum.

2435	40c. + 5c. Type **601**	50	35
2436	90c. + 5c. Mountain bike stunt	85	75
MS2437	Circular, 100 mm diameter. Nos. 2435/6	1·25	1·10

(b) Size 29×231/2. Self-adhesive.

2438	40c. + 5c. Boy on bike	40	30

602 "When Christ was born of Mary free"

2001. Christmas. Carols. Multicoloured. (a) Size 29×34 mm. Ordinary gum.

2439	40c. Type **602**	40	15
2440	80c. "Away in a manger"	70	40
2441	90c. "Joy to the world"	80	55
2442	$1.30 "Angels we have heard on high"	1·10	80
2443	$1.50 "O holy night"	1·25	1·00
2444	$2 "While shepherds watched"	1·50	1·50

(b) Size 21×26 mm. Self-adhesive.

2445	40c. Type **602**	40	30

603 Queen Elizabeth II at State Opening of Parliament, 1954

2001. Queen Elizabeth II's 75th Birthday. Multicoloured (except 40c.).

2446	40c. Type **603** (black and silver)	50	30
2447	80c. Queen Elizabeth II on walkabout, 1970	80	50
2448	90c. Queen Elizabeth II wearing Maori cloak, 1977	90	55
2449	$1.30 Queen Elizabeth II with bouquet, 1986	1·25	80
2450	$1.50 Queen Elizabeth II at Commonwealth Games, 1990	1·40	90
2451	$2 Queen Elizabeth II, 1997	1·60	1·25

604 Rockhopper Penguins

2001. New Zealand Penguins. Multicoloured.

2452	40c. Type **604**	50	30
2453	80c. Little penguin ("Little Blue Penguin")	75	50
2454	90c. Snares Island penguins ("Snares Crested Penguins")	85	60
2455	$1.30 Big-crested penguins ("Erect-crested Penguins")	1·10	85
2456	$1.50 Victoria penguins ("Fiord-land Crested Penguins")	1·25	1·10
2457	$2 Yellow-eyed penguins	1·60	1·40

605 Gandalf (Sir Ian McKellen) and Saruman (Christopher Lee)

2001. Making of The Lord of the Rings Film Trilogy (1st issue): The Fellowship of the Ring. Multicoloured. (a) Designs 24×50 mm or 50×24 mm.

2458	40c. Type **605**	60	30
2459	80c. The Lady Galadriel (Cate Blanchett)	1·10	60
2460	90c. Sam Gamgee (Sean Austin) and Frodo Baggins (Elijah Wood) (horiz)	1·10	75
2461	$1.30 Guardian of Rivendell	1·60	2·00
2462	$1.50 Strider (Viggo Mortensen)	1·75	2·50
2463	$2 Boromir (Sean Bean) (horiz)	2·25	3·50

(b) Designs 26×37 mm or 37×26 mm. Self-adhesive.

2464	40c. Type **605**	40	35
2465	80c. The Lady Galadriel (Cate Blanchett)	60	60
2466	90c. Sam Gamgee (Sean Austin) and Frodo Baggins (Elijah Wood) (horiz)	75	80
2467	$1.30 Guardian of Rivendell	1·25	1·75
2468	$1.50 Strider (Viggo Mortensen)	1·50	2·00
2469	$2 Boromir (Sean Bean) (horiz)	1·60	2·50

See also No. **MS**2490, 2652/63 and 2713/25.

606 "Christian Cullen" (harness racing)

2002. Chinese New Year ("Year of the Horse"). New Zealand Racehorses. Multicoloured.

2470	40c. Type **606**	30	30
2471	80c. "Lyell Creek" (harness racing)	50	50
2472	90c. "Yulestar" (harness racing)	55	55
2473	$1.30 "Sunline"	80	80
2474	$1.50 "Ethereal"	90	90
2475	$2 "Zabeel"	1·25	1·25
MS2476	127×90 mm. Nos. 2473/4	3·75	4·25

607 *Hygrocybe rubrocarnosa*

2002. Fungi. Multicoloured.

2477	40c. Type **607**	45	30
2478	80c. *Entoloma hochstetteri*	75	50
2479	90c. *Aseroe rubra*	85	60
2480	$1.30 *Hericium coralloides*	1·10	1·10
2481	$1.50 *Thaxterogaster porphyreus*	1·25	1·40
2482	$2 *Ramaria aureorhiza*	1·60	1·60
MS2483	114×104 mm. Nos. 2477/82	5·50	5·50

608 War Memorial Museum, Auckland

2002. Architectural Heritage. Multicoloured.

2484	40c. Type **608**	35	20
2485	80c. Stone Store, Kerikeri (25×30 mm)	60	50
2486	90c. Arts Centre, Christchurch (50×30 mm)	65	55
2487	$1.30 Government Buildings, Wellington (50×30 mm)	95	80
2488	$1.50 Dunedin Railway Station (25×30 mm)	1·10	1·00
2489	$2 Sky Tower, Auckland	1·25	1·25

2002. "Northpex 2002" Stamp Exhibition. Sheet 130×95 mm, containing Nos. 2458, 2461 and 2463. Multicoloured.

MS2490 40c. Gandalf (Sir Ian Mckellen) and Saruman (Christopher Lee); $1.30 Guardian of Rivendell; $2 Boromir (Sean Bean) (horiz)	6·00	6·00

No. **MS**2490 was sold at face value.

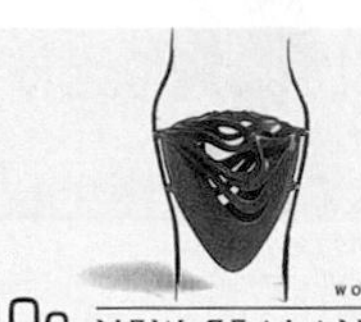

609 "Starfish Vessel" (wood sculpture) (Graeme Priddle)

2002. Artistic Crafts. Joint Issue with Sweden. Multicoloured.

2491	40c. Type **609**	35	30
2492	40c. Flax basket (Willa Rogers) (37×29 mm)	35	30
2493	80c. "Catch II" (clay bowl) (Raewyn Atkinson)	55	50
2494	90c. "Vessel Form" (silver brooch) (Gavin Hitchings)	60	55
2495	$1.30 Glass towers from "Immigration" series (Emma Camden)	85	85
2496	$1.50 "Pacific Rim" (clay vessel) (Merilyn Wiseman)	95	1·10
2497	$2 Glass vase (Ola and Maria Höglund) (37×29 mm)	1·25	1·40

Nos. 2492 and 2497 are additionally inscribed "JOINT ISSUE WITH SWEDEN".

610 *Brodie* (Anna Poland, Cardinal McKeefry School) (National Winner)

2002. Children's Book Festival. Stamp Design Competition. Designs illustrating books. Multicoloured.

2498	40c. Type **610**	30	35
2499	40c. *The Last Whale* (Hee Su Kim, Glendowie Primary School)	30	35
2500	40c. *Scarface Claw* (Jayne Bruce, Rangiora Borough School)	30	35
2501	40c. *Which New Zealand Bird?* (Teigan Stafford-Bush, Ararimu School)	30	35
2502	40c. *Which New Zealand Bird?* (Hazel Gilbert, Gonville School)	30	35
2503	40c. *The Plight of the Penguin* (Gerard Mackle, Temuka High School)	30	35
2504	40c. *Scarface Claw* (Maria Rodgers, Salford School)	30	35
2505	40c. *Knocked for Six* (Paul Read, Ararimu School)	30	35
2506	40c. *Grandpa's Shorts* (Jessica Hitchings, Ashleigh Bree, Malyna Sengdara and Aniva Kini, Glendene Primary School)	30	35
2507	40c. *Which New Zealand Bird?* (Olivia Duncan, Takapuna Intermediate School)	30	35
MS2508	230×90 mm. Nos. 2498/507	4·25	4·50

611 Queen Elizabeth the Queen Mother, 1992

2002. Queen Elizabeth the Queen Mother Commemoration.

2509	**611**	$2 multicoloured	2·00	1·60

612 Tongaporutu Cliffs, Taranaki

2002. Coastlines. Multicoloured. (a) Size 38×29 mm. Ordinary gum.

2510	40c. Type **612**	25	20
2511	80c. Lottin Point, East Cape	50	55
2512	90c. Curio Bay, Catlins	60	65
2513	$1.30 Kaikoura Coast	85	1·00
2514	$1.50 Meybille Bay, West Coast	95	1·50
2515	$2 Papanui Point, Raglan	1·25	1·60

(b) Size 28×21 mm. Self-adhesive.

2516	40c. Type **612**	30	30
2517	90c. Curio Bay, Catlins	85	1·10
2518	$1.50 Meybille Bay, West Coast	1·50	1·75

613 Basket of Fruit

2002. Children's Health. Healthy Eating. Multicoloured. (a) Ordinary gum.

2519	40c.+5c. Type **613**	50	55
2520	90c.+5c. Selection of vegetables	75	80
MS2521	90×75 mm. Nos. 2519/20 and as No. 2522 (22×26 mm)	1·75	2·00

(b) Self-adhesive.

2522	40c.+5c. Fruit and vegetables (22×26 mm)	30	35

2002. "Amphilex 2002" International Stamp Exhibition, Amsterdam. Sheet 130×95 mm, containing Nos. 2462/3. Multicoloured.

MS2523 $1.50 Strider (Viggo Mortensen); $2 Boromir (Sean Bean) (horiz)	2·00	2·00

No. **MS**2523 was sold at face value.

614 St. Werenfried, Tokaanu

2002. Christmas. Church Interiors. Multicoloured. (a) Size 35×35 mm. Ordinary gum.

2524	40c. Type **614**	25	15
2525	80c. St. David's, Christchurch	50	40
2526	90c. Orthodox Church of Transfiguration of Our Lord, Masterton	60	65
2527	$1.30 Cathedral of the Holy Spirit, Palmerston North	85	90
2528	$1.50 St. Paul's Cathedral, Wellington	95	1·10
2529	$2 Cathedral of the Blessed Sacrament, Christchurch	1·25	1·60

(b) Size 25×30 mm. Self-adhesive.

2530	40c. St. Werenfried, Tokaanu	30	30

615 *KZ 1* (racing yacht)

2002. Racing and Leisure Craft. Multicoloured.

2531	40c. Type **615**	35	30
2532	80c. *High 5* (ocean racing yacht)	65	55
2533	90c. *Gentle Spirit* (sports fishing and diving boat)	75	70
2534	$1.30 *North Star* (luxury motor cruiser)	1·00	1·00
2535	$1.50 *Ocean Runner* (powerboat)	1·25	1·40
2536	$2 *Salperton* (ocean-going yacht)	1·40	1·60
MS2537	140×80 mm. Nos. 2531/6	4·75	5·00

616 *Black Magic* (New Zealand) and *Luna Rossa* (Italy)

2002. America's Cup, 2003 (1st issue). Scenes from 2000 final, between New Zealand and Italy. Multicoloured.

2538	$1.30 Type **616**	95	90
2539	$1.50 Aerial view of race	1·00	1·00
2540	$2 Yachts turning	1·40	1·60
MS2541	140×80 mm. Nos. 2538/40	4·50	4·75

See also Nos. 2562/5.

2002. "Stampshow 02" International Stamp Exhibition, Melbourne. No. MS2541 with "Stampshow 02" emblem and inscription on the margin. Multicoloured.

MS2542	140×80 mm. Nos. 2538/40	3·75	4·00

617 Green-roofed Holiday Cottage and Paua Shell

2002. Holiday Homes. Multicoloured.

2543	40c. Type **617**	30	35
2544	40c. Red-roofed cottage and sunflower	30	35
2545	40c. White-roofed cottage and life-belt	30	35
2546	40c. Cottage with orange door, boat and fishing fly	30	35
2547	40c. Blue-roofed cottage and fish	30	35
2548	40c. Cottage and caravan	30	35

618 "The Nativity" (15th-cent painting in style of Di Baldese)

2002. New Zealand–Vatican City Joint Issue.

2549	**618** $1.50 multicoloured	1·25	1·40

2002. Making of The Lord of the Rings Film Trilogy (2nd issue): The Two Towers. As T 605. Multicoloured. (a) Designs 50×24 mm or 24×50 mm. Ordinary gum.

2550	40c. Aragorn (Viggo Mortenson) and Eowyn (Miranda Otto) (horiz)	50	30
2551	80c. Orc raider (horiz)	90	55
2552	90c. Gandalf the White (Sir Ian McKellen)	1·00	70
2553	$1.30 Easterling warriors (horiz)	1·25	1·25
2554	$1.50 Frodo (Elijah Wood)	1·40	1·40
2555	$2 Eowyn, Shield Maiden of Rohan (Miranda Otto) (horiz)	1·75	2·00

(b) Designs 37×26 mm or 26×37 mm. Self-adhesive.

2556	40c. Strider (Viggo Mortenson) and Eowyn (Miranda Otto) (horiz)	25	30
2557	80c. Orc raider (horiz)	55	50
2558	90c. Gandalf the White (Sir Ian McKellen)	60	65
2559	$1.30 Easterling warriors (horiz)	85	1·10
2560	$1.50 Frodo (Elijah Wood)	95	1·25
2561	$2 Eowyn, Shield Maiden of Rohan (Miranda Otto) (horiz)	1·25	1·75

2003. America's Cup (2nd issue). The Defence. As T 616. Multicoloured.

2562	40c. Aerial view of Team New Zealand yacht	25	30
2563	80c. Two Team New Zealand yachts	50	55
2564	90c. Team New Zealand yacht tacking	60	65
MS2565	140×80 mm. Nos. 2562/4	1·75	1·75

619 Shepherd with Flock in High Country

2003. Chinese New Year ("Year of the Sheep"). Sheep Farming. Multicoloured.

2566	40c. Type **619**	35	30
2567	90c. Mustering the sheep	65	55
2568	$1.30 Sheep in pen with sheep dog	1·10	1·10
2569	$1.50 Sheep shearing	1·25	1·40
2570	$2 Sheep shearing (different)	1·50	1·60
MS2571	125×85 mm. Nos. 2568 and 2570	2·75	2·75

620 Jon Trimmer in *Carmina Burana*

2003. 50th Anniv of Royal New Zealand Ballet. Scenes from past productions. Multicoloured.

2572	40c. Type **620**	35	30
2573	90c. *Papillon* (horiz)	75	65
2574	$1.30 *Cinderella*	1·10	1·10
2575	$1.50 *FrENZy*	1·25	1·40
2576	$2 *Swan Lake* (horiz)	1·50	1·60

621 Officer, Forest Rangers, 1860s

2003. New Zealand Military Uniforms. Multicoloured.

2577	40c. Type **621**	45	40
2578	40c. Lieutenant, Napier Naval Artillery Volunteers, 1890s	45	40
2579	40c. Officer, 2nd Regt, North Canterbury Mounted Rifles, 1900–10	45	40
2580	40c. Mounted Trooper, New Zealand Mounted Rifles, South Africa 1899–1902	45	40
2581	40c. Staff Officer, New Zealand Division, France, 1918	45	40
2582	40c. Petty Officer, Royal New Zealand Navy, 1914–18	45	40
2583	40c. Rifleman, New Zealand Rifle Brigade, France, 1916–18	45	40
2584	40c. Sergeant, New Zealand Engineers, 1939–45	45	40
2585	40c. Matron, Royal New Zealand Navy Hospital, 1940s	45	40
2586	40c. Private, New Zealand Women's Auxiliary Army Corps, Egypt, 1942	45	40
2587	40c. Pilot serving with R.A.F. Bomber Command, Europe, 1943	45	40
2588	40c. Fighter Pilot, No. 1 (Islands) Group, Royal New Zealand Air Force, Pacific, 1943	45	40
2589	40c. Driver, Women's Auxiliary Air Force, 1943	45	40
2590	40c. Gunner, 16th Field Regt, Royal New Zealand Artillery, Korea, 1950–53	45	40
2591	40c. Acting Petty Officer, H.M.N.Z.S. *Tamaki*, 1957	45	40
2592	40c. Scouts, New Zealand Special Air Service, Malaya, 1955–57	45	40
2593	40c. Canberra Pilot serving with R.A.F. Far East Command, Malaya, 1960	45	40
2594	40c. Infantrymen, 1st Bn, Royal New Zealand Infantry Regt, South Vietnam, 1960s	45	40
2595	40c. Infantryman, New Zealand Bn, UNTAET, East Timor, 2000	45	40
2596	40c. Monitor, Peace Monitoring Group, Bougainville, 2001	45	40

Nos. 2577/96 were printed together, se-tenant, with detailed descriptions of the designs printed on the reverse.

622 Ailsa Mountains

2003. New Zealand Landscapes. Each including the fern symbol after the country inscr. Multicoloured.

2597	5c. Geyser, Whakarewarewa, Rotorua	10	10
2598	10c. Central Otago	15	10
2599	20c. Rainbow Falls, Northland	25	20
2600	45c. Kaikoura	55	35
2601	50c. Type **622**	55	35
2602	50c. Lake Coleridge, Canterbury	55	35
2603	$1 Coromandel	1·00	65
2604	$1 Rangitoto Island, Auckland	1·60	1·50
2605	$1.35 Church of the Good Shepherd, Lake Tekapo	1·75	1·75
2606	$1.50 Arrowtown	2·00	1·00
2607	$2 Tongariro National Park	2·25	1·40
2608	$2.50 Abel Tasman National Park	2·50	1·60
2609	$3 Tongaporutu, Taranaki	3·00	2·50
2610	$5 Castlepoint Lighthouse	4·50	3·75

Nos. 2600, 2602, 2604 and 2606 also come self-adhesive.

623 Sir Edmund Hillary and Mount Everest

2003. 50th Anniv of Conquest of Everest. Multicoloured.

2616	40c. Type **623**	75	90
2617	40c. Climbers reaching summit and Tenzing Norgay	75	90

624 Buckingham Palace

2003. 50th Anniv of Coronation. As Nos. 714/18 (Coronation issue of 1953) but face values in decimal currency as T 624.

2618	**624**	40c. ultramarine	45	25
2619	-	90c. brown	80	70
2620	-	$1.30 red	1·25	1·25
2621	-	$1.50 blue	1·40	1·50
2622	-	$2 violet and ultramarine	1·60	1·60

DESIGNS—VERT: (as T **164**)—90c. Queen Elizabeth II; $1.50, Westminster Abbey. HORIZ: (as T **624**)—$1.30, Coronation State Coach; $2 St. Edward's Crown and Royal Sceptre.

625 New Zealand vs. South Africa Match, 1937

2003. Centenary of New Zealand Test Rugby. Multicoloured.

2623	40c. Type **625**	50	25
2624	90c. New Zealand vs. Wales match, 1963	75	70
2625	$1.30 New Zealand vs. Australia, 1985	1·10	1·10
2626	$1.50 New Zealand vs. France, 1986	1·25	1·40
2627	$1.50 All Blacks jersey	1·25	1·90
2628	$2 New Zealand vs. England, 1997	1·60	2·00
MS2629	100×180 mm. Nos. 2623/8	6·00	6·50

626 Papaaroha, Coromandel Peninsula

2003. New Zealand Waterways. Multicoloured.

2630	40c. Type **626**	45	25
2631	90c. Waimahana Creek, Chatham Islands	75	70
2632	$1.30 Blue Lake, Central Otago	1·25	1·25
2633	$1.50 Waikato River	1·40	1·50
2634	$2 Hooker River, Canterbury	1·60	1·75

627 Boy on Swing

2003. Children's Health. Playgrounds. Multicoloured. (a) Size 39×29 mm. Ordinary gum.

2635	40c.+5c. Type **627**	50	60
2636	90c.+5c. Girls playing hopscotch	90	1·00
MS2637	88×90 mm. Nos. 2635/6 and 40c.+5c. Girl on climbing frame	2·00	2·00

(b) Size 24×29 mm. Self-adhesive.

2638	40c.+5c. Girl on climbing frame	60	40

628 Benz Velo (1895)

2003. Veteran Vehicles. Multicoloured.

2639	40c. Type **628**	45	25
2640	90c. Oldsmobile (1903)	75	70
2641	$1.30 Wolseley (1911)	1·25	1·25
2642	$1.50 Talbot (1915)	1·40	1·50
2643	$2 Model T Ford (1915)	1·60	1·75

629 Christ Child in Crib

2003. Christmas Decorations. Multicoloured. (a) Size 30×30 mm. Ordinary gum.

2644	40c. Type **629**	55	15
2645	90c. Silver and gold bird	85	60
2646	$1.30 Silver candle	1·40	1·25
2647	$1.50 Bells	1·50	1·40
2648	$2 Angel	1·75	1·90

(b) Size 21×26 mm. Self-adhesive.

2649	40c. Type **629**	45	35
2650	$1 Filigree metalwork decoration with baubles	1·00	1·00

2003. "Bangkok 2003" World Philatelic Exhibition. Sheet, 110×80 mm, containing Nos. 2572/3 and 2576.

MS2651	40c. Type **620**; 90c. *Papillon* (horiz); $2 *Swan Lake* (horiz)	3·00	3·00

2003. Making of The Lord of the Rings Film Trilogy (3rd issue): The Return of the King. As T 605. Multicoloured. (a) Designs 24×49 mm or 49×50 mm. Ordinary gum.

2652	40c. Legolas	50	35
2653	80c. Frodo Baggins	85	70
2654	90c. Merry and Pippin (horiz)	95	75
2655	$1.30 Aragorn	1·25	1·25
2656	$1.50 Gandalf the White	1·50	1·50
2657	$2 Gollum (horiz)	2·00	2·75

(b) Designs 24×35 mm or 35×24 mm. Self-adhesive.

2658	40c. Legolas	50	35
2659	80c. Frodo Baggins	85	70
2660	90c. Merry and Pippin (horiz)	95	75
2661	$1.30 Aragorn	1·25	1·25
2662	$1.50 Gandalf the White	1·50	1·50
2663	$2 Gollum (horiz)	2·00	2·75

2003. "Welpex 2003" National Stamp Exhibition, Wellington. Sheet 120×100 mm, containing Nos. 2626/8.

MS2664	$1.50 New Zealand vs. France, 1986; $1.50 All Blacks jersey; $2 New Zealand vs. England, 1997	5·50	5·50

630 Hamadryas Baboon

2004. New Zealand Zoo Animals. Multicoloured. (a) Ordinary gum. Size 29×39 mm.

2665	40c. Type **630**	45	35
2666	90c. Malayan sun bear	85	70
2667	$1.30 Red panda	1·25	1·25
2668	$1.50 Ring-tailed lemur	1·40	1·40
2669	$2 Spider monkey	1·60	1·75
MS2670	125×90 mm. Nos. 2668/9	3·00	3·00

No. **MS**2670 commemorates Chinese New Year, "Year of the Monkey".

(b) Self-adhesive. Size 24×29 mm.

2671	40c. Type **631**	45	35

2004. Hong Kong 2004 International Stamp Exhibition. Sheet, 110×80 mm, containing Nos. 2627/8.

MS2672	$1.50 All Blacks jersey; $2 New Zealand vs. England, 1997	3·50	3·50

631 New Zealand Team

2004. Rugby Sevens. Multicoloured.

2673	40c. Type **631**	45	35
2674	90c. Hong Kong team	85	70
2675	$1.50 Hong Kong Stadium	1·40	1·40
2676	$2 Westpac Stadium, Wellington	1·75	2·00
MS2677	125×85 mm. Nos. 2673/6	4·00	4·00

Stamps of the same design were issued by Hong Kong.

632 Parliament Building, Auckland, 1854

2004. 150th Anniv of First Official Parliament in New Zealand.

2678	**632**	40c. purple and black	45	35
2679	-	45c. purple and black	55	60
2680	-	90c. lilac and black	85	70
2681	-	$1.30 grey and black	1·25	1·25
2682	-	$1.50 blue and black	1·40	1·40
2683	-	$2 green and black	1·60	1·75
MS2684		186×65 mm. Nos. 2678/82	5·00	5·00

DESIGNS:45c. As No. 2678; 90c. Parliament Buildings, Wellington, 1865; $1.30 Parliament Buildings, Wellington, 1899; $1.50 Parliament House, Wellington, 1918; $2 The Beehive, Wellington, 1977.

633

2004. "Draw it Yourself" Postcard Labels. Multicoloured. Self-adhesive.

2685	$1.50 Type **633**	2·50	2·75
2686	$1.50 Rosine with "New Zealand Post" at bottom left	2·50	2·75
2687	$1.50 As Type **633** but emerald	2·50	2·75
2688	$1.50 Reddish violet with "New Zealand Post" at bottom left	2·50	2·75

634 Mountain Oysters

2004. Wild Food Postcard Labels. Multicoloured. Self-adhesive.

2689	$1.50 Type **634**	2·50	3·00
2690	$1.50 Huhu grubs	2·50	3·00
2691	$1.50 Possum pate	2·50	3·00

635 Local Man outside Post Office on Tractor

2004. Kiwi Characters Postcard Labels. Multicoloured. Self-adhesive.

2692	$1.50 Type **635**	2·50	3·00
2693	$1.50 Children on horseback	2·50	3·00
2694	$1.50 Elderly couple outside their home	2·50	3·00

636 Kinnard Haines Tractor

2004. Historic Farm Equipment. Multicoloured.

2695	45c. Type **636**	45	25
2696	90c. Fordson F tractor with plough	80	65
2697	$1.35 Burrell traction engine	1·25	1·40
2698	$1.50 Threshing mill	1·25	1·40
2699	$2 Duncan's Seed Drill	1·60	1·75

637 "Dragon Fish"

2004. World of Wearable Arts. Multicoloured.

2701	45c. Type **637**	45	24
2702	90c. "Persephone's Descent" (man in armour costume)	80	65
2703	$1.35 "Meridian" (woman in silk costume)	1·25	1·40
2704	$1.50 "Taunga Ika" (woman in net costume)	1·25	1·40
2705	$2 "Cailleach Na Mara" (woman in sea witch costume)	1·60	1·75

638 Magnolia

2004. Garden Flowers. Multicoloured.

2706	45c. Type **638**	45	25
2707	90c. Helleborus	85	65
2708	$1.35 Nerine	1·25	1·40
2709	$1.50 Rhododendron	1·25	1·40
2710	$2 Delphinium	1·60	1·75
MS2711	160×65 mm. Nos. 2706/2710	4·75	5·00

The 45c. stamp in No. **MS**2711 was impregnated with the fragrance of Magnolia.

2004. Salon du Timbre International Stamp Exhibition, Paris. Sheet 125×95 mm, containing designs from MS2664 and No. 2676.

MS2712	$1.50 New Zealand vs. France 1986, $1.50 All Blacks jersey; $2 Westpac Stadium	3·50	3·75

639

2004. Emergency 5c. Provisional Stamp.

2713	**639**	5c. blue and vermilion	1·50	1·50

640 Skippers Canyon (The Ford of Bruinen)

2004. Making of The Lord of the Rings Film Trilogy (4th issue): Home of Middle Earth. Multicoloured. Designs 40×30 mm. (a) Ordinary gum.

2714	45c. Type **640**	35	40
2715	45c. Arwen facing Black Riders	35	40
2716	90c. Mount Olympus (South of Rivendell)	65	70
2717	90c. Gimli and Legolas	65	70
2718	$1.50 Erewhon (Edoras)	1·10	1·25
2719	$1.50 Gandalf the White, Legolas, Gimli and Aragorn riding to Rohan	1·10	1·25
2720	$2 Tongariro (Emyn Muil, Mordor)	1·50	1·60
2721	$2 Frodo and Sam	1·50	1·60
MS2722	100×180 mm. Nos. 2714/21	7·25	7·50

(b) Designs 29×24 mm. Self-adhesive.

2723	45c. Skippers Canyon (The Ford of Bruinen)	35	40
2724	45c. Arwen facing Black Riders	35	40
2725	90c. Mount Olympus (South of Rivendell)	65	70
2726	90c. Gimli and Legolas	65	70

641 John Walker winning 1500 Metre Race

2004. Olympic Games, Athens. Gold Medal Winners. Multicoloured. Self-adhesive.

2727	45c. Type **641**	60	40
2728	90c. Yvette Williams (long jump)	95	70
2729	$1.50 Ian Ferguson and Paul MacDonald (kayaking)	1·60	1·60
2730	$2 Peter Snell (800 metre race)	1·75	1·75

2004. World Stamp Exhibition, Singapore. Sheet 125×95 mm containing Nos. 2717/19. Multicoloured.

MS2731	90c. Gimley and Legolas; 90c. Mount Olympus (South of Rivendell); $1.50 Gandalf the White, Legolas, Gimley and Aragorn riding to Rohan; $1.50 Erewhon (Edoras)	3·50	4·00

2004. Tourism (1st series). As T 622. Multicoloured.

2732	$1.50 The Bath House, Rotorua	1·25	1·40
2733	$1.50 Pohutu Geyser, Rotorua	1·25	1·40
2734	$1.50 Hawke's Bay	1·25	1·40
2735	$1.50 Lake Wakatipu, Queenstown	1·25	1·40
2736	$1.50 Mitre Peak, Milford Sound	1·25	1·40
2737	$1.50 Kaikoura	1·25	1·40

See also Nos. 2868/73.

643 Christmas Dinner

644 Christmas Dinner

2004. Christmas. Multicoloured. Designs 49×49 mm. (a) Ordinary gum.

2742	45c. Type **643**	50	20
2743	90c. Traditional Maori meal	80	50
2744	$1.35 Barbecued prawns and salmon	1·25	1·25
2745	$1.50 Pie and salad	1·25	1·50
2746	$2 Plum pudding and pavlova	1·60	2·00

(b) Vert designs as T 644. Self-adhesive.

2747	45c. Type **644**	4·00	40
2748	90c. Traditional Maori meal	80	70
2749	$1 Christmas cake and cards	95	1·00

2004. "Baypex 2004 Hawke's Bay Stamp Show". Sheet 130×70 mm, containing Nos. 1934f and 2733. Multicoloured.

MS2750	$1.50 Hawke's Bay, $3 Cape Kidnappers	4·00	4·75

645 Whitewater Rafting

2004. Extreme Sports. Multicoloured.

2751	45c. Type **645**	50	25
2752	90c. Snowsports	80	65
2753	$1.35 Skydiving	1·25	1·25
2754	$1.50 Jet boating	1·25	1·60
2755	$2 Bungy jumping	1·60	1·75

646 Sheep

2005. Farmyard Animals and Chinese New Year ("Year of the Rooster"). Multicoloured. (a) Ordinary gum.

2757	45c. Type **646**	45	40
2758	90c. Dogs	80	70
2759	$1.35 Pigs	1·25	1·25
2760	$1.50 Rooster	1·25	1·40
2761	$2 Rooster perched on farm equipment	1·60	1·75
MS2762	126×90 mm. Nos. 2760/2761	3·50	4·25

(b) Size 24×30 mm. Self-adhesive.

2763	45c. Sheep	45	40

647 Beneficiaries (Centenary of Rotary International)

2005. Anniversaries of Organisations. Multicoloured.

2764	45c. Type **647**	45	40
2765	45c. Rural development (50th Anniv of the Lions)	45	40
2766	45c. Canoeists (150th Anniv of YMCA)	45	40

642 Children playing in the Sea

2004. Children's Health. A Day at the Beach. Multicoloured. (a) Size 30×40 mm. Ordinary gum.

2738	45c.+5c. Type **642**	35	40
2739	90c.+5c. People in dinghy and swimmer	65	70
MS2740	102×90 mm. Nos. 2738/9 and 45c.+5c. Children fishing (25×30 mm)	1·40	1·50

(b) Size 24×29 mm. Self-adhesive.

2741	45c.+5c. Children fishing	35	40

2767 $1.50 Building development (Centenary of Rotary International) 1·25 1·50
2768 $1.50 Miniature train (50th Anniv of the Lions) 1·25 1·50
2769 $1.50 Beneficiaries jumping (150th Anniv of YMCA) 1·25 1·50
MS2770 130×100 mm. Nos. 2764/9 and central gutter 4·50 5·25

648 1855 Full Face Queen, London Print (No. 1)

2005. 150th Anniv of New Zealand Stamps (1st issue). Stamps of 1855–1905. Multicoloured.
2771 45c. Type **648** 45 25
2772 90c. 1873 Newspaper (Nos. 143/5) 80 70
2773 $1.35 1891 Government Life (No. L 5) 1·25 1·10
2774 $1.50 1989 Pictorial, Mt. Cook (No. 259) 1·40 1·50
2775 $2 1901 Universal Postage (No. 277) 1·60 1·75
MS2776 160×80 mm. Nos. 2771/75 5·00 5·50
See also Nos. 2777/2781 and 2791/**MS**2796.

2005. 150th Anniv of New Zealand Stamps (2nd issue). Stamps of 1905–1955. As T 648. Multicoloured. Ordinary gum.
2777 45c. 1906 New Zealand Exhibition (No. 371) 45 25
2778 90c. 1931 Health (No. 546) 80 70
2779 $1.35 1935 Airmail (No. 571) 1·25 1·10
2780 $1.50 1946 Peace (No. 676) 1·40 1·50
2781 $2 1954 Queen Elizabeth II (No. 736) 1·60 1·75
MS2782 160×80 mm. Nos. 2766/70 5·00 5·50

(b) Designs 25×30 mm. Self-adhesive.
2783 45c. As No. 2777 50 65
2784 90c. As No. 2778 75 85

2005. Pacific Explorer World Stamp Exhibition, Sydney.
MS2785 109×90 mm. Nos. 2775 and 2780 3·25 3·50

649 Cafe, 1910s

2005. Cafe Culture. Multicoloured. Self-adhesive.
2786 45c. Type **649** 45 30
2787 90c. Cafe, 1940s 80 70
2788 $1.35 Cafe, 1970s 1·25 1·25
2789 $1.50 Tables outside cafe on pavement, 1990s 1·25 1·40
2790 $2 Internet cafe, 2005 1·60 1·75

2005. 150th Anniv of New Zealand Stamps (3rd issue). Stamps of 1955—2005. As T 648. Multicoloured.
2791 45c. 1965 50th Anniversary of the Gallipoli Landing (No. 827) 45 25
2792 90c. 1988 Round Kiwi (No. 1490) 80 70
2793 $1.35 1990 The Achievers Katherine Sheppard (No. 1550) 1·25 1·25
2794 $1.50 1994 Maori Myths Maui (No. 1807) 1·40 1·50
2795 $2 2003 Centenary of New Zealand Test Rugby (No. 2627) 1·60 1·75
MS2796 160×80 mm. Nos. 2791/5 5·00 5·50

650 All Blacks Jersey

2005. DHL New Zealand Lions Rugby Series. Self-adhesive.
2797 **650** 45c. black and grey 55 65
2798 - 45c. multicoloured 55 65
2799 - $1.50 black and grey 1·25 1·50
2800 - $1.50 multicoloured 1·25 1·50
DESIGNS: No. 2797, Type **650**; 2798, Red Lions jersey; 2799, As No. 2797; No. 2800, As No. 2798.

651 Kiwi

2005. Personalised Stamps. Multicoloured.
2801 45c. Type **651** 45 55
2802 45c. Pohutukawa (native Christmas tree) 45 55
2803 45c. Champagne glasses 45 55
2804 45c. Balloons 45 55
2805 45c. Wedding bands 45 55
2806 45c. Gift box 45 55
2807 45c. Baby's hand 45 55
2808 $1.50 Globe 1·25 1·40
2809 $2 As Type **651** 1·60 1·75
2810 $2 Fern 1·60 1·75

652 Kakapo ("Relies heavily on camouflage for defence")

2005. Endangered Species. Kakapo. Designs showing the Kakpo with different facts inscribed. Multicoloured.
2811 45c. Type **652** 70 60
2812 45c. "Night Parrot unique to New Zealand" 70 60
2813 45c. "Nocturnal bird living on the forest floor" 70 60
2814 45c. "Endangered – only 86 known surviving" 70 60

653 Child and Horse

2005. Children's Health. Pets. Multicoloured. (a) Size 30×40 mm. Ordinary gum.
2815 45c.+5c. Type **653** 55 55
2816 90c.+5c. Child holding rabbit 90 95
MS2817 100×90 mm. Nos. 2815/16 and 45c.+5c. Children and dog (25×30 mm) 2·50 2·50

(b) Size 25×30 mm. Self-adhesive.
2818 45c.+5c. Children and dog 50 55

2005. Taipei 2005 International Stamp Exhibition. Sheet, 110×90 mm, containing Nos. 2733 and 2737.
MS2819 $1.50 Kaikoura; $1.50 Pohutu Geyser, Rotorua 2·50 2·75

654 Baby Jesus

2005. Christmas. Multicoloured. (a) 35×35 mm. Ordinary gum.
2820 45c. Type **654** 40 15
2821 90c. Mary and Joseph 75 55
2822 $1.35 Shepherd 1·25 1·10
2823 $1.50 Wise Men 1·40 1·50
2824 $2 Star 1·60 2·00

(b) Size 24×29 mm. Self-adhesive.
2825 45c. Type **654** 45 35
2826 $1 Gifts on straw 85 85

655 King Kong

2005. King Kong (film). Multicoloured.
2827 45c. Type **655** 40 35
2828 90c. Carl Denham 75 70
2829 $1.35 Ann Darrow 1·25 1·10
2830 $1.50 Jack Driscoll 1·40 1·50
2831 $2 Ann Darrow and Jack Driscoll 1·60 1·75
MS2832 180×65 mm. Nos. 2827/31 4·75 5·50

2005. National Stamp Show, Auckland. Sheet, 120×90 mm, containing Nos. 2774, 2780 and 2794.
MS2833 $1.50 1989 Pictorial, Mt Cook (No. 259); $1.50 1946 Peace (No. 676); $1.50 1994 Maori Myths – Maui (No. 1807) 4·75 5·50

656 Lucy opening the Wardrobe

2005. Making of The Chronicles of Narnia: The Lion the Witch and the Wardrobe (film). Multicoloured. (a) Ordinary gum.
2834 45c. Type **656** 40 25
2835 90c. Lucy, Edmund, Peter and Susan in snowy forest (horiz) 75 70
2836 $1.35 The White Witch tempting Edmund with Turkish delight (horiz) 1·25 1·10
2837 $1.50 Dissenters turned to stone statues in courtyard of White Witch's castle 1·40 1·60
2838 $2 Lucy and body of Aslan (horiz) 1·60 1·75

(b) As Nos. 2834/8 but smaller. Self-adhesive.
MS2839 200×70 mm. 45c. Type **656** (25×35 mm); 90c. As No. 2835 (35×25 mm); $1.35 As No. 2836 (35×25 mm); $1.50 As No. 2837 (25×35 mm); $2 As No. 2838 (35×25 mm) 6·00 7·00

657 Labrador Retriever Guide Dog

2006. Chinese New Year ("Year of the Dog"). Multicoloured. (a) Ordinary gum.
2840 45c. Type **657** 50 25
2841 90c. German Shepherd Dog 90 70
2842 $1.35 Jack Russell Terrier 1·40 1·25
2843 $1.50 Golden Retriever 1·50 1·90
2844 $2 Huntaway (New Zealand Sheepdog) 1·75 2·00
MS2845 124×89 mm. Nos. 2843/4 5·50 6·00

(b) Size 25×30 mm. Self-adhesive.
2846 45c. Type **657** 50 45

658 Street Scene, c. 1930

2006. 75th Anniv of Hawke's Bay Earthquake. Multicoloured.
2848 45c. Type **658** 55 55
2849 45c. Aerial view of devastated city of Napier 55 55
2850 45c. Aerial view with roofless church and intact Public Trust Building, Napier 55 55
2851 45c. Fire engine and crew 55 55
2852 45c. HMS *Veronica* 55 55
2853 45c. Sailors from HMS *Veronica* clearing debris 55 55
2854 45c. Red Cross nurses with hospital patient 55 55
2855 45c. Rescue services 55 55
2856 45c. Abandoned vehicles on broken road ("Devastation") 55 55
2857 45c. Outdoor hospital ward, Botanical Gardens, Napier ("Medical services") 55 55
2858 45c. Emergency mail plane 55 55
2859 45c. Refugees on road 55 55
2860 45c. Refugee tents, Nelson Park 55 55
2861 45c. Makeshift cooking facilities, Hastings 55 50
2862 45c. Maori women ("Community spirit") 55 55
2863 45c. Refugees boarding train 55 55
2864 45c. Reconstruction work ("Building industry") 55 55
2865 45c. Hastings Street rebuilt in Art Deco style, 1933 55 55
2866 45c. Carnival procession ("Celebrations") 55 55
2867 45c. Entrance to National Tobacco Company building, Ahuriri, 2005 55 55
Nos. 2849/50 form a composite design showing an aerial view of Napier after the earthquake.

2006. Tourism (2nd series). As T 622. Multicoloured.
2868 $1.50 Lake Wanaka 1·40 1·60
2869 $1.50 Mount Taranaki 1·40 1·60
2870 $1.50 Halfmoon Bay, Stewart Island 1·40 1·60
2871 $1.50 Franz Josef Glacier, West Coast 1·40 1·60
2872 $1.50 Huka Falls, Taupo 1·40 1·60
2873 $1.50 Cathedral Cove, Coromandel 1·40 1·60

659 Queen Elizabeth II

2006. 80th Birthday of Queen Elizabeth II.
2874 **659** $5 multicoloured 5·00 5·00
MS2875 105×100 mm. No. 1272 of Jersey; $5 Type **659** (sold at $17.50) 13·00 15·00
No. **MS**2875 is identical to **MS**1273 of Jersey.

660 Champagne Glasses

2006. Personalised Stamps. Multicoloured.
2876 45c. Type **660** 45 50
2877 45c. Buzzy Bee (toy) 45 50
2878 45c. Silver fern 45 50
2879 45c. Pohutukawa flower 45 50
2880 45c. Christmas star decorations 45 50
2881 45c. Engagement and wedding rings 45 50
2882 45c. Red rose 45 50
2883 $1.50 As No. 2878 1·25 1·40
2884 $2 As No. 2879 1·60 1·75
2885 $2 As No. 2880 1·60 1·75

2006. Washington 2006 World Philatelic Exhibition. Sheet, 120×80 mm containing designs as Nos. 2809/10 but without imprint date.
MS2886 $2 Fern; $2 Type **651** 4·50 4·50

661 Wind Farm, Tararua, Palmerston North

2006. Renewable Energy. Multicoloured.
2887 45c. Type **661** 75 25
2888 90c. Roxburgh Dam, Central Otago (hydro) 1·25 90
2889 $1.35 Biogas production, Waikato 1·60 1·50
2890 $1.50 Wairakei Geothermal Power Station 1·90 2·25
2891 $2 Solar-powered lighthouse, Cape Reinga (vert) 2·25 3·00

662 "5" and Tomatoes

2006. Children's Health. "5+ A Day" Healthy Eating Campaign. Multicoloured. (a) Ordinary gum.
2892 45c.+5c. Type **662** (30×40 mm) 75 60
2893 90c.+10c. "+" and oranges (30×40 mm) 1·25 1·25
2894 $1.35 "a" and garlic (30×30 mm) 1·60 1·60
2895 $1.50 "DAY" and kiwi fruit (40×30 mm) 1·90 2·25
2896 $2 Hand silhouette and red cabbage (30×40 mm) 2·25 2·75
MS2897 120×90 mm. Nos. 2892/6 7·50 8·50

(b) Self-adhesive.
2898 45c.+5c. Type **662** (25×30 mm) 75 75

663 Gold Panning, c. 1880s

2006. Gold Rush. Multicoloured.
2899 45c. Type **663** 75 25
2900 90c. Settlement at Kurunui Creek, Thames, c. 1868 (horiz) 1·40 90
2901 $1.35 Chinese prospectors at Tuapeka, Otago, c. 1900s (horiz) 1·75 1·50
2902 $1.50 Last Otago gold escort at Roxburgh, 1901 (horiz) 1·90 2·50
2903 $2 Waterfront at Dunedin, c. 1900s (horiz) 2·25 3·00
MS2904 125×90 mm. As Nos. 2899/903 but "NEW ZEALAND" on stamp and fern symbol in gold 8·50 9·50

664 Decorated Silver Fern (Hanna McLachlan)

2006. Christmas. Designs showing winning entries in children's stamp design competition "What Christmas Means to Me". Multicoloured. Size 34×34 mm. (a) Ordinary gum.
2905 45c. Type **664** 50 15
2906 45c. Angel appearing to shepherds and magi (Isla Hewitt) 50 60
2907 45c. Extended family around Christmas tree (Caitlin Davidson) 50 60
2908 45c. Virgin Mary and baby Jesus (Maria Petersen) 50 60
2909 45c. Beach and pohutakawa tree (Deborah Yoon) 50 60
2910 45c. New Zealand wood pigeon and Christmas star (Hannah Webster) 50 60
2911 90c. Santa hat on kiwi fruit (Pierce Higginson) 1·00 60
2912 $1.35 KIwlana Christmas trees (Rosa Tucker) 1·25 1·00
2913 $1.50 Pattern of four pohutukawa flowers (Sylvie Webby) 1·40 1·75
2914 $2 Camping at Christmas (Gemma Baldock) 1·75 2·00

(b) Size 24×29 mm. Self-adhesive.
2915 45c. Type **664** 50 25
2916 $1.50 As No. 2913 1·40 1·50

665 Dragon Boat Festival

2006. Summer Festivals. Multicoloured.
2917 45c. Type **665** 75 40
2918 90c. Race day 1·40 90
2919 $1.35 Teddy bears' picnic 1·75 1·50
2920 $1.50 Outdoor concert 1·90 2·50
2921 $2 Jazz festival 2·25 2·75
MS2922 185×80 mm. Nos. 2917/21 8·00 8·00

2006. Kiwipex 2006 National Stamp Exhibition, Christchurch. Sheet 120×90 mm.
MS2932 As Nos. 2809/10 but without imprint date (sold at $5) 6·50 7·50
This sheet was sold at $5, a premium of $1 above the face value. The premium funded the NZ Philatelic Trust.

2006. Belgica '06 International Stamp Exhibition, Brussels. Sheet 120×90 mm.
MS2924 Nos. 2883×2 and 2884 6·50 7·50

666 Opening Ceremony, 1957

2007. 50th Anniv of Scott Base, Antarctica. Multicoloured.
2925 45c. Type **666** 1·00 40
2926 90c. Scott Base, 1990 1·75 90
2927 $1.35 Aerial view of Scott Base, 2000 2·00 1·75
2928 $1.50 "SCOTT BASE" sign 2·50 3·00
2929 $2 Scott Base, 2005 3·00 3·25

667 Kunekune Piglet

2007. Chinese New Year ("Year of the Pig"). Multicoloured.
2930 45c. Type **667** 75 25
2931 90c. Kunekune pig 1·40 90
2932 $1.35 Arapawa pig 1·75 1·60
2933 $1.50 Auckland Island pig 1·90 2·50
2934 $2 Kunekune pig, young sow "Ruby" 2·25 2·75
MS2935 125×90 mm. Nos. 2932/3 4·25 4·25

668 Tuatara

2007. Native Wildlife. Multicoloured. Phosphorised frame. Self-adhesive.
2936 45c. Type **668** 75 40
2937 90c. Kiwi 1·40 90
2938 $1.35 Hamilton's frog 1·75 1·60
2939 $1.50 Yellow-eyed penguin 2·50 2·50
2940 $2 Hector's dolphin 2·50 3·00

2007. Northland 2007 National Stamp Exhibition, Whangarei. Sheet 119×80 mm.
MS2941 Nos. 2884 and 2891 7·00 7·50

669 Scouts of 1908 and Lt. Col. David Cossgrove (NZ Scouts founder)

2007. Centenaries. Multicoloured.
2942 50c. Type **669** 1·00 1·00
2943 50c. Dr.Truby King (founder of Plunket Society) and nurse with baby, 1920s 1·00 1·00
2944 50c. All Golds, first New Zealand rugby league team, 1907 1·00 1·00
2945 50c. Sister Suzanne Aubert (founder) and classroom at Home of Compassion, 1907 1·00 1·00
2946 $1 Parents with baby, 2007 (Plunket Society) 1·50 90
2947 $1.50 Elderly lady and carer, 2007 (Home of Compassion) 2·25 2·25
2948 $2 Kiwi rugby league team, 2007 3·50 4·00
2949 $2 Scouts abseiling, 2007 3·50 4·00
Centenaries: Nos. 2942, 2949 World Scout Movement; 2943, 2946 Plunket Society; 2944, 2948 Rugby League in New Zealand; 2945, 2947 Home of Compassion.

2007. Personalised Stamps. As Nos. 2876/82 but new values. Multicoloured.
2950 50c. Buzzy Bee (toy) 70 70
2951 50c. Pohutukawa flower 70 70
2952 50c. Engagement and wedding rings 70 70
2953 50c. Silver fern 70 70
2954 50c. Type **660** 70 70
2955 50c. Red rose 70 70
2956 50c. Christmas star decorations 70 70

670 Southern Cross and 0.5m Zeiss Telescope at Stardome Observatory, Auckland

2007. Southern Skies. Multicoloured.
2957 50c. Type **670** 1·00 45
2958 $1 Pleiades and 1m McLellan telescope, Mt. John Observatory, Tekapo 1·50 1·00
2959 $1.50 Trifid Nebula and 24cm telescope, Ward Observatory, Wanganui 2·50 2·25
2960 $2 Southern Pinwheel and 1.8m MOA telescope, Mt. John Observatory 3·00 3·50
2961 $2.50 Large Magellanic Cloud and 11m Southern African large telescope 3·75 4·50

671 "good as gold"

2007. Classic Kiwi
2962 50c. Type **671** 65 65
2963 50c. "sweet as" 65 65
2964 50c. "she'll be right" 65 65
2965 50c. "hissy fit" 65 65
2966 50c. "sparrow fart" 65 65
2967 50c. Kiwi and "cuz" 65 65
2968 50c. "away laughing" 65 65
2969 50c. "tiki tour" 65 65
2970 50c. "away with the fairies" 65 65
2971 50c. "wop-wops" 65 65
2972 50c. "hard yakka" 65 65
2973 50c. "cods wallop" 65 65
2974 50c. "boots and all" 65 65
2975 50c. "shark and taties" 65 65
2976 50c. "knackered" 65 65
2977 50c. "laughing gear" 65 65
2978 50c. "everyman and his dog" 65 65
2979 50c. "bit of a dag" 65 65
2980 50c. "dreaded lurgy" 65 65
2981 50c. "rark up" 65 65
The shiny black portions at the right of Nos. 2962/81 are printed in thermochromic ink which fades temporarily when exposed to heat, revealing translations of the Kiwi slang on the stamps.

672 Electric Fence (Bill Gallagher), 1969

2007. "Clever Kiwis". New Zealand Inventions. Multicoloured.
2982 50c. Type **672** 60 30
2983 $1 Spreadable butter (Norris and Illingworth) 1·25 1·10
2984 $1.50 Mountain buggy, 1992 2·00 2·00
2985 $2 Jet boat (Bill Hamilton) 3·25 3·50
2986 $2.50 Tranquilliser gun (Colin Murdoch), 1950s 3·75 4·00

2007. Bangkok 2007 20th Asian International Stamp Exhibition. Sheet 80×70 mm.
MS2987 Nos. 2735/6 4·00 4·00

2007. Huttpex 2007 Stampshow (National Exhibition), Lower Hutt. Sheet 120×90 mm.
MS2988 Nos. 2960/1 5·50 5·50

673 Girl releasing Peace Dove

2007. Children's Health. Peaceful World. T 673 and similar vert designs. Multicoloured. (a) Size 30×40 mm. Ordinary gum.
2989 50c.+10c. Type **673** 35 35
2990 $1+10c. Boy holding Japanese crane 1·75 1·75
MS2991 100×90 mm. 50c.+10c. Girls with peace lily (24×29 mm) and Nos. 2989/90 3·00 3·00

(b) Size 24×29 mm. Self-adhesive.
2992 50c.+10c. Girls with peace lily 1·00 1·00

674 Queen Elizabeth II and Prince Philip, c. 2007

2007. Diamond Wedding of Queen Elizabeth II and Prince Philip. Multicoloured.
2993 50c. Type **674** 50 50
2994 $2 On their wedding day, 1947 2·75 2·75
MS2995 110×90 mm. Nos. 2993/4 3·25 3·25

675 Christmas Symbols (Sione Vao)

2007. Christmas. Showing winning entries in children's stamp design competition 'Christmas Symbols'. Multicoloured. (a) Ordinary gum.
2996 50c. Type **675** 60 20
2997 $1 Robin wearing Santa hat (Reece Cateley) 1·10 60
2998 $1.50 Baby Jesus (Emily Wang) 2·25 2·00
2999 $2 Beach cricket (Alexandra Eathorne) 3·00 3·25
3000 $2.50 Fantail (Jake Hooper) 3·75 4·50

(b) Self-adhesive. Size 24×29 mm.
3001 50c. As Type **675** 60 50
3002 $1.50 As No. 2997 1·75 1·75

676 'GO YOU GOOD THING'

2007. Personalised Stamps. Multicoloured.
3003 50c. Type **676** 75 75
3004 50c. 'Look Who it is!' 75 75
3005 50c. 'Love Always' 75 75
3006 50c. 'THANKS A MILLION' 75 75
3007 50c. 'WE'VE GOT NEWS' 75 75
3008 50c. 'Wish you were here' 75 75
3009 $1 'Time to Celebrate' 1·40 1·40
3010 $1 'Kia Ora' 1·40 1·40
3011 $1.50 'You gotta love Christmas' 2·25 2·25
3012 $2 Chinese inscription 3·00 3·00

677 Dusky Sound, Fiordland

2008. Underwater Reefs. Multicoloured. (a) Ordinary gum. Designs 39×29 mm.

3013	50c. Type **677**	75	30
3014	$1 *Callanthias australis* (splendid perch) and *Ecklonia radiata* (common kelp), Mayor Island, Bay of Plenty	1·50	1·25
3015	$1.50 Hydrocoral *Errina novaezelandiae* (red coral), Fiordland	2·25	2·50
3016	$2 *Diadema palmeri* (diadema urchin), Volkner Rocks, White Island, Bay of Plenty	3·00	3·50
MS3017	120×80 mm. Nos. 3013/16	6·75	6·75

(b) Self-adhesive. Size 29×24 mm.

3018	50c. Type **677**	75	75
3019	$1 As No. 3014	1·40	1·40

678 Rabbits

2008. Chinese New Year ('Year of the Rat'). Pocket Pets. Multicoloured.

3020	50c. Type **678**	1·00	30
3021	$1 Guinea pigs	1·75	1·25
3022	$1.50 Rats	2·50	3·00
3023	$2 Mice	3·25	3·50
MS3024	125×90 mm. Nos. 3022/3	5·75	6·50

679 Drought, 1997–98

2008. Weather Extremes. Multicoloured.

3025	50c. Type **679**	75	75
3026	50c. Pedestrians in gale, Auckland, March 2007	75	75
3027	$1 Storm waves, Evans Bay, Wellington, January 2001	1·40	1·40
3028	$1.50 Flooded farmland, Hikurangi, 2007	2·25	2·25
3029	$2 Snow storm, Ohai, Southland, May 2001	2·75	2·75
3030	$2.50 Heat, Matarangi beach, Coromandel, 2005	3·75	3·75

2008. Taipei 2008 21st Asian International Stamp Exhibition. Sheet 120×90 mm.

MS3031	No. 3012 and as No. 3023	5·75	5·75

680 Sapper John Luamanu and Baby Daughter, ANZAC Day Parade, 2007

2008. ANZAC (1st series). Multicoloured.

3032	50c. Type **680**	85	75
3033	50c. Auckland Infantry Battalion landing at Gallipoli, 25 April 1915	85	75
3034	$1 New Zealand soldiers on Western Front, April 1918	1·60	1·40
3035	$1.50 Sling Camp and chalk kiwi on Salisbury Plain, England, 1919	2·50	2·50
3036	$2 Maori Battalion performing haka, Helwan, Egypt, June 1941	3·00	3·25
3037	$2.50 161 Battery, Nui Dat, Vietnam, 1965–71	4·00	4·25

681 *Miro Whero, Miro Ma, Miro Pango*

2008. 150th Years of Kingitanga (Maori King) Movement. Designs showing art by Fred Graham. Multicoloured.

3038	50c. Type **681**	75	40
3039	$1.50 *He Piko He Taniwha*	2·00	2·25
3040	$2.50 *Kia Mau* (horiz)	3·75	4·00

682 The Pevensie Children playing in the Surf

2008. Making of The Chronicles of Narnia: Prince Caspian (film). Multicoloured.

3041	50c. Type **682**	1·00	45
3042	$1 Queen Susan	1·75	1·25
3043	$1.50 High King Peter	2·75	2·75
3044	$2 Prince Caspian	3·25	3·50

683 'Ranginui' (sky)

2008. Matariki (Maori New Year). Multicoloured.

3045	50c. Type **683**	65	50
3046	50c. Te Moana Nui A Kiwa	65	50
3047	$1 Papatuanuku	1·25	1·10
3048	$1.50 Whakapapa	2·25	2·25
3049	$2 Takoha	2·75	2·75
3050	$2.50 Te Tau Hou	3·75	3·75
MS3050	150×90 mm. Nos. 3045/50	10·50	10·50

684 Girl riding Bicycle ('INSPIRE')

2008. Children's Health. Multicoloured. (a) Ordinary gum.

3052	50c.+10c. Type **684**	70	70
3053	$1+10c. Boy kayaking ('PASSION')	1·40	1·40
MS3054	140×90 mm. 50c. +10c. Boy with arms outstretched in triumph (34×32 mm) and Nos. 3052/3	3·00	3·00

(b) Self-adhesive.

3055	50c.+10c. Boy with arms outstretched in triumph ('EXCEL') (34×32 mm)	70	70

685 Rower ('CELEBRATE')

2008. Olympic Games, Beijing. Multicoloured.

3056	50c. Type **685**	1·00	85
3057	50c. Cyclist ('PASSION')	1·50	85
3058	$1 Kayaker ('SUCCEED')	1·75	1·13
3059	$2 Athlete ('MOTIVATE')	3·25	3·50

686 'a' is for Aotearoa

2008. The A to Z of New Zealand. Multicoloured.

3060	50c. Type **686**	70	70
3061	50c. B is for Beehive (Parliament House, Wellington)	70	70
3062	50c. C is for Cook (Captain Cook)	70	70
3063	50c. D is for Dog (from Footrot Flats cartoon strip)	70	70
3064	50c. E is for Edmonds (Thomas Edmonds)	70	70
3065	50c. F is for Fantail (bird)	70	70
3066	50c. G Is for Goodnight Kiwi (TV cartoon)	70	70
3067	50c. H is for Haka	70	70
3068	50c. I is for Interislander (ferry)	70	70
3069	50c. J is for Jelly Tip (ice cream)	70	70
3070	50c. K is for Kia Ora	70	70
3071	50c. L is for log o'wood (Ranfurly Shield rugby trophy)	70	70
3072	50c. M is for Mudpools	70	70
3073	50c. N is for Nuclear Free	70	70
3074	50c. O is for O.E. (overseas experience)	70	70
3075	50c. P is for Pinetree (All Black player Colin Meads)	70	70
3076	50c. Q is for Quake (earthquakes)	70	70
3077	50c. R is for Rutherford (nuclear physicist Sir Ernest Rutherford)	70	70
3078	50c. S is for Southern Cross	70	70
3079	50c. T is for Tiki (carved by Lewis Gardiner)	70	70
3080	50c. U is for Upham (Captain Charles Upham's Victoria Cross)	70	70
3081	50c. V is for Vote (suffragette Kate Sheppard)	70	70
3082	50c. W is for Weta (model of insect)	70	70
3083	50c. X is for x-treme sports	70	70
3084	50c. Y is for Yarn	70	70
3085	50c. Z is for Zeeland (explorer Abel Tasman)	70	70

687 Last Spike Ceremony, Manganui-o-te-Ao, 1908

2008. Centenary of the North Island Main Trunk Railway Line. Multicoloured.

3086	50c. Type **687**	75	40
3087	$1 KA 947 class steam locomotive on display at Taumarunui, 1958	1·40	1·10
3088	$1.50 Steam hauled goods train on Makatote Viaduct, 1963	2·00	2·00
3089	$2 Steam hauled goods train climbing the Raurimu Spiral, 1964	2·75	3·25
3090	$2.50 EF powered 'Overlander' crossing Hapuawhenua Viaduct, 2003	3·75	4·25

2008. WIPA08 International Stamp Exhibition, Vienna. Sheet 121×85 mm.

MS3091	Nos. 3046 and 3048/9	4·50	4·75

688 Nativity

2008. Christmas (1st issue). Multicoloured. (a) Ordinary gum.

3092	50c. Type **688**	60	20
3093	$1 Holy Family	1·10	60
3094	$1.50 Mary and baby Jesus	1·75	2·00

(b) Self-adhesive. Size 24×29 mm.

3095	50c. As Type **688**	60	50
3096	$1.50 As No. 3094	1·60	1·60

689 Sheep wearing Santa Hat and Jandals (Kirsten Fisher-Marsters)

2008. Christmas (2nd issue). T 689 and similar square designs showing winning entries in children's stamp design competition 'Kiwi Christmas'. Multicoloured.

3097	50c. Type **689**	60	20
3098	$2 Pohutukawa flowers and koru (Tamara Jenkin)	2·25	2·50
3099	$2.50 Kiwi wearing Santa hat (Molly Bruhns)	2·50	2·75

2008. 90th Anniv of the End of World War I. Sheet 150×90 mm. Multicoloured.

MS3100	Nos. 3033/5	4·50	4·75

690 Sir Edmund Hillary

2008. Sir Edmund Hillary Commemoration. Multicoloured.

3101	50c. Type **690**	75	40
3102	$1 Edmund Hillary and Tenzing Norgay during first ascent of Mt. Everest, 1953	1·25	1·10
3103	$1.50 On tracked vehicle, Trans-Antarctic Expedition, 1955–8	1·90	1·90
3104	$2 Sir Edmund Hillary (founder of Himalayan Trust, 1960) with Nepalese children	2·50	2·75
3105	$2.50 Appointed to the Order of the Garter, 1995	2·75	3·00

2008. Tarapex 2008 National Stamp Exhibition, New Plymouth. Sheet 138×86 mm. Multicoloured.

MS3106	As Nos. 2609 and 2869 but without imprint dates	5·00	5·00

691 Pencarrow Lighthouse

2009. Lighthouses of New Zealand. Multicoloured.

3107	50c. Type **691**	80	45
3108	$1 Dog Island Lighthouse	1·14	1·00
3109	$1.50 Cape Brett Lighthouse	2·25	2·50
3110	$2 Cape Egmont Lighthouse	3·00	3·25
3111	$2.50 Cape Reinga Lighthouse	3·50	3·75

Nos. 3107/11 commemorate the 150th anniversary of New Zealand's first lighthouse (Pencarrow Head).

692 Lunar Ox Symbol

2009. Chinese New Year ('Year of the Ox'). Multicoloured.

3112	50c. Type **692**	80	65
3113	$1 Ox	1·40	1·14
3114	$2 Chinese lanterns and Auckland Harbour Bridge	2·75	3·25
MS3115	Nos. 3112/14	4·50	4·75

693 Scott Dixon in Race Car

2009. New Zealand Champions of Motorsport. (a) Ordinary gum.

3116 50c. Type **693** 1·00 45
3117 $1 Bruce McLaren in Formula One race car 1·75 1·25
3118 $1.50 Ivan Mauger on speedway motorcycle 2·50 2·50
3119 $2 Denny Hulme in race car 3·25 3·50
3120 $2.50 Hugh Anderson on Grand Prix motorcycle 3·75 4·25
MS3121 Nos. 3116x20 11·00 11·00

3122 50c. As Type **693** 1·00 1·00
3123 $1 As No. 3117 1·50 1·50

694 Giant Moa

2009. Giants of New Zealand. Multicoloured.

3124 50c. Type **694** 1·00 55
3125 $1 Colossal squid 1·75 1·20
3126 $1.50 Southern right whale 2·75 2·50
3127 $2 Giant eagle 3·25 3·50
3128 $2.50 Giant weta 3·75 4·25
MS3129 179×90 mm. Nos. 3124/8 11·00 12·00

2009. International Polar Year 2007–2009. Sheet 120×80 mm. Multicoloured.

MS3130 As No. 2871×2 but without imprint dates 5·50 5·50

695 Funeral Procession of the Unknown Warrior, Wellington, 2004

2009. ANZAC (2nd series). 'Comrades in Arms'. Multicoloured.

3131 50c. Type **695** 90 75
3132 50c. NZ (Maori) Pioneer Battalion on break from trench improvement, World War I 90 75
3133 $1 No. 75 (NZ) Squadron RAF and Wellington bomber, World War II 1·60 1·40
3134 $1.50 HMS *Achilles* (Leander class cruiser), World War II 2·25 2·25
3135 $2 Kayforce gun crew in action, Korea, 1 April 1952 2·75 3·00
3136 $2.50 Soldiers of ANZAC Battalion boarding RAAF Iroquois helicopter, Vietnam, 23 March 1968 3·75 4·00

2009. China 2009 World Stamp Exhibition, Luoyang, China. Sheet 95×90 mm. Multicoloured.

MS3137 Nos. 3010, 3012 and 3113 5·25 5·50

696 Pedestrians crossing Bridge before its opening to Traffic, 1959

2009. 50th Anniv of Auckland Harbour Bridge. Multicoloured.

3138 50c. Type **696** 75 40
3139 $1 Auckland Harbour Bridge (with two extra lanes) in 2009 1·25 1·10
3140 $1.50 Auckland Harbour Bridge in 1961 2·25 2·50
3141 $2 Auckland Harbour Bridge at night, 2009 2·75 3·00

697 Heitiki from 'Te Maori' Exhibition, 1984

2009. Matariki (Maori New Year). Multicoloured. (a) Self-adhesive.

3143 50c. Type 697 75 45
3144 $1 Heitiki by Raponi 1·40 1·10
3145 $1.50 Heitiki made from corian by Rangi Kipa 2·25 2·25
3146 $1.80 Female heitiki made from greenstone 2·50 2·50
3147 $2 Female heitiki, c. 1849, from the Museum of New Zealand 3·00 3·25
3148 $2.30 Heitiki made from paraoa by Rangi Hetet, 1991 3·50 3·75

(b) Ordinary gum.

MS3149 150×90 mm. As Nos. 3143/8 12·00 12·00

2009. New Zealand Landscapes (2nd series). As T 622. Multicoloured. (a) Ordinary gum.

3150 30c. Tolaga Bay 75 45
3151 $1.80 Russell 3·00 3·00
3152 $2.30 Lake Wanaka 3·50 3·50
3153 $2.80 Auckland 3·50 3·75
3154 $3.30 Rakaia River 4·25 4·25
3155 $4 Wellington 5·50 6·00

(b) Self-adhesive.

3156 $1.80 As No. 3151 2·75 3·00

698 Lighthouse (Cape Reinga) and Angler

2009. A Tiki Tour of New Zealand. Sheet 99×280 mm containing T 698 and similar square designs. Multicoloured.

MS3157 Type **698**; Hole in the Rock Tour (Cape Brett); Maui snaring the sun (Maori legend); Yachting; Sky Tower (Auckland) and surf boat; Marlin fishing; Waikato rugby (Mooloos); Rower, statue of shearer and Maori carving; Pohutukawa tree, east coast style whare (meeting house), surfing and horse-riding; Mt. Taranaki; Gumboot and wind turbines; Gannet (Cape Kidnappers); Tribute state (Greymouth) and Municipal Building (Westport); Grapes, fly-fishing and glass blowing; Richard Seddon statue (Parliament) and windsurfer; Mount Cook lily and statue of Mackenzie's dog (Lake Tekapo); Roadside crayfish caravan (Kaikoura) and Neil Dawson's Chalice sculpture (Christchurch); Whale watching; Crayfish, black robin and fishing boat (Chatham Islands); Milfound Sound and jetboat (Shotover river); 'Wings over Wanaka' (biplane); Kakapo; Curling; Stewart Island shag and chain sculpture (Rakiura track, Oban) 16·00 16·00

No. **MS**3157 contains 24 stamps and one stamp-size label, the backgrounds forming a composite design of a map of New Zealand.

699 1996 Child Safety 40c.+5c. Stamp

2009. 80th Anniv of Children's Health Stamps. Multicoloured. (a) Ordinary gum.

3158 50c.+10c. Type **699** 1·50 1·50
3159 $1+10c. 1932 Hygeia 1d.+1d. Health stamp 2·00 2·00
MS3160 100×90 mm. 50c.+10c. 1943 Princess Elizabeth 2d.+1d. Health stamp (25x30 mm) (p 14×14½) and as Nos. 3158/9 (p 14) 3·25 3·25

700 Beach Cricket

2009. KiwiStamps. Multicoloured. Self-adhesive.

3162 (–) Type **700** 80 80
3163 (–) Kiwi fruit 80 80
3164 (–) State Highway 1 road sign 80 80
3165 (–) Windfarm and umbrella blown inside out 80 80
3166 (–) Lawnmower 80 80
3167 (–) Caravan 80 80
3168 (–) Flying duck wall ornaments 80 80
3169 (–) Fish and chips at the beach 80 80
3170 (–) Swanndri jacket on barbed wire fence 80 80
3171 (–) Sausage on fork and barbecue 80 80

Nos. 3162/71c were all inscr 'KiwiStamp' and were valid for Standard Post medium letters in New Zealand.

701 Three Shepherds

2009. Christmas (1st issue). Multicoloured. (a) Ordinary gum.

3172 50c. Type **701** 75 45
3173 $1 Mary, Joseph and Infant Jesus 1·50 1·25
3174 $1.80 Three magi with gifts 2·50 3·00

(b) Self-adhesive. Size 30×25 mm.

3175 50c. As Type **701** 75 75
3176 $1.80 As No. 3174 2·25 2·25

702 Seaside Chair and Pohutukawa Tree (Felix Wang)

2009. Christmas (2nd issue). T 702 and similar square designs showing winning entries in children's stamp design competition 'What do you love about Christmas?'. Multicoloured.

3177 50c. Type **702** 75 45
3178 $2.30 New Zealand pigeon wearing Christmas hat (Danielle Aldworth) 3·00 3·25
3179 $2.80 Christmas presents (Apun Bakshi) 4·25 4·50

2009. Timpex 2009 National Stamp Exhibition, Timaru. Sheet 170×92 mm. Multicoloured.

MS3180 As Nos. 3101/2 and 3105 (all p 14) and specimen stamp as Type **501** (p 14½×15) 6·50 6·50

No. **MS**3180 was sold for $6.50, with a $2.50 surcharge to fund the Philatelic Trust.

703 Sir Peter Blake ('Inspirational Leader')

2009. Sir Peter Blake (yachtsman) Commemoration. Multicoloured.

3181 50c. Type **703** 75 45
3182 $1 Sir Peter Blake at wheel and yacht ('Whitbread Round the World Yachtsman') 1·40 1·25
3183 $1.80 Sir Peter Blake using winch and catamaran ('Jules Verne Trophy Record Breaker') 2·25 2·25
3184 $2.30 Sir Peter Blake, Americas Cup trophy and yacht *New Zealand* ('Passionate Kiwi') 3·00 3·25
3185 $2.80 Sir Peter Blake and yacht *Seamaster* on expedition in Antarctica ('Environmentalist') 4·00 4·25
MS3186 160×58 mm. Nos. 3181/5 11·00 11·00

704 Lunar Tiger Symbol

2010. Chinese New Year. Year of the Tiger. Multicoloured

3187 50c. Type **704** 1·00 75
3188 $1 Tiger 1·90 1·90
3189 $1.80 Head of tiger 2·75 2·75
3190 $2.30 Beehive (Parliament House, Wellington) 3·75 4·00
MS3191 150x90 mm. Nos. 3187/90 8·50 8·50

705 Heitiki

2010. Personalised Stamps. Sheet 94x82 mm. Multicoloured.

MS3192 $1.80 Type **705**; $2.30 As Type **660**; $2.30 Engagement and wedding rings; $2.30 Pohtukawa flower 13·00 13·00

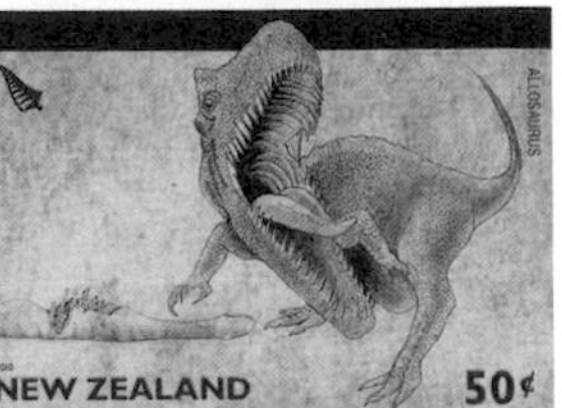

706 Allosaurus

2010. Dinosaurs of New Zealand. Multicoloured. (a) Ordinary gum.

3193 50c. Type **706** 95 85
3194 $1 Anhanguera 2·25 2·25
3195 $1.80 Titanosaurus 3·00 3·00
3196 $2.30 Moanasaurus 3·75 3·75
3197 $2.80 Mauisaurus 4·50 4·50

(b) Self-adhesive. Sheet 230×200 mm.

MS3198 As Nos. 3193/7 13·00 13·00

707 ANZAC Soldier

2010. ANZAC (3rd series). Remembrance. Multicoloured.

3199 50c. Type **707** 1·00 1·00
3201 $1 Posthumous VC Award Ceremony for Second Lieutenant Te Moana-Nui-a-Kiwa Ngarimu, Ruatoria, 1943 1·75 1·75
3202 $1.80 Nurses laying wreath, Cairo Cemetery, ANZAC Day, 1940 2·75 2·75
3203 50c. Gallipoli veterans marching, ANZAC Day, 1958 1·00 1·00
3203 $2.30 ANZAC War Memorial, Port Said, Egypt, 1932 3·50 3·50
3204 $2.80 Veteran at Sangro War Cemetery, Italy, 2004 4·00 4·00

708 Peony and Pohutukawa Flowers

2010. Expo 2010, Shanghai, China. Multicoloured.

3205 50c. Type **708** 95 95
3206 $1 Maori Kaitiaki (carved by Lyonel Grant for New Zealand pavilion) and Chinese Fu Dog 1·75 1·75
3207 $1.80 Pan Gu (Chinese creation story) and Tane creating world of light (Maori legend) 2·25 2·25

3208 $2.30 Shanghai and Auckland skylines 2·50 2·50
3209 $2.80 Jade cong (Chinese good luck symbol) and jade heitiki 2·75 2·75
MS3210 180×140 mm. As Nos. 3205/9 9·00 9·50

Nos. 3205/9 have text in English and Chinese printed on the back of the stamps.

Stamps from **MS**3210 do not have text printed on the reverse.

2010. London 2010 Festival of Stamps. Sheet 130×90 mm. Multicoloured.
MS3211 Nos. 3199 and 3203/4 9·00 9·00

709 Manu Aute

2010. Matariki
3212 50c. Type **709** 75 75
3213 $1 Manu patiki (vert) 2·00 2·00
3214 $1.80 Manu taratahi (vert) 2·75 2·75
3215 $2.30 Upoko tangata 3·25 3·25
MS3216 150×90 mm. Nos. 3215/18 8·75 8·75

710 Centenary Series Jersey

2010. Centenary of Maori Rugby. Multicoloured.
3217 50c. Type **710** 1·00 1·00
3218 $1.80 Centenary logo 2·75 2·75
MS3219 160×90 mm. Nos. 3220/1 3·75 3·75

711 Monarch Butterfly

2010. Children's Health. Butterflies

(a) Ordinary gum
3220 50c.+10c. Type **711** 1·50 1·50
3221 $1+10c. Tussock butterfly 1·50 1·50
MS3222 166×95 mm. 50c.+10c. Boulder copper butterfly (26×30 mm) and Nos. 3220/1 3·50 3·50

(b) Self-adhesive. Size 25x30 mm. Die-cut perf 9½x10
3223 Boulder copper butterfly 1·50 1·50

712 Silver Fern (All Blacks emblem)

2010. All Blacks (national rugby team)
3224 **712** 60c. black 1·00 1·00
3225 **712** $1.90 black 2·75 2·75
MS3226 90×78 mm. As Nos. 3224/5 but 35×20 mm (p 15×14½) and Nos. 3224/5 3·75 3·75

2010. New Zealand Landscapes (3rd series). Multicoloured.

(a) Ordinary gum. Phosphorised paper
3227 $1.20 Mitre Peak, Milford Sound 1·60 1·60
3228 $1.90 Queenstown 2·75 2·75
3229 $2.40 Lake Rotorua 3·75 3·75
3230 $2.90 Kaikoura 4·50 4·50
3231 $3.40 River Avon at Christchurch 5·50 5·50

(b) Self-adhesive. Phosphor frame
3232 $1.20 As No. 3227 1·75 1·75
3233 $1.90 As No. 3228 3·00 3·00

713 Emblem

2010. Rugby World Cup, New Zealand (2011)
3234 **713** 60c. multicoloured 1·00 1·00
3235 **713** $1.90 multicoloured 3·00 3·00
MS3236 91×79 mm. As Nos. 3234/5 but 35×20 mm (p 15×14½) and Nos. 3234/5 7·75 7·75

2010. Personalised Stamps. Multicoloured.
MS3237 60c.×8 As Type **660**; Buzzy Bee (toy); Silver fern; Pohutukawa flower; Engagement and wedding rings; Red rose; As Type **705**; Teddy bear 5·50 5·50
MS3238 94×82 mm. $1.90 As Type **705**; $2.40 As Type **660**; $2.40 Engagement and wedding rings; $2.40 Pohutukawa fllower 16·00 16·00

714 Tane Mahuta (oldest tree), Kerikeri Stone Store and Treaty House at Waitangi

2010. 'New Zealand A Slice of Heaven'. Multicoloured.
MS3239 60c.×25 Type **714**; Fountain and waterfront, Oriental Bay, Wellington; Octagon Plaza with Dunedin Cathedral and St. Paul's Church, Dunedin; Auckland Ferry Terminal; The Beehive, Wellington; Sky Tower, Auckland; One Tree Hill, Auckland; Mt. Ruapehu and Waikato River; Hot air balloons shaped as sheep, cow's head and kiwi; Christchurch Cathedral and River Avon; Horse race; Rural garage, coffee shop and church; Mt. Cook, helicopter and plane; War memorial, ploughed field and lake shore; Lake Taupo, Huka Falls and bridge; Champagne Pool, geysers, mud pools and marae; Rugby match; Queenstown, Lake Wakatipu and the Remarkables Range; Skiers, biplane, glider and golf course; Shotover River and Skippers Suspension Bridge; Seaside caravan park; Titahi Bay boatsheds; Hawke's Bay vineyard; Farm with sheep in pens; Nugget Point 24·00 24·00

The stamps and margins of No. **MS**3239 form a composite design.

715 1960 2d. 'The Adoration of the Shepherds' (Rembrandt) Stamp

2010. Christmas. 50th Anniv of New Zealand Christmas Stamps. Multicoloured.

(a) Phosphorised paper.
3240 60c. Type **715** 1·00 1·00
3241 $1.20 1970 3c. stamp showing 'The Holy Family' stained glass window from Invercargill Presbyterian Church 2·75 2·75
3242 $1.90 1979 35c. Pohutukawa tree stamp 1·00 1·00
3243 $2.40 1983 45c. 'The Glory of Christmas' stamp showing star and flowers 4·00 4·00
3244 $2.90 2000 40c. Virgin Mary and Baby Jesus stamp 4·75 4·75

(b) Self-adhesive. Size 25x30 mm
3245 60c. As Type **715** 1·00 1·00
3246 $1.90 As No. 3242 4·00 4·00

716 Surf Lifeguard with Rescue Tube

2010. Centenary of Surf Life Saving. Multicoloured.
3247 60c. Type **716** 1·10 1·10
3248 Type **716** Lifeguards in inflatable rescue boat (IRB) 2·20 2·20
3249 $1.90 Ski paddlers in Surf Life Saving Championships 2·75 2·75
3250 $2.40 Surf boat 3·75 3·75
3251 $2.90 March past of lifeguards in 1930s surf carnival 5·00 5·00

2010. Palmpex 2010 National Stamp Exhibition, Palmerston North. Sheet 150×90 mm
MS3252 No. 2090*b*×3 7·50 7·50

717 Rabbit Symbol

2010. Chinese New Year. Year of the Rabbit. Multicoloured.
3253 60c. Type **717** 1·10 1·10
3254 $1.20 Chinese style rabbit 1·90 1·90
3255 $1.90 Leaping rabbit 3·25 3·25
3256 $2.40 Christchurch Cathedral and Chinese kite 3·75 3·75
MS3257 150×90 mm. Nos. 3253/6 10·00 10·00

2011. INDIPEX 2011 World Philatelic Exhibition, New Delhi. Multicoloured.
MS3258 Nos. 3227/9 9·00 9·00

718 Whakaeke (choreographed entrance)

2011. Kapa Haka (Maori performing arts). Multicoloured.

(a) Self-adhesive
3259 60c. Type **718** 1·10 1·10
3260 60c. Poi (dancer swinging taupo ball on flax cord) 1·10 1·10
3261 $1.20 Waiata-a-ringa (action songs) 2·25 2·25
3262 $1.90 Haka 3·25 3·25
3263 $2.40 Whakawatea (choreographed exit) 3·75 3·75
3264 $2.90 Moteatea (traditional chant) 4·50 4·50

(b) Ordinary gum
MS3265 150×90 mm. As Nos. 3259/64 16·00 16·00

719 Prince William and Miss Catherine Middleton

2011. Royal Wedding. Multicoloured.
3266 $2.40 Type **719** 4·00 4·00
3267 $2.40 Prince William and Miss Catherine Middleton embracing 4·00 4·00
MS3268 135×91 mm. Nos. 3266/7 8·00 8·00

720 Hokey Pokey (vanilla and crunchy toffee ice cream)

2011. KiwiStamps. Multicoloured.
3269 (–) Type **720** 95 95
3270 (–) Kiwi road sign 95 95
3271 (–) Beach 95 95
3272 (–) Trout fishing 95 95
3273 (–) Mountain biking 95 95

721 Charles Heaphy, 11 February 1864, Waikato, New Zealand

2011. Victoria Cross. The New Zealand Story. Multicoloured.
3274 60c. Type **721** 1·00 1·00
3275 60c. William James Hardham, 28 January 1901, South Africa 1·00 1·00
3276 60c. Cyril Royston Guyton Bassett, 7 August 1915, Gallipoli 1·00 1·00
3277 60c. Donald Forrester Brown,15 September 1916, High Wood, France 1·00 1·00
3278 60c. Samuel Frickleton, 7 June 1917, Messines, Belgium 1·00 1·00
3279 60c. Leslie Wilton Andrew, 31 July 1917, La Basse Ville, France 1·00 1·00
3280 60c. Henry James Nicholas, 3 December 1917, Polderboek, Belgium 1·00 1·00
3281 60c. Richard Charles Travis, 24 July 1918, Hébuterne, France 1·00 1·00
3282 60c. Samuel Forsyth, 24 August 1918, Grévillers, France 1·00 1·00
3283 60c. Reginald Stanley Judson, 26 August 1918, Bapaume, France 1·00 1·00
3284 60c. Harry John Laurent, 12 September 1918, Gouzeaucourt Wood, France 1·00 1·00
3285 60c. James Crichton, 30 September 1918, Crevecoeur, France 1·00 1·00
3286 60c. John Gildroy Grant, 1 September 1918, Bancourt, France 1·00 1·00
3287 60c. James Edward Allen Ward, 7 July 1941, on operations over Holland 1·00 1·00
3288 60c. Charles Hazlitt Upham, 22–30 May 1941, Crete and 14–15 July 1942, Western Desert 1·00 1·00
3289 60c. Alfred Clive Hulme, 20–28 May 1941, Crete 1·00 1·00
3290 60c. John Daniel Hinton, 28–19 April 1941, Greece 1·00 1·00
3291 60c. Keith Elliott, 15 July 1942, Western Desert 1·00 1·00
3292 60c. Moana-Nui-a-Kiwa Ngarimu, 26–27 March 1943, Tunisia 1·00 1·00
3293 60c. Lloyd Allen Trigg, 11 August 1943, sea patrol, Atlantic Ocean 1·00 1·00
3294 60c. Leonard Henry Trent, 3 May 1943, on operation over Holland 1·00 1·00
3295 60c. Victoria Cross of New Zealand (awarded to Bill Henry Apiata, 2004, Afghanistan) 1·00 1·00

722 Humpback Whale

2011. 'Beyond the Coast'

MS3296 60c.×10 Type **722**; White-faced storm petrel (horiz); John dory (horiz); Yellowfin tuna (horiz); Hammerhead shark (horiz); Kingfish (horiz); Lord Howe coralfish; Snapper (horiz); Arrow squid (horiz); Orange roughy (horiz) $1.90 Yellow moray eel (horiz); $1.90 King crab		16·00	16·00

The stamps and margins of **MS**3296 form a composite design showing marine life from the surface to the sea bed.

EXPRESS DELIVERY STAMPS

E1

1903

E1	**E1**	6d. red and violet	38·00	23·00

E2 Express Mail Delivery Van

1939

E6	**E2**	6d. violet	1·50	1·75

LIFE INSURANCE DEPARTMENT

L1

1891

L13	**L 1**	½d. purple	75·00	4·00
L14	**L 1**	1d. blue	75·00	75
L9	**L 1**	2d. brown	£110	3·75
L4	**L 1**	3d. brown	£275	35·00
L5	**L 1**	6d. green	£375	75·00
L6	**L 1**	1s. pink	£600	£140

1905. Similar type but "V.R." omitted.

L37	½d. green	7·00	9·00
L22	1d. blue	£250	30·00
L38	1d. red	3·25	2·00
L26	1½d. black	45·00	8·50
L27	1½d. brown	1·50	3·00
L21	2d. brown	£1400	£120
L28	2d. purple	55·00	30·00
L29	2d. yellow	10·00	2·75
L30	3d. brown	50·00	38·00
L35	3d. red	18·00	24·00
L41	6d. pink	20·00	35·00

L3 Castlepoint Lighthouse

1947. Lighthouses.

L42	**L 3**	½d. green and orange	2·25	70
L43	-	1d. olive and blue	1·75	1·25
L44	-	2d. blue and black	2·75	1·00
L45	-	2½d. black and blue	9·50	13·00
L46	-	3d. mauve and blue	4·00	1·00
L47	-	4d. brown and orange	4·25	1·75
L48	-	6d. brown and blue	4·00	2·75
L49	-	1s. brown and blue	4·00	3·75

LIGHTHOUSES—HORIZ: 1d. Taiaroa; 2d. Cape Palliser; 6d. The Brothers. VERT: 2½d. Cape Campbell; 3d. Eddystone; 4d. Stephens Island; 1s. Cape Brett.

1967. Decimal currency. Stamps of 1947–65 surch.

L50a	1c. on 1d. (No. L43)	1·00	5·00
L51	2c. on 2½d. (No. L45)	8·00	14·00
L52	2½c. on 3d. (No. L46)	1·25	4·00
L53	3c. on 4d. (No. L47)	2·75	5·00
L54	5c. on 6d. (No. L48)	75	6·50
L55a	10c. on 1s. (No. L49)	75	4·00

L13 Moeraki Point Lighthouse

1969

L56	**L 13**	½c. yellow, red and violet	65	1·50
L57	-	2½c. blue, green and buff	50	1·00
L58	-	3c. stone, yellow & brn	50	60
L59	-	4c. green, ochre and blue	50	75
L60	-	8c. multicoloured	40	2·00
L61	-	10c. multicoloured	40	2·00
L62	-	15c. multicoloured	40	1·25

DESIGNS—HORIZ: 2½c. Puysegur Point Lighthouse; 4c. Cape Egmont Lighthouse. VERT: 3c. Baring Head Lighthouse; 8c. East Cape; 10c. Farewell Spit; 15c. Dog Island Lighthouse.

1978. No. L57 surch 25c.

L63	25c. on 2½c. blue, green and buff	75	1·75

5c N.Z.GOVERNMENT LIFE INSURANCE OFFICE

L17

1981

L64	**L17**	5c. multicoloured	10	10
L65	**L17**	10c. multicoloured	10	10
L66	**L17**	20c. multicoloured	15	15
L67	**L17**	30c. multicoloured	25	25
L68	**L17**	40c. multicoloured	30	30
L69	**L17**	50c. multicoloured	30	35

OFFICIAL STAMPS

1891. Optd O.P.S.O.

O1	**3**	½d. pink		£800
O2	**13**	½d. black		£650
O13	**23**	½d. green		£650
O4	**10**	1d. pink		£650
O19	**42**	1d. red		£700
O6	**9**	2d. mauve		£700
O8	**16**	2½d. blue		£700
O14	**26**	2½d. blue (A)		£1000
O21	**26**	2½d. blue (B)		£750
O22	**28**	3d. brown		£900
O16	**24**	4d. blue and brown		£900
O11	**19**	5d. black		£900
O17a	**30**	5d. brown		£850
O12	**8**	6d. brown (No. 224b)		£1100
O18	**32**	8d. blue		£1100
O23	**34**	1s. red		£2250
O24	**35**	2s. green		£3250

Optd OFFICIAL

1907. Pictorials.

O59	**23**	½d. green	13·00	75
O61a	**25**	2d. purple	8·50	1·60
O63	**28**	3d. brown	50·00	1·75
O64	**31**	6d. red	£200	23·00
O65	**34**	1s. orange	£100	20·00
O66	**35**	2s. green	85·00	£120
O67	-	5s. red (No. 329)	£160	£190

1907. "Universal" type.

O60b	**42**	1d. red	20·00	70

1908

O70	**50**	1d. red	70·00	4·25
O72	**31**	6d. red (No. 254)	£170	35·00

1910. King Edward VII etc.

O73	**51**	½d. green	13·00	40
O78	**53**	1d. red	4·00	10
O74	**51**	3d. brown	14·00	80
O75	**51**	6d. red	19·00	5·50
O76	**51**	8d. blue	12·00	29·00
O77	**51**	1s. orange	55·00	17·00

1913. Queen Victoria.

O82	**F4**	2s. blue	65·00	60·00
O83	**F4**	5s. green	90·00	£130
O84	**F4**	£1 red	£600	£550

1915. King George V.

O88	**62**	½d. green	1·25	20
O90	**62**	1½d. grey	5·50	1·00
O91	**62**	1½d. brown	5·00	30
O98	**62**	2d. yellow	2·50	50
O99	**62**	3d. brown	6·50	70
O101	**62**	4d. violet	14·00	5·50
O102	**62**	6d. red	5·00	75
O103	**62**	8d. brown	65·00	£190
O104	**62**	9d. green	42·00	38·00
O105b	**62**	1s. orange	7·00	2·00

1927. King George V.

O111	**71**	1d. red	2·00	20
O112	**71**	2s. blue	85·00	£120

1933. "Arms".

O113	**F6**	5s. green	£275	£325

Optd Official

1936. "Arms".

O133aw	5s. green	40·00	6·00

1936. As 1935.

O120	**81**	½d. green	7·50	4·50
O115	-	1d. red (No. 557)	7·00	1·25
O122	**83**	1½d. brown	38·00	4·75
O123	-	2d. orange (No. 580)	9·00	10
O124a	**85**	2½d. brown and grey	14·00	21·00
O125	**86**	3d. brown	48·00	3·50
O126c	**87**	4d. black and brown	6·00	1·00
O127c	**89**	6d. red	15·00	40
O128a	-	8d. brown (No. 586b)	8·50	16·00
O130	**91**	9d. red and black	20·00	22·00
O131b	-	1s. green (No. 588)	38·00	3·00
O132d	**93**	2s. olive	48·00	11·00

1938. King George VI.

O134	**108**	½d. green	24·00	2·25
O135	**108**	½d. orange	2·50	4·25
O136	**108**	1d. red	28·00	15
O137	**108**	1d. green	5·00	10
O138	**108**	1½d. brown	75·00	23·00
O139	**108**	1½d. red	16·00	9·50
O152	**108**	2d. orange	4·75	10
O140	**108**	3d. blue	5·00	10
O153	**108**	4d. purple	4·75	3·25
O154	**108**	6d. red	18·00	50
O155	**108**	8d. violet	8·00	6·50
O156	**108**	9d. brown	9·00	6·50
O157a	-	1s. brown and red (No. 686b)	8·50	9·00
O158	-	2s. orange and green (No. 688)	35·00	16·00

1940. Centenary stamps.

O141	½d. green	3·00	35
O142	1d. brown and red	7·50	10
O143	1½d. blue and mauve	5·00	2·00
O144	2d. green and brown	8·00	10
O145	2½d. green and blue	5·00	2·75
O146	3d. purple and red	8·00	1·00
O147	4d. brown and red	40·00	1·50
O148	6d. green and violet	32·00	1·50
O149	8d. black and red	35·00	17·00
O150	9d. olive and red	14·00	4·00
O151	1s. green	48·00	3·00

O6 Queen Elizabeth II

1954

O159a	**O6**	1d. orange	50	20
O160	**O6**	1½d. brown	3·75	5·00
O161a	**O6**	2d. green	40	30
O162	**O6**	2½d. olive	3·00	1·50
O163a	**O6**	3d. red	40	10
O164b	**O6**	4d. blue	1·00	50
O165	**O6**	9d. red	9·00	3·00
O166	**O6**	1s. purple	1·25	30
O167	**O6**	3s. slate	22·00	40·00

1959. Surch.

O169	2½d. on 2d. green	1·25	2·00
O168	6d. on 1½d. brown	50	1·10

POSTAGE DUE STAMPS

D1

1899

D9	**D1**	½d. red and green	3·75	16·00
D14	**D1**	1d. red and green	17·00	3·00
D15	**D1**	2d. red and green	55·00	8·00
D12	**D1**	3d. red and green	14·00	5·00
D16	**D1**	4d. red and green	35·00	17·00
D6	**D1**	5d. red and green	28·00	45·00
D7	**D1**	6d. red and green	38·00	40·00
D2	**D1**	8d. red and green	60·00	85·00
D8	**D1**	10d. red and green	75·00	£100
D3	**D1**	1s. red and green	65·00	90·00
D4	**D1**	2s. red and green	£120	£150

D2

1902

D18	**D2**	½d. red and green	2·00	3·00
D30	**D2**	1d. red and green	3·75	80
D22a	**D2**	2d. red and green	6·00	3·00
D36	**D2**	3d. red and green	15·00	48·00

D3

1939

D41	**D3**	½d. green	5·00	5·00
D42	**D3**	1d. red	2·75	3·00
D43	**D3**	2d. blue	6·00	2·75
D47aw	**D3**	3d. brown	9·00	17·00

POSTAL FISCAL STAMPS

F4

1882

F98	**F4**	2s. blue	50·00	7·00
F99	**F4**	2s.6d. brown	65·00	8·00
F100	**F4**	3s. mauve	£130	10·00
F102	**F4**	5s. green	£140	13·00
F108	**F4**	10s. brown	£225	24·00
F123	**F4**	£1 red	£325	80·00

The above are revenue stamps authorised for use as postage stamps as there were no other postage stamps available in these denominations. Other values in this and similar types were mainly used for revenue purposes.

F6 "Arms" Type

1931. Various frames.

F191	**F6**	1s.3d. yellow	22·00	3·50
F192	**F6**	1s.3d. yellow and black	9·00	3·25
F193	**F6**	2s.6d. brown	12·00	1·40
F194	**F6**	4s. red	29·00	2·00
F195	**F6**	5s. green	24·00	1·25
F196	**F6**	6s. red	45·00	3·25
F197	**F6**	7s. blue	50·00	6·00
F198	**F6**	7s.6d. grey	75·00	80·00
F153	**F6**	8s. violet	32·00	35·00
F154	**F6**	9s. orange	32·00	29·00
F155	**F6**	10s. red	24·00	10·00
F156	**F6**	12s.6d. purple	£150	£150
F202	**F6**	15s. green	65·00	21·00
F203	**F6**	£1 pink	30·00	3·75
F159	**F6**	25s. blue	£550	£750
F160	**F6**	30s. brown	£350	£190
F161	**F6**	35s. yellow	£4500	£5000
F206w	**F6**	£2 violet	£150	22·00
F207	**F6**	£2 10s. red	£400	£425
F208w	**F6**	£3 green	£200	50·00
F165	**F6**	£3 10s. red	£1800	£2000
F210	**F6**	£4 blue	£250	£170
F167	**F6**	£4 10s. grey	£1600	£1800
F211w	**F6**	£5 blue	£300	60·00

1939. Surch in bold figures.

F212	**F 6**	3/6 on 3s.6d. green	21·00	7·00
F214	**F 6**	5/6 on 5s.6d. lilac	65·00	24·00
F215	**F 6**	11/- on 11s. yellow	£100	48·00
F216	**F 6**	22/- on 22s. red	£425	£190
F186	**F 6**	35/- on 35s. orange	£750	£400

Pt. 15

NICARAGUA

A republic of Central America, independent since 1821.

1862. 100 centavos = 1 peso (paper currency).
1912. 100 centavos de cordoba = 1 peso de cordoba (gold currency).
1925. 100 centavos = 1 cordoba.
1990. Currency Reform. 150000 (old) cordoba = 1 (new) cordoba

2 Volcanoes

1862. Perf or roul.

13	**2**	1c. brown	1·80	1·40
4	**2**	2c. blue	4·00	1·50
14	**2**	5c. black	3·25	2·00
18	**2**	10c. red	3·50	2·50
19	**2**	25c. green	3·50	3·50

5

1882

20	**5**	1c. green	25	30
21	**5**	2c. red	25	30
22	**5**	5c. blue	25	30
23	**5**	10c. violet	30	85
24	**5**	15c. yellow	65	17·00
25	**5**	20c. grey	1·00	4·50
26	**5**	50c. violet	1·30	9·25

6 Steam Locomotive and Telegraph Key

1890

27	**6**	1c. brown	20	30
28	**6**	2c. red	20	30
29	**6**	5c. blue	20	25
30	**6**	10c. grey	20	30
31	**6**	20c. red	20	1·90
32	**6**	50c. violet	20	5·25
33	**6**	1p. brown	30	8·00
34	**6**	2p. green	30	
35	**6**	5p. red	30	
36	**6**	10p. orange	30	

7

1891

37	**7**	1c. brown	35	40
38	**7**	2c. red	35	40
39	**7**	5c. blue	35	30
40	**7**	10c. grey	35	50
41	**7**	20c. lake	35	2·75
42	**7**	50c. violet	35	5·25
43	**7**	1p. sepia	35	5·25
44	**7**	2p. green	35	9·25
45	**7**	5p. red	35	
46	**7**	10p. orange	35	

8 First Sight of the New World

1892. Discovery of America.

47	**8**	1c. brown	35	40
48	**8**	2c. red	35	30
49	**8**	5c. blue	35	30
50	**8**	10c. grey	35	30
51	**8**	20c. red	35	3·00
52	**8**	50c. violet	35	7·75
53	**8**	1p. brown	35	7·75
54	**8**	2p. green	35	9·25
55	**8**	5p. red	35	
56	**8**	10p. orange	35	

9 Volcanoes

1893

57	**9**	1c. brown	35	30
58	**9**	2c. red	35	30
59	**9**	5c. blue	35	30
60	**9**	10c. grey	35	30
61	**9**	20c. brown	35	2·40
62	**9**	50c. violet	35	4·75
63	**9**	1p. brown	35	7·25
64	**9**	2p. green	35	9·25
65	**9**	5p. red	35	
66	**9**	10p. orange	35	

10

1894

67	**10**	1c. brown	35	20
68	**10**	2c. red	35	30
69	**10**	5c. blue	35	20
70	**10**	10c. grey	35	30
71	**10**	20c. red	35	2·50
72	**10**	50c. violet	35	5·00
73	**10**	1p. brown	35	7·25
74	**10**	2p. green	35	13·00
75	**10**	5p. brown	35	16·00
76	**10**	10p. orange	35	

11

1895

77	**11**	1c. brown	25	30
78	**11**	2c. red	25	30
79	**11**	5c. blue	25	30
80	**11**	10c. grey	25	30
81	**11**	20c. red	25	3·25
82	**11**	50c. violet	25	5·25
83	**11**	1p. brown	25	5·25
84	**11**	2p. green	25	8·25
85	**11**	5p. red	25	11·50
86	**11**	10p. orange	25	

12 Map of Nicaragua

1896. Date "1896".

90A	**12**	1c. violet	35	1·00
91A	**12**	2c. green	35	50
92A	**12**	5c. red	35	30
93A	**12**	10c. blue	60	50
94A	**12**	20c. brown	3·50	4·25
95A	**12**	50c. grey	70	8·25
96A	**12**	1p. black	95	11·50
97A	**12**	2p. red	95	16·00
98A	**12**	5p. blue	1·10	18·00

1897. As T 12, dated "1897".

99A	1c. violet	60	50
100A	2c. green	60	50
101A	5c. red	60	30
102A	10c. blue	6·75	85
103A	20c. brown	3·00	4·00
104A	50c. grey	9·50	9·75
105A	1p. black	9·50	14·00
106A	2p. red	21·00	20·00
107A	5p. blue	21·00	43·00

13 Arms of Republic of Central America

1898

108	**13**	1c. brown	30	40
109	**13**	2c. grey	30	40
110	**13**	4c. lake	30	50
122	**13**	5c. olive	26·00	50
112	**13**	10c. purple	16·00	60
113	**13**	15c. blue	40	1·50
114	**13**	20c. blue	10·50	2·00
115	**13**	50c. yellow	10·50	10·00
116	**13**	1p. blue	40	16·00
117	**13**	2p. brown	20·00	22·00
118	**13**	5p. orange	26·00	32·00

14

1899

126	**14**	1c. green	20	40
127	**14**	2c. brown	20	30
128	**14**	4c. red	40	40
129	**14**	5c. blue	20	30
130	**14**	10c. orange	20	30
131	**14**	15c. brown	20	70
132	**14**	20c. green	40	80
133	**14**	50c. red	20	3·00
134	**14**	1p. orange	30	9·00
135	**14**	2p. violet	30	20·00
136	**14**	5p. blue	30	25·00

15 Mt. Momotombo

1900

137	**15**	1c. red	50	20
138	**15**	2c. orange	50	20
139	**15**	3c. green	85	30
140	**15**	4c. olive	1·00	30
184	**15**	5c. red	50	25
185	**15**	5c. blue	50	25
142	**15**	6c. red	14·50	5·00
186	**15**	10c. mauve	1·60	20
144	**15**	15c. blue	8·25	70
145	**15**	20c. brown	8·25	70
146	**15**	50c. lake	7·25	1·10
147	**15**	1p. yellow	12·50	4·00
148	**15**	2p. red	10·50	2·40
149	**15**	5p. black	10·50	3·00

1901. Surch 1901 and value.

151	**15**	2c. on 1p. yellow	5·25	3·00
169	**15**	3c. on 6c. red	6·25	4·50
163	**15**	4c. on 6c. red	5·25	4·00
173	**15**	5c. on 1p. yellow	7·75	6·50
152	**15**	10c. on 5p. black	6·75	4·50
168	**15**	10c. on 2p. red	5·75	4·00
153	**15**	20c. on 2p. red	7·75	7·50
176	**15**	20c. on 5p. black	5·25	3·50

1901. Postage Due stamps of 1900 optd 1901 Correos.

177	**D16**	1c. red	1·00	40
178	**D16**	2c. orange	85	40
179	**D16**	5c. blue	1·00	60
180	**D16**	10c. violet	1·30	1·10
181	**D16**	20c. brown	1·30	1·30
182	**D16**	30c. green	1·00	1·10
183	**D16**	50c. lake	1·00	1·10

1902. Surch 1902 and value.

187	**15**	15c. on 2c. orange	2·10	80
188	**15**	30c. on 1c. red	1·00	2·20

27 Pres. Santos Zelaya

1903. 10th Anniv of Revolution against Sacaza and 1st election of Pres. Zelaya.

189	**27**	1c. black and green	40	50
190	**27**	2c. black and red	70	50
191	**27**	5c. black and blue	40	50
192	**27**	10c. black and orange	40	90
193	**27**	15c. black and lake	60	2·00
194	**27**	20c. black and violet	60	2·00
195	**27**	50c. black and olive	60	5·00
196	**27**	1p. black and brown	60	6·00

1904. Surch 15 Centavos.

200	**15**	15c. on 10c. mauve	4·25	2·50

1904. Surch Vale, value and wavy lines.

203	**15**	5c. on 10c. mauve	1·90	30
204		15c. on 10c. mauve	30	30

1905. No. 186 surch 5 CENTS.

205	5c. on 10c. mauve	60	40

37 Arms

1905

206	**37**	1c. green	30	20
207	**37**	2c. red	30	20
208	**37**	3c. violet	40	30
280	**37**	3c. orange	40	20
209	**37**	4c. orange	40	30
281	**37**	4c. violet	40	20
282	**37**	5c. blue	40	20
211	**37**	6c. grey	60	40
283	**37**	6c. brown	3·00	1·50
212	**37**	10c. brown	95	30
284	**37**	10c. lake	95	20
213	**37**	15c. olive	85	40
285	**37**	15c. black	95	20
214	**37**	20c. lake	60	40
286	**37**	20c. olive	95	20
215	**37**	50c. orange	3·00	1·50
287	**37**	50c. green	1·30	40
216	**37**	1p. black	1·60	1·50
288	**37**	1p. yellow	1·30	40
217	**37**	2p. green	1·60	2·00
289	**37**	2p. red	1·30	40
218	**37**	5p. violet	1·90	2·50

1906. Surch Vale (or VALE) and value in one line.

292	2c. on 3c. orange	1·60	1·30
293	5c. on 20c. olive	40	30
247A	10c. on 2c. red	1·60	50
223B	10c. on 3c. violet	4·75	4·50
248A	10c. on 4c. orange	1·60	30
291B	10c. on 15c. black	1·30	30
250B	10c. on 20c. lake	2·40	90
252A	10c. on 50c. orange	2·10	1·60
234	10c. on 2p. green	21·00	13·00
235	10c. on 5p. violet	£100	70·00
226B	15c. on 1c. green	30	20
229A	20c. on 2c. red	60	30
230A	20c. on 5c. blue	70	50
236	35c. on 6c. grey	3·00	2·20
232A	50c. on 6c. grey	30	50
238	1p. on 5p. violet	43·00	25·00

51

1908. Fiscal stamps as T 51 optd CORREO–1908 or surch VALE and value also.

260	**51**	1c. on 5c. yellow	40	30
261	**51**	2c. on 5c. yellow	50	30
262	**51**	4c. on 5c. yellow	70	40
256	**51**	5c. yellow	60	40
257	**51**	10c. blue	50	30
263	**51**	15c. on 50c. green	60	40
264	**51**	35c. on 50c. green	4·25	1·00
258	**51**	1p. brown	50	2·00
259	**51**	2p. grey	50	2·50

50

1908. Fiscal stamps as T 50 optd CORREOS–1908 or surch VALE and value also.

268	50	2c. orange	3·50	2·00
269	50	4c. on 2c. orange	1·90	90
270	50	5c. on 2c. orange	1·60	60
271	50	10c. on 2c. orange	1·60	30

1909. Surch CORREOS–1909 VALE and value.

273	51	1c. on 50c. green	4·25	1·60
274	51	2c. on 50c. green	7·25	3·00
275	51	4c. on 50c. green	7·25	3·00
276	51	5c. on 50c. green	4·25	1·80
277	51	10c. on 50c. green	1·10	80

1910. Surch Vale and value in two lines.

296	37	2c. on 3c. orange	95	50
300	37	2c. on 4c. violet	30	20
301	37	5c. on 20c. olive	30	20
302	37	10c. on 15c. black	40	20
303	37	10c. on 50c. green	30	20
299	37	10c. on 1p. yellow	95	40
305	37	10c. on 2p. red	60	50

1911. Surch Correos 1911 (or CORREOS 1911) and value.

307	51	2c. on 5p. blue	40	40
312	51	5c. on 2p. grey	1·60	1·00
308	51	5c. on 10p. pink	85	40
309	51	10c. on 25c. lilac	40	30
310	51	10c. on 2p. grey	40	30
311	51	35c. on 1p. brown	40	30

1911. Surch VALE POSTAL de 1911 and value.

313	5c. on 25c. lilac	1·60	1·30
314	5c. on 50c. green	5·25	5·00
315	5c. on 5p. blue	7·25	7·00
317	5c. on 50p. red	5·25	5·00
318	10c. on 50c. green	1·60	50

64

1911. Railway tickets as T 64, with fiscal surch on the front, further surch for postal use. (a) Surch vale CORREO DE 1911 and value on back.

319	64	2c. on 5c. on 2nd class blue	30	30
320	64	05c. on 5c. on 2nd class blue	30	30
321	64	10c. on 5c. on 2nd class blue	30	30
322	64	15c. on 10c. on 1st class red	40	40

(b) Surch vale CORREO DE 1911 and value on front.

322c	2c. on 5c. on 2nd class blue	6·25	6·00
322d	05c. on 5c. on 2nd class blue	£160	£160
322e	10c. on 5c. on 2nd class blue	60·00	80·00
322f	15c. on 10c. on 1st class red	16·00	16·00

(c) Surch CORREO and value on front.

323	2c. on 10c. on 1st class red	1·60	1·50
324	20c. on 10c. on 1st class red	5·75	5·00
325	50c. on 10c. on 1st class red	10·50	10·00

(d) Surch Correo Vale 1911 and value on front.

326	2c. on 10c. on 1st class red	30	30
328	5c. on 5c. on 2nd class blue	1·40	1·30
327	5c. on 10c. on 1st class red	30	30
330	10c. on 10c. on 1st class red	1·60	1·20

(e) Surch Vale CORREO DE 1911 and value on back.

331a	5c. on 10c. on 1st class red	21·00	
332	10c. on 10c. on 1st class red	13·50	

(f) Surch CORREO Vale 10 cts. 1911 and bar obliterating oficial on front.

333	10c. on 10c. on 1st class red	1·20	1·00

70

71

1912

337	70	1c. green	40	20
338	70	2c. red	50	20
339	70	3c. brown	40	20
340	70	4c. purple	40	20
341	70	5c. black and blue	30	20
342	70	6c. brown	40	1·20
343	70	10c. brown	30	20
344	70	15c. violet	30	20
345	70	20c. brown	30	20
346	70	25c. black and green	40	20
347	71	35c. brown and green	2·50	1·80
348	70	50c. blue	1·30	50
349	70	1p. orange	1·80	2·50
350	70	2p. green	1·90	3·00
351	70	5p. black	4·75	4·50

1913. Surch Vale 15 cts Correos 1913.

352	71	15c. on 35c. brown & green	40	30

1913. Surch VALE 1913 and value in "centavos de cordoba". A. On stamps of 1912 issue.

353	70	½c. on 3c. brown	50	40
354	70	½c. on 15c. violet	30	20
355	70	½c. on 1p. orange	30	30
356	70	1c. on 3c. brown	85	60
357	70	1c. on 4c. purple	30	20
358	70	1c. on 50c. blue	30	20
359	70	1c. on 5p. black	30	20
360	70	2c. on 4c. purple	40	30
361	70	2c. on 20c. brown	4·25	5·00
362	70	2c. on 25c. black & green	40	20
363	71	2c. on 35c. brown & green	30	50
364	70	2c. on 50c. blue	30	20
365	70	2c. on 2p. green	20	20
366	70	3c. on 6c. brown	20	20

B. On Silver Currency stamps of 1912 (Locomotive type).

367	Z1	½c. on 2c. red	60	50
368	Z1	1c. on 3c. brown	50	30
369	Z1	1c. on 4c. red	50	30
370	Z1	1c. on 6c. red	40	20
371	Z1	1c. on 20c. blue	50	20
372	Z1	1c. on 25c. black & green	50	30
384	Z1	2c. on 1c. green	7·75	1·50
373	Z1	2c. on 25c. black & green	4·00	5·00
374	Z1	5c. on 35c. black & green	50	40
375	Z1	5c. on 50c. olive	50	40
376	Z1	6c. on 1p. orange	50	20
377	Z1	10c. on 2p. brown	50	40
378	Z1	1p. on 5p. green	40	40

1914. No. 352 surch with new value and Cordoba and thick bar over old surch.

385	71	½c. on 15c. on 35c.	30	20
386	71	1c. on 15c. on 35c.	30	20

1914. Official stamps of 1913 surch with new value and thick bar through "OFICIAL".

387	70	1c. on 25c. blue	50	30
388	71	1c. on 35c. blue	40	30
389	70	1c. on 1p. blue	30	20
391	70	2c. on 50c. blue	40	20
392	70	2c. on 2p. blue	40	20
393	70	5c. on 5p. blue	30	20

79 National Palace, Managua

80 Leon Cathedral

1914. Various frames.

394	79	½c. blue	85	20
395	79	1c. green	85	20
396	80	2c. orange	85	20
397	79	3c. brown	1·30	30
398	80	4c. red	1·30	40
399	79	5c. grey	50	20
400	80	6c. sepia	9·25	6·00
401	80	10c. yellow	95	20
402	79	15c. violet	6·25	2·00
403	80	20c. grey	11·50	6·00
404	79	25c. orange	1·60	50
405	80	50c. blue	1·40	40

See also Nos. 465/72, 617/27 and 912/24.

1915. Surch VALE 5 cts. de Cordoba 1915.

406	5c. on 6c. sepia	1·60	40

1918. Stamps of 1914 surch Vale centavos de cordoba.

407	80	½c. on 6c. sepia	4·25	1·50
408	80	½c. on 10c. yellow	2·50	30
409	79	½c. on 15c. violet	2·50	60
410	79	½c. on 25c. orange	5·25	2·00
411	80	½c. on 50c. blue	2·50	30
440	80	1c. on 2c. orange	1·60	30
413	79	1c. on 3c. brown	3·00	30
414	80	1c. on 6c. sepia	13·50	5·00
415	80	1c. on 10c. yellow	25·00	8·00
416	79	1c. on 15c. violet	4·75	80
418	80	1c. on 20c. grey	2·50	30
420	79	1c. on 25c. orange	4·75	1·00
421	80	1c. on 50c. blue	14·50	4·50
422	80	2c. on 4c. red	2·50	30
423	80	2c. on 6c. sepia	25·00	8·00
424	80	2c. on 10c. yellow	25·00	5·00
425	80	2c. on 20c. grey	13·50	3·50
426	79	2c. on 25c. orange	5·75	40
427	80	5c. on 6c. sepia	10·50	4·50
428	79	5c. on 15c. violet	3·50	60

1919. Official stamps of 1915 surch Vale centavo de cordoba and with bar through "OFICIAL".

444	80	½c. on 2c. blue	50	20
445	80	½c. on 4c. blue	1·30	20
446	79	1c. on 3c. blue	1·30	30
432	79	1c. on 25c. blue	1·60	30
433	80	2c. on 50c. blue	1·60	30
443a	80	10c. on 20c. blue	1·40	40

1921. Official stamps of 1913 optd Particular and wavy lines through "OFICIAL".

441	70	1c. blue	1·60	60
442	70	5c. blue	1·60	40

1921. No. 399 surch Vale medio centavo.

447	79	½c. on 5c. black	85	80

1921. Official stamp of 1915 optd Particular R de C and bars.

448	79	1c. blue	6·75	3·00

1921. Official stamps of 1915 surch Vale un centavo R de C and bars.

449	79	1c. on 5c. blue	1·80	70
450	80	1c. on 6c. blue	85	30
451	80	1c. on 10c. blue	1·20	30
452	79	1c. on 15c. blue	2·10	30

90

1921. Fiscal stamps as T 23 surch R de C Vale and new value.

453	90	1c. on 1c. red and black	20	20
454	90	1c. on 2c. green and black	20	20
455	90	1c. on 4c. orange and black	20	20
456	90	1c. on 15c. blue and black	20	20

No. 456 is inscr "TIMBRE TELEGRAFICO".

1921. Independence Centenary.

457	-	½c. black and blue	1·00	1·00
458	91	1c. black and green	1·00	1·00
459	-	2c. black and red	1·00	1·00
460	-	5c. black and violet	1·00	1·00
461	-	10c. black and orange	1·00	1·00
462	-	25c. black and yellow	1·00	1·00
463	-	50c. black and violet	1·00	1·00

DESIGNS: ½c. Arce; 2c. Larreinaga; 5c. F. Chamorro; 10c. Jerez; 25c. J. P. Chamorro; 50c. Dario.

1922. Surch Vale un centavo R. de C.

464	80	1c. on 10c. yellow	30	30

1922. As Nos. 394, etc, but colours changed.

465	79	½c. green	20	20
466	79	1c. violet	20	20
467	80	2c. red	20	20
468	79	3c. olive	20	20
469	80	6c. brown	20	20
470	79	15c. brown	50	20
471	80	20c. brown	70	20
472	80	1cor. brown	1·20	50

Nos. 465/72 are size 27×22¾ mm.
For later issues of these types, see Nos. 617/27 and 912/24.

1922. Optd R. de C.

473	79	1c. violet	30	20

91 Jose C. del Valle

1922. Independence issue of 1921 surch R. de C. Vale un centavo.

474	91	1c. on 1c. black and green	1·00	1·00
475	-	1c. on 5c. black and violet	1·00	1·00
476	-	1c. on 10c. black and orange	1·00	60
477	-	1c. on 25c. black and yellow	1·00	50
478	-	1c. on 50c. black and violet	50	30

94

1922. Surch Nicaragua R. de C. Vale un cent.

479	94	1c. yellow	20	20
480	94	1c. mauve	20	20
481	94	1c. blue	20	20

1922. Surch Vale 0.01 de Cordoba in two lines.

482	80	1c. on 10c. yellow	1·00	40
483	80	2c. on 10c. yellow	1·00	30

1923. Surch Vale 2 centavos de cordoba in three lines.

484	79	1c. on 5c. black	1·30	20
485	80	2c. on 10c. yellow	1·30	20

1923. Optd Sello Postal.

486	-	½c. black and blue (No. 457)	7·75	7·50
487	91	1c. black and green	2·50	90

1923. Independence issue of 1921 surch R. de C. Vale un centavo de cordoba.

488	1c. on 2c. black and red	70	70
489	1c. on 5c. black and violet	85	20
490	1c. on 10c. black and orange	30	30
491	1c. on 25c. black and yellow	40	40
492	1c. on 50c. black and violet	30	20

1923. Fiscal stamp optd R. de C.

493	90	1c. red and black	20	20

1924. Optd R. de C. 1924 in two lines.

494	79	1c. violet	20	20

99 F. Hernandez de Cordoba

1924. 400th Anniv of Foundation of Leon and Granada.

495	99	1c. green	1·60	30
496	99	2c. red	1·60	30
497	99	5c. blue	1·00	30
498	99	10c. brown	1·00	40

1925. Optd R. de C. 1925 in two lines.

499	79	1c. violet	30	30

1927. Optd Resello 1927.

525	79	½c. green	30	20
528	79	1c. violet (No. 466)	20	20
555	79	1c. violet (No. 473)	30	30
532	80	2c. red	20	20
533	79	3c. green	30	20
537	80	4c. red	32·00	23·00
539	79	5c. grey	1·00	30
542	80	6c. brown	13·50	11·00
543	80	10c. yellow	30	20
545	79	15c. brown	85	30
547	80	20c. brown	50	30
549	79	25c. orange	85	30
551	80	50c. blue	40	20
553	80	1cor. brown	1·30	40

1928. Optd Resello 1928.

559	79	½c. green	30	20
560	79	1c. violet	20	20
561	80	2c. red	20	20
562	79	3c. green	40	15
563	80	4c. red	40	20
564	79	5c. grey	20	20
565	80	6c. brown	20	20
566	80	10c. yellow	30	20
567	79	15c. brown	40	30
568	80	20c. brown	50	30
569	79	25c. orange	85	30
570	80	50c. blue	1·30	20
571	80	1cor. brown	1·30	40

1928. Optd Correos 1928.

574	**79**	½c. green	30	20
575	**79**	1c. violet	20	10
576	**79**	3c. olive	75	25
577	**80**	4c. red	35	20
578	**79**	5c. grey	30	20
579	**80**	6c. brown	45	20
580	**80**	10c. yellow	55	25
581	**79**	15c. brown	1·80	25
582	**80**	20c. brown	1·90	25
583	**79**	25c. orange	1·90	25
584	**80**	50c. blue	1·90	25
585	**80**	1cor. brown	4·75	2·20

1928. No. 577 surch Vale 2 cts.

586	2c. on 4c. red	1·20	35

1928. Fiscal stamp as T 90, but inscr "TIMBRE TELEGRAFICO" and surch Correos 1928 Vale and new value.

587	**90**	1c. on 5c. blue and black	30	20
588	**90**	2c. on 5c. blue and black	30	20
589	**90**	3c. on 5c. blue and black	30	20

1928. Obligatory Tax. No. 587 additionally optd R. de T.

590	1c. on 5c. blue and black	65	25

1928. As Nos. 465/72 but colours changed.

591	**79**	½c. red	40	20
592	**79**	1c. orange	40	20
593	**80**	2c. green	40	20
594	**79**	3c. purple	40	25
595	**80**	4c. brown	40	25
596	**79**	5c. yellow	40	20
597	**80**	6c. blue	40	25
598	**80**	10c. blue	85	25
599	**79**	15c. red	1·30	45
600	**80**	20c. green	1·30	45
601	**79**	25c. purple	26·00	5·50
602	**80**	50c. brown	3·25	90
603	**80**	1cor. violet	6·00	2·75

See also Nos. 617/27 and 912/24.

106

1928

604	**106**	1c. purple	35	25
647	**106**	1c. red	35	25

For 1c. green see No. 925.

1929. Optd R. de C.

605	**79**	1c. orange	30	20
628	**79**	1c. olive	30	20

1929. Optd Correos 1929.

606	½c. green	30	20

1929. Optd Correos 1928.

607	**99**	10c. brown	75	55

1929. Fiscal stamps as T 90, but inscr "TIMBRE TELEGRAFICO". A. Surch Correos 1929 R. de C. C$ 0.01 vert.

613	**90**	1c. on 5c. blue and black	30	20

B. Surch Correos 1929 and value.

611	1c. on 10c. green and black	30	20
612	2c. on 5c. blue and black	30	20

C. Surch Correos 1929 and value vert and R. de C. or R. de T. horiz.

608	1c. on 5c. blue and black (R. de T.)	30	20
609	2c. on 5c. blue and black (R. de T.)	20	20
610	2c. on 5c. blue and black (R. de C.)	23·00	1·30

1929. Air. Optd Correo Aereo 1929. P.A.A.

614	**79**	25c. sepia	2·00	2·00
615	**79**	25c. orange	1·70	1·60
616	**79**	25c. violet	1·20	70

1929. As Nos. 591/603 but colours changed.

617	**79**	1c. green	20	20
618	**79**	3c. blue	30	20
619	**80**	4c. blue	35	20
620	**79**	5c. brown	35	20
621	**80**	6c. drab	50	35
622	**80**	10c. brown	55	20
623	**79**	15c. red	90	25
624	**80**	20c. orange	1·40	45
625	**79**	25c. violet	30	20
626	**80**	50c. green	50	20
627	**80**	1cor. yellow	4·00	1·20

See also Nos. 912/24.

112 Mt. Momotombo

1929. Air.

629	**112**	15c. purple	20	20
630	**112**	20c. green	35	35
631	**112**	25c. olive	45	35
632	**112**	50c. sepia	75	70
633	**112**	1cor. red	95	90

See also Nos. 926/30.

1930. Air. Surch Vale and value.

634	15c. on 25c. olive	45	35
635	20c. on 25c. olive	75	70

114 G.P.O. Managua

1930. Opening of the G.P.O., Managua.

636	**114**	½c. sepia	1·40	1·30
637	**114**	1c. red	1·40	1·30
638	**114**	2c. orange	95	90
639	**114**	3c. orange	1·90	1·80
640	**114**	4c. yellow	1·90	1·80
641	**114**	5c. olive	2·75	2·75
642	**114**	6c. green	2·75	2·75
643	**114**	10c. black	3·00	2·75
644	**114**	25c. blue	6·00	5·75
645	**114**	50c. blue	9·25	9·00
646	**114**	1cor. violet	28·00	27·00

1931. Optd 1931 and thick bar obliterating old overprint "1928".

648	**99**	10c. brown (No. 607)	75	1·80

1931. No. 607 surch C$ 0.02.

649	2c. on 10c. brown	60	1·10

1931. Optd 1931 and thick bar.

650	2c. on 10c. brown (No. 498)	75	2·10

1931. Air. Nos. 614/16 surch 1931 Vale and value.

651	**79**	15c. on 25c. sepia	£160	£150
652	**79**	15c. on 25c. orange	60·00	60·00
653	**79**	15c. on 25c. violet	16·00	16·00
654	**79**	20c. on 25c. violet	9·25	9·00

1931. Optd 1931.

656	**79**	½c. green	35	20
657	**79**	1c. olive	35	20
665	**79**	1c. orange (No. 605)	30	20
658	**80**	2c. red	35	20
659	**79**	3c. blue	35	20
660	**79**	5c. yellow	3·75	2·75
661	**79**	5c. sepia	1·20	45
662	**79**	15c. orange	1·30	55
663	**79**	25c. sepia	12·00	7·25
664	**79**	25c. violet	4·50	3·00

1931. Air. Surch 1931 and value.

666	**80**	15c. on 20c. on 25c. olive (No. 635)	9·75	9·25
667	**80**	15c. on 25c. olive	6·25	6·00
668	**80**	15c. on 50c. sepia	55·00	55·00
669	**80**	15c. on 1cor. red	95·00	90·00

120 G.P.O. before and after the Earthquake

1932. G.P.O. Reconstruction Fund.

670	**120**	½c. green (postage)	1·80	1·70
671	**120**	1c. brown	2·20	2·10
672	**120**	2c. red	1·80	1·70
673	**120**	3c. blue	1·80	1·70
674	**120**	4c. blue	1·80	1·70
675	**120**	5c. brown	2·20	2·10
676	**120**	6c. brown	2·20	2·10
677	**120**	10c. brown	3·75	2·75
678	**120**	15c. red	5·25	3·00
679	**120**	20c. orange	3·75	3·75
680	**120**	25c. violet	3·75	3·75
681	**120**	50c. green	3·75	3·75
682	**120**	1cor. yellow	7·50	7·25
683	**120**	15c. mauve (air)	1·80	1·70
684	**120**	20c. green	2·00	2·00
685	**120**	25c. brown	7·00	6·75
686	**120**	50c. brown	9·25	8·75
687	**120**	1cor. red	14·50	14·00

1932. Air. Surch Vale and value.

688	**112**	30c. on 50c. sepia	1·50	1·50
689	**112**	35c. on 50c. sepia	1·50	1·50
690	**112**	40c. on 1cor. red	1·70	1·60
691	**112**	55c. on 1cor. red	1·70	1·60

For similar surcharges on these stamps in different colours see Nos. 791/4 and 931/4.

1932. Air. International Air Mail Week. Optd Semana Correo Aereo Internacional 11–17 Septiembre 1932.

692	15c. violet	75·00	70·00

1932. Air. Inauguration of Inland Airmail Service. Surch Inauguracion Interior 12 Octubre 1932 Vale C$0.08.

693	8c. on 1cor. red	20·00	20·00

1932. Air. Optd Interior–1932 or surch Vale and value also.

705	**120**	25c. brown	9·25	9·00
706	**120**	32c. on 50c. brown	9·25	9·00
707	**120**	40c. on 1cor. red	7·50	7·25

1932. Air. Nos. 671, etc, optd Correo Aereo Interior in one line and 1932, or surch Vale and value also.

694	1c. brown	21·00	20·00
695	2c. red	19·00	18·00
696	3c. blue	9·25	9·00
697	4c. blue	10·00	9·75
698	5c. brown	9·25	9·00
699	6c. brown	9·25	9·00
700	8c. on 10c. brown	9·25	9·00
701	16c. on 20c. orange	9·25	9·00
702	24c. on 25c. violet	9·25	9·00
703	50c. green	9·25	9·00
704	1cor. yellow	9·25	9·00

1932. Air. Surch Correo Aereo Interior–1932 in two lines and Vale and value below.

710	**80**	1c. on 2c. red	2·30	2·20
711	**79**	2c. on 3c. blue	2·30	2·20
712	**80**	3c. on 4c. blue	2·30	2·20
713	**79**	4c. on 5c. sepia	2·30	2·20
714	**80**	5c. on 6c. brown	2·30	2·20
715	**80**	6c. on 10c. brown	2·30	2·20
716	**79**	8c. on 15c. orange	2·30	2·20
717	**80**	16c. on 20c. orange	2·30	2·20
718	**79**	24c. on 25c. violet	4·75	4·50
719	**79**	25c. on 25c. violet	4·75	4·50
720	**80**	32c. on 50c. green	4·75	4·50
721	**80**	40c. on 50c. green	4·75	4·50
722	**80**	50c. on 1cor. yellow	1·60	1·60
723	**80**	100c. on 1cor. yellow	2·30	2·20

127 Wharf, Port San Jorge

128 La Chocolata Cutting

1932. Opening of Rivas Railway.

726	**127**	1c. yellow (postage)	15·00
727	-	2c. red	15·00
728	-	5c. sepia	15·00
729	-	10c. brown	15·00
730	-	15c. yellow	15·00
731	**128**	15c. violet (air)	19·00
732	-	20c. green	19·00
733	-	25c. brown	19·00
734	-	50c. sepia	19·00
735	-	1cor. red	19·00

DESIGNS—HORIZ: 2c. El Nacascolo Halt; 5c. Rivas Station; 10c. San Juan del Sur; 15c. (No. 730), Arrival platform at Rivas; 20c. El Nacascolo; 25c. La Cuesta cutting; 50c. San Juan del Sur quay; 1cor. El Estero.

1932. Surch Vale and value in words.

736	**79**	1c. on 3c. blue	35	15
737	**80**	2c. on 4c. blue	30	15

130 Railway Construction

1932. Opening of Leon-Sauce Railway.

739	-	1c. yellow (postage)	15·00
740	-	2c. red	15·00
741	-	5c. sepia	15·00
742	**130**	10c. brown	15·00
743	-	15c. yellow	15·00
744	-	15c. violet (air)	19·00
745	-	20c. green	19·00
746	-	25c. brown	19·00
747	-	50c. sepia	19·00
748	-	1cor. red	19·00

DESIGNS—HORIZ: 1c. El Sauce; 2c., 15c. (No. 744), Bridge at Santa Lucia; 5c. Santa Lucia; 15c. (No. 743), Santa Lucia cutting; 20c. Santa Lucia River Halt; 25c. Malpaicillo Station; 50c. Railway panorama; 1cor. San Andres.

1933. Surch Resello 1933 Vale and value in words.

749	**79**	1c. on 3c. blue	20	20
750	**79**	1c. on 5c. sepia	20	20
751	**80**	2c. on 10c. brown	20	20

133 Flag of the Race

1933. 441st Anniv of Columbus' Departure from Palos. Roul.

753	**133**	½c. green (postage)	1·70	1·60
754	**133**	1c. green	1·40	1·30
755	**133**	2c. red	1·40	1·30
756	**133**	3c. red	1·40	1·30
757	**133**	4c. orange	1·40	1·30
758	**133**	5c. yellow	1·70	1·60
759	**133**	10c. brown	1·90	1·80
760	**133**	15c. brown	1·90	1·80
761	**133**	20c. blue	1·90	1·80
762	**133**	25c. blue	1·90	1·80
763	**133**	30c. violet	4·75	4·50
764	**133**	50c. purple	4·75	4·50
765	**133**	1cor. brown	4·75	4·50
766	**133**	1c. brown (air)	1·40	1·30
767	**133**	2c. purple	1·40	1·30
768	**133**	4c. violet	2·30	2·20
769	**133**	5c. blue	2·30	2·20
770	**133**	6c. blue	2·30	2·20
771	**133**	8c. brown	1·10	1·10
772	**133**	15c. brown	1·10	1·10
773	**133**	20c. yellow	2·30	2·20
774	**133**	25c. orange	2·30	2·20
775	**133**	50c. red	2·30	2·20
776	**133**	1cor. green	11·00	11·00

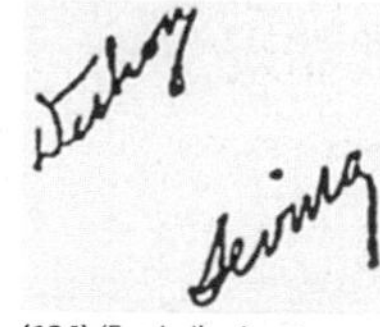

(134) (Facsimile signatures of R. E. Deshon, Minister of Transport and J. R. Sevilla, P.M.G.)

1933. Optd with T 134.

777	**79**	½c. green	45	20
778	**79**	1c. green	20	10
779	**80**	2c. red	65	20
780	**79**	3c. blue	20	10
781	**80**	4c. blue	30	20
782	**79**	5c. brown	30	10
783	**80**	6c. drab	35	25
784	**80**	10c. brown	35	20
785	**79**	15c. red	45	25
786	**80**	20c. orange	65	45
787	**79**	25c. violet	75	35
788	**80**	50c. green	1·20	70
789	**80**	1cor. yellow	6·50	2·30

1933. No. 605 optd with T 134.

790	**79**	1c. orange	35	20

1933. Air. Surch Vale and value.

791	**112**	30c. on 50c. orange	30	20
792	**112**	35c. on 50c. blue	45	20
793	**112**	40c. on 1cor. yellow	45	20
794	**112**	55c. on 1cor. green	55	20

135 Lake Xolotlan

1933. Air. International Airmail Week.

795	**135**	10c. brown	1·40	1·30
796	**135**	15c. violet	1·40	1·30
797	**135**	25c. red	1·40	1·30
798	**135**	50c. blue	1·40	1·30

(136)

1933. Air. Inland service. Colours changed. Surch as T 136 and optd with T 134.

799	**80**	1c. on 2c. green	20	10
800	**79**	2c. on 3c. olive	20	10
801	**80**	3c. on 4c. red	20	10
802	**79**	4c. on 5c. blue	20	10
803	**80**	5c. on 6c. blue	20	10
804	**80**	6c. on 10c. sepia	20	10
805	**79**	8c. on 15c. brown	20	20
806	**80**	16c. on 20c. brown	20	20
807	**79**	24c. on 25c. red	20	20
808	**79**	25c. on 25c. orange	20	20
809	**80**	32c. on 50c. violet	20	20
810	**80**	40c. on 50c. green	30	20
811	**80**	50c. on 1cor. yellow	30	20
812	**80**	1cor. on 1cor. red	1·20	90

1933. Obligatory Tax. As No. 647 optd with T 134. Colour changed.

813	**106**	1c. orange	35	20

1934. Air. Surch Servicio Centroamericano Vale 10 centavos.

814	**112**	10c. on 20c. green	35	25
815	**112**	10c. on 25c. olive	30	25

See also No. 872.

1935. Optd Resello 1935. (a) Nos. 778/9.

816	**79**	1c. green	20	20
817	**80**	2c. red	20	20

(b) No. 813 but without T 134 opt.

818	**106**	1c. orange	30	20

1935. No. 783 surch Vale Medio Centavo.

819	**80**	½c. on 6c. brown	35	20

1935. Optd with T 134 and RESELLO – 1935 in a box.

820	**79**	½c. green	20	20
821	**80**	½c. on 6c. brown (No. 819)	20	20
822	**79**	1c. green	30	20
823	**80**	2c. red	65	20
824	**80**	2c. red (No. 817)	30	20
825	**79**	3c. blue	30	20
826	**80**	4c. blue	30	20
827	**79**	5c. brown	30	20
828	**80**	6c. drab	30	20
829	**80**	10c. brown	75	20
830	**79**	15c. red	20	20
831	**80**	20c. orange	1·20	20
832	**79**	25c. violet	45	20
833	**80**	50c. green	55	20
834	**80**	1cor. yellow	65	20

1935. Obligatory Tax. No. 605 optd with RESELLO – 1935 in a box.

835	**79**	1c. orange	95·00	

1935. Obligatory Tax. Optd RESELLO – 1935 in a box. (a) No. 813 without T 134 opt.

836	**106**	1c. orange	35	20

(b) No. 818.

868		1c. orange	30	20

1935. Air. Nos. 799/812 optd with RESELLO – 1935 in a box.

839	**80**	1c. on 2c. green	20	20
840	**79**	2c. on 3c. olive	20	20
879	**80**	3c. on 4c. red	20	20
880	**79**	4c. on 5c. blue	20	20
881	**80**	5c. on 6c. blue	20	20
882	**80**	6c. on 10c. sepia	20	20
883	**79**	8c. on 15c. brown	20	20
884	**80**	16c. on 20c. brown	20	20
847	**79**	24c. on 25c. red	45	25
848	**79**	25c. on 25c. orange	30	25
849	**80**	32c. on 50c. violet	20	20
850	**80**	40c. on 50c. green	95	65
851	**80**	50c. on 1cor. yellow	65	25
852	**80**	1cor. on 1cor. red	1·50	90

1935. Air. Optd with RESELLO – 1935 in a box. (a) Nos. 629/33.

853A	**112**	15c. purple	55	20
873	**112**	20c. green	35	25
855A	**112**	25c. green	65	55
856A	**112**	50c. sepia	65	55
857A	**112**	1cor. red	55	55

(b) Nos. 791/4.

858A	30c. on 50c. orange	65	55
859A	35c. on 50c. blue	65	55
860A	40c. on 1cor. yellow	65	55
861A	55c. on 1cor. green	65	55

(c) Nos. 814/5.

862A	10c. on 20c. green	£550	£500
863A	10c. on 25c. olive	55	45

1935. Optd with RESELLO – 1935 in a box.

864	**79**	½c. green (No. 465)	20	20
865	**79**	1c. green (No. 617)	20	20
866	**80**	2c. red (No. 467)	60	20
867	**79**	3c. blue (No. 618)	20	20

1936. Surch Resello 1936 Vale and value.

869	1c. on 3c. blue (No. 618)	20	20
870	2c. on 5c. brown (No. 620)	20	20

1936. Air. Surch Servicio Centroamericano Vale diez centavos and RESELLO – 1935 in a box.

871	**112**	10c. on 25c. olive	30	25

1936. Obligatory Tax. No. 818 optd 1936.

874	**106**	1c. orange	75	25

1936. Obligatory Tax. No. 605 optd with T 134 and 1936.

875	**79**	1c. orange	75	25

1936. Air. No. 622 optd Correo Aereo Centro-Americano Resello 1936.

876	**80**	10c. brown	30	25

1936. Air. Nos. 799/800 and 805 optd Resello 1936.

885		1c. on 2c. green	20	20
886	**79**	2c. on 3c. olive	20	20
887	**79**	8c. on 15c. brown	30	25

1936. Optd with or without T 37, surch 1936 Vale and value.

888		½c. on 15c. red	20	20
889	**80**	1c. on 4c. blue	30	20
890	**79**	1c. on 5c. brown	30	20
891	**80**	1c. on 6c. drab	35	20
892	**79**	1c. on 15c. red	30	20
893	**80**	1c. on 20c. orange	20	20
895	**80**	2c. on 10c. brown	30	20
896	**79**	2c. on 15c. red	95	70
897	**80**	2c. on 20c. orange	45	25
898	**79**	2c. on 25c. violet	35	20
900	**80**	2c. on 50c. green	35	25
901	**80**	2c. on 1cor. yellow	35	20
902	**80**	3c. on 4c. blue	65	45

1936. Optd Resello 1936.

903	**79**	3c. blue (No. 618)	35	20
904	**79**	5c. brown (No. 620)	30	20
905	**80**	10c. brown (No. 784)	45	35

1936. Air. Surch 1936 Vale and value.

906	**112**	15c. on 50c. brown	20	20
907	**112**	15c. on 1cor. red	20	20

1936. Fiscal stamps surch RECONSTRUCCION COMUNICACIONES 5 CENTAVOS DE CORDOBA and further surch Vale dos centavos Resello 1936.

908	**90**	1c. on 5c. green	35	20
909	**90**	2c. on 5c. green	35	20

1936. Obligatory Tax. Fiscal stamps surch RECONSTRUCCION COMUNICACIONES 5 CENTAVOS DE CORDOBA and further surch. (a) 1936 R. de C. Vale Un Centavo.

910	1c. on 5c. green	35	25

(b) Vale un centavo R. de C. 1936.

911	1c. on 5c. green	45	25

1937. Colours changed. Size 27×22¾ mm.

912	**79**	½c. black	20	20
913	**79**	1c. red	20	20
914	**80**	2c. blue	20	20
915	**79**	3c. brown	20	20
916	**80**	4c. yellow	20	20
917	**79**	5c. red	20	20
918	**80**	6c. violet	20	20
919	**80**	10c. green	20	20
920	**79**	15c. green	20	20
921	**80**	20c. brown	45	20
922	**79**	25c. orange	45	20
923	**80**	50c. brown	45	20
924	**80**	1cor. blue	65	25

1937. Obligatory Tax. Colour changed.

925	**106**	1c. green	30	20

1937. Air. Colours changed.

926	**112**	15c. orange	20	20
927	**112**	20c. red	20	20
928	**112**	25c. black	30	20
929	**112**	50c. violet	30	20
930	**112**	1cor. orange	65	25

1937. Air. Surch Vale and value. Colours changed.

931	30c. on 50c. red	30	20
932	35c. on 50c. olive	30	20
933	40c. on 1cor. green	30	20
934	55c. on 1cor. blue	30	20

1937. Air. Surch Servicio Centroamericano Vale Diez Centavos.

949	10c. on 1cor. red	30	20

1937. Air. No. 805 (without T 134) optd 1937.

950	**79**	8c. on 15c. brown	45	25

142 Baseball Player

1937. Obligatory Tax. For 1937 Central American Olympic Games. Optd with ball in red under "OLIMPICO".

951	**142**	1c. red	45	20
952	**142**	1c. yellow	45	20
953	**142**	1c. blue	45	20
953a	**142**	1c. green	45	20
MS953b		134×90 mm. Nos. 951/3a	4·75	4·50

1937. Nos. 799/809 optd Habilitado 1937.

954	**80**	1c. on 2c. green	20	20
955	**79**	2c. on 3c. olive	20	20
956	**80**	3c. on 4c. red	20	20
957	**79**	4c. on 5c. blue	20	20
958	**80**	5c. on 6c. blue	20	20
959	**80**	6c. on 10c. brown	20	20
960	**79**	8c. on 15c. brown	20	20
961	**80**	16c. on 20c. brown	20	20
962	**79**	24c. on 25c. red	20	20
963	**79**	25c. on 25c. orange	30	20
964	**80**	32c. on 50c. violet	30	25

144 Presidential Palace, Managua

1937. Air. Inland.

965	**144**	1c. red	20	20
966	**144**	2c. blue	20	20
967	**144**	3c. olive	20	20
968	**144**	4c. black	20	20
969	**144**	5c. purple	20	20
970	**144**	6c. brown	20	20
971	**144**	8c. violet	20	20
972	**144**	16c. orange	20	20
973	**144**	24c. yellow	20	20
974	**144**	25c. green	30	20

145 Nicaragua

1937. Air. Abroad.

975	**145**	10c. green	20	20
976	**145**	15c. blue	20	20
977	**145**	20c. yellow	20	20
978	**145**	25c. violet	20	20
979	**145**	30c. red	30	20
980	**145**	50c. orange	35	20
981	**145**	1cor. olive	70	55

146 Presidential Palace

1937. Air. Abroad. 150th Anniv of U.S. Constitution.

982	-	10c. blue and green	1·90	1·10
983	**146**	15c. blue and orange	1·90	1·30
984	-	20c. blue and red	1·10	1·10
985	-	25c. blue and brown	1·10	1·10
986	-	30c. blue and green	1·10	1·10
987	-	35c. blue and yellow	60	60
988	-	40c. blue and green	50	50
989	-	45c. blue and purple	50	45
990	-	50c. blue and mauve	50	45
991	-	55c. blue and green	50	45
992	-	75c. blue and green	50	45
993	-	1cor. red and blue	1·10	60

DESIGNS: 10c. Children's Park, Managua; 20c. S. America; 25c. C. America; 30c. N. America; 35c. Lake Tiscapa; 40c. Pan-American motor-road; 45c. Priniomi Park; 50c. Piedrecitas Park; 55c. San Juan del Sur; 75c Rio Tipitapa; 1cor. Granade landscape.

146b Diriangen

1937. Air. Day of the Race.

993a	**146b**	1c. green (inland)	20	20
993b	**146b**	4c. lake	20	20
993c	**146b**	5c. violet	30	25
993d	**146b**	8c. blue	30	25
993e	**146b**	10c. brown (abroad)	20	20
993f	**146b**	15c. blue	20	20
993g	**146b**	20c. pink	30	25

147 Letter Carrier

1937. 75th Anniv of Postal Administration.

994	**147**	½c. green	20	20
995	-	1c. mauve	20	20
996	-	2c. brown	20	20
997	-	3c. violet	20	20
998	-	5c. blue	20	20
999	-	7½c. red	55	35

DESIGNS: 1c. Mule transport; 2c. Diligence; 3c. Yacht; 5c. Packet steamer; 7½c. Steam mail train.

147a Gen. Tomas Martinez

1938. Air. 75th Anniv of Postal Administration.

999a	**147a**	1c. blk & orge (inland)	25	25
999b	**147a**	5c. black and violet	25	25
999c	**147a**	8c. black and blue	35	35
999d	**147a**	16c. black and brown	35	35
999e	-	10c. blk & grn (abroad)	35	25
999f	-	15c. black and blue	35	35
999g	-	25c. black and violet	50	50
999h	-	50c. black and red	60	60

DESIGNS: 10c. to 50c. Gen. Anastasio Somoza.

1938. Surch 1938 and Vale, new value in words and Centavos.

1000	**79**	3c. on 25c. orange	25	25
1001	**80**	5c. on 50c. brown	35	25
1002	**80**	6c. on 1 cor. blue	25	25

149 Dario Park

150 Lake Managua

151 President Somoza

1939

No.	Type	Description	Mint	Used
1003	**149**	1½c. green (postage)	25	10
1004	**149**	2c. red	25	10
1005	**149**	3c. blue	25	10
1006	**149**	6c. brown	25	10
1007	**149**	7½c. green	25	10
1008	**149**	10c. brown	35	25
1009	**149**	15c. orange	35	25
1010	**149**	25c. violet	35	25
1011	**149**	50c. green	35	35
1012	**149**	1cor. yellow	75	50
1013	**150**	2c. blue (air: inland)	25	25
1014	**150**	3c. olive	25	25
1015	**150**	8c. mauve	25	25
1016	**150**	16c. orange	25	25
1017	**150**	24c. yellow	25	25
1018	**150**	32c. green	25	25
1019	**150**	50c. red	25	25
1020	**151**	10c. brown (air: abroad)	25	25
1021	**151**	15c. blue	25	25
1022	**151**	20c. yellow	25	25
1023	**151**	25c. violet	25	25
1024	**151**	30c. red	25	25
1025	**151**	50c. orange	35	25
1026	**151**	1cor. olive	45	45

1939. Nos. 920/1. Surch Vale un Centavo 1939.

No.	Type	Description	Mint	Used
1027	**79**	1c. on 15c. green	25	25
1028	**80**	1c. on 20c. brown	25	25

153 Will Rogers and Managua Airport

1939. Air. Will Rogers Commemorative. Inscr "WILL ROGERS/1931/1939".

No.	Type	Description	Mint	Used
1029	**153**	1c. green	25	25
1030	-	2c. red	25	25
1031	-	3c. blue	25	25
1032	-	4c. blue	25	25
1033	-	5c. red	25	25

DESIGNS: 2c. Rogers at Managua; 3c. Rogers in P.A.A. hut; 4c. Rogers and U.S. Marines; 5c. Rogers and street in Managua.

156 Senate House and Pres. Somoza

1940. Air. President's Visit to U.S.A. (a) Inscr "AEREO INTERIOR".

No.	Type	Description	Mint	Used
1034		4c. brown	25	25
1035	**156**	8c. brown	25	25
1036	-	16c. green	25	25
1037	**156**	20c. mauve	60	35
1038	-	32c. red	25	25

(b) Inscr "CORREO AEREO INTERNACIONAL".

No.	Type	Description	Mint	Used
1039		25c. blue	25	25
1040		30c. black	25	25
1041	**156**	50c. red	60	45
1042	-	60c. green	60	35
1043	-	65c. brown	60	35
1044	-	90c. olive	80	35
1045	-	1cor. violet	1·20	70

DESIGNS: 4c., 16c., 25c., 30c., 65c., 90c. Pres. Somoza addressing Senate; 32c., 60c., 1cor. Portrait of Pres. Somoza between symbols of Nicaragua and New York World's Fair.

158 L. S. Rowe, Statue of Liberty and Union Flags

1940. Air. 50th Anniv of Pan-American Union.

No.	Type	Description	Mint	Used
1046	**158**	1cor.25 multicoloured	95	80

159 First Issue of Nicaragua and Sir Rowland Hill

1941. Air. Centenary of First Adhesive Postage stamps.

No.	Type	Description	Mint	Used
1047	**159**	2cor. brown	3·00	1·10
1048	**159**	3cor. blue	10·00	1·70
1049	**159**	5cor. red	28·00	4·00

1941. Surch Servicio ordinario Vale Diez Centavos de Cordoba.

No.	Type	Description	Mint	Used
1050	**153**	10c. on 1c. green	25	25

161 Rube Dario

1941. 25th Death Anniv of Ruben Dario (poet).

No.	Type	Description	Mint	Used
1051	**161**	10c. red (postage)	45	20
1052	**161**	20c. mauve (air)	35	20
1053	**161**	35c. green	40	25
1054	**161**	40c. orange	45	25
1055	**161**	60c. blue	80	35

1943. Surch Servicio Ordinario Vale Diez Centavos.

No.	Type	Description	Mint	Used
1056	**153**	10c. on 1c. green	4·75	25

162 "V" for Victory

1943. Victory.

No.	Type	Description	Mint	Used
1057	**162**	10c. red and violet (postage)	25	25
1058	**162**	30c. red and brown	25	25
1059	**162**	40c. red and green (air)	35	25
1060	**162**	60c. red and blue	35	25

163 Red Cross

164 Red Cross Workers and Wounded

1944. Air. 80th Anniv of Int Red Cross Society.

No.	Type	Description	Mint	Used
1061	**163**	25c. red	95	45
1062	-	50c. bistre	1·20	70
1063	**164**	1cor. green	2·30	2·00

DESIGN—VERT: 50c. Two Hemispheres.

165 Columbus and Lighthouse 166 Columbus's Fleet and Lighthouse

1945. Honouring Columbus's Discovery of America and Erection of Columbus Lighthouse near Trujillo City, Dominican Republic.

No.	Type	Description	Mint	Used
1064	**165**	4c. black & green (postage)	25	20
1065	**165**	6c. black and orange	35	30
1066	**165**	8c. black and red	45	40
1067	**165**	10c. black and blue	55	45
1068	**166**	20c. grey and green (air)	25	20
1069	**166**	35c. black and red	40	30
1070	**166**	75c. pink and green	60	45
1071	**166**	90c. blue and red	95	80
1072	**166**	1cor. blue and black	1·00	40
1073	**166**	2cor.50 red and blue	2·40	2·40

168 Roosevelt as a Stamp Collector

1946. President Roosevelt Commemorative Inscr "HOMENAJE A ROOSEVELT".

No.	Type	Description	Mint	Used
1074	**168**	4c. green & black (postage)	20	20
1075	-	8c. violet and black	30	30
1076	-	10c. blue and black	40	40
1077	-	16c. red and black	50	50
1078	-	32c. brown and black	40	40
1079	-	50c. grey and black	40	40
1080	-	25c. orange & black (air)	30	20
1081	-	75c. red and black	40	30
1082	-	1cor. green and black	50	50
1083	-	3cor. violet and black	4·25	4·00
1084	-	5cor. blue and black	6·25	6·00

DESIGNS—portraying Roosevelt. HORIZ: 8c., 25c. with Churchill at the Atlantic Conference; 16c., 1cor. with Churchill, De Gaulle and Giraud at the Casablanca Conference; 32c., 3cor. with Churchill and Stalin at the Teheran Conference. VERT: 10c., 75c. Signing Declaration of War against Japan; 50c., 5cor. Head of Roosevelt.

171 Managua Cathedral

172 G.P.O., Managua

1947. Managua Centenary. Frames in black.

No.	Type	Description	Mint	Used
1085	**171**	4c. red (postage)	20	20
1086	-	5c. blue	30	20
1087	-	6c. green	30	20
1088	-	10c. olive	30	20
1089	-	75c. brown	30	30
1090	-	5c. violet (air)	20	20
1091	**172**	20c. green	20	20
1092	-	35c. orange	20	20
1093	-	90c. purple	40	30
1094	-	1cor. brown	60	50
1095	-	2cor.50 purple	1·70	1·50

DESIGNS—POSTAGE (as Type **171**): 5c. Health Ministry; 6c. Municipal Building; 10c. College; 75c. G.P.O., Managua. AIR (as Type **172**): 5c. College; 35c. Health Ministry; 90c. National Bank; 1cor. Municipal Building; 2cor.50, National Palace.

173 San Cristobal Volcano

174 Ruben Dario Monument, Managua

1947. (a) Postage.

No.	Type	Description	Mint	Used
1096	**173**	2c. orange and black	20	20
1097	-	3c. violet and black	20	20
1098	-	4c. grey and black	30	20
1099	-	5c. red and black	60	30
1100	-	6c. green and black	30	20
1101	-	8c. brown and black	40	20
1102	-	10c. red and black	60	30
1103	-	20c. blue and black	2·10	50
1104	-	30c. purple and black	1·60	50
1105	-	50c. red and black	3·50	1·00
1106	-	1cor. brown and black	1·20	60

DESIGNS—as Type **173**: 3c. Lion on Ruben Dario's tomb, Leon Cathedral; 4c. Race stand; 5c. Soldiers' Monument; 6c. Sugar cane; 8c. Tropical fruits; 10c. Cotton; 20c. Horses; 30c. Coffee plant; 50c. Prize bullock; 1cor. Agricultural landscape.

(b) Air.

No.	Type	Description	Mint	Used
1107	**174**	5c. red and green	20	20
1108	-	6c. orange and black	20	20
1109	-	8c. brown and red	20	20
1110	-	10c. blue and brown	20	20
1111	-	20c. orange and blue	30	30
1112	-	25c. green and red	40	40
1113	-	35c. brown and black	30	30
1114	-	50c. black and violet	40	30
1115	-	1cor. red and black	85	80
1116	-	1cor.50 green and red	85	80
1117	-	5cor. red and brown	6·75	6·50
1118	-	10cor. brown and violet	5·25	5·00
1119	-	25cor. yellow and green	10·50	10·00

DESIGNS—As Type **174**: 6c. Baird's tapir; 8c. Highway and Lake Managua; 10c. Genizaro Dam; 20c. Ruben Dario Monument, Managua; 25c. Sulphur Lagoon, Nejapa; 35c. Managua Airport; 50c. Mouth of Rio Prinzapolka; 1cor. Thermal Baths, Tipitapa; 1cor.50, Rio Tipitapa; 5cor. Embassy building; 10cor. Girl carrying basket of fruit; 2cor. Franklin D. Roosevelt Monument, Managua.

175 Softball

176 Pole-vaulting

177 Tennis

1949. 10th World Amateur Baseball Championships. (a) Postage as T 175/6.

No.	Type	Description	Mint	Used
1120	**175**	1c. brown	20	20
1121	-	2c. blue	85	20
1122	**176**	3c. green	30	20
1123	-	4c. purple	20	20
1124	-	5c. orange	50	20
1125	-	10c. green	50	20
1126	-	15c. red	85	20
1127	-	25c. blue	85	20
1128	-	35c. green	1·30	30
1129	-	40c. violet	1·90	30
1130	-	60c. black	2·10	40
1131	-	1cor. red	2·50	1·30
1132	-	2cor. purple	4·75	2·50
MS1132a		Thirteen sheets 140×105 or 105×140 mm (vert designs). Nos. 1120/32 in blocks of four	£120	£120

DESIGNS—VERT: 2c. Scout; 5c. Cycling; 25c. Boxing; 35c. Basketball. HORIZ: 4c. Diving; 10c. Stadium; 15c. Baseball; 40c. Yachting; 60c. Table tennis; 1cor. Football; 2cor. Tennis.

(b) Air as T 177.

1133	177	1c. red	20	20
1134	-	2c. black	20	20
1135	-	3c. red	20	20
1136	-	4c. black	20	20
1137	-	5c. blue	30	20
1138	-	15c. green	95	20
1139	-	25c. purple	2·10	30
1140	-	30c. brown	1·90	30
1141	-	40c. violet	50	30
1142	-	75c. mauve	4·75	2·75
1143	-	1cor. blue	5·25	1·50
1144	-	2cor. olive	2·10	1·80
1145	-	5cor. green	2·50	2·40
MS1145a Thirteen sheets each 125×115 mm. Nos. 1133/45 in blocks of four			£200	£200

DESIGNS—SQUARE: 2c. Football; 3c. Table tennis; 4c. Stadium; 5c. Yachting; 15c. Basketball; 25c. Boxing; 30c. Baseball; 40c. Cycling; 75c. Diving; 1cor. Pole-vaulting; 2cor. Scout; 5cor. Softball.

178 National Stadium, Managua

1949. Obligatory Tax stamps. Stadium Construction Fund.

1146	178	5c. blue	40	20
1146a	178	5c. red	40	20
MS1146b 87×97 mm. No. 1146 in block of four			5·25	5·00

179 Rowland Hill **180** Heinrich von Stephan

1950. 75th Anniv of U.P.U. Frames in black.

1147	179	20c. red (postage)	20	20
1148	-	25c. green	30	20
1149	-	75c. blue	50	30
1150	-	80c. green	30	30
1151	-	4cor. blue	1·00	90
MS1151a Five sheets each 114×126 mm. Nos. 1147/51 in blocks of four			36·00	35·00

DESIGNS—VERT: 25c. Portrait as Type **180**; 75c. Monument, Berne; 80c., 4cor. Obverse and reverse of Congress Medal.

1152		16c. red (air)	20	20
1153	180	20c. orange	20	20
1154	-	25c. black	30	30
1155	-	30c. red	40	30
1156	-	85c. green	60	50
1157	-	1cor.10 brown	60	50
1158	-	2cor.14 green	2·50	2·40
MS1158a Seven sheets each 126×114 mm. Nos. 1152/8 in blocks of four			41·00	40·00

DESIGNS—HORIZ: 16c. Rowland Hill; 25, 30c. U.P.U. Offices, Berne; 85c. Monument, Berne; 1cor.10 and 2cor.14,Obverse and reverse of Congress Medal.

181 Queen Isabella and Columbus's Fleet **182** Isabella the Catholic

1952. 500th Birth Anniv of Isabella the Catholic.

1159		10c. mauve (postage)	20	20
1160	181	96c. blue	85	80
1161	-	98c. red	85	80
1162	-	1cor.20 brown	1·00	1·00
1163	182	1cor.76 purple	1·30	1·30
MS1163a 160×128 mm. Nos. 1159/63			4·25	4·00

1164		2cor.30 red (air)	2·30	2·20
1165	-	2cor.80 orange	2·10	2·00
1166	-	3cor. green	2·30	2·20
1167	181	3cor.30 blue	2·30	2·20
1168	-	3cor.60 green	2·75	2·50
MS1168a 160×128 mm. Nos. 1164/8			11·50	11·00

DESIGNS—VERT: 10c., 3cor.60, Queen facing right; 98c., 3cor. Queen and "Santa Maria"; 1cor.20, 2cor.80, Queen and Map of Americas.

183 O.D.E.C.A. Flag

1953. Foundation of Organization of Central American States.

1169	183	4c. blue (postage)	20	20
1170	-	5c. green	20	20
1171	-	6c. brown	20	20
1172	-	15c. olive	30	20
1173	-	50c. sepia	30	30
1174	-	20c. red (air)	20	20
1175	183	25c. blue	20	20
1176	-	30c. brown	20	20
1177	-	60c. green	30	30
1178	-	1cor. purple	70	70

DESIGNS: 5c., 1cor. Map of C. America; 6c., 20c. Hands holding O.D.E.C.A. arms; 15c., 30c. Five presidents of C. America; 50c., 60c. Charter and flags.

184 Pres. Solorzano **185** Pres. Arguello

1953. Presidential Series. Portraits in black. (a) Postage. As T 184.

1179	184	4c. red	20	20
1180	-	6c. blue (D. M. Chamorro)	20	20
1181	-	8c. brown (Diaz)	20	20
1182	-	15c. red (Somoza)	20	20
1183	-	50c. green (E. Chamorro)	20	20

(b) Air. As T 185.

1184	185	4c. red	20	20
1185	-	5c. orange (Moncada)	20	20
1186	-	20c. blue (J. B. Sacasa)	20	20
1187	-	25c. blue (Zelaya)	20	20
1188	-	30c. lake (Somoza)	20	20
1189	-	35c. green (Martinez)	20	20
1190	-	40c. plum (Guzman)	30	20
1191	-	45c. olive (Cuadra)	30	30
1192	-	50c. red (P. J. Chamorro)	30	20
1193	-	60c. blue (Zavala)	30	30
1194	-	85c. brown (Cardenas)	40	40
1195	-	1cor.10 purple (Carazo)	50	50
1196	-	1cor.20 bistre (R. Sacasa)	50	50

186 Sculptor and U.N. Emblem

1954. U.N.O. Inscr "HOMENAJE A LA ONU".

1197	186	3c. drab (postage)	20	20
1198	A	4c. green	20	20
1199	B	5c. green	20	20
1200	C	15c. green	95	20
1201	D	1cor. turquoise	85	30
1202	E	3c. red (air)	20	20
1203	F	4c. orange	20	20
1204	C	5c. red	20	20
1205	D	30c. pink	1·00	30
1206	B	2cor. red	1·70	1·00
1207	A	3cor. brown	2·50	1·80
1208	186	5cor. purple	3·00	2·40

DESIGNS: A, Detail from Nicaragua's coat of arms; B, Globe; C, Candle and Nicaragua's Charter; D, Flags of Nicaragua and U.N.; E, Torch; F, Trusting hands.

187 Capt. D. L. Ray **188** North American Sabre

1954. National Air Force. Frames in black. (a) Postage. Frames as T 187.

1209	187	1c. black	20	20
1210	-	2c. black	20	20
1211	-	3c. myrtle	20	20
1212	-	4c. orange	20	20
1213	-	5c. green	20	20
1214	-	15c. turquoise	20	20
1215	-	1cor. violet	20	20

(b) Air. Frames as T 188.

1216		10c. black	20	20
1217	188	15c. black	20	20
1218	-	20c. mauve	20	20
1219	-	25c. red	20	20
1220	-	30c. blue	20	20
1221	-	50c. blue	50	50
1222	-	1cor. green	40	30

DESIGNS—POSTAGE: 2c. North American Sabre; 3c. Douglas Boston; 4c. Consolidated Liberator; 5c. North American Texan trainer; 15c. Pres. Somoza; 1cor. Emblem. AIR: 10c. D. L. Ray; 20c. Emblem; 25c. Hangars; 30c. Pres. Somoza; 50c. North American Texan trainers; 1cor. Lockheed Lightning airplanes.

189 Rotary Slogans

1955. 50th Anniv of Rotary International.

1223	189	15c. orange (postage)	20	20
1224	A	20c. olive	20	20
1225	B	35c. violet	30	20
1226	C	40c. red	30	20
1227	D	90c. black	50	40
MS1227a 127×102 mm. Nos. 1223/7			5·25	5·00

1228		1c. red (air)	20	20
1229	A	2c. blue	20	20
1230	C	3c. green	20	20
1231	189	4c. violet	20	20
1232	B	5c. brown	20	20
1233	B	25c. turquoise	20	20
1234	189	30c. black	20	20
1235	C	45c. mauve	40	30
1236	A	50c. green	40	30
1237	D	1cor. blue	50	40
MS1237a 127×102 mm. Nos. 1233/7			10·50	10·00

DESIGNS—VERT: A, Clasped hands; B, Rotarian and Nicaraguan flags; D, Paul P. Harris. HORIZ: C, World map and winged emblem.

1956. National Exhibition. Surch Conmemoracion Exposicion Nacional Febrero 4-16, 1956 and value.

1238	5c. on 6c. brown (No. 1171) (postage)	20	20
1239	5c. on 6c. black & bl (No. 1180)	20	20
1240	5c. on 8c. brn & blk (No. 1101)	20	20
1241	15c. on 35c. violet (No. 1225)	20	20
1242	15c. on 80c. grn & blk (No. 1150)	20	20
1243	15c. on 90c. black (No. 1227)	20	20
1244	30c. on 35c. black and green (No. 1189) (air)	20	20
1245	30c. on 45c. blk & ol (No. 1191)	20	20
1246	30c. on 45c. mauve (No. 1235)	20	20
1247	2cor. on 5cor. purple (No. 1208)	1·00	1·00

190a

1956. Obligatory Tax. Social Welfare Fund.

1247a	190a	5c. blue	20	20

191 Gen. J. Dolores Estrada

1956. Cent of War of 1856. Inscr as in T 191.

1248	-	5c. brown (postage)	20	20
1249	-	10c. lake	20	20
1250	-	15c. grey	20	20
1251	-	25c. red	20	20
1252	-	50c. purple	40	20
1253	191	30c. red (air)	20	20
1254	-	60c. brown	20	20
1255	-	1cor.50 green	30	30
1256	-	2cor.50 blue	40	40
1257	-	10cor. orange	2·50	2·00

DESIGNS—VERT: 5c. Gen. M. Jerez; 10c. Gen. F. Chamorro; 50c. Gen. J. D. Estrada; 1cor.50, E. Mangalo; 10cor. Commodore H. Paulding. HORIZ: 15c. Battle of San Jacinto; 25c. Granada in flames; 60c. Bas-relief; 2cor.50, Battle of Rivas.

192 President Somoza

1957. Air. National Mourning for Pres. G. A. Somoza. Various frames. Inscr as in T 192. Centres in black.

1258		15c. black	20	20
1259		30c. blue	30	30
1260	192	2cor. violet	1·00	1·00
1261	-	3cor. olive	2·10	2·00
1262	-	5cor. sepia	3·50	3·50

193 Scout and Badge **194** Clasped Hands, Badge and Globe

1957. Birth Centenary of Lord Baden-Powell.

1263	193	10c. olive & vio (postage)	20	20
1264	-	15c. sepia and purple	20	20
1265	-	20c. brown and blue	20	20
1266	-	25c. brown and turquoise	30	20
1267	-	50c. olive and red	40	40
MS1267a 127×102 mm. Nos. 1263/7. Imperf			3·00	3·00

1268	194	3c. olive and red (air)	20	20
1269	-	4c. blue and brown	20	20
1270	-	5c. brown and green	20	20
1271	-	6c. drab and violet	20	20
1272	-	8c. red and black	20	20
1273	-	30c. black and green	30	30
1274	-	40c. black and blue	30	30
1275	-	75c. sepia and purple	30	30
1276	-	85c. grey and red	40	40
1277	-	1cor. brown and green	50	50
MS1277a 127×102 mm. Nos. 1273/7. Imperf			5·25	5·00

DESIGNS—VERT: 4c. Scout badge; 5c., 15c. Wolf cub; 6c. Badge and flags; 8c. Badge and emblems of scouting 20c. Scout; 25., 1cor. Lord Baden-Powell; 30., 50c. Joseph A. Harrison; 75c. Rover Scout; 85c. Scout. HORIZ: 40c. Presentation to Pres. Somoza.

195 Pres. Luis Somoza

1957. Election of Pres. Somoza. Portrait in brown. (a) Postage. Oval frame.

1278	195	10c. red	20	20
1279	195	15c. blue	20	20
1280	195	35c. purple	30	20
1281	195	50c. brown	40	20
1282	195	75c. green	70	60

(b) Air. Rectangular frame.

1283	20c. blue	20	20
1284	25c. mauve	20	20
1285	30c. sepia	20	20
1286	40c. turquoise	30	30
1287	2cor. violet	1·30	1·30

197 Archbishop of Managua **196** Managua Cathedral

1957. Churches and Priests. Centres in olive.

1288	**196**	5c. green (postage)	20	20
1289	-	10c. purple	20	20
1290	**197**	15c. blue	20	20
1291	-	20c. sepia	20	20
1292	-	50c. green	20	20
1293	-	1cor. violet	30	30
1294	**197**	30c. green (air)	20	20
1295	**196**	60c. brown	20	20
1296	-	75c. blue	20	20
1297	-	90c. red	30	30
1298	-	1cor.50 turquoise	50	50
1299	-	2cor. purple	70	70

DESIGNS—HORIZ: As Type **196**: 20, 90c. Leon Cathedral; 50c., 1cor.50, La Merced, Granada Church. VERT: As Type **197**: 10, 75c. Bishop of Nicaragua; 1, 2cor. Father Mariano Dubon.

198 "Honduras" (freighter)

1957. Nicaraguan Merchant Marine Commemoration. Inscr as in T 198.

1300	**198**	4c. black, blue and myrtle (postage)	25	15
1301	-	5c. violet, blue and brown	25	15
1302	-	6c. black, blue and red	25	15
1303	-	10c. black, green and sepia	25	15
1304	-	15c. brown, blue and red	30	20
1305	-	50c. brown, blue and violet	40	30
1306	-	25c. purple, blue and ultramarine (air)	25	20
1307	-	30c. grey, buff and brown	25	20
1308	-	50c. bistre, blue and violet	35	25
1309	-	60c. black, turquoise and purple	40	35
1310	-	1cor. black, blue and red	50	45
1311	-	2cor.50 brown, blue and black	1·60	1·50

DESIGNS: 5c. Gen. A. Somoza, founder of Mamenic (National) Shipping Line, and "Guatemala" (freighter); 6c. "Guatemala"; 10c. "Salvador" (freighter); 15c. Freighter between hemispheres; 25c. "Managua" (freighter); 30c. Ship's wheel and world map; 50c. (No. 1305), Hemispheres and ship; 50c. (No. 1308), Mamenic Shipping Line flag; 60c. "Costa Rica" (freighter); 1cor. "Nicarao" (freighter); 2cor.50, Map, freighter and flag.

199 Exhibition Emblem

1958. Air. Brussels International Exn. Inscr "EXPOSICION MUNDIAL DE BELGICA 1958".

1312	**199**	25c. black, yellow & green	20	20
1313	-	30c. multicoloured	20	20
1314	-	45c. black, ochre and blue	25	20
1315	**199**	1cor. black, blue and dull purple	30	30
1316	-	2cor. multicoloured	40	40
1317	-	10cor. sepia, purple and blue	1·90	1·80
MS1317a		130×119 mm. Nos. 1312/17	14·50	14·00

DESIGNS: As Type **199**: 30c., 20cor. Arms of Nicaragua; 45c., 10cor. Nicaraguan pavilion.

200 Emblems of C. American Republics

1958. 17th Central American Lions Convention. Inscr as in T 200. Emblems (5c., 60c.) multicoloured; Lions badge (others) in blue, red, yellow (or orange and buff).

1318	**200**	5c. blue (postage)	20	20
1319	-	10c. blue and orange	20	20
1320	-	20c. blue and green	20	20
1321	-	50c. blue and purple	30	30
1322	-	75c. blue and mauve	50	40
1323	-	1cor.50 blue, salmon and drab	70	60
MS1323a		157×90 mm. Nos. 1318/23	3·00	3·00
1324		30c. blue and orange (air)	20	20
1325	**200**	60c. blue and pink	30	30
1326	-	90c. blue	40	30
1327	-	1cor.25 blue and olive	50	40
1328	-	2cor. blue and green	85	70
1329	-	3cor. blue, red and violet	1·20	1·20
MS1329a		157×90 mm. Nos. 1324/9	4·75	4·50

DESIGNS—HORIZ: 10c., 1cor.25, Melvin Jones; 20, 30c. Dr. T. A. Arias; 50, 90c. Edward G. Barry; 75c., 2cor. Lions emblem; 1cor.50, 3cor. Map of C. American Isthmus.

201 Arms of La Salle

1958. Brothers of the Nicaraguan Christian Schools Commemoration. Inscr as in T 201.

1330	**201**	5c. red, blue and yellow (postage)	20	20
1331	-	10c. sepia, blue and green	20	20
1332	-	15c. sepia, brown & bistre	20	20
1333	-	20c. black, red and bistre	20	20
1334	-	50c. sepia, orange & bis	20	20
1335	-	75c. sepia, turquoise & green	30	30
1336	-	1cor. black, violet & bis	40	40
1337	**201**	30c. blue, red & yellow (air)	20	20
1338	-	60c. sepia, purple & grey	30	30
1339	-	85c. black, red and blue	30	30
1340	-	90c. black, green & ochre	40	40
1341	-	1cor.25 black, red and ochre	60	50
1342	-	1cor.50 sepia, green and grey	70	60
1343	-	1cor.75 black, brn & bl	85	70
1344	-	2cor. sepia, green & grey	1·00	1·00

DESIGNS—HORIZ: 10, 60c. Managua Teachers Institute. VERT: 15, 85c. De La Salle (founder); 20, 90c. Brother Carlos; 50c., 1cor.50, Brother Antonio; 75c., 1cor.25, Brother Julio; 1cor., 1cor.75, Brother Argeo; 2cor. Brother Eugenio.

202 U.N. Emblem

1958. Inauguration of UNESCO Headquarters Building, Paris. Inscr as in T 202.

1345	**202**	10c. blue & mauve (postage)	20	20
1346	-	15c. mauve and blue	20	20
1347	-	25c. brown and green	20	20
1348	-	40c. black and red	20	20
1349	-	45c. mauve and blue	20	20
1350	**202**	50c. green and brown	20	20
MS1350a		85×103 mm. Nos. 1345/50	1·00	1·00
1351		60c. blue and mauve (air)	20	20
1352		75c. brown and green	30	30
1353		90c. green and brown	30	30
1354		1cor. mauve and blue	30	30
1355		3cor. red and black	75	75
1356		5cor. blue and mauve	1·20	1·10
MS1356a		85×103 mm. Nos. 1351/6	4·25	4·00

DESIGNS—VERT: 15c. Aerial view of H.Q. 25, 45c. Facade composed of letters "UNESCO"; 40c. H.Q. and Eiffel Tower. In oval vignettes—60c. As 15c.; 75c., 5cor. As 25c.; 90c., 3cor. As 40c.; 1cor. As Type **202**.

203

204

1959. Obligatory Tax. Consular Fiscal stamps surch. Serial Nos. in red.

1357	**203**	5c. on 50c. blue	30	20
1358	**204**	5c. on 50c. blue	30	20

205

1959. Obligatory Tax.

1359	**205**	5c. blue	30	20

206 Cardinal Spellman with Pope John XXIII

1959. Cardinal Spellman Commemoration.

1360	**206**	5c. flesh & green (postage)	20	20
1361	**A**	10c. multicoloured	20	20
1362	**B**	15c. red, black and green	20	20
1363	**C**	20c. yellow and blue	20	20
1364	**D**	25c. red and blue	20	20
MS1364a		116×128 mm. Nos. 1360/4	70	70
1365	**E**	30c. blue, red & yell (air)	20	20
1366	**206**	35c. bronze and orange	20	20
1367	**A**	1cor. multicoloured	30	30
1368	**B**	1cor.5 red and black	30	30
1369	**C**	1cor.50 yellow and blue	30	30
1370	**D**	2cor. blue, violet and red	50	50
1371	**E**	5cor. multicoloured	1·40	1·00
MS1371a		116×128 mm. Nos. 1365/71. Perf or imperf	4·25	4·00

DESIGNS—VERT: A, Cardinal's Arms; B, Cardinal; D, Cardinal wearing sash. HORIZ: C, Cardinal and Cross; E, Flags of Nicaragua, Vatican City and U.S.A.

207 Abraham Lincoln

1960. 150th Birth Anniv of Abraham Lincoln. Portrait in black.

1372	**207**	5c. red (postage)	20	20
1373	**207**	10c. green	20	20
1374	**207**	15c. orange	20	20
1375	**207**	1cor. purple	30	30
1376	**207**	2cor. blue	40	30
MS1376a		152×116 mm. Nos. 1372/6. Imperf	1·20	1·20
1377		30c. blue (air)	20	20
1378		35c. red	20	20
1379		70c. purple	20	20
1380		1cor.5 green	30	30
1381		1cor.50 violet	40	40
1382	-	5cor. ochre and black	1·30	1·30
MS1382a		152×116 mm. Nos. 1377/82. Imperf	3·75	3·75

DESIGN—HORIZ: 5cor. Scroll inscr "Dar al que necesite—A. Lincoln".

1960. Air. 10th Anniv of San Jose (Costa Rica) Philatelic Society. Optd X Aniversario Club FilatelicoS. J.—C. R.

1383		2cor. red (No. 1206)	85	80
1384		2cor.50 blue (No. 1256)	85	80
1385		3cor. green (No. 1166)	1·10	1·10

1960. Red Cross Fund for Chilean Earthquake Relief. Nos. 1372/82 optd Resello and Maltese Cross. Portrait in black.

1386	**207**	5c. red (postage)	20	20
1387	**207**	10c. green	20	20
1388	**207**	15c. orange	20	20
1389	**207**	1cor. purple	30	20
1390	**207**	2cor. blue	50	40
1391	**207**	30c. blue (air)	20	20
1392	**207**	35c. red	20	20
1393	**207**	70c. purple	20	20
1394	**207**	1cor.5 green	30	30
1395	**207**	1cor.50 violet	40	40
1396	-	5cor. ochre and black	1·30	1·20

210

1961. Air. World Refugee Year. Inscr "ANO MUNDIAL DEL REFUGIADO".

1397		2cor. multicoloured	50	40
1398	**210**	5cor. ochre, blue & green	1·00	80
MS1398a		100×70 mm. Nos. 1397/8	3·00	3·00

DESIGN: 2cor. Procession of refugees.

211 Pres. Roosevelt, Pres. Somoza and Officer

1961. Air. 20th Anniv of Nicaraguan Military Academy.

1399	**211**	20c. multicoloured	20	20
1400	-	25c. red, blue and black	20	20
1401	-	30c. multicoloured	20	20
1402	-	35c. multicoloured	20	20
1403	-	40c. multicoloured	20	20
1404	-	45c. black, flesh and red	20	20
1405	**211**	60c. multicoloured	20	20
1406	-	70c. multicoloured	20	20
1407	-	1cor.5 multicoloured	30	30
1408	-	1cor.50 multicoloured	30	30
1409	-	2cor. multicoloured	40	40
1410	-	5cor. black, flesh & grey	90	85
MS1410a		Two sheets each 160×100 mm. Nos. 1399/1404 and 1405/10. Imperf	3·75	3·50

DESIGNS—VERT: 25, 70c. Flags; 35c., 1cor.50, Standard bearers; 40c., 2cor. Pennant and emblem. HORIZ: 30c., 1cor.5 Group of officers; 45c., 5cor. Pres. Somoza and Director of Academy.

1961. Air. Consular Fiscal stamps as T 203/4 with serial Nos. in red, surch Correo Aereo and value.

1411		20c. on 50c. blue	20	20
1412		20c. on 1cor. olive	20	20
1413		20c. on 2cor. green	20	20
1414		20c. on 3cor. red	20	20
1415		20c. on 5cor. red	20	20
1416		20c. on 10cor. violet	20	20
1417		20c. on 20cor. brown	20	20
1418		20c. on 50cor. brown	20	20
1419		20c. on 100cor. lake	20	20

213 I.J.C. Emblem and Global Map of the Americas

1961. Air. Junior Chamber of Commerce Congress.

1420		2c. multicoloured	20	20
1421		3c. black and yellow	20	20
1422		4c. multicoloured	20	20
1423		5c. black and red	20	20
1424		6c. multicoloured	20	20
1425		10c. multicoloured	20	20
1426		15c. black, green and blue	20	20
1427		30c. black and blue	20	20
1428		35c. multicoloured	20	20
1429		70c. black, red and yellow	20	20
1430		1cor.5 multicoloured	30	30
1431		5cor. multicoloured	85	85

DESIGNS—HORIZ: 2c., 15c. Type **213**; 4c., 35c. "J.C.I." upon Globe. VERT: 3c., 30c. I.J.C. emblem; 5c., 70c. Scroll; 6c., 1cor.5, Handclasp; 10c., 5cor. Regional map of Nicaragua.

1961. Air. 1st Central American Philatelic Convention, San Salvador. Optd Convencion Filatelica–Centro–America–Panama–San Salvador–27 Julio 1961.

1432	**158**	1cor.25 multicoloured	50	50

215 R. Cabezas

1961. Air. Birth Centenary of Cabezas.

1433	**215**	20c. blue and orange	20	20
1434	-	40c. purple and blue	20	20
1435	-	45c. sepia and green	20	20
1436	-	70c. green and brown	30	20
1437	-	2cor. blue and pink	30	30
1438	-	10cor. purple and turquoise	1·70	1·30

DESIGNS—HORIZ: 40c. Map and view of Cartago; 45c. 1884 newspaper; 70c. Assembly outside building; 2cor. Scroll; 10cor. Map and view of Masaya.

216 Official Gazettes

1961. Centenary of Regulation of Postal Rates.

1439	**216**	5c. brown and turquoise	20	20
1440	-	10c. brown and green	20	20
1441	-	15c. brown and red	20	20

DESIGNS: 10c. Envelopes and postmarks; 15c. Martinez and Somoza.

1961. Air. Dag Hammarskjold Commemoration. Nos. 1351/6 optd Homenaje a Hammarskjold Sept. 18-1961.

1442	60c. blue and mauve	30	30
1443	75c. brown and green	30	30
1444	90c. green and brown	30	30
1445	1cor. mauve and blue	30	30
1446	3cor. red and black	85	80
1447	5cor. blue and mauve	1·90	1·80

1962. Air. Surch RESELLO C$ 1.00.

1449	**207**	1cor. on 1cor.5 black and green	20	20
1448	-	1cor. on 1cor.10 brown (No. 1157)	20	20

See also Nos. 1498/1500a, 1569/70, 1608/14, 1669/76 and 1748/62.

219 "Cattleya skinneri"

1962. Obligatory Tax. Nicaraguan Orchids. Mult.

1450	5c. Type **219**	30	30
1451	5c. "Bletia roezlii"	30	30
1452	5c. "Sobralia pleiantha"	30	30
1453	5c. "Lycaste macrophylla"	30	30
1454	5c. "Schomburgkia tibicinus"	30	30
1455	5c. "Maxillaria tenuifolia"	30	30
1456	5c. "Stanhopea ecornuta"	30	30
1457	5c. "Oncidium ascendens" and "O. cebolleta"	30	30
1458	5c. "Cycnoches egertonianum"	30	30
1459	5c. "Hexisia bidentata"	30	30

220 UNESCO "Audience"

1962. Air. 15th Anniv of UNESCO.

1460	**220**	2cor. multicoloured	40	30
1461	-	5cor. multicoloured	85	80
MS1461a		90×65 mm. Nos. 1460/1. Imperf	1·60	1·50

DESIGN: 5cor. U.N. and UNESCO emblems.

1962. Air. Malaria Eradication. Nos. 1425, 1428/31 optd with mosquito surrounded by LUCHA CONTRA LA MALARIA.

1462	10c.	30	30
1463	35c.	40	30
1464	70c.	50	40
1465	1cor.5	60	50
1466	5cor.	1·20	1·50

221a Reproduction of Nos. 1/2 and Early Postmarks (image scaled to 64% of original size)

1962. Air. Centenary of First Nicaraguan Postage Stamps. Sheet 85×95 mm. Imperf.

MS1466a	**221a**	7cor. multicoloured	3·00	3·00

222 Arms of Nueva Segovia

1962. Urban and Provincial Arms. Arms mult; inscr black; background colours below.

1467	**222**	2c. mauve (postage)	20	20
1468	-	3c. blue	20	20
1469	-	4c. lilac	20	20
1470	-	5c. yellow	20	20
1471	-	6c. brown	20	20
1472	**222**	30c. red (air)	20	20
1473	-	50c. orange	20	20
1474	-	1cor. green	20	20
1475	-	2cor. grey	40	40
1476	-	5cor. blue	1·00	1·00

ARMS: 3c., 50c. Leon; 4c., 1cor. Managua; 5c., 2cor. Granada; 6c., 5cor. Rivas.

223 Liberty Bell

1963. Air. 150th Anniv of Independence.

1477	**223**	30c. drab, blue & black	25	20

224 Blessing

1963. Air. Death Tercentenary of St. Vincent de Paul and St. Louise de Marillac.

1478	-	60c. black and orange	20	20
1479	**224**	1cor. olive and orange	30	20
1480	-	2cor. black and red	60	50

DESIGNS—VERT: 60c. "Comfort" (St. Louise and woman). HORIZ: 2cor. St. Vincent and St. Louise.

225 "Map Stamp"

1963. Air. Central American Philatelic Societies Federation Commemoration.

1481	**225**	1cor. blue and yellow	30	20

226 Cross on Globe

1963. Air. Ecumenical Council, Vatican City.

1482	**226**	20c. red and yellow	20	20

227 Ears of Wheat

1963. Air. Freedom from Hunger.

1483	**227**	10c. green and light green	20	20
1484	-	25c. sepia and yellow	30	20

DESIGN: 25c. Barren tree and campaign emblem.

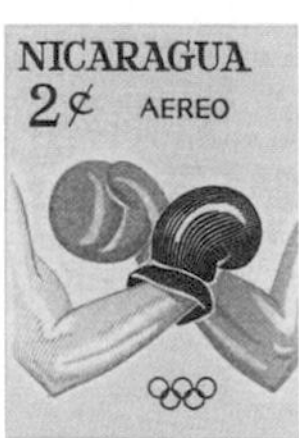

228 Boxing

1963. Air. Sports. Multicoloured.

1485	2c. Type **228**	20	20
1486	3c. Running	20	20
1487	4c. Underwater harpooning	20	20
1488	5c. Football	20	20
1489	6c. Baseball	20	20
1490	10c. Tennis	30	20
1491	15c. Cycling	30	20
1492	20c. Motor-cycling	30	20
1493	35c. Chess	40	30
1494	60c. Angling	50	30
1495	1cor. Table-tennis	60	40
1496	2cor. Basketball	85	90
1497	5cor. Golf	2·50	2·00

1964. Air. Surch Resello or RESELLO (1500a) and value.

1498	-	5c. on 6c. (No. 1424)	30	20
1499	-	10c. on 30c. (No. 1365)	50	20
1500	**207**	15c. on 30c.	70	30
1500a	**201**	20c. on 30c.	20	20

See also Nos. 1448/9, 1569/70, 1608/14 and 1669/76.

1964. Optd CORREOS.

1501	5c. multicoloured (No. 1451)	20	20

231 Flags

1964. Air. "Centro America".

1502	**231**	40c. multicoloured	30	30

232 "Alliance Emblem"

1964. Air. "Alliance for Progress". Multicoloured.

1503	5c. Type **232**	20	20
1504	10c. Red Cross post (horiz)	20	20
1505	15c. Highway (horiz)	20	20
1506	20c. Ploughing (horiz)	20	20
1507	25c. Housing (horiz)	20	20
1508	30c. Presidents Somoza and Kennedy and Eugene Black (World Bank) (horiz)	20	20
1509	35c. School and adults (horiz)	20	20
1510	40c. Chimneys (horiz)	30	20

233 Map of Member Countries

1964. Air. Central American "Common Market". Multicoloured.

1511	15c. Type **233**	20	20
1512	25c. Ears of wheat	20	20
1513	40c. Cogwheels	20	20
1514	50c. Heads of cattle	20	20

1964. Air. Olympic Games, Tokyo. Nos. 1485/7, 1489 and 1495/6 optd OLIMPIADAS TOKYO - 1964.

1515	2c. Type **108**	20	20
1516	3c. Running	20	20
1517	4c. Underwater harpooning	20	20
1518	6c. Baseball	20	20
1519	1cor. Table-tennis	2·30	2·20
1520	2cor. Basketball	3·00	3·00

235 Rescue of Wounded Soldier

1965. Air. Red Cross Centenary. Multicoloured.

1521	20c. Type **235**	20	20
1522	25c. Blood transfusion	20	20
1523	40c. Red Cross and snowbound town	30	20
1524	10cor. Red Cross and map of Nicaragua	2·30	1·60

236 Statuettes

1965. Air. Nicaraguan Antiquities. Multicoloured.

1525	5c. Type **236**	30	25
1526	10c. Totem	30	25
1527	15c. Carved dog (horiz)	30	25
1528	20c. Composition of "objets d'art"	30	25
1529	25c. Dish and vase (horiz)	30	25
1530	30c. Pestle and mortar	30	25
1531	35c. Statuettes (different) (horiz)	30	25
1532	40c. Deity	30	25
1533	50c. Wine vessel and dish	30	25
1534	60c. Bowl and dish (horiz)	30	25
1535	1cor. Urn	50	30

237 Pres. Kennedy

1965. Air. Pres. Kennedy Commemorative.

1536	**237**	35c. black and green	25	20
1537	**237**	75c. black and mauve	40	25
1538	**237**	1cor.10 black and blue	50	35
1539	**237**	2cor. black and brown	1·30	90
MS1539a		Four sheets each 90×116 mm. Nos. 1536/9 in blocks of four. Imperf	8·75	8·50

238 A. Bello

1965. Air. Death Centenary of Andres Bello (poet and writer).
1540 **238** 10c. black and brown 20 20
1541 **238** 15c. black and blue 20 20
1542 **238** 45c. black and purple 20 20
1543 **238** 80c. black and green 20 20
1544 **238** 1cor. black and yellow 30 30
1545 **238** 2cor. black and grey 50 50

1965. 9th Central American Scout Camporee. Nos. 1450/9 optd with scout badge and CAMPOREE SCOUT 1965.
1546 5c. multicoloured 40 40
1547 5c. multicoloured 40 40
1548 5c. multicoloured 40 40
1549 5c. multicoloured 40 40
1550 5c. multicoloured 40 40
1551 5c. multicoloured 40 40
1552 5c. multicoloured 40 40
1553 5c. multicoloured 40 40
1554 5c. multicoloured 40 40
1555 5c. multicoloured 40 40
MS1555a 127×102 mm. Sheet No. **MS**1277a optd **CAMPOREE SCOUT 1965** on each stamp 12·00 12·00

240 Sir Winston Churchill

1966. Air. Churchill Commemorative.
1556 **240** 20c. mauve and black 20 20
1557 - 35c. green and black 20 20
1558 - 60c. ochre and black 20 20
1559 - 75c. red 30 30
1560 - 1cor. purple 50 40
1561 **240** 2cor. violet, lilac & black 70 60
1562 - 3cor. blue and black 1·00 90
MS1563 99×95 mm. Nos. 1558/61. Imperf 2·10 2·00
DESIGNS—HORIZ: 35c., 1cor. Churchill broadcasting. VERT: 60c., 3cor. Churchill crossing the Rhine; 75c. Churchill in Hussars' uniform.

241 Pope John XXIII

1966. Air. Closure of Vatican Ecumenical Council. Multicoloured.
1564 20c. Type **241** 20 20
1565 35c. Pope Paul VI 20 20
1566 1cor. Archbishop Gonzalez y Robleto 30 20
1567 2cor. St. Peter's, Rome 40 30
1568 3cor. Papal arms 70 60

1967. Air. Nos. 1533/4 surch RESELLO and value.
1569 10c. on 50c. multicoloured 20 20
1570 15c. on 60c. multicoloured 20 20
See also Nos. 1448/9, 1498/1500a, 1608/14 and 1669/76.

243 Dario and Birthplace

1967. Air. Birth Centenary of Ruben Dario (poet). Designs showing Dario and view. Multicoloured.
1571 5c. Type **243** 20 20
1572 10c. Monument, Managua 20 20
1573 20c. Leon Cathedral (site of Dario's tomb) 20 20
1574 40c. Allegory of the centaurs 20 20
1575 75c. Allegory of the mute swans 30 20
1576 1cor. Roman triumphal march 30 20
1577 2cor. St. Francis and the wolf 40 30
1578 5cor. "Faith" opposing "Death" 1·00 95
MS1579 Two sheets each 130×107 mm. Nos. 1571/4 and 1575/8 5·75 5·50

244 "Megalura peleus"

1967. Air. Butterflies. Multicoloured.
1580 5c. "Heliconius petiveranua" (vert) 30 20
1581 10c. "Colaenis julia" (vert) 30 20
1582 15c. Type **244** 30 20
1583 20c. "Aneyluris jurgensii" 40 30
1584 25c. "Thecla regalis" 40 30
1585 30c. "Doriana thia" (vert) 40 30
1586 35c. "Lymnias pixae" (vert) 50 40
1587 40c. "Metamorpho dido" 50 40
1588 50c. "Papilio arcas" (vert) 50 40
1589 60c. "Ananea cleomestra" 60 50
1590 1cor. "Victorina epaphaus" (vert) 85 60
1591 2cor. "Prepona demophon" 1·00 80

245 McDivitt and White

1967. Air. Space Flight of McDivitt and White. Multicoloured.
1592 5c. Type **245** 30 30
1593 10c. Astronauts and "Gemini 5" on launching pad 30 30
1594 15c. "Gemini 5" and White in Space 30 30
1595 20c. Recovery operation at sea 30 30
1596 35c. Type **245** 30 30
1597 40c. As 10c. 30 30
1598 75c. As 15c. 30 30
1599 1cor. As 20c. 40 40

246 National Flower of Costa Rica

1967. Air. 5th Year of Central American Economic Integration. Designs showing national flowers of Central American countries. Multicoloured.
1600 40c. Type **246** 30 20
1601 40c. Guatemala 30 20
1602 40c. Honduras 30 20
1603 40c. Nicaragua 30 20
1604 40c. El Salvador 30 20

247 Presidents Diaz and Somoza

1968. Air. Visit of Pres. Diaz of Mexico.
1605 - 20c. black 20 20
1606 **247** 40c. olive 30 20
1607 - 1cor. brown 40 20
DESIGNS—VERT: 20c. Pres. Somoza greeting Pres. Diaz; 1cor. Pres. Diaz of Mexico.

1968. Surch RESELLO and value.
1608 5c. on 6c. (No. 1180) (postage) 60 60
1609 5c. on 6c. (No. 1471) 60 60
1610 5c. on 6c. (No. 1424) (air) 30 20
1611 5c. on 6c. (No. 1489) 30 20
1612 **156** 5c. on 8c. (No. 1035) 30 20
1614 - 1cor. on 1cor.50 (No. 1369) 30 20
See also Nos. 1448/9, 1498/1500a, 1569/70 and 1669/76.

249 Mangoes

1968. Air. Nicaraguan Fruits. Multicoloured.
1615 5c. Type **249** 30 20
1616 10c. Pineapples 30 20
1617 15c. Oranges 30 20
1618 20c. Pawpaws 30 20
1619 30c. Bananas 30 20
1620 35c. Avocado pears 30 20
1621 50c. Water-melons 30 20
1622 75c. Cashews 30 20
1623 1cor. Sapodilla plums 50 30
1624 2cor. Cocoa beans 85 50

250 "The Crucifixion" (Fra Angelico)

1968. Air. Religious Paintings. Multicoloured.
1625 10c. Type **250** 20 20
1626 15c. "The Last Judgement" (Michelangelo) (vert) 20 20
1627 35c. "The Beautiful Gardener" (Raphael) (vert) 20 20
1628 2cor. "The Spoliation of Christ" (El Greco) (vert) 60 50
1629 3cor. "The Conception" (Murillo) (vert) 85 60
MS1630 100×80 mm. 5cor. "The Crucifixion" (Dali) 3·50 3·50

1968. Air. Pope Paul's Visit to Bogota. Nos. 1625/8 optd Visita de S. S. Paulo VI C. E. de Bogota 1968.
1631 **250** 10c. multicoloured 20 20
1632 - 15c. multicoloured 20 20
1633 - 35c. multicoloured 30 30
1634 - 2cor. multicoloured 60 50

252 Basketball

1969. Air. Olympic Games, Mexico. Mult.
1635 10c. Type **252** 20 20
1636 15c. Fencing (horiz) 20 20
1637 20c. High-diving 20 20
1638 35c. Running 20 20
1639 50c. Hurdling (horiz) 30 30
1640 75c. Weightlifting 30 30
1641 1cor. Boxing (horiz) 40 40
1642 2cor. Football 1·00 80
MS1643 100×120 mm. Nos. 1639/42 2·50 2·50

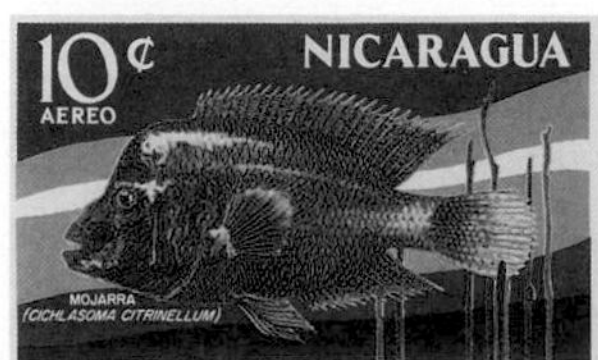

253 Midas Cichlid

1969. Air. Fishes. Multicoloured.
1644 10c. Type **253** 30 20
1645 15c. Moga cichlid 30 20
1646 20c. Common carp 30 20
1647 30c. Tropical gar 30 20
1648 35c. Swordfish 30 20
1649 50c. Big-mouthed sleeper 30 20
1650 75c. Atlantic tarpon 30 20
1651 1cor. Lake Nicaragua shark 40 30
1652 2cor. Sailfish 60 40
1653 3cor. Small-toothed sawfish 1·00 65
MS1654 83×137 mm. Nos. 1650/3 4·25 4·00

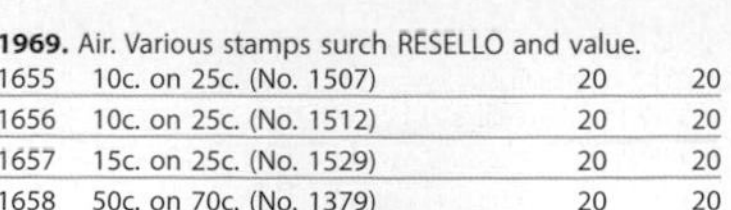
1969. Air. Various stamps surch RESELLO and value.
1655 10c. on 25c. (No. 1507) 20 20
1656 10c. on 25c. (No. 1512) 20 20
1657 15c. on 25c. (No. 1529) 20 20
1658 50c. on 70c. (No. 1379) 20 20

255 Scenery, Tower and Emblem

1969. Air. "Hemisfair" (1968) Exhibition.
1659 **255** 30c. blue and red 20 20
1660 **255** 35c. purple and red 20 20
1661 **255** 75c. red and blue 20 20
1662 **255** 1cor. purple and black 30 25
1663 **255** 2cor. purple and green 55 50
MS1664 75×111 mm. Nos. 1659/60, 1662/3. Perf or imperf 1·60 1·50

1969. Various stamps surch. (a) Optd CORREO.
1665 5c. (No. 1450) 60 60
1666 5c. (No. 1453) 60 60
1667 5c. (No. 1454) 60 60
1668 5c. (No. 1459) 60 60

(b) Optd RESELLO and surch.
1669 10c. on 25c. (No. 1529) 20 20
1670 10c. on 30c. (No. 1324) 20 20
1671 10c. on 30c. (No. 1427) 20 20
1672 10c. on 30c. (No. 1530) 20 20
1673 15c. on 35c. (No. 1531) 20 20
1674 20c. on 30c. (No. 1307) 20 20
1675 20c. on 30c. (No. 1401) 20 20
1676 20c. on 35c. (No. 1509) 20 20

258 "Minerals"

1969. Air. Nicaraguan Products. Multicoloured.
1677 5c. Type **258** 20 20
1678 10c. "Fish" 20 20
1679 15c. "Bananas" 20 20
1680 20c. "Timber" 20 20
1681 35c. "Coffee" 30 20
1682 40c. "Sugar-cane" 30 20
1683 60c. "Cotton" 30 20
1684 75c. "Rice and Maize" 30 20
1685 1cor. "Tobacco" 40 25
1686 2cor. "Meat" 65 45

1969. 50th Anniv of I.L.O. Obligatory tax stamps. Nos. 1450/9, optd O.I.T. 1919-1969.
1687 5c. multicoloured 30 30
1688 5c. multicoloured 30 30
1689 5c. multicoloured 30 30
1690 5c. multicoloured 30 30
1691 5c. multicoloured 30 30
1692 5c. multicoloured 30 30
1693 5c. multicoloured 30 30
1694 5c. multicoloured 30 30
1695 5c. multicoloured 30 30
1696 5c. multicoloured 30 30

260 Girl carrying Tinaja

1970. Air. 8th Inter-American Savings and Loans Conference, Managua.
1697 **260** 10c. multicoloured 20 20
1698 **260** 15c. multicoloured 20 20
1699 **260** 20c. multicoloured 20 20
1700 **260** 35c. multicoloured 20 20
1701 **260** 50c. multicoloured 20 20
1702 **260** 75c. multicoloured 30 20
1703 **260** 1cor. multicoloured 50 30
1704 **260** 2cor. multicoloured 85 50

261 Pele (Brazil)

1970. World Football "Hall of Fame" Poll-winners. Multicoloured.

1705	5c. Type **261** (postage)	30	30
1706	10c. Puskas (Hungary)	30	30
1707	15c. Matthews (England)	30	30
1708	40c. Di Stefano (Argentina)	30	30
1709	2cor. Facchetti (Italy)	1·00	80
1710	3cor. Yashin (Russia)	1·30	1·00
1711	5cor. Beckenbauer (West Germany)	1·60	1·30
1712	20c. Santos (Brazil) (air)	30	30
1713	80c. Wright (England)	40	30
1714	1cor. Flags of 16 World Cup finalists	50	40
1715	4cor. Bozsik (Hungary)	1·40	1·00
1716	5cor. Charlton (England)	1·60	1·30

262 Torii (Gate)

1970. Air. EXPO 70, World Fair, Osaka, Japan.

1717	**262**	25c. multicoloured	20	20
1718	**262**	30c. multicoloured	20	20
1719	**262**	35c. multicoloured	20	20
1720	**262**	75c. multicoloured	30	20
1721	**262**	1cor.50 multicoloured	50	30
1722	**262**	3cor. multicoloured	85	80
MS1723		108×78 mm. Nos. 1720/2. Imperf	1·90	1·50

263 Module and Astronauts on Moon

1970. Air. "Apollo 11" Moon Landing (1969). Mult.

1724	35c. Type **263**	20	20
1725	40c. Module landing on Moon	20	20
1726	60c. Astronauts with U.S. flag	20	20
1727	75c. As 40c.	30	20
1728	1cor. As 60c.	40	20
1729	2cor. Type **263**	70	40

264 F. D. Roosevelt

1970. Air. 25th Death Anniv of Franklin D. Roosevelt.

1730	**264**	10c. black	20	20
1731	-	15c. brown and black	20	20
1732	-	20c. green and black	20	20
1733	**264**	35c. purple and black	20	20
1734	-	50c. brown	20	20
1735	**264**	75c. blue	20	20
1736	-	1cor. red	30	20
1737	-	2cor. black	60	40

PORTRAITS: 15c., 1cor. Roosevelt with stamp collection; 20c., 50c., 2cor. Roosevelt (full-face).

265 "The Annunciation" (Grunewald)

1970. Air. Christmas. Paintings. Multicoloured.

1738	10c. Type **265**	15	15
1739	10c. "The Nativity" (detail, El Greco)	15	15
1740	10c. "The Adoration of the Magi" (detail, Durer)	15	15
1741	10c. "Virgin and Child" (J. van Hemessen)	15	15
1742	10c. "The Holy Shepherd" (Portuguese School, 16th cent)	15	15
1743	15c. Type **265**	15	15
1744	20c. As No. 1739	15	15
1745	35c. As No. 1740	20	20
1746	75c. As No. 1741	25	20
1747	1cor. As No. 1742	30	25

1971. Surch RESELLO and new value.

1748	30c. on 90c. black (No. 1227) (postage)	21·00	20·00
1749	10c. on 1cor.5 red, black & red (No. 1368) (air)	30	30
1750	10c. on 1cor.5 mult (No. 1407)	30	30
1751	10c. on 1cor.5 mult (No. 1430)	30	30
1752	15c. on 1cor.50 green and red (No. 1116)	40	40
1753	15c. on 1cor.50 green (No. 1255)	40	40
1754	15c. on 1cor.50 yellow and blue (No. 1369)	40	40
1755	15c. on 1cor.50 black and violet (No. 1381)	40	40
1756	20c. on 85c. black and red (No. 1276)	50	50
1757	20c. on 85c. black, red and blue (No. 1339)	50	50
1758	25c. on 90c. black, green and ochre (No. 1440)	70	70
1759	30c. on 1cor.10 black and purple (No. 1195)	95	90
1760	40c. on 1cor.10 brown and black (No. 1157)	1·10	1·10
1761	40c. on 1cor.50 mult (No. 1408)	1·10	1·10
1762	1cor. on 1cor.10 black and blue (No. 1538)	3·00	2·75

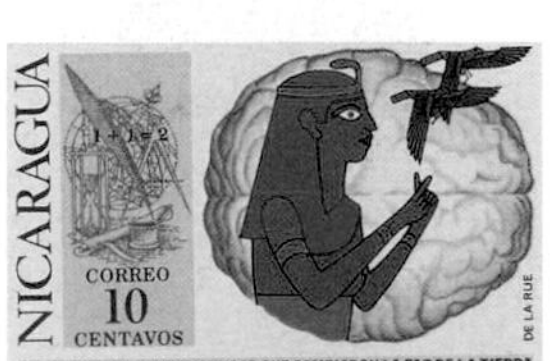

266 Basic Mathematical Equation

1971. Scientific Formulae. "The Ten Mathematical Equations that changed the Face of the Earth". Multicoloured.

1763	10c. Type **266** (postage)	15	15
1764	15c. Newton's Law	15	15
1765	20c. Einstein's Law	30	25
1766	1cor. Tsiolkovsky's Law	1·00	60
1767	2cor. Maxwell's Law	2·10	1·30
1768	25c. Napier's Law (air)	20	15
1769	30c. Pythagoras' Law	30	20
1770	40c. Boltzmann's Law	40	20
1771	1cor. Broglie's Law	95	40
1772	2cor. Archimedes' Law	1·60	80

267 Peace Emblem

1971. "Is There a Formula for Peace?".

1773	**267**	10c. blue and black	15	15
1774	**267**	15c. blue, black and violet	15	15
1775	**267**	20c. blue, black & brown	15	15
1776	**267**	40c. blue, black and green	30	25
1777	**267**	50c. blue, black & purple	40	40
1778	**267**	80c. blue, black and red	60	60
1779	**267**	1cor. blue, black & green	85	80
1780	**267**	2cor. blue, black & violet	1·60	1·50

268 Montezuma Oropendola

1971. Air. Nicaraguan Birds. Multicoloured.

1781	10c. Type **268**	30	20
1782	15c. Turquoise-browed motmot	30	20
1783	20c. White-throated magpie-jay	30	20
1784	25c. Scissor-tailed flycatcher	30	20
1785	30c. Spotted-breasted oriole (horiz)	30	20
1786	35c. Rufous-naped wren	30	20
1787	40c. Great kiskadee	40	30
1788	75c. Red-legged honeycreeper (horiz)	50	30
1789	1cor. Great-tailed grackle (horiz)	60	30
1790	2cor. Belted kingfisher	1·00	40

269 "Moses with the Tablets of the Law" (Rembrandt)

1971. "The Ten Commandments". Paintings. Multicoloured.

1791	10c. Type **269** (postage)	15	15
1792	15c. "Moses and the Burning Bush" (Botticelli) (1st Commandment)	15	15
1793	20c. "Jepthah's Daughter" (Degas) (2nd Commandment) (horiz)	15	15
1794	30c. "St. Vincent Ferrer preaching in Verona" (Morone) (3rd Commandment) (horiz)	15	15
1795	35c. "Noah's Drunkenness" (Michelangelo) (4th Commandment) (horiz)	25	20
1796	40c. "Cain and Abel" (Trevisani) (5th Commandment) (horiz)	25	25
1797	50c. "Joseph accused by Potiphar's Wife" (Rembrandt) (6th Commandment)	35	30
1798	60c. "Isaac blessing Jacob" (Eeckhout) (7th Commandment) (horiz)	50	50
1799	75c. "Susannah and the Elders" (Rubens) (8th Commandment) (horiz)	85	80
1800	1cor. "Bathsheba after her Bath" (Rembrandt) (9th Commandment) (air)	1·00	50
1801	2cor. "Naboth's Vineyard" (Smetham) (10th Commandment)	1·60	80

270 U Thant and Pres. Somoza

1971. Air. 25th Anniv of U.N.O.

1802	**270**	10c. brown and red	15	15
1803	**270**	15c. green and emerald	15	15
1804	**270**	20c. blue and light blue	15	15
1805	**270**	25c. red and purple	20	15
1806	**270**	30c. brown and orange	20	15
1807	**270**	40c. green and grey	20	20
1808	**270**	1cor. green and sage	30	25
1809	**270**	2cor. brown & light brown	75	45

1972. Olympic Games, Munich. Nos. 1709, 1711, 1713 and 1716 surch OLIMPIADAS MUNICH 1972, emblem and value or optd only (5cor.).

1810	40c. on 2cor. multicoloured (postage)	15	15
1811	50c. on 3cor. multicoloured	20	15
1812	20c. on 80c. mult (air)	15	15
1813	60c. on 4cor. multicoloured	20	15
1814	5cor. multicoloured	1·20	1·00

272 Figurine and Apoyo Site on Map

1972. Air. Pre-Columbian Art. A. H. Heller's Pottery Discoveries. Multicoloured.

1815	10c. Type **272**	15	15
1816	15c. Cana Castilla	15	15
1817	20c. Catarina	15	15
1818	25c. Santa Helena	15	15
1819	30c. Mombacho	15	15
1820	35c. Tisma	15	15
1821	40c. El Menco	15	15
1822	50c. Los Placeres	20	15
1823	60c. Masaya	20	20
1824	80c. Granada	25	20
1825	1cor. Las Mercedes	35	25
1826	2cor. Nindiri	65	45

273 "Lord Peter Wimsey" (Dorothy Sayers)

1972. Air. 50th Anniv of International Criminal Police Organization (INTERPOL). Famous Fictional Detectives. Multicoloured.

1827	5c. Type **273**	20	15
1828	10c. "Philip Marlowe" (Raymond Chandler)	20	15
1829	15c. "Sam Spade" (D. Hammett)	30	15
1830	20c. "Perry Mason" (Erle Stanley Gardner)	30	15
1831	25c. "Nero Wolfe" (Rex Stout)	30	15
1832	35c. "C. Auguste Dupin" (Edgar Allan Poe)	35	20
1833	40c. "Ellery Queen" (F. Dannay and M. Lee)	35	25
1834	50c. "Father Brown" (G. K. Chesterton)	45	25
1835	60c. "Charlie Chan" (Earl D. Biggers)	55	40
1836	80c. "Inspector Maigret" (Georges Simenon)	65	50
1837	1cor. "Hercule Poirot" (Agatha Christie)	95	70
1838	2cor. "Sherlock Holmes" (A. Conan Doyle)	1·70	1·30

274 "The Shepherdess and her Brothers"

1972. Air. Christmas. Scenes from Legend of the Christmas Rose. Multicoloured.

1839	10c. Type **274**	15	15
1840	15c. Adoration of the Wise Men	15	15
1841	20c. Shepherdess crying	15	15
1842	35c. Angel appears to Shepherdess	15	15
1843	40c. Christmas Rose	15	15
1844	60c. Shepherdess thanks angel for roses	20	20
1845	80c. Shepherdess takes roses to Holy Child	20	20
1846	1cor. Holy Child receiving roses	30	20
1847	2cor. Nativity scene	50	45
MS1848	132×132 mm. Nos. 1839/47	2·30	2·20

275 Sir Walter Raleigh and Elizabethan Galleon

1973. Air. Causes of the American Revolution. Multicoloured.

No.	Description	Unused	Used
1849	10c. Type **275**	15	15
1850	15c. Signing "Mayflower Compact"	15	15
1851	20c. Acquittal of Peter Zenger (vert)	15	15
1852	25c. Acclaiming American resistance (vert)	15	15
1853	30c. Revenue stamp (vert)	15	15
1854	35c. "Serpent" slogan—"Join or die"	40	20
1855	40c. Boston Massacre (vert)	40	20
1856	50c. Boston Tea-party	40	40
1857	60c. Patrick Henry on trial (vert)	40	40
1858	75c. Battle of Bunker Hill	50	40
1859	80c. Declaration of Independence	60	40
1860	1cor. Liberty Bell	85	50
1861	2cor. US seal (vert)	1·60	1·00

1973. Nos. 1450/54, 1456 and 1458/9 optd CORREO.

No.	Type	Description	Unused	Used
1862	**219**	5c. multicoloured	30	25
1863	-	5c. multicoloured	30	25
1864	-	5c. multicoloured	30	25
1865	-	5c. multicoloured	30	25
1866	-	5c. multicoloured	30	25
1867	-	5c. multicoloured	30	25
1868	-	5c. multicoloured	30	25
1869	-	5c. multicoloured	30	25

277 Baseball, Player and Map

1973. Air. 20th International Baseball Championships, Managua (1972).

No.	Type	Description	Unused	Used
1870	**277**	15c. multicoloured	25	15
1871	**277**	20c. multicoloured	25	15
1872	**277**	40c. multicoloured	25	20
1873	**277**	10cor. multicoloured	2·10	1·80
MS1874		105×134 mm. Nos. 1870/3	3·00	3·00

278 Givenchy, Paris

1973. World-famous Couturiers. Mannequins. Mult.

No.	Description	Unused	Used
1875	1cor. Type **278** (postage)	30	30
1876	2cor. Hartnell, London	60	50
1877	5cor. Balmain, Paris	1·60	1·20
1878	10c. Lourdes, Nicaragua (air)	20	15
1879	15c. Halston, New York	20	15
1880	20c. Pino Lancetti, Rome	20	15
1881	35c. Madame Gres, Paris	20	15
1882	40c. Irene Galitzine, Rome	20	15
1883	80c. Pedro Rodriguez, Barcelona	30	20
MS1884	170×170 mm. Nos. 1875/82	4·25	4·00

279 Diet Chart

1973. Air. Child Welfare. Multicoloured.

No.	Description	Unused	Used
1885	5c.+5c. Type **279**	15	15
1886	10c.+5c. Senora Samoza with baby, and Children's Hospital	15	15
1887	15c.+5c. "Childbirth"	15	15
1888	20c.+5c. "Immunization"	15	15
1889	30c.+5c. Water purification	15	15
1890	35c.+5c. As No. 1886	15	15
1891	50c.+10c. Alexander Fleming and "Antibiotics"	20	20
1892	60c.+15c. Malaria control	20	20
1893	70c.+10c. Laboratory analysis	20	20
1894	80c.+20c. Gastroenteritis	30	30
1895	1cor.+50c. As No. 1886	40	40
1896	2cor. Pediatric surgery	50	50

280 Virginia and Father

1973. Christmas. "Does Santa Claus exist?" (Virginia O'Hanlon's letter to American "Sun" newspaper). Multicoloured.

No.	Description	Unused	Used
1897	2c. Type **280** (postage)	15	15
1898	3c. Text of letter	15	15
1899	4c. Reading the reply	15	15
1900	5c. Type **280**	15	15
1901	15c. As 3c.	15	15
1902	20c. As 4c.	15	15
1903	1cor. Type **280** (air)	30	30
1904	2cor. As 3c.	60	60
1905	4cor. As 4c.	1·10	1·10
MS1906	197×143 mm. Nos. 1903/5	4·25	4·00

No **MS**1906 has an inscription in English on the reverse.

281 Churchill making Speech, 1936

1974. Birth Cent of Sir Winston Churchill.

No.	Type	Description	Unused	Used
1907	**281**	2c. multicoloured (postage)	15	15
1908	-	3c. black, blue and brown	15	15
1909	-	4c. multicoloured	15	15
1910	-	5c. multicoloured	15	15
1911	-	10c. brown, green & blue	15	15
1912	-	5cor. multicoloured (air)	1·40	1·40
1913	-	6cor. black, brown & bl	1·90	1·80
MS1914		Two sheets each 85×64 mm. (a) 4cor. black, yellow and green; (b) 4cor. multicoloured	3·00	3·00

DESIGNS: 3c. "The Four Churchills" (wartime cartoon); 4c. Candle, cigar and "Action" stickers; 5c. Churchill, Roosevelt and Stalin at Yalta; 10c. Churchill landing in Normandy, 1944; 5cor. Churchill giving "V" sign; 6cor. "Bulldog Churchill" (cartoon); **MS**1914 (a) Churchill and 10 Downing Street; (b) Churchill House of Parliament.

282 Presentation of World Cup to Uruguay, 1930

1974. World Cup Football Championship. Mult.

No.	Description	Unused	Used
1915	1c. Type **282** (postage)	15	15
1916	2c. Victorious Italian team, 1934	15	15
1917	3c. Presentation of World Cup to Italy, 1938	15	15
1918	4c. Uruguay's winning goal, 1950	15	15
1919	5c. Victorious West Germany, 1954	15	15
1920	10c. Rejoicing Brazilian players, 1958	15	15
1921	15c. Brazilian player holding World Cup, 1962	15	15
1922	20c. Queen Elizabeth II presenting Cup to Bobby Moore, 1966	15	15
1923	25c. Victorious Brazilian players, 1970	15	15
1924	10cor. Football and flags of participating countries, 1974 (air)	3·00	2·75
MS1925	Two sheets each 115×112 mm. (a) 4cor. As 10c.; (b) 5cor. As 20c	3·50	3·50

283 "Malachra sp."

1974. Wild Flowers and Cacti. Multicoloured.

No.	Description	Unused	Used
1926	2c. Type **283** (postage)	15	15
1927	3c. "Paguira insignis"	15	15
1928	4c. "Convolvulus sp."	15	15
1929	5c. "Pereschia autumnalis"	15	15
1930	10c. "Ipomea tuberosa"	15	15
1931	15c. "Hibiscus elatus"	15	15
1932	20c. "Plumeria acutifolia"	15	15
1933	1cor. "Centrosema sp." (air)	30	30
1934	3cor. "Hylocereus undatus"	70	60

284 Nicaraguan 7½c. Stamp of 1937

1974. Centenary of U.P.U.

No.	Type	Description	Unused	Used
1935	**284**	2c. red, green & blk (postage)	15	15
1936	-	3c. blue, green and black	15	15
1937	-	4c. multicoloured	15	15
1938	-	5c. brown, mauve & blk	15	15
1939	-	10c. red, brown and black	15	15
1940	-	20c. green, blue and black	15	15
1941	-	40c. multicoloured (air)	20	20
1942	-	3cor. green, black & pink	95	90
1943	-	5cor. blue, black and lilac	1·40	1·40
MS1944		108×128 mm. 1cor. As 20c.; 2cor. As 4c.; 4cor. Jet Airliner over Globe (horiz). Imperf	3·00	3·00

DESIGNS—VERT: 3c. 5c. stamp of 1937; 5c. 2c. stamp of 1937; 10c. 1c. stamp of 1937; 20c. ½c. stamp of 1937; 40c. 10c. stamp of 1961; 5cor. 4cor. U.P.U. stamp of 1950. HORIZ: 4c. 10c. air stamp of 1934; 3cor. 85c. U.P.U. air stamp of 1950.

1974. Air West Germany's Victory in World Cup Football Championships. Nos. 1924 and MS1925 optd TRIUMFADOR ALEMMANIA OCCIDENTAL.

No.	Description	Unused	Used
1945	10cr. multicoloured	3·00	2·50
MS1946	Two sheets each 115×112 mm	4·00	4·00

286 Tamandua

1974. Nicaraguan Fauna. Multicoloured.

No.	Description	Unused	Used
1947	1c. Type **286** (postage)	15	15
1948	2c. Puma	15	15
1949	3c. Common raccoon	15	15
1950	4c. Ocelot	15	15
1951	5c. Kinkajou	15	15
1952	10c. Coypu	15	15
1953	15c. Collared peccary	15	15
1954	20c. Baird's tapir	15	15
1955	3cor. Red brocket (air)	1·00	80
1956	5cor. Jaguar	1·60	1·00

287 "Prophet Zacharias"

1975. Christmas. 500th Birth Anniv of Michelangelo. Multicoloured.

No.	Description	Unused	Used
1957	1c. Type **287** (postage)	15	15
1958	2c. "Christ amongst the Jews"	15	15
1959	3c. "The Creation of Man" (horiz)	15	15
1960	4c. Interior of Sistine Chapel, Rome	15	15
1961	5c. "Moses"	15	15
1962	10c. "Mouscron Madonna"	15	15
1963	15c. "David"	15	15
1964	20c. "Doni Madonna"	15	15
1965	40c. "Madonna of the Steps" (air)	15	15
1966	80c. "Pitti Madonna"	20	20
1967	2cor. "Christ and Virgin Mary"	40	40
1968	5cor. "Michelangelo" (self-portrait)	1·20	1·00
MS1969	101×87 mm. Nos. 1967/8. Imperf	3·00	3·00

288 Giovanni Martinelli ("Othello")

1975. Great Opera Singers. Multicoloured.

No.	Description	Unused	Used
1970	1c. Type **288** (postage)	15	15
1971	2c. Tito Gobbi ("Simone Boccanegra")	15	15
1972	3c. Lotte Lehmann ("Der Rosenkavalier")	15	15
1973	4c. Lauritz Melchlor ("Parsifal")	15	15
1974	5c. Nellie Melba ("La Traviata")	15	15
1975	15c. Jussi Bjoerling ("La Boheme")	15	15
1976	20c. Birgit Nilsson ("Turandot")	15	15
1977	25c. Rosa Ponselle ("Norma") (air)	15	15
1978	35c. Guiseppe de Luca ("Rigoletto")	15	15
1979	40c. Joan Sutherland ("La Figlia del Reggimiento")	15	15
1980	50c. Enzio Pinza ("Don Giovanni")	15	15
1981	60c. Kirsten Flagstad ("Tristan and Isolde")	30	20
1982	80c. Maria Callas ("Tosca")	40	25
1983	2cor. Fyodor Chaliapin ("Boris Godunov")	85	45
1984	5cor. Enrico Caruso ("La Juive")	2·00	1·00
MS1985	137×119 mm. 1cor. As 80c.; Nos. 1983/4. Perf or imperf	4·25	4·00

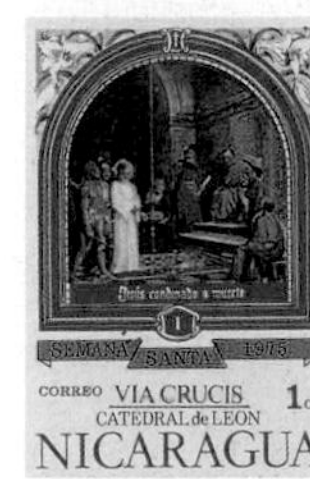

289 The First Station

1975. Easter. The 14 Stations of the Cross.

No.	Type	Description	Unused	Used
1986	**289**	1c. multicoloured (postage)	15	15
1987	-	2c. multicoloured	15	15
1988	-	3c. multicoloured	15	15
1989	-	4c. multicoloured	15	15
1990	-	5c. multicoloured	15	15
1991	-	15c. multicoloured	15	15
1992	-	20c. multicoloured	15	15
1993	-	25c. multicoloured	15	15
1994	-	35c. multicoloured	15	15
1995	-	40c. multicoloured (air)	15	15
1996	-	50c. multicoloured	15	15
1997	-	80c. multicoloured	20	20
1998	-	1cor. multicoloured	25	20
1999	-	5cor. multicoloured	1·20	1·00

DESIGNS: 2c. to 5cor. Different Stations of the Cross.

290 "The Spirit of 76"

1975. Bicentenary of American Independence (1st series). Multicoloured.

No.	Description	Unused	Used
2000	1c. Type **290** (postage)	15	15
2001	2c. Pitt addressing Parliament	15	15
2002	3c. Paul Revere's Ride (horiz)	15	15
2003	4c. Demolishing statue of George III (horiz)	15	15
2004	5c. Boston Massacre	15	15
2005	10c. Tax stamp and George III 3d. coin (horiz)	15	15
2006	15c. Boston Tea Party (horiz)	15	15
2007	20c. Thomas Jefferson	15	15
2008	25c. Benjamin Franklin	15	15
2009	30c. Signing of Declaration of Independence (horiz)	15	15

2010	35c. Surrender of Cornwallis at Yorktown (horiz)	20	20
2011	40c. Washington's Farewell (horiz) (air)	20	15
2012	50c. Washington addressing Congress (horiz)	25	15
2013	2cor. Washington arriving for Presidential Inauguration (horiz)	1·00	80
2014	5cor. Statue of Liberty and flags	2·10	1·90
MS2015	133×128 mm. 7cor. As 1c. Perf or imperf	3·00	3·00

See also Nos. 2506/**MS**2072.

291 Saluting the Flag

1975. "Nordjamb 75" World Scout Jamboree, Norway. Multicoloured.

2016	1c. Type **291** (postage)	10	10
2017	2c. Scout canoe	10	10
2018	3c. Scouts shaking hands	10	10
2019	4c. Scout preparing meal	10	10
2020	5c. Entrance to Nicaraguan camp	10	10
2021	20c. Scouts meeting	20	20
2022	35c. Aerial view of camp (air)	20	20
2023	40c. Scouts making music	20	20
2024	1cor. Camp-fire	50	20
2025	10cor. Lord Baden-Powell	2·20	1·70
MS2026	Two sheets each 126×112 mm. (a) 2cor. as 4c. and 3cor. as 2c. (Perf); (b) 2cor. as 5c. and 3cor. as 1cor. (Imperf)	3·00	3·00

292 President Somoza

1975. President Somoza's New Term of Office, 1974–81.

2027	**292**	20c. multicoloured (postage)	15	15
2028	**292**	40c. multicoloured	15	15
2029	**292**	1cor. multicoloured (air)	30	30
2030	**292**	10cor. multicoloured	2·10	1·90
2031	**292**	20cor. multicoloured	4·25	3·50

293 "Chess Players" (L. Carracci)

1975. Chess. Multicoloured.

2032	1c. Type **293** (postage)	15	15
2033	2c. "Arabs playing Chess" (Delacroix)	15	15
2034	3c. "Cardinals playing Chess" (V. Marais-Milton)	15	15
2035	4c. "Duke Albrecht V of Bavaria and Anna of Austria at Chess" (H. Muelich) (vert)	15	15
2036	5c. "Chess game" (14th-century Persian manuscript)	15	15
2037	10c. "Origins of Chess" (India, 1602)	15	15
2038	15c. "Napoleon playing Chess in Schonbrunn Palace in 1809" (A. Uniechowski) (vert)	15	15
2039	20c. "The Chess Game in the House of Count Ingenheim" (J.E. Hummel)	15	15
2040	40c. "The Chess-players" (T. Eakins) (air)	20	15
2041	2cor. Fischer v Spassky match, Reykjavik, 1972	1·00	60
2042	5cor. "William Shakespeare and Ben Jonson playing Chess" (K. van Mander)	1·90	1·30
MS2043	142×67 mm. Nos. 2041/2 Perf or imperf	4·25	4·00

294 Choir of King's College, Cambridge

1975. Christmas. Famous Choirs. Multicoloured.

2044	1c. Type **294** (postage)	15	15
2045	2c. Abbey Choir, Einsledeln	15	15
2046	3c. Regensburg Cathedral choir	15	15
2047	4c. Vienna Boys' choir	15	15
2048	5c. Sistine Chapel choir	15	15
2049	15c. Westminster Cathedral choir	15	15
2050	20c. Mormon Tabernacle choir	15	15
2051	50c. School choir, Montserrat (air)	15	15
2052	1cor. St. Florian children's choir	30	20
2053	2cor. "Little Singers of the Wooden Cross" (vert)	40	30
2054	5cor. Pope with choristers of Pueri Cantores	1·20	1·00
MS2055	163×127 mm. 10cor. First performance of "Stille Nacht", Obendorf Church, Austria, 1818 (40×47 mm). Imperf	11·50	11·00

295 "The Smoke Signal" (F. Remington)

1976. Bicent of American Revolution (2nd series). "200 Years of Progress". Multicoloured.

2056	1c. Type **295** (postage)	10	10
2057	1c. Houston Space Centre	10	10
2058	2c. Lighting candelabra, 1976	10	10
2059	2c. Edison's lamp and houses	10	10
2060	3c. "Agriculture 1776"	10	10
2061	3c. "Agriculture 1976"	10	10
2062	4c. Harvard College, 1776	10	10
2063	4c. Harvard University, 1976	10	10
2064	5c. Horse and carriage	10	10
2065	5c. Boeing 747-100 airliner	10	10
2066	80c. Philadelphia, 1776 (air)	20	20
2067	80c. Washington, 1976	20	20
2068	2cor.75 "Bonhomme Richard" (American frigate) (John Paul Jones's flagship) and H.M.S. "Seraphis" (frigate), Battle of Flamborough Head	85	60
2069	2cor.75 U.S.S. "Glenard Phipscomp" (nuclear submarine)	85	60
2070	4cor. Wagon train	1·00	75
2071	4cor. Amtrak gas turbine train, 1973	1·00	75
MS2072	140×111 mm. 10cor. George Washington and Family; 10cor. President Ford and Family	6·25	6·00

296 Italy, 1968

1976. Olympic Games, Victors in Rowing and Sculling. Multicoloured.

2073	1c. Denmark 1964 (postage)	10	10
2074	2c. East Germany 1972	10	10
2075	3c. Type **296**	10	10
2076	4c. Great Britain 1936	10	10
2077	5c. France 1952 (vert)	10	10
2078	35c. U.S.A. 1920 (vert)	20	10
2079	55c. Russia 1956 (vert) (air)	20	20
2080	70c. New Zealand 1972 (vert)	20	20
2081	90c. New Zealand 1968	30	20
2082	20cor. U.S.A. 1956	4·75	4·00
MS2083	157×109 mm. 10cor. First Women's Rowing "Eights" Event; part of U.S.A. crew, 1976 (39×52 mm)	3·25	3·00

1976. Air. East Germany Victory in Rowing Event at Montreal Olympics. Nos. 2082 and MS2083 optd REPUBLICA DEMOCRATIC ALEMANA VENCEDOR EN. 1976.

2084	20cor. multicoloured	5·25	3·50
MS2085	157×109 mm. 10cor. multicoloured	2·50	2·00

298 Buce Jenner

1976. Air. Decathlon Winner at Montreal Olympics.

MS2086	**298** 165×165 mm. 25cor. multicoloured	6·25	6·00

299 Mauritius 1847 2d. "Post Office"

1976. Rare and Famous Stamps. Multicoloured.

2087	1c. Type **299** (postage)	10	10
2088	2c. Western Australia 1854 "Inverted Mute Swan"	10	10
2089	3c. Mauritius 1847 1d. "Post Office"	10	10
2090	4c. Jamaica 1920 1s. inverted frame	10	10
2091	5c. U.S 1918 24c. inverted aircraft	10	10
2092	10c. Swiss 1845 Basel "Dove"	20	10
2093	25c. Canada 1959 Seaway inverted centre	20	10
2094	40c. Hawaiian 1851 2c. "Missionary" (air)	20	20
2095	1cor. G.B. 1840 "Penny Black"	20	20
2096	2cor. British Guiana 1850 1c. black on magenta	40	40
2097	5cor. Honduras 1925 airmail 25c. on 10c.	1·10	95
2098	10cor. Newfoundland 1919 "Hawker" airmail stamp	2·00	1·80
MS2099	140×101 mm. 4cor. Nicaragua 1881 "Grey-town" cover with G.B./ Nicaragua stamps	2·10	2·00

300 Olga Nunez de Saballos (Member of Parliament)

1977. Air. International Women's Year. Multicoloured.

2100	35c. Type **300**	15	15
2101	1cor. Josefa Toledo de Aguerri (educator)	30	30
2102	10cor. Hope Portocarreo de Samoza (President's wife)	2·30	2·00

1977. 50th Anniv of National Guard. Designs as MS1410a with revised inscription "1927–1977 Aniversario Guardia Nacional de Nicaragua".

MS2103	Two sheets each 160×100 mm. Nos. 1399/1404 and 1405/10. Imperf	4·00	3·75

301 "Graf Zeppelin" in Hangar

1977. 75th Anniv of First Zeppelin Flight. Mult.

2104	1c. Type **301** (postage)	15	15
2105	2c. "Graf Zeppelin" in flight	15	15
2106	3c. Giffard's steam-powered dirigible airship, 1852	15	15
2107	4c. "Graf Zeppelin" in mooring hangar	15	15
2108	5c. "Graf Zeppelin" on ground	15	15
2109	35c. Astra airship "Ville de Paris" (air)	20	20
2110	70c. "Schwaben"	30	20
2111	3cor. "Graf Zeppelin" over Lake Constance	1·00	80
2112	10cor. LZ-2 on Lake Constance	3·25	2·50
MS2113	101×65 mm. 20cor. Mooring crew handling "Graf Zeppelin". Perf or imperf	7·25	5·00

302 Lindbergh and Map

1977. 50th Anniv of Lindbergh's Transatlantic Flight. Multicoloured.

2114	1c. Type **302** (postage)	15	15
2115	2c. Map and "Spirit of St. Louis"	15	15
2116	3c. Charles Lindbergh (vert)	15	15
2117	4c. "Spirit of St. Louis" crossing Atlantic	15	15
2118	5c. Charles Lindbergh standing by "Spirit of St. Louis"	15	15
2119	20c. Lindbergh, route and "Spirit of St. Louis"	15	15
2120	55c. Lindbergh landing in Nicaragua (1928) (air)	20	20
2121	80c. "Spirit of St. Louis" and route map	30	20
2122	2cor. "Spirit of St. Louis" flying along Nicaraguan coast	50	30
2123	10cor. Passing Momotombo (Nicaragua)	2·50	2·00
MS2124	124×80 mm. 20cor. "Spirit of St. Louis" in flight	6·25	5·00

303 Christmas Festival

1977. Christmas. Scenes from Tchaikovsky's "Nutcracker" Suite. Multicoloured.

2125	1c. Type **303**	15	15
2126	2c. Doll's dance	15	15
2127	3c. Clara and snowflakes	15	15
2128	4c. Snow fairy and prince	15	15
2129	5c. Snow fairies	15	15
2130	15c. Sugar fairy and prince	15	15
2131	40c. Waltz of the Flowers	15	15
2132	90c. Chinese dance	30	30
2133	1cor. Senora Bonbonierre	40	30
2134	10cor. Arabian dance	2·50	2·20
MS2135	130×109 mm. 20cor. Finale (air)	5·25	5·00

304 "Mr. and Mrs. Andrews". (Gainsborough)

1978. Paintings. Multicoloured.

2136	1c. Type **304** (postage)	10	10
2137	2c. "Giovanna Bacelli" (Gainsborough)	10	10
2138	3c. "Blue Boy" (Gainsborough)	10	10
2139	4c. "Francis I" (Titian)	10	10
2140	5c. "Charles V at Battle of Muhlberg" (Titian)	10	10
2141	25c. "Sacred Love" (Titian)	20	10
2142	5cor. "Hippopotamus and Crocodile Hunt" (Rubens) (air)	1·20	1·00
2143	10cor. "Duke of Lerma on Horseback" (Rubens)	2·50	2·00
MS2144	130×105 mm. 20cor. Rubens (from painting of Rubens and Isabella Brandt)	5·25	4·50

305 Gothic Portal with Rose Window, Small Basilica of St. Francis

1978. 750th Anniv of Canonisation of St. Francis of Assisi. Multicoloured.

2145	1c. Type **305** (postage)	10	10
2146	2c. St. Francis preaching to birds	10	10
2147	3c. Painting of St. Francis	10	10
2148	4c. Franciscan genealogical tree	10	10

2149 5c. Portiuncola 10 10
2150 15c. Autographed blessing 10 10
2151 25c. Windows of Large Basilica 10 10
2152 80c. St. Francis and wolf (air) 20 15
2153 10cor. St. Francis 2·10 1·80
MS2154 121×105 mm. 20cor. Our Lady of Conception (patron saint of Nicaragua) 4·25 3·50

306 Locomotive No. 6, 1921

1978. Centenary of Railway. Multicoloured.
2155 1c. Type **306** (postage) 25 20
2156 2c. Lightweight cargo locomotive 25 20
2157 3c. Steam locomotive No. 10, 1909 25 20
2158 4c. Baldwin steam locomotive No. 31, 1906 25 20
2159 5c. Baldwin steam locomotive No. 21, 1911 25 20
2160 15c. Presidential Pullman coach 30 20
2161 35c. Steam locomotive No. 33, 1907 (air) 40 20
2162 4cor. Baldwin steam locomotive No. 36, 1907 1·70 1·20
2163 10cor. Juniata steam locomotive, 1914, U.S.A. 2·75 2·00
MS2164 140×107 mm. 20cor. Map of Nicaraguan railway system 7·25 5·00

307 Mongol Warriors ("Michael Strogoff")

1978. 150th Birth Anniv of Jules Verne. Mult.
2165 1c. Type **307** (postage) 10 10
2166 2c. Sea scene ("The Mysterious Island") 10 10
2167 3c. Sea monsters ("Journey to the Centre of the Earth") 10 10
2168 4c. Balloon and African elephant ("Five Weeks in a Balloon") 10 10
2169 90c. Submarine ("Twenty Thousand Leagues Under the Sea") (air) 30 20
2170 10cor. Balloon, Indian, steam locomotive and elephant ("Around the World in Eighty Days") 2·10 1·80
MS2171 113×87 mm. 20cor. Space ship ("From Earth to Moon") 6·25 5·00

308 Icarus

1978. 75th Anniv of History of Aviation. First Powered Flight. Multicoloured.
2172 1c. Type **308** (postage) 10 10
2173 2c. Montgolfier balloon (vert) 10 10
2174 3c. Wright Flyer I 10 10
2175 4c. Orville Wright in Wright Type A (vert) 10 10
2176 55c. Vought-Sikorsky VS-300 helicopter prototype (air) 30 20
2177 10cor. Space Shuttle 1·60 1·20
MS2178 143×114 mm. 20cor. "Flyer" III 6·25 5·00

309 Ernst Ocwirk and Alfredo di Stefano

1978. World Cup Football Championship, Argentina. Multicoloured.
2179 20c. Type **309** (postage) 15 15
2180 25c. Ralk Edstrom and Oswaldo Piazza 15 15
2181 50c. Franz Beckenbauer and Dennis Law (air) 20 20
2182 5cor. Dino Zoff and Pele 1·60 1·00
MS2183 102×77 mm. 20cor. Dominique Rocheteau and Johan Neeskens 6·25 5·00

310 "St. Peter" (Goya)

1978. Christmas. Multicoloured.
2184 10c. Type **310** (postage) 10 10
2185 15c. "St. Gregory" (Goya) 15 10
2186 3cor. "The Apostles John and Peter" (Durer) (air) 50 40
2187 10cor. "The Apostles Paul and Mark" (Durer) 1·70 1·20
MS2188 143×104 mm. 20cor. "The Child with Garland" (Durer) 4·25 3·50

311 San Cristobal

1978. Volcanoes and Lakes. Multicoloured.
2189 5c. Type **311** (postage) 10 10
2190 5c. Lake de Cosiguina 10 10
2191 20c. Telica 15 10
2192 20c. Lake Jiloa 15 10
2193 35c. Cerro Negro (air) 20 20
2194 35c. Lake Masaya 20 20
2195 90c. Momotombo 30 20
2196 90c. Lake Asososca 30 20
2197 1cor. Mombacho 30 20
2198 1cor. Lake Apoyo 30 20
2199 10cor. Concepcion 2·30 1·50
2200 10cor. Lake Tiscapa 2·30 1·50

312 General O'Higgins

1979. Air. Birth Bicentenary of Bernardo O'Higgins (liberation hero).
2201 **312** 20cor. multicoloured 5·25 4·00

313 Ginger Plant and Broad-tailed Hummingbird

1979. Air. Flowers. Multicoloured.
2202 50c. Type **313** 30 20
2203 55c. Orchids 30 20
2204 70c. Poinsettia 30 20
2205 80c. "Poro poro" 30 20
2206 2cor. "Morpho cypris" (butterfly) and Guayacan flowers 40 30
2207 4cor. Iris 85 60

314 Children with football

315 Indian Postal Runner

316 Einstein and Albert Schweitzer

317 Loggerhead Turtle

1980. Year of Liberation (1979) and Nicaragua's Participation in Olympic Games. Unissued stamps overprinted. (a) International Year of the Child. Mult.
2208 20c. Children on roundabout (postage) 30 20
2209 90c. Type **314** (air) 1·00 1·00
2210 2cor. Children with stamp albums 2·10 2·00
2211 2cor.20 Children playing with toy steam train and aircraft 12·50 12·00
2212 10cor. Baseball 4·25 4·00
MS2213 130×105 mm. 5cor. As No. 2211 (30×47 mm); 15cor. Dr. Hermann Gmeiner (30×47 mm) 50·00 50·00

(b) Death Centenary of Sir Rowland Hill. Mult.
2214 20c. Type **315** (postage) 1·10 1·10
2215 35c. Pony express 2·30 2·20
2216 1cor. Pre-stamp letter (horiz) 4·75 4·50
2217 1cor.80 Sir Rowland Hill examining sheet of Penny Black stamps (air) 8·25 8·00
2218 2cor.20 Penny Blacks (horiz) 10·50 10·00
2219 5cor. Nicaraguan Zeppelin flight cover (horiz) 23·00 22·00
MS2220 130×105 mm. 20cor. Sir Rowland Hill and Indian postal runner (36×47 mm) 50·00 50·00

(c) Birth Centenary of Albert Einstein (physicist). Multicoloured.
2221 5c. Type **316** (postage) 70 70
2222 10c. Einstein and equation 2·00 90
2223 15c. Einstein and 1939 World Fair pavilion 1·60 1·50
2224 20c. Einstein and Robert Oppenheimer 1·90 1·80
2225 25c. Einstein in Jerusalem 2·50 2·50
2226 1cor. Einstein and Nobel Prize medal (air) 7·75 7·50
2227 2cor.75 Einstein and space exploration 17·00 16·00
2228 10cor. Einstein and Mahatma Gandhi 50·00 50·00
MS2229 130×105 mm. 5cor. Einstein at work (53×36 mm); 15cor. As No. 2228 (53×36 mm) 41·00 40·00

(d) Endangered Turtles. Multicoloured.
2230 90c. Type **317** 6·25 6·00
2231 2cor. Leatherback turtle 10·50 10·00
2232 2cor.20 Ridley turtle 11·50 11·00
2233 10cor. Hawksbill turtle 36·00 35·00
MS2234 150×105 mm. 5cor. As No. 2231 (51×32 mm); 15cor. Green turtles (51×32 mm) 41·00 40·00

318 Rigoberto Lopez Perez and Crowds pulling down Statue

1980. 1st Anniv of the Revolution. Multicoloured.
2235 40c. Type **318** 10 10
2236 75c. Street barricade 10 10
2237 1cor. "Learn to Read" emblem (vert) 20 10
2238 1cor.25 German Pomares Ordonez and jungle fighters 30 20
2239 1cor.85 Victory celebrations (vert) 40 20
2240 2cor.50 Carlos Fonesca and camp-fire 50 40
2241 5cor. Gen. Augusto Sandino and flag (vert) 1·20 1·00
MS2242 118×90 mm. 10cor. Nicaraguan landscape 6·25 5·00

1980. Literacy Year. Unissued stamps optd 1980 ANO DE LA ALFABETIZACION. (a) International Year of the Child. As Nos. 2208/12.
2243 - 20c. Children on roundabout (postage) 1·80 1·70
2244 **314** 90c. Children with football (air) 1·80 1·70
2245 - 2cor. Children with stamp albums 1·80 1·70
2246 - 2cor.20 Children playing with toy steam train and airplane 23·00 22·00
2247 - 10cor. Baseball 8·25 8·00
MS2248 105×90 mm. 10cor. Dr. Hermann Gmeiner 41·00 40·00

(b) Death Centenary of Sir Rowland Hill. Nos. 2214/16.
2249 **315** 20c. Indian postal runner 1·20 1·20
2250 - 35c. Pony express 1·20 1·20
2251 - 1cor. Pre-stamp letter (horiz) 1·20 1·20
MS2252 83×100 mm. 10cor. Penny Black and Nicaraguan 2c. stamp 12·50 12·00

(c) Birth Centenary of Albert Einstein (physicist). As Nos. 2221/8.
2253 5c. Optd **"YURI GAGARIN/12/IV/1961/LER HOMBRE EN EL ESPACIO"** (postage) 6·25 6·00
2254 10c. Optd **"LURABA 1981"** and space shuttle 6·25 6·00
2255 15c. Optd **"SPACE SHUTTLE"** and craft 6·25 6·00
2256 20c. Optd **ANO DE LA ALFABETIZACION** 6·25 6·00
2257 25c. Optd **"16/VII/1969/LER HOMBRE A LA LUNA"** and **"APOLLO XI"** 6·25 6·00
2258 1cor. Optd As No. 2256 (air) 6·25 6·00
2259 2cor.75 Optd As No. 2256 6·25 6·00
2260 10cor. Optd **"LUNOJOD 1"** and vehicle 6·25 6·00
MS2261 111×85 mm. 10cor. Einstein at work £100 £100

(d) Air. Endangered Species. Turtles. As Nos. 2230/3. Multicoloured.
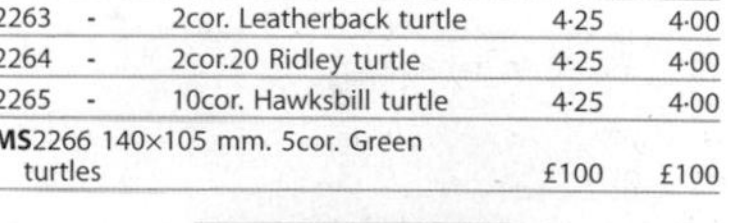
2262 **317** 90c. Loggerhead turtle 4·25 4·00
2263 - 2cor. Leatherback turtle 4·25 4·00
2264 - 2cor.20 Ridley turtle 4·25 4·00
2265 - 10cor. Hawksbill turtle 4·25 4·00
MS2266 140×105 mm. 5cor. Green turtles £100 £100

320 Resplendent Quetzal

1981. "WIPA" 1981 International Stamp Exhibition, Vienna. Sheet 93×55 mm.
MS2267 **320** 10cor. multicoloured 3·00 2·20

321 Footballer and El Molinon Stadium

1981. World Cup Football Championship, Spain. (1st issue). Venues. Multicoloured.
2268 5c. Type **321** 10 10
2269 20c. Sanchez Pizjuan, Seville 10 10
2270 25c. San Mames, Bilbao 10 10
2271 30c. Vincent Calderon, Madrid 15 10
2272 50c. R.C.D. Espanol, Barcelona 15 10
2273 4cor. New Stadium, Valladolid 50 30
2274 5cor. Balaidos, Vigo 65 35
2275 10cor. Santiago Bernabeu, Madrid 1·40 80
MS2276 65×79 mm. 10cor. Nou Camp, Barcelona (36×28 mm) 2·10 1·50
See also Nos. 2325/MS2332.

322 Adult Education

1981. 2nd Anniv of Revolution. Multicoloured.

2277	50c. Type **322** (postage)	15	10
2278	2cor.10 Workers marching (air)	30	30
2279	3cor. Roadbuilding and container ship	45	30
2280	6cor. Medical services	85	50

323 Allegory of Revolution

1981. 20th Anniv of Sandinista National Liberation Front. Multicoloured.

2281	50c. Type **323** (postage)	15	10
2282	4cor. Sandinista guerrilla (air)	60	40

324 Postman

1981. 12th Postal Union of the Americas and Spain Congress, Managua. Multicoloured.

2283	50c. Type **324** (postage)	10	10
2284	2cor.10 Pony Express (air)	30	20
2285	3cor. Postal Headquarters, Managua	50	20
2286	6cor. Government building, globe and flags of member countries	1·00	50

325 Reliefs depicting Bulgarian History (image scaled to 51% of original size)

1981. Air. 1300th Anniv of Bulgarian State. Sheet 96×70 mm. Imperf.

MS2287	**325** 10cor. multicoloured	3·00	2·00

326 "Nymphaea capensis"

1981. Water Lilies. Multicoloured.

2288	50c. Type **326** (postage)	15	10
2289	1cor. "Nymphaea daubenyana"	20	15
2290	1cor.20 "Nymphaea Marliacea Chromat"	30	20
2291	1cor.80 "Nymphaea Dir. Geo. T. Moore"	40	20
2292	2cor. "Nymphaea lotus"	50	30
2293	2cor.50 "Nymphaea B.G. Berry"	60	40
2294	10cor. "Nymphaea Gladstoniana" (air)	2·10	1·00

327 Giant Panda

1981. Air. "Philatokyo 81 International Stamp Exhibition". Sheet 100×61 mm.

MS2295	**327** 10cor. multicoloured	2·10	1·80

328 Cardinal Tetra

1981. Tropical Fishes. Multicoloured.

2296	50c. Type **328** (postage)	15	10
2297	1cor. Guppy	20	15
2298	1cor.85 Striped headstander	30	20
2299	2cor.10 Skunk corydoras	40	20
2300	2cor.50 Black-finned pearlfish	50	30
2301	3cor.50 Long-finned killie (air)	60	40
2302	4cor. Red swordtail	85	50

329 Frigate

1981. Air. "Espamer 81 Stamp Exhibition, Buenos Aires". Sheet 98×59 mm.

MS2303	**329** 10cor. multicoloured	2·10	1·80

330 Lineated Woodpecker

1981. Birds. Multicoloured.

2304	50c. Type **330** (postage)	30	20
2305	1cor.20 Keel-billed toucan (horiz)	40	20
2306	1cor.80 Finsch's conure (horiz)	50	30
2307	2cor. Scarlet macaw	50	30
2308	3cor. Slaty-tailed trogon (air)	60	30
2309	4cor. Violet sabrewing (horiz)	75	40
2310	6cor. Blue-crowned motmot	1·10	70

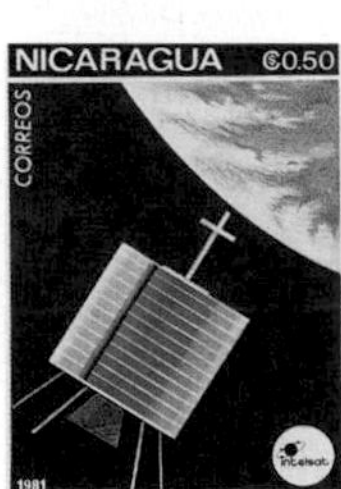

331 Satellite in Orbit

1981. Satellite Communications. Multicoloured.

2311	50c. Type **331** (postage)	15	10
2312	1cor. "Intelsat IVA"	20	15
2313	1cor.50 "Intelsat V" moving into orbit	30	20
2314	2cor. Rocket releasing "Intelsat V"	30	30
2315	3cor. Satellite and Space Shuttle (air)	60	40
2316	4cor. "Intelsat V" and world maps	1·00	50
2317	5cor. Tracking stations	1·30	60

332 Steam Locomotive at Lake Granada

1981. Locomotives. Multicoloured.

2318	50c. Type **332** (postage)	15	10
2319	1cor. Vulcan Iron Works steam locomotive No. 35, 1946	30	15
2320	1cor.20 Baldwin steam locomotive No. 21, 1911 (inscribed "Philadelphia Iron Works")	35	20
2321	1cor.80 Steam crane, 1909	50	30
2322	2cor. General Electric Model "U10B" diesel locomotive, 1960s	60	30
2323	2cor.50 German diesel railbus, 1954 (dated "1956")	70	40
2324	6cor. Japanese-built diesel railbus, 1967 (air)	1·90	70

333 Heading Ball

1982. World Cup Football Championship, Spain (2nd issue). Multicoloured.

2325	5c. Type **333** (postage)	15	10
2326	20c. Running with ball	15	10
2327	25c. Running with ball (different)	15	10
2328	2cor.50 Saving goal	40	35
2329	3cor.50 Goalkeeper diving for ball (horiz)	60	40
2330	4cor. Kicking ball (air)	70	40
2331	10cor. Tackle (horiz)	1·40	80
MS2332	98×61 mm. 10cor. Goalkeeper attempting save (39×31 mm)	3·00	2·00

334 Cocker Spaniel

1982. Pedigree Dogs. Multicoloured.

2333	5c. Type **334** (postage)	10	10
2334	20c. Alsatian	15	10
2335	25c. English setter	15	10
2336	2cor.50 Brittany spaniel	50	30
2337	3cor. Boxer (air)	60	35
2338	3cor.50 Pointer	60	40
2339	6cor. Collie	90	60

335 Satellite Communications

1982. Air. I.T.U. Congress.

2340	**335** 25cor. multicoloured	4·25	3·00

336 "Dynamine myrrhina"

1982. Butterflies. Multicoloured.

2341	50c. Type **336** (postage)	15	10
2342	1cor.20 "Eunica alcmena"	30	20
2343	1cor.50 "Callizona acesta"	30	20
2344	2cor. "Adelpha leuceria"	40	30
2345	3cor. "Parides iphidamas" (air)	75	30
2346	3cor.50 "Consul hippona"	90	40
2347	4cor. "Morpho peleides"	1·10	40

337 Laika and Rocket

1982. Space Exploration. Multicoloured.

2348	5c. Type **337** (postage)	10	10
2349	15c. Satellite (vert)	10	10
2350	50c. "Apollo–Soyuz" link	15	10
2351	1cor.50 Satellite	30	20
2352	2cor.50 Docking in space	50	30
2353	5cor. Russian space station (air)	85	40
2354	6cor. Space shuttle "Columbia" (vert)	1·00	50

338 Mailcoach

1982. Centenary of U.P.U. Membership. Mult.

2355	50c. Type **338** (postage)	15	10
2356	1cor.20 "Victoria" (packet steamer)	25	15
2357	3cor.50 Steam locomotive, 1953 (air)	50	30
2358	10cor. Boeing 727-100 airliner	1·50	90

339 Cyclists

1982. 14th Central American and Caribbean Games. Multicoloured.

2359	10c. Type **339** (postage)	10	10
2360	15c. Swimming (horiz)	10	10
2361	25c. Basketball	10	10
2362	50c. Weightlifting	15	10
2363	2cor.50 Handball (air)	50	30
2364	3cor. Boxing (horiz)	60	40
2365	9cor. Football (horiz)	2·10	1·00
MS2366	65×90 mm. 10cor. Baseball (30×39 mm)	2·50	1·50

340 Balloon

1982. Air. "Philexfrance 82 International Stamp Exhibition, Paris". Sheet 79×91 mm.

MS2367	**340** 15cor. multicoloured	3·00	2·00

341 Washington passing through Trenton

1982. 250th Birth Anniv of George Washington. Multicoloured.

2368	50c. Mount Vernon, Washington's house (39×49 mm) (postage)	15	10
2369	1cor. Washington signing the Constitution (horiz)	25	20
2370	2cor. Type **341**	40	25
2371	2cor.50 Washington crossing the Delaware (horiz) (air)	50	30
2372	3cor.50 Washington at Valley Forge (horiz)	65	40
2373	4cor. Washington at the Battle of Trenton	85	40
2374	6cor. Washington at Princeton	1·20	60

342 Carlos Fonseca, Dove and Flags

1982. 3rd Anniv of Revolution. Multicoloured.

2375	50c. Type **342** (postage)	15	10
2376	2cor.50 Ribbons forming dove (vert) (air)	50	30
2377	1cor. Augusto Sandino and dove (vert)	70	40
2378	6cor. Dove	1·20	60

343 "Vase of Flowers" (R. Penalba)

1982. Paintings. Multicoloured.

2379	25c. Type **343** (postage)	10	10
2380	50c. "El Gueguense" (M. Garcia) (horiz)	10	10
2381	1cor. "The Couple" (R. Perez)	20	10
2382	1cor.20 "Canales Valley" (A. Mejias) (horiz)	20	10
2383	1cor.85 "Portrait of Senora Castellon" (T. Jerez)	40	20
2384	2cor. "The Vendors" (L. Cerrato)	40	25
2385	9cor. "Sitting Woman" (A. Morales) (horiz) (air)	2·30	1·10
MS2386	86×64 mm. 10cor. "Roosters" (P. Ortiz) (horiz)	2·50	1·50

344 Lenin and Dimitrov, Moscow, 1921

1982. Birth Centenary of Georgi Dimitrov (Bulgarian statesman). Multicoloured.

2387	50c. Type **344** (postage)	10	10
2388	2cor.50 Dimitrov & Todor Yikov, Sofia, 1946 (air)	45	30
2389	4cor. Dimitrov and flag	75	50

345 Ausberto Narvaez

1982. 26th Anniv of State of Resistance Movement. Multicoloured.

2390	50c. Type **345** (postage)	10	10
2391	2cor.50 Cornelio Silva	50	30
2392	4cor. Rigoberto Lopez Perez (air)	60	45
2393	6cor. Edwin Castro	1·00	65

346 Old Ruins at Leon

1982. Tourism. Multicoloured.

2394	50c. Type **346** (postage)	10	10
2395	1cor. Ruben Dario Theatre and Park, Managua	20	10
2396	1cor.20 Independence Square, Granada	35	20
2397	1cor.80 Corn Island	35	20
2398	2cor. Carter Santiago Volcano, Masaya	45	30
2399	2cor.50 El Coyotepe Fortress, Masaya (air)	45	30
2400	3cor.50 Luis A. Velazquez Park, Managua	55	45

347 Karl Marx and View of Trier

1982. Death Centenary of Karl Marx. Mult.

2401	1cor. Type **347** (postage)	20	10
2402	4cor. Marx and grave in Highgate Cemetery (air)	75	45

348 Stacking Cane and Fruit

1982. World Food Day. Multicoloured.

2403	50c. Picking Fruit (horiz)	20	20
2404	1cor. Type **348**	20	20
2405	2cor. Cutting sugar cane (horiz)	35	25
2406	10cor. F.A.O. and P.A.N. emblems (horiz)	1·50	1·30

349 "Santa Maria"

1982. 490th Anniv of Discovery of America. Multicoloured.

2407	50c. Type **349** (postage)	20	10
2408	1cor. "Nina"	25	20
2409	1cor.50 "Pinta"	35	20
2410	2cor. Columbus and fleet	45	30
2411	2cor.50 Fleet and map of route (air)	50	30
2412	4cor. Arrival in America	75	40
2413	7cor. Death of Columbus	1·30	85
MS2414	71×56 mm. 10cor. "Santa Maria" (vert)	2·75	1·60

350 "Lobelia laxiflora"

1982. Woodland Flowers. Multicoloured.

2415	50c. Type **350** (postage)	10	10
2416	1cor.20 "Bombacopsis quinata"	25	20
2417	1cor.80 "Mimosa albida"	40	25
2418	2cor. "Epidendrum alatum"	40	25
2419	2cor.50 Passion flower "Pasiflora foetida" wrongly inscr "Pasiflora" (air)	40	25
2420	3cor.50 "Clitoria sp."	60	40
2421	5cor. "Russelia sarmentosa"	85	50

351 "Micrurus lemniscatus"

1982. Reptiles. Multicoloured.

2422	10c. Type **351** (postage)	10	10
2423	50c. Common iguana "Iguana iguana" (horiz)	20	10
2424	2cor. "Lachesis muta" (snake) (horiz)	45	30
2425	2cor.50 Hawksbill turtle "Eretmochelys imbricata" (horiz) (air)	90	30
2426	3cor. Boa constrictor "Constrictor constrictor"	1·10	35
2427	3cor.50 American crocodile "Crocodilus acutus" (horiz)	1·20	40
2428	5cor. Diamond-back rattlesnake "Sistrurus catenatus" (horiz)	1·90	65

352 Tele-cor Building, Managua

1982. Telecommunications Day. Multicoloured.

2429	1cor. Type **352** (postage)	20	10
2430	50c. Interior of radio transmission room (air)	10	10

353 Girl with Dove

1983. Air. Non-Aligned States Conference.

2431	**353**	4cor. multicoloured	85	45

354 Jose Marti and Birthplace

1983. 130th Birth Anniv of Jose Marti (Cuban revolutionary).

2432	**354**	1cor. multicoloured	30	15

355 Boxing

1983. Olympic Games, Los Angeles (1st issue). Multicoloured.

2433	50c. Type **355** (postage)	25	10
2434	1cor. Gymnastics	25	15
2435	1cor.50 Running	30	20
2436	2cor. Weightlifting	40	20
2437	4cor. Discus (air)	75	40
2438	5cor. Basketball	95	45
2439	6cor. Cycling	1·20	65
MS2440	60×88 mm. 15cor. Sailing (31×39 mm)	3·00	1·60

See also Nos. 2609/**MS**2616.

356 "Neomarica coerulea"

1983. Flowers.

2441	**356**	1cor. blue	20	10
2442	-	1cor. violet	20	10
2443	-	1cor. mauve	20	10
2444	-	1cor. brown	20	10
2445	-	1cor. green	20	10
2446	-	1cor. blue	20	10
2447	-	1cor. green	20	10
2448	-	1cor. green	20	10
2449	-	1cor. mauve	20	10
2450	-	1cor. red	20	10
2451	-	1cor. grey	20	10
2452	-	1cor. yellow	20	10
2453	-	1cor. brown	20	10
2454	-	1cor. purple	20	10
2455	-	1cor. green	20	10
2456	-	1cor. black	20	10

DESIGNS: No. 2442, "Tabebula ochraceae"; 2443, "Laella sp"; 2444, "Plumeria rubra"; 2445, "Brassavola nodosa"; 2446, "Stachytarpheta indica"; 2447, "Cochiospermum sp"; 2448, "Malvaviscus arboreus"; 2449, "Telecoma stans"; 2450, "Hibiscus rosa-sinensis"; 2451, "Cattleya lueddemanniana"; 2452, "Tagetes erecta"; 2453, "Senecio sp"; 2454, "Sobralia macrantha"; 2455, "Thumbergia alata"; 2456, "Bixa orellana".

See also Nos. 2739/54, 2838/53 and 3087/3102.

357 Momotombo Geothermal Electrical Plant

1983. Air. Energy.

2457	**357**	2cor.50 multicoloured	50	35

358 Map of Nicaragua and Girl picking Coffee

1983. Papal Visit.

2458	-	50c. red, black and blue (postage)	20	10
2459	**358**	1cor. multicoloured	30	20
2460	-	4cor. multicoloured (air)	1·00	60
2461	-	7cor. multicoloured	1·50	85
MS2462		80×66 mm. 15cor. multicoloured (31×39 mm)	3·25	1·90

DESIGNS: 50c. Demonstrating crowd; 4cor. Pres. Cordova Rivas and Pope John Paul II; 7cor. Pope outside Managua Cathedral; Pope John Paul II.

359 "Xilophanes chiron"

1983. Moths. Multicoloured.

2463	15c. Type **359** (postage)	25	10
2464	50c. "Protoparce ochus"	25	10
2465	65c. "Pholus lasbruscae"	25	10
2466	1cor. "Amphypterus gannascus"	25	15
2467	1cor.50 "Pholus licaon"	30	20
2468	2cor. "Agrius cingulata"	40	25
2469	10cor. "Rothschildia jurulla" (vert) (air)	2·00	1·10

360 La Recoleccion Church, Leon

1983. Monuments. Multicoloured.

2470	50c. Subtiava Church, Leon (horiz) (postage)	10	10
2471	1cor. La Inmaculada Castle, Rio San Juan (horiz)	25	10
2472	2cor. Type **360**	40	20
2473	4cor. Ruben Dario Monument, Managua (air)	80	45

361 Passenger Carriage

1983. Railway Wagons. Multicoloured.

2474	15c. Type **361** (postage)	10	10
2475	65c. Goods wagon No. 1034	25	10
2476	1cor. Tanker wagon No. 931	30	15
2477	1cor.50 Xolotlan hopper wagon	35	15
2478	4cor. Railcar (air)	75	40
2479	5cor. Tipper truck	85	50
2480	7cor. Railbus	1·50	70

362 Helping Earthquake Victim

1983. Red Cross. Multicoloured.

2481	50c. Aiding flood victims (horiz) (postage)	10	10
2482	1cor. Placing stretcher patient into ambulance (horiz)	20	10
2483	4cor. Type **362** (air)	75	40
2484	5cor. Doctor examining wounded soldier (horiz)	85	65

363 Raising Telephone Pole

1983. World Communications Year.

2485	**363**	1cor. multicoloured	25	15

364 Ibex

1983. Air. "Tembal 83 International Stamp Exhibition, Basel". Sheet 79×64 mm.

MS2486	**364** 15cor. multicoloured	2·50	1·50

365 Basketball

1983. 9th Pan-American Games. Multicoloured.

2487	15c. Basketball (horiz) (postage)	15	10
2488	50c. Water polo (horiz)	15	10
2489	65c. Running (horiz)	20	10
2490	1cor. Type **365**	20	10
2491	2cor. Weightlifting	45	25
2492	7cor. Fencing (horiz) (air)	1·20	70
2493	8cor. Gymnastics (horiz)	1·30	75
MS2494	75×85 mm. 15cor. Boxing (39×31 mm)	2·50	1·30

366 Boeing 727-100

1983. Air. "Expo Filnic National Stamp Exhibition". Sheet 79×60 mm.

MS2495	**366** 10cor. multicoloured	2·50	1·30

367 Container Ship being Unloaded

1983. 4th Anniv of Revolution. Multicoloured.

2496	1cor. Type **367**	20	10
2497	2cor. Telcor building, Leon	45	25

368 Carlos Fonseca

1983. Founders of Sandinista National Liberation Front. Multicoloured.

2498	50c. Escobar, Navarro, Ubeda, Pomares and Ruiz (postage)	10	10
2499	1cor. Santos Lopez, Borge, Buitrago and Mayorga	20	10
2500	4cor. Type **368** (air)	85	50

369 Simon Bolivar on Horseback

1983. Birth Bicentenary of Simon Bolivar. Mult.

2501	50c. Bolivar and Sandinista guerrilla	10	10
2502	1cor. Type **369**	20	10

370 Jaguar

1983. Air. "Brasiliana 83 International Stamp Exhibition, Rio de Janeiro. Sheet 95×65 mm.

MS2503	**370** 15cor. multicoloured	5·50	2·50

371 Movements of a Pawn

1983. Chess. Multicoloured.

2504	15c. Type **371** (postage)	15	10
2505	65c. Knight's movements	20	10
2506	1cor. Bishop's movements	20	10
2507	2cor. Rook's movements	35	25
2508	4cor. Queen's movements (air)	65	45
2509	5cor. King's movements	85	50
2510	7cor. Game in progress	1·20	70

372 Speed Skating

1983. Winter Olympic Games, Sarajevo (1984) (1st issue). Multicoloured.

2511	50c. Type **372** (postage)	10	10
2512	1cor. Slalom	20	10
2513	1cor.50 Luge	25	20
2514	2cor. Ski jumping	35	25
2515	4cor. Figure skating (air)	65	40
2516	5cor. Downhill skiing	85	50
2517	6cor. Biathlon	1·10	60
MS2518	51×80 mm. 15cor. Ice hockey (31×39 mm)	2·75	1·70

373 Soldiers with German Shepherd Dog

1983. Armed Forces.

2519	**373**	4cor. multicoloured	65	45

374 "Madonna of the Chair"

1983. 500th Birth Anniv of Raphael. Multicoloured.

2520	50c. Type **374** (postage)	10	10
2521	1cor. "Esterhazy Madonna"	20	10
2522	1cor.50 "Sistine Madonna"	30	15
2523	2cor. "Madonna of the Linnet"	35	20
2524	4cor. "Madonna of the Meadow" (air)	75	45
2525	5cor. "Madonna of the Garden"	95	50
2526	6cor. "Adoration of the Kings"	1·10	70
MS2527	86×123 mm. 15cor. "Foligno Madonna"	2·75	1·30

375 Pottery Idol

1983. Archaeological Finds. Multicoloured.

2528	50c. Type **375** (postage)	10	10
2529	1cor. Pottery dish with ornamental lid	20	10
2530	2cor. Vase with snake design	35	25
2531	4cor. Pottery dish (air)	85	45

376 Metal being poured into Moulds

1983. Nationalization of Mines. Multicoloured.

2532	1cor. Type **376** (postage)	20	10
2533	4cor. Workers and mine (air)	85	60

377 Radio Operator and Sinking Liner

1983. "Fracap '83" Congress of Radio Amateurs of Central America and Panama. Multicoloured.

2534	1cor. Type **377**	30	15
2535	4cor. Congress emblem and town destroyed by earthquake	75	45

378 Tobacco

1983. Agrarian Reform.

2536	**378**	1cor. green	20	15
2537	-	2cor. orange	35	25
2538	-	4cor. brown	75	40
2539	-	5cor. blue	85	50
2540	-	6cor. lavender	1·10	60
2541	-	7cor. purple	1·30	70
2542	-	8cor. purple	1·30	80
2543	-	10cor. brown	1·70	95

DESIGNS: 2cor. Cotton; 4cor. Maize; 5cor. Sugar; 6cor. Cattle; 7cor. Rice; 8cor. Coffee; 10cor. Bananas.

See also Nos. 2755/62 and 2854/61.

379 Fire Engine with Ladder

1983. Fire Engines. Multicoloured.

2544	50c. Type **379** (postage)	15	10
2545	1cor. Water tanker	20	15
2546	6cor. Crew vehicle, 1930	1·10	60
2547	1cor.50 Pump with extension fire hoses (air)	35	20
2548	2cor. Pump with high-pressure tank	45	25
2548a	4cor. Water tanker	60	40
2549	5cor. Fire engine, 1910	95	50

380 Jose Marti and General Sandino

1983. Nicaragua–Cuba Solidarity. Multicoloured.

2550	1cor. Type **380** (postage)	20	10
2551	4cor. Teacher, doctor and welder (air)	75	45

381 "Adoration of the Shepherds" (Hugo van der Gaes)

1983. Christmas. Multicoloured.

2552	50c. Type **381** (postage)	10	10
2553	1cor. "Adoration of the Kings" (Domenico Ghirlandaio)	20	10
2554	2cor. "Adoration of the Shepherds" (El Greco)	35	25
2555	7cor. "Adoration of the Kings" (Konrad von Soest) (air)	1·10	50

382 Anniversary Emblem

1984. Air. 25th Anniv of Cuban Revolution.

2557	**382**	4cor. red, blue and black	75	50
2558	-	6cor. multicoloured	1·10	70

DESIGN: 6cor. Fidel Castro and Che Guevara.

383 Bobsleigh

1984. Winter Olympic Games, Sarajevo. Mult.

2559	50c. Type **383** (postage)	10	10
2560	50c. Biathlon	10	10
2561	1cor. Slalom	20	10
2562	1cor. Speed skating	20	10
2563	4cor. Skiing (air)	75	45
2564	5cor. Ice-dancing	95	60
2565	10cor. Ski-jumping	1·60	85
MS2566	64×73 mm. 15cor. Ice hockey (31×35 mm)	3·75	1·90

384 Chinchilla

1984. Cats. Multicoloured.

2567	50c. Type **384** (postage)	30	15
2568	50c. Longhaired white	30	15
2569	1cor. Red tabby	35	15
2570	2cor. Tortoiseshell	45	25
2571	4cor. Burmese	95	45
2572	3cor. Siamese (air)	75	45
2573	7cor. Longhaired silver	1·40	80

385 National Arms

1984. 50th Death Anniv of Augusto Sandino. Mult.

2574	1cor. Type **385** (postage)	30	15
2575	4cor. Augusto Sandino (air)	95	45

386 Blanca Arauz

1984. International Women's Day.

2576	**386**	1cor. multicoloured	20	15

387 Sunflower

1984. Agricultural Flowers. Multicoloured.

2577	50c. Type **387** (postage)	30	15
2578	50c. "Poinsettia pulcherrima"	30	15
2579	1cor. "Cassia alata"	35	15
2580	1cor. "Antigonon leptopus"	35	15
2581	3cor. "Bidens pilosa" (air)	55	35
2582	4cor. "Althaea rosea"	75	45
2583	5cor. "Rivea corymbosa"	95	60

388 "Soyuz"

1984. Space Anniversaries. Multicoloured.

2584	50c. Type **388** (15th anniv of "Soyuz 6", "7" and "8" flights) (postage)	10	10
2585	50c. "Soyuz" (different) (15th anniv of "Soyuz 6", "7" and "8" flights)	10	10
2586	1cor. "Apollo 11" approaching Moon (15th anniv of 1st manned landing)	20	15
2587	2cor. "Luna I" (25th anniv of 1st Moon satellite)	45	25
2588	3cor. "Luna II" (25th anniv of 1st Moon landing) (air)	65	45
2589	4cor. "Luna III" (25th anniv of 1st photographs of far side of Moon)	85	60
2590	9cor. Rocket (50th anniv of Korolev's book on space flight)	1·80	85

389 "Noli me Tangere" (detail)

1984. 450th Death Anniv of Correggio (artist). Multicoloured.

2591	50c. Type **389** (postage)	10	10
2592	50c. "Madonna of St. Jerome" (detail)	10	10
2593	1cor. "Allegory of Virtue"	20	15
2594	2cor. "Allegory of Pleasure"	35	25
2595	3cor. "Ganymedes" (detail) (air)	55	35
2596	5cor. "The Danae" (detail)	85	50
2597	8cor. "Leda and the Swan" (detail)	1·30	85
MS2598	116×81 mm. 15cor. "St. John the Evangelist"	3·25	1·50

390 Daimler, 1886

1984. 150th Birth Anniv of Gottlieb Daimler (automobile designer). Multicoloured.

2599	1cor. Type **390** (postage)	20	10
2600	1cor. Abadal, 1914 (horiz)	20	10
2601	2cor. Ford, 1903	45	25
2602	2cor. Renault, 1899	45	25
2603	3cor. Rolls Royce, 1910 (horiz) (air)	55	45
2604	4cor. Metallurgique, 1907 (horiz)	75	50
2605	7cor. Bugatti "Mod 40" (horiz)	1·30	60

391 "Cardinal Infante Dom Fernando"

1984. Air. "Espana 84 International Stamp Exhibition, Madrid". Sheet 76×98 mm.

MS2606	**391** 15cor. multicoloured	3·75	1·70

392 Mail Transport

1984. Air. 19th Universal Postal Union Congress Philatelic Salon, Hamburg.

2607	15cor. Type **392**	3·25	1·70
MS2608	101×60 mm. 5cor. Zeppelin "Bodensee"	4·00	2·20

393 Basketball

1984. Olympic Games, Los Angeles (2nd issue). Multicoloured.

2609	50c. Type **393** (postage)	20	10
2610	50c. Volleyball	20	10
2611	1cor. Hockey	30	15
2612	2cor. Tennis (air)	35	25
2613	3cor. Football (horiz)	55	45
2614	4cor. Water polo (horiz)	75	50
2615	9cor. Soccer (horiz)	1·90	85
MS2616	105×67 mm. 15cor. Baseball (horiz)	2·75	1·70

394 Horses and Carriage

1984. Air. "Expofilnic 84 National Stamp Exhibition". Sheet 86×66 mm.

MS2617	**394** 15cor. multicoloured	2·30	1·70

395 Rural Construction Site

1984. 5th Anniv of Revolution. Multicoloured.

2618	5c. Type **395** (postage)	20	10
2619	1cor. Diesel locomotive, Pacific–Atlantic line	45	25
2620	4cor. Ploughing with oxen and tractor (Agrarian reform) (air)	65	35
2621	7cor. State Council building	1·30	60

396 "Children defending Nature" (Pablo Herrera Berrios)

1984. UNESCO Environmental Protection Campaign. Multicoloured.

2622	50c. Type **396** (postage)	20	10
2623	1cor. Living and dead forests	30	15
2624	2cor. Fisherman and dried river bed	45	25
2625	10cor. Hands holding plants (vert) (air)	1·90	1·00

397 Red Cross Airplane and Ambulance

1984. 50th Anniv of Nicaraguan Red Cross. Mult.

2626	1cor. Type **397** (postage)	30	15
2627	7cor. Battle of Solferino (125th anniv) (air)	1·20	60

398 "Discovery"

1984. Air. "Ausipex 84 International Stamp Exhibition, Melbourne". Sheet 74×94 mm.

MS2628	**398** 15cor. multicoloured	2·10	1·25

399 Ventura Escalante and Dominican Republic Flag

1984. Baseball. Multicoloured.

2629	50c. Type **399** (postage)	20	15
2630	50c. Danial Herrera and Mexican flag	20	15
2631	1cor. Adalberto Herrera and Venezuelan flag	30	20
2632	1cor. Roberto Clemente and Nicaraguan flag	30	20
2633	3cor. Carlos Colas and Cuban flag (air)	55	45
2634	4cor. Stanley Cayasso and Argentinian flag	80	50
2635	5cor. Babe Ruth and U.S.A. flag	1·00	60

400 Central American Tapir

1984. Wildlife Protection. Multicoloured.

2636	25c. Type **400** (postage)	30	15
2637	25c. Young tapir	30	15
2638	3cor. Close-up of tapir (air)	95	45
2639	4cor. Mother and young	1·30	50

401 Football in 1314

1985. World Cup Football Championship, Mexico (1986) (1st issue). Multicoloured.

2640	50c. Type **401** (postage)	20	10
2641	50c. Football in 1500	20	10
2642	1cor. Football in 1872	30	15
2643	1cor. Football in 1846	30	15
2644	2cor. Football in 1883 (air)	35	25
2645	4cor. Football in 1890	55	35
2646	6cor. Football in 1953	95	50
MS2647	92×81 mm. 10cor. Footballers	2·30	1·30

See also Nos. 2731/**MS**2738 and 2812/**MS**2819.

402 "Strobilomyces retisporus"

1985. Fungi. Multicoloured.

2648	50c. Type **402** (postage)	20	10
2649	50c. "Boletus calopus"	20	10
2650	1cor. "Boletus luridus"	30	15
2651	1cor. "Xerocomus illudens" (air)	30	15
2652	4cor. "Gyrodon merulioides"	75	35
2653	5cor. "Tylopilus plumbeoviolaceus"	95	45
2654	8cor. "Gyroporus castaneus"	1·40	70

403 Postal Runner and Map

1985. 13th Postal Union of the Americas and Spain Congress. Multicoloured.

2655	1cor. Type **403** (postage)	50	15
2656	7cor. Casa Aviocar mail plane over map (air)	2·50	50

404 Cyclist

1985. Air. "Olymphilex 85 International Stamp Exhibition, Lausanne". Sheet 53×82 mm.

MS2657	**404** 15cor. multicoloured	2·00	1·00

405 Cuban Crocodile

1985. Air. "Espamer 85 International Stamp Exhibition, Havana". Sheet 94×60 mm.

MS2658	**405** 10cor. multicoloured	1·40	85

406 Steam Locomotive, Oldenburg

1985. 150th Anniv of German Railway. Mult.

2659	1cor. Type **406** (postage)	30	15
2660	1cor. Electric locomotive, Prussia	30	15
2661	9cor. Steam locomotive No. 88, Prussia (air)	1·00	45
2662	9cor. Double-deck tram	1·00	45
2663	15cor. Steam locomotive, Wurttemberg	1·70	70
2664	21cor. Steam locomotive, Germany	2·30	1·00
MS2665	80×60 mm. 42cor. Steam engine with tender (35×26 mm)	6·50	4·00

The miniature sheets also commemorates centenary of Nicaraguan railways.

407 Douglas, 1928

1985. Centenary of Motor Cycle. Multicoloured.

2666	50c. Type **407** (postage)	35	15
2667	50c. FN, 1928	35	15
2668	1cor. Puch, 1938	45	25
2669	2cor. Wanderer, 1939 (air)	55	35
2670	4cor. Honda, 1949	1·20	45
2671	5cor. BMW, 1984	1·50	60
2672	7cor. Honda, 1984	2·00	85

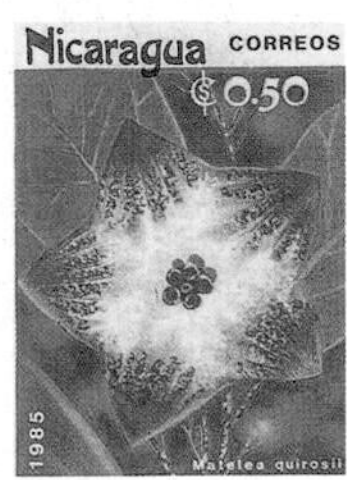

408 "Matelea quirosii"

1985. Flowers. Multicoloured.

2673	50c. Type **408** (postage)	35	15
2674	50c. "Ipomea nil"	35	15
2675	1cor. "Lysichitum americanum"	45	25
2676	2cor. "Clusia sp." (air)	85	35
2677	4cor. "Vanilla planifolia"	1·70	50
2678	7cor. "Stemmadenia obovata"	2·75	85

409 "Capitulation of German Troops" (P. Krivonogov)

1985. 40th Anniv of End of World War II. Mult.

2679	9cor.50 Type **409** (postage)	1·00	50
2680	28cor. Woman behind barbed wire and Nuremberg trial (air)	3·25	1·60

410 Lenin and Red Flag

1985. 115th Birth Anniv of Lenin. Multicoloured.

2681	4cor. Type **410**	45	15
2682	21cor. Lenin addressing crowd	2·30	1·00

411 Bassett Hound

1985. "Argentina 85 International Stamp Exhibition, Buenos Aires. Sheet 76×96 mm.

MS2683	**411** 75cor. multicoloured (4.47)	4·75	2·50

412 Victoria de Julio Sugar Factory

1985. Air. 6th Anniv of Revolution. Multicoloured.

2684	9cor. Type **412**	1·10	70
2685	9cor. Soldier and flag	1·10	70

413 Common Pheasant

1985. Domestic Birds. Multicoloured.

2686	50c. Type **413**	30	15
2687	50c. Hen	30	15
2688	1cor. Helmeted guineafowl	35	20
2689	2cor. Swan goose	75	25
2690	6cor. Ocellated turkey	2·00	85
2691	8cor. Duck	2·75	1·30

414 Luis A. Delgadillo

1985. International Music Year. Multicoloured.

2692	1cor. Type **414** (postage)	30	15
2693	1cor. Masked dancer with floral headdress	30	15
2694	9cor. Masked procession (air)	1·10	45
2695	9cor. Crowd outside church	1·10	45
2696	15cor. Masked dancer in brimmed hat	1·50	70
2697	21cor. Procession resting	2·20	1·20

415 Zeledon

1985. Air. Birth Centenary of Benjamin Zeledon.

2698	**415** 15cor. multicoloured	1·40	70

416 Dunant and Lifeboat

1985. 75th Death Anniv of Henri Dunant (founder of Red Cross). Multicoloured.

2699	3cor. Type **416**	30	15
2700	15cor. Dunant and Ilyushin Il-86 and Tupolev Tu-154 aircraft	1·10	60

417 Fire Engine

1985. 6th Anniv of SINACOI Fire Service. Mult.

2701	1cor. Type **417** (postage)	30	15
2702	1cor. Fire station	30	15
2703	1cor. Engine with water jet	30	15
2704	3cor. Foam tender (air)	55	25
2705	9cor. Airport fire engine	95	35
2706	15cor. Engine at fire	1·40	60
2707	21cor. Fireman in protective clothing	1·90	85

418 Halley, Masaya Volcano and Comet

1985. Appearance of Halley's Comet. Mult.

2708	1cor. Type **418** (postage)	30	15
2709	3cor. Armillary sphere and 1910 trajectory	35	20
2710	3cor. "Venus" space probe and Tycho Brahe underground observatory	35	20
2711	9cor. Habermel's astrolabe and comet's path through solar system (air)	1·10	25
2712	15cor. Hale Telescope, Mt. Palomar, and Herschel's telescope	1·90	50
2713	21cor. Galileo's telescope and sections through telescopes of Newton, Cassegrain and Ritchey	2·50	85

419 Tapir eating

1985. Protected Animals. Baird's Tapir. Mult.

2714	1cor. Type **419** (postage)	30	15
2715	3cor. Tapir in water (air)	65	20
2716	5cor. Tapir in undergrowth	1·10	45
2717	9cor. Mother and calf	1·90	60

420 "Rosa spinosissima"

1986. Wild Roses. Multicoloured.

2718	1cor. Type **420**	20	15
2719	1cor. Dog rose ("R. canina")	20	15
2720	3cor. "R. eglanteria"	30	20
2721	5cor. "R. rubrifolia"	35	25
2722	9cor. "R. foetida"	55	35
2723	100cor. "R. rugosa"	4·25	1·60

421 Crimson Topaz

1986. Birds. Multicoloured.

2724	1cor. Type **421**	20	15
2725	3cor. Orange-billed nightingale thrush	30	20
2726	3cor. Troupial	30	20
2727	5cor. Painted bunting	35	25
2728	10cor. Frantzius's nightingale thrush	55	35
2729	21cor. Great horned owl	1·10	60
2730	75cor. Great kiskadee	3·00	1·70

422 Footballer and Statue

1986. World Cup Football Championship, Mexico (2nd issue). Multicoloured.

2731	1cor. Type **422** (postage)	10	10
2732	1cor. Footballer and sculptured head	10	10
2733	3cor. Footballer and water holder with man as stem (air)	20	15
2734	3cor. Footballer and sculpture	20	15
2735	5cor. Footballer and sculptured head (different)	30	20
2736	9cor. Footballer and sculpture (different)	35	25
2737	100cor. Footballer and sculptured snake's head	3·00	1·40
MS2738	83×93 mm. 100cor. Footballer's leg and ball	3·25	1·70

1986. (a) Flowers. As Nos. 2441/56 but values changed.

2739	5cor. blue	35	15
2740	5cor. violet	35	15
2741	5cor. purple	35	15
2742	5cor. orange	35	15
2743	5cor. green	35	15
2744	5cor. blue	35	15
2745	5cor. green	35	15
2746	5cor. green	35	15
2747	5cor. mauve	35	15
2748	5cor. red	35	15
2749	5cor. grey	35	15
2750	5cor. orange	35	15
2751	5cor. brown	35	15
2752	5cor. brown	35	15
2753	5cor. green	35	15
2754	5cor. black	35	15

DESIGNS: No. 2739, Type **356**; 2740, "Tabebula ochraceae"; 2741, "Laelia sp"; 2742, Frangipani ("Plumeria rubra"); 2743, "Brassavola nodosa"; 2744, "Strachytarpheta indica"; 2745, "Cochlospermum sp"; 2746, "Malvaviscus arboreus"; 2747, "Tecoma stans"; 2748, Chinese hibiscus ("Hibiscus rosa-sinensis"); 2749, "Cattleya lueddemanniana"; 2750, African marigold ("Tagetes erecta"); 2751, "Senecio sp"; 2752, "Sobralia macrantha"; 2753, "Thumbergia alata"; 2754, "Bixa orellana".

(b) Agrarian Reform. As T 378.

2755	1cor. brown	20	10
2756	9cor. violet	30	15
2757	15cor. purple	45	20
2758	21cor. red	55	30
2759	33cor. orange	80	45
2760	42cor. green	1·00	60
2761	50cor. brown	1·30	70
2762	100cor. blue	2·20	1·70

DESIGNS: 1cor. Type **378**; 9cor. Cotton; 15cor. Maize; 21cor. Sugar; 33cor. Cattle; 42cor. Rice; 50cor. Coffee; 100cor. Bananas.

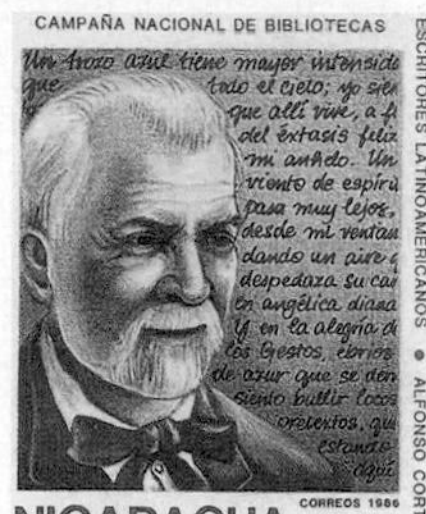

423 Alfonso Cortes

1986. National Libraries. Latin American Writers. Multicoloured.

2763	1cor. Type **423** (postage)	10	10
2764	3cor. Azarias H. Pallais	20	15
2765	3cor. Salomon de la Selva	20	15
2766	5cor. Ruben Dario	30	20
2767	9cor. Pablo Neruda	35	25
2768	15cor. Alfonso Reyes (air)	45	35
2769	100cor. Pedro Henriquez Urena	3·25	1·50

424 Great Britain Penny Black and Nicaragua 1929 25c. Stamp

1986. Air. 125th Anniv of Nicaraguan Stamps. Designs showing G.B. Penny Black and Nicaragua stamps.

2770	**424**	30cor. multicoloured	95	25
2771	-	40cor. brown, black and grey	1·10	45
2772	-	50cor. red, black and grey	1·30	60
2773	-	100cor. blue, black and grey	2·75	1·10

DESIGNS: 40c. 1903 1p. stamp; 50c. 1892 5p. stamp; 1p. 1862 2c. stamp.

425 Sapodilla

1986. 40th Anniv of F.A.O. Multicoloured.

2774	1cor. Type **425** (postage)	20	10
2775	1cor. Maranon	20	10
2776	3cor. Tree-cactus	30	15
2777	3cor. Granadilla	30	15
2778	5cor. Custard-apple (air)	35	20
2779	21cor. Melocoton	95	35
2780	100cor. Mamey	3·50	1·50

426 Rainbow and Globe

1986. Air. International Peace Year. Multicoloured.

2781	5cor. Type **426**	20	10
2782	10cor. Dove and globe	35	15

427 Lockheed L-1011 TriStar 500

1986. "Stockholmia 86" International Stamp Exhibition. Multicoloured.

2783	1cor. Type **427** (postage)	20	10
2784	1cor. Yakovlev Yak-40	20	10
2785	3cor. B.A.C. One Eleven	30	15
2786	3cor. Boeing 747-100	30	15
2787	9cor. Airbus Industrie A300 (air)	45	25
2788	15cor. Tupolev Tu-154	65	35
2789	100cor. Concorde (vert)	3·25	1·50
MS2790	60×73 mm. 100cor. SAAb "FAirchild 340" (39×31 mm)	3·75	1·70

428 "Pinta" and 16th-century Map

1986. 500th Anniv (1992) of Discovery of America by Columbus (1st issue). Multicoloured.

2791	1cor. Type **428** (postage)	30	15
2792	1cor. "Santa Maria" and "Nina"	30	15
2793	9cor. Juan de la Cosa (air)	35	20
2794	9cor. Christopher Columbus	35	20
2795	21cor. King and Queen of Spain	1·00	45
2796	100cor. Courtiers behind Columbus and Indians	4·25	1·50
MS2797	Two sheets each 155×80 mm. (a) Nos. 2971/2; (b) Nos. 2793/6	10·50	9·75

The designs of the same value and Nos. 2795/6 were printed together in se-tenant pairs within their sheets, Nos. 2791/2 and 2795/6 forming composite designs.

See also Nos. 2911/16.

429 Fonseca and Flags

1986. Air. 25th Anniv of Sandinista Front and 10th Death Anniv of Carlos Fonseca (co-founder).

2798	**429**	15cor. multicoloured	35	15

430 Rhinoceros

1986. Air. Endangered Animals. Multicoloured.

2799	15cor. Type **430**	45	15
2800	15cor. Zebra	45	15
2801	25cor. Elephant	75	35
2802	25cor. Giraffe	75	35
2803	50cor. Tiger	1·60	80
2804	50cor. Mandrill	1·60	80

431 "Theritas coronata"

1986. Butterflies. Multicoloured.

2805	10cor. Type **431** (postage)	45	15
2806	15cor. "Salamis cacta" (air)	75	25
2807	15cor. "Charayes nitebis"	75	25
2808	15cor. "Papilio maacki"	75	25
2809	25cor. "Palaeochrysophonus hippothoe"	1·20	50
2810	25cor. "Euphaedro cyparissa"	1·20	50
2811	30cor. "Ritra aurea"	1·40	60

432 Player and French Flag

1986. Air. World Cup Football Championship, Mexico (3rd issue). Finalists. Multicoloured. Designs showing footballers and national flags.

2812	10cor. Type **432**	45	15
2813	10cor. Argentina	45	15
2814	10cor. West Germany	45	15
2815	15cor. England	75	25
2816	15cor. Brazil	75	25
2817	25cor. Spain	95	35
2818	50cor. Belgium (horiz)	1·90	80
MS2819	95×65 mm. 100cor. Players	4·25	1·70

433 Ernesto Mejia Sanchez

1987. Ruben Dario Cultural Order of Independence. Multicoloured.

2820	10cor. Type **433** (postage)	25	15
2821	10cor. Fernando Gordillo	25	15
2822	10cor. Francisco Perez Estrada	25	15
2823	15cor. Order medal (air)	35	20
2824	30cor. Julio Cortazar	75	45
2825	60cor. Enrique Fernandez Morales	1·50	85

434 Ice Hockey

1987. Winter Olympic Games, Calgary (1988). Multicoloured.

2826	10cor. Type **434** (postage)	35	15
2827	10cor. Speed skating	35	15
2828	15cor. Downhill skiing (air)	55	15
2829	15cor. Figure skating	55	15
2830	20cor. Shooting	75	25
2831	30cor. Slalom	1·30	45
2832	40cor. Ski jumping	1·70	70
MS2833	75×66 mm. 110cor. Ice hockey (different) (39×31 mm)	3·75	3·00

435 Development

1987. UNICEF Child Survival Campaign. Multicoloured.

2834	10cor. Type **435** (postage)	45	15
2835	25cor. Vaccination (air)	85	45
2836	30cor. Oral rehydration therapy	1·20	50
2837	50cor. Breast-feeding	1·70	85

1987. (a) Flowers. As Nos. 2441/56 and 2739/54 but values changed.

2838	10cor. blue	35	15
2839	10cor. violet	35	15
2840	10cor. purple	35	15
2841	10cor. red	35	15
2842	10cor. green	35	15
2843	10cor. blue	35	15
2844	10cor. green	35	15
2845	10cor. green	35	15
2846	10cor. mauve	35	15
2847	10cor. red	35	15
2848	10cor. green	35	15
2849	10cor. orange	35	15
2850	10cor. brown	35	15
2851	10cor. purple	35	15
2852	10cor. turquoise	35	15
2853	10cor. black	35	15

DESIGNS: No. 2838, Type **356**; 2839, "Tabebula ochraceae"; 2840, "Laelia sp"; 2841, Frangipani; 2842, "Brassavola nodosa"; 2843, "Stachytarpheta indica"; 2844, "Cochlospermum sp"; 2845, "Malvaviscus arboreus"; 2846, "Tecoma stans"; 2847, Chinese hibiscus; 2848, "Cattleya lueddermanniana"; 2849, African marigold; 2850, "Senecio sp"; 2851, "Sobralla macrantha"; 2852, "Thumbergia alata"; 2853, "Bixa orellana".

(b) Agrarian Reform. As T 378. Dated "1987".

2854	10cor. brown	30	15
2855	10cor. violet	30	15
2856	15cor. purple	45	25
2857	25cor. red	65	45
2858	30cor. orange	85	60
2859	50cor. brown	1·30	95
2860	60cor. green	1·60	1·30
2861	100cor. blue	2·50	1·90

DESIGNS: No. 2854, Type **378**; 2855, Cotton; 2856, Maize; 2857, Sugar; 2858, Cattle; 2859, Coffee; 2860, Rice; 2861, Bananas.

436 Flags and Buildings

1987. 77th Interparliamentary Conf, Managua.

2862	**436**	10cor. multicoloured	20	10

437 "Mammuthus columbi"

1987. Prehistoric Animals. Multicoloured.

2863	10cor. Type **437** (postage)	80	15
2864	10cor. Triceratops	35	15
2865	10cor. Dimetrodon	35	15
2866	15cor. Uintaterium (air)	65	25
2867	15cor. Dinichthys	65	25
2868	30cor. Pteranodon	1·40	45
2869	40cor. Tilosaurus	1·90	50

438 Tennis Player

1987. "Capex 87" International Stamp Exhibition, Toronto.

2870	10cor. multicoloured (Type **438**) (postage)	45	15
2871	10cor. mult	45	15
2872	15cor. mult (male player) (air)	65	20
2873	15cor. mult (female player)	65	20
2874	20cor. multicoloured	75	25
2875	30cor. multicoloured	1·40	45
2876	40cor. multicoloured	1·90	50
MS2877	49×60 mm. 110cor. multicoloured (31×39 mm)	3·75	3·25

DESIGNS: Nos. 2871/**MS**2877, Various tennis players.

439 Dobermann Pinscher

1987. Dogs. Multicoloured.

2878	10cor. Type **439** (postage)	30	15
2879	10cor. Bull mastiff	30	15
2880	15cor. Japanese spaniel (air)	55	20
2881	15cor. Keeshond	55	20
2882	20cor. Chihuahua	95	25
2883	30cor. St. Bernard	1·40	45
2884	40cor. West Gotha spitz	1·90	70

440 Modern Wooden Houses

1987. Air. International Year of Shelter for the Homeless. Multicoloured.

2885	20cor. Type **440**	55	25
2886	30cor. Modern brick-built houses	95	45

441 Levski

1987. Air. 150th Birth Anniv of Vasil Levski (revolutionary).

2887	**441**	30cor. multicoloured	85	35

442 "Opuntia acanthocarpa major"

1987. Cacti. Multicoloured.

2888	10cor. Type **442** (postage)	35	15
2889	10cor. "Lophocereus schottii"	35	15
2890	10cor. "Echinocereus engelmanii"	35	15
2891	20cor. Saguaros (air)	85	35
2892	20cor. "Lemaireocereus thurberi"	85	35
2893	30cor. "Opuntia fulgida"	1·30	50
2894	50cor. "Opuntia ficus indica"	1·90	80

443 High Jumping

1987. 10th Pan-American Games, Indiana. Mult.

2895	10cor. Type **443** (postage)	30	15
2896	10cor. Handball	30	15
2897	15cor. Running (air)	45	20
2898	15cor. Gymnastics	45	20
2899	20cor. Baseball	75	25
2900	30cor. Synchronized swimming (vert)	1·10	45
2901	40cor. Weightlifting (vert)	1·40	60
MS2902	57×67 mm 110cor. Gymnastics (different) (31×39 mm)	3·25	2·50

444 Television Tower, East Berlin

1987. Air. 750th Anniv of Berlin. Sheet 69×96 mm.

MS2903	**443**	130cor. multicoloured	3·75	1·70

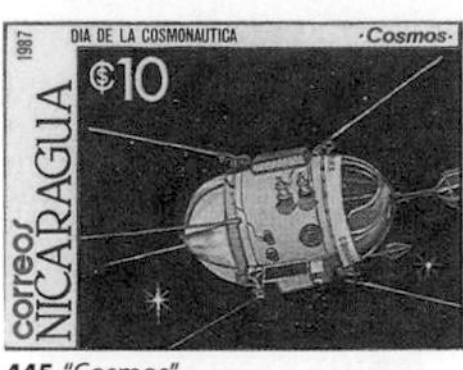

445 "Cosmos"

1987. Cosmonautics Day. Multicoloured.

2904	10cor. Type **445** (postage)	35	15
2905	10cor. "Sputnik"	35	15
2906	15cor. "Proton" (air)	65	20
2907	25cor. "Luna"	1·00	25
2908	25cor. "Meteor"	1·00	25
2909	30cor. "Electron"	1·10	45
2910	50cor. "Mars-1"	1·60	75

446 Native Huts and Terraced Hillside

1987. Air. 500th Anniv (1992) of Discovery of America by Columbus (2nd issue). Mult.

2911	15cor. Type **446**	65	15
2912	15cor. Columbus's fleet	65	15
2913	20cor. Spanish soldiers in native village	75	25
2914	30cor. Mounted soldiers killing natives	1·10	45
2915	40cor. Spanish people and houses	1·50	60
2916	50cor. Church and houses	1·70	75

447 Tropical Gar

1987. World Food Day. Fishes. Multicoloured.

2917	10cor. Type **447** (postage)	45	15
2918	10cor. Atlantic tarpon ("Tarpon atlanticus")	45	15
2919	10cor. Jaguar guapote ("Cichlasoma managuense")	45	15
2920	15cor. Banded astyanax ("Astyana fasciatus") (air)	75	35
2921	15cor. Midas cichlid ("Cichlasoma citrimellum")	75	35
2922	20cor. Wolf cichlid	1·20	45
2923	50cor. Lake Nicaragua shark	2·40	85

448 Lenin

1987. 70th Anniv of Russian Revolution. Mult.

2924	10cor. Type **448** (postage)	35	15
2925	30cor. "Aurora" (cruiser) (horiz) (air)	95	35
2926	50cor. Russian arms	1·40	60

449 "Nativity"

1987. Christmas. Details of Painting by L. Saenz. Multicoloured.

2927	10cor. Type **449**	30	15
2928	20cor. "Adoration of the Magi"	55	20
2929	25cor. "Adoration of the Magi" (close-up detail)	65	25
2930	50cor. "Nativity" (close-up detail)	1·40	50

1987. Surch.

2931	**435**	400cor. on 10cor. mult (postage)	1·40	50
2932	-	600cor. on 50cor. mult (No. 2837)	1·60	60
2933	-	1000cor. on 25cor. mult (No. 2835)	2·20	90
2934	-	5000cor. on 30cor. mult (No. 2836)	2·75	1·10
2935	**440**	200cor. on 20cor. multicoloured (air)	2·50	1·10
2936	-	3000cor. on 30cor. mult (No. 2886)	80	30

451 Cross-country Skiing

1988. Winter Olympic Games, Calgary. Mult.

2937	10cor. Type **451**	30	15
2938	10cor. Rifle-shooting (horiz)	30	15
2939	15cor. Ice hockey	55	20
2940	20cor. Ice skating	85	35
2941	25cor. Downhill skiing	1·10	45
2942	30cor. Ski jumping (horiz)	2·10	50
2943	40cor. Slalom	1·60	70
MS2944	66×74 mm. 100cor. Ice skating (pairs) (39×27 mm)	4·25	3·25

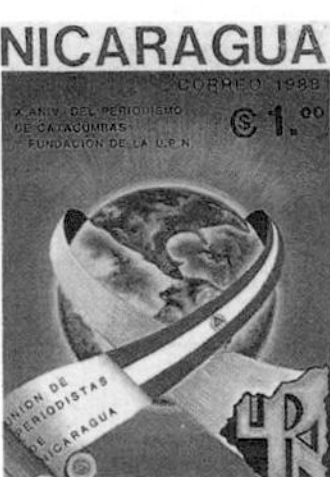

452 Flag around Globe

1988. 10th Anniv of Nicaragua Journalists' Association. Multicoloured.

2945	1cor. Type **452** (postage)	35	15
2946	5cor. Churches of St. Francis Xavier, Sandino and Fatima, Managua, and speaker addressing journalists (42×27 mm) (air)	95	45

453 Basketball

1988. Olympic Games, Seoul. Multicoloured.

2947	10cor. Type **453**	30	15
2948	10cor. Gymnastics	30	15
2949	15cor. Volleyball	55	20
2950	20cor. Long jumping	85	35
2951	25cor. Football	1·10	45
2952	30cor. Water polo	1·20	50
2953	40cor. Boxing	1·80	70

MS2954	70×60 mm. 100cor. Baseball (39×31 mm)	4·25	3·25

454 Brown Bear

1988. Mammals and their Young. Multicoloured.

2955	10c. Type **454** (postage)	10	10
2956	15c. Lion	20	15
2957	25c. Cocker spaniel	25	20
2958	50c. Wild boar	30	25
2959	4cor. Cheetah (air)	1·30	35
2960	7cor. Spotted hyena	1·80	80
2961	8cor. Red fox	2·10	85
MS2962	61×71 mm. 15cor. Kittens (31×39 mm)	4·25	3·25

455 Slide Tackle

1988. "Essen '88" International Stamp Fair and European Football Championship, Germany. Mult.

2963	50c. Type **455** (postage)	20	10
2964	1cor. Footballers	30	15
2965	2cor. Lining up shot (vert) (air)	45	20
2966	3cor. Challenging for ball (vert)	75	25
2967	4cor. Heading ball (vert)	1·10	35
2968	5cor. Tackling (vert)	1·40	45
2969	6cor. Opponent winning possession	1·60	50
MS2970	58×71 mm. 15cor. Players challenging goalkeeper (31×39 mm)	4·25	3·25

456 Bell JetRanger III (image scaled to 72% of original size)

1988. "Finlandia 88" International Stamp Exhibition, Helsinki. Helicopters. Multicoloured.

2971	4cor. Type **456** (postage)	35	10
2972	12cor. MBB-Kawasaki BK-117A-3 (air)	35	15
2973	16cor. Boeing-Vertol B-360	55	20
2974	20cor. Agusta A.109 MR11	70	25
2975	24cor. Sikorsky S-61N	85	30
2976	28cor. Aerospatiale SA.365 Dauphin 2	95	35
2977	56cor. Sikorsky S-76 Spirit	2·00	70
MS2978	97×52 mm. 120cor. "NH-90" (39×31 mm)	4·25	3·25

457 Flags and Map

1988. 9th Anniv of Revolution. Multicoloured.

2979	1cor. Type **457** (postage)	30	15
2980	5cor. Landscape and hands releasing dove (air)	95	35

458 Casimiro Sotelo Montenegro

1988. Revolutionaries.

2981	**458**	4cor. blue (postage)	20	10
2982	-	12cor. mauve (air)	30	10
2983	-	16cor. green	35	15
2984	-	20cor. red	45	20
2985	-	24cor. brown	55	25
2986	-	28cor. violet	65	35
2987	-	50cor. red	1·10	55
2988	-	100cor. purple	2·20	1·10

DESIGNS: 12cor. Ricardo Morales Aviles; 16cor. Silvio Mayorga Delgado; 20cor. Pedro Arauz Palacios; 24cor. Oscar A. Turcios Chavarrias; 28cor. Julio C. Buitrago Urroz; 50cor. Jose B. Escobar Perez; 100cor. Eduardo E. Contreras Escobar.

459 "Acacia baileyana"

1988. Flowers. Multicoloured.

2989	4cor. Type **459** (postage)	20	10
2990	12cor. "Anigozanthos manglesii" (air)	35	15
2991	16cor. "Telopia speciosissima"	45	20
2992	20cor. "Eucalyptus ficifolia"	60	25
2993	24cor. "Boronia heterophylla"	70	30
2994	28cor. "Callistemon speciosus"	80	40
2995	30cor. "Nymphaea caerulea" (horiz)	90	45
2996	50cor. "Clianthus formosus"	1·30	60

460 West Indian Fighting Conch

1988. Molluscs. Multicoloured.

2997	4cor. Type **460** (postage)	30	10
2998	12cor. Painted polymita (air)	35	15
2999	16cor. Giant sundial	55	20
3000	20cor. Japanese baking oyster	75	25
3001	24cor. Yoka star shell	1·00	35
3002	28cor. Gawdy frog shell	1·10	40
3003	50cor. Mantled top	1·90	60

461 Zapotecan Funeral Urn

1988. 500th Anniv (1992) of Discovery of America by Columbus (3rd issue). Multicoloured.

3004	4cor. Type **461** (postage)	25	10
3005	12cor. Mochican ceramic seated figure (air)	45	15
3006	16cor. Mochican ceramic head	60	20
3007	20cor. Tainan ceramic vessel	75	25
3008	28cor. Nazcan vessel (horiz)	95	35
3009	100cor. Incan ritual pipe (horiz)	2·75	1·10
MS3010	100×65 mm. 120cor. Aztec ceramic head (39×31 mm)	4·25	3·25

462 "Chrysina macropus"

1988. Beetles. Multicoloured.

3011	4cor. Type **462** (postage)	30	10
3012	12cor. "Plusiotis victoriana" (air)	35	15
3013	16cor. "Ceratotrupes bolivari"	60	20
3014	20cor. "Gymnetosoma stellata"	80	25
3015	24cor. "Euphoria lineoligera"	1·00	35
3016	28cor. "Euphoria candezei"	1·10	45
3017	50cor. "Sulcophanaeus chryseicollis"	1·90	55

463 Dario

1988. Air. Centenary of Publication of "Blue" by Ruben Dario.

3018	**463**	25cor. multicoloured	1·20	25

464 Simon Bolivar, Jose Marti, Gen. Sandino and Fidel Castro

1989. Air. 30th Anniv of Cuban Revolution.

3019	**464**	20cor. multicoloured	1·10	25

465 Pochomil Tourist Centre

1989. Tourism. Multicoloured.

3020	4cor. Type **465** (postage)	20	10
3021	12cor. Granada Tourist Centre (air)	45	15
3022	20cor. Olof Palme Convention Centre	65	20
3023	24cor. Masaya Volcano National Park	70	25
3024	28cor. La Boquita Tourist Centre	90	30
3025	30cor. Xiloa Tourist Centre	1·00	35
3026	50cor. Managua Hotel	1·50	60
MS3027	101×50 mm. 160cor. Beach, Montelimar International Tourist Centre (39×31 mm)	4·25	3·25

466 Footballers

1989. Air. World Cup Football Championship, Italy (1990).

3028	**466**	100cor. multicoloured	20	15
3029	-	200cor. multicoloured	25	20
3030	-	600cor. multicoloured	30	25
3031	-	1000cor. multicoloured	45	30
3032	-	2000cor. multicoloured	95	45
3033	-	3000cor. multicoloured	1·40	50
3034	-	5000cor. multicoloured	2·10	70
MS3035		90×70 mm. 9000cor. multicoloured (31×39 mm)	4·25	3·00

DESIGNS: 200cor. to 9000cor. Different footballers.

467 Downhill Skiing

1989. Air. Winter Olympic Games, Albertville (1992) (1st issue). Multicoloured.

3036	50cor. Type **467**	45	10
3037	300cor. Ice hockey	50	15
3038	600cor. Ski jumping	55	20
3039	1000cor. Ice skating	65	25
3040	2000cor. Biathlon	90	35
3041	3000cor. Slalom	1·20	45
3042	5000cor. Skiing	1·60	60
MS3043	86×65 mm. 9000cor. Two-man bobsleighing (31×39 mm)	3·50	2·50

See also Nos. 3184/**MS**3191.

468 Water Polo

1989. Air. Olympic Games, Barcelona (1992). Mult.

3044	100cor. Type **468**	45	10
3045	200cor. Running	50	15
3046	600cor. Diving	55	20
3047	1000cor. Gymnastics	65	25
3048	2000cor. Weightlifting	90	35
3049	3000cor. Volleyball	1·20	45
3050	5000cor. Wrestling	1·60	60
MS3051	80×60 mm. 9000cor. Hockey (31×39 mm)	3·50	2·50

See also Nos. 3192/**MS**3199.

469 Procession of States General at Versailles

1989. "Philexfrance 89" International Stamp Exhibition, Paris, and Bicentenary of French Revolution. Multicoloured.

3052	50cor. Type **469** (postage)	20	10
MS3053	66×96 mm. 9000cor. Words and score of "The Marseille" (28×36 mm)	4·75	4·00
3054	300cor. Oath of the Tennis Court (36×28 mm) (air)	30	15
3055	600cor. "The 14th of July" (29×40 mm)	35	20
3056	1000cor. Tree of Liberty (36×28 mm)	50	25
3057	2000cor. "Liberty guiding the People" (Eugene Delacroix) (29×40 mm)	95	35
3058	3000cor. Storming the Bastille (36×28 mm)	1·50	50
3059	5000cor. Lafayette taking oath (28×36 mm)	2·40	80

470 American Darter

1989. Air. "Brasiliana 89" International Stamp Exhibition, Rio de Janeiro. Birds. Multicoloured.

3060	100cor. Type **470**	20	15
3061	200cor. Swallow-tailed kite	25	15
3062	600cor. Turquoise-browed motmot	30	20
3063	1000cor. Painted redstart	45	25
3064	2000cor. Great antshrike (horiz)	95	35
3065	3000cor. Northern royal flycatcher	1·40	50
3066	5000cor. White-flanked antwren (horiz)	2·30	85
MS3067	61×91 mm. 9000cor. Yellow-crowned amazon (31×39 mm)	3·75	2·20

471 Anniversary Emblem

1989. Air. 10th Anniv of Revolution. Multicoloured.

3068	300r. Type **471**	20	15
MS3069	97×77 mm. 9000cor. Concepcion volcano (36×28 mm)	3·25	2·20

472 Animal-shaped Vessel

1989. Air. America. Pre-Columbian Artefacts.

3070	**472**	2000cor. multicoloured	85	25

Currency Reform. 150000 (old) cordoba = 1 (new) cordoba

The following issues, denominated in the old currency, were distributed by agents but were not issued (each set consists of seven values and is dated "1990"):

"London 90" International Stamp Exn. Ships
World Cup Football Championship, Italy
Olympic Games, Barcelona (1992)
Fungi
Winter Olympic Games, Albertville (1992)

473 Little Spotted Kiwi

1991. "New Zealand 1990" International Stamp Exhibition, Auckland. Birds. Multicoloured.

3071	5c. Type **473**	20	10
3072	5c. Takahe	20	10
3073	10c. Red-fronted parakeet	30	15
3074	20c. Weka rail	45	25
3075	30c. Kagu (vert)	85	45
3076	60c. Kea	1·60	85
3077	70c. Kakapo	1·90	1·10
MS3078	90×68 mm. 1cor.51 Black swan (40×31 mm)	4·75	3·25

474 Jaguar

1991. 45th Anniv of Food and Agriculture Organization. Animals. Multicoloured.

3079	5c. Type **474**	20	10
3080	5c. Ocelot (vert)	20	10
3081	10c. Black-handed spider monkey (vert)	30	15
3082	20c. Baird's tapir	50	20
3083	30c. Nine-banded armadillo	90	35
3084	60c. Coyote	1·80	80
3085	70c. Two-toed sloth	2·00	90

475 Dr. Chamorro

1991. Dr. Pedro Joaquin Chamorro (campaigner for an independent Press).

3086	**475**	2cor.25 multicoloured	1·10	45

1991. Flowers. As T 356 but with currency inscribed in "oro".

3087	-	1cor. blue	40	15
3088	-	2cor. green	85	15
3089	-	3cor. brown	1·30	15
3090	-	4cor. purple	1·70	15
3091	-	5cor. red	2·10	20
3092	-	6cor. green	2·30	20
3093	**356**	7cor. blue	3·00	20
3094	-	8cor. green	3·25	20
3095	-	9cor. green	3·75	25
3096	-	10cor. violet	4·25	25
3097	-	11cor. mauve	4·75	25
3098	-	12cor. yellow	5·00	30
3099	-	13cor. red	5·50	30
3100	-	14cor. green	5·75	30
3101	-	15cor. mauve	6·25	35
3102	-	16cor. black	6·75	35

DESIGNS: 1cor. "Stachytarpheta indica"; 2cor. "Cochlospermum sp."; 3cor. "Senecio sp."; 4cor. "Sobralia macrantha"; 5cor. Frangipani; 6cor. "Brassavola nodosa"; 8cor. "Malvaviscus arboreus"; 9cor. "Cattleya lueddemanniana"; 10cor. "Tabebula ochraceae"; 11cor. "Laelia sp."; 12cor. African marigold; 13cor. Chinese hibiscus; 14cor. "Thumbergia alata"; 15cor. "Tecoma stans"; 16cor. "Bixa orellana".

476 Steam Locomotive, 1920s, Peru

1991. Steam Locomotives of South and Central America. Multicoloured.

3103	25c. Type **476**	20	15
3104	25c. Locomotive No. 508, 1917, Bolivia	20	15
3105	50c. Class N/O locomotive, 1910s, Argentina	35	20
3106	1cor.50 Locomotive, 1952, Chile	60	35
3107	2cor. Locomotive No. 61, 1944, Colombia	80	45
3108	3cor. Locomotive No. 311, 1947, Brazil	1·20	50
3109	3cor.50 Locomotive No. 60, 1910, Paraguay	1·40	80
MS3110	Two sheets each 100×70 mm. (a) 7cor.50 Guatemala; (b) 7cor.50 Nicaragua	7·00	5·25

477 Match Scene (West Germany versus Netherlands)

1991. West Germany, Winners of World Cup Football Championship (1990). Multicoloured.

3111	25c. Type **477**	10	10
3112	25c. Match scene (West Germany versus Colombia) (vert)	10	10
3113	50c. West German players and referee	20	15
3114	1cor. West German players forming wall (vert)	45	20
3115	1cor.50 Diego Maradona (Argentina) (vert)	70	35
3116	3cor. Argentinian players and Italian goalkeeper (vert)	1·50	65
3117	3cor.50 Italian players	1·80	80
MS3118	100×70 mm. 7cor.50 West German team celebrating with World Cup trophy	3·50	1·90

478 "Prepona praeneste"

1991. Butterflies. Multicoloured.

3119	25c. Type **478**	10	10
3120	25c. "Anartia fatima"	10	10
3121	50c. "Eryphanis aesacus"	25	15
3122	1cor. "Heliconius melpomene"	45	20
3123	1cor.50 "Chlosyne janais"	70	25
3124	3cor. "Marpesia iole"	1·40	65
3125	3cor.50 Rusty-tipped page	1·80	85
MS3126	100×70 mm. 7cor.50 Emperor	3·50	1·90

479 Dove and Cross

1991. 700th Anniv of Swiss Confederation.

3127	**479**	2cor.25 red, black and yellow	1·10	80

480 Yellow-headed Amazon

1991. "Rainforest is Life". Fauna. Multicoloured.

3128	2cor.25 Type **480**	95	45
3129	2cor.25 Keel-billed toucan	95	45
3130	2cor.25 Scarlet macaw	95	45
3131	2cor.25 Resplendent quetzal	95	45
3132	2cor.25 Black-handed spider monkey	95	45
3133	2cor.25 White-throated capuchin	95	45
3134	2cor.25 Three-toed sloth	95	45
3135	2cor.25 Chestnut-headed oropendola	95	45
3136	2cor.25 Violet sabrewing	95	45
3137	2cor.25 Tamandua	95	45
3138	2cor.25 Jaguarundi	95	45
3139	2cor.25 Boa constrictor	95	45
3140	2cor.25 Common iguana	95	45
3141	2cor.25 Jaguar	95	45
3142	2cor.25 White-necked jacobin	95	45
3143	2cor.25 "Doxocopa clothilda" (butterfly)	95	45
3144	2cor.25 "Dismorphia deione" (butterfly)	95	45
3145	2cor.25 Golden arrow-poison frog	95	45
3146	2cor.25 "Callithomia hezia" (butterfly)	95	45
3147	2cor.25 Chameleon	95	45

Nos. 3128/47 were issued together, se-tenant, forming a composite design.

481 "Isochilus major"

1991. Orchids. Multicoloured.

3148	25c. Type **481**	10	10
3149	25c. "Cycnoches ventricosum"	10	10
3150	50c. "Vanilla odorata"	25	15
3151	1cor. "Helleriella nicaraguensis"	45	25
3152	1cor.50 "Barkeria spectabilis"	65	35
3153	3cor. "Maxillaria hedwigae"	1·30	60
3154	3cor.50 "Cattleya aurantiaca"	1·50	1·20
MS3155	100×70 mm. 7cor.50 *Psygmorchis pusilla* (27×41 mm)	3·25	1·90

482 Concepcion Volcano

1991. America (1990).

3156	**482**	2cor.25 multicoloured	1·10	50

483 Warehouse and Flags

1991. 30th Anniv of Central American Bank of Economic Integration.

3157	**483**	1cor.50 multicoloured	75	50

484 "The One-eyed Man"

1991. Death Centenary (1990) of Vincent van Gogh (painter). Multicoloured.

3158	25c. Type **484**	10	10
3159	25c. "Head of Countrywoman with Bonnet"	10	10
3160	50c. "Self-portrait"	30	15
3161	1cor. "Vase with Carnations and other Flowers"	45	20
3162	1cor.50 "Vase with Zinnias and Geraniums"	70	25
3163	3cor. "Portrait of Tanguy Father"	1·40	55
3164	3cor.50 "Portrait of a Man" (horiz)	1·60	70
MS3165	127×102 mm. 7cor.50 "Footpath with Poplars". Imperf	3·00	1·80

485 Painting by Rafaela Herrera (1st-prize winner)

1991. National Children's Painting Competition.

3166	**485**	2cor.25 multicoloured	1·10	45

486 Golden Pavilion

1991. "Phila Nippon '91" International Stamp Exhibition, Tokyo. Multicoloured.

3167	25c. Type **486**	10	10
3168	50c. Himaji Castle	25	15
3169	1cor. Head of Bunraku doll	35	20
3170	1cor.50 Japanese cranes	65	25
3171	2cor.50 Phoenix pavilion	1·00	45
3172	3cor. "The Guardian" (statue)	1·30	50
3173	3cor.50 Kabuki actor	1·50	70
MS3174	100×71 mm. 7cor.50 Mizusashi vase	3·00	2·40

487 Turquoise-browed Motmot

1992. Birds. Multicoloured.

3175	50c. Type **487**	20	15
3176	75c. Collared trogon	30	15
3177	1cor. Broad-billed motmot	35	20
3178	1cor.50 Wire-tailed manakin	55	25
3179	1cor.75 Paradise tanager (horiz)	75	35
3180	2cor.25 Resplendent quetzal	1·40	65
3181	2cor.25 Black-spotted bare-eye	1·40	65
MS3182	Two sheets each 100×70 mm. (a) 7cor.50 Crimson-rumped toucanet; (b) 7cor.50 Spotted antbird	7·00	5·25

488 Columbus's Fleet

1992. America (1991). Voyages of Discovery.

3183	**488**	2cor.25 multicoloured	1·10	65

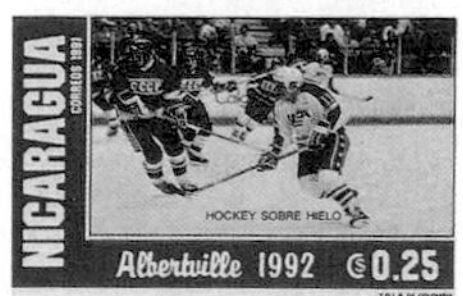

489 Ice Hockey

1992. Winter Olympic Games, Albertville (2nd issue). Multicoloured.

3184	25c. Type **489**	20	10
3185	25c. Four-man bobsleighing	20	10
3186	50c. Skiing (vert)	30	15
3187	1cor. Speed skating	45	25
3188	1cor.50 Cross-country skiing	70	35
3189	3cor. Double luge	1·40	65
3190	3cor.50 Ski jumping (vert)	1·50	80
MS3191	100×70 mm. 7cor.50 Skiing. Imperf	3·00	1·70

490 Fencing

1992. Olympic Games, Barcelona (2nd issue) Mult.

3192	25c. Type **490**	20	15
3193	25c. Throwing the javelin (horiz)	20	15
3194	50c. Basketball	30	20
3195	1cor.50 Running	70	35
3196	2cor. Long jumping	90	45
3197	3cor. Running	1·30	50
3198	3cor.50 Show jumping	1·40	80
MS3199	100×70 mm. 7cor.50 Canoeing. Imperf	3·00	1·70

491 Ceramic Vase with Face (Lorenza Pineda Co-operative)

1992. Contemporary Arts and Crafts. Mult.

3200	25c. Type **491**	20	15
3201	25c. Ceramic spouted vessel (Jose Oritz) (horiz)	20	15
3202	50c. Blue-patterned ceramic vase (Elio Gutierrez)	30	20
3203	1cor. "Christ" (Jose de los Santos)	45	25
3204	1cor.50 "Family" (sculpture, Erasmo Moya)	70	35
3205	3cor. "Bird-fish" (Silvio Chavarria Co-operative) (horiz)	1·40	75
3206	3cor.50 Filigree ceramic vessel (Maria de los Angeles Bermudez)	1·50	80
MS3207	100×70 mm., 7cor.50 Masks (Jose Flores). Imperf	3·00	1·70

492 "Picnic Table with Three Objects" (Alejandro Arostegui)

1992. Contemporary Paintings. Multicoloured.

3208	25c. Type **492**	20	15
3209	25c. "Prophetess of the New World" (Alberto Ycaza)	20	15
3210	50c. "Flames of Unknown Origin" (Bernard Dreyfus) (horiz)	30	20
3211	1cor.50 "Owl" (Orlando Sobalvarro) (horiz)	70	35
3212	2cor. "Pegasus at Liberty" (Hugo Palma) (horiz)	90	45
3213	3cor. "Avocados" (Omar d'Leon) (horiz)	1·30	65
3214	3cor.50 "Gueguense" (Carlos Montenegro)	1·40	80
MS3215	100×71 mm. 7cor.50 "Shipment" (Federico Nordalm). Imperf	3·00	1·70

493 Rivoli's Hummingbird

1992. 2nd U.N. Conference on Environment and Development, Rio de Janeiro. Tropical Forest Wildlife. Multicoloured.

3216	1cor.50 Type **493**	60	35
3217	1cor.50 Harpy eagle ("Aguila arpia")	60	35
3218	1cor.50 Orchid	60	35
3219	1cor.50 Keel-billed toucan and morpho butterfly	60	35
3220	1cor.50 Resplendent quetzal	60	35
3221	1cor.50 Guardabarranco	60	35
3222	1cor.50 Howler monkey ("Mono aullador")	60	35
3223	1cor.50 Sloth ("Perezoso")	60	35
3224	1cor.50 Squirrel monkey ("Mono ardilla")	60	35
3225	1cor.50 Blue and yellow macaw ("Guacamaya")	60	35
3226	1cor.50 Emerald boa and scarlet tanager	60	35
3227	1cor.50 Poison-arrow frog	60	35
3228	1cor.50 Jaguar	60	35
3229	1cor.50 Anteater	60	35
3230	1cor.50 Ocelot	60	35
3231	1cor.50 Coati	60	35

Nos. 3216/31 were issued together, se-tenant, forming a composite design of a forest.

494 Fabretto with Children

1992. Father Fabretto, "Benefactor of Nicaraguan Children".

3232	**494**	2cor.25 multicoloured	1·00	45

495 "Nicaraguan Identity" (Claudia Gordillo)

1992. Winning Entry in Photography Competition.

3233	**495**	2cor.25 multicoloured	1·00	45

496 "The Indians of Nicaragua" (Milton Jose Cruz)

1992. Winning Entry in Children's Painting Competition.

3234	**496**	2cor.25 multicoloured	1·00	45

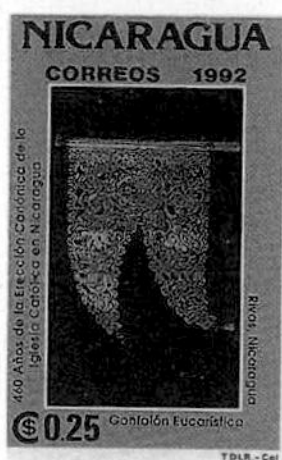

497 Eucharistical Banner

1993. 460th Anniv of Catholic Church in Nicaragua. Multicoloured.

3235	25c. Type **497**	20	15
3236	50c. "Shrine of the Immaculate Conception"	30	20
3237	1cor. 18th-century document	45	25
3238	1cor.50 16th-century baptismal font	70	40
3239	2cor. "The Immaculate Conception"	90	45
3240	2cor.25 Monsignor Diego Alvarez Osorio (1st Bishop of Leon)	1·00	55
3241	3cor. "Christ on the Cross"	1·30	70

498 Rivas Cross, 1523

1993. America (1992). 500th Anniv of Discovery of America by Columbus.

3242	**498**	2cor.25 multicoloured	1·00	45

499 Cathedral

1993. Inauguration of Cathedral of the Immaculate Conception of Mary, Managua. Multicoloured.

3243	3cor. Type **499**	1·10	50
3244	4cor. Cross, Virgin Mary and map of Nicaragua (2nd Provincial Council)	1·50	70

Nos. 3243/4 were issued together, se-tenant, forming a composite design.

500 Emblem and Voters queueing outside Poll Station

1993. 23rd General Assembly of Organization of American States.

3245	**500**	3cor. multicoloured	1·40	80

501 Anniversary Emblem

1993. 90th Anniv of Pan-American Health Organization.

3246	**501**	3cor. multicoloured	1·40	80

502 "Sonatina" (Alma Iris Perez)

1993. Winning Entry in Children's Painting Competition.

3247	**502**	3cor. multicoloured	1·20	85

503 Racoon Buttterflyfish

1993. Butterflyfishes. Multicoloured.

3248	1cor.50 Type **503**	55	30
3249	1cor.50 Rainford's butterflyfish ("Chaetodon rainfordi")	55	30
3250	1cor.50 Mailed butterflyfish ("Chaetodon reticulatus")	55	30
3251	1cor.50 Thread-finned butterflyfish ("Chaetodon auriga")	55	30
3252	1cor.50 Pennant coralfish ("Heniochus acuminatus")	55	30
3253	1cor.50 Dark-banded butterflyfish ("Coradion fulvocinctus")	55	30
3254	1cor.50 Mirror butterflyfish ("Chaetodon speculum")	55	30
3255	1cor.50 Lined butterflyfish ("Chaetodon lineolatus")	55	30
3256	1cor.50 Bennett's butterflyfish ("Chaetodon bennetti")	55	30
3257	1cor.50 Black-backed butterflyfish ("Chaetodon melanotus")	55	30
3258	1cor.50 Golden butterflyfish ("Chaetodon aureus")	55	30
3259	1cor.50 Saddle butterflyfish ("Chaetodon ephippium")	55	30
3260	1cor.50 Pyramid butterflyfish ("Hemitaurichthys polylepis")	55	30
3261	1cor.50 Dotted butterflyfish ("Chaetodon semeion")	55	30
3262	1cor.50 Klein's butterflyfish ("Chaetodon kleinii")	55	30
3263	1cor.50 Copper-banded butterflyfish ("Chelmon rostratus")	55	30

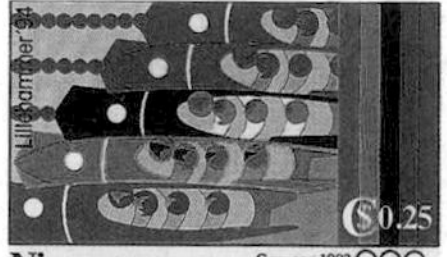

504 Four-man Bobsleigh

1993. Multicoloured. (a) Winter Olympic Games, Lillehammer, Norway (1994).

3264	25c. Type **504**	20	10
3265	25c. Skiing	20	10
3266	50c. Speed skating	30	15
3267	1cor.50 Ski jumping	70	40
3268	2cor. Women's figure skating	90	45
3269	3cor. Pairs' figure skating	1·30	70
3270	3cor.50 Shooting (biathlon)	1·40	90

(b) Olympic Games, Atlanta (1996).

3271	25c. Swimming	20	10
3272	25c. Diving	20	10
3273	50c. Long distance running	30	15
3274	1cor. Hurdling	70	40
3275	1cor.50 Gymnastics	90	45
3276	3cor. Throwing the javelin	1·30	70
3277	3cor.50 Sprinting	1·40	90
MS3278	Two sheets each 100×70 mm. (a) 7cor.50 Flags; (b) 7cor.50 Olympic torch and hands	6·75	4·25

505 "Bromeliaceae sp."

1994. Tropical Forest Flora and Fauna. Mult.

3279	2cor. Type **505**	75	45
3280	2cor. Sparkling-tailed humming-bird ("Tilmatura dupontii")	75	45
3281	2cor. "Anolis biporcatus" (lizard)	75	45
3282	2cor. Lantern fly ("Fulgara laternaria")	75	45
3283	2cor. Sloth ("Bradypus sp.")	75	45
3284	2cor. Ornate hawk eagle ("Spizaetus ornatus")	75	45
3285	2cor. Lovely cotinga ("Cotinga amabilis")	75	45
3286	2cor. Schegel's lance-head snake ("Bothrops schlegelii")	75	45
3287	2cor. "Odontoglossum sp." (orchid) and bee	75	45
3288	2cor. Red-eyed tree frog ("Agalychnis callidryas")	75	45
3289	2cor. "Heliconius sapho" (butterfly)	75	45
3290	2cor. Passion flower ("Passiflora vitifolia")	75	45
MS3291	Two sheets each 105×77 mm. (a) 10cor. Agouti; (b) 10cor. "Melinaea lilies" (butterfly)	8·50	5·25

Nos. 3279/90 were issued together, se-tenant, forming a composite design.

506 Tomas Brolin (Sweden)

1994. World Cup Football Championship, U.S.A. Players.

3292	50c. Type **506**	30	15
3293	1cor. Jan Karas (Poland) and Antonio Luiz Costa (Brazil)	45	30
3294	1cor. Maxime Bossis and Michel Platini (France)	45	30
3295	1cor.50 Harold Schumacher (Germany)	75	40
3296	2cor. Andoni Zubizarreta (Spain)	95	50
3297	2cor.50 Lothar Matthaeus (Germany) and Diego Maradona (Argentine Republic)	1·20	70
3298	3cor.50 Bryan Robson (England) and Carlos Santos (Portugal)	1·60	85
MS3299	71×100 mm. 10cor. Carlos Valderrama (Colombia)	5·00	3·50

507 "Four in One" (Julio Lopez)

1994. Contemporary Arts. Multicoloured.

3300	50c. Rush mat (Rosalia Sevilla) (horiz)	15	10
3301	50c. Type **507**	15	10
3302	1cor. Ceramic church (Auxiliadora Bush)	35	25
3303	1cor. Statuette of old woman (Indiana Robleto)	35	25
3304	2cor.50 "Santiago" (Jose de los Santos)	85	45
3305	3cor. "Gueguense" (Ines Gutierrez de Chong)	1·00	60
3306	4cor. Ceramic hornet's nest (Elio Gutierrez)	1·30	75
MS3307	100×70 mm. 10cor. "Metate" (grinding stone) (Saul Carballo). Imperf	3·75	2·30

508 "Callicore patelina"

1994. "Hong Kong '94" International Stamp Exhibition. Butterflies. Multicoloured.

3308	1cor.50 Type **508**	50	30
3309	1cor.50 "Chlosyne narva"	50	30
3310	1cor.50 Giant brimstone ("Anteos maerula")	50	30
3311	1cor.50 Diadem ("Marpesia petreus")	50	30
3312	1cor.50 "Pierella helvetia"	50	30
3313	1cor.50 "Eurytides epidaus"	50	30
3314	1cor.50 Doris ("Heliconius doris")	50	30
3315	1cor.50 "Smyrna blomfildia"	50	30
3316	1cor.50 "Eueides lybia olympia"	50	30
3317	1cor.50 "Adelpha heraclea"	50	30
3318	1cor.50 "Heliconius hecale zuleika"	50	30
3319	1cor.50 "Parides montezuma"	50	30
3320	1cor.50 "Morpho polyphemus"	50	30
3321	1cor.50 "Eresia alsina"	50	30
3322	1cor.50 "Prepona omphale octavia"	50	30
3323	1cor.50 "Morpho grenadensis"	50	30

509 "The Holy Family" (anonymous)

1994. Christmas (1993). Paintings. Multicoloured.

3324	1cor. Type **509**	25	15
3325	4cor. "Nativity" (Lezamon)	1·10	50

510 Sculpture

1994. Chontal Culture Statuary. Multicoloured, colour of frame given.

3326	**510**	50c. yellow	15	10
3327	-	50c. yellow	15	10
3328	-	1cor. emerald	35	25
3329	-	1cor. green	35	25
3330	-	2cor.50 blue	85	45
3331	-	3cor. blue	1·00	60
3332	-	4cor. green	1·50	75
MS3333		100×70 mm. 10cor. Twin totems. Imperf	3·00	1·40

DESIGNS: 50c. (3327) to 10cor. Different sculptures.

511 "Virgin of Nicaragua" (Celia Lacayo)

1994. Contemporary Paintings. Multicoloured.

3334	50c. Type **511**	15	10
3335	50c. "Woman embroidering" (Guillermo Rivas Navas)	15	10
3336	1cor. "Couple dancing" (June Beer)	35	25
3337	1cor. "Song of Peace" (Alejandro Canales)	35	25
3338	2cor.50 "Sapodilla Plums" (Genaro Lugo) (horiz)	85	45
3339	3cor. "Figure and Fragments" (Leonel Vanegas)	1·00	60
3340	4cor. "Eruption of Agua Volcano" (Asilia Guillen) (horiz)	1·30	75
MS3341	100×70 mm. 10cor. "Still-life" (Alejandro Alonso Rochi). Imperf	3·00	1·40

512 Nicolas Copernicus and Satellite

1994. Astronomers. Multicoloured.

3342	1cor.50 Type **512**	45	25
3343	1cor.50 Tycho Brahe and astronomers	45	25
3344	1cor.50 Galileo Galilei and "Galileo" space probe	45	25
3345	1cor.50 Sir Isaac Newton and telescope	45	25
3346	1cor.50 Edmond Halley, space probe and Halley's Comet	45	25
3347	1cor.50 James Bradley and Greenwich Observatory	45	25
3348	1cor.50 William Herschel and telescope	45	25
3349	1cor.50 John Goodricke and Algol (star)	45	25
3350	1cor.50 Karl Friedrich Gauss and Gottingen Observatory	45	25
3351	1cor.50 Friedrich Bessel and 1838 star telescope	45	25
3352	1cor.50 William Cranch Bond (wrongly inscr "Granch") and Harvard College Observatory	45	25
3353	1cor.50 Sir George Airy and stellar disk	45	25
3354	1cor.50 Percival Lowell and Flagstaff Observatory, Arizona, U.S.A.	45	25
3355	1cor.50 George Hale (wrongly inscr "Halle") and solar spectroscope	45	25
3356	1cor.50 Edwin Hubble and Hubble telescope	45	25
3357	1cor.50 Gerard Kuiper and Miranda (Uranus moon)	45	25
MS3358	144×84 mm. 10cor. Nicolas Copernicus and interstellar probe	3·25	2·50

Nos. 3342/57 were issued together, se-tenant, forming a composite design.

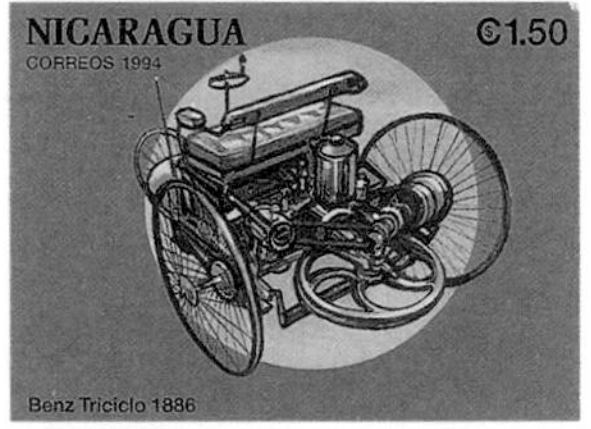

513 1886 Benz Tricycle

1994. Automobiles. Multicoloured.

3359	1cor.50 Type **513**	45	25
3360	1cor.50 1909 Benz Blitzen	45	25
3361	1cor.50 1923 Mercedes Benz 24/100/140	45	25
3362	1cor.50 1928 Mercedes Benz SSK	45	25
3363	1cor.50 1934 Mercedes Benz 500K Cabriolet	45	25
3364	1cor.50 1949 Mercedes Benz 170S	45	25
3365	1cor.50 1954 Mercedes Benz W196	45	25
3366	1cor.50 1954 Mercedes Benz 300SL	45	25
3367	1cor.50 1896 Ford Quadricycle	45	25
3368	1cor.50 1920 Ford taxi cab	45	25
3369	1cor.50 1928 Ford Roadster	45	25
3370	1cor.50 1932 Ford V-8	45	25
3371	1cor.50 1937 Ford V-8 78	45	25
3372	1cor.50 1939 Ford 91 Deluxe Tudor Sedan	45	25
3373	1cor.50 1946 Ford V-8 Sedan Coupe	45	25
3374	1cor.50 1958 Ford Custom 300	45	25
MS3375	120×84 mm. 10cor. Henry Ford, 1903 Ford Model A, Karl Benz and 1897 5CH	3·75	2·20

514 Hugo Eckener and Count Ferdinand von Zeppelin

1994. Zeppelin Airships. Multicoloured.

3376	1cor.50 Type **514**	45	25
3377	1cor.50 "Graf Zeppelin" over New York, 1928	45	25
3378	1cor.50 "Graf Zeppelin" over Tokyo, 1929	45	25
3379	1cor.50 "Graf Zeppelin" over Randolph Hearst's villa, 1929	45	25
3380	1cor.50 Charles Lindbergh, Hugo Eckener and "Graf Zeppelin" at Lakehurst, 1929	45	25
3381	1cor.50 "Graf Zeppelin" over St. Basil's Cathedral, Moscow (wrongly inscr "Santra Sofia")	45	25
3382	1cor.50 "Graf Zeppelin" over Paris, 1930	45	25
3383	1cor.50 "Graf Zeppelin" over Cairo, Egypt, 1931	45	25
3384	1cor.50 "Graf Zeppelin" over Arctic Sea	45	25
3385	1cor.50 "Graf Zeppelin" over Rio de Janeiro, 1932	45	25
3386	1cor.50 "Graf Zeppelin" over St. Paul's Cathedral, London, 1935	45	25
3387	1cor.50 "Graf Zeppelin" over St. Peter's Cathedral, Rome	45	25
3388	1cor.50 "Graf Zeppelin" over Swiss Alps	45	25
3389	1cor.50 "Graf Zeppelin over Brandenburg Gate, Berlin	45	25
3390	1cor.50 Hugo Eckener piloting "Graf Zeppelin"	45	25
3391	1cor.50 Captain Ernest Lehman, "Graf Zeppelin" and Dornier Do-X flying boat	45	25
MS3392	Two sheets each 96×69 mm. (a) 10cor. Hugo Eckener and *Graf Zeppelin*; (b) 10cor. Count Ferdinand von Zeppelin and Airship	6·50	4·25

515 Gabriel Horvilleur

1994. Nicaraguan Philatelists. Multicoloured.

3393	1cor. Type **515**	35	25
3394	3cor. Jose Cuadra	1·00	60
3395	4cor. Alfredo Pertz	1·30	75

516 August 21 1955 Sighting at Kentucky

1994. Alien Sightings. Eight sheets each 105×75 mm containing horiz designs as T 516.

MS3396	Eight sheets. (a) 60cor. Type **516**; (b) 60cor. September 19 1961 sighting, New Hampshire, USA; (c) 60cor. 28 July 1965 sighting, Argentina; (d) 60cor. May 8 1973 sighting, Texas, USA; (e) 60cor. September 22 1976 sighting, Canary Islands; (f) 60cor. October 26 1978 sighting, Pennsylvania, USA; (g) 60cor. November 7 1989 sighting, Kansas, USA; (h) 61cor. July 21 1991 sighting, Missouri, USA	£140	£140

517 "Poponjoche" (Thelma Gomez)

1994. 1st Nicaraguan Tree Conference.

3397	**517**	4cor. multicoloured	1·20	75

518 Conference Emblem

1994. 2nd International Conference on New and Restored Democracies, Managua.

No.	Description	Unused	Used
3398	**518** 3cor. multicoloured	1·00	60

518a Chocolate Point Himalayan

1994. Cats. Two sheets containing T 518a and similar vert designs. Multicoloured.

No.	Description	Unused	Used
MS3399	(a) 146×203 mm. 1cor.50×12, Type **518a**; Somali; American shorthair; Russian blue; Scottish fold; Persian; Egyptian mau; Blue cream Manx; Blue Birman; Seal point Balinese; Blue oriental shorthair; Persian; Angora; Siamese; Two seal point Birman kittens; Devon rex. (b) 136×100 mm. 15cor. Golden Persian (38×50 mm). Set of 2 sheets	13·00	13·00

The stamps of **MS**3399a form a composite design.

519 Pulpit, Leon Cathedral

1994. Religious Art. Multicoloured.

No.	Description	Unused	Used
3400	50c. Type **519**	15	10
3401	50c. "St. Anna" (porcelain figure), Chinandega Church	15	10
3402	1cor. "St. Joseph and Child" (porcelain figure), St. Peter's Church, Rivas	35	25
3403	1cor. "St. James", Jinotepe Church	35	25
3404	2cor.50 Gold chalice, Subtiava Temple, Leon	85	45
3405	3cor. Processional cross, Niquinohomo Church, Masaya	1·00	60
3406	4cor. "Lord of Miracles" (crucifix), Lord of Miracles Temple, Managua	1·30	75
MS3407	100×70 mm. 10cor. Silver altar hanging, St. Peter's Church, Rivas. Imperf	3·25	2·30

520 Mascot and Emblem

1994. 32nd World Amateur Baseball Championship.

No.	Description	Unused	Used
3408	**520** 4cor. multicoloured	1·40	1·30

520a "Verdad" (Aparicio Arthola)

1994. Sculpture. Multicoloured.

No.	Description	Unused	Used
3409	50c. Type **520a**	20	10
3410	1cor. "Buho" (Oelando Sobalvarro)	35	25
3411	1cor.50 "Pequeno Lustrador" (Noel Flores Castro)	55	40
3412	2cor. "Exodo II" (Miguel Angel Abarca)	85	60
3413	2cor.50 "Raza" (Fernando Saravia)	1·00	75
3414	3cor. "Dolor Incognito" (Edith Gron)	1·20	90
3415	4cor. "Garza" (Ernesto Cardenal)	1·60	1·10
MS3416	Two sheets, each 70×100 mm. (a) 15cor. "Atlante" (Jorge Navas Cordonero). Imperf. (b) 15cor. "Maternidad" (Rodrigo Penalba). Imperf. Set of 2 sheets	6·00	6·00

521 Mt. Sorak

1994. "Philakorea 1994" International Stamp Exhibition, Seoul. Views of South Korea. Mult.

No.	Description	Unused	Used
3417	1cor.50 Type **521**	45	25
3418	1cor.50 Bronze Statue of Kim Yu-Shin	45	25
3419	1cor.50 Woedolgae (solitary rock)	45	25
3420	1cor.50 Stream, Mt. Hallasan, Cheju Island	45	25
3421	1cor.50 Mirukpong and Pisondae	45	25
3422	1cor.50 Ch'onbuldong Valley	45	25
3423	1cor.50 Bridge of the Seven Nymphs	45	25
3425	1cor.50 Piryong Waterfall	25	10
MS3425	106×76 mm. 10cor. Child surrounded by food on first birthday	2·75	2·50

522 Piano on Stage

1994. 25th Anniv of Ruben Dario National Theatre, Managua.

No.	Description	Unused	Used
3426	**522** 3cor. multicoloured	1·10	85

523 Tyrannosaurus Rex

1994. Prehistoric Animals. Multicoloured.

No.	Description	Unused	Used
3427	1cor.50 Type **523**	45	25
3428	1cor.50 Plateosaurus	45	25
3429	1cor.50 Pteranodon	45	25
3430	1cor.50 Camarasaurus	45	25
3431	1cor.50 Euplocephalus	45	25
3432	1cor.50 Sacuanjoche	45	25
3433	1cor.50 Deinonychus	45	25
3434	1cor.50 Chasmosaurus	45	25
3435	1cor.50 Dimorphodon	45	25
3436	1cor.50 Ametriorhynchids	45	25
3437	1cor.50 Ichthyosaurus	45	25
3438	1cor.50 Pterapsis and compsognathus	45	25
3439	1cor.50 Cephalopod	45	25
3440	1cor.50 Archelon	45	25
3441	1cor.50 Griphognatus and gyroptychius	45	25
3442	1cor.50 Plesiosaur and nautiloid	45	25

Nos. 3427/42 were issued together, se-tenant, forming a composite design.

523a Chapel, Granada

1994. Cultural Heritage. Multicoloured.

No.	Description	Unused	Used
3443	50c. Type **523a**	20	10
3444	1cor. San Francisco Convent, Granada (horiz)	35	25
3445	1cor.50 Santiago tower, Leon	55	40
3446	2cor. Santa Ana parish church, Nindiri (horiz)	85	60
3447	2cor.50 Santa Ana parish church, Nandaime	1·00	75
3448	3cor. Arched doorway, Los Leones, Granada (horiz)	1·20	90
3449	4cor. La Inmaculada Concepcion castle, Rio San Juan (horiz)	1·60	1·10
MS3450	100×70 mm. 15cor. San Jacinto hacienda, Managua. Imperf	6·00	6·00

523b Rai (Brazil)

1994. World Cup Football Championships, USA. Three sheets containing T 523 and similar multicoloured designs showing players.

No.	Description	Unused	Used
MS3451	(a) 149×120 mm. 3cor.×8, Type **523b**; Freddy Rincon (Colombia); Luis Garcia (Mexico); Thomas Dooley (USA); Franco Barest (Italy); Tony Meola (USA); Enzo Francescoli (Uruguay); Roy Wegerle (USA). (b) 70×100 mm. 10cor. Faustino Asprilla (Colombia). (c) 106×76 mm. 10cor. Aldolfo Valencia (Colombia) (horiz). Set of 3 sheets	15·00	15·00

524 Hawker Typhoon 1B

1994. 50th Anniv of D-Day. Multicoloured.

No.	Description	Unused	Used
3452	3cor. Type **524**	1·10	70
3453	3cor. Douglas C-47 Skytrain transport dropping paratroops	1·10	70
3454	3cor. H.M.S. "Mauritius" (cruiser) bombarding Houlgate, Normandy	1·10	70
3455	3cor. Formation of Mulberry Harbours to transport supplies to beach	1·10	70
3456	3cor. British AVRE Churchill tank	1·10	70
3457	3cor. Tank landing craft	1·10	70

525 Renate Stecher (women's 200 m, 1972)

1994. Centenary of International Olympic Committee. Gold Medal Winners. Multicoloured.

No.	Description	Unused	Used
3458	3cor.50 Type **525**	1·70	1·00
3459	3cor.50 Cassius Clay (Muhammad Ali) (boxing, 1960)	1·70	1·00
MS3460	106×76 mm. 10cor. Claudia Pechstein (5000 metres speed skating, 1994)	3·75	3·75

526 Detachment of Command module "Eagle"

1994. 25th Anniv of First Manned Moon Landing. Multicoloured.

No.	Description	Unused	Used
3461	3cor. Type **526**	95	50
3462	3cor. Launch of "Saturn V", Cape Canaveral, Florida	95	50
3463	3cor. Command module orbiting Moon	95	50
3464	3cor. Footprint on Moon	95	50
3465	3cor. Primary space capsule separating	95	50
3466	3cor. Command module	95	50
3467	3cor. Lunar module landing on Moon	95	50
3468	3cor. Astronaut on Moon	95	50
MS3469	Two sheets each 81×116 mm. (a) 10cor. Buzz Aldrin, Neil Armstrong and Michael Collins (crew) (46×28 mm); (b) 10cor. Astronaut on Moon saluting American flag (28×46 mm)	7·50	7·50

527 "The Death Cart" (Erick Joanello Montoya)

1994. 1st Prize in Children's Painting Competition.

No.	Description	Unused	Used
3470	**527** 4cor. multicoloured	1·40	85

528 Black-crowned Night Heron

1994. Woodland Animals. Multicoloured.

No.	Description	Unused	Used
3471	2cor. Type **528**	65	35
3472	2cor. Scarlet macaw ("Ara macao")	65	35
3473	2cor. Cattle egrets ("Bubulcus ibis") (wrongly inscr "Bulbulcus")	65	35
3474	2cor. American black vultures ("Coragyps atratus")	65	35
3475	2cor. Brazilian rainbow boa ("Epicrates cenchria")	65	35
3476	2cor. Red-legged honeycreepers ("Cyanerpes cyaneus")	65	35
3477	2cor. Plain chachalaca ("Ortalis vetula")	65	35
3478	2cor. Sloth ("Bradypus griseus")	65	35
3479	2cor. Jaguar ("Felis onca")	65	35
3480	2cor. American darter ("Anhinga anhinga")	65	35
3481	2cor. Baird's tapir ("Tapirus bairdi")	65	35
3482	2cor. Anteater ("Myrmecophaga jubata")	65	35
3483	2cor. Iguana ("Iguana iguaana")	65	35
3484	2cor. Snapping turtle ("Chelydra serpentina")	65	35
3485	2cor. Red-billed whistling ducks ("Dendrocygna autumnalis")	65	35
3486	2cor. Ocelot ("Felis pardalis")	65	35
MS3487	100×70 mm. 15cor. American anhingas (as central motif of No. 3462)	4·25	4·25

Nos. 3471/86 were issued together, se-tenant, forming a composite design.

529 "The Kid" (dir. Charlie Chaplin)

1994. Centenary of Motion Pictures. Multicoloured.

3488 2cor. Type **529** 65 35
3489 2cor. "Citizen Kane" (dir. Orson Welles) 65 35
3490 2cor. "Lawrence of Arabia" (dir. David Lean) 65 35
3491 2cor. "Ivan the Terrible" (dir. Sergio Eisenstein) 65 35
3492 2cor. "Metropolis" (dir. Fritz Lang) 65 35
3493 2cor. "The Ten Commandments" (dir. Cecil B. De Mille) 65 35
3494 2cor. "Gandhi" (dir. Richard Attenborough) 65 35
3495 2cor. "Casablanca" (dir. Michael Curtiz) 65 35
3496 2cor. "Platoon" (dir. Oliver Stone) 65 35
3497 2cor. "The Godfather" (dir. Francis Ford Coppola) 65 35
3498 2cor. "2001: A Space Odyssey" (dir. Stanley Kubrick) 65 35
3499 2cor. "The Ocean Depths" (dir. Jean Renoir) 65 35
MS3500 80×109 mm. 15cor. "Gone with the Wind" (dir. Victor Fleming) 4·75 4·75

530 "Discovery of America"

1994. 15th Death Anniv of Rodrigo Penalba (artist). Multicoloured.

3501 50c. Type **530** 20 10
3502 1cor. "Portrait of Mauricio" 35 15
3503 1cor.50 "Portrait of Franco" 55 25
3504 2cor. "Portrait of Mimi Hammer" 75 35
3505 2cor.50 "Seated Woman" 95 45
3506 3cor. "Still-life" (horiz) 1·10 50
3507 4cor. "Portrait of Maria Augusta" 1·50 70
MS3508 70×100 mm. 15cor. "Entrance to Anticoli" (66×96 mm). Imperf 3·75 3·75

531 Hen and Cock

1994. Endangered Species. The Highland Guan. Multicoloured.

3509 50c. Type **531** 20 10
3510 1cor. Cock 35 15
3511 2cor.50 Hen 1·00 50
3512 3cor. Cock and hen (different) 1·20 60
MS3513 100×70 mm. 15cor. Heads of cock and hen 5·75 5·75

532 M.W. Jung

1995. Korea Baseball Championship. Eight sheets, each 147×200 mm containing T 532 and similar vert designs showing players and team emblems. Multicoloured.

MS3514 (a) 3cor.50×9, Type **532**; K.K. Kim; H.J. Kim; M.T. Chung; Pacific Dolphins emblem; B.W. An; D.G. Yoon; S.D. Choi; D.K. Kim. (b) 3cor.50×9, J.H. Jang; Y.D. Han; K.D. Lee; J.S. Park; Hanwha Eagles emblem; M.C. Jeong; J.W. Song; J.G. Kang; D.S. Koo. (c) 3cor.50×9, R.J. Park; K.J. Cho; K.T. Kim; W.H. Kim; Raiders emblem; I.H. Baik; S.K. Park; K.L. Kim; J.S. Park. (d) 3cor.50×9, J.I. Ryu; S.Y. Kim; S.R. Kim; B.C. Dong; Samsung Lions emblem; K.W. Kang; C.S. Park; J.H. Yang; T.H. Kim.(e) 3cor.50×9, D.H. Han; Y.S. Kim; J.H. Yoo; Y.B. Seo; LG Twins emblem; J.H. Park; S.H. Lee; D.S. Kim; J.H. Kim. (f) 3cor.50×9, H.K. Yoon; D.H. Park; H.K. Joo; E.G. Kim; Lotte Giants emblem; J.T. Park; P.S. Kong; J.S. Yeom; M.H. Kim. (g) 3.50×9, D.Y Sun; J.B. Lee; J.S. Kim; S.H. Kim; Haitai Tigers emblem; G.C. Lee; G.H. Cho; S.H. Kim (different); S.C. Lee. (h) 3cor.50×9, M.S. Lee; C.S. Park; H.S. Lim; K.W. Kim; OB Bears emblem; J.S. Kim; T.H. Kim; H.S. Kim; S.J. Kim. Set of 8 sheets 95·00 95·00

533 "Avanzamos Hacia El Siglo 21" (Maria Jose Zamora)

1995. FUNCOD (environmental organization) Art Prize. Multicoloured.

3515 1cor. Type**533** 35 15
3516 2cor. "Naturaleza Muerta" (Rafael Castellon) 65 35
3517 4cor. "Aguas Cautivas" (Alvaro Gutierrez) 1·40 70

534 Greater Bird of Paradise (*Paradisaea apoda*)

1995. Birds. Two sheets containing T 534 and similar vert designs. Multicoloured.

MS3518 (a) 120×164 mm. 2cor.×12, Type **534**; *Dryocopus galeatus*; Montezuma oropendola (*Psarocolius Montezuma*); Black-capped kingfisher (*Halcyon pileata*); White-throated magpie jay (*Calocitta Formosa*); Green-winged macaw (*Ara chloroptera*); Eastern rosella (*Platycercus eximius*); Palawan peacock pheasant (*Polyplectron emphanum*); Red-legged seriema (*Cariama cristata*); Hoatzin (*Opisthocomus hoatzin*); Blue-bellied roller (*Coracias cyanogaster*). (b) 75×102 mm. 10cor. *Dryocopus galeatus* (different). Set of 2 sheets 10·00 10·00

The stamps of **MS**3518a form a composite design.

535 Hovercraft

1995. British–Nicaraguan San Juan River Expedition.

3519 **535** 4cor. multicoloured 1·40 85

536 "Fiesta de Boaco" (Ernesto Brown)

1995. Centenary of Boaco City.

3520 **536** 4cor. multicoloured 1·40 85

537 Villa Rivas and Cannon

1995. 275th Anniv of Villa Rivas. 160th Anniv of Rivas City.

3521 **537** 3cor. multicoloured 1·10 70

538 Louis Pasteur

1995. Death Centenary of Louis Pasteur (research scientist).

3522 **538** 4cor. multicoloured 1·40 85

539 Crocodile

1995. Fauna. Three sheets containing T 541 and similar multicoloured designs.

MS3523 (a) 140×100 mm. 2cor.50×9, Type **539**; Opossum; Peccary; Paca; Tree frog; Iguana; Scarlet macaw; Capybara; Vampire bat. (b) 110×80 mm. 15cor. Jaguar (vert). (c) 110×80 mm. 15cor. Ornate hawk eagle (vert). Set of 3 sheets 10·50 10·50

540 "Children love Nature" (Brenda Gutierrez)

1995. Winning Design in Children's Drawing Competition.

3524 **540** 3cor. multicoloured 1·10 70

541 Carlos Drummond De Andrade

1995. Twentieth Century Writers. Sheet 112×210 mm containing T 541 and similar vert designs showing writers and their country flags. Multicoloured.

MS3525 3cor.×12, Type **541**; Cesar Vallejo; Jorge Luis Borges; James Joyce; Marcel Proust; William Faulkner; Vladimir Maiakovski; Ezra Pound; Franz Kafka; T.S. Eliot; Rainer Maria Rilke; Federico Garcia Lorca 11·00 11·00

542 Child and Maize

1995. 50th Anniv of United Nations Food and Agriculture Organization (FAO).

3526 **542** 4cor. multicoloured 1·40 85

543 "Ferry Boat"

1995. Paintings by Armando Morales. Multicoloured.

3527 50c. Type **543** 20 10
3528 1cor. "Oliverio Castaneda" (vert) 35 15
3529 1cor. 50 "Desnudo Sentado" (vert) 55 25
3530 2cor. "Las Senoritas de Puerto Cabezas" 75 35
3531 2cor. 50 "El Automovil de la Compania" (vert) 95 45
3532 3cor. "Paisaje Taurino" (vert) 1·10 50
3533 4cor. "Anonas" 1·50 70
MS3534 100×70 mm. 15cor. "Mujer Dormida". Imperf 4·25 4·25

544 Doves and UN Flag

1995. 50th Anniv of United Nations. Multicoloured.

3535 3cor. Type **544** 95 45
3536 4cor. Lion and lamb 1·10 50
3537 5cor. Dove sitting on UN helmet 1·40 70
MS3538 70×100 mm. 10cor. Dove and children 3·50 3·50

Nos. 3535/7 were issued together, se-tenant, forming a composite design.

545 African Map Butterfly (*Cyrestis Camillus*)

1995. Butterflies. Two sheets containing T 545 and similar multicoloured designs.

MS3539 (a) 138×125 mm. 2cor.50×12, Type **545**; Lilac beauty (*Salamis cacta*); Giant charaxes (*Charaxes castor*); Beautiful monarch (*Danaus Formosa*); Red swallowtail (*Graphium ridleyanus*); Hewitson's forest blue (*Hewitsonia boisduvali*); Club-tailed charaxes (*Charaxes zoolina*); *Kalima cymodoce*; Blue spot commodore (*Precis westermanni*); African giant swallowtail (*Papilio antimachus*); Red glider (*Cymothoe sangaris*); Giant blue swallowtail (*Papilio zalmoxis*). (b) 106×76 mm. *Danaus Formosa* (vert). Set of 2 sheets 13·50 13·50

The stamps of **MS**3539a form a composite design.

546 Paul Harris (founder) and Emblem

1995. 90th Anniv of Rotary International (charitable organization). Multicoloured.

3540 15cor. Type **546** 6·00 4·00
MS3541 106×76 mm. 25cor. Emblems from 1905 and 1995 8·50 8·50

547 Michael Jordan (basketball)

1995. Olympic Games, Atlanta. Three sheets containing T 547 and similar vert designs. Multicoloured.

MS3542	(a) 110×100 mm. 5cor.×6, Type **547**; Heike Henkel (high jump); Linford Christie (running); Vitaly Chterchbo (gymnastic); Heike Drechsler (long jump); Mark Tewksbury (swimming). (b) 112×78 mm. 20cor. Pierre de Coubertin (founder) and Runner. (c) 112×78 mm. 20cor. Javelin throw and Pierre de Coubertin (horiz). Set of 3 sheets	19·00	19·00

548 John Lennon

1995. 15th Death Anniv of John Lennon (musician).

3543	**548** 2cor. multicoloured	75	50

549 Stylized Nativity

1995. Christmas.

3544	**549** 4cor. multicoloured	1·40	85

550 Otto Meyerhof (medicine, 1922)

1995. Centenary of the Nobel Prize. Five sheets containing T 550 and similar vert designs showing prize winners. Multicoloured.

MS3545	(a) 102×180 mm. 2cor.50×9, Type **550**; Leon Bourgeois (peace, 1920); James Frank (physics, 1925); Leo Esaki (physics, 1973); Miguel Angel Asturias (literature, 1967); Henri Bergson (literature, 1927); Friedrich Bergius (chemistry, 1931); Klaus von Klitzing (physics, 1985); Eisaku Sato (peace, 1974). (b) 130×179 mm. 2cor.50×2, Wilhelm Rontgen (physics, 1901); Theodor Mommsen (literature, 1902); Philipp von Lenard (physics, 1905); Walther Nernst (chemistry, 1920); Hans Spemann (medicine,1935); Jean-Paul Sartre (literature, 1964); T.S. Eliot (literature, 1948); Albert Camus (literature, 1957); Ludwig Quidde (peace, 1927); Werner Heisenberg (physics, 1932); Joseph Brodsky (literature, 1987); Carl von Ossietzky (peace, 1935). (c) 107×76 mm.15cor. Johannes Stark (physics, 1919). (d) 107×76 mm. 15cor. Sin-itiro Tomonaga (physics, 1965). (e) 107×76 mm. 15cor. Oscar Arias Sanchez (peace, 1987)	30·00	30·00

The stamps of **MS**3545a/b, respectively, each form a composite design.

551 *Cattleya downiana*

1995. Orchids. Three sheets containing T 551 and similar horiz designs. Multicoloured.

MS3546	(a) 139×95 mm. 2cor.50×9, Type **551**; *Odontoglossum maculatum; Barkeria Lindleyana; Rossioglossum grande; Brassavola digbyana* (inscr "Brassavp");*Miltonia Schroederiana; Oncidium ornithorhynchum; Odontoglossum cervantesii; Chysis Tricostata*. (b) 139×95 mm. 3cor.×9, *Lycaste Auburn; Lemboglossum cordatum; Cyrtochilum macranthum; Miltassia Aztec; Masdevallia ignea; Oncidium Sniffen; Brassolaeliocattleya; Ascocenda; Phalaenopsis*. (c) 106×76 mm. 15cor. *Odontoglossum uro-skinneri*. Set of 3 sheets	20·00	20·00

The stamps of **MS**3546b form a composite design.

552 Russian Revolution (1917)

1995. 20th-century Events. Multicoloured.

3547	30cor. Type **552**	85	50
3548	30cor. Chinese revolution (1945)	85	50
3549	30cor. Creation of United Nations (1945)	85	50
3550	30cor. Destruction of Berlin wall (1989)	85	50
3551	30cor. World War I (inscr "1914—17") (vert)	85	50
3552	30cor. Creation of Israel (1948) (vert)	85	50
3553	30cor. World War II (vert)	85	50
3554	30cor. Vatican Council (1962—5) (vert)	85	50
3555	30cor. Hiroshima atomic bomb (1945)	85	50
3556	30cor. Vietnam war (1962—73)	85	50
3557	30cor. Gulf war (1991); End of apartheid (1991)	85	50
3558	3 cor. End of apartheid (1991)	9·25	5·50

553 Beyer-Garrat Locomotive, South Africa

1996. Trains. Multicoloured.

3559	2cor. Type **553**	75	45
3560	2cor. Beyer-Garrat locomotive, Rhodesia	75	45
3561	2cor. Mombasa mail train, Uganda	75	45
3562	2cor. Class 31 steam locomotive, East Africa	75	45
3563	2cor. Red steam locomotive, East Africa	75	45
3564	2cor. Electric locomotive, South Africa	75	45
3565	4cor. Plusmarquista 440 No. 999, USA	1·10	70
3566	4cor. Class 638 4.6.2. Pacific, Australia	1·10	70
3567	4cor. 2 .10.2 locomotive *Baldwin*, Bolivia	1·10	70
3568	4cor. Vulcan 4.8.4. locomotive, China	1·10	70
3569	4cor. Paris—Orleans 4.6.2. Pacific, France	1·10	70
3570	4cor. Class 062-4.6.4., Japan	1·10	70
MS3571	Three sheets, each 104×74 mm. Size 85×28 mm. (a) 15cor. Trans Siberian cargo train. (b) 15cor. Midland 4.4.0. compound steam locomotive, UK. (c) 15cor. Steam locomotive, Russia	15·00	15·00

554 Allied Troops crossing Rhine

1996. 50th Anniv (1995) of End of World War II. Multicoloured.

3572	3cor. Type **554**	85	50
3573	3cor. Winston Churchill, Franklin Roosevelt and Joseph Stalin	85	50
3574	3cor. American soldiers raising flag	85	50
3575	3cor. Marine infantry entering Okinawa	85	50
3576	3cor. American and Russian troops	85	50
3577	3cor. Freeing prisoners	85	50
3578	3cor. United Nations treaty	85	50
3579	3cor. American fleet entering Tokyo port	85	50
MS3580	110×80 mm. 10cor. German fighter aircraft	3·75	3·75

555 Pope John Paul II

1996. Visit of Pope John Paul II to Nicaragua.

3581	**555** 5cor. multicoloured	1·90	1·30

556 *Mayflower*

1996. Ships. Multicoloured.

3582	2cor. Type **556**	75	50
3583	2cor. *Young America*	75	50
3584	2cor. *Preussen*	75	50
3585	2cor. Pirate ship	75	50
3586	2cor. *Cutty Sark*	75	50
3587	2cor. Pirate barque	75	50
3588	2cor. Galleon	75	50
3589	2cor. Inscr "El Sol Real"	75	50
3590	2cor. *Santa Maria*	75	50
3591	2cor. HMS *Bountyt*	75	50
3592	2cor. *El Presidente*	75	50
3593	2cor. Inscr "El Principe Guillermo"	75	50
3594	2cor. *Vuelo Nublado*	75	50
3595	2cor. Nile sail boat	75	50
3596	2cor. *Europa*	75	50
3597	2cor. *Vasa*	75	50
3598	2cor. Junk	75	50
3599	2cor. *San Gabriel*	75	50
MS3600	Two sheets, each 100×70 mm. (a) 15cor. Junk (vert). (b) 15cor. *Passat* (vert)	9·75	9·75

557 Collie carrying Lead

1996. Dogs. Multicoloured.

3601	1cor. Type **557**	35	25
3602	1cor. Cairn terrier wearing neckerchief	35	25
3603	2cor. Otter hound holding biscuit	75	50
3604	2cor. Puppy with ball	75	50
3605	3cor. Bulldog	1·10	80
3606	3cor. Siberian husky	1·10	80
3607	4cor. Beagle carrying newspaper	1·40	1·00
3608	4cor. Dalmatian puppy and kitten	1·40	1·00
MS3609	Two sheets. (a) 104×73 mm. 16cor. Chihuahua (b) 73×104 mm. 16cor. Poodle	10·00	10·00

558 Indira Gandhi

1996. United Nations' Fourth Women's Conference. Famous Women. Multicoloured.

3610	2cor. Type **558**	75	50
3611	2cor. Madame Chaing Kai-Shek	75	50
3612	2cor. Mother Teresa	75	50
3613	2cor. Marie Curie	75	50
3614	2cor. Margaret Thatcher	75	50
3615	2cor. Eleanor Roosevelt	75	50
3616	2cor. Eva Peron	75	50
3617	2cor. Golda Meir	75	50
3618	2cor. Violetta Barrios de Chamorro	75	50
MS3619	Three sheets, each 127×102 mm. (a) 15cor. Valentina Tereshkova (vert). (b) 15cor. Aung San Suu Kyi (vert). (c) 15cor. Jacqueline Kennedy Onassis (vert)	15·00	15·00

559 Lou Gehrig

1996. Baseball. Multicoloured.

3620	4cor. Type **559**	1·10	80
3621	4cor. Rogers Hornby	1·10	80
3622	4cor. Mike Schmidt	1·10	80
3623	4cor. Honus Wagner	1·10	80
3624	4cor. Ty Cobb	1·10	80
3625	4cor. Roberto Clemente	1·10	80
3626	4cor. Babe Ruth	1·10	80
3627	4cor. Johnny Bench	1·10	80
3628	4cor. Tom Seaver	1·10	80
MS3629	130×97 mm. 10cor. Reggie Jackson	9·25	9·25

560 Takehide Nakatani (judo gold medallist—1964)

1996. Olympic Games, Atlanta. Multicoloured.

3630	1cor. Type **560**	30	15
3631	2cor. Olympic stadium, Japan 1964	55	35
3632	2cor.50 Basketball	75	45
3633	2cor.50 Baseball	75	45
3634	2cor.50 Boxing	75	45
3635	2cor.50 Hurdling	75	45
3636	2cor.50 Judo	75	45
3637	2cor.50 Handball	75	45
3638	2cor.50 Volleyball	75	45
3639	2cor.50 Water polo	75	45
3640	2cor.50 Tennis	75	45
3641	3cor. Al Oerter (discus gold medallist—1956, 1960, 1964 and 1968) (vert)	85	50
3642	10cor. Olympic rings and early athlete	2·75	2·90

561 Andrew Maynard

1996. Boxing Gold Medallists. Multicoloured.

No.	Type	Description	Mint	Used
3643		2cor.50 Type **561**	75	50
3644		2cor.50 Rudi Fink	75	50
3645		2cor.50 Peter Lessov	75	50
3646		2cor.50 Angel Herrera	75	50
3647		2cor.50 Patrizio Oliva	75	50
3648		2cor.50 Armando Martinez	75	50
3649		2cor.50 Slobodan Kacar	75	50
3650		2cor.50 Teofilo Stevenson	75	50
3651		2cor.50 George Foreman	75	50
MS3652		107×76 mm. 25cor. Cassius Clay (horiz)	8·50	8·50

Nos. 3643/51 were issued together, se-tenant, with the background forming a composite design.

562 Bay

1996. Horses. Multicoloured.

No.	Type	Description	Mint	Used
3653		1cor. Type **562**	35	25
3654		2cor. Liver chestnut	75	50
3655		2cor.18 th-century Persian light cavalry harness	75	50
3656		2cor.15 th-century Italian harness	75	50
3657		2cor.15 th-century German horse armour	75	50
3658		2cor.17 th-century Turkish light cavalry harness	75	50
3659		2cor.50 Bright bay with black and white socks	95	65
3660		3cor. Dark bay	1·10	70
3661		3cor. Chestnut with pale mane and tail and white socks (vert)	1·10	70
3662		4cor. Yellow dun	1·60	1·10
3663		4cor. Black with white socks and snip	1·60	1·10
MS3664		105×75 mm. 16cor. Dappled grey	5·50	5·50
MS3665		101×71 mm. 25cor. 16th-century German horse armour	8·50	8·50

563 Shark

1996. Marine Life. Multicoloured.

No.	Type	Description	Mint	Used
MS3666		(a) Two sheets, each 151×111 mm. (i) 2cor.50×9, Type **563**; Diver and hammer-head shark; Moray eel; Mackerel; Mackerel and hammer-head shark; Butterfly fish; Spotted grouper; Squid; Manta ray. (ii) 2cor.50×9, Butterfly fish; Barracuda; Manatee; Medusa; Octopus; Yellow comber; Lemon shark; Squirrel fish; Red snapper. (b) Two sheets, each 106×76 mm. (i) 20cor. Angelfish. (ii) 20cor. Striped butterfly fish Set of 4 sheets	28·00	28·00

The stamps and margins of **MS**3665a form composite designs.

564 Flags and Emblem

1996. Central American Integration System.

No.	Type	Description	Mint	Used
3667	**564**	5cor. multicoloured	2·00	1·40

565 Rat

1996. New Year. Year of the Ox. China 96 International Stamp Exhibition (MS3680). Multicoloured.

No.	Type	Description	Mint	Used
3668		2cor. Type **565**	55	35
3669		2cor. Ox	55	35
3670		2cor. Tiger	55	35
3671		2cor. Rabbit	55	35
3672		2cor. Dragon	55	35
3673		2cor. Snake	55	35
3674		2cor. Horse	55	35
3675		2cor. Goat	55	35
3676		2cor. Monkey	55	35
3677		2cor. Rooster	55	35
3678		2cor. Dog	55	35
3679		2cor. Pig	55	35
MS3680		100×141 mm. 4cor. Pagoda	1·70	1·70
MS3681		188×128 mm. 10cor. Ox (81×48 mm)	4·00	4·00

567 "Paisaje con Bolsa" (Frederico Nordalm)

1996

No.	Type	Description	Mint	Used
3682	**566**	4cor. multicoloured	1·40	1·10

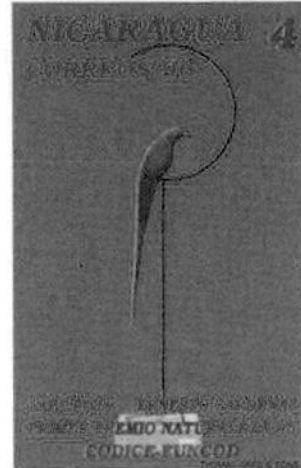

566 "Lapa Roja" (Ernesto Cardenal)

1996. Nicaragua—Taiwan Diplomatic Relations. Multicoloured.

No.	Type	Description	Mint	Used
3683		10cor. Type **567**	1·90	1·50
3684		20cor. President Lee Tang (Taiwan) and President Violetta Barrios de Chamorro (Nicaragua) (horiz)	3·75	3·00

568 Violeta Chamorro

1997. Violeta Barrios de Chamorro (president 1990–1996). Self-adhesive.

No.	Type	Description	Mint	Used
3685	**568**	3cor. multicoloured	1·10	80

569 House and Garden

1997. 60th Anniv of Plan Internacional. Self-adhesive.

No.	Type	Description	Mint	Used
3686	**569**	7cor.50 multicoloured	3·00	1·90

570 "Noctorno con dos Figuras" (Alejandro Arostegui)

1998. Art.

No.	Type	Description	Mint	Used
3687	**570**	7cor.50 multicoloured	2·40	1·70

571 Map of India and Flag

1998. 50th Anniv (1997) of Indian Independence .

No.	Type	Description	Mint	Used
3688	**571**	3cor. multicoloured	65	45
3689	**571**	9cor. multicoloured	1·90	1·30

572 Mombacho Volcano

1998. National Parks. Multicoloured.

No.	Type	Description	Mint	Used
3690		1cor.50 Type **572**	30	20
3691		2cor.50 La Flor	55	40
3692		3cor. Zapatera archipelago	65	45
3693		3cor.50 Miraflor	75	50
3694		5cor. Cosiguina volcano	1·00	75
3695		6cor.50 Masaya volcano	1·40	95
3696		7cor.50 Juan Venado Island	1·50	1·10
3697		8cor. Rio Escalante Chacocente	1·70	1·20
3698		10cor. Mountains (national system of protected areas)	1·90	1·50
MS3699		65×95 mm. 12cor. Bosawas. Imperf	2·75	2·75

573 Footprints

1998. Centenary Huellas de Acahualinca (Footprints of Acahualinca) Museum.

No.	Type	Description	Mint	Used
3700	**573**	3cor.50 multicoloured	75	50

574 "Descendimiento"

1998. 90th Birth Anniv of Rodrigo Penalba (artist). Multicoloured.

No.	Type	Description	Mint	Used
3701		2cor.50 Type **574**	55	40
3702		3cor.50 "Victoria y Piere"	75	50
3703		5cor. "Maternidad"	1·00	75
MS3704		95×65 mm. 10cor. "El gueguense" Imperf	2·00	2·00

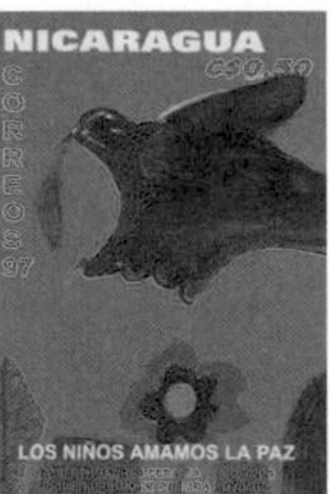

575 Dove (Yamileth Flores Peralta)

1998. Winning Design in Children's Painting Competition.

No.	Type	Description	Mint	Used
3705	**575**	50c. multicoloured	20	10

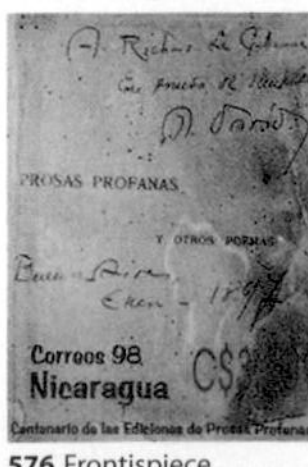

576 Frontispiece

1998. Centenary of Publication of "Prosas Profanos". Ruben Garcia Sarmiento Felix (Ruben Dario) (poet) Commemoration. Multicoloured.

No.	Type	Description	Mint	Used
3706		3cor.50 Type **576**	75	40
3707		5cor. Ruben Dario	1·10	75

577 "Vaca y Malinche" (Bayron Gomez Chavarria)

1998. Naturaleza 98 (art and culture).

No.	Type	Description	Mint	Used
3708	**577**	3cor.50 multicoloured	75	50

578 Post Box

1998. Stamp Day.

No.	Type	Description	Mint	Used
3709	**578**	6cor.50 multicoloured	1·40	95

579 "Dialogo de Nicaragua" (painting)

1998. Meeting between Nicarao Chief and Gil Gonzalez Davila (Spanish explorer).

No.	Type	Description	Mint	Used
3710	**579**	5cor. multicoloured	1·00	75

580 Lolita Soriano de Guerrero (founder of (Leoncio Saenz) Lola Soriano Grammar school)

1998. America. Famous Women. Multicoloured.

No.	Type	Description	Mint	Used
3711		3cor.50 Type **580**	75	90
3712		7cor.50 Violeta Barrios de Chamorro (president 1990—1996)	1·60	1·10

581 "50", Emblem and Faces

1998. 50th Anniv of Universal Declaration of Human Rights.

No.	Type	Description	Mint	Used
3713	**581**	12cor. multicoloured	2·30	1·80

582 The Nativity (clay)

1998. Christmas. Multicoloured.

No.	Type	Description	Mint	Used
3714		50c. Type **582**	10	10
3715		1cor. Jesus (carved gourd)	20	15
3716		2cor. The Nativity (statues) (horiz)	35	30
3717		3cor. Modern Nativity (painting) (horiz)	65	45
MS3718		95×65 mm. 7cor.50 Hark the Herald Angels. Imperf	1·70	1·70

583 Managua before the Earthquake

1998. 25th (1997) Anniv of Managua Earthquake. Multicoloured.

3719	3cor. Type **583**	65	45
3720	7cor.50 After the earthquake (horiz)	1·70	1·10
MS3721	65×95 mm.10cor.50 Clock and stylized buildings	2·30	2·30

584 Diana, Princess of Wales

1999. Diana, Princess of Wales Commemoration. Multicoloured.

3722	5cor. Type **584**	1·10	70
3723	7cor.50 Wearing tiara	1·70	1·20
3724	10cor. Wearing drop earrings	2·30	1·60

585 *Metamorpha stelenes*

1999. Butterflies. Multicoloured.

3725	2cor. Type **585**;	55	35
3726	2cor. *Erateina staudinger*	55	35
3727	2cor. *Premolis semirufa*	55	35
3728	2cor. Inscr "Heliconius eisini"	55	35
3729	2cor. Inscr "Phoebis phlea"	55	35
3730	2cor. *Dione juno*	55	35
3731	2cor. *Helicopis cupido*	55	35
3732	2cor. Inscr "Catonephele numili"	55	35
3733	2cor. *Anteos clorinde*	55	35
3734	3cor.50 Inscr "Papilionidae ornithoptera alexandrae"	75	50
3735	8cor. Inscr "Nymphalidae cepheutychia cephus"	1·80	1·30
3736	9cor. Inscr "Nymphalidae eryphanis polyxena"	1·90	1·30
3737	9cor. Inscr "Nymphalidae callicore maimuna"	1·90	1·30
3738	9cor. Inscr "Nymphalidae hypolimmas salmacis"	1·90	1·30
3739	9cor. Inscr "Nymphalidae precis octavia"	1·90	1·30
3740	9cor. Inscr "Papilionidae troides-brookiana"	1·90	1·30
3741	9cor. Inscr "Nymphalidae cithaerias esmeralda"	1·90	1·30
3742	9cor. Inscr "Papilionidae parides coon"	1·90	1·30
3743	9cor. Inscr "Nymphalidae heliconius"	1·90	1·30
3744	9cor. Inscr "Nymphalidae morpho rhetenor"	1·90	1·30
3745	12cor.50 Inscr "Pieridae phoebis philea"	2·75	1·90
MS3746	110×85 mm. 15cor. Inscr "Papiliomidae papilio glaucus"	2·75	2·75
MS3747	110×80 mm. 25cor. Inscr "Thecla coronata"	4·50	4·50
MS3748	105×72 mm. Inscr "Ufefheisa bela"	4·50	4·50

Nos. 3736/44 were issued together, se-tenant, forming a composite design.

586 *Eudyptes chrysocome*

1999. Sea Birds. Multicoloured.

3749	5cor. Type **586**	1·00	70
3749a	5cor.50 Inscr "Speniscus magellanious"	1·00	70
3756	6cor. Inscr "Speniscus magellanious"	1·10	80
3756a	6cor. Pygoscelis Antarctica	1·10	80
3757	6cor. Inscr "Phalacrocorax punctatus featherstoni" (horiz)	1·20	85
3758	2cor. *Phalacrocorax bougainvillii* (horiz)	1·20	85
3759	6cor. *Anhinga anhinga* (horiz)	1·20	85
3760	6cor. *Phalacrocorax punctatus punctatus* (horiz)	1·20	80
3761	6cor. *Phalacrocorax sulcirostris* (horiz)	1·20	85
3762	6cor. *Pelicanus occidentalis* (horiz)	1·20	85
3763	7cor.50 Inscr "Magadyptes antipodes"	1·50	1·00
MS3764	Two sheets, each 85×110 mm (a) 12cor. Inscr "Pygos papua". (b) 12cor. *Aptenodytes forsteri*	4·75	4·75

587 *Eagle* (1851)

1999. Ships. Multicoloured.

3765	2cor. Type **587**	35	25
3766	3cor. HMS *Rodney* (1830) (31×40 mm)	55	35
3767	3cor. *Boyne* (1700) (31×40 mm)		
3768	3cor. *Castor* (1800) (31×40 mm)	55	35
3769	3cor. *Mutin* (1800) (31×40 mm)	55	35
3770	3cor. *Britannia* (1820) (31×40 mm)	55	35
3771	3cor. *Goulden Leeuw* (1600) (31×40 mm)	55	35
3772	3cor. *Hercules* (1600) (31×40 mm)	55	35
3773	3cor. *Resolotion* (1667) (31×40 mm)	55	35
3774	3cor. *Royal George* (1756) (31×40 mm)	55	35
3775	3cor. HMS *Vanguard* (Inscr "Vaguard") (1700) (31×40 mm)	55	35
3776	3cor. *Prince Royal* (1600) (31×40 mm)	55	35
3777	3cor. *Zeven Provincien* (1600) (31×40 mm)	55	35
3778	4cor. *Contest* (1800)	75	50
3779	5cor. *Architect* (1847—8)	1·00	65
3780	10cor. *Edward O'Brien* (1863)	2·00	1·60
MS3781	Two sheets, each 115×84 mm (a) 15cor. *Pamir* (1905). (b) 15cor. *Great Expedition* (1700)	6·00	6·00

588 Sordes

1999. Pre-Historic Animals. Multicoloured.

3782	5cor. Type **588**	1·00	65
3783	5cor. Dimorphodon	1·00	65
3784	5cor. Anurognathus	1·00	65
3785	5cor. Rhamphorynchus	1·00	65
3786	5cor. Pterodaustro	1·00	65
3787	5cor. Pteranodon	1·00	65
3788	6cor. Macroplata	1·20	85
3789	6cor. Coelurus	1·20	85
3790	6cor. Inscr "Stegosaurus"	1·20	85
3791	6cor. Corythosaurus	1·20	85
3792	6cor. Inscr "Thadeosaurus"	1·20	85
3793	6cor. Inscr "Brachsaurus"	1·20	85
MS3794	Two sheets, each 115×84 mm (a) 12cor. Platecarpus. (b) 12cor. Pterodactylus	4·75	4·75

Nos. 3782/7 and 3788/93 were issued together, se-tenant, with enlarged illustrated margins, the whole, in each case, forming a composite design.

589 *Anteos clorinde*

1999. Fauna and Flora. Multicoloured.

3795	5cor. Type **589**	95	65
3796	5cor. Palm tree (vert)	95	65
3797	5cor. *Phaethon lepturus* (vert)	95	65
3798	5cor. *Cinlocerthia ruficauda* (vert)	95	65
3799	5cor. *Myadestes genbarbis* (vert)	95	65
3800	5cor. *Rosa sinesis* (vert)	95	65
3801	5cor. *Cyanophaia bicolor* (vert)	95	65
3802	5cor. *Delphinus delphinus* (vert)	95	65
3803	5cor. *Anolis carolinensis* (vert)	95	65
3804	5cor. *Dynastes titvus* (vert)	95	65
3805	5cor. *Iguana iguana* (vert)	95	65
3806	5cor. *Prepona meander* (vert)	95	65
3809	6cor. *Coereba flaveola*	1·20	80
3810	7cor.50 *Rynchops niger*	1·50	1·00
3811	7cor.50 *Chaetodon striatus*	1·50	1·00
MS3812	100×70 mm. 10cor. *Anisotremus virginicus*	1·90	1·90
MS3813	70×100 mm. 10cor. *Ceryle torquata* (vert)	1·90	1·90

Nos. 3796/808 were issued together, se-tenant, with enlarged illustrated margins, the whole forming a composite design.

590 U25B Rock Island No. 213 General Electric Locomotive (1960)

1999. Railways. Multicoloured.

3814	1cor. Type **590**	20	15
3815	5cor. C-630 Century Santa Fe Railroad Alco (1965)	1·00	75
3816	5cor. CR Alco RS11 No. 7610 (1956)	1·00	75
3817	5cor. Metra No. 167 GE EMD F40 (1983)	1·00	75
3818	5cor. British Columbia Railways GF6C	1·00	75
3819	5cor. Amtrak GE EMD AEM7 No. 908 (1981)	1·00	75
3820	5cor. C-40-9 Norfolk Southern No. 8845 GE EMD (1986)	1·00	75
3821	5cor. C-630 No. 5308 "Big Alco" Reading RR (1967)	1·00	75
3823	6cor. British Columbia Railways General Motors GF6C (1983)	1·20	80
3824	6cor. Alco Indian Railways WDM C-C (1962)	1·20	80
3825	6cor. Clyde Engineering GM Powerhouse Class 421 No. 42106 Australia (1982)	1·20	80
3826	6cor. Clyde Engineering GM Powerhouse Class M821 No. 8136 Australia (1986)	1·20	80
3827	6cor. Via Canada LRC BB Alco No. 6903 (1982)	1·20	80
3828	6cor. Clyde Engineering Victorian Railways GM class X No. X49 (1966)	1·20	80
3830	6cor.50 General Motors Class DD 41 AX Centennial DD Union Pacific (1969)	1·30	90
3831	7cor.50 F Series BB EMD Maryland DOT No. 7185	1·50	1·00
MS3832	Two sheets, each 116×76 mm (a) 15cor. Queen Victoria. (b) 15cor. Donald A. Smith drives the "Last Spike", Canadian and Pacific Railway (vert)	6·00	6·00

591 *Tricholoma ustaloides*

1999. Fungi. Multicoloured.

3833	5cor. Type **591**	1·10	70
3834	5cor. *Tricholoma pardinum*	1·10	70
3835	5cor. *Amanita echinocephala*	1·10	70
3836	5cor. *Tricholoma saponaceum*	1·10	70
3837	5cor. *Amanita inaurata*	1·10	70
3838	5cor. *Amanita rubescens*	1·10	70
3839	7cor.50 *Amanita*;	1·50	1·00
3840	7cor.50 Inscr "Cryptotrama asprata"	1·50	1·00
3841	7cor.50 *Amanita gemmata*	1·50	1·00
3842	7cor.50 *Cathelasma imperiale*	1·50	1·00
3843	7cor.50 *Collybia fuslpes*	1·50	1·00
3844	7cor.50 *Collybia butyracea*	1·50	1·00
MS3845	Two sheets, each 100×70 mm. (a) 12cor.50 *Tricholomopsis rutilans*. (b) 12cor.50 *Tricholoma virgatum*	4·75	4·75

592 *Cattleya skinneri*

1999. Orchids. Multicoloured.

3846	2cor. Type **592**	35	25
3847	3cor. *Odontoglossum rossii*	55	35
3848	3cor. *Cattleya aurantiaca*	55	35
3849	3cor. *Encyclia cordigera*	55	35
3850	3cor. *Phragmipedium besseae*	55	35
3851	3cor. *Brassavola nodosa*	55	35
3852	3cor. *Cattleya forbesii*	55	35
3853	3cor. *Barkeria spectabilis*	55	35
3854	3cor. *Dracula erythrochaete*	55	35
3855	3cor. *Cochleanthes discolor*	55	35
3856	3cor. *Encyclia cochleata*	55	35
3857	3cor. *Lycaste aromatica*	55	35
3858	3cor. *Brassia maculate*	55	35
3859	4cor. *Lycaste aromatica* (different)	85	50
3860	5cor. *Odontoglossum cervantesii*	1·00	65
3861	10cor. *Brassia verrucosa*	2·00	1·60
MS3862	Two sheets, each 85×110 mm. (a) 25cor. *Odontoglossum rossii* (different). (b) 25cor. *Phragmipedium longifolium*	10·00	10·00

593 Fishing Boats, Puerto Cabezas

1999. Nicaragua—Japan Friendship. Multicoloured.

MS3863	150×120 mm. 3cor.50 Type **593**; 5cor. Grain production; 6cor. Japanese school; 7cor.50 Pan American Highway bridge; 8cor. Japanese aqueduct, Managua; 9cor. Japan—Nicaragua Friendship Hospital	9·25	9·25

594 Tiberius Cavallo (early researcher into gases)

1999. Ballooning. Multicoloured.

3864	12cor. Type **594**	2·50	1·80
3865	12cor. *Breitling Orbiter 3* (1990)	2·50	1·80
3866	12cor. Bertrand Piccard and Brian Jones (balloonists)	2·50	1·80
3867	12cor. Brian Jones (captain)	2·50	1·80
3868	12cor. *Breitling Orbiter 3* (first non-stop circumnavigation of the world, 1999)	2·50	1·80
3869	12cor. Bertrand Picard (co-pilot)	2·50	1·80
3870	12cor. *Breitling Orbiter 3* over Alps	2·50	1·80
3871	12cor. Leonardo da Vinci (experiments with heavier than air)	2·50	1·80
3872	12cor. Bertrand Piccard and Brian Jones (different)	2·50	1·50
3873	12cor. *Solo Spirit 3* (first crossing of South Atlantic, 1998)	2·50	1·80
3874	12cor. *BreitlingOrbiter 3* emblem	2·50	1·80
3875	12cor. ICO Global (1998)	2·50	1·80
MS3876	Three sheets, each 70×100 mm. (a) 25cor. Pilatre de Rozier (first manned flight). (b) 25cor. Madame Thible (first woman solo balloon flight). (c) 25cor. J. A. C. Charles (early balloon producer)	17·00	17·00
MS3877	100×70 mm. 25cor. Jean Pierre Blanchard (balloon pioneer)	5·50	5·50

595 Bank Building, Washington

1999. 40th Anniv of Inter-American Development Bank.
3878 **595** 7cor.50 multicoloured 1·60 1·10

596 Dove carrying Olive Branch

1999. America. New Millennium without Arms.
3879 **596** 7cor.50 multicoloured 1·70 1·20

597 Theatre at Night

1999. 30th Anniv of Ruben Dario Theatre.
3880 **597** 7cor.50 multicoloured 1·90 1·30

598 Municipal Building, Grenada

1999. 475th Anniv of Grenada (3872/7) and Leon (3878/83). Multicoloured.
3881 3cor.50 Type **598** 75 50
3882 3cor.50 Guadalupe Church, Central Plaza 75 50
3883 3cor.50 Houses with verandas, Gral 75 50
3884 3cor.50 Ponciano Corral 75 50
3885 3cor.50 Casa de los Leones 75 50
3886 3cor.50 Colonial and neo-classical buildings, El Consulado 75 50
3887 7cor.50 Leon Cathedral 1·70 1·20
3888 7cor.50 Municipal theatre 1·70 1·20
3889 7cor.50 La Recoleccion Church 1·70 1·20
3890 7cor. Ruben Dario Archive Musuem 1·70 1·20
3891 7cor.50 TELCOR building 1·70 1·20
3892 7cor.50 Cural de Subtiava 1·70 1·20

599 Building

1999. 125th Anniv of Universal Postal Union.
3893 **599** 7cor.50 multicoloured 1·90 1·30

600 Azawakh Dog

2000. Dogs and Cats. Multicoloured.
3894 1cor. Type **600** 30 15
3895 2cor. Chihuahua dog 55 35
3896 2cor.50 Chocolate colour point Birman cat (horiz) 65 45
3897 3cor. Norwegian forest cat (horiz) 75 50
3898 6cor. Clumber spaniel 1·60 1·10
3899 6cor. Australian sheepdog 1·60 1·10
3900 6cor. German wire-haired pointer 1·60 1·10
3901 6cor. Dog with long ears and rough coat 1·60 1·10
3902 6cor. Ibizan hound 1·60 1·10
3903 6cor. Norwegian elkhound 1·60 1·10
3904 6cor. Italian blue colour point 1·60 1·10
3905 6cor. Turkish longhair 1·60 1·10
3906 6cor. Incr "Tiffany Rojo" 1·60 1·10
3907 6cor. Longhair 1·60 1·10
3908 6cor. Inscr "Calico Pelocorto sin Pedigree" 1·60 1·10
3909 6cor. Oriental blue 1·60 1·10
MS3910 110×86 mm. 12cor. Burmese cat (57×42 mm) 3·25 3·25
MS3911 86×110 mm. 12cor. Braque de Bourbonnais (42×57 mm) 3·25 3·25

601 Queen Elizabeth

2000. Birth Centenary of Queen Elizabeth, Queen Mother. Two sheets, each 151×155 mm containing T 601 and similar vert designs. Multicoloured.
MS3912 (a) 10cor.×4, Type **601**; Seated facing right; With King George VI ; Wearing blue hat. (b) Wearing tiara, facing left (38×51 mm) 17·00 17·00

602 Bristol F2B

2000. Aviation. Multicoloured.
3913 7cor.50 Montgolfier balloon (41×60 mm) 1·90 1·30
3914 7cor.50 Type **602** 1·90 1·30
3915 7cor.50 Inscr "Provost Jet" 1·90 1·30
3916 7cor.50 Inscr "Hunter" 1·90 1·30
3917 7cor.50 Wessex helicopter 1·90 1·30
3918 7cor.50 Inscr "Redwing II Trainer" (41×60 mm) 1·90 1·30
3919 7cor.50 Montgolfier balloon (41×60 mm) (different) 1·90 1·30
3920 7cor.50 Hawker Hart 1·90 1·30
3921 7cor.50 Westland Lysander
3922 7cor.50 ; British Aerospace Harrier 1·90 1·30
3923 7cor.50 VC10 1·90 1·30
3924 7cor.50 Bleriot and De Havilland Fox Moth (41×60 mm) 1·90 1·30
MS3925 Two sheets, each 86×110 mm. (a) 25cor. Spartan Arrow and De Havilland Tiger Moth. (b) 25cor. Tiger Moth and Spartan Arrow (different) 13·00 13·00

603 British Rail Class 470 APT-P

2000. Railways. Showing locomotives. Multicoloured.
3926 3cor. Type **603** 75 50
3927 3cor. Swedish State Railways Class DM3 75 50
3928 3cor. New Zealand Railways Class EW 165 75 50
3929 3cor. British Rail Class 87 75 50
3930 3cor. British Rail Class 40 75 50
3931 3cor. Swiss Class GE6/6 Crocodile 75 50
3932 3cor. Spanish Railways Class 277 No. 1737 75 50
3933 3cor. B-23-7 Metro North Commuter 75 50
3934 3cor. Long Island EMD DE30 75 50
3935 3cor. General Motors EMD F40 PHM-2C 75 50
3936 3cor. Pennsylvania Railroad GG1 75 50
3937 3cor. New Jersey Transit MK GP40 FH-2 75 50
3938 3cor. Amtrak EMD F59 PHI 75 20
3939 4cor. Swedish State Railways X-2000 Tilting Express 1·00 70
3940 5cor. New South Wales XPT 1·30 75
3941 10cor. British Rail HST 125 2·75 1·90
MS3942 110×86 mm. 25cor. British Rail Class 44 6·50 6·50
MS3943 86×110 mm. 25cor. Metra EMD P69PN-AC 6·50 6·50

604 Great White Shark

2000. Marine Life. Multicoloured.
3944 3cor.50 Type **604** 95 65
3945 5cor. Humpback whale 1·30 95
3946 6cor. Sea turtle 1·60 1·10
3947 9cor. Sperm whale 2·40 1·60
MS3948 Two sheets, each 163×89 mm. (a) 7cor.50×6, Bridled burrfish; Manta ray; Black grouper; Tiger grouper; Moray eel; Atlantic squid. (b) 7cor.50×6, Hawksbill turtle; Jellyfish; Reef shark; Reef turtle; Dolphin; Stingray 24·00 24·00
MS3949 Two sheets, each 85×110 mm. (a) 25cor. Tiger shark. (b) 25cor. Dolphins 13·00 13·00

The stamps and margins of **MS**3948a/b form composite designs.

605 *Cotinga amabilis*

2000. Birds. Multicoloured.
3950 5cor. Type **605** 1·30 95
3951 7cor.50 *Galbula ruficauda* 1·90 1·30
3952 10cor. *Guiraca caerulea* 2·50 1·80
3953 12cor.50 *Momotus momoto* 3·50 2·50
MS3954 157×108 mm. 3cor.×10, *Ara macao; Amazona ochrocephala; Chloroceryleamericana; Archilocus colubris; Pharamachrus mocinno; Ramphastossalfuratus; Coereba flaveola; Piculus rubiginosus; Passerina ciris; Busarella nigricollis* 8·00 8·00
MS3955 Two sheets, each 85×110 mm. (a) 25cor. *Aulacorhynchus prasinus.* (b) 25cor. *Megaceryle alcyon* 13·00 13·00

The stamps and margins of **MS**3954 form a composite design.

606 Recovery of Spacecraft

2000. Space Exploration. Multicoloured.
3956 5cor. Type **6061** 30 95
3957 5cor. Earth from space 1·30 95
3958 5cor. Malcolm Scott Carpenter in dinghy 1·30 95
3959 5cor. Helicopter rescue of Alan Shepherd 1·30 95
3960 5cor. USS *Intrepid* (rescue craft) 1·30 95
3961 5cor. Launch of *Friendship 7* 1·30 95
3962 5cor. *Mercury 9* splash down 1·30 95
3963 5cor. *Mercury 6* suspended from helicopter 1·30 95
MS3964 123×187 mm. All vert. 5cor.×8, Donald Kent Slayton; Malcolm Scott Carpenter; Walter Marty Schirra; John Herschel Glenn; Leroy Gordon Cooper; Virgil Ivan Grissom; Mercury Redstone-3 spacecraft; Alan Shepherd 10·00 10·00
MS3965 85×115 mm. 25cor. John Glenn (different) (vert) 6·50 6·50
MS3966 115×85 mm. 25cor. Alan Shepherd (different) 6·50 6·50

The stamps and margins of **MS**3964 form a composite design.

607 Pope Leo XIII

2000. 20th Century Popes. Multicoloured.
3967 3cor. Type **607** 75 50
3968 3cor. Worker with raised arm (Leo XIII's proclamation of worker's rights) 75 50
3969 3cor. Pius X 75 50
3970 3cor. Monk holding harp (Pius X's revision of ecclesiastical music) 75 50
3971 3cor. Benedict XV 75 50
3972 3cor. Joan of Arc (Benedict XV's campaign for the canonization of Joan of Arc) 75 50
3973 3cor. Pius XI 75 50
3974 3cor. Radio and globe (establishment of Radio Vatican) 75 50
3975 3cor. John XXIII 75 50
3976 3cor. Peace symbol 75 50
3977 3cor. Paul VI 75 50
3978 3cor. Paul VI's flag 75 50
3979 3cor. John Paul I 75 50
3980 3cor. Lamb and cross (symbol of Papal humility) 75 50
3981 3cor. John Paul II 75 50
3982 3cor. Globe and hands holding dove (symbol of John Paul II's ministry) 75 50
MS3983 Two sheets, each 108×115 mm. (a) 25cor. Pope John XXIII (38×51 mm). (b) 25cor. Pope John Paul II (38×51 mm) 13·00 13·00

608 *Heliconius cydno galanthus*

2000. Butterflies. Multicoloured.
3984 9cor. *Catonephele numilla esite* 2·00 1·40
3985 9cor. *Marpesia marcella* 2·00 1·40
3986 9cor. *Heliconius hecalesia* 2·00 1·40
3987 9cor. *Acinote thalia anteas* 2·00 1·40
3988 9cor. *Boxocopa larentia cherubina* 2·00 1·40
3989 9cor. *Napeogenes tolosa mombachoensis* 2·00 1·40
3990 9cor. Type **608** 2·00 1·40
3991 9cor. *Nessaea aglaura* 2·00 1·40
3992 9cor. *Godyris zavaleta sosunga* 2·00 1·40
3993 9cor. *Caligo atreusdionysos* 2·00 1·40
3994 9cor. *Morpho amonte* 2·00 1·40
3995 9cor. *Eryphanis polyxena lycomedon* 2·00 1·40
MS3996 Two sheets, each 106×75 mm. (a) 25cor. *Papillo garamas.* (b) 25cor. *Cithaerias menader* 13·00 13·00

609 Indira Ghandhi

2000. Twentieth Century Leaders. Multicoloured.
3997 5cor. Type **609** 1·30 95
3998 5cor. Indira Ghandi, soldier and elephant (57×43 mm) 1·30 95
3999 5cor. Ronald Reagan (57×43 mm) 1·30 95
4000 5cor. Ronald Reagan and flags 1·30 95
4001 5cor. Vladimir Lenin 1·30 95
4002 5cor. Vladimir Lenin and national symbols (57×43 mm) 1·30 95
4003 5cor. Charles de Gaulle (57×43 mm) 1·30 95
4004 5cor. Charles de Gaulle wearing uniform 1·30 95
4005 5cor. Kemal Ataturk 1·30 95
4006 5cor. Kemal Ataturk and national flag (57×43 mm) 1·30 95
4007 5cor. John F. Kennedy (57×43 mm) 1·30 95

4008	5cor. John F. Kennedy and space craft	1·30	95
4009	5cor. Winston Churchill	1·30	95
4010	5cor. Winston Churchill wearing uniform (57×43 mm)	1·30	95
4011	5cor. Jomo Kenyatta (57×43 mm)	1·30	95
4012	5cor. Jomo Kenyatta and mountains	1·30	95
MS4013	76×105 mm. 25cor. Chiang Kai-Shek	6·50	6·50
MS4014	105×76 mm. 25cor. Theodore Roosevelt	6·50	6·50

610 Founder Members

2000. Charitable Organizations. Lions Club International (4015/20) or Rotary International (4021/6). Multicoloured.

4015	5cor. Type **610**	1·30	95
4016	5cor. Headquarters building, Chicago	1·30	95
4017	5cor. Helen Keller	1·30	95
4018	5cor. Koffi Annan (United Nations Secretary General) and Kajit Haadanananda (Lions Club president)	1·30	95
4019	5cor. Melvin Jones (founder)	1·30	95
4020	5cor. Andre de Villiers (design a "Peace Poster" winner)	1·30	95
4021	7cor. Clowns and children (vert)	1·90	1·30
4022	7cor. Nurse giving Polio vaccine drops (vert)	1·90	1·30
4023	7cor. Women using water pump, Burkina Faso (vert)	1·90	1·30
4024	7cor. Women attending literacy class, Nepal (vert)	1·90	1·30
4025	7cor. Transport for people with physical disabilities (vert)	1·90	1·30
4026	7cor. Campaign to reduce urban violence, Northern Ireland	1·90	1·30
MS4027	Two sheets, each 114×101 mm. (a) 25cor. Melvin Jones (vert). (b) 25cor. Rotary International emblem (vert)	13·00	13·00

611 Puente El Tamarindo

2001. Nicaragua—Japan Friendship. Bridges. Sheet 150×141 mm containing T 611 and similar horiz designs. Multicoloured.

MS4028 6cor.50 Type **611**; 7cor.50 Puente Ochomogo; 9cor. Puente Gil Gonzalez; 10cor. Puente Las Lajas; 12cor. Puente Rio Negro 12·00 12·00

612 Globe

2001. Stamp Day.

4029	**612**	6cor.50 multicoloured	1·60	1·10

613 Ruins, Leon Viejo

2001. America. World Heritage.

4030	**613**	10cor. multicoloured	2·00	1·40

615 *Ramphastos swaisonii* (inscr "Rtamphastos")

2001. Fauna. Sheet 111×110 mm containing T 615 and similar vert designs. Multicoloured.

MS4032 5cor. Type **615**; 6cor.50 *Amazona auropalliata*; 8cor.*Buteo magnirostris*; 9cor. *Ateles geoffroy* (Inscr "Atteles");10cor. *Leopardus wiedii*; 12cor. *Puma concolor* 6·50 6·50

The stamps and margins of **MS**4032 form a composite design.

616 Children

2001. 50th Anniv of SOS Children's Villages.

4033	**616**	5cor.50 multicoloured	1·00	85

617 Cardinal Obando Bravo

2002. Cardinal Miguel Obando Bravo (archbishop of Managua).

4034	**617**	6cor.50 multicoloured	1·10	95

621 Early Village and Ships

2002. 500th Anniv of Discovery of Nicaragua. Multicoloured.

4038	7cor.50 Type **621**	1·40	1·30

622 Josemaria Escriva

2002. Birth Centenary of Josemaria Escriva de la Balaguer (founder of Opus Dei (religious organization)).

4040	**622**	2cor.50 multicoloured	45	45

623 Children enclosing Book

2002. America. Literacy Campaign.

4041	**623**	7cor.50 multicoloured	1·40	1·30

624 Puertos de Nicaragua-Corinto

2002. Ports.

4042	**624**	5cor. multicoloured	95	85

625 Central Market during the Earthquake and SNPMAD (disaster organization) Emblem

2002. 30th Anniv of Managua Earthquake. Multicoloured.

4043	3cor.50 Type **625**	65	60
4044	7cor.50 Managua Cathedral (vert)	1·40	1·30

626 Duke and Duchess of Luxembourg

2003. 1st Visit of Duke and Duchess of Luxembourg.

4045	**626**	12cor. multicoloured	2·30	2·20

627 "En Diriamba de Nicaragua, capturaronme amigo" (Roger Perez De la Rocha)

2003. Art. Multicoloured.

4046	3cor. Type **627**	45	45
4047	5cor. "San Gabriel Arcangel" (Orlando Sobalvarro)	75	70
4048	6cor.50 "Ave Fenex" (Alejandro Arostegul)	1·00	95
4049	7cor.50 "Abstraccion de frutas" (Leonel Vanegas)	1·10	1·00
4050	8cor. "Suite en Turquesa y azules" (Bernard Dreyfus) (horiz)	1·20	1·10
4051	9cor. "Ana III" (Armando Morales) (horiz)	1·40	1·30
4052	10cor. "Coloso IV" (Arnoldo Guillen) (horiz)	1·50	1·40

628 Pope John Paul II

2003. 25th Anniv of Pontificate of Pope John Paul II. Sheet 85×110 mm containing T 628 and similar vert design. Multicoloured.

MS4053 3cor. Type **628**; 10cor. Wearing mitre 2·00 2·00

629 Hospicio San Juan de Dios Leon

2003. Centenary of La Salle Christian Education. Multicoloured.

4055	3cor. Type **629**	45	45
4056	5cor. Octavio de Jesus (vert)	75	70
4057	6cor.50 Bodran Marie (vert)	1·00	95
4058	7cor.50 Agustin Herve (vert)	1·10	1·00
4059	9cor. Vauthier de Jesus (vert)	1·40	1·30
4060	10cor. Father Mariano Dubón (vert)	1·50	1·40
MS4060a	97×66 mm. 12cor. John Baptist de la Salle (founder) (vert)	1·90	1·70

630 *Fulgora laternaria*

2003. Insects. Two sheets, each 111×110 mm containing T 630 and similar horiz designs. Multicoloured.

MS4061 (a) 6cor.50×6 Type **630**; *Acraephia perspicillata; Copidocephala guttata;. Pterodictya reticularis; Phrictus quinquepartitus; Odontoptera carrenoi* (b) 8cor.×6 *Golofa pizarro; Phanaeus pyrois* (Inscr "Phaneus"); *Plusiotis aurigans; Polyphylla concurrens; Dynastes hercules septentrionalis; Phanaeus demon excelsus* (Inscr "Phaneus") 5·00 5·00

The stamps of **MS**4061a/b respectively form composite background design.

632 *Victoria*

2003. River Boat Mail Transportation. Steam Boats. Multicoloured.

4080	3cor. Type **632**	45	45
4081	5cor. *Irma*	75	70
4082	6cor.50 *Hollenbeck*	1·00	95
4083	7cor.50 *Managua*	1·10	1·00

633 *Corytophanes cristatus*

2003. America. Fauna and Flora. Multicoloured.

4084	10cor. Type **633**	1·50	1·40
4085	12cor. *Guaiacum sanctum*	1·80	1·60

634 Beachfront

2003. 150th Anniv of San Juan del Sur Port.

4086	**634**	10cor. multicoloured	1·50	1·40

635 Model AA (1936)

2003. Toyota Cars. Multicoloured.

4087	7cor.50 Type **635**	1·10	1·00
4088	7cor.50 AB Phaeton (1936)	1·10	1·00
4089	7cor.50 Model SA (1947)	1·10	1·00
4090	7cor.50 Model BJ (1951)	1·10	1·00
4091	7cor.50 Crown RSD (1955)	1·10	1·00
4092	7cor.50 Model FJ28VA	1·10	1·00

636 Ruben Dario and Book Cover

2004. Centenary of "Tierras Solares" by Ruben Dario.

4093	**636**	10cor. multicoloured	1·50	1·40

637 *Tabebuia rosea*

2004. Flowering Trees. Multicoloured.

4094	3cor. Type **637**	45	45
4095	5cor. *Cassia fistula*	75	70
4096	6cor.50 *Delonix regia*	1·00	95

638 Cerro Kilambe Nature Reserve

2004. America. Environmental Protection. Multicoloured.

4097	7cor.50 Type **638**	1·10	1·00
4098	7cor.50 Bosawas Rio Bocay reserve	1·10	1·00

639 Hurdling

2004. Olympic Games, Athens. Multicoloured.

4099	7cor.50 Type **639**	1·10	1·00
4100	10cor. Swimming	1·50	1·40
4101	12cor. Shooting	1·90	1·70

640 Judo and Kickboxing

2004. Central American Student Games, Managua. Multicoloured.

4102	3cor. Type **640**	45	45
4103	5cor. Football and baseball	75	70
4104	6cor.50 High jump and swimming	95	85

641 *Selenidera spectabilis*

2004. Birds. Multicoloured.

4105	5cor. Type **641**	75	70
4106	6cor.50 *Nycticorax nycticorax*	1·00	95
4107	7cor.50 *Caracara plancus*	1·10	1·00
4108	10cor. *Myiozetetes similes*	1·50	1·40

642 Station Building

2004. Granada Railway Station.

4109	**642**	3cor. multicoloured	45	45

643 Mambacho Volcano Reserve

2004. Tourism. Multicoloured.

4110	7cor.50 Type **643**	1·10	1·00
4111	7cor.50 Tapou river, San Juan river wildlife reserve	1·10	1·00

644 "Frutas Ocultas" (Federico Nordalm)

2004. Contemporary Art. Multicoloured.

4112	3cor. Type **644**	45	45
4113	7cor.50 "Nicaraguapa" (Efren Medina) (vert)	1·10	1·00
4114	10cor. "Bambues" (Genaro Lugo)	1·50	1·40

645 Mary (statue)

2004. 150th Anniv of Dogma of Immaculate Conception of Virgin Mary.

4115	**645**	3cor. multicoloured	45	45

646 Pablo Neruda

2004. Birth Centenary of Neftalí Ricardo Reyes Basoalto (Pablo Neruda) (winner of Nobel Prize for Literature, 1971).

4116	**646**	7cor.50 multicoloured	1·10	1·00

No. 4117 and Type **647** are left for Birth Centenary of Ruben Dario issued on 7 February 2005, not yet received.

No. 4118/21 and Type **648** are left for Centenary of Festival issued on 4 May 2007, not yet received.

649 Village

2007. Towards a Mine-free Nicaragua. 15th Anniv of Assistance Program for Demining in Central America (PADCA).

4122	**649**	19cor. multicoloured	2·75	2·50

No. 4123/6 and Type **650** are left for Augusto Sandino Commemoration issued on 18 May 2007, not yet received.

651 *Casmerodius albus* (great egret)

2007. Environmental Protection. Multicoloured.

4127	4cor.50 Type **651**	75	70
4128	11cor.50 *Amazilia tzacatl* (rufous-tailed hummingbird)	1·70	1·50
4129	13cor.50 *Jacana spinosa* (northern jacana)	2·10	1·90
4130	14cor.50 Rio Mico	2·30	2·00

No. 4131/4 and Type **652** are left for Alphabet issued on 9 October 2007, not yet received.

653 Puerto Corinto

2009. Ports. Multicoloured.

4135	1cor. Type **653**	15	10
4136	2cor. Puerto El Rama	25	20
4137	5cor. Puerto de Granada	85	75
4138	10cor. Puerto San Juan del Sur	1·60	1·50
4139	15cor. Puerto Sandino	2·20	2·00
4140	25cor. Puerto Salvador Allende	3·75	3·50

654 Sandino Monument

2009. Augusto Nicolas Calderon Sandino (revolutionary leader) Commemoration. Multicoloured.

4141	10cor. Type **654**	1·60	1·50
4142	10cor. With his wife Blanca Arauz	1·60	1·50

655 Victor Raul Haya de la Torre

2009. 30th Death Anniv of Victor Raul Haya de la Torre (Peruvian political leader).

4143	**655**	12cor. multicoloured	1·80	1·60

656 Augusto Sandino

2009. 30th Anniv of Revolution. Multicoloured

4144	4cor. Type **656**	55	50
4145	5cor. Day of Triumph–19th July 1979	75	70
4146	60cor. Insurrection	8·00	7·00

657 Nurse examing Child

2009. 50th Anniv of National Institute of Social Security. Multicoloured.

4147	4cor. Type **657** (protection of children)	55	50
4148	14cor. Hands, flag and anniversary emblem (solidarity)	2·00	1·80
4149	16cor. Elderly woman and carer (protection of the elderly)	2·40	2·20
4150	25cor. Man wearing mask (risk assessment)	3·50	3·00

SILVER CURRENCY

The following were for use in all places on the Atlantic coast of Nicaragua where the silver currency was in use. This currency was worth about 50c. to the peso.

Earlier issues (overprints on Nicaraguan stamps) were also issued for Zelaya. These are listed in the Stanley Gibbons Part 15 (Central America) Catalogue.

Z1 Steam Locomotive

1912

Z1	**Z1**	1c. green	1·20	75
Z2	**Z1**	2c. red	80	55
Z3	**Z1**	3c. brown	1·20	75
Z4	**Z1**	4c. lake	1·20	55
Z5	**Z1**	5c. blue	1·20	55
Z6	**Z1**	6c. red	4·75	2·75
Z7	**Z1**	10c. grey	1·20	1·10
Z8	**Z1**	15c. lilac	1·20	1·10
Z9	**Z1**	20c. blue	1·20	1·10
Z10	**Z1**	25c. black and green	1·80	1·70
Z11	**Z1**	35c. black and brown	2·30	1·70
Z12	**Z1**	50c. green	2·30	1·70
Z13	**Z1**	1p. orange	3·50	2·00
Z14	**Z1**	2p. brown	4·75	3·25
Z15	**Z1**	5p. green	20·00	7·25

OFFICIAL STAMPS

Overprinted FRANQUEO OFICIAL.

1890. Stamps of 1890.

O37	**6**	1c. blue	35	40
O38	**6**	2c. blue	35	40
O39	**6**	5c. blue	35	40
O40	**6**	10c. blue	35	50
O41	**6**	20c. blue	35	85
O42	**6**	50c. blue	35	1·00
O43	**6**	1p. blue	35	1·60
O44	**6**	2p. blue	35	2·10
O45	**6**	5p. blue	35	3·00
O46	**6**	10p. blue	35	5·25

7

1891. Stamps of 1891.

O47	**7**	1c. green	35	45
O48	**7**	2c. green	35	45
O49	**7**	5c. green	35	45
O50	**7**	10c. green	35	45
O51	**7**	20c. green	35	70
O52	**7**	50c. green	35	1·30
O53	**7**	1p. green	35	1·60
O54	**7**	2p. green	35	1·70
O55	**7**	5p. green	35	3·00
O56	**7**	10p. green	35	5·25

8 First Sight of the New World

1892. Stamps of 1892.

O57	**8**	1c. brown	35	40
O58	**8**	2c. brown	35	40
O59	**8**	5c. brown	35	40
O60	**8**	10c. brown	35	40
O61	**8**	20c. brown	35	85
O62	**8**	50c. brown	35	1·10
O63	**8**	1p. brown	35	1·60
O64	**8**	2p. brown	35	3·00
O65	**8**	5p. brown	35	3·50
O66	**8**	10p. brown	35	5·75

1893. Stamps of 1893.

O67	**9**	1c. black	35	40
O68	**9**	2c. black	35	40
O69	**9**	5c. black	35	40
O70	**9**	10c. black	35	40
O71	**9**	20c. black	35	60
O72	**9**	25c. black	35	80
O73	**9**	50c. black	35	1·00
O74	**9**	1p. black	35	1·70
O75	**9**	2p. black	35	2·50
O76	**9**	5p. black	35	3·50
O77	**9**	10p. black	35	5·75

1894. Stamps of 1894.

O78	**10**	1c. orange	45	40
O79	**10**	2c. orange	45	40
O80	**10**	5c. orange	45	40
O81	**10**	10c. orange	45	40
O82	**10**	20c. orange	45	65
O83	**10**	50c. orange	45	1·20
O84	**10**	1p. orange	45	1·70
O85	**10**	2p. orange	45	2·75
O86	**10**	5p. orange	2·75	4·00
O87	**10**	10p. orange	2·75	5·25

1895. Stamps of 1895.

O88A	**11**	1c. green	25	40
O89A	**11**	2c. green	25	40
O90A	**11**	5c. green	25	40
O91A	**11**	10c. green	25	40
O92A	**11**	20c. green	25	60
O93A	**11**	50c. green	25	1·20
O94A	**11**	1p. green	25	1·70
O95A	**11**	2p. green	25	2·10
O96A	**11**	5p. green	25	3·00
O97A	**11**	10p. green	25	5·25

1896. Stamps of 1896, dated "1896", optd FRANQUEO OFICIAL in oval frame.

O99A	**12**	1c. red	2·50	3·00
O100A	**12**	2c. red	2·50	3·00
O101A	**12**	5c. red	2·50	3·00
O102A	**12**	10c. red	2·50	3·00
O103A	**12**	20c. red	3·25	3·00
O104A	**12**	50c. red	5·25	5·25
O105A	**12**	1p. red	12·50	12·50
O106A	**12**	2p. red	12·50	12·50
O107A	**12**	5p. red	17·00	17·00

1896. Nos. D99/103 handstamped Franqueo Oficial.

O108A	**D13**	1c. orange		7·25
O109A	**D13**	2c. orange		7·25
O110A	**D13**	5c. orange		5·25
O111A	**D13**	10c. orange		5·25
O112A	**D13**	20c. orange		5·25

1897. Stamps of 1897, dated "1897", optd FRANQUEO OFICIAL in oval frame.

O113A	**12**	1c. red	3·25	3·25
O114A	**12**	2c. red	3·25	3·25
O115A	**12**	5c. red	3·25	3·25
O116A	**12**	10c. red	3·25	3·25
O117A	**12**	20c. red	3·25	3·25
O118A	**12**	50c. red	5·25	5·25
O119A	**12**	1p. red	12·50	12·50
O120A	**12**	2p. red	12·50	12·50
O121A	**12**	5p. red	17·00	17·00

1898. Stamps of 1898 optd FRANQUEO OFICIAL in oval frame.

O124	**13**	1c. red	3·50	3·50
O125	**13**	2c. red	3·50	3·50
O126	**13**	4c. red	3·50	3·50
O127	**13**	5c. red	2·50	2·50
O128	**13**	10c. red	4·00	4·00
O129	**13**	15c. red	6·00	6·00
O130	**13**	20c. red	6·00	6·00
O131	**13**	50c. red	8·50	8·50
O132	**13**	1p. red	11·00	11·00
O133	**13**	2p. red	11·00	11·00
O134	**13**	5p. red	11·00	11·00

1899. Stamps of 1899 optd FRANQUEO OFICIAL in scroll.

O137	**14**	1c. green	30	1·00
O138	**14**	2c. brown	30	1·00
O139	**14**	4c. red	30	1·00
O140	**14**	5c. blue	30	55
O141	**14**	10c. orange	20	1·00
O142	**14**	15c. brown	30	2·00
O143	**14**	20c. green	30	3·00
O144	**14**	50c. red	30	3·00
O145	**14**	1p. orange	30	10·00
O146	**14**	2p. violet	30	10·00
O147	**14**	5p. blue	30	16·00

O16

1900

O148	**O16**	1c. purple	60	60
O149	**O16**	2c. orange	50	50
O150	**O16**	4c. olive	60	60
O151	**O16**	5c. blue	1·30	50
O152	**O16**	10c. violet	1·30	40
O153	**O16**	20c. brown	1·00	40
O154	**O16**	50c. lake	1·30	50
O155	**O16**	1p. blue	3·50	2·50
O156	**O16**	2p. orange	4·25	4·00
O157	**O16**	5p. black	5·25	5·00

1903. Stamps of 1900 surch OFICIAL and value, with or without ornaments.

O197	**15**	1c. on 10c. mauve	40	40
O198	**15**	2c. on 3c. green	40	50
O199	**15**	4c. on 3c. green	1·60	1·50
O200	**15**	4c. on 10c. mauve	1·60	1·50
O201	**15**	5c. on 3c. green	25	25

1903. Surch.

O202	**O16**	10c. on 20c. brown	30	30
O203	**O16**	30c. on 20c. brown	30	30
O204	**O16**	50c. on 20c. brown	60	40

O38

1905

O219	**O38**	1c. green	30	30
O220	**O38**	2c. red	30	30
O221	**O38**	5c. blue	30	30
O222	**O38**	10c. brown	30	30
O223	**O38**	20c. orange	30	30
O224	**O38**	50c. olive	30	30
O225	**O38**	1p. lake	30	30
O226	**O38**	2p. violet	30	30
O227	**O38**	5p. black	30	30

1907. Surch Vale 10 c.

O239	10c. on 1c. green	1·00	1·00
O241	10c. on 2c. red	26·00	25·00
O243	20c. on 2c. red	26·00	20·00
O245	50c. on 1c. green	2·10	2·00
O247	50c. on 2c. red	16·00	15·00

1907. Surch Vale 20 cts or Vale $1.00.

O249	20c. on 1c. green	1·60	1·50
O250	$1 on 2c. red	2·10	2·00
O251	$2 on 2c. red	2·10	2·50
O252	$3 on 2c. red	2·50	2·00
O253	$4 on 5c. blue	2·50	2·50

1907. No. 206 surch OFICIAL and value.

O256	**49**	10c. on 1c. green	16·00	13·00
O257	**49**	15c. on 1c. green	16·00	13·00
O258	**49**	20c. on 1c. green	16·00	13·00
O259	**49**	50c. on 1c. green	16·00	13·00
O260	**49**	1p. on 1c. green	16·00	13·00
O261	**49**	2p. on 1c. green	16·00	13·00

1907. Fiscal stamps as T 50 surch 10 cts. CORREOS 1907 OFICIAL 10 CTS.

O262	**50**	10c. on 2c. orange	20	20
O263	**50**	35c. on 1c. blue	20	20
O264	**50**	70c. on 1c. blue	20	20
O266	**50**	1p. on 2c. orange	20	20
O267	**50**	2p. on 2c. orange	20	20
O268	**50**	3p. on 5c. brown	20	20
O269	**50**	4p. on 5c. brown	20	20
O270	**50**	5p. on 5c. brown	30	30

1908. Stamp of 1905 surch OFICIAL VALE and value.

O271	**37**	10c. on 3c. violet	16·00	15·00
O272	**37**	15c. on 3c. violet	16·00	15·00
O273	**37**	20c. on 3c. violet	16·00	15·00
O274	**37**	35c. on 3c. violet	16·00	15·00
O275	**37**	50c. on 3c. violet	16·00	15·00

1908. Fiscal stamps as T 50 surch as last but dated 1908.

O276	**50**	10c. on 1c. blue	85	60
O277	**50**	10c. on 2c. orange	1·20	70
O278	**50**	35c. on 1c. blue	85	60
O279	**50**	35c. on 2c. orange	1·20	70
O280	**50**	50c. on 1c. blue	85	60
O281	**50**	50c. on 2c. orange	1·20	70
O282	**50**	70c. on 2c. orange	1·20	70
O283	**50**	1p. on 1c. blue	41·00	40·00
O284	**50**	1p. on 2c. orange	1·20	70
O285	**50**	2p. on 1c. blue	1·00	80
O286	**50**	2p. on 2c. orange	1·20	70

1909. Stamps of 1905 optd OFICIAL.

O290	**37**	10c. lake	30	20
O291	**37**	15c. black	85	60
O292	**37**	20c. olive	1·20	80
O293	**37**	50c. green	1·70	1·10
O294	**37**	1p. yellow	1·90	1·30
O295	**37**	2p. red	3·00	2·20

1911. Stamps of 1905 optd OFICIAL and surch Vale and value.

O296	5c. on 3c. orange	7·25	7·00
O297	10c. on 4c. violet	6·25	6·00

1911. Railway tickets, surch Timbre Fiscal Vale 10 ctvs. further surch for official postal use. Printed in red.
(a) Surch Correo oficial Vale and value on front.

O334	**64**	10c. on 10c. on 1st class	3·00	3·00
O335	**64**	15c. on 10c. on 1st class	3·00	3·00
O336	**64**	20c. on 10c. on 1st class	3·00	3·00
O337	**64**	50c. on 10c. on 1st class	4·25	4·00
O338	**64**	$1 on 10c. on 1st class	5·25	7·00
O339	**64**	$2 on 10c. on 1st class	6·25	12·00

(b) Surch CORREO OFICIAL and new value on front.

O340	10c. on 10c. on 1st class	26·00	25·00
O341	15c. on 10c. on 1st class	26·00	25·00
O342	20c. on 10c. on 1st class	26·00	25·00
O343	50c. on 10c. on 1st class	19·00	18·00

(c) No. 322 surch on front Correo Oficial Vale 1911 and new value and with 15 cts. on back obliterated by heavy bar.

O344	5c. on 10c. on 1st class	5·25	7·00
O345	10c. on 10c. on 1st class	6·25	8·00
O346	15c. on 10c. on 1st class	7·25	9·00
O347	20c. on 10c. on 1st class	7·25	10·00
O348	50c. on 10c. on 1st class	9·25	11·00

(d) No. 322 surch on front Correo Oficial 1912 and new value and with the whole surch on back obliterated.

O349	5c. on 10c. on 1st class	10·50	10·00
O350	10c. on 10c. on 1st class	10·50	10·00
O351	15c. on 10c. on 1st class	10·50	10·00
O352	20c. on 10c. on 1st class	10·50	10·00
O353	25c. on 10c. on 1st class	10·50	10·00
O354	50c. on 10c. on 1st class	10·50	10·00
O355	$1 on 10c. on 1st class	10·50	10·00

1913. Stamps of 1912 optd OFICIAL.

O356	**70**	1c. blue	20	20
O357	**70**	2c. blue	20	20
O358	**70**	3c. blue	20	20
O359	**70**	4c. blue	20	20
O360	**70**	5c. blue	20	20
O361	**70**	6c. blue	20	20
O362	**70**	10c. blue	20	20
O363	**70**	15c. blue	20	20
O364	**70**	20c. blue	20	20
O365	**70**	25c. blue	30	30
O366	**71**	35c. blue	40	40
O367	**70**	50c. blue	1·90	1·80
O368	**70**	1p. blue	50	50
O369	**70**	2p. blue	60	60
O370	**70**	5p. blue	70	70

1915. Optd OFICIAL.

O406	**79**	1c. blue	20	20
O407	**80**	2c. blue	20	20
O408	**79**	3c. blue	30	20
O409	**80**	4c. blue	20	20
O410	**79**	5c. blue	20	20
O411	**80**	6c. blue	20	20
O412	**80**	10c. blue	30	30
O413	**79**	15c. blue	30	30
O414	**80**	20c. blue	30	30
O415	**79**	25c. blue	50	50
O416	**80**	50c. blue	85	80

1925. Optd Oficial or OFICIAL.

O513	**79**	½c. green	20	20
O514	**79**	1c. violet	20	20
O515	**80**	2c. red	20	20
O516	**79**	3c. olive	20	20
O517	**80**	4c. red	20	20
O518	**79**	5c. black	20	20
O519	**80**	6c. brown	20	20
O520	**80**	10c. yellow	20	20
O521	**79**	15c. brown	20	20
O522	**80**	20c. brown	20	20
O523	**79**	25c. orange	30	30
O524	**80**	50c. blue	40	40

1929. Air. Official stamps of 1925 additionally optd Correo Aereo.

O618	**79**	25c. orange	65	65
O619	**80**	50c. blue	85	80

1931. Stamp of 1924 surch OFICIAL C$ 0.05 Correos 1928.

O651	**99**	5c. on 10c. brown	30	20

1931. No. 648 additionally surch OFICIAL and value.

O652	5c. on 10c. brown	30	20

1931. Stamps of 1914 optd 1931 (except 6c., 10c.), and also optd OFICIAL.

O670	**79**	1c. olive (No. 762)	20	20
O707	**80**	2c. red	7·00	6·75
O671	**79**	3c. blue	20	20
O672	**79**	5c. sepia	20	20
O673	**80**	6c. brown	30	25
O674	**80**	10c. blue (No. 697)	1·50	1·40
O675	**80**	10c. brown	30	25
O710	**79**	15c. orange	95	90
O711	**79**	25c. sepia	95	90
O712	**79**	25c. violet	2·00	2·00

1932. Air. Optd Correo Aereo OFICIAL only.

O688		15c. orange	55	55
O689	**80**	20c. orange	65	65
O690	**79**	25c. violet	65	65
O691	**80**	50c. green	75	70
O692	**80**	1cor. yellow	1·10	1·10

1932. Air. Optd 1931 Correo Aereo OFICIAL.

O693	**79**	25c. sepia	47·00	45·00

1932. Optd OFICIAL.

O694		1c. olive	20	20
O695	**80**	2c. red	20	20
O696	**79**	3c. blue	20	20
O697	**80**	4c. blue	20	20
O698	**79**	5c. sepia	30	25
O699	**80**	6c. brown	30	20
O700	**80**	10c. brown	30	20
O701	**79**	15c. orange	50	25
O702	**80**	20c. orange	80	35
O703	**79**	25c. violet	2·30	70
O704	**80**	50c. green	30	20
O705	**80**	1cor. yellow	35	25

1933. 441st Anniv of Columbus's Departure from Palos. As T 133, but inscr "CORREO OFICIAL". Roul.

O777	1c. yellow	1·80	1·70
O778	2c. yellow	1·80	1·70
O779	3c. brown	1·80	1·70
O780	4c. brown	1·80	1·70
O781	5c. brown	1·80	1·70
O782	6c. blue	2·30	2·20
O783	10c. violet	2·30	2·20
O784	15c. purple	2·30	2·20
O785	20c. green	2·30	2·20
O786	25c. green	3·00	3·00
O787	50c. red	3·75	3·50
O788	1cor. red	5·25	5·00

1933. Optd with T 134 and OFICIAL.

O814	**79**	1c. green	20	20
O815	**80**	2c. red	20	20
O816	**79**	3c. blue	20	20
O817	**80**	4c. blue	20	20
O818	**79**	5c. brown	20	20
O819	**80**	6c. grey	20	20
O820	**80**	10c. brown	20	20
O821	**79**	15c. red	20	20
O822	**80**	20c. orange	20	20
O823	**79**	25c. violet	20	20
O824	**80**	50c. green	20	20
O825	**80**	1cor. yellow	45	25

1933. Air. Optd with T 134 and CORREO Aereo OFICIAL.

O826	**79**	15c. violet	30	25
O827	**80**	20c. green	30	25
O828	**79**	25c. olive	30	25
O829	**80**	50c. green	35	35
O830	**80**	1cor. red	60	50

1935. Nos. O814/25 optd RESELLO – 1935 in a box.

O864A	**79**	1c. green	30	25
O865A	**80**	2c. red	30	25
O866A	**79**	3c. blue	30	25
O867A	**80**	4c. blue	30	25
O868A	**79**	5c. brown	30	25
O869A	**80**	6c. grey	30	25
O870A	**80**	10c. brown	30	25
O871A	**79**	15c. red	30	25
O872A	**80**	20c. orange	30	25
O873A	**79**	25c. violet	30	25
O874A	**80**	50c. green	30	25
O875A	**80**	1cor. yellow	35	35

1935. Air. Nos. O826/30 optd RESELLO – 1935 in a box.

O877	**79**	15c. violet	30	25
O878	**80**	20c. green	30	25
O879	**79**	25c. olive	30	30
O880	**80**	50c. green	90	90
O881	**80**	1cor. red	90	90

(O141)

1937. Nos. 913, etc, optd with Type O 141.

O935	**79**	1c. red	20	20
O936	**80**	2c. blue	20	20
O937	**79**	3c. brown	30	25
O938	**79**	5c. red	35	25
O939	**80**	10c. green	65	35
O940	**79**	15c. green	95	55
O941	**79**	25c. orange	1·10	70
O942	**80**	50c. brown	1·40	90
O943	**80**	1cor. blue	2·75	1·30

1937. Air. Nos. 926/30 optd with Type O 141.

O944	**112**	15c. orange	1·10	55
O945	**112**	20c. red	1·10	55
O946	**112**	25c. black	1·10	70
O947	**112**	50c. violet	1·10	70
O948	**112**	1cor. orange	1·10	70

O151 Islets in the Great Lake

1939

O1020	**O151**	2c. red	35	35
O1021	**O151**	3c. blue	35	35
O1022	**O151**	6c. brown	35	35
O1023	**O151**	7½c. green	35	35
O1024	**O151**	10c. brown	35	35
O1025	**O151**	15c. orange	35	35
O1026	**O151**	25c. violet	45	45
O1027	**O151**	50c. green	60	60

O152 Pres. Somoza

1939. Air.

O1028	**O152**	10c. brown	35	35
O1029	**O152**	15c. blue	35	35
O1030	**O152**	20c. yellow	35	35
O1031	**O152**	25c. violet	35	35
O1032	**O152**	30c. red	45	45
O1033	**O152**	50c. orange	80	80
O1034	**O152**	1cor. olive	1·50	1·50

O175 Managua Airport

1947. Air.

O1120	**O175**	5c. brown and black	30	30
O1121	-	10c. blue and black	30	30
O1122	-	15c. violet and black	30	30
O1123	-	20c. orange & black	30	30
O1124	-	25c. blue and black	30	30
O1125	-	50c. red and black	30	30
O1126	-	1cor. grey and black	50	50
O1127	-	2cor.50 brown and black	1·60	1·50

DESIGNS: 10c. Sulphur lagoon, Nejapa; 15c. Ruben Dario Monument, Managua; 20c. Baird's tapir; 25c. Genizaro Dam; 50c. Thermal baths, Tipitapa; 1cor. Highway and Lake Managua; 2cor.50, Franklin D. Roosevelt Monument, Managua.

O181 U.P.U. Offices, Berne

1950. Air. 75th Anniv of U.P.U. Inscr as in Type O 181. Frames in black.

O1159		5c. purple	20	20
O1160		10c. green	20	20
O1161		25c. purple	30	30
O1162	**O181**	50c. orange	30	30
O1163	-	1cor. blue	30	30
O1164	-	2cor.60 black	2·50	2·50
MSO1165		Six sheets each 121×96 mm. Nos. O1159/64 in blocks of four	25·00	25·00

DESIGNS—HORIZ: 5c. Rowland Hill; 10c. Heinrich von Stephan; 25c. Standehaus, Berne; 1cor. Monument, Berne; 2cor.60, Congress Medal.

1961. Air. Consular Fiscal stamps as T 203/4 with serial Nos. in red, surch Oficial Aereo and value.

O1448	10c. on 1cor. olive	20	20
O1449	15c. on 20cor. brown	20	20
O1450	20c. on 100cor. lake	20	20
O1451	25c. on 50c. blue	20	20
O1452	35c. on 50cor. brown	20	20
O1453	50c. on 3cor. red	20	20
O1454	1cor. on 2cor. green	30	30
O1455	2cor. on 5cor. red	50	50
O1456	5cor. on 10cor. violet	1·20	1·20

POSTAGE DUE STAMPS

D13

1896

D99A	**D13**	1c. orange	65	1·60
D100A	**D13**	2c. orange	65	1·60
D101A	**D13**	5c. orange	65	1·60
D102A	**D13**	10c. orange	65	1·60
D103A	**D13**	20c. orange	65	1·60
D104A	**D13**	30c. orange	65	1·60
D105A	**D13**	50c. orange	65	1·60

1897

D108A	1c. violet	65	1·50
D109A	2c. violet	65	1·50
D110A	5c. violet	65	1·50
D111A	10c. violet	65	1·50
D112A	20c. violet	1·50	1·90
D113A	30c. violet	65	1·50
D114A	50c. violet	65	1·50

1898

D124	1c. green	30	2·00
D125	2c. green	30	2·00
D126	5c. green	30	2·00
D127	10c. green	30	2·00
D128	20c. green	30	2·00
D129	30c. green	30	2·00
D130	50c. green	30	2·00

1899

D137	1c. red	30	2·00
D138	2c. red	30	2·00
D139	5c. red	30	2·00
D140	10c. red	30	2·00
D141	20c. red	30	2·00
D142	50c. red	30	2·00

D16

1900

D146	**D16**	1c. red	1·20	
D147	**D16**	2c. orange	1·20	
D148	**D16**	5c. blue	1·20	
D149	**D16**	10c. violet	1·20	
D150	**D16**	20c. brown	1·20	
D151	**D16**	30c. green	2·30	
D152	**D16**	50c. lake	2·30	

APPENDIX

The following stamps have either been issued in excess of postal needs, or have not been available to the public in reasonable quantities at face value. Such stamps may later be given full listings if there is evidence of regular postal use. Miniature sheets and imperforate stamps are excluded from this listing.

1996

Fauna. 2cor.×12. 2cor×12.
Animals. 2cor.50×12.; 2cor.50×9; 2cor.50×6.

Pt. 6, Pt. 14

NIGER

Area south of the Sahara. In 1920 was separated from Upper Senegal and Niger to form a separate colony. From 1944 to 1959 used the stamps of French West Africa.

In 1958 Niger became an autonomous republic within the French Community and on 3 August 1960 an independent republic.

100 centimes = 1 franc.

1921. Stamps of Upper Senegal and Niger optd TERRITOIRE DU NIGER.

1	**7**	1c. violet and purple	35	3·75
2	**7**	2c. purple and grey	45	3·50
3	**7**	4c. blue and black	1·10	5·75
4	**7**	5c. chocolate and brown	75	2·50
5	**7**	10c. green and light green	2·30	4·25
25	**7**	10c. pink on blue	1·40	6·00
6	**7**	15c. yellow and brown	80	3·50
7	**7**	20c. black and purple	1·50	4·00
8	**7**	25c. green and black	1·30	3·25
9	**7**	30c. carmine and red	3·00	6·00
26	**7**	30c. red and green	1·10	4·75
10	**7**	35c. violet and red	1·90	4·75
11	**7**	40c. red and grey	1·60	5·00
12	**7**	45c. brown and blue	1·20	7·25
13	**7**	50c. blue and ultramarine	2·00	5·50
27	**7**	50c. blue and grey	1·20	5·25
28	**7**	60c. red	1·50	4·00
14	**7**	75c. brown and yellow	1·60	8·25
15	**7**	1f. purple and brown	1·50	5·50
16	**7**	2f. blue and green	1·90	8·75
17	**7**	5f. black and violet	2·30	8·50

1922. Stamps of 1921 surch.

18	25c. on 15c. yellow & brown	1·10	7·25
19	25c. on 2f. blue and green	2·30	6·25
20	25c. on 5f. black and violet	1·70	5·75
21	60 on 75c. violet on pink	85	4·50
22	65 on 45c. brown and blue	2·50	8·50
23	85c. on 75c. brown & yellow	2·50	9·50
24	1f.25 on 1f. light blue & blue	1·40	8·50

3 Wells

4 Canoe on River Niger

5 Zinder Fort

1926

29	**3**	1c. green and purple	35	2·50
30	**3**	2c. red and grey	10	3·50
31	**3**	3c. brown and mauve	10	4·25
32	**3**	4c. black and brown	35	5·00
33	**3**	5c. green and red	55	3·00
34	**3**	10c. green and blue	10	80
35	**3**	15c. light green and green	1·00	3·50
36	**3**	15c. red and lilac	35	4·25
37	**4**	20c. brown and blue	40	5·50
38	**4**	25c. pink and black	90	2·50
39	**4**	30c. light green and green	2·30	4·75
40	**4**	30c. mauve and yellow	1·40	5·00
41	**4**	35c. blue and red on blue	1·00	4·00
42	**4**	35c. green and deep green	2·00	7·25
43	**4**	40c. grey and purple	10	2·30
44	**4**	45c. mauve and yellow	1·40	5·00
45	**4**	45c. green and turquoise	1·30	8·00
46	**4**	50c. green and red on green	35	30
47	**4**	55c. brown and red	2·30	8·25
48	**4**	60c. brown and red	65	7·75
49	**4**	65c. red and green	1·50	4·75
50	**4**	70c. red and green	2·30	8·25
51	**4**	75c. mauve and green on pink	1·80	5·00
52	**4**	80c. green and purple	2·30	8·00
53	**4**	90c. red and carmine	1·90	8·25
54	**4**	90c. green and red	2·00	6·25
55	**5**	1f. green and red	7·00	13·00
56	**5**	1f. orange and red	2·30	3·00
57	**5**	1f. red and green	1·70	7·00
58	**5**	1f.10 green and brown	6·00	12·00
59	**5**	1f.25 red and green	2·50	3·00
60	**5**	1f.25 orange and red	3·25	8·00
61	**5**	1f.40 brown and mauve	2·50	8·50
62	**5**	1f.50 light blue and blue	1·40	2·00
63	**5**	1f.60 green and brown	2·50	8·75
64	**5**	1f.75 brown and mauve	2·75	3·75
65	**5**	1f.75 ultramarine and blue	1·80	8·75
66	**5**	2f. brown and orange	1·80	2·00
67	**5**	2f.25 ultramarine and blue	2·50	6·75
68	**5**	2f.50 brown	3·50	6·50
69	**5**	3f. grey and mauve	2·00	1·60
70	**5**	5f. black and purple on pink	1·30	2·50
71	**5**	10f. mauve and lilac	1·80	4·25
72	**5**	20f. orange and green	2·75	6·25

1931. "Colonial Exhibition" key types inscr "NIGER".

73	**E**	40c. green	7·00	10·00
74	**F**	50c. mauve	5·50	8·50
75	**G**	90c. red	5·00	14·00
76	**H**	1f.50 blue	9·25	14·00

4a

1937. International Exhibition, Paris.

77	**4a**	20c. violet	1·20	5·75
78	**4a**	30c. green	1·30	6·25
79	**4a**	40c. red	90	4·75
80	**4a**	50c. brown and agate	1·00	4·00
81	**4a**	90c. red	1·10	3·50
82	**4a**	1f.50 blue	90	4·25
MS82a		120×100 mm. 3f. mauve Imperf	12·00	24·00

1938. Int Anti-cancer Fund. As T 17a of Oceanic Settlements.

83	1f.75+50c. blue	14·00	50·00

4b

1939. Caille.

84	**4b**	90c. orange	80	3·75
85	**4b**	2f. violet	75	1·60
86	**4b**	2f.25 blue	65	4·25

1939. New York World's Fair. As T 17b of Oceanic Settlements.

87	1f.25 red	2·00	5·75
88	2f.25 blue	80	7·00

1939. 150th Anniv of French Revolution. As T 17c of Oceanic Settlements.

89	45c.+25c. green and black	10·00	23·00
90	70c.+30c. brown and black	10·00	23·00
91	90c.+35c. orange and black	10·00	23·00
92	1f.25+1f. red and black	10·00	23·00
93	2f.25+2f. blue and black	10·00	23·00

4c

1940. Air.

94	**4c**	1f.90 blue	2·30	4·25
95	**4c**	2f.90 red	1·40	4·75
96	**4c**	4f.50 green	2·30	5·00
97	**4c**	4f.90 olive	1·60	6·50
98	**4c**	6f.90 orange	1·90	4·00

1941. National Defence Fund. Surch SECOURS NATIONAL and additional value.

98a	**4**	+1f. on 50c. green and red on green	6·00	9·50
98b	**4**	+2f. on 80c. green & pur	8·75	19·00
98c	**5**	+2f. on 1f.50 lt blue & bl	17·00	27·00
98d	**5**	+3f. on 2f. brown & orge	12·00	27·00

5a Zinder Fort

1942. Marshal Petain issue.

98e	**5a**	1f. green	65	5·50
98f	**5a**	2f.50 blue	75	5·50

5b Weighing Baby

1942. Air. Colonial Child Welfare Fund.

98g	-	1f.50+3f.50 green	80	6·00
98h	-	2f.+6f. brown	90	6·00
98i	**5b**	3f.+9f. red	1·00	5·50

DESIGNS: 49×28 mm: 1f.50, Maternity Hospital, Dakar; 2f. Dispensary, Mopti.

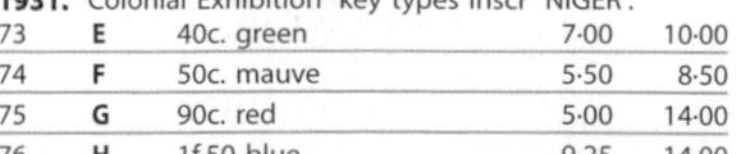

5c "Vocation"

1942. Air. Imperial Fortnight.

98j	**5c**	1f.20+1f.80 blue and red	1·40	7·25

5e

1942. Air. As T 5e but inscr "NIGER" at foot.

98k	**5e**	50f. red and yellow	3·00	7·00

7 Giraffes

8 Carmine Bee Eater

1959. Wild Animals and Birds. Inscr "PROTECTION DE LA FAUNE".

99	-	50c. turquoise, green and black (postage)	1·80	5·25
100	-	1f. multicoloured	1·80	5·25
101	-	2f. multicoloured	1·80	5·25
102	-	5f. mauve, black and brown	2·75	2·30
103	-	7f. red, black and green	5·25	5·00
104	-	10f. multicoloured	3·00	3·00
105	-	15f. sepia and turquoise	3·00	3·00
106	-	20f. black and violet	2·75	2·30
107	**7**	25f. multicoloured	3·00	2·30
108	**7**	30f. brown, bistre and green	2·50	2·75
109	-	50f. blue and brown	16·00	4·00
110	-	60f. sepia and green	20·00	7·50
111	-	85f. brown and bistre	7·50	4·75
112	-	100f. bistre and green	13·00	4·50
113	**8**	200f. multicoloured (air)	55·00	25·00
114	-	500f. green, brown and blue	23·00	23·00

DESIGNS—As Type **7**: HORIZ: 50c., 10f. African manatee. VERT: 1, 2f. Crowned cranes; 5, 7f. Saddle-bill stork; 15, 20f. Barbary sheep; 50, 60f. Ostriches; 85, 100f. Lion. As Type **8**: VERT: 500f. Game animals.

8a

1960. 10th Anniv of African Technical Co-operation Commission.

115	**8a**	25f. brown and ochre	1·80	4·50

9 Conseil de l'Entente Emblem

1960. 1st Anniv of Conseil de l'Entente.

116	**9**	25f. multicoloured	1·80	4·50

1960. Independence. No. 112 surch 200 F Independance 3-8-60.

117		200f. on 100f. bistre and green	13·50	13·50

11 Pres. Diori Hamani

1960

118	**11**	25f. black and bistre	60	45

12 U.N. Emblem and Niger Flag

1961. Air. 1st Anniv of Admission into U.N.

119	**12**	25f. red, green and orange	65	35
120	**12**	100f. green, red and emerald	2·40	1·20

12a

1962. Air. "Air Afrique" Airline.

121	**12a**	100f. violet, black and brown	1·90	95

12b

1962. Malaria Eradication.

122	**12b**	25f.+5f. brown	75	75

13 Athletics

1962. Abidjan Games, 1961. Multicoloured.

123	15f. Boxing and cycling (vert)	45	25
124	25f. Basketball and football (vert)	60	30
125	85f. Type **13**	1·80	80

13a

1962. 1st Anniv of Union of African and Malagasy States.

126	**13a**	30f. mauve	95	60

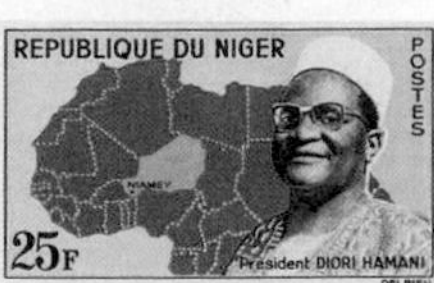

14 Pres. Hamani and Map

1962. 4th Anniv of Republic.

127	**14**	25f. multicoloured	60	35

14a

1963. Freedom from Hunger.

128	**14a**	25f.+5f. purple, brn & olive	75	75

15 Running

1963. Dakar Games.

129	-	15f. brown and blue	45	25
130	**15**	25f. red and brown	60	25
131	-	45f. black and green	1·10	55

DESIGNS—HORIZ: 15f. Swimming. VERT: 45f. Volleyball.

16 Agadez Mosque

1963. Air. 2nd Anniv of Admission to U.P.U. Multicoloured.

132	50f. Type **16**	1·20	45
133	85f. Gaya Bridge	1·90	80
134	100f. Presidential Palace, Niamey	2·00	1·00

17 Wood-carving

1963. Traditional Crafts. Multicoloured.

135	5f. Type **17** (postage)	30	20
136	10f. Skin-tanning (horiz)	35	20
137	25f. Goldsmith	60	30
138	30f. Mat-making (horiz)	1·00	45
139	85f. Potter	2·40	1·20
140	100f. Canoe building (horiz) (47×27 mm) (air)	3·00	1·60

17a

1963. Air. African and Malagasy Posts and Telecommunications Union.

141	**17a**	85f. multicoloured	1·50	80

1963. Air. Red Cross Centenary. Optd with cross and Centenaire de la Croix-Rouge in red.

142	**12**	25f. red, green and orange	90	60
143	**12**	100f. green, red and emerald	2·20	1·10

19 Costume Museum

1963. Opening of Costume Museum, Niamey. Vert costume designs. Multicoloured.

144	15f. Berber woman	35	25
145	20f. Haussa woman	55	25
146	25f. Tuareg woman	75	30
147	30f. Tuareg man	85	30
148	60f. Djerma woman	2·00	80
149	85f. Type **19**	2·20	1·00

20 "Europafrique"

1963. Air. European–African Economic Convention.

150	**20**	50f. multicoloured	4·25	3·00

21 Groundnut Cultivation

1963. Air. Groundnut Cultivation Campaign.

151	**21**	20f. blue, brown and green	55	30
152	-	45f. brown, blue and green	1·10	50
153	-	85f. multicoloured	2·00	1·00
154	-	100f. olive, brown and blue	2·50	1·30
MS154a		130×100 mm. Nos. 151/4	7·75	7·75

DESIGNS: 45f. Camel transport; 85f. Fastening sacks; 100f. Dispatch of groundnuts by lorry.

21a

1963. Air. 1st Anniv of "Air Afrique" and DC-8 Service Inauguration.

155	**21a**	50f. multicoloured	1·00	65

22 Man and Globe

1963. 15th Anniv of Declaration of Human Rights.

156	**22**	25f. blue, brown and green	75	40

23 "Telstar"

1964. Air. Space Telecommunications.

157	**23**	25f. olive and violet	50	25
158	-	100f. green and purple	1·60	1·10

DESIGN: 100f. "Relay".

24 "Parkinsonia aculeata"

1964. Flowers. Multicoloured.

159	5f. Type **24**	80	45
160	10f. "Russelia equisetiformis"	75	45
161	15f. "Lantana camara"	1·20	60
162	20f. "Agryeia nervosa"	1·20	60
163	25f. "Luffa cylindrica"	1·30	60
164	30f. "Hibiscus rosa-sinensis"	1·80	70
165	45f. "Plumierai rubra"	2·75	1·30
166	50f. "Catharanthus roseus"	3·00	1·40
167	60f. "Caesalpinia pulcherrima"	4·50	1·70

Nos. 164/7 have "REPUBLIQUE DU NIGER" at the top and the value at bottom right.

25 Statue, Abu Simbel

1964. Air. Nubian Monuments Preservation.

168	**25**	25f. green and brown	95	65
169	**25**	30f. brown and blue	1·50	90
170	**25**	50f. blue and purple	2·75	1·70

26 Globe and "Tiros" Satellite

1964. Air. World Meteorological Day.

171	**26**	50f. brown, blue and green	1·30	85

27 Sun Emblem and Solar Flares

1964. International Quiet Sun Years.

172	**27**	30f. red, violet and sepia	75	50

28 Convoy of Lorries

1964. O.M.N.E.S. (Nigerian Mobile Medical and Sanitary Organization) Commemoration.

173	**28**	25f. orange, olive and blue	55	15
174	-	30f. multicoloured	70	25
175	-	50f. multicoloured	95	45
176	-	60f. purple, orange & turq	1·20	1·40

DESIGNS: 30f. Tending children; 50f. Tending women; 60f. Open-air laboratory.

29 Rocket, Stars and Stamp Outline

1964. Air. "PHILATEC 1964" Int Stamp Exn, Paris.

177	**29**	50f. mauve and blue	1·30	80

30 European, African and Symbols of Agriculture and Industry

1964. Air. 1st Anniv of European–African Economic Convention.

178	**30**	50f. multicoloured	1·00	65

31 Pres. Kennedy

1964. Air. Pres. Kennedy Commemoration.

179	**31**	100f. multicoloured	2·30	1·70
MS179a		90×129 mm. No. 179 in block of four	6·75	6·50

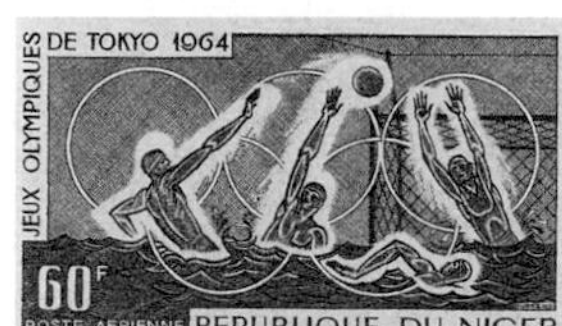

32 Water-polo

1964. Air. Olympic Games, Tokyo.

180	**32**	60f. brown, deep green and purple	1·00	80
181	-	85f. brown, blue and red	2·00	95
182	-	100f. blue, red and green	2·20	1·10
183	-	250f. blue, brown and green	5·00	2·75
MS183a		191×100 mm. Nos. 180/3	13·00	13·00

DESIGNS—HORIZ: 85f. Relay-racing. VERT: 100f. Throwing the discus; 250f. Athlete holding Olympic Torch.

32a

1964. French, African and Malagasy Co-operation.

184	**32a**	50f. brown, orange and violet	1·00	60

33 Azawak Tuareg Encampment

1964. Native Villages. Multicoloured.

185	15f. Type **33**	30	25
186	20f. Songhai hut	45	25
187	25f. Wogo and Kourtey tents	45	25
188	30f. Djerma hut	50	25
189	60f. Šorkawa fishermen's encampment	1·20	40
190	85f. Hausa urban house	1·80	60

34 Doctors and Patient and Microscope Slide

1964. Anti-leprosy Campaign.

191	**34**	50f. multicoloured	95	60

35 Abraham Lincoln

1965. Death Centenary of Abraham Lincoln.

192	**35**	50f. multicoloured	95	70

36 Instruction by "Radio-Vision"

1965. "Human Progress". Inscr as in T 36.

193	**36**	20f. brown, yellow and blue	45	25
194	-	25f. sepia, brown and green	55	25
195	-	30f. purple, red and green	80	40
196	-	50f. purple, blue and brown	1·10	50

DESIGNS: 25f. Student; 30f. Adult class; 50f. Five tribesmen ("Alphabetization").

37 Ader's Telephone

1965. I.T.U. Centenary.

197	**37**	25f. black, lake and green	75	25
198	-	30f. green, purple and red	95	40
199	-	50f. green, purple and red	1·30	70

DESIGNS: 30f. Wheatstone's telegraph; 50f. "Telautographe".

38 Pope John XXIII

1965. Air. Pope John Commemoration.

200	**38**	100f. multicoloured	1·80	1·00

39 Hurdling

1965. 1st African Games, Brazzaville.

201	**39**	10f. purple, green & brown	30	15
202	-	15f. red, brown and grey	50	25
203	-	20f. purple, blue and green	60	25
204	-	30f. purple, green and lake	95	25

DESIGNS—VERT: 15f. Running; 30f. Long-jumping. HORIZ: 20f. Pole-vaulting.

40 "Capture of Cancer" (the Crab)

1965. Air. Campaign against Cancer.

205	**40**	100f. brown, black & green	1·80	1·10

41 Sir Winston Churchill

1965. Air. Churchill Commemoration.

206	**41**	100f. multicoloured	1·80	1·10

42 Interviewing

1965. Radio Club Promotion.

207	**42**	30f. brown, violet and green	45	25
208	-	45f. red, black and buff	75	25
209	-	50f. multicoloured	95	40
210	-	60f. purple, blue and ochre	90	45

DESIGNS—VERT: 45f. Recording; 50f. Listening to broadcast. HORIZ: 60f. Listeners' debate.

43 "Agricultural and Industrial Workers"

1965. Air. International Co-operation Year.

211	**43**	50f. brown, black and bistre	1·00	55

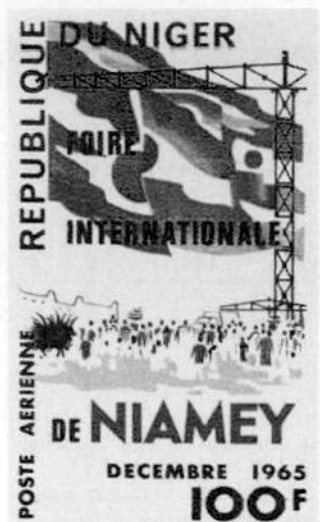

44 Fair Scene and Flags

1965. Air. International Fair, Niamey.

212	**44**	100f. multicoloured	1·50	95

45 Dr. Schweitzer and Diseased Hands

1966. Air. Schweitzer Commemoration.

213	**45**	50f. multicoloured	1·30	70

46 "Water Distribution and Control"

1966. Int Hydrological Decade Inauguration.

214	**46**	50f. blue, orange and violet	1·00	45

47 Weather Ship "France I"

1966. Air. 6th World Meteorological Day.

215	**47**	50f. green, purple and blue	1·50	70

48 White and "Gemini" Capsule

1966. Air. Cosmonauts.

216	**48**	50f. black, brown and green	1·20	60
217	-	50f. blue, violet and orange	1·20	60

DESIGN: No. 217, Leonov and "Voskhod" capsule.

49 Head-dress and Carvings

1966. World Festival of Negro Arts, Dakar.

218	**49**	30f. black, brown and green	60	35
219	-	50f. violet, brown and blue	95	50
220	-	60f. lake, violet and brown	1·00	60
221	-	100f. black, red and blue	1·90	95

DESIGNS: 50f. Carved figures and mosaics; 60f. Statuettes, drums and arch; 100f. Handicrafts and church.

50 "Diamant" Rocket and Gantry

1966. Air. French Space Vehicles. Multicoloured designs each showing different satellites.

222		45f. Type **50**	90	55
223		60f. "A 1" (horiz)	1·20	65
224		90f. "FR 1" (horiz)	1·50	85
225		100f. "D 1" (horiz)	2·00	1·20

51 Goalkeeper saving Ball

1966. World Cup Football Championship.

226	-	30f. red, brown and blue	80	25
227	**51**	50f. brown, blue and green	1·10	40
228	-	60f. blue, purple and bistre	1·40	70

DESIGNS—VERT: 30f. Player dribbling ball; 60f. Player kicking ball.

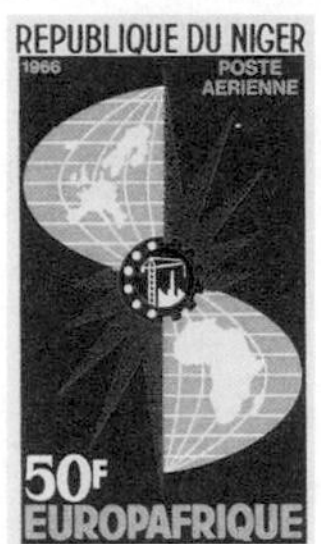

52 Cogwheel Emblem and Hemispheres

1966. Air. Europafrique.

229	**52**	50f. multicoloured	1·00	60

53 Parachutist

1966. 5th Anniv of National Armed Forces. Mult.

230		20f. Type **53**	45	25
231		30f. Soldiers with standard (vert)	55	25
232		45f. Armoured patrol vehicle (horiz)	80	45

53a

1966. Air. Inauguration of DC-8F Air Services.

233	**53a**	30f. olive, black and grey	75	40

54 Inoculating cattle

1966. Campaign for Prevention of Cattle Plague.

234	**54**	45f. black, brown and blue	1·50	70

55 "Voskhod 1"

1966. Air. Astronautics.

235	**55**	50f. blue, indigo and lake	95	55
236	-	100f. violet, blue and lake	2·00	1·10

DESIGN—HORIZ: 100f. "Gemini 6" and "7".

56 UNESCO "Tree"

1966. 20th Anniv of UNESCO.

237	**56**	50f. multicoloured	95	45

57 Japanese Gate, Atomic Symbol and Cancer ("The Crab")

1966. Air. International Cancer Congress, Tokyo.

238	**57**	100f. multicoloured	1·70	1·00

58 Furnace

1966. Malbaza Cement Works.

239	**58**	10f. blue, orange and brown	30	10
240	-	20f. blue and green	50	20
241	-	30f. brown, grey and blue	65	25
242	-	50f. indigo, brown and blue	95	40

DESIGNS—HORIZ: 20f. Electrical power-house; 30f. Works and cement silos; 50f. Installation for handling raw materials.

59 Niamey Mosque

1967. Air.

243	**59**	100f. blue, green and grey	2·00	1·10

60 Durer (self-portrait)

1967. Air. Paintings. Multicoloured.

244		50f. Type **60**	1·30	90
245		100f. David (self-portrait)	2·30	1·30
246		250f. Delacroix (self-portrait)	5·50	3·00

See also Nos. 271/2 and 277/9.

61 Red-billed Hornbill

1967. Birds.

247	**61**	1f. bistre, red and green (postage)	25	15
248	-	2f. black, brown and green	25	15
249	-	30f. multicoloured	75	40
249a	-	40f. purple, orange and green	3·50	1·10
250	-	45f. brown, green and blue	1·40	45
250a	-	65f. yellow, brown & pur	3·75	90
251	-	70f. multicoloured	2·40	80
251a	-	250f. blue, purple and green (48×27 mm) (air)	3·75	2·10

BIRDS: 2f. Lesser pied kingfishers; 30f. Common gonolek; 40f. Red bishop; 45f., 65f. Little masked weaver; 70f. Chestnut-bellied sandgrouse; 250f. Splendid glossy starlings.

62 Bobsleigh Course, Villard-de-Lans

1967. Grenoble—Winter Olympics Town (1968).

252	**62**	30f. brown, blue and green	55	30
253	-	45f. brown, blue and green	95	45
254	-	60f. brown, blue and green	1·00	65
255	-	90f. brown, blue and green	1·70	90

DESIGNS: 45f. Ski-jump, Autrans; 60f. Ski-jump, St. Nizier du Moucherotte; 90f. Slalom course, Chamrousse.

63 Family and Lions Emblem

1967. 50th Anniv of Lions International.

256	**63**	50f. blue, red and green	95	55

64 Weather Ship

1967. Air. World Meteorological Day.

257	**64**	50f. red, black and blue	1·80	95

65 View of World Fair

1967. Air. World Fair, Montreal.

258	**65**	100f. black, blue and purple	1·70	70

66 I.T.Y. Emblem and Jet Airliner

1967. International Tourist Year.

259	**66**	45f. violet, green and purple	75	45

67 Scouts around Campfire

1967. World Scout Jamboree, Idaho, U.S.A.

260	**67**	30f. brown, lake and blue	55	25
261	-	45f. blue, brown and orange	95	30
262	-	80f. lake, slate and bistre	1·50	55

DESIGNS—HORIZ: 45f. Jamboree emblem and scouts. VERT: 80f. Scout cooking meal.

68 Audio-Visual Centre

1967. Air. National Audio-Visual Centre, Niamey.

263	**68**	100f. violet, blue and green	1·50	75

69 Carrying Patient

1967. Nigerian Red Cross.

264	**69**	45f. black, red and green	95	30
265	-	50f. black, red and green	1·00	45
266	-	60f. black, red and green	1·40	50

DESIGNS: 50f. Nurse with mother and child; 60f. Doctor giving injection.

70 "Europafrique"

1967. Europafrique.

267	**70**	50f. multicoloured	95	45

71 Dr. Konrad Adenauer

1967. Air. Adenauer Commemoration.

268	**71**	100f. brown and blue	2·20	1·00
MS269		120×161 mm. No. 268 in block of four	10·00	10·00

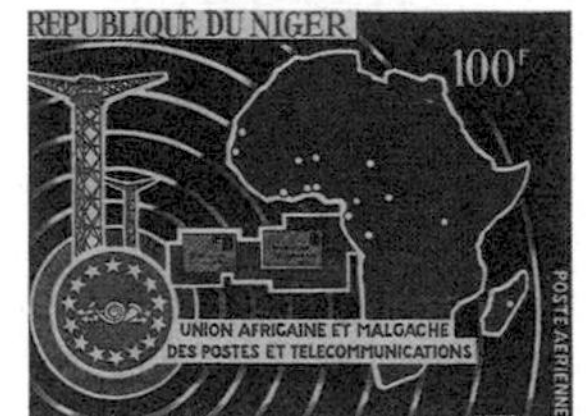

71a

1967. Air. 5th Anniv of African and Malagasy Post and Telecommunications Union (U.A.M.P.T.).

270	**71a**	100f. violet, green and red	1·70	75

1967. Air. Death Centenary of Jean Ingres (painter). Paintings by Ingres. As T 60. Multicoloured.

271	100f. "Jesus among the Doctors" (horiz)	3·00	1·50
272	150f. "Jesus restoring the Keys to St. Peter" (vert)	4·50	2·20

72 African Women

1967. U.N. Women's Rights Commission.

273	**72**	50f. brown, yellow and blue	95	45

72a

1967. 5th Anniv of West African Monetary Union.

274	**72a**	30f. green and purple	55	25

73 Nigerian Children

1967. Air. 21st Anniv of UNICEF.

275	**73**	100f. brown, blue and green	2·00	1·30

74 O.C.A.M. Emblem

1968. Air. O.C.A.M. Conference, Niamey.

276	**74**	100f. orange, green and blue	1·50	70

1968. Air. Paintings (self-portraits). As T 60. Multicoloured.

277	50f. J.-B. Corot	1·50	70
278	150f. Goya	1·50	55
279	200f. Van Gogh	3·50	1·40

75 Allegory of Human Rights

1968. Human Rights Year.

280	**75**	50f. indigo, brown and blue	1·20	55

76 Breguet 27 Biplane over Lake

1968. Air. 35th Anniv of 1st France–Niger Airmail Service.

281	**76**	45f. blue, green and mauve	1·20	45
282	-	80f. slate, brown and blue	1·80	70
283	-	100f. black, green and blue	2·75	95

DESIGNS—Potez 25TOE biplane: 80f. On ground; 100f. In flight.

77 "Joyous Health"

1968. 20th Anniv of W.H.O.

284	**77**	50f. indigo, blue and brown	75	35

78 Cyclists of 1818 and 1968

1968. Air. 150th Anniv of Bicycle.

285	**78**	100f. green and red	2·30	90

79 Beribboned Rope

1968. Air. 5th Anniv of Europafrique.

286	**79**	50f. multicoloured	95	55

80 Fencing

1968. Air. Olympic Games, Mexico.

287	**80**	50f. purple, violet and green	80	50
288	-	100f. black, purple and blue	1·50	70
289	-	150f. purple and orange	2·20	95
290	-	200f. blue, brown and green	3·00	1·70
MS291		240×104 mm. Nos. 287/90	10·00	10·00

DESIGNS—VERT: 100f. High-diving; 150f. Weight-lifting. HORIZ: 200f. Horse-jumping.

81 Woodland Kingfisher

1969. Birds. Dated "1968". Multicoloured.

292	5f. African grey hornbill (postage)	45	35
293	10f. Type **81**	55	35
294	15f. Senegal coucal	1·10	40
295	20f. Rose-ringed parakeets	1·20	55
296	25f. Abyssinian roller	1·90	50
297	50f. Cattle egret	2·75	1·00
298	100f. Violet starling (27×49 mm) (air)	5·25	1·90

See also Nos. 372/7, 567/8 and 714/15.

82 Mahatma Gandhi

1968. Air. "Apostles of Non-Violence".

299	**82**	100f. black and yellow	1·50	80
300	-	100f. black and turquoise	1·50	80
301	-	100f. black and grey	1·60	80
302	-	100f. black and orange	1·50	80
MS303		120×160 mm. Nos. 299/302	8·75	8·75

PORTRAITS: No. 300, President Kennedy; No. 301, Martin Luther King; No. 302, Robert F. Kennedy.

82a "Pare, Minister of the Interior" (J. L. La Neuville)

1968. Air. "Philexafrique" Stamp Exhibition, Abidjan (Ivory Coast, 1969) (1st issue).

304	**82a**	100f. multicoloured	3·75	3·75

83 Arms of the Republic

1968. Air. 10th Anniv of Republic.

305	**83**	100f. multicoloured	1·80	75

83a "Napoleon as First Consul" (Ingres)

1969. Air. Napoleon Bonaparte. Birth Bicentenary. Multicoloured.

306	50f. Type **83a**	2·50	1·40
307	100f. "Napoleon visiting the plague victims of Jaffa" (Gros)	3·75	2·10
308	150f. "Napoleon Enthroned" (Ingres)	6·00	2·20
309	200f. "The French Campaign" (Meissonier)	8·00	4·00

83b Giraffes and stamp of 1926

1969. Air. "Philexafrique" Stamp Exhibition, Abidjan, Ivory Coast (2nd issue).

310	**83b**	50f. brown, blue and orange	3·50	2·10

84 Boeing 707 over Rain-cloud and Anemometer

1969. Air. World Meteorological Day.

311	**84**	50f. black, blue and green	95	55

85 Workers supporting Globe

1969. 50th Anniv of I.L.O.

312	**85**	30f. red and green	60	30
313	**85**	50f. green and red	95	50

86 Panhard and Levassor (1909)

1969. Air. Veteran Motor Cars.

314	**86**	25f. green	75	40
315	-	45f. violet, blue and grey	95	40
316	-	50f. brown, ochre and grey	1·70	55
317	-	70f. purple, red and grey	2·50	90
318	-	100f. green, brown and grey	3·00	1·10

DESIGNS: 45f. De Dion Bouton 8 (1904); 50f. Opel "Doktor-wagen" (1909); 70f. Daimler (1910); 100f. Vermorel 12/16 (1912).

87 Mother and Child

1969. 50th Anniv of League of Red Cross Societies.

319	**87**	45f. red, brown and blue	95	30
320	-	50f. red, grey and green	1·00	45
321	-	70f. red, brown and ochre	1·50	65

DESIGNS—VERT: 70f. Man with Red Cross parcel. HORIZ: 50f. Symbolic Figures, Globe and Red Crosses.

88 Mouth and Ear

1969. 1st French Language Cultural Conf, Niamey.

322	**88**	100f. multicoloured	1·50	70

89 School Building

1969. National School of Administration.

323	**89**	30f. black, green and orange	55	30

1969. Air. 1st Man on the Moon. No. 114 optd L'HOMME SUR LA LUNE JUILLET 1969 APOLLO 11 and moon module.

324	500f. green, brown and blue	10·00	10·00

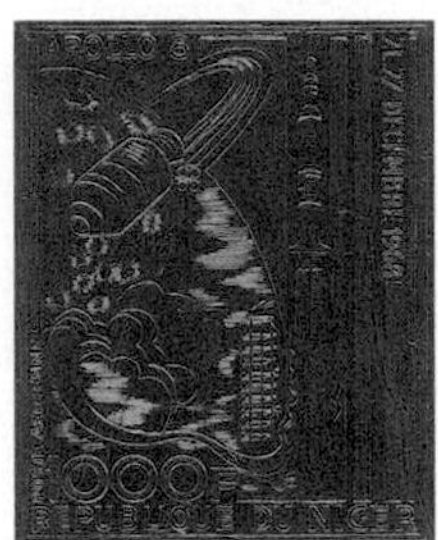
91 "Apollo 8" and Rocket

1969. Air. Moon Flight of "Apollo 8". Embossed on gold foil.

325	**91**	1000f. gold	25·00	25·00

91a

1969. 5th Anniv of African Development Bank.

326	**91a**	30f. brown, green and violet	75	30

92 Child and Toys

1969. Air. International Toy Fair, Nuremburg.

327	**92**	100f. blue, brown and green	1·70	75

93 Linked Squares

1969. Air. "Europafrique".

328	**93**	50f. yellow, black and violet	95	45

94 Trucks crossing Sahara

1969. Air. 45th Anniv of "Croisiere Noire" Trans-Africa Expedition.

329	**94**	50f. brown, violet & mauve	1·40	55
330	-	100f. violet, red and blue	2·50	80
331	-	150f. multicoloured	3·50	1·40
332	-	200f. green, indigo and blue	5·25	1·80

DESIGNS: 100f. Crossing the mountains; 150f. African children and expedition at Lake Victoria; 200f. Route Map, European greeting African and Citroen truck.

94a Aircraft, Map and Airport

1969. 10th Anniv of Aerial Navigation Security Agency for Africa and Madagascar (A.S.E.C.N.A.).

333	**94a**	100f. red	1·60	85

95 Classical Pavilion

1970. National Museum.

334	**95**	30f. blue, green and brown	45	25
335	-	45f. blue, green and brown	75	25
336	-	50f. blue, brown and green	80	35
337	-	70f. brown, blue and green	95	55
338	-	100f. brown, blue and green	1·50	80

DESIGNS: 45f. Temporary exhibition pavilion; 50f. Audio-visual pavilion; 70f. Local musical instruments gallery; 100f. Handicrafts pavilion.

96 Niger Village and Japanese Pagodas

1970. Air. "EXPO 70" World Fair, Osaka, Japan (1st issue).

339	**96**	100f. multicoloured	1·50	70

97 Hypodermic "Gun" and Map

1970. One Hundred Million Smallpox Vaccinations in West Africa.

340	**97**	50f. blue, purple and green	95	45

98 Education Symbols

1970. Air. International Education Year.

341	**98**	100f. slate, red and purple	1·50	70

99 Footballer

1970. World Cup Football Championship, Mexico.

342	**99**	40f. green, brown and purple	95	35
343	-	70f. purple, brown and blue	1·30	55
344	-	90f. red and black	1·80	70

DESIGNS: 70f. Football and Globe; 90f. Two footballers.

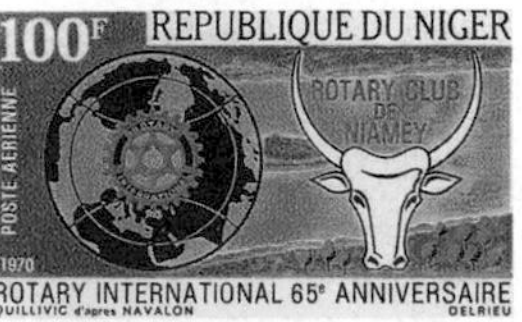

100 Rotary Emblems

1970. Air. 65th Anniv of Rotary International.

345	**100**	100f. multicoloured	1·80	80

101 Bay of Naples and Niger Stamp

1970. Air. 10th "Europafrique" Stamp Exn, Naples.

346	**101**	100f. multicoloured	1·50	65

102 Clement Ader's "Avion III" and Modern Airplane

1970. Air. Aviation Pioneers.

347	**102**	50f. grey, blue and red	1·00	45
348	-	100f. red, grey and blue	2·10	70
349	-	150f. lt brown, brn & grn	2·50	1·10
350	-	200f. red, bistre and violet	3·25	1·60
351	-	250f. violet, grey and red	4·50	1·90

DESIGNS: 100f. Joseph and Etienne Montgolfier balloon and rocket; 150f. Isaac Newton and gravity diagram; 200f. Galileo and rocket in planetary system; 250f. Leonardo da Vinci's drawing of a "flying machine" and Chanute's glider.

103 Cathode Ray Tube illuminating Books, Microscope and Globe

1970. Air. World Telecommunications Day.

352	**103**	100f. brown, green and red	1·70	75

1970. Inauguration of New U.P.U. Headquarters Building, Berne. As T 81 of New Caledonia.

353	30f. red, slate and brown	55	25
354	60f. violet, red and blue	95	45

1970. Air. Safe Return of "Apollo 13". Nos. 348 and 350 optd Solidarite Spatiale Apollo XIII 11-17 Avril 1970.

355	100f. red, slate and blue	1·50	70
356	200f. red, bistre and violet	2·75	1·10

105 U.N. Emblem, Man, Woman and Doves

1970. Air. 25th Anniv of U.N.O.

357	**105**	100f. multicoloured	1·50	70
358	**105**	150f. multicoloured	2·20	1·10

106 Globe and Heads

1970. Air. International French Language Conference, Niamey. Die-stamped on gold foil.

359	**106**	250f. gold and blue	5·25	5·25

107 European and African Women

1970. Air. "Europafrique".

360	**107**	50f. red and green	95	45

108 Japanese Girls and "EXPO 70" Skyline

1970. Air. "EXPO 70" World Fair, Osaka, Japan. (2nd issue).

361	**108**	100f. purple, orange & grn	1·30	65
362	-	150f. blue, brown & green	2·20	95

DESIGN: 150f. "No" actor and "EXPO 70" by night.

109 Gymnast on Parallel Bars

1970. Air. World Gymnastic Championships, Ljubljana.

363	**109**	50f. blue	75	45
364	-	100f. green	1·70	75
365	-	150f. purple	2·50	1·10
366	-	200f. red	3·00	1·50

GYMNASTS—HORIZ: 100f. Gymnast on vaulting-horse; 150f. Gymnast in mid-air. VERT: 200f. Gymnast on rings.

1970. Air. Moon Landing of "Luna 16". Nos. 349 and 351 surch LUNA 16 – Sept. 1970 PREMIERS PRELEVEMENTS AUTOMATIQUES SUR LA LUNE and value.

367	100f. on 150f. light brown, brown and green	2·00	80
368	200f. on 250f. violet, grey and red	4·00	1·60

111 Beethoven, Keyboard and Manuscripts

1970. Air. Birth Bicentenary of Beethoven. Mult.

369	100f. Type **111**	2·00	70
370	150f. Beethoven and allegory, "Hymn of Joy"	2·75	1·00

112 John F. Kennedy Bridge, Niamey

1970. Air. 12th Anniv of Republic.

371	**112**	100f. multicoloured	1·80	75

1971. Birds. Designs similar to T 81. Variously dated between 1970 and 1972. Multicoloured.

372	5f. African grey hornbill	30	25
373	10f. Woodland kingfisher	30	25
374	15f. Senegal coucal	65	40
375	20f. Rose-ringed parakeet	1·30	40
376	35f. Broad-tailed paradise whydah	2·50	70
377	50f. Cattle egret	6·50	1·80

The Latin inscription on No. 377 is incorrect, reading "Bulbucus ibis" instead of "Bubulcus ibis".

See also Nos. 714/15.

114 Pres. Nasser

1971. Air. Death of Pres. Gamal Nasser (Egyptian statesman). Multicoloured.

378	100f. Type **114**	1·20	50
379	200f. Nasser waving	2·30	1·10

115 Pres. De Gaulle

1971. Air. De Gaulle Commemoration. Embossed on gold foil.

380	**115**	1000f. gold	90·00	90·00

116 "MUNICH" and Olympic Rings

1971. Air. Publicity for 1972 Olympic Games, Munich.

381	**116**	150f. purple, blue & green	2·20	95

117 "Apollo 14" leaving Moon

1971. Air. Moon Mission of "Apollo 14".

382	**117**	250f. green, orange & blue	3·75	2·00

118 Symbolic Masks

1971. Air. Racial Equality Year.

383	**118**	100f. red, green and blue	1·30	70
384	-	200f. brown, green & blue	3·00	1·10

DESIGN: 200f. "Peoples" and clover-leaf emblem.

119 Niamey on World Map

1971. 1st Anniv of French-speaking Countries Co-operative Agency.

385	**119**	40f. multicoloured	80	55

120 African Telecommunications Map

1971. Air. Pan-African Telecommunications Network.

386	**120**	100f. multicoloured	1·00	50

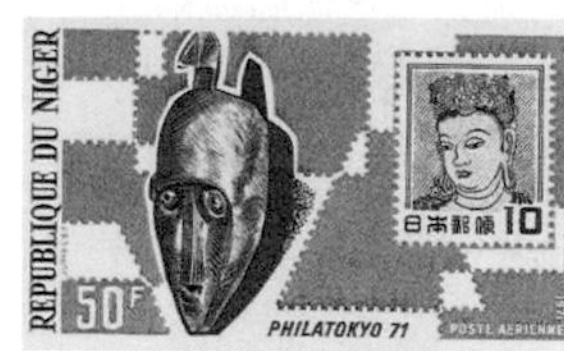

121 African Mask and Japanese Stamp

1971. Air. "PHILATOKYO 71" International Stamp Exhibition, Japan.

387	**121**	50f. olive, purple and green	1·00	50
388	-	100f. violet, red and green	1·80	75

DESIGN: 100f. Japanese scroll painting and Niger stamp.

122 "Longwood House, St. Helena" (C. Vernet)

1971. Air. 150th Anniv of Napoleon's Death. Paintings. Multicoloured.

389	150f. Type **122**	2·75	95
390	200f. "Napoleon's Body on his Camp-bed" (Marryat)	4·25	1·40

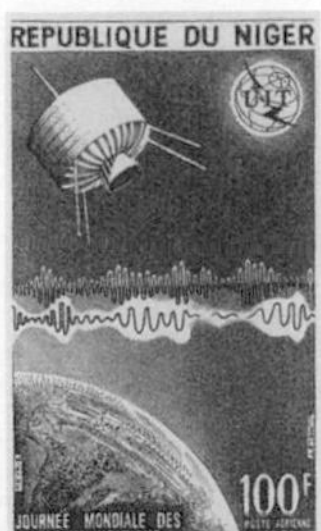

123 Satellite, Radio Waves, and Globe

1971. Air. World Telecommunications Day.

391	**123**	100f. multicoloured	1·80	75

124 Pierre de Coubertin and Discus-throwers

1971. Air. 75th Anniv of Modern Olympic Games.

392	**124**	50f. red and blue	95	35
393	-	100f. multicoloured	1·60	65
394	-	150f. blue and purple	2·50	1·20

DESIGNS—VERT: 100f. Male and female athletes holding torch. HORIZ: 150f. Start of race.

125 Scout Badges and Mount Fuji

1971. 13th World Scout Jamboree, Asagiri, Japan.

395	**125**	35f. red, purple and orange	55	25
396	-	40f. brown, plum and green	55	25
397	-	45f. green, red and blue	95	40
398	-	50f. green, violet and red	90	40

DESIGNS—VERT: 40f. Scouts and badge; 45f. Scouts converging on Japan. HORIZ: 50f. "Jamboree" in rope, and marquee.

126 "Apollo 15" on Moon

1971. Air. Moon Mission of "Apollo 15".

399	**126**	150f. blue, violet & brown	2·20	1·10

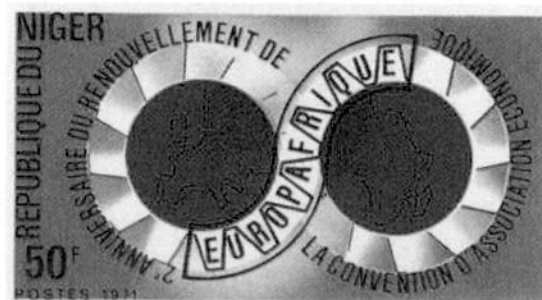

127 Linked Maps

1971. 2nd Anniv of Renewed "Europafrique" Convention, Niamey.

400	**127**	50f. multicoloured	1·00	50

128 Gouroumi (Hausa)

1971. Musical Instruments.

401	**128**	25f. brown, green and red	40	10
402	-	30f. brown, violet & green	55	25
403	-	35f. blue, green and purple	65	45
404	-	40f. brown, orange & grn	95	40
405	-	45f. ochre, brown and blue	1·30	60
406	-	50f. brown, red and black	1·70	70

DESIGNS: 30f. Molo (Djerma); 35f. Garaya (Hausa); 40f. Godjie (Djerma-Sonrai); 45f. Inzad (Tuareg); 50f. Kountigui (Sonrai).

129 De Gaulle in Uniform

1971. Air. 1st Death Anniv of Gen. Charles De Gaulle (French statesman).

407	**129**	250f. multicoloured	11·50	6·75

129a U.A.M.P.T. H.Q. and Rural Scene

1971. Air. 10th Anniv of African and Malagasy Posts and Telecommunications Union.

408	**129a**	100f. multicoloured	1·50	70

130 "Audience with Al Hariri" (Baghdad, 1237)

1971. Air. Moslem Miniatures. Multicoloured.

409	100f. Type **130**	1·50	70
410	150f. "Archangel Israfil" (Iraq, 14th-cent) (vert)	2·50	95
411	200f. "Horsemen" (Iraq, 1210)	3·50	1·80

131 Louis Armstrong

1971. Air. Death of Louis Armstrong (American jazz musician). Multicoloured.

412	100f. Type **131**	2·20	70
413	150f. Armstrong playing trumpet	3·25	1·10

132 "Children of All Races"

1971. 25th Anniv of UNICEF.

414	**132**	50f. multicoloured	75	50

133 "Adoration of the Magi" (Di Bartolo)

1971. Air. Christmas. Paintings. Multicoloured.

415	100f. Type **133**	1·50	60
416	150f. "The Nativity" (D. Ghirlandaio) (vert)	2·20	95
417	200f. "Adoration of the Shepherds" (Perugino)	3·00	1·30

134 Presidents Pompidou and Hamani

1972. Air. Visit of Pres. Pompidou of France.

418	**134**	250f. multicoloured	8·25	5·00

135 Ski "Gate" and Cherry Blossom

1972. Air. Winter Olympic Games, Sapporo, Japan.

419	**135**	100f. violet, red and green	1·50	70
420	-	150f. red, purple and violet	2·30	1·00
MS421		130×100 mm. Nos. 419/20	4·00	4·00

DESIGN—HORIZ: 150f. Snow crystals and Olympic flame.

135a "The Masked Ball"

1972. Air. UNESCO "Save Venice" Campaign.

422	**135a**	50f. multicoloured (vert)	1·40	55
423	-	100f. multicoloured (vert)	2·50	90
424	-	150f. multicoloured (vert)	3·75	1·30
425	-	200f. multicoloured	4·50	1·70

DESIGNS: Nos. 422/5 depict various details of Guardi's painting, "The Masked Ball".

136 Johannes Brahms and Music

1972. Air. 75th Death Anniv of Johannes Brahms (composer).

426	**136**	100f. green, myrtle and red	2·10	70

137 Saluting Hand

1972. Air. Int Scout Seminar, Cotonou, Dahomey.

427	**137**	150f. violet, blue & orange	2·00	70

138 Star Symbol and Open Book

1972. International Book Year.

428	**138**	35f. purple and green	55	25
429	-	40f. blue and lake	80	30

DESIGN: 40f. Boy reading, 16th-century galleon and early aircraft.

139 Heart Operation

1972. Air. World Heart Month.

430	**139**	100f. brown and red	1·80	70

140 Bleriot XI crossing the Channel, 1909

1972. Air. Milestones in Aviation History.

431	**140**	50f. brown, blue and lake	1·20	45
432	-	75f. grey, brown and blue	1·80	70
433	-	100f. ultramarine, blue and purple	3·50	1·60

DESIGNS: 75f. Lindbergh crossing the Atlantic in "Spirit of St. Louis"; 100f. First flight of Concorde, 1969.

141 Satellite and Universe

1972. Air. World Telecommunications Day.

434	**141**	100f. brown, purple & red	1·70	65

142 Boxing

1972. Air. Olympic Games, Munich. Sports and Munich Buildings.

435	**142**	50f. brown and blue	80	30
436	-	100f. brown and green	1·30	60
437	-	150f. brown and red	2·00	95
438	-	200f. brown and mauve	3·00	1·20
MS439		200×100 mm. Nos. 435/438	7·75	7·75

DESIGNS—VERT: 100f. Long-jumping; 150f. Football. HORIZ: 200f. Running.

143 A. G. Bell and Telephone

1972. Air. 50th Death Anniv of Alexander Graham Bell (inventor of telephone).

440	**143**	100f. blue, purple and red	1·50	50

144 "Europe on Africa" Map

1972. Air. "Europafrique" Co-operation.

441	**144**	50f. red, green and blue	75	30

145 Herdsman and Cattle

1972. Medicinal Salt-ponds at In-Gall. Multicoloured.

442	35f. Type **145**	1·00	35
443	40f. Cattle in salt-pond	1·80	40

146 Lottery Wheel

1972. 6th Anniv of National Lottery.

444	**146**	35f. multicoloured	75	45

147 Postal Runner

1972. Air. U.P.U. Day. Postal Transport.

445	**147**	50f. brown, green and lake	1·00	45
446	-	100f. green, blue and lake	1·50	70
447	-	150f. green, violet and lake	2·50	90

DESIGNS: 100f. Rural mail van; 150f. Loading Fokker Friendship mail plane.

147a

1972. 10th Anniv of West African Monetary Union.

448	**147a**	40f. grey, violet and brown	75	40

1972. Air. Gold Medal Winners. Munich Olympic Games. Nos. 435/8 optd with events and names, etc.

449	**142**	50f. brown and blue	80	35
450	-	100f. brown and green	1·30	60
451	-	150f. brown and red	2·10	80
452	-	200f. brown and mauve	2·75	1·20

OVERPRINTS: 50f. **WELTER CORREA MEDAILLE D'OR**; 100f. **TRIPLE SAUT SANEIEV MEDAILLE D'OR**; 150f. **FOOTBALL POLOGNE MEDAILLE D'OR**; 200f. **MARATHON SHORTER MEDAILLE D'OR.**

148 "The Raven and the Fox"

1972. Air. Fables of Jean de la Fontaine.
453 **148** 25f. black, brown & green 1·30 45
454 - 50f. brown, green & purple 2·50 70
455 - 75f. brown, green & brown 3·75 1·40
DESIGNS: 50f. "The Lion and the Rat"; 75f. "The Monkey and the Leopard".

149 Astronauts on Moon

1972. Air. Moon Flight of "Apollo 17".
456 **149** 250f. multicoloured 4·50 1·80

150 Dromedary Race

1972. Niger Sports.
457 **150** 35f. purple, red and blue 1·20 60
458 - 40f. lake, brown and green 1·50 85
DESIGN: 40f. Horse race.

151 Pole Vaulting

1973. 2nd African Games, Lagos, Nigeria. Mult.
459 35f. Type **151** 45 40
460 40f. Basketball 50 40
461 45f. Boxing 75 40
462 75f. Football 1·00 50

152 "Young Athlete"

1973. Air. Antique Art Treasures.
463 **152** 50f. red 75 35
464 - 100f. violet 1·50 55
DESIGN: 100f. "Head of Hermes".

153 Knight and Pawn

1973. World Chess Championships, Reykjavik, Iceland.
465 **153** 100f. green, blue and red 3·50 1·40

154 "Abutilon pannosum"

1973. Rare African Flowers. Multicoloured.
466 30f. Type **154** 1·00 45
467 45f. "Crotalaria barkae" 1·20 45
468 60f. "Dichrostachys cinerea" 1·60 55
469 80f. "Caralluma decaisneana" 2·20 70

155 Interpol Badge

1973. 50th Anniv of International Criminal Police Organization (Interpol).
470 **155** 50f. multicoloured 75 30

156 Scout with Radio

1973. Air. Scouting in Niger.
471 **156** 25f. brown, green and red 45 25
472 - 50f. brown, green and red 95 25
473 - 100f. brown, green and red 1·50 70
474 - 150f. brown, green and red 2·10 85
DESIGNS: 50f. First aid; 100f. Care of animals; 150f. Care of the environment.

157 Hansen and Microscope

1973. Centenary of Dr. Hansen's Discovery of Leprosy Bacillus.
475 **157** 50f. brown, green and blue 1·30 50

158 Nurse tending Child

1973. 25th Anniv of W.H.O.
476 **158** 50f. brown, red and blue 75 30

159 "The Crucifixion" (Hugo van der Goes)

1973. Air. Easter. Paintings. Multicoloured.
477 50f. Type **159** 95 25
478 100f. "The Deposition" (Cima de Conegliano) (horiz) 1·70 75
479 150f. "Pieta" (Bellini) (horiz) 2·40 85

160 Douglas DC-8 and Mail Van

1973. Air. Stamp Day.
480 **160** 100f. brown, red and green 2·00 75

161 W.M.O. Emblem and "Weather Conditions"

1973. Air. Centenary of W.M.O.
481 **161** 100f. brown, red and green 1·50 70

162 "Crouching Lioness" (Delacroix)

1973. Air. Paintings by Delacroix. Multicoloured.
482 150f. Type **162** 3·25 1·60
483 200f. "Tigress and Cub" 5·25 2·75

163 Crocodile

1973. Wild Animals from "Park W".
484 **163** 25f. multicoloured 70 25
485 - 35f. grey, gold and black 90 40
486 - 40f. multicoloured 1·20 40
487 - 80f. multicoloured 2·20 60
DESIGNS: 35f. African elephant; 40f. Hippopotamus; 80f. Warthog.

164 Eclipse over Mountain

1973. Total Eclipse of the Sun.
488 **164** 40f. violet 75 45

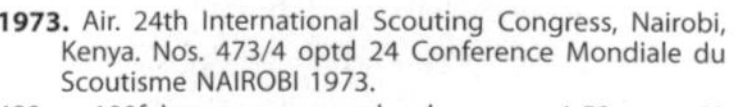
1973. Air. 24th International Scouting Congress, Nairobi, Kenya. Nos. 473/4 optd 24 Conference Mondiale du Scoutisme NAIROBI 1973.
489 100f. brown, green and red 1·50 60
490 150f. brown, green and red 2·20 85

166 Palomino

1973. Horse-breeding. Multicoloured.
491 50f. Type **166** 1·20 55
492 75f. French trotter 1·60 80
493 80f. English thoroughbred 2·00 90
494 100f. Arab thoroughbred 2·50 1·10

1973. Pan-African Drought Relief. African Solidarity. No. 436 surch SECHERESSE SOLIDARITE AFRICAINE and value.
495 **145** 100f. on 35f. multicoloured 2·00 1·40

168 Rudolf Diesel and Oil Engine

1973. 60th Death Anniv of Rudolf Diesel (engineer).
496 **168** 25f. blue, purple and grey 80 35
497 - 50f. grey, green and blue 1·50 55
498 - 75f. blue, black and mauve 2·20 90
499 - 125f. blue, red and green 3·25 1·40
DESIGNS: 50f. Series "BB 100" diesel locomotive; 75f. Type "060-DB1" diesel locomotive, France; 125f. Diesel locomotive No. 72004, France.

168a

1973. African and Malagasy Posts and Telecommunications Union.
500 **168a** 100f. red, green and brown 1·20 75

168b African Mask and Old Town Hall, Brussels

1973. Air. African Fortnight, Brussels.
501 **168b** 100f. purple, blue and red 1·50 70

169 T.V. Set and Class

1973. Schools Television Service.
502 **169** 50f. black, red and blue 95 40

1973. 3rd International French Language and Culture Conf, Liege. No. 385 optd 3e CONFERENCE DE LA FRANCOPHONIE LIEGE OCTOBRE 1973.
503 **110** 40f. multicoloured 95 40

171 "Apollo"

1973. Classical Sculptures.

504	**171**	50f. green and brown	1·70	55
505	-	50f. black and brown	1·70	55
506	-	50f. brown and red	1·70	55
507	-	50f. purple and red	1·70	55

DESIGNS: No. 505, "Atlas"; No. 506, "Hercules"; No. 507, "Venus".

172 Bees and Honeycomb

1973. World Savings Day.

508	**172**	40f. brown, red and blue	95	40

173 "Food for the World"

1973. Air. 10th Anniv of World Food Programme.

509	**173**	50f. violet, red and blue	95	45

174 Copernicus and "Sputnik 1"

1973. Air. 500th Birth Anniv of Copernicus (astonomer).

510	**174**	150f. brown, blue and red	2·20	95

175 Pres. John Kennedy

1973. Air. 10th Death Anniv of U.S. President Kennedy.

511	**175**	100f. multicoloured	1·50	70
MS512 80×100 mm. 200f. multicoloured			3·00	3·00

176 Kounta Songhai Blanket

1973. Niger Textiles. Multicoloured.

513		35f. Type **176**	80	40
514		40f. Tcherka Snghai blanket (horiz)	1·20	55

177 Barges on River Niger

1974. Air. 1st Anniv of Ascent of Niger by "Fleet of Hope".

515	**177**	50f. blue, green and red	1·20	70
516	-	75f. purple, blue and green	1·80	70

DESIGN: 75f. "Barban Maza" (tug) and barge.

178 Lenin

1974. Air. 50th Death Anniv of Lenin.

517	**178**	50c. brown	2·20	80

179 Slalom Skiing

1974. Air. 50th Anniv of Winter Olympic Games.

518	**179**	200f. red, brown and blue	3·75	1·40

180 Newly-born Baby

1974. World Population Year.

519	**180**	50f. multicoloured	75	40

181 Footballers and "Global" Ball

1974. Air. World Cup Football Championship, West Germany.

520	**181**	75f. violet, black & brown	70	45
521	-	150f. brown, green & turq	1·50	85
522	-	200f. blue, orange & green	2·10	1·50
MS523 130×100 mm. 250f. green, bistre and brown			3·75	3·75

DESIGNS: 150f. to 250f. Football scenes similar to Type **181**.

182 "The Crucifixion" (Grunewald)

1974. Air. Easter. Paintings. Multicoloured.

524		50f. Type **182**	80	40
525		75f. "Avignon Pieta" (attributed to E. Quarton)	1·20	55
526		125f. "The Entombment" (G. Isenmann)	1·90	75

183 Class 230K Locomotive, 1948, France and Locomotive No. 5511, 1938, U.S.A.

1974. Famous Railway Locomotives of the Steam Era.

527	**183**	50f. green, black and violet	1·30	55
528	-	75f. green, black & brown	2·00	75
529	-	100f. multicoloured	2·75	1·30
530	-	150f. brown, black and red	4·00	1·40

DESIGNS: 75f. Class 21 locomotive, 1893, France; 100f. Locomotive, 1866, U.S.A. and "Mallard", Great Britain; 150f. Marc Seguin locomotive, 1829, France and Stephenson's "Rocket", 1829.

184 Map of Member Countries

1974. 15th Anniv of Conseil de l'Entente.

531	**184**	40f. multicoloured	90	45

185 Knights

1974. Air. 21st Chess Olympiad, Nice.

532	**185**	50f. brown, blue & indigo	2·10	90
533	-	75f. purple, brown & green	2·50	1·10

DESIGN: 75f. Kings.

186 Marconi and "Elettra" (steam yacht)

1974. Birth Centenary of Guglielmo Marconi (radio pioneer).

534	**186**	50f. blue, brown & mauve	95	45

187 Astronaut on Palm of Hand

1974. Air. 5th Anniv of 1st Landing on Moon.

535	**187**	150f. brown, blue & indigo	2·00	90

188 Tree on Palm of Hand

1974. National Tree Week.

536	**188**	35f. turquoise, grn & brn	95	50

189 "The Rhinoceros" (Longhi)

1974. Air. Europafrique.

537	**189**	250f. multicoloured	8·50	4·25

190 Camel Saddle

1974. Handicrafts.

538	**190**	40f. red, blue and brown	75	30
539	-	50f. blue, red and brown	95	45

DESIGN: 50f. Statuettes of horses.

1974. Air. West Germany's Victory in World Cup Football Championships. No. MS523 optd R.F.A. HOLLANDE 1.

MS540 130×100 mm. **181** 250f. green, bistre and brown			3·75	3·75

192 Frederic Chopin

1974. 125th Death Anniv of Frederic Chopin.

541	**192**	100f. black, red and blue	2·10	80

1974. Beethoven's Ninth Symphony Commemoration. As T 192.

542		100f. lilac, blue and indigo	2·10	80

DESIGN: 100f. Beethoven.

193 European Woman and Douglas DC-8 Airliners

1974. Air. Centenary of U.P.U.

No.	Type	Description	Mint	Used
543	**193**	50f. turquoise, grn & pur	95	40
544	-	100f. blue, mauve & ultram	2·00	70
545	-	150f. brown, blue & indigo	2·20	1·10
546	-	200f. brown, orange & red	3·00	1·30

DESIGNS: 100f. Japanese woman and electric locomotives; 150f. American Indian woman and liner; 200f. African woman and road vehicles.

194 "Skylab" over Africa

1974. Air. "Skylab" Space Laboratory.

No.	Type	Description	Mint	Used
547	**194**	100f. violet, brown & blue	1·50	60

195 Don-don Drum

1974

No.	Type	Description	Mint	Used
548	**195**	60f. purple, green and red	1·40	70

196 Tree and Compass Rose

1974. 1st Death Anniv of Tenere Tree (desert landmark).

No.	Type	Description	Mint	Used
549	**196**	50f. brown, blue and ochre	3·00	1·40

197 "Virgin and Child" (Correggio)

1974. Air. Christmas. Multicoloured.

No.	Type	Description	Mint	Used
550		100f. Type **197**	1·50	55
551		150f. "Virgin and Child, and St. Hilary" (F. Lippi)	2·30	80
552		200f. "Virgin and Child" (Murillo)	3·00	1·40

198 "Apollo" Spacecraft

1975. Air. "Apollo–Soyuz" Space Test Project.

No.	Type	Description	Mint	Used
553	**198**	50f. green, red and blue	80	45
554	-	100f. grey, red and blue	1·20	60
555	-	150f. purple, plum & blue	2·00	85

DESIGNS: 100f. "Apollo" and "Soyuz" docked; 150f. "Soyuz" spacecraft.

199 European and African Women

1975. Air. Europafrique.

No.	Type	Description	Mint	Used
556	**199**	250f. brown, purple & red	3·75	1·90

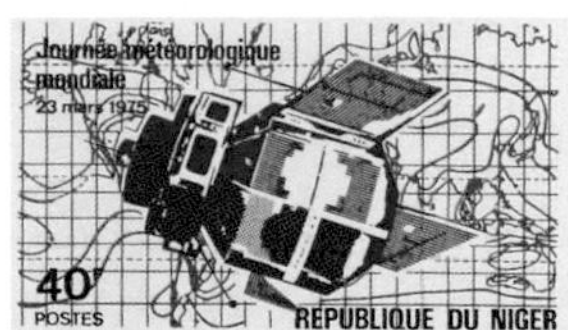

200 Communications Satellite and Weather Map

1975. World Meteorological Day.

No.	Type	Description	Mint	Used
557	**200**	40f. red, black and blue	75	40

201 "Christ in the Garden of Olives" (Delacroix)

1975. Air. Easter. Multicoloured.

No.	Type	Description	Mint	Used
558		75f. Type **201**	1·00	45
559		125f. "The Crucifixion" (El Greco) (vert)	1·80	75
560		150f. "The Resurrection" (Limousin) (vert)	2·30	95

202 Lt-Col. S. Kountche, Head of State

1975. Air. 1st Anniv of Military Coup.

No.	Type	Description	Mint	Used
561	**202**	100f. multicoloured	1·50	75

203 "City of Truro", 1903, Great Britain

1975. Famous Locomotives. Multicoloured.

No.	Type	Description	Mint	Used
562		50f. Type **203**	1·40	45
563		75f. Class 05 steam locomotive No. 003, 1937, Germany	2·00	50
564		100f. "General", 1855, U.S.A. (dated "1863")	2·75	90
565		125f. Series BB 15000 electric locomotive, 1971, France	4·00	1·40

1975. Birds. As Nos. 296 and 298, but dated "1975". Multicoloured.

No.	Type	Description	Mint	Used
567		25f. Abyssinian roller (postage)	1·80	55
568		100f. Violet starlings (air)	3·25	1·10

205 "Zabira" Leather Bag

1975. Niger Handicrafts. Multicoloured.

No.	Type	Description	Mint	Used
569		35f. Type **205**	45	25
570		40f. Chequered rug	55	40
571		45f. Flower pot	75	45
572		60f. Gourd	1·20	55

206 African Woman and Child

1975. International Women's Year.

No.	Type	Description	Mint	Used
573	**206**	50f. blue, brown and red	95	45

207 Dr. Schweitzer and Lambarene Hospital

1975. Birth Centenary of Dr. Albert Schweitzer.

No.	Type	Description	Mint	Used
574	**207**	100f. brown, green & black	1·70	85

208 Peugeot, 1892

1975. Early Motor-cars.

No.	Type	Description	Mint	Used
575	**208**	50f. blue and mauve	1·20	55
576	-	75f. purple and blue	1·70	70
577	-	100f. mauve and green	2·50	90
578	-	125f. green and red	3·00	1·30

DESIGNS: 75f. Daimler, 1895; 100f. Fiat, 1899; 125f. Cadillac, 1903.

209 Tree and Sun

1975. National Tree Week.

No.	Type	Description	Mint	Used
579	**209**	40f. green, orange and red	95	45

210 Boxing

1975. Traditional Sports.

No.	Type	Description	Mint	Used
580	**210**	35f. brown, orange & black	55	25
581	-	40f. brown, green & black	75	30
582	-	45f. brown, blue and black	75	45
583	-	50f. brown, red and black	85	50

DESIGNS—VERT: 40f. Boxing; 50f. Wrestling. HORIZ: 45f. Wrestling.

211 Leontini Tetradrachme

1975. Ancient Coins.

No.	Type	Description	Mint	Used
584	**211**	50f. grey, blue and red	80	25
585	-	75f. grey, blue and mauve	1·10	45
586	-	100f. grey, orange and blue	1·60	55
587	-	125f. grey, purple & green	2·20	85

COINS: 75f. Athens tetradrachme; 100f. Himer diadrachme; 125f. Gela tetradrachme.

212 Putting the Shot

1975. Air. "Pre-Olympic Year". Olympic Games, Montreal (1976).

No.	Type	Description	Mint	Used
588	**212**	150f. brown and red	2·00	80
589	-	200f. red, chestnut and brown	2·50	1·10

DESIGN: 200f. Gymnastics.

213 Starving Family

1975. Pan-African Drought Relief.

No.	Type	Description	Mint	Used
590	**213**	40f. blue, brown & orange	90	50
591	-	45f. brown and blue	2·20	1·10
592	-	60f. blue, green and orange	1·30	65

DESIGNS: 45f. Animal skeletons; 60f. Truck bringing supplies.

214 Trading Canoe crossing R. Niger

1975. Tourism. Multicoloured.

593	40f. Type **214**	80	45
594	45f. Boubon Camp entrance	95	45
595	50f. Boubon Camp view	1·00	55

215 U.N. Emblem and Peace Dove

1975. Air. 30th Anniv of U.N.O.

596	**215**	100f. light blue and blue	1·30	55

216 "Virgin of Seville" (Murillo)

1975. Air. Christmas. Multicoloured.

597	50f. Type **216**	75	40
598	75f. "Adoration of the Shepherds" (Tintoretto) (horiz)	1·20	55
599	125f. "Virgin with Angels" (Master of Burgo d'Osma)	1·80	1·10

1975. Air. "Apollo–Soyuz" Space Link. Nos. 533/5 optd JONCTION 17 Juillet 1975.

600	**198**	50f. green, red and blue	80	35
601	-	100f. grey, red and blue	1·20	60
602	-	150f. purple, plum & blue	1·80	60

218 "Ashak"

1976. Literacy Campaign. Multicoloured.

603	25f. Type **218**	30	10
604	30f. "Kaska"	30	25
605	40f. "Iccee"	35	25
606	50f. "Tuuri-nya"	45	25
607	60f. "Lekki"	65	25

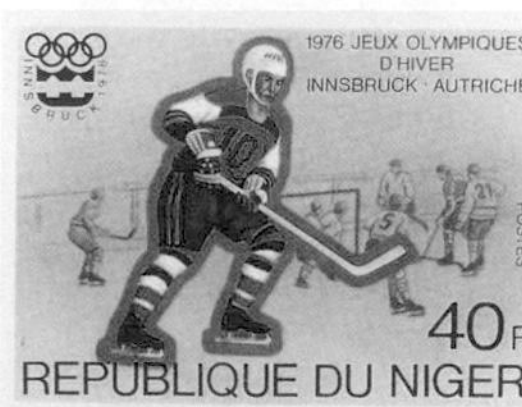

219 Ice Hockey

1976. Winter Olympic Games, Innsbruck, Austria. Multicoloured.

608	40f. Type **219** (postage)	45	25
609	50f. Tobogganing	60	30
610	150f. Ski-jumping	1·80	65
611	200f. Figure-skating (air)	1·80	80
612	300f. Cross-country skiing	2·75	1·20
MS613	117×78 mm. 500f. Speed Ice-skating	5·25	2·20

220 Early Telephone and Satellite

1976. Telephone Centenary.

614	**220**	100f. orange, blue & green	1·50	70

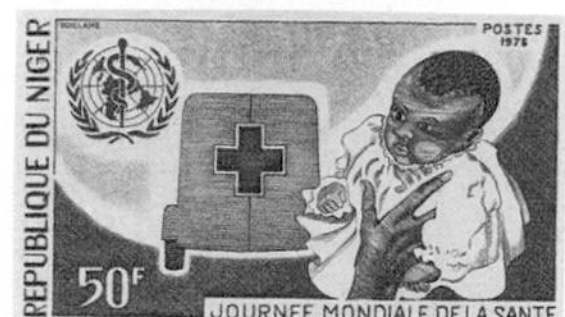

221 Baby and Ambulance

1976. World Health Day.

615	**221**	50f. red, brown and purple	95	30

222 Washington crossing the Delaware (after Leutze)

1976. Bicentenary of American Revolution. Mult.

616	40f. Type **222** (postage)	40	10
617	50f. First soldiers of the Revolution	55	25
618	150f. Joseph Warren – martyr of Bunker Hill (air)	1·20	40
619	200f. John Paul Jones aboard the "Bonhomme Richard"	2·00	80
620	300f. Molly Pitcher – heroine of Monmouth	2·75	1·20
MS621	128×97 mm. 500f. "Soldiers' farewell; the beginning of the revolution" (after F. Darley)	5·25	2·10

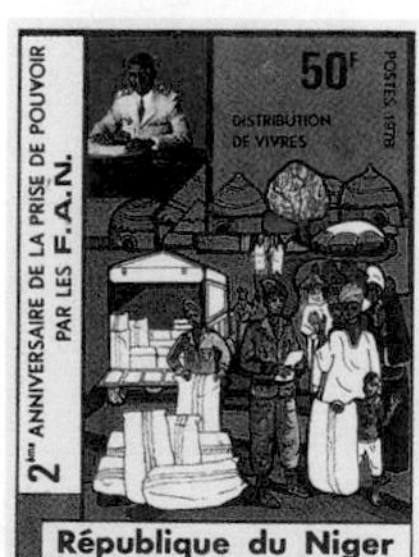

223 Distribution of Provisions

1976. 2nd Anniv of Military Coup. Multicoloured.

622	50f. Type **223**	55	25
623	100f. Soldiers with bulldozer (horiz)	1·20	55

224 "Hindenburg" crossing Lake Constance

1976. Air. 75th Anniv of Zeppelin Airships. Multicoloured.

624	40f. Type **224**	55	20
625	50f. LZ-3 over Wurzberg	75	25
626	150f. L-9 over Friedrichshafen	2·20	60
627	200f. LZ-2 over Rothenburg (vert)	2·75	80
628	300f. "Graf Zeppelin II" over Essen	3·75	95
MS629	129×103 mm. 500f. "LZ-127" crossing Alps	6·00	2·00

225 "Europafrique" Symbols

1976. "Europafrique".

630	**225**	100f. multicoloured	1·50	70

226 Plant Cultivation

1976. Communal Works. Multicoloured.

631	25f. Type **226**	30	25
632	30f. Harvesting rice	40	25

227 Boxing

1976. Olympic Games, Montreal. Multicoloured.

633	40f. Type **227**	35	15
634	50f. Basketball	50	15
635	60f. Football	60	15
636	80f. Cycling (horiz)	95	25
637	100f. Judo (horiz)	1·20	45
MS638	194×79 mm. 150f. Athletics (horiz)	2·00	90

228 Motobecane "125"

1976. Motorcycles.

639	**228**	50f. violet, brown & turq	85	30
640	-	75f. green, red & turquoise	1·20	50
641	-	100f. brown, orange & pur	1·90	70
642	-	125f. slate, olive and black	2·20	1·10

DESIGNS: 75f. Norton "Challenge"; 100f. B.M.W. "903"; 125f. Kawasaki "1000".

229 Cultivation Map

1976. Operation "Sahel Vert". Multicoloured.

643	40f. Type **229**	45	25
644	45f. Tending plants (vert)	60	25
645	60f. Planting sapling (vert)	1·00	35

1976. International Literacy Day. Nos. 603/7 optd JOURNEE INTERNATIONALE DE L'ALPHABETISATION.

646	**218**	25f. multicoloured	30	15
647	-	30f. multicoloured	30	15
648	-	40f. multicoloured	40	25
649	-	50f. multicoloured	45	25
650	-	60f. multicoloured	55	25

231 Basket Making

1976. Niger Women's Association. Multicoloured.

651	40f. Type **231**	55	25
652	45f. Hairdressing (horiz)	60	40
653	50f. Making pottery	85	40

232 Wall Paintings

1976. "Archaeology". Multicoloured.

654	40f. Type **232**	2·20	55
655	50f. Neolithic statuettes	2·50	55
656	60f. Dinosaur skeleton	4·50	80

233 "The Nativity" (Rubens)

1976. Air. Christmas. Multicoloured.

657	50f. Type **233**	80	25
658	100f. "Holy Night" (Correggio)	1·50	65
659	150f. "Adoration of the Magi" (David) (horiz)	2·30	1·10

234 Benin Ivory Mask

1977. 2nd World Festival of Negro-African Arts, Lagos.

660	**234**	40f. brown	55	25
661	-	50f. blue	95	45

DESIGNS—HORIZ: 50f. Nigerian stick dance.

235 Students in Class

1977. Alphabetization Campaign.

662	**235**	40f. multicoloured	45	25
663	**235**	50f. multicoloured	55	30
664	**235**	60f. multicoloured	95	35

236 Examining Patient

1977. Village Health. Multicoloured.

665	40f. Type **236**	60	25
666	50f. Examining baby	95	45

237 Rocket Launch

1977. "Viking" Space Mission. Multicoloured.

667	50f. Type **237** (postage)	55	25
668	80f. "Viking" approaching Mars (horiz)	95	30
669	100f. "Viking" on Mars (horiz) (air)	95	25
670	150f. Parachute descent	1·30	50
671	200f. Rocket in flight	1·90	95
MS672	104×77 mm. 400f. "Viking" landing on Mars (horiz)	3·75	1·50

238 Marabou Stork

1977. Fauna Protection.

673	**238**	80f. sepia, bistre and red	2·30	1·00
674	-	90f. brown and turquoise	2·50	1·00

DESIGN: 90f. Bushbuck.

239 Satellite and Weather Symbols

1977. World Meteorological Day.

675	**239**	100f. blue, black & turq	1·50	70

240 Gymnastic Exercise

1977. 2nd Youth Festival, Tahoua. Multicoloured.

676	40f. Type **240**	50	30
677	50f. High jumping	75	45
678	80f. Choral ensemble	1·10	55

241 Red Cross and Children playing

1977. World Health Day. Child Immunization Campaign.

679	**241**	80f. red, mauve and orange	95	40

242 Fly, Dagger, and W.H.O. Emblem in Eye

1977. Fight against Onchocerciasis (blindness caused by worm infestation).

680	**242**	100f. blue, grey and red	1·30	70

243 Guirka Tahoua Dance

1977. "Popular Arts and Traditions". Multicoloured.

681	40f. Type **243**	65	40
682	50f. Maifilafili Gaya	95	45
683	80f. Naguihinayan Loga	4·25	60

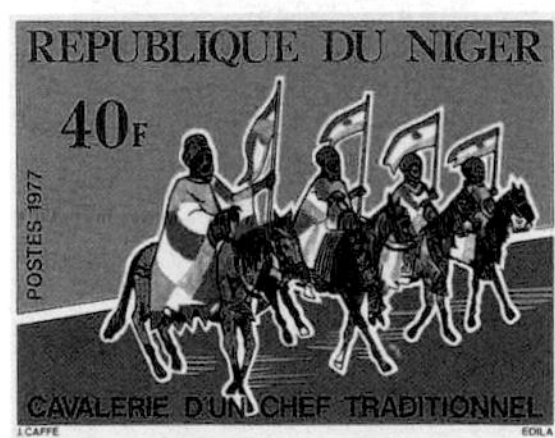

244 Four Cavalrymen

1977. Chiefs' Traditional Cavalry. Multicoloured.

684	40f. Type **244**	80	30
685	50f. Chieftain at head of cavalry	95	45
686	60f. Chieftain and cavalry	1·30	70

245 Planting Crops

1977. "Operation Green Sahel" (recovery of desert).

687	**245**	40f. multicoloured	75	40

246 Albert John Luthuli (Peace, 1960)

1977. Nobel Prize Winners. Multicoloured.

688	50f. Type **246**	45	25
689	80f. Maurice Maeterlinck (Literature, 1911)	95	25
690	100f. Allan L. Hodgkin (Medicine, 1963)	1·00	30
691	150f. Albert Camus (Literature, 1957)	1·60	45
692	200f. Paul Ehrlich (Medicine, 1908)	2·00	60
MS693	117×80 mm. 500f. Theodore Roosevelt (Peace, 1906)	5·50	1·60

247 Mao Tse-tung

1977. 1st Death Anniv of Mao Tse-tung (Chinese leader).

694	**247**	100f. black and red	3·50	1·80

248 Vittorio Pozzo (Italy)

1977. World Football Cup Elimination Rounds. Multicoloured.

695	40f. Type **248**	45	10
696	50f. Vincente Feola, Spain	50	25
697	80f. Aymore Moreira, Portugal	75	25
698	100f. Sir Alf Ramsey, England	1·30	45
699	200f. Helmut Schoen, West Germany	2·10	65
MS700	117×78 mm. 500f. Sepp Herberger (Germany)	5·50	2·10

249 Horse's Head and Parthenon

1977. UNESCO Commemoration.

701	**249**	100f. blue, red and pale blue	2·00	90

250 Carrying Water

1977. Women's Work. Multicoloured.

702	40f. Type **250**	55	25
703	50f. Pounding maize	65	40

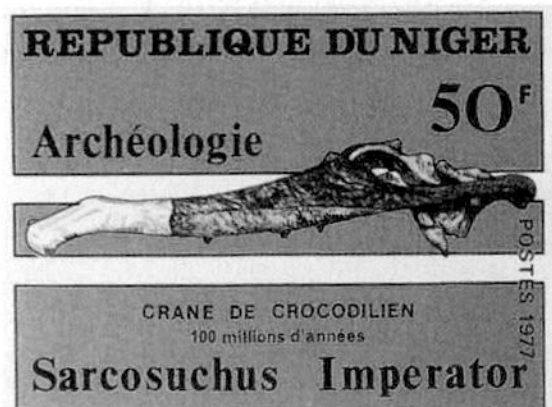

251 Crocodile Skull

1977. Archaeology. Multicoloured.

704	50f. Type **251**	1·30	70
705	80f. Neolithic tools	1·80	1·10

252 Paul Follereau and Leper

1978. 25th Anniv of World Leprosy Day.

706	**252**	40f. red, blue and orange	55	25
707	-	50f. black, red and orange	70	35

DESIGN—HORIZ: 50f. Follereau and two lepers.

253 "The Assumption"

1978. 400th Birth Anniv of Peter Paul Rubens. Paintings. Multicoloured.

708	50f. Type **253**	45	15
709	70f. "The Artist and his Friends" (horiz)	55	25
710	100f. "History of Maria de Medici"	1·00	40
711	150f. "Alathea Talbot"	1·70	55
712	200f. "Portrait of the Marquise de Spinola"	2·30	70
MS713	85×111 mm. 500f. "St. Ildofonse and the Virgin"	6·00	1·70

1978. As Nos. 376/7 but redrawn and background colour of 35f. changed to blue, 35f. undated, 50f. dated "1978".

714	35f. Broad-tailed paradise whydah	2·20	70
715	50f. Cattle egret	1·80	60

The 50f. is still wrongly inscribed "Balbucus".

254 Putting the Shot

1978. National Schools and University Sports Championships. Multicoloured.

716	40f. Type **254**	35	15
717	50f. Volleyball	45	25
718	60f. Long-jumping	55	25
719	100f. Throwing the javelin	95	40

255 Nurse assisting Patient

1978. Niger Red Cross.

720	**255**	40f. multicoloured	45	25

256 Station and Dish Aerial

1978. Goudel Earth Receiving Station.

721	**256**	100f. multicoloured	1·00	65

257 Football and Flags of Competing Nations

1978. World Cup Football Championship, Argentina. Multicoloured.

722	40f. Type **257**	35	10
723	50f. Football in net	70	25
724	100f. Globe and goal	1·00	30
725	200f. Tackling (horiz)	1·80	75
MS726	102×78 mm. 300f. Footballer and globe	3·00	1·60

258 "Fireworks"

1978. Air. 3rd African Games, Algiers. Multicoloured.

727	40f. Type **258**	45	25
728	150f. Olympic rings emblem	1·60	80

259 Niamey Post Office

1978. Niamey Post Office. Multicoloured.

729	40f. Type **259**	40	25
730	60f. Niamey Post Office (different)	55	40

260 Aerial View of Water-works

1978. Goudel Water-works.

731	**260**	100f. multicoloured	1·00	60

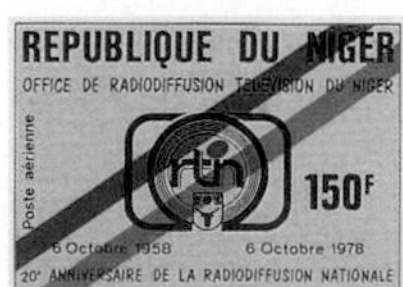

261 R.T.N. Emblem

1978. Air. 20th Anniv of Niger Broadcasting.

732	**261**	150f. multicoloured	1·50	85

262 Golden Eagle and Oldenburg 2g. Stamp of 1859

1978. Air. "Philexafrique" Stamp Exhibition, Libreville, Gabon (1st issue) and Int Stamp Fair, Essen, West Germany. Multicoloured.

733	100f. Type **262**	2·75	2·10
734	100f. Giraffes and Niger 1959 2f. stamp	2·75	2·10

See also Nos. 769/70.

263 Giraffe

1978. Endangered Animals. Multicoloured.

735	40f. Type **263**	1·00	35
736	50f. Ostrich	1·60	45
737	70f. Cheetah	2·30	60
738	150f. Scimitar oryx (horiz)	4·75	1·10
739	200f. Addax (horiz)	7·00	1·60
740	300f. Hartebeest (horiz)	9·25	2·20

1978. World Cup Football Championship Finalists. Nos. 695/9 optd.

741	**248**	40f. multicoloured	45	25
742	-	50f. multicoloured	60	25
743	-	80f. multicoloured	1·00	40
744	-	100f. multicoloured	1·20	70
745	-	200f. multicoloured	2·30	1·10
MS746		117×78 mm. 500f. Optd as No. 745	5·50	5·25

OVERPRINTS: 40f. **EQUIPE QUATRIEME: ITALIE**; 50f. **EQUIPE TROISIEME: BRESIL**; 80f. **EQUIPE SECONDE: PAYS BAS**; 100f. **EQUIPE VAINQUEUR: ARGENTINE**. 200 f; **ARGENTINE - PAYS BAS 3 - 1**.

265 Dome of the Rock, Jerusalem

1978. Palestinian Welfare.

747	**265**	40f.+5f. multicoloured	55	40

266 Laying Foundation Stone, and View of University

1978. Air. Islamic University of Niger.

748	**266**	100f. multicoloured	95	55

267 Tinguizi

1978. Musicians. Multicoloured.

749	100f. Type **267**	1·20	65
750	100f. Chetima Ganga (horiz)	1·20	65
751	100f. Dan Gourmou	1·20	65

268 "The Homecoming" (Daumier)

1979. Paintings. Multicoloured.

752	50f. Type **268**	95	25
753	100f. "Virgin in Prayer" (Durer)	95	25
754	150f. "Virgin and Child" (Durer)	1·50	45
755	200f. "Virgin and Child" (Durer) (different)	2·00	65
MS756	103×78 mm. 500f. "Virgin and Child with Garland"	6·00	1·80

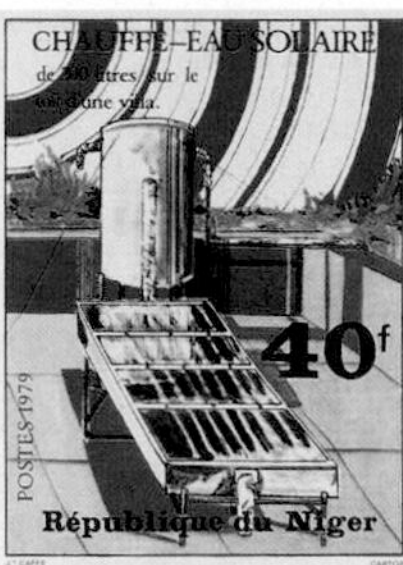

269 Feeder Tanks

1979. Solar Energy. Multicoloured.

757	40f. Type **269**	45	25
758	50f. Solar panels on house roofs (horiz)	55	40

270 Langha Contestants

1979. Traditional Sports. Multicoloured.

759	40f. Type **270**	45	25
760	50f. Langha contestants clasping hands	55	30

271 Children with Building Bricks

1979. International Year of the Child. Multicoloured.

761	40f. Type **271**	45	20
762	100f. Children with book	1·00	30
763	150f. Children with model airplane	1·80	60

272 Rowland Hill, Peugeot Mail Van and French "Ceres" Stamp of 1849

1979. Death Centenary of Sir Rowland Hill. Mult.

764	40f. Type **272**	50	20
765	100f. Canoes and Austrian newspaper stamp, 1851	1·20	30
766	150f. "DC-3" aircraft & U.S. "Lincoln" stamp, 1869	1·80	45
767	200f. Advanced Passenger Train (APT), Great Britain and Canada 7½d. stamp, 1857	2·20	65
MS768	119×81 mm. 400f. French electric train and Niger 75c. stamp, 1926	4·50	1·70

273 Zabira Decorated Bag and Niger 45f. Stamp, 1965

1979. "Philexafrique 2" Exhibition, Gabon (2nd issue).

769	**273**	50f. multicoloured	1·50	1·10
770	-	150f. blue, red and carmine	3·75	2·10

DESIGN: 150f. Talking Heads, world map, satellite and U.P.U. emblem.

274 Alcock and Brown Statue and Vickers Vimy Aircraft

1979. 60th Anniv of First Transatlantic Flight.

771	**274**	100f. multicoloured	1·30	45

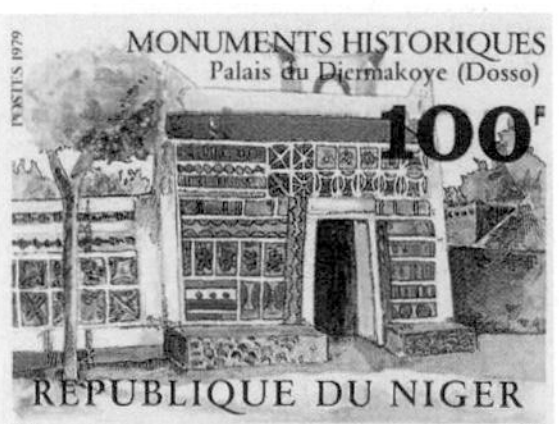

275 Djermakoye Palace

1979. Historic Monuments.

772	**275**	100f. multicoloured	1·00	60

276 Bororos in Festive Headdress

1979. Annual Bororo Festival. Multicoloured.

773	45f. Type **276**	50	45
774	60f. Bororo women in traditional costume (vert)	70	45

277 Boxing

1979. Pre-Olympic Year.

775	**277**	45f. multicoloured	20	10
776	-	100f. multicoloured	1·00	30
777	-	150f. multicoloured	1·50	45
778	-	250f. multicoloured	2·50	65
MS779		117×79 mm. 500f. multicoloured	4·50	1·60

DESIGNS: 100f. to 500f. Various boxing sheets.

278 Class of Learner-drivers

1979. Driving School.

780	**278**	45f. multicoloured	55	40

279 Douglas DC-10 over Map of Niger

1979. Air. 20th Anniv of ASECNA (African Air Safety Organization).

781	**279**	150f. multicoloured	1·20	40

1979. "Apollo 11" Moon Landing. Nos. 667/8, 670/1 optd alunissage apollo XI juillet 1969 and lunar module.

782	50f. Type **237** (postage)	45	25
783	80f. "Viking" approaching Mars (horiz)	80	45
784	150f. Parachute descent (air)	1·50	80
785	200f. Rocket in flight	2·00	1·10
MS786	104×77 mm. 400f. "Viking" landing on Mars (horiz)	4·00	4·00

281 Four-man Bobsleigh

1979. Winter Olympic Games, Lake Placid (1980). Multicoloured.

787	40f. Type **281**	45	15
788	60f. Downhill skiing	55	25
789	100f. Speed skating	95	40
790	150f. Two-man bobsleigh	1·50	55
791	200f. Figure skating	2·00	70
MS792	116×78 mm. 300f. Cross-country skiing	3·25	1·40

282 Le Gaweye Hotel

1980. Air.

793	**282**	100f. multicoloured	95	55

283 Sultan and Court

1980. Sultan of Zinder's Court. Multicoloured.

794	45f. Type **283**	45	25
795	60f. Sultan and court (different)	55	25

284 Chain Smoker and Athlete

1980. World Health Day. Anti-smoking Campaign.

796	**284**	100f. multicoloured	95	60

285 Walking

1980. Olympic Games, Moscow. Multicoloured.

797	60f. Throwing the javelin	60	20
798	90f. Type **285**	1·00	25
799	100f. High jump (horiz)	1·20	45
800	300f. Running (horiz)	2·75	90
MS801	105×79 mm. 500f. High jumping (different)	4·50	1·60

1980. Winter Olympic Games Medal Winners. Nos. 787/MS792 optd.

802	**281**	40f. **VAINQUEUR R.D.A.**	45	25
803	-	60f. **VAINQUEUR STENMARK SUEDE**	55	25
804	-	100f. **VAINQUEUR HEIDEN Etats-Unis**	95	55
805	-	150f. **VAINQUEURS SCHERER-BENZ Suisse**	1·40	75
806	-	200f. **VAINQUEUR COUSINS Grande Bretagne**	2·10	95
MS807		116×78 mm. 300f. **VAINQUEUR ZIMIATOV/U.R.S.S**	3·25	3·00

287 Village Scene

1980. Health Year.

808	**287**	150f. multicoloured	1·40	75

288 Class 150 (first locomotive in Japan, 1871)

1980. Steam Locomotives. Multicoloured.

809	45f. Type **288**	55	30
810	60f. "Fred Merril", 1848, U.S.A.	75	35
811	90f. Series 61, 1934, Germany	1·10	40
812	100f. Type P2, 1900, Prussia	1·40	70
813	130f. "Aigle", 1846, France	2·10	85
MS814	105×92 mm. 425f. "Rocket"	5·75	5·75

289 Steve Biko and Map of Africa

1980. 4th Death Anniv of Steve Biko (South African Anti-apartheid Worker).

815	**289**	150f. multicoloured	1·20	85

1980. Olympic Medal Winners. Nos. 787/MS801 optd.

816	**285**	60f. **KULA (URSS)**	55	25
817	-	90f. **DAMILANO (IT)**	95	35
818	-	100f. **WZSOLA (POL)**	1·20	40
819	-	300f. **YIFTER (ETH)**	2·75	1·20
MS820		105×79 mm. 500f. *WESSIG (RDA)*	4·00	3·50

291 Footballer

1980. World Cup Football Championship, Spain (1982). Various designs showing Football.

821	**291**	45f. multicoloured	35	15
822	-	60f. multicoloured	45	15
823	-	90f. multicoloured	95	25
824	-	100f. multicoloured	95	40
825	-	130f. multicoloured	1·10	40
MS826		113×91 mm. 425f. multicoloured	4·50	1·50

292 U.A.P.T. Emblem

1980. 5th Anniv of African Posts and Telecommunications Union.

827	**292**	100f. multicoloured	95	60

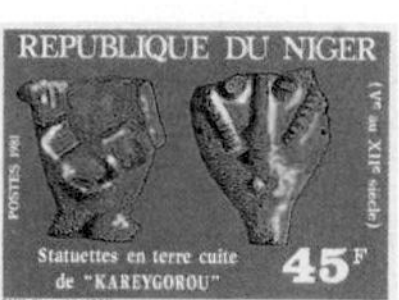

293 Earthenware Statuettes

1981. Kareygorou Culture Terracotta Statuettes. Multicoloured.

828	45f. Type **293**	35	25
829	60f. Head (vert)	55	25
830	90f. Head (different) (vert)	80	40
831	150f. Three heads	1·50	70

294 "Self-portrait"

1981. Paintings by Rembrandt. Multicoloured.

832	60f. Type **294**	70	25
833	90f. "Portrait of Hendrickje at the Window"	90	25
834	100f. "Portrait of an Old Man"	1·00	40
835	130f. "Maria Trip"	1·50	40
836	200f. "Self-portrait" (different)	2·00	70
837	400f. "Portrait of Saskia"	4·00	1·40

295 Ostrich

1981. Animals. Multicoloured.

839	10f. Type **295**	80	30
840	20f. Scimitar oryx	40	30
841	25f. Addra gazelle	45	30
842	30f. Arabian bustard	1·30	55
843	60f. Giraffe	85	35
844	150f. Addax	2·00	75

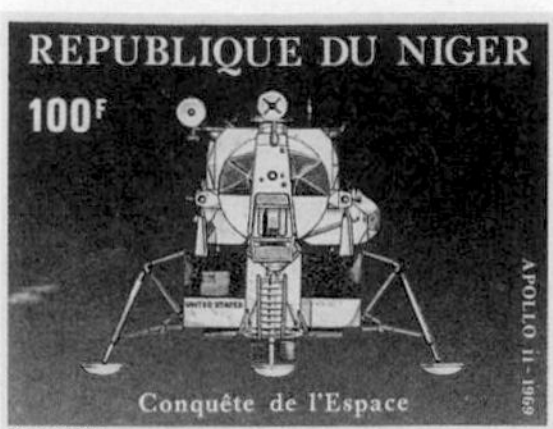

296 "Apollo 11"

1981. Air. Conquest of Space. Multicoloured.

845	100f. Type **296**	95	45
846	150f. Boeing 747 SCA carrying space shuttle	1·40	45
847	200f. Rocket carrying space shuttle	1·80	70
848	300f. Space shuttle flying over planet	2·75	95
MS848a	101×78 mm. 500f. Space shuttle returning to Earth	4·50	1·70

297 Tanks

1981. 7th Anniv of Military Coup.

849	**297**	100f. multicoloured	95	60

298 Disabled Archer

1981. International Year of Disabled People.

850	**298**	50f. dp brown, red & brown	95	35
851	-	100f. brown, red and green	1·30	65

DESIGN: 100f. Disabled draughtsman.

299 Ballet Mahalba

1981. Ballet Mahalba. Multicoloured.

852	100f. Type **299**	95	55
853	100f. Ballet Mahalba (different)	95	55

300 "Portrait of Olga in an Armchair"

1981. Air. Birth Centenary of Pablo Picasso (artist). Multicoloured.

854	60f. Type **300**	75	25
855	90f. "The Family of Acrobats"	1·00	40
856	120f. "The Three Musicians"	1·50	55
857	200f. "Paul on a Donkey"	2·50	80
858	400f. "Young Girl drawing in an Interior" (horiz)	4·25	1·40

301 Mosque and Ka'aba

1981. 15th Centenary of Hejira.

859	301	100f. multicoloured	95	55

302 Carriage

1981. British Royal Wedding.

860	302	150f. multicoloured	1·30	45
861	-	200f. multicoloured	2·00	60
862	-	300f. multicoloured	2·75	85
MS863 117×78 mm. 400f. multicoloured			3·75	1·50

DESIGNS: 200f. to 400f. Similar designs showing carriages.

303 Sir Alexander Fleming

1981. Birth Centenary of Sir Alexander Fleming (discoverer of Penicillin).

864	303	150f. blue, brown and green	2·50	1·10

304 Pen-nibs, Envelope, Flower and U.P.U. Emblem

1981. International Letter Writing Week.

865	304	65f. on 45f. blue and red	60	30
866	-	85f. on 60f. blue, orange and black	95	50

DESIGN: 85f. Quill, hand holding pen and U.P.U. emblem.

305 Crops, Cattle and Fish

1981. World Food Day.

867	305	100f. multicoloured	95	55

306 Tackling

1981. World Cup Football Championship, Spain (1982). Multicoloured.

868	40f. Type **306**	40	15
869	65f. Goalkeeper fighting for ball	55	15
870	85f. Passing ball	80	30
871	150f. Running with ball	1·50	55
872	300f. Jumping for ball	2·75	95
MS873 103×78 mm. 500f. Running for ball		4·50	1·70

307 Peugeot, 1912

1981. 75th Anniv of French Grand Prix Motor Race. Multicoloured.

874	20f. Type **307**	45	25
875	40f. Bugatti, 1924	60	25
876	65f. Lotus-Climax, 1962	95	30
877	85f. Georges Boillot	1·20	55
878	150f. Phil Hill	2·30	70
MS879 119×96 mm. 450f. United States Grand Prix, 1967		6·50	2·30

308 "Madonna and Child" (Botticelli)

1981. Christmas. Various Madonna and Child Paintings by named artists. Multicoloured.

880	100f. Type **308**	95	45
881	200f. Botticini	1·80	70
882	300f. Botticini (different)	2·75	1·00

309 Children watering Plants

1982. School Gardens. Multicoloured.

883	65f. Type **309**	60	30
884	85f. Tending plants and examining produce	90	50

310 Arturo Toscanini (conductor, 25th death anniv)

1982. Celebrities' Anniversaries. Multicoloured.

885	120f. Type **310**	1·70	55
886	140f. "Fruits on a Table" (Manet, 150th birth anniv) (horiz)	1·70	80
887	200f. "L'Estaque" (Braque, birth centenary) (horiz)	2·75	1·00
888	300f. George Washington (250th birth anniv)	3·75	1·30
889	400f. Goethe (poet, 150th death anniv)	5·00	1·70
890	500f. Princess of Wales (21st birthday)	5·50	2·00
MS891 80×104 mm. 500f. Princess of Wales (different)		4·50	1·70

311 Palace of Congresses

1982. Palace of Congresses.

892	311	150f. multicoloured	1·50	85

312 Martial Arts

1982. 7th Youth Festival, Agadez. Multicoloured.

893	65f. Type **312**	55	25
894	100f. Traditional wrestling	95	60

313 Planting a Tree

1982. National Re-afforestation Campaign. Multicoloured.

895	150f. Type **313**	1·50	55
896	200f. Forest and desert	1·80	85

314 Scouts in Pirogue

1982. 75th Anniv of Boy Scout Movement. Mult.

897	65f. Type **314**	75	25
898	85f. Scouts in inflatable dinghy	1·00	25
899	130f. Scouts in canoe	1·30	55
900	200f. Scouts on raft	1·90	75
MS901 80×104 mm. 400f. Scouts on beach		4·00	2·00

315 Map of Africa showing Member States

1982. Economic Community of West African States.

902	315	200f. yellow, black and blue	1·80	90

316 Casting Net

1982. Niger Fishermen. Multicoloured.

903	65f. Type **316**	75	40
904	85f. Net fishing	95	55

1982. Birth of Prince William of Wales. Nos. 860/MS863 optd NAISSANCE ROYALE 1982.

905	302	150f. multicoloured	1·30	60
906	-	200f. multicoloured	2·00	85
907	-	300f. multicoloured	2·75	1·10
MS908 117×78 mm. 400f. multicoloured			3·75	3·50

318 Hands reaching towards Mosque

1982. 13th Islamic Foreign Ministers Meeting, Niamey.

909	318	100f. multicoloured	95	55

319 "Flautist"

1982. Norman Rockwell Paintings. Multicoloured.

910	65f. Type **319**	60	30
911	85f. "Clerk"	95	30
912	110f. "Teacher and Pupil"	1·20	35
913	150f. "Girl Shopper"	1·50	60

320 World Map and Satellite

1982. I.T.U. Delegates' Conference, Nairobi.

914	320	130f. blue, light blue and black	1·20	70

1982. World Cup Football Championship Winners. Nos. 868/MS873 optd.

915	40f. Type **306**	40	15
916	65f. Goalkeeper fighting for ball	55	25
917	85f. Passing ball	75	40
918	150f. Running with ball	1·50	60
919	300f. Jumping for ball	2·75	1·40
MS920 103×78 mm. 500f. Running for ball		4·50	4·50

OVERPRINTS: 40f. **1966 VAINQUEUR GRANDE - BRETAGNE**; 65f. **1970 VAINQUEUR BRESIL**; 85f. **1974 VAINQUEUR ALLEMAGNE (RFA)**; 150f. **1978 VAINQUEUR ARGENTINE**; 300f. **1982 VAINQUEUR ITALIE**. 500f. **ITALIE-ALLEMAGNE (RFA) 3 1**.

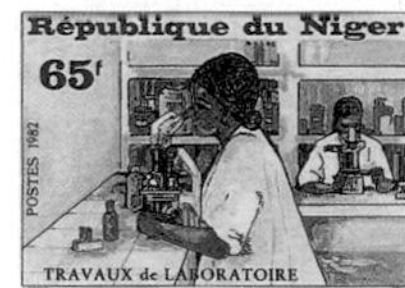

322 Laboratory Workers with Microscopes

1982. Laboratory Work. Multicoloured.

921	65f. Type **322**	75	60
922	115f. Laboratory workers	1·20	80

323 "Adoration of the Kings"

1982. Air. Christmas. Paintings by Rubens. Multicoloured.

923	200f. Type **323**	1·80	45
924	300f. "Mystic Marriage of St. Catherine"	2·75	1·30
925	400f. "Virgin and Child"	4·00	1·10

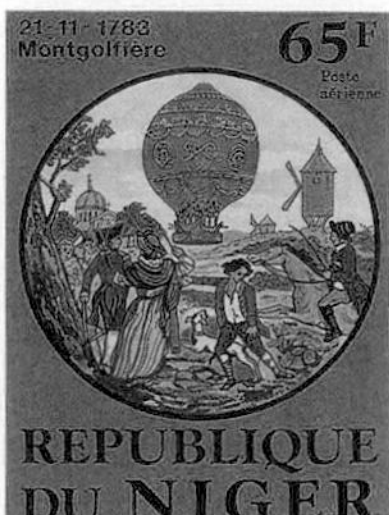

324 Montgolfier Balloon

1983. Air. Bicent of Manned Flight. Mult.

926	65f. Type **324**	55	25
927	85f. Charles's hydrogen balloon	55	25
928	200f. Goodyear Aerospace airship (horiz)	95	25
929	250f. Farman H.F.III biplane (horiz)	1·50	40
930	300f. Concorde	1·80	70
931	500f. "Apollo 11" spacecraft	2·75	80

No. 928 is wrongly inscribed "Zeppelin".

325 Harvesting Rice

1983. Self-sufficiency in Food. Multicoloured.

932	65f. Type **325**	3·75	90
933	85f. Planting rice	5·50	1·10

326 E.C.A. Anniversary Emblem

1983. 25th Anniv of Economic Commission for Africa.

934	**326** 120f. multicoloured	1·20	65
935	**326** 200f. multicoloured	1·80	90

327 "The Miraculous Draught of Fishes"

1983. 500th Birth Anniv of Raphael. Multicoloured.

936	65f. Type **327**	55	20
937	85f. "Grand Ducal Madonna" (vert)	75	20
938	100f. "The Deliverance of St. Peter"	95	35
939	150f. "Sistine Madonna" (vert)	1·40	55
940	200f. "The Fall on the Way to Calvary" (vert)	1·70	65
941	300f. "The Entombment"	2·50	90
942	400f. "The Transfiguration" (vert)	3·50	1·10
943	500f. "St. Michael fighting the Dragon" (vert)	4·75	1·40

328 Surveying

1983. The Army in the Service of Development. Multicoloured.

944	85f. Type **328**	75	45
945	150f. Road building	1·50	70

329 Palace of Justice

1983. Palace of Justice, Agadez.

946	**329** 65f. multicoloured	55	25

330 Javelin

1983. Air. Olympic Games, Los Angeles. Mult.

947	85f. Type **330**	75	25
948	200f. Shotput	1·80	60
949	250f. Throwing the hammer (vert)	2·30	80
950	300f. Discus	2·75	90
MS951	104×80 mm. 500f. Shotput (different)	4·50	1·70

331 Rural Post Vehicle

1983. Rural Post Service. Multicoloured.

952	65f. Type **331**	55	25
953	100f. Post vehicle and map	95	45

332 Dome of the Rock

1983. Palestine.

954	**332** 65f. multicoloured	75	30

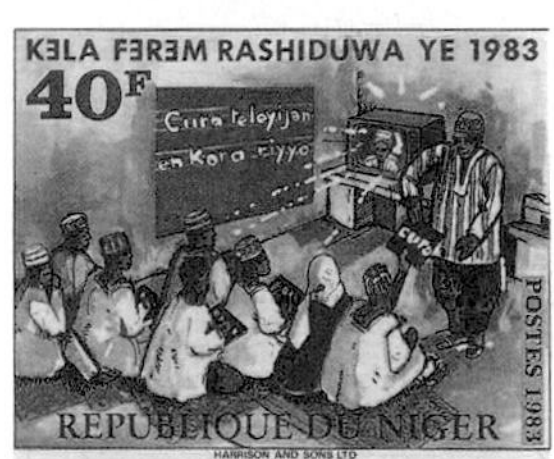

333 Class watching Television

1983. International Literacy Day. Multicoloured.

955	40f. Type **333**	45	10
956	65f. Teacher at blackboard (vert)	55	25
957	85f. Learning weights (vert)	95	45
958	100f. Outdoor class	95	55
959	150f. Woman reading magazine (vert)	1·50	70

334 Three Dancers

1983. 7th Dosso Dance Festival. Multicoloured.

960	65f. Type **334**	60	35
961	85f. Four dancers	95	55
962	120f. Two dancers	1·30	70

335 Post Van

1983. World Communications Year. Multicoloured.

963	80f. Type **335**	75	60
964	120f. Sorting letters	1·00	60
965	150f. W.C.Y. emblem (vert)	1·50	75

336 Television Antenna and Solar Panel

1983. Solar Energy in the Service of Television. Multicoloured.

966	85f. Type **336**	75	40
967	130f. Land-rover and solar panel	1·20	55

337 "Hypolimnas misippus"

1983. Butterflies. Multicoloured.

968	75f. Type **337**	1·00	45
969	120f. "Papilio demodocus"	1·50	70
970	250f. "Vanessa antiopa"	2·75	90
971	350f. "Charexes jasius"	3·75	1·40
972	500f. "Danaus chrisippus"	6·25	2·10

338 "Virgin and Child with Angels"

1983. Air. Christmas. Paintings by Botticelli. Multicoloured.

973	120f. Type **338**	1·20	50
974	350f. "Adoration of the Magi" (horiz)	3·75	1·00
975	500f. "Virgin of the Pomegranate"	4·50	1·80

339 Samariya Emblem

1984. Samariya.

976	**339** 80f. black, orange & green	75	45

340 Running

1984. Air. Olympic Games, Los Angeles. Mult.

977	80f. Type **340**	75	25
978	120f. Pole vault	1·00	25
979	140f. High jump	1·50	40
980	200f. Triple jump (vert)	1·70	55
981	350f. Long jump (vert)	3·50	1·30
MS982	104×79 mm. 500f. Hurdles	4·50	1·50

341 Boubon's Tetra

1984. Fish.

983	**341** 120f. multicoloured	2·75	80

342 Obstacle Course

1984. Military Pentathlon. Multicoloured.

984	120f. Type **342**	1·20	60
985	140f. Shooting	1·40	90

343 Radio Station

1984. New Radio Station.

986	**343** 120f. multicoloured	1·20	55

344 Flags, Agriculture and Symbols of Unity and Growth

1984. 25th Anniv of Council of Unity.

987	**344** 65f. multicoloured	60	35
988	**344** 85f. multicoloured	95	55

345 "Paris" (early steamer)

1984. Ships. Multicoloured.

989	80f. Type **345**	75	25
990	120f. "Jacques Coeur" (full-rigged ship)	95	40
991	150f. "Bosphorus" (full-rigged ship)	1·50	55
992	300f. "Comet" (full-rigged ship)	2·75	85

346 Daimler

1984. Motor Cars. Multicoloured.

993	100f. Type **346**	1·20	25
994	140f. Renault	1·40	45
995	250f. Delage "D 8"	2·40	80
996	400f. Maybach "Zeppelin"	3·75	1·40

347 "Rickmer Rickmers" (full-rigged ship)

1984. Universal Postal Union Congress, Hamburg.

997	**347** 300f. blue, brown and green	4·00	2·30

348 Cattle

1984. Ayerou Market. Multicoloured.

998	80f. Type **348**	95	60
999	120f. View of market	1·40	85

349 Viper

1984

1000	**349**	80f. multicoloured	1·20	70

350 Carl Lewis (100 and 200 m)

1984. Air. Olympic Games Medal Winners. Multicoloured.

1001	80f. Type **350**	70	35
1002	120f. J. Cruz (800 m)	1·20	50
1003	140f. A. Cova (10,000 m)	1·40	65
1004	300f. Al Joyner (Triple jump)	2·75	1·20
MS1005	101×78 mm. 500f. D. Mogenburg (high jump) (horiz)	4·50	2·75

351 Emblem

1984. 10th Anniv of Economic Community of West Africa.

1006	**351**	80f. multicoloured	75	45

352 Emblem and Extract from General Kountche's Speech

1984. United Nations Disarmament Decennials.

1007	**352**	400f. black and green	3·75	1·70
1008	**352**	500f. black and blue	4·25	2·50

353 Football

1984. Air. Preliminary Rounds of World Cup Football Championship, Mexico.

1009	**353**	150f. multicoloured	1·50	60
1010	-	250f. multicoloured	2·50	1·00
1011	-	450f. multicoloured	4·00	1·70
1012	-	500f. multicoloured	4·50	2·00

DESIGNS: 250 to 500f. Footballing scenes.

354 "The Visitation" (Ghirlandaio)

1984. Air. Christmas. Multicoloured.

1013	100f. Type **354**	95	40
1014	200f. "Virgin and Child" (Master of Saint Verdiana)	2·00	85
1015	400f. "Virgin and Child" (J. Koning)	3·75	1·80

1984. Drought Relief. Nos. 895/6 optd Aide au Sahel 84.

1016	150f. multicoloured	1·70	1·10
1017	200f. multicoloured	2·20	1·50

356 Organization Emblem

1985. 10th Anniv of World Tourism Organization.

1018	**356**	100f. black, orange and green	1·00	55

357 Breast-feeding Baby

1985. Infant Survival Campaign. Multicoloured.

1019	85f. Type **357**	85	40
1020	110f. Feeding baby and changing nappy	1·20	60

358 Black-necked Stilt

1985. Air. Birth Centenary of John J. Audubon (ornithologist). Multicoloured.

1021	110f. Type **358**	1·20	50
1022	140f. Greater flamingo (vert)	1·50	65
1023	200f. Atlantic puffin	2·00	90
1024	350f. Arctic tern (vert)	3·75	1·60

1985. International Exhibitions. Nos. MS814, MS848, MS879, MS901 and MS951 variously optd.

MS1025	Five sheets. (a) 400f. **MOPHILA'85 HAMBOURG**; (b) 425f. **TSUKUBA EXPO '85**. (c) 450f. **Italia '85 ROME** and emblem; (d) 500f. **ARGENTINA '85 BUENOS AIRES** and emblem; (e) 500f. **OLYMPHILEX '85 LAUSANNE** and emblem	26·00	26·00

360 Profile and Emblem

1985. 15th Anniv of Technical and Cultural Co-operation Agency.

1026	**360**	110f. brown, red & violet	95	55

361 Dancers

1985. 8th Niamey Festival. Multicoloured.

1027	85f. Type **361**	75	55
1028	110f. Four dancers (vert)	95	70
1029	150f. Dancers (different)	1·50	85

362 Wolf ("White Fang") and Jack London

1985. International Youth Year. Multicoloured.

1030	85f. Type **362**	95	35
1031	105f. Woman with lion and Joseph Kessel	95	50
1032	250f. Capt. Ahab harpooning white whale ("Moby Dick")	2·75	1·10
1033	450f. Mowgli on elephant ("Jungle Book")	4·25	1·80

363 Two Children on Leaf

1985. "Philexafrique" Stamp Exhibition, Lome, Togo (1st issue). Multicoloured.

1034	200f. Type **363**	2·00	1·40
1035	200f. Mining	2·00	1·40

See also Nos. 1064/5.

364 "Hugo with his Son Francois" (A. de Chatillon)

1985. Death Centenary of Victor Hugo (writer).

1036	**364**	500f. multicoloured	5·75	2·20

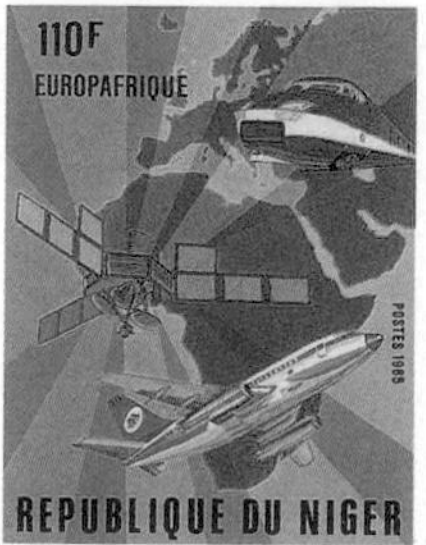

365 French Turbotrain TGV 001, Satellite and Boeing 737 on Map

1985. Europafrique.

1037	**365**	110f. multicoloured	1·20	60

366 Addax

1985. Endangered Animals. Multicoloured.

1038	50f. Type **366**	2·75	40
1039	60f. Addax (different) (horiz)	3·25	55
1040	85f. Two scimitar oryxes (horiz)	4·75	70
1041	110f. Oryx	7·50	95

367 "Oedaleus sp" on Millet

1985. Vegetation Protection. Multicoloured.

1042	85f. Type **367**	1·00	40
1043	110f. "Dysdercus volkeri" (beetle)	1·40	70
1044	150f. Fungi attacking sorghum and millet (horiz)	1·80	80
1045	210f. Sudan golden sparrows in tree	2·50	1·10
1046	390f. Red-billed queleas in tree	4·50	2·50

368 Cross of Agadez

1985

1047	**368**	85f. green	75	25
1048	-	110f. brown	1·00	30

DESIGN: 110f. Girl carrying water jar on head.

369 Arms, Flags and Agriculture

1985. 25th Anniv of Independence.

1049	**369**	110f. multicoloured	1·20	60

370 Baobab

1985. Protected Trees. Multicoloured.

1050	110f. Type **370**	1·20	70
1051	210f. "Acacia albida"	2·00	1·40
1052	390f. Baobab (different)	4·25	2·20

371 Man watching Race

1985. Niamey–Bamako Powerboat Race. Mult.

1053	110f. Type **371**	1·00	50
1054	150f. Helicopter and powerboat	1·50	75
1055	250f. Powerboat and map	2·50	1·40

1985. "Trees for Niger". As Nos. 1050/2 but new values and optd DES ARBRES POUR LE NIGER.

1056	**370**	30f. multicoloured	55	45
1057	-	85f. multicoloured	1·00	70
1058	-	110f. multicoloured	1·60	90

373 "Boletus"

1985. Fungi. Multicoloured.

1059	85f. Type **373**	1·00	45
1060	110f. "Hypholoma fasciculare"	1·50	55
1061	200f. "Coprinus comatus"	2·20	95
1062	300f. "Agaricus arvensis" (horiz)	3·75	1·60
1063	400f. "Geastrum fimbriatum" (horiz)	4·50	2·20

374 First Village Water Pump

1985. "Philexafrique" Stamp Exhibition, Lome, Togo (2nd issue). Multicoloured.

1064	250f. Type **374**	2·50	1·60
1065	250f. Handicapped youths playing dili (traditional game)	2·50	1·60

375 "Saving Ant" and Savings Bank Emblem

1985. World Savings Day.

1066	**375**	210f. multicoloured	2·00	1·10

376 Gouroumi

1985. Musical Instruments. Multicoloured.

1067	150f. Type **376**	1·50	90
1068	210f. Gassou (drums) (horiz)	2·20	1·30
1069	390f. Algaita (flute)	3·75	2·20
MS1070	114×79 mm. 500f. Biti (drums) (horiz)	5·00	4·25

377 "The Immaculate Conception"

1985. Air. Christmas. Paintings by Murillo. Mult.

1071	110f. "Madonna of the Rosary"	95	40
1072	250f. Type **377**	2·30	1·00
1073	390f. "Virgin of Seville"	3·75	1·60

378 Comet over Paris, 1910

1985. Air. Appearance of Halley's Comet. Multicoloured.

1074	110f. Type **378**	1·00	45
1075	130f. Comet over New York	1·20	50
1076	200f. "Giotto" satellite	2·00	80
1077	300f. "Vega" satellite	3·00	1·20
1078	390f. "Planet A" space probe	4·00	1·60

379 National Identity Card

1986. Civil Statutes Reform. Each black, green and orange.

1079	85f. Type **379**	85	40
1080	110f. Civil registration emblem	1·20	55

380 Road Signs

1986. Road Safety Campaign.

1081	**380**	85f. black, yellow and red	80	40
1082	-	110f. black, red and green	1·20	55

DESIGN: 110f. Speed limit sign, road and speedometer ("Watch your speed").

381 Oumarou Ganda (film producer)

1986. Honoured Artists. Multicoloured.

1083	60f. Type **381**	55	25
1084	85f. Idi na Dadaou	75	45
1085	100f. Dan Gourmou	95	55
1086	130f. Koungoui (comedian)	1·40	80

382 Martin Luther King

1986. Air. 18th Death Anniv of Martin Luther King (human rights activist).

1087	**382**	500f. multicoloured	4·50	2·20

383 Footballer and 1970 40f. Stamp

1986. Air. World Cup Football Championship, Mexico. Multicoloured.

1088	130f. Type **383**	1·20	45
1089	210f. Footballer and 1970 70f. stamp	1·80	85
1090	390f. Footballer and 1970 90f. stamp	4·00	1·50
1091	400f. Footballer and Mexican figure on "stamp"	4·00	1·50
MS1092	102×78 mm. 500f. Footballer and trophy on "stamp"	4·50	3·00

384 Statue and F. A. Bartholdi

1986. Air. Centenary of Statue of Liberty.

1093	**384**	300f. multicoloured	3·00	1·50

385 Truck

1986. "Trucks of Hope". Multicoloured.

1094	85f. Type **385**	1·00	45
1095	110f. Mother and baby (vert)	1·30	60

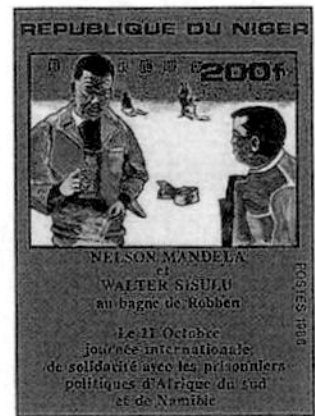

386 Nelson Mandela and Walter Sisulu

1986. International Solidarity with S. African and Namibian Political Prisoners Day. Multicoloured.

1096	200f. Type **386**	2·20	1·00
1097	300f. Nelson Mandela	3·75	1·40

387 Food Co-operatives

1986. 40th Anniv of F.A.O. Multicoloured.

1098	50f. Type **387**	45	25
1099	60f. Anti-desertification campaign	55	40
1100	85f. Irrigation	95	55
1101	100f. Rebuilding herds of livestock	95	55
1102	110f. Reafforestation	1·20	70

388 Trees and Woman with Cooking Pots

1987. "For a Green Niger". Multicoloured.

1103	85f. Type **388**	1·00	45
1104	110f. Trees, woman and cooking pots (different)	1·30	65

389 "Sphodromantis sp."

1987. Protection of Vegetation. Useful Insects. Multicoloured.

1105	85f. Type **389**	1·10	70
1106	110f. "Delta sp."	1·50	90
1107	120f. "Cicindela sp."	2·00	1·10

390 Transmitter, Map and Woman using Telephone

1987. Liptako–Gourma Telecommunications Network.

1108	**390**	110f. multicoloured	1·00	70

391 Morse Key and Operator, 19th-century

1987. 150th Anniv of Morse Telegraph. Mult.

1109	120f. Type **391**	1·00	55
1110	200f. Samuel Morse (inventor) (vert)	1·80	80
1111	350f. Morse transmitter and receiver	3·25	1·60

392 Tennis Player

1987. Olympic Games, Seoul (1988). Multicoloured.

1112	85f. Type **392**	75	60
1113	110f. Pole vaulter	1·00	60
1114	250f. Footballer	2·50	1·20
MS1115	120×90 mm. 500f. Runner	4·50	4·00

393 Ice Hockey

1987. Winter Olympic Games, Calgary (1988) (1st issue). Multicoloured.

1116	85f. Type **393**	75	55
1117	110f. Speed skating	1·20	55
1118	250f. Figure skating (pairs)	2·30	1·20
MS1119	120×87 mm. 500f. Downhill skiing (51×30 mm)	4·50	4·00

See also Nos. 1146/**MS**1150.

394 Long-distance Running

1987. African Games, Nairobi. Multicoloured.

1120	85f. Type **394**	75	55
1121	110f. High jumping	95	55
1122	200f. Hurdling	2·00	95
1123	400f. Javelin throwing	3·75	1·90

395 Chief's Stool, Sceptre and Crown

1987. 10th Anniv of National Tourism Office. Multicoloured.

1124	85f. Type **395**	75	45
1125	110f. Nomad, caravan and sceptre handle	95	55
1126	120f. Houses	1·20	60
1127	200f. Bridge over River Niger	2·00	1·00

396 Yaama Mosque at Dawn

1987. Aga Khan Prize.

1128	**396**	85f. multicoloured	75	55
1129	-	110f. multicoloured	95	55
1130	-	250f. multicoloured	2·75	1·20

DESIGNS: 110, 250f. Yaama mosque at various times of the day.

397 Court Building

1987. Appeal Court, Niamey. Multicoloured.

1131	85f. Type **397**	75	45
1132	110f. Front entrance	95	55
1133	140f. Side view	1·50	80

398 "Holy Family of the Sheep" (Raphael)

1997. Christmas. Multicoloured.

1134	110f. Type **398** (postage)	1·30	65
MS1135	1235×92 mm. 500f. "Adoration of the Magi" (detail) (Hans Memling) (30×51 mm) (air)	4·75	4·75

399 Water Drainage

1988. Health Care. Multicoloured.

1136	85f. Type **399**	1·20	80
1137	110f. Modern sanitation	1·50	85
1138	165f. Refuse collection	2·50	1·10

400 Singer and Band

1988. Award of Dan-Gourmou Music Prize.

1139	**400**	85f. multicoloured	1·50	90

1988. Winter Olympic Games Winners. Nos. 1116/18 optd.

1140	85f. **Medaille d'or URSS**	75	55
1141	110f. **Medaille d'or 5.000-10.000 m GUSTAFSON (Suede)**	95	70
1142	250f. **Medaille d'or E. GOR-DEEVA - S. GRINKOV URSS**	2·75	1·50

402 New Great Market, Niamey

1988

1143	**402**	85f. multicoloured	95	55

403 Mother and Child

1988. UNICEF Child Vaccination Campaign and 40th Anniv of W.H.O. Multicoloured.

1144	85f. Type **403**	80	55
1145	110f. Doctor and villagers	1·20	80

404 Kayak

1988. Air. Olympic Games, Seoul (2nd issue) and 125th Birth Anniv of Pierre de Coubertin (founder of modern Olympic Games). Multicoloured.

1146	85f. Type **404**	95	30
1147	165f. Rowing (horiz)	1·50	55
1148	200f. Two-man kayak (horiz)	2·00	70
1149	600f. One-man kayak	5·50	2·20
MS1150	105×80 mm. 750f. One-man kayak (different)	7·25	4·00

405 Emblem

1988. 25th Anniv of Organization of African Unity.

1151	**405**	85f. multicoloured	95	45

406 Team working

1988. Dune Stabilization.

1152	**406**	85f. multicoloured	1·20	70

407 Anniversary Emblem

1988. 125th Anniv of International Red Cross.

1153	**407**	85f. multicoloured	80	40
1154	**407**	110f. multicoloured	1·20	60

409 Emblem

1989. Niger Press Agency.

1159	**409**	85f. black, orange & grn	95	40

410 Couple, Globe and Laboratory Worker

1989. Campaign against AIDS.

1160	**410**	85f. multicoloured	85	35
1161	**410**	110f. multicoloured	1·30	55

411 Radar, Tanker and Signals

1989. 30th Anniv of International Maritime Organization.

1162	**411**	100f. multicoloured	95	45
1163	**411**	120f. multicoloured	1·30	65

412 General Ali Seybou (Pres.)

1989. 15th Anniv of Military Coup. Mult.

1164	85f. Type **412**	75	35
1165	110f. Soldiers erecting flag	1·00	55

413 Eiffel Tower

1989. "Philexfrance 89" International Stamp Exhibition, Paris. Multicoloured.

1166	100f. Type **413**	95	60
1167	200f. Flags on stamps	2·00	85

414 "Planting a Tree of Liberty"

1989. Bicentenary of French Revolution.

1168	**414**	250f. multicoloured	3·00	1·60

415 Telephone Dial, Radio Mast, Map and Stamp

1989. 30th Anniv of West African Posts and Telecommunications Association.

1169	**415**	85f. multicoloured	95	45

1989 – 20ème Anniversaire du Premier Homme sur la Lune

416 "Apollo 11" Launch

1989. Air. 20th Anniv of First Manned Landing on Moon. Multicoloured.

1170	200f. Type **416**	1·80	75
1171	300f. Crew	2·75	1·00
1172	350f. Astronaut and module on lunar surface	3·25	1·20
1173	400f. Astronaut and U.S. flag on lunar surface	3·75	1·40

417 Emblem

1989. 25th Anniv of African Development Bank.

1174	**417**	100f. multicoloured	1·10	50

418 Before and After Attack, and "Schistocerca gregaria"

1989. Locusts.

1175	**418**	85f. multicoloured	1·20	70

419 Auguste Lumiere and 1st Cine Performance, 1895

1989. 35th Death Anniv of Auguste Lumiere and 125th Birth Anniv of Louis Lumiere (photo-graphy pioneers). Multicoloured.

1176	150f. Type **419**	1·70	80
1177	250f. Louis Lumiere and first cine-camera, 1894	2·75	1·40
1178	400f. Lumiere brothers and first colour cine-camera, 1920	4·75	2·00

420 Tractor, Map and Pump

1989. 30th Anniv of Agriculture Development Council.

1179	**420**	75f. multicoloured		23·00

421 Zinder Regional Museum

1989. Multicoloured.. Multicoloured..

No.	Description	Mint	Used
1180	85f. Type **421**		23·00
1181	145f. Carawan	80·00	
1182	165f. Temet dunes	80·00	

422 "Russelia equisetiformis"

1989. Flowers. Multicoloured.

No.	Description	Mint	Used
1183	10f. Type **422**	15	10
1184	20f. "Argyreia nervosa"	30	10
1185	30f. "Hibiscus rosa-sinensis"	30	25
1186	50f. "Catharanthus roseus"	50	25
1187	100f. "Cymothoe sangaris" (horiz)	1·30	55

423 Emblem

1990. 10th Anniv of Pan-African Postal Union.

No.	Type	Description	Mint	Used
1188	**423**	120f. multicoloured	1·20	60

424 Adults learning Alphabet

1990. International Literacy Year. Multicoloured.

No.	Description	Mint	Used
1189	85f. Type **424**	80	35
1190	110f. Adults learning arithmetic	1·20	50

425 Emblem

1990. 20th Anniv of Islamic Conference Organization.

No.	Type	Description	Mint	Used
1191	**425**	85f. multicoloured	95	45

426 Footballers and Florence

1990. Air. World Cup Football Championship, Italy. Multicoloured.

No.	Description	Mint	Used
1192	130f. Type **426**	1·20	55
1193	210f. Footballers and Verona	2·00	70
1194	500f. Footballers and Bari	4·75	80
1195	600f. Footballers and Rome	5·25	1·40

427 Leland and Child

1990. Mickey Leland (American Congressman) Commemoration.

No.	Type	Description	Mint	Used
1196	**427**	300f. multicoloured	2·75	1·40
1197	**427**	500f. multicoloured	4·75	2·20

428 Emblem

1990. 1st Anniv of National Movement for the Development Society.

No.	Type	Description	Mint	Used
1198	**428**	85f. multicoloured	95	45

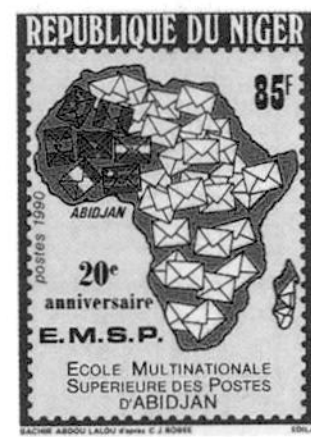

429 Flags and Envelopes on Map

1990. 20th Anniv of Multinational Postal Training School, Abidjan.

No.	Type	Description	Mint	Used
1199	**429**	85f. multicoloured	95	50

430 Gymnastics

1990. Olympic Games, Barcelona (1992). Mult.

No.	Description	Mint	Used
1200	85f. Type **430**	75	30
1201	110f. Hurdling	1·20	35
1202	250f. Running	2·30	1·00
1203	400f. Show jumping	3·75	1·40
1204	500f. Long jumping	4·75	1·70
MS1205	92×70 mm. 600f. Cycling	5·75	4·25

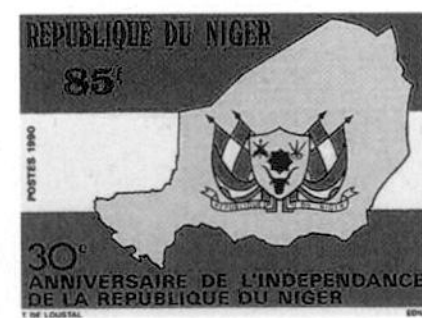

431 Arms, Map and Flag

1990. 30th Anniv of Independence.

No.	Type	Description	Mint	Used
1206	**431**	85f. multicoloured	80	40
1207	**431**	110f. multicoloured	1·20	60

432 Emblem

1990. 40th Anniv of United Nations Development Programme.

No.	Type	Description	Mint	Used
1208	**432**	100f. multicoloured	95	45

433 The Blusher

1991. Butterflies and Fungi. Multicoloured.

No.	Description	Mint	Used
1209	85f. Type **433** (postage)	1·00	25
1210	110f. "Graphium pylades" (female)	1·10	25
1211	200f. "Pseudacraea hostilia"	2·30	65
1212	250f. Cracked green russula	2·50	80
1213	400f. "Boletus impolitus" (air)	3·75	1·30
1214	500f. "Precis octavia"	4·50	1·20
MS1215	98×85 mm. 600f. "Pseudacraea boisduvali" (female) and "Chanterelle" ("Cantharellus cibarius") (29×37 mm)	6·00	3·75

434 Christopher Columbus and "Santa Maria"

1991. 540th Birth of Christopher Columbus. Mult.

No.	Description	Mint	Used
1216	85f. Type **434** (postage)	80	25
1217	110f. 15th-century Portuguese caravel	1·00	25
1218	200f. 16th-century four-masted caravel	1·80	60
1219	250f. "Estremadura" (Spanish caravel), 1511	2·50	75
1220	400f. "Vija" (Portuguese caravel), 1600 (air)	3·75	90
1221	500f. "Pinta"	4·50	1·30
MS1222	108×68 mm. 600f. "Nina"	6·50	4·00

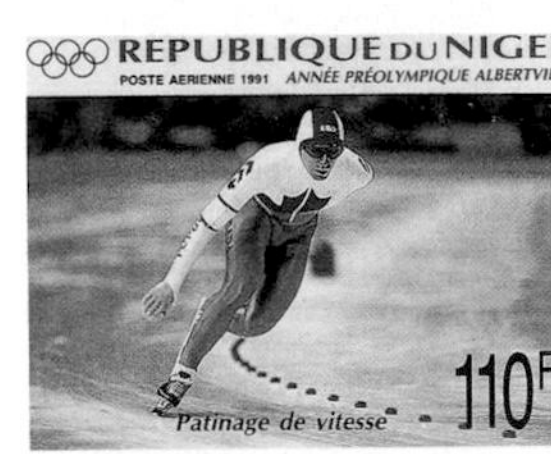

435 Speed Skating

1991. Winter Olympic Games, Albertville (1992). Multicoloured.

No.	Description	Mint	Used
1223	110f. Type **435**	1·10	45
1224	300f. Ice-hockey	2·75	1·30
1225	500f. Women's downhill skiing	4·50	1·80
1226	600f. Two-man luge	5·25	1·80

436 Flag and Boy holding Stone

1991. Palestinian "Intifada" Movement.

No.	Type	Description	Mint	Used
1227	**436**	110f. multicoloured	1·20	55

437 Hairstyle

1991. Traditional Hairstyles. Multicoloured.

No.	Description	Mint	Used
1228	85f. Type **437**	2·00	55
1229	110f. Netted hairstyle	1·50	45
1230	165f. Braided hairstyle	2·20	75
1231	200f. Plaited hairstyle	2·50	1·00

438 Boubon Market

1991. African Tourism Year. Multicoloured.

No.	Description	Mint	Used
1232	85f. Type **438**	85	35
1233	110f. Timia waterfalls (vert)	1·20	55
1234	130f. Ruins at Assode	1·50	70
1235	200f. Tourism Year emblem (vert)	2·50	1·10

439 Anatoly Karpov and Gary Kasparov

1991. Anniversaries and Events. Multicoloured.

No.	Description	Mint	Used
1236	85f. Type **439** (World Chess Championship) (postage)	75	25
1237	110f. Ayrton Senna and Alain Prost (World Formula 1 motor racing championship)	1·20	40
1238	200f. Reading of Declaration of Human Rights and Comte de Mirabeau (bicentenary of French Revolution)	1·80	40
1239	250f. Dwight D. Eisenhower, Winston Churchill and Field-Marshal Montgomery (50th anniv of America's entry into Second World War)	5·00	1·10
1240	400f. Charles de Gaulle and Konrad Adenauer (28th anniv of Franco-German Co-operation Agreement) (air)	5·50	90
1241	500f. Helmut Kohl and Brandenburg Gate (2nd anniv of German reunification)	6·00	1·10
MS1242	119×56 mm. 600f. Pope John Paul II (visit to Africa)	6·25	6·25

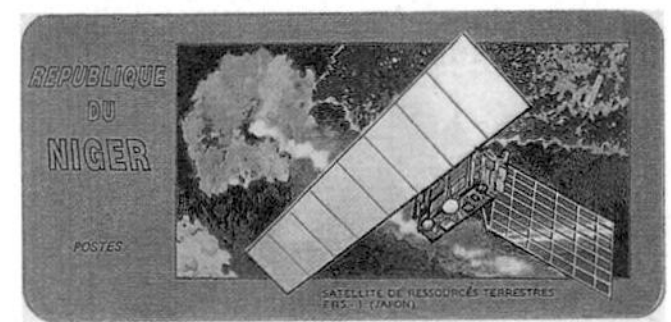

440 Japanese "ERS-1" Satellite

1991. Satellites and Transport. Multicoloured.

No.	Description	Mint	Used
1243	85f. Type **440** (postage)	75	25
1244	110f. Japanese satellite observing Aurora Borealis	95	25
1245	200f. Louis Favre and "BB 415" diesel locomotive	2·20	45
1246	250f. "BB-BB 301" diesel locomotive	2·75	70
1247	400f. "BB 302" diesel locomotive (air)	4·25	90
1248	500f. Lockheed Stealth fighter-bomber and Concorde	4·50	1·10
MS1249	120×86 mm. 600f. George Nagelmacker and "Orient Express"	6·00	3·75

441 Crowd and Emblem on Map

1991. National Conference (to determine new constitution).

No.	Type	Description	Mint	Used
1250	**441**	85f. multicoloured	95	45

442 Timberless House

1992

1251	**442**	85f. multicoloured	95	45

443 Couple adding Final Piece to Globe Jigsaw

1992. World Population Day. Multicoloured.

1252	85f. Type **443**	85	45
1253	110f. Children flying globe kite (after Robert Parker)	1·20	50

444 Columbus and Fleet

1992. 500th Anniv of Discovery of America by Columbus.

1254	**444**	250f. multicoloured	2·75	1·20

445 Zaleye

1992. 2nd Death Anniv of Hadjia Haqua Issa (Zaleye) (singer).

1255	**445**	150f. multicoloured	1·50	70

446 Conference Emblem

1992. International Nutrition Conference, Rome.

1256	**446**	145f. multicoloured	1·50	70
1257	**446**	350f. multicoloured	3·50	1·50

447 College Emblem

1993. 30th Anniv of African Meteorology and Civil Aviation College.

1258	**447**	110f. blue, black & green	95	55

448 Girl planting Sapling

1993. Anti-desertification Campaign.

1259	**448**	85f. multicoloured	75	55
1260	**448**	165f. multicoloured	1·70	80

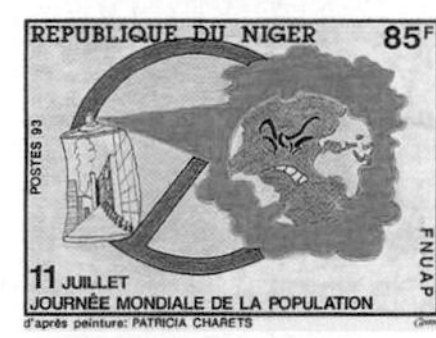

449 Aerosol spraying Globe (Patricia Charets)

1993. World Population Day. Children's Drawings. Multicoloured.

1261	85f. Type **449**	85	45
1262	110f. Tree and person with globe as head looking at high-rise tower blocks (Mathieu Chevrault)	1·20	70

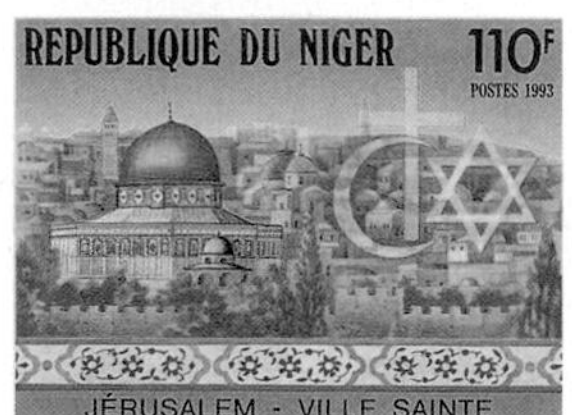

450 Jerusalem

1993. "Jerusalem, Holy City".

1268	**450**	110f. multicoloured	1·20	70

451 People of Different Races

1994. Award of Nobel Peace Prize to Nelson Mandela and F. W. de Klerk (South African statesmen).

1269	**451**	270f. multicoloured	1·50	80

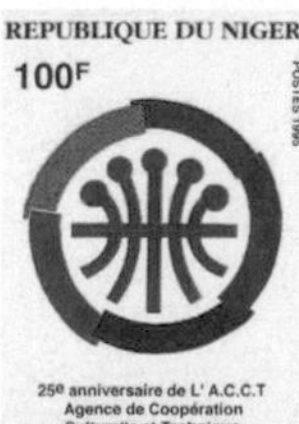

452 Emblem

1995. 25th Anniv of ACCT (cooperation and cultural agency).

1270	**452**	100f. multicoloured	

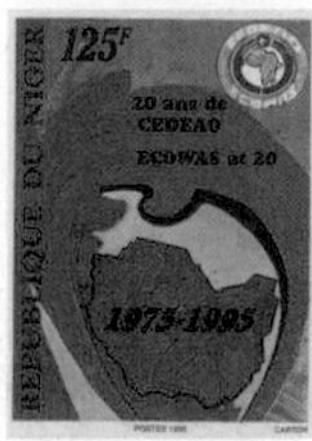

453 Map enclosing Figures

1995. 20th Anniv ECOWAS Commission.

1271	**453**	125f. multicoloured	

454 Replenishment of Stock

1995. Agriculture. Multicoloured.

1272	125f. Type **454**
1273	300f. Irrigation

455 Emblem

1995. 30th Anniv of African Development Bank.

1274	**455**	300f. emerald and scarlet

456 Donkey Cart

1995. Children's Drawings. Multicoloured.

1275	500f. Type **456**
1276	1000f. Courtesan's Mount

457 Race Car

1997. Agades–Dakar Rally. Multicoloured.

1277	125f. Type **457**
1278	175f. Quad bike
1279	300f. Lorry
1280	500f. Motor cycle
MS1281	113×117 mm. Nos. 1277/80

458 *Tockus nastus* (grey hornbill)

1997. Birds. Multicoloured.

1282	5f. Type **458**
1283	15f. *Psittacula krameri* (ring-necked parakeet)
1284	25f. *Coracias abyssinica* (Abyssinian roller)
1285	35f. *Bubulcus ibis* (inscr 'Bubulcus ibis') (cattle egret)

459 Abdou Moumouni Dioffo

1998. Abdou Moumouni Dioffo (university president) Commemoration.

1286	**459**	125f. multicoloured

461 Ibrahim Bare Mainassara

1998. Ibrahim Bare Mainassara (president 1996–1999).

1290	**461**	500f. multicoloured

Nos. 1287/9 and Type **460** have been left for 'Flowers', issued on 17 June 1998, not yet received

462 Woman and Cloth

1998. FIMA NIGER 98–International African Fashion Festival, Tiguidit and Agades. Multicoloured.

1291	175f. Type **462**
1292	225f. Woman and desert

463 1849 20c. Stamp of France (As No. 6)

1999. 150th Anniv of First French Stamp.

1293	**463**	200f. multicoloured

464 Couple and Farmer

1999. 40th Anniv of Council for Rural Development.

1294	**464**	150f. multicoloured
1295	**464**	175f. multicoloured

465 Tracks in Sand

2000. International Day against Deserts and Desertification. Multicoloured.

1296	150f. Type **465**
1297	200f. Figures and scrub
1298	225f. Open landscape

466 Air Mountains, Chiriet

2001

1299	**466**	150f. multicoloured

467 Emblem

2001. International Year of Volunteers.

1300	467	150f. multicoloured		

468 Cow's Head

2002

1301	468	50f. multicoloured		

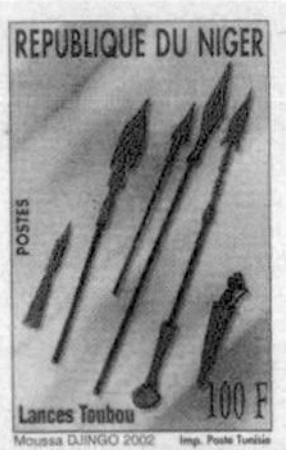

469 Tobou Spears

2002

1302	469	100f. multicoloured		

470 Birds

2002

1303	470	225f. multicoloured		

OFFICIAL STAMPS

O13 Djerma Women

1962. Figures of value in black.

O121	O13	1f. violet	10	10
O122	O13	2f. green	10	10
O123	O13	5f. blue	10	10
O124	O13	10f. red	30	10
O125	O13	20f. blue	30	25
O126	O13	25f. orange	30	25
O127	O13	30f. blue	45	25
O128	O13	35f. green	55	40
O129	O13	40f. brown	55	40
O130	O13	50f. slate	55	40
O131	O13	60f. turquoise	75	45
O132	O13	85f. turquoise	1·00	45
O133	O13	100f. purple	1·20	45
O134	O13	200f. blue	2·50	95

1988. As Type O 13, but figures of value in same colour as remainder of design.

O1155	5f. blue	10	10
O1156	10f. red	20	15
O1157	15f. yellow	15	15
O1158	20f. blue	30	15
O1159	45f. orange	45	25
O1160	50f. green	60	25

POSTAGE DUE STAMPS

1921. Postage Due stamps of Upper Senegal and Niger "Figure" key-type optd TERRITOIRE DU NIGER.

D18	M	5c. green	45	6·25
D19	M	10c. red	65	6·25
D20	M	15c. grey	60	6·00
D21	M	20c. brown	35	4·00
D22	M	30c. blue	90	4·75
D23	M	50c. black	1·30	5·75
D24	M	60c. orange	1·30	9·00
D25	M	1f. violet	1·40	6·00

D6 Zinder Fort

1927

D73	D6	2c. red and blue	20	4·25
D74	D6	4c. black and orange	20	3·25
D75	D6	5c. violet and yellow	35	4·25
D76	D6	10c. violet and red	20	3·25
D77	D6	15c. orange and green	35	5·75
D78	D6	20c. sepia and red	35	3·50
D79	D6	25c. sepia and black	35	3·75
D80	D6	30c. grey and violet	65	6·50
D81	D6	50c. red on green	55	8·00
D82	D6	60c. orange & lilac on bl	45	7·25
D83	D6	1f. violet & blue on blue	1·10	4·25
D84	D6	2f. mauve and red	1·70	8·50
D85	D6	3f. blue and brown	2·00	9·25

D13 Cross of Agadez

1962

D123	D13	50c. green	15	15
D124	D13	1f. violet	15	15
D125	D13	2f. myrtle	15	15
D126	A	3f. mauve	15	15
D127	A	5f. green	30	25
D128	A	10f. orange	30	25
D129	B	15f. blue	30	25
D130	B	20f. red	30	25
D131	B	50f. brown	50	50

DESIGNS: A, Cross of Iferouane; B, Cross of Tahoua.

D450 Cross of Iferouane

1993

D1263	D450	5f. multicoloured	10	10
D1264	D450	10f. orange and black	10	10
D1265	-	15f. multicoloured	10	10
D1266	-	20f. mve, yell & blk	15	15
D1267	-	50f. multicoloured	45	40

DESIGN: 15 to 50f. Cross of Tahoua.

APPENDIX

The following stamps have either been issued in excess of postal needs, or have not been available to the public in reasonable quantities at face value. Such stamps may later be given full listings if there is evidence of regular postal use. Miniature sheets and imperporate stamps are excluded from this listing.

1994

Entertainers. 175, 300, 400, 600, 700f.×2; 750f.; 800f.×2

1996

World Scout Jamboree, Netherlands. 350, 500f.
90th Anniv of Rotary International.150, 200f.×2; 700, 900, 1000f.
80th Anniv of Lions International. 300, 600f.
50th Anniv of United Nations and UNICEF. 150, 22, 475, 550f.
Red Cross. 250, 400f.
Winter Olympic Games, Nagano (1st issue). Overprinted in red or blue. 85, 200, 400, 500f.
Sport. 300, 450, 500, 700f.
Olympic Games, Atlanta. 250, 350, 400, 600f.
Football World Cup, France. 125f.; 175f.; 750f.; 1000f.
Winter Olympic Games, Nagano (2nd issue). 125, 175, 700, 800f.
Traditional Musical Instruments. 125, 175f.
Butterflies. 150f, 200, 750, 800f.

1997

Chinese New Year. Year of the Ox. 500f.×2

1998

Diana, Princess of Wales. 180f.×4
Gazelles. 250f.×4
Birds. 5, 15, 25, 35f.

Pt. 1

NIGER COAST PROTECTORATE

A district on the west coast of Africa. In 1900 became part of Southern Nigeria.

12 pence = 1 shilling; 20 pence = 1 pound.

1892. Stamps of Gt. Britain (Queen Victoria) optd BRITISH PROTECTORATE OIL RIVERS.

1	71	½d. red	18·00	10·00
2	57	1d. lilac	10·00	9·00
3	73	2d. green and red	30·00	8·00
4	74	2½d. purple and blue	7·00	2·25
5	78	5d. purple and blue	16·00	6·50
6	82	1s. green	65·00	85·00

1893. Half of No. 2 surch ½d.

7	57	½d. on half of 1d. lilac	£160	£140

1893. Nos. 1 to 6 surch in words (½d., 1s.) or figures (others).

20	73	½d. on 2d. green and red	£450	£250
21	74	½d. on 2½d. purple on blue	£350	£180
37	73	1s. on 2d. green and red	£450	£350
40	73	5s. on 2d. green and red	£9000	£11000
41	78	10s. on 5d. purple and blue	£6500	£9500
42	82	20s. on 1s. green	£140000	

13

1893. Various frames with "OIL RIVERS" barred out and "NIGER COAST" above.

45	13	½d. red	8·00	8·00
46b	13	1d. blue	6·00	3·50
47d	13	2d. green	19·00	14·00
48	13	2½d. red	12·00	3·50
49b	13	5d. lilac	17·00	13·00
50	13	1s. black	14·00	12·00

14

1894. Various frames.

66	14	½d. green	5·00	1·50
67d	14	1d. red	2·50	2·75
68	14	2d. red	2·50	2·00
69	14	2½d. blue	7·50	2·25
55a	14	5d. purple	7·50	5·50
71	14	6d. brown	7·00	6·50
72	14	1s. black	15·00	29·00
73b	14	2s.6d. brown	22·00	90·00
74b	14	10s. violet	£120	£200

1894. Surch with large figures.

58	½ on half 1d. (No. 46)	£1100	£375
59	1 on half 2d. (No. 2)	£1700	£375

1894. No. 67 bisected and surch.

64	½d. on half of 1d. red	£3250	£500

1894. Surch ONE HALF PENNY and bars.

65	½d. on 2½d. blue	£400	£225

Pt. 1

NIGERIA

A former British colony on the west coast of Africa, comprising the territories of Northern and Southern Nigeria and Lagos. Attained full independence within the British Commonwealth in 1960 and became a Federal Republic in 1963.

The Eastern Region (known as Biafra (q.v.)) seceded in 1967, remaining independent until overrun by Federal Nigerian troops during January 1970.

1914. 12 pence = 1 shilling; 20 shillings = 1 pound.
1973. 100 kobo = 1 naira.

1

1914

15	1	½d. green	1·25	40
16b	1	1d. red	1·75	35
17	1	1½d. orange	7·00	15
18	1	2d. grey	1·50	7·00
20	1	2d. brown	2·50	15
21	1	2½d. blue	1·00	9·50
5a	1	3d. purple on yellow	1·50	2·75
22	1	3d. violet	6·00	3·25
23	1	3d. blue	9·00	1·00
24	1	4d. black and red on yellow	65	55
25a	1	6d. purple	7·00	8·00
26	1	1s. black on green	3·50	2·00
9	1	2s.6d. black and red on blue	16·00	6·50
10	1	5s. green and red on yellow	18·00	55·00
11d	1	10s. green and red on green	35·00	£110
12a	1	£1 purple and black on red	£190	£225

1935. Silver Jubilee. As T 143a of Newfoundland.

30	1½d. blue and grey	80	1·50
31	2d. green and blue	1·75	1·75
32	3d. brown and blue	3·25	19·00
33	1s. grey and purple	6·50	38·00

3 Apapa Wharf 11 Victoria–Buea Road

1936

34	3	½d. green	1·50	1·40
35	-	1d. red	50	40
36	-	1½d. brown	2·00	40
37	-	2d. black	50	80
38	-	3d. blue	2·00	1·50
39	-	4d. brown	2·00	2·00
40	-	6d. violet	50	60
41	-	1s. green	1·75	4·75
42	11	2s.6d. black and blue	5·00	30·00
43	-	5s. black and green	15·00	45·00
44	-	10s. black and grey	75·00	£110
45	-	£1 black and orange	95·00	£170

DESIGNS—VERT: 1d. Cocoa; 1½d. Tin dredger; 2d. Timber industry; 3d. Fishing village; 4d. Cotton ginnery; 6d. Habe minaret; 1s. Fulani cattle. HORIZ: 5s. Oil palms; 10s. River Niger at Jebba; £1 Canoe pulling.

1937. Coronation. As T 143b of Newfoundland.

46	1d. red	1·00	2·50
47	1½d. brown	2·50	3·00
48	3d. blue	2·50	5·00

15 King George VI

1938

49	15	½d. green	10	10
50a	15	1d. red	75	30
50b	15	1d. lilac	10	20
51a	15	1½d. brown	10	10
52	15	2d. black	10	2·75
52ab	15	2d. red	10	50
52b	15	2½d. orange	10	2·75
53	15	3d. blue	10	10
53b	15	3d. black	15	2·50
54	15	4d. orange	50·00	3·50
54a	15	4d. blue	15	4·00
55	15	6d. purple	40	10
56a	15	1s. olive	1·00	10
57	15	1s.3d. blue	1·00	30
58b	-	2s.6d. black and blue	2·75	3·50
59c	-	5s. black and orange	7·00	4·00

DESIGNS: 2s.6d., 5s. As Nos. 42 and 44 but with portrait of King George VI.

1946. Victory. As T 4a of Pitcairn Islands.

60	1½d. brown	35	10
61	4d. blue	35	2·25

1948. Royal Silver Wedding. As T 4b/c of Pitcairn Islands.

62	1d. mauve	35	30
63	5s. orange	15·00	20·00

1949. U.P.U. As T 4d/g of Pitcairn Islands.

64	1d. purple	15	30
65	3d. blue	1·25	3·75
66	6d. purple	30	3·75
67	1s. olive	50	2·00

1953. Coronation. As T 4h of Pitcairn Islands.

68	1½d. black and green	50	10

18 Old Manilla Currency

26 Victoria Harbour

29 New and Old Lagos

1953

69	18	½d. black and orange	15	30
70	-	1d. black and bronze	20	10
71	-	1½d. turquoise	50	40
72	-	2d. black and ochre	4·00	30
72cb	-	2d. slate	4·75	40
73	-	3d. black and purple	55	10
74	-	4d. black and blue	2·50	20
75	-	6d. brown and black	30	10
76	-	1s. black and purple	50	10
77	26	2s.6d. black and green	12·00	1·00
78	-	5s. black and orange	4·25	1·40
79	-	10s. black and brown	20·00	3·00
80	29	£1 black and violet	30·00	14·00

DESIGNS—HORIZ (As Type **18**): 1d. Bornu horsemen; 1½d. "Groundnuts"; 2d. "Tin"; 3d. Jebba Bridge and R. Niger; 4d. "Cocoa"; 1s. "Timber". (As Type **26**): 5s. "Palm oil"; 10s. "Hides and skins". VERT (As Type **18**): 6d. Ife bronze.

1956. Royal Visit. No. 72 optd ROYAL VISIT 1956.

81	2d. black and ochre	40	30

31 Victoria Harbour

1958. Centenary of Victoria, S. Cameroons.

82	31	3d. black and purple	20	30

32 Lugard Hall

1959. Attainment of Self-government. Northern Region of Nigeria.

83	32	3d. black and purple	25	10
84	-	1s. black and green	75	60

DESIGN: 1s. Kano Mosque.

35 Legislative Building

1960. Independence Commemoration.

85	35	1d. black and red	10	10
86	-	3d. black and blue	15	10
87	-	6d. green and brown	20	20
88	-	1s.3d. blue and yellow	40	20

DESIGNS—As Type **35**: 3d. African paddling canoe; 6d. Federal Supreme Court. LARGER (40×24 mm): 1s.3d. Dove, torch and map.

39 Groundnuts 48 Central Bank

1961

89	39	½d. green	10	60
90	-	1d. violet	80	10
91	-	1½d. red	80	2·25
92	-	2d. blue	30	10
93	-	3d. green	40	10
94	-	4d. blue	40	2·00
95	-	6d. yellow and black	80	10
96	-	1s. green	4·50	10
97	-	1s.3d. orange	1·50	10
98	48	2s.6d. black and yellow	2·75	15
99	-	5s. black and green	65	1·25
100	-	10s. black and blue	3·75	4·25
101	-	£1 black and red	13·00	18·00

DESIGNS—VERT (as Type **39**): 1d. Coal mining; 1½d. Adult education; 2d, Pottery; 3d. Oyo carver; 4d. Weaving; 6d. Benin mask; 1s. Yellow casqued hornbill; 1s.3d. Camel train. HORIZ (as Type **48**: 5s. Nigeria Museum; 10s. Kano airport; £1 Lagos railway station.

52 Globe and Diesel-electric Locomotive

1961. Admission into U.P.U. Inscr as in T 52.

102	52	1d. orange and blue	30	10
103	-	3d. olive and black	30	10
104	-	1s.3d. blue and red	80	20
105	-	2s.6d. green and blue	85	2·00

DESIGNS: 3d. Globe and mail van; 1s.3d. Globe and Bristol 175 Britannia aircraft; 2s.6d. Globe and liner.

56 Coat of Arms

1961. 1st Anniv of Independence.

106	56	3d. multicoloured	10	10
107	-	4d. green and orange	20	50
108	-	6d. green	30	10
109	-	1s.3d. grey and blue	35	10
110	-	2s.6d. green and blue	40	1·75

DESIGNS—HORIZ: 4d. Natural resources map; 6d. Nigerian eagle; 1s 3d. Eagles in flight; 2s.6d. Nigerians and flag.

61 "Health"

1962. Lagos Conf of African and Malagasy States.

111	61	1d. bistre	10	10
112	-	3d. purple	10	10
113	-	6d. green	15	10
114	-	1s. brown	20	10
115	-	1s.3d. blue	25	20

DESIGNS: Map and emblems symbolising Culture (3d.); Commerce (6d.); Communications (1s.); Co-operation (1s.3d.).

66 Malaria Eradication Emblem and Parasites

1962. Malaria Eradication.

116	66	3d. green and red	15	10
117	-	6d. blue and purple	20	10
118	-	1s.3d. mauve and blue	20	10
119	-	2s.6d. blue and brown	30	90

DESIGNS (embodying emblem): 6d. Insecticide-spraying; 1s.3d. Aerial spraying; 2s.6d. Mother, child and microscope.

70 National Monument

1962. 2nd Anniv of Independence.

120	70	3d. green and blue	10	10
121	-	5s. red, green and violet	1·00	1·00

DESIGN—VERT: 5s. Benin bronze.

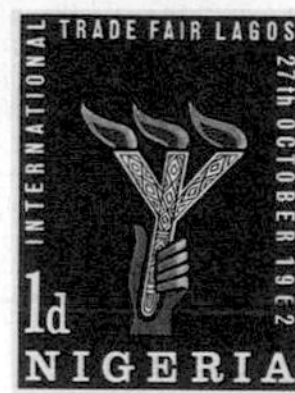

72 Fair Emblem

1962. International Trade Fair, Lagos.

122	72	1d. red and olive	10	10
123	-	6d. black and red	15	10
124	-	1s. black and brown	15	10
125	-	2s.6d. yellow and blue	60	20

DESIGNS—HORIZ: 6d. "Cogwheels of Industry"; 1s. "Cornucopia of Industry"; 2s.6d. Oilwells and tanker.

76 "Arrival of Delegates"

1962. 8th Commonwealth Parliamentary Conference, Lagos.

126	76	2½d. blue	15	1·10
127	-	4d. blue and rose	15	30
128	-	1s.3d. sepia and yellow	20	20

DESIGNS—HORIZ: 4d. National Hall. VERT: 1s.3d. Mace as Palm Tree.

80 Tractor and Maize

1963. Freedom from Hunger.

129		3d. olive	1·75	20
130	80	6d. mauve	2·00	20

DESIGN—VERT: 3d. Herdsman.

81 Mercury Capsule and Kano Tracking Station

1963. "Peaceful Use of Outer Space".

No.	Type	Description	Unused	Used
131	**81**	6d. blue and green	25	10
132	-	1s.3d. black and turquoise	35	20

DESIGN: 1s.3d. Satellite and Lagos Harbour.

83 Scouts shaking Hands

1963. 11th World Scout Jamboree. Marathon.

No.	Type	Description	Unused	Used
133	**83**	3d. red and bronze	30	20
134	-	1s. black and red	95	80
MS134a		93×95 mm. Nos. 133/4	1·75	1·75

DESIGN: 1s. Campfire.

85 Emblem and First Aid Team

1963. Centenary of Red Cross.

No.	Type	Description	Unused	Used
135	**85**	3d. red and blue	60	10
136	-	6d. red and green	80	10
137	-	1s.3d. red and sepia	1·00	70
MS137a		102×102 mm. No. 137 (block of four)	8·50	11·00

DESIGNS: 6d. Emblem and "Hospital Services"; 1s.3d. Patient and emblem.

88 President Azikiwe and State House

1963. Republic Day.

No.	Type	Description	Unused	Used
138	**88**	3d. olive and green	10	10
139	-	1s.3d. brown and sepia	10	10
140	-	2s.6d. turquoise and blue	15	15

The buildings on the 1s.3d. and the 2s.6d. are the Federal Supreme Court and the Parliament Building respectively.

90 "Freedom of worship"

1963. 15th Anniv of Declaration of Human Rights.

No.	Type	Description	Unused	Used
141		3d. red	10	10
142	**90**	6d. green	15	10
143	-	1s.3d. blue	30	10
144	-	2s.6d. purple	45	30

DESIGNS—HORIZ: 3d. (Inscr "1948–1963"), Charter and broken whip. VERT: 1s.3d. "Freedom from Want"; 2s.6d. "Freedom of Speech".

93 Queen Nefertari

1964. Nubian Monuments Preservation.

No.	Type	Description	Unused	Used
145	**93**	6d. olive and green	50	10
146	-	2s.6d. brown, olive & green	1·75	2·25

DESIGN: 2s.6d. Rameses II.

95 President Kennedy

1964. Pres. Kennedy Memorial Issue.

No.	Type	Description	Unused	Used
147	**95**	1s.3d. lilac and black	30	15
148	-	2s.6d. multicoloured	40	65
149	-	5s. multicoloured	70	1·75
MS149a		154×135 mm. No. 149 (block of four). Imperf	7·00	12·00

DESIGNS: 2s.6d. Kennedy and flags; 5s. Kennedy (U.S. coin head) and flags.

98 President Azikiwe

1964. 1st Anniv of Republic.

No.	Type	Description	Unused	Used
150	**98**	3d. brown	10	10
151	-	1s.3d. green	35	10
152	-	2s.6d. green	70	90

DESIGNS—25×42 mm: 1s.3d. Herbert Macaulay; 2s.6d. King Jaja of Opobo.

101 Boxing Gloves

1964. Olympic Games, Tokyo.

No.	Type	Description	Unused	Used
153	**101**	3d. sepia and green	45	10
154	-	6d. green and blue	60	10
155	-	1s.3d. sepia and olive	1·00	15
156	-	2s.6d. sepia and brown	1·75	3·75
MS156a		102×102 mm. No. 156 (block of four). Imperf	3·00	4·25

DESIGNS—HORIZ: 6d. High-jumping. VERT: 1s.3d. Running. TRIANGULAR (60×30 mm): 2s.6d. Hurdling.

105 Scouts on Hill-top

1965. 50th Anniv of Nigerian Scout Movement.

No.	Type	Description	Unused	Used
157	**105**	1d. brown	10	10
158	-	3d. red, black and green	15	10
159	-	6d. red, sepia and green	25	20
160	-	1s.3d. brown, yellow and deep green	40	85
MS160a		76×104 mm. No. 160 (block of four). Imperf	5·00	8·50

DESIGNS: 3d. Scout badge on shield; 6d. Scout badges; 1s.3d. Chief Scout and Nigerian scout.

109 "Telstar"

1965. International Quiet Sun Years.

No.	Type	Description	Unused	Used
161	**109**	6d. violet and turquoise	15	15
162	-	1s.3d. green and lilac	15	15

DESIGN: 1s.3d. Solar satellite.

111 Native Tom-tom and Modern Telephone

1965. Centenary of I.T.U.

No.	Type	Description	Unused	Used
163	**111**	3d. black, red and brown	30	10
164	-	1s.3d. black, green & blue	2·50	1·00
165	-	5s. multicoloured	6·50	7·00

DESIGNS—VERT: 1s.3d. Microwave aerial. HORIZ: 5s. Telecommunications satellite and part of globe.

114 I.C.Y. Emblem and Diesel-hydraulic Locomotive

1965. International Co-operation Year.

No.	Type	Description	Unused	Used
166	**114**	3d. green, red and orange	3·00	20
167	-	1s. black, blue and lemon	3·00	40
168	-	2s.6d. green, blue & yellow	9·00	7·00

DESIGNS: 1s. Students and Lagos Teaching Hospital; 2s.6d. Kainji (Niger) Dam.

117 Carved Frieze

1965. 2nd Anniv of Republic.

No.	Type	Description	Unused	Used
169	**117**	3d. black, red and yellow	10	10
170	-	1s.3d. brown, green & blue	25	10
171	-	5s. brown, sepia and green	60	1·25

DESIGNS—VERT: 1s.3d. Stone Images at Ikom; 5s. Tada bronze.

121 African Elephants

1965

No.	Type	Description	Unused	Used
172		½d. multicoloured	1·00	2·75
173	**121**	1d. multicoloured	50	15
174	-	1½d. multicoloured	8·00	9·50
222a	-	2d. multicoloured	1·00	1·75
176	-	3d. multicoloured	1·25	30
177a	-	4d. multicoloured	30	10
178	-	6d. multicoloured	2·00	40
179	-	9d. blue and red	3·00	60
227	-	1s. multicoloured	2·50	20
181	-	1s.3d. multicoloured	8·50	1·75
182	**227**	2s.6d. light brown, buff and brown	75	2·00
183	-	5s. chestnut, yellow and brown	1·75	3·50
184	-	10s. multicoloured	6·50	3·25
185	-	£1 multicoloured	17·00	9·00

DESIGNS—VERT (as T **121**): ½d. Lion and cubs; 6d. Saddle-bill stork. (26½×46 mm): 10s. Hippopotamus. HORIZ (as T **121**): 1½d. Splendid sunbird; 2d. Village weaver and red-headed malimbe; 3d. Cheetah; 4d. Leopards; 9d. Grey parrots. (46×26½ mm): 1s. Blue-breasted kingfishers; 1s.3d. Crowned cranes; 2s.6d. Kobs; 5s. Giraffes; £1 African buffalo.

The 1d., 3d., 4d., 1s., 1s.3d., 2s.6d., 5s. and £1 exist optd **F.G.N.** (Federal Government of Nigeria) twice in black. They were prepared in November 1968 as official stamps, but the scheme was abandoned. Some stamps held at a Head Post Office were sold in error and passed through the post. The Director of Posts then decided to put limited supplies on sale, but they had no postal validity.

1966. Commonwealth Prime Ministers' Meeting, Lagos. Optd COMMONWEALTH P. M. MEETING 11. JAN. 1966.

No.	Type	Description	Unused	Used
186	**48**	2s.6d. black and yellow	30	30

135 Y.W.C.A. Emblem and H.Q., Lagos

1966. Diamond Jubilee of Nigerian Y.W.C.A.

No.	Type	Description	Unused	Used
187	**135**	4d. multicoloured	15	10
188	**135**	9d. multicoloured	15	60

137 Telephone Handset and Linesman

1966. 3rd Anniv of Republic.

No.	Type	Description	Unused	Used
189	-	4d. green	10	10
190	**137**	1s.6d. black, brown & violet	30	50
191	-	2s.6d. multicoloured	1·00	2·25

DESIGNS—VERT: 4d. Dove and flag. HORIZ: 2s.6d. North Channel Bridge over River Niger, Jebba.

139 "Education, Science and Culture"

1966. 20th Anniv of UNESCO.

No.	Type	Description	Unused	Used
192	**139**	4d. black, lake and orange	65	20
193	**139**	1s.6d. black, lake & turq	2·75	3·50
194	**139**	2s.6d. black, lake and pink	3·75	8·50

140 Children drinking

1966. Nigerian Red Cross.

No.	Type	Description	Unused	Used
195	**140**	4d.+1d. black, vio & red	30	30
196	-	1s.6d.+3d. multicoloured	55	3·75
197	-	2s.6d.+3d. multicoloured	65	4·25

DESIGNS—VERT: 1s.6d. Tending patient. HORIZ: 2s.6d. Tending casualties and badge.

143 Surveying

1967. Int Hydrological Decade. Mult.

No.	Type	Description	Unused	Used
198		4d. Type **143**	10	10
199		2s.6d. Water gauge on dam (vert)	25	1·50

145 Globe and Weather Satellite

1967. World Meteorological Day.

No.	Type	Description	Unused	Used
200	**145**	4d. mauve and blue	15	10
201	-	1s.6d. black, yellow & blue	65	90

DESIGN: 1s.6d. Passing storm and sun.

147 Eyo Masqueraders

1967. 4th Anniv of Republic. Multicoloured.

202		4d. Type **147**	15	10
203		1s.6d. Crowds watching acrobat	50	1·50
204		2s.6d. Stilt dancer (vert)	75	3·50

150 Tending Sick Animal

1967. Rinderpest Eradication Campaign.

205	**150**	4d. multicoloured	15	10
206	**150**	1s.6d. multicoloured	55	1·50

151 Smallpox Vaccination

1968. 20th Anniv of W.H.O.

207	**151**	4d. mauve and black	15	10
208	-	1s.6d. orange, lemon & blk	55	1·00

DESIGN: 1s.6d. African and mosquito.

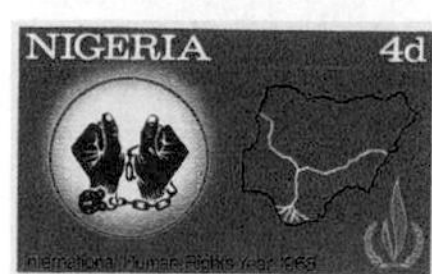

153 Chained Hands and Outline of Nigeria

1968. Human Rights Year.

209	**153**	4d. blue, black and yellow	10	10
210	-	1s.6d. green, red and black	20	1·00

DESIGN—VERT: 1s.6d. Nigerian flag and Human Rights emblem.

155 Hand grasping at Doves of Freedom

1968. 5th Anniv of Federal Republic.

211	**155**	4d. multicoloured	10	10
212	**155**	1s.6d. multicoloured	20	20

156 Map of Nigeria and Olympic Rings

1968. Olympic Games, Mexico.

213	**156**	4d. black, green and red	20	10
214	-	1s.6d. multicoloured	80	30

DESIGN: 1s.6d. Nigerian athletes, flag and Olympic rings.

158 G.P.O., Lagos

1969. Inauguration of Philatelic Service.

215	**158**	4d. black and green	10	10
216	**158**	1s.6d. black and blue	20	50

159 Yakubu Gowon and Victoria Zakari

1969. Wedding of General Gowon.

217	**159**	4d. brown and green	10	10
218	**159**	1s.6d. black and green	90	30

160 Bank Emblem and "5th Anniversary"

1969. 5th Anniv of African Development Bank.

233	**160**	4d. orange, black and blue	10	10
234	-	1s.6d. yellow, black and purple	20	1·25

DESIGN: 1s.6d. Bank emblem and rays.

162 I.L.O. Emblem

1969. 50th Anniv of I.L.O.

235	**162**	4d. black and violet	10	10
236	-	1s.6d. green and black	75	1·50

DESIGN: 1s.6d. World map and I.L.O. emblem.

164 Olumo Rock

1969. International Year of African Tourism.

237	**164**	4d. multicoloured	15	10
238	-	1s. black and green	20	10
239	-	1s.6d. multicoloured	1·25	95

DESIGNS—VERT: 1s. Traditional musicians; 1s.6d. Assob Falls.

167 Symbolic Tree

1970. "Stamp of Destiny". End of Civil War.

240	**167**	4d. gold, blue and black	10	10
241	-	1s. multicoloured	10	10
242	-	1s.6d. green and black	15	10
243	-	2s. multicoloured	20	20

DESIGNS—VERT: 1s. Symbolic wheel; 1s.6d. United Nigerians supporting map. HORIZ: 2s. Symbolic torch.

168 U.P.U. Headquarters Building

1970. New U.P.U. Headquarters Building.

244	**168**	4d. violet and yellow	10	10
245	**168**	1s.6d. blue and indigo	40	20

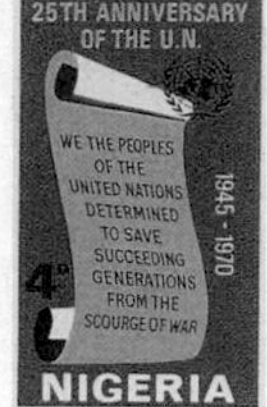

169 Scroll

1970. 25th Anniv of United Nations.

246	**169**	4d. brown, buff and black	10	10
247	-	1s.6d. blue, brown & gold	30	20

DESIGN: 1s.6d. U.N. Building.

170 Oil Rig

1970. 10th Anniv of Independence.

248		2d. Type **170**	25	10
249		4d. University graduate	15	10
250		6d. Durbar horsemen	30	10
251		9d. Servicemen raising flag	40	10
252		1s. Footballer	40	10
253		1s.6d. Parliament building	40	40
254		2s. Kainji Dam	70	90
255		2s.6d. Agricultural produce	70	1·10

171 Children and Globe

1971. Racial Equality Year. Multicoloured.

256		4d. Type **171**	10	10
257		1s. Black and white men uprooting "Racism" (vert)	10	10
258		1s.6d. "The World in Black and White" (vert)	15	75
259		2s. Black and white men united	15	1·50

172 Ibibio Face Mask

1971. Antiquities of Nigeria.

260	**172**	4d. black and blue	10	10
261	-	1s.3d. brown and ochre	15	30
262	-	1s.9d. green, brown & yell	20	1·25

DESIGNS: 1s.3d. Benin bronze; 1s.9d. Ife bronze.

173 Children and Symbol

1971. 25th Anniv of UNICEF.

263	**173**	4d. multicoloured	10	10
264	-	1s.3d. orange, red & brn	15	40
265	-	1s.9d. turquoise and deep turquoise	15	1·00

DESIGNS: Each with UNICEF symbol: 1s.3d. Mother and child; 1s.9d. Mother carrying child.

174 Mast and Dish Aerial

1971. Opening of Nigerian Earth Satellite Station.

266	**174**	4d. multicoloured	15	10
267	-	1s.3d. green, blue & black	25	50
268	-	1s.9d. brown, orange & blk	25	1·00
269	-	3s. mauve, black and purple	45	2·00

DESIGNS: Nos. 267/9 as Type **174**, but showing different views of the Satellite Station.

175 Trade Fair Emblem

1972. All-Africa Trade Fair.

270	**175**	4d. multicoloured	10	10
271	-	1s.3d. lilac, yellow & gold	15	35
272	-	1s.9d. yellow, orange & blk	15	1·60

DESIGNS—HORIZ: 1s.3d. Map of Africa with pointers to Nairobi. VERT: 1s.9d. Africa on globe.

176 Traffic

1972. Change to Driving on the Right.

273	**176**	4d. orange, brown & black	50	10
274	-	1s.3d. multicoloured	1·25	70
275	-	1s.9d. multicoloured	1·25	1·25
276	-	3s. multicoloured	1·75	3·00

DESIGNS: 1s.3d. Roundabout; 1s.9d. Highway; 3s. Road junction.

177 Nok Style Terracotta Head

1972. All-Nigeria Arts Festival. Multicoloured.

277		4d. Type **177**	10	10
278		1s.3d. Bronze pot from Igbo-Ukwu	25	60
279		1s.9d. Bone harpoon (horiz)	30	1·75

178 Hides and Skins

1973

290	**178**	1k. multicoloured	10	20
281	-	2k. multicoloured	35	10
292	-	3k. multicoloured	15	10
282a	-	5k. multicoloured	50	10
294	-	7k. multicoloured	30	1·25
295	-	8k. multicoloured	40	10
344	-	10k. multicoloured	1·25	20
297	-	12k. black, green and blue	30	3·25
298	-	15k. multicoloured	30	60
299	-	18k. multicoloured	50	30
300	-	20k. multicoloured	65	30
301	-	25k. multicoloured	85	45

302	-	30k. black, yellow & blue	40	1·50
303	-	35k. multicoloured	6·00	4·25
288a	-	50k. multicoloured	50	90
305	-	1n. multicoloured	50	75
306	-	2n. multicoloured	75	2·00

DESIGNS—HORIZ: 2k. Natural gas tanks; 3k. Cement works; 5k. Cattle-ranching; 7k. Timber mill; 8k. Oil refinery; 10k. Cheetahs, Yankari Game Reserve; 12k. New Civic Building; 15k. Sugar-cane harvesting; 20k. Vaccine production; 25k. Modern wharf; 35k. Textile machinery; 1n. Eko Bridge; 2n. Teaching Hospital, Lagos. VERT: 18k. Palm oil production; 30k. Argungu Fishing Festival; 50k. Pottery.

179 Athlete

1973. 2nd All-African Games, Lagos.

307	**179**	5k. lilac, blue and black	15	10
308	-	12k. multicoloured	25	50
309	-	18k. multicoloured	45	1·00
310	-	25k. multicoloured	50	1·50

DESIGNS—HORIZ: 12k. Football; 18k. Table tennis. VERT: 25k. National stadium.

180 All-Africa House, Addis Ababa

1973. 10th Anniv of O.A.U. Multicoloured.

311	5k. Type **180**	10	10
312	18k. O.A.U. flag (vert)	30	40
313	30k. O.A.U. emblem and symbolic flight of ten stairs (vert)	50	80

181 Dr. Hansen

1973. Cent of Discovery of Leprosy Bacillus.

314	**181**	5k.+2k. brown, pink and black	30	1·00

182 W.M.O. Emblem and Weather-vane

1973. Centenary of I.M.O./W.M.O.

315	**182**	5k. multicoloured	30	10
316	**182**	30k. multicoloured	1·50	2·25

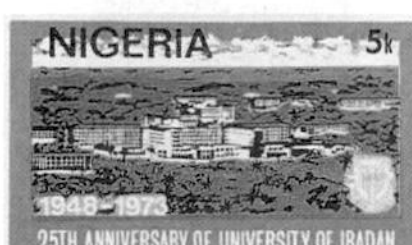
183 University Complex

1973. 25th Anniv of Ibadan University. Multicoloured.

317	5k. Type **183**	10	10
318	12k. Students' population growth (vert)	15	20
319	18k. Tower and students	25	35
320	30k. Teaching Hospital	35	65

184 Lagos 1d. Stamp of 1874

1974. Stamp Centenary.

321	-	5k. green, orange & black	15	10
322	-	12k. multicoloured	30	40
323	**184**	18k. green, mauve & black	50	70
324	-	30k. multicoloured	1·50	2·00

DESIGNS: 5k. Graph of mail traffic growth; 12k. Northern Nigeria £25 stamp of 1904; 30k. Forms of mail transport.

185 U.P.U. Emblem on Globe

1974. Centenary of U.P.U.

325	**185**	5k. blue, orange and black	15	10
326	-	18k. multicoloured	2·00	60
327	-	30k. brown, green & black	1·75	1·75

DESIGNS: 18k. World transport map; 30k. U.P.U. emblem and letters.

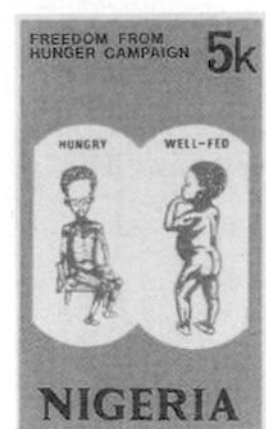
186 Starving and Well-fed Children

1974. Freedom from Hunger Campaign.

328	**186**	5k. green, buff and black	10	10
329	-	12k. multicoloured	30	50
330	-	30k. multicoloured	80	1·75

DESIGNS—HORIZ: 12k. Poultry battery. VERT: 30k. Water-hoist.

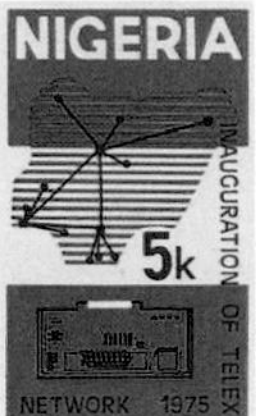
187 Telex Network and Teleprinter

1975. Inauguration of Telex Network.

331	**187**	5k. black, orange & green	10	10
332	-	12k. black, yellow & brn	20	20
333	-	18k. multicoloured	30	30
334	-	30k. multicoloured	50	50

DESIGNS: 12, 18, 30k. are as Type **187** but with the motifs arranged differently.

188 Queen Amina of Zaria

1975. International Women's Year.

335	**188**	5k. green, yellow and blue	35	10
336	**188**	18k. purple, blue & mauve	1·00	80
337	**188**	30k. multicoloured	1·25	1·60

190 Alexander Graham Bell

1976. Centenary of Telephone.

355	**190**	5k. multicoloured	10	10
356	-	18k. multicoloured	40	55
357	-	25k. blue, light blue and brown	70	1·00

DESIGNS—HORIZ: 18k. Gong and modern telephone system. VERT: 25k. Telephones, 1876 and 1976.

191 Child writing

1976. Launching of Universal Primary Education.

358	**191**	5k. yellow, violet & mauve	10	10
359	-	18k. multicoloured	45	75
360	-	25k. multicoloured	70	1·00

DESIGNS—VERT: 18k. Children entering school; 25k. Children in class.

192 Festival Emblem

1976. 2nd World Black and African Festival of Arts and Culture, Nigeria.

361	**192**	5k. gold and brown	35	10
362	-	10k. brown, yellow & blk	35	55
363	-	12k. multicoloured	80	90
364	-	18k. yellow, brown & blk	90	90
365	-	30k. red and black	1·00	1·50

DESIGNS: 10k. National Arts Theatre; 12k. African hair-styles; 18k. Musical instruments; 30k. "Nigerian arts and crafts".

193 General Murtala Muhammed and Map of Nigeria

1977. 1st Death Anniv of General Muhammed (Head of State). Multicoloured.

366	5k. Type **193**	10	10
367	18k. General in dress uniform (vert)	20	35
368	30k. General in battle dress (vert)	30	70

194 Scouts saluting

1977. 1st All-African Scout Jamboree, Jos, Nigeria. Multicoloured.

369	5k. Type **194**	15	10
370	18k. Scouts cleaning street (horiz)	60	70
371	25k. Scouts working on farm (horiz)	70	1·25
372	30k. Jamboree emblem and map of Africa (horiz)	80	2·00

195 Trade Fair Complex

1977. 1st Lagos Int Trade Fair.

373	**195**	5k. black, blue and green	10	10
374	-	18k. black, blue and purple	20	25
375	-	30k. multicoloured	30	45

DESIGNS: 18k. Globe and Trade Fair emblem; 30k. Weaving and basketry.

196 Map showing Nigerian Universities

1978. Global Conference on Technical Co-operation between Developing Countries, Buenos Aires.

376	**196**	5k. multicoloured	10	10
377	-	12k. multicoloured	15	15
378	-	18k. multicoloured	25	25
379	-	30k. yellow, violet & black	45	60

DESIGNS: 12k. Map of West African highways and telecommunications; 18k. Technologists undergoing training; 30k. World map.

197 Microwave Antenna

1978. 10th World Telecommunications Day.

380	**197**	30k. multicoloured	50	60

198 Students on "Operation Feed the Nation"

1978. "Operation Feed the Nation" Campaign. Multicoloured.

381	5k. Type **198**	10	10
382	18k. Family backyard farm	20	20
383	30k. Plantain farm (vert)	35	60

199 Mother with Infected Child

1978. Global Eradication of Smallpox.

384	**199**	5k. black, brown and lilac	15	10
385	-	12k. multicoloured	25	40
386	-	18k. black, brown & yell	40	45
387	-	30k. black, silver and pink	55	1·40

DESIGNS—HORIZ: 12k. Doctor and infected child; 18k. Group of children being vaccinated. VERT: 30k. Syringe.

200 Nok Terracotta Human Figure, Bwari (900 B.C.–100 A.D.)

1978. Antiquities.

388	**200**	5k. black, blue and red	10	10
389	-	12k. multicoloured	15	10
390	-	18k. black, blue and red	20	15
391	-	30k. multicoloured	25	20

DESIGNS—HORIZ: 12k. Igbo-Ukwu bronze snail shell, Igbo Isaiah (9th-century A.D.). VERT: 18k. Ife bronze statue of a king (12th–15th century A.D.); 30k. Benin bronze equestrian figure (about 1700 A.D.).

201 Anti-Apartheid Emblem

1978. International Anti-Apartheid Year.

392	**201**	18k. black, yellow and red	15	15

202 Wright Brothers and Wright Type A

1978. 75th Anniv of Powered Flight.

393	**202**	5k. multicoloured	20	10
394	-	18k. black, blue and light blue	60	20

DESIGN: 18k. Nigerian Air Force formation.

203 Murtala Muhammed Airport

1979. Opening of Murtala Muhammed Airport.
395 **203** 5k. black, grey and blue 40 30

204 Child with Stamp Album

1979. 10th Anniv of National Philatelic Service.
396 **204** 5k. multicoloured 10 20

205 Mother and Child

1979. International Year of the Child. Multicoloured.
397 5k. Type **205** 10 10
398 18k. Children studying 35 30
399 25k. Children playing (vert) 40 50

206 Trainee Teacher making Audio Visual Aid Materials

1979. 50th Anniv of International Bureau of Education. Multicoloured.
400 10k. Type **206** 10 10
401 30k. Adult education class 25 30

207 Necom House

1979. 50th Anniv of Consultative Committee of International Radio.
402 **207** 10k. multicoloured 15 30

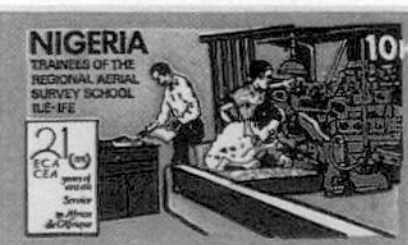

208 Trainees of the Regional Air Survey School, Ile-Ife

1979. 21st Anniv of Economic Commission for Africa.
403 **208** 10k. multicoloured 20 30

209 Football Cup and Map of Nigeria

1980. African Cup of Nations Football Competition, Nigeria. Multicoloured.
404 10k. Type **209** 20 10
405 30k. Footballer (vert) 60 50

210 Wrestling

1980. Olympic Games, Moscow.
406 **210** 10k. multicoloured 10 10
407 - 20k. black and green 10 10
408 - 30k. black, orange & blue 15 15
409 - 45k. multicoloured 20 20
DESIGNS—VERT: 20k. Long jump; 45k. Netball. HORIZ: 30k. Swimming.

211 Figures supporting O.P.E.C. Emblem

1980. 20th Anniv of O.P.E.C. (Organization of Petroleum Exporting Countries).
410 **211** 10k. black, blue and yellow 15 10
411 - 45k. black, blue and mauve 70 60
DESIGN—VERT: 45k. O.P.E.C. emblem and globe.

212 Tank Locomotive No. 2, Wushishi Tramway

1980. 25th Anniv of Nigerian Railway Corporation. Multicoloured.
412 10k. Type **212** 75 10
413 20k. Loading goods train 1·00 85
414 30k. Freight train 1·40 1·25

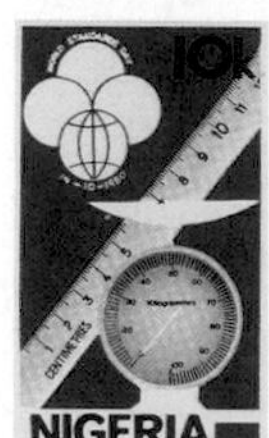

213 Metric Scales

1980. World Standards Day.
415 **213** 10k. red and black 10 10
416 - 30k. multicoloured 35 40
DESIGN—HORIZ: 30k. Quality control.

214 "Communication" Symbols and Map of West Africa

1980. 5th Anniv of Economic Community of West African States.
417 **214** 10k. black, orange & olive 10 10
418 - 25k. black, green and red 30 10
419 - 30k. black, yellow & brn 20 15
420 - 45k. black, turquoise & bl 25 25
DESIGNS: 25k. "Transport"; 30k. "Agriculture"; 45k. "Industry".

215 Disabled Woman sweeping

1981. International Year for Disabled Persons.
421 **215** 10k. multicoloured 20 10
422 - 30k. black, brown and blue 65 65
DESIGN: 30k. Disabled man filming.

216 President launching "Green Revolution" (food production campaign)

1981. World Food Day.
423 **216** 10k. multicoloured 10 10
424 - 25k. black, yellow & green 20 50
425 - 30k. multicoloured 25 55
426 - 45k. black, brown & yell 45 85
DESIGNS—VERT: 25k. Food crops; 30k. Harvesting tomatoes. HORIZ: 45k. Pig farming.

217 Rioting in Soweto

1981. Anti-Apartheid Movement.
427 **217** 30k. multicoloured 35 55
428 - 45k. black, red and green 50 1·25
DESIGN—VERT: 45k. "Police brutality".

218 "Preservation of Wildlife"

1982. 75th Anniv of Boy Scout Movement. Multicoloured.
429 30k. Type **218** 50 55
430 45k. Lord Baden-Powell taking salute 75 1·25

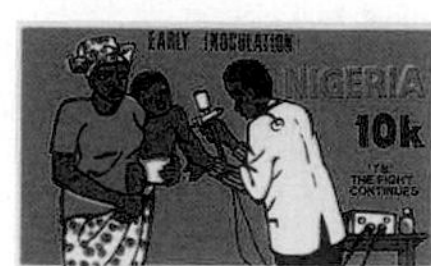

219 Early Inoculation

1982. Centenary of Robert Koch's Discovery of Tubercle Bacillus.
431 **219** 10k. multicoloured 20 15
432 - 30k. black, brown and green 50 65
433 - 45k. black, brown and green 80 1·75
DESIGNS—HORIZ: 30k. Technician and microscope. VERT: 45k. Patient being X-rayed.

220 "Keep Your Environment Clean"

1982. 10th Anniv of U.N. Conference on Human Environment.
434 **220** 10k. multicoloured 10 10
435 - 20k. orange, grey and black 20 40
436 - 30k. multicoloured 35 60
437 - 45k. multicoloured 55 85
DESIGNS: 20k. "Check air pollution"; 30k. "Preserve natural environment"; 45k. "Reafforestation concerns all".

221 "Salamis parhassus"

1982. Nigerian Butterflies. Multicoloured.
438 10k. Type **221** 15 10
439 20k. "Iterus zalmoxis" 30 30
440 30k. "Cymothoe beckeri" 40 40
441 45k. "Papilio hesperus" 70 1·25

222 Carving of "Male and Female Twins"

1982. 25th Anniv of National Museum. Multicoloured.
442 10k. Type **222** 10 10
443 20k. Royal bronze leopard (horiz) 20 35
444 30k. Soapstone seated figure 35 90
445 45k. Wooden helmet mask 50 1·75

223 Three Generations

1983. Family Day. Multicoloured.
446 10k. Type **223** 15 10
447 30k. Parents with three children (vert) 50 65

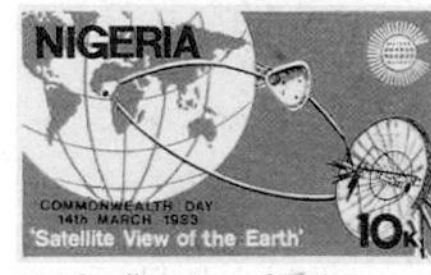

224 Satellite View of Globe

1983. Commonwealth Day.
448 **224** 10k. brown and black 10 10
449 - 25k. multicoloured 20 30
450 - 30k. black, purple and grey 75 35
451 - 45k. multicoloured 35 45
DESIGNS—HORIZ: 25k. National Assembly Buildings. VERT: 30k. Drilling for oil; 45k. Athletics.

225 Corps Members on Building Project

1983. 10th Anniv of National Youth Service Corps. Multicoloured.
452 10k. Type **225** 15 10
453 25k. On the assault-course (vert) 30 30
454 30k. Corps members on parade 40 40

226 Postman on Bicycle

1983. World Communications Year. Multicoloured.
455 10k. Type **226** 15 10
456 25k. Newspaper kiosk (horiz) 30 45
457 30k. Town crier blowing elephant tusk (horiz) 35 80
458 45k. T.V. newsreader (horiz) 45 1·10

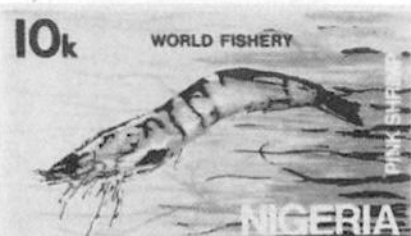

227 Pink Shrimp

1983. World Fishery Resources.
459 **227** 10k. red, blue and black 15 10
460 - 25k. multicoloured 30 40
461 - 30k. multicoloured 30 45
462 - 45k. multicoloured 40 70
DESIGNS: 25k. Long-necked croaker; 30k. Barracuda; 45k. Fishing techniques.

228 On Parade

1983. Centenary of Boys' Brigade and 75th Anniv of Founding in Nigeria. Multicoloured.

463		10k. Type **228**	40	10
464		30k. Members working on cassava plantation (horiz)	1·50	1·50
465		45k. Skill training (horiz)	2·25	2·75

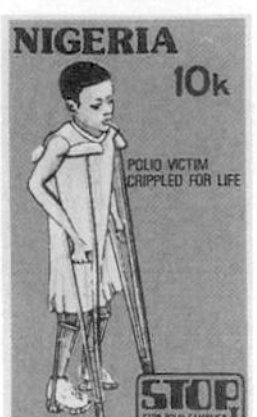

229 Crippled Child

1984. Stop Polio Campaign.

466	**229**	10k. blue, black and brown	20	15
467	-	25k. orange, black & yell	40	75
468	-	30k. red, black and brown	60	1·10

DESIGNS—HORIZ: 25k. Child receiving vaccine. VERT: 30k. Healthy child.

230 Waterbuck

1984. Nigerian Wildlife.

469	**230**	10k. green, brown & black	15	10
470	-	25k. multicoloured	30	50
471	-	30k. brown, black & green	40	90
472	-	45k. blue, orange & black	45	1·50

DESIGNS—HORIZ: 25k. Hartebeest; 30k. African buffalo. VERT: 45k. Diademed monkey.

231 Obverse and Reverse of 1969 £1 Note

1984. 25th Anniv of Nigerian Central Bank.

473	**231**	10k. multicoloured	20	10
474	-	25k. brown, black & green	45	70
475	-	30k. red, black and green	55	85

DESIGNS: 25k. Central Bank; 30k. Obverse and reverse of 1959 £5 note.

232 Boxing

1984. Olympic Games, Los Angeles. Mult.

476		10k. Type **232**	15	10
477		25k. Discus-throwing	35	50
478		30k. Weightlifting	40	60
479		45k. Cycling	60	90

233 Irrigation Project, Lesotho

1984. 20th Anniv of African Development Bank.

480	**233**	10k. multicoloured	15	10
481	-	25k. multicoloured	30	50
482	-	30k. black, yellow and blue	35	60
483	-	45k. black, brown and blue	1·75	90

DESIGNS—HORIZ: 25k. Bomi Hills Road, Liberia; 30k. School building project, Seychelles; 45k. Coal mining, Niger.

234 Pin-tailed Whydah

1984. Rare Birds. Multicoloured.

484		10k. Type **234**	75	20
485		25k. Spur-winged plover	1·50	70
486		30k. Red bishop	1·50	1·75
487		45k. Double-spurred francolin	1·75	2·50

235 Boeing 747 Airliner taking-off

1984. 40th Anniv of International Civil Aviation Organization. Multicoloured.

488		10k. Type **235**	40	10
489		45k. Boeing 707 airliner circling globe	1·50	2·25

236 Office Workers and Clocks ("Punctuality")

1985. "War against Indiscipline". Mult.

490		20k. Type **236**	30	35
491		50k. Cross over hands passing banknotes ("Discourage Bribery")	55	75

237 Footballers receiving Flag from Major-General Buhari

1985. International Youth Year. Mult.

492		20k. Type **237**	30	20
493		50k. Girls of different tribes with flag (vert)	55	70
494		55k. Members of youth organizations with flags (vert)	55	80

238 Rolling Mill

1985. 25th Anniv of Independence. Mult.

495		20k. Type **238**	25	10
496		50k. Map of Nigeria	40	40
497		55k. Remembrance Arcade	40	50
498		60k. Eleme, first Nigerian oil refinery	1·00	1·50
MS499		101×101 mm. Nos. 495/8	5·00	6·50

239 Globe and O.P.E.C. Emblem

1985. 25th Anniv of Organization of Petroleum Exporting Countries.

500	**239**	20k. blue and red	75	35
501	-	50k. black and blue	1·50	75

DESIGN—HORIZ: 50k. World map and O.P.E.C. emblem.

240 Waterfall

1985. World Tourism Day. Multicoloured.

502		20k. Type **240**	35	10
503		50k. Pottery, carved heads and map of Nigeria (horiz)	45	50
504		55k. Calabash carvings and Nigerian flag	45	50
505		60k. Leather work	45	55

241 Map of Nigeria and National Flag

1985. 40th Anniv of United Nations Organization and 25th Anniv of Nigerian Membership.

506	**241**	20k. black, green and blue	20	10
507	-	50k. black, blue and red	35	85
508	-	55k. black, blue and red	35	95

DESIGNS—HORIZ: 50k. United Nations Building, New York; 55k. United Nations logo.

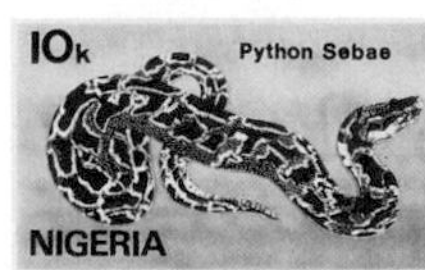

242 Rock Python

1986. African Reptiles.

509	**242**	10k. multicoloured	30	10
510	-	20k. black, brown and blue	50	90
511	-	25k. multicoloured	50	1·00
512	-	30k. multicoloured	50	1·00

DESIGNS: 20k. Long snouted crocodile; 25k. Gopher tortoise; 30k. Chameleon.

243 Social Worker with Children

1986. Nigerian Life. Multicoloured.

513		1k. Type **243**	10	20
514		2k. Volkswagen motor assembly line (horiz)	10	20
515		5k. Modern housing estate (horiz)	10	20
516		10k. Harvesting oil palm fruit	10	10
517		15k. Unloading freighter (horiz)	15	10
518		20k. "Tecoma stans" (flower)	15	10
519		25k. Hospital ward (horiz)	15	10
519a		30k. Birom dancers (horiz)	15	10
520		35k. Telephonists operating switchboard (horiz)	15	10
521		40k. Nkpokiti dancers	15	10
522		45k. Hibiscus (horiz)	15	10
523a		50k. Post Office counter (horiz)	1·00	10
524		1n. Stone quarry (horiz)	15	15
525a		2n. Students in laboratory (horiz)	20	10
525ba		10n. Lekki Beach (horiz)	20	15
525c		20n. Ancient wall, Kano (horiz)	5·50	1·75
525d		50n. Rock bridge (horiz)	5·00	3·50
525e		100n. Ekpe masquerader	3·00	3·25
525f		500n. National Theatre (horiz)	8·00	8·50

244 Emblem and Globe

1986. International Peace Year. Mult.

526		10k. Type **244**	20	10
527		20k. Hands of five races holding globe	60	1·50

245 "Goliathus goliathus" (beetle)

1986. Nigerian Insects. Multicoloured.

528		10k. Type **245**	30	10
529		20k. "Vespa vulgaris" (wasp)	40	40
530		25k. "Acheta domestica" (cricket)	45	90
531		30k. "Anthrenus verbasci" (beetle)	55	1·50
MS532		119×101 mm. Nos. 528/31	4·50	6·50

246 Oral Rehydration Therapy

1986. 40th Anniv of UNICEF.

533	**246**	10k. multicoloured	30	10
534	-	20k. black, brown & yell	40	40
535	-	25k. multicoloured	45	70
536	-	30k. multicoloured	55	1·00

DESIGNS: 20k. Immunization; 25k. Breast-feeding; 30k. Mother and child.

247 Stylized Figures on Wall ("International Understanding")

1986. 25th Anniv of Nigerian Institute of International Affairs.

537	**247**	20k. black, blue and green	50	50
538	-	30k. multicoloured	75	1·25

DESIGN—VERT: 30k. "Knowledge" (bronze sculpture).

248 Freshwater Clam

1987. Shells.

539	**248**	10k. multicoloured	65	10
540	-	20k. black, brown and pink	1·00	1·75
541	-	25k. multicoloured	1·00	2·00
542	-	30k. multicoloured	1·25	2·50

DESIGNS: 20k. Periwinkle; 25k. Bloody cockle (inscr "BLOODY COCKLE"); 30k. Mangrove oyster.

249 "Clitoria ternatea"

1987. Nigerian Flowers.
543 **249** 10k. multicoloured 10 10
544 - 20k. brown, yellow and green 15 25
545 - 25k. multicoloured 15 45
546 - 30k. multicoloured 20 1·00
DESIGNS: 20k. "Hibiscus tiliaceus"; 25k. "Acanthus montanus"; 30k. "Combretum racemosum".

250 Doka Hairstyle

1987. Women's Hairstyles.
547 **250** 10k. black, brown and grey 10 10
548 - 20k. multicoloured 15 30
549 - 25k. black, brown and red 20 55
550 - 30k. multicoloured 20 1·00
DESIGNS: 20k. Eting; 25k. Agogo; 30k. Goto.

251 Family sheltering under Tree

1987. International Year of Shelter for the Homeless. Multicoloured.
551 20k. Type **251** 15 15
552 30k. Family and modern house 15 90

252 Red Cross Worker distributing Food

1988. 125th Anniv of International Red Cross. Multicoloured.
553 20k. Type **252** 65 30
554 30k. Carrying patient to ambulance 65 1·75

253 Doctor vaccinating Baby

1988. 40th Anniv of W.H.O. Multicoloured.
555 10k. Type **253** 25 10
556 20k. W.H.O. logo and outline map of Nigeria 60 60
557 30k. Doctor and patients at mobile clinic 60 60

254 O.A.U. Logo

1988. 25th Anniv of Organization of African Unity.
558 **254** 10k. brown, green & orge 15 15
559 - 20k. multicoloured 15 15
DESIGN: 20k. Four Africans supporting map of Africa.

255 Pink Shrimp

1988. Shrimps.
560 **255** 10k. multicoloured 20 10
561 - 20k. black and green 30 15
562 - 25k. black, red and brown 30 25
563 - 30k. orange, brown & blk 30 60
MS564 120×101 mm. Nos. 560/3 1·50 2·00
DESIGNS: 20k. Tiger shrimp; 25k. Deepwater roseshrimp; 30k. Estuarine prawn.

256 Weightlifting

1988. Olympic Games, Seoul. Multicoloured.
565 10k. Type **256** 25 10
566 20k. Boxing 35 35
567 30k. Athletics (vert) 50 65

257 Banknote Production Line (image scaled to 64% of original size)

1988. 25th Anniv of Nigerian Security Printing and Minting Co. Ltd.
568 **257** 10k. multicoloured 10 10
569 - 20k. black, silver and green 20 20
570 - 25k. multicoloured 30 30
571 - 30k. multicoloured 50 50
DESIGNS—HORIZ (As T **257**): 20k. Coin production line. VERT (37×44 mm): 25k. Montage of products; 30k. Anniversary logos.

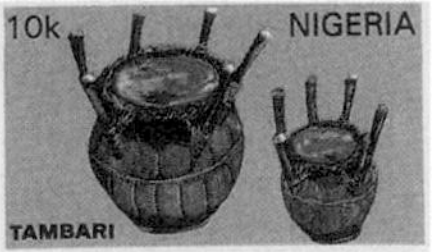
258 Tambari

1989. Nigerian Musical Instruments.
572 **258** 10k. multicoloured 10 10
573 - 20k. multicoloured 20 20
574 - 25k. brown, green & black 30 30
575 - 30k. brown and black 50 50
DESIGNS: 20k. Kundung; 25k. Ibid; 30k. Dundun.

259 Construction of Water Towers, Mali

1989. 25th Anniv of African Development Bank. Multicoloured.
576 10k. Type **259** 10 10
577 20k. Paddy field, Gambia 15 15
578 25k. Bank Headquarters, Abidjan, Ivory Coast 25 25
579 30k. Anniversary logo (vert) 35 35

260 Lighting Campfire

1989. 70th Anniv of Nigerian Girl Guides Association. Multicoloured.
580 10k. Type **260** 30 10
581 20k. Guide on rope bridge (vert) 70 60

261 Etubom Costume

1989. Traditional Costumes. Multicoloured.
582 10k. Type **261** 40 10
583 20k. Fulfulde 45 25
584 25k. Aso-Ofi 50 85
585 30k. Fuska Kura 60 1·75

262 Dove with Letter and Map of Africa

1990. 10th Anniv of Pan African Postal Union. Multicoloured.
586 10k. Type **262** 25 10
587 20k. Parcel and map of Africa 50 50

263 Oil Lamps

1990. Nigerian Pottery.
588 **263** 10k. black, brown & violet 10 10
589 - 20k. black, brown & violet 20 20
590 - 25k. brown and violet 25 25
591 - 30k. multicoloured 35 35
MS592 120×100 mm. Nos. 588/91 80 90
DESIGNS: 20k. Water pots; 25k. Musical pots; 50k. Water jugs.

264 Teacher and Class

1990. International Literacy Year.
593 **264** 20k. multicoloured 20 10
594 - 30k. brown, blue & yellow 30 30
DESIGN: 30k. Globe and book.

265 Globe and OPEC Logo

1990. 30th Anniv of the Organization of Petroleum Exporting Countries. Multicoloured.
595 10k. Type **265** 10 10
596 20k. Logo and flags of member countries (vert) 20 20
597 25k. World map and logo 25 25
598 30k. Logo within inscription "Co-operation for Global Energy Security" (vert) 35 35

266 Grey Parrot

1990. Wildlife. Multicoloured.
599 20k. Type **266** 20 10
600 30k. Roan antelope 20 10
601 1n.50 Grey-necked bald crow ("Rockfowl") 60 80
602 2n.50 Mountain gorilla 85 1·25
MS603 118×119 mm. Nos. 599/602 1·75 2·25

267 Eradication Treatment

1991. National Guineaworm Eradication Day. Multicoloured.
604 10k. Type **267** 15 10
605 20k. Women collecting water from river (horiz) 25 25
606 30k. Boiling pot of water 25 25

268 Hand holding Torch (Progress)

1991. Organization of African Unity Heads of State and Governments Meeting, Abuja. Each showing outline map of Africa. Multicoloured.
607 20k. Type **268** 15 10
608 30k. Cogwheel (Unity) 20 25
609 50k. O.A.U. flag (Freedom) 20 45

269 National Flags

1991. Economic Community of West African States Summit Meeting, Abuja. Multicoloured.
610 20k. Type **269** 15 10
611 50k. Map showing member states 30 45

270 Electric Catfish

1991. Nigerian Fishes. Multicoloured.
612 10k. Type **270** 15 10
613 20k. Nile perch 25 25
614 30k. Nile mouthbrooder ("Talapia") 35 35
615 50k. Sharp-toothed catfish 50 55
MS616 121×104 mm. Nos. 612/15 1·75 2·00

271 Telecom '91 Emblem

1991. "Telecom '91" 6th World Telecommunication Exhibition, Geneva.
617 **271** 20k. black, green and violet 30 10
618 - 50k. multicoloured 40 30
DESIGN—VERT: 50k. Emblem and patchwork.

272 Boxing

1992. Olympic Games, Barcelona (1st issue). Multicoloured.

619	50k. Type **272**	15	15
620	1n. Nigerian athlete winning race	25	25
621	1n.50 Table tennis	35	35
622	2n. Taekwondo	45	45
MS623	120×117 mm. Nos. 619/22	1·75	2·00

See also No. 624.

273 Football

1992. Olympic Games, Barcelona (2nd issue).

624	**273**	1n.50 multicoloured	50	50

274 Blood Pressure Gauge

1992. World Health Day. Multicoloured.

625	50k. Type **274**	15	15
626	1n. World Health Day '92 emblem	20	20
627	1n.50 Heart and lungs	30	30
628	2n. Interior of heart	45	45
MS629	123×111 mm. Nos. 625/8	1·10	1·25

275 Map of World and Stamp on Globe

1992. "Olymphilex '92" Olympic Stamp Exhibition, Barcelona. Multicoloured.

630	50k. Type **275**	20	10
631	1n.50 Examining stamps	40	40
MS632	120×109 mm. Nos. 630/1	1·60	1·75

276 Gathering Plantain Fruit

1992. 25th Anniv of International Institute of Tropical Agriculture.

633	**276**	50k. multicoloured	10	10
634	-	1n. multicoloured	15	15
635	-	1n.50 black, brown & grn	20	20
636	-	2n. multicoloured	25	25
MS637		121×118 mm. Nos. 633/6	1·25	1·50

DESIGNS—VERT: 1n.50, Harvesting cassava tubers; 2n. Stacking yams. HORIZ: 1n. Tropical foods.

277 Centre Emblem

1992. Commissioning of Maryam Babangida National Centre for Women's Development.

638	**277**	50k. gold, emerald and green	10	10
639	-	1n. multicoloured	15	15
640	-	1n.50 multicoloured	20	20
641	-	2n. multicoloured	30	30

DESIGNS—VERT: 1n. Women working in fields; 2n. Woman at loom. HORIZ: 1n.50, Maryam Babangida National Centre.

All examples of No. 641 are without a "NIGERIA" inscription.

278 Healthy Food and Emblem

1992. International Conference on Nutrition, Rome. Multicoloured.

642	50k. Type **278**	10	10
643	1n. Child eating	15	15
644	1n.50 Fruit (vert)	20	20
645	2n. Vegetables	25	25
MS646	120×100 mm. Nos. 642/5	1·50	1·75

279 Sabada Dance

1992. Traditional Dances. Multicoloured.

647	50k. Type **279**	10	10
648	1n. Sato	15	15
649	1n.50 Asian Ubo Ikpa	20	20
650	2n. Dundun	25	25
MS651	126×107 mm. Nos. 647/50	1·50	1·75

280 African Elephant

1993. Wildlife. Multicoloured.

652	1n.50 Type **280**	1·75	40
653	5n. Stanley crane (vert)	2·25	50
654	20n. Roan antelope	3·00	2·50
655	30n. Lion	3·50	3·75

281 Suburban Garden

1993. World Environment Day. Multicoloured.

656	1n. Type **281**	10	10
657	1n.50 Water pollution	15	10
658	5n. Forest road	50	60
659	10n. Rural house	90	1·25

282 Oni Figure

1993. 50th Anniv of National Museums and Monuments Commission. Multicoloured.

660	1n. Type **282**	10	10
661	1n.50 Bronze head of Queen Mother	10	10
662	5n. Bronze pendant (horiz)	30	50
663	10n. Nok head	70	1·00

283 "Bulbophyllum distans"

1993. Orchids. Multicoloured.

664	1n. Type **283**	10	25
665	1n.50 "Eulophia cristata"	15	25
666	5n. "Eulophia horsfalli"	45	55
667	10n. "Eulophia quartiniana"	1·00	1·25
MS668	103×121 mm. Nos. 664/7	1·75	2·25

284 Children in Classroom and Adults carrying Food

1994. International Year of the Family. Mult.

669	1n.50 Type **284**	10	10
670	10n. Market	1·00	1·50

285 Hand with Tweezers holding 1969 4d. Philatelic Service Stamp

1994. 25th Anniv of Nat Philatelic Service. Mult.

671	1n. Type **285**	10	10
672	1n.50 Philatelic Bureau	15	10
673	5n. Stamps forming map of Nigeria	45	60
674	10n. Philatelic counter	1·00	1·40

286 "I Love Stamps"

1994. 120th Anniv of First Postage Stamps in Nigeria. Multicoloured.

675	1n. Type **286**	10	10
676	1n.50 "I Collect Stamps"	15	10
677	5n. 19th-century means of communication	45	60
678	10n. Lagos stamp of 1874	1·00	1·40

287 Magnifying Glass over Globe

1994. "Philakorea '94" International Stamp Exhibition, Seoul.

679	**287**	30n. multicoloured	1·75	2·40
MS680		127×115 mm. **287** 30n. multicoloured	2·25	4·00

288 Geryon Crab

1994. Crabs. Multicoloured.

681	1n. Type **288**	10	10
682	1n.50 Spider crab	10	10
683	5n. Red spider crab	45	45
684	10n. Geryon maritae crab	90	1·25

289 Sewage Works

1994. 30th Anniv of African Development Bank. Multicoloured.

685	1n.50 Type **289**	15	10
686	30n. Development Bank emblem and flowers	1·75	2·40

290 Letterbox

1995. 10th Anniv of Nigerian Post and Telecommunication Corporations. Multicoloured.

687	1n. Type **290**	10	10
688	1n.50 Letter showing "1 JAN 1985" postmark (horiz)	10	10
689	5n. Nipost and Nitel emblems (horiz)	30	45
690	10n. Mobile telephones	60	1·00

291 Woman preparing Food

1995. Family Support Programme. Multicoloured.

691	1n. Type **291**	10	10
692	1n.50 Mother teaching children	10	10
693	5n. Family meal	30	45
694	10n. Agricultural workers and tractor	60	1·00

292 "Candlestick" Telephone

1995. Cent of First Telephone in Nigeria. Mult.

695	1n.50 Type **292**	10	10
696	10n. Early equipment	60	1·00

293 F.A.O. Emblem

1995. 50th Anniv of F.A.O. Multicoloured.

697	1n.50 Type **293**	10	10
698	30n. Fishing canoes	1·90	2·75

294 "Justice" and 50th Anniversary Emblem

1995. 50th Anniv of United Nations. Multicoloured.

699	1n. Type **294**	10	10
700	1n.50 Toxic waste (horiz)	10	10
701	5n. Tourist hut (horiz)	30	40
702	10n. Nigerian armoured car on U.N. duty (horiz)	1·25	1·40

295 Container Ship in Dock

1996. 10th Anniv of Niger Dock. Multicoloured.

703	5n. Type **295**	35	30
704	10n. "Badagri" (tourist launch) on crane	65	60
705	20n. Shipping at dock	1·00	1·50
706	30n. "Odoragushin" (ferry)	1·50	2·50

296 Scientist and Crops

1996. 21st Anniv of E.C.O.W.A.S. (Economic Community of West African States). Multicoloured.

707	5n. Type **296**	30	30
708	30n. Queue at border crossing	1·50	2·50

297 Judo

1996. Olympic Games, Atlanta. Multicoloured.

709	5n. Type **297**	35	30
710	10n. Tennis	80	60
711	20n. Relay race	1·00	1·50
712	30n. Football	1·50	2·25

298 Nigerian Flag and Exhibition Emblem

1996. "ISTANBUL '96" International Stamp Exhibition.

713	**298**	30n. mauve, green and black	1·50	2·25

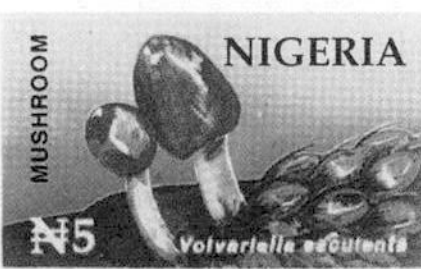

299 "Volvariella esculenta"

1996. Fungi. Multicoloured.

714	5n. Type **299**	45	30
715	10n. "Lentinus subnudus"	90	60
716	20n. "Tricholoma lobayensis"	1·00	1·50
717	30n. "Pleurotus tuber-regium"	1·25	2·25

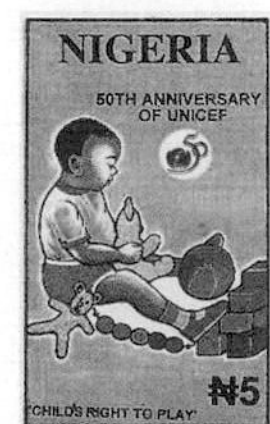

300 Boy with Toys

1996. 50th Anniv of UNICEF. Multicoloured.

718	5n. Type **300**	30	30
719	30n. Girl reading book (horiz)	1·50	2·50

301 Literacy Logo

1996. 5th Anniv of Mass Literacy Commission.

720	**301**	5n. emerald, green and black	30	30
721	-	30n. emerald, green and black	1·50	2·50

DESIGN: 30n. Hands holding book and literacy logo.

302 Three Footballers

1998. World Cup Football Championship, France. Multicoloured.

722	5n. Type **302**	25	30
723	10n. Player with ball (vert)	55	60
724	20n. Player receiving ball (vert)	1·10	1·25
725	30n. Two opposing players	1·60	2·50

303 University Tower and Complex

1998. 50th Anniv of Ibadan University. Mult.

726	5n. Type **303**	25	30
727	30n. Anniversary logo and University crest	1·60	2·50

304 Ship and Logo

1998. 8th Anniv of Economic Community of West African States Military Arm (ECOMOG). Multicoloured.

728	5n. Type **304**	25	30
729	30n. Logo and original member states	1·25	1·75
730	50n. Current member states	2·25	3·50

305 Caged Steam Locomotive

1999. Centenary of Nigerian Railway Corporation. Multicoloured.

731	5n. Type **305**	25	30
732	10n. Iddo Terminus	55	60
733	20n. Diesel locomotive No. 2131	1·10	1·25
734	30n. Passenger train pulling into station	1·60	2·50

306 Football and Globe

1999. 11th World Youth Football Championship, Nigeria. Multicoloured.

735	5n.+5n. Type **306**	15	20
736	10n.+5n. Player throwing ball	20	25
737	20n.+5n. Player scoring goal	35	50
738	30n.+5n. Map of Nigeria showing venues	50	70
739	40n.+5n. World Youth Football Championship logo	60	80
740	50n.+5n. Player being tackled	75	90
MS741	120×115 mm. Nos. 735/40	2·50	3·00

307 Sea Life and F.E.P.A. Emblem

1999. 10th Anniv of Federal Environmental Protection Agency. Multicoloured.

742	5n. Type **307**	30	30
743	10n. Forest	65	60
744	20n. Monkeys	1·40	1·10
745	30n. Villagers and wildlife	2·75	2·75

308 Nicon Emblem

1999. 30th Anniv of Nicon Insurance Corporation. Multicoloured.

746	5n. Type **308**	25	30
747	30n. Emblem and Nicon Building (horiz)	1·00	1·75

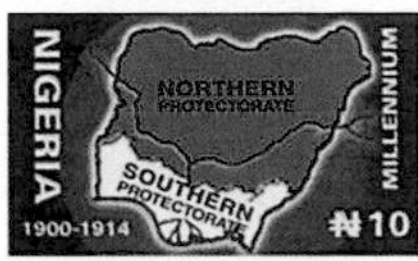

309 Map of Nigeria in 1900

2000. New Millennium (1st Issue). Multicoloured.

748	10n. Type **309**	45	15
749	20n. Map of Nigeria in 1914	65	40
750	30n. Coat of arms	70	80
751	40n. Map of Nigeria in 1996	1·00	1·40

See also Nos. 786/9.

310 Sunshine Hour Recorder

2000. 50th Anniv of World Meteorological Organization.

752	**310**	10n. multicoloured	15	15
753	-	30n. brown and blue	55	75

DESIGN—HORIZ: 30n. Meteorological station.

311 "Freedom of the Press"

2000. Return to Democracy. Multicoloured.

754	10n. Type **311**	20	15
755	20n. "Justice for All" (horiz)	35	30
756	30n. Parliamentary Mace	55	55
757	40n. President Olusegun Obasanjo	75	1·10
MS758	99×109 mm. Nos. 754/7	1·75	1·90

312 Boxing

2000. Olympic Games, Sydney. Multicoloured.

759	10n. Type **312**	20	15
760	20n. Weightlifting	35	30
761	30n. Women's football	55	55
762	40n. Men's football	75	1·10
MS763	136×118 mm. Nos. 759/62	1·75	1·90

313 Obafemi Awolowo

2000. 40th Anniv of Nigeria's Independence.

764	**313**	10n. black, emerald and green	20	15

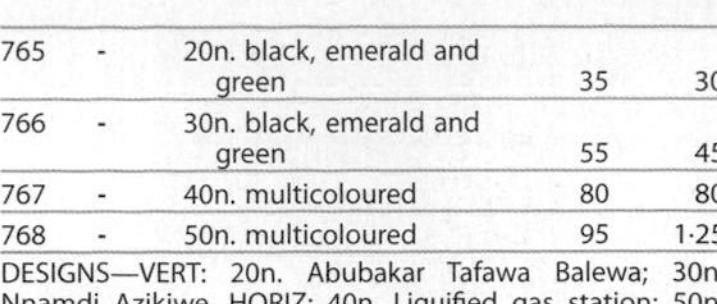

765	-	20n. black, emerald and green	35	30
766	-	30n. black, emerald and green	55	45
767	-	40n. multicoloured	80	80
768	-	50n. multicoloured	95	1·25

DESIGNS—VERT: 20n. Abubakar Tafawa Balewa; 30n. Nnamdi Azikiwe. HORIZ: 40n. Liquified gas station; 50n. Container ships.

314 Hug Plum

2001. Fruits. Multicoloured.

769	20n. Type **314**	55	30
770	30n. White star apple	65	40
771	40n. African breadfruit	85	85
772	50n. Akee apple	95	1·40

315 *Daily Times* Headquarters, Lagos

2001. 75th Anniv of The Daily Times of Nigeria. Multicoloured.

773	20n. Type **315**	40	30
774	30n. First issue of *Nigerian Daily Times*, 1926	55	45
775	40n. *Daily Times* printing works, Lagos	75	80
776	50n. *Daily Times* masthead, 1947	90	1·25

316 Broad-tailed Paradise Whydah

2001. Wildlife. Multicoloured.

777	10n. Type **316**	20	15
778	15n. Fire-bellied woodpecker	25	20
779	20n. Grant's zebra (horiz)	25	20
780	25n. Aardvark (horiz)	30	25
781	30n. Preuss's guenon (monkey)	35	30
782	40n. Great ground pangolin (horiz)	50	40
783	50n. Pygmy chimpanzee (*Pan paniscus*) (horiz)	70	70
784	100n. Red-eared guenon (monkey)	1·25	1·25

317 "Children encircling Globe" (Urska Golob)

2001. U.N. Year of Dialogue among Civilisations.

785	**317**	20n. multicoloured	50	50

318 Map of Nigeria and Dove

2002. New Millennium (2nd issue). Multicoloured.

786	20n. Type **318**	40	30
787	30n. Globe and satellite dish	55	40
788	40n. Handshake across flag in shape of Nigeria	95	90
789	50n. Two overlapping hearts	85	1·25

319 Kola Nuts

2002. Cash Crops. Multicoloured.

790 20n. Type **319** 30 25
791 30n. Oil palm 40 35
792 40n. Cassava 50 50
793 50n. Maize (vert) 60 70

320 Nigerian Player dribbling Ball

2002. World Cup Football Championship, Japan and Korea. Multicoloured.

794 20n. Type **320** 30 25
795 30n. Footballs around Globe 40 35
796 40n. Footballer's legs and World Cup Trophy (horiz) 50 55
797 50n. World Cup Trophy 60 70

321 Nurse caring for Patient

2003. World AIDS Day. Multicoloured.

798 20n. Type **321** 30 20
799 50n. Counselling on AIDS 70 80

322 Girl and Boy in Class

2003. Universal Basic Education. Multicoloured.

800 20n. Type **322** 40 20
801 50n. Boy writing in book (horiz) 1·00 1·25

2003. 8th All Africa Games, Abuja. Multicoloured.

802 20n. Type **323** 40 20
803 30n. High jump (horiz) 50 35
804 40n. Taekwondo (horiz) 70 80
805 50n. Long jump 80 1·00
MS806 172×98 mm. Nos. 802/5 2·25 2·50

324 Logo and Map of Nigeria

2003. Commonwealth Heads of Government Meeting, Abuja. Multicoloured.

807 20n. Type **324** 40 20
808 50n. Logo (vert) 1·00 1·25

325 Female with Cubs

2003. Endangered Species. Side-Striped Jackal. Multicoloured.

809 20n. Type **325** 35 20
810 40n. Adult jackal 65 40
811 80n. Two jackals 1·25 1·40
812 100n. Adult jackal (with head lowered, looking through grass) 1·50 2·00

326 Athletes

2004. Olympic Games, Athens. Multicoloured.

813 50n. Type **326** 80 90
814 120n. Basketball 2·00 2·25

327 Children carrying Water and Food (Zainab Jalloh)

2004. Children's Day. Multicoloured.

815 50n. Type **327** 70 45
816 90n. Book with lightening bolt and hand-cuffed hands (Jessica Umaru) (horiz) 1·25 1·40
817 120n. Skulls, outline of Nigeria and forbidden weapons (Chinonso Chukwougor)(horiz) 1·50 2·00
818 150n. Skull smoking, drugs and alcohol (Sanusi Omolola) 1·75 2·25
MS819 170×104 mm. Nos. 815/18 4·75 5·50

328 Emblems in "100"

2005. Centenary of Rotary International. Mult.

820 50n. Type **328** 70 50
821 120n. Map of world and Rotary and centenary emblems 1·50 2·00

329 Outline of Stamp

2005. 131st Year of Commemorative Postage Stamps. Multicoloured.

823 50n. Type **329** 70 50
824 90n. Outlines of Nigeria and postage stamp 1·25 90
825 120n. "1874 2005" and Nigerian flag in outline map 1·50 1·75
826 150n. 1961 3d. 1st anniv of independence and 2002 50n. maize stamps 1·75 2·00

330 Nipost Emblem and Globe

2005. World Summit on the Information Society, Tunis. Multicoloured.

827 20n. Type **330** 30 20
828 50n. Motorcycle courier, satellite dish and globe (vert) 70 80
829 120n. Type **330** 1·75 2·00

331 Prof. Chinua Achebe (novelist)

2006. Nigerian Personalities. Multicoloured.

830 20n. Type **331** 30 20
831 40n. Alhaji Abubakar Imam (journalist and writer) 50 55
832 50n. Prof. Wole Soyinka (dramatist and writer) 60 70
833 50n. Prof. Ayodele Awojobi (engineer and educationist) (vert) 60 70
834 50n. Prof. Gabriel Oyibo (mathematician and physicist) (vert) 60 70
835 50n. As No. 833 (vert) 60 70
836 100n. As No. 833 (vert) 1·50 1·75
837 120n. As No. 834 (vert) 1·75 1·90
838 150n. As No. 835 (vert) 2·75 3·00

332 International Conference Centre, Abuja

2006. 52nd Commonwealth Parliamentary Conference, Abuja. Sheet 159×97 mm containing T 332 and similar horiz design. Multicoloured. Imperf.

839 20n. Type **332** 30 20
840 50n. National Assembly Building, Abuja 70 70
MS841 159×97 mm. 20n. As Type **332**; 50n. As No. 840. Imperf 1·25 1·25

Stamps from **MS**841 differ slightly from the sheet stamps in design. The 20n. from **MS**841 has a smaller face value in white and the inscription "NIGERIA International Conference Centre" in a grey panel. The 50n. from **MS**841 has the face value in green (red on No. 840) and the inscription "NIGERIA National Assembly" on a white background (green panel on No. 840).

333 Queen Elizabeth II on Visit to Nigeria, 2003

2006. 80th Birthday of Queen Elizabeth II. Multicoloured.

842 20n. Type **333** 50 25
843 50n. Queen Elizabeth II (vert) 90 1·00

334 Agbani Darego

2006. Crowning of Miss Nigeria Agbani Darego as Miss World 2001. Multicoloured.

844 20n. Type **334** 35 25
845 50n. Agbani Darego and world map (horiz) 65 75

335 Entrance to Abuja and Fireworks

2006. 10th Anniv of Abuja. Multicoloured.

846 20n. Type **335** 35 25
847 50n. Emblem inside outline map (vert) 65 75

336 Emblem and Outline Map

2006. 143rd Extraordinary OPEC Conference, Abuja.

848 **336** 50n. multicoloured 65 75

337 Mungo Park and Memorial to Park

2007. Death Bicentenary (2006) of Mungo Park (explorer). Multicoloured.

849 20n. Type **337** 25 25
850 50n. Mungo Park and river Niger (horiz) 75 75

338 CBAAC and FESTAC '77 Emblems and Richard Lander, Jebba

2007. 30th Anniv of FESTAC '77 2nd World Black and African Festival of Arts and Culture, Lagos.

851 **338** 50n. multicoloured 1·00 1·00

338a Fulani Man, north-west Nigeria

2007. 24th UPU Congress, Nairobi. Ceremonial Costumes

851a 20n. Type **338a** 35 35
851b 20n. Igbo couple, south-east Nigeria 35 35
851c 30n. South Zone costume 55 55
851d 30n. Tiv couple, north-central Nigeria (horiz) 55 55
851e 50n. North East Zone costume 80 80
851f 50n. Yoruba couple, south-west Nigeria 80 80
MS851g 100×164 mm. Nos. 851*a/f*. Imperf 3·50 3·50

The horiz stamp No. 851*d* is laid vertically within **MS**851*g*

339 Silverback (adult male) Gorilla

2008. Endangered Species. Cross River Gorilla (Gorilla gorilla diehli). Multicoloured.

852 20n. Type **339** 30 30
853 50n. Silverback with female and baby (horiz) 75 75
854 100n. Baby riding on female's back (horiz) 1·50 1·50
855 150n. Head of gorilla 2·20 2·20

340 Hands and Money ('Treasury Looting kills the Economy')

2008. EFCC (Economic and Financial Crimes Commission) Anti-Corruption Campaign. Multicoloured.

856 20n. Type **340** 30 30
857 50n. Stop sign and 'LET'S FIX NIGERIA' 75 75
858 100n. Clasped hands and 'UNITED WE WIN' 1·50 1·50

341 Athletes breaking Finish Tape

2008. Olympic Games, Beijing. Multicoloured.

859 20n. Type **341** 30 30
860 50n. Footballer scoring goal 75 75
861 100n. Wrestling (vert) 1·50 1·50

342 Overloaded Vehicle

2008. 20th Anniv of the Federal Road Safety Commission Nigeria

862	**342**	50n. multicoloured	55	55

343 Emblem

2009. 30th Anniv of the Nigerian Institute of Advanced Legal Studies

863	**343**	50n. multicoloured	55	55

No. 864, T **344** are left for 30th Anniv of the Pan African Postal Union, issued 8 January 2010, not yet received

345 Pres. Umaru Musa Yar'Adua and Nigerian Flag

2010. Tenth Anniv of Return to Democracy

865	50n. Type **345**	55	55
866	50n. Scales, mace and lawyer's wig ('The Rule of Law') (vert)	55	55

POSTAGE DUE STAMPS

D1

1959

D1	**D1**	1d. orange	15	1·00
D2	**D1**	2d. orange	20	1·00
D3	**D1**	3d. orange	25	1·50
D4	**D1**	6d. orange	25	5·00
D5	**D1**	1s. black	50	6·50

1961

D6	1d. red	15	40
D7	2d. blue	20	45
D8	3d. green	25	60
D9	6d. yellow	30	1·40
D10	1s. blue	50	2·25

1973. As Type D 1.

D11	2k. red	10	10
D12	3k. blue	10	10
D13	5k. yellow	10	10
D14	10k. green	10	10

Pt. 1

NIUAFO'OU

A remote island, part of the Kingdom of Tonga, with local autonomy.

100 seniti = 1 pa'anga.

1 Map of Niuafo'ou

1983

1	**1**	1s. stone, black and red	30	90
2	**1**	2s. stone, black and green	30	90
3	**1**	3s. stone, black and blue	30	90
4	**1**	3s. stone, black and brown	30	90
5	**1**	5s. stone, black and purple	40	90
6	**1**	6s. stone, black and blue	40	90
7	**1**	9s. stone, black and green	40	90
8	**1**	10s. stone, black and blue	40	90
9	**1**	13s. stone, black and green	65	90
10	**1**	15s. stone, black and brown	70	1·25
11	**1**	20s. stone, black and blue	75	1·25
12	**1**	29s. stone, black and purple	1·00	80
13	**1**	32s. stone, black and green	1·00	90
14	**1**	47s. stone, black and red	1·40	1·40

1983. No. 820 of Tonga optd NIUAFO'OU KINGDOM OF TONGA or surch also.

15	1p. on 2p. green and black	2·50	3·50
16	2p. green	3·50	5·00

2a SPIA De Havilland D.H.C. 6 Turin Otter 300

1983. Inauguration of Niuafo'ou Airport.

17	**2a**	29s. multicoloured	1·50	1·00
18	**2a**	1p. multicoloured	3·00	3·25

1983. As T 1, but without value, surch.

19	3s. stone, black and blue	30	50
20	5s. stone, black and blue	30	50
21	32s. stone, black and blue	1·75	1·25
22	2p. stone, black and blue	8·50	10·00

4 Eruption of Niuafo'ou

1983. 25th Anniv of Re-settlement. Mult.

23	5s. Type **4**	60	55
24	29s. Lava flow	1·25	1·00
25	32s. Islanders fleeing to safety	1·40	1·00
26	1p.50 Evacuation by canoe	4·00	6·00

5 Purple Swamphen

1983. Birds of Niuafo'ou.

27	**5**	1s. black and mauve	1·25	1·25
28	-	2s. black and blue	1·25	1·25
29	-	3s. black and green	1·25	1·25
30	-	5s. black and yellow	1·50	1·25
31	-	6s. black and orange	1·75	1·60
32	-	9s. multicoloured	2·00	1·25
33	-	10s. multicoloured	2·00	2·00
34	-	13s. multicoloured	2·50	1·60
35	-	15s. multicoloured	2·50	2·50
36	-	20s. multicoloured	2·75	2·75
37	-	29s. multicoloured	2·75	1·50
38	-	32s. multicoloured	2·75	1·60
39	-	47s. multicoloured	3·25	2·25
40	-	1p. multicoloured	6·00	8·50
41	-	2p. multicoloured	8·00	12·00

DESIGNS—VERT (22×29 mm): 2s. White collared kingfisher; 3s. Red-headed parrot finch; 5s. Buff-banded rail ("Banded Rail"); 6s. Polynesian scrub hen ("Niuafo'ou megapode"); 9s. Green honeyeater; 10s. Purple swamphen (different). (22×36 mm): 29s. Red-headed parrot finch (different); 32s. White-collared kingfisher (different). (29×42 mm): 1p. As 10s. HORIZ (29×22 mm): 13s. Buff-banded rail ("Banded Rail") (different): 15s. Polynesian scrub hen (different). (36×22 mm): 20s. As 13s.; 47s. As 15s. (42×29 mm): 2p. As 15s.

6 Green Turtle

1984. Wildlife and Nature Reserve. Mult.

42	29s. Type **6**	70	70
43	32s. Insular flying fox (vert)	70	70
44	47s. Humpback whale	3·50	1·75
45	1p.50 Polynesian scrub hen ("Niuafo'ou megapode") (vert)	5·50	7·50

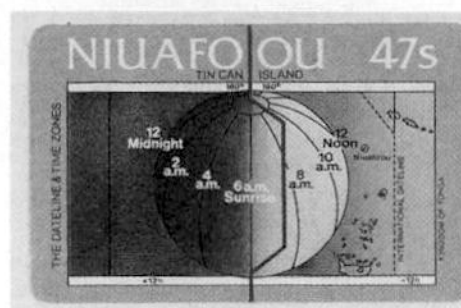

7 Diagram of Time Zones

1984. Cent of International Dateline. Mult.

46	47s. Type **7**	75	50
47	2p. Location map showing Niuafo'ou	2·75	3·50

8 Australia 1913 £2 Kangaroo Definitive

1984. "Ausipex" International Stamp Exhibition, Melbourne. Multicoloured.

48	32s. Type **8**	75	60
49	1p.50 Niuafo'ou 1983 10s. map definitive	2·25	3·00
MS50	90×100 mm. As Nos. 48/9, but without exhibition logo and with face value at foot	1·75	2·50

9 Dutch Brass Band entertaining Tongans

1985. 400th Birth Anniv of Jacob Le Maire (discoverer of Niuafo'ou).

51	**9**	13s. brown, yellow & orange	25	40
52	-	32s. brown, yellow and blue	55	60
53	-	47s. brown, yellow and green	75	80
54	-	1p.50 brown, cinnamon and yellow	2·25	3·00
MS55		90×90 mm. 1p.50 brown, light brown and blue. Imperf	1·50	2·00

DESIGNS: 32s. Tongans preparing kava; 47s. Tongan canoes and outriggers; 1p.50, "Eendracht" at anchor off Tafahi Island.

10 "Ysabel", 1902

1985. Mail Ships. Multicoloured.

56B	9s. Type **10**	35	55
57A	13s. "Tofua I", 1908	70	55
58B	47s. "Mariposa", 1934	1·10	1·60
59B	1p.50 "Matua", 1936	2·50	4·00

11 Preparing to fire Rocket

1985. Niuafo'ou Rocket Mails. Multicoloured.

60B	32s. Type **11**	1·00	80
61A	42s. Rocket in flight	1·25	1·00
62B	57s. Ship's crew watching rocket's descent	1·60	1·40
63A	1p.50 Islanders reading mail	3·50	4·50

12 Halley's Comet, 684 A.D.

1986. Appearance of Halley's Comet. Multicoloured.

64	42s. Type **12**	5·00	3·00
65	42s. Halley's Comet, 1066, from Bayeux Tapestry	5·00	3·00
66	42s. Edmond Halley	5·00	3·00
67	42s. Halley's Comet, 1910	5·00	3·00
68	42s. Halley's Comet, 1986	5·00	3·00
69	57s. Type **12**	5·00	3·50
70	57s. As No. 65	5·00	3·50
71	57s. As No. 66	5·00	3·50
72	57s. As No. 67	5·00	3·50
73	57s. As No. 68	5·00	3·50

Nos. 64/8 and 69/73 were printed together, se-tenant, forming composite designs.

1986. Nos. 32/9 surch.

74	4s. on 9s. Green honeyeater	85	2·50
75	4s. on 10s. Purple swamphen	85	2·50
76	42s. on 13s. Buff-banded rail ("Banded Rail")	3·00	2·00
77	42s. on 15s. Polynesian scrub hen	3·00	2·00
78	57s. on 29s. Red-headed parrot finch	3·50	2·25
79	57s. on 32s. White-collared kingfisher	3·50	2·25
80	2p.50 on 20s. Buff-banded rail ("Banded Rail")	11·00	13·00
81	2p.50 on 47s. Polynesian scrub hen	11·00	13·00

13a Peace Corps Surveyor and Pipeline

1986. "Ameripex '86" International Stamp Exhibition, Chicago. 25th Anniv of United States Peace Corps. Multicoloured.

82	57s. Type **13a**	1·25	1·25
83	1p.50 Inspecting crops	2·25	3·00
MS84	90×90 mm. Nos. 82/3, magnifying glass and tweezers. Imperf	3·75	5·00

14 Swimmers with Mail

1986. Centenary of First Tonga Stamps. Designs showing Niuafo'ou mail transport. Multicoloured.

85	42s. Type **14**	90	90
86	57s. Collecting tin can mail	1·10	1·10
87	1p. Ship firing mail rocket	2·00	2·50
88	2p.50 "Collecting the Mails" (detail) (C. Mayger)	3·50	4·75
MS89	135×80 mm. No. 88	5·00	7·00

15 Woman with Nourishing Foods ("Eat a balanced diet")

1987. Red Cross. Preventive Medicine. Mult.

90	15s. Type **15**	60	60
91	42s. Nurse with baby ("Give them post-natal care")	1·60	1·60
92	1p. Man with insecticide ("Insects spread disease")	2·50	3·25
93	2p.50 Boxer ("Say no to alcohol, drugs, tobacco")	4·00	5·50

16 Hammerhead

1987. Sharks. Multicoloured.

94	29s. Type **16**	2·00	1·75
95	32s. Tiger shark	2·00	1·75
96	47s. Grey nurse shark	2·50	2·25
97	1p. Great white shark	4·00	6·00
MS98	90×90 mm. 2p. Shark and fishes	11·00	12·00

17 Capt. E. C. Musick and Sikorsky S.42A Flying Boat "Samoan Clipper"

1987. Air Pioneers of the South Pacific. Multicoloured.

99	42s. Type **17**	2·50	1·60
100	57s. Capt. J. W. Burgess and Short S. 30 modified "G" Class flying boat "Aotearoa"	2·75	1·75
101	1p.50 Sir Charles Kingsford Smith and Fokker F.VIIa/3m "Southern Cross"	5·00	4·50
102	2p. Amelia Earhart and Lockheed 10E Electra	5·50	6·00

18 Polynesian Scrub Hen and 1983 1s. Map Definitive

1988. 5th Annivs of First Niuafo'ou Postage Stamp (42, 57s.) and Niuafo'ou Airport Inauguration (1, 2p.). Multicoloured.

103	42s. Type **18**	1·00	75
104	57s. As Type **18**, but with stamp at left	1·00	95
105	1p. Concorde and 1983 Airport Inauguration 29s. stamp	5·50	3·25
106	2p. As 1p. but with stamp at left	6·00	4·00

19 Sailing Ship and Ship's Boat

1988. Bicentenary of Australian Settlement. Sheet 115×110 mm containing T 19 and similar vert designs. Multicoloured.

MS107 42s. Type **19**; 42s. Aborigines; 42s. Early settlement; 42s. Marine and convicts; 42s. Sheep station; 42s. Mounted stockman; 42s. Kangaroos and early Trans Continental locomotive; 42s. Kangaroos and train carriages; 42s. Flying Doctor aircraft; 42s. Cricket match; 42s. Wicket and Sydney skyline; 42s. Fielders and Sydney Harbour Bridge — 38·00 35·00

Each horizontal strip of 4 within No. **MS**107 shows a composite design.

20 Audubon's Shearwaters and Blowholes, Houma, Tonga

1988. Islands of Polynesia. Multicoloured.

108	42s. Type **20**	1·50	95
109	57s. Brown kiwi at Akaroa Harbour, New Zealand	2·25	1·40
110	90s. Red-tailed tropic birds at Rainmaker Mountain, Samoa	2·50	2·50
111	2p.50 Laysan albatross at Kapoho Volcano, Hawaii	4·75	6·00

21 Sextant

1989. Bicentenary of Mutiny on the Bounty. Sheet 115×110 mm containing T 21 and similar vert designs. Multicoloured.

MS112 42s. Type **21**; 42s. Capt. Bligh; 42s. Lieutenant, 1787; 42s. Midshipman, 1787; 42s. Tahitian woman and contemporary newspaper; 42s. Breadfruit plant; 42s. Pistol and extract from "Mutiny on the Bounty"; 42s. Book illustration of Bligh cast adrift; 42s. Profile of Tahitian woman and extract from contemporary newspaper; 42s. Signatures of "Bounty officers"; 42s. Fletcher Christian; 42s. Tombstone of John Adams, Pitcairn Island — 17·00 16·00

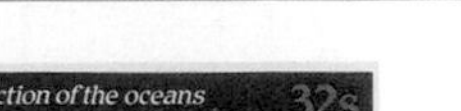

22 Spiny Hatchetfish

1989. Fishes of the Deep. Multicoloured.

113	32s. Type **22**	85	1·00
114	42s. Snipe eel	1·00	1·00
115	57s. Viperfish	1·25	1·50
116	1p.50 Football anglerfish	3·00	4·00

23 Formation of Earth's Surface

1989. The Evolution of the Earth. Multicoloured. (a) Size 27×35½ mm.

117	1s. Type **23**	50	80
118	2s. Cross-section of Earth's crust	50	80
119	5s. Volcano	60	80
120	10s. Cross-section of Earth during cooling	60	80
120a	13s. Gem stones	1·50	70
121	15s. Sea	60	70
122	20s. Mountains	60	70
123	32s. River gorge	75	50
124	42s. Early plant life, Silurian era	90	55
124a	45s. Early marine life	1·25	90
125	50s. Fossils and Cambrian lifeforms	1·00	80
126	57s. Carboniferous forest and coal seams	1·25	80
126a	60s. Dinosaurs feeding	2·00	1·25
126b	80s. Tyrannosaurus and triceratops fighting	2·50	1·75

(b) Size 25½×40 mm.

127	1p. Dragonfly and amphibians, Carboniferous era	1·75	1·75
128	1p.50 Dinosaurs, Jurassic era	3·00	3·00
129	2p. Archaeopteryx and mammals, Jurassic era	3·25	3·25
130	5p. Human family and domesticated dog, Pleistocene era	5·00	6·00
130a	10p. Mammoth and sabre-tooth tiger	10·00	12·00

24 Astronaut on Moon and Newspaper Headline

1989. "World Stamp Expo '89" International Stamp Exhibition, Washington.

131	**24**	57s. multicoloured	2·00	1·50

1989. 20th Universal Postal Union Congress, Washington. Miniature sheet, 185×150 mm, containing designs as Nos. 117/20, 121/4, 125/6 and 127/30, but wuth U.P.U. emblem at top right and some new values.

MS132 32s.×5 (as Nos. 117/20, 121); 42s.×5 (as Nos. 122/4, 125/6); 57s.×5 (as Nos. 127/30, 131) — 23·00 24·00

25 Lake Vai Lahi

1990. Niuafo'ou Crater Lake. Multicoloured.

133	42s. Type **25**	70	1·00
134	42s. Islands in centre of lake	70	1·00
135	42s. South-west end of lake and islet	70	1·00
136	1p. Type **25**	1·40	1·60
137	1p. As No. 134	1·40	1·60
138	1p. As No. 135	1·40	1·60

Nos. 133/8 were printed together in se-tenant strips of each value, forming a composite design.

26 Penny Black and Tin Can Mail Service

1990. 150th Anniv of the Penny Black. Mult.

139	42s. Type **26**	1·25	1·00
140	57s. U.S.A. 1847 10c. stamp	1·40	1·25
141	75s. Western Australia 1854 1d. stamp	1·60	2·00
142	2p.50 Mafeking Siege 1900 1d. stamp	5·00	6·00

27 Humpback Whale surfacing

1990. Polynesian Whaling. Multicoloured.

143	15s. Type **27**	2·25	1·75
144	42s. Whale diving under canoe	2·75	1·90
145	57s. Tail of Blue whale	3·00	1·90
146	2p. Old man and pair of whales	8·00	9·00
MS147	120×93 mm. 1p. Pair of whales (38×30 mm)	10·00	11·00

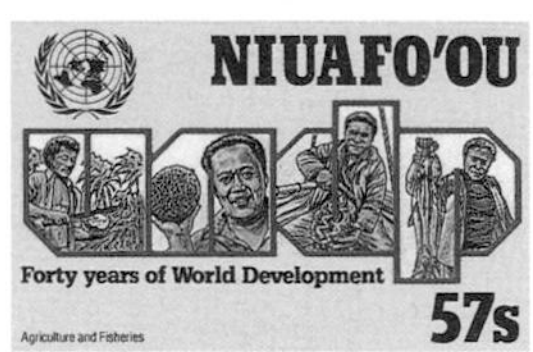

27a Agriculture and Fisheries

1990. 40th Anniv of U.N. Development Programme. Multicoloured.

148	57s. Type **27a**	90	1·40
149	57s. Education	90	1·40
150	2p.50 Healthcare	3·25	4·00
151	2p.50 Communications	3·25	4·00

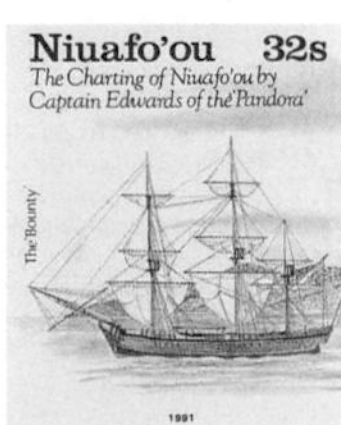

28 H.M.S. "Bounty"

1991. Bicentenary of Charting of Niuafo'ou. Multicoloured.

152	32s. Type **28**	1·25	1·75
153	42s. Chart of "Pandora's" course	1·40	1·75
154	57s. H.M.S. "Pandora" (frigate)	1·75	1·75
MS155	120×93 mm. 2p. Capt. Edwards of the "Pandora"; 3p. Capt. Bligh of the "Bounty"	13·00	14·00

1991. Ornithological and Scientific Expedition to Niuafo'ou. No. MS147 surch 1991 ORNITHOLOGICAL AND SCIENTIFIC EXPEDITION T $1.

MS156	120×93 mm. 1p. on 1p. multicoloured	3·25	4·00

30 Longhorned Beetle Grub

1991. Longhorned Beetle. Multicoloured.

157	42s. Type **30**	80	1·00
158	57s. Adult beetle	90	1·00
159	1p.50 Grub burrowing	2·75	3·25
160	2p.50 Adult on tree trunk	4·00	4·50

31 Heina meeting the Eel

1991. Christmas. The Legend of the Coconut Tree. Multicoloured.

161	15s. Type **31**	65	75
162	42s. Heina crying over the eel's grave	1·25	1·25
MS163	96×113 mm. 15s. Type **31**; 42s. No. 162; 1p.50, Heina's son collecting coconuts; 3p. Milk flowing from coconut	9·00	10·00

31a Columbus

1992. 500th Anniv of Discovery of America by Columbus. Sheet 119×109 mm. containing vert designs as T 31a. Multicoloured.

MS164 57s. Columbus; 57s. Queen Isabella and King Ferdinand; 57s. Columbus being blessed by Abbot of Palos; 57s. 15th-century compass; 57s. Wooden traverse, windrose and the "Nina"; 57s. Bow of "Santa Maria"; 57s. Stern of "Santa Maria"; 57s. The "Pinta"; 57s. Crew erecting cross; 57s. Sailors and Indians; 57s. Columbus reporting to King and Queen; 57s. Coat of Arms — 22·00 24·00

31b American Battleship Ablaze, Pearl Harbor

1992. 50th Anniv of War in the Pacific. Multicoloured.

165	42s. Type **31b**	1·60	1·60
166	42s. Destroyed American Douglas B-18 Bolo aircraft, Hawaii	1·60	1·60
167	42s. Newspaper and Japanese Mitsubishi A6M Zero-Sen fighter	1·60	1·60
168	42s. Pres. Roosevelt signing Declaration of War	1·60	1·60
169	42s. Japanese T95 light tank and Gen. MacArthur	1·60	1·60
170	42s. Douglas SBD Dauntless dive bomber and Admiral Nimitz	1·60	1·60
171	42s. Bren gun and Gen. Sir Thomas Blamey	1·60	1·60
172	42s. Australian mortar crew, Kokoda	1·60	1·60
173	42s. U.S.S. "Mississippi" in action and Maj. Gen. Julian C. Smith	1·60	1·60
174	42s. U.S.S. "Enterprise" (aircraft carrier)	1·60	1·60
175	42s. American marine and Maj. Gen. Curtis Lemay	1·60	1·60
176	42s. Boeing B-29 Superfortress bomber and Japanese surrender, Tokyo Bay	1·60	1·60

Nos. 165/76 were printed together, se-tenant, forming a composite design.

31c King Taufa'ahau Tupou IV and Queen Halaevalu During Coronation

1992. 25th Anniv of the Coronation of King Tupou IV.

177	31c	45s. multicoloured	75	75
178	-	80s. multicoloured	1·50	1·75
179	-	80s. black and brown	1·50	1·75
180	-	80s. multicoloured	1·50	1·75
181	-	2p. multicoloured	2·50	3·00

DESIGNS—(34×23 mm): No. 177, Type **31c**. (48×35 mm): No. 178, King Tupou IV and Tongan national anthem; 179, Extract from Investiture ceremony; 180, Tongan choir; 181, As 45s.

Nos. 177/81 show the King's first name incorrectly spelt as "Tauf'ahau".

32 Male and Female Scrub Hens searching for Food

1992. Endangered Species. Polynesian Scrub Hen. Multicoloured.

182	45s. Type **32**	1·00	1·25
183	60s. Female guarding egg	1·25	1·40
184	80s. Chick	1·60	1·75
185	1p.50 Head of male	2·75	3·50

33 1983 2s. Map Definitive and 1993 60s. Dinosaur Definitive

1993. 10th Anniv of First Niuafo'ou Stamp. Multicoloured.

186	60s. Type **33**	1·25	1·40
187	80s. 1983 5s. definitive and 1993 80s. dinosaurs definitive	1·50	1·75

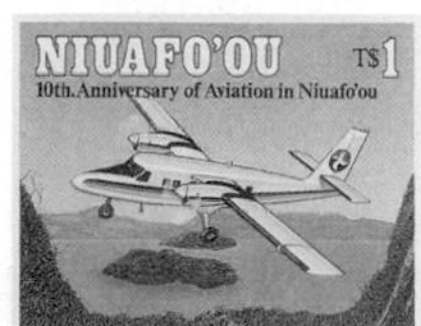
34 De Havilland Twin Otter 200/300 of South Pacific Island Airways

1993. 10th Anniv of First Flight to Niuafo'ou. Multicoloured.

188	1p. Type **34**	1·50	2·00
189	2p.50 De Havilland Twin Otter 200/300 of Friendly Islands Airways	3·50	4·50

34a King Tupou IV and "Pangai" (patrol boat)

1993. 75th Birthday of King Taufa'ahau Tupou IV. Multicoloured.

190	45s. Type **34a**	55	65
191	80s. King Tupou IV and musical instruments (38½×51 mm)	1·25	1·75
192	80s. King Tupou IV and sporting events (38½×51 mm)	1·25	1·75
193	80s. King Tupou IV with De Havilland Twin Otter 200/300 airplane and telecommunications	1·25	1·75
194	2p. As 45s. but larger (38½×51 mm)	2·75	3·25

35 Blue-crowned Lorikeets

1993. Natural History of Lake Vai Lahi. Multicoloured.

195	60s. Type **35**	1·00	1·25
196	60s. White-tailed tropic bird and reef heron	1·00	1·25
197	60s. Black admiral (butterfly) and Niuafo'ou coconut beetle	1·00	1·25
198	60s. Niuafo'ou dragonfly, pacific black ducks and Niuafo'ou moths	1·00	1·25
199	60s. Niuafo'ou megapode	1·00	1·25

Nos. 195/9 were printed together, se-tenant, forming a composite design.

35a "Crater Lake Megapode and Volcano" (Paea Puletau)

1993. Children's Painting Competition Winners.

200	35a	10s. multicoloured	50	1·00
201	-	10s. black and grey	50	1·00
202	-	1p. multicoloured	3·50	3·75
203	-	1p. multicoloured	3·50	3·75

DESIGNS: Nos. 200 and 202, Type **35a**; Nos. 201 and 203, "Ofato Beetle Grubs of Niuafo'ou" (Peni Finau).

36 "Scarabaeidea"

1994. Beetles. Multicoloured.

204	60s. Type **36**	85	1·00
205	80s. "Coccinellidea"	1·10	1·40
206	1p.50 "Cerambycidea"	2·00	2·50
207	2p.50 "Pentatomidae"	3·75	4·25

37 Stern of H.M.S. "Bounty"

1994. Sailing Ships. Multicoloured.

208	80s. Type **37**	1·75	2·25
209	80s. Bow of H.M.S. "Bounty"	1·75	2·25
210	80s. H.M.S. "Pandora" (frigate)	1·75	2·25
211	80s. Whaling ship	1·75	2·25
212	80s. Trading schooner	1·75	2·25

38 Blue-crowned Lory and Lava Flows

1994. Volcanic Eruptions on Niuafo'ou. Multicoloured.

213	80s. Type **38**	1·25	1·75
214	80s. Pacific ducks over lava flows	1·25	1·75
215	80s. Megapodes and palm trees	1·25	1·75
216	80s. White-tailed tropic birds and inhabitants	1·25	1·75
217	80s. Reef heron and evacuation, 1946	1·25	1·75

Nos. 213/17 were printed together, se-tenant, forming a composite design.

1995. Visit South Pacific Year '95. Save the Whales. Nos. 143/6 surch SAVE THE WHALES VISIT SOUTH PACIFIC YEAR '95, emblem and value.

218	60s. on 42s. Whale diving under canoe	2·00	1·75
219	80s. on 15s. Type **27**	2·25	2·25
220	80s. on 57s. Tail of blue whale	2·25	2·25
221	2p. on 2p. Old man and pair of whales	4·25	4·50
MS222	120×93 mm. 1p.50 on 1p. Pair of whales (38×30 mm)	3·50	4·25

39a American Marine

1995. 50th Anniv of End of World War II in the Pacific.

223	39a	60s. yellow, black and blue	1·40	1·60
224	-	60s. yellow, black and blue	1·40	1·60
225	-	60s. yellow, black and blue	1·40	1·60
226	-	60s. yellow, black and blue	1·40	1·60
227	-	60s. yellow, black and blue	1·40	1·60
228	39a	80s. yellow, black and red	1·40	1·60
229	-	80s. yellow, black and red	1·40	1·60
230	-	80s. yellow, black and red	1·40	1·60
231	-	80s. yellow, black and red	1·40	1·60
232	-	80s. yellow, black and red	1·40	1·60

DESIGNS: Nos. 224 and 229, Marine firing and side of tank; 225 and 230, Tank; 226 and 231, Marines leaving landing craft; 227 and 232, Beach assault and palm trees.

Nos. 223/32 were printed together, se-tenant, forming two composite designs.

39b Dinosaurs Feeding

1995. "Singapore '95" International Stamp Exhibitions. Designs showing exhibition emblem. Multicoloured.

233	45s. Type **39b** (as No. 126a)	1·00	1·50
234	60s. Tyrannosaurus fighting Triceratops (as No. 126b)	1·00	1·50
MS235	110×70 mm. 2p. Plesiosaurus	2·50	3·50

39c Great Wall of China (image scaled to 57% of original size)

1995. Beijing International Coin and Stamp Show '95. Sheet 143×87 mm.

MS236 **39c**	1p.40 multicoloured	2·25	3·00

39d St. Paul's Cathedral and Searchlights

1995. 50th Anniv of United Nations and End of Second World War.

237	39d	60s. multicoloured	1·25	1·75
238	-	60s. black and blue	1·25	1·75
239	-	60s. multicoloured	1·25	1·75
240	-	80s. multicoloured	1·50	1·75
241	-	80s. blue and black	1·50	1·75
242	-	80s. multicoloured	1·50	1·75

DESIGNS—HORIZ: No. 239, Concorde; 240, Allied prisoners of war and Burma Railway; 242, Mt. Fuji and express train. VERT—25×35 mm: Nos. 238 and 241, U.N. anniversary emblem.

40 Charles Ramsay and Swimmers with Poles

1996. Tin Can Mail Pioneers. Multicoloured.

243	45s. Type **40**	90	90
244	60s. Charles Ramsay and encounter with shark	1·25	1·25
245	1p. Walter Quensell and transferring mail from canoes to ship	2·00	2·00
246	3p. Walter Quensell and Tin Can Mail cancellations	6·50	6·00

40a Cave Painting, Lake Village and Hunter

1996. 13th Congress of International Union of Prehistoric and Protohistoric Sciences, Forli, Italy. Multicoloured.

247	1p. Type **40a**	2·25	2·25
248	1p. Egyptians with Pyramid, Greek temple, and Romans with Colosseum	2·25	2·25

40b Dolls, Model Truck and Counting Balls

1996. 50th Anniv of UNICEF. Children's Toys. Multicoloured.

249	80s. Type **40b**	1·75	2·00
250	80s. Teddy bear, tricycle and model car	1·75	2·00
251	80s. Book, model helicopter, pedal car and roller skates	1·75	2·00

Nos. 249/51 were printed together, se-tenant, forming a composite design.

41 Island and Two Canoes

1996. 50th Anniv of Evacuation of Niuafo'ou. Multicoloured.

No.	Description	Mint	Used
252	45s. Type **41**	85	1·10
253	45s. Erupting volcano and canoes	85	1·10
254	45s. End of island, volcanic cloud and canoe	85	1·10
255	45s. Family and livestock in outrigger canoe	85	1·10
256	45s. Islanders reaching "Matua" (inter-island freighter)	85	1·10
257	60s. Type **41**	95	1·10
258	60s. As No. 253	95	1·10
259	60s. As No. 254	95	1·10
260	60s. As No. 255	95	1·10
261	60s. As No. 256	95	1·10

Nos. 252/6 and 257/61 respectively were printed together, se-tenant, forming the same composite design.

42 Plankton

1997. The Ocean Environment.

No.	Type	Description	Mint	Used
262	**42**	60s. multicoloured	1·00	1·00
263	-	80s. multicoloured	1·25	1·25
264	-	1p.50 multicoloured	2·25	2·50
265	-	2p.50 multicoloured	3·00	3·50

DESIGNS: 80s. to 2p.50, Different plankton.

42a Black-naped Tern

1997. "Pacific '97" International Stamp Exhibition, San Francisco. Sheet 85×110 mm.

No.	Description	Mint	Used
MS266	**42a** 2p. multicoloured	3·00	3·75

42b King and Queen on Wedding Day

1997. King and Queen of Tonga's Golden Wedding and 30th Anniv of Coronation. Multicoloured.

No.	Description	Mint	Used
267	80s. Type **42b**	1·75	1·75
268	80s. King Tupou in Coronation robes	1·75	1·75
MS269	82×70 mm. 5p. King Tupou with pages (horiz)	7·00	7·50

43 Blue-crowned Lory Nestlings

1998. Endangered Species. Blue-crowned Lory. Multicoloured.

No.	Description	Mint	Used
270	10s. Type **43**	1·50	1·50
271	55s. Feeding on flowers	3·00	1·25
272	80s. Perched on branch	4·00	2·00
273	3p. Pair on branch	8·00	9·00
MS274	160×112 mm. Nos. 270/3×2	30·00	30·00

1998. Diana, Princess of Wales Commemoration. Sheet, 145×70 mm, containing vert designs as T 91 of Kiribati. Multicoloured.

No.	Description	Mint	Used
MS275	10s. Princess Diana in tartan jacket, 1987; 80s. Wearing white dress, 1992; 1p. Wearing check jacket, 1993; 2p.50, Wearing black jacket (sold at 4p.40+50s. charity premium)	4·25	6·00

43a King Taufa'ahau Tupou IV

1998. 80th Birthday of King Taufa'ahau Tupou IV.

No.	Type	Description	Mint	Used
276	**43a**	2p.70 multicoloured	2·50	3·25

43b Tiger and Top Left Quarter of Clock Face

1998. Chinese New Year ("Year of the Tiger"). Sheet, 126×85 mm, containing horiz designs as T 43b, each showing tiger and quarter segment of clock face. Multicoloured.

No.	Description	Mint	Used
MS277	55s. Type **43b**; 80s. Top right quarter; 1p. Bottom left quarter; 1p. Bottom right quarter	4·00	4·75

No. **MS**277 also includes "SINGPEX '98" Stamp Exhibition, Singapore emblem on the sheet margin.

43c "Amphiprion melanopus"

1998. International Year of the Ocean. Multicoloured.

No.	Description	Mint	Used
278	10s. Type **43c**	40	50
279	55s. "Amphiprion perideraion"	80	90
280	80s. "Amphiprion chrysopterus"	1·00	1·10

43d Angel playing lute (inscr in Tongan)

1998. Christmas. Multicoloured.

No.	Description	Mint	Used
281	20s. Type **43d**	80	55
282	55s. Angel playing violin (inscr in English)	1·25	60
283	1p. Children and bells (inscr in Tongan)	1·75	1·90
284	1p.60 Children and candles (inscr in English)	2·50	4·00

43e Rabbit on Hind Legs

1999. Chinese New Year ("Year of the Rabbit"). Sheet 126×85 mm, containing horiz designs as T 43e, showing rabbits and segments of flower (each red, yellow and grey).

No.	Description	Mint	Used
MS285	10s. Type **43e**; 55s. Rabbit facing left; 80s. Rabbit facing right; 1p. Two rabbits	2·75	3·50

44 "Eendracht" (Le Maire)

1999. Early Explorers. Multicoloured.

No.	Description	Mint	Used
286	80s. Type **44**	2·50	1·25
287	2p.70 Tongiaki (outrigger canoe)	3·75	4·50
MS288	120×72 mm. Nos. 286/7	6·00	7·00

No. **MS**288 also includes the "Australia '99" emblem on the sheet margin.

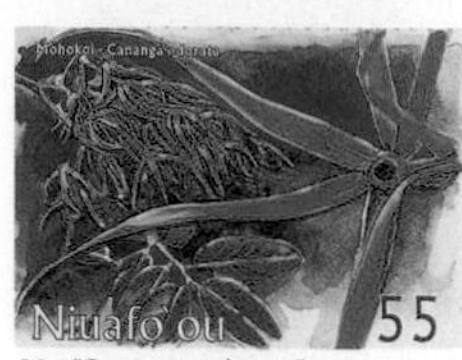

44a "Cananga odorata"

1999. Fragrant Flowers. Multicoloured.

No.	Description	Mint	Used
289	55s. Type **44a**	75	60
290	80s. "Gardenia tannaensis" (vert)	1·00	80
291	1p. "Coleus amboinicus" (vert)	1·40	1·50
292	2p.50 "Hernandia moerenhoutiana"	2·75	3·75

45 Dove over Tafahi Island

2000. New Millennium. Sheet, 120×80 mm, containing T 45 and similar vert design. Multicoloured.

No.	Description	Mint	Used
MS293	1p. Type **45**; 2p.50, Kalia (traditional canoe) passing island	3·50	4·00

45a Dragon in the Sky

2000. Chinese New Year ("Year of the Dragon"). Sheet, 126×85 mm, containing horiz designs as T 46a. Multicoloured.

No.	Description	Mint	Used
MS294	10s. Type **45a**; 55s. Dragon in the sky (facing left); 80s. Sea dragon (facing right); 1p. Sea dragon (facing left)	2·25	2·75

45b Queen Elizabeth the Queen Mother

2000. "The Stamp Show 2000" International Stamp Exhibition, London. Queen Elizabeth the Queen Mother's 100th Birthday. Sheet, 105×71 mm, containing designs as T 45b.

No.	Description	Mint	Used
MS295	1p.50, Type **45b**; 2p.50, Queen Salote Tupou III of Tonga	3·50	4·00

46 Tongan Couple

2000. "EXPO 2000" World Stamp Exhibition, Anaheim, U.S.A. Space Communications. Sheet, 120×90 mm, containing T 46 and similar vert designs. Multicoloured.

No.	Description	Mint	Used
MS296	10s. Type **46**; 2p.50, Telecom dish aerial; 2p.70, "Intelsat" satelite	4·50	5·50

47 *Jamides bochus* (butterfly)

2000. Butterflies. Multicoloured.

No.	Description	Mint	Used
297	55s. Type **47**	95	80
298	80s. *Hypolimnas bolina*	1·40	1·25
299	1p. *Eurema hecabe aprica*	1·60	1·60
300	2p.70 *Danaus plexippus*	3·25	4·00

48 Snake

2001. Chinese New Year ("Year of the Snake") and "Hong Kong 2001" Stamp Exhibition. Sheet, 125×87 mm, containing horiz designs as T 48 showing decorative snakes.

No.	Description	Mint	Used
MS301	10s. multicoloured; 55s. multicoloured; 80s. multicoloured; 1p. multicoloured	3·00	3·25

49 Seale's Flying Fish

2001. Fishes. Multicoloured.

No.	Description	Mint	Used
302	80s. Type **49**	1·75	1·25
303	1p. Swordfish	1·90	1·75
304	2p.50 Skipjack tuna	3·75	4·50
MS305	121×92 mm. Nos. 302/4	7·00	7·50

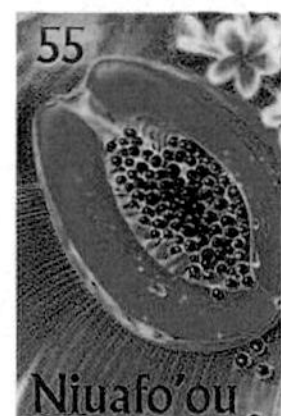

50 Pawpaw

2001. Tropical Fruit. Sheet, 120×67 mm, containing T 50 and similar vert designs. Multicoloured.

No.	Description	Mint	Used
MS306	55s. Type **50**; 80s. Limes; 1p. Mango; 2p.50, Bananas	4·25	5·50

51 Barn Owl in Flight

2001. Barn Owls. Multicoloured.

No.	Description	Mint	Used
307	10s. Type **51**	50	60
308	55s. Adult feeding young in nest	1·25	55
309	2p.50 Adult and fledglings in nest	2·50	2·75
310	2p.70 Barn owl in palm tree	2·50	2·75
MS311	170×75 mm. Nos. 307/10	6·00	6·50

51a Queen Elizabeth with Princess Elizabeth, Coronation, 1937

2002. Golden Jubilee. Sheet 162×95 mm, containing designs as T 51a.

No.	Description	Mint	Used
MS312	15s. brown, violet and gold; 90s. multicoloured; 1p.20, multicoloured; 1p.40, multicoloured; 2p.25, multicoloured	8·50	9·00

DESIGNS—HORIZ (as Type **51a**): 15s. Type **51a**; 90s. Queen Elizabeth in lilac outfit; 1p.20, Princess Elizabeth in garden; 1p.40, Queen Elizabeth in red hat and coat. VERT (38×51 mm): 2p.25, Queen Elizabeth after Annigoni.

51b Two Horses with Foal

2002. Chinese New Year ("Year of the Horse"). Sheet, 126×89 mm, containing vert designs as T 51b. Multicoloured.

MS313	65s. Two horses with foal; 80s. Horse drinking from river; 1p. Horse standing in river; 2p.50 Horse and foal on river bank	6·00	6·50

52 Polynesian Scrub Fowl with Eggs

2002. Polynesian Scrub Fowl. Multicoloured.

314	15s. Type **52**	30	50
315	70s. Two birds on rocks	90	90
316	90s. Polynesian scrub fowl by tree (vert)	1·10	1·10
317	2p.50 Two birds in undergrowth (vert)	2·25	2·75
MS318	72×95 mm. Nos. 316/17	4·50	5·00

53 Octopus (*Octopus vulgaris*)

2002. Cephalopods. Multicoloured.

319	80s. Type **53**	1·40	1·00
320	1p. Squid (*Sepioteuthis lessoniana*)	1·50	1·40
321	2p.50 Nautilus (*Nautilus belauensis*)	3·75	4·50
MS322	120×83 mm. Nos. 319/21	7·00	8·00

54 CASA C-212 Aviocar

2002. Mail Planes. Sheet, 140×80 mm, containing T 54 and similar horiz designs. Multicoloured.

MS323	80s. Type **54**; 1p.40 Britten-Norman Islander; 2p.50 DHC 6-300 Twin Otter	8·00	8·50

54a Ram

2003. Chinese New Year ("Year of the Sheep"). Sheet 128×88 mm, containing horiz designs as T 54a.

MS324	65s. Type **54a**, 80s. Three ewes; 1p. Three black-faced ewes; 2p.50 Two ewes	6·00	6·50

54b Queen Elizabeth II

2004. 50th Anniv of Coronation.

325	**54b**	90s. purple, blue and bistre	90	80
326	-	1p.20 green, blue and bistre	1·40	1·25
327	-	1p.40 blue, purple and bistre	1·60	1·50
328	-	2p.50 multicoloured	3·25	4·00

DESIGNS: 1p.20 Queen Elizabeth II on throne; 1p.40 Queen Salote in open-top car; 2p.50 Queen Salote.

54c Spider Monkey

2004. Chinese New Year ("Year of the Monkey"). Sheet 95×85 mm containing horiz designs as T 54c. Each azure, black and scarlet.

MS329	60s. Spider monkey; 80s; Ring-tailed Lemur; 1p. Cotton-top tamarin; 2p.50 White-cheeked gibbon	5·50	6·50

55 King George Tupou II (1893–1918)

2004. Royal Succession. Multicoloured.

330	30s. King George Tupou I (1875–93)	40	40
331	65s. Type **55**	70	70
332	80s. Queen Salote Tupou III (1918–65)	80	80
333	$3.05 King Taufa'ahau Tupou IV (1965–)	3·00	4·25
MS334	160×65 mm. Nos. 330/3	5·50	6·00

Stamps in the same designs were also issued by Tonga.

56 Pawpaw Tree

2004. Fruit Trees. Multicoloured.

335	45s. Type **56**	70	60
336	60s. Banana tree	85	85
337	80s. Coconut tree	1·00	1·00
338	1p.80 Lime tree	2·25	2·75

57 Mary and Baby Jesus

2004. Christmas. Multicoloured.

339	15s. Type **57**	35	40
340	90s. Mary and Joseph on the way to Bethlehem	1·00	80
341	1p.20 The Shepherds	1·40	1·50
342	2p.60 The Three Wise Men	2·75	3·50

58 Rooster and Hen

2005. Chinese New Year ("Year of the Rooster"). Sheet 95×85 mm, containing T 58 and similar horiz designs. Multicoloured.

MS343	65s. Type **58**; 80s. Rooster, hen and three chicks; 1p. Rooster, hen and chick; 2p.50 Rooster and hen on nest	5·50	6·00

NIUE

Pt. 1

One of the Cook Is. group in the S. Pacific. A dependency of New Zealand, the island achieved local self-government in 1974.

1902. 12 pence = 1 shilling; 20 shillings = 1 pound.
1967. 100 cents = 1 dollar.

1902. T 42 of New Zealand optd NIUE only.

1	**42**	1d. red	£300	£300

Stamps of New Zealand surch **NIUE.** and value in native language.

1902. Pictorials of 1898 etc.

8	**23**	½d. green	1·00	1·00
9	**42**	1d. red	60	1·00
2	**26**	2½d. blue (B)	1·50	4·00
13	**28**	3d. brown	9·50	5·00
14	**31**	6d. red	13·00	11·00
16	**34**	1s. orange	38·00	45·00

1911. King Edward VII stamps.

17	**51**	½d. green	50	50
18	**51**	6d. red	2·00	7·00
19	**51**	1s. orange	6·50	48·00

1917. Dominion and King George V stamps.

21	**53**	1d. red	19·00	5·50
22	**62**	3d. brown	50·00	95·00

1917. Stamps of New Zealand (King George V, etc) optd NIUE. only.

23		½d. green	70	2·50
24	**53**	1d. red	10·00	10·00
25	**62**	1½d. grey	1·00	2·25
26	**62**	1½d. brown	70	6·50
28a	**62**	2½d. blue	1·25	11·00
29a	**62**	3d. brown	1·25	1·50
30a	**62**	6d. red	4·75	24·00
31a	**62**	1s. orange	2·50	27·00

1918. Stamps of New Zealand optd NIUE.

33	**F4**	2s. blue	16·00	32·00
34	**F4**	2s.6d. brown	22·00	48·00
35	**F4**	5s. green	25·00	50·00
37b	**F4**	10s. red	90·00	£150
37	**F4**	£1 red	£170	£250

1920. Pictorial types as Cook Islands (1920), but inscr "NIUE".

38	**9**	½d. black and green	3·75	3·75
45	-	1d. black and red	1·75	1·00
40	-	1½d. black and red	2·75	14·00
46	-	2½d. black and blue	4·25	11·00
41	-	3d. black and blue	1·25	15·00
47	**7**	4d. black and violet	7·00	20·00
42	-	6d. brown and green	3·00	18·00
43	-	1s. black and brown	3·00	18·00

1927. Admiral type of New Zealand optd NIUE.

49	**71**	2s. blue	18·00	32·00

1931. No. 40 surch TWO PENCE.

50	2d. on 1½d. black and red	4·25	1·00

1931. Stamps of New Zealand (Arms types) optd NIUE.

83	**F6**	2s.6d. brown	3·50	10·00
84	**F6**	5s. green	11·00	11·00
53	**F6**	10s. red	35·00	£110
86	**F6**	£1 pink	60·00	75·00

1932. Pictorial stamps as Cook Islands (1932) but inscr additionally "NIUE".

89	**20**	½d. black and green	50	4·00
56	-	1d. black and red	1·00	50
64	**22**	2d. black and brown	50	1·75
92	-	2½d. black and blue	60	1·25
93	-	4d. black and blue	4·25	1·00
67	-	6d. black and orange	70	75
61	-	1s. black and violet	2·25	5·00

1935. Silver Jubilee. As Nos. 63, 92 and 67, with colours changed, optd SILVER JUBILEE OF KING GEORGE V. 1910-1935.

69	1d. red	60	3·50
70	2½d. blue	4·00	12·00
71	6d. green and orange	3·50	7·00

1937. Coronation. New Zealand stamps optd NIUE.

72	**106**	1d. red	30	10
73	**106**	2½d. blue	40	1·50
74	**106**	6d. orange	40	20

1938. As 1938 issue of Cook Islands, but inscr "NIUE COOK ISLANDS".

95	**29**	1s. black and violet	1·50	85
96	**30**	2s. black and brown	8·50	3·00
97	-	3s. blue and green	15·00	7·00

1940. As No. 132 of Cook Islands but inscr "NIUE COOK ISLANDS".

78	**32**	3d. on 1½d. black and purple	75	20

1946. Peace. New Zealand stamps optd NIUE (twice on 2d.).

98	**132**	1d. green	40	10
99	-	2d. purple (No. 670)	40	10
100	-	6d. brown & red (No. 674)	40	80
101	**139**	8d. black and red	50	80

18 Map of Niue

19 H.M.S. "Resolution"

1950

113	**18**	½d. orange and blue	10	1·50
114	**19**	1d. brown and green	2·25	2·50
115	-	2d. black and red	1·25	2·00
116	-	3d. blue and violet	10	20
117	-	4d. olive and purple	10	20
118	-	6d. green and orange	1·00	1·25
119	-	9d. orange and brown	15	1·40
120	-	1s. purple and black	15	20
121	-	2s. brown and green	5·00	5·00
122	-	3s. blue and black	5·00	5·00

DESIGNS—HORIZ: 2d. Alofi landing; 3d. Native hut; 4d. Arch at Hikutavake; 6d. Alofi bay; 1s. Cave, Makefu. VERT: 9d. Spearing fish; 2s. Bananas; 3s. Matapa Chasm.

1953. Coronation. As Types of New Zealand but inscr "NIUE".

123	**164**	3d. brown	65	40
124	**168**	6d. grey	95	40

26

1967. Decimal Currency. (a) Nos. 113/22 surch.

125	**17**	½c. on ½d.	10	10
126	**19**	1c. on 1d.	1·10	15
127	-	2c. on 2d.	10	10
128	-	2½c. on 3d.	10	10
129	-	3c. on 4d.	10	10
130	-	5c. on 6d.	10	10
131	-	8c. on 9d.	10	10
132	-	10c. on 1s.	10	10
133	-	20c. on 2s.	35	1·50
134	-	30c. on 3s.	65	1·50

(b) Arms type of New Zealand without value, surch as in T 26.

135	**26**	25c. brown	30	55
136	**26**	50c. green	70	80
137	**26**	$1 mauve	45	1·25
138	**26**	$2 pink	50	2·00

1967. Christmas. As T 278 of New Zealand but inscr "NIUE".

139	2½c. multicoloured	10	10

1969. Christmas. As No. 905 of New Zealand but inscr "NIUE".

140	2½c. multicoloured	10	10

27 "Pua"

1969. Flowers. Multicoloured; frame colours given.

141	**27**	½c. green	10	10
142	-	1c. red	10	10
143	-	2c. olive	10	10
144	-	2½c. brown	10	10
145	-	3c. blue	10	10
146	-	5c. red	10	10
147	-	8c. violet	10	10
148	-	10c. yellow	10	10
149	-	20c. blue	35	1·50
150	-	30c. green	1·10	2·00

DESIGNS: 1c. "Golden Shower"; 2c. Flamboyant; 2½c. Frangipani; 3c. Niue crocus; 5c. Hibiscus; 8c. "Passion Fruit"; 10c. "Kampui"; 20c. Queen Elizabeth II (after Anthony Buckley); 30c. Tapeu orchid.

For 20c. design as 5c. see No. 801.

37 Kalahimu

1970. Indigenous Edible Crabs. Mult.
151 3c. Type **37** 10 10
152 5c. Kalavi 10 10
153 30c. Unga 30 25

1970. Christmas. As T 314 of New Zealand, but inscr "NIUE".
154 2½c. multicoloured 10 10

38 Outrigger Canoe, and Fokker F.27 Friendship over Jungle

1970. Opening of Niue Airport. Multicoloured.
155 3c. Type **38** 10 20
156 5c. "Tofua II" (cargo liner) and Fokker F.27 Friendship over harbour 15 20
157 8c. Fokker F.27 Friendship over airport 15 30

39 Spotted Triller

1971. Birds. Multicoloured.
158 5c. Type **39** 15 35
159 10c. Purple-capped fruit dove 40 20
160 20c. Blue-crowned lory 60 20

1971. Christmas. As T 325 of New Zealand, but inscr "Niue".
161 3c. multicoloured 10 10

40 Niuean Boy

1971. Niuean Portraits. Multicoloured.
162 4c. Type **40** 10 10
163 6c. Girl with garland 10 20
164 9c. Man 10 40
165 14c. Woman with garland 15 80

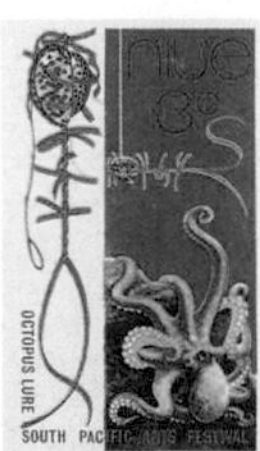
41 Octopus Lure

1972. South Pacific Arts Festival, Fiji. Multicoloured.
166 3c. Type **41** 10 10
167 5c. War weapons 15 15
168 10c. Sika throwing (horiz) 20 15
169 25c. Vivi dance (horiz) 30 25

42 Alofi Wharf

1972. 25th Anniv of South Pacific Commission. Multicoloured.
170 4c. Type **42** 10 10
171 5c. Medical services 15 10
172 6c. Schoolchildren 15 10
173 18c. Dairy cattle 25 20

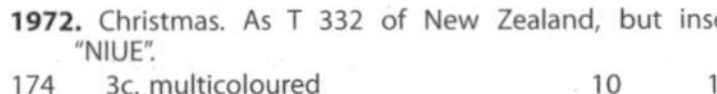

1972. Christmas. As T 332 of New Zealand, but inscr "NIUE".
174 3c. multicoloured 10 10

43 Silver Sweeper

1973. Fishes. Multicoloured.
175 8c. Type **43** 25 25
176 10c. Peacock hind ("Loi") 25 30
177 15c. Yellow-edged lyretail ("Malau") 30 40
178 20c. Ruby snapper ("Palu") 30 45

44 "Large Flower Piece" (Jan Brueghel)

1973. Christmas. Flower studies by the artists listed. Multicoloured.
179 4c. Type **44** 10 10
180 5c. Bollongier 10 10
181 10c. Ruysch 20 20

45 Capt. Cook and Bowsprit

1974. Bicent of Capt. Cook's Visit. Mult.
182 2c. Type **45** 20 20
183 3c. Niue landing place 20 20
184 8c. Map of Niue 20 30
185 20c. Ensign of 1774 and Administration Building 30 65

46 King Fataaiki

1974. Self-government. Multicoloured.
186 4c. Type **46** 10 15
187 8c. Annexation Ceremony, 1900 10 15
188 10c. Legislative Assembly Chambers (horiz) 10 15
189 20c. Village meeting (horiz) 15 25

47 Decorated Bicycles

1974. Christmas. Multicoloured.
190 3c. Type **47** 10 10
191 10c. Decorated motorcycle 10 10
192 20c. Motor transport to church 20 30

48 Children going to Church

1975. Christmas. Multicoloured.
193 4c. Type **48** 10 10
194 5c. Child with balloons on bicycle 10 10
195 10c. Balloons and gifts on tree 20 20

49 Hotel Buildings

1975. Opening of Tourist Hotel. Mult.
196 8c. Type **49** 10 10
197 20c. Ground-plan and buildings 20 20

50 Preparing Ground for Taro

1976. Food Gathering. Multicoloured.
198 1c. Type **50** 10 10
199 2c. Planting taro 10 10
200 3c. Banana gathering 10 10
201 4c. Harvesting taro 10 10
202 5c. Gathering shellfish 30 10
203 10c. Reef fishing 10 10
204 20c. Luku gathering 15 15
205 50c. Canoe fishing 20 60
206 $1 Coconut husking 25 80
207 $2 Uga gathering 45 1·40

See also Nos. 249/58 and 264/73.

51 Water

1976. Utilities. Multicoloured.
208 10c. Type **51** 10 10
209 15c. Telecommunications 15 15
210 20c. Power 15 15

52 Christmas Tree, Alofi

1976. Christmas. Multicoloured.
211 9c. Type **52** 15 15
212 15c. Church service, Avatele 15 15

53 Queen Elizabeth II and Westminster Abbey

1977. Silver Jubilee. Multicoloured.
213 $1 Type **53** 60 50
214 $2 Coronation regalia 80 75
MS215 72×104 mm. Nos. 213/14 1·10 1·60

Stamps from the miniature sheet have a blue border.

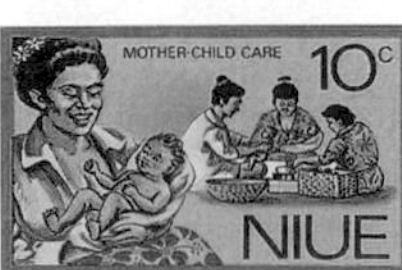

54 Child Care

1977. Personal Services. Multicoloured.
216 10c. Type **54** 15 10
217 15c. School dental clinic 20 20
218 20c. Care of the aged 20 20

55 "The Annunciation"

1977. Christmas. Paintings by Rubens. Multicoloured.
219 10c. Type **55** 20 10
220 12c. "Adoration of the Magi" 20 15
221 20c. "Virgin in a Garland" 35 40
222 35c. "The Holy Family" 55 90
MS223 82×129 mm. Nos. 219/22 1·10 1·25

1977. Nos. 198/207, 214, 216 and 218 surch.
224 12c. on 1c. Type **50** 25 25
225 16c. on 2c. Planting taro 30 30
226 20c. on 3c. Banana gathering 30 40
227 35c. on 4c. Harvesting taro 30 45
228 40c. on 5c. Gathering shellfish 30 50
229 60c. on 20c. Luku gathering 30 55
230 70c. on $1 Coconut husking 30 55
231 85c. on $2 Uga gathering 30 60
232 $1.10 on 10c. Type **22** 30 60
233 $2.60 on 20c. Care of the aged 50 70
234 $3.20 on $2 Coronation regalia 60 80

57 "An Island View in Atooi"

1978. Bicent of Discovery of Hawaii. Paintings by John Webber. Multicoloured.
235 12c. Type **57** 85 40
236 16c. "A View of Karakaooa, in Owhyhee" 95 50
237 20c. "An Offering before Capt. Cook in the Sandwich Islands" 1·00 60
238 30c. "Tereoboo, King of Owhyhee bringing presents to Capt. Cook" 1·10 70
239 35c. "A Canoe in the Sandwich Islands, the rowers masked" 1·25 80
MS240 121×121 mm. Nos. 235/9 4·75 2·75

58 "The Deposition of Christ" (Caravaggio)

1978. Easter. Paintings from the Vatican Galleries. Multicoloured.
241 10c. Type **58** 20 10
242 20c. "The Burial of Christ" (Bellini) 40 25
MS243 102×68 mm. Nos. 241/2 1·00 1·00

1978. Easter. Children's Charity. Designs as Nos. 241/2 in separate miniature sheets 64×78 mm, each with a face value of 70c.+5c.
MS244 As Nos. 241/2 Set of 2 sheets 1·00 2·00

59 Flags of Niue and U.K.

1978. 25th Anniv of Coronation. Mult.
245 $1.10 Type **59** 60 90
246 $1.10 Coronation portrait by Cecil Beaton 60 90
247 $1.10 Queen's personal flag for New Zealand 60 90
MS248 87×98 mm. Nos. 245/7 with white borders 2·50 1·50

1978. Designs as Nos. 198/207 but margin colours changed and silver frame.

249	12c. Type **50**	20	20
250	16c. Planting taro	20	20
251	30c. Banana gathering	30	25
252	35c. Harvesting taro	30	30
253	40c. Gathering shellfish	40	40
254	60c. Reef fishing	40	35
255	75c. Luku gathering	40	40
256	$1.10 Canoe fishing	50	80
257	$3.20 Coconut husking	60	90
258	$4.20 Uga gathering	65	95

60 "Festival of the Rosary"

1978. Christmas. 450th Death Anniv of Durer. Multicoloured.

259	20c. Type **60**	40	20
260	30c. "The Nativity"	50	30
261	35c. "Adoration of the Magi"	60	35
MS262	143×82 mm. Nos. 259/61	1·50	2·00

1978. Christmas. Children's Charity. Designs as Nos. 259/61 in separate miniature sheets 74×66 mm., each with a face value of 60c.+5c.

MS263	As Nos. 259/61 Set of 3 sheets	1·00	2·00

1979. Air. Designs as Nos. 249/58 but gold frames and additionally inscr "AIRMAIL".

264	15c. Planting taro	20	15
265	20c. Banana gathering	20	15
266	23c. Harvesting taro	25	15
267	50c. Canoe fishing	65	20
268	90c. Reef fishing	65	35
269	$1.35 Type **50**	65	1·50
270	$2.10 Gathering shellfish	65	1·75
271	$2.60 Luku gathering	65	1·75
272	$5.10 Coconut husking	80	1·75
273	$6.35 Uga gathering	80	1·75

61 "Pieta" (Gregorio Fernandez)

1979. Easter. Paintings. Multicoloured.

274	30c. Type **61**	30	25
275	35c. "Burial of Christ" (Pedro Roldan)	35	25
MS276	82×82 mm. Nos. 274/5	1·00	1·00

1979. Easter. Children's Charity. Designs as Nos. 274/5 in separate miniature sheets 86×69 mm., each with a face value of 70c.+5c.

MS277	As Nos. 274/5 Set of 2 sheets	1·10	1·75

62 "The Nurse and Child" (Franz Hals)

1979. International Year of the Child. Details of Paintings. Multicoloured.

278	16c. Type **62**	20	15
279	20c. "Child of the Duke of Osuna" (Goya)	20	20
280	30c. "Daughter of Robert Strozzi" (Titian)	35	35
281	35c. "Children eating Fruit" (Murillo)	45	40
MS282	80×115 mm. Nos. 278/81	1·25	2·25

1979. International Year of the Child. Children's Charity. Designs as Nos. 278/81 in separate miniature sheets 99×119 mm, each with a face value of 70c.+5c.

MS283	As Nos. 278/81 Set of 4 sheets	1·00	1·50

63 Penny Black Stamp

1979. Death Cent of Sir Rowland Hill. Mult.

284	20c. Type **63**	15	15
285	20c. Sir Rowland Hill and original Bath mail coach	15	15
286	30c. Basel 1845 2½r. stamp	15	20
287	30c. Sir Rowland Hill and Alpine village coach	15	20
288	35c. U.S.A. 1847 5c. stamp	20	20
289	35c. Sir Rowland Hill and "Washington" (first transatlantic U.S.A. mail vessel)	20	20
290	50c. France 1849 20c. stamp	25	20
291	50c. Sir Rowland Hill and French Post Office railway van, 1849	25	20
292	60c. Bavaria 1849 1k. stamp	25	20
293	60c. Sir Rowland Hill and Bavarian coach with mail	25	20
MS294	143×149 mm. Nos. 284/93	2·00	2·75

The two versions of each value were issued se-tenant within the sheet, forming composite designs.

64 Cook's Landing at Botany Bay

1979. Death Bicentenary of Captain Cook. Multicoloured.

295	20c. Type **64**	55	30
296	30c. Cook's men during a landing on Erromanga	75	40
297	35c. H.M.S. "Resolution" and H.M.S. "Discovery" in Queen Charlotte's Sound	85	45
298	75c. Death of Captain Cook, Hawaii	1·50	70
MS299	104×80 mm. Nos. 295/8	3·75	2·50

65 Launch of "Apollo 11"

1979. 10th Anniv of First Manned Moon Landing. Multicoloured.

300	30c. Type **65**	35	20
301	35c. Lunar module on Moon	45	25
302	60c. Sikorsky Sea King helicopter, recovery ship and command module after splashdown	90	40
MS303	120×82 mm. Nos. 300/2	1·25	1·60

Stamps from No. **MS**303 have the inscription in gold on a blue panel.

66 "Virgin of Tortosa" (P. Serra)

1979. Christmas. Paintings. Multicoloured.

304	20c. Type **66**	10	10
305	25c. "Virgin with Milk" (R. di Mur)	15	15
306	30c. "Virgin and Child" (S. di G. Sassetta)	20	20
307	50c. "Virgin and Child" (J. Huguet)	25	25
MS308	95×113 mm. Nos. 304/7	75	1·25

1979. Christmas Children's Charity. Designs as Nos. 304/7 in separate miniature sheets, 49×84 mm, each with a face value of 85c.+5c.

MS309	As Nos. 304/7 Set of 4 sheets	1·00	2·00

1980. Hurricane Relief. Surch HURRICANE RELIEF Plus 2c. (a) On Nos. 284/93 HURRICANE RELIEF spread over each se-tenant pair.

310	**63**	20c.+2c. multicoloured	20	40
311	-	20c.+2c. multicoloured (No. 285)	20	40
312	-	30c.+2c. multicoloured (No. 286)	25	45
313	-	30c.+2c. multicoloured (No. 287)	25	45
314	-	35c.+2c. multicoloured (No. 288)	30	50
315	-	35c.+2c. multicoloured (No. 289)	30	50
316	-	50c.+2c. multicoloured (No. 290)	35	65
317	-	50c.+2c. multicoloured (No. 291)	35	65
318	-	60c.+2c. multicoloured (No. 292)	35	70
319	-	60c.+2c. multicoloured (No. 293)	35	70

(b) On Nos. 295/8.

320	**64**	20c.+2c. multicoloured	40	50
321	-	30c.+2c. multicoloured	40	60
322	-	35c.+2c. multicoloured	40	65
323	-	75c.+2c. multicoloured	70	1·10

(c) On Nos. 300/2.

324	**65**	30c.+2c. multicoloured	25	40
325	-	35c.+2c. multicoloured	25	45
326	-	60c.+2c. multicoloured	50	75

(d) On Nos. 304/7.

327	**66**	20c.+2c. multicoloured	20	35
328	-	25c.+2c. multicoloured	20	40
329	-	30c.+2c. multicoloured	20	45
330	-	50c.+2c. multicoloured	30	70

68 "Pieta" (Bellini)

1980. Easter. "Pieta". Paintings. Mult.

331	25c. Type **68**	20	15
332	30c. Botticelli	25	20
333	35c. A. van Dyck	25	20
MS334	75×104 mm. As Nos. 331/3, but each with additional premium of **+ 2c.**	55	90

The premiums on No. **MS**334 were used to support Hurricane Relief.

1980. Easter. Hurricane Relief. Designs as Nos. 331/3 in separate miniature sheets, 75×52 mm, each with a face value of 85c.+5c.

MS335	As Nos. 331/3 Set of 3 sheets	1·00	1·50

69 Ceremonial Stool, New Guinea

1980. South Pacific Festival of Arts, New Guinea. Multicoloured.

336	20c. Type **69**	10	10
337	20c. Ku-Tagwa plaque, New Guinea	10	10
338	20c. Suspension hook, New Guinea	10	10
339	20c. Ancestral board, New Guinea	10	10
340	25c. Platform post, New Hebrides	10	10
341	25c. Canoe ornament, New Ireland	10	10
342	25c. Carved figure, Admiralty Islands	10	10
343	25c. Female with child, Admiralty Islands	10	10
344	30c. The God A'a, Rurutu (Austral Islands)	15	15
345	30c. Statue of Tangaroa, Cook Islands	15	15
346	30c. Ivory pendant, Tonga	15	15
347	30c. Tapa (Hiapo) cloth, Niue	15	15
348	35c. Feather box (Waka), New Zealand	15	15
349	35c. Hei-Tiki amulet, New Zealand	15	15
350	35c. House post, New Zealand	15	15
351	35c. Feather image of god Ku, Hawaii	15	15
MS352	Four sheets, each 86×124 mm. (a) Nos. 336, 340, 344, 348; (b) Nos. 337, 341, 345, 349; (c) Nos. 338, 342, 346, 350; (d) Nos. 339, 343, 347, 351. Each stamp with an additional premium of 2c. Set of 4 sheets	1·50	2·00

1980. "Zeapex '80" International Stamp Exhibition, Auckland. Nos. 284/93 optd (A) ZEAPEX'80 AUCKLAND or (B) NEW ZEALAND STAMP EXHIBITION and emblem.

353	**63**	20c. multicoloured (A)	20	15
354	-	20c. multicoloured (B)	20	15
355	-	30c. multicoloured (A)	20	15
356	-	30c. multicoloured (B)	20	15
357	-	35c. multicoloured (A)	20	15
358	-	35c. multicoloured (B)	20	15
359	-	50c. multicoloured (A)	25	20
360	-	50c. multicoloured (B)	25	20
361	-	60c. multicoloured (A)	25	20
362	-	60c. multicoloured (B)	25	20
MS363		143×149 mm. Nos. 353/62, each additionally surcharged **+ 2c.**	2·50	2·00

72 Queen Elizabeth the Queen Mother

1980. 80th Birthday of The Queen Mother.

364	**72**	$1.10 multicoloured	80	1·50
MS365		55×80 mm. **72** $3 multicoloured	1·00	1·75

73 100 m Dash

1980. Olympic Games, Moscow.

366	**73**	20c. multicoloured	20	15
367	-	20c. multicoloured	20	15
368	-	25c. multicoloured	20	20
369	-	25c. multicoloured	20	20
370	-	30c. multicoloured	25	20
371	-	30c. multicoloured	25	20
372	-	35c. multicoloured	25	25
373	-	35c. multicoloured	25	25
MS374		119×128 mm. Nos. 366/73, each stamp including premium of 2c.	1·00	1·00

DESIGNS: No. 367, Allen Wells, Great Britain (winner 100 m dash); 368, 400 m freestyle 369, Ines Diers (winner, D.D.R.); 370, Soling Class; 371, Winner, Denmark; 372, Football; 373, Winner, Czechoslovakia.

Nos. 366/7, 368/9, 370/1 and 372/3 were printed se-tenant in pairs each pair forming a composite design. On the 25c. and 35c. stamps the face value is at right on the first design and at left on the second in each pair. For the 30c. No. 370 has a yacht with a green sail at left and No. 371 a yacht with a red sail.

74 "The Virgin and Child"

1980. Christmas.

375	**74**	20c. multicoloured	15	15
376	-	25c. multicoloured	15	15
377	-	30c. multicoloured	20	20
378	-	35c. multicoloured	20	20
MS379		87×112 mm. Nos. 375/8	85	1·25

DESIGNS: 25c. to 35c. Various Virgin and Child paintings by Andrea del Sarto.

1980. Christmas. Children's Charity. Designs as Nos. 375/8 in separate miniature sheets 62×84 mm, each with a face value of 80c.+5c.

MS380	As Nos. 375/8 Set of 4 sheets	1·25	1·75

75 "Phalaenopsis sp."

1981. Flowers (1st series). Multicoloured.

381	2c. Type **75**	10	10
382	2c. Moth orchid	10	10
383	5c. "Euphorbia pulcherrima"	10	10
384	5c. Poinsettia	10	10
385	10c. "Thunbergia alata"	10	10
386	10c. Black-eyed Susan	10	10
387	15c. "Cochlospermum hibis-coides"	15	15
388	15c. Buttercup tree	15	15
389	20c. "Begonia sp."	20	20
390	20c. Begonia	20	20
391	25c. "Plumeria sp."	25	25
392	25c. Frangipani	25	25
393	30c. "Strelitzia reginae"	25	30
394	30c. Bird of Paradise	25	30
395	35c. "Hibiscus syriacus"	25	30
396	35c. Rose of Sharon	25	30
397	40c. "Nymphaea sp."	30	35
398	40c. Water lily	30	35
399	50c. "Tibouchina sp."	35	45
400	50c. Princess flower	35	45
401	60c. "Nelumbo sp."	45	55
402	60c. Lotus	45	55
403	80c. "Hybrid hibiscus"	55	75
404	80c. Yellow hibiscus	55	75
405	$1 Golden shower tree ("cassia fistula")	75	1·00
406	$2 "Orchid var"	3·00	2·50
407	$3 "Orchid sp."	3·25	3·50
408	$4 "Euphorbia pulcherrima poinsettia"	1·75	4·00
409	$6 "Hybrid hibiscus"	2·25	6·00
410	$10 Scarlet hibiscus ("hibiscus rosa-sinensis")	3·50	9·00

Nos. 405/10 are larger, 47×35 mm.
See also Nos. 527/36.

76 "Jesus Defiled" (El Greco)

1981. Easter. Details of Paintings. Mult.

425	35c. Type **76**	40	30
426	50c. "Pieta" (Fernando Gallego)	60	50
427	60c. "The Supper of Emmaus" (Jacopo de Pontormo)	65	55
MS428	69×111 mm. As Nos. 425/7, but each with charity premium of 2c.	1·00	1·75

1981. Easter. Children's Charity. Designs as Nos. 425/7 in separate miniature sheets 78×86 mm, each with a face value of 80c.+5c.

MS429	As Nos. 425/7 Set of 3 sheets	1·00	2·00

77 Prince Charles

1981. Royal Wedding. Multicoloured.

430	75c. Type **77**	25	60
431	95c. Lady Diana Spencer	30	70
432	$1.20 Prince Charles and Lady Diana Spencer	30	80
MS433	78×85 mm. Nos. 430/2	2·00	2·50

78 Footballer Silhouettes

1981. World Cup Football Championship, Spain (1982).

434	**78**	30c. green, gold and blue	20	20
435	-	30c. green, gold and blue	20	20
436	-	30c. green, gold and blue	20	20
437	-	35c. blue, gold and orange	20	20
438	-	35c. blue, gold and orange	20	20
439	-	35c. blue, gold and orange	20	20
440	-	40c. orange, gold and green	20	20
441	-	40c. orange, gold and green	20	20
442	-	40c. orange, gold and green	20	20
MS443		162×122 mm. 30c.+3c., 35c.+3c., 40c.+3c. (each×3). As Nos. 434/42	1·60	2·00

DESIGNS—Various footballer silhouettes: 435, gold figure 3rd from left; 436, gold figure 4th from left; 437, gold figure 3rd from left; 438, gold figure 4th from left; 439, gold figure 2nd from left; 440, gold figure 3rd from left displaying close control; 441, gold figure 2nd from left; 442, gold figure 3rd from left, heading.

1982. International Year for Disabled Persons. Nos. 430/2 surch +5c.

444	75c.+5c. Type **77**	50	85
445	95c.+5c. Lady Diana Spencer	60	1·00
446	$1.20+5c. Prince Charles and Lady Diana	60	1·25
MS447	78×85 mm. As Nos. 444/6, with each surcharged **+ 10c.**	1·75	4·50

80 "The Holy Family with Angels" (detail)

1981. Christmas. 375th Birth Anniv of Rembrandt. Multicoloured.

448	20c. Type **80**	65	45
449	35c. "Presentation in the Temple"	85	55
450	50c. "Virgin and Child in Temple"	95	1·10
451	60c. "The Holy Family"	1·25	1·50
MS452	79×112 mm. Nos. 448/51	3·25	3·75

1982. Christmas. Children's Charity. Designs as Nos. 448/51 in separate miniature sheets 66×80 mm, each with a face value of 80c.+5c.

MS453	As Nos. 448/51 Set of 4 sheets	2·00	2·50

1982. 21st Birthday of Princess of Wales. Multicoloured.

454	50c. Type **81**	40	55
455	$1.25 Prince and Princess of Wales	60	90
456	$2.50 Princess of Wales	1·50	1·40
MS457	81×101 mm. Nos. 454/6	4·75	3·50

The stamps from No. **MS**457 are without white borders.

1982. Birth of Prince William of Wales (1st issue). Nos. 430/3 optd.

458	75c. Type **77**	1·50	2·00
459	75c. Type **77**	1·50	2·00
460	95c. Lady Diana Spencer	2·50	2·50
461	95c. Lady Diana Spencer	2·50	2·50
462	$1.20 Prince Charles and Lady Diana Spencer	2·50	2·75
463	$1.20 Prince Charles and Lady Diana Spencer	2·50	2·75
MS464	78×85 mm. Nos. 430/2	6·00	6·00

OVERPRINTS: Nos. 458, 460 and 462 **COMMEMORATING THE ROYAL BIRTH 21 JUNE 1982**; 459, 461 and 463 **BIRTH OF PRINCE WILLIAM OF WALES 21 JUNE 1982**; **MS**464 **PRINCE WILLIAM OF WALES 21 JUNE 1982.**

81 Prince of Wales

1982. Birth of Prince William of Wales (2nd issue). As Nos. 454/6, but with changed inscriptions. Multicoloured.

465	50c. Type **81**	50	65
466	$1.25 Prince and Princess of Wales	1·00	1·25
467	$2.50 Princess of Wales	4·00	3·25
MS468	81×101 mm. As Nos. 465/7	7·00	5·50

83 Infant

1982. Christmas. Paintings of Infants by Bronzion, Murillo and Boucher.

469	**83**	40c. multicoloured	1·50	80
470	-	52c. multicoloured	1·60	95
471	-	83c. multicoloured	2·50	2·50
472	-	$1.05 multicoloured	2·75	2·75
MS473		110×76 mm. Designs as Nos. 469/72 (each 31×27 mm), but without portrait of Princess and Prince William	5·00	2·75

84 Prince and Princess of Wales with Prince William

1982. Christmas. Children's Charity. Sheet 72×58 mm.

MS474	**84** 80c.+5c. multicoloured	1·50	1·50

85 Prime Minister Robert Rex

1983. Commonwealth Day. Multicoloured.

475	70c. Type **85**	50	55
476	70c. H.M.S. "Resolution" and H.M.S. "Adventure" off Niue, 1774	50	55
477	70c. Passion flower	50	55
478	70c. Limes	50	55

86 Scouts signalling

1983. 75th Anniv of Boy Scout Movement and 125th Birth Anniv of Lord Baden-Powell. Multicoloured.

479	40c. Type **86**	35	40
480	50c. Planting sapling	45	50
481	83c. Map-reading	85	90
MS482	137×90 mm. As Nos. 479/81, but each with premium of 3c.	1·25	1·75

1983. 15th World Scout Jamboree, Alberta, Canada. Nos. 479/81 optd XV WORLD JAMBOREE CANADA.

483	40c. Type **86**	35	40
484	50c. Planting sapling	45	50
485	83c. Map-reading	85	90
MS486	137×90 mm. As Nos. 483/5, but each with premium of 3c.	1·60	1·75

88 Black Right Whale

1983. Protect the Whales. Multicoloured.

487	12c. Type **88**	75	65
488	25c. Fin whale	95	80
489	35c. Sei whale	1·50	1·25
490	40c. Blue whale	1·75	1·50
491	58c. Bowhead whale	1·90	1·60
492	70c. Sperm whale	2·25	1·75
493	83c. Humpback whale	2·50	2·25
494	$1.05 Minke whale	3·00	2·50
495	$2.50 Grey whale	4·25	4·00

89 Montgolfier Balloon, 1783

1983. Bicentenary of Manned Flight. Mult.

496	25c. Type **89** (postage)	55	25
497	40c. Wright Brothers Flyer I, 1903	1·40	45
498	58c. Airship "Graf Zeppelin", 1928	1·50	60
499	70c. Boeing 247, 1933	1·75	85
500	83c. "Apollo 8", 1968	1·75	1·00
501	$1.05 Space shuttle "Columbia", 1982	2·00	1·40
MS502	118×130 mm. Nos. 496/501 (air)	3·00	3·25

90 "The Garvagh Madonna"

1983. Christmas. 500th Birth Anniv of Raphael. Multicoloured.

503	30c. Type **90**	95	40
504	40c. "Madonna of the Granduca"	1·00	45
505	58c. "Madonna of the Goldfish"	1·40	60
506	70c. "The Holy Family of Francis I"	1·60	70
507	83c. "The Holy Family with Saints"	1·75	80
MS508	120×114 mm. As Nos. 503/7 but each with a premium of 3c.	3·25	2·75

1983. Various stamps surch. (a) Nos. 393/4, 399/404 and 407.

509	52c. on 30c. "Strelitzia reginae"	70	45
510	52c. on 30c. Bird of paradise	70	45
511	58c. on 50c. "Tibouchina sp."	70	55
512	58c. on 50c. Princess flower	70	55
513	70c. on 60c. "Nelumbo sp."	85	60
514	70c. on 60c. Lotus	85	60
515	83c. on 80c. "Hybrid hibiscus"	1·00	75
516	83c. on 80c. Yellow hibiscus	1·00	75
517	$3.70 on $3 "Orchid sp."	6·00	3·25

(b) Nos. 431/2 and 455/6.

518	$1.10 on 95c. Lady Diana Spencer	2·50	2·25
519	$1.10 on $1.25 Prince and Princess of Wales	1·50	2·00
520	$2.60 on $1.20 Prince Charles and Lady Diana	3·00	3·50
521	$2.60 on $2.50 Princess of Wales	2·75	3·25

1983. Christmas. 500th Birth Anniv of Raphael. Children's Charity. Designs as Nos. 503/7 in separate miniature sheets, 65×80 mm, each with face value of 85c.+5c.

MS522	As Nos. 503/7 Set of 5 sheets	3·50	3·25

91 Morse Key Transmitter

1984. World Communications Year. Multicoloured.

523	40c. Type **91**	30	35
524	52c. Wall-mounted phone	40	45
525	83c. Communications satellite	60	65
MS526	114×90 mm. Nos. 523/5	1·10	1·50

92 "Phalaenopsis sp."

1984. Flowers (2nd series). Multicoloured.

527	12c. Type **92**	25	15
528	25c. "Euphorbia pulcherrima"	35	20
529	30c. "Cochlospermum hibiscoides"	40	25
530	35c. "Begonia sp."	40	25
531	40c. "Plumeria sp."	50	30
532	52c. "Strelitzia reginae"	65	40
533	58c. "Hibiscus syriacus"	70	45
534	70c. "Tibouchina sp."	1·00	60
535	83c. "Nelumbo sp."	1·10	70
536	$1.05 "Hybrid hibiscus"	1·25	85
537	$1.75 "Cassia fistula"	2·00	1·50
538	$2.30 "Orchid var"	4·50	2·00
539	$3.90 "Orchid sp."	6·00	4·00
540	$5 "Euphorbia pulcherrima poinsettia"	5·00	4·50
541	$6.60 "Hybrid hibiscus"	6·00	6·00
542	$8.30 "Hibiscus rosa-sinensis"	8·00	7·00

Nos. 537/42 are larger, 39×31 mm.

93 Discus throwing

1984. Olympic Games, Los Angeles. Multicoloured.

547	30c. Type **93**	25	30
548	35c. Sprinting (horiz)	30	35
549	40c. Horse racing (horiz)	35	40
550	58c. Boxing (horiz)	50	55
551	70c. Javelin-throwing	60	65

94 Koala

1984. "Ausipex" International Stamp Exhibition, Melbourne. (a) Designs showing Koala Bears.

552	**94**	25c. multicoloured (postage)	70	50
553	-	35c. multicoloured	80	55
554	-	40c. multicoloured	90	60
555	-	58c. multicoloured	1·00	85
556	-	70c. multicoloured	1·25	1·00

(b) Vert designs showing Kangaroos.

557	83c. multicoloured (air)	1·50	1·25
558	$1.05 multicoloured	1·75	1·60
559	$2.50 multicoloured	3·00	4·00
MS560	110×64 mm. $1.75 Wallaby; $1.75 Koala bear	4·00	4·00

See also Nos. **MS**566/7.

1984. Olympic Gold Medal Winners, Los Angeles. Nos. 547/51 optd.

561	30c. Type **93**	65	30
562	35c. Sprinting	70	35
563	40c. Horse racing	75	35
564	58c. Boxing	80	50
565	70c. Javelin-throwing	85	60

OPTS: 30c. **Discus Throw Rolf Danneberg Germany**; 35c. **1,500 Metres Sebastian Coe Great Britain**; 40c. **Equestrian Mark Todd New Zealand**; 58c. **Boxing Tyrell Biggs United States**; 70c. **Javelin Throw Arto Haerkoenen Finland**.

1984. "Ausipex" International Stamp Exhibition, Melbourne (2nd issue). Designs as Nos. 552/60 in miniature sheets of six or four. Multicoloured.

MS566	109×105 mm. Nos. 552/6 and $1.75 Koala bear (as No. **MS**560)	6·00	4·75
MS567	80×105 mm. Nos. 557/9 and $1.75 Wallaby (as No. **MS**560)	6·00	4·75

96 Niue National Flag and Premier Sir Robert Rex

1984. 10th Anniv of Self-government. Mult.

568	40c. Type **96**	1·10	50
569	58c. Map of Niue and Premier Rex	1·10	60
570	70c. Premier Rex receiving proclamation of self-government	1·10	70
MS571	110×83 mm. Nos. 568/70	2·00	2·00
MS572	100×74 mm. $2.50 As 70c. (50×30 mm)	2·00	2·00

1984. Birth of Prince Henry. Nos. 430 and 454 surch $2 Prince Henry 15. 9. 84.

573	$2 on 50c. Type **81**	2·50	2·75
574	$2 on 75c. Type **77**	2·50	2·75

98 "The Nativity" (A. Vaccaro)

1984. Christmas. Multicoloured.

575	40c. Type **98**	70	35
576	58c. "Virgin with Fly" (anon, 16th-century)	85	50
577	70c. "The Adoration of the Shepherds" (B. Murillo)	95	60
578	80c. "Flight into Egypt" (B. Murillo)	1·10	70
MS579	115×111 mm. As Nos. 575/8 but each stamp with a 5c. premium	2·50	2·25
MS580	Four sheets, each 66×98 mm. As Nos. 575/8, but each stamp 30×42 mm. with a face value of 95c.+10c. Set of 4 sheets	3·75	3·00

99 House Wren

1985. Birth Bicentenary of John J. Audubon (ornithologist). Multicoloured.

581	40c. Type **99**	2·75	1·00
582	70c. Veery	3·00	1·60
583	83c. Grasshopper sparrow	3·25	2·00
584	$1.50 Henslow's sparrow	3·50	2·25
585	$2.50 Vesper sparrow	5·00	4·25
MS586	Five sheets, each 54×60 mm. As Nos. 581/5 but each stamp 34×26 mm with a face value of $1.75 and without the commemorative inscription Set of 5 sheets	13·00	8·50

100 The Queen Mother in Garter Robes

1985. Life and Times of Queen Elizabeth the Queen Mother. Multicoloured.

587	70c. Type **100**	1·50	1·50
588	$1.15 In open carriage with the Queen	1·60	1·60
589	$1.50 With Prince Charles during 80th birthday celebrations	1·75	1·75
MS590	70×70 mm. $3 At her desk in Clarence House (38×35 mm)	6·50	2·75

See also No. **MS**627.

1985. South Pacific Mini Games, Rarotonga. Nos. 547/8 and 550/1 surch MINI SOUTH PACIFIC GAMES, RAROTONGA and emblem.

591	52c. on 70c. Javelin throwing	40	55
592	83c. on 58c. Boxing	65	80
593	95c. on 35c. Sprinting	75	90
594	$2 on 30c. Type **93**	1·50	2·00

1985. Pacific Islands Conference, Rarotonga. Nos. 475/8 optd PACIFIC ISLANDS CONFERENCE, RAROTONGA and emblem.

595	70c. Type **85**	55	75
596	70c. "Resolution" and "Adventure" off Niue, 1774	55	75
597	70c. Passion flower	55	75
598	70c. Limes	55	75

Nos. 595 also shows an overprinted amendment to the caption which now reads **Premier Sir Robert Rex K.B.E.**.

103 "R. Strozzi's Daughter" (Titian)

1985. International Youth Year. Mult.

599	58c. Type **103**	2·25	90
600	70c. "The Fifer" (E. Manet)	2·50	1·00
601	$1.15 "Portrait of a Young Girl" (Renoir)	3·25	1·90
602	$1.50 "Portrait of M. Berard" (Renoir)	3·50	2·50
MS603	Four sheets, each 63×79 mm. As Nos. 599/602 but each with a face value of $1.75+10c. Set of 4 sheets	15·00	11·00

104 "Virgin and Child"

1985. Christmas. Details of Paintings by Correggio. Multicoloured.

604	58c. Type **104**	1·75	85
605	85c. "Adoration of the Magi"	2·00	1·40
606	$1.05 "Virgin with Child and St. John"	2·50	2·50
607	$1.45 "Virgin and Child with St. Catherine"	3·00	3·50
MS608	83×123 mm. As Nos. 604/7 but each stamp with a face value of 60c.+10c.	3·00	2·75
MS609	Four sheets, each 80×90 mm. 65c. Type **104**; 95c. As No. 605; $1.20, As No. 606; $1.75, As No. 607 (each stamp 49×59 mm). Imperf Set of 4 sheets	4·00	4·00

105 "The Constellations" (detail)

1986. Appearance of Halley's Comet. Designs showing details from ceiling painting "The Constellations" by Giovanni de Vecchi. Nos. 611/13 show different spacecraft at top left. Multicoloured.

610	60c. Type **105**	50	50
611	75c. "Vega" spacecraft	65	65
612	$1.10 "Planet A" spacecraft	90	90
613	$1.50 "Giotto" spacecraft	1·25	1·25
MS614	125×91 mm. As Nos. 610/13 but each stamp with a face value of 95c.	4·75	4·25

Stamps from No. **MS**614 are without borders.

106 Queen Elizabeth II and Prince Philip

1986. 60th Birthday of Queen Elizabeth II. Multicoloured.

615	$1.10 Type **106**	80	1·00
616	$1.50 Queen and Prince Philip at Balmoral	1·00	1·25
617	$2 Queen at Buckingham Palace	1·50	1·75
MS618	110×70 mm. As Nos. 615/17, but each stamp with a face value of 75c.	2·75	3·25
MS619	58×89 mm. $3 Queen and Prince Philip at Windsor Castle	3·50	4·25

107 U.S.A. 1847 Franklin 5c. Stamp and Washington Sculpture, Mt. Rushmore, U.S.A.

1986. "Ameripex '86" International Stamp Exhibition, Chicago. Multicoloured.

620	$1 Type **107**	3·50	3·50
621	$1 Flags of Niue and U.S.A. and Mt. Rushmore sculptures	3·50	3·50

Nos. 620/1 were printed together, se-tenant, forming a composite design.

108 "Statue under Construction, Paris, 1883" (Victor Dargaud)

1986. Centenary of Statue of Liberty. Multicoloured.

622	$1 Type **108**	2·00	2·00
623	$2.50 "Unveiling of Statue of Liberty" (Edmund Morand)	2·75	3·50
MS624	107×73 mm. As Nos. 622/3, but each stamp with a face value of $1.25	2·50	3·00

See also No. **MS**648.

109 Prince Andrew, Miss Sarah Ferguson and Westminster Abbey

1986. Royal Wedding.

625	**109**	$2.50 multicoloured	3·25	3·50
MS626		106×68 mm. $5 Prince Andrew and Miss sarah Ferguson (43×30 mm)	7·50	8·00

1986. 86th Birthday of Queen Elizabeth the Queen Mother. Nos. 587/9 in miniature sheet, 109×83 mm.

MS627	Nos. 587/9	13·00	12·00

110 Great Egret

1986. "Stampex '86" Stamp Exhibition, Adelaide. Australian Birds. Multicoloured.

No.	Description	Unused	Used
628	40c. Type **110**	3·00	1·75
629	60c. Painted finch (horiz)	3·25	2·00
630	75c. Australian king parrot	3·50	2·25
631	80c. Variegated wren (horiz)	3·75	2·50
632	$1 Peregrine falcon	4·25	2·75
633	$1.65 Azure kingfisher (horiz)	6·00	4·00
634	$2.20 Budgerigars	6·50	6·00
635	$4.25 Emu (horiz)	8·00	7·50

111 "Virgin and Child" (Perugino)

1986. Christmas. Paintings from Vatican Museum. Multicoloured.

No.	Description	Unused	Used
636	80c. Type **111**	2·25	2·00
637	$1.15 "Virgin of St. N. dei Frari" (Titian)	2·50	2·25
638	$1.80 "Virgin with Milk" (Lorenzo di Credi)	3·75	3·75
639	$2.60 "Madonna of Foligno" (Raphael)	4·50	5·50
MS640	87×110 mm. As Nos. 636/9, but each stamp with a face value of $1.50	9·00	6·00
MS641	70×100 mm. $7.50 As No. 639, but 27×43 mm	8·00	9·00

1986. Visit of Pope John Paul II to South Pacific. Nos. 636/9 surch CHRISTMAS VISIT TO SOUTH PACIFIC OF POPE JOHN PAUL II NOVEMBER 21 24 1986.

No.	Description	Unused	Used
642	80c.+10c. Type **111**	3·25	2·50
643	$1.15+10c. "Virgin of St. N. dei Frari" (Titian)	3·75	3·00
644	$1.80+10c. "Virgin with Milk" (Lorenzo di Credi)	5·50	4·00
645	$2.60+10c. "Madonna of Foligno" (Raphael)	6·50	5·00
MS646	87×110 mm. As Nos. 642/5, but each stamp with a face value of $1.50+10c.	16·00	12·00
MS647	70×100 mm. $7.50+50c. As No. 645, but 27×43 mm	16·00	12·00

112a Sailing Ship under Brooklyn Bridge

1987. Centenary of Statue of Liberty (1986) (2nd issue). Two sheets, each 122×122 mm, containing T 112a and similar multicoloured designs.

No.	Description	Unused	Used
MS648	Two sheets. (a) 75c. Type **112a**; 75c. Restoring Statue's flame; 75c. Steam-cleaning Statue's torch; 75c. "Esmerelda" (children cadet barquentine) off Manhattan; 75c. Cadet barque at dusk. (b) 75c. Statue of Liberty at night (vert); 75c. Statue at night (side view) (vert); 75c. Cleaning Statue's crown (vert); 75c. Statue at night (rear view) (vert); 75c. Cleaning a finial (vert) Set of 2 sheets	8·00	9·00

113 Boris Becker, Olympic Rings and Commemorative Coin

1987. Olympic Games, Seoul (1988). Tennis (1st issue). Designs showing Boris Becker in play.

No.	Description	Unused	Used
649	**113** 80c. multicoloured	2·75	2·00
650	- $1.15 multicoloured	3·00	2·25
651	- $1.40 multicoloured	3·25	2·50
652	- $1.80 multicoloured	4·00	3·25

1987. Olympic Games, Seoul (1988). Tennis (2nd issue). As T 113 but showing Steffi Graf.

No.	Description	Unused	Used
653	85c. multicoloured	3·00	1·75
654	$1.05 multicoloured	3·25	2·00
655	$1.30 multicoloured	3·50	2·25
656	$1.75 multicoloured	3·75	2·75

1987. Royal Ruby Wedding. Nos. 616/17 surch 40TH WEDDING ANNIV. 4.85.

No.	Description	Unused	Used
657	$4.85 on $1.50 Queen and Prince Philip at Balmoral	4·75	4·50
658	$4.85 on $2 Queen at Buckingham Palace	4·75	4·50

115 "The Nativity"

1987. Christmas. Religious Paintings by Durer. Multicoloured.

No.	Description	Unused	Used
659	80c. Type **115**	1·50	1·25
660	$1.05 "Adoration of the Magi"	1·75	1·75
661	$2.80 "Celebration of the Rosary"	3·25	3·75
MS662	100×140 mm. As Nos. 659/61, but each size 48×37 mm with a face value of $1.30	8·50	4·50
MS663	90×80 mm. $7.50 As No. 661, but size 51×33 mm	8·50	7·00

Nos. 659/61 each include detail of an angel with lute as in T **115**.

Stamps from the miniature sheets are without this feature.

116 Franz Beckenbauer in Action

1988. West German Football Victories. Mult.

No.	Description	Unused	Used
664	20c. Type **116**	70	70
665	40c. German "All Star" team in action	90	90
666	60c. Bayern Munich team with European Cup, 1974	1·10	1·10
667	80c. World Cup match, England, 1966	1·40	1·40
668	$1.05 World Cup match, Mexico, 1970	1·60	1·60
669	$1.30 Beckenbauer with pennant, 1974	2·00	2·00
670	$1.80 Beckenbauer and European Cup, 1974	2·25	2·25

1988. Steffi Graf's Tennis Victories. Nos. 653/6 optd.

No.	Description	Unused	Used
671	85c. mult (optd **Australia 24 Jan 88 French Open 4 June 88**)	2·50	1·50
672	$1.05 multicoloured (optd **Wimbledon 2 July 88 U S Open 10 Sept. 88**)	3·00	1·75
673	$1.30 multicoloured (optd **Women's Tennis Grand Slam: 10 September 88**)	3·00	1·90
674	$1.75 mult (optd **Seoul Olympic Games Gold Medal Winner**)	3·25	2·10

118 Angels

1988. Christmas. Details from "The Adoration of the Shepherds" by Rubens. Multicoloured.

No.	Description	Unused	Used
675	60c. Type **118**	1·75	1·50
676	80c. Shepherds	2·00	1·75
677	$1.05 Virgin Mary	2·75	2·50
678	$1.30 Holy Child	3·50	3·00
MS679	83×103 mm. $7.20 The Nativity (38×49 mm)	6·00	7·50

119 Astronaut and "Apollo 11" Emblem

1989. 20th Anniv of First Manned Landing on Moon. Multicoloured.

No.	Description	Unused	Used
680	$1.50 Type **119**	5·50	4·50
681	$1.50 Earth and Moon	5·50	4·50
682	$1.50 Astronaut and "Apollo 11" emblem	5·50	4·50
MS683	160×64 mm. As Nos. 680/2, but each stamp with a face value of $1.15	5·50	5·00

120 Priests

1989. Christmas. Details from "Presentation in the Temple" by Rembrandt. Multicoloured.

No.	Description	Unused	Used
684	70c. Type **120**	3·25	2·75
685	80c. Virgin and Christ Child in Simeon's arms	3·25	2·75
686	$1.05 Joseph	3·75	3·25
687	$1.30 Simeon and Christ Child	4·25	3·75
MS688	84×110 mm. $7.20 "Presentation in the Temple" (39×49 mm)	13·00	13·00

121 Fritz Walter

1990. World Cup Football Championship, Italy. German Footballers. Multicoloured.

No.	Description	Unused	Used
689	80c. Type **121**	2·50	2·50
690	$1.15 Franz Beckenbauer	2·75	2·75
691	$1.40 Uwe Seeler	3·00	3·00
692	$1.80 German team emblem and signatures of former captains	4·00	4·00

122 "Merchant Maarten Looten" (Rembrandt)

1990. 150th Anniv of the Penny Black. Rembrandt Paintings. Multicoloured.

No.	Description	Unused	Used
693	80c. Type **122**	3·50	2·50
694	$1.05 "Rembrandt's Son Titus with Pen in Hand"	3·75	3·00
695	$1.30 "The Shipbuilder and his Wife"	4·00	3·25
696	$1.80 "Bathsheba with King David's Letter"	4·25	3·50
MS697	82×143 mm. As Nos. 693/6, but each with a face value of $1.50	7·50	7·50

123 Queen Elizabeth the Queen Mother

1990. 90th Birthday of Queen Elizabeth the Queen Mother.

No.	Description	Unused	Used
698	**123** $1.25 multicoloured	4·75	4·00
MS699	84×64 mm. **123** $7 multicoloured	14·00	12·00

124 "Adoration of the Magi" (Dirk Bouts)

1990. Christmas. Religious Paintings. Mult.

No.	Description	Unused	Used
700	70c. Type **124**	3·00	2·75
701	80c. "Holy Family" (Fra Bartolommeo)	3·25	3·00
702	$1.05 "Nativity" (Memling)	3·50	3·50
703	$1.30 "Adoration of the Kings" (Bruegel the Elder)	4·50	4·50
MS704	100×135 mm. $7.20 "Virgin and Child Enthroned" (detail, Cosimo Tura)	11·00	12·00

1990. "Birdpex '90" Stamp Exhibition, Christchurch, New Zealand. No. 410 optd Birdpex '90 and logo.

No.	Description	Unused	Used
705	$10 Scarlet hibiscus	12·00	13·00

1991. 65th Birthday of Queen Elizabeth II. No. 409 optd SIXTY FIFTH BIRTHDAY QUEEN ELIZABETH II.

No.	Description	Unused	Used
706	$6 "Hybrid hibiscus"	13·00	12·00

1991. 10th Wedding Anniv of Prince and Princess of Wales. Nos. 430/2 optd TENTH ANNIVERSARY.

No.	Description	Unused	Used
707A	75c. Type **77**	2·25	1·75
708A	95c. Lady Diana Spencer	3·25	2·75
709A	$1.20 Prince Charles and Lady Diana	3·25	2·75

129 "The Virgin and Child with Sts. Jerome and Dominic" (Lippi)

1991. Christmas. Religious Paintings. Mult.

No.	Description	Unused	Used
710	20c. Type **129**	1·50	1·00
711	50c. "The Isenheim Altarpiece" (M. Grunewald)	2·50	2·00
712	$1 "The Nativity" (G. Pittoni)	3·75	3·50
713	$2 "Adoration of the Kings" (J. Brueghel the Elder)	5·00	6·50
MS714	79×104 mm. $7 "Adoration of the Sheperds" (G. Reni)	12·00	13·00

130 Buff-banded Rail

1992. Birds. Multicoloured.

718 20c. Type **130** 1·75 80
719 50c. Red-tailed tropic bird 2·00 1·10
720 70c. Purple swamphen 2·75 1·25
721 $1 Pacific pigeon 3·00 1·75
722 $1.50 White-collared kingfisher 2·50 2·25
723 $2 Blue-crowned lory 2·50 2·50
724 $3 Purple-capped fruit dove 2·50 3·00
726 $5 Barn owl 6·00 5·50
727 $7 Longtailed koel ("Cockoo") (48½×35 mm) 5·50 7·50
728 $10 Reef heron (48½×35 mm) 8·00 10·00
729 $15 Spotted triller ("Polynesian Triller") (48½×35 mm) 11·00 14·00

131 Columbus before King Ferdinand and Queen Isabella

1992. 500th Anniv of Discovery of America by Columbus. Multicoloured.

731 $2 Type **131** 3·50 3·00
732 $3 Fleet of Columbus 6·00 5·50
733 $5 Claiming the New World for Spain 7·00 6·50

132 Tennis and $10 Commemorative Coin

1992. Olympic Games, Barcelona. Mult.

734 $2.50 Type **132** 6·00 5·00
735 $2.50 Olympic flame and national flags 6·00 5·00
736 $2.50 Gymnastics and different $10 coin 6·00 5·00
MS737 152×87 mm. $5 Water polo 12·00 12·00

1992. 6th Festival of Pacific Arts, Rarotonga. Nos. 336/51 surch $1.

738 $1 on 20c. Type **69** 1·00 1·00
739 $1 on 20c. Ku-Tagwa plaque, New Guinea 1·00 1·00
740 $1 on 20c. Suspension hook, New Guinea 1·00 1·00
741 $1 on 20c. Ancestral board, New Guinea 1·00 1·00
742 $1 on 25c. Platform post, New Hebrides 1·00 1·00
743 $1 on 25c. Canoe ornament, New Ireland 1·00 1·00
744 $1 on 25c. Carved figure, Admiralty Islands 1·00 1·00
745 $1 on 25c. Female with child, Admiralty Islands 1·00 1·00
746 $1 on 30c. The God A'a, Rurutu, Austral Islands 1·00 1·00
747 $1 on 30c. Statue of Tangaroa, Cook Islands 1·00 1·00
748 $1 on 30c. Ivory pendant, Tonga 1·00 1·00
749 $1 on 30c. Tapa (Hiapo) cloth, Niue 1·00 1·00
750 $1 on 35c. Feather box (Waka), New Zealand 1·00 1·00
751 $1 on 35c. Hei-Tiki amulet, New Zealand 1·00 1·00
752 $1 on 35c. House post, New Zealand 1·00 1·00
753 $1 on 35c. Feather image of god Ku, Hawaii 1·00 1·00

134 "St. Catherine's Mystic Marriage" (detail) (Memling)

1992. Christmas.

754 **134** 20c. multicoloured 1·50 75
755 - 50c. multicoloured 2·25 1·50
756 - $1 multicoloured 3·25 3·00
757 - $2 multicoloured 4·75 5·50
MS758 87×101 mm. $7 multicoloured (as 50c., but larger (36×47 mm) 12·00 13·00

DESIGNS: 50c., $1, $2 Different details from "St. Catherine's Mystic Marriage" by Hans Memling.

135 Queen on Official Visit

1992. 40th Anniv of Queen Elizabeth II's Accession. Multicoloured.

759 70c. Type **135** 2·50 1·75
760 $1 Queen in green evening dress 3·00 2·25
761 $1.50 Queen in white embroidered evening dress 3·50 2·75
762 $2 Queen with bouquet 4·00 3·25

136 Rough-toothed Dolphin

1993. Endangered Species. South Pacific Dolphins. Multicoloured.

763 20c. Type **136** 1·25 90
764 50c. Fraser's dolphin 2·00 1·60
765 75c. Pantropical spotted dolphin 2·50 2·75
766 $1 Risso's dolphin 3·00 3·50

1993. Premier Sir Robert Rex Commemoration. Nos. 568/70 optd 1909 IN MEMORIAM 1992 SIR ROBERT R REX K.B.E. or surch also.

767 40c. Type **96** 2·50 2·50
768 58c. Map of Niue and Premier Rex 2·50 2·50
769 70c. Premier Rex receiving proclamation of self-government 2·50 2·50
770 $1 on 40c. Type **96** 2·75 2·75
771 $1 on 58c. Map of Niue and Premier Rex 2·75 2·75
772 $1 on 70c. Premier Rex receiving proclamation of self-government 2·75 2·75

138 Queen Elizabeth II in Coronation Robes and St. Edward's Crown

1993. 40th Anniv of Coronation.

773 **138** $5 multicoloured 13·00 12·00

139 "Virgin of the Rosary" (detail) (Guido Reni)

1993. Christmas.

774 **139** 20c. multicoloured 85 75
775 - 70c. multicoloured 2·00 1·25
776 - $1 multicoloured 2·25 1·50
777 - $1. 50 multicoloured 3·00 3·50
778 - $3 multicoloured (32×47 mm) 4·75 6·50

DESIGNS: 70c. to $3 Different details of "Virgin of the Rosary" (Reni).

140 World Cup and Globe with Flags of U.S.A. and Previous Winners

1994. World Cup Football Championship, U.S.A.

779 **140** $4 multicoloured 6·50 7·50

141 "Apollo 11" and Astronaut on Moon

1994. 25th Anniv of First Manned Moon Landing. Multicoloured.

780 $2.50 Type **141** 6·00 6·00
781 $2.50 Astronaut and flag 6·00 6·00
782 $2.50 Astronaut and equipment 6·00 6·00

142 "The Adoration of the Kings" (Jan Gossaert)

1994. Christmas. Religious Paintings. Multicoloured.

783 70c. Type **142** 1·00 1·25
784 70c. "Madonna and Child with Sts. John and Catherine" (Titian) 1·00 1·25
785 70c. "The Holy Family and Shepherd" (Titian) 1·00 1·25
786 70c. "The Virgin and Child with Saints" (Gerard David) 1·00 1·25
787 $1 "The Adoration of the Shepherds" (cherubs detail) (Poussin) 1·25 1·50
788 $1 "The Adoration of the Shepherds" (Holy Family detail) (Poussin) 1·25 1·50
789 $1 "Madonna and Child with Sts. Joseph and John" (Sebastiano) 1·25 1·50
790 $1 "The Adoration of the Kings" (Veronese) 1·25 1·50

143 Long John Silver and Jim Hawkins ("Treasure Island")

1994. Death Centenary of Robert Louis Stevenson (author). Multicoloured.

791 $1.75 Type **143** 4·50 3·50
792 $1.75 Transformation of Dr. Jekyll ("Dr. Jekyll and Mr. Hyde") 4·50 3·50
793 $1.75 Attack on David Balfour ("Kidnapped") 4·50 3·50
794 $1.75 Robert Louis Stevenson, tomb and inscription 4·50 3·50

1996. Nos. 720 and 722 surch.

795 50c. on 70c. Purple swamphen 7·00 4·00
796 $1 on $1.50 White-collared kingfisher 8·00 6·50

145 Tapeu Orchid

1996. Flowers. Multicoloured.

797 70c. Type **145** 80 80
798 $1 Frangipani 1·00 1·00
799 $1.20 "Golden Shower" 1·40 1·75
800 $1.50 "Pua" 1·90 2·50

1996. Redrawn design as No. 146.

801 20c. red and green 1·75 1·25

146 "Jackfish" (yacht)

1996. Sailing Ships. Multicoloured.

802 70c. Type **146** 1·10 1·10
803 $1 "Jennifer" (yacht) 1·60 1·60
804 $1.20 "Mikeva" (yacht) 1·90 2·00
805 $2 "Eye of the Wind" (cadet brig) 2·50 3·00

147 "Desert Star" (ketch)

1996. "Taipei '96" International Philatelic Exhibition, Taiwan. Sheet 90×80 mm.

MS806 **147** $1.50 multicoloured 2·00 2·50

148 "Acropora gemmifera"

1996. Corals. Multicoloured.

807 20c. Type **148** 70 70
808 50c. "Acropora nobilis" 1·00 75
809 70c. "Goniopora lobata" 1·25 85
810 $1 "Sylaster sp." 1·50 1·25
811 $1.20 "Alveopora catalai" 1·75 1·75
812 $1.50 "Fungia scutaria" 2·00 2·00
813 $2 "Porites solida" 2·50 2·75
814 $3 "Millepora sp." 3·25 3·75
815 $4 "Pocillopora eydouxi" 3·75 4·50
816 $5 "Platygyra pini" 4·00 4·75

149 Ox

1997. "HONG KONG '97" International Stamp Exhibition. Chinese New Year ("Year of the Ox"). Sheet 120×90 mm.

MS817 **149** $1.50 multicoloured 1·50 2·25

150 Steps to Lagoon

1997. Island Scenes. Multicoloured.

818	$1 Type **150**	1·25	1·50
819	$1 Islands in lagoon	1·25	1·50
820	$1 Beach with rocks in foreground	1·25	1·50
821	$1 Over-hanging rock on beach	1·25	1·50

Nos. 818/21 were printed together, se-tenant, forming a composite design.

151 Humpback Whale

1997. Whales (1st series). Multicoloured.

822	20c. Type **151**	50	45
823	$1 Humpback whale and calf (vert)	1·25	1·25
824	$1.50 Humpback whale surfacing (vert)	1·75	2·00
MS825	120×90 mm. Nos. 822/4	3·00	3·50

No. **MS**825 shows the "Pacific '97" International Stamp Exhibition, San Francisco, emblem on the margin.

See also Nos. 827/9.

152 Niue 1902 Ovpt on New Zealand 1d.

1997. "Aupex '97" Stamp Exhibition, Auckland (1st issue). Sheet 136×90 mm.

MS826	**152** $2+20c. multicoloured	2·10	2·50

1997. Whales (2nd series). As T 151. Multicoloured.

827	50c. Killer whale (vert)	85	85
828	70c. Minke whale (vert)	1·00	1·00
829	$1.20 Sperm whale (vert)	1·25	1·25

153 Niue 1918–29 Overprint on New Zealand £1

1997. "Aupex '97" Stamp Exhibition, Auckland (2nd issue). Sheet 90×135 mm.

MS830	**153** $2+20c. multicoloured	1·90	2·50

154 Floral Display in Woven Basket

1997. Christmas. Floral Displays. Multicoloured.

831	20c. Type **154**	45	40
832	50c. Display in white pot	70	60
833	70c. Display in white basket	90	90
834	$1 Display in purple vase	1·25	1·50

1998. Diana, Princess of Wales Commemoration. Sheet 145×70 mm, containing vert designs as T 91 of Kiribati. Multicoloured.

MS835	20c. Wearing white jacket, 1992; 50c. Wearing pearl-drop earrings, 1988; $1 In raincoat, 1990; $2 With Mother Theresa, 1992 (sold at $3.70+50c. charity premium)	3·00	3·50

155 Divers and Turtle

1998. Diving. Multicoloured.

836	20c. Type **155**	45	45
837	70c. Diver exploring coral reef	75	75
838	$1 Exploring underwater chasm (vert)	90	90
839	$1.20 Divers and coral fronds	1·10	1·25
840	$1.50 Divers in cave	1·40	1·75

157 Pacific Black Duck

1998. Coastal Birds (1st series). Multicoloured.

841	20c. Type **157**	70	60
842	70c. White tern ("Fairy Tern")	1·25	80
843	$1 Great frigate bird (vert)	1·25	1·10
844	$1.20 Pacific golden plover ("Lesser Golden Plover")	1·40	1·50
845	$2 Common noddy ("Brown Noddy")	2·00	2·50

See also Nos. 875/8.

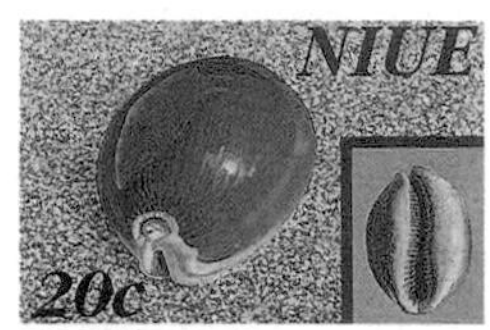

158 Golden Cowrie

1998. Shells. Multicoloured.

846	20c. Type **158**	40	30
847	70c. Cowrie shell	75	65
848	$1 Spider conch	1·00	1·00
849	$5 Helmet shell	5·00	7·00

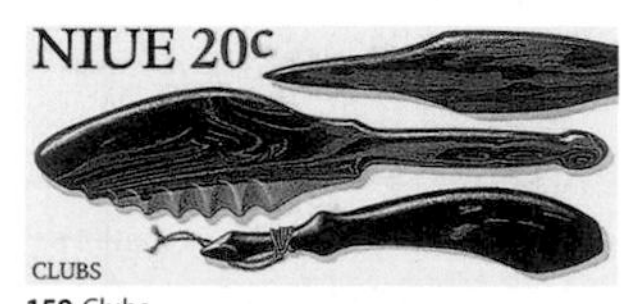

159 Clubs

1998. Ancient Weapons. Multicoloured.

850	20c. Type **159**	40	30
851	$1.20 Three spears (59×24 mm)	1·00	1·00
852	$1.50 Five spears (59×24 mm)	1·25	1·75
853	$2 Throwing stones	1·50	2·25

160 Outrigger Canoe (first migration of Niue Fekai)

1999. "Australia '99" World Stamp Exhibition, Melbourne. Maritime History. Each blue.

854	70c. Type **160**	70	60
855	$1 H.M.S. "Resolution" (Cook)	1·25	1·00
856	$1.20 "John Williams" (missionary sailing ship)	1·40	1·60
857	$1.50 Captain James Cook	1·60	2·00

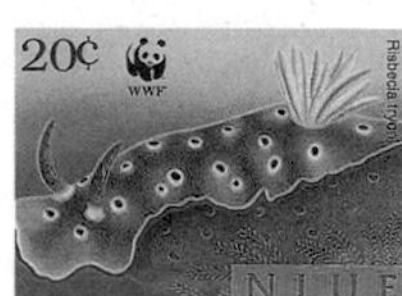

161 "Risbecia tryoni"

1999. Endangered Species. Nudibranchs. Mult.

858	20c. Type **161**	45	40
859	$1 "Chromodoris lochi"	1·10	1·00
860	$1.20 "Chromodoris elizabethina"	1·25	1·40
861	$1.50 "Chromodoris bullocki"	1·50	2·00
MS862	190×105 mm. Nos. 858/61×2	6·50	8·00

162 Togo Chasm

1999. Scenic Views. Multicoloured.

863	$1 Type **162**	1·10	1·00
864	$1.20 Matapa Chasm	1·25	1·25
865	$1.50 Tufukia (horiz)	1·50	2·00
866	$2 Talava Arches (horiz)	1·75	2·50

163 Shallow Baskets

1999. Woven Baskets. Multicoloured.

867	20c. Type **163**	70	90
868	70c. Tray and bowl	80	1·10
869	$1 Tall basket and deep bowls (44×34 mm)	1·00	1·40
870	$3 Tall basket and shallow bowls (44×34 mm)	2·10	2·50

164 Children, Yachts and Forest

1999. 25th Anniv of Self-Government. Sheet, 120×74 mm, containing T 164 and similar horiz design. Multicoloured.

MS871	20c. Type **164**; $5 Scuba diver, young child and sunset	4·00	5·00

165 Family and Man in Canoe

1999. New Millennium. Multicoloured.

872	20c. Type **165**	1·00	1·25
873	70c. People pointing up	1·60	1·90
874	$4 Diver and man in traditional dress	2·75	3·25

Nos. 872/4 were printed together, se-tenant, with the backgrounds forming a composite design.

166 Purple-capped Fruit Dove

2000. Coastal Birds (2nd series). Multicoloured.

875	20c. Type **166**	45	40
876	$1 Purple swamphen	1·00	90
877	$1.20 Barn owl	1·40	1·40
878	$2 Blue-crowned lory	1·75	2·25

167 Queen Elizabeth the Queen Mother

2000. 100th Birthday of Queen Elizabeth the Queen Mother and 18th Birthday of Prince William. Multicoloured.

879	$1.50 Type **167**	1·75	1·75
880	$3 Queen Elizabeth the Queen Mother and Prince William (horiz)	2·50	3·25

168 Pole Vault

2000. Olympic Games, Sydney. Multicoloured.

881	50c. Type **168**	60	45
882	70c. Diving	75	65
883	$1 Hurdling	1·10	1·10
884	$3 Gymnastics	2·25	3·25

169 Couple in Traditional Costumes

2000. Island Dances. Multicoloured.

885	20c. Type **169**	45	70
886	70c. Woman in red costume	80	1·10
887	$1.50 Woman in white costume	1·25	1·40
888	$3 Child in costume made of leaves	1·75	1·90

Nos. 885/8 were printed together, se-tenant, with the backgrounds forming a composite design of flowers.

170 New Zealand Overprinted 1d. of 1902

2001. Centenary of First Niue Stamps. Multicoloured.

889	70c. Type **170**	75	75
890	$3 New Zealand overprinted £1 stamp of 1918–29	2·00	2·75

171 Large Green-banded Blue

2001. Butterflies. Multicoloured.

891	20c. Type **171**	40	35
892	70c. Leafwing	80	70
893	$1.50 Cairns birdwing	1·25	1·40
894	$2 Meadow argus	1·50	2·00

172 Green Turtle

2001. Turtles. Multicoloured.

895	50c. Type **172**	60	60
896	$1 Hawksbill turtle	1·00	1·00
897	$3 Green turtle on beach	2·50	3·00

173 Coconut Crab emerging from Sea

2001. Coconut Crabs. Multicoloured.

898	20c. Type **173**	40	30
899	70c. Crab on beach with coconut palms	80	70
900	$1.50 Crab climbing coconut palm	1·25	1·50
901	$3 Crab with coconut	2·50	3·00

174 Government Offices

2001. Centenary of Annexation to New Zealand. Multicoloured.

902	$1.50 Type **174**	1·25	1·40
903	$2 New Zealand Commissioner and Niue Chief	1·50	2·00

175 Three Wise Men

2001. Christmas. Multicoloured.

904	20c. Type **175**	35	25
905	70c. Dove	80	60
906	$1 Angel	1·10	90
907	$2 Star	2·00	2·50

2002. World Wildlife Fund. No. 858 surch $10.00.

908	$10 on 20c. *Risbecia tryoni*	10·00	10·00

177 Great Clam

2002. Great Clam. Multicoloured.

909	50c. Type **177**	50	50
910	70c. Clam with black spots around opening	65	65
911	$1 Clam with barnacles attached	90	90
912	$1.50 Clam with white coral attached	1·40	1·60
MS913	163×101 mm. Nos. 909/12, each×2	6·00	7·00

178 Cadillac Eldorado (1953)

2003. Centenary of the Cadillac. Multicoloured.

MS916	115×155 mm. $1.50 Type **178**; $1.50 Cadillac Eldorado (2002); $1.50 Cadillac Eldorado (1967); $1.50 Cadillac Sedan DeVille (1961)	6·00	6·50
MS917	108×82 mm. $4 Cadillac Seville (1978)	5·00	5·50

179 Corvette Convertible (1954)

2003. 50th Anniv of the Corvette. Multicoloured.

MS918	117×156 mm. $1.50 Type **179**; $1.50 Corvette (1979); $1.50 Corvette Convertible (1956); $1.50 Corvette Stingray (1964)	6·00	6·50
MS919	109×82 mm. $4 Corvette (1979)	5·00	5·50

180 Queen Elizabeth II

2003. Golden Jubilee. Multicoloured.

MS920	147×78 mm. $1.50 Type **180**; $1.50 Wearing tiara; $1.50 Wearing Imperial State Crown	4·00	4·50
MS921	97×68 mm. $4 Holding bouquet	4·00	4·50

181 Nicholas Frantz (1927)

2003. Centenary of Tour de France Cycle Race. Multicoloured.

MS922	156×96 mm. $1.50 Type **181**; $1.50 Nicholas Frantz (1928); $1.50 Maurice De Waele (1929); $1.50 Andre Leducq wearing round neck t-shirt (1930)	5·00	6·00
MS923	106×76 mm. $4 Andre Leducq wearing collared shirt (1930)	4·00	4·50

182 Prince William

2003. 21st Birthday of Prince William. Two sheets containing T 182 and similar vert designs. Multicoloured.

MS924	147×78 mm. $1.50 Wearing suit and white spotted tie; $1.50 Type **182**; $1.50 Wearing suit and square patterned tie	6·00	6·50
MS925	68×98 mm. $4 Wearing blue patterned shirt	6·00	6·50

183 Boeing 737-200

2003. Centenary of Powered Flight. Two sheets containing T 183 and similar horiz designs. Multicoloured.

MS926	107×176 mm. 80c. Type **183**; 80c. Boeing Stratocruiser; 80c. Boeing Model SA-307B; 80c. Douglas DC-2; 80c. Wright Flyer 1; 80c. DeHavilland D.H.4A	6·00	6·50
MS927	106×76 mm. $4 Boeing 767	6·00	6·50

184 Wrinkled Hornbill

2004. Birds. Two sheets containing T 184 and similar multicoloured designs.

MS928	79×104 mm. $1.50 Type **184**; $1.50 Toco toucan; $1.50 Roseate spoonbill; $1.50 Blue and yellow ("Gold") macaw	6·00	6·50
MS929	52×76 mm. $3 Green-winged Macaw (horiz)	5·50	6·00

185 Garibaldi Fish

2004. Fish. Two sheets containing T 185 and similar horiz designs. Multicoloured.

MS930	104×79 mm. $1.50 Type **185**; $1.50 Golden dddamselfish; $1.50 Squarespot anthias; $1.50 Orange-fin anemonefish	6·00	6·50
MS931	76×52 mm. $3 Maculosus angel	4·50	5·00

186 *Agrias beata*

2004. Butterflies. Two sheets containing T 186 and similar horiz designs. Multicoloured.

MS932	104×79 mm. $1.50 Type **186**; $1.50 *Papilio blume*; $1.50 *Cethosia bibbis*; $1.50 *Cressida Cressida*	5·50	6·00
MS933	52×76 mm. $3 *Morpho rhetenor rhetenor*	5·00	5·50

187 Allied Air Forces

2004. 60th Anniv of D-Day Landings. Two sheets containing T 187 and similar horiz designs. Multicoloured.

MS934	140×100 mm. $1.50 Type **187**; $1.50 Allied naval guns; $1.50 Paratroopers; $1.50 Advance of Allies	4·75	5·50
MS935	98×68 mm. $3 Landing on Normandy	3·25	3·75

188 520 Class 4-8-4, Australia

2004. Bicentenary of Steam Locomotives. Two sheets containing T 188 and similar horiz designs. Multicoloured.

MS936	200×103 mm. $1.50 Type **188**; $1.50 FEF-2 Class 4-8-4, U.S.A; $1.50 Royal Scot Class 4-6-0, Great Britain; $1.50A4 Class 4-6-2, Great Britain	6·50	7·00
MS937	100×70 mm. $3 Class GS-4 4-8-4, U.S.A	4·50	5·00

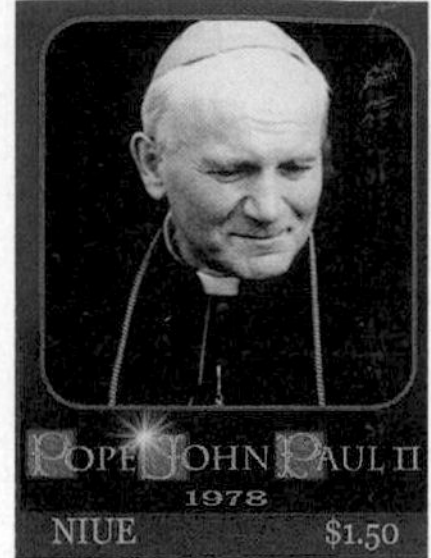

189 Pope John Paul II

2004. 25th Anniv of the Pontificate of Pope John Paul II. Sheet 126×198 mm containing T 189 and similar vert designs.

MS938	$1.50 Type **189**; $1.50 Waving; $1.50 At the Wailing Wall; $1.50 Holding Crucifix	5·00	5·50

190 Lily

2004. United Nations International Year of Peace. Flowers. Sheet 139×177 mm containing T 190 and similar vert designs. Multicoloured.

MS939	75c. Type **190**; 75c. Thistle; 75c. Lily of the Valley; 75c. Rose; 75c. Garland flower; 75c. Crocus; 75c. Lotus; 75c. Iris	5·00	5·50

191 Pope John Paul II

2005. Pope John Paul II Commemoration.

940	**191** $2 multicoloured	2·75	2·75

192 Children

2005. Centenary of Rotary International. Multicoloured.

MS941	132×95 mm. (a) $1.50 Type **192**; $1.50 Paul Harris (founder); $1.50 Carlo Ravizza (President 1999–2000). (b) $3 Jonas Salk (polio vaccine)	10·00	11·00

The two left-hand stamps within **MS**941 form a composite background design showing children.

193 D-Day Invasion, Normandy

2005. 60th Anniv of VE Day. Multicoloured.

942	$1.25 Type **193**	2·00	2·00
943	$1.25 "Monty's Double", Lt. Meyrick Clifton-James, R.A.P. Corps	2·00	2·00
944	$1.25 RAF Hawker Typhoon over French coast	2·00	2·00
945	$1.25 Allied war cemetery, St. Laurent-sur-Mer	2·00	2·00
MS946	70×99 mm. $3 Sir Winston Churchill	6·00	6·00

194 Entertaining the Troops in the Pacific

2005. 60th Anniv of VJ Day. Multicoloured.

947	75c. Type **194**	1·25	1·25
948	75c. Reading letters from home, USS *Argonaut*, August 1942	1·25	1·25
949	75c. Japan surrenders, USS *Missouri*, 1945	1·25	1·25
950	75c. A toast to peace, Naval Air Station, South Carolina	1·25	1·25
951	75c. Entertainment at sea	1·25	1·25
952	75c. Headline "Japs Sign, 6-Yr. War Ends"	1·25	1·25
MS953	99×70 mm. $3 Franklin Delano Roosevelt (US President 1932–45) (vert)	5·00	5·50

195 Frank Bauman, 2002

2005. 75th Anniv of the First World Cup Football Championship, Uruguay. Designs showing players from German World Cup teams. Multicoloured.

954	$1.50 Type **195**	2·50	2·50
955	$1.50 Marcus Babbel, 1998	2·50	2·50
956	$1.50 Dietmar Hamann, 2002	2·50	2·50
MS957	123×105 mm. $3 Christian Worns, 2004	5·00	5·50

196 Hans Christian Andersen

2005. Birth Bicentenary of Hans Christian Andersen (writer). Multicoloured.

958	$1.50 Type **196**	2·50	2·50
959	$1.50 In profile, facing right	2·50	2·50
960	$1.50 Holding book	2·50	2·50
MS961	70×100 mm. $3 In profile, facing left	2·20	2·50

197 Pope Benedict XVI

2005. Inauguration of Pope Benedict XVI.

962	**197**	$1.50 multicoloured	2·50	2·50

198 *Life Study of a Young Man pulling a Rope* (detail)

2007. 400th Birth Anniv (2006) of Rembrandt Harmenszoon van Rijn. Multicoloured.

963	75c. Type **198**	1·25	1·25
964	$1.25 *Self-Portrait*	2·25	2·25
965	$1.50 *Joseph Telling His Dreams*	3·00	3·00
966	$2 *The Blindness of Tobit*	3·50	3·50
MS967	70×99 mm. $3 *Christ in the Storm on the Lake of Galilee*. Imperf	6·25	6·25

199 Young Queen Elizabeth II

2007. 80th Birthday (2006) of Queen Elizabeth II. Multicoloured.

968	$1.50 Type **199**	3·00	3·00
969	$1.50 Wearing pale pink jacket	3·00	3·00
970	$1.50 Speaking, wearing orange-brown dress	3·00	3·00
971	$1.50 In recent years, wearing white	3·00	3·00
MS972	120×120 mm. $3 In recent years, wearing violet dress	6·25	6·25

200 Elvis Presley

2007. 50th Anniv of Purchase of Gracelands by Elvis Presley. Multicoloured.

973	$1.50 Type **200**	3·00	3·00
974	$1.50 Seated, playing guitar	3·00	3·00
975	$1.50 Standing, playing guitar and singing	3·00	3·00
976	$1.50 Standing, holding guitar	3·00	3·00

201 *Stardust* at Kennedy Space Center

2007. Space Anniversaries. Multicoloured. (a) Stardust Spacecraft's encounter with Comet Wild 2, [2004].

977	$1 Type **201**	2·00	2·00
978	$1 *Stardust* Dust Collector with Aerogel	2·00	2·00
979	$1 *Stardust* Navigation Camera	2·00	2·00
980	$1 *Stardust* Whipple Shield	2·00	2·00
981	$1 Cometary and Interstellar Dust Analyzer	2·00	2·00
982	$1 *Stardust* and Comet Wild 2	2·00	2·00

(b) NASA Future Projects (artists renditions).

983	$1.50 Astrobiology Field Laboratory	3·00	3·00
984	$1.50 Deep-Drill Lander	3·00	3·00
985	$1.50 Mars Science Laboratory	3·00	3·00
986	$1.50 The Phoenix Lander	3·00	3·00

202 Palaha Cave

2007. Island Scenes. Multicoloured.

987	20c. Type **202**	40	40
988	70c. White pua flowers	1·10	1·10
989	$1 Talava Natural Arch	2·00	2·00
990	$1.20 Avaiki Pool	2·25	2·25
991	$1.50 Coral rock spears	3·00	3·00
992	$2 Humpback whale	3·50	3·50
993	$3 Spinner dolphins	65	6·25

203 Diana, Princess of Wales

2007. 20th Death Anniv of Diana, Princess of Wales. Multicoloured.

994	$1 Type **203**	2·00	2·00
995	$1 Wearing tiara and black evening dress	2·00	2·00
996	$1 Wearing green, with chin cupped in hand	2·00	2·00
997	$1 As Type **203** but in close-up	2·00	2·00
998	$1 As No. 995 but in close-up	2·00	2·00
999	$1 As No. 996 but head and shoulders photograph	2·00	2·00
MS1000	70×100 mm. $3 Wearing black dress, with hand resting on chin	6·25	6·25

204 Queen Elizabeth II and Duke of Edinburgh

2007. Diamond Wedding of Queen Elizabeth II and Duke of Edinburgh. Multicoloured.

1001	$1 Type **204**	2·00	2·00
1002	$1 Queen Elizabeth wearing green dress and hat	2·00	2·00
MS1003	100×70 mm. $3 Queen Elizabeth and Duke of Edinburgh waving (horiz)	6·25	6·25

205 Final Landing of Concorde F-BVFC at Toulouse

2007. Concorde. Multicoloured.

1004	$1 Type **205** (bistre frame)	2·00	2·00
1005	$1 Crew waving to crowd from cockpit (grey frame)	2·00	2·00
1006	$1 As Type **205** but olive frame	2·00	2·00
1007	$1 As No. 1005 but brown frame	2·00	2·00
1008	$1 As Type **205** (grey frame)	2·00	2·00
1009	$1 As No. 1005 but blue frame	2·00	2·00
1010	$1 Concorde G-BOAD on ground (grey background, blue tint to aircraft)	2·00	2·00
1011	$1 Concorde G-BOAD in flight (natural colours)	2·00	2·00
1012	$1 As No. 1010 but brown background	2·00	2·00
1013	$1 As No. 1011 but lilac tint	2·00	2·00
1014	$1 As No. 1010 but drab background	2·00	2·00
1015	$1 As No. 1011 but blue tint	2·00	2·00

Nos. 1004/9 show the last flight of Concorde F-BVFC from Paris to Toulouse on 27 June 2003.

Nos. 1010/15 show the final flight of Concorde G-BOAD from London Heathrow Airport to New York on 10 November 2003.

206 Marilyn Monroe

2007. 80th Birth Anniv of Marilyn Monroe (actress). Multicoloured.

1016	$1.50 Type **206**	3·00	3·00
1017	$1.50 Smiling, looking over shoulder	3·00	3·00
1018	$1.50 Wearing halter-neck dress	3·00	3·00
1019	$1.50 Speaking, wearing black	3·00	3·00
1020	$1.50 Half-profile, looking to her left	3·00	3·00
1021	$1.50 Close-up of face	3·00	3·00
1022	$1.50 Wearing pale blouse with stand-up collar	3·00	3·00
1023	$1.50 Head and neck portrait	3·00	3·00

207 Marriage of John Rolfe to Pocahontas

2007. 400th Anniv of Jamestown, Virginia, USA. Multicoloured.

1024	$1 Type **207**	2·00	2·00
1025	$1 First settlers reach Jamestown (on board ship)	2·00	2·00
1026	$1 Tobacco plant imported by John Rolfe	2·00	2·00
1027	$1 Captain John Smith	2·00	2·00
1028	$1 Jamestown Tercentenary Monument	2·00	2·00
1029	$1 Map of Jamestown	2·00	2·00
MS1030	100×70 mm. $3 Queen Elizabeth II and Prince Philip at Jamestown Settlement	6·25	6·25

208 Pope Benedict XVI

2007. 80th Birthday of Pope Benedict XVI.

1031	**208**	70c. multicoloured	1·10	1·10

209 Ferrari 166FL, 1949

2007. 60th Anniv of Ferrari Motor Company. Multicoloured.

1032	$1 Type **209**	2·00	2·00
1033	$1 512 TR, 1991	2·00	2·00
1034	$1 Challenge Stradale, 2003	2·00	2·00
1035	$1 F1 87/88C, 1988	2·00	2·00
1036	$1 F2007, 2007	2·00	2·00
1037	$1 Ferrari Headquarters, Italy	2·00	2·00

210 Coconut Palm

2009. Niue Scenes. Multicoloured.

1038	10c. Type **210**	30	30
1039	20c. Sunset over the sea	60	60
1040	30c. Humpback whale	75	75
1041	50c. Rainbow over dead tree and rainforest	90	90
1042	$1 Hio Beach	1·75	1·75
1043	$1.20 Talava Arches	2·50	2·50
1044	$1.40 Limu Pools	2·75	2·75
1045	$1.70 Limestone caves	3·00	3·00
1046	$2 Snorkelling in Limu Pools	3·25	3·25
1047	$3 Coastline	3·75	3·75
1048	$5 Liku Cave	6·00	6·00
MS1049	150×80 mm. Nos. 1038/43	6·00	6·00
MS1050	150×80 mm. Nos. 1044/8	14·00	14·00

211 'Devotion to the Lord', Ekalesia Millennium Hall

2009. Christmas. Stained Glass Windows. Multicoloured.

1051	30c. Type **211**	75	75
1052	80c. Dove, Lakepa Ekalesia Church	1·50	1·50
1053	$1.20 Chalice and bread, Lakepa Ekalesia Church	2·50	2·50
1054	$1.40 'Steward of the Lord', Ekalesia Millennium Hall	2·75	2·75
MS1055	148×80 mm. Nos. 1051/4. Phosphorised paper	6·75	6·75

OFFICIAL STAMPS

1985. Nos. 409/10 and 527/42 optd O.H.M.S.

O1	12c. Type **92**	35	30
O2	25c. "Euphorbia pulcherrima"	40	35
O3	30c. "Cochlospermum hibiscoides"	45	35
O4	35c. "Begonia sp."	50	40
O5	40c. "Plumeria sp."	50	45
O6	52c. "Strelitzia reginae"	60	50
O7	58c. "Hibiscus syriacus"	60	55
O8	70c. "Tibouchina sp."	75	70
O9	83c. "Nelumbo sp."	90	80
O10	$1.05 "Hybrid hibiscus"	1·25	1·00
O11	$1.75 "Cassia fistula"	1·75	1·75
O12	$2.30 Orchid var.	5·50	2·75
O13	$3.90 Orchid sp.	6·00	4·25
O14	$4 "Euphorbia pulcherrima poinsettia"	5·50	6·00
O15	$5 "Euphorbia pulcherrima poinsettia"	5·50	6·00
O16	$6 "Hybrid hibiscus"	8·00	9·00
O17	$6.60 "Hybrid hibiscus"	8·00	9·00
O18	$8.30 "Hibiscus rosa-sinensis"	9·00	10·00
O19	$10 Scarlet hibiscus	10·00	11·00

1993. Nos. 718/29 optd O.H.M.S.

O20	20c. Type **130**	1·75	1·50
O21	50c. Red-tailed tropic bird	2·25	1·75
O22	70c. Purple swamphen	3·00	2·00
O23	$1 Pacific pigeon	3·25	2·00
O24	$1.50 White-collared kingfisher	4·00	3·00
O25	$2 Blue-crowned lory	4·00	3·25
O26	$3 Crimson-crowned fruit dove	2·75	3·50
O27	$5 Barn owl	9·50	6·50
O28	$7 Longtailed cuckoo (48½×35 mm)	6·50	8·50
O29	$10 Eastern reef heron (48½×35 mm)	7·50	10·00
O30	$15 Spotted triller ("Polynesian Triller") (48½×35 mm)	16·00	18·00

Pt. 1

NORFOLK ISLAND

A small island East of New South Wales, administered by Australia until 1960 when local government was established.

1947. 12 pence = 1 shilling; 20 shillings = 1 pound.
1966. 100 cents = $1 Australian.

1 Ball Bay

1947

1	1	½d. orange	85	60
2	1	1d. violet	50	60
3	1	1½d. green	50	70
4	1	2d. mauve	55	40
5	1	2½d. red	80	30
6	1	3d. brown	70	70
6a	1	3d. green	12·00	8·50
7	1	4d. red	1·75	40
8	1	5½d. blue	70	30
9	1	6d. brown	70	30
10	1	9d. pink	1·25	40
11	1	1s. green	70	40
12	1	2s. brown	1·00	1·25
12a	1	2s. blue	14·00	9·00

2 Warder's Tower

22 Red-tailed Tropic Bird

12 "Hibiscus insularis"

17 Queen Elizabeth II (after Annigoni) and Cereus

4 Old Stores (Crankmill)

1953

24	12	1d. green	15	10
25	-	2d. red and green	20	10
26	-	3d. green	70	15
13	2	3½d. red	1·00	90
27	-	5d. purple	55	20
14	-	6½d. green	2·25	3·50
15	4	7½d. blue	1·50	3·00
28	-	8d. red	80	50
16	-	8½d. brown	1·75	4·75
29	17	9d. blue	80	45
17	-	10d. violet	1·00	75
30	-	10d. brown and violet	1·25	1·00
31	-	1s. on 1d. red	80	35
32	-	2s. brown	4·00	1·00
33	-	2s. on 5d. violet	1·00	40
34	-	2s. on 8d. brown and green	2·25	55
18	-	5s. brown	35·00	8·50
35	-	5s. brown and green	2·75	75
36	22	10s. green	26·00	32·00

DESIGNS—VERT: 2d. "Lagunaria patersonii"; 5d. Lantana; 8d. Red hibiscus; 8½d. Barracks entrance; 10d. Salt house; 1s.1d. Fringed hibiscus; 2s. Solander's petrel; 2s.5d. Passion-flower; 2s.8d. Rose apple. HORIZ: 3d. White tern; 6½d. Airfield; 5s. Bloody Bridge.

For Nos. 25 and 28 with face values in decimal currency see Nos. 600/1.

8 Norfolk Is. Seal and Pitcairners Landing

1956. Cent of Landing of Pitcairners on Norfolk Is.

19	8	3d. green	75	40
20	8	2s. violet	1·25	1·00

1958. Surch.

21	4	7d. on 7½d. blue	1·25	1·00
22	-	8d. on 8½d. brown (No. 16)	1·25	1·00

1959. 150th Anniv of Australian P.O. No. 331 of Australia surch NORFOLK ISLAND 5D.

23	143	5d. on 4d. slate	35	30

1960. As Nos. 13 and 14/15 but colours changed and surch.

37	2	1s.1d. on 3½d. blue	2·00	1·00
38	2	2s.5d. on 6½d. turquoise	3·00	1·00
39	4	2s.8d. on 7½d. sepia	7·00	6·00

26 Queen Elizabeth II and Map

1960. Introduction of Local Government.

40	26	2s.8d. purple	4·50	6·50

27 Open Bible and Candle

1960. Christmas.

41	27	5d. mauve	40	50

28 Open Prayer Book and Text

1961. Christmas.

42	28	5d. blue	30	70

29 Stripey

1962. Fishes.

43	29	6d. sepia, yellow and green	60	25
44	-	11d. orange, brown and blue	1·00	80
45	-	1s. blue, pink and olive	60	25
46	-	1s.3d. blue, brown and green	1·00	2·00
47	-	1s.6d. sepia, violet and blue	1·25	80
48	-	2s.3d. multicoloured	2·50	80

DESIGNS: 11d. Gold-mouthed emperor; 1s. Surge wrasse ("Po'ov"); 1s.3d. Seachub ("Dreamfish"); 1s.6d. Giant grouper; 2s.3d. White trevally.

30 "Madonna and Child"

1962. Christmas.

49	30	5d. blue	45	80

31 "Peace on Earth ..."

1963. Christmas.

50	31	5d. red	40	70

32 Overlooking Kingston

1964. Multicoloured.. Multicoloured..

51	5d. Type **32**	60	60
52	8d. Kingston	1·00	1·50
53	9d. The Arches (Bumboras)	1·00	30
54	10d. Slaughter Bay	1·00	30

33 Norfolk Pine

1964. 50th Anniv of Norfolk Island as Australian Territory.

55	33	5d. black, red and orange	40	15
56	33	8d. black, red and green	40	1·10

34 Child looking at Nativity Scene

1964. Christmas.

57	34	5d. multicoloured	30	40

1965. 50th Anniv of Gallipoli Landing. As T 22 of Nauru, but slightly larger (22×34½ mm).

58	5d. brown, black and green	15	10

35 Nativity Scene

1965. Christmas.

59	35	5d. multicoloured	15	10

38 "Hibiscus insularis"

1966. Decimal Currency. As earlier issue but with values in cents and dollars. Surch in black on silver tablets obliterating old value as in T 38.

60	38	1c. on 1d.	20	10
61	-	2c. on 2d. (No. 25)	20	10
62	-	3c. on 3d. (No. 26)	75	90
63	-	4c. on 5d. (No. 27)	25	10
64	-	5c. on 8d. (No. 28)	30	10
65	-	10c. on 10d. (No. 30)	1·00	15
66	-	15c. on 1s.1d. (No. 31)	50	1·00
67	-	20c. on 2s. (No. 32)	2·75	3·00
68	-	25c. on 2s.5d. (No. 33)	1·00	40
69	-	30c. on 2s.8d. (No. 34)	1·00	50
70	-	50c. on 5s. (No. 35)	1·75	75
71	22	$1 on 10s.	2·50	2·50

39 Headstone Bridge

1966. Multicoloured.. Multicoloured..

72	7c. Type **39**	40	15
73	9c. Cemetery Road	40	15

41 St. Barnabas' Chapel (interior)

1966. Centenary of Melanesian Mission. Mult.

74	4c. Type **41**	10	10
75	25c. St. Barnabas' Chapel (exterior)	20	20

43 Star over Philip Island

1966. Christmas.

76	43	4c. multicoloured	10	10

44 H.M.S. "Resolution", 1774

1967. Multicoloured.. Multicoloured..

77	1c. Type **44**	10	10
78	2c. "La Boussole" and "L'Astrolabe", 1788	15	10
79	3c. H.M.S. "Supply" (brig), 1788	15	10
80	4c. H.M.S. "Sirius" (frigate), 1790	75	10
81	5c. "Norfolk" (sloop), 1798	20	10
82	7c. H.M.S. "Mermaid" (survey cutter), 1825	20	10
83	9c. "Lady Franklin" (full-rigged ship), 1853	20	10

84	10c. "Morayshire" (full-rigged transport), 1856	20	50
85	15c. "Southern Cross" (missionary ship), 1866	50	30
86	20c. "Pitcairn" (missionary schooner), 1891	60	40
87	25c. "Black Billy" (Norfolk Island whaleboat), 1895	1·50	75
88	30c. "Iris" (cable ship), 1907	1·50	2·00
89	50c. "Resolution" (schooner), 1926	2·50	2·75
90	$1 "Morinda" (freighter), 1931	3·00	2·75

45 Lions Badge and 50 Stars

1967. 50th Anniv of Lions International.

91	**45**	4c. black, green and yellow	10	10

46 Prayer of John Adams and Candle

1967. Christmas.

92	**46**	5c. black, olive and red	10	10

47 Queen Elizabeth II

1968

93	**47**	3c. black, brown and red	10	10
94	**47**	4c. black, brown and green	10	10
95	**47**	5c. black, brown and violet	10	10
95a	**47**	6c. black, brown and lake	30	60

59 Avro Type 691 Lancastrian and Douglas DC-4 Aircraft

1968. 21st Anniv of QANTAS Air Service, Sydney–Norfolk Island.

96	**59**	5c. black, red and blue	15	10
97	**59**	7c. brown, red and turquoise	15	10

60 Bethlehem Star and Flowers

1968. Christmas.

98	**60**	5c. multicoloured	10	10

61 Captain Cook, Quadrant and Chart of Pacific Ocean

1969. Captain Cook Bicentenary (1st issue). Observation of the transit of Venus across the Sun from Tahiti.

99	**61**	10c. multicoloured	10	10

See also Nos. 118/19, 129, 152/5, 200/2 and 213/14.

62 Van Diemen's Land, Norfolk Island and Sailing Cutter

1969. 125th Anniv of Annexation of Norfolk Island to Van Diemen's Land.

100	**62**	5c. multicoloured	10	10
101	**62**	30c. multicoloured	50	1·00

63 "The Nativity" (carved mother-of- pearl plaque)

1969. Christmas.

102	**63**	5c. multicoloured	10	10

64 New Zealand Grey Flyeater

1970. Birds. Multicoloured.

103	1c. Scarlet robin (vert)	30	10
104	2c. Golden whistler (vert)	30	40
105	3c. Type **64**	30	10
106	4c. Long-tailed koels	60	10
107	5c. Red-fronted parakeet (vert)	1·50	60
108	7c. Long-tailed triller (vert)	45	10
109	9c. Island thrush	70	10
110	10c. Boobook owl (vert)	1·75	3·00
111	15c. Norfolk Island pigeon (vert)	1·25	65
112	20c. White-chested white-eye	6·00	3·50
113	25c. Norfolk Island parrots (vert)	1·25	40
114	30c. Collared grey fantail	6·00	2·00
115	45c. Norfolk Island starlings	1·00	80
116	50c. Crimson rosella (vert)	1·25	2·00
117	$1 Sacred kingfisher	7·00	10·00

65 Cook and Map of Australia

1970. Captain Cook Bicentenary (2nd issue). Discovery of Australia's East Coast. Mult.

118	5c. Type **65**	15	10
119	20c. H.M.S. "Endeavour" and aborigine	40	10

66 First Christmas Service, 1788

1970. Christmas.

120	**66**	5c. multicoloured	10	10

67 Bishop Patteson, and Martyrdom of St. Stephen

1971. Death Cent of Bishop Patteson. Multicoloured.

121	6c. Type **67**	10	35
122	6c. Bible, Martyrdom of St. Stephen and knotted palm-frond	10	35
123	10c. Bishop Patteson and stained glass	10	35
124	10c. Cross and Bishop's Arms	10	35

68 Rose Window, St. Barnabas Chapel, Kingston

1971. Christmas.

125	**68**	6c. multicoloured	10	10

69 Map and Flag

1972. 25th Anniv of South Pacific Commission.

126	**69**	7c. multicoloured	15	20

70 "St. Mark" (stained glass window) (All Saints, Norfolk Is.)

1972. Christmas.

127	**70**	7c. multicoloured	10	10

71 Cross and Pines (stained-glass window, All Saints Church)

1972. Cent of First Pitcairner-built Church.

128	**71**	12c. multicoloured	10	10

72 H.M.S. "Resolution" in the Antarctic

1973. Capt. Cook Bicentenary (3rd issue). Crossing of the Antarctic Circle.

129	**72**	35c. multicoloured	2·25	2·25

73 Child and Christmas Tree

1973. Christmas. Multicoloured.

130	7c. Type **73**	20	10
131	12c. Type **73**	25	10
132	35c. Fir trees and star	70	90

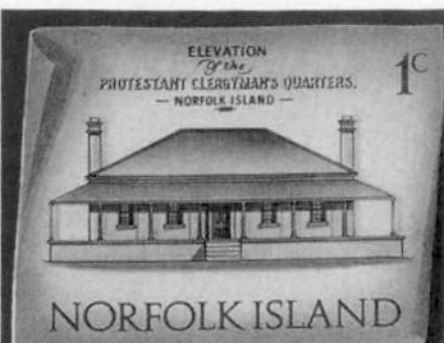

74 Protestant Clergyman's Quarters

1973. Historic Buildings. Multicoloured.

133	1c. Type **74**	10	10
134	2c. Royal Engineers' Office	10	10
135	3c. Double Quarters for Free Overseers	25	1·00
136	4c. Guard House	20	20
137	5c. Entrance to Pentagonal Gaol	25	15
138	7c. Pentagonal Gaol	35	35
139	8c. Prisoners' Barracks	1·25	2·25
140	10c. Officers' Quarters, New Military Barracks	50	55
141	12c. New Military Barracks	50	30
142	14c. Beach Stores	50	70
143	15c. The Magazine	1·25	50
144	20c. Entrance, Old Military Barracks	50	1·00
145	25c. Old Military Barracks	1·25	1·50
146	30c. Old Stores (Crankmill)	50	60
147	50c. Commissariat Stores	50	2·00
148	$1 Government House	1·00	4·00

75 Royal Couple and Map

1974. Royal Visit.

149	**75**	7c. multicoloured	40	20
150	**75**	25c. multicoloured	70	80

76 Chichester's De Havilland Gipsy Moth Seaplane "Madame Elijah"

1974. 1st Aircraft Landing on Norfolk Island.

151	**76**	14c. multicoloured	75	70

77 "Captain Cook" (engraving by J. Basire)

1974. Capt. Cook Bicentenary (4th issue). Discovery of Norfolk Is. Multicoloured.

152	7c. Type **77**	55	65
153	10c. H.M.S. "Resolution" (H. Roberts)	1·00	1·25
154	14c. Norfolk Island pine	75	1·25
155	25c. "Norfolk Island flax" (G. Raper)	75	1·50

78 Nativity Scene (pearl-shell pew carving)

1974. Christmas.

156	**78**	7c. multicoloured	15	10
157	**78**	30c. multicoloured	60	75

79 Norfolk Pine

1974. Centenary of Universal Postal Union. Multicoloured. Imperf. Self-adhesive.

158	10c. Type **79**	35	50
159	15c. Offshore islands	45	50
160	35c. Crimson rosella and sacred kingfisher	1·00	85
161	40c. Pacific map	1·00	95
MS162	106×101 mm. Map of Norfolk Is. cut-to-shape with reduced size replicas of Nos. 158/61	20·00	24·00

80 H.M.S. "Mermaid" (survey cutter)

1975. 150th Anniv of Second Settlement. Multicoloured.

163	10c. Type **80**	40	1·10
164	35c. Kingston, 1835 (from painting by T. Seller)	60	1·25

81 Star on Norfolk Island Pine

1975. Christmas.

165	**81**	10c. multicoloured	15	10
166	**81**	15c. multicoloured	20	10
167	**81**	35c. multicoloured	30	35

82 Memorial Cross

1975. Cent of St. Barnabas Chapel. Mult.

168	30c. Type **82**	20	15
169	60c. Laying foundation stone, and Chapel in 1975	40	40

83 Launching of "Resolution"

1975. 50th Anniv of Launching of "Resolution" (schooner). Multicoloured.

170	25c. Type **83**	25	40
171	45c. "Resolution" at sea	40	70

84 Whaleship "Charles W. Morgan"

1976. Bicent of American Revolution. Mult.

172	18c. Type **84**	20	35
173	25c. Thanksgiving Service	20	35
174	40c. Boeing B-17 Flying Fortress over Norfolk Island	30	85
175	45c. California quail	45	85

85 Antarctic Tern and Sun

1976. Christmas.

176	**85**	18c. multicoloured	25	15
177	**85**	25c. multicoloured	35	20
178	**85**	45c. multicoloured	50	50

86 "Vanessa ita"

1977. Butterflies and Moths. Multicoloured.

179	1c. Type **86**	10	40
180	2c. "Utetheisa pulchelloides"	10	40
181	3c. "Agathia asterias"	10	20
182	4c. "Cynthia kershawi"	10	60
183	5c. "Leucania loreyimima"	15	1·10
184	10c. "Hypolimnas bolina"	30	1·10
185	15c. "Pyrrhorachis pyrrhogona"	30	30
186	16c. "Austrocarea iocephala"	30	30
187	17c. "Pseudocoremia christiani"	35	30
188	18c. "Cleora idiocrossa"	35	30
189	19c. "Simplicia caeneusalis"	35	30
190	20c. "Austrocidaria ralstonae"	40	30
191	30c. "Hippotion scrofa"	50	75
192	40c. "Papilio amynthor (ilioneus)"	50	40
193	50c. "Tiracola plagiata"	50	1·00
194	$1 "Precis villida"	60	75
195	$2 "Cepora perimale"	75	1·40

87 Queen's View, Kingston

1977. Silver Jubilee.

196	**87**	25c. multicoloured	35	30

88 Hibiscus Flowers and Oil Lamp

1977. Christmas.

197	**88**	18c. multicoloured	15	10
198	**88**	25c. multicoloured	15	10
199	**88**	45c. multicoloured	30	35

89 Captain Cook (from a portrait by Nathaniel Dance)

1978. Capt. Cook Bicentenary (5th issue). Discovery of Hawaii. Multicoloured.

200	18c. Type **89**	30	20
201	25c. Discovery of northern Hawaiian islands	30	30
202	80c. British flag against island background	60	70

90 Guide Flag and Globe

1978. 50th Anniv of Girl Guides. Multicoloured. Imperf. Self-adhesive.

203	18c. Type **90**	25	45
204	25c. Trefoil and scarf badge	30	55
205	35c. Trefoil and Queen Elizabeth	45	75
206	45c. Trefoil and Lady Baden-Powell	55	75

91 St. Edward's Crown

1978. 25th Anniv of Coronation. Mult.

207	25c. Type **91**	15	15
208	70c. Coronation regalia	40	45

92 View of Duncombe Bay with Scout at Camp Fire

1978. 50th Anniv of Boy Scout Movement. Multicoloured. Imperf. Self-adhesive.

209	20c. Type **92**	30	45
210	25c. View from Kingston and emblem	35	55
211	35c. View of Anson Bay and Link Badge	50	90
212	45c. Sunset scene and Lord Baden-Powell	55	95

93 Chart showing Route of Arctic Voyage

1978. Captain Cook Bicentenary (6th issue). Northernmost Voyages. Multicoloured.

213	25c. Type **93**	30	30
214	90c. "H.M.S. "Resolution" and H.M.S. "Discovery" in Pack Ice" (Webber)	80	80

94 Poinsettia and Bible

1978. Christmas. Multicoloured.

215	20c. Type **94**	15	10
216	30c. Native oak and bible	20	15
217	55c. Hibiscus and bible	30	30

95 Cook and Village of Staithes near Marton

1978. 250th Birth Anniv of Captain Cook. Multicoloured.

218	20c. Type **95**	30	25
219	80c. Cook and Whitby Harbour	70	1·25

96 H.M.S. "Resolution"

1979. Death Bicent of Captain Cook. Mult.

220	20c. Type **96**	25	30
221	20c. Cook (statue)	25	30
222	40c. Cook's death	30	50
223	40c. Cook's death (different)	30	50

Nos. 220/1 were issued se-tenant, in horizontal pairs throughout the sheet, forming a composite design. A chart of Cook's last voyage is shown in the background. Nos. 222/3 were also issued se-tenant, the horizontal pair forming a composite design taken from an aquatint by John Cleveley.

97 Assembly Building

1979. First Norfolk Island Legislative Assembly.

224	**97**	$1 multicoloured	50	50

98 Tasmania 1853 1d. Stamp and Sir Rowland Hill

1979. Death Centenary of Sir Rowland Hill.

225	**98**	20c. blue and brown	20	10
226	-	30c. red and grey	25	15
227	-	55c. violet and indigo	40	30
MS228		142×91 mm. No. 227	55	1·25

DESIGNS: 30c. Great Britain 1841 1d. red; 55c. 1947 "Ball Bay" 1d. stamp.

99 I.Y.C. Emblem and Map of Pacific showing Norfolk Island as Pine Tree

1979. International Year of the Child.

229	**99**	80c. multicoloured	40	45

100 Emily Bay

1979. Christmas.

230	**100**	15c. multicoloured	15	15
231	-	20c. multicoloured	15	15
232	-	30c. multicoloured	15	15
MS233		152×83 mm. Nos. 230/2	1·00	1·40

DESIGNS: 20, 30c. Different scenes.

Nos. 230/2 were printed together, se-tenant, forming a composite design.

101 Lions International Emblem

1980. Lions Convention.

234	**101**	50c. multicoloured	35	30

102 Rotary International Emblem

1980. 75th Anniv of Rotary International.

235	**102**	50c. multicoloured	35	30

103 De Havilland Gipsy Moth Seaplane "Madame Elijah"

1980. Airplanes. Multicoloured.

236	1c. Hawker Siddeley H.S.748	15	20
237	2c. Type **103**	15	20
238	3c. Curtis P-40E Kittyhawk I	15	20
239	4c. Chance Vought F4U-1 Corsair	15	30
240	5c. Grumman TBF Avenger	15	30
241	15c. Douglas SBD-5 Dauntless	30	30
242	20c. Cessna 172D Skyhawk	30	30
243	25c. Lockheed 414 Hudson	30	35
244	30c. Lockheed PV-1 Ventura	40	2·00
245	40c. Avro Type 685 York	50	55
246	50c. Douglas DC-3	65	65
247	60c. Avro Type 691 Lancastrian	75	75
248	80c. Douglas DC-4	1·00	1·00
249	$1 Beech 200 Super King Air	1·00	1·00
250	$2 Fokker F.27 Friendship	2·00	3·00
251	$5 Lockheed C-130 Hercules	2·25	2·00

104 Queen Elizabeth the Queen Mother

1980. 80th Birthday of The Queen Mother.

252	**104**	22c. multicoloured	20	20
253	**104**	60c. multicoloured	35	40

105 Red-tailed Tropic Birds

1980. Christmas. Birds. Multicoloured.

254	15c. Type **105**	30	25
255	22c. White terns	30	25
256	35c. White-capped noddys	30	25
257	60c. White terns (different)	40	45

106 "Morayshire" and View of Norfolk Island

1981. 125th Anniv of Pitcairn Islanders' Migration to Norfolk Island. Multicoloured.

258	5c. Type **106**	15	15
259	35c. Islanders arriving ashore	40	30
260	60c. View of new settlement	60	45
MS261	183×127 mm. Nos. 258/60	1·00	1·25

107 Wedding Bouquet from Norfolk Island

1981. Royal Wedding. Multicoloured.

262	35c. Type **107**	15	15
263	55c. Prince Charles at horse trials	25	25
264	60c. Prince Charles and Lady Diana Spencer	25	35

108 Uniting Church in Australia

1981. Christmas. Churches. Multicoloured.

265	18c. Type **108**	10	10
266	24c. Seventh Day Adventist Church	15	15
267	30c. Church of the Sacred Heart	15	20
268	$1 St. Barnabas Chapel	35	70

109 Pair of White-chested White-Eyes

1981. White-chested White-Eye ("Silvereye"). Mult.

269	35c. Type **109**	25	35
270	35c. Bird on nest	25	35
271	35c. Bird with egg	25	35
272	35c. Parents with chicks	25	35
273	35c. Fledgelings	25	35

110 Aerial view of Philip Island

1982. Philip and Nepean Islands. Mult.

274	24c. Type **110**	20	20
275	24c. Close-up view of Philip Island landscape	20	20
276	24c. Gecko ("Phyllodactylus guentheri"), Philip Island	20	20
277	24c. Sooty tern, Philip Island	20	20
278	24c. Philip Island hibiscus ("hibiscus insularis")	20	20
279	35c. Aerial view of Nepean Island	20	25
280	35c. Close-up view of Nepean Island landscape	20	25
281	35c. Gecko ("phyllodactylus guentheri"), Nepean Island	20	25
282	35c. Blue-faced boobies, Nepean Island	20	25
283	35c. "Carpobrotus glaucescens" (flower), Nepean Island	20	25

111 Sperm Whale

1982. Whales.

284	**111**	24c. multicoloured	50	35
285	-	55c. multicoloured	70	95
286	-	80c. black, mauve & stone	80	2·00

DESIGNS: 55c. Black right whale; 80c. Humpback whale.

112 "Diocet", Wrecked 20 April 1873

1982. Shipwrecks. Multicoloured.

287	24c. H.M.S. "Sirius", wrecked 19 March 1790	50	50
288	27c. Type **112**	50	50
289	35c. "Friendship", wrecked 17 May 1835	90	80
290	40c. "Mary Hamilton", wrecked 6 May 1873	90	1·25
291	55c. "Fairlie", wrecked 14 February 1840	1·25	1·25
292	65c. "Warrigal", wrecked 18 March 1918	1·25	2·25

113 R.N.Z.A.F. Lockheed 414 Hudson dropping Christmas Supplies, 1942

1982. Christmas. 40th Anniv of First Supply-plane Landings on Norfolk Island (Christmas Day 1942). Multicoloured.

293	27c. Type **113**	80	35
294	40c. R.N.Z.A.F. Lockheed 414 Hudson landing Christmas supplies 1942	1·00	65
295	75c. Christmas, 1942	1·25	2·00

114 50th (Queen's Own) Regiment

1982. Military Uniforms. Multicoloured.

296	27c. Type **114**	25	35
297	40c. 58th (Rutlandshire) Regiment	30	75
298	55c. 80th (Staffordshire Volunteers) Battalion Company	35	95
299	65c. 11th (North Devonshire) Regiment	40	1·25

115 "Panaeolus papilionaceus"

1983. Fungi. Multicoloured.

300	27c. Type **115**	30	35
301	40c. "Coprinus domesticus"	40	50
302	55c. "Marasmius niveus"	45	70
303	65c. "Cymatoderma elegans var lamellatum"	50	85

116 Beechcraft 18

1983. Bicentenary of Manned Flight. Mult.

304	10c. Type **116**	15	15
305	27c. Fokker F.28 Fellowship	25	35
306	45c. French military Douglas C-54	40	60
307	75c. Sikorsky S-61N helicopter	60	95
MS308	105×100 mm. Nos. 304/7	1·40	2·50

117 St. Matthew

1983. Christmas. 150th Birth Anniv of Sir Edward Burne-Jones.

309	5c. Type **117**	10	10
310	24c. St. Mark	20	30
311	30c. Jesus Christ	25	40
312	45c. St. Luke	35	55
313	85c. St. John	55	1·10

DESIGNS: showing stained glass windows from St. Barnabas Chapel, Norfolk Island.

118 Cable Ship "Chantik"

1983. World Communications Year. ANZCAN Cable. Multicoloured.

314	30c. Type **118**	25	40
315	45c. "Chantik" during in-shore operations	30	55
316	75c. Cable ship "Mercury"	40	95
317	85c. Diagram of cable route	40	1·10

119 Popwood

1984. Flowers. Multicoloured.

318	1c. Type **119**	30	70
319	2c. Strand morning glory	40	70
320	3c. Native phreatia	45	70
321	4c. Philip Island wisteria	45	70
322	5c. Norfolk Island palm	50	70
323	10c. Evergreen	50	70
324	15c. Bastard oak	50	70
325	20c. Devil's guts	50	70
326	25c. White oak	50	80
327	30c. Ti	50	1·00
328	35c. Philip Island hibiscus	50	1·00
329	40c. Native wisteria	50	1·25
330	50c. Native jasmine	55	1·25
331	$1 Norfolk Island hibiscus	60	1·75
332	$3 Native oberonia	70	3·00
333	$5 Norfolk Island pine	1·00	3·50

120 Morwong

1984. Reef Fishes. Multicoloured.

334	30c. Type **120**	20	45
335	45c. Black-spotted goatfish	25	65
336	75c. Surgeonfish	30	1·10
337	85c. Three-striped butterflyfish	35	1·40

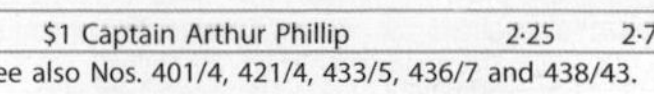

121 Owl with Eggs

1984. Boobook Owl. Multicoloured.

338	30c. Type **121**	75	90
339	30c. Fledgeling	75	90
340	30c. Young owl on stump	75	90
341	30c. Adult on branch	75	90
342	30c. Owl in flight	75	90

122 1953 7½d. and 1974 Cook Bicent 10c. Stamps

1984. "Ausipex" International Stamp Exhibition, Melbourne. Multicoloured.

343	30c. Type **122**	25	35
344	45c. John Buffett commemorative postal stationery envelope	35	75
345	75c. Design from Presentation Pack for 1982 Military Uniforms issue	50	1·75
MS346	151×93 mm. Nos. 343/5	4·50	5·50

123 Font, Kingston Methodist Church

1984. Christmas. Centenary of Methodist Church on Norfolk Island. Multicoloured.

347	5c. Type **123**	10	30
348	24c. Church service in Old Barracks, Kingston, late 1800s	20	40
349	30c. The Revd. & Mrs. A. H. Phelps and sailing ship	20	45
350	45c. The Revd. A. H. Phelps and First Congregational Church, Chester, U.S.A.	25	65
351	85c. Interior of Kingston Methodist Church	40	1·40

124 The Revd. Nobbs teaching Pitcairn Islanders

1984. Death Centenary of Revd. George Hunn Nobbs (leader of Pitcairn community). Multicoloured.

352	30c. Type **124**	20	45
353	45c. The Revd. Nobbs with sick islander	25	65
354	75c. Baptising baby	35	1·10
355	85c. Presented to Queen Victoria, 1852	45	1·40

125 "Fanny Fisher"

1985. 19th-Century Whaling Ships (1st series). Multicoloured.

356	5c. Type **125**	30	50
357	33c. "Costa Rica Packet"	60	55
358	50c. "Splendid"	1·00	1·50
359	90c. "Onward"	2·75	5·00

See also Nos. 360/3.

1985. 19th-Century Whaling Ships (2nd series). As T 125. Multicoloured.

360	15c. "Waterwitch"	50	80
361	20c. "Canton"	55	90
362	60c. "Aladdin"	1·00	2·00
363	80c. "California"	1·00	2·50

126 The Queen Mother (from photo by Norman Parkinson)

1985. Life and Times of Queen Elizabeth the Queen Mother. Multicoloured.

364	5c. The Queen Mother (from photo by Dorothy Wilding)	10	10
365	33c. With Princess Anne at Trooping the Colour	25	25
366	50c. Type **126**	40	55
367	90c. With Prince Henry at his christening (from photo by Lord Snowdon)	60	1·00
MS368	91×73 mm. $1 With Princess Anne at Ascot Races	2·50	2·00

127 "Swimming"

1985. International Youth Year. Children's Paintings. Multicoloured.

369	33c. Type **127**	40	40
370	50c. "A Walk in the Country"	70	85

128 Prize-winning Cow and Owner

1985. 125th Anniv of Royal Norfolk Island Agricultural and Horticultural Show. Mult.

371	80c. Type **128**	60	80
372	90c. Show exhibits	65	90
MS373	132×85 mm. Nos. 371/2	2·25	3·00

129 Shepherds with Flock

1985. Christmas. Multicoloured.

374	27c. Type **129**	30	30
375	33c. Mary and Joseph with donkey	35	40
376	50c. The Three Wise Men	60	65
377	90c. The Nativity	1·00	1·25

130 Long-spined Sea Urchin

1986. Marine Life. Multicoloured.

378	5c. Type **130**	10	10
379	33c. Blue starfish	25	35
380	55c. Southern eagle ray	40	85
381	75c. Snowflake moray	55	1·50
MS382	100×95 mm. Nos. 378/81	2·50	4·00

131 "Giotto" Spacecraft

1986. Appearance of Halley's Comet. Mult.

383	$1 Type **131**	50	1·50
384	$1 Halley's Comet	50	1·50

Nos. 383/4 were printed together, se-tenant, forming a composite design.

132 Isaac Robinson (U.S. Consul 1887–1908)

1986. "Ameripex '86" International Stamp Exhibition, Chicago. Multicoloured.

385	33c. Type **132**	30	35
386	50c. Ford "Model T" (first vehicle on island) (horiz)	40	50
387	80c. Statue of Liberty	40	1·10
MS388	125×100 mm. Nos. 385/7	1·00	2·25

No. 387 also commemorates the Centenary of the Statue of Liberty.

133 Princess Elizabeth and Dog

1986. 60th Birthday of Queen Elizabeth II. Multicoloured.

389	5c. Type **133**	10	10
390	33c. Queen Elizabeth II	40	35
391	80c. Opening Norfolk Island Golf Club	1·90	1·60
392	90c. With Duke of Edinburgh in carriage	1·25	1·60

134 Stylized Dove and Norfolk Island

1986. Christmas.

393	**134**	30c. multicoloured	25	30
394	**134**	40c. multicoloured	30	45
395	**134**	$1 multicoloured	70	1·50

135 British Convicts, 1787

1986. Bicentenary (1988) of Norfolk Island Settlement (1st issue). Governor Phillip's Commission. Multicoloured.

396	36c. Type **135**	65	35
397	55c. Judge passing sentence of transportation	1·25	85
398	90c. Governor Phillip meeting Home Secretary (inscr "Home Society")	2·25	3·75
399	90c. As No. 398, but correctly inscr "Home Secretary"	2·00	3·75
400	$1 Captain Arthur Phillip	2·25	2·75

See also Nos. 401/4, 421/4, 433/5, 436/7 and 438/43.

136 Stone Tools

1986. Bicentenary (1988) of Norfolk Island Settlement (2nd issue). Pre-European Occupation. Multicoloured.

401	36c. Type **136**	35	85
402	36c. Bananas and taro	35	85
403	36c. Polynesian outrigger canoe	35	85
404	36c. Maori chief	35	85

137 Philip Island from Point Ross

1987. Norfolk Island Scenes. Multicoloured.

405	1c. Cockpit Creek Bridge	50	1·50
406	2c. Cemetery Bay Beach	50	1·50
407	3c. Island guesthouse	50	1·50
408	5c. Type **137**	30	1·00
409	15c. Cattle in pasture	80	2·00
410	30c. Rock fishing	30	1·25
411	37c. Old Pitcairner-style house	1·40	2·00
412	40c. Shopping centre	35	1·25
413	50c. Emily Bay	45	1·25
414	60c. Bloody Bridge	2·00	3·00
415	80c. Pitcairner-style shop	1·75	2·75
416	90c. Government House	1·25	2·25
417	$1 Melanesian Memorial Chapel	1·00	1·75
418	$2 Convict Settlement, Kingston	1·25	3·50
419	$3 Ball Bay	2·00	5·00
420	$5 Northern cliffs	2·50	7·00

1987. Bicentenary of Norfolk Island Settlement (1988) (3rd issue). The First Fleet. As T 135. Multicoloured.

421	5c. Loading supplies, Deptford	50	75
422	55c. Fleet leaving Spithead	2·00	2·50
423	55c. H.M.S. "Sirius" leaving Spithead	2·00	2·25
424	$1 Female convicts below decks	2·25	3·00

Nos. 422/3 were printed together, se-tenant, forming a composite design.

138 Male Red-fronted Parakeet

1987. Red-fronted Parakeet ("Green Parrot"). Multicoloured.

425	5c. Type **138**	2·00	2·00
426	15c. Adult with fledgeling and egg	2·50	2·50
427	36c. Young parakeets	2·75	2·75
428	55c. Female parakeet	3·75	3·75

139 Christmas Tree and Restored Garrison Barracks

1987. Christmas. Multicoloured.

429	30c. Type **139**	30	30
430	42c. Children opening presents	45	55
431	58c. Father Christmas with children	60	1·00
432	63c. Children's party	70	1·25

1987. Bicentenary of Norfolk Island Settlement (1988) (4th issue). Visit of La Perouse (navigator). As T 135. Multicoloured.

433	37c. La Perouse with King Louis XVI	95	55
434	90c. "L'Astrolabe" and "La Boussole" off Norfolk Island	2·75	3·00
435	$1 "L'Astrolabe" wrecked in Solomon Islands	2·75	3·00

1988. Bicentenary of Norfolk Island Settlement (5th issue). Arrival of First Fleet at Sydney. As T 135. Multicoloured.

436	37c. Ship's cutter approaching Port Jackson	1·75	75
437	$1 Landing at Sydney Cove	3·25	3·75

1988. Bicentenary of Norfolk Island Settlement (6th issue). Foundation of First Settlement. As T 135. Multicoloured.

438	5c. Lt. Philip Gidley King	20	50
439	37c. Raising the flag, March 1788	85	75
440	55c. King exploring	1·75	1·50
441	70c. Landing at Sydney Bay, Norfolk Island	2·00	2·50
442	90c. H.M.S. "Supply" (brig)	2·25	2·75
443	$1 Sydney Bay settlement, 1788	2·25	2·75

140 Airliner, Container Ship and Sydney Harbour Bridge

1988. "Sydpex '88" National Stamp Exhibition, Sydney. Multicoloured.

444	37c. Type **140**	55	1·25
445	37c. Exhibition label under magnifying glass (horiz)	55	1·25
446	37c. Telephone and dish aerial	55	1·25
MS447	118×84 mm. Nos. 444/6	6·00	7·00

141 Flowers and Decorations

1988. Christmas. Multicoloured.

448	30c. Type **141**	30	40
449	42c. Flowers	40	70
450	58c. Fishes and beach	50	85
451	63c. Norfolk Island	55	1·00

142 Pier Store and Boat Shed

1988. Restored Buildings from the Convict Era. Multicoloured.

452	39c. Type **142**	30	40
453	55c. Royal Engineers Building	40	50
454	90c. Old Military Barracks	60	1·40
455	$1 Commissariat Store and New Military Barracks	65	1·40

143 "Lamprima aenea"

1989. Endemic Insects. Multicoloured.

456	39c. Type **143**	65	40
457	55c. "Insulascirtus nythos"	90	75
458	90c. "Caedicia araucariae"	1·40	2·25
459	$1 "Thrincophora aridela"	1·60	2·25

144 H.M.S. "Bounty" off Tasmania

1989. Bicentenary of the Mutiny on the "Bounty". Multicoloured.

460	5c. Type **144**	60	60
461	39c. Mutineers and Polynesian women, Pitcairn Island	1·75	1·25
462	55c. Lake Windermere, Cumbria (Christian's home county)	2·25	2·25
463	$1.10 "Mutineers casting Bligh adrift" (Robert Dodd)	3·50	4·50
MS464	110×85 mm. 39c. No. 461; 90c. Isle of Man 1989 Mutiny 35p., No. 414; $1 Pitcairn Islands 1989 Settlement Bicent 90c., No. 345	6·00	7·00

145 Norfolk Island Flag

1989. 10th Anniv of Internal Self-government. Multicoloured.

465	41c. Type **145**	90	55
466	55c. Old ballot box	95	65
467	$1 Norfolk Island Act, 1979	1·75	2·25
468	$1.10 Island crest	1·75	3·25

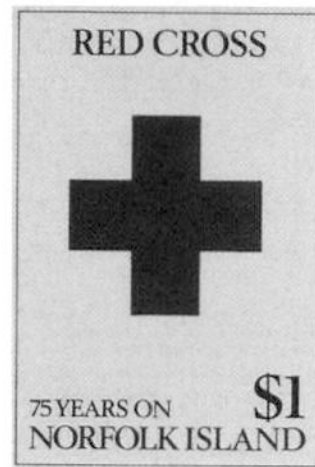

146 Red Cross

1989. 75th Anniv of Red Cross on Norfolk Island.

469	**146**	$1 red and blue	3·00	3·25

147 "Gethsemane"

1989. Christmas. Designs showing opening lines of hymns and local scenes. Multicoloured.

470	36c. Type **147**	80	40
471	60c. "In the Sweet Bye and Bye"	1·50	2·00
472	75c. "Let the Lower Lights be Burning"	2·00	3·25
473	80c. "The Beautiful Stream"	2·00	3·25

148 John Royle (first announcer)

1989. 50th Anniv of Radio Australia. Designs each showing Kingston buildings. Mult.

474	41c. Type **148**	95	70
475	65c. Radio waves linking Australia and Norfolk Island	1·75	2·50
476	$1.10 Anniversary kookaburra logo	2·75	4·50

149 H.M.S. "Bounty" on fire, Pitcairn Island, 1790

1990. History of the Norfolk Islanders (1st series). Settlement on Pitcairn Island. Mult.

477	70c. Type **149**	2·50	3·00
478	$1.10 Arms of Norfolk Island	2·75	3·50

See also Nos. 503/4 and 516/17.

150 H.M.S. "Sirius" striking Reef

1990. Bicentenary of Wreck of H.M.S. "Sirius". Multicoloured.

479	41c. Type **150**	1·50	2·00
480	41c. H.M.S. "Sirius" failing to clear bay	1·50	2·00
481	65c. Divers at work on wreck	2·00	3·00
482	$1 Recovered artifacts and chart of site	2·25	3·25

Nos. 479/80 were printed together, se-tenant, forming a composite design.

151 Unloading Lighter, Kingston

152 "Ile de Lumiere" (freighter)

1990. Ships.

483	**151**	5c. brown	20	50
484	**151**	10c. brown	20	50
485	-	45c. multicoloured	1·00	60
486	-	50c. multicoloured	1·00	1·00
487	-	65c. multicoloured	1·00	1·25
488	**152**	70c. multicoloured	1·00	1·25
489	-	75c. multicoloured	1·50	2·00
490	-	80c. multicoloured	1·50	2·25
491	-	90c. multicoloured	1·50	2·25
492	-	$1 multicoloured	1·50	2·00
493	-	$2 multicoloured	1·75	3·50
494	-	$5 multicoloured	3·25	7·00

DESIGNS—As T **152**: 45c. "La Dunkerquoise" (French patrol vessel); 50c. "Dmitri Mendeleev" (Russian research vessel); 65c. "Pacific Rover" (tanker); 75c. "Norfolk Trader" (freighter); 80c. "Roseville" (transport); 90c. "Kalia" (container ship); $1 "Bounty" (replica); $2 H.M.A.S. "Success" (supply ship); $5 H.M.A.S. "Whyalla" (patrol vessel).

153 Santa on House Roof

1990. Christmas. Multicoloured.

499	38c. Type **153**	65	45
500	43c. Santa at Kingston Post Office	70	50
501	65c. Santa over Sydney Bay, Kingston (horiz)	1·50	2·25
502	85c. Santa on Officers' Quarters (horiz)	1·75	2·75

154 William Charles Wentworth

1990. History of the Norfolk Islanders (2nd series). The First Generation.

503	**154**	70c. brown and cinnamon	1·25	1·50
504	-	$1.20 brown and cinnamon	2·00	2·50

DESIGN: $1.20, Thursday October Christian.

155 Adult Robin and Chicks in Nest

1990. "Birdpex '90" Stamp Exhibition, Christchurch, New Zealand. Scarlet Robin. Multicoloured.

505	65c. Type **155**	1·25	1·50
506	$1 Hen on branch	1·75	2·00
507	$1.20 Cock on branch	1·75	2·25
MS508	70×90 mm. $1 Hen; $1 Cock and hen	4·50	4·75

Each inscribed "Norfolk Island Robin".

156 Map of Norfolk Island

1991. Ham Radio Network. Multicoloured.

509	43c. Type **156**	1·25	70
510	$1 Globe showing Norfolk Island	2·75	3·00
511	$1.20 Map of south-west Pacific	2·75	4·00

157 Display in "Sirius" Museum

1991. Norfolk Island Museums. Mult.

512	43c. Type **157**	70	65
513	70c. 19th-century sitting room, House Museum (horiz)	1·25	2·75
514	$1 Carronade, "Sirius" Museum (horiz)	1·60	3·25
515	$1.20 Reconstructed jug and beaker, Archaeological Museum	1·60	4·00

158 H.M.S. "Pandora" wrecked on Great Barrier Reef (1791)

1991. History of the Norfolk Islanders (3rd series). Search for the "Bounty". Multicoloured.

516	$1 Type **158**	2·75	2·50
517	$1.20 H.M.S. "Pandora" leaving bay	2·75	3·00

159 Hibiscus and Island Scene

1991. Christmas.

518	**159**	38c. multicoloured	70	45
519	**159**	43c. multicoloured	80	55
520	**159**	65c. multicoloured	1·25	2·00
521	**159**	85c. multicoloured	1·50	2·50

NORFOLK ISLAND 43c

160 Tank and Soldier in Jungle

1991. 50th Anniv of Outbreak of Pacific War. Multicoloured.

522	43c. Type **160**	1·25	65
523	70c. Boeing B-17 Flying Fortress on jungle airstrip	2·25	2·75
524	$1 Warships	2·75	3·50

161 Coat of Arms

1992. 500th Anniv of Discovery of America by Columbus. Multicoloured.

525	45c. Type **161**	85	55
526	$1.05 "Santa Maria"	2·00	2·75
527	$1.20 Columbus and globe	2·50	3·25

162 Deployment Map

1992. 50th Anniv of Battle of the Coral Sea. Multicoloured.

528	45c. Type **162**	1·25	60
529	70c. H.M.A.S. "Australia" (cruiser)	2·00	2·50
530	$1.05 U.S.S. "Yorktown" (aircraft carrier)	2·75	3·50

1992. 50th Anniv of Battle of Midway. As T 162. Multicoloured.

531	45c. Battle area	1·25	60
532	70c. Consolidated PBY-5 Catalina flying boat over task force	2·00	2·50
533	$1.05 Douglas SBD Dauntless dive bomber and "Akagi" (Japanese aircraft carrier) burning	2·75	3·50

1992. 50th Anniv of Battle of Guadalcanal. As T 162. Multicoloured.

534	45c. American troops landing (horiz)	1·25	60
535	70c. Machine-gun crew (horiz)	2·00	2·50
536	$1.05 Map of Pacific with Japanese and American flags (horiz)	4·50	3·50

163 Norfolk Pines above Ball Bay

1992. Christmas. Multicoloured.

537	40c. Type **163**	70	40
538	45c. Headstone Creek	75	45
539	75c. South side of Ball Bay	1·50	2·25
540	$1.20 Rocky Point Reserve	2·00	3·00

164 Boat Shed and Flaghouses, Kingston

1993. Tourism. Historic Kingston. Mult.

541	45c. Type **164**	70	1·00
542	45c. Old Military Barracks	70	1·00
543	45c. All Saints Church	70	1·00
544	45c. Officers' Quarters	70	1·00
545	45c. Quality Row	70	1·00

Nos. 541/5 were printed together, se-tenant, forming a composite design.

165 Fire Engine

1993. Emergency Services. Multicoloured.

546	45c. Type **165**	1·00	60
547	70c. Cliff rescue squad	1·10	1·75
548	75c. Ambulance	1·40	1·90
549	$1.20 Police car	2·50	3·00

166 Blue Sea Lizard ("Glaucus atlanticus")

1993. Nudibranchs. Multicoloured.

550	45c. Type **166**	80	55
551	45c. Ocellate nudibranch ("Phyllidia ocellata")	80	55
552	75c. "Bornella sp."	1·25	1·75
553	85c. "Glossodoris rubroannolata"	1·50	2·25
554	95c. "Halgerda willeyi"	1·75	2·50
555	$1.05 "Ceratosoma amoena"	1·75	3·00

167 Christmas Wreath

1993. Christmas.

556	**167**	40c. multicoloured	60	50
557	**167**	45c. multicoloured	60	50
558	**167**	75c. multicoloured	85	1·50
559	**167**	$1.20 multicoloured	1·50	3·00

168 Maori Stone Clubs

1993. Bicentenary of Contact with New Zealand. Multicoloured.

560	70c. Type **168**	1·00	1·50
561	$1.20 First Maori map of New Zealand, 1793	1·75	2·75

169 Alvaro de Saavedra, Route Map and "Florida"

1994. Pacific Explorers. Multicoloured.

562	5c. Vasco Nunez de Balboa, map and "Barbara"	75	1·00
563	10c. Ferdinand Magellan, map and "Vitoria"	1·00	1·00
564	20c. Juan Sebastian del Cano, map and "Vitoria"	1·40	1·25
565	50c. Type **169**	1·50	1·00
566	70c. Ruy Lopez de Villalobos, map and "San Juan"	1·75	1·50
567	75c. Miguel Lopez de Legaspi, map and "San Lesmes"	1·75	1·75
568	80c. Sir Francis Drake, map and "Golden Hind"	1·75	1·75
569	85c. Alvaro de Mendana, map and "Santiago"	1·75	1·75
570	90c. Pedro Fernandes de Quiros, map and "San Pedro y Pablo"	1·75	1·75
571	$1 Luis Baez de Torres, map and "San Pedrico"	1·75	1·75
572	$2 Abel Tasman, map and "Heemskerk"	2·25	3·00
573	$5 William Dampier, map and "Cygnet"	4·25	6·50
MS574	100×80 mm. $1.20 "Golden Hind" (Drake) (32×52 mm)	4·50	5·00

170 Sooty Tern

1994. Sea Birds. Multicoloured.

575	45c. Type **170**	95	1·25
576	45c. Red-tailed tropic bird	95	1·25
577	45c. Australian gannet	95	1·25
578	45c. Wedge-tailed shearwater	95	1·25
579	45c. Masked booby	95	1·25

Nos. 575/9 were printed together, se-tenant, forming a composite design.

171 House and Star

1994. Christmas. Multicoloured. Self-adhesive.

580	45c. Type **171**	80	55
581	75c. Figures from stained-glass windows	1·50	2·00
582	$1.20 Rainbow and "The Church of God" (missionary sailing ship)	2·50	3·50

172 Chevrolet, 1926

1995. Vintage Motor Vehicles. Multicoloured.

583	45c. Type **172**	75	55
584	75c. Ford Model "A", 1928	1·00	1·75
585	$1.05 Ford Model "A A/C", 1929	1·40	2·00
586	$1.20 Ford Model "A", 1930	1·60	2·25

173 Tail Flukes of Humpback Whale

1995. Humpback Whale Conservation. Multicoloured.

587	45c. Type **173**	1·00	55
588	75c. Mother and calf	1·50	2·00
589	$1.05 Whale breaching (vert)	1·75	2·50
MS590	107×84 mm. $1.20 Humpback whale (29×49 mm)	2·50	3·25

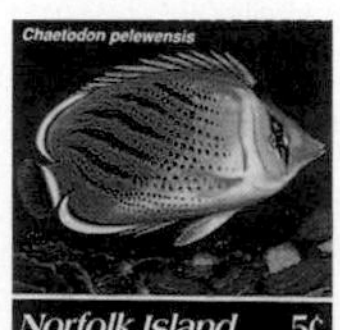

174 Dot-and-Dash Butterflyfish

1995. Butterflyfishes. Multicoloured.

591	5c. Type **174**	30	75
592	45c. Blue-spotted butterflyfish	85	50
593	$1.20 Three-belted butterflyfish	2·25	2·75
594	$1.50 Three-finned butterflyfish	2·50	3·25

1995. "JAKARTA '95" Stamp Exhibition, Indonesia. No. MS590 optd "Selamat Hari Merdeka" and emblem on sheet margin in gold.

MS595	107×84 mm. $1.20 Humpback whale	1·75	2·75

175 International 4×4 Refueller, 1942

1995. Second World War Vehicles. Multicoloured.

596	5c. Type **175**	30	75
597	45c. Ford Sedan, 1942	75	45
598	$1.20 Ford 3 ton tipper, 1942	2·00	2·50
599	$2 D8 caterpillar with scraper	3·00	4·00

1995. Flower designs as 1960 issues, but with face values in decimal currency.

600	5c. pink and green (as No. 25)	20	35
601	5c. red (as No. 28)	20	35

176 Servicing Fighter

1995. 50th Anniv of End of Second World War in the Pacific. Multicoloured.

602	5c. Type **176**	40	1·00
603	45c. Sgt. Tom Derrick, VC (vert)	85	45
604	75c. Gen. Douglas MacArthur (vert)	1·50	1·50
605	$1.05 Girls celebrating victory	2·25	2·25
606	$10 Pacific War medals (50×30 mm)	19·00	23·00

The $10 also includes the "Singapore '95" International stamp exhibition logo.

177 Peace Dove and Anniversary Emblem

1995. Christmas. 50th Anniv of United Nations. Each including U.N. anniversary emblem.

607	**177**	45c. gold and blue	60	45
608	-	75c. gold and violet	1·00	1·50
609	-	$1.05 gold and red	1·40	2·25
610	-	$1.20 gold and green	1·60	2·50

DESIGNS: 75c. Star of Bethlehem; $1.05, Symbolic candles on cake; $1.20, Olive branch.

178 Skink on Bank

1996. Endangered Species. Skinks and Geckos. Multicoloured.

611	5c. Type **178**	60	85
612	5c. Gecko on branch	60	85
613	45c. Skink facing right	80	85
614	45c. Gecko on flower	80	85

179 Sopwith Pup Biplane and Emblem

1996. 75th Anniv of Royal Australian Air Force. Aircraft. Multicoloured.

615	45c. Type **179**	60	60
616	45c. Wirraway fighter	60	60
617	75c. F-111C jet fighter	1·00	1·50
618	85c. F/A-18 Hornet jet fighter	1·10	1·60

180 Rat

1996. Chinese New Year ("Year of the Rat"). Sheet 100×75 mm.

MS619	**180** $1 black, red and brown	1·50	2·25

181 "Naticarlus oncus"

1996. Shells. Multicoloured.

620	45c. Type **181**	70	85
621	45c. "Janthina janthina"	70	85
622	45c. "Cypraea caputserpentis"	70	85
623	45c. "Argonauta nodosa"	70	85

182 Shopping

1996. Tourism. Multicoloured.

624	45c. Type **182**	50	50
625	75c. Celebrating Bounty Day	1·00	1·00
626	$2.50 Horse riding	3·75	4·50
627	$3.70 Unloading lighter	4·50	5·75

183 The Nativity

1996. Christmas. Multicoloured.

628	45c. Type **183**	50	50
629	45c. Star and boat sheds	50	50
630	75c. Star, bungalow and ox	90	1·50
631	85c. Star, fruit, flowers and ox	1·10	1·75

184 Coat of Arms

1997

632	**184**	5c. blue and yellow	25	35
633	-	5c. brown	25	35

DESIGN: No. 633, Great Seal of Norfolk Island.

185 Calf

1997. Beef Cattle. Sheet 67×67 mm.

MS634	**185** $1.20 multicoloured	2·00	2·75

1997. "HONG KONG '97" International Stamp Exhibition. As No. MS634, but with exhibition emblem on sheet margin.

MS635	67×67 mm. **185** $1.20 multi-coloured	3·25	4·00

186 "Cepora perimale"

1997. Butterflies. Multicoloured.

636	75c. Type **186**	1·10	1·00
637	90c. "Danaus chrysippus"	1·40	1·60
638	$1 "Danaus hamata"	1·40	1·60
639	$1.20 "Danaus plexippus"	1·50	2·25

187 Dusky Dolphins

1997. Dolphins. Multicoloured.

640	45c. Type **187**	75	60
641	75c. Common dolphin and calf	1·25	1·40
MS642	106×80 mm. $1.05 Dolphin	2·75	3·25

1997. "Pacific '97" International Stamp Exhibition, San Francisco. As No. MS642, but with exhibition emblem on sheet margin.

MS643	106×80 mm. $1.05 Dolphin	3·75	4·50

188 Ball Bay, Norfolk Island

1997. 50th Anniv of Norfolk Island Stamps. Multicoloured.

644	$1 Type **188**	1·25	2·00
645	$1.50 1947 2d. stamp	1·25	2·00
646	$8 Ball Bay and 1947 2s. bistre stamp (90×45 mm)	7·50	12·00

188a Queen Elizabeth II

1997. Golden Wedding of Queen Elizabeth and Prince Philip. Multicoloured.

647	20c. Type **188a**	50	60
648	25c. Prince Philip in carriage-driving trials	50	60
649	25c. Prince Philip	55	65
650	50c. Queen in phaeton at Trooping the Colour	70	80
MS651	110×70 mm. $1.50 Queen Elizabeth and Prince Philip in landau (horiz)	2·25	2·75

Nos. 647/8 and 649/50 were each printed together, se-tenant, with the backgrounds forming composite designs.

189 Royal Yacht "Britannia" leaving Hong Kong

1997. Return of Hong Kong to China. Sheet 126×91 mm.

MS652	**189** 45c. multicoloured	1·00	1·50

No. **MS**652 is inscribed "Brittania" in error.

190 Christmas Tree

1997. Annual Festivals. Multicoloured.

653	45c. Type **190**	60	45
654	75c. Fireworks (New Year's Eve)	90	1·25
655	$1.20 Rose (Valentine's Day)	1·40	2·00

191 Oriental Pearl T.V. Tower, Shanghai

1997. "Shanghai '97" International Stamp and Coin Exhibition, shanghai. Sheet 103×138 mm.

MS656	**191** 45c. multicoloured	1·00	1·50

192 Tiger Mask

1998. Chinese New Year ("Year of the Tiger"). Sheet 75×95 mm.

MS657	**192** 45c. multicoloured	1·00	1·50

193 "Pepper"

1998. Cats. Multicoloured.

658	45c. Type **193**	65	65
659	45c. "Tabitha" at window	65	65
660	75c. "Midnight"	85	1·25
661	$1.20 "Rainbow" with flower pot	1·25	1·75

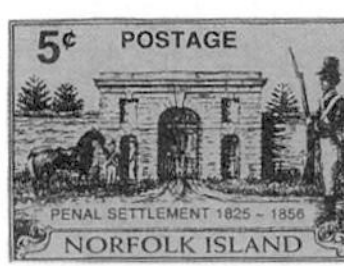

194 Entrance to Pentagonal Gaol

1998

662	**194**	5c. black and blue	25	35
663	-	5c. black and green	25	35

DESIGN: No. 663, Ruined First Settlement cottage.

194a Princess Diana with Bouquet, 1991

1998. Diana, Princess of Wales Commemoration. Multicolured.

664	45c. Type **194a**	50	50
MS665	145×70 mm. 45c. Wearing blue and white dress, 1989; 45c. Wearing pearl earrings, 1990; 45c. No. 664; 45c. Wearing striped dress (sold at $1.80+45c. charity premium)	1·25	2·00

195 Tweed Trousers

1998. Reef Fishes. Multicoloured.

666	10c. Type **195**	30	40
667	20c. Conspicuous angelfish	55	50
668	30c. Moon wrasse	65	50
669	45c. Wide-striped clownfish	75	50
670	50c. Racoon butterflyfish	80	80
671	70c. Artooti (juvenile)	1·00	1·00
672	75c. Splendid hawkfish	1·00	1·00
673	85c. Scorpion fish	1·25	1·25
674	90c. Orange fairy basslet	1·25	1·25
675	$1 Sweetlips	1·25	1·25
676	$3 Moorish idol	2·75	3·50
677	$4 Gold-ribbon soapfish	3·25	4·25
MS678	110×85 mm. $1.20 Shark (29×39 mm)	1·50	2·00

Nos. 672 and 675 are incorrectly inscribed "Splendid Hawkefish" and "Sweetlip".

196 Hammer Throwing

1998. 16th Commonwealth Games, Kuala Lumpur.

679	**196**	75c. red and black	85	1·10
680	-	95c. violet and black	1·00	1·40
681	-	$1.05 mauve and black	1·10	1·50
MS682		80×100 mm. 85c. green and black	1·00	1·50

DESIGNS—HORIZ: 95c. Trap shooting. VERT: 85c. Flag bearer; $1.05, Lawn bowls.

197 "Norfolk" (sloop)

1998. Bicentenary of the Circumnavigation of Tasmania by George Bass and Matthew Flinders.

683	**197** 45c. multicoloured	1·90	1·25
MS684	101×69 mm. **197** $1.20 multicoloured	4·00	4·50

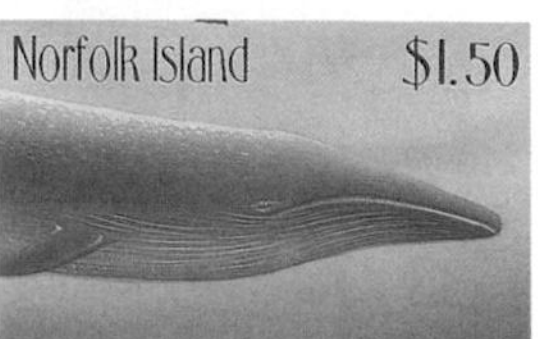

198 Blue whale

1998. Whales of the Southern Oceans (joint issue with Namibia and South Africa). Sheet 103×70 mm.

MS685	**198** $1.50 multicoloured	1·90	2·75

199 "Peace on Earth"

1998. Christmas. Multicoloured.

686	45c. Type **199**	55	50
687	75c. "Joy to the World"	85	80
688	$1.05 "A Season of Love"	1·25	1·75
689	$1.20 "Light of the World"	1·25	1·75

200 Short S.23 Sandringham (flying boat)

1999. Aircraft. Each red and green.

690	5c. Type **200**	30	45
691	5c. DC-4 "Norfolk Trader"	30	45

201 Soft Toy Rabbit

1999. Chinese New Year ("Year of the Rabbit"). Sheet 80×100 mm.

MS692	**201** 95c. multicoloured	1·00	1·75

202 Hull of "Resolution" under Construction

1999. "Australia '99" International Stamp Exhibition, Melbourne. Schooner "Resolution". Multicoloured.

693	45c. Type **202**	1·50	1·50
694	45c. After being launched	1·50	1·50
695	45c. In Emily Bay	1·50	1·50
696	45c. Off Cascade	1·50	1·50
697	45c. Alongside at Auckland	1·50	1·50

203 Pacific Black Duck

1999. "iBRA '99" International Stamp Exhibition, Nuremburg. Sheet 80×100 mm.

MS698	**203** $2.50 multicoloured	4·75	5·50

204 Solander's Petrel in Flight

1999. Endangered Species. Solander's Petrel ("Providence Petrel"). Multicoloured.

699	75c. Type **204**	2·25	1·50
700	$1.05 Head of Solander's petrel (horiz)	2·75	2·00
701	$1.20 Adult and fledgling (horiz)	3·00	3·00
MS702	130×90 mm. $4.50 Solander's petrel in flight (35×51 mm)	8·50	9·50

See also No. **MS**738.

205 "Cecile Brunner" Rose

1999. Roses. Multicoloured.

703	45c. Type **205**	60	40
704	75c. Green rose	85	90
705	$1.05 "David Buffett" rose	1·25	1·75
MS706	60×81 mm. $1.20 "A Country Woman" Rose	1·40	2·00

No. **MS**706 also commemorates the 50th anniversary of the Country Women's Association on Norfolk Island.

1999. "China '99" International Stamp Exhibition, Beijing. No. MS692 with "China '99" logo optd on the margin in red.

MS707	80×100 mm. 95c. Type **201**	1·75	2·25

206 Pottery

1999. Handicrafts of Norfolk Island. Multicoloured.

708	45c. Type **206**	70	70
709	45c. Woodcarving	70	70
710	75c. Quilting	1·25	1·25
711	$1.05 Basket-weaving	1·50	2·00

206a Inspecting Bomb Damage, Buckingham Palace, 1940

1999. "Queen Elizabeth the Queen Mother's Century". Multicoloured (except $1.20).

712	45c. Type **206a**	70	70
713	45c. At Abergeldy Castle sale of work, 1955	70	70
714	75c. Queen Mother, Queen Elizabeth and Prince William, 1994	95	95
715	$1.20 Inspecting the King's Regiment (black)	1·50	1·75
MS716	145×70 mm. $3 Queen Elizabeth, 1937, and Amy Johnson's flight to Australia, 1930	3·50	3·75

207 Bishop George Augustus Selwyn

1999. Christmas. 150th Anniv of Melanesian Mission. Multicoloured (except 75c.).

717	45c. Type **207**	1·50	1·75
718	45c. Bishop John Coleridge Patteson	1·50	1·75
719	75c. "150 YEARS MELANESIAN MISSION" (black)	1·75	1·90
720	$1.05 Stained-glass windows	2·00	2·25
721	$1.20 "Southern Cross" (missionary ship) and religious symbols	2·25	2·50

Nos. 717/21 were printed together, se-tenant, with the backgrounds forming a composite design.

208 Basket of Food (Thanksgiving)

2000. Festivals.

722	**208**	5c. black and blue	20	30
723	-	5c. black and blue	20	30

DESIGN: No. 723, Musician playing guitar (Country Music Festival).

209 Dragon

2000. Chinese New Year ("Year of the Dragon"). Sheet 106×86 mm.

MS724	**209** $2 multicoloured	1·75	2·50

210 Domestic Goose

2000. Ducks and Geese. Multicoloured.

725	45c. Type **210**	1·00	70
726	75c. Pacific black duck	1·75	1·25
727	$1.05 Mallard drake	2·00	2·25
728	$1.20 Aylesbury duck	2·00	2·25

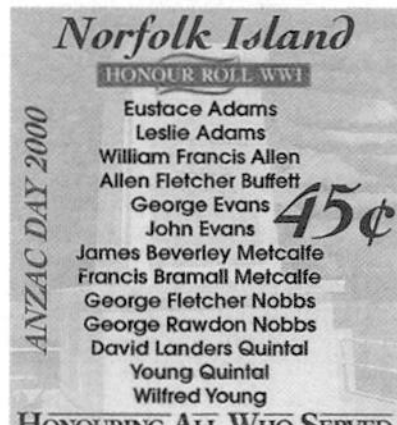

211 Honour Roll for First World War

2000. Anzac Day. Multicoloured.

729	45c. Type **211**	1·25	1·00
730	75c. Honour rolls for Second World War and Korea	1·75	1·75

212 Young Boy, Shipwright and Whaleboat

2000. "Whaler Project 2000". Two sheets, each 96×76 mm, containing T 212. Multicoloured.

MS731	**212** $4 multicoloured	6·50	7·50
MS732	$4 mult ("THE STAMP SHOW 2000" and Crown Agents logos added in gold) Imperf	7·00	8·00

213 Captain William Bligh and Bounty

2000. "Bounty" Day. Multicoloured.

733	45c. Type **213**	1·75	1·00
734	75c. Fletcher Christian and Tahiti	2·00	1·75

214 Turtle

2000. 8th Festival of Pacific Arts, New Caledonia. Multicoloured. (a) Size 24×29 mm. Self-adhesive.

735	45c. Urn and swat	1·50	1·00

(b) Sheet 130×70 mm.

MS736	75c. Type **214**; $1.05 Traditional mosaic; $1.20 Mask and spearhead; $2 Decorated utensils	7·00	6·50

215 Malcolm Champion (Olympic Gold Medal Winner, Stockholm, 1912)

2000. "Olymphilex 2000" International Stamp Exhibition, Sydney. Sheet 120×70 mm.

MS737	**215** $3 multicoloured	6·00	5·00

2000. "Canpex 2000" National Stamp Exhibition, Christchurch, New Zealand. Sheet 120×90 mm.

MS738	$2.40 No. 701×2	5·50	4·50

216 Sun over Pines

2000. Christmas. Multicoloured.

739	45c. Type **216**	1·25	45
740	75c. Candle over pines	1·75	80
741	$1.05 Moon over pines	2·25	2·00
742	$1.20 Star over pines	2·50	2·50

217 "Norfolk Island in 1825 and 2001" (Jessica Wong and Mardi Pye)

2000. New Millennium. Children's drawings. Mult.

743	45c. Type **217**	1·60	1·25
744	45c. "Seabirds over Norfolk Island" (Roxanne Spreag)	1·60	1·25
745	75c. "Trees and Clothes" (Tara Grube)	2·50	2·00
746	75c. "Underwater Scene" (Thomas Greenwood)	2·50	2·00

218 Red-fronted Parakeet ("Green Parrot")

2001. Green Parrot.

747	**218**	5c. red and green	30	55

219 Purple Swamphen

2001. Chinese New Year "Year of the Snake" and International Stamp Exhibition, Hong Kong.

No.	Type	Description	Unused	Used
748	**219**	45c. multicoloured	2·00	1·75
MS749		110×70 mm. $2.30 Norfolk Island eel and purple swamphen (as Type **219**, but without country inscr and face value). Imperf	3·25	3·75

220 "Old Clothes"

2001. Centenary of Australian Federation. Cartoons from The Bulletin Magazine. Multicoloured.

No.	Description	Unused	Used
750	45c. Type **220**	65	70
751	45c. "Tower of Babel"	65	70
752	45c. "The Political Garotters"	65	70
753	45c. "Promises, Promises!"	65	70
754	45c. "The Gout of Federation"	65	70
755	45c. "The Federal Spirit"	65	70
756	75c. "Australia Faces the Dawn"	80	90
757	$1.05 "The Federal Capital Question"	1·00	1·40
758	$1.20 "The Imperial Fowl-Yard"	1·10	1·50

221 Satellite over China

2001. Invercargill "Stamp Odyssey 2001" National Stamp Exhibition, New Zealand. Sheet, 136×105 mm, containing T 221 and similar vert designs. Multicoloured.

No.	Description	Unused	Used
MS759	75c. Type **221**; 75c. Satellite over Pacific; 75c. Satellite over Australia	3·00	3·00

222 Woman and Child in Victorian Dress

2001. Bounty Day.

No.	Type	Description	Unused	Used
760	**222**	5c. black and green	20	30

223 *Jasminium simplicifolium*

2001. Perfume from Norfolk Island. Multicoloured.

No.	Description	Unused	Used
761	45c. Type **223**	60	35
762	75c. Girl's face in perfume bottle	80	70
763	$1.05 Girl and roses	1·00	1·10
764	$1.20 Taylor's Road, Norfolk Island	1·10	1·25
765	$1.50 Couple shopping for perfume	1·25	1·50
MS766	145×98 mm. $3 Girl and perfume bottle ("NORFOLK ISLAND" in two lines) (60×72 mm)	3·00	3·50

Nos. 761/5 were printed on paper impregnated with the Jasmine fragrance.

224 Whaleboat

2001. Local Boats. Multicoloured.

No.	Description	Unused	Used
768	45c. Type **224**	1·00	50
769	$1 Motor launch	2·00	1·90
770	$1 Family rowing boat (horiz)	2·00	1·90
771	$1.50 Sailing cutter (horiz)	2·25	2·25

No. 768 also comes self-adhesive.

225 Australian Soldiers playing Cards

2001. Centenary of Australian Army. B.C.O.F. Japan.

No.	Type	Description	Unused	Used
773	**225**	45c. brown and blue	1·10	1·10
774	-	45c. brown and blue	1·10	1·10
775	-	$1 brown and green	2·50	1·90
776	-	$1 brown and green	2·50	1·90

DESIGNS: No. 774, Christmas float; 775, Birthday cake; 776, Australian military policeman directing traffic.

226 Miamiti (cartoon owl) holding Island Flag

2001. 6th South Pacific Mini Games (1st issue).

No.	Type	Description	Unused	Used
777	**226**	10c. brown and green	35	35

See also Nos. 794/5.

227 Strawberry Guava

2001. Christmas. Island Plants. Each incorporating carol music. Multicoloured.

No.	Description	Unused	Used
778	45c. Type **227**	1·00	75
779	45c. Poinsettia	1·00	75
780	$1 Christmas croton	1·75	1·50
781	$1 Hibiscus	1·75	1·50
782	$1.50 Indian shot	2·25	2·25

No. 779 is inscribed "Pointsettia" in error.

228 Sacred Kingfisher

2002. "Nuffka" (Sacred Kingfisher).

No.	Type	Description	Unused	Used
783	**228**	10c. deep blue and blue	50	55

229 Red-tailed Tropic Bird

2002. Cliff Ecology. Multicoloured.

No.	Description	Unused	Used
784	45c. Type **229**	1·25	60
785	$1 White oak blossom	2·25	2·00
786	$1 White oak tree	2·25	2·00
787	$1.50 Eagle ray	2·50	2·50

229a Elizabeth Duchess of York with Princesses Elizabeth and Margaret, 1930

2002. Golden Jubilee.

No.	Type	Description	Unused	Used
788	**229a**	45c. black, red and gold	1·00	50
789	-	75c. multicoloured	1·25	90
790	-	$1 black, red and gold	1·50	1·25
791	-	$1.50 multicoloured	2·25	2·25
MS792		162×95 mm. Nos. 788/91 and $3 multicoloured	6·50	7·50

DESIGNS:—HORIZ: 75c. Queen Elizabeth in multicoloured hat, 1977; $1 Queen Elizabeth wearing Imperial State Crown, Coronation 1953; $1.50, Queen Elizabeth at Windsor Horse Show, 2000. VERT (38×51 mm)— $3 Queen Elizabeth after Annigoni.

Designs as Nos. 788/91 in No. **MS**792 omit the gold frame around each stamp and the "Golden Jubilee 1952-2002" inscription.

230 Derelict Steam Engine

2002. Restoration of Yeaman's Mill Steam Engine.

No.	Type	Description	Unused	Used
793	**230**	$4.50 multicoloured	8·00	7·50

231 Miamiti (cartoon owl) running

2002. 6th South Pacific Mini Games (2nd issue). Multicoloured.

No.	Description	Unused	Used
794	50c. Type **231**	1·50	75
795	$1.50 Miamiti playing tennis	2·75	3·00

232 Lawn Bowls Player

2002. Bounty Bowls Tournament.

No.	Type	Description	Unused	Used
796	**232**	10c. black and green	30	30

233 *Streblorrhiza speciosa*

2002. Phillip Island Flowers. Multicoloured.

No.	Description	Unused	Used
797	10c. Type **233**	30	40
798	20c. *Plumbago zeylanica*	35	20
799	30c. *Canavalia rosea*	55	30
800	40c. *Ipomea pes-caprae*	55	45
801	45c. *Hibiscus insularis*	60	45
802	50c. *Solanum laciniatum*	1·00	45
803	95c. *Phormium tenax*	1·00	1·00
804	$1 *Lobelia anceps*	1·25	1·00
805	$1.50 *Carpobrotus glaucescens*	2·50	2·25
806	$2 *Abutilon julianae*	2·50	2·75
807	$3 *Wollastonia biflora*	3·50	3·25
808	$5 *Oxalis corniculata*	6·00	6·50

No. 797 is inscribed "specioca" in error.

234 Running

2002. 17th Commonwealth Games, Manchester. Multicoloured.

No.	Description	Unused	Used
809	10c. Type **234**	45	50
810	45c. Cycling (horiz)	2·50	70
811	$1 Lawn bowls	1·75	1·50
812	$1.50 Shooting (horiz)	2·50	2·50

235 Adult Sperm Whale and Calf

2002. Norfolk Island—New Caledonia Joint Issue. Operation Cetaces (marine mammal study). Multicoloured.

No.	Description	Unused	Used
813	$1 Type **235**	2·25	1·75
814	$1 Sperm whale attacked by giant squid	2·25	1·75

A similar set was issued by New Caledonia.

236 White Tern incubating Egg

2002. Christmas. White Tern. Multicoloured.

No.	Description	Unused	Used
815	45c. Type **236**	1·25	80
816	45c. White tern chick	1·25	80
817	$1 Two White terns in flight	2·00	1·40
818	$1.50 White tern landing	2·75	3·00

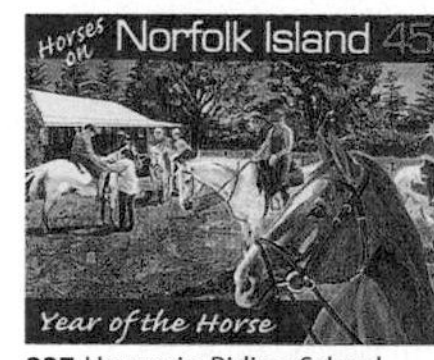

237 Horses in Riding School

2003. Horses on Norfolk Island. Multicoloured.

No.	Description	Unused	Used
819	45c. Type **237**	1·10	1·00
820	45c. Mares and foals in paddock	1·10	1·00
821	45c. Showjumpers	1·10	1·00
822	75c. Racehorses	1·40	1·40
823	75c. Draught horses	1·40	1·40

238 Old Warehouse Buildings at Seashore

2003. Photographic Scenes of Norfolk Island (1st series). Multicoloured.

No.	Description	Unused	Used
824	50c. Type **238**	1·25	60
825	95c. Beached boat (with rainbow markings) and sandy shore	2·00	1·50
826	$1.10 Grazing cattle and pine trees	2·25	1·60
827	$1.65 Sandy shore and headland with single pine tree	3·25	3·00

See also Nos. 859/62.

239 "Southern Prize"

2003. Day Lilies. Multicoloured.

No.	Description	Unused	Used
828	50c. Type **239**	65	70
829	50c. "Becky Stone"	65	70
830	50c. "Cameroons"	65	70
831	50c. "Chinese Autumn"	65	70
832	50c. "Scarlet Orbit"	65	70

833 50c. "Ocean Rain" 65 70
834 50c. "Gingerbread Man" 65 70
835 50c. "Pink Corduroy" 65 70
836 50c. "Elizabeth Hinrichsen" 65 70
837 50c. "Simply Pretty" 65 70

240 Maeve and Gil Hitch

2003. 1st Norfolk Island Writer's Festival. Black, violet and lilac (Nos. 838/9 and 844/5) or multicoloured (Nos. 840/3).
838 10c. Type **240** 60 30
839 10c. Alice Buffett 60 70
840 10c. Nan Smith 60 70
841 10c. Archie Bigg 60 70
842 50c. Colleen McCullough 60 70
843 50c. Peter Clarke 60 70
844 50c. Bob Tofts 60 70
845 50c. Merval Hoare 60 70

241 Seashore with Trees and Stream

2004. Island Landscapes. Multicoloured.
846 50c. Type **241** 1·40 1·25
847 50c. Sandy shore with wooden post and small boat 1·40 1·25
848 50c. Rocky bay with pine trees on headland 1·40 1·25
849 50c. Grazing cattle, pine trees and ruined building 1·40 1·25

242 Queen Elizabeth II wearing Imperial State Crown

2003. 50th Anniv of Coronation.
MS850 115×85 mm. 10c. Type **242** (black, deep violet and violet); $3 Queen wearing flowered hat and dress (multicoloured) 4·50 5·00

243 Globe ("Peace on Earth")

2003. Christmas. Multicoloured.
851 50c. Type **243** 1·25 75
852 50c. Bird and rainbow ("Joy to the World") 1·25 75
853 $1.10 Heart-shaped Christmas present ("Give the gift of Love") 2·25 1·50
854 $1.65 Candle ("Trust in Faith") 3·00 3·75

244 De Havilland D.H.60G Gipsy Moth Floatplane (first aircraft at Norfolk Island, 1931)

2003. Centenary of Powered Flight. Multicoloured (except Type 244).
855 50c. Type **244** (black, brown and violet) 1·50 70
856 $1.10 Boeing 737 (Norfolk Island–Australia service) 2·50 1·50
857 $1.65 Douglas DC-4 (passenger service 1949–977) 3·75 3·75
MS858 110×83 mm. $1.65 Wright *Flyer I*, 1903 (47×29 mm) 4·50 4·00

245 Timbers from Prow of Boat and Houses

2004. Photographic Scenes of Norfolk Island (2nd series). Multicoloured.
859 50c. Type **245** 1·25 70
860 95c. Waterfall 2·25 1·50
861 $1.10 Cattle and pine trees 2·25 1·60
862 $1.65 Beach and headland at sunset 3·50 3·50

246 Whale Shark

2004. Sharks. Multicoloured.
863 10c. Type **246** 55 60
864 50c. Hammerhead shark 1·50 50
865 $1.10 Tiger shark 2·75 1·60
866 $1.65 Bronze whaler shark 4·00 3·25

247 Golden Orb Spider

2004. Spiders. Multicoloured.
867 50c. Type **247** 1·00 75
868 50c. Community spider 1·00 75
869 $1 St. Andrews Cross 1·60 1·40
870 $1.65 Red-horned spider 2·50 3·00
MS871 120×80 mm. $1.50 Red-horned spider (48×40 mm) 2·50 3·00

248 Loading Cargo into Light Craft

2004. Werken Dar Shep. Multicoloured.
872 50c. Type **248** 1·00 60
873 $1.10 Transporting cargo 1·75 1·50
874 $1.65 Two light craft 2·25 3·00
MS875 130×85 mm. $1.65 Craft moored alongside dock 3·00 3·25

249 Apple Blossom

2004. Hippeastrums. Multicoloured.
876 50c. Type **249** 80 85
877 50c. Carnival 80 85
878 50c. Cherry blossom 80 85
879 50c. Lilac wonder 80 85
880 50c. Millennium star 80 85
881 50c. Cocktail 80 85
882 50c. Milady 80 85
883 50c. Pacific sunset 80 85
884 50c. Geisha girl 80 85
885 50c. Lady Jane 80 85

250 Three Children

2004. 25th Anniv of Quota International (humanitarian organisation). Sheet 135×73 mm containing T 250 and similar horiz designs. Multicoloured.
MS886 50c. Type **250**; $1.10 Feet painted with "WE CARE"; $1.65 Boy drawing "Quota" in sand 5·00 5·00

2004. Perfume from Norfolk Island. Special Edition. No. MS766 optd with SPECIAL EDITION.
MS887 145×98 mm. $3 Girl and perfume bottle 3·00 3·75

252 Tree and "Twas the Night Before Christmas"

2004. Christmas. Designs showing Christmas tree and excerpt of carol.
890 **252** 50c. green and silver 75 70
891 - 50c. lilac and silver 75 70
892 - $1.10 carmine and silver 1·50 1·40
893 - $1.65 orange and silver 2·25 3·00
DESIGNS: No. 890, Type **252**; 891, "Silent Night"; 892, "Twelve Days of Christmas"; 893, "Oh Holy Night".

253 Sacred Kingfisher

2004. Sacred Kingfisher. Multicoloured.
894 50c. Type **253** 1·10 75
895 50c. Two sacred kingfishers 1·10 75
896 $1 Sacred kingfisher perched 2·00 1·60
897 $2 Sacred kingfisher from back 3·75 4·25
MS898 130×158 mm. Nos. 894/7, each ×2 13·00 16·00

251 Tree Fern

2004. Norfolk Island Palm and Fern.
888 **251** 10c. green and black 20 30
889 - 10c. yellow and black 20 30
DESIGNS: No. 888, Type **251**; 889, Palm.

254 Coat of Arms and Flag

2004. 25th Anniv of Self-Government.
899 **254** $5 multicoloured 6·25 7·50

255 Boat Race

2005. Centenary of Rotary International (humanitarian organisation). Multicoloured.
900 50c. Type **255** 75 75
901 50c. Tree planting (vert) 75 75
902 $1.20 Paul Harris (founder) 1·50 1·40
903 $1.80 Rotary Youth Leadership Awards (vert) 2·25 2·75
MS904 110×80 mm. $2 District 9910 (Rotary community) 3·00 3·75

256 Tea Cup, 1856

2005. Norfolk Island Museum, Kingston. Multicoloured.
905 50c. Type **256** 1·00 65
906 50c. Salt cellar from HMS *Bounty*, 1856 1·00 65
907 $1.10 Medicine cups, 1825–55 1·75 1·40
908 $1.65 Stoneware jar, 1825–55 2·50 2·75

257 Polynesian Explorer and Voyaging Canoe

2005. Pacific Explorers. Multicoloured.
909 50c. Type **257** 70 50
910 $1.20 *Vitoria* (Magellan) 1·60 1·60
911 $1.80 Captain Cook ashore at Norfolk Island and HMS *Resolution* 2·40 2·75
MS912 140×85 mm. $2 Early map of Pacific (45×31 mm) 2·75 3·00

No. **MS**912 also commemorates Pacific Explorer 2005 World Stamp Expo, Sydney.

258 Branka House

2005. Old Island Houses. Multicoloured.
913 50c. Type **258** 60 55
914 50c. Greenacres 60 55
915 $1.20 Ma Annas 1·40 1·40
916 $1.80 Naumai 2·00 2·75

259 Red-tailed Tropic Bird

2005. Seabirds of Norfolk Island. Multicoloured.
917 10c. Type **259** 15 20
918 25c. White tern 30 35
919 40c. Sooty tern 50 40
920 50c. Australasian gannet 60 40
921 70c. Black-winged petrel 75 65
922 $1 Black noddy 1·10 1·10
923 $1.50 Grey ternlet 1·50 1·25
924 $2 Masked booby 2·00 2·25
925 $3 Wedge-tailed shearwater 3·00 3·25
926 $5 White-necked petrel 5·50 5·75
MS927 (a) 65×90 mm. $2.50 Sooty tern in flight. (b) 100×70 mm. $4 Red-tailed tropic bird (horiz). Set of 2 sheets 9·00 6·75

260 "Marjory Brown"

2005. Hibiscus Varieties. Multicoloured.

928	50c. Type **260**	60	70
929	50c. "Aloha"	60	70
930	50c. "Pulau Tree"	60	70
931	50c. "Ann Miller"	60	70
932	50c. "Surfrider"	60	70
933	50c. "Philip Island"	60	70
934	50c. "Rose of Sharon"	60	70
935	50c. "D. J. O'Brien"	60	70
936	50c. "Elaine's Pride"	60	70
937	50c. "Castle White"	60	70
938	50c. Skeleton Hibiscus	60	70
939	50c. "Pink Sunset"	60	70

261 Anson Bay

2005. Christmas. Multicoloured.

940	50c. Type **261**	75	40
941	$1.20 Cascade Bay	1·60	1·40
942	$1.80 Ball Bay	2·25	3·00

262 Drummer

2005. Norfolk Island Jazz Festival. Multicoloured.

943	50c. Type **262**	75	50
944	$1.20 Saxophone player	1·60	1·40
945	$1.80 Guitarist and pine tree	2·25	3·00

263 Baton and Norfolk Island Pines

2006. Commonwealth Games Queen's Baton Relay on Norfolk Island. Multicoloured.

946	$1.50 Type **263**	2·25	2·25
947	$1.50 Prow of ship and girl carrying baton	2·25	2·25

264 Shooting

2006. Commonwealth Games. Multicoloured.

948	50c. Type **264**	70	50
949	$1.50 Lawn bowls	1·50	1·50
950	$2 Squash	2·00	3·00

265 HMS *Bounty* at Portsmouth, 1789

2006. 150th Anniv of Migration of Pitcairn Islanders to Norfolk Island (1st issue). Departure from Pitcairn Island. Designs showing scenes from cyclorama on Norfolk Island depicting the "Bounty" story. Multicoloured.

951	50c. Type **265**	1·25	1·00
952	50c. Collecting breadfruit at Tahiti	1·25	1·00
953	$1.20 Capt. Bligh cast adrift in Bounty's launch	2·50	2·00
954	$1.50 Burning of HMS *Bounty* at Pitcairn Island	3·00	3·00
955	$1.80 Pitcairn Islanders arriving at Norfolk Island, 1856	3·25	3·25

266 Re-enactment Procession

2006. 150th Anniv of Migration of Pitcairn Islanders to Norfolk Island (2nd issue). Arrival on Norfolk Island. Designs showing Bounty Day re-enactment and celebrations. Multicoloured.

956	10c. Type **266**	60	60
957	30c. Laying wreath at war memorial	1·00	60
958	50c. Honouring ancestors	1·25	1·00
959	50c. Community picnic	1·25	1·00
960	$4 Bounty ball	7·00	7·50

267 Hat with Decorated Brim

2006. Traditional Hats. Multicoloured.

961	50c. Type **267** (blue)	1·25	1·10
962	50c. Hat with pale woven band (blue)	1·25	1·10
963	50c. Hat with flowers on brim (green)	1·25	1·10
964	50c. Plain hat (green)	1·25	1·10
965	50c. Hat with white decoration around brim (violet)	1·25	1·10
966	50c. Plain hat (different) (violet)	1·25	1·10

268 "Wal"

2006. Dogs of Norfolk Island ("Year of the Dog"). Multicoloured.

967	10c. Type **268**	70	55
968	50c. "Axel"	1·50	75
969	$1 "Wag"	2·25	1·40
970	$2.65 "Gemma"	6·00	5·50

269 Norfolk Island Central School, Middlegate, c. 1906

2006. Centenary of Norfolk Island Central School, Middlegate. Multicoloured.

971	$2 Type **269**	5·50	4·75
972	$2 Norfolk Island Central School, Middlegate, 2006	5·50	4·75

270 Adult and Juvenile Boobies enclosed in Bauble

2006. Christmas. Multicoloured.

973	50c. Type **270**	1·25	80
974	50c. Prow of boat and houses in bauble and fish decoration	1·25	80
975	$1.20 Old Military Barracks, Kingston, in bauble and star decoration	2·50	1·60
976	$1.80 Hibiscus flower in bauble and bird decoration	3·75	3·25

271 *Lantana camara*

2007. Weed Flowers. Multicoloured.

977	50c. Type **271**	1·25	90
978	50c. *Ageratina riparia* (Crofton weed)	1·25	90
979	$1.20 *Ipomoea cairica* (morning glory)	2·50	1·75
980	$1.80 *Solanum mauritianum* (wild tobacco)	3·75	3·25

272 Sea Kayaking

2007. Adventure Sports. Multicoloured.

981	50c. Type **272**	1·25	90
982	50c. Wind surfing	1·25	90
983	$1.20 Mountain biking	2·50	1·75
984	$1.80 Surfing	3·75	3·25

273 Kentia Palms

2007. Kentia Palm Seed Harvest. Sheet 82×82 mm containing T 273 and similar multicoloured designs and one label.

MS985	50c. Type **273**; 50c. Dog guarding buckets of palm seeds (horiz); 50c. Emptying bucket into wooden crates (horiz); 50c. Kentia palm tree laden with seeds	4·25	4·00

274 The Violin Teacher and Government House

2007. Ghosts of Norfolk Island. Multicoloured.

986	10c. Type **274**	35	40
987	50c. Ghosts in graveyard	1·25	75
988	$1 Emily (lady in white) at Kingston Pier	2·50	1·75
989	$1.80 Officer on guard at entrance to Barracks	3·75	3·25

275 Queen Victoria

2007. 120th Anniv of Queen Victoria Scholarship at Norfolk Island Central School. Self-adhesive.

990	**275**	10c. multicoloured	30	35
991	**275**	$5 multicoloured (25×32 mm)	11·00	8·50

276 Squash player

2007. South Pacific Games, Samoa. Multicoloured.

992	50c. Type **276**	1·00	75
993	$1 Golf	1·75	1·40
994	$1.20 Netball player	1·75	1·75
995	$1.80 Athlete running	2·75	3·25
MS996	115×90 mm. $2 Emblem	3·00	3·00

277 HMS *Sirius* and *Supply* off Kingston

2007. Bicentenary of Transfer of First Convict Settlement to Tasmania. Multicoloured.

997	10c. Type **277**	40	30
998	50c. Shipping Signal, Kingston	1·25	75
999	$1.20 First Settlement, Kingston	2·50	1·75
1000	$1.80 *Lady Nelson* leaving for Tasmania, 1807	3·75	3·25

278 Two Children ('friendship')

2007. 30th Anniv of Banyan Park Play Centre. Multicoloured.

1001	50c. Type **278**	1·25	75
1002	$1 Four children ('Community')	2·00	1·40
1003	$1.20 Three children playing ('Play grow learn together')	2·25	1·60
1004	$1.80 Two children reading book ('read books')	3·75	2·75

279 Young Norfolk Island Pine

2007. Christmas. 'Fairy Lights'. Multicoloured.

1005	10c. Type **279**	1·25	75
1006	$1.20 Back of Melanesian Chapel	2·50	1·60
1007	$1.80 Old lighter on Kingston foreshore	3·75	2·50

280 Ford Falcon XP, 1965

2008. Classic Cars. Each showing car and photograph of Norfolk Island scene. Multicoloured.

1008	50c. Type **280**	1·25	75
1009	$1 Chevrolet Styleline, 1952	2·25	1·40
1010	$1.20 Pontiac Silver Arrow, 1953	2·50	1·75
1011	$1.80 Rolls Royce Silver Shadow, 1971	3·75	3·50

281 Andre Nobbs

2008. Faces of Norfolk Island. Portraits by Adam Jauczius. Multicoloured.

1012	50c. Type **281**	1·00	75
1013	$1 Darlene Buffett	1·75	1·40
1014	$1.20 Colin Lindsay Buffett ('Boonie')	1·90	1·60
1015	$1.80 Tania Grube and her baby son	2·75	2·75

282 Limousin Cross Calf

2008. Calves. Multicoloured.

1016	50c. Type **282**	1·00	75
1017	$1 Murray Grey	1·90	1·40
1018	$1.20 Poll Hereford	2·00	1·60
1019	$1.80 Brahman cross	2·75	2·75

283 Gravestone

2008. A Jewish Resting Place

1020	**283**	50c. multicoloured	1·25	75
1021	–	$1.20 multicoloured	2·25	1·75
1022	–	$1.80 multicoloured	3·00	3·25

2008. Israel 2008 World Stamp Championship, Tel-Aviv. Sheet 103×80 mm containing stamp as T **283** but 30×40 mm, optd World Championship Israel 2008 Tel-Aviv 14–21 May and emblem on right-hand sheet margin.

MS1023 Jewish gravestone	5·00	3·50

284 Past and Present Members

2008. 25th Anniv of St. John's Ambulance in Norfolk Island. Multicoloured.

1024	30c. Type **284**	75	45
1025	40c. Re-enactment: putting casualty in recovery position	90	60
1026	95c. Re-enactment: loading casualty into ambulance	2·25	1·50
1027	$4 Re-enactment: taking casualty into hospital	7·25	6·25

285 Netted Brakefern

2008. Rare Ferns. Multicoloured.

1028	20c. Type **285**	70	30
1029	20c. *Pteris zahlbruckneriana*	70	30
1030	50c. Robinsonia	1·25	75
1031	50c. *Asplenium australasicum f. robinsonii*	1·25	75
1032	80c. Hanging fork fern	1·75	1·25
1033	80c. *Tmesipteris norfolkensis*	1·75	1·25
1034	$2 King fern	3·50	2·75
1035	$2 *Marattia salicina*	3·50	2·75

286 *Norfolk* (sloop), 1798

2008. Ships built on Norfolk Island. Multicoloured.

1036	50c. Type **286**	1·25	75
1037	$1.20 *Resolution* (schooner), 1925	2·50	1·75
1038	$1.80 *Endeavour* (schooner), 1808	3·50	2·50

287 Royal Engineers Cottage, Store and Guard Houses from Second Settlement

2008. 'Isles of Exile'. Multicoloured.

1039	25c. Type **287**	60	35
1040	55c. Commissariat Stores	1·25	80
1041	$1.75 Cemetery	3·25	2·50
1042	$2.50 Aerial view of Pentagonal Gaol from the Second Settlement	4·75	3·25

288 Child at Prayer

2008. Christmas. Multicoloured.

1043	55c. Type **288**	1·25	80
1044	$1.40 Virgin Mary and baby Jesus	2·75	2·00
1045	$2.05 Three Magi carrying gifts	4·25	2·75

289 Fish Mosaic

2009. Norfolk Island Mosaics. Multicoloured. (a) Ordinary gum.

1046	5c. Type **289**	15	10
1047	15c. Lily	35	25
1048	55c. Red-tailed tropic bird	1·00	85
1049	$1.40 Tree	3·25	2·10

(b) Self-adhesive.

1050	15c. Sea turtle (Jasmine Kiernan)	25	25
1051	15c. Starfish on urn (Jeannie Sheridan)	25	25

2009. Norfolk Island Cattle (2nd series). Cattle Breeds. As T 282. Multicoloured.

1052	15c. Shorthorn	25	25
1053	55c. South Devon	1·00	85
1054	$1.40 Norfolk Blue	2·50	2·25
1055	$2.05 Lincoln Red	3·50	3·25
MS1056	110×84 mm. $5 Young cattle in pasture	8·00	8·00

290 *Gyrodon* sp.

2009. Fungi of Norfolk Island. Multicoloured.

1057	15c. Type **290**	25	25
1058	55c. *Stereum ostrea*	1·00	85
1059	$1.40 *Cymatoderma elegans* var *lamellatum*	2·50	2·25
1060	$2.05 *Chlorophyllum molybdites*	3·50	3·25
MS1061	130×71 mm. Nos. 1057/60	6·50	6·50

291 Bridled Nailtail Wallaby

2009. Species at Risk. Multicoloured.

1062	55c. Type **291**	1·40	95
1063	55c. Norfolk Island green parrot	1·40	95
1064	55c. Subantarctic fur seal	1·40	95
1065	55c. Christmas Island blue-tailed skink	1·40	95
1066	55c. Green turtle	1·40	95
MS1067	150×85 mm. Nos. 3247 and 3249/51 of Australia and No. 1063	5·75	5·75

Similar designs were issued by Australia.

No. **MS**1067 is identical to No. **MS**3252 of Australia. Nos. 1062/**MS**1067 of Norfolk Island and Nos. 3247/**MS**3252 of Australia were all issued on August 2010.

292 Grey Fantail

2009. Bush Birds. Multicoloured.

1068	15c. Type **292**	35	25
1069	55c. Pacific robin	1·10	90
1070	$1.40 Golden whistler	2·75	2·40
1071	$2.05 Sacred kingfisher	3·50	3·50

293 Children in Bounty Day Dress, Gavel, Handshake and Flags of Norfolk Island, Commonwealth Parliamentary Association and Australia

2009. 30th Anniv of Self-Government (Norfolk Island Legislative Assembly).

1072	**293**	$10 multicoloured	18·00	16·00

294 St. Mathew, St. Barnabas Chapel

2009. Christmas. Stained Glass Windows from St. Barnabas Chapel and All Saints Church. Multicoloured.

1073	15c. Type **294**	35	25
1074	50c. Rose window, St. Barnabas Chapel	1·10	85
1075	$1.45 Christ in Glory, All Saints Church, Kingston	2·75	2·50
1076	$2.10 Memorial window to missionaries at St. Barnabas Chapel	4·00	3·50

295 Pottery from Second Convict Settlement

2010. Artefacts from Norfolk Island's Museums. Multicoloured.

1077	5c. Type **295**	15	10
1078	55c. Polynesian ivory fish hook, c.1450	1·50	1·00
1079	$1.10 Regimental badge	2·10	1·40
1080	$1.45 Brass wall fitting from wreck of HMS *Sirius*	2·75	2·00
1081	$1.65 Bottles from Convict Settlement's hospital	3·25	2·75
1082	$2.10 The Bounty Ring	3·75	3·25

296 Pacific Jewel

2010. Cruise Ships to Norfolk Island. Multicoloured.

1083	55c. Type **296**	1·40	95
1084	$1.45 *Pacific Sun*	2·00	1·40
1085	$1.65 *Pacific Pearl*	3·25	2·75
1086	$1.75 *Pacific Dawn*	3·50	2·75
1087	$2.10 RMS *Strathaird*	4·25	3·50

297 Pitcairn Island Girls on Norfolk Island, 1857

2010. 'They came aboard the *Morayshire*'. Multicoloured.

1088	55c. Type **297**	1·40	95
1089	$1.10 Pitcairn Islanders aboard the *Morayshire*, 1856	1·75	1·10
1090	$1.45 Pitcairn Island men on Norfolk Island, 1861	2·75	2·00
1091	$2.75 Naomi and Jane Nobbs	5·50	5·00

298 Blessing of the Boats

2010. History of Whaling in Norfolk Island. Multicoloured.

1092	60c. Type **298**	1·00	60
1093	60c. Launching boat from shore	1·00	60
1094	$1.20 Women on cliff tops burning fires to guide boats back to shore	2·25	1·75
1095	$3 Whale products	5·75	5·00

299 Crimson Rosella

2010. Christmas. Parrots. Multicoloured.

1096	15c. Type **299**	35	20
1097	55c. Crimson rosella and Norfolk Island green parrot	1·40	95
1098	60c. Norfolk Island green parrot and wrapped present	1·60	1·00
1099	$1.30 Crimson rosella with ribbon and bauble in beak	2·40	2·00

300 Bowler holding Trophy

2010. World Bowls Champion of Champions. Multicoloured.

1100	60c. Type **300**	1·40	95
1101	$1.50 Bowler	3·00	2·40
1102	$2.20 Bowls and jack	4·75	4·00

301 Construction of St. Barnabas Chapel, 1880

2010. 130th Anniv of St. Barnabas Chapel. Multicoloured.

MS1103 60c.×3 Type **301**; St. Barnabas Chapel and congregation; Chapel wall and builders	3·75	3·75

Pt. 1

NORTH BORNEO

A territory in the north of the Island of Borneo in the China Sea, formerly under the administration of the British North Borneo Company. A Crown Colony since 1946. Joined Malaysia in 1963 and renamed Sabah in 1964.

100 cents = 1 dollar (Malayan).

1

1883. "POSTAGE NORTH BORNEO" at top.

8	**1**	½c. mauve	£100	£180
9	**1**	1c. orange	£180	£325
10	**1**	2c. brown	38·00	32·00
11	**1**	4c. pink	17·00	50·00
12	**1**	8c. green	20·00	50·00
13	**1**	10c. blue	42·00	60·00

1883. Surch 8 Cents. vert.

2	8c. on 2c. brown	£1300	£800

1883. Surch EIGHT CENTS.

3	8c. on 2c. brown	£500	£190

Where there are three price columns, prices in the second column are for postally used stamps and those in the third column are for stamps cancelled with black bars.

4

5

1883. Inscr "NORTH BORNEO".

4	**4**	50c. violet	£170	£250	35·00
5	**5**	$1 red	£150	£225	16·00

For these designs with "BRITISH" in place of value in words at top, see Nos. 46/7.

1886. Optd and Revenue.

14	**1**	½c. mauve	£170	£250
15	**1**	10c. blue	£225	£275

1886. Surch in words and figures.

18	3c. on 4c. pink	£120	£130
19	5c. on 8c. green	£130	£130

9

10

13

19

1886. Inscr "BRITISH NORTH BORNEO".

22	**9**	½c. red	3·75	17·00	
24	**9**	1c. orange	2·00	13·00	
25	**9**	2c. brown	2·00	11·00	
26	**9**	4c. pink	4·50	17·00	
27	**9**	8c. green	27·00	26·00	
28	**9**	10c. blue	11·00	38·00	
45	**10**	25c. blue	80·00	85·00	75
46	-	50c. violet	£110	£130	75
47	-	$1 red	45·00	£110	75
48	**13**	$2 green	£180	£200	1·50
49	**19**	$5 purple	£325	£350	8·50
50	-	$10 brown	£325	£375	12·00

DESIGNS: 50c. As Type **4**; $1, As Type **5**. $10 As Type **19** but with different frame.

14

1888. Inscr "POSTAGE & REVENUE".

36b	**14**	½c. red	1·50	7·00	60
37	**14**	1c. orange	5·00	5·50	50
38b	**14**	2c. brown	6·00	22·00	50
39	**14**	3c. violet	2·50	12·00	50
40	**14**	4c. pink	10·00	42·00	50
41	**14**	5c. grey	2·75	27·00	50
42	**14**	6c. red	15·00	27·00	50
43a	**14**	8c. green	25·00	32·00	50
44b	**14**	10c. blue	6·50	21·00	50

1890. Surch in words.

51	**10**	2c. on 25c. blue	70·00	90·00
52	**10**	8c. on 25c. blue	95·00	£120

1891. Surch in figures and words.

63	**14**	1c. on 4c. pink	26·00	14·00
64	**14**	1c. on 5c. grey	7·00	6·00
54	**9**	6c. on 8c. green	£9000	£4500
55	**14**	6c. on 8c. green	25·00	10·00
56	**9**	6c. on 10c. blue	60·00	22·00
57	**14**	6c. on 10c. blue	£190	26·00
65	**10**	8c. on 25c. blue	£150	£160

24 Dyak Chief

25 Sambar Stag ("Cervus unicolor")

26 Sago Palm

27 Great Argus Pheasant

28 Arms of the Company

29 Malay Prau

30 Estuarine Crocodile

31 Mt. Kinabalu

32 Arms of the Company with Supporters

1894

66	**24**	1c. black and bistre	1·25	9·50	50
69	**25**	2c. black and red	5·50	4·25	50
70	**26**	3c. green and mauve	2·75	8·50	50
72	**27**	5c. black and red	14·00	11·00	60
73a	**28**	6c. black and brown	4·50	18·00	60
74	**29**	8c. black and lilac	6·50	11·00	60
75a	**30**	12c. black and blue	29·00	80·00	2·50
78	**31**	18c. black and green	28·00	50·00	2·00
79c	**32**	24c. blue and red	23·00	70·00	2·00

1894. As Nos. 47, etc, but inscr "THE STATE OF NORTH BORNEO".

81	25c. blue	9·00	30·00	1·00
82	50c. violet	42·00	60·00	2·00
83	$1 red	12·00	28·00	1·25
84	$2 green	23·00	75·00	2·50
85	$5 purple	£275	£325	16·00
86	$10 brown	£300	£350	15·00

1895. No. 83 surch in figures and words.

87	4 cents on $1 red	7·00	1·50	50
88	10 cents on $1 red	26·00	1·75	50
89	20 cents on $1 red	48·00	17·00	50
90	30 cents on $1 red	42·00	32·00	1·50
91	40 cents on $1 red	55·00	60·00	1·50

37 Orang-utan

41 Sun Bear

43 Borneo Steam Train

1897. As 1894 issue with insertion of native inscriptions.

92a	**24**	1c. black and bistre	11·00	2·75	40
94a	**25**	2c. black and red	25·00	1·50	40
95	**25**	2c. black and green	65·00	2·00	60
97	**26**	3c. green and mauve	25·00	3·00	50
98	**37**	4c. black and green	9·50	—	1·50
99	**37**	4c. black and red	40·00	10·00	50
100a	**27**	5c. black & orange	£110	2·00	70
101a	**28**	6c. black and brown	48·00	4·25	50
103	**29**	8c. black and brown	13·00	38·00	1·00
104	**41**	10c. brown and grey	£130	55·00	3·25
106b	**30**	12c. black and blue	£140	35·00	1·50
107	**43**	16c. green & brown	£130	90·00	3·25
108	**31**	18c. black and green	29·00	75·00	3·25
110b	**31**	18c. black & green*	£100	12·00	1·50
109	**32**	24c. blue and red*	26·00	90·00	3·25
111b	**32**	24c. blue and red*	48·00	55·00	3·00

*No. 110b is inscribed "POSTAGE & REVENUE" at the sides instead of "POSTAL REVENUE" as in No. 108. No. 111b has the words "POSTAGE & REVENUE" at the sides below the Arms; these words were omitted in No. 109.

1899. Stamps of 1897 and Nos. 81/6 surch 4 CENTS.

112a	4c. on 5c. black and orange	40·00	10·00
113	4c. on 6c. black and brown	19·00	24·00
114	4c. on 8c. black and lilac	16·00	10·00
115	4c. on 12c. black and blue	32·00	13·00
116	4c. on 18c. black and green (110)	17·00	14·00
117	4c. on 24c. blue and red (111)	35·00	18·00
118	4c. on 25c. blue	5·50	8·50
119	4c. on 50c. violet	21·00	16·00
121	4c. on $1 red	5·50	12·00
122	4c. on $2 green	5·50	13·00
125	4c. on $5 purple	7·00	16·00
126	4c. on $10 brown	7·00	16·00

1901. Stamps of 1897 and Nos. 81/6 optd BRITISH PROTECTORATE.

127a	1c. black and bistre	2·50	1·75	30
128	2c. black and green	5·50	1·00	30
129	3c. green and mauve	1·75	5·50	30
130	4c. black and red	9·00	1·00	30
131a	5c. black and orange	14·00	2·75	30
132b	6c. black and brown	4·00	15·00	70
133	8c. black and lilac	4·25	3·75	50
134	10c. brown and grey	80·00	5·00	1·00
135	12c. black and blue	60·00	12·00	1·50
136	16c. green and brown	£170	35·00	2·25
137	18c. black & green (110b)	15·00	25·00	1·25
138	24c. blue and red (111b)	16·00	40·00	1·50
139	25c. blue	2·00	10·00	50
140	50c. violet	2·75	11·00	55
142	$1 red	6·50	38·00	2·00
143	$2 green	38·00	£100	2·75
144	$5 purple (with full point)	£325	£500	9·00
184	$5 purple (without full point)	£1300	£1500	9·50
145	$10 brown (with full point)	£550	£850	11·00
185	$10 brown (without full point)	£1800	—	9·50

1904. Stamps of 1897 and Nos. 81/6 surch 4 cents.

146	4c. on 5c. blk & orge	50·00	55·00	12·00
147	4c. on 6c. black & brn	7·00	21·00	12·00
148	4c. on 8c. blk & lilac	16·00	26·00	12·00
149	4c. on 12c. black & bl	40·00	40·00	12·00
150	4c. on 18c. black and green (110b)	14·00	38·00	12·00
151a	4c. on 24c. bl & red (111b)	20·00	50·00	12·00
152	4c. on 25c. blue	4·75	25·00	12·00
153	4c. on 50c. violet	5·50	38·00	12·00
154	4c. on $1 red	6·00	48·00	12·00
155	4c. on $2 green	6·00	48·00	12·00
156	4c. on $5 purple	12·00	48·00	12·00
157	4c. on $10 brown	12·00	48·00	12·00

51 Malayan Tapir

52 Traveller's Tree

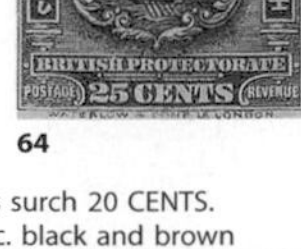
64

1909. No. 177 is surch 20 CENTS.

277	**51**	1c. black and brown	1·00	70	
160	**52**	2c. black and green	1·00	70	30
278	**52**	2c. black and red	85	60	
162	-	3c. black and red	3·25	2·75	50
279	-	3c. black and green	3·00	75	
280	-	4c. black and red	50	10	
281	-	5c. black and brown	6·00	2·75	
282	-	6c. black and green	10·00	90	
283	-	8c. black and red	4·75	50	
284	-	10c. black and blue	4·25	90	
285	-	12c. black and blue	24·00	80	
174	-	16c. black and brown	26·00	7·00	1·00
175	-	18c. black and green	£130	32·00	1·00
177	-	20c. on 18c. blk & grn	7·00	1·00	30
176	-	24c. black and mauve	28·00	3·50	1·75
289	**64**	25c. black and green	16·00	4·25	
179	-	50c. black and blue	18·00	5·50	2·25
180	-	$1 black and brown	18·00	4·00	4·00
181	-	$2 black and lilac	75·00	17·00	5·50
182	-	$5 black and red	£160	£130	32·00
183	-	$10 black and orange	£550	£600	95·00

DESIGNS—As T **51**: 3c. Jesselton railway station; 4c. Sultan of Sulu, his staff and W. C. Cowie, first Chairman of the Company; 5c. Asiatic elephant; 8c. Ploughing with buffalo; 24c. Dwarf cassowary. As T **52**: 6c. Sumatran rhinoceros; 10c. Wild boar; 12c. Palm cockatoo; 16 c Rhinoceros hornbill; 18 c Banteng. As T **64** but Arms with supporters: $5, $10.

1916. Stamps of 1909 surch.

186	2c. on 3c. black and red	30·00	15·00
187	4c. on 6c. black and olive	30·00	21·00
188	10c. on 12c. black and blue	60·00	70·00

(68)

1916. Nos. 277 etc, optd with T 68.

189	1c. black and brown	7·50	35·00
203	2c. black and green	27·00	50·00
191	3c. black and red	27·00	50·00
192	4c. black and red	5·50	32·00
193	5c. black and brown	50·00	55·00
206	6c. black and green	65·00	80·00
207	8c. black and red	29·00	55·00
196	10c. black and blue	55·00	70·00
197	12c. black and blue	£100	£100
198	16c. black and brown	£110	£110
199	20c. on 18c. black and green	55·00	£100
200	24c. black and mauve	£130	£130
201	25c. black and green	£350	£425

1918. Nos. 159, etc, surch RED CROSS TWO CENTS.

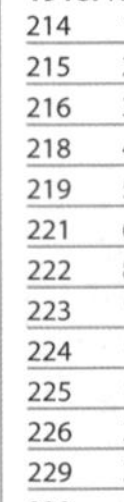

214	1c.+2c. black and brown	3·50	14·00
215	2c.+2c. black and green	1·00	8·50
216	3c.+2c. black and red	14·00	19·00
218	4c.+2c. black and red	70	5·00
219	5c.+2c. black and brown	8·00	29·00
221	6c.+2c. black and olive	5·00	29·00
222	8c.+2c. black and red	5·50	11·00
223	10c.+2c. black and blue	8·00	27·00
224	12c.+2c. black and blue	21·00	55·00
225	16c.+2c. black and brown	22·00	45·00
226	24c.+2c. black and mauve	22·00	45·00
229	25c.+2c. black and green	10·00	45·00
230	50c.+2c. black and blue	12·00	45·00
231	$1+2c. black and brown	50·00	55·00
232	$2+2c. black and lilac	75·00	95·00
233	$5+2c. black and red	£425	£600
234	$10+2c. black and orange	£475	£650

The premium of 2c. on each value was for Red Cross Funds.

1918. Nos. 159, etc. surch FOUR CENTS and a red cross.

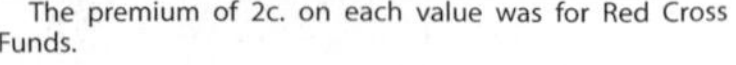

235	1c.+4c. black and brown	60	5·00
236	2c.+4c. black and green	65	8·00
237	3c.+4c. black and red	1·00	3·75
238	4c.+4c. black and red	40	4·75
239	5c.+4c. black and brown	2·00	23·00
240	6c.+4c. black and olive	1·90	12·00

241	8c.+4c. black and red	1·25	9·50
242	10c.+4c. black and blue	3·75	12·00
243	12c.+4c. black and blue	14·00	14·00
244	16c.+4c. black and brown	8·00	16·00
245	24c.+4c. black and mauve	11·00	20·00
246	25c.+4c. black and green	9·00	50·00
248	50c.+4c. black and blue	15·00	45·00
249	$1+4c. black and brown	23·00	60·00
250	$2+4 c black and lilac	55·00	80·00
251	$5+4c. black and red	£300	£400
252	$10+4c. black and orange	£375	£450

The premium of 4c. on each value was for Red Cross Funds.

1922. Nos. 159, etc, optd MALAYA-BORNEO EXHIBITION 1922.

253	1c. black and brown	20·00	70·00
255	2c. black and green	2·50	26·00
256	3c. black and red	16·00	65·00
257	4c. black and red	3·75	48·00
258	5c. black and brown	9·50	65·00
260	6c. black and green	10·00	70·00
261	8c. black and red	8·50	45·00
263	10c. black and blue	20·00	65·00
265	12c. black and blue	13·00	21·00
267	16c. black and brown	27·00	75·00
268	20c. on 18c. black and green	28·00	90·00
270	24c. black and mauve	50·00	75·00
274	25c. black and green	12·00	65·00
275	50c. black and blue	17·00	70·00

1923. No. 280 surch THREE CENTS and bars.

276	3c. on 4c. black and red	2·75	6·00

73 Head of a Murut

76 Mount Kinabalu

1931. 50th Anniv of North Borneo Company.

295	**73**	3c. black and green	1·50	80
296	-	6c. black and orange	17·00	3·25
297	-	10c. black and red	4·50	13·00
298	**76**	12c. black and blue	4·75	8·00
299	-	25c. black and violet	40·00	35·00
300	-	$1 black and green	27·00	£110
301	-	$2 black and brown	48·00	£110
302	-	$5 black and purple	£160	£500

DESIGNS—VERT: 6c. Orang-utan; 10c. Dyak warrior; $1, $2, $5 Arms. HORIZ: 25c. Clouded leopard.

81 Buffalo Transport

82 Palm Cockatoo

1939

303	**81**	1c. green and brown	4·75	2·50
304	**82**	2c. purple and blue	5·00	2·50
305	-	3c. blue and green	6·00	2·75
306	-	4c. green and violet	14·00	1·00
307	-	6c. blue and red	13·00	14·00
308	-	8c. red	18·00	2·25
309	-	10c. violet and green	40·00	7·50
310	-	12c. green and blue	45·00	8·00
311	-	15c. green and brown	35·00	13·00
312	-	20c. violet and blue	24·00	7·50
313	-	25c. green and brown	35·00	15·00
314	-	50c. brown and violet	38·00	14·00
315	-	$1 brown and red	£120	23·00
316	-	$2 violet and olive	£200	£150
317	-	$5 indigo and blue	£600	£375

DESIGNS—VERT: 3c. Native; 4c. Proboscis monkey; 6c. Mounted Bajaus; 10c. Orang-utan; 15c. Dyak; $1, $2 Arms. HORIZ: 8c. Map of Eastern Archipelago; 12c. Murut with blow-pipe; 20c. River scene; 25c. Native boat; 50c. Mt. Kinabalu; $5 Arms with supporters.

1941. Optd WAR TAX.

318	**81**	1c. green and brown	2·75	4·50
319	**82**	2c. purple and blue	11·00	4·75

1945. British Military Administration. Stamps of 1939 optd BMA.

320	**81**	1c. green and brown	16·00	2·25
321	**82**	2c. purple and blue	14·00	2·00
322	-	3c. blue and green	1·25	1·25
323	-	4c. green and violet	20·00	16·00
324	-	6c. blue and red	1·25	1·25
325	-	8c. red	3·00	75
326	-	10c. violet and green	3·00	40
327	-	12c. green and blue	6·00	3·75
328	-	15c. green and brown	2·00	1·00
329	-	20c. violet and blue	7·00	2·75
330	-	25c. green and brown	7·00	1·75
331	-	50c. brown and violet	5·00	2·75
332	-	$1 brown and red	55·00	40·00
333	-	$2 violet and olive	60·00	42·00
334	-	$5 indigo and blue	30·00	18·00

1947. Stamps of 1939 optd with Crown over GR monogram and bars obliterating "THE STATE OF" and "BRITISH PROTECTORATE".

335	**81**	1c. green and brown	15	1·00
336	**82**	2c. purple and blue	2·00	1·00
337	-	3c. blue and green	15	1·00
338	-	4c. green and violet	70	1·00
339	-	6c. blue and red	25	20
340	-	8c. red	30	20
341	-	10c. violet and green	1·50	40
342	-	12c. green and blue	3·50	2·75
343	-	15c. green and brown	2·25	30
344	-	20c. violet and blue	4·00	85
345	-	25c. green and brown	3·00	50
346	-	50c. brown and violet	3·50	85
347	-	$1 brown and red	14·00	1·75
348	-	$2 violet and olive	19·00	18·00
349	-	$5 indigo and blue	32·00	25·00

1948. Silver Wedding. As T 4b/c of Pitcairn Islands.

350	8c. red	30	80
351	$10 mauve	29·00	35·00

1949. U.P.U. As T 4d/g of Pitcairn Islands.

352	8c. red	60	30
353	10c. brown	3·25	1·75
354	30c. brown	1·25	1·75
355	55c. blue	1·25	2·75

100 Mt. Kinabalu

102 Coconut Grove

1950

356	**100**	1c. brown	15	1·25
357	-	2c. blue	15	50
358	**102**	3c. green	15	15
359	-	4c. purple	15	10
360	-	5c. violet	15	10
361	-	8c. red	1·25	85
362	-	10c. purple	1·75	15
363	-	15c. blue	2·00	65
364	-	20c. brown	2·50	10
365	-	30c. buff	5·50	30
366	-	50c. red ("JESSLETON")	1·75	4·50
366a	-	50c. red ("JESSELTON")	16·00	3·25
367	-	$1 orange	6·00	1·00
368	-	$2 green	13·00	20·00
369	-	$5 green	22·00	30·00
370	-	$10 blue	60·00	90·00

DESIGNS—VERT: 4c. Hemp drying; 5c. Cattle at Kota Belud; 30c. Suluk river canoe; 50c. Clock tower, Jesselton; $1 Bajau horsemen. HORIZ: 2c. Musician; 8c. Map; 10c. Log pond; 15c. Malay prau, Sandakan; 20c. Bajau chief; $2 Murut with blowpipe; $5 Net fishing; $10, King George VI and arms.

1953. Coronation. As T 4h of Pitcairn Islands.

371	10c. black and red	2·00	1·00

1954. As 1950 but with portrait of Queen Elizabeth II.

372	1c. brown	10	30
373	2c. blue	1·25	15
374	3c. green	4·00	2·00
375	4c. purple	1·75	20
376	5c. violet	1·00	10
377	8c. red	1·25	30
378	10c. purple	30	10
379	15c. blue	1·00	10
380	20c. brown	50	15
381	30c. buff	3·25	20
382	50c. red (No. 366a)	5·50	20
383	$1 orange	6·50	20
384	$2 green	13·00	1·25
385	$5 green	10·00	32·00
386	$10 blue	28·00	35·00

117 Malay Prau

1956. 75th Anniv of Foundation of British North Borneo Co. Inscr "CHARTER 1ST NOVEMBER 1881".

387	-	10c. black and red	1·25	40
388	**117**	15c. black and brown	45	30
389	-	35c. black and green	45	1·50
390	-	$1 black and slate	65	2·50

DESIGNS—HORIZ: 10c. Borneo Railway, 1902; 35c. Mt. Kinabalu. VERT: $1 Arms of Chartered Company.

120 Sambar Stag

1961

391	**120**	1c. green and red	20	10
392	-	4c. olive and orange	1·00	90
393	-	5c. sepia and violet	30	10
394	-	6c. black and turquoise	75	40
395	-	10c. green and red	1·25	10
396	-	12c. brown and myrtle	50	10
397	-	20c. turquoise and blue	4·00	10
398	-	25c. black and red	1·25	1·50
399	-	30c. sepia and olive	1·25	20
400	-	35c. slate and brown	2·50	2·50
401	-	50c. green and bistre	2·25	20
402	-	75c. blue and purple	16·00	90
403	-	$1 brown and green	13·00	80
404	-	$2 brown and slate	35·00	3·75
405	-	$5 green and purple	38·00	22·00
406	-	$10 red and blue	50·00	50·00

DESIGNS—HORIZ: 4c. Sun bear; 5c. Clouded leopard; 6c. Dusun woman with gong; 10c. Map of Borneo; 12c. Banteng; 20c. Butterfly orchid; 25c. Sumatran rhinoceros; 30c. Murut with blow-pipe; 35c. Mt. Kinabalu; 50c. Dusun and buffalo transport; 75c. Bajau horseman. VERT: $1 Orang-utan; $2 Rhinoceros hornbill; $5 Crested wood partridge; $10 Arms of N. Borneo.

1963. Freedom from Hunger. As T 20a of Pitcairn Islands.

407	12c. blue	1·50	75

POSTAGE DUE STAMPS

Overprinted POSTAGE DUE.

1895. Issue of 1894.

D2	**25**	2c. black and red	24·00	24·00	2·75
D3	**26**	3c. green & mve	6·00	16·00	1·25
D5	**27**	5c. black and red	60·00	29·00	3·50
D6a	**28**	6c. black & brn	22·00	50·00	3·00
D7	**29**	8c. black and lilac	55·00	50·00	3·25
D8b	**30**	12c. black & blue	70·00	50·00	3·25
D10	**31**	18c. black & grn	70·00	60·00	4·50
D11b	**32**	24c. blue and red	32·00	55·00	4·00

1897. Issue of 1897.

D12	**25**	2c. black and red	9·00	9·00
D13	**25**	2c. black & green	75·00	†
D14	**26**	3c. green & mve	35·00	†
D16a	**26**	4c. black and red	75·00	†
D17a	**27**	5c. black & orge	24·00	50·00
D18	**28**	6c. black & brn	8·00	40·00
D20	**29**	8c. black & lilac	9·50	†
D21a	**30**	12c. black & blue	£150	†
D22	**31**	18c. black and green (No. 108)	†	†
D23	**31**	18c. black and green (No. 110b)	85·00	†
D24	**32**	24c. blue and red (No. 109)	—	†
D25	**32**	24c. blue and red (No. 111b)	50·00	†

1902. Issue of 1901.

D37	1c. black and bistre	—	†	30·00
D38	2c. black and green	28·00	4·25	30
D39	3c. green and mauve	7·50	4·00	30
D40	4c. black and red	23·00	6·50	30
D41	5c. black and orange	45·00	5·00	30
D42	6c. black and brown	24·00	11·00	40
D43	8c. black and lilac	27·00	4·75	40
D45	10c. brown and grey	£130	25·00	1·60
D46	12c. black and blue	42·00	22·00	3·75
D47	16c. green & brown	85·00	27·00	3·75
D48	18c. black and green	17·00	21·00	1·50
D49	24c. blue and red	17·00	32·00	3·75

1919. Issue of 1909.

D52	2c. black and green	11·00	75·00
D66	2c. black and red	75	1·75
D77	3c. black and green	9·00	35·00
D55	4c. black and red	1·00	1·25
D57	5c. black and brown	9·50	30·00
D80	6c. black and olive	7·50	2·50
D62	8c. black and red	1·50	1·50
D63	10c. black and blue	16·00	19·00
D64	12c. black and blue	70·00	55·00
D65a	16c. black and brown	26·00	55·00

POSTAGE DUE

D2 Crest of the Company

1939

D85	**D2**	2c. brown	7·00	80·00
D86	**D2**	4c. red	8·00	£110
D87	**D2**	6c. violet	29·00	£150
D88	**D2**	8c. green	35·00	£300
D89	**D2**	10c. blue	80·00	£450

For later issues see **SABAH**.

JAPANESE OCCUPATION

1942. Stamps of North Borneo optd as T 1 of Japanese Occupation of Brunei. (a) Issue of 1939.

J1	**81**	1c. green and brown	£180	£225
J2	**82**	2c. purple and blue	£190	£250
J3	-	3c. blue and green	£150	£250
J4a	-	4c. green and violet	60·00	£130
J5	-	6c. blue and red	£170	£300
J6	-	8c. red	£225	£190
J7	-	10c. violet and green	£200	£300
J8	-	12c. green and blue	£225	£450
J9	-	15c. green and brown	£190	£450
J10	-	20c. violet and blue	£250	£550
J11	-	25c. green and brown	£250	£600
J12	-	50c. brown and violet	£325	£650
J13	-	$1 brown and red	£375	£800
J14	-	$2 violet and olive	£550	£1000
J15	-	$5 blue	£700	£1100

(b) War Tax Issue of 1941.

J16	**81**	1c. green and brown	£700	£300
J17	**82**	2c. purple and blue	£1800	£600

2 Mt. Kinabalu

3 Borneo Scene

1943

J18	**2**	4c. red	26·00	55·00
J19	**3**	8c. blue	22·00	50·00

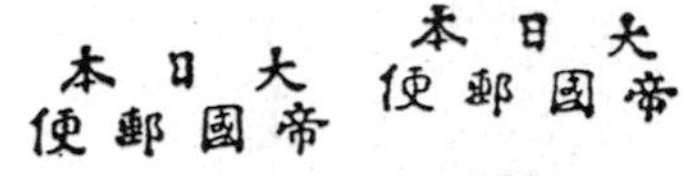

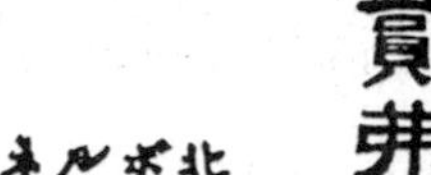

(4) ("Imperial Japanese Postal Service, North Borneo")

(5) ("Imperial Japanese Postal Service, North Borneo")

1944. Optd with T 4. (a) On stamps of North Borneo.

J20	**81**	1c. green and brown	7·00	12·00
J21	**82**	2c. purple and blue	7·50	9·00
J22	-	3c. blue and green	7·00	10·00
J23	-	4c. green and violet	14·00	22·00
J24	-	6c. blue and red	10·00	6·50
J25	-	8c. red	10·00	17·00
J26	-	10c. violet and green	8·50	13·00
J27	-	12c. green and blue	15·00	13·00
J28	-	15c. green and brown	15·00	16·00
J29	-	20c. violet and blue	30·00	50·00
J30	-	25c. green and brown	30·00	50·00
J31	-	50c. brown and violet	80·00	£120
J32	-	$1 brown and red	95·00	£150

(b) On stamps of Japanese Occupation of North Borneo.

J21a	2c. purple and blue (J2)	£425	
J22a	3c. blue and green (J3)	£425	
J25a	8c. red (J6)	£425	
J26b	10c. violet and green (J7)	£225	£425
J27a	12c. green and blue (J8)	£425	
J28a	15c. green and brown (J9)	£425	

1944. No. J1 surch with T 5.

J33	**81**	$2 on 1c. green and brown	£4750	£4000

(6)

1944. No. 315 of North Borneo surch with T 6.

J34	$5 on $1 brown and red	£4250	£3000

1944. Stamps of Japan optd as bottom line in T 4.

J35	**126**	1s. brown	8·50	30·00
J36	**84**	2s. red	7·50	26·00
J37	-	3s. green (No. 319)	8·50	30·00
J38	**129**	4s. green	16·00	24·00

J39	-	5s. red (No. 396)	13·00	27·00
J40	-	6s. orange (No. 322)	20·00	28·00
J41	-	8s. violet (No. 324)	6·50	28·00
J42	-	10s. red (No. 399)	12·00	28·00
J43	-	15s. blue (No. 401)	12·00	28·00
J44	-	20s. blue (No. 328)	80·00	90·00
J45	-	25s. brown (No. 329)	55·00	80·00
J46	-	30s. blue (No. 330)	£180	95·00
J47	-	50s. olive and brown (No. 331)	75·00	75·00
J48	-	1y. brown (No. 332)	80·00	£100

Pt. 7

NORTH GERMAN CONFEDERATION

The North German Confederation was set up on 1 January 1868, and comprised the postal services of Bremen, Brunswick, Hamburg Lubeck, Mecklenburg (both), Oldenburg, Prussia (including Hanover, Schleswig-Holstein with Bergedorf and Thurn and Taxis) and Saxony.

The North German Confederation joined the German Reichspost on 4 May 1871, and the stamps of Germany were brought into use on 1 January 1872.

Northern District: 30 groschen = 1 thaler.
Southern District: 60 kreuzer = 1 gulden.

1

1868. Roul or perf. (a) Northern District.

19	1	¼g. mauve	19·00	21·00
22	1	⅓g. green	6·75	3·75
23	1	½g. orange	6·75	4·75
25	1	1g. red	5·25	2·10
27	1	2g. blue	9·50	2·75
29	1	5g. bistre	11·50	13·50

(b) Southern District.

30		1k. green	17·00	13·50
13		2k. orange	75·00	75·00
33		3k. red	9·50	4·25
36		7k. blue	15·00	16·00
18		18k. bistre	48·00	85·00

The 1k. to 18k. have the figures in an oval.

3

1869. Perf.

38	3	10g. grey	£425	85·00
39	-	30g. blue	£325	£180

The frame of the 30g. is rectangular.

OFFICIAL STAMPS

O5

1870. (a) Northern District.

O40	O 5	¼g. black and brown	37·00	60·00
O41	O 5	⅓g. black and brown	12·50	26·00
O42	O 5	½g. black and brown	3·75	5·25
O43	O 5	1g. black and brown	3·75	2·75
O44	O 5	2g. black and brown	9·50	6·25

(b) Southern District.

O45		1k. black and grey	42·00	£350
O46		2k. black and grey	£110	£1200
O47		3k. black and grey	32·00	65·00
O48		7k. black and grey	60·00	£375

Pt.. 10

NORTH INGERMANLAND

Stamps issued during temporary independence of this Russian territory, which adjoins Finland.

100 pennia = 1 mark.

1 18th-century Arms of Ingermanland

1920

1	1	5p. green	3·25	5·00
2	1	10p. red	3·25	5·00
3	1	25p. brown	3·25	5·00
4	1	50p. blue	3·25	5·00
5	1	1m. black and red	43·00	50·00
6	1	5m. black and purple	£200	£180
7	1	10m. black and brown	£350	£275

4 Gathering Crops

1920. Inscr as in T 2.

8	-	10p. blue and green	6·00	9·00
9	-	30p. green and brown	6·00	9·00
10	-	50p. brown and blue	6·00	9·00
11	-	80p. grey and red	6·00	9·00
12	4	1m. grey and red	27·00	44·00
13	-	5m. red and violet	13·50	21·00
14	-	10m. violet and brown	13·50	21·00

DESIGNS—VERT: 10p. Arms; 30p. Reaper; 50p. Ploughing; 80p. Milking. HORIZ: 5m. Burning church; 10m. Zither players.

Pt. 10

NORTH WEST RUSSIA

Issues made for use by the various Anti-Bolshevist Armies during the Russian Civil War, 1918-20.

100 kopeks = 1 rouble.

NORTHERN ARMY

1 "OKCA" = Osobiy Korpus Severnoy Armiy—(trans "Special Corps, Northern Army")

1919. As T 1 inscr "OKCA".

1	1	5k. purple	15	40
2	1	10k. blue	15	40
3	1	15k. yellow	15	40
4	1	20k. red	15	40
5	1	50k. green	15	40

NORTH-WESTERN ARMY

Сѣв. Зап.
Армія

(2)

1919. Arms types of Russia optd as T 2. Imperf or perf.

6	22	2k. green	3·00	8·75
16	22	3k. red	2·75	5·50
7	22	5k. lilac	3·00	8·75
8	23	10k. blue	6·00	13·50
9	10	15k. blue and brown	6·75	8·75
10	14	20k. red and blue	6·00	9·25
11	10	20k. on 14k. red and blue	£300	
12	10	25k. violet and green	6·25	8·50
13	14	50k. green and purple	9·50	13·00
14	15	1r. orange & brown on brn	22·00	31·00
17	11	3r.50 green and red	44·00	55·00
18	22	5r. blue on green	35·00	44·00
19	11	7r. pink and green	£130	£180
15	20	10r. grey and red on yellow	90·00	£110

1919. No. 7 surch.

20	22	10k. on 5k. lilac	6·75	8·75

WESTERN ARMY

1919. Stamps of Latvia optd with Cross of Lorraine in circle with plain background. Imperf. (a) Postage stamps.

21	1	3k. lilac	44·00	55·00
22	1	5k. red	44·00	55·00
23	1	10k. blue	£150	£275
24	1	20k. orange	44·00	55·00
25	1	25k. grey	44·00	55·00
26	1	35k. brown	44·00	55·00
27	1	50k. violet	44·00	55·00
28	1	75k. green	44·00	90·00

(b) Liberation of Riga issue.

29	4	5k. red	44·00	55·00
30	4	15k. green	22·00	44·00
31	4	35k. brown	22·00	55·00

1919. Stamps of Latvia optd with Cross of Lorraine in circle with burele background and characters 3. A (= "Z. A."). Imperf. (a) Postage stamps.

32	1	3k. lilac	5·00	10·50
33	1	5k. red	5·00	10·50
34	1	10k. blue	£130	£225
35	1	20k. orange	10·00	16·00
36	1	25k. grey	31·00	65·00
37	1	35k. brown	22·00	31·00
38	1	50k. violet	22·00	31·00
39	1	75k. green	22·00	31·00

(b) Liberation of Riga issue.

40	4	5k. red	3·50	8·75
41	4	15k. green	3·50	8·75
42	4	35k. brown	3·50	8·75

1919. Arms type of Russia surch with Cross of Lorraine in ornamental frame and LP with value in curved frame. Imperf or perf.

43	22	10k. on 2k. green	6·75	8·75
44	23	30k. on 4k. red	8·75	10·50
45	22	40k. on 5k. lilac	6·75	8·75
46	23	50k. on 10k. blue	6·75	8·75
47	10	70k. on 15k. blue and brown	6·75	8·75
48	14	90k. on 20k. red and blue	13·50	18·00
49	10	1r. on 25k. violet and green	6·75	8·75
50	10	1r.50 on 35k. green & brown	55·00	70·00
51	14	2r. on 50k. green and purple	13·50	18·00
52	10	4r. on 70k. red and brown	22·00	32·00
53	15	6r. on 1r. orange, brown on brown	31·00	44·00
54	22	20k. on 3k. red	24·00	37·00
56	11	10r. on 3r.50 green & pur	90·00	90·00

Pt. 1

NORTHERN NIGERIA

A British protectorate on the west coast of Africa. In 1914 incorporated into Nigeria.

12 pence = 1 shilling; 20 shillings = 1 pound.

1

1900

1	1	½d. mauve and green	5·00	16·00
2	1	1d. mauve and red	3·75	4·25
3	1	2d. mauve and yellow	15·00	55·00
4	1	2½d. mauve and blue	12·00	38·00
5	1	5d. mauve and brown	27·00	60·00
6	1	6d. mauve and violet	27·00	45·00
7	1	1s. green and black	27·00	80·00
8	1	2s.6d. green and blue	£170	£550
9	1	10s. green and brown	£325	£850

1902. As T 1, but portrait of King Edward VII.

10	½d. purple and green	2·00	1·00
11	1d. purple and red	3·00	75
12	2d. purple and yellow	2·00	3·00
13	2½d. purple and blue	1·50	9·50
14	5d. purple and brown	5·00	5·50
15	6d. purple and violet	14·00	5·00
16	1s. green and black	5·00	6·00
17	2s.6d. green and blue	11·00	65·00
18	10s. green and brown	48·00	55·00

1910. As last. New colours etc.

28	½d. green	2·00	1·25
29	1d. red	3·00	1·25
30	2d. grey	7·00	2·75
31	2½d. blue	2·50	7·00
32	3d. purple on yellow	3·75	75
34	5d. purple and green	5·00	13·00
35a	6d. purple	5·00	6·00
36	1s. black and green	3·25	75
37	2s.6d. black and red on blue	14·00	35·00
38	5s. green and red on yellow	26·00	75·00
39	10s. green and red on green	50·00	48·00

5

1912

40	5	½d. green	3·00	60
41	5	1d. red	3·00	60
42	5	2d. grey	4·50	11·00
43	5	3d. purple on yellow	2·25	1·25
44	5	4d. black and red on yellow	1·25	2·25
45	5	5d. purple and olive	4·00	14·00
46	5	6d. purple and violet	4·00	4·25
47	5	9d. purple and red	2·00	12·00
48	5	1s. black on green	4·50	2·25
49	5	2s.6d. black and red on blue	7·00	55·00
50	5	5s. green and red on yellow	24·00	80·00
51	5	10s. green and red on green	40·00	48·00
52	5	£1 purple and black on red	£180	£110

Pt. 1

NORTHERN RHODESIA

A British territory in central Africa, north of the Zambesi. From 1954 to 1963 part of the central African Federation and using the stamps of Rhodesia and Nyasaland (q.v.). A new constitution was introduced on 3 January 1964, with internal self-government and independence came on 24 October 1964 when the country was renamed Zambia (q.v.).

12 pence = 1 shilling; 20 shillings = 1 pound.

1

1925. The shilling values are larger and the view is in first colour.

1	1	½d. green	1·75	80
2	1	1d. brown	1·75	10
3	1	1½d. red	3·50	30
4	1	2d. orange	3·75	10
5	1	3d. blue	3·75	1·25
6	1	4d. violet	6·50	50
7	1	6d. grey	6·50	40
8	1	8d. purple	6·50	55·00
9	1	10d. olive	6·50	50·00
10	1	1s. orange and black	3·75	1·75
11	1	2s. brown and blue	23·00	32·00
12	1	2s.6d. black and green	24·00	15·00
13	1	3s. violet and blue	32·00	23·00
14	1	5s. grey and violet	45·00	19·00
15	1	7s.6d. purple and black	£130	£225
16	1	10s. green and black	85·00	85·00
17	1	20s. red and purple	£200	£250

1935. Silver Jubilee. As T 143a of Newfoundland.

18	1d. blue and olive	1·50	1·50
19	2d. green and blue	2·25	2·75
20	3d. brown and blue	4·00	9·00
21	6d. grey and purple	8·00	1·75

1937. Coronation. As T 143b of Newfoundland.

22	1½d. red	30	50
23	2d. brown	40	50
24	3d. blue	60	1·25

1938. As 1925, but with portrait of King George VI facing right and "POSTAGE & REVENUE" omitted.

25	½d. green	10	10
26	½d. brown	2·00	1·50
27	1d. brown	20	20
28	1d. green	1·00	2·00
29	1½d. red	50·00	75
30	1½d. orange	30	10
31	2d. orange	50·00	1·75
32	2d. red	1·50	50
33	2d. purple	45	1·50
34	3d. blue	50	30
35	3d. red	50	3·00
36	4d. violet	40	40
37	4½d. blue	2·75	10·00
38	6d. grey	40	10
39	9d. violet	2·75	9·50
40	1s. orange and black	4·00	60
41	2s.6d. black and green	10·00	6·00
42	3s. violet and blue	22·00	16·00
43	5s. grey and violet	22·00	16·00

44	10s. green and black	27·00	27·00
45	20s. red and purple	65·00	70·00

1946. Victory. As T 8a of Pitcairn Islands.

46	1½d. orange	1·00	1·50
47	2d. red	10	50

1948. Silver Wedding. As T 8b/c of Pitcairn Islands.

48	1½d. orange	30	10
49	20s. red	65·00	70·00

1949. U.P.U. As T 8d/g of Pitcairn Islands.

50	2d. red	20	75
51	3d. blue	2·00	3·00
52	6d. grey	1·00	2·00
53	1s. orange	75	1·50

5 Cecil Rhodes and Victoria Falls

1953. Birth Centenary of Cecil Rhodes.

54	**5**	½d. brown	55	1·50
55	**5**	1d. green	45	1·50
56	**5**	2d. mauve	60	30
57	**5**	4½d. blue	45	3·50
58	**5**	1s. orange and black	1·00	4·75

6 Arms of the Rhodesias and Nyasaland

1953. Rhodes Centenary Exhibition.

59	**6**	6d. violet	70	1·25

1953. Coronation. As T 8h of Pitcairn Islands.

60	1½d. black and orange	70	20

1953. As 1938 but with portrait of Queen Elizabeth II facing left.

61	½d. brown	65	10
62	1d. green	65	10
63	1½d. orange	1·25	10
64	2d. purple	1·25	10
65	3d. red	80	10
66	4d. violet	1·25	2·00
67	4½d. blue	1·50	4·25
68	6d. grey	1·25	10
69	9d. violet	1·25	4·25
70	1s. orange and black	70	10
71	2s.6d. black and green	13·00	8·00
72	5s. grey and purple	14·00	14·00
73	10s. green and black	11·00	32·00
74	20s. red and purple	29·00	38·00

9 Arms

1963. Arms black, gold and blue; portrait and inscriptions black; background colours given.

75	**9**	½d. violet	70	1·25
76	**9**	1d. blue	1·50	10
77	**9**	2d. brown	70	10
78	**9**	3d. yellow	75	10
79	**9**	4d. green	70	30
80	**9**	6d. green	1·00	10
81	**9**	9d. bistre	70	1·60
82	**9**	1s. purple	50	10
83	**9**	1s.3d. purple	2·25	10
84	**9**	2s. orange	2·50	5·00
85	**9**	2s.6d. lake	2·50	2·25
86	**9**	5s. mauve	10·00	8·50
87	**9**	10s. mauve	16·00	21·00
88	**9**	20s. blue	20·00	38·00

Nos. 84/88 are larger (27×23 mm).

POSTAGE DUE STAMPS

D1

1929

D1	**D1**	1d. black	2·50	2·50
D2	**D1**	2d. black	5·50	3·00
D3	**D1**	3d. black	3·00	26·00
D4	**D1**	4d. black	9·50	38·00

D2

1963

D5	**D2**	1d. orange	2·75	5·00
D6	**D2**	2d. blue	2·75	4·25
D7	**D2**	3d. lake	2·75	7·00
D8	**D2**	4d. blue	2·75	12·00
D9	**D2**	6d. purple	9·00	9·50
D10	**D2**	1s. green	10·00	27·00

For later issues see **ZAMBIA**.

Pt. 11

NORWAY

In 1814 Denmark ceded Norway to Sweden, from 1814 to 1905 the King of Sweden was also King of Norway after which Norway was an independent Kingdom.

1855. 120 skilling = 1 speciedaler.
1877. 100 ore = 1 krone.

1

1855. Imperf.

1	**1**	4s. blue	£5000	80·00

3 King Oscar I

1856. Perf.

4	**3**	2s. yellow	£550	95·00
6	**3**	3s. lilac	£300	60·00
7	**3**	4s. blue	£275	9·50
11	**3**	8s. red	£950	28·00

4

1863

12	**4**	2s. yellow	£550	£130
13	**4**	3s. lilac	£425	£275
21	**4**	4s. blue	£180	9·75
17	**4**	8s. pink	£600	36·00
18	**4**	24s. brown	34·00	85·00

5

1867

22	**5**	1s. black	60·00	37·00
23	**5**	2s. buff	20·00	37·00
26	**5**	3s. lilac	£275	80·00
27	**5**	4s. blue	85·00	8·00
29	**5**	8s. red	£400	34·00

6

1872. Value in "Skilling".

33	**6**	1s. green	11·50	21·00
36	**6**	2s. blue	12·50	44·00
39	**6**	3s. red	50·00	7·50
42	**6**	4s. mauve	30·00	40·00
44	**6**	6s. brown	£350	39·00
45	**6**	7s. brown	41·00	48·00

10 With background shading

A

1877. Letters without serifs as Type A. Value in "ore".

47	**10**	1ore brown	6·00	5·25
83	**10**	2ore brown	3·50	4·75
84c	**10**	3ore orange	46·00	4·50
52	**10**	5ore blue	60·00	11·50
85d	**10**	5ore green	39·00	1·40
86a	**10**	10ore red	38·00	1·60
55	**10**	12ore green	80·00	14·00
75b	**10**	12ore brown	21·00	16·00
76	**10**	20ore brown	£110	13·00
87	**10**	20ore blue	70·00	2·20
88	**10**	25ore mauve	13·00	11·00
61	**10**	35ore green	17·00	9·50
62	**10**	50ore purple	39·00	7·75
63	**10**	60ore blue	38·00	7·50

9 King Oscar II

1878

68	**9**	1k. green and light green	25·00	8·50
69	**9**	1k.50 blue and ultramarine	55·00	32·00
70	**9**	2k. brown and pink	35·00	19·00

1888. Surch 2 ore.

89a	**6**	2ore on 12ore brown	2·00	1·90

D

1893. Letters with serifs as Type D.

133	**10**	1ore drab	75	45
134	**10**	2ore brown	50	30
135	**10**	3ore orange	65	30
136	**10**	5ore green	3·75	25
529	**10**	5ore purple	50	20
138	**10**	7ore green	1·10	25
139	**10**	10ore red	5·00	20
140	**10**	10ore green	16·00	45
529a	**10**	10ore grey	50	20
141	**10**	12ore violet	85	1·10
143	**10**	15ore blue	12·50	30
530	**10**	15ore brown	50	20
144	**10**	20ore blue	5·75	25
530a	**10**	20ore green	2·20	20
146	**10**	25ore mauve	35·00	35
147	**10**	25ore red	10·50	65
531	**10**	25ore blue	20	20
148	**10**	30ore grey	7·25	40
149	**10**	30ore blue	16·00	4·25
119	**10**	35ore green	11·00	6·25
150	**10**	35ore brown	13·00	30
151	**10**	40ore green	7·50	40
152	**10**	40ore blue	55·00	25
531b	**10**	50ore purple	20	20
154	**10**	60ore blue	34·00	55
531c	**10**	60ore orange	30	20
531d	**10**	70ore orange	30	25
531e	**10**	80ore brown	30	20
531f	**10**	90ore brown	30	25

See also Nos. 279 etc and 1100/3.

1905. Surch.

122	**5**	1k. on 2s. buff	28·00	32·00
123	**5**	1k.50 on 2s. buff	55·00	75·00
124	**5**	2k. on 2s. buff	60·00	65·00

1906. Surch.

162	**10**	5ore on 25ore mauve	85	60
125	**6**	15ore on 4s. mauve	5·00	4·25
126	**6**	30ore on 7s. brown	8·25	7·50

15 King Haakon VII

1907

127	**15**	1k. green	28·00	27·00
128	**15**	1½k. blue	75·00	75·00
129	**15**	2k. red	£110	95·00

16 King Haakon VII

1910

155a	**16**	1k. green	60	20
156	**16**	1½k. blue	2·40	75
157	**16**	2k. red	3·00	95
158	**16**	5k. violet	5·00	4·75

17 Constitutional Assembly (after O. Wergeland)

1914. Centenary of Independence.

159	**17**	5ore green	1·10	40
160	**17**	10ore red	3·00	40
161	**17**	20ore blue	8·25	5·50

19

1922

163	**19**	10ore green	24·00	45
164	**19**	20ore purple	43·00	20
165	**19**	25ore red	44·00	55
166	**19**	45ore blue	4·75	85

20

1925. Air. Amundsen's Polar Flight.

167	**20**	2ore brown	3·00	3·00
168	**20**	3ore orange	6·00	4·00
169	**20**	5ore mauve	12·50	11·50
170	**20**	10ore green	15·00	14·50
171	**20**	15ore blue	16·00	19·00
172	**20**	20ore mauve	18·00	21·00
173	**20**	25ore red	7·25	5·00

21

1925. Annexation of Spitzbergen.

183	**21**	10ore green	8·50	7·75
184	**21**	15ore blue	8·50	4·25
185	**21**	20ore purple	8·50	1·20
186	**21**	45ore blue	8·50	5·50

22

1926. Size 16×19½ mm.

187	**22**	10ore green	90	20
187a	**22**	14ore orange	1·50	2·20
188	**22**	15ore brown	1·10	20
189	**22**	20ore purple	60·00	20
189a	**22**	20ore red	1·80	20
190	**22**	25ore red	19·00	1·90
190a	**22**	25ore brown	1·90	20
190b	**22**	30ore blue	2·10	25
191	**22**	35ore brown	£120	20
191a	**22**	35ore violet	3·25	30
192	**22**	40ore blue	7·75	95
193	**22**	40ore grey	2·75	20
194	**22**	50ore pink	3·00	20
195	**22**	60ore blue	3·00	20

For stamps as Type **22** but size 17×21 mm, see Nos. 284, etc.

1927. Surcharged with new value and bar.

196		20ore on 25ore red	6·00	1·20
197	**19**	30ore on 45ore blue	21·00	1·20
198	**21**	30ore on 45ore blue	5·50	4·75

24 Akershus Castle

1927. Air.

199a	**24**	45ore blue (with frame-lines)	8·75	2·75
323	**24**	45ore blue (without frame-lines)	1·10	30

25 Ibsen

1928. Ibsen Centenary.

200	**25**	10ore green	10·50	1·70
201	**25**	15ore brown	4·50	2·50
202	**25**	20ore red	5·75	45
203	**25**	30ore blue	6·50	3·00

1929. Postage Due stamps optd Post Frimerke (204/6 and 211) or POST and thick bar (others).

204	**D12**	1ore brown	40	80
205	**D12**	4ore mauve (No. D96a)	40	45
206	**D12**	10ore green	2·10	2·10
207	**D12**	15ore brown	3·25	3·50
208	**D12**	20ore purple	1·40	55
209	**D12**	40ore blue	3·75	80
210	**D12**	50ore purple	12·50	6·75
211	**D12**	100ore yellow	3·50	2·50
212	**D12**	200ore violet	5·50	3·00

28 Abel

1929. Death Cent of N. H. Abel (mathematician).

213	**28**	10ore green	4·50	65
214	**28**	15ore brown	4·00	1·30
215	**28**	20ore red	1·70	35
216	**28**	30ore blue	2·50	1·60

1929. Surch 14 ORE 14.

217	**5**	14ore on 2s. buff	3·00	3·25

30 St. Olaf (sculpture, Brunlanes Church)

31 Nidaros Trondhjem Cathedral

32 Death of St. Olaf (after P. N. Arbo)

1930. 9th Death Centenary of St. Olaf.

219	**30**	10ore green	16·00	45
220	**31**	15ore sepia and brown	1·20	45
221	**30**	20ore red	1·60	35
222	**32**	30ore blue	6·75	2·75

33 North Cape and "Bergensfjord" (liner)

1930. Norwegian Tourist Association Fund. Size 35½×21½ mm.

223	**33**	15ore+25ore brown	2·30	2·75
224	**33**	20ore+25ore red	42·00	33·00
225	**33**	30ore+25ore blue	95·00	75·00

For smaller stamps in this design see Nos. 349/51, 442/66 and 464/6.

34 Radium Hospital

1931. Radium Hospital Fund.

226	**34**	20ore+10ore red	17·00	5·00

35 Bjornson

1932. Birth Cent of Bjornstjerne Bjornson (writer).

227	**35**	10ore green	14·00	45
228	**35**	15ore brown	1·60	1·10
229	**35**	20ore red	1·90	30
230	**35**	30ore blue	3·50	2·40

36 L. Holberg

1934. 250th Birth Anniv of Holberg (writer).

231	**36**	10ore green	3·50	45
232	**36**	15ore brown	85	65
233	**36**	20ore red	19·00	30
234	**36**	30ore blue	4·00	2·20

37 Dr. Nansen

1935. Nansen Refugee Fund.

235	**37**	10ore+10ore green	3·75	3·50
236	**37**	15ore+10ore brown	8·25	9·00
237	**37**	20ore+10ore red	4·00	1·90
238	**37**	30ore+10ore blue	8·75	8·50

See also Nos. 275/8.

38 No background shading

1937

279	**38**	1ore green	25	20
280	**38**	2ore brown	25	20
281	**38**	3ore orange	25	20
282	**38**	5ore mauve	30	20
283	**38**	7ore green	35	20
413	**38**	10ore grey	70	20
285	**38**	12ore violet	75	1·40
414	**38**	15ore green	1·70	55
415	**38**	15ore brown	60	20
416	**38**	20ore brown	3·75	1·80
417	**38**	20ore green	35	20
531a	**38**	40ore brown	20	20

1937. As T 22, but size 17×21 mm.

284	**22**	10ore green	45	20
286	**22**	14ore orange	2·30	3·25
287	**22**	15ore green	1·40	20
288a	**22**	20ore red	50	20
289	**22**	25ore brown	2·00	20
289a	**22**	25ore red	70	20
290	**22**	30ore blue	2·50	20
290a	**22**	30ore grey	8·75	20
291	**22**	35ore violet	3·25	20
292	**22**	40ore grey	2·75	20
292a	**22**	40ore blue	4·75	20
293	**22**	50ore purple	2·20	20
293a	**22**	55ore orange	29·00	20
294	**22**	60ore blue	3·00	20
294a	**22**	80ore brown	28·00	25

38b King Haakon VII

1937

255	**38b**	1k. green	30	20
256	**38b**	1k.50 blue	1·20	2·75
257	**38b**	2k. red	75	8·25
258	**38b**	5k. purple	6·50	42·00

39 Reindeer

41 Joelster in Sunnfjord

1938. Tourist Propaganda.

262	**39**	15ore brown	60	55
263	-	20ore red	60	30
264	**41**	30ore blue	60	35

DESIGN—As T **39** but VERT: 20ore, Stave Church, Borgund.

42 Queen Maud

1939. Queen Maud Children's Fund.

267	**42**	10ore+5ore green	65	9·25
268	**42**	15ore+5ore brown	65	9·25
269	**42**	20ore+5ore red	65	7·25
270	**42**	30ore+5ore blue	65	11·00

43 Lion Rampant

1940

271	**43**	1k. green	1·30	20
272	**43**	1½k. blue	2·50	45
273	**43**	2k. red	3·75	1·10
274	**43**	5k. purple	4·25	4·25

See also Nos. 318/21.

44 Dr. Nansen

1940. National Relief Fund.

275	**44**	10ore+10ore green	2·50	3·25
276	**44**	15ore+10ore brown	3·50	4·25
277	**44**	20ore+10ore red	75	1·10
278	**44**	30ore+10ore blue	1·80	2·50

46 Femboring (fishing boat) and Iceberg

1941. Haalogaland Exhibition and Fishermen's Families Relief Fund.

295	**46**	15ore+10ore blue	1·60	4·75

47 Colin Archer (founder) and Lifeboat "Colin Archer"

1941. 50th Anniv of National Lifeboat Institution.

296	**47**	10ore+10ore green	1·30	1·90
297	**47**	15ore+10ore brown	1·60	2·40
298	-	20ore+10ore red	55	65
299	-	30ore+10ore blue	4·00	5·75

DESIGN—VERT: 20ore, 30ore, "Osloskoyta" (lifeboat).

48 Soldier and Flags

1941. Norwegian Legion Support Fund.

300	**48**	20ore+80ore red	50·00	70·00

1941. Stamps of 1937 optd V (= Victory).

301B	**38**	1ore green	35	3·75
302B	**38**	2ore brown	35	6·25
303B	**38**	3ore orange	35	3·75
304B	**38**	5ore mauve	35	40
305A	**38**	7ore green	70	3·50
306B	**22**	10ore green	35	25
307B	**38**	12ore violet	1·10	14·00
308A	**22**	14ore orange	1·70	13·00
309A	**22**	15ore green	85	1·00
310B	**22**	20ore red	30	25
311B	**22**	25ore brown	60	50
312B	**22**	30ore blue	1·20	2·20
313A	**22**	35ore violet	1·70	85
314B	**22**	40ore grey	90	60
315B	**22**	50ore purple	1·70	2·40
316A	**22**	60ore blue	1·80	1·60
317B	**43**	1k. green	1·60	55
318B	**43**	1½k. blue	6·00	13·50
319B	**43**	2k. red	17·00	42·00
320B	**43**	5k. purple	30·00	£100

1941. As No. 413, but with "V" incorporated in the design.

321	10ore green	1·20	10·00

51 Oslo University

1941. Centenary of Foundation of Oslo University Building.

322	**51**	1k. green	33·00	44·00

52 Queen Ragnhild's Dream **53** Stiklestad Battlefield

1941. 700th Death Anniv of Snorre Sturlason (historian).

324	**52**	10ore green	40	25
325	-	15ore brown	40	45
326	-	20ore red	40	20
327	-	30ore blue	1·30	1·60
328	-	50ore violet	95	1·30
329	**53**	60ore blue	1·40	1·40

DESIGNS (illustrations from "Sagas of Kings")—As T **53**: 15ore Einar Tambarskjelve at Battle of Svolder; 30ore King Olav II sails to his wedding; 50ore Svipdag's men enter Hall of the Seven Kings. As T **52**: 20ore Snorre Sturlason.

55 Vidkun Quisling

1942. (a) Without opt.

330	**55**	20ore+30ore red	4·50	19·00

(b) Optd 1-2-1942.

331		20ore+30ore red	4·50	19·00

See also No. 336.

56 Rikard Nordraak 57 Embarkation of the Viking Fleet

1942. Birth Centenary of Rikard Nordraak (composer).

332	**56**	10ore green	1·10	1·70
333	**57**	15ore brown	1·10	1·70
334	**56**	20ore red	1·10	1·70
335	-	30ore blue	1·10	1·70

DESIGN—As Type **57**: 30ore Mountains across sea and two lines of the National Anthem.

1942. War Orphans' Relief Fund. As T 55 but inscr "RIKSTINGET 1942".

336	20ore+30ore red	45	4·75

58 J. H. Wessel

1942. Birth Bicentenary of Wessel (poet).

337	**58**	15ore brown	25	30
338	**58**	20ore red	25	30

59 Reproduction of Types **55** and **1**

1942. Inaug of European Postal Union, Vienna.

339	**59**	20ore red	25	95
340	**59**	30ore blue	40	1·90

60 "Sleipner" (Destroyer)

1943

341	**60**	5ore purple	25	20
342	-	7ore green	35	30
343	**60**	10ore green	25	20
344	-	15ore green	95	95
345	-	20ore red	25	20
346	-	30ore blue	1·10	1·10
347	-	40ore green	1·10	1·10
348	-	60ore blue	1·10	1·10

DESIGNS: 7ore, 30ore Merchant ships in convoy; 15ore Airman; 20ore "Vi Vil Vinne" (We will win) written on the highway; 40ore Soldiers on skis; 60ore King Haakon VII.

For use on correspondence posted at sea on Norwegian merchant ships and (in certain circumstances) from Norwegian camps in Gt. Britain during the German Occupation of Norway. After liberation all values were put on sale in Norway.

1943. Norwegian Tourist Association Fund. As T 33, but reduced to 27×21 mm.

349	**33**	15ore+25ore brown	75	1·20
350	**33**	20ore+25ore red	1·40	2·20
351	**33**	30ore+25ore blue	1·40	2·20

61 Edvard Grieg

1943. Birth Centenary of Grieg (composer).

352	**61**	10ore green	30	25
353	**61**	20ore red	30	25
354	**61**	40ore green	30	30
355	**61**	60ore blue	30	30

62 Soldier's Emblem

1943. Soldiers' Relief Fund.

356	**62**	20ore+30ore red	50	5·00

63 Fishing Station

1943. Winter Relief Fund.

357	**63**	10ore+10ore green	90	5·75
358	-	20ore+10ore red	90	5·75
359	-	40ore+10ore grey	90	5·75

DESIGNS: 20ore Mountain scenery; 40ore Winter landscape.

64 Sinking of "Baroy" (freighter)

1944. Shipwrecked Mariners' Relief Fund.

360	**64**	10ore+10ore green	70	5·75
361	-	15ore+10ore brown	70	5·75
362	-	20ore+10ore red	70	5·75

DESIGNS—HORIZ: 15ore "Sanct Svithun" (cargo liner) attacked by Bristol Type 142 Blenheim Mk IV airplane. VERT: 20ore Sinking of "Irma" (freighter).

65 Gran's Bleriot XI "Nordsjoen"

1944. 30th Anniv of First North Sea Flight, by Tryggve Gran.

363	**65**	40ore blue	50	3·00

66 Girl Spinning

1944. Winter Relief Fund. Inscr as in T 66.

364	**66**	5ore+10ore mauve	55	5·25
365	-	10ore+10ore green	55	5·25
366	-	15ore+10ore purple	55	5·25
367	-	20ore+10ore red	55	5·25

DESIGNS: 10ore Ploughing; 15ore Tree felling; 20ore Mother and children.

67 Arms

1945

368	**67**	1½k. blue	2·00	55

68 Henrik Wergeland

1945. Death Centenary of Wergeland (poet).

369	**68**	10ore green	25	25
370	**68**	15ore brown	85	90
371	**68**	20ore red	25	25

69 Red Cross Sister

1945. Red Cross Relief Fund and Norwegian Red Cross Jubilee.

372	**69**	20ore+10ore red	60	60

70 Folklore Museum Emblem

1945. 50th Anniv of National Folklore Museum.

373	**70**	10ore green	65	40
374	**70**	20ore red	1·00	40

71 Crown Prince Olav

1946. National Relief Fund.

375	**71**	10ore+10ore green	55	45
376	**71**	15ore+10ore brown	55	45
377	**71**	20ore+10ore red	65	45
378	**71**	30ore+10ore blue	1·80	1·40

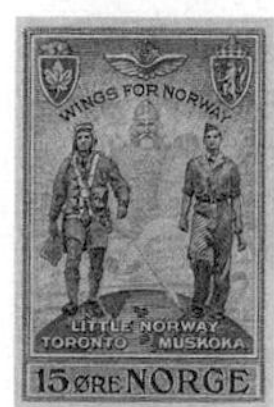

72 "R.N.A.F."

1946. Honouring Norwegian Air Force trained in Canada.

379	**72**	15ore red	60	80

73 King Haakon VII

1946

380	**73**	1k. green	1·90	20
381	**73**	1½k. blue	4·00	20
382	**73**	2k. brown	32·00	20
383	**73**	5k. violet	22·00	65

74 Fridtjof Nansen, Roald Amundsen and "Fram"

1947. Tercentenary of Norwegian Post Office.

384	-	5ore mauve	50	20
385	-	10ore green	50	20
386	-	15ore brown	90	20
387	-	25ore red	65	20
388	-	30ore grey	1·20	20
389	-	40ore blue	3·00	20
390	-	45ore violet	2·50	60
391	-	50ore brown	3·75	45
392	**74**	55ore orange	6·00	30
393	-	60ore grey	4·75	1·20
394	-	80ore brown	5·50	55

DESIGNS: 5ore Hannibal Sehested (founder of postal service) and Akershus Castle; 10ore "Postal-peasant"; 15ore Admiral Tordenskiold and 18th-century warship; 25ore Christian M. Falsen; 30ore Cleng Peerson and "Restaurationen" (emigrant sloop), 1825; 40ore "Constitutionen" (paddle-steamer), 1827; 45ore First Norwegian locomotive "Caroline"; 50ore Svend Foyn and "Spes et Fides" (whale catcher); 60ore Coronation of King Haakon and Queen Maud in Nidaros Cathedral; 80ore King Haakon and Oslo Town Hall.

75 Petter Dass

1947. Birth Tercentenary of Petter Dass (poet).

395	**75**	25ore red	80	65

76 King Haakon VII

1947. 75th Birthday of King Haakon VII.

396	**76**	25ore orange	55	55

77 Axel Heiberg

1948. 50th Anniv of Norwegian Forestry Society and Birth Centenary of Axel Heiberg (founder).

397	**77**	25ore red	85	50
398	**77**	80ore brown	1·80	30

1948. Red Cross. Surch 25+5 and bars.

399	**69**	25+5 ore on 20+10 ore red	80	75

1949. Nos. 288a and 292a surch.

400	**22**	25ore on 20ore red	40	20
401	**22**	45ore on 40ore blue	3·00	55

80 A. L. Kielland

1949. Birth Centenary of Alexander L. Kielland (author).

402	**80**	25ore red	1·50	30
403	**80**	40ore blue	1·50	55
404	**80**	80ore brown	2·00	85

81 Symbolising Universe **82** Pigeons and Globe

1949. 75th Anniv of U.P.U.

405	**81**	10ore green and purple	50	45
406	**82**	25ore red	50	30
407	-	40ore blue	50	45

DESIGN—37×21 mm: 40ore Dove, globe and signpost.

84 King Harald Haardraade and Oslo Town Hall

1950. 900th Anniv of Founding of Oslo.

408	**84**	15ore green	60	55
409	**84**	25ore red	60	30
410	**84**	45ore blue	65	55

85 Child with Flowers

1950. Infantile Paralysis Fund.

411	**85**	25ore+5ore red	1·70	1·50
412	**85**	45ore+5ore blue	6·25	6·00

87 King Haakon VII

1950

418	**87**	25ore red	60	20
419	**87**	25ore grey	17·00	20
419a	**87**	25ore green	1·10	20
420	**87**	30ore grey	7·75	65
421	**87**	30ore red	60	20
422a	**87**	35ore red	4·25	20
422b	**87**	40ore purple	1·70	1·80
423	**87**	45ore blue	1·70	1·80
424	**87**	50ore brown	3·75	20
425	**87**	55ore orange	1·70	1·10
426	**87**	55ore blue	1·30	50
427	**87**	60ore blue	13·50	20
427a	**87**	65ore blue	1·10	30
427b	**87**	70ore brown	11·00	25
428	**87**	75ore purple	2·20	25
429	**87**	80ore brown	3·00	30
430	**87**	90ore orange	1·30	25

"NOREG" on the stamps was the spelling advocated by Arne Garborg.

88 Arne Garborg (after O. Rusti)

1951. Birth Centenary of Garborg (author).

431	**88**	25ore red	55	30
432	**88**	45ore blue	2·20	2·20
433	**88**	80ore brown	2·20	1·70

89 Ice Skater

1951. 6th Winter Olympic Games. Inscr "OSLO 1952".

434	**89**	15ore+5ore green	2·75	2·75
435	-	30ore+10ore red	2·75	2·75
436	-	55ore+20ore blue	10·00	9·75

DESIGNS—As T **89**: 30ore Ski jumping. 38×21 mm: 55ore Winter landscape.

1951. Surch in figures.

437	**87**	30ore on 25ore red	55	20
440	**38**	20ore on 15ore green	50	20

92 King Haakon VII

1952. 80th Birthday of King Haakon.

438	**92**	30ore scarlet and red	35	30
439	**92**	55ore blue and grey	85	75

94 "Supplication"

1953. Anti-cancer Fund.

441	**94**	30ore+10ore red and cream	2·00	1·90

1953. Norwegian Tourist Association Fund. As T 33 but smaller 27½×21 mm.

442	**33**	20ore+10ore green	9·50	9·25
464	**33**	25ore+10ore green	5·00	5·00
443	**33**	30ore+15ore red	9·50	9·25
465	**33**	35ore+15ore red	6·50	6·25
444	**33**	55ore+25ore blue	14·50	13·50
466	**33**	65ore+25ore blue	3·75	3·50

95 Medieval Sculpture

1953. 8th Cent of Archbishopric of Nidaros.

445	**95**	30ore red	85	50

96 Stephenson Locomotive on Hoved Railway, 1854, and Horse-drawn Sledge

1954. Centenary of Norwegian Railways.

446	**96**	20ore green	80	40
447	-	30ore red	80	30
448	-	55ore blue	1·60	1·00

DESIGNS: 30ore Diesel-hydraulic express train; 55ore Alfred Andersen (engine driver) in locomotive cab.

97 C. T. Nielsen (first Director)

1954. Centenary of Telegraph Service.

449	**97**	20ore black and green	35	35
450	-	30ore red	35	30
451	-	55ore blue	80	75

DESIGNS: 30ore Radio masts at Tryvannshogda; 55ore Telegraph lineman on skis.

98 "Posthorn" Type Stamp

1955. Norwegian Stamp Centenary.

452		20ore blue and green	45	45
453	**98**	30ore deep red and red	35	25
454	-	55ore blue and grey	75	60

DESIGNS: 20ore Norway's first stamp; 55ore "Lion" type stamp.

1955. Stamp Cent and Int Stamp Exn, Oslo. Nos. 452/4 with circular opt OSLO NORWEX.

455		20ore blue and green	10·00	9·75
456	**98**	30ore deep red and red	10·00	9·75
457	-	55ore blue and grey	10·00	9·75

Nos. 455/7 were only on sale at the Exhibition P.O. at face plus 1k. entrance fee.

100 King Haakon and Queen Maud

1955. Golden Jubilee of King Haakon.

458	**100**	30ore red	35	25
459	**100**	55ore blue	50	45

101 Crown Princess Martha

1956. Crown Princess Martha Memorial Fund.

460	**101**	35ore+10ore red	1·20	1·20
461	**101**	65ore+10ore blue	3·00	3·00

101a Whooper Swans

1956. Northern Countries' Day.

462	**101a**	35ore red	60	55
463	**101a**	65ore blue	60	60

102 Jan Mayen Island (after aquarell, H. Mohn)

103 Map of Spitzbergen

1957. Int Geophysical Year. Inscr "INTERN. GEOFYSISK AR 1957–1958".

467	**102**	25ore green	45	40
468	**103**	35ore red and grey	45	25
469	-	65ore green and blue	45	40

DESIGN—VERT: 65ore Map of Antarctica showing Queen Maud Land.

104 King Haakon VII

1957. 85th Birthday of King Haakon.

470	**104**	35ore red	35	25
471	**104**	65ore blue	70	75

105 King Olav V **106** King Olav V

1958

472	**105**	25ore green	1·00	20
473	**105**	30ore violet	1·70	20
474	**105**	35ore red	65	25
474a	**105**	35ore green	4·00	20
475	**105**	40ore red	85	20
475a	**105**	40ore grey	3·25	1·20
476	**105**	45ore red	1·00	20
477	**105**	50ore brown	5·25	20
478	**105**	50ore red	6·75	20
479	**105**	55ore grey	1·70	95
480	**105**	60ore violet	4·00	85
481	**105**	65ore blue	2·00	40
482	**105**	80ore brown	11·00	55

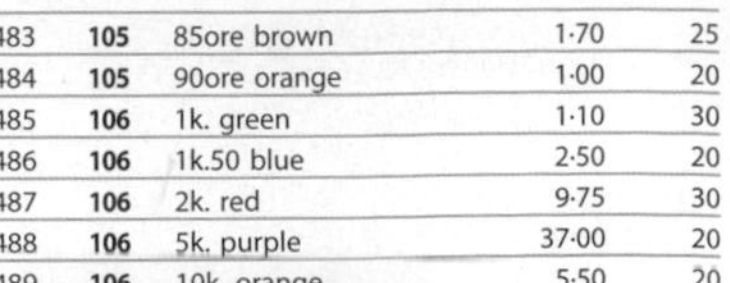

483	**105**	85ore brown	1·70	25
484	**105**	90ore orange	1·00	20
485	**106**	1k. green	1·10	30
486	**106**	1k.50 blue	2·50	20
487	**106**	2k. red	9·75	30
488	**106**	5k. purple	37·00	20
489	**106**	10k. orange	5·50	20

107 Asbjorn Kloster (founder)

1959. Cent of Norwegian Temperance Movement.

490	**107**	45ore brown	55	30

108 Society's Centenary Medal

1959. 150th Anniv of Royal Norwegian Agricultural Society.

491	**108**	45ore brown and red	45	40
492	**108**	90ore grey and blue	1·50	1·60

109 Sower

1959. Centenary of Norwegian Royal College of Agriculture.

493	**109**	45ore black and brown	65	40
494	-	90ore black and blue	1·20	1·10

DESIGN—VERT: 90ore Ears of corn.

110 White Anemone

1960. Tuberculosis Relief Funds.

495	**110**	45ore+10ore yellow, green and red	2·50	2·40
496	-	90ore+10ore mult	6·50	6·25

DESIGN: 90ore Blue anemone.

111 Society's Original Seal

1960. Bicentenary of Royal Norwegian Society of Scientists.

497	**111**	45ore red on grey	55	45
498	**111**	90ore blue on grey	1·40	1·40

112 Refugee Mother and Child

1960. World Refugee Year.

499	**112**	45ore+25ore black and pink	4·25	4·00
500	**112**	90ore+25ore blk & bl	7·50	7·25

113 Viking Longship

1960. Norwegian Ships.

501	**113**	20ore black and grey	1·20	90
502	-	25ore black and green	85	85
503	-	45ore black and red	85	55
504	-	55ore black and brown	2·20	2·20
505	-	90ore black and blue	2·75	1·90

SHIPS: 25ore Hanse kogge; 45ore "Skomvaer" (barque); 55ore "Dalfon" (tanker); 90ore "Bergensfjord" (liner).

113a Conference Emblem

1960. Europa.

506	**113a**	90ore blue	70	65

113b Douglas DC-8

1961. 10th Anniv of Scandinavian Airlines System (SAS).

507	**113b**	90ore blue	75	60

114 Throwing the Javelin

1961. Centenary of Norwegian Sport.

508	**114**	20ore brown	55	55
509	-	25ore green	55	55
510	-	45ore red	55	45
511	-	90ore mauve	1·00	95

DESIGNS: 25ore Ice skating; 45ore Ski jumping; 90ore Yachting.

115 Haakonshallen Barracks and Rosencrantz Tower

1961. 700th Anniv of Haakonshallen, Bergen.

512	**115**	45ore black and red	45	30
513	**115**	1k. black and green	65	30

116 Oslo University

1961. 150th Anniv of Oslo University.

514	**116**	45ore red	45	30
515	**116**	1k.50 blue	75	30

117 Nansen

1961. Birth Centenary of Fridtjof Nansen (polar explorer).

516	**117**	45ore black and red	50	35
517	**117**	90ore black and blue	95	90

118 Amundsen, "Fram" and Dog-team

1961. 50th Anniv of Amundsen's Arrival at South Pole.

518	**118**	45ore red and grey	60	45
519	-	90ore deep blue and blue	1·10	95

DESIGN: 90ore Amundsen's party and tent at South Pole.

119 Frederic Passy and Henri Dunant (winners in 1901)

1961. Nobel Peace Prize.

520	**119**	45ore red	35	30
521	**119**	1k. green	1·30	40

120 Prof. V. Bjerknes

1962. Birth Centenary of Prof. Vilhelm Bjerknes (physicist).

522	**120**	45ore black and red	35	30
523	**120**	1k.50 black and blue	90	35

121 Etrich/Rumpler Taube Monoplane "Start"

1962. 50th Anniv of Norwegian Aviation.

524	**121**	1k.50 brown and blue	2·30	50

122 Branch of Fir, and Cone

1962. Cent of State Forestry Administration.

525	**122**	45ore grey, black and red	50	50
526	**122**	1k. grey, black and green	5·25	35

123 Europa "Tree"

1962. Europa.

527	**123**	50ore red	55	55
528	**123**	90ore blue	1·40	1·30

125 Reef Knot

1962

531g	-	25ore green	30	25
532	-	30ore drab	3·50	3·25
532a	-	30ore green	40	25
533	**125**	35ore green	20	20
533a	-	40ore red	3·50	20
534	-	40ore green	20	20
534a	-	45ore green	55	55
535	**125**	50ore red	3·25	20
535a	**125**	50ore grey	25	20
536	-	55ore brown	55	55
536a	**125**	60ore green	9·25	25
537a	**125**	60ore red	1·30	30
537b	-	65ore violet	2·50	20
538	**125**	65ore red	25	15
538a	**125**	70ore brown	25	20
539	-	75ore green	25	15
539a	-	80ore purple	8·50	2·20
539b	-	80ore brown	20	15
540	-	85ore brown	40	25
540a	-	85ore buff	30	25
540b	-	90ore blue	30	20
541	-	100ore violet	60	25
541a	-	100ore red	35	15
542	-	110ore red	30	20
542a	-	115ore brown	85	35
543	-	120ore blue	35	30
543a	-	125ore red	40	20
544	-	140ore blue	50	30
544a	-	750ore brown	2·10	25

DESIGNS: 25, 40, 90, 100 (2), 110, 120, 125ore, Runic drawings; 30, 45, 55, 75, 85ore, Ear of wheat and Atlantic cod; 65 (537b), 80, 140ore, "Stave" (wooden) church and "Aurora Borealis"; 115ore Fragment of Urnes stave-church; 750ore Sigurd Farnesbane (the Dragon killer) and Regin (the blacksmith), portal from Hylestad stave-church.

126 Camilla Collett

1963. 150th Birth Anniv of Camilla Collett (author).

545	**126**	50ore red	50	30
546	**126**	90ore blue	1·10	1·30

127 Boatload of Wheat

1963. Freedom from Hunger.

547	**127**	25ore bistre	35	30
548	**127**	35ore green	65	60
549	-	50ore red	55	45
550	-	90ore blue	1·10	1·10

DESIGN—37½×21 mm: 50, 90ore Birds carrying food on cloth.

128 River Mail Boat

1963. Tercentenary of Southern-Northern Norwegian Postal Services.

551	**128**	50ore red	80	75
552	-	90ore blue	2·20	2·20

DESIGN: 90ore Femboring (Northern sailing vessel).

129 Ivar Aasen

1963. 150th Birth Anniv of Ivar Aasen (philologist).

553	**129**	50ore red and grey	35	30
554	**129**	90ore blue and grey	1·20	1·20

The note after No. 433 re "NOREG" also applies here.

130 "Co-operation"

1963. Europa.

555	**130**	50ore orange and purple	75	55
556	**130**	90ore green and blue	2·30	1·80

131 "Herringbone" Pattern

1963. 150th Anniv of Norwegian Textile Industry.

557	**131**	25ore green and bistre	55	55
558	**131**	35ore ultramarine and blue	1·00	95
559	**131**	50ore purple and red	55	45

132 Edvard Munch (self-portrait)

1963. Birth Centenary of Edvard Munch (painter and engraver).

560	**132**	25ore black	25	25
561	-	35ore green	30	30
562	-	50ore brown	45	25
563	-	90ore blue and indigo	60	60

DESIGNS (woodcuts)—HORIZ: 35ore "Fecundity"; 50ore "The Solitaries". VERT: 90ore "The Girls on the Bridge".

133 Eilert Sundt (founder)

1964. Centenary of Oslo Workers' Society.

564	**133**	25ore green	50	40
565	-	50ore purple	50	20

DESIGN: 50ore Beehive emblem of O.W.S.

134 C. M. Guldberg and P. Waage (chemists)

1964. Centenary of Law of Mass Action.

566	**134**	35ore green	55	45
567	**134**	55ore stone	1·40	1·30

135 Eidsvoll Manor

1964. 150th Anniv of Norwegian Constitution.

568	**135**	50ore grey and red	60	40
569	-	90ore black and blue	1·50	1·40

DESIGN: 90ore Storting (Parliament House), Oslo.

On 1 June 1964 a stamp depicting the U.N. refugee emblem and inscr "PORTO BETALT ... LYKKEBREVET 1964' was put on sale. It had a franking value of 50ore but was sold for 2k.50, the balance being for the Refugee Fund. In addition, each stamp bore a serial number representing participation in a lottery which took place in September. The stamp was on sale until 15 July and had validity until 10 August.

136 Harbour Scene

1964. Cent of Norwegian Seamen's Mission.

570	**136**	25ore green and yellow	55	45
571	**136**	90ore blue and cream	1·50	1·40

137 Europa "Flower"

1964. Europa.

572	**137**	90ore deep blue and blue	3·25	2·75

138 H. Anker and O. Arvesen (founders)

1964. Cent of Norwegian Folk High Schools.

573	**138**	50ore pink	55	40
574	**138**	90ore blue	2·00	1·90

The note after No. 433 re "NOREG" also applies here.

139 "Radio-telephone"

1965. Centenary of I.T.U.

575	**139**	60ore purple	55	25
576	-	90ore grey	1·00	1·00

DESIGN: 90ore "T.V. transmission".

140 Dove of Peace and Broken Chain

1965. 20th Anniv of Liberation.

577	**140**	30ore+10ore brown, green and sepia	35	30
578	-	60ore+10ore blue and red	45	40

DESIGN: 60ore Norwegian flags.

141 Mountain Landscapes

1965. Centenary of Norwegian Red Cross.

579	**141**	60ore brown and red	55	45
580	-	90ore blue and red	3·25	3·00

DESIGN: 90ore Coastal view.

142 Europa "Sprig"

1965. Europa.

581	**142**	60ore red	80	35
582	**142**	90ore blue	1·80	1·60

143 St. Sunniva and Bergen Buildings

1965. Bicentenary of Harmonien Philharmonic Society.

583	-	30ore black and green	45	30
584	**143**	90ore black and blue	1·10	1·10

DESIGN—VERT: 30ore St. Sunniva.

144 Rondane Mountains (after H. Sohlberg)

1965. Rondane National Park.

585	**144**	1k.50 blue	1·80	30

145 "Rodoy Skier" (rock carving)

1966. World Skiing Championships, Oslo. Inscr "VM OSLO 1966".

586	**145**	40ore brown	90	75
587	-	55ore green	1·30	1·30
588	-	60ore brown	50	35
589	-	90ore blue	1·30	1·30

DESIGNS—HORIZ: 55ore Ski jumper; 60ore Cross-country skier. VERT: 90ore Holmenkollen ski jumping tower, Oslo.

146 "The Bible"

1966. 150th Anniv of Norwegian Bible Society.

590	**146**	60ore red	45	30
591	**146**	90ore blue	90	1·10

147 Guilloche Pattern

1966. 150th Anniv of Bank of Norway.

592	**147**	30ore green	50	45
593	-	60ore red (Bank building)	25	25

No. 593 is size 27½×21 mm.

148 J. Sverdrup (after C. Krohg)

1966. 150th Birth Anniv of Johan Sverdrup (statesman).

594	**148**	30ore green	50	45
595	**148**	60ore purple	30	25

149 Europa "Ship"

1966. Europa.

596	**149**	60ore red	55	35
597	**149**	90ore blue	1·60	1·20

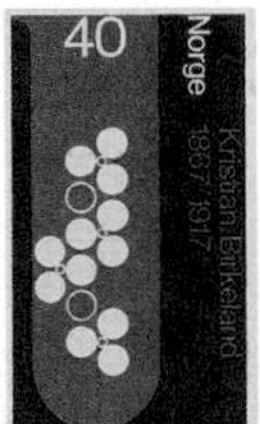

150 Molecules in Test-tube

1966. Birth Centenaries of S. Eyde (industrialist) (1966) and K. Birkeland (scientist) (1967), founders of Norwegian Nitrogen Industry.

598	**150**	40ore blue and light blue	1·40	1·10
599	-	55ore mauve and red	1·70	1·40

DESIGN: 55ore Ear of wheat and conical flask.

151 E.F.T.A. Emblem

1967. European Free Trade Association.

600	**151**	60ore red	45	30
601	**151**	90ore blue	1·70	1·40

152 "Owl" and Three Swords

1967. 150th Anniv of Higher Military Training.

602	**152**	60ore brown	55	55
603	**152**	90ore green	2·00	1·90

153 Cogwheels

1967. Europa.

604	**153**	60ore deep plum, plum and purple	80	30
605	**153**	90ore deep violet, violet and blue	1·30	1·30

154 Johanne Dybwad

1967. Birth Centenary of J. Dybwad (actress).

606	**154**	40ore blue	45	30
607	**154**	60ore red	45	30

155 I. Skrefsrud (missionary and founder)

1967. Centenary of Norwegian Santal Mission.

608	**155**	60ore brown	40	20
609	-	90ore blue	90	85

DESIGN—HORIZ: 90ore Ebenezer Church, Benagaria, Santal, India.

156 Climbers on Mountain-top

1968. Centenary of Norwegian Mountain Touring Association.

610	**156**	40ore brown	90	85
611	-	60ore red	70	20
612	-	90ore blue	1·10	1·10

DESIGNS: 60ore Mountain cairn and scenery; 90ore Glitretind peak.

157 "The Blacksmiths"

1968. Norwegian Handicrafts.

613	**157**	65ore brown, black & red	45	30
614	**157**	90ore brown, black & blue	1·10	1·10

158 Vinje

1968. 150th Birth Anniv of Aasmund Vinje (poet).

615	**158**	50ore brown	50	45
616	**158**	65ore red	30	20

See note below No. 433.

159 Cross and Heart

1968. Centenary of Norwegian Lutheran Home Mission Society.

617	**159**	40ore red and green	2·30	2·20
618	**159**	65ore red and violet	45	20

160 Cathinka Guldberg (first deaconess)

1968. Centenary of Deaconess House, Oslo.

619	**160**	50ore blue	45	40
620	**160**	65ore red	45	20

161 K. P. Arnoldson and F. Bajer

1968. Nobel Peace Prize Winners of 1908.

621	**161**	65ore brown	45	40
622	**161**	90ore blue	95	90

161a Viking Ships (from old Swedish coin)

1969. 50th Anniv of Northern Countries' Union.

623	**161a**	65ore red	45	35
624	**161a**	90ore blue	1·00	95

162 Transport

1969. Centenary of "Rutebok for Norge" ("Communications of Norway") and Road Safety Campaign.

625	**162**	50ore green	70	60
626	-	65ore red and green	40	20

DESIGN: 65ore Pedestrian-crossing.

163 Colonnade

1969. Europa.

627	**163**	65ore black and red	80	25
628	**163**	90ore black and blue	1·80	1·10

164 J. Hjort and Atlantic Cod Eggs

1969. Birth Centenary of Professor Johan Hjort (fisheries pioneer).

629	**164**	40ore brown and blue	75	70
630	-	90ore blue and green	2·00	1·80

DESIGN: 90ore Hjort and polyp.

165 Traena Islands

1969

631	**165**	3k.50 black	1·20	20

166 King Olav V

1969

632	**166**	1k. green	50	20
633	**166**	1k.50 blue	55	20
634	**166**	2k. red	70	20
635	**166**	5k. blue	1·70	20
636	**166**	10k. brown	4·50	20
637	**166**	20k. brown	7·75	30
637a	**166**	50k. green	12·50	35

167 "Mother and Child"

1969. Birth Centenary of Gustav Vigeland (sculptor).

638	**167**	65ore black and red	40	25
639	-	90ore black and blue	80	80

DESIGN: 90ore "Family" (sculpture).

168 Punched Cards

1969. Bicentenary of 1st National Census. Mult.

640	65ore Type **168**	45	30
641	90ore "People" (diagram)	90	85

169 Queen Maud

1969. Birth Centenary of Queen Maud.

642	**169**	65ore purple	45	25
643	**169**	90ore blue	80	80

170 Wolf ("Canis lupus")

1970. Nature Conservation Year.

644	**170**	40ore brown and blue	1·00	95
645	-	60ore grey and brown	1·80	1·30
646	-	70ore brown and blue	1·00	65
647	-	100ore brown and blue	1·50	1·40

DESIGNS—VERT: 60ore Pale pasque flower ("Pulsatilla vernalis"); 70ore Voringsfossen Falls. HORIZ: 100ore White-tailed sea eagle ("Haliaeetus albicilla").

171 "V" Symbol

1970. 25th Anniv of Liberation.

648	**171**	70ore red and violet	1·30	55
649	-	100ore blue and green	1·60	1·30

DESIGN—HORIZ: 100ore Merchant ships in convoy.

172 "Citizens"

1970. 900th Anniv of Bergen.

650	**172**	40ore green	1·20	80
651	-	70ore purple	1·80	45
652	-	1k. blue	1·50	1·50

DESIGNS: 70ore "City between the Mountains"; 1k. "Ships".

173 Hands reaching for Globe

1970. 25th Anniv of United Nations.

653	**173**	70ore red	2·00	60
654	**173**	100ore green	1·40	1·30

174 G. O. Sars

1970. Norwegian Zoologists.

655	**174**	40ore brown	1·00	95
656	-	50ore lilac	1·00	75
657	-	70ore brown	1·00	45
658	-	100ore blue	1·00	95

ZOOLOGISTS: 50ore Hans Strom; 70ore J. E. Gunnerus; 100ore Michael Sars.

175 Ball-game

1970. Centenary of Central School of Gymnastics, Oslo.

659	**175**	50ore brown and blue	50	40
660	-	70ore brown and red	80	20

DESIGN—HORIZ: 70ore "Leapfrog" exercise.

176 Tonsberg's Seal c. 1340

1971. 1100th Anniv of Tonsberg.

661	**176**	70ore red	45	30
662	**176**	100ore blue	1·00	70

177 Parliament House, Oslo

1971. Centenary of Introduction of Annual Parliamentary Sessions.

663	**177**	70ore lilac and red	40	30
664	**177**	100ore green and blue	1·00	75

178 "Helping Hand"

1971. "Help for Refugees".

665	**178**	50ore green and black	45	45
666	**178**	70ore red and black	35	20

179 "Hauge addressing Followers" (A. Tidemand)

1971. Birth Centenary of Hans Nielson Hauge (church reformer).

667	**179**	60ore black	45	45
668	**179**	70ore brown	35	20

180 Bishop welcoming Worshippers

1971. 900th Anniv of Oslo Bishopric.

669	-	70ore black and red	40	35
670	**180**	1k. black and blue	1·10	95

DESIGN—VERT: 70ore Masons building first church.

181 Roald Amundsen and Treaty Emblem

1971. 10th Anniv of Antarctic Treaty.

671	**181**	100ore red and blue	2·50	1·80

182 "The Preacher and the King"

1971. Norwegian Folk Tales. Drawings by Erik Werenskiold.

672	-	40ore black and green	50	35
673	**182**	50ore black and blue	50	25
674	-	70ore black and purple	45	25

DESIGNS—VERT: 40ore "The Farmer and the Woman"; 70ore "The Troll and the Girl".

183 Anniversary Symbol

1972. 150th Anniv of Norwegian Savings Banks.

675	**183**	80ore gold and red	40	25
676	**183**	1k.20 gold and blue	95	75

184 3s. "Posthorn" Stamp

1972. Centenary of Norwegian "Posthorn" Stamps.

677	**184**	80ore red and brown	55	30
678	**184**	1k. blue and violet	55	45
MS679		120x71 mm. Nos. 677/8 (sold at 2k.50)	5·00	5·50

185 Alstad "Picture" Stone (detail)

1972. 1100th Anniv of Norway's Unification. Relics.

680	**185**	50ore green	55	55
681	-	60ore brown	1·10	85
682	-	80ore red	1·10	40
683	-	1k.20 blue	1·20	1·20

DESIGNS: 60ore Portal, Hemsedal Church (detail); 80ore Figurehead of Oseberg Viking ship; 1k.20, Sword-hilt (Lodingen).

186 King Haakon VII

1972. Birth Centenary of King Haakon VII.

684	**186**	80ore red	2·20	45
685	**186**	1k.20 blue	1·10	95

187 "Joy" (Ingrid Ekrem)

1972. "Youth and Leisure".

686	**187**	80ore mauve	60	20
687	-	1k.20 blue	1·10	1·10

DESIGN: 1k.20, "Solidarity" (Ole Instefjord).

1972. "Interjunex 1972" Stamp Exhibition, Oslo. Nos. 686/7 optd INTERJUNEX 72.

688	**187**	80ore mauve	2·40	2·30
689	-	1k.20 blue	2·40	2·30

189 "Maud"

1972. Norwegian Polar Ships.

690	**189**	60ore olive and green	1·10	95
691	-	80ore red and black	1·50	45
692	-	1k.20 blue and red	1·50	1·20

DESIGNS: 80ore "Fram" (Amundsen and Nansen's ship); 1k.20, "Gjoa".

190 "Little Man"

1972. Norwegian Folk Tales. Drawings of Trolls by Th. Kittelsen.

693	**190**	50ore black and green	55	20
694	-	60ore black and blue	60	45
695	-	80ore black and pink	60	20

TROLLS: 60ore "The troll who wonders how old he is"; 80ore "Princess riding on a bear".

191 Dr. Hansen and Bacillus Diagram

1973. Centenary of Hansen's Identification of Leprosy Bacillus.

696	**191**	1k. red and blue	45	25
697	-	1k.40 blue and red	1·10	95

DESIGN: 1k.40, As Type **191** but bacillus as seen in modern microscope.

192 Europa "Posthorn"

1973. Europa.

698	**192**	1k. red, scarlet and carmine	1·50	35
699	**192**	1k.40 emerald, green and blue	3·00	1·10

192a "The Nordic House", Reykjavik

1973. Nordic Countries' Postal Co-operation.

700	**192a**	1k. multicoloured	80	50
701	**192a**	1k.40 multicoloured	90	85

193 King Olav V

1973. King Olav's 70th Birthday.

702	**193**	1k. brown and purple	90	25
703	**193**	1k.40 brown and blue	90	80

194 J. Aall

1973. Birth Centenary of Jacob Aall (industrialist).

704	**194**	1k. purple	50	30
705	**194**	1k.40 blue	85	80

195 Bone Carving

1973. Lapp Handicrafts.

706	**195**	75ore brown and cream	50	35
707	-	1k. red and cream	60	25
708	-	1k.40 black and blue	80	70

DESIGNS: 1k. Detail of weaving; 1k.40, Detail of tin-ware.

196 Yellow Wood Violet

1973. Mountain Flowers. Multicoloured.

709	65ore Type **196**	35	30
710	70ore Rock speedwell	50	55
711	1k. Mountain heath	50	25

197 Land Surveying

1973. Bicent of Norwegian Geographical Society.

712	**197**	1k. red	40	30
713	-	1k.40 blue	90	85

DESIGN: 1k.40, Old map of Hestbraepiggene (mountain range).

198 Lindesnes

1974. Norwegian Capes.

714	**198**	1k. green	70	50
715	-	1k.40 blue	2·00	1·90

DESIGN: 1k.40, North Cape.

199 "Bridal Procession on Hardanger Fjord" (A. Tidemand and H. Gude)

1974. Norwegian Paintings. Multicoloured.

716	1k. Type **199**	50	30
717	1k.40 "Stugunoset from Filefjell" (J. Dahl)	70	65

200 Gulating Law Manuscript, 1325

1974. 700th Anniv of King Magnus Lagaboter National Legislation.

718	**200**	1k. red and brown	50	25
719	-	1k.40 blue and brown	90	85

DESIGN: 1k.40, King Magnus Lagaboter (sculpture in Stavanger Cathedral).

201 Trees and Saw Blade

1974. Industrial Accident Prevention.

720	**201**	85ore green, deep green and emerald	1·90	1·80
721	-	1k. carmine, red and orange	1·00	40

DESIGN: 1k. Flower and cogwheel.

202 J. H. L. Vogt

1974. Norwegian Geologists.

722	**202**	65ore brown and green	35	30
723	-	85ore brown and purple	1·30	1·20
724	-	1k. brown and orange	40	25
725	-	1k.40 brown and blue	1·00	95

DESIGNS: 85ore V. M. Goldschmidt; 1k. Th. Kjerulf; 1k.40, W. C. Brogger.

203 Buildings of the World

1974. Centenary of Universal Postal Union.

726	**203**	1k. brown and green	35	20
727	-	1k.40 blue and brown	90	85

DESIGN: 1k.40, People of the World.

204 Detail of Chest of Drawers

1974. Norwegian Folk Art. Rose Painting. Mult.

728	85ore Type **204**	50	50
729	1k. Detail of cupboard	50	35

205 Woman Skier, 1900

1975. Norwegian Skiing.

730	**205**	1k. red and green	55	25
731	-	1k.40 blue and brown	75	65

DESIGN: 1k.40, Skier making telemark turn.

206 "Three Women with Ivies" Gate, Vigeland Park, Oslo

1975. International Women's Year.

732	**206**	1k.25 violet and purple	35	20
733	**206**	1k.40 ultramarine and blue	75	65

207 Nusfjord Fishing Harbour, Lofoten Islands

1975. European Architectural Heritage Year.

734	**207**	1k. green	55	55
735	-	1k.25 red	50	30
736	-	1k.40 blue	85	65

DESIGNS: 1k.25, Old Stavanger; 1k.40, Roros.

208 Norwegian 1k. Coin, 1875 (Monetary Convention)

1975. Cent of Monetary and Metre Conventions.

737	**208**	1k.25 red	50	20
738	-	1k.40 blue	70	65

DESIGN: 1k.40, O. J. Broch (original Director of the International Bureau of Weights and Measures) (Metre Convention).

209 Camping and Emblem

1975. World Scout Jamboree, Lillehammer. Mult.

739	1k.25 Type **209**	50	20
740	1k.40 Skiing and emblem	1·00	85

210 Colonist's Peat House

1975. 150th Anniv of First Emigrations to America.

741	**210**	1k.25 brown	50	20
742	-	1k.40 blue	80	65

DESIGNS: 1k.40, C. Peerson and extract from letter to America, 1874.

211 "Templet" (Temple Mountain), Tempelfjord, Spitzbergen

1975. 50th Anniv of Norwegian Administration of Spitzbergen.

743	**211**	1k. grey	60	45
744	-	1k.25 purple	60	20
745	-	1k.40 blue	1·20	1·20

DESIGNS: 1k.25, Miners leaving pit; 1k.40, Polar bear.

212 "Television Screen" (T. E. Johnsen)

1975. 50th Anniv of Norwegian Broadcasting System. Multicoloured.

746	1k.25 Type **212**	35	20
747	1k.40 Telecommunications antenna (N. Davidsen) (vert)	75	65

213 "The Annunciation"

1975. Paintings from "Altaket" (wooden vault) of "Al" Stave Church, Hallingdal.

748	80ore Type **213**	30	30
749	1k. "The Visitation"	45	35
750	1k.25 "The Nativity" (30×38 mm)	35	20
751	1k.40 "The Adoration" (30×38 mm)	55	55

214 "Halling" (folk dance)

1976. Norwegian Folk Dances. Multicoloured.

752	80ore Type **214**	55	55
753	1k. "Springar"	55	30
754	1k.25 "Gangar"	55	20

215 Silver Sugar Caster, Stavanger, 1770

1976. Centenary of Oslo Museum of Applied Art.

755	**215**	1k.25 brown, red and pink	40	30
756	-	1k.40 lilac, blue and azure	65	65

DESIGN: 1k.40, Goblet, Nostetangen Glass-works, 1770.

216 Bishop's "Mitre" Bowl, 1760

1976. Europa. Early Products of Herrebo Potteries, Halden.

757	**216**	1k.25 red and mauve	55	25
758	-	1k.40 ultramarine & blue	1·10	95

DESIGN: 1k.40, Decorative plate, 1760.

217 "The Pulpit", Lyse Fjord

1976. Norwegian Scenery. Multicoloured.

759	1k. Type **217**	55	55
760	1k.25 Peak of Gulleplet ("The Golden Apple"), Balestrand, Sognefjord	75	25

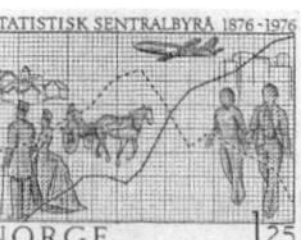

218 Social Development Graph

1976. Cent of Norwegian Central Bureau of Statistics.

761	**218**	1k.25 red	35	20
762	-	2k. blue	70	35

DESIGN: 2k. National productivity graph.

219 Olav Duun and Cairn, Dun Mountain, Joa Island, Namsen Fjord

1976. Birth Centenary of Olav Duun (novelist).

763	**219**	1k.25 multicoloured	40	25
764	**219**	1k.40 multicoloured	75	75

220 "Slindebirkin" (T. Fearnley)

1976. Norwegian Paintings. Multicoloured.

765	1k.25 Type **220**	45	20
766	1k.40 "Gamle Furutraer" (L. Hertervig)	80	75

221 Details of "April"

1976. Tapestry from Baldishol Stave Church. Mult.

767	80ore Type **221**	35	30
768	1k. Detail of "May"	40	30
769	1k.25 "April" and "May" section of tapestry (48×30 mm)	45	20

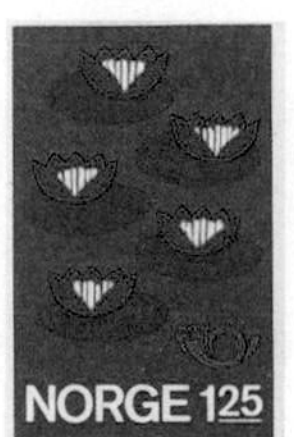

222 Five Water-lilies

1977. Nordic Countries Co-operation in Nature Conservation and Environment Protection.

770	**222**	1k.25 multicoloured	45	30
771	**222**	1k.40 multicoloured	65	65

223 Akershus Castle, Oslo

1977

772	-	1k. green	25	20
773	-	1k.10 purple	40	20
774	**223**	1k.25 red	30	15
775	-	1k.30 brown	35	20
776	-	1k.40 lilac	45	25
777	-	1k.50 red	40	15
778	-	1k.70 green	50	45
779	-	1k.75 green	45	20
780	-	1k.80 blue	45	35
781	-	2k. red	45	20
782	-	2k.20 blue	60	45
783	-	2k.25 violet	65	35
784	-	2k.50 red	55	15
785	-	2k.75 red	80	65
786	-	3k. blue	65	25
787	-	3k.50 violet	90	35

DESIGNS—HORIZ: 1k. Austraat Manor; 1k.10, Trondenes Church, Harstad; 1k.30, Steinviksholm Fortress, Asen Fjord; 1k.40, Ruins of Hamar Cathedral; 2k.20, Tromsdalen Church; 2k.50, Loghouse, Breiland; 2k.75, Damsgard Palace, Laksevag, near Bergen; 3k. Ruins of Selje Monastery; 3k.50, Lindesnes lighthouse. VERT: 1k.50, Stavanger Cathedral; 1k.70, Rosenkrantz Tower, Bergen; 1k.75, Seamen's commemoration hall, Stavern; 1k.80, Torungen lighthouses, Arendal; 2k. Tofte royal estate, Dovre; 2k.25, Oscarshall (royal residence), Oslofjord.

224 Hamnoy, Lofoten Islands

1977. Europa. Multicoloured.

795	1k.25 Type **224**	65	30
796	1k.80 Huldrefossen, Nordfjord (vert)	1·00	85

225 Spruce

1977. Norwegian Trees.

797	**225**	1k. green	40	30
798	-	1k.25 brown	50	30
799	-	1k.80 black	55	55

DESIGNS: 1k.25, Fir; 1k.80, Birch.

See note below No. 433.

226 "Constitutionen" (paddle-steamer) at Arendal

1977. Norwegian Coastal Routes.

800	**226**	1k. brown	35	25
801	-	1k.25 red	65	25
802	-	1k.30 green	1·30	1·10
803	-	1k.80 blue	75	60

DESIGNS: 1k.25, "Vesteraalen" (coaster) off Bodo; 1k.30, "Kong Haakon" and "Dronningen" at Stavanger, 1893 (ferries); 1k.80, "Nordstjernen" and "Harald Jarl" (ferries).

227 "From the Herring Fishery" (after photo by S. A. Borretzen)

1977. Fishing Industry.

804	**227**	1k.25 brown on orange	50	20
805	-	1k.80 blue on blue	65	60

DESIGN: 1k.80, Saithe and fish hooks.

See note below No. 433.

228 "Saturday Evening" (H. Egedius)

1977. Norwegian Paintings. Multicoloured.

806	1k.25 Type **228**	35	30
807	1k.80 "Forest Lake in Lower Telemark" (A. Cappelen)	75	70

229 "David with the Bells"

1977. Miniatures from the Bible of Aslak Bolt. Mult.

808	80ore Type **229**	30	20
809	1k. "Singing Friars"	35	20
810	1k.25 "The Holy Virgin with the Child" (34×27 mm)	40	20

230 "Peer and the Buck Reindeer" (after drawing by P. Krohg for "Peer Gynt")

1978. 150th Birth Anniv of Henrik Ibsen (dramatist).

811	**230**	1k.25 black and stone	35	25
812	-	1k.80 multicoloured	70	65

DESIGN: 1k.80, Ibsen (after E. Werenskiold).

231 Heddal Stave Church, Telemark

1978. Europa.

813	**231**	1k.25 brown and orange	85	35
814	-	1k.80 green and blue	1·40	90

DESIGN: 1k.80, Borgund stave church, Sogn.

232 Lenangstindene and Jaegervasstindene, Troms

1978. Norwegian Scenery. Multicoloured.

815	1k. Type **232**	55	25
816	1k.25 Gaustatoppen, Telemark	60	20

233 King Olav in Sailing-boat

1978. 75th Birthday of King Olav V.

817	**233**	1k.25 brown	45	20
818	-	1k.80 violet	75	65

DESIGN—VERT: 1k.80, King Olav delivering royal speech at opening of Parliament.

234 Amundsen's Polar Flight Stamp of 1925

1978. "Norwex 80" International Stamp Exhibition (1st issue).

819	**234**	1k.25 green and grey	65	65
820	**234**	1k.25 blue and grey	65	65
821	-	1k.25 green and grey	65	65
822	-	1k.25 blue and grey	65	65
823	**234**	1k.25 purple and grey	65	65
824	**234**	1k.25 red and grey	65	65
825	-	1k.25 purple and grey	65	65
826	-	1k.25 blue and grey	65	65

DESIGNS: Nos. 821/2, 825/6, Annexation of Spitzbergen stamp of 1925.

On Nos. 819/26 each design incorporates a different value of the 1925 issues.

See also Nos. **MS**847 and **MS**862.

235 Willow Pipe Player

1978. Musical Instruments.

827	**235**	1k. green	30	20
828	-	1k.25 red	35	20
829	-	1k.80 blue	60	50
830	-	7k.50 grey	2·75	30
831	-	15k. brown	3·75	30

DESIGNS: 1k.25, Norwegian violin; 1k.80, Norwegian zither; 7k.50, Ram's horn; 15k. Jew's harp.

See note below No. 433.

236 Wooden Doll, c. 1830

1978. Christmas. Antique Toys from Norwegian Folk Museum. Multicoloured.

835	80ore Type **236**	30	25
836	1k. Toy town, 1896/7	40	25
837	1k.25 Wooden horse from Torpo, Hallingdal	35	20

237 Ski Jumping at Huseby, 1879

1979. Centenary of Skiing Competitions at Huseby and Holmenkollen.

838	**237**	1k. green	40	30
839	-	1k.25 red	45	20
840	-	1k.80 blue	70	60

DESIGNS: 1k.25, Crown Prince Olav ski jumping at Holmenkollen, 1922; 1k.80, Cross-country skiing at Holmenkollen, 1976.

238 "Portrait of Girl" (M. Stoltenberg)

1979. International Year of the Child. Mult.

841	1k.25 Type **238**	40	25
842	1k.80 "Portrait of Boy" (H. C. F. Hosenfelder)	70	65

239 Road to Briksdal Glacier

1979. Norwegian Scenery. Multicoloured.

843	1k. Type **239**	45	25
844	1k.25 Skjernoysund, near Mandal	55	25

240 Falkberget (after Harald Dal)

1979. Birth Centenary of Johan Falkberget (novelist).

845	**240**	1k.25 brown	45	25
846	-	1k.80 blue	60	60

DESIGN: 1k.80, "Ann-Magritt and the Hovi Bullock" (statue by Kristofer Leirdal).

241 Dornier Do-J Wal Flying Boat N-25

1979. "Norwex 80" International Stamp Exhibition, Oslo (2nd issue). Arctic Aviation. Sheet 113×91 mm containing T 241 and similar horiz designs, each black, yellow and ultramarine.

MS847 1k.25 Type **241** (Amundsen and Ellsworth, 1925); 2k. Airship N.1 *Norge* (Amundsen, Ellsworth and Nobile, 1926); 2k.80, Loening OA-2 amphibian *Live Eriksson* (Thor Solberg, 1935); 4k. Douglas DC-7C *Reider Viking* (first scheduled flight over North Pole, 1957) (sold at 15k.) 4·75 4·50

242 Steam Train on Kylling Bridge, Verma, Romsdal

1979. Norwegian Engineering.

848	**242**	1k.25 black and brown	40	15
849	-	2k. black and blue	60	25
850	-	10k. brown and bistre	2·75	45

DESIGNS: 2k. Vessingsjo Dam, Nea, Sor- Trondelag; 10k. Statfjord A offshore oil drilling and production platform.

243 Glacier Buttercup ("Ranunculus glacialis")

1979. Flowers. Multicoloured.

851	80ore Type **243**	35	20
852	1k. Alpine cinquefoil ("Potentilla crantzii")	35	20
853	1k.25 Purple saxifrage ("Saxifraga oppositifolia")	45	20

See also Nos. 867/8.

244 Leaf and Emblems

1980. Centenary of Norwegian Christian Youth Association. Multicoloured.

854	1k. Type **244**	30	25
855	1k.80 Plant and emblems	65	60

245 Oystercatcher Chick ("Haematopus ostralegus")

1980. Birds (1st series). Multicoloured.

856	1k. Type **245**	30	20
857	1k. Mallard chick ("Anas platyrhynchos")	30	20
858	1k.25 White-throated dipper ("Cinclus cinclus")	40	20
859	1k.25 Great tit ("Parus major")	40	20

See also Nos. 869/72, 894/5 and 914/15.

246 Telephone and Dish Aerial

1980. Centenary of Norwegian Telephone Service.

860	**246**	1k.25 brown, purple & bl	35	25
861	-	1k.80 multicoloured	75	70

DESIGN: 1k.80, Erecting a telephone pole.

247 *Bergen* (paddle-steamer)

1980. "Norwex 80" International Stamp Exhibition, Oslo (3rd issue). Sheet 113×90 mm containing T 247 and similar horiz designs.

MS862 1k.25, red and black; 2k. yellow and black; 2k.80, yellow, green and black; 4k. dull blue and black (sold at 15k.) 4·75 4·50

DESIGNS: 2k. Steam locomotive and carriages, 1900; 2k.80, Motor coach, 1940; 4k. Boeing 737 and Douglas DC-9 aircraft.

248 "Vulcan as an Armourer" (Hassel Jerverk after Bech)

1980. Nordic Countries' Postal Co-operation. Cast-iron Stove Ornaments.

863	**248**	1k.25 brown	35	25
864	-	1k.80 violet	70	65

DESIGN: 1k.80, "Hercules at a burning Altar" (Moss Jerverk after Henrich Bech).

249 "Jonsokbal" (Nikolai Astrup)

1980. Norwegian Paintings. Multicoloured.

865	1k.25 Type **249**	35	25
866	1k.80 "Seljefloyten" (Christian Skredsvig)	70	65

1980. Flowers. As T 243. Multicoloured.

867	80ore Rowan berries ("Sorbus aucparia")	30	25
868	1k. Dog rose hips ("Rosa canina")	30	25

1981. Birds (2nd series). As T 245. Multicoloured.

869	1k.30 Lesser white-fronted goose ("Anser erythropus")	40	30
870	1k.30 Peregrine falcon ("Falco peregrinus")	40	30
871	1k.50 Atlantic puffin ("Fratercula arctica")	50	25
872	1k.50 Black guillemot ("Cepphus grylle")	50	25

250 Cow

1981. Centenary of Norwegian Milk Producers' National Association. Multicoloured.

873	1k.10 Type **250**	40	20
874	1k.50 Goat	45	20

See note below No. 433.

251 "The Mermaid" (painting by Kristen Aanstad on wooden dish from Hol)

1981. Europa. Multicoloured.

875	1k.50 Type **251**	65	30
876	2k.20 "The Proposal" (painting by Ola Hansson on box from Nes)	1·00	85

See note below No. 433.

252 Weighing Anchor

1981. Sailing Ship Era.

877	**252**	1k.30 green	40	30
878	-	1k.50 red	45	25
879	-	2k.20 blue	65	55

DESIGNS—VERT: 1k.50, Climbing the rigging. HORIZ: 2k.20, "Christian Radich" (cadet ship).

253 "Skibladner" (paddle-steamer)

1981. Norwegian Lake Shipping.

880	**253**	1k.10 brown	45	20
881	-	1k.30 green	55	45
882	-	1k.50 red	55	25
883	-	2k.30 blue	80	45

DESIGNS: 1k.30, "Victoria" (ferry); 1k.50, "Faemund II" (ferry); 2k.30, "Storegut" (train ferry).

254 Handicapped People as Part of Community

1981. International Year of Disabled Persons.

884	**254**	1k.50 pink, red and blue	50	25
885	-	2k.20 blue, deep blue and red	60	50

DESIGN: 2k.20, Handicapped and non-handicapped people walking together.

255 "Interior in Blue" (Harriet Backer)

1981. Norwegian Paintings. Multicoloured.

886	1k.50 Type **255**	35	25
887	1k.70 "Peat Moor on Jaeren" (Kitty Lange Kielland)	65	60

256 Hajalmar Branting and Christian Lange

1981. Nobel Peace Prize Winners of 1921.

888	**256**	5k. black	1·40	30

257 "One of the Magi" (detail from Skjak tapestry, 1625)

1981. Tapestries. Multicoloured.

889	1k.10 Type **257**	30	25
890	1k.30 "Adoration of Christ" (detail, Skjak tapestry, 1625)	30	30
891	1k.50 "Marriage in Cana" (pillow slip from Storen, 18th century) (29×36 mm)	45	20

258 Ski Sticks

1982. World Ski Championships, Oslo.

892	**258**	2k. red and blue	45	25
893	-	3k. blue and red	70	45

DESIGN: 3k. Skis.

1982. Birds (3rd series). As T 245. Multicoloured.

894	2k. Bluethroat ("Luscinia svecica")	50	25
895	2k. European robin ("Erithacus rubecula")	50	25

259 Nurse

1982. Anti-tuberculosis Campaign. Mult.

896	2k. Type **259**	45	20
897	3k. Microscope	70	60

See note below No. 433.

260 King Haakon VII disembarking from "Heimdal" after Election, 1905

1982. Europa.

898	**260**	2k. brown	1·70	30
899	-	3k. blue	1·90	45

DESIGN: 3k. Crown Prince Olav greeting King Haakon VII after liberation, 1945.

261 "Girls from Telemark" (Erik Werenskiold)

1982. Norwegian Paintings. Multicoloured.

900	1k.75 Type **261**	50	40
901	2k. "Tone Veli by Fence" (Henrik Sorenson) (vert)	50	25

See note below No. 433.

262 Consecration Ceremony, Nidaros Cathedral, Trondheim

1982. 25th Anniv of King Olav V's Reign.

902	**262**	3k. violet	1·00	75

263 "Bjornstjerne Bjornson on Balcony at Aulestad" (Erik Werenskiold)

1982. Writers' Birth Anniversaries. Multicoloured.

903	1k.75 Type **263** (150th anniv)	60	30
904	2k. "Sigrid Undset" (after A. C. Svarstad) (birth centenary)	60	20

264 Construction of Letter "A"

1982. Centenary of Graphical Union of Norway.
905 **264** 2k. yellow, green and black 50 30
906 - 3k. multicoloured 75 50
DESIGN: 3k. Offset litho printing rollers.

265 Fridtjof Nansen

1982. 1922 Nobel Peace Prize Winner.
907 **265** 3k. blue 1·00 40
See note below No. 433.

266 "Christmas Tradition" (Adolf Tidemand)

1982. Christmas.
908 **266** 1k.75 multicoloured 45 25

267 Buhund (farm dog)

1983. Norwegian Dogs. Multicoloured.
909 2k. Type **267** 70 40
910 2k.50 Elkhound 80 20
911 3k.50 Lundehund (puffin hunter) 1·10 60
See note below No. 433.

268 Mountain Scenery

1983. Nordic Countries' Postal Co-operation. "Visit the North". Multicoloured.
912 2k.50 Type **268** 60 25
913 3k.50 Fjord scenery 1·20 65

1983. Birds (4th series). As T 245. Mult.
914 2k.50 Barnacle goose ("Branta leucopsis") 85 25
915 2k.50 Little auk ("Alle alle") 85 25

269 Edvard Grieg with Concerto in A minor

1983. Europa.
916 **269** 2k.50 red 1·70 30
917 - 3k.50 blue and green 2·40 75
DESIGN—VERT: 3k.50, Statue of Niels Henrik Abel (mathematician) by Gustav Vigeland.

270 Arrows forming Posthorn

1983. World Communications Year. Multicoloured.
918 2k.50 Type **270** 60 25
919 3k.50 Arrows circling globe 1·00 60

271 King Olav V and Royal Birch, Molde

1983. 80th Birthday of King Olav V.
920 **271** 5k. green 1·70 35

272 Lie

1983. 150th Birth Anniv of Jonas Lie (author).
921 **272** 2k.50 red 70 25

273 Northern Femboring

1983. North Norwegian Ships.
922 **273** 2k. blue and brown 75 40
923 - 3k. brown and blue 1·10 60
DESIGNS: 3k. Northern jekt.
See note below No. 433.

274 "The Sleigh Ride" (Axel Ender)

1983. Christmas. Multicoloured.
924 2k. Type **274** 75 30
925 2k.50 "The Guests are arriving" (Gustav Wendel) 80 30

275 Post Office Counter

1984. Postal Work. Multicoloured.
926 2k. Type **275** 65 30
927 2k.50 Postal sorting 65 20
928 3k.50 Postal delivery 1·10 55

276 Freshwater Fishing

1984. Sport Fishing.
929 **276** 2k.50 red 60 20
930 - 3k. green 65 45
931 - 3k.50 blue 1·00 45
DESIGNS: 3k. Atlantic salmon fishing; 3k.50, Sea fishing.

277 Magnetic Meridians and Parallels

1984. Birth Bicentenary of Christopher Hansteen (astronomer and geophysicist).
932 **277** 3k.50 blue 1·00 45
933 - 5k. red 1·30 30
DESIGN—VERT: 5k. Portrait of Hansteen by Johan Gorbitz.

278 Bridge

1984. Europa. 25th Anniv of European Post and Telecommunications Conference.
934 **278** 2k.50 multicoloured 1·10 30
935 **278** 3k.50 multicoloured 2·50 75

279 Vegetables, Fruit and Herbs

1984. Centenary of Norwegian Horticultural Society. Multicoloured.
936 2k. Type **279** 65 30
937 2k.50 Rose and garland of flowers 70 25

280 Honey Bees

1984. Centenaries of Norwegian Beekeeping Society and Norwegian Poultry-breeding Society. Mult.
938 2k.50 Type **280** 70 25
939 2k.50 Leghorn cock 70 25
See note below No. 433.

281 Holberg (after J. M. Bernigeroth)

1984. 300th Birth Anniv of Ludvig Holberg (writer).
940 **281** 2k.50 red 75 25

282 Children reading

1984. 150th Anniv of "Norsk Penning-Magazin" (1st weekly magazine in Norway).
941 **282** 2k.50 purple, blue and red 60 25
942 - 3k.50 orange and violet 80 45
DESIGN: 3k.50, 1st edition of "Norsk Penning-Magazin".

283 Entering Parliamentary Chamber, 2 July 1884

1984. Cent of Norwegian Parliament.
943 **283** 7k.50 brown 3·00 85

284 Karius and Baktus (tooth decay bacteria)

1984. Characters from Stories by Thorbjorn Egner. Multicoloured.
944 2k. Type **284** 1·10 25
945 2k. The tree shrew playing guitar 1·10 25
946 2k.50 Kasper, Jesper and Jonatan (Rovers) in Kardemomme Town 1·20 20
947 2k.50 Chief Constable Bastian 1·20 20

285 Mount Sagbladet (Saw Blade)

1985. Antarctic Mountains. Multicoloured.
948 2k.50 Type **285** 1·00 25
949 3k.50 Mount Hoggestabben (Chopping Block) 1·30 65

286 Return of Crown Prince Olav, 1945

1985. 40th Anniv of Liberation.
950 **286** 3k.50 red and blue 1·30 55

287 Kongsten Fort

1985. 300th Anniv of Kongsten Fort.
951 **287** 2k.50 multicoloured 1·10 25

288 Bronze Cannon, 1596

1985. Artillery Anniversaries. Multicoloured.
952 3k. Type **288** (300th anniv of Artillery) 1·00 55
953 4k. Cannon on sledge carriage, 1758 (bicentenary of Artillery Officers Training School) 1·30 45

289 "Boy and Girl" (detail)

1985. International Youth Year. Sculptures in Vigeland Park, Oslo. Multicoloured.
954 2k. Type **289** 65 30
955 3k.50 Bronze fountain (detail) 1·10 60
See note below No. 433.

290 Torgeir Augundsson (fiddler)

1985. Europa. Music Year.

956	**290**	2k.50 red	1·10	30
957	-	3k.50 blue	3·00	65

DESIGN: 3k.50, Ole Bull (composer and violinist).

291 Workers at Glomfjord

1985. Centenary of Electricity in Norway.

958	**291**	2k.50 red and scarlet	80	20
959	-	4k. blue and green	1·20	40

DESIGN: 4k. Men working on overhead cable.

292 Ekofisk Centre

1985. Stamp Day. Norwegian Working Life (1st series). Offshore Oil Industry. Sheet 112×91 mm containing T 292 and similar horiz designs. Multicoloured.

MS960 2k.+1k. Type **292**; 2k.+1k. Drilling rig *Treasure Scout* and supply ship *Odin Viking*; 2k.+1k. Towing *Stratfjord C* platform to oil field, 1984; 2k.+1k. Drilling team on rig *Neptuno Nordraug* — 5·25 — 6·50

See also Nos. **MS**989 and **MS**1012.

293 Carl Deichman on Book Cover

1985. Bicentenary of Public Libraries.

961	**293**	2k.50 sepia and brown	95	25
962	-	10k. green	3·75	55

DESIGN—HORIZ: 10k. Library interior.

294 Wreath

1985. Christmas. Multicoloured.

963	2k. Type **294**	1·50	25
964	2k.50 Northern bullfinches	1·40	25

295 "Berghavn" (dredger)

1985. 250th Anniv of Port Authorities and Bicentenary of Hydrography in Norway.

965	**295**	2k.50 purple, orange & bl	1·40	25
966	-	5k. blue, green and brown	65	25

DESIGN: 5k. Sextant and detail of chart No. 1 of Lt. F.C. Grove showing Trondheim sealane, 1791.

296 Sun

1986

967	**296**	2k.10 orange and brown	1·50	10
968	-	2k.30 green and blue	75	25
970	-	2k.70 pink and red	80	25
971	-	4k. blue and green	1·10	30

DESIGNS: 2k.30, Atlantic cod and herring; 2k.70, Flowers; 4k. Star ornaments.

297 Marksman in Prone Position

1986. World Biathlon Championships. Mult.

977	2k.50 Type **297**	70	25
978	3k.50 Marksman standing to take aim	1·00	65

298 Industry and Countryside

1986. Europa. Multicoloured.

979	2k.50 Type **298**	1·10	25
980	3k.50 Dead and living forest, mountains and butterflies	2·30	80

299 Stone Cutter

1986. Centenary of Norwegian Craftsmen's Federation.

981	**299**	2k.50 lake and red	85	25
982	-	7k. blue and red	2·75	65

DESIGN: 7k. Carpenter.

300 Moss

1986. Nordic Countries' Postal Co-operation. Twinned Towns. Multicoloured.

983	2k.50 Type **300**	85	25
984	4k. Alesund	1·30	50

See note below No. 433.

301 Hans Polson Egede (missionary) and Map

1986. Birth Anniversaries.

985	**301**	2k.10 brown and red	60	55
986	-	2k.50 red, green and blue	65	25
987	-	3k. brown and red	90	40
988	-	4k. purple and lilac	1·10	40

DESIGNS: 2k.10, Type **301** (300th anniv); 2k.50, Herman Wildenvey (poet) and poem carved in wall at Stavern (centenary); 3k. Tore Ojasaeter (poet) and old cupboard from Skjak (centenary); 4k. Engebret Soot (engineer) and lock gates, Orje (centenary).

See note below No. 433.

302 Timber being debarked and cut

1986. Stamp Day. Norwegian Working Life (2nd series). Paper Industry. Sheet 113×91 mm containing T 302 and similar horiz designs. Multicoloured.

MS989 2k.50+1k. Type **302**; 2k.50+1k. Boiling plant; 2k.50+1k. Paper factory; 2k.50+1k. Paper being dried and rolled into bales — 7·25 — 7·00

303 "Olav Kyrre founds Diocese in Nidaros"

1986. Christmas. Stained Glass Windows by Gabriel Kielland in Nidaros Cathedral, Trondheim. Multicoloured.

990	2k.10 Type **303**	90	35
991	2k.50 "The King and the Peasant at Sul"	1·00	25

304 Doves

1986. International Peace Year.

992	**304**	15k. red, blue and green	6·25	65

305 Numeral

1987

993	**305**	3k.50 yellow, red and blue	1·00	60
994	**305**	4k.50 blue, yellow & green	1·30	45

306 Wooden Building

1987. Europa. Multicoloured.

1000	2k.70 Type **306**	1·60	30
1001	4k.50 Building of glass and stone	1·90	45

307 The Final Vote

1987. 150th Anniv of Laws on Local Councils (granting local autonomy).

1002	**307**	12k. green	4·50	60

308 Rehabilitation Centre, Mogadishu

1987. Norwegian Red Cross in Somalia. Sheet 113×92 mm.

MS1003 **308** 4k.50 multicoloured — 1·80 — 1·70

309 Funnel-shaped Chanterelle ("Cantharellus tubaeformis")

1987. Fungi (1st series). Multicoloured.

1004	2k.70 Type **309**	1·00	25
1005	2k.70 The gypsy ("Rozites caperata")	1·00	25

See also Nos. 1040/1 and 1052/3.

310 Bjornstad Farm from Vaga

1987. Centenary of Sandvig Collections, Maihaugen.

1006	**310**	2k.70 sepia and brown	80	25
1007	-	3k.50 purple and blue	1·20	60

DESIGN: 3k.50, "Horse and Rider" (wooden carving, Christen Erlandsen Listad).

311 Valevag Churchyard

1987. Birth Centenary of Fartein Valen (composer).

1008	**311**	2k.30 blue and green	75	60
1009	-	4k.50 brown	1·30	35

DESIGN—VERT: 4k.50, Fartein Valen.

See note below No. 433.

312 "Storm at Sea" (Christian Krohg)

1987. Paintings. Multicoloured.

1010	2k.70 Type **312**	85	25
1011	5k. "The Farm" (Gerhard Munthe)	1·70	40

313 Eggs and Alevin

1987. Stamp Day. Norwegian Working Life (3rd series). Atlantic Salmon Farming. Sheet 113×91 mm containing T 313 and similar horiz designs. Multicoloured.

MS1012 2k.30+50ore Type **313**; 2k.70+50ore Hatching tanks and parr; 3k.50+50ore Marine stage; 4k.50+50ore Harvested salmon — 7·00 — 6·75

314 Cat with Children making Decorations

1987. Christmas. Multicoloured.

1013	2k.30 Type **314**	1·00	40
1014	2k.70 Dog with children making gingersnaps	1·10	25

315 Dales Pony

1987. Native Ponies.

1015	**315**	2k.30 deep brown, green and brown	80	60
1016	-	2k.70 buff, brown & blue	80	25
1017	-	4k.50 brown, red and blue	1·30	45

DESIGNS: 2k.70, Fjord pony; 4k.50, Nordland pony.

See note below No. 433.

2.90
NORGE · NOREG

316 Western Capercaillie

1988. Wildlife.

1018		2k.60 deep brown, brown and green	80	25
1019	**316**	2k.90 black, brn & grn	1·00	20
1020	-	3k. brown, grey and green	1·00	20
1021	-	3k.20 ultramarine, green and blue	1·00	20
1022	-	3k.80 brown, blue & blk	1·30	25
1023	-	4k. brown, red and green	1·30	25
1024	-	4k.50 brown, green & bl	1·20	25
1025	-	5k.50 brown, grey & grn	1·40	30
1026	-	6k.40 brown, blk & grn	1·80	50

DESIGNS: 2k.60, Fox; 3k. Stoat; 3k.20, Mute swan; 3k.80, Reindeer; 4k. Eurasian red squirrel; 4k.50, Beaver; 5k.50, Lynx; 6k.40, Tengmalm's owl.

317 Band

1988. Centenary of Salvation Army in Norway. Multicoloured.

1035	2k.90 Type **317**	85	25
1036	4k.80 Othilie Tonning (early social worker) and Army nurse	1·70	65

318 Building Fortress

1988. Military Anniversaries.

1037	**318**	2k.50 green	85	30
1038	-	2k.90 brown	1·00	20
1039	-	4k.60 blue	1·50	60

DESIGNS: 2k.50, Type **318** (300th anniv of Defence Construction Service); 2k.90, Corps members in action (centenary of Army Signals corps); 4k.60, Making pontoon bridge (centenary of Engineer Corps).

1988. Fungi (2nd series). As T 309. Mult.

1040	2k.90 Wood blewits ("Lepista nuda")	95	20
1041	2k.90 "Lactarius deterrimus"	95	20

319 Globe

1988. European Campaign for Interdependence and Solidarity of North and South.

1042	**319**	25k. multicoloured	7·75	1·00

320 King Olav V

1988. 85th Birthday of King Olav V. Multicoloured.

1043	2k.90 Type **320**	1·00	25
MS1044	121×91 mm. 2k.90 King Olav arriving as baby; 2k.90 Type **320**; 2k.90 King Olav at Holmenkollen	3·75	3·50

321 "Prinds Gustav" (paddle-steamer)

1988. Europa. Transport and Communications.

1045	**321**	2k.90 black, red and blue	1·10	30
1046	-	3k.80 blue, red & yellow	3·25	1·10

DESIGN: 3k.80, Heroybrua Bridge.

322 King Christian IV

1988. 400th Anniv of Christian IV's Accession to Danish and Norwegian Thrones.

1047	**322**	2k.50 black, stone & vio	1·10	25
1048	-	10k. multicoloured	3·50	45

DESIGN: 10k. 1628 silver coin and extract from decree on mining in Norway.

323 Handball

1988. Stamp Day. Sport. Sheet 113×91 mm containing T 323 and similar horiz designs. Multicoloured.

MS1049	2k.90 Type **323**; 2k.90 Football; 2k.90 Basketball; 2k.90 Volleyball (sold at 15k.)	7·00	7·25

324 Ludvig with Ski Stick

1988. Christmas. Multicoloured.

1050	2k.90 Type **324**	1·00	20
1051	2k.90 Ludvig reading letter	1·00	20

1989. Fungi (3rd series). As T 309. Multicoloured.

1052	3k. Chanterelle ("Cantharellus cibarius")	95	20
1053	3k. Butter mushroom ("Suillus luteus")	95	20

325 Start and Finish of Race

1989. World Cross-country Championship, Stavanger.

1054	**325**	5k. multicoloured	1·60	40

326 Vardo

1989. Town Bicentenaries.

1055	**326**	3k. blue, red & light blue	90	20
1056	-	4k. purple, blue & orange	1·10	55

DESIGN: 4k. Hammerfest.

327 Setesdal Woman

1989. Nordic Countries' Postal Co-operation. Traditional Costumes. Multicoloured.

1057	3k. Type **327**	1·00	25
1058	4k. Kautokeino man	1·50	85

328 Children making Snowman

1989. Europa. Children's Games. Multicoloured.

1059	3k.70 Type **328**	1·50	80
1060	5k. Cat's cradle	2·75	80

See note below No. 433.

329 Rooster and Cover of 1804 First Reader

1989. 250th Anniv of Primary Schools.

1061	**329**	2k.60 multicoloured	1·00	40
1062	-	3k. brown	95	20

DESIGN: 3k. Pocket calculator and child writing.

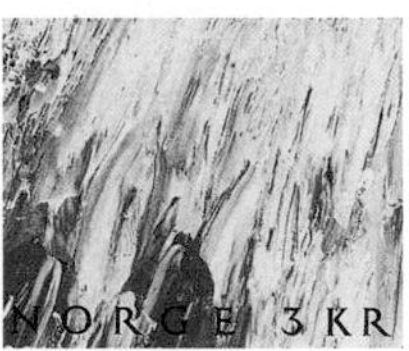

330 "Impressions of the Countryside" (detail)

1989. Stamp Day. Sheet 107×85 mm. containing T 330 and similar horiz designs, forming a composite design of the painting by Jakob Weidemann.

MS1063	3k.×4 multicoloured (sold at 15k.)	6·75	6·50

331 Bjorg Eva Jensen (300m. speed skating 1980)

1989. Winter Olympic Games, Lillehammer (1994) (1st issue). Norwegian Gold Medallists. Sheet 113×91 mm containing T 331 and similar horiz designs. Multicoloured.

MS1064	4k. Type **331**; 4k. Eirik Kvalfoss (biathlon, 1984); 4k. Tom Sandberg (combined cross-country and ski-jumping, 1984); 4k. Women's team (10km cross-country relay, 1984) (sold at 20k.)	7·00	6·75

See also Nos. **MS**1083, **MS**1097, **MS**1143, 1150/1, **MS**1157, 1169/70 and 1175/80.

332 Arnulf Overland (poet, centenary)

1989. Writers' Birth Anniversaries.

1065	**332**	3k. red and blue	1·00	20
1066	-	25k. blue, orange & green	6·75	95

DESIGN: 25k. Hanna Winsnes (pseudonym Hugo Schwartz) (bicentenary).

333 Star Decoration

1989. Christmas. Tree Decorations. Mult.

1067	3k. Type **333**	1·00	20
1068	3k. Bauble	1·00	20

334 Larvik Manor

1989. Manor Houses.

1069	**334**	3k. brown	90	20
1070	-	3k. green	90	20

DESIGN: No. 1070, Rosendal Barony.

335 Emblem

1990. Winter Cities Events, Tromso.

1071	**335**	5k. multicoloured	1·60	40

336 Common Spotted Orchid ("Dactylorhiza fuchsii")

1990. Orchids (1st series). Multicoloured.

1072	3k.20 Type **336**	75	20
1073	3k.20 Dark red helleborine ("Epipactis atrorubens")	75	20

See also Nos. 1141/2.

337 Merchant Navy, Airforce, Home Guard, "Moses" (coastal gun) and Haakon VII's Monogram

1990. 50th Anniv of Norway's Entry into Second World War. Multicoloured.

1074	3k.20 Type **337**	1·10	25
1075	4k. Second Battle of Narvik, 1940	1·40	60

338 Penny Black

1990. 150th Anniv of the Penny Black. Sheet 113×91 mm containing T 338 and similar vert design.

MS1076	5k. Type **338**; 5k. First Norwegian stamp (sold at 15k.)	5·50	5·25

339 Trondheim Post Office

1990. Europa. Post Office Buildings. Mult.

1077	3k.20 Type **339**	1·50	30
1078	4k. Longyearbyen Post Office	3·25	80

340 "Tordenskiold" (from print by J. W. Tegner after Balthazar Denner)

1990. 300th Birth Anniv of Admiral Tordenskiold (Peter Wessel). Multicoloured.

1079	3k.20 Type **340**	95	25
1080	5k. Tordenskiold's coat-of-arms	1·40	50

341 Svendsen

1990. 150th Birth Anniv of Johan Svendsen (composer and conductor).

1081	**341**	2k.70 black and red	90	60
1082	-	15k. brown and yellow	4·75	85

DESIGN: 15k. Svendsen Monument (Stinius Fredriksen), Oslo.

342 Thoreleif Haug (cross-country skiing, 1924)

1990. Winter Olympic Games, Lillehammer (1994) (2nd issue). Norwegian Gold Medallists. Sheet 113×91 mm containing T 342 and similar horiz designs. Multicoloured.

MS1083 4k. Type **342**; 4k. Sonja Henie (figure skating, 1928, 1932, 1936); 4k. Ivar Ballangrud (speed skating, 1928, 1936); 4k. Hjalmar Andersen (speed skating, 1952) (sold at 20k.) 6·75 6·50

343 "Children and Snowman" (Ragni Engstrom Nilsen)

1990. Christmas. Children's Prize-winning Drawings. Multicoloured.

1084	3k.20 Type **343**	85	20
1085	3k.20 "Christmas Church" (Jorgen Ingier)	85	20

344 Nobel Medal and Soderblom

1990. 60th Anniv of Award of Nobel Peace Prize to Nathan Soderblom, Archbishop of Uppsala.

1086	**344**	30k. brown, blue and red	7·25	90

345 Plan and Elevation of Container Ship and Propeller

1991. Centenaries of Federation of Engineering Industries (1989) and Union of Iron and Metal Workers.

1087	**345**	5k. multicoloured	1·30	45

346 Satellite transmitting to Tromso

1991. Europa. Europe in Space. Mult.

1088	3k.20 Type **346**	1·90	30
1089	4k. Rocket leaving Andoya rocket range	5·25	75

See note below No. 433.

347 Christiansholm Fortress (late 17th- century)

1991. 350th Anniv of Kristiansand. Each black, blue and red.

1090	3k.20 Type **347**	1·10	25
1091	5k.50 Present day view of Christiansholm Fortress	1·50	35

348 Fountain, Vigeland Park, Oslo

1991. Nordic Countries' Postal Co-operation. Tourism. Multicoloured.

1092	3k.20 Type **348**	1·10	25
1093	4k. Globe, North Cape Plateau	1·80	1·10

349 "Skomvaer III" (lifeboat)

1991. Centenary of Norwegian Society for Sea Rescue.

1094	**349**	3k.20 brown, black & grn	1·10	35
1095	-	27k. brown, grey & purple	6·75	1·50

DESIGN—VERT: 27k. "Colin Archer" (first lifeboat).

350 Engraving on Steel

1991. Stamp Day. Stamp Engraving. Sheet 113×91 mm containing T 350 and similar horiz designs.

MS1096 2k.70 Type **350**; 3k.20 Engraver using magnifying glass; 4k. Engraver's hands seen through magnifying glass; 5k. Positive impression of engraving and burin (sold at 20k.) 5·75 6·00

351 Birger Ruud (ski jumping, 1932, 1936; downhill, 1936)

1991. Winter Olympic Games, Lillehammer (1994) (3rd issue). Norwegian Gold Medallists. Sheet 113×91 mm containing T 351 and similar horiz designs. Multicoloured.

MS1097 4k. Type **351**; 4k. Johann Grottumsbraten (cross-country skiing, 1928, 1932); 4k. Knut Johannesen (speed skaing, 1960, 1964); 4k. Magnar Solberg (biathlon, 1960, 1968, 1972) (sold at 20k.) 6·50 6·25

352 Posthorn

1991

1098	**352**	1k. black and orange	25	20
1099	**352**	2k. red and green	45	20
1100	**352**	3k. green and blue	65	20
1101	**352**	4k. red and orange	85	20
1102	**352**	5k. blue and green	1·10	25
1103	**352**	6k. red and green	1·30	20
1104	**352**	7k. blue and brown	1·50	25
1105	**352**	8k. green and purple	1·70	30
1106	**352**	9k. brown and blue	1·90	40

353 Guisers with Goat Head

1991. Christmas. Guising. Multicoloured.

1120	3k.20 Type **353**	80	20
1121	3k.20 Guisers with lantern	80	20

354 Queen Sonja **355** King Harald **356** King Harald

1992

1122	**354**	2k.80 lake, purple & red	85	20
1123	**354**	3k. green, deep green and turquoise	85	40
1124	**355**	3k.30 blue, ultramarine and light blue	1·00	20
1125	**355**	3k.50 black and grey	95	45
1127	**355**	4k.50 deep red and red	1·00	55
1128	**355**	5k.50 brown, sepia & blk	1·30	65
1129	**355**	5k.60 orange, red and vermilion	1·50	35
1131	**355**	6k.50 emerald, green and turquoise	1·70	45
1132	**355**	6k.60 maroon, purple and brown	2·00	35
1133	**355**	7k.50 violet, lilac and purple	1·60	1·00
1134	**355**	8k.50 chestnut, deep brown and brown	1·90	1·30
1135	**356**	10k. green	2·50	40
1438	**356**	20k. violet	4·25	50
1138	**356**	30k. blue	6·50	60
1139	**356**	50k. green	10·00	1·30

1992. Orchids (2nd series). As T 336. Mult.

1141	3k.30 Lady's slipper orchid ("Cypripedium calceolus")	85	20
1142	3k.30 Fly orchid ("Ophrys insectifera")	85	20

357 Hallgeir Brenden (cross-country skiing, 1952, 1956)

1992. Winter Olympic Games, Lillehammer (4th issue). Norwegian Gold Medallists. Sheet 113×91 mm containing T 357 and similar horiz designs. Multicoloured.

MS1143 4k. Type **357**; 4k. Arnfinn Bergmann (ski jumping, 1952); 4k. Stein Eriksen (super slalom, 1952); 4k. Simon Slattvik (combined, 1952) (sold at 20k.) 6·50 6·25

358 "Restaurationen" (emigrant sloop)

1992. Europa. 500th Anniv of Discovery of America by Columbus. Transatlantic Ships. Multicoloured.

1144	3k.30 Type **358**	1·50	50
1145	4k.20 "Stavangerfjord" (liner) and American skyline	2·10	75

See note below No. 433.

359 Norwegian Pavilion, Rainbow and Ship

1992. "Expo '92" World's Fair, Seville. Mult.

1146	3k.30 Type **359**	90	25
1147	5k.20 Mountains, rainbow, fish and oil rig	1·50	55

360 Molde

1992. 250th Anniversaries of Molde and Kristiansund.

1148	**360**	3k.30 blue, green & brn	1·00	25
1149	-	3k.30 blue, brown & lt bl	1·00	25

DESIGN: No. 1149, Kristiansund.

361 Banners and Lillehammer Buildings

1992. Winter Olympic Games, Lillehammer (1994) (5th issue). Multicoloured.

1150	3k.30 Type **361**	80	25
1151	4k.20 Flags	1·20	55

362 Flask with Etched Figures (Serre Petersen)

1992. Stamp Day. Sheet 113×91 mm containing T 362 and similar horiz designs. Multicoloured.

MS1152 2k.80 Type **362**; 3k.30 Monogrammed carafe; 4k.20 Cut-glass salad bowl; 5k.20 Engraved goblet (Heinrich Gottlieb Kohler) (sold at 20k.) 5·75 5·50

363 Gnomes below Pillar Box

1992. Christmas. Christmas card designs by Otto Moe. Multicoloured.

1153	3k.30 Type **363**	80	20
1154	3k.30 Gnome posting letter	80	20

364 Orange-tip ("Anthocaris cardamines")

1993. Butterflies (1st series). Multicoloured.

1155	3k.50 Type **364**	80	20
1156	3k.50 Small tortoiseshell ("Aglais urticae")	80	20

See also Nos. 1173/4.

365 Finn Chr. Jagge (slalom)

1993. Winter Olympic Games, Lillehammer (1994) (6th issue). Norwegian Gold Medallists at 1992 Games. Sheet 113×91 mm containing T 365 and similar horiz designs. Multicoloured.

MS1157	4k.50 Type **365**; 4k.50 Bjorn Daehlie (cross-country skiing); 4k.50 Geir Karlstad (speed skating); 4k.50 Vegard Ulvang (cross-country skiing)	6·75	6·25

366 Grieg

1993. 150th Birth Anniv of Edvard Grieg (composer). Multicoloured.

1158	3k.50 Type **366**	90	25
1159	5k.50 "Spring"	2·00	45

367 Two-man Kayak on Lake

1993. Nordic Countries' Postal Co-operation. Tourist Activities. Multicoloured.

1160	4k. Type **367**	1·10	50
1161	4k.50 White-water rafting	1·70	55

368 Richard With (founder) and "Vesteraalen"

1993. Centenary of Express Coaster Service.

1162	**368**	3k.50 blue, violet and red	90	25
1163	-	4k.50 multicoloured	1·20	45

DESIGN: 4k.50, "Kong Harald".

369 Handball

1993. Sports Events. Multicoloured.

1164	3k.50 Type **369** (Women's World Championship, Norway)	90	25
1165	5k.50 Cycling (World Championships, Oslo and Hamar)	1·30	45

370 Johann Castberg (politician)

1993. Centenary of Workforce Protection Legislation.

1166	**370**	3k.50 brown and blue	90	25
1167	-	12k. blue and brown	3·25	55

DESIGN: 12k. Betzy Kjelsberg (first woman factory inspector).

371 Deail of Altarpiece (Jakob Klukstad), Lesja Church

1993. Stamp Day. Wood Carvings of Acanthus Leaves. Sheet 113×91 mm containing T 371 and similar horiz designs. Multicoloured.

MS1168	3k. Type **371**; 3k.50 Detail of dresser (Ola Teigeroen); 4k.50 Detail of Fliksaker chest (Jens Strammerud); 5k.50 Detail of pulpit, Our Saviour's Church, Oslo (sold at 21k.)	5·75	5·50

372 Torch Bearer on Skis

1993. Winter Olympic Games, Lillehammer (1994) (7th issue). Morgedal–Lillehammer Torch Relay. Multicoloured.

1169	3k.50 Type **372**	85	30
1170	3k.50 Lillehammer	85	30

Nos. 1169/70 were issued together, se-tenant, forming a composite design.

373 Store Mangen Chapel

1993. Christmas. Multicoloured.

1171	3k.50 Type **373**	75	20
1172	3k.50 Stamnes church, Sandnessjoen	80	15

1994. Butterflies (2nd series). As T 364. Mult.

1173	3k.50 Northern clouded yellow ("Colias hecla")	80	20
1174	3k.50 Freya's fritillary ("Clossiana freija")	80	20

374 Flags

1994. Winter Olympic Games, Lillehammer (8th issue). Multicoloured.

1175	3k.50 Type **374**	85	20
1176	3k.50 Flags (different)	85	20
1177	3k.50 Lillehammer (church) and rings	85	20
1178	3k.50 Lillehammer (ski jump) and rings	85	20
1179	4k.50 Flags of European countries	1·10	45
1180	5k.50 Flags of non-European countries	1·30	55

Nos. 1175/8 were issued together, se-tenant, forming a composite design.

375 Cross-country Skiing

1994. Paralympic Games, Lillehammer. Mult.

1181	4k.50 Type **375**	1·10	60
1182	5k.50 Downhill skiing	1·10	50

376 King Christian VII's Signature and Seal

1994. Bicentenary of Tromso.

1183	**376**	3k.50 red, bistre & brn	95	20
1184	-	4k.50 blue, yellow and light blue	1·30	55

DESIGN: 4k.50, Tromsdalen church.

377 Mount Floy Incline Railway Cars, Bergen

1994. Tourism. Multicoloured.

1185	4k. Type **377**	95	45
1186	4k.50 "Svolvaer Goat" (rock formation), Lofoten	1·20	55
1187	5k.50 Beacon, World's End, Tjome	1·30	50

378 Osterdal Farm Buildings

1994. Cent of Norwegian Folk Museum, Bygdoy.

1188	**378**	3k. multicoloured	75	30
1189	-	3k.50 blue, yellow and purple	1·00	30

DESIGN: 3k.50, Horse-drawn sleigh, 1750 (Torsten Hoff).

379 Technological Symbols and Formula ("Glass Flasks")

1994. EUREKA (European technology co-operation organization) Conference of Ministers, Lillehammer. Multicoloured.

1190	4k. Type **379**	1·10	55
1191	4k.50 Technological symbols ("Electronic Chips")	1·70	60

380 Electric Tram and Street Plan of Oslo, 1894

1994. Centenary of Electric Trams. Multicoloured.

1192	3k.50 Type **380**	1·00	25
1193	12k. Articulated tram and Oslo route map	3·25	1·00

381 Engraved Brooch

1994. Stamp Day. Jewellery. Sheet 113×91 mm containing T 381 and similar horiz designs. Multicoloured.

MS1194	3k. Type **381**; 3k.50 Silver and gem studded brooch; 4k.50 "Rings" brooch; 5k.50 Brooch with medallions and central stone (sold at 21k.)	6·25	6·00

382 Sledge

1994. Christmas.

1195	**382**	3k.50 red and black	75	25
1196	-	3k.50 ultramarine, blue and black	75	25

DESIGN: No. 1196, Kick-sledge.

383 Cowberry ("Vaccinium vitis-idaea")

1995. Wild Berries (1st Series). Multicoloured.

1197	3k.50 Type **383**	75	35
1198	3k.50 Bilberry ("Vaccinium myrtillus")	75	35

See also Nos. 1224/5.

384 Swan Pharmacy, Bergen

1995. 400th Anniv of Norwegian Pharmacies. Multicoloured.

1199	3k.50 Type **384**	1·00	30
1200	25k. Scales, pestle and mortar and ingredients	6·50	1·40

385 German Commander saluting Terje Rollem (Home Guard commander)

1995. 50th Anniv of Liberation of Norway.

1201	**385**	3k.50 silver, green and black	90	30
1202	-	4k.50 silver, blue and black	1·20	80
1203	-	5k.50 silver, red and black	1·40	65

DESIGNS: 4k.50, King Haakon VII and family returning to Norway; 5k.50, Children waving Norwegian flags.

386 Old Moster Church

1995. Millenary of Christianity in Norway. Multicoloured.

1204	3k.50 Type **386**	95	30
1205	15k. Slettebakken Church, Bergen	3·75	1·50

387 Skudeneshavn

1995. Nordic Countries' Postal Co-operation. Tourism. Multicoloured.

1206	4k. Type **387**	85	60
1207	4k.50 Hole in the Hat (coastal rock formation)	1·00	75

388 Flagstad as Isolde

1995. Birth Centenary of Kirsten Flagstad (opera singer). Multicoloured.

1208	3k.50 Type **388**	95	30
1209	5k.50 Flagstad in scene from "Lohengrin" (Wagner)	1·40	50

389 Disputants in Conflict

1995. Bicentenary of Conciliation Boards. Multicoloured.

1210	7k. Type **389**	1·80	80
1211	12k. Disputants in conciliation with mediator	3·00	1·20

390 Letter and Vice-regent Hannibal Sehested (founder)

1995. 350th Anniv (1997) of Norwegian Postal Service (1st issue). Multicoloured.

1212 3k.50 Type **390** (letter post, 1647) 85 50
1213 3k.50 Wax seal (registered post, 1745) 85 50
1214 3k.50 Postmarks (1845) 85 50
1215 3k.50 Banknotes, coins and money orders (transfer of funds, 1883) 85 50
1216 3k.50 Editions of "Norska Intelligenz-Sedler" and "Arkiv" (newspapers and magazines, 1660) 85 50
1217 3k.50 Address label, cancellations and "Constitutionen" (paddle-steamer) (parcel post, 1827) 85 50
1218 3k.50 Stamps (1855) 85 50
1219 3k.50 Savings book (Post Office Savings Bank, 1950) 85 50

The dates are those of the introduction of the various services.

See also Nos. 1237/44 and 1283/90.

391 Trygve Lie (first Secretary-General) and Emblem

1995. 50th Anniv of U.N.O. Multicoloured.

1220 3k.50 Type **391** 95 25
1221 5k.50 Relief worker, water pump and emblem 1·40 50

392 Woolly Hat

1995. Christmas. Multicoloured.

1222 3k.50 Type **392** 75 30
1223 3k.50 Mitten 75 30

1996. Wild Berries (2nd series). As T 383. Multicoloured.

1224 3k.50 Wild strawberries ("Fragaria vesca") 75 30
1225 3k.50 Cloudberries ("Rubus chamaemorus") 75 30

393 Advent Bay

1996. Svalbard Islands. Multicoloured.

1226 10k. Type **393** 2·50 80
1227 20k. Polar bear 5·00 1·60

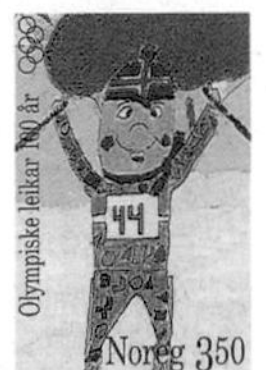

394 Cross-country Skier (Hakon Paulsen)

1996. Centenary of Modern Olympic Games. Children's Drawings. Multicoloured.

1228 3k.50 Type **394** 95 30
1229 5k.50 Athlete (Emil Tanem) 1·40 55

395 Besseggen

1996. Tourism. UNESCO World Heritage Sites. Multicoloured.

1230 4k. Type **395** 80 60
1231 4k.50 Stave church, Urnes 95 1·00
1232 5k.50 Rock carvings, Alta 1·20 45

See also Nos. 1291/3.

396 Steam Train, Urskog-Holand Line

1996. Railway Centenaries. Multicoloured.

1233 3k. Type **396** 70 45
1234 4k.50 Steam train, Setesdal line 1·00 70

397 Location Map and Height Indicator

1996. Natural Gas Production at Troll, near Bergen. Multicoloured.

1235 3k.50 Type **397** 80 35
1236 25k. Planned route map of pipelines to Europe for next 200 years 6·00 2·75

398 Postal Courier crossing Mountains

1996. 350th Anniv (1997) of Postal Service (2nd issue). Multicoloured.

1237 3k.50 Type **398** 95 65
1238 3k.50 "Framnaes" (fjord steamer) 95 65
1239 3k.50 Postal truck in Oslo 95 65
1240 3k.50 Taking mail on board Junkers W-34 "Ternen" (seaplane) on Jonsvatn Lake, Trondheim 95 65
1241 3k.50 Loading mail train at East Station, Oslo 95 65
1242 3k.50 Rural postman at Mago farm, Nittedal 95 65
1243 3k.50 Serving customer, Elverum post office 95 65
1244 3k.50 Computer, letters and globe 95 65

399 Leif Juster, Sean Connery, Liv Ullmann and Olsen Gang

1996. Centenary of Motion Pictures. Multicoloured.

1245 3k.50 Type **399** 80 40
1246 5k.50 Wenche Foss, Jack Fjeldstad, Marilyn Monroe, blood and gun 1·30 55
1247 7k. Charlie Chaplin in "Modern Times", Ottar Gladvedt, Laurel and Hardy and Marlene Dietrich 1·70 80

400 Left Detail of Embroidery

1996. Christmas. Embroidery Details from Telemark Folk Costume. Multicoloured.

1248 3k.50 Type **400** 75 40
1249 3k.50 Right detail 75 40

Nos. 1248/9 were issued together, se-tenant, forming a composite design.

401 Skram

1996. 150th Birth Anniv of Amalie Skram (writer).

1250 **401** 3k.50 red 95 35
1251 - 15k. violet and red 3·75 1·40

DESIGN: 15k. Scene from dramatisation of "People of Hellemyr".

402 Posthorn

1997. Multicoloured, colour of oval given.

1252 **402** 10ore red 25 20
1253 **402** 20ore blue 25 20
1254 **402** 30ore orange 25 20
1255 **402** 40ore black 25 20
1256 **402** 50ore green 25 20

403 Coltsfoot

1997. Flowers. Multicoloured.

1259 3k.20 Red clover 75 30
1260 3k.40 Marsh marigold 75 25
1261 3k.60 Red campion 75 40
1262 3k.70 Type **403** 85 30
1263 3k.80 Wild pansy 85 35
1264 4k. Wood anemone 85 35
1265 4k.30 Lily of the valley 1·10 50
1266 4k.50 White clover 1·00 60
1267 5k. Harebell 1·10 65
1268 5k.40 Oeder's lousewort 1·20 70
1269 5k.50 Hepatica 1·20 50
1270 6k. Ox-eye daisy 1·30 45
1271 7k. Yellow wood violet 1·50 75
1272 7k.50 Pale pasque flower 1·70 85
1273 8k. White water-lily 1·70 55
1274 13k. Purple saxifrage 3·00 95
1275 14k. Globe flower 3·00 1·50
1276 25k. Melancholy thistle 5·25 2·20

404 Bumble Bee

1997. Insects (1st series). Multicoloured.

1277 3k.70 Type **404** 75 30
1278 3k.70 Ladybird 75 30

See also Nos. 1306/7.

405 Ski Jumping

1997. World Nordic Skiing Championships, Trondheim. Multicoloured.

1279 3k.70 Type **405** 90 40
1280 5k. Speed skiing 1·20 60

406 King Harald (photo by Erik Johansen)

1997. 60th Birthdays of King Harald and Queen Sonja. Multicoloured.

1281 3k.70 Type **406** 85 30
1282 3k.70 Queen Sonja and King Harald (photo by Knut Falch) (horiz) 85 30

407 Hammer, Plumb Line and Hook (post-war reconstruction)

1997. 350th Anniv of Postal Service (3rd issue). Post-war History. Multicoloured.

1283 3k.70 Type **407** 85 65
1284 3k.70 "Kon Tiki" (replica of balsa raft) (Thor Heyerdahl's expedition from Peru to Polynesia, 1947) 85 65
1285 3k.70 Grouse feather (official bird of Rondane National Park (first National Park, 1962)) 85 65
1286 3k.70 Hands of man and woman (Welfare State (introduction of National Insurance, 1967)) 85 65
1287 3k.70 Drilling platform, Ekofisk oil field (discovery of oil in Norwegian sector of North Sea, 1969) 85 65
1288 3k.70 Grete Waitz (first women's world Marathon champion, 1983) 85 65
1289 3k.70 Askoy Bridge, 1992 (communications) 85 65
1290 3k.70 Crown Prince Haakon Magnus lighting Olympic flame (Winter Olympic Games, Lillehammer, 1994) 85 65

1997. Tourism. As T 395. Multicoloured.

1291 4k.30 Roros 85 85
1292 5k. Faerder Lighthouse 1·10 95
1293 6k. Nusfjord 1·30 65

408 University, Cathedral, Statue of King Olav, City Gate and Broadcasting Tower

1997. Millenary of Trondheim. Multicoloured.

1294 3k.70 Type **408** 1·00 30
1295 12k. Trees, mine, King Olav, pilgrims, burning buildings and harbour 3·00 1·50

409 Gerhardsen and Storting (Parliament House)

1997. Birth Centenary of Einar Gerhardsen (Prime Minister 1945–51, 1955–63 and 1963–65).

1296 **409** 3k.70 black, stone and red 1·00 35
1297 - 25k. black, flesh and green 6·00 3·00

DESIGN: 25k. Gerhardsen, mountain, factory and electricity pylon.

410 Thematic Subjects

1997. Inauguration of National Junior Stamp Club. Multicoloured.

1298 3k.70 Type **410** 85 35
1299 3k.70 Thematic subjects including fish and tiger 85 35

411 Harald Saeverud (composer)

1997. Birth Centenaries.

1300 **411** 10k. blue 2·75 1·20
1301 - 15k. green 3·75 1·40

DESIGN: 15k. Tarjei Vesaas (writer).

412 Dass in Rowing Boat

1997. 350th Birth Anniv of Petter Dass (priest and poet). Multicoloured.

1302 **412** 3k.20 blue and brown 80 45
1303 - 3k.70 green, blue and brown 95 50

DESIGN: 3k.70, Dass and Alstahaug Church.

413 Golden Calendar Stick Symbols against Candle Flames

1997. Christmas. Multicoloured. Self-adhesive.

1304 3k.70 Type **413** 80 45
1305 3k.70 Silver calendar stick symbols against night sky 80 45

1998. Insects (2nd series). As T 404. Multicoloured.

1306 3k.80 Dragonfly 85 40
1307 3k.80 Grasshopper 85 40

414 Roses

1998. St. Valentine's Day. Self-adhesive.

1308 **414** 3k.80 multicoloured 1·00 40

415 "Hornelen" (passenger and mail steamer)

1998. Nordic Countries' Postal Co-operation. Ships.

1309 **415** 3k.80 blue and green 1·00 55
1310 - 4k.50 green and blue 1·50 1·10

DESIGN: No. 1310, "Kommandoren" (passenger catamaran).

416 Holmenkollen Ski Jump, Oslo

1998. Tourist Sights. Multicoloured.

1311 3k.80 Type **416** 80 55
1312 4k.50 Fisherman, Alesund Harbour 1·00 65
1313 5k.50 Mt Hamaroyskaftet 1·30 1·00

417 Egersund Harbour

1998. Bicentenary of Egersund.

1314 **417** 3k.80 blue and pink 1·00 50
1315 - 6k. blue and mauve 1·50 75

DESIGN: No. 1315, Egersund ceramics.

418 Silver

1998. Minerals. Multicoloured.

1316 3k.40 Type **418** 90 55
1317 5k.20 Cobalt 1·30 65

419 "Water Rider" (Frans Widerberg)

1998. Contemporary Art. Multicoloured.

1318 6k. Type **419** 1·50 75
1319 7k.50 "Red Moon" (carpet, Synnove Anker Aurdal) 1·80 95
1320 13k. "King Haakon VII" (sculpture, Nils Aas) 3·00 1·40

420 Hopscotch

1998. Children's Games (1st series). Multicoloured.

1321 3k.80 Type **420** 95 50
1322 5k.50 Throwing coins at a stick 1·40 95

See also Nos 1355/6.

421 Boeing 747, Douglas DC-3 and Junkers Ju 52/3m Airliners

1998. Inauguration of Oslo Airport, Gardermoen. Multicoloured.

1323 3k.80 Type **421** 1·00 50
1324 6k. Boeing 737 airliner and map of former approaches to Gardermoen Airport 1·50 70
1325 24k. Terminal building, control tower and wings drawn by Leonardo da Vinci 5·75 2·75

422 Main Entrance and Guard

1998. 150th Anniv of Royal Palace, Oslo.

1326 **422** 3k.40 purple 85 65
1327 - 3k.80 blue, pink and yellow 95 50

DESIGN: 3k.80, Main front of palace.

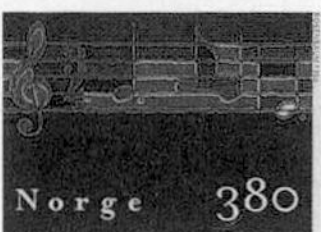

423 Music Score

1998. Christmas. Multicoloured. Self-adhesive.

1328 3k.80 Type **423** (red background) 85 45
1329 3k.80 Music score (blue background) 85 45

424 Cheese Slicer (Thor Bjorklund)

1999. Norwegian Inventions. Self-adhesive.

1330 **424** 3k.60 black and blue 80 35
1331 - 4k. black and red 90 40
1332 - 4k.20 black and green 85 65

DESIGNS: 4k. Paper clip (Johan Vaaler); 4k.20 Aerosol can (Erik Rotheim).

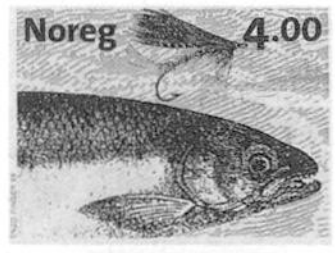

425 Salmon and Fly

1999. Fishes and Fishing Flies. Multicoloured. Self-adhesive.

1333 4k. Type **425** 85 40
1334 4k. Cod and fly 85 40

426 Heart blowing Flowers out of Posthorn

1999. St. Valentine's Day.

1335 **426** 4k. multicoloured 85 40

427 "The Pioneer" (statue, Per Palle Storm)

1999. Centenary of Norwegian Confederation of Trade Unions.

1336 **427** 4k. multicoloured 85 45

428 Poland v Norway, Class B Championship, 1998

1999. World Ice Hockey Championships, Norway. Multicoloured.

1337 4k. Type **428** 85 50
1338 7k. Switzerland v Sweden, Class A Championship, 1998 1·50 90

429 Mute Swans

1999. Tourism. Multicoloured.

1339 4k. Type **429** 85 70
1340 5k. Hamar Cathedral 1·10 85
1341 6k. Sami man from Troms 1·30 1·00

430 Emigration

1999. "Norway 2000" (1st issue). Norwegian History. Multicoloured.

1342 4k. Type **430** 85 60
1343 6k. King Olav and Bible (conversion to Christianity, 11th century) 1·30 85
1344 14k. Medal of King Christian IV and quarry workers (union of Norway and Denmark) 3·00 1·60
1345 26k. Oslo at Beier Bridge, 1850s (industrialization) 5·25 2·75

431 Horse Ferry, Amli, East Agder, 1900

1999. "Norway 2000" (2nd issue). Photographs of Everyday Life. Multicoloured.

1346 4k. Type **431** 85 50
1347 4k. Men hewing rock during construction of Valdres railway line, 1900 85 50
1348 4k. Taxi driver Aarseth Odd filling up car with petrol, Kleive, 1930 85 50
1349 4k. Dairymaid Mathea Isaksen milking cow, Karmoy, 1930 85 50
1350 4k. Haymakers, Hemsedal, 1943 85 50
1351 4k. Cross-country skier Dagfinn Knutsen, 1932 85 50
1352 4k. "Bolgen" (coastal fishing boat), Varanger Fjord, 1977 85 50
1353 4k. Boy Jon Andre Koch holding football, 1981 85 50
MS1354 136×148 mm. Nos. 1346/53 6·75 6·50

432 Skateboarding

1999. Children's Games (2nd series). Multicoloured.

1355 4k. Type **432** 85 45
1356 6k. Inline skating 1·20 1·00

433 Wenche Foss and Per Haugen in "An Ideal Husband" (Oscar Wilde)

1999. Centenary of National Theatre.

1357 **433** 3k.60 purple and orange 90 85
1358 - 4k. ultramarine and blue 85 65

DESIGN: 4k. Toralv Maurstad and Tore Segelcke in "Per Gynt" (Henrik Ibsen).

434 Family bringing in Logs

1999. Christmas. Multicoloured. Self-adhesive.

1359 4k. Type **434** 85 45
1360 4k. Family sitting by window 85 45

435 "Sunset" (Sverre Simonsen)

1999. Year 2000. Winning entries in photographic competition. Multicoloured. Self-adhesive.

1361 4k. Type **435** 1·00 60
1362 4k. "Winter Nights" (Poul Christensen) 1·00 60

436 Eye within Heart

2000. St. Valentine's Day.

1363 **436** 4k. multicoloured 85 55

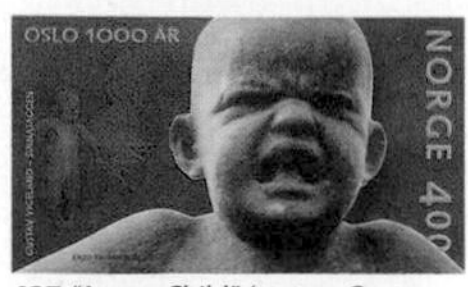

437 "Angry Child" (statue, Gustav Vigeland)

2000. Millenary of Oslo City. Multicoloured.

1364 4k. Type **437** 85 60
1365 6k. Christian IV statue 1·30 95
1366 8k. City Hall and clock face 1·70 1·10
1367 27k. Oslo Stock Exchange and Mercury (statue) 5·75 3·00

438 Golden Eagle

2000. Endangered Species. Multicoloured.

1368 5k. Type **438** 1·10 70
1369 6k. European moose 1·30 90
1370 7k. Sperm whale 1·50 1·00

439 "Power and Energy"

2000. "EXPO 2000" World's Fair, Hanover, Germany. Paintings by Marianne Heske. Mult.

1371 4k.20 "The Quiet Room" 1·10 65
1372 6k.30 Type **439** 1·50 80

440 Cadets, 1750

2000. 250th Anniv of Royal Norwegian Military Academy.

1373 **440** 3k.60 multicoloured 90 85
1374 - 8k. blue, yellow and red 1·70 1·20

DESIGN: 8k. Cadets, 2000.

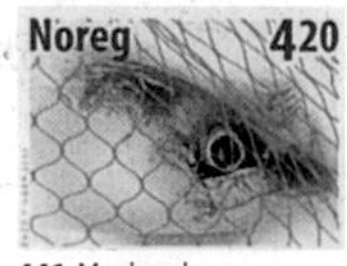

441 Mackerel

2000. Fishes. Multicoloured. Self-adhesive.

1375 4k.20 Type **441** 85 40
1376 4k.20 Herring 85 40

442 Spaceman (May-Therese Vorland)

2000. "Stampin the Future". Winning Entries in Children's International Painting Competition. Multicoloured.

1377 4k.20 Type **442** 85 55
1378 6k.30 Rocket and Earth (Jann Fredrik Ronning) 1·30 85

443 "Monument to Log Drivers" (sculpture, Trygve M. Barstad)

2000. Millennium of Skien City. Multicoloured.

1379 4k.20 Type **443** 85 55
1380 15k. Skien Church 3·25 2·00

444 Laestadius, Lifelong Saxifrage and Laestadius Poppy

2000. Birth Bicentenary of Lars Levi Laestadius (clergyman and botanist).

1381 **444** 5k. multicoloured 1·10 85

445 Nils og Blamann with Goat and Cart

2000. Cartoon Characters. Multicoloured. Self-adhesive.

1382 4k.20 Type **445** 85 60
1383 4k.20 Soldier No. 91 Stomperud and birds 85 60

446 Woven Altar Piece, Hamaroy Church

2000. Altar Pieces. Multicoloured.

1384 3k.60 Type **446** 85 65
1385 4k.20 Ski Church 85 65

2000

1388 **352** 1k. multicoloured 25 25
1389 **352** 2k. multicoloured 45 35
1389a **352** 3k. multicoloured 65 85
1389b **352** 5k. multicoloured 1·10 70
1390 **352** 6k. multicoloured 1·30 75
1391 **352** 7k. multicoloured 1·50 1·60
1392 **352** 9k. multicoloured 1·90 1·00

447 Sekel Rose

2001. Roses (1st series). Multicoloured. Self-adhesive.

1395 4k.50 Type **447** 95 55
1396 4k.50 Namdal rose 95 55

See also Nos 1418/19 and 1491/2.

448 Place Mat

2001. Crafts (1st series). Multicoloured. Self-adhesive.

1397 4k. Type **448** 80 50
1398 4k.50 Pot with lid 95 55
1399 7k. Bunad (woven cloth) 1·50 85

See also Nos. 1415/17.

449 Aase Bye

2001. Thespians (1st series).

1400 **449** 4k. black and brown 80 65
1401 - 4k.50 black and blue 95 55
1402 - 5k.50 black and brown 1·20 65
1403 - 7k. black and purple 1·50 1·00
1404 - 8k. black and grey 1·70 1·00

DESIGNS: 4k.50, Per Aabel; 5k.50, Alfred Maurstad; 7k. Lillebil Ibsen; 8k. Tore Segelcke.

See also Nos 1410/14 and 1450/4.

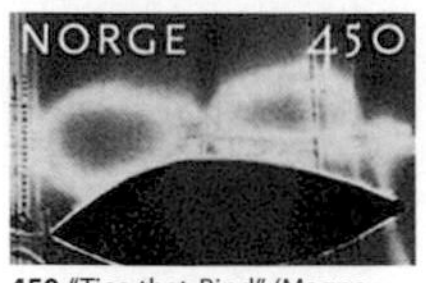

450 "Ties that Bind" (Magne Furuholmen)

2001. St. Valentine's Day.

1405 **450** 4k.50 multicoloured 95 60

451 Whitewater Kayaking

2001. Sports. Multicoloured. Self-adhesive.

1406 4k.50 Type **451** 95 60
1407 7k. Rock climbing 1·50 65

452 Tuba Player

2001. Centenary of School Bands. Multicoloured.

1408 4k.50 Type **452** 95 60
1409 9k. Majorette 1·90 1·20

453 Lalla Carlsen

2001. Thespians (2nd series). Multicoloured.

1410 5k. Type **453** 1·10 80
1411 5k.50 Leif Juster 1·20 80
1412 7k. Kari Diesen 1·50 1·00
1413 9k. Arvid Nilssen 1·90 1·20
1414 10k. Einar Rose 2·20 1·40

2001. Crafts (2nd series). As T 449. Multicoloured.

1415 5k. Wooden drinking vessel 1·20 65
1416 6k.50 Crocheted doll's clothing 1·40 65
1417 8k.50 Knitted woollen hat 2·00 1·30

454 Rose "Heidekonigin"

2001. Roses (2nd series). Multicoloured. Self-adhesive.

1418 5k.50 Type **454** 1·40 65
1419 5k.50 Rose "Old Master" 1·40 65

Nos. 1418/19 are impregnated with the scent of roses.

455 Old Bank of Norway

2001. Norwegian Architecture. Multicoloured.

1420 5k.50 Type **455** 1·20 55
1421 8k.50 Ivar Aasen Centre 1·90 1·00

456 Kittens

2001. Pets. Multicoloured.

1422 5k.50 Type **456** 1·20 75
1423 7k.50 Goat 1·60 1·00

457 Aung San Suu Kyi (Burmese opposition leader), 1991

2001. Centenary of Nobel Prizes. Peace Prize Winners (Nos. 1424/5 and 1427). Multicoloured.

1424 5k.50 Type **457** 1·30 65
1425 5k.50 Nelson Mandela (South African President), 1993 1·30 65
1426 7k. Alfred Nobel (Prize Fund founder) 1·50 85
1427 7k. Henry Dunant (founder of Red Cross), 1901 1·50 85
1428 9k. Fridtjof Nansen (Norwegian organizer for League of Nations refugee relief), 1922 2·00 1·30
1429 9k. Mikhail Gorbachev (Soviet President), 1990 2·00 1·30
1430 10k. Martin Luther King (Civil Rights leader), 1964 2·20 1·40
1431 10k. Rigoberta Menchu Tum (Guatemalan Civil Rights leader), 1992 2·20 1·40
MS1432 170×64 mm. No. 1426 2·30 1·90

Dates are those on which the Prize was awarded.

458 Snow-covered Trees and Lights

2001. Northern Lights. Multicoloured.

1433 5k. Type **458** 1·10 80
1434 5k.50 Lights and reindeer 1·20 85

459 Gingerbread Man

2001. Christmas. Multicoloured. Self-adhesive.

1435 5k.50 Type **459** 1·20 55
1436 5k.50 Gingerbread house 1·20 55

460 Tordis Maurstad

2002. Thespians (3rd series). Showing caricatures by Arne Roar Lund.

1450 **460** 5k. black and lilac 1·10 80
1451 - 5k.50 black and grey 1·20 80
1452 - 7k. black and green 1·50 1·00
1453 - 9k. black and green 1·90 1·30
1454 - 10k. black and brown 2·20 1·50

DESIGNS: 5k.50 Rolf Just Nilsen; 7k. Lars Tvinde; 9k. Henry Gleditsch; 10k. Norma Balean.

461 Boys tackling

2002. Centenary of Norwegian Football Association (1st issue). Multicoloured. Self-adhesive.

1455 5k.50 Type **461** 1·40 75
1456 5k.50 German referee Peter Hertel and player 1·40 75
1457 5k.50 Girls tackling 1·40 75

1458	5k.50 Boy kicking ball	1·40	75

See also Nos. 1469/**MS**1475.

462 Scene from "Askeladden and the Good Helpers" (animated film by Ivo Caprino)

2002. Fairytale Characters. Multicoloured. Self-adhesive.

1459	5k.50 Type **462**	1·20	75
1460	9k. Giant troll (drawing by Theodor Kittelsen)	2·10	1·30

463 "Monument to Whaling" (Sivert Donali)

2002. Nordic Countries' Postal Co-operation. Modern Art. Sculptures. Multicoloured.

1461	7k.50 Type **463**	1·60	1·20
1462	8k.50 "Throw" (Kåre Groven)	1·80	1·30

464 Holmestrand

2002. City Charter Anniversaries. Multicoloured.

1463	5k.50 Type **464** (300th anniv)	1·20	85
1464	5k.50 Kongsberg (200th anniv)	1·30	85

465 Abel

2002. Birth Bicentenary of Niels Henrik Abel (mathematician). Multicoloured.

1465	5k.50 Type **465**	1·80	1·80
1466	22k. Mathematical rosette	7·00	6·25

466 Johan Borgen

2002. Writers' Birth Centenaries. Portraits by Nils Aas.

1467	**466**	11k. yellow and green	2·50	1·60
1468	-	20k. green and blue	4·50	2·75

DESIGN: 20k. Nordahl Grieg.

467 Norwegian Team (Olympic Games, Berlin, 1936)

2002. Centenary of Norwegian Football Association (2nd issue). Multicoloured.

1469	5k. Type **467**	1·10	80
1470	5k.50 No. 9 player and Brazil No. 4 player (World Cup, France, 1998)	1·20	80
1471	5k.50 Norway and U.S.A. women players (Olympic Games, Sydney, 2000)	1·20	80
1472	7k. Player capturing ball from Sweden No. 11 player (Norway–Sweden, 1960)	1·50	1·30
1473	9k. Player with chevron sleeves (Norway–England, 1981)	2·00	1·50
1474	10k. Winning team members (Rosenborg–Milan (Champions League, 1996))	2·20	1·60
MS1475	140×127 mm. Nos. 1469/74	10·00	9·75

468 Clown on Tightrope

2002. Europa. Circus. Multicoloured.

1476	5k.50 Type **468**	1·30	85
1477	8k.50 Elephant, horse and chimpanzee	2·10	1·40

2002. "Nordia 2002" Nordic Stamp Exhibition, Kristiansand. Nos. 1465/6 surch NORDIC 2002.

1478	5k.50 multicoloured	2·00	2·00
1479	22k. multicoloured	7·00	6·50

470 Landstad on Horseback and Frontispiece of "Norske Folkeviser"

2002. Birth Bicentenary of Magnus Brostrup Landstad (folk-song collector and hymn writer). Multicoloured.

1480	5k. Type **470**	1·20	85
1481	5k.50 Landstad and frontispiece of Kirkefalmebog	1·30	85

471 Straw Heart-shaped Decoration

2002. Christmas. Multicoloured. Self-adhesive.

1482	5k.50 Type **471**	1·20	75
1483	5k.50 Paper star-shaped decoration	1·20	75

472 "Nordmandens Krone" (Kare Espolin Johnson)

2003. Graphic Art (1st series). Multicoloured.

1484	5k. Type **472**	1·20	80
1485	8k.50 "Bla Hester" (Else Hagen)	2·00	1·60
1486	9k. "Dirigent og Solist" (Niclas Gulbrandsen)	2·10	1·60
1487	11k. "Olympia" (Svein Strand)	2·50	2·00
1488	22k. "Still Life XVII" (Rigmor Hansen)	5·00	4·25

See also Nos. 1515/16.

473 Heart

2003. St. Valentine.

1489	**473**	5k.50 multicoloured	1·50	85

474 Doudji Knife Handle (Havard Larsen)

2003. Crafts. Coil stamp. Self-adhesive.

1490	**474**	5k.50 multicoloured	1·50	75

475 Rose "Grand Prix"

2003. Roses (3rd series). Multicoloured. Self-adhesive.

1491	5k.50 Type **475**	1·30	75
1492	5k.50 Rose "Champagne"	1·30	75

476 Operating Theatre

2003. 400th Anniv of Public Health Service. Multicoloured.

1493	5k.50 Type **476**	1·30	75
1494	7k. Doctor examining baby	1·70	1·20

477 Forest Troll

2003. Fairytale Characters (2nd series). Showing drawings by Theodor Kittelsen. Self-adhesive. Multicoloured.

1495	5k.50 Type **477**	1·50	75
1496	9k. Water sprite (horiz)	2·10	1·40

478 Hand and Violin

2003. Bergen International Festival. Multicoloured.

1497	5k.50 Type **478**	1·30	75
1498	10k. Children's faces	2·50	1·50

479 Child holding Bread

2003. World Refugee Day. Multicoloured.

1499	5k.50 Type **479**	1·30	75
1500	10k. Refugees	2·50	1·50

480 Crown Prince Olav as a Child

2003. Birth Centenary of King Olav V (1903–1991). Multicoloured.

1501	5k.50 Type **480**	1·30	85
1502	8k.50 Crown Prince Olav and Crown Princess Martha	2·10	1·20
1503	11k. King Olav V	2·50	1·50
MS1504	170×101 mm. Nos. 1501/3	6·25	6·00

481 Baby

2003. Greetings Stamps. Multicoloured. Self-adhesive.

1505	5k.50 Type **481**	1·20	85
1506	5k.50 Hand wearing ring	1·20	85
1507	5k.50 Lily	1·20	85
1508	5k.50 Couple	1·20	85
1509	5k.50 Children and cake	1·20	85

482 Dagbladet (Per Krohg)

2003. Europa. Poster Art. Multicoloured.

1510	8k.50 Type **482**	1·50	1·30
1511	9k. Winter Olympics, Oslo (Knut Yran)	2·00	1·50
1512	10k. Music festival (Willibald Storn)	2·20	1·80

483 Bjornstjerne Bjornson (literature, 1903)

2003. Norwegian Nobel Prize Winners (1st series). Multicoloured.

1513	11k. Type **483**	2·40	2·00
1514	22k. Lars Onsager (chemistry, 1968)	5·00	4·50

See also Nos. 1549/50.

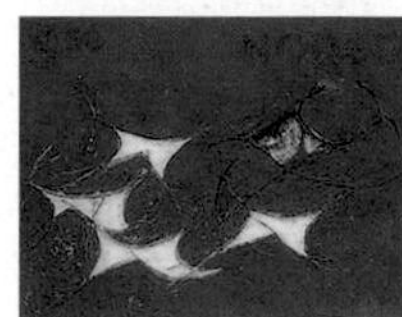

484 "Goatherd and Goats" (Rolf Nesch)

2003. Graphic Art (2nd series). Multicoloured.

1515	5k. Type **484**	1·30	95
1516	5k.50 "Winter Landscape 1980" (Terje Grostad)	1·30	1·00

485 Santa Claus

2003. Christmas. Self-adhesive gum. Multicoloured.

1517	5k.50 Type **485**	1·20	80
1518	5k.50 Present	1·20	80

486 Coronet Medusa (*Periphylla periphylla*)

2004. Marine Life (1st series). Multicoloured. Self-adhesive.

1519	5k.50 Type **486**	1·50	1·10
1520	6k. Catfish (*Anarhichas lupus*)	1·60	1·10
1521	9k. Little cuttlefish (*Sepiola atlantica*)	2·75	2·10

See also Nos. 1576/7, 1608, 1621/2, 1649 and 1658/61.

487 Couple

2004. Greetings Stamps. Self-adhesive gum. Each green and grey.

1522	6k. Type **487**	1·80	1·20
1523	6k. Globe	1·80	1·20

488 "Idyll" (Christian Skredsbvig)

2004. Painters' Birth Anniversaries. Multicoloured.

1524	6k. Type **488** (150th anniv)	1·70	1·20
1525	9k.50 "Stetind in Fog" (Peder Balke) (bicentenary)	2·75	2·00
1526	10k.50 "Workers' Protest" (Reidar Aulie) (centenary)	3·00	2·20

489 Heart

2004. St. Valentine's Day.

1527	**489**	6k. multicoloured	1·50	1·30

490 Cyclist

2004. Europa. Holidays. Multicoloured.

1528	6k. Type **490**	1·70	1·30
1529	7k.50 Canoeist	2·00	1·60
1530	9k.50 Skiers	2·50	2·00

491 Otto Sverdrup

2004. 150th Birth Anniv of Otto Sverdrup (polar explorer). Each purple and buff.

1531	6k. Type **491**	1·60	1·30
1532	9k.50 *Fram* (polar research ship)	2·50	2·10
MS1533	166×60 mm. Nos. 1541/2 plus 1 label	4·00	3·75

No. **MS**1533 was issued with a stamp-sized label showing design of Greenland stamp.

Stamps of similar designs were issued by Greenland and Canada.

492 Sea God Njord

2004. Nordic Mythology. Multicoloured.

1534	7k.50 Type **492**	1·90	1·60
1535	10k.50 Balder's funeral	2·75	2·50
MS1536	106×70 mm. Nos. 1544/5	4·75	4·50

Stamps of a similar theme were issued by Aland Islands, Denmark, Faeroe Islands, Finland, Greenland, Iceland and Sweden.

493 Princess Ingrid Alexandra

2004. Birth of Princess Ingrid Alexandra of Norway. Sheet 94×61 mm.

MS1537	6k. multicoloured	1·80	1·80

494 Steam Locomotive, Koppang Station

2004. 150th Anniv of Norwegian Railways. Multicoloured.

1538	6k. Type **494**	1·70	1·60
1539	7k.50 Passengers and staff, Dovre station	2·10	2·00
1540	9k.50 Early diesel locomotive, Flatmark halt	2·75	2·50
1541	10k.50 Airport Express locomotive	3·25	3·00

495 Hakon Hakonsson

2004. 800th Birth Anniv of Hakon Hakonsson (Viking leader). Multicoloured.

1542	12k. Type **495**	3·25	3·00
1543	22k. Outline of Hakon's hall and sword	6·00	5·75

496 Smiley (emblem)

2004. Youth Stamps. Multicoloured.

1544	6k. Type **496**	1·60	1·50
1545	9k. Badges	2·50	2·10

497 Ship's Prow and Barrels

2004. Centenary of Archaeological Discovery, Oseberg. Multicoloured.

1546	7k.50 Type **497**	2·30	2·00
1547	9k.50 Sled	3·00	2·75
1548	12k. Bed	3·50	3·25

2004. Norwegian Nobel Prize Winners (2nd series). As T 483. Multicoloured.

1549	5k.50 Odd Hassel (chemistry, 1969)	1·60	1·40
1550	6k. Christian Lous Lange (peace, 1921)	1·70	1·60

498 "Friends" (Hanne Soteland)

2004. Christmas. Winning Designs in UNICEF Painting Competition. Multicoloured. Self-adhesive.

1551	6k. Type **498**	1·70	1·60
1552	6k. "Caring" (Synne Amalie Lund Kallak)	1·70	1·60

499 Princesses and Guard

2005. 150th Birth Anniv of Erik Werenskiold (artist). Illustrations from "The Three Princesses in the Blue Hill" fairytale by Peter Christen Asbjornsen and Jorgen Moe. Multicoloured.

1553	7k.50 Type **499**	2·20	1·80
1554	9k.50 Royal cradle	2·50	2·30

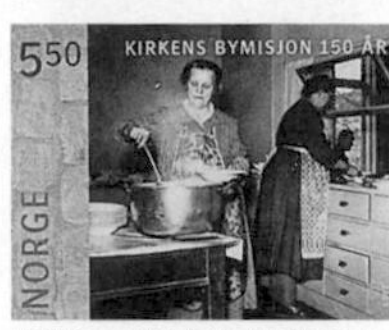

500 Soup Kitchen, Møllergata (1953)

2005. 150th Anniv of Church City Missions (humanitarian organization). Multicoloured.

1555	5k.50 Type **500**	1·60	1·40
1556	6k. Ministers giving communion at street service, Oslo	1·60	1·50

501 Heart and "Nar du er Borte" (poem by Tor Jonsson)

2005. St. Valentine's Day.

1557	**501**	6k. carmine and silver	1·70	1·50

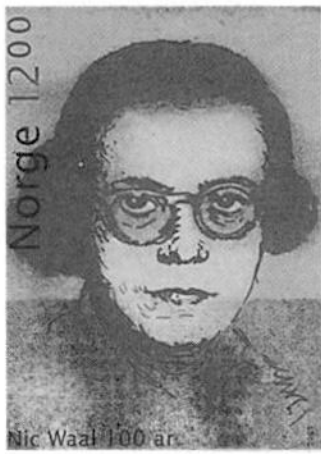

502 Caroline (Nic) Waal

2005. Birth Centenaries. Multicoloured.

1558	12k. Type **502** (first child psychiatrist)	3·50	3·00
1559	22k. Aase Gruda Skard (first child psychologist)	6·25	5·50

503 "City of the Future" (Maja Anna Marszalek)

2005. Winning Entries in Children's Drawing Competition. Multicoloured.

1560	6k. Type **503**	1·70	1·50
1561	7k.50 "The Modern Classroom" (Tobias Abrahamsen)	2·20	1·90

504 Fjord, Geiranger

2005. Tourism. Self-adhesive. Multicoloured.

1562	6k. Type **504**	1·70	1·50
1563	9k.50 Kjosfossen, Flam	2·50	2·30
1564	10k.50 Polar bear, Svalbard	3·00	2·75

505 Prime Minister Christian Michelsen (Norway)

2005. Centenary of Dissolution of Union with Sweden. Multicoloured.

1565	6k. Type **505**	1·70	1·50
1566	7k.50 King Haakon VII (Sweden)	2·20	1·90
MS1567	162×94 mm. Nos. 1565/56	4·00	3·50

506 King Haakon VII taking Oath (1905)

2005. 20th-century Events. Multicoloured.

1568	6k. Type **506**	2·10	1·70
1569	6k. Crown Prince Olav riding through Oslo (1945)	2·10	1·70
1570	6k. King Olav V appearing on first Norwegian television broadcast (1960)	2·10	1·70
1571	6k. Prime Minister Trygve Bratteli opening Ekofisk oilfield (1971)	2·10	1·70
1572	9k. Kjetil Rekdal scoring winning goal in World Cup match against Brazil (1998)	2·10	1·70

507 *Christian Radich*

2005. Ships. Multicoloured.

1573	6k. Type **507**	2·00	1·80
1574	9k.50 *Sorlandet*	3·00	2·75
1575	10k.50 *Statsraad Lehmkuhl*	3·25	3·00

508 Killer Whale (*Orcinus orca*)

2005. Marine Life (2nd series). Multicoloured. Self-adhesive.

1576	**A**	(5k.50) Type **508**	1·80	2·00
1577	**B**	(6k.) Sea anemone (*Urticina eques*)	2·00	1·80

509 Jomfruland Lighthouse

2005. Lighthouses. Self-adhesive. Multicoloured.

1578	(6k.) Type **509**	2·00	1·80
1579	(6k.) Tranoy	2·00	1·80

510 Thortveitite (rare mineral)

2005. Centenary of Geological Society. Mult.

1580	5k.50 Type **510**	1·80	1·60
1581	6k. Drilling rig, ship, continental shelf, stylized rock section and *Lamprocyclas maritalis*	2·00	1·80

511 Transmitting Apparatus

2005. 150th Anniv of Telegraph in Norway. Multicoloured.

1582	6k. Type **511**	2·10	1·80
1583	10k.50 Girl using mobile phone	3·25	3·00

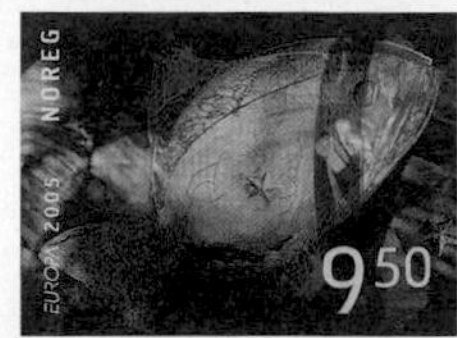

512 Fish

2005. Europa. Gastronomy. Multicoloured.

1584	9k.50 Type **512**	3·00	2·75
1585	10k.50 Decorated table	3·25	3·00

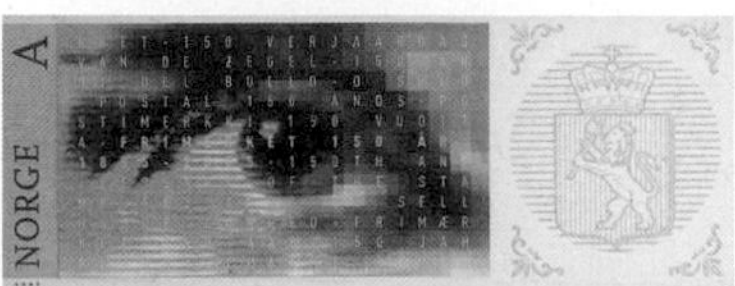

513 Eye and "150th Anniversary" (image scaled to 71% of original size)

2005. 150th Anniv of Norwegian Stamps. Mult.

1586	(6k.) Type **513**	1·80	1·60
MS1587	170×60 mm. (6k.) Type **513**; 12k. First stamp and woman writing letter	5·50	4·75

514 King Haakon holding Crown Prince Olav and Prime Minister Christian Michelsen

2005. Centenary of Norwegian Royal House. Multicoloured.

1588	6k. Type **514**	1·80	1·60
1589	6k. King Harald VII and Crown Prince Haakon holding Princess Ingrid Alexandra	1·80	1·60

515 Gingerbread Christmas Tree

2005. Christmas. Multicoloured. Self-adhesive.

1590	(6k.) Type **515**	1·80	1·60
1591	(6k.) Spiced oranges	1·80	1·60

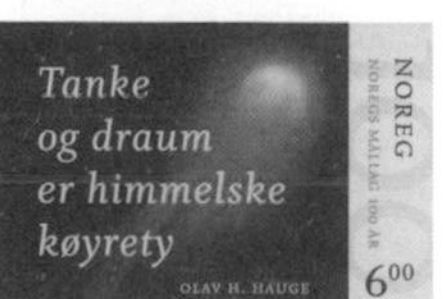

516 Comet and "Tanke og draum er himmelske køyrety" (Olav Hauge)

2006. Centenary of Language Society.

1592	**516**	6k. multicoloured	1·80	1·60

517 Kari Traa performing Iron Cross

2006. Winter Olympic Games, Turin. Multicoloured.

1593	6k. Type **517**	1·80	1·60
1594	22k. Elinar Bjørndalen (biathlete)	6·25	5·75

518 Heart and Blossom

2006. St. Valentine's Day.

1595	**518**	A (6k.) multicoloured	1·80	1·60

519 Flower

2006. Greetings Stamps. Multicoloured. Self-adhesive.

1596	A (6k.) Type **519**	1·90	1·70
1597	A (6k.) Baby	1·90	1·70
1598	A (6k.) Heart and rings	1·90	1·70
1599	A (6k.) Cake	1·90	1·70

520 Lifeguard carrying Victim

2006. Centenary of Lifesaving Society. Mult.

1600	10k. Type **520**	2·75	2·50
1601	10k.50 Baby swimming	3·00	2·50

521 Shaman's Drum (detail)

2006. Nordic Mythology. Sheet 105×70 mm containing T 521 and similar horiz design. Multicoloured.

MS1602	A (6k.) Type **521**; 10k.50 Fafnir (dragon) (carved door panel)	4·75	4·50

Stamps of a similar theme were issued by Aland Islands, Denmark, Faroe Islands, Finland, Greenland, Iceland and Sweden.

522 Lynx

2006. Wildlife. Multicoloured.

1603	6k.50 Type **522**	1·90	1·80
1604	8k.50 Capercaillie	2·50	2·30
1605	10k. Golden eagle	3·00	2·75
1606	10k.50 Artic fox	3·25	3·00
1607	13k. Mountain hare	3·75	3·50

523 *Polycera quadrilineata*

2006. Marine Life. (3rd series). Self-adhesive.

1608	**523**	10k. multicoloured	3·00	2·75

524 Shopper c. 1947

2006. Centenary of Cooperative Movement.

1609	**524**	6k.50 multicoloured	1·90	1·80

525 *Skibladner*

2006. Tourism. Multicoloured. Self-adhesive.

1610	6k.50 Type **525**	1·90	1·80
1611	6k.50 Maihaugen, Lillehammer	1·90	1·80
1612	8k.50 Kirkenporten, Nordkapp	2·50	2·10
1613	8k.50 Nordkapp	2·50	2·40
1614	10k.50 Bryggen, Bergen	3·25	3·00
1615	10k.50 Atlanterhavsveien	3·25	3·00

526 Surveying c. 1906

2006. Centenary of Prince Albert I of Monaco's Expedition to Svalbard, Arctic Circle and Establishment of Longyearbyen and Stoke Norske Coal Mining Company. Multicoloured.

1616	6k.50 Type **526**	2·00	1·80
1617	8k.50 Coal transport terminal	1·80	2·50
1618	22k. Longyearbyen today	6·50	6·25
MS1619	171×100 mm. Nos. 1616/18	10·50	10·00

527 Dove

2006. Personalised Stamp. Self-adhesive.

1620	**527**	A (6k.50) multicoloured	1·75	85

528 Sea urchin (*Strongylocentrotus droebachiensis*)

2006. Marine Life. (4th series). Multicoloured. Self-adhesive.

1621	B (6k.) Type **528**	1·70	1·50
1622	A (6k.50) Cuckoo wrasse (*Labrus bimaculatus*)	1·80	1·60

529 On Parade

2006. 150th Anniv of King's Guard. Multicoloured.

1623	6k.50 Type **529**	1·80	1·60
1624	13k. Field training	3·50	3·25
MS1625	178×65 mm. Nos. 1623/4	5·25	5·00

530 Lantern

2006. Personalised Stamp. Self-adhesive.

1626	**530**	A (6k.50) multicoloured	1·80	1·60

531 Children and Tree

2006. Christmas. Multicoloured. Self-adhesive.

1627	A (6k.50) Type **531**	1·80	1·60
1628	A (6k.50) Snowman	1·80	1·60

532 Circle of Children

2006. Europa. Integration. Multicoloured.

1629	8k.50 Type **532**	2·40	3·50
1630	13k. Children and ball	2·10	3·25

533 Heart

2007. St. Valentine's Day.

1631	**533**	A (6k.50) multicoloured	1·80	1·60

534 Petter Solberg driving Subaru Impreza

2007. Motor Sport. Norway Winter Rally. Multicoloured.

1632	A (6k.50) "Innland" Type **534**	1·80	1·60
1633	A (8k.50) "Europa" Henning Solberg driving Peugeot 307	2·50	2·20
1634	A (10k.50) "Verden" Thomas Schie driving Ford Focus	3·00	2·75
MS1635	170×100 mm. Nos. 1632/4	7·00	6·75

No. 1632 was for use on priority domestic mail, 1633 was for use on priority mail within Europe and 1634 was for use on worldwide priority mail.

535 King Harald V

2007. 70th Birthday of King Harald V.

1636	**535**	6k.50 multicoloured	1·80	1·60

536 Water Samples and CTD Machine

2007. International Polar Year. Sheet 170×100 mm containing T 536 and similar horiz design. Multicoloured.

MS1637	170×100 mm. 10k.50 Type **536**; 13k. *Svalbard* (research ship) and antenna	6·50	6·25

537 Hedgehog

2007. Wildlife. Multicoloured.

1638	12k. Type **537**	3·25	3·00
1639	22k. Red squirrel	6·00	5·75

538 Arms, *Dionne* (barque), Customs House and Perfume Bottle

2007. Bicentenary of Porgrunn. Value expressed by letter.

1640	**538**	A "Innland" (7k.) mult	1·90	1·70

No. 1640 was for use on Priority mail within Norway.

539 Free Fall over Voss

2007. Tourism. Multicoloured. Self-adhesive.
1641 A "Innland" (7k.) Type **539** 2·00 1·80
1642 A "Innland" (7k.) Cyclists on Old Navvy Road, Finse 2·00 1·80
1643 A "Europa" (9k.) Houses, Roros 2·50 2·30
1644 A "Europa" (9k.) River, Fredrikstad 2·50 2·30
1645 A "Verden" (11k.) House and bay, Portor 3·00 2·75
1646 A "Verden" (11k.) View from sea, Reine 3·00 2·75

Nos. 1641/2 was for use on priority domestic mail, 1643/4 was for use on priority mail within Europe and 1645/6 was for use on priority mail worldwide.

540 "Et Overfall" (An Attack)

2007. 150th Birth Anniv of Theodor Kittelsen (artist). Multicoloured.
1647 A "Europa" (9k.) Type **540** 2·50 2·20
1648 A "Verden" (11k.) "For tidlig Nedkomst" (Premature Delivery) 3·00 2·50

Nos. 1647 was for use on priority mail within Europe and 1648 was for use on priority mail worldwide.

541 Mackerel (*Scomber scombrus*)

2007. Marine Life (5th series). Multicoloured. Self-adhesive.
1649 **541** 11k. multicoloured 3·00 2·50

542 Scouts and Knots

2007. Europa. Centenary of Scouting. Multicoloured.
1650 9k. Type **542** 2·50 2·20
1651 11k. Camp 3·00 2·50

543 Church of Our Lady, Trondheim

2007. Architectural Anniversaries. Multicoloured.
1652 14k. Type **543** (800th anniv) 3·50 3·25
1653 23k. Vardohus Fortress (700th anniv) 6·50 6·25

544 Ona Lighthouse

2007. Lighthouses. Multicoloured. Self-adhesive.
1654 (7k.) Type **544** 2·00 1·80
1655 (7k.) Tungeneset 2·00 1·80

See also Nos. 1578/9.

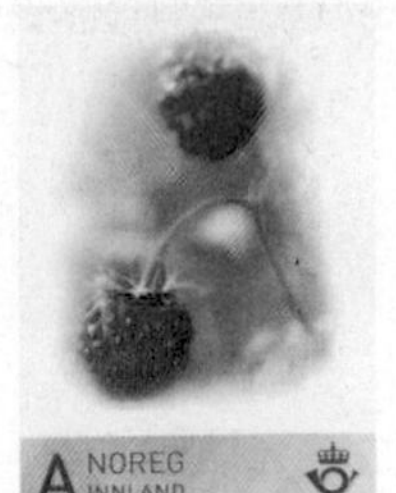

545 Strawberries

2007. Personalised Stamp. Self-adhesive.
1656 **545** (7k.) multicoloured 2·00 1·80

546 'Ingen tanke er tenkt fo den er stot i ord' (Inge Loning)

2007. Centenary of Riksmaal (language) Society.
1657 **546** 7k. multicoloured 2·00 1·80

547 *Pandalus montagui*

2007. Marine Life (6th series). Mlticoloured. Self-adhesive.
1658 (7k.) Type **547** 2·30 2·00
1659 (7k.) *Homarus gammarus* 2·30 2·00
1660 (7k.) *Cancer pagurus* 2·30 2·00
1661 (7k.) *Galathea strigosa* 2·30 2·00

548 Halldis Moren

2007. Birth Centenary of Halldis Moren Vesaas (poet and translator).
1662 **548** 23k. bronze, black and gold 6·50 6·25

549 Reindeer

2007. Personal Stamp. Self-adhesive A-Priority Domestic Stamp.
1663 **549** (7k.) blue and vermilion 2·30 2·00

No. 1663 was inscr 'A INNLAND'.

550 Star

2007. Christmas. A-Priority Domestic Stamps. Multicoloured. Self-adhesive.
1664 (7k.) Type **550** 2·30 2·00
1665 (7k.) Three Wise Men 2·30 2·00

Nos. 1664/5 were inscr 'A INNLAND'.

551 Academy Building and Machinery

2007. Scientific Anniversaries. Multicoloured.
1666 14k. Type **551** (250th anniv of Kongsberg Mining Academy) 4·25 4·00
1667 14k. Molecule and microscope (150th anniv of Academy of Science and Letters) 4·25 4·00

552 'Love'

2008. St Valentine's Day. Multicoloured. (a) Inscr 'INNLAND A'.
1668 (7k.) Type **552** 2·30 2·00

(b) Inscr 'EUROPA A'.
1669 (9k.) Letter, roses and doves 3·00 2·75

No. 1668 was for use on domestic mail and No. 1669 for use on mail within Europe.

553 Elk

2008. Wildlife. Multicoloured.
1670 11k. Type **553** 2·75 2·75
1671 14k. Brown bear 4·25 4·25
1672 23k. Wolf 7·00 7·00

554 Thorleif Haug

2008. Centenary of Norwegian Ski Federation. Multicoloured. Self adhesive.
1673 A (7k.) Type **554** (Olympic cross country and Nordic gold medallist–1924) 2·00 2·00
1674 A (7k.) Espen Bredesen (Olympic hill gold medallist–1994) 2·00 2·00
1675 A (7k.) Children skiing 2·00 2·00
1676 A (7k.) Kjetil Andre Aamodt (four times Olympic alpine gold medallist) 2·00 2·00

555 Harald Fairhair and Snofrid

2008. Norse Mythology. Mythological Places. Sheet 105×70 mm containing T 555 and similar horiz design. Multicoloured.
MS1677 A (70k.)×2, Type **555**; Snøhetta (home of giants) in Dovre mountains 25·00 25·00

The stamps and margins of **MS**1677 form a composite design.

556 Building Facade

2008. Inauguration of New Opera House, Oslo.
1678 **556** A (7k.) multicoloured 2·00 2·00

557 Frederick Stang

2008. Birth Bicentenaries. Multicoloured.
1679 A (7k.) Type **557** (politician) 2·00 2·00
1680 A (7k.) Henrick Wergland (lyricist) 2·00 2·20

558 Oslo Harbour

2008. Tourism. Multicoloured. Self-adhesive. (a) Inscr 'INNLAND A'.
1681 A (7k.) Type **558** 2·00 2·00
1682 A (7k.) *Divers* (sculpture) (Ola Enstad) 2·00 2·00

(b) Inscr 'EUROPA A'.
1683 A (9k.) The Blade, Molladalen (Sunnmore alps) 2·20 2·20
1684 A (9k.) Wedged boulder, Kjerag plateau, Lyse Fjord 2·20 2·20

556 Building Facade

(c) Inscr 'VERDEN A'.
1685 A (11k.) Yacht and Lyngør lighthouse 2·75 2·75
1686 A (11k.) Houses, Lyngor 2·75 2·75

Nos. 1681/2 was for use on priority domestic mail, 1683/4 was for use on priority mail within Europe and 1685/6 was for use on priority mail worldwide.

559 *Boroysund*

2008. Transportation Centenaries.
1687 7k. olive and brown 2·00 2·00
1688 9k. indigo and crimson 2·20 2·20
1689 25k. brown and blue 6·25 6·25
1690 30k. lilac and green 9·50 9·50

DESIGNS: 7k. Type **559**; 9k. *Oster* (ice breaker and transport ship); 25k. French Unic 1907 bus and driver; 30k. Thamshavn electric railway locomotive and train.

560 *Dancer in a Cultural Landscape* (composed photograph by Marcel Lelienhof)

2008. Stavanger–European Capital of Culture, 2008. Multicoloured.
1691 7k. Type **560** 2·00 2·00
1692 14k. *Swords in Rock* (sculpture by Fritz Roed) 4·00 4·00
1693 23k. 'Eye' (character from *The Thousandth Heart* (musical)) (vert) 7·50 7·50

561 Andreas Thorkildsen (javelin)

2008. Olympic Games, Beijing. Multicoloured.
1694 9k. Type **561** 3·00 7·50
1695 23k. Gro Hammerseng (handball) 7·50 7·50

562 New Post Logo

2008. Personalised Stamp.
1696 **562** A (7k.) multicoloured 2·25 2·25

No. 1696 was for use on priority domestic mail, and originally sold for 7k.

2008. Stavanger–European Capital of Culture, 2008. As T 560. Multicoloured.
MS1697 170×65 mm. Nos. 1691/3 14·00 14·00

563 *I revolusjonens forgard* (Arne Ekeland)

2008. Norwegian Art. Multicoloured. Self-adhesive.

1698	A (7k.) Type **563**	2·25	2·25
1699	A (7k.) *Svalbardmotiv* (Kare Tveter)	2·25	2·25
1700	A (7k.) *Komposisjon i rodt* (Inge Sitter)	2·25	2·25
1701	A (7k.) *Fra Sagorsk ca 1985* (Terje Bergstad)	2·25	2·25

No. 1698/701 were for use on priority domestic mail, and originally sold for 7k.

564 Gnomes and Amperhaugen Farm

2008. Christmas. Multicoloured. Self-adhesive.

1702	A (7k.) Type **564**	2·25	2·25
1703	A (7k.) Gnome looking down on Nordre Lien farm	2·25	2·25

Nos. 1702/3 were for use on priority domestic mail, and originally sold for 7k.

2009. Norwegian Art (2nd series). Self-adhesive Coil Stamps. As T 563. Multicoloured.

1704	B (7k.50) *Sommernatt til E.M.* (Kjell Nupen)	2·25	2·25
1705	12k. *Lyset ved pinsetider* (Irmo Salo Jæger)	3·00	3·00

No. 1704 were for use on economy domestic mail, and originally sold for 7k.50.

565 Roe Deer

2009. Wildlife. Multicoloured.

1706	11k.50 Type **565**	3·00	3·00
1707	15k.50 Reindeer	4·25	4·25
1708	25k. Willow grouse	6·25	6·25

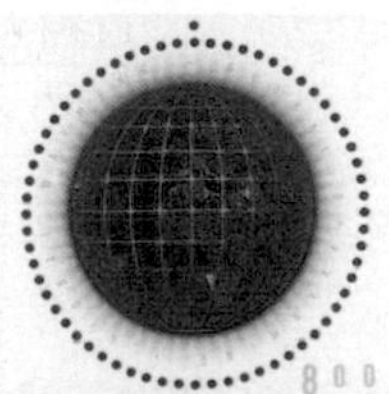

566 Over-heated Globe

2009. Preserve Polar Regions and Glaciers. Sheet 120×80 mm containing T 566 and similar circular design. Multicoloured.

MS1709	8k.×2, Type **566**; Polar ice	5·00	5·00

567 Hepatica

2009. Personal Stamp. Self-adhesive.

1710 **567**	A (8k.) multicoloured	2·50	2·50

No. 1710 was for use on priority domestic mail, and originally sold for 8k.

568 Bergen Railway Line

2009. Tourism. Self-adhesive Booklet Stamps. Multicoloured.

1711	A (8k.) Type **568**	2·75	2·75
1712	A (8k.) Locomotive in snow	2·75	2·75
1713	A (10k.) Stottafjorden, Meloy, Nordland	3·25	3·25
1714	A (10k.) Revtangen, Kiepp, Rogaland	3·25	3·25
1715	A (12k.) Bleik, Andoya, Nordland	4·00	4·00
1716	A (12k.) Kennesteinen, Vagsoy, Sogh og Fjordane	4·00	4·00

Nos. 1711/12 were for use on priority domestic mail, and originally sold for 8k. Nos. 1713/14 were for use on priority mail within Europe, and originally sold for 10k. Nos. 1715/16 were for use on priority worldwided mail, and originally sold for 12k.

569 Procession

2009. 150th Anniv of National Anthem.

1717 **569**	12k. multicoloured	4·00	4·00

570 Telephone Kiosk (designed by Georg Fasting, 1932)

2009. Norwegian Year of Cultural Heritage. Coil stamps. Multicoloured. Self-adhesive.

1718	(8k.) Type **570**	2·75	2·75
1719	(8k.) Kurer radio (1950)	2·75	2·75

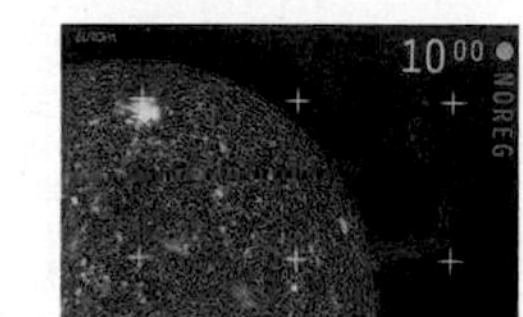

571 Explosion on Sun's Surface

2009. Europa. Astronomy. Multicolured.

1720	10k. Type **571**	3·00	3·00
1721	12k. Moon	4·00	4·00
MS1722	156×108 mm. Nos. 1720/1	7·00	7·00

572 Symbols of Development

2009. Bicentenary of Royal Norwegian Society for Development.

1723 **572**	12k. multicoloured	4·50	4·50

573 *Kobben* (1909)

2009. Centenary of Naval Submarines. Multicoloured.

1724	14k.50 Type **573**	5·00	5·00
1725	15k.50 Modern Ula class submarine	6·00	6·00

574 Knut Hamsun

2009. 150th Birth Anniv of Knut Hamsun (writer and winner of 1920 Nobel Prize for Literature).

1726 **574**	25k. deep claret, silver and gold	8·50	8·50

575 Roald Stensby

2009. Norwegian Rock Pioneers. Multicoloured. Self-adhesive.

1727	A (8k.) Type **575**	3·00	3·00
1728	A (8k.) Rocke-Pelle (Per Hartvig)	3·00	3·00
1729	A (8k.) Jan Rhode	3·00	3·00
1730	A (8k.) Per 'Elvis' Granberg	3·00	3·00

576 Cruise Ship

2009. Centenary of Shipowners' Association.

1731 **576**	15k.50 multicoloured	4·50	4·50

577 Man with Guide Dog and White Stick

2009. Centenary of Norwegian Association of the Blind and Partially Sighted.

1732 **577**	8k. vermillon	3·25	3·25

No. 1732 is embossed with Braille letters.

578 Apple

2009. Christmas. Booklet Stamps. Multicoloured. Self-adhesive.

1733	A (8k.) Type **578**	3·00	3·00
1734	A (8k.) Star	3·00	3·00

Nos. 1733/4 were for use on priority domestic mail, and originally sold for 8k.

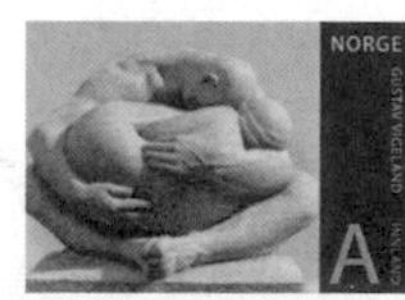

579 *Woman on a Man's Lap* (Gustav Vigeland)

2009. Modern Art. Multicoloured. Self-adhesive.

1735	A (8k.) Type **579**	3·00	3·00
1736	A (8k.) *Crow* (Nils Aas)	3·00	3·00
1737	A (8k.) *Birds in Flight* (Arnold Haukeland)	3·00	3·00
1738	A (8k.) *Granite Head on Side* (Kristian Blystad)	3·00	3·00

No. 1735/8 were for use on priority domestic mail, and originally sold for 8k.

580 *Mann som drikker* (Per Salle Storm)

2010. Modern Art. Self-adhesive.

1739 **580**	13k. multicoloured	4·75	4·75

581 Otter

2010. Fauna. Multicoloured.

1740	15k. Type **581**	3·50	3·50
1741	16k. Lemming	4·75	4·75
1742	26k. Wolverine	13·00	13·00

582 Ole Bull (violinist)

2010. Birth Bicentenaries. Multicoloured. Self-adhesive.

1743	A (8k.) Type **582**	3·00	3·00
1744	A (8k.) Peter Andreas Munch (historian)	3·00	3·00

No. 1743/4 were for use on priority domestic mail, and originally sold for 8k.

583 Fish on Drying Rack, Lofoten

2010. Norden. Life at the Coast

MS1745	multicoloured	4·00	4·00

Stamps of a similar theme were issued by Denmark, Greenland, Faröe Islands, Finland, Iceland, Aland Islands and Sweden.

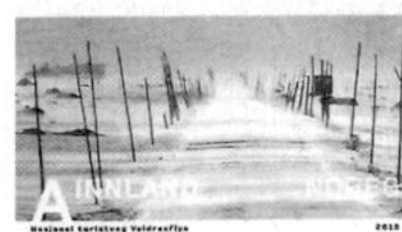

584 Valdresflya

2010. Tourism. Multicoloured.

1746	A INNLAND (8k.50) Type **584**	3·00	3·00
1747	A INNLAND (8k.50) Gamle Strynefjellsveien	3·00	3·00
1748	A EUROPA (11k.) Sognfjellet	3·75	3·75
1749	A EUROPA (11k.) Trollstigen	3·75	3·75
1750	A VERDA (13k.) Helgelandsky-sten Nord	4·75	4·75
1751	A VERDA (13k.) Lofoten	4·75	4·75

Nos. 1746/7 were for use on priority domestic mail, and originally sold for 8k.50

Nos. 1748/9 were for use on priority mail within Europe, and originally sold for 11k

Nos. 1750/1 were for use on priority worldwide mail, and originally sold for 13k.

585 Heather

2010. Personal Stamp

1752	A INNLAND (8k.50 multicoloured	4·00	4·00

586 Jahn Teigen

2010. Eurovision Song Contest Performers. Multicoloured.

1753	A INNLAND (8k.50) Type **586**	3·25	3·25
1754	A INNLAND (8k.50) Alexander Rybak	3·25	3·25
1755	A INNLAND (8k.50) Secret Garden	3·25	3·25
1756	A INNLAND (8k.50) Bobbysocks	3·25	3·25

587 Nils Petter Molvær (trumpeter)

2010. 50th (2011) Anniv of Molde Jazz Festival

1757	**587**	13k. black and turquoise-blue	4·50	4·50

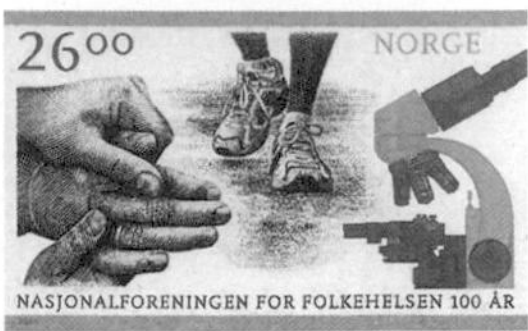

588 Hands, Feet and Microscope

2010. Centenary of Norwegian National Health Association

1758	**588**	26k. multicoloured	9·25	9·25

589 Bjørnen Teodor, Komekameratene,Pompel & Piltand Titten Tei (children's television)

2010. 50th Anniv of Norwegian Television. Multicoloured.

Coil stamps. Self-adhesive

1759	A INNLAND (8k.50) Type **489**	3·00	3·00
1760	A INNLAND (8k.50) Trond Kirkvåg as *Skremmer'n*, Robert Stolenberg as *Narvestad*, Rolv Wesenlund as *Fleksnes* and Trond-Viggo Torgesen as *Vaktmester'n* (comedy)	3·00	3·00
1761	A INNLAND (8k.50) Erik Diesen, Dan Børge Åkerø, Ivar Dyrhaug and Anne Grosvald (entertainment)	3·00	3·00
1762	A INNLAND (8k.50) Arne Scheie, Ingrid Espelid Høvig, Erik Bye and Ragnhild Sælthun Fjørtoft (personalities)	3·00	3·00

Miniature sheet. Ordinary gum

MS1763 120×80 mm. A INNLAND (8k.50)×2, As Type **589** and As No. 1762	6·00	6·00

590 Norwegian University of Technology and Science, Gloshaugen (centenary)

2010. Anniversaries. Multicoloured.

1764	8k.50 Type **590**	3·25	3·25
1765	13k. Society seal and building, Klavskinnet, Trondheim (Royal Norwegian Society of Science and Letters (250th anniv))	4·50	4·50

591 'YTRINGSFRIHET' (freedom of speech)

2010. Centenary of Norwegian Press Association and Norwegian Media Businesses' Association

1766	**591**	11k. multicoloured	4·00	4·00

592 Boatswain Mikel Våge aboard Stavanger (1973)

2010. Centenary of Norwegian Seafarers' Union

1767	**592**	16k. multicoloured	5·75	5·75

Nos. 1768/9 and Type **593** are left for DKNVS and NTNU Anniversaries issue on 15 September 2010, not yet received.

2010. Posthorn. Multicoloured, colour of oval given.

1770	4k. royal blue	1·75	1·75
1771	8k. deep carmine-red	2·75	2·75
1772	30k. reddish lilac	11·00	11·00

594 Christmas Goat

2010. Christmas. Multicoloured.

1773	A (8k.50) Type **594**	3·25	3·25
1774	A (8k.50) Candlestick with candles	3·25	3·25

Nos. 1773/4 were both inscribed 'INNLAND' and were for use on priority domestic mail, and originally sold for 8k.60.

595 In the Sledge

2010. Europa. Multicoloured.

1176	A(11k.) Father, Mother, Grandmother and children approaching cottage	4·50	4·50
1775	A(8k.50) Type **595**	2·75	2·75

Nos. 1775 was inscribed 'INNLAND' and was for use on priority domestic mail, and originally sold for 8k.60 No. 1776 was inscribed 'EUROPA' and were for use on priority European mail, and originally sold for 11k.

596 Athletes

2011. 150th Anniv of Norwegian Confederation of Sports

1777	14k. multicoloured	7·75	7·75

597 Polar Bear

2011. Fauna. Multicoloured.

1778	17k. Type **597**	12·00	12·00
1779	27k. Musk ox	16·00	16·00

OFFICIAL STAMPS

O22

1925

O187	**O22**	5ore mauve	1·20	1·10
O188	**O22**	10ore green	45	25
O189	**O22**	15ore blue	2·50	2·40
O190	**O22**	20ore purple	40	25
O191	**O22**	30ore grey	4·25	4·50
O192	**O22**	40ore blue	3·00	1·20
O193	**O22**	60ore blue	5·00	4·75

1929. Surch 2 2.

O219	2ore on 5ore mauve	85	85

O36

1933

O231	**O36**	2ore brown	60	1·60
O243	**O36**	5ore purple	2·10	1·60
O233	**O36**	7ore orange	5·75	4·75
O245	**O36**	10ore green	85	40
O235	**O36**	15ore green	65	55
O247	**O36**	20ore red	1·10	35
O237	**O36**	25ore brown	65	60
O238	**O36**	30ore blue	85	65
O248	**O36**	35ore violet	80	45
O249	**O36**	40ore grey	1·20	50
O250	**O36**	60ore blue	1·30	80
O241	**O36**	70ore brown	1·70	2·40
O242	**O36**	100ore blue	3·00	2·10

O39

1937

O267	**O39**	5ore mauve	40	25
O268	**O39**	7ore orange	60	55
O269	**O39**	10ore green	25	25
O270	**O39**	15ore brown	40	25
O271	**O39**	20ore red	25	25
O260	**O39**	25ore brown	1·40	65
O273	**O39**	25ore red	25	20
O261	**O39**	30ore blue	90	75
O275	**O39**	30ore grey	95	40
O276	**O39**	35ore purple	60	25
O277	**O39**	40ore grey	65	25
O278	**O39**	40ore blue	4·25	30
O279	**O39**	50ore lilac	95	30
O280	**O39**	60ore blue	65	25
O281	**O39**	100ore blue	1·30	25
O282	**O39**	200ore orange	2·40	30

O58 Quisling Emblem

1942

O336	**O58**	5ore mauve	40	1·80
O337	**O58**	7ore orange	40	1·80
O338	**O58**	10ore green	15	30
O339	**O58**	15ore brown	2·50	13·00
O340	**O58**	20ore red	15	30
O341	**O58**	25ore brown	5·00	19·00
O342	**O58**	30ore blue	3·25	19·00
O343	**O58**	35ore purple	3·25	10·00
O344	**O58**	40ore grey	20	30
O345	**O58**	60ore blue	3·00	11·00
O346	**O58**	1k. blue	3·00	15·00

1949. Surch 25 and bar.

O402	**O39**	25ore on 20ore red	35	30

O89

1951

O434	**O89**	5ore mauve	1·20	15
O435	**O89**	10ore grey	1·00	15
O436	**O89**	15ore brown	1·20	65
O437	**O89**	30ore red	75	15
O438	**O89**	35ore brown	1·10	50
O439	**O89**	60ore blue	1·30	20
O440	**O89**	100ore violet	1·90	40

O99

1955

O458	**O99**	5ore purple	20	20
O459	**O99**	10ore grey	20	15
O460	**O99**	15ore brown	55	1·80
O461	**O99**	20ore green	40	20
O736	**O99**	25ore green	20	20
O463	**O99**	30ore red	2·10	70
O464	**O99**	30ore green	2·20	20
O465	**O99**	35ore red	45	15
O466	**O99**	40ore lilac	85	15
O467	**O99**	40ore green	45	40
O468	**O99**	45ore red	1·50	15
O469	**O99**	50ore brown	2·50	20
O470	**O99**	50ore red	1·80	30
O471	**O99**	50ore blue	50	20
O738	**O99**	50ore grey	20	15
O473	**O99**	60ore red	65	20
O739	**O99**	60ore blue	1·10	3·50
O475	**O99**	65ore red	1·40	25
O476	**O99**	70ore brown	4·75	85
O477	**O99**	70ore red	30	20
O478	**O99**	75ore purple	13·00	11·50
O479	**O99**	75ore green	75	45
O481	**O99**	80ore brown	60	15
O741	**O99**	80ore red	35	15
O482	**O99**	85ore brown	55	1·60
O483	**O99**	90ore orange	1·30	20
O484	**O99**	1k. violet	1·30	15
O485	**O99**	1k. red	30	20
O486	**O99**	1k.10 red	60	80
O744	**O99**	1k.25 red	85	20
O745	**O99**	1k.30 purple	1·10	1·50
O746	**O99**	1k.50 red	50	30
O747	**O99**	1k.75 green	1·50	1·40
O748	**O99**	2k. green	1·20	25
O749	**O99**	2k. red	1·20	25
O750	**O99**	3k. violet	1·50	55
O488	**O99**	5k. violet	5·50	70
O752	**O99**	5k. blue	1·30	25

POSTAGE DUE STAMPS

D12

1889. Inscr "at betale" and "PORTOMAERKE".

D95	**D12**	1ore green	65	80
D96a	**D12**	4ore mauve	85	45
D97	**D12**	10ore red	2·75	45
D98	**D12**	15ore brown	1·30	80
D99	**D12**	20ore blue	1·70	45
D94	**D12**	50ore purple	3·75	1·50

1922. Inscr "a betale" and "PORTOMERKE".

D162	4ore purple	6·75	10·00
D163	10ore green	4·25	1·40
D164	20ore purple	5·00	2·75
D165	40ore blue	8·50	85
D166	100ore yellow	34·00	7·50
D167	200ore violet	43·00	18·00

Pt. 6

NOSSI-BE

An island north-west of Madagascar, declared a French protectorate in 1840. In 1901 it became part of Madagascar and Dependencies.

100 centimes = 1 franc.

1889. Stamp of French Colonies, "Peace and Commerce" type, surch.

8	**H**	25c. on 40c. red on yellow	£2250	£800

1889. Stamps of French Colonies, "Commerce" type, surch.

4	**J**	5c. on 10c. black on lilac	£2750	£800
2	**J**	5c. on 20c. red on green	£3000	£850
6	**J**	15 on 20c. red on green	£2750	£800
7	**J**	25 on 30c. brown on drab	£2750	£650
9	**J**	25 on 40c. red on yellow	£2250	£650

1890. Stamps of French Colonies, "Commerce" type, surch. (a) N S B 0 25.

10	0 25 on 20c. red on green	£325	£225
11	0 25 on 75c. red on pink	£275	£225
12	0 25 on 1f. green	£325	£225

(b) N S B 25 c.

13	25c. on 20c. red on green	£325	£225
14	25c. on 75c. red on pink	£325	£225
15	25c. on 1f. green	£325	£225

(c) N S B 25 in frame.

16	25 on 20c. red on green	£750	£550
17	25 on 75c. red on pink	£750	£550
18	25 on 1f. green	£750	£550

1893. Stamps of French Colonies, "Commerce" type, surch NOSSI-BE and bar over value in figures.

36	25 on 20c. red on green	60·00	60·00
37	50 on 10c. black on lilac	65·00	60·00
38	75 on 15c. blue	£225	£170
39	1f. on 5c. green	£120	£100

1893. Stamps of French Colonies, "Commerce" type, optd Nossi Be.

40a	10c. black on lilac	40·00	9·25
41	15c. blue	40·00	12·00
42	20c. red on green	£425	28·00

1894. "Tablet" key-type inscr "NOSSI-BE" in red (1, 5, 15, 25, 75c., 1f.) or blue (others).

44	**D**	1c. black on blue	1·90	1·70
45	**D**	2c. brown on buff	2·50	3·50
46	**D**	4c. brown on grey	3·00	3·50
47	**D**	5c. green on green	3·25	3·00
48	**D**	10c. black on lilac	3·25	5·25
49	**D**	15c. blue	14·00	4·50
50	**D**	20c. red on green	11·00	10·50
51	**D**	25c. black on pink	14·00	12·50
52	**D**	30c. brown on drab	11·00	20·00
53	**D**	40c. red on yellow	17·00	23·00
54	**D**	50c. red on pink	6·00	7·75
55	**D**	75c. brown on orange	34·00	27·00
56	**D**	1f. green	11·00	46·00

POSTAGE DUE STAMPS

1891. Stamps of French Colonies, "Commerce" type, surch NOSSI-BE chiffre-taxe A PERCEVOIR and value.

D19	**J**	0.20 on 1c. black on blue	£275	£200
D20	**J**	0.30 on 2c. brown on buff	£275	£200
D21	**J**	0.35 on 4c. brown on grey	£300	£225
D22	**J**	0.35 on 20c. red on green	£325	£225
D23	**J**	0.50 on 30c. brn on drab	£110	85·00
D24	**J**	1f. on 35c. black on orge	£180	£140

1891. Stamps of French Colonies, "Commerce" type, surch Nossi-Be A PERCEVOIR and value.

D25	5c. on 20c. red on green	£140	£140
D33	0.10 on 5c. green	33·00	19·00
D26	10c. on 15c. blue on blue	£150	£150
D27	15c. on 10c. black on lilac	£140	£140
D34	0.15 on 20c. red on green	40·00	42·00
D28	25c. on 5c. green on green	£140	£140
D35	0.25 on 75c. red on pink	£425	£425

Pt. 1

NOVA SCOTIA

An eastern province of the Dominion of Canada, whose stamps it now uses.

Currency: As Canada.

1

2 Emblem of the United Kingdom

1851. Imperf.

1	**1**	1d. brown	£2500	£425
4	**2**	3d. blue	£900	£140
5	**2**	6d. green	£4750	£500
8	**2**	1s. purple	£18000	£3250

3

4

1863. Perf.

10	**3**	1c. black	4·25	18·00
23	**3**	2c. purple	4·75	13·00
13	**3**	5c. blue	£475	24·00
14	**4**	8½c. green	4·50	50·00
28	**4**	10c. red	5·00	35·00
17	**4**	12½c. black	35·00	30·00

Pt. 1

NYASALAND PROTECTORATE

A British Protectorate in central Africa. Formerly known as British Central Africa. From 1954 to 1963 part of the Central African Federation using the stamps of Rhodesia and Nyasaland (q.v.). From July 1964 independent within the Commonwealth under its new name of Malawi.

12 pence = 1 shilling; 20 shillings = 1 pound.

1891. Stamps of Rhodesia optd B.C.A.

1	**1**	1d. black	12·00	8·50
2	**1**	2d. green and red	12·00	4·00
3	**1**	4d. brown and black	12·00	5·50
5	**1**	6d. blue	15·00	8·00
6	**1**	8d. red and blue	19·00	29·00
7	**1**	1s. brown	24·00	17·00
8	**1**	2s. red	40·00	55·00
9	**1**	2s.6d. purple	70·00	90·00
10	**1**	3s. brown and green	80·00	80·00
11	**1**	4s. black and red	80·00	90·00
12	**1**	5s. yellow	95·00	95·00
13	**1**	10s. green	£170	£200
14	-	£1 blue	£900	£650
15	-	£2 red	£1100	£1300
16	-	£5 olive	£1700	
17	-	£10 brown	£4000	£4750

1892. Stamps of Rhodesia surch B.C.A. and value in words.

18	**1**	3s. on 4s. black and red	£350	£350
19	**1**	4s. on 5s. yellow	90·00	90·00

1895. No. 2 surch ONE PENNY. and bar.

20	1d. on 2d. green and red	24·00	50·00

5 Arms of the Protectorate

1895. The 2s.6d. and higher values are larger.

32	**5**	1d. black	3·25	8·00
33	**5**	2d. black and green	17·00	5·00
34	**5**	4d. black and orange	27·00	17·00
35	**5**	6d. black and blue	40·00	13·00
36	**5**	1s. black and red	40·00	22·00
37	**5**	2s.6d. black and mauve	£170	£140
38	**5**	3s. black and yellow	£150	60·00
39	**5**	5s. black and olive	£200	£200
29	**5**	£1 black and orange	£1100	£450
40	**5**	£1 black and blue	£1000	£500
30	**5**	£10 black and orange	£6000	£4000
31	**5**	£25 black and green	£12000	

7 Arms of the Protectorate

1897. The 2s.6d. and higher values are larger.

43	**7**	1d. black and blue	3·25	1·25
57d	**7**	1d. purple and red	2·50	50
44	**7**	2d. black and yellow	2·00	2·00
45	**7**	4d. black and red	6·50	1·50
57e	**7**	4d. purple and olive	8·50	11·00
46	**7**	6d. black and green	55·00	4·25
58	**7**	6d. purple and brown	5·50	3·00
47	**7**	1s. black and purple	11·00	7·00
48	**7**	2s.6d. black and blue	80·00	42·00
49	**7**	3s. black and green	£275	£300
50	**7**	4s. black and red	90·00	95·00
50a	**7**	10s. black and olive	£225	£250
51	**7**	£1 black and purple	£400	£180
52	**7**	£10 black and yellow	£6500	£2250

1897. No. 49 surch ONE PENNY.

53	1d. on 3s. black and green	9·00	13·00

10

1898

56a	**10**	1d. red and blue (imperf)	£5000	£180
57	**10**	1d. red and blue (perf)	£4250	29·00

11

1903. The 2s.6d. and higher values are larger.

68	**11**	1d. grey and red	8·00	2·75
60	**11**	2d. purple	3·50	1·00
61	**11**	4d. green and black	2·50	9·00
62	**11**	6d. grey and brown	3·75	2·00
62b	**11**	1s. grey and blue	4·75	13·00
63	**11**	2s.6d. green	60·00	95·00
64	**11**	4s. purple	85·00	85·00
65	**11**	10s. green and black	£180	£250
66	**11**	£1 grey and red	£300	£190
67	**11**	£10 grey and blue	£6500	£4000

13

14

1908

73	**13**	½d. green	1·75	2·25
74	**13**	1d. red	7·00	1·00
75	**13**	3d. purple on yellow	1·50	4·25
76	**13**	4d. black and red on yellow	1·50	1·50
77	**13**	6d. purple	4·25	11·00
72	**13**	1s. black on green	3·50	15·00
78	**14**	2s.6d. black and red on blue	65·00	95·00
79	**14**	4s. red and black	95·00	£150
80	**14**	10s. green and red on green	£180	£275
81	**14**	£1 purple and black on red	£550	£650
82	**14**	£10 purple and blue	£9500	£6500

1913. As 1908, but portrait of King George V.

100	½d. green	2·25	50
101	1d. red	2·50	50
102	1½d. orange	3·25	17·00
103	2d. grey	2·00	50
89	2½d. blue	2·25	7·00
90	3d. purple on yellow	6·00	4·50
91	4d. black and red on yellow	2·00	2·50
107	6d. purple	3·50	3·25
93a	1s. black on green	5·50	1·50
109	2s. purple and blue on blue	18·00	12·00
94	2s.6d. black and red on blue	11·00	19·00
111	4s. red and black	20·00	38·00
112	5s. green and red on yellow	50·00	85·00
113	10s. green and red on green	£110	£110
98	£1 purple and black on red	£200	£150
99e	£10 purple and blue	£3500	£1700

17 King George V and Symbol of the Protectorate

1934

114	**17**	½d. green	75	1·25
115	**17**	1d. brown	75	75
116	**17**	1½d. red	75	3·00
117	**17**	2d. grey	80	1·25
118	**17**	3d. blue	3·00	1·75
119	**17**	4d. mauve	4·50	3·50
120	**17**	6d. violet	2·50	50
121	**17**	9d. olive	7·00	9·00
122	**17**	1s. black and orange	18·00	14·00

1935. Silver Jubilee. As T 143a of Newfoundland.

123	1d. blue and grey	1·00	2·00
124	2d. green and blue	1·00	1·50
125	3d. brown and blue	8·50	20·00
126	1s. grey and purple	25·00	55·00

1937. Coronation. As T 143b of Newfoundland.

127	½d. green	30	2·25
128	1d. brown	50	1·50
129	2d. grey	50	3·25

1938. As T 17 but with head of King George VI and "POSTAGE REVENUE" omitted.

130	½d. green	30	2·50
130a	½d. brown	10	2·50
131	1d. brown	4·00	30
131a	1d. green	30	2·25
132	1½d. red	7·50	6·50
132a	1½d. grey	30	7·50
133	2d. grey	8·00	1·25
133a	2d. red	30	1·75
134	3d. blue	1·00	1·50
135	4d. mauve	2·75	2·00
136	6d. violet	2·75	2·00
137	9d. olive	3·00	5·00
138	1s. black and orange	3·50	3·25

1938. As T 14 but with head of King George VI facing right.

139	2s. purple and blue on blue	10·00	17·00
140	2s.6d. black and red on blue	14·00	19·00
141	5s. green and red on yellow	55·00	30·00
142	10s. green and red on green	55·00	70·00
143	£1 purple and black on red	48·00	45·00

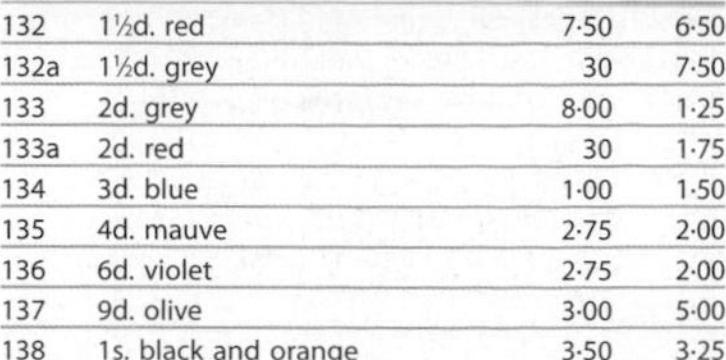

20 Lake Nyasa

21 King's African Rifles

1945

144	**20**	½d. black and brown	50	10
145	**21**	1d. black and green	20	70
160	-	1d. brown and green	50	30
146	-	1½d. black and grey	30	50
147	-	2d. black and red	1·50	85
148	-	3d. black and blue	30	30
149	-	4d. black and red	2·00	80
150	-	6d. black and violet	3·00	90
151	**20**	9d. black and olive	3·50	3·00
152	-	1s. blue and green	3·75	20
153	-	2s. green and purple	9·50	5·50
154	-	2s.6d. green and blue	9·50	7·00
155	-	5s. purple and blue	7·00	6·50
156	-	10s. red and green	20·00	18·00
157	-	20s. red and black	27·00	32·00

DESIGNS—HORIZ: 1½d., 6d. Tea estate; 2d., 1s., 10s. Map of Nyasaland; 4d., 2s.6d. Tobacco; 5s., 20s. Badge of Nyasaland. VERT: 1d. (No. 160), Leopard and sunrise; 3d., 2s. Fishing village.

1946. Victory. As T 8a of Pitcairn Islands.

158	1d. green	20	30
159	2d. red	30	30

1948. Silver Wedding. As T 8b/c of Pitcairn Islands.

161	1d. green	15	10
162	10s. mauve	18·00	27·00

1949. U.P.U. As T 8d/g of Pitcairn Islands.

163	1d. green	30	20
164	3d. blue	2·25	4·25
165	6d. purple	50	70
166	1s. blue	30	50

27 Arms in 1891 and 1951

1951. Diamond Jubilee of Protectorate.

167	**27**	2d. black and red	1·25	1·50
168	**27**	3d. black and blue	1·25	1·50
169	**27**	6d. black and violet	1·50	2·00
170	**27**	5s. black and blue	5·00	7·00

1953. Rhodes Centenary Exhibition. As T 6 of Northern Rhodesia.

171	6d. violet	50	30

1953. Coronation. As T 4h of Pitcairn Islands.

172	2d. black and orange	70	80

29 Grading Cotton

1953. As 1945 but with portrait of Queen Elizabeth II as in T 29. Designs as for corresponding values except where stated.

173	**20**	½d. black and brown	10	1·50
174	-	1d. brn & grn (as No. 160)	65	40
175	-	1½d. black and grey	20	1·90
176a	-	2d. black and orange	40	30
177	**29**	2½d. green and black	20	50

178	-	3d. black and red (as 4d.)	30	20
179	-	4½d. black and blue (as 3d.)	40	40
180	-	6d. black and violet	1·00	1·50
181	20	9d. black and olive	1·00	2·50
182	-	1s. blue and green	3·50	50
183	-	2s. green and red	3·00	3·75
184	-	2s.6d. green and blue	4·00	6·00
185	-	5s. purple and blue	9·00	6·00
186	-	10s. red and green	7·50	19·00
187	-	20s. red and black	22·00	32·00

30

1963. Revenue stamps optd POSTAGE as in T 30 or surch also.

188	30	½d. on 1d. blue	30	30
189	30	1d. green	30	10
190	30	2d. red	30	30
191	30	3d. blue	30	10
192	30	6d. purple	30	10
193	30	9d. on 1s. red	40	25
194	30	1s. purple	45	10
195	30	2s.6d. black	1·25	2·75
196	30	5s. brown	3·25	2·00
197	30	10s. olive	5·50	8·50
198	30	£1 violet	5·50	8·50

32 Mother and Child

34 Tea Industry

1964

199	32	½d. violet	10	30
200	-	1d. black and green	10	10
201	-	2d. brown	10	10
202	-	3d. brown, green and bistre	10	10
203	-	4d. blue and yellow	20	30
204	34	6d. purple, green and blue	70	70
205	-	1s. brown, blue and yellow	15	10
206	-	1s.3d. bronze and brown	3·75	10
207	-	2s.6d. brown and blue	3·25	50
208	-	5s. blue, green, yellow & blk	1·50	1·75
209	-	10s. green, salmon and black	2·50	3·25
210	-	£1 brown and yellow	7·00	14·00

DESIGNS—HORIZ (as Type **32**): 1d. Chambo (fish); 2d. Zebu bull; 3d. Groundnuts; 4d. Fishing. (As Type **34**): 1s. Timber; 1s.3d. Turkish tobacco industry; 2s.6d. Cotton industry; 5s. Monkey Bay, Lake Nyasa; 10s. Forestry, Afzelia. VERT (as Type **34**): £1 Nyala.

POSTAGE DUE STAMPS

1950. As Type D 1 of Gold Coast, but inscr "NYASALAND".

D1	1d. red	4·00	32·00
D2	2d. blue	18·00	32·00
D3	3d. green	17·00	6·00
D4	4d. purple	30·00	60·00
D5	6d. orange	42·00	£160

For later issues see **MALAWI**.

Pt. 9

NYASSA COMPANY

In 1894 Portugal granted a charter to the Nyassa Company to administer an area in the Northern part of Mozambique, including the right to issue its own stamps. The lease was terminated in 1929 and the administration was transferred to Mozambique whose stamps were used there.

1898. 1000 reis = 1 milreis.
1913. 100 centavos = 1 escudo.

1898. "Figures" and "Newspaper" key-types inscr "MOCAMBIQUE" optd NYASSA.

1	V	2½r. brown	3·75	3·50
2	R	5r. orange	3·75	3·50
3	R	10r. mauve	3·75	3·50
4	R	15r. brown	3·75	3·50
5	R	20r. lilac	3·75	3·50
6	R	25r. green	3·75	3·50
7	R	50r. blue	3·75	3·50
8	R	75r. pink	4·50	4·25
9	R	80r. green	4·50	4·25
10	R	100r. brown on buff	4·50	4·25
11	R	150r. red on pink	14·00	13·00
12	R	200r. blue on blue	8·25	7·50
13	R	300r. blue on brown	8·25	7·50

1898. "King Carlos" key-type inscr "MOCAMBIQUE" optd NYASSA.

14	S	2½r. grey	2·50	2·50
15	S	5r. red	2·50	2·50
16	S	10r. green	2·50	2·50
17	S	15r. brown	3·50	2·75
18	S	20r. lilac	3·50	2·75
19	S	25r. green	3·50	2·75
20	S	50r. blue	3·50	2·75
21	S	75r. pink	3·75	3·50
22	S	80r. mauve	4·50	2·50
23	S	100r. blue on blue	4·50	2·50
24	S	150r. brown on yellow	4·50	2·50
25	S	200r. purple on pink	4·75	2·75
26	S	300r. blue on pink	6·25	2·75

2 Giraffe

3 Dromedaries

1901

27	2	2½r. brown and black	2·30	1·20
28	2	5r. violet and black	2·30	1·20
29	2	10r. green and black	2·30	1·20
30	2	15r. brown and black	2·30	1·20
31	2	20r. red and black	2·30	1·50
32	2	25r. orange and black	2·30	1·50
33	2	50r. blue and black	2·30	1·50
34	3	75r. red and black	2·75	1·90
35	3	80r. bistre and black	2·75	1·90
36	3	100r. brown and black	2·75	1·90
37	3	150r. brown and black	3·25	2·20
38	3	200r. green and black	3·25	2·20
39	3	300r. green and black	3·25	2·20

1903. (a) Surch in figures and words.

40		65r. on 80r. mauve and black	2·10	1·60
41		115r. on 150r. brown & black	2·10	1·60
42		130r. on 300r. green & black	2·10	1·60
		(b) Optd PROVISORIO.		
43	2	15r. brown and black	2·10	1·60
44	2	25r. orange and black	2·10	1·60

1910. Optd PROVISORIO and surch in figures and words.

50		5r. on 2½r. brown and black	2·20	1·80
51	3	50r. on 100r. bistre and black	2·20	1·80

9 Dromedaries

12 Vasco de Gama's Flagship "Sao Gabriel"

1911. Optd REPUBLICA.

53	9	2½r. violet and black	2·10	1·30
54	9	5r. black	2·10	1·30
55	9	10r. green and black	2·10	1·30
56	-	20r. red and black	2·10	1·30
57	-	25r. brown and black	2·10	1·30
58	-	50r. blue and black	2·10	1·30
59	-	75r. brown and black	2·10	1·30
60	-	100r. brown & black on green	2·10	1·30
61	-	200r. green & black on orge	2·30	2·10
62	12	300r. black on blue	5·00	3·50
63	12	400r. brown and black	5·75	4·00
64	12	500r. violet and green	7·50	6·25

DESIGNS—HORIZ: 20, 25, 50r. Common zebra. VERT: 75, 100, 200r. Giraffe.

1918. Surch REPUBLICA and value in figures. (a) Stamps of 1901.

65	2	¼c. on 2½c. brown and black	£275	£200
66	2	½c. on 5r. violet and black	£275	£200
67	2	1c. on 10r. green and black	£275	£200
68	2	1½c. on 15r. brown and black	4·50	2·30
69	2	2c. on 20r. red and black	2·75	2·10
70	2	3½c. on 25r. orange and black	2·75	2·10
71	2	5c. on 50r. blue and black	2·75	2·10
72	3	7½c. on 75r. red and black	2·75	2·10
73	3	8c. on 80r. mauve and black	2·75	2·10
74	3	10c. on 100r. bistre and black	2·75	2·10
75	3	15c. on 150r. brown & black	4·50	4·25
76	3	20c. on 200r. green and black	4·25	4·25
77	3	30c. on 300r. green and black	6·75	5·00
		(b) Nos. 43/4 and 40/2.		
78	2	1½c. on 15r. brown and black	8·50	6·50
79	2	3½c. on 25r. orange and black	3·25	2·10
80	3	40c. on 65r. on 80r.	38·00	35·00
81	3	50c. on 115r. on 150r.	5·50	4·25
82	3	1E. on 130r. on 300r.	5·50	4·25

1921. Stamps of 1911 surch in figures and words.

83A	9	¼c. on 2½r. violet and black	3·25	3·25
85A	9	½c. on 5r. black	3·25	3·25
86A	9	1c. on 10r. green and black	3·25	3·25
87A	12	1½c. on 300r. black on blue	3·25	3·25
88A	-	2c. on 20r. red and black	3·25	3·25
89A	-	2½c. on 25r. brown and black	3·25	3·25
90A	12	3c. on 400r. brown & black	3·25	3·25
91A	-	5c. on 50r. blue and black	3·25	3·25
92A	-	7½c. on 75r. brown & black	3·25	3·25
93A	-	10c. on 100r. brown and black on green	3·25	3·25
94A	12	12c. on 500r. violet & green	3·25	3·25
95A	-	20c. on 200r. green and black on orange	3·25	3·25

16 Giraffe

19 Common Zebra

1921

96	16	¼c. purple	1·90	1·40
97	16	½c. blue	1·90	1·40
98	16	1c. black and green	1·90	1·40
99	16	1½c. orange and black	1·90	1·40
100	-	2c. black and red	1·90	1·40
101	-	2½c. green and black	1·90	1·40
102	-	4c. red and black	1·90	1·40
103	-	5c. black and blue	1·90	1·40
104	-	6c. violet and black	1·90	1·40
123	-	7½c. brown and black	1·50	1·20
124	-	8c. green and black	1·50	1·20
125	-	10c. brown and black	1·50	1·20
126	-	15c. red and black	1·50	1·20
127	-	20c. blue and black	1·50	1·20
110	19	30c. brown and black	1·90	1·40
111	19	40c. blue and black	1·90	1·40
112	19	50c. green and black	1·90	1·40
113	19	1e. brown and black	1·90	1·40
114	-	2e. black and brown	6·25	5·00
115	-	5e. brown and blue	5·75	4·50

DESIGNS—As Type **16**: 2c. to 6c. Vasco da Gama; 7½c. to 20c. Vasco da Gama's flagship "Sao Gabriel". As Type **19**: 2, 5e. Native dhow.

CHARITY TAX STAMPS

The notes under this heading in Portugal also apply here.

1925. Marquis de Pombal Commem. Nos. C327/9 of Mozambique optd NYASSA.

C141	C22	15c. brown	12·50	10·00
C142	-	15c. brown	12·50	10·00
C143	C 25	15c. brown	12·50	10·00

POSTAGE DUE STAMPS

D21 "Sao Gabriel"

1924

D132	-	½c. green	4·50	3·50
D133	-	1c. blue	4·50	3·50
D134	-	2c. red	4·50	3·50
D135	-	3c. red	4·50	3·50
D136	D21	5c. brown	4·50	3·50
D137	D21	6c. brown	4·50	3·50
D138	D21	10c. purple	4·50	3·50
D139	-	20c. red	4·50	3·50
D140	-	50c. purple	4·50	3·50

DESIGNS: ½c., 1c. Giraffe; 2c., 3c. Common zebra; 20c., 50c. Vasco da Gama.

1925. De Pombal stamps of Mozambique, Nos. D327/9, optd NYASSA.

D144	C22	30c. brown	15·00	15·00
D145	-	30c. brown	15·00	15·00
D146	C25	30c. brown	15·00	15·00

Pt. 6

OBOCK

A port and district on the Somali Coast. During 1894 the administration was moved to Djibouti, the capital of French Somali Coast, and the Obock post office was closed.

1892. Stamps of French Colonies, "Commerce" type, optd OBOCK.

1	J	1c. black on blue	55·00	60·00
2	J	2c. brown on buff	60·00	65·00
12	J	4c. brown on grey	14·00	22·00
13	J	5c. green on green	20·00	20·00
14	J	10c. black on lilac	25·00	42·00
15	J	15c. blue	14·00	32·00
16	J	20c. red on green	65·00	60·00
17	J	25c. black on pink	21·00	30·00
8	J	35c. black on orange	£325	£325
18	J	40c. red on buff	60·00	65·00
19	J	75c. red on pink	£250	£225
20	J	1f. green	70·00	70·00

1892. Nos. 14, 15, 17 and 20 surch.

39	1 on 25c. black on red	11·00	13·00
40	2 on 10c. black on lilac	80·00	65·00
41	2 on 15c. blue	8·25	30·00
42	4 on 15c. blue	12·00	42·00
43	4 on 25c. black on red	12·00	10·00
44	5 on 25c. black on red	30·00	40·00
45	20 on 10c. black on lilac	95·00	95·00
46	30 on 10c. black on lilac	£100	£100
47	35 on 25c. black on red	£100	80·00
48	75 on 1f. olive	£100	£110
49	5f. on 1f. olive	£700	£600

1892. "Tablet" key-type inscr "OBOCK" in red (1, 5, 15, 25, 75c., 1f.) or blue (others).

50	D	1c. black on blue	4·75	5·25
51	D	2c. brown on buff	2·75	3·75
52	D	4c. brown on grey	2·50	1·80
53	D	5c. green on green	7·00	9·00
54	D	10c. black on lilac	9·00	12·00
55	D	15c. blue	25·00	17·00
56	D	20c. red on green	40·00	48·00
57	D	25c. black on pink	36·00	42·00
58	D	30c. brown on drab	29·00	26·00
59	D	40c. red on yellow	21·00	18·00
60	D	50c. red on pink	16·00	16·00
61	D	75c. brown on orange	50·00	22·00
62	D	1f. green	40·00	60·00

5

1893

63	**5**	2f. grey	70·00	70·00
64	**5**	5f. red	£130	£130

The 5f. stamp is larger than the 2f.

6

7

1894

65	**6**	1c. black and red	75	90
66	**6**	2c. red and green	2·30	1·70
67	**6**	4c. red and orange	1·40	1·20
68	**6**	5c. green and brown	2·10	1·40
69	**6**	10c. black and green	5·50	3·75
70	**6**	15c. blue and red	2·30	1·20
71	**6**	20c. orange and purple	7·75	1·40
72	**6**	25c. black and blue	9·00	2·75
73	**6**	30c. yellow and green	20·00	9·25
74	**6**	40c. orange and green	10·00	7·25
75	**6**	50c. red and blue	8·25	4·50
76	**6**	75c. lilac and orange	11·00	6·50
77	**6**	1f. olive and purple	9·25	8·25
78	**7**	2f. orange and lilac	£130	£130
79	**7**	5f. red and blue	£120	£120
80	**7**	10f. lake and red	£150	£150
81	**7**	25f. blue and brown	£750	£750
82	**7**	50f. green and lake	£800	£800

Length of sides of Type **7**: 2f. 37 mm; 5f. 42 mm; 10f. 46 mm; 25, 50f. 49 mm.

POSTAGE DUE STAMPS

1892. Postage Due stamps of French Colonies optd OBOCK.

D25	**U**	1c. black	65·00	70·00
D26	**U**	2c. black	55·00	65·00
D27	**U**	3c. black	55·00	70·00
D28	**U**	4c. black	48·00	60·00
D29	**U**	5c. black	18·00	13·00
D30	**U**	10c. black	60·00	60·00
D31	**U**	15c. black	30·00	44·00
D32	**U**	20c. black	36·00	55·00
D33	**U**	30c. black	55·00	60·00
D34	**U**	40c. black	75·00	75·00
D35	**U**	60c. black	95·00	95·00
D36	**U**	1f. brown	£170	£170
D37	**U**	2f. brown	£180	£180
D38	**U**	5f. brown	£350	£350

For later issues see **DJIBOUTI**.

Pt. 6

OCEANIC SETTLEMENTS

Scattered French islands in the E. Pacific Ocean, including Tahiti and the Marquesas.

In 1957 the Oceanic Settlements were renamed French Polynesia.

1892. "Tablet" key-type.

1	**D**	1c. black and red on blue	80	1·00
2	**D**	2c. brown and blue on buff	1·50	1·70
3	**D**	4c. brown and blue on grey	2·75	2·75
14	**D**	5c. green and red	2·75	1·60
5	**D**	10c. black and blue on lilac	22·00	12·50
15	**D**	10c. red and blue	3·25	1·40
6	**D**	15c. blue and red	20·00	11·50
16	**D**	15c. grey and red	5·75	4·75
7	**D**	20c. red and blue on green	16·00	14·00
8	**D**	25c. black and red on pink	42·00	28·00
17	**D**	25c. blue and red	23·00	13·00
9	**D**	30c. brown and blue on drab	16·00	16·00
18	**D**	35c. black and red on yellow	7·75	8·25
10	**D**	40c. red and blue on yellow	£110	£100
19	**D**	45c. black and red on green	6·00	7·00
11	**D**	50c. red and blue on pink	8·00	10·50
20	**D**	50c. brown and red on blue	£200	£225
12	**D**	75c. brown and red on orange	12·50	15·00
13	**D**	1f. green and red	16·00	18·00

2 Tahitian Woman

3 Kanakas

4 Valley of Fautaua

1913

21	**2**	1c. brown and violet	30	45
22	**2**	2c. grey and brown	55	1·10
23	**2**	4c. blue and orange	90	1·50
24	**2**	5c. light green and green	1·70	1·70
46	**2**	5c. black and blue	1·30	2·50
25	**2**	10c. orange and red	3·00	1·90
47	**2**	10c. light green and green	2·75	4·25
48	**2**	10c. purple and red on blue	2·75	3·50
25a	**2**	15c. black and orange	2·50	2·75
26	**2**	20c. violet and black	85	3·75
49	**2**	20c. green	2·30	6·00
50	**2**	20c. brown and red	3·25	4·00
27	**3**	25c. blue and ultramarine	4·00	3·00
51	**3**	25c. red and violet	2·10	2·30
28	**3**	30c. brown and grey	6·75	8·25
52	**3**	30c. red and carmine	2·75	9·00
53	**3**	30c. red and black	2·50	2·75
54	**3**	30c. green and blue	3·50	6·00
29	**3**	35c. red and green	2·30	3·50
30	**3**	40c. green and black	2·40	2·50
31	**3**	45c. red and orange	2·50	4·75
32	**3**	50c. black and brown	13·00	15·00
55	**3**	50c. blue and ultramarine	2·30	3·00
56	**3**	50c. blue and grey	2·20	2·10
57	**3**	60c. black and green	1·90	6·25
58	**3**	65c. mauve and brown	5·00	4·50
33	**3**	75c. violet and purple	3·00	3·50
59	**3**	90c. mauve and red	15·00	29·00
34	**4**	1f. black and red	4·00	2·75
60	**4**	1f.10 brown and mauve	4·25	6·25
61	**4**	1f.40 violet and brown	7·50	8·00
62	**4**	1f.50 light blue and blue	17·00	11·50
35	**4**	2f. green and brown	7·25	7·00
36	**4**	5f. blue and violet	11·50	25·00

1915. "Tablet" key-type optd E F O 1915 and bar.

37	**D**	10c. red	2·10	4·50

1915. Red Cross. No. 37 surch 5c and red cross.

38		10c.+5c. red	15·00	34·00

1915. Red Cross. Surch 5c and red cross.

41	**2**	10c.+5c. orange and red	3·75	6·25

1916. Surch.

42		10c. on 15c. black and orange	2·75	3·00
71	**4**	20f. on 5f. mauve and red	26·00	25·00
67	**4**	25c. on 2f. green and brown	1·00	8·00
68	**4**	25c. on 5f. blue and violet	1·00	8·00
63	**3**	60 on 75c. brown and blue	55	2·75
64	**4**	65 on 1f. brown and blue	1·90	4·50
65	**4**	85 on 1f. brown and blue	1·60	3·50
66	**3**	90 on 75c. mauve and red	3·25	5·50
69	**4**	1f.25 on 1f. ultramarine & bl	85	3·50
70	**4**	1f.50 on 1f. light blue & blue	3·25	3·25

1921. Surch 1921 and new value.

43	**2**	05 on 2c. grey and brown	40·00	40·00
44	**3**	10 on 45c. red and orange	50·00	50·00
45	**2**	25 on 15c. black and orange	6·25	12·00

1924. Surch 45c. 1924.

72		45c. on 10c. orange and red	5·25	8·25

1926. Surch in words.

73	**4**	3f. on 5f. blue and grey	2·75	4·00
74	**4**	10f. on 5f. black and green	5·50	6·25

13 Papetoia Bay

1929

75	**13**	3f. sepia and green	7·50	8·00
76	**13**	5f. sepia and blue	10·50	18·00
77	**13**	10f. sepia and red	32·00	50·00
78	**13**	20f. sepia and mauve	43·00	55·00

1931. "International Colonial Exhibition", Paris, key-types.

79	**E**	40c. black and green	7·50	11·50
80	**F**	50c. black and mauve	8·00	14·00
81	**G**	90c. black and red	8·00	16·00
82	**H**	1f.50 black and blue	8·00	11·50

14 Spearing Fish

15 Tahitian Girl

16 Native Gods

1934

83	**14**	1c. black	20	2·10
84	**14**	2c. red	20	2·75
85	**14**	3c. blue	30	6·25
86	**14**	4c. orange	20	5·75
87	**14**	5c. mauve	35	3·00
88	**14**	10c. brown	25	3·75
89	**14**	15c. green	25	4·50
90	**14**	20c. red	35	4·00
91	**15**	25c. blue	1·60	2·75
92	**15**	30c. green	2·20	6·75
93	**15**	30c. orange	65	4·50
94	**16**	35c. green	3·25	11·00
95	**15**	40c. mauve	55	5·75
96	**15**	45c. red	12·00	18·00
97	**15**	45c. green	2·20	7·50
98	**15**	50c. violet	75	1·40
99	**15**	55c. blue	6·50	16·00
100	**15**	60c. black	1·00	4·00
101	**15**	65c. brown	5·75	5·50
102	**15**	70c. pink	3·25	7·00
103	**15**	75c. olive	8·75	12·50
104	**15**	80c. purple	2·50	7·75
105	**15**	90c. red	1·40	3·25
106	**16**	1f. brown	1·50	2·75
107	**16**	1f.25 purple	12·00	11·50
108	**16**	1f.25 red	2·20	7·25
109	**16**	1f.40 orange	1·80	7·00
110	**16**	1f.50 blue	1·70	2·10
111	**16**	1f.60 violet	1·90	7·50
112	**16**	1f.75 green	10·00	9·00
113	**16**	2f. red	95	3·25
114	**16**	2f.25 blue	2·20	7·50
115	**16**	2f.50 black	2·30	7·00
116	**16**	3f. orange	1·30	8·00
117	**16**	5f. mauve	2·00	8·00
118	**16**	10f. green	1·90	10·50
119	**16**	20f. brown	2·00	11·00
MS126a		120x100 mm. 3f. emerald-green, Imperf	32·00	65·00

17 Flying Boat

1934. Air.

120	**17**	5f. green	2·00	5·50

1937. International Exhibition, Paris. As Nos. 168/73 of St.-Pierre et Miquelon.

121	20c. violet	2·50	4·00
122	30c. green	2·50	4·00
123	40c. red	2·10	3·50
124	50c. brown	3·25	3·50
125	90c. red	3·50	4·50
126	1f.50 blue	4·00	6·25

17a Pierre and Marie Curie

1938. International Anti-cancer Fund.

127	**17a**	1f.75+50c. blue	12·50	23·00

17b

1939. New York World's Fair.

128	**17b**	1f.25 red	2·00	4·00
129	**17b**	2f.25 blue	2·00	4·00

17c Storming the Bastille

1939. 150th Anniv of French Revolution.

130	**17c**	45c.+25c. green and black (postage)	17·00	29·00
131	**17c**	70c.+30c. brown & black	17·00	29·00
132	**17c**	90c.+35c. orange & black	17·00	29·00
133	**17c**	1f.25+1f. red and black	17·00	29·00
134	**17c**	2f.25+2f. blue and black	17·00	29·00
135	**17c**	5f.+4f. black & orge (air)	42·00	50·00

1941. Adherence to General de Gaulle. Optd FRANCE LIBRE. (a) Nos. 75/8.

136	**13**	3f. brown and green	5·25	9·75
137	**13**	5f. brown and blue	5·25	15·00
138	**13**	10f. brown and red	16·00	28·00
139	**13**	20f. brown and mauve	80·00	£130

(b) Nos. 106 and 115/19.

140	**16**	1f. brown	4·00	16·00
141	**16**	2f.50 black	4·00	21·00
142	**16**	3f. red	4·50	21·00
143	**16**	5f. mauve	5·25	20·00
144	**16**	10f. green	42·00	90·00
145	**16**	20f. brown	40·00	90·00

(c) Air stamp of 1934.

146	**17**	5f. green	3·75	6·50

19 Polynesian Travelling Canoe

19a Airplane

1942. Free French Issue. (a) Postage.

147	**19**	5c. brown	20	6·75
148	**19**	10c. blue	20	4·25
149	**19**	25c. green	55	6·75
150	**19**	30c. red	35	5·75
151	**19**	40c. green	35	6·75
152	**19**	80c. purple	75	6·75

153	19	1f. mauve	80	1·40
154	19	1f.50 red	1·30	4·75
155	19	2f. black	1·30	2·30
156	19	2f.50 blue	1·60	7·25
157	19	4f. violet	1·20	5·00
158	19	5f. yellow	1·10	4·00
159	19	10f. brown	2·30	4·75
160	19	20f. green	2·10	7·00

(b) Air. As T 19a.

161	1f. orange	1·80	5·75
162	1f.50 red	1·80	6·50
163	5f. purple	2·00	7·75
164	10f. black	2·50	8·50
165	25f. blue	3·25	10·00
166	50f. green	4·00	10·00
167	100f. red	3·75	10·00

19b

1944. Mutual Aid and Red Cross Funds.

168	19b	5f.+20f. blue	1·10	9·00

1945. Surch in figures.

169	19	50c. on 5c. brown	55	7·00
170	19	60c. on 5c. brown	70	7·00
171	19	70c. on 5c. brown	60	7·50
172	19	1f.20 on 5c. brown	85	7·00
173	19	2f.40 on 25c. green	1·10	7·25
174	19	3f. on 25c. green	1·00	4·00
175	19	4f.50 on 25c. green	1·60	8·00
176	19	15f. on 2f.50 blue	1·40	6·25

20a Felix Eboue

1945. Eboue.

177	20a	2f. black	30	7·25
178	20a	25f. green	1·60	9·50

20b "Victory"

1946. Air. Victory.

179	20b	8f. green	1·10	9·25

20c Legionaries by Lake Chad

1946. Air. From Chad to the Rhine.

180	20c	5f. red	1·60	8·25
181	-	10f. brown	1·30	10·00
182	-	15f. green	1·60	9·50
183	-	20f. red	2·00	9·00
184	-	25f. purple	2·10	9·25
185	-	50f. black	2·20	13·00

DESIGNS: 10f. Battle of Koufa; 15f. Tank Battle, Mareth; 20f. Normandy Landings; 25f. Liberation of Paris; 50f. Liberation of Strasbourg.

21 Mooréa Coastline

22 Tahitian Girl

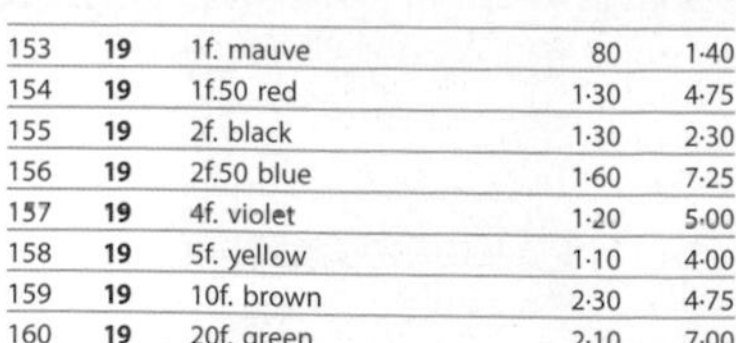

23 Wandering Albatross over Mooréa

1948. (a) Postage as T 21/22.

186	21	10c. brown	35	55
187	21	30c. green	45	60
188	21	40c. blue	60	4·25
189	-	50c. lake	60	3·50
190	-	60c. olive	55	5·25
191	-	80c. blue	65	6·50
192	-	1f. lake	2·75	1·10
193	-	1f.20 blue	2·75	7·25
194	-	1f.50 blue	1·10	3·00
195	22	2f. brown	2·75	90
196	22	2f.40 lake	3·25	8·00
197	22	3f. violet	8·50	80
198	22	4f. blue	2·50	70
199	-	5f. brown	3·75	1·80
200	-	6f. blue	3·75	90
201	-	9f. brown, black and red	4·25	7·00
202	-	10f. olive	4·00	55
203	-	15f. red	5·75	1·40
204	-	20f. blue	5·75	80
205	-	25f. brown	5·50	1·70

(b) Air. As T 23.

206		13f. light blue and deep blue	7·50	5·75
207	23	50f. lake	28·00	18·00
208	-	100f. violet	17·00	12·50
209	-	200f. blue	44·00	25·00

DESIGNS: As T **22**: 50c. to 80c. Kanaka fisherman; 9f. Bora-Bora girl; 1f. to 1f.50, Faa village; 5, 6, 10f. Bora-Bora and Pandanus pine; 15f. to 25f. Polynesian girls. As T **23**: 13f. Pahia Peak and palms; 100f. Airplane over Mooréa; 200f. Wandering albatross over Maupiti Island.

24a People of Five Races, Aircraft and Globe

1949. Air. 75th Anniv of U.P.U.

210	24a	10f. blue	12·50	21·00

24b Doctor and Patient

1950. Colonial Welfare.

211	24b	10f.+2f. green and blue	7·50	9·25

24c

1952. Centenary of Military Medals.

212	24c	3f. violet, yellow and green	10·50	10·50

25 "Nafea" (after Gauguin)

1953. Air. 50th Death Anniv of Gauguin (painter).

213	25	14f. sepia, red and turquoise	50·00	70·00

25a Normandy Landings, 1944

1954. Air. 10th Anniv of Liberation.

214	25a	3f. green and turquoise	11·50	11·50

26 Schooner in Dry Dock, Papeete

1956. Economic and Social Development Fund.

215	26	3f. turquoise	2·30	2·30

POSTAGE DUE STAMPS

1926. Postage Due stamps of France surch Etabts Francais de l'Oceanie 2 francs a percevoir (No. D80) or optd Etablissements Francais de l'Oceanie (others).

D73	D11	5c. blue	65	3·25
D74	D11	10c. brown	65	2·75
D75	D11	20c. olive	1·20	3·25
D76	D11	30c. red	1·50	3·50
D77	D11	40c. red	2·75	5·25
D78	D11	60c. green	2·75	4·75
D79	D11	1f. red on yellow	2·75	5·25
D80	D11	2f. on 1f. red	3·00	5·75
D81	D11	3f. mauve	10·50	17·00

D14 Fautaua Falls

1929

D82	D14	5c. brown and blue	65	2·50
D83	D14	10c. green and orange	65	3·00
D84	D14	30c. red and brown	1·60	3·50
D85	D14	50c. brown and green	1·50	3·00
D86	D14	60c. green and violet	3·25	5·75
D87	-	1f. mauve and blue	3·00	4·50
D88	-	2f. brown and red	2·10	4·00
D89	-	3f. green and blue	2·30	4·75

DESIGN: 1 to 3f. Polynesian man.

D24

1948

D210	D24	10c. green	20	1·90
D211	D24	30c. brown	20	2·75
D212	D24	50c. red	35	2·75
D213	D24	1f. blue	95	2·75
D214	D24	2f. green	95	3·50
D215	D24	3f. red	1·90	4·00
D216	D24	4f. violet	2·00	4·50
D217	D24	5f. mauve	2·75	5·00
D218	D24	10f. blue	3·75	6·25
D219	D24	20f. lake	5·25	7·50

For later issues see **FRENCH POLYNESIA**.

Pt. 7

OLDENBURG

A former Grand Duchy in North Germany. In 1867 it joined the North German Federation.

72 grote = 1 thaler

1

1852. Imperf.

2	1	1/30th. black on blue	£475	37·00
5	1	1/15th. black on red	£1100	£110
8	1	1/10th. black on yellow	£1100	£130
1	1	1/3sgr. black on green	£1700	£1300

2

1859. Imperf.

17	2	1/4g. yellow	£400	£4750
10	2	1/3g. black on green	£3250	£3750
19	2	1/3g. green	£650	£1200
21	2	1/2g. brown	£550	£700
11	2	1g. black on blue	£950	60·00
23	2	1g. blue	£325	£200
15	2	2g. black on red	£1300	£800
26	2	2g. red	£600	£600
16	2	3g. black on yellow	£1300	£800
28	2	3g. yellow	£600	£600

3

1862. Roul.

30	3	1/3g. green	£275	£250
32	3	1/2g. orange	£275	£130
42	3	1g. red	25·00	75·00
36	3	2g. blue	£275	65·00
39	3	3g. bistre	£275	70·00

Pt. 19

OMAN (SULTANATE)

In January 1971, the independent Sultanate of Muscat and Oman was renamed Sultanate of Oman.

NOTE. Labels inscribed "State of Oman" or "Oman Imamate State" are said to have been issued by a rebel administration under the Imam of Oman. There is no convincing evidence that these labels had any postal use within Oman and they are therefore omitted. They can be found, however, used on covers which appear to emanate from Amman and Baghdad.

1971. 1000 baizas = 1 rial saidi.
1972. 1000 baizas = 1 rial omani.

1971. Nos. 110/21 of Muscat and Oman optd SULTANATE of OMAN in English and Arabic.

122	12	5b. purple	12·00	55
142	12	10b. brown	40·00	23·00
124	12	20b. brown	16·00	85
125	A	25b. black and violet	2·10	55
126	A	30b. black and blue	3·25	95
127	A	40b. black and orange	4·00	1·10
128	14	50b. mauve and blue	5·25	1·50
129	B	75b. green and brown	8·00	2·00
130	C	100b. blue and orange	10·50	3·50
131	C	1/4r. brown and green	27·00	8·50
132	E	1/2r. violet and red	55·00	15·00
133	F	1r. red and violet	£120	30·00

19 Sultan Qabus and Buildings ("Land Development")

1971. National Day. Multicoloured.

134	F	10b. Type **19**	2·75	45
135	F	40b. Sultan in military uniform and Omanis ("Freedom")	10·50	95
136	F	50b. Doctors and patients ("Health Services")	14·00	1·60
137	F	100b. Children at school ("Education")	27·00	5·25

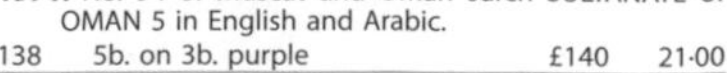

1971. No. 94 of Muscat and Oman surch SULTANATE of OMAN 5 in English and Arabic.

138	5b. on 3b. purple	£140	21·00

21 Child in Class

1971. 25th Anniv of UNICEF.

139	21	50b.+25b. multicoloured	32·00	7·00

22 Book Year Emblem

1972. International Book Year.

140	22	25b. multicoloured	25·00	3·25

سلطنة عمان

25 B ٢٥ ب

(24)

1972. Nos. 102 of Muscat and Oman and 127 of Oman optd with T 24.

145		25b. on 40b. black and orange	£160	£160
144		25b. on 1r. blue and orange	£160	£160

26 Matrah, 1809

1972

158	26	5b. multicoloured	40	10
147	26	10b. multicoloured	1·50	30
148	26	20b. multicoloured	1·80	30
149	26	25b. multicoloured	2·40	30
150	-	30b. multicoloured	3·00	30
151	-	40b. multicoloured	3·00	30
152	-	50b. multicoloured	4·00	50
153	-	75b. multicoloured	9·25	1·00
154	-	100b. multicoloured	12·50	1·60
155	-	¼r. multicoloured	29·00	3·25
156	-	½r. multicoloured	55·00	9·75
157	-	1r. multicoloured	85·00	20·00

DESIGNS—26×21 mm: 30b. to 75b. Shinas, 1809. 42×25 mm: 100b. to 1r. Muscat, 1809.

29 Government Buildings

1973. Opening of Ministerial Complex.

170	29	25b. multicoloured	3·50	1·30
171	29	100b. multicoloured	12·50	3·25

30 Oman Crafts (dhow building)

1973. National Day. Multicoloured.

172		15b. Type **30**	2·00	60
173		50b. Seeb International Airport	9·75	2·50
174		65b. Dhow and tanker	10·50	2·50
175		100b. "Ship of the Desert" (camel)	14·50	4·00

31 Aerial View of Port

1974. Inauguration of Port Qabus.

176	31	100b. multicoloured	15·00	5·25

32 Map on Open Book

1974. Illiteracy Eradication Campaign. Mult.

177		25b. Type **32**	3·50	60
178		100b. Hands reaching for open book (vert)	11·50	3·50

33 Sultan Qabus bin Said and Emblems

1974. Centenary of U.P.U.

179	33	100b. multicoloured	3·50	2·10

34 Arab Scribe

1975. "Eradicate Illiteracy".

180	34	25b. multicoloured	9·25	3·00

35 New Harbour, Mina Raysoot

1975. National Day. Multicoloured.

181		30b. Type **35**	1·30	70
182		50b. Stadium and map	2·75	80
183		75b. Water desalination plant	3·50	1·50
184		100b. Television station	5·00	2·40
185		150b. Satellite Earth station and map	7·25	3·50
186		250b. Telecommunications symbols and map	13·50	7·25

36 Arab Woman and Child with Nurse

1975. International Women's Year. Mult.

187		75b. Type **36**	3·00	1·20
188		150b. Mother and children (vert)	5·25	2·40

37 Presenting Colours and Opening of Seeb–Nizwa Highway

1976. National Day. Multicoloured.

201		25b. Type **37**	1·10	35
202		40b. Parachutists and harvesting	3·25	75
203		75b. Agusta-Bell AB-212 helicopters and Victory Day procession	6·25	1·60
204		150b. Road construction and Salalah T.V. Station	7·75	2·75

38 Great Bath, Moenjodaro

1977. "Save Moenjodaro" Campaign.

205	38	125b. multicoloured	7·25	3·25

39 A.P.U. Emblem

1977. 25th Anniv of Arab Postal Union.

206	39	30b. multicoloured	3·75	1·00
207	39	75b. multicoloured	7·25	3·00

40 Coffee Pots

1977. National Day. Multicoloured.

208		40b. Type **40**	1·50	55
209		75b. Earthenware pots	3·25	1·00
210		100b. Khor Rori inscriptions	5·50	1·50
211		150b. Silver jewellery	8·50	2·00

1978. Surch in English and Arabic.

212		40b. on 150b. mult (No. 185)	£400	£325
213		50b. on 150b. mult (No. 188)	£450	£450
214		75b. on 250b. mult (No. 186)	£2000	£450

42 Mount Arafat, Pilgrims and Kaaba

1978. Pilgrimage to Mecca.

215	42	40b. multicoloured	6·00	2·50

43 Jalali Fort

1978. National Day. Forts. Multicoloured.

216		20b. Type **43**	1·10	35
217		25b. Nizwa Fort	1·20	45
218		40b. Rostaq Fort	3·00	80
219		50b. Sohar Fort	3·25	90
220		75b. Bahla Fort	4·00	1·50
221		100b. Jibrin Fort	6·00	2·00

44 World Map, Koran and Symbols of Arab Achievements

1979. The Arabs.

222	44	40b. multicoloured	2·50	65
223	44	100b. multicoloured	5·00	1·50

45 Child on Swing

1979. International Year of the Child.

224	45	40b. multicoloured	3·75	2·50

46 Gas Plant

1979. National Day. Multicoloured.

225		25b. Type **46**	2·75	90
226		75b. Dhow and modern trawler	8·25	2·75

47 Sultan Qabus on Horseback

1979. Armed Forces Day. Multicoloured.

227		40b. Type **47**	6·00	1·80
228		100b. Soldier	12·50	4·00

48 Mosque, Mecca

1980. 1400th Anniv of Hegira. Multicoloured.

229		50b. Type **48**	5·00	1·20
230		150b. Mosque and Kaaba	8·50	3·75

49 Bab Alkabir

1980. National Day. Multicoloured.

231		75b. Type **49**	2·30	1·20
232		100b. Corniche	3·00	2·00
233		250b. Polo match	6·25	5·00
234		500b. Omani women	12·00	9·00

50 Sultan and Naval Patrol Boat

1980. Armed Forces Day. Multicoloured.

235		150b. Type **50**	6·25	3·25
236		750b. Sultan and mounted soldiers	32·00	15·00

51 Policewoman helping Children across Road

1981. National Police Day. Multicoloured.

237 50b. Type **51** 3·75 1·10

238 100b. Police bandsmen 4·25 2·20

239 150b. Mounted police 5·00 3·25

240 ½r. Police headquarters 14·50 10·00

1981. Nos. 231, 234 and 235/6 surch POSTAGE and new value in English and Arabic.

241 **50** 20b. on 150b. multicoloured 4·25 90

242 - 30b. on 750b. multicoloured 5·50 1·30

243 **49** 50b. on 75b. multicoloured 6·75 2·20

244 - 100b. on 500b. multicoloured 11·00 3·75

53 Sultan's Crest

1981. Welfare of Blind.

245 **53** 10b. black, blue and red 26·00 3·00

54 Palm Tree, Fishes and Wheat

1981. World Food Day.

246 **54** 50b. multicoloured 6·75 2·75

55 Pilgrims at Prayer

1981. Pilgrimage to Mecca.

247 **55** 50b. multicoloured 8·25 3·50

56 Al Razha

1981. National Day. Multicoloured.

248 160b. Type **56** 5·75 3·25

249 300b. Sultan Qabus bin Said 9·75 5·00

57 Muscat Port, 1981

1981. Retracing the Voyage of Sinbad. Mult.

250 50b. Type **57** 2·50 1·20

251 100b. The "Sohar" (replica of medieval dhow) 5·25 3·00

252 130b. Map showing route of voyage 6·25 4·00

253 200b. Muscat Harbour, 1650 8·75 5·75

MS254 172×130 mm. Nos. 250/3 41·00 21·00

58 Parachute-drop

1981. Armed Forces Day. Multicoloured.

255 100b. Type **58** 7·25 3·50

256 400b. Missile-armed corvettes 18·00 8·75

59 Police Launch

1982. National Police Day. Multicoloured.

257 50b. Type **59** 3·00 1·50

258 100b. Royal Oman Police Band at Cardiff 6·25 3·00

60 "Nerium mascatense"

1982. Flora and Fauna. Multicoloured.

259 5b. Type **60** 30 20

260 10b. "Dionysia mira" 30 20

261 20b. "Teucrium mascatense" 60 25

262 25b. "Geranium mascatense" 60 30

263 30b. "Cymatium boschi" (horiz) 90 40

264 40b. Eloise's acteon (horiz) 90 40

265 50b. Teulere's cowrie (horiz) 1·00 60

266 75b. Lovely cowrie (horiz) 1·30 90

267 100b. Arabian chukar (25×33 mm) 4·50 1·50

268 ¼r. Hoopoe (25×33 mm) 11·50 6·25

269 ½r. Arabian tahr (25×39 mm) 13·50 8·75

270 1r. Arabian oryx (25×39 mm) 23·00 16·00

Nos. 259/62 show flowers, Nos. 263/6 shells, Nos. 267/8 birds and Nos. 269/70 animals.

61 Palm Tree

1982. Arab Palm Tree Day. Multicoloured.

271 40b. Type **61** 4·75 2·30

272 100b. Palm tree and nuts 9·75 3·50

62 I.T.U. Emblem

1982. I.T.U. Delegates Conference, Nairobi.

273 **62** 100b. multicoloured 10·50 4·00

63 Emblem and Cups

1982. Municipalities Week.

274 **63** 40b. multicoloured 7·25 3·00

64 State Consultative Council Inaugural Session

1982. National Day. Multicoloured.

275 40b. Type **64** 4·00 2·10

276 100b. Petroleum refinery 8·25 3·50

65 Sultan meeting Troops

1982. Armed Forces Day. Multicoloured.

277 50b. Type **65** 4·00 2·10

278 100b. Mounted army band 8·25 4·00

66 Police Motorcyclist and Headquarters

1983. National Police Day.

279 **66** 50b. multicoloured 7·25 2·50

67 Satellite, W.C.Y. Emblem and Dish Aerial

1983. World Communications Year.

280 **67** 50b. multicoloured 6·25 3·00

68 Bee Hives

1983. Bee-keeping. Multicoloured.

281 50b. Type **68** 4·50 3·50

282 50b. Bee collecting nectar 4·50 3·50

Nos. 281/2 were issued together, se-tenant, each pair forming a composite design.

69 Pilgrims at Mudhalfa

1983. Pilgrimage to Mecca.

283 **69** 40b. multicoloured 10·50 3·50

70 Emblem, Map and Sultan

1983. Omani Youth Year.

284 **70** 50b. multicoloured 7·25 3·00

71 Sohar Copper Mine

1983. National Day. Multicoloured.

285 50b. Type **71** 4·50 2·30

286 100b. Sultan Qabus University and foundation stone 8·75 4·50

72 Machine Gun Post

1983. Armed Forces Day.

287 **72** 100b. multicoloured 8·25 3·00

73 Police Cadets Parade

1984. National Police Day.

288 **73** 100b. multicoloured 9·25 3·50

74 Footballers and Cup

1984. 7th Arabian Gulf Cup Football Tournament. Multicoloured.

289 40b. Type **74** 3·50 1·70

290 50b. Emblem and pictograms of footballers 5·75 2·40

75 Stoning the Devil

1984. Pilgrimage to Mecca.

291 **75** 50b. multicoloured 6·25 2·75

76 New Central Post Office and Automatic Sorting Machine

1984. National Day. Multicoloured.

292 130b. Type **76** 6·75 3·25

293 160b. Map of Oman with telecommunications symbols 8·75 4·00

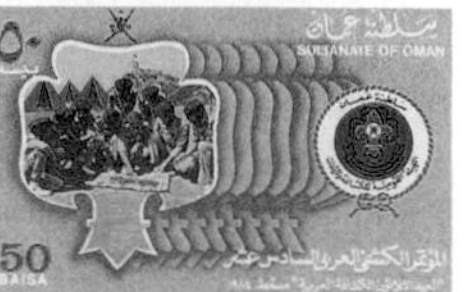

77 Scouts reading Map

1984. 16th Arab Scouts Conference, Muscat. Multicoloured.

294	50b. Scouts pegging tent	2·10	70
295	50b. Type **77**	2·10	70
296	130b. Scouts assembled round flag	6·25	2·20
297	130b. Scout, cub, guide, brownie and scout leaders	6·25	2·20

78 Sultan, Jet Fighters and "Al Munassir" (landing craft)

1984. Armed Forces Day.

298	**78**	100b. multicoloured	10·50	4·50

79 Bell 214ST Helicopter lifting Man from "Al-Ward" (tanker)

1985. National Police Day.

299	**79**	100b. multicoloured	9·25	4·00

80 Al-Khaif Mosque and Tent, Mina

1985. Pilgrimage to Mecca.

300	**80**	50b. multicoloured	5·25	1·80

81 I.Y.Y. Emblem and Youth holding Olive Branches

1985. International Youth Year. Mult.

301	50b. Type **81**	3·00	1·10
302	100b. Emblem and young people at various activities	5·25	2·40

82 Palace before and after Restoration

1985. Restoration of Jabrin Palace. Mult.

303	100b. Type **82**	3·50	2·10
304	250b. Restored ceiling	8·75	5·75

83 Drummers

1985. International Omani Traditional Music Symposium.

305	**83**	50b. multicoloured	5·75	2·10

84 Scenes of Child Care and Emblem

1985. UNICEF Child Health Campaign.

306	**84**	50b. multicoloured	4·50	1·70

85 Flags around Map of Gulf

1985. 6th Supreme Council Session of Gulf Co-operation Council, Muscat. Multicoloured.

307	40b. Type **85**	3·00	1·30
308	50b. Portraits of rulers of Council member countries	3·75	1·50

86 Sultan Qabus University and Students

1985. National Day. Multicoloured.

309	20b. Type **86**	1·50	1·00
310	50b. Tractor and oxen ploughing field	3·00	2·10
311	100b. Port Qabus cement factory and Oman Chamber of Commerce	5·25	3·00
312	200b. Road bridge, Douglas DC-10 airliner and communications centre	8·75	5·75
313	250b. Portrait of Sultan Qabus (vert)	10·50	6·75

87 Military Exercise at Sea

1985. Armed Forces Day.

314	**87**	100b. multicoloured	9·25	2·40

88 Red-tailed Butterflyfish

1985. Marine Life. Multicoloured.

315	20b. Type **88**	60	20
316	50b. Black-finned melon butterflyfish	1·20	50
317	100b. Gardiner's butterflyfish	1·80	1·20
318	150b. Narrow-barred Spanish mackerel	2·75	2·10
319	200b. Lobster (horiz)	4·00	2·75

89 Frankincense Tree

1985. Frankincense Production.

320	**89**	100b. multicoloured	1·30	1·30
321	**89**	3r. multicoloured	38·00	33·00

90 Camel Corps Member

1986. National Police Day.

322	**90**	50b. multicoloured	5·75	1·80

91 Cadet Barquentine "Shabab Oman", 1986

1986. Participation of "Shabab Oman" in Statue of Liberty Centenary Celebrations. Multicoloured.

323	50b. "Sultana" (full-rigged sailing ship), 1840	4·50	1·70
324	100b. Type **91**	6·75	3·00
MS325	162×128 mm. Nos. 323/4 (sold at 250b.)	26·00	14·50

92 Crowd around Holy Kaaba

1986. Pilgrimage to Mecca.

326	**92**	50b. multicoloured	4·00	1·60

93 Scouts erecting Tent

1986. 17th Arab Scout Camp, Salalah. Multicoloured.

327	50b. Type **93**	3·00	1·20
328	100b. Scouts making survey	5·25	2·40

94 Sports Complex

1986. Inauguration of Sultan Qabus Sports Complex.

329	**94**	100b. multicoloured	4·00	2·10

95 Mother and Baby, Emblem and Tank on Globe

1986. International Peace Year.

330	**95**	130b. multicoloured	3·50	1·80

96 Al-Sahwa Tower

1986. National Day. Multicoloured.

331	50b. Type **96**	1·80	1·00
332	100b. Sultan Qabus University (inauguration)	4·25	2·10
333	130b. 1966 stamps and F.D.C. cancellation (20th anniv of first Oman stamp issue) (57×27 mm)	5·25	2·50

97 Camel Corps

1987. National Police Day.

334	**97**	50b. multicoloured	4·00	1·80

98 Family

1987. Arabian Gulf Social Work Week.

335	**98**	50b. multicoloured	3·00	1·20

99 Aqueduct

1987. International Environment Day. Mult.

336	50b. Greater flamingoes	3·00	1·00
337	130b. Type **99**	5·25	1·50

100 Crowd around Holy Kaaba

1987. Pilgrimage to Mecca. Multicoloured.

338	50b. Type **100**	1·70	1·10
339	50b. Al-Khaif Mosque and tents, Mina	1·70	1·10
340	50b. Stoning the Devil	1·70	1·10
341	50b. Pilgrims at Mudhalfa	1·70	1·10
342	50b. Pilgrims at prayer	1·70	1·10
343	50b. Mount Arafat, pilgrims and Kaaba	1·70	1·10

101 Examples of Work and Hand holding Cup

1987. 3rd Municipalities Month.

344	**101**	50b. multicoloured	2·50	1·10

102 Marine Science and Fisheries Centre

1987. National Day. Multicoloured.

345	50b. Type **102**	1·20	80
346	130b. Royal Hospital	3·50	2·00

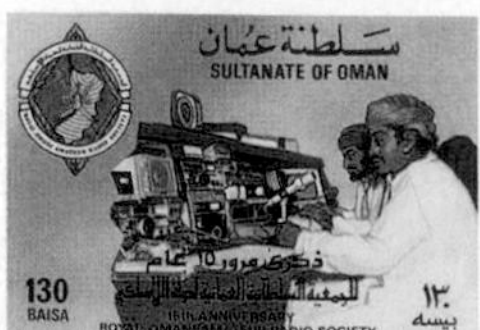

103 Radio Operators

1987. 15th Anniv of Royal Omani Amateur Radio Society.

347	**103**	130b. multicoloured	3·50	1·80

104 Weaver

1988. Traditional Crafts. Multicoloured.

348	50b. Type **104**	1·30	80
349	100b. Potter	2·00	1·10
350	150b. Halwa maker	2·75	1·80
351	200b. Silversmith	3·25	2·10
MS352	165×135 mm. Nos. 348/51 (sold at 600b.)	18·00	12·50

105 Show Jumping

1988. Olympic Games, Seoul. Multicoloured.

353	100b. Type **105**	1·70	1·10
354	100b. Hockey	1·70	1·10
355	100b. Football	1·70	1·10
356	100b. Running	1·70	1·10
357	100b. Swimming	1·70	1·10
358	100b. Shooting	1·70	1·10
MS359	160×160 mm. Nos. 353/8 (sold at 700b.)	23·00	17·00

106 Emblem

1988. 40th Anniv of W.H.O. "Health for All".

360	**106**	100b. multicoloured	2·50	1·50

107 Tending Land and Crops

1988. National Day. Agriculture Year. Mult.

361	100b. Type **107**	1·80	1·30
362	100b. Livestock	1·80	1·30

108 Dhahira Region (woman's)

1989. Costumes. Multicoloured.

363	30b. Type **108**	1·00	50
364	40b. Eastern region (woman's)	1·30	80
365	50b. Batinah region (woman's)	1·50	1·00
366	100b. Interior region (woman's)	3·00	2·10
367	130b. Southern region (woman's)	4·00	3·00
368	150b. Muscat region (woman's)	4·50	3·25
369	200b. Dhahira region (man's)	2·30	1·80
370	¼r. Eastern region (man's)	3·00	2·50
371	½r. Southern region (man's)	5·25	5·00
372	1r. Muscat region (man's)	10·50	9·25
MS373	210×145 mm. Nos. 363/8 (sold at 700b.)	18·00	15·00
MS374	210×145 mm. Nos. 369/72 (sold at 2r.)	31·00	24·00

109 Fishing

1989. National Day. Agriculture Year. Mult.

375	100b. Type **109**	1·50	1·00
376	100b. Agriculture	1·50	1·00

110 Flags and Omani State Arms

1989. 10th Supreme Council Session of Arab Co-operation Council, Muscat. Multicoloured.

377	50b. Type **110**	90	70
378	50b. Council emblem and Sultan Qabus	90	70

111 Emblem and Map

1990. 5th Anniv (1989) of Gulf Investment Corporation.

379	**111**	50b. multicoloured	2·50	1·20
380	**111**	130b. multicoloured	3·50	1·80

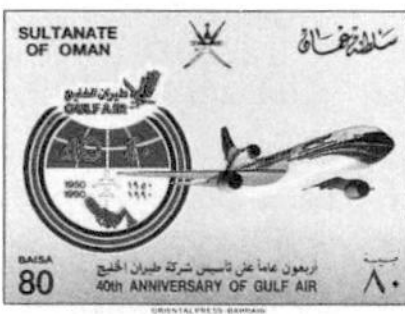

112 Emblem and Douglas DC-10 Airliner

1990. 40th Anniv of Gulf Air.

381	**112**	80b. multicoloured	5·25	2·10

113 Map

1990. Omani Ophiolite Symposium, Muscat.

382	**113**	80b. multicoloured	1·30	90
383	**113**	150b. multicoloured	2·75	2·00

114 Ahmed bin Na'aman al-Ka'aby (envoy), "Sultana" and Said bin Sultan al-Busaidi

1990. 150th Anniv of First Omani Envoy's Journey to U.S.A.

384	**114**	200b. multicoloured	3·00	2·00

115 Sultan Qabus Rose

1990. 20th Anniv of Sultan Qabus's Accession.

385	**115**	200b. multicoloured	3·00	2·00

116 National Day Emblem

1990. National Day.

386	**116**	100b. red and green on gold foil	1·80	1·00
387	-	200b. green and red on gold foil	3·75	2·10
MS388		160×114 mm. Nos. 386/7 (sold at 500b.)	7·75	7·75

DESIGN: 200b. Sultan Qabus.

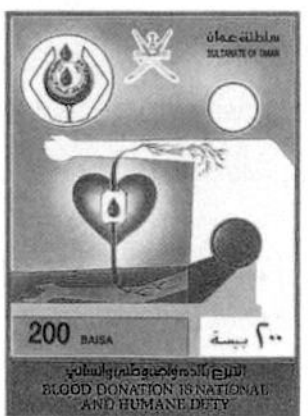

117 Donor and Recipient

1991. Blood Donation.

389	**117**	50b. multicoloured	80	60
390	**117**	200b. multicoloured	3·50	2·00

118 Industrial Emblems

1991. National Day and Industry Year. Mult.

391	100b. Type **118**	3·50	1·20
392	200b. Sultan Qabus	5·75	2·40
MS393	172×123 mm. Nos. 391/2 (sold at 400b.)	9·25	5·75

119 Weapons, Military Transport and Sultan Qabus

1991. Armed Forces Day.

394	**119**	100b. multicoloured	2·50	1·30

120 Interior of Museum and National Flags

1992. Inaug of Omani-French Museum, Muscat.

395	**120**	100b. multicoloured	2·10	1·30
MS396		141×100 mm. No. 395 (sold at 300b.)	13·50	6·75

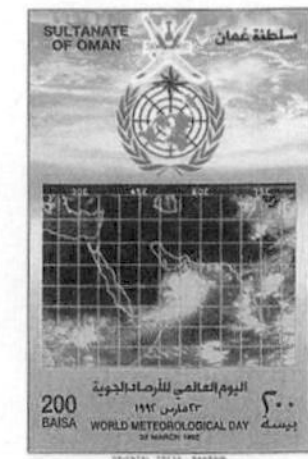

121 Satellite Picture of Asia

1992. World Meteorological Day.

397	**121**	220b. multicoloured	3·50	2·40

122 Emblem and Hands

1992. World Environment Day.

398	**122**	100b. multicoloured	2·30	1·30

123 Emblem and Hands protecting Handicapped Child

1992. Welfare of Handicapped Children.

399	**123**	70b. multicoloured	1·80	90

124 Sultan Qabus and Books

1992. Publication of Sultan Qabus "Encyclopedia of Arab Names".

400	**124**	100b. multicoloured	2·50	1·40

125 Sultan Qabus, Factories and Industry Year Emblem

1992. National Day. Multicoloured.

401	100b. Type **125**	2·75	1·80
402	200b. Sultan Qabus and Majlis As'shura (Consultative Council) emblem	4·50	2·75

126 Mounted Policemen and Sultan Qabus

1993. National Police Day.

403	**126**	80b. multicoloured	2·10	1·10

127 Census Emblem

1993. Population, Housing and Establishments Census.

404	**127**	100b. multicoloured	2·10	1·30

128 Frigate and Sultan Qabus presenting Colours

1993. Navy Day.

405	**128**	100b. multicoloured	3·00	1·50

129 Youth Year Emblem

1993. National Day and Youth Year. Mult.

406	100b. Type **129**	2·10	1·50
407	200b. Sultan Qabus	3·50	2·10

130 Scout Headquarters and Emblem

1993. 61st Anniv of Scouting in Oman (408) and 10th Anniv of Sultan Qabus as Chief Scout (409). Multicoloured.

408	100b. Type **130**	1·50	1·30
409	100b. Scout camp and Sultan Qabus	1·30	1·30

Nos. 408/9 were issued together, se-tenant, forming a composite design.

131 Sei Whale and School of Dolphins

1993. Whales and Dolphins in Omani Waters. Multicoloured.

410	100b. Type **131**	3·00	1·80
411	100b. Sperm whale and dolphins	3·00	1·80
MS412	160×120 mm. Nos. 410/11 (sold at 400b.)	39·00	28·00

Nos. 410/11 were issued together, se-tenant, forming a composite design.

132 Water Drops and Falaj (ancient water system)

1994. World Water Day.

413	**132**	50b. multicoloured	1·50	80

133 Municipality Building

1994. 70th Anniv of Muscat Municipality.

414	**133**	50b. multicoloured	2·10	1·00

134 Centenary Emblem and Sports Pictograms

1994. Centenary of International Olympic Committee.

415	**134**	100b. multicoloured	16·00	8·25

135 Emblem

1994. National Day. Multicoloured.

416	50b. Type **135**	1·00	70
417	50b. Sultan Qabus	1·00	70

136 Airplane and Emblem

1994. 50th Anniv of I.C.A.O.

418	**136**	100b. multicoloured	6·25	3·00

137 Arms

1994. 250th Anniv of Al-Busaid Dynasty. Multicoloured.

419	50b. Type **137** dated "1744–1775"	1·60	60
420	50b. Type **137** dated "1775–1779"	1·60	60
421	50b. Type **137** dated "1779–1792"	1·60	60
422	50b. Type **137** dated "1792–1804"	1·60	60
423	50b. Type **137** dated "1804–1807"	1·60	60
424	50b. Said bin Sultan (1807–1856)	1·60	60
425	50b. Type **137** dated "1856–1866"	1·60	60
426	50b. Type **137** dated "1866–1868"	1·60	60
427	50b. Type **137** dated "1868–1871"	1·60	60
428	50b. Turki bin Said (1871–1888)	1·60	60
429	50b. Feisal bin Turki (1888–1913)	1·60	60
430	50b. Taimur bin Feisal (1913–1932)	1·60	60
431	50b. Arms, Sultan Qabus and family tree	1·60	60
432	50b. Said bin Taimur (1932–1970)	1·60	60
433	50b. Sultan Qabus (1970–)	1·60	60
MS434	140×110 mm. 200d. As No. 431. Imperf	5·25	3·50

138 Meeting

1995. Open Parliament.

435	**138**	50b. multicoloured	1·80	1·00

139 Emblem and National Colours

1995. 50th Anniv of Arab League.

436	**139**	100b. multicoloured	2·10	1·00

140 Anniversary Emblem

1995. 50th Anniv of U.N.O.

437	**140**	100b. multicoloured	3·50	1·50

141 Sultan Qabus in Robes

1995. National Day. Multicoloured.

438	50b. Type **141**	1·40	80
439	100b. Sultan Qabus in military uniform	2·20	1·00
MS440	150×110 mm. Nos. 438/9 (sold at 300b.)	5·25	4·00

142 Council Emblem

1995. 16th Supreme Council Session of Gulf Co-operation Council, Oman. Multicoloured.

441	100b. Type **142**	2·75	1·30
442	200b. Sultan Qabus, members' flags and map	4·00	2·00

143 Ash'shashah

1996. Omani Sailing Vessels. Multicoloured.

443	50b. Type **143**	30	20
444	100b. Al-Battil	70	60
445	200b. Al-Boum	1·30	1·20
446	250b. Al-Badan	1·70	1·40
447	350b. As'sanbuq	2·50	2·10
448	450b. Al-Galbout	3·00	2·50
449	650b. Al-Baghlah	4·00	3·75
450	1r. Al-Ghanjah	7·00	5·75

144 Emblem, Poppy Head, Skull-like Face smoking Cigarette and Syringe

1996. United Nations Decade against Drug Abuse.

451	**144**	100b. multicoloured	21·00	15·00

145 Shooting

1996. Olympic Games, Atlanta. Multicoloured.

452	100b. Type **145**	5·75	3·00
453	100b. Swimming	5·75	3·00
454	100b. Cycling	5·75	3·00
455	100b. Running	5·75	3·00

Nos. 452/5 were issued together, se-tenant, forming a composite design.

146 Tournament Emblem and Flags of Participating Countries

1996. 13th Arabian Gulf Cup Football Championship.

456	**146**	100b. multicoloured	2·10	1·20

147 Sultan Qabus and Sur (left detail)

1996. National Day. Multicoloured.

457	50b. Type **147**	1·10	90
458	50b. Sultan Qabus and Sur (right detail)	1·10	90

Nos. 457/8 were issued together, se-tenant, forming a composite design.

148 Mother with Children

1996. 50th Anniv of UNICEF.

459	**148**	100b. multicoloured	1·70	1·10

149 Nakl Fort

1997. Tourism. Multicoloured.

460	100b. Type **149**	2·00	1·50
461	100b. Wadi Tanuf (waterfall in centre of stamp)	2·00	1·50
462	100b. Fort on Muthrah Corniche	2·00	1·50
463	100b. Wadi Dayqah Dam	2·00	1·50
464	100b. Bahla fort (overlooking tree-covered plain)	2·00	1·50
465	100b. Wadi Darbut waterfall (near top of stamp)	2·00	1·50

150 Sultan Qabus and Dhofar Waterfalls

1997. National Day. Multicoloured.

466	100b. Type **150**	2·00	1·50
467	100b. Sultan Qabus seated by waterfalls	2·00	1·50

151 Guide Activities

1997. 25th Anniv of Oman Girl Guides.

468	**151**	100b. multicoloured	2·20	1·50

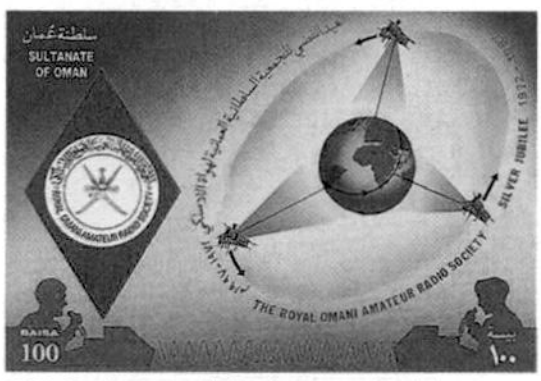
152 Society and Anniversary Emblems

1997. 25th Anniv of Royal Omani Amateur Radio Society.

469	**152**	100b. multicoloured	3·25	2·00

153 Dagger and Sheath

1998. Al-Khanjar Assaidi. Multicoloured, background colours given.

470	**153**	50b. green	80	65
471	**153**	50b. red	80	65
471a	**153**	80b. yellow	1·60	1·20
472	**153**	100b. violet	2·00	1·50
473	**153**	200b. brown	3·25	2·50

154 Car, Traffic Lights, Hand and Police Motor Cycle

1998. Gulf Co-operation Council Traffic Week.

474	**154**	100b. multicoloured	7·75	4·00

155 Sohar Fort

1998. Tourism. Multicoloured.

475	100b. Type **155**	2·20	1·60
476	100b. Wadi Shab	2·20	1·60
477	100b. Nizwa town	2·20	1·60
478	100b. Eid celebration (religious holiday)	2·20	1·60
479	100b. View of river	2·20	1·60
480	100b. Three young girls by an aqueduct	2·20	1·60

156 Exhibition Emblem

1998. 4th Arab Gulf Countries Stamp Exhibition, Muscat.

481	**156**	50b. multicoloured	1·10	80

157 U.P.U. Emblem and Doves

1998. World Stamp Day.

482	**157**	100b. multicoloured	1·70	1·50

158 Year Emblem

1998. National Day. Year of the Private Sector. Multicoloured.

483	100b. Sultan Qabus	4·25	2·75
484	100b. Type **158**	4·25	2·75
MS485	160×80 mm. Nos. 483/4	30·00	30·00

159 Map and Container Ship at Quayside

1998. Inauguration of Salalah Port Container Terminal.

486	**159**	50b. multicoloured	4·50	2·20

160 Sultan Qabus, Dove and Olive Branch

1998. International Peace Award.

487	**160**	500b. multicoloured	17·00	12·50

161 Military Aircraft and Sultan Qabus

1999. 40th Anniv of Royal Air Force of Oman.

488	**161**	100b. multicoloured	2·75	1·70

162 African Monarch

1999. Butterflies. Multicoloured.

489	100b. Type **162**	2·75	2·00
490	100b. Chequered swallowtail (*Papilio demoleus*)	2·75	2·00
491	100b. Blue pansy (*Precis orithya*)	2·75	2·00
492	100b. Yellow pansy (*Precis hierta*)	2·75	2·00
MS493	110×110 mm. Nos. 489/92	28·00	17·00

163 Longbarbel Goatfish

1999. Marine Life. Multicoloured.

494	100b. Type **163**	1·50	1·10
495	100b. Red-eyed round herring (*Etrumeus teres*)	1·50	1·10
496	100b. Brown-spotted grouper (*Epinephelus chlorostigma*)	1·50	1·10
497	100b. Blue-spotted emperor (*Lethrinus lentjan*)	1·50	1·10
498	100b. Blood snapper (*Lutjanus erythropterus*)	1·50	1·10
499	100b. Wahoo (*Acanthocybium solandri*)	1·50	1·10
500	100b. Long-tailed tuna (*Thunnus tonggol*)	1·50	1·10
501	100b. Crimson jobfish (*Pristipomoides filamentosus*)	1·50	1·10
502	100b. Yellow-finned tuna (*Thunnus albacares*)	1·50	1·10
503	100b. Cultured shrimp (*Penaeus indicus*)	1·50	1·10
504	100b. Pharaoh cuttlefish (*Sepia pharaonis*)	1·50	1·10
505	100b. Tropical rock lobster (*Panulirus homarus*)	1·50	1·10

164 Sand Cat

1999. Wildlife. Multicoloured.

506	100b. Type **164**	1·50	1·10
507	100b. Genet	1·50	1·10
508	100b. Leopard	1·50	1·10
509	100b. Sand fox	1·50	1·10
510	100b. Caracal lynx	1·50	1·10
511	100b. Hyena	1·50	1·10
MS512	175×96 mm. Nos. 506/11	33·00	22·00

165 Globe and Emblem

1999. 125th Anniv of Universal Postal Union.

513	**165**	200b. multicoloured	2·20	2·20

166 Sultan Qabus and Musicians

1999. National Day. Multicoloured.

514	100b. Type **166**	2·20	1·50
515	100b. Sultan Qabus and horsemen	2·20	1·50

Nos. 514/15 were issued together, se-tenant, forming a composite design.

167 Sultan Qabus, Globe and "2000"

2000. New Year. Sheet 80×95 mm.

MS516	500b. multicoloured	14·50	11·00

168 Water Droplet and Dried Earth

2000. World Water Week.

517	**168**	100b. multicoloured	1·70	1·10

169 Emblem, Airplane and Silhouette of Bird

2000. 50th Anniv of Gulf Air.

518	**169**	100b. multicoloured	2·00	1·10

170 Crimson-tip Butterfly (*Colotis danae*)

2000. Butterflies. Multicoloured.

519	100b. Type **170**	2·00	1·10
520	100b. *Anaphaeis aurota*	2·00	1·10
521	100b. *Tarucus rosaceus*	2·00	1·10
522	100b. Long-tailed blue (*Lampides boeticus*)	2·00	1·10
MS523	110×110 mm. Nos. 519/22	25·00	13·50

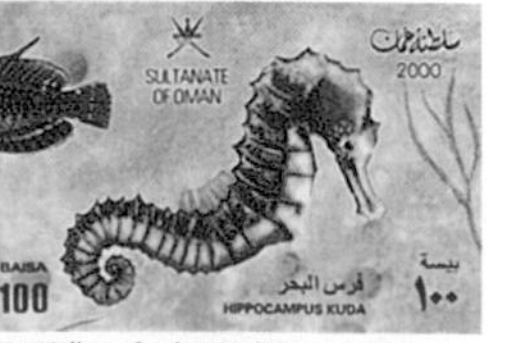
171 Yellow Seahorse (*Hippocampus kuda*)

2000. Marine Life. Multicoloured.

524	100b. Type **171**	2·75	1·30

525	100b. Yellow boxfish (*Ostracion cubicus*)	2·75	1·30
526	100b. Japanese pineconefish (*Monocentris japonica*)	2·75	1·30
527	100b. Broad-barred lionfish (*Pterois antennata*)	2·75	1·30
528	100b. *Rhinecanthus assasi*	2·75	1·30
529	100b. Blue-spotted stingray (*Taeniura lymma*)	2·75	1·30
MS530	130×125 mm. Nos. 524/9	22·00	11·00

172 Arabian Tahr

2000. Mammals. Multicoloured.

531	100b. Type **172**	2·00	1·20
532	100b. Nubian ibex	2·00	1·20
533	100b. Arabian oryx	2·00	1·20
534	100b. Arabian gazelle	2·00	1·20
MS535	130×96 mm. Nos. 531/4	19·00	11·00

173 Emblem

2000. Olympic Games, Sydney. Multicoloured.

536	100b. Type **173**	2·10	1·70
537	100b. Running	2·10	1·70
538	100b. Swimming	2·10	1·70
539	100b. Rifle-shooting	2·10	1·70
MS540	121×100 mm. Nos. 536/9	28·00	17·00

174 Sultan Qabus

2000. National Day. Multicoloured.

541	100b. Type **174**	1·90	1·10
542	100b. Sitting	1·90	1·10
543	100b. Wearing uniform including red beret	1·90	1·10
544	100b. Wearing (white) naval uniform	1·90	1·10
545	100b. Anniversary emblem	1·90	1·10
546	100b. Wearing (beige) police uniform	1·90	1·10
MS547	175×120 mm. Nos. 541/6	13·50	7·75

175 Egret and Sea Birds

2001. Environment Day. Sheet 83×46 mm.

MS548 **175**	200b. multicoloured	13·50	11·00

176 Dagger and Sheath

2001. Al-Khanjar A'suri. Multicoloured, background colours given. (a) Size 24×27 mm.

549	**176**	50b. red	65	55
550	**176**	80b. yellow	1·10	1·00

(b) Size 26×34 mm.

551	100b. blue	1·30	1·20
552	200b. white	2·50	2·20
MS553	80×100 mm. Nos. 549/552	7·75	5·00

177 Child and Tank

2001. Al Aqsa Uprising. Sheet 105×100 mm.

MS554 **177**	100b. multicoloured	6·75	2·20

178 Children encircling Globe

2001. United Nations Year of Dialogue among Civilizations.

555	**178**	200b. multicoloured	5·50	3·25

179 Globe, Tree, Map and Sunrise

2001. National Day. Year of the Environment. Multicoloured.

556	100b. Type **179**	1·70	1·10
557	100b. Sunrise and Sultan Qabas	1·70	1·10

Nos. 556/7 were issued together, se-tenant, forming a composite design.

180 *Cerithium caeruleum*

2001. Shells. Multicoloured.

558	100b. Type **180**	1·30	1·10
559	100b. *Nassarius coronatus*	1·30	1·10
560	100b. *Cerithdea cingulata*	1·30	1·10
561	100b. *Epitoneum pallash*	1·30	1·10

181 Necklace

2001. Traditional Jewellery. Four sheets, each 71×71 mm containing T 181 and similar multicoloured designs.

MS562	(a) 100b. Type **181**; (b) 100b. Necklace with barred pendant (horiz) (63×28 mm); (c) 100b. "Mazrad" necklace (circular) (38×38 mm); (d) 100b. Hair decoration (triangular) (64×32 mm)	17·00	11·00

182 Map enclosed in Circle

2001. 22nd Supreme Session of Gulf Co-operation Council, Oman. Multicoloured.

563	50b. Type **182**	90	55
564	100b. Sultan Qabas	1·90	1·10

183 Interior of Dome

2002. Inauguration of Sultan Qabus Grand Mosque, Baushar. Multicoloured.

565	50b. Type **183**	1·00	55
566	50b. Dome	1·00	55
567	50b. Entrance	1·00	55
568	50b. Decorated roof	1·00	55
MS569	120×90 mm. 100b. Aerial view of mosque. Imperf	5·50	2·20

184 Olive Ridley Turtle

2002. Turtles. Multicoloured.

570	100b. Type **184**	1·70	1·10
571	100b. Atlantic green turtle	1·70	1·10
572	100b. Hawksbill	1·70	1·10
573	100b. Loggerhead	1·70	1·10
MS574	130×98 mm. Nos. 570/3. Imperf	11·00	7·75

185 Adult and Child's Hands

2002. Early Intervention for Children with Special Needs. Ordinary or self-adhesive gum.

575	**185**	100b. multicoloured	3·25	1·70

186 Sultan Qabus and Cheetah (image scaled to 62% of original size)

2002. National Day. Year of the Environment. Sheet 100×80 mm.

MS577 **186**	100b. multicoloured	5·50	3·25

187 Collared Dove (*Streptopelia decaocto*)

2002. Birds. Multicoloured.

578	50b. Type **187**	1·10	55
579	50b. Black-headed tchagra (*Tchagra senegala*)	1·10	55
580	50b. Ruppell's weaver (*Ploceus galbula*)	1·10	55
581	50b. Bonelli's eagle (*Hieraetus fasciatus*)	1·10	55
582	50b. White-eyed bulbul (*Pycnontus xanthopygos*)	1·10	55
583	50b. Northern eagle owl (*Bubo bubo*)	1·10	55
584	50b. Dunn's lark (*Eremalauda dunni*)	1·10	55
585	50b. Cape dikkop (*Burhinus capensis*)	1·10	55
586	50b. Graceful prinia (*Prinia gracilis*)	1·10	55
587	50b. Indian grey francolin (*Francolinus pondicerianus*)	1·10	55
588	50b. Tristram's grackle (*Onychognathus tristramii*)	1·10	55
589	50b. Red-wattled plover (*Vanellus indicus* (inscr "Hoplopterus indicus"))	1·10	55
590	50b. House crow (*Corvus splendens*)	1·10	55
591	50b. Houbara bustard (*Chlamydotis undulate*)	1·10	55
592	50b. White-collared kingfisher (*Halcyon chloris*)	1·10	55
593	50b. Crowned sand grouse (*Pterocles coronatus*)	1·10	55

188 Muscat Gate and Festival Emblem

2003. Muskat Festival.

594	**188**	100b. multicoloured	1·70	1·10

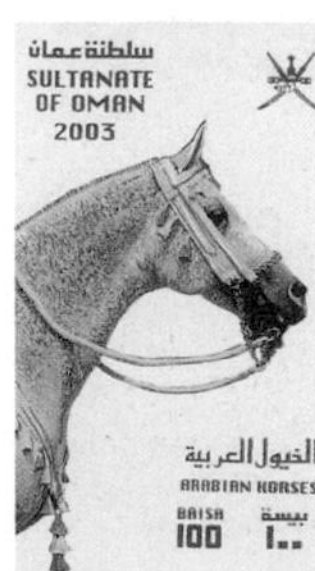

189 Horse's Head

2003. Arabian Horses. Four sheets, each 95×80 mm containing T 189 and similar vert designs. Multicoloured.

MS595	(a) 100b. Type **189**; (b) 100b. Chestnut; (c) 100b. Grey; (d) 100b. Wearing tasselled breast harness	9·00	5·50

190 Chinese and Omani Buildings (image scaled to 70% of original size)

2003. 25th Anniv of Oman—China Diplomatic Relations.

596	**190**	70b. multicoloured	1·70	1·10

191 Census Emblem

2003. National Census. Multicoloured.

597	50b. Type **191**	90	55
598	50b. Emblem and numbers	90	55

192 Dove, Globe and Hands

2003. International Day of Peace.

599	**192**	200b. multicoloured	2·20	2·00

193 Emblem

2003. Organization of Islamic Conference.

600	**193**	100b. multicoloured	1·10	1·00

194 Emblem

2003. SANAD (Self-employment and national autonomous development) Project. (a) Self-adhesive gum.

601	**194**	100b. multicoloured	1·20	1·10

(b) Miniature sheet. Ordinary gum.

MS602	120×95 mm. **194** 100b. multicoloured	1·80	1·80

195 Illuminated Manuscript

2003. Manuscripts. Multicoloured.

603	100b. Type **195**	1·20	1·20
604	100b. Mathematical drawing	1·20	1·20
605	100b. Compass	1·20	1·20
606	100b. Diagram	1·20	1·20
MS607	151×122 mm. 50b. ×4, Showing ships; As No. 606; As No. 603; Script enclosed in circle	2·40	2·40

Nos. 603/6 were issued together, se-tenant forming a composite design.

196 Sultan Qabus

2003. National Day. Multicoloured.

608	50b. Type **196**	60	55
609	50b. Wearing dark robe facing left	60	55
610	50b. Wearing white robe and multicoloured turban	60	55
611	50b. Wearing white turban facing right	60	55

197 *Anogeissus* (inscr "dhoafrica")

2004. Flowers. Multicoloured.

612	50b. Type **197**	60	55
613	50b. *Tecomella undulate*	60	55
614	50b. *Euyrops pinifolius*	60	55
615	50b. *Aloe dhofarensis*	60	55
616	50b. *Cleome glaucescens*	60	55
617	50b. *Cassia italica*	60	55
618	50b. *Cibirhiza dhofarensis*	60	55
619	50b. *Ipomoea nil*	60	55
620	50b. *Viola cinera*	60	55
621	50b. *Dyschoriste dalyi*	60	55
622	50b. *Calotropis procera*	60	55
623	50b. *Lavandula dhofarensis*	60	55
624	50b. *Teucrium mascatense*	60	55
625	50b. *Capparis mucronifolia*	60	55
626	50b. *Geranium mascatense*	60	55
627	50b. *Convolvulus arvensis*	60	55

198 Emblem

2004. Centenary of FIFA (Federation Internationale de Football Association).

628	**198**	250b. multicoloured	3·00	2·75

199 Leopard

2004. Arabian Leopard. Multicoloured.

629	50b. Type **199**	65	65
630	50b. Two leopards	65	65
631	50b. Leopard facing left	65	65
632	50b. Leopard with raised paw	65	65

Nos. 629/32 were issued together, se-tenent, forming a composite design.

200 *Montipora*

2004. Corals. Multicoloured.

633	100b. Type **200**	1·30	1·30
634	100b. *Porites*	1·30	1·30
635	100b. *Acropora*	1·30	1·30
636	100b. *Cycloeris*	1·30	1·30

201 Dove holding Olive Branch

2004. International Day of Peace. Multicoloured.

637	50b. Type **201**	40	40
638	100b. Doves becoming olive branch and globe	80	80

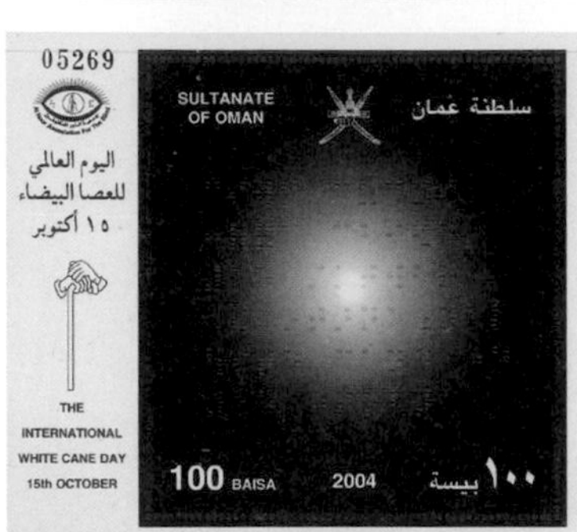

202 Sun in Black Sky (image scaled to 42% of original size)

2004. International White Cane Day. Sheet 118×105 mm.

MS639	100b. black	3·25	3·25

No. **MS**639 was embossed with Braille letters.

203 Emblem

2004. 10th Gulf Cooperation Council Stamp Exhibition, Muscat. Ordinary or self-adhesive gum.

640	**203**	50c. multicoloured	1·00	1·00

204 Sultan Qabus

2004. National Day. Multicoloured.

642	100b. Type **204**	1·30	1·30
643	100b. Facing left	1·30	1·30
644	100b. Wearing blue turban facing right	1·30	1·30
645	100b. Wearing pink turban facing right	1·30	1·30

205 Oasis (Al Masarrat Water Supply Scheme)

2004. Al Masarrat and Ash'Sharqiyah Water Supply Schemes. Multicoloured.

646	50b. Type **205**	65	65
647	50b. Oasis (Ash'Sharqiyah Water Supply Scheme)	65	65

Nos. 646/7 were issued together, se-tenant, forming a composite design.

206 Children and Rescue Workers

2005. Civil Defence. Multicoloured.

648	50b. Type **206**	65	65
649	100b. Fire fighters and rescue team	1·30	1·30

207 Blood Droplet and Arm

2005. International Blood Donor Day.

650	**207**	100b. multicoloured	1·30	1·30

208 Animals and Census Recorders

2005. Agricultural Census. Multicoloured.

651	100b. Type **208**	1·30	1·30
652	100b. Recorder, farmer, palm and shrub	1·30	1·30

Nos. 651/2 were issued together, se-tenant, forming a composite design.

209 Emblem and Faces

2005. World Information Society Summit, Tunis.

653	**209**	100b. multicoloured	1·30	1·30

210 Aircraft and Satellite Dishes

2005. National Day. Multicoloured.

654	100b. Type **210**	1·30	1·30
655	100b. Helicopter and cavalry	1·30	1·30
656	100b. Sultan Qabus	1·30	1·30
657	100b. Musicians and dancers	1·30	1·30
658	100b. Aircraft, ship and tanks	1·30	1·30
659	100b. Castle and inlet	1·30	1·30
660	100b. Clock tower and computers	1·30	1·30
661	100b. Emblem	1·30	1·30
662	100b. Woodlands	1·30	1·30
663	100b. Oil refinery	1·30	1·30

2005. Al-Khanjar A'suri. Multicoloured, background colours given. Size 27×35 mm.

664	**176**	250b. green	3·25	3·25
665	**176**	300b. mauve	4·00	4·00
666	**176**	400b. ochre	5·25	5·25

211 Flag

2006. 25th Anniv of Gulf Co-operation Council. Multicoloured.

667	100b. Type **211**	5·25	5·25
MS668	165×105 mm. 500b. Flags of member states. Imperf	21·00	21·00

Stamps of similar designs were issued by Kuwait, Bahrain, Qatar, Saudi Arabia and United Arab Emirates.

212 Emblem

2006. Muscat–Arab Capital of Culture, 2006. Sheet 100×60 mm.

MS669	100b. multicoloured	2·50	2·50

213 Boy and Flowers

2006. International Day of Tourism. Multicoloured.

670	100b. Type **213**	1·20	1·20
671	100b. Musicians	1·20	1·20
672	100b. Beach	1·20	1·20
673	100b. Nomads and textiles	1·20	1·20

214 Emblem

2006. Postal Service.

674	**214**	100b. ultramarine and silver	1·30	1·30
675	**214**	250b. ultramarine and silver	3·25	3·25

The No. 675 is as No. 674 but with the colours reversed.

215 Sultan Qaboos

2006. National Day.

676	**215**	100b. multicoloured	1·30	1·30

216 Cultural Symbols

2006. Sultan Qaboos Prize for Cultural Innovation.

677	**216**	250b. multicoloured	3·25	3·25

217 Refinery and Tanker

2007. 40th Anniv of Oil Exports. Multicoloured.

678	100b. Type **217**	1·30	1·30
679	100b. Refinery, well head and pipeline	1·30	1·30

Nos. 678/9 were issued together, se-tenant, forming a composite design.

218 Emblem

2007. Symposium on Sustainable Agriculture.

680	**218**	100b. multicoloured	1·30	1·30

219 Sultan Qaboos

2007. National Day.

681	**219**	100b. multicoloured	1·30	1·30

220 Khasab Castle

2007. Tourism. Multicoloured.

682	100b. Type **220**	1·30	1·30
683	100b. Shop keeper	1·30	1·30
684	100b. Children reading	1·30	1·30
685	100b. Entrance and cannon	1·30	1·30

221 Modern and Early Scouts

2007. Centenary of World Scouting. 75th Anniv of Scouting in Oman.

686	**221**	250b. multicoloured	3·25	3·25

Pt. 1

ORANGE FREE STATE (ORANGE RIVER COLONY)

British possession 1848–54. Independent 1854–99. Annexed by Great Britain, 1900. Later a province of the Union of South Africa.

12 pence = 1 shilling; 20 shillings = 1 pound.

1

1869

48	1	½d. brown	5·50	50
84	1	½d. yellow	2·50	35
2	1	1d. brown	17·00	45
68	1	1d. purple	4·00	30
50	1	2d. mauve	19·00	30
51	1	3d. blue	6·00	2·00
19	1	4d. blue	4·00	3·50
7	1	6d. red	16·00	2·00
87	1	1s. brown	27·00	1·50
9	1	1s. orange	60·00	1·50
20	1	5s. green	10·00	15·00

1877. Surch in figures.

75	½d. on 3d. blue	8·00	4·50
36	½d. on 5s. green	22·00	4·75
54	1d. on 3d. blue	8·50	60
57	1d. on 4d. blue	35·00	9·50
22	1d. on 5s. green	60·00	26·00
53	2d. on 3d. blue	50·00	2·00
67	2½d. on 3d. blue	19·00	70
83	2½d. on 3d. blue	9·00	80
40	3d. on 4d. blue	42·00	20·00
12	4d. on 6d. red	£200	32·00

1896. Surch Halve Penny.

77	½d. on 3d. blue	1·00	50

1900. Surch V.R.I. and value in figures.

112	½d. on ½d. orange	30	20
113	1d. on 1d. purple	30	20
114	2d. on 2d. mauve	2·25	30
104	2½d. on 3d. blue (No. 83)	20·00	18·00
117	3d. on 3d. blue	80	30
118	4d. on 4d. blue	3·00	3·75
108	6d. on 6d. red	40·00	35·00
120	6d. on 6d. blue	70	40
121	1s. on 1s. brown	7·50	45
122	5s. on 5s. green	9·00	12·00

1900. Stamps of Cape of Good Hope optd ORANGE RIVER COLONY.

133	**17**	½d. green	50	10
134	**17**	1d. red	2·00	10
135	**6**	2½d. blue	2·75	35

1902. No. 120 surch 4d and bar.

136	1	4d. on 6d. blue	1·50	1·50

1902. Surch E. R. I. 6d.

137	6d. on 6d. blue	4·75	15·00

1902. No. 20 surch One Shilling and star.

138	1s. on 5s. green	9·00	22·00

38 King Edward VII, Springbok and Gnu

1903

148	**38**	½d. green	13·00	75
140	**38**	1d. red	6·50	10
141	**38**	2d. brown	8·50	80
142	**38**	2½d. blue	4·00	80
143	**38**	3d. mauve	9·50	1·00
150	**38**	4d. red and green	4·50	4·25
145	**38**	6d. red and mauve	8·50	1·00
146	**38**	1s. red and brown	40·00	2·25
147	**38**	5s. blue and brown	£100	27·00

MILITARY FRANK STAMP

M1

1899

M1	**M1**	(–) black on yellow	24·00	55·00

POLICE FRANK STAMPS

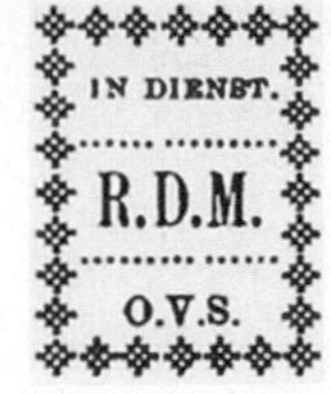

PF1

1896

PF2	**PF1**	(–) black	£150	£200

PF2

1899

PF3	**PF2**	(–) black on yellow	£130	£150

Pt. 1

ORCHHA

A state of Central India. Now uses Indian stamps.

12 pies = 1 anna; 16 annas = 1 rupee.

1

1913. Imperf.

1	1	½a. green	40·00	£130
2	1	1a. red	20·00	£225

2

1914. Imperf.

3a	2	¼a. blue	40	5·50
4	2	½a. green	55	7·50
5	2	1a. red	2·50	8·50
6	2	2a. brown	4·50	24·00
7a	2	4a. yellow	9·00	48·00

3 Maharaja Vir Singh II

1935

8b	3	¼a. purple and grey	50	4·75
9	3	½a. grey and green	50	3·75
10	3	¾a. mauve and green	50	2·75
11	-	1a. green and brown	50	4·00
12	3	1¼a. grey and mauve	50	4·00
13	3	1½a. brown and red	50	3·75
14	3	2a. blue and orange	50	3·75
15	3	2½a. brown and orange	65	4·25
16	3	3a. blue and mauve	65	4·00
17	3	4a. purple and green	65	6·00
18	3	6a. black and buff	70	6·50
19	3	8a. brown and purple	2·25	8·50
20	3	12a. green and purple	1·00	8·50
21	3	12a. blue and purple	42·00	£130
22	3	1r. brown and green	1·00	9·50
24	3	2r. brown and yellow	3·00	27·00
25	3	3r. black and blue	1·50	28·00
26	3	4r. black and brown	3·00	32·00
27	3	5r. blue and purple	3·00	35·00
28	-	10r. green and red	7·00	45·00
29	-	15r. black and green	12·00	£100
30	-	25r. orange and blue	16·00	£110

DESIGN: 1a., 10r. to 25r. As Type **3**, but inscr "POSTAGE & REVENUE". There are two different versions of the portrait for the 1r. value.

5 Maharaja Vir Singh II

1939

31	**5**	¼a. brown	6·00	£110
32	**5**	½a. green	5·00	80·00

33	**5**	¾a. blue	7·00	£130
34	**5**	1a. red	5·00	26·00
35	**5**	1¼a. blue	6·00	£130
36	**5**	1½a. mauve	6·00	£160
37	**5**	2a. red	5·00	95·00
38	**5**	2½a. green	7·50	£300
39	**5**	3a. violet	7·50	£150
40	**5**	4a. slate	8·50	35·00
41	**5**	8a. mauve	12·00	£300
42	-	1r. green	24·00	£650
43	-	2r. violet	65·00	£900
44	-	5r. orange	£200	£2500
45	-	10r. green	£800	£4000
46	-	15r. lilac	£20000	
47	-	25r. purple	£14000	

The rupee values are larger (25×30 mm) and have different frame.

Pt. 1

PAHANG

A state of the Federation of Malaya, incorporated in Malaysia in 1963.

100 cents = 1 dollar (Straits or Malayan).

1889. Nos. 52/3 and 63 of Straits Settlements optd PAHANG.

4a	2c. red	10·00	11·00
2	8c. orange	£1800	£1800
3	10c. grey	£225	£275

1891. No. 68 of Straits Settlements surch PAHANG Two CENTS.

7	2c. on 24c. green	£250	£275

9 Tiger

1891

11	**9**	1c. green	4·25	3·25
12	**9**	2c. red	4·50	3·75
13	**9**	5c. blue	11·00	48·00

10 Tiger

1895

14	**10**	3c. purple and red	9·50	2·75
15	**10**	4c. purple and red	17·00	16·00
16	**10**	5c. purple and yellow	45·00	23·00

1897. No. 13 divided, and each half surch.

18	**9**	2c. on half of 5c. blue	£1500	£400
18d	**9**	3c. on half of 5c. blue	£1500	£400

1898. Stamps of Perak optd Pahang.

19	**44**	10c. purple and orange	24·00	27·00
20	**44**	25c. green and red	85·00	£170
21	**44**	50c. purple and black	£475	£550
22	**44**	50c. green and black	£275	£400
23	**45**	$1 green	£375	£550
24	**45**	$5 green and blue	£1600	£2750

1898. Stamp of Perak surch Pahang Four cents.

25	**44**	4c. on 8c. purple and blue	8·00	8·00

1899. No. 16 surch Four cents.

28	**10**	4c. on 5c. purple and yellow	21·00	70·00

15 Sultan Sir Abu Bakar

1935

29	**15**	1c. black	20	40
30	**15**	2c. green	2·75	50
31a	**15**	3c. green	22·00	22·00
32	**15**	4c. orange	70	50
33	**15**	5c. brown	70	10
34	**15**	6c. red	25·00	1·75
35	**15**	8c. grey	60	10
36	**15**	8c. red	6·50	75·00
37	**15**	10c. purple	1·75	10
38	**15**	12c. blue	5·00	1·25
39	**15**	15c. blue	35·00	70·00
40	**15**	25c. purple and red	2·50	1·50
41	**15**	30c. purple and orange	1·25	1·10
42	**15**	40c. red and purple	1·00	2·00
43	**15**	50c. black on green	5·00	1·50
44	**15**	$1 black and red on blue	5·00	8·00
45	**15**	$2 green and red	30·00	42·00
46	**15**	$5 green and red on green	12·00	85·00

1948. Silver Wedding. As T 8b/c of Pitcairn Islands.

47	10c. violet	15	60
48	$5 green	25·00	42·00

1949. U.P.U. As T 8d/g of Pitcairn Islands.

49	10c. purple	30	25
50	15c. blue	1·10	1·50
51	25c. orange	35	2·50
52	50c. black	70	3·50

16 Sultan Sir Abu Bakar

1950

53	**16**	1c. black	10	10
54	**16**	2c. orange	20	10
55	**16**	3c. green	30	80
56	**16**	4c. brown	2·50	10
57a	**16**	5c. purple	50	15
58	**16**	6c. grey	50	30
59	**16**	8c. red	50	1·50
60	**16**	8c. green	1·00	75
61	**16**	10c. mauve	25	10
62	**16**	12c. red	2·00	1·25
63	**16**	15c. blue	75	10
64	**16**	20c. black and green	1·00	2·75
65	**16**	20c. blue	3·00	10
66	**16**	25c. purple and orange	50	10
67	**16**	30c. red and purple	3·25	35
68	**16**	35c. red and purple	1·00	25
69	**16**	40c. red and purple	3·00	7·50
70	**16**	50c. black and blue	1·50	10
71	**16**	$1 blue and purple	3·00	3·25
72	**16**	$2 green and red	14·00	27·00
73	**16**	$5 green and brown	70·00	95·00

1953. Coronation. As T 8h of Pitcairn Islands.

74	10c. black and purple	2·50	10

1957. As Nos. 92/102 of Kedah but inset portrait of Sultan Sir Abu Bakar.

75	1c. black	10	10
76	2c. red	10	10
77	4c. sepia	10	10
78	5c. lake	10	10
79	8c. green	2·75	2·25
80	10c. sepia	1·25	10
81	10c. purple	3·75	30
82	20c. blue	2·25	20
83	50c. black and blue	45	75
84	$1 blue and purple	11·00	2·25
85	$2 green and red	8·50	9·00
86	$5 brown and green	12·00	15·00

17 "Vanda hookeriana"

1965. As Nos. 115/21 of Kedah but with inset portrait of Sultan Sir Abu Bakar as in T 17.

87	**17**	1c. multicoloured	10	1·25
88	-	2c. multicoloured	10	1·25
89	-	5c. multicoloured	15	10
90	-	6c. multicoloured	30	1·25
91	-	10c. multicoloured	20	10
92	-	15c. multicoloured	1·00	10
93	-	20c. multicoloured	1·60	40

The higher values used in Pahang were Nos. 20/7 of Malaysia (National Issue).

18 "Precis orithya"

1971. Butterflies. As Nos. 124/30 of Kedah, but with portrait of Sultan Sir Abu Bakar as in T 18.

96	1c. multicoloured	20	1·75
97	2c. multicoloured	50	2·00
98	5c. multicoloured	1·00	50
99	6c. multicoloured	1·50	2·25
100	10c. multicoloured	1·00	30
101 **18**	15c. multicoloured	1·75	10
102 -	20c. multicoloured	2·00	50

The higher values in use with this Issue were Nos. 64/71 of Malaysia (National Issues).

19 Sultan Haji Ahmad Shah

1975. Installation of the Sultan.

103	**19**	10c. green, lilac and gold	50	1·25
104	**19**	15c. black, yellow and green	60	10
105	**19**	50c. black, blue and green	1·75	4·25

1977. As Nos. 97/8, 100/102 but with portrait of Sultan Haji Ahmad Shah.

106	-	2c. multicoloured	70·00	65·00
107	-	5c. multicoloured	70	1·25
108	-	10c. multicoloured	1·00	75
109	**18**	15c. multicoloured	1·00	30
110	-	20c. multicoloured	4·00	2·00

20 "Rhododendron scortechinii"

1979. Flowers. As Nos. 135/41 of Kedah but with portrait of Sultan Haji Ahmad Shah as in T 20.

111	1c. "Rafflesia hasseltii"	10	1·00
112	2c. "Pterocarpus indicus"	10	1·00
113	5c. "Lagerstroemia speciosa"	10	30
114	10c. "Durio zibethinus"	15	10
115	15c. "Hibiscus rosa-sinensis"	15	10
116	20c. Type **20**	20	10
117	25c. "Etlingera elatior" (inscr "Phaeomeria speciosa")	40	40

21 Rice

1986. As Nos. 152/8 of Kedah but with portrait of Sultan Ahmad Shah as in T 21.

125	1c. Coffee	10	25
126	2c. Coconuts	10	35
127	5c. Cocoa	15	10
128	10c. Black pepper	15	10
129	15c. Rubber	25	10
130	20c. Oil palm	25	15
131	30c. Type **21**	30	15

2002. As T 21 but redenominated in 'sen'. Multicoloured.

132	30s. Rice	2·00	10

22 *Nelumbium nelumbo* (sacred lotus)

2007. Garden Flowers. As Nos. 210/15 of Johore, but with portrait of Sultan Ahmad Shah and Arms of Pahang as in T 22. Multicoloured.

133	5s. Type **22**	10	10
134	10s. *Hydrangea macrophylla*	15	10
135	20s. *Hippeastrum reticulatum*	25	15
136	30s. *Bougainvillea*	40	20
137	40s. *Ipomoea indica*	50	30
138	50s. *Hibiscus rosa-sinensis*	65	35
MS139	100×85 mm. Nos. 133/8	2·00	1·25
MS139	100×85 mm. Nos. 133/8	2·00	1·25

Pt. 17

PAKHOI

An Indo-Chinese Post Office in China, closed in 1922.

1903. Stamps of Indo-China, "Tablet" key-type, surch PACKHOI and value in Chinese.

1	**D**	1c. black and red on blue	21·00	24·00
2	**D**	2c. brown and blue on buff	9·25	12·00
3	**D**	4c. brown and blue on grey	6·50	13·50
4	**D**	5c. green and red	2·75	3·75
5	**D**	10c. red and blue	2·30	4·50
6	**D**	15c. grey and red	3·25	6·50
7	**D**	20c. red and blue on green	11·00	11·00
8	**D**	25c. blue and red	7·00	18·00
9	**D**	25c. black and red on pink	6·50	11·50
10	**D**	30c. brown and blue on drab	20·00	32·00
11	**D**	40c. red and blue on yellow	80·00	90·00
12	**D**	50c. red and blue on pink	£325	£325
13	**D**	50c. brown and red on blue	95·00	£120
14	**D**	75c. brown and red on orange	95·00	£120
15	**D**	1f. green and red	£100	£120
16	**D**	5f. mauve and blue on lilac	£130	£130

1906. Stamps of Indo-China surch PAK-HOI and value in Chinese.

17	**8**	1c. green	3·75	3·00
18	**8**	2c. red on yellow	2·30	2·00
19	**8**	4c. mauve on blue	2·75	2·30
20	**8**	5c. green	6·25	1·60
21	**8**	10c. red	3·25	2·30
22	**8**	15c. brown on blue	10·00	10·50
23	**8**	20c. red on green	4·75	3·25
24	**8**	25c. blue	4·25	5·75
25	**8**	30c. brown on cream	9·25	5·00
26	**8**	35c. black on yellow	5·25	4·75
27	**8**	40c. black on grey	5·25	7·00
28	**8**	50c. olive on green	17·00	10·00
29	**D**	75c. brown on orange	90·00	95·00
30	**8**	1f. green	50·00	44·00
31	**8**	2f. brown on yellow	65·00	70·00
32	**D**	5f. mauve on lilac	£130	£130
33	**8**	10f. red on green	£130	£130

1908. Stamps of Indo-China (Native types) surch PAKHOI and value in Chinese.

34	**10**	1c. black and brown	1·40	75
35	**10**	2c. black and brown	1·00	1·20
36	**10**	4c. black and blue	1·50	1·70
37	**10**	5c. black and green	1·80	2·00
38	**10**	10c. black and red	1·80	5·75
39	**10**	15c. black and violet	3·00	6·00
40	**11**	20c. black and violet	2·75	7·00
41	**11**	25c. black and blue	3·25	8·50
42	**11**	30c. black and brown	3·00	11·50
43	**11**	35c. black and green	3·25	11·50
44	**11**	40c. black and brown	3·00	11·50
45	**11**	50c. black and red	3·75	11·50
46	**12**	75c. black and orange	11·00	17·00
47	-	1f. black and red	17·00	23·00
48	-	2f. black and green	28·00	50·00
49	-	5f. black and blue	£110	£130
50	-	10f. black and violet	£130	£130

1919. As last, surch in addition in figures and words.

51	**10**	⅖c. on 1c. black and green	45	6·25
52	**10**	⅘c. on 2c. black and brown	1·30	7·75
53	**10**	1⅗c. on 4c. black and blue	1·10	6·75
54	**10**	2c. on 5c. black and green	2·50	7·25
55	**10**	4c. on 10c. black and red	5·00	5·50
56	**10**	6c. on 15c. black and violet	3·25	7·75
57	**11**	8c. on 20c. black and violet	7·00	7·00
58	**11**	10c. on 25c. black and blue	6·75	9·00
59	**11**	12c. on 30c. black & brown	3·25	4·25
60	**11**	14c. on 35c. black and green	4·00	3·75
61	**11**	16c. on 40c. black & brown	3·75	4·50
62	**11**	20c. on 50c. black and red	5·75	5·50
63	**12**	30c. on 75c. black & orange	4·25	9·75
64	-	40c. on 1f. black and red	21·00	32·00
65	-	80c. on 2f. black and green	8·50	13·50
66	-	2pi. on 5f. black and blue	13·00	20·00
67	-	4pi. on 10f. black and violet	50·00	60·00

Pt. 1

PAKISTAN

A Dominion created in 1947 from territory with predominantly Moslem population in Eastern and Western India. Became an independent Islamic Republic within the British Commonwealth in 1956. The eastern provinces declared their independence in 1971 and are now known as Bangladesh.

On 30 January 1972 Pakistan left the Commonwealth but rejoined on 1 October 1989.

1947. 12 pies = 1 anna; 16 annas = 1 rupee.
1961. 100 paisa = 1 rupee.

1947. King George VI stamps of India optd PAKISTAN.

1	**100a**	3p. grey	30	10
2	**100a**	½a. purple	30	10
3	**100a**	9p. green	30	10
4	**100a**	1a. red	30	10
5	**101**	1½a. violet	1·25	10
6	**101**	2a. red	30	20
7	**101**	3a. violet	35	20
8	**101**	3½a. blue	1·00	2·25
9	**102**	4a. brown	35	20
10	**102**	6a. green	1·00	1·25
11	**102**	8a. violet	45	60
12	**102**	12a. red	1·00	20
13	-	14a. purple (No. 277)	3·25	3·50
14	**93**	1r. grey and brown	3·50	1·25
15	**93**	2r. purple and brown	3·50	3·50
16	**93**	5r. green and blue	7·00	5·00
17	**93**	10r. purple and claret	7·00	8·00
18	**93**	15r. brown and green	80·00	£110
19	**93**	25r. violet and purple	85·00	75·00

3 Constituent Assembly Building, Karachi

1948. Independence.

20	**3**	1½a. blue	1·25	2·00
21	-	2½a. green	1·25	20
22	-	3a. brown	1·25	35
23	-	1r. red	1·25	70

DESIGNS—HORIZ: 2½a. Entrance to Karachi Airport; 3a. Gateway to Lahore Fort. VERT: 1r. Crescent and Stars in foliated frame.

7 Scales of Justice

9 Lloyds Barrage

12 Salimullah Hostel, Dacca University

13 Khyber Pass

1948. Designs with crescent moon pointing to right.

24	**7**	3p. red	10	10
25	**7**	6p. violet	1·25	10
26	**7**	9p. green	50	10
27	-	1a. blue	15	50
28	-	1½a. green	15	10
29	-	2a. red	3·25	70
30	**9**	2½a. green	4·50	9·50
31	-	3a. green	7·50	1·00
32	**9**	3½a. blue	4·75	5·50
33	**9**	4a. brown	1·00	10
34	-	6a. blue	2·00	50
35	-	8a. black	1·00	1·50
36	-	10a. red	6·00	12·00
37	-	12a. red	7·50	1·00
38	**12**	1r. blue	15·00	10
39	**12**	2r. brown	20·00	75
40a	**12**	5r. red	12·00	25
41b	**13**	10r. mauve	18·00	2·75
42	**13**	15r. green	18·00	25·00
210b	**13**	25r. violet	5·50	7·50

DESIGNS—VERT (as Type **7**): 1a., 1½a., 2a. Star and Crescent; 6a., 8a., 12a. Karachi Port Trust. HORIZ (as Type **12**): 3a., 10a. Karachi Airport.

1949. As 1948 but with crescent moon pointing to left.

44	1a. blue	4·00	85
45a	1½a. green	3·50	10
46a	2a. red	5·50	10
47	3a. green	16·00	1·00
48	6a. blue	17·00	2·50
49	8a. black	17·00	2·50
50	10a. red	25·00	3·75
51	12a. red	25·00	60

16

1949. 1st Death Anniv of Mohammed Ali Jinnah.

52	**16**	1½a. brown	2·50	1·50
53	**16**	3a. green	2·50	1·50
54	-	10a. black	7·00	8·00

DESIGN: 10a. inscription reads "QUAID-I-AZAM MOHAMMAD ALI JINNAH" etc.

17 Pottery

1951. 4th Anniv of Independence.

55	**17**	2½a. red	1·75	1·25
56	-	3a. purple	1·00	10
57	**17**	3½a. blue (A)	1·25	7·00
57a	-	3½a. blue (B)	3·50	5·00
58	-	4a. green	1·00	10
59	-	6a. orange	1·00	10
60	-	8a. sepia	4·50	25
61	-	10a. violet	2·00	2·25
62	-	12a. slate	2·00	10

DESIGNS—VERT: 3, 12a. Airplane and hour-glass; 4, 6a. Saracenic leaf pattern. HORIZ: 8, 10a. Archway and lamp.

(A) has Arabic fraction on left as in Type **17**, (B) has it on right.

For similar 3½a. see No. 88.

21 "Scinde Dawk" Stamp and Ancient and Modern Transport

1952. Cent of "Scinde Dawk" Issue of India.

63	**21**	3a. green on olive	1·00	85
64	**21**	12a. brown on salmon	1·25	15

22 Kaghan Valley

24 Tea Plantation, East Pakistan

1954. 7th Anniv of Independence.

65	**22**	6p. violet	10	10
66	-	9p. blue	3·50	2·50
67	-	1a. red	10	10
68	-	1½a. red	10	10
69	**24**	14a. myrtle	4·00	10
70	-	1r. green	11·00	10
71	-	2r. orange	2·75	10

DESIGNS—HORIZ (as Type **22**): 9p. Mountains, Gilgit; 1a. Badshahi Mosque, Lahore. (As Type **24**): 1r. Cotton plants, West Pakistan; 2r. Jute fields and river, East Pakistan. VERT (as Type **22**): 1½a. Mausoleum of Emperor Jehangir, Lahore.

29 View of K2

1954. Conquest of K2 (Mount Godwin-Austen).

72	**29**	2a. violet	40	30

30 Karnaphuli Paper Mill, East Bengal

1955. 8th Anniv of Independence.

73	**30**	2½a. red (A)	50	1·40
73a	-	2½a. red (B)	65	1·40
74	-	6a. blue	1·00	10
75	-	8a. violet	3·75	10
76	-	12a. red and orange	4·00	10

DESIGNS: 6a. Textile mill, W. Pakistan; 8a. Jute mill, E. Pakistan; 12a. Main Sui gas plant.

(A) has Arabic fraction on left as in Type **30**, (B) has it on right.

For similar 2½a. see No. 87.

1955. 10th Anniv of U.N. Nos. 68 and 76 optd TENTH ANNIVERSARY UNITED NATIONS 24.10.55.

77	1½a. red	1·50	5·00
78	12a. red and orange	50	3·50

35 Map of West Pakistan

1955. West Pakistan Unity.

79	**35**	1½a. green	80	1·50
80	**35**	2a. brown	65	10
81	**35**	12a. red	1·50	50

36 Constituent Assembly Building, Karachi

1956. Republic Day.

82	**36**	2a. green	80	10

37

1956. 9th Anniv of Independence.

83	**37**	2a. red	65	10

38 Map of East Pakistan

1956. 1st Session of National Assembly of Pakistan at Dacca.

84	**38**	1½a. green	40	1·50
85	**38**	2a. brown	40	10
86	**38**	12a. red	40	1·25

41 Orange Tree

1957. 1st Anniv of Republic.

87	-	2½a. red	20	10
88	-	3½a. blue	30	10
89	**41**	10r. green and orange	80	20

DESIGNS: 2½a. as Type **30** without value in Arabic at right; 3½a. as Type **17** without value in Arabic at right.

42 Pakistani Flag

1957. Centenary of Struggle for Independence (Indian Mutiny).

90	**42**	1½a. green	50	10
91	**42**	12a. blue	1·25	10

43 Pakistani Industries

1957. 10th Anniv of Independence.

92	**43**	1½a. blue	20	30
93	**43**	4a. salmon	45	1·50
94	**43**	12a. mauve	45	50

44 Coconut tree

1958. 2nd Anniv of Republic.

95	**44**	15r. red and purple	3·00	3·00

45

1958. 20th Death Anniv of Mohammed Iqbal (poet).

96	**45**	1½a. olive and black	55	1·00
97	**45**	2a. brown and black	55	10
98	**45**	14a. turquoise and black	90	10

46 U.N. Charter and Globe

1958. 10th Anniv of Declaration of Human Rights.

99	**46**	1½a. turquoise	10	10
100	**46**	14a. sepia	45	10

1958. Scout Jamboree. Optd PAKISTAN BOY SCOUT 2nd NATIONAL JAMBOREE CHITTAGONG Dec. 58-Jan. 59.

101	**22**	6p. violet	20	10
102	-	8a. violet (No. 75)	40	10

1959. Revolution Day. No. 74 optd REVOLUTION DAY Oct. 27, 1959.

103	6a. blue	80	10

49 "Centenary of An Idea"

1959. Red Cross Commemoration.
104 **49** 2a. red and green 30 10
105 **49** 10a. red and blue 55 10

50 Armed Forces Badge

1960. Armed Forces Day.
106 **50** 2a. red, blue and green 50 10
107 **50** 14a. red and blue 1·00 10

51 Map of Pakistan

1960
108 **51** 6p. purple 40 10
109 **51** 2a. red 60 10
110 **51** 8a. green 1·25 10
111 **51** 1r. blue 2·00 10

52 "Uprooted Tree"

1960. World Refugee Year.
112 **52** 2a. red 20 10
113 **52** 10a. green 30 10

53 Punjab Agricultural College

1960. Golden Jubilee of Punjab Agricultural College, Lyallpur.
114 **53** 2a. blue and red 10 10
115 - 8a. green and violet 20 10
DESIGN: 8a. College arms.

55 "Land Reforms, Rehabilitation and Reconstruction"

1960. Revolution Day.
116 **55** 2a. green, pink and brown 10 10
117 **55** 14a. green, yellow and blue 50 75

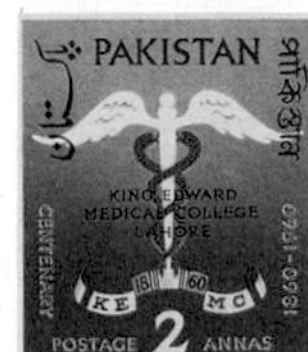

56 Caduceus

1960. Centenary of King Edward Medical College, Lahore.
118 **56** 2a. yellow, black and blue 50 10
119 **56** 14a. green, black and red 1·75 1·00

57 "Economic Co-operation"

1960. Int Chamber of Commerce C.A.F.E.A. Meeting, Karachi.
120 **57** 14a. brown 50 20

58 Zam-Zama Gun, Lahore ("Kim's Gun" after Rudyard Kipling)

1960. 3rd Pakistan Boy Scouts' National Jamboree, Lahore.
121 **58** 2a. red, yellow and green 80 20

1961. Surch in "PAISA".
122 - 1p. on 1½a. red (No. 68) 40 10
123 **7** 2p. on 3p. red 10 10
124 **51** 3p. on 6p. purple 15 10
125 - 7p. on 1a. red (No. 67) 40 10
126 **51** 13p. on 2a. red 40 10
127 **37** 13p. on 2a. red 30 10
See also Nos. 262/4.

60 Khyber Pass

61 Shalimar Gardens, Lahore

62 Chota Sona Masjid (gateway)

1961
170 **60** 1p. violet 10 10
132 **60** 2p. red 1·00 10
133 **60** 3p. purple 75 10
173 **60** 5p. blue 10 10
135 **60** 7p. green 2·00 10
175 **61** 10p. brown 10 10
176 **61** 13p. violet 10 10
176a **61** 15p. purple 20 10
176b **61** 20p. green 30 10
138 **61** 25p. blue 5·50 10
178 **61** 40p. purple 15 30
179 **61** 50p. green 15 10
141 **61** 75p. red 40 70
142 **61** 90p. green 70 70
204 **62** 1r. red 1·00 10
144 **62** 1r.25 violet 75 80
206 **62** 2r. orange 1·00 15
207 **62** 5r. green 5·50 1·00

1961. Lahore Stamp Exn. No. 110 optd LAHORE STAMP EXHIBITION 1961 and emblem.
145 **51** 8a. green 1·00 1·75

64 Warsak Dam and Power Station

1961. Completion of Warsak Hydro-electric Project.
146 **64** 40p. black and blue 60 10

65 Narcissus

1961. Child Welfare Week.
147 **65** 13p. turquoise 50 10
148 **65** 90p. mauve 1·25 20

66 Ten Roses

1961. Co-operative Day.
149 **66** 13p. red and green 40 10
150 **66** 90p. red and blue 85 90

67 Police Crest and "Traffic Control"

1961. Police Centenary.
151 **67** 13p. silver, black and blue 50 10
152 **67** 40p. silver, black and red 1·00 20

68 Locomotive "Eagle", 1861

1961. Railway Centenary.
153 **68** 13p. green, black and yellow 75 80
154 - 50p. yellow, black and green 1·00 1·50
DESIGN: 50p. Diesel locomotive No. 20 and tracks forming "1961".

1962. 1st Karachi–Dacca Jet Flight. No. 87 surch with Boeing 720B airliner and FIRST JET FLIGHT KARACHI–DACCA 13 Paisa.
155 13p. on 2½a. red 1·75 1·25

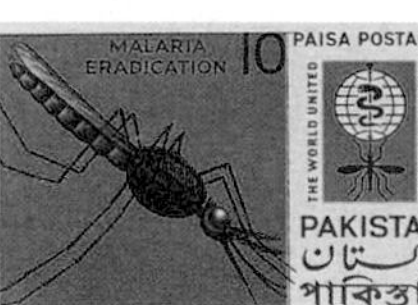

71 "Anopheles sp." (mosquito)

1962. Malaria Eradication.
156 **71** 10p. black, yellow and red 35 10
157 - 13p. black, lemon and red 35 10
DESIGN: 13p. Mosquito pierced by blade.

73 Pakistan Map and Jasmine

1962. New Constitution.
158 **73** 40p. green, turquoise & grey 70 10

74 Football

1962. Sports.
159 **74** 7p. black and blue 10 10
160 - 13p. black and green 60 1·50
161 - 25p. black and purple 20 10
162 - 40p. black and brown 2·00 2·50
DESIGNS: 13p. Hockey; 25p. Squash; 40p. Cricket.

78 Marble Fruit Dish and Bahawalpuri Clay Flask

1962. Small Industries.
163 **78** 7p. lake 10 10
164 - 13p. green 2·50 2·50
165 - 25p. violet 10 10
166 - 40p. green 10 10
167 - 50p. red 10 10
DESIGNS: 13p. Sports equipment; 25p. Camelskin lamp and brassware; 40p. Wooden powder-bowl and basket-work; 50p. Inlaid cigarette-box and brassware.

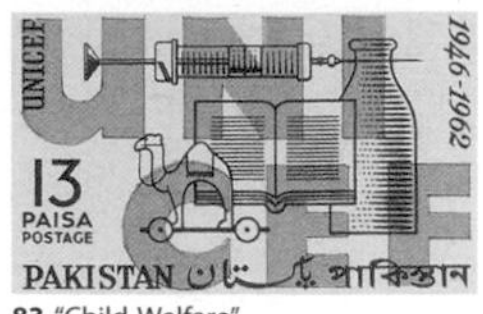

83 "Child Welfare"

1962. 16th Anniv of UNICEF.
168 **83** 13p. black, blue and purple 35 10
169 **83** 40p. black, yellow and blue 35 10

1963. Pakistan U.N. Force in West Irian. Optd U.N. FORCE W. IRIAN.
182 **61** 13p. violet 10 1·00

85 "Dancing" Horse, Camel and Bull

1963. National Horse and Cattle Show.
183 **85** 13p. blue, sepia and pink 10 10

86 Wheat and Tractor

1963. Freedom from Hunger.
184 **86** 13p. brown 3·00 10
185 - 50p. bistre 4·50 55
DESIGN: 50p. Lifting rice.

1963. 2nd International Stamp Exhibition, Dacca. Surch 13 PAISA INTERNATIONAL DACCA STAMP EXHIBITION 1963.
186 **51** 13p. on 2a. red 50 50

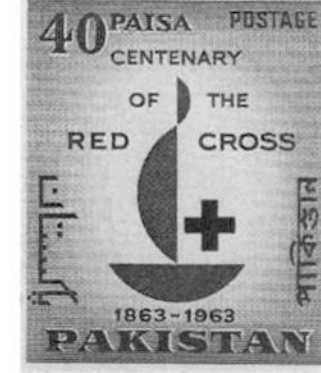

89 Centenary Emblem

1963. Centenary of Red Cross.
187 **89** 40p. red and olive 2·00 15

90 Paharpur

1963. Archaeological Series.
188 **90** 7p. blue 55 10
189 - 13p. sepia 55 10
190 - 40p. red 90 10
191 - 50p. violet 95 10
DESIGNS—VERT: 13p. Moenjodaro. HORIZ: 40p. Taxila; 50p. Mainamati.

1963. Centenary of Pakistan Public Works Department. Surch 100 YEARS OF P.W.D. OCTOBER, 1963 13.
192 **60** 13p. on 3p. purple 10 10

95 Ataturk's Mausoleum

1963. 25th Death Anniv of Kemal Ataturk.

193 **95** 50p. red 50 10

96 Globe and UNESCO Emblem

1963. 15th Anniv of Declaration of Human Rights.

194 **96** 50p. brown, red and blue 40 10

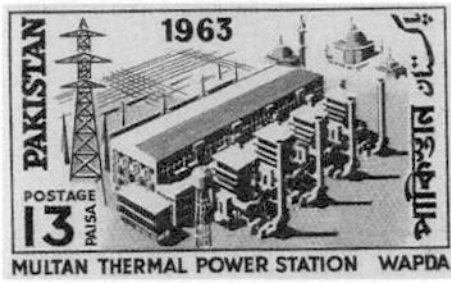

97 Thermal Power Installations

1963. Completion of Multan Thermal Power Station.

195 **97** 13p. blue 10 10

99 Temple of Thot, Queen Nefertari and Maids

1964. Nubian Monuments Preservation.

211 **99** 13p. blue and red 30 10

212 - 50p. purple and black 70 10

DESIGN: 50p. Temple of Abu Simbel.

101 "Unisphere" and Pakistan Pavilion

1964. New York World's Fair.

213 **101** 13p. blue 10 10

214 - 1r.25 blue and orange 40 20

DESIGN—VERT: 1r.25, Pakistan Pavilion on "Unisphere".

103 Shah Abdul Latif's Mausoleum

1964. Death Bicentenary of Shah Abdul Latif of Bhit.

215 **103** 50p. blue and red 1·00 10

104 Mausoleum of Quaid-i-Azam

1964. 16th Death Anniv of Mohammed Ali Jinnah (Quaid-i-Azam).

216 **104** 15p. green 1·00 10

217 - 50p. green 2·25 10

DESIGN: 50p. As Type **104**, but 26½×31½ mm.

106 Bengali and Urdu Alphabets

1964. Universal Children's Day.

218 **106** 15p. brown 10 10

107 University Building

1964. 1st Convocation of the West Pakistan University of Engineering and Technology, Lahore.

219 **107** 15p. brown 10 10

108 "Help the Blind"

1965. Blind Welfare.

220 **108** 15p. blue and yellow 20 10

109 I.T.U. Emblem and Symbols

1965. Centenary of I.T.U.

221 **109** 15p. purple 1·50 30

110 I.C.Y. Emblem

1965. International Co-operation Year.

222 **110** 15p. black and blue 50 15

223 **110** 50p. green and yellow 1·50 40

111 "Co-operation"

1965. 1st Anniv of Regional Development Co-operation Pact. Multicoloured.

224 15p. Type **111** 20 10

225 50p. Globe and flags of Turkey, Iran and Pakistan (54¾×30¾ mm) 1·10 10

113 Soldier and Tanks

1965. Pakistan Armed Forces. Multicoloured.

226 7p. Type **113** 75 30

227 15p. Naval Officer and "Tughril" (destroyer) 1·50 10

228 50p. Pilot and Lockheed F-104C Starfighters 2·50 30

116 Army, Navy and Air Force Crests

1966. Armed Forces Day.

229 **116** 15p. blue, green and buff 1·00 10

117 Atomic Reactor, Islamabad

1966. Inauguration of Pakistan's 1st Atomic Reactor.

230 **117** 15p. black 10 10

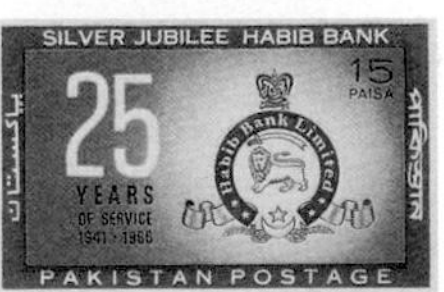

118 Bank Crest

1966. Silver Jubilee of Habib Bank.

231 **118** 15p. green, orange & sepia 10 10

119 Children

1966. Universal Children's Day.

232 **119** 15p. black, red and yellow 10 10

120 UNESCO Emblem

1966. 20th Anniversary of UNESCO.

233 **120** 15p. multicoloured 3·75 30

121 Flag, Secretariat Building and President Ayub

1966. Islamabad (new capital).

234 **121** 15p. multicoloured 35 10

235 **121** 50p. multicoloured 65 10

122 Avicenna

1966. Foundation of Health and Tibbi Research Institute.

236 **122** 15p. green and salmon 40 10

123 Mohammed Ali Jinnah

1966. 90th Birth Anniv of Mohammed Ali Jinnah.

237 **123** 15p. black, orange & blue 15 10

238 - 50p. black, purple and blue 35 10

DESIGN: 50p. Same portrait as 15p. but different frame.

124 Tourist Year Emblem

1967. International Tourist Year.

239 **124** 15p. black, blue and brown 10 10

125 Emblem of Pakistan T.B. Association

1967. Tuberculosis Eradication Campaign.

240 **125** 15p. red, sepia and brown 10 10

126 Scout Salute and Badge

1967. 4th National Scout Jamboree.

241 **126** 15p. brown and purple 15 10

127 "Justice"

1967. Cent of West Pakistan High Court.

242 **127** 15p. multicoloured 10 10

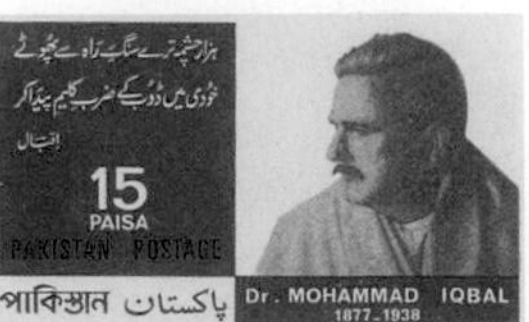

128 Dr. Mohammed Iqbal (philosopher)

1967. Iqbal Commemoration.

243 **128** 15p. sepia and red 15 10

244 **128** 1r. sepia and green 35 10

129 Hilal-i-Isteqlal Flag

1967. Award of Hilal-i-Isteqlal (for Valour) to Lahore, Sialkot and Sargodha.

245 **129** 15p. multicoloured 10 10

130 "20th Anniversary"

1967. 20th Anniv of Independence.

246 **130** 15p. red and green 10 10

131 "Rice Exports"

1967. Pakistan Exports. Multicoloured.

247 10p. Type **131** 10 15

248 15p. Cotton plant, yarn and textiles (vert) (27×45 mm) 10 10

249 50p. Raw jute, bale and bags (vert) (27×45 mm) 20 15

134 Clay Toys

1967. Universal Children's Day.

250 **134** 15p. multicoloured 10 10

135 Shah and Empress of Iran and Gulistan Palace, Teheran

1967. Coronation of Shah Mohammed Riza Pahlavi and Empress Farah of Iran.

251 **135** 50p. purple, blue and ochre 1·00 10

136 "Each For All–All for Each"

1967. Co-operative Day.

252 **136** 15p. multicoloured 10 10

137 Mangla Dam

1967. Indus Basin Project.

253 **137** 15p. multicoloured 10 10

138 Crab pierced by Sword

1967. The Fight Against Cancer.

254 **138** 15p. red and black 70 10

139 Human Rights Emblem

1968. Human Rights Year.

255 **139** 15p. red and blue 10 15

256 **139** 50p. red, yellow and grey 10 15

140 Agricultural University, Mymensingh

1968. First Convocation of East Pakistan Agricultural University.

257 **140** 15p. multicoloured 10 10

141 W.H.O. Emblem

1968. 20th Anniv of W.H.O.

258 **141** 15p. orange and green 10 15

259 **141** 50p. orange and blue 10 15

142 Kazi Nazrul Islam (poet, composer and patriot)

1968. Nazrul Islam Commemoration.

260 **142** 15p. sepia and yellow 35 15

261 **142** 50p. sepia and red 65 15

1968. Nos. 56, 74 and 61 surch.

262 4p. on 3a. purple 1·00 1·75

263 4p. on 6a. blue 1·25 1·75

264 60p. on 10a. violet 1·00 35

144 Children running with Hoops

1968. Universal Children's Day.

265 **144** 15p. multicoloured 10 10

145 National Assembly

1968. "A Decade of Development".

266 **145** 10p. multicoloured 10 10

267 - 15p. multicoloured 10 10

268 - 50p. multicoloured 2·00 20

269 - 60p. blue, purple and red 50 35

DESIGNS: 15p. Industry and Agriculture; 50p. Army, Navy and Air Force; 60p. Minaret and atomic reactor plant.

149 Chittagong Steel Mill

1969. Pakistan's First Steel Mill, Chittagong.

270 **149** 15p. grey, blue and olive 10 10

150 "Family"

1969. Family Planning.

271 **150** 15p. purple and blue 10 10

151 Olympic Gold Medal and Hockey Player

1969. Olympic Hockey Champions.

272 **151** 15p. multicoloured 75 50

273 **151** 1r. multicoloured 2·25 1·00

152 Mirza Ghalib and Lines of Verse

1969. Death Centenary of Mirza Ghalib (poet).

274 **152** 15p. multicoloured 20 15

275 **152** 50p. multicoloured 50 15

The lines of verse on No. 275 are different from those in Type **152**.

153 Dacca Railway Station

1969. 1st Anniv of New Dacca Railway Station.

276 **153** 15p. multicoloured 30 10

154 I.L.O. Emblem and "1919–1969"

1969. 50th Anniv of I.L.O.

277 **154** 15p. buff and green 10 10

278 **154** 50p. brown and red 40 10

155 "Lady on Balcony" (18th-cent Mogul)

1969. 5th Anniv of Regional Co-operation for Development. Miniatures. Multicoloured.

279 20p. Type **155** 15 10

280 50p. "Kneeling Servant" (17th-cent Persian) 15 10

281 1r. "Suleiman the Magnificent holding Audience" (16th-cent Turkish) 20 10

158 Eastern Refinery, Chittagong

1969. 1st East Pakistan Oil Refinery.

282 **158** 20p. multicoloured 10 10

159 Children playing outside "School"

1969. Universal Children's Day.

283 **159** 20p. multicoloured 10 10

160 Japanese Doll and P.I.A. Air Routes

1969. Inauguration of P.I.A. Pearl Route, Dacca–Tokyo.

284 **160** 20p. multicoloured 40 10

285 **160** 50p. multicoloured 60 40

161 "Reflection of Light" Diagram

1969. Millenary Commemorative of Ibn-al-Haitham (physicist).

286 **161** 20p. black, yellow and blue 10 10

162 Vickers Vimy and Karachi Airport

1969. 50th Anniv of 1st England–Australia Flight.

287 **162** 50p. multicoloured 1·00 35

163 Flags, Sun Tower and Expo Site Plan

1970. "Expo-70" World Fair, Osaka.
288 **163** 50p. multicoloured 20 30

164 New U.P.U. H.Q. Building

1970. New U.P.U. Headquarters Building.
289 **164** 20p. multicoloured 15 10
290 **164** 50p. multicoloured 25 25

165 U.N. H.Q. Building

1970. 25th Anniv of United Nations. Mult.
291 20p. Type **165** 10 10
292 50p. U.N. emblem 15 20

167 I.E.Y. Emblem, Book and Pen

1970. International Education Year.
293 **167** 20p. multicoloured 10 10
294 **167** 50p. multicoloured 20 20

168 Saiful Malook Lake (Pakistan)

1970. 6th Anniv of Regional Co-operation for Development. Multicoloured.
295 20p. Type **168** 15 10
296 50p. Seeyo-Se-Pol Bridge, Esfahan (Iran) 20 10
297 1r. View from Fethiye (Turkey) 20 15

171 Asian Productivity Symbol

1970. Asian Productivity Year.
298 **171** 50p. multicoloured 20 20

172 Dr. Maria Montessori

1970. Birth Centenary of Dr. Maria Montessori (educationist).
299 **172** 20p. multicoloured 15 10
300 **172** 50p. multicoloured 15 30

173 Tractor and Fertilizer Factory

1970. 10th Near East F.A.O. Regional Conference, Islamabad.
301 **173** 20p. green and brown 15 50

174 Children and Open Book

1970. Universal Children's Day.
302 **174** 20p. multicoloured 15 10

175 Pakistan Flag and Text

1970. Elections for National Assembly.
303 **175** 20p. green and violet 15 10

1970. Elections for Provincial Assemblies. As No. 303 but inscr "PROVINCIAL ASSEMBLIES".
304 20p. green and red 15 10

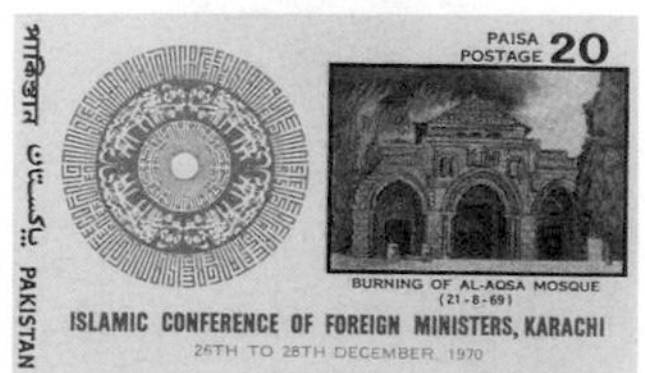

176 Conference Crest and burning Al-Aqsa Mosque

1970. Conference of Islamic Foreign Ministers, Karachi.
305 **176** 20p. multicoloured 15 15

177 Coastal Embankments

1971. East Pakistan Coastal Embankments Project.
306 **177** 20p. multicoloured 15 15

178 Emblem and United Peoples of the World

1971. Racial Equality Year.
307 **178** 20p. multicoloured 10 15
308 **178** 50p. multicoloured 20 45

179 Maple Leaf Cement Factory, Daudkhel

1971. 20th Anniv of Colombo Plan.
309 **179** 20p. brown, black & violet 10 10

180 Chaharbagh School (Iran)

1971. 7th Anniv of Regional Co-operation for Development. Multicoloured.
310 10p. Selimiye Mosque (Turkey) (horiz) 10 15
311 20p. Badshahi Mosque, Lahore (horiz) 20 25
312 50p. Type **180** 30 35

181 Electric Train and Boy with Toy Train

1971. Universal Children's Day.
313 **181** 20p. multicoloured 1·75 50

182 Horseman and Symbols

1971. 2500th Anniv of Persian Monarchy.
314 **182** 10p. multicoloured 25 30
315 **182** 20p. multicoloured 35 40
316 **182** 50p. multicoloured 50 75

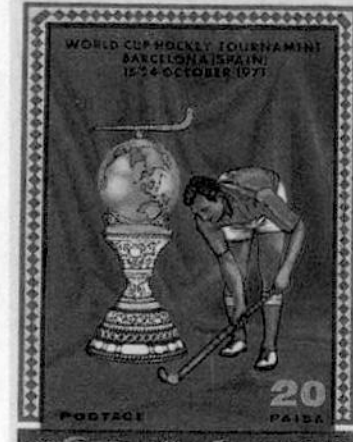

183 Hockey-player and Trophy

1971. World Cup Hockey Tournament, Barcelona.
317 **183** 20p. multicoloured 1·75 1·00

184 Great Bath, Moenjodaro

1971. 25th Anniv of UNESCO and Campaign to save the Moenjodaro Excavations.
318 **184** 20p. multicoloured 20 30

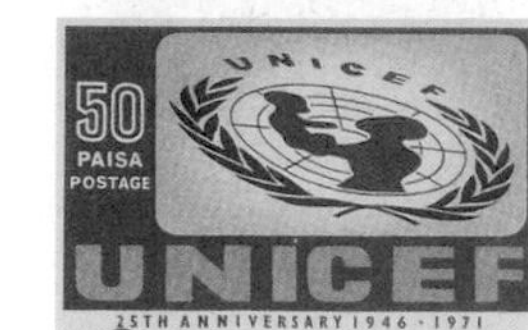

185 UNICEF Symbol

1971. 25th Anniv of UNICEF.
319 **185** 50p. multicoloured 30 60

186 King Hussein and Jordanian Flag

1971. 50th Anniv of Hashemite Kingdom of Jordan.
320 **186** 20p. multicoloured 15 20

187 Badge of Hockey Federation and Trophy

1971. Hockey Championships Victory.
321 **187** 20p. multicoloured 2·50 1·00

188 Reading Class

1972. International Book Year.
322 **188** 20p. multicoloured 20 40

189 View of Venice

1972. UNESCO Campaign to Save Venice.
323 **189** 20p. multicoloured 30 40

190 E.C.A.F.E. Emblem and Discs

1972. 25th Anniv of E.C.A.F.E.

324 **190** 20p. multicoloured 15 30

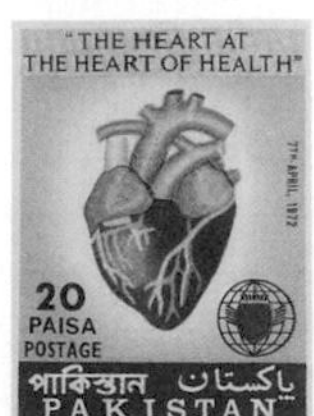

191 Human Heart

1972. World Health Day.

325 **191** 20p. multicoloured 20 30

192 "Only One Earth"

1972. U.N. Conference on the Human Environment, Stockholm.

326 **192** 20p. multicoloured 20 30

193 "Fisherman" (Cevat Dereli)

1972. 8th Anniv of Regional Co-operation for Development. Multicoloured.

327 10p. Type **193** 20 20
328 20p. "Iranian Woman" (Behzad) 35 25
329 50p. "Will and Power" (A. R. Chughtai) 55 70

194 Mohammed Ali Jinnah and Tower

1972. 25th Anniv of Independence. Mult.

330 10p. Type **194** 10 10
331 20p. "Land Reform" (74×23½) 20 30
332 20p. "Labour Reform" (74×23½) 20 30
333 20p. "Education Policy" (74×23½) 20 30
334 20p. "Health Policy" (74×23½) 20 30
335 60p. National Assembly Building (46×28 mm) 25 40

195 Donating Blood

1972. National Blood Transfusion Service.

336 **195** 20p. multicoloured 20 30

196 People and Squares

1972. Centenary of Population Census.

337 **196** 20p. multicoloured 20 20

197 Children from Slums

1972. Universal Children's Day.

338 **197** 20p. multicoloured 20 30

198 People and Open Book

1972. Education Week.

339 **198** 20p. multicoloured 20 30

199 Nuclear Power Plant

1972. Inauguration of Karachi Nuclear Power Plant.

340 **199** 20p. multicoloured 20 40

200 Copernicus in Observatory

1973. 500th Birth Anniv of Nicholas Copernicus (astronomer).

341 **200** 20p. multicoloured 20 30

201 Moenjodaro Excavations

1973. 50th Anniv of Moenjodaro Excavations.

342 **201** 20p. multicoloured 20 30

202 Elements of Meteorology

1973. Centenary of I.M.O./W.M.O.

343 **202** 20p. multicoloured 30 40

203 Prisoners-of-war

1973. Prisoners-of-war in India.

344 **203** 1r.25 multicoloured 1·75 2·50

204 National Assembly Building and Constitution Book

1973. Constitution Week.

345 **204** 20p. multicoloured 70 65

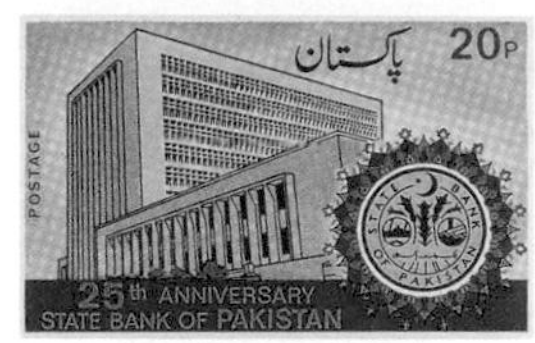

205 Badge and State Bank Building

1973. 25th Anniv of Pakistan State Bank.

346 **205** 20p. multicoloured 15 30
347 **205** 1r. multicoloured 30 50

206 Lut Desert Excavations (Iran)

1973. 9th Anniv of Regional Co-operation for Development. Multicoloured.

348 20p. Type **206** 30 20
349 60p. Main Street, Moenjodaro (Pakistan) 55 50
350 1r.25 Mausoleum of Antiochus I (Turkey) 75 1·25

207 Constitution Book and Flag

1973. Independence Day and Enforcement of the Constitution.

351 **207** 20p. multicoloured 15 30

208 Mohammed Ali Jinnah (Quaid-i-Azam)

1973. 25th Death Anniv of Mohammed Ali Jinnah.

352 **208** 20p. green, yellow & black 15 30

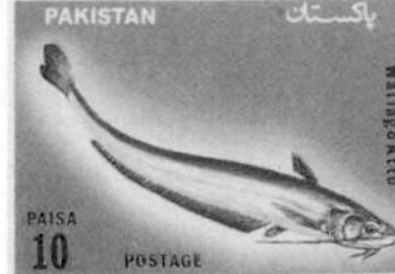

209 Wallago

1973. Fishes. Multicoloured.

353 10p. Type **209** 1·10 1·10
354 20p. Rohu 1·25 1·25
355 60p. Mozambique mouthbrooder 1·40 1·40
356 1r. Catla 1·40 1·40

210 Children's Education

1973. Universal Children's Day.

357 **210** 20p. multicoloured 15 40

211 Harvesting

1973. 10th Anniv of World Food Programme.

358 **211** 20p. multicoloured 60 40

212 Ankara and Kemal Ataturk

1973. 50th Anniv of Turkish Republic.

359 **212** 50p. multicoloured 45 35

213 Boy Scout

1973. National Silver Jubilee Jamboree.

360 **213** 20p. multicoloured 1·75 50

214 "Basic Necessities"

1973. 25th Anniv of Declaration of Human Rights.

361 **214** 20p. multicoloured 30 40

215 Al-Biruni and Nandana Hill

1973. Al-Biruni Millennium Congress.

362 **215** 20p. multicoloured 50 20
363 **215** 1r.25 multicoloured 1·25 90

216 Dr. Hansen, Microscope and Bacillus

1973. Centenary of Hansen's Discovery of Leprosy Bacillus.
364 **216** 20p. multicoloured 1·00 80

218 Conference Emblem

1974. World Population Year.
365 **217** 20p. multicoloured 10 10
366 **217** 1r.25 multicoloured 30 40

217 Family and Emblem

1974. Islamic Summit Conference, Lahore. Multicoloured.
367 20p. Type **218** 10 10
368 65p. Emblem on "Sun" (42×30 mm) 25 60
MS369 102×102 mm. Nos. 367/8. Imperf 1·50 4·75

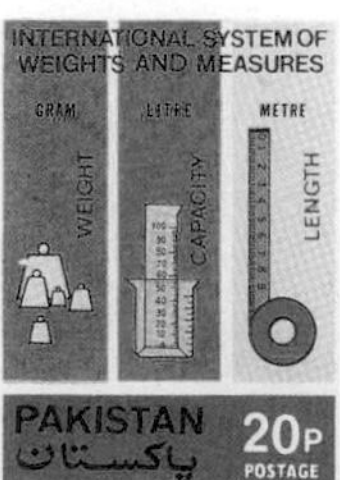

219 Units of Weight and Measurement

1974. Adoption of Int Weights and Measures System.
370 **219** 20p. multicoloured 15 25

220 "Chand Chauthai" Carpet, Pakistan

1974. 10th Anniversary of Regional Co-operation for Development. Multicoloured.
371 20p. Type **220** 20 15
372 60p. Persian carpet, 16th-century 40 55
373 1r.25 Anatolian carpet, 15th-century 65 1·25

221 Hands protecting Sapling

1974. Tree Planting Day.
374 **221** 20p. multicoloured 50 60

222 Torch and Map

1974. Namibia Day.
375 **222** 60p. multicoloured 50 80

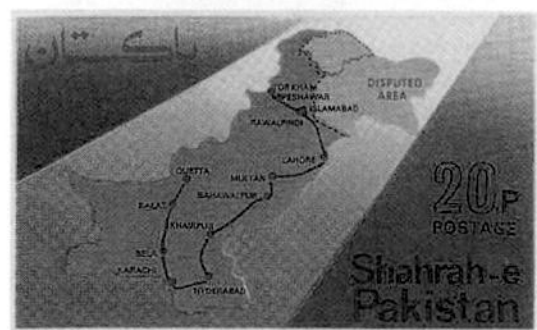

223 Highway Map

1974. Shahrah-e-Pakistan (Pakistan Highway).
376 **223** 20p. multicoloured 1·25 1·00

224 Boy at Desk

1974. Universal Children's Day.
377 **224** 20p. multicoloured 30 40

225 U.P.U. Emblem

1974. Centenary of U.P.U. Multicoloured.
378 20p. Type **225** 20 20
379 2r.25 U.P.U. emblem, Boeing 707 and mail-wagon (30×41 mm) 55 1·40
MS380 100×101 mm. Nos. 378/9. Imperf 1·25 5·00

226 Liaquat Ali Khan

1974. Liaquat Ali Khan (First Prime Minister of Pakistan).
381 **226** 20p. black and red 30 40

227 Dr. Mohammed Iqbal (poet and philosopher)

1974. Birth Centenary of Dr. Iqbal (1977) (1st issue).
382 **227** 20p. multicoloured 30 40
See also Nos. 399, 433 and 445/9.

228 Dr. Schweitzer and River Scene

1975. Birth Centenary of Dr. Albert Schweitzer.
383 **228** 2r.25 multicoloured 4·50 3·25

229 Tourism Year Symbol

1975. South East Asia Tourism Year.
384 **229** 2r.25 multicoloured 60 1·00

230 Assembly Hall, Flags and Prime Minister Bhutto

1975. 1st Anniv of Islamic Summit Conference, Lahore.
385 **230** 20p. multicoloured 35 35
386 **230** 1r. multicoloured 75 1·40

231 "Scientific Research"

1975. International Women's Year. Mult.
387 20p. Type **231** 25 25
388 2r.25 Girl teaching woman ("Adult Education") 1·25 2·00

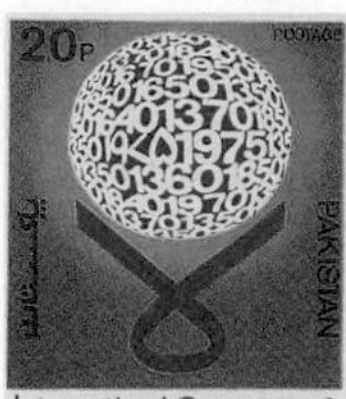

232 "Globe" and Algebraic Symbol

1975. International Congress of Mathematical Sciences, Karachi.
389 **232** 20p. multicoloured 50 60

233 Pakistani Camel-skin Vase

1975. 11th Anniv of Regional Co-operation for Development. Multicoloured.
390 20p. Type **233** 30 30
391 60p. Iranian tile (horiz) 60 1·00
392 1r.25 Turkish porcelain vase 90 1·50

234 Sapling and Dead Trees

1975. Tree Planting Year.
393 **234** 20p. multicoloured 35 70

235 Black Partridge

1975. Wildlife Protection (1st series).
394 **235** 20p. multicoloured 1·25 35
395 **235** 2r.25 multicoloured 4·00 4·75
See also Nos. 400/1, 411/12, 417/18, 493/6, 560, 572/3, 581/2, 599, 600, 605, 621/2, 691, 702, 752, 780/3, 853 and 1027.

236 "Today's Girls"

1975. Universal Children's Day.
396 **236** 20p. multicoloured 30 50

237 Hazrat Amir Khusrau, Sitar and Tabla (image scaled to 71% of original size)

1975. 700th Birth Anniv of Hazrat Amir Khusrau (poet and musician).
397 **237** 20p. multicoloured 20 50
398 **237** 2r.25 multicoloured 80 2·00

238 Dr. Mohammed Iqbal

1975. Birth Cent (1977) of Dr. Iqbal (2nd issue).

399	**238**	20p. multicoloured	30	50

239 Urial (wild sheep)

1975. Wildlife Protection (2nd series).

400	**239**	20p. multicoloured	30	30
401	**239**	3r. multicoloured	1·75	3·25

240 Moenjodaro Remains

1976. "Save Moenjodaro" (1st issue). Multicoloured.

402	10p. Type **240**	65	80
403	20p. Remains of houses	75	90
404	65p. The Citadel	75	90
405	3r. Well inside a house	75	90
406	4r. The "Great Bath"	85	1·00

See also Nos. 414 and 430.

241 Dome and Minaret of the Rauza-e-Mubarak

1976. International Congress on Seerat.

407	**241**	20p. multicoloured	15	20
408	**241**	3r. multicoloured	55	90

242 Alexander Graham Bell and Dial

1976. Telephone Centenary.

409	**242**	3r. multicoloured	1·25	2·00

243 College Arms within "Sun"

1976. Cent of National College of Arts, Lahore.

410	**243**	20p. multicoloured	30	50

244 Common Peafowl

1976. Wildlife Protection (3rd series).

411	**244**	20p. multicoloured	1·00	35
412	**244**	3r. multicoloured	3·50	4·50

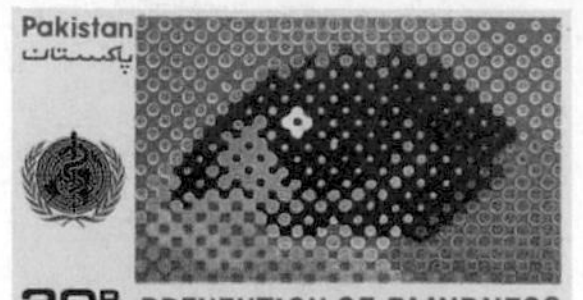

245 Human Eye

1976. Prevention of Blindness.

413	**245**	20p. multicoloured	1·00	70

246 Unicorn and Ruins

1976. "Save Moenjodaro" (2nd series).

414	**246**	20p. multicoloured	30	40

247 Jefferson Memorial

1976. Bicent of American Revolution. Mult.

415	90p. Type **247**	75	60
416	4r. "Declaration of Independence" (47×36 mm)	3·00	5·00

248 Ibex

1976. Wildlife Protection (4th series).

417	**248**	20p. multicoloured	30	35
418	**248**	3r. multicoloured	1·25	2·50

249 Mohammed Ali Jinnah

1976. 12th Anniv of Regional Co-operation for Development. Multicoloured.

419	20p. Type **249**	65	90
420	65p. Reza Shah the Great (Iran)	65	90
421	90p. Kemal Ataturk (Turkey)	65	90

250 Urdu Text

1976. Birth Cent of Mohammed Ali Jinnah (1st issue). (a) Type 250.

422	**250**	5p. black, blue and yellow	20	25
423	**250**	10p. black, yellow & pur	20	25
424	**250**	15p. black and blue	20	25
425	**250**	1r. black, yellow and blue	30	30

251 Mohammed Ali Jinnah and Wazir Mansion

(b) Type 251. Background Buildings given. Mult.

426	20p. Type **251**	20	25
427	40p. Sind Madressah	20	25
428	50p. Minar Qarardad-e-Pakistan	20	25
429	3r. Mausoleum	45	50

See also No. 436.

252 Dancing-girl, Ruins and King Priest (image scaled to 66% of original size)

1976. "Save Moenjodaro" (3rd series).

430	**252**	65p. multicoloured	35	80

253 U.N. Racial Discrimination Emblem

1976. U.N. Decade to Combat Racial Discrimination.

431	**253**	65p. multicoloured	30	60

254 Child in Maze and Basic Services

1976. Universal Children's Day.

432	**254**	20p. multicoloured	60	60

255 Verse from "Allama Iqbal"

1976. Birth Centenary (1977) of Dr. Iqbal (3rd issue).

433	**255**	20p. multicoloured	15	30

256 Mohammed Ali Jinnah giving Scout Salute

1976. Quaid-i-Azam Centenary Jamboree.

434	**256**	20p. multicoloured	1·00	60

257 Children Reading

1976. Children's Literature.

435	**257**	20p. multicoloured	65	65

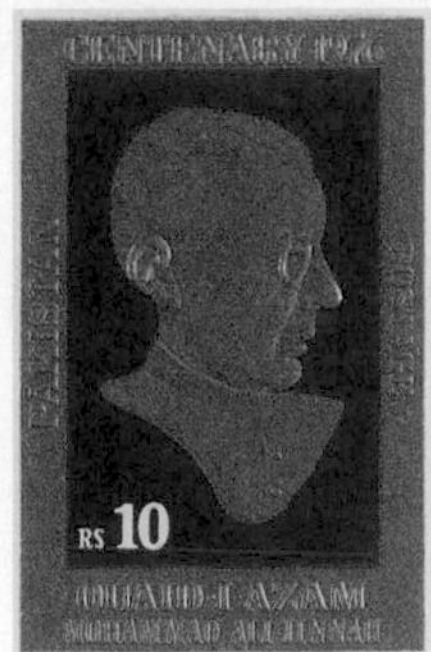

258 Mohammed Ali Jinnah

1976. Birth Centenary of Mohammed Ali Jinnah (2nd issue).

436	**258**	10r. green and gold	2·75	3·50

259 Rural Family

1977. Social Welfare and Rural Development Year.

437	**259**	20p. multicoloured	40	20

260 Turkish Vase, 1800 B.C.

1977. 13th Anniv of Regional Co-operation for Development.

438	**260**	20p. orange, blue & black	45	10
439	-	65p. multicoloured	65	40
440	-	90p. multicoloured	90	1·50

DESIGNS: 60p. Pakistani toy bullock cart from Moenjodaro; 90p. Pitcher with spout from Sialk Hill, Iran.

261 Forest

1977. National Tree Plantation Campaign.

441	**261**	20p. multicoloured	20	30

262 Desert Scene

1977. U.N. Conference on Desertification, Nairobi.

442	**262**	65p. multicoloured	1·25	45

263 "Water for Children of the World"

1977. Universal Children's Day.

443	**263**	50p. multicoloured	40	30

264 Aga Khan III

1977. Birth Centenary of Aga Khan III.

444	**264**	2r. multicoloured	55	1·00

265 Iqbal and Spirit of the Poet Roomi (from painting by Behzad)

1977. Birth Centenary of Dr. Mohammed Iqbal (4th issue). Multicoloured.

445	20p. Type **265**	60	70
446	65p. Iqbal looking at Jamalud-din Afghani and Saeed Haleem Pasha at prayer (Behzad)	60	70
447	1r.25 Urdu verse	65	75
448	2r.25 Persian verse	70	85
449	3r. Iqbal	75	95

266 The Holy "Khana-Kaaba" (House of God, Mecca)

1977. Haj (pilgrimage to Mecca).

450	**266**	65p. multicoloured	30	30

267 Rheumatic Patient and Healthy Man

1977. World Rheumatism Year.

451	**267**	65p. blue, black and yellow	30	20

268 Woman in Costume of Rawalpindi-Islamabad

1978. Indonesia–Pakistan Economic and Cultural Co-operation Organization.

452	**268**	75p. multicoloured	30	20

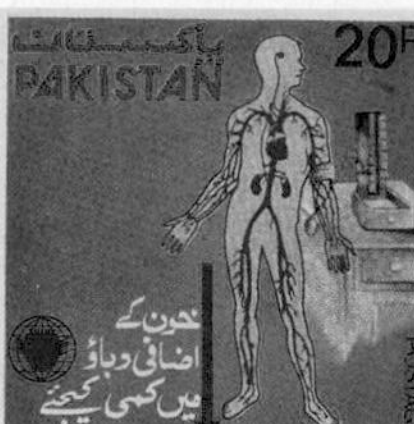

269 Human Body and Sphygmomanometer

1978. World Hypertension Month.

453	**269**	20p. multicoloured	25	10
454	-	2r. multicoloured	75	90

The 2r. value is as Type **269** but has the words "Down with high blood pressure" instead of the Urdu inscription at bottom left.

270 Henri Dunant

1978. 150th Birth Anniv of Henri Dunant (founder of the Red Cross).

455	**270**	1r. multicoloured	1·00	20

271 Red Roses (Pakistan)

1978. 14th Anniv of Regional Co-operation for Development. Roses. Multicoloured.

456	20p. Type **271**	35	25
457	90p. Pink roses (Iran)	50	35
458	2r. Yellow rose (Turkey)	75	50

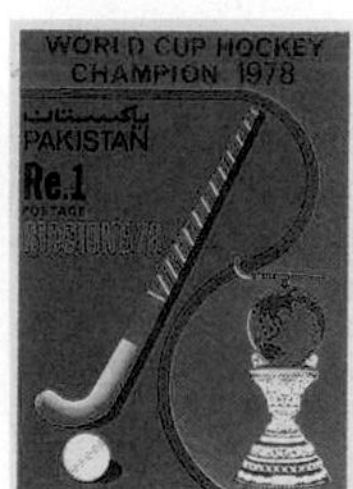

272 "Pakistan, World Cup Hockey Champions"

1978. "Riccione '78" International Stamp Fair. Multicoloured.

459	1r. Type **272**	1·25	25
460	2r. Fountain at Piazza Turismo	50	35

273 Cogwheels within Globe Symbol

1978. U.N. Technical Co-operation amongst Developing Countries Conference.

461	**273**	75p. multicoloured	25	20

274 St. Patrick's Cathedral, Karachi

1978. Centenary of St. Patrick's Cathedral, Karachi. Multicoloured.

462	1r. Type **274**	15	10
463	2r. Stained glass window	30	30

275 Minar-i-Qarardad-e-Pakistan

1978

464	**275**	2p. green	10	10
465	**275**	3p. black	10	10
466	**275**	5p. blue	10	10
467	-	10p. blue and turquoise	10	10
468	-	20p. green	60	10
469	-	25p. green and mauve	1·25	10
470	-	40p. blue and mauve	10	10
471	-	50p. lilac and green	30	10
472	-	60p. black	10	10
473b	-	75p. red	1·75	10
474	-	90p. mauve and blue	30	10
475	-	1r. green	60	10
476	-	1r.50 orange	20	10
477	-	2r. red	20	10
478	-	3r. blue	20	10
479	-	4r. black	20	10
480	-	5r. brown	20	10

DESIGNS—HORIZ (25×20 mm): 10p. to 90p. Tractor. VERT (21×25 mm): 1r. to 5r. Mausoleum of Ibrahim Khan Makli, Thatta.

277 Emblem and "United Races" Symbol

1978. International Anti-Apartheid Year.

481	**277**	1r. multicoloured	15	15

278 Maulana Mohammad Ali Jauhar

1978. Birth Centenary of Maulana Mohammad Ali Jauhar (patriot).

482	**278**	50p. multicoloured	50	20

279 Panavia MRCA Tornado, De Havilland Dragon Rapide and Wright Flyer I

1978. 75th Anniv of Powered Flight. Mult.

483	65p. Type **279**	1·00	1·75
484	1r. McDonnell Douglas Phantom II, Lockheed Tristar 500 and Wright Flyer I	1·10	1·75
485	2r. North American X-15, Tupolev Tu-104 and Wright Flyer I	1·25	2·00
486	2r.25 Mikoyan Gurevich MiG-15, Concorde and Wright Flyer I	1·25	2·25

280 "Holy Koran illuminating Globe" and Raudha-e-Mubarak (mausoleum)

1979. "12th Rabi-ul-Awwal" (Prophet Mohammed's birthday).

487	**280**	20p. multicoloured	40	15

281 "Aspects of A.P.W.A."

1979. 30th Anniv of A.P.W.A. (All Pakistan Women's Association).

488	**281**	50p. multicoloured	75	15

282 Tippu Sultan Shaheed of Mysore

1979. Pioneers of Freedom (1st series). Multicoloured.

490	10r. Type **282**	75	1·60
491	15r. Sir Syed Ahmad Khan	1·00	2·25
492	25r. Altaf Hussain Hali	1·50	2·25

See also Nos. 757, 801/27, 838/46, 870/2, 904/6, 921/8, 961/2, 1007, 1019/20 and 1075/7.

283 Himalayan Monal Pheasant

1979. Wildlife Protection (5th series). Pheasants. Multicoloured.

493	20p. Type **283**	1·25	60
494	25p. Kalij pheasant	1·25	80
495	40p. Koklass pheasant	1·60	1·75
496	1r. Cheer pheasant	3·00	2·00

284 "Pakistan Village Scene" (Ustad Bakhsh)

1979. 15th Anniv of Regional Co-operation for Development. Multicoloured.

497	40p. Type **284**	20	25
498	75p. "Iranian Goldsmith" (Kamal al Molk)	20	25
499	1r.60 "Turkish Harvest" (Namik Ismail)	25	30

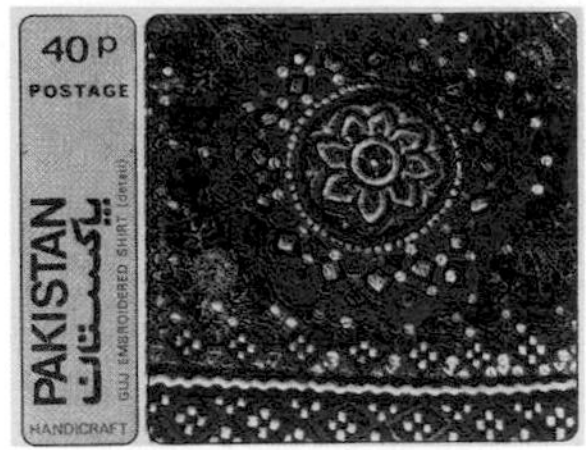

285 Guj Embroidered Shirt (detail)

1979. Handicrafts (1st series). Multicoloured.

500	40p. Type **285**	20	20
501	1r. Enamel inlaid brass plate	25	25
502	1r.50 Baskets	30	30
503	2r. Chain-stitch embroidered rug (detail)	40	40

See also Nos. 578/9, 595/6 and 625/8.

286 Children playing on Climbing-frame

1979. S.O.S. Children's Village, Lahore.

504	**286**	50p. multicoloured	40	40

287 "Island" (Z. Maloof)

1979. International Year of the Child. Children's Paintings. Multicoloured.

505	40p. Type **287**	15	15
506	75p. "Playground" (R. Akbar)	25	25
507	1r. "Fairground" (M. Azam)	25	25
508	1r.50 "Hockey Match" (M. Tayyab)	30	30
MS509	79×64 mm. 2r. "Child looking at Faces in the Sky" (M. Mumtaz) (vert). Imperf	1·00	2·00

288 Warrior attacking Crab

1979. "Fight Against Cancer".

510	**288**	40p. black, yellow and purple	70	70

289 Pakistan Customs Emblem

1979. Centenary of Pakistan Customs Service.

511	**289**	1r. multicoloured	30	30

290 Boeing 747-200 and Douglas DC-3 Airliners

1980. 25th Anniv of Pakistan International Air Lines.

512	**290**	1r. multicoloured	1·75	90

291 Islamic Pattern

1980

513	**291**	10p. green and yellow	10	10
514	**291**	15p. deep green and green	20	10
515	**291**	25p. violet and red	30	50
516	**291**	35p. red and green	40	1·00
517	-	40p. red and brown	40	10
518	-	50p. violet and green	40	50
519	-	80p. green and black	60	50

The 40 to 80p. values also show different Islamic patterns, the 40p. being horizontal and the remainder vertical.

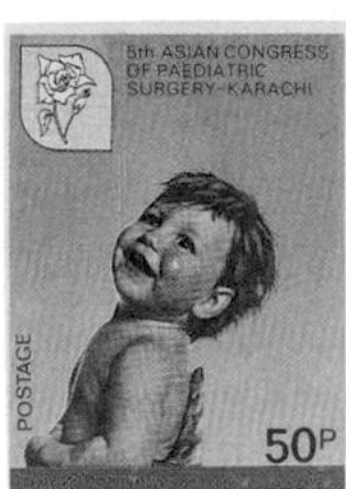

292 Young Child

1980. 5th Asian Congress of Paediatric Surgery, Karachi.

530	**292**	50p. multicoloured	75	1·50

293 Conference Emblem

1980. 11th Islamic Conference of Foreign Ministers, Islamabad.

531	**293**	1r. multicoloured	1·25	75

294 Karachi Port (image scaled to 71% of original size)

1980. Centenary of Karachi Port Authority.

532	**294**	1r. multicoloured	1·75	2·00

1980. "Riccione 80" International Stamp Exhibition. Nos. 505/8 optd RICCIONE 80.

533	**287**	40p. multicoloured	30	80
534	-	75p. multicoloured	40	90
535	-	1r. multicoloured	45	90
536	-	1r.50 multicoloured	60	1·10

296 College Emblem with Old and New Buildings

1980. 75th Anniv of Command and Staff College, Quetta.

537	**296**	1r. multicoloured	20	15

1980. World Tourism Conference, Manila. No. 496 optd WORLD TOURISM CONFERENCE MANILA 80.

538	1r. Cheer pheasant	1·25	40

298 Birth Centenary Emblem

1980. Birth Cent of Hafiz Mahmood Shairani.

539	**298**	40p. multicoloured	30	1·00

299 Shalimar Gardens, Lahore

1980. Aga Khan Award for Architecture.

540	**299**	2r. multicoloured	40	1·75

300 Rising Sun

1980. 1400th Anniv of Hegira (1st issue). Multicoloured.

541	40p. Type **300**	15	10
542	2r. Ka'aba and symbols of Moslem achievement (33×33 mm)	40	45
543	3r. Holy Koran illuminating the World (30×54 mm)	55	80
MS544	106×84 mm. 4r. Candles. Imperf	60	1·00

See also No. 549.

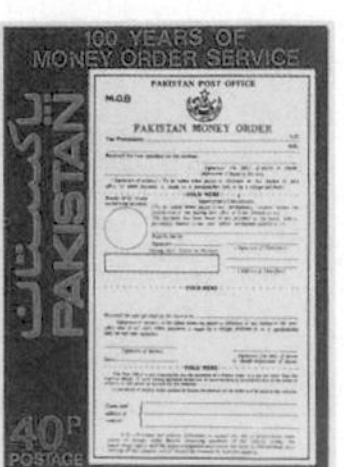

301 Money Order Form

1980. Centenary of Money Order Service.

545	**301**	40p. multicoloured	20	60

302 Postcards encircling Globe

1980. Centenary of Postcard Service.

546	**302**	40p. multicoloured	20	60

303 Heinrich von Stephan and U.P.U. Emblem

1981. 150th Birth Anniv of Heinrich von Stephan (U.P.U. founder).

547	**303**	1r. multicoloured	30	20

304 Aircraft and Airmail Letters

1981. 50th Anniv of Airmail Service.

548	**304**	1r. multicoloured	75	20

305 Mecca

1981. 1400th Anniv of Hegira (2nd issue).

549	**305**	40p. multicoloured	20	60

306 Conference Emblem and Afghan Refugees

1981. Islamic Summit Conference (1st issue). Multicoloured.

550	40p. Type **306**	30	15
551	40p. Conference emblem encircled by flags and Afghan refugees (28×58 mm)	30	15
552	1r. Type **306**	50	15
553	1r. As No. 551	50	15
554	2r. Conference emblem and map showing Afghanistan (48×32 mm)	65	50

307 Conference Emblem

1981. Islamic Summit Conference (2nd issue). Multicoloured.

555	40p. Type **307**	15	15
556	40p. Conference emblem and flags (28×46 mm)	15	15
557	85p. Type **307**	20	40
558	85p. As No. 556	20	40

308 Kemal Ataturk

1981. Birth Centenary of Kemal Ataturk (Turkish statesman).

559	**308**	1r. multicoloured	50	15

309 Green Turtle

1981. Wildlife Protection (6th series).

560	**309**	40p. multicoloured	1·25	40

310 Dome of the Rock

1981. Palestinian Welfare.

561	**310**	2r. multicoloured	1·25	60

311 Malubiting West

1981. Mountain Peaks (1st series). Karakoram Range. Multicoloured.

562	40p. Type **311**	40	40
563	40p. Malubiting West (24×31 mm)	40	40
564	1r. Haramosh	55	75
565	1r. Haramosh (24×31 mm)	55	75
566	1r.50 K6	70	1·00
567	1r.50 K6 (24×31 mm)	70	1·00
568	2r. K2, Broad Peak, Gasherbrum 4 and Gasherbrum 2	70	1·40
569	2r. K2 (24×31 mm)	70	1·40

See also Nos. 674/5.

312 Pakistan Steel "Furnace No. 1"

1981. 1st Firing of Pakistan Steel "Furnace No. 1", Karachi.

570	**312**	40p. multicoloured	20	10
571	**312**	2r. multicoloured	60	1·75

313 Western Tragopan

1981. Wildlife Protection (7th series).

572	**313**	40p. multicoloured	2·25	75
573	-	2r. multicoloured	4·25	4·25

DESIGN: 2r. As Type **313** but with background showing a winter view.

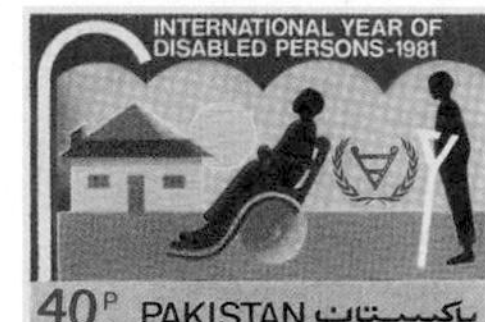

314 Disabled People and I.Y.D.P. Emblem

1981. International Year for Disabled Persons.

574	**314**	40p. multicoloured	30	50
575	**314**	2r. multicoloured	1·10	1·75

315 World Hockey Cup below Flags of participating Countries

1982. Pakistan—World Cup Hockey Champions. Multicoloured.

576	1r. Type **315**	2·00	1·50
577	1r. World Hockey Cup above flags of participating countries	2·00	1·50

316 Camel Skin Lamp

1982. Handicrafts (2nd series). Multicoloured.

578	1r. Type **316**	70	80
579	1r. Hala pottery	70	80

See also Nos. 595/6.

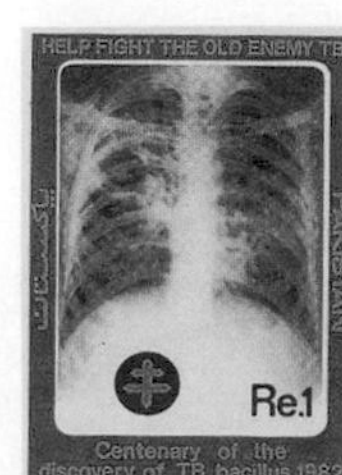

317 Chest X-Ray of Infected Person

1982. Centenary of Robert Koch's Discovery of Tubercle Bacillus.

580	**317**	1r. multicoloured	1·25	1·50

318 Indus Dolphin

1982. Wildlife Protection (8th series).

581	**318**	40p. multicoloured	1·50	1·50
582	-	1r. multicoloured	3·00	2·50

DESIGN: 1r. As Type **318** but with design reversed.

319 "Apollo–Soyuz" Link-up, 1975

1982. Peaceful Use of Outer Space.

583	**319**	1r. multicoloured	2·00	1·25

320 Sukkur Barrage

1982. 50th Anniv of Sukkur Barrage.

584	**320**	1r. multicoloured	30	30

321 Pakistan National Flag and Stylized Sun

1982. Independence Day. Multicoloured.

585	40p. Type **321**	20	30
586	85p. Map of Pakistan and stylized torch	45	1·25

1982. "Riccione '82" Stamp Exhibition. No. 584 optd RICCIONE-82.

587	1r. multicoloured	20	20

323 Arabic Inscription and University Emblem

1982. Centenary of the Punjab University.

588	**323**	40p. multicoloured	1·25	1·00

324 Scout Emblem and Tents

1983. 75th Anniv of Boy Scout Movement.

589	**324**	2r. multicoloured	50	50

325 Laying Pipeline

1983. Inaug of Quetta Natural Gas Pipeline Project.

590	**325**	1r. multicoloured	30	30

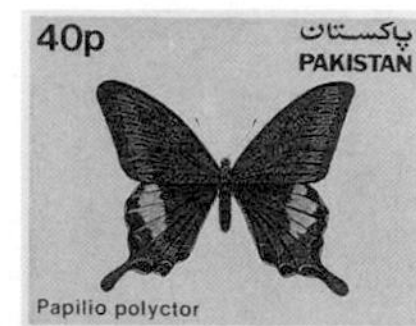

326 "Papilio polyctor"

1983. Butterflies. Multicoloured.

591	40p. Type **326**	1·25	20
592	50p. "Atrophaneura aristolochiae"	1·50	20
593	60p. "Danaus chrysippus"	1·75	60
594	1r.50 "Papilio demoleus"	2·50	2·25

1983. Handicrafts (3rd series). As T 316. Multicoloured.

595	1r. Five flower motif needle-work, Sind	15	15
596	1r. Straw mats	15	15

327 School of Nursing and University Emblem

1983. Presentation of Charter to Aga Khan University, Karachi.

597	**327**	2r. multicoloured	1·75	2·00

328 Yak Caravan crossing Zindiharam-Darkot Pass, Hindu Kush

1983. Trekking in Pakistan.

598	**328**	1r. multicoloured	1·50	1·50

329 Marsh Crocodile

1983. Wildlife Protection (9th series).

599	**329**	3r. multicoloured	3·50	2·00

330 Goitred Gazelle

1983. Wildlife Protection (10th series).

600	**330**	1r. multicoloured	2·50	2·00

331 Floral Design

1983. 36th Anniv of Independence. Mult.

601 60p. Type **331** 10 10
602 4r. Hand holding flaming torch 40 45

332 Traditional Weaving, Pakistan

1983. Indonesian–Pakistan Economic and Cultural Co-operation Organization, 1969–1983. Mult.

603 2r. Type **332** 20 25
604 2r. Traditional weaving, Indonesia 20 25

333 "Siberian Cranes" (Great White Cranes) (Sir Peter Scott)

1983. Wildlife Protection (11th series).

605 **333** 3r. multicoloured 3·75 3·25

334 W.C.Y. Emblem

1983. World Communications Year. Multicoloured.

606 2r. Type **334** 20 25
607 3r. W.C.Y. emblem (different) (33×33 mm) 30 35

335 Farm Animals

1983. World Food Day. Multicoloured.

608 3r. Type **335** 1·50 1·75
609 3r. Fruit 1·50 1·75
610 3r. Crops 1·50 1·75
611 3r. Sea food 1·50 1·75

336 Agriculture Produce and Fertilizer Factory

1983. National Fertilizer Corporation.

612 **336** 60p. multicoloured 20 30

337 Lahore, 1852

1983. National Stamp Exn, Lahore. Mult.

613 60p. Musti Durwaza Dharmsala 60 75
614 60p. Khabgha 60 75
615 60p. Type **337** 60 75
616 60p. Summan Burj Hazuri 60 75
617 60p. Flower Garden, Samadhi Northern Gate 60 75
618 60p. Budda Darya, Badshahi Masjid 60 75

338 Winner of "Enterprise" Event

1983. Yachting Champions, Asian Games, Delhi. Multicoloured.

619 60p. Type **338** 1·75 1·75
620 60p. Winner of "OK" Dinghy event 1·75 1·75

339 Snow Leopard

1984. Wildlife Protection (12th series).

621 **339** 40p. multicoloured 1·75 90
622 **339** 1r.60 multicoloured 4·75 6·00

340 Jahangir Khan (World Squash Champion)

1984. Squash.

623 **340** 3r. multicoloured 2·25 1·75

341 P.I.A. Boeing 707 Airliner

1984. 20th Anniv of Pakistan International Airways Service to China.

624 **341** 3r. multicoloured 5·00 5·50

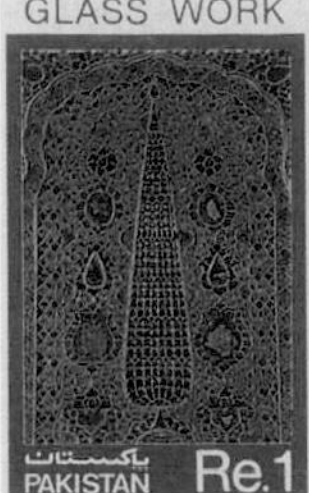

342 Glass-work

1984. Handicrafts (4th series). Multicoloured, frame colours given.

625 **342** 1r. blue 30 20
626 - 1r. red 30 20
627 - 1r. green 30 20
628 - 1r. violet 30 20

DESIGNS: showing glass-work in Sheesh Mahal, Lahore Fort. Nos. 627/8 are horizontal designs.

343 Attock Fort

1984. Forts.

629 5p. black and purple 40 60
630 10p. black and red 40 10
631 15p. violet and brown 75 10
632 **343** 20p. black and violet 1·50 10
633 - 50p. brown and red 1·50 10
634 - 60p. light brown & brown 1·25 10
635 - 70p. blue 1·50 10
636 - 80p. brown and red 1·50 10

DESIGNS: 5p. Kot Diji Fort; 10p. Rohtas Fort; 15p. Bala Hissar Fort; 50p. Hyderabad Fort; 60p. Lahore Fort; 70p. Sibi Fort; 80p. Ranikot Fort.

344 Shah Rukn i Alam's Tomb, Multan

1984. Aga Khan Award for Architecture.

647 **344** 60p. multicoloured 2·50 2·75

345 Radio Mast and Map of World

1984. 20th Anniv of Asia–Pacific Broadcasting Union.

648 **345** 3r. multicoloured 1·00 60

346 Wrestling

1984. Olympic Games, Los Angeles. Mult.

649 3r. Type **346** 1·25 1·50
650 3r. Boxing 1·25 1·50
651 3r. Athletics 1·25 1·50
652 3r. Hockey 1·25 1·50
653 3r. Yachting 1·25 1·50

347 Jasmine (National flower) and Inscription

1984. Independence Day. Multicoloured.

654 60p. Type **347** 10 10
655 4r. Symbolic torch 45 50

348 Gearwheel Emblem and Flags of Participating Nations

1984. Pakistan International Trade Fair.

656 **348** 60p. multicoloured 1·00 30

349 Interior of Main Dome

1984. Tourism Convention, Shahjahan Mosque, Thatta. Multicoloured.

657 1r. Type **349** 50 60
658 1r. Brick and glazed tile work 50 60
659 1r. Gateway 50 60
660 1r. Symmetrical archways 50 60
661 1r. Interior of a dome 50 60

350 Bank Emblem in Floral Pattern

1984. 25th Anniv of United Bank Ltd.

662 **350** 60p. multicoloured 1·00 1·00

351 Conference Emblem

1984. 20th United Nations Conference of Trade and Development.

663 **351** 60p. multicoloured 80 40

352 Postal Life Insurance Emblem within Hands

1984. Centenary of Postal Life Insurance. Multicoloured.

664 60p. Type **352** 70 15
665 1r. "100" and Postal Life Insurance emblem 90 15

353 Bull (wall painting)

1984. UNESCO Save Moenjadoro Campaign. Multicoloured.

666		2r. Type **353**	1·40	1·00
667		2r. Bull (seal)	1·40	1·00

354 International Youth Year Emblem and "75"

1985. 75th Anniv of Girl Guide Movement.

668	**354**	60p. multicoloured	3·25	1·50

355 Smelting Ore

1985. Inauguration of Pakistan Steel Corporation. Multicoloured.

669		60p. Type **355**	65	25
670		1r. Pouring molten steel from ladle (28×46 mm)	1·10	25

356 Map of Pakistan and Rays of Sun

1985. Presidential Referendum of 19 December 1984.

671	**356**	60p. multicoloured	1·75	55

357 Ballot Box and Voting Paper

1985. March Elections. Multicoloured.

672		1r. Type **357**	65	15
673		1r. Minar-e-Qarardad-e-Pakistan Tower, and word "Democracy" (31×43 mm)	65	15

1985. Mountain Peaks (2nd series). As T 311. Multicoloured.

674		40p. Rakaposhi (Karakoram Range)	1·75	75
675		2r. Nangaparbat (Western Himalayas)	3·75	6·00

358 Trophy and Medals from Olympic Games 1984, Asia Cup 1985 and World Cup 1982

1985. Pakistan Hockey Team "Grand Slam" Success.

676	**358**	1r. multicoloured	2·50	2·25

359 King Edward Medical College

1985. 125th Anniv of King Edward Medical College, Lahore.

677	**359**	3r. multicoloured	1·75	1·00

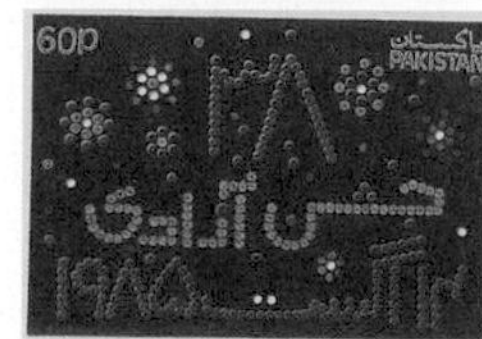

360 Illuminated Inscription in Urdu

1985. Independence Day. Multicoloured.

678		60p. Type **360**	65	1·00
679		60p. Illuminated "XXXVIII" (inscr in English)	65	1·00

361 Sind Madressah-tul-Islam, Karachi

1985. Centenary of Sind Madressah-tul-Islam (theological college), Karachi.

680	**361**	2r. multicoloured	1·75	1·00

362 Jamia Masjid Mosque by Day

1985. Inauguration of New Jamia Masjid Mosque, Karachi. Multicoloured.

681		1r. Type **362**	90	50
682		1r. Jamia Masjid illuminated at night	90	50

363 Lawrence College, Murree

1985. 125th Anniv of Lawrence College, Murree.

683	**363**	3r. multicoloured	2·50	2·25

364 United Nations Building, New York

1985. 40th Anniv of United Nations Organization. Multicoloured.

684		1r. Type **364**	30	15
685		2r. U.N. Building and emblem	40	60

365 Tents and Jamboree Emblem

1985. 10th National Scout Jamboree.

686	**365**	60p. multicoloured	2·25	2·50

366 Islamabad

1985. 25th Anniv of Islamabad.

687	**366**	3r. multicoloured	2·50	1·00

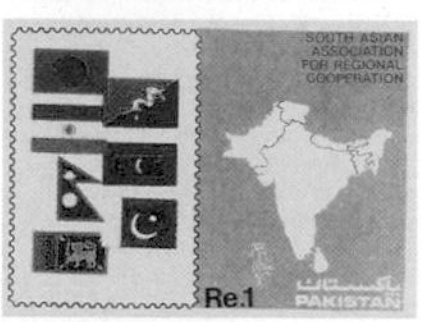

367 Map of S.A.A.R.C. Countries and National Flags

1985. 1st Summit Meeting of South Asian Association for Regional Co-operation, Dhaka, Bangladesh. Multicoloured.

688		1r. Type **367**	1·50	4·00
689		2r. National flags (39×39 mm)	75	2·00

368 Globe and Peace Dove

1985. 25th Anniv of U.N. General Assembly's Declaration on Independence for Colonial Territories.

690	**368**	60p. multicoloured	1·00	60

369 Peregrine Falcon

1986. Wildlife Protection (13th series). Peregrine Falcon.

691	**369**	1r.50 multicoloured	4·25	4·25

370 A.D.B.P. Building, Islamabad

1986. 25th Anniv of Agricultural Development Bank of Pakistan.

692	**370**	60p. multicoloured	1·75	50

371 Government S.E. College

1986. Centenary of Government Sadiq Egerton College, Bahawalpur.

693	**371**	1r. multicoloured	2·75	50

372 Emblem and Bar Graph

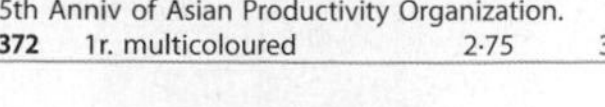

1986. 25th Anniv of Asian Productivity Organization.

694	**372**	1r. multicoloured	2·75	30

373 "1947 1986"

1986. 39th Anniv of Independence. Multicoloured.

695		80p. Type **373**	1·50	25
696		1r. Illuminated inscription in Urdu	1·50	25

374 Open Air Class

1986. International Literacy Day.

697	**374**	1r. multicoloured	1·75	30

375 Mother and Child

1986. UNICEF Child Survival Campaign.

698	**375**	80p. multicoloured	2·25	65

376 Aitchison College

1986. Centenary of Aitchison College, Lahore.

699	**376**	2r.50 multicoloured	2·50	1·25

377 Two Doves carrying Olive Branches

1986. International Peace Year.

700	**377**	4r. multicoloured	60	75

378 Table Tennis Players

1986. 4th Asian Cup Table Tennis Tournament, Karachi.

701	**378**	2r. multicoloured	2·00	1·00

379 Argali

1986. Wildlife Protection (14th series). Argali.

702	**379**	2r. multicoloured	3·00	3·00

380 Selimiye Mosque, Edirne, Turkey

1986. "Ecophilex '86" International Stamp Exhibition, Islamabad. Multicoloured.

703	3r. Type **380**	1·40	1·60
704	3r. Gawhar Shad Mosque, Mashhad, Iran	1·40	1·60
705	3r. Grand Mosque, Bhong, Pakistan	1·40	1·60

381 St. Patrick's School

1987. 125th Anniv of St. Patrick's School, Karachi.

706	**381**	5r. multicoloured	3·00	1·50

382 Mistletoe Flowerpecker and Defence Symbols

1987. Post Office Savings Bank Week. Multicoloured.

707	5r. Type **382**	1·10	1·25
708	5r. Spotted pardalote and laboratory apparatus	1·10	1·25
709	5r. Black-throated blue warbler and agriculture symbols	1·10	1·25
710	5r. Red-capped manakin and industrial skyline	1·10	1·25

383 New Parliament House, Islamabad

1987. Inauguration of New Parliament House, Islamabad.

711	**383**	3r. multicoloured	50	60

384 Opium Poppies and Flames

1987. Campaign Against Drug Abuse.

712	**384**	1r. multicoloured	75	30

385 Flag and National Anthem Score

1987. 40th Anniv of Independence. Mult.

713	80p. Type **385**	1·40	20
714	3r. Text of speech by Mohammed Ali Jinnah, Minar-e-Qardad-e-Pakistan Tower and arms	1·60	80

386 Hawker Tempest Mk II

1987. Air Force Day. Military Aircraft. Mult.

715	3r. Type **386**	1·50	1·50
716	3r. Hawker Fury	1·50	1·50
717	3r. Supermarine Attacker	1·50	1·50
718	3r. North American F-86 Sabre	1·50	1·50
719	3r. Lockheed F-104C Starfighter	1·50	1·50
720	3r. Lockheed C-130 Hercules	1·50	1·50
721	3r. Shenyang/Tianjin F-6	1·50	1·50
722	3r. Dassault Mirage III	1·50	1·50
723	3r. North American A-5A Vigilante	1·50	1·50
724	3r. General Dynamics F-16 Fighting Falcon	1·50	1·50

387 Pasu Glacier

1987. Pakistan Tourism Convention. Views along Karakoram Highway. Multicoloured.

725	1r.50 Type **387**	60	55
726	1r.50 Apricot trees	60	55
727	1r.50 Karakoram Highway	60	55
728	1r.50 View from Khunjerab Pass	60	55

388 Shah Abdul Latif Bhitai Mausoleum

1987. Shah Abdul Latif Bhitai (poet) Commem.

729	**388**	80p. multicoloured	30	30

389 D. J. Sind Science College, Karachi

1987. Centenary of D. J. Sind Science College, Karachi.

730	**389**	80p. multicoloured	20	20

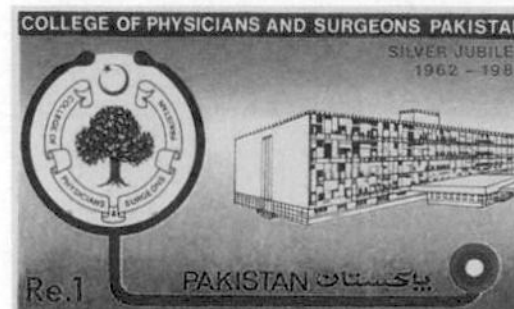

390 College Building

1987. 25th Anniv of College of Physicians and Surgeons.

731	**390**	1r. multicoloured	2·25	30

391 Homeless People, Houses and Rising Sun

1987. International Year of Shelter for the Homeless.

732	**391**	3r. multicoloured	50	50

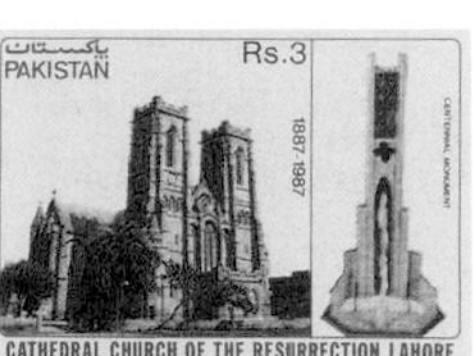

392 Cathedral Church of the Resurrection, Lahore

1987. Centenary of Cathedral Church of the Resurrection, Lahore.

733	**392**	3r. multicoloured	50	50

393 Honeycomb and Arms

1987. 40th Anniv of Pakistan Post Office.

734	**393**	3r. multicoloured	50	50

394 Corporation Emblem

1987. Radio Pakistan's New Programme Schedules.

735	**394**	80p. multicoloured	20	15

395 Jamshed Nusserwanjee Mehta and Karachi Municipal Corporation Building

1988. Birth Centenary (1986) of Jamshed Nusserwanjee Mehta (former President of Karachi Municipal Corporation).

736	**395**	3r. multicoloured	50	50

396 Leprosy Symbols within Flower

1988. World Leprosy Day.

737	**396**	3r. multicoloured	75	50

397 W.H.O. Building, Geneva

1988. 40th Anniv of W.H.O.

738	**397**	4r. multicoloured	60	50

398 Globe

1988. 125th Anniv of Int Red Cross and Crescent.

739	**398**	3r. multicoloured	50	50

399 Crescent, Leaf Pattern and Archway

1988. Independence Day.

740	**399**	80p. multicoloured	10	10
741	**399**	4r. multicoloured	45	50

400 Field Events

1988. Olympic Games, Seoul. Multicoloured.

742	10r. Type **400**	1·10	1·10
743	10r. Track events	1·10	1·10
744	10r. Jumping and pole vaulting	1·10	1·10
745	10r. Gymnastics	1·10	1·10
746	10r. Table tennis, tennis, hockey and baseball	1·10	1·10
747	10r. Volleyball, football, basket-ball and handball	1·10	1·10
748	10r. Wrestling, judo, boxing and weightlifting	1·10	1·10
749	10r. Shooting, fencing and archery	1·10	1·10
750	10r. Water sports	1·10	1·10
751	10r. Equestrian events and cycling	1·10	1·10

401 Markhor

1988. Wildlife Protection (15th series).

752	**401**	2r. multicoloured	65	50

402 Islamia College, Peshawar

1988. 75th Anniv of Islamia College, Peshawar.

753	**402**	3r. multicoloured	50	50

403 Symbols of Agriculture, Industry and Education with National Flags

1988. South Asian Association for Regional Co-operation 4th Summit Meeting, Islamabad. Multicoloured.

754	25r. Type **403**	1·50	1·50
755	50r. National flags on globe and symbols of communications (33×33 mm)	4·50	3·25
756	75r. Stamps from member countries (52×29 mm)	3·50	4·50

1989. Pioneers of Freedom (2nd series). As T 282. Multicoloured.

757	3r. Maulana Hasrat Mohani	45	45

404 Logo

1989. "Adasia 89" 16th Asian Advertising Congress, Lahore.

758	**404**	1r. multicoloured ("Pakistan" in yellow)	1·10	1·40
759	**404**	1r. multicoloured ("Pakistan" in blue)	1·10	1·40
760	**404**	1r. multicoloured ("Pakistan" in white)	1·10	1·40

405 Zulfikar Ali Bhutto

1989. 10th Death Anniv of Zulfikar Ali Bhutto (statesman). Multicoloured.

761	1r. Type **405**	40	10
762	2r. Zulfikar Ali Bhutto (different)	60	50

406 "Daphne" Class Submarine

1989. 25 Years of Pakistan Navy Submarine Operations. Multicoloured.

763	1r. Type **406**	1·50	1·75
764	1r. "Fleet Snorkel" class submarine	1·50	1·75
765	1r. "Agosta" class submarine	1·50	1·75

407 "The Oath of the Tennis Court" (David)

1989. Bicentenary of French Revolution.

766	**407**	7r. multicoloured	1·75	1·50

408 Pitcher, c. 2200 B.C.

1989. Archaeological Artefacts. Terracotta pottery from Baluchistan Province. Mult.

767	1r. Type **408**	30	30
768	1r. Jar, c. 2300 B.C.	30	30
769	1r. Vase, c. 3600 B.C.	30	30
770	1r. Jar, c. 2600 B.C.	30	30

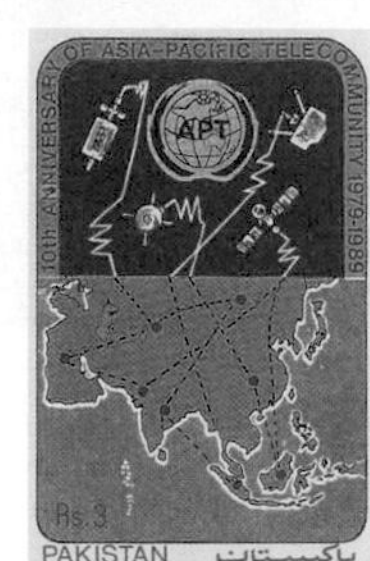

409 Satellites and Map of Asian Telecommunications Network

1989. 10th Anniv of Asia–Pacific Telecommunity.

771	**409**	3r. multicoloured	50	50

410 Container Ship at Wharf

1989. Construction of Integrated Container Terminal, Port Qasim.

772	**410**	6r. multicoloured	3·00	4·00

411 Mohammed Ali Jinnah

1989

773	**411**	1r. multicoloured	80	10
774	**411**	1r.50 multicoloured	90	50
775	**411**	2r. multicoloured	1·00	30
776	**411**	3r. multicoloured	1·25	50
777	**411**	4r. multicoloured	1·50	70
778	**411**	5r. multicoloured	1·50	70

412 Mausoleum of Shah Abdul Latif Bhitai

1989. 300th Birth Anniv of Shah Abdul Latif Bhitai (poet).

779	**412**	2r. multicoloured	1·00	70

413 Asiatic Black Bear

1989. Wildlife Protection (16th series). Asiatic Black Bear. Multicoloured.

780	4r. Type **413**	90	1·10
781	4r. Bear among boulders	90	1·10
782	4r. Standing on rock	90	1·10
783	4r. Sitting by trees	90	1·10

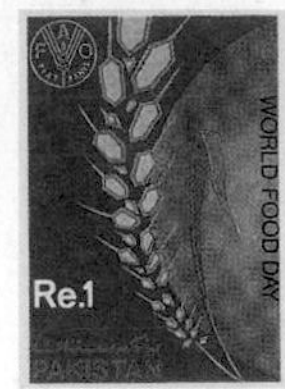

414 Ear of Wheat encircling Globe

1989. World Food Day.

784	**414**	1r. multicoloured	60	35

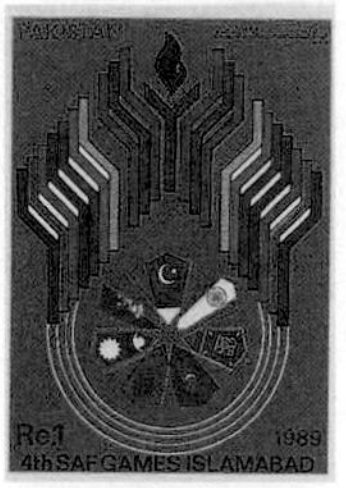

415 Games Emblem and Flags of Member Countries

1989. 4th South Asian Sports Federation Games, Islamabad.

785	**415**	1r. multicoloured	35	35

416 Patchwork Kamblee (cloth) entering Gate of Heaven

1989. 800th Birth Anniv of Baba Farid (Muslim spiritual leader).

786	**416**	3r. multicoloured	50	50

417 Pakistan Television Logo

1989. 25th Anniv of Television Broadcasting in Pakistan.

787	**417**	3r. multicoloured	50	50

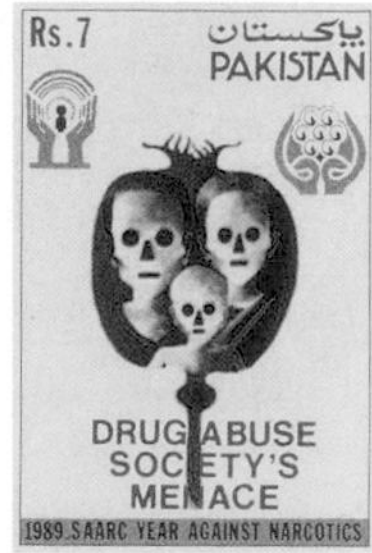

418 Family of Drug Addicts in Poppy Bud

1989. South Asian Association for Regional Co-operation Anti-Drugs Campaign.

788	**418**	7r. multicoloured	2·25	1·40

419 Murray College, Sialkot

1989. Centenary of Murray College, Sialkot.

789	**419**	6r. multicoloured	1·50	1·25

420 Government College, Lahore

1989. 125th Anniv of Government College, Lahore.

790	**420**	6r. multicoloured	1·00	1·25

421 Fields, Electricity Pylons and Rural Buildings

1989. 10th Anniv of Centre for Asia and Pacific Integrated Rural Development.

791	**421**	3r. multicoloured	1·00	75

422 Emblem and Islamic Patterns

1990. 20th Anniv of Organization of the Islamic Conference.

792	**422**	1r. multicoloured	1·75	40

423 Hockey Match

1990. 7th World Hockey Cup, Lahore.

793	**423**	2r. multicoloured	4·50	4·25

424 Mohammed Iqbal addressing Crowd and Liaquat Ali Khan taking Oath

1990. 50th Anniv of Passing of Pakistan Resolution. Multicoloured.

794	1r. Type **424**	1·00	1·25
795	1r. Maulana Mohammad Ali Jauhar and Mohammed Ali Jinnah with banner	1·00	1·25
796	1r. Women with Pakistan flag, and Mohammed Ali Jinnah taking Governor-General's oath, 1947	1·00	1·25
797	7r. Minar-i-Qarardad-e-Pakistan Monument and Resolution in Urdu and English (86×42 mm)	2·50	3·00

Nos. 794/6 were printed together, se-tenant, forming a composite design.

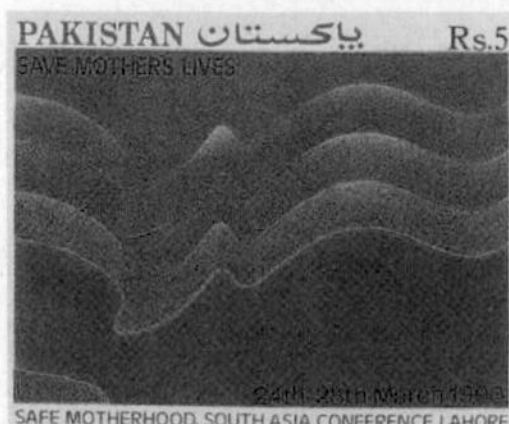

425 Pregnant Woman resting

1990. "Safe Motherhood" South Asia Conference, Lahore.
798 **425** 5r. multicoloured 1·00 1·25

426 "Decorated Verse by Ghalib" (Shakir Ali)

1990. Painters of Pakistan (1st series). Shakir Ali.
799 **426** 1r. multicoloured 2·25 1·25
See also Nos. 856/7.

427 Satellite in Night Sky

1990. Launch of "Badr I" Satellite.
800 **427** 3r. multicoloured 3·50 3·50

428 Allama Mohammed Iqbal

1990. Pioneers of Freedom (3rd series). Each brown and green.
801 1r. Type **428** 40 45
802 1r. Mohammed Ali Jinnah 40 45
803 1r. Sir Syed Ahmad Khan 40 45
804 1r. Nawab Salimullah 40 45
805 1r. Mohtarma Fatima Jinnah 40 45
806 1r. Aga Khan III 40 45
807 1r. Nawab Mohammad Ismail Khan 40 45
808 1r. Hussain Shaheed Suhrawardy 40 45
809 1r. Syed Ameer Ali 40 45
810 1r. Nawab Bahadur Yar Jung 40 45
811 1r. Khawaja Nazimuddin 40 45
812 1r. Maulana Obaidullah Sindhi 40 45
813 1r. Sahibzada Abdul Qaiyum Khan 40 45
814 1r. Begum Jahanara Shah Nawaz 40 45
815 1r. Sir Ghulam Hussain Hidayatullah 40 45
816 1r. Qazi Mohammad Isa 40 45
817 1r. Sir M. Shahnawaz Khan Mamdot 40 45
818 1r. Pir Sahib of Manki Sharif 40 45
819 1r. Liaquat Ali Khan 40 45
820 1r. Maulvi A. K. Fazl-ul-Haq 40 45
821 1r. Allama Shabbir Ahmad Usmani 40 45
822 1r. Sadar Abdur Rab Nishtar 40 45
823 1r. Bi Amma 40 45
824 1r. Sir Abdullah Haroon 40 45
825 1r. Chaudhry Rahmat Ali 40 45
826 1r. Raja Sahib of Mahmudabad 40 45
827 1r. Hassanally Effendi 40 45
See also Nos. 838/46, 870/2, 904/6, 921/8, 961/2, 1007, 1019/20 and 1075/7.

429 Cultural Aspects of Indonesia and Pakistan

1990. Indonesia–Pakistan Economic and Cultural Co-operation Organization.
828 **429** 7r. multicoloured 3·50 3·50

430 Globe, Open Book and Pen

1990. International Literacy Year.
829 **430** 3r. multicoloured 1·00 1·50

431 College Crests

1990. Joint Meeting between Royal College of Physicians, Edinburgh, and College of Physicians and Surgeons, Pakistan.
830 **431** 2r. multicoloured 60 75

432 Children and Globe

1990. U.N. World Summit for Children, New York.
831 **432** 7r. multicoloured 75 1·25

433 Girl within Members' Flags

1990. South Asian Association for Regional Co-operation Year of Girl Child.
832 **433** 2r. multicoloured 70 75

434 Paper passing over Rollers

1990. 25th Anniv of Security Papers Limited.
833 **434** 3r. multicoloured 4·50 2·50

435 Civil Defence Worker protecting Islamabad

1991. International Civil Defence Day.
834 **435** 7r. multicoloured 1·75 1·75

436 Logo and Flags of Member Countries

1991. South and West Asia Postal Union Commemoration.
835 **436** 5r. multicoloured 1·60 1·90

437 Globe and Figures

1991. World Population Day.
836 **437** 10r. multicoloured 1·90 2·50

438 Mentally Handicapped Athlete

1991. Pakistan Participation in Special Olympic Games.
837 **438** 7r. multicoloured 1·75 2·50

1991. Pioneers of Freedom (4th series). As T **428**. Each brown and green.
838 1r. Maulana Zafar Ali Khan 70 80
839 1r. Maulana Mohamed Ali Jauhar 70 80
840 1r. Chaudhry Khaliquzzaman 70 80
841 1r. Hameed Nizami 70 80
842 1r. Begum Ra'ana Liaquat Ali Khan 70 80
843 1r. Mirza Abol Hassan Ispahani 70 80
844 1r. Raja Ghazanfar Ali Khan 70 80
845 1r. Malik Barkat Ali 70 80
846 1r. Mir Jaffer Khan Jamali 70 80

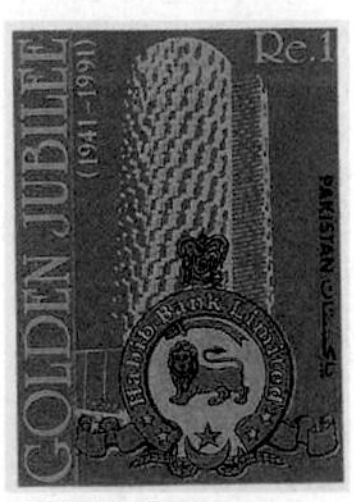

439 Habib Bank Headquarters and Emblem

1991. 50th Anniv of Habib Bank.
847 **439** 1r. multicoloured 1·25 25
848 **439** 5r. multicoloured 3·75 4·00

440 St. Joesph's Convent School

1991. 130th Anniv (1992) of St. Joesph's Convent School, Karachi.
849 **440** 5r. multicoloured 4·00 4·00

441 Emperor Sher Shah Suri

1991. Emperor Sher Shah Suri (founder of road network) Commemoration.
850 **441** 5r. multicoloured 2·25 2·50
MS851 92×80 mm. 7r. Emperor on horseback and portrait as Type **441**. Imperf 1·75 2·75

442 Jinnah Antarctic Research Station

1991. Pakistan Scientific Expedition to Antarctica.
852 **442** 7r. multicoloured 3·00 2·75

443 Houbara Bustard

1991. Wildlife Protection (17th series).
853 **443** 7r. multicoloured 2·50 2·75

444 Mosque

1991. 300th Death Anniv of Hazrat Sultan Bahoo.
854 **444** 7r. multicoloured 2·25 3·00

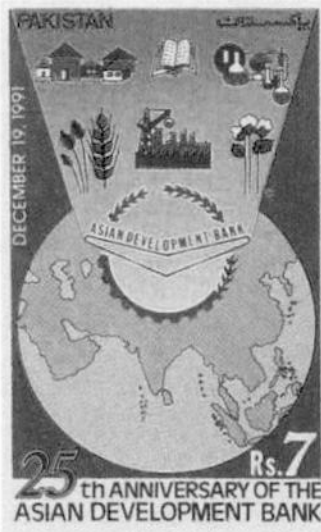

445 Development Symbols and Map of Asia

1991. 25th Anniv of Asian Development Bank.
855 **445** 7r. multicoloured 3·25 3·25

1991. Painters of Pakistan (2nd series). As T **426**. Multicoloured.
856 1r. "Procession" (Haji Muhammad Sharif) 2·50 1·75
857 1r. "Women harvesting" (Ustad Allah Bux) 2·50 1·75

446x 446 American Express Travellers Cheques of 1891 and 1991 (image scaled to 73% of original size)

1991. Centenary of American Express Travellers Cheques.

858	**446**	7r. multicoloured	1·75	2·50

447 Flag, Banknote and Banking Equipment

1992. 1st Anniv of Muslim Commercial Bank Privatization. Multicoloured.

859	1r. Type **447**	20	10
860	7r. Flag with industrial and commercial scenes	1·25	1·40

448 Imran Khan (team captain) and Trophy

1992. Pakistan's Victory in World Cricket Championship. Multicoloured.

861	2r. Type **448**	70	70
862	5r. Trophy and national flags (horiz)	1·50	1·50
863	7r. Pakistani flag, trophy and symbolic cricket ball	1·75	2·00

449 "Rehber-1" Rocket and Satellite View of Earth

1992. International Space Year. Mult.

864	1r. Type **449**	40	10
865	2r. Satellite orbiting Earth and logo	60	60

450 Surgical Instruments

1992. Industries. Multicoloured.

866	10r. Type **450**	1·25	1·60
867	15r. Leather goods	1·75	2·50
868	25r. Sports equipment	2·75	3·50

451 Globe and Symbolic Family

1992. Population Day.

869	**451**	6r. multicoloured	1·00	1·25

1992. Pioneers of Freedom (5th series). As T 428. Each brown and green.

870	1r. Syed Suleman Nadvi	1·40	1·60
871	1r. Nawab Iftikhar Hussain Khan Mamdot	1·40	1·60
872	1r. Maulana Muhammad Shibli Naumani	1·40	1·60

452 Scout Badge and Salute

1992. 6th Islamic Scout Jamboree and 4th Islamic Scouts Conference. Multicoloured.

873	6r. Type **452**	50	75
874	6r. Conference centre and scout salute	50	75

453 College Building

1992. Centenary of Islamia College, Lahore.

875	**453**	3r. multicoloured	70	75

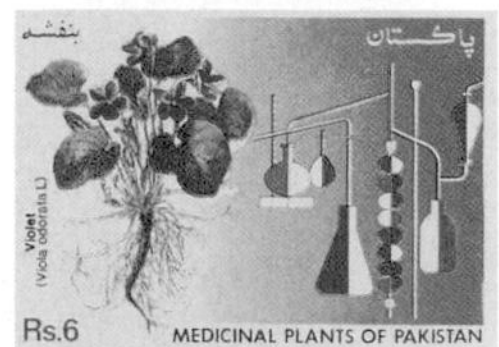

454 "Viola odorata" (flower) and Symbolic Drug Manufacture

1992. Medicinal Plants (1st series).

876	**454**	6r. multicoloured	3·25	2·25

See also Nos. 903, 946, 1010, 1026, 1037, 1099, 1123, 1142, 1159, 1185 and 1333/4.

455 Emblem

1992. Extraordinary Ministerial Council Session of Economic Co-operation Organization, Islamabad.

877	**455**	7r. multicoloured	1·00	1·75

456 Emblems and Field

1992. International Conference on Nutrition, Rome.

878	**456**	7r. multicoloured	70	1·25

457 Alhambra Palace, Granada, Spain

1992. Cultural Heritage of Muslim Granada.

879	**457**	7r. multicoloured	1·00	1·50

Type A. "Rs.5" at right with rainbow 8 mm beneath "P" of "PAKISTAN"
Type B. "Rs.5" at right with rainbow 2 mm beneath "P"
Type C. "Rs.5" at left with rainbow 2 mm beneath "N" of "PAKISTAN"
Type D. "Rs.5" at left with rainbow 8 mm beneath "N"

458 Mallard

1992. Water Birds. Multicoloured.

880	5r. Type **458** (A)	60	70
881	5r. Type **458** (B)	60	70
882	5r. Type **458** (C)	60	70
883	5r. Type **458** (D)	60	70
884	5r. Greylag goose (A)	60	70
885	5r. As No. 884 (B)	60	70
886	5r. As No. 884 (C)	60	70
887	5r. As No. 884 (D)	60	70
888	5r. Gadwall (A)	60	70
889	5r. As No. 888 (B)	60	70
890	5r. As No. 888 (C)	60	70
891	5r. As No. 888 (D)	60	70
892	5r. Common shelduck (A)	60	70
893	5r. As No. 892 (B)	60	70
894	5r. As No. 892 (C)	60	70
895	5r. As No. 892 (D)	60	70

Four different versions of designs as T **458**:

Nos. 880/95 were printed together, se-tenant, each horizontal row having a composite design of a rainbow.

459 Baluchistan Costume

1993. Women's Traditional Costumes. Multicoloured.

896	6r. Type **459**	1·25	1·50
897	6r. Punjab	1·25	1·50
898	6r. Sindh	1·25	1·50
899	6r. North-west Frontier Province	1·25	1·50

460 Clasped Hands and Islamic Symbols

1993. 21st Conference of Islamic Foreign Ministers, Karachi.

900	**460**	1r. multicoloured	75	10
901	**460**	6r. multicoloured	2·25	2·75

461 I.T.U. Emblem

1993. 25th Anniv of World Telecommunication Day.

902	**461**	1r. multicoloured	1·50	30

1993. Medicinal Plants (2nd issue). As T 454. Multicoloured.

903	6r. Fennel and symbolic drug manufacture	3·50	2·75

1993. Pioneers of Freedom (6th series). As T 428. Each brown and red.

904	1r. Ghulam Mohammad Bhurgri	1·40	1·40
905	1r. Ahmed Yar Khan	1·40	1·40
906	1r. Mohammad Pir Sahib Zakori Sharif	1·40	1·40

462 College Building and Arms

1993. Centenary of Gordon College, Rawalpindi.

907	**462**	2r. multicoloured	2·25	2·00

463 Juniper Forest

1993. Campaign to Save the Juniper Forest, Ziarat.

907a	**463**	1r. multicoloured	2·00	35
908	**463**	7r. multicoloured	4·00	3·50

464 Globe, Produce and Emblem

1993. World Food Day.

909	**464**	6r. multicoloured	1·50	1·60

465 Burn Hall Institution, Abbottabad

1993. 50th Anniv of Burn Hall Institutions.

910	**465**	7r. multicoloured	3·00	3·25

466 Peace Dove carrying Letter and National Flags

1993. South and West Asia Postal Union Commemoration.

911	**466**	7r. multicoloured	3·00	3·25

467 Congress Emblem

1993. Pakistan College of Physicians and Surgeons International Medical Congress.

912	**467**	1r. multicoloured	2·50	40

468 Wazir Mansion (birthplace)

1993. 45th Death Anniv of Mohammed Ali Jinnah.

913	**468**	1r. multicoloured	2·00	30

469 Emblem and National Flag

1994. 75th Anniv of I.L.O.

914	**469**	7r. multicoloured	1·75	2·75

470 Ratan Jot (flower)

1994. Ratification of International Biological Diversity Convention. Multicoloured.

915	6r. Type **470**	50	65
916	6r. Wetlands habitat	50	65
917	6r. Golden mahseer ("Tor puttitora") (fish)	50	65
918	6r. Brown bear	50	65

471 Silhouette of Family and Emblem

1994. International Year of the Family.

919	**471**	7r. multicoloured	80	1·00

472 Symbolic Globe and Logo

1994. World Population Day.

920	**472**	7r. multicoloured	1·00	1·00

1994. Pioneers of Freedom (7th series). As T 428. Each brown and green.

921	1r. Nawab Mohsin-Ul-Mulk	35	45
922	1r. Sir Shahnawaz Bhutto	35	45
923	1r. Nawab Viqar-Ul-Mulk	35	45
924	1r. Pir Ilahi Bux	35	45
925	1r. Sheikh Abdul Qadir	35	45
926	1r. Dr. Sir Ziauddin Ahmed	35	45
927	1r. Jam Mir Ghulam Qadir Khan	35	45
928	1r. Sardar Aurangzeb Khan	35	45

473 Hala Pottery, Pakistan

1994. Indonesia–Pakistan Economic and Cultural Co-operation Organization. Multicoloured.

929	10r. Type **473**	2·00	2·50
930	10r. Lombok pottery, Indonesia	2·00	2·50

474 Boy writing and Globe

1994. International Literacy Day.

931	**474**	7r. multicoloured	1·00	1·25

475 Mohammed Ali Jinnah and Floral Pattern

1994

932	**475**	1r. multicoloured	35	10
933	**475**	2r. multicoloured	50	10
934	**475**	3r. multicoloured	65	10
935	**475**	4r. multicoloured	70	10
936	**475**	5r. multicoloured	75	15
937	**475**	7r. multicoloured	1·00	20
938	**475**	10r. multicoloured	80	30
939	**475**	12r. multicoloured	90	60
940	**475**	15r. multicoloured	1·00	80
941	**475**	20r. multicoloured	1·10	1·00
942	**475**	25r. multicoloured	1·25	1·25
943	**475**	30r. multicoloured	1·40	1·40

476 Gateway and Emblem

1994. 2nd South Asian Association for Regional Co-operation and 12th National Scout Jamborees, Quetta.

944	**476**	7r. multicoloured	1·00	1·10

477 Engraver

1994. 1st Int Festival of Islamic Artisans at Work.

945	**477**	2r. multicoloured	1·50	60

478 Henbane

1994. Medicinal Plants (3rd issue).

946	**478**	6r. multicoloured	1·00	1·00

479 Abu-l Kasim Firdausi (poet)

1994. Millenary of "Shah Namah" (poem).

947	**479**	1r. multicoloured	35	15

480 Museum Building

1994. Centenary of Lahore Museum.

948	**480**	4r. multicoloured	60	80

481 World Cup Trophies for 1971, 1978, 1982 and 1994

1994. Victory of Pakistan in World Cup Hockey Championship.

949	**481**	5r. multicoloured	1·00	1·00

482 Tourist Attractions

1995. 20th Anniv of World Tourism Organization.

950	**482**	4r. multicoloured	1·25	1·40

483 Khan Khushal of Khattak and Army

1995. Khan Khushal of Khattak (poet) Commemoration.

951	**483**	7r. multicoloured	2·25	2·25

484 E.C.O. Emblem

1995. 3rd Economic Co-operation Organization Summit, Islamabad.

952	**484**	6r. multicoloured	1·50	1·50

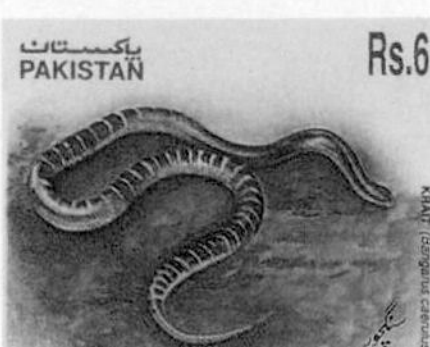

485 Common Indian Krait

1995. Snakes. Multicoloured.

953	6r. Type **485**	70	90
954	6r. Indian cobra	70	90
955	6r. Indian python	70	90
956	6r. Russell's viper	70	90

486 Globe and Environments

1995. Earth Day.

957	**486**	6r. multicoloured	70	80

487 Victoria Carriage, Karachi

1995. Traditional Transport.

958	**487**	5r. multicoloured	1·00	1·00

488 Prime Minister Tansu Ciller of Turkey and Rose

1995. 1st Muslim Women Parliamentarians' Conference, Islamabad. Multicoloured.

959	5r. Type **488**	1·00	1·50
960	5r. Prime Minister Benazir Bhutto and jasmine	1·00	1·50

1995. Pioneers of Freedom (8th series). As T 428. Each brown and green.

961	1r. Maulana Shaukat Ali	80	70
962	1r. Chaudhry Ghulam Abbas	80	70

489 Oil Sardine

1995. Fishes. Multicoloured.

963	6r. Type **489**	70	85
964	6r. Mozambique mouthbrooder ("Tilapia")	70	85
965	6r. Brown trout	70	85
966	6r. Rohu	70	85

490 "Erasmia pulchella"

1995. Butterflies. Multicoloured.

967	6r. Type **490**	70	90
968	6r. "Callicore astarte" (inscr "Catogramme")	70	90
969	6r. "Ixias pyrene"	70	90
970	6r. "Heliconius"	70	90

491 Major Raja Aziz Bhatti Shaheed and Medal

1995. Defence Day.

971	**491**	1r.25 multicoloured	2·00	1·50

492 Presentation Convent School, Rawalpindi

1995. Centenary of Presentation Convent School, Rawalpindi.

972	**492**	1r.25 multicoloured	1·50	1·00

493 Women Soldiers, Golfer and Scientist

1995. 4th World Conference on Women, Peking. Multicoloured.

973	1r.25 Type **493**	30	45
974	1r.25 Women graduates, journalist, computer operator and technicians	30	45
975	1r.25 Sewing machinist and women at traditional crafts	30	45
976	1r.25 Army officer and women at traditional tasks	30	45

494 "Louis Pasteur in Laboratory" (Edelfelt)

1995. Death Centenary of Louis Pasteur (chemist).

977	**494**	5r. multicoloured	1·00	1·00

495

1995

978	**495**	5p. blue, orange and brown	15	20
979	**495**	15p. orange, violet and brown	40	20
980	**495**	25p. blue, mauve and purple	50	10
981	**495**	75p. green, brown and deep brown	1·25	10

496 Liaquat Ali Khan

1995. Birth Centenary (1995) of Liaquat Ali Khan (statesman).

987	**496**	1r.25 multicoloured	1·00	40

497 Village and Irrigated Fields

1995. 50th Anniv of F.A.O.

988	**497**	1r.25 multicoloured	1·00	40

498 Pakistani Soldier treating Somali Refugees

1995. 50th Anniv of United Nations.

989	**498**	7r. multicoloured	1·25	1·60

499 Education Emblem

1995. 80th Anniv (1993) of Kinnaird College for Women, Lahore.

990	**499**	1r.25 multicoloured	1·00	40

500 Hand holding Book, Eye and Pen Nib

1995. International Conference of Writers and Intellectuals, Islamabad.

991	**500**	1r.25 multicoloured	1·00	40

501 Children holding Hands and S.A.A.R.C. Logo

1995. 10th Anniv of South Asian Association for Regional Co-operation.

992	**501**	1r.25 multicoloured	60	30

502 Jet Skier

1995. National Water Sports Gala, Karachi. Multicoloured.

993	1r.25 Type **502**	35	45
994	1r.25 Local punts	35	45
995	1r.25 Sailboard	35	45
996	1r.25 Water skier	35	45

503 Mortar Board and Books

1995. 20th Anniv of Allama Iqbal Open University.

997	**503**	1r.25 multicoloured	60	30

504 Balochistan Quetta University Building

1995. 25th Anniv of Balochistan Quetta University.

998	**504**	1r.25 multicoloured	60	30

505 Zulfikar Ali Bhutto,Flag and Crowd

1996. 17th Death Anniv of Zulfikar Ali Bhutto (former Prime Minister). Multicoloured.

999	1r.25 Type **505**	1·25	20
1000	4r. Zulfikar Ali Bhutto and flag (53×31 mm)	2·75	2·25
MS1001	118×74 mm. 8r. Zulfikar Ali Bhutto and crowd. Imperf	2·25	2·50

506 Wrestling

1996. Olympic Games, Atlanta. Multicoloured.

1002	5r. Type **506**	65	80
1003	5r. Boxing	65	80
1004	5r. Pierre de Coubertin	65	80
1005	5r. Hockey	65	80
MS1006	112×100 mm. 25r. Designs as Nos. 1002/5, but without face values. Imperf	3·00	3·75

1996. Pioneers of Freedom (9th series). Allama Abdullah Yousuf Ali. As T 428.

1007	1r. brown and green	40	20

507 G.P.O. Building, Lahore

1996. Restoration of G.P.O. Building, Lahore.

1008	**507**	5r. multicoloured	50	60

508 Symbolic Open Book and Text

1996. International Literacy Day.

1009	**508**	2r. multicoloured	40	30

509 Yarrow

1996. Medicinal Plants (4th series).

1010	**509**	3r. multicoloured	1·75	1·00

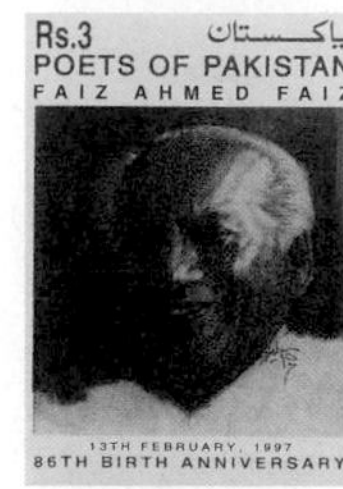

510 Faiz Ahmed Faiz

1997. 86th Birth Anniv of Faiz Ahmed Faiz (poet).

1011	**510**	3r. multicoloured	60	60

511 Golden Jubilee and O.I.C. Emblems

1997. Special Summit Conference of Organization of Islamic Countries commemorating 50th anniv of Pakistan.

1012	**511**	2r. multicoloured	35	35

512 Amir Timur

1997. 660th Birth Anniv of Timur (founder of Timurid Empire).

1013	**512**	3r. multicoloured	60	60

513 Jalal-al-din Moulana Rumi

1997. Pakistan–Iran Joint Issue.

1014	3r. Type **513**	60	65
1015	3r. Allama Mohammad Iqbal (poet)	50	65

514 Apple

1997. Fruit.

1016	**514**	2r. multicoloured	35	35

515 People on Globe

1997. World Population Day.
1017 **515** 2r. multicoloured 35 35

516 Stylized Dove of Peace

1997. 40th Anniv of Co-operation between International Atomic Energy Agency and Pakistan Atomic Energy Corporation.
1018 **516** 2r. multicoloured 70 35

1997. Pioneers of Freedom (10th series). As T 428. Each brown and green.
1019 1r. Mohammad Ayub Khuhro 75 75
1020 1r. Begum Salma Tassaduq Hussain 75 75

517 Mohammed Ali Jinnah

1997. 50th Anniv of Independence. Multicoloured.
1021 3r. Type **517** 60 70
1022 3r. Allama Mohammad Iqbal 60 70
1023 3r. Mohtarma Fatima Jinnah 60 70
1024 3r. Liaquat Ali Khan 60 70

518 College Building

1997. 75th Anniv of Lahore College for Women.
1025 **518** 3r. multicoloured 1·50 1·00

519 Garlic

1997. Medicinal Plants (5th series).
1026 **519** 2r. multicoloured 1·50 65

520 Himalayan Monal Pheasant

1997. Wildlife Protection (18th series).
1027 **520** 2r. multicoloured 2·25 1·25

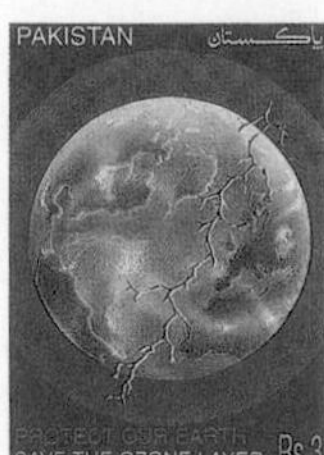

521 Globe and Cracked Ozone Layer

1997. Save Ozone Layer Campaign.
1028 **521** 3r. multicoloured 1·60 1·25

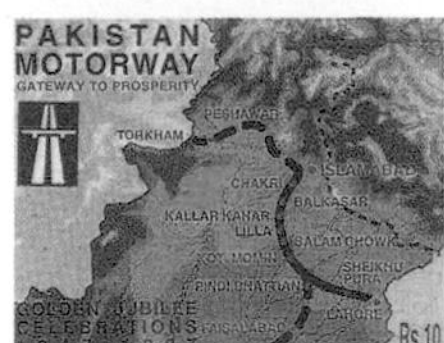

522 Map of Pakistan Motorway Project

1997. Pakistan Motorway Project.
1029 **522** 10r. multicoloured 2·25 2·50
MS1030 117×97 mm. No. 1029 (sold at 15r.) 2·75 3·00

523 Emblem and Disabled People

1997. International Day for the Disabled.
1031 **523** 4r. multicoloured 1·50 1·00

524 Karachi Grammar School

1997. 150th Anniv of Karachi Grammar School.
1032 **524** 2r. multicoloured 1·50 70

525 Mirza Ghalib

1998. Birth Bicentenary (1997) of Mirza Ghalib (poet).
1033 **525** 2r. multicoloured 60 30

No. 1033 is inscr "DEATH ANNIVERSARY".

526 Servicemen, Pakistan Flag and "50"

1998. 50th Anniv (1997) of Armed Forces.
1034 **526** 7r. multicoloured 1·00 1·00

527 Sir Syed Ahmed Khan

1998. Death Centenary of Sir Syed Ahmed Khan (social reformer).
1035 **527** 7r. brown, green & stone 1·00 1·25

528 Olympic Torch and Sports

1998. 27th National Games, Peshawar.
1036 **528** 7r. multicoloured 1·00 1·10

529 Thornapple

1998. Medicinal Plants (6th series).
1037 **529** 2r. multicoloured 1·50 55

530 Silver Jubilee Emblem

1998. 25th Anniv of Senate.
1038 **530** 2r. multicoloured 30 15
1039 **530** 5r. multicoloured 70 85

531 Mohammed Ali Jinnah

1998
1039a **531** 1r. red and black 15 10
1040 **531** 2r. blue and red 25 10
1041 **531** 3r. green and brown 30 10
1042 **531** 4r. purple and orange 40 10
1043 **531** 5r. brown and green 40 10
1044 **531** 6r. green and blue 50 20
1045 **531** 7r. red and violet 60 25

532 College Building

1998. Cent of Government College, Faisalabad.
1046 **532** 5r. multicoloured 70 70

533 "Mohammed Ali Jinnah" (S. Akhtar)

1998. 50th Death Anniv of Mohammed Ali Jinnah.
1047 **533** 15r. multicoloured 2·25 2·50
MS1048 72×100 mm. **533** 15r. multicoloured (sold at 20r.) 2·50 3·00

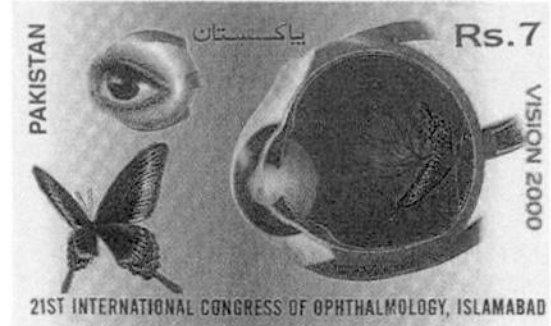

534 Cross-section of Eye

1998. 21st International Ophthalmology Congress, Islamabad.
1049 **534** 7r. multicoloured 1·50 1·50

535 United Nations Emblems and Bukhari

1998. Birth Centenary of Syed Ahmed Shah Patrus Bukhari.
1050 **535** 5r. multicoloured 1·25 1·00

536 Map, "50 years" and Stamps

1998. 50th Anniv of Philately in Pakistan.
1051 **536** 6r. multicoloured 65 65

537 Mother and Child

1998. World Food Day.
1052 **537** 6r. multicoloured 75 75

538 Dr. Abdus Salam

1998. Scientists of Pakistan (1st series). Dr. Abdus Salam.
1053 **538** 2r. multicoloured 50 25

See also No. 1068.

539 Satellite Dish Aerial

1998. "Better Pakistan" Development Plan. Mult.

1054		2r. Type **539**	45	55
1055		2r. Combine harvester	45	55
1056		2r. Airliner	45	55
1057		2r. Children and doctor	45	55

540 Globe and Human Rights Emblem

1998. 50th Anniv of Universal Declaration of Human Rights.

1058	**540**	6r. multicoloured	1·25	1·25

541 Pakistani Woman carrying Water Pot

1998. 50th Anniv of UNICEF in Pakistan. Multicoloured.

1059		2r. Type **541**	30	40
1060		2r. Woman reading	30	40
1061		2r. Woman with goitre	30	40
1062		2r. Young boy receiving oral vaccine	30	40

542 Earth seen from Space

1998. International Year of the Ocean.

1063	**542**	5r. multicoloured	1·25	1·00

543 Marchers and Route Map

1998. Qaumi Parcham March, Khyber to Chaghi.

1064	**543**	2r. multicoloured	40	25

544 Centenary Logo

1999. Centenary of Saudi Dynasty of Saudi Arabia. Multicoloured.

1065		2r. Type **544**	30	10
1066		15r. As Type **544**, but with mosaic pattern in corners	1·75	2·00
MS1067		73×100 mm. 15r. No. 1066 (sold at 20r.)	2·50	3·00

545 Dr. Salimuz Zaman Siddiqui

1999. Scientists of Pakistan (2nd series). Dr. Salimuz Zaman Siddiqui.

1068	**545**	5r. multicoloured	60	60

546 Mountains and Pakistan Flag

1999. "Atoms for Peace".

1069	**546**	5r. multicoloured	60	60

547 Plan and View of Mosque

1999. Completion of Data Darbar Mosque Complex, Lahore.

1070	**547**	7r. multicoloured	75	1·00

548 Fasting Buddha Statue (drapery on left knee)

1999. Archaeological Heritage. Multicoloured.

1071		7r. Type **548**	70	85
1072		7r. Fasting Buddha (drapery on right knee)	70	85
MS1073		107×90 mm. Nos. 1071/2 (sold at 25r.)	2·25	3·00

No. **MS**1073 includes the "China '99" International Stamp Exhibition, Beijing, logo on the margin.

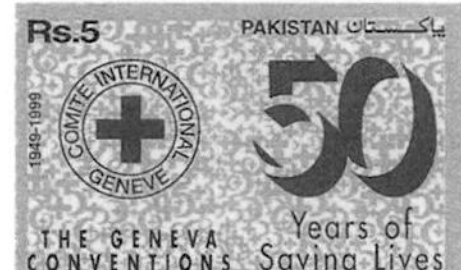

549 Red Cross International Committee Emblem and "50"

1999. 50th Anniv of Geneva Conventions.

1074	**549**	5r. red and black	60	50

1999. Pioneers of Freedom (11th series). As T 428. Each brown and green.

1075		2r. Maulana Abdul Hamid Badayuni	45	50
1076		2r. Chaudhry Muhammad Ali	45	50
1077		2r. Sir Adamjee Haji Dawood	45	50

550 Ustad Nusrat Fateh Ali Khan

1999. Ustad Nusrat Fateh Ali Khan (musician) Commemoration.

1078	**550**	2r. multicoloured	1·25	60

551 Islamic Development Bank Building

1999. 25th Anniv of Islamic Development Bank.

1079	**551**	5r. multicoloured	1·00	1·00

552 Crowd celebrating

1999. 50th Anniv of People's Republic of China. Multicoloured.

1080		2r. Type **552**	20	20
1081		15r. Bust of Mao Tse-tung (Chinese leader) and emblem (horiz)	1·25	1·75

553 "Enterprise" Sailing Dinghy

1999. 9th Asian Sailing Championship. Sailing Craft. Multicoloured.

1082		2r. Type **553**	50	50
1083		2r. "470" dinghy	50	50
1084		2r. "Optimist" dinghy	50	50
1085		2r. "Laser" dinghy	50	50
1086		2r. "Mistral" sailboard	50	50

554 "Optimist" Sailing Dinghies

1999. 10th Asian "Optimist" Sailing Championship.

1087	**554**	2r. multicoloured	60	40

555 U.P.U. Emblem

1999. 125th Anniv of Universal Postal Union.

1088	**555**	10r. multicoloured	1·00	1·25

556 Hakim Mohammed Said

1999. 1st Death Anniv of Hakim Mohammed Said.

1089	**556**	5r. multicoloured	60	60

557 National Bank of Pakistan Building

1999. 50th Anniv of National Bank of Pakistan.

1090	**557**	5r. multicoloured	1·25	70

558 Evolution of the "Shell" Emblem

1999. Centenary of Shell in Pakistan.

1091	**558**	4r. multicoloured	1·25	75

559 Profiles of Children in "10"

1999. 10th Anniv of United Nations Rights of the Child Convention.

1092	**559**	2r. emerald, green and red	30	30

560 Science Equipment, Books and Computer

1999. 25th Anniv of Allama Iqbal Open University. Multicoloured.

1093		2r. Type **560**	20	15
1094		3r. Scholastic symbols as Type **560**	30	30
1095		5r. Map of Pakistan	1·25	90

561 Josh Malihabadi

1999. Birth Centenary of Josh Malihabadi (poet).

1096	**561**	5r. multicoloured	60	60

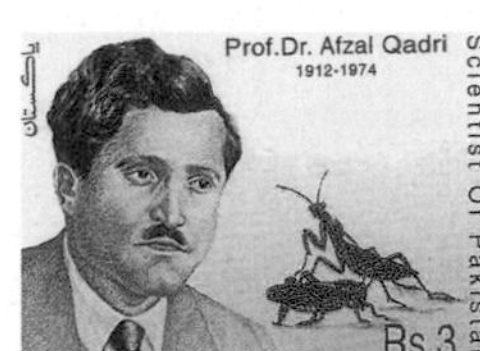

562 Dr. Afzal Qadri and Locusts

1999. 25th Death Anniv of Dr. Afzal Qadri (scientist).

1097	**562**	3r. multicoloured	60	40

563 Ghulam Bari Aleeg

1999. 50th Death Anniv of Ghulam Bari Aleeg (writer).

1098	**563**	5r. multicoloured	1·00	65

564 Plantain

1999. Medicinal Plants (7th series).
1099 **564** 5r. multicoloured 1·75 1·00

565 Mosque (image scaled to 72% of original size)

1999. Eid-ul-Fitr Greetings.
1100 **565** 2r. multicoloured 40 25
1101 **565** 15r. multicoloured 2·50 3·00

566 Woman and Young Boy

2000. 25th Anniv of S.O.S. Children's Villages in Pakistan.
1102 **566** 2r. multicoloured 65 30

567 Racing Cyclists

2000. Centenary of International Cycling Union.
1103 **567** 2r. multicoloured 1·75 80

568 Doves

2000. Pakistan Convention on Human Rights and Human Dignity.
1104 **568** 2r. multicoloured 60 30

569 College Building

2000. Centenary of Edwardes College, Peshawar.
1105 **569** 2r. multicoloured 60 30

570 Mahomed Ali Habib

2000. Mahomed Ali Habib (founder of Habib Bank Ltd) Commemoration.
1106 **570** 2r. multicoloured 60 30

571 Emblems and Symbols

2000. 50th Anniv of Institute of Cost and Management Accountants. Multicoloured.
1107 2r. Type **571** 30 20
1108 15r. Emblems, graph, keyboard and globe 2·00 2·50

572 Ahmed Jaffer

2000. 10th Death Anniv of Ahmed Jaffer (prominent businessman).
1109 **572** 10r. multicoloured 1·25 1·25

573 "Sarfaroshaane Tehreeke Pakistan" (detail)

2000. "Sarfaroshaane Tehreeke Pakistan" (painting). Showing different details. Multicoloured.
1110 5r. Type **573** 50 55
1111 5r. Bullock carts with tree in foreground 50 55
1112 5r. Bullock carts and crowd carrying Pakistan flag 50 55
1113 5r. Unloading bullock cart 50 55

574 Captain Muhammad Sarwar

2000. Defence Day. Showing winners of Nishan-e-Haider medal. Multicoloured.
1114 5r. Type **574** 1·00 1·00
1115 5r. Major Tufail Muhammad 1·00 1·00
See also No. 1173/4.

575 Athletics

2000. Olympic Games, Sydney. Multicoloured.
1116 4r. Type **575** 70 70
1117 4r. Hockey 70 70
1118 4r. Weightlifting 70 70
1119 4r. Cycling 70 70

576 Emblem and Building

2000. 125th Anniv of National College of Arts, Lahore.
1120 **576** 5r. multicoloured 55 65

577 Conference Emblem

2000. "Creating the Future" Business Conference.
1121 **577** 5r. multicoloured 1·00 75

578 Exhibition Emblem

2000. "Ideas 2000" International Defence Exhibition and Seminar.
1122 **578** 7r. multicoloured 1·25 1·25

579 Liquorice

2000. Medicinal Plants (8th series).
1123 **579** 2r. multicoloured 1·50 65

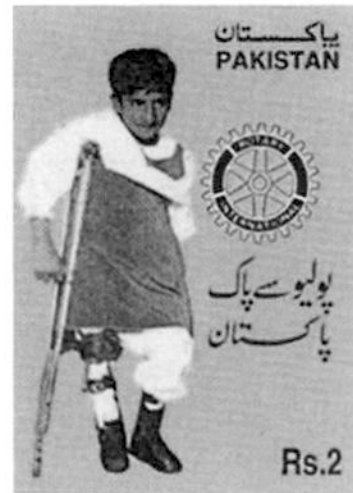

580 Crippled Child and Rotary Emblem

2000. "A World Without Polio" Campaign.
1124 **580** 2r. multicoloured 60 25

581 Refugee Family and Emblems

2000. 50th Anniv of United Nations High Commissioner for Refugees.
1125 **581** 2r. multicoloured 35 25

582 Hafeez Jalandhri

2001. Birth Centenary of Hafeez Jalandhri (poet).
1126 **582** 2r. multicoloured 1·00 40

583 Habib Bank AG Zurich Head Office

2001. Habib Bank AG Zurich Commemoration.
1127 **583** 5r. multicoloured 1·50 1·25

584 Chashma Nuclear Power Station

2001. Opening of Chashma Nuclear Power Station.
1128 **584** 4r. multicoloured 1·25 1·00

585 S.A.F. Games Emblem

2001. 9th S.A.F. Games, Islamabad.
1129 **585** 4r. multicoloured (blue background) 75 80
1130 **585** 4r. multicoloured (pink background) 75 80

586 "Ma Gu's Birthday Offering"

2001. 50th Anniv of Pakistan–China Friendship. Multicoloured.
1131 4r. Type **586** 70 80
1132 4r. "Two Pakistani Women drawing Water" 70 80
1133 4r. Girls in traditional Yugur and Hunza costumes 70 80
No. 1131 is inscribed "BIRTTHDAY" in error.

587 Mohammad Ali Jinnah

2001. 125th Birth Anniv of Mohammad Ali Jinnah ("Quaid-e-Azam") (1st issue).
1134 **587** 4r. multicoloured 60 80
See also Nos. 1152/6.

2001. Defence Day. As T 574 showing winners of Nishan-e-Haider medal. Multicoloured.
1135 4r. Major Shabbir Sharif Shaheed 75 75
1136 4r. Major Mohammad Akram Shaheed 75 75

588 Goat Emblem and Traditional Architecture

2001. Sindh Festival, Karachi.
1137 **588** 4r. yellow, black and green 60 60

589 Khawaja Ghulam Farid

2001. Death Centenary of Khawaja Ghulam Farid (poet).
1138 **589** 5r. multicoloured 60 60

590 "Children encircling Globe"(Urska Golob)

2001. U.N. Year of Dialogue among Civilizations.
1139 **590** 4r. multicoloured 50 50

591 Syed Imitaz Ali Taj

2001. Syed Imitaz Ali Taj (writer) Commemoration.
1140 **591** 5r. multicoloured 60 60

592 Pres. Saparmurat Niyazov of Turkmenistan

2001. 10th Anniv of Turkmenistan Independence.
1141 **592** 5r. multicoloured 60 60

593 Peppermint

2001. Medicinal Plants (9th series).
1142 **593** 4r. multicoloured 2·00 1·25

594 Convent of Jesus and Mary, Lahore

2001. 125th Anniv of Convent of Jesus and Mary, Lahore.
1143 **594** 4r. multicoloured 1·00 75

595 Dr. Ishtiaq Husain Qureshi

2001. 20th Death Anniv of Dr. Ishtiaq Husain Qureshi (historian).
1144 **595** 4r. multicoloured 50 50

596 Blue Throat

2001. Birds. Multicoloured.
1145 4r. Type **596** 1·25 1·25
1146 4r. Hoopoe 1·25 1·25
1147 4r. Pin-tailed sandgrouse 1·25 1·25
1148 4r. Magpie robin 1·25 1·25

597 Handshake beneath Flags of U.A.E. and Pakistan

2001. 30th Anniv of Diplomatic Relations between Pakistan and United Arab Emirates. Multicoloured.
1149 5r. Type **597** 50 25
1150 30r. Pres. Sheikh Zayed bin Sultan Al Nahyan of U.A.E. and Mohammed Ali Jinnah (horiz) 3·25 4·00

598 Nishtar Medical College, Multan

2001. 50th Anniv of Nishtar Medical College, Multan.
1151 **598** 5r. multicoloured 70 55

599 Mohammad Ali Jinnah taking Oath as Governor General, 1947

2001. 125th Birth Anniv of Mohammad Ali Jinnah ("Quaid-e-Azam") (2nd issue). Multicoloured.
1152 4r. Type **599** 30 35
1153 4r. Opening State Bank, Karachi, 1948 30 35
1154 4r. Taking salute, Peshawar, 1948 30 35
1155 4r. Inspecting guard of honour, 1948 (55×27 mm) 30 35
1156 4r. With anti-aircraft gun crew, 1948 (55×27 mm) 30 35

600 Troops and Ordnance

2001. 50th Anniv of Pakistan Ordnance Factories.
1157 **600** 4r. multicoloured 1·00 60

601 Samandar Khan Samandar

2002. Samandar Khan Samandar (poet) Commemoration.
1158 **601** 5r. multicoloured 60 60

602 Hyssop

2002. Medicinal Plants (10th series).
1159 **602** 5r. multicoloured 1·75 1·25

603 Statues of Buddha

2002. 50th Anniv of Diplomatic Relations between Pakistan and Japan.
1160 **603** 5r. multicoloured 50 50

604 Pakistan and Kyrgyzstan Flags

2002. 10th Anniv of Diplomatic Relations between Pakistan and Kyrgyzstan.
1161 **604** 5r. multicoloured 50 50

605 Anwar Ratol Mangoes

2002. Fruits of Pakistan. Mangoes. Multicoloured.
1162 4r. Type **605** 65 75
1163 4r. Dusehri mangoes 65 75
1164 4r. Chaunsa mangoes 65 75
1165 4r. Sindhri mango 65 75

606 Begum Noor us Sabah

2002. 55th Independence Day Celebrations. Political Figures. Multicoloured.
1166 4r. Type **606** 60 75
1167 4r. I. Chundrigar 60 75
1168 4r. Habib Ibrahim Rahimtoola 60 75
1169 4r. Qazi Mureed Ahmed 60 75

607 Children with Animals and Pakistan Flag

2002. World Summit on Sustainable Development, Johannesburg. Multicoloured.
1170 4r. Type **607** 50 50
1171 4r. Mountain and cartoon character (37×37 mm) 50 50

608 Mohammad Aly Rangoonwala (politician/philanthropist)

2002. Mohammad Aly Rangoonwala Commem.
1172 **608** 4r. multicoloured 60 50

2002. Defence Day. As T 574 showing winners of Nishan-e-Haider medal. Multicoloured.
1173 4r. Lance Naik Muhammad Mahfuz Shaheed 70 70
1173b 4r. Sawar Muhammad Hussain Shaheed 70 70

609 Muhammad Iqbal in Academic Gown

2002. 125th Birth Anniv of Muhammad Iqbal (writer). Multicoloured.
1174 4r. Type **609** 50 50
1175 4r. Muhammad Iqbal in library 50 50

610 "Eid Mubarak"

2002. Eid-ul-Fitr Festival.
1176 **610** 4r. multicoloured 50 50

611 Hakim Muhammad Hassan Qarshi and Plants

2002. Hakim Muhammad Hassan Qarshi (pioneer of Tibb homeopathic medicine) Commemoration.
1177 **611** 4r. multicoloured 1·00 55

612 Red-legged Partridge, Markhor and White Flowers

2003. National Philatelic Exhibition, Karachi.
1178 **612** 4r. multicoloured 1·50 1·10

613 Anniversary Emblem

2003. 50th Anniv of Pakistan Academy of Sciences.
1179 **613** 4r. multicoloured 70 70

614 Minaret Emblem

2003. Centenary Celebrations of North West Frontier Province.
1180 **614** 4r. multicoloured 60 60

615 Golden Jubilee Emblem

2003. 50th Anniv of Pakistan Council of Scientific and Industrial Research, Islamabad.
1181 **615** 4r. brown, green and yellow 60 60

616 Prof. A. B. A. Haleem

2003. Prof. A. B. A. Haleem (1st Vice Chancellor of Karachi University) Commemoration.
1182 **616** 2r. multicoloured 55 35

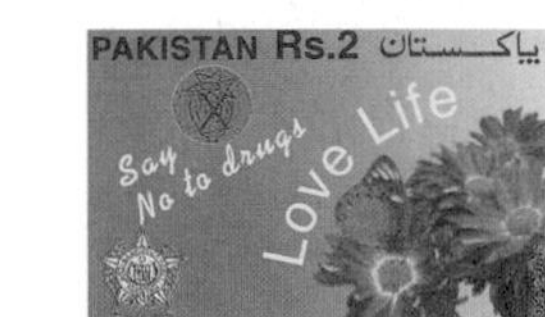

617 Flowers and Anti Narcotics Force Badge

2003. "Say No to Drugs".
1183 **617** 2r. multicoloured 1·00 55

618 Sir Syed Memorial, Islamabad

2003. Sir Syed Memorial, Islamabad.
1184 **618** 2r. multicoloured 45 30

619 *Rosa damascene*

2003. Medicinal Plants (11th series).
1185 **619** 2r. multicoloured 1·50 65

620 Fatima Jinnah

2003. 110th Birth Anniv of Fatima Jinnah (politician and campaigner for women's rights).
1186 **620** 4r. multicoloured 55 45

621 Abdul Rahman (PO employee killed in raid, 2002)

2003. Commemorations. Multicoloured.
1187 2r. Type **621** 35 35
1188 2r. M. A. Rahim (trade union leader and philanthropist) 35 35

622 Moulana Abdul Sattar Khan Niazi (politician, 88th)

2003. Birth Anniversaries. Multicoloured.
1189 2r. Type **622** 40 50
1190 2r. Muhammad Yousaf Khattak (politician, 86th) 40 50
1191 2r. Moulana Muhammad Ismail Zabeeh (politician, centenary) 40 50

623 Emblem

2003. United Nations Literacy Decade.
1192 **623** 1r. multicoloured 20 20

624 Pilot Officer Rashid Minhas and Nishan-e-Haider Medal

2003. 32nd Death Anniv of Pilot Officer Rashid Minhas.
1193 **624** 2r. multicoloured 1·25 55

625 Pakistan Academy of Letters, Islamabad

2003. 25th Anniv of Pakistan Academy of Letters (2001).
1194 **625** 2r. multicoloured 40 25

626 Karakoram Highway

2003. 25th Anniv of Karakoram Highway.
1195 **626** 2r. multicoloured 1·00 50

627 Nanga Parbat

2003. 50th Anniv of First Ascent of Nanga Parbat Mountain.
1196 **627** 2r. multicoloured 1·00 50

628 PAF Public School, Sargodha

2003. 50th Anniv of PAF Public School, Sargodha.
1197 **628** 4r. multicoloured 1·25 1·00

629 Leather Coats

2003. Achievement of 10 Billion US Dollar Exports Target, 2002–3. Multicoloured.
1198 1r. Type **629** 35 40
1199 1r. Towels 35 40
1200 1r. Readymade garments 35 40
1201 1r. Cargo ship being loaded by crane, Port Qasim 35 40
1202 1r. Fisheries 35 40
1203 1r. Yarn 35 40
1204 1r. Sports equipment 35 40
1205 1r. Fabrics 35 40
1206 1r. Furniture 35 40
1207 1r. Surgical instruments 35 40
1208 1r. Gems and jewellery 35 40
1209 1r. Leather goods 35 40
1210 1r. Information technology 35 40
1211 1r. Rice 35 40
1212 1r. Auto parts 35 40
1213 1r. Carpets 35 40
1214 1r. Marble and granite 35 40
1215 1r. Fruits 35 40
1216 1r. Cutlery 35 40
1217 1r. Engineering goods 35 40

630 Boy in Wheelchair with Boy and Girl

2003. International Day for Disabled.
1218 **630** 2r. multicoloured 1·00 50

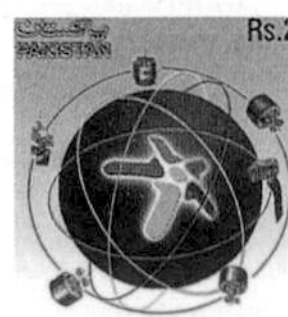

631 Globe

2003. World Summit on the Information Society, Geneva (Switzerland) and Tunis (Tunisia).
1219 **631** 2r. multicoloured 75 40

632 Khalid Class Submarine (Agosta 90B)

2003. Submarine Construction in Pakistan. Multicoloured.
1220 1r. Type **632** 75 25
1221 2r. Khalid Class submarine (Agosta 90B) and Pakistan flag (horiz) 1·50 85

633 Pakistan Air Force Plane, Siachen, 1988–90

2003. Centenary of Powered Flight. Pakistan Air Force. Multicoloured.
1222 2r. Type **633** 80 80
1223 2r. Old and modern Pakistan Air Force planes 80 80

634 Emblem

2004. 12th Summit Meeting of South Asian Association for Regional Co-operation, Islamabad.
1224 **634** 4r. multicoloured 50 50

635 Sadiq Public School, Bahawalpur

2004. 50th Anniv of Sadiq Public School, Bahawalpur.
1225 **635** 4r. multicoloured 60 50

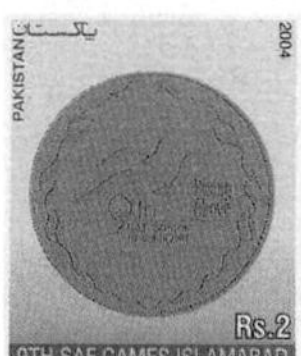

636 South Asian Federation Games Medal

2004. 9th South Asian Federation (S.A.F.) Games, Islamabad. Multicoloured.
1226 2r. Type **636** 35 40
1227 2r. Sprinting 35 40
1228 2r. Squash 35 40
1229 2r. Boxing 35 40
1230 2r. Wrestling 35 40
1231 2r. Judo 35 40
1232 2r. Javelin throwing 35 40
1233 2r. Football 35 40
1234 2r. Rowing 35 40
1235 2r. Shooting 35 40
1236 2r. Shot-putting 35 40
1237 2r. Badminton 35 40
1238 2r. Weight lifting 35 40
1239 2r. Volleyball 35 40
1240 2r. Table tennis 35 40
1241 2r. Swimming 35 40

637 Justice Pir Muhammad Karam Shah Al-Azhari

2004. Justice Pir Muhammad Karam Shah Al-Azhari Commemoration.

1242 **637** 2r. multicoloured 50 25

638 Cadet College, Hasanabdal

2004. 50th Anniv of Cadet College, Hasanabdal.

1243 **638** 4r. multicoloured 50 50

639 Central Library, Bahawalpur

2004. 80th Anniv of Central Library, Bahawalpur.

1244 **639** 2r. multicoloured 40 25

640 Bhong Mosque, Rahim Yar Khan

2004. Bhong Mosque.

1245 **640** 4r. multicoloured 70 60

641 Footballer and FIFA Emblem

2004. Centenary of FIFA (Federation Internationale de Football Association). Multicoloured.

1246 5r. Type **641** 75 75

1247 5r. FIFA emblem 75 75

1248 5r. As No. 1246 with stadium background extended behind FIFA emblem 75 75

642 Silk Road alongside Indus River

2004. Silk Road. Multicoloured.

1249 4r. Type **642** 50 50

1250 4r. Silk Road and Haramosh Peak (vert) 50 50

643 Juniper Forest and Emblems

2004. 50th Anniv of Sui Southern Gas Company. Protecting National Heritage.

1251 **643** 4r. multicoloured 60 55

644 K2

2004. 50th Anniv of First Ascent of K2. Multicoloured.

1252 5r. Type **644** 60 60

MS1253 **1253** 96×64 mm. 30r. Views of K2. Imperf 2·75 3·50

645 Running

2004. Olympic Games, Athens. Multicoloured.

1254 5r. Type **645** 55 55

1255 5r. Boxing 55 55

1256 5r. Hockey 55 55

1257 5r. Wrestling 55 55

646 Muhammad Ali Jinnah

647

648 Muhammad Ali Jinnah

649

2004. 57th Anniv of Independence.

1258 **646** 5r. multicoloured 45 45

1259 **647** 5r. multicoloured 45 45

1260 **648** 5r. multicoloured 45 45

1261 **649** 5r. multicoloured 45 45

Nos. 1258/61 each show Muhammad Ali Jinnah beside Urdu text, which differs on each stamp.

650 Maulvi Abdul Haq

2004. Maulvi Abdul Haq (scholar) Commemoration.

1262 **650** 4r. multicoloured 40 40

651 Calligraphic Dove with Olive Branch and Emblem

2004. 4th International Calligraphy and Calligraph-Art Exhibition and Competition.

1263 **651** 5r. multicoloured 40 40

652 Striped Gourami

2004. Fish. Multicoloured.

1264 2r. Type **652** 55 55

1265 2r. Black widow 55 55

1266 2r. Yellow dwarf cichlid 55 55

1267 2r. Tiger barb 55 55

1268 2r. Neon tetra 55 55

653 Training for Handicapped

2004. 50th Anniv of Japan's International Co-Operation and Assistance. Multicoloured.

1269 5r. Type **653** 75 75

1270 5r. Polio eradication 75 75

1271 5r. Ghazi Barotha hydropower 75 75

1272 5r. Friendship tunnel (Kohat) 75 75

MS1273 128×68 mm. 30r. Looking down Friendship Tunnel and designs as Nos. 269/72 2·75 3·50

654 Children and Daffodils

2004. Year of Child Welfare and Rights.

1274 **654** 4r. multicoloured 45 45

655 Open University Emblems

2004. 30th Anniv of Allama Iqbal Open University, Islamabad.

1275 **655** 20r. multicoloured 1·50 2·00

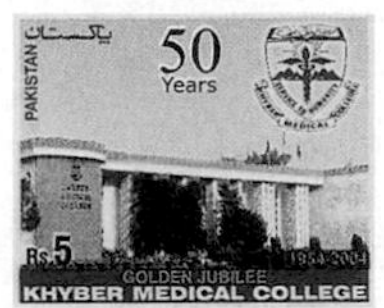

656 Khyber Medical College

2004. Centenary of Khyber Medical College.

1276 **656** 5r. multicoloured 60 50

657 Prof. Ahmed Ali

2005. 95th Birth Anniv of Prof. Ahmed Ali.

1277 **657** 5r. multicoloured 50 50

658 Allama Iqbal (Pakistani), Mihai Emineseu (Romanian) and Monument

2005. Pakistani and Romanian Poets. Multicoloured.

1278 5r. Type **658** 70 70

1279 5r. Allama Iqbal, Mihai Emineseu and book title 70 70

659 Saadat Hasan Manto

2005. 50th Death Anniv of Saadat Hasan Manto (short story writer).

1280 **659** 5r. multicoloured 45 45

660 Muhammad Ali Jinnah and Tempest II Airplane

2005. Air Force. Multicoloured.

1281 5r. Type **660** 1·00 1·00

1282 5r. Visit of Muhammad Ali Jinnah to the Air Force academy (vert) 1·00 1·00

1283 5r. Fighter plane and air force base facilities 1·00 1·00

1284 5r. Roundel and fighter plane 1·00 1·00

661 Command and Staff College

2005. Centenary of Command and Staff College, Quetta.

1285 **661** 5r. multicoloured 50 50

662 Muhammad Ali Jinnah and Mustafa Kemal Atatürk

2005. 85th Anniversary of Turkish Grand National Assembly. Multicoloured.

1286 10r. Type **662** 1·00 1·40

1287 10r. Mustafa Kemal Atatürk 1·00 1·40

663 Institute of Business Administration, Karachi

2005. 50th Anniv of Institute of Business Administration, Karachi. Multicoloured.

1288 3r. Type **663** 50 50

1289 3r. Entrance to Institute 50 50

664 Entrance

2005. 95th Anniv of Islamia High School, Quetta. Paper with fluorescent fibres.

1290 **664** 5r. multicoloured 50 50

665 Akhtar Shairani

2005. Birth Centenary of Akhtar Shairani (poet).

1291 **665** 5r. multicoloured 50 50

666 Emblem

2005. World Summit on the Information Society, Tunis.

1292	**666**	5r. multicoloured	50	50

667 Abdul Rehman Baba

2005. Abdul Rehman Baba (poet) Commemoration.

1293	**667**	5r. multicoloured	50	50

668 Marathon Runners

2005. Lahore Marathon.

1294	**668**	5r. multicoloured	50	50

669 *Lepiota procera*

2005. Mushrooms. Multicoloured.

1295	5r. Type **669**	75	75
1296	5r. *Tricholoma gambosum*	75	75
1297	5r. *Amanita caesarea*	75	75
1298	5r. *Cantharellus cibarius*	75	75
1299	5r. *Boletus luridus*	75	75
1300	5r. *Morchella vulgaris*	75	75
1301	5r. *Amanita vaginata*	75	75
1302	5r. *Agaricus arvensis*	75	75
1303	5r. *Coprinus comatus*	75	75
1304	5r. *Clitocybe geotropa*	75	75

669a 'HELP EARTHQUAKE VICTIMS'

2005. President's Relief Fund for Earthquake Victims. Sheet 174×147 mm. Multicoloured.

MS1304a	Type **669a** and 17 stamp size labels (sold for 100r.)	3·25	3·25

No. **MS**1304a the sheet was sold at 100r., a premium of 60r. for the President's Relief Fund for Earthquake Victims.

670 Silhouettes and Sports Equipment

2005. International Year of Sports and Physical Education.

1305	**670**	5r. multicoloured	50	50

671 Emblem and Clasped Hands

2005. 20th Anniv of South Asian Association for Regional Co-operation.

1306	**671**	5r. multicoloured	50	50

672 Khwaja Sarwar Hasan

2005. Khwaja Sarwar Hasan (founder of Pakistan Institute of International Affairs) Commemoration.

1307	**672**	5r. multicoloured	50	50

673 Emblem and Silhouettes of Children

2005. 30th Anniv of SOS Children's Villages of Pakistan.

1308	**673**	5r. multicoloured	50	50

674 Emblem and Players

2005. 20th World Men's Team Squash Championship, Islamabad.

1309	**674**	5r. multicoloured	1·00	60

675 Supreme Court Building

2006. 50th Anniv of Supreme Court of Pakistan. Multicoloured.

1310	4r. Type **675**	60	30
1311	15r. Supreme Court at night	2·25	2·75

676 Muhammed Ali Jinnah inspecting Troops and Tanks

2006. Muhammad Ali Jinnah's visit to Armoured Corps Centre, Nowshera, 1948. Multicoloured.

1312	5r. Type **676**	50	50
1313	5r. Col. Stroud (Commandant), Muhammad Ali Jinnah and Begum Ra'na Liaquat Ali Khan	50	50

677 Begum Ra'na Liaquat Ali Khan

2006. Birth Centenary (2005) of Begum Ra'na Liaquat Ali Khan.

1314	**677**	4r. multicoloured	60	50

678 Gurdwara Dera Sahib, Lahore

2006. 400th Death Anniv of Arjun Dev Ji (Sikh Guru).

1315	**678**	5r. multicoloured	65	60

679 Polo at Shandur Pass

2006. Shandur Polo Festival, Chitral.

1316	**679**	5r. multicoloured	1·00	75

680 Hanna Lake, Quetta

2006. "Visit Pakistan 2006". Lakes. Multicoloured.

1317	5r. Type **680**	70	70
1318	5r. Lake Payee, Kaghan	70	70
1319	5r. Lake Saiful Maluk, Kaghan	70	70
1320	5r. Lake Dudi Pat Sar, Kaghan	70	70

681 Prof. Shakir Ali

2006. Painters of Pakistan. Each showing the artist and one of their paintings. Multicoloured.

1321	4r. Type **681**	55	55
1322	4r. Anna Molka Ahmed	55	55
1323	4r. Sadequain	55	55
1324	4r. Ali Imam	55	55
1325	4r. Zubeida Agha	55	55
1326	4r. Laila Shahzada	55	55
1327	4r. Ahmed Parvez	55	55
1328	4r. Bashir Mirza	55	55
1329	4r. Zahooral Akhlaque	55	55
1330	4r. Askari Mian Irani	55	55

682 Centenary Emblem

2006. Centenary of Hamdard Services.

1331	**682**	5r. multicoloured	60	50

683 New Houses under Construction

2006. 1st Anniv of Earthquake.

1332	**683**	5r. multicoloured	60	50

684 Aloe Vera

2006. Medicinal Plants (12th series). Multicoloured.

1333	5r. Type **684**	90	90
1334	5r. Chamomilla (vert)	90	90

685 UN Emblem

2006. United Nations International Anti-Corruption Day.

1335	**685**	5r. multicoloured	60	60

686 Baltit Fort, Karimabad

2006. 10thth Anniv of Baltit Heritage Trust.

1336	**686**	15r. multicoloured	2·25	2·75

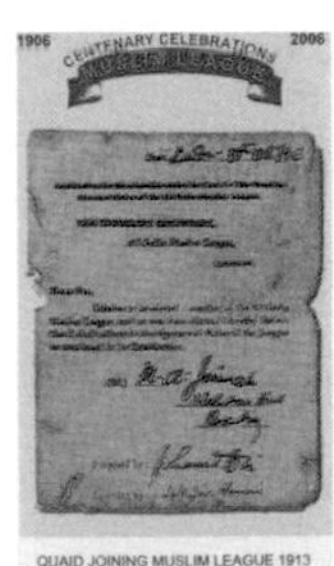

687 Muhammed Ali Jinnah joins Muslim League, 1913

2006. Centenary of the Muslim League. Multicoloured.

1337	4r. Type **687**	50	50
1338	4r. Muhammed Ali Jinnah ("Quaid") in 1937	50	50
1339	4r. Addressing Lucknow Session, 1937	50	50
1340	4r. With Fatima Jinnah and youth and women of Muslim League, 1938	50	50
1341	4r. Hoisting Muslim League flag, Manto Park, Lahore, 1940	50	50
1342	4r. Addressing Lahore session, 1940	50	50
1343	4r. Ballot box and crowd (election victory, 1945–6)	50	50
1344	4r. Addressing first Constituent Assembly, 1947	50	50

688 Old KMC Building, Karachi

2007. 75th Anniv of Inauguration of KMC (Karachi Municipal Corporation) Building.

1345	**688**	10r. multicoloured	1·50	1·50

689 Cadet College, Petaro and Arms

2007. 50th Anniv of Cadet College, Petaro.
1346 **689** 10r. multicoloured 1·00 1·00

690 Women at Work

2007. International Women's Day.
1347 **690** 10r. multicoloured 1·00 1·00

691 Hugh Catchpole

2007. Birth Centenary of Hugh Catchpole (educationist).
1348 **691** 10r. multicoloured 1·00 1·00

692 Emblem

2007. 'Launch of New Vision of Pakistan Post'.
1349 **692** 4r. vermilion and yellow 1·00 1·00

693 JF-17 Thunder

2007. Pakistan Air Force Defence Day.
1350 **693** 5r. multicoloured 1·50 1·00

694 Members Flags and Map

2007. ECO (Economic Co-operation Organization) Postal Authorities Conference, Ankara (2006).
1351 **694** 10r. multicoloured 1·75 1·50

No. 1351 is inscr '650 Rials I.R. Iran' at top left and the country name 'PAKISTAN' is missing from the stamp.

695 National Assembly Building

2007. Completion of Five Years Term of National Assembly of Pakistan.
1352 **695** 15r. multicoloured 1·50 1·75

696 Church Building, Medallion and Nave

2007. Centenary of Catholic Cathedral Church, Lahore.
1353 **696** 5r. multicoloured 1·00 1·00

697 Zulfikar Ali Bhutto, Benazir Bhutto and Crowd

2008. 29th Death Anniv of Zulfikar Ali Bhutto.
1354 **697** 4r. multicoloured 1·25 1·00
MS1355 106×70 mm. **696** 20r. multicoloured. Imperf 2·00 2·50

698 Benazir Bhutto

2008. 55th Birth Anniv of Benazir Bhutto (Prime Minister of Pakistan 1988–90, 1993–6). Multicoloured.
1356 4r. Type **698** 1·25 1·00
1357 5r. Benazir Bhutto waving (34×56 mm) 1·25 1·00
MS1358 67×98 mm. 20r. As No. 1357. Imperf 2·00 2·50

699 Girls in Class and Rebuilt School

2008. 3rd Anniv of Earthquake.
1359 **699** 4r. multicoloured 1·25 1·00

700 Benazir Bhutto

2008. United Nations Human Rights Award for Benazir Bhutto.
1360 **700** 4r. multicoloured 1·25 1·00

701 Benazir Bhutto and Pakistan Flag

2008. 1st Death Anniv of Benazir Bhutto.
1361 **701** 4r. multicoloured 1·25 1·00
MS1362 99×67 mm. **701** 20r. multicoloured. Imperf 2·00 2·50

702 Members Flags

2009. Tenth ECO Summit, Tehran, Iran.
1363 **702** 5r. multicoloured 1·00 1·00

703 Deodar

2009. National Year of the Environment. Multicoloured.
1364 5r. Type **703** 45 50
1365 5r. Chukar 45 50
1366 5r. Markhor 45 50
1367 5r. Jasmine 45 50

704 Entrance to 'Habib Education Centre'

2009. 50th Anniv of Habib Public School, Karachi.
1368 **704** 5r. multicoloured 1·00 1·00

705 High School Building, Karachi

2009. 150th Anniv of Bai Virbaiji Soparivala Parsi High School, Karachi.
1369 **705** 5r. multicoloured 1·00 1·00

706 KCCI Building, Karachi

2009. 75th Anniv of Karachi Chamber of Commerce and Industry Building.
1370 **706** 4r. multicoloured 1·00 1·00

707 Ahmad Nadeem Qasmi

2009. Ahmad Nadeem Qasmi (Urdu poet and writer) Commemoration.
1371 **707** 5r. multicoloured 1·00 1·00

708 Prime Minister holding Refugee Baby

2009. Prime Minister's Relief Fund for Swat Refugees. Sheet 174×153 mm. Multicoloured.
MS1372 5r.×8 Type **708** and 17 stamp size labels (sold for 100r.) 1·00 1·00

No. **MS**1372 was sold for 100r., a premium of 60r. for the Prime Minister's Relief Fund for Swat Refugees.

709 St. Patrick's Cathedral, Karachi, Gurdwara Dera Sahib, Lahore and Hindu Temple, Taxila

2010. Minorities Week
1373 **709** 5r. multicoloured 1·00 1·00

No. 1373 is incorrectly inscr 'ST. PATARICS'.

710 Teacher, Students and National Flag

2009. Independence Day.
1374 **710** 5r. multicoloured 1·00 1·00

711 Mausoleum of Hazrat Musa Pak Shaheed

2009. Mausoleum of Hazrat Musa Pak Shaheed.
1375 **711** 5r. multicoloured 1·00 1·00

712 Peace Dove

2009. 'United for Peace'.
1376 **712** 5r. dull violet, azure and black 1·00 1·00

713 National Flags of Pakistan and Philippines

2009. 60th Anniv of Diplomatic Relations between Pakistan and the Philippines.
1377 **713** 5r. multicoloured 1·00 1·00

714 Sun, Chinese Flag and Outline Map of China

2009. 60th Anniv of the People's Republic of China.

1378	**714**	5r. multicoloured	1·00	1·00

715 Aseefa Bhutto Zardari and Benazir Bhutto

2009. 'Polio Free Pakistan Mother's Vision Daughter's Mission'. Multicoloured.

1379	5r. Type **715**	1·00	1·00
1379a	5r. As Type **715** but country name in Urdu and all other inscriptions in English	1·00	1·00

716 Mr. Yousaf Raza Gillani, Chief Ministers, Cabinet Members and Portrait of Benazir Bhutto

2010. Seventh National Finance Commission Award

1380	**716**	8r. multicoloured	1·00	1·00

717 Gwadar Port

2010. Aghaz-e-Haqooq-e-Balochistan (government development package for Balochistan)

1381	**717**	8r. multicoloured	1·00	1·00

718 Pakistan Flag and Navy Rifle Insignia

2010. 50th Anniv of the Pakistan Navy Rifle Association

1382	**718**	10r. multicoloured	1·00	1·00

719 War Memorial, Nowshera

2010. Conferment of Hilal-i-Eissar on Cities of Nowshera, Peshawar, Swabi, Mardan and Charsadda. Multicoloured.

1383	5r. Type **719**	50	50
1384	5r. Islamia College, Peshawar	50	50
1385	5r. Judicial Complex, Swabi	50	50
1386	5r. Takht-e-Barhi, Mardan	50	50
1387	5r. Sugar mills, Charsadda	50	50

Nos. 1383/7 were printed together, *se-tenant*, as horizontal strips of five stamps in sheets of 40 (4×10).

Type **720** is vacant.

721 OICCI Building

2010. 150th Anniv of the Overseas Investors Chamber of Commerce and Industry

1388	**721**	8r. multicoloured	1·00	1·00

OFFICIAL STAMPS

1947. King George VI Official stamps of India optd PAKISTAN.

O1	**O20**	3p. slate	3·00	2·50
O2	**O20**	½a. purple	60	10
O3	**O20**	9p. green	5·50	4·50
O4	**O20**	1a. red	60	10
O5	**O20**	1½a. violet	60	10
O6	**O20**	2a. orange	60	40
O7	**O20**	2½a. violet	8·50	12·00
O8	**O20**	4a. brown	1·50	1·75
O9	**O20**	8a. violet	2·00	3·25
O10	**93**	1r. slate and brown (No. O138)	1·25	3·25
O11	**93**	2r. purple and brown (No. O139)	8·50	8·00
O12	**93**	5r. green and blue (No. O140)	28·00	55·00
O13	**93**	10r. purple and red (No. O141)	80·00	£140

1948. Optd SERVICE. Crescent moon pointing to right.

O14	**7**	3p. red	10	10
O15	**7**	6p. violet	10	10
O37	**7**	9p. green	10	10
O17	-	1a. blue	3·75	10
O18	-	1½a. green	3·50	10
O19	-	2a. red	1·50	10
O20	-	3a. green	26·00	15·00
O21	**9**	4a. brown	2·25	10
O22	-	8a. black	2·75	10·00
O23	**12**	1r. blue	1·50	10
O42	**12**	2r. brown	5·00	30
O61	**12**	5r. red	7·50	15
O26	**13**	10r. mauve	22·00	65·00

1949. Optd SERVICE. Crescent moon pointing to left.

O38	1a. blue	10	10
O39	1½a. green	10	10
O40	2a. red	20	10
O30	3a. green	38·00	6·50
O31	8a. black	55·00	24·00

1951. 4th Anniv of Independence. As Nos. 56, 58 and 60 but inscr "SERVICE" instead of "PAKISTAN POSTAGE".

O32	3a. purple	8·50	10·00
O33	4a. green	2·25	10
O34	8a. sepia	9·00	5·50

1954. 7th Anniv of Independence. Nos. 65/71 optd SERVICE.

O53	6p. violet	10	10
O54	9p. blue	10	10
O55	1a. red	10	10
O56	1½a. red	10	10
O57	14a. myrtle	50	4·25
O58	1r. green	50	10
O51	2r. orange	4·50	15

1955. 8th Anniv of Independence. Nos. 74/5 optd SERVICE.

O63	6a. blue	15	10
O64	8a. violet	15	10

1959. 9th Anniv of Independence. Optd SERVICE.

O65	**37**	2a. red	10	10

1961. 1st Anniv of Republic. Optd SERVICE.

O62	**41**	10r. green and orange	7·00	9·00

1961. Optd SERVICE.

O66	**51**	8a. green	20	10
O67	**51**	1r. blue	20	10

1961. New currency. Provisional stamps. Nos. 122 etc. optd SERVICE.

O68	-	1p. on 1½a. red	10	10
O69	**7**	2p. on 3p. red	10	10
O70	**51**	3p. on 6p. purple	10	10
O71	-	7p. on 1a. red	10	10
O72	**51**	13p. on 2a. red	10	10
O73	**37**	13p. on 2a. red	10	10

1961. Definitive issue optd SERVICE.

O74	**60**	1p. violet	10	10
O75	**60**	2p. red	10	10
O79	**60**	3p. purple	10	10
O94	**60**	5p. blue	10	10
O81	**60**	7p. green	10	10
O82	**61**	10p. brown	10	10
O83	**61**	13p. violet	10	10
O98	**61**	15p. purple	10	2·00
O99	**61**	20p. green	10	40
O100	**61**	25p. blue	20·00	5·00
O85	**61**	40p. purple	10	10
O102	**61**	50p. turquoise	10	15
O87	**61**	75p. red	20	10
O104	**61**	90p. green	13·00	8·00
O88	**62**	1r. red	35	10
O89	**62**	2r. orange	1·50	20
O90	**62**	5r. green	4·25	7·00

1979. Optd SERVICE.

O109	**275**	2p. green	10	30
O110	-	3p. black	10	30
O111	-	5p. blue	10	30
O112	**275**	10p. blue and turquoise	10	30
O113	-	20p. green (No. 468)	10	10
O114	-	25p. green and mauve (No. 489)	10	10
O115	-	40p. blue and mauve (No. 470)	30	10
O116	-	50p. lilac and green (No. 471)	10	10
O117	-	60p. black (No. 472)	1·00	10
O118	-	75p. red (No. 473)	1·00	10
O119	-	1r. green (No. 475)	2·25	10
O120	-	1r.50 orange (No. 476)	20	30
O121	-	2r. red (No. 477)	20	10
O122	-	3r. blue (No. 478)	30	30
O123	-	4r. black (No. 479)	3·50	50
O124	-	5r. brown (No. 480)	3·50	50

1980. As Nos. 513/19 but inscr "SERVICE".

O125	**291**	10p. green and yellow	1·00	10
O126	**291**	15p. deep green & green	1·00	10
O127	**291**	25p. violet and red	15	1·00
O128	**291**	35p. red and green	20	1·50
O129	-	40p. red and brown	1·00	10
O130	-	50p. red and green	20	60
O131	-	80p. green and black	30	1·50

1984. Nos. 629/30 and 632/6 optd SERVICE.

O132		5p. black and purple	10	60
O133		10p. black and red	15	40
O135	**343**	20p. black and violet	30	40
O136	-	50p. brown and red	40	40
O137	-	60p. lt brown & brown	45	50
O138	-	70p. blue	50	70
O139	-	80p. brown and red	55	70

1989. No. 773 optd SERVICE.

O140	**411**	1r. multicoloured	5·00	85

O7 State Bank of Pakistan Building, Islamabad

1990

O141	**O7**	1r. red and green	15	10
O142	**O7**	2r. red and pink	25	15
O143	**O7**	3r. red and blue	35	15
O144	**O7**	4r. red and brown	45	15
O145	**O7**	5r. red and purple	50	15
O146	**O7**	10r. red and brown	1·25	40

Pt. 22

PALAU

Formerly part of the United States Trust Territory of the Pacific Islands, Palau became an autonomous republic on 1 January 1981. Until 1983 it continued to use United States stamps.

Palau became an independent republic on 1 October 1994.

100 cents = 1 dollar.

1 Preamble to Constitution

1983. Inaug of Postal Independence. Mult.

1	20c. Type **1**	80	70
2	20c. Natives hunting (design from Koror meeting house)	80	70
3	20c. Preamble to Constitution (different)	80	70
4	20c. Three fishes (design from Koror meeting house)	80	70

2 Palau Fruit Dove

1983. Birds. Multicoloured.

5	20c. Type **2**	65	55
6	20c. Morning bird	65	55
7	20c. Palau white-eye (inscr "Giant White-eye")	65	55
8	20c. Palau fantail	65	55

3 Map Cowrie

1983. Marine Life. Multicoloured.

9	1c. Sea fan	30	20
10	3c. Type **3**	30	20
11	5c. Jellyfish	30	20
12	10c. Hawksbill turtle	30	20
13	13c. Giant clam	30	20
14	14c. Trumpet triton	45	40
15	20c. Parrotfish	50	45
16	22c. Indo-Pacific hump-headed ("Bumphead") parrotfish	80	70
17	25c. Soft coral and damselfishes	85	75
17a	28c. Chambered nautilus	75	65
18	30c. Dappled sea cucumber	75	65
18a	33c. Sea anemone and anemonefishes ("Clownfish")	1·20	1·00
19	37c. Sea urchin	85	75
19a	39c. Green sea turtle	1·30	1·10
19b	44c. Sailfish	1·50	1·30
20	50c. Starfish	1·20	1·00
21	$1 Common squid	2·30	2·00
22	$2 Dugong	6·25	5·25
23	$5 Pink sponge	14·50	12·50
24	$10 Spinner dolphin	28·00	24·00

4 Humpback Whale

1983. World Wildlife Fund. Whales. Mult.

25	20c. Type **4**	1·50	1·30
26	20c. Blue whale	1·50	1·30
27	20c. Fin whale	1·50	1·30
28	20c. Sperm whale	1·50	1·30

5 "Spear fishing at New Moon"

1983. Christmas. Paintings by Charlie Gibbons. Mult.

29	20c. Type **5**	75	65
30	20c. "Taro Gardening"	75	65
31	20c. "First Child Ceremony"	75	65
32	20c. "Traditional Feast at the Bai"	75	65
33	20c. "Spear Fishing from Red Canoe"	75	65

6 King Abba Thulle

1983. Bicentenary of Captain Henry Wilson's Voyage to Palau.

34	**6**	20c. brown, blue & deep blue	75	65
35	-	20c. brown, blue & deep blue	75	65

36	-	20c. brown, blue & deep blue	75	65
37	-	20c. brown, blue & deep blue	75	65
38	-	20c. brown, blue & deep blue	75	65
39	-	20c. brown, blue & deep blue	75	65
40	-	20c. brown, blue & deep blue	75	65
41	-	20c. brown, blue & deep blue	75	65

DESIGNS—VERT: No. 37, Ludec (King Abba Thulle's wife); 38, Capt. Henry Wilson; 41, Prince Lee Boo. HORIZ: (47×20 mm): 35, Mooring in Koror; 36, Village scene in Pelew Islands; 39, Approaching Pelew; 40, Englishman's camp on Ulong.

7 Trumpet Triton

1984. Sea Shells (1st series). Multicoloured.

42	20c. Type **7**	75	65
43	20c. Horned helmet	75	65
44	20c. Giant clam	75	65
45	20c. Laciniate conch	75	65
46	20c. Royal oak ("cloak") scallop	75	65
47	20c. Trumpet triton (different)	75	65
48	20c. Horned helmet (different)	75	65
49	20c. Giant clam (different)	75	65
50	20c. Laciniate conch (different)	75	65
51	20c. Royal oak ("cloak") scallop (different)	75	65

Nos. 43/6 have mauve backgrounds, Nos. 48/51 blue backgrounds.

See also Nos. 145/9, 194/8, 231/5, 256/60 and 515/19.

8 White-tailed Tropic Bird

1984. Air. Birds. Multicoloured.

52	40c. Type **8**	1·50	1·30
53	40c. White tern (inscr "Fairy Tern")	1·50	1·30
54	40c. White-capped noddy (inscr "Black Noddy")	1·50	1·30
55	40c. Black-naped tern	1·50	1·30

9 "Oroolong" (Wilson's schooner)

1984. 19th Universal Postal Union Congress Philatelic Salon, Hamburg. Multicoloured.

56	40c. Type **9**	1·20	1·10
57	40c. Missionary ship "Duff"	1·20	1·10
58	40c. German expeditionary steamer "Peiho"	1·20	1·10
59	40c. German gunboat "Albatros"	1·20	1·10

10 Spear Fishing

1984. "Ausipex 84" International Stamp Exhibition, Melbourne. Fishing. Multicoloured.

60	20c. Type **10**	60	50
61	20c. Kite fishing	60	50
62	20c. Underwater spear fishing	60	50
63	20c. Net fishing	60	50

11 Mountain Apple

1984. Christmas. Multicoloured.

64	20c. Type **11**	60	50
65	20c. Beach morning glory	60	50
66	20c. Turmeric	60	50
67	20c. Plumeria	60	50

12 Chick

1985. Birth Bicentenary of John J. Audubon (ornithologist). Designs showing Audubon's Shearwater. Multicoloured.

68	22c. Type **12** (postage)	1·20	1·10
69	22c. Head of shearwater	1·20	1·10
70	22c. Shearwater flying	1·20	1·10
71	22c. Shearwater on lake	1·20	1·10
72	44c. "Audubon's Shearwater" (Audubon) (air)	2·50	2·30

13 Borotong (cargo canoe)

1985. Traditional Canoes and Rafts. Multicoloured.

73	22c. Type **13**	80	70
74	22c. Kabekl (war canoe)	80	70
75	22c. Olechutel (bamboo raft)	80	70
76	22c. Kaeb (racing/sailing canoe)	80	70

14 Boy with Guitar

1985. International Youth Year. Multicoloured.

77	44c. Type **14**	1·20	1·10
78	44c. Boy with fishing rod	1·20	1·10
79	44c. Boy with baseball bat	1·20	1·10
80	44c. Boy with spade	1·20	1·10

Nos. 77/80 were issued together se-tenant, each block forming a composite design showing a ring of children of different races.

15 Raising German Flag at Palau, 1885, and German 1880 20pf. Stamp

1985. Air. Centenary of Vatican Treaty (granting German trading privileges in Caroline Islands). Multicoloured.

81	44c. Type **15**	1·40	1·20
82	44c. Early German trading post, Angaur, and Marshall Islands 1899 5pf. overprinted stamp	1·40	1·20
83	44c. Abai (village meeting house) and Caroline Islands 1901 5m. yacht stamp	1·40	1·20
84	44c. "Cormoran" (German cruiser), 1914, and Caroline Islands 1901 40pf. yacht stamp	1·40	1·20

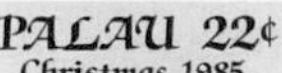

16 Mother cuddling Child

1985. Christmas. Multicoloured.

85	14c. Mother with child on lap	50	45
86	22c. Type **16**	75	65
87	33c. Mother supporting child in arms	1·20	1·00
88	44c. Mother lifting child in air	1·60	1·40

17 Consolidated Catalina Amphibian over Natural Bridge

1985. Air. 50th Anniv of First Trans-Pacific Airmail Flight. Multicoloured.

89	44c. Type **17**	1·20	1·10
90	44c. Douglas DC-6B approaching Airai–Koror Passage	1·20	1·10
91	44c. Grumman Albatross flying boat over Airai Village	1·20	1·10
92	44c. Douglas DC-4 landing at Airai	1·20	1·10
MS93	85×69 mm. $1 Martin M-130 flying boat "China Clipper" on first flight (postage)	3·75	3·25

18 Comet and Kaeb, 1758

1985. Appearance of Halley's Comet. Multicoloured.

94	44c. Type **18**	1·20	1·10
95	44c. Comet and U.S.S. "Vincennes", 1835	1·20	1·10
96	44c. Comet and "Scharnhorst" (German cruiser), 1910	1·20	1·10
97	44c. Comet and tourist cabin cruiser, 1986	1·20	1·10

19 Micronesian Flycatchers

1986. Songbirds. Multicoloured.

98	44c. Type **19** ("Mangrove Flycatchers")	1·20	1·10
99	44c. Cardinal honeyeaters	1·20	1·10
100	44c. Blue-faced parrot finches	1·20	1·10
101	44c. Grey-brown white-eye ("Dusky White-eye") and bridled white eye	1·20	1·10

20 Spear Fisherman

1986. "Ameripex '86" International Stamp Exhibition, Chicago. Sea and Reef World. Multicoloured.

102	14c. Type **20**	1·10	65
103	14c. Olechutel (native raft)	1·10	65
104	14c. Kaebs (sailing canoes)	1·10	65
105	14c. Rock islands and sailfish	1·10	65
106	14c. Inter-island ferry and two-winged flyingfishes	1·10	65
107	14c. Bonefishes	1·10	65
108	14c. Jacks	1·10	65
109	14c. Japanese mackerel	1·10	65
110	14c. Sailfishes	1·10	65
111	14c. Barracuda	1·10	65
112	14c. Undulate triggerfishes	1·10	65
113	14c. Dolphin (fish)	1·10	65
114	14c. Spear fisherman with grouper	1·10	65
115	14c. Manta ray	1·10	65
116	14c. Striped marlin	1·10	65
117	14c. Black-striped parrotfishes	1·10	65
118	14c. Red-breasted wrasse	1·10	65
119	14c. Malabar blood snappers	1·10	65
120	14c. Malabar blood snapper and clupeid ("Herring") school	1·10	65
121	14c. Dugongs	1·10	65
122	14c. Powder-blue surgeonfishes	1·10	65
123	14c. Spotted eagle ray	1·10	65
124	14c. Hawksbill turtle	1·10	65
125	14c. Needlefishes	1·10	65
126	14c. Tuna	1·10	65
127	14c. Octopus	1·10	65
128	14c. Anemonefishes ("Clown-fish")	1·10	65
129	14c. Squid	1·10	65
130	14c. Groupers	1·10	65
131	14c. Moorish idols	1·10	65
132	14c. Queen conch and starfish	1·10	65
133	14c. Diadem soldierfishes	1·10	65
134	14c. Starfish and stingrays	1·10	65
135	14c. Lionfish	1·10	65
136	14c. Emperor angelfishes	1·10	65
137	14c. Saddle butterflyfishes	1·10	65
138	14c. Spiny lobster	1·10	65
139	14c. Mangrove crab	1·10	65
140	14c. Giant clam ("Tridacna gigas")	1·10	65
141	14c. Moray	1·10	65

Nos. 102/41 are each inscribed on the back (over the gum) with the name of the subject featured on the stamp.

Nos. 102/41 were printed together, se-tenant, forming a composite design.

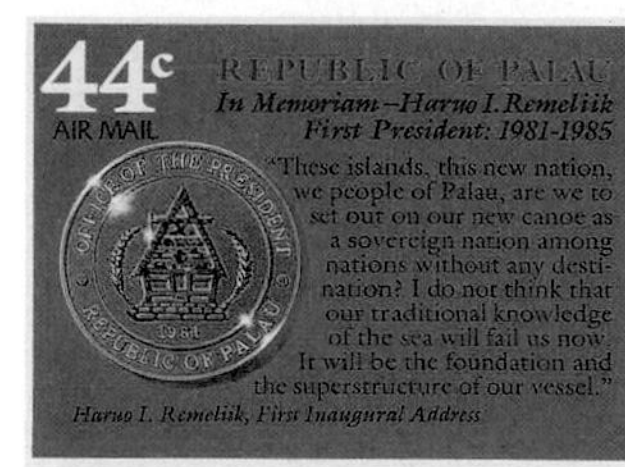

21 Presidential Seal

1986. Air. Haruo I. Remeliik (first President) Commemoration. Multicoloured.

142	44c. Type **21**	1·60	1·40
143	44c. Kabeki (war canoe) passing under Koror–Babeldaob Bridge	1·60	1·40
144	44c. Presidents Reagan and Remeliik	1·60	1·40

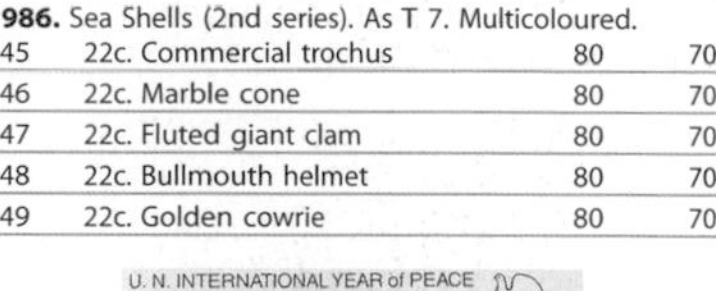

1986. Sea Shells (2nd series). As T 7. Multicoloured.

145	22c. Commercial trochus	80	70
146	22c. Marble cone	80	70
147	22c. Fluted giant clam	80	70
148	22c. Bullmouth helmet	80	70
149	22c. Golden cowrie	80	70

23 Crab inhabiting Soldier's rusting Helmet

1986. International Peace Year. Multicoloured.

150	22c. Type **23** (postage)	85	75
151	22c. Marine life inhabiting airplane	85	75
152	22c. Rusting tank behind girl	85	75
153	22c. Abandoned assault landing craft, Airai	85	75
154	22c. Statue of Liberty, New York (centenary) (air)	1·50	1·30

24 Gecko

1986. Reptiles. Multicoloured.

155	22c. Type **24**	95	80
156	22c. Emerald tree skink	95	80
157	22c. Estuarine crocodile	95	80
158	22c. Leatherback turtle	95	80

25 Girl with Guitar and Boy leading Child on Goat

1986. Christmas. Multicoloured.

159	22c. Type **25**	60	50
160	22c. Boys singing and girl carrying flowers	60	50
161	22c. Mother holding baby	60	50
162	22c. Children carrying baskets of fruit	60	50
163	22c. Girl with white terns	60	50

Nos. 159/63 were issued together, se-tenant, forming a composite design.

26 Tailed Jay on Soursop

1987. Butterflies (1st series). Multicoloured.

164	44c. Type **26**	1·20	1·00
165	44c. Common mormon on sweet orange	1·20	1·00
166	44c. Common eggfly on swamp cabbage	1·20	1·00
167	44c. Oleander butterfly on fig	1·20	1·00

See also Nos. 223/6.

27 Bat flying

1987. Air. Palau Fruit Bat. Multicoloured.

168	44c. Type **27**	1·20	1·10
169	44c. Bat hanging from branch	1·20	1·10
170	44c. Bat feeding	1·20	1·10
171	44c. Head of bat	1·20	1·10

28 *Ixora casei*

1987. Flowers. Multicoloured.

172	1c. Type **28**	30	20
173	3c. *Lumnitzera littorea*	30	20
174	5c. *Sonneratia alba*	30	20
175	10c. Woody vine	30	20
176	14c. *Bikkia palauensis*	30	20
177	15c. *Limophila aromatica*	35	25
178	22c. *Bruguiera gymnorhiza*	60	50
179	25c. *Fragraea ksid*	75	65
180	36c. *Ophiorrhiza palauensis*	95	80
181	39c. *Cerbera manghas*	1·00	90
182	44c. *Samadera indica*	1·20	1·10
183	45c. *Maesa canfieldiae*	1·30	1·10
184	50c. *Dolichandrone spathacea*	1·50	1·30
185	$1 *Barringtonia racemosa*	3·00	2·50
186	$2 *Nepenthes mirabilis*	5·75	5·00
187	$5 Orchid	14·50	12·50
188	$10 Bouquet of mixed flowers	25·00	21·00

29 Babeldaob

1987. "Capex '87" International Stamp Exhibition, Toronto. Multicoloured.

190	22c. Type **29**	75	65
191	22c. Floating Garden Islands	75	65
192	22c. Rock Island	75	65
193	22c. Koror	75	65

1987. Sea Shells (3rd series). As T 7. Multicoloured.

194	22c. Black-striped triton	80	70
195	22c. Tapestry turban	80	70
196	22c. Adusta murex	80	70
197	22c. Little fox mitre	80	70
198	22c. Cardinal mitre	80	70

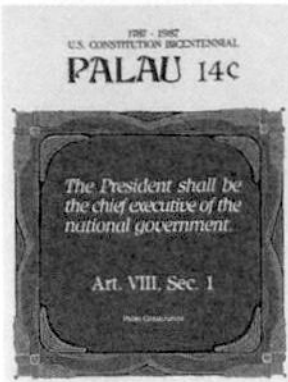

31 "The President shall be the chief executive ..."

1987. Bicentenary of United States of America Constitution. Multicoloured.

199	14c. Type **31**	30	20
200	14c. Palau and U.S. Presidents' seals (24×37 mm)	30	20
201	14c. "The executive power shall be vested ..."	30	20
202	22c. "The legislative power of Palau ..."	60	50
203	22c. Palau Olbiil Era Kelulau and U.S. Senate seals (24×37 mm)	60	50
204	22c. "All legislative powers herein granted ..."	60	50
205	44c. "The judicial power of Palau ..."	1·10	95
206	44c. Palau and U.S. Supreme Court seals (24×37 mm)	1·10	95
207	44c. "The judicial power of the United States ..."	1·10	95

The three designs of the same value were printed together in se-tenant strips, the top stamp of each strip bearing extracts from the Palau Constitution and the bottom stamp extracts from the U.S. Constitution.

32 Japanese Mobile Post Office and 1937 Japan ½s. Stamp

1987. Links with Japan. Multicoloured.

208	14c. Type **32**	45	40
209	22c. Phosphate mine and Japan 1942 5s. stamp	65	55
210	33c. Douglas DC-2 flying over Badrulchau monuments and Japan 1937 2s.+2s. stamp	95	80
211	44c. Japanese Post Office, Koror, and Japan 1927 10s. stamp	1·20	1·10
MS212	80×94 mm. $1 Japanese visitors at the Aviator's Grave, Japanese Cemetery, Peleliu	3·25	3·00

33 Huts, White Tern and Outrigger Canoes

1987. Christmas. Multicoloured.

213	22c. Type **33**	75	65
214	22c. Flying white tern carrying twig	75	65
215	22c. Holy Family in kaeb	75	65
216	22c. Angel and kaeb	75	65
217	22c. Outrigger canoes and hut	75	65

Nos. 213/17 were issued together, se-tenant, forming a composite design; each stamp bears a verse of the carol "I Saw Three Ships".

34 Snapping Shrimp and Watchman Goby

1987. 25th Anniv of World Ecology Movement. Multicoloured.

218	22c. Type **34**	80	70
219	22c. Mauve vase sponge and sponge crab	80	70
220	22c. Lemon ("Pope's") damselfish and blue-streaked cleaner wrasse	80	70
221	22c. Clown anemonefishes and sea anemone	80	70
222	22c. Four-coloured nudibranch and banded coral shrimp	80	70

1988. Butterflies (2nd series). As T 26.

223	44c. Orange tiger on "Tournefotia argentia"	1·10	95
224	44c. Swallowtail on "Citrus reticulata"	1·10	95
225	44c. Lemon migrant on "Crataeva speciosa"	1·10	95
226	44c. "Appias ada" (wrongly inscr "Colias philodice") on "Crataeva speciosa"	1·10	95

35 Whimbrel

1988. Ground-dwelling Birds. Multicoloured.

227	44c. Type **35**	1·10	95
228	44c. Chinese little bittern ("Yellow Bittern")	1·10	95
229	44c. Nankeen ("Rufous Night Heron")	1·10	95
230	44c. Buff-banded rail ("Banded Rail")	1·10	95

1988. Sea Shells (4th series). As T 7. Mult.

231	25c. Striped engina	80	70
232	25c. Ivory cone	80	70
233	25c. Plaited mitre	80	70
234	25c. Episcopal mitre	80	70
235	25c. Isabelle cowrie	80	70

36 Palauan Kaeb

1988. 5th Anniv of Palau Postal Independence and "Finlandia 88" International Stamp Exhibition, Helsinki. Sheet 149×97 mm containing T 36 and similar horiz designs. Multicoloured.

MS236	25c. Type **36**; 25c. Spanish "Vizcaya" class cruiser; 25c. German cruiser "Cormoran"; 25c. Japanese street mailbox, Koror Museum; 25c. U.S Trust Territory freighter at Malakal; 25c. Koror Post Office	4·25	3·75

37 Baseball

1988. Olympic Games, Seoul. Multicoloured.

237	25c.+5c. Type **37**	75	65
238	25c.+5c. Running	75	65
239	45c.+5c. Diving	1·80	1·60
240	45c.+5c. Swimming	1·80	1·60

38 Man's Head and Artwork for Finlandia'88 Stamp

1988. 10th Anniv of U.S. Possessions Philatelic Society. "Praga 88" International Stamp Exhibition, Czechoslovakia. Sheet 149×97 mm containing T 38 and similar horiz designs. Multicoloured.

MS241	45c. Type **38**; 45c. Society emblem; 45c. Artwork for first set of Palau stamps; 45c. Artwork for "China Clipper" miniature sheet; 45c. Man examining cover and boy holding envelope; 45c. Woman cancelling cover	7·25	6·25

39 Angel Violinist and Singing Cherubs

1988. Christmas. Multicoloured.

242	25c. Type **39**	75	65
243	25c. Angels and children singing	75	65
244	25c. Children adoring child	75	65
245	25c. Angels and birds flying	75	65
246	25c. Running children and angels playing trumpets	75	65

Nos. 242/6 were issued together, se-tenant, forming a composite design.

40 Ammonite and Cross Section of Palauan Nautilus

1988. Chambered Nautilus. Sheet 133×121 mm containing T 40 and similar designs.

MS247	25c. multicoloured (Type **40**); 25c. brown, black and black (Palauan bai symbols for nautilus) (25×53 mm); 25c. multicoloured (Palauan nautilas in cage); 25c. multicoloured (Different species); 25c. multicoloured (Releasing tagged nautilus)	4·25	3·75

41 Nicobar Pigeon

1989. Endangered Birds. Multicoloured.

248	45c. Type **41**	1·20	1·10
249	45c. Palau ground dove	1·20	1·10
250	45c. Marianas scrub hen	1·20	1·10
251	45c. Palau scops owl	1·20	1·10

42 False Chanterelle

1989. Fungi. Multicoloured.

252	45c. Type **42** (inscr "Gilled Auricularia)	1·30	1·10
253	45c. Black fellows' bread ("Rock mushroom")	1·30	1·10
254	45c. Chicken mushroom ("Polyporous")	1·30	1·10
255	45c. Veiled stinkhorn	1·30	1·10

43 Robin-redbreast Triton

1989. Sea Shells (5th series). Multicoloured.

256	25c. Type **43**	80	70
257	25c. Hebrew cone	80	70
258	25c. Tadpole triton	80	70
259	25c. Lettered cone	80	70
260	25c. Rugose mitre	80	70

44 Cessna 207 Stationair 7

1989. Air. Aircraft. Multicoloured.

261	36c. Type **44**	95	80
262	39c. Embraer Bandeirante airliner	1·00	90
264	45c. Boeing 727 jetliner	1·40	1·20

No. 261 is wrongly inscribed "Skywagon".

45 "Little Bird amidst Chrysanthemum" (Ando Hiroshige)

1989. Emperor Hirohito of Japan Commemoration. Sheet 67×101 mm.

MS266	**45** $1 multicoloured	3·25	3·00

46 Jettison of Third Stage

1989. 20th Anniv of First Manned Landing on Moon. Multicoloured.

267	25c. Type **46**	65	55
268	25c. Command Module adjusting position	65	55
269	25c. Lunar Excursion Module "Eagle" docking	65	55
270	25c. Space module docking	65	55
271	25c. Propulsion for entry into lunar orbit	65	55
272	25c. Third stage burn	65	55
273	25c. Command Module orbiting Moon	65	55
274	25c. Command Module and part of "Eagle"	65	55
275	25c. Upper part of "Eagle" on Moon	65	55
276	25c. Descent of "Eagle"	65	55
277	25c. Nose of rocket	65	55
278	25c. Reflection in Edwin "Buzz" Aldrin's visor	65	55
279	25c. Neil Armstrong and flag on Moon	65	55
280	25c. Footprints and astronaut's oxygen tank	65	55
281	25c. Upper part of astronaut descending ladder	65	55
282	25c. Launch tower and body of rocket	65	55
283	25c. Survival equipment on Aldrin's space suit	65	55
284	25c. Blast off from lunar surface	65	55
285	25c. View of Earth and astronaut's legs	65	55
286	25c. Leg on ladder	65	55
287	25c. Lift off	65	55
288	25c. Spectators at launch	65	55
289	25c. Capsule parachuting into Pacific	65	55
290	25c. Re-entry	65	55
291	25c. Space Module jettison	65	55
292	$2.40 "Buzz" Aldrin on Moon (photo by Neil Armstrong) (34×47 mm)	7·00	6·00

Nos. 267/91 were issued together, se-tenant, forming a composite design.

47 Girl as Astronaut

1989. Year of the Young Reader. Multicoloured.

293	25c. Type **47**	60	50
294	25c. Boy riding dolphin	60	50
295	25c. Cheshire Cat in tree	60	50
296	25c. Mother Goose	60	50
297	25c. Baseball player	60	50
298	25c. Girl reading	60	50
299	25c. Boy reading	60	50
300	25c. Mother reading to child	60	50
301	25c. Girl holding flowers listening to story	60	50
302	25c. Boy in baseball strip	60	50

48 Bridled Tern

1989. "World Stamp Expo '89" International Stamp Exhibition, Washington D.C. Stilt Mangrove. Multicoloured.

303	25c. Type **48**	80	70
304	25c. Lemon migrant (inscr "Sulphur Butterfly")	80	70
305	25c. Micronesian flycatcher ("Mangrove Flycatcher")	80	70
306	25c. White-collared kingfisher	80	70
307	25c. Fruit bat	80	70
308	25c. Estuarine crocodile	80	70
309	25c. Nankeen ("Rufous Night Heron")	80	70
310	25c. Stilt mangrove	80	70
311	25c. Bird's nest fern	80	70
312	25c. Beach hibiscus tree	80	70
313	25c. Common eggfly (butterfly)	80	70
314	25c. Dog-faced watersnake	80	70
315	25c. Mangrove jingle shell	80	70
316	25c. Palau bark cricket	80	70
317	25c. Periwinkle and mangrove oyster	80	70
318	25c. Jellyfish	80	70
319	25c. Flat-headed grey ("Striped") mullet	80	70
320	25c. Mussels, sea anemones and algae	80	70
321	25c. Pajama cardinalfish	80	70
322	25c. Black-tailed snappers	80	70

Nos. 303/22 are each inscribed on the back (over the gum) with the name of the subject featured on the stamp.

Nos. 303/22 were issued together, se-tenant, forming a composite design.

49 Angels, Sooty Tern and Audubon's Shearwater

1989. Christmas. Carol of the Birds. Mult.

323	25c. Type **49**	80	70
324	25c. Palau fruit dove and angel	80	70
325	25c. Madonna and child, cherub and birds	80	70
326	25c. Angel, blue-faced parrot finch, Micronesian flycatcher and cardinal honeyeater	80	70
327	25c. Angel, Micronesian flycatcher and black-headed gulls	80	70

Nos. 323/7 were printed together, se-tenant, forming a composite design.

50 Pink Coral

1990. Soft Corals. Multicoloured.

328	25c. Type **50**	80	70
329	25c. Mauve coral	80	70
330	25c. Yellow coral	80	70
331	25c. Orange coral	80	70

See also Nos. 392/5.

51 Siberian Rubythroat

1990. Forest Birds. Multicoloured.

332	45c. Type **51**	1·20	1·10
333	45c. Palau bush warbler	1·20	1·10
334	45c. Micronesian starling	1·20	1·10
335	45c. Common cicdabird ("Cicadabird")	1·20	1·10

52 Prince Lee Boo, Capt. Henry Wilson and H.M.S. "Victory"

1990. "Stamp World London 90" International Stamp Exhibition. Prince Lee Boo's Visit to England, 1784, and 150th Anniv of the Penny Black. Multicoloured.

336	25c. Type **52**	65	55
337	25c. St. James's Palace	65	55
338	25c. Rotherhithe Docks	65	55
339	25c. Oroolong House, Devon (Capt. Wilson's home)	65	55
340	25c. Vincenzo Lunardi's balloon	65	55
341	25c. St. Paul's Cathedral	65	55
342	25c. Prince Lee Boo's grave	65	55
343	25c. St. Mary's Church, Rotherhithe	65	55
344	25c. Memorial tablet to Prince Lee Boo	65	55
MS345	115×85 mm. $1 Penny Black (vert)	3·00	2·50

53 "Corymborkis veratrifolia"

1990. "Expo 90" International Garden and Greenery Exposition, Osaka. Orchids. Multicoloured.

346	45c. Type **53**	1·20	1·00
347	45c. "Malaxis setipes"	1·20	1·00
348	45c. "Dipodium freycinetianum"	1·20	1·00
349	45c. "Bulbophyllum micronesiacum"	1·20	1·00
350	45c. "Vanda teres"	1·20	1·00

54 Plane Butterfly on Beach Sunflower

1990. Butterflies. Multicoloured.

351	45c. Type **54**	1·20	1·00
352	45c. Painted lady on coral tree	1·20	1·00
353	45c. "Euploea nemertes" on sorcerer's flower	1·20	1·00
354	45c. Meadow argus (inscr "Buckeye") on beach pea	1·20	1·00

55 White Tern, Pacific Golden Plover and Sanderling

1990. Lagoon Life. Multicoloured.

355	25c. Type **55**	60	50
356	25c. Bidekill fisherman	60	50
357	25c. Yacht and insular halfbeaks	60	50
358	25c. Palauan kaebs	60	50
359	25c. White-tailed tropic bird	60	50
360	25c. Spotted eagle ray	60	50
361	25c. Great barracudas	60	50
362	25c. Reef needlefish	60	50
363	25c. Reef needlefish and black-finned reef ("Reef Blacktip") shark	60	50
364	25c. Hawksbill turtle	60	50
365	25c. Six-feelered threadfins and octopus	60	50
366	25c. Narrow-banded batfish and six-feelered threadfins	60	50
367	25c. Lionfish and six-feelered threadfins	60	50
368	25c. Snowflake moray and six-feelered threadfins	60	50
369	25c. Inflated and uninflated porcupinefishes and six-feelered threadfins	60	50
370	25c. Regal angelfish, blue-streaked cleaner wrasse, blue sea star and corals	60	50
371	25c. Clown triggerfish and spotted garden eels	60	50
372	25c. Anthias and spotted garden eels	60	50
373	25c. Sail-finned snapper ("Bluelined sea bream"), blue-green chromis, blue ("Sapphire") damselfish and spotted garden eel	60	50
374	25c. Masked ("Orange-spine") unicornfish and ribbon-striped ("White-tipped") soldierfish	60	50
375	25c. Slatepencil sea urchin and leopard sea cucumber	60	50
376	25c. Pacific partridge tun (shell)	60	50
377	25c. Mandarin fish and spotted garden eel	60	50
378	25c. Tiger cowrie	60	50
379	25c. Feather starfish and orange-finned anemonefish	60	50

Nos. 355/79 were printed together, se-tenant, forming a composite design.

56 *Delphin*, 1890, and Card

1990. Pacifica. Mail Transport. Multicoloured.

380	45c. Type **56**	1·70	1·50
381	45c. Right-hand half of card flown on 1951 inaugural U.S. civilian airmail flight and forklift unloading mail from Boeing 727	1·70	1·50

Nos. 380/1 were issued together, se-tenant, forming a composite design.

57 Girls singing and Boy with Butterfly

1990. Christmas. Multicoloured.

382	25c. Type **57**	75	65
383	25c. White terns perching on girl's songbook	75	65
384	25c. Girl singing and boys playing flute and guitar	75	65
385	25c. Couple with baby	75	65
386	25c. Three girls singing	75	65

58 Consolidated B-24S Liberator Bombers over Peleliu

1990. 46th Anniv of U.S. Action in Palau Islands during Second World War.

387	45c. Type **58**	1·50	1·30
388	45c. Landing craft firing rocket barrage	1·50	1·30
389	45c. 1st Marine division attacking Peleliu	1·50	1·30
390	45c. U.S. Infantryman and Palauan children	1·50	1·30
MS391	105×53 mm. $1 U.S.S. "Peleiu" (helicopter carrier) (50× 38 mm)	3·50	3·00

1991. Hard Corals. As T 50.

392	30c. Staghorn coral	90	75
393	30c. Velvet leather coral	90	75
394	30c. Van Gogh's cypress coral	90	75
395	30c. Violet lace coral	90	75

59 Statue of Virgin Mary, Nkulangelul Point

1991. Angaur, The Phosphate Island. Mult.

396	30c. Type **59**	90	75
397	30c. Angaur Post Office opening day cancellation and kaeb (sailing canoe) (41×27 mm)	90	75
398	30c. Billfish and Caroline Islands 40pf. "Yacht" stamp (41×27 mm)	90	75
399	30c. Steam locomotive at phosphate mine	90	75
400	30c. Lighthouse Hill and German copra freighter	90	75
401	30c. Dolphins and map showing phosphate mines (41×27 mm)	90	75
402	30c. Estuarine crocodile (41×27 mm)	90	75
403	30c. Workers cycling to phosphate plant	90	75
404	30c. Freighter loading phosphate	90	75
405	30c. Hammerhead shark and German overseer (41×27 mm)	90	75
406	30c. Angaur cancellation and Marshall Islands 10pf. "Yacht" stamp (41×27 mm)	90	75
407	30c. Rear Admiral Graf von Spee and "Scharnhorst" (German cruiser)	90	75
408	30c. "Emden" (German cruiser) and Capt. Karl von Muller	90	75
409	30c. Crab-eating macaque (41×27 mm)	90	75
410	30c. Sperm whale (41×27 mm)	90	75
411	30c. H.M.A.S. "Sydney" (cruiser) shelling radio tower	90	75

Nos. 396/411 were issued together, se-tenant, with the centre block of eight stamps forming a composite design of a map of the island.

60 Moorhen

1991. Birds. Multicoloured.

412	1c. Palau bush warbler	25	15
413	4c. Type **60**	25	15
414	6c. Buff-banded rail ("Banded Rail")	25	15
415	19c. Palau fantail	45	35
416	20c. Micronesian flycatcher ("Mangrove Flycatcher")	45	35
417	23c. Purple swamphen	55	35
418	29c. Palau fruit dove	75	50
419	35c. Crested tern	95	65
420	40c. Reef herons (inscr "Pacific Reef-Heron")	1·10	70
421	45c. Micronesian pigeon	1·20	80
422	50c. Great frigate bird	1·40	90
423	52c. Little pied cormorant	1·40	1·00
424	75c. Jungle nightjar	2·00	1·40
425	95c. Cattle egret	2·75	1·70
426	$1.34 Sulphur-crested cockatoo	3·00	2·30
427	$2 Blue-faced parrot finch	4·50	3·50
428	$5 Eclectus parrots	11·00	9·00
429	$10 Palau bush warblers feeding chicks (51×28 mm)	22·00	17·00

61 Pope Leo XIII and 19th-century Spanish and German Flags

1991. Centenary of Christianity in Palau Islands. Multicoloured.

432	29c. Type **61**	80	70
433	29c. Ibedul Ilengelekei and Church of the Sacred Heart, Koror, 1920	80	70
434	29c. Marino de la Hoz, Emilio Villar and Elias Fernandez (Jesuit priests executed in Second World War)	80	70
435	29c. Centenary emblem and Fr. Edwin G. McManus (compiler of Palauan–English dictionary)	80	70
436	29c. Present Church of the Sacred Heart, Koror	80	70
437	29c. Pope John Paul II and Palau and Vatican flags	80	70

62 Pacific White-sided Dolphin

1991. Pacific Marine Life. Multicoloured.

438	29c. Type **62**	90	75
439	29c. Common dolphin	90	75
440	29c. Rough-toothed dolphin	90	75
441	29c. Bottle-nosed dolphin	90	75
442	29c. Common (inscr "Harbor") porpoise	90	75
443	29c. Head and body of killer whale	90	75
444	29c. Tail of killer whale, spinner dolphin and yellow-finned tuna	90	75
445	29c. Dall's porpoise	90	75
446	29c. Finless porpoise	90	75
447	29c. Map of Palau Islands and bottle-nosed dolphin	90	75
448	29c. Dusky dolphin	90	75
449	29c. Southern right whale dolphin	90	75
450	29c. Striped dolphin	90	75
451	29c. Fraser's dolphin	90	75
452	29c. Peale's dolphin	90	75
453	29c. Spectacled porpoise	90	75
454	29c. Spotted dolphin	90	75
455	29c. Hourglass dolphin	90	75
456	29c. Risso's dolphin	90	75
457	29c. Hector's dolphin	90	75

63 McDonnell Douglas Wild Weasel Fighters

1991. Operation Desert Storm (liberation of Kuwait). Multicoloured.

458	20c. Type **63**	55	45
459	20c. Lockheed Stealth fighter-bomber	55	45
460	20c. Hughes Apache helicopter	55	45
461	20c. "M-109 TOW" missile on "M998 HMMWV" vehicle	55	45
462	20c. President Bush of U.S.A.	55	45
463	20c. M2 "Bradley" tank	55	45
464	20c. U.S.S. "Ranger" (aircraft carrier)	55	45
465	20c. "Pegasus" (patrol boat)	55	45
466	20c. U.S.S. "Wisconsin" (battleship)	55	45
467	$2.90 Sun, dove and yellow ribbon	7·00	6·25
MS468	101×127 mm. No. 467	7·75	7·00

64 Bai Gable

1991. 10th Anniv of Republic of Palau and Palau–Pacific Women's Conference, Koror. Bai (community building) Decorations. Mult. Imperf (self-adhesive) (50c.), perf (others).

469	29c. Type **64** (postage)	80	70
470	29c. Interior of bai (left side) (32×48 mm)	80	70
471	29c. Interior of bai (right side) (32×48 mm)	80	70
472	29c. God of construction	80	70
473	29c. Bubuu (spider) (value at left) (30×23 mm)	80	70
474	29c. Delerrok, the money bird (facing right) (31×23 mm)	80	70
475	29c. Delerrok (facing left) (31×23 mm)	80	70
476	29c. Bubuu (value at right) (30×23 mm)	80	70
477	50c. Bai gable (as in Type **64**) (24×51 mm) (air)	2·00	1·70

Nos. 469/76 were issued together, se-tenant, Nos. 470/1 forming a composite design.

65 Bear's-paw Clam, China Clam, Fluted Giant Clam and "Tridacna derasa"

1991. Conservation and Cultivation of Giant Clams. Multicoloured.

478	50c. Type **65**	1·40	1·20
479	50c. Symbiotic relationship between giant clam and "Symbiodinium microadriaticum"	1·40	1·20
480	50c. Hatchery	1·40	1·20
481	50c. Diver measuring clams in sea-bed nursery	1·40	1·20
482	50c. Micronesian Mariculture Demonstration Center, Koror (108×16 mm)	1·40	1·20

66 "Silent Night, Holy Night!"

1991. Christmas. Multicoloured.

483	29c. Type **66**	75	65
484	29c. "All is calm, all is bright;"	75	65
485	29c. "Round yon virgin mother and child!"	75	65
486	29c. "Holy Infant, so tender and mild,"	75	65
487	29c. "Sleep in heavenly peace."	75	65

Nos. 483/7 were issued together, se-tenant, forming a composite design.

67 Flag, Islands and Children

1991. 25th Anniv of Presence of United States Peace Corps in Palau. Children's paintings.

488	29c. Type **67**	80	70
489	29c. Volunteers arriving by airplane	80	70
490	29c. Health care	80	70
491	29c. Fishing	80	70
492	29c. Agriculture	80	70
493	29c. Education	80	70

68 *Zuiho Maru* (commercial trochus shell breeding and marine research)

1991. "Phila Nippon '91" International Stamp Exhibition, Tokyo. Japanese Heritage in Palau. Multicoloured.

494	29c. Type **68**	80	70
495	29c. Man carving story board (traditional arts)	80	70
496	29c. Tending pineapple crop (agricultural training)	80	70
497	29c. Klidm (stone carving), Koror (archaeological research)	80	70
498	29c. Teaching carpentry and building design	80	70
499	29c. Kawasaki "Mavis" flying boat (air transport)	80	70
MS500	71×102 mm. $1 Map, yellow-finned tuna and 1941 cancellation	4·00	3·75

69 Mitsubishi Zero-Sen attacking Shipping at Pearl Harbor

1991. Pacific Theatre in Second World War (1st issue). Multicoloured.

501	29c. Type **69**	85	80
502	29c. U.S.S. "Nevada" underway from Pearl Harbor	85	80
503	29c. U.S.S. "Shaw" exploding at Pearl Harbor	85	80
504	29c. Douglas Dauntless dive bombers attacking Japanese carrier "Akagi"	85	80
505	29c. U.S.S. "Wasp" sinking off Guadalcanal	85	80
506	29c. Battle of Philippine Sea	85	80
507	29c. Landing craft storming Saipan Beach	85	80
508	29c. U.S. 1st Cavalry on Leyte	85	80
509	29c. Battle of Bloody Nose Ridge, Peleliu	85	80
510	29c. U.S. troops landing at Iwo Jima	85	80

See also Nos. 574/83, 601/10 and 681/90.

70 *Troides criton*

1992. Butterflies. Multicoloured.

511	50c. Type **70**	1·30	1·30
512	50c. *Alcides zodiaca*	1·30	1·30
513	50c. *Papilio poboroi*	1·30	1·30
514	50c. *Vindula arsinoe*	1·30	1·30

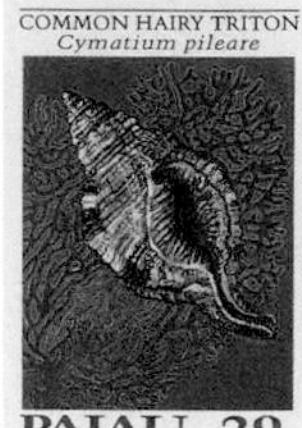

71 Common Hairy Triton

1992. Sea Shells (6th series). Multicoloured.

515	29c. Type **71**	80	75
516	29c. Eglantine cowrie	80	75
517	29c. Sulcate swamp cerith	80	75
518	29c. Black-spined murex	80	75
519	29c. Black-mouth moon	80	75

72 Christopher Columbus

1992. Age of Discovery from Columbus to Drake. Multicoloured.

520	29c. Type **72**	80	75
521	29c. Ferdinand Magellan	80	75
522	29c. Sir Francis Drake	80	75
523	29c. Cloud blowing northerly wind	80	75
524	29c. Compass rose	80	75
525	29c. Dolphin and "Golden Hind" (Drake's ship)	80	75
526	29c. Corn cobs and "Santa Maria" (Columbus's ship)	80	75
527	29c. Mythical fishes	80	75
528	29c. Betel palm, cloves and black pepper	80	75
529	29c. "Vitoria" (Magellan's ship), Palau Islands, Audubon's shearwater and crested tern	80	75
530	29c. White-tailed tropic bird, bicoloured parrotfish, pine-apple and potatoes	80	75
531	29c. Compass	80	75
532	29c. Mythical sea monster	80	75
533	29c. Paddles and astrolabe	80	75
534	29c. Parallel ruler, divider and Inca gold treasure	80	75
535	29c. Backstaff	80	75
536	29c. Cloud blowing southerly wind	80	75
537	29c. Amerigo Vespucci	80	75
538	29c. Francisco Pizarro	80	75
539	29c. Vasco Nunez de Balboa	80	75

With the exception of Nos. 523 and 536 each stamp is inscribed on the back (over the gum) with the name of the subject featured on the stamp.

Nos. 520/39 were issued together, se-tenant, the backgrounds forming a composite design of the hemispheres.

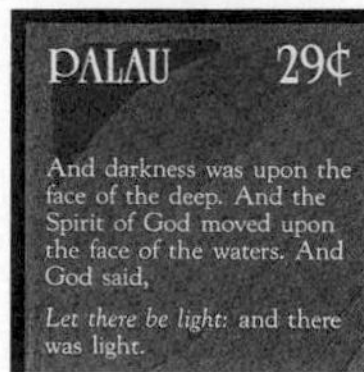

73 "And darkness was upon the face of the deep ..."

1992. 2nd U.N. Conference on Environment and Development, Rio de Janeiro. The Creation of the World from the Book of Genesis, Chapter 1. Multicoloured.

540	29c. Type **73**	80	75
541	29c. Sunlight	80	75
542	29c. "Let there be a firmament in the midst of the waters, ..."	80	75
543	29c. Sky and clouds	80	75
544	29c. "Let the waters under the heaven ..."	80	75
545	29c. Tree	80	75
546	29c. Waves and sunlight (no inscr)	80	75
547	29c. Waves and sunlight ("... and it was good.")	80	75
548	29c. Waves and clouds (no inscr)	80	75
549	29c. Waves and clouds ("... and it was so.")	80	75
550	29c. Plants on river bank (no inscr)	80	75
551	29c. Plants on river bank ("... and it was good.")	80	75
552	29c. "Let there be lights in the firmament ..."	80	75
553	29c. Comet, planet and clouds	80	75
554	29c. "Let the waters bring forth abundantly the moving creature ..."	80	75
555	29c. Great frigate bird and red-tailed tropic bird flying and collared lory on branch	80	75
556	29c. "Let the earth bring forth the living creature after his kind ..."	80	75
557	29c. Woman, man and rainbow	80	75
558	29c. Mountains ("... and it was good.")	80	75
559	29c. Sun and hills	80	75
560	29c. Killer whale and fishes	80	75
561	29c. Fishes ("... and it was good.")	80	75
562	29c. Elephants and squirrel	80	75
563	29c. Orchard and cat ("... and it was very good.")	80	75

Nos. 540/63 were issued together, se-tenant, forming six composite designs each covering four stamps.

74 Greg Louganis (diving)

1992. Olympic Games, Barcelona. Six sheets, each 80×110 mm containing horiz design as T 74 showing outstanding competitors.

MS564 Six sheets. (a) 50c. Type **74**; (b) 50c. Dawn Fraser (swimming); (c) 50c. Carl Lewis (track and field); (d) 50c. Bob Beamon (long jumping); (e) 50c. Olga Korbutt (gymnast); (f) 50c. Dick Fosbury (high jumping) 7·75 7·50

75 Presley and Dove

1992. 15th Death Anniv of Elvis Presley (entertainer). Multicoloured.

565	29c. Type **75**	1·00	90
566	29c. Presley and dove's wing	1·00	90
567	29c. Presley in yellow cape	1·00	90
568	29c. Presley in white and red shirt (¾ face)	1·00	90
569	29c. Presley singing into microphone	1·00	90
570	29c. Presley crying	1·00	90
571	29c. Presley in red shirt (¾ face)	1·00	90
572	29c. Presley in purple shirt (full face)	1·00	90
573	29c. Presley (left profile)	1·00	90

76 Grumman Avenger

1992. Air. Pacific Theatre in Second World War (2nd issue). Aircraft. Multicoloured.

574	50c. Type **76**	1·30	1·20
575	50c. Curtiss P-40C of the Flying Tigers fighters	1·30	1·20
576	50c. Mitsubishi Zero-Sen fighter	1·30	1·20
577	50c. Hawker Hurricane Mk I fighter	1·30	1·20
578	50c. Consolidated Catalina flying boat	1·30	1·20
579	50c. Curtiss Hawk 75 fighter	1·30	1·20
580	50c. Boeing Flying Fortress bomber	1·30	1·20
581	50c. Brewster Buffalo fighter	1·30	1·20
582	50c. Vickers Supermarine Walrus flying boat	1·30	1·20
583	50c. Curtiss Kittyhawk I fighter	1·30	1·20

77 "Thus Every Beast"

1992. Christmas. "The Friendly Beasts" (carol). Multicoloured.

584	29c. Type **77**	80	75
585	29c. "By Some Good Spell"	80	75
586	29c. "In the Stable Dark was Glad to Tell"	80	75
587	29c. "Of the Gift He Gave Emanuel" (angel on donkey)	80	75
588	29c. "The Gift He Gave Emanuel" (Palau fruit doves)	80	75

78 Dugong

1993. Animals. Multicoloured.

589	50c. Type **78**	1·30	1·20
590	50c. Blue-faced booby ("Masked Booby")	1·30	1·20
591	50c. Crab-eating macaque	1·30	1·20
592	50c. New Guinea crocodile	1·30	1·20

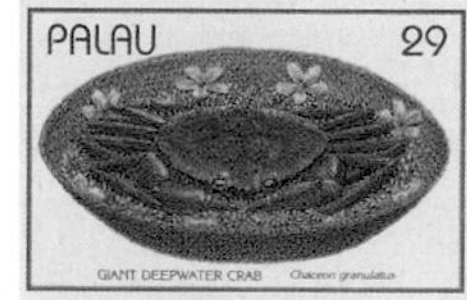

79 Giant Deepwater Crab

1993. Seafood. Multicoloured.

593	29c. Type **79**	80	75
594	29c. Scarlet shrimp	80	75
595	29c. Smooth nylon shrimp	80	75
596	29c. Armed nylon shrimp	80	75

80 Oceanic White-tipped Shark

1993. Sharks. Multicoloured.

597	50c. Type **80**	1·30	1·20
598	50c. Great hammerhead	1·30	1·20
599	50c. Zebra ("Leopard") shark	1·30	1·20
600	50c. Black-finned reef shark	1·30	1·20

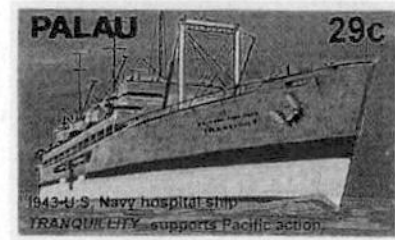

81 U.S.S. "Tranquility" (hospital ship)

1993. Pacific Theatre in Second World War (3rd issue). Multicoloured.

601	29c. Capture of Guadalcanal	1·00	95
602	29c. Type **81**	1·00	95
603	29c. New Guineans drilling	1·00	95
604	29c. Americans land in New Georgia	1·00	95
605	29c. U.S.S. "California" (battleship)	1·00	95
606	29c. Douglas Dauntless dive bombers over Wake Island	1·00	95
607	29c. Flame-throwers on Tarawa	1·00	95
608	29c. American advance on Makin	1·00	95
609	29c. North American B-25 Mitchells bomb Simpson Harbour, Rabaul	1·00	95
610	29c. Aerial bombardment of Kwajalein	1·00	95

82 Girl with Goat

1993. Christmas. Multicoloured.

611	29c. Type **82**	80	75
612	29c. Children with garlands and goats	80	75
613	29c. Father Christmas	80	75
614	29c. Musicians and singer	80	75
615	29c. Family carrying food	80	75

83 Pterosaur

1993. Monsters of the Pacific. Multicoloured.

616	29c. Type **83**	80	75
617	29c. Outrigger canoe	80	75
618	29c. Head of plesiosaur	80	75
619	29c. Pterosaur and neck of plesiosaur	80	75
620	29c. Pterosaur (flying towards left)	80	75
621	29c. Giant crab	80	75
622	29c. Tentacles of squid and two requiem sharks	80	75
623	29c. Hammerhead shark, tentacle of squid and neck of plesiosaur	80	75
624	29c. Head of lake serpent	80	75
625	29c. Hammerhead shark and neck of serpent	80	75
626	29c. Squid ("Kraken")	80	75
627	29c. Manta ray, tentacles of squid and body of plesiosaur	80	75
628	29c. Three barracudas and body of plesiosaur	80	75
629	29c. Angelfishes and serpent's claw	80	75
630	29c. Octopus and body of serpent	80	75
631	29c. Nautilus and body of plesiosaur	80	75
632	29c. Moorish idols (two striped fishes)	80	75
633	29c. Lionfish	80	75
634	29c. Squid	80	75
635	29c. Requiem shark and body of kronosaur	80	75
636	29c. Zebra shark and sea-bed	80	75
637	29c. Squid and sea-bed	80	75
638	29c. Giant nautilus and tail of serpent	80	75
639	29c. Head of kronosaur	80	75
640	29c. Lionfish, body of kronosaur and sea-bed	80	75

Nos. 616/40 were issued together, se-tenant, forming a composite design.

84 "After Child-birth Ceremony" (Charlie Gibbons)

1993. International Year of Indigenous Peoples. Multicoloured.

641	29c. Type **84**	1·30	1·10
642	29c. "Village in Early Palau" (Charlie Gibbons)	1·30	1·10

MS643 112×96 mm. $290 "Quarrying of Stone Money" (storyboard carving, Ngiraibuuch Skebong) (37×50 mm) 7·75 7·50

85 Flukes of Whale's Tail

1993. Jonah and The Whale. Multicoloured.

644	29c. Type **85**	80	75
645	29c. Bird and part of fluke	80	75
646	29c. Two birds	80	75
647	29c. Kaeb (canoe)	80	75
648	29c. Sun, birds and dolphin	80	75
649	29c. Shark and whale's tail	80	75
650	29c. Shoal of brown fishes and part of whale	80	75
651	29c. Hammerhead shark, shark's tail and fishes	80	75
652	29c. Dolphin (fish) and shark's head	80	75
653	29c. Dolphin and fishes	80	75
654	29c. Scombroid and other fishes and part of whale	80	75
655	29c. Two turtles swimming across whale's body	80	75
656	29c. Shoal of pink fishes and whale's back	80	75
657	29c. Spotted eagle ray, manta ray and top of whale's head	80	75
658	29c. Two groupers and shoal of small brown fishes	80	75
659	29c. Jellyfish and wrasse (blue fish)	80	75
660	29c. Wrasse, other fishes and whale's dorsal fin	80	75
661	29c. Whale's eye and corner of mouth	80	75
662	29c. Opened mouth	80	75
663	29c. Jonah	80	75
664	29c. Convict tang (yellow and black striped fish) and brain corals on sea bed	80	75
665	29c. Hump-headed bannerfishes and sea anenome	80	75
666	29c. Undulate triggerfish (blue-striped) and corals on sea bed	80	75
667	29c. Brown and red striped fish, corals and part of whale's jaw	80	75
668	29c. Two groupers (spotted) on sea bed	80	75

Nos. 644/68 were issued together, se-tenant, forming a composite design.

86 Alfred's Manta

1994. "Hong Kong '94" International Stamp Exhibition. Rays. Multicoloured.

669	40c. Type **86**	1·00	95
670	40c. Spotted eagle ray	1·00	95
671	40c. Coachwhip stingray	1·00	95
672	40c. Black-spotted stingray	1·00	95

87 Crocodile's Head

1994. The Estuarine Crocodile. Multicoloured.

673	20c. Type **87**	1·20	1·10
674	20c. Hatchling and eggs	1·20	1·10
675	20c. Crocodile swimming underwater	1·20	1·10
676	20c. Crocodile half-submerged	1·20	1·10

88 Red-footed Booby

1994. Sea Birds. Multicoloured.

677	50c. Type **88**	1·30	1·20
678	50c. Great frigate bird	1·30	1·20
679	50c. Brown booby	1·30	1·20
680	50c. Little pied cormorant	1·30	1·20

89 U.S. Marines capture Kwajalein

1994. Pacific Theatre in Second World War (4th issue). Multicoloured.

681	29c. Type **89**	1·10	1·00
682	29c. Aerial bombardment of Japanese airbase, Truk	1·10	1·00
683	29c. U.S.S. 284 "Tullibee" (submarine) (Operation Desecrate)	1·10	1·00
684	29c. Landing craft storming Saipan beach	1·10	1·00
685	29c. Shooting down Japanese Mitsubishi Zero-Sen bombers, Mariana Islands (Turkey Shoot)	1·10	1·00
686	29c. Liberated civilians, Guam	1·10	1·00
687	29c. U.S. troops taking Peleliu	1·10	1·00
688	29c. Securing Angaur	1·10	1·00
689	29c. General Douglas MacArthur	1·10	1·00
690	29c. U.S. Army memorial	1·10	1·00

90 Allied Warships

1994. 50th Anniv of D-day (Allied Landings in Normandy). Multicoloured.

691	50c. C-47 transport aircraft dropping paratroopers	1·60	1·50
692	50c. Type **90**	1·60	1·50
693	50c. Troops disembarking from landing craft	1·60	1·50
694	50c. Tanks coming ashore	1·60	1·50
695	50c. Sherman tank crossing minefield	1·60	1·50
696	50c. Aircraft attacking German positions	1·60	1·50
697	50c. Gliders dropping paratroops behind lines	1·60	1·50
698	50c. Pegasus Bridge	1·60	1·50
699	50c. Allied forces pushing inland	1·60	1·50
700	50c. Beach at end of 6 June 1944	1·60	1·50

91 Baron Pierre de Coubertin (founder of modern games)

1994. Centenary of International Olympic Committee. Multicoloured.

701	29c. Type **91**	90	90
MS702	Six sheets each 110×80 mm. (a) 50c. Anne-Marie Moser (skater) (vert); (b) 50c. James Craig (ice hockey) (vert); (c) $1 Eric Heiden (speed skater) (vert); (d) $1 Nancy Kerrigan (ice skater); (f) $2 Dan Jansen (speed skater) holding child and flowers	16·00	15·00

92 Top of "Saturn V" Rocket and Command and Lunar Modules joined

1994. 25th Anniv of First Manned Moon Landing. Multicoloured.

703	29c. Type **92**	80	75
704	29c. Lunar module preparing to land (side view)	80	75
705	29c. Lunar module leaving surface (top view)	80	75
706	29c. Command module (view of circular end)	80	75
707	29c. Earth viewed from Moon	80	75
708	29c. "Saturn V" third stage	80	75
709	29c. Neil Armstrong descending ladder to lunar surface	80	75
710	29c. Footprint in lunar surface	80	75
711	29c. Alan Shepard and lunar module on Moon	80	75
712	29c. Command module separating from service module	80	75
713	29c. "Saturn V" second stage (rocket Inscr "USA USA")	80	75
714	29c. Rear view of "Apollo 17" astronaut at Splitrock Valley of Taurus-Littrow	80	75
715	29c. Lunar module reflected in visor of Edwin Aldrin	80	75
716	29c. James Irwin and David Scott raising flag on "Apollo 15" mission	80	75
717	29c. Command module descending with parachutes deployed	80	75
718	29c. "Saturn V" lifting off from Kennedy Space Center	80	75
719	29c. "Apollo 17" astronaut Harrison Schmitt collecting lunar surface samples with shovel	80	75
720	29c. "Apollo 16" astronaut John Young and lunar rover vehicle	80	75
721	29c. "Apollo 12" astronaut Charles Conrad collecting samples with machine	80	75
722	29c. Command module after splashdown	80	75

Nos. 703/22 were issued together, se-tenant, forming a composite design.

93 Sail-finned Goby

1994. "Philakorea 1994" International Stamp Exhibition, Seoul. Philatelic Fantasies. Designs showing named animal with various postal items. Multicoloured.

723	29c. Type **93** (postage)	1·00	95
724	29c. Black-saddled ("Sharp-nose") puffers	1·00	95
725	29c. Lightning butterflyfish	1·00	95
726	29c. Clown anemonefish	1·00	95
727	29c. Parrotfish	1·00	95
728	29c. Narrow-banded batfish	1·00	95
729	29c. Clown triggerfish	1·00	95
730	29c. Twin-spotted wrasse	1·00	95
731	40c. Palau fruit bat	1·30	1·30
732	40c. Crocodile	1·30	1·30
733	40c. Dugong	1·30	1·30
734	40c. Banded sea snake	1·30	1·30
735	40c. Bottle-nosed dolphin	1·30	1·30
736	40c. Hawksbill turtle	1·30	1·30
737	40c. Common octopus	1·30	1·30
738	40c. Manta ray	1·30	1·30
739	50c. Palau fantail and chicks (air)	1·60	1·50
740	50c. Banded crake	1·60	1·50
741	50c. Grey-rumped ("Island") swiftlets	1·60	1·50
742	50c. Micronesian kingfisher	1·60	1·50
743	50c. Red-footed booby	1·60	1·50
744	50c. Great frigate bird	1·60	1·50
745	50c. Palau scops owl	1·60	1·50
746	50c. Palau fruit dove	1·60	1·50

1994. 50th Anniv of American Invasion of Peleliu. No. MS391 optd 50th ANNIVERSARY INVASION OF PELEUU SEPTEMBER 1994.

MS747	105×53 mm. $1 multicoloured	3·25	3·25

95 Micronesian Monument (Henrik Starcke), U.N. Headquarters

1994. Attainment of Independence. Multicoloured.

748	29c. Type **95**	80	75
749	29c. Presidential seal	80	75
750	29c. Pres. Kuniwo Nakamura of Palau and Pres. William Clinton of United States shaking hands (56×41 mm)	80	75
751	29c. Palau and United States flags	80	75
752	29c. Score of "Belau Er Kid" (national anthem)	80	75

Nos. 748/52 were issued together, se-tenant, forming a composite design.

96 Mickey and Minnie Mouse at Airport

1994. Tourism. Walt Disney cartoon characters. Multicoloured.

753	29c. Type **96**	85	80
754	29c. Goofy on way to hotel	85	80
755	29c. Donald Duck on beach	85	80
756	29c. Minnie Mouse and Daisy Duck learning Ngloik (dance)	85	80
757	29c. Mickey and Minnie rafting to natural bridge	85	80
758	29c. Uncle Scrooge finding stone money in Babeldaob Jungle	85	80
759	29c. Goofy and napoleon wrasse after collision	85	80
760	29c. Minnie visiting clam garden	85	80
761	29c. Grandma Duck weaving basket	85	80
MS762	Three sheets each 127×101 mm. (a) $1 Mickey diving on shipwreck; (b) $1 Donald visiting Airai Bai on Babeldaob; (c) $2.90 Pluto and Mickey visiting Second World War aircraft wreck	18·00	17·00

97 Tebruchel in Mother's Arms

1994. International Year of the Family. Illustrating story of Tebruchel. Multicoloured.

763	20c. Type **97**	55	50
764	20c. Tebruchel's father (kneeling on beach)	55	50
765	20c. Tebruchel as youth	55	50
766	20c. Tebruchel's wife (standing on beach)	55	50
767	20c. Tebruchel with catch of fish	55	50
768	20c. Tebruchel's pregnant wife sitting in house	55	50
769	20c. Tebruchel's aged mother in dilapidated house	55	50
770	20c. Tebruchel's aged father (standing)	55	50
771	20c. Tebruchel holding first child	55	50
772	20c. Tebruchel's wife (sitting on beach mat)	55	50
773	20c. Tebruchel with aged mother	55	50
774	20c. Tebruchel's father (sitting cross-legged) and wife holding child	55	50

Nos. 763/74 were issued together, se-tenant, forming a composite design.

98 Wise Men and Cherubs

1994. Christmas. "O Little Town of Bethlehem" (carol). Multicoloured.

775	29c. Type **98**	80	75
776	29c. Angel, shepherds with sheep and cherub	80	75
777	29c. Angels and Madonna and Child	80	75
778	29c. Angels, Bethlehem and shepherd with sheep	80	75
779	29c. Cherubs and Palau fruit doves	80	75

Nos. 775/9 were issued together, se-tenant, forming a composite design.

99 Bora Milutinovic (coach)

1994. World Cup Football Championship, U.S.A. Multicoloured.

780	29c. Type **99**	80	75
781	29c. Cle Kooiman	80	75
782	29c. Ernie Stewart	80	75
783	29c. Claudio Reyna	80	75
784	29c. Thomas Dooley	80	75
785	29c. Alexi Lalas	80	75
786	29c. Dominic Kinnear	80	75
787	29c. Frank Klopas	80	75
788	29c. Paul Caligiuri	80	75
789	29c. Marcelo Balboa	80	75
790	29c. Cobi Jones	80	75
791	29c. U.S.A. flag and World Cup trophy	80	75
792	29c. Tony Meola	80	75
793	29c. John Doyle	80	75
794	29c. Eric Wynalda	80	75
795	29c. Roy Wegerle	80	75
796	29c. Fernando Clavijo	80	75
797	29c. Hugo Perez	80	75
798	29c. John Harkes	80	75
799	29c. Mike Lapper	80	75
800	29c. Mike Sorber	80	75
801	29c. Brad Friedel	80	75
802	29c. Tab Ramos	80	75
803	29c. Joe-Max Moore	80	75
804	50c. Babeto (Brazil)	1·20	1·10
805	50c. Romario (Brazil)	1·20	1·10
806	50c. Franco Baresi (Italy)	1·20	1·10
807	50c. Roberto Baggio (Italy)	1·20	1·10
808	50c. Andoni Zubizarreta (Spain)	1·20	1·10
809	50c. Oleg Salenko (Russia)	1·20	1·10
810	50c. Gheorghe Hagi (Rumania)	1·20	1·10
811	50c. Dennis Bergkamp (Netherlands)	1·20	1·10
812	50c. Hristo Stoichkov (Bulgaria)	1·20	1·10
813	50c. Tomas Brolin (Sweden)	1·20	1·10
814	50c. Lothar Matthaus (Germany)	1·20	1·10
815	50c. Arrigo Sacchi (Italy coach), Carlos Alberto Parreira (Brazil coach), flags and World Cup trophy	1·20	1·10

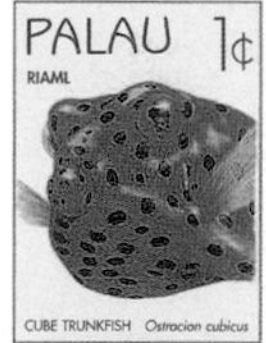

100 Yellow Boxfish ("Cube Trunkfish")

1995. Fishes. Multicoloured.

816	1c. Type **100**	25	20
817	2c. Lionfish	25	20
818	3c. Scarlet-finned ("Long-jawed") squirrelfish	25	20
819	4c. Harlequin ("Longnose") filefish	25	20
820	5c. Ornate butterflyfish	25	20
821	10c. Yellow seahorse	25	20
822	20c. Magenta dottyback (22×30 mm)	45	40
823	32c. Reef lizardfish (22×30 mm)	65	55
824	50c. Multibarred goatfish	1·10	90
825	55c. Barred blenny	1·30	95
826	$1 Fingerprint pufferfish	2·30	1·90
827	$2 Long-nosed hawkfish	4·50	3·75
828	$3 Mandarin fish	6·50	5·75
829	$5 Palette ("Blue") surgeonfish	11·00	9·75
830	$10 Coral hind (47×30 mm)	23·00	20·00
836	20c. Magenta dottyback (17½×21 mm)	25	15
837	32c. Reef lizardfish (17½×21 mm)	40	30

101 Presley

1995. 60th Birth Anniv of Elvis Presley (entertainer). Multicoloured.

838	32c. Type **101**	90	85
839	32c. Presley wearing white shirt and blue jacket	90	85
840	32c. Presley with microphone and flower	90	85
841	32c. Presley wearing blue shirt and jumper	90	85
842	32c. Presley with rose	90	85
843	32c. Presley with brown hair wearing white shirt	90	85
844	32c. Presley wearing blue open-necked shirt	90	85
845	32c. Presley (in green shirt) singing	90	85
846	32c. Presley as boy (with fair hair)	90	85

102 Grey-rumped ("Palau") Swiftlets

1995. Air. Birds. Multicoloured.

847	50c. Type **102**	1·30	1·20
848	50c. Barn swallows	1·30	1·20
849	50c. Jungle nightjar	1·30	1·20
850	50c. White-breasted wood swallow	1·30	1·20

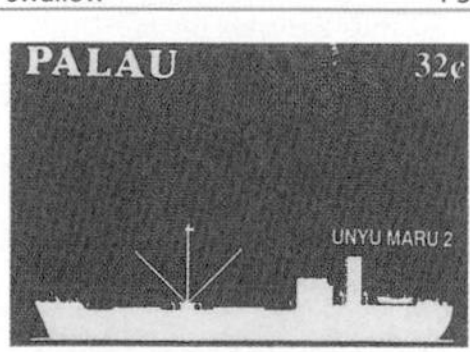

103 "Unyu Maru 2" (tanker)

1995. Japanese Fleet Sunk off Rock Islands (1944). Multicoloured.

851	32c. Type **103**	85	80
852	32c. "Wakatake" (destroyer)	85	80
853	32c. "Teshio Maru" (freighter)	85	80
854	32c. "Raizan Maru" (freighter)	85	80
855	32c. "Chuyo Maru" (freighter)	85	80
856	32c. "Shinsei Maru" (No. 18 freighter)	85	80
857	32c. "Urakami Maru" (freighter)	85	80
858	32c. "Ose Maru" (tanker)	85	80
859	32c. "Iro" (tanker)	85	80
860	32c. "Shosei Maru" (freighter)	85	80
861	32c. Patrol Boat 31	85	80
862	32c. "Kibi Maru" (freighter)	85	80
863	32c. "Amatsu Maru" (tanker)	85	80
864	32c. "Gozan Maru" (freighter)	85	80
865	32c. "Matuei Maru" (freighter)	85	80
866	32c. "Nagisan Maru" (freighter)	85	80
867	32c. "Akashi" (repair ship)	85	80
868	32c. "Kamikazi Maru" (freighter)	85	80

Nos. 851/68 were issued together, se-tenant, forming a composite design.

104 "Pteranodon sternbergi"

1995. 25th Anniv of Earth Day. Prehistoric Winged Animals. Multicoloured.

869	32c. Type **104**	85	80
870	32c. "Pteranodon ingens"	85	80
871	32c. Pterodactyls	85	80
872	32c. Dorygnathus	85	80
873	32c. Dimorphodon	85	80
874	32c. Nyctosaurus	85	80
875	32c. "Pterodactylus kochi"	85	80
876	32c. Ornithodesmus	85	80
877	32c. "Diatryma" sp.	85	80
878	32c. Archaeopteryx	85	80
879	32c. Campylognathoides	85	80
880	32c. Gallodactylus	85	80
881	32c. Batrachognathus	85	80
882	32c. Scaphognathus	85	80
883	32c. Peteinosaurus	85	80
884	32c. "Ichthyornis" sp.	85	80
885	32c. Ctenochasma	85	80
886	32c. Rhamphorhynchus	85	80

Nos. 869/86 were issued together, se-tenant, forming a composite design.

105 Fairey Delta 2

1995. Research and Experimental Jet-propelled Aircraft. Multicoloured.

887	50c. Type **105**	1·30	1·20
888	50c. B-70 Valkyrie	1·30	1·20
889	50c. Douglas X-3 Stiletto	1·30	1·20
890	50c. Northrop/Nasa HL-10	1·30	1·20
891	50c. Bell XS-1	1·30	1·20
892	50c. Tupolev Tu-144	1·30	1·20
893	50c. Bell X-1	1·30	1·20
894	50c. Boulton Paul P.111	1·30	1·20
895	50c. EWR VJ 101C	1·30	1·20
896	50c. Handley Page HP-115	1·30	1·20
897	50c. Rolls Royce TMR "Flying Bedstead"	1·30	1·20
898	50c. North American X-15	1·30	1·20
MS899	$2 Concorde (84×28 mm) (postage)	5·00	4·75

106 Scuba Gear

1995. Submersibles. Multicoloured.

900	32c. Type **106**	85	80
901	32c. Cousteau midget submarine "Denise"	85	80
902	32c. Jim suit	85	80
903	32c. Beaver IV	85	80
904	32c. "Ben Franklin"	85	80
905	32c. U.S.S. "Nautilus" (submarine)	85	80
906	32c. Deep Rover	85	80
907	32c. Beebe bathysphere	85	80
908	32c. "Deep Star IV"	85	80
909	32c. U.S. Navy Deep Submergence Rescue Vehicle	85	80
910	32c. "Aluminaut" (aluminium submarine)	85	80
911	32c. "Nautile"	85	80
912	32c. "Cyana"	85	80
913	32c. French Navy (F.N.R.S.) bathyscaphe	85	80
914	32c. Woods Hole Oceanographic Institute's "Alvin"	85	80
915	32c. "Mir I" (research submarine)	85	80
916	32c. "Archimede" (bathyscaphe)	85	80
917	32c. "Trieste" (bathyscaphe)	85	80

Nos. 900/917 were issued together, se-tenant, forming a composite design.

107 Dolphins, Diver and Pufferfish

1995. "Singapore'95" International Stamp Exhibition. Marine Life. Multicoloured.

918	32c. Type **107**	80	75
919	32c. Turtle and diver	80	75
920	32c. Grouper, anemonefish and crab on sea-bed (emblem on right)	80	75
921	32c. Parrotfish, lionfish and angelfish (emblem on left)	80	75

108 Dove in Helmet (Peace)

1995. 50th Annivs of U.N.O. and F.A.O. Mult.

922	60c. Type **108**	1·50	1·40
923	60c. Ibedul Gibbons (Palau chief) in flame (human rights)	1·50	1·40
924	60c. Palau atlas in open book (education)	1·50	1·40
925	60c. Bananas in tractor (agriculture)	1·50	1·40
MS926	Two sheets each 116×83 mm. (a) $2 National flag and Palau fruit dove; (b) $2 Irrigation of crops and anniversary emblem (FAO) (vert)	9·75	9·00

Nos. 922/5 were issued together, se-tenant, the centre of each block forming a composite design of the U.N. emblem.

109 Palau Fruit Doves

1995. 1st Anniv of Independence. Each showing Palau national flag. Multicoloured.

927	20c. Type **109**	50	45
928	20c. Rock Islands	50	45
929	20c. Map of Palau islands	50	45
930	20c. Orchid and hibiscus	50	45
931	32c. Raccoon butterflyfish, soldierfish and conch shell	80	75

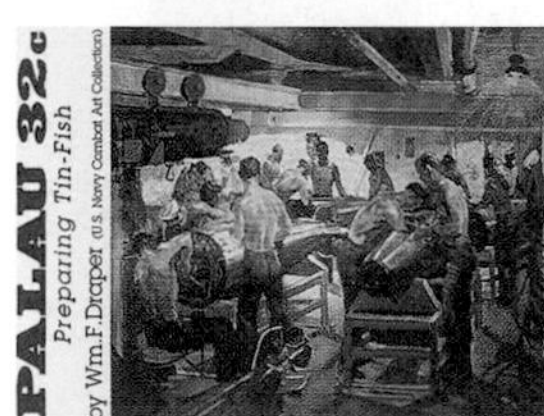

110 "Preparing Tin-Fish" (William Draper)

1995. 50th Anniv of the End of Second World War. Multicoloured.

932	32c. Type **110**	80	75
933	32c. "Hellcat's Take-off into Palau's Rising Sun" (Draper)	80	75
934	32c. "Dauntless Dive Bombers over Malakal Harbor" (Draper)	80	75
935	32c. "Planes Return from Palau" (Draper)	80	75
936	32c. "Communion Before Battle" (Draper)	80	75
937	32c. "The Landing" (Draper)	80	75
938	32c. "First Task Ashore" (Draper)	80	75
939	32c. "Fire Fighters save Flak-torn Pilot" (Draper)	80	75
940	32c. "Young Marine Headed for Peleliu" (Tom Lea)	80	75
941	32c. "Peleliu" (Lea)	80	75
942	32c. "Last Rites" (Lea)	80	75
943	32c. "The Thousand Yard Stare" (Lea)	80	75
944	60c. "Admiral Chester W. Nimitz" (Albert Murray) (vert)	1·80	1·70
945	60c. "Admiral William F. Halsey" (Murray) (vert)	1·80	1·70
946	60c. "Admiral Raymond A. Spruance" (Murray) (vert)	1·80	1·70
947	60c. "Vice-Admiral Marc A. Mitscher" (Murray) (vert)	1·80	1·70
948	60c. "General Holland M. Smith" (Murray) (vert)	1·80	1·70
MS949	129×90 mm. $3 Nose art on B-29 bomber Bock's Car (38×24½ mm)	7·25	6·75

111 Angel with Animals

1995. Christmas. "We Three Kings of Orient Are" (carol). Multicoloured.

950	32c. Type **111**	80	75

951 32c. Two wise men 80 75
952 32c. Shepherd at crib 80 75
953 32c. Wise man and shepherd 80 75
954 32c. Children with goat 80 75

Nos. 950/4 were issued together, se-tenant, forming a composite design.

112 Mother and Young in Feeding Area

1995. Year of the Sea Turtle. Multicoloured.

955 32c. Type **112** 85 80
956 32c. Young adult females meeting males 85 80
957 32c. Sun, cockerel in tree and mating area 85 80
958 32c. Woman and hatchlings 85 80
959 32c. Couple and nesting area 85 80
960 32c. House and female swimming to lay eggs 85 80

Nos. 955/60 were issued together, se-tenant, forming a composite design of the turtle's life cycle.

113 Lennon

1995. 15th Death Anniv of John Lennon (entertainer).

961 **113** 32c. multicoloured 1·20 1·10

114 Rats leading Procession

1996. Chinese New Year. Year of the Rat. Multicoloured.

962 10c. Type **114** 55 50
963 10c. Three rats playing instruments 55 50
964 10c. Rats playing tuba and banging drum 55 50
965 10c. Family of rats outside house 55 50

MS966 131×63 mm. 60c. Family of rats outside house and rats playing tuba and banging drum (56×42 mm); (b) 60c. Rats playing instruments and leading procession (56×42 mm) (air) 2·75 2·50

Nos. 962/5 were issued together, se-tenant, forming a composite design of a procession.

115 Girls

1996. 50th Anniv of UNICEF. Each showing three children. Multicoloured.

967 32c. Type **115** 75 70
968 32c. Girl in centre wearing lei around neck 75 70
969 32c. Girl in centre wearing headscarf 75 70
970 32c. Boy in centre and girls holding bunches of grass 75 70

Nos. 967/70 were issued together, se-tenant, forming a composite design of the children around a globe and the UNICEF emblem.

116 Basslet and Vermiculate Parrotfish ("P")

1996. Underwater Wonders. Illuminated letters spelling out PALAU. Multicoloured.

971 32c. Type **116** 75 70
972 32c. Yellow-striped cardinalfish ("A") 75 70
973 32c. Pair of atoll butterflyfish ("L") 75 70
974 32c. Starry moray and slate-pencil sea urchin ("A") 75 70
975 32c. Blue-streaked cleaner wrasse and coral hind ("Grouper") ("U") 75 70

117 Ferdinand Magellan and "Vitoria"

1996. "CAPEX'96" International Stamp Exhibition, Toronto, Canada. Circumnavigators. Multicoloured. (a) POSTAGE

976 32c. Type **117** (postage) 75 70
977 32c. Charles Wilkes and U.S.S. "Vincennes" (sail frigate) 75 70
978 32c. Joshua Slocum and "Spray" (yacht) 75 70
979 32c. Ben Carlin and "Half-Safe" (amphibian) 75 70
980 32c. Edward Beach and U.S.S. "Triton" (submarine) 75 70
981 32c. Naomi James and "Express Crusader" (yacht) 75 70
982 32c. Sir Ranulf Fiennes and snow vehicle 75 70
983 32c. Rick Hansen and wheelchair 75 70
984 32c. Robin Knox-Johnson and "Enza New Zealand" (catamaran) 75 70

MS985 Two sheets each 110×80 mm. (a) $3 Sir Francis Chichester and "Gypsy Moth IV" (yacht); (b) $3 Bob Martin, Mark Sullivan and Troy Bradley and "Odyssey" (helium balloon) 14·50 13·50

(b) AIR

986 60c. Lowell Smith and Douglas world cruiser seaplanes (air) 1·50 1·40
987 60c. Ernst Lehmann and "Graf Zeppelin" (dirigible airship) 1·50 1·40
988 60c. Wiley Post and Lockheed Vega "Winnie Mae" 1·50 1·40
989 60c. Yuri Gagarin and "Vostok I" (spaceship) 1·50 1·40
990 60c. Jerrie Mock and Cessna 180 "Spirit of Columbus" 1·50 1·40
991 60c. H. Ross Perot jnr. and Bell LongRanger III helicopter "Spirit of Texas" 1·50 1·40
992 60c. Brooke Knapp and Gulfstream III "The American Dream" 1·50 1·40
993 60c. Jeana Yeager and Dick Rutan and "Voyager" 1·50 1·40
994 60c. Fred Lasby and Piper Commanche 1·50 1·40

118 Simba, Nala and Timon ("The Lion King")

1996. Disney Sweethearts. Multicoloured.

995 1c. Type **118** 25 10
996 2c. Georgette, Tito and Oliver ("Oliver & Company") 25 10
997 3c. Duchess, O'Malley and Marie ("The Aristocats") 25 10
998 4c. Bianca, Jake and Polly ("The Rescuers Down Under") 25 10
999 5c. Tod, Vixey and Copper ("The Fox and the Hound") 25 10
1000 6c. Thumper, Flower and their Sweethearts ("Bambi") 25 10
1001 60c. As No. 995 1·80 1·70
1002 60c. Bernard, Bianca and Mr. Chairman ("The Rescuers") 1·80 1·70
1003 60c. As No. 996 1·80 1·70
1004 60c. As No. 997 1·80 1·70
1005 60c. As No. 998 1·80 1·70
1006 60c. As No. 999 1·80 1·70
1007 60c. Robin Hood, Maid Marian and Alan-a-Dale ("Robin Hood") 1·80 1·70
1008 60c. As No. 1000 1·80 1·70
1009 60c. Pongo, Perdita and the Puppies ("101 Dalmatians") 1·80 1·70

MS1010 Two sheets each 110×131 mm. (a) $2 Bambi and Faline; (b) $2 Lady ("Lady and the Tramp") (vert) 11·50 10·50

119 Hakeem Olajuwan (basketball)

1996. Centenary of Modern Olympic Games and Olympic Games, Atlanta. Multicoloured.

1011 32c. Type **119** 80 75
1012 32c. Pat McCormick (gymnastics) 80 75
1013 32c. Jim Thorpe (pentathlon and decathlon) 80 75
1014 32c. Jesse Owens (athletics) 80 75
1015 32c. Tatyana Gutsu (gymnastics) 80 75
1016 32c. Michael Jordan (basketball) 80 75
1017 32c. Fu Mingxia (diving) 80 75
1018 32c. Robert Zmelik (decathlon) 80 75
1019 32c. Ivan Pedroso (long jumping) 80 75
1020 32c. Nadia Comaneci (gymnastics) 80 75
1021 32c. Jackie Joyner-Kersee (long jumping) 80 75
1022 32c. Michael Johnson (running) 80 75
1023 32c. Kristin Otto (swimming) 80 75
1024 32c. Vitai Scherbo (gymnastics) 80 75
1025 32c. Johnny Weissmuller (swimming) 80 75
1026 32c. Babe Didrikson (track and field athlete) 80 75
1027 32c. Eddie Tolan (track athlete) 80 75
1028 32c. Krisztina Egerszegi (swimming) 80 75
1029 32c. Sawao Kato (gymnastics) 80 75
1030 32c. Aleksandr Popov (swimming) 80 75
1031 40c. Fanny Blankers-Koen (track and field athlete) (vert) 90 85
1032 40c. Bob Mathias (decathlon) (vert) 90 85
1033 60c. Torchbearer entering Wembley Stadium, 1948 1·50 1·40
1034 60c. Entrance to Olympia Stadium, Athens, and flags 1·50 1·40

Nos. 1011/30 were issued together, se-tenant, forming a composite design of the athletes and Olympic rings.

120 The Creation

1996. 3000th Anniv of Jerusalem. Illustrations by Guy Rowe from "In Our Image: Character Studies from the Old Testament". Mult.

1035 20c. Type **120** 45 40
1036 20c. Adam and Eve 45 40
1037 20c. Noah and his Wife 45 40
1038 20c. Abraham 45 40
1039 20c. Jacob's Blessing 45 40
1040 20c. Jacob becomes Israel 45 40
1041 20c. Joseph and his Brethren 45 40
1042 20c. Moses and Burning Bush 45 40
1043 20c. Moses and the Tablets 45 40
1044 20c. Balaam 45 40
1045 20c. Joshua 45 40
1046 20c. Gideon 45 40
1047 20c. Jephthah 45 40
1048 20c. Samson 45 40
1049 20c. Ruth and Naomi 45 40
1050 20c. Saul anointed 45 40
1051 20c. Saul denounced 45 40
1052 20c. David and Jonathan 45 40
1053 20c. David and Nathan 45 40
1054 20c. David mourns 45 40
1055 20c. Solomon praying 45 40
1056 20c. Solomon judging 45 40
1057 20c. Elijah 45 40
1058 20c. Elisha 45 40
1059 20c. Job 45 40
1060 20c. Isaiah 45 40
1061 20c. Jeremiah 45 40
1062 20c. Ezekiel 45 40
1063 20c. Nebuchadnezzar's Dream 45 40
1064 20c. Amos 45 40

121 Nankeen Night Heron

1996. Birds over Palau Lagoon. Multicoloured.

1065 50c. Eclectus parrot (female) ("lakkotsiang") 1·20 1·10
1066 50c. Type **121** 1·20 1·10
1067 50c. Micronesian pigeon ("Belochel") 1·20 1·10
1068 50c. Eclectus parrot (male) ("lakkotsiang") 1·20 1·10
1069 50c. White tern ("Sechosech") 1·20 1·10
1070 50c. Common noddy ("Mechadelbedaoch") 1·20 1·10
1071 50c. Nicobar pigeon ("Laib") 1·20 1·10
1072 50c. Chinese little bittern ("Cheloteachel") 1·20 1·10
1073 50c. Little pied cormorant ("Deroech") 1·20 1·10
1074 50c. Black-naped tern ("Kerkirs") 1·20 1·10
1075 50c. White-tailed tropic bird ("Dudek") 1·20 1·10
1076 50c. Sulphur-crested cockatoo ("lakkotsiang") (white bird) 1·20 1·10
1077 50c. White-capped noddy ("Bedaoch") 1·20 1·10
1078 50c. Bridled tern ("Bedebedchakl") 1·20 1·10
1079 50c. Reef heron (grey) ("Sechou") 1·20 1·10
1080 50c. Grey-tailed tattler ("Kekereielderariik") 1·20 1·10
1081 50c. Reef heron (white) ("Sechou") 1·20 1·10
1082 50c. Audubon's shearwater ("Ochaieu") 1·20 1·10
1083 50c. Black-headed gull ("Oltirakladial") 1·20 1·10
1084 50c. Ruddy turnstone ("Omechederiibabad") 1·20 1·10

Nos. 1065/84 were issued together, se-tenant, forming a composite design.

122 Lockheed U-2

1996. Spy Planes. Multicoloured.

1085 40c. Type **122** 1·00 95
1086 40c. General Dynamics EF-111A 1·00 95
1087 40c. Lockheed YF-12A 1·00 95
1088 40c. Lockheed SR-71 1·00 95
1089 40c. Teledyne Ryan Tier II Plus 1·00 95
1090 40c. Lockheed XST 1·00 95
1091 40c. Lockheed ER-2 1·00 95
1092 40c. Lockheed F-117A Nighthawk 1·00 95
1093 40c. Lockheed EC-130E 1·00 95
1094 40c. Ryan Firebee 1·00 95
1095 40c. Lockheed Martin/Boeing Darkstar 1·00 95
1096 40c. Boeing E-3A Sentry 1·00 95

MS1097 120×90 mm. $3 Northrop B-2A Stealth Bomber (41×56 mm) 7·75 7·25

123 "The Birth of a New Nation"

1996. 2nd Anniv of Independence. Illustrations from "Kirie" by Koh Sekiguchi. Multicoloured.
1098 20c. Type **123** 50 45
1099 20c. "In the Blue Shade of Trees" 50 45

124 Pandanus

1996. Christmas. "O Tannenbaum" (carol). Decorated Trees. Multicoloured.
1100 32c. Type **124** 80 75
1101 32c. Mangrove 80 75
1102 32c. Norfolk Island pine 80 75
1103 32c. Papaya 80 75
1104 32c. Casuarina 80 75
Nos. 1100/4 were issued together, se-tenant, forming a composite design.

125 "Viking I" in Orbit (½-size illustration) (image scaled to 64% of original size)

1996. Space Missions to Mars. Multicoloured.
1105 32c. Type **125** 80 75
1106 32c. "Viking I" emblem (top half) 80 75
1107 32c. "Mars Lander" firing de-orbit engines 80 75
1108 32c. "Viking I" emblem (bottom half) 80 75
1109 32c. Phobos (Martian moon) 80 75
1110 32c. "Mars Lander" entering Martian atmosphere 80 75
1111 32c. "Mariner 9" (first mission, 1971) 80 75
1112 32c. Parachute opens for landing and heat shield jettisons 80 75
1113 32c. Projected U.S./Russian manned spacecraft, 21st century (top half) 80 75
1114 32c. "Lander" descent engines firing 80 75
1115 32c. Projected U.S./Russian spacecraft (bottom half) 80 75
1116 32c. "Viking I Lander" on Martian surface, 1976 80 75
MS1117 Two sheets each 98×78 mm. (a) $3 Mars Rover (projected 1997 mission) (37×30 mm); (b) $3 Water probe (projected 1999 mission) 14·50 13·50
Nos. 1105/16 were issued together, se-tenant, forming several composite designs.

126 Northrop XB-35 Bomber

1996. Oddities of the Air. Aircraft Designs. Multicoloured.
1118 60c. Type **126** 1·50 1·40
1119 60c. Leduc O.21 1·50 1·40
1120 60c. Convair Model 118 flying car 1·50 1·40
1121 60c. Blohm und Voss BV 141 1·50 1·40
1122 60c. Vought V-173 1·50 1·40
1123 60c. McDonnell XF-85 Goblin 1·50 1·40
1124 60c. North American F-82B Twin Mustang fighter 1·50 1·40
1125 60c. Lockheed XFV-1 vertical take-off fighter 1·50 1·40
1126 60c. Northrop XP-79B 1·50 1·40
1127 60c. Saunders Roe SR/A1 flying boat fighter 1·50 1·40
1128 60c. "Caspian Sea Monster" hovercraft 1·50 1·40
1129 60c. Grumman X-29 demonstrator 1·50 1·40
MS1130 $3 Martin Marieeta X-24B (84×28 mm) 7·75 7·25

127 Ox Cart

1997. Chinese New Year. Year of the Ox. Sheet 76×106 mm.
MS1131 **127** $2 multicoloured 5·25 4·75

128 Emblem

1997. 50th Anniv of South Pacific Commission. Sheet 103×70 mm.
MS1132 **128** $1 multicoloured 2·40 2·30

129 Pemphis

1997. "Hong Kong '97" Stamp Exhibition. Flowers. Multicoloured.
1133 1c. Type **129** 25 15
1134 2c. Sea lettuce 25 15
1135 3c. Tropical almond 25 15
1136 4c. Guettarda 25 15
1137 5c. Pacific coral bean 25 15
1138 32c. Black mangrove 80 75
1139 32c. Cordia 80 75
1140 32c. Lantern tree 80 75
1141 32c. Palau rock-island flower 80 75
1142 50c. Fish-poison tree 1·20 1·10
1143 50c. Indian mulberry 1·20 1·10
1144 50c. Pacific poison-apple 1·20 1·10
1145 50c. "Ailanthus" sp. 1·20 1·10
1146 $3 Sea hibiscus (73×48 mm) 7·25 6·75

130 "Apollo 15" Command Module splashing-down

1997. Bicentenary of the Parachute. Multicoloured. (a) POSTAGE
1147 32c. Type **130** (postage) 80 75
1148 32c. Skydiving team in formation (40×23 mm) 80 75
1149 32c. Cargo drop from airplane 80 75
1150 32c. Parasailing (40×23 mm) 80 75
1151 32c. Parachutist falling to earth 80 75
1152 32c. Parachute demonstration team (40×23 mm) 80 75
1153 32c. Parachutist falling into sea 80 75
1154 32c. Drag-racing car (40×23 mm) 80 75
MS1155 Two sheets. (a) 72×102 mm. $2 Training tower, Fort Benning, Georgia (27×84 mm); (b) 102×72 mm. $2 "Funny Car" safety parachute (56×42 mm) 12·00 11·50

(b) AIR
1156 60c. Parachuting demonstration (air) 1·50 1·40
1157 60c. "The Blue Flame" (world land-speed record attempt) (40× 23 mm) 1·50 1·40
1158 60c. Atmospheric Re-entry Demonstrator (capsule with three canopies) 1·50 1·40
1159 60c. Spies parachuting behind enemy lines during Second World War (40×23 mm) 1·50 1·40
1160 60c. Andre Jacquerin Garnerin's first successful parachute descent (from balloon), 1797 1·50 1·40
1161 60c. C-130E airplane demonstrating Low Altitude Parachute Extraction System (airplane and capsule with four canopies) (40×23 mm) 1·50 1·40
1162 60c. U.S. Army parachutist flying parafoil 1·50 1·40
1163 60c. Parachute (one canopy) slowing high performance airplane (40×23 mm) 1·50 1·40

131 Pacific Black Duck beneath Banana Tree

1997. Palau's Avian Environment. Multicoloured.
1164 20c. Type **131** 50 45
1165 20c. Pair of red junglefowl beneath calamondin (clustered orange fruits) 50 45
1166 20c. Nicobar pigeon in parinari tree (single orange fruits) 50 45
1167 20c. Cardinal honeyeater in wax apple tree (clustered brown fruits) 50 45
1168 20c. Purple swamphen and Chinese little bittern amid taro plants 50 45
1169 20c. Eclectus parrot in pangi football fruit tree (single brown fruits) 50 45
1170 20c. Micronesian pigeon in rambutan (clustered red fruits) 50 45
1171 20c. Micronesian starlings in mango tree (clustered green fruits) 50 45
1172 20c. Fruit bat in breadfruit tree 50 45
1173 20c. White-collared kingfisher in coconut palm (with sailing dinghy) 50 45
1174 20c. Palau fruit dove in sweet orange tree (single green fruits) 50 45
1175 20c. Chestnut mannikins flying around sour-sop tree and nest 50 45

132 Himeji Temple, Japan

1997. 50th Anniv of UNESCO. Multicoloured.
1176 32c. Type **132** 85 80
1177 32c. Kyoto, Japan 85 80
1178 32c. Pagoda roofs, Himeji Temple (white inscr at left) 85 80
1179 32c. Garden, Himeji Temple 85 80
1180 32c. Path and doorway, Himeji Temple 85 80
1181 32c. Pagoda roofs, Himeji Temple (white inscr at right) 85 80
1182 32c. Roof ridge and decoration, Himeji Temple 85 80
1183 32c. Inscribed post and veranda, Himeji Temple 85 80
1184 60c. Ceiling, Augustusburg Castle, Germany (horiz) 1·50 1·40
1185 60c. Augustusburg Castle (horiz) 1·50 1·40
1186 60c. Falkenlust Castle, Germany (horiz) 1·50 1·40
1187 60c. Roman ruins, Trier, Germany (horiz) 1·50 1·40
1188 60c. House, Trier (horiz) 1·50 1·40
MS1189 Two sheets each 127×102 mm. (a) $2 Tree trunk, Yakushims, Japan (horiz); (b) $2 Forest, Shirakami-Sanchi, Japan (horiz) 10·50 9·75

133 Darago, Philippines

1997. "Pacific 97" International Stamp Exhibition, San Francisco. Volcano Goddesses of the Pacific. Multicoloured.
1190 32c. Type **133** 90 85
1191 32c. Fuji, Japan 90 85
1192 32c. Pele, Hawaii 90 85
1193 32c. Pare and Hutu, Polynesia 90 85
1194 32c. Dzalarhons, Haida tribe, North America 90 85
1195 32c. Chuginadak, Aleutian Islands, Alaska 90 85

134 "Swallows and Peach Blossoms under a Full Moon"

1997. Birth Bicentenary of Ando Hiroshige (Japanese painter). Multicoloured.
1196 32c. Type **134** 95 90
1197 32c. "Parrot on a Flowering Branch" 95 90
1198 32c. "Crane and Rising Sun" 95 90
1199 32c. "Cock, Unbrella and Morning Glories" 95 90
1200 32c. "Titmouse hanging Head Downward on a Camellia Branch" 95 90
MS1201 Two sheets each 102×127 mm. (a) $2 Kingfisher and Iris; (b) $2 "Falcon on a Pine Tree with Rising Sun" 10·00 9·25

135 Bai (community building)

1997. 3rd Anniv of Independence.
1202 **135** 32c. multicoloured 80 75

136 "Albatross" (U.S.A.)

1997. Oceanic Research. Research Vessels (1203/11) or Personalities (MS1212). Multicoloured.

1203 32c. Type **136** 80 75
1204 32c. "Mabahiss" (Egypt) 80 75
1205 32c. "Atlantis II" (U.S.A.) 80 75
1206 32c. Hans Hass's "Xarifa" (schooner) 80 75
1207 32c. "Meteor" (Germany) 80 75
1208 32c. "Egabras III" (U.S.A.) 80 75
1209 32c. "Discoverer" (U.S.A.) 80 75
1210 32c. "Kaiyo" (Japan) 80 75
1211 32c. "Ocean Defender" (Great Britain) 80 75
MS1212 Three sheets each 110×80 mm. (a) $2 Jacques-Yves Cousteau (undersea researcher) (looking to right); (b) $2 Cousteau wearing diving suit (vert); (c) $2 Pete Seeger (folk singer and ecologist) (vert) 16·00 14·50

137 "I Can Read by Myself"

1997. Literacy Campaign. Walt Disney cartoon characters. Multicoloured.

1213 1c. Type **137** 20 15
1214 2c. "Start Them Young" 20 15
1215 3c. "Share your Knowledge" 20 15
1216 4c. "The insatiable Reader" 20 15
1217 5c. "Reading is the ultimate Luxury" 20 15
1218 10c. "Real Men read" 20 15
1219 32c. "Exercise your Right to Read" 80 75
1220 32c. As No. 1217 80 75
1221 32c. As No. 1215 80 75
1222 32c. As No. 1214 80 75
1223 32c. "Reading is fundamental" 80 75
1224 32c. As No. 1216 80 75
1225 32c. "Reading Time is Anytime" 80 75
1226 32c. As No. 1218 80 75
1227 32c. Type **137** 80 75
MS1228 Two sheets. (a) 139×114 mm. $2 Daisy Duck carrying books ("The Library is for Everyone"); (b) $3 Mickey Mouse holding book ("Books are Magical") 13·50 12·50

138 Boy and Girl

1997. Christmas. "Some Children See Him" (carol). Multicoloured.

1229 32c. Type **138** 80 75
1230 32c. Asian boy and white girl 80 75
1231 32c. Madonna and Child behind boy and girl 80 75
1232 32c. White girl and Oriental children 80 75
1233 32c. Asian boy and Palauan girl 80 75

Nos. 1229/33 were issued together, se-tenant, forming a composite design.

139 Diana, Princess of Wales

1997. Diana, Princess of Wales Commemoration.

1234 **139** 60c. multicoloured 1·50 1·40

140 Tiger (paper cutting)

1998. Chinese New Year. Year of the Tiger. Two sheets each 92×117 mm.

MS1235 Two sheets. (a) 50c. Type **140**; (b) 50c. Tiger (toy) 3·00 2·75

141 Nucleus of Galaxy M100

1998. Hubble Space Telescope. Multicoloured.

1236 32c. Type **141** 80 75
1237 32c. Top of Hubble telescope 80 75
1238 32c. Astronaut on robot arm 80 75
1239 32c. Astronaut fixing new camera to telescope 80 75
1240 32c. Astronaut in cargo space of shuttle "Endeavour" 80 75
1241 32c. Hubble released after repair 80 75
MS1242 Three sheets each 71×110 mm. (a) $2 Edwin Hubble (astronomer); (b) $2 Hubble telescope; (c) $2 Astronauts servicing Hubble telescope 15·00 14·00

142 Mother Teresa

1998. Mother Teresa (founder of Missionaries of Charity) Commemoration. Portraits of Mother Teresa. Multicoloured.

1243 60c. Type **142** 1·50 1·40
1244 60c. Facing right 1·50 1·40
1245 60c. Wearing cross 1·50 1·40
1246 60c. Wearing cardigan 1·50 1·40

143 Ladybird Remotely Operated Vehicle, Japan

1998. International Year of the Ocean. Deep-sea Robots. Multicoloured.

1247 32c. Type **143** 80 75
1248 32c. Slocum Glider 80 75
1249 32c. "Hornet" 80 75
1250 32c. "Scorpio" 80 75
1251 32c. "Odyssey" Autonomous Underwater Vehicle 80 75
1252 32c. Jamstec Survey System launcher, Japan 80 75
1253 32c. "Scarab II" (servicer of undersea telephone cables) 80 75
1254 32c. U.S. Navy torpedo finder 80 75
1255 32c. Jamstec Survey System vehicle, Japan 80 75
1256 32c. Cetus tether for undersea cables 80 75
1257 32c. Deep-sea remotely operated vehicle 80 75
1258 32c. Abe (autonomous benthic explorer) 80 75
1259 32c. OBSS 80 75
1260 32c. Remote controlled vehicle 225G "Swimming Eyeball" (for inspection of undersea oil rigs) 80 75
1261 32c. Japanese Underwater Remotely Operated Vehicle 80 75
1262 32c. Benthos remotely piloted vehicle 80 75
1263 32c. Curv III (cable-controlled underwater research vehicle) 80 75
1264 32c. "Smartie", Great Britain 80 75
MS1265 Two sheets each 88×118 mm. (a) $2 "Dolphin 3K", Japan; (b) $2 "Jason jr." 10·50 9·50

1998. "Israel 98" International Stamp Exhibition, Tel Aviv. Nos. 1035/64 optd with emblem.

1266 20c. multicoloured 50 45
1267 20c. multicoloured 50 45
1268 20c. multicoloured 50 45
1269 20c. multicoloured 50 45
1270 20c. multicoloured 50 45
1271 20c. multicoloured 50 45
1272 20c. multicoloured 50 45
1273 20c. multicoloured 50 45
1274 20c. multicoloured 50 45
1275 20c. multicoloured 50 45
1276 20c. multicoloured 50 45
1277 20c. multicoloured 50 45
1278 20c. multicoloured 50 45
1279 20c. multicoloured 50 45
1280 20c. multicoloured 50 45
1281 20c. multicoloured 50 45
1282 20c. multicoloured 50 45
1283 20c. multicoloured 50 45
1284 20c. multicoloured 50 45
1285 20c. multicoloured 50 45
1286 20c. multicoloured 50 45
1287 20c. multicoloured 50 45
1288 20c. multicoloured 50 45
1289 20c. multicoloured 50 45
1290 20c. multicoloured 50 45
1291 20c. multicoloured 50 45
1292 20c. multicoloured 50 45
1293 20c. multicoloured 50 45
1294 20c. multicoloured 50 45
1295 20c. multicoloured 50 45

145 Hut

1998. The Legend of Orachel. Multicoloured.

1296 40c. Type **145** 95 90
1297 40c. Outrigger canoes moored by hut 55 45
1298 40c. Hut and man in canoe 95 90
1299 40c. Bird in tree 95 90
1300 40c. Front half of three-man canoe 95 90
1301 40c. Rear half of canoe and head of snake 95 90
1302 40c. Crocodile, fishes and coral 95 90
1303 40c. Shark and fishes 95 90
1304 40c. Turtle, jellyfish and body of snake 95 90
1305 40c. Underwater bai (community building) 95 90
1306 40c. Orachel swimming underwater and fishes 95 90
1307 40c. Coral, fishes and seaweed 95 90

146 Footballer

1998. World Cup Football Championship, France. Multicoloured.

1308 50c. Type **146** 1·20 1·10
1309 50c. Player in blue and white striped shirt 1·20 1·10
1310 50c. Player in green shirt and white shorts 1·20 1·10
1311 50c. Player in white shirt and blue shorts 1·20 1·10
1312 50c. Player in green shirt and black shorts 1·20 1·10
1313 50c. Player in red short-sleeved shirt 1·20 1·10
1314 50c. Player in yellow shirt and blue shorts 1·20 1·10
1315 50c. Player in red long-sleeved shirt 1·20 1·10
MS1316 70×64 mm. $3 Pele being tackled 7·25 6·75

147 Scuba Fishing

1998. 4th Micronesian Islands Games, Palau. Multicoloured.

1317 32c. Type **147** 80 75
1318 32c. Spear throwing 80 75
1319 32c. Swimming 80 75
1320 32c. Coconut throwing 80 75
1321 32c. Games emblem 80 75
1322 32c. Coconut tree climbimg 80 75
1323 32c. Canoe racing 80 75
1324 32c. Coconut husking 80 75
1325 32c. Diving 80 75

148 Rudolph and other Reindeer

1998. Christmas. "Rudolph the Red Nosed Reindeer" (carol). Multicoloured.

1326 32c. Type **148** 80 75
1327 32c. Two reindeer and girl in yellow dress 80 75
1328 32c. Two reindeer, boy and girl 80 75
1329 32c. Two reindeer, girl in long pink dress and star 80 75
1330 32c. Father Christmas and sleigh 80 75

Nos. 1326/30 were issued together, se-tenant, forming a composite design.

149 Princess Dot (ant)

1998. "A Bug's Life" (computer animated film). Multicoloured.

1331 20c. Type **149** 55 50
1332 20c. Heimlich (caterpillar), Francis (ladybird) and Slim (stick insect) 55 50
1333 20c. Hopper (grasshopper) 55 50
1334 20c. Princess Atta (ant) 55 50
1335 32c. Princess Atta and Flick (ant) in boat 85 80
1336 32c. Princess Atta and Flick sitting on heart 85 80
1337 32c. Flick with Princess Atta sitting on leaf 85 80
1338 32c. Flick handing Princess Atta a flower 85 80
1339 50c. Butterfly, Heimlich, Francis and other bugs (horiz) 1·20 1·10
1340 50c. Slim, Francis and Heimlich (horiz) 1·20 1·10
1341 50c. Manny (praying mantis) (horiz) 1·20 1·10
1342 50c. Francis (horiz) 1·20 1·10
1343 60c. Slim and Flick juggling 1·60 1·50

1344	60c. Francis on cycle, Heimlich and Slim	1·60	1·50
1345	60c. Manny hynotizing Flick	1·60	1·50
1346	60c. Manny, Rosie (spider) and other bugs	1·60	1·50
MS1347	Four sheets. (a) 127×102 mm. $2 Slim, Francis and Heimlich (75×50 mm); (b)127×102 mm. $2 Princess Atta and Flick (horiz); (c) 127×102 mm. $2 Butterfly; (d) 102×127 mm. $2 Francis, Flick and Heimlich (75×50 mm)	22·00	20·00

150 Group Photograph of Astronauts, 1962

1999. John Glenn's Return to Space. Multicoloured.

1348	60c. Type **150**	1·50	1·40
1349	60c. Glenn in space helmet (looking straight ahead)	1·50	1·40
1350	60c. Group photograph of five astronauts	1·50	1·40
1351	60c. Glenn in space helmet (head turned to left)	1·50	1·40
1352	60c. Glenn in civilian suit	1·50	1·40
1353	60c. Glenn in space helmet (eyes looking right)	1·50	1·40
1354	60c. Glenn with Pres. John Kennedy	1·50	1·40
1355	60c. Glenn in space suit (bare-headed) ("John Glenn, 1962")	1·50	1·40
1356	60c. Glenn (head raised)	1·50	1·40
1357	60c. "Discovery" (space shuttle) on launch pad	1·50	1·40
1358	60c. Glenn and two fellow astronauts with three NASA employees	1·50	1·40
1359	60c. Glenn (wearing glasses and looking straight ahead)	1·50	1·40
1360	60c. "Discovery" in hangar	1·50	1·40
1361	60c. Glenn in space suit (bare-headed) ("John Glenn")	1·50	1·40
1362	60c. Glenn (wearing glasses and looking down)	1·50	1·40
1363	60c. Glenn in space suit and inner helmet	1·50	1·40
MS1364	Two sheets. (a) 80×120 mm. $2 Glenn in 1962 (28×41 mm); (b) 110×90 mm $2 Glenn in 1998 (28×41 mm)	10·50	9·50

151 Rachel Carson (naturalist)

1999. Environmental Heroes of the 20th Century. Multicoloured.

1365	33c. Type **151**	80	75
1366	33c. Ding Darling (President of U.S. National Wildlife Federation, 1936)	80	75
1367	33c. David Brower	80	75
1368	33c. Jacques Cousteau (oceanologist)	80	75
1369	33c. Roger Tory Peterson (ornithologist)	80	75
1370	33c. Prince Philip, Duke of Edinburgh (President of World Wide Fund for Nature)	80	75
1371	33c. Joseph Wood Krutch	80	75
1372	33c. Aldo Leopold	80	75
1373	33c. Dian Fossey (zoologist) (wrongly inscr "Diane")	80	75
1374	33c. Al Gore	80	75
1375	33c. Sir David Attenborough (naturalist and broadcaster)	80	75
1376	33c. Paul MacCready (aeronautical engineer) (wrongly inscr "McCready")	80	75
1377	33c. Sting	80	75
1378	33c. Paul Winter	80	75
1379	33c. Ian MacHarg	80	75
1380	33c. Denis Hayes	80	75

152 "Soyuz" Spacecraft

1999. "Mir" Space Station. Multicoloured.

1381	33c. Type **152**	80	75
1382	33c. "Specktr" science module	80	75
1383	33c. Rear of space shuttle	80	75
1384	33c. "Kuant 2" scientific and air lock module	80	75
1385	33c. "Kristall" technological module	80	75
1386	33c. Front of "Atlantis" (space shuttle) and docking module	80	75
MS1387	Four sheets each 76×108 mm. (a) $2 Cosmonaut Valery Polyakov watching from "Mir", 1995; (b) $2 Shannon Lucid and Yury Usachov, 1996; (c) $2 Anatoly Solovyov inspecting damage to "Mir", 1997; (d) $2 Charles Precourt and Talgat Musabayev, 1998	19·00	18·00

153 Haruo Remeliik

1999

1388	**153**	1c. multicoloured	25	15
1389	-	2c. multicoloured	25	15
1390	-	20c. multicoloured	50	45
1391	-	22c. multicoloured	55	50
1392	-	33c. multicoloured	80	75
1393	-	50c. multicoloured	1·20	1·10
1394	-	55c. multicoloured	1·30	1·20
1395	-	60c. multicoloured	1·50	1·40
1396	-	70c. violet and deep violet	1·70	1·60
1397	-	77c. multicoloured	1·80	1·70
1398	-	80c. green and emerald	1·90	1·80
1399	-	$3.20 multicoloured	7·25	7·25
1400	-	$12.25 rose and red	30·00	28·00

DESIGNS: 2c. Lazarus Salii; 20c. Charlie Gibbons; 22c. Admiral Raymond Spuance; 33c. Pres. Kuniwo Nakamura; 50c. Admiral William Halsey; 55c. Colonel Lewis Puller; 60c. Franklin Roosevelt (US President 1933–45); 70c. General Douglas MacArthur; 77c. Harry Truman (US President 1945–53); 80c. Admiral Chester W. Nimitz; $3.20 Jimmy Carter (US President 1977–81); $12.25 President John F. Kennedy.

154 Leatherback Turtle

1999. Endangered Reptiles and Amphibians. Multicoloured.

1405	33c. Type **154**	80	75
1406	33c. Kemp's Ridley turtle	80	75
1407	33c. Green turtles	80	75
1408	33c. Marine iguana	80	75
1409	33c. Table Mountain ghost frog	80	75
1410	33c. Spiny turtle	80	75
1411	33c. Hewitt's ghost frog	80	75
1412	33c. Geometric tortoise	80	75
1413	33c. Limestone salamander	80	75
1414	33c. Desert rain frog	80	75
1415	33c. Cape plantanna	80	75
1416	33c. Long-toed tree frog	80	75
MS1417	Two sheets each 110×80 mm. (a) $2 Hawksbill Turtle; (b) $2 Marine crocodile	9·75	9·00

155 Caroline Islands 1901 5 and 20pf. Stamps and Golsdorf Steam Railway Locomotive

1999. "iBRA '99" International Stamp Exhibition, Nuremberg, Germany. Multicoloured.

1418	55c. Type **155**	1·40	1·30
1419	55c. Caroline Islands 1901 5m. yacht stamp and carriage of Leipzig–Dresden Railway	1·40	1·30
MS1420	160×106 mm. $2 Caroline Islands 1900 3pf. Stamp on cover	4·75	4·50

156 "Mars Global Surveyor" in Orbit

1999. Space Missions to Mars. Multicoloured.

1421	33c. Type **156**	85	80
1422	33c. "Mars Climate" Orbiter	85	80
1423	33c. "Mars Polar" Lander	85	80
1424	33c. "Deep Space 2"	85	80
1425	33c. "Mars Surveyor 2001" Orbiter	85	80
1426	33c. "Mars Surveyor 2001" Lander	85	80
MS1427	Four sheets, each 76×111 mm. (a) $2 "Mars Global Surveyor"; (b) $2 "Mars Climate" Orbiter; (c) "Mars Polar" Lander; (d) $2 "Mars Surveyor 2001" Lander	20·00	19·00

Nos. 1421/6 were issued together, se-tenant, forming a composite design.

157 "Banza natida"

1999. Earth Day. Pacific Insects. Multicoloured.

1428	33c. Type **157**	90	85
1429	33c. "Drosophila heteroneura" (fruit-fly)	90	85
1430	33c. "Nesomicromus lagus"	90	85
1431	33c. "Megalagrian leptodemus"	90	85
1432	33c. "Pseudopsectra cookeorum"	90	85
1433	33c. "Ampheida neocaledonia"	90	85
1434	33c. "Pseudopsectra swezeyi"	90	85
1435	33c. "Deinacrida heteracantha"	90	85
1436	33c. Beech forest butterfly	90	85
1437	33c. Hercules moth	90	85
1438	33c. Striped sphinx moth	90	85
1439	33c. Tussock butterfly	90	85
1440	33c. Weevil	90	85
1441	33c. Bush cricket	90	85
1442	33c. Longhorn beetle	90	85
1443	33c. "Abathrus bicolor"	90	85
1444	33c. "Stylogymnusa subantartica"	90	85
1445	33c. Moth butterfly	90	85
1446	33c. "Paraconosoma naviculare"	90	85
1447	33c. Cairn's birdwing ("Ornithoptera priamus")	90	85

158 Launch 1R (living quarters)

1999. International Space Station, 1998–2004. Multicoloured.

1448	33c. Type **158**	85	80
1449	33c. Launch 14A (final solar arrays)	85	80
1450	33c. Launch 8A (mechanical arm)	85	80
1451	33c. Launch 1J (Japanese experiment module)	85	80
1452	33c. Launch 1E (Colombus Orbital Facility laboratory)	85	80
1453	33c. Launch 16A (habitation module)	85	80
MS1454	Four sheets each 76×111 mm. (a) $2 Complete International Space Station; (b) $2 Commander Bob Cabana and Sergei Krikalev; (c) $2 Crew of Flight 2R (horiz); (d) $2 X-38 Crew Return Vehicle (horiz)	20·00	19·00

159 William Gibson

1999. The Information Age: Visionaries in the Twentieth Century. Multicoloured.

1455	33c. Type **159**	90	85
1456	33c. Danny Hillis	90	85
1457	33c. Steve Wozntak	90	85
1458	33c. Steve Jobs	90	85
1459	33c. Nolan Bushnell	90	85
1460	33c. John Warnock	90	85
1461	33c. Ken Thompson	90	85
1462	33c. Al Shugart	90	85
1463	33c. Rand and Robyn Miller	90	85
1464	33c. Nicolas Negroponte	90	85
1465	33c. Bill Gates	90	85
1466	33c. Arthur C. Clarke	90	85
1467	33c. Marshall McLuhan	90	85
1468	33c. Thomas Watson Jr	90	85
1469	33c. Gordon Moore	90	85
1470	33c. James Gosling	90	85
1471	33c. Sabeer Bhatia and Jack Smith	90	85
1472	33c. Esther Dyson	90	85
1473	33c. Jerry Young and David Filo	90	85
1474	33c. Jeff Bezos	90	85
1475	33c. Bob Kahn	90	85
1476	33c. Jaron Lanier	90	85
1477	33c. Andy Grove	90	85
1478	33c. Jim Clark	90	85
1479	33c. Bob Metcalfe	90	85

160 "Women Divers"

1999. 150th Death Anniv of Katsushika Hokusai (Japanese artist). Multicoloured.

1480	33c. Type **160**	90	85
1481	33c. "Bull and Parasol"	90	85
1482	33c. Drawing of bare-breasted woman	90	85
1483	33c. Drawing of fully-clothed woman (sitting)	90	85
1484	33c. "Japanese Spaniel"	90	85
1485	33c. "Porter in Landscape"	90	85
1486	33c. "Bacchanalian Revelry" (musician in bottom right corner)	90	85
1487	33c. "Bacchanalian Revelry" (different)	90	85
1488	33c. Drawing of woman (crouching)	90	85
1489	33c. Drawing of woman (reclining on floor)	90	85

1490	33c. "Ox-herd" (ox)	90	85
1491	33c. "Ox-herd" (man on bridge)	90	85
MS1492	Two sheets each 102×73 mm. (a) $2 "At Swan Lake in Shainani"; (b) $2 "Mount Fuji in a Thunderstorm" (vert)	10·00	9·75

161 Queen Mother and Attendants

1999. "Queen Elizabeth the Queen Mother's Century".

1493	**161**	60c. black and gold	1·60	1·50
1494	-	60c. black and gold	1·60	1·50
1495	-	60c. multicoloured	1·60	1·50
1496	-	60c. multicoloured	1·60	1·50
MS1497		152×154 mm. $2 black	6·50	6·25

DESIGNS: No. 1494, Queen Mother with corgi dog; 1495, Queen Mother in pink coat and hat; 1496, Queen Mother in yellow evening dress and tiara. 37×49 mm—Queen Mother holding open book.

162 Launch of Rocket

1999. 30th Anniv of First Manned Moon Landing. Multicoloured.

1498	33c. Type **162**	85	80
1499	33c. Spacecraft above Earth and Moon's surface	85	80
1500	33c. Astronaut descending ladder	85	80
1501	33c. Distant view of rocket launch	85	80
1502	33c. Astronaut planting flag on Moon	85	80
1503	33c. "Apollo 11" crew members	85	80
MS1504	Four sheets each 78×101 mm. (a) $2 Rocket on launch-pad; (b) $2 Astronaut descending ladder (different); (c) $2 Lunar module; (d) $2 Splash down	21·00	20·00

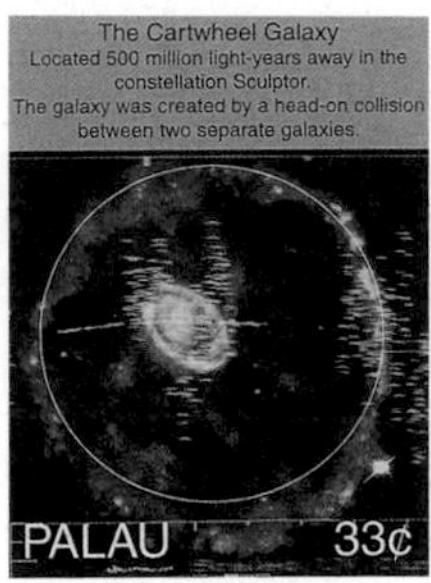

163 Cartwheel Galaxy

1999. Images from Space: Hubble Telescope. Multicoloured.

1505	33c. Type **163**	85	80
1506	33c. Stingray Nebula	85	80
1507	33c. Planetary Nebula NGC 3918	85	80
1508	33c. Cat's Eye Nebula	85	80
1509	33c. Galaxy NGC 7742	85	80
1510	33c. Eight-burst Nebula	85	80
MS1511	Four sheets each 77×100 mm. (a) $2 Supernova 1987-A; (b) Saturn (infrared aurora); (c) $2 Planetary Nebula M2-9; (d) $2 Eta Carinae	21·00	20·00

164 Calves and Chickens

1999. Christmas. "Puer Nobis" (carol). Mult.

1512	20c. Type **164**	55	50
1513	20c. Donkey, geese and rabbit	55	50
1514	20c. Child Jesus, cats and lambs	55	50
1515	20c. Geese, goat and sheep	55	50
1516	20c. Donkey and cockerel	55	50

Nos. 1512/16 were issued together, se-tenant, forming a composite design.

165 "Keep Safe"

1999. "How to Love Your Dog". Multicoloured.

1517	33c. Type **165**	90	85
1518	33c. Girl with puppies (Show affection)	90	85
1519	33c. Dog asleep (A place of one's own)	90	85
1520	33c. Girl with Scottish terrier (Communicate)	90	85
1521	33c. Dog eating (Good food)	90	85
1522	33c. Vet examining dog (Annual check-up)	90	85
1523	33c. Girl with prone dog (Teach rules)	90	85
1524	33c. Dog with disc (Exercise and play)	90	85
1525	33c. Dog with basket (Let him help)	90	85
1526	33c. Dog with heart on collar (Unconditional love)	90	85
MS1527	Two sheets each 100×69 mm. (a) $2 Puppies (Love is a gentle thing); (b) $2 Puppy (Pleasure of your company)	10·50	9·75

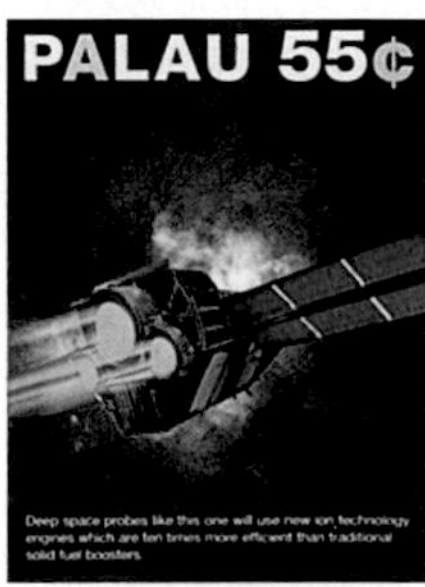

166 Deep Space Probe

2000. Projected Space Probes. Multicoloured.

1528	55c. Type **166**	1·30	1·20
1529	55c. Piggy back probe	1·30	1·20
1530	55c. Deep space telescope probe	1·30	1·20
1531	55c. Space probe on course to rendezvous with comet	1·30	1·20
1532	55c. Yellow space probe orbiting planet	1·30	1·20
1533	55c. Deep space probe with advanced onboard artificial intelligence	1·30	1·20
MS1534	Four sheets each 98×138 mm. (a) $2 Space probe in storm (horiz); (b) $2 Insect-shaped lander (horiz); (c) $2 Space probe with dish aerial; (d) Secondary probe disengaging from parent probe	21·00	20·00

167 Native Brazilian Indians, 1800

2000. New Millennium (1st series). The Nineteenth Century 1800–1850. Multicoloured.

1535	20c. Type **167**	55	50
1536	20c. Broken manacles (Haiti slave revolt, 1800)	55	50
1537	20c. Napoleon I (assumption of title of Emperor of France, 1804)	55	50
1538	20c. Shaka (Zulu leader)	55	50
1539	20c. Monster (publication of *Frankenstein* (novel) by Mary Shelley, 1818)	55	50
1540	20c. Simon Bolivar (revolutionary)	55	50
1541	20c. Camera (development of photography)	55	50
1542	20c. Dripping tap (introduction of water purification system, 1829)	55	50
1543	20c. Steam locomotive (inauguration in Great Britain of first passenger-carrying railway, 1830)	55	50
1544	20c. Discovery of electromagnetic induction by Michael Faraday, 1831	55	50
1545	20c. First use of anaesthesia in surgery by Crawford Williamson Long, 1842	55	50
1546	20c. Morse key (transmission of first message by Samuel Morse, 1844)	55	50
1547	20c. Poster (first convention on Women's Rights, Seneca Falls, U.S.A., 1848)	55	50
1548	20c. Karl Marx (publication of the *Communist Manifesto*), 1848	55	50
1549	20c. Charles Darwin's (naturalist) voyage on *Beagle* (56×36 mm)	55	50
1550	20c. Revolution in Germany, 1848	55	50
1551	20c. Commencement of Taiping Rebellion, China, 1850	55	50

There are a number of errors in the stamp inscriptions and descriptions.

See also Nos. 1552/68, 1691/1702 and 1741/57.

168 Lech Walesa and Shipyard Workers

2000. New Millennium (2nd series). The Twentieth Century 1980–1989. Multicoloured.

1552	20c. Type **168** (foundation of Solidarity (trade union), 1980)	55	50
1553	20c. First photographic image taken by *Voyager I* of Saturn, 1980	55	50
1554	20c. Election of Ronald Reagan as President of the United States of America, 1980	55	50
1555	20c. A.I.D.S. virus (identification of A.I.D.S.)	55	50
1556	20c. Marriage of Prince Charles and Lady Diana Spencer, 1981	55	50
1557	20c. Production of the compact disc, 1983	55	50
1558	20c. Leak of poisonous gas from insecticide plant, Bhopal, India, 1984	55	50
1559	20c. Inauguration of Pai's Pyramid, 1984	55	50
1560	20c. Mikhail Gorbachev elected Secretary General of the Soviet Communist Party, 1985	55	50
1561	20c. Explosion at the Chernobyl nuclear power plant, 1986	55	50
1562	20c. Explosion of space shuttle *Challenger*, 1986	55	50
1563	20c. Klaus Barbie, ((former chief of German Gestapo in France) sentenced to life imprisonment), 1987	55	50
1564	20c. Salman Rushdie (author) (publication of *The Satanic Verses*, 1988)	55	50
1565	20c. Election of Benazir Bhutto as Prime Minister of Pakistan, 1988	55	50
1566	20c. Tiananmen Square (student demonstrations, 1989)	55	50
1567	20c. Demonstrators breaching Berlin Wall, 1989 (59×39 mm)	55	50
1568	20c. Development of the World Wide Web	55	50

169 Dragon

2000. Chinese New Year. Year of the Dragon. Sheet 80×60 mm.

MS1569	**169** $2 multicoloured	5·50	5·00

170 Bill Clinton (1992–2000)

2000. Former United States Presidents.

1570	**170**	$1 black and brown	2·75	2·50
1571	-	$2 black and blue	5·50	5·00
1572	-	$3 black and mauve	8·25	7·25
1574	-	$5 black and brown	13·50	12·50
1575	-	$11.75 black and brown (40×23 mm)	31·00	28·00

DESIGNS: $2 Ronald Reagan (1980–88); $3 Gerald Ford (1974–76); $5 George Bush (1988–92); $11.75 John F. Kennedy (1960–63).

171 Australopithecine (Southern Ape species, Africa)

2000. Pre-historic Discoveries of the 20th-Century. Multicoloured.

1580	20c. Type **171**	55	50
1581	20c. Australopithecine skull	55	50
1582	20c. Homo habilis using hand axe	55	50
1583	20c. Hand-axe	55	50
1584	20c. Homo habilis skull	55	50
1585	20c. Australo pithecine skeleton "Lucy"	55	50
1586	20c. Archaic Homo sapien skull	55	50
1587	20c. Diapithicine skull	55	50
1588	20c. Homo erectus family	55	50
1589	20c. Wood hut	55	50
1590	20c. Australopithecine ethopis skull	55	50
1591	20c. Homo sapien	55	50
1592	20c. Homo sapien skull	55	50
1593	20c. Discovery of Taung Baby, 1924	55	50
1594	20c. Homo erectus skull	55	50
1595	20c. Louis Leaky (archaeologist)	55	50
1596	20c. Neanderthal skull	55	50
1597	20c. Neanderthal man	55	50
1598	20c. Development of the fully bipedal foot	55	50
1599	20c. Raymond Dart (discoverer of Taung Baby)	55	50

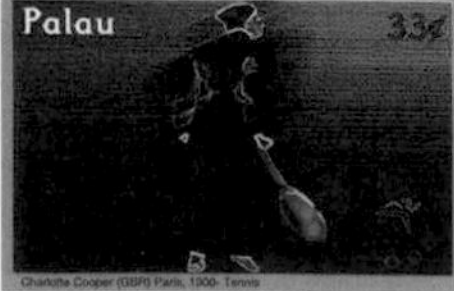

172 Tennis Player

2000. Olympic Games, Sydney. Multicoloured.

1600	33c. Type **172**	95	85
1601	33c. Shot put	95	85
1602	33c. Greek flag and stadium	95	85
1603	33c. Ancient Olympic athletes	95	85

173 Re-usable Launch Vehicle

2000. Projected Unmanned Craft and Space Exploration. Multicoloured.

1604	33c. Type **173**	90	80
1605	33c. Single stage vertical take-off craft	90	80
1606	33c. Robotic rocket plane	90	80
1607	33c. Single-stage craft	90	80
1608	33c. Fully-automated deep-space exploration craft	90	80
1609	33c. Magnetohydrodynamics-powered launch craft	90	80
MS1610	Four sheets, each 100×135 mm. (a) $2 Spacecraft taking-off (privately funded launch craft); (b) $2 Emergency crew return craft using parachutes (horiz); (c) $2 Interplanetary space craft (horiz); (d) $2 Space shuttle leaving space station	22·00	20·00

174 Banded Crake (*Rallina eurizonoides*)

2000. Birds. Multicoloured.

1611	20c. Type **174**	55	50
1612	20c. Micronesian kingfisher (*Halcyon cinnamomina*)	55	50
1613	20c. Little pied cormorant (*Phalacrocorax melanoleucos*)	55	50
1614	20c. Eastern reef heron (*Egretta sacra*)	55	50
1615	20c. Nicobar pigeon (*Caloenas nicobarica*)	55	50
1616	20c. Rufous night heron (*Nycticorax caledonicus*)	55	50
1617	33c. Palau ground dove (*Gallicolumba canifrons*)	90	80
1618	33c. Palau scops owl (*Pyrroglaux podargina*)	90	80
1619	33c. Mangrove flycatcher (*Cyornis rufigastra*) (wrongly inscr "Pyrrboglaux podargina")	90	80
1620	33c. Palau bushwarbler (*Cettia annae*)	90	80
1621	33c. Palau fantail (*Rhipidura lepida*)	90	80
1622	33c. Morning bird (*Celluricincla tenebrosa*)	55	50
MS1623	Two sheets, each 76×126 mm. (a) $2 Palau whiteeye (*Megazosterops palauensis*) (horiz); (b) $2 Palau fruit-dove (*Ptilinopus pelewensis*) (horiz)	11·00	9·75

No. 1611 is inscribed "Slatey-legged Crake" and No. 1614 "Pacific reef egret" both in error. There are also several errors in the Latin names.

175 Booker T. Washington (educationist)

2000. 20th-Century Personalities. Multicoloured.

1624	33c. Type **175**	90	80
1625	33c. Buckmeister Fuller (inventor and designer)	90	80
1626	33c. Marie Curie (physicist)	90	80
1627	33c. Walt Disney (animator and producer)	90	80
1628	33c. Franklin D. Roosevelt (32nd United States President)	90	80
1629	33c. Henry Ford (car manufacturer)	90	80
1630	33c. Betty Friedan (author and feminist leader)	90	80
1631	33c. Sigmund Freud (founder of psychoanalysis)	90	80
1632	33c. Mahatma Ghandi (Indian leader)	90	80
1633	33c. Mikhail Gorbachev (Soviet President)	90	80
1634	33c. Stephan Hawkings (theoretical physicist)	90	80
1635	33c. Martin Luther King Jr. (civil rights leader)	90	80
1636	33c. Toni Morrison (writer)	90	80
1637	33c. Georgia O'Keeffe (artist)	90	80
1638	33c. Rosa Parks (civil rights activist)	90	80
1639	33c. Carl Sagan (astronomer)	90	80
1640	33c. Jonas Salk (immunologist)	90	80
1641	33c. Sally Ride (astronaut and astrophysicist)	90	80
1642	33c. Nikola Tesla (electrical engineer and physicist)	90	80
1643	33c. Wilbur and Orville Wright (aviation pioneer)	90	80

176 Reef Bass (*Pseudogramma gregoryi*)

2000. Marine Life of the Atlantic and Pacific Oceans. Multicoloured.

1644	20c. Type **176**	60	55
1645	20c. Great white shark (*Carcharodon carcharias*)	60	55
1646	20c. Sharptail eel (*Myrichthys breviceps*)	60	55
1647	20c. Sailfish (*Istiophorus platypterus*)	60	55
1648	20c. Southern stingray (*Dasyatis americana*)	60	55
1649	20c. Ocean triggerfish (*Canthidermis sufflamen*)	60	55
1650	55c. Scalloped hammerhead (*Sphyrna lewini*) (vert)	1·70	1·50
1651	55c. White-tipped reef shark (*Triaenodon obesus*) (vert)	1·70	1·50
1652	55c. Moon jellyfish (*Aurelia aurita*) (vert)	1·70	1·50
1653	55c. Lionfish (*Pterois volitans*) (vert)	1·70	1·50
1654	55c. Seahorse (*Hippocampus abdominalis*) (vert)	1·70	1·50
1655	55c. Spotted eagle ray (*Aetobatus narinari*) (vert)	1·70	1·50
MS1656	Two sheets, each 110×85 mm. (a) $2 Short bigeye (*Pristigenys alta*) (vert); (b) $2 Gaff-topsail catfish (*Bagre marinus*) (vert)	12·00	11·00

177 Prawn

2000. Marine Life. Multicoloured.

1657	33c. Type **177**	1·00	90
1658	33c. Deep sea angler	1·00	90
1659	33c. Rooster fish	1·00	90
1660	33c. Grenadier	1·00	90
1661	33c. *Platyberix opalescens*	1·00	90
1662	33c. Lantern fish	1·00	90
1663	33c. Emperor angelfish	1·00	90
1664	33c. Nautilus	1·00	90
1665	33c. Moorish idol	1·00	90
1666	33c. Seahorse	1·00	90
1667	33c. Clown triggerfish	1·00	90
1668	33c. Clown fish	1·00	90
MS1669	Two sheets, each 106×75 mm. (a) $2 Giant squid; (b) $2 Manta ray	12·00	11·00

178 James Watson (co-discoverer of structure of D.N.A.)

2000. Advances in Science and Medicine. Multicoloured.

1670	33c. Type **178**	1·00	90
1671	33c. Har Gobing Khorana and Robert Holley (work on genetic code)	1·00	90
1672	33c. Hamilton Smith and Werner Arber (discovered restriction enzymes)	1·00	90
1673	33c. Centrifugation machine and D.N.A. double helix	1·00	90
1674	33c. Richard Roberts (discovered R.N.A. splicing and split genes)	1·00	90
1675	33c. Maurice Wilkins (co-discoverer of structure of D.N.A.)	1·00	90
1676	33c. D.N.A. double helix	1·00	90
1677	33c. Frederick Sanger and Walter Gilbert (developed methods for determining nucleotide sequences for D.N.A. molecules)	1·00	90
1678	33c. Kary Mullis (discovered polymerase chain reaction)	1·00	90
1679	33c. D.N.A. double helix and frogs (mapping location of genes)	1·00	90
1680	33c. Francis Crick (co-discoverer of structure of D.N.A.)	1·00	90
1681	33c. Marshall Nirenberg (work on genetic code)	1·00	90
1682	33c. Daniel Nathans (discovered restriction enzymes)	1·00	90
1683	33c. Harold Varmus and Michael Bishop (identified several genes involved in cancer)	1·00	90
1684	33c. Phillip Sharp (discovered polymerase chain reaction)	1·00	90
1685	33c. Sheep (cloning sheep to produce Dolly, 1997)	1·00	90
1686	33c. D.N.A. being separated by electrophoresis	1·00	90
1687	33c. Paul Berg (first developed methods for cloning genes, 1980)	1·00	90
1688	33c. Michael Smith and D.N.A. (discovered polymerase chain reaction)	1·00	90
1689	33c. D.N.A. and deer (human genome project)	1·00	90
MS1690	Two sheets, each 97×117 mm. (a) $2 Dolly (cloned sheep) (37×50 mm). (b) $2 D.N.A. and deer (37×50 mm)	12·00	11·00

179 Hourglass and Map of South East Asia

2000. New Millennium (3rd series). Multicoloured.

1691	20c. Type **179**	60	55
1692	20c. Hourglass and map of North America	60	55
1693	20c. Hourglass and map of Europe	60	55
1694	20c. Hourglass and map of Australia	60	55
1695	20c. Hourglass and map of South America	60	55
1696	20c. Hourglass and map of Africa	60	55
1697	55c. Clock face and clouds (vert)	1·70	1·50
1698	55c. Clock face and building façade (vert)	1·70	1·50
1699	55c. Clock face and coastline (vert)	1·70	1·50
1700	55c. Clock face and farm buildings (vert)	1·70	1·50
1701	55c. Clock face and forest (vert)	1·70	1·50
1702	55c. Clock face and desert (vert)	1·70	1·50

180 American Bald Eagle

2000. Endangered Species. Multicoloured.

1703	33c. Type **180**	1·00	90
1704	33c. Small whorled pogonia	1·00	90
1705	33c. Arctic peregrine falcon	1·00	90
1706	33c. Golden lion tamarin	1·00	90
1707	33c. American alligator	1·00	90
1708	33c. Brown pelican	1·00	90
1709	33c. Aleutian Canada goose	1·00	90
1710	33c. Western grey kangaroo	1·00	90
1711	33c. Palau scops owl	1·00	90
1712	33c. Jocotoco antpitta	1·00	90
1713	33c. Orchid	1·00	90
1714	33c. Red lechwe	1·00	90
MS1715	Two sheets, each 120×92 mm. (a) $2 Lahontan cutthroat trout (horiz); (b) $2 Leopard	12·00	11·00

181 Rhamphorhynchus

2000. Dinosaurs. Multicoloured.

1716	20c. Type **181**	60	55
1717	20c. Ceratosaurus	60	55
1718	20c. Apatosaurus	60	55
1719	20c. Stegosaurus	60	55
1720	20c. Archaeopteryx	60	55
1721	20c. Allosaurus	60	55
1722	33c. Parasaurolophus	1·00	90
1723	33c. Pteranodonrus	1·00	90
1724	33c. Tyrannosaurus	1·00	90
1725	33c. Triceratops	1·00	90
1726	33c. Ankylosaurus	1·00	90
1727	33c. Velociraptor	1·00	90
MS1728	Two sheets, each 94×71 mm. (a) $2 Jurassic landscape; (b) $2 Cretaceous landscape	12·00	11·00

Nos. 1716/21 and 1722/7 were each issued together, se-tenant, forming a composite design.

182 Lebaudy–Juillot Airship Le Jaune

2000. Centenary of First Zeppelin Flight and Airship Development. Multicoloured.

1729	55c. Type **182**	1·70	1·50
1730	55c. Forlanini airship *Leonardo DaVinci*	1·70	1·50
1731	55c. Thomas Baldwin's airship U.S. Military No. 1, 1908	1·70	1·50
1732	55c. Astra-Torres 1	1·70	1·50
1733	55c. Rear of Astra-Torres 1 and Parseval PL VII	1·70	1·50
1734	55c. Rear of Parseval PL VII and Lebaudy airship *Liberte*	1·70	1·50
MS1735	Two sheets, each 110×85 mm. (a) $2 Santos-Dumont airship Ballon No. 9 La Badaleuse; (b) $2 Santos-Dumont Ballon No. 6 circling Eiffel Tower	12·00	11·00

Nos. 1729/34 were issued together, se-tenant, forming a composite design.

183 Duke and Duchess of York

2000. 100th Birthday of Queen Elizabeth the Queen Mother. Multicoloured.

1736	55c. Type **183**	1·70	1·50
1737	55c. As Duchess of York wearing cloche hat	1·70	1·50
1738	55c. Wearing green floral hat	1·70	1·50
1739	55c. Wearing blue hat	1·70	1·50
MS1740	99×84 mm. $2 Wearing yellow coat and hat	6·00	5·50

184 Viking Diver attacking Danish Ship

2000. New Millennium (4th series). Development of Diving Equipment. Multicoloured.

1741	33c. Type **184**	1·10	1·00
1742	33c. Issa (12th-century Arab diver)	1·10	1·00
1743	33c.15 th-century salvage diver using breathing tube	1·10	1·00
1744	33c. 17 th-century diver wearing leather suit and carrying halberd	1·10	1·00
1745	33c. Edmund Halley's wooden diving bell, 1690	1·10	1·00
1746	33c. David Bushnell's diving bell Turtle, 1776	1·10	1·00
1747	33c. Diver wearing suit and Siebe helmet,1819	1·10	1·00
1748	33c. *Hunley* (Confederate submarine)	1·10	1·00
1749	33c. Argonaut (first underwater salvage vehicle), 1899	1·10	1·00
1750	33c. John Williamson's underwater filming vehicle photosphere, 1914	1·10	1·00
1751	33c. Diver wearing brass helmet, weighted boots, with air supply and safety lines (circa 1930)	1·10	1·00
1752	33c. William Beebe and Otis Barton's bathysphere, 1934	1·10	1·00
1753	33c. Coelacanth (prehistoric fish previously thought extinct)	1·10	1·00
1754	33c. Italian divers on chariot planting explosive charges on ship hull during World War II	1·10	1·00
1755	33c. *Trieste* (bathyscaphe) (record dive by Jaques Picard and Lt. Don Walsh, 1960)	1·10	1·00
1756	33c. *Alvin* (submersible) surveying thermal vents in Galapagos Rift (1977) (60×40 mm)	1·10	1·00
1757	33c. Sylvia Earle wearing Jim Suit, 1979	1·10	1·00

185 "Dancers" (S. Adelbai)

2000. 8th Pacific Arts Festival, Noumea, New Caledonia. Sheet 192×153 mm containing T 185 and similar horiz designs. Multicoloured.

MS1758 33c. Type **185**; 33c. "Storyboard Art" (D. Inabo); 33c. "Traditional Money" (M. Takeshi); 33c. "Clay Lamp and Bowl" (W. Watanabe); 33c. "Meeting House" (P. Tiakl); "Outrigger Canoe" (S. Adelbai); 33c. "Weaver" (M. Vitarelli); 33c. "Rock Island Scene" (W. Marcil); 33c. "Contemporary Music" (J. Imetuker) 9·00 8·25

186 Turtle Shell Bracelet

2000. 45th Anniv of Belau National Museum. Multicoloured.

1759	33c. Type **186**	1·00	90
1760	33c. Bust (sculpture) (H. Hijikata)	1·00	90
1761	33c. "Turtle Shell Women's Money"	1·00	90
1762	33c. "Cherecheroi" (T. Suzuki)	1·00	90
1763	33c. Money jar (B. Sylvester)	1·00	90
1764	33c. "Prince Lebu" (Ichikawa)	1·00	90
1765	33c. "Beach at Lild" (H. Hijikata)	1·00	90
1766	33c. Traditional mask	1·00	90
1767	33c. Taro platter (T. Rebluud)	1·00	90
1768	33c. "Meresebang" (Ichikawa)	1·00	90
1769	33c. Woman and child (sculpture) (B. Sylvester)	1·00	90
1770	33c. "Birth Ceremony" (I. Kishigawa)	1·00	90

187 Top of Head

2000. 80th Birthday of Pope John Paul II. Sheet 158×243 mm containing T 187 and similar vert designs showing collage of miniature religious photographs. Multicoloured, country inscription and face value at left (a) or right (b).

MS1771 50c. Type **187**; 50c. Ear (a); 50c. Neck and collar (a); 50c. Shoulder (a); 50c. Forehead (b); 50c. Forehead and eye (b); 50c. Nose and cheek (b); 50c. Hands (b) 12·00 11·00

No. **MS**1771 was issued with the stamps arranged in two vertical columns separated by a gutter also containing miniature photographs. When viewed as a whole, the miniature sheet forms a portrait of Pope John Paul II.

188 Face enclosed by Snake

2000. Chinese New Year. Year of the Snake. Two sheets, each 69×99 mm containing T 188 and similar horiz design.

MS1772 (a) 60c. Type **188**; (b) 60c. Face with snake head-dress 3·50 3·25

189 Indian Red Admiral (*Vanessa indica*)

2000. Butterflies. Multicoloured.

1773	33c. Type **189**	1·10	95
1774	33c. Chequered swallowtail (*Papilio demoleus*)	1·10	95
1775	33c. Yamfly (*Loxura atymnus*)	1·10	95
1776	33c. Fiery jewel (*Hypochrysops ignite*)	1·10	95

MS1777 Four sheets. (a) 119×134 mm. 33c. Cairn's birdwing (*Ornithoptera priamus*); 33c. Meadow argus (*Junonia villida*); 33c. Orange albatross (*Appias nero*); 33c. Glasswing (*Acraea andromacha*); 33c. Beak butterfly (*Libythea geoffroyi*); 33c. Great eggfly (*Hypolimnas bolina*); (b) 119×134 mm. 33c. Large green-banded blue (*Danis danis*); 33c. Union jack (*Delias mysis*); 33c. Broad-bordered grass yellow (*Eurema brigitta*); 33c. Striped blue crow (*Euploea mulciber*); 33c. Red lacewing (*Cethosia bibles*); 33c. Palmfly (*Elyminias hypermnestra*) (inscr "Elyminas agondas"); (c) 107×77 mm. $2 Clipper (*Parthenos Sylvia*); (d) 107×77 mm. $2 Blue triangle (*Graphium sarpedon*) 24·00 22·00

190 Little Kingfisher

2000. Flora and Fauna. Four sheets containing T 190 and similar multicoloured designs.

MS1778 (a) 132×80 mm. 33c. Type **190**; 33c. Mangrove snake; 33c. Bats and breadfruit; 33c. Giant tree frog; 33c. Giant centipede; 33c. Crab-eating macaque; (b) 90×112 mm. 33c. Giant spiral ginger; 33c. Good luck plant; 33c. Leaves and green coconuts; 33c. Orchid and butterfly; 33c. Crocodile; 33c. Orchid; (c) 120×93 mm. $2 Claw and mouth of land crab (vert); (d) 119×93 mm. $2 Head and fin of fish 24·00 22·00

2001. As T 153 with additional imprint date at foot. Multicoloured.

1779	1c. Type **153**	25	20
1780	11c. As No. 1389	40	35
1781	60c. As No. 1395	1·90	1·70

191 "Washing the Copybook" (Torii Kiyomitsu)

2001. Japanese Art. Six sheets containing T 191 and similar vert designs. Multicoloured.

MS1795 (a) 161×120 mm. 60c. ×5 Type **191**; "Woman playing Shamisen and woman reading letter" (Iwasa Matabei); "Ichikawa Danjuro (actor) as Samurai" (Katasukawa Shunsho); "Gentleman entertained by courtesans" (Torrii Kiyonaga); "Geisha at teahouse" (Torrii Kiyonaga); (b) 161×120 mm. 60c. ×5 "Preparing Sashimi" (Kitagawa Utamaro); "Sanogawa Ichimatsu and Onoe Kikugoro (actors) in Plum Blossoms and Young Herbs" (Ishikawa Toyonobu); "Courtesan adjusting her comb" (Kaigetsudo Dohan); "Nakamura Tomijuro (actor) as woman dancing" (Katsukawa Shunsho); "Woman with poem card and writing brush" (Yashima Gakutei); (c) 187×113 mm. 60c. ×6 "Kitano Shrine, Kyoto" (Anon.); (d) 91×104 mm. $2 "Raiko attacks demon kite" (detail, Totoya Hokkei); (e) 123×105 mm. $2 "Beauty writing letter" (detail, Kaigetsudo Doshin) (28×42 mm); (e) 150×102 mm. $2 "Fireworks at Ikenohata" (detail, Kobayashi Kiyochika) (28×42 mm) 47·00 43·00

No. **MS**1795c was made up of six stamps, each stamp forming part of the composite design of the painting.

192 *Teracotona euprepia*

2001. Moths. Multicoloured.

1796	20c. Type **192**	60	55
1797	21c. Basker (*Euchromia lethe*)	75	70
1798	80c. White-lined sphinx (*Hyles lineate*)	2·50	2·30
1799	$1 Isabella Tiger Moth (*Pyrrharctia Isabella*) (Inscr "Pyrrrharctia")	3·25	2·75

MS1800 (a) 133×115 mm. 34c. ×6 Cinnabar moth (*Tyria jacobeae*); Beautiful tiger moth (*Amphicallia bellatrix*); Garden tiger moth (*Arctia caja*); *Zygaena occitanica*; Jersey tiger moth (*Euplagia quadripunctaria*); *Utetheisa ornatrix*; (b) 133×115 mm. 70c. ×6 Milionia isodoxa (inscr "Milonia"); *Cephonodes kingi*; *Anaphe panda*; Io moth (*Automeris io*); Tau emperor (*Aglia tau*); Lime hawk moth (*Mimas tiliae*); (c) 98×71 mm. $2 Owl moth (*Brahmaea wallichii*); (d) 98×71 mm. $2 Isabel moth (*Graellsia isabellae*) (inscr "Graaellsia") 31·00 28·00

193 Ivo Andric (1961)

2001. Centenary of the First Nobel Prize for Literature. Six sheets containing T 193 and similar vert designs. Multicoloured.

MS1801 (a) 148×209 mm. 34c. ×6 Type **193**; Eyvind Johnson (1974); Salvatore Quasimodo (1959); Mikhael Sholokhov (1965); Pablo Neruda (1971); Saul Bellow (1976); (b) 148×209 mm. 70c. ×6 Boris Pasternak (1958); Francois Mauriac (1952); Frans Eemil Sillanpaa (1939); Roger Martin du Gard (1937); Pearl Buck (1938); Andre Gide (1947); (c) 148×209 mm. 80c. ×6 Karl Gjellerup (1917); Anatole France (1921); Sinclair Lewis (1930); Jacinto Benavente (1922); John Galsworthy (1932); Erik A. Karlfeldt (1931); (d) 108×128 mm. $2 Bertrand Russell (1950); (e) 108×128 mm. $2 Luigi Pirandello (1934); (f) 108×128 mm. $2 Harry Martinson (1974) 50·00 47·00

194 Communal Meeting House (Bai)

2001. Christmas. Multicoloured.

1802	20c. Type **194**	75	70
1803	34c. No. 1786	1·20	1·10

195 Foot and Football (1950)

2001. History of Football World Cup Championships. Poster Designs. Four sheets containing T 195 and similar vert designs. Multicoloured.

MS1804 (a) 154×109 mm. 34c. ×6 Type **195**; Goalkeeper and ball (1954); Ball enclosed in scarf of flags (1958); Globe and ball (1962); Championship mascot (1966); Silhouette of ball (1970); (b) 154×109 mm. Player with raised arms (1978); Stylized player (1982); Silhouette of player against statues (1986); Amphitheatre (1990); "94", ball and player (1994); Championship emblem (1998); (c) 88×75 mm. $2 Trophy (detail); (d) 88×75 mm. $2 "Uruguay" (1930) 34·00 32·00

196 "Groom taking Horses to Pasture" (Han Kan)

2001. Sheet 200×136 mm containing T 196. Multicoloured.

MS1805 60c.×4 Type **196** 7·75 7·25

197 Yellow-faced Mynah (*Mino dumontii*)

2001. Birds. Four sheets containing T 197 and similar vert designs. Multicoloured.

MS1806 (a) 120×120 mm. 55c. ×6 Type **197**; Red-breasted pitta (*Pitta erythogaster*); Red-bearded Bee-eater (*Nyctyornis amictus*); Superb fruit dove (*Ptilinopus superbus*); Coppersmith barbet (*Megalaima haemacephala*); Diard's trogon (*Harpactes diardii*); (b) 120×120 mm. 60c. ×6 Spectacled monarch (*Monarcha trivirgatus*); Blue-tailed pitta (*Pitta guajana*) (inscr "Banded pitta"); Rufous-backed kingfisher (*Ceyx rufidorsa*); Scarlet robin (*Petroica multicolour*); Golden whistler (*Pachycephala pectoralis*); Mid-mountain rail babbler (*Ptilorrhoa castanonota*) (inscr "Jewel babbler"); (c) 105×75 mm. $2 River kingfisher (*Alcedo atthis*); (d) 105×75 mm. $2 Asiatic paradise flycatcher (*Tersiphone paradise*) 34·00 32·00

198 Seagull on Rock

2002. Inauguration of Japanese sponsored Koror—Babeldaob Bridge. Multicoloured.

No.	Description	Unused	Used
1807	20c. Type **198**	70	65
1808	20c. Palm tree on island	70	65
1809	20c. Three palm trees on island	70	65
1810	20c. Rocks and prow of boat	70	65
1811	20c. Boat, bird and island	70	65
1812	20c. Shoreline	70	65
1813	20c. Two people in row boat	70	65
1814	20c. Buoy and birds	70	65
1815	20c. Birds and dolphin's tail	70	65
1816	20c. Dolphins	70	65
1817	20c. Boy on raft	70	65
1818	20c. Two men wading	70	65
1819	20c. Man fishing	70	65
1820	20c. Bridge supports	70	65
1821	20c. Cyclist and part of car	70	65
1822	20c. Car	70	65
1823	20c. Two people and bridge supports	70	65
1824	20c. Motor boat and truck	70	65
1825	20c. Coach	70	65
1826	20c. Base of bridge support	70	65
1827	20c. Canoe paddle and two birds	70	65
1828	20c. One bird	70	65
1829	20c. Top of sail and base of bridge	70	65
1830	20c. Treetops, motorcyclist and palm trees	70	65
1831	20c. Two pelicans on rock	70	65
1832	20c. Bird's wing, rock and canoes	70	65
1833	20c. Prow of canoe and motor boat	70	65
1834	20c. Rear of boat and rear of outrigger canoe	70	65
1835	20c. Outrigger canoe	70	65
1836	20c. Jet ski, boat slip and base of trees	70	65
1837	34c. No. 1807	1·10	1·00
1838	34c. No. 1808	1·10	1·00
1839	34c. No. 1809	1·10	1·00
1840	34c. No. 1810	1·10	1·00
1841	34c. No. 1811	1·10	1·00
1842	34c. No. 1812	1·10	1·00
1843	34c. No. 1813	1·10	1·00
1844	34c. No. 1814	1·10	1·00
1845	34c. No. 1815	1·10	1·00
1846	34c. No. 1816	1·10	1·00
1847	34c. No. 1817	1·10	1·00
1848	34c. No. 1808	1·10	1·00
1849	34c. No. 1819	1·10	1·00
1850	34c. No. 1820	1·10	1·00
1851	34c. No. 1821	1·10	1·00
1852	34c. No. 1822	1·10	1·00
1853	34c. No. 1823	1·10	1·00
1854	34c. No. 1824	1·10	1·00
1855	34c. No. 1825	1·10	1·00
1856	34c. No. 1826	1·10	1·00
1857	34c. No. 1827	1·10	1·00
1858	34c. No. 1828	1·10	1·00
1859	34c. No. 1829	1·10	1·00
1860	34c. No. 1830	1·10	1·00
1861	34c. No. 1831	1·10	1·00
1862	34c. No. 1832	1·10	1·00
1863	34c. No. 1833	1·10	1·00
1864	34c. No. 1834	1·10	1·00
1865	34c. No. 1835	1·10	1·00
1866	34c. No. 1836	1·10	1·00

Nos. 1807/36 and 1837/66, respectively, each form a composite design of Koror and Babeldaob islands, the bridge and bay.

199 Statue of Liberty wrapped in Flag

2002. "United We Stand" Support for Victims of Terrorist Attacks on World Trade Centre, New York.

No.	Type	Description	Unused	Used
1867	**199**	$1 multicoloured	3·00	3·00

200 Queen Elizabeth II

2002. Golden Jubilee. 50th Anniv of Queen Elizabeth II's Accession to the Throne. Two sheets containing T 200 and similar square designs. Multicoloured.

MS1868 (a) 132×100 mm. 80c. ×4, Type **200**; Queen Elizabeth wearing flowered hat; Prince Phillip; Wearing tiara and diamond jewellery. (b) 76×109 mm. $2 Queen Elizabeth with hand extended. Set of 2 sheets 16·00 15·00

201 Grey-backed White Eye

2002. Birds. Multicoloured.

No.	Description	Unused	Used
1869	1c. Type **201**	25	20
1870	2c. Great frigate bird	25	20
1871	3c. Eclectus parrot	25	20
1872	4c. Red-footed booby	25	20
1873	5c. Cattle egret	25	20
1874	10c. Cardinal honey eater	30	30
1875	11c. Blue-faced parrot-finch	30	30
1876	15c. Rufous fantail	45	45
1877	20c. White-faced storm petrel	60	60
1878	21c. Willie wagtail	60	60
1879	23c. Black-headed gull	70	65
1879a	26c. Great tit	85	80
1879b	50c. Pale white-eye	1·20	1·10
1880	50c. Sanderling	1·50	1·50
1881	57c. White-tailed tropicbird	1·70	1·60
1882	70c. Rainbow lorikeet	2·20	2·00
1883	80c. Moorhen	2·50	2·30
1884	$1 Buff-banded rail	3·00	3·00
1885	$2 *Esacus magnirostris*	6·25	5·75
1886	$3 Common tern	9·25	8·75
1887	$3.50 Ruddy turnstone	11·00	10·00
1888	$3.95 White-collared kingfisher	12·50	11·50
1889	$5 Sulphur-crested cockatoo	15·00	14·50
1890	$10 Swallow	31·00	29·00

202 *Euanthe sanderiana*

2002. Flowers. Multicoloured.

No.	Description	Unused	Used
1891	20c. Type **202**	60	60
1892	34c. *Ophiorrhiza palauensis*	1·10	1·00
1893	60c. *Cerbera manghas*	1·90	1·70
1894	80c. Inscr "Mendinillia pterocaula"	2·50	2·30

MS1895 Four sheets. (a) 87×158 mm. 60c. ×6, *Bruguiera gymnorhiza*; *Samadera indica* (inscr "indical"); Inscr "Maesa canfieldiae"; *Lumnitzera litorea*; *Dolichandrone palawense*; Orchid (inscr "Limnophila aromatica"). (b) 96×171 mm. 60c. ×6 *Sonneratia alba*; *Barringtonia racemosa*; *Ixora casei*; *Tristellateia australasiae*; *Nepenthes mirabilisi*; *Limnophila aromaticai*. (c) 100×90 mm. $2 *Fagraea ksid*. (d) 100×90 mm. $2 *Cerbera manghas* (horiz). Set of 4 sheets 35·00 33·00

The stamps and margins of **MS**1895a/b, respectively, each form a composite design.

203 Great Dane

2002. Dogs and Cats. Four sheets containing T 203 and similar multicoloured designs.

MS1896 Two sheets (a/b), each 199×105 mm. (a) Dogs. 50c. ×6, Type **203**; Whippet; Bedlington terrier; Golden retriever; Papillon; Doberman. (b) Cats. 50c. ×6, Persian Himalayan; Norwegian Forest Cat; Havana; Exotic shorthair; Persian; Maine coon. Two sheets (c/d), each 105×75 mm. (c) $2 British shorthair cat. (d) $2 Shetland sheepdog 31·00 29·00

204 Male Super-G Skier

2002. Winter Olympic Games, Salt Lake City (1st issue). Multicoloured.

No.	Description	Unused	Used
1897	$1 Type **204**	3·00	2·75
1898	$1 Female Super-G skier	3·00	2·75
MS1899	88×119 mm. Nos. 1897/8	6·25	5·75

See also Nos. 1918/**MS**1920.

205 Mount Fuji, Japan

2002. International Year of Mountains. Two sheets containing T 205 and similar horiz designs. Multicoloured.

MS1900 (a) 152×112 mm. 80c. ×4 Type **205**; Mount Everest, Nepal/China; Mount Owen, USA; Mount Huascaran, Peru (inscr "Huascarran", Nepal). (b) 90×68 mm. $2 Mount Eiger, Switzerland. Set of 2 sheets 16·00 15·00

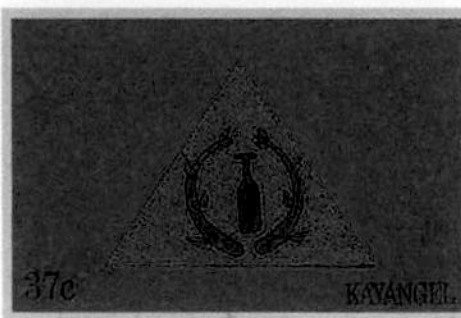

206 Kayangel

2002. 21st Anniv of Constitutional Day. Showing flags of Palau states.

No.	Type	Description	Unused	Used
1901	**206**	37c. multicoloured	1·20	1·10
1902	-	37c. red, ultramarine and black	1·20	1·10
1903	-	37c. multicoloured	1·20	1·10
1904	-	37c. multicoloured	1·20	1·10
1905	-	37c. blue, yellow and black	1·20	1·10
1906	-	37c. multicoloured	1·20	1·10
1907	-	37c. yellow, blue and black	1·20	1·10
1908	-	37c. multicoloured	1·20	1·10
1909	-	37c. scarlet, ultramarine and black	1·20	1·10
1910	-	37c. green and black	1·20	1·10
1911	-	37c. black, green and ultramarine	1·20	1·10
1912	-	37c. multicoloured	1·20	1·10
1913	-	37c. multicoloured	1·20	1·10
1914	-	37c. multicoloured	1·20	1·10
1915	-	37c. multicoloured	1·20	1·10
1916	-	37c. ultramarine, scarlet and black	1·20	1·10
1917	-	37c. blue and black	1·20	1·10

DESIGNS: Type **206**; Ngarchelong; Ngaraard; Ngardmau; Ngaremlengui; Ngiwal; Republic of Palau; Ngatpang; Melekeor; Ngchesar; Aimeliik; Airai; Koror; Peleliu; Angaur; Sonsorol; Hatohobei.

207 Male Super-G Skier

2002. Winter Olympic Games, Salt Lake City (2nd issue). Multicoloured.

No.	Description	Unused	Used
1918	$1 Type **207**	3·00	2·75
1919	$1 Female Super-G skier	3·00	2·75
MS1920	88×119 mm. Nos. 1918/19	6·25	5·75

Nos. 1918/**MS**1920 differ from 1897/**MS**1899, in the design of the Olympic rings.

208 Fish

2002. International Year of Eco Tourism. Two sheets containing T 208 and similar vert designs. Multicoloured.

MS1921 (a) 108×144 mm. 60c. ×6, Type **208**; Ray; Sea slug; Angelfish (different); Turtle; Nautilus. (b) 76×104 mm. $2 Canoeist. Set of 2 sheets 17·00 16·00

The stamps and margins of **MS**1921a/b, respectively, each form a composite design.

209 "Bando Shuka as the Courtesan Shirato" (Utagawa Kunisada)

2002. Japanese Art. Five sheets containing T 209 and similar multicoloured designs.

MS1922 (a) 190×143 mm. 60c. ×6, Type **209**; "Ichikawa Danjuro VII as Sugawara No Michizane" (Utagawa Kunisada); "Sawamura Sojuro III as Oboshi Yuranosuke" (Utagawa Toyokuni); "Kataoka Nizaemon Vii as Fujiwara Shihei" (Utagawa Toyokuni); "Portrait of Nakamura Noshio II" (Utagawa Kunimasa); "Kawarazaki Gon-Nosuke as Daroku" (Toyohara Kunichika). (b) 177×110 mm. 80c. ×4, "Gaslight Hall" (Kobayashi Kiyochika) (horiz); "Cherry Blossom at Night at Shin Yoshiwara" (Inoue Yasuji) (horiz); "Night Rain at Oyama" (Utagawa Toyokuni II) (horiz); "Kintai Bridge" (Keisai Eisen) (horiz). (c) 150×127 mm. 80c. ×4, "Bush-clover Branch and Sweetfish" (Utagawa Kuniyoshi) (28×89 mm); "Catfish" (Utagawa Kuniyoshi) (28×89 mm); "Scene at Takanawa" (Keisai Eisen) (28×89 mm); "Ochanomizu" (Keisai Eisen) (28×89 mm). (d) 105×85 mm. $2 "Okane, Strong Woman of Omi" (Utagawa Kuniyoshi). Imperf. (e) 105×85 mm. $2 "Scenes on the Banks of the Oumaya River" (Utagawa Kuniyoshi). Imperf 44·00 41·00

210 Wimpy

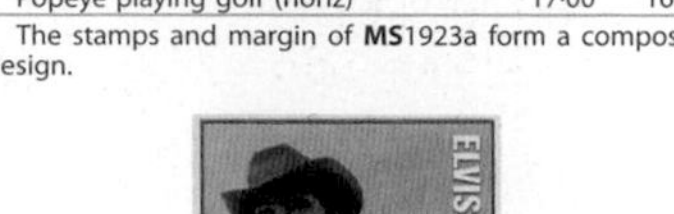

2002. Popeye (cartoon character created by Elzie Segar). Two sheets containing T 210 and similar multicoloured designs showing characters.

MS1923 (a) 198×128 mm. 60c. ×6, Type **210**; Swee'pea; Popeye; Marlin; Jeep; Brutus (Bluto). (b) 125×92 mm. $2 Popeye playing golf (horiz) 17·00 16·00

The stamps and margin of **MS**1923a form a composite design.

211 Elvis Presley

2002. 25th Death Anniv of Elvis Presley (entertainer). Sheet 156×152 mm containing T 211 similar vert designs. Multicoloured.

MS1924 37c. ×6, Type **211**; Seated holding guitar; Wearing white jacket and black hat; Standing holding two-necked electric guitar; Holding acoustic guitar; Wearing open-necked shirt 7·25 7·00

212 "Presentation of Jesus in the Temple" (detail) (Perugino)

2002. Christmas. Paintings.Multicoloured.

1925 23c. Type **212** 70 65

1926 37c. "Madonna and Child enthroned between Angels and Saints" (Domenico Chirlandio) 1·20 1·10

1927 60c. "Maesta, Madonna and Child" (Simone Martini) 1·90 1·70

1928 80c. "Sacred Conversation" (Giovanni Bellini (inscr "Giovanna")) (horiz) 2·50 2·30

1929 $1 "Nativity" (Domenico Ghirlandaio) (horiz) 3·00 3·00

MS1930 104×78 mm. $2 "Sacred Conversation" (detail) (horiz) 6·25 5·75

213 Teddy Bear dressed as Accountant

2002. Centenary of the Teddy Bear. Sheet 149×194 mm containing T 213 and imilar vert designs showing dressed bears.

MS1931 60c. ×4, Type **213**; Computer programmer; Business woman; Lawyer 7·75 7·25

No.**MS**1931 was cut around in the shape of a teddy bear.

214 Queen Elizabeth Queen Mother

2002. Queen Elizabeth the Queen Mother Commemoration. Two sheets containing T 214 and similar multicoloured designs. Multicoloured.

MS1932 (a) 140×156 mm. 80c. ×4, Type **214**; Wearing pearls; Wearing purple outfit; Wearing tiara and sash (b) 108×82 mm. $2 Wearing flowered hat. Set of 2 sheets 16·00 15·00

215 Rock Climbing

2003. 20th World Scout Jamboree, Thailand. Multicoloured.

1933/8 60c. ×6; Type **215**; Emblem and penknife; Rope knots; Cub Scout; Square Knot; Boy Scout 10·50 9·25

MS1939 100×72 mm. $2 Robert Baden-Powell (founder) (vert) 6·25 5·75

216 *Lethocerus grandis*

2003. Flora and Fauna. Multicoloured.

1940-1945 60c. ×6 Type **216**; *Cyrtotrachelus;Lytta vesicatoria; Aulacocylus; Phalacrognathus mulleri; Mormolyce phyllodes* 10·50 9·25

1946-1951 60c. ×6 *Murex brevifrons; Charonia variegate; Tonna galea; Strombus gigas; Tonna maculova; Cassis madagasariensis* 10·50 9·25

1952-1957 60c. ×6 *Phalaenopsis grex; Cattlya loddigesii; Phalaenopsis; Dendrobium; Laelia anceps; Cymbidium* 10·50 9·25

MS1958 Three sheets. (a) 70×96 mm. $2 *Catacanthus incarnates*. (b) 66×96 mm. $2 *Cymatium femorale*. (c) 66×96 mm. $2 *Vanda rothchidiana* (horiz). Set of 3 sheets 19·00 17·00

217 White Goat

2003. New Year. "Year of the Ram" (stamps show goats and sheep). Multicoloured.

1959-1961 37c. ×3 Type **217**; Sheep with curved horns; Angora goat 3·25 3·00

218 Charles Lindbergh, Donald Hall

2003. 75th Anniv of First Transatlantic Flight. Sheet 135×118 mm containing T 218 and similar horiz designs. Multicoloured.

1962-1967 60c.×6, Type **218**; *Spirit of St. Louis; Spirit of St. Louis* on Curtis Field; *Spirit of St. Louis* airborne; Arriving in Paris; Ticker tape parade, New York 10·50 9·25

219 Diana, Princess of Wales

2003. Anniversaries. Three sheets, each 136×96 mm containing T 219 and similar multicoloured designs.

MS1968 (a) Diana, Princess of Wales (5th death anniv). 80c.×4, Type **219** (India); Wearing orange outfit (Canada); Wearing blue-patterned outfit (Egypt); Facing left (Italy). (b) John F. Kennedy (40th death anniv). 80c.×4, Wearing naval uniform; Facing left; Facing right; Holding ship's wheel. (c) Ronald Reagan (92nd birth anniv). 80c.×4, As young man, horses at right (horiz); In middle age, horses at left (horiz); As older man, one horse (horiz); Facing left, two horses (horiz) 30·00 28·00

Nos. **MS**1968a/c, respectively, each form a composite design.

220 David Brown

2003. Columbia Space Shuttle Commemoration. Sheet 184×146 mm containing T 220 and similar vert designs. Multicoloured.

MS1969 37c.×7, Type **220**; Rick Husband; Laurel Blair Salton Clark; Kalpana Chawla; Michael Anderson; William McCool; Ilan Ramon 8·00 7·75

The stamps and margin of No. **MS**1969 form a composite design.

221 Queen Elizabeth II

2003. 50th Anniv of Coronation (2002) of Queen Elizabeth II. Two sheets containing T 221 and similar vert designs. Multicoloured.

MS1970 (a) 161×104 mm. $1×3, Type **221**; Wearing pink dress; Wearing Order of the Garter robes. (b) 71×106 mm. Wearing tiara and robe 15·00 14·50

The stamps and margins of Nos. **MS**1970a/b, respectively, each form a composite design.

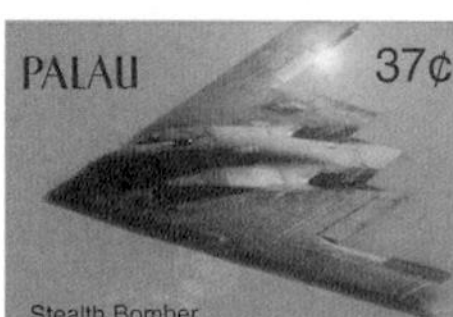

222 Stealth Bomber

2003. Military Action in Iraq. Sheet 136×136 mm containing T 222 and similar horiz designs. Multicoloured.

1971-1976 37c.×6, Type **222**; F-18 fighter; M1 Abrams tank; 203 mm M 110s artillery; *Donald Cook* (destroyer); Tomahawk missile 6·50 6·00

223 Prince William

2003. 21st Birthday of Prince William. Multicoloured.

1977-1979 $1×3, Type **223**; As baby; Wearing dark sweater 8·00 7·50

MS1980 68×98 mm. $2 As baby in Princess Diana's arms 6·25 5·75

224 Henri Pelissier

2003. Centenary of Tour de France Cycle Race. Multicoloured.

1981-1984 60c.×4, Type **224** (1923); Ottavio Bottecchia (1924); Ottavio Bottecchia (1925); Lucien Buysse (1926) 6·75 6·00

MS1985 161×100 mm. $2 Philippe Thys (1920) 6·25 5·75

225 Fokker 70

2003. Centenary of Powered Flight. Two sheets containing T 225 and similar horiz designs. Multicoloured.

MS1986 (a) 108×175 mm. 55c.×6, Type **225**; Boeing 747 217B; Curtiss T-32 *Condor*; Vickers Viscount; *Wright Flyer III*; Avro Ten Achilles. (b) 106×76 mm. $2 *Wright Flyer III* (different) 17·00 16·00

226 "Blue and Silver: Trouville"

2003. Death Centenary of James McNeil Whistler (artist). Multicoloured.

1987 37c. Type **226** 1·20 1·10

1988 55c. "The Last of Old Westminster" 1·70 1·60

1989 60c. "Wapping" 1·90 1·70

1990 $1 "Cremorne Gardens" 3·00 3·00

MS1991 Two sheets. (a) 186×97 mm. Size 36×72 mm. 80c.×4, "Arrangement in Flesh Colour and Black: Portrait of Theodore Duret"; "Arrangement in White and Black"; "Harmony in Pink and Grey: Portrait of Lady Meux"; "Arrangement in Black and Gold; Comte Robert de Montesquiou-Fezensac". (b) 114×88 mm. $2 "Portrait of the Artist's Mother" (vert) 16·00 15·00

227 Apes (clown)

2003. Circus. Two sheets containing T 227 and similar vert designs. Multicoloured.

MS1992 (a) 120×195 mm. Clowns. 80c.×4, Type **227**; Mo Lite; Gigi; Buttons. (b) 147×218 mm. Performers. 80c.×4, Performing dogs; Trapeze artiste; Performing goat; Balancing act 20·00 19·00

228 "Madonna Della Melagrana" (Sandro Botticelli)

2003. Christmas. Multicoloured.

1993	37c. Type **228**	1·20	1·10
1994	60c. "Madonna del Magnificat" (Sandro Botticelli)	1·90	1·70
1995	80c. "Madonna and Child with the Saints and the Angels" (Andrea del Sarto)	2·50	2·30
1996	$1 "La Madonna del Roseto" (Sandro Botticelli)	3·00	3·00
MS1997	106×84 mm. $2 "Madonna and Child with Angels and Saints" (Domenico Ghirlandaio)	6·25	5·75

229 Mating Turtles

2004. Turtles. Two sheets containing T 229 and similar horiz designs. Multicoloured.

MS1998 (a) 146×107 mm. 60c.×6, Type **229**; Laying eggs; Hatching; Hatchlings going to sea; Growing up; Returning. (b) 100×87 mm. $2 Turtle 17·00 16·00

The stamps and margins of Nos. **MS**1998a/b, respectively, each form a composite design.

230 "The Connoisseur" (1962)

2004. 25th Death Anniv of Norman Rockwell (artist). Two sheets containing T 230 and similar multicoloured designs.

MS1999 (a) 146×177 mm. 80c.×4, Type **230**; "Artist facing Blank Canvas" (Deadline) (1938); "Art Critic" (1955); Stained glass (1960). (b) 95×102 mm. $2 "Painting Tavern Sign" (1926) (horiz) 16·00 15·00

231 "Antonia Zarate" (Francisco Jose de Goya y Lucientes)

2004. Treasures of Hermitage Museum, St. Petersburg. Multicoloured.

2000	37c. Type **231**	1·20	1·10
2001	55c. "Portrait of a Lady" (Antonio Correggio)	1·70	1·60
2002	80c. "Portrait of Count Olivarez" (Diego Velasquez)	2·50	2·30
2003	$1 "Portrait of a Young Man with a Lace Collar" (Rembrandt Harmensz van Rijn)	3·00	3·00
MS2004	62×81 mm. $2 "Family Portrait" (Anthony van Dyck). Imperf	6·25	5·75

232 Coral Hind

2004. Marine Life (1st issue). Two sheets containing T 232 and similar horiz designs. Multicoloured.

MS2005 (a) 146×107 mm. 55c.×6, Type **232**; Octopus; Manta ray; Dugong; Crab; Grouper. (b) 100×87 mm. $2 Grey reef shark 17·00 16·00

Nos. **MS**2005a/b, respectively each form a composite design. See also Nos. 2031/6.

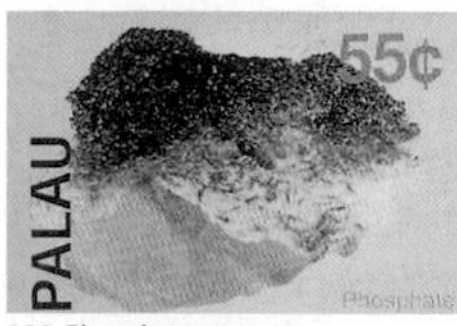

233 Phosphate

2004. Minerals. Two sheets containing T 233 and similar horiz designs. Multicoloured.

MS2006 (a) 146×107 mm. 55c.×6, Type **233**; Antimony; Limonite; Chalcopyrite (inscr "Calcopyrite"); Bauxite; Manganite. (b) 100×87 mm. $2 Gold 3 17·00 16·00

234 "Dora Maar" (1938)

2004. 30th Death Anniv of Pablo Picasso (artist). Two sheets containing T 234 and similar vert designs.

MS2007 (a) 180×130 mm. 80c.×4, Type **234**; "The Yellow Sweater" (1939); "Woman in Green" (1944); "Woman in Armchair" (1941). (b) 52×82 mm. $2 "Woman dressing her Hair" (1940). Imperf 16·00 15·00

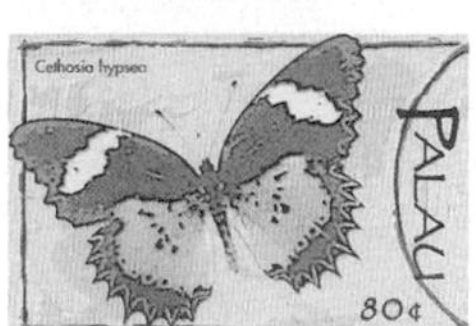

235 *Cethosia hypsea*

2004. Fauna. Six sheet containing T 235 and similar multicoloured.

MS2008 (a) 154×119 mm. Butterflies. 80c.×4 Type **235**; *Cethosia myrina*; *Charaxes durnfordi*; Charaxes nitebis. (b) 154×119 mm. Snakes. 80c.×4, Bull snake; Garter snake; Yellow-lipped sea snake; Yellow-bellied sea snake. (c) 154×119 mm. Birds. 80c.×4, Blue-faced parrot finch (vert); Mangrove flycatcher (vert); Palau swiftlet (vert); Bridled white-eye (vert). (d) 105×76 mm. $2 Inscr "Charaxes nitesbis". (e) 105×76 mm. $2 Glass frog (f) 105×76 mm. $2 Dusky white-eye 49·00 46·00

236 "Green Bamboo and White Ape" (Ren Yu) (detail)

2004. New Year. Year of the Monkey. Mulitcoloured.

2009	50c. Type **236**	1·50	1·50
MS2010	71×100 mm. $1 "Green Bamboo and White Ape" (Ren Yu) (24×80 mm)	3·00	3·00

237 Orsachel (M. Takeshi)

2004. 9th Pacific Arts Festival. Multicoloured.

2011-2020	26c.×10, Type **237**; Flute (Sim Adelbai); Rur (W. Watanabe); Bamboo Raft (P. Tiaki); Story Telling (A. Murret); Yek (A. Imetuker); Canoe House (W. Marsil); Carving Axe (W. Watanabe); Weaving (W. Marsil); Dancing Props (Sam Adelbai)	7·50	7·00
2021-2030	37c.×10, Ongall (P. Tiaki); Bai (S. Weers); Taro Plant (S. Smaserui); Toluk (W. Watanabe); Medicinal Plants (S. Smaserui); War Canoe (M. Takeshi); Painting (Sim Adelbai); Ponding Taro (A. Imetuker); Llengel (M. Takeshi); Speer Technique (A. Imeuker)	10·50	10·00

238 Cuttle Fish

2004. Marine Life (2nd issue). Multicoloured.

2031-2036	26c.×6, Type **238**; Pennant coralfish (inscr "Longfin bannerfish") (*Heniochus acuminatus*); Red sponge and medusa worm; Sea slug (*Risbecia tryoni*); Emperor angel fish; Sea slug (*Chromodoris coi*)	4·00	3·50
2037-2042	37c.×6, Spotted eagle ray (*Aetobatis narinari*); Jelly fish (*Mastigias*); Nautilus (*Nautilus belauensis*); Grey reef shark (*Carcharhinus amblyrhynchos*); Tunicales; Manta ray (*Manta birostris*)	7·50	11·00
MS2043	Two sheets (a) 107×66 mm. $2 Pink anemonefish (*Amphiprion perideraion*). (b) 77×107 mm. $2 Fire (inscr "Dusky") anemonefish (*Amphiprion melanopus*)	12·50	11·50

239 Dove holding Olive Branch

2004. International Year of Peace. Two sheets containing T 239 and similar multicoloured designs.

MS2044 (a) 68×99 mm. $2 Type **239**; (b) 148×87 mm. $3×3, Mahatma Gandhi; Nelson Mandela; Martin Luther King 34·00 32·00

240 Early Greek Athletes

2004. Olympic Games, Athens. Multicoloured.

2045	37c. Type **240**	1·20	1·10
2046	55c. Gold medals (Atlanta, 1996)	1·70	1·60
2047	80c. Sigfrid Edstrom (IOC president 1942–1952) (vert)	2·50	2·30
2048	$1 Women footballers	3·00	3·00

241 Landing Craft LCA 1377

2004. 60th Anniv of D-Day (the Normandy invasion). Two sheets containing T 241 and similar horiz designs. Multicoloured.

MS2049 (a) 136×136 mm. 50c.×6, Type **241**; Landing craft, infantry: LCVP (landing craft, vehicle and personnel); Conning tower, Submarine U 309; HMS *Begonia*; HMS *Roberts*. (b) 97×77 mm. $2 LST (tank landing ship) 15·00 14·50

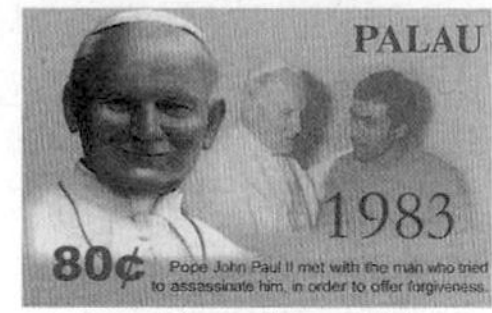

242 Pope John Paul II and Mehmet Ali Agca (Turkish man who shot and wounded Pope John Paul II)

2004. 25th Anniv of Pontificate of Pope John Paul II (2003). Sheet 95×117 mm containing T 242 and similar horiz designs. Multicoloured.

MS2050 80c.×4, Type **242**; Facing left (visit to Poland); Wearing shawl (concert, Ischia); With Patriach Zakka 10·00 9·50

243 Rinus Michels

2004. European Football Championship. Two sheets containing T 243 and similar multicoloured designs.

MS2051 (a) 147×86 mm. 80c.×4, Type **243**; Rinat Dasaev; Marco van Basten; Olympiastadion, Berlin. (b) 98×85 mm. Netherlands team, 1988 Cup Winners (51×38 mm) 16·00 15·00

The stamps and margin of Nos. **MS**1267a/b, respectively, form composite designs.

244 Deng Xiaoping

2004. Birth Centenary of Deng Xiaoping (leader of China, 1978–89). Sheet 97×67 mm.

MS2052 **244** $2 multicoloured 6·25 5·75

245 "Babe" Ruth

2004. Centenary of World Series Baseball Championships. George Herman (Babe) Ruth Commemoration. Multicoloured.

2053	37c. Type **245**	1·20	1·10
2054	37c. Facing right	1·20	1·10

246 Locomotive ATSF 315

2004. Bicentenary of Steam Locomotives. Multicoloured.

2055-2058	26c.×4, Type **246**; Amtrak 464; Electric rail car N52; Diesel electric locomotive SD70MAC	3·25	3·25
2059-2062	50c.×4, Locomotive CS SO2002; Locomotive P 36 NO032; Locomotive SW600; Steam locomotive (inscr "Gambler LNV 9703 440 NG")	5·75	5·75
2063-2036	80c.×4, Birney n62 Interurban; Steam locomotive (inscr "c 62-2-103103"); Locomotive (inscr "WRMO 2007"); ATSF 314 Santa Fe	10·00	10·00

MS2067 Three sheets. (a) 100×70 mm. $2 *Eurostar*. (b) 98×68 mm. $2 Locomotive CN 5700. (c) 101×70 mm. $2 *Royal Hudson* 2860 (vert) 19·00 17·00

247 Hadrosaurus

2004. Dinosaurs. Four sheets containing T 247 and similar multicoloured designs.
MS2068 (a) 154×119 mm. 26c.×4, Kritosaurus (vert); Tricerotops (vert); Hypselosaurus (vert); Yingshanosaurus (vert). (b) 154×119 mm. 80c.×4, Type **247**; Pterodaustro; Agilisaurus; Amargasaurus. (c) 106×76 mm. $2 Archaeopteryx. (d) 106×76 mm. $2 Ornithomimus 23·00 21·00

The stamps and margins of **MS**2068a/d, respectively, each form composite designs.

248 Diego Maradona (Argentina)

2004. Centenary of FIFA (Federation Internationale de Football Association). Two sheets containing T 248 and similar horiz designs showing players. Multicoloured.
MS2069 (a) 193×97 mm. 80c.×4, Type **248**; David Seaman (England); Andreas Brehme (Germany); Paul Ince (England). (b) 108×87 mm. $2 Fernando Redondo (Argentina) 16·00 15·00

249 Kevin Garnett

2004. Basketball Players. Multicoloured.

2070	26c. Type **249**	85	80
2071	26c. Tim Duncan	85	80
2072	26c. Chris Bosh	85	80

250 "Virgin and Child" (Quentin Metsys (Massys))

2004. Christmas. Multicoloured.

2073	37c. Type **250**	1·20	1·10
2074	60c. "Virgin and Child" (Adolphe William Bouguereau)	1·90	1·70
2075	80c. "Madonna and Child" (William Dyce)	2·50	2·30
2076	$1 Madonna and child (Carlo Crivelli)	3·00	3·00

MS2077 76×107 mm. $2 Madonna and child (Peter Paul Rubens) (vert) 6·25 5·75

251 Fruit and Vegetables

2004. 5th Anniv of Diplomatic Relations with Republic of China (Taiwan). Multicoloured.
2078–2081 80c.×4, Type **251**; Destroyer; Ngarachamayong Cultural Centre; Belau National Museum 9·00 8·25

252 Rooster

2005. New Year. Year of the Rooster. Multicoloured.

2082	50c. Type **252**	1·50	1·50
2083	50c. As No. 2082 but design reversed	1·50	1·50

253 "Battle of Trafalgar" (Thomas Luny)

2005. Bicentenary of Battle of Trafalgar. Multicoloured.

2084	37c. Type **253**	1·20	1·10
2085	55c. *Redoubtable* surrendering (painting)	1·70	1·60
2086	80c. *Victory* firing on *Redoubtable* (painting)	2·50	2·30
2087	$1 "*Victory* returning Home" (J. M. W. Turner)	3·00	3·00

MS2088 86×122 mm. $2 Nelson wounded (painting) 6·25 5·75

254 Emblem

2005. Centenary of Rotary International. Sheet 120×110 mm containing T 254 and similar vert designs. Multicoloured.
MS2089 80c.×4, Type **254**; Rotary centennial bell; Flags; James Wheeler Davidson (rotary pioneer) 10·00 9·50

255 Book Cover for "Andersen Fairy Tales"

2005. Birth Bicentenary of Hans Christian Andersen (writer). Book covers. Multicoloured.
2090–2092 $1×3, Type **255**; *The Ugly Duckling*; *Tales of Hans Christian Andersen* 8·00 8·00

MS2093 67×97 mm. $2 *The Little Match Girl* 6·25 5·75

256 Friedrich Von Schiller

2005. Death Bicentenary of Friedrich Von Schiller (writer). Multicoloured.
MS2094 116×142 mm. $1×3, Type **256**; Facing right; Standing 9·25 8·75
MS2095 53×72 mm. $2 Facing left 6·25 5·75

257 Pilots reviewing Route

2005. 60th Anniv of End of World War II. Multicoloured.

2096–2099	80c.×4, Type **257**; "Dambuster" crew; Ground crew; Lancaster bomber over Mohne Dam ("Dambuster" raid—May 16/17 1945)	9·00	8·50
2100–2103	80c.×4, Russian tanks; Tank commanders; Russian and German tanks; Destroyed German tank (Kursk Battle—July 1943)	9·00	8·50

MS2104 Two sheets, each 107×97 mm. (a) $2 Squadron 617 Leader Guy Gibson and "Bouncing bomb" ("Dambuster" raid). (b) $2 Russian troops and destroyed German tank (Kursk Battle) 12·50 11·50

258 Audie Murphy

2005. 60th Anniv of Victory in Japan Day (VJ day—15 August 1945). Multicoloured.
2105–2108 80c.×4, Type **258**; John F. Kennedy; Admiral Chester William Nimitz; US Marines recapture Guam 9·00 8·25

MS2109 100×70 mm. $2 Sailors returning home (horiz) 6·25 5·75

259 *Nautilus* ("20000 Leagues under the Sea")

2005. Death Centenary of Jules Verne (writer). Two sheets containing T 259 and similar multicoloured designs.
MS2110 145×56 mm. $1×3, Type **259**; Cliff face ("Mysterious Island"); Dinosaurs ("Journey to the Centre of the Earth") 9·25 8·75
MS2111 56×145 mm. $2 Air balloon ("Around the World in Eighty Days") (vert) 6·25 5·75

260 Seagulls

2005. EXPO 2005, Aichi, Japan. Multicoloured.
2112–2115 80c.×4, Type **260**; Cosmos; Koala bear; Baby in incubator 9·00 8·25

261 Tepukei

2005. Boats. Two sheets containing T 261 and similar horiz designs. Multicoloured.
MS2116 203×173 mm. 80c.×4, Type **261**; Tainui; Palaun canoe; Yap outrigger 10·00 9·50
MS2117 89×101 mm. $2 *Kon-tiki* 6·25 5·75

262 Pope John Paul II

2005. Pope John Paul II Commemoration.
2118 **262** $1 multicoloured 3·00 3·00

263 Elvis Presley

2005. 70th Birth Anniv of Elvis Presley (entertainer). Multicoloured.

2119	80c. Type **263**	2·50	2·30
2120–2123	80c.×4, Facing right (blue); As No. 2119 (green); As No. 2119 (yellow); As No. 2119 (red)	11·00	10·50

264 2002 World Cup Final (Brazil–Germany)

2005. 75th Anniv of World Cup Football Championship. Multicoloured.

2124–2126	$1×3 Type **264**; Lothar Matthaus (Germany) holding trophy; Gerd Muller (top scorer)	8·00	8·00
2126a–2126c	$1×3 1954 Final game; 1966 Final; 1974 Final **MS**2127 Two sheets (a) 100×70 mm. $2 Franz Beckenbauer (German player and manager) (43×29 mm). (b) 140×90 mm. $2 Sepp Herberger (German coach) (50×38 mm)	8·00	8·00

265 1939 5c. Vatican City Stamp

2005. Vacant See.
2128 **265** 37c. multicoloured 1·20 1·10

266 "Wildeve Rose"

2005. Taipei 2005 International Stamp Exhibition. Roses. Multicoloured.
2129–2133 80c.×4, Type **266**; "Graham Thomas"; "Crocus"; "Tess of the d'Urbervilles" 9·00 8·25

267 Decorated Wooden Bowl

2005. 50th Anniv of Belau National Museum. Multicoloured.

2134- 2143 10c.×3 Type **267**; Potsherds; Bowl containing people; Model of native dwelling; Ebonised lidded pot with string handle; Cannon; Man on ship (drawing); Local crafts (drawing); Bird shaped pot; Platter with carved supports 11·00 10·00

268 Pope Benedict XVI

2005

2144 **268** 80c. multicoloured 2·50 2·30

269 Madonna and Child (Daniel Seghers)

2005. Christmas. Designs showing paintings of the Madonna and Child, painters' names given. Multicoloured.

2145 37c. Type **269** 1·20 1·10
2146 60c. Raphael 1·90 1·70
2147 80c. Gerard David 2·50 2·30
2148 $1 Raphael (different) 3·00 3·00
MS2149 66×96 mm. $2 Bartolme Esteban Murillo 6·25 5·75

270 Dog

2006. New Year. Year of the Dog.

2150 **270** 50c. multicoloured 1·50 1·50

271 *Haematopus bachmani*

2006. Birds. Multicoloured.

2151 24c. Type **271** 75 75
2152 39c. *Ardea herodias* (vert) 1·20 1·20

272 *Nautilius belaunensis*

2006. Endangered Species. Nautilius belaunensis. Multicoloured.

2153 63c. Type **272** 2·00 1·90
2154 63c. Nautilus and coral 2·00 1·90
2155 63c. Two nautilus facing right 2·00 1·90
2156 63c. Two nautilus facing left 2·00 1·90

2006. 20th Anniv of First Postal Sheetlet. Sea and Reef World. As T 20. Multicoloured.

2157- 2196 8c.×40 As Type **20**; As No. 103; As No. 104; As No. 105; As No. 106; As No. 107; As No. 108; As No. 109; As No. 110; As No. 111; As No. 112; As No. 113; As No. 114; As No. 115; As No. 116; As No. 117; As No. 118; As No. 119; As No. 120; As No. 121; As No. 122; As No. 123; As No. 124; As No. 125; As No. 126; As No. 127; As No. 128; As No. 129; As No. 130; As No. 131; As No. 132; As No. 133; As No. 134; As No. 135; As No. 136; As No. 137; As No. 138; As No. 139; As No. 140; As No. 141 16·00 16·00

Nos. 2157/96 were each inscribed on the back, over the gum, with the name of the subject featured on the stamp. Nos. 2157/96 were issued together, se-tenant, forming a composite design of a reef.

273 "Marriage of Figaro"

2006. 250th Birth Anniv of Wolfgang Amadeus Mozart (composer and musician). Sheet 100×70 mm.

MS2197 **273** $2 multicoloured 6·25 5·75

274 Queen Elizabeth II

2006. 80th Birthday of Queen Elizabeth II. Designs showing Queen Elizabeth II. Multicoloured.

2198 84c. Type **274** 2·75 2·50
2199 84c. As young woman 2·75 2·50
2200 84c. Facing front wearing pendant earrings 2·75 2·50
2201 84c. Facing left 2·75 2·50
MS2202 126×126 mm. $2 Wearing sleeveless frock looking right 6·25 5·75

275 "Old Man in a Fur Hat"

2006. 400th Birth Anniv of Rembrandt Harmenszoon van Rijn (artist). Paintings. Multicoloured.

2203 $1 Type **275** 3·00 3·00
2204 $1 "Head of a Man" 3·00 3·00
2205 $1 "An Old Man in a Cap" 3·00
2206 $1 "Portrait of an Old Man" 3·00 3·00
MS2207 70×100 mm. $2 "Saskia with a Veil". Imperf 6·25 5·75

276 First Flight of Space Shuttle *Columbia*

2006. Space Exploration. Multicoloured.

2208 75c. Type **276** (25th anniv of first flight of space shuttle *Columbia*) 2·30 2·20
2209 75c. Shuttle left 2·30 2·20
2210 75c. Shuttle right 2·30 2·20
2211 75c. Shuttle inscribed "Young. Crippen" 2·30 2·20
2212 75c. Robert Crippen (astronaut) 2·30 2·20
2213 75c. Commander John Young 2·30 2·20
2214 75c. *Viking I* and Mars (30th anniv of *Viking I* Mars landing) (horiz) 2·30 2·20
2215 75c. *Viking I* on the Moon (horiz) 2·30 2·20
2216 75c. *Viking I* (horiz) 2·30 2·20
2217 75c. Solar panels (horiz) 2·30 2·20
2218 75c. Observatory (horiz) 2·30 2·20
2219 75c. Mars surface (horiz) 2·30 2·20
2220 $1 International Space Station upper left (horiz) 3·00 3·00
2221 $1 International Space Station upper right (horiz) 3·00 3·00
2222 $1 International Space Station lower left (horiz) 3·00 3·00
2223 $1 International Space Station lower right (horiz) 3·00 3·00
MS2224 (a) 68×98 mm. $2 *Sputnik I*. (b) 68×98 mm. $2 *Columbia*. (c) 68×98 mm. $2 Walking on the moon (*Apollo 11* moon landing) 19·00 17·00

Nos. 2220/3 were issued in se-tenant, with an enlarged top margin, forming a composite design of the space station.

277 English Literacy

2006. 40th Anniv of Peace Corps in Palau. Multicoloured.

2225 75c. Type **277** 2·30 2·20
2226 75c. Sea turtle conservation 2·30 2·20
2227 75c. Swim camp 2·30 2·20
2228 75c. Reef survey 2·30 2·20

278 Tin Soldier

2006. Christmas. Tree Decorations. Multicoloured.

2229 84c. Type **278** 2·75 2·50
2230 84c. Father Christmas 2·75 2·50
2231 84c. Doll with tall knitted hat 2·75 2·50
2232 84c. Mice 2·75 2·50

279 Concorde over New York

2006. 10th Anniv of Concorde's Record Flight from New York to London. Multicoloured.

2233 75c. Type **279** 2·30 2·20
2234 75c. Over London 2·30 2·20
2235 75c. Tail bumper wheel 2·30 2·20
2236 75c. Drop down nose 2·30 2·20

280 Elvis Presley

2007. 30th Death Anniv of Elvis Presley (entertainer). Multicoloured.

2237 39c. Type **280** 1·20 1·20
2238 39c. Facing front 1·20 1·20
2239 39c. Wearing dark shirt 1·20 1·20
2240 39c. Wearing light shirt facing left 1·20 1·20
2241 39c. Wearing hat 1·20 1·20
2242 39c. Wearing sweater, facing left, looking down 1·20 1·20
2243 39c. At microphone, loose tie and dog wearing hat 1·20 1·20
2244 39c. At microphone, wearing light jacket 1·20 1·20
2245 39c. Back view holding guitar 1·20 1·20

Nos. 2243/5 were issued together, se-tenant, forming a composite background design.

281 Marilyn Monroe

2007. 70th Birth (2006) Anniv of Marilyn Monroe (entertainer). Multicoloured.

2246 84c. Type **281** 2·75 2·50
2247 84c. Wearing long earrings, hair to right 2·75 2·50
2248 84c. Wearing necklace 2·75 2·50
2249 84c. Wearing earrings, hair brushed back 2·75 2·50

282 Dove, Flag and Globe

2007. Centenary of Scouting. Multicoloured.

2250 $1 Type **282** 3·00 3·00
2251 $1 As No. 2250 3·00 3·00
2252 $1 As No. 2250 3·00 3·00
MS2253 112×81 mm. $2 Robert Baden Powell (founder) (vert) 6·25 5·75

Nos. 2251/2 are as No. 2250 but with colour changed.

283 *Entoloma hochstetteri*

2007. Fungi. Multicoloured.

2254 $1 Type **283** 3·00 3·00
2255 $1 *Aseroe rubra* 3·00 3·00
2256 $1 *Omphalotus nidiformis* 3·00 3·00
2257 $1 *Amanita* 3·00 3·00
MS2258 100×70 mm. $2 *Aseroe rubra* (different) (horiz) 6·25 5·75

284 "Pig" (Xu Beihong)

2007. New Year. Year of the Pig.

2259 **284** 75c. multicoloured 2·30 2·20

285 Bell 206B Jetranger III

2007. Centenary of First Helicopter Flight. Multicoloured.

2260	10c. Type **285**	30	30
2261	19c. McDonnell Douglas MD500D	60	60
2262	20c. McDonnell Douglas AH-64A Apache	60	60
2263	22c. Aerospatiale AS 332 Super Puma	70	65
2264	75c. Aerospatiale AS 355F-1 Twin Squirrel	2·30	2·20
2265	84c. MBB Eurocopter BO105DB/4	2·75	2·50
2266	$1 Sikorsky MH-53J Pave Low III	3·00	3·00
MS2267	102×72 mm. $2 Boeing Helicopters 234LR Chinook	6·25	5·75

286 Palau Owl

2007. Birds of Palau. Multicoloured.

2268	50c. Type **286**	1·50	1·50
2269	50c. Palau fruit dove	1·50	1·50
2270	50c. Palau ground dove	1·50	1·50
2271	50c. Morning bird	1·50	1·50
2272	50c. Palau megapode	1·50	1·50
2273	50c. Rusty-capped kingfisher	1·50	1·50
2274	50c. Mangrove flycatcher	1·50	1·50
2275	50c. Palau fantail	1·50	1·50
2276	50c. Palau bush warbler	1·50	1·50
2277	50c. Giant white-eye	1·50	1·50
2278	50c. Dusky white-eye	1·50	1·50
2279	50c. Palau swift	1·50	1·50

287 Fiddler Crab

2007. Crabs of Palau. Multicoloured.

2280	$1 Type **287**	3·00	3·00
2281	$1 Ghost crab	3·00	3·00
2282	$1 Coconut crab	3·00	3·00
2283	$1 Land crab	3·00	3·00

288 Chelbucheb

2007. Udoud Money Beads. Sheet 127×150 mm containing T 288 and similar vert designs. Multicoloured.

MS2284	50c.×6, Type **288**; Kluk; Two long beads; Kidait; Lek; Chelbucheb (different)	9·25	8·75

289 Praying Mantis

2007. Kids and Wildlife. Sheet 127×150 mm containing T 289 and similar vert designs. Multicoloured.

MS2285	75c.×4, Type **289**; Boy holding lobster; Boy with fruit bat; Two dolphins	9·25	8·75

No. **MS**2285 also contains four stamp size labels, two of which, with the upper and lower central stamps, form composite designs of a boy with a praying mantis and a boy feeding two dolphins respectively.

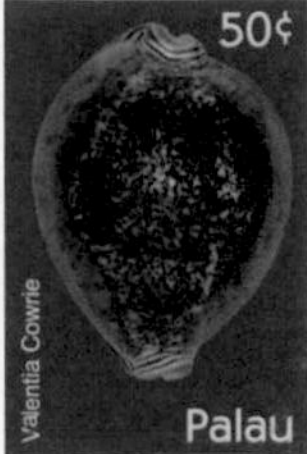

290 Valentia Cowrie

2007. Cowries. Two sheets containing T 290 and similar vert designs. Multicoloured.

MS2286	102×153 mm. 50c.×6, Type **290**; Leucodon cowrie; Golden cowrie; Tiger cowrie; Ovum cowrie; Guttata cowrie	9·25	8·75
MS2287	100×70 mm. $2 Triton horn	6·25	5·75

291 Engagement of Princess Elizabeth and Lt. Philip Mountbatten

2007. Diamond Wedding Anniv of Queen Elizabeth II and Prince Philip. Sheet 150×100 mm containing T 291 and similar horiz designs. Multicoloured.

MS2288	60c.×6, Type **291**×3; Princess Elizabeth and Prince Philip on honeymoon×3;	11·00	10·50

292 Red-billed Leiothrix (*Leiothrix lutea*)

2007. Birds of South East Asia. Two sheets containing T 292 and similar horiz designs. Multicoloured.

MS2289	130×108 mm. 80c.×4, Type **292**; Greater necklaced laughing-thrush (*Garrulax pectoralis*) (not identified on stamp); Wahnes' parotia (*Parotia wahnesi*); White-bellied yuhina (*Yuhina zantholeuca*)	10·00	9·50
MS2290	100×70 mm. $2 Wilson's bird of paradise (*Cicinnurus respublica*)	6·25	5·75

293 Longhorn Cowfish (inscr 'Box Fish') (*Lactoria cornuta*)

2007. Tropical Fish. Two sheets containing T 293 and similar horiz designs. Multicoloured.

MS2291	108×130 mm. 80c.×4, Type **293**; Copper band butterfly fish (*Chelmon rostratus*); Long nosed hawkfish (*Oxycirrhites typus*); Emperor angelfish (*Pomacanthus imperator*)	12·50	11·50
MS2292	70×100 mm. $2 Firefish (*Nemateleotris magnifica*)	6·25	5·75

294 *Plumeria*

2007. Flowers of South East Asia. Two sheets containing T 294 and similar horiz designs. Multicoloured.

MS2293	130×108 mm. $1×4, Type **294**; *Streptosolen jamesonii*; *Heliconia pseudoaemygdiana*; *Manaita*	12·50	11·50
MS2294	100×70 mm. $2 Spider lily (*Hymenocallis occidentalis*)	6·25	5·75

295 Pope Benedict XVI

2007. Enthronement of Pope Benedict XVI.

2295	**295**	41c. multicoloured	1·30	1·20

296 Princess Diana

2007. Tenth Death Anniv of Princess Diana. Two sheets containing T 296 and similar vert designs. Multicoloured.

MS2296	150×101 mm. 90c.×4, Type **296**;Wearing pearl necklace; Facing left, longer hair; Facing right, large pearl earring	11·00	10·50
MS2297	100×70 mm. $2 Wearing hat with veil	6·25	5·75

297 *Troides amphrysus*

2007. Butterflies. Multicoloured.

2298	2c. Type **297**	15	15
2299	3c. Inscr 'Paraeronia boebera'	15	15
2300	4c. *Delias catisa*	15	15
2301	5c. *Chilasa clytia*	25	20
2302	11c. *Ornithoptera goliath*	40	35
2303	15c. Insc 'Graphium delesseru'	45	45
2304	20c. *Euploea*	60	60
2305	23c. *Papilio euchenor*	70	65
2306	26c. *Ornithoptera tithonus*	85	80
2307	41c. *Hypolimnas misippus*	1·30	1·20
2308	45c. *Delias meeki*	1·40	1·30
2309	50c. *Papilio ulysses*	1·50	1·50
2310	75c. *Ornithoptera croseus*	2·30	2·20
2311	90c. *Trogonoptera brookiana*	3·00	2·75
2312	$1 *Idea lynceus*	3·00	3·00
2313	$2 *Parantica weiskei*	6·25	5·75
2314	$3 *Graphium weiskei*	9·25	8·75
2315	$4 *Ornithoptera goliath* (different)	12·50	11·50
2316	$5 *Attacus lorquini*	15·00	14·50
2317	$10 *Delias henningia*	31·00	29·00

298 Elvis Presley

2007. 30th Death Anniv of Elvis Presley. Two sheets containing T 298 and similar vert designs. Multicoloured.

MS2318	195×132 mm. 75c.×6, Type **298**; Holding guitar, mauve overlay; As Type **298**, greenish silver suit, olive-brown country and value imprint; Holding guitar, claret overlay; As Type **298**, silver suit, new blue country and value imprint; Holding guitar, orange-yellow/yellow-orange overlay	14·00	13·00
MS2319	100×70 mm. 75c.×6, Wearing dark grey shirt; Wearing green shirt; Wearing reddish shirt, eyes closed; As Type **298**, gold suit, white background; Standing wearing white shirt; Standing wearing blackish lilac suit	14·00	13·00

299 Eduardo Sevilla, Nicaragua

2007. United Nations General Assembly adoption of Holocaust Remembrance Resolution No. 60/7 (1 November 2005). Sheet 198×158 mm containing T 299 and similar vert designs. Multicoloured.

MS2320	50c.×8, Type **299**; Aminu Bashir Wali, Nigeria; Stuart Beck, Palau; Ricardo Alberto Arias, Panama; Robert Aisi, Papua New Guinea; Eladio Loizaga, Paraguay; Jorge Voto-Bernales, Peru; Ban-Ki Moon, Secretary General	12·50	11·50

300 Baubles

2007. Christmas. T 300 and similar vert designs. Multicoloured.

2321	22c. Type **301**	70	65
2322	26c. Green bauble	85	80
2323	41c. Blue baubles	1·30	1·20
2324	90c. Orange bauble with red bow	3·00	2·75

301 '32nd America's cup' and Yachts

2007. 32nd America's Cup. Designs showing emblem and yachts. Multicoloured.

2325	26c. Type **300**	85	80
2326	80c. Yacht with black and red keel, yellow-orange emblem	2·50	2·30
2327	$1.14 Yacht with inscribed dark blue keel, turquoise-green emblem	3·75	3·50
2328	$2 Yacht crowded with rescued crew, scarlet-vermilion emblem	6·25	5·75

Nos. 2325/8 were printed, *se-tenant*, in horizontal or vertical strips of four stamps within sheets of 16.

302 Rat

2008. Chinese New Year. Year of the Rat.

2329	**302**	50c. multicoloured	1·50	1·50

303 Crowd and 'Kennedy for President' Poster

2008. 45th Death Anniv of John F. Kennedy. Sheet 132×110 mm containing T 303 and similar vert designs. Multicoloured.

MS2330 90c.×4, Type **303**; John F. Kennedy reaching down into crowd; Speaking from podium; Speaking into microphones	11·00	10·50

304 1908 Fencing Poster

2008. History of the Olympic Games. London–1908. Sheet 178×102 mm containing T 304 and similar vert designs. Multicoloured.

MS2331 50c.×4, Type **304**; 1908 Olympic Games poster; Wyndham Halswelle–track gold medalist; Dorando Pietri–marathon runner	6·25	5·75

305 National Democracy Memorial Hall

2008. Sites and Scenes of Taiwan. Two sheets containing T 305 and similar horiz designs. Multicoloured.

MS2332 100×108 mm. 50c.×4, Type **305**; Chinese ornamental garden, Taipei; Taipei 101 tower and city-scape; Eastern coast	6·25	5·75
MS2333 100×70 mm. $2 Illuminated temple in southern Taiwan (51×47 mm)	6·25	5·75

306 Entrance to the City of David (image scaled to 49% of original size)

2008. World Stamp Championship, Israel. Sheet 100×110 mm.

MS2334 multicoloured	9·25	8·75

307 Edmund Hillary and Prince Charles

2008. Sir Edmund Percival Hillary (first man to reach the summit of Mount Everest) Commemoration. Sheet 131×118 mm containing T 307 and similar horiz designs. Multicoloured.

MS2335 90c.×4, Type **307**; Facing left; With Lokendra Bahdur Chand (prime minister of Nepal); With cockatoo on shoulder	11·00	10·50

308 Pope Benedict XVI

2008. Visit of Pope Benedict XVI to the USA. Sheet 127×177 mm containing T 308 and similar horiz designs showing Pope Benedict XVI. Multicoloured

MS2336 90c.×4, Type **308**; As Type **308**, red smudge, central left shoulder; As Type **308**, two red smudges, front and rear of left shoulder; As Type **308**, heavier red strip, leaching into margin	11·00	10·50

Nos. 2337/40 and Type **309** are vacant.

310 Barack Obama

2009. Inauguration of President Barack Obama

MS2341 133×100 mm. 94c.×4, Type **310**; Facing left; Facing right; With hand raised	11·00	11·00
MS2342 111×80 mm. $2 Facing left with presidential seal in background (38×51 mm)	6·25	6·25

311 Ox

2009. Chinese New Year. Year of the Ox. Multicoloured.

MS2343 94c.×4, Type **311**×2; As Type **311** but with white central inscriptions×2	11·00	11·00

Pt. 1

PALESTINE

A territory at the extreme east of the Mediterranean Sea, captured from the Turks by Great Britain in 1917 and under Military Occupation until 1920. It was a British Mandate of the League of Nations from 1923 to May 1948 when the State of Israel was proclaimed.

1918. 10 milliemes = 1 piastre.
1927. 1,000 mills = £P1.

1

1918

3	1	1p. blue	2·00	2·00

5MILLIEMES

(2)

1918. Surch with T 2.

4	5m. on 1p. blue	7·50	2·25

3 "E.E.F." = Egyptian Expeditionary Force

1918

5	3	1m. brown	30	40
6	3	2m. green	30	45
7	3	3m. brown	50	35
8	3	4m. red	35	40
9a	3	5m. orange	65	30
10	3	1p. blue	50	25
11	3	2p. olive	3·25	60
12	3	5p. purple	3·75	2·50
13	3	9p. ochre	12·00	7·50
14	3	10p. blue	12·00	4·50
15	3	20p. grey	16·00	20·00

Nos. 1/15 were also valid in Transjordan, Cilicia, Lebanon and Syria.

فلسطين

PALESTINE

פלשתינה א״י

(4)

1920. Optd with T 4.

71	1m. brown	2·00	30
61	2m. green	3·00	30
72	2m. yellow	2·75	30
62	3m. brown	3·25	30
73	3m. blue	3·00	15
74	4m. red	3·00	20
64	5m. orange	3·50	30
76	6m. green	2·75	30
77	7m. brown	2·75	30
78	8m. red	2·75	30
65	1p. blue	2·75	35
79	1p. grey	3·25	30
80	13m. blue	3·75	15
66	2p. olive	4·25	40
82	5p. purple	5·50	1·25
87	9p. ochre	9·00	9·00
88	10p. blue	7·50	3·00
26	20p. grey	35·00	50·00
89	20p. violet	9·00	5·50

9 Rachel's Tomb

10 Dome of the Rock

11 Citadel, Jerusalem

12 Sea of Galilee

1927

90	9	2m. blue	2·75	10
91	9	3m. green	1·75	10
92	10	4m. red	9·00	1·25
104	10	4m. purple	3·00	10
93	11	5m. orange	4·25	10
94a	10	6m. green	1·50	20
95	11	7m. red	11·00	60
105	11	7m. violet	1·00	10
96	10	8m. brown	18·00	6·00
106	10	8m. red	1·25	20
97	9	10m. grey	2·00	10
98	10	13m. blue	17·00	30
107	10	13m. brown	3·50	10
108a	10	15m. blue	5·50	40
99a	11	20m. olive	2·25	15
100	12	50m. purple	2·75	30
101	12	90m. bistre	75·00	60·00
102	12	100m. blue	2·25	70
103	12	200m. violet	8·00	5·00
109	12	250m. brown	7·50	3·50
110	12	500m. red	7·50	3·00
111	12	£P1 black	10·00	3·50

POSTAGE DUE STAMPS

D1

1920

D1	D1	1m. brown	21·00	30·00
D2	D1	2m. green	17·00	10·00
D3	D1	4m. red	10·00	10·00
D4	D1	8m. mauve	7·00	7·00
D5	D1	13m. blue	6·00	6·50

D2

1924

D6	D2	1m. brown	90	2·00
D7	D2	2m. yellow	4·00	1·75
D8	D2	4m. green	2·00	1·25
D9	D2	8m. red	3·00	90
D10	D2	13m. blue	2·75	2·50
D11	D2	5p. violet	13·00	1·75

1928. As Type D 2, but inscr "MIL" instead of "MILLIEME".

D12	1m. brown	2·50	85
D13	2m. yellow	3·50	60
D14	4m. green	4·00	1·60
D15	6m. brown	18·00	5·00
D16	8m. red	2·75	1·50
D17	10m. grey	1·50	60
D18	13m. blue	4·50	2·50
D19	20m. olive	4·50	1·25
D20	50m. violet	4·50	1·75

Pt. 19

PALESTINIAN AUTHORITY

Following negotiations in Oslo, during which the Israeli government recognized the Palestine Liberation Organization as representing the Arab inhabitants of those areas occupied by Israel since 1967 and the P.L.O. accepted Israel's right to exist within secure borders, an agreement was signed in Washington on 13 September 1993 under which there was to be limited Palestinian self-rule in the Gaza Strip and in an enclave around Jericho on the West Bank. Further talks followed, leading to the Cairo Agreement of 4 May 1994, which inaugurated Palestinian Authority rule in Gaza and Jericho.

Under the Taba Accord of 28 September 1995 the Israeli army progressively withdrew from much of the remainder of the West Bank, which was then placed under Palestinian Authority administration.

1000 fils = 1 dinar

CURRENCY Israeli currency continued to be used in the Palestinian Authority areas. The first stamp issues had face values in mils, the currency of the Palestine Mandate period, but the Israeli authorities objected to this notional currency with the result that the face values were subsequently shown in the Jordanian currency of 1000 fils = 1 dinar.

PA1 Monument from Hisham Palace, Jericho

1994. Multicoloured.. Multicoloured..

PA1	5m. Type PA **1**	10	10
PA2	10m. Type PA **1**	10	10
PA3	20m. Type PA **1**	10	10
PA4	30m. Church of the Holy Sepulchre, Jerusalem	15	15
PA5	40m. As No. PA4	20	20
PA6	50m. As No. PA4	25	25
PA7	75m. As No. PA4	35	35
PA8	125m. Flags of Palestinian Authority	45	45
PA9	150m. As No. PA8	60	60
PA10	250m. As No. PA8	1·20	1·20
PA11	300m. As No. PA8	1·50	1·50
PA12	500m. Flags of Palestinian Authority (51×29 mm)	2·10	2·10
PA13	1000m. Dome of the Rock, Jerusalem (51×29 mm)	4·75	4·75

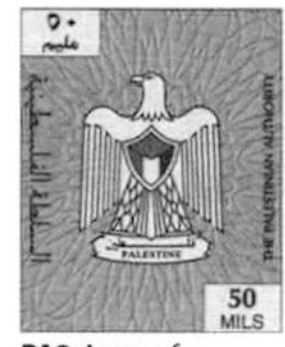

PA2 Arms of Palestinian Authority

1994

PA14	**PA2**	50m. yellow	25	25
PA15	**PA2**	100m. green	35	35
PA16	**PA2**	125m. blue	45	45
PA17	**PA2**	200m. orange	95	95
PA18	**PA2**	250m. yellow	1·20	1·20
PA19	**PA2**	400m. purple	1·70	1·70

PA3 Prime Minister Rabin of Israel and Chairman Arafat of P.L.O. with Pres. Clinton

1994. Gaza and Jericho Peace Agreement. Sheet 105×70 mm.

MSPA20 PA **3** 750m.+250m. multicoloured	4·75	4·75

PA4 "Land of My Dreams" (Ibrahim Hazimeh)

1995. 50th Anniv of Arab League. Sheet 105×70 mm.

MSPA21 PA **4** 750f.+250f. multicoloured	4·75	4·75

1995. Award of Nobel Peace Prize to Yasser Arafat, Yitzhak Rabin and Shimon Peres. No. MSPA20 surch FILS English and Arabic.

MSPA22 PA **3** 740f.+250f. multicoloured	5·75	5·75

NEW CURRENCY. From No. PA23 the face values are expressed as 1000 fils = 1 Jordanian dinar.

PA6 Palestine Mandate 1927 2m. Stamp

1995. Palestine Postal History.

PA23	**PA6**	150f. green and black	70	70
PA24	-	350f. orange and black	1·60	1·60
PA25	-	500f. red and black	2·10	2·10

DESIGNS: 350f. Palestine Mandate 1927; 5m. stamp; 500f. Palestine Mandate 1932; 8m. stamp.

PA7 Woman in Embroidered Costume

1995. Traditional Palestinian Women's Costumes. Multicoloured.

PA26	250f. Type PA **7**	1·20	1·20
PA27	300f. Woman carrying basket	1·40	1·40
PA28	550f. Woman in cloak	2·75	2·75
PA29	900f. Woman in veiled head-dress	4·00	4·00

1995. Nos. PA1/13 surch FILS in English and Arabic.

PA30	**PA1**	5f. on 5m. mult	10	10
PA31	**PA1**	10f. on 10m. mult	10	10
PA32	**PA1**	20f. on 20m. mult	10	10
PA33	-	30f. on 30m. mult	15	15
PA34	-	40f. on 40m. mult	20	20
PA35	-	50f. on 50m. mult	25	25
PA36	-	75f. on 75m. mult	35	35
PA37	-	125f. on 125m. mult	45	45
PA38	-	150f. on 150m. mult	60	60
PA39	-	250f. on 250m. mult	1·20	1·20
PA40	-	300f. on 300m. mult	1·50	1·50
PA41	-	500f. on 500m. mult	2·10	2·10
PA42	-	1000f. on 1000m. mult	4·75	4·75

PA9

1995. Handstamped Fils within circle in English and Arabic, twice on each stamp. As Type PA**9**. (a) On Nos. PA1/13.

PA43	**PA1**	5f. on 5m. mult	10	10
PA44	**PA1**	10f. on 10m. mult	10	10
PA45	**PA1**	20f. on 20m. mult	10	10
PA46	-	30f. on 30m. mult	15	15
PA47	-	40f. on 40m. mult	20	20
PA48	-	50f. on 50m. mult	25	25
PA49	-	75f. on 75m. mult	35	35
PA50	-	125f. on 125m. mult	45	45
PA51	-	150f. on 150m. mult	60	60
PA52	-	250f. on 250m. mult	1·20	1·20
PA53	-	300f. on 300m. mult	1·50	1·50
PA54	-	500f. on 500m. mult	2·10	2·10
PA55	-	1000f. on 1000m. mult	4·75	4·75

(b) On Nos. PA14/19.

PA56	**PA2**	50f. on 50m. yellow	25	25
PA57	**PA2**	100f. on 100m. green	35	35
PA58	**PA2**	125f. on 125m. blue	45	45
PA59	**PA2**	200f. on 200m. orange	95	95
PA60	**PA2**	250f. on 250m. yellow	1·20	1·20
PA61	**PA2**	400f. on 400m. purple	1·70	1·70
MSPA62 PA **3** 750f.+250f. on 750m.+250m. multicoloured			5·75	5·75

PA10 Bethlehem (old print)

1995. Christmas. Multicoloured.

PA63	10f. Type PA**10**	15	15
PA64	20f. Manger Square, Bethlehem	20	20
PA65	50f. Entrance to Church of the Nativity (vert)	25	25
PA66	100f. Pope John Paul II with Yasser Arafat	70	70
PA67	1000f. Site of the Nativity	6·50	6·50

PA11 Yasser Arafat

1996

PA68	**PA11**	10f. black and lilac	10	10
PA69	**PA11**	20f. black and yellow	20	20
PA70	**PA11**	50f. black and blue	25	25
PA71	**PA11**	100f. black and green	60	60
PA72	**PA11**	1000f. black & brown	5·25	5·25

PA12 Summer Palace, Peking

1996. Int Stamp Exhibitions and Fairs. Mult.

PA73	20f. Type PA **12** ("China '96")	25	25
PA74	50f. Hagia Sofia Mosque, Istanbul ("Istanbul '96")	35	35
PA75	100f. Villa Hugel, Essen (Essen stamp fair)	60	60
PA76	1000f. Modern skyline, Toronto ("Capex '96")	5·75	5·75

PA13 Crowd of Palestinians

1996. 1st Presidential Legislative and Presidential Elections. Sheet 105×70 mm.

MSPA77 PA **13** 1250f. multicoloured	7·00	7·00

PA14 Boxing

1996. Olympic Games, Atlanta. Multicoloured.

PA78	30f. Type PA **14**	15	15
PA79	40f. Olympic medal of 1896	25	25
PA80	50f. Running	35	35
PA81	150f. Olympic flame and flag	80	80
PA82	1000f. Palestinian Olympic Committee emblem	6·00	6·00
PAPA83	140×105 mm. Nos. PA78 and PA80/1	4·75	4·75

PA15 Poppy

1996. Flowers and Fruits. Multicoloured.

PA84	10f. Type PA**15**	10	10
PA85	25f. Hibiscus	15	15
PA86	100f. Thyme	60	60
PA87	150f. Lemon	95	95
PA88	750f. Orange	4·75	4·75
MSPA89	105×70 mm. 1000f. Olive	5·75	5·75

PA 16 Three Wise Men

1996. Christmas. Sheet 165×105 mm containing Type PA 16 and similar square designs. Multicoloured.

MSPA90 150f. Type PA **16**; 350f. Bethlehem; 500f. Shepherds; 750f. The Nativity	9·25	9·25

No. **MS**PA90 form a composite design.

PA17 Great Tits

1997. Birds. Multicoloured.

PA91	25f. Type PA **17**	35	35
PA92	75f. Blue rock thrushes	45	45
PA93	150f. Golden orioles	1·00	1·00
PA94	350f. Hoopoes	2·20	2·20
PA95	600f. Peregrine falcons	3·00	3·00

PA18 Gaza

1997. Palestinian Towns in 1839. Each brown and black.

PA96	350f. Type PA **18**	1·50	1·50
PA97	600f. Hebron	2·50	2·50

PA19 Chinese Junk

1997. Return of Hong Kong to China. Sheet 140X90 mm.

MSPA98 PA **19** 225f. multicoloured	1·20	1·20

PA20 Yasser Arafat and Wischnewski

1997. Friends of Palestine (1st series). Hans-Jurgen Wischnewski (German politician). Multicoloured.

PA99	600f. Type PA **20**	2·10	2·10
PA100	600f. Wischnewski congratulating Yasser Arafat	2·10	2·10

See also Nos. PA103/4.

PA21 "The Young Jesus in the Temple" (Anton Wollenek)

1997. Christmas.

PA101	**PA21** 350f. multicoloured	1·30	1·30
PA102	**PA21** 700f. multicoloured	2·50	2·50

PA22 Mother Teresa and Street Scene

1997. Friends of Palestine (2nd series). Mother Teresa (founder of Missionaries of Charity). Multicoloured.

PA103	600f. Type PA **22**	2·10	2·10
PA104	600f. Mother Teresa with Yasser Arafat	2·10	2·10

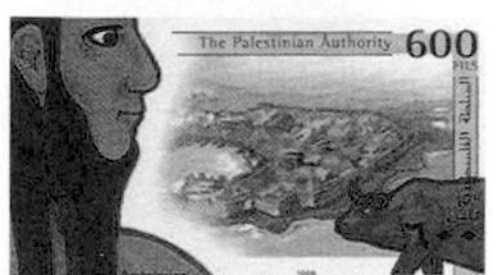

PA23 Baal, Tyre and Bull

1998. Baal (Canaanite god). Sheet 72×109 mm.

MSPA105	PA **23** 600f. multicoloured	3·00	3·00

PA24 Hare and Palm Tree

1998. Mosaics from Jabalia. Multicoloured.

PA106	50f. Type PA **24**	35	35
PA107	125f. Goat, hare and hound	80	80
PA108	200f. Lemon tree and baskets	1·30	1·30
PA109	400f. Lion	2·30	2·30

PA25 Sea Onion

1998. Medicinal Plants. Multicoloured.

PA110	40f. Type PA **25**	15	15
PA111	80f. "Silybum marianum"	35	35
PA112	500f. "Foeniculum vulgare"	2·10	2·10
PA113	800f. "Inula viscosa"	3·50	3·50

PA 26 Emblem

1998. Admission of Palestinian Authority as Non-voting Member to United Nations Organization. Sheet 82×65 mm.

MSPA114	PA **26** 700f. multicoloured	3·25	3·25

PA27 Bonelli's Eagle

1998. Birds of Prey. Multicoloured.

PA115	20f. Type PA **27**	15	15
PA116	60f. Northern hobby ("Hobby")	25	25
PA117	340f. Verreaux's eagle	1·40	1·40
PA118	600f. Bateleur	2·50	2·50
PA119	900f. Common buzzard ("Buzzard")	3·75	3·75

PA 28 Southern Swallowtail (Papilio alexanor)

1998. Butterflies. Sheet 106×84 mm containing Type PA28 and similar horiz designs. Multicoloured.

MSPA120	100f. Type PA **28**; 200f. African monarch; 300f. *Gonepteryx cleopatra*; 400f. *Melanargia titea*	5·50	5·50

PA 29 Ornamental Star

1998. Christmas. Sheet 90×140 mm.

MSPA121	PA **29** 1000f. multicoloured	5·00	5·00

PA 30 Yasser Arafat and U.S. Pres Clinton signing Agreement

1999. Wye River Middle East Peace Agreement. Sheet 83×65 mm.

MSPA122	PA **30** 900f. multicoloured	4·00	4·00

PA31 Control Tower

1999. Inauguration of Gaza International Airport. Multicoloured.

PA123	80f. Type PA **31**	25	25
PA124	300f. Fokkar F.27 Friendship airliner (horiz)	1·00	1·00
PA125	700f. Terminal building (horiz)	2·75	2·75

PA32 Peking ("China'99")

1999. International Stamp Exhibitions and Anniversary. Multicoloured.

PA126	20f. Type PA **32**	25	25
PA127	80f. Melbourne ("Australia 99")	35	35
PA128	260f. Nuremberg ("iBRA'99")	1·30	1·30
PA129	340f. Paris ("Philexfrance 99")	1·60	1·60
PA130	400f. Emblem and landscape (face value at right) (125th anniv of U.P.U.)	1·70	1·70
PA131	400f. As No. PA130 but face value at left	1·70	1·70

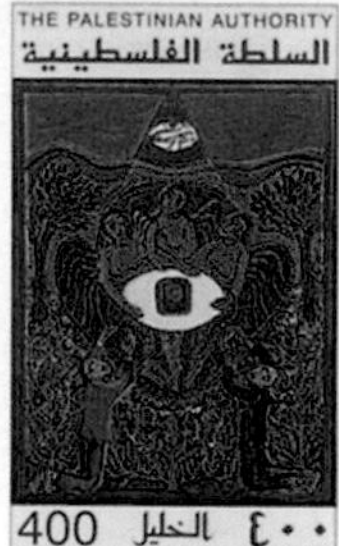

PA33 Relief by Anton Wollenek

1999. Hebron.

PA132	**PA33** 400f. multicoloured	1·90	1·90
PA133	**PA33** 500f. multicoloured	2·50	2·50

PA34 Horse and Foal

1999. Arabian Horses. Multicoloured.

PA134	25f. Type PA **34**	25	25
PA135	75f. Black horse	35	35
PA136	150f. Horse rearing	70	70
PA137	350f. Horse trotting	1·60	1·60
PA138	800f. Brown horse	4·25	4·25

PA35 Madonna and Child

1999. Christmas (1st series).

PA139	**PA35** 60f. blue, black and ochre	20	20
PA140	**PA35** 80f. multicoloured	25	25
PA141	**PA35** 100f. multicoloured	35	35
PA142	**PA35** 280f. multicoloured	95	95
PA143	**PA35** 300f. multicoloured	1·00	1·00
PA144	**PA35** 400f. multicoloured	1·40	1·40
PA145	**PA35** 500f. multicoloured	1·90	1·90
PA146	**PA35** 560f. multicoloured	2·10	2·10

See also Nos. PA147/57.

PA36 Nativity

1999. Christmas (2nd series). Designs with frames and face values in colours indicated.

PA147	**PA36** 200f. multicoloured (black)	35	35
PA148	**PA36** 200f. multicoloured (silver)	1·00	1·00
PA149	**PA36** 280f. multicoloured (white)	45	45
PA150	**PA36** 280f. multicoloured (silver)	1·40	1·40
PA151	- 380f. multicoloured (black)	60	60
PA152	- 380f. multicoloured (silver)	1·70	1·70
PA153	- 460f. multicoloured (white)	75	75
PA154	- 460f. multicoloured (silver)	2·20	2·20
PA155	- 560f. multicoloured (lemon)	95	95
PA156	- 560f. multicoloured (silver)	3·50	3·50
PA157	**PA 36** 2000f. multicoloured	8·25	8·25

DESIGNS: 380, 460f. Adoration of the Magi; 560f. Flight into Egypt.

PA 37 Palestine Sunbird

1999. Sheet 105×70 mm.

MSPA158	PA **37** 750f. multicoloured	3·50	3·50

PA 38 *The Last Supper*

2000. Easter. Paintings by Giotto di Bondone. Multicoloured.

PA159	150f. Type PA **38**	45	45
PA160	200f. As Type PA **38**	70	70
PA161	750f. *Lamentation*	95	95
PA162	800f. As No. PA161	1·40	1·40
PA163	1000r. *Crucificion*	2·30	2·30
MSPA164	155×98 mm. 2000f. As No. PA163.	8·25	8·25

No. **MS**PA164 has the outline of the cross embossed in gold foil.

PA 39 Landscape

2000. Children's Drawings. Multicoloured.

PA165	50f. Type PA **39**	35	35
PA166	100f. Two boys	45	45
PA167	350f. Buildings	1·50	1·50
PA168	400f. Woman crying	2·00	2·00

PA 40 Pope John Paul II and Yassar Arafat

2000. Papal Visit. Multicoloured.

PA169	500f. Type PA **40**	1·70	1·70
PA170	600f. Pope John Paul II	2·10	2·10
PA171	750f. With hand on Yassar Arafat	2·50	2·50
PA172	800f. Looking at crib	3·00	3·00
PA173	1000r. Talking to Yassar Arafat	3·50	3·50

2000. Bethlehem 2000.As Type PA 36. Multicoloured.

PA174	2000f. As No. PA157 but face value at top left	7·00	7·00
PA175	2000f. As **MS**PA164 but inscription in white (horiz)	7·00	7·00
PA176	2000f. *Madonna and Child* (Fra Angelico)	7·00	7·00

PA 41 Yasser Arafat and Gerhard Schroder (German Chancellor)

2000. Yasser Arafat's Visit to Germany. Multicoloured.

PA177	200f. Type PA **41**	80	80
PA178	300f. With President Johannes Rau	1·30	1·30

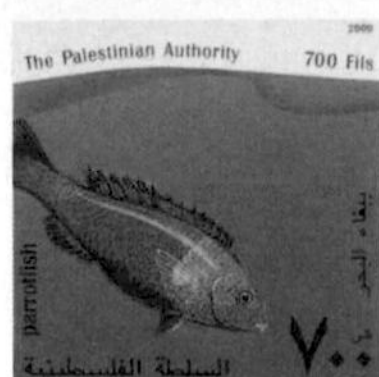

PA 42 Parrotfish

2000. Marine Fauna. Sheet 175×105 mm containing Type PA 42 and similar square designs. Multicoloured.

MSPA179	700f.×8, Type PA **42**; Mauve stinger; Ornate wrasse; Rainbow wrasse; Redstarfish; Common octopus; Purple sea urchin; Striated hermit crab	19·00	19·00

The stamps and margins of **MS**PA179 form a composite design of the seabed.

PA 43 *Blue Madonna*

2000. Sheet 70×110 mm.

MSPA180	multicoloured	3·50	3·50

PA 44 *Nativity* (Gentile da Fabriano)

2000. Christmas. Multicoloured.

PA181	100f. Type PA 44	25	25
PA182	150f. *Adoration of the Magi* (Gentile da Fabriano)	60	60
PA183	250f. *Annunciation* (Fra Angelico)	95	95
PA184	350f. *Madonna and Child* (Fra Angelico) (As No. PA176) (vert)	1·40	1·40
PA185	500f. As Type PA **44**	1·70	1·70
PA186	1000f. As No. PA184 (vert)	3·25	3·25
MSPA187	56×71 mm. As No. PA184	7·25	7·25

No. **MS**PA187 has halos and dress decoration embossed in gold foil.

PA 45 *Christ carrying the Cross* (Fra Angelico)

2000. Easter. Multicoloured.

PA188	150f. Type PA **45**	60	60
PA189	200f. As Type PA **45**	70	70
PA190	300f. *Removing Christ from the Cross* (Fra Angelico)	1·30	1·30
PA191	350f. As No. PA190	1·60	1·60
MSPA192	155×98 mm. 2000f. *Crucificion* (Giotto di Bondone) (vert).	7·25	7·25

No. **MS**PA192 has the figure of Christ embossed in gold foil.

PA 46 Palestine Authority and Organization for African Unity

2001. International Co-operation. Designs showing Palestine flag conjoined with other organizations. Multicoloured.

PA193	50f. Type PA **46**	25	25
PA194	100f. Organisation of the Islamic Conference	45	45
PA195	200f. European Union	70	70
PA196	500f. Arab League	1·70	1·70

PA 47 *Jerusalem after Rain*

2001. Art for Peace. Sheet 127×138 mm containing Type PA 47 and similar vert designs showing paintings by Ibrahim Hazimeh. Multicoloured.

MSPA197	350f. Type PA **47**; 550f. *Mysticism*; 850f. *Ramallah*; 900f. *Remembrance*	9·25	9·25

PA 48 Scene from *Aladdin and the Wonderful Lamp*

2001. Tales from the Arabian Nights. Designs showing scenes from the stories. Multicoloured.

PA198	300f. Type PA **48**	95	95
PA199	450f. *Adventures of Sinbad*	1·50	1·50
PA200	650f. *The Enchanted Horse'*	2·30	2·30
PA201	800f. *Ali Baba and the Forty Thieves*	2·75	2·75

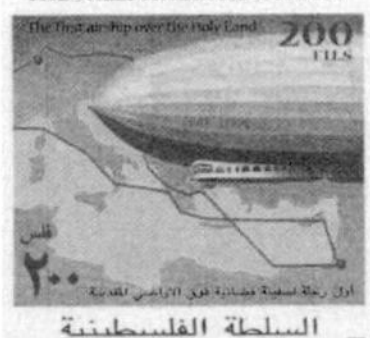

PA 49 Airship and Map of Route

2001. 70th Anniv of Flight of Graf Zeppelin (LZ-127) over Palestine. Multicoloured.

PA202	200f. Type PA **49**	95	95
PA203	600f. Airship over Palestine	2·50	2·50

PA 50 Male Displaying

2001. Houbara Bustard (Chlamydotis undulata). Multicoloured.

PA204	350f. Type PA **50**	1·70	1·70
PA205	350f. Chick	1·70	1·70
PA206	750f. Female	3·50	3·50
PA207	750f. Male	3·50	3·50

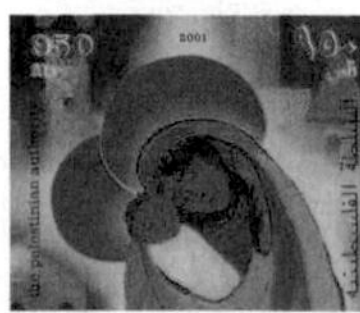

PA 51 Madonna and Child

2001. Peace for Bethlehem. Sheet 90×90 mm.

MSPA208	multicoloured	3·50	3·50

PA 52 Woman

2002. Traditional Costumes. Designs showing women wearing traditional dress. Multicoloured.

PA209	50f. Type PA **52**	25	25
PA210	100f. Wearing tall headdress and yellow skirt	45	45
PA211	500f. White head veil and panelled skirt	2·10	2·10

PA 53 Jerusalem

2002. Historic City Views. Multicoloured.

PA212	450f. Type PA **53**	1·70	1·70
PA213	650f. El-Eizariya	2·30	2·30
PA214	850f. Nablus	3·00	3·00

PA 54 Madonna and Child

2002. Christmas. Sheet 98×85 mm.

MSPA215	multicoloured	3·75	3·75

PA 55 Prickly Pear

2003. Flora. Multicoloured.

PA216	550f. Type PA **55**	2·00	2·00
PA217	600f. Euphorbia	2·20	2·20
PA218	750f. Agave (century plant)	2·75	2·75
MSPA219	110×66 mm. Nos. PA216/18	7·25	7·25

PA 56 Olive Tree

2003. Trees. Multicoloured.

PA220	300f. Type PA **56**	1·40	1·40
PA221	700f. Blessing tree	2·75	2·75

PA 57 Al-Azhar University, Gaza

2003. Universities. Multicoloured.

PA222	250f. Type PA **57**	95	95
PA223	650f. Hebron University	2·30	2·30
PA224	800f. Arab American University, Jenin	3·00	3·00

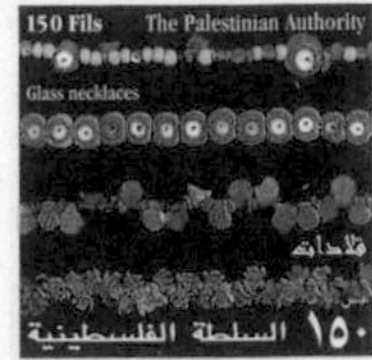

PA 58 Glass Necklace

2003. Handicrafts. Multicoloured.

PA225	150f. Type PA **58**	70	70
PA226	200f. Headdress	80	80
PA227	450f. Embroidery	2·00	2·00
PA228	500f. Embroidery on costume	2·30	2·30
PA229	950f. Head veil	4·25	4·25

PA 59 Madonna and Child

2004. Christmas. Sheet 100×75 mm.

MSPA230	multicoloured	5·00	5·00

PA 60 Yasser Arafat and Jaques Chirac (French president 1995–2007)

2004. Friends of Peace. Sheet 100×100 mm containing Type PA 60 and similar horiz design. Multicoloured.

MSPA231	200f.×2, Type PA **60**×2; 450f.×2, Jaques Chirac×2	6·50	6·50

PA 61 Town

2005. 60th Anniv of Arab League. Sheet 105×70 mm.

MSPA232	**PA 61** 750f. multicoloured	3·75	3·75

PA 62 Mahmud Darwish

2008. Visit (2007) of Mahmud Darwish (Palestinian writer).

PA233	**PA 62** 350f. multicoloured	1·70	1·70

PA 63 Emblem and Skyline

2009. Al Quds–Arab Capital of Culture. Multicoloured.

PA237	100f. Type PA **63**	
PA238	150f. As Type PA **63**	
PA239	500f. Type PA **63**	
PA240	1000f. Emblem (central, large)	

Nos. PA234/6 are left for additions to Visit (2007) of Mahmud Darwish (Palestinian writer).

Pt. 15

PANAMA

Country situated on the C. American isthmus. Formerly a State or Department of Colombia, Panama was proclaimed an independent republic in 1903.

1878. 100 centavos = 1 peso.
1906. 100 centesimos = 1 balboa.

1 Coat of Arms

1878. Imperf. The 50c. is larger.

1A	**1**	5c. green	31·00	37·00
2A	**1**	10c. blue	80·00	80·00
3A	**1**	20c. red	44·00	35·00
4B	**1**	50c. yellow	17·00	

3 Map

1887. Perf.

5	**3**	1c. black on green	1·20	95
6	**3**	2c. black on pink	1·80	1·40
7	**3**	5c. black on blue	1·20	35
7a	**3**	5c. black on grey	1·40	45
8	**3**	10c. black on yellow	1·40	45
9	**3**	20c. black on lilac	1·70	55
10	**3**	50c. brown	2·50	1·20

5 Map of Panama

1892

12a	**5**	1c. green	30	30
12b	**5**	2c. red	50	30
12c	**5**	5c. blue	2·10	65
12d	**5**	10c. orange	40	30
12e	**5**	20c. violet	65	45
12f	**5**	50c. brown	70	45
12g	**5**	1p. lake	7·25	4·25

1894. Surch HABILITADO 1894 and value.

13		1c. on 2c. red	70	45
15	**3**	5c. on 20c. black on lilac	3·50	1·90
18	**3**	10c. on 50c. brown	3·75	3·75

1903. Optd REPUBLICA DE PANAMA.

70B	**5**	1c. green	95	95
36B	**5**	2c. red	1·30	1·20
72B	**5**	5c. blue	1·30	1·00
38A	**5**	10c. orange	2·75	2·50
39A	**5**	20c. violet	5·25	4·50
40B	**5**	50c. brown	12·50	9·25
75B	**3**	50c. brown	31·00	26·00
41B	**5**	1p. lake	65·00	50·00

1903. Optd PANAMA twice.

53	**5**	1c. green	30	30
54	**5**	2c. red	30	30
55	**5**	5c. blue	40	30
56	**5**	10c. orange	40	30
64	**5**	20c. violet	6·25	6·00
65	**5**	50c. brown	12·50	12·00
66	**5**	1p. lake	15·00	15·00

1904. Optd Republica de Panama.

94		1c. green	50	45
97		2c. red	60	55
98		5c. blue	60	55
99		10c. orange	60	55
100		20c. violet	60	55
103	**3**	50c. brown	3·75	3·75
104	**5**	1p. lake	18·00	16·00

38 Map of Panama

1905

151	**38**	½c. orange	1·20	55
136	**38**	1c. green	75	55
137	**38**	2c. red	1·20	65

1906. Surch PANAMA twice and new value and thick bar.

138	**5**	1c. on 20c. violet	30	30
139	**5**	2c. on 50c. brown	30	30
140	**5**	5c. on 1p. lake	70	45

41 Panamanian Flag

42 Vasco Nunez de Balboa

43 F. de Cordoba

44 Arms of Panama

45 J. Arosemena

46 M. J. Hurtado

47 J. de Obaldia

1906

142	**41**	½c. multicoloured	75	65
143	**42**	1c. black and green	75	65
144	**43**	2c. black and red	1·10	65
145	**44**	2½c. red	1·10	65
146	**45**	5c. black and blue	1·30	65
147	**46**	8c. black and purple	1·60	1·20
148	**47**	10c. black and violet	1·60	65
149	-	25c. black and brown	3·75	2·00
150	-	50c. black	9·75	6·50

DESIGNS: 25c. Tomas Herrera; 50c. Jose de Fabrega.

48 Balboa

49 De Cordoba

50 Arms

51 Arosemena

52 Hurtado

53 Obaldia

1909

152	**48**	1c. black and green	1·20	95
153	**49**	2c. black and red	1·20	55
154	**50**	2½c. red	1·60	55
155	**51**	5c. black and blue	2·10	55
156	**52**	8c. black and purple	9·75	5·50
157	**53**	10c. black and purple	4·00	2·00

56 Balboa viewing Pacific Ocean

1913. 400th Anniv of Discovery of Pacific Ocean.

160	**56**	2½c. yellow and green	1·90	75

57 Balboa reaches the Pacific

1915. Panama Exhibition and Opening of Canal.

161	-	½c. black and olive	50	35
162	-	1c. black and green	1·10	35
163	**57**	2c. black and red	85	35
164	-	2½c. black and red	1·20	45
165	-	3c. black and violet	1·70	65
166	-	5c. black and blue	2·40	45
167	-	10c. black and orange	2·30	85
168	-	20c. black and brown	11·50	3·50

DESIGNS: ½c. Chorrera Falls; 1c. Relief Map of Panama Canal; 2½c. Cathedral ruins, Old Panama; 3c. Palace of Arts, National Exhibition; 5c. Gatun Locks; 10c. Culebra Cut; 20c. Archway, S. Domingo Monastery.

62 Balboa Docks

1918. Views of Panama Canal.

178		12c. black and violet	17·00	6·50
179		15c. black and blue	11·50	4·00
180		24c. black and brown	17·00	4·00
181	**62**	50c. black and orange	34·00	24·00
182	-	1b. black and violet	42·00	28·00

DESIGNS: 12c. "Panama" (cargo liner) in Gaillard Cut, north; 15c. "Panama" in Gaillard Cut, south; 24c. "Cristobal" (cargo liner) in Gatun Locks; 1b. "Nereus" (U.S. Navy collier) in Pedro Miguel Locks.

1919. 400th Anniv of Founding of City of Panama. No. 164 surch 1519 1919 2 CENTESIMOS 2.

183	2c. on 2½c. black and red	50	50

64 Arms of Panama

65 Vallarino

68 Bolivar's Speech

1921. Independence Centenary. Dated "1821 1921".

184	**64**	½c. orange	85	30
185	**65**	1c. green	1·20	30
186	-	2c. red ("Land Gate", Panama City)	1·40	30
187	**65**	2½c. red (Bolivar)	3·00	1·50
188	-	3c. violet (Cervantes statue)	3·00	1·50
189	**68**	5c. blue	3·00	55
190	**65**	8c. olive (Carlos Ycaza)	10·50	4·00
191	-	10c. violet (Government House 1821–1921)	7·25	1·90
192	-	15c. blue (Balboa statue)	8·75	2·40
193	-	20c. brown (Los Santos Church)	15·00	4·00
194	**65**	24c. sepia (Herrera)	15·00	4·75
195	-	50c. black (Fabrega)	27·00	9·25

70 Hurtado

1921. Birth Centenary of Manuel Jose Hurtado (writer).

196	**70**	2c. green	70	65

1923. No. 164 surch 1923 2 CENTESIMOS 2.

197	2c. on 2½c. black and red	50	45

72

1924

198	**72**	½c. orange	30	20
199	**72**	1c. green	30	20
200	**72**	2c. red	30	20
201	**72**	5c. blue	60	25
202	**72**	10c. violet	70	30
203	**72**	12c. olive	85	45
204	**72**	15c. blue	1·10	45
205	**72**	24c. brown	2·10	65
206	**72**	50c. orange	5·25	1·20
207	**72**	1b. black	7·75	2·75

73 Simon Bolivar

74 Statue of Bolivar

75 Congress Hall, Panama

1926. Bolivar Congress.

208	**73**	½c. orange	60	30
209	**73**	1c. green	60	30
210	**73**	2c. red	75	35
211	**73**	4c. grey	95	45
212	**73**	5c. blue	1·50	65
213	**74**	8c. purple	2·40	1·00
214	**74**	10c. violet	1·70	95
215	**74**	12c. olive	2·75	1·40
216	**74**	15c. blue	3·50	1·70
217	**74**	20c. brown	7·25	2·40
218	**75**	24c. slate	8·75	2·40
219	**75**	50c. black	14·50	6·50

78 "Spirit of St. Louis" over Map

1928. Lindbergh's Flying Tour.

222	-	2c. red on rose	40	30
223	**78**	5c. blue on green	60	45

DESIGN—VERT: 2c. "Spirit of St. Louis" over Old Panama with opt **HOMENAJE A LINDBERGH**.

1928. 25th Anniv of Independence. Optd 1903 NOV 3 BRE 1928.

224	**70**	2c. green	30	30

1929. Air. No. E226 surch with Fokker Universal airplane and CORREO AEREO 25 25 VEINTICINCO CENTESIMOS.

225	**E81**	25c. on 10c. orange	1·20	95

1929. Air. Nos. E226/7 optd CORREO AEREO or additionally surch with new value in CENTESIMOS.

238	5c. on 10c. orange	60	55
228	10c. orange	60	55
268	10c. on 20c. brown	95	65
229	15c. on 10c. orange	60	55
269	20c. brown	1·20	65
230	25c. on 20c. brown	1·30	1·10

83

1930. Air.

231	**83**	5c. blue	25	20
232	**83**	5c. orange	30	30
233	**83**	7c. red	30	30
234	**83**	8c. black	30	30
235	**83**	15c. green	40	30
236	**83**	20c. red	60	30
237	**83**	25c. blue	75	75

1930. No. 182 optd with airplane and CORREO AEREO.

239	1b. black and violet	21·00	16·00

87

1930. Air.

244	**87**	5c. blue	30	30
245	**87**	10c. orange	40	30
246	**87**	30c. violet	6·25	4·25
247	**87**	50c. red	1·70	55
248	**87**	1b. black	6·25	4·25

1930. Bolivar's Death Centenary. Surch 1830 - 1930 17 DE DICIEMBRE UN CENTESIMO.

249	**73**	1c. on 4c. grey	30	25

89 Seaplane over Old Panama

1931. Air. Opening of service between Panama City and western provinces.

250	**89**	5c. blue	95	1·10

1932. Optd HABILITADA or surch also.

251	**64**	½c. orange (postage)	50	25
252	**73**	½c. orange	30	25
253	**73**	1c. green	50	25
270	**68**	1c. on 5c. blue	50	45
254	**73**	2c. red	50	25
255	**73**	5c. blue	95	50
256	-	10c. violet (No. 191)	1·40	85
258	**74**	10c. on 12c. olive	1·40	85
259	**74**	10c. on 15c. blue	1·20	65
257	**74**	20c. brown	2·50	2·00
260	**83**	20c. on 25c. blue (air)	6·75	80

92 Manuel Amador Guerrero

1932. Birth Centenary of Dr. Guerrero (first president of republic).

261	**92**	2c. red	50	30

95 National Institute

1934. 25th Anniv of National Institute.

262	-	1c. green	1·20	65
263	-	2c. red	1·20	60
264	-	5c. blue	1·50	1·10
265	**95**	10c. brown	3·50	2·00
266	-	12c. green	5·75	2·20
267	-	15c. blue	7·75	2·75

DESIGNS—VERT: 1c. J. D. de Obaldia; 2c. E. A. Morales; 5c. Sphinx and Quotation from Emerson. HORIZ: 12c. J. A. Facio; 15c. P. Arosemena.

(98)

1936. Birth Centenary of Pablo Arosemena. (a) Postage. Surch as T 98, but without CORREO AEREO.

271	**72**	2c. on 24c. brown	75	75

(b) Air. Surch with T 98.

272	5c. on 50c. orange	1·40	1·10

100 Urraca Monument

99 Custom House Ruins, Portobelo

1936. 4th Spanish–American Postal Congress (1st issue). Inscr "IV CONGRESO POSTAL AMERICO–ESPANOL".

273	**99**	½c. orange (postage)	60	40
274	-	1c. green	60	30
275	-	2c. red	60	30
276	-	5c. blue	85	55
277	-	10c. violet	1·90	95
278	-	15c. blue	1·90	1·00
279	-	20c. red	2·10	1·90
280	-	25c. brown	3·75	2·40
281	-	50c. orange	8·25	6·00
282	-	1b. black	19·00	17·00

DESIGNS: 1c. "Panama" (Old tree); 2c. "La Pollera" (woman in costume); 5c. Bolivar; 10c. Ruins of Old Panama Cathedral; 15c. Garcia y Santos; 20c. Madden Dam; 25c. Columbus; 50c. "Resolute" (liner) in Gaillard Cut; 1b. Panama Cathedral.

283	**100**	5c. blue (air)	75	55
284	-	10c. orange	85	75
285	-	20c. red	2·10	1·90
286	-	30c. violet	3·75	3·00
287	-	50c. red	8·75	7·00
288	-	1b. black	10·50	7·50

DESIGNS—HORIZ: 10c. "Man's Genius Uniting the Oceans"; 20c. Panama; 50c. San Pedro Miguel Locks; 1b. Courts of Justice. VERT: 30c. Balboa Monument.

1937. 4th Spanish–American Postal Congress (2nd issue). Nos. 273/88 optd UPU.

289	**99**	½c. orange (postage)	40	35
290	-	1c. green	50	30
291	-	2c. red	50	30
292	-	5c. blue	75	35
293	-	10c. violet	1·30	45
294	-	15c. blue	5·75	4·00
295	-	20c. red	2·10	1·90
296	-	25c. brown	3·00	1·90
297	-	50c. orange	9·75	8·00
298	-	1b. black	18·00	12·00
299	**99**	5c. blue (air)	50	45
300	-	10c. orange	75	60
301	-	20c. red	1·90	1·30
302	-	30c. violet	5·00	4·00
303	-	50c. red	20·00	19·00
304	-	1b. black	24·00	19·00

1937. Optd 1937-38.

305	**73**	½c. orange	1·30	1·20
306	**65**	1c. green	40	35
307	**73**	1c. green	40	35
308	**70**	2c. green	50	45
309	**73**	2c. red	60	55

1937. Surch 1937-38 and value.

310	-	2c. on 4c. grey	75	55
311	**78**	2c. on 8c. olive	75	75
312	**74**	2c. on 8c. purple	75	55
313	**74**	2c. on 10c. violet	75	65
314	**74**	2c. on 12c. olive	75	55
315	-	2c. on 15c. blue (No. 192)	75	75
316	**65**	2c. on 24c. sepia	75	1·00
317	**65**	2c. on 50c. black	75	55

1937. Air. Optd CORREO AEREO or surch also.

318	**73**	5c. blue	95	95
319	**74**	5c. on 15c. blue	95	95
320	**74**	5c. on 20c. brown	95	95
321	**75**	5c. on 24c. slate	95	95
322	**62**	5c. on 1b. black and violet	95	55
323	-	10c. on 10c. violet (No. 191)	2·10	1·80
324	**75**	10c. on 50c. black	3·00	2·40

105 Fire-Engine

106 Firemen's Monument

107 Fire-Brigade Badge

1937. 50th Anniv of Fire Brigade.

325	-	½c. orange (postage)	2·30	45
326	-	1c. green	2·30	45
327	-	2c. red	2·30	55
328	**105**	5c. blue	4·25	65
329	**106**	10c. violet	7·75	1·60
330	-	12c. green	12·50	2·40
331	**107**	5c. blue (air)	3·75	75
332	-	10c. orange	5·25	1·40
333	-	20c. red	7·75	1·00

DESIGNS—VERT: ½c. R. Arango; 1c. J. A. Guizado; 10c. (No. 332), F. Arosemena; 12c. D. H. Brandon; 20c. J. G. Duque. HORIZ: 2c. House on fire.

108 Basketball Player

1938. Air. Central American and Caribbean Olympic Games.

334	**108**	1c. red	2·40	45
335	-	2c. green (Baseball player) (horiz)	2·40	30
336	-	7c. grey (Swimmer) (horiz)	3·50	50
337	-	8c. brown (Boxers) (horiz)	3·50	50
338	-	15c. blue (Footballer)	5·25	2·50

MS339	140×140 mm. Nos. 334/8 (sold at 35c.)	21·00	20·00

1938. Opening of Aguadulce Normal School, Santiago. Optd NORMAL DE SANTIAGO JUNIO 5 1938 or surch also.

340	**72**	2c. red (postage)	50	40
341	**87**	7c. on 30c. violet (air)	60	55
342	**83**	8c. on 15c. green	60	55

111 Old Panama Cathedral and Statue of Liberty

1938. 150th Anniv of U.S. Constitution. Flags in red, white and blue.

343	**111**	1c. black and green (postage)	40	35
344	**111**	2c. black and red	60	30
345	**111**	5c. black and blue	85	35
346	**111**	12c. black and olive	1·50	1·10
347	**111**	15c. black and blue	1·90	1·70
348	**111**	7c. black and grey (air)	40	35
349	**111**	8c. black and blue	60	55
350	**111**	15c. black and brown	75	55
351	**111**	50c. black and orange	8·75	7·00
352	**111**	1b. black	8·75	7·00

Nos. 343/7 are without the Douglas DC-3 airliner.

112 Pierre and Marie Curie

1939. Obligatory Tax. Cancer Research Fund. Dated "1939".

353	**112**	1c. red	70	25
354	**112**	1c. green	70	25
355	**112**	1c. orange	70	25
356	**112**	1c. blue	70	25

113 Gatun Locks

1939. 25th Anniv of Opening of Panama Canal.

357	**113**	½c. yellow (postage)	40	25
358	-	1c. green	60	25
359	-	2c. red	70	25
360	-	5c. blue	1·10	30
361	-	10c. violet	1·30	45
362	-	12c. olive	1·30	60
363	-	15c. blue	1·30	1·00
364	-	50c. orange	3·00	1·80
365	-	1b. brown	6·25	3·75

DESIGNS: 1c. "Santa Elena" (liner) in Pedro Miguel Locks; 2c. Allegory of canal construction; 5c. "Rangitata" (liner) in Culebra Cut; 10c. Panama canal ferry; 12c. Aerial view; 15c. Gen. Gorgas; 50c. M. A. Guerrero; 1b. Woodrow Wilson.

366	1c. red (air)	50	25
367	2c. green	50	25
368	5c. blue	70	25
369	10c. violet	75	30
370	15c. blue	1·70	40
371	20c. red	4·25	1·90
372	50c. brown	5·25	95
373	1b. black	7·75	5·00

PORTRAITS: 1c. B. Porras; 2c. Wm. H. Taft; 5c. P. J. Sosa; 10c. L. B. Wise; 15c. A. Reclus; 20c. Gen. Goethals; 50c. F. de Lesseps; 1b. Theodore Roosevelt.

115 Flags of American Republics

1940. Air. 50th Anniv of Pan-American Union.

374	**115**	15c. blue	50	35

1940. Air. No. 370 surch 55.

375	5c. on 15c. blue	30	30

No. 363 surch AEREO SIETE.

376	7c. on 15c. blue	50	30

No. 371 surch SIETE.

377	7c. on 20c. red	50	30

No. 374 surch 8–8.

378	8c. on 15c. blue	50	30

1941. Obligatory Tax. Cancer Research Fund. Optd LUCHA CONTRA EL CANCER.

379	**72**	1c. green	1·70	1·00

1941. Enactment of New Constitution. (a) Postage. Optd CONSTITUCION 1941.

380	½c. orange	40	30
381	1c. green	40	30
382	2c. red	40	30
383	5c. blue	60	30
384	10c. violet	85	55
385	15c. blue	1·80	75
386	50c. orange	6·75	3·75
387	1b. black	15·00	6·50

(b) Air. Surch CONSTITUCION 1941 AEREO and value in figures.

388	**E81**	7c. on 10c. orange	1·10	1·00
389	**72**	15c. on 24c. brown	2·50	2·40

(c) Air. Optd CONSTITUCION 1941.

390	83	20c. red	2·10	2·00
391	87	50c. red	6·25	4·00
392	87	1b. black	14·50	10·00

1941. Obligatory Tax. Cancer Research Fund. Dated "1940".

393	112	1c. red	70	30
394	112	1c. green	70	30
395	112	1c. orange	70	30
396	112	1c. blue	70	30

120a "Liberty"

1942. Telegraph stamps as T 120a optd or surch. (a) Optd CORREOS 1942 and (No. 397) surch 2c.

397	2c. on 5c. blue	1·80	65
398	10c. violet	1·50	1·20

(b) Air. Optd CORREO AEREO 1942.

399	20c. brown	4·25	3·25

123 Flags of Panama and Costa Rica

1942. 1st Anniv of Revised Frontier Agreement between Panama and Costa Rica.

400	123	2c. red (postage)	40	35
401	123	15c. green (air)	75	30

1942. Obligatory Tax. Cancer Research Fund. Dated "1942".

402	112	1c. violet	60	30

127 Balboa reaches Pacific

129 J. D. Arosemena Normal School

1942. (a) Postage stamps.

403	-	½c. red, blue and violet	30	30
404	-	½c. blue, orange and red	30	30
405	-	1c. green	30	30
406	-	1c. red	30	30
407	-	2c. red ("ACARRERO")	30	30
408	-	2c. red ("ACARREO")	1·00	30
409	-	2c. black and red	30	30
410	127	5c. black and blue	30	30
411	-	5c. blue	50	30
412	-	10c. orange and red	70	30
413	-	10c. orange and purple	1·10	30
414	-	15c. black and blue	1·30	65
415	-	15c. black	95	35
416	-	50c. black and red	2·75	1·20
417	-	1b. black	3·75	1·20

DESIGNS—VERT: ½c. National flag; 1c. Farm girl; 10c. Golden Altar, Church of St. Jose; 50c. San Blas Indian woman and child. HORIZ: 2c. Oxen drawing sugar cart; 15c. St. Thomas's Hospital; 1b. National highway.

(b) Air.

418		2c. red	95	30
419		7c. red	95	30
420		8c. black and brown	30	30
421		10c. black and blue	30	30
422		15c. violet	50	30
423		15c. grey	50	30
424	129	20c. brown	70	30
425	129	20c. green	50	30
426	-	50c. green	1·30	45
427	-	50c. red	7·75	3·75
428	-	50c. blue	3·75	1·20
429	-	1b. orange, yellow and black	3·00	95

DESIGNS—HORIZ: 2c., 7c. Black marlin; 8c., 10c. Gate of Glory, Portobelo; 15c. Taboga Is; 50c. Fire Brigade H.Q., Panama City; 1b. Idol (Golden Beast).

1943. Obligatory Tax. Cancer Research Fund. Dated "1943".

433	112	1c. green	60	30
434	112	1c. red	60	30
435	112	1c. orange	60	30
436	112	1c. blue	60	30

131 A. G. Melendez

1943. Air.

437	131	3b. grey	5·75	5·50
438	-	5b. blue (T. Lefevre)	8·75	8·50

1945. Obligatory Tax. Cancer Research Fund. Dated "1945".

439	112	1c. red	1·60	35
440	112	1c. green	1·60	35
441	112	1c. orange	1·60	35
442	112	1c. blue	1·60	35

1946. Obligatory Tax. Cancer Research Fund. Surch CANCER B/. 0.01 1947.

443	72	1c. on ½c. orange	1·20	30
444	72	1c. on 1c. green	1·20	30
445	-	1c. on ½c. red, blue and violet (No. 403)	1·10	30
446	72	1c. on 12c. olive	1·10	35
447	72	1c. on 24c. brown	1·10	35

1947. Air. Surch AEREO 1947 and value.

448	-	5c. on 7c. red (No. 419)	30	30
449	83	5c. on 8c. black	30	30
450	-	5c. on 8c. black and brown (No. 420)	30	30
451	83	10c. on 15c. green	60	55
452	-	10c. on 15c. violet (422)	30	30

134 Flag of Panama

135 National Theatre

1947. 2nd Anniv of National Constitutional Assembly.

453	134	2c. red, deep red and blue (postage)	25	20
454	-	5c. blue	25	25
455	135	8c. violet (air)	50	30

DESIGN—As Type **134**: 5c. Arms of Panama.

1947. Cancer Research Fund. Dated "1947".

456	112	1c. red	1·40	25
457	112	1c. green	1·40	25
458	112	1c. orange	1·40	25
459	112	1c. blue	1·40	25

1947. Surch HABILITADA CORREOS and value.

460	83	½c. on 8c. black	10	10
461	-	½c. on 8c. black and brown (No. 420)	20	20
462	-	1c. on 7c. red (No. 419)	20	20
463	135	2c. on 8c. violet	40	20

1947. Surch Habilitada CORREOS B/. 0.50.

464	72	50c. on 24c. brown	2·10	1·80

138 J. A. Arango

1948. Air. Honouring members of the Revolutionary Junta of 1903.

465	-	3c. black and blue	50	30
466	138	5c. black and brown	50	30
467	-	10c. black and orange	50	30
468	-	15c. black and red	50	30
469	-	20c. black and red	85	65
470	-	50c. black	1·50	95
471	-	1b. black and green	4·75	3·25
472	-	2b. black and yellow	10·50	7·50

PORTRAITS—HORIZ: 3c. M. A. Guerrero; 10c. F. Boyd; 15c. R. Arias. VERT: 20c. M. Espinosa; 50c. Carlos Arosemena (engineer); 1b. N. de Obarrio; 2b. T. Arias.

140 Firemen's Monument

1948. 50th Anniv of Colon Fire Brigade.

473	140	5c. black and red	70	25
474	-	10c. black and orange	95	35
475	-	20c. black and blue	1·90	65
476	-	25c. black and brown	1·90	1·00
477	-	50c. black and violet	3·75	1·00
478	-	1b. black and green	5·25	2·00

DESIGNS—HORIZ: 10c. Fire engine; 20c. Fire hose; 25c. Fire Brigade Headquarters. VERT: 50c. Commander Walker; 1b. First Fire Brigade Commander.

142 F. D. Roosevelt and J. D. Arosemena

144 Roosevelt Monument, Panama

1948. Air. Homage to F. D. Roosevelt.

479	142	5c. black and red	30	20
480	-	10c. orange	40	35
481	144	20c. green	50	45
482	-	50c. black and blue	75	75
483	-	1b. black	1·90	1·50

DESIGNS—HORIZ: 10c. Woman with palm symbolizing "Four Freedoms"; 50c. Map of Panama Canal. VERT: 1b. Portrait of Roosevelt.

147 Cervantes

148 Monument to Cervantes

1948. 400th Birth Anniv of Cervantes.

484	147	2c. black and red (postage)	85	30
485	148	5c. black and blue (air)	60	30
486	-	10c. black and mauve	95	35

DESIGN—HORIZ: 10c. Don Quixote and Sancho Panza (inscr as Type **148**).

1949. Air. Jose Gabriel Duque (philanthropist). Birth Centenary. No. 486 optd "CENTENARIO DE JOSE GABRIEL DUQUE" "18 de Enero de 1949".

487	10c. black and mauve	75	65

1949. Obligatory Tax. Cancer Research Fund. Surch LUCHA CONTRA EL CANCER and value.

488	142	1c. on 5c. black and red	70	30
489	-	1c. on 10c. orange (No. 480)	70	30

1949. Incorporation of Chiriqui Province Cent. Stamps of 1930 and 1942 optd 1849 1949 CHIRIQUI CENTENARIO. (a) On postage stamps as No. 407. (i) Without surcharge.

491	2c. red	30	30

(ii) Surch 1 UN CENTESIMO 1 also.

490	1c. on 2c. red	30	30

(b) Air.

492	-	2c. red (No. 418)	30	30
493	83	5c. blue	30	30
494	-	15c. grey (No. 423)	75	75
495	-	50c. red (No. 427)	3·00	2·75

1949. 75th Anniv of U.P.U. Stamps of 1930 and 1942/3 optd 1874 1949 U.P.U. No. 625 is also surch B/0.25.

496		1c. green (No. 405) (postage)	30	20
497		2c. red (No. 407)	50	30
498	127	5c. blue	75	45
499	-	2c. red (No. 418) (air)	30	30
500	83	5c. orange	95	65
501	-	10c. black and blue (No. 421)	95	75
502	131	25c. on 3b. grey	1·40	1·30
503	-	50c. red (No. 427)	4·25	4·00

1949. Cancer Research Fund. Dated "1949".

504	112	1c. brown	2·10	30

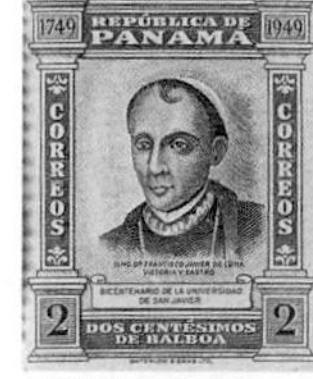

153 Father Xavier

154 St. Xavier University

1949. Bicentenary of Founding of St. Xavier University.

505	153	2c. black and red (postage)	30	30
506	154	5c. black and blue (air)	50	30

155 Dr. Carlos J. Finlay

156 "Aedes aegypti"

1950. Dr. Finlay (medical research worker).

507	155	2c. black and red (postage)	50	30
508	156	5c. black and blue (air)	1·70	75

1950. Death Centenary of San Martin. Optd CENTENARIO del General (or Gral.) Jose de San Martin 17 de Agosto de 1950 or surch also. The 50c. is optd AEREO as well.

509	-	1c. green (No. 405) (postage)	30	30
510	-	2c. on ½c. blue, orange and red (No. 404)	30	30
511	127	5c. black and blue	40	30
512	-	2c. red (No. 418) (air)	60	35
513	83	5c. orange	70	45
514	-	10c. black & blue (No. 421)	70	55
515	83	25c. blue	1·10	95
516	-	50c. black & violet (No. 477)	2·10	1·60

158 Badge

159 Stadium

1950. Obligatory Tax. Physical Culture Fund. Dated "1950".

517		1c. black and red	1·70	45
518	158	1c. black and blue	1·70	45
519	159	1c. black and green	1·70	45
520	-	1c. black and orange	1·70	45
521	-	1c. black and violet	1·70	45

DESIGNS—VERT: No. 520, as Type **159** but medallion changed and incorporating four "F"s; 521, Discus thrower. HORIZ: No. 517, as Type **159** but front of stadium.

1951. Birth Tercentenary of Jean-Baptiste de La Salle (educational reformer). Optd Tercer Centenario del Natalicio de San Juan Baptista de La Salle. 1651-1951.

522	2c. black and red (No. 409)	30	30
523	5c. blue (No. 411)	50	30

1952. Air. Surch AEREO 1952 and value.

524	2c. on 10c. black and blue (No. 421)	30	30
525	5c. on 10c. black and blue (No. 421)	40	35
526	1b. on 5b. blue (No. 438)	31·00	30·00

1952. Surch 1952 and figure of value.

527	1c. on ½c. (No. 404)	30	30

Air. Optd AEREO also.

528	5c. on 2c. (No. 408)	30	30
529	25c. on 10c. (No. 413)	1·40	1·40

164 Isabella the Catholic

1952. 500th Birth Anniv of Isabella the Catholic.

530	164	1c. black & grn (postage)	50	30
531	164	2c. black and red	50	30
532	164	5c. black and blue	50	30
533	164	10c. black and violet	75	35
534	164	4c. black and orange (air)	50	30
535	164	5c. black and olive	50	30
536	164	10c. black and buff	70	35
537	164	25c. black and slate	1·80	35
538	164	50c. black and brown	2·75	85
539	164	1b. black	8·00	3·75

1953. Surch B/.0.01 1953.

540	1c. on 10c. (No. 413)	30	30
541	1c. on 15c. black (No. 415)	30	30

1953. Air. No. 421 surch 5 1953.

542	5c. on 10c. black and blue	50	30

167 Masthead of "La Estrella"

1953. Air. Centenary of "La Estrella de Panama", Newspaper.

543	167	5c. red	30	30
544	167	10c. blue	50	35

168 Pres. and Senora Amador Guerrero

1953. 50th Anniv of Panama Republic.

545	-	2c. violet (postage)	50	25
546	168	5c. orange	60	25
547	-	12c. purple	1·40	25
548	-	20c. indigo	2·40	40
549	-	50c. yellow	3·75	95
550	-	1b. blue	5·50	2·10

DESIGNS—VERT: 2c. Blessing the flat; 50c. Old Town Hall. HORIZ: 12c. J. A. Santos and J. De La Ossa; 20c. Revolutionary council; 1b. Obverse and reverse of coin.

551	2c. blue (air)	50	25
552	5c. green	50	25
553	7c. grey	60	25
554	25c. black	3·75	1·00
555	50c. brown	2·40	1·20
556	1b. orange	5·50	2·40

DESIGNS—VERT: 2c. Act of Independence. HORIZ: 5c. Pres. and Senora Remon Cantera; 7c. Girl in national costume; 25c. National flower; 50c. Salazar, Huertas and Domingo; 1b. National dance.

1954. Surch in figures.

557	-	3c. on 1c. red (No. 406) (postage)	25	25
558	167	1c. on 5c. red (air)	25	25
559	167	1c. on 10c. blue	25	25

170 Gen. Herrera at Conference Table

1954. Death Centenary of Gen. Herrera.

560	-	3c. violet (postage)	25	20
561	170	6c. green (air)	25	20
562	-	1b. black and red	3·75	2·75

DESIGNS—VERT: 3c. Equestrian statue. HORIZ: 1b. Cavalry charge.

171 Rotary Emblem and Map

1955. Air. 50th Anniv of Rotary International.

563	171	6c. violet	25	20
564	171	21c. red	70	40
565	171	1b. black	5·50	3·50

172 Tocumen Airport

1955

566	172	½c. brown	50	20

173 President Remon Cantera

1955. National Mourning for Pres. Remon Cantera.

567	173	3c. black & pur (postage)	25	20
568	173	6c. black and violet (air)	25	20

174 V. de la Guardia y Azala and M. Chiaria

1955. Centenary of Cocle Province.

569	174	5c. violet	40	20

175 F. de Lesseps

1955. 150th Birth Anniv of De Lesseps (engineer).

570	175	3c. lake on pink (postage)	60	20
571	-	25c. blue on blue	2·40	1·60
572	-	50c. violet on lilac	3·00	1·80
573	-	5c. myrtle on green (air)	40	20
574	-	1b. black and mauve	5·25	2·75

DESIGNS—VERT: 5c. P. J. Sosa; 50c. T. Roosevelt. HORIZ: 25c. First excavations for Panama Canal; 1b. "Ancon I" (first ship to pass through canal) and De Lesseps.

1955. Air. No. 564 surch.

575	171	15c. on 21c. red	60	45

177 Pres. Eisenhower (United States)

178 Bolivar Statue

1956. Air. Pan-American Congress, Panama and 30th Anniv of First Congress.

576	-	6c. black and blue	50	30
577	-	6c. black and bistre	50	30
578	-	6c. black and green	50	30
579	-	6c. sepia and green	50	30
580	-	6c. green and yellow	50	30
581	-	6c. green and violet	50	30
582	-	6c. blue and lilac	50	30
583	-	6c. green and purple	50	30
584	-	6c. blue and olive	50	30
585	-	6c. sepia and yellow	50	30
586	-	6c. blue and sepia	50	30
587	-	6c. green and mauve	50	30
588	-	6c. sepia and red	50	30
589	-	6c. green and blue	50	30
590	-	6c. sepia and blue	50	30
591	-	6c. black and orange	50	30
592	-	6c. sepia and grey	50	30
593	-	6c. black and pink	50	30
594	177	6c. blue and red	50	30
595	-	6c. blue and grey	50	30
596	-	6c. green and brown	50	30
597	178	20c. grey	1·30	90
598	-	50c. green	1·90	1·60
599	-	1b. sepia	4·50	2·75

PRESIDENTIAL PORTRAITS as Type **177**: No. 576, Argentina; 577, Bolivia; 578, Brazil; 579, Chile; 580, Colombia; 581, Costa Rica; 582, Cuba; 583, Dominican Republic; 584, Ecuador; 585, Guatemala; 586, Haiti; 587, Honduras; 588, Mexico; 589, Nicaragua; 590, Panama; 591, Paraguay; 592, Peru; 593, Salvador; 595, Uruguay; 596, Venezuela. As Type **178**—HORIZ: No. 598, Bolivar Hall. VERT: No. 599, Bolivar Medallion.

179 Arms of Panama City

1956. 6th Inter-American Congress of Municipalities, Panama City.

600	179	3c. green (postage)	25	20
601	-	25c. red (air)	70	45
602	-	50c. black	1·40	1·10

MS603 125×76 mm. Nos. 600/2. Imperf (sold at 85c.) 3·25 3·25

DESIGNS: 25c. Stone bridge, Old Panama; 50c. Town Hall, Panama.

180 Pres. Carlos A. Mendoza

1956. Birth Centenary of Pres. Carlos A. Mendoza.

604	180	10c. green and red	40	25

182 Dr. Belisario Porras

1956. Birth Centenary of Dr. Porras.

605	-	15c. grey (postage)	75	30
606	182	25c. blue and red	1·20	65
607	-	5c. green (air)	30	25
608	-	15c. red	50	30

DESIGNS—HORIZ: 15c. (No. 605), National Archives; 15c. (No. 608), St. Thomas's Hospital. VERT: 5c. Porras Monument.

183 Isthmus Highway

1957. 7th Pan-American Highway Congress.

609	183	3c. green (postage)	30	20
610	-	10c. black (air)	30	20
611	-	20c. black and blue	70	55
612	-	1b. green	3·00	2·75

MS613 85c. No. **MS**603 optd **VII CONGRESO INTERAMERICANO DE CARRETERAS 1957** 17·00 17·00

DESIGNS—VERT: 10c. Highway under construction; 20c. Darien Forest; 1b. Map of Pan-American Highway.

1957. Air. Surch 1957 x 10c x.

614	173	10c. on 6c. black & violet	30	25

185 Manuel E. Batista

1957. Birth Centenary of Manuel Espinosa Batista (independence leader).

615	185	5c. blue and green	25	20

186 Portobelo Castle

1957. Air. Buildings. Centres in black.

616	186	10c. grey	30	25
617	-	10c. purple	30	25
618	-	10c. violet	30	25
619	-	10c. grey and green	30	25
620	-	10c. blue	30	25
621	-	10c. brown	30	25
622	-	10c. orange	30	25
623	-	10c. light blue	30	25
624	-	1b. red	3·00	1·90

DESIGNS—HORIZ: No. 617, San Jeronimo Castle; 618, Portobelo Customs-house; 619, Panama Hotel; 620, Pres. Remon Cantera Stadium; 621, Palace of Justice; 622, Treasury; 623, San Lorenzo Castle. VERT: No. 624, Jose Remon Clinics.

1957. Surch 1957 and value.

625	172	1c. on ½c. brown	20	20
626	172	3c. on ½c. brown	25	20

1958. Air. Surch 1958 and value.

627	170	5c. on 6c. green	35	20

189 U.N. Emblem

1958. Air. 10th Anniv of U.N.O.

628	189	10c. green	25	20
629	189	21c. blue	50	30
630	189	50c. orange	1·30	1·00
631	-	1b. red, blue and grey	2·50	1·90

MS632 127×102 mm. Nos. 628/31. Imperf (sold at 2b.) 6·75 6·50

DESIGN: 1b. Flags of Panama and United Nations.

1958. No. 547 surch 3c 1958.

633	3c. on 12c. purple	25	20

191 Flags Emblem

1958. 10th Anniv of Organization of American States. Emblem (T 191) multicoloured within yellow and black circular band; background colours given below.

634	191	1c. grey (postage)	25	20
635	191	2c. green	25	20
636	191	3c. red	30	20
637	191	7c. blue	30	25
638	191	5c. blue (air)	25	20
639	191	10c. red	30	25
640	-	50c. black, yellow and grey	75	75
641	191	1b. black	2·40	1·90

DESIGN—VERT: 50c. Headquarters building.

192 Brazilian Pavilion

1958. Brussels International Exhbition.

642	192	1c. green & yellow (postage)	20	20
643	-	3c. green and blue	25	20
644	-	5c. slate and brown	25	25
645	-	10c. brown and blue	30	25
646	-	15c. violet and grey (air)	30	30
647	-	50c. brown and slate	75	75
648	-	1b. turquoise and lilac	1·70	1·70

MS649 130×105 mm. Nos. 642/8 (sold at 2b.) 5·75 5·50

DESIGNS—PAVILIONS: As Type **192**: 3c. Argentina; 5c. Venezuela; 10c. Great Britain; 15c. Vatican City; 50c. United States; 1b. Belgium.

193 Pope Pius XII

1959. Pope Pius XII Commemoration.

650	**193**	3c. brown (postage)	25	20
651	-	5c. violet (air)	25	25
652	-	30c. mauve	70	45
653	-	50c. grey	95	75
MS654 127×86 mm. Nos. 650/3. Imperf (sold at 1b.)			2·40	2·30

PORTRAITS (Pope Pius XII): 5c. when Cardinal; 30c. wearing Papal tiara; 50c. enthroned.

194 Children on Farm

1959. Obligatory Tax. Youth Rehabilitation Institute. Size 35×24 mm.

655	**194**	1c. grey and red	25	20

195 U.N. Headquarters, New York

1959. 10th Anniv of Declaration of Human Rights.

656	**195**	3c. olive & brown (postage)	25	20
657	-	15c. green and orange	45	30
658	-	5c. blue and green (air)	25	20
659	-	10c. brown and grey	30	25
660	-	20c. slate and brown	30	30
661	-	50c. blue and green	85	75
662	**195**	1b. blue and red	1·70	1·70

DESIGNS: 5c., 15c. Family looking towards light; 10c., 20c. U.N. emblem and torch; 50c. U.N. flag.

1959. 8th Latin-American Economic Commission Congress. Nos. 656/61 optd 8A REUNION C.E.P.A.L. MAYO 1959 or surch also.

663		3c. olive and brown (postage)	20	20
664	-	15c. green and orange	45	25
665	-	5c. blue and green (air)	25	25
666	-	10c. brown and grey	30	25
667	-	20c. slate and brown	50	30
668	-	1b. on 50c. blue and green	2·40	2·30
MS669 No. **MS**654, but larger in two lines (sold at 1b.)			6·75	6·50

197 J. A. Facio

1959. 50th Anniv of National Institute.

670		3c. red (postage)	20	20
671		13c. green	50	25
672		21c. blue	75	40
673	**197**	5c. black (air)	20	20
674	-	10c. black	25	20

DESIGNS—VERT: 3c. E. A. Morales (founder); 10c. Ernesto de la Guardia, Nr; 13c. A. Bravo. HORIZ: 21c. National Institute building.

1959. Obligatory Tax. Youth Rehabilitation Institute. As No. 655, but colours changed and inscr "1959".

675	**194**	1c. green and black	25	20
676	**194**	1c. blue and black	25	20

See also No. 690.

198 Football

1959. 3rd Pan-American Games, Chicago. Inscr "III JUEGOS DEPORTIVOS PANAMERICANOS".

677	**198**	1c. green & grey (postage)	20	20
678	-	3c. brown and blue	40	20
679	-	20c. brown and green	1·80	1·10
680	-	5c. brown and black (air)	40	30
681	-	10c. brown and grey	75	40
682	-	50c. brown and blue	3·00	1·70

DESIGNS: 3c. Swimming; 5c. Boxing; 10c. Baseball; 20c. Hurdling; 50c. Basketball.

1960. Air. World Refugee Year. Nos. 554/6 optd NACIONES UNIDAS ANO MUNDIAL. REFUGIADOS. 1959–1960.

683		25c. black	95	30
684		50c. brown	1·40	45
685		1b. orange	2·10	1·50

200 Administration Building

1960. Air. 25th Anniv of National University.

686	**200**	10c. green	25	20
687	-	21c. blue	60	25
688	-	25c. blue	85	45
689	-	30c. black	1·10	50

DESIGNS: 21c. Faculty of Science; 25c. Faculty of Medicine; 30c. Statue of Dr. Octavio Mendez Pereira (first rector) and Faculty of Law.

1960. Obligatory Tax. Youth Rehabilitation Institute. As No. 655 but smaller (32×22 mm) and inscr "1960".

690	**194**	1c. grey and red	20	20

202 Fencing

1960. Olympic Games.

691	**202**	3c. purple & violet (postage)	25	20
692	-	5c. green and turquoise	50	20
693	-	5c. red and orange (air)	25	20
694	-	10c. black and bistre	60	30
695	-	25c. deep blue and blue	1·30	70
696	-	50c. black and brown	2·50	1·30
MS697 127×76 mm. Nos. 695/6. Imperf (sold at 80c.)			4·75	4·75

DESIGNS—VERT: 5c. (No. 692), Football; (No. 693), Basketball; 25c. Javelin-throwing; 50c. Runner with Olympic Flame. HORIZ: 10c. Cycling.

204 "Population"

1960. Air. 6th National Census (5c.) and Central American Census.

698	**204**	5c. black	20	20
699	-	10c. brown	25	25

DESIGN: 10c. Two heads and map.

205 Boeing 707 Airliner

1960. Air.

700	**205**	5c. blue	25	20
701	**205**	10c. green	30	20
702	**205**	20c. brown	50	30

206 Pastoral Scene

1961. Agricultural Census (16th April).

703	**206**	3c. turquoise	25	20

206a U.N. Emblem

1961. Air. 15th Anniv of United Nations (1960). Sheet 65×77 mm. Imperf.

MS704 80c. cerise and black		2·50	2·40

207 Helen Keller School

1961. 25th Anniv of Lions Club.

705	-	3c. blue (postage)	25	20
706	**207**	5c. black (air)	25	25
707	-	10c. green	35	25
708	-	21c. blue, red and yellow	40	30

DESIGNS: 3c. Nino Hospital; 10c. Children's Colony, Verano; 21c. Lions emblem, arms and slogan.

1961. Air. Obligatory Tax. Youth Rehabilitation Fund. Surch 1 c "Rehabilitacion de Menores".

709		1c. on 10c. black and bistre (No. 694)	25	20
710	**205**	1c. on 10c. green	25	20

1961. Air. World Refugee Year (1959–60). Sheet No. MS704 optd with uprooted oak emblem and ANO DE LOS REFUGIADOS.

MS711 80c. cerise and black		4·50	4·50

1961. Air. Surch HABILITAD. en and value.

712	**200**	1c. on 10c. green	25	20
713	-	1b. on 25c. blue and blue (No. 695)	2·50	2·40

210 Flags of Costa Rica and Panama

1961. Meeting of Presidents of Costa Rica and Panama.

715	**210**	3c. red and blue (postage)	25	20
716	-	1b. black and gold (air)	3·00	2·50

DESIGN: 1b. Pres. Chiari of Panama and Pres. Echandi of Costa Rica.

211 Girl using Sewing-machine

1961. Obligatory Tax. Youth Rehabilitation Fund.

717	**211**	1c. violet	25	20
718	**211**	1c. yellow	25	20
719	**211**	1c. green	25	20
720	**211**	1c. blue	25	20
721	**211**	1c. purple	25	20
722	-	1c. mauve	25	20
723	-	1c. grey	25	20
724	-	1c. blue	25	20
725	-	1c. orange	25	20
726	-	1c. red	25	20

DESIGN: Nos. 722/6, Boy sawing wood.

212 Campaign Emblem

1961. Air. Malaria Eradication.

727	**212**	5c.+5c. red	1·40	95
728	**212**	10c.+10c. blue	1·40	95
729	**212**	15c.+15c. green	1·40	95

213 Dag Hammarskjold

1961. Air. Death of Dag Hammarskjold.

730	**213**	10c. black and grey	35	20

1962. Air. (a) Surch Vale B/.0.15.

731	**200**	15c. on 10c. green	40	30

(b) No. 810 surch XX over old value and VALE B/.1.00.

732		1b. on 25c. deep blue and blue	3·00	1·50

214 Arms of Panama

1962. 3rd Central American Inter-Municipal Co-operation Assembly.

733	**214**	3c. red, yellow and blue (postage)	30	30
734	-	5c. black and blue (air)	30	25

DESIGN—HORIZ: 5c. City Hall, Colon.

215 Mercury on Cogwheel

1962. 1st Industrial Census.

735	**215**	3c. red	20	20

1962. Surch VALE and value with old value obliterated.

736	**212**	10c. on 5c.+5c. red	1·50	1·10
737	**212**	20c. on 10c.+10c. blue	2·30	2·20

217 Social Security Hospital

1962. Opening of Social Security Hospital, Panama City.

738	**217**	3c. black and red	25	20

218 Colon Cathedral

1962. "Freedom of Worship". Inscr "LIBERTAD DE CULTOS". Centres in black.

No.	Type	Description	Mint	Used
739	-	1c. red and blue (postage)	20	20
740	-	2c. red and cream	20	20
741	-	3c. blue and cream	25	20
742	-	5c. red and green	25	25
743	-	10c. green and cream	30	25
744	-	10c. mauve and blue	30	25
745	-	15c. blue and green	35	30
746	218	20c. red and pink	60	35
747	-	25c. green and pink	70	50
748	-	50c. blue and pink	1·30	65
749	-	1b. violet and cream	2·75	2·00

DESIGNS—HORIZ: 1c. San Francisco de Veraguas Church; 3c. David Cathedral; 25c. Orthodox Greek Temple; 1b. Colon Protestant Church. VERT: 2c. Panama Old Cathedral; 5c. Nata Church; 10c. Don Bosco Temple; 15c. Virgin of Carmen Church; 50c. Panama Cathedral.

No.	Description	Mint	Used
750	5c. violet and flesh (air)	20	20
751	7c. light mauve and mauve	25	20
752	8c. violet and blue	25	20
753	10c. violet and salmon	25	20
754	10c. green and purple	25	25
755	15c. red and orange	35	25
756	21c. sepia and blue	60	50
757	25c. blue and pink	70	45
758	30c. mauve and blue	75	55
759	50c. purple and green	1·10	75
760	1b. blue and salmon	2·20	1·50
MS761	132×107 mm. Nos. 747/8, 757 and 759. Imperf	6·25	6·00

DESIGNS—HORIZ: 5c. Cristo Rey Church; 7c. San Miguel Church; 21c. Canal Zone Synagogue; 25c. Panama Synagogue; 50c. Canal Zone Protestant Church. VERT: 8c. Santuario Church; 10c. Los Santos Church; 15c. Santa Ana Church; 30c. San Francisco Church; 1b. Canal Zone Catholic Church.

1962. Air. 9th Central American and Caribbean Games, Jamaica. Nos. 693 and 695 optd "IX JUEGOS C.A. Y DEL CARIBE KINGSTON - 1962" or surch also.

No.	Description	Mint	Used
762	5c. red and orange	20	20
764	10c. on 25c. deep blue & blue	70	45
765	15c. on 25c. deep blue & blue	85	60
766	20c. on 25c. deep blue & blue	95	65
763	25c. deep blue and blue	1·10	90

220 Thatcher Ferry Bridge nearing Completion

1962. Opening of Thatcher Ferry Bridge, Canal Zone.

No.	Type	Description	Mint	Used
767	220	3c. black and red (postage)	25	20
768	-	10c. black and blue (air)	25	20

DESIGN: 10c. Completed bridge.

221 Col. Glenn and Capsule "Friendship 7"

1962. Air. Col. Glenn's Space Flight.

No.	Type	Description	Mint	Used
769	221	5c. red	20	20
770	-	10c. yellow	40	30
771	-	31c. blue	1·60	95
772	-	50c. green	1·90	1·40
MS773		77×110 mm. Nos. 769/72. Imperf (sold at 1b.)	4·25	4·25

DESIGNS—HORIZ: "Friendship": 10c. Over Earth; 31c. In space. VERT: 50c. Col. Glenn.

222 U.P.A.E. Emblem

1963. Air. 50th Anniv of Postal Union of Americas and Spain.

No.	Type	Description	Mint	Used
774	222	10c. multicoloured	40	20

223 Water Exercise

1963. 75th Anniv of Panama Fire Brigade.

No.	Type	Description	Mint	Used
775	223	1c. black & green (postage)	20	20
776	-	3c. black and blue	25	20
777	-	5c. black and red	30	20
778	-	10c. black and orange (air)	40	25
779	-	15c. black and purple	50	30
780	-	21c. blue, gold and red	95	75

DESIGNS: 3c. Brigade officers; 5c. Brigade president and advisory council; 10c. "China" pump in action, 1887; 15c. "Cable 14" station and fire-engine; 21c. Fire Brigade badge.

1963. Air. Red Cross Cent (1st issue). Nos. 769/71 surch with red cross 1863 1963 and premium.

No.	Type	Description	Mint	Used
781	215	5c.+5c. red	1·60	1·50
782	-	10c.+10c. yellow	3·50	3·00
783	-	31c.+15c. blue	3·50	3·00

See also No. 797.

225 F.A.O. Emblem

1963. Air. Freedom from Hunger.

No.	Type	Description	Mint	Used
784	225	10c. red and green	40	30
785	225	15c. red and blue	50	40

1963. Air. 22nd Central American Lions Convention. Optd "XXII Convencion Leonistica Centroamericana Panama, 18-21 Abril 1963".

No.	Type	Description	Mint	Used
786	207	5c. black	75	20

1963. Air. Surch HABILITADO Vale B./0.04.

No.	Type	Description	Mint	Used
789	200	4c. in 10c. green	30	20

1963. Air. Nos. 743 and 769 optd AEREO vert.

No.	Description	Mint	Used
790	10c. green and cream	30	20
791	20c. brown and green	70	40

1963. Air. Freedom of the Press. No. 693 optd LIBERTAD DE PRENSA 20-VIII-63.

No.	Description	Mint	Used
792	5c. red and orange	30	20

1963. Air. Visit of U.S. Astronauts to Panama. Optd "Visita Astronautas Glenn-Schirra Sheppard Cooper a Panama" or surch also.

No.	Type	Description	Mint	Used
793	221	5c. red	3·50	3·25
794	221	10c. on 5c. red	4·75	4·75
MS795		77×100 mm. No. **MS**773 (sold at 1b.)	55·00	50·00

1963. Air. Surch HABILITADO 10c.

No.	Description	Mint	Used
796	10c. on 5c. red	9·75	9·25

1963. Air. Red Cross Centenary (2nd issue). No. 781 surch "Centenario Cruz Roja Internacional 10c" with premium obliterated.

No.	Description	Mint	Used
797	10c. on 5c.+5c. red	7·75	6·00

1963. Surch VALE and value.

No.	Type	Description	Mint	Used
798	217	4c. on 3c. black and red (postage)	25	20
799	-	4c. on 3c. black, blue and cream (No. 741)	25	20
800	220	4c. on 3c. black and red	25	20
801	-	4c. on 3c. black and blue (No. 776)	25	20
802	182	10c. on 25c. blue and red	45	25
803	-	10c. on 25c. blue (No. 688) (air)	35	20

234 Pres. Orlich (Costa Rica) and Flags

1963. Presidential Reunion, San Jose (Costa Rica). Multicoloured. Presidents and flags of their countries.

No.	Description	Mint	Used
804	1c. Type **234** (postage)	20	20
805	2c. Somoza (Nicaragua)	20	20
806	3c. Villeda (Honduras)	25	20
807	4c. Chiari (Panama)	30	25
808	5c. Rivera (El Salvador) (air)	30	30
809	10c. Ydigoras (Guatemala)	60	35
810	21c. Kennedy (U.S.A.)	1·60	1·20

235 Innsbruck

1963. Winter Olympic Games, Innsbruck.

No.	Description	Mint	Used
811	½c. red and blue (postage)	20	10
812	1c. red, brown and turquoise	20	10
813	3c. red and blue	60	25
814	4c. red, brown and green	70	30
815	5c. red, brown and mauve (air)	85	35
816	15c. red, brown and blue	1·60	95
817	21c. red, brown and myrtle	2·75	1·40
818	31c. red, brown and blue	3·75	2·40
MS819	100×65 mm. Nos. 817/18 but colours changed. Imperf	21·00	20·00

DESIGNS: ½c. (expressed "B/0.005"), 3c. Type **235**; 1, 4c. Speed-skating; 5c. to 31c. Skiing (slalom).

236 Vasco Nunez de Balboa

1964. 450th Anniv of Discovery of Pacific Ocean.

No.	Type	Description	Mint	Used
820	236	4c. green on flesh (postage)	25	20
821	236	10c. violet on pink (air)	30	30

237 Boy Scout

1964. Obligatory Tax for Youth Rehabilitation Institute.

No.	Type	Description	Mint	Used
822	237	1c. red	25	20
823	237	1c. grey	25	20
824	237	1c. light blue	25	20
825	237	1c. olive	25	20
826	237	1c. violet	25	20
827	-	1c. brown	25	20
828	-	1c. orange	25	20
829	-	1c. turquoise	25	20
830	-	1c. violet	25	20
831	-	1c. yellow	25	20

DESIGN: Nos. 827/31, Girl guide.

238 St. Paul's Cathedral, London

1964. Air. Ecumenical Council, Vatican City (1st issue). Cathedrals. Centres in black.

No.	Description	Mint	Used
832	21c. red (Type **238**)	1·50	1·10
833	21c. blue (Kassa, Hungary)	1·50	1·10
834	21c. green (Milan)	1·50	1·10
835	21c. black (St. John's, Poland)	1·50	1·10
836	21c. brown (St. Stephen's, Vienna)	1·50	1·10
837	21c. brown (Notre Dame, Paris)	1·50	1·10
838	21c. violet (Moscow)	1·50	1·10
839	21c. violet (Lima)	1·50	1·10
840	21c. red (Stockholm)	1·50	1·10
841	21c. mauve (Cologne)	1·50	1·10
842	21c. bistre (New Delhi)	1·50	1·10
843	21c. deep turquoise (Basel)	1·50	1·10
844	21c. green (Toledo)	1·50	1·10
845	21c. red (Metropolitan, Athens)	1·50	1·10
846	21c. olive (St. Patrick's, New York)	1·50	1·10
847	21c. green (Lisbon)	1·50	1·10
848	21c. turquoise (Sofia)	1·50	1·10
849	21c. deep brown (New Church, Delft, Netherlands)	1·50	1·10
850	21c. deep sepia (St. George's Patriarchal Church, Istanbul)	1·50	1·10
851	21c. blue (Basilica, Guadalupe, Mexico)	1·50	1·10
852	1b. blue (Panama)	8·25	7·00
853	2b. green (St. Peter's, Rome)	15·00	13·00
MS854	198×138 mm. Nos. 832, 837/8, 846 and 852/3. Imperf (sold at 3b.85)	16·00	16·00

See also Nos. 822/**MS**888.

1964. As Nos. 749 and 760 but colours changed and optd HABILITADA.

No.	Description	Mint	Used
855	1b. black, red & blue (postage)	3·00	2·30
856	1b. black, green & yellow (air)	3·25	2·75

1964. Air. No. 756 surch VALE B/. 0.50.

No.	Description	Mint	Used
857	50c. on 21c. black, sepia and blue	1·90	1·20

241 Discus-thrower

1964. Olympic Games, Tokyo.

No.	Description	Mint	Used
858	½c. ("B/0.005") purple, red, brown and green (postage)	15	15
859	1c. multicoloured	20	15
860	5c. black, red and olive (air)	40	30
861	10c. black, red and yellow	70	35
862	21c. multicoloured	1·40	75
863	50c. multicoloured	2·50	1·50
MS864	66×95 mm. No. 863	21·00	20·00

DESIGNS: ½c. Type **241**; 1c. Runner with Olympic Flame; 5c. to 50c. Olympic Stadium, Tokyo, and Mt. Fuji.

1964. Air. Nos. 692 and 742 surch Aereo B/.0.10.

No.	Description	Mint	Used
865	10c. on 5c. green and turquoise	35	20
866	10c. on 5c. black, red and green	35	20

243 Space Vehicles (Project "Apollo")

1964. Space Exploration. Multicoloured.

No.	Description	Mint	Used
867	½c. ("B/0.005") Type **243** (postage)	15	10
868	1c. Rocket and capsule (Project "Gemini")	15	10
869	5c. W. M. Schirra (air)	35	35
870	10c. L. G. Cooper	60	45
871	21c. Schirra's capsule	1·30	1·10
872	50c. Cooper's capsule	6·25	4·50
MS873	60×95 mm. No. 872	21·00	19·00

1964. No. 687 surch Correos B/. 0.10.

No.	Description	Mint	Used
874	10c. on 21c. blue	35	25

245 Water-skiing

1964. Aquatic Sports. Multicoloured.

No.	Description	Mint	Used
875	½c. ("B/0.005") Type **245** (postage)	25	20
876	1c. Underwater swimming	25	20
877	5c. Fishing (air)	35	25
878	10c. Sailing (vert)	1·90	65
879	21c. Speedboat racing	3·50	1·20
880	31c. Water polo at Olympic Games, 1964	4·50	1·50
MS881	95×65 mm. No. 880	21·00	19·00

1964. Air. Ecumenical Council, Vatican City (2nd issue). Stamps of 1st issue optd 1964. Centres in black.

882		21c. red (No. 832)	1·20	75
883		21c. green (No. 834)	1·20	75
884		21c. olive (No. 836)	1·20	75
885		21c. deep sepia (No. 850)	1·20	75
886		1b. blue (No. 852)	4·50	3·25
887		2b. green (No. 853)	9·25	7·50
MS888		No. **MS**854 optd **1964** and coat-of-arms (sold at 3b.65)	80·00	80·00

247 General View

1964. Air. New York's World Fair.

889	**247**	5c. black and yellow	60	45
890	-	10c. black and red	1·40	1·10
891	-	15c. black and green	2·40	1·50
892	-	21c. black and blue	3·50	2·75
MS893		127×76 mm. No. 892	5·75	5·50

DESIGNS: 10c., 15c. Fair pavilions (different); 21c. Unisphere.

248 Eleanor Roosevelt

1964. Mrs. Eleanor Roosevelt Commemoration.

894	**248**	4c. black and red on yellow (postage)	30	20
895	**248**	20c. black and green on buff (air)	50	35
MS896		87×76 mm. Nos. 894/5Imperf (sold at 25c.)	2·00	1·90

249 Dag Hammarskjold

1964. Air. U.N. Day.

897	**249**	21c. black and blue	1·20	75
898	-	21c. blue and black	1·20	75
MS899		98×80 mm. No. 897/8. Imperf	6·25	6·00

DESIGN: No. 898, U.N. Emblem.

250 Pope John XXIII

1964. Air. Pope John Commemoration.

900	**250**	21c. black and bistre	95	65
901	-	21c. mult (Papal Arms)	95	65
MS902		97×80 mm. Nos. 900/1	9·25	8·75

251 Slalom Skiing Medals

1964. Winter Olympic Winners' Medals. Medals in gold, silver and bronze.

903	**251**	½c. ("B/0.005") turquoise (postage)	20	10
904	-	1c. deep blue	20	10
905	-	2c. brown	25	15
906	-	3c. mauve	50	20
907	-	4c. lake	75	40
908	-	5c. violet (air)	60	50
909	-	6c. blue	75	65
910	-	7c. violet	1·30	1·00
911	-	10c. green	1·90	1·60
912	-	21c. red	2·10	1·80
913	-	31c. blue	3·75	3·25
MS914		142×103 mm. Nos. 911/13	21·00	20·00

DESIGNS—Medals for: 1c., 7c. Speed-skating; 2c., 21c. Bobsleighing; 3c., 10c. Figure-skating; 4c. Ski-jumping; 5c., 6c., 31c. Cross-country skiing. Values in the same design show different medal-winners and country names.

252 Red-billed Toucan

1965. Birds. Multicoloured.

915		1c. Type **252** (postage)	70	20
916		2c. Scarlet macaw	70	20
917		3c. Woodpecker sp.	1·10	20
918		4c. Blue-grey tanager (horiz)	1·10	20
919		5c. Troupial (horiz) (air)	1·50	45
920		10c. Crimson-backed tanager (horiz)	2·75	45

253 Red Snapper

1965. Marine Life. Multicoloured.

921		1c. Type **253** (postage)	40	20
922		2c. Dolphin (fish)	40	20
923		8c. Shrimp (air)	50	20
924		12c. Smooth hammerhead	65	35
925		13c. Sailfish	75	45
926		25c. Lined seahorse (vert)	1·50	75

254 Double Daisy and Emblem

1966. Air. 50th Anniv of Junior Chamber of Commerce. Flowers. Multicoloured: background colour given.

927	**254**	30c. mauve	95	45
928	-	30c. flesh (Hibiscus)	95	45
929	-	30c. olive (Mauve orchid)	95	45
930	-	40c. green (Water lily)	1·40	45
931	-	40c. blue (Gladiolus)	1·40	45
932	-	40c. pink (White orchid)	1·40	45

Each design incorporates the Junior Chamber of Commerce Emblem.

1966. Surch. (a) Postage.

933	13c. on 25c. (No. 747)	50	30

(b) Air.

934	3c. on 5c. (No. 680)	30	30
935	13c. on 25c. (No. 695)	50	35

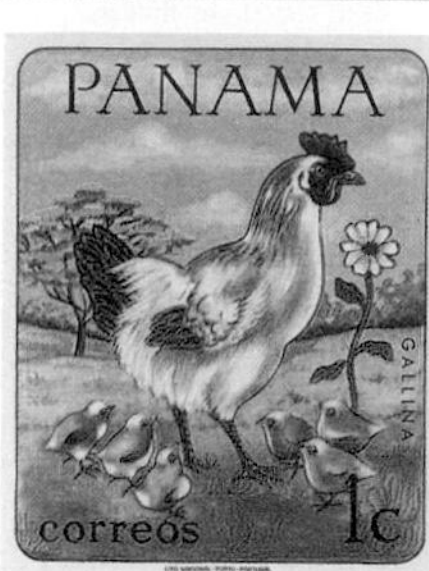

256 Chicken

1967. Domestic Animals. Multicoloured.

936	1c. Type **256** (postage)	10	10
937	3c. Cockerel	10	10
938	5c. Pig (horiz)	20	10
939	8c. Cow (horiz)	30	20
940	10c. Pekingese dog (air)	50	35
941	13c. Zebu (horiz)	60	35
942	30c. Cat	1·20	80
943	40c. Horse (horiz)	1·40	95

257 American Darter

1967. Wild Birds. Multicoloured.

944	½c. Type **257**	1·10	20
945	1c. Resplendent quetzal	1·10	20
946	3c. Turquoise-browed motmot	1·30	30
947	4c. Red-necked aracari (horiz)	1·50	30
948	5c. Chestnut-fronted macaw	1·90	30
949	13c. Belted kingfisher	7·25	1·20

258 "Deer" (F. Marc)

1967. Wild Animals. Paintings. Multicoloured.

950	1c. Type **258** (postage)	10	10
951	3c. "Cougar" (F. Marc) (vert)	10	10
952	5c. "Monkeys" (F. Marc)	20	10
953	8c. "Fox" (F. Marc)	40	10
954	10c. "St. Jerome and the Lion" (Durer) (vert) (air)	40	30
955	13c. "The Hare" (Durer) (vert)	60	35
956	20c. "Lady with the Ermine" (Da Vinci) (vert)	85	45
957	30c. "The Hunt" (Delacroix)	1·30	75

259 Map of Panama and People

1969. National Population Census.

958	**259**	5c. blue	30	30
959	-	10c. purple	45	20

DESIGN—VERT: 10c. People and map of the Americas.

260 Cogwheel

1969. 50th Anniv of Rotary Int in Panama.

960	**260**	13c. black, yellow and blue	45	20

261 Cornucopia and Map

1969. 1st Anniv of 11 October Revolution.

961	**261**	10c. multicoloured	40	20

262 Tower and Map

1969

962	**262**	3c. black and orange	15	10
963	-	5c. green	20	10
964	-	8c. brown	25	20
965	-	13c. black and green	35	20
966	-	20c. brown	50	30
967	-	21c. yellow	50	35
968	-	25c. green	70	35
969	-	30c. black	85	55
970	-	34c. brown	1·10	55
971	-	38c. blue	1·20	55
972	-	40c. yellow	1·40	75
973	-	50c. black and purple	1·50	90
974	-	59c. purple	2·10	95

DESIGNS—HORIZ: 5c. Peasants; 13c. Hotel Continental; 25c. Del Rey Bridge; 34c. Panama Cathedral; 38c. Municipal Palace; 40c. French Plaza; 50c. Thatcher Ferry Bridge; 59c. National Theatre. VERT: 8c. Nata Church; 20c. Virgin of Carmen Church; 21c. Altar, San Jose Church; 30c. Dr. Arosemena statue.

263 Discus-thrower and Stadium

1970. 11th Central American and Caribbean Games, Panama (1st series).

975	**263**	1c. multicoloured (postage)	15	10
976	**263**	2c. multicoloured	15	10
977	**263**	3c. multicoloured	15	10
978	**263**	5c. multicoloured	15	10
979	**263**	10c. multicoloured	20	20
980	**263**	13c. multicoloured	30	20
981	-	13c. multicoloured	35	20
982	**263**	25c. multicoloured	1·00	75
983	**263**	30c. multicoloured	1·20	80
984	-	13c. multicoloured (air)	1·00	40
985	-	30c. multicoloured	1·20	80

DESIGNS—VERT: No. 981, "Flor del Espirited Santo" (flowers); 985, Indian girl. HORIZ: No. 984, Thatcher Ferry Bridge and palm.

See also Nos. 986/94.

264 J. D. Arosemena and Stadium

1970. Air. 11th Central American and Caribbean Games, Panama (2nd series). Multicoloured.

986	1c. Type **264**	15	15
987	2c. Type **264**	15	15
988	3c. Type **264**	15	15
989	5c. Type **264**	20	15
990	13c. Basketball	45	20
991	13c. New Gymnasium	45	20
992	13c. Revolution Stadium	45	20
993	13c. Panamanian couple in festive costume	45	20
994	30c. Eternal Flame and stadium	1·20	65
MS995	85×75 mm. No. 994. Imperf	2·10	2·00

265 A. Tapia and M. Sosa (first comptrollers)

1971. 40th Anniv of Panamanian Comptroller-General's Office. Multicoloured.

996	3c. Comptroller-General's Building (1970) (vert)	15	10
997	5c. Type **265**	15	10
998	8c. Comptroller-General's emblem (vert)	20	15
999	13c. Comptroller-General's Building (1955–70)	25	15

266 "Man and Alligator"

1971. Indian Handicrafts.

1000	**266**	8c. multicoloured	80	25

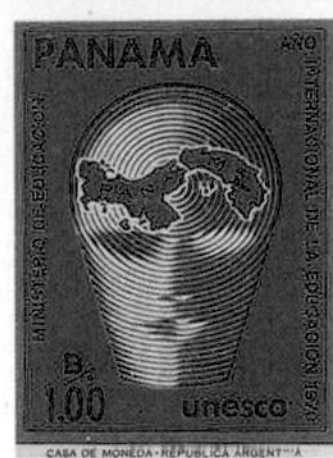

267 Map of Panama on I.E.Y. Emblem

1971. International Education Year.

1001	**267**	1b. multicoloured	3·50	3·00

268 Astronaut on Moon

1971. Air. "Apollo 11" and "Apollo 12" Moon Missions. Multicoloured.

1002	13c. Type **268**	60	40
1003	13c. "Apollo 12" astronauts	60	40

269 Panama Pavilion

1971. Air. "EXPO 70" World Fair, Osaka, Japan.

1004	**269**	10c. multicoloured	25	25

270 Conference Text and Emblem

1971. 9th Inter-American Loan and Savings Association Conference, Panama City.

1005	**270**	25c. multicoloured	95	75

271 Panama Flag

1971. Air. American Tourist Year. Multicoloured.

1006	5c. Type **271**	15	10
1007	13c. Map of Panama and Western Hemisphere	45	25

272 New U.P.U. H.Q. Building

1971. Inauguration of New U.P.U. Headquarters Building, Berne. Multicoloured.

1008	8c. Type **272**	25	10
1009	30c. U.P.U. Monument, Berne (vert)	1·00	75

273 Cow and Pig

1971. 3rd Agricultural Census.

1010	**273**	3c. multicoloured	25	20

274 Map and "4S" Emblem

1971. "4S" Programme for Rural Youth.

1011	**274**	2c. multicoloured	20	20

275 Gandhi

1971. Air. Birth Centenary (1969) of Mahatma Gandhi.

1012	**275**	10c. multicoloured	70	40

276 Central American Flags

1971. Air. 150th Anniv of Central American States' Independence from Spain.

1013	**276**	13c. multicoloured	35	25

277 Early Panama Stamp

1971. Air. 2nd National, Philatelic and Numismatic Exhibition, Panama.

1014	**277**	8c. blue, black and red	25	20

278 Altar, Nata Church

1972. Air. 450th Anniv of Nata Church.

1015	**278**	40c. multicoloured	85	75

279 Telecommunications Emblem

1972. Air. World Telecommunications Day.

1016	**279**	13c. black, blue & lt blue	50	40

280 "Apollo 14" Badge

1972. Air. Moon Flight of "Apollo 14".

1017	**280**	13c. multicoloured	85	60

281 Children on See-saw

1972. 25th Anniv (1971) of UNICEF. Mult.

1018	1c. Type **281** (postage)	10	10
1019	5c. Boy sitting by kerb (vert) (air)	15	10
1020	8c. Indian mother and child (vert)	25	25
1021	50c. UNICEF emblem (vert)	1·30	65
MS1022	86×75 mm. No. 1021. Imperf	1·70	1·70

282 Tropical Fruits

1972. Tourist Publicity. Multicoloured.

1023	1c. Type **282** (postage)	10	10
1024	2c. "Isle of Night"	10	10
1025	3c. Carnival float (vert)	15	10
1026	5c. San Blas textile (air)	15	15
1027	8c. Chaquira (beaded collar)	25	15
1028	25c. Ruined fort, Portobelo	80	60
MS1029	96×120 mm. Nos. 1026 and 1028. Imperf	3·50	2·50

283 Map and Flags

1973. Obligatory Tax. Panama City Post Office Building Fund. 7th Bolivar Games.

1030	**283**	1c. black	20	15

284 Baseball Players

1973. Air. 7th Bolivar Games.

1031	**284**	8c. red and yellow	25	15
1032	-	10c. black and blue	25	20
1033	-	13c. multicoloured	35	25
1034	-	25c. black, red and green	70	35
1035	-	50c. multicoloured	1·50	80
1036	-	1b. multicoloured	3·00	1·50

DESIGNS—VERT: 10c. Basketball; 13c. Flaming torch. HORIZ: 25c. Boxing; 50c. Panama map and flag, Games emblem and Bolivar; 1b. Games' medals.

1973. U.N. Security Council Meeting, Panama City. Various stamps surch O.N.U. in laurel leaf, CONSEJO DE SEGURIDAD 15 - 21 Marzo 1973 and value.

1037	8c. on 59c. (No. 974) (postage)	15	15
1038	10c. on 1b. (No. 1001)	20	15
1039	13c. on 30c. (No. 969)	35	20
1040	13c. on 40c. (No. 1015) (air)	45	25

286 Farming Co-operative

1973. Obligatory Tax. Post Office Building Fund.

1041	**286**	1c. green and red	45	25
1042	-	1c. grey and red	45	25
1043	-	1c. yellow and red	45	25
1044	-	1c. orange and red	45	25
1045	-	1c. blue and red	45	25

DESIGNS: No. 1042, Silver coins; 1043, V. Lorenzo; 1044, Cacique Urraca; 1045, Post Office building.

See also Nos. 1061/2.

287 J. D. Crespo (educator)

1973. Famous Panamanians. Multicoloured.

1046	3c. Type **287** (postage)	15	10
1047	5c. Isabel Obaldia (educator) (air)	15	10
1048	8c. N. V. Jaen (educator)	25	20
1049	10c. "Forest Scene" (Roberto Lewis, painter)	35	25
1050	13c. R. Miro (poet)	50	25
1051	13c. "Portrait of a Lady" (M. E. Amador, painter)	50	25
1052	20c. "Self-Portrait" (Isaac Benitez, painter)	70	40
1053	21c. M. A. Guerrero (statesman)	80	50
1054	25c. Dr. B. Porras (statesman)	85	50
1055	30c. J. D. Arosemena (statesman)	1·00	60
1056	34c. Dr. O. M. Pereira (writer)	1·10	70
1057	38c. Dr. R. J. Alfaro (writer)	1·30	80

1973. Air. 50th Anniv of Isabel Obaldia Professional School. Nos. 1047, 1054 and 1056 optd 1923 1973 Godas de Oro Escuela Profesional Isabel Herrera Obaldia and EP emblem.

1058	5c. multicoloured	15	10
1059	25c. multicoloured	85	50
1060	34c. multicoloured	1·10	85

1974. Obligatory Tax. Post Office Building Fund. As Nos. 1044/5.

1061	1c. orange	45	25
1062	2c. blue	45	25

1974. Surch VALE and value.

1063	5c. on 30c. black (No. 969) (postage)	15	15
1064	10c. on 34c. brown (No. 970)	25	15
1065	13c. on 21c. yellow (No. 967)	25	20
1066	1c. on 25c. multicoloured (No. 1028) (air)	10	10
1067	3c. on 20c. mult (No. 1052)	10	10
1068	8c. on 38c. mult (No. 1057)	20	15
1069	10c. on 34c. mult (No. 1056)	25	20
1070	13c. on 21c. mult (No. 1053)	25	20

290 Women's upraised Hands

1975. Air. International Women's Year.

1071	**290**	17c. multicoloured	70	40

291 Bayano Dam

1975. Air. 7th Anniv of October 1968 Revolution.

1073	**291**	17c. black, brown & blue	70	40
1074	-	27c. blue and green	95	65
1075	-	33c. multicoloured	1·10	75

DESIGNS—VERT: 27c. Victoria sugar plant, Veraguas, and sugar cane. HORIZ: 33c. Tocumen International Airport.

1975. Obligatory Tax. Various stamps surch VALE PRO EDIFICIO and value.

1076	1c. on 30c. black (No. 969) (postage)	25	20

1077		1c. on 40c. yellow (No. 972)	25	20
1078		1c. on 50c. black and purple (No. 973)	25	20
1079		1c. on 30c. mult (No. 1009)	25	20
1080	282	1c. on 1c. multicoloured	25	20
1081	-	1c. on 2c. multicoloured (No. 1024)	25	20
1082	278	1c. on 40c. mult (air)	25	20
1083	-	1c. on 25c. mult (No. 1028)	25	20
1084	-	1c. on 25c. mult (No. 1052)	25	20
1085	-	1c. on 20c. mult (No. 1054)	25	20
1086	-	1c. on 30c. mult (No. 1055)	25	20

1975. Obligatory Tax. Post Office Building Fund. As No. 1045.

1087	1c. red	45	25

294 Bolivar and Thatcher Ferry Bridge

1976. 150th Anniv of Panama Congress (1st issue). Multicoloured.

1088	6c. Type **294** (postage)	15	10
1089	23c. Bolivar Statue (air)	60	25
1090	35c. Bolivar Hall, Panama City (horiz)	95	40
1091	41c. Bolivar and flag	1·00	75

295 "Evibacus princeps"

1976. Marine Fauna. Multicoloured.

1092	2c. Type **295** (postage)	45	20
1093	3c. "Ptitosarcus sinuosus" (vert)	45	20
1094	4c. "Acanthaster planci"	45	20
1095	7c. "Oreaster reticulatus"	45	25
1096	17c. Porcupinefish (vert) (air)	85	35
1097	27c. "Pocillopora damicornis"	1·30	50
MS1098	100×100 mm. 1b. *Mithrax spinossimus*. Imperf	5·25	5·00

296 "Simon Bolivar"

1976. 150th Anniv of Panama Congress (2nd issue). Designs showing details of Bolivar Monument or flags of Latin-American countries. Multicoloured.

1099	20c. Type **296**	60	60
1100	20c. Argentina	60	60
1101	20c. Bolivia	60	60
1102	20c. Brazil	60	60
1103	20c. Chile	60	60
1104	20c. "Battle scene"	60	60
1105	20c. Colombia	60	60
1106	20c. Costa Rica	60	60
1107	20c. Cuba	60	60
1108	20c. Ecuador	60	60
1109	20c. El Salvador	60	60
1110	20c. Guatemala	60	60
1111	20c. Guyana	60	60
1112	20c. Haiti	60	60
1113	20c. "Congress assembly"	60	60
1114	20c. "Liberated people"	60	60
1115	20c. Honduras	60	60
1116	20c. Jamaica	60	60
1117	20c. Mexico	60	60
1118	20c. Nicaragua	60	60
1119	20c. Panama	60	60
1120	20c. Paraguay	60	60
1121	20c. Peru	60	60
1122	20c. Dominican Republic	60	60
1123	20c. "Bolivar and standard-bearer"	60	60
1124	20c. Surinam	60	60
1125	20c. Trinidad and Tobago	60	60
1126	20c. Uruguay	60	60
1127	20c. Venezuela	60	60
1128	20c. "Indian Delegation"	60	60
MS1129	81×122 mm. 30c. Bolivar and flag-bearer; 30c. Top of Monument; 40c. Inscribed tablet. Perf or Imperf	3·50	3·25

297 Nicanor Villalaz (designer of Panama Arms)

1976. Villalaz Commemoration.

1130	297	5c. blue	25	20

298 National Lottery Building, Panama City

1976. "Progressive Panama".

1131	298	6c. multicoloured	25	20

299 Cerro Colorado, Copper Mine

1976. Air.

1132	299	23c. multicoloured	50	25

300 Contadora Island

1977. Tourism.

1133	300	3c. multicoloured	25	20

301 Secretary-General of Pan-American Union, A. Orfila

1978. Signing of Panama–U.S.A. Treaty. Mult.

1134	3c. Type **301**	15	15
1135	23c. Treaty signing scene (horiz)	60	25
1136	40c. President Carter	1·00	60
1137	50c. Gen. O. Torrijos of Panama	1·30	90

Nos. 1134 and 1136/7 were issued together se-tenant in horizontal stamps of three showing Treaty signing as No. 1135.

302 Signing Ratification of Panama Canal Treaty

1978. Ratification of Panama Canal Treaty.

1138	302	3c. multicoloured	15	10
1139	-	5c. multicoloured	20	10
1140	-	35c. multicoloured	95	40
1141	-	41c. multicoloured	1·00	50

DESIGNS: 5, 35, 41c. As Type **302**, but with the design of the Ratification Ceremony spread over the three stamps, issued as a se-tenant strip in the order 5c. (29×39 mm), 41c. (44×39 mm), 35c. (29×39 mm).

303 Colon Harbour and Warehouses

1978. 30th Anniv of Colon Free Zone.

1142	303	6c. multicoloured	25	20

304 Children's Home and Melvin Jones

1978. Birth Centenary of Melvin Jones (founder of Lions International).

1143	304	50c. multicoloured	1·30	85

305 Pres. Torrijos, "Flavia" (liner) and Children

1979. Return of Canal Zone. Multicoloured.

1144	3c. Type **305**	25	15
1145	23c. Presidents Torrijos and Carter, liner and flags of Panama and U.S.A.	60	35

306 "75" and Bank Emblem

1979. 75th Anniv of National Bank.

1146	306	6c. black, red and blue	25	20

307 Rotary Emblem

1979. 75th Anniv of Rotary International.

1147	307	17c. blue and yellow	45	35

308 Children inside Heart

1979. International Year of the Child.

1148	308	50c. multicoloured	1·30	60

309 U.P.U. Emblem and Globe

1979. 18th Universal Postal Union Congress, Rio de Janeiro.

1149	309	35c. multicoloured	85	65

310 Colon Station

1980. Centenary of Trans-Panamanian Railway.

1150	310	1c. purple and lilac	15	10

311 Postal Headquarters, Balboa (inauguration)

1980. Anniversaries and Events.

1151	311	3c. multicoloured	15	10
1152	-	6c. multicoloured	20	10
1153	-	17c. multicoloured	45	25
1154	-	23c. multicoloured	50	25
1155	-	35c. blue, black and red	85	40
1156	-	41c. pink and black	1·00	50
1157	-	50c. multicoloured	1·10	65

DESIGNS—HORIZ: 17c. Map of Central America and flags (census of the Americas); 23c. Tourism and Convention Centre (opening); 35c. Bank emblem (Inter-American Development Bank, 25th anniv); 41c. F. de Lesseps (Panama Canal cent); 50c. Olympic Stadium, Moscow (Olympic Games). VERT: 6c. National flag (return of Canal Zone).

1980. Olympic Games, Lake Placid and Moscow. (a) Optd 1980 LAKE PLACID MOSCU and venue emblems.

1158	20c. (No. 1099)	1·30	1·20
1160	20c. (1101)	1·30	1·20
1162	20c. (1103)	1·30	1·20
1164	20c. (1105)	1·30	1·20
1166	20c. (1107)	1·30	1·20
1168	20c. (1109)	1·30	1·20
1170	20c. (1111)	1·30	1·20
1172	20c. (1113)	1·30	1·20
1174	20c. (1115)	1·30	1·20
1176	20c. (1117)	1·30	1·20
1178	20c. (1119)	1·30	1·20
1180	20c. (1121)	1·30	1·20
1182	20c. (1123)	1·30	1·20
1184	20c. (1125)	1·30	1·20
1186	20c. (1127)	1·30	1·20

(b) Optd with Lake Placid Olympic emblems and medals total of country indicated.

1159	20c. "**ALEMANIA D.**" (1100)	1·30	1·20
1161	20c. "**AUSTRIA**" (1102)	1·30	1·20
1163	20c. "**SUECIA**" (1104)	1·30	1·20
1165	20c. "**U.R.S.S.**" (1106)	1·30	1·20
1167	20c. "**ALEMANIA F.**" (1108)	1·30	1·20
1169	20c. "**ITALIA**" (1110)	1·30	1·20
1171	20c. "**U.S.A.**" (1112)	1·30	1·20
1173	20c. "**SUIZA**" (1114)	1·30	1·20
1175	20c. "**CANADA/GRAN BRETANA**" (1116)	1·30	1·20
1177	20c. "**NORUEGA**" (1118)	1·30	1·20
1179	20c. "**LICHTENSTEIN**" (1120)	1·30	1·20
1181	20c. "**HUNGRIA/BULGARIA**" (1122)	1·30	1·20
1183	20c. "**FINLANDIA**" (1124)	1·30	1·20
1185	20c. "**HOLANDA**" (1126)	1·30	1·20
1187	20c. "**CHECOS-LOVAQUIA/FRANCIA**" (1128)	1·30	1·20

Nos. 1158, etc, occur on 1st, 3rd and 5th rows and Nos. 1159, etc, occur on the others.

(c) Lake Placid and Moscow and venue with Olympic rings.

1188	20c. (No. 1099)	1·30	1·20
1190	20c. (1101)	1·30	1·20
1192	20c. (1103)	1·30	1·20
1194	20c. (1105)	1·30	1·20
1196	20c. (1107)	1·30	1·20
1198	20c. (1109)	1·30	1·20
1200	20c. (1111)	1·30	1·20
1202	20c. (1113)	1·30	1·20

1204 20c. (1115) 1·30 1·20
1206 20c. (1117) 1·30 1·20
1208 20c. (1119) 1·30 1·20
1210 20c. (1121) 1·30 1·20
1212 20c. (1123) 1·30 1·20
1214 20c. (1125) 1·30 1·20
1216 20c. (1127) 1·30 1·20

(d) Optd with country names as indicated.
1189 20c. "**RUSIA/ALEMANIA D.**" (1101) 1·30 1·20
1191 20c. "**SUECIA/FINLANDIA**" (1102) 1·30 1·20
1193 20c. "**GRECIA/BELGICA/INDIA**" (1104) 1·30 1·20
1195 20c. "**BULGARIA/CUBA**" (1106) 1·30 1·20
1197 20c. "**CHECOS-LOVAQUIA/ YUGOSLAVIA**" (1108) 1·30 1·20
1199 20c. "**ZIMBAWE/COREA DEL NORTE/MONGOLIA**" (1110) 1·30 1·20
1201 20c. "**ITALIA/HUNGRIA**" (1112) 1·30 1·20
1203 20c. "**AUSTRALIA/DINAMARCA**" (1114) 1·30 1·20
1205 20c. "**TANZANIA/MEXICO/ HOLANDA**" (1116) 1·30 1·20
1207 20c. "**RUMANIA/FRANCIA**" (1118) 1·30 1·20
1209 20c. "**BRASIL/ETIOPIA**" (1120) 1·30 1·20
1211 20c. "**IRLANDA/UGANDA/VEN-EZUELA**" (1122) 1·30 1·20
1213 20c. "**GRAN BRETANA/POLO-NIA**" (1124) 1·30 1·20
1215 20c. "**SUIZA/ESPANA/AUSTRIA**" (1126) 1·30 1·20
1217 20c. "**JAMAICA/LIBANO/GUY-ANA**" (1128) 1·30 1·20
MS1218 No. **MS**1129 optd in gold 30c. with Olympic emblems; 30c. with Concorde and Lindbergh's aircraft; 40c. with Apollo I and space shuttle 30·00 29·00

Nos. 1188, etc, occur on 1st, 3rd and 5th rows and Nos. 1189, etc, on the others.

1980. Medal Winners at Winter Olympic Games, Lake Placid. (a) Optd with 1980, medals and venue emblems.
1219 20c. 1980 medals and venue and emblems (No. 1099) 1·30 1·20
1221 20c. As No. 1219 (1101) 1·30 1·20
1223 20c. As No. 1219 (1103) 1·30 1·20
1225 20c. As No. 1219 (1105) 1·30 1·20
1227 20c. As No. 1219 (1107) 1·30 1·20
1229 20c. As No. 1219 (1109) 1·30 1·20
1231 20c. As No. 1219 (1111) 1·30 1·20
1233 20c. As No. 1219 (1113) 1·30 1·20
1235 20c. As No. 1219 (1115) 1·30 1·20
1237 20c. As No. 1219 (1117) 1·30 1·20
1239 20c. As No. 1219 (1119) 1·30 1·20
1241 20c. As No. 1219 (1121) 1·30 1·20
1243 20c. As No. 1219 (1123) 1·30 1·20
1245 20c. As No. 1219 (1125) 1·30 1·20
1247 20c. As No. 1219 (1127) 1·30 1·20

(b) Optd with 1980 medals and venue emblems and Olympic torch and country indicated.
1220 20c. "**ALEMANIA D.**" (1100) 1·30 1·20
1222 20c. "**AUSTRIA**" (1102) 1·30 1·20
1224 20c. "**SUECIA**" (1104) 1·30 1·20
1226 20c. "**U.R.S.S.**" (1106) 1·30 1·20
1228 20c. "**ALEMANIA F.**" (1108) 1·30 1·20
1230 20c. "**ITALIA**" (1110) 1·30 1·20
1232 20c. "**U.S.A.**" (1112) 1·30 1·20
1234 20c. "**SUIZA**" (1114) 1·30 1·20
1236 20c. "**CANADA/GRAN BRE-TANA**" (1116) 1·30 1·20
1238 20c. "**NORUEGA**" (1118) 1·30 1·20
1240 20c. "**LICHTENSTEIN**" (1120) 1·30 1·20
1242 20c. "**HUNGRIA/BULGARIA**" (1122) 1·30 1·20
1244 20c. "**FINLANDIA**" (1124) 1·30 1·20
1246 20c. "**HOLANDIA**" (1126) 1·30 1·20
1248 20c. "**CHECOS-LOVAQUIA/ FRANCIA**" (1128) 1·30 1·20

Nos. 1219, etc, occur on 1st, 3rd and 5th rows and Nos. 1220, etc, on the others.

1980. World Cup Football Championship, Argentina (1978) and Spain (1980). Optd with: A. Football cup emblems. B. "ESPAMER 80" and "Argentina '78" emblems and inscriptions "ESPANA '82/ CAMPEONATO/MUNDIAL DE FUTBOL". C. World Cup Trophy and "ESPANA '82.". D. "ESPANA 82/Football/ Argentina '78/BESPAMER '80 MADRID". E. FIFA globes emblem and "ESPANA '82/ARGENTINA '78/ESPANA '82". F. With ball and inscription as for B.
1249 20c. No. 1099 (A, C, E) 1·30 1·20
1250 20c. No. 1100 (B, D, F) 1·30 1·20
1251 20c. No. 1101 (A, C, E) 1·30 1·20
1252 20c. No. 1102 (B, D, F) 1·30 1·20
1253 20c. No. 1103 (A, C, E) 1·30 1·20
1254 20c. No. 1104 (B, D, F) 1·30 1·20
1255 20c. No. 1105 (A, C, E) 1·30 1·20
1256 20c. No. 1106 (B, D, F) 1·30 1·20
1257 20c. No. 1107 (A, C, E) 1·30 1·20
1258 20c. No. 1108 (B, D, F) 1·30 1·20
1259 20c. No. 1109 (A, C, E) 1·30 1·20
1260 20c. No. 1110 (B, D, F) 1·30 1·20
1261 20c. No. 1111 (A, C, E) 1·30 1·20
1262 20c. No. 1112 (B, D, F) 1·30 1·20
1263 20c. No. 1113 (A, C, E) 1·30 1·20
1264 20c. No. 1114 (B, D, F) 1·30 1·20
1265 20c. No. 1115 (A, C, E) 1·30 1·20
1266 20c. No. 1116 (B, D, F) 1·30 1·20
1267 20c. No. 1117 (A, C, E) 1·30 1·20
1268 20c. No. 1118 (B, D, F) 1·30 1·20
1269 20c. No. 1119 (A, C, E) 1·30 1·20
1270 20c. No. 1120 (B, D, F) 1·30 1·20
1271 20c. No. 1121 (A, C, E) 1·30 1·20
1272 20c. No. 1122 (B, D, F) 1·30 1·20
1273 20c. No. 1123 (A, C, E) 1·30 1·20
1274 20c. No. 1124 (B, D, F) 1·30 1·20
1275 20c. No. 1125 (A, C, E) 1·30 1·20
1276 20c. No. 1126 (B, D, F) 1·30 1·20
1277 20c. No. 1127 (A, C, E) 1·30 1·20
1278 20c. No. 1128 (B, D, F) 1·30 1·20
MS1279 No. **MS**1129 optd in silver. 30c. with World Cup embelms; 30c. with "Viking-Mars" emblem and space shuttle; 40c. with Zeppelin 30·00 29·00

318 Boys in Children's Village

1980. Obligatory Tax. Children's Village. Mult.
1280 2c. Type **318** 20 20
1281 2c. Boy with chicks 20 20
1282 2c. Working in the fields 20 20
1283 2c. Boys with pig 20 20
MS1284 154×170 mm. 2c. Type **318**; 2c. Boys cleaning cages; 2c. As No. 1160; 2c. Woodwork (sold at 1b.) 13·00 12·50

319 Jean Baptiste de la Salle and Map showing La Salle Schools

1981. Education in Panama by the Christian Schools.
1285 **319** 17c. blue, black and red 45 25

320 Louis Braille

1981. International Year of Disabled People.
1286 **320** 23c. multicoloured 50 25

321 Statue of the Virgin

1981. 150th Anniv of Apparition of Miraculous Virgin to St. Catharine Laboure.
1287 **321** 35c. multicoloured 85 50

322 Crimson-backed Tanager

1981. Birds. Multicoloured.
1288 3c. Type **322** 95 25
1289 6c. Chestnut-fronted macaw (vert) 95 25
1290 41c. Violet sabrewing (vert) 4·25 90
1291 50c. Keel-billed toucan 5·25 1·10

323 "Boy feeding Donkey" (Ricardo Morales)

1981. Obligatory Tax. Christmas. Children's Village. Multicoloured.
1292 2c. Type **323** 20 20
1293 2c. "Nativity" (Enrique Daniel Austin) 20 20
1294 2c. "Bird in Tree" (Jorge Gonzalez) 20 20
1295 2c. "Church" (Eric Belgrane) 20 20
MS1296 131×140 mm. 2c. The Wise Men (Eliecer Antonio Osorio); 2c. Nativity (Ricardo Correoso); 2c. House (Samuel Carter Ruiz); 2c. Family in House (John A. Calvo) (sold for 5b.) 14·00 13·00

324 Banner

1981. National Reaffirmation.
1297 **324** 3c. multicoloured 15 10

325 General Herrera

1982. 1st Death Anniv of General Omar Torrijos Herrera. Multicoloured.
1298 5c. Aerial view of Panama (postage) 15 10
1299 6c. Colecito army camp 15 10
1300 17c. Bayano river barrage 45 25
1301 50c. Felipillo engineering works 1·30 75
1302 23c. Type **325** (air) 60 35
1303 35c. Security Council reunion 95 50
1304 41c. Gen. Omar Torrijos airport 1·10 60
MS1305 84×75 mm. No. 1302 (sold at 1b.) 3·00 3·00

326 Ricardo J. Alfaro

1982. Birth Cent of Ricardo J. Alfaro (statesman).
1306 **326** 3c. black, mauve and blue (postage) 20 15
1307 - 17c. black and mauve (air) 45 25
1308 - 23c. multicoloured 60 35

DESIGNS: 17c. Profile of Alfaro wearing spectacles (as humanist); 23c. Portrait of Alfaro (as lawyer).

328 Pig Farming

1982. Obligatory Tax. Christmas. Children's Village. Multicoloured.
1309 2c. Type **328** 20 20
1310 2c. Gardening 20 20
1311 2c. Metalwork (horiz) 20 20
1312 2c. Bee-keeping (horiz) 20 20
MS1313 Two sheets each 70×95 mm.(a) 2b. Football and classroom; (b) 2b. Scouts and musicians. Imperf 34·00 33·00

329 Pele (Brazilian footballer)

1982. World Cup Football Championship, Spain. Multicoloured.
1314 50c. Italian team (horiz) (postage) 1·40 60
1315 23c. Football emblem and map of Panama (air) 70 25
1316 35c. Type **329** 95 40
1317 41c. World Cup Trophy 1·30 50
MS1318 85×75 mm. No. 1316. Imperf (sold at 1b.) 13·00 12·50

330 Chamber of Trade Emblem

1983. "Expo Comer" Chamber of Trade Exhibition.
1319 **330** 17c. lt blue, blue, & gold 50 35

331 Dr. Nicolas Solano

1983. Air. Birth Centenary (1982) of Dr. Nicolas Solano (anti-tuberculosis pioneer).
1320 **331** 23c. brown 50 35

332 Pope John Paul II giving Blessing

1983. Papal Visit. Multicoloured.
1321 6c. Type **332** (postage) 45 25
1322 17c. Pope John Paul II 80 35
1323 35c. Pope and map of Panama (air) 1·60 50

333 Map of Americas and Sunburst

1983. 24th Assembly of Inter-American Development Bank Governors.
1324 **333** 50c. light blue, blue and gold 1·30 60

334 Simon Bolivar

1983. Birth Bicentenary of Simon Bolivar.
1325 **334** 50c. multicoloured 1·30 60

MS1326 85×75 mm. **334** 1b. multicoloured. Imperf 2·75 2·10

335 Postal Union of the Americas and Spain Emblem

1983. World Communications Day. Mult.

1327	30c. Type **335**	80	40
1328	40c. W.C.Y. emblem	1·00	60
1329	50c. Universal Postal Union emblem	1·30	75
1330	60c. "Flying Dove" (Alfredo Sinclair)	1·60	90
MS1331	150×150 mm. 1b. As Nos. 1327/30. Imperf	2·75	2·75

336 Moslem Mosque

1983. Freedom of Worship. Multicoloured.

1332	3c. Type **336**	15	15
1333	5c. Bahai temple	15	15
1334	6c. Church of St. Francis of the Mountains, Veraguas	25	15
1335	17c. Shevet Ahim synagogue	70	35

337 "The Annunciation" (Dagoberto Moran)

1983. Obligatory Tax. Christmas. Children's Village. Multicoloured.

1336	2c. Type **337**	30	20
1337	2c. Church and houses (Leonidas Molinar) (vert)	30	20
1338	2c. Bethlehem and star (Colon Olmedo Zambrano) (vert)	30	20
1339	2c. Flight into Egypt (Hector Ulises Velasquez) (vert)	30	20
MS1340	Two sheets each 70×95 mm. (a) 2b. As Nos. 1336/7; (b) 2b. As Nos. 1338/9	14·50	14·00

338 Ricardo Miro (writer)

1983. Famous Panamanians. Multicoloured.

1341	1c. Type **338**	15	15
1342	3c. Richard Newman (educationalist)	15	15
1343	5c. Cristobal Rodriguez (politician)	15	15
1344	6c. Alcibiades Arosemena (politician)	15	15
1345	35c. Cirilo Martinez (educationalist)	1·00	50

339 "Rural Architecture" (Juan Manuel Cedero)

1983. Paintings. Multicoloured.

1346	1c. Type **339**	10	10
1347	1c. "Large Nude" (Manuel Chong Neto)	10	10
1348	3c. "On another Occasion" (Spiros Vamvas)	10	10
1349	6c. "Punta Chame" (Guillermo Trujillo)	15	10
1350	28c. "Neon Light" (Alfredo Sinclair)	70	40
1351	35c. "The Prophet" (Alfredo Sinclair) (vert)	85	60
1352	41c. "Highland Girls" (Al Sprague) (vert)	1·00	65
1353	1b. "One Morning" (Ignacio Mallol Pibernat)	2·50	1·70

340 Tonosi Double Jug

1984. Archaeological Finds. Multicoloured.

1354	30c. Type **340**	1·10	50
1355	40c. Dish on stand	1·30	65
1356	50c. Jug decorated with human face (vert)	1·60	85
1357	60c. Waisted bowl (vert)	1·90	1·00
MS1358	85×75 mm. 1b. As No. 1355. Imperf	2·50	2·50

341 Boxing

1984. Olympic Games, Los Angeles. Mult.

1359	19c. Type **341**	85	40
1360	19c. Baseball	85	40
1361	19c. Basketball (vert)	85	40
1362	19c. Swimming (vert)	85	40

342 Roberto Duran

1984. Roberto Duran (boxer) Commem.

1363	**342**	26c. multicoloured	70	40

343 Shooting

1984. Olympic Games, Los Angeles (2nd series). Multicoloured.

1364	6c. Type **343** (postage)	15	15
MS1365	75×85 mm. 1b. Running (53×26 mm)	3·00	2·75
1366	30c. Weightlifting (air)	85	50
1367	37c. Wrestling	1·00	65
1368	1b. Long jump	3·00	1·80

344 "Pensive Woman" (Manuel Chong Neto)

1984. Paintings. Multicoloured.

1369	1c. Type **344**	10	10
1370	3c. "The Child" (Alfredo Sinclair) (horiz)	10	10
1371	6c. "A Day in the Life of Rumalda" (Brooke Alfaro) (horiz)	15	10
1372	30c. "Highlanders" (Al Sprague)	85	50
1373	37c. "Ballet Interval" (Roberto Sprague) (horiz)	1·00	65
1374	44c. "Wood on Chame Head" (Guillermo Trujillo) (horiz)	1·30	85
1375	50c. "La Plaza Azul" (Juan Manuel Cedeno) (horiz)	1·50	90
1376	1b. "Ira" (Spiros Vamvas) (horiz)	3·00	1·80

345 Map, Pres. Torrijos Herrera and Liner in Canal Lock

1984. 5th Anniv of Canal Zone Postal Sovereignty.

1377	**345**	19c. multicoloured	80	50

346 Emblem as Seedling

1984. Air. World Food Day.

1378	**346**	30c. red, green and blue	1·30	60

347 Boy

1984. Obligatory Tax. Christmas. Children's Village. Multicoloured.

1379	2c. Type **347**	25	25
1380	2c. Boy in tee-shirt	25	25
1381	2c. Boy in checked shirt	25	25
1382	2c. Cub scout	25	25
MS1383	75×84 mm. 4×2c. Designs showing children (sold at 2b.)	5·50	5·50

348 American Manatee

1984. Animals. Each in black.

1384	3c. Type **348** (postage)	10	10
1385	30c. "Tayra" (air)	1·40	85
1386	44c. Jaguarundi	1·90	1·20
1387	50c. White-lipped peccary	2·20	1·50
MS1388	75×85 mm. 1b. Three-toed sloth (*Bradypus griseus*) (vert)	4·75	4·50

349 Copper One Centesimo Coins, 1935

1985. Coins. Multicoloured.

1389	3c. Type **349** (postage)	10	10
1390	3c. Silver ten centesimo coins, 1904	10	10
1391	3c. Silver five centesimo coins, 1916	25	15
1392	30c. Silver 50 centesimo coins, 1904 (air)	1·30	85
1393	37c. Silver half balboa coins, 1962	1·60	1·00
1394	44c. Silver balboa coins, 1953	1·90	1·20

350 Figures on Map reaching for Dove

1985. Contadora Peace Movement.

1395	**350**	10c. multicoloured	45	25
1396	**350**	20c. multicoloured	85	35
1397	**350**	30c. multicoloured	1·30	60
MS1398		85×75 mm. 1b. multicoloured (Dove over flags on map) (air)	4·25	4·25

351 Tanker in Dock

1985. 70th Anniv of Panama Canal.

1399	**351**	19c. multicoloured	1·10	50

352 Scouts with Statue of Christ

1985. Obligatory Tax. Christmas. Children's Village. Multicoloured.

1400	2c. Type **352**	25	25
1401	2c. Children holding cards spelling "Feliz Navidad"	25	25
1402	2c. Children holding balloons	25	25
1403	2c. Group of cub scouts	25	25
MS1404	95×70 mm. Nos. 1400/3. Perf or imperf (sold at 2b.)	14·00	13·00

353 "40" on Emblem

1986. 40th Anniv (1985) of U.N.O.

1405	**353**	23c. multicoloured	80	35

354 Boys in Cab of Crane

1986. International Youth Year (1985).

1406	**354**	30c. multicoloured	1·00	45

355 "Awaiting Her Turn" (Al Sprague)

1986. Paintings. Multicoloured.

1407	3c. Type **355**	10	10
1408	5c. "Aerobics" (Guillermo Trujillo) (horiz)	15	10
1409	19c. "House of Cardboard" (Eduardo Augustine)	80	35
1410	30c. "Tierra Gate" (Juan Manuel Cedeno) (horiz)	1·30	60
1411	36c. "Supper for Three" (Brood Alfaro)	1·50	65
1412	42c. "Tenderness" (Alfredo Sinclair)	1·70	75
1413	50c. "Lady of Character" (Manuel Chong Neto)	2·20	90
1414	60c. "Calla Lilies No. 1" (Maigualida de Diaz) (horiz)	2·75	1·20

356 Atlapa Convention Centre

1986. Miss Universe Contest. Multicoloured.

1415	23c. Type **356**	80	35
1416	60c. Emblem	2·10	90

357 Comet and Globe

1986. Appearance of Halley's Comet.

No.	Type	Description	Mint	Used
1417	357	23c. multicoloured	80	35
1418	-	30c. blue, brown and yellow	1·00	45
MS1419		75×85 mm. 1b. multicoloured. Imperf	4·00	3·75

DESIGNS: 30c., 1b. Panama la Vieja Cathedral tower.

358 Angels

1986. Obligatory Tax. 20th Anniv of Children's Village. Children's drawings. Multicoloured.

No.	Description	Mint	Used
1420	2c. Type **358**	45	25
1421	2c. Cupids	45	25
1422	2c. Indians	45	25
1423	2c. Angels (different)	45	25
MS1424	75×85 mm. 2b. Dancers (54×62 mm). Perf or imperf	5·50	5·50

359 Basketball

1986. 15th Central American and Caribbean Games, Santiago. Multicoloured.

No.	Description	Mint	Used
1425	20c. Type **359**	60	30
1426	23c. Sports	70	35

360 Argentina Player

1986. World Cup Football Championship, Mexico. Multicoloured.

No.	Description	Mint	Used
1427	23c. Type **360**	85	30
1428	30c. West Germany player	1·00	40
1429	37c. West Germany and Argentina players	1·30	55
MS1430	75×85 mm. 1b. Ball and players legs	3·00	3·00

361 Crib

1986. Christmas. Multicoloured.

No.	Description	Mint	Used
1431	23c. Type **361**	70	30
1432	36c. Tree and presents	1·10	55
1433	42c. As No. 1432	1·30	60

364 Headquarters Building

365 Mountain Rose

366 Octavio Menendez Pereira (founder) and Anniversary Monument

368 Heinrich Schutz

362 Dove and Globe

369 Development Projects

370 Horse-drawn Fire Pump, 1887, and Modern Appliance

371 Wrestling

372 "Adoration of the Magi" (Albrecht Nentz)

373 Distressed Family and Poor Housing

374 Heart falling into Crack

1986. International Peace Year. Multicoloured.

No.	Type	Description	Mint	Used
1434		8c. Type **362**	25	15
1435		19c. Profiles and emblem	60	35

363 Mask

1987. Tropical Carnival. Multicoloured.

No.	Description	Mint	Used
1436	20c. Type **363**	60	40
1437	35c. Sun with eye mask	1·30	65
MS1438	75×85 mm. 1b. As No. 363. Imperf	3·00	2·00

1987. 50th Anniv (1985) of Panama Lions Club.

No.	Type	Description	Mint	Used
1439	364	37c. multicoloured	1·30	65

1987. Flowers and Birds. Multicoloured.

No.	Description	Mint	Used
1440	3c. Type **365**	15	10
1441	5c. Blue-grey tanager (horiz)	15	10
1442	8c. Golden cup	25	10
1443	15c. Tropical kingbird (horiz)	50	25
1444	19c. "Barleria micans" (flower)	70	35
1445	23c. Brown pelican (horiz)	80	40
1446	30c. "Cordia dentata" (flower)	1·10	60
1447	36c. Rufous pigeon (horiz)	1·50	65

1987. 50th Anniv (1986) of Panama University.

No.	Type	Description	Mint	Used
1448	366	19c. multicoloured	60	35

367 Emblem in "40"

1987. 40th Anniv (1985) of F.A.O.

No.	Type	Description	Mint	Used
1449	367	10c. brown, yellow and black	25	15
1450	367	45c. brown, green and black	1·50	85

1987. Composers and 7th Anniv (1986) of National Theatre.

No.	Type	Description	Mint	Used
1451	368	19c. multicoloured	50	35
1452	-	30c. green, mauve & brown	85	60
1453	-	37c. brown, blue and deep blue	1·00	70
1454	-	60c. green, yellow & black	1·70	1·20

DESIGNS—HORIZ: 30c. National Theatre. VERT: 37c. Johann Sebastian Bach; 60c. Georg Friedrich Handel.

1987. 25th Anniv (1986) of Inter-American Development Bank.

No.	Type	Description	Mint	Used
1455	369	23c. multicoloured	70	40

1987. Centenary of Fire Service. Multicoloured.

No.	Description	Mint	Used
1456	25c. Type **370**	1·20	40
1457	35c. Fireman carrying boy	1·70	65

1987. 10th Pan-American Games, Indianapolis. Mult.

No.	Description	Mint	Used
1458	15c. Type **371**	70	25
1459	25c. Tennis (vert)	95	40
1460	30c. Swimming	1·20	60
1461	41c. Basketball (vert)	1·70	85
1462	60c. Cycling (vert)	2·40	1·10
MS1463	74×84 mm. 1b. Weightlifting	3·50	3·50

1987. Christmas. Multicoloured.

No.	Description	Mint	Used
1464	22c. Type **372**	70	40
1465	35c. "The Virgin adored by Angels" (Matthias Grunewald)	1·10	65
1466	37c. "Virgin and Child" (Konrad Witz)	1·10	75

1987. International Year of Shelter for the Homeless. Multicoloured.

No.	Description	Mint	Used
1467	45c. Type **373**	1·30	85
1468	50c. Happy family and stylized modern housing	1·40	90

1988. Anti-drugs Campaign.

No.	Type	Description	Mint	Used
1469	374	10c. red and orange	25	15
1470	374	17c. red and green	60	25
1471	374	25c. red and blue	95	40

375 Hands and Sapling

1988. Reafforestation Campaign.

No.	Type	Description	Mint	Used
1472	375	35c. deep green and green	1·10	60
1473	375	40c. red and purple	1·30	65
1474	375	45c. brown and bistre	1·50	75

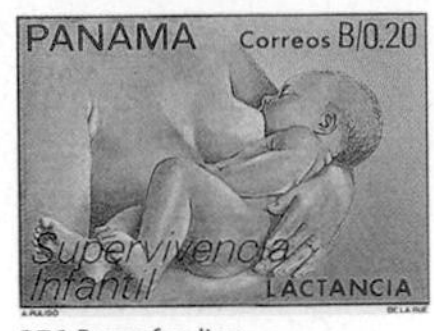

376 Breastfeeding

1988. UNICEF Infant Survival Campaign. Mult.

No.	Description	Mint	Used
1475	20c. Type **376**	60	40
1476	31c. Vaccination	1·10	65
1477	45c. Children playing by lake (vert)	1·70	1·00

377 Rock Beauty and Cuban Hogfish

1988. Fishes. Multicoloured.

No.	Description	Mint	Used
1478	7c. Type **377**	25	15
1479	35c. French angelfish	1·10	65
1480	60c. Black-barred soldierfish	1·90	1·20
1481	1b. Spotted drum	3·25	1·60

378 Emblem and Clasped Hands

1988. 75th Anniv of Girl Guide Movement.

No.	Type	Description	Mint	Used
1482	378	35c. multicoloured	1·00	75

379 "Virgin with Donors"

1988. Christmas. Anonymous Paintings from Museum of Colonial Religious Art. Mult.

No.	Description	Mint	Used
1483	17c. Type **379** (postage)	60	35
1484	45c. "Virgin of the Rosary with St. Dominic"	1·50	85
1485	35c. "St. Joseph with the Child" (air)	1·10	65

380 Athletes and Silver Medal (Brazil)

1989. Seoul Olympic Games Medals. Mult.

No.	Description	Mint	Used
1486	17c. Type **380** (postage)	50	35
1487	25c. Wrestlers and gold medal (Hungary)	80	50
1488	60c. Weightlifter and gold medal (Turkey)	1·90	1·20
MS1489	120×80 mm. 1b. Swimmer	3·50	3·50

1490 35c. Boxers and bronze medal (Colombia) (air) 1·10 65

381 St. John Bosco

1989. Death Centenary of St. John Bosco (founder of Salesian Brothers). Multicoloured.

1491 10c. Type **381** 25 15
1492 20c. Menor Basilica and St. John with people 60 40

382 Anniversary Emblem

1989. 125th Anniv of Red Cross Movement.

1493 **382** 40c. black and red 1·30 85
1494 - 1b. multicoloured 3·00 1·60

DESIGN: 1b. Red Cross workers putting patient in ambulance.

383 "Ancon I" (first ship through Canal)

1989. Air. 75th Anniv of Panama Canal.

1495 **383** 35c. red, black and yellow 1·30 75
1496 - 60c. multicoloured 1·90 1·10

DESIGN: 60c. Modern tanker.

384 Barriles Ceremonial Statue

1989. America. Pre-Columbian Artefacts. Mult.

1497 20c. Type **384** 1·10 85
1498 35c. Ceramic vase 2·75 2·00

385 "March of the Women on Versailles" (engraving)

1989. Bicent of French Revolution. Mult.

1499 25c. Type **385** (postage) 1·10 60
1500 35c. "Storming the Bastille" (air) 1·60 85
1501 45c. Birds 2·10 1·10

386 "Holy Family"

1989. Christmas. Multicoloured.

1502 17c. Type **386** 70 35
1503 35c. 1988 crib in Cathedral 1·50 65
1504 45c. "Nativity" 1·90 95

The 17 and 45c. show children's paintings.

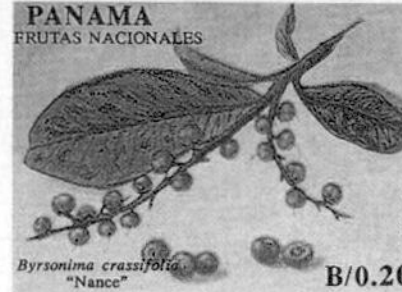

387 "Byrsonima crassifolia"

1990. Fruit. Multicoloured.

1505 20c. Type **387** 50 40
1506 35c. "Bactris gasipaes" 1·10 65
1507 40c. "Anacardium occidentale" 1·50 80

388 Sinan

1990. 88th Birthday of Rogelio Sinan (writer).

1508 **388** 23c. brown and blue 70 45

389 Pond Turtle

1990. Reptiles. Multicoloured.

1509 35c. Type **389** 1·40 85
1510 45c. Olive loggerhead turtle 1·70 1·10
1511 60c. Red-footed tortoise 2·40 1·40

390 Carrying Goods on Yoke (after Oviedo)

1990. America.

1512 **390** 20c. brown, light brown and gold 1·40 50
1513 - 35c. multicoloured 2·20 1·10

DESIGN—VERT: 35c. Warrior wearing gold chest ornament and armbands.

391 Dr. Guillermo Patterson, jun., "Father of Chemistry"

1990. Chemistry in Panama.

1514 **391** 25c. black and turquoise 95 65
1515 - 35c. multicoloured 1·30 90
1516 - 45c. multicoloured 1·60 1·20

DESIGNS: 35c. Evaporation experiment; 45c. Books and laboratory equipment.

392 In Sight of Land

1991. America. 490th Anniv of Discovery of Panama Isthmus by Rodrigo Bastidas.

1517 **392** 35c. multicoloured 1·40 90

393 St. Ignatius

1991. 450th Anniv of Society of Jesus and 500th Birth Anniv of St. Ignatius de Loyola (founder).

1518 **393** 20c. multicoloured 60 50

394 Declaration of Women's Right to Vote

1991. 50th Anniv of First Presidency of Dr. Arnulfo Arias Madrid.

1519 **394** 10c. brown, stone & gold 35 25
1520 - 10c. brown, stone & gold 35 25

DESIGN: No. 1520, Department of Social Security headquarters.

395 "Glory to God ..." (Luke 2:14) and Score of "Gloria in Excelsis"

1991. Christmas. Multicoloured.

1521 35c. Type **395** 1·10 90
1522 35c. Nativity 1·10 90

396 Adoration of the Kings

1992. Epiphany.

1523 **396** 10c. multicoloured 25 25

397 Family and Housing Estate

1992. "New Lives" Housing Project.

1524 **397** 5c. multicoloured 25 25

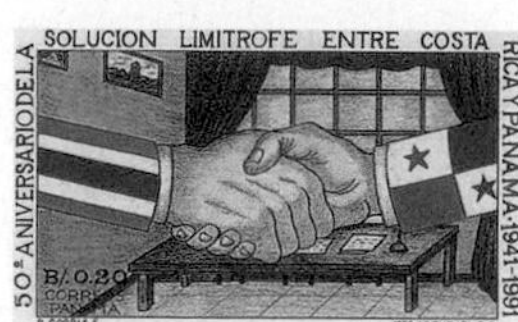

398 Costa Rican and Panamanian shaking Hands

1992. 50th Anniv (1991) of Border Agreement with Costa Rica. Multicoloured.

1525 20c. Type **398** 60 50
1526 40c. Map showing Costa Rica and Panama 1·10 1·00
1527 50c. Presidents Calderon and Arias and national flags 1·40 1·20

399 Pollutants and Hole over Antarctic

1992. "Save the Ozone Layer".

1528 **399** 40c. multicoloured 1·70 1·00

400 Exhibition Emblem

1992. "Expocomer 92" 10th International Trade Exhibition, Panama City.

1529 **400** 10c. multicoloured 25 25

401 Portrait

1992. 1st Death Anniv of Dame Margot Fonteyn (ballet dancer). Portraits by Pietro Annigoni. Multicoloured.

1530 35c. Type **401** 85 85
1531 45c. On stage 1·10 1·10

402 Maria Olimpia de Obaldia

1992. Birth Centenary of Maria Olimpia de Obaldia (poet).

1532 **402** 10c. multicoloured 25 25

403 Athletics Events and Map of Spain

1992. Olympic Games, Barcelona.

1533 **403** 10c. multicoloured 25 25

404 Paca

1992. Endangered Animals.

1534 **404** 5c. brown, stone & black 25 15
1535 - 10c. black, brn & stone 50 40
1536 - 15c. brown, blk & stone 80 60
1537 - 20c. multicoloured 1·00 75

DESIGNS: 10c. Harpy eagle; 15c. Jaguar; 20c. Iguana.

405 Zion Baptist Church, Bocas del Toro

1992. Centenary of Baptist Church in Panama.
1538 **405** 20c. multicoloured 60 50

406 Columbus's Fleet

1992. America. 500th Anniv of Discovery of America by Columbus. Multicoloured.
1539 20c. Type **406** 60 50
1540 35c. Columbus planting flag 1·10 90

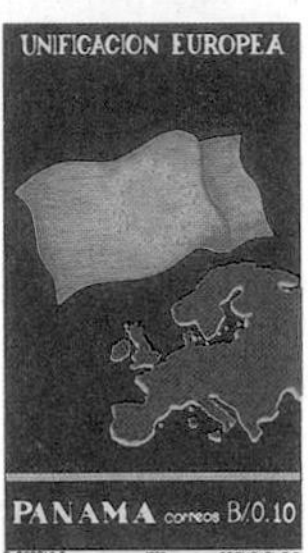

407 Flag and Map of Europe

1992. European Single Market.
1541 **407** 10c. multicoloured 35 25

408 Mascot

1992. "Expo '92" World's Fair, Seville.
1542 **408** 10c. multicoloured 25 25

409 Occupations

1992. American Workers' Health Year.
1543 **409** 15c. multicoloured 45 40

410 Angel and Shepherds

1992. Christmas. Multicoloured.
1544 20c. Type **410** 60 50
1545 35c. Mary and Joseph arriving at Bethlehem 1·10 90

411 Jesus lighting up the Americas

1993. 500th Anniv (1992) of Evangelization of the American Continent.
1546 **411** 10c. multicoloured 25 25

412 Woman on Crutches and Wheelchair-bound Man

1993. National Day of Disabled Persons.
1547 **412** 5c. multicoloured 25 15

413 Herrera (bust)

1993. 32nd Death Anniv of Dr. Jose de la Cruz Herrera (essayist).
1548 **413** 5c. multicoloured 25 15

414 Nutritious Foods and Emblems

1993. International Nutrition Conference, Rome.
1549 **414** 10c. multicoloured 25 25

415 Caravel and Columbus in Portobelo Harbour

1994. 490th Anniv (1992) of Columbus's Fourth Voyage and Exploration of the Panama Isthmus.
1550 **415** 50c. multicoloured 1·50 1·30

416 Panama Flag and Greek Motifs

1995. 50th Anniv of Greek Community in Panama. Multicoloured.
1551 20c. Type **416** 50 50
MS1552 100×50 mm. 75c. Acropolis, Athens; 75c. Greek Orthodox Church, Panama (horiz) 4·25 4·25

1995. Various stamps surch.
1553 - 20c. on 23c. multicoloured (1459) 50 40
1554 **373** 25c. on 45c. multicoloured 70 50
1555 - 30c. on 45c. multicoloured (1510) 85 55
1556 **375** 35c. on 45c. brown and bistre 95 65
1557 - 35c. on 45c. multicoloured (1477) 1·00 70
1558 - 40c. on 41c. multicoloured (1461) 1·10 80
1559 - 50c. on 60c. multicoloured (1511) 1·70 1·00
1560 - 1b. on 50c. multicoloured (1480) 3·00 1·90

418 Chinese Family and House

1996. Chinese Presence in Panama. 142nd Anniv of Arrival of First Chinese Immigrants. Multicoloured.
1561 60c. Type **418** 2·20 1·50
MS1562 90×78 mm. 1b.50 Motifs for winter, spring, summer and autumn. Imperf 4·75 4·50

419 The King's Bridge from the North (16th century)

1996. 475th Anniv (1994) of Founding by the Spanish of Panama City. Multicoloured.
1563 15c. Type **419** 45 40
1564 20c. City arms, 1521 (vert) 60 50
1565 25c. Plan of first cathedral 80 65
1566 35c. Present-day ruins of Cathedral of the Assumption of Our Lady 1·20 90

420 "60", Campus and Emblem

1996. 60th Anniv of Panama University.
1567 **420** 40c. multicoloured 1·20 1·10

421 Anniversary Emblem

1996. 75th Anniv of Panama Chapter of Rotary International.
1568 **421** 5b. multicoloured 14·50 13·00

422 Great Tinamou

1996. America (1993). Endangered Species.
1569 **422** 20c. multicoloured 1·00 50

423 Northern Coati

1996. Mammals. Multicoloured.
1570 25c. Type **423** 70 65
1571 25c. Collared anteater ("Tamandua mexicana") 70 65
1572 25c. Two-toed anteater ("Cyclopes didactylus") 70 65
1573 25c. Puma 70 65

424 De Lesseps

1996. Death Centenary of Ferdinand, Vicomte de Lesseps (builder of Suez Canal).
1574 **424** 35c. multicoloured 1·10 90

425 "50" and Emblem

1996. 50th Anniv of U.N.O.
1575 **425** 45c. multicoloured 1·40 1·20

426 Emblem and Motto

1996. 25th Anniv (1993) of Panama Chapter of Kiwanis International.
1576 **426** 40c. multicoloured 1·20 1·10

427 Bello

1996. 25th Anniv (1995) of Andres Bello Covenant for Education, Science, Technology and Culture.
1577 **427** 35c. multicoloured 1·10 90

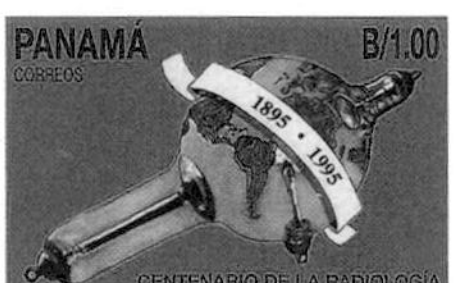

428 World Map on X-ray Equipment

1996. Centenary of Discovery of X-rays by Wilhelm Rontgen.
1578 **428** 1b. multicoloured 3·00 2·75

429 Madonna and Child

1996. Christmas.
1579 **429** 35c. multicoloured 1·10 90

430 Diesel Train and Panama Canal

1996. America (1994). Postal Transport.
1580 **430** 30c. multicoloured 85 85

431 "Panama, More than a Canal" (C. Gonzalez)

1997. 20th Anniv of Torrijos–Carter Treaty (transferring Control of Canal Zone to Panama in Year 2000). Multicoloured.
1581 20c. Type **431** 60 60
1582 30c. "A Curtain of Our Flag" (A. Siever) (vert) 95 90
1583 45c. "Perpetual Steps" (R. Martinez) 1·40 1·30
1584 50c. Kurt Waldheim (U.N. Secretary-General), President Carter of U.S.A. and President Torrijos of Panama at signing ceremony 1·60 1·50
MS1585 127×102 mm. 3, 40, 50c. Composite design as No. 1584 (sold at 1b.50) 1·75 1·40

432 Pedro Miguel Locks

1997. World Congress on Panama Canal. Mult.
1586 45c. Type **432** 1·40 1·30
1587 45c. Miraflores Locks 1·40 1·30
MS1588 100×75 mm. 1b.50 Gatun Locks (75×30 mm) 4·75 4·50

433 "Gandhi Spinning" (P. Biswas)

1997. 50th Anniv of Independence of India.
1589 **433** 50c. multicoloured 1·60 1·40

434 Crocodile on Rock

1997. The American Crocodile. Multicoloured.
1590 25c. Type **434** 70 50
1591 25c. Looking across water 70 50
1592 25c. Two crocodiles 70 50
1593 25c. Head with mouth open 70 50

435 Mary and Joseph searching for Lodgings

1997. Christmas.
1594 **435** 35c. multicoloured 1·10 85

436 Fire Engines from 1941 and 1948

1997. Centenary of Colon City Fire Brigade.
1595 **436** 20c. multicoloured 60 45

437 "Eleutherodactylus biporcatus" (robber frog)

1997. Frogs. Multicoloured.
1596 25c. Type **437** 80 50
1597 25c. "Hyla colymba" (tree frog) 80 50
1598 25c. "Hyla rufitela" (tree frog) 80 50
1599 25c. "Nelsonephryne aterrima" 80 50

438 Women wearing Polleras

1997. America (1996). Traditional Costumes.
1600 **438** 20c. multicoloured 60 40

439 Arosemena

1997. Death Centenary of Justo Arosemena (President, 1855–56).
1601 **439** 40c. multicoloured 1·30 1·10

440 Emblem

1997. 85th Anniv of Colon Chamber of Commerce, Agriculture and Industry.
1602 **440** 1b. multicoloured 3·00 2·75

441 Douglas DC-3

1997. 50th Anniv of Panamanian Aviation Company. Multicoloured.
1603 35c. Type **441** 1·00 85
1604 35c. Martin 4-0-4 1·00 85
1605 35c. Avro HS-748 1·00 85
1606 35c. Lockheed L-188 Electra 1·00 85
1607 35c. Boeing 727-100 1·00 85
1608 35c. Boeing 737-200 Advanced 1·00 85

442 Wailing Wall

1997. 3000th Anniv of Jerusalem. Multicoloured.
1609 20c. Type **442** 60 40
1610 25c. Service in the Basilica of the Holy Sepulchre 80 60
1611 60c. Dome of the Rock 1·70 1·50
MS1612 100×75 mm. 2b.50 Motifs of Nos. 1609/11 4·75 4·50

443 Building Facade and Emblem

1998. 50th Anniv of Organization of American States.
1613 **443** 40c. multicoloured 1·30 1·10

444 Central Avenue, San Felipe

1998. Tourism. Multicoloured.
1614 10c. Type **444** 25 10
1615 20c. Tourists in rainforest 60 40
1616 25c. Gatun Locks, Panama Canal (horiz) 80 60
1617 35c. Panama City (horiz) 1·10 90
1618 40c. San Jeronimo Fort, San Felipe de Portobelo (horiz) 1·30 1·10
1619 45c. Rubber raft, River Chagres (horiz) 1·50 1·20
1620 60c. Beach, Dog's Island, Kuna Yala (horiz) 1·90 1·70

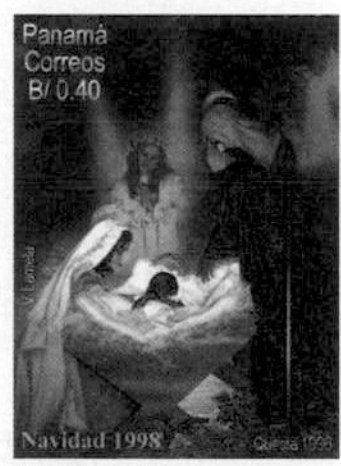

445 Nativity

2000. Christmas.
1621 **445** 40c. multicoloured 1·40 1·20

446 Pavilion

2000. "World Expo'98" World's Fair, Lisbon, Portugal.
1622 **446** 45c. multicoloured 1·60 1·30

447 Harpy Eagle (L. Melillo)

2000. The Harpy Eagle. Entries in painting competition by named artist.
1623 **447** 20c. black and green 70 50
1624 - 20c. multicoloured 70 50
1625 - 20c. multicoloured 70 50
1626 - 20c. multicoloured 70 50
DESIGNS: No. 1624, J. JimEnez; 1625, S. Castro; 1626, J. Ramos.

448 Emblem

2000. 40th Anniv of Business Executives' Association.
1627 **448** 50c. multicoloured 2·20 1·70

449 Emblem

2000. 50th Anniv of Colon Free Trade Zone.
1628 **449** 15c. multicoloured 70 50

450 Emblem

2000. 50th Anniv of Universal Declaration of Human Rights.
1629 **450** 15c. multicoloured 70 50

451 *Platyphora haroldi*

2000. Beetles. Multicoloured.
1630 30c. Type **451** 1·10 90
1631 30c. *Stilodes leopard*a 1·10 90
1632 30c. *Stilodes fuscolineata* 1·10 90
1633 30c. *Platyphora boucardi* 1·10 90

452 Cruise Ship

2000. Return of Control of Panama Canal to Panama (1999). Multicoloured.
1634 20c. Type **452** 95 75
1635 35c. Cruise ship at lock gate 1·60 1·40
1636 40c. View down canal 1·70 1·50
1637 45c. Cruise ship passing through lock 2·10 1·80

453 Constructing Canal

2000. 85th Anniv of Panama Canal. Multicoloured.
1638 40c. Type **453** 1·90 1·70
1639 40c. Construction of canal (different) 1·90 3·75
MS1640 106×56 mm. 1b.50 View of canal at early stage of construction 7·25 7·25

454 Crowd and Madrid wearing surgical mask

2001. Birth Centenary of Dr. Arnulfo Arias Madrid.

1641	**454**	20c. black and brown	70	50
1642	-	20c. black and sepia	70	50
1643	-	30c. multicoloured	95	75
1644	-	30c. multicoloured	95	75

DESIGNS: No. 1642, Crowd and Madrid holding glasses; 1643, Flag, building façade and Madrid; 1644, Crowd and Madrid.

Nos. 1641/25 and 1643/4 respectively were each issued together, se-tenant, forming a composite design.

455 Baby Jesus

2001. Year 2000.

1645	**455**	20c. multicoloured	85	65

456 Crowned Globe, Rainbow and Birds (D. Ortega)

2001. "Dreaming of the Future". Winning Entries in Stamp Design Competition. Multicoloured.

1646	20c. Type **456**	85	65
1647	20c. Globe in flower (L. Guerra)	85	65
MS1648	105×54 mm. 75c. Tree, birds, globe and children (J. Aguilar) (horiz); 75c. Blue birds holding ribbons, globe and children holding hands (S. Sitton) (horiz)	6·50	6·50

457 Angel and Baby Jesus

2001. Christmas.

1649	**457**	35c. multicoloured	80	60

458 Banco General Tower (Carlos Medina)

2001. Architecture of 1990s. Multicoloured.

1650	35c. Type **458**	1·60	1·30
1651	35c. Los Delfines condominium (Edwin Brown)	1·60	1·30
MS1652	104×54 mm. 75c. Circular building (Ricardo Moreno and Jesus Santamaria) (horiz); 75c. Building with three gables (Ricardo Moreno and Jesus Santamaria) (horiz)	6·50	6·50

459 *Psychopsis krameriana*

2001. Orchids. Multicoloured.

1653	35c. Type **459**	1·60	1·30
1654	35c. *Cattleya dowiana*	1·60	1·30
MS1655	104×54 mm. 75c. *Peristeria elata*; 75c. *Miltoniopsis roezlii*	6·50	6·50

460 1878 50c. Sovereign State and 1904 1c. Republic of Panama Stamps

2001. 18th U. P. A. E. P. Congress, Panama.

1656	**460**	5b. multicoloured	22·00	21·00

461 Hospital Buildings and Dr Jaime de la Guardia (founder)

2001. 50th Anniv of San Fernando Clinical Hospital.

1657	**461**	20c. multicoloured	85	65

462 Pres. Moscoso and Cornucopia

2002. Mireya Moscoso, First Woman President of Panama. (1st issue).

1658	**462**	35c. multicoloured	1·60	1·30

See also No. 1720.

463 Couple and Drums

2002. Christmas, 2001. Multicoloured.

1659	60c. Type **463**	2·20	2·00
1660	1b. Hat, instruments and candles	4·00	3·50
1661	2b. Vase, gourds and holly	7·75	5·75

464 Helmeted Warrior (allegorical painting)

2002. 180th Anniv of Independence. Multicoloured.

1662	15c. Type **464**	60	40
1663	15c. Woman charioteer (allegorical painting)	60	40

465 San Lorenzo Castle

2002. America.Cultural Heritage. Multicoloured.

1664	15c. Type **465**	70	50
1665	15c. Panama city	70	50
1666	1b. 50 Metropolitan Cathedral church (horiz)	6·25	4·25
1667	1b. 50 Portobelo fortifications (horiz)	6·25	4·25

466 Natives and Ship

2002. 500th Anniv of Discovery of Panama Isthmus. Multicoloured.

1668	50c. Type **466**	1·90	1·70
1669	5b. Native woman and Spanish conquistador	19·00	17·00

467 Spaniard and Natives (allegorical painting)

2002. Artistic Treasures of Las Garzas Palace. Painting by Robert Lewis. Multicoloured.

1670	5c. Type **467**	25	15
1671	5c. Battle scene	25	15
1672	5c. Mythical figures	25	15
1673	5c. Spanish women	25	15

468 *Montastraea annularis*

2002. Corals. Multicoloured.

1674	10c. Type **468**	35	25
1675	10c. *Pavona chiriquiensis*	35	25
1676	1b. *Siderastrea glynni*	3·75	3·25
1677	2b. *Pocillopora*	7·50	6·50

469 *Ophioderes maternal*

2002. Butterflies and Moths. Multicoloured.

1678	10c. Type **469**	45	25
1679	10c. *Rhuda focula*	45	25
1680	1b. *Morpho peleides*	4·25	3·25
1681	2b. *Tarchon felderi*	8·50	6·50

470 "100" enclosing Jean Baptiste de La Salle (founder) and Children

2003. Air. Centenary of La Salle Christian Schools.

1682	**470**	5b. multicoloured	16·00	13·00

471 Nata Church

2003. Air. 480th Anniv of Nata.

1683	**471**	1b. multicoloured	3·00	2·50

472 Girl and Nativity Figures

2003. Christmas (2002).

1684	**472**	15c. multicoloured	50	35

473 Children

2003. America. Literacy Campaign.

1685	**473**	45c. multicoloured	1·40	1·20

474 Clara Gonzalez de Behringer

2003. Famous Women. Clara Gonzalez de Behringer (first woman lawyer).

1686	**474**	30c. multicoloured	1·00	85

475 "Colon" (steam locomotive)

2003. Air. First Transcontinental Railway. Multicoloured.

1687	40c. Type **475**	1·30	1·10
1688	50c. Locomotive in station (vert)	1·60	1·40

476 Columbus Monument

2003. 150th Anniv of Colon City (2002).

1689	**476**	15c. multicoloured	50	35

477 Spanish Soldiers and Native Americans

2003. Air. 500th Anniv of Santa Maria de Belen.

1690	**477**	1b.50 multicoloured	4·75	4·25

478 Christopher Columbus and his Ships

2003. Air. 500th Anniv of Fourth Voyage of Christopher Columbus (2002).

1691 **478** 2b. multicoloured 6·50 5·00

479 Luis Russell

2003. Birth Centenary of Luis Russell (musician).

1692 **479** 10c. multicoloured 35 15

480 Muse of Music (statue)

2003. Artistic Treasures of National Theatre. Multicoloured.

1693 5c. Type **480** (postage) 15 10
1694 5c. Muse of theatre (statue) 15 10

(b) Size 40×30 mm.

1695 50c. Decorated balcony (air) 1·60 1·40
1696 60c. Portico and decorated ceiling 1·80 1·60

481 Village and Woman's Face

2003. Kuna Indians of San Blas Archipelago. Multicoloured.

1697 50c. Type **481** 1·60 1·40
1698 50c. Couple wearing traditional costume (vert) 1·60 1·40
1699 60c. Traditional dance 1·90 1·60
1700 60c. Woman's hands sewing mola (traditional cloth) 1·90 1·60
MS1701 100×50 mm. 1b.50 Fish (mola design) (50×46 mm) 5·50 5·50

482 Josemaria Escriva de Balaguer

2003. Birth Centenary (2002)of Josemaria Escriva de Balaguer (founder of Opus Dei (religious organization).

1702 **482** 10c. multicoloured 35 15

483 Hospital Building and St. Tomas de Villanueva (founder)

2003. Air. Panamanian Medicine Multicoloured.

1703 50c. Type **483** (300th anniv of St. Tomas Hospital) 1·60 1·40
1704 50c. Building facade and William Crawford Gorgas (founder) (75th anniv of Gorgas Medical Institute) 1·60 1·40

484 Necklaces

2003. Air. Pollera (Latin American folk costume) Jewellery. Multicoloured.

1705 45c. Type **484** 1·40 1·20
1706 60c. Broaches 1·80 1·60

485 National Arms

2003. Centenary of Panama Republic (1st issue). Multicoloured.

1707 5c. Type **485** 15 10
1708 10c. National flag 35 15
1709 15c. Manuel Amador Guerrero (president, 1903) 50 35
1710 15c. Mireya Mascoso (president, 2003) 50 35
1711 25c. Act of Independence 80 60
1712 30c. Sterculia apetala 1·00 85
1713 30c. Peristeria elata 1·00 85
1714 35c. Revolutionary junta 1·20 95
1715 45c. Constitutional conference members 1·40 1·20

See also No. 1717.

486 Harpy Eagle (*Harpia harpia*) and Harlequin Frog (*Atelopus varius*)

2003. America. Endangered Species.

1716 **486** 2b. multicoloured 6·50 5·00

487 Panama City and Nativity

2003. Centenary of Panama Republic (2nd issue). Christmas.

1717 **487** 10c. multicoloured 35 15

488 Building Facade

2003. 150th Anniv of "La Estrella" Newspaper.

1718 **488** 40c. multicoloured 1·30 1·10

489 Panama City and Emblems

2003. Panama City, Ibero-American Cultural Capital, 2003.

1719 **489** 5c. multicoloured 15 10

490 Pres. Moscoso and Cornucopia

2004. Mireya Moscoso, First Woman President of Panama (2nd issue).

1720 **490** 35c. multicoloured 1·10 90

491 Don Quixote and Sanco Panza (based on drawing by Salvador Dali)

2007. 400th (2005) Anniv of Publication of El Ingenioso Hidalgo Don Quixote de la Mancha (novel) by Miguel de Cervantes.

1721 **491** 45c. multicoloured 1·50 1·50

492 Building Facade

2007. 50th Anniv of Augustinians in Panama.

1722 **492** 35c. multicoloured 1·30 1·30

493 Red-backed Squirrel Monkey

2007. Red-backed Squirrel Monkey (Saimiri oerstedi). Multicoloured.

1723 20c. Type **493** 75 75
1724 20c. Mother and baby 75 75
1725 20c. Two monkeys 75 75
1726 20c. Monkey chewing stick and mother with baby 75 75

Nos. 1723/6 were issued together, se-tenant, forming a composite design.

494 Pope John Paul II (image scaled to 65% of original size)

2007. Pope John Paul II and Pope Benedict XVI. Sheet 150×100 mm containing Type 494 and similar vert design. Multicoloured.

MS1727 50c.×2, Type **494**; Pope Benedict XVI 3·25 3·25

495 Children looking at Atlas

2007. Tourism includes People. National Secretariat for Social Integration of Disabled Persons of Panama (SENADIS).

1728 **495** 5c. multicoloured 15 15

496 'Crossing the Isthmus'

2007. 150th (2005) Anniv of Panama Canal Railway. Multicoloured.

1729 20c. Type **496** 75 75
1730 30c. Locomotive 1·20 1·20

497 Diablico Sucio

2008. Tourism. Multicoloured.

1731 15c. Type **497** 60 60
1732 20c. Salto de la Chorrera (vert) 75 75
1733 25c. Sarigua Park 90 90
1734 35c. Ancient pots 1·30 1·30
1735 45c. Casa Fuerte de San Fernando 1·50 1·50
1736 60c. Colonial buildings (vert) 3·50 3·50

ACKNOWLEDGEMENT OF RECEIPT STAMPS

1898. Handstamped A. R. COLON COLOMBIA.

AR24 **5** 5c. blue 6·75 5·75
AR27 **5** 10c. orange 12·00 11·50

1902. Handstamped AR in circle.

AR32 5c. blue 5·75 5·50
AR33 10c. orange 11·50 11·00

1903. No. AR169 of Colombia handstamped AR in circle.

AR34 **AR 60** 5c. red 23·00 22·00

AR37

1904

AR135 **AR 37** 5c. blue 1·20 95

1916. Optd A.R.

AR177 **50** 2½c. red 1·20 95

EXPRESS LETTER STAMPS

1926. Optd EXPRESO.

E220 **57** 10c. black and orange 9·75 3·75
E221 **57** 20c. black and brown 11·50 3·75

E81 Cyclist Messenger

1929

E226 **E 81** 10c. orange 1·40 1·10
E227 **E 81** 20c. brown 5·25 3·25

INSURANCE STAMPS

1942. Surch SEGURO POSTAL HABILITADO and value.

IN430 5c. on 1b. black (No. 373) 60 55
IN431 10c. on 1b. brown (No. 365) 95 95
IN432 25c. on 50c. brown (No. 372) 2·50 2·40

POSTAGE DUE STAMPS

D58 San Geronimo Castle Gate, Portobelo

1915

D169	**D58**	1c. brown	3·75	95
D170	-	2c. brown	5·75	75
D171	-	4c. brown	7·75	1·50
D172	-	10c. brown	5·75	2·00

DESIGNS—VERT: 2c. Statue of Columbus. HORIZ: 4c. House of Deputies. VERT: 10c. Pedro J. Sosa.

No. D169 is wrongly inscr "CASTILLO DE SAN LORENZO CHAGRES".

D86

1930

D240	**D86**	1c. green	1·20	75
D241	**D86**	2c. red	1·20	75
D242	**D86**	4c. blue	1·70	95
D243	**D86**	10c. violet	1·70	95

R4

1888

R12	**R4**	10c. black on grey	9·25	7·50

1897. Handstamped R COLON in circle.

R22	**5**	10c. orange	6·75	6·25

REGISTRATION STAMPS

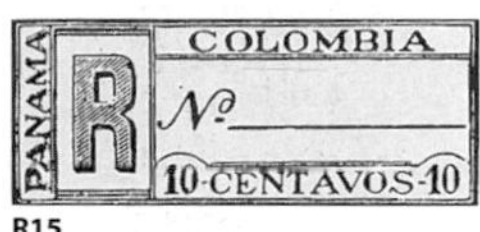

R15

1900

R29	**R15**	10c. black on blue	5·75	4·75
R30	**R15**	10c. red	39·00	22·00

1902. No. R30 surch by hand.

R31	20c. on 10c. red	23·00	18·00

1903. Type R 85 of Colombia optd REPUBLICA DE PANAMA.

R42A	20c. red on blue	60·00	50·00
R43A	20c. blue on blue	60·00	50·00

1903. Nos. R42/3 surch.

R46	10c. on 20c. red on blue	75·00	70·00
R47	10c. on 20c. blue on blue	75·00	70·00

1904. Optd PANAMA.

R60	**5**	10c. orange	3·75	3·00

1904. Type R 6 of Colombia surch Panama 10 and bar.

R67	10c. on 20c. red on blue	90·00	85·00
R68	10c. on 20c. blue on blue	70·00	60·00

1904. Type R 85 of Colombia optd Republica de Panama.

R106	20c. red on blue	6·75	6·50

R35

1904

R133	**R35**	10c. green	1·20	55

1916. Stamps of Panama surch R 5 cts.

R175	**46**	5c. on 8c. black & purple	4·00	3·50
R176	**52**	5c. on 8c. black & purple	4·75	2·40

TOO LATE STAMPS

1903. Too Late stamp of Colombia optd REPUBLICA DE PANAMA.

L44A	**L86**	5c. violet on red	14·50	10·00

L36

1904

L134	**L36**	2½c. red	1·20	75

1910. Typewritten optd Retardo.

L158	**50**	2½c. red	£140	£110

1910. Optd RETARDO.

L159	2½c. red	70·00	55·00

1916. Surch RETARDO UN CENTESIMO.

L173	**38**	1c. on ½c. orange	1·20	1·10

APPENDIX

The following stamps have either been issued in excess of postal needs or have not been available to the public in reasonable quantites at face value. Such stamps may later be given full listing if there is evidence of regular postal use.

1964

Satellites. Postage 1/2, 1c.; Air 5, 10, 21, 50c.

1965

Tokyo Olympic Games Medal Winners. Postage 1/2, 1, 2, 3, 4c.; Air 5, 6, 7, 10, 21, 31c.
Space Research. Postage 1/2, 1, 2, 3c.; Air 5, 10, 11, 31c.
400th Birth Anniv of Galileo. Air 10, 21c.
Peaceful Uses of Atomic Energy. Postage 1/2, 1, 4c.; Air 6, 10, 21c.
Nobel Prize Medals. Air 10, 21c.
Pres. John Kennedy. Postage 1/2, 1c.; Air 10+5c., 21+10c., 31+15c.

1966

Pope Paul's Visit to U.N. in New York. Postage 1/2, 1c.; Air 5, 10, 21, 31c.
Famous Men. Postage 1/2c.; Air 10, 31c.
Famous Paintings. Postage 1/2c.; Air 10, 31c.
World Cup Football Championship. Postage 1/2, 1/2c.; Air 10, 10, 21, 21c.
Italian Space Research. Postage 1/2, 1c.; Air 5, 10, 21c.
Centenary of I.T.U. Air 31c.
World Cup Winners. Optd on 1966 World Cup Issue. Postage 1/2, 1/2c.; Air 10, 10, 21, 21c.
Religious Paintings. Postage 1/2, 1, 2, 3c.; Air 21, 21c.
Churchill and Space Research. Postage 1/2c.; Air 10, 31c.
3rd Death Anniv of Pres. John Kennedy. Postage 1/2, 1c.; Air 10, 31c.
Jules Verne and Space Research. Postage 1/2, 1c.; Air 5, 10, 21, 31c.

1967

Religious Paintings. Postage 1/2, 1c.; Air 5, 10, 21, 31c.
Mexico Olympics. Postage 1/2, 1c.; Air 5, 10, 21, 31c.
Famous Paintings. Postage 5c.x3; Air 21c.x3.
Goya's Paintings. Postage 2, 3, 4c.; Air 5, 8, 10, 13, 21c.

1968

Religious Paintings. Postage 1, 1, 3c.; Air 4, 21, 21c.
Mexican President's Visit. Air 50c., 1b.
Winter Olympic Games, Grenoble. Postage 1/2, 1c.; Air 5, 10, 21, 31c.
Butterflies. Postage 1/2, 1, 3, 4c.; Air 5, 13c.
Ship Paintings. Postage 1/2, 1, 3, 4c.; Air 5, 13c.
Fishes. Postage 1/2, 1, 3, 4c.; Air 5, 13c.
Winter Olympic Medal Winners. Postage 1, 2, 3, 4, 5, 6, 8c.; Air 13, 30c.
Paintings of Musicians. Postage 5, 10, 15, 20, 25, 30c.
Satellite Transmissions from Panama T.V. (a) Olympic Games, Mexico. Optd on 1964 Satellites issue. Postage 1/2c.; Air 50c. (b) Pope Paul's Visit to Latin America. Postage 1/2c.; Air 21c. (c) Panama Satellite Transmissions. Inauguration. (i) optd on Space Research issue of 1965. Postage 5c.; Air 31c. (ii) optd on Churchill and Space Research issue of 1966. Postage 1/2c.; Air 10c.
Hunting Paintings. Postage 1, 3, 5, 10c.; Air 13, 30c.
Horses and Jockeys. Postage 5, 10, 15, 20, 25, 30c.
Mexico Olympics. Postage 1, 2, 3, 4, 5, 6, 8c.; Air 13, 30c.

1969

1st International Philatelic and Numismatic Exhibition. Optd on 1968 Issue of Mexican President's Visit. Air 50c., 1b.
Telecommunications Satellites. Air 5, 10, 15, 20, 25, 30c.
Provisionals. Surch "Decreto No. 112 (de 6 de marzo de 1969)" and new values on No. 781 and 10c.+5c. and 21c.+10c. of 1965 Issue of 3rd Death Anniv of Pres. John Kennedy. Air 5c. on 5c.+5c., 5c. on 10c.+5c., 10c. on 21c.+10c.
Pope Paul VI Visit to Latin America. Religious Paintings. Postage 1, 2, 3, 4, 5c.; Air 6, 7, 8, 10c.

Pt. 8

PAPAL STATES

Parts of Italy under Papal rule till 1870 when they became part of the Kingdom of Italy.

1852. 100 bajoochi = 1 scudo.
1866. 100 centesimi = 1 lira.

1

2

1852. Papal insignia as in T 1 and 2 in various shapes and frames. Imperf.

2	½b. black on grey	£750	70·00
5	½b. black on lilac	80·00	£160
10	1b. black on green	£110	£110
11	2b. black on green	£275	21·00
14	2b. black on white	20·00	95·00
15	3b. black on brown	£225	80·00
16	3b. black on yellow	21·00	£140
17	4b. black on brown	£8000	95·00
19	4b. black on yellow	£300	95·00
20	5b. black on pink	£300	21·00
22	6b. black on lilac	£1600	£275
23	6b. black on grey	£1100	90·00
25	7b. black on blue	£1800	90·00
26	8b. black on white	£700	55·00
27	50b. blue	£18000	£2000
29	1s. pink	£4500	£3750

1867. Same types. Imperf.

30	2c. black on green	£140	£325
32	3c. black on grey	£1800	£2250
33	5c. black on blue	£225	£300
34	10c. black on red	£1900	£110
35	20c. black on red	£225	£140
36	40c. black on yellow	£225	£225
37	80c. black on pink	£225	£600

1868. Same types. Perf.

42	2c. black on green	16·00	95·00
43	3c. black on grey	65·00	£4000
45	5c. black on blue	37·00	85·00
46	10c. black on orange	5·25	19·00
49	20c. black on mauve	6·50	43·00
50	20c. black on red	3·75	18·00
52	40c. black on yellow	13·00	£120
55	80c. black on pink	65·00	£450

Pt. 1

PAPUA

The eastern portion of the island of New Guinea, to the North of Australia, a territory of the Commonwealth of Australia, now combined with New Guinea. Australian stamps were used after the Japanese defeat in 1945 until the combined issue appeared in 1952.

12 pence = 1 shilling; 20 shilling = 1 pound.

(Formerly BRITISH NEW GUINEA)

1 Lakatoi (native canoe) with Hanuabada Village in Background

1901

9	**1**	½d. black and green	18·00	3·75
10	**1**	1d. black and red	7·50	2·00
11	**1**	2d. black and violet	11·00	4·25
12	**1**	2½d. black and blue	24·00	12·00
13	**1**	4d. black and brown	35·00	55·00
6	**1**	6d. black and green	60·00	35·00
7	**1**	1s. black and orange	70·00	70·00
8	**1**	2s.6d. black and brown	£650	£550

1906. Optd Papua.

38	½d. black and green	17·00	20·00
39	1d. black and red	7·50	5·00
40	2d. black and violet	4·50	2·25
42	4d. black and brown	45·00	65·00
43	6d. black and green	42·00	45·00
19	1s. black and orange	22·00	38·00
24	2½d. black and blue	6·00	15·00
37	2s.6d. black and brown	42·00	65·00

6

1907

66	**6**	½d. black and green	2·25	4·00
94	**6**	1d. black and red	1·75	1·25
68	**6**	2d. black and purple	6·50	8·00
51a	**6**	2½d. black and blue	11·00	6·50
63	**6**	4d. black and brown	4·75	9·00
80	**6**	6d. black and green	8·50	7·50
81	**6**	1s. black and orange	8·50	20·00
82	**6**	2s.6d. black and brown	45·00	50·00

1911

84a	½d. green	70	2·25
85	1d. red	1·25	75
86	2d. mauve	3·00	75
87	2½d. blue	6·00	8·50
88	4d. olive	2·25	11·00
89	6d. brown	3·75	5·00
90	1s. yellow	9·50	15·00
91	2s.6d. red	38·00	45·00

1916

93	½d. green and olive	80	1·00
95	1½d. blue and brown	1·50	80
96	2d. purple and red	1·75	75
97	2½d. green and blue	4·75	12·00
98	3d. black and turquoise	3·50	1·75
99	4d. brown and orange	2·50	5·00
100	5d. grey and brown	4·25	16·00
101	6d. purple	3·25	9·50
127	9d. lilac and violet	4·50	35·00
102	1s. brown and olive	4·25	7·00
128	1s.3d. lilac and blue	7·50	35·00
103	2s.6d. red and pink	23·00	40·00
104	5s. black and green	50·00	48·00
105	10s. green and blue	£150	£170

1917. Surch ONE PENNY.

106a	1d. on ½d. green	1·00	1·25
107	1d. on 2d. mauve	12·00	15·00
108	1d. on 2½d. blue	1·25	3·75
109	1d. on 4d. green	1·75	4·50
110	1d. on 6d. brown	8·50	19·00
111	1d. on 2s.6d. red	1·50	6·00

1929. Air. Optd AIR MAIL.

114	3d. black and turquoise	1·00	7·50

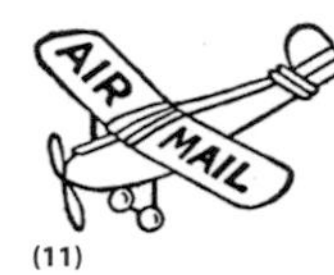

(11)

1930. Air. Optd with T 11.

118	3d. black and turquoise	1·00	6·00
119	6d. purple	5·50	14·00
120	1s. brown and olive	4·25	13·00

1931. Surch in words or figures and words.

122	2d. on 1½d. blue and brown	1·00	2·00
125	5d. on 1s. brown and olive	1·00	2·00
126	9d. on 2s.6d. red and pink	5·50	8·50
123	1s.3d. on 5d. black and green	4·25	9·00

15 Motuan Girl

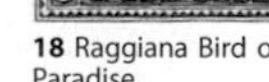

18 Raggiana Bird of Paradise

20 Native Mother and Child

1932

130	**15**	½d. black and orange	2·75	3·25
131	-	1d. black and green	2·75	60
132	-	1½d. black and red	3·00	8·00
133	**18**	2d. red	11·00	30
134	-	3d. black and blue	3·25	6·50
135	**20**	4d. olive	9·50	9·50
136	-	5d. black and green	4·50	3·00
137	-	6d. brown	7·50	5·50
138	-	9d. black and violet	10·00	21·00
139	-	1s. green	6·00	8·50
140	-	1s.3d. black and purple	15·00	27·00
141	-	2s. black and green	15·00	24·00
142	-	2s.6d. black and mauve	25·00	38·00
143	-	5s. black and brown	60·00	55·00
144	-	10s. violet	£120	£110
145	-	£1 black and grey	£225	£180

DESIGNS—VERT (as T **15**): 1d. Chieftain's son; 1½d. Tree houses; 3d. Papuan dandy; 5d. Masked dancer; 9d. Shooting fish; 1s. Ceremonial platform; 1s.3d. Lakatoi; 2s. Papuan art; 2s.6d. Pottery-making; 5d. Native policeman; £1 Delta house. VERT (as T **18**): 6d. Papuan mother. HORIZ: (as T **20**): 10s. Lighting fire.

31 Hoisting the Union Jack

1934. 50th Anniv of Declaration of British Protectorate. Inscr "1884 1834".

146	**31**	1d. green	1·50	3·50
147	-	2d. red	2·00	3·00
148	**31**	3d. blue	2·00	3·00
149	-	5d. purple	11·00	18·00

DESIGN: 2d., 5d. Scene on H.M.S. "Nelson".

1935. Silver Jubilee. Optd HIS MAJESTY'S JUBILEE 1910 1935 (1910 – 1935 on 2d.).

150		1d. black & green (No. 131)	1·50	3·25
151	**18**	2d. red	5·50	6·00
152	-	3d. black and blue (No. 134)	3·25	3·25
153	-	5d. black & green (No. 136)	3·25	3·25

35 King George VI

1937. Coronation.

154	**35**	1d. green	45	20
155	**35**	2d. red	45	1·25
156	**35**	3d. blue	45	1·25
157	**35**	5d. purple	45	1·75

36 Port Moresby

1938. Air. 50th Anniv of Declaration of British Possession.

158	**36**	2d. red	3·00	3·50
159	**36**	3d. blue	3·00	2·50
160	**36**	5d. green	3·00	3·75
161	**36**	8d. red	6·00	23·00
162	**36**	1s. mauve	23·00	25·00

37 Natives poling Rafts

1939. Air.

163	**37**	2d. red	3·50	7·50
164	**37**	3d. blue	3·50	13·00
165	**37**	5d. green	3·50	2·50
166	**37**	8d. red	8·00	4·50
167	**37**	1s. mauve	13·00	10·00
168	**37**	1s.6d. olive	30·00	40·00

OFFICIAL STAMPS

1931. Optd O S.

O55	**6**	½d. green and olive	2·50	4·75
O56a	**6**	1d. black and red	5·00	14·00
O57	**6**	1½d. blue and brown	1·60	12·00
O58	**6**	2d. brown and purple	5·00	15·00
O59	**6**	3d. black and turquoise	2·50	22·00
O60	**6**	4d. brown and orange	2·50	18·00
O61	**6**	5d. grey and brown	6·00	38·00
O62	**6**	6d. purple and red	4·00	8·50
O63	**6**	9d. lilac and violet	30·00	48·00
O64	**6**	1s. brown and olive	9·00	30·00
O65	**6**	1s.3d. lilac and blue	30·00	48·00
O66	**6**	2s.6d. red and pink	48·00	95·00

Pt. 1

PAPUA NEW GUINEA

Combined territory on the island of New Guinea administered by Australia under trusteeship. Self-government was established during 1973.

1952. 12 pence = 1 shilling; 20 shillings = 1 pound.
1966. 100 cents = $1 Australian.
1975. 100 toea = 1 kina.

1 Matschie's Tree Kangaroo

7 Kiriwina Chief House

1952

1	**1**	½d. green	30	10
2	-	1d. brown	20	10
3	-	2d. blue	35	10
4	-	2½d. orange	3·00	50
5	-	3d. myrtle	50	10
6	-	3½d. red	50	10
6a	-	3½d. black	6·00	90
18	-	4d. red	60	10
19	-	5d. green	60	10
7	**7**	6½d. purple	1·25	10
20	-	7d. green	2·25	10
8	-	7½d. blue	2·50	1·00
21	-	8d. blue	60	1·00
9	-	9d. brown	2·50	40
10	-	1s. green	1·50	10
11	-	1s.6d. myrtle	2·75	60
22	-	1s.7d. brown	5·50	3·00
12	-	2s. blue	2·50	10
23	-	2s.5d. red	1·50	1·00
13	-	2s.6d. purple	2·50	40
24	-	5s. red and olive	3·50	1·00
14	-	10s. slate	32·00	13·00
15	-	£1 brown	35·00	14·00

DESIGNS—VERT (as T **1**): 1d. Buka head-dresses; 2d. Native youth; 2½d. Greater bird of paradise; 3d. Native policeman; 3½d. Papuan head-dress; 4d., 5d. Cacao plant. (As T **7**): 7½d. Kiriwina Yam house; 1s.6d. Rubber tapping; 2s. Sepik dancing masks; 5s. Coffee beans; £1 Papuan shooting fish. HORIZ (as T **7**): 7, 8d. Klinki plymill; 9d. Copra making; 1s. Lakatoi; 1s.7d., 2s.5d. Cattle; 2s.6d. Native shepherd and flock; 10s. Map of Papua and New Guinea.

1957. Nos. 4, 1 and 10 surch.

16		4d. on 2½d. orange	1·25	10
25	**1**	5d. on ½d. green	75	10
17		7d. on 1s. green	40	10

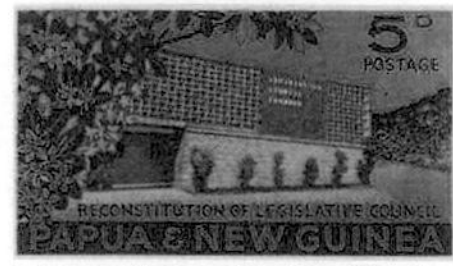

23 Council Chamber, Port Moresby

1961. Reconstitution of Legislative Council.

26	**23**	5d. green and yellow	75	25
27	**23**	2s.3d. green and salmon	2·00	1·50

24 Female, Goroka, New Guinea

26 Female Dancer

39 Waterfront, Port Moresby

28 Traffic Policeman

1961

28	**24**	1d. lake	70	10
29	-	3d. blue	30	10
47	**39**	8d. green	30	15
30	**26**	1s. green	1·00	15
31	-	2s. purple	45	15
48	-	2s.3d. blue	30	30
32	**28**	3s. green	1·00	2·00

DESIGNS—As Type **24**: 3d. Tribal elder, Tari, Papua. As Type **39**: 2s.3d. Piaggio P-166B Portofino aircraft landing at Tapini. As Type **26**: 2s. Male dancer.

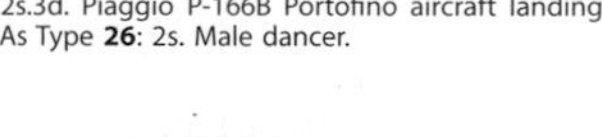

29 Campaign Emblem

1962. Malaria Eradication.

33	**29**	5d. lake and blue	30	15
34	**29**	1s. red and brown	50	25
35	**29**	2s. black and green	60	70

30 Map of South Pacific

1962. 5th South Pacific Conference, Pago Pago.

36	**30**	5d. red and green	50	15
37	**30**	1s.6d. violet and yellow	75	70
38	**30**	2s.6d. green and blue	75	1·40

31 Throwing the Javelin

1962. 7th British Empire and Commonwealth Games, Perth.

39	**31**	5d. brown and blue	20	10
40	-	5d. brown and orange	20	10
41	-	2s.3d. brown and green	70	75

SPORTS—As T **31**: No. 40, High jump. 32×23 mm: No. 41, Runners.

34 Raggiana Bird of Paradise

37 Queen Elizabeth II

36 Rabaul

1963

42	**34**	5d. yellow, brown and sepia	70	10
43	-	6d. red, brown and grey	50	1·00
44	**36**	10s. multicoloured	9·50	4·50
45	**37**	£1 brown, gold and green	1·25	1·75

DESIGN—As Type **34**: 6d. Common phalanger.

38 Centenary Emblem

1963. Centenary of Red Cross.

46	**38**	5d. red, grey and green	75	10

40 Games Emblem

1963. 1st South Pacific Games, Suva.

49	**40**	5d. brown	10	10
50	**40**	1s. green	30	60

41 Watam Head

1964. Native Artefacts. Multicoloured.

51	11d. Type **41**	25	10
52	2s.5d. Watam head (different)	30	1·75
53	2s.6d. Bosmun head	30	10
54	5s. Medina head	35	20

45 Casting Vote

1964. Common Roll Elections.

55	**45**	5d. brown and drab	10	10
56	**45**	2s.3d. brown and blue	20	25

46 "Health Centres"

1964. Health Services.

57	**46**	5d. violet	10	10
58	-	8d. green	10	10
59	-	1s. blue	15	10
60	-	1s.2d. red	20	35

DESIGNS: 8d. "School health"; 1s. "Infant child and maternal health"; 1s.2d. "Medical training".

50 Striped Gardener Bowerbird

1964. Multicoloured.. Multicoloured..

61	1d. Type **50**	50	10
62	3d. Adelbert bowerbird	50	10
63	5d. Blue bird of paradise	55	10
64	6d. Lawes's parotia	60	10
65	8d. Black-billed sicklebill	1·00	20
66	1s. Emperor of Germany bird of paradise	1·50	10
67	2s. Brown sicklebill	60	30
68	2s.3d. Lesser bird of paradise	60	85
69	3s. Magnificent bird of paradise	60	1·25

70		5s. Twelve-wired bird of paradise	6·00	1·00
71		10s. Magnificent riflebird	1·75	6·50

Nos. 66/71 are larger, 25½×36½ mm.

61 Canoe Prow

1965. Sepik Canoe Prows in Port Moresby Museum.

72	**61**	4d. multicoloured	30	10
73	-	1s.2d. multicoloured	1·00	1·75
74	-	1s.6d. multicoloured	30	10
75	-	4s. multicoloured	40	50

Each show different carved prows as Type **61**.

61a "Simpson and his Donkey"

1965. 50th Anniv of Gallipoli Landing.

76	**61a**	2s.3d. brown, black & green	20	10

65 Urban Plan and Native House

1965. 6th South Pacific Conference, Lae.

77	**65**	6d. multicoloured	10	10
78	-	1s. multicoloured	10	10

No. 78 is similar to Type **65** but with the plan on the right and the house on the left. Also "URBANISATION" reads downwards.

66 Mother and Child

1965. 20th Anniv of U.N.O.

79	**66**	6d. sepia, blue and turquoise	10	10
80	-	1s. brown, blue and violet	10	10
81	-	2s. blue, green and olive	10	10

DESIGNS—VERT: 1s. Globe and U.N. emblem; 2s. U.N. emblem and globes.

69 "Papilio ulysses"

1966. Decimal Currency. Butterflies. Mult.

82		1c. Type **69**	40	1·00
83		3c. "Cyrestis acilia"	40	1·00
84		4c. "Graphium weiskei"	40	1·00
85		5c. "Terinos alurgis"	40	10
86		10c. "Ornithoptera priamus" (horiz)	50	30
86a		12c. "Euploea callithoe" (horiz)	2·75	2·25
87		15c. "Papilio euchenor" (horiz)	1·00	80
88		20c. "Parthenos sylvia" (horiz)	50	25
89		25c. "Delias aruna" (horiz)	70	1·25
90		50c. "Apaturina erminea" (horiz)	10·00	1·25
91		$1 "Doleschallia dascylus" (horiz)	2·00	2·25
92		$2 "Ornithoptera paradisea" (horiz)	5·00	9·00

80 "Molala Harai"

1966. Folklore. Elema Art (1st series).

93	**80**	2c. black and red	10	10
94	-	7c. black, yellow and blue	10	65
95	-	30c. black, red and green	15	15
96	-	60c. black, red and yellow	40	65

DESIGNS: 7c. "Marai"; 30c. "Meavea Kivovia"; 60c. "Toivita Tapaivita".

84 Throwing the Discus

1966. South Pacific Games, Noumea. Mult.

97		5c. Type **84**	10	10
98		10c. Football	15	10
99		20c. Tennis	20	40

87 "Mucuna novoguineensis"

1966. Flowers. Multicoloured.

100		5c. Type **87**	15	10
101		10c. "Tecomanthe dendrophila"	15	10
102		20c. "Rhododendron macgregoriae"	20	10
103		60c. "Rhododendron konori"	50	1·40

91 "Fine Arts"

1967. Higher Education. Multicoloured.

104		1c. Type **91**	10	10
105		3c. "Surveying"	10	10
106		4c. "Civil Engineering"	10	10
107		5c. "Science"	10	10
108		20c. "Law"	10	10

96 "Sagra speciosa"

1967. Fauna Conservation (Beetles). Mult.

109		5c. Type **96**	15	10
110		10c. "Eupholus schoenherri"	15	10
111		20c. "Sphingnotus albertisi"	25	10
112		25c. "Cyphogastra albertisi"	25	10

100 Laloki River

1967. Laloki River Hydro-electric Scheme, and "New Industries". Multicoloured.

113		5c. Type **100**	10	10
114		10c. Pyrethrum	10	10
115		20c. Tea plant	15	10
116		25c. Type **100**	15	10

103 Air Attack at Milne Bay

1967. 25th Anniv of Pacific War. Multicoloured.

117		2c. Type **103**	10	50
118		5c. Kokoda Trail (vert)	10	10
119		20c. The Coast watchers	25	10
120		50c. Battle of the Coral Sea	80	70

107 Papuan Lory

1967. Christmas. Territory Parrots. Mult.

121		5c. Type **107**	20	10
122		7c. Pesquet's parrot	25	90
123		20c. Dusky lory	30	10
124		25c. Edward's fig parrot	35	10

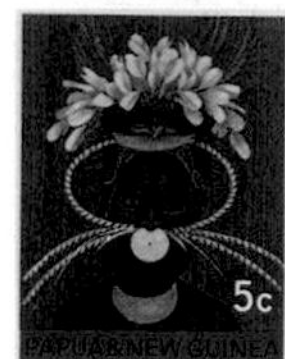

111 Chimbu Head-dress

1968. "National Heritage". Designs showing different Head-dresses. Multicoloured.

125		5c. Type **111**	10	10
126		10c. Southern Highlands (horiz)	15	10
127		20c. Western Highlands (horiz)	15	10
128		60c. Chimbu (different)	40	45

115 "Hyla thesaurensis"

1968. Fauna Conservation (Frogs). Mult.

129		5c. Type **115**	15	10
130		10c. "Hyla iris"	15	20
131		15c. "Ceratobatrachus guentheri"	15	30
132		20c. "Nyctimystes narinosa"	20	60

119 Human Rights Emblem and Papuan Head-dress (abstract)

1968. Human Rights Year. Multicoloured.

133		5c. Type **119**	10	10
134		10c. Human Rights in the World (abstract)	10	10

121 Leadership (abstract)

1968. Universal Suffrage. Multicoloured.

135		20c. Type **121**	15	20
136		25c. Leadership of the Community (abstract)	15	30

123 Common Egg Cowrie

1968. Sea Shells. Multicoloured.

137		1c. Type **123**	10	10
138		3c. Laciniate conch	30	1·25
139		4c. Lithograph cone	20	1·25
140		5c. Marbled cone	25	10
141		7c. Episcopal mitre	35	10
142		10c. "Cymbiola rutila ruckeri"	45	10
143		12c. Checkerboard bonnet	1·25	2·00
144		15c. Scorpion conch	60	1·00
145		20c. Fluted giant clam or scale tridacna	70	10
146		25c. Camp pitar venus	70	1·75
147		30c. Ramose murex	70	1·00
148		40c. Chambered or pearly nautilus	75	1·25
149		60c. Trumpet triton	70	50
150		$1 Manus green papuina	1·00	60
151		$2 Glory of the sea cone	10·00	1·50

138 Tito Myth

1969. Folklore. Elema Art (2nd series).

152	**138**	5c. black, yellow and red	10	60
153	-	5c. black, yellow and red	10	60
154	-	10c. black, grey and red	15	60
155	-	10c. black, grey and red	15	60

DESIGNS: No. 153, Iko Myth; 154, Luvuapo Myth; 155, Miro Myth.

142 "Fireball" Class Dinghy

1969. 3rd South Pacific Games, Port Moresby.

156	**142**	5c. black	10	10
157	-	10c. violet	10	20
158	-	20c. green	15	30

DESIGNS—HORIZ: 10c. Swimming pool, Boroko; 20c. Games arena, Konedobu.

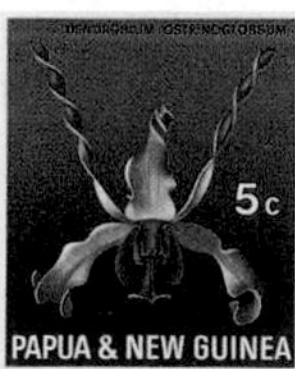

145 "Dendrobium ostrinoglossum"

1969. Flora Conservation (Orchids). Multicoloured.

159		5c. Type **145**	25	10
160		10c. "Dendrobium lawesii"	25	70
161		20c. "Dendrobium pseudofrigidum"	30	90
162		30c. "Dendrobium conanthum"	30	70

149 Bird of Paradise

1969

162a	**149**	2c. blue, black and red	10	65
163	**149**	5c. green, brown & orge	10	10

150 Native Potter

1969. 50th Anniv of I.L.O.

164	**150**	5c. multicoloured	10	10

151 Tareko

1969. Musical Instruments.

165	**151**	5c. multicoloured	10	10
166	-	10c. black, green & yellow	10	10
167	-	25c. black, yellow & brown	15	15
168	-	30c. multicoloured	25	15

DESIGNS: 10c. Garamut; 25c. Iviliko; 30c. Kundu.

155 Prehistoric Ambun Stone

1970. "National Heritage". Multicoloured.

169	5c. Type **155**	10	10
170	10c. Masawa canoe of Kula Circuit	10	10
171	25c. Torres' map, 1606	40	15
172	30c. H.M.S. "Basilisk" (paddle-sloop), 1873	65	25

159 King of Saxony Bird of Paradise

1970. Fauna Conservation. Birds of Paradise. Mult.

173	5c. Type **159**	40	15
174	10c. King bird of paradise	40	45
175	15c. Raggiana bird of paradise	55	80
176	25c. Sickle-crested bird of paradise	65	50

163 Douglas DC-6B and Mt. Wilhelm

1970. Australian and New Guinea Air Services. Multicoloured.

177	5c. Type **163**	25	30
178	5c. Lockheed Electra and Mt. Yule	25	30
179	5c. Boeing 727-100 and Mt. Giluwe	25	30
180	5c. Fokker Friendship and Manam Island	25	30
181	25c. Douglas DC-3 and Matupi Volcano	35	40
182	30c. Boeing 707 and Hombrom's Bluff	35	60

169 N. Miklouho-Maclay (scientist) and Effigy

1970. 42nd A.N.Z.A.A.S. Congress, Port Moresby. Multicoloured.

183	5c. Type **169**	10	10
184	10c. B. Malinowski (anthropologist) and native hut	20	10
185	15c. T. Salvadori (ornithologist) and double-wattled cassowary	70	25
186	20c. F. R. R. Schlechter (botanist) and flower	40	25

A.N.Z.A.A.S. = Australian–New Zealand Association for the Advancement of Science.

170 Wogeo Island Food Bowl

1970. Native Artefacts. Multicoloured.

187	5c. Type **170**	10	10
188	10c. Lime pot	20	10
189	15c. Albom sago storage pot	20	10
190	30c. Manus island bowl (horiz)	25	30

171 Eastern Highlands Dwelling

1971. Native Dwellings. Multicoloured.

191	5c. Type **171**	10	10
192	7c. Milne Bay stilt dwelling	15	90
193	10c. Purari Delta dwelling	15	10
194	40c. Sepik dwelling	25	90

172 Spotted Phalanger

1971. Fauna Conservation. Multicoloured.

195	5c. Type **172**	30	10
196	10c. Long-fingered possum	30	10
197	15c. Feather-tailed possum	40	80
198	25c. Long-tailed echidna	60	80
199	30c. Ornate tree kangaroo (horiz)	60	50

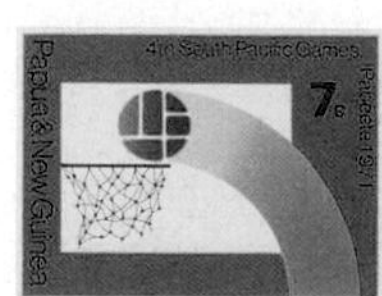

173 "Basketball"

1971. 4th South Pacific Games, Papeete. Mult.

200	7c. Type **173**	10	10
201	14c. "Sailing"	15	20
202	21c. "Boxing"	15	30
203	28c. "Athletics"	15	40

174 Bartering Fish for Vegetables

1971. Primary Industries. Multicoloured.

204	7c. Type **174**	10	10
205	9c. Man stacking yams	15	30
206	14c. Vegetable market	25	10
207	30c. Highlanders cultivating garden	45	65

175 Sia Dancer

1971. Native Dancers. Multicoloured.

208	7c. Type **175**	20	10
209	9c. Urasena dancer	20	20
210	20c. Siassi Tubuan dancers (horiz)	50	75
211	28c. Sia dancers (horiz)	65	90

176 Papuan Flag over Australian Flag

1971. Constitutional Development.

212	**176**	7c. multicoloured	30	10
213	-	7c. multicoloured	30	10

DESIGN: No. 213, Crest of Papua New Guinea and Australian coat of arms.

177 Map of Papua New Guinea and Flag of South Pacific Commission

1972. 25th Anniv of South Pacific Commission.

214	**177**	15c. multicoloured	45	55
215	-	15c. multicoloured	45	55

DESIGN: No. 215, Man's face and flag of the Commission.

178 Turtle

1972. Fauna Conservation (Reptiles). Mult.

216	7c. Type **178**	35	10
217	14c. Rainforest dragon	50	1·25
218	21c. Green python	55	1·50
219	30c. Salvador's monitor	60	1·25

179 Curtiss MF-6 Seagull and "Eureka" (schooner)

1972. 50th Anniv of Aviation. Multicoloured.

220	7c. Type **179**	40	10
221	14c. De Havilland D.H.37 and native porters	60	1·25
222	20c. Junkers G.31 and gold dredger	70	1·25
223	25c. Junkers F-13 and mission church	70	1·25

180 New National Flag

1972. National Day. Multicoloured.

224	7c. Type **180**	20	10
225	10c. Native drum	25	25
226	30c. Trumpet triton	45	50

181 Rev. Copland King

1972. Christmas. Missionaries. Multicoloured.

227	7c. Type **181**	25	40
228	7c. Rev. Dr. Flierl	25	40
229	7c. Bishop Verjus	25	40
230	7c. Pastor Ruatoka	25	40

182 Mt. Tomavatur Station

1973. Completion of Telecommunications Project, 1968–72. Multicoloured.

231	7c. Type **182**	15	20
232	7c. Mt. Kerigomma Station	15	20
233	7c. Sattelburg Station	15	20
234	7c. Wideru Station	15	20
235	9c. Teleprinter	15	20
236	30c. Network map	35	50

Nos. 235/6 are larger, 36×26 mm.

183 Queen Carola's Parotia

1973. Birds of Paradise. Multicoloured.

237	7c. Type **183**	80	35
238	14c. Goldie's bird of paradise	1·75	1·00
239	21c. Ribbon-tailed bird of paradise	2·00	1·50
240	28c. Princess Stephanie's bird of paradise	2·00	2·00

Nos. 239/40 are size 18×49 mm.

184 Wood Carver

1973. Multicoloured.. Multicoloured..

241	1c. Type **184**	10	10
242	3c. Wig-makers	30	10
243	5c. Mt. Bagana	55	10
244	6c. Pig exchange	80	1·50
245	7c. Coastal village	20	10
246	8c. Arawe mother	25	30
247	9c. Fire dancers	20	20
248	10c. Tifalmin hunter	40	10
249	14c. Crocodile hunters	35	70
250	15c. Mt. Elimbari	50	30
251	20c. Canoe-racing, Manus	60	40
252	21c. Making sago	30	1·00
253	25c. Council House	30	45
254	28c. Menyamya bowmen	30	1·00
255	30c. Shark-snaring	50	50
256	40c. Fishing canoes, Madang	30	40
257	60c. Tapa cloth-making	40	50
258	$1 Asaro Mudmen	45	1·10
259	$2 Enga "Sing Sing"	1·75	6·00

185 Stamps of German New Guinea, 1897

1973. 75th Anniv of Papua New Guinea Stamps.

260	**185**	1c. multicoloured	10	15
261	-	6c. indigo, blue and silver	15	30
262	-	7c. multicoloured	15	30
263	-	9c. multicoloured	15	30

264	-	25c. orange and gold	30	80
265	-	30c. plum and silver	30	90

DESIGNS—As Type **185**: 6c. 2 mark stamp of German New Guinea, 1900; 7c. Surcharged registration label of New Guinea, 1914. 46×35 mm: 9c. Papuan 1s. stamp, 1901. 45×38 mm: 25c. ½d. stamp of New Guinea, 1925; 30c. Papuan 10s. stamp, 1932.

186 Native Carved Heads

1973. Self-government.

266	**186**	7c. multicoloured	30	15
267	**186**	10c. multicoloured	50	65

187 Queen Elizabeth II (from photo by Karsh)

1974. Royal Visit.

268	**187**	7c. multicoloured	25	15
269	**187**	30c. multicoloured	75	1·50

188 Blyth's Hornbill

1974. Birds' Heads. Multicoloured.

270	7c. Type **188**	1·00	70
271	10c. Double-wattled cassowary (33×49 mm)	1·75	3·00
272	30c. New Guinea harpy eagle	3·25	7·50

189 "Dendrobium bracteosum"

1974. Flora Conservation. Multicoloured.

273	7c. Type **189**	30	10
274	10c. "D. anosmum"	40	60
275	20c. "D. smillieae"	50	1·40
276	30c. "D. insigne"	60	1·75

190 Motu Lakatoi

1974. National Heritage. Canoes. Multicoloured.

277	7c. Type **190**	30	10
278	10c. Tami two-master morobe	30	55
279	25c. Aramia racing canoe	60	3·00
280	30c. Buka Island canoe	60	1·00

191 1-toea Coin

1975. New Coinage. Multicoloured.

281	1t. Type **191**	10	30
282	7t. New 2t. and 5t. coins	20	10
283	10t. New 10t. coin	20	30
284	20t. New 20t. coin	30	70
285	1k. New 1k. coin	90	4·00

SIZES: 10, 20t. As Type **191**; 7t., 1k. 45×26 mm.

192 "Ornithoptera alexandrae"

1975. Fauna Conservation (Birdwing Butterflies). Multicoloured.

286	7t. Type **192**	25	10
287	10t. "O. victoriae"	30	65
288	30t. "O. allottei"	60	2·00
289	40t. "O. chimaera"	75	3·50

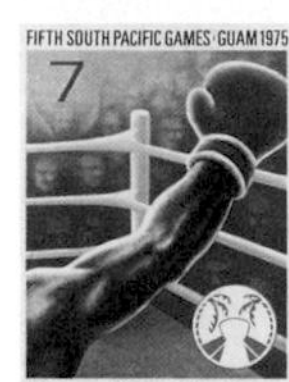

193 Boxing

1975. 5th South Pacific Games, Guam. Mult.

290	7t. Type **193**	10	10
291	20t. Running	15	30
292	25t. Basketball	30	45
293	30t. Swimming	30	50

194 Map and National Flag

1975. Independence. Multicoloured.

294	7t. Type **194**	20	10
295	30t. Map and National emblem	40	65
MS296	116×58 mm. Nos. 294/5	1·10	1·75

195 M.V. "Bulolo"

1976. Ships of the 1930s. Multicoloured.

297	7t. Type **195**	20	10
298	15t. M.V. "Macdhui"	30	30
299	25t. M.V. "Malaita"	35	65
300	60t. S.S. "Montoro"	50	2·50

196 Rorovana Carvings

1976. Bougainville Art. Multicoloured.

301	7t. Type **196**	10	10
302	20t. Upe hats	20	35
303	25t. Kapkaps	25	1·50
304	30t. Canoe paddles	30	80

197 Rabaul House

1976. Native Dwellings. Multicoloured.

305	7t. Type **197**	10	10
306	15t. Aramia house	15	20
307	30t. Telefomin house	25	60
308	40t. Tapini house	25	1·75

198 Landscouts

1976. 50th Annivs of Survey Flight and Scouting in Papua New Guinea. Multicoloured.

309	7t. Type **198**	15	10
310	10t. De Havilland D.H.50A seaplane	15	20
311	15t. Seascouts	20	40
312	60t. De Havilland D.H.50A seaplane on water	60	3·00

199 Father Ross and New Guinea Highlands

1976. William Ross Commemoration.

313	**199**	7t. multicoloured	40	15

200 Picture Wrasse

1976. Fauna Conservation (Tropical Fish). Mult.

314	5t. Type **200**	15	10
315	15t. Emperor angelfish	25	45
316	30t. Six-blotched hind	40	80
317	40t. Thread-finned butterflyfish	45	1·10

201 Man from Kundiawa

202 Headdress, Wasara Tribe

1977. Headdresses. Multicoloured.

318	1t. Type **201**	10	10
319	5t. Masked dancer, Abelam area of Maprik	10	10
320	10t. Headdress from Koiari	20	15
321	15t. Woman with face paint, Hanuabada	20	20
322	20t. Orokaiva dancer	30	30
323	25t. Haus Tambaran dancer, Abelam area of Maprik	25	30
324	30t. Asaro Valley headdress	25	35
325	35t. Singsing costume, Garaina	25	45
326	40t. Waghi Valley headdress	25	35
327	50t. Trobriand Island dancer	30	60
328	1k. Type **202**	40	1·50
329	2k. Headdress, Meko tribe	75	3·00

SIZES: 1, 5, 20t. 25×31 mm; 35, 40t. 23×38 mm; 1k. 28×35 mm; 2k. 33×23 mm; others 26×26 mm.

203 National Flag and Queen Elizabeth II

1977. Silver Jubilee. Multicoloured.

330	7t. Type **203**	20	10
331	15t. The Queen and national emblem	25	35
332	35t. The Queen and map of P.N.G.	40	70

204 White-breasted Ground Pigeon

1977. Fauna Conservation (Birds). Mult.

333	5t. Type **204**	25	10
334	7t. Victoria crowned pigeon	25	10
335	15t. Pheasant pigeon	50	65
336	30t. Orange-fronted fruit dove	70	1·10
337	50t. Banded imperial pigeon	1·00	3·50

205 Guides and Gold Badge

1977. 50th Anniv of Guiding in Papua New Guinea. Multicoloured.

338	7t. Type **205**	20	10
339	15t. Guides mapping	25	20
340	30t. Guides washing	40	50
341	35t. Guides cooking	40	60

206 Kari Marupi Myth

1977. Folklore. Elema Art (3rd series).

342	**206**	7t. multicoloured	15	10
343	-	20t. multicoloured	35	35
344	-	30t. red, blue and black	40	75
345	-	35t. red, yellow and black	40	75

DESIGNS: 20t. Savoripi clan myth; 30t. Oa-Laea myth; 35t. Oa-Iriarapo myth.

207 Blue-tailed Skink

1978. Fauna Conservation (Skinks). Mult.

346	10t. Type **207**	20	10
347	15t. Green tree skink	25	25
348	35t. Crocodile skink	30	70
349	40t. New Guinea blue-tongued skink	45	85

208 "Roboastra arika"

1978. Sea Slugs. Multicoloured.

350	10t. Type **208**	20	10
351	15t. "Chromodoris fidelis"	25	30
352	35t. "Flabellina macassarana"	45	85
353	40t. "Chromodoris marginata"	50	1·00

209 Present Day Royal Papua New Guinea Constabulary

1978. History of Royal Papua New Guinea Constabulary. Uniformed Police and Constabulary Badges. Multicoloured.

354	10t. Type **209**	20	10
355	15t. Mandated New Guinea Constabulary, 1921–41	25	15
356	20t. British New Guinea Armed Constabulary, 1890–1906	25	40
357	25t. German New Guinea Police, 1899–1914	30	45
358	30t. Royal Papua and New Guinea Constabulary, 1906–64	30	60

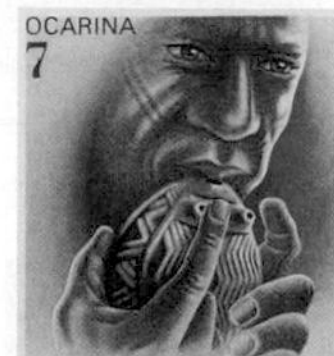

210 Ocarina

1979. Musical Instruments. Mult.

359	7t. Type **210**	10	10
360	20t. Musical bow (horiz)	20	20
361	28t. Launut	25	30
362	35t. Nose flute (horiz)	30	45

211 East New Britain Canoe Prow

1979. Traditional Canoe Prows and Paddles. Mult.

363	14t. Type **211**	20	15
364	21t. Sepik war canoe	30	25
365	25t. Trobriand Island canoe	30	30
366	40t. Milne Bay canoe	40	60

212 Katudababila (waist belt)

1979. Traditional Currency. Multicoloured.

367	7t. Type **212**	10	10
368	15t. Doga (chest ornament)	20	30
369	25t. Mwali (armshell)	35	55
370	35t. Soulava (necklace)	45	75

213 "Aenetus cyanochlora"

1979. Fauna Conservation. Moths. Multicoloured.

371	7t. Type **213**	20	10
372	15t. "Celerina vulgaris"	30	35
373	20t. "Alcidis aurora" (vert)	30	75
374	25t. "Phyllodes conspicillator"	35	1·00
375	30t. "Lyssa patroclus" (vert)	40	1·00

214 "The Right to Affection and Love"

1979. International Year of the Child. Mult.

376	7t. Type **214**	10	10
377	15t. "The right to adequate nutrition and medical care"	15	15
378	30t. "The right to play"	20	20
379	60t. "The right to a free education"	45	60

215 "Post Office Service"

1980. Admission to U.P.U. (1979). Multicoloured.

380	7t. Type **215**	10	10
381	25t. "Wartime mail"	25	25
382	35t. "U.P.U. emblem	35	40
383	40t. "Early postal services"	40	50

216 Detail from Betrothal Ceremony Mural, Minj District, Western Highlands Province

1980. South Pacific Festival of Arts.

384	**216**	20t. yellow, orange & blk	15	45
385	-	20t. mult (two figures, left-hand in black and yellow; right-hand in black, yellow and red)	15	45
386	-	20t. mult (two figures, left-hand in black and orange; right-hand in black)	15	45
387	-	20t. mult (two figures, one behind the other)	15	45
388	-	20t. mult (one figure)	15	45

DESIGNS: Nos. 385/8, further details of Betrothal Ceremony.

Nos. 384/8 were issued together in horizontal se-tenant strips of five within the sheet, forming a composite design.

217 Family being Interviewed

1980. National Census. Multicoloured.

389	7t. Type **217**	10	10
390	15t. Population symbol	15	15
391	40t. Papua New Guinea map	30	40
392	50t. Heads symbolizing population growth	35	50

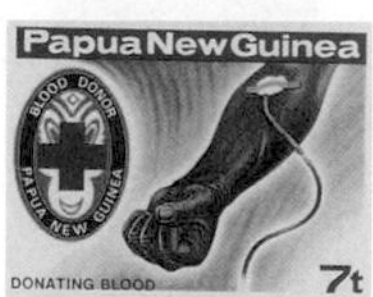

218 Donating Blood

1980. Red Cross Blood Bank. Multicoloured.

393	7t. Type **218**	15	10
394	15t. Receiving transfusion	20	20
395	30t. Map of Papua New Guinea showing blood transfusion centres	25	25
396	60t. Blood and its components	40	60

219 Dugong

1980. Mammals. Multicoloured.

397	7t. Type **219**	10	10
398	30t. New Guinea marsupial cat (vert)	30	45
399	35t. Tube-nosed bat (vert)	30	45
400	45t. Rufescent bandicoot	40	55

220 White-headed Kingfisher

1981. Kingfishers. Multicoloured.

401	3t. Type **220**	25	80
402	7t. Forest kingfisher	25	10
403	20t. Sacred kingfisher	30	50
404	25t. White-tailed kingfisher (26×46 mm)	30	85
405	60t. Blue-winged kookaburra	60	3·50

221 Native Mask

1981

406	**221**	2t. violet and orange	10	20
407	-	5t. red and green	10	20

DESIGN: 5t. Hibiscus flower.

222 Mortar Team

1981. Defence Force. Multicoloured.

408	7t. Type **222**	15	10
409	15t. Douglas DC-3 and aircrew	25	25
410	40t. "Aitape" (patrol boat) and seamen	35	65
411	50t. Medical team examining children	35	75

223 M.A.F. (Missionary Aviation Fellowship) Cessna Super Skywagon

1981. "Mission Aviation". Multicoloured.

412	10t. Type **223**	20	10
413	15t. Catholic mission British Aircraft Swallow "St. Paulus"	25	15
414	20t. S.I.L. (Summer Institute of Linguistics) Hiller 12E helicopter	25	25
415	30t. Lutheran mission Junkers F-13	35	40
416	35t. S.D.A. (Seventh Day Adventist Church) Piper PA-23 Aztec	35	55

224 Scoop Net Fishing

1981. Fishing. Multicoloured.

417	10t. Type **224**	15	10
418	15t. Kite fishing	20	30
419	30t. Rod fishing	30	50
420	60t. Scissor net fishing	55	85

225 Buhler's Papuina

1981. Land Snail Shells. Multicoloured.

421	5t. Type **225**	10	10
422	15t. Yellow naninia	20	25
423	20t. Adonis papuina and Hermoine papuina	20	35
424	30t. Hinde's papuina and New Pommeranian papuina	30	50
425	40t. "Papuina strabo"	40	80

226 Lord Baden-Powell and Flag-raising Ceremony

1981. 75th Anniv of Boy Scout Movement. Mult.

426	15t. Type **226**	20	15
427	25t. Scout leader and camp	20	30
428	35t. Scout and hut building	20	45
429	50t. Percy Chaterton and Scouts administering first aid	30	75

227 Yangoru and Boiken Bowls, East Sepik

1981. Native Pottery. Multicoloured.

430	10t. Type **227**	10	10
431	20t. Utu cooking pot and small Gumalu pot, Madang	20	30
432	40t. Wanigela pots, Northern (37×23 mm)	40	55
433	50t. Ramu Valley pots, Madang (37×23 mm)	45	80

228 "Eat Healthy Foods"

1982. Food and Nutrition. Multicoloured.

434	10t. Type **228**	10	10
435	15t. Protein foods	20	30
436	30t. Protective foods	40	55
437	40t. Energy foods	45	70

229 "Stylophora sp."

1982. Multicoloured.. Multicoloured..

438	1t. Type **229**	10	20
439	3t. "Dendrophyllia sp." (vert)	60	1·75
440	5t. "Acropora humilis"	15	10
441	10t. "Dendronephthya sp." (vert)	80	1·00
442	12t. As 10t.	3·50	6·00
443	15t. "Distichopora sp."	20	20
444	20t. "Isis sp" (vert)	90	25
445	25t. "Acropora sp." (vert)	50	50
446	30t. "Dendronephthya sp." (different) (vert)	1·25	90
447	35t. "Stylaster elegans" (vert)	1·25	50
448	40t. "Antipathes sp." (vert)	1·25	1·75
449	45t. "Turbinarea sp." (vert)	2·00	1·00
450	1k. "Xenia sp."	1·00	85
451	3k. "Distichopora sp." (vert)	2·25	3·50
452	5k. Raggiana bird of paradise (33×33 mm)	7·00	10·00

230 Missionaries landing on Beach

1982. Centenary of Catholic Church in Papua New Guinea. Mural on Wall of Nordup Catholic Church, East New Britain. Multicoloured.

457	10t. Type **230**	20	75
458	10t. Missionaries talking to natives	20	75
459	10t. Natives with slings and spears ready to attack	20	75

Nos. 457/9 were issued together, se-tenant, forming a composite design.

231 Athletics

1982. Commonwealth Games and "Anpex 82" Stamp Exhibition, Brisbane. Multicoloured.

460 10t. Type **231** 15 10
461 15t. Boxing 20 25
462 45t. Rifle-shooting 40 70
463 50t. Bowls 45 75

232 National Flag

1983. Commonwealth Day. Multicoloured.

464 10t. Type **232** 15 10
465 15t. Basket-weaving and cabbage-picking 20 30
466 20t. Crane hoisting roll of material 25 35
467 50t. Lorries and ships 60 75

233 Transport Communications

1983. World Communications Year. Multicoloured.

468 10t. Type **233** 30 10
469 25t. "Postal service" 50 25
470 30t. "Telephone service" 55 30
471 60t. "Transport service" 1·10 90

234 "Chelonia depressa"

1984. Turtles. Multicoloured.

472 5t. Type **234** 20 10
473 10t. "Chelonia mydas" 25 10
474 15t. "Eretmochelys imbricata" 30 30
475 20t. "Lepidochelys olivacea" 40 35
476 25t. " Caretta caretta" 45 50
477 40t. "Dermochelys coriacea" 60 75

235 Avro Type 618 Ten "Faith in Australia"

1984. 50th Anniv of First Airmail Australia–Papua New Guinea. Multicoloured.

478 20t. Type **235** 40 30
479 25t. De Havilland Dragon Express "Carmania" 40 45
480 40t. Westland Widgeon 50 80
481 60t. Consolidated PBY-5 Catalina flying boat 70 1·25

236 Parliament House

1984. Opening of New Parliament House.

482 **236** 10t. multicoloured 30 30

237 Ceremonial Shield and Club, Central Province

1984. Ceremonial Shields. Multicoloured.

483 10t. Type **237** 20 10
484 20t. Ceremonial shield, West New Britain 30 35
485 30t. Ceremonial shield, Madang Province 45 75
486 50t. Ceremonial shield, East Sepik 75 3·00

See also Nos. 558/61.

238 H.M.S. "Nelson" at Port Moresby, 1884

1984. Centenary of Protectorate Proclamations for British New Guinea and German New Guinea. Multicoloured.

487 10t. Type **238** 35 55
488 10t. Papua New Guinea flag and Port Moresby, 1884 35 55
489 45t. Papua New Guinea flag and Rabaul, 1884 50 1·90
490 45t. German warship "Elizabeth" at Rabaul, 1884 50 1·90

Nos. 487/8 and 489/90 were issued in se-tenant pairs, each pair forming a composite picture.

239 Fergusson Island

1985. Tourist Scenes. Multicoloured.

491 10t. Type **239** 25 10
492 25t. Sepik River 50 60
493 40t. Chimbu Gorge (horiz) 75 1·50
494 60t. Dali Beach, Vanimo (horiz) 1·25 2·00

1985. No. 408 surch 12t.

495 **222** 12t. on 7t. multicoloured 60 75

241 Dubu Platform, Central Province

1985. Ceremonial Structures. Multicoloured.

496 15t. Type **241** 35 15
497 20t. Tamuniai house, West New Britain 50 50
498 30t. Traditional yam tower, Trobriand Island 65 80
499 60t. Huli grave, Tari 1·00 1·75

242 Head of New Britain Collared Sparrow Hawk

1985. Birds of Prey. Multicoloured.

500 12t. Type **242** 60 1·40
501 12t. New Britain collared sparrow hawk in flight 60 1·40
502 30t. Doria's goshawk 75 1·50
503 30t. Doria's goshawk in flight 75 1·50
504 60t. Long-tailed honey buzzard 95 2·00
505 60t. Long-tailed honey buzzard in flight 95 2·00

244 Early Postcard, Aerogramme, Inkwell and Spectacles

1985. 10th Anniv of Independence.

506 **243** 12t. multicoloured 60 1·00

243 National Flag and Parliament House

1985. Centenary of Papua New Guinea Post Office. Multicoloured.

507 12t. Type **244** 45 10
508 30t. Queensland 1897 1d. die with proof and modern press printing stamps 1·10 1·00
509 40t. Newspaper of 1885 announcing shipping service and loading mail into aircraft 1·75 2·25
510 60t. Friedrich-Wilhelmshafen postmark of 1892 and Port Moresby F.D.C. postmark of 9 October 1985 2·00 3·75
MS511 As Nos. 507/10, but designs continue on sheet margins 6·00 7·00

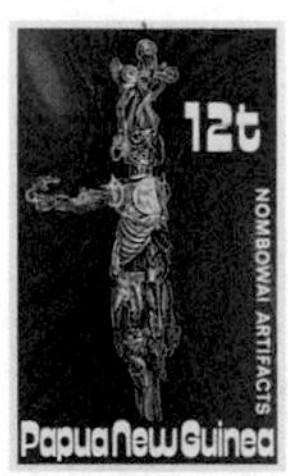

245 Figure with Eagle

1985. Nombowai Wood Carvings. Mult.

512 12t. Type **245** 50 10
513 30t. Figure with clam shell 1·25 75
514 60t. Figure with dolphin 2·00 3·00
515 80t. Figure of woman with cockerel 2·50 5·00

246 Valentine or Prince Cowrie

1986. Sea Shells. Multicoloured.

516 15t. Type **246** 60 15
517 35t. Bulow's olive 1·25 1·40
518 45t. Parkinson's olive 1·50 2·25
519 70t. Golden cowrie 2·00 5·75

246a Princess Elizabeth in A.T.S. Uniform, 1945

1986. 60th Birthday of Queen Elizabeth II. Mult.

520 15t. Type **246a** 15 15
521 35t. Silver Wedding Anniversary photograph (by Patrick Lichfield), Balmoral, 1972 20 40
522 50t. Queen inspecting guard of honour, Port Moresby, 1982 40 85
523 60t. On board Royal Yacht "Britannia", Papua New Guinea, 1982 65 1·00
524 70t. At Crown Agents' Head Office, London, 1983 40 1·25

247 Rufous Fantail

1986. "Ameripex '86" International Stamp Exhibition, Chicago. Small Birds (1st series). Multicoloured.

525 15t. Type **247** 90 30
526 35t. Streaked berry pecker 1·75 1·25
527 45t. Red-breasted pitta 1·90 1·25
528 70t. Olive-yellow robin (vert) 2·50 6·50

See also Nos. 597/601.

248 Martin Luther nailing Theses to Cathedral Door, Wittenberg and Modern Lutheran Pastor

1986. Centenary of Lutheran Church in Papua New Guinea. Multicoloured.

529 15t. Type **248** 60 15
530 70t. Early church, Finschhafen, and modern Martin Luther Chapel, Lae Seminary 1·90 3·75

249 "Dendrobium vexillarius"

1986. Orchids. Multicoloured.

531 15t. Type **249** 95 20
532 35t. "Dendrobium lineale" 2·00 75
533 45t. "Dendrobium johnsoniae" 2·00 1·10
534 70t. "Dendrobium cuthbertsonii" 2·75 6·00

250 Maprik Dancer

1986. Papua New Guinea Dancers. Multicoloured.

535 15t. Type **250** 80 15
536 35t. Kiriwina 1·60 80
537 45t. Kundiawa 1·75 1·10
538 70t. Fasu 3·00 5·50

251 White-bonnet Anemonefish

1987. Anemonefish. Multicoloured.

539 17t. Type **251** 70 25
540 30t. Orange-finned anemonefish 1·10 1·10
541 35t. Fire anemonefish ("Tomato clownfish") 1·25 1·40
542 70t. Spine-cheeked anemonefish 1·75 6·50

252 "Roebuck" (Dampier), 1700

1987. Ships. Multicoloured.

543	1t. "La Boudeuse" (De Bougainville, 1768)	50	1·50
544	5t. Type **252**	1·00	2·00
545	10t. H.M.S. "Swallow" (Philip Carteret), 1767	1·25	2·00
546	15t. H.M.S. "Fly" (Blackwood), 1845	1·75	1·00
547	17t. As 15t.	1·75	75
548	20t. H.M.S. "Rattlesnake" (Owen Stanley), 1849	1·75	1·00
549	30t. "Vitiaz" (Maclay), 1871	1·75	2·50
550	35t. "San Pedrico" (Torres) and zabra, 1606	70	1·00
551	40t. "L'Astrolabe" (D'Urville), 1827	2·00	3·00
552	45t. "Neva" (D. Albertis), 1876	75	1·50
553	60t. Spanish galleon (Jorge de Meneses), 1526	2·25	4·00
554	70t. "Eendracht" (Schouten and Le Maire), 1616	1·75	2·75
555	1k. H.M.S. "Blanche" (Simpson), 1872	2·25	3·00
556	2k. "Merrie England" (steamer), 1889	2·50	3·00
557	3k. "Samoa" (German colonial steamer), 1884	2·75	6·00

For some of these designs redrawn for "Australia '99" World Stamp Exhibition see Nos. 857/60.

1987. War Shields. As T 237. Multicoloured.

558	15t. Gulf Province	20	25
559	35t. East Sepik	45	50
560	45t. Madang Province	55	60
561	70t. Telefomin	85	90

1987. No. 442 surch 15t.

562	15t. on 12t. "Dendronephthya sp." (vert)	65	65

254 "Protoreaster nodosus"

1987. Starfish. Multicoloured.

563	17t. Type **254**	55	25
564	35t. "Gomophia egeriae"	1·10	70
565	45t. "Choriaster granulatus"	1·25	80
566	70t. "Neoferdina ocellata"	1·75	3·50

255 Cessna Stationair 6 taking off, Rabaraba

1987. Aircraft in Papua New Guinea. Mult.

567	15t. Type **255**	1·25	25
568	35t. Britten Norman Islander over Hombrum Bluff	2·00	90
569	45t. De Havilland Twin Otter 100 over Highlands	2·00	1·00
570	70t. Fokker F.28 Fellowship over Madang	3·00	7·00

256 Pre-Independence Policeman on Traffic Duty and Present-day Motorcycle Patrol

1988. Centenary of Royal Papua New Guinea Constabulary. Multicoloured.

571	17t. Type **256**	45	25
572	35t. British New Guinea Armed Constabulary, 1890, and Governor W. MacGregor	80	50
573	45t. Police badges	90	65
574	70t. German New Guinea Police, 1888, and Dr. A Hahl (founder)	1·50	1·75

257 Lakatoi (canoe) and Sydney Opera House

1988. "Sydpex '88" Nat Stamp Exn, Sydney.

575	**257** 35t. multicoloured	80	1·25

258 Papua New Guinea Flag on Globe and Fireworks

1988. Bicent of Australian Settlement. Mult.

576	35t. Type **258**	75	1·25
577	35t. Australian flag on globe and fireworks	75	1·25
MS578	90×50 mm. Nos. 576/7	1·50	2·25

Nos. 576/7 were printed together, se-tenant, forming a composite design.

259 Male and Female Butterflies in Courtship

1988. Endangered Species. "Ornithoptera alexandrae" (butterfly). Multicoloured.

579	5t. Type **259**	1·00	2·00
580	17t. Female laying eggs and mature larva (vert)	2·00	40
581	25t. Male emerging from pupa (vert)	2·75	4·00
582	35t. Male feeding	3·25	3·50

260 Athletics

1988. Olympic Games, Seoul. Multicoloured.

583	17t. Type **260**	30	30
584	45t. Weightlifting	70	70

261 "Rhododendron zoelleri"

1989. Rhododendrons. Multicoloured.

585	3t. Type **261**	10	10
586	20t. "Rhododendron cruttwellii"	50	30
587	60t. "Rhododendron superbum"	1·25	1·50
588	70t. "Rhododendron christianae"	1·50	2·00

263 Writing Letter

1989. Int Letter Writing Week. Multicoloured.

589	20t. Type **263**	30	30
590	35t. Stamping letter	55	50
591	60t. Posting letter	90	1·10
592	70t. Reading letter	1·10	1·60

264 Village House, Buka Island, North Solomons

1989. Traditional Dwellings. Multicoloured.

593	20t. Type **264**	40	35
594	35t. Tree house, Koiari, Central Province	70	60
595	60t. Longhouse, Lauan, New Ireland	1·25	1·50
596	70t. Decorated house, Basilaki, Milne Bay	1·50	1·75

265 Tit Berrypecker (female)

1989. Small Birds (2nd issue). Multicoloured.

597	20t. Type **265**	1·00	1·25
598	20t. Tit berrypecker (male)	1·00	1·25
599	35t. Blue-capped babbler	1·50	80
600	45t. Black-throated robin	1·50	1·00
601	70t. Large mountain sericornis	2·25	3·00

1989. No. 539 surch 20t.

602	20t. on 17t. Type **251**	60	70

266 Motu Motu Dancer, Gulf Province

1989. Traditional Dancers. Multicoloured.

603	20t. Type **266**	65	35
604	35t. Baining, East New Britain	1·10	90
605	60t. Vailala River, Gulf Province	2·00	2·50
606	70t. Timbunke, East Sepik Province	2·00	3·00

267 Hibiscus, People going to Church and Gope Board

1989. Christmas. Designs showing flowers and carved panels. Multicoloured.

607	20t. Type **267**	40	20
608	35t. Rhododendron, Virgin and Child and mask	60	40
609	60t. D'Albertis creeper, Christmas candle and war shield	1·25	1·75
610	70t. Pacific frangipani, peace dove and flute mask	1·40	2·25

268 Guni Falls

1990. Waterfalls. Multicoloured.

611	20t. Type **268**	60	35
612	35t. Rouna Falls	85	75
613	60t. Ambua Falls	1·40	1·50
614	70t. Wawoi Falls	1·60	2·00

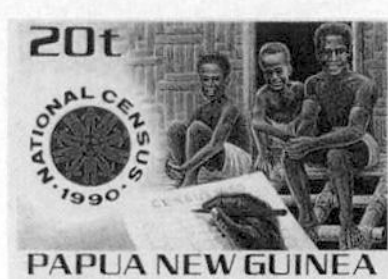

269 Boys and Census Form

1990. National Census. Multicoloured.

615	20t. Type **269**	40	30
616	70t. Family and census form	1·50	2·50

270 Gwa Pupi Dance Mask

1990. Gogodala Dance Masks. Multicoloured.

617	20t. Type **270**	80	30
618	35t. Tauga paiyale	1·25	70
619	60t. A: ga	2·00	3·25
620	70t. Owala	2·00	3·75

271 Sepik and Maori Kororu Masks

1990. "New Zealand 1990" International Stamp Exhibition, Auckland.

621	**271** 35t. multicoloured	75	1·00

272 Dwarf Cassowary and Great Spotted Kiwi

1990. 150th Anniv of Treaty of Waitangi. Mult.

622	20t. Type **272**	1·25	50
623	35t. Double-wattled cassowary and brown kiwi	1·50	1·50

273 Whimbrel

1990. Migratory Birds. Multicoloured.

624	20t. Type **273**	85	40
625	35t. Sharp-tailed sandpiper	1·25	80
626	60t. Ruddy turnstone	2·25	3·25
627	70t. Terek sandpiper	2·50	3·25

274 Jew's Harp

1990. Musical Instruments. Multicoloured.

628	20t. Type **274**	60	30
629	35t. Musical bow	90	50
630	60t. Wantoat drum	1·75	2·25

631 70t. Gogodala rattle 1·75 2·50

275 Weigman's Papuina

1991. Land Shells. Multicoloured.
632 21t. Type **275** 65 30
633 40t. "Papuina globula" and "Papuina azonata" 1·00 85
634 50t. "Planispira deaniana" 1·40 1·60
635 80t. Chance's papuina and golden-mouth papuina 2·00 2·75

276 Magnificent Riflebird

1991. Birds of Paradise. Multicoloured. (a) Face values shown as "t" or "K".
636 1t. Type **276** 15 40
637 5t. Loria's bird of paradise 20 40
638 10t. Sickle-crested bird of paradise 20 40
639 20t. Wahnes' parotia 50 30
640 21t. Crinkle-collared manucode 1·75 30
641 30t. Goldie's bird of paradise 30 40
642 40t. Wattle-billed bird of paradise 50 50
643 45t. King bird of paradise 5·50 80
644 50t. Short-tailed paradigalla bird of paradise 50 55
645 60t. Queen Carola's parotia 8·50 2·75
646 90t. Emperor of Germany bird of paradise 9·00 4·00
647 1k. Magnificent bird of paradise 1·75 1·75
648 2k. Superb bird of paradise 1·90 2·00
649 5k. Trumpet bird 2·25 6·50
650 10k. Lesser bird of paradise (32×32 mm) 6·00 11·00

(b) Face values shown as "T".
650a 21t. Crinkle-collared manucode 1·00 40
650b 45t. King bird of paradise 2·00 1·00
650c 60t. Queen Carola's parotia 2·25 2·25
650d 90t. Emperor of Germany bird of paradise 2·75 3·50

For designs as Nos. 642, 644 and 647/8 but without "1992 BIRD OF PARADISE" at foot, see Nos. 704/7.

277 Cricket

1991. 9th South Pacific Games. Multicoloured.
651 21t. Type **277** 1·75 40
652 40t. Athletics 1·50 1·00
653 50t. Baseball 1·75 2·25
654 80t. Rugby Union 2·75 4·00

278 Cathedral of St. Peter and St. Paul, Dogura

1991. Cent of Anglican Church in Papua New Guinea. Multicoloured.
655 21t. Type **278** 70 30
656 40t. Missionaries landing, 1891, and Kaieta shrine 1·40 1·40
657 80t. First church and Modawa tree 2·25 3·50

279 Rambusto Headdress, Manus Province

1991. Tribal Headdresses. Multicoloured.
658 21t. Type **279** 60 30
659 40t. Marawaka, Eastern Highlands 1·10 1·40
660 50t. Tufi, Oro Province 1·25 2·25
661 80t. Sina Sina, Simbu Province 2·00 4·50

280 "Nina"

1992. 500th Anniv of Discovery of America by Columbus and "EXPO '92" World's Fair, Seville. Multicoloured.
662 21t. Type **280** 60 30
663 45t. "Pinta" 1·25 1·00
664 60t. "Santa Maria" 1·75 2·00
665 90t. Christopher Columbus and ships 2·25 3·50

281 Canoe Prow Shield, Bamu

1992. "World Columbian Stamp Expo '92", Chicago. Sheet, 110×80 mm, containing Nos. 664/5.
MS666 60t. "Santa Maria"; 90t. Christopher Columbus and ships (sold at 1k. 70) 4·25 5·50

1992. Papuan Gulf Artifacts. Multicoloured.
667 21t. Type **281** 40 30
668 45t. Skull rack, Kerewa 85 75
669 60t. Ancestral figure, Era River 1·25 1·50
670 90t. Gope (spirit) board, Urama 1·60 2·75

282 Papuan Infantryman

1992. 50th Anniv of Second World War Campaigns in Papua New Guinea. Multicoloured.
671 21t. Type **282** 60 30
672 45t. Australian militiaman 1·25 90
673 60t. Japanese infantryman 1·75 2·25
674 90t. American infantryman 2·50 3·75

283 "Hibiscus tiliaceus"

1992. Flowering Trees. Multicoloured.
675 21t. Type **283** 65 30
676 45t. "Castanospermum australe" 1·50 1·00
677 60t. "Cordia subcordata" 2·50 2·75
678 90t. "Acacia auriculiformis" 2·75 4·00

284 Three-striped Dasyure

1993. Mammals. Multicoloured.
679 21t. Type **284** 40 30
680 45t. Striped bandicoot 90 80
681 60t. Dusky black-eared giant rat 1·25 1·50
682 90t. Painted ringtail possum 1·75 2·75

285 Rufous Wren Warbler

1993. Small Birds. Multicoloured.
683 21t. Type **285** 45 30
684 45t. Superb pitta 90 80
685 60t. Mottled whistler 1·25 1·50
686 90t. Slaty-chinned longbill 1·60 2·75

1993. "Taipei '93" Asian Int Stamp Exn, Taiwan. Nos. 683/6 optd TAIPEI'93 and emblem.
687 21t. Type **285** 75 30
688 45t. Superb pitta 1·40 80
689 60t. Mottled whistler 1·60 2·75
690 90t. Slaty-chinned longbill 2·00 4·50

287 Thread-finned Rainbowfish

1993. Freshwater Fishes. Multicoloured.
691 21t. Type **287** 60 30
692 45t. Peacock gudgeon 1·25 80
693 60t. Northern rainbowfish 1·60 2·25
694 90t. Popondetta blue-eye 2·25 4·50

288 Blue Bird of Paradise

1993. "Bangkok '93" Asian International Stamp Exhibition, Thailand. Sheet 100×65 mm.
MS695 **288** 2k. multicoloured 6·00 8·00

289 Douglas DC-3

1993. 20th Anniv of Air Niugini. Multicoloured.
696 21t. Type **289** 75 25
697 45t. Fokker F.27 Friendship 1·75 70
698 60t. De Havilland D.H.C.7 Dash Seven 2·00 2·25
699 90t. Airbus Industrie A310 2·75 4·50

290 Girl holding Matschie's Tree Kangaroo

1994. Matschie's (Huon Gulf) Tree Kangaroo. Mult.
700 21t. Type **290** 35 25
701 45t. Adult male 90 60
702 60t. Female with young in pouch 1·25 1·75
703 90t. Adolescent on ground 1·90 3·50

1994. "Hong Kong '94 International Stamp Exhibition. Designs as Nos. 642, 644 and 647/8, but without "1992 BIRD OF PARADISE" at foot. Multicoloured.
704 40t. Yellow-breasted bird of paradise 85 1·25
705 50t. Short-tailed paradigalla bird of paradise 1·25 1·50
706 1k. Magnificent bird of paradise 2·00 2·75
707 2k. Superb bird of paradise 3·00 4·00

1994. Nos. 541 and 551 surch.
708 21t. on 35t. Fire anemonefish 6·00 50
709 1k.20 on 40t. "L'Astrolabe" (D'Urville) 1·50 1·50

292 Hagen Axe, Western Highlands

1994. Artifacts. Multicoloured.
710 1t. Type **292** 10 70
711 2t. Telefomin shield, West Sepik 10 70
712 20t. Head mask, Gulf Province 80 50
713 21t. Kanganaman stool, East Sepik 1·00 10
714 45t. Trobriand lime gourd, Milne Bay 50 25
715 60t. Yuat River flute stopper, East Sepik 1·00 30
716 90t. Tami Island dish, Morobe 60 40
717 1k. Kundu (drum), Ramu River estuary 3·75 2·50
723 5k. Gogodala dance mask, Western Province 1·75 1·90
724 10k. Malanggan mask, New Ireland 4·00 4·25

293 Ford Model "T", 1920

1994. Historical Cars. Multicoloured.
725 21t. Type **293** 35 25
726 45t. Chevrolet "490", 1915 35 25
727 60t. Austin "7", 1931 1·25 1·75
728 90t. Willys jeep, 1942 1·90 3·50

294 Grizzled Tree Kangaroo

1994. "Phila Korea '94" International Stamp Exhibition, Seoul. Tree Kangaroos. Sheet 106×70 mm, containing T 294 and similar vert design. Multicoloured.
MS729 90t. Type **294**; 1k.20, Doria's tree kangaroo 3·00 3·50

1994. Surch.
730 - 5t. on 35t. mult (No. 604) 1·00 75
731 - 5t. on 35t. mult (No. 629) 14·00 10·00
732 **271** 10t. on 35t. mult 22·00 5·50
733 - 10t. on 35t. mult (No. 623) 10·00 3·50
734 - 21t. on 80t. mult (No. 635) 42·00 75
735 - 50t. on 35t. mult (No. 612) 27·00 13·00
736 - 50t. on 35t. mult (No. 618) 90·00 18·00
737 - 65t. on 70t. mult (No. 542) 2·00 1·40
738 - 65t. on 70t. mult (No. 616) 2·00 1·40
739 - 1k. on 70t. mult (No. 614) 17·00 5·00
740 - 1k. on 70t. mult (No. 620) 2·00 3·00

297 "Daphnis hypothous pallescens"

1994. Moths. Multicoloured.

741	21t. Type **297**	35	25
742	45t. "Tanaorhinus unipuncta"	80	65
743	60t. "Neodiphthera sciron"	1·10	1·50
744	90t. "Parotis marginata"	1·60	2·50

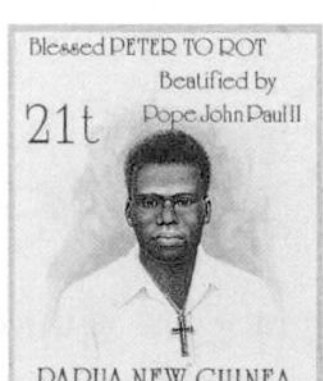

298 Peter To Rot

1995. Beatification of Peter To Rot (catechist) and Visit of Pope John Paul II. Multicoloured.

745	21t. Type **298**	1·00	1·00
746	1k. on 90t. Pope John Paul II	2·50	2·50

No. 746 was not issued without surcharge.

299 Airliner over Holiday Village

1995. Tourism. Multicoloured.

747	21t. "Melanesian Discoverer" (cruise ship) and launch	90	1·25
748	21t. Tourist taking photo of traditional mask	90	1·25
749	50t. on 45t. Type **299**	1·50	2·75
750	50t. on 45t. Holiday homes	1·50	1·75
751	65t. on 60t. Tourists and guide crossing river	1·75	2·00
752	65t. on 60t. White water rafting	1·75	2·00
753	1k. on 90t. Scuba diver and "Chertan" (launch)	2·00	2·50
754	1k. on 90t. Divers and wreck of aircraft	2·00	2·50

Nos. 749/54 were not issued without surcharge.

1995. Nos. 643, 646, 650b, 650d and 692/4 surch 21t.

755	21t. on 45t. King bird of paradise (643)	1·50	1·00
756	21t. on 90t. Emperor of Germany bird of paradise (646)	1·50	1·00
757	21t. on 45t. King bird of paradise (650b)	5·00	3·00
758	21t. on 90t. Emperor of Germany bird of paradise (650d)	6·50	1·00
759	21t. on 45t. Peacock gudgeon	55	40
760	21t. on 60t. Northern rainbowfish	1·50	2·00
761	21t. on 90t. Popondetta blue-eye	55	60

302 "Lentinus umbrinus" **302a** "Lentinus umbrinus"

1995. Fungi. Multicoloured.

762	25t. Type **302**	45	30
763	50t. "Amanita hemibapha"	80	80
764	65t. "Boletellus emodensis"	95	1·25
765	1k. "Ramaria zippellii"	1·60	2·25
765a	25t. Type **302a**	1·00	60

On Type **302a** the fungi illustration is larger, 26×32 mm instead of 27×30½ mm, face value and inscriptions are in a different type and there is no imprint date at foot.

303 Anniversary Emblem and Map of Papua New Guinea

1995. 20th Anniv of Independence. Multicoloured.

766	21t. Type **303**	30	25
767	50t. Emblem and lines on graph	70	80
768	1k. As 50t.	1·40	2·25

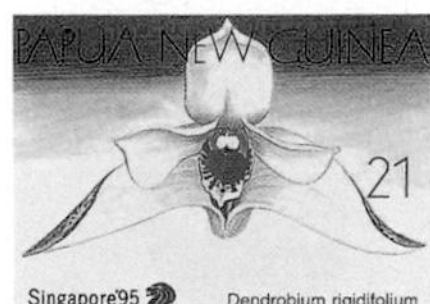

304 "Dendrobium rigidifolium"

1995. "Singapore '95" International Stamp Exhibition. Orchids. Sheet 150×95 mm, containing T 304 and similar horiz designs. Multicoloured.

MS769	21t. Type **304**; 45t. "Dendrobium convolutum"; 60t. "Dendrobium spectabile"; 90t. "Dendrobium tapiniense" (sold at 3k.)	1·25	1·50

305 Pig

1995. Chinese New Year ("Year of the Pig"). Sheet 150×95 mm.

MS770	**305** 3k. multicoloured	3·50	3·75

No. **MS**770 is inscribed "BEIJING '95" on the sheet margin.

306 Volcanic Eruption, Tavarvur

1995. 1st Anniv of Volcanic Eruption, Rabaul.

771	**306** 2k. multicoloured	1·25	1·60

307 "Zosimus aeneus"

1995. Crabs. Multicoloured.

772	21t. Type **307**	40	25
773	50t. "Cardisoma carnifex"	75	60
774	65t. "Uca tetragonon"	90	1·25
775	1k. "Eriphia sebana"	1·25	2·00

308 Pesquet's Parrot

1996. Parrots. Multicoloured.

776	25t. Type **308**	1·50	30
777	50t. Rainbow lory	2·00	65
778	65t. Green-winged king parrot	2·25	1·75
779	1k. Red-winged parrot	2·75	3·75

309 "Lagriomorpha indigacea"

1996. Beetles. Multicoloured.

780	25t. Type **309**	15	15
781	50t. "Eupholus geoffroyi"	20	25
782	65t. "Promechus pulcher"	30	40
783	1k. "Callistola pulchra"	45	70

310 Guang Zhou Zhong Shang Memorial Hall

1996. "China '96" 9th Asian International Stamp Exhibition, Peking. Sheet 105×70 mm.

MS784	**310** 70t. multicoloured	75	1·00

311 Rifle-shooting

1996. Olympic Games, Atlanta. Multicoloured.

785	25t. Type **311**	15	15
786	50t. Athletics	25	20
787	65t. Weightlifting	30	35
788	1k. Boxing	45	70

312 Air Traffic Controller

1996. Centenary of Radio. Multicoloured.

789	25t. Type **312**	15	15
790	50t. Radio disc-jockey	25	20
791	65t. Dish aerials	30	35
792	1k. Early radio transmitter	45	70

313 Dr. Sun Yat-sen

1996. "TAIPEI '96" 10th Asian International Stamp Exhibition, Taiwan. Sheet 105×70 mm, containing T 313 and similar vert design. Multicoloured.

MS793	65t. Type **313**; 65t. Dr. John Guise (former speaker of Papua New Guinea House of Assembly)	1·75	2·00

314 "Hibiscus rosa-sinensis"

1996. Flowers. Multicoloured.

794	1t. Type **314**	10	20
795	5t. "Bougainvillea spectabilis"	10	20
796	10t. "Thunbergia fragrans" (vert)	10	20
797	20t. "Caesalpinia pulcherrima" (vert)	15	20
798	25t. "Hoya sp." (vert)	15	15
799	30t. "Heliconia spp." (vert)	15	15
800	50t. "Amomum goliathensis" (vert)	25	20
801	65t. "Plumeria rubra"	35	25
802	1k. "Mucuna novoguineensis"	60	60

315 Ox and National Flag

1997. "HONG KONG '97" International Stamp Exhibition. Sheet 130×90 mm.

MS808	**315** 1k.50 multicoloured	1·00	1·25

316 Gogodala Canoe Prow

1997. Canoe Prows. Multicoloured.

809	25t. Type **316**	15	15
810	50t. East New Britain	25	20
811	65t. Trobriand Island	35	35
812	1k. Walomo	50	70

1997. Golden Wedding of Queen Elizabeth and Prince Philip. As T 87 of Kiribati. Multicoloured.

813	25t. Prince Philip on polo pony, 1972	25	35
814	25t. Queen Elizabeth at Windsor Polo Club	25	35
815	50t. Prince Philip carriage-driving, 1995	40	55
816	50t. Queen Elizabeth and Prince Edward on horseback	40	55
817	1k. Prince Philip waving and Peter and Zara Phillips on horseback	75	1·00
818	1k. Queen Elizabeth waving and Prince Harry on horseback	75	1·00
MS819	105×71 mm. 2k. Queen Elizabeth and Prince Philip in landau (horiz)	1·40	1·60

Nos. 813/14, 815/16 and 818/19 respectively were printed together, se-tenant, with the backgrounds forming composite designs.

317 Air Niugini Airliner over Osaka

1997. Inaugural Air Niugini Port moresby to Osaka Flight. Sheet 110×80 mm.

MS820	**317** 3k. multicoloured	1·50	1·75

318 "Pocillopora woodjonesi"

1997. Pacific Year of the Coral Reef. Corals. Mult.

821	25t. Type **318**	15	15
822	50t. "Subergorgia mollis"	25	20
823	65t. "Oxypora glabra"	35	35
824	1k. "Turbinaria reinformis"	60	70

319 Greater Sooty Owl

1998. Birds. Multicoloured.

825	25t. Type **319**	50	20
826	50t. Wattled brush turkey	70	45
827	65t. New Guinea grey-headed goshawk	80	1·00

828	1k. Forest bittern	1·25	2·25

1998. Diana, Princess of Wales Commemoration. Sheet, 145×70 mm, containing vert designs as T 91 or Kiribati. Multicoloured.

MS829 1k., Wearing pink jacket, 1992; 1k. Wearing purple dress; 1988; 1k. wearing tartan jacket, 1990; 1k. Carrying bouquets, 1990 (sold at 4k.+50t. charity premium) 1·50 1·60

320 Mother Teresa and Child

1998. Mother Teresa Commemoration. Mult.

830	65t. Type **320**	80	80
831	1k. Mother Teresa	80	80

1998. No. 774 surch 25t.

832	25t. on 65t. "Uca tetragonon"	60	25

322 "Daphnis hypothous pallescens"

1998. Moths. Multicoloured.

833	25t. Type **322**	20	15
834	50t. "Theretra polistratus"	40	25
835	65t. "Psilogramma casurina"	55	50
836	1k. "Meganoton hyloicoides"	1·00	1·50

323 "Coelogyne fragrans"

1998. Orchids. Multicoloured.

837	25t. Type **323**	20	15
838	50t. "Den cuthbertsonii"	30	20
839	65t. "Den vexillarius "var" retroflexum"	40	40
840	1k. "Den finisterrae"	65	75

324 Weightlifting

1998. 16th Commonwealth Games, Kuala Lumpur, Malaysia. Multicoloured.

841	25t. Type **324**	20	15
842	50t. Lawn bowls	25	20
843	65t. Rugby Union	35	35
844	1k. Squash	60	75

325 Double Kayak

1998. Sea Kayaking World Cup, Manus Island. Multicoloured.

845	25t. Type **325**	20	15
846	50t. Running	30	20
847	65t. Traditional canoe and modern kayak	40	40
848	1k. Single kayak and stylized bird of paradise	65	75

326 The Holy Child

1998. Christmas. Multicoloured.

849	25t. Type **326**	20	15
850	50t. Mother breast-feeding baby	30	20
851	65t. Holy Child and tribal elders	40	40
852	1k. Map of Papua New Guinea and festive bell	65	75

1999. "Australia '99" World Stamp Exhibition, Melbourne. Designs as Nos. 543, 552 and 556/7, showing ships, redrawn to include exhibition emblem at top right and with some face values changed. Multicoloured.

853	25t. "La Boudeuse" (De Bougainville) (as No. 543)	20	15
854	50t. "Neva" (D'Albertis) (as No. 552)	30	20
855	65t. "Merrie England" (steamer) (as No. 556)	40	40
856	1k. "Samoa" (German colonial steamer) (as No. 557)	60	75

MS857 165×110 mm. 5t. H.M.S. "Rattlesnake" (Owen Stanley) (as No. 548); 10t. H.M.S. "Swallow" (Philip Carteret) (as No. 545); 15t. "Roebuck" (Dampier) (as No. 544); 20t. H.M.S. "Blanche" (SImpson) (as No. 55); 30t. "Vitaz" (Maclay) (as No. 549); 40t. "San Pedrico" (Torres) and zabra (as No. 550); 60t. Spanish galleon (Jorge de Meneses) (as No. 553); 1k.20, "L' Astrolabe" (D' Urville) (as No. 551) 1·50 1·75

No. 855 is inscribed "Merrir England" in error. Of the designs in No. **MS**857 the 5t. is inscribed "Simpson Blanche 1872", 10t. "Carterel", 15t. "Dampien", 40t. "eabra" and 60t. "Menesis", all in error.

327 German New Guinea 1900 Yacht Type 2m. Stamp

1999. "iBRA '99" International Stamp Exhibition, Nuremberg. Multicoloured.

858	1k. Type **327**	55	65
859	1k. German New Guinea 1897 3pf. and 5pf. optd on Germany	55	65

328 Father Jules Chevalier

1999. "PhilexFrance '99" International Stamp Exhibition, Paris. Famous Frenchmen. Mult.

860	25t. Type **328**	20	15
861	50t. Bishop Alain-Marie	30	20
862	65t. Joseph-Antoine d'Entrecasteaux (explorer)	40	40
863	1k. Louis de Bougainville (explorer)	65	75

329 Hiri Claypot and Traditional Dancer

1999. Hiri Moale Festival. Multicoloured (except No. MS686).

864	25t. Type **329**	20	15
865	50t. Three dancers	30	20
866	65t. Hiri Lagatoi (trading canoe) and dancer	40	40
867	1k. Hiri Sorcerer and dancer	65	75

MS868 140×64 mm. 1k. Hiri Sorcerer (deep blue and blue); 1k. Hiri Claypot (deep purple and blue); 1k. Hiri Lagatoi (green and blue) 1·00 1·10

330 Lap-top Computer, Globe and Watch

1999. New Millennium. Modern Technology. Each showing Globe. Multicoloured.

869	25t. Type **330**	20	15
870	50t. Globe within concentric circles	35	25
871	65t. Compact disc, web site and man using computer	50	45
872	1k. Keyboard, dish aerial and solar eclipse	70	90

331 *Turbo petholatus*

2000. Sea Shells. Multicoloured.

873	25t. Type **331**	20	15
874	50t. *Charonia tritonis*	35	20
875	65t. *Cassis cornuta*	50	45
876	1k. *Ovula ovum*	75	95

332 Rabbit

2000. Chinese New Year ("Year of the Rabbit") (1999). Sheet, 145×70 mm, containing T 332 and similar vert designs. Multicoloured.

MS877 65t. Type **332**; 65t. Light brown rabbit running; 65t. White rabbit grinning; 65t. Pink rabbit hiding behind grass knoll 1·50 1·75

333 Shell

2000. 25th Anniv of Independence. Multicoloured.

878	25t. Type **333**	30	15
879	50t. Raggiana bird of Paradise	50	30
880	65t. Ornament	70	50
881	1k. Red bird of Paradise perched on spear and drums	1·10	1·25

MS882 145×75 mm. Nos. 878/81 2·40 2·50

334 Athletics

2000. Olympic Games, Sydney. Multicoloured.

883	25t. Type **334**	25	15
884	50t. Swimming	40	30
885	65t. Boxing	50	50
886	1k. Weightlifting	80	95

MS887 80×90 mm. 3k. Runner with Olympic Torch (34×45 mm) (sold at 3k.50) 2·25 2·75

No. **MS**887 includes the "Olymphilex 2000" stamp exhibition logo on the sheet margin.

335 Queen Mother in Yellow Coat and Hat

2000. Queen Elizabeth the Queen Mother's 100th Birthday. Multicoloured.

888	25t. Type **335**	25	15
889	50t. Queen Mother with bouquet of roses	45	30
890	65t. Queen Mother in green coat	55	50
891	1k. Lady Elizabeth Bowes-Lyon	80	1·00

336 Comb-crested Jacana

2001. Water Birds. Multicoloured.

892	35t. Type **336**	20	15
893	70t. Masked lapwing	40	30
894	90t. Australian white ibis	50	40
895	1k.40 Black-tailed godwit	95	1·10

337 Cessna 170 Aircraft

2001. 50th Anniv of Mission Aviation Fellowship. Multicoloured.

896	35t. Type **337**	25	15
897	70t. Auster Autocar	50	35
898	90t. Cessna 260	70	50
899	1k.40 Twin Otter	1·25	1·60

338 Flags of China and Papua New Guinea

2001. 25th Anniv of Diplomatic Relations between Papua New Guinea and China. Multicoloured.

900	10t. Type **338**	10	10
901	50t. Dragon and bird of paradise	30	20
902	2k. Tian An Men (Gate of Heavenly Peace), Beijing, and Parliament House, Port Moresby	1·10	1·40

2001. Nos. 745, 862, 866, 871 and 883 surch.

903	50t. on 21t. Type **248**	2·00	65
904	50t. on 25t. Type **334**	40	30
905	50t. on 65t. Compact disc, web site and man using computer	40	30
906	2k.65 on 65t. Joseph-Antoine d'Entrecasteaux	2·25	2·50
907	2k.65 on 65t. Hiri Lagatoi (trading canoe) and dancer	2·25	2·50

341 Flag of Enga Province

2001. Provincial Flags. Multicoloured.

908	10t. Type **341**	20	20
909	15t. Simbu Province	20	20
910	20t. Manus Province	20	20
911	50t. Central Province	50	20
912	2k. New Ireland Province	1·75	1·75
913	5k. Sandaun Province	3·00	4·00

2002. Golden Jubilee. As T 211 of St. Helena.

914	1k.25 multicoloured	50	50
915	1k.45 multicoloured	60	65
916	2k. black, brown and gold	90	1·00

917 2k.65 multicoloured 1·10 1·40

MS918 162×95 mm. Nos. 914/17 and 5k. multicoloured 4·25 4·75

DESIGNS—HORIZ:1k.25, Queen Elizabeth with Princesses Elizabeth and Margaret, 1941; 1k.45, Queen Elizabeth in evening dress, 1975; 2k. Princess Elizabeth, Duke of Edinburgh and children, 1951; 2k.65, Queen Elizabeth at Henley-on-Thames. VERT (38×51 mm)—5k. Queen Elizabeth after Annigoni.

Designs as Nos. 914/17 in No. MS918 omit the gold frame around each stamp and the "Golden Jubilee 1952–2002" inscription.

342 Lakotoi (trading canoe) and Hanuabada Village

2002. Centenary of First Papuan Stamps (2001).

919 **342** 5t. black and mauve 10 20
920 **342** 15t. black and brown 25 20
921 **342** 20t. black and blue 30 20
922 **342** 1k.25 black and brown 75 70
923 **342** 1k.45 black and green 75 70
924 **342** 10k. black and orange 5·00 6·00
MS925 127×99 mm. Nos. 919/24 6·50 7·50

The design of Type **342** is adapted from that of the first Papua issue of 1901.

343 Queen Elizabeth with Princess Elizabeth in South Africa

2002. Queen Elizabeth the Queen Mother Commemoration. Multicoloured (No. 929) or black and blue (others).

926 2k. Type **343** 1·10 1·10
927 2k. Queen Elizabeth with Princess Elizabeth at Balmoral, 1951 1·10 1·10
928 2k. Queen Mother at Sandown races, 2001 (26×30 mm) 1·10 1·10
929 2k. Queen Mother with Irish Guards, 1988 (41×30 mm) 1·10 1·10
930 2k. Queen Mother at the Derby, 1988 (26×30 mm) 1·10 1·10
931 2k. Queen Mother at Ascot races, 1966 1·10 1·10
932 2k. King George VI with Queen Elizabeth at Balmoral, 1951 1·10 1·10

MS933 Two sheets, each 65×101 mm. (a) 3k. Queen Mother at Lord Linley's wedding, 1993; 3k. At Aintree racecourse, 1991 (wearing brooch). (b) 3k. Lady Elizabeth Bowes-Lyon as a young girl; 3k. Queen Mother on Remembrance Day, 1988 (each 26×40 mm) 7·00 7·50

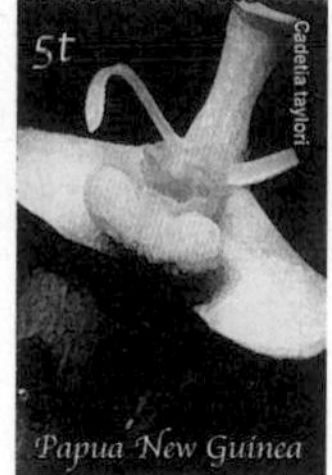

344 *Cadetia taylori*

2002. Orchids

934 5t. Type **344** 10 30
935 30t. *Dendrobium anosmum* 30 20
936 45t. *Dendrobium bigibbum* 40 25
937 1k.25 *Dendrobium cuthbertsonii* 75 60
938 1k.45 *Spiranthes sinensis* 80 70
939 2k.65 *Thelymitra carnea* 1·50 2·00

MS940 135×135 mm. 2k. *Dendrobium bracteosum*; 2k. *Calochilus campestris*; 2k. *Anastomus oscitans*; 2k. *Thelymitra carnea*; 2k. *Dendrobium macrophyllum*; 2k. *Dendrobium johnsoniae* (all horiz) 7·00 7·50
MS940a 8·00 8·00

345 *Ornithoptera chimaera*

2002. Birdwing Butterflies. Multicoloured.

941 50t. Type **345** 50 40
942 50t. *Ornithoptera goliath* 50 40
943 1k.25 *Ornithoptera meridionalis* 1·00 70
944 1k.45 *Ornithoptera paradisea* 1·10 75
945 2k.65 *Ornithoptera victoriae* 2·00 2·25
946 5k. *Ornithoptera alexandrae* 3·75 4·50

346 Globe covered in National Flags and New York Skyline

2002. "United We Stand". Support for Victims of 11 September 2001 Terrorist Attacks. Sheet 174×123 mm.

MS947 **346** 50t.×4 multicoloured 1·60 1·75

347 Mt. Wilhelm, Papua New Guinea

2003. International Year of Mountains. Multicoloured.

948 50t. Type **347** 30 20
949 1k.25 Matterhorn, Switzerland 70 60
950 1k.45 Mount Fuji, Japan 85 70
951 2k.65 Massif des Aravis, France 1·50 2·00

348 Sago Storage Pot

2003. Clay Pots. Multicoloured.

952 65t. Type **348** 40 25
953 1k. Smoking pot 60 40
954 1k.50 Water jar 80 70
955 2k.50 Water jar on stand 1·25 1·50
956 4k. Ridge pot 1·90 2·50

349 Papuan Scout Troop

2003. 20th World Scout Jamboree, Thailand. Multicoloured.

957 50t. Type **349** 35 20
958 1k.25 Scouts in workshop 75 55
959 1k.45 Scouts on wooden platform with banner 85 65
960 2k.65 Scouts 1·50 2·25

350 Princess Elizabeth

2003. 50th Anniv of Coronation.

961 **350** 65t. brown, bistre and black 50 40
962 - 65t. deep lilac, lilac and black 50 40
963 - 1k.50 deep blue, blue and black 90 65
964 - 2k. deep purple, purple and black 1·10 1·00
965 - 2k.50 black and grey 1·60 1·75
966 - 4k. brown, cinnamon and black 2·50 3·00

MS967 146×116 mm. 2k. multicoloured; 2k. multicoloured; 2k. multicoloured; 2k. multicoloured; 2k. multicoloured; 2k. multicoloured 6·00 7·00
MS968 97×67 mm. 8k. multicoloured 5·50 6·50

DESIGNS: No. 962, Queen Elizabeth II in Coronation robes and crown; 963, Queen wearing white evening dress, sash and tiara; 964, Queen seated, wearing tiara; 965, Queen in Coronation robes, with Imperial State Crown and sceptre; 966, Princess Elizabeth as teenager; MS967, Princess Elizabeth aged 21; Queen wearing diadem, 1952; Wearing hat with blue flowers, c. 1958; Wearing tiara, c. 1970; Wearing red hat with black bow, c. 1985; Wearing black robes and hat with white cockade, c. 1992; MS968, Wearing garter robes (from painting by Annigoni).

351 Prince William

2003. 21st Birthday of Prince William of Wales. Multicoloured.

969 65t. Type **351** 65 55
970 65t. Wearing red and blue t-shirt 65 55
971 1k.50 As toddler 1·50 1·10
972 2k. Wearing grey jacket and blue tie 1·75 1·25
973 2k.50 Prince William 2·25 2·50
974 4k. Playing polo 3·75 4·50

MS975 146×116 mm. 2k. As toddler; 2k. Wearing sunglasses; 2k. Wearing blue jacket and tie (facing forwards); 2k. Wearing blue jacket and tie (facing right); 2k. Wearing blue shirt; 2k. Wearing black and yellow t-shirt 6·00 7·00
MS976 95×66 mm. 8k. Prince William 5·50 6·50

352 Gabagaba Village

2003. Coastal Villages. Multicoloured.

977 65t. Type **352** 50 45
978 65t. Wanigela (Koki) 50 45
979 1k.50 Tubuserea 1·10 80
980 2k. Hanuabada 1·25 95
981 2k.50 Barakau 1·50 1·75
982 4k. Porebada 2·50 3·25

353 Orville Wright circling Fort Myer, Virginia, 1908

2003. Centenary of Powered Flight. Multicoloured (except No. MS987).

983 65t. Type **353** 60 40
984 1k.50 Orville Wright piloting "Baby Grand" biplane, Belmont New York, 1910 1·25 80
985 2k.50 Wilbur Wright holding anemometer, Pau, France, 1909 2·25 2·50
986 4k. Wilbur Wright piloting Wright Model A, Pau, France, 1909 3·75 4·50

MS987 176×96 mm. 2k.50 Wright *Flyer I* outside hangar, Kitty Hawk, North Carolina, 1903 (multicoloured); 2k.50 Wright *Flyer I* rolled out from hangar (black, grey and brown); 2k.50 Wright *Flyer I* being prepared for takeoff (black, green and brown); 2k.50 Wright *Flyer I* taking off, 1903 (multicoloured) 5·50 6·50
MS988 105×76 mm. 10k. Wright *Flyer I*, 1903 5·50 6·50

354 Matschie's Tree Kangaroo

2003. Endangered Species. Tree Kangaroos. Multicoloured.

989 65t. Grizzled tree kangaroo 90 1·00
990 1k.50 Type **354** 1·25 1·50
991 2k.50 Doria's tree kangaroo 1·75 2·00
992 4k. Goodfellow's tree kangaroo 2·50 2·75

MS993 168×127 mm. As Nos. 989/92, each ×2, but without white margins 10·00 12·00

355 Indo-Pacific Hump-backed Dolphin

2003. Protected Species. Dolphins. Multicoloured.

994 65t. Type **355** 60 50
995 65t. Two Indo-Pacific bottlenose dolphins 60 50
996 1k.50 Indo-Pacific bottlenose dolphin leaping 1·25 85
997 2k. Irrawaddy dolphin 1·50 1·50
998 2k.50 Indo-Pacific hump-backed dolphin leaping 1·75 2·00
999 4k. Irrawaddy dolphin with diver 2·75 3·50

MS1000 147×112 mm. 1k.50 Indo-Pacific hump-backed dolphin; 1k.50 Indo-Pacific bottlenose dolphin; 1k.50 Two Indo-Pacific bottlenose dolphins; 1k.50 Irrawaddy dolphin with diver; 1k.50 Irrawaddy dolphin; 1k.50 Indo-Pacific hump-backed dolphin 5·50 6·50

2004. Nos. 977/8 surch.

1001 70t. on 65t. Type **352** 1·00 65
1002 70t. on 65t.Wanigela (Koki) 1·00 65

357 Lake Wanam Rainbowfish

2004. Freshwater Fish. Multicoloured.

1003 70t. Type **357** 55 65
1004 70t. Kokoda mogurnda 55 65
1005 1k. Sepik grunter 70 50
1006 2k.70 Papuan black bass 1·75 1·50
1007 4k.60 Lake Tebera rainbowfish 2·50 2·75
1008 20k. Wichmann's mouth almighty 10·00 12·00

358 Ankylosaurus

2004. Prehistoric Animals. Multicoloured.

1009 70t. Type **358** 60 40
1010 1k. Oviraptor 70 50
1011 2k. Tyranosaurus 1·25 95
1012 2k.65 Gigantosaurus 1·50 1·50
1013 2k.70 Centrosaurus 1·50 1·50
1014 4k.60 Carcharodontsaurus 2·50 3·25

MS1015 146×106 mm. 1k.50 Edmontonia; 1k.50 Struthiomimus; 1k.50 Psittacosaurus; 1k.50 Gastonia; 1k.50 Shunosaurus; 1k.50 Iguanadon 5·50 6·50
MS1016 116×86 mm. 7k. Afrovenator 4·00 4·50

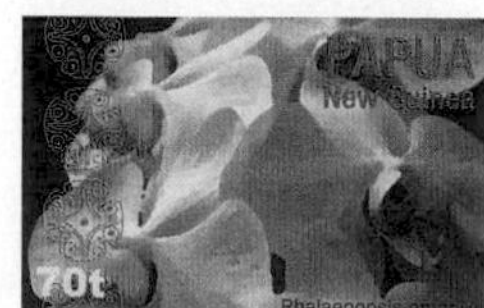

359 *Phalaenopsis amabilis*

2004. Orchids. Multicoloured.

1017 70k. Type **359** 60 40
1018 1k. *Phaius tankervilleae* 70 50
1019 2k. *Bulbophyllum macranthum* 1·25 95
1020 2k.65 *Dendrobium rhodostictum* 1·50 1·50
1021 2k.70 *Diplocaulobium ridleyanum* 1·50 1·50
1022 4k.60 *Spathoglottis papuana* 2·50 3·25

MS1023 146×106 mm. 2k. *Dendrobium cruttwellii*; 2k. *Dendrobium coeloglossum*; 2k. *Dendrobium alaticaulinum*; 2k. *Dendrobium Obtusisepalum*; 2k. *Dendrobium johnsoniae*; 2k. *Dendrobium insigne* 6·00 7·00

MS1024	116×86 mm. 7k. *Dendrobium biggibum*	4·00	4·50

360 Headdress from East Sepik Province

2004. Local Headdresses. Multicoloured.

1025	70t. Type **360**	55	65
1026	70t. Simbu Province	55	65
1027	2k.65 Southern Highlands Province	1·50	1·50
1028	2k.70 Western Highlands Province	1·50	1·50
1029	4k.60 Eastern Highlands Province	2·50	3·25
1030	5k. Central Province	2·50	3·25

2004. No. 910 and Nos. 994/5 surch.

1031	5t. on 20t. Manus Province (910)	25	40
1032	70t. on 65t. Type **355** (994)	1·00	70
1033	70t. on 65t. Two Indo-Pacific bottlenose dolphins (995)	1·00	70

363 Swimming

2004. Olympic Games, Athens. Multicoloured.

1034	70t. Type **363**	50	30
1035	2k.65 Weight lifting (vert)	1·25	1·50
1036	2k.70 "The Torch Race" (Greek art) (vert)	1·25	1·50
1037	4k.60 Olympic poster, Helsinki 1952 (vert)	2·25	2·75

364 Papua New Guinea Football Player

2004. Centenary of FIFA (Federation Internationale de Football Association). Multicoloured.

1038	70t. Type **364**	50	30
1039	2k.65 Shooting at goal	1·25	1·50
1040	2k.70 Two players	1·25	1·50
1041	4k.60 Players and referee	2·25	2·75
MS1042	165×85 mm. 2k.50 Bruno Conti, Italy; 2k.50 Oliver Kahn, Germany; 2k.50 Mario Kempes, Argentina; 2k.50 Bobby Moore, England (51×20 mm)	5·50	6·50
MS1043	93×76 mm. 10k. Bobby Robson, England (51×20 mm)	5·50	6·50

365 Flag of East New Britain Province

2004. Provincial Flags. Multicoloured.

1044	70t. Type **365**	60	50
1045	70t. Madang Province	60	50
1046	2k.65 Eastern Highlands Province	1·75	1·75
1047	2k.70 Morobe Province	1·75	1·75
1048	4k.60 Milne Bay Province	2·75	3·00
1049	10k. East Sepik Province	5·50	6·50

366 *Phalium areola*

2004. Sea Shells. Multicoloured.

1050	70t. Type **366**	55	50
1051	70t. *Conus auratus*	55	50
1052	2k.65 *Oliva miniacea*	1·60	1·60
1053	2k.70 *Lambis chiragra*	1·60	1·60
1054	4k.60 *Conus suratensis*	2·50	2·75
1055	10k. *Architectonica perspective*	5·50	6·50

2005. Nos. 1003/4 and 1025/6 surch 75t.

1056	75t. on 70t. Type **357**	1·00	80
1057	75t. on 70t. Kokoda mogurnda	1·00	80
1058	75t. on 70t. Type **360**	1·00	80
1059	75t. on 70t. Simbu Province	1·00	80

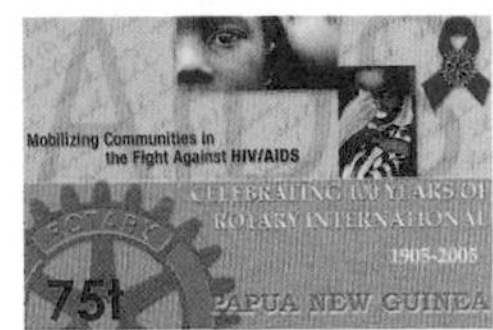

369 Little Egret

2005. Coastal Birds. Multicoloured.

1060	5t. Type **369**	40	60
1061	75t. White-faced heron	1·25	75
1062	75t. Nankeen night heron	1·25	75
1063	3k. Crested tern	2·25	2·75
1064	3k.10 Bar-tailed godwit	2·25	2·75
1065	5k.20 Little pied heron	3·75	4·50

370 Children, Handwriting and Rotary Emblem

2005. Centenary of Rotary International (Humanitarian organisation). Multicoloured.

1066	75t. Type **370**	90	35
1067	3k. Child and PolioPlus emblem	2·00	2·25
1068	3k.10 Co-Founders of the first Rotary club	2·00	2·25
1069	4k. Silvester Schiele (1st Rotary Pres.) (vert)	2·50	2·75
1070	4k. Paul Harris (Founder of Rotary International) (vert)	2·50	2·75
1071	4k. Three children (vert)	2·50	2·75
1072	5k.20 Chicago skyline	2·75	3·25
MS1073	107×74 mm. 10k. Globe and "Mankind is our Business" (vert)	5·50	6·50

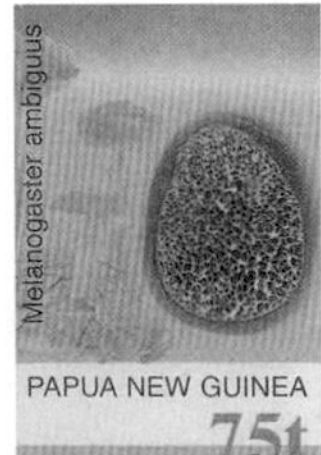

371 Lady in Pink

2005. Frangipani Flowers. Multicoloured.

1074	75t. Type **371**	1·00	65
1075	75t. Evergreen	1·00	65
1076	1k. Carmine flush	1·40	65
1077	3k. *Cultivar acutifolia*	2·50	2·75
1078	3k.10 American beauty	2·50	2·75
1079	5k.20 Golden kiss	3·25	3·75

372 *Melanogaster ambiguus*

2005. Mushrooms. Multicoloured.

1080	75t. Type **372**	75	45
1081	75t. *Gymnopilus spectabilis*	75	45
1082	2k. *Amanita muscaria*	1·40	1·40
1083	2k. *Amanita rubescens*	1·40	1·40
1084	2k. *Suillus luteus*	1·40	1·40
1085	2k. *Stropharia cubensis*	1·40	1·40
1086	2k. *Aseroe rubra*	1·40	1·40
1087	2k. *Psilocybe aucklandii*	1·40	1·40
1088	3k.10 *Microporus xanthopus*	2·25	2·50
1089	5k.20 *Psilocybe subcubensis*	3·25	3·75
MS1090	100×70 mm. 10k. *Mycena pura*	5·50	6·50

373 *Promechus pulcher*

2005. Beetles. Multicoloured.

1091	75t. Type **373**	85	85
1092	75t. *Callistola pulchra*	85	85
1093	1k. *Lagriomorpha indigacea*	1·00	85
1094	3k. *Hellerhinus papuanus*	2·50	2·75
1095	3k.10 *Aphorina australis*	2·50	2·75
1096	5k.20 *Bothricara pulchella*	4·00	4·50

374 Pope John Paul II on Visit to Papua New Guinea

2005. Pope John Paul II Commemoration. Multicoloured. Country name and value colour given.

1097	**374**	2k. blue	2·25	2·25
1098	**374**	2k. green	2·25	2·25
1099	**374**	2k. orange	2·25	2·25
1100	**374**	2k. mauve	2·25	2·25

375 Flag of Southern Highlands Province

2005. Provincial Flags. Multicoloured.

1101	75t. Type **375**	1·00	65
1102	75t. Gulf Province	1·00	65
1103	1k. North Solomons Province	1·40	65
1104	3k. Oro Province	3·00	3·25
1105	3k.10 Western Highlands Province	3·00	3·25
1106	5k.20 Western Province	4·75	5·50

376 Ruddy Somali (inscr "Rudy")

2005. Cats and Dogs. Multicoloured.

1107	75t. Type **376**	1·00	65
1108	75t. Balinese seal lynx point	1·00	65
1109	3k. Sphynx brown mackerel tabby and white	3·00	3·25
1110	3k.10 Korat blue	3·00	3·25
1111	5k.20 Bengal brown spotted tabby	4·75	5·50
MS1112	232×100 mm. 2k.50 Yorkshire terrier; 2k.50 Basenji; 2k.50 Neapolitan mastiff (wrongly inscr "Msastiff"); 2k.50 Poodle	8·00	8·50
MS1113	100×70 mm. 10k. Boston terrier (horiz)	8·00	8·50

The stamps and margins of No. **MS**1112 form a composite background design spelling "DOGS".

377 Adult Literacy Class

2006. 50th Anniv of SIL (Summer Institute of Linguistics). Multicoloured.

1114	80t. Type **377**	90	45
1115	80t. Postmarking letters (Postal Services)	90	45
1116	1k. Dr. Jim Dean (first director of SIL Papua New Guinea Branch, 1956–64)	1·10	45
1117	3k.20 Learning to read in mother tongue (Tokples Preschools)	2·50	2·75
1118	3k.25 Rural people and aircraft (SIL Aviation)	2·50	2·75
1119	5k.35 SIL worker teaching woman to use sewing machine (Community Development)	3·75	4·25

378 Queen with President Bill Clinton

2006. 80th Birthday of Queen Elizabeth II. Two sheets each 162×152 mm containing T 378 and similar vert designs. Multicoloured.

MS1120	(a) 80t. Type **378**; 3k.20 Dancing with Pres. Gerald Ford; 3k.25 At banquet with Pres. Ronald Reagan; 5k.35 With Pres. George Bush. (b) 2k.50 Wearing polka dot dress; 2k.50 Line engraving of Queen; 2k.50 Line engraving of Queen (facing left); 2k.50 With Queen Mother	18·00	19·00

379 "Spirit House" (interior of Sepik Haus Tambaran)

2006. Contemporary Art in Papua New Guinea (1st series). Multicoloured.

1121	5t. Type **379**	25	50
1122	80t. "Rhythm and Harmony" (two heads)	1·25	65
1123	80t. "The Chief" (man with nose ring)	1·25	65
1124	3k.20 "Reaching out to the People"	3·00	3·25
1125	3k.25 "Protecting our Women"	3·00	3·25
1126	5k.35 "Man as Art"	4·50	5·50

See also Nos. 1214/**MS**1220.

380 Stylised England Player

2006. World Cup Football Championship, Germany. Sheet 127×102 mm containing T 380 and similar horiz designs showing cartoon players and team colours. Multicoloured.

MS1127	80t. Type **380**; 3k.20 Germany; 3k.25 Argentina; 5k.35 Australia	9·75	11·00

381 "50th Anniversary" Emblem

2006. 50th Anniv of the Salvation Army in Papua New Guinea. Multicoloured.

1128	5t. Type **381**	25	50
1129	80t. Papua New Guinea and Salvation Army flags	1·40	60
1130	1k. Lt. Ian Cutmore and Major Keith Baker (pioneer officers, 1956)	1·40	60
1131	3k.20 Colonels Andrew and Julie Kalai (first Papua New Guinean commanders)	3·25	3·50
1132	3k.25 Kei Geno (first Papua New Guinean convert)	3·25	3·50
1133	5k.35 Lt. Dorothy Elphick (pioneer officer in Highlands) holding baby	4·50	5·50

2006. Nos. 1050/1 surch 80t.

No.	Description	Mint	Used
1134	80t. on 70t. Type **366**	80	70
1135	80t. on 70t. *Conus auratus*	80	70

383 *Delias iltis*

2006. Butterflies. Multicoloured.

No.	Description	Mint	Used
1136	80t. Type **383**	1·40	50
1137	3k.20 *Ornithoptera paradisea*	3·50	3·50
1138	3k.25 *Taenaris catops*	3·50	3·50
1139	5k.35 *Papilio ulysses autolycus*	5·00	5·50

384 Black Whipsnake

2006. Snakes of Papua New Guinea. Multicoloured.

No.	Description	Mint	Used
1140	5t. Type **384**	25	50
1141	80t. Papuan taipan	1·25	50
1142	2k. Smooth-scaled death adder	1·90	1·75
1143	3k.20 Papuan blacksnake	3·00	3·00
1144	3k.25 New Guinea small-eyed snake	3·00	3·00
1145	5k.35 Eastern brownsnake	4·00	4·50

385 Elvis Presley

2006. Elvis Presley Commemoration. Multicoloured.

No.	Description	Mint	Used
1146	80t. Type **385**	1·25	50
1147	3k.20 Holding microphone, wearing red shirt	3·00	3·00
1148	3k.25 Wearing white jacket and bow tie	3·00	3·00
1149	5k.35 Playing guitar	4·75	5·50
MS1150	127×190 mm. 80t. Wearing gold suit, "Elvis Gold Records–Volume 2"; 3k.20 Aged 2, "Elvis Country"; 3k.25 Playing piano, "His Hand in Mine"; 5k.35 "King Creole" (all 50×37 mm)	11·00	12·00
MS1151	100×70 mm. 10k. Holding three teddy bears	8·50	8·50

The stamps within No. **MS**1150 all show album covers.

386 Mango

2007. Tropical Fruits. Multicoloured.

No.	Description	Mint	Used
1152	5t. Type **386**	25	50
1153	85t. Pineapple	1·25	65
1154	85t. Watermelon	1·25	65
1155	3k.35 Guava	3·00	3·00
1156	3k.35 Pawpaw	3·00	3·00
1157	5k.35 Lemon	4·50	5·50

387 Hawksbill Turtle

2007. Endangered Marine Turtles. Multicoloured.

No.	Description	Mint	Used
1158	10t. Type **387**	30	40
1159	35t. Flatback turtle (adult)	60	60
1160	85t. Loggerhead turtle	1·10	1·10
1161	3k. Leatherback turtle (adult)	3·25	3·25
1162	3k.35 Green turtle (adult)	3·25	3·25
1163	5k.35 Olive Ridley turtle (adult on beach)	4·50	5·50
MS1164	176×96 mm. 85t. Flatback turtle hatchling; 3k. Leatherback turtle hatchling reaching sea; 3k.35 Young green turtle emerging from egg; 5k.35 Young Olive Ridley turtle swimming	11·00	11·00

388 Scouts on Parade

2007. Centenary of Scouting. Multicoloured.

No.	Description	Mint	Used
1165	10t. Type **388**	35	40
1166	85t. Papua New Guinea scouts in procession	1·25	75
1167	3k.35 Papua New Guinea scouts seated on ground	3·25	3·25
1168	5k.35 Papua New Guinea scout leaders	4·75	5·50
MS1169	177×98 mm. Nos. 1165/8	8·50	9·00
MS1170	116×86 mm. 10k. Lord Baden-Powell (founder) (vert)	8·50	9·00

389 Handshake and Scales of Justice (Joshua Weka)

2007. National Stamp Design Competition. Designs showing winning entries. Multicoloured.

No.	Description	Mint	Used
1171	5t. Type **389** ('A Just, Safe & Secure Society for all')	20	50
1172	30t. Open book between totem poles (David Moripi) ('Prosperity through self reliance')	45	30
1173	85t. AIDS ribbon and outline map (Kokenu Makita) ('STOP Aids Now')	1·25	75
1174	3k. Saluting policemen, arms and scales of justice (Tenison Paki) ('Crime Reduction')	3·25	3·25
1175	3k.35 Nurse and mother breast feeding baby (Kopoi Boi) ('Infant Care & Child Immunization')	3·25	3·25
1176	5k.35 Teacher and tribesmen in classroom (Paul Gemis) ('Minimizing illiteracy')	4·75	5·50

No. 1176 is incorrectly spelled 'iliteracy'.

390 *Den. conanthum* and *Den. lasianthera*

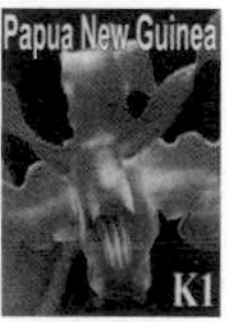

391 Pale Yellow Orchid with Mauve Lip

2007. Personalised Stamps. Orchids of Papua New Guinea. Multicoloured. (a) As T 390.

No.	Description	Mint	Used
1177	85t. Type **390**	1·25	75
1178	3k. *Dendrobium conanthum* Schltr	3·25	3·25
1179	3k.35 *Dendrobium lasianthera* var May River Red	3·25	3·25
1180	5k.35 *Dendrobium wulaiense* Howcroft	5·00	5·50

(b) As T 391.

No.	Description	Mint	Used
1181	1k. Type **391**	1·10	1·10
1182	1k. Cream orchid with twisted petals and mauve lip	1·10	1·10
1183	1k. White orchids	1·10	1·10
1184	1k. Orchid with mauve lip and white and pink petals	1·10	1·10
1185	1k. White orchid with deep red markings on petals	1·10	1·10
1186	1k. Yellow orchid with brownish shading	1·10	1·10
1187	1k. Pale mauve orchid with deep mauve lip	1·10	1·10
1188	1k. White Stanhopea orchid with yellow blotch in throat and reddish veining	1·10	1·10
1189	1k. Pale pink orchid with mauve veining on lip	1·10	1·10
1190	1k. Many bloomed red-brown orchid	1·10	1·10
1191	1k. Yellow orchid with greenish column	1·10	1·10
1192	1k. Greenish orchid with dark shading	1·10	1·10

392 Separated Siamese Twins Eustina and Eustocia Bosin, 1996

2007. 50th Anniv of First Rotary Club in Papua New Guinea. Multicoloured.

No.	Description	Mint	Used
1193	85t. Type **392** (ROMAC medical aid for children)	1·00	60
1194	3k.35 Distribution of insecticide treated mosquito nets	3·25	3·25
1195	5k. List of Papua New Guinea Rotary Clubs	3·75	4·00
1196	5k.35 Rotary members and container of donated goods	4·25	4·50
MS1197	146×106 mm. Nos. 1193/6	12·00	12·00

393 Lady Diana Spencer, 1965

2007. 10th Death Anniv of Diana, Princess of Wales. Multicoloured.

No.	Description	Mint	Used
MS1198	130×100 mm. 85t. Type **393**; 2k.45 Lady Diana Spencer, 1971; 3k.35 Lady Diana Spencer, 1981; 5k.35 Princess Diana, 1983	10·50	10·50
MS1199	70×100 mm. 10k. Princess Diana	9·75	9·75

394 Queen Elizabeth II and Prince Philip

2007. Diamond Wedding of Queen Elizabeth II and Prince Philip. Multicoloured.

No.	Description	Mint	Used
1200	2t. Type **394** (mauve border)	1·90	1·90
1201	2k. Queen Elizabeth II (mauve border)	1·90	1·90
1202	2k. As No. 1201 (lavender border)	1·90	1·90
1203	2k. As Type **394** (lavender border)	1·90	1·90
1204	2k. As Type **394** (stone border)	1·90	1·90
1205	2k. As No. 1201 (stone border)	1·90	1·90
MS1206	70×100 mm. 10k. Princess Elizabeth and Philip Mountbatten, c. 1949	9·00	9·00

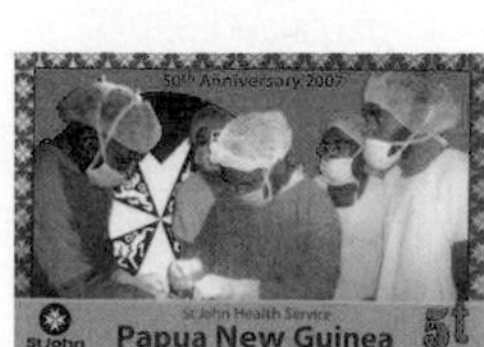

395 St. John Health Service

2007. 50th Anniv of St. John Ambulance in Papua New Guinea. Multicoloured.

No.	Description	Mint	Used
1207	5t. Type **395**	25	50
1208	20t. St. John Blood Service	60	40
1209	85t. St. John Blind Service	1·40	75
1210	1k. St. John Ambulance Service	1·50	90
1211	3k.35 St. John Volunteer Service	4·00	4·00
1212	5k.35 The Order of St. John	6·00	6·50
MS1213	186×114 mm. Nos. 1207/12	12·50	12·50

396 'Blended Culture' (Oro Gagara)

2007. Contemporary Art in Papua New Guinea (2nd series). Multicoloured.

No.	Description	Mint	Used
1214	5t. Type **396**	25	50
1215	30t. Tribesman – Western Province	50	35
1216	85t. 'The Sorcerer – Cultural Initiation' (Begesin/Madang)	1·10	60
1217	3k. 'Blended Culture' (Hewa Wigman)	3·25	3·25
1218	3k.35 'Pigs into Python – Legend' (Bukawa, Morobe Province)	3·25	3·25
1219	5k.35 Tolai masks – East New Britain Province	5·50	6·00
MS1220	186×114 mm. Nos. 1214/19 (sold at 12k.55)	12·50	12·50

No. **MS**1220 was sold at 12k.55, a discount of 35t. over the face value.

397 Papuan Hornbill

2008. Protected Birds. Multicoloured.

No.	Description	Mint	Used
1221	10t. Type **397**	50	50
1222	50t. Osprey	1·25	80
1223	85t. New Guinea harpy eagle	1·75	85
1224	3k. Victoria crowned pigeon	4·00	4·50
MS1225	145×101 mm. Nos. 1221/3; 1k. Palm cockatoo; No. 1224; 5k.35 Great white egret	10·50	10·50
MS1226	115×86 mm. 10k. Palm cockatoo	11·00	11·00

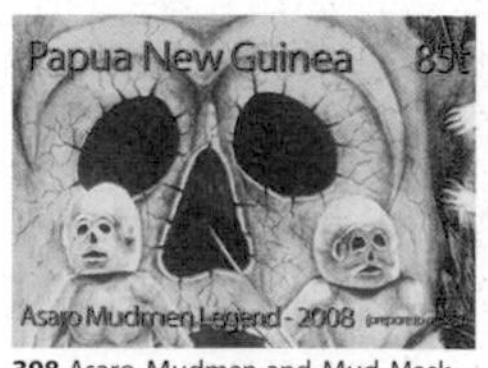

398 Asaro Mudmen and Mud Mask

2008. Asaro Mudmen Legend. Multicoloured.

No.	Description	Mint	Used
1227	85t. Type **398**	1·25	65
1228	3k. Mudmen hiding in bushes	3·25	3·25
1229	3k.35 Firing arrows at enemy	3·25	3·25
1230	5k.35 Enemy tribe fleeing believing mudmen are ghosts	5·50	6·00
MS1231	176×80 mm. Nos. 1227/30	12·00	12·00
MS1232	115×86 mm. 10k. As Type **398**	10·00	10·00

399 *Sarcophyton* sp. (leather coral)

2008. Marine Biodiversity. Multicoloured.

No.	Description	Mint	Used
1233	85t. Type **399**	1·25	65
1234	3k. *Chromodoris kunei*	3·25	3·25
1235	3k.35 *Lambis scorpius* (scorpion spider snail)	3·25	3·25
1236	5k.35 *Clatheia mima* (veined sponge)	5·50	6·00
MS1237	85t. *Astropyga radiata* (radiant sea urchin); 3k. *Phyllidia varicosa*; 3k.35 *Nephtheis fascicularis* (sea squirt); 5k.35 *Celerina heffernani* (Heffernan's sea star)	12·00	12·00
MS1238	116×85 mm. 10k. *Euphyllia cristata* (white grape coral)	10·00	10·00

400 Weightlifting

2008. Olympic Games, Beijing. Multicoloured.

1239 1k.40 Type **400** 1·60 1·60
1240 1k.40 Diving 1·60 1·60
1241 1k.40 Hurdling 1·60 1·60
1242 1k.40 Boxing 1·60 1·60

401 Papua New Guinea and EU Flags

2008. 30 Years of Papua New Guinea – European Union Partnership. Multicoloured; background colours given.

1243 **401** 85t. grey 1·25 75
1244 **401** 3k. yellow 3·25 3·25
1245 **401** 3k.35 rose 3·25 3·25
1246 **401** 5k.35 blue 5·00 6·00
MS1247 100×120 mm. As Nos. 1243/6 11·50 12·00
MS1248 85×85 mm. 10k. blue 10·00 10·00

Stamps from **MS**1247 have dark blue borders at foot. Nos. 1243/6 have dark blue borders at foot with white patterns.

402 *Long Hair*

2008. Pioneer Art by Akis (Timothy Akis). Multicoloured.

1249 85t. Type **402** 1·00 60
1250 3k. *Alone* 3·25 3·25
1251 3k.35 *Woman with Cassowary and Child* 3·25 3·25
1252 5k.35 *Man shooting Cassowary* 5·50 6·50
MS1253 128×155 mm. 85t. *Five Men in their Gardens* (top portion); 3k. Crocodile woman; 3k.35 *Five Men in their Gardens* (bottom portion); 5k.35 Two-headed man 12·50 12·50
MS1254 80×90 mm. 10k. *Flying Fox* 10·00 10·00

The 3k. and 5k.35 values from **MS**1253 form a complete drawing: *The Crocodile Woman and Two-headed Man.*

403 Headdress

2008. Traditional Headdress. Multicoloured.

1255 85t. Type **403** 90 90
1256 3k. Headdress with red feathers and white plume 3·25 3·25
1257 3k.35 Headdress with white feathers and brown plume 3·75 3·75
1258 5k.35 Man wearing headdress of white feathers with brown markings 5·75 5·75
MS1259 145×105 mm. 85t. Man wearing headdress with light brown plumes; 3k. Headdress with shells and dark red feathers; 3k. 35 Man with white painted face wearing black and white headdress; 5k.35 Red headdress 13·50 13·50
MS1260 86×115 mm. 10k. Red and yellow headdress with white feathers 10·50 10·50

404 Marilyn Monroe

2008. Marilyn Monroe Commemoration. Multicoloured.

MS1261 100×140 mm. 85c. Type **404**; 3k. Looking over shoulder; 3k.35 Smiling at camera; 5k.35 With hand raised to face 13·50 13·50
MS1262 100×70 mm. 10k. Looking out of car window 10·50 10·50

405 *Paradisaea guilielmi*

2008. Birds of Paradise. Previously issued designs as Nos. 64, 66/7, 69, 173/4, 176 and 239/40 redrawn with new values and inscriptions as T 405. Multicoloured.

1263 85t. Type **405** (66) 1·10 1·10
1264 3k. *Parotia lawesi* (64) 3·25 3·25
1265 3k.35 *Epimachus meyeri* (67) 3·25 3·25
1266 5k.35 *Diphyllodes magnificus* (69) 5·50 5·50
MS1267 146×106 mm. 85t. *Astrapia stephaniae* (240); 3k. *Cnemophilus macgregorii* (176); 3k.35 *Pteridophora albertii* (173); 5k.35 *Astrapia mayeri* (239) 12·00 12·00
MS1268 116×86 mm. 10k. *Cicinnurus regius* (174) 10·00 10·00

406 Tunnel drilling

2008. Mining. Multicoloured.

1269 85t. Type **406** 1·10 1·10
1270 3k. Mine truck (Logistics) 3·25 3·25
1271 3k.35 Refinery 3·25 3·25
1272 5k.35 Gold bars 5·50 5·50
MS1273 145×105 mm. 85t. Open pit mining; 3k. Conveyor belt; 3k.35 Plant site; No. 1272 12·00 12·00
MS1274 116×86 mm. 10k. Close up of gold bar 10·00 10·00

407 'HIV and the Workplace'

2008. World AIDS Day. Multicoloured.

1275 5t. Type **407** 15 20
1276 10t. 'Voluntary Counselling and Testing' 35 40
1277 50t. Condom ('Role of Men and Women') 60 65
1278 85t. Teaching children about HIV/AIDS ('Education') 1·10 1·10
1279 1k. 'Eradicating Stigma and Discrimination' 1·20 1·20
1280 2k. 'Living with the Virus' 2·00 2·00
1281 3k. Couple ('Care, Support and the Role of Family') 3·25 3·25
1282 3k.70 AIDS ribbons in pattern ('Building Leadership') 3·50 3·50
1283 6k. Anti-AIDS drugs and fruit ('Health and Nutrition') 6·50 6·50
MS1284 146×106 mm. As Nos. 1278 and 1281/3 but 42×28 mm 15·00 15·00
MS1285 115×86 mm. 10k. As No. 1279 but 42×28 mm 10·00 10·00

408 The Nativity ('Joy to the World')

2008. Christmas. Multicoloured.

1286 85t. Type **408** 1·10 1·10
1287 3k. Santa riding reindeer ('Ho ho ho... Merry Christmas') 3·25 3·25
1288 3k.35 Book and candle ('Amazing Grace') 3·25 3·25
1289 5k.35 Book and bell ('Jingle Bells') 5·50 5·50
MS1290 146×106 mm. 85t. 'The Journey to Bethlehem'; 3k. Native huts and Christmas star ('Silent Night'); 3k.35 Shepherds following Star ('Behold that Star'); 5k.35 Three Papuan men carrying gifts ('The 3 Wise Men') 12·00 12·00
MS1291 116×86 mm. 10k. Wrapped Christmas gift 10·00 10·00

409 *Bixa orellana*

2009. Plants. Multicoloured.

1292 85t. Type **409** 1·10 1·10
1293 3k. Perfume tree (*Cananga odorata*) 3·25 3·25
1294 3k.70 Beach kalofilum (*Calophyllum inophyllum*) 3·75 3·75
1295 6k. *Macaranga tenarius* 6·50 6·50
MS1296 146×106 mm. 85t. Native frangipani (*Hymenosporum flavum*); 3k. Ten cent flower (*Fagraea berteriana*); 3k.70 Beach terminali (*Terminalia catappa*); 6k. Red beech (*Dillenia alata*) 15·00 15·00
MS1297 111×66 mm. 10k. Beach convolvulus or morning glory (*Ipomoea pes-caprae*) 10·00 10·00

410 *Albericus siegfriedi*

2009. Frogs. Multicoloured.

1298 85t. Type **410** 1·10 1·10
1299 3k. *Cophixalus nubicola* 3·25 3·25
1300 3k.70 *Nyctimystes pulcher* 3·75 3·75
1301 6k. *Sphenophryne cornuta* 6·50 6·50
MS1302 146×113 mm. 85t. *Litoria sauroni*; 3k. *Litoria prora*; 3k.70 *Litoria multiplica*; 6k. *Litoria pronimia* 14·50 14·50
MS1303 117×93 mm. 10k. *Oreophyrne* sp. 10·00 10·00

411 *Chota*

2009. 'Pioneer Art' (2nd series) by David Lasisi. Multicoloured.

1304 85t. Type **411** 1·75 1·75
1305 3k. *Stability* 4·25 4·25
1306 3k.70 *Taumirmir* 5·00 5·00
1307 6k. *The Moieties* 7·75 7·75
MS1308 146×107 mm. 85t. *Like a Log being Adrifted*; 3k. *Lasisi*; 3k.70 *Lupa*; 6k. *InMemory of Marker Craftsman* 19·00 19·00
MS1309 116×86 mm. 10k. *Trapped by Cobweb of Stinging Pain* 12·00 12·00

412 Vessel (lian or Zun) with Design of Deities, Animals and Masks (265–316)

2009. China 2009 World Stamp Exhibition, Luoyang. Multicoloured.

1310 5t. Type **412** 30 30
1311 10t. *Evening in the Peach and Plum Garden* (Li Bai) (1644–1911) 45 45
1312 85t. Reliquary with Buddhist figures (960–1127) 1·25 1·25
1313 1k. Pink peony 1·60 1·60
1314 3k. Brick relief figure (1279–1368) 3·75 3·75
1315 3k.70 Round tray with scroll designs (206BCE–8CE) 4·75 4·75
1316 6k. Plate in shape of two peach halves with design of two foxes (618–907) 7·75 7·75
MS1317 108×154 mm. As Nos. 1310/15 but with different background design. P 14½×14 19·00 19·00
MS1318 70×101mm. 6k. Two pink peonies (44×44 mm) 8·50 8·50

Nos. 1310/15 all show the right hand part of a plate at left of the stamp. The stamps within **MS**1317 each have a background showing part of the plate design.

413 Fish ('Sustainable Income & Food Security')

2009. Coral Triangle. Multicoloured.

1319 85t. Type **413** 1·10 1·10
1320 3k. Green turtle 3·50 3·50
1321 3k.70 Mangroves 4·75 4·75
1322 6k. Coral reefs 7·75 7·75
MS1323 146×106 mm. 85t. Dolphin; 3k. Green turtle; 3k.70 Reef fish; 6k. Killer whale 17·00 17·00
MS1324 116×87 mm. 10k. Grouper 12·00 12·00

MS1324 contains four triangular stamps laid tête-beche, the stamps and margins forming a composite background design showing a coral reef and fish.

414 Guides helping Trekker down Steep Slope

2009. Kokoda Trail. Multicoloured.

1325 85t. Type **414** 1·00 1·00
1326 3k. Crossing Vabuyavi River 3·25 3·25
1327 3k.70 Waterfall near Abuari 4·50 4·50
1328 6k. Trekkers crossing Lake Myola 1 7·25 7·25
MS1329 146×106 mm. 85t. Crossing Emune River; 3k. Entering Imita Ridge; Crossing Alo Creek; 6k. Camping at Templeton's Crossing No. 2 16·00 16·00
MS1330 86×116 mm. 10k. 'Golden Staircase', Imita Ridge 12·00 12·00

415 Black-bellied Bat (*Melanycteris melanops*)

2009. Bats of Papua New Guinea. Multicoloured.

1331 85t. Type **415** 1·10 1·10
1332 3k. Least blossom bat (*Macroglossus minimus*) 3·50 3·50
1333 3k.70 Sanborn's broad-nosed bat (*Scotorepens sanborni*) 4·75 4·75
1334 6k. Mantled mastiff bat (*Otomops secundus*) 7·75 7·75

MS1335 146×106 mm. 85t. Trident leaf-nosed bat (*Aselliscus tricuspidatus*); 3k. Flower-faced bat (*Anthopsornatus*); 3k.70 Eastern horseshoe bat (*Phinolophus megaphyllus*); 6k. Greater tubed-nose bat (*Nyctimene aello*) 17·00 17·00

MS1336 116×86 mm. 10k. Bougainville's fruit bat (*Pteralopex anceps*) 12·00 12·00

416 Abraham Lincoln

2009. International Day of Non-Violence. Multicoloured.

1337 85t. Type **416** 1·00 1·00
1338 3k. Princess Diana 3·25 3·25
1339 3k.70 Nelson Mandela 4·50 4·50
1340 6k. Pres. Barack Obama (facing left) 7·25 7·25

MS1341 106×146 mm. 85t. As No. 1340; 3k. Martin Luther King; 3k.70 Mahatma Gandhi; 6k. As No. 1338 16·00 16·00

MS1342 86×116 mm. 10k. Pres Barack Obama (facing right) (37×51 mm) 12·00 12·00

417 Mt. Vulcan, Rabaul

2009. Volcanoes. Multicoloured.

1343 85t. Type **417** 1·00 1·00
1344 3k. Foreshore with buildings and Mt. Tavurvur, Rabaul 3·25 3·25
1345 3k.70 Mt. Bagana, Bougainville 4·50 4·50
1346 6k. Forest and volcano, Manam Island, Madang 7·25 7·25

MS1347 146×106 mm. 85t. Mt. Tavurvur, Rabaul, emitting black smoke; 3k. Volcano, Manam Island, Madang; 3k.70 Mt. Tavurvur, Rabaul, emitting black cloud; 6k. Mt. Ulawun, Rabaul 16·00 16·00

MS1348 116×86 mm. 10k. Mt. Tavurvur, Rabaul, erupting red lava at sunset 12·00 12·00

418 Oil Palm Fruitlets

2009. Oil Palm Farming. Multicoloured.

1349 85t. Type **418** 1·00 1·00
1350 3k. Oil palm nursery 3·25 3·25
1351 3k.70 Bunches of oil palm fruit 4·50 4·50
1352 6k. Collection of fruit by lorry 7·75 7·75

MS1353 146×106 mm. 85t. Irrigation of oil palm seedlings; 3k. As No. 1351; 3k.70 Loose fruits; 6k. Oil palm mill 16·00 16·00

MS1354 116×86 mm. 10k. Hand holding fruitlets 12·00 12·00

419 Canoe, Mortlock Island, North Solomon Province

2009. Traditional Canoes. Multicoloured.

1355 85t. Type **419** 1·10 1·10
1356 3k. Manus Province 2·50 2·50
1357 3k.70 Bilbil, Madang Province 3·75 3·75
1358 6k. Central Province 5·75 5·75

MS1359 146×106 mm. 85t. Kimbe, West New Britain Province; 3k. Vuvulu Island, East Sepik Province; 3k.70 Suau Island, Milne Bay Province; 6k. Mailu, Central Province 16·50 16·50

MS1360 116×86 mm. 10k. Gogodala, Western Province 12·00 12·00

420 Engagement Dance, Western Highlands Province

2009. Traditional Dance (Romance). Multicoloured.

1361 1k. Type **420** 1·25 1·25
1362 3k. Bride Price Dance, Central Province 3·25 3·25
1363 4k.65 Engagement Dance, Manus Province 4·25 4·25
1364 6k.30 Tobriand Love Dance, Milne Bay Province 8·00 8·00

MS1365 146×107 mm. 1k. Courtship Dance, Chimbu Province; 3k. Engagement Dance, Enga Province; 4k.65 Engagement Dance, Central Province; 6k.30 Womanhood, Central Province 16·75 16·75

MS1366 116×86 mm. 10k. Tobriand Love Dance, Milne Bay Province 12·00 12·00

421 *Fish Man*

2010. Pioneer Art (3rd series) by Jakupa Ako. Multicoloured.

1367 1k. Type **421** 1·25 1·25
1368 3k. *Story Board* (vert) 3·25 3·25
1369 4k.65 *Hunting Trip* (vert) 4·25 4·25
1370 6k.30 *Warrior* (vert) 8·00 8·00

MS1371 106×146 mm. 1k. *Bird Art*; 3k. *Bird Eating*; 4k.65 *Bird Nest*; 6k.30 *Marsupial* (all vert) 8·00 8·00

MS1372 116×86 mm. 10k. *Spirit Mask* (vert) 12·00 12·00

422 *Bohadschia similis* ('Chalkfish')

2010. Sea Cucumbers (Beche-de-Mer).Multicoloured.

1373 1k. Type **422** 95 95
1374 3k. *Holothuria* (*Microthele*) *fuscopunctata* ('Elephant trunk fish') 2·50 2·50
1375 4k.65 *Stichopus hermanni* ('Curryfish') 3·75 3·75
1376 6k.30 *Bohadschia argus* ('Tigerfish') 5·50 5·50

MS1377 146×106 mm. 1k. *Actinopyga mauritiana* ('Surf redfish'); 3k. *Holothuria* (*Halodeima*) *atra* ('Lollyfish'); 4k.65 *Bohadschia vitiensis* ('Brown sandfish'); 6k.30 *Holothuria scabra* ('Sandfish') 12·00 12·00

MS1378 86×116 mm. 10k. *Holothuria* (*Halodeima*) *edulis* ('Pinkfish') 8·25 8·25

423 Huene Island

2010. Climate Change. Sinking Islands (Carterets). Multicoloured.

1379 1k. Type **423** 1·00 1·00
1380 3k. Upsurge of sea through man made barriers 2·25 2·25
1381 4k.65 Flooded forest ('Saltwater Intrusion') 3·75 3·75
1382 6k.30 Uprooted tree and branches at forest edge ('Saltwater Claims') 5·25 5·25

MS1383 146×106 mm. 1k. Dwindling Island; 3k. Uprooted tree on beach ('Saltwater Claims'); 4k.65 Storm surge and erosion; 6k.30 Man made barriers 12·50 12·50

MS1384 116×86 mm. 10k. Divided atolls 8·25 8·25

424 Nelumbium nelumbo (sacred lotus)

2010. Centenary of Girl Guiding.. Multicoloured.

1385 1k. Type **424** 1·00 1·00
1386 3k. Creating wash bowl stand for badge work 2·25 2·25
1387 4k.65 Trainer teaching knots at Guide Leaders training 3·75 3·75
1388 6k.30 Brownies displaying their badge work 5·25 5·25

MS1389 146×107 mm. 1k. Lady Kala Olewale, Second PNG Chief Commissioner, 1980s–90s; 3k. Lady Christian Chartterton, founder of Guiding in PNG, 1927; 4k.65 Princess Anne's visit to PNG, 1970; 6k.30 Enny Moaitz, first PNG Chief Commissioner, 1970s–80s 12·50 12·50

MS1390 117×86 mm. 10k. Lady Olave Baden-Powell, World Chief Guide, 1930–77 8·25 8·25

425 Australian Soldiers on Kokoda Trail, 1942

2010. Kokoda Trail Campaign, World War II. Multicoloured.

1391 1k. Type **425** 1·40 1·40
1392 1k. Papua New Guineans helping wounded soldiers along trail, 1942 1·40 1·40
1393 1k. Trekker, guide and memorial 1·40 1·40
1394 4k.65 Veterans at Kokoda Isurava Memorial 4·50 4·50
1395 4k.65 Kokoda veterans 4·50 4·50

MS1396 160×90 mm. Nos. 1391/5 13·00 13·00

Stamps in the same designs were issued by Australia on the same date. .

426 Elderly Man holding Infant and Children ('Young and Old')

2010. National Census 2010. Multicoloured.

1397 1k. Type **426** 1·40 40
1398 1k. 'Youths' 1·40 1·40
1399 3k. Village women with produce ('Villagers') 2·75 2·75
1400 3k. Working mother with baby from town and village houses ('Infants') 2·75 2·75

MS1401 145×106 mm. 1k. Davau Pre-School class and teacher, Ugabega, National Capital District ('School Kids'); 1k. 'Elderly men'; 3k. Women from Deacon Mothers of Mahuru United Church, National Capital District ('Elderly women'); 3k. People outside Post PNG, Boroko ('All walks of life') 8·25 8·25

427 Summer Palace, Wenchang Tower

2010. Expo 2010, Shanghai, China. Multicoloured.

1402 1k. Type **427** 1·00 1·00
1403 3k. Ballet dancer, Shanghai International Culture and Art Festival 2·50 2·50
1404 4k.65 Oriental Pearl Tower, Pudong, Shanghai 3·25 3·25
1405 6k.30 Chinese acrobatic performers (two men) 5·25 5·25

MS1406 131×181 mm. 5t. As Type **427**; 10t. As No. 1403; 85t. As No. 1404; 3k. Chinese acrobatic performers (three women); 3k.70 As No. 1405; 6k. Ancient Chinese building 8·00 8·00

MS1407 100×70 mm. 10k. Tower, Suzhou 11·00 11·00

428 Female Angler

2010. Game Fishing. Multicoloured.

1408 1k. Type **428** 1·00 1·00
1409 3k. Anglers with sailfish 2·25 2·25
1410 4k.65 Anglers with 25kg sailfish 3·75 3·75
1411 6k.30 Angler with 10kg barramundi 5·25 5·25

MS1412 146×106 mm. 1k. Game fishing boat; 3k. Angler; 4k.65 Angler with 14kg wahoo; 6k.30 Angler with 11kg barramundi 12·00 12·00

MS1413 86×116 mm. 10k. Irene Robinson with world record catch (2.6kg blue fin trevally on 4kg line) 8·00 8·00

429 Coffee Tree with Cherries

2010. Coffee. Multicoloured.

1414 15t. Type **429** 50 50
1415 1k. Coffee nursery (budding) 1·10 1·10
1416 4k.65 Coffee green cherries 2·75 2·75
1417 6k.30 Coffee red cherries 5·00 5·00

MS1418 146×107 mm. 1k. Harvesting coffee; 3k. Coffee fermentation; 4k.65 Coffee drying parchment; 6k.30 Coffee green beans 11·50 11·50

MS1419 116×86 mm. 10k. Coffee cherries 8·00 8·00

430 Macgregor's Gardener Bowerbird (*Amblyornis macgregoriae*)

2010. Bowerbirds. Multicoloured.

1420 5t. Type **430** 50 50
1421 1k. Flame bowerbird (*Sericulus aureus*) (male with bower) 1·10 1·10
1422 4k.65 Archbold's bowerbird (*Archboldia papuensis*) 2·75 2·75
1423 6k.30 Adelbert regent bowerbird (*Sericulus bakeri*) 5·00 5·00

MS1424 106×146 mm. 1k. Flame bowerbird (*Sericulus aureus*) (pair); 3k. Yellow-fronted gardener bowerbird (*Amblyornis flavifrons*); 4k.65 Vogelkop gardener bowerbird (*Amblyornis inornatus*); 6k.30 Lauterbach's bowerbird (*Chlamydera lautabachi*) 11·50 11·50

MS1425 86×116 mm. 10k. Flame bowerbird (*Sericulus aureus*) (close-up of male) 8·00 8·00

431 Rugby Sevens

2010. 19th Commonwealth Games, Delhi. Multicoloured.

1426	1k. Type **431**	1·00	1·00
1427	3k. Boxing	2·25	2·25
1428	4k.65 Netball	3·75	3·75
1429	6k.30 Hurdling	5·25	5·25
MS1431	87×116 mm. 10k. Tennis	8·00	8·00

No. **MS**1430 is left for a miniature sheet not yet received.

432 *Dendrobium lasianthera* 'May River Red'

2010. Orchids. Multicoloured.

1432	1k. Type **432**	95	95
1433	3k. *Dendrobium violaceoflavens* J. J. Smith	2·40	2·40
1434	4k.65 *Dendrobium mirbelianum* var. Vanimo	4·00	4·00
1435	6k.30 *Dendrobium helix*	4·75	4·75
MS1436	146×106 mm. 1k. *Dendrobium nindii* W. Hill; 3k. *Dendrobium* sp. *aff. D. gouldii Reichb.f.*; 4k.65 *Dendrobium gouldii Reichb.f.* var. Bougainville White; 6k.30 *Dendrobium discolor* var. pink Bensbach	12·00	12·00
MS1437	116×87 mm. 10k. *Dendrobium lasianthera* var. Sepik Blue	8·00	8·00

433 Mother Teresa, New Delhi, 1997

2010. Birth Centenary of Mother Teresa (founder of Missionaries of Charity). Multicoloured.

1438	1k. Type **433**	95	95
1439	3k. On visit to Rome, Italy, 1971	2·40	2·40
1440	4k.65 Mother Teresa in 1988	4·00	4·00
1441	6k.30 Arriving in Bhopal, India, 1984	4·75	4·75

434 Pope John Paul II meeting Pilgrims, Czestochowa

2010. Fifth Death Anniv of Pope John Paul II. Multicoloured.

MS1442	112×152 mm. 5t. Type **434**; 10t. In Nigeria; 1k. In Poland (giving blessing); 3k. In Poland (wearing mitre); 4k.65 Greeting Easter crowds, St. Peter's Square, Rome; 6k.30 In England	12·00	12·00

435 Pope Benedict XVI

2010. Fifth Anniv of Pontificate of Pope Benedict XVI

MS1443	**435** 10k. multicoloured	9·50	9·50

436 *Nephila pilipes*

2010. Spiders. Multicoloured.

1444	1k. Type **436**	1·00	1·00
1445	3k. *Argiope aemula*	2·25	2·25
1446	4k.65 *Gasterocantha* (black and yellow spider)	3·75	3·75
1447	6k.30 *Cyrtophora moluccensis*	5·75	5·75
MS1448	106×146 mm. 1k. *Leucauge celebesiana*; 3k. *Holconia*; 4k.65 *Gasterocantha* (black and white spider); 6k.30 *Ocrisiona*	12·50	12·50
MS1449	86×116 mm. 10k. *Nephila pilipes* (different)	8·25	8·25

437 Warrior with Bow and Arrow, Western Highlands Province

2010. Traditional Dance (2nd series). War. Multicoloured.

1450	50t. Type **437**	55	55
1451	1k.05 Simbu warrior with spear, Chimbu Province	1·00	1·00
1452	5k. Warrior with spear and shield, Western Highlands Province	3·50	3·50
1453	7k. Mudman with bow and arrow, Eastern Highlands Province	6·00	6·00
MS1454	86×116 mm. 10k. Tasman Island knife dancer, North Solomons Province	8·25	8·25

438 Emerald Tree Monitor (Varanus prasinus)

2011. Monitor Lizards. Multicoloured.

1455	1k.05 Type **438**	1·00	1·00
1456	5k. Papuan argus monitor (*Varanus panoptes horni*)	3·50	3·50
1457	5k. Papuan Monitor (*Varanus salvadori*)	3·50	3·50
1458	7k. Blue-tailed monitor (*Varanus doreanus*) (head and front foot)	6·00	6·00
MS1459	146×107 mm. 1k.05 Blue-tailed monitor (*Varanus doreanus*); 2k. Spotted tree monitor (*Varanus similis*); 5k. Mangrove monitor (*Varanus indicus*); 5k. Peach-throat monitor (*Varanus jobiensis*)	10·50	10·50
MS1460	116×86 mm. 5k. Papuan argus monitor (*Varanus panoptes horni*) (head)	4·00	4·00

POSTAGE DUE STAMPS

1960. Stamps of 1952 surch POSTAL CHARGES and value.

D2	1d. on 6½d. purple	2·50	4·00
D3	3d. on ½d. green	3·00	1·25
D1	6d. on 7½d. blue (A)	£800	£425
D4	6d. on 7½d. blue (B)	32·00	5·50
D5	1s.3d. on 3½d. black	2·50	1·25
D6	3s. on 2½d. orange	10·00	2·25

In (A) value and "POSTAGE" is obliterated by a solid circle and a series of "IX's" but these are omitted in (B).

D3

1960

D7	**D3**	1d. orange	65	75
D8	**D3**	3d. brown	70	75
D9	**D3**	6d. blue	75	40
D10	**D3**	9d. red	75	1·75
D11	**D3**	1s. green	75	50
D12	**D3**	1s.3d. violet	1·00	1·25
D13	**D3**	1s.6d. blue	3·50	5·50
D14	**D3**	3s. yellow	1·50	50

Pt. 20

PARAGUAY

A republic in the centre of S. America, independent since 1811.

1870. 8 reales = 1 peso.
1878. 100 centavos = 1 peso.
1944. 100 centimos = 1 guarani.

1

1870. Various frames. Values in "reales". Imperf.

1	**1**	1r. red	4·50	8·25
3	**1**	2r. blue	90·00	£100
4	**1**	3r. black	£160	£180

1878. Handstamped with large 5. Imperf.

5	**1**	5c. on 1r. red	£100	£130
9	**1**	5c. on 2r. blue	£500	£425
13	**1**	5c. on 3r. black	£600	£600

7

1879. Prepared for use but not issued (wrong currency). Values in "reales". Perf.

14	**7**	5r. orange	80	
15	**7**	10r. brown	95	

1879. Values in "centavos". Perf.

16	**7**	5c. brown	1·20	1·10
17	**7**	10c. green	3·75	3·75

1881. Handstamped with large figures.

18	**7**	1 on 10c. green	17·00	16·00
19	**7**	2 on 10c. green	17·00	16·00

1881. As T 1 (various frames), but value in "centavos". Perf.

20	**1**	1c. blue	90	85
21a	**1**	2c. red	65	95
22	**1**	4c. brown	65	65

1884. No. 1 handstamped with large 1. Imperf.

23	**1**	1c. on 1r. red	7·25	7·00

13

1884. Perf.

24	**13**	1c. green	65	85
25	**13**	2c. red	50	55
26	**13**	5c. blue	75	70

24

1887

32	**24**	1c. green	20	15
33a	**24**	2c. red	25	15
34	**24**	5c. blue	25	15
35	**24**	7c. brown	65	50
36	**24**	10c. mauve	55	35
37	**24**	15c. orange	55	35
38	**24**	20c. pink	55	35
50	**24**	40c. blue	2·40	1·20
51	**24**	60c. orange	1·00	55
52	**24**	80c. blue	90	55
53	**24**	1p. green	90	55

25

1889. Imperf or perf.

40	**25**	15c. purple	1·80	1·50

27 C. Rivarola

1892

42	**27**	1 CENTAVOS grey	20	10
54	**27**	1 CENTAVO grey	20	10
43	-	2c. green	20	10
44	-	4c. red	20	10
57	-	5c. purple	20	20
46	-	10c. violet	20	20
47	-	14c. brown	55	55
48	-	20c. red	90	55
49	-	30c. green	1·30	85
84	-	1p. blue	45	20

PORTRAITS: 2c. S. Jovellano; 4c. J. Bautista Gil; 5c. H. Uriarte; 10c. C. Barreiro; 14c. Gen. B. Caballero; 20c. Gen. P. Escobar; 30c. J. Gonzales; 1p. J. B. Egusquisa.

1892. 400th Anniv of Discovery of America. No. 46 optd 1492 12 DE OCTUBRE 1892 in oval.

41		10c. violet	6·00	2·75

1895. Surch PROVISORIO 5.

59	**24**	5c. on 7c. brown	55	55

30

1896. Telegraph stamps as T 30 surch CORREOS 5 CENTAVOS in oval.

60	**30**	5c. on 2c. brown, blk & grey	55	30
61	**30**	5c. on 4c. orange, blk & grey	55	30

1898. Surch Provisorio 10 Centavos.

63	**24**	10c. on 15c. orange	55	45
62	**24**	10c. on 40c. blue	20	20

1900. Telegraph stamps as T 30 surch with figures of value twice and bar.

64	**30**	5c. on 30c. green, blk & grey	1·80	1·20
65	**30**	10c. on 50c. lilac, blk & grey	4·00	2·75

39

1900

76	**39**	1c. green	20	20
67	**39**	2c. grey	20	20
73	**39**	2c. pink	45	20
68	**39**	3c. brown	20	20
78	**39**	4c. blue	20	20
69	**39**	5c. green	20	20
74	**39**	5c. brown	45	20
79	**39**	5c. lilac	20	20
80	**39**	8c. brown	35	30
71	**39**	10c. red	35	20
72	**39**	24c. blue	55	55
82	**39**	28c. orange	75	65
83	**39**	40c. blue	65	55

1902. Surch Habilitado en and new values.

88	-	1c. on 14c. brown (No. 47)	30	20
91	-	1c. on 1p. blue (No. 84)	30	25
86	**39**	5c. on 8c. brown (No. 80)	35	25
87	**39**	5c. on 28c. orange (No. 82)	35	25
89	**24**	5c. on 60c. orange (No. 51)	35	25
90	**24**	5c. on 80c. blue (No. 52)	30	25
85	**39**	20c. on 24c. blue (No. 72)	35	20

46

1903

92	**46**	1c. grey	30	25
93	**46**	2c. green	30	25
94a	**46**	5c. blue	45	25
95	**46**	10c. brown	45	25
96	**46**	20c. red	45	25
97	**46**	30c. blue	55	25
98	**46**	60c. violet	1·30	85

47

1903

99	**47**	1c. green	30	25
100	**47**	2c. orange	30	25
101	**47**	5c. blue	30	25
102	**47**	10c. violet	30	25
103	**47**	20c. green	90	45
104	**47**	30c. blue	1·00	25
105	**47**	60c. brown	1·10	65

48

1904

106	**48**	10c. blue	35	20

1904. End of successful Revolt against Govt. (begun in August). Surch PAZ 12 Dic. 1904. 30 centavos.

107	**48**	30c. on 10c. blue	55	30

50

51 National Palace, Asuncion

1905

108	**50**	1c. orange	35	25
109	**50**	1c. red	35	25
110	**50**	1c. blue	35	25
112	**50**	2c. green	41·00	
113	**50**	2c. red	35	25
114	**50**	5c. blue	35	25
116	**50**	5c. yellow	35	25
117	**50**	10c. brown	35	25
118	**50**	10c. green	35	25
119	**50**	10c. blue	35	25
120	**50**	20c. lilac	45	25
121	**50**	20c. brown	45	25
122	**50**	20c. green	35	25
123	**50**	30c. blue	45	25
124	**50**	30c. grey	45	25
125	**50**	30c. lilac	55	25
126	**50**	60c. brown	35	25
128	**50**	60c. pink	5·00	2·75
129	**51**	1p. black and red	1·80	95
130	**51**	1p. black and brown	65	30
131	**51**	1p. black and green	65	30
132	**51**	2p. black and blue	35	25
133	**51**	2p. black and red	45	25
134	**51**	2p. black and brown	35	25
135	**51**	5p. black and red	1·10	65
136	**51**	5p. black and blue	1·10	65
137	**51**	5p. black and green	1·10	65
138	**51**	10p. black and brown	1·10	65
139	**51**	10p. black and blue	1·00	65
141	**51**	20p. black and green	2·40	2·20
142	**51**	20p. black and yellow	2·40	2·20
143	**51**	20p. black and purple	2·40	2·20

1907. Surch Habilitado en and value and bars.

159	**50**	5c. on 1c. blue	30	25
145	**50**	5c. on 2c. green	35	25
160	**50**	5c. on 2c. red	30	25
172	**39**	5c. on 28c. orange	1·80	1·50
173	**39**	5c. on 40c. blue	55	45
162	**50**	5c. on 60c. pink	30	25
163	**50**	5c. on 60c. brown	30	25
175	**50**	20c. on 1c. blue	30	25
177	**50**	20c. on 2c. red	5·00	3·75
180	**24**	20c. on 2c. red	3·50	2·75
178	**50**	20c. on 30c. blue	2·10	2·00
179	**50**	20c. on 30c. lilac	30	25

1907. Official stamps surch Habilitado en, value and bars. Where not otherwise stated, the design is as T 50 but with "OFICIAL" below the lion.

149	-	5c. on 10c. brown	30	25
150	-	5c. on 10c. lilac	30	25
164	-	5c. on 10c. green	30	25
181	**24**	5c. on 15c. orange (No. O63)	3·75	2·30
151	-	5c. on 20c. green	55	45
152	-	5c. on 20c. lilac	55	45
166	-	5c. on 20c. brown	55	45
167	-	5c. on 20c. pink	55	45
182	**24**	5c. on 20c. pink (No. O64)	55·00	45·00
154	-	5c. on 30c. blue	30	25
157	**46**	5c. on 30c. blue (No. O104)	1·80	1·50
168	-	5c. on 30c. grey	30	25
169	-	5c. on 30c. yellow	30	25
183	**24**	5c. on 50c. grey (No. O65)	24·00	17·00
155	-	5c. on 60c. brown	30	25
158	**46**	5c. on 60c. violet (No. O105)	65	45
171	-	5c. on 60c. blue	30	25
174	**46**	20c. on 5c. blue (No. O101)	2·10	1·70
184	**24**	20c. on 5c. blue (No. O60)	2·10	1·70

1907. Official stamps, as T 50 and 51 with "OFICIAL" added, optd Habilitado and one bar.

146	5c. grey	55	25
148	5c. blue	55	25
185	1p. black and orange	55	55
186	1p. black and red	45	30

1907. Official stamps, as T 51 with "OFICIAL" added, surch Habilitado 1908 UN CENTAVO and bar.

188	1c. on 1p. black and red	30	25
189	1c. on 1p. black and brown	6·50	3·25

1908. Optd 1908.

190	**50**	1c. green	15	15
191	**50**	5c. yellow	15	15
192	**50**	10c. brown	20	20
193	**50**	20c. orange	15	15
194	**50**	30c. red	30	25
195	**50**	60c. mauve	25	25
196	**51**	1p. blue	25	25

1909. Optd 1909.

197	**50**	1c. blue	35	35
198	**50**	1c. red	30	25
199	**50**	5c. green	30	25
200	**50**	5c. orange	30	25
201	**50**	10c. red	30	25
202	**50**	10c. brown	30	25
203	**50**	20c. lilac	30	25
204	**50**	20c. yellow	35	30
205	**50**	30c. brown	75	65
206	**50**	30c. blue	65	55

62

1910

207	**62**	1c. brown	30	25
208	**62**	5c. lilac	30	25
209	**62**	5c. green	30	25
210	**62**	5c. blue	30	25
211	**62**	10c. green	30	25
212	**62**	10c. violet	30	25
213	**62**	10c. red	30	25
214	**62**	20c. red	30	25
215	**62**	50c. red	45	25
216	**62**	75c. blue	30	25

1911. No. 216 perf diagonally and each half used as 20c.

217	**62**	20c. (½ of 75c.) blue	30	20

63

1911. Independence Centenary.

218	**63**	1c. black and olive	20	10
219	**63**	2c. black and blue	20	20
220	**63**	5c. black and red	35	20
221	**63**	10c. brown and blue	35	20
222	**63**	20c. blue and olive	35	20
223	**63**	50c. blue and lilac	65	30
224	**63**	75c. purple and olive	65	30

1912. Surch Habilitada en VEINTE and thin bar.

225	**62**	20c. on 50c. red	30	20

65

1913

226	**65**	1c. black	30	10
227	**65**	2c. orange	30	10
228	**65**	5c. mauve	30	10
229	**65**	10c. green	30	10
230	**65**	20c. red	30	10
231	**65**	40c. red	30	10
232	**65**	75c. blue	30	10
233	**65**	80c. yellow	30	10
234	**65**	1p. blue	30	10
235	**65**	1p.25 blue	30	20
236	**65**	3p. green	30	20

1918. No. D242 surch HABILITADO EN 0.05 1918 and bar.

237	5c. on 40c. brown	30	25

1918. Nos. D239/42 optd HABILITADO 1918.

238	5c. brown	20	20
239	10c. brown	20	20
240	20c. brown	30	20
241	40c. brown	30	20

1918. Surch HABILITADO EN 0.30 1918 and bar.

242	**65**	30c. on 40c. red	10	10

1920. Surch HABILITADO en, value and 1920.

243	**65**	50c. on 80c. yellow	20	20
244	**65**	1p.75 on 3p. green	1·10	95

1920. Nos. D243/4 optd HABILITADO 1920 or surch also.

245	1p. brown	35	25
246	1p. on 1p.50 brown	35	25

72 Parliament House, Asuncion

1920. Jubilee of Constitution.

247	**72**	50c. black and red	35	25
248	**72**	1p. black and blue	1·00	45
249	**72**	1p.75 black and blue	20	25
250	**72**	3p. black and yellow	1·50	25

1920. Surch 50.

251	**65**	50 on 75c. blue	45	25

1921. Surch 50 and two bars.

252	**62**	50 on 75c. blue	30	25
253	**65**	50 on 75c. blue	30	25

75

1922

254	**75**	50c. blue and red	30	20
255	**75**	1p. brown and blue	30	20

77 Starting-point of Conspirators

1922. Independence.

256	**77**	1p. blue	35	10
258	**77**	1p. blue and red	35	25
259	**77**	1p. grey and purple	35	25
260	**77**	1p. grey and orange	35	25
257	**77**	5p. purple	55	30
261	**77**	5p. brown and blue	55	30
262	**77**	5p. black and green	55	30
263	**77**	5p. blue and red	55	30

Between 1922 and 1936 many regular postage stamps were overprinted **C** (= Campana—country), these being used at post offices outside Asuncion but not for mail sent abroad. The prices quoted are for whichever is the cheapest.

1924. Surch Habilitado en, value and 1924.

265	**65**	50c. on 75c. blue	30	25
266	**65**	$1 on 1p.25 blue	30	25
267	-	$1 on 1p.50 brown (No. D244)	30	25

80 Map

1924

268	**80**	1p. blue	20	10
269	**80**	2p. red	35	10
270	**80**	4p. blue	45	30

81 Gen. Jose E. Diaz

1925

271	**81**	50c. red	10	10
272	**81**	1p. blue	10	10
273	**81**	1p. green	20	10

82 Columbus

1925

274	**82**	1p. blue	20	10

1926. Surch Habilitado en and new value.

275	**62**	1c. on 5c. blue	10	10
276	**62**	$0.02 on 5c. blue	10	10
277	**65**	7c. on 40c. red	30	15
278	**65**	15c. on 75c. blue	10	10
279	**50**	$0.50 on 60c. purple (No. 195)	30	25
280	-	$0.50 on 75c. blue (No. O243)	20	10
281	-	$1.50 on 1p.50 brown (No. D244)	30	20
282	**80**	$1.50 on 4p. blue	20	10

86

87 P. J. Caballero

88 Paraguay

89 Cassel Tower, Asuncion

90 Columbus

1927

283	**86**	1c. red	10	10
284	**86**	2c. orange	10	10
285	**86**	7c. lilac	10	10
286	**86**	7c. green	10	10
287	**86**	10c. green	10	10
288	**86**	10c. red	10	10
290	**86**	10c. blue	10	10
291	**86**	20c. blue	10	10
292	**86**	20c. purple	10	10
293	**86**	20c. violet	10	10
294	**86**	20c. pink	10	10
295	**86**	50c. blue	10	10
296	**86**	50c. red	20	20
299	**86**	50c. mauve	10	10
300	**86**	50c. pink	10	10
323	**86**	50c. orange	10	10
326	**86**	50c. green	10	10
301	**86**	70c. blue	20	20
304	**87**	1p. orange	10	10
328	**87**	1p. green	10	10
329	**87**	1p. red	10	10
330	**87**	1p. purple	10	10
331	**87**	1p. blue	10	10
332	**87**	1p. violet	10	10
307	**88**	1p.50 pink	20	10
333	**88**	1p.50 brown	10	10
334	**88**	1p.50 lilac	10	10
335	**88**	1p.50 blue	10	10
308	-	2p.50 bistre	10	10
337	-	2p.50 violet	10	10
310	-	3p. red	20	45
311	-	3p. violet	10	10
338	-	3p. grey	20	10
312	**89**	5p. brown	55	45
314	**89**	5p. orange	20	10
340	**89**	5p. violet	15	10
315	**90**	10p. red	1·70	75
317	**90**	10p. blue	1·70	75
318	**88**	20p. red	3·75	3·00
319	**88**	20p. green	3·75	3·00
320	**88**	20p. purple	3·75	3·00

DESIGNS—As Type **87**: 2p.50, Fulgencio Yegros; 3p. V. Ignacio Yturbe.

92 Arms of De Salazarde Espinosa, founder of Asuncion

1928. Foundation of Asuncion, 1537.

342	**92**	10p. purple	1·90	1·30

93 Pres. Hayes of U.S.A. and Villa Hayes

1928. 50th Anniv of Hayes's Decision to award Northern Chaco to Paraguay.

343	**93**	10p. brown	9·25	4·25
344	**93**	10p. grey	9·25	4·25

1929. Air. Surch Correo Aereo Habilitado en and value.

357	**86**	$0.95 on 7c. lilac	30	25
358	**86**	$1.90 on 20c. blue	30	25
345	-	$2.85 on 5c. purple (No. O239)	1·10	95
348	-	$3.40 on 3p. grey (No. 338)	2·75	1·60
359	**80**	$3.40 on 4p. blue	35	25
360	**80**	$4.75 on 4p. blue	65	65
346	-	$5.65 on 10c. green (No. O240)	75	55
361	-	$6.80 on 3p. grey (No. 338)	75	75
349	**80**	$6.80 on 4p. blue	2·75	1·60
347	-	$11.30 on 50c. red (No. O242)	1·10	75
350	**89**	$17 on 5p. brown (A)	2·75	1·60
362	**89**	$17 on 5p. brown (B)	2·20	2·10

On No. 350 (A) the surcharge is in four lines, and on No. 362 (B) it is in three lines.

95

1929. Air.

352	**95**	2.85p. green	35	20
353	-	5.65p. brown	1·10	55
354	-	5.65p. red	55	30
355	-	11.30p. purple	75	55
356	-	11.30p. blue	35	30

DESIGNS: 5.65p. Carrier pigeon; 11.30p. Stylized airplane.

1930. Air. Optd CORREO AEREO or surch also in words.

363	**86**	5c. on 10c. green	30	25
364	**86**	5c. on 70c. blue	30	25
365	**86**	10c. green	35	20
366	**86**	20c. blue	35	20
367	**87**	20c. on 1p. red	35	25
368	**86**	40c. on 50c. orange	35	25
369	**87**	1p. green	75	75
370	-	3p. grey (No. 338)	75	75
371	**90**	6p. on 10p. red	1·30	1·10
372	**88**	10p. on 20p. red	5·50	5·25
373	**88**	10p. on 20p. purple	5·50	5·25

101

103

1930. Air.

374	**101**	95c. blue on blue	55	30
375	**101**	95c. red on pink	55	30
376	-	1p.90 purple on blue	55	30
377	-	1p.90 red on pink	55	30
378	**103**	6p.80 black on blue	55	30
379	**103**	6p.80 green on pink	55	30

DESIGN: 1p.90, Asuncion Cathedral.

104 Declaration of Independence

1930. Air. Independence Day.

380	**104**	2p.85 blue	55	30
381	**104**	3p.40 green	55	25
382	**104**	4p.75 purple	55	25

105

1930. Red Cross Fund.

383	**105**	1p.50+50c. blue	2·20	1·30
384	**105**	1p.50+50c. red	2·20	1·30
385	**105**	1p.50+50c. lilac	2·20	1·30

106 Portraits of Archbishop Bogarin

1930. Consecration of Archbishop Bogarin.

386	**106**	1p.50 blue	2·20	1·60
387	**106**	1p.50 red	2·20	1·60
388	**106**	1p.50 violet	2·20	1·60

1930. Surch Habilitado en CINCO.

389	**86**	5c. on 7c. green	10	10

108 Planned Agricultural College at Ypacarai

1931. Agricultural College Fund.

390	**108**	1p.50+50c. blue on red	65	65

109 Arms of Paraguay

1931. 60th Anniv of First Paraguay Postage Stamps.

391	**109**	10p. brown	1·20	55
392	**109**	10p. red on blue	1·20	55
393	**109**	10p. blue on red	1·20	55
395	**109**	10p. grey	1·00	45
396	**109**	10p. blue	35	30

110 Gunboat "Paraguay"

1931. Air. 60th Anniv of Constitution and Arrival of new Gunboats.

397	**110**	1p. red	20	20
398	**110**	1p. blue	20	20
399	**110**	2p. orange	35	30
400	**110**	2p. brown	35	30
401	**110**	3p. green	75	75
402	**110**	3p. blue	75	75
403	**110**	3p. red	65	65
404	**110**	6p. green	1·10	1·10
405	**110**	6p. mauve	1·10	1·10
406	**110**	6p. blue	1·10	1·10
407	**110**	10p. red	1·10	3·75
408	**110**	10p. green	2·40	2·10
409	**110**	10p. blue	1·90	1·80
410	**110**	10p. brown	2·75	2·75
411	**110**	10p. pink	2·75	2·75

1931. As T 110.

412	1p.50 violet	55	30
413	1p.50 blue	35	30

DESIGN: Gunboat "Humaita".
No. 413 is optd with large **C**.

112 War Memorial

113 Orange Tree and Yerba Mate

114 Yerba Mate

115 Palms

116 Yellow-headed Caracara

1931. Air.

414	**112**	5c. blue	20	10
415	**112**	5c. green	15	20
416	**112**	5c. red	35	20
417	**112**	5c. purple	10	10
418	**113**	10c. violet	20	20
419	**113**	10c. red	20	20
420	**113**	10c. brown	20	10
421	**113**	10c. blue	10	10
422	**114**	20c. red	20	10
423	**114**	20c. blue	35	30
424	**114**	20c. green	30	10
425	**114**	20c. brown	10	10
426	**115**	40c. green	30	20
426a	**115**	40c. blue	20	10
426b	**115**	40c. red	35	25
427	**116**	80c. blue	55	30
428	**116**	80c. green	35	25
428a	**116**	80c. red	30	25

1931. Air. Optd with airship "Graf Zeppelin" and Correo Aereo "Graf Zeppelin" or surch also.

429	**80**	3p. on 4p. blue	17·00	16·00
430	**80**	4p. blue	17·00	16·00

118 Farm Colony

1931. 50th Anniv of Foundation of San Bernardino.

431	**118**	1p. green	35	25
432	**118**	1p. red	35	25

1931. New Year. Optd FELIZ ANO NUEVO 1932.

433	**106**	1p.50 blue	2·00	2·00
434	**106**	1p.50 red	2·00	2·00

120 "Graf Zeppelin"

1932. Air.

435	**120**	4p. blue	3·25	3·25
436	**120**	8p. red	3·75	3·75
437	**120**	12p. green	5·00	5·00
438	**120**	16p. purple	6·50	6·50
439	**120**	20p. brown	6·50	6·50

121 Red Cross H.Q.

1932. Red Cross Fund.

440	**121**	50c.+50c. pink	65	55

122 (Trans: "Has been, is and will be")

1932. Chaco Boundary Dispute.

441	**122**	1p. purple	30	20
442	**122**	1p.50 pink	30	20
443	**122**	1p.50 brown	30	20
444	**122**	1p.50 green	30	20
445	**122**	1p.50 blue	30	20

Nos. 443/5 are optd with a large **C**.

1932. New Year. Surch CORREOS FELIZ ANO NUEVO 1933 and value.

446	**120**	50c. on 4p. blue	35	25
447	**120**	1p. on 8p. red	75	65
448	**120**	1p.50 on 12p. green	75	65
449	**120**	2p. on 16p. purple	75	65
450	**120**	5p. on 20p. brown	1·90	1·50

124 "Graf Zeppelin" over Paraguay

125 "Graf Zeppelin" over Atlantic

1933. Air. "Graf Zeppelin" issue.

451	**124**	4p.50 blue	2·20	1·50
452	**124**	9p. red	3·75	2·75
453	**124**	13p.50 green	3·75	2·75
454	**125**	22p.50 brown	10·00	7·50
455	**125**	45p. violet	13·00	13·00

126 Columbus's Fleet

1933. 441st Anniv of Departure of Columbus from Palos. Maltese Crosses in violet.

456	**126**	10c. olive and red	35	30
457	**126**	20c. blue and lake	35	30
458	**126**	50c. red and green	35	30
459	**126**	1p. brown and blue	45	45
460	**126**	1p.50 green and blue	55	55
461	**126**	2p. green and sepia	75	75
462	**126**	5p. lake and olive	1·70	1·60
463	**126**	10p. sepia and blue	1·70	1·60

127 G.P.O., Asuncion

1934. Air.

464	**127**	33p.75 blue	2·20	1·90
466	**127**	33p.75 green	2·75	2·10
467	**127**	33p.75 brown	75	75
468	**127**	33p.75 red	2·00	1·90

1934. Air. Optd 1934.

469	**124**	4p.50 blue	2·20	1·90
470	**124**	9p. red	2·75	2·10
471	**124**	13p.50 green	7·75	7·00
472	**125**	22p.50 brown	6·00	5·25
473	**125**	45p. violet	11·00	9·00

1935. Air. Optd 1935.

474	**124**	4p.50 red	2·75	1·90
475	**124**	9p. green	3·75	2·10
476	**124**	13p.50 brown	7·75	7·00
477	**125**	22p.50 purple	6·00	5·25
478	**125**	45p. blue	11·00	9·00

131 Tobacco Plant

1935. Air.

479	**131**	17p. brown	11·00	3·25
480	**131**	17p. red	21·00	5·75
481	**131**	17p. blue	14·50	3·75
482	**131**	17p. green	8·75	2·10

132 Church of the Incarnation

1935. Air.

483	**132**	102p. red	6·00	3·50
485	**132**	102p. blue	3·75	2·75
486	**132**	102p. brown	3·75	2·75
487	**132**	102p. violet	2·00	1·50
487a	**132**	102p. orange	1·80	1·30

1937. Air. Surch Habilitado en and value in figures.

488	**127**	$24 on 33p.75 blue	75	55
489	**132**	$65 on 102p. grey	2·00	1·40
490	**132**	$84 on 102p. green	2·00	1·20

134 Arms of Asuncion

1937. 4th Centenary of Asuncion (1st issue).

491	**134**	50c. purple and violet	35	25
492	**134**	1p. green and bistre	35	25
493	**134**	3p. blue and red	35	25
494	**134**	10p. yellow and red	35	25
495	**134**	20p. grey and blue	35	25

135 Monstrance

1937. 1st National Eucharistic Congress.

496	**135**	1p. red, yellow and blue	35	25
497	**135**	3p. red, yellow and blue	35	25
498	**135**	10p. red, yellow and blue	35	25

136 Oratory of the Virgin of Asuncion

1938. 4th Centenary of Asuncion (2nd issue).

499	**136**	5p. olive	35	30
500	**136**	5p. red	55	30
501	**136**	11p. brown	55	45

137 Asuncion

1939. Air.

502	**137**	3p.40 blue	75	75
503	**137**	3p.40 green	45	30
504	**137**	3p.40 brown	45	30

138 J. E. Diaz

1939. Reburial in National Pantheon of Ashes of C. A. Lopez and J. E. Diaz.

505	**138**	2p. brown and blue	45	30
506	-	2p. brown and blue	45	30

DESIGN—VERT: No. 506, C. A. Lopez.

139 Pres. Caballero and Senator Decoud

1939. 50th Anniv of Asuncion University.

507	-	50c. blk & orge (postage)	20	10
508	-	1p. black and blue	45	20
509	-	2p. black and red	65	30
510	**139**	5p. black and blue	90	55
511	**139**	28p. black and red (air)	10·00	9·50
512	**139**	90p. black and green	12·00	11·50

DESIGN: Nos. 507/9, Pres. Escobar and Dr. Zubizarreta.

140 Coats of Arms

141 Pres. Baldomir and Flags of Paraguay and Uruguay

1939. Chaco Boundary Peace Conference, Buenos Aires (1st issue).

513	**140**	50c. blue (postage)	45	30
514	**141**	1p. olive	35	20
515	**A**	2p. green	45	30
516	**B**	3p. brown	90	65
517	**C**	5p. orange	65	45
518	**D**	6p. violet	1·80	1·40
519	**E**	10p. brown	1·30	85
520	**F**	1p. brown (air)	20	20
521	**140**	3p. blue	35	20
522	**E**	5p. olive	35	30
523	**D**	10p. violet	45	30
524	**C**	30p. orange	65	45
525	**B**	50p. brown	1·10	65
526	**A**	100p. green	1·50	1·40
527	**141**	200p. green	8·75	5·75
528	-	500p. black	22·00	21·00

DESIGNS (flag on right is that of country named): A, Benavides (Peru); B, Eagle (USA); C, Alessandri (Chile); D, Vargas (Brazil); E, Ortiz (Argentina); F, Figure of "Peace" (Bolivia); 500p. (30×40 mm), Map of Chaco frontiers.

See also Nos. 536/43.

143 Arms of New York

144 Asuncion–New York Air Route

1939. New York World's Fair.

529	**143**	5p. red (postage)	45	30
530	**143**	10p. blue	90	65
531	**143**	11p. green	1·30	1·10
532	**143**	22p. grey	1·80	1·40
533	**144**	30p. brown (air)	8·25	5·25
534	**144**	80p. orange	10·00	9·50
535	**144**	90p. violet	13·00	13·00

145 Soldier

147 Waterfall

1940. Chaco Boundary Peace Conference, Buenos Aires (2nd issue). Inscr "PAZ DEL CHACO".

536	**145**	50c. orange	35	20
537	-	1p. purple	35	20
538	-	3p. green	35	20
539	-	5p. brown	35	20
540	-	10p. mauve	35	20
541	-	20p. blue	65	45
542	-	50p. green	1·50	65
543	**147**	100p. black	3·25	2·10

DESIGNS: As Type **145**: VERT: 1p. Water-carrier; 5p. Ploughing with oxen. HORIZ: 3p. Cattle Farming. As Type **147**: VERT: 10p. Fishing in the Paraguay River. HORIZ: 20p. Bullock-cart; 50p. Cattle-grazing.

148 Western Hemisphere

1940. 50th Anniv of Pan-American Union.

544	**148**	50c. orange (postage)	10	10
545	**148**	1p. green	20	20
546	**148**	5p. blue	35	30
547	**148**	10p. brown	1·20	1·20
548	**148**	20p. red (air)	55	45
549	**148**	70p. blue	1·40	55
550	**148**	100p. green	1·70	1·60
551	**148**	500p. violet	7·25	5·75

149 Reproduction of Paraguay No. 1

1940. Cent of First Adhesive Postage Stamps. Inscr "CENTENARIO DEL SELLO POSTAL 1940".

552	**149**	1p. purple and green	75	30
553	-	5p. brown and green	1·00	45
554	-	6p. blue and brown	2·20	95
555	-	10p. black and red	2·20	1·50

DESIGNS: 5p. Sir Rowland Hill; 6p., 10p. Early Paraguayan stamps.

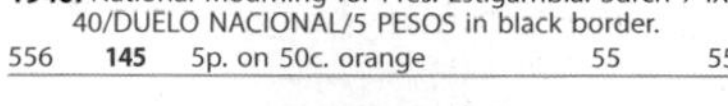

1940. National Mourning for Pres. Estigarribia. Surch 7-IX-40/DUELO NACIONAL/5 PESOS in black border.

556	**145**	5p. on 50c. orange	55	55

152 Dr. Francia

1940. Death Centenary of Dr. Francia (dictator).

557	**152**	50c. red	40	25
558	-	50c. purple	40	25
559	**152**	1p. green	40	25
560	-	5p. blue	40	25

PORTRAIT: Nos. 558 and 560, Dr. Francia seated in library.

1941. Visit of President Vargas of Brazil. Optd Visita al Paraguay Agosto de 1941.

560a	6p. violet (No. 518)	55	55

154 Our Lady of Asuncion

1941. Mothers' Fund.

561	**154**	7p.+3p. brown	45	35
562	**154**	7p.+3p. violet	45	35
563	**154**	7p.+3p. red	45	35
564	**154**	7p.+3p. blue	45	35

1942. Nos. 520/2 optd Habilitado and bar(s).

565	-	1p. brown	45	30
566	**140**	3p. blue	45	30
567	-	5p. olive	45	30

156 Arms of Paraguay

1942

568	**156**	1p. green	35	25
569	**156**	1p. orange	35	20
570	**156**	7p. blue	35	20
571	**156**	7p. brown	35	20

For other values as Type **156** see Nos. 631, etc.

158 Irala's Vision

1942. 4th Centenary of Asuncion.

572	-	2p. green (postage)	1·20	55
573	**158**	5p. red	1·20	55
574	-	7p. blue	1·20	55
575	-	20p. purple (air)	1·00	55
576	**158**	70p. brown	2·75	1·70
577	-	500p. olive	7·75	5·25

DESIGNS—VERT: 2p., 20p. Indian hailing ships; 7p., 500p. Irala's Arms.

160 Columbus sighting America

161 Pres. Morinigo and Symbols of Progress

1943. 450th Anniv of Discovery of America by Columbus.

578	**160**	50c. violet	35	25
579	**160**	1p. brown	35	25
580	**160**	5p. green	65	30
581	**160**	7p. blue	35	25

1943. Three Year Plan.

582	**161**	7p. blue	20	20

NOTE: From No. 583 onwards, the currency having been changed, the letter "c" in the value description indicates "centimos" instead of "centavos".

1944. St. Juan Earthquake Fund. Surch U.P.A.E. Adhesion victimas San Juan y Pueblo Argentino centimos and bar.

583	**E**	10c. on 10p. brown (No. 519)	75	55

1944. No. 311 surch Habilitado en un centimo.

584		1c. on 3p. violet	35	25

1944. Surch 1944/5 Centimos 5.

585	**160**	5c. on 7p. blue	30	15
586	**161**	5c. on 7p. blue	30	15

164 Primitive Indian Postmen

181 Jesuit Relics of Colonial Paraguay

1944

587	**164**	1c. black (postage)	10	15
588	-	2c. brown	20	15
589	-	5c. olive	2·20	30
590	-	7c. blue	65	45
591	-	10c. green	90	55
592	-	15c. blue	90	55
593	-	50c. black	1·20	85
594	-	1g. red	3·75	2·10

DESIGNS—HORIZ: 2c. Ruins of Humaita Church; 7c. Marshal Francisco S. Lopez; 1g. Ytororo Heroes' Monument. VERT: 5c. First Paraguayan railway locomotive; 10c. "Tacuary" (paddle-steamer); 15c. Port of Asuncion; 50c. Meeting place of Independence conspirators.

595	-	1c. blue (air)	10	10
596	-	2c. green	20	20
597	-	3c. purple	45	30
598	-	5c. green	35	30
599	-	10c. violet	55	45
600	-	20c. brown	1·70	1·30
601	-	30c. blue	75	65
602	-	40c. olive	1·30	1·20
603	-	70c. red	1·80	1·60
604	**181**	1g. orange	2·75	2·75
605	-	2g. brown	4·50	3·75
606	-	5g. brown	11·00	10·50
607	-	10g. blue	28·00	27·00

DESIGNS—HORIZ: 1c. Port of Asuncion; 2c. First telegraphic apparatus in S. America; 3c. Paddle-steamer "Tacuary"; 5c. Meeting place of Independence Conspirators; 10c. Antequera Monument; 20c. First Paraguayan railway locomotive; 40c. Government House. VERT: 30c. Ytororo Heroes' Monument; 70c. As Type **164** but vert: 2g. Ruins of Humaita Church; 5g. Oratory of the Virgin; 10g. Marshal Francisco S. Lopez.

See also Nos. 640/51.

1945. No. 590 surch with figure 5 over ornaments deleting old value.

608		5c. on 7c. blue	35	20

186 Clasped Hands and Flags

1945. President Morinigo's Goodwill Visits. Designs of different sizes inscr "CONFRATERNIDAD" between crossed flags of Paraguay and another American country, mentioned in brackets. (a) Postage.

609	**186**	1c. green (Panama)	10	10
610	**186**	3c. red (Venezuela)	20	20
611	**186**	5c. grey (Ecuador)	20	20
612	**186**	2g. brown (Peru)	2·75	2·75

(b) Air.

613		20c. orange (Colombia)	55	55
614		40c. olive (Bolivia)	55	55
615		70c. red (Mexico)	55	55
616		1g. blue (Chile)	1·10	1·10
617		2g. violet (Brazil)	1·70	1·60
618		5g. green (Argentina)	3·25	3·25
619		10g. brown (U.S.A.)	22·00	21·00

The 5 and 10g. are larger, 32×28 and 33½×30 mm respectively.

1945. Surch 1945 5 Centimos 5.

620	**160**	5c. on 7p. blue	55	45
621	**161**	5c. on 7p. blue	45	45
622	-	5c. on 7p. blue (No. 590)	90	45

1945. Surch 1945 and value.

623	**154**	2c. on 7p.+3p. brown	35	20
624	**154**	2c. on 7p.+3p. violet	35	20
625	**154**	2c. on 7p.+3p. red	35	20
626	**154**	2c. on 7p.+3p. blue	35	20
627	**154**	5c. on 7p.+3p. brown	40	20
628	**154**	5c. on 7p.+3p. violet	40	20
629	**154**	5c. on 7p.+3p. red	40	20
630	**154**	5c. on 7p.+3p. blue	40	20

1946. As T 156 but inscr "U.P.U." at foot.

631	**156**	5c. grey	35	20
631a	**156**	5c. pink	35	20
631b	**156**	5c. brown	35	20
686	**156**	10c. blue	35	20
687	**156**	10c. pink	35	20
631c	**156**	30c. green	35	20
631d	**156**	30c. brown	35	20
775	**156**	45c. green	35	25
631e	**156**	50c. mauve	35	20
776	**156**	50c. purple	35	25
858	**156**	70c. brown	35	25
777	**156**	90c. blue	35	25
778	**156**	1g. violet	35	25
860	**156**	1g.50 mauve	35	25
814	**156**	2g. ochre	35	25
780	**156**	2g.20 mauve	35	25
781	**156**	3g. brown	35	25
782	**156**	4g.20 green	35	25
862	**156**	4g.50 blue	35	25
816	**156**	5g. red	35	25
689	**156**	10g. orange	1·10	75
784	**156**	10g. green	35	25
818	**156**	12g.45 green	35	25
819	**156**	15g. orange	35	25
786	**156**	20g. blue	55	30
820	**156**	30g. bistre	55	30
812	**156**	50g. brown	35	20
821	**156**	100g. blue	1·50	1·20

See also Nos. 1037/49.

1946. Surch 1946 5 Centimos 5.

632	**154**	5c. on 7p.+3p. brown	1·20	95
633	**154**	5c. on 7p.+3p. violet	1·20	95
634	**154**	5c. on 7p.+3p. red	1·20	95
635	**154**	5c. on 7p.+3p. blue	1·20	95

1946. Air. Surch 1946 5 Centimos 5.

636		5c. on 20c. brown (No. 600)	1·80	1·70
637		5c. on 30c. blue (No. 601)	1·80	1·70
638		5c. on 40c. olive (No. 602)	1·80	1·70
639		5c. on 70c. red (No. 603)	1·80	1·70

1946. As Nos. 587/607 but colours changed and some designs smaller.

640	-	1c. red (postage)	15	10
641	-	2c. violet	20	15
642	**164**	5c. blue	30	15
643	-	10c. orange	45	25
644	-	15c. olive	55	35
645	**181**	50c. green	1·10	55
646	-	1g. blue	1·70	1·10

DESIGNS—VERT: 1c. Paddle-steamer "Tacuary"; 1g. Meeting place of Independence Conspirators. HORIZ: 2c. First telegraphic apparatus in S. America; 10c. Antequera Monument; 15c. Ytororo Heroes' Monument.

647		10c. red (air)	20	20
648		20c. green	35	30
649		1g. brown	1·10	1·10
650		5g. purple	3·25	3·25
651		10g. red	17·00	16·00

DESIGNS—VERT: 10c. Ruins of Humaita Church. HORIZ: 20c. Port of Asuncion; 1g. Govt. House; 5g. Marshal Francisco S. Lopez; 10g. Oratory of the Virgin.

189 Marshal Francisco Lopez

1947. Various frames.

652	**189**	1c. violet (postage)	15	15
653	**189**	2c. red	15	15
654	**189**	5c. green	20	20
655	**189**	15c. blue	20	20
656	**189**	50c. green	1·20	1·20
657	**189**	32c. red (air)	20	20
658	**189**	64c. brown	55	55
659	**189**	1g. blue	1·10	1·10
660	**189**	5g. purple and blue	2·75	2·75
661	**189**	10g. green and red	5·50	5·25

190 Archbishop of Paraguay

1947. 50th Anniv of Archbishopric of Paraguay.

662	**190**	2c. grey (postage)	10	10
663	-	5c. red	20	20
664	-	10c. black	35	20
665	-	15c. green	65	55
666	-	20c. black (air)	20	20
667	-	30c. grey	35	30
668	-	40c. mauve	55	55
669	**190**	70c. red	55	55
670	-	1g. lake	75	75
671	-	2g. red	2·20	2·10
672	**190**	5g. slate and red	3·75	3·75
673	-	10g. brown and green	6·50	6·50

DESIGNS: 5, 20c., 10g. Episcopal Arms; 10, 30c, 1g. Sacred Heart Monument; 15, 40c., 2g. Vision of projected monument.

194 Torchbearer

1948. Honouring the "Barefeet" (political party). Badge in red and blue.

674	**194**	5c. red (postage)	20	20
675	**194**	15c. orange	35	30
676	**194**	69c. green (air)	1·20	1·40
677	**194**	5g. blue	8·75	5·25

195 C. A. Lopez, J. N. Gonzalez and "Paraguari" (freighter)

1948. Centenary of Paraguay's Merchant Fleet. Centres in black, red and blue.

678	**195**	2c. orange	10	10
679	**195**	5c. blue	20	10
680	**195**	10c. black	30	10
681	**195**	15c. violet	45	15
682	**195**	50c. green	55	20
683	**195**	1g. red	65	45

1949. Air. National Mourning for Archbishop of Paraguay. Surch DUELO NACIONAL 5 CENTIMOS 5.

684	**190**	5c. on 70c. red	35	30

1949. Air. Aid to Victims of Ecuadorean Earthquake. No. 667 surch AYUDA AL ECUADOR 5 + 5 and two crosses.

685		5c.+5c. on 30c. slate	35	30

198 "Postal Communications"

1950. Air. 75th Anniv of U.P.U.

691	**198**	20c. violet and green	75	45
692	**198**	30c. brown and purple	1·10	65
693	**198**	50c. green and grey	1·70	85
694	**198**	1g. brown and blue	2·20	1·10
695	**198**	5g. black and red	5·50	2·75

199 President Roosevelt

1950. Air. Honouring F. D. Roosevelt. Flags in red and blue.

696	**199**	20c. orange	35	30
697	**199**	30c. black	35	30
698	**199**	50c. purple	35	30
699	**199**	1g. green	35	30
700	**199**	5g. blue	65	65

1951. 1st Economic Congress of Paraguay. Surch PRIMER CONGRESO DE ENTIDADES ECONOMICAS DEL PARAGUAY 18-IV-1951 and shield over a block of four stamps.

700a	**156**	5c. pink	35	20
700b	**156**	10c. blue	55	30
700c	**156**	30c. green	90	65

Prices are for single stamps. Prices for blocks of four, four times single prices.

200 Columbus Lighthouse

201 Urn

1952. Columbus Memorial Lighthouse.

701	**200**	2c. brown (postage)	40	35
702	**200**	5c. blue	40	35
703	**200**	10c. pink	40	35
704	**200**	15c. blue	40	35
705	**200**	20c. purple	40	35
706	**200**	50c. orange	40	35
707	**200**	1g. green	40	35
708	**201**	10c. blue (air)	40	35
709	**201**	20c. green	40	35
710	**201**	30c. purple	40	35
711	**201**	40c. pink	40	35
712	**201**	50c. bistre	40	35
713	**201**	1g. blue	40	35
714	**201**	2g. orange	40	35
715	**201**	5g. lake	55	55

202 Isabella the Catholic

1952. Air. 500th Birth Anniv of Isabella the Catholic.

716	**202**	1g. blue	35	30
717	**202**	2g. brown	45	45
718	**202**	5g. green	90	85
719	**202**	10g. purple	2·20	2·10

203 S. Pettirossi (aviator)

1954. Pettirossi Commemoration.

720	**203**	5c. blue (postage)	55	30
721	**203**	20c. red	55	30
722	**203**	50c. purple	55	30
723	**203**	60c. violet	55	30
724	**203**	40c. brown (air)	55	30
725	**203**	55c. green	55	30
726	**203**	80c. blue	55	30
727	**203**	1g.30 grey	55	30

204 San Roque Church, Asuncion

1954. Air. San Roque Church Centenary.

728	**204**	20c. red	20	15
729	**204**	30c. purple	20	15
730	**204**	50c. blue	20	15
731	**204**	1g. purple and brown	35	25
732	**204**	1g. black and brown	35	25
733	**204**	1g. green and brown	35	25
734	**204**	1g. orange and brown	35	25
735	**204**	5g. yellow and brown	55	45
736	**204**	5g. olive and brown	55	45
737	**204**	5g. violet and brown	55	45
738	**204**	5g. buff and brown	55	45
MS738a		Two sheets each 124×108 mm. Nos. 731/4 and 735/8. No gum	9·00	9·00

205 Marshal Lopez, C. A. Lopez and Gen. Caballero

1954. National Heroes.

739	**205**	5c. violet (postage)	10	10
740	**205**	20c. blue	10	10
741	**205**	50c. mauve	10	10
742	**205**	1g. brown	15	10
743	**205**	2g. green	35	30
744	**205**	5g. violet (air)	45	30
745	**205**	10g. olive	90	75
746	**205**	20g. grey	1·40	1·20
747	**205**	50g. pink	3·00	3·00
748	**205**	100g. blue	10·00	9·50

206 Presidents Stroessner and Peron

1955. Visit of President Peron. Flags in red and blue.

749	**206**	5c. brown & buff (postage)	10	10
750	**206**	10c. lake and buff	10	10
751	**206**	50c. grey	20	10
752	**206**	1g.30 lilac and buff	35	30
753	**206**	2g.20 blue and buff	65	65
754	**206**	60c. olive and buff (air)	10	10
755	**206**	2g. green	45	30
756	**206**	3g. red	45	30
757	**206**	4g.10 mauve and buff	65	55

207 Trinidad Campanile

1955. Sacerdotal Silver Jubilee of Mgr. Rodriguez.

758	**207**	5c. brown (postage)	40	35
759	-	20c. brown	40	35
760	-	50c. brown	40	35
761	-	2g.50 green	40	35
762	-	5g. brown	40	35
763	-	15g. green	40	35
764	-	25g. green	75	45
765	**207**	2g. blue (air)	40	35
766	-	3g. green	40	35
767	-	4g. green	40	35
768	-	6g. brown	40	35
769	-	10g. red	40	35
770	-	20g. brown	40	35
771	-	30g. green	55	45
772	-	50g. blue	65	55

DESIGNS—HORIZ: 20c., 3g. Cloisters in Trinidad; 5, 10g. San Cosme Portico; 15, 20g. Church of Jesus. VERT: 50c., 4g. Cornice in Santa Maria; 2g.50, 6g. Santa Rosa Tower; 25, 30g. Niche in Trinidad; 50g. Trinidad Sacristy.

208 Angel and Marching Soldiers

209 Soldier and Flags

1957. Chaco Heroes. Inscr "HOMENAJE A LOS HEROES DEL CHACO". Flags in red, white and blue.

787	**208**	5c. green (postage)	35	30
788	**208**	10c. red	35	30
789	**208**	15c. blue	35	30
790	**208**	20c. purple	35	30
791	**208**	25c. black	35	30
792	-	30c. blue	35	30
793	-	40c. black	35	30
794	-	50c. lake	35	30
795	-	1g. turquoise	35	30
796	-	1g.30 blue	35	30
797	-	1g.50 purple	35	30
798	-	2g. green	35	30
799	**209**	10c. blue (air)	35	30
800	**209**	15c. purple	35	30
801	**209**	20c. red	35	30
802	**209**	25c. blue	35	30
803	**209**	50c. turquoise	35	30
804	**209**	1g. red	35	30
805	-	1g.30 purple	35	30
806	-	1g.50 blue	35	30
807	-	2g. green	35	30
808	-	4g.10 vermilion and red	35	30
809	-	5g. black	35	30
810	-	10g. turquoise	35	30
811	-	25g. blue	45	30

DESIGNS—HORIZ: Nos. 792/8, Man, woman and flags; 805/11, "Paraguay" and kneeling soldier.

212 R. Gonzalez and St. Ignatius

1958. 4th Centenary of St. Ignatius of Loyola.

822	**212**	50c. green	35	30
823	-	50c. brown	35	30
824	-	1g.50 violet	35	30
825	-	3g. blue	35	30
826	**212**	6g.25 red	35	30

DESIGNS—VERT: 50c. brown; 3g. Statue of St. Ignatius. HORIZ: 1g.50, Jesuit Fathers' house, Antigua.

See also Nos. 1074/81.

213 President Stroessner

1958. Re-election of Pres. Stroessner. Portrait in black.

827	**213**	10c. red (postage)	10	10
828	**213**	15c. violet	10	10
829	**213**	25c. green	10	10
830	**213**	30c. lake	10	10
831	**213**	50c. mauve	10	10
832	**213**	75c. blue	10	10
833	**213**	5g. turquoise	20	15
834	**213**	10g. brown	65	55
835	**213**	12g. mauve (air)	75	65
836	**213**	18g. orange	90	75
837	**213**	23g. brown	1·20	1·10
838	**213**	36g. green	1·90	1·60
839	**213**	50g. olive	2·20	2·10
840	**213**	65g. grey	3·75	3·25

1959. Nos. 758/72 surch with star enclosed by palm leaves and value.

841	1g.50 on 5c. ochre (postage)	10	10
842	1g.50 on 20c. brown	10	10
843	1g.50 on 50c. purple	10	10
844	3g. on 2g.50 olive	10	10
845	6g.25 on 5g. brown	15	15
846	20g. on 15g. turquoise	65	65
847	30g. on 25g. green	1·00	95
848	4g. on 2g. blue (air)	20	10
849	12g.45 on 3g. olive	45	30
850	18g.15 on 6g. brown	65	55
851	23g.40 on 10g. red	90	65
852	34g.80 on 20g. bistre	1·20	95
853	36g. on 4g. green	1·40	95
854	43g.95 on 30g. green	1·70	1·10
855	100g. on 50g. blue	3·75	2·30

215 U.N. Emblem

1959. Air. Visit of U.N. Secretary-General.

856	**215**	5g. blue and orange	90	65

216 U.N. Emblem and Map of Paraguay

1959. Air. U.N. Day.

857	**216**	12g.45 orange and blue	45	30

217 Football

1960. Olympic Games, Rome. Inscr "1960".

863	**217**	30c. red & green (postage)	40	35
864	**217**	50c. purple and blue	40	35
865	**217**	75c. green and orange	40	35
866	**217**	1g.50 violet and green	40	35
867	-	12g.45 blue and red (air)	40	35
868	-	18g.15 green and purple	40	35
869	-	36g. red and green	65	65

DESIGN—AIR: Basketball.

218 "Uprooted Tree"

1960. World Refugee Year (1st issue).

870	**218**	25c. pink and green (postage)	45	35
871	**218**	50c. green and red	45	35
872	**218**	70c. brown and mauve	55	35
873	**218**	1g.50 blue and deep blue	55	35
874	**218**	3g. grey and brown	1·10	85
875	-	4g. pink and green (air)	90	75
876	-	12g.45 green and blue	1·80	1·30
877	-	18g.15 orange and red	2·40	1·40
878	-	23g.40 blue and red	2·75	2·75

DESIGN—AIR. As Type **218** but with "ANO MUNDIAL" inscr below tree.

See also Nos. 971/7.

219 U.N. Emblem

1960. "Human Rights". Inscr "DERECHOS HUMANOS".

879	**219**	1g. red and blue (postage)	40	35
880	-	3g. orange and blue	40	35
881	-	6g. orange and green	40	35
882	-	20g. yellow and red	40	35
MS882a		140×95 mm. Nos. 879/82	6·00	6·00
883	**219**	40g. blue and red (air)	45	45
884	-	60g. red and green	55	55
885	-	100g. red and blue	1·30	1·30
MS885a		140×95 mm. Nos. 883/5	22·00	22·00

DESIGNS: 3g., 60g. Hand holding scales; 6g. Hands breaking chain; 20g., 100g. "Freedom flame".

220 U.N. Emblem and Flags

1960. U.N. Day. Flags and inscr in blue and red.

886	**220**	30c. blue (postage)	40	35
887	**220**	75c. yellow	40	35
888	**220**	90c. mauve	40	35
889	**220**	3g. orange (air)	40	35
890	**220**	4g. green	40	35

221 Bridge with Arms of Brazil and Paraguay

1961. Inauguration of International Bridge between Brazil and Paraguay.

891	**221**	15c. green (postage)	10	10
892	**221**	30c. blue	10	10
893	**221**	50c. orange	10	10
894	**221**	75c. blue	10	10
895	**221**	1g. violet	10	10
896	-	3g. red (air)	35	20
897	-	12g.45 lake	65	55
898	-	18g.15 green	75	65
899	-	36g. blue	1·50	1·30
MS899a		125×181 mm. Nos. 896/9. Imperf	3·25	3·25

DESIGN—HORIZ: Nos. 896/9, Aerial view of bridge.

222 Timber Truck

1961. Paraguayan Progress. Inscr "PARAGUAY EN MARCHA".

No.	Type	Description	Mint	Used
900	**222**	25c. red & green (postage)	10	10
901	-	90c. yellow and blue	10	10
902	-	1g. red and orange	10	10
903	-	2g. green and pink	10	10
904	-	5g. violet and green	35	20
905	**222**	12g.45 blue and buff (air)	65	55
906	-	18g.15 violet and buff	90	75
907	-	22g. blue and orange	1·00	85
908	-	36g. yellow, green and blue	1·70	1·50

DESIGNS: 90c., 2g., 18g.15, Motorized timber barge; 1, 5, 22g. Radio mast; 36g. Boeing 707 jetliner.

223 P. J. Caballero, J. G. R. de Francia and F. Yegros

1961. 150th Anniv of Independence. (a) 1st issue.

No.	Type	Description	Mint	Used
909	**223**	30c. green (postage)	10	10
910	**223**	50c. mauve	10	10
911	**223**	90c. violet	10	10
912	**223**	1g.50 blue	10	10
913	**223**	3g. bistre	10	10
914	**223**	4g. blue	20	10
915	**223**	5g. brown	20	20
916	-	12g.45 red (air)	55	30
917	-	18g.15 blue	65	55
918	-	23g.40 green	90	75
919	-	30g. violet	1·10	85
920	-	36g. red	1·40	1·30
921	-	44g. brown	1·80	1·40

DESIGN: Nos. 916/21, Declaration of Independence.

224 "Chaco Peace"

(b) 2nd issue. Inscr "PAZ DEL CHACO".

No.	Type	Description	Mint	Used
922	**224**	25c. red (postage)	10	10
923	**224**	30c. green	10	10
924	**224**	50c. brown	10	10
925	**224**	1g. violet	10	10
926	**224**	2g. blue	10	10
927	-	3g. blue (air)	55	45
928	-	4g. purple	65	55
929	-	100g. green	3·75	3·25

DESIGN: Nos. 927/9, Clasped hands.

225 Puma

(c) 3rd issue.

No.	Type	Description	Mint	Used
930	**225**	75c. violet (postage)	90	30
931	**225**	1g.50 brown	90	30
932	**225**	4g.50 green	90	30
933	**225**	10g. blue	90	30
934	-	12g.45 purple (air)	2·75	1·70
935	-	18g.15 blue	2·75	2·10
936	-	34g.80 brown	5·00	3·75

DESIGN: Nos. 934/6, Brazilian tapir.

226 Arms of Paraguay

(d) 4th issue.

No.	Type	Description	Mint	Used
937	**226**	15c. blue (postage)	35	30
938	**226**	25c. red	35	30
939	**226**	75c. green	35	30
940	**226**	1g. red	35	30
941	**226**	3g. brown (air)	35	30
942	**226**	12g.45 mauve	35	30
943	**226**	36g. turquoise	75	75

The air stamps have a background pattern of horiz lines.

227 Grand Hotel, Guarani

(e) 5th issue.

No.	Type	Description	Mint	Used
944	**227**	50c. grey (postage)	35	30
945	**227**	1g. green	35	30
946	**227**	4g.50 violet	35	30
947	-	3g. brown (air)	35	30
948	-	4g. blue	35	30
949	-	18g.15 orange	45	45
950	-	36g. red	75	75

The air stamps are similar to Type **227** but inscr "HOTEL GUARANI" in upper left corner. See also Nos. 978/85 and 997/1011.

228 Racquet, Net and Balls

1961. 28th South American Tennis Championships, Asuncion (1st issue). Centres multicoloured; border colours given.

No.	Type	Description	Mint	Used
951	**228**	35c. pink (postage)	10	10
952	**228**	75c. yellow	10	10
953	**228**	1g.50 blue	10	10
954	**228**	2g.25 turquoise	15	15
955	**228**	4g. grey	30	25
MS955a		105×160 mm. Nos. 951/5 in block of 4 with colours changed. Imperf	29·00	28·00
956	**228**	12g.45 orange (air)	1·00	95
957	**228**	20g. orange	1·90	1·80
958	**228**	50g. orange	4·75	4·50

See also Nos. 978/85.

229

1961. "Europa".

No.	Type	Description	Mint	Used
959	**229**	50c. red, blue and mauve	55	20
960	**229**	75c. red, blue and green	55	20
961	**229**	1g. red, blue and brown	55	20
962	**229**	1g.50 red, blue & lt blue	55	20
963	**229**	4g.50 red, blue and yellow	1·30	55
MS963a		180×139 mm. Nos. 959/63. Imperf	29·00	29·00

230 Comm. Alan Shepard and Solar System

1961. Commander Shepard's Space Flight.

No.	Type	Description	Mint	Used
964	-	10c. brown and blue (postage)	35	10
965	-	25c. mauve and blue	35	10
966	-	50c. orange and blue	35	10
967	-	75c. green and blue	35	10
968	**230**	18g.15 blue and green (air)	13·00	6·50
969	**230**	36g. blue and orange	13·00	6·50
970	**230**	50g. blue and mauve	18·00	7·50
MS970a		124×94 mm. No. 970	33·00	33·00

DESIGN—HORIZ: Nos. 964/7, Comm. Shepard.

231

1961. World Refugee Year (2nd issue).

No.	Type	Description	Mint	Used
971	**231**	10c. deep blue and blue (postage)	10	10
972	**231**	25c. purple and orange	10	10
973	**231**	50c. mauve and pink	10	10
974	**231**	75c. blue and green	10	10
975	-	18g.15 red and brown (air)	75	75
976	-	36g. green and red	1·90	1·80
977	-	50g. orange and green	2·40	2·30
MS977a		119×80 mm. No. 977	19·00	19·00

Nos. 975/7 have a different background and frame.

232 Tennis-player

1962. 150th Anniv of Independence (6th issue) and 28th South American Tennis Championships, Asuncion (2nd issue).

No.	Type	Description	Mint	Used
978	**232**	35c. blue (postage)	1·00	30
979	**232**	75c. violet	1·00	30
980	**232**	1g.50 brown	1·00	30
981	**232**	2g.25 green	1·00	30
982	-	4g. red (air)	1·00	30
983	-	12g.45 purple	1·00	30
984	-	20g. turquoise	1·90	65
985	-	50g. brown	2·75	1·10

Nos. 982/5 show tennis-player using backhand stroke.

233 Scout Bugler

1962. Boy Scouts Commemoration.

No.	Type	Description	Mint	Used
986	**233**	10c. green & pur (postage)	10	10
987	**233**	20c. green and red	10	10
988	**233**	25c. green and brown	10	10
989	**233**	30c. green and emerald	10	10
990	**233**	50c. green and blue	10	10
991	-	12g.45 mauve & blue (air)	1·20	1·20
992	-	36g. mauve and green	3·50	3·50
993	-	50g. mauve and yellow	5·00	4·75
MS993a		128×101 mm. No. 993	19·00	19·00

DESIGN: Nos. 991/3, Lord Baden-Powell.

234 Pres. Stroessner and the Duke of Edinburgh

1962. Air. Visit of Duke of Edinburgh.

No.	Type	Description	Mint	Used
994	**234**	12g.45 blue, buff & green	35	30
995	**234**	18g.15 blue, pink and red	35	30
996	**234**	36g. blue, yellow & brown	65	65
MS996a		130×80 mm. No. 995	10·00	10·00

235 Map of the Americas

1962. 150th Anniv of Independence (7th issue) and Day of the Americas.

No.	Type	Description	Mint	Used
997	**235**	50c. orange (postage)	35	30
998	**235**	75c. blue	35	30
999	**235**	1g. violet	35	30
1000	**235**	1g.50 green	35	30
1001	**235**	4g.50 red	35	30
1002	-	20g. mauve (air)	35	30
1003	-	50g. orange	75	75

DESIGN: 20g., 50g. Hands supporting Globe.

236 U.N. Emblem

1962. 150th Anniv of Independence (8th issue).

No.	Type	Description	Mint	Used
1004	**236**	50c. brown (postage)	10	10
1005	**236**	75c. purple	10	10
1006	**236**	1g. blue	10	10
1007	**236**	2g. brown	10	10
1008	-	12g.45 violet (air)	65	65
1009	-	18g.15 green	1·10	1·10
1010	-	23g.40 red	1·50	1·50
1011	-	30g. red	1·80	1·70

DESIGN: Nos. 1008/11, U.N. Headquarters, New York.

237 Mosquito and W.H.O. Emblem

1962. Malaria Eradication.

No.	Type	Description	Mint	Used
1012	**237**	30c. black, blue and pink (postage)	10	10
1013	**237**	50c. black, green & bistre	10	10
1014	-	75c. black, bistre and red	10	10
1015	-	1g. black, bistre and green	10	10
1016	-	1g.50 black, bistre & brown	10	10
1017	**237**	3g. black, red & blue (air)	10	10
1018	**237**	4g. black, red and green	10	10
1019	-	12g.45 black, grn & brn	55	45
1020	-	18g.15 black, red and purple	1·30	75
1021	-	36g. black, blue and red	3·25	2·10
MS1021a		105×70 mm. No. 1021	22·00	22·00

DESIGN: Nos. 1014/16, 1019/21, Mosquito on U.N. emblem, and microscope.

238 Football Stadium

1962. World Cup Football Championship, Chile.

1022	**238**	15c. brown & yell (postage)	10	10
1023	**238**	25c. brown and green	10	10
1024	**238**	30c. brown and violet	10	10
1025	**238**	40c. brown and orange	10	10
1026	**238**	50c. brown and green	10	10
1027	-	12g.45 black, red and violet (air)	1·20	55
1028	-	18g.15 black, brn & vio	1·90	75
1029	-	36g. black, grey & brown	3·50	1·40
MS1029a		105×70 mm. No. 1029	33·00	32·00

DESIGN—HORIZ: Nos. 1027/9, Footballers and Globe.

239 "Lago Ypoa" (freighter)

1962. Paraguayan Merchant Marine Commem.

1030	**239**	30c. brown (postage)	45	45
1031	-	90c. blue	45	45
1032	-	1g.50 purple	45	45
1033	-	2g. green	45	45
1034	-	4g.20 blue	45	45
1035	-	12g.45 red (air)	45	45
1036	-	44g. blue	75	65

DESIGNS—HORIZ: 90c. Freighter; 1g.50, "Olympo" (freighter); 2g. Freighter (diff); 4g.20, "Rio Apa" (freighter). VERT: 12g.45, 44g. Ship's wheel.

1962. As Nos. 631, etc, but with taller figures of value.

1037	**156**	50c. blue	45	30
1038	**156**	70c. lilac	45	30
1039	**156**	1g.50 violet	45	30
1040	**156**	3g. blue	45	30
1041	**156**	4g.50 brown	45	30
1042	**156**	5g. mauve	45	30
1043	**156**	10g. mauve	45	30
1044	**156**	12g.45 blue	45	30
1045	**156**	15g.45 red	45	30
1046	**156**	18g.15 purple	45	30
1047	**156**	20g. brown	45	30
1048	**156**	50g. brown	65	30
1049	**156**	100g. grey	1·40	75

241 Gen. A. Stroessner

1963. Re-election of Pres. Stroessner to Third Term of Office.

1050	**241**	50c. brown and drab (postage)	45	45
1051	**241**	75c. brown and pink	45	45
1052	**241**	1g.50 brown and mauve	45	45
1053	**241**	3g. brown and green	45	45
1054	**241**	12g.45 red and pink (air)	45	45
1055	**241**	18g.15 green and pink	45	45
1056	**241**	36g. violet and pink	1·50	95

242 Popes Paul VI, John XXIII and St. Peter's

1964. Popes Paul VI and John XXIII.

1057	**242**	1g.50 yellow and red (postage)	10	10
1058	**242**	3g. green and red	10	10
1059	**242**	4g. brown and red	10	10
1060	-	12g.45 olive & grn (air)	55	45
1061	-	18g.15 green and violet	75	55
1062	-	36g. green and blue	2·75	1·90

DESIGNS: Nos. 1060/2, Cathedral, Asuncion.

243 Arms of Paraguay and France

1964. Visit of French President.

1063	**243**	1g.50 brown (postage)	10	10
1064	-	3g. blue	10	10
1065	**243**	4g. grey	15	10
1066	-	12g.45 violet (air)	45	45
1067	**243**	18g.15 green	65	65
1068	-	36g. red	2·75	1·90

DESIGNS: 3, 12g.45, 36g. Presidents Stroessner and De Gaulle.

245 Map of the Americas

1965. 6th Reunion of the Board of Governors of the Inter-American Development Bank. Optd Centenario de la Epopeya Nacional 1,864–1,870 as in T 245.

1069	**245**	1g.50 green (postage)	35	30
1070	**245**	3g. pink	35	30
1071	**245**	4g. blue	35	30
1072	**245**	12g.45 brown (air)	35	30
1073	**245**	36g. violet	1·00	65

The overprint refers to the National Epic of 1864–70, the war with Argentina, Brazil and Uruguay and this inscription occurs on many other issues from 1965 onwards.

Nos. 1069/73 without the overprint were not authorized.

246 R. Gonzalez and St. Ignatius

1966. 350th Anniv of Founding of San Ignacio Guazu Monastery.

1074	**246**	15c. blue (postage)	35	30
1075	**246**	25c. blue	35	30
1076	**246**	75c. blue	35	30
1077	**246**	90c. blue	35	30
1078	-	3g. brown (air)	35	30
1079	-	12g.45 brown	35	30
1080	-	18g.15 brown	45	45
1081	-	23g.40 brown	45	45

DESIGNS: Nos. 1078/81, Jesuit Fathers' house, Antigua.

For similar stamps with different inscriptions, see Nos. 822, 824 and 826.

247 Ruben Dario

1966. 50th Death Anniv of Ruben Dario (poet).

1082	**247**	50c. blue	10	10
1083	**247**	70c. brown	10	10
1084	**247**	1g.50 lake	10	10
1085	**247**	3g. violet	10	10
1086	**247**	4g. turquoise	10	10
1087	**247**	5g. black	10	10
1088	-	12g.45 blue (air)	35	20
1089	-	18g.15 violet	55	45
1090	-	23g.40 brown	65	55
1091	-	36g. green	1·00	75
1092	-	50g. red	1·70	1·20

DESIGNS: Nos. 1088/92, Open book inscr "Paraguay de Fuego ..." by Dario.

248 Lions' Emblem on Globe

1967. 50th Anniv of Lions International.

1093	**248**	50c. violet (postage)	35	30
1094	**248**	70c. blue	35	30
1095	-	1g.50 blue	35	30
1096	-	3g. brown	35	30
1097	-	4g. blue	35	30
1098	-	5g. brown	35	30
1099	-	12g.45 brown (air)	35	30
1100	-	18g.15 violet	35	30
1101	-	23g.40 purple	35	30
1102	-	36g. blue	45	30
1103	-	50g. red	55	30

DESIGNS—VERT: 1g.50, 3g. M. Jones; 4, 5g. Lions headquarters, Chicago. HORIZ: 12g.45, 18g.15, Library–"Education"; 23g.40, 36g., 50g. Medical laboratory–"Health".

249 W.H.O. Emblem

1968. 20th Anniv of W.H.O.

1104	**249**	3g. turquoise (postage)	10	10
1105	**249**	4g. purple	10	10
1106	**249**	5g. brown	10	10
1107	**249**	10g. violet	10	10
1108	-	36g. brown (air)	90	45
1109	-	50g. red	1·00	65
1110	-	100g. blue	2·20	1·30

DESIGN—VERT: Nos. 1108/10, W.H.O. emblem on scroll.

250

1969. World Friendship Week.

1111	**250**	50c. red	10	10
1112	**250**	70c. blue	10	10
1113	**250**	1g.50 brown	10	10
1114	**250**	3g. mauve	10	10
1115	**250**	4g. green	10	10
1116	**250**	5g. violet	10	10
1117	**250**	10g. purple	35	10

251

1969. Air. Campaign for Houses for Teachers.

1118	**251**	36g. blue	1·10	55
1119	**251**	50g. brown	1·30	1·10
1120	**251**	100g. red	5·00	4·00

252 Pres. Lopez

1970. Death Centenary of Pres. F. Solano Lopez.

1121	**252**	1g. brown (postage)	35	30
1122	**252**	2g. violet	35	30
1123	**252**	3g. pink	35	30
1124	**252**	4g. red	35	30
1125	**252**	5g. blue	35	30
1126	**252**	10g. green	35	30
1127	**252**	15g. blue (air)	35	30
1128	**252**	20g. brown	35	30
1129	**252**	30g. green	35	30
1130	**252**	40g. purple	45	30

253 Paraguay 2r. Stamp of 1870

1970. Centenary of First Paraguayan Stamps.

1131	**253**	1g. red (postage)	10	10
1132	**A**	2g. blue	10	10
1133	**B**	3g. brown	10	10
1134	**253**	5g. violet	10	10
1135	**A**	10g. lilac	35	20
1136	**B**	15g. purple (air)	55	45
1137	**253**	30g. green	1·20	85
1138	**A**	36g. red	1·30	1·10

DESIGNS: First Paraguay stamps. A, 1r.; B, 3r.

254 Teacher and Pupil

1971. International Education Year–UNESCO.

1139	**254**	3g. blue (postage)	10	10
1140	**254**	5g. lilac	10	10
1141	**254**	10g. green	10	10
1142	**254**	20g. red (air)	45	30
1143	**254**	25g. mauve	55	45
1144	**254**	30g. brown	65	55
1145	**254**	50g. green	1·20	75

255 UNICEF Emblem

1972. 25th Anniv of UNICEF.

1146	**255**	1g. brown (postage)	35	30
1147	**255**	2g. blue	35	30
1148	**255**	3g. red	35	30
1149	**255**	4g. purple	35	30
1150	**255**	5g. green	35	30
1151	**255**	10g. purple	35	30
1152	**255**	20g. blue (air)	35	30
1153	**255**	25g. green	35	30
1154	**255**	30g. brown	35	30

256 Acaray Dam

1972. Tourist Year of the Americas.

1155	**256**	1g. brown (postage)	10	10
1156	-	2g. brown	10	10
1157	-	3g. blue	10	10
1158	-	5g. red	10	10
1159	-	10g. green	30	10
1160	-	20g. red (air)	45	30
1161	-	25g. grey	65	45
1162	-	50g. lilac	1·30	85
1163	-	100g. mauve	2·40	1·70

DESIGNS: 2g. Statue of Lopez; 3g. Friendship Bridge; 5g. Rio Tebicuary Bridge; 10g. Grand Hotel, Guarani; 20g. Motor coach; 25g. Social Service Institute Hospital; 50g. Liner "Presidente Stroessner"; 100g. Lockheed Electra airliner.

257 O.E.A. Emblem

1973. 25th Anniv of Organization of American States (O.E.A.).

1164	**257**	1g. mult (postage)	10	10
1165	**257**	2g. multicoloured	10	10
1166	**257**	3g. multicoloured	10	10
1167	**257**	4g. multicoloured	10	10
1168	**257**	5g. multicoloured	10	10
1169	**257**	10g. multicoloured	20	10
1170	**257**	20g. multicoloured (air)	35	10
1171	**257**	25g. multicoloured	55	10
1172	**257**	50g. multicoloured	1·30	10
1173	**257**	100g. multicoloured	2·20	10

258 Exhibition Emblem

1973. International Industrial Exhibition, Paraguay.

1174	**258**	1g. brown (postage)	35	30
1175	**258**	2g. red	35	30
1176	**258**	3g. blue	35	30
1177	**258**	4g. green	35	30
1178	**258**	5g. lilac	35	30
1179	**258**	20g. mauve (air)	35	30
1180	**258**	25g. red	35	30

259 Carrier Pigeon with Letter

1975. Centenary of U.P.U.

1181	**259**	1g. violet & blk (postage)	10	10
1182	**259**	2g. red and black	10	10
1183	**259**	3g. blue and black	10	10
1184	**259**	5g. blue and black	10	10
1185	**259**	10g. purple and black	35	10
1186	**259**	20g. brown & black (air)	65	30
1187	**259**	25g. green and black	75	30

260 Institute Buildings

1976. Inauguration (1974) of Institute of Higher Education.

1188	**260**	5g. violet, red and black (postage)	10	10
1189	**260**	10g. blue, red and black	20	10
1190	**260**	30g. brn, red & blk (air)	65	55

261 Rotary Emblem

1976. 70th Anniv of Rotary International.

1191	**261**	3g. blue, bistre and black (postage)	10	10
1192	**261**	4g. blue, bistre and mauve	10	10
1193	**261**	25g. blue, bistre and green (air)	75	45

262 Woman and I.W.Y. Emblem

1976. International Women's Year.

1194	**262**	1g. brown & blue (postage)	35	30
1195	**262**	2g. brown and red	35	30
1196	**262**	20g. brown & green (air)	35	30

263 Black Palms

1977. Flowering Plants and Trees. Multicoloured.

1197	2g. Type **263** (postage)	35	25
1198	3g. Mburucuya flowers	35	25
1199	20g. Marsh rose (tree) (air)	1·00	55

264 Nanduti Lace

1977. Multicoloured.. Multicoloured..

1200	1g. Type **264** (postage)	30	25
1201	5g. Nanduti weaver	30	25
1202	25g. Lady holding jar (air)	45	45

265 F. S. Lopez

1977. 150th Birth Anniv of Marshal Francisco Solano Lopez.

1203	**265**	10g. brown (postage)	35	60
1204	**265**	50g. blue (air)	75	55
1205	**265**	100g. green	1·50	1·10

266 General Bernardino Caballero National College

1978. Cent of National College of Asuncion.

1206	**266**	3g. red (postage)	10	10
1207	**266**	4g. blue	10	10
1208	**266**	5g. violet	10	10
1209	**266**	20g. brown (air)	45	20
1210	**266**	25g. purple	55	30
1211	**266**	30g. green	65	45

267 Marshal Jose F. Estigarribia, Trumpeter and Flag

1978. "Salon de Bronce" Commemoration.

1212	**267**	3g. purple, blue and red (postage)	10	10
1213	**267**	5g. violet, blue and red	10	10
1214	**267**	10g. grey, blue and red	20	10
1215	**267**	20g. green, bl & red (air)	35	20
1216	**267**	25g. violet, blue and red	45	30
1217	**267**	30g. purple, blue and red	55	30

268 Congress Emblem

1979. 22nd Latin American Tourism Congress, Asuncion.

1218	**268**	10g. black, blue and red (postage)	35	30
1219	**268**	50g. black, blue and red (air)	55	45

269 Spanish Colonial House, Pilar

1980. Bicentenary of Pilar City.

1220	**269**	5g. mult (postage)	10	10
1221	**269**	25g. multicoloured (air)	55	10

270 Boeing 707

1980. Inauguration of Paraguayan Airlines Boeing 707 Service.

1222	**270**	20g. mult (postage)	55	10
1223	**270**	100g. multicoloured (air)	2·40	1·30

271 Seminary, Communion Cup and Bible

1981. Air. Centenary of Metropolitan Seminary, Asuncion.

1224	**271**	5g. blue	10	10
1225	**271**	10g. brown	20	10
1226	**271**	25g. green	55	30
1227	**271**	50g. black	1·10	75

272 U.P.U. Monument, Berne

1981. Centenary of Admission to U.P.U.

1228	**272**	5g. red and black (postage)	10	10
1229	**272**	10g. mauve and black	20	10
1230	**272**	20g. green and black (air)	45	20
1231	**272**	25g. red and black	55	30
1232	**272**	50g. blue and black	1·10	65

273 St. Maria Mazzarello

1981. Air. Death Centenary of Mother Maria Mazzarello (founder of Daughters of Mary).

1233	**273**	20g. green and black	35	30
1234	**273**	25g. red and black	35	30
1235	**273**	50g. violet and black	55	45

274 Stroessner and Bridge over River Itaipua

1983. 25th Anniv of President Stroessner City.

1236	**274**	3g. green, blue & blk (postage)	10	10
1237	**274**	5g. red, blue and black	10	10
1238	**274**	10g. violet, blue and black	10	10
1239	**274**	20g. grey, blue & blk (air)	35	20
1240	**274**	25g. purple, blue & black	55	30
1241	**274**	50g. blue, grey and black	90	65

275 Sun and Map of Americas

1985. Air. 25th Anniv of Inter-American Development Bank.

1242	**275**	3g. orange, yellow & pink	30	25
1243	**275**	5g. orange, yellow & mauve	30	25
1244	**275**	10g. orange, yellow & mauve	30	25
1245	**275**	50g. orange, yellow & brown	30	25
1246	**275**	65g. orange, yellow & bl	30	25
1247	**275**	95g. orange, yellow & green	30	25

276 U.N. Emblem

1986. Air. 40th Anniv of U.N.O.

1248	**276**	5g. blue and brown	30	25
1249	**276**	10g. blue and grey	30	25
1250	**276**	50g. blue and black	30	25

277 1886 1c. Stamp

1986. Centenary of First Official Stamp.

1251	**277**	5g. deep blue, brown and blue (postage)	20	20
1252	**277**	15g. deep blue, brown and blue	20	20
1253	**277**	40g. deep blue, brown and blue	45	20
1254	-	65g. blue, green and red (air)	65	20
1255	-	100g. blue, green and red	1·10	30
1256	-	150g. blue, green and red	1·90	65

DESIGNS: 65, 100, 150g. 1886 7c. stamp.

278 Integration of the Nations Monument, Colmena

1986. Air. 50th Anniv of Japanese Immigration. Multicoloured.

1257	5g. La Colmena vineyards (horiz)	20	10
1258	10g. Flowers of cherry tree and lapacho (horiz)	20	10
1259	20g. Type **278**	20	10

279 Caballero, Stroessner and Road

1987. Centenary of National Republican Association (Colorado Party).

1260	**279**	5g. multicoloured (postage)	10	10
1261	**279**	10g. multicoloured	10	10
1262	**279**	25g. multicoloured	10	10
1263	-	150g. multicoloured (air)	75	65
1264	-	170g. multicoloured	90	75
1265	-	200g. multicoloured	1·10	85

DESIGN: 150 to 200g. Gen. Bernardino Caballero (President 1881–86 and founder of party), Pres. Alfredo Stroessner and electrification of countryside.

280 Emblem of Visit

1988. Visit of Pope John Paul II.

1266	**280**	10g. blue and black (postage)	20	20
1267	**280**	20g. blue and black	20	20
1268	**280**	50g. blue and black	20	20
1269	-	100g. multicoloured (air)	65	45
1270	-	120g. multicoloured	75	55
1271	-	150g. multicoloured	90	75

DESIGN—HORIZ: 100 to 150g. Pope and Caacupe Basilica.

281 Silver Mate

1988. Air. Centenary of New Germany Colony. Multicoloured.

1272	90g. Type **281**	65	45
1273	105g. Mate ("Ilex paraguayensis") plantation	65	55
1274	120g. As No. 1273	75	65

1988. Air. 75th Anniv of Paraguay Philatelic Centre. No. 1249 optd * 75o ANIVERSARIO DE FUNDACION CENTRO FILATELICO DEL PARAGUAY 15 JUNIO-1913 - 1988.

1275	**276**	10g. blue and grey	20	20

283 Pres. Stroessner and Government Palace

1988. Air. Re-election of President Stroessner.

1276	**283**	200g. multicoloured	55	45
1277	**283**	500g. multicoloured	1·50	1·50
1278	**283**	1000g. multicoloured	2·75	2·75

1989. "Parafil 89" Stamp Exhibition. Nos. 1268 and 1270 optd PARAFIL 89.

1279	**280**	50g. blue and black (postage)	4·00	3·75
1280	-	120g. multicoloured (air)	9·25	9·00

285 Green-winged Macaw

1989. Birds. Multicoloured.

1281	50g. Type **285** (postage)	20	10
1282	100g. Brazilian merganser (horiz) (air)	35	20
1283	300g. Greater rhea (horiz)	75	55
1284	500g. Toco toucan (horiz)	1·30	1·10
1285	1000g. Bare-faced curassow (horiz)	2·40	2·10
1286	2000g. Wagler's macaw and blue and yellow macaw	4·75	4·25

286 Anniversary Emblem

1990. Centenary of Organization of American States. Multicoloured.

1287	50g. Type **286**	20	10
1288	100g. Organization and anniversary emblems (vert)	45	30
1289	200g. Map of Paraguay	90	65

287 Basket

1990. America. Pre-Columbian Life. Mult.

1290	150g. Type **287** (postage)	75	55
1291	500g. Guarani post (air)	2·50	1·70

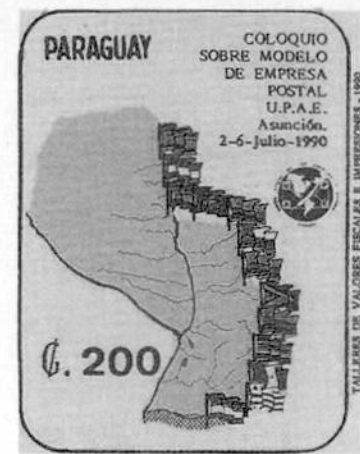

288 Flags on Map

1990. Postal Union of the Americas and Spain Colloquium. Multicoloured.

1292	200g. Type **288**	90	45
1293	250g. First Paraguay stamp	1·00	55
1294	350g. Paraguay 1990 America first day cover (horiz)	1·50	65

289 Planned Building

1990. Centenary of National University. Mult.

1295	300g. Type **289**	1·30	95
1296	400g. Present building	1·80	1·40
1297	600g. Old building	2·75	2·10

290 Guarambare Church

1990. Franciscan Churches. Multicoloured.

1298	50g. Type **290**	20	10
1299	100g. Yaguaron Church	45	30
1300	200g. Ita Church	90	65

1991. Visit of King and Queen of Spain. Nos. 1290/1 optd Vista de sus Majestades Los Reyes de Espana 22-24 Octubre 1990.

1301	**287**	150g. mult (postage)	65	55
1302	-	500g. multicoloured (air)	2·20	1·70

292 "Human Rights" (Hugo Pistilli)

1991. 40th Anniv of United Nations Development Programme. Multicoloured.

1303	50g. Type **292**	20	10
1304	100g. "United Nations" (sculpture, Hermann Guggiari)	45	30
1305	150f. First Miguel de Cervantes prize, awarded to Augusto Roa Bastos, 1989	65	55

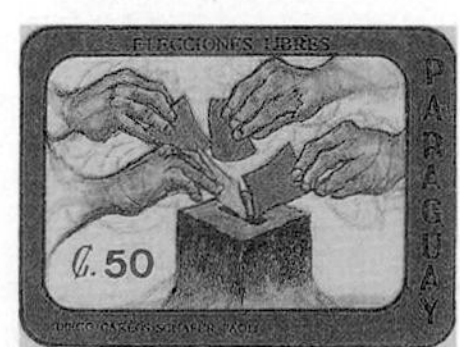

294 Hands and Ballot Box (free elections)

1991. Democracy. Multicoloured.

1308	50g. Type **294** (postage)	25	10
1309	100g. Sun (State and Catholic Church) (vert)	30	15
1310	200g. Arrows and male and female symbols (human rights) (vert)	60	40
1311	300g. Dove and flag (freedom of the press) (vert) (air)	95	75
1312	500g. Woman and child welcoming man (return of exiles)	2·40	1·30
1313	3000g. Crowd with banners (democracy)	9·50	8·25

295 Julio Manuel Morales (gynaecologist)

1991. Medical Professors.

1314	**295**	50g. mult (postage)	25	10
1315	-	100g. multicoloured	30	15
1316	-	200g. multicoloured	60	45
1317	-	300g. brown, black & green	95	75
1318	-	350g. brown, black and green (air)	1·10	90
1319	-	500g. multicoloured	1·70	1·30

DESIGNS: 100g. Carlos Gatti (surgeon); 200g. Gustavo Gonzalez (symptomatologist); 300g. Juan Max Boettner (physician and musician); 350g. Juan Boggino (pathologist); 500g. Andres Barbero (founder of Paraguayan Red Cross).

1991. "Espamer '91" Spain–Latin America Stamp Exhibition, Buenos Aires. Nos. 1298/1300 optd ESPAMER 91 BUENOS AIRES 5 14 Jul and Conquistador in oval.

1323	50g. multicoloured	35	20
1324	100g. multicoloured	40	30
1325	200g. multicoloured	70	55

298 Ruy Diaz de Guzman (historian)

1991. Writers and Musicians. Multicoloured.

1326	50g. Type **298** (postage)	25	15
1327	100g. Maria Talavera (war chronicler) (vert)	35	20
1328	150g. Augusto Roa Bastos (writer and 1989 winner of Miguel de Cervantes Prize) (vert)	60	45
1329	200g. Jose Asuncion Flores (composer of "La Guarania") (vert) (air)	85	65
1330	250g. Felix Perez Cardozo (harpist and composer)	1·10	90
1331	300g. Juan Carlos Moreno Gonzalez (composer)	1·30	1·00

299 Battle of Tavare

1991. America. Voyages of Discovery. Mult.

1332	100g. Type **299** (postage)	45	35
1333	300g. Arrival of Domingo Martinez de Irala in Paraguay (air)	1·40	1·00

300 "Compass of Life" (Alfredo Moraes)

1991. Paintings. Multicoloured.

1334	50g. Type **300** (postage)	25	15
1335	100g. "Callejon Illuminated" (Michael Burt)	35	20
1336	150g. "Arete" (Lucy Yegros)	60	45
1337	200g. "Itinerants" (Hugo Bogado Barrios) (air)	85	65
1338	250g. "Travellers without a Ship" (Bernardo Ismachoviez)	1·10	90
1339	300g. "Guarani" (Lotte Schulz)	1·30	1·00

301 Chaco Peccary

1992. Endangered Mammals. Multicoloured.

1340	50g. Type **301**	25	15
1341	100g. Ocelot (horiz)	35	20
1342	150g. Brazilian tapir	60	45
1343	200g. Maned wolf	85	65

302 Geometric Design, Franciscan Church, Caazapa

1992. 500th Anniv of Discovery of America by Columbus (1st series). Church Roof Tiles. Mult.

1344	50g. Type **302**	25	15
1345	100g. Church, Jesuit church, Trinidad	35	20
1346	150g. Missionary ship, Jesuit church, Trinidad	60	45
1347	200g. Plant, Franciscan church, Caazapa	85	65

See also Nos. 1367/71.

1992. "Granada '92" International Thematic Stamp Exhibition. Nos. 1344/7 optd GRANADA '92 and emblem.

1348	50g. multicoloured	25	10
1349	100g. multicoloured	35	20
1350	150g. multicoloured	85	35
1351	200g. multicoloured	95	45

304 Malcolm L. Norment (founder) and Emblem

1992. 68th Anniv of Paraguay Leprosy Foundation. Multicoloured.

1352	50g. Type **304**	35	20
1353	250g. Gerhard Hansen (discoverer of leprosy bacillus)	1·10	90

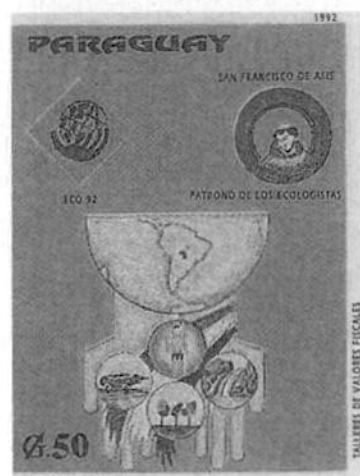

305 Southern Hemisphere and Ecology Symbols on Hands

1992. 2nd United Nations Conference on Environment and Development, Rio de Janeiro. Multicoloured.

1354	50g. Type **305**	30	20
1355	100g. Butterfly and chimneys emitting smoke	35	30
1356	250g. Tree and map of South America on globe	1·10	90

306 Factories and Cotton (economy)

1992. National Population and Housing Census. Multicoloured.

1357	50g. Type **306**	30	20
1358	200g. Houses (vert)	85	65
1359	250g. Numbers and stylized people (population) (vert)	1·10	90
1360	300g. Abacus (education)	1·30	1·00

307 Football

1992. Olympic Games, Barcelona. Multicoloured.

1361	50g. Type **307**	25	15
1362	100g. Tennis	35	20
1363	150g. Running	60	45
1364	200g. Swimming (horiz)	85	65
1365	250g. Judo	1·10	90
1366	350g. Fencing (horiz)	1·40	1·20

308 Brother Luis Bolanos

1992. 500th Anniv of Discovery of America by Columbus (2nd series). Evangelists. Mult.

1367	50g. Type **308** (translator of Catechism into Guarani and founder of Guarani Christian settlements)	30	20
1368	100g. Brother Juan de San Bernardo (Franciscan and first Paraguayan martyr)	35	30
1369	150g. St. Roque Gonzalez de Santa Cruz (Jesuit missionary and first Paraguayan saint)	60	45
1370	200g. Fr. Amancio Gonzalez (founder of Melodia settlement)	85	65
1371	250g. Mgr. Juan Sinforiano Bogarin (first Archbishop of Asuncion) (vert)	1·10	90

309 Fleet approaching Shore

1992. America. 500th Anniv of Discovery of America by Columbus. Multicoloured.

1372	150g. Type **309** (postage)	70	55
1373	350g. Christopher Columbus (vert) (air)	1·50	1·20

1992. 30th Anniv of United Nations Information Centre in Paraguay. Nos. 1354/6 optd NACIONES UNIDAS 1992 - 30 ANOS CENTRO INFORMACION OUN EN PARAGUAY.

1374	50g. multicoloured	30	20
1375	100g. multicoloured	35	30
1376	250g. multicoloured	1·10	90

1992. Christmas. Nos. 1367/9 optd Navidad 92.

1377	50g. multicoloured	30	20
1378	100g. multicoloured	35	30
1379	150g. multicoloured	60	45

1992. "Parafil 92" Paraguay–Argentina Stamp Exhibition, Buenos Aires. Nos. 1372/3 optd PARAFIL 92.

1380	150g. multicoloured (postage)	35	20
1381	350g. multicoloured (air)	95	55

313 Planting and Hoeing

1992. 50th Anniv of Pan-American Agricultural Institute. Multicoloured.

1382	50g. Type **313**	30	20
1383	100g. Test tubes	35	30
1384	200g. Cotton plant in cupped hands	85	65
1385	250g. Cattle and maize plant	1·10	90

314 Yolanda Bado de Artecona

1992. Centenary of Paraguayan Writers' College. Multicoloured.

1386	50g. Type **314**	30	20
1387	100g. Jose Ramon Silva	35	30
1388	150g. Abelardo Brugada Valpy	60	45
1389	200g. Tomas Varela	85	65
1390	250g. Jose Livio Lezcano	1·10	90
1391	300g. Francisco I. Fernandez	1·20	1·00

315 Members' Flags and Map of South America

1993. 1st Anniv (1992) of Treaty of Asuncion forming Mercosur (common market of Argentina, Brazil, Paraguay and Uruguay). Multicoloured.

1392	50g. Type **315**	30	20
1393	350g. Flags encircling globe showing map of South America	1·40	1·20

316 Orange Flowers (Gilda Hellmers)

1993. 50th Anniv of St. Isabel Leprosy Association. Flower paintings by artists named. Multicoloured.

1394	50g. Type **316**	30	20
1395	200g. Luis Alberto Balmelli	85	65
1396	250g. Lili del Monico	1·10	90
1397	350g. Brunilde Guggiari	1·40	1·20

317 Goethe (after J. Lips) and Manuscript of Poem

1993. Centenary of Goethe College.

1398	**317**	50g. brown, black & blue	30	20
1399	-	200g. multicoloured	85	65

DESIGN: 200g. Goethe (after J. Tischbein).

1993. "Brasiliana 93" International Stamp Exhibition, Rio de Janeiro. Nos. 1398/9 optd BRASILIANA 93.

1400	50g. brown, black and blue	30	20
1401	200g. multicoloured	85	65

319 Palace (Michael Burt)

1993. Centenary (1992) of Los Lopez (Government) Palace, Asuncion. Paintings of palace by artists named. Multicolured.

1402	50g. Type **319**	30	20
1403	100g. Esperanza Gill	35	30
1404	200g. Emili Aparici	85	65
1405	250g. Hugo Bogado Barrios (vert)	1·10	90

320 Couple sitting on Globe and Emblem

1993. 35th Anniv of World Friendship Crusade.

1406	**320**	50g. black, blue and mauve	30	20
1407	-	100g. multicoloured	35	30
1408	-	200g. multicoloured	85	65
1409	-	250g. multicoloured	1·10	90

DESIGNS: 100g. Dr. Ramon Artemio Bracho (founder), map of Americas and emblem; 200g. Children and sun emerging from cloud; 250g. Couple hugging and emblem.

1993. Inauguration of President Juan Carlos Wasmosy. Nos. 1402/5 optd TRANSMISION DEL MANDO PRESIDENCIAL GRAL. ANDRES RODRIGUEZ ING. JUAN C. WASMOSY 15 DE AGOSTO 1993.

1410	50g. multicoloured	30	20
1411	100g. multicoloured	35	30
1412	200g. multicoloured	85	65
1413	250g. multicoloured	1·10	90

322 "Church of the Incarnation" (Juan Guerra Gaja)

1993. Centenary of Church of the Incarnation. Paintings. Multicoloured.

1414	50g. Type **322**	25	10
1415	350g. "Church of the Incarnation" (Hector Blas Ruiz) (horiz)	1·20	55

323 Bush Dog

1993. America. Endangered Animals. Mult.

1416	250g. Type **323** (postage)	1·70	55
1417	50g. Great anteater (air)	1·10	45

1993. 80th Anniv of World Food Programme. Nos. 1383/4 optd '30 ANOS DEL PROGRAMA MUNDIAL DE ALIMENTOS' and emblem.

1418	100g. multicoloured	30	10
1419	200g. multicoloured	60	35

325 Children Carol-singing

1993. Christmas. Multicoloured.

1420	50g. Type **325**	25	10
1421	250g. Wise men following star	70	45

326 Boy and Girl Scouts

1993. 80th Anniv of Paraguay Scouts Association. Multicoloured.

1422	50g. Type **326**	25	10
1423	100g. Boy scouts in camp	30	15
1424	200g. Lord Robert Baden-Powell (founder of Scouting movement)	60	35
1425	250g. Girl scout with flag	70	45

327 Cecilio Baez

1994. Centenary of First Graduation of Lawyers from National University, Asuncion.

1426	**327**	50g. red and crimson	30	20
1427	-	100g. yellow and orange	35	30
1428	-	250g. yellow and green	45	35
1429	-	500g. blue and deep blue	95	75

DESIGNS—VERT: 100g. Benigno Riquelme. HORIZ: 250g. Emeterio Gonzalez; 500g. J. Gaspar Villamayor.

328 Basketball

1994. 50th Anniv of Phoenix Sports Association. Multicoloured.

1430	50g. Type **328**	30	20
1431	200g. Football	35	30
1432	250g. Pedro Andres Garcia Arias (founder) and tennis (horiz)	60	35

329 Penalty Kick

1994. World Cup Football Championship, U.S.A. Multicoloured.

1433	250g. Type **329**	45	20
1434	500g. Tackle	1·10	45
1435	1000g. Dribbling ball past opponent	2·00	1·00

330 Runner

1994. Centenary of International Olympic Committee. Multicoloured.

1436	350g. Type **330**	70	55
1437	400g. Athlete lighting Olympic Flame	85	65

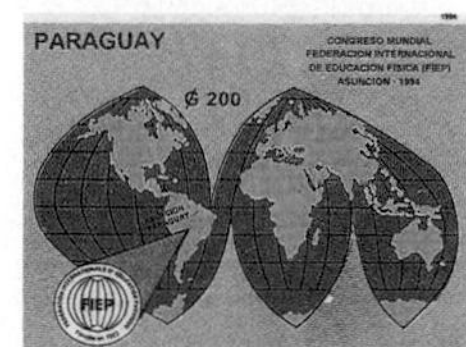

331 World Map and Emblem

1994. World Congress of International Federation for Physical Education, Asuncion. Multicoloured.

1438	200g. Type **331**	60	45
1439	1000g. Family exercising and flag (vert)	3·00	2·40

1994. Brazil, Winners of World Cup Football Championship. Nos. 1433/5 optd BRASIL Campeon Mundial de Futbol Estados Unidos '94.

1440	250g. multicoloured	70	55
1441	500g. multicoloured	1·50	1·20
1442	1000g. multicoloured	3·00	2·40

1994. 25th Anniv of First Manned Moon Landing. No. 1407 optd 25 Anos, Conquista de la Luna por el hombre 1969 - 1994.

1443	100g. multicoloured	35	20

334 Barrios

1994. 50th Death Anniv of Agustin Pio Barrios Mangore (guitarist). Multicoloured.

1444	250g. Type **334**	70	55
1445	500g. Barrios wearing casual clothes and a hat	1·50	1·20

335 Police Commandant, 1913

1994. 151st Anniv of Police Force. Multicoloured.

1446	50g. Type **335**	35	20
1447	250g. Carlos Bernardino Cacabelos (first Commissioner) and Pedro Nolasco Fernandez (first Chief of Asuncion Police Dept)	70	55

336 Maguari Stork

1994. "Parafil 94" Stamp Exhibition. Birds. Mult.

1448	100g. Type **336**	60	35
1449	150g. Yellow-billed cardinal	95	45
1450	400g. Green kingfisher (vert)	2·40	1·00
1451	500g. Jabiru (vert)	3·00	1·20

337 Nicolas Copernicus and Eclipse

1994. Total Eclipse of the Sun, November 1994. Astronomers. Multicoloured.

1452	50g. Type **337**	35	20
1453	200g. Johannes Kepler and sun dial, St. Cosmas and Damian Jesuit settlement	70	55

338 Steam Locomotive

1994. America. Postal Transport. Multicoloured.

1454	100g. Type **338**	40	30
1455	1000g. Express mail motor cycle	3·50	2·75

339 Mother and Child

1994. International Year of the Family. Details of paintings by Olga Blinder. Multicoloured.

1456	50g. Type **339**	35	20
1457	250g. Mother and children	85	65

340 Holy Family and Angels

1994. Christmas. Ceramic Figures. Multicoloured.

1458	150g. Type **340**	45	35
1459	700g. Holy Family (vert)	2·40	1·80

341 Red Cross Workers and Dr. Andres Barbero (founder)

1994. 75th Anniv of Paraguay Red Cross. Mult.

1460	150g. Scouts, anniversary emblem and Henri Dunant (founder of International Red Cross)	45	35
1461	700g. Type **341**	2·40	1·80

342 Sculpture by Herman Guggiari and Pope John Paul II

1994. 90th Anniv of San Jose College. Mult.

1462	200g. Type **342**	60	45

1463	250g. College entrance and Pope John Paul II	85	55

343 Pasteur and Hospital Facade

1995. Paraguayan Red Cross. Death Centenary of Louis Pasteur (chemist) and Centenary of Clinical Hospital.

1464	**343**	1000g. multicoloured	2·40	1·50

344 Couple

1995. Anti-AIDS Campaign. Multicoloured.

1465	500g. Type **344**	1·30	75
1466	1000g. Sad and happy blood droplets	2·40	1·50

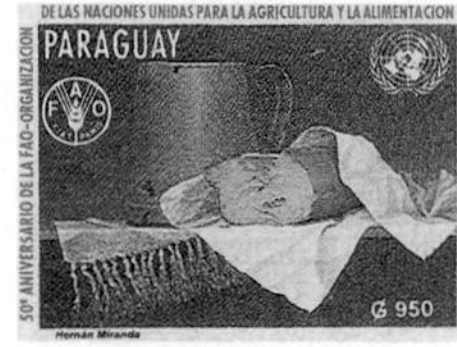

345 Jug and Loaf

1995. 50th Anniv of F.A.O. Paintings by Hernan Miranda. Multicoloured.

1467	950g. Type **345**	2·20	1·40
1468	2000g. Melon and leaf	5·00	2·75

346 Olive-backed Warbler

1995. 5th Neo-tropical Ornithological Congress, Asuncion. Multicoloured.

1469	100g. Type **346**	45	35
1470	200g. Swallow-tailed manakin	60	35
1471	600g. Troupial	2·00	90
1472	1000g. Hooded siskin	3·00	1·50

347 River Monday Rapids

1995. 5th International Town, Ecology and Tourism Symposium. Multicoloured.

1473	1150g. Type **347**	1·90	1·20
1474	1300g. Aregua railway station	2·10	1·30

348 "100"

1995. Centenary of Volleyball.

1475	348	300g. multicoloured	50	25
1476	-	600g. blue and black	1·00	60
1477	-	1000g. multicoloured	1·70	1·10

DESIGNS: 600g. Ball hitting net; 1000g. Hands, ball and net.

349 Macizo, Acahay

1995. America. Environmental Protection. Mult.

1478	950g. Type **349**	3·00	1·10
1479	2000g. Tinfunque Reserve, Chaco (vert)	5·50	2·40

350 Anniversary Emblem

1995. 50th Anniv of U.N.O. Multicoloured.

1480	200g. Type **350**	35	25
1481	3000g. Stylized figures supporting emblem	5·25	3·25

351 Couple holding Star

1995. Christmas. Multicoloured.

1482	200g. Type **351**	35	25
1483	1000g. Crib	2·00	1·30

352 Marti and "Hedychium coronarium"

1995. Birth Cent of Jose Marti (revolutionary). Multicoloured.

1484	200g. Type **352**	35	25
1485	1000g. Marti, Cuban national flag and "Hedychium coronarium" (horiz)	2·00	1·30

353 "Railway Station" (Asuncion)

1996. 25th Latin American and Caribbean Forum of Lions International. Paintings by Esperanza Gill. Multicoloured.

1486	200g. Type **353**	35	25
1487	1000g. "Viola House"	2·00	1·30

354 "Cattleya nobilior"

1996. Orchids. Multicoloured.

1488	100g. Type **354**	30	10
1489	200g. "Oncidium varicosum"	35	25
1490	1000g. "Oncidium jonesianum" (vert)	1·70	95
1491	1150g. "Sophronitis cernua"	2·00	1·10

355 Emblems and Gymnast on "Stamp"

1996. Centenary of Modern Olympic Games and Olympic Games, Atlanta. Multicoloured.

1492	500g. Type **355**	85	45
1493	1000g. Emblems and runner on "stamp"	1·70	95

356 Bosco, Monks and Boys

1996. Centenary of Salesian Brothers in Paraguay. Multicoloured.

1494	200g. Type **356**	35	25
1495	300g. Madonna and Child, Pope John Paul II and St. John Bosco (vert)	50	35
1496	1000g. St. John Bosco (founder) and map	1·70	1·40

357 Family Outing (Silvia Cacares Baez)

1996. 50th Anniv of UNICEF. Multicoloured.

1497	1000g. Type **357**	1·70	1·40
1498	1300g. Families (Cinthia Perez Alderete)	2·20	1·90

358 Pope John Paul II, Caacupe Cathedral and Virgin

1996. Our Lady of Caacupe. Multicoloured.

1499	200g. Type **358**	35	30
1500	1300g. Pope John Paul II, floodlit cathedral and Virgin (horiz)	2·20	1·90

359 Woman

1996. America. Traditional Costumes. Mult.

1501	500g. Type **359**	85	70
1502	1000g. Couple	1·80	1·40

360 Boxes and Food

1996. International Year for Eradication of Poverty. Multicoloured.

1503	1000g. Type **360**	1·70	1·40
1504	1150g. Boy with boxes and food (vert)	2·00	1·70

361 Mother and Baby

1996. Christmas. Multicoloured.

1505	200g. Type **361**	35	30
1506	1000g. Mother with smiling child	1·70	95

362 "Eryphanis automedon"

1997. Butterflies. Multicoloured.

1507	200g. Type **362**	60	35
1508	500g. "Dryadula phaetusa"	1·80	45
1509	1000g. "Vanessa myrinna"	3·00	95
1510	1150g. Rare tiger	3·75	1·10

363 First Government Palace (legislative building)

1997. Buildings. Multicoloured.

1511	200g. Type **363**	35	30
1512	1000g. Patri Palace (postal headquarters)	2·00	1·10

364 Crucifix, Piribebuy

1997. Year of Jesus Christ.

1513	364	1000g. multicoloured	1·70	95

365 Summit Emblem

1997. 11th Group of Rio Summit Meeting, Asuncion.

1514	365	1000g. multicoloured	1·80	1·20

366 Cactus

1997. "The Changing Climate—Everyone's Concern". Plants. Multicoloured.

1515	300g. Type **366**	60	35
1516	500g. "Bromelia balansae" (vert)	85	60
1517	1000g. "Monvillea kroenlaini"	1·80	1·20

367 Tiger Cat

1997. 1st Mercosur (South American Common Market), Chile and Bolivia Stamp Exhibition, Asuncion. Mammals. Multicoloured.

1518	200g. Type **367**	25	10
1519	1000g. Black howler monkey (vert)	1·80	1·20
1520	1150g. Paca	2·10	1·30

368 Members' Flags and Southern Cross

1997. 6th Anniv of Mercosur (South American Common Market).

1521	368	1000g. multicoloured	1·80	1·20

369 Postman and Letters circling Globe

1997. America. The Postman. Multicoloured.

1522	1000g. Type **369**	2·75	1·20
1523	1150g. Weather and terrain aspects of postal delivery and postman (horiz)	3·00	1·40

370 Neri Kennedy (javelin)

1997. 50th Anniv of National Sports Council. Multicoloured.

1524	200g. Type **370**	35	30
1525	1000g. Ramon Milciades Gimenez Gaona (discus)	2·20	1·30

1997. "Mevifil '97" First International Exhibition of Philatelic Audio-visual and Computer Systems, Buenos Aires, Argentina. Nos. 1446/7 optd MEVIFIL '97.

1526	50g. multicoloured	85	60
1527	250g. multicoloured	4·25	2·40

372 Mother and Child (Olga Blinder)

1997. Christmas. Multicoloured.

1528 200g. Type **372** 25 10
1529 1000g. Mother and child (Hernan Miranda) 1·80 1·20

373 Boy

1997. "Children of the World with AIDS". Children's Paintings. Multicoloured.

1530 500g. Type **373** 85 60
1531 1000g. Girl 1·80 1·20

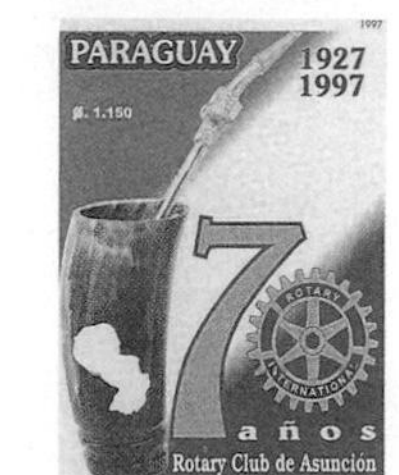

374 Drinking Vessel and Emblem forming "70"

1997. 70th Anniv of Asuncion Rotary Club.

1532 **374** 1150g. multicoloured 2·10 1·30

375 Julio Cesar Romero (1986 World Cup team member)

1998. World Cup Football Championship, France. Multicoloured.

1533 200g. Type **375** 25 10
1534 500g. Carlos Gamarra (World Cup team member) tackling opponent 85 60
1535 1000g. World Cup team (horiz) 1·80 1·20

376 Silver Tetra

1998. Fishes. Multicoloured.

1536 200g. Type **376** 60 35
1537 300g. Spotted sorubim 85 35
1538 500g. Dorado 1·30 60
1539 1000g. Pira jagua 2·75 1·20

377 Painting by Carlos Colombino

1998. Paintings by artists named. Multicoloured.

1540 200g. Type **377** 25 10
1541 300g. Felix Toranzos 60 35
1542 400g. Edith Gimenez 75 45
1543 1000g. Ricardo Migliorisi (horiz) 1·80 1·20

378 Cep

1998. Fungi. Multicoloured.

1544 400g. Type **378** 80 50
1545 600g. Parasol mushroom 1·00 60
1546 1000g. Collared earthstar 1·90 1·20

379 Carlos Lopez's House, Botanical and Zoological Gardens, Asuncion

1998. 50th Anniv of Organization of American States. Multicoloured.

1547 500g. Type **379** 90 60
1548 1000g. Villa Palmerola, Aregua 1·90 1·20

380 Door of Sanctuary, Caazapa Church

1998. 400th Anniv of Ordination of First Paraguayan Priests by Brother Hernando de Trejo y Sanabria. Multicoloured.

1549 400g. Type **380** 80 50
1550 1700g. Statue of St. Francis of Assisi, Atyra Church (horiz) 3·50 2·20

382 Ruins of the Mission of Jesus, Itapua

1998. Mercosur (South American Common Market) Heritage Sites.

1554 **382** 5000g. multicoloured 10·50 6·75

383 Serafina Davalos (first female lawyer in Paraguay) and National College

1998. America. Famous Women. Multicoloured.

1555 1600g. Type **383** 3·50 2·10
1556 1700g. Adela Speratti (first director) and Teachers' Training College 3·75 2·20

384 Abstract (Carlos Colombino)

1998. 50th Anniv of Universal Declaration of Human Rights. Multicoloured.

1557 500g. Type **384** 90 60
1558 1000g. Man on crutches (after Joel Filartiga) 1·90 1·20

385 Crib

1998. Christmas. Multicoloured.

1559 300g. Type **385** 65 35
1560 1600g. Crib (different) (vert) 3·50 2·10

386 Coral Cobra

1999. Reptiles. Multicoloured.

1561 100g. Type **386** 25 10
1562 300g. Ground lizard 65 35
1563 1600g. Red-footed tortoise 3·50 2·10
1564 1700g. Paraguay caiman 3·75 2·20

1999. "Chaco Peace 99" Stamp Exhibition, Paraguay and Bolivia. No. 1542 optd 1era. Exposicion Filatelica Paraguayo-Boliviana PAZ DEL CHACO 99.

1565 400g. multicoloured 90 50

388 Painting by Ignacio Nunes Soler

1999. Paintings. Showing paintings by named artists.

1566 500g. Type **388** 90 60
1567 1600g. Modesto Delgado Rodas 2·75 1·80

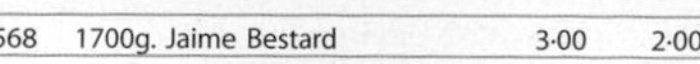
1568 1700g. Jaime Bestard 3·00 2·00

389 Carlos Humberto Parades being tackled

1999. American Cup Football Championship, Paraguay. Multicoloured.

1569 300g. Type **389** 50 25
1570 500g. South American Football Federation Building, Luque, Paraguay (horiz) 90 50
1571 1900g. Feliciano Caceres Stadium, Luque (horiz) 3·50 2·10

390 Toucan

1999. 50th Anniv of S.O.S. Children's Villages. Multicoloured.

1572 1700g. Type **390** 2·75 1·60
1573 1900g. Toucan (different) (vert) 3·00 1·90

391 Government Palace

1999. Assassination of Dr. Luis Marua Argana (Vice-president, 1998–99). Multicoloured.

1574 100g. Type **391** 25 10
1575 500g. Dr. Argana (vert) 65 40
1576 1500g. Crowd before National Congress building 2·30 1·40

392 *Cochlospermum regium*

1999. Medicinal Plants. Multicoloured.

1577 600g. Type **392** 95 50
1578 700g. *Borago officinalis* 1·00 65
1579 1700g. *Passiflora cincinnata* 2·50 1·50

393 "The Man who carries the Storm"

1999. America. A New Millennium without Arms. Showing paintings by Ricardo Migliorisi. Mult.

1580 1500g. Type **393** 2·10 1·40
1581 3000g. "The Man who dominates the Storm" (vert) 4·75 3·25

394 "Couple" (Olga Blinder)

1999. International Year of the Elderly. Mult.

1582 1000g. Type **394** 1·50 1·00

1583	1900g. "Old Woman" (Marma de los Reyes Omella Herrero) (vert)	3·00	1·90

395 "Mother and Child" (Manuel Viedma)

1999. Christmas. Multicoloured.

1584	300g. Type **395**	55	25
1585	1600g. "Nativity" (Federico Ordinana)	2·40	1·50

396 *Tabebuia impetiginosa*

1999. Centenary of Pedro Juan Caballero City. Multicoloured.

1586	1000g. Type **396**	1·50	1·00
1587	1600g. *Tabebuia pulcherrima* (vert)	2·40	1·50

397 Oratory of the Virgin Our Lady of the Assumption and National Mausoleum

1999. 40th Anniv of Inter-American Development Bank. Multicoloured.

1588	600g. Type **397**	95	65
1589	700g. Government Palace	1·10	75

398 Carmen Casco de Lara Castro and "Conjunction" (bronze sculpture, Domingo Rivarola)

2000. International Women's Day. Carmen Casco de Lara Castro (founder of National Commission for Human Rights). Multicoloured.

1590	400g. Type **398**	65	40
1591	2000g. Carmen Casco de Lara Castro and "Violation" (bronze sculpture, Gustavo Beckelman)	3·25	2·20

399 Hydroelectric Dam, Yacyreta, and Marsh Deer

2000. "EXPO 2000" World's Fair, Hanover, Germany. Showing bi-lateral development projects. Multicoloured.

1592	500g. Type **399** (Paraguay–Argentine Republic)	80	50
1593	2500g. Hydroelectric dam, Itaipu and Brazilian tapir (Paraguay–Brazil)	4·00	2·75

400 Students and Pope John Paul II

2000. Centenary of the Daughters of Maria Auxiliadora College. Multicoloured.

1594	600g. Type **400**	95	65
1595	2000g. College building	3·25	2·20

401 Footballers chasing Ball

2000. Olympic Games, Sydney. Multicoloured.

1596	2500g. Type **401**	4·00	2·75
1597	3000g. Francisco Rojas Soto (athlete), Munich Olympics, 1972 (horiz)	4·75	3·25

402 Adult Hands protecting Child (Nahuel Moreno Lezcano)

2000. 10th Anniv of United Nations Convention on the Rights of the Child. Multicoloured.

1598	1500g. Type **402**	2·10	1·40
1599	1700g. Hand prints (Claudia Alessandro Irala Chavez) (horiz)	2·75	1·60

403 Firemen attending to Fire

2000. 95th Anniv of Fire Service. Multicoloured.

1600	100g. Type **403**	25	15
1601	200g. Badge and fireman wearing 1905 dress uniform	40	20
1602	1500g. Firemen attending fire (horiz)	2·10	1·40
1603	1600g. Firemen using hose (horiz)	2·40	1·50

404 Stretch of Road from San Bernardino to Altos

2000. Road Development Scheme. Multicoloured.

1604	500g. Type **404**	80	50
1605	3000g. Gaspar Rodriguez de Francia motorway	4·75	3·25

405 Signpost and Emblem

2000. America. AIDS Awareness Campaign. Mult.

1606	1500g. Type **405**	2·10	1·40
1607	2500g. Ribbon emblem on noughts and crosses grid	4·00	2·75

406 "Love and Peace" (metal sculpture, Hugo Pistilli)

2000. International Year of Culture and Peace. Multicoloured.

1608	500g. Type **406**	80	50
1609	2000g. "For Peace" (metal sculpture, Herman Guggiari)	3·25	2·20

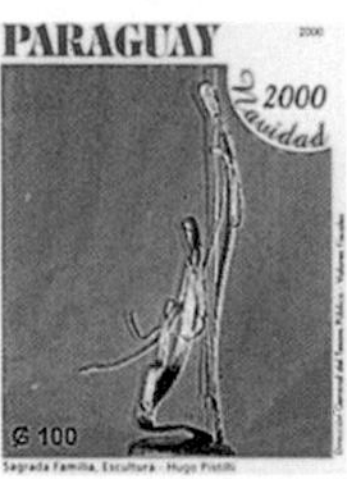

407 "Holy Family" (metal sculpture, Hugo Pistilli)

2000. Christmas. Multicoloured.

1610	100g. Type **407**	25	15
1611	500g. Poem, pen and Jose Luis Appleyard (poet and writer)	80	50
1612	2000g. Nativity (crib firgures) (horiz)	3·25	2·20

408 Country Woman (sculpture, Behage)

2000. Art. Multicoloured.

1613	200g. Type **408**	40	20
1614	1500g. Drinking vessels (Quintin Velazquez) (horiz)	2·10	1·40
1615	2000g. Silver orchid brooch (Quirino Torres)	3·25	2·20

409 Flores

2000. 30th Birth Anniv (2002) of Jose Asuncion Flores (musician). Multicoloured.

1616	100g. Type **409**	25	15
1617	1500g. Violin	2·10	1·40
1618	2500g. Trombone	4·00	2·75

410 Presidents of Argentina, Brazil, Paraguay and Uruguay signing Treaty

2001. 10th Anniv of Asuncion Treaty (cooperation treaty). Multicoloured.

1619	500g. Type **410**	80	50
1620	2500g. Map of South America (vert)	4·00	2·75

411 *Opuntia*

2001. Cacti. Multicoloured.

1621	2000g. Type **411**	3·25	2·20
1622	2500g. *Cerus stenogonus*	4·00	2·75

412 Three Players

2001. Under 20's Football Championship, Argentina. Multicoloured.

1623	2000g. Type **412**	3·25	2·20
1624	2500g. Two players (vert)	4·00	2·75

413 Holando Cow (Friesian)

2001. Cattle. Multicoloured.

1625	200g. Type **413**	40	20
1626	500g. Nelore bull (Brahmin)	80	50
1627	1500g. Pampa Chaqueno bull	2·10	1·40

414 Donkey Riders (Josefina Pla)

2001. Xylographs (wood engravings).

1628	**414**	500g. multicoloured	85	55
1629	-	500g. multicoloured (vert)	85	55
1630	-	1500g. black, green and lemon	2·20	1·50
1631	-	2000g. multicoloured	3·50	2·40

DESIGNS: 500g. Type **414**; 500g. Women (Leonor Cecotto); 1500g. Frog (Jacinta Rivero); 2000g. (Livio Abramo).

415 Eichu (Pleiades)

2001. Guarani (Native Americans) Mythology. Multicoloured.

1632	100g. Type **415**	30	15
1633	600g. Mborevi Rape (Milky Way)	95	70

1634 1600g. Jagua Ho'u Jasy (Eclipse of the moon) 2·50 1·70

416 Inocencio Lezcano

2001. Teachers' Day. Multicoloured.
1635 200g. Type **416** 40 20
1636 1600g. Ramon Cardozo 2·50 1·70

417 Jesuit Mission Ruins, Trinidad and St. Ignacio de Loyola (statue)

2001. America. Cultural Heritage. Multicoloured.
1637 500g. Type **417** 85 55
1638 2000g. Ruins (different) 3·50 2·40
Nos. 1637/8 were issued together, se-tenant, in strips of two stamps and two labels, the whole forming a composite design.

418 Children encircling Globe

2001. United Nations Year of Dialogue among Civilization.
1639 **418** 3000g. multicoloured 4·75 3·50

419 Dough Nativity (Gladys Feliciangeli)

2001. Christmas. Multicoloured.
1640 700g. Type **419** 1·10 85
1641 4000g. Clay and banana leaf Nativity (Mercedes Servin) 6·25 4·25

420 World Trade Buildings, New York

2001. "No to Terrorism". Multicoloured.
1642 700g. Type **420** 1·10 85
1643 5000g. Chain links changing to doves and flags (horiz) 7·50 5·50

421 *Passiflora carulea*

2001. 10th Anniv of Mercosur (South American Common Market).
1644 **421** 4000g. multicoloured 6·25 4·25

422 Tree Frog (*Phyllomedusa sauvagei*)

2002. Scout Jamboree, Loma Plata.
1645 **422** 6000g. multicoloured 9·00 7·00

423 Rowers, Club Building and Cormorant

2002. Centenary of "El Mbigua" (cormorant) Social Club.
1646 **423** 700g. multicoloured 1·10 85

424 "The Pieta" (statue)

2002. 25th Anniv of Juan de Salzar Cultural Centre, Asuncion. Multicoloured.
1647 2500g. Type **424** 4·25 3·00
1648 5000g. St. Michael (statue) 7·50 5·50

425 Team Members

2002. Football World Cup Championships, Japan and South Korea. Multicoloured.
1649 3000g. Type **425** 4·75 3·50
1649a 3000g. As Type **425** but with no inscription 4·75 3·50
1649b 5000g. Players celebrating 7·50 5·50

426 Mennonite Church, Filadelfia

2002. 75th Anniv of Arrival of Mennonite Christians. Multicoloured.
1650 2000g. Type **426** 3·50 2·40
1651 4000g. Church, Loma Plata 6·25 4·25

427 Criollo Mare and Foal

2002. Horses. Multicoloured.
1652 700g. Type **427** 1·10 85
1653 1000g. Quarto de Milla 1·50 1·10
1654 6000g. Arabian 9·00 7·00

428 Players holding Cup

2002. Centenary of Olimpia Football Club.
1655 **428** 700g. multicoloured 1·10 85

429 *Stevia rebaudiana*

2002. Centenary of Pan American Health Organization. Multicoloured.
1656 4000g. Type **429** 6·25 4·25
1657 5000g. *Ilex paraguayensis* 7·50 5·50

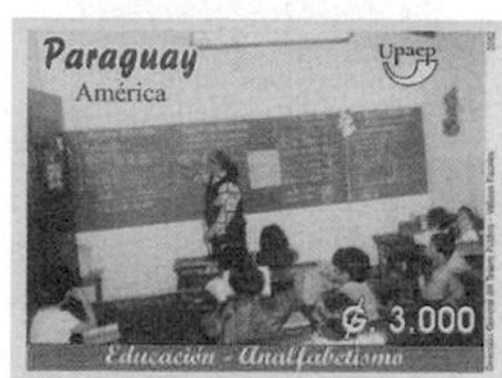

432 Teacher and Class

2002. America. Literacy Campaign. Multicoloured.
1661 3000g. Type **432** 4·75 3·50
1662 6000g. Children playing 9·00 7·00

435 San Antonio Church and Saint Anthony (statue)

2003. Centenary of San Antonio District.
1667 **435** 700g. multicoloured 1·10 85

436 Decorated Plate and Josefina Pla

2003. Birth Centenary of Josefina Pla (ceramist and writer). Multicoloured.
1668 700g. Type **436** 1·10 85
1669 6000g. Josefina Pla and engraving 9·00 7·00

437 Blue-fronted Amazon (*Amazona aestiva*)

2003. Parrots. Multicoloured.
1670 1000g. Type **437** 1·50 1·10
1671 2000g. Monk parrot (*Myiopsitta monachus*) 3·50 2·40
1672 4000g. White-eyed conure (*Aratinga leucophtalmus*) 6·25 4·25

438 Legislative Palace

2003. Inauguration of New Legislative Palace.
1674 **438** 4000g. multicoloured 6·25 4·25
No. 1673 is vacant.

439 Pope John Paul II and Our Lady of Ascuncion Church

2003. 25th Anniv of Pontificate of Pope John Paul II.
1675 **439** 6000g. multicoloured 9·00 7·00

440 Pig

2003. Domestic Animals. Multicoloured.
1676 1000g. Type **440** 1·40 1·00
1677 3000g. Sheep 4·50 3·25
1678 8000g. Goat 9·75 7·75

441 Sweets

2003. Gastronomy. Multicoloured.
1679 700g. Type **441** 1·00 80
1680 2000g. Sopa Paraguaya (cake) 3·25 2·30
1681 3000g. Chipa (bread) 4·50 3·25

442 Julio Correa

2003. Folklorists. Multicoloured.
1682 700g. Type **442** 1·00 80
1683 1000g. Emilano Rivarola Fernadez 1·40 1·00

1684 2000g. Manuel Ortiz Guerrero 3·25 2·30

443 La Golondriana

2003. National Dances. Multicoloured.
1685 700g. Type **443** 1·00 80
1686 3000g. Polca 4·50 3·25
1687 4000g. Galopera 5·75 4·00

444 Footballers

2003. Centenary of Guarani Football Club.
1688 **444** 700g. multicoloured 1·00 80

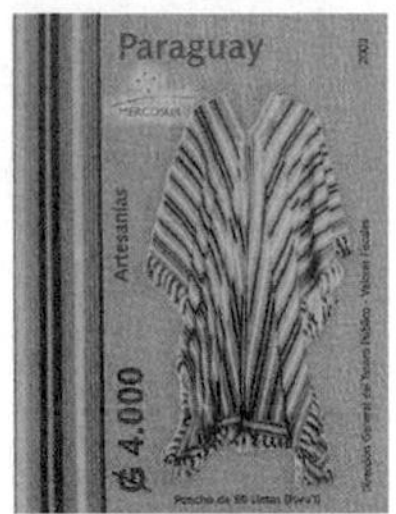

445 Poncho Para i (60 stripe poncho)

2003. Mercosur. Crafts. Multicoloured.
1689 4000g. Type **445** 5·75 4·00
1690 5000g. Shirt made from Ao Poi fabric 7·25 5·25

446 Flight into Egypt

2003. Christmas. Patchwork designs made by Santa Maria de Fe Mission. Multicoloured.
1691 700g. Type **446** 1·00 80
1692 1000g. Shepherd and star 1·40 1·00
1693 4000g. Holy Family 5·75 4·00

447 Footballers

2003. Futsal (Indoor Football) Championship, Sol de America Stadium, Asuncion, Paraguay. Multicoloured.
1694 4000g. Type **447** 5·75 4·00
1695 5000g. Two players 7·25 5·25

2003. Paraguay's Qualification for Futsal World Cup Championship, Taiwan . Nos. 1694/5 optd PARAGUAY CAMPEON MUNDIAL. Multicoloured.
1696 4000g. As Type **447** 5·75 4·00
1697 5000g. As No. 1695 7·25 5·25

449 *Cordia bordasii*

2003. America. Endangered Species. Multicoloured.
1698 1000g. Type **449** 1·40 1·00
1699 5000g. *Chorisia insignis* 7·25 5·25
1700 5000g. *Bulnesia sarmientoi* 7·25 5·25

450 Anahi (C. Gomez)

2004. Comics written by Robin Wood. Mult.
1701 1000g. Type **450** 1·40 1·00
1702 3000g. Nippur de Lagash (L. Olivera) 4·50 3·25
1703 5000g. Dago (A. Salinas) 7·25 5·25

451 Footballer

2004. Centenary of National Football Team.
1704 **451** 700g. multicoloured 1·00 80

452 Statues, Alter Piece, San Jose Church

2004. Centenary of San Jose College, Asuncion.
1705 **452** 700g. multicoloured 1·00 80

453 Pablo Neruda (statue) (Hugo Pistilli)

2004. Birth Centenary of Ricardo Eliecer Neftali Reyes Basoalto. (Pablo Neruda) (writer).
1706 **453** 5000g. multicoloured 7·25 5·25

454 Monday Waterfall

2004. Tourism. Multicoloured.
1707 700g. Type **454** 1·00 80

1708 6000g. Tobati 8·50 6·50

455 Asuncion (fresco) (Jose Laterza Parodi)

2004. Museum of Independence. Multicoloured.
1709 700g. Type **455** 1·00 80
1710 5000g. Museum building 7·25 5·25

456 Abstract (Enrique Careaga)

2004. Centenary of Museo del Barro (art museum). Multicoloured.
1711 2000g. Type **456** 3·25 2·30
1712 3000g. Female figure (Mercedes Noguera) (vert) 4·50 3·25
1713 4000g. Crucified Christ (Jesuit Mission) (vert) 5·75 4·00

457 Jose Flores and Musical Score

2004. Birth Centenary of Jose Asuncion Flores (composer).
1714 **457** 5000g. multicoloured 7·25 5·25

458 Camello Locomotive (1911)

2004. 150th Anniv of Railways. Multicoloured.
1715 2000g. Type **458** 3·25 2·30
1716 3000g. El Coqueto locomotive (1911) (horiz) 4·50 3·25
MS1717 117×82 mm. 6000g. Sapucai locomotive (1886) (50×40 mm) 8·50 8·50

459 *Procias nudicollis*

2004. America. Environmental Protection. Mult.
1718 6000g. Type **459** 8·50 6·50
MS1719 117×82 mm. 6000g. *Ceratophys cranwelli* (50×40 mm) 8·50 8·50

460 Ocelot (*Felis pardalis*)

2004. Mercosur. Aquifer Conservation. Mult.
1720 2000g. Type **460** 3·25 2·30
1721 4000g. Giant anteater (*Myrmecophaga tridactyla*), Hippopotamus (*Hydrochoerus hydrochaeris*) and crested screamer (*Chauna torquata*) 5·75 4·00

461 Maize (Zea mays)

2004. Agricultural Crops. Multicoloured.
1722 2000g. Type **461** 3·25 2·30
1723 4000g. Cotton (*Gossypium hirsutum*) 5·75 4·00
1724 6000g. Soya bean (*Glicine max*) 8·50 6·50

462 Mary and Jesus

2004. Christmas. Paintings by Ricardo Migliorisi. Multicoloured.
1725 3000g. Type **462** 4·50 3·25
1726 5000g. Angel (vert) 7·25 5·25

463 1870 3r. Stamp and Emblem

2004. 40th Anniv of Latin American Parliament.
1727 **463** 4000g. multicoloured 5·75 4·00

464 Turbines

2004. 30th Anniv of Paraguay—Brazil Hydro-Electric Generation (ITAIPU). Multicoloured.
1728 4000g. Type **464** 5·75 4·00
1729 5000g. Dam (vert) 7·25 5·25

2005. Pope John Paul II Commemoration (1st issue). No. 1713 optd S.S. JUNA PABLO II EN LA GLORIA DE DIOS 2 ABRIL 2005. Multicoloured.
1730 4000g. Crucified Christ (Jesuit Mission) 5·75 4·00

See also No. 1742.

466 La Santisima Trinidad de Paraná Ruins

2005. Centenary of Rotary International. Mult.

1731	3000g. Type **466**	4·50	3·25
1732	4000g. Statue (vert)	5·75	4·00

467 Building and Jose Gaspar Rodríguez de Francia (1st post-independence leader)

2005. Bicentenary of Casa Castelvi.

1733	**467**	5000g. multicoloured	7·25	5·25

468 Orchestra and Herminio Gimenez

2005. Birth Centenary of Herminio Gimenez (composer).

1734	**468**	700g. multicoloured	1·00	80

469 Building Facade

2005. 1st Anniv of El Cabildo National Cultural Centre.

1735	**469**	1000g. multicoloured	1·40	1·00

470 Monument to the Pioneers

2005. 75th Anniv of Fernheim Mennonite Colony. Multicoloured.

1736	5000g. Type **470**	7·25	5·25
MS1737	116×82 mm. 6000g. Ox cart (50×40 mm)	8·50	8·50

471 Team Members (1955)

2005. Centenary of Club Libertad Football Club.

1738	**471**	700g. multicoloured	1·00	80

472 Don Quixote and Sancho Panza

2005. 400th Anniv of Don Quixote De La Mancha novel by Miguel de Cervantes Saavedra.

1739	**472**	8000g. multicoloured	9·75	7·75

473 Herib Campos Cervera

2005. Mercosur. Writers. Multicoloured.

1740	3000g. Type **473**	4·50	3·25
1741	5000g. Gabriel Casaccia	7·25	5·25

474 Pope John Paul II

2005. Pope John Paul II Commemoration (2nd issue).

1742	**474**	2000g. multicoloured	3·25	2·30

475 Chains, Bird and Justice (statue)

2005. Truth and Justice.

1743	**475**	8000g. multicoloured	9·75	7·75

476 Elderly Women

2005. America. Struggle against Poverty. Mult.

1744	5000g. Type **476**	7·25	5·25
1745	6000g. Man mending shoes	8·50	6·50

477 Cats

2005. Cats and Dogs. Multicoloured.

1746	2000g. Type **477**	3·25	2·30
1747	2000g. Samoyed dog	3·25	2·30
1748	3000g. White shorthair cat	4·50	3·25
1749	3000g. Inscr "German dog"	4·50	3·25

478 Branislava Susnik and Chamacoco Bracelet

2005. Anthropologists. Multicoloured.

1750	1000g. Type **478**	1·40	1·00
1751	2000g. Miguel Chase-Sardi and Nivacle poncho	3·25	2·30
1752	8000g. Leon Cadogan and Mbya basket	9·75	7·75

479 Lucy Aguero (athlete)

2005. International Year of Sports Education. Multicoloured.

1753	5000g. Type **479**	7·25	5·25
MS1754	116×81 mm. 6000g. Carlos Franco (golfer) (50×40 mm)	8·50	8·50

480 Angels

2005. Christmas. Multicoloured.

1755	700g. Type **480**	1·00	80
1756	5000g. The Nativity	7·25	5·25

481 Dam and Plant

2005. Yacyreta Hydroelectric Plant. Multicoloured.

1757	3000g. Type **481**	4·50	3·25
1758	5000g. Aerial view of plant	7·25	5·25

482 Monumento a Las Residentas (statue) (Francisco Javier Baez Rolon)

2005. 150th Anniv of Ministry of Defence. Multicoloured.

1759	700g. Type **482**	1·00	80
1760	1000g. Ministry of Defence building	1·40	1·00

483 Karl Benz Vehicle, 1886

2006. 50th Anniv of Paraguay—Germany Chamber of Commerce.

1761	**483**	8000g. multicoloured	9·75	7·75

484 Paraguay Team

2006. World Cup Football Championship, Germany. Multicoloured.

1762	3000g. Type **484**	4·50	3·25
1763	5000g. Emblem and trophy	7·25	5·25

485 Eiffel Tower and Pot

2006. 50th Anniv of Asuncion French Alliance.

1764	**485**	8000g. multicoloured	9·75	7·75

486 Miguel de Cervantes Saavedra and Letter, 1616

2006. 50th Anniv of Cervantes Grammar School.

1765	**486**	700g. multicoloured	1·00	80

488 *Cattleya* (orchid)

2006. Centenary of Commercial School.

1767	**488**	700g. multicoloured	1·00	80

489 *Junonia evarete*

2005. 70th Anniv of Japanese Immigration. Butterflies. Multicoloured.

1768	1000g. Type **489**	1·40	1·00
1769	2000g. *Anartia jatrophae*	3·25	2·30
1770	3000g. *Agraulis vanillae*	4·50	3·25
MS1771	116×83 mm. 6000g. *Danaus plexippus* (50×40 mm)	8·50	8·50

490 Surfacing Route 10

2006. 30th Anniv of OPEC International Development Fund.

1772	**490**	8000g. multicoloured	9·75	7·75

491 Virgin of Schoenstatt (inscr "Schoenstant")

2006. 25th Anniv of Tuparenda Sanctuary.

1773	**491**	700g. multicoloured	1·00	80

492 Windmills

2006. America. Energy Conservation. Multicoloured.

1774	5000g. Type **492**	7·25	5·25
1775	6000g. Solar panels	8·50	6·50

493 Livestock

2006. 30th Anniv of Veterinary and Agricultural School. Multicoloured.

1776	4000g. Type **493** (veterinary faculty)	5·75	4·00
1777	4000g. Symbols of agriculture (agricultural faculty)	5·75	4·00

494 Building and Monument

2006. 90th Anniv of Confederacion Sudamericana de Futbol (CONMEBOL).

1778	**494**	8000g. multicoloured	9·75	7·75

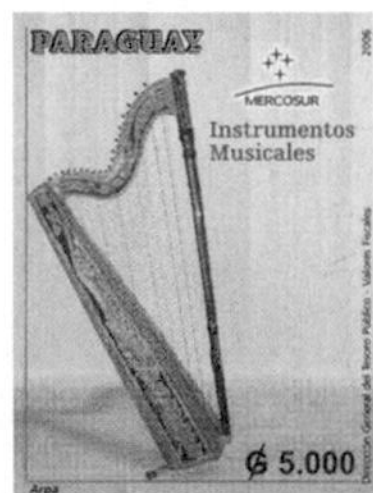

495 Harp

2006. Mercosur. Musical Instruments. Mult.

1779	5000g. Type **495**	7·25	5·25
1780	6000g. Guitar	8·50	6·50

496 Nuestra Senora de la Asuncion Cathedral

2006. Christmas. Mmulticoloured.

1781	4000g. Type **496**	5·75	4·00
1782	6000g. Santisima Trinidad Church (horiz)	8·50	6·50

497 Battle Area

2007. 80th Death Anniv of Adolfo Rojas Silva (casualty during 'Chaco War'). Multicoloured.

1783	4000g. Type **497**	5·75	4·00
1784	6000g. Adolfo Rojas Silva (vert)	8·50	6·50

498 Flower

2007. 50th Anniv of B'nai B'rith Organization (Jewish service organization) in Paraguay.

1785	**498**	8000g. multicoloured	9·75	7·75

499 Parrot

2007. Asuncion 2007–Americas Conference.

1786	**499**	8000g. multicoloured	9·75	7·75

500 Smoky Atmosphere

2007. Freedom from Tobacco Day. Multicoloured.

1787	5000g. Type **500**	7·25	5·25
1788	6000g. Clean atmosphere (vert)	8·50	6·50

501 Masks

2007. 25th Anniv of Arlequin Theatre.

1789	**501**	700g. multicoloured	1·00	80

502 *Felis pardalis* (ocelot)

2007. Inter-American Philatelic Association. Chaco National Park. Multicoloured.

1790	700g. Type **502**	1·00	80
1791	8000g. Postman riding ox	9·75	7·75

503 Horse-drawn Cart (inscr 'Sulki')

2007. 45th Anniv of Paraguay–Korea Diplomatic Relations. Multicoloured.

1792	1000g. Type **503**	1·40	1·00
1793	2000g. Covered horse-drawn cart (inscr 'Carumbe')	3·25	2·30
1794	3000g. Ox cart (vert)	4·50	3·25
MS1795	116×81 mm. 6000g. Mugungfa (Korean national flower) (50×40 mm)	8·50	8·50

504 Taipei 101 Tower

2007. 50th Anniv of Paraguay–Republic of China (Taiwan) Friendship.

1796	**504**	7000g. multicoloured	9·00	7·25

505 Tree and Building

2007. 25th Anniv of Paraguay–Indonesia Diplomatic Relations.

1797	**505**	11000g. multicoloured	13·00	10·50

506 Bull

2007. 40th Anniv of SENASCA (veterinary services). Multicoloured.

1798	5000g. Type **506**	7·25	5·25
1799	7000g. Vet, cattle and prize bull (horiz)	9·00	7·25

507a Celebration

2007. America. Education for All

1800 **507a**	5000g. Type **507a**	1·50	1·10
1800a	6000g. Teacher and pupils		

508a Nautilus Building

2007. Mercosur. Architecture. Multicoloured.

1801	6000g. Type **508a**	6·00	6·50
1802	7000g. Barro Museum (horiz)	8·50	6·50

509 martin McMahon

General Martin McMahon Commemoration.

1803	700g. **509** multicoloured	1·00	80

510 Anniversary Emblem

40th Anniv of Peace Corps.

1804	7000g. **510** multicoloured	9·00	7·25

511 Scouts and Campfire

Centenary of Scouting. Multicoloured.

1805	700g. Type **511**	1·00	80
1806	6000g. Girl scout	8·50	6·50

512 Stadium Façade

Inauguration of New Stadium.

1807	700g. **512** multicoloured	1·00	80

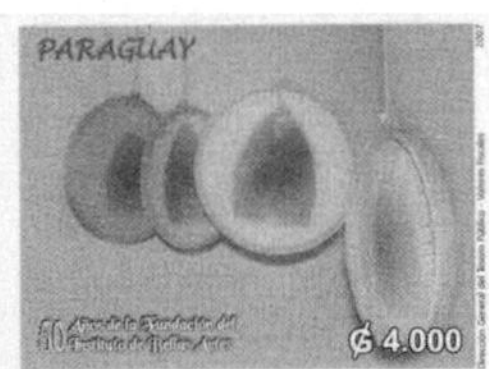

513 Pendants (Engelberto Gimenez Legal)

2007. 50th Anniv of Institute of Fine Arts. Multicoloured.

1808	4000g. Type **513**	5·75	4·00
1809	8000g. Hands releasing bird (sculpture) (Hugo Pistilli) (vert)	9·75	7·75

No. 1803 and Type **509** have been left for 'General McMahon', issued on 19 Sept 2007, not yet received.

No. 1804 and Type **510** have been left for '40th Anniv of Peace Corps', issued on19 Sept 2007, not yet received.

Nos. 1805/6 and Type **511** have been left for 'Boy Scouts', issued on 11 Oct 2007, not yet received.

No. 1807 and Type **512** have been left for 'Stadium', issued on 22 October 2007, not yet received.

514 Gabriel Casaccia

2007. Birth Centenary of Gabriel Casaccia Bibolini (writer).
1810 **514** 8000g. multicoloured 9·75 7·75

515 Fronds

2007. Christmas. Multicoloured.
1811 700g. Type **515** 1·00 80
1812 8000g. The Nativity 9·75 7·75

516 Emblem and Marco Aguayo

2007. 15th Anniv of Marco Aguayo AIDS Foundation. Multicoloured.
1813 1000g. Type **516** 9·75 7·75
1814 8000g. Emblem (different) 1·40 1·10

517 Nu Guarza Parks

2007. National Parks. Multicoloured.
1815 3000g. Type **517** 4·50 3·25
MS1816 117×82 mm. 6000g. *Alouatta caraya* (50×40 mm) (rouletted) 8·50 6·50

518 Tree in Desert

2007. International Year of Deserts and Desertification.
1817 **518** 7000g. multicoloured 9·00 7·25

519 Flower

40th Anniv of Nasta Advertising.
1818 700g. Type **519** 1·00 80
1819 5000g. Stylized tulip (vert) 7·25 5·25

520 Emblem

2008. 80th Anniv of Asunción Rotary Club. Multicoloured.
1820 2000g. Type **520** 3·25 2·30
1821 8000g. Parkland (Martin Luis Vallejos Cuevas) (horiz) 9·75 7·75

522 *Coryphospingus cucullatus* (red crested finch)

2008. Mercosur. Birds. Multicoloured.
1822 5000g. Type **522** 6·25 5·25
1823 6000g. *Pitangus sulpphuratus* (great kiskadee) 8·25 6·25

523 Building Facade

2008. 125th Anniv of Fundacion del Anteo Paraguayo.
1824 **523** 700g. multicoloured 1·00 80

524 Celebration

2008. America. Festivals.
1825 **524** 11000g. multicoloured 12·00 10·50

525 Signing

2008. 30th Anniv (2007) of Torrijos-Carter Treaties (two treaties signed by the United States and Panama guaranteeing Panama control of Panama Canal after 1999). Multicoloured.
1826 700g. Type **525** 1·00 80
1827 7000g. Pres. Omar Torrijos, Pres. Jimmy Carter and Panama Canal 9·00 7·25

526 Scouts and Tent

2008. 70th Anniv of Scouting in Paraguay. Multicoloured.
1828 3000g. Type **526** 4·25 3·25
1829 4000g. Capitan Figan troop

527 Virgin and Child

2008. Christmas. Multicoloured.
1830 700g. Type **527** 1·00 80
1831 5000g. Holy Family 7·25 5·25

528 Cathedral and Cotton

2008. 250th Anniv of Corniel Oviedo City. Multicoloured.
1832 3000g. Type **528** 4·25 3·25
1833 7000g. Approach to city 9·00 7·25

529 Pres. Hayes

2008. 130th Anniv of Pres. Hayes' Arbitration.
1834 **529** 1000g. multicoloured 1·40 1·00

530 Children and Flower

2008. 25th Anniv of SOS Children's Village, Zeballos Cue. Multicoloured.
1835 2000g. Type **530** 3·25 2·30
1836 7000g. Emblem 9·00 7·25

531 Harpist

2008. Year of the Harp.
1837 **531** 5000g. multicoloured 7·25 5·25

OFFICIAL STAMPS

O14

O19

O20

1886. Various types as O 14, O 19 and O 20 optd OFICIAL. (a) Imperf.
O32 1c. orange 3·50 3·50
O33 2c. violet 3·50 3·50
O34 5c. orange 3·50 3·50
O35 7c. green 3·50 3·50
O36 10c. brown 3·50 3·50
O37 15c. blue 3·50 3·50
O38 20c. lake 3·50 3·50

(b) New colours. Perf.
O39 1c. green 55 55
O40 2c. red 55 55
O41 5c. blue 55 55
O42 7c. orange 55 55
O43 10c. lake 55 55
O44 15c. brown 55 55
O45 20c. blue 55 55

1889. Stamp of 1889 surch OFICIAL and value. Perf.
O47 **25** 1 on 15c. purple 2·50 2·40
O48 **25** 2 on 10c. purple 2·50 2·40

1889. Stamp of 1889 surch OFICIAL and value. Imperf.
O49 **25** 3 on 15c. purple 2·50 2·40
O50 **25** 5 on 15c. brown 2·50 2·40

1890. Stamps of 1887 optd OFICIAL or Oficial.
O58 **24** 1c. green 20 20
O59 **24** 2c. red 20 20
O60 **24** 5c. blue 20 20
O61 **24** 7c. brown 4·00 1·80
O55 **24** 10c. mauve 35 30
O63 **24** 15c. orange 35 20
O64 **24** 20c. pink 75 30
O65 **24** 50c. grey 65 30
O86 **24** 1p. green 35 30

O37

1901
O73 **O37** 1c. blue 65 60
O74 **O37** 2c. red 10 10
O75 **O37** 4c. brown 10 10
O76 **O37** 5c. green 10 10
O77 **O37** 8c. brown 20 20
O78 **O37** 10c. red 35 20
O79 **O37** 20c. blue 45 30

1903. Stamps of 1903, optd OFICIAL.
O99 **46** 1c. grey 35 30
O100 **46** 2c. green 35 30
O101 **46** 5c. blue 35 30
O102 **46** 10c. brown 35 30
O103 **46** 20c. red 35 30
O104 **46** 30c. blue 35 30
O105 **46** 60c. violet 35 30

1904. As T 50, but inscr "OFICIAL".
O106 1c. green 20 10
O107 1c. olive 90 15
O108 1c. orange 35 15
O109 1c. red 45 20
O110 2c. orange 20 15
O111 2c. green 20 15
O112 2c. red 1·40 45
O113 2c. grey 75 30
O114 5c. blue 35 20
O116 5c. grey 1·40 1·20
O117 10c. lilac 20 10
O118 20c. lilac 1·20 75

1913. As T 65, but inscr "OFICIAL".
O237 1c. grey 35 30
O238 2c. orange 35 30
O239 5c. purple 35 30
O240 10c. green 35 30
O241 20c. red 35 30
O242 50c. red 35 30
O243 75c. blue 35 30
O244 1p. blue 35 30
O245 2p. yellow 35 30

1935. Optd OFICIAL.
O474 **86** 10c. blue 35 30
O475 **86** 50c. mauve 35 30
O476 **87** 1p. orange 35 30
O477 **122** 1p.50 green 35 30
O478 - 2p.50 violet (No. 337) 35 30

1940. 50th Anniv of Asuncion University. As T 139, inscr "SERVICIO OFICIAL", but portraits of Pres. Escobar and Dr. Zubizarreta.
O513 50c. black and red 35 30
O514 1p. black and red 35 30
O515 2p. black and blue 35 30
O516 5p. black and blue 35 30
O517 10p. black and blue 35 30
O518 50p. black and orange 55 55

POSTAGE DUE STAMPS

D48

1904
D106 **D48** 2c. green 55 55
D107 **D48** 4c. green 55 55
D108 **D48** 10c. green 55 55
D109 **D48** 20c. green 55 55

1913. As T 65, but inscr "DEFICIENTE".

D237	1c. brown	45	45
D238	2c. brown	45	45
D239	5c. brown	45	45
D240	10c. brown	45	45
D241	20c. brown	45	45
D242	40c. brown	45	45
D243	1p. brown	45	45
D244	1p.50 brown	45	45

APPENDIX

The following stamps have either been issued in excess of postal needs or have not been available to the public in reasonable quantities at face value. Such stamps may later be given full listing if there is evidence of regular postal use.

1962

Manned Spacecraft. Postage 15, 25, 30, 40, 50c.; Air 12g.45, 18g.15, 36g.
Previous Olympic Games (1st series). Vert designs. Postage 15, 25, 30, 40, 50c.; Air 12g.45, 18g.15, 36g.
Vatican Council. Postage 50, 70c., 1g.50, 2, 3g.; Air 5, 10g., 12g.45, 18g.15, 23g.40, 36g.
Europa. Postage 4g.; Air 36g.
Solar System. Postage 10, 20, 25, 30, 50c.; Air 12g.45, 36g., 50g.

1963

Previous Olympic Games (2nd series). Horiz designs. Postage 15, 25, 30, 40, 50c.; Air 12g.45, 18g.15, 36g.
Satellites and Space Flights. Vert designs. Postage 10, 20, 25, 30, 50c.; Air 12g.45, 36, 50g.
Previous Winter Olympic Games. Postage 10, 20, 25, 30, 50c.; Air 12g.45, 36, 50g.
Freedom from Hunger. Postage 10, 25, 50, 75c.; Air 18g.15, 36, 50g.
"Mercury" Space Flights. Postage 15, 25, 30, 40, 50c.; Air 12g.45, 18g.15, 50g.
Winter Olympic Games. Postage 15, 25, 30, 40, 50c.; Air 12g.45, 18g.15, 50g.

1964

Tokyo Olympic Games. Postage 15, 25, 30, 40, 50c.; Air 12g.45, 18g.15, 50g.
Red Cross Centenary. Postage 10, 25, 30, 50c.; Air 18g.15, 36, 50g.
"Gemini", "Telstar" and "Apollo" Projects. Postage 15, 25, 30, 40, 50c.; Air 12g.45, 18g.15, 50g.
Spacecraft Developments. Postage 15, 25, 30, 40, 50c.; Air 12g.45, 18g.15, 50g.
United Nations. Postage 15, 25, 30, 40, 50c.; Air 12g.45, 18g.15, 50g.
American Space Research. Postage 10, 15, 20, 30, 40c.; Air 12g.45+6g., 18g.15+9g., 20g.+20g.
Eucharistic Conference. Postage 20g.+10g., 30g.+15g., 50g.+25g., 100g.+50g.
Pope John Memorial Issue. Postage 20g.+10g., 30g.+15g., 50g.+25g., 100g.+50g.

1965

Scouts. Postage 10, 15, 20, 30, 50c.; Air 12g.45, 18g.15, 36g.
Tokyo Olympic Games Medals. Postage 15, 25, 30, 40, 50c.; Air 12g.45, 18g.15, 50g.
Famous Scientists. Postage 10, 15, 20, 30, 40c.; Air 12g.45+6g., 18g.15+9g., 20g.+20g.
Orchids and Trees. Postage 20, 30, 90c., 1g.50, 4g.50.; Air 3, 4, 66g.
Kennedy and Churchill. Postage 15, 25, 30, 40, 50c.; Air 12g.45, 18g.15, 50g.
I.T.U. Centenary. Postage 10, 15, 20, 30, 40c.; Air 12g.45+6g., 18g.15+9g., 20g.+10g.
Pope Paul VI. Visit to United Nations. Postage 10, 15, 20, 30, 50c.; Air 12g.45, 18g.15, 36g.

1966

"Gemini" Space Project. Postage 15, 25, 30, 40, 50c.; Air 12g.45, 18g.15, 50g.
Events of 1965. Postage 10, 15, 20, 30, 50c.; Air 12g.45, 18g.15, 36g.
Mexico Olympic Games. Postage 10, 15, 20, 30, 50c.; Air 12g.45, 18g.15, 36g.
German Space Research. Postage 10, 15, 20, 30, 50c.; Air 12g.45, 18g.15, 36g.
Famous Writers. Postage 10, 15, 20, 30, 50c.; Air 12g.45, 18g.15, 36g.
Italian Space Research. Postage 10, 15, 20, 30, 50c.; Air 12g.45, 18g.15, 36g.
Moon Missions. Postage 10, 15, 20, 30, 50c.; Air 12g.45, 18g.15, 36g.
Sports Commemorative Issue. Postage 10, 15, 20, 30, 50c.; Air 12g.45, 18g.15, 36g.
3rd Death Anniv of Pres. John Kennedy. Postage 10, 15, 20, 30, 50c.; Air 12g.45, 18g.15, 36g.
Famous Paintings. Postage 10, 15, 20, 30, 50c.; Air 12g.45, 18g.15, 36g.

1967

Religious Paintings. Postage 10, 15, 20, 30, 50c.; Air 12g.45, 18g.15, 36g.
16th-century. Religious Paintings. Postage 10, 15, 20, 30, 50c.; Air 12g.45, 18g.15, 36g.
Impressionist Paintings. Postage 10, 15, 20, 30, 50c.; Air 12g.45, 18g.15, 36g.
European Paintings of 17th and 18th Cent. Postage 10, 15, 20, 25, 30, 50c.; Air 12g.45, 18g.15, 36g.
Birth Anniv of Pres. John Kennedy. Postage 10, 15, 20, 25, 30, 50c.; Air 12g.45, 18g.15, 36g.
Sculpture. Postage 10, 15, 20, 25, 30, 50c.; Air 12g.45, 18g.15, 50g.
Mexico Olympic Games. Archaeological Relics. Postage 10, 15, 20, 25, 30, 50c.; Air 12g.45, 18g.15, 36g.

1968

Religious Paintings. Postage 10, 15, 20, 25, 30, 50c.; Air 12g.45, 18g.15, 36g.
Winter Olympic Games, Grenoble. Paintings. Postage 10, 15, 20, 25, 30, 50c.; Air 12g.45, 18g.15, 36g.
Paraguayan Stamps from 1870–1970. Postage 10, 15, 20, 25, 30, 50c.; Air 12g.45, 18g.15, 36g.
Mexico Olympic Games, Paintings of Children. Postage 10, 15, 20, 25, 30, 50c.; Air 12g.45, 18g.15, 36g. (Sailing ship and Olympic Rings).
Visit of Pope Paul VI to Eucharistic Congress. Religious Paintings. Postage 10, 15, 20, 25, 30, 50c.; Air 12g.45, 18g.15, 36g.
Important Events of 1968. Postage 10, 15, 20, 25, 30, 50c.; Air 12g.45, 18g.15, 50g.

1969

Gold Medal Winners of 1968 Mexico Olympic Games. Postage 10, 15, 20, 25, 30, 50c.; Air 12g.45, 18g.15, 50g.
Int. Projects in Outer Space. Postage 10, 15, 20, 25, 30, 50c.; Air 12g.45, 18g.15, 50g.
Latin American Wildlife. Postage 10, 10, 15, 15, 20, 20, 25, 25, 30, 30, 50, 50, 75, 75 c; Air 12g.45×2, 18g.15×2.
Gold Medal Winners in Olympic Football, 1900–1968. Postage 10, 15, 20, 25, 30, 50, 75c.; Air 12g.45, 18g.15.
Paraguayan Football Champions, 1930–1966. Postage 10, 15, 20, 25, 30, 50, 75c.; Air 12g.45, 18g.15.
Paintings by Goya. Postage 10, 15, 20, 25, 30, 50, 75c.; Air 12g.45, 18g.15.
Christmas. Religious Paintings. Postage 10, 15, 20, 25, 30, 50, 75c.; Air 12g.45, 18g.15.

1970

Moon Walk. Postage 10, 15, 20, 25, 30, 50, 75c.; Air 12g.45, 18g.15.
Easter. Paintings. Postage 10, 15, 20, 25, 30, 50, 75c.; Air 12g.45, 18g.15.
Munich Olympic Games. Postage 10, 15, 20, 25, 30, 50, 75c.; Air 12g.45, 18g.15.
Paintings from the Pinakothek Museum in Munich. Postage 10, 15, 20, 25, 30, 50, 75c.; Air 12g.45, 18g.15.
"Apollo" Space Programme. Postage 10, 15, 20, 25, 30, 50, 75c.; Air 12g.45, 18g.15.
Space Projects in the Future. Postage 10, 15, 20, 25, 30, 50, 75c.; Air 12g.45, 18g.15.
"Expo 70" World Fair, Osaka, Japan. Japanese Paintings. Postage 10, 15, 20, 25, 30, 50, 75c.; Air 12g.45, 18g.15, 50g.
Flower Paintings. Postage 10, 15, 20, 25, 30, 50, 75c.; Air 12g.45, 18g.15, 50g.
Paintings from Prado Museum, Madrid. Postage 10, 15, 20, 25, 30, 50, 75c.; Air 12g.45, 18g.15, 50g.
Paintings by Durer. Postage 10, 15, 20, 25, 30, 50, 75c.; Air 12g.45, 18g.15, 50g.

1971

Christmas 1970/71. Religious Paintings. Postage 10, 15, 20, 25, 30, 50, 75c.; Air 12g.45, 18g.15, 50g.
Munich Olympic Games, 1972. Postage 10, 15, 20, 25, 30, 50, 75c.; Air 12g.45, 18g.15, 50g.
Paintings of Horses and Horsemen. Postage 10, 15, 20, 25, 30, 50, 75c.; Air 12g.45, 18g.15, 50g.
Famous Paintings from the Louvre, Paris. Postage 10, 15, 20, 25, 30, 50, 75c.; Air 12g.45, 18g.15, 50g.
Paintings in the National Museum, Asuncion. Postage 10, 15, 20, 25, 30, 50, 75c.; Air 12g.45, 18g.15, 50g.
Hunting Paintings. Postage 10, 15, 20, 25, 30, 50, 75c.; Air 12g.45, 18g.15, 50g.
Philatokyo '71, Stamp Exhibition, Tokyo. Japanese Paintings. Postage 10, 15, 20, 25, 30, 50, 75c.; Air 12g.45, 18g.15, 50g.
Winter Olympic Games, Sapporo, 1972. Japanese Paintings. Postage 10, 15, 20, 25, 30, 50, 75c.; Air 12g.45, 18g.15, 50g.
150th Death Anniv of Napoleon. Paintings. Postage 10, 15, 20, 25, 30, 50, 75c.; Air 12g.45, 18g.15, 50g.
Famous Paintings from the Dahlem Museum, Berlin. Postage 10, 15, 20, 25, 30, 50, 75c.; Air 12g.45, 18g.15, 50g.

1972

Locomotives (1st series). Postage 10, 15, 20, 25, 30, 50, 75c.; Air 12g.45, 18g.15, 50g.
Winter Olympic Games, Sapporo. Postage 10, 15, 20, 25, 30, 50, 75c.; Air 12g.45, 18g.15, 50g.
Racing Cars. Postage 10, 15, 20, 25, 30, 50, 75c.; Air 12g.45, 18g.15, 50g.
Famous Sailing Ships. Postage 10, 15, 20, 25, 30, 50, 75c.; Air 12g.45, 18g.15, 50g.
Famous Paintings from the Vienna Museum. Postage 10, 15, 20, 25, 30, 50, 75c.; Air 12g.45, 18g.15, 50g.
Famous Paintings from the Asuncion Museum. Postage 10, 15, 20, 25, 30, 50, 75c.; Air 12g.45, 18g.15, 50g.
Visit of the Argentine President to Paraguay. Postage 10, 15, 20, 25, 30, 50, 75c.; Air 12g.45, 18g.15.
Visit of President of Paraguay to Japan. Postage 10, 15, 20, 25, 30, 50, 75c.; Air 12g.45, 18g.15.
Paintings of Animals and Birds. Postage 10, 15, 20, 25, 30, 50, 75c.; Air 12g.45, 18g.15.
Locomotives (2nd series). Postage 10, 15, 20, 25, 30, 50, 75c.; Air 12g.45, 18g.15.
South American Fauna. Postage 10, 15, 20, 25, 30, 50, 75c.; Air 12g.45, 18g.15.

1973

Famous Paintings from the Florence Museum. Postage 10, 15, 20, 25, 30, 50, 75c.; Air 5, 10, 20g.
South American Butterflies. Postage 10, 15, 20, 25, 30, 50, 75c.; Air 5, 10, 20g.
Cats. Postage 10, 15, 20, 25, 30, 50, 75c.; Air 5, 10, 20g.
Portraits of Women. Postage 10, 15, 20, 25, 30, 50, 75c.; Air 5, 10, 20g.
World Cup Football Championship, West Germany (1974) (1st issue). Postage 10, 15, 20, 25, 30, 50, 75c.; Air 5, 10, 20g.
Paintings of Women. Postage 10, 15, 20, 25, 30, 50, 75c.; Air 5, 10, 20g.
Birds. Postage 10, 15, 20, 25, 30, 50, 75c.; Air 5, 10, 20g.
"Apollo" Moon Missions and Future Space Projects. Postage 10, 15, 20, 25, 30, 50, 75c.; Air 5, 10, 20g.
Visit of Pres. Stroessner to Europe and Morocco. Air 5, 10, 25, 50, 150g.
Folk Costume. Postage 25, 50, 75c., 1g., 1g.50, 1g.75, 2g.25.
Flowers. Postage 10, 20, 25, 30, 40, 50, 75c.

1974

World Cup Football Championship, West Germany (2nd issue). Air 5, 10, 20g.
Roses. Postage 10, 15, 20, 25, 30, 50, 75c.
Famous Paintings from the Gulbenkian Museum, New York. Postage 10, 15, 20, 25, 30, 50, 75 c; Air 5, 10, 20g.
U.P.U. Centenary. Postage 10, 15, 20, 25, 30, 50, 75c.; Air 5, 10, 20g.
Famous Masterpieces. Postage 10, 15, 20, 25, 30, 50, 75c.; Air 5, 10, 20g.
Visit of Pres. Stroessner to France. Air 100g.
World Cup Football Championship, West Germany (3rd issue). Air 4, 5, 10g.
Ships. Postage 5, 10, 15, 20, 25, 35, 40, 50c.
Events of 1974. Air 4g. (U.P.U.), 5g. (President of Chile's visit), 10g. (President Stroessner's visit to South Africa).
Centenary of U.P.U. Air 4, 5, 10, 20g.

1975

Paintings. Postage 5, 10, 15, 20, 25, 35, 40, 50c.
Christmas (1974). Postage 5, 10, 15, 20, 25, 35, 40, 50c.
"Expo '75" Okinawa, Japan. Air 4, 5, 10g.
Paintings from National Gallery, London. Postage 5, 10, 15, 20, 25, 35, 40, 50c.
Dogs. Postage 5, 10, 15, 20, 25, 35, 40, 50c.
South American Fauna. Postage 5, 10, 15, 20, 25, 35, 40, 50c.
"Espana '75". Air 4, 5, 10g.
500th Birth Anniv of Michelangelo. Postage 5, 10, 15, 20, 25, 35, 40, 50c.; Air 4, 5, 10g.
Winter Olympic Games, Innsbruck (1976). Postage 1, 2, 3, 4, 5g.; Air 10, 15, 20g.
Olympic Games, Montreal (1976). Gold borders. Postage 1, 2, 3, 4, 5g.; Air 10, 15, 20g.
Various Commemorations. Air 4g. (Zeppelin), 5g. (1978 World Cup), 10g. (Nordposta Exhibition).
Bicent (1976) of American Revolution (1st issue). Paintings of Sailing Ships. Postage 5, 10, 15, 20, 25, 35, 40, 50c.
Bicent (1976) of American Revolution (2nd issue). Paintings. Postage 5, 10, 15, 20, 25, 35, 40, 50c.
Bicent (1976) of American Revolution (3rd issue). Lunar Rover and American Cars. Air 4, 5, 10g.
Various Commemorations. Air 4g. (Concorde), 5g. (Lufthansa), 10g. ("Exfilmo" and "Espamer" Stamp Exhibitions).
Paintings by Spanish Artists. Postage 1, 2, 3, 4, 5g.; Air 10, 15, 20g.

1976

Holy Year. Air 4, 5, 10g.
Cats. Postage 5, 10, 15, 20, 25, 35, 40, 50c.
Railway Locomotives (3rd series). Postage 1, 2, 3, 4, 5g.; Air 10, 15, 20g.
Butterflies. Postage 5, 10, 15, 20, 25, 35, 40, 50c.
Domestic Animals. Postage 1, 2, 3, 4, 5g.; Air 10, 15, 20g.
Bicent of American Revolution (4th issue) and U.S. Postal Service. Postage 1, 2, 3, 4, 5g.; Air 10, 15, 20g.
"Paintings and Planets". Postage 1, 2, 3, 4, 5g.; Air 10, 15, 20g.
Ship Paintings. Postage 1, 2, 3, 4, 5g.; Air 10, 15, 20g.
German Ship Paintings (1st issue). Postage 1, 2, 3, 4, 5g.; Air 10, 15, 20g.
Bicentenary of American Revolution (5th issue). Paintings of Cowboys and Indians. Postage 1, 2, 3, 4, 5g.; Air 10, 15, 20g.
Gold Medal Winners. Olympic Games, Montreal. Postage 1, 2, 3, 4, 5g.; Air 10, 15, 20g.
Paintings by Titian. Postage 1, 2, 3, 4, 5g.; Air 10, 15, 20g.
History of the Olympics. Postage 1, 2, 3, 4, 5g.; Air 10, 15, 20g.

1977

Paintings by Rubens (1st issue). Postage 1, 2, 3, 4, 5g.; Air 10, 15, 20g.
Bicent of American Revolution (6th issue). Astronautics. Postage 1, 2, 3, 4, 5g.; Air 10, 15, 20g.
"Luposta 77" Stamp Exn. Zeppelin and National Costumes. Postage 1, 2, 3, 4, 5g.; Air 10, 15, 20g.
History of Aviation. Postage 1, 2, 3, 4, 5g.; Air 10, 15, 20g.
Paintings. Postage 1, 2, 3, 4, 5g.; Air 10, 15, 20g.
German Ship Paintings (2nd issue). Postage 1, 2, 3, 4, 5g.; Air 10, 15, 20g.
Nobel Prize-winners for Literature. Postage 1, 2, 3, 4, 5g.; Air 10, 15, 20g.
History of World Cup (1st issue). Postage 1, 2, 3, 4, 5g.; Air 10, 15, 20g.
History of World Cup (2nd issue). Postage 1, 2, 3, 4, 5g.; Air 10, 15, 20g.

1978

Paintings by Rubens (2nd issue). Postage 1, 2, 3, 4, 5g.; Air 10, 15, 20g.
Chess Olympiad, Buenos Aires. Paintings of Chess Games. Postage 1, 2, 3, 4, 5g.; Air 10, 15, 20g.
Paintings by Jordaens. Postage 3, 4, 5, 6, 7, 8, 20g.; Air 10, 25g.
450th Death Anniv of Durer (1st issue). Postage 3, 4, 5, 6, 7, 8, 20g.; Air 10, 25g.
Paintings by Goya. Postage 3, 4, 5, 6, 7, 8, 20g.; Air 10, 25g.
Astronautics of the Future. Postage 3, 4, 5, 6, 7, 8, 20g.; Air 10, 25g.
Racing Cars. Postage 3, 4, 5, 6, 7, 8, 20g.; Air 10, 25g.
Paintings by Rubens (3rd issue). Postage 3, 4, 5, 6, 7, 8, 20g.; Air 10, 25g.
25th Anniv of Queen Elizabeth's Coronation (reproduction of stamps). Postage 3, 4, 5, 6, 7, 8, 20g.; Air 10, 25g.
Paintings and Stamp Exhibition Emblems. Postage 3, 4, 5, 6, 7, 8, 20g.; Air 10, 25g.
Various Commemorations. Air 75g. (Satellite Earth Station), 500g. (Coat of Arms), 1000g. (Pres. Stroessner).
International Year of the Child (1st issue). Snow White and the Seven Dwarfs. Postage 3, 4, 5, 6, 7, 8, 20g.; Air 10, 25g.
Military Uniforms. Postage 3, 4, 5, 6, 7, 8, 20g.; Air 10, 25g.

1979

World Cup Football Championship, Argentina. Postage 3, 4, 5, 6, 7, 8, 20g.; Air 10, 25g.
Christmas (1978). Paintings of Madonnas. Postage 3, 4, 5, 6, 7, 8, 20g.; Air 10, 25g.
History of Aviation. Postage 3, 4, 5, 6, 7, 8, 20g.; Air 10, 25g.
450th Death Anniv of Durer (2nd issue). Postage 3, 4, 5, 6, 7, 8, 20g.; Air 10, 25g.
Death Centenary of Sir Rowland Hill (1st issue). Reproduction of Stamps. Postage 3, 4, 5, 6, 7, 8, 20g.; Air 10, 25g.
International Year of the Child (2nd issue). Cinderella. Postage 3, 4, 5, 6, 7, 8, 20g.; Air 10, 25g.
Winter Olympic Games, Lake Placid (1980). Postage 3, 4, 5, 6, 7, 8, 20g.; Air 10, 25g.
Sailing Ships. Postage 3, 4, 5, 6, 7, 8, 20g.; Air 10, 25g.
International Year of the Child (3rd issue). Cats. Postage 3, 4, 5, 6, 7, 8, 20g.; Air 10, 25g.
International Year of the Child (4th issue). Little Red Riding Hood. Postage 3, 4, 5, 6, 7, 8, 20g.; Air 10, 25g.
Olympic Games, Moscow (1980). Greek Athletes. Postage 3, 4, 5, 6, 7, 8, 20g.; Air 10, 25g.
Centenary of Electric Locomotives. Postage 3, 4, 5, 6, 7, 8, 20g.; Air 10, 25g.

1980

Death Centenary of Sir Rowland Hill (2nd issue). Military Aircraft. Postage 3, 4, 5, 6, 7, 8, 20 g; Air 10, 25g.
Death Centenary of Sir Rowland Hill (3rd issue). Stamps. Postage 3, 4, 5, 6, 7, 8, 20g.; Air 10, 25g.
Winter Olympic Games Medal Winners (1st issue). Postage 3, 4, 5, 6, 7, 8, 20g.; Air 10, 25g.
Composers. Scenes from Ballets. Postage 3, 4, 5, 6, 7, 8, 20g.; Air 20, 25g.
International Year of the Child (1979) (5th issue). Christmas. Postage 3, 4, 5, 6, 7, 8, 20g.; Air 10, 25g.
Exhibitions. Paintings of Ships. Postage 3, 4, 5, 6, 7, 8, 20g.; Air 10, 25g.
World Cup Football Championship, Spain (1982) (1st issue). Postage 3, 4, 5, 6, 7, 8, 20g.; Air 10, 25g.
World Chess Championship, Merano. Postage 3, 4, 5, 6, 7, 8, 20g.; Air 10, 25g.

1981

Winter Olympic Games Medal Winners (2nd issue). Postage 25, 50c., 1, 2, 3, 4, 5g.; Air 5, 10, 30g.
International Year of the Child (1979) (6th issue). Children and Flowers. Postage 10, 25, 50, 100, 200, 300, 400g.; Air 75, 500, 1000g.
"WIPA 1981" International Stamp Exhibition, Vienna. 1980 Composers stamp optd. Postage 4g.; Air 10g.
Wedding of Prince of Wales (1st issue). Postage 25, 50c., 1, 2, 3, 4, 5g.; Air 5, 10, 30g.
Costumes and Treaty of Itaipu. Postage 10, 25, 50, 100, 200, 300, 400g.
Paintings by Rubens. Postage 25, 50c., 1, 2, 3, 4, 5g.
Anniversaries and Events. Air 5g. (250th birth anniv of George Washington), 10g. (80th birthday of Queen Mother), 30g. ("Philatokyo '81").
Flight of Space Shuttle. Air 5, 10, 30g.
Birth Bicentenary of Ingres. Postage 25, 50c., 1, 2, 3, 4, 5g.
World Cup Football Championship, Spain (1982) (2nd issue). Air 5, 10, 30g.
Birth Centenary of Picasso. Postage 25, 50c., 1, 2, 3, 4, 5g.
"Philatelia '81" International Stamp Exhibition, Frankfurt. Picasso stamps optd. Postage 25, 50c., 1, 2, 3, 4g.
"Espamer '81" International Stamp Exhibition. Picasso stamps optd. Postage 25, 50c., 1, 2, 3, 4g.
Wedding of Prince of Wales (2nd issue). Postage 25, 50c., 1, 2, 3, 4, 5g.; Air 5, 10, 30g.
International Year of the Child (1979) (7th issue). Christmas. Postage 25, 50c., 1, 2, 3, 4, 5g.
Christmas. Paintings. Air 5, 10, 30g.

1982

International Year of the Child (1979) (8th issue). Puss in Boots. Postage 25, 50c., 1, 2, 3, 4, 5g.
World Cup Football Championship, Spain (3rd issue). Air 5, 10, 30g.
75th Anniv of Boy Scout Movement and 125th Birth Anniv of Lord-Baden Powell (founder). Postage 25, 50c., 1, 2, 3, 4, 5g.; Air 5, 10, 30g.
"Essen 82" International Stamp Exhibition, 1981 International Year of the Child (7th issue) Christmas stamps optd. Postage 25, 50c., 1, 2, 3, 4g.
Cats. Postage 25, 50c., 1, 2, 3, 4, 5g.
Chess paintings. Air 5, 10, 30g.
"Philexfrance 82" International Stamp Exhibition. 1981 Ingres stamps optd. Postage 25, 50c., 1, 2, 3g.
World Cup Football Championship, Spain (4th issue). Postage 25, 50c., 1, 2, 3, 4, 5g.; Air 5, 10, 30g.
"Philatelia 82" International Stamp Exhibition, Hanover. 1982 Cats issue optd. Postage 25, 50c., 1, 2, 3, 4, 5g.
500th Birth Anniv of Raphael (1st issue). Postage 25, 50c., 1, 2, 3, 4, 5g.
500th Birth Anniv of Raphael (2nd issue) and Christmas (1st issue). Postage 25, 50c., 1, 2, 3, 4, 5g.
World Cup Football Championship Results. Air 5, 10, 30g.
Christmas (2nd issue). Paintings by Rubens. Air 5, 10, 30g.
Paintings by Durer. Life of Christ. Postage 25, 50c., 1, 2, 3, 4, 5g.
500th Birth Anniv of Raphael (3rd issue) and Christmas (3rd issue). Air 5, 10, 30g.

1983

Third International Railways Congress, Malaga (1982). Postage 25, 50c., 1, 2, 3, 4, 5g.
Racing Cars. Postage 25, 50c., 1, 2, 3, 4, 5g.
Paintings by Rembrandt. Air 5, 10, 30g.
German Astronautics. Air 5, 10, 30g.
Winter Olympic Games, Sarajevo (1984). Postage 25, 50c., 1, 2, 3, 4, 5g.
Bicentenary of Manned Flight. Air 5, 10, 30g.
Pope John Paul II. Postage 25, 50c., 1, 2, 3, 4, 5g.
Olympic Games, Los Angeles (1984). Air 5, 10, 30g.
Veteran Cars. Postage 25, 50c., 1, 2, 3, 4, 5g.; Air 5, 10, 30g.
"Brasiliana '83" International Stamp Exhibition and 52nd F.I.P. Congress (1st issue). 1982 World Cup (4th issue) stamps optd. Postage 25, 50c., 1, 2, 3, 4g.
"Brasiliana '83" International Stamp Exhibition and 52nd F.I.P. Congress (2nd issue). 1982 Raphael/Christmas stamps optd. Postage 25, 50c., 1, 2, 3, 4g.
Aircraft Carriers. Postage 25, 50c., 1, 2, 3, 4, 5g.
South American Flowers. Air 5, 10, 30g.
South American Birds. Postage 25, 50c., 1, 2, 3, 4, 5g.
25th Anniv of International Maritime Organization. Air 5, 10, 30g.
"Philatelia '83" International Stamp Exhibition, Dusseldorf. 1983 International Railway Congress stamps optd. Postage 25, 50c., 1, 2, 3, 4g.
"Exfivia - 83" International Stamp Exn, Bolivia. 1982 Durer paintings optd. Postage 25, 50c., 1, 2, 3, 4g.
Flowers, Postage 10, 25g.; Chaco soldier, Postage 50g.; Dams, Postage 75g; Air 100g.; President, Air 200g.

1984

Bicent of Manned Flight. Postage 25, 50c., 1, 2, 3, 4, 5g.
World Communications Year. Air 5, 10, 30g.
Dogs. Postage 25, 50c., 1, 2, 3, 4, 5g.
Olympic Games, Los Angeles. Air 5, 10, 30g.
Animals. Postage 10, 25, 50, 75g.
1983 Anniversaries. Air 100g. (birth bicentenary of Bolivar), 200g. (76th anniv of boy scout movement).
Christmas (1983) and New Year. Postage 25, 50c., 1, 2, 3, 4, 5g.
Winter Olympic Games, Sarajevo. Air 5, 10, 30g.
Troubador Knights. Postage 25, 50c., 1, 2, 3, 4, 5g.
World Cup Football Championship, Spain (1982) and Mexico (1986). Air 5, 10, 30g.
International Stamp Fair, Essen. 1983 Racing Cars stamps optd. Postage 25, 50c., 1, 2, 3, 4g.
Extinct Animals. Postage 25, 50c., 1, 2, 3, 4, 5g.
60th Anniv of International Chess Federation. Air 5, 10, 30g.
19th Universal Postal Union Congress Stamp Exhibition, Hamburg (1st issue). Sailing Ships. Postage 25, 50c., 1, 2, 3, 4, 5g.
19th Universal Postal Union Congress Stamp Exhibition, Hamburg (2nd issue). Troubadour Knights stamp optd. Postage 5g.
Leaders of the World. British Railway Locomotives. Postage 25, 50c., 1, 2, 3, 4, 5g.
50th Anniv of First Lufthansa Europe–South America Direct Mail Flight. Air 5, 10, 30g.
30th Anniv of Presidency of Alfredo Stroessner. Dam stamp optd. Air 100g.
"Ausipex 84" International Stamp Exhibition, Melbourne. 1974 U.P.U. Centenary stamps optd. Postage 10, 15, 20, 25, 30, 50, 75c.
"Phila Korea 1984" International Stamp Exhibition, Seoul. Olympic Games, Los Angeles, and Extinct Animals stamps optd. Postage 5g.; Air 30g.
German National Football Championship and Sindelfingen Stamp Bourse. 1974 World Cup stamps (1st issue) optd. Postage 10, 15, 20, 25, 30, 50, 75c.
Cats. Postage 25, 50c., 1, 2, 3, 4, 5g.
Winter Olympic Games Medal Winners. Air 5, 10, 30g.
Centenary of Motor Cycle. Air 5, 10, 30g.

1985

Olympic Games Medal Winners. Postage 25, 50c., 1, 2, 3, 4, 5g.
Christmas (1984). Costumes. Air 5, 10, 30g.
Fungi. Postage 25, 50c., 1, 2, 3, 4, 5g.
Participation of Paraguay in Preliminary Rounds of World Cup Football Championship. Air 5, 10, 30g.
"Interpex 1985" and "Stampex 1985" Stamp Exhibitions. 1981 Queen Mother's Birthday stamp optd. Postage 10g.×2.
International Federation of Aero-Philatelic Societies Congress, Stuttgart. 1984 Lufthansa Europe–South America Mail Flight stamp optd. Air 10g.
Paraguayan Animals and Extinct Animals. Postage 25, 50c., 1, 2, 3, 4, 5g.
"Olymphilex 85" Olympic Stamps Exhibition, Lausanne. 1984 Winter Olympics Games Medal Winners stamp optd. Postage 10g.
"Israphil 85" International Stamp Exhibition, Tel Aviv. 1982 Boy Scout Movement stamp optd. Postage 5g.
Music Year. Air 5, 10, 30g.
Birth Bicentenary of John J. Audubon (ornithologist). Birds. Postage 25, 50c., 1, 2, 3, 4, 5g.
Railway Locomotives. Air 5, 10, 30g.
"Italia '85" International Stamp Exhibition, Rome (1st issue). 1983 Pope John Paul II stamp optd. Postage 5g.
50th Anniv of Chaco Peace (1st issue). 1972 Visit of Argentine President stamp optd. Postage 30c.
"Mophila 85" Stamp Exhibition, Hamburg. 1984 U.P.U. Congress Stamp Exhibition (1st issue) stamp optd. Postage 5g.
"Lupo 85" Stamp Exhibition, Lucerne. 1984 Bicentenary of Manned Flight stamp optd. Postage 5g.
"Expo 85" World's Fair, Tsukuba. 1981 "Philatokyo '81" stamp optd. Air 30g.
International Youth Year. Mark Twain. Postage 25, 50c., 1, 2, 3, 4, 5g.
75th Death Anniv of Henri Dunant (founder of Red Cross). Air 5, 10, 30g.
150th Anniv of German Railways (1st issue). Postage 25, 50c., 1, 2, 3, 4, 5g.
International Chess Federation Congress, Graz. Air 5, 10, 30g.
50th Anniv of Chaco Peace (2nd issue) and Government Achievements. Postage 10, 25, 50, 75g.; Air 100, 200g.
Paintings by Rubens. Postage 25, 50c., 1, 2, 3, 4, 5g.
Explorers and their Ships. Air 5, 10, 30g.
"Italia '85" International Stamp Exhibition, Rome (2nd issue). Paintings. Air 5, 10, 30g.

1986

Paintings by Titian. Postage 25, 50c., 1, 2, 3, 4, 5g.
International Stamp Fair, Essen. 1985 German Railways stamps optd. Postage 25, 50c., 1, 2, 3, 4g.
Fungi. Postage 25, 50c., 1, 2, 3, 4, 5g.
"Ameripex '86" International Stamp Exhibition, Chicago. Air 5, 10, 30g.
Lawn Tennis (1st issue). Inscriptions in black or red. Air 5, 10, 30g.
Centenary of Motor Car. Postage 25, 50c., 1, 2, 3, 4, 5g.
Appearance of Halley's Comet. Air 5, 10, 30g.
Qualification of Paraguay for World Cup Football Championship Final Rounds, Mexico (1st issue). Postage 25, 50c., 1, 2, 3, 4, 5g.
Tenth Pan-American Games, Indianapolis (1987). 1985 Olympic Games Medal Winners stamp optd. Postage 5g.
Maybach Cars. Postage 25, 50c., 1, 2, 3, 4, 5g.
Freight Trains. Air 5, 10, 30g.
Qualification of Paraguay for World Cup Football Championship Final Rounds (2nd issue). Air 5, 10, 30g.
Winter Olympic Games, Calgary (1988) (1st issue). 1983 Winter Olympic Games stamp optd. Postage 5g.
Centenary of Statue of Liberty. Postage 25, 50c., 1, 2, 3, 4, 5g.
Dogs. Postage 25, 50c., 1, 2, 3, 4, 5g.
150th Anniv of German Railways (2nd issue). Air 5, 10, 30g.
Lawn Tennis (2nd issue). Postage 25, 50c., 1, 2, 3, 4, 5g.
Visit of Prince Hitachi of Japan. 1972 Visit of President of Paraguay to Japan stamps optd. Postage 10, 15, 20, 25, 30, 50, 75c.
International Peace Year. Paintings by Rubens. Air 5, 10, 30g.
Olympic Games, Seoul (1988) (1st issue). Postage 25, 50c., 1, 2, 3, 4, 5g.
27th Chess Olympiad, Dubai. 1982 Chess Paintings stamp optd. Air 10g.

1987

World Cup Football Championship, Mexico (1986) and Italy (1990). Air 5, 10, 20, 25, 30g.
12th Spanish American Stamp and Coin Exhibition, Madrid, and 500th Anniv of Discovery of America by Columbus. 1975 South American Fauna and 1983 25th Anniv of I.M.O. stamps optd. Postage 15, 20, 25, 35, 40g.; Air 10g.
Tennis as Olympic Sport. 1986 Lawn Tennis (1st issue) stamps optd. Air 10, 30g.
Olympic Games, Barcelona (1992). 1985 Olympic Games Medal Winners stamps optd. Postage 25, 50c., 1, 2, 3, 4g.
"Olymphilex '87" Olympic Stamps Exhibition, Rome. 1985 Olympic Games Medal Winners stamp optd. Postage 5g.
Cats. Postage 1, 2, 3, 5, 60g.
Paintings by Rubens (1st issue). Postage 1, 2, 3, 5, 60g.
Saloon Cars. Air 5, 10, 20, 25, 30g.
National Topics. Postage 10g. (steel plant), 25g. (Franciscan monk), 50g. (400th anniv of Ita and Yaguaron), 75g. (450th Anniv of Asuncion); Air 100g. (airliner), 200g. (Pres. Stroessner).
"Capex 87" International Stamp Exhibition, Toronto. Cats stamps optd. Postage 1, 2, 3, 5g.
500th Anniv of Discovery of America by Columbus. Postage 1, 2, 3, 5, 60g.
Winter Olympic Games, Calgary (1988) (2nd issue). Air 5, 10, 20, 25, 30g.
Centenary of Colorado Party. National Topics and 1978 Pres. Stroessner stamps optd. Air 200, 1000g.
750th Anniv of Berlin (1st issue) and "Luposta '87" Air Stamps Exhibition, Berlin. Postage 1, 2, 3, 5, 60g.
Olympic Games, Seoul (1988) (2nd issue). Air 5, 10, 20, 25, 30g.
Rally Cars. Postage 1, 2, 3, 5, 60g.
"Exfivia 87" Stamp Exhibition, Bolivia. National Topics stamps optd. Postage 75g.; Air 100g.
"Olymphilex '88" Olympic Stamps Exhibition, Seoul. 1986 Olympic Games, Seoul (1st issue) stamps optd. Postage 2, 3, 4, 5g.
"Philatelia '87" International Stamp Exhibition, Cologne. 1986 Lawn Tennis (2nd issue) stamps optd. Postage 25, 50c., 1, 2, 3, 4g.
Italy–Argentina Match at Zurich to Launch 1990 World Cup Football Championship, Italy. 1986 Paraguay Qualification (2nd issue) stamps optd. Air 10, 30g.
"Exfilna '87" Stamp Exhibition, Gerona. 1986 Olympic Games, Seoul (1st issue) stamps optd. Postage 25, 50c.
Spanish Ships. Postage 1, 2, 3, 5, 60g.
Paintings by Rubens (2nd issue). Air 5, 10, 20, 25, 30g.
Christmas. Air 5, 10, 20, 25, 30g.
Winter Olympic Games, Calgary (1988) (3rd issue). Postage 1, 2, 3, 5, 60g.

1988

150th Anniv of Austrian Railways. Air 5, 10, 20, 25, 30g.
"Aeropex 88" Air Stamps Exhibition, Adelaide, 1987. 750th Anniv of Berlin and "Luposta '87" stamps optd. Postage 1, 2, 3, 5g.
"Olympex" Stamp Exhibition, Calgary. 1987 Winter Olympic Games (3rd issue) stamps optd. Postage 1, 2, 3g.
Olympic Games, Seoul (3rd issue). Equestrian Events. Postage 1, 2, 3, 5, 60g.
Space Projects. Air 5, 10, 20, 25, 30g.
750th Anniv of Berlin (2nd issue). Paintings. Postage 1, 2, 3, 5, 60g.
Visit of Pope John Paul II. Postage 1, 2, 3, 5, 60g.
"Lupo Wien 88" Stamp Exhibition, Vienna. 1987 National Topics stamp optd. Air 100g.
World Wildlife Fund. Extinct Animals. Postage 1, 2, 3, 5g.
Paintings in West Berlin State Museum. Air 5, 10, 20, 25, 30g.
Bicentenary of Australian Settlement. 1981 Wedding of Prince of Wales (1st issue) optd. Postage 25, 50c., 1, 2g.
History of World Cup Football Championship (1st issue). Air 5, 10, 20, 25, 30g.
New Presidential Period, 1988–1993. 1985 Chaco Peace and Government Achievements issue optd. Postage 10, 25, 50, 75g.; Air 100, 200g.
Olympic Games, Seoul (4th issue). Lawn Tennis and Medal. Postage 1, 2, 3, 5, 60g.
Calgary Winter Olympics Gold Medal Winners. Air 5, 10, 20, 25, 30g.
History of World Cup Football Championship (2nd issue). Air 5, 10, 20, 25, 30g.
"Prenfil '88" International Philatelic Press Exhibition, Buenos Aires. "Ameripex '86" stamp optd. Air 30g.
"Philexfrance 89" International Stamp Exhibition, Paris. 1985 Explorers stamp optd. Air 30g.

Pt. 8

PARMA

A former Grand Duchy of N. Italy, united with Sardinia in 1860 and now part of Italy.

100 centesimi = 1 lira.

1 Bourbon "fleur-de-lis"

1852. Imperf.

2	1	5c. black on yellow	£150	£170
11	1	5c. yellow	£9000	£850
4	1	10c. black	£150	£170
5	1	15c. black on pink	£4250	80·00
13	1	15c. red	£12000	£250
7	1	25c. black on purple	£18000	£275
14	1	25c. brown	£12000	£475
9	1	40c. black on blue	£2750	£450

2

1857. Imperf.

17	2	15c. red	£425	£425
19	2	25c. purple	£700	£225
20	2	40c. blue	£120	£650

3

1859. Imperf.

28	3	5c. green	£3250	£4500
29	3	10c. brown	£1400	£850
32	3	20c. blue	£1400	£250
33	3	40c. red	£800	£9500
35	3	80c. yellow	£8500	

NEWSPAPER STAMPS

1853. As T 3. Imperf.

N1	6c. black on pink	£2250	£475
N3	9c. black on blue	£1300	£28000

Pt. 1

PATIALA

A "convention" state in the Punjab, India.

12 pies = 1 anna; 16 annas = 1 rupee.

1884. Stamps of India (Queen Victoria) with curved opt PUTTIALLA STATE vert.

1	23	½a. turquoise	5·00	4·75
2	-	1a. purple	65·00	90·00
3	-	2a. blue	15·00	16·00
4	-	4a. green (No. 96)	£110	£130
5	-	8a. mauve	£500	£1400
6	-	1r. grey (No. 101)	£170	£800

1885. Stamps of India (Queen Victoria) optd PUTTIALLA STATE horiz.

7	23	½a. turquoise	3·00	30
11	-	1a. purple	75	30
8	-	2a. blue	13·00	1·75
9	-	4a. green (No. 96)	5·50	4·25
12	-	8a. mauve	40·00	80·00
10	-	1r. grey (No. 101)	30·00	£100

Stamps of India optd PATIALA STATE.

1891. Queen Victoria.

32	40	3p. red	30	15
13	23	½a. turquoise (No. 84)	75	10
33	-	½a. green (No. 114)	1·00	75
14	-	9p. red	1·00	2·25
15	-	1a. purple	1·40	30
34	-	1a. red	2·50	2·25
17	-	1a.6p. brown	2·00	2·25
18	-	2a. blue	2·50	30
20	-	3a. orange	3·00	75
21	-	4a. green (No. 95)	4·00	1·00
23	-	6a. brown (No. 80)	3·50	15·00
26	-	8a. mauve	5·50	16·00
27	-	12a. purple on red	4·00	16·00
28	37	1r. green and red	8·00	60·00
29	38	2r. red and orange	£180	£1100
30	38	3r. brown and green	£225	£1200
31	38	5r. blue and violet	£275	£1200

1903. King Edward VII.

35	3p. grey	40	10
37	½a. green (No. 122)	1·10	15
38	1a. red (No. 123)	2·50	10
39	2a. lilac	2·50	65
40	3a. orange	2·00	35
41	4a. olive	3·75	1·50
42	6a. bistre	4·50	13·00
43	8a. mauve	4·25	3·00
44	12a. purple on red	10·00	32·00
45	1r. green and red	6·00	7·00

1912. King Edward VII. Inscr "INDIA POSTAGE & REVENUE".

46	½a. green (No. 149)	40	25
47	1a. red (No. 150)	1·75	1·00

1912. King George V. Optd in two lines.

48	55	3p. grey	25	10
49	56	½a. green	1·00	20
50	57	1a. red	1·75	20
61	57	1a. brown	2·75	50
51	58	1½a. brown (A)	50	55
52	59	2a. purple	1·75	1·50
53	62	3a. orange	3·00	2·00
62	62	3a. blue	3·75	12·00
54	63	4a. olive	4·00	3·50
55	64	6a. ochre	3·00	4·50
56	65	8a. mauve	4·00	3·75
57	66	12a. red	5·00	10·00
58	67	1r. brown and green	13·00	18·00
59	67	2r. red and brown	16·00	£160
60	67	5r. blue and violet	45·00	£275

1928. King George V. Optd in one line.

63	55	3p. grey	2·00	10
64	56	½a. green	25	10
75	79	½a. green	1·00	30
65	80	9p. green	2·25	1·00
66	57	1a. brown	75	25
76	81	1a. brown	1·10	20
67	82	1a.3p. mauve	3·25	15
68	70	2a. lilac	1·75	40
77	59	2a. red	40	1·50
69	61	2a.6p. orange	6·00	3·50
70	62	3a. blue	3·25	3·00
78w	62	3a. red	5·50	11·00
71	71	4a. green	7·00	2·25
79	63	4a. olive	2·00	3·50
72	65	8a. mauve	9·00	4·25
73	66	1r. brown and green	8·00	13·00
74w	66	2r. red and orange	12·00	70·00

1937. King George VI. Optd in one line.

80	91	3p. grey	18·00	35
81	91	½a. brown	8·00	50
82	91	9p. green	5·00	1·00
83	91	1a. red	2·75	20
84	92	2a. red	1·75	12·00
85	-	2a.6p. violet	8·00	28·00
86	-	3a. green	9·50	12·00
87	-	3a.6p. blue	9·00	32·00
88	-	4a. brown	26·00	21·00
89	-	6a. green	32·00	75·00
90	-	8a. violet	35·00	55·00
91	-	12a. red	30·00	85·00
92	93	1r. grey and brown	35·00	50·00
93	93	2r. purple and brown	35·00	£140
94	93	5r. green and blue	42·00	£325
95	93	10r. purple and red	65·00	£475
96	93	15r. brown and green	£170	£800
97	93	25r. grey and purple	£180	£800

1943. King George VI. Optd PATIALA only. (a) Issue of 1938.

98	94	3p. grey	18·00	3·25
99	94	½a. brown	6·50	2·75
100	94	9p. green	£450	12·00
101	94	1a. red	32·00	3·00
102	93	1r. grey and brown	18·00	80·00

(b) Issue of 1940.

103	92	3p. grey	3·00	15
104	92	½a. mauve	4·00	15
105	92	9p. green	1·75	15
106	92	1a. red	3·00	10
107	101	1a.3p. bistre	1·75	4·00
108a	101	1½a. violet	14·00	6·00
109	101	2a. red	8·00	50
110	101	3a. violet	8·00	3·25
111	101	3½a. blue	19·00	45·00
112	102	4a. brown	13·00	4·75
113	102	6a. green	6·00	38·00
114	102	8a. violet	5·00	15·00
115	102	12a. purple	35·00	£100

OFFICIAL STAMPS

Overprinted SERVICE.

1884. Nos. 1 to 3 (Queen Victoria).

O1	23	½a. turquoise	24·00	40
O2	-	1a. purple	1·00	10
O3	-	2a. blue	£6500	£130

1885. Nos. 7, 11 and 8 (Queen Victoria).

O6	23	½a. turquoise	2·00	10
O5	-	1a. purple	2·25	10
O7	-	2a. blue	1·00	40

1891. Nos. 13 to 28 and No. 10 (Queen Victoria).

O8	23	½a. turquoise (No. 13)	75	10
O9	-	1a. purple	7·50	10
O20	-	1a. red	1·50	10
O10a	-	2a. blue	4·00	3·25
O12	-	3a. orange	3·50	4·00
O13a	-	4a. green	3·25	30
O15	-	6a. brown	2·50	35
O16	-	8a. mauve	4·25	1·75
O18	-	12a. purple on red	3·25	60
O19	-	1r. grey	3·25	65
O21	37	1r. green and red	6·50	10·00

1903. Nos. 36 to 45 (King Edward VII).

O22	3p. grey	50	10
O24	½a. green	1·00	10
O25	1a. red	60	10
O26	2a. lilac	80	25
O28	3a. brown	4·50	3·50
O29	4a. olive	3·50	20
O30	8a. mauve	2·25	75
O32	1r. green and red	2·50	80

1907. Nos. 46/7 (King Edward VII). Inscr "INDIA POSTAGE & REVENUE".

O33	½a. green	50	20
O34	1a. red	75	10

1913. Official stamps of India (King George V). Optd PATIALA STATE in two lines.

O35	**55**	3p. grey	10	20
O36	**56**	½a. green	10	10
O37	**57**	1a. red	10	10
O38	**57**	1a. brown	8·00	1·00
O39	**59**	2a. mauve	1·00	1·00
O40	**63**	4a. olive	50	35
O41	**64**	6a. bistre	2·25	2·50
O42	**65**	8a. mauve	55	70
O43	**67**	1r. brown and green	1·40	1·40
O44	**67**	2r. red and brown	20·00	55·00
O45	**67**	5r. blue and violet	18·00	28·00

1927. Postage stamps of India (King George V) optd PATIALA STATE SERVICE in two lines.

O47	**55**	3p. grey	10	10
O48	**56**	½a. green	1·00	55
O58	**79**	½a. green	10	10
O49	**57**	1a. brown	15	10
O59	**81**	1a. brown	35	30
O50	**82**	1a.3p. mauve	40	10
O51	**70**	2a. purple	30	30
O52	**70**	2a. red	30	35
O60	**59**	2a. red	15	30
O53w	**61**	2½a. orange	1·50	80
O54	**71**	4a. green	50	30
O62	**63**	4a. olive	3·75	1·75
O55w	**65**	8a. purple	1·25	80
O56w	**66**	1r. brown and green	2·75	3·50
O57	**66**	2r. red and orange	17·00	50·00

1938. Postage stamps of India (King George VI) optd PATIALA STATE SERVICE.

O63	**91**	½a. brown	1·00	20
O64	**91**	9p. green	14·00	80·00
O65	**91**	1a. red	1·00	40
O66	**93**	1r. grey and brown	1·00	9·00
O67	**93**	2r. purple and green	8·50	5·00
O68	**93**	5r. green and blue	18·00	80·00

1939. Surch 1A SERVICE 1A.

O69w	**82**	1a. on 1¼a. mauve	11·00	3·25

1940. Official stamps of India optd PATIALA.

O71	**O20**	3p. grey	1·75	10
O72	**O20**	½a. brown	5·00	10
O73	**O20**	½a. purple	1·25	10
O74	**O20**	9p. green	1·60	50
O75	**O20**	1a. red	3·50	10
O76	**O20**	1a.3p. bistre	1·40	25
O77	**O20**	1½a. violet	8·00	1·50
O78	**O20**	2a. orange	10·00	35
O79	**O20**	2½a. violet	4·00	1·00
O80	**O20**	4a. brown	2·00	2·50
O81	**O20**	8a. violet	7·50	6·00

1940. Postage stamps of India (King George VI) optd PATIALA SERVICE.

O82	**93**	1r. slate and brown	5·00	11·00
O83	**93**	2r. purple and brown	15·00	80·00
O84	**93**	5r. green and blue	26·00	95·00

Pt. 1

PENANG

A British Settlement which became a state of the Federation of Malaya, incorporated in Malaysia in 1963.

100 cents = 1 dollar (Straits or Malayan).

1948. Silver Wedding. As T 4b/c of Pitcairn Islands.

1	10c. violet	30	20
2	$5 brown	38·00	38·00

1949. As Nos. 278/92 of Straits Settlement.

3	1c. black	1·75	20
4	2c. orange	1·50	20
5	3c. green	60	1·00
6	4c. brown	50	10
7	5c. purple	4·75	3·75
8	6c. grey	2·00	20
9	8c. red	1·25	5·50
10	8c. green	5·00	3·25
11	10c. mauve	50	10
12	12c. red	5·00	10·00
13	15c. blue	2·00	30
14	20c. black and green	3·00	1·50
15	20c. blue	4·00	1·25
16	25c. purple and orange	3·25	1·50
17	35c. red and purple	4·50	1·25
18	40c. red and purple	4·75	16·00
19	50c. black and blue	6·00	20
20	$1 blue and purple	20·00	3·25
21	$2 green and red	23·00	2·00
22	$3 green and brown	48·00	3·00

1949. U.P.U. As T 4d/g of of Pitcairn Islands.

23	10c. purple	20	10
24	15c. blue	2·50	3·75
25	25c. orange	45	3·75
26	30c. black	1·50	3·50

1953. Coronation. As T 4h of Pitcairn Islands.

27	10c. black and purple	2·00	10

1954. As T 1 of Malacca, but inscr "PENANG".

28	1c. black	10	70
29	2c. orange	50	30
30	4c. brown	2·00	10
31	5c. mauve	2·00	4·50
32	6c. grey	20	80
33	8c. green	40	3·50
34	10c. purple	20	10
35	12c. red	40	3·50
36	20c. blue	50	10
37	25c. purple and orange	40	10
38	30c. red and purple	40	10
39	35c. red and purple	70	60
40	50c. black and blue	75	10
41	$1 blue and purple	3·00	30
42	$2 green and red	17·00	3·75
43	$5 green and brown	48·00	3·75

1957. As Nos. 92/102 of Kedah, but inset portrait of Queen Elizabeth II.

44	1c. black	10	1·50
45	2c. red	10	1·00
46	4c. sepia	10	10
47	5c. lake	10	30
48	8c. green	3·00	2·25
49	10c. brown	30	10
50	20c. blue	1·00	40
51	50c. black and blue	2·00	70
52	$1 blue and purple	9·50	1·00
53	$2 green and red	21·00	18·00
54	$5 brown and green	26·00	14·00

1 Copra

1960. As Nos. 44/54, but with inset Arms of Penang as in T 1.

55	1c. black	10	1·60
56	2c. red	10	1·60
57	4c. brown	10	10
58	5c. lake	10	10
59	8c. green	2·75	4·50
60	10c. purple	30	10
61	20c. blue	55	10
62	50c. black and blue	30	30
63	$1 blue and purple	7·50	1·75
64	$2 green and red	10·00	8·50
65	$5 brown and green	14·00	8·50

2 "Vanda hookeriana"

1965. As Nos. 115/21 of Kedah, but with Arms of Penang inset and inscr "PULAU PINANG" as in T 2.

66	**2**	1c. multicoloured	10	1·25
67	-	2c. multicoloured	10	1·25
68	-	5c. multicoloured	55	10
69	-	6c. multicoloured	30	1·25
70	-	10c. multicoloured	20	10
71	-	15c. multicoloured	1·00	10
72	-	20c. multicoloured	1·60	30

The higher values used in Penang were Nos. 20/7 of Malaysia (National Issues).

3 "Valeria valeria"

1971. Butterflies. As Nos. 124/30 of Kedah but with Arms of Penang inset and inscr "pulau pinang" as in T 3.

75		1c. multicoloured	40	2·00
76		2c. multicoloured	70	2·00
77		5c. multicoloured	1·50	40
78		6c. multicoloured	1·50	2·00
79		10c. multicoloured	1·50	15
80		15c. multicoloured	1·50	10
81	**3**	20c. multicoloured	1·75	60

The higher values in use with this issue were Nos. 64/71 of Malaysia (National Issues).

4 "Etlingera elatior" (inscr "Phaeomeria speciosa")

1979. Flowers. As Nos. 135/41 of Kedah, but with Arms of Penang and inscr "pulau pinaug" as in T 4.

86	1c. "Rafflesia hasseltii"	10	1·00
87	2c. "Pterocarpus indicus"	10	1·00
88	5c. "Lagerstroemia speciosa"	10	35
89	10c. "Durio zibethinus"	15	10
90	15c. "Hibiscus rosa-sinensis"	15	10
91	20c. "Rhododendron scorte-chinii"	20	10
92	25c. Type **4**	40	30

1986. As Nos. 152/8 of Kedah but with Arms of Penang and inscr "PULAU PINANG" as in T 5.

100	1c. Coffee	10	30
101	2c. Coconuts	10	35
102	5c. Type **5**	15	10
103	10c. Black pepper	15	10
104	15c. Rubber	25	10
105	20c. Oil palm	25	15
106	30c. Rice	30	15

2003. As T 5 but redenominated in 'sen'. Multicoloured.

107	30s. Rice	1·75	10

6 *Nelumbium nelumbo* (sacred lotus)

2007. Garden Flowers. As Nos. 210/15 of Johore, but with Arms of Penang as in T 6. Multicoloured.

108	5s. Type **6**	10	10
109	10s. *Hydrangea macrophylla*	15	10
110	20s. *Hippeastrum reticulatum*	25	15
111	30s. *Bougainvillea*	40	20
112	40s. *Ipomoea indica*	50	30
113	50s. *Hibiscus rosa-sinensis*	65	35
MS114	100×85 mm.Nos. 108/13	2·10	1·25

Pt. 1

PENRHYN ISLAND

One of the Cook Islands in the South Pacific. A dependency of New Zealand. Used Cook Islands stamps until 1973 when further issues for use in the Northern group of the Cook Islands issues appeared.

A. NEW ZEALAND DEPENDENCY

1902. Stamps of New Zealand (Pictorials) surch PENRHYN ISLAND. and value in native language.

4	**23**	½d. green	80	11·00
10	**42**	1d. red	1·25	7·50
1	**26**	2½d. blue (No. 249)	8·00	9·00
14	**28**	3d. brown	10·00	32·00
15	**31**	6d. red	15·00	48·00
16a	**34**	1s. orange	42·00	42·00

1914. Stamps of New Zealand (King Edward VII) surch PENRHYN ISLAND. and value in native language.

19	**51**	½d. green	80	9·50
22	**51**	6d. red	23·00	75·00
23	**51**	1s. orange	42·00	£100

1917. Stamps of New Zealand (King George V) optd PENRHYN ISLAND.

28	**62**	½d. green	1·00	2·00
29	**62**	1½d. grey	6·50	24·00
30	**62**	1½d. brown	60	24·00
24a	**62**	2½d. blue	2·00	9·00
31	**62**	3d. brown	4·00	35·00
26a	**62**	6d. red	5·00	21·00
27a	**62**	1s. orange	12·00	35·00

1920. Pictorial types as Cook Islands (1920), but inscr "PENRHYN".

32	**9**	½d. black and green	1·00	22·00
33	-	1d. black and red	1·50	15·00
34	-	1½d. black and violet	6·50	19·00
40	-	2½d. brown and black	10·00	38·00
35	-	3d. black and red	2·50	12·00
36	-	6d. brown and red	3·25	20·00
37	-	1s. black and blue	10·00	26·00

B. PART OF COOK ISLANDS

1973. Nos. 228/9, 231, 233/6, 239/40 and 243/5 of Cook Is. optd PENRHYN NORTHERN or PENRHYN ($1, 2).

41B	1c. multicoloured	10	10
42B	2c. multicoloured	10	10
43B	3c. multicoloured	20	10
44B	4c. multicoloured	10	10
45B	5c. multicoloured	10	10
46B	6c. multicoloured	15	30
47B	8c. multicoloured	20	40
48B	15c. multicoloured	30	50
49B	20c. multicoloured	1·50	80
50B	50c. multicoloured	50	1·75
51B	$1 multicoloured	50	2·00
52B	$2 multicoloured	50	2·25

1973. Nos. 450/2 of Cook Is. optd PENRHYN NORTHERN.

53	**138**	25c. multicoloured	30	20
54	-	30c. multicoloured	30	20
55	-	50c. multicoloured	30	20

10 "Ostracion sp."

1974. Fishes. Multicoloured.

56	½c. Type **10**	50	75
57	1c. "Monodactylus argenteus"	70	75
58	2c. "Pomacanthus imperator"	80	75
59	3c. "Chelmon rostratus"	80	50
60	4c. "Chaetodon ornatissimus"	80	50
61	5c. "Chaetodon melanotus"	80	50
62	8c. "Chaetodon raffessi"	80	50
63	10c. "Chaetodon ephippium"	85	50
64	20c. "Pygoplites diacanthus"	1·75	50
65	25c. "Heniochus acuminatus"	1·75	50
66	60c. "Plectorhynchus chaetodonoides"	2·50	90
67	$1 "Balistipus undulatus"	3·25	1·25
68	$2 Bird's-eye view of Penrhyn	3·00	12·00
69	$5 Satellite view of Australasia	3·00	5·00

Nos. 68/9 are size 63×25 mm.

11 Penrhyn Stamps of 1902

1974. Cent of Universal Postal Union. Mult.

70	25c. Type **11**	20	45
71	50c. Stamps of 1920	35	55

12 "Adoration of the Kings" (Memling)

1974. Christmas. Multicoloured.

72	5c. Type **12**	20	30
73	10c. "Adoration of the Shepherds" (Hugo van der Goes)	25	30
74	25c. "Adoration of the Magi" (Rubens)	40	45
75	30c. "The Holy Family" (Borgianni)	45	65

13 Churchill giving "V" sign

1974. Birth Cent of Sir Winston Churchill.

76	**13**	30c. brown and gold	35	85
77	-	50c. green and gold	45	90

DESIGN: 50c. Full-face portrait.

1975. "Apollo–Soyuz" Space Project. Optd KIA ORANA ASTRONAUTS and emblem.

78	$5 Satellite view of Australasia	1·50	2·50

15 "Virgin and Child" (Bouts)

1975. Christmas. Paintings of the "Virgin and Child" by artists given below. Multicoloured.

79	7c. Type **15**	40	10
80	15c. Leonardo da Vinci	70	20
81	35c. Raphael	1·10	35

16 "Pieta"

1976. Easter. 500th Birth Anniv of Michelangelo.

82	**16**	15c. brown and gold	25	15
83	-	20c. lilac and gold	30	15
84	-	35c. green and gold	40	20
MS85		112×72 mm. Nos. 82/4	85	1·25

DESIGNS: Nos. 83/4 show different views of the "Pieta".

17 "Washington crossing the Delaware" (E. Leutze)

1976. Bicentenary of American Revolution.

86	**17**	30c. multicoloured	25	15
87	-	30c. multicoloured	25	15
88	-	30c. multicoloured	25	15
89	-	50c. multicoloured	30	20
90	-	50c. multicoloured	30	20
91	-	50c. multicoloured	30	20
MS92		103×103 mm. Nos. 86/91	1·25	1·25

DESIGNS: Nos. 86/88, "Washington crossing the Delaware" (E. Leutze); Nos. 89/91, "The Spirit of '76" (A. M. Willard).

Nos. 86/88 and 89/91 were each printed together, se-tenant, forming a composite design of the complete painting. Type **17** shows the left-hand stamp of the 30c. design.

18 Running

1976. Olympic Games, Montreal. Multicoloured.

93	25c. Type **18**	25	15
94	30c. Long jumping	30	15
95	75c. Throwing the javelin	55	25
MS96	86×128 mm. Nos. 93/5	1·10	2·00

19 "The Flight into Egypt"

1976. Christmas. Durer Engravings.

97	**19**	7c. black and silver	15	10
98	-	15c. blue and silver	25	15
99	-	35c. violet and silver	35	25

DESIGNS: 15c. "Adoration of the Magi"; 35c. "The Nativity".

20 The Queen in Coronation Robes

1977. Silver Jubilee. Multicoloured.

100	50c. Type **20**	25	60
101	$1 The Queen and Prince Philip	35	65
102	$2 Queen Elizabeth II	50	80
MS103	128×87 mm. Nos. 100/2	1·00	1·50

Stamps from the miniature sheet have silver borders.

21 "The Annunciation"

1977. Christmas. Illustrations by J. S. von Carolsfeld.

104	**21**	7c. brown, purple and gold	40	15
105	-	15c. red, purple and gold	60	15
106	-	35c. deep green, green and gold	1·00	30

DESIGNS: 15c. "The Announcement to the Shepherds"; 35c. "The Nativity".

22 Iiwi

1978. Bicentenary of Discovery of Hawaii. Birds and Artefacts. Multicoloured.

107	20c. Type **22**	80	30
108	20c. Elgin cloak	80	30
109	30c. Apapane	90	40
110	30c. Feather image of a god	90	40
111	35c. Moorhen	90	45
112	35c. Feather cape, helmet and staff	90	45
113	75c. Hawaii O-o	1·50	80
114	75c. Feather image and cloak	1·50	80
MS115	Two sheets, each 78×119 mm. containing. (a) Nos. 107, 109, 111, 113. (b) Nos. 108, 110, 112, 114	5·00	7·00

23 "The Road to Calvary"

1978. Easter. 400th Birth Anniv of Rubens. Multicoloured.

116	10c. Type **23**	20	10
117	15c. "Christ on the Cross"	25	15
118	35c. "Christ with Straw"	45	25
MS119	87×138 mm. Nos. 116/18	1·00	1·60

Stamps from No. **MS**119 are slightly larger (28×36 mm).

1978. Easter. Children's Charity. Designs as Nos. 116/18 in separate miniature sheets, 49×68 mm, each with a face value of 60c.+5c.

MS120	As Nos. 116/18. Set of 3 sheets	1·00	1·50

24 Royal Coat of Arms

1978. 25th Anniv of Coronation.

121	**24**	90c. black, gold and mauve	30	60
122	-	90c. multicoloured	30	60
123	-	90c. black, gold and green	30	60
MS124		75×122 mm. Nos. 121/3	1·10	2·00

DESIGNS: No. 122, Queen Elizabeth II; No. 123, New Zealand coat of arms.

25 "Madonna of the Pear"

1978. Christmas. 450th Death Anniv of Albrecht Durer. Multicoloured.

125	30c. Type **25**	65	30
126	35c. "The Virgin and Child with St. Anne" (Durer)	65	30
MS127	101×60 mm. Nos. 125/6	1·00	1·25

26 Sir Rowland Hill and G.B. Penny Black Stamp

1979. Death Centenary of Sir Rowland Hill. Mult.

128	75c. Type **26**	40	55
129	75c. 1974 U.P.U. Centenary 25c. and 50c. commemoratives	40	55
130	90c. Sir Rowland Hill	45	70
131	90c. 1978 Coronation Anniversary 90c. commemorative	45	70
MS132	116×58 mm. Nos. 128/31	1·25	1·50

Stamps from No. **MS**132 have cream backgrounds.

27 Max and Moritz

1979. International Year of the Child. Illustrations from "Max and Moritz" stories by Wilhelm Busch. Multicoloured.

133	12c. Type **27**	15	15
134	12c. Max and Moritz looking down chimney	15	15
135	12c. Max and Moritz making off with food	15	15
136	12c. Cook about to beat dog	15	15
137	15c. Max sawing through bridge	20	15
138	15c. Pursuer approaching bridge	20	15
139	15c. Collapse of bridge	20	15
140	15c. Pursuer in river	20	15
141	20c. Baker locking shop	20	20
142	20c. Max and Moritz emerge from hiding	20	20
143	20c. Max and Moritz falling in dough	20	20
144	20c. Max and Moritz made into buns	20	20

28 "Christ carrying Cross" (Book of Ferdinand II)

1980. Easter. Scenes from 15th-cent Prayer Books. Multicoloured.

145	12c. Type **28**	15	20
146	20c. "The Crucifixion" (William Vrelant, Book of Duke of Burgundy)	20	25
147	35c. "Descent from the Cross" (Book of Ferdinand II)	30	45
MS148	111×65 mm. Nos. 145/7	55	1·00

Stamps from No. **MS**148 have cream borders.

1980. Easter. Children's Charity. Designs as Nos. 145/7 in separate miniature sheets 54×85 mm, each with a face value of 70c.+5c.

MS149	As Nos. 145/7. Set of 3 sheets	75	1·00

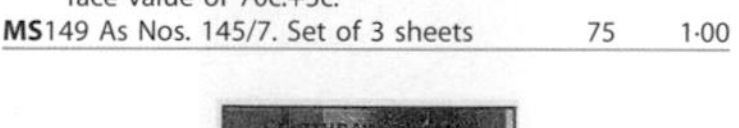

29 "Queen Elizabeth, 1937" (Sir Gerald Kelly)

1980. 80th Birthday of The Queen Mother.

150	**29** $1 multicoloured	1·00	1·25
MS151	55×84 mm. **29** $2.50 multicoloured	1·60	1·60

30 Falk Hoffman, East Germany (platform diving) (gold)

1980. Olympic Medal Winners. Multicoloured.

152	10c. Type **30**	30	10
153	10c. Martina Jaschke, East Germany (platform diving)	30	10
154	20c. Tomi Polkolainen, Finland (archery)	35	15
155	20c. Kete Losaberidse, U.S.S.R. (archery)	35	15
156	30c. Czechoslovakia (football)	35	20
157	30c. East Germany (football)	40	20
158	50c. Barbel Wockel, East Germany (200 m)	50	30
159	50c. Pietro Mennea, Italy (200 m)	50	30
MS160	150×106 mm. Nos. 152/9	1·40	1·75

Stamps from No. **MS**160 have gold borders.

31 "The Virgin of Counsellors" (Luis Dalmau)

1980. Christmas. Mult.

161	20c. Type **31**	15	15
162	35c. "Virgin and Child" (Serra brothers)	20	20
163	50c. "The Virgin of Albocacer" (Master of the Porciuncula)	30	30
MS164	135×75 mm. Nos. 161/3	1·50	1·50

1980. Christmas. Children's Charity. Design as Nos. 161/3 in separate miniature sheets, 54×77 mm, each with a face value of 70c.+5c.

MS165	As Nos. 161/3. Set of 3 sheets	1·00	1·50

32 Amatasi

1981. Sailing Craft and Ships (1st series). Mult.

166	1c. Type **32**	20	15
167	1c. Ndrua (canoe)	20	15
168	1c. Waka (canoe)	20	15
169	1c. Tongiaki (canoe)	20	15
170	3c. Va'a Teu'ua (canoe)	50	15
171	3c. "Vitoria" (Del Cano's ship)	50	15
172	3c. "Golden Hind" (Drake's ship)	50	15
173	3c. "La Boudeuse" (Bougainville's ship)	50	15
174	4c. H.M.S. "Bounty"	50	15
175	4c. "L'Astrolabe" (Dumont d'Urville's ship)	50	15
176	4c. "Star of India" (full-rigged ship)	50	15
177	4c. "Great Republic" (clipper)	50	15
178	6c. "Balcutha" (clipper)	50	20
179	6c. "Coonatto" (clipper)	50	20
180	6c. "Antiope" (clipper)	50	20
181	6c. "Taeping" (clipper)	50	20
182	10c. "Preussen" (full-rigged ship)	50	75
183	10c. "Pamir" (barque)	50	75
184	10c. "Cap Hornier" (full-rigged ship)	50	75
185	10c. "Patriarch" (clipper)	50	75
186	15c. Type **32**	50	85
187	15c. As No. 167	50	85
188	15c. As No. 168	50	85
189	15c. As No. 169	50	85
190	20c. As No. 170	50	85
191	20c. As No. 171	50	85
192	20c. As No. 172	50	85
193	20c. As No. 173	50	85
194	30c. As No. 174	50	95
195	30c. As No. 175	50	95
196	30c. As No. 176	50	95
197	30c. As No. 177	50	95
198	50c. As No. 178	1·00	1·75
199	50c. As No. 179	1·00	1·75
200	50c. As No. 180	1·00	1·75
201	50c. As No. 181	1·00	1·75
202	$1 As No. 182	2·50	1·50
203	$1 As No. 183	2·50	1·50
204	$1 As No. 184	2·50	1·50
205	$1 As No. 185	2·50	1·50
206	$2 "Cutty Sark" (clipper)	4·50	3·25
207	$4 "Mermerus" (clipper)	9·00	5·00
208	$6 H.M.S. "Resolution" and H.M.S. "Discovery" (Cook's ships)	15·00	12·00

Nos. 186/201 are 41×35 mm, Nos. 202/5 41×25 mm and Nos. 206/8 47×33 mm in size.

Nos. 181 and 201 are wrongly inscribed "TEAPING".

See also Nos. 337/55.

33 "Jesus at the Grove" (Veronese)

1981. Easter. Paintings. Multicoloured.

218	30c. Type **33**	40	20
219	40c. "Christ with Crown of Thorns" (Titian)	55	25
220	50c. "Pieta" (Van Dyck)	60	30
MS221	110×68 mm. Nos. 218/20	2·75	2·00

1981. Easter. Children's Charity. Designs as Nos. 218/20 in separate miniature sheets 70×86 mm, each with a face value of 70c.+5c.

MS222	As Nos. 218/20. Set of 3 sheets	1·00	1·50

34 Prince Charles as Young Child

1981. Royal Wedding. Multicoloured.

223	40c. Type **34**	15	35
224	50c. Prince Charles as schoolboy	15	40
225	60c. Prince Charles as young man	20	40
226	70c. Prince Charles in ceremonial Naval uniform	20	45
227	80c. Prince Charles as Colonel-in-Chief, Royal Regiment of Wales	20	45
MS228	99×89 mm. Nos. 223/7	1·00	2·00

1981. International Year for Disabled Persons. Nos. 223/7 surch +5c.

229	**34** 40c.+5c. multicoloured	15	50
230	- 50c.+5c. multicoloured	15	55
231	- 60c.+5c. multicoloured	20	55
232	- 70c.+5c. multicoloured	20	60
233	- 80c.+5c. multicoloured	20	65
MS234	99×89 mm. As Nos. 229/33, but 10c. premium on each stamp	80	2·50

35 Footballers

1981. World Cup Football Championship, Spain (1982). Multicoloured.

235	15c. Type **35**	20	15
236	15c. Footballer wearing orange jersey with black and mauve stripes	20	15
237	15c. Player in blue jersey	20	15
238	35c. Player in blue jersey	30	25
239	35c. Player in red jersey	30	25
240	35c. Player in yellow jersey with green stripes	30	25
241	50c. Player in orange jersey	40	35
242	50c. Player in mauve jersey	40	35
243	50c. Player in black jersey	40	35
MS244	113×151 mm. As Nos. 235/43, but each stamp with a premium of 3c.	4·75	2·50

36 "The Virgin on a Crescent"

1981. Christmas. Engravings by Durer.

245	**36** 30c. violet, purple and stone	90	1·00
246	- 40c. violet, purple and stone	1·25	1·40
247	- 50c. violet, purple and stone	1·50	1·75
MS248	134×75 mm. As Nos. 245/7, but each stamp with a premium of 2c.	2·00	2·25
MS249	Designs as Nos. 245/7 in separate miniature sheets, 58×85 mm, each with a face value of 70c.+5c. Set of 3 sheets	1·50	1·75

DESIGNS: 40c. "The Virgin at the Fence"; 50c. "The Holy Virgin and Child".

37 Lady Diana Spencer as Baby

1982. 21st Birthday of Princess of Wales. Multicoloured.

250	30c. Type **37**	30	30
251	50c. As young child	40	45
252	70c. As schoolgirl	60	60
253	80c. As teenager	70	80
254	$1.40 As a young lady	1·10	1·25
MS255	87×110 mm. Nos. 250/4	6·50	3·50

1982. Birth of Prince William of Wales (1st issue). Nos. 223/7 optd BIRTH OF PRINCE WILLIAM OF WALES 21 JUNE 1982.

256	40c. Type **34**	30	35
257	50c. Prince Charles as schoolboy	40	45
258	60c. Prince Charles as young man	45	55
259	70c. Prince Charles in ceremonial Naval uniform	50	60
260	80c. Prince Charles as Colonel-in-Chief, Royal Regiment of Wales	50	65
MS261	99×89 mm. Nos. 256/60	5·00	7·00

1982. Birth of Prince William of Wales (2nd issue). As Nos. 250/5 but with changed inscriptions. Multicoloured.

262	30c. As Type **37** (A)	30	30
263	30c. As Type **37** (B)	60	55
264	50c. As No. 251 (A)	60	55
265	50c. As No. 251 (B)	70	65
266	70c. As No. 252 (A)	90	80
267	70c. As No. 252 (B)	90	80
268	80c. As No. 253 (A)	95	85
269	80c. As No. 253 (B)	95	85
270	$1.40 As No. 254 (A)	1·40	1·25
271	$1.40 As No. 254 (B)	1·40	1·25
MS272	88×109 mm. As No. **MS**255 (c)	4·75	3·25

INSCR: A. "21 JUNE 1982. BIRTH OF PRINCE WILLIAM OF WALES"; B. "COMMEMORATING THE BIRTH OF PRINCE WILLIAM OF WALES"; C. "21 JUNE 1982. ROYAL BIRTH PRINCE WILLIAM OF WALES".

39 "Virgin and Child" (detail, Joos Van Cleve)

1982. Christmas. Details from Renaissance Paintings of "Virgin and Child". Multicoloured.

273	25c. Type **39**	30	40
274	48c. "Virgin and Child" (Filippino Lippi)	45	55
275	60c. "Virgin and Child" (Cima da Conegliano)	60	70
MS276	134×73 mm. As Nos. 273/5 but each with 2c. charity premium	1·00	2·00

1982. Christmas. Children's Charity. Designs as Nos. 273/5, but without frames, in separate miniature sheets, 60×85 mm, each with a face value of 70c.+5c.

MS277 As Nos. 273/5. Set of 3 sheets 1·25 1·60

40 Red Coral

1983. Commonwealth Day. Multicoloured.

278 60c. Type **40** 40 45
279 60c. Aerial view of Penrhyn atoll 40 45
280 60c. Eleanor Roosevelt on Penrhyn during Second World War 40 45
281 60c. Map of South Pacific 40 45

41 Scout Emblem and Blue Tropical Flower

1983. 75th Anniv of Boy Scout Movement. Multicoloured.

282 36c. Type **41** 1·50 60
283 48c. Emblem and pink flower 1·75 90
284 60c. Emblem and orange flower 1·75 1·00
MS285 86×46 mm. $2 As 48c., but with elements of design reversed 1·50 3·00

1983. 15th World Scout Jamboree, Alberta, Canada. Nos. 282/4 optd XV WORLD JAMBOREE CANADA 1983.

286 36c. Type **41** 1·25 45
287 48c. Emblem and pink flower 1·50 60
288 60c. Emblem and orange flower 1·60 75
MS289 86×46 mm. $2 As 48c., but with elements of design reversed 1·50 3·50

43 School of Sperm Whales

1983. Whale Conservation. Multicoloured.

290 8c. Type **43** 1·00 70
291 15c. Harpooner preparing to strike 1·40 95
292 35c. Whale attacking boat 2·00 1·40
293 60c. Dead whales marked with flags 3·00 2·00
294 $1 Dead whales on slipway 3·75 3·00

44 "Mercury" (cable ship)

1983. World Communications Year. Multicoloured.

295 36c. Type **44** 80 35
296 48c. Men watching cable being laid 85 45
297 60c. "Mercury" (different) 1·10 60
MS298 115×90 mm. As Nos. 295/7 but each with charity premium of 3c. 1·25 1·60

On No. **MS**298 the values are printed in black and have been transposed with the World Communications Year logo.

1983. Various stamps surch. (a) Nos. 182/5, 190/7 and 206.

299 18c. on 10c. "Preussen" 1·25 50
300 18c. on 10c. "Pamir" 1·25 50
301 18c. on 10c. "Cap Hornier" 1·25 50
302 18c. on 10c. "Patriarch" 1·25 50
303 36c. on 20c. Va'a Teu'ua 1·50 70
304 36c. on 20c. "Vitoria" 1·50 70
305 36c. on 20c. "Golden Hind" 1·50 70
306 36c. on 20c. "La Boudeuse" 1·50 70
307 36c. on 30c. H.M.S. "Bounty" 1·50 70
308 36c. on 30c. "L'Astrolabe" 1·50 70
309 36c. on 30c. "Star of India" 1·50 70
310 36c. on 30c. "Great Republic" 1·50 70
311 $1.20 on $2 "Cutty Sark" 5·00 2·00

(b) Nos. 252/3.

312 72c. on 70c. Princess Diana as schoolgirl 4·00 1·50
313 96c. on 80c. Princess Diana as teenager 4·00 1·75

1983. Nos. 225/6, 268/9, 253 and 208 surch.

314 48c. on 60c. Prince Charles as young man 3·75 1·75
315 72c. on 70c. Prince Charles in ceremonial Naval uniform 4·25 1·90
316 96c. on 80c. As No. 253 (inscr "21 JUNE 1982 ...") 3·00 1·10
317 96c. on 80c. As No. 253 (inscr "COMMEMORATING ...") 2·00 1·10
318 $1.20 on $4.40 As young lady 3·50 1·60
319 $5.60 on $6 H.M.S. "Resolution" and "Discovery" 18·00 10·00

45 George Cayley's Airship Design, 1837

1983. Bicentenary of Manned Flight. Mult. A. Inscr "NORTHERN COOK ISLANDS".

320A 36c. Type **45** 1·50 80
321A 48c. Dupuy de Lome's man-powered airship, 1872 1·75 90
322A 60c. Santos Dumont's airship "Ballon No. 6", 1901 2·00 1·25
323A 96c. Lebaudy-Juillot's airship, No. 1 "La Jaune", 1902 2·75 1·75
324A $1.32 Airship LZ-127 "Graf Zeppelin", 1929 3·25 2·50
MS325A 113×138 mm. Nos. 320A/4A 6·50 11·00

B. Corrected spelling optd in black on silver over original inscription.

320B 36c. Type **45** 40 35
321B 48c. Dupuy de Lome's man-powered airship, 1872 50 45
322B 60c. Santos Dumont's airship "Ballon No. 6", 1901 55 50
323B 96c. Lebaudy-Juillot's airship No. 1 "La Jaune", 1902 80 80
324B $1.32 Airship LZ-127 "Graf Zeppelin", 1929 1·10 1·10
MS325B 113×138 mm. Nos. 320B/4B 2·25 4·25

46 "Madonna in the Meadow"

1983. Christmas. 500th Birth Anniv of Raphael. Multicoloured.

326 36c. Type **46** 60 40
327 42c. "Tempi Madonna" 60 40
328 48c. "The Smaller Cowper Madonna" 80 50
329 60c. "Madonna della Tenda" 95 60
MS330 87×115 mm. As Nos. 326/9 but each with a charity premium of 3c. 2·00 2·50

1983. Nos. 266/7, 227 and 270 surch.

331 72c. on 70c. As No. 252 (inscr "21 JUNE 1982 ...") 2·00 80
332 72c. on 70c. As No. 252 (inscr "COMMEMORATING ...") 1·25 60
333 96c. on 80c. Prince Charles as Colonel-in-Chief, Royal Regiment of Wales 2·00 65
334 $1.20 on $1.40 As No. 254 (inscr "21 JUNE 1982 ...") 2·25 70
335 $1.20 on $1.40 As No. 254 (inscr "COMMEMORATING ...") 1·75 65

1983. Christmas. 500th Birth Anniv of Raphael. Children's Charity. Designs as Nos. 326/9 in separate miniature sheets, 65×84 mm, each with a face value of 75c.+5c.

MS336 As Nos. 326/9. Set of 4 sheets 1·75 3·00

47 Waka

1984. Sailing Craft and Ships (2nd series). Multicoloured.

337 2c. Type **47** 70 70
338 4c. Amatasi 70 70
339 5c. Ndrua 70 70
340 8c. Tongiaki 70 70
341 10c. "Vitoria" 70 70
342 18c. "Golden Hind" 1·25 70
343 20c. "La Boudeuse" 80 70
344 30c. H.M.S. "Bounty" 1·25 70
345 36c. "L'Astrolabe" 1·00 70
346 48c. "Great Republic" 1·00 70
347 50c. "Star of India" 1·00 70
348 60c. "Coonatto" 1·00 70
349 72c. "Antiope" 1·00 70
350 80c. "Balcutha" 1·00 70
351 96c. "Cap Hornier" 1·00 85
352 $1.20 "Pamir" 2·50 1·40
353 $3 "Mermerus" (41×31 mm) 5·00 3·00
354 $5 "Cutty Sark" (41×31 mm) 5·50 5·00
355 $9.60 H.M.S. "Resolution" and H.M.S. "Discovery" (41×31 mm) 22·00 23·00

48 Olympic Flag

1984. Olympic Games, Los Angeles. Mult.

356 35c. Type **48** 30 35
357 60c. Olympic torch and flags 50 55
358 $1.80 Ancient athletes and Coliseum 1·00 1·60
MS359 103×86 mm. As Nos. 356/8 but each with a charity premium of 5c. 1·90 2·50

49 Penrhyn Stamps of 1978, 1979 and 1981

1984. "Ausipex" International Stamp Exhibition, Melbourne. Multicoloured.

360 60c. Type **49** 50 75
361 $1.20 Location map of Penrhyn 1·00 1·25
MS362 90×90 mm. As Nos. 360/1, but each with a face value of 96c. 1·75 2·00

1984. Birth of Prince Harry. Nos. 223/4 and 250/1 surch $2 Birth of Prince Harry 15 Sept. 1984.

363 $2 on 30c. Type **37** 1·40 1·50
364 $2 on 40c. Type **34** 1·40 1·50
365 $2 on 50c. Prince Charles as schoolboy 1·40 1·50
366 $2 on 50c. Lady Diana as young child 1·40 1·50

51 "Virgin and Child" (Giovanni Bellini)

1984. Christmas. Paintings of the Virgin and Child by different artists. Multicoloured.

367 36c. Type **51** 60 35
368 48c. Lorenzo di Credi 75 45
369 60c. Palma the Older 80 50
370 96c. Raphael 1·00 80
MS371 93×118 mm. As Nos. 367/70, but each with a charity premium of 5c. 2·00 3·00

1984. Christmas. Children's Charity. Designs as Nos. 367/70, but without frames, in separate miniature sheets 67×81 mm, each with a face value of 96c.+10c.

MS372 As Nos. 367/70. Set of 4 sheets 2·50 3·50

52 Harlequin Duck

1985. Birth Bicentenary of John J. Audubon (ornithologist). Multicoloured.

373 20c. Type **52** 2·00 1·75
374 55c. Sage grouse 2·75 2·75
375 65c. Solitary sandpiper 3·00 3·00
376 75c. Dunlin 3·25 3·50
MS377 Four sheets, each 70×53 mm. As Nos. 373/6, but each with a face value of 95c. 9·00 6·50

Nos. 373/6 show original paintings.

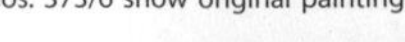

53 Lady Elizabeth Bowes-Lyon, 1921

1985. Life and Times of Queen Elizabeth the Queen Mother. Each violet, silver and yellow.

378 75c. Type **53** 40 65
379 95c. With baby Princess Elizabeth, 1926 50 80
380 $1.20 Coronation Day, 1937 65 1·00
381 $2.80 On her 70th birthday 1·25 2·00
MS382 66×90 mm. $5 The Queen Mother 2·40 3·25

See also No. **MS**403.

54 "The House in the Wood"

1985. International Youth Year. Birth Centenary of Jacob Grimm (folklorist). Multicoloured.

383 75c. Type **54** 2·75 2·50
384 95c. "Snow-White and Rose-Red" 3·00 2·75
385 $1.15 "The Goose Girl" 3·25 3·00

55 "The Annunciation"

1985. Christmas. Paintings by Murillo. Mult.

386 75c. Type **55** 1·25 1·25
387 $1.15 "Adoration of the Shepherds" 1·75 1·75
388 $1.80 "The Holy Family" 2·50 2·50
MS389 66×131 mm. As Nos. 386/8, but each with a face value of 95c. 2·75 3·00
MS390 Three sheets, each 66×72 mm. As Nos. 386/8, but with face values of $1.20, $1.45 and $2.75. Set of 3 sheets 4·50 4·75

56 Halley's Comet

1986. Appearance of Halley's Comet. Design showing details of the painting "Fire and Ice" by Camille Rendal. Multicoloured.
391 $1.50 Type **56** 2·25 1·50
392 $1.50 Stylized "Giotto" spacecraft 2·25 1·50
MS393 108×43 mm. $3 As Nos. 391/2 (104×39 mm). Imperf 2·25 2·50

Nos. 391/2 were printed together, forming a composite design of the complete painting.

57 Princess Elizabeth aged Three, 1929, and Bouquet

1986. 60th Birthday of Queen Elizabeth II. Multicoloured.
394 95c. Type **57** 1·50 80
395 $1.45 Profile of Queen Elizabeth and St. Edward's Crown 2·00 1·25
396 $2.50 Queen Elizabeth aged three and in profile with Imperial State Crown (56×30 mm) 2·50 2·00

58 Statue of Liberty under Construction, Paris

1986. Centenary of Statue of Liberty. Each black, gold and green.
397 95c. Type **58** 65 70
398 $1.75 Erection of Statue, New York 1·10 1·25
399 $3 Artist's impression of Statue, 1876 2·10 2·25

See also No. **MS**412.

59 Prince Andrew and Miss Sarah Ferguson

1986. Royal Wedding. Multicoloured.
400 $2.50 Type **59** 3·50 3·50
401 $3.50 Profiles of Prince Andrew and Miss Sarah Ferguson 4·00 4·00

1986. "Stampex '86" Stamp Exhibition, Adelaide. No. MS362 surch $2 in black on gold.
MS402 $2 on 96c. × 2 6·00 7·00

The "Stampex '86" exhibition emblem is overprinted on the sheet margin.

1986. 86th Birthday of Queen Elizabeth the Queen Mother. Nos. 378/81 in miniature sheet, 90×120 mm.
MS403 Nos. 378/81 12·00 11·00

61 "Adoration of the Shepherds"

1986. Christmas. Engravings by Rembrandt. Each brown, ochre and gold.
404 65c. Type **61** 1·75 1·75
405 $1.75 "Virgin and Child" 3·00 3·00
406 $2.50 "The Holy Family" 4·25 4·25
MS407 120×87 mm. As Nos. 404/6, but each size 31×39 mm with a face value of $1.50 13·00 10·00

1986. Visit of Pope John Paul II to South Pacific. Nos. 404/6 surch SOUTH PACIFIC VISIT 21 TO 24 NOVEMBER 1986 +10c.
408 65c.+10c. Type **61** 4·50 2·75
409 $1.75+10c. "Virgin and Child" 6·00 4·00
410 $2.50+10c. "The Holy Family" 7·00 4·25
MS411 120×87 mm. As Nos. 408/10, but each size 31×39 mm with a face value of $1.50+10c. 20·00 12·00

1987. Centenary of Statue of Liberty (1986) (2nd issue). Two sheets, each 122×122 mm, containing multicoloured designs as T 112a of Niue.
MS412 Two sheets. (a) 65c. Head and torch of Statue; 65c. Torch at sunset; 65c. Restoration workers with flag; 65c. Statue and Manhattan skyline; 65c. Workers and scaffolding. (b) 65c. Workers on Statue crown (horiz); 65c. Aerial view of Ellis Island (horiz); 65c. Ellis Island Immigration Centre (horiz); 65c. View from Statue to Ellis Island and Manhattan (horiz); 65c. Restoration workers (horiz). Set of 2 sheets 7·50 11·00

1987. Royal Ruby Wedding. Nos. 68/9 optd Fortieth Royal Wedding Anniversary 1947–87.
413 $2 Birds-eye view of Penrhyn 2·00 2·25
414 $5 Satellite view of Australasia 3·50 4·25

65 "The Garvagh Madonna"

1987. Christmas. Religious Paintings by Raphael. Multicoloured.
415 95c. Type **65** 1·50 1·50
416 $1.60 "The Alba Madonna" 2·00 2·00
417 $2.25 "The Madonna of the Fish" 3·00 3·00
MS418 91×126 mm. As Nos. 415/17, but each with a face value of $1.15 15·00 15·00
MS419 70×86 mm. $4.80 As No. 417, but size 36×39 mm. 15·00 15·00

1988. Olympic Games, Seoul. Multicoloured.
420 55c. Type **66** 75 65
421 95c. Pole vaulting (vert) 1·25 1·00
422 $1.25 Shot putting 1·50 1·40
423 $1.50 Lawn tennis (vert) 2·50 1·75
MS424 110×70 mm. As Nos. 421 and 423, but each with a face value of $2.50 4·00 5·00

66 Athletics

1988. Olympic Gold Medal Winners, Seoul. Nos. 420/3 optd.
425 55c. Type **66** (optd **CARL LEWIS UNITED STATES 100 METERS**) 80 60
426 95c. Pole vaulting (optd **LOUISE RITTER UNITED STATES HIGH JUMP**) 1·25 90
427 $1.25 Shot putting (optd **ULF TIMMERMANN EAST GERMANY SHOT-PUT**) 1·50 1·25
428 $1.50 Lawn tennis (optd **STEFFI GRAF WEST GERMANY WOMEN'S TENNIS**) 5·00 1·75
MS429 110×70 mm. $2.50 As No. 421 (optd **JACKIE JOYNER-KERSEE United States Heptathlon**); $2.50 As No. 423 (optd **STEFFI GRAF West Germany Women's Tennis MILOSLAV MECIR Czechoslovakia Men's Tennis**) 5·50 5·50

67 "Virgin and Child"

1988. Christmas. Designs showing different "Virgin and Child" paintings by Titian.
430 **67** 70c. multicoloured 90 90
431 - 85c. multicoloured 1·00 1·00
432 - 95c. multicoloured 1·25 1·25
433 - $1.25 multicoloured 1·50 1·50
MS434 100×80 mm. $6.40 As type **67**, but diamond-shaped (57×57 mm) 6·00 7·00

68 Neil Armstrong stepping onto Moon

1989. 20th Anniv of First Manned Moon Landing. Multicoloured.
435 55c. Type **68** 1·60 70
436 75c. Astronaut on Moon carrying equipment 1·75 85
437 95c. Conducting experiment on Moon 2·25 1·10
438 $1.25 Crew of "Apollo 11" 2·50 1·40
439 $1.75 Crew inside "Apollo 11" 2·75 1·90

69 Virgin Mary

1989. Christmas. Details from "The Nativity" by Durer. Multicoloured.
440 55c. Type **69** 80 80
441 70c. Christ Child and cherubs 90 90
442 85c. Joseph 1·25 1·25
443 $1.25 Three women 1·60 1·60
MS444 88×95 mm. $6.40 "The Nativity" (31×50 mm) 6·50 7·50

70 Queen Elizabeth the Queen Mother

1990. 90th Birthday of Queen Elizabeth the Queen Mother.
445 **70** $2.25 multicoloured 2·50 2·50
MS446 85×73 mm. **70** $7.50 multicoloured 14·00 14·00

71 "Adoration of the Magi" (Veronese)

1990. Christmas. Religious Paintings. Multicoloured.
447 55c. Type **71** 1·00 1·00
448 70c. "Virgin and Child" (Quentin Metsys) 1·40 1·40
449 85c. "Virgin and Child Jesus" (Hugo van der Goes) 1·60 1·60
450 $1.50 "Adoration of the Kings" (Jan Gossaert) 2·50 2·50
MS451 108×132 mm. $6.40 "Virgin and Child with Saints, Francis, John the Baptist, Zenobius and Lucy" (Domenico Veneziano) 8·00 9·00

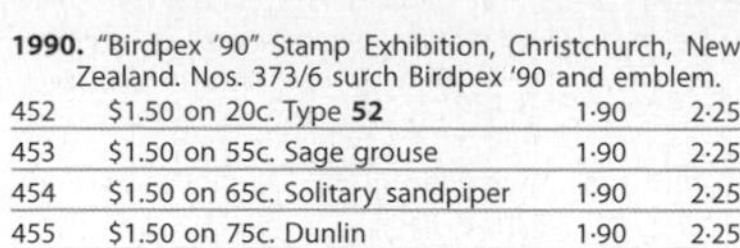
1990. "Birdpex '90" Stamp Exhibition, Christchurch, New Zealand. Nos. 373/6 surch Birdpex '90 and emblem.
452 $1.50 on 20c. Type **52** 1·90 2·25
453 $1.50 on 55c. Sage grouse 1·90 2·25
454 $1.50 on 65c. Solitary sandpiper 1·90 2·25
455 $1.50 on 75c. Dunlin 1·90 2·25

1991. 65th Birthday of Queen Elizabeth II. No. 208 optd COMMEMORATING 65th BIRTHDAY OF H.M. QUEEN ELIZABETH II.
456 $6 H.M.S. "Resolution" and "Discovery", 1776–80 12·00 13·00

74 "The Virgin and Child with Saints" (G. David)

1991. Christmas. Religious Paintings. Multicoloured.
457 55c. Type **74** 1·00 1·00
458 85c. "Nativity" (Tintoretto) 1·50 1·50
459 $1.15 "Mystic Nativity" (Botticelli) 1·75 1·75
460 $1.85 "Adoration of the Shepherds" (B. Murillo) 2·75 3·25
MS461 79×103 mm. $6.40 "The Madonna of the Chair" (Raphael) (vert) 12·00 13·00

74a Running

1992. Olympic Games, Barcelona. Multicoloured.
462 75c. Type **74a** 1·60 1·60
463 95c. Boxing 1·75 1·75
464 $1.15 Swimming 2·00 2·00
465 $1.50 Wrestling 2·25 2·25

75 Marquesan Canoe

1992. 6th Festival of Pacific Arts, Rarotonga. Multicoloured.
466 $1.15 Type **75** 1·60 1·60
467 $1.75 Tangaroa statue from Rarotonga 2·00 2·00
468 $1.95 Manihiki canoe 2·25 2·25

1992. Royal Visit by Prince Edward. Nos. 466/8 optd ROYAL VISIT.
469 $1.15 Type **75** 3·00 2·50
470 $1.75 Tangaroa statue from Rarotonga 4·00 3·50
471 $1.95 Manihiki canoe 4·25 4·00

76 "Virgin with Child and Saints" (Borgognone)

1992. Christmas. Religious Paintings by Ambrogio Borgognone. Multicoloured.
472 55c. Type **76** 75 75
473 85c. "Virgin on Throne" 1·10 1·10
474 $1.05 "Virgin on Carpet" 1·40 1·40
475 $1.85 "Virgin of the Milk" 2·25 2·25
MS476 101×86 mm. $6.40 As 55c., but larger (36×46 mm) 8·00 9·00

77 Vincente Pinzon and "Nina"

1992. 500th Anniv of Discovery of America by Columbus. Multicoloured.

477		$1.15 Type **77**	2·50	2·50
478		$1.35 Martin Pinzon and "Pinta"	2·75	2·75
479		$1.75 Christopher Columbus and "Santa Maria"	3·50	3·50

78 Queen Elizabeth II in 1953

1993. 40th Anniv of Coronation.

480	**78**	$6 multicoloured	6·50	8·50

79 Bull-mouth Helmet

1993. Marine Life. Multicoloured.

481		5c. Type **79**	30	50
482		10c. Daisy coral	35	50
483		15c. Hydroid coral	45	50
484		20c. Feather-star	50	50
485		25c. Sea star	50	50
486		30c. Varicose nudibranch	50	50
487		50c. Smooth sea star	70	70
488		70c. Black-lip pearl oyster	1·00	1·00
489		80c. Four-coloured nudibranch	1·00	1·00
490		85c. Prickly sea cucumber	1·00	1·00
491		90c. Organ pipe coral	1·00	1·00
492		$1 Blue sea lizard	1·00	2·00
493		$2 Textile cone shell	1·50	2·75
494		$3 Starfish	2·25	2·75
495		$5 As $3	3·75	4·50
496		$8 As $3	5·00	6·50
497		$10 As $3	10·00	11·00

Nos. 494/7 are larger, 47×34 mm, and include a portrait of Queen Elizabeth II at top right.

80 "Virgin on Throne with Child" (detail) (Tura)

1993. Christmas.

499	**80**	55c. multicoloured	1·00	1·00
500	-	85c. multicoloured	1·50	1·50
501	-	$1.05 multicoloured	1·75	1·75
502	-	$1.95 multicoloured	2·75	3·00
503	-	$4.50 mult (32×47 mm)	6·00	7·00

DESIGNS: 80c. to $4.50, Different details from "Virgin on Throne with Child" (Cosme Tura).

81 Neil Armstrong stepping onto Moon

1994. 25th Anniv of First Manned Moon Landing.

504	**81**	$3.25 multicoloured	7·50	8·00

82 "The Virgin and Child with Sts. Paul and Jerome" (Vivarini)

1994. Christmas. Religious Paintings. Multicoloured.

505		90c. Type **82**	1·10	1·25
506		90c. "The Virgin and Child with St. John" (Luini)	1·10	1·25
507		90c. "The Virgin and Child with Sts. Jerome and Dominic" (Lippi)	1·10	1·25
508		90c. "Adoration of the Shepherds" (Murillo)	1·10	1·25
509		$1 "Adoration of the Kings" (detail of angels) (Reni)	1·10	1·25
510		$1 "Madonna and Child with the Infant Baptist" (Raphael)	1·10	1·25
511		$1 "Adoration of the Kings" (detail of manger) (Reni)	1·10	1·25
512		$1 "Virgin and Child" (Borgognone)	1·10	1·25

83 Battleship Row burning, Pearl Harbor

1995. 50th Anniv of End of Second World War. Multicoloured.

513		$3.75 Type **83**	9·00	8·00
514		$3.75 Boeing B-25 Superfortress "Enola Gay" over Hiroshima	9·00	8·00

84 Queen Elizabeth the Queen Mother at Remembrance Day Ceremony

1995. 95th Birthday of Queen Elizabeth the Queen Mother.

515	**84**	$4.50 multicoloured	10·00	9·50

85 Anniversary Emblem, United Nations Flag and Headquarters

1995. 50th Anniv of United Nations.

516	**85**	$4 multicoloured	4·50	6·00

86 Loggerhead Turtle

1995. Year of the Sea Turtle. Multicoloured.

517		$1.15 Type **86**	1·75	2·00
518		$1.15 Hawksbill turtle	1·75	2·00
519		$1.65 Olive ridley turtle	2·25	2·50
520		$1.65 Green turtle	2·25	2·50

87 Queen Elizabeth II and Rose

1996. 70th Birthday of Queen Elizabeth.

521	**87**	$4.25 multicoloured	5·00	6·50

88 Olympic Flame, National Flags and Sports

1996. Centenary of Modern Olympic Games.

522	**88**	$5 multicoloured	6·50	8·00

89 Royal Wedding, 1947

1997. Golden Wedding of Queen Elizabeth and Prince Philip.

523	**89**	$3 multicoloured	4·25	3·75
MS524 42×28 mm. **89** $4 multicoloured			4·25	5·00

90 Diana, Princess of Wales with Sons

1998. Diana, Princess of Wales Commemoration.

525	**90**	$1.50 multicoloured	1·10	1·75
MS526 70×100 mm. **90** $3.75 multicoloured			2·50	4·00

1998. Children's Charities. No. MS526 surch +$1 CHILDREN'S CHARITIES.

MS527 70×100 mm. **90** $3.75+$1 multicoloured			4·50	5·50

1999. New Millennium. Nos. 466/8 optd KIA ORANA THIRD MILLENNIUM.

528		$1.15 Type **75**	1·25	1·25
529		$1.75 Tangaroa statue from Rarotonga	1·60	1·60
530		$1.95 Manihiki canoe	1·75	1·75

90a King George VI and Queen Elizabeth on Wedding Day

2000. Queen Elizabeth the Queen Mother's 100th Birthday.

531	**90a**	$2.50 purple and brown	2·75	2·75
532	-	$2.50 brown	2·75	2·75
533	-	$2.50 green and brown	2·75	2·75
534	-	$2.50 blue and brown	2·75	2·75
MS535 72×100 mm. $10 multicoloured			9·50	10·00

DESIGNS: No. 532, Queen Elizabeth with young Princess Elizabeth; 533, Royal Family in 1930; 534, Queen Elizabeth with Princesses Elizabeth and Margaret; **MS**535, Queen Elizabeth wearing blue gown.

90b Ancient Greek Javelin-throwers

2000. Olympic Games, Sydney. Multicoloured.

536		$2.75 Type **90b**	2·40	2·50
537		$2.75 Modern javelin-thrower	2·40	2·50
538		$2.75 Ancient Greek discus-thrower	2·40	2·50
539		$2.75 Modern discus-thrower	2·40	2·50
MS540 90×99 mm. $3.50 Cook Islands Olympic Torch Relay runner in traditional costume (vert)			3·25	4·00

91 Ocean Sunfish

2003. Endangered Species. Ocean Sunfish.

541	**91**	80c. multicoloured	1·40	1·60
542	-	90c. multicoloured	1·40	1·60
543	-	$1.15 multicoloured	1·60	1·90
544	-	$1.95 multicoloured	2·00	2·75

DESIGNS: 90c. to $1.95, Ocean sunfish.

91a Statue of Liberty

2003. "United We Stand". Support for Victims of 11 September 2001 Terrorist Attacks. Multicoloured.

MS545 75×109 mm. **91a** $1.50×4 Statue of Liberty, Twin Towers and flags of USA and Cook Islands			5·50	6·50

92 Pope John Paul II

2005. Pope John Paul II Commemoration.

546	**92**	$1.45 multicoloured	2·50	2·50

93 Pacific Reef Egrets (white and dark grey morphs)

2008. WWF Pacific Reef-egret (Egretta sacra). Multicoloured.

547	80c. Type **93**	1·75	1·90
548	90c. Egret (dark grey morph) on shore	1·75	1·90
549	$1.15 Egret (white morph) in flight	1·90	2·00
550	$1.95 Egret (dark grey morph) at nest with chicks	2·25	2·50

94 Striped Dolphin

2010. Endangered Species. Striped Dolphin (*Stenella coeruleoalba*). Multicoloured.

551	80c. Type **94**	1·50	1·60
552	90c. Two striped dolphins	1·50	1·60
553	$1.10 Striped dolphin (swimming to right)	1·75	1·90
554	$1.20 School of dolphins	1·75	1·90

2011. Royal Engagement. Multicoloured designs as T **299** of Cook Islands

555	55c. Prince William laying wreath at the Cenotaph, London, 2009	85	85
556	50c. Prince William competing in Chakravarty Cup, Beaufort Polo Club	85	85
557	50c. Kate Middleton, Prince William in background	85	85
558	50c. Prince William	85	85
559	50c. Kate Middleton	85	85
560	50c. Prince William and Kate Middleton	85	85
561	50c. Kate Middleton wearing black hat	85	85
562	50c. Prince William (head and shoulders)	85	85
563	50c. Prince William and Kate Middleton (facing each other)	85	85
564	50c. Engagement ring on Kate Middleton's hand	85	85
565	$2 Prince William arriving at Imperial War Museum for 'Night of Heroes' event, 15 December 2009	16·00	16·00
566	$2 Kate Middleton (wearing white jacket) at wedding of Rose Astor and Hugh van Cutsem, Burford	16·00	16·00
MS567	108×70 mm. Nos. 565/6	35·00	35·00
MS568	144×93 mm. $8.10 Prince William and Kate Middleton (38×50 mm)	6·75	6·72
MS569	58×95 mm. $11 As No. 565 (38×50 mm)	13·50	13·50
MS570	58×95 mm. $11 As No. 566 (38×50 mm)	13·50	13·50

OFFICIAL STAMPS

1978. Optd or surch O.H.M.S.

O1	1c. multicoloured (No. 57)	15	10
O2	2c. multicoloured (No. 58)	15	10
O3	3c. multicoloured (No. 59)	25	10
O4	4c. multicoloured (No. 60)	25	10
O5	5c. multicoloured (No. 61)	30	10
O6	8c. multicoloured (No. 62)	35	15
O7	10c. multicoloured (No. 63)	40	15
O8	15c. on 60c. mult (No. 66)	45	25
O9	18c. on 60c. mult (No. 66)	50	25
O10	20c. multicoloured (No. 64)	50	25
O11	25c. multicoloured (No. 65)	55	30
O12	30c. on 60c. mult (No. 66)	55	35
O13	50c. multicoloured (No. 89)	90	55
O14	50c. multicoloured (No. 90)	90	55
O15	50c. multicoloured (No. 91)	90	55
O16	$1 multicoloured (No. 101)	2·25	45
O17	$2 multicoloured (No. 102)	4·00	50

1985. Nos. 206/8, 278/81, 337/47 and 349/55 optd O.H.M.S. or surch also.

O18	2c. Type **47**	70	80
O19	4c. Amatasi	70	80
O20	5c. Ndrua	70	80
O21	8c. Tongiaki	70	80
O22	10c. "Vitoria"	70	80
O23	18c. "Golden Hind"	2·00	90
O24	20c. "La Boudeuse"	1·75	90
O25	30c. H.M.S. "Bounty"	2·75	1·00
O26	40c. on 36c. "L'Astrolabe"	1·75	90
O27	50c. "Star of India"	1·75	90
O28	55c. on 48c. "Great Republic"	1·75	90
O39	65c. on 60c. Type **40**	80	1·00
O40	65c. on 60c. Aerial view of Penrhyn atoll	80	1·00
O41	65c. on 60c. Eleanor Roosevelt on Penrhyn during Second World War	80	1·00
O42	65c. on 60c. Map of South Pacific	80	1·00
O29	75c. on 72c. "Antiope"	2·50	1·60
O30	75c. on 96c. "Cap Hornier"	2·50	1·60
O31	80c. "Balcutha"	2·50	1·60
O32	$1.20 "Pamir"	2·75	1·60
O33	$2 "Cutty Sark"	5·00	3·25
O34	$3 "Mermerus"	4·25	3·50
O35	$4 "Mermerus"	5·50	5·00
O36	$5 "Cutty Sark"	8·00	6·50
O37	$6 H.M.S. "Resolution" and H.M.S. "Discovery"	11·00	9·50
O38	$9.60 H.M.S. "Resolution" and H.M.S. "Discovery"	14·00	13·00

1998. Nos. 481/93 optd O.H.M.S.

O43	5c. Type **79**	35	50
O44	10c. Daisy coral	35	50
O45	15c. Hydroid coral	50	50
O46	20c. Feather-star	50	50
O47	25c. Sea star	50	50
O48	30c. Varicose nudibranch	50	50
O49	50c. Smooth sea star	70	70
O50	70c. Black-lip pearl oyster	1·00	1·00
O51	80c. Four-coloured nudibranch	1·00	1·00
O52	85c. Prickly sea cucumber	1·00	1·00
O53	90c. Organ pipe coral	1·00	1·00
O54	$1 Blue sea lizard	1·00	1·00
O55	$2 Textile cone shell	1·75	2·00

Pt. 1

PERAK

A state of the Federation of Malaya, incorporated in Malaysia in 1963.

100 cents = 1 dollar (Straits or Malayan).

Stamps of Straits Settlement optd or surch.

1878. No. 11 optd with crescent and star and P in oval.

1	2c. brown	£2000	£1700

1880. Optd PERAK.

10	**9**	2c. brown	22·00	75·00
17	**9**	2c. red	6·00	3·75

1883. Surch 2 CENTS PERAK.

16	2c. on 4c. red	£700	£275

1886. No. 63a surch ONE CENT PERAK. (a) Without full point.

29	1c. on 2c. red	4·00	15·00

(b) With final full point.

26	1c. on 2c. red	65·00	85·00

1886. No. 63a surch 1 CENT PERAK.

28	1c. on 2c. red	£170	£170

1886. No. 63a surch One CENT PERAK.

33b	1c. on 2c. red	2·75	3·25

1889. No. 17 surch ONE CENT (with full point).

41	1c. on 2c. red	£325	£130

1891. Surch PERAK One CENT.

57	1c. on 2c. red	2·25	10·00
43	1c. on 6c. lilac	55·00	30·00

1891. Surch PERAK Two CENTS.

48	2c. on 24c. green	25·00	14·00

42 Tiger

1892

61	**42**	1c. green	2·25	15
62	**42**	2c. red	1·75	30
63	**42**	2c. orange	50	5·50
64	**42**	5c. blue	3·25	7·50

1895. Surch 3 CENTS.

65	3c. red	3·75	4·25

44 Tiger

45 Elephants

1895

66	**44**	1c. purple and green	2·75	50
67	**44**	2c. purple and brown	3·25	50
68	**44**	3c. purple and red	3·25	50
69	**44**	4c. purple and red	15·00	5·00
70	**44**	5c. purple and yellow	7·00	55
71	**44**	8c. purple and blue	45·00	65
72	**44**	10c. purple and orange	15·00	50
73	**44**	25c. green and red	£200	12·00
74	**44**	50c. purple and black	48·00	45·00
75	**44**	50c. green and black	£225	£170
76	**45**	$1 green	£275	£225
77	**45**	$2 green and red	£400	£350
78	**45**	$3 green and yellow	£500	£500
79	**45**	$5 green and blue	£550	£550
80	**45**	$25 green and orange	£9000	£3750

1900. Surch in words.

81	**44**	1c. on 2c. purple and brown	60	2·25
82	**44**	1c. on 4c. purple and red	1·00	15·00
83	**44**	1c. on 5c. purple and yellow	2·75	18·00
84	**44**	3c. on 8c. purple and blue	8·00	14·00
85	**44**	3c. on 50c. green and black	4·50	9·00
86	**45**	3c. on $1 green	55·00	£150
87	**45**	3c. on $2 green and red	45·00	85·00

50 Sultan Iskandar

1935

88	**50**	1c. black	2·25	10
89	**50**	2c. green	2·25	10
90	**50**	4c. orange	2·50	10
91	**50**	5c. brown	75	10
92	**50**	6c. red	11·00	4·50
93	**50**	8c. grey	1·00	10
94	**50**	10c. purple	80	15
95	**50**	12c. blue	4·00	1·00
96	**50**	25c. purple and red	3·00	1·00
97	**50**	30c. purple and orange	4·00	1·50
98	**50**	40c. red and purple	6·00	5·00
99	**50**	50c. black on green	7·50	1·25
100	**50**	$1 black and red on blue	2·50	1·25
101	**50**	$2 green and red	32·00	7·00
102	**50**	$5 green and red on green	£120	35·00

51 Sultan Iskandar

1938

103	**51**	1c. black	15·00	10
104	**51**	2c. green	10·00	10
105	**51**	2c. orange	3·50	19·00
106a	**51**	3c. green	30·00	11·00
107	**51**	4c. orange	40·00	10
108	**51**	5c. brown	6·50	10
109	**51**	6c. red	27·00	10
110	**51**	8c. grey	32·00	10
111	**51**	8c. red	1·00	85·00
112	**51**	10c. purple	38·00	10
113	**51**	12c. blue	26·00	1·00
114	**51**	15c. blue	4·25	13·00
115	**51**	25c. purple and red	50·00	3·25
116	**51**	30c. purple and orange	10·00	2·25
117	**51**	40c. red and purple	50·00	2·00
118	**51**	50c. black on green	32·00	75
119	**51**	$1 black and red on blue	£140	24·00
120	**51**	$2 green and red	£180	70·00
121	**51**	$5 green and red on green	£325	£375

1948. Silver Wedding. As T 4b/c of Pitcairn Islands.

122	10c. violet	15	10
123	$5 green	23·00	40·00

1949. U.P.U. As T 4d/g of Pitcairn Islands.

124	10c. purple	15	10
125	15c. blue	1·50	2·00
126	25c. orange	30	5·50
127	50c. black	1·25	3·50

52 Sultan Yussuf 'Izzuddin Shah

1950

128	**52**	1c. black	10	10
129	**52**	2c. orange	20	10
130	**52**	3c. green	4·50	10
131	**52**	4c. brown	80	10
132	**52**	5c. purple	50	2·50
133	**52**	6c. grey	40	10
134	**52**	8c. red	2·25	2·25
135	**52**	8c. green	1·25	1·00
136	**52**	10c. purple	20	10
137	**52**	12c. red	1·25	6·00
138	**52**	15c. blue	1·25	10
139	**52**	20c. black and green	1·75	65
140	**52**	20c. blue	1·00	10
141	**52**	25c. purple and orange	1·00	10
142	**52**	30c. red and purple	2·50	20
143	**52**	35c. red and purple	1·50	25
144	**52**	40c. red and purple	7·00	6·00
145	**52**	50c. black and blue	7·00	10
146	**52**	$1 blue and purple	7·00	1·00
147	**52**	$2 green and red	18·00	7·00
148	**52**	$5 green and brown	42·00	24·00

1953. Coronation. As T 4h of Pitcairn Islands.

149	10c. black and purple	2·00	10

1957. As Nos. 92/102 of Kedah, but portrait of Sultan Yussuf Izzuddin Shah.

150	1c. black	10	20
151	2c. orange	30	1·00
152	4c. brown	20	10
153	5c. lake	20	10
154	8c. green	2·00	3·50
155	10c. sepia	2·50	10
156	10c. purple	7·50	10
157	20c. blue	2·25	10
158a	50c. black and blue	40	10
159	$1 blue and purple	6·50	40
160	$2 green and red	4·00	5·00
161a	$5 brown and green	16·00	8·00

53 Sultan Idris Shah

1963. Installation of Sultan of Perak.

162	**53**	10c. multicoloured	10	10

54 "Vanda hookeriana"

1965. As Nos. 115/21 of Kedah, but with inset portrait of Sultan Idris as in T 54.

163	**54**	1c. multicoloured	10	50
164	-	2c. multicoloured	10	70
165	-	5c. multicoloured	10	10
166	-	6c. multicoloured	15	40
167	-	10c. multicoloured	15	10
168	-	15c. multicoloured	80	10
169	-	20c. multicoloured	1·25	10

The higher values used in Perak were Nos. 20/7 of Malaysia (National Issues).

55 "Delias ninus"

1971. Butterflies. As Nos. 124/30 of Kedah, but with portrait of Sultan Idris as in T 55.

172	**55**	1c. multicoloured	40	2·00
173	-	2c. multicoloured	1·00	2·00
174	-	5c. multicoloured	1·25	10
175	-	6c. multicoloured	1·25	2·00
176	-	10c. multicoloured	1·25	10
177	-	15c. multicoloured	1·00	10

178	-	20c. multicoloured	1·75	30

The higher values in use with this issue were Nos. 64/71 of Malaysia (National Issues).

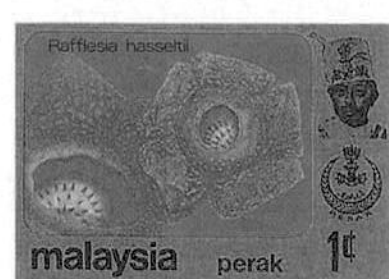
56 "Rafflesia hasseltii"

1979. Flowers. As Nos. 135/41 of Kedah but with portrait of Sultan Idris as in T 56.

184		1c. Type **56**	10	85
185		2c. "Pterocarpus indicus"	10	85
186		5c. "Lagerstroemia speciosa"	10	20
187		10c. "Durio zibethinus"	15	10
188		15c. "Hibiscus rosa-sinensis"	15	10
189		20c. "Rhododendron scorte-chinii"	20	10
190		25c. "Etlingera elatior" (inscr"Phaeomeria speciosa")	40	20

57 Coffee

1986. As Nos. 152/8 of Kedah but with portrait of Sultan Azlan Shah as in T 57.

198		1c. Type **57**	10	25
199		2c. Coconuts	10	35
200		5c. Cocoa	15	10
201		10c. Black pepper	15	10
202		15c. Rubber	25	10
203		20c. Oil palm	25	15
204		30c. Rice	30	15

58 *Nelumbium nelumbo* (sacred lotus)

2007. Garden Flowers. As Nos. 210/15 of Johore, but with portrait of Sultan Azlan Shah and Arms of Penang as in T 58. Multicoloured.

205		5s. Type **58**	10	10
206		10s. *Hydrangea macrophylla*	15	10
207		20s. *Hippeastrum reticulatum*	25	15
208		30s. *Bougainvillea*	40	20
209		40s. *Ipomoea indica*	50	30
210		50s. *Hibiscus rosa-sinensis*	65	35
MS211		100×85 mm. Nos. 205/10	2·00	1·25
MS211		100×85 mm. Nos. 205/10	2·00	1·25

OFFICIAL STAMPS

1889. Stamps of Straits Settlements optd P.G.S.

O1	**30**	2c. red	6·00	8·00
O2	**30**	4c. brown	25·00	28·00
O3	**30**	6c. lilac	32·00	55·00
O4	**30**	8c. orange	45·00	65·00
O5	**38**	10c. grey	75·00	75·00
O6	**30**	12c. blue	£250	£300
O7	**30**	12c. purple	£250	£325
O9	**30**	24c. green	£200	£225

1894. No. 64 optd Service.

O10		5c. blue	£100	1·00

1895. No. 70 optd Service.

O11	**31**	5c. purple and yellow	3·00	50

Pt. 1

PERLIS

A state of the Federation of Malaya, incorporated in Malaysia in 1963.

100 cents = 1 dollar (Straits or Malayan).

1948. Silver Wedding. As T 4b/c of Pitcairn Islands.

1		10c. violet	30	2·75
2		$5 brown	29·00	48·00

1949. U.P.U. As T 4d/g of Pitcairn Islands.

3		10c. purple	30	2·25
4		15c. blue	1·25	4·75
5		25c. orange	45	4·00
6		50c. black	1·00	3·75

1 Raja Syed Putra

1951

7	**1**	1c. black	20	1·00
8	**1**	2c. orange	75	80
9	**1**	3c. green	1·75	4·50
10	**1**	4c. brown	1·75	1·75
11	**1**	5c. purple	1·00	4·00
12	**1**	6c. grey	1·50	2·75
13	**1**	8c. red	4·25	8·50
14	**1**	8c. green	2·75	3·50
15	**1**	10c. purple	1·25	50
16	**1**	12c. red	2·75	6·50
17	**1**	15c. blue	6·00	8·00
18	**1**	20c. black and green	4·50	12·00
19	**1**	20c. blue	1·50	1·25
20	**1**	25c. purple and orange	2·50	4·25
21	**1**	30c. red and purple	2·25	15·00
22	**1**	35c. red and purple	3·50	8·00
23	**1**	40c. red and purple	5·50	32·00
24	**1**	50c. black and blue	5·00	7·50
25	**1**	$1 blue and purple	8·50	28·00
26	**1**	$2 green and red	21·00	65·00
27	**1**	$5 green and brown	75·00	£140

1953. Coronation. As T 4h of Pitcairn Islands.

28		10c. black and purple	1·50	3·00

1957. As Nos. 92/102 of Kedah, but inset portrait of Raja Syed Putra.

29		1c. black	10	30
30		2c. red	10	30
31		4c. brown	10	30
32		5c. lake	10	10
33		8c. green	2·00	1·75
34		10c. brown	1·50	2·25
35		10c. purple	11·00	4·50
36		20c. blue	4·00	5·50
37		50c. black and blue	1·50	4·00
38		$1 blue and purple	11·00	15·00
39		$2 green and red	11·00	9·00
40		$5 brown and green	14·00	12·00

2 "Vanda hookeriana"

1965. As Nos. 115/21 of Kedah, but with inset portrait of Tunku Bendahara Abu Bakar as in T 2.

41	**2**	1c. multicoloured	10	1·00
42	-	2c. multicoloured	10	1·50
43	-	5c. multicoloured	15	40
44	-	6c. multicoloured	65	1·50
45	-	10c. multicoloured	65	40
46	-	15c. multicoloured	1·00	40
47	-	20c. multicoloured	1·00	1·75

The higher values used in Perlis were Nos. 20/7 of Malaysia (National Issues).

3 "Danaus melanippus"

1971. Butterflies. As Nos. 124/30 of Kedah, but with portrait of Raja Syed Putra as in T 3.

48		1c. multicoloured	20	1·25
49	**3**	2c. multicoloured	40	2·25
50	-	5c. multicoloured	1·25	1·25
51	-	6c. multicoloured	1·50	3·00
52	-	10c. multicoloured	1·50	1·25
53	-	15c. multicoloured	1·50	50
54	-	20c. multicoloured	1·50	2·50

The higher values in use with this issue were Nos. 64/71 of Malaysia (National Issues).

4 Raja Syed Putra

1971. 25th Anniv of Installation of Raja Syed Putra.

56	**4**	10c. multicoloured	30	2·25
57	**4**	15c. multicoloured	30	75
58	**4**	50c. multicoloured	80	4·25

5 "Pterocarpus indicus"

1979. Flowers. As Nos. 135/41 of Kedah, but with portrait of Raja Syed Putra as in T 5.

59		1c. "Rafflesia hasseltii"	10	1·00
60		2c. Type **5**	10	1·00
61		5c. "Lagerstroemia speciosa"	10	1·00
62		10c. "Durio zibethinus"	15	30
63		15c. "Hibiscus rosa-sinensis"	15	10
64		20c. "Rhododendron scorte-chinii"	20	10
65		25c. "Etlingera elatior" (inscr "Phaeomeria speciosa")	40	85

6 Coconuts

1986. As Nos. 152/8 of Kedah, but with portrait of Raja Syed Putra as in T 6.

73		1c. Coffee	10	50
74		2c. Type **6**	10	50
75		5c. Cocoa	15	40
76		10c. Black pepper	20	15
77		15c. Rubber	30	10
78		20c. Oil palm	30	15
79		30c. Rice	40	15

7 Raja Syed Putra and Aspects of Perlis

1995. 50th Anniv of Raja Syed Putra's Accession. Multicoloured.

80		30c. Type **7**	75	50
81		$1 Raja Syed Putra and Palace	2·25	3·50

8 *Nelumbium nelumbo* (sacred lotus)

2007. Garden Flowers. As Nos. 210/15 of Johore, but with portrait of Raja Tuanku Syed Sirajuddin and Arms of Perlis as in T 8. Multicoloured.

82		5s. Type 8	10	10
83		10s. *Hydrangea macrophylla*	15	10
84		20s. *Hippeastrum reticulatum*	25	15
85		30s. *Bougainvillea*	40	20
86		40s. *Ipomoea indica*	50	30
87		50s. *Hibiscus rosa-sinensis*	65	35
MS88		100×85. Nos. 82/7	2·00	1·25

Pt. 20

PERU

A republic on the N.W. coast of S. America independent since 1821.

1857. 8 reales = 1 peso.
1858. 100 centavos = 10 dineros = 5 pesetas = 1 peso.
1874. 100 centavos = 1 sol.
1985. 100 centimos = 1 inti.
1991. 100 centimos = 1 sol.

7

1858. T 7 and similar designs with flags below arms. Imperf.

5	**7**	½ peso yellow	£2750	£375
8	**7**	1d. blue	£180	10·50
13	**7**	1 peseta red	£250	27·00

8

1862. Various frames. Imperf.

14	**8**	1d. red	14·50	4·50
20	**8**	1d. green	19·00	3·75
16	**8**	1 peseta, brown	£120	37·00
22	**8**	1 peseta, yellow	£150	55·00

10 Vicuna 13 14

1866. Various frames. Perf.

17	**10**	5c. green	10·50	95
18	-	10c. red	10·50	2·30
19	-	20c. brown	35·00	7·00

See also No. 316.

1871. 20th Anniv of First Railway in Peru (Callao–Lima–Chorillos). Imperf.

21a	**13**	5c. red	£130	43·00

1873. Roul by imperf.

23	**14**	2c. blue	50·00	£325

15 Sun-god 16 20

21

1874. Various frames. Perf.

24	**15**	1c. orange	90	65
25a	**16**	2c. violet	1·10	85
26	**16**	5c. blue	1·40	45
27	**16**	10c. green	45	30
28	**16**	20c. red	3·50	1·10
29	**20**	50c. green	15·00	4·25
30	**21**	1s. pink	2·40	2·30

For further stamps in these types, see Nos. 278, 279/84 and 314/5.

(24)

1880. Optd with T 24.

36	**15**	1c. green	90	65
37	**16**	2c. red	1·80	1·10
39	**16**	5c. blue	3·50	1·70
40	**20**	50c. green	46·00	28·00
41	**21**	1s. red	70·00	50·00

1881. Optd as T 24, but inscr "LIMA" at foot instead of "PERU".

42	**15**	1c. green	1·30	95
43	**16**	2c. red	24·00	15·00
44	**16**	5c. blue	2·75	1·30
286	**16**	10c. green	2·00	1·90
45	**20**	50c. green	£750	£425
46	**21**	1s. red	£140	90·00

(27) Arms of Chile

1881. Optd with T 27.

57	15	1c. orange	45	85
58	16	2c. violet	45	3·50
59	16	2c. red	1·40	15·00
60	16	5c. blue	50·00	55·00
61	16	10c. green	45	1·40
62	16	20c. red	70·00	£110

(28)

1882. Optd with T 27 and 28.

63	15	1c. green	45	70
64	16	5c. blue	70	70
66	20	50c. red	1·40	1·70
67	21	1s. blue	3·00	3·75

1883. Optd with T 28 only.

200	15	1c. green	2·20	2·10
201	16	2c. red	2·20	6·50
202	16	5c. blue	3·50	3·50
203	20	50c. pink	55·00	
204	21	1s. blue	55·00	

(28a)

1883. Handstamped with T 28a only.

206	15	1c. orange	1·30	1·10
210	16	5c. blue	13·00	7·00
211	16	10c. green	1·30	1·10
216	20	50c. green	6·00	4·25
220	21	1s. red	9·25	8·00

1883. Optd with T 24 and 28a, the inscription in oval reading "PERU".

223	20	50c. green	2·10	£110
225	21	1s. red	£250	£160

1883. Optd with T 24 and 28a, the inscription in oval reading "LIMA".

227	15	1c. green	7·25	7·00
228	16	2c. red	7·75	7·50
232	16	5c. blue	11·00	10·00
234	20	50c. green	£250	£150
236	21	1s. red	£275	£275

1883. Optd with T 28 and 28a.

238	15	1c. green	90	85
241	16	2c. red	1·70	1·30
246	16	5c. blue	2·20	1·60

1884. Optd CORREOS LIMA and sun.

277		5c. blue	45	25

1886. Re-issue of 1866 and 1874 types.

278	15	1c. violet	90	30
314	15	1c. red	65	30
279	16	2c. green	1·30	30
315	16	2c. blue	55	30
280	16	5c. orange	1·00	45
316	16	5c. lake	2·20	85
281	16	10c. black	65	30
317	-	10c. orange (Llamas)	1·00	55
282	16	20c. blue	8·75	1·10
318	-	20c. blue (Llamas)	10·50	2·30
283	20	50c. red	2·75	1·10
284	21	1s. brown	2·20	85

71 Pres. R. M. Bermudez

1894. Optd with T 71.

294	15	1c. orange	1·00	65
295	15	1c. green	65	55
296c	16	2c. violet	40	35
297	16	2c. red	65	55
298	16	5c. blue	4·50	2·75
299	16	10c. green	65	55
300	20	50c. green	2·40	2·00

1894. Optd with T 28 and 71.

301	16	2c. red	55	45
302	16	5c. blue	1·80	85
303	20	50c. red	70·00	43·00
304	21	1s. blue	£170	£150

73

1895. Installation of Pres. Nicolas de Pierola.

328	73	1c. violet	1·90	1·10
329	73	2c. green	1·90	1·10
330	73	5c. yellow	1·90	1·10
331	73	10c. blue	1·90	1·10
332	-	20c. orange	1·90	1·30
333	-	50c. blue	10·00	7·00
334	-	1s. lake	55·00	36·00

Nos. 332/4 are larger (30×36 mm) and the central device is in a frame of laurel.

See also Nos. 352/4.

75 Atahualpa **76** Pizarro

77 General de la Mar

1896

335	75	1c. blue	90	30
336	75	1c. green	90	30
337	75	2c. blue	90	30
338	75	2c. red	90	30
340	76	5c. green	1·30	30
341	76	5c. blue	90	55
342	76	10c. yellow	1·70	45
343	76	10c. black	1·70	30
344	76	20c. orange	3·50	45
345	77	50c. red	8·75	1·60
346	77	1s. red	13·00	1·60
347	77	2s. lake	3·50	1·20

1897. No. D31 optd FRANQUEO.

348	D 22	1c. brown	90	75

82 Suspension Bridge at Paucartambo **83** Pres. D. Nicolas de Pierola

1897. Opening of New Postal Building. Dated "1897".

349	82	1c. blue	1·20	55
350	-	2c. brown	1·20	30
351	83	5c. red	1·70	55

DESIGN: 2c. G.P.O. Lima.

1899. As Nos. 328/34, but vert inscr replaced by pearl ornaments.

352	73	22c. green	55	30
353	-	5s. red	2·75	2·75
354	-	10s. green	£850	£600

84 President Eduardo Lopez de Romana

1900

357	84	22c. black and green	13·00	1·30

85 Admiral Grau

1901. Advent of the Twentieth Century.

358	85	1c. black and green	1·70	45
359	-	2c. black and red	1·70	45
360	-	5c. black and lilac	1·70	45

PORTRAITS: 2c. Col. Bolognesi; 5c. Pres. Romana.

90 Municipal Board of Health Building

1905

361	90	12c. black and blue	1·70	45

1907. Surch.

362		1c. on 12c. black and blue	35	30
363		2c. on 12c. black and blue	65	45

97 Bolognesi Monument **98** Admiral Grau

99 Llama **101** Exhibition Buildings

103 G.P.O., Lima

1907

364	97	1c. black and green	55	30
365	98	2c. purple and red	55	30
366	99	4c. olive	9·25	1·30
367	-	5c. black and blue	1·00	30
368	101	10c. black and brown	1·70	45
369	-	20c. black and green	39·00	75
370	103	50c. black	39·00	1·60
371	-	1s. green and violet	£200	3·75
372	-	2s. black and blue	£200	£160

DESIGNS—VERT: As Type **98**: 5c. Statue of Bolivar. (24×33 mm): 2c. Columbus Monument. HORIZ: As Type **101**: 20c. Medical School, Lima. (33×24 mm): 1s. Grandstand, Santa Beatrice Race-course, Lima.

107 Columbus

1909. Portraits.

373		1c. grey (Manco Capac)	35	15
374	107	2c. green	35	15
375	-	4c. red (Pizarro)	45	30
376	-	5c. purple (San Martin)	35	15
377	-	10c. blue (Bolivar)	75	30
378	-	12c. blue (de la Mar)	1·70	30
379	-	20c. brown (Castilla)	1·90	45
380	-	50c. orange (Grau)	8·25	55
381	-	1s. black and lake (Bolognesi)	17·00	65

See also Nos. 406/13, 431/5, 439/40 and 484/9.

1913. Surch UNION POSTAL 8 Cts. Sud Americana in oval.

382	90	8c. on 12c. black and blue	90	30

1915. As 1896, 1905 and 1907, surch 1915 and value.

383	75	1c. on 1c. green	28·00	23·00
384	97	1c. on 1c. black and green	1·10	1·10
385	98	1c. on 2c. purple and red	1·70	1·60
387	99	1c. on 4c. green	3·25	2·75
386	76	1c. on 10c. black	1·70	1·30
388	101	1c. on 10c. black & brown	1·70	1·30
389	101	2c. on 10c. black & brown	£170	£130
390	90	2c. on 12c. black and blue	45	30
391	-	2c. on 20c. black and green (No. 369)	22·00	21·00
392	103	2c. on 50c. black	3·25	3·25

1916. Surch VALE, value and 1916.

393		1c. on 12c. blue (378)	35	15
394		1c. on 20c. brown (379)	35	15
395		1c. on 50c. orange (380)	35	15
396		2c. on 4c. red (375)	35	15
397		10c. on 1s. black & lake (381)	75	55

1916. Official stamps of 1909 optd FRANQUEO 1916 or surch VALE 2 Cts also.

398	O108	1c. red	20	15
399	O108	2c. on 50c. olive	35	15
400	O108	10c. brown	35	15

1916. Postage Due stamps of 1909 surch FRANQUEO VALE 2 Cts. 1916.

401	D109	2c. on 1c. brown	65	65
402	D109	2c. on 5c. brown	20	15
403	D109	2c. on 10c. brown	20	15
404	D109	2c. on 50c. brown	20	15

1917. Surch Un Centavo.

405		1c. on 4c. (No. 375)	55	55

1918. Portraits as T 107.

406		1c. black & orge (San Martin)	35	10
407		2c. black and green (Bolivar)	35	10
408		4c. black and red (Galvez)	45	30
409		5c. black and blue (Pardo)	45	30
410		8c. black and brown (Grau)	1·30	45
411		10c. black and blue (Bolognesi)	55	30
412		12c. black and lilac (Castilla)	1·70	30
413		20c. black and green (Caceres)	2·10	30

126 Columbus at Salamanca University

1918

414	126	50c. black and brown	8·25	55
415a	-	1s. black and green	21·00	75
416	-	2s. black and blue	35·00	1·10

DESIGNS: 1s. Funeral of Atahualpa; 2s. Battle of Arica.

129 A. B. Leguia

1920. New Constitution.

417	129	5c. black and blue	35	30
418	129	5c. black and brown	35	30

130 San Martin **131** Oath of Independence

132 Admiral Cochrane **137** J. Olaya

1921. Centenary of Independence.

419	130	1c. brown (San Martin)	35	15
420	130	2c. green (Arenales)	55	30
421	130	4c. red (Las Heras)	1·90	65
422	131	5c. brown	45	15
423	132	7c. violet	1·90	65

424	130	10c. blue (Guisse)	1·90	65
425	130	12c. black (Vidal)	4·50	75
426	130	20c. black and red (Leguia)	4·50	75
427	130	50c. violet and purple (S. Martin Monument)	13·00	3·75
428	131	1s. green and red (San Martin and Leguia)	19·00	8·00

1923. Surch CINCO Centavos 1923.

429	5c. on 8c. black & brn (No. 410)	75	55

1924. Surch CUATRO Centavos 1924.

430	4c. on 5c. (No. 409)	55	15

1924. Portraits as T 107. Size 18½×23 mm.

431	2c. olive (Rivadeneyra)	35	10
432	4c. green (Melgar)	35	10
433	8c. black (Iturregui)	3·25	3·25
434	10c. red (A. B. Leguia)	35	10
435	15c. blue (De la Mar)	1·00	30
439	1s. brown (De Saco)	15·00	1·60
440	2s. blue (J. Leguia)	39·00	8·00

1924. Monuments.

436	137	20c. blue	1·70	30
437	137	20c. yellow	2·75	30
438	-	50c. purple (Bellido)	8·25	45

See also Nos. 484/9.

139 Simon Bolivar

140

1924. Cent of Battle of Ayacucho. Portraits of Bolivar.

441		2c. olive	35	10
442	139	4c. green	45	20
443	139	5c. black	2·20	20
444	140	10c. red	35	10
445	-	20c. blue	2·20	30
446	-	50c. lilac	5·50	1·10
447	-	1s. brown	13·00	4·25
448	-	2s. blue	35·00	18·00

1925. Surch DOS Centavos 1925.

449	137	2c. on 20c. blue	1·70	1·10

1925. OptdPlebiscito.

450	10c. red (No. 434)	1·70	1·70

143 The Rock of Arica

1925. Obligatory Tax. Tacna–Arica Plebiscite.

451	143	2c. orange	1·10	30
452	143	5c. blue	2·75	75
453	143	5c. red	1·40	55
454	143	5c. green	1·30	55
455	-	10c. brown	5·50	23·00
456	-	50c. green	35·00	17·00

DESIGNS—HORIZ: 39×30 mm: 10c. Soldiers with colours. VERT: 27×33 mm: 50c. Bolognesi Statue.

146 The Rock of Arica

1927. Obligatory Tax. Figures of value not encircled.

457	146	2c. orange	1·10	30
458	146	2c. brown	1·10	30
459	146	2c. blue	1·10	30
460	146	2c. violet	1·10	30
461	146	2c. green	1·10	30
462	146	20c. red	5·50	1·80

1927. Air. Optd Servicio Aereo.

463	9	50c. purple (No. 438)	50·00	26·00

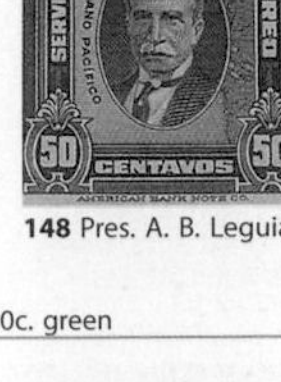

148 Pres. A. B. Leguia

1927. Air.

464	148	50c. green	1·10	55

149 The Rock of Arica

1928. Obligatory Tax. Plebiscite Fund.

465	149	2c. mauve	55	20

1929. Surch Habilitada 2 Cts. 1929.

466	-	2c. on 8c. (No. 410)	1·30	1·30
468	137	15c. on 20c. (No. 437)	1·30	1·30

1929. Surch Habilitada 2 centavos 1929.

467	2c. on 8c. (No. 410)	1·30	1·30

1930. Optd Habilitada Franqueo.

469	149	2c. mauve	55	55

1930. Surch Habilitada 2 Cts. 1930.

470	137	2c. on 20c. yellow	55	55

1930. Surch Habilitada Franqueo 2 Cts. 1930.

471	148	2c. on 50c. green	55	55

156 Arms of Peru

157 Lima Cathedral

1930. 6th (inscribed "seventh") Pan-American Child Congress.

472	156	2c. green	1·70	75
473	157	5c. red	3·75	2·10
474	-	10c. blue	2·20	1·60
475	-	50c. brown	31·00	19·00

DESIGNS—HORIZ: 10c. G.P.O., Lima. VERT: 50c. Madonna and Child.

1930. Fall of Leguia Govt. No. 434 optd with Arms of Peru or surch with new value in four corners also.

477	2c. on 10c. red	35	20
478	4c. on 10c. red	35	20
479	10c. red	35	20
476	15c. on 10c. red	35	20

159 Simon Bolivar

1930. Death Centenary of Bolivar.

480	159	2c. brown	55	55
481	159	4c. red	90	65
482	159	10c. green	45	30
483	159	15c. grey	90	85

1930. As T 107 and 137 but smaller, 18×22 mm.

484	-	2c. olive (Rivadeneyra)	45	30
485	-	4c. green (Melgar)	45	30
486	-	15c. blue (De la Mar)	1·30	30
487	137	20c. yellow (Olaya)	2·10	30
488	-	50c. purple (Bellido)	2·10	45
489	-	1s. brown (De Saco)	3·25	55

1931. Obligatory Tax. Unemployment Fund. Surch Habilitada Pro Desocupados 2 Cts.

490	159	2c. on 4c. red	1·80	75
491	159	2c. on 10c. green	75	75
492	159	2c. on 15c. grey	75	75

161 Pizarro

162 The Old Stone Bridge, Lima

1931. 1st Peruvian Philatelic Exhibition.

493	161	2c. slate	2·10	1·80
494	161	4c. brown	2·10	1·80
495	162	10c. red	2·10	1·80
496	162	10c. green and mauve	2·10	1·80
497	161	15c. green	2·10	1·80
498	162	15c. red and grey	2·10	1·80
499	162	15c. blue and orange	2·10	1·80

163 Manco Capac

164 Oil Well

1931

500	163	2c. olive	35	10
501	164	4c. green	65	30
502	-	10c. orange	1·70	10
503	-	15c. blue	2·00	30
504	-	20c. yellow	8·25	30
505	-	50c. lilac	8·25	30
506	-	1s. brown	20·00	1·40

DESIGNS—VERT: 10c. Sugar Plantation; 15c. Cotton Plantation; 50c. Copper Mines. 1s. Llamas. HORIZ: 20c. Guano Islands.

170

1931. Obligatory Tax. Unemployment Fund.

507	170	2c. green	10	10
508	170	2c. red	10	10

171 Arms of Piura

1932. 4th Centenary of Piura.

509	171	10c. blue (postage)	8·25	8·00
510	171	15c. violet	8·25	8·00
511	171	50c. red (air)	26·00	23·00

172 Parakas

1932. 400th Anniv of Spanish Conquest of Peru. Native designs.

512	172	10c. purple (22×19½ mm)	35	10
513	-	15c. lake (25×19½ mm)	65	30
514	-	50c. brown (19½×22 mm)	1·50	30

DESIGNS: 15c. Chimu; 50c. Inca.

175 Arequipa and El Misti

176 Pres. Sanchez Cerro

1932. 1st Anniv of Constitutional Government.

515	175	2c. blue	20	55
527	175	2c. black	20	10
528	175	2c. green	20	10
516	175	4c. brown	20	10
529	175	4c. orange	20	10
517	176	10c. red	28·00	16·00
530	-	10c. red	75	10
518	-	15c. blue	55	10
531	-	15c. mauve	55	10
519	-	20c. lake	75	10
532	-	20c. violet	75	20
520	-	50c. green	1·10	20
521	-	1s. orange	11·00	1·60
533	-	1s. brown	11·00	1·10

DESIGNS—VERT: 10c. (No. 530), Statue of Liberty; 15c. to 1s. Bolivar Monument, Lima.

178 Blacksmith

1932. Obligatory Tax. Unemployment Fund.

522	178	2c. grey	20	10
523	178	2c. violet	35	10

179 Monument of 2nd May to Battle of Callao

1933. Obligatory Tax. Unemployment Fund.

524	179	2c. violet	20	10
525	179	2c. orange	20	10
526	179	2c. purple	20	10

181 Hawker Hart Bomber

1934. Air.

534	181	2s. blue	6·50	65
535	181	5s. brown	15·00	1·20

1934. Obligatory Tax. Unemployment Fund. Optd Pro-Desocupados. (a) In one line.

536	176	2c. green	20	10
585	-	2c. purple (No. 537)	10	10

(b) In two lines.

566	2c. purple (No. 537)	20	10

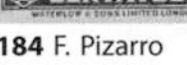

184 F. Pizarro

185 Coronation of Huascar

186 The Inca

1934

537	-	2c. purple	20	10
538	-	4c. green	20	10
539	184	10c. red	20	10

540	**184**	15c. blue	55	20
541	**185**	20c. blue	75	20
542	**185**	50c. brown	1·10	20
543	**186**	1s. violet	11·00	1·10

DESIGNS: 2, 4c. show the scene depicted in Type **189**.

187 Lake of the Marvellous Cure **188** Grapes

1935. Tercentenary of Founding of Ica.

544	-	4c. black	35	1·40
545	**187**	5c. red	45	1·40
546	**188**	10c. mauve	6·50	3·25
547	**187**	20c. green	2·20	2·10
548	-	35c. red	11·00	8·00
549	-	50c. brown and orange	7·75	7·00
550	-	1s. red and violet	22·00	17·00

DESIGNS—HORIZ: 4c. City of Ica; 50c. Don Diego Lopez and King Philip IV of Spain. VERT: 35c. Cotton blossom; 1s. Supreme God of the Nazcas.

189 Pizarro and "The Thirteen"

192 Funeral of Atahualpa

1935. 4th Centenary of Founding of Lima.

551	**189**	2c. brown (postage)	55	30
552	-	4c. violet	55	65
553	-	10c. red	55	30
554	-	15c. blue	1·10	75
555	**189**	20c. grey	2·20	95
556	-	50c. green	3·25	1·90
557	-	1s. blue	6·00	3·75
558	-	2s. brown	14·50	10·00

DESIGNS—HORIZ: 4c. Lima Cathedral. VERT: 10c., 50c. Miss L. S. de Canevaro; 15c., 2s. Pizarro; 1s. The "Tapada" (a veiled woman).

559	**192**	5c. green (air)	35	20
560	-	35c. brown	45	45
561	-	50c. yellow	90	75
562	-	1s. purple	1·70	1·20
563	-	2s. orange	2·75	2·30
564	**192**	5s. purple	11·00	7·00
565	**189**	10s. blue	44·00	30·00

DESIGNS—HORIZ: 35c. Airplane near San Cristobal Hill; 50c., 1s. Airplane over Avenue of Barefoot Friars. VERT: 2s. Palace of Torre Tagle.

207 "San Cristobal" (caravel)

1936. Callao Centenary.

567	**207**	2c. black (postage)	75	30
568	-	4c. green	75	30
569	-	5c. brown	75	30
570	-	10c. blue	75	30
571	-	15c. green	75	30
572	-	20c. brown	1·00	30
573	-	50c. lilac	1·90	55
574	-	1s. olive	12·00	1·80
575	-	2s. purple	20·00	9·00
576	-	5s. red	28·00	19·00
577	-	10s. brown and red	65·00	55·00
578	-	35c. slate (air)	3·25	1·80

DESIGNS—HORIZ: 4c. La Punta Naval College; 5c. Independence Square, Callao; 10c. Aerial view of Callao; 15c. "Reina del Pacifico" (liner) in Callao Docks and Custom House; 20c. Plan of Callao, 1746; 35c. "La Callao" (locomotive); 1s. Gunboat "Sacramento"; 10s. Real Felipe Fortifications. VERT: 50c. D. Jose de la Mar; 2s. Don Jose de Velasco; 5s. Fort Maipo and miniature portraits of Galvez and Nunez.

1936. Obligatory Tax. St. Rosa de Lima Cathedral Construction Fund. Optd "Ley 8310".

579	**179**	2c. purple	10	10

1936. Surch Habilitado and value in figures and words.

580	-	2c. on 4c. green (No. 538) (postage)	35	20
581	**185**	10c. on 20c. blue	35	20
582	**186**	10c. on 1s. violet	55	55
583	**181**	5c. on 2s. blue (air)	55	30
584	**181**	25c. on 5s. brown	1·10	55

211 Guanay Cormorants

217 Mail Steamer "Inca" on Lake Titicaca

1936

586	**211**	2c. brown (postage)	75	30
616	**211**	2c. green	1·00	30
587	-	4c. brown	75	30
617	-	4c. black	45	30
618	-	10c. red	35	30
619	-	15c. blue	45	30
590	-	20c. black	90	30
620	-	20c. brown	35	30
591	-	50c. yellow	3·25	85
621	-	50c. grey	1·00	30
592	-	1s. purple	6·50	1·10
622	-	1s. blue	1·90	30
593	-	2s. blue	13·00	2·75
623	-	2s. violet	4·50	85
594	-	5s. blue	13·00	2·75
595	-	10s. brown and violet	75·00	37·00

DESIGNS—VERT: 4c. Oil well; 10c. Inca postal runner; 1s. G.P.O., Lima; 2s. M. de Amat y Junyent; 5s. J. A. de Pando y Riva; 10s. J. D. Condemarin. HORIZ: 15c. Paseo de la Republica, Lima; 20c. Municipal Palace and Natural History Museum; 50c. University of San Marcos, Lima.

596		5c. green (air)	35	20
625	**217**	15c. blue	35	20
598		20c. grey	1·50	20
626	-	20c. green	1·00	30
627	-	25c. red	45	10
628	-	30c. brown	1·50	10
600		35c. brown	2·75	2·30
601		50c. yellow	45	30
629	-	50c. red	65	10
630	-	70c. green	1·00	85
603		80c. black	6·50	5·00
631	-	80c. green	1·30	55
604		1s. blue	4·75	45
632	-	1s. brown	2·40	30
605		1s.50 brown	7·75	5·25
633	-	1s.50 orange	4·75	45
606		2s. blue	13·00	7·50
634	-	2s. green	9·25	75
607		5s. green	17·00	3·50
608		10s. brown and red	£130	£110

DESIGNS—HORIZ: 5c. La Mar Park; 20c. Native recorder player and llama; 30c. Chuquibambilla ram; 25, 35c. J. Chavez; 50c. Mining Area; 70c. Ford "Tin Goose" airplane over La Punta; 1s. Steam train at La Cima; 1s.50, Aerodrome at Las Palmas, Lima. 2s. Douglas DC-2 mail plane; 5s. Valley of R. Inambari. VERT: 80c. Infiernillo Canyon, Andes; 10s. St. Rosa de Lima.

223 St. Rosa de Lima

1937. Obligatory Tax. St. Rosa de Lima Construction Fund.

609	**223**	2c. red	15	10

1937. Surch Habilit. and value in figures and words. (a) Postage.

610		1s. on 2s. blue (593)	3·25	3·25
		(b) Air.		
611		15c. on 30c. brown (599)	65	45
612		15c. on 35c. brown (600)	65	45
613		15c. on 70c. green (630)	4·50	3·50
614		25c. on 80c. black (603)	4·50	3·50
615		1s. on 2s. blue (606)	7·75	6·50

225 Bielovucic over Lima **226** Jorge Chavez

1937. Air. Pan-American Aviation Conference.

635	**225**	10c. violet	65	20
636	**226**	15c. green	90	20
637	-	25c. brown	65	20
638	-	1s. black	3·00	2·10

DESIGNS—As T **225**: 25c. Limatambo Airport; 1s. Peruvian air routes.

229 "Protection" (by John Q. A. Ward)

1938. Obligatory Tax. Unemployment Fund.

757c	**229**	2c. brown	10	10

230 Children's Holiday Camp

1938. Designs as T 230.

693	**230**	2c. green	55	30
694	-	4c. brown	55	30
642	-	10c. red	35	10
696	-	15c. blue	55	30
727	-	15c. turquoise	35	10
644	-	20c. purple	20	10
740	-	20c. violet	35	10
698	-	50c. blue	55	30
741	-	50c. brown	35	10
699	-	1s. purple	65	30
742	-	1s. brown	65	10
700	-	2s. green	1·70	30
731	-	2s. blue	1·90	30
701	-	5s. brown and violet	10·50	95
732	-	5s. purple and blue	1·90	65
702	-	10s. blue and black	13·00	1·30
733	-	10s. black and green	5·50	1·30

DESIGNS—VERT: 4c. Chavin pottery; 10c. Automobile roads in Andes; 20c. (2) Industrial Bank of Peru; 1s. (2) Portrait of Toribio de Luzuriaga; 5s. (2) Chavin Idol. HORIZ: 15c. (2) Archaeological Museum, Lima; 50c. (2) Labourers' homes at Lima; 2s. (2) Fig Tree; 10s. (2) Mt. Huascaran.

240 Monument on Junin Plains

1938. Air. As T 240.

650		5c. brown	20	10
743	-	5c. green	20	10
651	**240**	15c. brown	20	10
652	-	20c. red	55	30
653	-	25c. green	20	10
654	-	30c. orange	20	10
735	-	30c. red	20	10
655	-	50c. green	45	30
656	-	70c. grey	65	30
736	-	70c. blue	35	10
657	-	80c. green	1·20	30
737	-	80c. red	1·30	45
658	-	1s. green	10·00	4·25
705	-	1s.50 violet	75	30
738	-	1s.50 purple	90	55
660	-	2s. red and blue	3·75	95
661	-	5s. purple	18·00	1·70
662	-	10s. blue and green	70·00	38·00

DESIGNS—VERT: 20c. Rear-Admiral M. Villar; 70c. (No. 656, 736), Infiernillo Canyon; 2s. Stele from Chavin Temple. HORIZ: 5c. People's restaurant, Callao; 25c. View of Tarma; 30c. Ica River irrigation system; 50c. Port of Iquitos; 80c. Mountain roadway; 1s. Plaza San Martin, Lima; 1s.50, Nat. Radio Station, San Miguel; 5s. Ministry of Public Works; 10s. Heroe's Crypt, Lima.

248 Seal of City of Lima

1938. 8th Pan-American Congress, Lima.

663		10c. grey (postage)	65	45
664	**248**	15c. gold, blue, red & blk	1·10	55
665	-	1s. brown	2·75	1·60

DESIGNS (39×32½ mm): 10c. Palace and Square, 1864; 1s. Palace, 1938.

666		25c. blue (air)	90	65
667		1s.50 lake	2·40	1·90
668		2s. black	1·50	75

DESIGNS—VERT: 26×37 mm: 25c. Torre Tagle Palace. HORIZ: 39×32½ mm: 1s.50, National Congress Building, Lima; 2s. Congress Presidents, Ferreyros, Paz Soldan and Arenas.

1940. No. 642 surch Habilitada 5 cts.

669		5c. on 10c. red	20	10

251 National Broadcasting Station

1941. Optd FRANQUEO POSTAL.

670	**251**	50c. yellow	3·25	15
671	**251**	1s. violet	3·25	30
672	**251**	2s. green	5·25	85
673	**251**	5s. brown	31·00	8·50
674	**251**	10s. mauve	46·00	7·00

1942. Air. No. 653 surch Habilit 0.15.

675		15c. on 25c. green	1·70	20

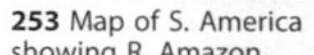

253 Map of S. America showing R. Amazon **254** Francisco de Orellana

255 Francisco Pizarro

1943. 400th Anniv of Discovery of R. Amazon.

676	-	2c. red	35	10
677	**254**	4c. grey	35	10
678	**255**	10c. brown	35	10
679	**253**	15c. blue	65	30
680	-	20c. olive	35	30
681	-	25c. orange	2·20	55
682	**254**	30c. red	55	30
683	**253**	50c. green	55	45
685	-	70c. violet	2·75	1·30
686	-	80c. blue	2·75	1·30
687	-	1s. brown	5·50	75
688	**255**	5s. black	11·00	5·00

DESIGNS—As Type **254**: 2, 70c. Portraits of G. Pizarro and Orellana in medallion; 20, 80c. G. Pizarro. As Type **253**: 25c., 1s. Orellana's Discovery of the R. Amazon.

1943. Surch with Arms of Peru (as Nos. 483, etc) above 10 CTVS.

689		10c. on 10c. red (No. 642)	20	10

257 Samuel Morse

1944. Centenary of Invention of Telegraphy.

691	**257**	15c. blue	35	30
692	**257**	30c. brown	1·00	30

1946. Surch Habilitada S/o 0.20.

706	20c. on 1s. purple (No. 699)	75	30

259

261

1947. 1st National Tourist Congress, Lima. Unissued designs inscr "V Congreso Pan Americano de Carreteras 1944" optd Habilitada I Congreso Nac. de Turismo Lima–1947.

707	**259**	15c. black and red	65	30
708	-	1s. brown	1·10	45
709	-	1s.35 green	1·10	45
710	**261**	3s. blue	2·00	75
711	-	5s. green	4·50	1·60

DESIGNS—VERT: 1s. Mountain road; 1s.35, Forest road. HORIZ: 5s. Road and house.

1947. Air. 1st Peruvian Int Airways Lima–New York Flight. Optd with PIA badge and PRIMER VUELO LIMA - NUEVA YORK.

712	5c. brown (No. 650)	55	20
713	50c. green (No. 655)	55	30

263 Basketball Players

1948. Air. Olympic Games.

714	-	1s. blue	4·00	2·75
715	**263**	2s. brown	5·50	3·50
716	-	5s. green	9·25	5·75
717	-	10s. yellow	11·00	7·00
MS717a		116×151 mm. Nos. 714/17	50·00	50·00

DESIGNS: 1s. Map showing air route from Peru to Great Britain; 5s. Discus thrower; 10s. Rifleman.

No. 714 is inscr "AEREO" and Nos. 715/17 are optd **AEREO**.

The above stamps exist overprinted **MELBOURNE 1956** but were only valid for postage on one day.

1948. Air. Nos. 653, 736 and 657 surch Habilitada S/o. and value.

722	5c. on 25c. green	20	10
723	10c. on 25c. green	20	10
718	10c. on 70c. blue	35	10
719	15c. on 70c. blue	35	10
720	20c. on 70c. blue	35	10
724	30c. on 80c. green	1·10	65
721	55c. on 70c. blue	35	10

263a

263b

1949. Anti-tuberculosis Fund. Surch Decreto Ley No. 18 and value.

724a	**263a**	3c. on 4c. blue	1·10	10
724b	**263b**	3c. in 10c. blue	1·10	10

264 Statue of Admiral Grau

1949

726	**264**	10c. blue and green	35	10

264a "Education"

1950. Obligatory Tax. National Education Fund.

851	**264a**	3c. lake (16½×21 mm)	10	10
897	**264a**	3c. lake (18×21½ mm)	20	10

265 Park, Lima

1951. Air. 75th Anniv of U.P.U. Unissued stamps inscr "VI CONGRESO DE LA UNION POSTAL DE LAS AMREICAS Y ESPANA-1949" optd U.P.U. 1874-1949.

745	**265**	5c. green	10	10
746	-	30c. red and black	20	10
747	-	55c. green	20	10
748	-	95c. turquoise	20	15
749	-	1s.50 red	35	30
750	-	2s. blue	35	30
751	-	5s. red	4·00	3·25
752	-	10s. violet	5·25	4·50
753	-	20s. blue and brown	8·75	7·00

DESIGNS: 30c. Peruvian flag; 55c. Huancayo Hotel; 95c. Ancash Mtns; 1s.50, Arequipa Hotel; 2s. Coaling Jetty; 5s. Town Hall, Miraflores; 10s. Congressional Palace; 20s. Pan-American flags.

1951. Air Surch HABILITADA S/o. 0.25.

754	25c. on 30c. red (No. 735)	20	10

1951. Surch HABILITADA S/. and figures.

755	1c. on 2c. (No. 693)	20	10
756	5c. on 15c. (No. 727)	20	10
757	10c. on 15c. (No. 727)	20	10

268 Obrero Hospital, Lima

1951. 5th Pan-American Highways Congress. Unissued "VI CONGRESO DE LA UNION POSTAL" stamps, optd V Congreso Panamericano de Carreteras 1951.

758	-	2c. green	35	10
759	**268**	4c. red	35	10
760	-	15c. grey	35	10
761	-	20c. brown	35	10
762	-	50c. purple	35	10
763	-	1s. blue	55	30
764	-	2s. blue	90	30
765	-	5s. red	2·20	2·10
766	-	10s. brown	4·00	2·10

DESIGNS—HORIZ: 2c. Aguas Promenade; 50c. Archiepiscopal Palace, Lima; 1s. National Judicial Palace; 2s. Municipal Palace; 5s. Lake Llanganuco, Ancash. VERT: 15c. Inca postal runner; 20c. Old P.O., Lima; 10s. Machu-Picchu ruins.

269 Father Tomas de San Martin and Capt. J. de Aliaga

1951. Air. 4th Cent of S. Marcos University.

767	**269**	30c. black	35	30
768	-	40c. blue	35	30
769	-	50c. mauve	35	30
770	-	1s.20 green	35	30
771	-	2s. grey	1·40	30
772	-	5s. multicoloured	3·00	30

DESIGNS: 40c. San Marcos University; 50c. Santo Domingo Convent; 1s.20, P. de Peralto Barnuevo, Father Tomas de San Martin and Jose Baquijano; 2s. Toribio Rodriguez, Jose Hipolito Unanue and Jose Cayetano Heredia; 5s. University Arms in 1571 and 1735.

270 Engineer's School

1952. (a) Postage.

774		2c. purple	10	10
775		5c. green	10	10
776		10c. green	20	10
777		15c. grey	10	10
777a		15c. brown	65	10
829	-	20c. brown	20	10
779	**270**	25c. red	20	10
779a	**270**	25c. green	65	10
780	-	30c. blue	20	10
780a	-	30c. red	35	10
830	-	30c. mauve	20	10
831	-	50c. purple	20	10
924	-	50c. green	35	10
782	-	1s. brown	55	10
782a	-	1s. blue	55	10
783	-	2s. turquoise	1·10	10
783a	-	2s. grey	1·10	10

DESIGNS—As Type **270**: HORIZ: 2c. Hotel, Tacna; 5c. Tuna fishing boat and indigenous fish; 10c. View of Matarani; 15c. Steam train; 30c. Public Health and Social Assistance. VERT: 20c. Vicuna. Larger (35×25 mm): HORIZ: 50c. Inca maize terraces; 1s. Inca ruins, Paramonga Fort; 2s. Agriculture Monument, Lima.

(b) Air.

784	40c. green	10	10
785	75c. brown	1·50	30
834	80c. red	35	10
786	1s.25 blue	35	10
787	1s.50 red	45	30
788	2s.20 blue	2·20	45
789	3s. brown	1·90	65
835	3s. green	1·10	45
836	3s.80 orange	2·20	55
790	5s. brown	1·50	30
791	10s. brown	3·75	85
838	10s. red	2·20	65

DESIGNS—As Type **270**. HORIZ: 40c. Gunboat "Maranon"; 1s.50, Housing Complex. VERT: 75c., 80c. Colony of Guanay cormorants. Larger (25×25 mm.): HORIZ: 1s.25, Corpac-Limatambo Airport; 2s.20, 3s.80, Inca Observatory, Cuzco; 5s. Garcilaso (portrait). VERT: 3s. Tobacco plant, leaves and cigarettes; 10s. Manco Capac Monument (25×37 mm).

See also Nos. 867, etc.

271 Isabella the Catholic

272 "Santa Maria", "Pinta" and "Nina"

1953. Air. 500th Birth Anniv of Isabella the Catholic.

792	**271**	40c. red	20	10
793	**272**	1s.25 green	65	15
794	**271**	2s.15 purple	1·10	55
795	**272**	2s.20 black	1·30	65

273

1954. Obligatory Tax. National Marian Eucharistic Congress Fund. Roul.

796	**273**	5c. blue and red	35	10

274 Gen. M. Perez Jimenez

1956. Visit of President of Venezuela.

797	**274**	25c. brown	10	10

275 Arms of Lima and Bordeaux

1957. Air. Exhibition of French Products, Lima.

798	**275**	40c. lake, blue and green	20	10
799	-	50c. black, brown & green	20	10
800	-	1s.25 deep blue, green and blue	55	45
801	-	2s.20 brown and blue	90	65

DESIGNS—HORIZ: 50c. Eiffel Tower and Lima Cathedral; 1s.25, Admiral Dupetit-Thouars and frigate "La Victorieuse"; 2s.20, Exhibition building, Pres. Prado and Pres. Coty.

276 1857 Stamp

1957. Air. Centenary of First Peruvian Postage Stamp.

802		5c. black and grey	10	10
803	**276**	10c. turquoise and mauve	10	10
804	-	15c. brown and green	10	10
805	-	25c. blue and yellow	10	10
806	-	30c. brown and chocolate	10	10
807	-	40c. ochre and black	20	10
808	-	1s.25 brown and blue	75	55
809	-	2s.20 red and blue	1·10	75
810	-	5s. red and mauve	2·40	75
811	-	10s. violet and green	4·50	85

DESIGNS: 5c. Pre-stamp Postmarks; 15c. 1857 2r. stamp; 25c. 1d. 1858; 30c. 1p. 1858 stamp; 40c. ½ peso 1858 stamp; 1s.25, J. Davila Condemarin, Director of Posts, 1857; 2s.20, Pres. Ramon Castilla; 5s. Pres. D. M. Prado; 10s. Various Peruvian stamps in shield.

277 Carlos Paz Soldan (founder)

1958. Air. Centenary of Lima–Callao Telegraph Service.

812	**277**	40c. brown and red	20	10
813	-	1s. green	35	20
814	-	1s.25 blue and purple	55	30

DESIGNS—VERT: 1s. Marshal Ramon Castilla. HORIZ: 1s.25, Pres. D. M. Prado and view of Callao.

No. 814 also commemorates the political centenary of the Province of Callao.

278 Flags of France and Peru

1958. Air. "Treasures of Peru" Exhibition, Paris.

815	**278**	50c. red, blue & deep blue	10	10
816	-	65c. multicoloured	15	15
817	-	1s.50 brown, purple & bl	35	20
818	-	2s.50 purple, turq & grn	65	30

DESIGNS—HORIZ: 65c. Lima Cathedral and girl in national costume; 1s.50, Caballero and ancient palace. VERT: 2s.50, Natural resources map of Peru.

279 Father Martin de Porras Velasquez

1958. Air. Birth Centenary of D. A. Carrion Garcia (patriot).

819	**279**	60c. multicoloured	10	10
820	-	1s.20 multicoloured	15	10
821	-	1s.50 multicoloured	20	10
822	-	2s.20 black	65	65

DESIGNS—VERT: 1s.20, D. A. Carrion Garcia. 1s.50, J. H. Unanue Pavon. HORIZ: 2s.20, First Royal School of Medicine (now Ministry of Government Police, Posts and Telecommunications).

280 Gen. Alvarez Thomas

1958. Air. Death Centenary of Gen. Thomas.

823	**280**	1s.10 purple, red & bistre	20	15
824	**280**	1s.20 black, red and bistre	55	55

281 Association Emblems

1958. Air. 150th Anniv of Advocates' College, Lima. Emblems in bistre and blue.

825	**281**	80c. green	20	10
826	**281**	1s.10 red	20	10
827	**281**	1s.20 blue	35	10
828	**281**	1s.50 purple	35	10

292 Symbol of Eucharist

1960. Obligatory Tax. 6th National Eucharistic Congress Fund.

839	**282**	10c. multicoloured	20	10
839a	**282**	10c. blue and red	35	10

283

1960. Air. World Refugee Year.

840	**283**	80c. multicoloured	55	55
841	**283**	4s.30 multicoloured	1·00	95
MS841a		150×100 mm. Nos. 840/1. Imperf (sold at 15s.)	17·00	17·00

284 Sea Bird bearing Map

1960. Air. International Pacific Fair, Lima.

842	**284**	1s. multicoloured	3·75	45

285 Congress Emblem

1960. 6th National Eucharistic Congress, Piura.

843	**285**	50c. red, black and blue	20	20
844	-	1s. multicoloured (Eucharistic symbols)	55	30

286 1659 Coin

1961. Air. 1st National Numismatic Exhibition, Lima.

845		1s. grey and brown	55	30
846	**286**	2s. grey and blue	55	30

DESIGNS: 1s. 1659 coin.

287 "Amazonas"

1961. Air. Centenary of World Tour of Cadet Sailing Ship "Amazonas".

847	**287**	50c. green and brown	20	10
848	**287**	80c. red and purple	35	10
849	**287**	1s. black and green	55	15

288 Globe, Moon and Stars

1961. Air. I.G.Y.

850	**288**	1s. multicoloured	1·40	65

289 Olympic Torch

1961. Air. Olympic Games, 1960.

852	**289**	5c. blue and black	90	55
853	**289**	10s. red and black	2·00	1·30
MS853a		100×80 mm. Nos. 852/3. Imerf	28·00	28·00

290 "Balloon"

1961. Christmas and New Year.

854	**290**	20c. blue	55	30

291 Fair Emblem

1961. Air. 2nd International Pacific Fair, Lima.

855	**291**	1s. multicoloured	35	30

292 Symbol of Eucharist

1962. Obligatory Tax. 7th National Eucharistic Congress Fund. Roul.

857	**292**	10c. blue and yellow	10	10

293 Sculptures "Cahuide" and "Cuauhtemoc"

1962. Air. Peruvian Art Treasures Exhibition, Mexico 1960. Flags red and green.

859	**293**	1s. red	20	10
860	-	2s. turquoise	45	30
861	-	3s. brown	65	55

DESIGNS: 2s. Tupac-Amaru and Hidalgo; 3s. Presidents Prado and Lopez.

294 Frontier Maps

1962. Air. 20th Anniv of Ecuador–Peru Border Agreement.

862	**294**	1s.30 black & red on grey	35	30
863	**294**	1s.50 multicoloured	35	30
864	**294**	2s.50 multicoloured	65	65

295 The Cedar, Pomabamba

1962. Centenary of Pomabamba and Pallasca Ancash.

865	**295**	1s. green and red (postage)	55	30
866	-	1s. black and grey (air)	35	10

DESIGN: No. 866, Agriculture, mining, etc, Pallasca Ancash (31½×22 mm.).

1962. As Nos. 774/91 but colours and some designs changed and new values. (a) Postage.

867		20c. purple	20	10
921		20c. red	35	10
922		30c. blue (as No. 776)	35	10
923		40c. orange (as No. 784)	35	10
871		60c. black (as No. 774)	55	10
925		1s. red	35	10

(b) Air.

873		1s.30 ochre (as No. 785)	75	20
874		1s.50 purple	55	10
875		1s.80 blue (as No. 777)	55	20
876		2s. green	55	10
926		2s.60 green (as No. 783)	1·00	30
877		3s. purple	55	10
927		3s.60 purple (as No. 789)	1·40	45
878		4s.30 orange	1·30	30
928		4s.60 orange (as No. 788)	1·50	55
879		5s. green	1·30	35
880		10s. blue	2·75	75

296 "Man"

1963. Air. Chavin Excavations Fund. Pottery.

881	-	1s.+50c. grey and pink	35	30
882	-	1s.50+1s. grey and blue	55	55
883	-	3s.+2s.50 grey & green	65	95
884	**296**	4s.30+3s. grey and green	1·70	1·60
885	-	6s.+4s. grey and olive	2·00	1·90

FIGURES—HORIZ: 1s. "Griffin"; 1s.50, "Eagle"; 3s. "Cat". VERT: 6s. "Deity".

297 Campaign and Industrial Emblems

1963. Freedom from Hunger.

886	**297**	1s. bistre and red (postage)	20	10
887	**297**	4s.30 bistre and green (air)	1·40	75

298 Henri Dunant and Centenary Emblem

1964. Air. Red Cross Centenary.

888	**298**	1s.30+70c. multicoloured	55	55
889	**298**	4s.30+1s.70 multicoloured	1·10	1·10

299 Chavez and Wing

1964. Air. 50th Anniv of Jorge Chavez's Trans-Alpine Flight.

890	**299**	5s. blue, purple and brn	90	45

300 Alliance Emblem

1964. "Alliance for Progress". Emblem black, green and blue.

891	**300**	40c. black & yell (postage)	10	10
892	-	1s.30 black & mauve (air)	20	10
893	**300**	3s. black and blue	75	55

DESIGN—HORIZ: 1s.30, As Type **300**, but with inscription at right.

301 Fair Poster

1965. Air. 3rd International Pacific Fair, Lima.

894	**301**	1s. multicoloured	10	10

302 Net, Flag and Globe

1965. Air. Women's World Basketball Championships, Lima.

895	**302**	1s.30 violet and red	75	30
896	**302**	4s.30 bistre and red	1·70	75

303 St. Martin de Porras (anonymous)

1965. Air. Canonization of St. Martin de Porras (1962). Paintings. Multicoloured.

898	1s.30 Type **303**	35	10
899	1s.80 "St. Martin and the Miracle of the Animals" (after painting by Camino Brent)	45	20
900	4s.30 "St. Martin and the Angels" (after painting by Fausto Conti)	90	85

Porras is wrongly spelt "Porres" on the stamps.

304 Fair Emblem

1965. 4th International Pacific Fair, Lima.

901	**304**	1s.50 multicoloured	35	15
902	**304**	2s.50 multicoloured	35	20
903	**304**	3s.50 multicoloured	45	30

305 Father Christmas and Postmarked Envelope

1965. Christmas.

904	**305**	20c. black and red	20	10
905	**305**	50c. black and green	45	30
906	**305**	1s. black and blue	75	55

The above stamps were valid for postage only on November 2nd. They were subsequently used as postal employees' charity labels.

1966. Obligatory Tax. Journalists' Fund. (a) Surch HABILITADO "Fondo del Periodista Peruano" Ley 16078 S/o. 0.10.

907	**264a**	10c. on 3c. (No. 897)	35	20

(b) Surch Habilitado "Fondo del Periodista Peruano" Ley 16078 S/. 0.10.

909	10c. on 3c. (No. 897)	35	20

1966. Obligatory Tax. Journalists' Fund. No. 857 optd Periodista Peruano LEY 16078.

910	**292**	10c. blue and yellow	10	10

1966. Nos. 757c, 851 and 897 surch XX Habilitado S/. 0.10.

911	**229**	10c. on 2c. brown	10	10
912	**264a**	10c. on 3c. lake (No. 897)	10	10
912b	**264a**	10c. on 3c. lake (No. 851)	1·30	20

312 2nd May Monument and Battle Scene

1966. Air. Centenary of Battle of Callao. Mult.

913	1s.90 Type **312**	65	30
914	3s.60 Monument and sculpture	75	45
915	4s.60 Monument and Jose Galvez	1·30	55

313 Funerary Mask

1966. Gold Objects of Chimu Culture. Multicoloured.

916	1s.90+90c. Type **313**	1·20	1·20
917	2s.60+1s.30 Ceremonial knife (vert)	1·50	1·50
918	3s.60+1s.80 Ceremonial urn	2·20	2·10
919	4s.60+2s.30 Goblet (vert)	3·00	2·75
920	20s.+10s. Ear-ring	12·00	11·50

314 Civil Guard Emblem

1966. Air. Civil Guard Centenary Multicoloured.

929	90c. Type **314**	10	10
930	1s.90 Emblem and activities of Civil Guard	55	20

315 Map and Mountains

1966. Opening of Huinco Hydro-electric Scheme.

931	**315**	70c. black, deep blue and blue (postage)	35	20
932	**315**	1s.90 black, blue and violet (air)	35	20

316 Globe

1967. Air. Peruvian Photographic Exhibition, Lima.

933	-	2s.60 red and black	35	20
934	-	3s.60 black and blue	45	55
935	**316**	4s.60 multicoloured	55	55

DESIGNS: 2s.60, "Sun" carving; 3s.60, Map of Peru within spiral.

317 Symbol of Construction

1967. Six-year Construction Plan.

936	**317**	90c. black, gold and mauve (postage)	35	15
937	**317**	1s.90 black, gold and ochre (air)	45	30

318 "St. Rosa" (from painting by A. Medoro)

1967. Air. 350th Death Anniv of St. Rosa of Lima. Designs showing portraits of St. Rosa by artists given below. Multicoloured.

938	1s.90 Type **318**	65	15
939	2s.60 C. Maratta	1·10	30
940	3s.60 Anon., Cusquena School	1·20	55

319 Vicuna within Figure "5"

1967. 5th International Pacific Fair, Lima.

941	**319**	1s. black, green and gold (postage)	20	10
942	**319**	1s. purple, black and gold (air)	35	20

320 Pen-nib made of Newspaper

1967. Obligatory Tax. Journalists' Fund.

943	**320**	10c. black and red	10	10

321 Wall Reliefs (fishes)

1967. Obligatory Tax. Chan-Chan Excavation Fund.

944	**321**	20c. black and blue	10	10
945	-	20c. black and mauve	10	10
946	-	20c. black and brown	10	10
947	-	20c. multicoloured	10	10
948	-	20c. multicoloured	10	10
949	-	20c. black and green	10	10

DESIGNS: No. 945, Ornamental pattern; No. 946, Carved "bird"; No. 947, Temple on hillside; No. 948, Corner of Temple; No. 949, Ornamental pattern (birds).

322 Lions' Emblem

1967. Air. 50th Anniv of Lions International.

950	**322**	1s.60 violet, blue and grey	45	30

323 Nazca Jug

1968. Air. Ceramic Treasures of Nazca Culture. Designs showing painted pottery jugs. Mult.

951	1s.90 Type **323**	65	30
952	2s.60 Falcon	75	55
953	3s.60 Round jug decorated with bird	75	55
954	4s.60 Two-headed snake	1·10	75
955	5s.60 Sea Bird	2·20	1·10

324 Alligator

1968. Gold Sculptures of Mochica Culture. Mult.

956	1s.90 Type **324**	2·20	45
957	2s.60 Bird (vert)	3·25	55
958	3s.60 Lizard	4·00	65
959	4s.60 Bird (vert)	4·75	65
960	5s.60 Jaguar	4·75	95

325 "Antarqui" (Airline Symbol)

1968. Air. 12th Anniv of APSA (Peruvian Airlines).

961	**325**	3s.60 multicoloured	55	30
962	-	5s.60 brown, black & red	75	55

DESIGN: 5s.60, Alpaca and stylized Boeing 747.

326 Human Rights Emblem

1968. Air. Human Rights Year.

963	**326**	6s.50 red, green & brown	55	55

327 "The Discus-thrower"

1968. Air. Olympic Games, Mexico.

964	**327**	2s.30 brown, blue & yell	35	10
965	**327**	3s.50 blue, red and green	35	20
966	**327**	5s. black, blue and pink	35	30
967	**327**	6s.50 purple, brown & bl	55	45
968	**327**	8s. blue, mauve and lilac	55	55
969	**327**	9s. violet, green and orange	55	65

328

1968. Obligatory Tax. Unissued stamps surch as in T 328.

970	**328**	20c. on 50c. violet, orange and black	90	85
971	**328**	20c. on 1s. blue, orange and black	90	85

1968. Obligatory Tax. Journalists' Fund. No. 897 surch Habilitado Fondo Periodista Peruano Ley 17050 S/. and value.

972	**264a**	20c. on 3c. lake	10	10

1968. Christmas. No. 900 surch PRO NAVIDAD Veinte Centavos R.S. 5-11-68.

973	20c. on 4s.30 multicoloured	65	55

331 Indian's Head and Wheat

1969. Unissued Agrarian Reform stamps, surch as in T 331. Multicoloured.

974		2s.50 on 90c. Type **331** (postage)	20	10
975		3s. on 90c. Man digging	35	20
976		4s. on 90c. As No. 975	45	30
977		5s.50 on 1s.90 Corn-cob and hand scattering cobs (air)	55	30
978		6s.50 on 1s.90 As No. 977	75	45

333 First Peruvian Coin (obverse and reverse)

1969. Air. 400th Anniv of 1st Peruvian Coinage.

979	**333**	5s. black, grey and yellow	55	20
980	**333**	5s. black, grey and green	55	20

334 Worker holding Flag and Oil Derrick

1969. Nationalization of International Petroleum Company's Oilfields and Refinery (9 October 1968).

981	**334**	2s.50 multicoloured	35	15
982	**334**	3s. multicoloured	35	20
983	**334**	4s. multicoloured	65	30
984	**334**	5s.50 multicoloured	65	30

335 Castilla Monument

1969. Air. Death Centenary of President Ramon Castilla.

985	**335**	5s. blue and green	55	30
986	-	10s. brown and purple	1·30	65

DESIGN—(21×37 mm): 10s. President Castilla.

336 Boeing 707, Globe and "Kon Tiki" (replica of balsa raft)

1969. 1st A.P.S.A. (Peruvian Airlines) Flight to Europe.

987	**336**	2s.50 mult (postage)	55	10
988	**336**	3s. multicoloured (air)	35	10
989	**336**	4s. multicoloured	55	15
990	**336**	5s.50 multicoloured	65	30
991	**336**	6s.50 multicoloured	65	55

337 Dish Aerial, Satellite and Globe

1969. Air. Inauguration of Lurin Satellite Telecommunications Station, Lima.

992	**337**	20s. multicoloured	2·20	1·10
MS993		110×81 mm. No. 992. Imperf	4·00	4·00

338 Captain Jose A. Quinones Gonzales (military aviator)

1969. Quinones Gonzales Commemoration.

994	**338**	20s. mult (postage)	2·75	1·30
995	**338**	20s. multicoloured (air)	2·75	1·30

339 W.H.O. Emblem

1969. Air. 20th Anniv (1968) of W.H.O.

996	**339**	5s. multicoloured	35	30
997	**339**	6s.50 multicoloured	45	30

340 Peasant breaking Chains

1969. Agrarian Reform Decree.

998	**340**	2s.50 deep blue, blue and red (postage)	10	10
999	**340**	3s. purple, lilac and black (air)	35	15
1000	**340**	4s. brown and light brown	55	30

341 Arms of the Inca Garcilaso de la Vega (historian)

1969. Air. Garcilaso de la Vega Commemoration.

1001	**341**	2s.40 black, silver & grn	20	10
1002	-	3s.50 black, buff and blue	35	15
1003	-	5s. multicoloured	55	20
MS1004		127×88 mm. Nos. 1001/1003. Imperf	1·90	1·90

DESIGNS: 3s.50, Title page, "Commentarios Reales", Lisbon, 1609; 5s. Inca Garcilaso de la Vega.

342 Admiral Grau and Ironclad Warship "Huascar"

1969. Navy Day.

1005	**342**	50s. multicoloured	5·50	3·25

343 "6" and Fair Flags

1969. 6th International Pacific Fair, Lima.

1006	**343**	2s.50 mult (postage)	55	10
1007	**343**	3s. multicoloured (air)	55	10
1008	**343**	4s. multicoloured	55	15

344 Father Christmas and Greetings Card

1969. Christmas.

1009	**344**	20c. black and red	35	20
1010	**344**	20c. black and orange	35	20
1011	**344**	20c. black and brown	35	20

345 Col. F. Bolognesi and Soldier

1969. Army Day.

1012	**345**	1s.20 black, gold and blue (postage)	35	10
1013	**345**	50s. black, gold and brown (air)	4·50	1·90

346 Arms of Amazonas

1970. Air. 150th Anniv (1971) of Republic (1st issue).

1014	**346**	10s. multicoloured	1·20	75

See also Nos. 1066/70, 1076/80 and 1081/90.

347 I.L.O. Emblem on Map

1970. Air. 50th Anniv of I.L.O.

1015	**347**	3s. deep blue and blue	35	10

348 "Motherhood"

1970. Air. 24th Anniv of UNICEF.

1016	**348**	5s. black and yellow	45	30
1017	**348**	6s.50 black and pink	65	45

349 "Puma" Jug

1970. Vicus Culture. Ceramic Art. Multicoloured.

1018		2s.50 Type **349** (postage)	75	10
1019		3s. Squatting warrior (statuette) (air)	1·10	30
1020		4s. Animal jug	1·10	30
1021		5s.50 Twin jugs	2·20	85
1022		6s.50 Woman with jug (statuette)	3·25	1·10

350 Ministry Building

1970. Ministry of Transport and Communications.

1023	**350**	40c. black and purple	35	10
1024	**350**	40c. black and yellow	35	10
1025	**350**	40c. black and grey	35	10
1026	**350**	40c. black and red	35	10
1027	**350**	40c. black and brown	35	10

351 Peruvian Anchovy

1970. Fishes. Multicoloured.

1028		2s.50 Type **351** (postage)	2·00	30
1029		2s.50 Chilean hake	2·00	30
1030		3s. Swordfish (air)	2·00	30
1031		3s. Yellow-finned tuna	2·00	30
1032		5s.50 Atlantic wolffish	2·00	30

352 Telephone and Skyline

1970. Air. Nationalization of Lima Telephone Service.

1033	**352**	5s. multicoloured	55	20
1034	**352**	10s. multicoloured	1·10	55

353 "Soldier and Farmer"

1970. Unity of Armed Forces and People.

1035	**353**	2s.50 mult (postage)	55	10
1036	**353**	3s. multicoloured (air)	55	20
1037	**353**	5s.50 multicoloured	1·10	20

354 U.N. Headquarters and Dove

1970. Air. 25th Anniv of U.N.O.

1038	**354**	3s. blue and light blue	35	30

355 Rotary Emblem

1970. Air. 50th Anniv of Lima Rotary Club.

1039	**355**	10s. gold, red and black	1·30	75

356 Military Parade (Army Staff College, Chorrillos)

1970. Military, Naval and Air Force Academies. Multicoloured.

No.	Description	Mint	Used
1040	2s.50 Type **356**	90	30
1041	2s.50 Parade, Naval Academy, La Punta	90	30
1042	2s.50 Parade, Air Force Officer Training School, Las Palmas	90	30

357 Puruchuco, Lima

1970. Tourism. Multicoloured.

No.	Description	Mint	Used
1043	2s.50 Type **357** (postage)	1·10	30
1044	3s. Chan-Chan-Trujillo, La Libertad (air)	1·10	30
1045	4s. Sacsayhuaman, Cuzco (vert)	1·30	30
1046	5s.50 Lake Titicaca, Pomata, Puno (vert)	1·90	45
1047	10s. Machu-Picchu, Cuzco (vert)	2·75	95
MS1048	127×95 mm. Nos. 1043/7. Imperf	5·50	5·50

358 Festival Procession

1970. Air. October Festival, Lima. Multicoloured.

No.	Description	Mint	Used
1049	3s. Type **358**	20	10
1050	4s. "The Cock-fight" (T. Nunez Ureta)	35	20
1051	5s.50 Altar, Nazarenas Shrine (vert)	65	45
1052	6s.50 "The Procession" (J. Vinatea Reinoso)	75	55
1053	8s. "The Procession" (Jose Sabogal) (vert)	1·10	65

359 "The Nativity" (Cuzco School)

1970. Christmas. Paintings by Unknown Artists. Multicoloured.

No.	Description	Mint	Used
1054	1s.20 Type **359**	35	20
1055	1s.50 "The Adoration of the Magi" (Cuzquena School)	35	20
1056	1s.80 "The Adoration of the Shepherds" (Peruvian School)	35	20

360 "Close Embrace" (petroglyph)

1971. Air. "Gratitude for World Help in Earthquake of May 1970".

No.	Type	Description	Mint	Used
1057	**360**	4s. olive, black and red	55	30
1058	**360**	5s.50 blue, flesh and red	55	30
1059	**360**	6s.50 grey, blue and red	55	30

361 "St. Rosa de Lima" (F. Laso)

1971. 300th Anniv of Canonization of St. Rosa de Lima.

No.	Type	Description	Mint	Used
1060	**361**	2s.50 multicoloured	35	10

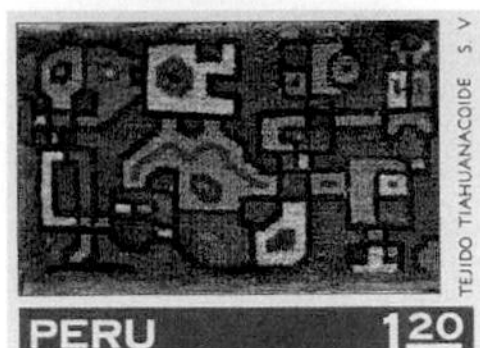

362 Tiahuanaco Fabric

1971. Ancient Peruvian Textiles.

No.	Type	Description	Mint	Used
1061	**362**	1s.20 mult (postage)	20	10
1062	-	2s.50 multicoloured	55	10
1063	-	3s. multicoloured (air)	1·10	20
1064	-	4s. pink, green & dp grn	1·10	30
1065	-	5s.50 multicoloured	1·70	55

DESIGNS—HORIZ: 2s.50, Chancay fabric; 4s. Chancay lace. VERT: 3s. Chancay tapestry; 5s.50, Paracas fabric.

363 M. Garcia Pumacahua

1971. 150th Anniv of Independence (2nd issue). National Heroes.

No.	Type	Description	Mint	Used
1066	**363**	1s.20 blk & red (postage)	10	10
1067	-	2s.50 black and blue	35	15
1068	-	3s. black and mauve (air)	15	15
1069	-	4s. black and green	35	20
1070	-	5s.50 black and brown	55	20

DESIGNS: 2s.50, F. Antonio de Zela; 3s. T. Rodriguez de Mendoza; 4s. J. P. Viscardo y Guzman; 5s.50, J. G. Condorcanqui, Tupac Amani.

See also Nos. 1076/80 and Nos. 1081/90.

364 Violet Amberjack (Nazca Culture)

1971. "Traditional Fisheries of Peru". Piscatorial Ceramics. Multicoloured.

No.	Description	Mint	Used
1071	1s.50 Type **364** (postage)	35	10
1072	3s.50 Pacific bonito (Chimu Inca) (air)	65	20
1073	4s. Peruvian anchovy (Mochica)	75	20
1074	5s.50 Chilian hake (Chimu)	1·20	55
1075	8s.50 Peruvian menhaden (Nazca)	1·80	1·10

1971. 150th Anniv of Independence. National Heroes (3rd issue). As T 363. Multicoloured.

No.	Description	Mint	Used
1076	1s.20 M. Melgar (postage)	10	10
1077	2s.50 J. Baquijano y Carrillo	35	20
1078	3s. J. de la Riva Aguero (air)	20	15
1079	4s. H. Unanue	35	15
1080	5s.50 F. J. de Luna Pizarro	55	20

366 Liberation Expedition Monument

1971. 150th Anniv of Independence (4th issue). As T 366. Multicoloured.

No.	Description	Mint	Used
1081	1s.50 M. Bastidas (postage)	20	10
1082	2s. J. F. Sanchez Carrion	20	10
1083	2s.50 M. J. Guise	35	20
1084	3s. F. Vidal (air)	20	20
1085	3s.50 J. de San Martin	35	20
1086	4s.50 Type **366**	35	20
1087	6s. "Surrender of the 'Numancia Battalion'" (horiz) (42×35 mm)	65	30
1088	7s.50 Alvarez de Arenales Monument (horiz) (42×39 mm)	75	55
1089	9s. Monument to Founders of the Republic, Lima (horiz) (42×39 mm)	75	55
1090	10s. "Proclamation of Independence" (horiz) (46×35 mm)	55	65

367 R. Palma (author and poet)

1971. Air. 150th Anniv of National Library.

No.	Type	Description	Mint	Used
1091	**367**	7s.50 black and brown	1·10	55

368 Weightlifting

1971. Air. 25th World Weightlifting Championships, Huampani, Lima.

No.	Type	Description	Mint	Used
1092	**368**	7s.50 black and blue	1·10	55

369 "Gongora portentosa"

1971. Peruvian Flora (1st series). Orchids. Mult.

No.	Description	Mint	Used
1093	1s.50 Type **369**	90	10
1094	2s. "Odontoglossum cristatum"	1·10	20
1095	2s.50 "Mormolyca peruviana"	1·10	10
1096	3s. "Trichocentrum pulchrum"	1·30	20
1097	3s.50 "Oncidium sanderae"	2·20	20

See also Nos. 1170/4 and 1206/10.

370 Family and Flag

1971. Air. 3rd Anniv of October 3rd Revolution.

No.	Type	Description	Mint	Used
1098	**370**	7s.50 black, red and blue	90	30
MS1099		110×82 mm. No. 1089. Imperf	2·75	2·75

371 Schooner "Sacramento" of 1821

1971. Air. 150th Anniv of Peruvian Navy and "Order of the Peruvian Sun".

No.	Type	Description	Mint	Used
1100	**371**	7s.50 blue and light blue	1·00	55
1101	-	7s.50 multicoloured	55	30

DESIGN: No. 1101, Order of the Peruvian Sun.

372 "Development and Liberation" (detail)

1971. 2nd Ministerial Meeting of "The 77" Group.

No.	Type	Description	Mint	Used
1102	**372**	1s.20 multicoloured (postage)	10	10
1103	-	3s.50 multicoloured	45	20
1104	-	50s. multicoloured (air)	6·50	2·30

DESIGNS—As Type **372**: 3s.50, 50s. Detail from the painting "Development and Liberation".

373 "Plaza de Armas, 1843" (J. Rugendas)

1971. "Exfilima" Stamp Exhibition, Lima.

No.	Type	Description	Mint	Used
1105	**373**	3s. black and green	65	30
1106	-	3s.50 black and pink	65	30

DESIGN: 3s.50, "Plaza de Armas, 1971" (C. Zeiter).

374 Fair Emblem

1971. Air. 7th International Pacific Fair, Lima.

No.	Type	Description	Mint	Used
1107	**374**	4s.50 multicoloured	55	20

375 Army Crest

1971. 150th Anniv of Peruvian Army.

No.	Type	Description	Mint	Used
1108	**375**	8s.50 multicoloured	1·30	55

376 "The Flight into Egypt"

1971. Christmas. Multicoloured.

No.	Description	Mint	Used
1109	1s.80 Type **376**	35	30
1110	2s.50 "The Magi"	55	30
1111	3s. "The Nativity"	65	30

377 "Fishermen" (J. Ugarte Elespuru)

1971. Social Reforms. Paintings. Multicoloured.

1112	3s.50 Type **377**	1·10	20
1113	4s. "Threshing Grain in Cajamarca" (Camilo Blas)	1·10	20
1114	6s. "Hand-spinning Huanca Native Women" (J. Sabogal)	1·70	20

378 Chimu Idol

1972. Peruvian Antiquities. Multicoloured.

1115	3s.90 Type **378**	1·10	20
1116	4s. Chimu statuette	1·10	20
1117	4s.50 Lambayeque idol	1·30	30
1118	5s.40 Mochica collar	1·30	30
1119	6s. Lambayeque "spider" pendant	1·80	55

379 Peruvian Bigeye

1972. Peruvian Fishes. Multicoloured.

1120	1s.20 Type **379** (postage)	55	20
1121	1s.50 Common guadana	55	20
1122	2s.50 Jack mackerel	1·20	20
1123	3s. Diabolico (air)	1·30	30
1124	5s.50 Galapagos hogfish	2·40	65

380 "Peruvian Family" (T. Nunez Ureta)

1972. Air. Education Reforms.

1125	**380**	6s.50 multicoloured	75	45

381 Mochica Warrior

1972. Peruvian Art (1st series). Mochica Ceramics. Multicoloured.

1126	1s.20 Type **381**	55	20
1127	1s.50 Warrior's head	55	20
1128	2s. Kneeling deer	1·20	20
1129	2s.50 Warrior's head (different)	1·30	20
1130	3s. Kneeling warrior	1·90	20

See also Nos. 1180/4.

382 White-tailed Trogon

1972. Air. Peruvian Birds. Multicoloured.

1131	2s. Type **382**	2·40	30
1132	2s.50 Amazonian umbrellabird	2·40	30
1133	3s. Andean cock of the rock	2·75	30
1134	6s.50 Red-billed toucan	5·00	55
1135	8s.50 Blue-crowned motmot	7·75	65

383 "The Harvest" (July)

1972. 400th Anniv of G. Poma de Ayala's "Inca Chronicles". Woodcuts.

1136	**383**	2s.50 black and red	1·90	30
1138	-	2s.50 black and pink	1·90	30
1140	-	2s.50 black and orange	1·90	30
1142	-	2s.50 black and brown	1·90	30
1144	-	2s.50 black and blue	1·90	30
1146	-	2s.50 black and mauve	1·90	30
1137	-	3s. black and green	1·90	30
1139	-	3s. black and blue	1·90	30
1141	-	3s. black and lilac	1·90	30
1143	-	3s. black and green	1·90	30
1145	-	3s. black and orange	1·90	30
1147	-	3s. black and yellow	1·90	30

DESIGNS: No. 1137, "Land Purification" (August); No. 1138, "Sowing" (September); No. 1139, "Invocation of the Rains" (October); No. 1140, "Irrigation" (November); No. 1141, "Rite of the Nobility" (December); No. 1142, "Maize Cultivation Rights" (January); No. 1143, "Ripening of the Maize" (February); No. 1144, "Birds in the Maize" (March); No. 1145, "Children as camp-guards" (April); No. 1146, "Gathering the harvest" (May); No. 1147, "Removing the harvest" (June).

384 "Quipu" on Map

1972. Air. "Exfibra 72" Stamp Exn, Rio de Janeiro.

1148	**384**	5s. multicoloured	1·00	30

385 "The Messenger"

1972. Air. Olympic Games, Munich.

1149	**385**	8s. multicoloured	1·10	55

386 Catacaos Woman

1972. Air. Provincial Costumes (1st series). Mult.

1150	2s. Tupe girl	35	20
1151	3s.50 Type **386**	1·30	55
1152	4s. Conibo Indian	1·50	65
1153	4s.50 Agricultural worker playing "quena" and drum	90	30
1154	5s. "Moche" (Trujillo) girl	75	30
1155	6s.50 Ocongate (Cuzco) man and woman	2·20	85
1156	8s. "Chucupana" (Ayacucho) girl	1·70	65
1157	8s.50 "Cotuncha" (Junin) girl	1·70	65
1158	10s. "Pandilla" dancer	1·70	75

See also Nos. 1248/9.

387 Ruins of Chavin (Ancash)

1972. Air. 25th Death Anniv Julio C. Tello (archaeologist). Multicoloured.

1159	1s.50 "Stone of the 12 Angles", Cuzco (vert)	55	10
1160	3s.50 Type **387**	75	20
1161	4s. Burial-tower, Sillustani (Puno) (vert)	75	20
1162	5s. Gateway, Chavin (Ancash)	1·10	30
1163	8s. "Wall of the 3 Windows", Machu Picchu (Cuzco)	1·80	55

388 "Territorial Waters"

1972. 4th Anniv of Armed Forces Revolution. Mult.

1164	2s. Agricultural Workers ("Agrarian Reform") (vert)	35	30
1165	2s.50 Type **388**	35	30
1166	3s. Oil rigs ("Nationalization of Petroleum Industry") (vert)	35	30

389 "The Holy Family" (wood-carving)

1972. Christmas. Multicoloured.

1167	1s.50 Type **389**	35	10
1168	2s. "The Holy Family" (carved Huamanga stone) (horiz)	35	20
1169	2s.50 "The Holy Family" (carved Huamanga stone)	35	20

390 "Ipomoea purpurea"

1972. Peruvian Flora (2nd series). Multicoloured.

1170	1s.50 Type **390**	55	20
1171	2s.50 "Amaryllis ferreyrae"	65	20
1172	3s. "Liabum excelsum"	90	20
1173	3s.50 "Bletia catenulata"	1·10	20
1174	5s. "Cantua buxifolia cantuta"	1·80	55

391 Inca Poncho

1973. Air. Ancient Inca Textiles.

1175	**391**	2s. multicoloured	55	20
1176	-	3s.50 multicoloured	75	30
1177	-	4s. multicoloured	75	30
1178	-	5s. multicoloured	75	55
1179	-	8s. multicoloured	1·90	55

DESIGNS: Nos. 1176/9, similar to T **391**.

392 Mochica Cameo and Cups

1973. Air. Peruvian Art (2nd series). Jewelled Antiquities. Multicoloured.

1180	1s.50 Type **392**	1·20	30
1181	2s.50 Gold-plated arms and hands (Lambayeque)	1·20	30
1182	4s. Bronze effigy (Mochica)	1·20	30
1183	5s. Gold pendants (Nazca)	1·50	65
1184	8s. Gold cat (Mochica)	2·75	75

393 Andean Condor

1973. Air. Fauna Protection (1st series). Mult.

1185	2s.50 Lesser rhea	1·90	30
1186	3s.50 Giant otter	2·75	55
1187	4s. Type **393**	55	20
1188	5s. Vicuna	75	45
1189	6s. Chilian flamingo	3·75	55
1190	8s. Spectacled bear	1·70	75
1191	8s.50 Bush dog (horiz)	3·75	75
1192	10s. Short-tailed chinchilla (horiz)	4·75	1·30

See also Nos. 1245/6.

394 "The Macebearer" (J. Sabogal)

1973. Air. Peruvian Paintings. Multicoloured.

1193	1s.50 Type **394**	35	20
1194	8s. "Yananacu Bridge" (E. C. Brent) (horiz)	1·10	30
1195	8s.50 "Portrait of a Lady" (D. Hernandez)	40	15
1196	10s. "Peruvian Birds" (T. N. Ureta)	1·80	55
1197	20s. "The Potter" (F. Laso)	2·75	1·10
1198	50s. "Reed Boats" (J. V. Reinoso) (horiz)	7·75	2·10

395 Basketball Net and Map

1973. Air. 1st World Basketball Festival.

1199	**395**	5s. green	65	30
1200	**395**	20s. purple	2·75	85

396 "Spanish Mayor on Horseback"

1973. 170th Birth Anniv of Pancho Fierro (painter). Multicoloured.

1201	1s.50 Type **396**	35	10
1202	2s. "Peasants"	35	10
1203	2s.50 "Father Abregu"	55	20

1204 3s.50 "Dancers" 55 20
1205 4s.50 "Esteban Arredondo on horseback" 1·30 65

1973. Air. Peruvian Flora (3rd series). Orchids. As T 390. Multicoloured.
1206 1s.50 "Lycaste reichenbachii" 1·50 30
1207 2s.50 "Masdevallia amabilis" 2·00 30
1208 3s. "Sigmatostalix peruviana" 2·10 30
1209 3s.50 "Porrogossum peruvianum" 2·75 30
1210 8s. "Oncidium incarum" 5·50 1·10

398 Fair Emblem (poster)

1973. Air. 8th International Pacific Fair, Lima.
1211 **398** 8s. red, black and grey 1·10 30

399 Symbol of Flight

1973. Air. 50th Anniv of Air Force Officers' School.
1212 **399** 8s.50 multicoloured 1·10 30

400 "The Presentation of the Child"

1973. Christmas. Paintings of the Cuzco School. Multicoloured.
1213 1s.50 Type **400** 20 10
1214 2s. "The Holy Family" (vert) 35 20
1215 2s.50 "The Adoration of the Kings" 35 30

401 Freighter "Ilo"

1973. Air. National Development. Multicoloured.
1216 1s.50 Type **401** 20 20
1217 2s.50 Trawlers 35 30
1218 8s. B.A.C. One Eleven 200 airliner and seagull 1·50 30

402 House of the Mulberry Tree, Arequipa

1974. Air. "Landscapes and Cities". Mult.
1219 1s.50 Type **402** 20 10
1220 2s.50 El Misti (peak), Arequipa 55 10
1221 5s. Giant puya, Cordillera Blanca, Ancash (vert) 75 20
1222 6s. Huascaran (peak), Cordillera Blanca, Ancash 1·10 20
1223 8s. Lake Querococha, Cordillera Blanca, Ancash 1·80 65

403 Peruvian 2c. Stamp of 1873

1974. Stamp Day and 25th Anniv of Peruvian Philatelic Association.
1224 **403** 6s. blue and grey 90 30

404 Room of the Three Windows, Machu Picchu

1974. Air. Archaeological Discoveries. Mult. (a) Cuzco Relics.
1225 3s. Type **404** 75 20
1226 5s. Baths of Tampumacchay 75 20
1227 10s. "Kencco" 1·10 20

(b) Dr. Tello's Discoveries at Chavin de Huantar. Stone carvings.
1228 3s. Mythological jaguar (vert) 1·10 20
1229 5s. Rodent ("Vizcacha") (vert) 2·20 65
1230 10s. Chavin warrior (vert) 2·20 65

405 Church of San Jeronimo, Cuzco

1974. Air. Architectural Treasures. Multicoloured.
1231 1s.50 Type **405** 90 30
1232 3s.50 Cathedral of Santa Catalina, Cajamarca 90 30
1233 5s. Church of San Pedro, Zepita, Puno (horiz) 1·30 30
1234 6s. Cuzco Cathedral 1·30 45
1235 8s.50 Wall of the Coricancha, Cuzco 2·20 55

406 "Colombia" Bridge, Tarapoto–Juanjui Highway

1974. "Structural Changes". Multicoloured.
1236 2s. Type **406** 20 10
1237 8s. Tayacaja hydro-electric scheme 1·10 55
1238 10s. Tablachaca dam 1·10 55

407 "Battle of Junin" (F. Yanez)

1974. 150th Anniv of Battle of Junin.
1239 **407** 1s.50 mult (postage) 20 20
1240 **407** 2s.50 multicoloured 35 30
1241 **407** 6s. multicoloured (air) 90 30

408 "Battle of Ayacucho" (F. Yanez)

1974. 150th Anniv of Battle of Ayacucho.
1242 **408** 2s. mult (postage) 20 20
1243 **408** 3s. multicoloured 35 30
1244 **408** 7s.50 multicoloured (air) 90 30

1974. Air. Fauna Protection (2nd series). As T 393. Multicoloured.
1245 8s. Red uakari 1·10 20
1246 20s. As 8s. 2·75 1·10

409 Chimu Gold Mask

1974. Air. 8th World Mining Congress, Lima.
1247 **409** 8s. multicoloured 1·90 30

1974. Air. Provincial Costumes (2nd series). As T 386. Multicoloured.
1248 5s. Horseman in "chalan" (Cajamarca) 55 20
1249 8s.50 As 5s. 1·10 55

410 Pedro Paulet and Spacecraft

1974. Air. Centenary of U.P.U. and Birth Centenary of Pedro E. Paulet (aviation scientist).
1250 **410** 8s. violet and blue 75 30

411 Copper Smelter, La Oroya

1974. Expropriation of Cerro de Pasco Mining Complex.
1251 **411** 1s.50 blue and deep blue 20 10
1252 **411** 3s. red and brown 55 20
1253 **411** 4s.50 green and grey 90 45

412 "Capitulation of Ayacucho" (D. Hernandez)

1974. Air. 150th Anniv of Spanish Forces' Capitulation at Ayacucho.
1254 **412** 3s.50 multicoloured 55 20
1255 **412** 8s.50 multicoloured 1·10 30
1256 **412** 10s. multicoloured 1·30 65

413 "Madonna and Child"

1974. Christmas. Paintings of the Cuzco Shool. Multicoloured.
1257 1s.50 Type **413** (postage) 20 20
1258 6s.50 "Holy Family" (air) 55 30

414 "Andean Landscape" (T. Nunez Ureta)

1974. Air. Andean Pact Communications Ministers' Meeting, Cali, Colombia.
1259 **414** 6s.50 multicoloured 65 45

415 Map and Civic Centre, Lima

1975. Air. 2nd General Conference of U.N. Organization for Industrial Development.
1260 **415** 6s. black, red and grey 55 20

1975. Air. Various stamps surch.
1261 - 1s.50 on 3s.60 purple (No. 927) 35 20
1262 - 2s. on 2s.60 green (No. 926) 35 20
1263 - 2s. on 3s.60 purple (No. 927) 35 20
1263a - 2s. on 3s.60 black and blue (No. 934) 35 20
1264 - 2s. on 4s.30 orange (No. 878) 45 20
1265 - 2s. on 4s.30 multicoloured (No. 900) 35 20
1266 - 2s. on 4s.60 orange (No. 928) 35 20
1267 - 2s.50 on 4s.60 orange (No. 928) 55 20
1268 - 3s. on 2s.60 green (No. 926) 45 20
1294 - 3s.50 on 4s.60 orange (No. 928) 20 20
1269 - 4s. on 2s.60 green (No. 926) 45 30
1270 - 4s. on 3s.60 purple (No. 927) 45 30
1271 - 4s. on 4s.60 orange (No. 928) 45 20
1295 - 4s.50 on 3s.80 orange (No. 836) 20 20
1272 - 5s. on 3s.60 purple (No. 927) 35 20
1273 - 5s. on 3s.80 orange (No. 836) 55 45
1296 - 5s. on 4s.30 orange (No. 878) 35 20
1277 **316** 6s. on 4s.60 multicoloured (No. 935) 65 30
1297 - 6c. on 4s.60 orange (No. 928) 55 20
1278 - 7s. on 4s.30 orange (No. 878) 45 30
1279 - 7s.50 on 3s.60 purple (No. 927) 75 45
1280 - 8s. on 3s.60 purple (No. 927) 1·00 30
1281 **271** 10s. on 2s.15 purple (No. 794) 75 30
1298 - 10s. on 2s.60 green (No. 926) 65 65
1282 - 10s. on 3s.60 purple (No. 927) 1·20 45
1283 - 10s. on 3s.60 multicoloured (No. 940) 1·10 45
1284 - 10s. on 4s.30 orange (No. 878) 55 30
1285 - 10s. on 4s.60 orange (No. 928) 1·10 30
1286 - 20s. on 3s.60 purple (No. 927) 1·10 65
1287 - 24s. on 3s.60 multicoloured (No. 953) 1·10 65
1288 - 28s. on 4s.60 multicoloured (No. 954) 2·20 1·10
1289 - 32s. on 5s.60 multicoloured (No. 955) 2·20 1·10
1290 - 50s. on 2s.60 green (No. 926) 5·50 1·80
1299 - 50s. on 3s.60 purple (No. 927) 1·30 2·10
1292 - 100s. on 3s.80 orange (No. 836) 5·50 3·75

417 Lima on World Map

1975. Air. Conference of Non-aligned Countries' Foreign Ministers, Lima.
1311 **417** 6s.50 multicoloured 1·10 30

418 Maria Parado de Bellido

1975. "Year of Peruvian Women" and International Women's Year. Multicoloured.

1312		1s.50 Type **418**	20	10
1313		2s. Micaela Bastidas (vert)	35	10
1314		2s.50 Juana Alarco de Dammert	35	10
1315		3s. I.W.Y. emblem (vert)	65	10

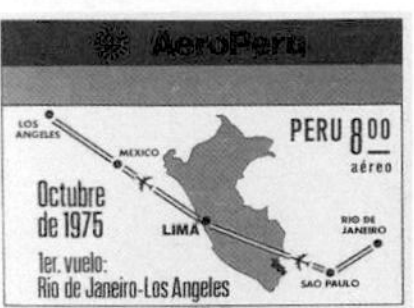

419 Route Map of Flight

1975. Air. 1st "Aero Peru" Flight, Rio de Janeiro–Lima–Los Angeles.

1316	**419**	8s. multicoloured	1·00	30

420 San Juan Macias

1975. Canonization of St. Juan Macias.

1317	**420**	5s. multicoloured	55	20

421 Fair Poster

1975. Air. 9th International Pacific Fair, Lima.

1318	**421**	6s. red, brown and black	75	30

422 Col. F. Bolognesi

1975. Air. 159th Birth Anniv of Colonel Francisco Bolognesi.

1319	**422**	20s. multicoloured	2·75	85

423 "Nativity"

1976. Air. Christmas (1975).

1320	**423**	6s. multicoloured	75	30

424 Louis Braille

1976. 150th Anniv of Braille System for Blind.

1321	**424**	4s.50 red, black and grey	55	20

426 Inca Postal Runner

1976. Air. 11th UPAE Congress, Lima.

1322	**426**	5s. black, brown and red	75	20

427 Map on Riband

1976. Air. Reincorporation of Tacna.

1323	**427**	10s. multicoloured	75	30

428 Peruvian Flag

1976. 1st Anniv of Second Phase of Revolution.

1324	**428**	5s. red, black and grey	35	20

429 Police Badge

1976. Air. 54th Anniv of Peruvian Special Police.

1325	**429**	20s. multicoloured	1·30	75

430 "Tree of Badges"

1976. Air. 10th Anniv of Bogota Declaration.

1326	**430**	10s. multicoloured	75	20

431 Chairman Pal Losonczi

1976. Air. Visit of Hungarian Head of State.

1327	**431**	7s. black and blue	75	30

432 "St. Francis of Assisi" (El Greco)

1976. 750th Death Anniv of St. Francis of Assisi.

1328	**432**	5s. brown and gold	75	20

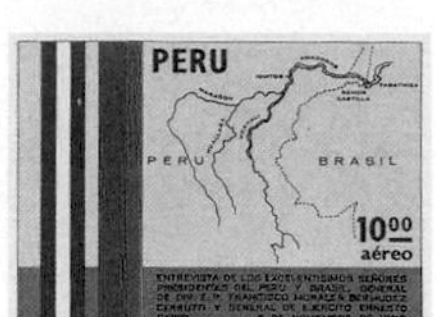

433 Map and National Colours

1976. Air. Meeting of Presidents of Peru and Brazil.

1329	**433**	10s. multicoloured	75	30

434 "Nativity"

1976. Christmas.

1330	**434**	4s. multicoloured	65	20

435 Military Monument and Symbols

1977. Air. Army Day.

1331	**435**	20s. black, buff and red	1·70	75

436 Map and Scroll

1977. Air. Visit of Peruvian President to Venezuela.

1332	**436**	12s. multicoloured	1·10	55

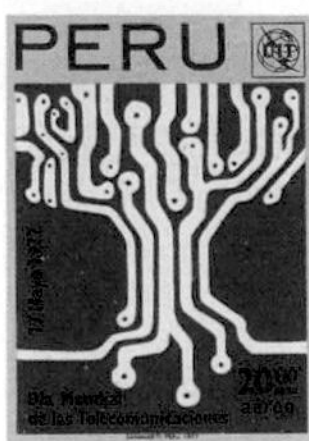

437 Printed Circuit

1977. Air. World Telecommunications Day.

1333	**437**	20s. red, black and silver	2·20	75

438 Inca Postal Runner

1977

1334	**438**	6s. black and turquoise (postage)	55	20
1335	**438**	8s. black and red	55	20
1336	**438**	10s. black and blue	55	55
1337	**438**	12s. black and green	55	55
1338	**438**	24s. black and red (air)	1·70	75
1339	**438**	28s. black and blue	2·75	75
1340	**438**	32s. black and brown	1·70	1·10

439 Petrochemical Plant, Map and Tanker

1977. Air. Bayovar Petrochemical Complex.

1341	**439**	14s. multicoloured	75	55

440 Arms of Arequipa

1977. Air. "Gold of Peru" Exhibition, Arequipa.

1342	**440**	10s. multicoloured	35	20

441 President Videla

1977. Air. Visit of President Videla of Argentina.

1343	**441**	36s. multicoloured	1·10	30

1977. Various stamps surch FRANQUEO and new value.

1344	**325**	6s. on 3s.60 multicoloured	75	55
1345	**325**	8s. on 3s.60 multicoloured	90	65
1347	**305**	10s. on 50c. black & grn	45	30
1346	-	10s. on 5s.60 brown, black and red (No. 962)	1·10	75
1348	**305**	20s. on 20c. black and red	90	55
1349	**305**	30s. on 1s. black and blue	1·20	75

444 Fair Emblem and Flags

1977. 10th International Pacific Fair.

1350	**444**	10s. multicoloured	35	20

445 Republican Guard Badge

1977. 58th Anniv of Republican Guard.

1351	**445**	12s. multicoloured	55	30

446 Admiral Miguel Grau

1977. Air. Navy Day.

1352	**446**	28s. multicoloured	75	45

447 "The Holy Family"

1977. Christmas. Multicoloured.

1353	8s. Type **447** (postage)	45	20
1354	20s. "The Adoration of the Shepherds" (air)	75	55

448 Open Book of Flags

1978. Air. 8th Meeting of Education Ministers.

1355	**448**	30s. multicoloured	10	10

449 Inca Head

1978

1356	**449**	6s. green (postage)	10	10
1357	**449**	10s. red	20	20
1358	**449**	16s. brown	45	45
1359	**449**	24s. mauve (air)	65	20
1360	**449**	30s. pink	75	20
1361	**449**	65s. blue	1·80	1·10
1362	**449**	95s. blue	2·75	1·10

450 Emblem and Flags of West Germany, Argentina, Austria and Brazil

1978. World Cup Football Championship, Argentina (1st issue). Multicoloured.

1367	10s. Type **450**	65	30
1368	10s. Emblem and flags of Hungary, Iran, Italy and Mexico	65	30
1369	10s. Emblem and flags of Scotland, Spain, France and Netherlands	65	30
1370	10s. Emblem and flags of Peru, Poland, Sweden and Tunisia	65	30

See also Nos. 1412/15.

451 Microwave Antenna

1978. Air. 10th World Telecommunications Day.

1371	**451**	50s. grey, deep blue and blue	1·20	1·20

1978. Various stamps surch Habilitado Dif.-Porte and value (Nos. 1372/4), Habilitado R.D. No. 0118 and value (Nos. 1377/8, 1381, 1384, 1390) or with value only (others).

1372	**229**	2s. on 2c. brown (postage)	20	20
1373	**229**	4s. on 2c. brown	20	20
1374	**229**	5s. on 2c. brown	20	20
1375	**313**	20s. on 1s.90+90c. multicoloured	1·10	1·10
1376	-	30s. on 2s.60+1s.30 multicoloured (No. 917)	1·10	1·10
1377	**229**	35s. on 2c. brown	1·70	1·60
1378	**229**	50s. on 2c. brown	5·50	5·25
1379	-	55s. on 3s.60+1s.80 multicoloured (No. 918)	1·70	1·60
1380	-	65s. on 4s.60+2s.30 multicoloured (No. 919)	1·70	1·60
1381	-	80s. on 5s.60 mult (No. 960)	1·40	1·40
1382	-	85s. on 20s.+10s. multicoloured (No. 920)	2·75	2·75
1383	-	25s. on 4s.60 mult (No. 954) (air)	55	45
1384	**316**	34s. on 4s.60 mult	55	45
1385	**302**	40s. on 4s.30 bistre and red	65	55
1386	**449**	45s. on 28s. green	1·10	55
1387	-	70s. on 2s.60 green (No. 926)	1·10	85
1388	**449**	75s. on 28s. green	1·70	1·10
1389	-	105s. on 5s.60 mult (No. 955)	2·40	1·60
1390	-	110s. on 3s.60 purple (No. 927)	2·75	65
1391	-	265s. on 4s.30 mult (No. 900)	4·00	3·75

The 28s. value as Type **449** was not issued without a surcharge.

1978. Surch SOBRE TASA OFICIAL and value.

1400	**229**	3s. on 2s. brown	20	20
1401	**229**	6s. on 2c. brown	20	20

456 San Martin

1978. Air. Birth Bicentenary of General Jose de San Martin.

1410	**456**	30s. multicoloured	75	75

457 Elmer Faucett and Stinson-Faucett F-19 and Boeing 727-200 Aircraft

1978. 50th Anniv of Faucett Aviation.

1411	**457**	40s. multicoloured	1·00	45

1978. World Cup Football Championship, Argentina (2nd issue). Multicoloured.

1412	16s. As Type **450**	65	45
1413	16s. As No. 1368	65	45
1414	16s. As No. 1369	65	45
1415	16s. As No. 1370	65	45

458 Nazca Bowl

1978

1416	**458**	16s. blue	55	20
1417	**458**	20s. green	55	20
1418	**458**	25s. green	65	20
1419	**458**	35s. red	1·10	30
1420	**458**	45s. brown	1·30	55
1421	**458**	50s. black	1·50	65
1422	**458**	55s. mauve	1·50	65
1423	**458**	70s. mauve	1·90	95
1424	**458**	75s. blue	2·10	75
1425	**458**	80s. brown	2·10	95
1426	**458**	200s. violet	5·25	3·25

459 Peruvian Nativity

1978. Christmas.

1436	**459**	16s. multicoloured	65	45

460 Ministry of Education, Lima

1979. National Education.

1437	**460**	16s. multicoloured	45	45

461 Queen Sophia and King Juan Carlos

1979. Air. Visit of King and Queen of Spain.

1438	**461**	75s. multicoloured	1·10	30

462 Red Cross Emblem

1979. Centenary of Peruvian Red Cross Society.

1439	**462**	16s. multicoloured	45	45

463 "Naval Battle of Iquique" (E. Velarde)

1979. Pacific War Centenary. Multicoloured.

1440	14s. Type **463**	45	45
1441	25s. "Col. Jose Joaquin Inclan" (vert)	65	30
1442	25s. "Arica Blockade-runner, the Corvette "Union""	1·00	45
1443	25s. "Heroes of Angamos"	1·00	45
1444	25s. "Lt. Col. Pedro Ruiz Gallo" (vert)	55	10
1445	85s. "Marshal Andres H. Caceres" (vert)	1·10	75
1446	100s. "Battle of Angamos" (T. Castillo)	1·20	75
1447	100s. "Battle of Tarapaca"	1·30	75
1448	115s. "Admiral Miguel Grau" (vert)	2·40	1·40
1449	200s. "Bolognesi's Reply" (Leppiani)	2·40	1·90
1450	200s. "Col. Francisco Bolognesi" (vert)	2·40	1·90
1451	200s. "Col. Alfonso Ugarte" (Morizani)	3·50	1·90

A similar 200s. value, showing the Crypt of the Fallen was on sale for a very limited period only.

464 Billiard Balls and Cue

1979. 34th World Billiards Championship, Lima.

1456	**464**	34s. multicoloured	65	45

465 Arms of Cuzco

1979. Inca Sun Festival, Cuzco.

1457	**465**	50s. multicoloured	1·40	45

466 Flag and Arch

1979. 50th Anniv of Reincorporation of Tacna into Peru.

1458	**466**	16s. multicoloured	65	45

1979. Surch in figures only.

1459	**229**	7s. on 2c. brown	45	45
1460	**229**	9s. on 2c. brown	45	45
1461	**229**	15s. on 2c. brown	45	45

468 Exposition Emblem

1979. 3rd World Telecommunications Exhibition, Geneva.

1467	**468**	15s. orange, blue and grey	45	45

469 Caduceus

1979. Int Stomatology Congress, Lima, and 50th Anniv of Peruvian Academy of Stomatology.

1468	**469**	25s. gold, black & turq	45	45

470 Fair Emblem on World Map

1979. 11th International Pacific Fair.

1469	**470**	55s. multicoloured	75	55

471 Regalia of Chimu Chief (Imperial period)

1979. Rafael Larco Herrera Museum of Archaeology.
1470 **471** 85s. multicoloured 2·00 65

472 Angel with Lute

1980. Christmas.
1471 **472** 25s. multicoloured 65 45

1980. Various stamps surch.
1472 **466** 20s. on 16s. multicoloured (postage) 45 45
1473 **463** 25s. on 14s. multicoloured 55 45
1474 **464** 65s. on 34s. multicoloured 1·00 75
1475 **458** 80s. on 70s. mauve 1·40 55
1476 **449** 35s. on 24s. mauve (air) 55 45
1477 **438** 45s. on 32s. black and brown 5·50 45

474 "Respect and Comply with the Constitution"

1980. Citizens' Duties.
1478 **474** 15s. turquoise 40 55
1479 - 20s. red 45 45
1480 - 25s. blue 45 45
1481 - 30s. mauve 45 45
1482 - 35s. black 45 45
1483 - 45s. green 55 45
1484 - 50s. brown 1·00 45
INSCRIPTIONS: 20s. "Honour your country and protect your interests"; 25s. "Comply with the elective process"; 30s. "Comply with your military service"; 35s. "Pay your taxes"; 45s. "Work and contribute to national progress"; 50s. "Respect the rights of others".

475 Ceramic Vase (Chimu Culture)

1980. Rafael Larco Herrera Archaeological Museum.
1485 **475** 35s. multicoloured 1·20 45

476 "Liberty" and Map of Peru

1980. Return to Democracy.
1486 **476** 25s. black, buff and red 65 45
1487 - 35s. black and red 90 45
DESIGN: 35s. Handshake.

477 Machu Picchu

1980. World Tourism Conference, Manila.
1488 **477** 25s. multicoloured 2·40 45

478 Rebellion Memorial, Cuzco (Joaquin Ugarte)

1980. Bicentenary of Tupac Amaru Rebellion.
1489 **478** 25s. multicoloured 45 30
See also No. 1503.

479 Nativity

1980. Christmas.
1490 **479** 15s. multicoloured 65 45

480 Bolivar and Flags

1981. 150th Death Anniv of Simon Bolivar.
1491 **480** 40s. multicoloured 55 30

1981. Various stamps surch.
1492 - 25s. on 35s. black and red (No. 1487) 35 20
1493 **482** 40s. on 25s. multicoloured 1·00 55
1494 **458** 85s. on 200s. violet 1·20 85
1495 - 100s. on 115s. mult (No. 1448) 1·30 95
1496 **482** 130s. on 25s. mult 1·00 55
1497 **482** 140s. on 25s. mult 1·00 55

482 Presidential Badge of Office, Laurel Leaves and Open Book

1981. Re-establishment of Constitutional Government.
1498 25s. multicoloured 65 45

483 Stone Head, Pallasca

1981
1499 **483** 30s. violet 75 45
1500 - 40s. blue 90 45
1501 - 100s. mauve 2·20 85
1502 - 140s. green 3·00 1·30
DESIGNS—VERT: 40s. Stone head, Huamachuco; 100s. Stone head (Chavin culture). HORIZ: 140s. Stone puma head (Chavin culture).

484 Tupac Amaru and Micaela Bastidas (sculptures by Miguel Boca Rossi)

1981. Bicentenary of Revolution of Tupac Amaru and Micaela Bastidas.
1503 **484** 60s. multicoloured 90 65

485 Post Box, 1859

1981. 50th Anniv of Postal and Philatelic Museum, Lima.
1504 **485** 130s. multicoloured 1·10 1·10

486 Map of Peru and I.Y.D.P. Emblem

1981. International Year of Disabled Persons.
1505 **486** 100s. violet, mauve and gold 1·50 75

487 Victor Raul Haya de la Torre (President of Constitutional Assembly)

1981. Constitution.
1506 **487** 30s. violet and grey 45 45

1981. No. 801 surch.
1507 30s. on 2s.20 brown & blue 55 55
1508 40s. on 2s.20 brown & blue 55 30

1981. 12th International Pacific Fair. No. 801 surch with 12 Feria Internacional del Pacifico 1981 140.
1509 140s. on 2s.20 brown & blue 2·00 1·30

490 Inca Messenger (drawing by Guaman Ponce de Ayala)

1981. Christmas.
1510 **490** 30s. black and mauve 1·70 30
1511 **490** 40s. black and red 1·30 65
1512 **490** 130s. black and green 3·25 75
1513 **490** 140s. black and blue 3·25 95
1514 **490** 200s. black and brown 5·00 1·30

1982. Various stamps surch Habilitado Franq. Postal and value (Nos. 1520/1) or with value only (others).
1515 **229** 10s. on 2c. brown (postage) 45 45
1516 - 10s. on 10c. red (No. 642) 35 20
1517 **292** 40s. on 10c. blue and yellow 35 20
1518 **273** 70s. on 5c. blue and red 45 30
1519 **264a** 80s. on 3c. lake 35 20
1520 **D 109** 80s. on 10c. green 35 20
1521 **O 108** 80s. on 10c. brown 35 20
1522 **292** 100s. on 10c. blue and yellow 45 45
1523 - 140s. on 50c. brown, yellow and red 55 45
1524 - 140s. on 1s. mult 55 45
1525 **264a** 150s. on 3c. lake 65 65
1526 **264a** 180s. on 3c. lake 65 65
1527 **264a** 200s. on 3c. lake 75 75
1528 **273** 280s. on 5c. blue and red 1·20 1·20
1529 - 40s. on 1s.25 blue and purple (No. 814) (air) 35 20
1530 - 100s. on 2s.20 brown and blue (No. 801) 55 55
1531 - 240s. on 1s.25 blue and purple (No. 814) 1·30 1·30
Nos. 1523/4 are surcharged on labels for the Seventh Eucharistic Congress which previously had no postal validity.

493 Inca Pot

1982. Indian Ceramics.
1532 **493** 40s. orange 90 30
1533 **493** 80s. lilac 2·20 85
1534 - 80s. red 2·20 65
1535 **493** 180s. green 5·25 95
1536 - 240s. blue 3·00 1·20
1537 - 280s. violet 4·25 1·60
DESIGNS: 80s., (No. 1534), 240, 280s. Nazca fish ceramic.

494 Jorge Basadre (after Oscar Lopez Aliaga)

1982. Jorge Basadre (historian) Commemoration.
1538 **494** 100s. black and green 45 30

495 Julio C. Tello (bust, Victoria Macho)

1982. Birth Centenary of Julio C. Tello (archaeologist).
1539 **495** 200s. green and blue 90 55

496 Championship Emblem

1982. 9th World Women's Volleyball Championship, Peru.
1540 **496** 80s. red and black 35 30

497 Disabled Person in Wheelchair

1982. Rights for the Disabled Year.
1541 **497** 200s. blue and red 1·10 30

498 Andres A. Caceres Medallion

1982. Centenary of Brena Campaign.

1542	**498**	70s. brown and grey	35	30

499 Footballers

1982. World Cup Football Championship, Spain.

1543	**499**	80s. multicoloured	1·00	30

500 Congress Emblem

1982. 16th Int Latin Notaries Congress, Lima.

1544	**500**	500s. black, gold and red	1·70	1·10

501 Bull (clay jar)

1982. Handicrafts Year.

1545	**501**	200s. red, brown and black	65	30

502 Pedro Vilcapaza

1982. Death Bicentenary of Pedro Vilcapaza (Indian leader).

1546	**502**	240s. brown and black	75	55

503 Jose Davila Condemarin (after J. Y. Pastor)

1982. Death Centenary of Jose Davila Condemarin (Director General of Posts).

1547	**503**	150s. black and blue	45	45

504 "Nativity" (Hilario Mendivil)

1982. Christmas.

1548	**504**	280s. multicoloured	90	85

505 Centre Emblem and Hand holding Potatoes

1982. 10th Anniv of International Potato Centre.

1549	**505**	240s. brown and grey	75	55

506 Arms of Piura

1982. 450th Anniv of San Miguel de Piura.

1550	**506**	280s. multicoloured	1·10	75

507 Microscope

1982. Centenary of Discovery of Tubercule Bacillus.

1551	**507**	240s. green	75	75

508 "St. Theresa of Avila" (Jose Espinoza de los Monteros)

1983. 400th Death Anniv of St. Theresa of Avila.

1552	**508**	100s. multicoloured	35	30

509 Civil Defence Badge and Interlocked Hands

1983. 10th Anniv of Civil Defence System.

1553	**509**	100s. blue, orange & blk	35	30

510 Silver Shoe

1983. "Peru, Land of Silver".

1554	**510**	250s. silver, black & blue	75	55

511 Map of Signatories and 200 Mile Zone

1983. 30th Anniv of Santiago Declaration.

1555	**511**	280s. brown, blue & black	1·10	75

512 Boeing 747-200

1983. 25th Anniv of Lima–Bogota Airmail Service.

1556	**512**	150s. multicoloured	75	20

513 "75"

1983. 75th Anniv of Lima and Callao State Lotteries.

1557	**513**	100s. blue and purple	35	20

514 Cruiser "Almirante Grau"

1983. Peruvian Navy. Multicoloured.

1558	150s. Type **514**	1·00	30
1559	350s. Submarine "Ferre"	2·75	65

1983. Various stamps surch.

1560	**493**	100s. on 40s. orange	1·40	20
1561	**498**	100s. on 70s. brown and grey	1·40	20
1562	**496**	100s. on 80s. red and black	1·40	20
1563	**502**	100s. on 240s. brown and black	1·40	20
1564	**505**	100s. on 240s. ochre, deep brown and brown	1·40	20
1565	**507**	100s. on 240s. green	1·40	20
1566	**506**	150s. on 280s. mult	1·80	65
1567	**511**	150s. on 280s. brown, blue and black	1·80	65
1568	**504**	200s. on 280s. mult	2·75	75
1569	**493**	300s. on 180s. green	4·25	1·30
1570	**493**	400s. on 180s. green	5·00	1·60
1571	**499**	500s. on 80s. mult	6·50	1·80

516 Simon Bolivar

1983. Birth Bicentenary of Simon Bolivar.

1572	**516**	100s. blue and black	90	30

517 "Virgin and Child" (Cuzquena School)

1983. Christmas.

1573	**517**	100s. multicoloured	1·20	30

518 Fair Emblem

1983. 14th International Pacific Fair.

1574	**518**	350s. multicoloured	1·20	65

519 W.C.Y. Emblem

1984. World Communications Year.

1575	**519**	700s. multicoloured	2·75	1·30

520 Leoncio Prado

1984. Death Centenary (1983) of Colonel Leoncio Prado.

1576	**520**	150s. bistre and brown	75	20

521 Container Ship "Presidente Jose Pardo" at Wharf

1984. Peruvian Industry.

1577	**521**	250s. purple	75	30
1578	-	300s. blue	90	30

DESIGN: 300s. "Presidente Jose Pardo" (container ship).

522 Ricardo Palma

1984. 150th Birth Anniv (1983) of Ricardo Palma (writer).

1579	**522**	200s. violet	55	20

523 Pistol Shooting

1984. Olympic Games, Los Angeles.

1580	**523**	500s. mauve and black	1·10	55
1581	-	750s. red and black	1·70	75

DESIGN: 750s. Hurdling.

524 Arms of Callao

1984. Town Arms.

1582	**524**	350s. grey	65	20
1583	-	400s. brown	1·50	30
1584	-	500s. brown	2·00	30

DESIGNS: 400s. Cajamarca; 500s. Ayacucho.

525 Water Jar

1984. Wari Ceramics (1st series).

1585	**525**	100s. brown	90	30
1586	-	150s. brown	90	30
1587	-	200s. brown	90	30

DESIGNS: 150s. Llama; 200s. Vase.
See also Nos. 1616/18.

526 Hendee's Woolly Monkeys

1984. Fauna.

1588	**526**	1000s. multicoloured	2·75	75

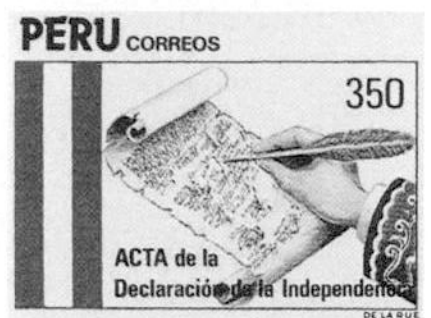

527 Signing Declaration of Independence

1984. Declaration of Independence.

1589	**527**	350s. black, brown & red	75	30

528 General Post Office, Lima

1984. Postal Services.

1590	**528**	50s. olive	35	30

529 "Canna edulis"

1984. Flora.

1591	**529**	700s. multicoloured	1·30	55

530 Grau (after Pablo Muniz)

1984. 150th Anniv of Admiral Miguel Grau. Mult.

1592	600s. Type	1·30	30
1593	600s. Battle of Angamos (45×35 mm)	1·30	30
1594	600s. Grau's seat, National Congress	1·30	30
1595	600s. "Battle of Iquique" (Guillermo Spier) (45×35 mm)	1·30	30

531 Hipolito Unanue

1984. 150th Death Anniv (1983) of Hipolito Unanue (founder of School of Medicine).

1596	**531**	50s. green	55	10

532 Destroyer "Almirante Guise"

1984. Peruvian Navy.

1597	**532**	250s. blue	1·00	30
1598	-	400s. turquoise and blue	1·00	30

DESIGN: 400s. River gunboat "America".

533 "The Adoration of the Shepherds"

1984. Christmas.

1599	**533**	1000s. multicoloured	75	55

534 Belaunde

1984. Birth Centenary (1983) of Victor Andres Belaunde (diplomat).

1600	**534**	100s. purple	55	10

535 Street in Cuzco

1984. 450th Anniv of Founding of Cuzco by the Spanish.

1601	**535**	1000s. multicoloured	1·20	55

536 Fair Emblem

1984. 15th International Pacific Fair, Lima.

1602	**536**	1000s. blue and red	1·20	55

537 "Foundation of Lima" (Francisco Gonzalez Gamarra)

1985. 450th Anniv of Lima.

1603	**537**	1500s. multicoloured	2·75	65

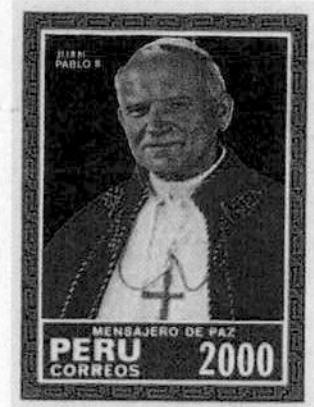

538 Pope John Paul II

1985. Papal Visit.

1604	**538**	2000s. multicoloured	3·00	55

539 Dish Aerial, Huancayo

1985. 15th Anniv (1984) of Entel Peru (National Telecommunications Enterprise).

1605	**539**	1100s. multicoloured	1·30	45

540 Jose Carlos Mariategui

1985. 60th Death Anniv (1984) of Jose Carlos Mariategui (writer).

1606	**540**	800s. red	65	30

541 Emblem

1985. 25th Meeting of American Airforces Co-operation System.

1607	**541**	400s. multicoloured	65	20

542 Captain Quinones

1985. 44th Death Anniv of Jose Abelardo Quinones Gonzales (airforce captain).

1608	**542**	1000s. multicoloured	1·20	45

543 Arms of Huancavelica

1985

1609	**543**	700s. orange	1·00	45

See also Nos. 1628/9.

544 Globe and Emblem

1985. 14th Latin-American Air and Space Regulations Days, Lima.

1610	**544**	900s. blue	75	30

545 Francisco Garcia Calderon (head of 1881 Provisional Government)

1985. Personalities.

1611	**545**	500s. green	55	20
1612	-	800s. green	65	30

DESIGN: 800s. Oscar Miro Quesada (philosopher and jurist).

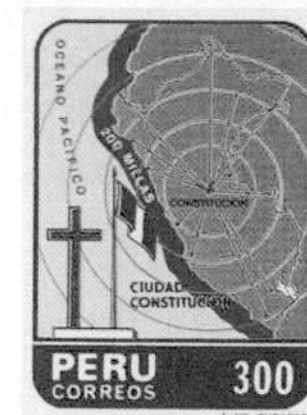

546 Cross, Flag and Map

1985. 1st Anniv of Constitucion City.

1613	**546**	300s. multicoloured	75	45

547 General Post Office, Lima

1985. Postal Services.

1614	**547**	200s. grey	75	45

548 Society Emblem, Satellite and Radio Equipment

1985. 55th Anniv of Peruvian Radio Club.

1615	**548**	1300s. blue and orange	1·20	45

549 Robles Moqo Style Cat Vase

1985. Wari Ceramics (2nd series).

1616	**549**	500s. brown	45	45
1617	-	500s. brown	45	45
1618	-	500s. brown	45	45

DESIGNS: No. 1617, Cat, Huaura style; No. 1618, Llama's head, Robles Moqo Style.

550 St. Francis's Monastery, Lima

1985. Tourism Day.
1619 **550** 1300s. multicoloured 75 20

551 Title Page of "Doctrina Christiana"

1985. 400th Anniv of First Book printed in South America.
1620 **551** 300s. black and stone 90 30

552 Emblem and Curtiss "Jenny" Airplane

1985. 40th Anniv of I.C.A.O.
1621 **552** 1100s. black, blue and red 1·00 45

553 Humboldt Penguin

1985. Fauna.
1622 **553** 1500s. multicoloured 1·30 20

554 "Virgin and Child" (Cuzquena School)

1985. Christmas.
1623 **554** 2i.50 multicoloured 1·10 30

555 Postman lifting Child

1985. Postal Workers' Christmas and Children's Restaurant Funds.
1624 **555** 2i.50 multicoloured 75 45

556 Cesar Vallejo

1986. Poets.
1625 **556** 800s. blue 65 30
1626 - 800s. brown 65 30
DESIGN: No. 1626, Jose Santos Chocano.

557 Arms

1986. 450th Anniv of Trujillo.
1627 **557** 3i. multicoloured 1·20 45

1986. Town Arms. As T 543.
1628 700s. blue 1·00 45
1629 900s. brown 1·40 45
DESIGNS: 700s. Huanuco; 900s. Puno.

558 Stone Carving of Fish

1986. Restoration of Chan-Chan.
1630 **558** 50c. multicoloured 1·10 30

559 "Hymenocallis amancaes"

1986. Flora.
1631 **559** 1100s. multicoloured 1·00 45

560 Alpaca and Textiles

1986. Peruvian Industry.
1632 **560** 1100s. multicoloured 1·00 45

561 St. Rosa de Lima (Daniel Hernandez)

1986. 400th Birth Anniv of St. Rosa de Lima.
1633 **561** 7i. multicoloured 2·75 1·60

562 Daniel Alcides Carrion

1986. Death Centenary (1985) of Daniel Alcides Carrion.
1634 **562** 50c. brown 45 45

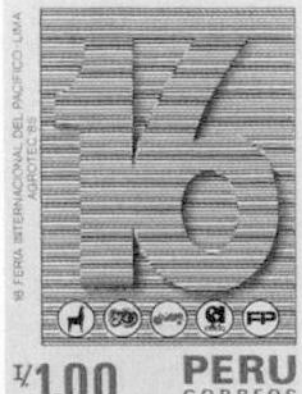

563 Emblems and "16"

1986. 16th International Pacific Fair, Lima.
1635 **563** 1i. multicoloured 75 45

564 Woman Handspinning and Boy in Reed Canoe

1986. International Youth Year.
1636 **564** 3i.50 multicoloured 75 55

565 Pedro Vilcapaza

1986. 205th Anniv of Vilcapaza Rebellion.
1637 **565** 50c. brown 55 10

566 U.N. Building, New York

1986. 40th Anniv (1985) of U.N.O.
1638 **566** 3i.50 multicoloured 1·30 55

567 Fernando and Justo Albujar Fayaque and Manuel Guarniz

1986. National Heroes.
1639 **567** 50c. brown 55 10

568 Nasturtium

1986. Flora.
1640 **568** 80c. multicoloured 55 10

569 Submarine "Casma (R-1)", 1926

1986. Peruvian Navy. Each blue.
1641 1i.50 Type **569** 1·10 45
1642 2i.50 Submarine "Abtao", 1954 1·50 45

570 Tinta Costumes, Canchis Province

1986. Costumes.
1643 **570** 3i. multicoloured 1·40 45

571 Sacsayhuaman Fort, Cuzco

1986. Tourism Day (1st issue).
1644 **571** 4i. multicoloured 2·00 75
See also No. 1654.

572 La Tomilla Water Treatment Plant

1986. 25th Anniv of Inter-American Development Bank.
1645 **572** 1i. multicoloured 45 45

573 "Datura candida"

1986. Flora.
1646 **573** 80c. multicoloured 55 20

574 Pope John Paul and Sister Ana

1986. Beatification of Sister Ana of the Angels Monteagudo.
1647 **574** 6i. multicoloured 2·40 85

575 Chavez, Bleriot XI and Simplon Range

1986. 75th Anniv of Trans-Alpine Flight by Jorge Chavez Dartnell.
1648 **575** 5i. multicoloured 1·70 85

576 Emblem

1986. National Vaccination Days.
1649 **576** 50c. blue 45 45

577 "Martyrs of Uchuraccay"

1986. Peruvian Journalists' Fund.
1650 **577** 1i.50 black and blue 55 20

578 "Canis nudus"

1986. Fauna.
1651 **578** 2i. multicoloured 1·30 55

579 Brigantine "Gamarra"

1986. Navy Day.
1652 **579** 1i. blue and light blue 1·00 45
1653 - 1i. blue and red 1·00 45
DESIGN: No. 1653, Battleship "Manco Capac".

580 Intihuatana Cuzco

1986. Tourism Day (2nd issue).
1654 **580** 4i. multicoloured 2·75 65

581 Institute Building

1986. 35th Anniv (1985) of Institute of Higher Military Studies.
1655 **581** 1i. multicoloured 45 20

582 Children

1986. Postal Workers' Christmas and Children's Restaurant Funds.
1656 **582** 2i.50 black and brown 75 55

583 White-winged Guan

1986. Fauna.
1657 **583** 2i. multicoloured 1·70 55

584 Galvez

1986. Birth Centenary (1985) of Jose Galvez Barrenechea (poet).
1658 **584** 50c. brown 45 45

585 "St. Joseph and Child" (Cuzquena School)

1986. Christmas.
1659 **585** 5i. multicoloured 2·10 1·20

586 Flags, and Hands holding Cogwheel

1986. 25th Anniv of "Senati" (National Industrial Training Organization).
1660 **586** 4i. multicoloured 1·30 85

587 Shipibo Costumes

1987. Christmas.
1661 **587** 3i. multicoloured 1·50 85

588 Harvesting Mashua

1987. World Food Day.
1662 **588** 50c. multicoloured 65 20

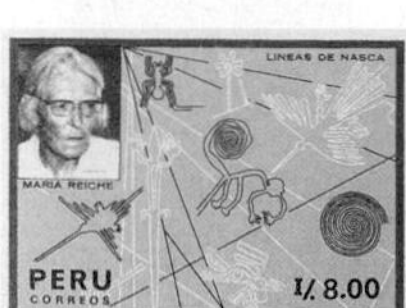

589 Dr. Reiche and Diagram of Nazca Lines

1987. Dr. Maria Reiche (Nazca Lines researcher).
1663 **589** 8i. multicoloured 3·50 1·70

590 Santos

1987. Mariano Santos (Hero of War of the Pacific).
1664 **590** 50c. violet 55 20

591 Show Jumping

1987. 50th Anniv of Peruvian Horse Club.
1665 **591** 3i. multicoloured 90 65

592 Salaverry

1987. 150th Death Anniv (1986) of General Felipe Santiago Salaverry (President, 1835–36).
1666 **592** 2i. multicoloured 90 45

593 Colca Canyon

1987. "Arequipa 87" National Stamp Exhibition.
1667 **593** 6i. multicoloured 1·00 75

594 1857 1 & 2r. Stamps

1987. "Amifil 87" National Stamp Exhibition, Lima.
1668 **594** 1i. brown, blue and grey 45 45

595 Arguedas

1987. 75th Birth Anniv (1986) of Jose Maria Arguedas (writer).
1669 **595** 50c. brown 45 45

596 Carving, Emblem and Nasturtium

1987. Centenary of Arequipa Chamber of Commerce and Industry.
1670 **596** 2i. multicoloured 45 20

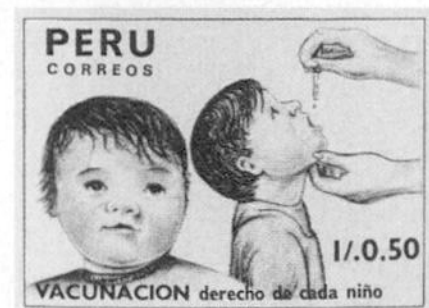

597 Vaccinating Child

1987. Child Vaccination Campaign.
1671 **597** 50c. red 45 45

598 De la Riva Aguero

1987. Birth Centenary (1985) of Jose de la Riva Aguero (historian).
1672 **598** 80c. brown 55 20

599 Porras Barrenechea

1987. 90th Birth Anniv of Raul Porras Barrenechea (historian).
1673 **599** 80c. brown 55 20

600 Footballers

1987. World Cup Football Championship, Mexico (1986).
1674 **600** 4i. multicoloured 1·00 55

601 Stone Carving of Man

1987. Restoration of Chan-Chan.
1675 **601** 50c. multicoloured 1·20 45

602 Comet and "Giotto" Space Probe .

1987. Appearance of Halley's Comet (1986).
1676 **602** 4i. multicoloured 1·90 55

603 Chavez

1987. Birth Centenary of Jorge Chavez Dartnell (aviator).
1677 **603** 2i. brown, ochre and gold 65 20

604 Osambela Palace

1987. 450th Birth Anniv of Lima.

1678	**604**	2i.50 multicoloured	65	20

605 Machu Picchu

1987. 75th Anniv (1986) of Discovery of Machu Picchu.

1679	**605**	9i. multicoloured	3·50	95

606 St. Francis's Church

1987. Cajamarca, American Historical and Cultural Site.

1680	**606**	2i. multicoloured	55	20

607 National Team, Emblem and Olympic Rings

1988. 50th Anniv (1986) of First Peruvian Participation in Olympic Games (at Berlin).

1681	**607**	1i.50 multicoloured	75	20

608 Children

1988. 150th Anniv of Ministry of Education.

1682	**608**	1i. multicoloured	1·00	55

609 Statue and Pope

1988. Coronation of Virgin of Evangelization, Lima.

1683	**609**	10i. multicoloured	1·00	55

610 Emblems

1988. Rotary International Anti-Polio Campaign.

1684	**610**	2i. blue, gold and red	55	20

611 Postman and Lima Cathedral

1988. Postal Workers' Christmas and Children's Restaurant Funds.

1685	**611**	9i. blue	1·10	30

612 Flags

1988. 1st Meeting of Eight Latin American Presidents of Contadora and Lima Groups, Acapulco, Mexico.

1686	**612**	9i. multicoloured	1·50	45

613 St. John Bosco

1988. Death Centenary of St. John Bosco (founder of Salesian Brothers).

1687	**613**	5i. multicoloured	45	45

614 Supply Ship "Humboldt" and Globe

1988. 1st Peruvian Scientific Expedition to Antarctica.

1688	**614**	7i. multicoloured	65	20

615 Clay Wall

1988. Restoration of Chan-Chan.

1689	**615**	4i. brown and black	55	20

616 Vallejo (after Picasso)

1988. 50th Death Anniv of Cesar Vallejo (poet).

1690	**616**	25i. black, yellow & brn	1·20	55

617 Journalists at Work

1988. Peruvian Journalists' Fund.

1691	**617**	4i. blue and brown	45	45

618 1908 2s. Columbus Monument Stamp

1988. "Exfilima 88" Stamp Exhibition, Lima, and 500th Anniv of Discovery of America by Christopher Columbus.

1692	**618**	20i. blue, pink and black	55	20

619 "17" and Guanaco

1988. 17th International Pacific Fair, Lima.

1693	**619**	4i. multicoloured	1·20	45

620 "Village Band"

1988. Birth Centenary of Jose Sabogal (painter).

1694	**620**	12i. multicoloured	45	45

621 Dogs

1988. "Canino '88" International Dog Show, Lima.

1695	**621**	20i. multicoloured	2·00	55

622 Silva and Score of "Splendour of Flowers"

1988. 50th Death Anniv (1987) of Alfonso de Silva (composer).

1696	**622**	20i. grey, deep brown and brown	75	30

623 Pope

1988. 2nd Visit of Pope John Paul II.

1697	**623**	50i. multicoloured	75	30

624 Volleyball

1988. Olympic Games, Seoul.

1698	**624**	25i. multicoloured	75	45

625 Volleyball

1988. Postal Workers' Christmas and Children's Restaurant Funds. Unissued stamp surch as in T 625.

1699	**625**	95i. on 300s. black and red	1·80	75

626 Ceramic Vase

1988. Chavin Culture. Unissued stamps surch as in T 626.

1700	**626**	40i. on 100s. red	1·50	65
1701	**626**	80i. on 10s. black	2·20	70

627 Map

1989. Forest Boundary Road. Unissued stamp surch as in T 627.

1702	**627**	70i. on 80s. green, black and blue	60	30

628 Arm

1989. Laws of the Indies. Unissued stamp surch as in T 628.

1703	**628**	230i. on 300s. brown	1·10	60

629 Huari Weaving

1989. Centenary of Credit Bank of Peru.

1704	**629**	500i. multicoloured	1·70	90

630 Special Postal Services Emblem

1989. Postal Services.

1705	**630**	50i. blue and green	45	35
1706	-	100i. red and pink	55	40

DESIGN: 100i. National Express Post emblem.

631 Newspaper Offices

1989. 150th Anniv of "El Comercio" (newspaper).
1707 **631** 600i. multicoloured 1·20 60

632 Garcilaso de la Vega

1989. 450th Birth Anniv of Garcilaso de la Vega (writer).
1708 **632** 300i. multicoloured 60 25

633 Emblem

1989. Express Mail Service.
1709 **633** 100i. red, blue and orange 45 35

634 Dr. Luis Loli Roca (founder of Journalists' Federation)

1989. Peruvian Journalists' Fund.
1710 **634** 100i. blue, deep blue and black 45 35

635 Relief of Birds

1989. Restoration of Chan-Chan.
1711 **635** 400i. multicoloured 2·40 1·10

636 Old Map of South America

1989. Centenary of Lima Geographical Society.
1712 **636** 600i. multicoloured 2·50 1·30

637 Painting

1989. 132nd Anniv of Society of Founders of Independence.
1713 **637** 300i. multicoloured 60 35

638 Lake Huacachina

1989. 3rd Meeting of Latin American Presidents of Contadora and Lima Groups, Ica.
1714 **638** 1300i. multicoloured 3·00 1·50

639 Children buying Stamps for Commemorative Envelopes

1989. Postal Workers' Christmas and Children's Restaurant Funds.
1715 **639** 1200i. multicoloured 60 25

640 "Corryocactus huincoensis"

1989. Cacti. Multicoloured.
1716 500i. Type **640** 60 45
1717 500i. "Haagocereus clavispinus" (vert) 60 45
1718 500i. "Loxanthocereus acanthurus" 60 45
1719 500i. "Matucana cereoides" (vert) 60 45
1720 500i. "Trichocereus peruvianus" (vert) 60 45

641 Vessel with Figure of Doctor examining Patient

1989. America. Pre-Columbian Ceramics. Mult.
1721 5000i. Type **641** 8·25 3·50
1722 5000i. Vessel with figure of surgeon performing cranial operation 8·25 3·50

642 Bethlehem Church

1990. Cajamarca, American Historical and Cultural Site.
1723 **642** 600i. multicoloured 1·80 1·20

643 Climber in Andes

1990. Huascaran National Park. Multicoloured.
1724 900i. Type **643** 70 45
1725 900i. Llanganuco Lake (horiz) 70 45
1726 1000i. "Puya raimondi" (plant) 85 60
1727 1000i. Snow-covered mountain peak (horiz) 85 60
1728 1100i. Huascaran Mountain (horiz) 95 70
1729 1100i. Andean condor over mountain slopes (horiz) 95 70

644 Pope and Virgin of Evangelization

1990. 2nd Visit of Pope John Paul II.
1730 **644** 1250i. multicoloured 1·10 45

645 "Agrias beata" (female)

1990. Butterflies. Multicoloured.
1731 1000i. Type **645** 2·40 95
1732 1000i. "Agrias beata" (male) 2·40 95
1733 1000i. "Agrias amydon" (female) 2·40 95
1734 1000i. "Agrias sardanapalus" (female) 2·40 95
1735 1000i. "Agrias sardanapalus" (male) 2·40 95

646 Victor Raul Haya de la Torre (President of Constituent Assembly)

1990. 10th Anniv of Political Constitution.
1736 **646** 2100i. multicoloured 1·20 60

647 Emblem

1990. 40th Anniv of Peruvian Philatelic Association.
1737 **647** 300i. brown, blk & cream 60 35

648 Globe and Exhibition Emblem

1990. "Prenfil '88" International Philatelic Literature Exhibition, Buenos Aires.
1738 **648** 300i. multicoloured 35 25

649 "Republic" (Antoine-Jean Gros)

1990. Bicentenary of French Revolution. Paintings. Multicoloured.
1739 2000i. Type **649** 95 60
1740 2000i. "Storming the Bastille" (Hubert Robert) 95 60
1741 2000i. "Lafayette at the Festival of the Republic" (anon) 95 60
1742 2000i. "Jean Jacques Rousseau and Symbols of the Revolution" (E. Jeaurat) 95 60

650 "Founding Arequipa" (Teodoro Nunez Ureta)

1990. 450th Anniv of Arequipa.
1743 **650** 50000i. multicoloured 1·20 60

651 Pelado Island Lighthouse

1990. Peruvian Navy. Unissued stamps, each light blue and blue, surch as in T 651.
1744 110000i. on 200i. Type **651** 1·70 75
1745 230000i. on 400i. "Morona" (hospital ship) 3·50 1·50

652 Games Mascot

1990. 4th South American Games (1st issue). Multicoloured.
1746 110000i. Type **652** 1·20 60
1747 280000i. Shooting 2·75 1·80
1748 290000i. Athletics (horiz) 3·00 1·90
1749 300000i. Football 3·00 1·90

See also Nos. 1753/6.

653 1857 1r. Stamp and Container Ship

1990. 150th Anniv of Pacific Steam Navigation Company. Multicoloured. Self-adhesive.
1750 250000i. Type **653** 3·00 1·80
1751 350000i. 1857 2r. stamp and container ship 4·25 2·50

654 Postal Van

1990. Postal Workers' Christmas and Children's Restaurant Funds.
1752 **654** 310000i. multicoloured 3·50 1·80

1991. 4th South American Games (2nd issue). As T 652. Multicoloured.
1753 560000i. Swimming 4·25 2·50
1754 580000i. Show jumping (vert) 4·50 3·00
1755 600000i. Yachting (vert) 4·75 3·00
1756 620000i. Tennis (vert) 5·25 3·50

655 Maria Jesus Castaneda de Pardo

1991. Red Cross. Unissued stamp surch.
1757 **655** 0.15i/m. on 2500i. red 1·20 60

Note. "i/m" on No. 1757 onwards indicates face value in million intis.

656 Adelie Penguins, Scientist and Station

1991. 2nd Peruvian Scientific Expedition to Antarctica. Unissued stamps surch. Multicoloured.
1758 0.40i/m. on 50000i. Type **656** 4·25 1·90
1759 0.45i/m. on 80000i. Station and Pomarine skua 5·00 2·10
1760 0.50i/m. on 100000i. Whale, map and station 5·50 2·50

657 "Siphoonandra elliptica" (plant No. 1 in University herbarium)

1991. 300th Anniv of National University of St. Anthony Abad del Cusco. Multicoloured.
1761 10c. Type **657** 40 25
1762 20c. Bishop Manuel de Mollinedo y Angulo (first Chancellor) 95 60
1763 1s. University arms 4·75 3·00

658 "Virgin of the Milk"

1991. Postal Workers' Christmas and Children's Restaurant Funds. Paintings by unknown artists. Multicoloured.
1764 70c. Type **658** 4·25 3·00
1765 70c. "Divine Shepherdess" 4·25 3·00

659 Lake

1991. America (1990). The Natural World. Mult.
1766 0.50i/m. Type **659** 3·00 1·80
1767 0.50i/m. Waterfall (vert) 3·00 1·80

660 Sir Rowland Hill and Penny Black

1992. 150th Anniv (1990) of the Penny Black.
1768 **660** 0.40i/m. black, grey & bl 1·80 85

661 Arms and College

1992. 150th Anniv (1990) of Our Lady of Guadalupe College.
1769 **661** 0.30i/m. multicoloured 1·40 70

662 Arms

1992. 80th Anniv (1991) of Entre Nous Society, Lima (literature society for women).
1770 **662** 10c. multicoloured 35 25

663 Map

1992. Bolivia–Peru Presidential Meeting, Ilo.
1771 **663** 20c. multicoloured 95 60

664 Tacaynamo Idol

1992. Restoration of Chan-Chan.
1772 **664** 0.15i/m. multicoloured 1·30 70
See note below No. 1757.

665 Raimondi

1992. Death Centenary of Jose Antonio Raimondi (naturalist).
1773 **665** 0.30i/m. multicoloured 1·40 85
See note below No. 1757.

666 First Issue

1992. Bicentenary (1990) of "Diario de Lima" (newspaper).
1774 **666** 35c. black and yellow 1·40 85

667 Melgar

1992. Birth Bicentenary (1990) of Mariano Melgar (poet).
1775 **667** 60c. multicoloured 2·50 1·20

668 1568 Eight Silver Reales Coin

1992. 1st Peruvian Coinage.
1776 **668** 70c. multicoloured 2·50 1·20

669 Emblem

1992. 75th Anniv of Catholic University of Peru.
1777 **669** 90c. black and stone 3·50 1·80

670 Emblem

1992. 90th Anniv of Pan-American Health Organization. Self-adhesive. Imperf.
1778 **670** 3s. multicoloured 7·00 6·00

1992. Various stamps surch.
1779 - 40c. on 500i. multicoloured (1717) 10·50 4·75
1780 - 40c. on 500i. multicoloured (1718) 10·50 4·75
1781 - 40c. on 500i. multicoloured (1719) 10·50 4·75
1782 - 40c. on 500i. multicoloured (1720) 10·50 4·75
1783 **493** 50c. on 180s. green 1·30 85
1784 **648** 50c. on 300i. mult 12·00 5·25
1785 **645** 50c. on 1000i. mult 12·00 5·25
1786 - 50c. on 1000i. mult (1732) 12·00 5·25
1787 - 50c. on 1000i. mult (1733) 12·00 5·25
1788 - 50c. on 1000i. mult (1734) 12·00 5·25
1789 - 50c. on 1000i. mult (1735) 12·00 5·25
1790 **647** 1s. on 300i. brown, black and cream 22·00 6·00
1791 **644** 1s. on 1250i. mult 22·00 6·00
1792 **638** 1s. on 1300i. mult 3·00 1·80

672 "Virgin of the Spindle" (painting, Santa Clara Monastery, Cuzco)

1993. Self-adhesive. Imperf.
1793 **672** 80c. multicoloured 3·00 1·30

673 Gold Figures

1993. Sican Culture (1st series). Multicoloured. Self-adhesive. Imperf.
1794 2s. Type **673** 5·00 3·00
1795 5s. Gold foil figure (vert) 13·00 6·00
See also Nos. 1814/15.

674 Incan Gold Decoration and Crucifix on Chancay Robe

1993. 500th Anniv of Evangelization of Peru.
1796 **674** 1s. multicoloured 3·50 1·50

675 "The Marinera" (Monica Rojas)

1993. Paintings of Traditional Scenes. Multicoloured. Self-adhesive. Imperf.
1797 1s.50 Type **675** 5·25 2·40
1798 1s.50 "Fruit Sellers" (Angel Chavez) 5·25 2·40

676 "Madonna and Child" (statue)

1993. Centenary (1991) of Salesian Brothers in Peru. Self-adhesive. Imperf.
1799 **676** 70c. multicoloured 2·10 95

677 Francisco Pizarro and Spanish Galleon

1993. America (1991). Voyages of Discovery. Multicoloured.
1800 90c. Type **677** 2·00 1·20
1801 1s. Spanish galleon and route map of Pizarros' second voyage 2·40 1·40
Nos. 1800/1 were issued together, se-tenant, forming a composite design.

678 Gold Mask

1993. Jewels from Funerary Chamber of "Senor of Sipan" (1st series).
1802 **678** 50c. multicoloured 12·00 10·50
See also Nos. 1830/1.

679 Escriva

1993. 1st Anniv of Beatification of Josemaria Escriva (founder of Opus Dei). Self-adhesive. Imperf.

1803 **679** 30c. multicoloured 95 40

680 Cherry Blossom and Nazca Lines Hummingbird

1993. 120th Anniv of Diplomatic Relations and Peace, Friendship, Commerce and Navigation Treaty with Japan. Multicoloured.

1804 1s.50 Type **680** 4·25 1·80

1805 1s.70 Peruvian and Japanese children and Mts. Huascaran (Peru) and Fuji (Japan) 4·25 2·00

681 Sea Lions

1993. Stamp Exhibitions. Multicoloured.

1806 90c. Type **681** ("Amifil '93" National Stamp Exhibition, Lima) 2·40 95

1807 1s. Blue and yellow macaw ("Brasiliana '93" International Stamp Exhibition, Rio de Janeiro) (vert) 2·50 1·20

682 Delgado

1993. Birth Centenary of Dr. Honorio Delgado (psychiatrist and neurologist). Self-adhesive. Imperf.

1808 **682** 50c. brown 1·70 70

683 Morales Macedo

1993. Birth Centenary of Rosalia de Lavalle de Morales Macedo (founder of Society for Protection of Children and of Christian Co-operation Bank). Self-adhesive. Imperf.

1809 **683** 80c. orange 3·00 1·30

684 "The Sling" (Quechua Indians)

1993. Ethnic Groups (1st series). Statuettes by Felipe Lettersten. Multicoloured. Self-adhesive. Imperf.

1810 2s. Type **684** 13·00 4·75

1811 3s.50 "Fire" (Orejon Indians) 15·00 7·75

See also Nos. 1850/1.

685 "20" on Stamp

1993. 20th International Pacific Fair.

1812 **685** 1s.50 multicoloured 6·50 3·50

686 "Virgin of Loreta"

1993. Christmas.

1813 **686** 1s. multicoloured 3·00 1·50

687 Artefacts from Tomb, Poma

1993. Sican Culture (2nd series). Multicoloured. Self-adhesive. Imperf.

1814 2s.50 Type **687** 12·00 7·00

1815 4s. Gold mask 19·00 10·50

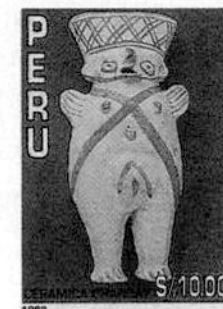

688 Ceramic Figure

1993. Chancay Culture. Multicoloured. Self-adhesive. Imperf.

1816 10s. Type **688** 47·00 24·00

1817 20s. Textile pattern (horiz) 95·00 47·00

689 "With AIDS There is No Tomorrow"

1993. International AIDS Day.

1818 **689** 1s.50 multicoloured 4·75 2·40

690 Computer Graphics

1994. 25th Anniv of National Council for Science and Technology. Self-adhesive. Imperf.

1819 **690** 1s. multicoloured 3·00 1·30

691 "The Bridge" (woodcut from "New Chronicle and Good Government" by Poma de Ayala)

1994. Self-adhesive. Imperf.

1820 **691** 20c. blue 1·20 45

1821 **691** 40c. orange 2·20 95

1822 **691** 50c. violet 3·00 1·20

For similar design see Nos. 1827/9.

1994. Multicoloured. Self-adhesive. Imperf.

1823 1s.50 Type **692** 4·25 2·10

1824 1s.50 Engraved silver and mate vessel (vert) 4·25 2·10

1825 3s. Figure of bull from Pucara 8·75 3·50

1826 3s. Glazed plate decorated with fishes 8·75 3·50

693 "The Bridge" (Poma de Ayala)

1994

1827 **693** 30c. brown 1·30 45

1828 **693** 40c. black 2·10 85

1829 **693** 50c. red 2·50 1·10

694 Gold Trinkets

1994. Jewels from Funerary Chamber of Senor de Sipan (2nd series). Multicoloured.

1830 3s. Type **694** 11·00 4·75

1831 5s. Gold mask (vert) 19·00 8·25

695 El Brujo

1994. Archaeology. El Brujo Complex, Trujillo.

1832 **695** 70c. multicoloured 2·00 95

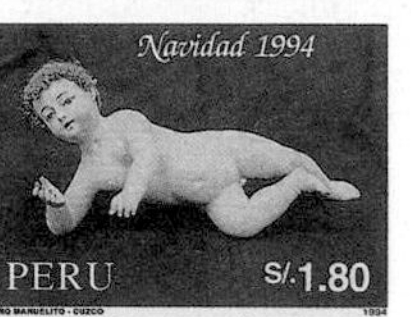

696 "Baby Emmanuel" (Cuzco sculpture)

1995. Christmas (1994). Multicoloured.

1833 1s.80 Type **696** 4·75 2·40

1834 2s. "Nativity" (Huamanga ceramic) 5·25 2·75

697 Brazilian Player

1995. World Cup Football Championship, U.S.A. (1994). Multicoloured.

1835 60c. Type **697** 1·20 70

1836 4s.80 Mascot, pitch and flags 9·50 6·00

698 Jauja–Huancayo Road

1995. 25th Anniv (1994) of Ministry of Transport, Communications, Housing and Construction.

1837 **698** 20c. multicoloured 35 30

699 Mochican Pot (Rafael Larco Herrera Museum of Archaeology)

1995. Museum Exhibits. Multicoloured.

1838 40c. Type **699** 1·30 60

1839 80c. Mochican gold and gemstone ornament of man with slingshot (Rafael Larco Herrera Museum of Archaeology, Lima) 2·50 95

1840 90c. Vessel in shape of beheaded man (National Museum) 3·00 1·20

700 Juan Parra del Reigo (poet) (after David Alfaro)

1995. Writers' Birth Centenaries (1994). Mult.

1841 90c. Type **700** 3·25 1·80

1842 90c. Jose Carlos Mariategui 3·25 1·80

701 Church

1995. 350th Anniv (1993) of Carmelite Monastery, Lima.

1843 **701** 70c. multicoloured 2·40 1·20

702 Violoncello and Music Stand

1995. Musical Instruments. Multicoloured.

1844 20c. Type **702** 60 35

1845 40c. Andean drum 1·30 85

703 Steam-powered Fire Engine

1995. Volunteer Firemen. Multicoloured.

1846 50c. Type **703** 1·80 1·40

1847 90c. Modern fire engine 3·00 2·40

704 Union Club and Plaza de Armas

1995. World Heritage Site. Lima. Multicoloured.

1848 90c. Type **704** 5·00 2·20

1849 1s. Cloisters of Dominican Monastery 5·75 2·50

705 "Bora Child"

1995. Ethnic Groups (2nd series). Statuettes by Felipe Lettersten. Multicoloured.

1850 1s. Type **705** 3·25 2·00

1851 1s.80 "Aguaruna Man" 6·00 3·50

706 Woman fishing

1995. 30th Anniv (1993) of World Food Programme.

1852	**706**	1s.80 multicoloured	5·50	3·50

707 Potato Plant

1995. The Potato. Multicoloured.

1853	1s.80 Type **707**	5·50	3·50
1854	2s. Mochican ceramic of potato tubers	6·50	4·25

708 Reed Sailing Canoe

1995. Tourism and Ecology. Lake Titicaca.

1855	**708**	2s. multicoloured	6·50	4·75

709 Great Horned Owl

1995. Endangered Animals. Multicoloured.

1856	1s. Type **709**	4·25	3·00
1857	1s.80 Jaguar on branch (horiz)	5·50	4·25

710 Anniversary Emblem

1995. 25th Anniv of Andean Development Corporation.

1858	**710**	5s. multicoloured	15·00	10·50

711 Ollantaytambo

1995. World Tourism Day.

1859	**711**	5s.40 multicoloured	21·00	12·00

712 Ancient Letterbox, Head Post Office

1995. World Post Day.

1860	**712**	1s.80 multicoloured	5·25	3·50

713 Columbus landing on Beach

1995. America (1992 and 1993). Multicoloured.

1861	1s.50 Type **713** (500th anniv of discovery of America)	4·75	3·00
1862	1s.70 Guanaco (vert)	5·25	3·50

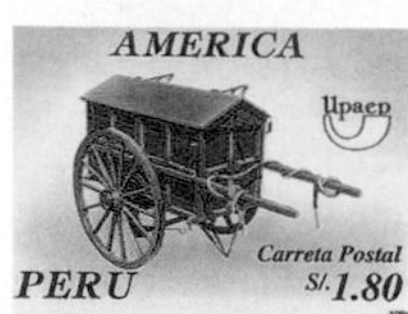

714 Cart

1995. America (1994). Postal Transport. Mult.

1863	1s.80 Type **714**	5·25	3·50
1864	2s. Post vans	6·00	3·75

715 Lima Cathedral (rear entrance)

1995. Doorways. Multicoloured.

1865	30c. Type **715**	1·10	70
1866	70c. St. Francis's Church (side entrance)	2·40	1·50

716 Peruvian Delegation, San Francisco Conference, 1945

1995. 50th Anniv of U.N.O.

1867	**716**	90c. multicoloured	3·00	1·80

717 Ceramic Church (National Culture Museum)

1995. Museum Exhibits. Multicoloured.

1868	20c. Type **717**	95	45
1869	20c. "St. John the Apostle" (figurine) (Riva Aguero Institute Museum of Popular Art)	95	45
1870	40c. "Allegory of Asia" (alabaster figurine) (National Culture Museum)	1·80	85
1871	50c. "Archangel Moro" (figurine) (Riva Aguero Institute Museum of Popular Art)	2·20	95

718 Lady Olave Baden-Powell (Girl Guides)

1995. Scouting. Multicoloured.

1872	80c. Type **718**	2·00	1·20
1873	1s. Lord Robert Baden Powell (founder of Boy Scouts)	2·50	1·80

Nos. 1872/3 were issued together, se-tenant, forming a composite design.

719 "Festejo"

1995. Folk Dances. Multicoloured.

1874	1s.80 Type **719**	5·25	3·50
1875	2s. "Marinera Limena" (horiz)	5·50	3·75

720 Stream in Sub- tropical Forest

1995. Manu National Park, Madre de Dios. Multicoloured.

1876	50c. Type **720**	7·00	4·75
1877	90c. American chamaeleon (horiz)	8·25	3·50

721 Toma de Huinco

1995. Electricity and Development. Multicoloured.

1878	20c. Type **721**	60	35
1879	40c. Antacoto Lake	1·20	85

722 St. Toribio de Mogrovejo (Archbishop of Lima)

1995. Saints. Multicoloured.

1880	90c. Type **722**	2·50	1·80
1881	1s. St. Francisco Solano (missionary)	2·75	1·90

723 Cultivating Crops

1996. 50th Anniv (1995) of F.A.O.

1882	**723**	60c. multicoloured	1·80	95

724 Crib

1996. Christmas (1995). Porcelain Figures. Multicoloured.

1883	30c. Type **724**	85	60
1884	70c. Three Wise Men (horiz)	1·90	1·30

725 Lachay National Park

1996. America (1995). Environmental Protection. Multicoloured.

1885	30c. Type **725**	1·20	60
1886	70c. Black caiman	2·40	1·30

726 "21"

1996. 21st International Pacific Fair, Lima.

1887	**726**	60c. multicoloured	1·70	95

727 Rifle Shooting

1996. Olympic Games, Barcelona (1992). Multicoloured.

1888	40c. Type **727**	95	60
1889	40c. Tennis	95	60
1890	60c. Swimming	1·40	95
1891	60c. Weightlifting	1·40	95

Nos. 1888/91 were issued together, se-tenant, forming a composite design of the sports around the games emblem.

728 Archaeological Find from Sipan

1996. "Expo'92" World's Fair, Seville.

1892	**728**	1s.50 multicoloured	7·75	3·50

729 Vallejo (after Gaston Garreu)

1996. Birth Centenary of Cesar Vallejo (writer).

1893	**729**	50c. black	2·10	1·10

730 Avenue of the Descalzos

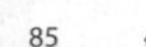

1996. UNESCO World Heritage Site. Lima.

1894	**730**	30c. brown and stone	85	45

731 "Kon Tiki" (replica of balsa raft)

1997. 50th Anniv of Thor Heyerdahl's "Kon Tiki" Expedition (voyage from Peru to Tuamoto Island, South Pacific).

1895	**731**	3s.30 multicoloured	7·00	4·75

732 Child

1997. 50th Anniv (1996) of UNICEF.

1896	**732**	1s.80 multicoloured	4·75	2·50

733 Owl

1997. Mochica Culture.

1897	**733**	20c. green	85	35
1898	-	30c. violet	1·30	55
1899	-	50c. black	2·20	85
1900	-	1s. orange	4·25	1·90
1901	-	1s.30 red	6·00	2·40
1902	-	1s.50 brown	6·50	3·00

DESIGNS—Vessels in shape of: 30c. Crayfish; 50c. Cormorant; 1s. Monkeys; 1s.30, Duck; 1s.50, Jaguar.

See also Nos. 1942/6.

734 Shooting

1997. Olympic Games, Atlanta, U.S.A. (1996). Multicoloured.

1903	2s.70 Type **734**	4·75	3·00
1904	2s.70 Volleyball	4·75	3·00
1905	2s.70 Boxing	4·75	3·00
1906	2s.70 Football	4·75	3·00

735 White-bellied Caique

1997. 25th Anniv of Peru Biology College.

1907	**735**	5s. multicoloured	8·75	6·25

736 Scout Badge and Tents

1997. 90th Anniv of Boy Scout Movement.

1908	**736**	6s.80 multicoloured	12·00	8·25

737 Man on Reed Raft

1997. 8th International Anti-corruption Conference, Lima.

1909	**737**	2s.70 multicoloured	4·75	3·00

738 Emblem

1997. 10th Anniv of Montreal Protocol (on reduction of use of chlorofluorocarbons).

1910	**738**	6s.80 multicoloured	18·00	9·50

739 Pectoral

1997. Funerary Chamber of "Senor of Sipan". Multicoloured.

1911	2s.70 Type **739**	7·00	3·50
1912	3s.30 Ear-cap (vert)	8·25	4·50
MS1913	80×59 mm. 10s. Open tomb	24·00	24·00

740 Von Stephan

1997. Death Centenary of Heinrich von Stephan (founder of U.P.U.).

1914	**740**	10s. multicoloured	24·00	24·00

741 Shipibo Woman

1997. America (1996). Traditional Costumes. Multicoloured.

1915	2s.70 Type **741**	6·50	3·50
1916	2s.70 Shipibo man	6·50	3·50

742 Inca Messenger

1997. America. The Postman. Multicoloured.

1917	2s.70 Type **742**	6·50	3·50
1918	2s.70 Modern postman	6·50	3·50

743 Castilla

1997. Birth Bicentenary of Ramon Castilla (President, 1845–51 and 1855–62).

1919	**743**	1s.80 multicoloured	5·00	2·75

744 Tennis

1997. 13th Bolivarian Games, Arequipa. Mult.

1920	2s.70 Type **744**	5·25	3·50
1921	2s.70 Football	5·25	3·50
1922	2s.70 Basketball	5·25	3·50
1923	2s.70 Volleyball	5·25	3·50

Nos. 1920/3 were issued together, se-tenant, containing a composite design of a ball in the centre.

745 River Kingfisher

1997. Manu National Park. Birds. Multicoloured.

1924	3s.30 Type **745**	6·00	4·25
1925	3s.30 Green woodpecker	6·00	4·25
1926	3s.30 Red crossbill	6·00	4·25
1927	3s.30 Eagle	6·00	4·25
1928	3s.30 Jabiru	6·00	4·25
1929	3s.30 Cuban screech owl	6·00	4·25

746 Concentric Circles over Map

1997. 30th Anniv of Treaty of Tlatelolco (banning nuclear weapons in Latin America and the Caribbean).

1930	**746**	20s. multicoloured	47·00	30·00

747 Map and Krill

1997. 8th Peruvian Scientific Expedition to Antarctica.

1931	**747**	6s. multicoloured	14·00	8·25

748 Holy Family

1997. Christmas.

1932	**748**	2s.70 multicoloured	6·50	3·75

749 Map, Emblem and Unanue

1997. 25th Anniv (1996) of Hipolito Unanue Agreement (health co-operation in Andes region).

1933	**749**	1s. multicoloured	2·40	1·30

750 Obverse and Reverse of 1897 1 Libra Coin

1997. Centenary of Gold Libra in Peru. Sheet 80×59 mm.

MS1934	**750**	10s. multicoloured	33·00	33·00

751 Facade

1997. Cent of Posts and Telegraph Headquarters.

1935	**751**	1s. multicoloured	2·40	1·30

752 School and Cadets

1998. Centenary of Chorrillos Military School.

1936	**752**	2s.70 multicoloured	6·50	3·50

753 Map and Emblem

1998. 50th Anniv of Organization of American States.

1937	**753**	2s.70 multicoloured	6·50	3·50

754 Cuzco Cathedral

1998. 25th Anniv of Aeroperu. Multicoloured.

1938	1s.50 Type **754**	3·75	2·10
1939	2s.70 Airbus Industrie A320 jetliner	7·00	4·00

755 "Paso Horse" (Enrique Arambur Ferreyros)

1998. 50th Anniv of National Association of Breeders and Owners of Paso Horses.

1940	**755**	2s.70 violet	7·75	4·25

756 Lima Cathedral

1998. Centenary of Restoration of Lima Cathedral.

1941	**756**	2s.70 red, yellow and black	6·00	3·50

1998. Mochica Culture. As Nos. 1897 and 1899/1902 but values and/or colours changed.

1942	1s. blue	4·25	1·50
1943	1s.30 purple	5·25	1·90
1944	1s.50 blue	6·50	2·30
1945	2s.70 bistre	11·00	4·50
1946	3s.30 black	13·00	4·75

DESIGNS: 1s.30, Type **733**; 1s.50, Jaguar; 2s.70, Cormorant; 3s.30, Duck.

758 Goalkeeper

1998. "Inti-Raymi" Inca Festival.

1947	**757**	5s. multicoloured	11·00	6·75

757 Ceremony, Sacsayhuaman, Cuzco

1998. World Cup Football Championship, France. Multicoloured.

1948	2s.70 Type **758**	6·00	3·50
1949	3s.30 Two players	6·50	4·25
MS1950	100×79 mm. 10s. Player kicking ball (horiz)	24·00	24·00

Nos. 1948/9 were issued together, se-tenant, forming a composite design.

759 Lloque Yupanqui

1998. Inca Chiefs (1st issue). Multicoloured.

1951	2s.70 Type **759**	8·75	6·75
1952	2s.70 Sinchi Roca	8·75	6·75
1953	9s.70 Mancoc Capau	31·00	27·00

See also Nos. 2008/11.

760 Soldiers

1998. Heroes of (River) Cenepa (Peru-Ecuador border dispute). Sheet 110×80 mm.

MS1954	**760**	10s. multicoloured	24·00	24·00

761 Fishermen (Moche sculpture) and Emblem

1998. International Year of the Ocean.

1955	**761**	6s.80 multicoloured	15·00	15·00

762 Bars of Music and Conductor's Hands

1998. 60th Anniv of National Symphony Orchestra.

1956	**762**	2s.70 multicoloured	6·00	4·75

763 Mother Teresa and Baby

1998. 1st Death Anniv of Mother Teresa (founder of Missionaries of Charity).

1957	**763**	2s.70 multicoloured	6·00	4·75

764 Children with Toys

1998. Peruvian Children's Foundation.

1958	**764**	8s.80 multicoloured	21·00	17·00

765 Princess of Ampato (Inca mummy)

1998. 3rd Anniv of Discovery by Johann Reinhard of Best Preserved Pre-Hispanic Corpse. Sheet 100×80 mm.

MS1959	**765**	10s. multicoloured	24·00	24·00

766 Tropical Forest

1998. Manu National Park.

1960	**766**	1s.50 multicoloured	3·50	2·75

767 1858 1 Dinero Stamp

1998. World Stamp Day.

1961	**767**	6s.80 multicoloured	14·00	12·00

768 Chabuca Granda (singer)

1998. America. Famous Women.

1962	**768**	2s.70 multicoloured	6·00	4·75

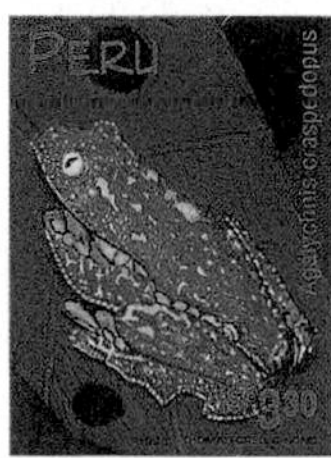
769 "Agalychnis craspedopus"

1998. Frogs. Multicoloured.

1963	3s.30 Type **769**	5·00	3·75
1964	3s.30 Amazonian horned frog ("Ceratophrys cornuta")	5·00	3·75
1965	3s.30 "Epipedobates macero"	5·00	3·75
1966	3s.30 "Phyllomedusa vaillanti" (leaf frog)	5·00	3·75
1967	3s.30 "Dendrobates biolat" (poison arrow frog)	5·00	3·75
1968	3s.30 "Hemiphractus probosci-deus" (horned frog)	5·00	3·75

Nos. 1963/8 were issued together, se-tenant, forming a composite design.

770 "Chulucanas Nativity" (Lizzy Lopez)

1998. Christmas.

1969	**770**	3s.30 multicoloured	5·00	3·75

771 Dove and Flags of Peru, Ecuador and Guarantor Countries

1998. Signing of Peru–Ecuador Peace Agreement, Brasilia.

1970	**771**	2s.70 multicoloured	4·75	3·75

772 Children on Hillside

1998. 50th Anniv of Universal Declaration of Human Rights.

1971	**772**	5s. multicoloured	6·50	5·25

773 Scout Badge and Tents

1999. 19th World Scout Jamboree, Chile. Multicoloured.

1972	5s. Type **773**	6·50	5·25
1973	5s. Emblem and tents	6·50	5·25

774 Emblem

1999. 50th Anniv of Peruvian Philatelic Association.

1974	**774**	2s.70 multicoloured	3·50	2·75

775 "Evening Walk"

1999. 120th Death Anniv of Pancho Fierro (artist). Multicoloured.

1975	2s.70 Type **775**	3·50	2·75
1976	3s.30 "The Sound of the Devil"	4·25	3·25

776 Dancer and Detail from Costume

1999. "Puno" (traditional dance).

1977	**776**	3s.30 multicoloured	4·25	3·25

1999. Mochica Culture. As Nos. 1943/46 but values and or colours changed.

1978	1s. red	1·40	1·10
1979	1s.50 blue	1·90	1·50
1980	1s.80 brown	2·40	1·90
1981	2s. orange	2·50	2·10

DESIGNS: Vessels in shape of—1s. Jaguar; 1s.50, Duck; 1s.80, Type **733**; 2s. Cormorant.

777 Inca blowing Conch Shell

1999. 25th Anniv of Peruvian Folklore Centre (CENDAF).

1982	**777**	1s.80 multicoloured	2·40	1·90

778 Malinowski and Train crossing Bridge

1999. Death Centenary of Ernest Malinowski (designer of iron bridge between Lima and La Oroya).
1983 **778** 5s. multicoloured 6·50 5·25

779 Sick and Healthy Hearts with Smiling Face

1999. Child Heart Care.
1984 **779** 2s.70 multicoloured 3·50 2·75

780 Origami Birds

1999. Centenary of Japanese Immigration.
1985 **780** 6s.80 multicoloured 8·75 7·00

781 Miner and Crowbars

1999. 50th Anniv of Milpo S.A. Mining Company.
1986 **781** 1s.50 multicoloured 1·90 1·50

782 Wildlife

1999. Flora and Fauna.
1987 **782** 5s. multicoloured 6·50 5·25
MS1988 79×98 mm. 10s. Jaguar, Manu National Park (horiz) 17·00 17·00

1999. Nos. 1888/91 surch.
1989 1s. on 40c. Rifle shooting 1·30 1·00
1990 1s. on 40c. Tennis 1·30 1·00
1991 1s. on 60c. Swimming 1·30 1·00
1992 1s. on 60c. Weightlifting 1·30 1·00
1993 1s.50 on 40c. Rifle shooting 1·90 1·50
1994 1s.50 on 40c. Tennis 1·90 1·50
1995 1s.50 on 60c. Swimming 1·90 1·50
1996 1s.50 on 60c. Weightlifting 1·90 1·50
1997 2s.70 on 40c. Rifle shooting 3·50 2·75
1998 2s.70 on 40c. Tennis 3·50 2·75
1999 2s.70 on 60c. Swimming 3·50 2·75
2000 2s.70 on 60c. Weightlifting 3·50 2·75
2001 3s.30 on 40c. Rifle shooting 4·25 3·25
2002 3s.30 on 40c. Tennis 4·25 3·25
2003 3s.30 on 60c. Swimming 4·25 3·25
2004 3s.30 on 60c. Weightlifting 4·25 3·25

1999. No. 1894 surch.
2005 2s.40 on 30c. brown and ochre 3·00 2·40

785 Penguin and Antarctic Vessel

1999. 40th Anniv of Antarctic Treaty.
2006 **785** 6s.80 multicoloured 10·00 8·00

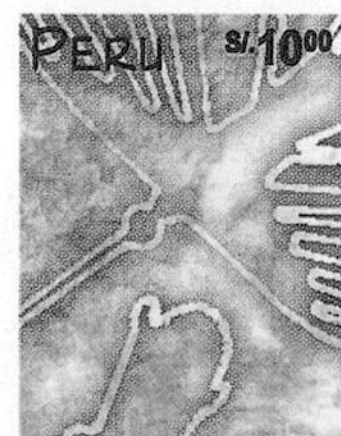

786 Bird

1999. Nazca Lines. Sheet 98×79 mm.
MS2007 **786** 10s. multicoloured 13·00 13·00

1999. Inca Chiefs (2nd issue). As T 759. Multicoloured.
2008 3s.30 Maita Capac 4·25 3·25
2009 3s.30 Inca Roca 4·25 3·25
2010 3s.30 Capac Yupanqui 4·25 3·25
2011 3s.30 Yahuar Huaca 4·25 3·25

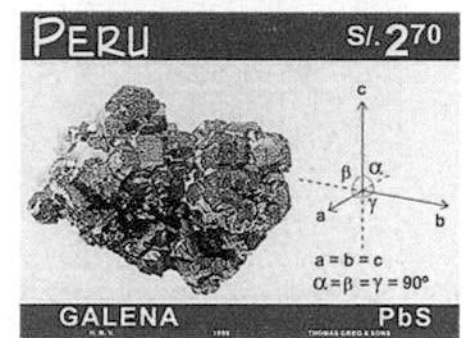

787 Galena

1999. Minerals. Multicoloured.
2012 2s.70 Type **787** 3·50 2·75
2013 3s.30 Scheelita 4·25 3·25
2014 5s. Virgotrigonia peterseni 6·50 5·25

788 Virgin of Carmen

1999
2015 **788** 3s.30 multicoloured 6·00 4·75

789 Building

1999. St. Catalina Monastery, Arequipa.
2016 **789** 2s.70 multicoloured 3·50 2·75

790 Emblem and Dragon

1999. 150th Anniv of Chinese Immigration to Peru.
2017 **790** 1s.50 red and black 3·25 2·50

791 Taking Pulse

1999. 25th Anniv of Peruvian Medical Society.
2018 **791** 1s.50 multicoloured 1·90 1·50

792 Emblem

1999. 125th Anniv of Universal Postal Union.
2019 **792** 3s.30 multicoloured 4·50 3·50

793 Sunflower growing out of Gun

1999. America. A New Millennium without Arms. Multicoloured.
2020 2s.70 Type **793** 3·50 2·75
2021 3s.30 Man emerging from Globe (horiz) 4·50 3·50

794 Woman with Fumigator

1999. Señor de los Milagros Festival, Lima. Multicoloured.
2022 1s. Type **794** 1·40 1·10
2023 1s.50 Procession 1·90 1·50

795 Young Child and Emblem

1999. 40th Anniv of Inter-American Development Bank.
2024 **795** 1s.50 multicoloured 1·90 1·50

796 *Pterourus zagreus chrysomelus*

1999. Butterflies. Multicoloured.
2025 3s.30 Type **796** 4·50 3·50
2026 3s.30 *Asterope buckleyi* 4·50 3·50
2027 3s.30 *Parides chabrias* 4·50 3·50
2028 3s.30 *Mimoides pausanias* 4·50 3·50
2029 3s.30 *Nessaea obrina* 4·50 3·50
2030 3s.30 *Pterourus zagreus zagreus* 4·50 3·50

797 Map of Cunhuime Sur Sub-sector

1999. 1st Anniv of Peru–Ecuador Border Peace Agreement. Multicoloured.
2031 1s. Type **797** 1·40 1·10
2032 1s. Map of Lagartococha-Gueppi sector 1·40 1·10
2033 1s. Map of Cusumasa Bumbuiza-Yaupi Santiago sub-sector (horiz) 1·40 1·10

798 Globe

1999. 5th Anniv of Serpost S.A. (Peruvian postal services).
2034 **798** 2s.70 multicoloured 3·50 2·75

799 Virgin of Belen

1999. Christmas.
2035 **799** 2s.70 multicoloured 4·50 3·50

800 Mujica and Factory

1999. Birth Centenary of Ricardo Bentin Mujica (industrialist).
2036 **800** 2s.70 multicoloured 3·50 2·75

801 Flags encircling Globe

2000. New Millennium. Sheet 79×99 mm.
MS2037 **801** 10s. multicoloured 13·00 13·00

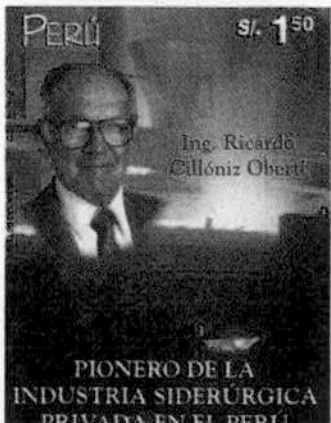

802 Oberti and Foundry

2000. Ricardo Cilloniz Oberti (founder of Peruvian steel industry).
2038 **802** 1s.50 multicoloured 1·90 1·50

803 Llamas

2000. Michell Group (Peruvian alpaca exporters). Multicoloured.

2039		1s.50 Type **803**	1·90	1·50
2040		1s.50 Llamas (different)	1·90	1·50

Nos. 2039/40 were issued together, se-tenant, forming a composite design.

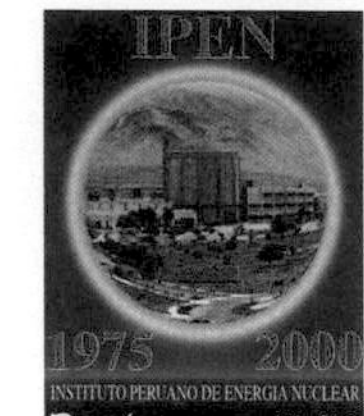

804 Power Station

2000. 25th Anniv of Peruvian Institute of Nuclear Energy (I.P.E.N.).

2041	**804**	4s. multicoloured	5·25	4·25

805 Miner

2000. Mining Industry. Multicoloured.

2042		1s. Type **805**	1·30	1·00
2043		1s. View of mine	1·30	1·00

Nos. 2042/3 were issued together, se-tenant, forming a composite design.

806 Stylized Outline of Peru

2000. 70th Anniv of Comptroller General of Republic.

2044	**806**	3s.30 multicoloured	4·50	3·50

807 Field and Emilio Guimoye Hernandez

2000. Poblete Agriculture Group.

2045	**807**	1s.50 multicoloured	1·90	1·50

808 Pupils carrying Flags

2000. National School Sports Games.

2046	**808**	1s.80 multicoloured	2·50	2·10

809 Machu Picchu

2000. World Heritage Sites.

2047	**809**	1s.30 multicoloured	1·90	1·60

810 Emblem

2000. Campaign Against Domestic Violence.

2048	**810**	3s.80 multicoloured	5·25	4·50

811 Emblem

2000. Year.

2049	**811**	3s.20 multicoloured	4·75	4·00

812 "Cataratas de Ahuashiyacu" (Susan Hidalgo Bacalla)

2000. Winning Entries in Students' Painting Competition. Multicoloured.

2050		3s.20 Type **812**	4·75	4·00
2051		3s.20 "Laguna Yarinacocha" (Mari Trini Ramos Vargas) (horiz)	4·75	4·00
2052		3s.80 "La Campina Arequipena" (Anibal Lajo Yanez) (horiz)	5·25	4·50

813 Member Flags and Emblem

2000. United Nations Millennium Summit, New York, U.S.A.

2053	**813**	3s.20 multicoloured	4·75	4·00

814 San Martín

2000. 150th Death Anniv of General Jose de San Martin.

2054	**814**	3s.80 multicoloured	5·25	4·50

815 Bus, Map of South America and Road

2000. 30th Anniv of Peru—North America Bus Route. Multicoloured.

2055		1s. Type **815**	1·50	1·30

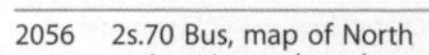

2056		2s.70 Bus, map of North America and road	3·75	3·25

Nos. 2055/6 were issued together, se-tenant, forming a composite design.

816 Cyclist

2000. Centenary of International Cycling Union.

2057	**816**	3s.20 multicoloured	4·75	4·00

817 Sun Dial

2000. 50th Anniv of World Meteorological Organization.

2058	**817**	1s.50 multicoloured	2·00	1·70

818 Western Leaf Lizard (*Tropidurus plica*)

2000. Lizards. Multicoloured.

2059		3s.80 Type **818**	5·25	4·50
2060		3s.80 Haitian ameiva (*Ameiva ameiva*)	5·25	4·50
2061		3s.80 Two-lined skink (*Mabouya bistriata*)	5·25	4·50
2062		3s.80 *Neusticurus ecpleopus*	5·25	4·50
2063		3s.80 Blue-lipped forest anole (*Anolis fuscoauratus*)	5·25	4·50
2064		3s.80 Horned wood lizard (*Enyalioides palpebralis*)	5·25	4·50

Nos. 2059/64 were issued together, se-tenant, forming a composite design.

819 *Matucana madisoniorum*

2000. Cacti.

2065	**819**	3s.80 multicoloured	5·25	4·50

820 Noriega and Space Shuttle

2000. Carlos Noriega (first Peruvian astronaut).

2066	**820**	3s.80 multicoloured	5·25	4·50

821 De Mendoza and Library

2000. 250th Birth Anniv Toribio Rodríguez de Mendoza.

2067	**821**	3s.20 multicoloured	4·75	4·00

822 Symbols of Ucayali

2000. Centenary of Ucayali Province.

2068	**822**	3s.20 multicoloured	4·75	4·00

823 Grape Vine and Flag

2000. Wines of Peru.

2069	**823**	3s.80 multicoloured	5·25	4·50

824 Flags on Watch Parts

2000. 20th Anniv of ALADI (Latin-American integration association).

2070	**824**	10s.20 multicoloured	18·00	18·00

825 Emblem

2000. 50th Anniv of Federation of Journalists.

2071	**825**	1s.50 multicoloured	2·10	1·70

826 Petrified Forest, Santa Cruz

2000

2072	**826**	1s.50 multicoloured	2·30	1·90

827 Male and Female Symbols

2000. America. Anti-AIDS Campaign.

2073	**827**	3s.80 multicoloured	5·50	4·50

828 Justice Palace, Trujillo

2000. New Judicial Powers.

2074	**828**	1s.50 multicoloured	2·10	1·70

829 Child at Table

2000. 90th Anniv of Peruvian Salvation Army.

2075	**829**	1s.50 multicoloured	2·10	1·70

830 Ribbon and Medal

2000. 50th Anniv of League against Cancer.

2076	**830**	1s.50 multicoloured	2·10	1·70

831 Steam Locomotive

2000. 150th Anniv of Peruvian Railways.

2077	**831**	1s.50 multicoloured	2·10	1·70

832 Monument, Parliament Building

2000. National Congress.

2078	**832**	3s.80 multicoloured	5·50	4·50

833 Doris Gibson (first editor)

2000. 50th Anniv of "Caretas" Magazine.

2079	**833**	3s.20 multicoloured	4·75	4·00

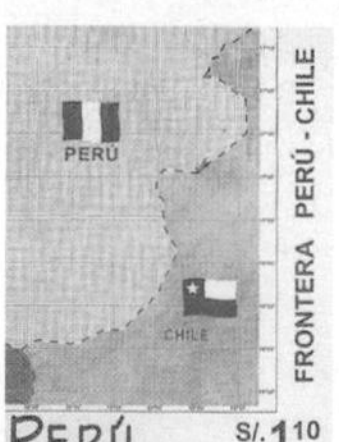

834 Map showing Peru—Chile Border

2000. National Borders. Multicoloured. Designs showing maps of borders.

2080	1s.10 Type **834**	1·70	1·40
2081	1s.50 Peru—Brazil	2·10	1·70
2082	2s.10 Peru—Colombia (horiz)	3·00	2·40
2083	3s.20 Peru—Ecuador (horiz)	4·75	4·00
2084	3s.80 Peru—Bolivia	5·50	4·50

835 Luis Alberto Sanchez

2000. Birth Centenary of Luis Alberto Sanchez (writer).

2085	**835**	3s.20 multicoloured	4·75	4·00

836 *Haageocereus acranthus*

2000. Cacti. Multicoloured.

2086	1s.10 Type **836**	1·70	1·40
2087	1s.50 *Cleistocactus xylorhizus*	2·10	1·70
2088	2s.10 *Mila caespitose*	3·00	2·40
2089	2s.10 *Haageocereus setosus* (horiz)	3·00	2·40
2090	3s.20 *Opuntia pachypus* (horiz)	4·75	4·00
2091	3s.80 *Haageocereus tenuis*	5·50	4·50

837 University Arms

2001. 450th Anniv of San Marco University.

2092	**837**	1s.50 multicoloured	2·10	1·70

838 Footballers

2001. Centenary of Club Alianza Lima (Lima football club). Multicoloured.

2093	3s.20 Type **838**	4·75	4·00
2094	3s.20 Two players and ball	4·75	4·00

Nos. 2093/4 were issued together, se-tenant, forming a composite design.

839 Symbols of Abuse and Family

2001. International Day against Drug Abuse.

2095	**839**	1s.10 multicoloured	1·70	1·40

840 Roque Saenz Pena

2001. 150th Birth Anniv of Roque Saenz Pena (Argentinean general).

2096	**840**	3s.80 multicoloured	5·50	4·50

841 Walls, Sun, Tree and Horseman

2001. Rio Lurin Valley.

2097	**841**	1s.10 multicoloured	1·70	1·40

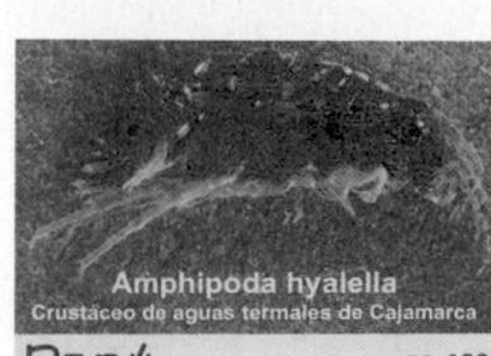

842 *Hyalella* (amphipod crustacean)

2001

2098	**842**	1s.80 multicoloured	2·50	2·10

843 Early Post Cart

2001. 70th Anniv of Post and Philately Museum.

2099	**843**	3s.20 multicoloured	4·75	4·00

844 Names of Participating Countries

2002. Ibero-American Conference, Lima.

2100	**844**	1s.10 black and scarlet	1·70	1·40
2101	-	2s.70 scarlet and orange	4·00	3·25

DESIGN: 2s.70, Triangle.

845 Ruins and Hand

2002. 150th Anniv of Peru—Costa Rica Diplomatic Relations. Multicoloured.

2102	1s.10 Type **845**	1·70	1·40
2103	2s.70 Hand and grassland	4·00	3·25

Nos. 2102/3 were issued, together, se-tenant, forming a composite design.

846 People from Many Races

2002. International Conference to Combat Racism.

2104	**846**	3s.80 multicoloured	5·50	4·50

847 Multicultural Symbols

2002. International Day of Indigenous Peoples.

2105	**847**	5s.80 multicoloured	8·00	6·75

848 Airplane and Passengers

2002. 50th Anniv of International Organization for Migration.

2106	**848**	3s.80 multicoloured	5·50	4·50

849 "100" enclosing Map of Americas

2002. Centenary of Pan American Health Organization.

2107	**849**	3s.20 multicoloured	4·75	4·00

850 Early University Building

2002. Centenary of La Molina Agricultural University. Multicoloured.

2108	1s.10 Type **850**	1·70	1·40
2109	2s.70 Modern building	4·00	3·25

851 Distillation Equipment

2002. Pisco (brandy) Distilling. Multicoloured.

2110	3s.20 Type **851**	4·75	4·00
2111	3s.80 Amphora	5·50	4·50
MS2112	100×80 mm. 10s. "Pisco Festival" (Jose Sabogal)	18·00	18·00

852 *Stanhopea*

2002. Orchids. Multicoloured.

2113	1s.50 Type **852**	2·10	1·70
2114	3s.20 *Chloraea pavoni*	4·75	4·00
2115	3s.80 *Psychopsis*	5·50	4·50

853 *Solanum stenotomum*

2002. Native Tuberous Plants. Multicoloured.

2116	1s.10 Type **853**	1·70	1·40
2117	1s.50 *Ipomea batatas*	2·10	1·70
2118	2s.10 *Ipomea purpurea*	3·00	2·40

854 Balcony, Osambela Palace

2002. America. Cultural Heritage. Multicoloured.

2119	2s.70 Type **854**	4·00	3·25
2120	5s.80 Balcony, Torre Tagle Palace	8·00	6·75

855 Flower enclosing Globe

2002. United Nations Year (2001) of Dialogue among Civilizations. Multicoloured.

2121	1s.50 Type **855**	2·10	1·70
2122	1s.80 Children encircling globe	2·50	2·10

856 Blue-faced Booby (*Sula dactiilatra*)

2002. Paracus National Reserve. Multicoloured.

2123	1s.10 Type **856**	1·70	1·40
2124	1s.50 Peruvian booby (*Sula variegate*) (horiz)	2·10	1·70
2125	3s.20 American oystercatcher (*Haematopus palliates*) (horiz)	4·75	4·00
2126	3s.80 *Grapus grapus* (crab) (horiz)	5·50	4·50

857 Giant Otter (*Pteronura brasiliensis*)

2002. Endangered Species. Sheet 80×100 mm.

MS2127	**857** 8s. multicoloured	14·50	14·50

858 Figure with Crab's Claws, Sipan

2002. Tourism. Archaeological Sites. Multicoloured.

2128	1s.50 Type **858**	2·10	1·70
2129	3s.20 Warrior (metal decoration), Sican	4·75	4·00
2130	3s.80 Gold pectoral decoration, Kuntur Wasi (horiz)	5·50	4·50
MS2131	80×100 mm. 10s.20 Los Pinchudos, Gran Pajaten (horiz)	18·00	18·00

859 La Zamacueca

2002. Peruvian Dances. Multicoloured.

2132	2s.10 Type **859**	3·00	2·50
2133	2s.70 El Alcatraz	4·00	3·25

860 Robert Baden Powell (founder of Scout movement)

2002. 90th Anniv of Peruvian Scouts. Multicoloured.

2134	3s.20 Type **860**	5·00	4·25
2135	3s.20 Juan Luis Rospigliosi (co-founder of Peruvian Scouts)	5·00	4·25
MS2136	100×80 mm. 10s.20 First Peruvian Scout group	19·00	19·00

Nos. 2134/5 were issued together, se-tenant, forming a composite design.

861 Globe and Postal Emblems

2002. Postal Services.

2137	**861** 20s. multicoloured	35·00	35·00

862 Viracocha

2002. Ancient Rulers (1st series). Multicoloured.

2138	1s.50 Type **862**	2·10	1·80
2139	2s.70 Pachacutec	4·00	3·25
2140	3s.20 Inca Yupanqui	5·00	4·25
2141	3s.80 Tupac Inca Yupanqui	5·75	4·75

See also Nos. 2191/3.

863 Peruvian Red-necked Owl Monkey (*Aotus nancymai* (inscr "nancymaea"))

2002. Primates. Multicoloured.

2142	3s.80 Type **863**	5·75	4·75
2143	3s.80 Grey monk saki (*Pithecia irrorata*)	5·75	4·75
2144	3s.80 Equatorial saki (*Pithecia aequatorialis*)	5·75	4·75
2145	3s.80 White-fronted capuchin (*Cebus albifrons*)	5·75	4·75
2146	3s.80 Bolivian squirrel monkey (*Saimiri boliviensis*)	5·75	4·75
2147	3s.80 Owl monkey (*Aotus vociferans*)	5·75	4·75

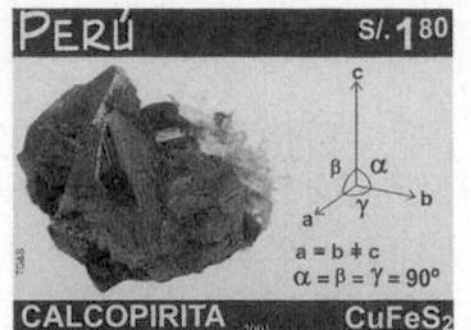

864 Chalcopyrite (CuFeS2)

2002. Minerals (1st series). Multicoloured.

2148	1s.80 Type **864**	2·75	2·20
2149	3s.20 Zinc sulphide (Zns)	5·00	4·25
2150	3s.20 Pyrargyrite (inscr "AgSbS3")	5·00	4·25

See also Nos. 2187/8.

865 Miguel Grau

2002. Miguel Grau (naval hero) Commemoration.

2151	**865** 3s.80 multicoloured	5·75	4·75

866 Spanish and Peruvian Flags and Coins

2002. Peru—Spain Business Conference.

2152	**866** 3s.80 multicoloured	5·75	4·75

867 Flags, Bridge and Map

2002. Peru—Bolivia Integrated Development Plan.

2153	**867** 3s.20 multicoloured	5·00	4·25

868 Andean and Amazonian People

2002. National Commission for Andean and Amazonian Peoples.

2154	**868** 1s.50 multicoloured	2·10	1·80

869 Fishermen

2002. 50th Anniv of National Fishing Society.

2155	**869** 3s.20 multicoloured	5·00	4·25

870 Alexander von Humboldt

2002. Bicentenary of Visit by Alexander von Humboldt (geologist).

2156	**870** 3s.20 multicoloured	5·00	4·25

871 Surveyor

2003. Centenary of Hydro-graphic Mapping.

2157	**871** 1s.10 multicoloured	1·70	1·40

872 Emblem

2003. 25th Anniv of Movimiento Manuela Ramos (organization for sexual equality).

2158	**872** 3s.80 scarlet and black	5·75	4·75

873 Transmitter

2003. 40th Anniv of RPP Radio.

2159	**873** 4s. multicoloured	6·00	5·00

874 Fernando Terry

2003. 1st Death Anniv of Fernando Belaunde Terry (president 1963—68 and 1980—1985).

2160	**874** 1s.60 multicoloured	2·30	1·90

875 Jose Maria Escriva de Balaguer

2003. Canonization of Jose Maria Escriva de Balaguer (founder of Opus Dei (religious organization)).

2161	**875** 1s.20 multicoloured	1·70	1·40

876 Teresa de la Cruz

2003. 50th Death Anniv of Teresa de la Cruz Candamo.

2162	**876** 4s. brown and yellow	6·00	5·00

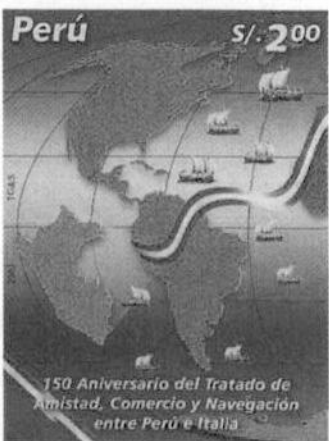

877 Map of the Americas

2003. 150th Anniv of Peru—Italy Treaty of Friendship and Trade. Multicoloured.

2163	2s. Type **877**	3·00	2·40

2164		2s. Map of Europe, Africa and Asia	3·00	2·40

Nos. 2163/4 were issued together, se-tenant, forming a composite design.

878 Emblems

2003. Serpente de Agua Exhibition (cultural project). Multicoloured.

2165		2s. Type **878**	3·00	2·40
2166		2s. Early and modern children	3·00	2·40

879 Emblem and Children

2003. 50th Anniv of UNESCO Associated Schools.

2167	**879**	1s.20 multicoloured	1·90	1·50

880 Four Birds

2003. Endangered Species. Andean Cock of the Rock (Rupicola peruviana). Multicoloured.

2168		2s. Type **880**	3·00	2·40
2169		2s. Single bird	3·00	2·40

Nos. 2168/9 were issued together, se-tenant, forming a composite design.

881 1570 Map (Diego Mendez)

2003. 150th Anniv of Peru—Panama Diplomatic Relations.

2170	**881**	4s. multicoloured	6·00	5·00

882 *Wright Flyer*, Orville and Wilbur Wright

2003. Centenary of Powered Flight. Multicoloured.

2171		4s.80 Type **882**	7·00	5·75
2172		4s.80 "Arriba siempre arriba hasta alcanzar la gloria"	1·60	95

Nos. 2171/2 were issued together, se-tenant, forming a composite design.

883 Musician and Notes

2003. Cajon (wooden box played as musical instrument).

2173	**883**	4s.80 multicoloured	7·00	5·75

884 Chess Board and Globe

2004. Chess.

2174	**884**	1s.20 multicoloured	1·90	1·50

885 Free-style Crawl

2004. Swimming.

2175	**885**	1s.20 multicoloured	1·90	1·50

886 Wheelchair User, Amputee and Boy using Crutches

2004. National Institute of Rehabilitation. Year of the Rights for the Disabled.

2176	**886**	1s.20 multicoloured	1·90	1·50

887 Antonio de Mendoza

2004. Viceroys. Multicoloured.

2177		1s.20 Type **887**	1·90	1·50
2178		1s.20 Andreas Hurtado de Mendoza	1·90	1·50
2179		1s.20 Deigo Lopez de Zuniga y Velasco	1·90	1·50
2180		4s.80 Blasco Nunez de Vela	7·00	5·75

888 The Nativity

2004. Christmas (2003).

2181	**888**	4s.80 multicoloured	6·75	5·50

889 Emblem

2004. 30th Anniv of Civil Defence Organization.

2182	**889**	4s.80 multicoloured	7·00	5·75

890 Cebiche (fish)

2004. Traditional Dishes.

2183	**890**	4s.80 multicoloured	7·00	5·75

891 *Chaubardia heteroclite*

2004. Orchids. Multicoloured.

2184		1s.20 Type **891**	1·90	1·50
2185		2s.20 *Cochleanthes amazonica* (incr "Cochleanther")	3·00	2·50
2186		4s.80 *Sobralia* (horiz)	7·00	5·75

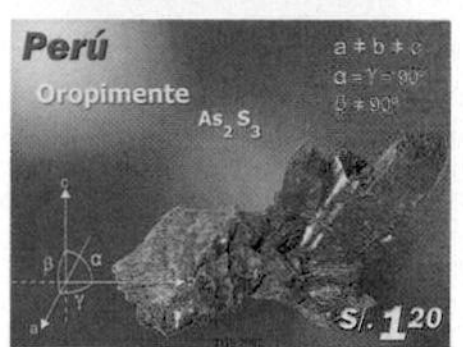

892 Orpiment

2004. Minerals (2nd series). Multicoloured.

2187		1s.20 Type **892**	1·90	1·50
2188		4s.80 Rodocrosita	7·00	5·75

893 St. Martin de Porres

2004. Peruvian Saints. Multicoloured.

2189		4s.80 Type **893**	7·00	5·75
2190		4s.80 St. Rosa de Lima (horiz)	7·00	5·75

2004. Ancient Rulers (2nd series). As T 862. Multicoloured.

2191		1s.20 Huascar	1·90	1·50
2192		1s.20 Atahualpa	1·90	1·50
2193		3s.20 Huayna Capac	7·00	5·75

894 Locomotive

2004. Railways. Multicoloured.

2194		1s.20 Type **894**	1·90	1·50
2195		4s.80 "Puente Galeros" viaduct	7·00	5·75

895 Marine Otter (*Lontra feline*) (inscr "Londra")

2004. Endangered Species. Multicoloured.

2196		1s.80 Type **895**	2·75	2·20
2197		1s.80 Ara couloni (vert)	2·75	2·20

896 Fire Fighters

2004. Fire Service. Multicoloured.

2198		2s.20 Type **896**	3·00	2·50
2199		2s.20 Fire appliance	3·00	2·50

897 Jorge Basadre

2004. Birth Centenary of Jorge Basadre Grohmann (writer) (2003).

2200	**897**	4s.80 indigo	7·00	5·75

898 *Matucana haynei*

2004. Cacti (2nd series). Multicoloured.

2201		1s.20 Type **898**	1·90	1·50
2202		1s.20 *Eriosyce islayensis*	1·90	1·50
2203		4s.80 *Pymaeocereus bylesianus* (inscr "Pigmaeocereus")	7·00	5·75

899 Gentoo Penguin (*Pygoscelis papua*) (inscr "Pygosceles")

2004. Antarctic Fauna. Multicoloured.

2204		1s.80 Type **899**	2·75	2·20
2205		1s.80 *Asteroidea*	2·75	2·20
2206		1s.80 *Leucocarbo atriceps* (horiz)	2·75	2·20

900 Tree and Children

2004. Environmental Awareness. Multicoloured.

2207		4s.80 Type **900** (Population Control Day)	7·00	5·75
2208		4s.80 Plants and animals (National Biological Diversity Day)	7·00	5·75

901 Stadium

2004. Football. Multicoloured.

2209		4s.80 Type **901** (50th anniv of National Stadium, Lima)	7·00	5·75
2210		4s.80 Players, emblem and trophy (World Cup Football Championships, Japan and South Korea (2002))	7·00	5·75

902 Ruben Vargas Ugarte (historian)

2004. Personalities. Multicoloured.

2211		4s.80 Type **902**	7·00	5·75
2212		4s.80 Jose Jimenez Borja (writer) (vert)	7·00	5·75

903 Glass

2004. Pisco Sour National Drink.

2213	**903**	4s.80 multicoloured	7·00	5·75

904 Daniel Carrion

2004. Daniel Alcides Carrion (medical student who died after inoculation experiment) Commemoration.

2214	**904**	4s.80 multicoloured	7·00	5·75

905 "Founding of Juaja" (Wenceslao Hinostroza)

2004. 470th Anniv of Founding of Juaja. Sheet 100×80 mm.

MS2215 **905**	7s. multicoloured	11·50	11·50

906 Alpaca

2004. Llamas. Multicoloured.

2216	20c. Type **906**	40	35
2217	30c. Vicuna	55	45
2218	40c. Guanaco	65	55
2219	50c. Llama	80	65

907 *Bothros roedingeri*

2004. Snakes. Multicoloured.

2220	1s.80 Type **907**	2·75	2·20
2221	1s.80 *Micrurus lemniscalus*	2·75	2·20
2222	1s.80 *Bothrops atrox*	2·75	2·20
2223	1s.80 *Bothrops microphtlalmus*	2·75	2·20
2224	1s.80 *Micrurus surinamensis*	2·75	2·20
2225	1s.80 *Bothrops barnetti*	2·75	2·20

Nos. 2220/5 were issued together, se-tenant, forming a composite design.

908 Mount Huascaran

2004. International Year of Mountains (2002). Sheet 100×80 mm.

MS2226 **908**	7s. multicoloured	11·50	11·50

909 Artefacts and Building

2004. Royal Tombs of Sipan Museum, Lambayeque.

2227	**909**	4s.80 multicoloured	7·00	5·75

910 Punta Capones Lighthouse

2004. Lighthouses (1st issue). Multicoloured.

2228	2s. Type **910**	3·00	2·40
2229	2s. Islas Chincha	3·00	2·40

See also Nos. 2286/7 and **MS**2404.

911 Fire Fighter

2004. 130th Anniv of Volunteer Fire Brigades.

2230	**911**	4s.80 multicoloured	7·00	5·75

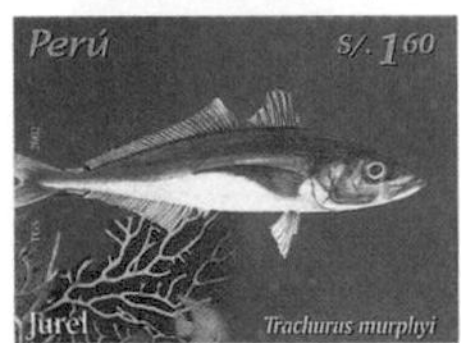

912 *Trachurus murphyi*

2004. Fish. Sheet 140×112 mm containing T 912 and similar horiz designs. Multicoloured.

MS2231	1s.60×5, Type **912**; *Mugil cephalus; Engraulis ringens; Odontesthes regia; Merluccius peruanus*	15·00	15·00

The stamps and margin of **MS**2231 form a composite design.

913 Cathedral Tower, Arequipa

2004. Tourism. Sheet 100×80 mm containing T 913 and similar multicoloured design.

MS2232	4s.×2, Type **913**; El Misti volcano	14·50	14·50

The stamps and margin of **MS**2232 form a composite design.

914 Solar Clock, Intihuatana

2004. World Heritage Site. Machu Picchu. Multicoloured.

2233	1s.20 Type **914**	1·90	1·50
2234	1s.20 Temple	1·90	1·50
2235	1s.20 Waterfall, Huayna Picchu	1·90	1·50
2236	4s.80 Ciudadela	7·00	5·75

915 *Myrciaria dubia*

2004. Medicinal Plants. Multicoloured.

2237	4s.80 Type **915**	7·00	5·75
2238	4s.80 *Lepidium meyenii*	7·00	5·75
2239	4s.80 *Uncaria tomentosa*	7·00	5·75

916 Map and Emblem

2004. Inter-American Development Bank Governors' Assembly Annual Reunion.

2240	**916**	4s.80 multicoloured	7·00	5·75

917 Italian Volpino Spitz

2004. Dogs. Multicoloured.

2241	4s.80 Type **917**	7·00	5·75
2242	4s.80 Peruvian Inca Orchid	7·00	5·75
2243	4s.80 Beauceron (Pastor de Beauce)	7·00	5·75
2244	4s.80 Italian Spinone	7·00	5·75

918 Huaylash

2004. Traditional Dances. Multicoloured.

2245	1s.20 Type **918**	1·90	1·50
2246	1s.20 Huayno	1·90	1·50

919 Scientists and Weather Map

2004. Preparation for "El Nino".

2247	**919**	4s.80 multicoloured	7·00	5·75

920 Paca Lake, Jauja

2004. Tourism. Multicoloured.

2248	4s.80 Type **920**	7·00	5·75
2249	4s.80 Banos del Inca (thermal springs), Cajamarca (vert)	7·00	5·75
2250	4s.80 Ballestas island, Paracas, Ica (vert)	7·00	5·75
2251	4s.80 Caballitos (handmade totora reed boats) (vert)	7·00	5·75

921 Santiago Apostol Church, Pomata

2004. Cultural Heritage.

2252	**921**	1s.80 multicoloured	2·75	2·20

922 Flower containing Children

2004. America. Literacy Campaign. Multicoloured.

2253	1s.20 Type **922**	1·90	1·50
2254	1s.20 Child and computer (horiz)	1·90	1·50

923 Aboriginal Footballer

2004. Americas' Cup Football Championship, Peru. Sheet 74×74 mm.

MS2255 **923**	5s. multicoloured	8·00	8·00

No. **MS**2255 was cut round in the shape of a football.

924 SR Orfeo

2004. Peruvian Gaited Horses. Multicoloured.

2256	1s.20 Type **924**	1·90	1·50
2257	1s.20 JyEP Pretencioso	1·90	1·50
2258	1s.20 MSP Morenita	1·90	1·50
2259	4s.80 Horse's head	7·00	5·75

925 Otter

2004. Endangered Species. Giant Otter (Pteronura brasiliensis). Sheet 90×115 mm containing T 925 and similar vert designs. Multicoloured.

MS2260	30c. Type **925**; 50c. Snarling; 1s.50 Eating fish; 1s.50 Mother and cubs	6·25	6·25

926 Living and Dead Trees

2004. America. Environmental Protection.

2261	**926**	4s.50 multicoloured	6·75	5·50

927 Central Railway (1870)

2004. National Railways. Multicoloured.

2262 5s. Type **927** 7·25 6·00

MS2263 80×60 mm. 10s. Train on Puente Infiernillo bridge (horiz) 19·00 19·00

928 Musical Instruments

2004. 60th Anniv of Cancion Criolla Day.

2264 **928** 5s. multicoloured 7·25 6·00

929 Pope John Paul II and Mother Teresa

2004. Canonization of Mother Teresa.

2265 **929** 5s. multicoloured 7·25 6·00

930 Anniversary Emblem

2004. Centenary of FIFA (Federation Internationale de Football Association).

2266 **930** 5s. multicoloured 7·25 6·00

931 Pope John Paul II

2004. 25th Anniv of Pope John Paul II's Pontificate.

2267 **931** 5s. multicoloured 7·25 6·00

932 Flora Tristan (women's rights activist)

2004. 25th Anniv of Women's Centre.

2268 **932** 5s. multicoloured 7·25 6·00

933 World Map and Exports

2004. Exporters Day.

2269 **933** 5s. multicoloured 7·25 6·00

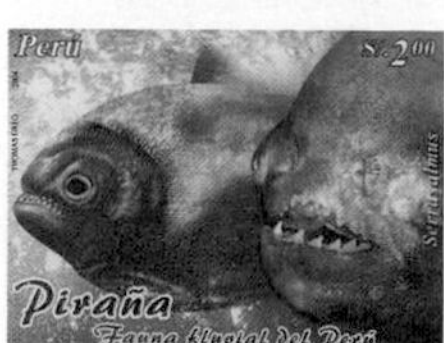

934 Piranha (*Serrasalmus*)

2004. Fish. Multicoloured.

2270 2s. Type **934** 3·00 2·40

2271 4s.50 La Plata river dolphin (*Pontoporia blainvillei*) 6·75 5·50

2272 5s. Pirarucu (*Arapaima gigas*) (vert) 7·25 6·00

935 "40"

2004. 40th Anniv of Latin American Parliament. Multicoloured.

2273 2s.50 Type **935** 3·75 3·00

2274 2s.50 Andres Townsend Escurra (first president) and flags 3·75 3·00

936 Couple

2004. Mochica Ceramics. Designs showing jugs. Multicoloured.

2275 4s.50 Type **936** 6·75 5·50

2276 4s.50 Couple (different) 6·75 5·50

2277 5s. Two animals (horiz) 7·25 6·00

937 Gavel and Regalia

2004. Bicentenary of Law College.

2278 **937** 5s. multicoloured 7·25 6·00

938 Envelope

2004. 10th Anniv of Serpost.

2279 **938** 5s. multicoloured 7·25 6·00

939 Juan Diego Florez

2004. Musicians. Sheet 121×95 mm containing T 939 and similar multicoloured designs.

MS2280 2s.×5, Type **939**; Susana Baca; Gian Marco; Eva Ayllon (horiz); Libido (horiz) 19·00 19·00

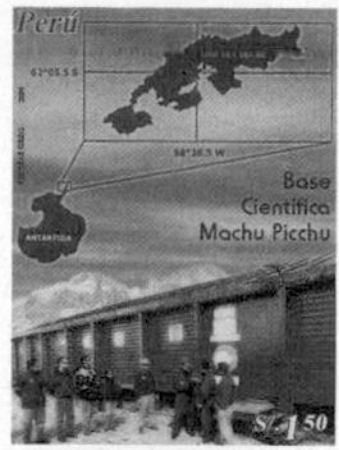

940 Machu Picchu Base

2004. Antarctic. Multicoloured.

2281 1s.50 Type **940** 2·10 1·80

2282 2s. *Megaptera novaeagliae* (horiz) 3·00 2·40

2283 4s.50 *Orcinus orca* (horiz) 6·75 5·50

941 Smilodon neogaeus

2004. Pre-historic Animals. Multicoloured.

2284 1s.80 Type **941** 2·75 2·20

2285 3s.20 Toxodon platensis 5·00 4·25

Nos. 2284/5 were issued together, se-tenant, forming a composite design.

2004. Lighthouses (2nd issue). As T 910. Multicoloured.

2286 4s.50 Pijuayal 6·75 5·50

2287 4s.50 Suana 6·75 5·50

942 The Nativity

2004. Christmas.

2288 **942** 5s. multicoloured 7·25 6·00

943 Flags

2004. Latin-American Presidential Summit.

2289 **943** 5s. multicoloured 7·25 6·00

944 Map and Battle of Ayacucho

2004. 180th Anniv of Battles. Multicoloured.

2290 1s.80 Type **944** 2·75 2·20

2291 3s.20 Battle of Junin 5·00 4·25

945 Emblem

2004. 50th Anniv of Art Museum, Lima.

2292 **945** 5s. multicoloured 7·25 6·00

946 Ruins

2004. Caral Archaeological Site. Sheet 80×60 mm.

MS2293 **946** 10s. multicoloured 19·00 19·00

947 *Cantua buxifolia*

2005. 40th Anniv of Las Leyendas Park. Multicoloured.

2294 5s. Type **947** 7·25 6·00

2295 5s. Puma (*Puma concolor*) 7·25 6·00

Nos. 2294/5 were issued together, se-tenant, forming a composite design.

948 Trophies and Emblem

2005. Cienciano Football Club—South American Cup Champions, 2003 and South American Recopa Champions, (2004).

2296 **948** 5s. multicoloured 7·25 6·00

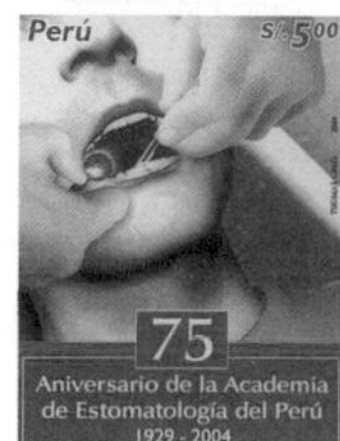

949 Dental Examination

2005. 75th Anniv (2004) of Stomatology Academy.

2297 **949** 5s. multicoloured 7·25 6·00

950 Children and Teacher

2005. Campaign for Rights and Responsibilities for Health.

2298 **950** 2s. multicoloured 3·00 2·40

951 San Cristobal Church, Huamanga

2005. Churches. Multicoloured.

2299 4s.50 Type **951** 6·75 5·50

2300 5s. Huancayo Cathedral 7·25 6·00

952 Don Ramon Castilla (president 1845—51 and 1855—62) and Slaves

2005. 150th Anniv of Abolition of Slavery.

2301	**952**	5s. crimson	7·25	6·00

953 Tank

2005. Armed Forces. Multicoloured.

2302	1s.80 Type **953**	2·75	2·20
2303	3s.20 Sukoi aircraft	5·00	4·25
2304	3s.20 Soldiers	5·00	4·25
2305	1s.80 Submarine	2·75	2·20
2306	1s.80 Mirage fighters and ship	2·75	2·20
2307	3s.20 Missile frigate	5·00	4·25

Nos. 2302/4 and 2305/7, respectively were issued together, se-tenant, forming a composite design.

954 *Eugenia stipitata*

2005. Fruit. Multicoloured.

2308	4s.50 Type **954**	6·75	5·50
2309	4s.50 *Maurita flexuosa*	6·75	5·50
2310	5s. *Solanum sessiliflorum* (vert)	7·25	6·00

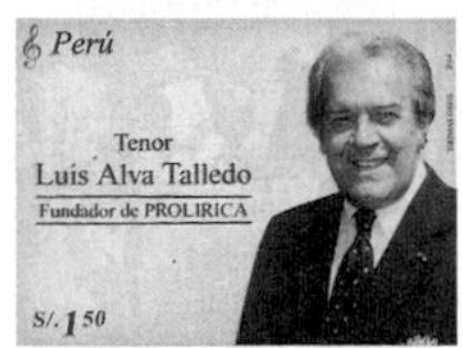

955 Luis Alva Talledo

2005. Luis Alva Talledo (singer and founder of Prolirica (music association)).

2311	**955**	1s.50 multicoloured	2·10	1·80

956 Northern Chestnut-tailed Ant Bird

2005. Allpahuayo-Mishana Reserve. Multicoloured.

2312	4s.50 Type **956**	6·75	5·50
2313	4s.50 *Mishana tyrannulet*	6·75	5·50
2314	4s.50 Tree frog	6·75	5·50
2315	4s.50 Iguana	6·75	5·50

Nos. 2312/15 were issued together, se-tenant, forming a composite design.

957 Soldier and Woman (Pancho Fierro)

2005. Art. Multicoloured.

2316	2s. Type **957**	3·00	2·40
2317	2s. Old woman, child, old man and woman wearing fur trimmed robe (Ignacio Merino)	3·00	2·40
2318	2s. Portrait of man (Daniel Hernandes)	3·00	2·40
2319	2s. Mountains and church (Camilo Blas)	3·00	2·40
2320	2s. Portrait of woman (Ricardo Grau)	3·00	2·40
2321	2s. Abstract (Fernando de Szyszlo)	3·00	2·40

958 Stone Carvings, Chavin de Huantar

2005. 180th Birth Anniv (2004) of Antonio Raimondi (scientist). Multicoloured.

2322	1s.80 Type **958**	2·75	2·20
2323	3s.20 Inca tern and bat	5·00	4·25
2324	4s.50 *Stanhophea*	6·75	5·50
2325	5s. Huallanca periwinkle fossil (*Roemoceras subplanum*)	7·25	6·00

959 White-winged Guan (*Penelope albipennis*)

2005. Rediscovery of White-winged Guan (presumed extinct) in Laquipampa Reserve. Sheet 81×60 mm.

MS2326	**959**	10s. multicoloured	19·00	19·00

960 Government Palace

2005. Architecture. Multicoloured.

2327	4s.50 Type **960**	6·75	5·50
2328	4s.50 Museum of Italian Art	6·75	5·50
2329	5s. Tourist and Entertainment Centre, Larco Mer	7·25	6·00
2330	5s. Mega Plaza	7·25	6·00

961 Paper Plane

2005. Postal Giros.

2331	**961**	5s. multicoloured	7·25	6·00

962 Pope John Paul II

2005. Pope John Paul II Commemoration.

2332	**962**	1s.80 multicoloured	2·75	2·20

963 Spain 1968 3p.50 Stamp (As T **393**) and Machica Medallion

2005. 50th Anniv of Europa Stamps. Showing stamps of Spain and Pre-historic gold ornaments. Multicoloured.

2333	2s. Type **963**	3·00	2·40
2334	2s. 1960 1p. (As No. 1355) and Chimu ceremonial accoutrements	3·00	2·40
2335	2s. 1969 3p.50 (As T **400**) and Mochica turquoise and Lapis Lazuli roundels	3·00	2·40
2336	2s. 1970 3p.50 (T **410**) and Mochica frontal decoration	3·00	2·40

964 Punta Malpelo, 1828

2005. Naval Victories. Designs showing naval battles. Multicoloured.

2337	2s. Type **964**	3·00	2·40
2338	2s. Callao, May, 1880	3·00	2·40
2339	2s. Collapse of *Covadonga*, December, 1880	3·00	2·40
2340	2s. Abtao, 1866	3·00	2·40
2341	2s. Iquique, 1879	3·00	2·40
2342	2s. Pedrera, 1911	3·00	2·40

Nos. 2337/42 were issued together, se-tenant, with the background forming a composite design of the battle.

965 Skull

2005. 35th Anniv of Medical College.

2343	**965**	5s.50 multicoloured	8·00	6·50

966 Gold Medallion

2006. Cultural Heritage. Cusco.

2344	**966**	5s.50 multicoloured	8·00	6·50

967 The Nativity

2006. Christmas (2005).

2345	**967**	5s.50 multicoloured	8·00	6·50

968 Sister Ana de los Angeles

2006. 400th Birth Anniv of Sister Ana de los Angeles Monteagudo.

2346	**968**	5s.50 multicoloured	8·00	6·50

969 Pope Benedict XVI

2006. Enthronement (2005) of Pope Benedict XVI. Multicoloured.

2347	2s.50 Type **969**	3·75	3·00
2348	2s.50 Giving blessing	3·75	3·00

970 Reading

2006. 400th (2005) Anniv of "Don Quixote de la Mancha" (novel by Miguel de Cervantes).

2349	**970**	5s. multicoloured	7·25	6·00

971 Children

2006. Centenary (2005) of Rotary International.

2350	**971**	5s.50 multicoloured	8·00	6·50

972 Child with Outstretched Hand

2006. America (2005). Struggle against Poverty.

2351	**972**	5s.50 multicoloured	8·00	6·50

973 Pichpichu

2006. Volcanoes. Multicoloured.

2352	2s.50 Type **973**	3·75	3·00
2353	2s.50 Chachani	3·75	3·00
2354	2s.50 Misti	3·75	3·00

974 Church Facade

2006. San Pedro Church, Lima. Multicoloured.

2355	2s.50 Type **974**	3·75	3·00
2356	2s.50 Interior	3·75	3·00

975 Academy Medallion

2006. Centenary (2005) of National History Academy.

2357	**975**	5s.50 multicoloured	8·00	6·50

976 Emblems

2006. 85th (2005) Anniv of YMCA.

2358	**976**	5s.50 multicoloured	8·00	6·50

977 Julio Tello

2006. 125th Birth Anniv (2005) of Julio Tello (anthropologist).

2359	**977**	5s. multicoloured	7·25	6·00

978 Emblems

2006. 75th (2005) Anniv of Contraloria General de la Republica.

2360	**978**	5s.50 multicoloured	8·00	6·50

979 Building Facade

2006. 150th Anniv of Cajamarca City.

2361	**979**	6s. multicoloured	8·75	7·25

980 Chupe de Camarones

2006. Food. Multicoloured.

2362	2s. Type **980**	3·00	2·40
2363	2s. Juane	3·00	2·40
2364	2s. Arroz con Pato	3·00	2·40
2365	2s. Rocoto Relleno	3·00	2·40

981 *Helliconius sara*

2006. Butterflies. Multicoloured.

2366	2s. Type **981**	3·00	2·40
2367	2s. *Morpho Achilles*	3·00	2·40
2368	2s. *Dryas iulia*	3·00	2·40
2369	2s. *Caligo eurilochus*	3·00	2·40

Nos. 2366/9 were issued together, se-tenant, forming a composite design.

982 Scouts

2006. XII Pan American Scout Jamboree. Multicoloured.

2370	2s. Type **982**	3·00	2·40
2371	2s. Scouts carrying flags	3·00	2·40

Nos. 2370/1 were issued together, se-tenant, forming a composite design.

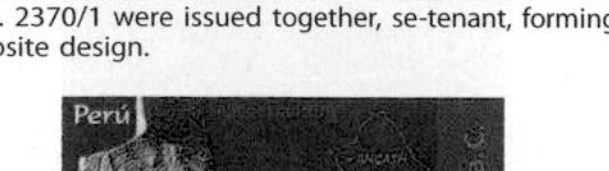

983 Ceramics, Chavin, 1200 BC

2006. Cultural Heritage. Multicoloured.

2372	6s. Type **983**	8·75	7·25
2373	6s. Mummy and textiles, Paracas, 500 BC	8·75	7·25

984 Los Hermanos Ayar

2006. Myths and Legends.

2374	**984**	6s. multicoloured	8·75	7·25

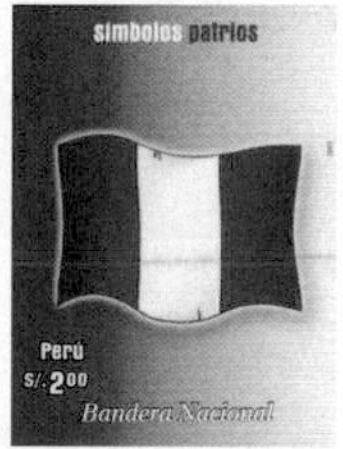

985 Flag

2006. National Symbols. Multicoloured.

2375	2s. Type **985**	3·00	2·40
2376	2s. Emblem	3·00	2·40
2377	2s. Hymn, Jose Bernado Alcedo (composer) and Jose de la Torre Ugarte (writer)	3·00	2·40

986 Discussion, Market, Child and Grower

2006. 50th (2005) Anniv of Caritas.

2378	**986**	5s.50 multicoloured	8·00	6·50

987 Lucuma

2006. Fruit. Multicoloured.

2379	6s. Type **987**	8·75	7·25
2380	6s. Chirimoya	8·75	7·25

988 Map of Highway

2006. Peru—Brazil Interoceanica Highway.

2381	**988**	6s. multicoloured	8·75	7·25

989 Alfredo Bryce Echenique

2006. Writers. Each brown.

2382	6s. Type **989**	8·75	7·25
2383	6s. Mario Vargas Llosa	8·75	7·25

990 Emblem

2006. 70th (2005) Anniv of Ministry of Health.

2384	**990**	6s. multicoloured	8·75	7·25

991 Emblem

2006. 25th (2005) Anniv of ALADI (Latin American integration association).

2385	**991**	6s. multicoloured	8·75	7·25

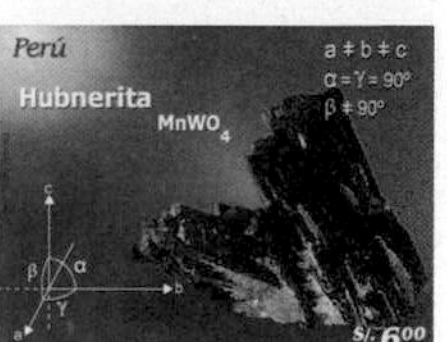

992 Hubnerite

2006. Minerals.

2386	**992**	6s. multicoloured	8·75	7·25

993 Chicha de Maiz Morado

2006. National Drink.

2387	**993**	6s. multicoloured	8·75	7·25

994 *Orestias*

2006. Fauna of Lake Titicaca. Multicoloured.

2388	5s.50 Type **994**	8·00	6·50
2389	5s.50 *Plegadis ridgwayi*	8·00	6·50
2390	5s.50 *Phoenicoparrus andinus*	8·00	6·50
2391	5s.50 *Telmatobius coleus*	8·00	6·50

Nos. 2388/91 were issued together, se-tenant, block forming a composite design.

995 Micaela Bastidas (freedom fighter)

2006. Precursor of Independence. Multicoloured.

2392	2s. Type **995**	3·00	2·40
2393	2s. Cusco Plaza	3·00	2·40

Nos. 2392/3 were issued together, se-tenant, forming a composite design.

996 *Pionopsitta barrabandi*

2006. Parrots. Multicoloured.

2394	5s.50 Type **996**	8·00	6·50
2395	5s.50 *Touit huetii* (Inscr "Tovit")	8·00	6·50
2396	5s.50 *Pionites melanocephala*	8·00	6·50
2397	5s.50 *Ara severa*	8·00	6·50
2398	5s.50 *Amazona festiva*	8·00	6·50
2399	5s.50 *Ara ararauna*	8·00	6·50

2006. Viceroys. As T 887. Multicoloured.

2400	5s.50 Francisco de Toledo	8·00	6·50
2401	5s.50 Martin Enriquez de Almansa	8·00	6·50
2402	5s.50 Fernando Torres y Portugal	8·00	6·50
2403	5s.50 Garcia Hurtado de Mendoza	8·00	6·50

2006. Lighthouses (3rd issue). Sheet 102×82 mm containing vert designs as T 910. Multicoloured.

MS2404 6s.×2, Isla Lobos de Tierra; Isla Blanca 20·00 20·00

997 Simon Bolivar

2006. 180th Anniv of El Peruano Newspaper.

2405	**997**	6s. multicoloured	8·75	7·25

998 Inscr "Tortolita moteada" (*Metriopelia ceciliae*)

2006. Birds. Multicoloured.

2406	6s. Type **998**	8·75	7·25
2407	6s. Inscr "Perlita de Iquitos" (*Polioptila clementsi*)	8·75	7·25
2408	6s. Inscr "Ganso Andino" (*Chloephaga melanoptera*)	8·75	7·25

999 Surfing

2006. Sofia Mulanovich World Champion Surfer—2004.

2409	5s.50 Type **999**	8·00	6·50
2410	5s.50 Holding trophy	8·00	6·50

1000 Early Steam Locomotive

2006. 150th (2005) Anniv of Lima—Callao Railway. Sheet 81×60 mm.

MS2411	**1000**	6s. multicoloured	9·00	9·00

1001 Chan Chan, Trujillo

2006. Tourism. Multicoloured.

2412	5s.50 Type **1001**	8·00	6·50
2413	5s.50 Sipan man, Lambayeque	8·00	6·50
2414	5s.50 Ventanas de Otuzco, Cajamarca	8·00	6·50
2415	5s.50 Kuelap fort, Amazonas	8·00	6·50
2416	5s.50 Rio Abiseo National Park, San Martin	8·00	6·50
2417	5s.50 Pacaya Samiria, Loreto	8·00	6·50

1002 Pope John Paul II

2006. Pope John Paul II's Visit to Peru. Designs showing Pope John Paul II. Multicoloured.

2418	2s. Type **1002**	3·00	2·40
2419	2s. With two nuns	3·00	2·40
2420	2s. With dignitaries	3·00	2·40
2421	2s. Wearing native poncho	3·00	2·40
2422	2s. Accepting straw hat	3·00	2·40
2423	2s. With statue of the Virgin	3·00	2·40
2424	2s. Wearing native hat	3·00	2·40
2425	2s. Waving to crowd	3·00	2·40

1003 Couple, Arequipa

2006. Carnival Costumes. Multicoloured.

2426	6s. Type **1003**	8·75	7·25
2427	6s. Devil masked dancer, Puno	8·75	7·25
2428	6s. Guitarist, Cajamarca	8·75	7·25

1004 Emblem

2006. National Air Force. Multicoloured.

2429	6s. Type **1004**	8·75	7·25
2430	6s. Pilot	8·75	7·25

1005 Arid and Irrigated Land

2006. International Year of Deserts and Desertification.

2431	**1005**	2s. multicoloured	3·00	2·40

1006 The Nativity and Cathedral Museum

2006. Christmas.

2432	**1006**	2s. multicoloured	3·00	2·40

1007 Mozart and Score

2006. 250th Birth Anniv of Wolfgang Amadeus Mozart.

2433	**1007**	5s.50 multicoloured	8·00	6·50

1008 Flags and Ball

2006. World Cup Football Championship, Germany.

2434	**1008**	8s.50 multicoloured	14·50	14·50

1009 Christopher Columbus

2006. 500th Death Anniv of Christopher Columbus.

2435	**1009**	6s. multicoloured	8·75	7·25

1010 Solar Energy Collection Panels

2006. America. Energy Conservation. Multicoloured.

2436	3s. Type **1010**	4·25	3·50
2437	5s.50 Gas	8·00	6·50

Nos. 2436/7 were issued together, se-tenant, forming a composite design.

1011 Giant Panda

2006. 35th Anniv of Peru–China Diplomatic Relations. Multicoloured.

2438	2s. Type **1011**	3·00	2·40
2439	2s. Guanaco	3·00	2·40
2440	2s. Machu Pichu mountain	3·00	2·40
2441	2s. Great Wall of China	3·00	2·40

Nos. 2438/41 were issued together, se-tenant, forming a composite design.

1012 As Type **162**

2006. 75th Anniv of First Stamp Exhibition in Peru.

2442	**1012**	8s.50 multicoloured	14·50	14·50

1013 Pirates

2007. Movies (1st issue). Piratas en el Callao (first 3D animated film in Peru). Multicoloured.

2443	2s. Type **1013**	3·00	2·40
2444	2s. Children	3·00	2·40

See also Nos. 2453/4.

1014 Abstract (painting) (Fernando de Szyszlo)

2007. Peruvian Artists. Multicoloured.

2445	2s.20 Type **1014**	3·00	2·50
2446	2s.20 Horse (sculpture) (Victor Delfin)	3·00	2·50

1015 Purussaurus Skull

2007. Fossils. Sheet 101×81 mm.

MS2447	8s.50 multicoloured	15·00	15·00

1016 Quena

2007. Musical Instruments of the Andes. Multicoloured.

2448	5s.50 Type **1016**	8·00	6·50
2449	5s.50 Zampona	8·00	6·50
2450	5s.50 Antara	8·00	6·50

1017 Toribio de Mogrovejo

2007. 400th Death Anniv of Toribio de Mogrovejo (Archbishop of Lima).

2451	**1017**	2s. purple	3·00	2·40

1018 Senor de los Milagros

2007. Religious Festivals. Sheet 90×110 mm containing T **1018** and similar vert designs. Multicoloured.

MS2452	5s.50×4 Type **1018**; Virgen de las Mercedes; Virgen de la Candelaria; Senor de Muruhuay	32·00	32·00

The stamps and margins of No. **MS**2452 share a composite background design.

1019 Flying Dragons

2007. Movies (2nd issue). Dragones. Destino de Fuego (animation based on book by Hernan Garrido Lecca). Multicoloured.

2453	2s. Type **1019**	3·00	2·40
2454	2s. Head of large dragon	3·00	2·40

1020 Clasped Hands

2007. 75th Anniv of National Jury of Elections.

2455	**1020**	2s.20 sepia	3·00	2·50

1021 Suspiro de Limena

2007. Gastronomy. Desserts. Multicoloured.

2456	2s.50 Type **1021**	3·75	3·00
2457	2s.50 Picarones	3·75	3·00
2458	2s.50 Mazamorra morada	3·75	3·00

1022 Perro Sin Pelo (Peruvian hairless dog)

2007. Dogs. Multicoloured.

2459	6s. Type **1022**	8·75	7·25
2460	6s. Dachshund	8·75	7·25
2461	6s. Samoyed	8·75	7·25
2462	6s. Siberian husky	8·75	7·25

Nos. 2459/62 were issued together, se-tenant, forming a composite design.

1023 San Augustin Church

2007. Cultural Heritage. Lima. Multicoloured.

2463	5s.50 Type **1023**	8·00	6·50
2464	5s.50 San Francisco Sacristy	8·00	6·50
2465	5s.50 Santa Apolonia	8·00	6·50
2466	5s.50 Metropolitan Cathedral	8·00	6·50

1024 Tambo Machay, Cusco

2007. Archaeology (1st issue). Inca Temples. Multicoloured.

2467	6s. Type **1024**	8·75	7·25
2468	6s. Pachacamac, Lima	8·75	7·25
2469	6s. Tambo Colorado, Ica	8·75	7·25

See also Nos. 2472/3.

1025 Felipe Pinglo Alva

2007. 70th (2006) Death Anniv of Felipe Pinglo Alva (singer and musician). Multicoloured.

2470	3s. Type **1025**	4·25	3·50
2471	3s. Photograph and guitar	4·25	3·50

Nos. 2470/1 were issued together, se-tenant, forming a composite design.

1026 Cat-shaped Pot and Gold Mask (Vicus c. 500BC)

2007. Archaeology (2nd issue). Multicoloured.

2472	6s. Type **1026**	8·75	7·25
2473	6s. Two anthropomorphic pots, decorated pot and jug (Salinar c. 200BC)	8·75	7·25

1027 Danza de los Negritos

2007. Traditional Costumes and Dances. Multicoloured.

2474	2s.50 Type **1027**	3·75	3·00
2475	2s.50 Danza de las Tijeras	3·75	3·00
2476	2s.50 Danza Capac Colla	3·75	3·00
2477	2s.50 Danza Diablada	3·75	3·00

Nos. 2474/7 were issued together, se-tenant, forming a composite design.

1028 Asparagus

2007. Exports. Multicoloured.

2478	6s. Type **1028**	8·75	7·25
2479	6s. Mangoes	8·75	7·25
2480	6s. Alpaca wool	8·75	7·25

1029 White Water Rafting (canoeing)

2007. Adventurous Sports. Multicoloured.

2481	6s. Type **1029**	8·75	7·25
2482	6s. Off road cycling (cycling)	8·75	7·25
2483	6s. Rock climbing (climbing)	8·75	7·25

1030 Provisional Headquarters of Chamber of Deputies

2007. 185th Anniv of First Constitutional Congress. Sheet 176×146 mm containing T 1030 and similar vert designs. Multicoloured.

MS2484	2s.50×8, Type **1030**; First constitutional congress; Former local court of the Inquisition, headquarters of the chamber of senators; Simon Bolivar (statue); Legislative Palace at night; Pasos Perdidos hall; Window showing 'Mother Peru'; Portico, Legislative Palace	29·00	29·00

2007. Viceroys. As T 887. Multicoloured.

2485	6s. Luis de Velasco	8·75	7·25
2486	6s. Gaspar de Zuniga y Acevedo	8·75	7·25
2487	6s. Juan de Mendoza y Luna	8·75	7·25
2488	6s. Francisco de Borja y Aragon	8·75	7·25

1031 Giuseppe Garibaldi

2007. Birth Bicentenary of Giuseppe Garibaldi (soldier and nationalist).

2489	**1031**	6s. multicoloured	8·75	7·25

1032 *Oncifelis colocolo* (pampas cat)

2007. Endangered Species. Multicoloured.

2490	3s. Type **1032**	4·25	3·50
2491	3s. *Lontra felina* (marine otter)	4·25	3·50
2492	6s. *Harpia harpyja* (harpy eagle)	8·75	7·25
2493	6s. *Odocoileus virginianus* (white-tailed deer)	8·75	7·25

Nos. 2490/3 were issued together, se-tenant, forming a composite design.

1033 Emblem

2007. Centenary of Scouting. Multicoloured.

2494	3s. Type **1033**	4·25	3·50
2495	3s. Robert Baden-Powell and world flags	4·25	3·50

1034 *Bixa orellana*

2007. Medicinal Plants. Multicoloured.

2496	2s.50 Type **1034**	3·75	3·00
2497	2s.50 *Cestrum auriculatum*	3·75	3·00
2498	2s.50 *Brugmansia suaveolens*	3·75	3·00
2499	2s.50 *Anacardium occidentale*	3·75	3·00
2500	2s.50 *Caesalpinia spinosa*	3·75	3·00
2501	2s.50 *Croton lechleri*	3·75	3·00

1035 Raul Maria Pereira and Postal Building

2007. 130th Birth Anniv of Raul Maria Pereira (artist and architect).

2502	**1035**	2s. multicoloured	3·00	2·40

A stamp of a similar design was issued by Portugal.

No. 2503 has been left for 'Victor de la Torre' Commemoration, issued on 16 August 2007, not yet received.

1036 Institute Building

2007. 60th Anniv of Riva–Aguero Institute. Sheet 100×81 mm.

MS2504	10s.50 multicoloured	19·00	19·00

1037 *Pyrocephalus rubinus* (vermilion flycatcher)

2007. Birds. Multicoloured.

2505	5s.50 Type **1037**	8·00	6·50
2506	5s.50 *Mimus longicaudatus* (long-tailed mockingbird)	8·00	6·50
2507	5s.50 *Coeraba flaveola* (bananaquit)	8·00	6·50
2508	5s.50 *Sarcoramphus papa* (king vulture)	8·00	6·50

1038 Band Members

2007. Centenary of National Band. Multicoloured.

2509	2s. Type **1037**	3·00	2·40
2510	8s.50 Band marching	14·50	12·00

1039 Symbols of Masons

2007. 125th Anniv of Grand Masonic Lodge.

2511	**1039**	6s.50 multicoloured	9·25	7·75

1040 Auburn Speedster 851 SC

2007. Classic Cars. Sheet 141×100 mm containing T 1040 and similar horiz designs. Multicoloured.

MS2512	3s.×5, Type **1040**; Inscr 'Clement Brass Phaeton 9 CV'; Dodge Brothers Special Pickup; Inscr 'Stutz BB Sedan Convertible Victoria'; Inscr 'Pierce Arrow 1603 Touring D 700'	21·00	21·00

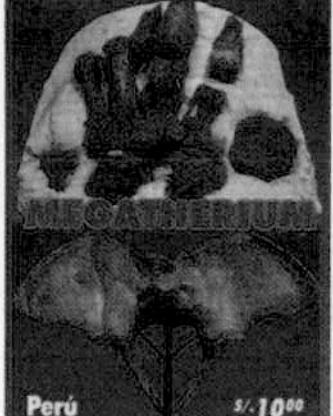

1041 Fossilized Bones

2007. Megatherium. Sheet 101×81 mm.

MS2513	multicoloured	17·00	17·00

1042 Map Outline and Service Personnel

2007. 50th Anniv of Joint Command of Armed Forces. Sheet 101×81 mm.

MS2514	multicoloured	21·00	21·00

1043 Courtyard

2007. 450th Anniv (2008) of Santa Clara Monastery, Cusco.

2515	**1043**	5s.50 multicoloured	8·00	6·50

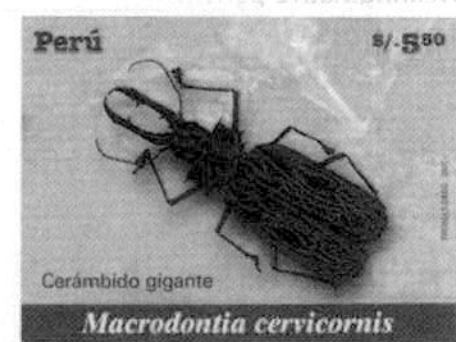

1044 *Macrodontia cervicornis*

2007. Terrestrial Invertebrates. Sheet 110×91 mm containing T 1044 and similar horiz designs. Multicoloured.

MS2516	5s.50×4, Type **1044**; *Dynastes hercules*; *Titanus giganteus*; *Megasoma*	24·00	24·00

1045 Angora

2007. Cats. Multicoloured.

2517	6s. Type **1045**	8·75	7·25
2518	6s. Persian	8·75	7·25
2519	6s. Bengal	8·75	7·25
2520	6s. Siamese	8·75	7·25

1046 Daniel Alcides Carrion

2007. 150th Birth Anniv of Daniel Alcides Carrion (medical student after whom Carrion's disease is named (died after self testing of theory)).

2521	**1046**	3s. brown	4·25	3·50

1047 Francisco Ruiz Lozano (first professor of mathematics)

2007. 350th Anniv of First Nautical Skills Academy.

2522 **1047** 5s.50 multicoloured 8·00 6·50

1048 Woman and Child reading

2007. America. Education for All. Multicoloured.

2523 5s.50 Type **1048** 8·00 6·50

2524 5s.50 Two children reading 8·00 6·50

1049 *Dictyophora indusiata* (inscr 'Dyctiophora indusiata')

2007. Fungi. Sheet 115×127 mm containing T 1049 and similar vert designs. Multicoloured.

MS2525 2s.50×4, Type **1049**; *Sepultaria arenicola*; *Marasmius haematocephalus*; *Marasmiellus volvatus* 15·00 15·00

1050 Bush Dog

2007. Endangered Species. Bush Dog (Speothos venaticus). Sheet 115×127 mm containing T 1050 and similar horiz designs. Multicoloured.

MS2526 2s.×2, Type **1050**; Two bush dogs; 5s.50×2, Preparing to pounce; Facing left 22·00 22·00

1051 Soldiers on Parade

2007. Architecture. Fortaleza del Real Felipe. Sheet 80×100 mm.

MS2527 multicoloured 8·75 7·25

1052 Merryweather Fire Appliance, 1908

2007. Centenary of Volunteer Firefighters. Multicoloured.

2528 3s. Type **1052** 4·25 3·50

2529 3s. Mack fire appliance, 1969 4·25 3·50

Nos. 2528/9 were issued together, se-tenant, forming a composite design.

1053 *Familia serrana* (Camilo Blas)

2007. Art.

2530 **1053** 6s. multicoloured 8·75 7·25

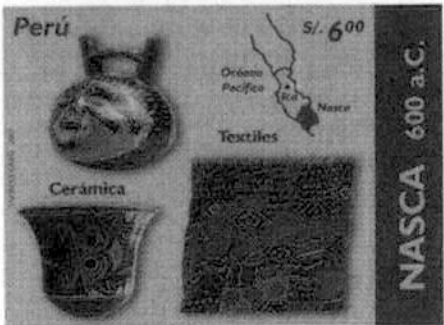

1054 Nasca Artefacts

2007. Cultural Heritage. Multicoloured.

2531 6s. Type **1054** 8·75 7·25

2532 7s. Mohica artefacts 11·00 9·00

1055 Cahuachi

2007. Archaeology. Sheet 100×80 mm.

MS2533 multicoloured 23·00 23·00

1056 Emblem

2007. Asia—Pacific Economic Cooperation Forum, 2008.

2534 **1056** 6s. multicoloured 8·75 7·25

1057 House on Stilts (Juan Chuquipiondo Mesia) (1st place)

2007. Winning Designs in Children's Painting Competition 'Flora and Fauna of My Region'. Multicoloured.

2535 2s. Type **1057** 3·00 2·40

2536 2s. Egret in swamp (Ruben Saavedra Cobenas) (2nd place) (vert) 3·00 2·40

1058 1857 1r. stamp (Type **1**)

2007. 150th Anniv of First Peruvian Stamps (1st series). Multicoloured.

2537 2s.50 Type **1058** 3·75 3·00

2538 2s.50 1857 2r. stamp (As Type **1**) 3·75 3·00

1059 Bronze Cross of Society of the Founders of Independence and Woman holding Arms of Peru

2007. 150th Anniv of Society of the Founders of Independence.

2539 **1059** 6s. multicoloured 8·75 7·25

1060 Iglesia de las Carmelitas (Church of the Carmelites)

2007. Chuirch Altars. Multicoloured.

2540 6s. Type **1060** 8·75 7·25

2541 8s.50 Catedral de Lima (Lima Cathedral) 14·50 12·00

1061 Litany of the Blessed Virgin

2007. Christmas.

2542 **1061** 6s.50 multicoloured 8·75 7·25

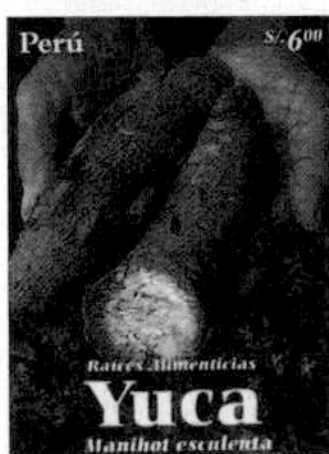

1062 Yuca

2007. Root Vegetables. Multicoloured.

2543 6s. Type **1062** 8·75 7·25

2544 6s. Yacon 8·75 7·25

1063 Pedro Paulet Mostajo (astrononautical pioneer)

2007. 1st Anniv of Launch of Paulet I Space Probe. Multicoloured.

2545 3s. Type **1063** 4·25 3·50

2546 3s. Paulet I on launch pad 4·25 3·00

Nos. 2545/6 were issued together, se-tenant, forming a composite design.

1064 Victor Raul Haya de la Torre

2008. Victor Raul Haya de la Torre Commemoration (American Popular Revolutionary Alliance founder).

2547 **1064** 3s. brown 4·25 3·00

1065 1858 1dinero Stamp (As Type **3**)

2008. 150th Anniv of First Peruvian Stamps (2nd series). Multicoloured.

2548 5s.50 Type **1065** 8·00 6·50

2549 5s.50 1858 1/2 peso stamp 8·00 6·50

2550 5s.50 1858 1dinero stamp 8·00 6·50

1066a Nun and Interior

2008. 300th Anniv of Santa Rosa de Santa Maria Convent.

2551 **1066a** 5s.50 **1066a** multicoloured 8·00 6·50

1067 Research Ship

2008. 20th Anniv of First Antarctic Expedition. Sheet 100×80 mm containing T 1067 and similar multicoloured design.

MS2552 10s.×2, Type **1067**; Scientists and crew (horiz) 33·00 33·00

Nos. 2548/50 and Type **1065** have been left for '150th Anniv of First Peruvian Stamps (2nd series)', issued on 10 March 2008, not yet recieved.

No. 2551 and Type **1066** have been left for '300th Anniv of Monastery' issued on 3 June 2008, not yet received.

1068 '100 Anos' and Violin

2008. Centenary of Philharmonic Orchestra. Multicoloured.

2553 3s. Type **1068** 4·25 3·50

2554 3s. Photograph of members 4·25 3·50

1069 Statue

2008. Bicentenary of Matias Maestro Cemetery. Multicoloured.

2555 6s.50 Type **1069** 9·25 7·75

2556 6s.50 Memorial (horiz) 9·25 7·75

No. 2553/4 and Type **1068** have been left for 'Centenary of Philharmonic Society' issued on 8 June 2008, not yet received.

2008. Viceroys. As T 887. Multicoloured.

2557 6s. Luis Enriquez de Guzman 8·75 7·25

2558 6s. Diego de Benavides y de la Cueva 8·75 7·25

2559 6s. Pedro Antonio Fernandez de Castro 8·75 7·25

2560 6s. Baltasar de la Cueva Enriquez 8·75 7·25

1070 Aboriginal (Inti Raymi (Festival of the Sun))

2008. America. Festivals. Multicoloured.

2561	6s.50 Type **1070**	9·25	7·75
2562	6s.50 Grapes and dancer (Festival de la Vendima)	9·25	7·75

1071 Postman and Customers

2008. Serpost–Ease of Exports.

2563	**1071**	10s. multicoloured	17·00	13·00

1072 Beibel

2008. Olympic Games, Beijing. Multicoloured.

2564	1s.40 Type **1072**	2·00	1·60
2565	1s.40 Jingjing	2·00	1·60
2566	1s.40 Yingying	2·00	1·60
2567	1s.40 Nini	2·00	1·60

1073 Ruins

2008. ALC–UE (Latin American and Caribbean—European Union Cooperation) Summit.

2568	**1073**	6s.50 vermilion and black	9·25	7·75

1074 Flags and Arms

2008. Euro-Latin American Parliamentary Assembly, Lima.

2569	**1074**	6s.50 multicoloured	9·25	7·75

1075 Aurelio Sosa

2008. Birth Centenary of Aurelio Miro Queseda Sosa (journalist and writer).

2570	2s.50 **1075** multic coloured	3·75	3·00

1076 Woman writing on Blackboard

2008. National Literacy Campaign.

2571	**1076**	2s.50 multicoloured	3·75	3·00

1077 Petra, Jordan

2008. New Seven Wonders of the World. Sheet 150x130 mm containing T **1077** and similar horiz designs.. Multicoloured.

MS2572	2s.50 Type **1077**; 2s.50 Machu Pichu, Peru; 2s.50 Great Wall, China; 2s.50 Christo Redentor, Brazil; 7s.50 Chichen Itza, Mexico; 10s. Colosseum, Rome; 10s.50 Taj Mahal, India	32·00	32·00

1078 Avocados

2008. Exports. Multicoloured.

2573	5s.50 Type **1078**	8·00	6·50
2574	5s.50 Olives	8·00	6·50
2575	5s.50 Cotton flowers	8·00	6·50

1079 *Phractocephalus hemioliopterus*

2008. Fish. Sheet 135×96 mm containing T 1079 and similar horiz designs. Multicoloured.

MS2576	3s.×5, Type **1079**; *Mylossoma duriventre; Piaractus brachypomus* (inscr 'braphypomus'); *Ageneiosus ucayalensis; Brycon melanopterus*	21·00	21·00

The stamps and margins of **MS**2576 form a composite design.

1080 Christ sat in Judgement

2008. The Last Judgement, Cathedral, Lima. Multicoloured.

2577	6s.50 Type **1080**	9·25	7·75
2578	6s.50 Angels and the damned	9·25	7·75
2579	6s.50 Christ holding sword and the damned	9·25	7·75
2580	6s.50 Christ, Saints and the saved	9·25	7·75

1081 Edwin Vasquez Cam

2008. 60th Anniv of Edwin Vasquez Cam's Olympic Gold Medal for Pistol Shooting.

2581	**1081**	6s. multicoloured	8·75	7·25

1082 *Espostoa mirabilis*

2008. Peruvian Cacti. Multicoloured.

2582	7s.50 Type **1082**	11·00	9·00
2583	7s.50 *Matucana oreodoxa*	11·00	9·00
2584	7s.50 *Melocactus onychacanthus*	11·00	9·00

1083 Javier Arias Stella

2008. Javier Arias Stella (scientist, politician, Minister of Health and Foreign Minister).

2585	**1083**	2s. multicoloured	3·00	2·40

1084 Girl and Potatoes

2008. International Year of Potato.

2586	**1084**	5s.50 multicoloured	8·00	6·50

1085 *Cattleya rex*

2008. Orchids. Multicoloured.

2587	7s. Type **1085**	10·50	8·50
2588	7s. *Cattleya maxima*	10·50	8·50

1086 Facade

2008. Centenary of Crypt of Heroes. Sheet 100×80 mm.

MS2589	multicoloured	17·00	17·00

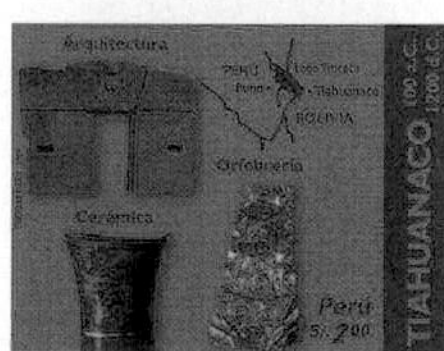

1087 Architecture, Ceramics and Silver, Tiahuanaco

2008. Cultural Heritage. Multicoloured.

2590	2s. Type **1087**	3·00	2·40
2591a	6s. Ceramics and metallurgy, Recuay	8·75	7·25

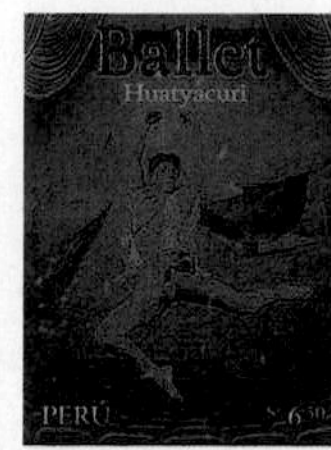

1088 *Huatyacuri* (ballet)

2008. Ballet and Theatre. Multicoloured.

2592	6s.50 Type **1088**	9·25	7·75
2593	6s.50 *Na Catita* (theatre)	9·25	7·75

1089 Mochica Ceramic

2008. 50th Anniv of Faculty of Medicine, National University of Trujillo.

2594	**1089**	6s. multicoloured	8·75	7·25

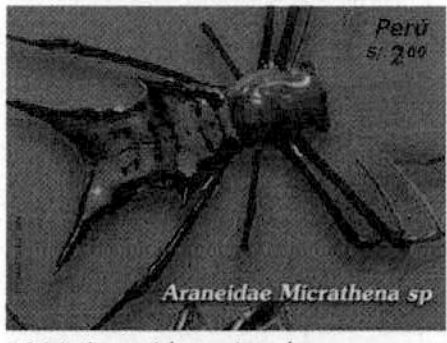

1090 *Araneidae micrathena*

2008. Spiders. Sheet 80x100 mm containing T **1090** and similar horiz designs.. Multicoloured.

MS2595	2s.x4 Type **1088**; *Lycosidae lyscosinae; Salticidae; Lycosidae aglaoctenus*	12·00	9·50

1091 1822 2r. Note

2008. 1st Currency of Independence. Sheet 80x100 mm containing T 1091 and similar horiz designs. Multicoloured.

MS2596	8s.50×2, Type **1091**; 1822 8r. peso	7·25	7·25

1092 Choquequirao

2008. Cultural Heritage. Choquequirao. Sheet 100×80 mm.

MS2597	multicoloured	17·00	17·00

1093 Portico

2008. 40th Anniv of Inquisition Museum. Multicoloured.

2598	6s. Type **1093**	8·75	7·25
2599	6s. Seated inquisitors	8·75	7·25

1094 Traffic Policeman

2008. Traffic Control Campaign.

2600	**1094**	6s.50 multicoloured	9·25	7·75

1095 Emblem

2008. 50th Anniv of Edgardo Rebagliati Martins National Hospital.
2601 **1095** 2s. multicoloured 3·00 2·40

1096 Textile

2008. Textiles. Manto Paracas. Multicoloured.
2602 6s. Type **1096** 8·75 7·25
2603 6s. Geometric shapes, red-brown background 8·75 7·25
2604 6s. Squares on black background, stylized figures in border 8·75 7·25
2605 6s. Ochre and brown background, stylized figures 8·75 7·25

1097 *Xenoglaux loweryi* (long-whiskered owlet)

2008. Endangered Species.
2606 **1097** 7s.50 multicoloured 11·00 9·00

1098 Cannabis Leaves and Crossed Bones (Carolina Luna Polo) (1st)

2008. Fight against Drug Abuse. Winning Designs in Children's Painting Competition. Multicoloured.
2607 2s. Type **1098** 3·00 2·40
2608 2s. Sad and happy children (Diego Gutierrez) (2nd) (horiz) 3·00 2·40

1099 The Nativity

2008. Christmas.
2609 **1099** 8s.50 multicoloured 13·00 11·00

1100 Presidents Alan Garcia Perez (Peru) and George W. Bush (USA)

2008. 1st Anniv of Peru–USA Trade Promotion Agreement.
2610 **1100** 6s. multicoloured 8·75 7·25

1101 Jeronimo de Loayza Gonzalez

2008. Jeronimo de Loayza Gonzalez (first archbishop of Lima) Commemoration.
2611 **1101** 2s. multicoloured 3·00 2·40

1102 Wiracocha

2008. Myths and Legends. Wiracocha (creator god). Sheet 152×76 mm containing T 1102 and similar horiz designs. multicoloured.
MS2612 2s.50×3, Type **1102**; Creating flowers; Walking through landscape 11·25 11·25

1103 Ice Cliffs, South Pole

2009. Preserve Polar Regions and Glaciers. Sheet 120×80 mm containing T 1103 and similar horiz designs. Multicoloured.
MS2613 2s.20×4, Type **1103**; Raising flag; Emblem of International Polar Year; Quelcayya glacier, Cusco 12·00 12·00

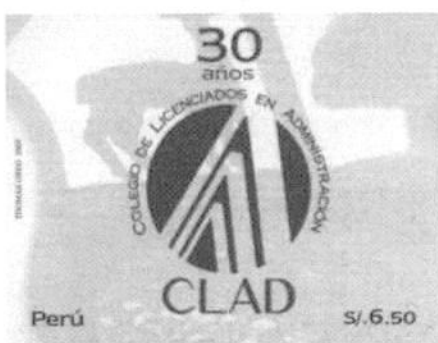

1104 Emblem

2009. 30th Anniv of Business Administration College
2614 **1104** 6s.50 multicoloured 9·00 7·25

1105 Sun and Planets

2009. International Heliophysical Year.
2615 **1105** 5s.50 multicoloured 9·00 6·50

1106 La Marina

2008. Lighthouses. Multicoloured.
2617 6s.50 Type **1106** 9·25 7·75
2618 6s.50 Muelle Darsena 9·25 7·75

1107 Sunflower

2009. Sunflowers. Multicoloured.
2619 2s.50 Type **1107** 3·75 3·00
2620 2s.50 Sunflower in frame 3·75 3·00

1108 Faces of Different Ethnicity and 'HONRADEZ'

2009. Honesty and Punctuality. Multicoloured.
2621 6s.50 Type **1108** 9·00 6·50
2622 6s.50 Torso with clock for face and 'PUNTUALIDAD' (vert) 9·00 6·50

1109 Symbols of Weather

2009. International Meteorological Day.
2623 **1109** 2s. multicoloured 3·00 2·40

1110 Canon del Colca

2009. Canyons. Multicoloured.
2624 2s. Type **1110** 3·00 2·40
2625 2s. Canon de Cotahuasi 3·00 2·40
2626 2s. Canon del Pato 3·00 2·40

Nos. 2624/6 were printed, se-tenant, forming a composite design.

1111 Parachutist

2009. Adventurous Sports. Parachuting. Multicoloured.
2627 7s. Type **1111** 12·00 10·00
2628 7s. Parachutist in close up 12·00 10·00

Nos. 2627/8 were printed, se-tenant forming a composite design.

1112 Boy riding Ox

2009. Chinese New Year. Year of the Ox. Multicoloured.
2629 2s.50 Type **1112** 3·75 3·00
2630 2s.50 Symbol and ox's head 3·75 3·00

1113 Hand holding Globe

2009. Earth Day.
2631 **1113** 5s.50 multicoloured 8·00 6·50

2009. Viceroys. As T **887**. Multicoloured.
2632 6s. Melchor de Linan y Cisneros 8·75 7·25
2633 6s. Melchor de Navarra y Rocafull 8·75 7·25
2634 6s. Melchor Portocarrero Lasso de la Vega 8·75 7·25
2635 6s. Manuel de Oms y de Santa Pau 8·75 7·25

No. 2636 and Type **1114** are left for 50th Anniv of Central University, issued on 30 April 2009, not yet received.

No. 2637/8 and Type **1115** are left for 400th Anniv of Royal Comments, issued on 30 April 2009, not yet received.

No. 2639/42 and Type **1116** are left for Endangered Species, issued on 4 May 2009, not yet received.

2009. First Currency of Independence. One sheet 80×100 mm containing multicoloured designs as T 1091.
MS2643 3s.×2, 1826 'Libertad Parada' (vert); Obverse 8·75 7·25

1117 Horse Riders (Munequeria Cusquena)

2009. Peruvian Crafts. Multicoloured.
2644 6s.50 Type **1117** 8·00 7·50
2645 6s.50 Retalbo (Retalbo Ayacuchano) 8·00 7·50
2646 6s.50 Bull (Torito de Pucara) 8·00 7·50

No. 2647 and Type **1118** are left for Dog, issued on 15 May 2009, not yet received.

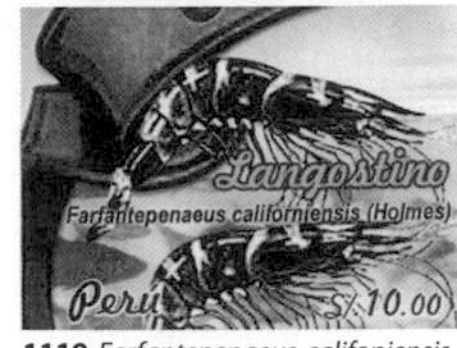

1119 *Farfantepenaeus califoniensis*

2009. Crustaceans. Multicoloured.
2648 10s. Type **1119** 15·00 15·00
2649 10s. *Sicyonia aliaffinis* 15·00 15·00
2650 10s. *Ucides occidentalis* 15·00 15·00
2651 10s. *Palinurus elephas* 15·00 15·00

Nos. 2648/51 were printed, se-tenant forming a composite design.

1120 Gateway and Bell Tower

2008. 80th Anniv of Santiago de Surco Municipality.
2652 **1120** 5s.50 multicoloured 8·00 6·50

1121 *Pisagua*

2009. Submarines. Multicoloured.
2653 2s.50 Type **1121** 3·75 3·00
2654 2s.50 *Arica* 3·75 3·00

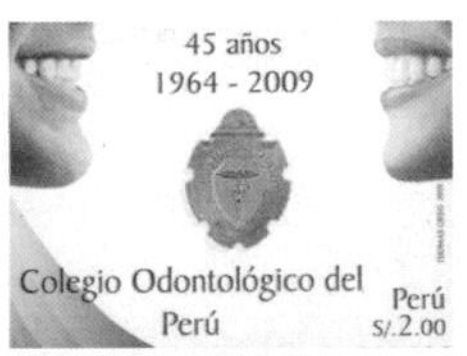

1122 Mouths and Emblem

2009. 45th Anniv of School of Dentistry.
2655 **1122** 2s. multicoloured 3·00 2·40

1123 Building

2009. 25th Anniv of Cusco as UNESCO World Heritage Site.
2656 **1123** 2s.50 multicoloured 3·75 3·00

1124 Emblem and Dog

2009. Rabies Awareness Day.
2657 **1124** 5s.50 multicoloured 8·00 6·50

1125 Louis Braille

2009. Birth Bicentenary of Louis Braille (inventor of Braille writing for the blind). Multicoloured.
2658 2s.50 Type **1125** 3·75 3·00
2659 2s.50 Braille letters 3·75 3·00

1126 Ceramics and Textiles

2009. Cultural Heritage. Multicoloured.
2660 2s. Type **1126** 3·00 2·40
2661 2s. Metals and textile 3·00 2·40

1127 Ciro Alegria

2009. Birth Centenary of Ciro Alegria (journalist, politician, and novelist).
2662 **1127** 2s.50 multicoloured 3·75 3·00

1128 Rock Formation

2009. Cumbemayo Archaeological Complex, Cajamarca.
2663 **1128** 7s.50 multicoloured 13·00 12·00

1129 Loreto River

2009. Rivers and Lakes. Multicoloured.
2664 2s.50 Type **1129** 3·75 3·00
2665 2s.50 Lake Titicaca 3·75 3·00

1130 Anniversary Emblem

2009. 60th Anniv of Philatelic Association.
2666 **1130** 2s. multicoloured 3·00 2·40

1131 Victor Raul Haya de la Torre

2009. 30th Death Anniv of Victor Raul Haya de la Torre (political leader).
2667 **1131** 2s. multicoloured 3·00 2·40

1133 Tacacho con cecina

2009. Peruvian Gastronomy. Sheet 95×135 mm containing T **1133** and similar horiz designs. Multicoloured.
MS2667a 3s.×5, Type **1133**; Ocupa; Cebiche de conchas negras; Picante de papa con cuy frito; Frejoles con cabrito 21·00 21·00

1134 Puente Inca de Qeswachaka

2009. Inca Path. Sheet 91×117 mm containing T **1134** and similar horiz designs. Multicoloured.
MS2668 6s. Type **1134**; 6s. Camino Inca Wanacaure; 6s. Escalerayoe, Lima; 7s.50 Quebrada Huarautambo, Pasco 35·00 35·00

1135 Presidents Alan Garcia of Peru and Hu Jintao of China

2009. Peru–China Commercial Agreement.
2669 **1135** 7s.50 multicoloured 11·00 9·00

1136 Guinea Pig

2009. Exports. Multicoloured.
2670 2s.50 Type **1136** 3·75 3·00
2671 2s.50 Coffee beans 3·75 3·00

1137 Baguatherium (Pyrotheria)

2009. Prehistoric Animals. Sheet 100×80 mm.
MS2672 **1137** 7s. multicoloured 12·00 10·00

1138 *Megalobulimus populirianus*

2009. Molluscs. Sheet 110×90 mm containing T 1138 and similar horiz designs. Multicoloured.
MS2673 6s.50×4, Type **1138**; *Megalobulimus capillaccus; Scutalus versicolor; Scutalus proteus* 35·00 35·00

1139 Symbols of China

2009. 160th Anniv of Chinese Immigration to Peru.
2674 **1139** 8s.50 multicoloured 11·00 9·25

1140 Building Façade

2009. National Museum of Archaeology, Anthropology and History.
2675 **1140** 5s.50 multicoloured 8·00 6·50

1141 *Actitis macularia* (spotted sandpiper)

2009. Birds. Sheet 110×91 mm containing T 1141 and similar horiz designs. Multicoloured.
MS2676 6s.×4, Type **1141**; *Glaucidium brasilianum* (ferruginous pygmy owl); *Numenius phaeopus* (whimbrel); *Egretta caerula* (little blue heron) 34·00 34·00

1142 Luciano Pavarotti

2009. Luciano Pavarotti (tenor) Commemoration.
2677 **1142** 10s.50 multicoloured 16·00 13·00

1143 Orchid and Parrot (Ahmed Lonia Heredia Perez)

2009. Protection of Environment. Winning Designs in Children's Painting Competition. Multicoloured.
2678 2s. Type **1143** 3·00 2·40
2679 2s. Hill as woman feeding hummingbird (Scarle Estefany Rojas Reategui) 3·00 2·40

1144 Virgen de Chapi

2009. Christmas.
2680 **1144** 2s.20 multicoloured 3·25 2·50

EXPRESS LETTER STAMPS

1908. Optd EXPRESO.
E373 **76** 10c. black 26·00 19·00
E382 - 10c. blue (No. 377) 24·00 20·00
E383 **101** 10c. black and brown 40·00 23·00

OFFICIAL STAMPS

1890. Stamps of 1866 optd GOBIERNO in frame.
O287 **15** 1c. violet 2·40 2·30
O324 **15** 1c. red 13·00 13·00
O288 **16** 2c. green 2·40 2·30
O325 **16** 2c. blue 13·00 13·00
O289 **16** 5c. orange 3·50 2·75
O326 **10** 5c. lake 11·00 11·00
O290 **16** 10c. black 1·90 1·20
O291 **16** 20c. blue 5·50 3·50
O327 **16** 20c. blue (as T **10**) 11·00 11·00
O292 **20** 50c. red 7·25 3·75
O293 **21** 1s. brown 9·25 8·00

1894. Stamps of 1894 (with "Head" optd) optd GOBIERNO in frame.
O305 **15** 1c. orange (No. 294) 40·00 34·00
O306 **15** 1c. green (No. 295) 2·40 2·30
O307 **16** 2c. violet (No. 296) 2·40 2·30
O308 **16** 2c. red (No. 297) 2·40 2·30
O309 **16** 5c. blue (No. 298) 19·00 16·00
O310 **16** 10c. green (No. 299) 6·00 5·75
O311 **20** 50c. green (No. 300) 9·25 9·00

1894. Stamps of 1894 (with "Head" and "Horseshoe" optd) optd GOBIERNO in frame.
O312 **16** 2c. red (No. 301) 3·50 3·50
O313 **16** 5c. blue (No. 302) 3·50 3·50

1896. Stamps of 1896 optd GOBIERNO.
O348 **75** 1c. blue 35 30
O349 **76** 10c. yellow 2·00 85
O350 **76** 10c. black 35 30
O351 **77** 50c. red 5·00 5·00

O108

1909
O382 **108** 1c. red 55 30
O385 **108** 10c. purple 90 45
O572 **108** 10c. brown 20 10
O573 **108** 50c. green 65 65

1935. Optd Servicio Oficial.
O567 **184** 10c. red 35 20

PARCEL POST STAMPS

P79

1895. Different frames.
P348 **79** 1c. purple 4·00 3·50
P349 **79** 2c. brown 5·50 3·75
P350 **79** 5c. blue 19·00 10·50
P351 **79** 10c. brown 24·00 18·00
P352 **79** 20c. pink 29·00 23·00
P353 **79** 50c. green 85·00 75·00

1903. Surch in words.
P361 1c. on 20c. pink 11·00 6·75
P362 1c. on 50c. green 11·00 10·00
P363 5c. on 10c. brown 70·00 55·00

POSTAGE DUE STAMPS

D22

D23

1874
D31 **D 22** 1c. brown 45 30
D32 **D 23** 5c. red 55 30
D33 **D 23** 10c. orange 65 30
D34 **D 23** 20c. blue 1·10 55
D35 **D 23** 50c. brown 17·00 6·50

1881. Optd with T 24 ("LIMA" at foot instead of "PERU").
D47 **D 22** 1c. brown 6·00 5·75
D48 **D 23** 5c. red 12·00 11·50
D49 **D 23** 10c. orange 12·00 11·50
D50 **D 23** 20c. blue 46·00 34·00

D51	**D 23**	50c. brown	£100	95·00

1881. Optd LIMA CORREOS in double-lined circle.

D52	**D 22**	1c. brown	9·25	9·25
D53	**D 23**	5c. red	11·00	10·50
D54	**D 23**	10c. orange	13·00	13·00
D55	**D 23**	20c. blue	55·00	38·00
D56	**D 23**	50c. brown	£130	£130

1883. Optd with T 24 (inscr "LIMA" instead of "PERU") and also with T 28a.

D247	**D 22**	1c. brown	9·25	6·50
D250	**D 23**	5c. red	17·00	16·00
D253	**D 23**	10c. orange	13·00	13·00
D256	**D 23**	20c. blue	£850	£850
D258	**D 23**	50c. brown	60·00	60·00

1884. Optd with T 28a only.

D259	**D 22**	1c. brown	90	85
D262	**D 23**	5c. red	90	85
D267	**D 23**	10c. orange	90	85
D269	**D 23**	20c. blue	1·90	85
D271	**D 23**	50c. brown	5·50	1·70

1894. Optd LIMA CORREOS in double-lined circle and with T 28a.

D275	**D 22**	1c. brown	31·00	31·00

1896. Optd DEFICIT.

D348		1c. brown (D31)	65	55
D349	**D 23**	5c. red (D32)	75	45
D350	**D 23**	10c. orange (D33)	1·00	65
D351	**D 23**	20c. blue (D34)	1·20	85
D352	**20**	50c. red (283)	1·30	85
D353	**21**	1s. brown (284)	1·90	1·20

1899. As T 73, but inscr "DEFICIT" instead of "FRANQUEO".

D355	5s. green	1·90	10·50
D356	10s. brown	£1700	£1700

1902. Surch DEFICIT and value in words.

D361	1c. on 10s. (D356)	75	75
D362	5c. on 10s. (354)	1·90	1·60

1902. Surch DEFICIT and value in words.

D363	**23**	1c. on 20c. (D34)	1·10	75
D364	**23**	5c. on 20c. (D34)	2·75	1·80

D109

1909

D382	**109**	1c. brown	90	30
D419	**109**	1c. purple	45	30
D420	**109**	2c. purple	45	30
D570	**109**	2c. brown	45	45
D383	**109**	5c. brown	90	30
D421	**109**	5c. purple	65	30
D384	**109**	10c. brown	1·10	45
D422	**109**	10c. purple	90	45
D571	**109**	10c. green	90	85
D385	**109**	50c. brown	1·70	45
D423	**109**	50c. purple	2·75	1·30
D424	**109**	1s. purple	13·00	5·25
D425	**109**	2s. purple	22·00	6·50

1935. Optd Deficit.

D568	-	2c. purple (No. 537)	1·30	45
D569	**184**	10c. red	1·30	45

Pt. 9, Pt. 22, Pt. 21

PHILIPPINES

A group of islands in the China Sea, E. of Asia, ceded by Spain to the United States after the war of 1898. Under Japanese Occupation from 1941 until 1945. An independent Republic since 1946.

1854. 20 cuartos = 1 real; 8 reales = 1 peso plata fuerte.
1864. 100 centimos = 1 peso plata fuerte.
1871. 100 centimos = 1 escudo (= 1/2 peso).
1872. 100 centimos = 1 peseta (=1/5peso).
1876. 1000 milesimas = 100 centavos or centimos = 1 peso.
1899. 100 cents = 1 dollar.
1906. 100 centavos = 1 peso.
1962. 100 sentimos = 1 piso.

SPANISH ADMINISTRATION

1 Queen Isabella II

1854. Imperf.

1	**1**	5c. red	£2500	£425
3	**1**	10c. red	£850	£300
5	**1**	1r. blue	£950	£325
7	**1**	2r. green	£1300	£225

On the 1r. the inscriptions are reversed.

4 Queen Isabella II

1859. Imperf.

13	**4**	5c. red	24·00	7·75
14	**4**	10c. pink	24·00	23·00

5 Queen Isabella II

1861. Larger lettering. Imperf.

17	**5**	5c. red	65·00	16·00

7

1863. Imperf.

19	**7**	5c. red	21·00	7·50
20	**7**	10c. red	65·00	65·00
21	**7**	1r. mauve	£1100	£650
22	**7**	2r. blue	£800	£550

8

1863. Imperf.

25	**8**	1r. green	£170	55·00

1864. As T 14 of Spain, but value in "centimos de peso". Imperf.

26	3⅛c. black on buff	5·25	2·75
27	6 2/8c. green on pink	5·25	1·60
28	12 4/8c. blue on pink	10·50	1·30
29	25c. red on pink	21·00	7·50
30	25c. red on white	16·00	4·75

1868. Optd HABILITADO POR LA NACION. (a) On 1854 to 1863 issues of Philippines.

41	**7**	5c. red	£100	55·00
53	**4**	10c. pink	£140	80·00
36		1r. green	70·00	29·00
42	**7**	1r. mauve	£950	£550
52	**1**	1r. blue	£3250	£1600
43	**7**	2r. blue	£800	£375

(b) On 1864 issues of Philippines.

31	**7**	3⅛c. black on buff	27·00	6·50
32	**7**	6 2/8c. green on pink	27·00	6·50
33	**7**	12 4/8c. blue on pink	70·00	37·00
34	**7**	25c. red	32·00	21·00

(c) On Nos. 10/11a of Cuba (as T 8 of Philippines).

44	1r. green	£275	£150
45	2r. red	£375	£150

12

1871

37	**12**	5c. blue	85·00	9·00
38	**12**	10c. green	11·50	7·75
39	**12**	20c. brown	£100	55·00
40	**12**	40c. red	£130	27·00

13 King Amadeo

1872

46	**13**	12c. pink	20·00	7·50
47	**13**	16c. blue	£190	49·00
48a	**13**	25c. grey	15·00	7·00
49	**13**	62c. mauve	46·00	13·00
50	**13**	1p.25 brown	85·00	41·00

14

1874

54	**14**	12c. grey	21·00	6·50
55	**14**	25c. blue	8·25	2·75
56	**14**	62c. pink	65·00	6·50
57	**14**	1p.25 brown	£350	95·00

15

1875. With rosettes each side of "FILIPINAS".

58	**15**	2c. pink	3·00	1·10
59	**15**	2c. blue	£325	£130
60	**15**	6c. orange	15·00	3·50
61	**15**	10c. blue	4·00	1·10
62	**15**	12c. mauve	4·25	1·10
63	**15**	20c. brown	27·00	4·50
64	**15**	25c. green	32·00	1·10

16

1878. Without rosettes.

65	**16**	25m. black	4·25	65
66	**16**	25m. green	95·00	41·00
67	**16**	50m. purple	48·00	17·00
68a	**16**	(62½m.) 0.0625 lilac	85·00	27·00
69	**16**	100m. red	£160	65·00
70	**16**	100m. green	15·00	3·75
71	**16**	125m. blue	7·00	65
72	**16**	200m. pink	49·00	9·25
74	**16**	250m. brown	19·00	3·75

1877. Surch HABILITADO 12 CS. PTA. in frame.

75	**15**	12c. on 2c. pink	£160	40·00
76	**16**	12c. on 25m. black	£160	40·00

1879. Surch CONVENIO UNIVERSAL DE CORREOS HABILITADO and value in figures and words.

78	2c. on 25m. green	80·00	15·00
79	8c. on 100m. red	55·00	10·00

1880. "Alfonso XII" key-type inscr "FILIPINAS".

97	**X**	1c. green	45	20
82a	**X**	2c. red	1·20	2·30
83	**X**	2½c. brown	11·50	2·30
95	**X**	2 4/8c. blue	85	30
99	**X**	50m. bistre	70	20
85	**X**	5c. grey	1·20	2·30
100	**X**	6c. brown	18·00	2·50
87	**X**	6 2/8c. green	8·50	13·00
88	**X**	8c. brown	60·00	30·00
89	**X**	10c. brown	4·75	2·30
90	**X**	10c. purple	9·50	19·00
91	**X**	10c. green	£600	£350
92	**X**	12 4/8c. pink	2·75	2·30
93	**X**	20c. brown	4·75	2·30
94	**X**	25c. brown	6·25	2·30

1881. "Alfonso XII" key-type inscr "FILIPINAS" with various circular surcharges. (a) HABILITADO U. POSTAL and value.

111		1c. on 2 4/8c. blue	1·20	75
102	**X**	10c. on 2 4/8c. blue	11·50	2·30

(b) HABILITADO CORREOS 2 CENTS. DE PESO.

101	**X**	2c. on 2½c. brown	5·75	2·30

(c) HABILITADO PA. U. POSTAL 8 CMOS.

106	**X**	8c. on 2c. red	11·50	2·75

(d) HABILITADO PA. CORREOS DE and value.

107	**X**	10c. cuartos on 2c. red	7·00	2·10
112	**X**	16 cuartos on 2 4/8c. blue	18·00	4·50
103	**X**	20c. on 8c. brown	15·00	5·25
113	**X**	1r. on 2c. red	11·50	4·50
109	**X**	1r. on 5c. lilac	9·50	4·00
110	**X**	1r. on 8c. brown	18·00	7·00
105	**X**	2r. on 2 4/8c. blue	9·50	2·75

25

29

30

31

1881. Fiscal and telegraph stamps. (a) with circular surch HABILITADO CORREOS, HABILITADO PARA CORREOS, HABILITADO PA. U. POSTAL or HABILITADO PA. CORREOS and value in figures and words.

115	**25**	2c. on 10 cuartos bistre	41·00	26·00
129	**29**	2c. on 200m. green	9·00	4·50
116	**25**	2 4/8c. on 10 cuartos bistre	5·75	1·30
117	**25**	2 4/8c. on 2r. blue	£300	£130
124	**25**	6 2/8c. on 12 4/8c. lilac	9·00	5·25
119	**25**	8c. on 10c. brown	£325	£250
118	**25**	8c. on 2r. blue	16·00	4·25
123	**25**	16 cmos. on 2r. blue	10·50	4·50
137	**31**	20c. on 150m. blue	27·00	22·00
134	**31**	20c. on 250m. blue	£550	£325
127	**25**	1r. on 10 cuartos bistre	21·00	7·50
121	**25**	1r. on 12 4/8c. lilac	15·00	7·00
130	**29**	1r. on 200m. green	£110	70·00
131	**29**	1r. on 1 peso green	55·00	27·00
132	**30**	1r. on 10 pesetas bistre	80·00	41·00
133	**31**	2r. on 250m. blue	18·00	5·75

(b) With two circular surcharges as above, showing two different values.

128	**25**	8c. on 2r. on 2r. blue	26·00	13·00
136	**31**	1r. on 20c. on 250m. blue	19·00	8·00

(c) Optd HABILITADO PARA CORREOS in straight lines.

122	**25**	10 cuartos bistre	£300	£130
126	**25**	1r. green	£160	£120

1887. Various stamps with oval surch UNION GRAL. POSTAL HABILITADO (No. 142) or HABILITADO PARA COMMUNICACIONES and new value. (a) "Alfonso XII" key-type inscr "FILIPINAS".

138	**X**	2 4/8c. on 1c. green	3·75	2·10
139	**X**	2 4/8c. on 5c. lilac	2·50	1·20
140	**X**	2 4/8c. on 50m. bistre	3·50	2·30
141	**X**	2 4/8c. on 10c. green	2·50	1·30
142	**X**	8c. on 2 4/8c. blue	1·50	85

34

(b) "Alfonso XII" key-type inscr "FILIPAS-IMPRESOS".

143	2 4/8c. on 1/8c. green	85	30

(c) Fiscal and telegraph stamps.

144	**29**	2 4/8c. on 200m. green	7·50	3·25
146	**34**	2 4/8c. on 1c. bistre	1·50	1·10
145	**29**	2 4/8c. on 20c. brown	20·00	9·00

1889. Various stamps with oval surch RECARGO DE CONSUMOS HABILITADO and new value. (a) "Alfonso XII" key-type inscr "FILIPINAS".

147	**X**	2 4/8c. on 1c. green	20	20
148	**X**	2 4/8c. on 2c. red	15	15
149	**X**	2 4/8c. on 2 4/8c. blue	10	10
150	**X**	2 4/8c. on 5c. lilac	15	15
151	**X**	2 4/8c. on 50m. bistre	15	15
152	**X**	2 4/8c. on 12 4/8c. pink	75	75

(b) "Alfonso XII" key-type inscr "FILIPAS-IMPRESOS".

160	2 4/8c. on 1/8c. green	20	20

(c) Fiscal and telegraph stamps.

153	**34**	2 4/8c. on 1c. bistre	40	40
154	**34**	2 4/8c. on 2c. red	40	40
155	**34**	2 4/8c. on 2 4/8c. brown	15	15
156	**34**	2 4/8c. on 5c. blue	15	15
157	**34**	2 4/8c. on 10c. green	15	15
158	**34**	2 4/8c. on 10c. mauve	80	70
159	**34**	2 4/8c.on 20c. mauve	30	30
161	-	17 4/8c. on 5p. green	75·00	

No. 161 is a fiscal stamp inscribed "DERECHO JUDICIAL" with a central motif as T **43** of Spain.

1890. "Baby" key-type inscr "FILIPINAS".

176	**Y**	1c. violet	1·40	45
188	**Y**	1c. red	27·00	11·50
197	**Y**	1c. green	3·75	1·10
162	**Y**	2c. red	20	20
177	**Y**	2c. violet	65	20
190	**Y**	2c. brown	30	20
198	**Y**	2c. blue	45	25
163	**Y**	2⅝c. blue	75	20
178	**Y**	2⅝c. grey	45	20
164	**Y**	5c. green	75	20
165	**Y**	5c. blue	75	20
199	**Y**	5c. brown	15·00	5·50
181	**Y**	6c. purple	45	20
192	**Y**	6c. red	2·75	1·30
166	**Y**	8c. green	45	20
182	**Y**	8c. blue	1·10	45
193	**Y**	8c. red	1·30	45
167	**Y**	10c. green	2·75	45
172	**Y**	10c. pink	1·20	35
202	**Y**	10c. brown	95	45
173	**Y**	12⅝c. green	30	20
184	**Y**	12⅝c. orange	1·20	20
185	**Y**	15c. brown	1·40	45
195	**Y**	15c. red	3·00	1·30
203	**Y**	15c. green	3·50	2·50
169	**Y**	20c. red	£140	70·00
186	**Y**	20c. brown	3·50	55
196	**Y**	20c. purple	32·00	11·50
204	**Y**	20c. orange	7·50	2·75
170	**Y**	25c. brown	10·50	2·10
175	**Y**	25c. blue	2·20	85
205	**Y**	40c. purple	32·00	9·25
206	**Y**	80c. red	43·00	30·00

1897. Surch HABILITADO CORREOS PARA 1897 and value in frame. (a) "Baby" key-type inscr "FILIPINAS".

212		5c. on 5c. green	7·50	4·25
208	**Y**	15c. on 15c. red	4·25	2·30
213		15c. on 15c. brown	6·50	3·75
209		20c. on 20c. purple	30·00	17·00
214		20c. on 20c. brown	10·50	6·50
210		20c. on 25c. brown	21·00	14·00

(b) "Alfonso XII" key-type inscr "FILIPINAS".

215	**X**	5c. on 5c. lilac	8·50	4·00

1898. "Curly Head" key-type inscr "FILIPNAS 1898 y 99".

217	**Z**	1m. brown	20	20
218	**Z**	2m. brown	20	20
219	**Z**	3m. brown	20	20
220	**Z**	4m. brown	13·00	2·50
221	**Z**	5m. brown	20	20
222	**Z**	1c. purple	20	20
223	**Z**	2c. green	20	20
224	**Z**	3c. brown	20	20
225	**Z**	4c. orange	21·00	15·00
226	**Z**	5c. red	45	20
227	**Z**	6c. blue	1·50	80
228	**Z**	8c. brown	70	20
229	**Z**	10c. red	2·75	1·50
230	**Z**	15c. grey	2·50	1·20
231	**Z**	20c. purple	2·50	1·80
232	**Z**	40c. lilac	1·50	1·20
233	**Z**	60c. black	6·50	4·00
234	**Z**	80c. brown	8·50	4·00
235	**Z**	1p. green	30·00	19·00
236	**Z**	2p. blue	43·00	23·00

STAMPS FOR PRINTED MATTER

1886. "Alfonso XII" key-type inscr "FILIPAS-IMPRESOS".

P138	**X**	1m. red	30	20
P139	**X**	⅛c. green	30	20
P140	**X**	2m. blue	30	20
P141	**X**	5m. brown	30	20

1890. "Baby" key-type inscr "FILIPAS-IMPRESOS".

P171	**Y**	1m. purple	20	20
P172	**Y**	⅛c. purple	20	20
P173	**Y**	2m. purple	20	20
P174	**Y**	5m. purple	20	20

1892. "Baby" key-type inscr "FILIPAS-IMPRESOS".

P192		1m. green	3·75	95
P193		⅛c. green	1·70	20
P194		2m. green	4·50	95
P191	**Y**	5m. green	£400	85·00

1894. "Baby" key-type inscr "FILIPAS-IMPRESOS".

P197	1m. grey	35	35
P198	⅛c. brown	35	35
P199	2m. grey	35	35
P200	5m. grey	35	35

1896. "Baby" key-type inscr "FILIPAS-IMPRESOS".

P205	1m. blue	45	20
P206	⅛c. blue	1·50	1·10
P207	2m. brown	55	20
P208	5m. blue	4·25	2·50

UNITED STATES ADMINISTRATION

1899. United States stamps of 1894 (No. 267 etc) optd PHILIPPINES.

252	-	1c. green	3·50	70
253	-	2c. red	2·30	1·00
255	-	3c. violet	9·00	1·40
256	-	4c. brown	34·00	6·25
257	-	5c. blue	9·00	1·10
258	-	6c. purple	45·00	8·50
259	-	8c. brown	45·00	9·00
260	-	10c. brown	34·00	5·00
262	-	15c. green	50·00	9·00
263	**83**	50c. orange	£160	45·00
264	-	$1 black	£550	£350
266	-	$2 blue	£550	£425
267	-	$5 green	£1000	£950

1903. United States stamps of 1902 optd PHILIPPINES.

268	**103**	1c. green	6·25	45
269	**104**	2c. red	9·00	1·40
270	**105**	3c. violet	85·00	16·00
271a	**106**	4c. brown	90·00	25·00
272	**107**	5c. blue	17·00	1·10
273	**108**	6c. lake	£100	28·00
274	**109**	8c. violet	55·00	18·00
275	**110**	10c. brown	32·00	2·75
276	**111**	13c. purple	45·00	20·00
277	**112**	15c. olive	75·00	18·00
278	**113**	50c. orange	£150	45·00
279	**114**	$1 black	£650	£350
280	**115**	$2 blue	£950	£950
281	**116**	$5 green	£1300	£5500

1904. United States stamp of 1903 optd PHILIPPINES.

282a	**117**	2c. red	8·00	2·75

45 Rizal

46 Arms of Manila

1906. Various portraits as T 45 and T 46.

337	**45**	2c. green	25	25
338	-	4c. red (McKinley)	25	25
339	-	6c. violet (Magellan)	35	25
340	-	8c. brown (Legaspi)	45	25
341	-	10c. blue (Lawton)	35	25
288	-	12c. red (Lincoln)	6·75	2·30
342	-	12c. orange (Lincoln)	35	35
289	-	16c. black (Sampson)	5·75	35
298	-	16c. green (Sampson)	4·00	1·40
344	-	16c. olive (Dewey)	1·10	25
290	-	20c. brown (Washington)	5·75	35
345	-	20c. yellow (Washington)	45	25
291	-	26c. brown (Carriedo)	8·00	2·75
346	-	26c. green (Carriedo)	55	55
292	-	30c. green (Franklin)	6·25	1·80
313	-	30c. blue (Franklin)	4·25	55
347	-	30c. grey (Franklin)	70	35
293	**46**	1p. orange	36·00	8·50
363a	**46**	1p. violet	5·75	5·00
294	**46**	2p. black	50·00	1·70
364	**46**	2p. brown	£400	£160
350	**46**	4p. blue	32·00	55
351	**46**	10p. green	65·00	6·25

Nos. 288, 289, 298, 290, 291, 292, 313, 293 and 294 exist perf only, the other values perf or imperf.

1926. Air. Madrid–Manila Flight. Stamps as last, optd AIR MAIL 1926 MADRID-MANILA and aeroplane propeller.

368	**45**	2c. green	18·00	18·00
369	**45**	4c. red	23·00	23·00
370	-	6c. violet	70·00	55·00
371	-	8c. brown	70·00	55·00
372	-	10c. blue	70·00	55·00
373	-	12c. orange	70·00	55·00
374	-	16c. green (Sampson)	£3750	£1800
375	-	16c. olive (Dewey)	90·00	90·00
376	-	20c. yellow	85·00	85·00
377	-	26c. green	85·00	85·00
378	-	30c. grey	85·00	85·00
383	**46**	1p. violet	£250	£225
379	**46**	2p. brown	£700	£375
380	**46**	4p. blue	£900	£650
381	**46**	10p. green	£1700	£850

49 Legislative Palace

1926. Inauguration of Legislative Palace.

384	**49**	2c. black and green	55	35
385	**49**	4c. black and red	55	35
386	**49**	16c. black and olive	1·10	90
387	**49**	18c. black and brown	1·10	90
388	**49**	20c. black and orange	1·70	1·40
389	**49**	24c. black and grey	2·30	90
390	**49**	1p. black and mauve	55·00	36·00

1928. Air. London–Orient Flight by British Squadron of Seaplanes. Stamps of 1906 optd L.O.F. (= London Orient Flight), 1928 and Fairey IIID seaplane.

402	**45**	2c. green	80	45
403	-	4c. red	90	70
404	-	6c. violet	2·75	2·30
405	-	8c. brown	3·25	2·50
406	-	10c. blue	3·25	2·50
407	-	12c. orange	4·50	3·50
408	-	16c. olive (Dewey)	4·00	2·30
409	-	20c. yellow	4·50	3·50
410	-	26c. green	13·50	8·00
411	-	30c. grey	13·50	8·00
412	**46**	1p. violet	65·00	34·00

54 Mayon Volcano

57 Vernal Falls, Yosemite National Park, California, wrongly inscr "PAGSANJAN FALLS"

1932

424	**54**	2c. green	70	80
425	-	4c. red	55	45
426	-	12c. orange	80	70
427	**57**	18c. red	32·00	11·50
428	-	20c. yellow	1·00	90
429	-	24c. violet	1·70	1·00
430	-	32c. brown	1·70	1·10

DESIGNS—HORIZ: 4c. Post Office, Manila; 12c. Freighters at Pier No. 7, Manila Bay; 20c. Rice plantation; 24c. Rice terraces; 32c. Baguio Zigzag.

1932. No. 350 surch in words in double circle.

431	**46**	1p. on 4p. blue	4·25	70
432	**46**	2p. on 4p. blue	7·50	90

1932. Air. Nos. 424/30 optd with Dornier Do-J flying boat "Gronland Wal" and ROUND-THE-WORLD FLIGHT VON GRONAU 1932.

433	2c. green	90	45
434	4c. red	90	45
435	12c. orange	1·40	70
436	18c. red	6·25	4·00
437	20c. yellow	3·75	2·00
438	24c. violet	3·75	2·00
439	32c. brown	2·75	2·00

1933. Air. Stamps of 1906 optd F. REIN MADRID-MANILA FLIGHT-1933 under propeller.

440	**45**	2c. green	55	45
441	-	4c. red	70	45
442	-	6c. violet	1·10	90
443	-	8c. brown	3·50	1·80
444	-	10c. blue	3·50	1·40
445	-	12c. orange	3·25	1·40
446	-	16c. olive (Dewey)	3·25	1·40
447	-	20c. orange	3·25	1·40
448	-	26c. green	3·50	1·80
449	-	30c. grey	3·50	2·30

1933. Air. Nos. 337 and 425/30 optd with AIR MAIL on wings of airplane.

450	2c. green	70	55
451	4c. red	35	25
452	12c. orange	55	25
453	20c. yellow	55	25
454	24c. violet	70	35
455	32c. brown	90	45

66 Baseball

1934. 10th Far Eastern Championship Games.

456	**66**	2c. brown	1·80	1·00
457	-	6c. blue	35	25
458	-	16c. purple	70	70

DESIGNS—VERT: 6c. Tennis; 16c. Basketball.

69 Dr. J. Rizal

72 Pearl Fishing

1935. Designs as T 69/70 in various sizes (sizes in millimetres).

459	2c. red (19×22)	25	25
460	4c. green (34×22)	25	25
461	6c. brown (22½×28)	25	25
462	8c. violet (34×22)	25	25
463	10c. red (34×22)	35	25
464	12c. black (34×22)	35	25
465	16c. blue (34×22)	35	25
466	20c. bistre (19×22)	35	25
467	26c. blue (34×22)	45	35
468	30c. red (34×22)	45	35
469	1p. black and orange (37×27)	2·75	2·00
470	2p. black and brown (37×27)	6·75	2·00
471	4p. black and blue (37×27)	6·75	4·00
472	5p. black and green (27×37)	17·00	4·00

DESIGNS: 4c. Woman, Carabao and Rice-stalks; 6c. Filipino girl; 10c. Fort Santiago; 12c. Salt springs; 16c. Magellan's landing; 20c. "Juan de la Cruz"; 26c. Rice terraces; 30c. Blood Compact; 1p. Barasoain Church; 2p. Battle of Manila Bay; 4p. Montalban Gorge; 5p. George Washington (after painting by John Faed).

COMMONWEALTH OF THE PHILIPPINES

83 "Temples of Human Progress"

1935. Inauguration of Commonwealth of the Philippines.

483	**83**	2c. red	25	25
484	**83**	6c. violet	25	25
485	**83**	16c. blue	35	35
486	**83**	36c. green	45	45
487	**83**	50c. brown	70	70

1935. Air. "China Clipper" Trans-Pacific Air Mail Flight. Optd P.I. U.S. INITIAL FLIGHT December-1935 and Martin M-130 flying boat.

488	10c. red (No. 463)	45	35
489	30c. red (No. 468)	70	70

85 J. Rizal y Mercado

1936. 75th Birth Anniv of Rizal.

490	**85**	2c. yellow	25	25
491	**85**	6c. blue	25	25
492	**85**	36c. brown	70	70

1936. Air. Manila–Madrid Flight by Arnaiz and Calvo. Stamps of 1906 surch MANILA-MADRID ARNACAL FLIGHT–1936 and value.

493	**45**	2c. on 4c. red	25	25
494	**45**	6c. on 12c. orange	25	25
495	**45**	16c. on 26c. green	35	35

1936. Stamps of 1935 (Nos. 459/72) optd COMMONWEALTH (2c., 6c., 20c.) or COMMONWEALTH (others).

496	2c. red	25	25
497	4c. green	70	5·75
526	6c. brown	25	25
527	8c. violet	25	25
528	10c. red	25	25
529	12c. black	25	25
530	16c. blue	25	25
531	20c. bistre	25	25
532	26c. blue	35	35
505	30c. red	55	25
534	1p. black and orange	70	25
535	2p. black and brown	5·75	90
508	4p. black and blue	34·00	6·75
509	5p. black and green	8·00	2·30

89 Manuel L. Quezon

1936. 1st Anniv of Autonomous Government.

510	**89**	2c. brown	25	25
511	**89**	6c. green	25	25
512	**89**	12c. blue	35	35

90 Philippine Is

1937. 33rd International Eucharistic Congress.

513	**90**	2c. green	25	25
514	**90**	6c. brown	25	25
515	**90**	12c. blue	25	25
516	**90**	20c. orange	35	25
517	**90**	36c. violet	55	55
518	**90**	50c. red	80	45

1937

522	**92**	10p. grey	6·00	2·50
523	**92**	20p. brown	4·00	2·00

92 Arms of Manila

1939. Air. 1st Manila Air Mail Exhibition. Surch FIRST AIR MAIL EXHIBITION Feb 17 to 19, 1939 and value.

548a	-	8c. on 26c. green (346)	90	55
549	**92**	1p. on 10p. grey	3·75	2·75

1939. 1st National Foreign Trade Week. Surch FIRST FOREIGN TRADE WEEK MAY 21-27, 1939 and value.

551	-	2c. on 4c. green (460)	25	25
552a	**45**	6c. on 26c. green (346)	1·10	35
553	**92**	50c. on 20p. brown	1·40	1·40

101 Triumphal Arch **102** Malacanan Palace

103 Pres. Quezon taking Oath of Office

1939. 4th Anniv of National Independence.

554	**101**	2c. green	25	25
555	**101**	6c. red	25	25
556	**101**	12c. blue	35	25
557	**102**	2c. green	25	25
558	**102**	6c. orange	25	25
559	**102**	12c. red	35	25
560	**103**	2c. orange	25	25
561	**103**	6c. green	25	25
562	**103**	12c. violet	35	25

104 Jose Rizal

1941

563	**104**	2c. green	25	55
623	-	2c. brown	35	25

In No. 623 the head faces to the right.

105 Filipino Vinta and Boeing 314 Flying Boat

1941. Air.

566	**105**	8c. red	2·50	70
567	**105**	20c. blue	3·25	55
568	**105**	60c. green	2·75	1·10
569	**105**	1p. sepia	1·10	55

For Japanese Occupation issues of 1941–45 see **JAPANESE OCCUPATION OF PHILIPPINE ISLANDS**.

1945. Victory issue. Nos. 496, 525/31, 505, 534 and 522/3 optd **VICTORY**.

610	2c. red	25	25
611	4c. green	25	25
612	6c. brown	35	25
613	8c. violet	35	25
614	10c. red	35	25
615	12c. black	25	25
616	16c. blue	45	25
617	20c. bistre	55	25
618	30c. red	70	55
619	1p. black and orange	2·00	45
620	10p. grey	70·00	17·00
621	20p. brown	65·00	18·00

INDEPENDENT REPUBLIC

111 "Independence"

1946. Proclamation of Independence.

625	**111**	2c. red	30	30
626	**111**	6c. green	60	30
627	**111**	12c. blue	90	45

1946. Optd PHILIPPINES 50TH ANNIVERSARY MARTYRDOM OF RIZAL 1896–1946.

628	**104**	2c. brown (No. 623)	30	20

113 Bonifacio Monument

1947

629	-	4c. brown	15	15
630	**113**	10c. red	15	15
631	-	12c. blue	20	15
632	-	16c. grey	1·60	95
633	-	20c. brown	45	15
634	-	50c. green	1·20	10
635	-	1p. violet	2·40	60

DESIGNS—VERT: 4c. Rizal Monument; 50c., 1p. Avenue of Palm Trees. HORIZ: 12c. Jones Bridge; 16c. Santa Lucia Gate; 20c. Mayon Volcano.

115 Manuel L. Quezon

1947

636	**115**	1c. green	15	10
MS637		64×85 mm. No. 636 in block of four. Imperf	1·50	1·50

116 Pres. Roxas taking Oath of Office

1947. 1st Anniv of Independence.

638	**116**	4c. red	20	15
639	**116**	6c. green	50	50
640	**116**	16c. purple	1·20	80

117 Presidents Quezon and Roosevelt

1947. Air.

641	**117**	6c. green	60	60
642	**117**	40c. orange	1·30	1·30
643	**117**	80c. blue	3·25	3·25

119 United Nations Emblem

1947. Conference of Economic Commission for Asia and Far East, Baguio. Imperf or perf.

648	**119**	4c. red and pink	1·60	1·60
649	**119**	6c. violet and light violet	2·40	2·40
650	**119**	12c. blue and light blue	2·75	2·75

121 General MacArthur

1948. 3rd Anniv of Liberation.

652	**121**	4c. violet	60	20
653	**121**	6c. red	1·10	75
654	**121**	16c. blue	1·60	75

122 Threshing Rice

1948. United Nations Food and Agriculture Organization Conference, Baguio.

655	**122**	2c. green & yell (postage)	90	60
656	**122**	6c. brown and stone	1·10	80
657	**122**	18c. blue and light blue	3·00	2·40
658	**122**	40c. red and pink (air)	15·00	8·00

125 Dr. Jose Rizal

1948

662	**125**	2c. green	20	15

126 Pres. Manuel Roxas

1948. President Roxas Mourning Issue.

663	**126**	2c. black	20	15
664	**126**	4c. black	35	20

127 Scout and Badge

1948. 25th Anniv of Philippine Boy Scouts. Perf or imperf.

665	**127**	2c. green and brown	1·10	60
666	**127**	4c. pink and brown	1·50	90

128 Sampaguita, National Flower

1948. Flower Day.

667	**128**	3c. green and black	35	30

130 Santos, Tavera and Kalaw

131 "Doctrina Christiana" (first book published in Philippines)

1949. Library Rebuilding Fund.

671	**130**	4c.+2c. brown	1·10	80
672	**131**	6c.+4c. violet	3·25	2·20
673	-	18c.+7c. blue	4·50	3·75

DESIGN—VERT: 18c. Title page of Rizal's "Noli Me Tangere".

132 U.P.U. Monument, Berne

1949. 75th Anniv of U.P.U.

674	**132**	4c. green	20	10
675	**132**	6c. violet	20	15
676	**132**	18c. blue	80	30
MS677		106×92 mm. Nos. 674/6. Imperf	1·50	1·50

133 General del Pilar at Tirad Pass

1949. 50th Death Anniv of Gen. Gregorio del Pilar.

678	**133**	2c. brown	15	15
679	**133**	4c. green	35	30

134 Globe

1950. 5th International Congress of Junior Chamber of Commerce.

680	**134**	2c. violet (postage)	20	10
681	**134**	6c. green	30	15
682	**134**	18c. blue	65	20
683	**134**	30c. orange (air)	50	20
684	**134**	50c. red	90	20

135 Red Lauan Trees

1950. 15th Anniv of Forestry Service.

685	**135**	2c. green	35	20
686	**135**	4c. violet	75	30

136 Franklin D. Roosevelt

1950. 25th Anniv of Philatelic Association.

687	**136**	4c. brown	30	20

688	**136**	6c. pink	60	35
689	**136**	18c. blue	1·30	95
MS690 61×51 mm. **136** 80c. green. Imperf			2·50	2·50

137 Lions Emblem

1950. "Lions" International Convention, Manila.

691	**137**	2c. orange (postage)	65	65
692	**137**	4c. lilac	1·00	1·00
693	**137**	30c. green (air)	1·00	75
694	**137**	50c. blue	1·10	1·00
MS695 91×88 mm. Nos. 693/4			2·20	2·20

138 President Quirino taking Oath of Office

1950. Pres. Quirino's Inauguration.

696	**138**	2c. red	15	10
697	**138**	4c. purple	15	15
698	**138**	6c. green	20	15

1950. Surch ONE CENTAVO.

699	**125**	1c. on 2c. green	15	10

140 Dove and Map

1950. Baguio Conference.

701	**140**	5c. green	30	20
702	**140**	6c. red	30	20
703	**140**	18c. blue	75	50

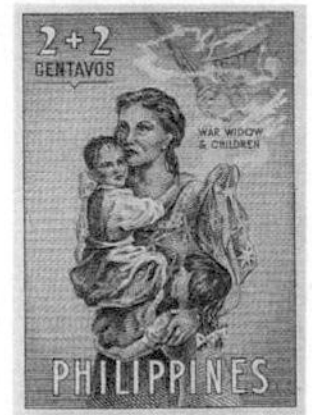

141 War Widow and Children

1950. Aid to War Victims.

704	**141**	2c.+2c. red	10	10
705	-	4c.+4c. violet	45	45

DESIGN: 4c. Disabled veteran.

142 Arms of Manila

1950. As T 142. Various arms and frames. (a) Arms inscr "MANILA".

706	5c. violet	60	50
707	6c. grey	50	35
708	18c. blue	60	50

(b) Arms inscr "CEBU".

709	5c. red	60	50
710	6c. brown	50	35
711	18c. violet	60	50

(c) Arms inscr "ZAMBOANGA".

712	5c. green	60	50
713	6c. brown	50	35
714	18c. blue	60	50

(d) Arms inscr "ILOILO".

715	5c. green	60	50
716	6c. violet	50	35
717	18c. blue	60	50

143 Soldier and Peasants

1951. Guarding Peaceful Labour. Perf or imperf.

718	**143**	5c. green	20	20
719	**143**	6c. purple	35	35
720	**143**	18c. blue	1·00	1·00

144 Philippines Flag and U.N. Emblem

1951. U.N. Day.

721	**144**	5c. red	90	35
722	**144**	6c. green	60	35
723	**144**	18c. blue	1·60	1·10

145 Statue of Liberty

1951. Human Rights Day.

724	**145**	5c. green	50	30
725	**145**	6c. orange	75	50
726	**145**	18c. blue	1·30	80

146 Schoolchildren

1952. 50th Anniv of Philippine Educational System.

727	**146**	5c. orange	60	50

147 M. L. Quezon

1952. Portraits.

728	**147**	1c. brown	15	15
729	-	2c. black (J. Abad Santos)	15	15
730	-	3c. red (A. Mabini)	15	15
731	-	5c. red (M. H. del Pilar)	15	15
732	-	10c. blue (Father J. Burgos)	15	15
733	-	20c. red (Lapu-Lapu)	30	15
734	-	25c. green (Gen. A. Luna)	45	20
735	-	50c. red (C. Arellano)	90	30
736	-	60c. red (A. Bonifacio)	1·00	45
737	-	2p. violet (G. L. Jaena)	3·25	1·10

149 Aurora A. Quezon

1952. Fruit Tree Memorial Fund.

742	**149**	5c.+1c. blue	15	15
743	**149**	6c.+2c. pink	45	45

See also No. 925.

150 Milkfish and Map of Oceania

1952. Indo-Pacific Fisheries Council.

744	**150**	5c. brown	1·20	75
745	**150**	6c. blue	75	60

151 "A Letter from Rizal"

1952. Pan-Asiatic Philatelic Exhibition, Manila.

746	**151**	5c. blue (postage)	65	15
747	**151**	6c. brown	65	20
748	**151**	30c. red (air)	1·30	1·10

152 Wright Park, Baguio City

1952. 3rd Lions District Convention.

749	**152**	5c. red	95	95
750	**152**	6c. green	1·30	1·10

153 F. Baltazar (poet)

1953. National Language Week.

751	**153**	5c. bistre	50	35

154 "Gateway to the East"

1953. International Fair, Manila.

752	**154**	5c. turquoise	35	15
753	**154**	6c. red	35	15

155 Pres. Quirino and Pres. Sukarno

1953. Visit of President to Indonesia. Flags in yellow, blue and red.

754	**155**	5c. blue, yellow and black	20	10
755	**155**	6c. green, yellow and black	30	30

156 Doctor examining patient

1953. 50th Anniv of Philippines Medical Association.

756	**156**	5c. mauve	30	30
757	**156**	6c. blue	45	35

1954. Optd FIRST NATIONAL BOY SCOUTS JAMBOREE APRIL 23-30, 1954 or surch also.

758	5c. red (No. 731)	1·30	1·10
759	18c. on 50c. green (No. 634)	2·20	1·60

158 Stamp of 1854, Magellan and Manila P.O.

1954. Stamp Centenary. Central stamp in orange.

760	**158**	5c. violet (postage)	80	60
761	**158**	18c. blue	1·60	1·30
762	**158**	30c. green	3·75	2·40
763	**158**	10c. brown (air)	1·60	1·30
764	**158**	20c. green	2·75	2·20
765	**158**	50c. red	5·50	4·75

159 Diving

1954. 2nd Asian Games, Manila.

766	-	5c. blue on blue (Discus)	90	65
767	**159**	18c. green on green	1·50	1·10
768	-	30c. red on pink (Boxing)	2·20	1·90

1954. Surch MANILA CONFERENCE OF 1954 and value.

769	**113**	5c. on 10c. red	20	15
770	-	18c. on 20c. brown (No. 633)	80	75

161 "Independence"

1954. Independence Commemoration.

771	**161**	5c. red	30	20
772	**161**	18c. blue	95	60

162 "The Immaculate Conception" (Murillo)

1954. Marian Year.

773	**162**	5c. blue	60	35

163 Mayon Volcano and Filipino Vinta

1955. 50th Anniv of Rotary International.

774	**163**	5c. blue (postage)	35	15
775	**163**	18c. red	1·30	65
776	**163**	50c. green (air)	2·50	1·10

164 "Labour"

1955. Labour-Management Congress, Manila.

777	**164**	5c. brown	1·50	60

165 Pres. Magsaysay

1955. 9th Anniv of Republic.

778	**165**	5c. blue	20	20
779	**165**	20c. red	75	75
780	**165**	30c. green	1·30	1·30

166 Lt. J. Gozar

1955. Air. Air Force Heroes.

781	**166**	20c. violet	80	15
782	-	30c. red (Lt. C. F. Basa)	1·30	30
783	**166**	50c. green	1·10	20
784	-	70c. blue (Lt. C. F. Basa)	1·90	1·30

167 Liberty Well

1956. Artesian Wells for Rural Areas.

785	**167**	5c. violet	35	35
786	**167**	20c. green	80	75

1956. 5th Conference of World Confederation of Organizations of the Teaching Profession. No. 731 optd WCOTP CONFERENCE MANILA.

787	5c. red	35	35

169 Nurse and War Victims

1956. 50th Anniv of Philippines Red Cross.

788	**169**	5c. violet and red	50	50
789	**169**	20c. brown and red	75	60

170 Monument (landing marker) in Leyte

1956. Liberation Commem. Perf or imperf.

790	**170**	5c. red	15	15

171 St. Thomas's University

1956. University of St. Thomas.

791	**171**	5c. brown and red	25	20
792	**171**	60c. brown and mauve	1·10	1·00

172 Statue of the Sacred Heart

1956. 2nd National Eucharistic Congress and Centenary of the Feast of the Sacred Heart.

793	**172**	5c. green	35	30
794	**172**	20c. pink	80	80

1956. Surch 5 5.

795	5c. on 6c. brown (No. 710)	15	15
796	5c. on 6c. brown (No. 713)	15	15
797	5c. on 6c. violet (No. 716)	15	15

174 Girl Guide, Badge and Camp

1957. Girl Guides' Pacific World Camp, Quezon City, and Birth Centenary of Lord Baden-Powell. Perf or imperf.

798	**174**	5c. blue	50	50

175 Pres. Ramon Magsaysay

1957. Death of Pres. Magsaysay.

799	**175**	5c. black	15	10

176 Sergio Osmena (Speaker) and First Philippine Assembly

1957. 50th Anniv of First Philippine Assembly.

800	**176**	5c. green	15	15

177 "The Spoliarium" after Juan Luna

1957. Birth Centenary of Juan Luna (painter).

801	**177**	5c. red	15	10

1957. Inauguration of President C. P. Garcia and Vice-President D. Macapagal. Nos. 732/3 surch GARCIA-MACAPAGAL INAUGURATION DEC. 30, 1957 and value.

802	5c. on 10c. blue	20	20
803	10c. on 20c. red	30	30

179 University of the Philippines

1958. Golden Jubilee of University of the Philippines.

804	**179**	5c. red	35	15

180 Pres. Garcia

1958. 12th Anniv of Republic.

805	**180**	5c. multicoloured	15	15
806	**180**	20c. multicoloured	60	45

181 Main Hospital Building, Quezon Institute

1958. Obligatory Tax. T.B. Relief Fund.

807	**181**	5c.+5c. green and red	20	20
808	**181**	10c.+5c. violet and red	45	45

182 The Immaculate Conception and Manila Cathedral

1958. Inauguration of Manila Cathedral.

809	**182**	5c. multicoloured	20	15

1959. Surch One Centavo.

810	1c. on 5c. red (No. 731)	15	10

1959. 14th Anniv of Liberation. Nos. 704/5 surch.

812	**141**	1c. on 2c.+2c. red	10	10
813	-	6c. on 4c.+4c. violet	15	15

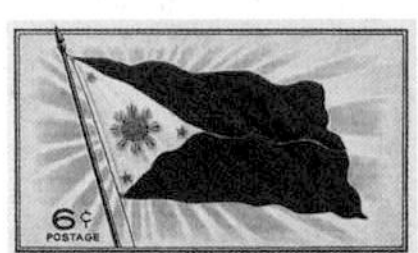

186 Philippines Flag

1959. Adoption of Philippine Constitution.

814	**186**	6c. red, blue and yellow	15	10
815	**186**	20c. red, blue and yellow	20	20

187 Bulacan Seal

1959. Provincial Seals. (a) Bulacan Seal and 60th Anniv of Malolos Constitution.

816	**187**	6c. green	15	10
817	**187**	20c. red	30	20

(b) Capiz Seal and 11th Death Anniv of Pres. Roxas.

818	6c. brown	10	10
819	25c. violet	30	30

The shield within the Capiz seal bears the inset portrait of Pres. Roxas.

(c) Bacolod Seal.

820	6c. green	15	10
821	10c. purple	20	15

188 Scout at Campfire

1959. 10th World Scout Jamboree, Manila.

822	**188**	6c.+4c. red on yellow (postage)	15	15
823	**188**	6c.+4c. red	35	35
824	-	25c.+5c. blue on yellow	60	60

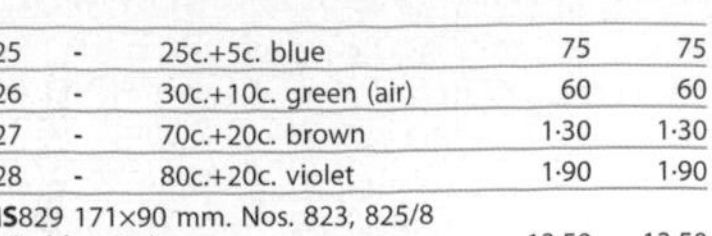

825	-	25c.+5c. blue	75	75
826	-	30c.+10c. green (air)	60	60
827	-	70c.+20c. brown	1·30	1·30
828	-	80c.+20c. violet	1·90	1·90

MS829 171×90 mm. Nos. 823, 825/8 (sold at 4p.) 12·50 12·50

DESIGNS: 25c. Scout with bow and arrow; 30c. Scout cycling; 70c. Scout with model airplane; 80c. Pres. Garcia with scout.

190 Bohol Sanatorium

1959. Obligatory Tax. T.B. Relief Fund. Nos. 807/8 surch HELP FIGHT T B with Cross of Lorraine and value and new design (T 190).

830	**181**	3c.+5c. on 5c.+5c.	20	20
831	**181**	6c.+5c. on 10c.+5c.	20	20
832	**190**	6c.+5c. green and red	20	20
833	**190**	25c.+5c. blue and red	45	35

191 Pagoda and Gardens at Camp John Hay

1959. 50th Anniv of Baguio.

834	**191**	6c. green	15	10
835	**191**	25c. red	35	20

1959. U.N. Day. Surch 6c UNITED NATIONS DAY.

836	**132**	6c. on 18c. blue	15	10

193 Maria Cristina Falls

1959. World Tourist Conference, Manila.

837	**193**	6c. green and violet	15	15
838	**193**	30c. green and brown	60	45

1959. No. 629 surch One and bars.

839	1c. on 4c. brown	15	10

195

1959. Centenary of Manila Athenaeum (school).

840	**195**	6c. blue	10	10
841	**195**	30c. red	50	35

196 Dr. Jose Rizal

1959

842	**196**	6c. blue	15	10

197 Book of the Constitution

1960. 25th Anniv of Philippines Constitution.

844	**197**	6c. brn & gold (postage)	15	15
845	**197**	30c. blue and silver (air)	45	30

198 Congress Building

1960. 5th Anniv of Manila Pact.

846	198	6c. green	10	10
847	198	25c. orange	45	35

199 Sunset, Manila Bay

1960. World Refugee Year.

848	199	6c. multicoloured	15	15
849	199	25c. multicoloured	45	30

200 North American F-86 Sabre and Boeing P-12 Fighters

1960. Air. 25th Anniv of Philippine Air Force.

850	200	10c. red	15	15
851	200	20c. blue	45	30

1960. Surch.

852	134	1c. on 18c. blue	20	15
853	161	5c. on 18c. blue	20	20
854	163	5c. on 18c. red	30	15
855	158	10c. on 18c. orange & blue	20	15
856	140	10c. on 18c. blue	30	20

202 Lorraine Cross

1960. 50th Anniv of Philippine Tuberculosis Society. Lorraine Cross and wreath in red and gold.

857	202	5c. green	15	10
858	202	6c. blue	15	10

1960. Obligatory Tax. T.B. Relief Fund. Surch 6+5 HELP PREVENT TB.

859	181	6c.+5c. on 5c.+5c. green and red	35	15

204 Pres. Quezon

1960

860	204	1c. green	15	10

205 Basketball

1960. Olympic Games.

861	205	6c. brown & grn (postage)	15	10
862	-	10c. brown and purple	20	15
863	-	30c. brown and orange (air)	60	50
864	-	70c. purple and blue	1·30	1·10

DESIGNS: 10c. Running; 30c. Rifle-shooting; 70c. Swimming.

206 Presidents Eisenhower and Garcia

1960. Visit of President Eisenhower.

865	206	6c. multicoloured	20	15
866	206	20c. multicoloured	50	30

207 "Mercury" and Globe

1961. Manila Postal Conference.

867	207	6c. multicoloured (postage)	15	10
868	207	30c. multicoloured (air)	35	30

1961. Surch 20 20.

869		20c. on 25c. green (No. 734)	30	15

1961. 2nd National Scout Jamboree, Zamboanga. Nos. 822/5 surch 2nd National Boy Scout Jamboree Pasonanca Park and value.

870		10c. on 6c.+4c. red on yellow	15	15
871		10c. on 6c.+4c. red	50	50
872		30c. on 25c.+5c. blue on yellow	35	35
873		30c. on 25c.+5c. blue	60	60

210 La Salle College

1961. 50th Anniv of La Salle College.

874	210	6c. multicoloured	15	10
875	210	10c. multicoloured	20	15

211 Rizal when Student, School and University Buildings

1961. Birth Centenary of Dr. Jose Rizal.

876	211	5c. multicoloured	10	10
877	-	6c. multicoloured	10	10
878	-	10c. brown and green	20	20
879	-	20c. turquoise and brown	30	30
880	-	30c. multicoloured	50	35

DESIGNS: 6c. Rizal and birthplace at Calamba, Laguna; 10c. Rizal, mother and father; 20c. Rizal extolling Luna and Hidalgo at Madrid; 30c. Rizal's execution.

1961. 15th Anniv of Republic. Optd IKA 15 KAARAWAN Republika ng Pilipinas Hulyo 4, 1961.

881	198	6c. green	20	20
882	198	25c. orange	45	45

213 Roxas Memorial T.B. Pavilion

1961. Obligatory Tax. T.B. Relief Fund.

883	213	6c.+5c. brown and red	35	15

214 Globe, Plan Emblem and Supporting Hand

1961. 7th Anniv of Admission of Philippines to Colombo Plan.

884	214	5c. multicoloured	10	10
885	214	6c. multicoloured	15	15

1961. Philippine Amateur Athletic Federation's Golden Jubilee. Surch with P.A.A.F. monogram and 6c PAAF GOLDEN JUBILEE 1911 1961.

886	200	6c. on 10c. red	20	20

216 Typist

1961. Government Employees' Association.

887	216	6c. violet and brown	20	10
888	216	10c. blue and brown	35	20

1961. Inauguration of Pres. Macapagal and Vice-Pres. Pelaez. Surch MACAPAGAL-PELAEZ DEC. 30, 1961 INAUGURATION 6c.

889		6c. on 25c. violet (No. 819)	15	10

1962. Cross obliterated by Arms and surch 6s.

890	181	6c. on 5c.+5c. green and red	15	15

220 Waling-Waling

1962. Orchids. Multicoloured.

892		5c. Type **220**	15	15
893		6c. White Mariposa	15	15
894		10c. "Dendrobium sanderii"	20	20
895		20c. Sanggumay	35	35

221 A. Mabini (statesman)

1962. New Currency.

896	-	1s. brown	10	10
897	221	3s. red	10	10
898	-	5s. red	10	10
899	-	6s. brown	15	10
900	-	6s. blue	15	10
901	-	10s. purple	15	10
902	-	20s. blue	20	10
903	-	30s. red	50	15
904	-	50s. violet	90	15
905	-	70s. blue	1·10	50
906	-	1p. green	2·20	45
907	-	1p. orange	75	35

PORTRAITS: 1s. M. L. Quezon; 5s. M. H. del Pilar; 6s. (2) J. Rizal (different); 10s. Father J. Burgos; 20s. Lapu-Lapu; 30s. Rajah Soliman; 50s. C. Arellano; 70s. S. Osmena; 1p. (No. 906) E. Jacinto; 1p. (No. 907) J. M. Panganiban.

225 Pres. Macapagal taking Oath

1962. Independence Day.

915	225	6s. multicoloured	15	10
916	225	10s. multicoloured	20	15
917	225	30s. multicoloured	35	20

226 Valdes Memorial T.B. Pavilion

1962. Obligatory Tax Stamps. T.B. Relief Fund. Cross in red.

918	226	6s.+5s. purple	15	15
919	226	30s.+5s. blue	45	30
920	226	70s.+5s. blue	1·00	90

1962. Malaria Eradication.

921	227	6s. multicoloured	15	15
922	227	10s. multicoloured	20	15
923	227	70s. multicoloured	1·50	1·10

227 Lake Taal

1962. Bicentenary of Diego Silang Revolt. No. 734 surch 1762 1962 BICENTENNIAL Diego Silang Revolt 20.

924		20s. on 25c. green	30	20

1962. No. 742 with premium obliterated.

925	149	5c. blue	20	15

230 Dr. Rizal playing Chess

1962. Rizal Foundation Fund.

926	230	6s.+4s. green and mauve	20	20
927	-	30s.+5s. blue and purple	50	50

DESIGN: 30s. Dr. Rizal fencing.

1963. Surch.

928	221	1s. on 3s. red	15	10
929	-	5s. on 6s. brown (No. 899)	15	15

1963. Diego Silang Bicentenary Art and Philatelic Exhibition, G.P.O., Manila. No. 737 surch 1763 1963 DIEGO SILANG BICENTENNIAL ARPHEX and value.

930		6c. on 2p. violet	15	15
931		20c. on 2p. violet	30	30
932		70c. on 2p. violet	90	75

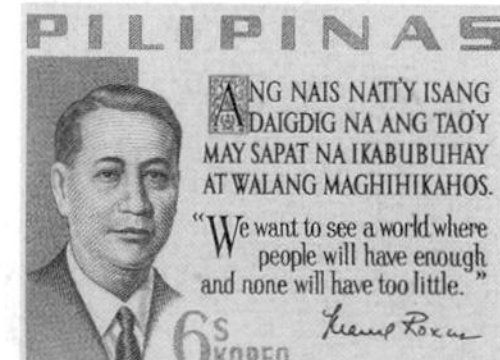

233 "We want to see ..." (Pres. Roxas)

1963. Presidential Sayings (1st issue).

933	233	6s. blue and black	15	10
934	233	30s. brown and black	45	15

See also Nos. 959/60, 981/2, 1015/16, 1034/5, 1055/6, 1148/9 and 1292/3.

234 Lorraine Cross on Map

1963. Obligatory Tax. T.B. Relief Fund. Cross in red.

935	**234**	6s.+5s. pink and violet	15	10
936	**234**	10s.+5s. pink and green	15	15
937	**234**	50s.+5s. pink & brown	75	50

235 Globe and Flags

1963. 1st Anniv of Asian-Oceanic Postal Union.

938	**235**	6s. multicoloured	15	15
939	**235**	20s. multicoloured	20	15

236 Centenary Emblem

1963. Red Cross Centenary. Cross in red.

940	**236**	5s. grey and violet	15	10
941	**236**	6s. grey and blue	15	15
942	**236**	20s. grey and green	45	20

237 Tinikling (dance)

1963. Folk Dances. Multicoloured.

943	5s. Type **237**	15	15
944	6s. Pandanggo sa Ilaw	15	15
945	10s. Itik-Itik	15	15
946	20s. Singkil	30	30

238 Pres. Macapagal and Philippine Family

1963. President's Social-Economic Programme.

947	**238**	5s. multicoloured	15	15
948	**238**	6s. multicoloured	15	15
949	**238**	20s. multicoloured	35	20

239 Presidents' Meeting

1963. Visit of President Mateos of Mexico.

950	**239**	6s. multicoloured	15	15
951	**239**	30s. multicoloured	45	15

240 Bonifacio and Flag

1963. Birth Cent of Andres Bonifacio (patriot).

952	**240**	5s. multicoloured	15	10
953	**240**	6s. multicoloured	15	15
954	**240**	25s. multicoloured	35	30

1963. 15th Anniv of Declaration of Human Rights. Sheet No. MS677 optd with UN ADOPTION OF HUMAN RIGHTS 15TH ANNIVERSARY DEC. 10, 1963, by Philippine Bureau of Printing.

MS955	106×92 mm	1·30	1·30

241 Harvester

1963. Freedom from Hunger.

956	**241**	6s. multicoloured (postage)	15	10
957	**241**	30s. multicoloured (air)	60	45
958	**241**	50s. multicoloured	95	75

1963. Presidential Sayings (2nd issue). As T 233 but with portrait and saying changed.

959	6s. black and violet	15	10
960	30s. black and green	35	15

PORTRAIT AND SAYING: Pres. Magsaysay, "I believe ...".

242 Bamboo Organ, Catholic Church, Las Pinas

1964. Las Pinas Organ Commemoration.

961	**242**	5s. multicoloured	15	10
962	**242**	6s. multicoloured	15	15
963	**242**	20s. multicoloured	45	20

243 A. Mabini (patriot)

1964. Birth Centenary of A. Mabini.

964	**243**	6s. gold and violet	15	10
965	**243**	10s. gold and brown	15	15
966	**243**	30s. gold and green	35	15

244 Negros Oriental T.B. Pavilion

1964. Obligatory Tax. T.B. Relief Fund. Cross in red.

967	**244**	5s.+5s. purple	15	10
968	**244**	6s.+5s. blue	15	10
969	**244**	30s.+5s. brown	45	30
970	**244**	70s.+5s. green	90	80

245 S.E.A.T.O. Emblems and Flags

1964. 10th Anniv of S.E.A.T.O.

971	**245**	6s. multicoloured	15	10
972	**245**	10s. multicoloured	20	15
973	**245**	25s. multicoloured	30	15

246 President signing the Land Reform Code

1964. Agricultural Land Reform Code. President and inscr at foot in brown, red and sepia.

974	**246**	3s. green (postage)	15	10
975	**246**	6s. blue	15	15
976	**246**	30s. brown (air)	35	20

247 Basketball

1964. Olympic Games, Tokyo. Sport in brown. Perf or imperf.

977	**247**	6s. blue and gold	15	15
978	-	10s. pink and gold	20	15
979	-	20s. yellow and gold	50	20
980	-	30s. green and gold	65	50

SPORTS: 10s. Relay-racing; 20s. Hurdling; 30s. Football.

1965. Presidential Sayings (3rd issue). As T 233 but with portrait and saying changed.

981	6s. black and green	15	15
982	30s. black and purple	35	15

PORTRAIT AND SAYING: Pres. Quirino, "So live ...".

248 Presidents Luebke and Macapagal

1965. Visit of President of German Federal Republic.

983	**248**	6s. multicoloured	15	10
984	**248**	10s. multicoloured	20	15
985	**248**	25s. multicoloured	35	30

249 Meteorological Emblems

1965. Cent of Philippines Meteorological Services.

986	**249**	6s. multicoloured	15	15
987	**249**	20s. multicoloured	15	15
988	**249**	50s. multicoloured	60	30

250 Pres. Kennedy

1965. John F. Kennedy (U.S. President) Commemoration.

989	**250**	6s. multicoloured	15	15
990	**250**	10s. multicoloured	20	15
991	**250**	30s. multicoloured	50	20

251 King Bhumibol and Queen Sirikit, Pres. Macapagal and Wife

1965. Visit of King and Queen of Thailand.

992	**251**	2s. multicoloured	10	10
993	**251**	6s. multicoloured	15	15
994	**251**	30s. multicoloured	50	20

252 Princess Beatrix and Mrs. Macapagal

1965. Visit of Princess Beatrix of the Netherlands.

995	**252**	2s. multicoloured	10	10
996	**252**	6s. multicoloured	15	15
997	**252**	10s. multicoloured	20	15

1965. Obligatory Tax. T.B. Relief Fund. Surch.

998	**244**	1s.+5s. on 6s.+5s.	15	10
999	**244**	3s.+5s. on 6s.+5s.	20	15

254 Hand holding Cross and Rosary

1965. 400th Anniv of Philippines Christianisation. Multicoloured.

1000	3s. Type **254** (postage)	15	10
1001	6s. Legaspi-Urdaneta, monument	20	10
1002	30s. Baptism of Filipinos by Father Urdaneta, Cebu (horiz) (48×27 mm) (air)	50	30
1003	70s. "Way of the Cross"-ocean map of Christian voyagers' route, Spain to the Philippines (horiz) (48×27 mm)	1·30	1·20
MS1004	170×105 mm. Nos. 1000/3. Imperf	3·00	3·00

256 Signing Agreement

1965. "MAPILINDO" Conference, Manila.

1005	**256**	6s. blue, red and yellow	15	15
1006	**256**	10s. multicoloured	15	15
1007	**256**	25s. multicoloured	45	20

The above stamps depict Pres. Sukarno of Indonesia, former Pres. Macapagal of the Philippines and Prime Minister Tunku Abdul Rahman of Malaysia.

257 Cyclists and Globe

1965. 2nd Asian Cycling Championships, Philippines.

1008	**257**	6s. multicoloured	10	10
1009	**257**	10s. multicoloured	20	15
1010	**257**	25s. multicoloured	45	30

1965. Inauguration of Pres. Marcos and Vice-Pres. Lopez. Nos. 926/7 surch MARCOS-LOPEZ INAUGURATION DEC. 30, 1965 and value.

1011	**230**	10s. on 6s.+4s.	20	20
1012	-	30s. on 30s.+5s.	50	50

259 Dr. A. Regidor

1966. Regidor (patriot) Commemoration.

1013	**259**	6s. blue	15	15
1014	**259**	30s. brown	30	20

1966. Presidential Sayings (4th issue). As T 233 but with portrait and saying changed.

1015	6s. black and red	15	10
1016	30s. black and blue	35	20

PORTRAIT AND SAYING: Pres. Aguinaldo, "Have faith ...".

1966. Campaign Against Smuggling. No. 900 optd HELP ME STOP SMUGGLING Pres. MARCOS.

1017		6s. blue	20	15

261 Girl Scout

1966. Silver Jubilee of Philippines Girl Scouts.

1018	**261**	3s. multicoloured	15	10
1019	**261**	6s. multicoloured	15	15
1020	**261**	20s. multicoloured	45	20

262 Pres. Marcos taking Oath

1966. Inauguration (1965) of Pres. Marcos.

1021	**262**	6s. multicoloured	15	15
1022	**262**	20s. multicoloured	15	15
1023	**262**	30s. multicoloured	30	20

263 Manila Seal and Historical Scenes

1966. Introduction of New Seal for Manila.

1024	**263**	6s. multicoloured	15	15
1025	**263**	30s. multicoloured	30	15

264 Bank Facade and 1 peso Coin

265 "Progress"

1966. 50th Anniv of Philippines National Bank. Mult.

1026		6s. Type **264**	15	10
1027		10s. Old and new bank buildings	20	15
MS1028		157×70 mm. **265** 70s. multicoloured	1·90	1·90

266 Bank Building

1966. 60th Anniv of Postal Savings Bank.

1029	**266**	6s. violet, yellow & green	15	10
1030	**266**	10s. red, yellow and green	20	15
1031	**266**	20s. blue, yellow & green	45	20

1966. Manila Summit Conference. Nos. 1021 and 1023 optd MANILA SUMMIT CONFERENCE 1966 7 NATIONS and emblem.

1032	**262**	6s. multicoloured	20	15
1033	**262**	30s. multicoloured	30	30

1966. Presidential Sayings (5th issue). As T 233 but with portrait and saying changed.

1034		6s. black and brown	15	10
1035		30s. black and blue	35	15

PORTRAIT AND SAYING: Pres. Laurel; "No one can love the Filipinos better ...".

1967. 50th Anniv of Lions International. Nos. 977/80 optd with Lions emblem and 50th ANNIVERSARY LIONS INTERNATIONAL 1967. Imperf.

1036	**247**	6c. blue and gold	15	15
1037	-	10c. pink and gold	20	15
1038	-	20c. yellow and gold	45	20
1039	-	30c. green and gold	65	65

269 "Succour" (after painting by F. Amorsolo)

1967. 25th Anniv of Battle of Bataan.

1040	**269**	5s. multicoloured	15	10
1041	**269**	20s. multicoloured	20	15
1042	**269**	2p. multicoloured	2·40	1·30

1967. Nos. 900 and 975 surch.

1043	-	4s. on 6s. blue	15	10
1044	**246**	5s. on 6s. blue	15	10

271 Stork-billed Kingfisher

1967. Obligatory Tax. T.B. Relief Fund. Birds. Multicoloured.

1045		1s.+5s. Type **271**	15	15
1046		5s.+5s. Rufous hornbill	20	20
1047		10s.+5s. Philippine eagle	35	20
1048		30s.+5s. Great-billed parrot	75	50

See also Nos. 1113/16.

272 Gen. MacArthur and Paratroopers landing on Corregidor

1967. 25th Anniv of Battle of Corregidor.

1049	**272**	6s. multicoloured	10	10
1050	**272**	5p. multicoloured	4·50	3·75

273 Bureau of Posts Building, Manila

1967. 65th Anniv of Philippines Bureau of Posts.

1051	**273**	4s. multicoloured	20	20
1052	**273**	20s. multicoloured	20	15
1053	**273**	50s. multicoloured	60	45

274 Escaping from Eruption

1967. Obligatory Tax. Taal Volcano Eruption (1965) (1st issue).

1054	**274**	70s. multicoloured	95	80

For compulsory use on foreign air mail where the rate exceeds 70s. in aid of Taal Volcano Rehabilitation Committee.

See also No. 1071.

1967. Presidential Sayings (6th issue). As T 233 but with portrait and saying changed.

1055		10s. black and blue	15	10
1056		30s. black and violet	35	15

PORTRAIT AND SAYING: Pres. Quezon. "Social justice is far more beneficial ...".

275 "The Holy Family" (Filipino version)

1967. Christmas.

1057	**275**	10s. multicoloured	20	15
1058	**275**	40s. multicoloured	50	45

276 Pagoda, Pres. Marcos and Chiang Kai-shek

1967. China–Philippines Friendship.

1059	**276**	5s. multicoloured	10	10
1060	-	10s. multicoloured	15	15
1061	-	20s. multicoloured	20	15

DESIGNS (with portraits of Pres. Marcos and Chiang Kai-shek): 10s. Gateway, Chinese Garden, Rizal Park, Luneta; 20s. Chinese Garden, Rizal Park, Luneta.

277 Ayala Avenue, Manila, Inaugural Ceremony and Rotary Badge

1968. 1st Anniv of Makati Centre Post Office, Manila.

1062	**277**	10s. multicoloured	15	15
1063	**277**	20s. multicoloured	20	20
1064	**277**	40s. multicoloured	60	60

1968. Surch.

1065	-	5s. on 6s. (No. 981)	15	10
1066	-	5s. on 6s. (No. 1034)	15	10
1067	**244**	10s. on 6s.+5s.	15	10

280 Calderon, Barasoain Church and Constitution

1968. Birth Centenary of Felipe G. Calderon (lawyer and author of Malolos Constitution).

1068	**280**	10s. multicoloured	15	10
1069	**280**	40s. multicoloured	60	45
1070	**280**	75s. multicoloured	1·20	1·10

281 Eruption

1968. Taal Volcano Eruption (1965) (2nd issue).

1071	**281**	70s. multicoloured	95	95

Two issues were prepared by an American Agency under a contract signed with the Philippine postal authority but at the last moment this contract was cancelled by the Philippine Government. In the meanwhile the stamps had been on sale in the U.S.A. but they were never issued in the Philippines and they had no postal validity.

They comprise a set for the Mexican Olympic Games in the values 1, 2, 3 and 15s. postage and 50, 75s., 1, 2p. airmail and a set in memory of J. F. Kennedy and Robert Kennedy in the values 1, 2, 3s. postage and 5, 10p. airmail.

282 "Philcomsat", Earth Station and Globe

1968. Inauguration of "Philcomsat"–POTC Earth Station, Tanay, Rizal, Luzon.

1072	**282**	10s. multicoloured	20	15
1073	**282**	40s. multicoloured	60	45
1074	**282**	75s. multicoloured	1·00	90

283 "Tobacco Production" (mural)

1968. Philippines Tobacco Industry.

1075	**283**	10s. multicoloured	15	15
1076	**283**	40s. multicoloured	60	50
1077	**283**	70s. multicoloured	1·10	90

284 "Kudyapi"

1968. St. Cecilia's Day. Musical Instruments. Mult.

1078		10s. Type **284**	10	10
1079		20s. "Ludag"	10	10
1080		30s. "Kulintangan"	25	20
1081		50s. "Subing"	35	35

285 Concordia College

1968. Centenary of Concordia Women's College.

1082	**285**	10s. multicoloured	10	10
1083	**285**	20s. multicoloured	15	10
1084	**285**	70s. multicoloured	50	35

286 Children singing Carols

1968. Christmas.

1085	**286**	10s. multicoloured	15	15
1086	**286**	40s. multicoloured	50	45
1087	**286**	75s. multicoloured	95	80

287 Philippine Tarsier

1969. Philippines Fauna. Multicoloured.

1088		2s. Type **287**	15	15
1089		10s. Tamarau	15	15
1090		20s. Water buffalo	20	20
1091		75s. Greater Malay chevrotain	1·30	1·00

288 President Aguinaldo and Cavite Building

1969. Birth Centenary of President Amilio Aguinaldo.

1092	**288**	10s. multicoloured	20	15
1093	**288**	40s. multicoloured	60	35
1094	**288**	70s. multicoloured	1·00	80

289 Rotary Emblem and "Bastion of San Andres"

1969. 50th Anniv of Manila Rotary Club.

1095	**289**	10s. mult (postage)	15	15
1096	**289**	40s. multicoloured (air)	45	30
1097	**289**	75s. multicoloured	95	75

290 Senator C. M. Recto

1969. Recto Commemoration.

1098	**290**	10s. purple	15	10

1969. Philatelic Week. No. 1051 optd PHILATELIC WEEK NOV. 24-30, 1968.

1099	**273**	4s. multicoloured	20	10

292 Jose Rizal College

1969. 50th Anniv of Jose Rizal College, Mandaluyong, Rizal.

1100	**292**	10s. multicoloured	15	15
1101	**292**	40s. multicoloured	60	45
1102	**292**	50s. multicoloured	90	65

1969. 4th National Boy Scout Jamboree, Palayan City. No. 1019 surch 4th NATIONAL BOY SCOUT JAMBOREE PALAYAN CITY–MAY, 1969 5s.

1103		5s. on 6s. multicoloured	20	15

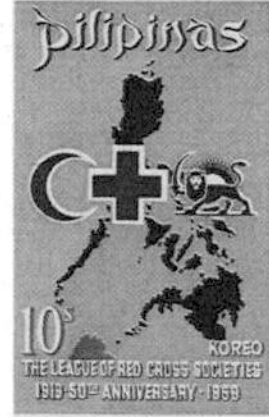

294 Red Cross Emblems and Map

1969. 50th Anniv of League of Red Cross Societies.

1104	**294**	10s. red, blue and grey	15	15
1105	**294**	40s. red, blue and cobalt	50	30
1106	**294**	75s. red, brown and buff	80	75

295 Pres. and Mrs. Marcos harvesting Rice

1969. "Rice for Progress".

1107	**295**	10s. multicoloured	15	15
1108	**295**	40s. multicoloured	50	35
1109	**295**	75s. multicoloured	80	75

296 "The Holy Child of Leyte" (statue)

1969. 80th Anniv of Return of the "Holy Child of Leyte" to Tacloban.

1110	**296**	5s. mult (postage)	15	10
1111	**296**	10s. multicoloured	15	15
1112	**296**	40s. multicoloured (air)	50	35

1969. Obligatory Tax. T.B. Relief Fund. Birds as T 271.

1113	1s.+5s. Common gold-backed woodpecker	20	15
1114	5s.+5s. Philippine trogon	20	15
1115	10s.+5s. Johnstone's (inscr "Mt. Apo") lorikeet	35	20
1116	40s.+5s. Scarlet (inscr "John-stone's") minivet	50	35

297 Bank Building

1969. Inauguration of Philippines Development Bank, Makati, Rizal.

1117	**297**	10s. black, blue and green	15	10
1118	**297**	40s. black, purple and green	90	45
1119	**297**	75s. black, brown & grn	1·30	95

298 "Philippine Birdwing"

1969. Philippine Butterflies. Multicoloured.

1120	10s. Type **298**	20	15
1121	20s. Tailed jay	30	20
1122	30s. Red Helen	50	30
1123	40s. Birdwing	80	45

299 Children of the World

1969. 15th Anniv of Universal Children's Day.

1124	**299**	10s. multicoloured	15	10
1125	**299**	20s. multicoloured	20	15
1126	**299**	30s. multicoloured	20	20

300 Memorial and Outline of Landing

1969. 25th Anniv of U.S. Forces' Landing on Leyte.

1127	**300**	5s. multicoloured	15	10
1128	**300**	10s. multicoloured	20	15
1129	**300**	40s. multicoloured	50	30

301 Cultural Centre

1969. Cultural Centre, Manila.

1130	**301**	10s. blue	15	15
1131	**301**	30s. purple	35	20

1969. Philatelic Week. Nos. 943/6 (Folk Dances) optd 1969 PHILATELIC WEEK or surch also.

1132	5s. multicoloured	15	15
1133	5s. on 6s. multicoloured	15	15
1134	10s. multicoloured	20	20
1135	10s. on 20s. multicoloured	20	20

303 Melchora Aquino

1969. 50th Death Anniv of Melchora Aquino, "Tandang Sora" (Grand Old Woman of the Revolution).

1136	**303**	10s. multicoloured	15	15
1137	**303**	20s. multicoloured	20	15
1138	**303**	30s. multicoloured	50	20

1969. 2nd-term Inaug of President Marcos. Surch PASINAYA, IKA-2 PANUNUNGKULAN PANGULONG FERDINAND E. MARCOS DISYEMBRE 30, 1969.

1139	**262**	5s. on 6s. multicoloured	20	10

305 Ladle and Steel Mills

1970. Iligan Integrated Steel Mills.

1140	**305**	10s. multicoloured	15	15
1141	**305**	20s. multicoloured	35	20
1142	**305**	30s. multicoloured	65	30

1970. Nos. 900, 962 and 964 surch.

1143	-	4s. on 6s. blue	15	10
1144	**242**	5s. on 6s. multicoloured	15	10
1145	**243**	5s. on 6s. multicoloured	15	10

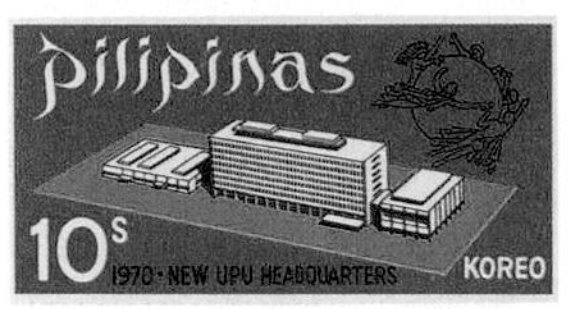

307 New U.P.U. Headquarters Building

1970. New U.P.U. Headquarters Building, Berne.

1146	**307**	10s. ultramarine, yellow and blue	15	15
1147	**307**	30s. blue, yellow and green	60	30

1970. Presidential Sayings (7th issue). As T 233 but with portrait and saying changed.

1148	10s. black and purple	15	10
1149	40s. black and green	35	15

PORTRAIT AND SAYING: Pres. Osmena, "Ante todo el bien de nuestro pueblo" ("The well-being of our nation comes above all").

308 Dona Julia V. de Ortigas and T.B. Society Headquarters

1970. Obligatory Tax. T.B. Relief Fund.

1150	**308**	1s.+5s. multicoloured	15	10
1151	**308**	5s.+5s. multicoloured	20	20
1152	**308**	30s.+5s. multicoloured	75	50
1153	**308**	70s.+5s. multicoloured	95	65

309 I.C.S.W. Emblem

1970. 15th Int Conference on Social Welfare.

1154	**309**	10s. multicoloured	15	15
1155	**309**	20s. multicoloured	30	20
1156	**309**	30s. multicoloured	60	20

310 "Crab" (after sculpture by A. Calder)

1970. "Fight Cancer" Campaign.

1157	**310**	10s. multicoloured	20	15
1158	**310**	40s. multicoloured	45	20
1159	**310**	50s. multicoloured	65	35

311 Scaled Tridacna

1970. Sea Shells. Multicoloured.

1160	5s. Type **311**	15	10
1161	10s. Royal spiny oyster	15	10
1162	20s. Venus comb murex	20	15
1163	40s. Glory-of-the-sea cone	60	35

1970. Nos. 986, 1024 and 1026 surch with new values in figures and words.

1164	**249**	4s. on 6s.	15	10
1165	**263**	4s. on 6s.	15	10
1166	**264**	4s. on 6s.	15	10

313 The "Hundred Islands" and Ox-cart

1970. Tourism (1st series). Multicoloured.

1167	10s. Type **313**	15	15
1168	20s. Tree-house, Pasonanca Park, Zamboanga City	20	15
1169	30s. "Filipino" (statue) and sugar plantation, Negros Island	30	30
1170	2p. Calesa (horse-carriage) and Miagao Church, Iloilo	1·90	1·20

See also Nos. 1186/9, 1192/5 and 1196/9.

314 Map of the Philippines

1970. Golden Jubilee of Philippine Pharmaceutical Association.

1171	**314**	10s. multicoloured	15	10
1172	**314**	50s. multicoloured	75	35

1970. U.P.U./A.O.P.U. Regional Seminar, Manila. No. 938 surch UPU-AOPU REGIONAL SEMINAR NOV. 23 - DEC. 5, 1970 TEN 10s.

1173	**235**	10s. on 6s. multicoloured	15	15

1970. Philatelic Week. No. 977 surch 1970 PHILATELIC WEEK 10s TEN.

1174	**247**	10s. on 6s. brown, blue and gold	15	10

317 Pope Paul VI and Map

1970. Pope Paul's Visit to the Philippines.

1175	**317**	10s. mult (postage)	15	15
1176	**317**	30s. multicoloured	30	20
1177	**317**	40s. multicoloured (air)	45	20

318 Mariano Ponce

1970

1178 **318** 10s. red 15 10
1179 - 15s. brown 15 10
1180 - 40s. red 35 10
1181 - 1p. blue 95 35

DESIGNS: 15s. Josefa Llanes Escoda; 40s. Gen. Miguel Malvar; 1p. Julian Felipe.

320 "PATA" Horse and Carriage

1971. 20th PATA Conference and Workshop, Manila.

1183 **320** 5s. multicoloured 15 10
1184 **320** 10s. multicoloured 15 15
1185 **320** 70s. multicoloured 50 35

1971. Tourism (2nd series). Views as T 313. Multicoloured.

1186 10s. Nayong Pilipino resort 10 10
1187 20s. Fish farm, Iloilo 15 10
1188 30s. Pagsanjan Falls 20 15
1189 5p. Watch-tower, Punta Cruz 1·80 1·60

321 Emblem and Family

1971. Regional Conference of International Planned Parenthood Federation for South-East Asia and Oceania.

1190 **321** 20s. multicoloured 15 10
1191 **321** 40s. multicoloured 20 15

1971. Tourism (3rd series). As T 313. Mult.

1192 10s. Aguinaldo pearl farm 15 15
1193 20s. Coral-diving, Davao 15 15
1194 40s. Taluksengay Mosque 20 20
1195 1p. Ifugao woman and Banaue rice-terraces 1·60 65

1971. Tourism (4th series). As T 313. Mult.

1196 10s. Cannon and Filipino vintas, Fort del Pilar 15 15
1197 30s. Magellan's Cross, Cebu City 15 15
1198 50s. "Big Jar", Calamba, Laguna (Rizal's birthplace) 30 20
1199 70s. Mayon Volcano and diesel train 1·60 45

1971. Surch FIVE 5s.

1200 **264** 5s. on 6s. multicoloured 15 10

323 G. A. Malcolm (founder) and Law Symbols

1971. 60th Anniv of Philippines College of Law.

1201 **323** 15s. mult (postage) 15 15
1202 **323** 1p. multicoloured (air) 80 75

324 Commemorative Seal

1971. 400th Anniv of Manila.

1203 **324** 10s. multicoloured (postage) 15 15
1204 **324** 1p. multicoloured (air) 1·20 80

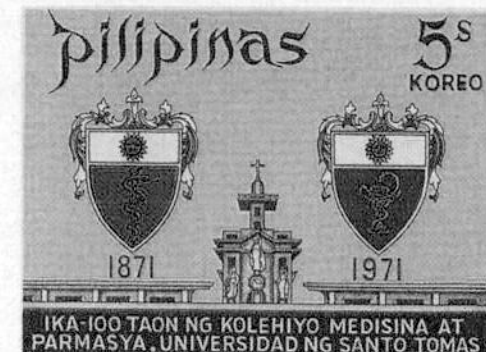

325 Arms of Faculties

1971. Centenaries of Faculties of Medicine and Surgery, and of Pharmacy, Santo Tomas University.

1205 **325** 5s. mult (postage) 15 10
1206 **325** 2p. multicoloured (air) 1·60 1·50

1971. University Presidents' World Congress, Manila. Surch MANILA MCMLXX1 CONGRESS OF UNIVERSITY PRESIDENTS 5s FIVE and emblem.

1207 **266** 5s. on 6s. violet, yellow and green 15 10

327 "Our Lady of Guia"

1971. 400th Anniv of "Our Lady of Guia", Ermita, Manila.

1208 **327** 10s. multicoloured 15 15
1209 **327** 75s. multicoloured 60 50

328 Bank and "Customers"

1971. 70th Anniv of First National City Bank.

1210 **328** 10s. multicoloured 15 15
1211 **328** 30s. multicoloured 30 20
1212 **328** 1p. multicoloured 75 60

1971. Surch in figure and word.

1213 **259** 4s. on 6s. blue 15 10
1214 **259** 5s. on 6s. blue 15 10

1971. Philatelic Week. Surch 1971 - PHILATELIC WEEK 5s FIVE.

1215 **266** 5s. on 6s. violet, yellow and green 15 10

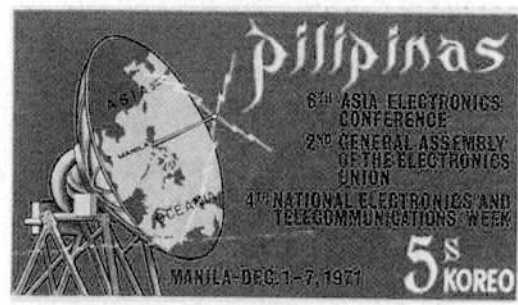

331 Dish Aerial and Events

1972. 6th Asian Electronics Conference, Manila (1971) and Related Events.

1216 **331** 5s. multicoloured 15 10
1217 **331** 40s. multicoloured 60 35

332 Fathers Burgos, Gomez and Zamora

1972. Centenary of Martyrdom of Fathers Burgos, Gomez and Zamora.

1218 **332** 5s. multicoloured 10 10
1219 **332** 60s. multicoloured 45 45

333 Human Organs

1972. 4th Asian–Pacific Gastro-enterological Congress, Manila.

1220 **333** 20s. mult (postage) 20 15
1221 **333** 40s. multicoloured (air) 45 35

1972. Surch 5s FIVE.

1222 **263** 5s. on 6s. multicoloured 15 10

1972. No. O914 with optd G.O. obliterated by bars.

1223 50s. violet 45 20

1972. Surch.

1224 **245** 10s. on 6s. multicoloured 15 10
1225 **251** 10s. on 6s. multicoloured 15 10
1226 - 10s. on 6s. black and red (No. 1015) 15 10

336 Memorial Gardens, Manila

1972. Tourism. "Visit Asean Lands" Campaign.

1227 **336** 5s. multicoloured 15 10
1228 **336** 50s. multicoloured 90 20
1229 **336** 60s. multicoloured 1·20 35

337 "KKK" Flag

1972. Evolution of Philippines' Flag.

1230 **337** 30s. red and blue 30 20
1231 - 30s. red and blue 30 20
1232 - 30s. red and blue 30 20
1233 - 30s. black and blue 30 20
1234 - 30s. red and blue 30 20
1235 - 30s. red and blue 30 20
1236 - 30s. red and blue 30 20
1237 - 30s. red and blue 30 20
1238 - 30s. black, red and blue 30 20
1239 - 30s. yellow, red and blue 30 20

FLAGS: No. 1231, Three "K"s in pyramid; No. 1232, Single "K"; No. 1233, "K", skull and crossbones; No. 1234, Three "K"s and sun in triangle; No. 1235, Sun and three "K"s; No. 1236, Ancient Tagalog "K" within sun; No. 1237, Face in sun; No. 1238, Tricolor; No. 1239, Present national flag—sun and stars within triangle, two stripes.

338 Mabol, Santol and Papaya

1972. Obligatory Tax. T.B. Relief Fund. Fruits. Mult.

1240 1s.+5s. Type **338** 10 10
1241 10s.+5s. Bananas, balimbang and mangosteen 15 15
1242 40s.+5s. Guava, mango, duhat and susongkalabac 30 30
1243 1p.+5s. Orange, pineapple, lanzones and sirhuelas 65 65

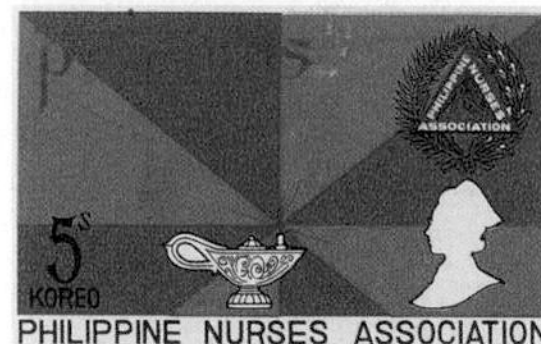

339 Bridled Parrotfish

1972. Fishes. Multicoloured.

1244 5s. Type **339** (postage) 15 10
1245 10s. Klein's butterflyfish 15 10
1246 20s. Moorish idol 20 15
1247 50s. Two-spined angelfish (air) 75 35

340 Bank Headquarters

1972. 25th Anniv of Philippines Development Bank.

1248 **340** 10s. multicoloured 15 10
1249 **340** 20s. multicoloured 15 15
1250 **340** 60s. multicoloured 60 35

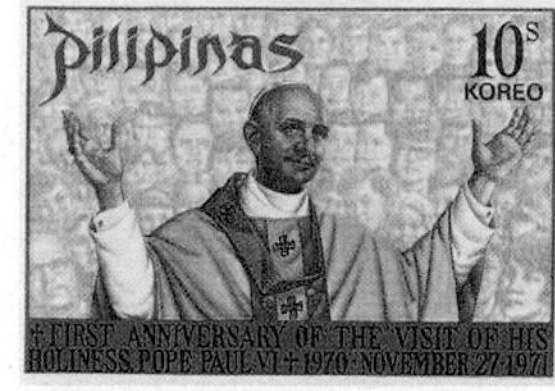

341 Pope Paul VI

1972. 1st Anniv of Pope Paul's Visit to Philippines.

1251 **341** 10s. mult (postage) 10 10
1252 **341** 50s. multicoloured 45 35
1253 **341** 60s. multicoloured (air) 60 60

1972. Various stamps surch.

1254 **240** 10s. on 6s. (No. 953) 15 10
1255 - 10s. on 6s. (No. 959) 15 10
1256 **250** 10s. on 6s. (No. 989) 15 10

343 "La Barca de Aqueronte" (Hidalgo)

1972. 25th Anniv of Stamps and Philatelic Division, Philippines Bureau of Posts. Filipino Paintings. Multicoloured.

1257 5s. Type **343** 10 10
1258 10s. "Afternoon Meal of the Rice Workers" (Amorsolo) 15 15
1259 30s. "Espana y Filipinas" (Luna) (27x60 mm) 20 20
1260 70s. "The Song of Maria Clara" (Amorsolo) 60 60

345 Heart on Map

344 Lamp, Emblem and Nurse

1972. 50th Anniv of Philippine Nurses Assn.

1261 **344** 5s. multicoloured 10 10
1262 **344** 10s. multicoloured 15 15
1263 **344** 70s. multicoloured 45 35

1972. World Heart Month.

1264 **345** 5s. red, green and violet 10 10
1265 **345** 10s. red, green and blue 15 10
1266 **345** 30s. red, blue and green 20 20

346 "The First Mass" (C. V. Francisco)

1972. 450th Anniv of 1st Mass in Limasawa (1971).

1267	**346**	10s. mult (postage)	15	15
1268	**346**	60s. multicoloured (air)	50	45

1972. Asia-Pacific Scout Conference, Manila. Various stamps surch ASIA PACIFIC SCOUT CONFERENCE NOV, 1972 and value.

1269	**233**	10s. on 6s. (No. 933)	15	10
1270	**240**	10s. on 6s. (No. 953)	15	10
1271	-	10s. on 6s. (No. 981)	15	10

348 Olympic Emblems and Torch

1972. Olympic Games, Munich.

1272	**348**	5s. multicoloured	10	10
1273	**348**	10s. multicoloured	15	15
1274	**348**	70s. multicoloured	60	45

1972. Philatelic Week. Nos. 950 and 983 surch 1972 PHILATELIC WEEK TEN 10s.

1275	**239**	10s. on 6s. multicoloured	15	10
1276	**248**	10s. on 6s. multicoloured	15	10

350 Manunggul Burial Jar

1972. Philippine Archaeological Discoveries. Multicoloured.

1277	10s. Type **350**	15	10
1278	10s. Ritual earthenware vessel	15	10
1279	10s. Metal pot	15	10
1280	10s. Earthenware vessel	15	10

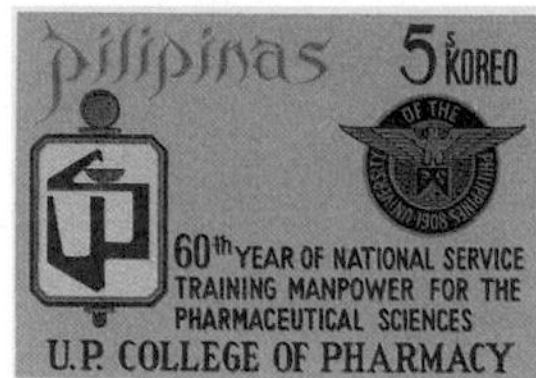

351 Emblems of Pharmacy and University of the Philippines

1972. 60th Anniv of National Training for Pharmaceutical Sciences, University of the Philippines.

1281	**351**	5s. multicoloured	10	10
1282	**351**	10s. multicoloured	15	15
1283	**351**	30s. multicoloured	20	15

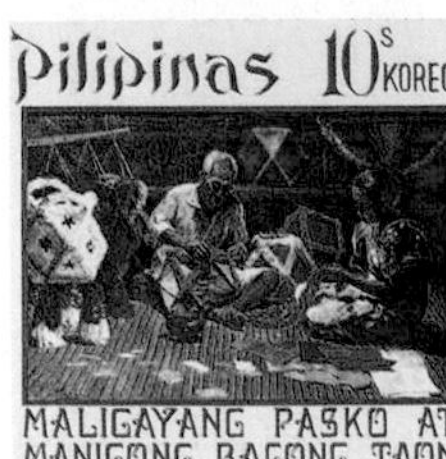

352 "The Lantern-makers" (J. Pineda)

1972. Christmas.

1284	**352**	10s. multicoloured	15	15
1285	**352**	30s. multicoloured	20	15
1286	**352**	50s. multicoloured	45	35

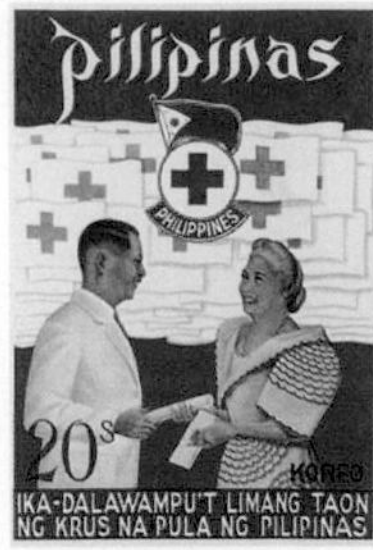

353 President Roxas and Wife

1972. 25th Anniv of Philippines Red Cross.

1287	**353**	5s. multicoloured	15	10
1288	**353**	20s. multicoloured	15	15
1289	**353**	30s. multicoloured	20	20

1973. Nos. 948 and 1005 surch 10s.

1290	**238**	10s. on 6s. multicoloured	15	10
1291	**256**	10s. on 6s. blue. red and yellow	15	10

1973. Presidential Sayings (8th issue). As T 233 but with portrait and saying changed.

1292	10s. black and bistre	15	10
1293	30s. black and mauve	35	15

PORTRAIT AND SAYING: 10s., 30s. Pres. Garcia, "I would rather be right than successful".

355 University Building

1973. 60th Anniv of St. Louis University, Baguio City.

1294	**355**	5s. multicoloured	10	10
1295	**355**	10s. multicoloured	10	10
1296	**355**	75s. multicoloured	60	50

356 Col. J. Villamor and Air Battle

1973. Villamor Commemoration.

1297	**356**	10s. multicoloured	15	10
1298	**356**	2p. multicoloured	1·30	1·30

1973. Various stamps surch.

1299	**252**	5s. on 6s. multicoloured	15	10
1300	**266**	5s. on 6s. violet, yellow and green	15	10
1301	**318**	15s. on 10s. red (No. O1182)	15	10

359 Actor and Stage Performance

1973. 1st "Third-World" Theatre Festival, Manila.

1302	**359**	5s. multicoloured	10	10
1303	**359**	10s. multicoloured	10	10
1304	**359**	50s. multicoloured	35	20
1305	**359**	70s. multicoloured	60	35

1973. President Marcos's Anti-smuggling Campaign. No. 1017 surch 5s.

1306	5s. on 6s. blue	15	10

1973. 10th Death Anniv of John F. Kennedy. No. 989 surch 5s.

1307	5s. on 6s. multicoloured	15	10

1973. Compulsory Tax Stamps. T.B. Relief Fund. Nos. 1241/2 surch.

1308	15s.+5s. on 10s.+5s. mult	15	15
1309	60s.+5s. on 40s.+5s. mult	45	45

363 Proclamation Scenes

1973. 75th Anniv of Philippine Independence.

1310	**363**	15s. multicoloured	15	15
1311	**363**	45s. multicoloured	20	20
1312	**363**	90s. multicoloured	65	65

364 M. Agoncillo (maker of first national flag)

1973. Perf or imperf.

1313	-	15s. violet	15	10
1314	**364**	60s. brown	35	35
1315	-	90s. blue	60	30
1316	-	1p.10 blue	75	35
1317	-	1p.50 red	95	80
1318	-	1p.50 brown	95	35
1319	-	1p.80 green	1·10	1·00
1320	-	5p. blue	3·00	3·00

DESIGNS: 15s. Gabriela Silang (revolutionary); 90s. Teodoro Yangco (businessman); 1p.10, Pio Valenzuela (physician); 1p.50 (No. 1317), Pedro Paterno (revolutionary); 1p.50 (No. 1318), Teodora Alonso (mother of Jose Rizal); 1p.80, E. Evangelista (revolutionary); 5p. F. M. Guerrero (writer).

For similar designs see Nos. 1455/8.

365 Imelda Marcos

1973. Projects Inaugurated by Sra Imelda Marcos.

1321	**365**	15s. multicoloured	15	15
1322	**365**	50s. multicoloured	30	30
1323	**365**	60s. multicoloured	35	35

366 Malakanyang Palace

1973. Presidential Palace, Manila.

1324	**366**	15s. mult (postage)	15	15
1325	**366**	50s. multicoloured	20	20
1326	**366**	60s. multicoloured (air)	35	35

367 Interpol Emblem

1973. 50th Anniv of International Criminal Police Organization (Interpol).

1327	**367**	15s. multicoloured	15	10
1328	**367**	65s. multicoloured	45	20

368 Scouting Activities

1973. Golden Jubilee of Philippine Boy Scouts. Perf or imperf.

1329	**368**	15s. bistre and green	15	15
1330	-	65s. blue and yellow	45	30

DESIGN: 65s. Scouts reading brochure.

369 Bank Emblem, Urban and Agricultural Landscapes

1974. 25th Anniv of Central Bank of the Philippines. Multicoloured.

1331	15s. Type **369**	15	10
1332	60s. Bank building, 1949	35	20
1333	1p.50 Bank complex, 1974	95	60

370 "Maria Clara" Costume

1974. Centenary of U.P.U. Philippine Costumes. Multicoloured.

1334	15s. Type **370**	15	15
1335	60s. "Balintawak"	35	20
1336	80s. "Malong"	60	30

1974. Philatelic Week (1973). No. 1303 surch 1973 PHILATELIC WEEK 15s.

1337	**359**	15s. on 10s. multicoloured	15	10

1974. 25th Anniv of Philippine "Lionism". Nos. 1297 and 1180 surch PHILIPPINE LIONISM 1949-1974 15s and Lions emblem.

1338	**356**	15s. on 10s. multicoloured	15	10
1339	-	45s. on 40s. red	20	20

373 Map of South-East Asia

1974. Asian Paediatrics Congress, Manila. Perf or imperf.

1340	**373**	30s. red and blue	20	15
1341	**373**	1p. red and green	60	35

374 Gen. Valdes and Hospital

1974. Obligatory Tax. T.B. Relief Fund. Perf or imperf.

1342	**374**	15s.+5s. green and red	15	15
1343	**374**	1p.10+5s. blue and red	35	30

1974. Nos. 974, 1024 and 1026 surch.

1344	**246**	5s. on 3s. green	15	10
1345	**263**	5s. on 6s. multicoloured	15	10
1346	**264**	5s. on 6s. multicoloured	15	10

378 W.P.Y. Emblem

1974. World Population Year. Perf or imperf.

1347	**378**	5s. black and orange	15	15
1348	**378**	2p. blue and green	1·10	60

379 Red Feather Emblem

1974. 25th Anniv of Community Chest Movement in the Philippines. Perf or imperf.

1349	**379**	15s. red and blue	15	15
1350	**379**	40s. red and green	20	15
1351	**379**	45s. red and brown	35	15

381 Sultan Mohammad Kudarat, Map, Malayan Prau and Order

1975. Sultan Kudarat of Mindanao Commem.

1352	**381**	15s. multicoloured	15	10

382 Association Emblem

1975. 25th Anniv of Philippine Mental Health Association. Perf or imperf.

1353	**382**	45s. green and orange	20	15
1354	**382**	1p. green and purple	45	30

383 Rafael Palma

1975. Birth Centenary of Rafael Palma (educationalist and statesman). Perf or imperf (15s.), perf (30s.).

1355	**383**	15s. green	20	15
1436	**383**	30s. brown	15	10

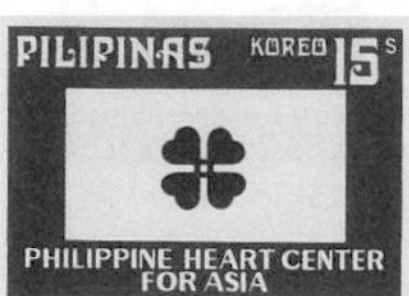

384 Heart Centre Emblem

1975. Inauguration of Philippine Heart Centre for Asia, Quezon City. Perf or imperf.

1356	**384**	15s. red and blue	15	15
1357	**384**	50s. red and green	20	20

385 Cadet in Full Dress, and Academy Building

1975. 70th Anniv of Philippine Military Academy.

1358	**385**	15s. multicoloured	15	15
1359	**385**	45s. multicoloured	45	20

387/9, 392/4 "Helping the Disabled"

1975. 25th Anniv (1974) of Philippines Orthopaedic Association. Perf or imperf.

1360	-	45s. green (inscr at left and top)	20	15
1361	**387**	45s. green	20	15
1362	**388**	45s. green	20	15
1363	**389**	45s. green	20	15
1364	-	45s. green (inscr at top and right)	20	15
1365	-	45s. green (inscr at left and bottom)	20	15
1366	**392**	45s. green	20	15
1367	**393**	45s. green	20	15
1368	**394**	45s. green	20	15
1369	-	45s. green (inscr at bottom and right)	20	15

DESIGNS—23×30 mm: Nos. 1360, 1364/5, 1369, Details of corners of the mural.

Nos. 1360/9 were issued together, se-tenant, forming a composite design.

1975. Nos. 1153 and 1342/3 surch.

1370	**374**	5s. on 15s.+5s. green and red	10	10
1371	**308**	60s. on 70s.+5s. multicoloured	35	20
1372	**374**	1p. on 1p.10+5s. blue and red	45	30

397 Planting Sapling

1975. Forest Conservation. Multicoloured.

1373	45s. Type **397**	20	15
1374	45s. Sapling and tree-trunks	20	15

398 Jade Vine

1975

1375	**398**	15s. multicoloured	15	10

399 Imelda Marcos and I.W.Y. Emblem

1975. International Women's Year. Perf or imperf.

1376	**399**	15s. black, blue & dp blue	15	15
1377	**399**	80s. black, blue and pink	45	35

400 Commission Badge

1975. 75th Anniv of Civil Service Commission. Perf or imperf.

1378	**400**	15s. multicoloured	15	15
1379	**400**	50s. multicoloured	30	20

401 Angat River Barrage

1975. 25th Anniv of International Irrigation and Drainage Commission. Perf or imperf.

1380	**401**	40s. blue and orange	20	15
1381	**401**	1p.50 blue and mauve	60	45

402 "Welcome to Manila"

1975. Centenary of Hong Kong and Shanghai Banking Corporation's Service in the Philippines.

1382	**402**	1p.50 multicoloured	1·30	35

403 N. Romualdez (legislator and writer)

1975. Birth Centenaries. Perf or imperf.

1383	**403**	60s. lilac	20	15
1384	-	90s. mauve	35	15

DESIGN: 90s. General G. del Pilar.

405 Boeing 747-100 Airliner and Martin M-130 Flying Boat

1975. 40th Anniv of First Trans-Pacific China Clipper Airmail Flight. San Francisco–Manila.

1385	**405**	60s. multicoloured	45	20
1386	**405**	1p.50 multicoloured	1·20	60

1975. Airmail Exn. Nos. 1314 and 1318 optd AIRMAIL EXHIBITION NOV 22-DEC 9.

1387	**364**	60s. brown	20	20
1388	-	1p.50 brown	65	65

407 APO Emblem

1975. 25th Anniv of APO Philatelic Society. Perf or imperf.

1389	**407**	5s. multicoloured	15	15
1390	**407**	1p. multicoloured	50	35

408 E. Jacinto

1975. Birth Centenary of Emilio Jacinto (military leader). Perf or imperf.

1391	**408**	65s. mauve	20	15

409 San Agustin Church

1975. Holy Year. Churches. Perf or imperf.

1392	**409**	20s. blue	15	15
1393	-	30s. black and yellow	15	15
1394	-	45s. red, pink and black	20	15
1395	-	60s. bistre, yellow & black	30	20

DESIGNS—HORIZ: 30s. Morong Church; 45s. Taal Basilica. VERT: 60s. San Sebastian Church.

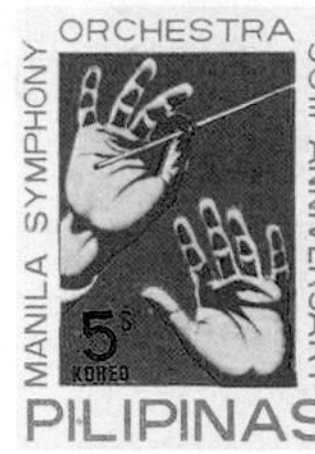

410 "Conducting" Hands

1976. 50th Anniv of Manila Symphony Orchestra.

1396	**410**	5s. multicoloured	10	10
1397	**410**	50s. multicoloured	35	30

411 Douglas DC-3 and DC-10

1976. 30th Anniv of Philippines Airlines (PAL).

1398	**411**	60s. multicoloured	30	15
1399	**411**	1p.50 multicoloured	1·20	65

412 Felipe Agoncillo (statesman)

1976. Felipe Agoncillo Commemoration.

1400	**412**	1p.60 black	95	20

413 University Building

1976. 75th Anniv of National University.

1401	**413**	45s. multicoloured	20	15
1402	**413**	60s. multicoloured	35	20

414 "Foresight Prevents Blindness"

1976. World Health Day.

1403	**414**	15s. multicoloured	15	10

415 Emblem on Book

1976. 75th Anniv of National Archives.

1404	**415**	1p.50 multicoloured	80	75

416 College Emblem and University Tower

1976. 50th Anniv of Colleges of Education and Science, Saint Thomas's University.

1405	**416**	15s. multicoloured	15	10
1406	**416**	50s. multicoloured	20	20

417 College Building

1976. 50th Anniv of Maryknoll College.

1407	**417**	15s. multicoloured	15	10
1408	**417**	1p.50 multicoloured	80	60

1976. Olympic Games, Montreal. Surch 15s Montreal 1976 21st OLYMPICS, CANADA and emblem.

1409	**348**	15s. on 10s. mult	15	10

419 Constabulary Headquarters, Manila

1976. 75th Anniv of Philippine Constabulary. Perf or imperf.

1410	**419**	15s. multicoloured	15	15
1411	**419**	60s. multicoloured	35	20

420 Land and Aerial Surveying

1976. 75th Anniv of Lands Bureau.

1412	**420**	80s. multicoloured	25	25

1976. Air. Bicentenary of American Revolution. No. MS1004 optd U.S.A. BICENTENNIAL 1776—1976 and individual stamps surch.

MS1413 170×105 mm. 5s. on 3s., 5s. on 6s., 15s. on 30s., 50s. on 70s. Imperf — 3·75 3·75

422 Badges of Banking Organizations

1976. International Monetary Fund and World Bank Joint Board of Governors Annual Meeting, Manila.

1414	**422**	60s. multicoloured	20	20
1415	**422**	1p.50 multicoloured	80	60

423 Virgin of Antipolo

1976. 350th Anniv of "Virgin of Antipolo".

1416	**423**	30s. multicoloured	15	15
1417	**423**	90s. multicoloured	35	35

1976. Philatelic Week. Surch 1976 PHILATELIC WEEK 30s.

1418	**355**	30s. on 10s. mult	15	15

425 "Going to Church"

1976. Christmas.

1419	**425**	15s. multicoloured	10	10
1420	**425**	30s. multicoloured	20	15

426 Facets of Education

1976. 75th Anniv of Philippine Educational System.

1421	**426**	30s. multicoloured	15	15
1422	**426**	75s. multicoloured	45	20

1977. Surch.

1423	1p.20 on 1p.10 blue (No. 1316)	60	35
1424	3p. on 5p. blue (No. 1320)	1·30	1·10

428 Jose Rizal

1977. Famous Filipinos. Multicoloured.

1425	30s. Type **428**	15	10
1426	2p.30 Dr. Galicano Apacible	95	65

429 Flags, Map and Emblem

1977. 15th Anniv of Asian–Oceanic Postal Union.

1427	**429**	50s. multicoloured	15	10
1428	**429**	1p.50 multicoloured	60	45

430 Worker and Cogwheels

1977. 10th Anniv of Asian Development Bank.

1429	**430**	90s. multicoloured	45	35
1430	**430**	2p.30 multicoloured	95	80

431 Commission Emblem

1977. National Rural Credit Commission.

1431	**431**	30s. multicoloured	15	10

432 Dutch Windmill and First Stamps of The Netherlands and the Philippines

1977. Air. "Amphilex77" International Stamp Exhibition, Amsterdam. Sheet 73×90 mm.

MS1432 7p.50 ×3, multicoloured — 11·00 11·00

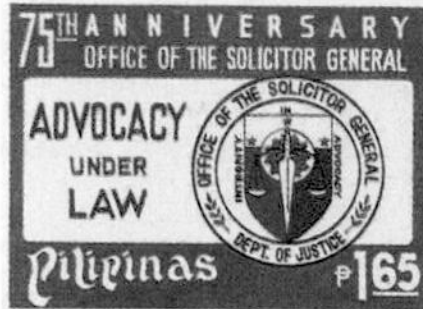

433 Solicitor-General's Emblem

1977. 75th Anniv of Office of Solicitor-General.

1433	**433**	1p.65 multicoloured	45	20

434 Conference Emblem

1977. World Law Conference, Manila.

1434	**434**	2p.20 multicoloured	75	30

435 A.S.E.A.N. Emblem

1977. 10th Anniv of Association of South East Asian Nationals (A.S.E.A.N.).

1435	**435**	1p.50 multicoloured	65	35

436 Cable Ship "Mercury" and Map

1977. Inauguration of OLUHO Cable (Okinawa–Luzon–Hong Kong).

1437	**436**	1p.30 multicoloured	60	35

437 President Marcos

1977. 60th Birthday of President Marcos.

1438	**437**	30s. multicoloured	15	10
1439	**437**	2p.30 multicoloured	1·00	65

438 People raising Flag

1977. 5th Anniv of "New Society".

1440	**438**	30s. multicoloured	15	10
1441	**438**	2p.30 multicoloured	1·00	65

439 Bishop Gregorio Aglipay (founder)

1977. 75th Anniv of Aglipayan Church.

1442	**439**	30s. multicoloured	15	10
1443	**439**	90s. multicoloured	35	20

440 Bull and early Spanish Stamps

1977. Air. "Espamer 77" International Stamp Exhibition, Barcelona. Sheet 75×90 mm.

MS1444 7p.50 ×3, multicoloured — 15·00 15·00

441 Fokker F.7 Trimotor "General New" and World Map

1977. 50th Anniv of 1st Pan-Am International Air Service.

1445	**441**	2p.30 multicoloured	95	60

442 Eight-pointed Star and Children

1977. Christmas.

1446	**442**	30s. multicoloured	15	10
1447	**442**	45s. multicoloured	20	15

1977. Philatelic Week. Surch 90s 1977 PHILATELIC WEEK.

1448	**407**	90s. on 1p. multicoloured	35	20

444 Scouts and Map of Philippines

1977. National Scout Jamboree.

1449	**444**	30s. multicoloured	50	15

445 University Badge

1978. 50th Anniv of Far Eastern University.

1450	**445**	30s. multicoloured	15	10

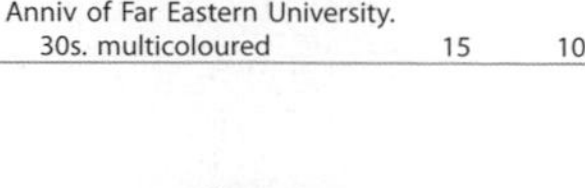

446 Sipa Player

1978. "Sipa" (Filipino ball game).

1451	**446**	5s. multicoloured	10	10
1452	-	10s. multicoloured	10	10
1453	-	40s. multicoloured	30	15
1454	-	75s. multicoloured	45	20

DESIGNS: Nos. 1452/4, Different players.

Nos. 1451/4 were issued together, se-tenant, forming a composite design.

447 Jose Rizal

1978

1455	**447**	30s. blue	15	10
1456	-	30s. mauve	15	10
1457	-	90s. green	20	10
1458	-	1p.20 red	35	15

DESIGNS: No. 1456, Rajah Kalantiaw (Panay chief); 1457, Lope K. Santos ("Father of Filipino grammar"); 1458, Gregoria de Jesus (patriot).

448 Arms of Meycauayan

1978. 400th Anniv of Meycauayan.

1459	**448**	1p.05 multicoloured	35	20

449 Horse-drawn Mail Cart

1978. "CAPEX 78" International Stamp Exhibition, Toronto. Multicoloured.

1460	2p.50 Type **449**	1·10	75
1461	5p. Filipino vinta (sailing canoe)	3·00	1·90
MS1462	Two sheets, each 90×73 mm, each containing 4 ×7p.50. (a) With blue backgrounds; (b) With green backgrounds	18·00	18·00

DESIGNS—36×22 mm : 7p.50 (i) As No. 1461; (ii) As No. 1460; (iii) Early staem locomotive; (iv) Schooner.

450 Andres Bonifacio Monument (Guillermo Tolentino)

1978. Andres Bonifacio Monument.

1463	**450**	30s. multicoloured	15	10

451 Knight, Rook and Globe

1978. World Chess Championship, Baguio City.

1464	**451**	30s. red and violet	15	10
1465	**451**	2p. red and violet	60	35

452 Miner

1978. 75th Anniv of Benguet Consolidated Mining Company.

1466	**452**	2p.30 multicoloured	1·20	45

453 Pres. Quezon

1978. Birth Centenary of Manuel L. Quezon (former President).

1467	**453**	30s. multicoloured	15	10
1468	**453**	1p. multicoloured	35	15

454 Law Association and Conference Emblems

1978. 58th Int Law Association Conf, Manila.

1469	**454**	2p.30 multicoloured	80	60

455 Pres. Osmena

1978. Birth Centenary of Sergio Osmena (former President).

1470	**455**	30s. multicoloured	15	10
1471	**455**	1p. multicoloured	35	20

456 Map of Cable Route and Cable Ship "Mercury"

1978. Inauguration of Philippines–Singapore Submarine Cable.

1472	**456**	1p.40 multicoloured	60	20

457 Basketball

1978. 8th Men's World Basketball Championship, Manila.

1473	**457**	30s. multicoloured	15	10
1474	**457**	2p.30 multicoloured	80	60

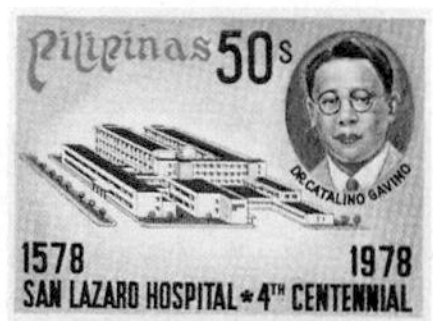

458 Dr. Catalino Gavino and Hospital

1978. 400th Anniv of San Lazaro Hospital.

1475	**458**	50s. multicoloured	20	10
1476	**458**	90s. multicoloured	35	20

459 Nurse vaccinating Child

1978. Global Eradication of Smallpox.

1477	**459**	30s. multicoloured	10	10
1478	**459**	1p.50 multicoloured	65	35

1978. Philatelic Week. No. 1391 surch 1978 PHILATELIC WEEK 60s.

1479	**408**	60s. on 65s. mauve	20	10

461 Man on Telephone, Map and Satellite

1978. 50th Anniv of Philippine Long Distance Telephone Company. Multicoloured.

1480	30s. Type **461**	10	10
1481	2p. Woman on telephone and globe	75	50

Nos. 1480/1 were issued together, se-tenant, forming a composite design.

462 Family travelling in Ox-drawn Cart

1978. Decade of the Filipino Child.

1482	**462**	30s. multicoloured	10	10
1483	**462**	1p.35 multicoloured	60	20

463 Spanish Colonial Church and Arms

1978. 400th Anniv of Agoo Town.

1484	**463**	30s. multicoloured	10	15
1485	**463**	45s. multicoloured	15	20

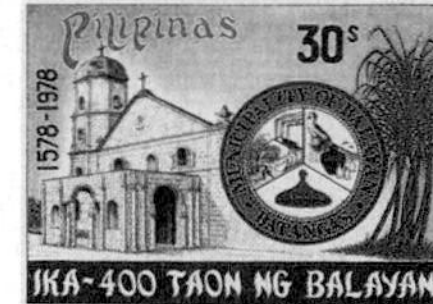

464 Church and Arms

1978. 400th Anniv of Balayan Town.

1486	**464**	30s. multicoloured	15	10
1487	**464**	90s. multicoloured	35	15

465 Dr. Sison

1978. Dr. Honoria Acosta Sison (first Filipino woman physician) Commemoration.

1488	**465**	30s. multicoloured	15	10

466 Family and Houses

1978. 30th Anniv of Declaration of Human Rights.

1489	**466**	30s. multicoloured	10	10
1490	**466**	3p. multicoloured	1·30	75

467 Melon butterflyfish

1978. Fishes. Multicoloured.

1491	30s. Type **467**	15	10
1492	1p.20 Black triggerfish	45	15
1493	2p.20 Picasso triggerfish	80	35
1494	2p.30 Copper-banded butterflyfish	80	45
1495	5p. Atoll butterflyfish ("Chaetodon mertensi")	1·80	1·00
1496	5p. Yellow-faced butterflyfish ("Euxiphipops xanthometapon")	1·80	1·00

468 Carlos P. Romulo

1979. 80th Anniv of Carlos P. Romulo (1st Asian President of U.N. General Assembly).

1497	**468**	30s. multicoloured	10	10
1498	**468**	2p. multicoloured	95	45

469 Cogwheel (Rotary Emblem)

1979. 60th Anniv of Manila Rotary Club.

1499	**469**	30s. multicoloured	10	10

1500	**469**	2p.30 multicoloured	70	25

470 Rosa Sevilla de Alvero

1979. Birth Centenary of Rosa Sevilla de Alvero (writer and educator).

1501	**470**	30s. mauve	10	10

471 Burning-off Gas and Map

1979. 1st Oil Production. Nido Complex, Palawan.

1502	**471**	30s. multicoloured	15	10
1503	**471**	45s. multicoloured	20	10

472 Merrill's Fruit Dove

1979. Birds. Multicoloured.

1504	30s. Type **472**	30	15
1505	1p.20 Brown tit-babbler	50	45
1506	2p.20 Mindoro zone-tailed (inscr "Imperial") pigeon	95	45
1507	2p.30 Steere's pitta	1·00	50
1508	5p. Koch's pitta and red-breasted pitta	2·20	1·20
1509	5p. Great eared nightjar	2·20	1·20

473 Association Emblem

1979. 25th Anniv of Association of Special Libraries of the Philippines.

1510	**473**	30s. green, black & yell	15	10
1511	**473**	75s. green, black & yell	30	10
1512	**473**	1p. green, black & orange	35	20

474 Conference Emblem

1979. 5th U.N. Conference on Trade and Development, Manila.

1513	**474**	1p.20 multicoloured	35	15
1514	**474**	2p.30 multicoloured	95	35

475 Malay Civet

1979. Animals. Multicoloured.

1515	30s. Type **475**	15	10
1516	1p.20 Crab-eating macaque	45	15
1517	2p.20 Javan pig	80	35
1518	2p.30 Leopard cat	80	45
1519	5p. Oriental small-clawed otter	1·80	1·00
1520	5p. Malayan pangolin	1·80	1·00

476 Dish Aerial

1979. World Telecommunications Day. Mult.

1521	90s. Type **476**	30	10
1522	1p.30 Hemispheres	45	20

477 Mussaenda "Dona Evangelina"

1979. Cultivated Mussaendas. Multicoloured.

1523	30s. Type **477**	15	10
1524	1p.20 "Dona Esperanza"	45	15
1525	2p.20 "Dona Hilaria"	80	35
1526	2p.30 "Dona Aurora"	80	45
1527	5p. "Gining Imelda"	1·80	1·00
1528	5p. "Dona Trining"	1·80	1·00

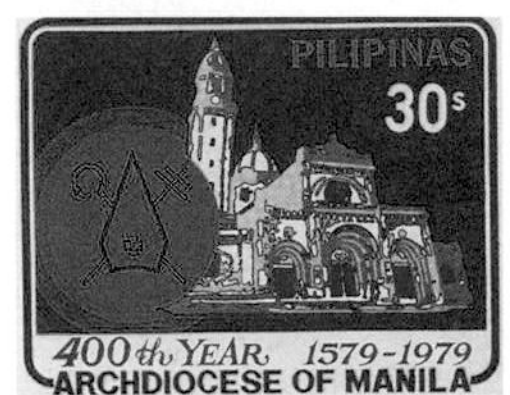

478 Manila Cathedral

1979. 400th Anniv of Archdiocese of Manila.

1529	**478**	30s. multicoloured	15	10
1530	**478**	75s. multicoloured	20	10
1531	**478**	90s. multicoloured	35	20

479 "Bagong Lakas" (patrol boat)

1979. Philippine Navy Foundation Day.

1532	**479**	30s. multicoloured	20	10
1533	**479**	45s. multicoloured	30	15

1979. Air. 1st Scout Philatelic Exhibition and 25th Anniv of 1st National Jamboree. Surch 1ST SCOUT PHILATELIC EXHIBITION JULY 4.14, 1979 QUEZON CITY AIRMAIL 90s.

1534	**188**	90s. on 6c.+4c. red on yellow	30	30
MS1535		171×90 mm. Nos. 823, 825/8 each surch **50s.**	2·75	2·75

481 Drug Addict breaking Manacles

1979. "Fight Drug Abuse" Campaign.

1536	**481**	30s. multicoloured	15	10
1537	**481**	90s. multicoloured	35	15
1538	**481**	1p.05 multicoloured	45	20

482 Afghan Hound

1979. Cats and Dogs. Multicoloured.

1539	30s. Type **482**	10	10
1540	90s. Tabby cats	35	15
1541	1p.20 Dobermann pinscher	45	20
1542	2p.20 Siamese cats	80	20
1543	2p.30 German shepherd dog	95	80
1544	5p. Chinchilla cats	1·80	95

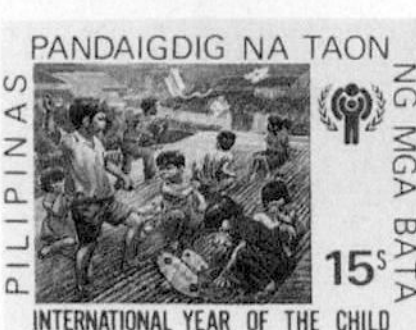

483 Children flying Kites

1979. International Year of the Child. Paintings by Rod Dayao. Multicoloured.

1545	15s. Type **483**	10	10
1546	20s. Boys fighting with catapults	15	10
1547	25s. Girls dressing-up	15	15
1548	1p.20 Boy playing policeman	35	20

484 Hands holding Emblems

1979. 80th Anniv of Methodism in the Philippines.

1549	**484**	30s. multicoloured	15	10
1550	**484**	1p.35 multicoloured	45	15

485 Anniversary Medal and 1868 Coin

1979. 50th Anniv of Philippine Numismatic and Antiquarian Society.

1551	**485**	30s. multicoloured	15	10

486 Concorde over Manila and Paris

1979. 25th Anniv of Air France Service to the Philippines. Multicoloured.

1552	1p.05 Type **486**	50	20
1553	2p.20 Concorde over monument	1·30	60

1979. Philatelic Week. Surch 1979 PHILATELIC WEEK 90s.

1554	**412**	90s. on 1p.60 black	35	15

488 "35" and I.A.T.A. Emblem

1979. 35th Annual General Meeting of International Air Transport Association, Manila.

1555	**488**	75s. multicoloured	30	15
1556	**488**	2p.30 multicoloured	95	65

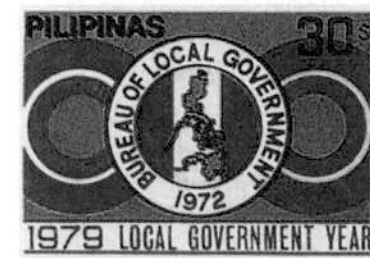

489 Bureau of Local Government Emblem

1979. Local Government Year.

1557	**489**	30s. multicoloured	15	15
1558	**489**	45s. multicoloured	20	65

490 Christmas Greetings

1979. Christmas. Multicoloured.

1559	30s. Type **490**	15	10
1560	90s. Stars	45	30

491 Rheumatism Victim

1980. 4th Congress of Southeast Asia and Pacific Area League Against Rheumatism, Manila.

1561	**491**	30s. multicoloured	15	10
1562	**491**	90s. multicoloured	50	20

492 Birthplace and MacArthur Memorial Foundation

1980. Birth Centenary of General Douglas MacArthur (U.S. Army Chief of Staff). Mult.

1563	30s. Type **492**	15	10
1564	75s. General MacArthur	35	15
1565	2p.30 Hat, pipe and glasses	1·30	75
MS1566	76×76 mm. 5p. Landing in the Philippines (horiz). Imperf	3·00	2·50

493 Columbus and Emblem

1980. 75th Anniv of Knights of Columbus Organization in Philippines.

1567	**493**	30s. multicoloured	15	10
1568	**493**	1p.35 multicoloured	80	45

494 Soldiers and Academy Emblem

1980. 75th Anniv of Philippine Military Academy.

1569	**494**	30s. multicoloured	15	10
1570	**494**	1p.20 multicoloured	75	30

495 Tirona, Benitez and University

1980. 60th Anniv of Philippine Women's University.

1571	**495**	30s. multicoloured	15	10
1572	**495**	1p.05 multicoloured	65	30

496 Boats and Burning City

1980. 75th Anniv of Rotary International. Details of painting by Carlos Francisco. Multicoloured.

1573	30s. Type **496**	15	10
1574	30s. Priest with cross, swordsmen and soldier	15	10
1575	30s. "K K K" flag and group around table	15	10
1576	30s. Man in midst of spearmen and civilian scenes	15	10
1577	30s. Reading the Constitution, soliders and U.S. and Philippine flags	15	10
1578	2p.30 Type **496**	1·30	60
1579	2p.30 As No. 1574	1·30	60
1580	2p.30 As No. 1575	1·30	60
1581	2p.30 As No. 1576	1·30	60
1582	2p.30 As No. 1577	1·30	60

Nos. 1573/7 and 1578/82 were issued together in se-tenant strips of five, each strip forming a composite design.

497 Mosque and Koran

1980. 600th Anniv of Islam in the Philippines.

1583	**497**	30s. multicoloured	15	10
1584	**497**	1p.30 multicoloured	75	30

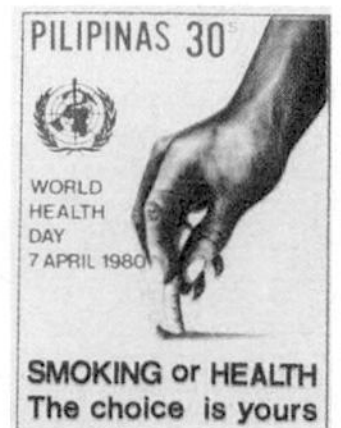

498 Hand stubbing out Cigarette

1980. World Health Day. Anti-smoking Campaign.

1585	**498**	30s. multicoloured	15	10
1586	**498**	75s. multicoloured	45	20

499 Scouting Activities and Badge

1980. 40th Anniv of Girl Scouting in the Philippines.

1587	**499**	30s. multicoloured	15	10
1588	**499**	2p. multicoloured	65	30

500 Jeepney

1980. Philippine Jeepneys (decorated jeeps). Multicoloured.

1589	30s. Type **500**	15	10
1590	1p.20 Side view of Jeepney	65	30

1980. 82nd Anniv of Independence. Surch PHILIPPINE INDEPENDENCE 82ND ANNIVERSARY 1898 1980.

1591	**412**	1p.35 on 1p.60 black	80	45
1592	**412**	1p.50 on 1p.80 green (No. 1319)	1·00	50

502 Association Emblem

1980. 7th General Conference of International Association of Universities, Manila.

1593	**502**	30s. multicoloured	15	10
1594	**502**	2p.30 multicoloured	1·30	1·30

503 Map and Emblems

1980. 46th Congress of International Federation of Library Associations and Institutions, Manila.

1595	**503**	30s. green and black	20	10
1596	**503**	75s. blue and black	45	20
1597	**503**	2p.30 red and black	1·50	80

504 Filipinos and Emblem

1980. 5th Anniv of Kabataang Barangay (national council charged with building the "New Society").

1598	**504**	30s. multicoloured	20	10
1599	**504**	40s. multicoloured	20	15
1600	**504**	1p. multicoloured	65	30

1980. Nos. 1433, 1501, 1536, 1557 and 1559 surch.

1601	**470**	40s. on 30s. mauve	20	10
1602	**481**	40s. on 30s. multicoloured	20	10
1603	**489**	40s. on 30s. multicoloured	20	10
1604	**490**	40s. on 30s. multicoloured	20	10
1605	**433**	2p. on 1p.65 mult	1·30	65

506 Sunset, Filipino Vinta and Conference Emblem

1980. World Tourism Conference, Manila.

1606	**506**	30s. multicoloured	20	15
1607	**506**	2p.30 multicoloured	1·40	80

507 Magnifying Glass and Stamps

1980. Postage Stamp Day.

1608	**507**	40s. multicoloured	20	15
1609	**507**	1p. multicoloured	65	30
1610	**507**	2p. multicoloured	1·30	65

508 U.N. Headquarters and Philippines Flag

1980. 35th Anniv of U.N.O.

1611	40s. Type **508**	30	15
1612	3p.20 U.N. Headquarters and U.N. and Philippines flags	1·90	1·30

509 Alabaster Murex

1980. Shells. Multicoloured.

1613	40s. Type **509**	20	15
1614	60s. Giant frog shell	35	20
1615	1p.20 Zambo's murex	65	30
1616	2p. Pallid carrier shell	1·30	60

510 Interpol Emblem on Globe

1980. 49th General Assembly of Interpol, Manila.

1617	**510**	40s. multicoloured	20	10
1618	**510**	1p. multicoloured	65	30
1619	**510**	3p.20 multicoloured	2·10	1·30

511 University and Faculty Emblems

1980. 75th Anniv of Central Philippine University. Multicoloured, background colour given.

1620	**511**	40s. blue	30	10
1621	**511**	3p.20 green	1·20	1·30

1980. Philatelic Week. No. 1377 surch 1980 PHILATELIC WEEK P1.20.

1622	**399**	1p.20 on 80s. black, blue and pink	60	30

513 Christmas Tree and Presents

1980. Christmas.

1623	**513**	40s. multicoloured	20	10

1981. Various stamps surch.

1624	**244**	10s. on 6s.+5s. blue	15	10
1625	**462**	10s. on 30s. mult	10	10
1626	**408**	40s. on 65s. mauve	20	10
1627	**458**	40s. on 90s. mult	20	10
1628	**481**	40s. on 90s. mult	20	10
1629	-	40s. on 90s. mult (No. 1560)	20	10
1630	**448**	40s. on 1p.05 mult	20	10
1631	**462**	40s. on 1p.35 mult	20	15
1632	**399**	85s. on 80s. black, blue and pink	50	30
1633	**408**	1p. on 65s. mauve	75	30
1634	**401**	1p. on 1p.50 blue and mauve	75	30
1635	**422**	1p. on 1p.50 mult	60	20
1636	-	1p.20 on 1p.50 brown (No. 1318)	75	35
1637	**433**	1p.20 on 1p.65 mult	75	35
1638	-	1p.20 on 1p.80 green (No. 1319)	75	35
1639	**401**	2p. on 1p.50 blue and mauve	1·30	60
1640	**434**	3p.20 on 2p.20 mult	1·90	1·00

1981. 30th Anniv of APO Philatelic Society. Surch NOV. 30, 1980 APO PHILATELIC SOCIETY PEARL JUBILEE 40s.

1641	**455**	40s. on 30s. mult	20	10

516 Von Stephan and U.P.U. Emblem

1981. 150th Birth Anniv of Heinrich von Stephan (founder of U.P.U.).

1642	**516**	3p.20 multicoloured	1·90	95

1981. Girl Scouts Camp. No. 1589 surch GSP RJASIA-PACIFIC REGIONAL CAMP PHILIPPINES DECEMBER 23, 1980 40s.

1643	**500**	40s. on 30s. mult	20	10

518 Pope John Paul II

1981. Papal Visit. Multicoloured.

1644	90s. Type **518**	50	20
1645	1p.20 Pope and cardinals	65	30
1646	2p.30 Pope blessing crowd (horiz)	1·30	65
1647	3p. Pope and Manila Cathedral (horiz)	1·60	80
MS1648	75×91 mm. 7p.50 Pope and map of Philippines	6·00	3·00

519 Parliamentary Debate

1981. Interparliamentary Union Meeting, Manila.

1649	**519**	2p. multicoloured	1·40	60
1650	**519**	3p.20 multicoloured	1·90	1·00

520 Monument

1981. Jose Rizal Monument, Luneta Park.

1651	**520**	40s. black, yellow & brn	20	10

521 President Aguinaldo's Car

1981. 50th Anniv of Philippine Motor Association. Multicoloured.

1652	40s. Type **521**	20	10
1653	40s. 1930 model car	20	10
1654	40s. 1937 model car	20	10
1655	40s. 1937 model car (different)	20	10

522 Bubble Coral

1981. Corals. Multicoloured.

1656	40s. Type **522**	20	10
1657	40s. Branching corals	20	10
1658	40s. Brain coral	20	10
1659	40s. Table coral	20	10

523 President Marcos and Flag

1981. Inauguration of President Marcos. Perf or imperf.

1660 **523** 40s. multicoloured 20 10

MS1661 78×78 mm. 5p. As No. 1660 but design smaller with inscriptions below. Imperf 3·00 1·30

524 St. Ignatius de Loyola (founder)

1981. 400th Anniv of Jesuits in the Philippines. Mult.

1662 40s. Type **524** 20 10

1663 40s. Dr. Jose P. Rizal and Intramuros Ateneo 20 10

1664 40s. Father Frederico Faura (director) and Manila Observatory 20 10

1665 40s. Father Saturnino Urios (missionary) and map of Mindanao 20 10

MS1666 89×89 mm. As Nos. 1662/5 but smaller. Imperf (sold at 2p.) 2·20 75

525 F. R. Castro

1981. Chief Justice Fred Ruiz Castro.

1667 **525** 40s. multicoloured 20 10

526 Pres. Ramon Magsaysay

1981

1668 - 1p. brown and black 65 30

1669 **526** 1p.20 brown and black 75 35

1670 - 2p. purple and black 1·40 60

DESIGNS: 1p. General Gregorio del Pilar; 2p. Ambrosio R. Bautista.

See also Nos. 1699/1704, 1807 etc. and 2031/3.

527 Man in Wheelchair

1981. International Year of Disabled Persons.

1671 **527** 40s. multicoloured 30 15

1672 **527** 3p.20 multicoloured 1·90 1·00

528 Early Filipino Writing

1981. 24th International Red Cross Conference.

1673 **528** 40s. black, red and bistre 15 10

1674 **528** 2p. black and red 1·30 50

1675 **528** 3p.20 black, red and mauve 1·90 90

529 Isabel II Gate, Manila

1981

1676 **529** 40s. black 20 10

530 Concert in Park

1981. Opening of Concert at Park 200.

1677 **530** 40s. multicoloured 20 10

1981. Philatelic Week. No. 1435 surch P120 1981 PHILATELIC WEEK.

1678 **435** 1p.20 on 1p.50 mult 75 35

532 Running

1981. 11th South-east Asian Games, Manila.

1679 **532** 40s. yellow, green & brn 20 10

1680 - 1p. multicoloured 75 30

1681 - 2p. multicoloured 1·50 60

1682 - 2p.30 multicoloured 1·50 65

1683 - 2p.80 multicoloured 1·80 80

1684 - 3p.20 violet and blue 1·90 1·00

DESIGNS: 1p. Cycling; 2p. President Marcos and Juan Antonio Samaranch (president of International Olympic Committee); 2p.30, Football; 2p.80, Shooting; 3p.20, Bowling.

533 Manila Film Centre

1982. Manila International Film Festival. Mult.

1685 40s. Type **533** 30 10

1686 2p. Front view of trophy 1·50 60

1687 3p.20 Side view of trophy 1·90 1·00

534 Carriedo Fountain

1982. Centenary of Manila Metropolitan Waterworks and Sewerage System.

1688 **534** 40s. blue 20 10

1689 **534** 1p.20 brown 75 35

535 Lord Baden-Powell (founder)

1982. 75th Anniv of Boy Scout Movement. Mult.

1690 40s. Type **535** 20 10

1691 2p. Scout 1·50 60

536 Embroidered Banner

1982. 25th Anniv of Children's Museum and Library Inc. Multicoloured.

1692 40s. Type **536** 20 10

1693 1p.20 Children playing 75 35

537 President Marcos presenting Sword of Honour

1982. Military Academy.

1694 **537** 40s. multicoloured 20 15

1695 **537** 1p. multicoloured 75 30

538 Soldier and Memorial

1982. Bataan Day.

1696 **538** 40s. multicoloured 20 10

1697 - 2p. multicoloured 1·50 60

MS1698 76×76 mm. 3p.20 purple and black. Imperf 2·20 1·60

DESIGNS: 2p. Doves and rifles; 3p.20, Field gun and flag.

1982. Portraits. As T 526.

1699 40s. blue 20 10

1700 1p. red 75 30

1701 1p.20 brown 75 35

1702 2p. mauve 1·30 60

1703 2p.30 purple 1·50 60

1704 3p.20 blue 1·90 1·00

DESIGNS: 40s. Isabelo de los Reyes (founder of first workers' union); 1p. Aurora Aragon Quezon (social worker and former First Lady); 1p.20, Francisco Dagohoy; 2p. Juan Sumulong (politician); 2p.30, Professor Nicanor Abelardo (composer); 3p.20, General Vicente Lim.

For these designs in other values, see Nos. 1811/15.

539 Worker with Tower Award

1982. Tower Awards (for best "Blue Collar" Workers). Multicoloured.

1705 40s. Type **539** (inscr "MANGGAGAWA") 20 10

1705d 40s. Type **539** (inscr "MANGAGAWA") 60 10

1706 1p.20 Cogwheel and tower award (inscr "MANGGAGAWA") 75 35

1706b 1p.20 As No. 1706 but inscr "Mangagawa" 1·25 20

541 Green Turtle

1982. 10th Anniv of United Nations Environment Programme. Multicoloured.

1707 40s. Type **541** 30 15

1708 3p.20 Philippine eagle 2·75 1·00

542 K.K.K. Emblem

1982. Inauguration of Kilusang Kabuhayan at Kaunlaran (national livelihood movement).

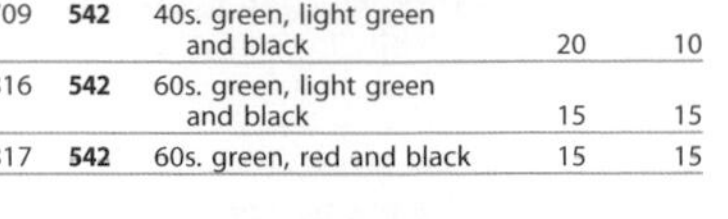
1709 **542** 40s. green, light green and black 20 10

1816 **542** 60s. green, light green and black 15 15

1817 **542** 60s. green, red and black 15 15

543 Chemistry Apparatus and Emblem

1982. 50th Anniv of Adamson University.

1710 **543** 40s. multicoloured 20 10

1711 **543** 1p.20 multicoloured 75 35

544 Dr. Fernando G. Calderon and Emblems

1982. 75th Anniv of College of Medicine, University of the Philippines.

1712 **544** 40s. multicoloured 30 15

1713 **544** 3p.20 multicoloured 1·90 1·00

545 President Marcos

1982. 65th Birthday of President Ferdinand Marcos.

1714 **545** 40s. multicoloured 20 10

1715 **545** 3p.20 multicoloured 1·90 1·00

MS1716 76×76 mm. Nos. 1714/15. Imperf 2·50 1·60

546 Hands supporting Family

1982. 25th Anniv of Social Security System.

1717 **546** 40s. black, orange & blue 20 10

1718 **546** 1p.20 black, orange and green 75 35

547 Emblem and Flags forming Ear of Wheat

1982. 15th Anniv of Association of South East Asian Nations.
1719 **547** 40s. multicoloured 20 10

548 St. Theresa of Avila

1982. 400th Death Anniv of St. Theresa of Avila. Multicoloured.
1720 40s. Type **548** 20 10
1721 1p.20 St. Theresa and map of Europe, Africa and Asia 75 35
1722 2p. As 1p.20 1·50 60

549 St. Isabel College

1982. 350th Anniv of St. Isabel College.
1723 **549** 40s. multicoloured 20 15
1724 **549** 1p. multicoloured 75 30

550 President Marcos signing Decree and Tenant Family

1982. 10th Anniv of Tenant Emancipation Decree.
1725a **550** 40s. green, brown and black (37×27 mm) 20 10
1726 **550** 40s. green, brown and black (32×22½ mm) 20 10

551 "Reading Tree"

1982. Literacy Campaign.
1727 **551** 40s. multicoloured 20 10
1728 **551** 2p.30 multicoloured 1·50 60

552 Helmeted Heads

1982. 43rd World Congress of Skal Clubs, Manila.
1729 40s. Type **552** 20 10
1730 2p. Head in feathered head-dress 1·50 60

553 Dancers with Parasols

1982. 25th Anniv of Bayanihan Folk Arts Centre. Multicoloured.
1731 40s. Type **553** 20 10
1732 2p.80 Dancers (different) 1·80 80

554 Dr. Robert Koch and Bacillus

1982. Cent of Discovery of Tubercule Bacillus.
1733 **554** 40s. red, blue and black 20 10
1734 **554** 2p.80 multicoloured 1·80 80

555 Father Christmas in Sleigh

1982. Christmas.
1735 **555** 40s. multicoloured 20 15
1736 **555** 1p. multicoloured 75 30

556 Presidential Couples and Flags

1982. State Visit of Pres. Marcos to United States.
1737 **556** 40s. multicoloured 15 15
1738 **556** 3p.20 multicoloured 1·30 90
MS1739 76×75 mm. Nos. 1737/8. Imperf 2·75 1·30

557 Woman with Sewing Machine

1982. U.N. World Assembly on Ageing.
1740a **557** 1p.20 green and orange 75 35
1741a - 2p. pink and blue 1·50 60
DESIGN: 2p. Man with carpentry tools.

558 Stamp and Magnifying Glass

1983. Philatelic Week.
1742 **558** 40s. multicoloured 20 10
1743 **558** 1p. multicoloured 45 30

559 Eulogio Rodriguez

1983. Birth Centenary of Eulogio Rodriguez (former President of Senate).
1744a **559** 40s. multicoloured 20 10
1745 **559** 1p.20 multicoloured 75 35

560 Symbolic Figure and Film Frame

1983. Manila International Film Festival.
1746a **560** 40s. multicoloured 20 10

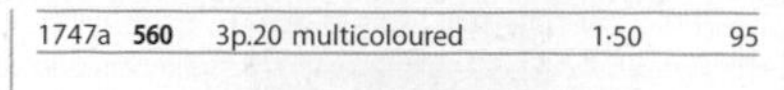
1747a **560** 3p.20 multicoloured 1·50 95

561 Monument

1983. 2nd Anniv of Beatification of Lorenzo Ruiz.
1748 **561** 40s. yellow, red and black 20 10
1749 **561** 1p.20 multicoloured 75 35

562 Early Printing Press

1983. 390th Anniv of First Local Printing Press.
1750 **562** 40s. green and black 20 10

563 Emblem and Ship

1983. 25th Anniv of International Maritime Organization.
1751 **563** 40s. red, black and blue 20 10

1983. 7th National Scout Jamboree. No. 1709 optd 7TH BSP NATIONAL JAMBOREE 1983.
1752 **542** 40s. green, light green and black 20 10

1983. Nos. 1360/9 surch 40s.
1753 - 40s. on 45c. green 20 10
1754 **387** 40s. on 45c. green 20 10
1755 **388** 40s. on 45c. green 20 10
1756 **389** 40s. on 45c. green 20 10
1757 - 40s. on 45c. green 20 10
1758 - 40s. on 45c. green 20 10
1759 **392** 40s. on 45c. green 20 10
1760 **393** 40s. on 45c. green 20 10
1761 **394** 40s. on 45c. green 20 10
1762 - 40s. on 45c. green 20 10

566 Calculator Keys

1983. 11th International Organization of Supreme Audit Institutions Congress.
1763 **566** 40s. blue, light blue and silver 20 10
1764 - 2p.80 multicoloured 1·80 80
MS1765 77×76 mm. Nos. 1763/4. Imperf 2·20 1·50
DESIGN: 2p.80, Congress emblem.

567 Smiling Children

1983. 75th Anniv of Philippine Dental Association.
1766 **567** 40s. green, mauve & brn 20 15

568 Detail of Statue

1983. 75th Anniv of University of the Philippines.
1767 **568** 40s. brown and green 20 15
1768 - 1p.20 multicoloured 65 30
DESIGN: 1p.20, Statue and diamond.

569 Yasuhiro Nakasone and Pres. Marcos

1983. Visit of Japanese Prime Minister.
1769 **569** 40s. multicoloured 20 15

570 Agriculture and Natural Resources

1983. 25th Anniv of National Science and Technology Authority. Multicoloured.
1770 40s. Type **570** 30 15
1771 40s. Heart, medical products and food (Health and nutrition) 30 15
1772 40s. Industrial complex and air (Industry and energy) 30 15
1773 40s. House, scientific equipment and book (Sciences and social science) 30 15

571 Globes and W.C.Y. Emblem

1983. World Communication Year.
1774 **571** 3p.20 multicoloured 1·90 90

572 Postman

1983. Bicent of Philippine Postal System.
1775 **572** 40s. multicoloured 20 15

573 Woman with Tambourine

1983. Christmas. Multicoloured.
1776 40s. Type **573** 20 15
1777 40s. Man turning spit (left side) 20 15
1778 40s. Pig on spit 20 15
1779 40s. Man turning spit (right side) 20 15
1780 40s. Man with guitar 20 15
MS1781 153×77 mm. Nos. 1776/80. Imperf 1·80 1·80

Nos. 1776/80 were issued together, se-tenant, forming a composite design.

574 University Activities

1983. 50th Anniv of Xavier University.

1782	**574**	40s. multicoloured	20	15
1783	**574**	60s. multicoloured	35	15

575 Woman casting Vote

1983. 50th Anniv of Female Suffrage.

1784	**575**	40s. multicoloured	20	15
1785	**575**	60s. multicoloured	35	15

576 Workers

1983. 50th Anniv of Ministry of Labour and Employment.

1786	**576**	40s. multicoloured	20	15
1787	**576**	60s. multicoloured	35	15

577 Cutting Stamp from Envelope

1983. Philatelic Week. Multicoloured.

1788	50s. Type **577**	45	15
1789	50s. Sorting stamps	45	15
1790	50s. Soaking stamps	45	15
1791	50s. Hinging stamp	45	15
1792	50s. Mounting stamp in album	15	15

578 Red-vented Cockatoo

1984. Parrots. Multicoloured.

1793	40s. Type **578**	60	30
1794	2p.30 Guaiabero	80	30
1795	2p.80 Mountain racket-tailed parrot	95	35
1796	3p.20 Great-billed parrot	1·20	35
1797	3p.60 Muller's parrot	1·50	75
1798	5p. Philippine hanging parrot	1·30	65

579 Princess Tarhata Kiram

1984. 5th Death Anniv of Princess Tarhata Kiram.

1799	**579**	3p. deep green, green and red	75	30

580 Nun and Congregation

1984. 300th Anniv of Religious Congregation of the Virgin Mary.

1800	**580**	40s. multicoloured	15	15
1801	**580**	60s. multicoloured	15	15

581 Dona Concha Felix de Calderon

1984. Birth Centenary of Dona Concha Felix de Calderon.

1802	**581**	60s. green and black	10	10
1803	**581**	3p.60 green and red	50	15

1984. Various stamps surch.

1804	**545**	60s. on 40s. multicoloured	15	15
1805	**558**	60s. on 40s. multicoloured	15	15
1806	-	3p.60 on 3p.20 blue (No. 1704)	95	30

1984. As Nos. 1700/4 but values changed, and new designs as T 526.

1807	60s. brown and black	15	10
1808	60s. violet and black	15	10
1809	60s. black	15	10
1889	60s. brown	20	10
1913	60s. blue	20	10
1914	60s. red	20	15
1811	1p.80 blue	20	15
1812	2p.40 purple	35	15
1813	3p. brown	35	15
1814	3p.60 red	50	15
1815	4p.20 purple	60	20

DESIGNS: No. 1807, General Artemio Ricarte; 1808, Teodoro M. Kalaw (politician); 1809, Carlos P. Garcia (4th President); 1913, Quintin Paredes (senator); 1889, Dr. Deogracias V. Villadolid; 1914, Santiago Fonacier (former Senator and army chaplain); 1811, General Vicente Lim; 1812, Professor Nicanor Abelardo; 1813, Francisco Dagohoy; 1814, Aurora Aragon Quezon; 1815, Juan Sumulong.

583 Manila

1984. 150th Anniv of Ayala Corporation.

1818	**583**	70s. multicoloured	15	10
1819	**583**	3p.60 multicoloured	35	15

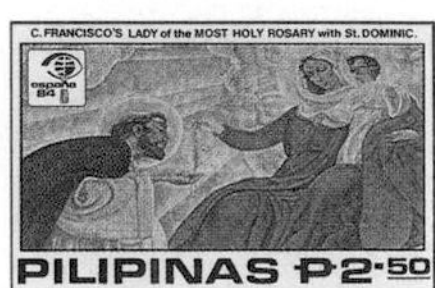

584 "Lady of the Most Holy Rosary with St. Dominic" (C. Francisco)

1984. "Espana 84" International Stamp Exhibition, Madrid. Multicoloured.

1820	2p.50 Type **584**	35	15
1821	5p. "Spoliarum" (Juan Luna)	80	35
MS1822	99×73 mm. 7p.50, As No. 1821; 7p.50, Virgin of Manila and Spanish galleon; 7p.50, Illustrations from Rizal's "The Monkey and the Turtle"; 7p.50, As No. 1820. Perf or imperf	8·00	8·00

585 Maria Paz Mendoza Guazon

1984. Birth Centenary of Dr. Maria Paz Mendoza Guazon.

1823	**585**	60s. red and blue	15	10
1824	**585**	65s. red, black and blue	15	10

586 "Adolias amlana"

1984. Butterflies. Multicoloured.

1825	60s. Type **586**	15	10
1826	2p.40 "Papilio daedalus"	50	20
1827	3p. "Prothoe franckii semperi"	65	30
1828	3p.60 Philippine birdwing	80	30
1829	4p.20 Lurcher	95	45
1830	5p. "Chilasa idaeoides"	1·30	50

1984. National Children's Book Day. Stamp from miniature sheet ("The Monkey and the Turtle") surch 7-17-84 NATIONAL CHILDREN'S BOOK DAY 20. Perf or imperf.

1831	7p.20 on 7p.50 multicoloured	15·00	8·75

1984. 420th Anniv of Philippine–Mexican Friendship. Stamp from miniature sheet (Virgin of Manila) surch 420TH PHIL-MEXICAN FRIENDSHIP 8-3-84 20. Perf or imperf.

1832	7p.20 on 7p.50 multicoloured	15·00	8·75

589 Running

1984. Olympic Games, Los Angeles. Multicoloured.

1833	60s. Type **589**	10	10
1834	2p.40 Boxing	45	20
1835	6p. Swimming	1·20	60
1836	7p.20 Windsurfing	1·50	80
1837	8p.40 Cycling	1·80	90
1838	20p. Running (woman athlete)	4·00	2·20
MS1839	87×129 mm. 6p. ×4, As Nos. 1834 and 1836/8	4·75	4·75

590 The Mansion

1984. 75th Anniv of Baguio City.

1840	**590**	1p.20 multicoloured	20	15

1984. 300th Anniv of Our Lady of Holy Rosary Parish. Stamp from miniature sheet ("Lady of the Most Holy Rosary") surch 9-1-84 300TH YR O.L. HOLY ROSARY PARISH 20. Perf or imperf.

1841	7p.20 on 7p.50 multicoloured	30·00	26·00

592 Electric Train on Viaduct

1984. Light Railway Transit.

1842	**592**	1p.20 multicoloured	45	15

593 Australian and Philippine Stamps and Koalas

1984. "Ausipex 84" International Stamp Exhibition, Melbourne.

1843	**593**	3p. multicoloured	60	30
1844	**593**	3p.60 multicoloured	75	30
MS1845		75×90 mm. **593** 20p. ×3, multicoloured	24·00	24·00

1984. National Museum Week. Stamp from miniature sheet (as No. 1821) surch NATIONAL MUSEUM WEEK 10-5-84 20. Perf or imperf.

1846	7p.20 on 7p.50 multicoloured	15·00	8·75

1984. Asia Regional Conference of Rotary International. No. 1728 surch 14-17 NOV. 84 R.I. ASIA REGIONAL CONFERENCE P1.20.

1847	**551**	1p.20 on 2p.30 mult	20	15

596 Gold Award

1984. Philatelic Week. Gold Award at "Ausipex 84" to Mario Que. Multicoloured.

1848	1p.20 Type **596**	20	15
1849	3p. Page of Que's exhibit	45	15

597 Caracao

1984. Water Transport. Multicoloured.

1850	60s. Type **597**	20	15
1851	1p.20 Chinese junk	20	15
1852	6p. Spanish galleon	1·30	60
1853	7p.20 Casco (Filipino cargo prau)	1·50	75
1854	8p.40 Early paddle-steamer	1·60	90
1855	20p. Modern liner	4·00	1·90

1984. No. MS1666 surch 3 00 with T 598.

MS1856	89×89 mm. 3p. on 2p. multicoloured	90	90

599 Anniversary Emblem

1984. 125th Anniv of Ateneo de Manila University.

1857	**599**	60s. blue and gold	20	15
1858	**599**	1p.20 blue and silver	35	20

600 Virgin and Child

1984. Christmas. Multicoloured.

1859	60s. Type **600**	15	10
1860	1p.20 Holy Family	35	20

601 Manila–Dagupan Steam Locomotive, 1892

1984. Rail Transport. Multicoloured.

No.	Description	Mint	Used
1861	60s. Type **601**	20	15
1862	1p.20 Light Rail Transit eletric train, 1984	20	15
1863	6p. Bicol express, 1955	1·30	60
1864	7p.20 Electric tram, 1905	1·50	75
1865	8p.40 Diesel commuter railcar, 1972	1·60	90
1866	20p. Horse tram, 1898	4·00	1·90

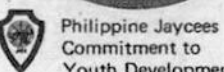

602 Abstract

1984. 10th Anniv of Philippine Jaycees' Ten Outstanding Young Men Awards. Abstracts by Raul Isidro. Multicoloured.

No.	Description	Mint	Used
1867	60s. brown background in circle	15	10
1868	60s. Type **602**	15	10
1869	60s. red background	15	10
1870	60s. blue and purple background	15	10
1871	60s. orange and brown background	15	10
1872	3p. As No. 1867	45	30
1873	3p. Type **602**	45	30
1874	3p. As No. 1869	45	30
1875	3p. As No. 1870	45	30
1876	3p. As No. 1871	45	30

603 Tobacco Plant and Dried Leaf

1985. 25th Anniv of Philippine Virginia Tobacco Administration.

No.	Type	Description	Mint	Used
1877	**603**	60s. multicoloured	15	10
1878	**603**	3p. multicoloured	60	30

1985. Philatelic Week, 1984. Nos. 1848/9 optd Philatelic Week 1984.

No.	Type	Description	Mint	Used
1879	**596**	1p.20 multicoloured	20	15
1880	-	3p. multicoloured	50	35

605 National Research Council Emblem

1985. 5th Pacific Science Association Congress.

No.	Type	Description	Mint	Used
1881	**605**	60s. black, blue and light blue	15	10
1882	**605**	1p.20 black, blue and orange	45	20

606 "Carmona retusa"

1985. Medicinal Plants. Multicoloured.

No.	Description	Mint	Used
1883a	60s. Type **606**	20	10
1884	1p.20 "Orthosiphon aristatus"	20	15
1885	2p.40 "Vitex negundo"	45	30
1886	3p. "Aloe barbadensis"	60	35
1887	3p.60 "Quisqualis indica"	1·30	45
1888	4p.20 "Blumea balsamifera"	90	50

607 "Early Bird" Satellite

1985. 20th Anniv of International Telecommunications Satellite Organization.

No.	Type	Description	Mint	Used
1896	**607**	60s. multicoloured	15	10
1897	**607**	3p. multicoloured	60	30

608 Piebalds

1985. Horses. Multicoloured.

No.	Description	Mint	Used
1898	60s. Type **608**	20	15
1899	1p.20 Palominos	20	15
1900	6p. Bays	1·30	60
1901	7p.20 Browns	1·50	75
1902	8p.40 Greys	1·60	90
1903	20p. Chestnuts	4·00	1·90
MS1904	123×84 mm. 8p.40 ×4, As Nos. 1899/1901 and 1903	8·75	8·75

609 Emblem

1985. 25th Anniv of National Tax Research Centre.

No.	Type	Description	Mint	Used
1905	**609**	60s. multicoloured	15	10

610 Transplanting Rice

1985. 25th Anniv of International Rice Research Institute, Los Banos. Multicoloured.

No.	Description	Mint	Used
1906	60s. Type **610**	15	10
1907	3p. Paddy fields	35	20

611 Image of Holy Child of Cebu

1985. 420th Anniv of Filipino–Spanish Treaty. Mult.

No.	Description	Mint	Used
1908	1p.20 Type **611**	20	15
1909	3p.60 Rajah Tupas and Miguel Lopez de Lagazpi signing treaty	45	15

1985. 10th Anniv of Diplomatic Relations with Chinese People's Republic. No. MS1661 optd 10th ANNIVERSARY PHILIPPINES AND PEOPLE'S REPUBLIC OF CHINA DIPLOMATIC RELATIONS 1975–1985.

No.	Description	Mint	Used
MS1910a	78×78 m. 5p. multicoloured	2·30	2·30

613 Early Anti-TB Label

1985. 75th Anniv of Philippine Tuberculosis Society. Multicoloured.

No.	Description	Mint	Used
1911	60s. Screening for TB, laboratory work, health education and inoculation	15	10
1912	1p.20 Type **613**	30	20

1985. 45th Anniv of Girl Scout Charter. No. 1409 surch 45th ANNIVERSARY GIRL SCOUT CHARTER, emblem and new value.

No.	Type	Description	Mint	Used
1917	**348**	2p.40 on 15s. on 10s. multicoloured	30	20
1918	**348**	4p.20 on 15s. on 10s. multicoloured	60	30
1919	**348**	7p.20 on 15s. on 10s. multicoloured	95	45

616 "Our Lady of Fatima"

1985. Marian Year. 2000th Birth Anniversary of Virgin Mary. Multicoloured.

No.	Description	Mint	Used
1920	1p.20 Type **616**	20	15
1921	2p.40 "Our Lady of Beaterio" (Juan Bueno Silva)	30	15
1922	3p. "Our Lady of Penafrancia"	35	20
1923	3p.60 "Our Lady of Guadalupe"	60	30

617 Family planting Tree

1985. Tree Week. International Year of the Forest.

No.	Type	Description	Mint	Used
1924	**617**	1p.20 multicoloured	20	15

618 Battle of Bessang Pass

1985. 40th Anniv of Bessang Pass Campaign.

No.	Type	Description	Mint	Used
1925	**618**	1p.20 multicoloured	20	15

619 Vicente Orestes Romualdez

1985. Birth Centenary of Vicente Orestes Romualdez (lawyer).

No.	Type	Description	Mint	Used
1926a	**619**	60s. blue	90	15
1927a	**619**	2p. mauve	1·20	35

620 Fishing

1985. International Youth Year. Children's Paintings. Multicoloured.

No.	Description	Mint	Used
1928	2p.40 Type **620**	30	15
1929	3p.60 Picnic	50	15

621 Banawe Rice Terraces

1985. World Tourism Organization Congress, Sofia, Bulgaria.

No.	Type	Description	Mint	Used
1930	**621**	2p.40 multicoloured	30	20

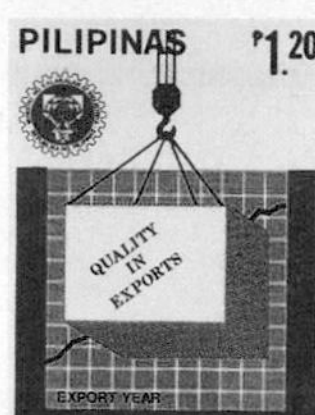

622 Export Graph and Crane lifting Crate

1985. Export Promotion Year.

No.	Type	Description	Mint	Used
1931	**622**	1p.20 multicoloured	20	15

1985. No. 1815 surch P360.

No.	Description	Mint	Used
1932	3p.60 on 4p.20 purple	75	35

624 Emblem and Dove with Olive Branch

1985. 40th Anniv of U.N.O.

No.	Type	Description	Mint	Used
1933	**624**	3p.60 multicoloured	45	20

625 Martin M-130 Flying Boat "China Clipper"

1985. 50th Anniv of First Trans-Pacific Commercial Flight (San Francisco–Manila). Multicoloured.

No.	Description	Mint	Used
1934	3p. Type **625**	35	20
1935	3p.60 Route map, "China Clipper" and anniversary emblem	50	20

1985. Philatelic Week. Nos. 1863/4 surch PHILATELIC WEEK 1985, No. 1937 further optd AIRMAIL.

No.	Description	Mint	Used
1936	60s. on 6p. mult (postage)	15	10
1937	3p. on 7p.20 mult (air)	60	30

627 Bible and Churches

1985. National Bible Week.

No.	Type	Description	Mint	Used
1938	**627**	60s. multicoloured	15	10
1939	**627**	3p. multicoloured	60	30

628 Panuluyan (enactment of search for an inn)

1985. Christmas. Multicoloured.

No.	Description	Mint	Used
1940	60s. Type **628**	15	10
1941	3p. Pagdalaw (nativity)	60	30

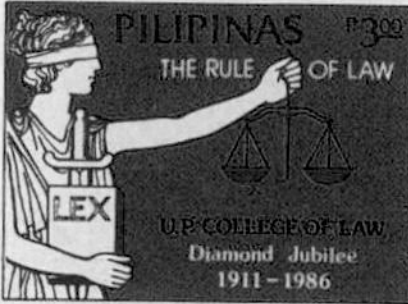

629 Justice holding Scales

1986. 75th Anniv of College of Law.

No.	Type	Description	Mint	Used
1942	**629**	60s. mauve and black	15	10
1943	**629**	3p. green, purple & black	60	30

See also No. 2009.

630 Rizal and "Noli Me Tangere"

1986. Centenary of Publication of "Noli Me Tangere" (Jose Rizal's first book).

1944	**630**	60s. violet	10	10
1945	-	1p.20 green	30	20
1946	-	3p.60 brown	65	30

DESIGNS: 1p.20, 3p.60, Rizal, "To the Flowers of Heidelberg" (poem) and Heidelberg University.

631 Douglas DC-3, 1946

1986. 45th Anniv of Philippine Airlines. Each red, black and blue.

1947		60s. Type **631**	15	15
1948		60s. Douglas DC-4 Skymaster, 1946	15	15
1949		60s. Douglas DC-6, 1948	15	15
1950		60s. Vickers Viscount 784, 1957	15	15
1951		2p.40 Fokker F.27 Friendship, 1960	50	20
1952		2p.40 Douglas DC-8-50, 1962	80	35
1953		2p.40 B.A.C. One Eleven 500, 1964	50	20
1954		2p.40 Douglas DC-10-30, 1974	50	20
1955		3p.60 Beech 18, 1941	75	35
1956		3p.60 Boeing 747-200, 1980	75	35

See also No. 2013.

632 Oil Refinery, Manila Bay

1986. 25th Anniv of Bataan Refinery Corporation.

1957	**632**	60s. silver and green	15	10
1958	-	3p. silver and blue	50	20

DESIGN—HORIZ: 3p. Refinery (different).

633 Emblem

1986. "Expo 86" World's Fair, Vancouver.

1959	**633**	60s. multicoloured	15	10
1960	**633**	3p. multicoloured	60	30

634 Emblem and Industrial and Agricultural Symbols

1986. 25th Anniv of Asian Productivity Organization.

1961	**634**	60s. black, green & orge	15	10
1962	**634**	3p. black, green & orange	60	30
1963	**634**	3p. brown (30×22 mm)	65	30

635 1906 2c. Stamp

1986. "Ameripex 86" Int Stamp Exhibition, Chicago.

1964	**635**	60s. green, black & yellow	15	10
1965	-	3p. bistre, black and green	60	30

DESIGN: 3p. 1935 20c. stamp.
See also No. 2006.

637 Corazon Aquino, Salvador Laurel and Hands

1986. "People Power". Multicoloured.

1966		60s. Type **637**	15	10
1967		1p.20 Radio antennae, helicopter and people	20	15
1968		2p.40 Religious procession	45	20
1969		3p. Crowds around soldiers in tanks	50	20
MS1970		76×76 mm. 7p.20, Crowd, Pres. Aquino and Vice-Pres. Laurel (42×32 mm). Imperf	2·20	2·20

638 Monument and Paco and Taft Schools

1986. 75th Anniv of First La Salle School in Philippines.

1971	**638**	60s. black, lilac and green	15	15
1972	-	2p.40 black, blue & grn	45	20
1973	-	3p. black, yellow & green	50	20
MS1974		75×75 mm. 7p.20, black and emerald. Imperf	4·50	4·50

DESIGNS: 2p.40, St. Miguel Febres Cordero and Paco school; 3p. St. Benilde and Taft school; 7p.20, Founding brothers of Paco school.

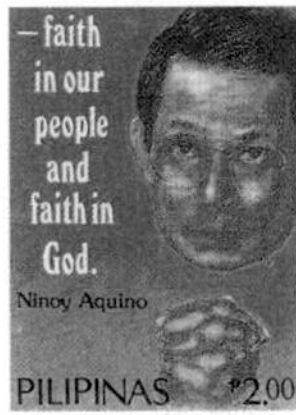

639 Aquino praying

1986. 3rd Death Anniv of Benigno S. Aquino, jun.

1975		60s. green	15	15
1976	**639**	2p. multicoloured	30	15
1977	-	3p.60 multicoloured	65	30
MS1978		75×75 mm. 10p. multicoloured. Imperf	2·50	2·50

DESIGNS: 27×36 mm (as T **526**—60s. Aquino. HORIZ (as T **639**)—3p.60 Aquino (different); 10p. Crowd and Aquino.
See also No. 2007.

640 "Vanda sanderiana"

1986. Orchids. Multicoloured.

1979		60s. Type **640**	15	10
1980		1p.20 "Epigeneium lyonii"	50	15
1981		2p.40 "Paphiopedilum philippinense"	90	20
1982		3p. "Amesiella philippinense"	1·10	20

641 "Christ carrying the Cross"

1986. 400th Anniv of Quiapo District.

1983	**641**	60s. red, black and mauve	15	10
1984	-	3p.60 blue, black & grn	60	30

DESIGN—HORIZ: 3p.60, Quiapo Church.

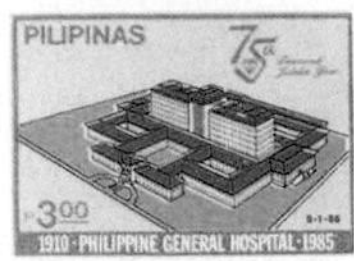

642 Hospital

1986. 75th Anniv of Philippine General Hospital.

1985	**642**	60s. multicoloured	15	15
1986	**642**	3p. multicoloured	50	20
2012	**642**	5p. brown	1·10	15

643 Comet and Earth

1986. Appearance of Halley's Comet. Multicoloured.

1987		60s. Type **643**	10	10
1988		2p.40 Comet, Moon and Earth	45	30

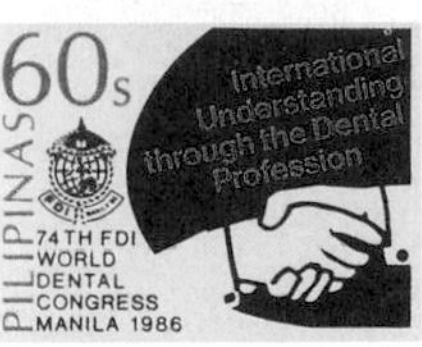

644 Handshake

1986. 74th International Dental Federation Congress, Manila. Multicoloured.

1989		60s. Type **644**	15	10
1990		3p. Jeepney, Manila	75	35

See also Nos. 2008 and 2011.

645 Emblem

1986. 75th Anniv of Manila Young Men's Christian Association.

1991	**645**	2p. blue	45	15
1992	**645**	3p.60 red	65	35
2058	**645**	4p. blue	70	45

646 Old and New Buildings

1986. 85th Anniv of Philippine Normal College.

1993	-	60s. multicoloured	15	10
1994	**646**	3p.60 yellow, brown & bl	90	45

DESIGN: 60s. Old and new buildings (different).

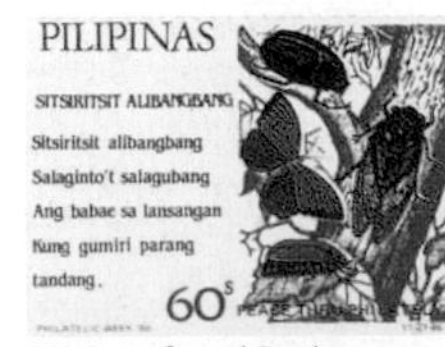

647 Butterfly and Beetles

1986. Philatelic Week and International Peace Year.

1995	**647**	60s. multicoloured	15	10
1996	-	1p. blue and black	20	15
1997	-	3p. multicoloured	75	35

DESIGNS—VERT: 1p. Peace Year emblem. HORIZ: 3p. Dragonflies.

648 Mother and Child

1986. Christmas. Multicoloured.

1998		60s. Type **648**	15	10
1999		60s. Couple with child and cow	15	10
2000		60s. Mother and child with doves	15	10
2001		1p. Mother and child receiving gifts (horiz)	30	15
2002		1p. Mother and child beneath arch (horiz)	30	15
2003		1p. Madonna and shepherd adoring child (horiz)	30	15
2004		1p. Shepherds and animals around child in manger (horiz)	30	15

1987. No. 1944 surch P100.

2005	**630**	1p. on 60s. violet	15	10

1987. As previous issues but smaller, 22×30 mm, 30×22 mm or 32×22 mm (5p.50), and values and colours changed.

2006	-	75s. green (As No. 1965)	15	10
2007	-	1p. blue (As No. 1975)	20	15
2008	**644**	3p.25 green	75	15
2009	**629**	3p.50 brown	80	15
2011	-	4p.75 green (As No. 1990)	1·10	15
2013	-	5p.50 blue (As No. 1956)	1·10	20

650 Manila Hotel, 1912

1987. 75th Anniv of Manila Hotel.

2014	**650**	1p. bistre and black	20	15
2015	-	4p. multicoloured	75	35
2016	-	4p.75 multicoloured	90	45
2017	-	5p.50 multicoloured	1·10	50

DESIGNS: 4p. Hotel; 4p.75, Lobby; 5p.50, Staff in ante-lobby.

651 Emblem

1987. 50th Anniv of International Eucharistic Congress, Manila. Multicoloured.

2018		75s. Type **651**	15	10
2019		1p. Emblem (different) (horiz)	30	15

652 Pres. Cory Aquino taking Oath

1987. Ratification of New Constitution.

2020	**652**	1p. multicoloured	20	15
2021	-	5p.50 blue and brown	1·20	60
2060	-	5p.50 green and brown (22×31 mm)	80	15

DESIGN: 5p.50, Constitution on open book and dove.

653 Dr. Jose P. Laurel (founder) and Tower

1987. 35th Anniv of Lyceum.

2022	**653**	1p. multicoloured	20	10
2023	**653**	2p. multicoloured	60	15

654 City Seal, Man with Philippine Eagle and Woman with Fruit

1987. 50th Anniv of Davao City.

2024	**654**	1p. multicoloured	15	10

655 Salary and Policy Loans

1987. 50th Anniv of Government Service Insurance System. Multicoloured.

2025	1p. Type **655**	20	15
2026	1p.25 Disability and medicare	20	15
2027	2p. Retirement benefits	35	20
2028	3p.50 Survivorship benefits	65	35

656 Emblem and People in Hand

1987. 50th Anniv of Salvation Army in Philippines.

2029	**656**	1p. multicoloured	30	10

657 Woman, Ballot Box and Map

1987. 50th Anniv of League of Women Voters.

2030	**657**	1p. blue and mauve	15	10

1987. As T 526.

2031	1p. green	15	10
2032	1p. blue	15	10
2033	1p. red	15	10
2034	1p. purple and red	15	10

DESIGNS: No. 2031, Gen. Vicente Lukban; 2032, Wenceslao Q. Vinzons; 2033, Brigadier-General Mateo M. Capinpin; 2034, Jesus Balmori.

658 Map and Flags as Leaves

1987. 20th Anniv of Association of South-East Asian Nations.

2035	**658**	1p. multicoloured	30	10

659 Man with Outstretched Arm

1987. Exports.

2036	**659**	1p. multicoloured	15	10
2037	-	2p. green, yellow & brn	30	15
2059	-	4p.75 blue and black	65	15

DESIGN: 2p., 4p.75, Man, cogwheel and factory.

660 Nuns, People and Crucifix within Flaming Heart

1967. 125th Anniv of Daughters of Charity in the Philippines.

2038	**660**	1p. blue, red and black	20	10

661 Statue and Stained Glass Window

1987. Canonization of Blessed Lorenzo Ruiz de Manila (first Filipino saint). Multicoloured.

2039	1p. Type **661**	20	15
2040	5p.50 Lorenzo Ruiz praying before execution	1·30	35
MS2041	56×56 mm. 8p. As No. 2040. Imperf	1·80	1·80

1987. No. 2012 surch P4.75.

2042	**642**	4p.75 on 5p. brown	95	15

663 Nun and Emblem

1987. 75th Anniv of Good Shepherd Sisters in Philippines.

2043	**663**	1p. multicoloured	20	10

664 Founders

1987. 50th Anniv of Philippines Boy Scouts.

2044	**664**	1p. multicoloured	20	10

665 Family with Stamp Album

1987. 50th Anniv of Philippine Philatelic Club.

2045	**665**	1p. multicoloured	20	10

666 Monks, Church and Wrecked Galleon

1987. 400th Anniv of Dominican Order in Philippines.

2046	**666**	1p. black, blue and orange	15	15
2047	-	4p.75 multicoloured	80	30
2048	-	5p.50 multicoloured	1·30	45

DESIGNS: 4p.75, J. A. Jeronimo Guerrero, Diego de Sta. Maria and Letran Dominican college; 5p.50, Pope and monks.

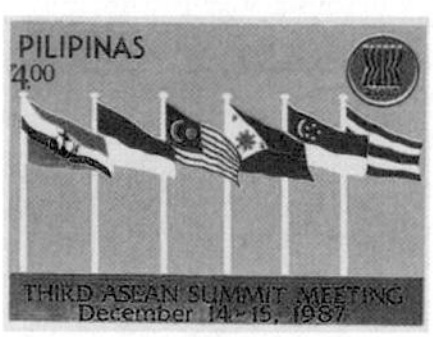

667 Flags

1987. 3rd Association of South-east Asian Nations Summit Meeting.

2049	**667**	4p. multicoloured	95	10

668 Dove with Letter

1987. Christmas. Multicoloured.

2050	1p. Type **668**	15	15
2051	1p. People and star decoration	15	15
2052	4p. Crowd going to church	80	20
2053	4p.75 Mother and children exchanging gifts	80	30
2054	5p.50 Children and bamboo cannons	1·20	30
2055	8p. Children at table bearing festive fare	1·50	50
2056	9p.50 Woman at table	1·60	65
2057	11p. Woman having Christmas meal	1·90	65

669 Emblem, Headquarters and Dr. Rizal

1987. 75th Anniv of Grand Lodge of Philippine Masons.

2061	**669**	1p. multicoloured	30	10

670 Foodstuffs in Split Globe

1987. 40th Anniv of U.N.O. Multicoloured.

2062	1p. Type **670** (International Fund for Agricultural Development)	20	15
2063	1p. Means of transport and communications (Asian and Pacific Transport and Communications Decade)	20	15
2064	1p. People and hands holding houses (International Year of Shelter for the Homeless)	20	15
2065	1p. Happy children playing musical instruments (World Health Day: UNICEF child vaccination campaign)	20	15

671 Official Seals and Gavel

1988. Opening Session of 1987 Congress. Mult.

2066	1p. Type **671**	20	10
2067	5p.50 Congress in session and gavel (horiz)	1·40	45

672 Children and Bosco

1988. Death Centenary of St. John Bosco (founder of Salesian Brothers).

2068	**672**	1p. multicoloured	15	10
2069	**672**	5p.50 multicoloured	1·20	45

673 Emblem

1988. Buy Philippine-Made Movement Month.

2070	**673**	1p. multicoloured	15	15

1988. Various stamps surch P 3.00.

2071	-	3p. on 3p.60 brown (No. 1946)	50	20
2072	**645**	3p. on 3p.60 red	60	20
2073	-	3p. on 3p.60 mult (No. 1977)	75	30
2074	-	3p. on 3p.60 blue, black and green (No. 1984)	50	20
2075	**646**	3p. on 3p.60 yellow, brown and blue	75	30

675 Envelope with Coded Addresses

1988. Postal Codes.

2076	**675**	60s. multicoloured	15	10
2077	**675**	1p. multicoloured	20	15

676 "Vesbius purpureus" (soldier bug)

1988. Insect Predators. Multicoloured.

2078	1p. Type **676**	15	10
2079	5p.50 "Campsomeris aurulenta" (dagger wasp)	1·10	45

677 Solar Eclipse

1988

2080	**677**	1p. multicoloured	15	10
2081	**677**	5p.50 multicoloured	1·20	45

678 Teodoro

1988. 101st Birth Anniv of Toribio Teodoro (industrialist).

2082	**678**	1p. cinnamon, brn & red	15	10
2083	**678**	1p.20 blue, brown & red	20	15

679 Emblem

1988. 75th Anniv of College of Holy Spirit.

2084	**679**	1p. brown, gold & black	15	10
2085	-	4p. brown, green & black	80	30

DESIGN: 4p. Arnold Janssen (founder) and Sister Edelwina (director, 1920–47).

680 Emblem

1988. Newly Restored Democracies International Conference.

2086	**680**	4p. blue, ultram & blk	95	30

681 Luna and Hidalgo

1988. National Juan Luna and Felix Resurreccion Hidalgo Memorial Exhibition.

2087	**681**	1p. black, yellow & brn	15	10
2088	**681**	5p.50 black, cinnamon and brown	1·00	35

682 Magat Dam, Ramon, Isabela

1988. 25th Anniv of National Irrigation Administration.

2089	**682**	1p. multicoloured	1·10	1·10
2090	**682**	5p.50 multicoloured	1·20	50

683 Scuba Diving, Siquijor

1988. Olympic Games, Seoul (1st issue). Multicoloured. Perf or imperf.

2091	1p. Type **683**	15	15
2092	1p.20 Big game fishing, Aparri, Cagayan	20	15
2093	4p. Yachting, Manila Central	75	45
2094	5p.50 Mountain climbing, Mt. Apo, Davao	1·10	65
2095	8p. Golfing, Cebu City	1·50	95
2096	11p. Cycling (Tour of Mindanao), Marawi City	2·20	1·30

See also Nos. 2113/18.

684 Headquarters, Plaza Santa Cruz, Manila

1988. Banking Anniversaries. Multicoloured.

2097	1p. Type **684** (50th anniv of Philippine International Commercial Bank)	15	15
2098	1p. Family looking at factory and countryside (25th anniv of Land Bank)	15	15
2099	5p.50 Type **684**	95	50
2100	5p.50 As No. 2098	95	50

1988. Various stamps surch.

2101	1p.90 on 2p.40 mult (No. 1968)	45	15
2102	1p.90 on 2p.40 black, blue and green (No. 1972)	45	15
2103	1p.90 on 2p.40 mult (No. 1981)	45	15
2104	1p.90 on 2p.40 mult (No. 1988)	45	15

686 Balagtas

1988. Birth Bicentenary of Francisco Balagtas Baltasco (writer). Each green, brown and yellow.

2105	1p. Type **686**	15	10
2106	1p. As Type **686** but details reversed	15	10

687 Hospital

1988. 50th Anniv of Quezon Institute (tuberculosis hospital).

2107	**687**	1p. multicoloured	15	15
2108	**687**	5p.50 multicoloured	1·00	60

688 Brown Mushroom

1988. Fungi. Multicoloured.

2109	60s. Type **688**	15	10
2110	1p. Rat's ear fungus	20	15
2111	2p. Abalone mushroom	35	20
2112	4p. Straw mushroom	90	45

689 Archery

1988. Olympic Games, Seoul (2nd issue). Multicoloured. Perf or imperf.

2113	1p. Type **689**	20	15
2114	1p.20 Tennis	20	15
2115	4p. Boxing	60	30
2116	5p.50 Athletics	90	45
2117	8p. Swimming	1·30	60
2118	11p. Cycling	1·80	95
MS2119	101×76 mm. 5p.50, Weightlifting; 5p.50, Basketball; 5p.50, Judo; 5p.50, Shooting. Imperf	4·50	4·50

690 Department of Justice

1988. Law and Justice Week.

2120	**690**	1p. multicoloured	15	10

691 Red Cross Work

1988. 125th Anniv of Red Cross.

2121	**691**	1p. multicoloured	15	15
2122	**691**	5p.50 multicoloured	1·00	50

692 Girl and Boy

1988. 50th Anniv of Christian Children's Fund.

2123	**692**	1p. multicoloured	15	10

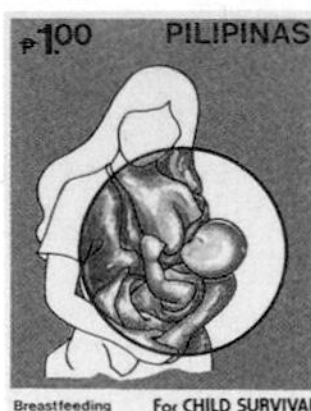

693 Map and Shrimps

1988. 50th Anniv of Bacolod City Charter.

2124	**693**	1p. multicoloured	15	10

694 Breastfeeding

1988. Child Survival Campaign. Multicoloured.

2125	1p. Type **694**	15	10
2126	1p. Growth monitoring	15	10
2127	1p. Immunization	15	10
2128	1p. Oral rehydration	15	10
2129	1p. Access for the disabled (U.N. Decade of Disabled Persons)	15	10

695 A. Aragon Quezon

1988. Birth Centenary of Aurora Aragon Quezon.

2130	**695**	1p. multicoloured	15	10
2131	**695**	5p.50 multicoloured	90	60

696 Post Office

1988. Philatelic Week. Multicoloured.

2132	1p. Type **696** (inscr "1938")	20	15
2132b	1p. Type **696** (inscr "1988")	35	15
2133	1p. Stamp counter	20	15
2134	1p. Fern and stamp displays	20	15
2135	1p. People looking at stamp displays	20	15

697 Sampaloc Branch Transmitter

1988. 10 Years of Technological Improvements by Philippine Long Distance Telephone Company.

2136	**697**	1p. multicoloured	15	10

698 Clasped Hands and Dove

1988. Christmas. Multicoloured.

2137	75s. Type **698**	15	15
2138	1p. Children making decorations (horiz)	15	15
2139	2p. Man carrying decorations on yoke (horiz)	30	20
2140	3p.50 Christmas tree	60	30
2141	4p.75 Candle and stars	80	35
2142	5p.50 Reflection of star forming heart (horiz)	95	45

699 Crowd with Banners

1988. Commission on Human Rights (2143) and 40th Anniv of Universal Declaration of Human Rights (2144). Multicoloured.

2143	1p. Type **699**	15	10
2144	1p. Doves escaping from cage	15	10

700 Church, 1776

1988. 400th Anniv of Malate. Multicoloured.

2145	1p. Type **700**	15	10
2146	1p. Our Lady of Remedies Church anniversary emblem and statue of Virgin (Eduardo Castrillo)	15	10
2147	1p. Church, 1880	15	10
2148	1p. Church, 1988	15	10

PILIPINAS P1.00
UST 1938-1988 GRADUATE SCHOOL 50th ANNIVERSARY

701 Statue and School

1988. 50th Anniv of University of Santo Tomas Graduate School.

2149	**701**	1p. multicoloured	15	10

702 Order's Activities

1989. 50th Anniv of Oblates of Mary Immaculate.

2150	**702**	1p. multicoloured	15	10

703 Miguel Ver (first leader)

1989. 47th Anniv of Recognition of Hunters ROTC Guerrilla Unit (formed by Military Academy and University students). Mult.

2151	1p. Type **703**	15	10
2152	1p. Eleuterio Adevoso (leader after Ver's death)	15	10

704 Foodstuffs and Paulino Santos

1989. 50th Anniv of General Santos City.

2153	**704**	1p. multicoloured	15	10

705 Sinulog

1989. "Fiesta Islands '89" (1st series). Mult.

2154	4p.75 Type **705**	95	35
2155	5p.50 Cenaculo (Lenten festival)	95	45
2156	6p.25 Iloilo Paraw Regatta	95	65

See also Nos. 2169/71, 2177/9, 2194/6 and 2210.

706 Tomas Mapua

1989. Birth Centenaries. Multicoloured.

2157	1p. Type **706**	15	10
2158	1p. Camilo Osias	15	10
2159	1p. Dr. Olivia Salamanca	15	10
2160	1p. Dr. Francisco Santiago	15	10
2161	1p. Leandro Fernandez	15	10

707 Adventure Pool

1989. 26th International Federation of Landscape Architects World Congress, Manila. Mult.

2162	1p. Type **707**	15	10
2163	1p. Paco Park	15	10
2164	1p. Street improvements in Malacanang area	15	10
2165	1p. Erosion control on upland farm	15	10

708 Palawan Peacock- Pheasant

1989. Environment Month. Multicoloured.

2166	1p. Type **708**	15	10
2167	1p. Palawan bear cat	15	10

709 Entrance and Statue of Justice

1989. Supreme Court.

2168	**709**	1p. multicoloured	30	15

1989. "Fiesta Islands '89" (2nd series). As T 705. Multicoloured.

2169	60s. Turumba	15	10
2170	75s. Pahiyas	15	15
2171	3p.50 Independence Day	50	30

710 Birds, Quill, "Noli Me Tangere" and Flags

1989. Bicentenary of French Revolution and Decade of Philippine Nationalism.

2172	**710**	1p. multicoloured	15	15
2173	**710**	5p.50 multicoloured	90	60

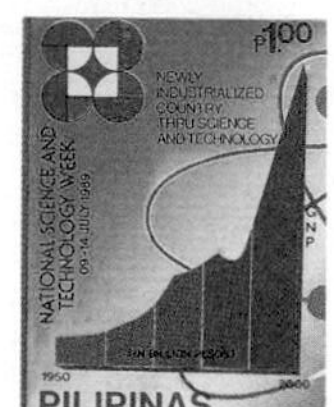

711 Graph

1989. National Science and Technology Week. Multicoloured.

2174	1p. Type **711**	15	10
2175	1p. "Man" (Leonardo da Vinci) and emblem of Philippine Science High School)	15	10

1989. New Constitution stamp of 1987 surch P4 75.

2176	4p.75 on 5p.50 green and brown (2060)	75	50

1989. "Fiesta Island 89" (3rd series). As T 705.

2177	1p. Pagoda Sa Wawa (carnival float)	15	15
2178	4p.75 Cagayan de Oro Fiesta	80	35
2179	5p.50 Penafrancia Festival	95	45

713 Monument, Flag, Civilian and Soldier

1989. 50th Anniv of National Defence Department.

2180	**713**	1p. multicoloured	20	10

714 Map and Satellite

1989. 10th Anniv of Asia–Pacific Telecommunity.

2181	**714**	1p. multicoloured	30	15

715 Annunciation

1989. Christmas. Multicoloured.

2182	60s. Type **715**	10	10
2183	75s. Mary and Elizabeth	15	10
2184	1p. Mary and Joseph travelling to Bethlehem	15	10
2185	2p. Search for an inn	30	20
2186	4p. Magi and star	65	45
2187	4p.75 Adoration of shepherds	75	50

716 Lighthouse, Liner and Lifebelt

1989. International Maritime Organization.

2188	**716**	1p. multicoloured	20	10

717 Spanish Philippines 1854 5c. and Revolutionary Govt 1898 2c. Stamps

1989. "World Stamp Expo '89" International Stamp Exhibition, Washington D.C. Multicoloured.

2189	1p. Type **717**	15	10
2190	4p. U.S. Administration 1899 50c. and Commonwealth 1935 6c. stamps	75	50
2191	5p.50 Japanese Occupation 1942 2c. and Republic 1946 6c. stamps	90	60

718 Teacher using Stamp as Teaching Aid

1989. Philatelic Week. Philately in the Classroom. Multicoloured.

2192	1p. Type **718**	15	10
2193	1p. Children working with stamps	15	10

1989. "Fiesta Islands '89" (4th series). As T 705.

2194	1p. Masked festival, Negros	15	15
2195	4p.75 Grand Canao, Baguio	80	35
2196	5p.50 Fireworks	95	45

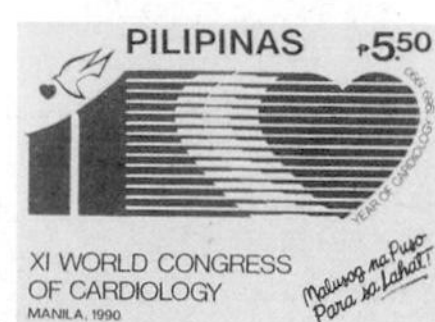

719 Heart

1990. 11th World Cardiology Congress, Manila.

2197	**719**	5p.50 red, blue and black	95	45

720 Glasses of Beer

1990. Centenary of San Miguel Brewery.

2198	**720**	1p. multicoloured	15	15
2199	**720**	5p.50 multicoloured	95	45

721 Houses and Family

1990. Population and Housing Census. Multicoloured, colours of houses given.

2200	**721**	1p. blue	15	10
2201	**721**	1p. pink	15	10

722 Scouts

1990. 50th Anniv of Philippine Girl Scouts.

2202	**722**	1p. multicoloured	35	10
2203	**722**	1p.20 multicoloured	35	15

723 Claro Recto (politician)

1990. Birth Centenaries. Multicoloured.

2204	1p. Type **723**	15	10
2205	1p. Manuel Bernabe (poet)	15	10
2206	1p. Guillermo Tolentino (sculptor)	15	10
2207	1p. Elpidio Quirino (President 1948–53)	15	10
2208	1p. Dr. Bienvenido Gonzalez (University President, 1937–51)	15	10

724 Badge and Globe

1990. 50th Anniv of Legion of Mary.

2209	**724**	1p. multicoloured	15	10

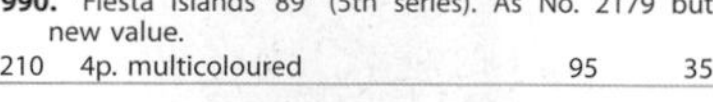

1990. "Fiesta Islands '89" (5th series). As No. 2179 but new value.

2210	4p. multicoloured	95	35

725 Torch

1990. 20th Anniv of Asian–Pacific Postal Training Centre.

2211	**725**	1p. multicoloured	15	15
2212	**725**	4p. multicoloured	65	35

726 Catechism Class

1990. National Catechetical Year.

2213	**726**	1p. multicoloured	15	10
2214	**726**	3p.50 multicoloured	60	35

727 Waling Waling Flowers

1990. 29th Orient and South-East Asian Lions Forum, Manila. Multicoloured.

2215	1p. Type **727**	20	15
2216	4p. Sampaguita flowers	65	30

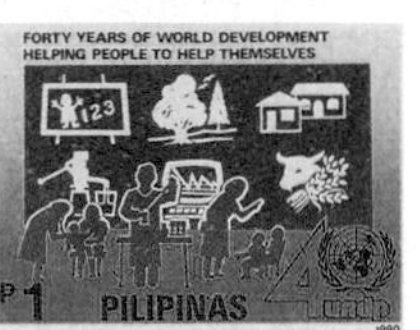

728 Areas for Improvement

1990. 40th Anniv of United Nations Development Programme.

2217	**728**	1p. multicoloured	15	10
2218	**728**	5p.50 multicoloured	90	60

729 Letters of Alphabet

1990. International Literacy Year.

2219	**729**	1p. green, orange & black	15	10
2220	**729**	5p.50 green, yellow & blk	90	60

730 "Laughter" (A. Magsaysay-Ho)

1990. Philatelic Week. Multicoloured.

2221	1p. "Family" (F. Amorsolo) (horiz)	20	15
2222	4p.75 "The Builders" (V. Edades)	1·20	60
2223	5p.50 Type **730**	1·40	75

731 Star

1990. Christmas. Multicoloured.

2224	1p. Type **731**	15	10
2225	1p. Stars within stars (blue background)	15	10
2226	1p. Red and white star	15	10
2227	1p. Gold and red star (green background)	15	10
2228	5p.50 Geometric star (Paskuhan Village, San Fernando)	15	10

732 Figures

1990. International White Cane Safety Day.

2229	**732**	1p. black, yellow and blue	20	15

733 La Solidaridad in 1990 and 1890 and Statue of Rizal

1990. Centenary of Publication of "Filipinas Dentro de Cien Anos" by Jose Rizal.

2230	**733**	1p. multicoloured	20	15

734 Crowd before Figure of Christ

1991. 2nd Plenary Council of the Philippines.

2231	**734**	1p. multicoloured	20	15

735 Tailplane and Stewardess

1991. 50th Anniv of Philippine Airlines.

2232	**735**	1p. mult (postage)	15	15
2233	**735**	5p.50 multicoloured (air)	95	60

736 Gardenia

1991. Flowers. Multicoloured.

2234	60s. Type **736**	10	10
2235	75s. Yellow bell	10	10
2236	1p. Yellow plumeria	15	15
2237	1p. Red plumeria	15	15
2238	1p. Pink plumeria	15	15
2239	1p. White plumeria	15	15
2475	1p. Yellow bell	10	10
2240	1p.20 Nerium	15	10
2241	3p.25 Ylang-ylang	60	35
2242	4p. Pink ixora	60	35
2243	4p. White ixora	60	35
2244	4p. Yellow ixora	60	35
2245	4p. Red ixora	60	35
2246	4p.75 Orange bougainvillea	65	45
2247	4p.75 Purple bougainvillea	65	45
2248	4p.75 White bougainvillea	65	45
2249	4p.75 Red bougainvillea	65	45
2250	5p. Canna	75	45
2251	5p.50 Red hibiscus	95	65
2252	5p.50 Yellow hibiscus	95	65
2253	5p.50 White hibiscus	95	65
2254	5p.50 Pink hibiscus	95	65

See also Nos. 2322/41.

737 Sheepshank

1991. 12th Asia–Pacific and 9th National Boy Scouts Jamboree. Multicoloured.

2255	1p. Reef knot	20	15
2256	4p. Type **737**	60	30
2257	4p.75 Granny knot	65	30
MS2258	88×82 mm. Nos. 2255/7. Imperf (sold at 16p.50)	3·00	3·00

738 Jorge Vargas

1991. Birth Centenaries. Multicoloured.

2259	1p. Type **738**	15	10
2260	1p. Ricardo Paras	15	10
2261	1p. Jose Laurel	15	10
2262	1p. Vicente Fabella	15	10
2263	1p. Maximo Kalaw	15	10

739 "Antipolo" (Carlos Francisco) and Score

1991. 400th Anniv of Antipolo.

2264	**739**	1p. multicoloured	20	15

740 Philippine Eagle

1991. Endangered Species. The Philippine Eagle. Multicoloured.

2265	1p. Type **740**	45	30
2266	4p.75 Eagle on branch	1·90	1·30
2267	5p.50 Eagle in flight	2·20	1·50
2268	8p. Eagle feeding chick	3·25	2·20

741 Emblem

1991. Centenary of Founding of Society of Lawyers (from 1904 Philippine Bar Association).

2269	**741**	1p. multicoloured	20	15

742 Flags and Induction Ceremony

1991. 50th Anniv of Induction of Philippine Reservists into United States Army Forces in the Far East. Background colours given where necessary in brackets. (a) T742.

2270	**742**	1p. multicoloured	20	15
MS2271		82×88 mm. **742** 16p. multicoloured. Imperf	2·75	2·75

743 First Regular Division Emblem

(b) Showing Division emblems.

2272	**743**	2p. red, black and yellow	20	15
2273	-	2p. multicoloured (yellow) (2nd Regular)	20	15
2274	-	2p. multicoloured (yellow) (11th)	20	15
2275	-	2p. blue, yellow and black (yellow) (21st)	20	15
2276	**743**	2p. red and black	20	15
2277	-	2p. black, blue and red (2nd Regular)	20	15
2278	-	2p. multicoloured (white) (11th)	20	15
2279	-	2p. blue, yellow and black (white) (21st)	20	15
2280	-	2p. multicoloured (yellow) (31st)	20	15
2281	-	2p. multicoloured (yellow) (41st)	20	15
2282	-	2p. multicoloured (yellow) (51st)	20	15
2283	-	2p. multicoloured (yellow) (61st)	20	15
2284	-	2p. red, blue and black (31st)	20	15
2285	-	2p. multicoloured (white) (41st)	20	15
2286	-	2p. blue, black and red (51st)	20	15
2287	-	2p. multicoloured (white) (61st)	20	15
2288	-	2p. multicoloured (yellow) (71st)	20	15
2289	-	2p. multicoloured (yellow) (81st)	20	15
2290	-	2p. multicoloured (yellow) (91st)	20	15
2291	-	2p. multicoloured (yellow) (101st)	20	15
2292	-	2p. multicoloured (white) (71st)	20	15
2293	-	2p. multicoloured (white) (81st)	20	15
2294	-	2p. multicoloured (white) (91st)	20	15
2295	-	2p. multicoloured (white) (101st)	20	15
2296	-	2p. blue, black and yellow (Bataan Force)	20	15
2297	-	2p. yellow, red and black (yellow) (Philippine)	20	15
2298	-	2p. multicoloured (yellow) (Air Corps)	20	15
2299	-	2p. black, blue and yellow (Offshore Patrol)	20	15
2300	-	2p. blue and black (Bataan Force)	20	15
2301	-	2p. yellow, red and black (white) (Philippine)	20	15
2302	-	2p. multicoloured (white) (Air Corps)	20	15
2303	-	2p. black and blue (Offshore Patrol)	20	15

Nos. 2272/2303 (all as T **743**) show divisional emblems.

744 Basilio

1991. Centenary of Publication of "El Filibusterismo" by Jose Rizal. Characters from the novel. Each red, blue and black.

2304	1p. Type **744**	15	15
2305	1p. Simoun	15	15
2306	1p. Father Florentino	15	15
2307	1p. Juli	15	15

745 St. John of the Cross

1991. 400th Death of St. John of the Cross. Multicoloured.

2308 Type **745** 20 15

MS2309 59×59 mm. 16p. St. John praying, signature and Type **745**. Imperf 4·50 4·50

746 Faces (Children's Fund)

1991. United Nations Agencies.

2310 **746** 1p. multicoloured 15 15

2311 - 4p. multicoloured 60 20

2312 - 5p.50 black, red and blue 80 35

DESIGNS: 4p. Hands supporting boatload of people (High Commissioner for Refugees); 5p.50, 1951 15c. and 1954 3c. U.N. stamps (40th anniv of Postal Administration).

747 "Bayanihan" (Carlos "Botong" Francisco)

1991. Philatelic Week. Multicoloured.

2313 2p. Type **747** 30 15

2314 7p. "Sari-Sari Vendor" (Mauro Malang Santos) 1·00 50

2315 8p. "Give Us This Day" (Vicente Manansala) 1·20 60

748 Gymnastics

1991. 16th South-East Asian Games, Manila. Multicoloured.

2316 2p. Type **748** 30 15

2317 2p. Gymnastics (emblem at bottom) 30 15

2318 6p. Arnis (martial arts) (emblem at left) (vert) 65 15

2319 6p. Arnis (emblem at right) (vert) 65 15

MS2320 Two sheets. (a) 90×60 mm. Nos. 2318/19. Imperf; (b) 65×98 mm. Nos. 2316/19 3·00 3·00

Designs of the same value were issued together, se-tenant, each pair forming a composite design.

1991. 1st Philippine Philatelic Convention, Manila. No. MS1698 surch p4.

MS2321 4p. on 3p.20 purple and black 1·10 1·10

1991. Flowers. As T 736. Multicoloured.

2322 1p.50 Type **736** 15 15

2323 2p. Yellow plumeria 20 20

2324 2p. Red plumeria 20 20

2325 2p. Pink plumeria 20 20

2326 2p. White plumeria 20 20

2327 3p. Nerium 30 30

2328 5p. Ylang-ylang 50 50

2329 6p. Pink ixora 60 60

2330 6p. White ixora 60 60

2331 6p. Yellow ixora 60 60

2332 6p. Red ixora 75 75

2333 7p. Orange bougainvillea 75 75

2334 7p. Purple bougainvillea 75 75

2335 7p. White bougainvillea 75 75

2336 7p. Red bougainvillea 80 80

2337 8p. Red hibiscus 80 80

2338 8p. Yellow hibiscus 80 80

2339 8p. White hibiscus 80 75

2340 8p. Pink hibiscus 80 80

2341 10p. Canna 1·00 1·00

750 Church

1991. Christmas. Children's Paintings. Mult.

2342 2p. Type **750** 20 15

2343 6p. Christmas present 65 45

2344 7p. Santa Claus and tree 75 50

2345 8p. Christmas tree and star 90 60

751 Player

1991. Centenary of Basketball. Multicoloured.

2346 2p. Type **751** 35 15

2347 6p. Basketball player and map (issue of first basketball stamp, 1934) (horiz) 90 30

2348 7p. Girls playing basketball (introduction of basketball in Philippines, 1904) (horiz) 1·00 35

2349 8p. Players 1·30 50

MS2350 Two sheets (a) 60×60 mm. Match scene. Imperf; (b) 73×101 mm. Nos. 2346/9 4·00 4·00

752 Monkey firing Cannon

1991. New Year. Year of the Monkey.

2351 **752** 2p. multicoloured 45 15

2352 **752** 6p. multicoloured 1·30 30

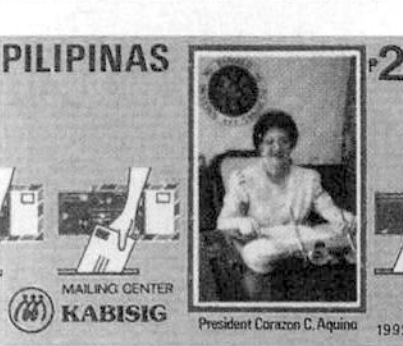

753 Pres. Aquino and Mailing Centre Emblem

1992. Kabisig Community Projects Organization. Multicoloured.

2353 2p. Type **753** 20 20

2354 6p. Housing 65 30

2355 7p. Livestock 80 35

2356 8p. Handicrafts 95 45

754 "Curcuma longa"

1992. Asian Medicinal Plants Symposium, Los Banos, Laguna. Multicoloured.

2357 2p. Type **754** 35 20

2358 6p. "Centella asiatica" 75 30

2359 7p. "Cassia alata" 90 35

2360 8p. "Ervatamia pandacaqui" 1·00 45

755 "Mahal Kita", Envelopes and Map

1992. Greetings Stamps. Multicoloured.

2361 2p. Type **755** 20 15

2362 2p. As No. 2361 but inscr "I Love You" 20 15

2363 6p. Heart and doves ("Mahal Kita") 75 35

2364 6p. As No. 2363 but inscr "I Love You" 75 35

2365 7p. Basket of flowers ("Mahal Kita") 80 35

2366 7p. As No. 2365 but inscr "I Love You" 80 35

2367 8p. Cupid ("Mahal Kita") 1·60 45

2368 8p. As No. 2367 but inscr "I Love You" 1·60 45

756 Philippine Pavilion and Couple Dancing

1992. "Expo '92" World's Fair, Seville. Mult.

2369 2p. Type **756** 20 15

2370 8p. Pavilion, preacher and conquistador holding globe 95 45

MS2371 63×76 mm. 16p. Pavilion (horiz). Imperf 1·90 1·90

757 "Our Lady of the Sun" (icon)

1992. 300th Anniv of Apparition of Our Lady of the Sun at Gate, Vaga Cavite.

2372 **757** 2p. multicoloured 20 15

2373 **757** 8p. multicoloured 95 45

758 Fish Farming

1992. 75th Anniv of Department of Agriculture. Multicoloured.

2374 2p. Type **758** 20 15

2375 2p. Pig farming 20 15

2376 2p. Sowing seeds 20 15

759 Race Horses and Emblem

1992. 125th Anniv of Manila Jockey Club.

2377 **759** 2p. multicoloured 20 15

MS2378 74×63 mm. **759** 8p. multicoloured. Imperf 95 95

760 Manuel Roxas (President, 1946–48)

1992. Birth Centenaries. Multicoloured.

2379 2p. Type **760** 20 15

2380 2p. Natividad Almeda-Lopez (judge) 20 15

2381 2p. Roman Ozaeta (judge) 20 15

2382 2p. Engracia Cruz-Reyes (women's rights campaigner and environmentalist) 20 15

2383 2p. Fernando Amorsolo (artist) 20 15

761 Queen, Bishop and 1978 30s. Stamp

1992. 30th Chess Olympiad, Manila. Mult.

2384 2p. Type **761** 20 15

2385 6p. King, queen and 1962 6s.+4s. stamp 65 45

MS2386 89×63 mm. 8p. Type **761**; 8p. As No. 2385. Imperf 1·80 1·80

762 Bataan Cross

1992. 50th Anniv of Pacific Theatre in Second World War. Multicoloured.

2387 2p. Type **762** 20 15

2388 6p. Map inside "W" 65 45

2389 8p. Corregidor eternal flame 95 65

MS2390 Two sheets. (a) 63×75 mm. 16p. Map of Bataan and cross; (b) 76×63 mm. 16p. Map of Corregidor and Eternal flame 3·00 3·00

763 President Aquino and President-elect Ramos

1992. Election of Fidel Ramos to Presidency.

2391 **763** 2p. multicoloured 30 15

764 "Dapitan Shrine" (Cesar Legaspi)

1992. Centenary of Dr. Jose Rizal's Exile to Dapitan. Multicoloured.

2392 2p. Type **764** 20 15

2393 2p. Portrait (after Juan Luna) (vert) 20 15

765 "Spirit of ASEAN" (Visit Asean Year)

1992. 25th Anniv of Association of South-East Asian Nations. Multicoloured.

2394 2p. Type **765** 20 15

2395 2p. "ASEAN Sea" (25th Ministerial Meeting and Postal Ministers' Conf) 20 15

2396 6p. Type **765** 65 45

2397 6p. As No. 2395 65 45

766 Member of the Katipunan

1992. Centenary of Katipunan ("KKK") (revolutionary organization). Multicoloured.

2398 2p. Type **766** 20 15

2399 2p. Revolutionaries 20 15

2400		2p. Plotting (horiz)	20	15
2401		2p. Attacking (horiz)	20	15

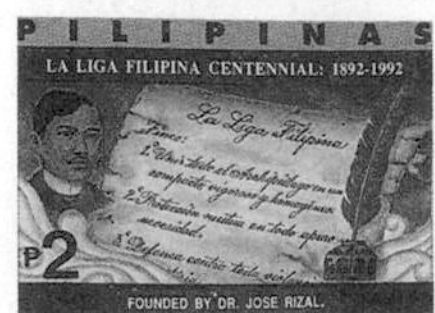

767 Dr. Jose Rizal, Text and Quill

1992. Centenary of La Liga Filipina.

2402	**767**	2p. multicoloured	20	15

768 Swimming

1992. Olympic Games, Barcelona. Multicoloured.

2403	2p. Type **768**	20	15
2404	7p. Boxing	75	50
2405	8p. Hurdling	90	60
MS2406	87×85 mm. 1p. Type **768**; 7p. No. 2404; 8p. No. 2405. Imperf	4·50	4·50

769 School, Emblem and Students

1992. Centenaries. Multicoloured.

2407	2p. Type **769** (Sisters of the Assumption in the Philippines)	20	15
2408	2p. San Sebastian's Basilica, Manila (centenary (1991) of blessing of fifth construction) (vert)	20	15

770 Masonic Symbols

1992. Centenary of Nilad Lodge (first Filipino Masonic Lodge).

2409	**770**	2p. black and green	20	15
2410	-	6p. multicoloured	65	45
2411	-	8p. multicoloured	90	60

DESIGNS: 6p. Antonio Luna and symbols; 8p. Marcelo del Pilar ("Father of Philippine Masonry") and symbols.

771 Ramos taking Oath

1992. Swearing in of President Fidel Ramos. Mult.

2412	2p. Type **771**	20	15
2413	8p. President taking oath in front of flag	95	45

772 Flamingo Guppy

1992. Freshwater Aquarium Fishes (1st series). Multicoloured.

2414	1p.50 Type **772**	15	10
2415	1p.50 Neon tuxedo guppy	15	10
2416	1p.50 King cobra guppy	15	10
2417	1p.50 Red-tailed guppy	15	10
2418	1p.50 Tiger lace-tailed guppy	15	10
2419	2p. Pearl-scaled goldfish	30	15
2420	2p. Red-capped goldfish	30	15
2421	2p. Lion-headed goldfish	30	15
2422	2p. Black moor goldfish	30	15
2423	2p. Bubble-eyed goldfish	30	15
2424	4p. Delta topsail platy ("Variatus")	60	60
2425	4p. Orange-spotted hi-fin platy	60	60
2426	4p. Red lyre-tailed swordtail	60	60
2427	4p. Bleeding heart hi-fin platy	60	60
MS2428	Two sheets. (a) 132×78 mm. 6p. Green discus; 6p. Brown discus; 7p. Red discus; 7p. Harald's blue discus; (b) 88×61 mm. 8p. Golden arowana. Imperf	2·50	2·50

See also Nos. 2543/**MS**2557.

1992. Philippines Stamp Exhibition, Taipeh, Taiwan. No. MS2428 optd PHILIPPINE STAMP EXHIBITION 1992 – TAIPEI.

MS2429	Two sheets. (a) 132×79 mm. 6p. ×2, 7p. ×2, multicoloured; (b) 88×61 mm. 8p. multicoloured	4·50	4·50

774 Couple

1992. Greetings Stamps. "Happy Birthday". Multicoloured.

2430	2p. Type **774**	20	15
2431	6p. Type **774**	65	45
2432	7p. Balloons and candles on birthday cake	75	50
2433	8p. As No. 2432	95	60

775 Melon, Beans, Tomatoes and Potatoes

1992. 500th Anniv of Discovery of America by Columbus. Multicoloured.

2434	2p. Type **775**	20	15
2435	6p. Maize and sweet potatoes	65	45
2436	8p. Pineapple, cashews, avocado and water melon	90	60

1992. Second National Philatelic Convention. No.MS2271 optd Second National Philatelic Convention Cebu, Philippines, Oct 22—24, 1992.

MS2437	16p. multicoloured	3·00	3·00

777 Figures around World Map

1992. International Nutrition Conference, Rome.

2438	**777**	2p. multicoloured	20	15

778 Mother and Child

1992. Christmas.

2439	**778**	2p. multicoloured	20	15
2440	-	6p. multicoloured	65	45
2441	-	7p. multicoloured	75	50
2442	-	8p. multicoloured	95	60

DESIGNS: 6p. to 8p. Various designs showing mothers and children.

1992. Inauguration of Postal Museum and Philatelic Library. No. MS1566 optd INAUGURATION OF THE PHILIPPINE POSTAL MUSEUM AND PHILTATELIC LIBRARY NOVEMBER 10 1992.

MS2443	76×76 mm. 5p. multicoloured	1·80	1·80

780 Family and Canoe

1992. Anti-drugs Campaign. Multicoloured.

2444	2p. Type **780**	20	15
2445	8p. Man carrying paddle, children and canoe	90	60

781 Damaged Trees

1992. Mt. Pinatubo Fund (for victims of volcanic eruption). Multicoloured.

2446	25s. Type **781**	10	10
2447	1p. Mt. Pinatubo erupting	10	10
2448	1p. Cattle in ash-covered field	10	10
2449	1p. Refugee settlement	10	10
2450	1p. People shovelling ash	10	10

782 Red Junglefowl

1992. New Year. Year of the Cock. Mult.

2451	2p. Type **782**	20	15
2452	6p. Maranao Sarimanok (mythical bird)	65	45
MS2453	98×87 mm. Nos. 2451/2 plus two labels. Perf or Imperf	90	90

1992. Philippine Stamp Exhibition, Taipeh. No. MS2453 optd PHILIPPPINE STAMP EHXIBIT TAIPEI DECEMBER 1—3 1992.

MS2454	98×87 mm. 2, 6p. multicoloured	1·80	1·80

784 Badges of 61st and 71st Divisions, Cebu Area Command

1992. Philippine Guerrilla Units of Second World War (1st series). Multicoloured.

2455	2p. Type **784**	20	15
2456	2p. Vinzon's Guerrillas and badges of 48th Chinese Guerrilla Squadron and 101st Division	20	15
2457	2p. Anderson's Command, Luzon Guerrilla Army Forces and badge of Bulacan Military Area	20	15
2458	2p. President Quezon's Own Guerrillas and badges of Marking's Fil-American Troops and Hunters ROTC Guerrillas	20	15

See also Nos. 2594/7, 2712/15 and 2809/12.

785 "Family" (Cesar Legaspi) (family ties)

1992. Philatelic Week. Multicoloured.

2459	2p. Type **785**	20	15
2460	6p. "Pounding Rice" (Nena Saguil) (hard work and industry)	65	45
2461	7p. "Fish Vendors" (Romeo Tabuena) (flexibility and adaptability)	75	50

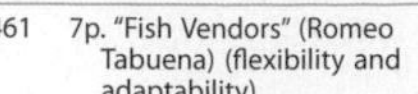

786 Black Shama

1992. Endangered Birds. Multicoloured. (a) As T 786.

2462	2p. Type **786**	20	15
2463	2p. Blue-headed fantail	20	15
2464	2p. Mindoro zone-tailed (inscr "Imperial") pigeon	20	15
2465	2p. Sulu hornbill	20	15
2466	2p. Red-vented (inscr "Philippine") cockatoo	20	15

(b) Size 29×39 mm.

2467	2p. Philippine trogon	20	20
2468	2p. Rufous hornbill	20	20
2469	2p. White-bellied black woodpecker	20	20
2470	2p. Spotted wood kingfisher	20	20

(c) Size 36×26½ mm.

2471	2p. Brahminy kite	20	20
2472	2p. Philippine falconet	20	20
2473	2p. Reef heron	20	20
2474	2p. Philippine duck (inscr "Mallard")	20	20

787 Flower (Jasmine)

1993. National Symbols. Multicoloured. (a) As T 787. "Pilipinas" in brown at top.

2476	1p. Type **787**	15	10
2571	2p. Flag	20	15
2478	6p. Leaf (palm)	65	45
2479	7p. Costume	75	50
2480	8p. Fruit (mango)	90	60

788 Flower (Jasmine)

(b) As T 788. "Pilipinas" in red at foot.

2481	60s. Tree	15	10
2512	1p. Flag	10	10
2513	1p. House	10	10
2514	1p. Costume	10	10
2515	1p. As No. 2481	10	10
2516	1p. Type **788**	10	10
2517	1p. Fruit	10	10
2518	1p. Leaf	10	10
2519	1p. Fish (milkfish)	10	10
2520	1p. Animal (water buffalo)	10	10
2521	1p. Bird (Philippine trogons)	10	10
2482	1p.50 As No. 2519	15	10
2565	2p. Hero (Dr. Jose Rizal)	20	15
2566	2p. As No. 2513	20	15
2567	2p. As No. 2514	20	15
2568	2p. Dance ("Tinikling")	20	15
2569	2p. Sport (Sipa)	20	15
2570	2p. As No. 2521	20	15
2572	2p. As No. 2520	20	15
2573	2p. Type **788**	20	15
2574	2p. As No. 2481	20	15
2575	2p. As No. 2517	20	15
2576	2p. As No. 2518	20	15
2577	2p. As No. 2519	20	15
2578	2p. As No. 2512	20	15
2644	3p. As No. 2520	15	15
2645	5p. As No. 2521	30	20
2646	6p. As No. 2518	35	15
2647	7p. As No. 2514	40	25
2486	8p. As No. 2517	1·00	60
2649	10p. As No. 2513	55	30

See also Nos. **MS**2663, 2717/19, **MS**2753, 2818/20, **MS**2906, 2973/5, **MS**3010, 3017/19, 3089/3092, 3093/7, 3103/5, **MS**3106, 3107/21, **MS**3178 and 3200/9.

789 "Euploea mulciber dufresne"

1993. Butterflies. Multicoloured. (a) As T 789.

2488 2p. Type **789** 20 15
2489 2p. "Cheritra orpheus" 20 15
2490 2p. "Delias henningia" 20 15
2491 2p. "Mycalesis ita" 20 15
2492 2p. "Delias diaphana" 20 15

(b) Size 28×35 mm.

2493 2p. "Papilio rumanzobia" 20 20
2494 2p. "Papilio palinurus" 20 20
2495 2p. "Trogonoptera trojana" 20 20
2496 2p. Tailed jay ("Graphium agamemnon") 20 20
MS2497 10p. "Papilio iowi", "Valeria boebera" and "Delias themis" 1·50 1·50

1993. Indopex 93 International Stamp Exhibition, Surabaya. No. MS2497 optd INDOPEX 93 INDONESIA PHILATELIC EXHIBITION 1993, 6th ASIAN INTERNATIONAL PHILATELIC EXHIBITION 29th MAY – 4th JUNE 1993 SURABAYA – INDONESIA.

MS2498 140×70 mm. 10p. multicoloured 2·20 2·20

791 Nicanor Abelardo

1993. Birth Centenaries. Multicoloured.

2499 2p. Type **791** 20 15
2500 2p. Pilar Hidalgo-Lim 20 15
2501 2p. Manuel Viola Gallego 20 15
2502 2p. Maria Ylagan-Orosa 20 15
2503 2p. Eulogio B. Rodriguez 20 15

792 Boxing and Judo

1993. 17th South-East Asian Games, Singapore. Multicoloured.

2504 2p. Weightlifting, archery, fencing and shooting (79×29 mm) 20 15
2505 2p. Type **792** 20 15
2506 2p. Athletics, cycling, gymnastics and golf (79×29 mm) 20 15
2507 6p. Table tennis, football, volleyball and badminton (79×29 mm) 65 45
2508 6p. Billiards and bowling 65 45
2509 6p. Swimming, water polo, yachting and diving (79×29 mm) 65 45
MS2510 84×96 mm. 10p. Basketball (vert) 3·00 3·00

1993. 46th Anniv of Philippine Air Force. No. MS2497 optd Towards the Year 2000, 46th PAF Anniversary 1 July 1993.

MS2511 140×70 mm. 10p. multicoloured 7·50 7·50

794 "Spathoglottis chrysantha"

1993. Orchids. Multicoloured.

2522 2p. Type **794** 20 15
2523 2p. "Arachnis longicaulis" 20 15
2524 2p. "Phalaenopsis mariae" 20 15
2525 2p. "Coelogyne marmorata" 20 15
2526 2p. "Dendrobium sanderae" 20 15
2527 3p. "Dendrobium serratilabium" 30 20
2528 3p. "Phalaenopsis equestris" 30 20
2529 3p. "Vanda merrillii" 30 20
2530 3p. "Vanda luzonica" 30 20
2531 3p. "Grammatophyllum martae" 30 20
MS2532 Two sheets, each 58×99 mm. (a) 8p. "Aerides quinquevulnera" (27×77 mm); (b) 8p. "Vanda lamellate" (27×77 mm). Imperf 90 90

1993. "Taipei '93" Asian Stamp Exhibition. No. MS2532 optd ASIAN INTERNATIONAL INVITATION STAMP EXHIBITION TAIPEI '93.

MS2533 Two sheets, each 58×99 mm. Perf. (a) 8p. multicoloured; (b) 8p. multicoloured. Imperf 90 90

796 Dog in Window ("Thinking of You")

1993. Greetings Stamps. Multicoloured.

2534 2p. Type **796** 20 15
2535 2p. As No. 2534 but inscr "Naaalala Kita" 20 15
2536 6p. Dog looking at clock ("Thinking of You") 65 45
2537 6p. As No. 2536 but inscr "Naaalala Kita" 65 45
2538 7p. Dog looking at calendar ("Thinking of You") 75 50
2539 7p. As No. 2538 but inscr "Naaalala Kita" 75 50
2540 8p. Dog with pair of slippers ("Thinking of You") 90 60
2541 8p. As No. 2540 but inscr "Naaalala Kita" 90 60

797 Palms and Coconuts

1993. "Tree of Life".

2542 **797** 2p. multicoloured 20 15

798 Albino Ryukin Goldfish

1993. Freshwater Aquarium Fishes (2nd series). Multicoloured. (a) As T 798.

2543 2p. Type **798** 20 15
2544 2p. Black oranda goldfish 20 15
2545 2p. Lion-headed goldfish 20 15
2546 2p. Celestial goldfish 20 15
2547 2p. Pompon goldfish 20 15
2548 2p. Paradise fish 20 15
2549 2p. Pearl gourami 20 15
2550 2p. Red-tailed black shark (carp) 20 15
2551 2p. Tiger barb 20 15
2552 2p. Cardinal tetra 20 15

(b) Size 29×39 mm.

2553 2p. Pearl-scaled freshwater angelfish 20 15
2554 2p. Zebra freshwater angelfish 20 20
2555 2p. Marble freshwater angelfish 20 20
2556 2p. Black freshwater angelfish 20 20
MS2557 Two sheets. (a) 138×78 mm. 3p. Neon Siamese fighting fish; 3p. Libby Siamese fighting fish; 3p. Split-tailed Siamese fighting fish; 3p. Butterfly Siamese fighting fish. Perf. (b) 87×60 mm. 6p. Albino oscar. Imperf 3·75 3·50

799 Map and Emblem

1993. Basic Petroleum and Minerals Inc. "Towards Self-sufficiency in Energy".

2558 **799** 2p. multicoloured 20 15

1993. "Bangkok '93" International Stamp Exhibition, Thailand. No. MS2557 optd QUEEN SIRIKIT NATIONAL CONVENTION CENTRE 1-10 OCTOBER 1993, BANGKOK WORLD PHILATELIC EXHIBITION 1993.

MS2559 Two sheets. (a) 3p. ×4, multicoloured; (b) 6p. multicoloured 7·50 7·50

801 Globe, Scales, Book and Gavel

1993. 16th Int Law Conference, Manila. Mult.

2560 2p. Type **801** 20 15
2561 6p. Globe, scales, gavel and conference emblem on flag of Philippines (vert) 65 45
2562 7p. Woman holding scales, conference building and globe 80 50
2563 8p. Fisherman pulling in nets and emblem (vert) 95 65

802 Our Lady of La Naval (statue) and Galleon

1993. 400th Anniv of Our Lady of La Naval.

2564 **802** 2p. multicoloured 20 15

803 Woman and Terraced Hillside

1993. International Year of Indigenous Peoples. Women in traditional costumes. Multicoloured.

2579 2p. Type **803** 20 15
2580 6p. Woman, plantation and mountain 65 45
2581 7p. Woman and mosque 80 50
2582 8p. Woman and Filipino vintas (sail canoes) 95 65

804 Trees

1993. Philatelic Week. "Save the Earth". Mult.

2583 2p. Type **804** 20 15
2584 6p. Marine flora and fauna 65 45
2585 7p. Dove and irrigation system 80 50
2586 8p. Effects of industrial pollution 95 65

805 1949 6c.+4c. Stamp and Symbols

1993. 400th Anniv of Publication of "Doctrina Christiana" (first book published in Philippines).

2587 **805** 2p. multicoloured 20 15

806 Moon-buggy and Society Emblem

1993. 50th Anniv of Filipino Inventors Society. Multicoloured.

2588 2p. Type **806** 20 15
2589 2p. Rice-harvesting machine 20 15

Nos. 2588/9 were issued together, se-tenant, forming a composite design.

807 Holy Family

1993. Christmas. Multicoloured.

2590 2p. Type **807** 20 15
2591 6p. Church goers 65 45
2592 7p. Cattle and baskets of food 80 50
2593 8p. Carol-singers 95 65

808 Northern Luzon

1993. Philippine Guerrilla Units of Second World War (2nd series). Multicoloured.

2594 2p. Type **808** 20 15
2595 2p. Bohol Area Command 20 15
2596 2p. Leyte Area Command 20 15
2597 2p. Palawan Special Battalion and Sulu Area Command 20 15

809 Dove over City (peace and order)

1993. "Philippines 2000" (development plan). Multicoloured.

2598 2p. Type **809** 20 15
2599 6p. Means of transport and communications 65 45
2600 7p. Offices, roads and factories (infrastructure and industry) 80 50
2601 8p. People from different walks of life (people empowerment) 95 65
MS2602 110×85 mm. 8p. Various motifs on themes of peace, transport and communication, infrastructure and industry and people power. Imperf 2·20 2·20

810 Shih Tzu

1993. New Year. Year of the Dog. Multicoloured.

2603 2p. Type **810** 20 15
2604 6p. Chow 65 45
MS2605 98×88 mm. Nos. 2603/4 plus two labels. Perf or imperf 1·50 1·50

811 Jamboree Emblem and Flags

1993. 1st Association of South-East Asian Nations Scout Jamboree, Makiling. Multicoloured.

No.	Description	Unused	Used
2606	2p. Type **811**	20	15
2607	6p. Scout at camp-site, flags and emblem	65	45
MS2608	86×86 mm. Nos. 2606/7	1·80	1·80

812 Club Emblem on Diamond

1994. 75th Anniv of Manila Rotary Club.

No.	Description	Unused	Used
2609	**812** 2p. multicoloured	20	15

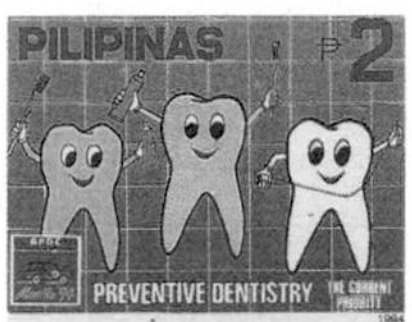

813 Teeth and Dental Hygiene Products

1994. 17th Asian–Pacific Dental Congress, Manila. Multicoloured.

No.	Description	Unused	Used
2610	2p. Type **813**	20	15
2611	6p. Teeth, flags of participating countries and teeth over globe with Philippines circled (vert)	65	45

814 "Acropora micropthalma"

1994. Corals. Multicoloured.

No.	Description	Unused	Used
2612	2p. Type **814**	20	15
2613	2p. "Seriatopora hystrix"	20	15
2614	2p. "Acropora latistella"	20	15
2615	2p. "Millepora tenella"	20	15
2616	2p. "Millepora tenella" (different)	20	15
2617	2p. "Pachyseris valenciennesi"	20	15
2618	2p. "Pavona decussata"	20	15
2619	2p. "Galaxea fascicularis"	20	15
2620	2p. "Acropora formosa"	20	15
2621	2p. "Acropora humilis"	20	15
2622	2p. "Isis sp." (vert)	20	20
2623	2p. "Plexaura sp." (vert)	20	20
2624	2p. "Dendronepthya sp." (vert)	20	20
2625	2p. "Heteroxenia sp." (vert)	20	20
MS2626	135×78 mm. 3p. "Xenia puertogalerae"; 3p. "Plexaura" sp. (different); 3p. "Dendrophyllia gracilis"; 3p. "Plerogyra sinuosa"	95	95

815 New Year Stamps of 1991 and 1992 bearing Exhibition Emblem

1994. "Hong Kong '94" Stamp Exhibition. Multicoloured.

No.	Description	Unused	Used
2627	2p. Type **815**	20	15
2628	6p. 1993 New Year stamps	65	45
MS2629	Two sheets, each 98×72 mm. (a) Nos. 2627/8 (blue margin); (b) Nos. 2627/8 (green margin)	90	90

816 Class of 1944 Emblem

1994. 50th Anniv of Philippine Military Academy Class of 1944.

No.	Description	Unused	Used
2630	**816** 2p. multicoloured	20	15

1994. Naphilcon 94 First National Philatelic Congress. As No. MS2626 but with additional inscription in the central gutter.

No.	Description	Unused	Used
MS2631	135×78 mm. 3p. ×4 multicoloured	1·40	1·40

817 Airplane over Harbour, Man and Cogwheel and Emblem

1994. Federation of Filipino–Chinese Chambers of Commerce and Industry.

No.	Description	Unused	Used
2632	**817** 2p. multicoloured	20	15

818 Stork carrying Baby ("Binabati Kita")

1994. Greetings Stamps. Multicoloured.

No.	Description	Unused	Used
2633	2p. Type **818**	20	15
2634	2p. As No. 2633 but inscr "Congratulations"	20	15
2635	2p. Bouquet ("Binabati Kita")	20	15
2636	2p. As No. 2635 but inscr "Congratulations"	20	15
2637	2p. Mortar board, scroll and books ("Binabati Kita")	20	15
2638	2p. As No. 2637 but inscr "Congratulations"	20	15
2639	2p. Bouquet, doves and heads inside heart ("Binabati Kita")	20	15
2640	2p. As No. 2639 but inscr "Congratulations"	20	15

819 Gloria Diaz (Miss Universe 1969)

1994. Miss Universe Beauty Contest. Multicoloured.

No.	Description	Unused	Used
2653	2p. Type **819**	20	15
2654	2p. Margie Moran (Miss Universe 1973)	20	15
2655	6p. Crown	65	45
2656	7p. Contestant	80	60
MS2657	90×80 mm. 8p. As No. 2653; 8p. As No. 2654	1·80	1·80

820 Antonio Molina (composer)

1994. Birth Centenaries. Multicoloured.

No.	Description	Unused	Used
2658	2p. Type **820**	20	15
2659	2p. Jose Yulo (Secretary of Justice)	20	15
2660	2p. Josefa Jara-Martinez (social worker)	20	15
2661	2p. Nicanor Reyes (accountant)	20	15
2662	2p. Sabino Padilla (judge)	20	15

1994. Centenary of Declaration of Philippine Independence (2nd issue). National Landmarks. Sheet 100×80 mm containing vert designs as T 788. Multicoloured.

No.	Description	Unused	Used
MS2663	2p. Aguinaldo Shrine; 2p. Barasoain Shrine; 3p. Rizal Shrine; 3p. Mabini Shrine	1·20	1·20

821 Map, Forest and Emblem (Baguio City)

1994. Export Processing Zones. Multicoloured.

No.	Description	Unused	Used
2664	2p. Type **821**	20	15
2665	2p. Cross on hilltop (Bataan)	20	15
2666	2p. Octagonal building (Mactan)	20	15
2667	2p. Aguinaldo Shrine (Cavite)	20	15
2668	7p. Map and products	80	50
2669	8p. Globe and products	95	65

Nos. 2264/7 and 2668/9 repectively were issued together, se-tenant, forming composite designs.

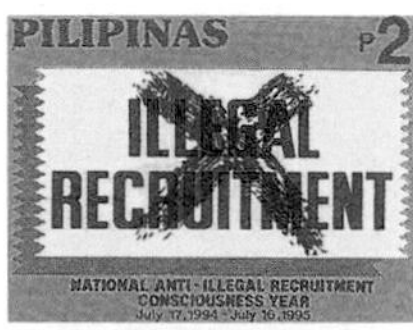

822 Cross through "ILLEGAL RECRUITMENT"

1994. Anti-illegal Recruitment Campaign.

No.	Description	Unused	Used
2670	**822** 2p. multicoloured	20	15

823 Palawan Bearcat

1994. Mammals. Multicoloured.

No.	Description	Unused	Used
2671	6p. Type **823**	75	45
2672	6p. Philippine tarsier	75	45
2673	6p. Malayan pangolin (inscr "Scaly Anteater")	75	45
2674	6p. Indonesian ("Palawan") porcupine	75	45
MS2675	96×67 mm. 12p. Visayan spotted deer (79×29 mm)	1·50	1·50

824 Glory of the Sea Cone ("Conus gloriamaris")

1994. "Philakorea 1994" International Stamp Exhibition, Seoul. Shells. Multicoloured.

No.	Description	Unused	Used
2676	2p. Type **824**	20	15
2677	2p. Striate cone ("Conus striatus")	20	15
2678	2p. Geography cone ("Conus geographus")	20	15
2679	2p. Textile cone ("Conus textile")	20	15
MS2680	Two sheets, each 88×78 mm. (a) 6p. Striate cone; 6p. "Conus marmoreus" (Marble cone); (b) 6p. Marble cone; 6p. Geography cone	1·50	1·50

1994. "Singpex '94" National Stamp Exhibition, Singapore. As No. MS2675 but additionally inscribed "Singpex '94 31 August–3 September 1994" and emblem.

No.	Description	Unused	Used
MS2681	96×67 mm. 12p. multicoloured	1·50	1·50

825 Sergio Osmena, Snr.

1994. 50th Anniv of Leyte Gulf Landings. Multicoloured.

No.	Description	Unused	Used
2682	2p. Type **825**	20	15
2683	2p. Soldiers landing at Palo	20	15
2684	2p. "Peace – A Better World" emblem	20	15
2685	2p. Carlos Romulo	20	15

Nos. 2682/5 were issued together, se-tenant, forming a composite design.

826 Family (International Year of the Family)

1994. Anniversaries and Event. Multicoloured.

No.	Description	Unused	Used
2686	2p. Type **826**	20	15
2687	6p. Workers (75th anniv of I.L.O.)	75	45
2688	7p. Aircraft and symbols of flight (50th anniv of I.C.A.O.)	90	60

827 Blue-naped Parrot

1994. "Aseanpex '94" Stamp Exhibition, Penang, Malaysia. Birds. Muilticoloured.

No.	Description	Unused	Used
2689	2p. Type **827**	20	15
2690	2p. Luzon bleeding heart ("Bleeding Heart Pigeon")	20	15
2691	2p. Palawan peacock-pheasant	20	15
2692	2p. Koch's pitta	20	15
MS2693	69×55 mm. 12p. Philippine eagle (vert)	1·50	1·50

828 Presidents Fidel Ramos and W. Clinton

1994. Visit of United States President William Clinton to Philippines.

No.	Description	Unused	Used
2694	**828** 2p. multicoloured	20	15
2695	**828** 8p. multicoloured	1·00	65

829 Convention Emblem

1994. Association of South-East Asian Nations Eastern Business Convention, Davao City.

No.	Description	Unused	Used
2696	**829** 2p. multicoloured	30	15
2697	**829** 6p. multicoloured	75	50

830 "Soteranna Puson y Quintos de Ventenilla" (Dionisio de Castro)

1994. Philatelic Week. Portraits. Multicoloured.

No.	Description	Unused	Used
2698	2p. Type **830**	30	1·70
2699	6p. "Quintina Castor de Sadie" (Simon Flores y de la Rosa)	75	50
2700	7p. "Portrait of the Artist's Mother" (Felix Hidalgo y Padilla)	90	60
2701	8p. "Una Bulaquena" (Juan Luna y Novicio)	1·00	65
MS2702	60×100 mm. 12p. "Cirilo and Severina Quaison Family" (Simon Flores y de la Rosa) (28½×79 mm)	1·50	1·50

831 Wreath

1994. Christmas. Multicoloured.

2703	2p. Type **831**	75	50
2704	6p. Angels	90	60
2705	7p. Bells	1·00	65
2706	8p. Christmas basket	1·00	65

832 Piggy Bank

1994. New Year. Year of the Pig. Multicoloured.

2707	2p. Type **832**	30	15
2708	6p. Pig couple	75	50
MS2709	98×88 mm. Nos. 2707/8 plus two labels. Perf or imperf	1·10	1·10

833 Raid on Prison

1994. 50th Anniversaries of Raid by Hunters ROTC Guerrillas on Psew Bilibi Prison and of Mass Escape by Inmates. Multicoloured.

2710	2p. Type **833**	20	15
2711	2p. Inmates fleeing	20	15

Nos. 2710/11 were issued together, se-tenant, forming a composite design.

834 East Central Luzon Guerrilla Area

1994. Philippine Guerrilla Units of Second World War (3rd series). Multicoloured.

2712	2p. Type **834**	20	15
2713	2p. Mindoro Provincial Battalion and Marinduque Guerrilla Force	20	15
2714	2p. Zambales Military District and Masbate Guerrilla Regiment	20	15
2715	2p. Samar Area Command	50	35

835 Ribbon on Globe

1994. National AIDS Awareness Campaign.

2716	**835**	2p. multicoloured	20	15

836 Flag

1994. Centenary of Declaration of Philippine Independence. Multicoloured.

2717	2p. Type **836**	20	15
2718	2p. Present state flag	20	15
2719	2p. Anniversary emblem	20	15

Nos. 2717/19 were issued together, se-tenant, forming a composite design.

837 Pope John Paul II and Manila Cathedral

1995. Papal Visit. Multicoloured.

2720	2p. Type **837** (400th anniv of Manila Archdiocese)	20	15
2721	2p. Pope and Cebu Cathedral (400th anniv of Diocese)	20	15
2722	2p. Pope and Caceres Cathedral (400th anniv of Diocese)	20	15
2723	2p. Pope and Nueva Segovia Cathedral (400th anniv of Diocese)	20	15
2724	2p. Pope, globe and Pope's arms	30	20
2725	6p. Pope and Federation of Asian Bishops emblem (6th Conference, Manila)	75	50
2726	8p. Pope, youths and emblem (10th World Youth Day)	1·00	65
MS2727	81×60 mm. 8p. Pope and President Fidel Ramos	1·00	1·00

1995. "Christypex '95" Philatelic Exhibition, Manila. No. MS2727 optd CHRISTYPEX '95 JANUARY 4-16, 1995 University of Santo Tomas, Manila PHILIPPINE PHILATELIC FEDERATION.

MS2728	81×60 mm. 8p. multicoloured	1·00	1·00

839 Landing Craft and Map

1995. 50th Anniv of Lingayen Gulf Landings. Multicoloured.

2729	2p. Type **839**	20	15
2730	2p. Map and emblems of 6th, 37th, 40th and 43rd army divisions	20	15

Nos. 2729/30 were issued together, se-tenant, forming a composite design.

840 Monument (Peter de Guzman) and Ruins of Intramuros (image scaled to 63% of original size)

1995. 50th Anniv of Battle for the Liberation of Manila. Multicoloured.

2731	2p. Type **840**	10	10
2732	8p. Monument and ruins of Legislative Building and Department of Agriculture	40	20

841 Diokno

1995. 8th Death Anniv of Jose Diokno (politician).

2733	**841**	2p. multicoloured	20	15

842 Anniversary Emblem and Ethnic Groups

1995. 75th Anniv of International School, Manila. Multicoloured.

2734	2p. Type **842**	20	15
2735	8p. Globe and cut-outs of children	1·00	65

843 Greater Malay Mouse Deer

1995. Mammals. Multicoloured.

2736	2p. Type **843**	20	15
2737	2p. Tamarau	20	15
2738	2p. Visayan warty pig	20	15
2739	2p. Palm civet	20	15
MS2740	89×80 mm. 8p. Flying lemur; 8p. Philippine deer	2·10	2·10

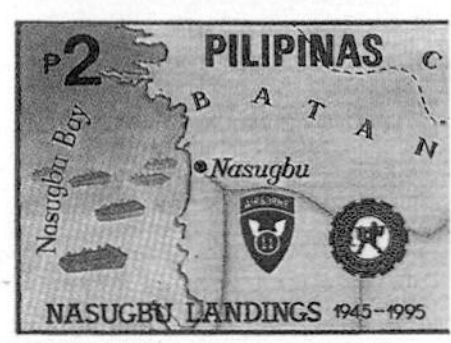

844 Nasugbu Landings

1995. 50th Anniversaries. Multicoloured.

2741	2p. Type **844**	20	15
2742	2p. Tagaytay Landings	20	15
2743	2p. Battle of Nichols Airbase and Fort McKinley	20	15

Nos. 2741/2 were issued together, se-tenant, forming a composite design.

845 Memorial

1995. 50th Anniv of Liberation of Baguio.

2744	**845**	2p. multicoloured	20	15

846 Cabanatuan Camp

1995. 50th Anniv of Liberation of Internment and Prisoner of War Camps. Multicoloured.

2745	2p. Type **846**	20	15
2746	2p. Entrance to U.S.T. camp	20	15
2747	2p. Los Banos camp	20	15

Nos. 2746/7 are wrongly inscribed "Interment".

847 Victorio Edades (artist)

1995. Birth Centenaries. Multicoloured.

2748	2p. Type **847**	20	15
2749	2p. Jovita Fuentes (opera singer)	20	15
2750	2p. Candido Africa (medical researcher)	20	15
2751	2p. Asuncion Arriola-Perez (politician)	20	15
2752	2p. Eduardo Quisumbing (botanist)	20	15

1995. Centenary of Declaration of Philippine Independence (3rd issue). 123rd Anniv of Cavite Mutiny. Sheet 100×80 mm. containing vert designs as T788.

MS2753	2p. Cavite shipyard; 2p. Centenary memorial; 3p. San Filipe fortress; 3p. Crisanto de los Reyes y Mendoza (death centenary)	1·30	80

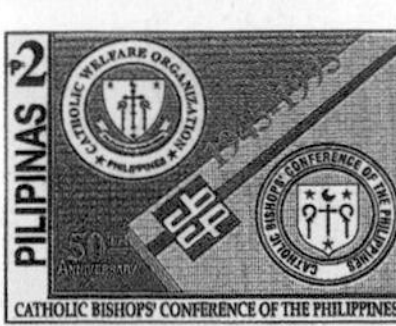

848 Emblems and Bible

1995. 50th Anniv of Philippine Catholic Bishops' Conference, Manila.

2754	**848**	2p. multicoloured	20	15

849 Ferrer

1995. 8th Death Anniv of Jaime Ferrer (administrator).

2755	**849**	2p. multicoloured	20	15

850 Neolithic Burial Jar, Manunggul

1995. Archaeology. Multicoloured.

2756	2p. Type **850**	20	15
2757	2p. Iron age secondary burial jar, Ayub Cave, Mindanao	20	15
2758	2p. Iron age secondary burial jar (different), Ayub Cave	20	15
2759	2p. Neolithic ritual drinking vessel, Leta-Leta Cave, Palawan	20	15
MS2760	100×70 mm. 12p. 14th–15th century double-spouted vessel and presentation tray, Laurel, Batangas (80×30 mm)	1·60	1·60

See also No.**MS**2767.

851 Philippine Eagle

1995. Adoption of the Philippine Eagle as National Bird. Sheet 69×55 mm.

MS2761	16p. multicoloured	2·20	2·20

852 Right Hand supporting Wildlife

1995. Association of South-East Asian Nations Environment Year. Multicoloured.

2762	2p. Type **852**	20	15
2763	2p. Left hand supporting wildlife	20	15
MS2764	89×78 mm. 6p. Type **852**; 6p. As No. 2766	1·60	1·60

Nos. 2762/3 were issued together, se-tenant, forming a composite design.

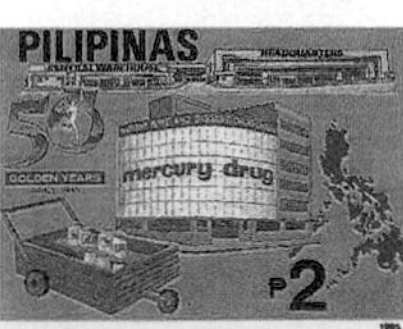

853 Anniversary Emblem, Buildings and Trolley

1995. 50th Anniv of Mercury Drug Corporation.

2765	**853**	2p. multicoloured	20	15

854 Parish Church

1995. 400th Anniv of Parish of Saint Louis Bishop, Lucban.

2766	**854**	2p. multicoloured	20	15

1995. "Jakarta 95" Asian Stamp Exhibition. As No.MS2760 but with additional inscription at foot.

MS2767		100×70 mm. 12p. multicoloured	1·60	1·60

855 Instructor and Pupils

1995. 25th Anniv of Asian-Pacific Postal Training Centre, Bangkok.

2768	**855**	6p. multicoloured	80	50

856 Crops and Child drinking from Well

1995. 50th Anniv of F.A.O.

2769	**856**	8p. multicoloured	1·10	75

857 Carlos Romulo

1995. 50th Anniv of U.N.O. Multicoloured.

2770	2p. Jose Bengzon (inscr "Cesar Bengzon")	55	55
2771	2p. Rafael Salas (Assistant Secretary General)	55	55
2772	2p. Salvador Lopez (Secretary)	55	55
2773	2p. Jose Ingles (Under-secretary)	55	55
MS2774	71×57 mm. 16p. Carlos Romulo (President of General Assembly)	2·20	2·20
2775	2p. Type **857**	20	15

No. 2770 depicts Jose Bengzon in error for his brother Cesar.

858 Anniversary Emblem

1995. 50th Anniv of Manila Overseas Press Club.

2779	**858**	2p. multicoloured	20	15

859 Eclipse

1995. Total Solar Eclipse.

2780	**859**	2p. multicoloured	20	15

860 Flag

1995. National Symbols. With blue barcode at top. "Pilipinas" in red. Variously dated. Multicoloured.

2781	2p. Flag ("Pillipinas" at top)	20	15
2782	2p. Hero (Jose Rizal)	20	15
2783	2p. House	20	15
2784	2p. Costume	20	15
2785	2p. Dance	20	15
2786	2p. Sport	20	15
2787	2p. Bird (Philippine eagle)	20	15
2788	2p. Type **860**	20	15
2789	2p. Animal (water buffalo)	20	15
2790	2p. Flower (jasmine)	20	15
2791	2p. Tree	20	15
2792	2p. Fruit (mango)	20	15
2793	2p. Leaf (palm)	20	15
2794	2p. Fish (milkfish)	20	15

For designs with barcode but "Pilipinas" in blue, see Nos. 2822/44.

861 "Two Igorot Women" (Victorio Edades)

1995. National Stamp Collecting Month (1st issue). Paintings by Filipino artists. Multicoloured.

2795	2p. Type **861**	30	15
2796	6p. "Serenade" (Carlos Francisco)	90	50
2797	7p. "Tuba Drinkers" (Vicente Manansala)	95	65
2798	8p. "Genesis" (Hernando Ocampo)	1·00	80
MS2799	99×70 mm. "The Builders" (Victorio Edades) (79×29 mm)	1·60	1·60

See also No. **MS**2805.

862 Tambourine

1995. Christmas. Musical instruments and Lines from Carols. Multicoloured.

2800	2p. Type **862**	20	15
2801	6p. Maracas	75	50
2802	7p. Guitar	95	65
2803	8p. Drum	1·20	80

863 Abacus and Anniversary Emblem

1995. 50th Anniv of Sycip Gorres Velayo & Co. (accountants).

2804	**863**	2p. multicoloured	20	15

864 Pres. Ramos signing Stamp Month Proclamation

1995. National Stamp Collecting Month (2nd issue). Sheet 80×60 mm.

MS2805	8p. multicoloured	1·10	1·10

865 Rat and Fireworks

1995. New Year. Year of the Rat. Multicoloured.

2806	2p. Type **865**	30	20
2807	6p. Model of rat	80	50
MS2808	98×88 mm. Nos. 2806/7 plus two greetings labels. Perf or imperf	1·20	1·20

866 Badge of Fil-American Irregular Troops Veterans Legion

1995. Philippine Guerrilla Units of Second World War (4th series). Multicoloured.

2809	2p. Type **866**	20	15
2810	2p. Badge of Bicol Brigade Veterans	20	15
2811	2p. Map of Fil-American Guerrilla forces (Cavite) and Hukbalahap unit (Pampanga)	20	15
2812	2p. Map of South Tarlac military district and Northwest Pampanga	20	15

867 Liberation of Panay and Romblon

1995. 50th Anniversaries. Multicoloured.

2813	2p. Type **867**	20	15
2814	2p. Liberation of Cebu	20	15
2815	2p. Battle of Ipo Dam	20	15
2816	2p. Battle of Bessang Pass	20	15
2817	2p. Surrender of General Yamashita	20	15

868 Jose Rizal

1995. Centenary of Declaration of Philippine Independence Revolutionaries. Multicoloured.

2818	2p. Type **868**	20	15
2819	2p. Andres Bonifacio	20	15
2820	2p. Apolinario Mabini	20	15

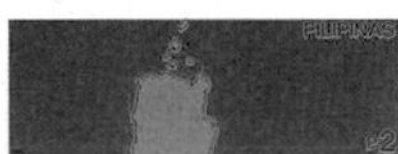

869 Top detail of Map of Islands

1995. 50th Anniv of End of Second World War. Dated "1995". Two sheets containing new designs as T 869 and previous designs. Multicoloured.

MS2821	Two sheets. (a) 177×139 mm. 2p. ×8, Nos. 2682/5, 2729/30 and 2741/2; 2p. ×4, As T **869** forming composite design of map of Philippine Islands (blue background). (b) 179×199 mm. 2p. ×13, Nos. 2710/11, 2731, 2743/7 and 2813/17; 2p. ×4 As T **869** forming composite design of map of Philippine Islands (green background); 2p. As No. 2732	8·00	8·00

1996. National Symbols. As T 860, with blue barcode at top. "Pilipinas" in blue. Variously dated. Multicoloured.

2822	1p. Flower (jasmine)	15	10
2823	1p.50 Fish (milkfish)	20	15
2823a	2p. Flower (jasmine)	30	30
2824	3p. Animal (water buffalo)	35	30
2825	4p. Flag ("Pilipinas" at top)	50	35
2826	4p. Hero (Jose Rizal)	50	35
2827	4p. House	50	35
2828	4p. Costume	50	35
2829	4p. Dance	50	35
2830	4p. Sport	50	35
2831	4p. Bird (Philippine eagle)	50	35
2832	4p. Type **860**	50	35
2833	4p. Animal (head of water buffalo) (dated "1995")	50	35
2834	4p. Flower (jasmine)	50	35
2835	4p. Tree	50	35
2836	4p. Fruit (mango)	50	35
2837	4p. Leaf (palm)	50	35
2838	4p. Fish (milkfish)	50	35
2839	4p. Animal (water buffalo) (dated "1996")	50	35
2840	5p. Bird (Philippine eagle)	75	1·20
2841	6p. Leaf (palm)	80	50
2842	7p. Costume	90	60
2843	8p. Fruit (mango)	1·10	75
2844	10p. House	1·40	90

870 "Treating Patient" (Manuel Baldemor)

1996. 23rd International Congress of Internal Medicine, Manila.

2856	**870**	2p. multicoloured	20	15

871 Walled City of Intramuros

1996. Centenary of Sun Life of Canada (insurance company). Multicoloured.

2857	2p. Type **871**	20	15
2858	8p. Manila Bay sunset	1·10	75

872 Pair of Eastern Rosella (birds) on Branch ("I Love You")

1996. Greetings Stamps. Multicoloured.

2859	2p. Type **872**	20	15
2860	2p. Eastern rosella (birds) ("Happy Valentine")	20	15
2861	6p. Cupid holding banner ("I Love You")	75	50
2862	6p. Cupid holding banner ("Happy Valentine")	75	50
2863	7p. Box of chocolates ("I Love You")	95	65
2864	7p. Box of chocolates ("Happy Valentine")	95	65
2865	8p. Butterfly and roses ("I Love You")	1·20	80
2866	8p. Butterfly and roses ("Happy Valentine")	1·20	80

Nos. 2861/2 were issued together, se-tenant, forming a composite design.

873 University Building and Map of Islands on Grid

1996. 50th Anniv of Gregorio Araneta University Foundation.

2867	**873**	2p. multicoloured	20	15

874 Hospital

1996. 50th Anniv of Santo Tomas University Hospital.

2868	**874**	2p. multicoloured	20	15

875 Racoon Butterflyfish

1996. Fishes (1st series). Multicoloured.

2869	4p. Type **875**	50	35
2870	4p. Clown triggerfish	50	35

2871	4p. Regal angelfish	50	35
2872	4p. Mandarin fish	50	35
2873	4p. Emperor angelfish	50	35
2874	4p. Japan surgeonfish ("Powder Brown Tang")	50	35
2875	4p. Blue-girdled ("Majestic") angelfish	50	35
2876	4p. Palette surgeonfish ("Blue tang")	50	35
2877	4p. Moorish idol	50	35
2878	4p. Yellow-tailed ("Two-band-ed") anemonefish	50	35

MS2879 Two sheets (a) 140×81 mm. 4p. Clown triggerfish; 4p. Blue and red angelfish; 4p. Regal angelfish; 4p. Yellow-tailed anemonefish. (b) 82×61 mm. 12p. Lionfish 1·60 1·60

See also Nos. 2885/**MS**95.

MS2880 Two sheets. No. **MS**2879 additionally inscr in right margin for "Indonesia 96" World Youth Stamp Exhibition, Bandung 1·60 1·60

No **MS**2879 commemorates "ASENPEX '96".
See also Nos. 2885/**MS**2895.

1996. Basketball Championship. No. MS2510 trimmed to 85×85 mm (to remove inscr at foot) and optd in bottom margin with PALARONG '96 PAMBANSA SOCSARGEN (SOUTH COTABATO, SARAGANI & GENERAL SANTOS CITY) APRIL 14-21, 1996.

MS2881 10p. multicoloured 1·30 1·30

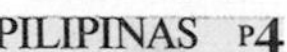

877 Francisco Ortigas

1996

2882 **877** 4p. multicoloured 50 35

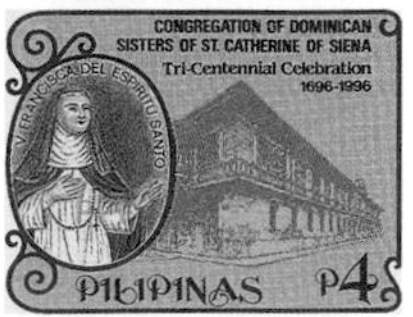

878 Mother Francisca and Convent

1996. 300th Anniv of Dominican Sisters of St. Catherine of Siena.

2883 **878** 4p. multicoloured 50 35

879 Nuclear Reactor

1996. Centenary of Discovery of Radioactivity by Antoine Henri Becquerel.

2884 **879** 4p. multicoloured 50 35

1996. Fishes (2nd series). As T 875. Multicoloured.

2885	4p. Spotted boxfish	50	35
2886	4p. Saddle ("Saddleback") butterflyfish	50	35
2887	4p. Sail-finned tang	50	35
2888	4p. Harlequin tuskfish	50	35
2889	4p. Clown wrasse	50	35
2890	4p. Yellow-faced ("Blue-faced") angelfish	50	35
2891	4p. Long-horned cowfish	50	35
2892	4p. Queen angelfish	50	35
2893	4p. Forceps ("Long-nosed") butterflyfish	50	35
2894	4p. Yellow tang	50	35

MS2895 Two sheets. (a) 133×80 mm. Nos. 2888, 2890 and 2892/3; (b) 136×74 mm. 4p. Purple fire goby; 4p. Yellow seahorse; 4p. Dusky bat-fish; 4p. Long-nosed hawkfish 4·50 4·50

1996. No. MS2895 additionally inscr in margin "CHINA 96–9th Asian International Exhibition" in English and Chinese and with exhibition emblem.

MS2896 Two sheets. (a) 133×80 mm. 4p. ×4 multicoloured. (b) 136×74 mm. 4p. ×4, multicoloured 4·50 4·50

(880)

1996. 10th Anniv of Young Philatelists' Society. Nos. 2471/4 optd with T 880.

2897	2p. multicoloured	20	20
2898	2p. multicoloured	20	20
2899	2p. multicoloured	20	20
2900	2p. multicoloured	20	20

881 Carlos Garcia (President, 1957–61)

1996. Birth Centenaries. Multicoloured.

2901	4p. Type **881**	50	35
2902	4p. Casimiro del Rosario (physicist)	50	35
2903	4p. Geronima Pecson (first woman senator)	50	35
2904	4p. Cesar Bengson (member of International Court of Justice)	50	35
2905	4p. Jose Corazon de Jesus (writer)	50	35

1996. Centenary of Declaration of Philippine Independence (6th issue). Centenary of Philippine Revolution. Sheet 100×80 mm containing vert designs as T 860 but with bar code sideways at right.

MS2906 4p. Cry of Pugadlawin; 4p. Battle of Pinaglabanan; 4p. Cry of Nueva Ecija; 4p. Battle of Binakayan 2·20 2·20

882 Satellite, Dish Aerial, Cock and Map

1996. 50th Anniv of ABS–CBN Broadcasting Services in Philippines. Multicoloured.

2907	4p. Type **882**	50	35
2908	8p. Cock, satellite and hemi-spheres	1·10	75

883 "M" and Heart

1996. "Convention City Manila".

2909 **883** 4p. multicoloured 50 35

884 Cojuangco

1996. Birth Centenary of Jose Cojuangco (entrepreneur and Corazon Aquino's father).

2910 **884** 4p. multicoloured 50 35

885 Brass Helmet and Top Hat

1996. 50th Anniv of Republic Day. Philippine–American Friendship Day. Multicoloured.

2911	4p. Type **885**	50	35
2912	8p. Philippine eagle and Ameri-can bald eagle	1·10	75

MS2913 60×80 mm. 16p. American and Philippine flags (27×37 mm) 2·20 2·20

886 Boxing

1996. Centenary of Modern Olympic Games. Mult.

2914	4p. Type **886**	50	35
2915	6p. Athletics	80	50
2916	7p. Swimming	95	65
2917	8p. Equestrian	1·10	75

MS2918 119×80 mm. 4p. ×4, Motifs as in Nos. 2914/17 but with different backgrounds and inscriptions differ-ently arranged 2·20 2·20

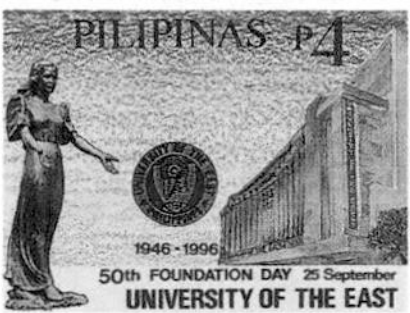

887 "Alma Mater" (statue, Guillermo Tolentino) and Manila Campus (after Florentino Concepcion)

1996. 50th Anniv of University of the East, Manila and Kalookan City.

2919 **887** 4p. multicoloured 50 35

888 "Dendrobium anosmum"

1996. Orchids. Multicoloured.

2920	4p. Type **888**	50	35
2921	4p. "Phalaenopsis equestris-alba"	50	35
2922	4p. "Aerides lawrenceae"	50	35
2923	4p. "Vanda javierii"	50	35
2924	4p. "Renanthera philippinensis"	50	35
2925	4p. "Dendrobium schuetzei"	50	35
2926	4p. "Dendrobium taurinum"	50	35
2927	4p. "Vanda lamellata"	50	35

MS2928 141×64 mm. 4p. "Coelogyne pandurata"; 4p. "Vanda merrilii" (vert); 4p. "Cymbidium aliciae" (vert); 4p. "Dendrobium topaziacum" (vert) 2·20 2·20

889 Emblem and Globe

1996. 6th Asia–Pacific International Trade Fair, Manila.

2929 **889** 4p. multicoloured 50 35

890 Children's Activities

1996. 50th Anniv of UNICEF. Multicoloured.

2930	4p. Type **890**	50	35
2931	4p. Windmills, factories, gen-erator, boy with radio and children laughing	50	35
2932	4p. Mother holding "sun" baby and children gardening	50	35
2933	4p. Wind blowing toy wind-mills, boy with electrical fan and children playing	50	35

MS2934 91×58 mm. 16p. Boy with anemometer, girl with testubes, boy with magnifying glass and girl with windmill (39×29 mm) 2·20 2·20

891 Fran's Fantasy "Aiea"

1996. "Taipeh 96" Asian Stamp Exhibition. Orchids. Multicoloured.

2935	4p. Type **891**	50	35
2936	4p. Malvarosa Green Goddess "Nani"	50	35
2937	4p. Ports of Paradise "Emerald Isle"	50	35
2938	4p. Mem. Conrada Perez "Nani"	50	35
2939	4p. Pokai Tangerine "Lea"	50	35
2940	4p. Mem. Roselyn Reisman "Diana"	50	35
2941	4p. C. Moscombe x Toshie Aoki	50	35
2942	4p. Mem. Benigno Aquino "Flying Aces"	50	35

MS2943 97×65 mm. 12p. Pamela Het-herington "Coronation", Living Gold "Erin Treasure" and Eleanor Spicer "White Bouquet"(79×29 mm) 1·60 1·60

892 Communications

1996. 4th Asia–Pacific Economic Co-operation Summit Conference, Subic. Multicoloured.

2944	4p. Type **892**	50	35
2945	6p. Open hands reaching towards sun (horiz)	80	50
2946	7p. Grass and buildings (horiz)	95	65
2947	8p. Members' flags lining path leading to emblem, city and sun	1·10	75

893 Philippine Nativity (Gilbert Miraflor)

1996. Christmas. Stamp design competition winning entries. Multicoloured.

2948	4p. Type **893**	50	35
2949	6p. Church (Stephanie Miljares) (horiz)	80	50
2950	7p. Carol singer with guitars (Mark Sales) (horiz)	95	65
2951	8p. Carol singers and statue of buffalo (Lecester Glaraga)	1·10	75

894 Perez

1996. Birth Centenary of Eugenio Perez (politician).

2952 **894** 4p. multicoloured 50 35

895 Carabao

1996. New Year. Year of the Ox. Multicoloured.

2953	4p. Type **895**	50	35
2954	6p. Tamaraw	80	50

MS2955 97×88 mm. Nos. 2953/4. Perf or imperf 1·30 1·30

896 Rizal aged 14

1996. "Aseanpex '96" Association of South-East Asian Nations Stamp Exhibition, Manila. Death Centenary of Dr. Jose Rizal (1st issue). Mult.

2956	4p. Type **896**	50	35
2957	4p. Rizal aged 18	50	35
2958	4p. Rizal aged 25	50	35
2959	4p. Rizal aged 31	50	35
2960	4p. Title page of "Noli Me Tangere" (first novel)	50	35
2961	4p. Gomburza and associates	50	35
2962	4p. "Oyang Dapitana" (sculpture by Rizal)	50	35
2963	4p. Bust by Rizal of Ricardo Carnicero (commandant of Dapitan)	50	35
2964	4p. Rizal's house at Calamba (horiz)	50	35
2965	4p. University of Santo Tomas, Manila (horiz)	50	35
2966	4p. Hotel de Oriente, Manila (horiz)	50	35
2967	4p. Dapitan during Rizal's exile (horiz)	50	35
2968	4p. Central University, Madrid (horiz)	50	35
2969	4p. British Museum, London (horiz)	50	35
2970	4p. Botanical Garden, Madrid (horiz)	50	35
2971	4p. Heidelberg, Germany (horiz)	50	35

MS2972 Four sheets, each 97×70 mm. (a) 12p. Cooking equipment and portrait as in T **896**; (b) 12p. Cooking equipment and portrait as in No. 2957; (c) 12p. No. 2958; (d) 12p. Cooking equipment and portrait as in No. 2959 — 6·50 6·50

See also No. 2976.

897 Father Mariano Gomez

1996. Centenary of Declaration of Philippine Independence. Execution of Secularist Priests, 1872. Multicoloured.

2973	4p. Type **897**	50	35
2974	4p. Father Jose Burgos	50	35
2975	4p. Father Jacinto Zamora	50	35

1997. "Hong Kong 97" Stamp Exhibition. Chinese Zodiac. Two sheets 161×100 mm containing previous New Year issues (some with changed face values). Multicoloured.

MS2977 Two sheets (a) 4p. ×5, As Nos. 2351, 2452, 2603, 2806 and 2953; (b) 6p. ×6, As Nos. 2352, 2451, 2604, 2708 and 2954 — 8·00 8·00

898 Rizal (poster)

1996. Death Centenary of Dr. Jose Rizal (2nd issue).

2976	**898**	4p. multicoloured	50	35

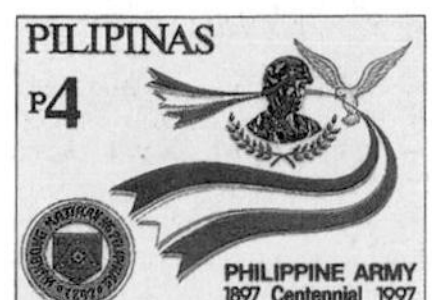

899 Soldier, Dove and National Colours

1997. Centenary of Philippine Army.

2978	**899**	4p. multicoloured	50	45

900 Ordination, Seminary, Priest prostrate before Altar and Priest at Devotions

1997. Bicentenary of Holy Rosary Seminary, Naga City.

2979	**900**	4p. multicoloured	50	45

1997. National Symbols. As T 788 (no bar code). "Pilipinas" in blue. Multicoloured.

2980	1p. Flower (jasmine)	30	15
2981	5p. Bird (Philippine eagle)	1·30	45
2982	6p. Leaf (palm)	1·50	60
2983	7p. Costume	1·80	65
2984	8p. Fruit (mango)	2·10	80
2985	10p. House	2·50	1·00

901 Volunteers attending Patient

1997. 50th Anniv of Philippine National Red Cross.

2986	**901**	4p. multicoloured	50	45

902 Insurance Services

1997. 50th Anniv of Philippine American Life Insurance Company.

2987	**902**	4p. multicoloured	50	45

903 Columns

1997. Centenary of Department of Finance.

2988	**903**	4p. multicoloured	50	45

904 Signatures and Globe

1997. 50th Anniv of J. Walter Thompson (Philippines) Inc. (advertising agency).

2989	**904**	4p. multicoloured	50	45

1997. "Pacific 97" International Stamp Exhibition, San Francisco. No. MS2913 optd World Philatelic Exhibition May 29 – June 8, 1997 San Francisco, California U.S.A. in the right margin and with exhibition emblem in the left margin.

MS2990 16p. multicoloured — 3·00 3·00

1997. National Symbol. As T 860 (with bar code). "Pilipinas" in black at foot. Multicoloured.

2991	4p. Gem (South Sea pearls)	50	45

906 Visayan Warty Pig

1997. Endangered Animals. Multicoloured.

2992	4p. Type **906**	60	50
2993	4p. Sow and young Visayan warty pig	60	50
2994	4p. Visayan spotted deer buck	60	50
2995	4p. Roe and young Visayan spotted deer	60	50

907 Founding Signatories

1997. 30th Anniv of Association of South-East Asian Nations. Multicoloured.

2996	4p. Type **907**	60	50
2997	4p. Flags of founding member nations	60	50
2998	6p. Members' flags as figures forming circle around ASEAN emblem	90	75
2999	6p. Members' flags encircling globe	90	75

908 Symbols of Education and Law, University Building and Graduate

1997. 50th Anniv of Manuel L. Quezon University.

3000	**908**	4p. multicoloured	50	4·50

909 Assembly Emblem

1997. 2nd World Scout Parliamentary Union General Assembly, Manila.

3001	**909**	4p. multicoloured	50	45

910 Isabelo Abaya

1997. Battle of Candon. Multicoloured.

3002	4p. Type **910**	50	45
3003	6p. Abaya rallying revolutionaries (horiz)	75	65

911 Roberto Regala (diplomat and lawyer)

1997. Birth Centenaries. Multicoloured.

3004	4p. Type **911**	50	45
3005	4p. Doroteo Espiritu (dentist)	50	45
3006	4p. Elisa Ochoa (nurse, first Congresswoman and 1930s' national tennis champion)	50	45
3007	4p. Mariano Marcos (politician)	50	45
3008	4p. Jose Romero (politician)	50	45

912 St. Theresa

1997. Death Centenary of St. Theresa of Lisieux.

3009	**912**	6p. multicoloured	75	65

1997. Centenary of Declaration of Phillipine Independence (8th issue). Revolutionaries. Sheet 100×80 mm containing vert designs as T 860 but with barcode sideways at right.

MS3010 4p. Edilberto Evangelista and battle of Zapota Bride; 4p. Vicente Alvarez; 4p. Fracisco del Castillo; 4p. Pantaleon Villegas — 2·20 2·20

913 "Homage to the Heroes of Bessang Pass" (Hernando Ruiz Ocampo)

1997. 50th Anniv of Stamp and Philatelic Division. Modern Art. Multicoloured.

3011	4p. Type **913**	45	45
3012	6p. "Jardin III" (Fernando Zobel)	75	65
3013	7p. "Abstraction" (Nena Saguil) (vert)	80	75
3014	8p. "House of Life" (Jose Joya) (vert)	95	90

MS3015 120×69 mm. 16p. "Dimension of Fear" (Jose Joya) (79×30 mm) — 1·90 1·90

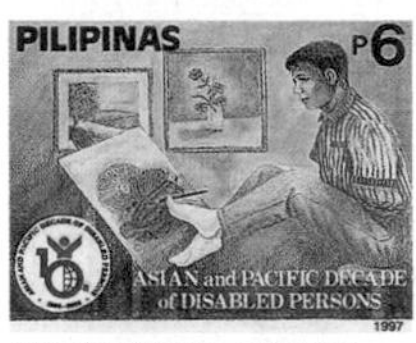

914 Man Painting with Feet

1997. Asian and Pacific Decade of Disabled Persons.

3016	**914**	6p. multicoloured	75	75

915 Bonifacio writing

1997. Centenary of Declaration of Philippine Independence. Statues of Andres Bonifacio. Multicoloured.

3017	4p. Type **915**	45	45
3018	4p. Bonifacio holding flag	45	45
3019	4p. Bonifacio holding sword	45	45

916 Von Stephan

1997. Death Centenary of Heinrich von Stephan (founder of U.P.U.).

3020	**916**	4p. multicoloured	50	50

917 Underwater Scene (image scaled to 63% of original size)

1997. International Year of the Reef.

3021	**917**	8p. multicoloured	1·00	1·00

MS3022 100×69 mm. **917** 16p. multicoloured — 2·10 2·10

918 "Adoration of the Magi"

1997. Christmas. Stained Glass Windows. Mult.

3023	4p. Type **918**	45	45
3024	6p. Mary, Jesus and Wise Men	75	75

3025 7p. Mary on donkey and Nativity 80 80
3026 8p. "Nativity" 95 95

919 Tiger

1997. New Year. Year of the Tiger. Multicoloured.
3027 4p. Type **919** 45 45
3028 6p. Head of tiger and tiger climbing rockface 65 65
MS3029 98×90 mm. Nos. 3027/8 plus two labels 1·10 1·10

920 "Dalagang Bukid" (Fernando Amorsolo)

1997. Stamp Collecting Month. Paintings. Multicoloured.
3030 4p. Type **920** 45 45
3031 6p. "Bagong Taon" (Arturo Luz) 75 75
3032 7p. "Jeepneys" (Vicente Manansala) (horiz) 80 80
3033 8p. "Encounter of the 'Nuestra Senora de Cavadonga' and the 'Centurion' " (Alfredo Carmelo) (horiz) 95 95
MS3034 102×60 mm. 16p. "Pista sa Nayon" (Carlos Francisco) (77×27 mm) 2·10 2·10

921 Hatch Grey

1997. Gamecocks. Multicoloured.
3035 4p. Type **921** 30 30
3036 4p. Spangled roundhead 30 30
3037 4p. Racey mug 30 30
3038 4p. Silver grey 30 30
3039 4p. Grey (vert) 30 30
3040 4p. Kelso (vert) 30 30
3041 4p. Bruner roundhead (vert) 30 30
3042 4p. Democrat (vert) 30 30
MS3043 Two sheets. (a) 55×69 mm. 12p. Cocks fighting (vert); (b) 99×59 mm. 16p. Cocks preparing to fight (79×29 mm) 2·10 2·10

922 Philippine Eagle

1997. National Symbols. Multicoloured.
3044 20p. Type **922** 1·50 1·50
3045 30p. Philippine eagle (different) 2·20 2·20
3046 50p. Philippine eagle (different) 3·75 3·75

923 Flag and Stars

1998. 50th Anniv of Art Association of the Philippines. Multicoloured.
3047 4p. Type **923** 45 45
3048 4p. Hand clasping paintbrushes 50 50

924 Mother Philippines, Club Building and Emblem

1998. Centenary of Club Filipino (social club).
3049 **924** 4p. multicoloured 45 45

925 Marie Eugenie

1998. Death Centenary of Blessed Marie Eugenie (founder of the Sisters of the Assumption).
3050 **925** 4p. multicoloured 45 45

926 Philippine and United States Flags

1998. 50th Anniv of Fulbright (student exchange) Program.
3051 **926** 4p. multicoloured 45 45

927 Emilio Jacinto

1998. Heroes of the Revolution. Multicoloured. White backgrounds. Blue barcode at foot.
3052 2p. Type **927** 20 15
3054 4p. Melchora Aquino 45 35
3055 4p. Jose Rizal 35 30
3056 5p. Antonio Luna 45 35
3057 8p. Marcelo del Pilar 60 50
3058 10p. Gregorio del Pilar 75 65
3059 11p. Andres Bonifacio 80 75
3060 13p. Apolinario Mabini 95 90
3061 15p. Emilio Aguinaldo 1·10 1·00
3062 18p. Juan Luna 1·30 1·20
See also Nos. 3179/88 and 3189/98.

928 Mt. Apo, Bagobo Woman, Orchids and Fruit

1998. 50th Anniv of Apo View Hotel, Davao City.
3070 **928** 4p. multicoloured 45 45

929 School and Emblem

1998. 75th Anniv of Philippine Cultural High School.
3071 **929** 4p. multicoloured 35 35

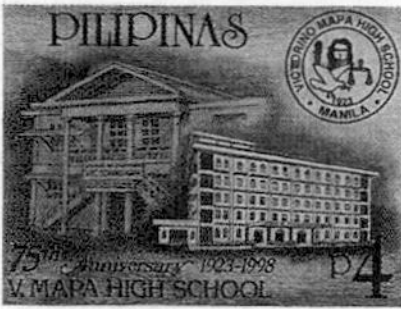

930 Old and Present School Buildings

1998. 75th Anniv of Victorino Mapa High School, San Rafael.
3072 **930** 4p. multicoloured 35 35

931 Lighthouse, Warship and Past and Present Uniforms

1998. Centenary of Philippine Navy.
3073 **931** 4p. multicoloured 35 35

932 University and Igorot Dancer

1998. 50th Anniv of University of Baguio.
3074 **932** 4p. multicoloured 35 35

933 Training Ship and Emblem

1998. 50th Anniv of Philippine Maritime Institute.
3075 **933** 4p. multicoloured 35 35

934 Forest, Palawan

1998. "EXPO '98" World's Fair, Lisbon. Mult.
3076 4p. Type **934** 35 35
3077 15p. Filipino vinta (sail canoe), Zamboanga (horiz) 1·10 1·10
MS3078 102×81 mm. 15p. Main Lobby of Philippine Pavilion (79×29 mm) 1·10 1·10

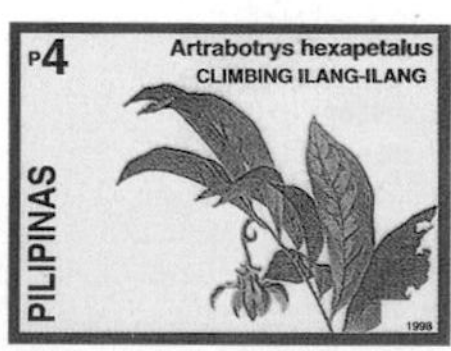

935 Climbing Ilang-ilang

1998. "Florikultura'98" International Garden Festival, San Fernando, Pampanga. Illustrations from "Flowers of the Philippines" by Manuel Blanco. Multicoloured.
3079 4p. Type **935** 30 30
3080 4p. "Hibiscus rosa-sinensis" 30 30
3081 4p. "Nerium oleander" 30 30
3082 4p. Arabian jasmine ("Jasminum sambac") 30 30
3083 4p. "Gardenia jasminoides" (vert) 30 30
3084 4p. Flame-of-the-forest ("Ixora coccinea") (vert) 30 30
3085 4p. Indian coral bean ("Erythrina indica") (vert) 30 30
3086 4p. "Abelmoschus moschatus" (vert) 30 30
MS3087 61×70 mm. 15p. "Medinilla magnifica" (vert) 3·00 3·00

936 City and Clark International Airport (image scaled to 63% of original size)

1998. Clark Special Economic Zone.
3088 **936** 15p. multicoloured 1·10 1·10

937 Manila Galleon

1998. Centenary of Declaration of Philippine Independence. Philippines–Mexico–Spain Friendship. Multicoloured.
3089 15p. Type **937** 65 50
3090 15p. Philippine woman with flag, Legaspi-Urdaneta Monument and galleon 1·10 1·10
3091 15p. Spanish and Philippine flags, Cebu Basilica (after M. Miguel) and "Holy Child" (statuette) 1·10 1·10
MS3092 145×90 mm. Nos. 3089/91 plus three labels 3·25 3·25

938 "Spoliarium" (Juan Luna)

1998. Centenary of Declaration of Philippine Independence. Multicoloured.
3093 4p. Type **938** 20 20
3094 8p. General Emilio Aguinaldo introducing Philippine national flag at Cavite 35 35
3095 16p. Execution of Jose Rizal, 1896 2·75 2·75
3096 16p. Andres Bonifacio and Katipunan monument 2·75 2·75
3097 20p. Barasoain Church (venue of first Philippine Congress, 1898) 3·25 3·25

939 Andres Soriano (accountant)

1998. Birth Centenaries. Multicoloured.
3098 4p. Type **939** 35 35
3099 4p. Tomas Fonacier (Univeristy dean and historian) 35 35
3100 4p. Josefa Escoda (founder of Filipino Girl Scouts and social reformer) 35 35
3101 4p. Lorenzo Tanada (politician) 35 35
3102 4p. Lazaro Francisco (writer) 35 35

940 Melchora Aquino

1998. Centenary of Declaration of Philippine Independence Women Revolutionaries. Mult.
3103 4p. Type **940** 20 20
3104 4p. Nazaria Lagos 20 20
3105 4p. Agueda Kahabagan 20 20

1998. Centenary of Philippine Independence (13th issue). Events of 1898. Sheet 100×80 mm containing vert designs as T 860 but with barcode sideways at right.
MS3106 4p. Cebu uprising; 4p. Negros uprising; 4p. Iligan uprising; 4p. Centenary emblem 1·20 1·20

1998. Centenary of Declaration of Philippine Independence (14th issue). Nos. 2644 (1993), 2825/32 and 2834/9 optd 1898 1998 KALAYAAN and emblem.
3107 3p. Animal (head of water buffalo) 30 30

3108	4p. Flag ("Pilipinas" at top)	30	30
3109	4p. Hero (Jose Rizal)	30	30
3110	4p. House	30	30
3111	4p. Costume	30	30
3112	4p. Dance	30	30
3113	4p. Sport	30	30
3114	4p. Bird (Philippine eagle)	30	30
3115	4p. Type **860**	30	30
3116	4p. Flower (jasmine)	30	30
3117	4p. Tree	30	30
3118	4p. Fruit (mango)	30	30
3119	4p. Leaf (palm)	30	30
3120	4p. Fish	30	30
3121	4p. Animal (water buffalo)	30	30

942 River Pasig

1998. River Pasig Environmental Campaign.

3122	**942** 4p. multicoloured	35	35

943 Bottle-nosed ("Bottlenose") Dolphin

1998. Marine Mammals. Multicoloured.

3123	4p. Type **943**	30	30
3124	4p. Humpback whale	30	30
3125	4p. Fraser's dolphin	30	30
3126	4p. Melon-headed whale	30	30
3127	4p. Minke whale	30	30
3128	4p. Striped dolphin	30	30
3129	4p. Sperm whale	30	30
3130	4p. Pygmy killer whale	30	30
3131	4p. Cuvier's beaked whale	30	30
3132	4p. Killer whale	30	30
3133	4p. Bottle-nosed ("Bottlenose") dolphin (different)	30	30
3134	4p. Spinner dolphin ("Long-snouted spinner dolphin")	30	30
3135	4p. Risso's dolphin	30	30
3136	4p. Finless porpoise	30	30
3137	4p. Pygmy sperm whale	30	30
3138	4p. Pantropical spotted dolphin	30	30
3139	4p. False killer whale	30	30
3140	4p. Blainville's beaked whale	30	30
3141	4p. Rough-toothed dolphin	30	30
3142	4p. Bryde's whale	30	30
MS3143	83×60 mm. 15p. Dugong	1·80	1·80

944 Coconuts and Products

1998. Centenary of Philippine Coconut Industry.

3144	**944** 4p. multicoloured	30	30

945 Grapes, Emblem and Nun

1998. 75th Anniv of Holy Spirit Adoration Sisters in the Philippines.

3145	**945** 4p. multicoloured	30	30

946 Child posting Letter

1998. Centenary of Postal Service. Multicoloured.

3146	6p. Type **946**	45	45
3147	6p. Globe and handshake	45	45
3148	6p. Philippine stamps, globe, airplane, galleon and building	45	45
3149	6p. Flags, dove and letters floating down to girl	45	45
MS3150	102×60 mm. 15p. Boy holding letter and letters encircling globe	1·00	1·00

947 Holly Wreath

1998. Christmas. Multicoloured.

3151	6p. Type **947**	45	45
3152	11p. Star wreath	75	75
3153	13p. Flower wreath	90	90
3154	15p. Bell wreath	1·00	1·00

948 2c. Postage Stamps

1998. "Philipinas 98" International Stamp Exhibition, Mandaluyong City. Six sheets each 121×60 mm containing horiz designs as T 948 showing 1898 Filipino Revolutionary Government Stamps. Multicoloured.

MS3155	Six sheets (a) 15p. Type **948** (blue background); (b) 15p. 2c. Postage and 1m. imperforate and perforate Printed Matter ("IMPRESOS") stamps; (c) 15p. 2 and 5c. Telegraph stamps; (d) 15p. 8c. Registered Letter ("CERTIFICADO") and 10c. Revenue ("RECIBOS") stamps; (e) 15p. Local issue and 5p. "LIBERTAD" stamp; (f) 15p. As No. **MS**3154a but imperforate and with green background	13·50	13·50

949 Person gagged with Barbed Wire

1998. 50th Anniv of Universal Declaration of Human Rights.

3156	**949** 4p. multicoloured	10	10

950 Papal Mitre

1998. Shells. Multicoloured.

3157	4p. Type **950**	30	30
3158	4p. "Vexillum citrinum"	30	30
3159	4p. "Rugose mitre" ("Vexillum rugosum")	30	30
3160	4p. "Volema carinifera"	30	30
3161	4p. "Teramachia dalli"	30	30
3162	4p. "Nassarius vitiensis"	30	30
3163	4p. "Cymbiola imperialis"	30	30
3164	4p. "Cymbiola aulica"	30	30
MS3165	97×70 mm. 8p. "Nassarius papillosus"; 8p. Trapezium horse conch ("Fasciolaria trapezium")	2·10	2·10

951 Sea Creatures (image scaled to 63% of original size)

1998. International Year of the Ocean.

3166	**951** 15p. multicoloured	45	35
MS3167	101×71 mm. No. 3166	1·80	1·80

952 Taking Oath

1998. Inauguration of President Joseph Ejercito Estrada. Multicoloured.

3168	6p. Type **952**	45	45
3169	15p. Inaugural speech	1·00	1·00

953 Rabbit

1998. New Year. Year of the Rabbit. Multicoloured.

3170	4p. Type **953**	30	30
3171	11p. Two rabbits	75	75
MS3172	97×89 mm. Nos. 3170/1 plus two labels. Perf or Imperf	2·00	2·00

954 "Dyesebel"

1998. National Stamp Collecting Month. Film Posters.

3173	**954** 6p. blue and black	45	45
3174	- 11p. brown and black	75	75
3175	- 13p. mauve and black	90	90
3176	- 15p. green and black	1·00	1·00
MS3177	58×101 mm. 15p. black	1·80	1·80

DESIGNS—As T **954** 11p. "Ang Sawa sa Lumang Simboryo"; 13p. "Prinsipe Amante"; 10p. (3176) "Anak Dalita". 26×76 mm—15p. (**MS**3177) "Siete Infantes de Lara".

955 "Noli Me Tangere" (Jose Rizal) (Pride in the Citizenry)

1998. Centenary of Declaration of Independence of Philippine Independence (15th issue). The Six Prides. Six sheets, each 84×90 mm containing vert designs as T 955. Multicoloured.

MS3178	Six sheets. (a) 15p. Type **955**; (b) 15p. Banaue Rice Terraces (engineering); (c) 15p. Monument and woman holding national flag (Filipino people); (d) 15p. Malay woman in traditional costume (heritage); (e) 15p. Woman decorating pot and scripts (literature); (f) 15p. Woman with eagle on arm (resources)	6·00	6·00

1998. Heroes of the Revolution. As Nos. 3052/62. Multicoloured. Blue barcode at foot. (a) Yellow backgrounds.

3179	6p. Type **927**	50	50
3180	6p. Melchora Aquino	50	50
3181	6p. Jose Rizal	50	50
3182	6p. Antonio Luna	50	50
3183	6p. Marcelo del Pilar	50	50
3184	6p. Gregorio del Pilar	50	50
3185	6p. Andres Bonifacio	50	50
3186	6p. Apolinario Mabini	50	50
3187	6p. Emilio Aguinaldo	50	50
3188	6p. Juan Luna	50	50

(b) Green backgrounds.

3189	15p. Type **927**	1·10	1·10
3190	15p. Melchora Aquino	1·10	1·10
3191	15p. Jose Rizal	1·10	1·10
3192	15p. Antonio Luna	1·10	1·10
3193	15p. Marcelo del Pilar	1·10	1·10
3194	15p. Gregorio del Pilar	1·10	1·10
3195	15p. Andres Bonifacio	1·10	1·10
3196	15p. Apolinario Mabini	1·10	1·10
3197	15p. Emilio Aguinaldo	1·10	1·10
3198	15p. Juan Luna	1·10	1·10

(c) Pink background.

3229	5p. Jose Rizal	35	35

956 Old and New Bank Emblems

1999. 50th Anniv of Central Bank of the Philippines.

3199	**956** 6p. multicoloured	35	35

957 Anniversary Emblem

1999. Centenary of Declaration of Philippine Independence. Multicoloured.

3200	6p. Type **957**	35	35
3201	6p. General Emilio Aguinaldo's house (site of declaration, June 1898)	35	35
3202	6p. Malolos Congress, Barasoain Church, Bulacan (ratification by regions of declaration, September 1898)	35	35
3203	6p. House in Western Negros (uprising of 5 November 1898)	35	35
3204	6p. Cry of Santa Barbara, Iloilo (inauguration of government, 17 November 1898)	35	35
3205	6p. Cebu City (Victory over Colonial Forces of Spain, December 1898)	35	35
3206	6p. Philippine flag and emblem (declaration in Butaan City of sovereignty over Mindanao, 17 January 1899)	35	35
3207	6p. Facade of Church (Ratification of Constitution, 22 January 1899)	35	35
3208	6p. Carnival procession, Malolos (Inauguration of Republic, 23 January 1899)	35	35
3209	6p. Barosoain Church and anniversary emblem	35	35

958 Scouts and Guides

1999

3210	5p. Type **958**	1·10	1·10
3211	5p. Children gardening	1·10	1·10

Nos. 3210/11 were originally issued as Savings Bank stamps in 1995, but were authorized for postal use from 16 January 1999.

959 Cruise Liner

1999. Centenary of Department of Transportation and Communication. Multicoloured.

3212	6p. Type **959**	35	35
3213	6p. Airplane	35	35
3214	6p. Air traffic control tower	35	35
3215	6p. Satellite dish aerial and bus	35	35
MS3216	114×70 mm. 15p. Globe, stamps, Philpost headquarters and letters (79×27 mm)	1·80	1·80

Nos. 3212/15 were issued together, se-tenant, forming a composite design.

960 San Juan del Monte Bridge

1999. Centenary of American–Filipino War.

3217	**960**	5p. multicoloured	35	35

961 General Emilio Aguinaldo and Academy Arms

1999. Centenary (1998) of Philippine Military Academy.

3218	**961**	5p. multicoloured	35	35

962 Green-backed Heron

1999. Birds. Multicoloured.

3219	5p. Type **962**	35	35
3220	5p. Common tern	35	35
3221	5p. Greater crested tern	35	35
3222	5p. Ruddy Turnstone	35	35
3223	5p. Black-winged stilt	35	35
3224	5p. Asiatic Dowitcher	35	35
3225	5p. Whimbrel	35	35
3226	5p. Reef heron	35	35
MS3227	84×71 mm. 8p, Spotted greenshank; 8p. Tufted duck	3·00	3·00
MS3228	84×71 mm. As No. **MS**3227 but with different margin and emblem and inscription for "Australia 99" World Stamp Exhibition, Melbourne	80	1·20

963 Man holding Crutches

1999. 50th Anniv of Philippine Orthopaedic Association.

3230	**963**	5p. multicoloured	35	35

964 Francisco Ortigas and Emblem

1999. 50th Anniv of Manila Lions Club.

3231	**964**	5p. multicoloured	35	35

965 Entrance to Garden

1999. La Union Botanical Garden, San Fernando.

3232	5p. Type **965**	35	35
3233	5p. Kiosk	35	35

Nos. 3232/3 were issued together, se-tenant, forming a composite design.

966 Gliding Tree Frog

1999. Frogs. Multicoloured.

3234	5p. Type **966**	35	35
3235	5p. Common forest frog	35	35
3236	5p. Woodworth's frog	35	35
3237	5p. Giant Philippine frog	35	35
MS3238	108×86 mm. 5p. Spiny tree frog; 5p. Truncate-toed chorus frog; 5p. Variable-backed frog	3·00	3·00

967 Manta Ray

1999. Marine Life. Multicoloured.

3239	5p. Type **967**	35	35
3240	5p. Painted rock lobster	35	35
3241	5p. Sea squirt	35	35
3242	5p. Banded sea snake	35	35
MS3243	111×88 mm. 5p. Sea grapes; 5p. Branching coral; 5p. Sea urchin	4·00	4·00

968 Nakpil

1999. Birth Centenary of Juan Nakpil (architect).

3244	**968**	5p. multicoloured	35	35

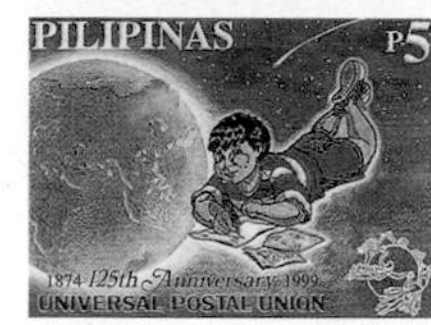

969 Child writing Letter and Globe

1999. 125th Anniv of Universal Postal Union. Multicoloured.

3245	5p. Type **969**	35	35
3246	15p. Girl with stamp album	1·10	1·10

970 Waling-Waling and Cattleya "Queen Sirikit'

1999. 50 Years of Philippines–Thailand Diplomatic Relations. Multicoloured.

3247	5p. Type **970**	35	35
3248	11p. As Type **970** but with flowers transposed	80	80

971 Child writing

1999. 150th Anniv of Mongol Pencils.

3249	**971**	5p. multicoloured	35	35

972 Emblem and Handicapped Children

1999. 75th Anniv of Masonic Charities for Handicapped Children.

3250	**972**	5p. multicoloured	35	35

973 Sampaguita and Rose of Sharon

1999. 50 Years of Philippines–South Korea Diplomatic Relations. Multicoloured.

3251	5p. Type **973**	35	35
3252	11p. As Type **973** but with flowers transposed	80	80

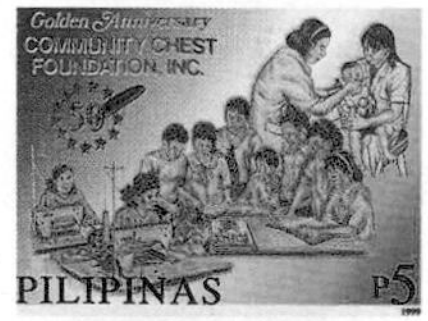

974 Teachers, Nurses and Machinists

1999. 50th Anniv of Community Chest Foundation.

3253	**974**	5p. multicoloured	35	35

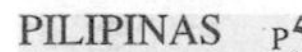

975 Dove, Fishes, Bread and Quotation from Isaiah

1999. Centenary of Philippine Bible Society.

3254	**975**	5p. multicoloured	35	35

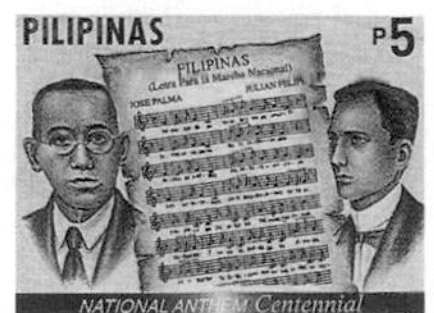

976 Score, Jose Palma (lyricist) and Julian Felipe (composer)

1999. Centenary of National Anthem.

3255	**976**	5p. multicoloured	35	35

977 St. Francis of Assisi and Parish Church

1999. 400th Anniv of St. Francis of Assisi Parish, Sariaya, Quezon.

3256	**977**	5p. multicoloured	35	35

1999. 25th Anniv of International Philippine Philatelic Society. No. MS3092 optd 25th ANNIVERSARY IPPS on each stamp and in the margins with anniversary inscr and emblems in silver.

MS3257	145×90 mm. Nos. 3089/91 plus three labels	3·50	3·50

979 Flags and Official Seal

1999. The Senate.

3258	**979**	5p. multicoloured	35	35

980 New Business, Arts and Sciences Faculty Building

1999. 60th Anniv of Chiang Kai Shek College, Manila.

3259	**980**	5p. multicoloured	45	45

981 School Building

1999. 50th Anniv of Tanza National High School.

3260	**981**	5p. multicoloured	45	45

982 St. Agustin Church, Paoay (World Heritage Day)

1999. United Nations Day. Multicoloured.

3261	5p. Type **982**	45	45
3262	11p. Elderly couple (International Year of the Older Person)	90	90
3263	15p. "Rizal Learns the Alphabet and Prayers from his Mother" (Miguel Galvez) (World Teachers' Day)	1·20	1·20

983 Angel

1999. Christmas. Multicoloured.

3264	5p. Type **983**	45	45
3265	11p. Angel holding star	90	90
3266	13p. Angel holding ribbon	1·10	1·10
3267	15p. Angel holding flowers	1·30	1·30
MS3268	141×95 mm. Nos. 3264/7	35	35

984 Tamaraw and Polar Bear

1999. 50 Years of Philippines–Canada Diplomatic Relations. Multicoloured.

3269	5p. Type **984**	45	45
3270	15p. As Type **984** but with animals transposed	1·30	1·30

985 Coliseum

1999. Renovation of Araneta Coliseum.

3271	**985**	5p. multicoloured	45	45

986 Sunrise

1999. 3rd Informal Summit of Association of South-east Asian Nations, Manila.

3272	**986**	5p. multicoloured	45	45
3273	**986**	11p. multicoloured	95	95

987 "Kristo" (Arturo Luz)

1999. National Stamp Collecting Month. Modern Sculptures. Multicoloured.

3274	5p. Type **987**	45	45
3275	11p. "Homage to Dodgie Laurel" (J. Elizalde Navarro)	90	90
3276	13p. "Hilojan" (Napoleon Abueva)	1·10	1·10
3277	15p. "Mother and Child" (Napoleon Abueva)	1·30	1·30
MS3278	100×90 mm. 5p. "Mother's Revenge" (Jose Rival); 15p. "El Ermitano" (Jose Rival) (horiz)	2·50	2·50

988 Dragon

1999. New Year. Year of the Dragon. Multicoloured.

3279	5p. Type **988**	45	45
3280	15p. Dragon amongst clouds	90	90
MS3281	98×88 mm. Nos. 3279/80 plus two labels. Perf or imperf	1·50	1·50

989 Gen. Gregorio H. del Pilar

1999. Centenary of the Battle of Tirad Pass.

3282	**989**	5p. multicoloured	45	45

990 *Paphiopedilum urbanianum*

1999. Orchids. Multicoloured.

3283	5p. Type **990**	45	45
3284	5p. *Phalaenopsis schilleriana*	45	45
3285	5p. *Dendrobium amethystoglossum*	45	45
3286	5p. *Paphiopedilum barbatum*	45	45
MS3287	132×83 mm. 5p. "Paphiopedilum haynaldianum" (horiz); 5p. "Phalaenopsis stuartiana" (horiz); 5p. "Trichoglottis brachiata" (horiz); 5p. "Ceratostylis rubra" (horiz)	1·80	1·80

991 General Licerio Geronimo

1999. Centenary of Battle of San Mateo.

3288	**991**	5p. multicoloured	45	45

992 Crowds around Soldiers in Tanks

1999. New Millennium (1st series). "People Power". Multicoloured.

3289	5p. Type **992**	45	45
3290	5p. Radio antennae, helicopters and people	45	45
3291	5p. Religious procession	45	45

Nos. 3289/91 were issued together, se-tenant, forming a composite design.

See also Nos. 3311/13, 3357/9 and 3394/6.

993 Woman holding Gender Signs

2000. 25th Anniv of National Commission on Role of Filipino Women.

3292	**993**	5p. multicoloured	45	45

994 Newspaper Headline and Headquarters

2000. Centenary of the Manila Bulletin (newspaper).

3293	**994**	5p. multicoloured	45	45

995 Manuel Roxas (1946–48)

2000. Presidential Office. Multicoloured.

3294	5p. Type **995**	45	45
3295	5p. Elpidio Quirino (1948–53)	45	45

996 Golfer, Sailing Boat and Swimmers

2000. 150th Anniv of La Union Province. Mult.

3296	5p. Type **996**	45	45
3297	5p. Tractor, building and worker	45	45
3298	5p. Government building	45	45
3299	5p. Airplane, bus, satellite dish, workers and bus	45	45

997 Joseph Ejercito Estrada (1998–2000)

2000. Presidential Office. Multicoloured.

3300	5p. Presidential seal (face value at top left)	35	35
3301	5p. Type **997**	35	35
3302	5p. Fidel V. Ramos (1992–98)	35	35
3303	5p. Corazon C. Aquino (1986–92)	35	35
3304	5p. Ferdinand E. Marcos (1965–86)	35	35
3305	5p. Diosdado Macapagal (1961–65)	35	35
3306	5p. Carlos P. Garcia (1957–61)	35	35
3307	5p. Ramon Magsaysay (1953–57)	35	35
3308	5p. Elpidio Quirino (1948–53)	35	35
3309	5p. Manuel Roxas (1946–48)	35	35

998 Workers and Emblem

2000. Centenary of the Civil Service Commission.

3310	**998**	5p. multicoloured	45	45

999 Golden Garuda, Palawan

2000. New Millennium (2nd series). Artefacts. Mult.

3311	5p. Type **999**	75	75
3312	5p. Sunrise at Pusan Point, Davao Oriental	75	75
3313	5p. Golden Tara, Agusan	75	75

1000 Outrigger Canoe, Boracay Island

2000. Tourist Sites. Multicoloured.

3314	5p. Type **1000**	35	35
3315	5p. Chocolate Hills, Bohol	35	35
3316	5p. El Nido Forest, Palawan	35	35
3317	5p. Vigan House, Ilocos Sur	35	35
MS3318	99×59 mm. 15p. Bananue rice terraces, Ifugao (79×29 mm)	1·80	1·80

1001 Great Wall of China and Chinese Phoenix

2000. 25th Anniv of Diplomatic Relations with Republic of China. Multicoloured.

3319	5p. Type **1001**	35	35
3320	11p. Banaue rice terraces and Philippine Sarimanok	80	80
MS3321	98×60 mm. 5p. Great Wall of China (39×29 mm); 11p. Banaue rice terraces (39×29 mm)	1·20	1·20

1002 Television and Emblem

2000. 50th Anniv of GMA Television and Radio Network.

3322	**1002**	5p. multicoloured	45	45

1003 Church Building

2000. 400th Anniv of St. Thomas de Aquinas Parish, Mangaldan.

3323	**1003**	5p. multicoloured	45	45

1004 Carlos P. Garcia

2000. Presidential Office. Multicoloured.

3324	10p. Type **1004**	90	90
3325	10p. Ramon Magsaysay	90	90
3326	11p. Ferdinand E. Marcos	95	95
3327	11p. Diosdado Macapagal	95	95
3328	13p. Corazon C. Aquino	1·00	1·00
3329	13p. Fidel V. Ramos	1·00	1·00
3330	15p. Joseph Ejercito Estrada	1·20	1·20
3331	15p. Presidential seal (face value at top right)	1·20	1·20

See also Nos. 3489/98.

1005 Memorial and Map

2000. Battle Centenaries. Multicoloured.

3332	5p. Type **1005** (Battle of Pulang Lupa)	45	45
3333	5p. Memorial and soldiers (Battle of Mabitac)	45	45
3334	5p. Sun and soldiers (Battles of Cagayan, Agusan Hill and Makahambus Hill) (vert)	45	45
3335	5p. Map, memorial and bamboo signalling device (Battle of Paye) (vert)	45	45

1006 Joseph Ejercito Estrada

2000. Presidential Office. Multicoloured.

3336	5p. Presidential seal	45	45
3337	5p. Type **1006**	45	45
3338	5p. Fidel V. Ramos	45	45
3339	5p. Corazon C. Aquino	45	45
3340	5p. Ferdinand E. Marcos	45	45
3341	5p. Diosdado Macapagal	45	45
3342	5p. Carlos P. Garcia	45	45
3343	5p. Ramon Magsaysay	45	45
3344	5p. Elpidio Quirino	45	45
3345	5p. Manuel Roxas	45	45

1007 Ornate Chequered Beetle

2000. Insects. Multicoloured.

3346	5p. Type **1007**	35	35
3347	5p. Sharpshooter bug	35	35
3348	5p. Milkweed bug	35	35
3349	5p. Spotted cucumber beetle	35	35
3350	5p. Green June beetle	35	35
3351	5p. Convergent ladybird beetle	35	35
3352	5p. Eastern hercules beetle	35	35
3353	5p. Harlequin cabbage bug	35	35
MS3354	Two sheets, each 99×19 mm. (a) Nos. 3346/9; (b) Nos. 3350/3	4·50	4·50

1008 St. Ferdinand Cathedral, Map and Emblem

2000. 50th Anniv of Lucena Diocese.

3355	**1008**	5p. multicoloured	50	50

1009 Nurses and Patients

2000. 50th Anniv of Occupational Health Nurses' Association.

3356	**1009**	5p. multicoloured	50	50

1010 Balanghai

2000. New Millennium (3rd series). Traditional Sea Craft. Multicoloured.

3357	5p. Type **1010**	45	45
3358	5p. Vinta	45	45
3359	5p. Caracoa	45	45

1011 Jars, Bank Note, Circuit Board, Computer Mouse and Emblem

2000. 50th Anniv of Equitable PCI Bank.

3360	**1011**	5p. multicoloured	50	50

1012 Ship, Globe, Airplane and Workers

2000. Year of Overseas Filipino Workers.

3361	**1012**	5p. multicoloured	50	50

1013 Pedro Poveda (founder), Buildings and Emblem

2000. 50th Anniv of the Teresian Association (international lay preacher association) in the Philippines.

3362	**1013**	5p. multicoloured	50	50

1014 Congress in Session

2000. House of Representatives.

3363	**1014**	5p. multicoloured	45	45

1015 Soldiers, Tank and Emblem

2000. 50th Anniv of Philippine Marine Corps.

3364	**1015**	5p. multicoloured	45	45

1016 Running

2000. Olympic Games, Sydney. Multicoloured.

3365	5p. Type **1016**	45	45
3366	5p. Archery	45	45
3367	5p. Rifle shooting	45	45
3368	5p. Diving	45	45
MS3369	100×85 mm. 5p. Boxing (horiz); 5p. Show jumping (horiz); 5p. Rowing (horiz); 5p. Taekwondo (horiz)	3·00	3·00

1017 Boy, Envelopes and Statue of Postman (image scaled to 63% of original size)

2000. Postal Service. Sheet 100×60 mm.

MS3370 **1017**	15p. multicoloured	1·20	1·20

1018 B'laan Woman's Blouse, Davao del Sur

2000. "Sheer Realities: Clothing and Power in 19th-century Philippines" Exhibition, Manila. Multicoloured.

3371	5p. Type **1018**	45	45
3372	5p. T'boli T'nalak abaca cloth, South Cotabato	45	45
3373	5p. Kalinga/Gaddang cotton loincloth, Cordilleras (vert)	45	45
3374	5p. Portrait of Leticia Jimenez (anon) (vert)	45	45
MS3375	101×70 mm. 5p. Portrait of Teodora Devera Ygnacio (Justiniano Asuncion); 15p. Tawsug silk sash, Sulu Archipelago	2·50	2·50

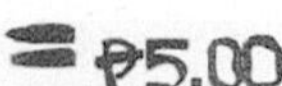
1019 Angel cradling Sunflowers

2000. Christmas. Multicoloured.

3376	5p. Type **1019**	45	45
3377	5p. As No. 3376 but inscribed "CHRISTMAS JUBILEUM"	45	45
3378	11p. Angel with basket of fruit and swag of leaves	90	90
3379	13p. Angel with basket of fruit on shoulder	1·00	1·00
3380	15p. Angel with garland of flowers	1·30	1·30

1020 1955 5c. Labour Management Congress Stamp

2000. 50th Anniv of Amateur Philatelists Organization Philatelic Society. Multicoloured.

3381	5p. Type **1020**	35	35
3382	5p. 1957 5c. Juan Luna birth centenary stamp (horiz)	35	35
3383	5p. 1962 5c. orchid stamp	35	35
3384	5p. 1962 6 + 4c. Rizal Foundation Fund stamp (horiz)	35	35

2000. No. 1977 surch P5.00.

3385	5p on 3p.60 multicoloured	35	35

1022 "Portrait of an Unknown Lady" (Juan Novicio Luna)

2000. Modern Art. Multicoloured.

3386	5p. Type **1022**	35	35
3387	11p. "Nude" (Jose Joya) (horiz)	80	80
3388	13p. "Lotus Odalisque" (Rodolfo Paras-Perez) (horiz)	90	90
3389	15p. "Untitled (Nude)" (Fernando Amorsolo) (horiz)	1·00	1·00
MS3390	100×80 mm. 15p. "The Memorial" (Cesar Legaspi) (79×29 mm)	2·50	2·50

1023 Snake

2000. New Year. Year of the Snake. Multicoloured.

3391	5p. Type **1023**	35	35
3392	11p. Snake	80	80
MS3393	98×88 mm. Nos. 3391/2. Perf or imperf	2·20	2·20

1024 Ships in Port (Trade and Industry)

2000. New Millennium (4th series). Multicoloured.

3394	5p. Type **1024**	35	35
3395	5p. Pupils and teacher (Education and Knowledge)	35	35
3396	5p. Globe, satellite, family using computer and woman using telephone (Communications and Technology)	35	35

1025 Pesos Fuertes (1st Philippines Banknote)

2001. 150th Anniv of Philippines Bank.

3397	**1025**	5p. multicoloured	35	35

1026 Eagle

2001. "Hong Kong 2001" International Stamp Exhibition. Flora and Fauna. Multicoloured.

3398	5p. Type **1026**	35	35
3399	5p. Philippine tarsier	35	35
3400	5p. "Talisman Cove" (flower)	35	35
3401	5p. Turtle	35	35
3402	5p. Tamaraw	35	35
MS3403	Five sheets, each 80×71 mm. (a) 11p. As Type **1026**. (b) 11p. As No. 3399. (c) 11p. As No. 3400. (d) 11p. As No. 3401. (e) 11p. As No. 3402	7·50	7·50

1027 Rizal

2001. 150th Birth Anniv of General Paciano Rizal.

3404	**1027**	5p. multicoloured	35	35

1028 Facade

2001. Centenary of San Beda College.

3405	**1028**	5p. multicoloured	35	35

1029 High Altar, St. Peter's Basilica, Rome

2001. 50th Anniv of Diplomatic Relations with Vatican City. Multicoloured.

3406	5p. Type **1029**	35	35
3407	15p. High altar, San Agustin Church, Manila	1·10	1·10
MS3408	90×71 mm. 15p. Adam; 15p. God	2·20	2·20

The two stamps in No. **MS**3408 form the composite design of "Creation of Adam" (Michaelangelo).

1030 Presidential Seal

2001. Multicoloured, background colour given.

3409	**1030**	5p. yellow	35	35
3410	**1030**	10p. green	80	80
3411	**1030**	11p. red	90	90
3412	**1030**	13p. black	1·10	1·10
3413	**1030**	15p. blue	1·30	1·30

1031 Our Lady of Manaoag

2001. 75th Anniv of Canonical Coronation of Our Lady of the Rosary of Manaoag.

3414	**1031**	5p. multicoloured	35	35

1032 Pres. Macapagal-Arroyo taking Presidential Oath

2001. President Gloria Macapagal-Arroyo. Multicoloured.

3415	5p. Type **1032**	35	35
3416	5p. Pres. Macapagal-Arroyo waving	35	35

1033 Sydney Opera House and Philippines Cultural Centre

2001. Philippine-Australia Diplomatic Relations. Multicoloured.

3417	5p. Type **1033**	35	35
3418	13p. As Type **1033** but with subjects transposed	1·10	1·10
MS3419	96×60 mm. 13p. Philippines Cultural Centre and Sydney Opera House (79×29 mm)	1·10	1·10

1034 Philippine Normal University

2001. University Centenaries. Multicoloured.

3420	5p. Type **1034**	35	35
3421	5p. Facade of Silliman University	35	35

1035 Scales of Justice and Court Building

2001. Centenary of Supreme Court.

3422	**1035** 5p. multicoloured	35	35

1036 Joaquin J. Ortega

2001. Anniversaries. Multicoloured.

3423	5p. Type **1036** (centenary of appointment as first Civil Governor of the Province of La Union)	35	35
3424	5p. Eugenio H. Lopez (business-man, birth centenary)	35	35

1037 Visayan Couple

2001. "PHILANIPPON '01" International Stamp Exhibition, Japan. Boxer Codex (manuscript depicting Philippine lifestyle during first century of Spanish contact). Multicoloured.

3425	5p. Type **1037**	45	45
3426	5p. Tagalog couple	45	45
3427	5p. Moros of Luzon (man wear-ing red tunic)	45	45
3428	5p. Moros of Luzon (woman wearing blue dress)	45	45
MS3429	82×107 mm. 5p. Tattooed Pintados; 5p. Pintados wearing costumes; 5p. Cagayan woman; 5p. Zambal	1·80	1·80

1038 Teachers and Thomas (transport)

2001. Centenary of Arrival of American Teachers. Multicoloured.

3430	5p. Type **1038**	45	45
3431	15p. Pupils and school building	1·30	1·30

1039 Emblem

2001. Centenary of Technology University, Manila.

3432	**1039** 5p. multicoloured	45	45

1040 Museum Artefacts

2001. Centenary of National Museum.

3433	**1040** 5p. multicoloured	45	45

1041 1901 Lands Management Charter, Modern Surveyors and Emblems

2001. Centenary of Lands Management Bureau.

3434	**1041** 5p. multicoloured	45	45

1042 Statue of St. Joseph and Seminary Building

2001. 400th Anniv of San Jose Seminary.

3435	**1042** 5p. multicoloured	45	45

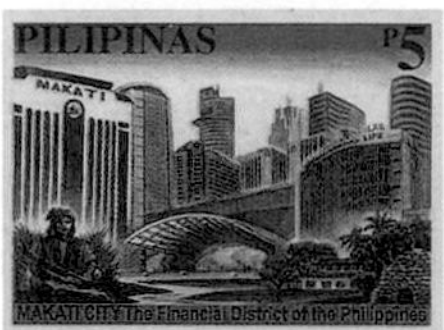

1043 Makati City Financial District

2001

3436	**1043** 5p. multicoloured	45	45

1044 Trumpet

2001. Musical Instruments. Multicoloured.

3437	5p. Type **1044**	45	45
3438	5p. Tuba	45	45
3439	5p. French horn	45	45
3440	5p. Trombone	45	45
MS3441	81×106 mm. VERT:—5p. ×4 Bass drum; Clarinet and oboe; Xylophone; Sousaphone	1·80	1·80

1045 Off Shore Production Platform

2001. Malampaya Deep Water Gas to Power Project. Multicoloured.

3442	5p. Type **1045**	45	45
3443	15p. As No. 3442 but with gold border	1·30	1·30

1046 Two Stylized Figures

2001. International Year of Volunteers.

3444	**1046** 5p. multicoloured	45	45

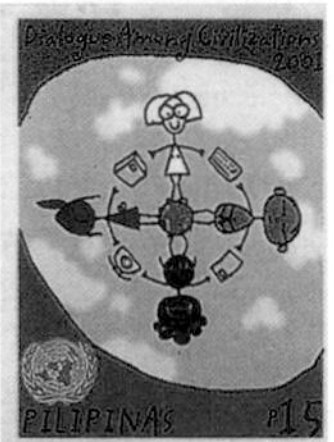

1047 Children surrounding globe

2001. United Nations Year of Dialogue among Civilizations.

3445	**1047** 15p. multicoloured	1·30	1·30

1048 Girls and Singers ("Herald Angels")

2001. Christmas.

3446	5p. Type **1048**	45	45
3447	11p. Boy and Christmas baubles ("Kumukutikutitap")	90	90
3448	13p. Children and lanterns ("Pasko ni Bitoy")	1·00	1·00
3449	15p. Children blowing trumpets ("Pasko na naman")	1·30	1·30

1049 William Tell Monument

2001. 150th Anniv of Philippines–Switzerland Diplomatic Relations. Multicoloured.

3450	5p. Type **1049**	45	45
3451	15p. Jose P. Rizal Monument	1·30	1·30
MS3452	98×62 mm. 15p. Mayon volcano and Matterhorn (horiz) (80×30 mm)	1·30	1·30

1050 St. George and Dragon

2001. Centenary of Solicitor General's Office.

3453	**1050** 5p. multicoloured	45	45

1051 "Puj" (Antonio Austria)

2001. National Stamp Collecting Month. Art. Multicoloured.

3454	5p. Type **1051**	45	45
3455	17p. "Hesus Nazereno" (Angelito Antonio)	1·40	1·40
3456	21p. "Three Women with Basket" (Anita Magsaysay-Ho) (vert)	1·60	1·60
3457	22p. "Church with Yellow back-ground" (Mauro Santos)	1·80	1·80
MS3458	102×74 mm. 22p. "Komedya ng Pakil" (Danilo Dalena) (80×30 mm)	1·80	1·80

1052 Couple (woman wearing brown apron)

2001. Inhabitants of Manila drawn by Jean Mallet. Multicoloured.

3462	5p. Couple in riding dress	45	45
3468	17p. Type **1052**	1·40	1·40
3469	21p. Couple (woman wearing blue apron)	1·60	1·60
3470	22p. Couple using pestles and mortar	1·80	1·80

1053 Red Horse

2001. New Year. Year of the Horse. Multicoloured.

3471	5p. Type **1053**	45	45
3472	17p. White horse	1·40	1·40
MS3473	100×89 mm. As Nos. 3471/2 plus 2 labels	1·80	1·80

No. **MS**3473 also exists imperforate.

1054 "Sanctification in Ordinary Life" (Godofredo F. Zapanta)

2002. Birth Centenary of Josemaria Escriva de Balaguer (founder of Opus Dei religious order).

3474	**1054** 5p. multicoloured	45	45

1055 St. Paul's Metropolitan Cathedral

2002. UNESCO World Heritage Sites, Vigan City, Ilocos Sur Province. Multicoloured.

3475	5p. Type **1055**	45	45
3476	22p. Calee Crisologo	1·90	1·90

1056 Salvador Araneta

2002. Birth Centenary of Salvador Araneta (nationalist politician and philanthropist).

3477	**1056** 5p. multicoloured	45	45

1057 "Manila Customs" (painting, Auguste Nicolas Vaillant)

2002. Centenary of Customs Bureau.

3478	**1057**	5p. multicoloured	45	45

1058 Envelope and "I Love You"

2002. St. Valentine's Day. Multicoloured.

3479	5p. Type **1058**	45	45
3480	5p. Couple enclosed in heart	45	45
3481	5p. Cat and dog	45	45
3482	5p. Air balloon	45	45

1059 "Image of the Resurrection" (detail, Fernando Amorsolo) and Hospital Façade

2002. Centenary of Baguio General Hospital and Medical Centre.

3483	**1059**	5p. multicoloured	45	45

1060 Pedro Calungsod

2002. 330th Death Anniv of Pedro Calungsod. Multicoloured.

3484	5p. Type **1060**	45	45
MS3485	102×72 mm. 22p. Pedro Calungsod holding crucifix. Imperf	1·80	1·80

1061 Virgin and Child (painting) and School Façade

2002. Centenary of Negros Occidental High School.

3486	**1061**	5p. multicoloured	45	45

1062 College Facade

2002. Centenary of La Consolacion College, Manila.

3487	**1062**	5p. multicoloured	45	45

1063 Stupa, Buddha and Lotus Blossom

2002. Vesak Day.

3488	**1063**	5p. multicoloured	45	45

1064 Gloria Macapagal-Arroyo (2001–)

2002. Presidential Office (2nd series). With blue barcode at foot. Multicoloured.

3489	5p. Type **1064**	45	45
3490	5p. Joseph Ejercito Estrada (1998–2000)	45	45
3491	5p. Fidel V. Ramos (1992–98)	45	45
3492	5p. Corazon C. Aquino (1986–92)	45	45
3493	5p. Ferdinand E. Marcos (1965–86)	45	45
3494	5p. Diosdado Macapagal (1961–65)	45	45
3495	5p. Carlos P. Garcia (1957–61)	45	45
3496	5p. Ramon Magsaysay (1953–57)	45	45
3497	5p. Elpidio Quirino (1948–1953)	45	45
3498	5p. Manuel Roxas (1946–1948)	45	45

1065 National Flag and School Façade

2002. Centenary of Cavite National High School.

3499	**1065**	5p. multicoloured	45	45

1066 Emblem and Cathedral Façade

2002. Centenary Iglesia Filipina Independiente (religious movement).

3500	**1066**	5p. multicoloured	45	45

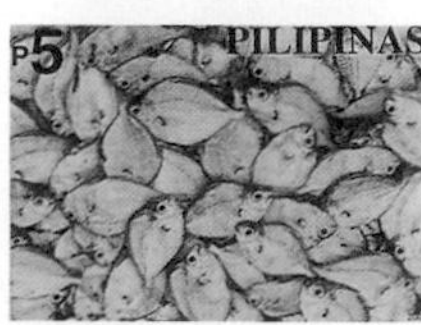

1067 Fish

2002. Marine Conservation. Multicoloured.

3501	5p. Type **1067**	45	45
3502	5p. Fish laid head to head	45	45
3503	5p. Edge of mangrove swamp	45	45
3504	5p. Hands holding minnows	45	45
MS3505	90×77 mm. 5p. ×4, Man using binoculars from catamaran (no fishing); Mangrove swamp (reforestation of mangroves); Divers (reef monitoring); Rows of seaweed (seaweed farming)	1·80	1·80

No. **MS**3505 has a brief description of each stamp in the lower margin.

1068 Edge of Mangrove Swamp

2002. Philakorea 2002 International Stamp Exhibition, Seoul. Two sheets, each 97×86 mm containing T 1068 and similar vert design. Multicoloured.

MS3506	(a) 5p. Type **1068**; 17p. As No. 3488 (b) As No. **MS**3506a but with gold horizontal band	1·60	1·60

2002. No. 2476 optd 3p.

3507	3p. on 60s. multicoloured	35	35

1070 Participating Countries' Flags surrounding Communication Mast

2002. TELMIN, TELSOM and ATRC Telecommunications Meetings held in Manila.

3508	**1070**	5p. multicoloured	45	45

1071 Kapitan Moy Building and Giant Shoe

2002. Shoe Manufacture in Marikina City.

3509	**1071**	5p. multicoloured	45	45

1072 Gerardo de Leon

2002. National Stamp Collecting Month. Multicoloured.

3510	5p. Type **1072** (filmmaker)	45	45
3511	17p. Francisca Reyes Aquino (folk dance researcher)	1·40	1·40
3512	21p. Pablo Antonio (architect)	1·60	1·60
3513	22p. Jose Garcia Villa (writer)	1·80	1·80
MS3514	100×74 mm. 22p. Honorata de la Rama (singer and actress) Imperf	1·80	1·80

1073 Kutsinta (rice cakes)

2002. Christmas. Multicoloured.

3515	5p. Type **1073**	45	45
3516	17p. Sapin-sapin (multilayered cake)	1·40	1·40
3517	21p. Bibingka (rice and coconut cake)	1·60	1·60
3518	22p. Puto bumbong (cylindrical rice cakes)	1·80	1·80

1074 Dove, Family and Crucifix

2002. 4th World Meeting of Families (papal initiative), Manila (1st issue).

3519	**1074**	11p. multicoloured	90	90

See also No. 3528.

1075 Antonio Pigafetta

2002. 480th Anniv of First Circumnavigation of the Globe (1st issue). Multicoloured.

3520	5p. Type **1075**	45	45
3521	5p. Ferdinand Magellan	45	45
3522	5p. Charles I coin and *Vitoria*	45	45
3523	5p. Sebastian *Eleano* and *Vitoria*	45	45

See also No. **MS**3530.

1076 Female Goat

2002. Year of the Goat. Multicoloured.

3524	5p. Type **1076**	45	45
3525	17p. Male goat	1·40	1·40
MS3526	99×88 mm. Nos. 3524/5. Perf or imperf	1·80	1·80

1077 Lyceum Building and Bust of Jose Laurel (founder)

2002. 50th Anniv of Philippines Lyceum.

3527	**1077**	5p. multicoloured	45	45

1078 Holy Family

2002. 4th World Meeting of Families, Manila (2nd issue).

3528	**1078**	5p. multicoloured	45	45

1079 Mt. Guiting (image scaled to 61% of original size)

2002. International Year of Mountains. Sheet 96×70 mm.

MS3529	**1079**	22p. multicoloured	1·80	1·80

1080 Charles I Coin and 16th-century Map (image scaled to 70% of original size)

2002. 480th Anniv of First Circumnavigation of the Globe (2nd issue). Sheet 104×85 mm. Imperf.

MS3530	**1080** 22p. multicoloured	1·80	1·80

1081 *Geodorum densiflorum*

2002. Orchids. (1st series). Multicoloured.

3531	5p. Type **1081**	45	45
3532	5p. *Nervilia plicata*	45	45
3533	5p. *Luisia teretifolia*	45	45
3534	5p. *Dendrobium Victoria-reginae*	45	45
MS3535	101×87 mm. 22p. *Grammatophylum scriptum*. Imperf	1·80	1·80

See also Nos. 3596/9.

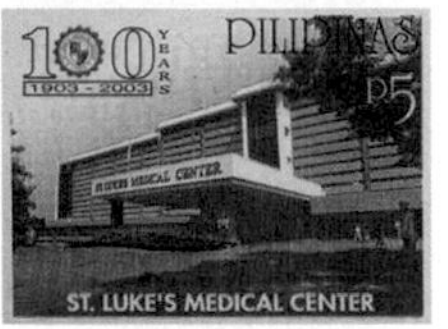

1082 Centre Buildings

2002. Centenary of St. Luke's Medical Centre, Manila.

3536	**1082** 5p. multicoloured	15	15

1083 University Facade and Emblem

2003. 75th Anniv of Far Eastern University.

3537	**1083** 5p. multicoloured	15	15

1084 20th-century Tram

2003. Centenary of Meralco (electric tram company).

3538	**1084** 5p. multicoloured	15	15

1085 Heart-shaped Strawberry and Postman

2003. St. Valentine's Day. Multicoloured.

3539	5p. Type **1085**	15	15
3540	17p. Three hearts	45	45
3541	21p. Heart-shaped rainbow	55	55
3542	22p. Butterflies and heart-shaped flowers	60	60

1086 Kennon Mountain Road

2003. Centenary of Japanese Construction Workers Arrival.

3543	**1086** 23p. multicoloured	60	60

1087 Emblem and School Building

2003. Centenary of La Union National High School.

3544	**1087** 5p. multicoloured	15	15

1088 Yakan Weaving

2003. Traditional Weaving (MS3544a/b) or Crafts (MS3544c). 50th Anniv of Summer Linguistics Institute. Three sheets, each 98×83 mm containing T 1087 and similar horiz designs. Multicoloured.

MS3545	(a) 15p. ×4, Type **1088**; Ifugao; Kagayanen; Bagbo Abaca; (b) 5p. ×2, Kalinga; Aklanon Pina; 17p. ×2, Tboli cross-stitch; Manobo beadwork (c) 11p. ×4, Ayta bow and arrows; Ibatan baskets; Palawano gong; Mindanao musical instruments. Set of 3 sheets	3·75	3·75

1089 Our Lady of Guadelupe (statue)

2003. 50th Anniv of Philippine—Mexico Diplomatic Relations. Multicoloured.

3546	5p. Type **1089**	15	15
3547	22p. Black Nazarene, Quiapo (statue)	60	60
MS3548	97×61 mm. 22p. Procession (80×30 mm)	60	60

1090 Apolinario Mabini carried in Litter

2003. Revolutionaries' Death Centenaries. Multicoloured.

3549	6p. Type **1090**	15	15
3550	6p. Luciano San Miguel	15	15

1091 *Dendrobium uniflorum*

2003. Orchids. Multicoloured. (a) Without Latin inscription.

3551	6p. Type **1091**	10	10
3552	9p. *Paphiopedilum urbanianum*	10	10
3553	17p. *Epigeneium lyonii*	10	10
3554	21p. *Thrixspermum subulatum*	10	10

(b) With Latin inscription.

3555	1p. *Liparis latifolia*	10	10
3556	2p. *Cymbidium finlaysonianum*	10	10
3557	3p. *Phalaenopsis philippinensis*	10	10
3558	4p. *Phalaenopsis fasiata*	10	10
3559	5p. *Spathoglotis plicata*	10	10
3560	6p. As No. 3551	15	15
3561	6p. *Phalaenopsis fuscata*	15	15
3562	6p. *Phalaenopsis stuartiana*	15	15
3563	6p. *Renanthera monachia*	15	15
3564	6p. *Aerides quinquevulnera*	15	15
3565	8p. *Phalaenopsis schilleriana*	20	20
3566	9p. *Phalaenopsis pulchra*	25	25
3567	10p. *Kingidium philippinennse*	25	25
3568	17p. As. No. 3553	45	45
3569	20p. *Phaius tankervillae*	50	50
3570	21p. As. No. 3554	55	55
3571	22p. *Trichoglottis philippinensis*	55	55

2003. No. 3409 surch.

3581	1p. on 5p. multicoloured	10	10
3582	6p. on 5p. multicoloured	15	15

1093 Flag, Doctors and Patient

2003. Centenary of Philippine Medical Association.

3583	**1093** 6p. multicoloured	15	15

1094 Woman carrying Corn

2003. 50th Anniv of Rural Banking.

3584	**1094** 6p. multicoloured	15	15

1095 Rizal Monument, Rizal Park, Fujian,People's Republic of China

2003. Jose Rizal (writer and reformer) Commemoration. Multicoloured.

3585	6p. Type **1095**	15	15
3586	17p. Pagoda and Jose Rizal (horiz)	45	45

1096 Madoura Ceramics Exhibition Poster (Pablo Picasso)

2003. Philippines—Spain Friendship Day. Multicoloured.

3587	6p. Type **1096**	15	15
3588	22p. "Flashback" (Jose Joya)	60	60

1097 "Early Traders" (Cesar Amorsolo)

2003. Centenary of Chamber of Commerce.

3589	**1097** 6p. multicoloured	15	15

1098 Mt. Makiling, Laguna

2003. Mountains. Multicoloured.

3590	6p. Type **1098**	15	15
3591	6p. Mt. Kanlaon	15	15
3592	6p. Mt. Kitangland	15	15
3593	6p. Mt. Mating-oy	15	15
MS3594	92×82 mm. 6p. ×4, Mt. Iraya; Mt. Hibok-Hibok; Mt. Apo; Mt. Sto Tomas	60	60

1099 Miners

2003. Centenary of Benguet Corporation.

3595	**1099** 6p. multicoloured	15	15

1100 Mariposa

2003. Orchids (2nd series). Multicoloured.

3596	30p. Type **1100**	80	80
3597	50p. Sanggumay	1·30	1·30
3598	75p. Lady's slipper	2·00	2·00
3599	100p. Waling-waling	2·60	2·75

1101 Maria Cristina Falls, Lanao Del Norte

2003. Waterfalls. Multicoloured.

3600	6p. Type **1101**	15	15
3601	6p. Pagsanjan, Laguna	15	15
3602	6p. Katibawasan, Camiguin Island	15	15
3603	6p. Bagongbong, Biliran	15	15

1102 Our Lady of Caysasay (statue)

2003. 400th Anniv of Blessed Virgin of the Immaculate Conception (Our Lady of Caysasay), found by Juan Maningcad.

3605	**1102** 6p. multicoloured	15	15

1103 Cornelio Villareal

2003. Birth Centenary of Cornelio Villareal (Speaker of the House).

3606 **1103** 6p. multicoloured 15 15

1104 Teacher and Pupil (statue)

2003. 75th Anniv of National Teachers College.

3607 **1104** 6p. multicoloured 15 15

1105 St. Francis and Parish Church

2003. 50th Anniv of Santurio de San Antonio Parish Church.

3608 **1105** 6p. multicoloured 15 15

2003. "No to Drugs" Campaign. Nos. 3409 and 3413 optd No To Drugs.

3609 6p. multicoloured (3409) 15 15

3610 15p. multicoloured (3413) 40 40

1107 Anniversary Emblem

2003. 50th Anniv of Federation of Free Farmers.

3611 **1107** 6p. multicoloured 15 15

1108 Boy sweeping away Drug Symbols (Nicole Caminian)

2003. "Youth against Drugs" Campaign. Winning Entries in Design a Stamp Competition. Multicoloured.

3612 6p. Type **1108** 15 15

3613 6p. Drug symbols behind "Stop" sign and children (Jarius Cabajar) 15 15

3614 6p. Children pasting over "Drug addiction" poster (Genevieve Lazarte) 15 15

3615 6p. Boy cutting down tree inscribed "Drugs" 15 15

1109 "Mano Po Ninong II" (Jes Pelino)

2003. Christmas. Multicoloured.

3616 6p. Type **1109** 15 15

3617 17p. "Himig at Kulay Ng Pasko" (Jes Pelino) (vert) 45 45

3618 21p. "Noche Buena" (Mamerto Ynigo) (vert) 55 55

3619 22p. "Karoling Sa" Jeepney" (Jes Pelino) 60 60

2003. No. 3409 surch 1p.

3620 1p. on 5p. multicoloured 10 10

2003. Nos. 3093/6 surch.

3621 17p. on 8p. multicoloured (3093) 45 45

3622 17p. on 8p. multicoloured (3094) 45 45

3623 22p. on 16p. multicoloured (3905) 60 60

3624 22p. on 16p. multicoloured (3906) 60 60

1112 Lake Buhi, Camarines Sur (image scaled to 61% of original size)

2003. International Year of Freshwater. Sheet 109×88 mm.

MS3625 22p. multicoloured 60 60

1113 Kenkoy (Tony Velasquez)

2003. National Stamp Collecting Month. Cartoon Characters. Multicoloured.

3626 6p. Type **1113** 15 15

3627 17p. Ikabod (Nonoy Marcelo) 45 45

3628 21p. Sakay N'Moy (Hugo Yonzon) (horiz) 55 55

3629 22p. Kalabog en Bosyo (Larry Alcaa) (horiz) 60 60

MS3630 101×70 mm. 22p. Hugo the sidewalk vendor (Rudolfo Ragodon) (80×30 mm) 60 60

1114 Shoreline at Sunset

2003. 75th Anniv of Philippines Camera Club.

3631 **1114** 6p. multicoloured 15 15

1115 First Philippines Stamps (image scaled to 61% of original size)

2003. Filipinas 2004 Stamp Exhibition. Six sheets, each 142×82 mm and with different background colours. Multicoloured.

MS3632 (a) 22p. Type **1115** (yellow background). (b) 22p. Type **1115** (green background). (c) 22p. Type **1115** (flesh). (d) 22p. Type **1115** (lavender). (e) 22p. Type **1115** (azure). (f) 22p. Type **1115** (pink) Set of 6 sheets 3·00 3·00

1116 Capuchin Monkey

2003. New Year. "Year of the Monkey". Multicoloured.

3633 6p. Type **1116** 15 15

3634 17p. Orangutan 45 45

MS3635 98×90 mm. Nos. 3632/3. Perf or imperf 60 60

1117 *Rebutia spinosissima*

2003. Cacti. Multicoloured.

3636 6p. Type **1117** 15 15

3637 6p. *Turbinicarpus alonsoi* 15 15

3638 6p. *Mammilaria spinosissima* 15 15

3639 6p. *Epithelantha bokei* 15 15

MS3640 100×100 mm. 6p. ×4, *Aloe humilis* (horiz); Inscr "Euphorbia golisana" (horiz); Inscr "Gymnocalycium spinosissima" (horiz); *Mammilaria spinosissima* (horiz) (dIfferent) 60 60

1118 Luneta Hotel

2003. Architectural Heritage. Multicoloured.

3641 6p. Type **1118** 15 15

3642 6p. Hong Kong—Shanghai bank 15 15

3643 6p. El Hogar 15 15

3644 6p. Regina building 15 15

MS3645 101×101 mm. 6p. ×4, Pangasinan Capitol (horiz); Metropolitan theatre (horiz); Philtrust (horiz); University of Manila (horiz) 60 60

1119 First Sisters

2004. Centenary of Sisters of St. Paul of Chartres.

3646 **1119** 6p. multicoloured 15 15

1120 Building Facade, Flag and Emblem

2004. 50th Anniv of Grepalife (Great Pacific Life Assurance Corporation).

3647 **1120** 6p. multicoloured 15 15

1121 University Facade and Anniversary Emblem

2004. Centenary of Polytechnic University, Manila.

3648 **1121** 6p. multicoloured 15 15

1122 1854 5 cuartos Stamp

2004. 150th Anniv of First Philippine Stamps. Designs showing 1854 stamps. Multicoloured.

3649 6p. Type **1122** 15 15

3650 6p.10 cuartos stamp 15 15

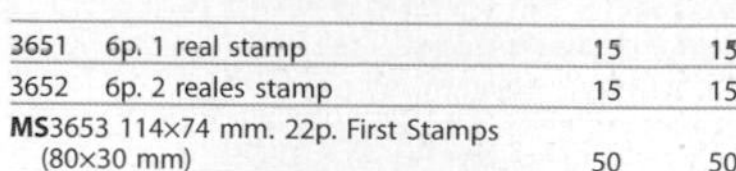

3651 6p. 1 real stamp 15 15

3652 6p. 2 reales stamp 15 15

MS3653 114×74 mm. 22p. First Stamps (80×30 mm) 50 50

1123 Brewer

2004. 150th Anniv of Tanduay Distillers.

3654 **1123** 6p. multicoloured 15 15

1124 Dornier DO-24TT Seaplane

2004. Centenary of Powered Flight (2003).

3655 **1124** 6p. multicoloured 15 15

3656 **1124** 6p. multicoloured 15 15

1125 President George W. Bush

2004. Visit of USA President George W. Bush to Philippines (18 October 2003). Multicoloured.

3657 6p. Type **1125** 15 15

3658 22p. Presidents George W. Bush and Gloria Macapagal-Arroyo 50 50

1126 Hands

2004. 50th Anniv of Pfizer (pharmaceutical company).

3659 **1126** 6p. multicoloured 15 15

1127 Our Lady of Piat (statue)

2004. 400th Anniv of the Arrival of Our Lady of Piat.

3660 **1127** 6p. multicoloured 15 15

1128 Inscr "Bantigue"

2004. Bonsai Trees. Multicoloured designs showing trees inscription given.

3661 6p. Type **1128** 15 15

3662 6p. Chinese elm 15 15

3663 6p. Bantigue with two stems in black tray 15 15

3664 6p. Bantigue in white pot 15 15

3665 6p. Balete sweeping down left 15 15

3666 6p. Balete leafless 15 15

3667 6p. Bantigue with large stem in orange pot 15 15

3668 6p. Mansanita 15 15

3669	6p. Bantigue (vert)	15	15
3670	6p. Kamuning Binangonan (vert)	15	15
3671	6p. Balete (vert)	15	15
3672	6p. Mulawinaso (vert)	15	15
3673	6p. Kamuning Binangonan multi-stemmed (vert)	15	15
3674	6p. Logwood (vert)	15	15
3675	6p. Kamuning Binangonan octagonal pot Bantolinao (vert)	15	15
MS3676	146×95 mm. 6p.×4, Lemonsito; Bougainvillea on stand; Bougainvillea in flower; Kalyos	60	60

1129 Rifle Shooting

2004. Olympic Games, Athens. Multicoloured.

3677	6p. Type **1129**	15	15
3678	17p. Taekwondo	35	35
3679	21p. Swimming	45	45
3680	22p. Archery	50	50
MS3681	60×61 mm. 22p. Boxing	50	50

1130 Tomas Cloma

2004. Birth Centenary of Tomas Cloma (maritime educationalist).

3682	**1130**	6p. multicoloured	15	15

1131 "Sandugo" (Carlos Francisco)

2004. 600th Birth Anniv of Miguel Lopez De Legazpi (first Governor General of Philippines).

3683	**1131**	6p. multicoloured	15	15

1132 Rat

2004. Lunar New Year. Multicoloured.

3684	6p. Type **1132**	15	15
3685	6p. Ox	15	15
3686	6p. Tiger	15	15
3687	6p. Pig	15	15
3688	6p. Rabbit	15	15
3689	6p. Dog	15	15
3690	6p. Dragon	15	15
3691	6p. Rooster	15	15
3692	6p. Snake	15	15
3693	6p. Monkey	15	15
3694	6p. Goat	15	15
3695	6p. Horse	15	15

1133 Building Facade

2004. Centenary of Manila University.

3696	**1133**	6p. multicoloured	15	15

1134 Decorated Tree

2004. Christmas. Decorated trees. Multicoloured.

3697	6p. Type **1134**	15	15
3698	17p. With red ribbons and bells	35	35
3699	21p. With poinsettia flowers	45	45
3700	22p. With white stems	50	50

1135 Intamuros, Manila

2004. Centenary of Filipino—Chinese Chamber of Commerce. Multicoloured.

3701	6p. Type **1135**	15	15
3702	6p. Great Wall, China	15	15

Nos. 3701/2 were issued together, se-tenant, forming a composite design.

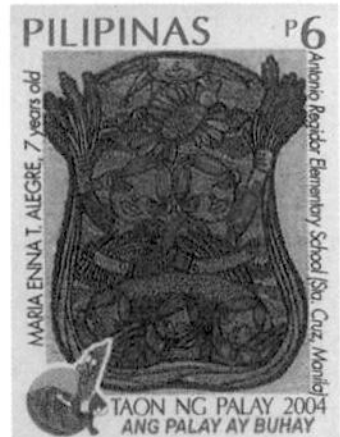

1136 People enclosed in Rice Grain (Maria Enna T. Alegre)

2004. International Year of Rice. Winning Entries in Design a Stamp Competition. Multicoloured.

3703	6p. Type **1136**	15	15
3704	6p. Woman, rice and family (Lady Fatima Velasco)	15	15
3705	6p. Boy amongst plants (Gary Manalo)	15	15
3706	6p. Dove, rice stalk and family (Michael Villadolid)	15	15
3707	6p. Rice grains (Ljian Delgado)	15	15
3708	6p. Doves and man cradling rice plant (Sean Pajaron)	15	15

1137 19th-century Facade

2004. 400th Anniv of San Augustin Church. Multicoloured.

3709	6p. Type **1137**	15	15
3710	6p. Modern facade	15	15

1138 Lapu-Lapu (Francisco Coching)

2004. Stamp Collecting Month. Comics. Multicoloured.

3711	6p. Type **1138**	15	15
3712	6p. El Vibora (Frederico Javinal)	15	15
3713	6p. Kulafu (Francisco Reyes) (horiz)	15	15
3714	6p. Darna (Nestor Redondo) (horiz)	15	15
MS3715	68×95 mm. 22p. Darna (Mats Revelo) (30×80 mm)	50	50

1139 Rooster

2004. New Year. Year of the Rooster. Multicoloured.

3716	6p. Type **1139**	15	15
3717	17p. Rooster (different)	35	35
MS3718	138×80 mm. Nos. 3416/17 each×2	1·00	1·00

1140 *Otus megalottis nigrorum*

2004. Owls. Multicoloured.

3719	6p. Type **1140**	15	15
3720	6p. *Ninox philippensis centralis*	15	15
3721	6p. *Mimizuku gurneyi*	15	15
3722	6p. *Bubo philippensis*	15	15

1141 Chapel and North Academy Cluster Building

2005. 50th Anniv of Liceo de Cagayan University.

3723	**1141**	6p. multicoloured	15	15

1142 Baguio Country Club, 1930

2005. Centenary of Baguio Country Club. Multicoloured.

3724	6p. Type **1142**	15	15
3725	6p. Modern building facade	15	15

1143 Christ, Manila Skyline and Emblem

2005. Centenary of the Seventh Day Adventists' Church in the Philippines.

3726	**1143**	6p. multicoloured	15	15

1144 *Arisbe decolour stratos*

2005. Butterflies. Multicoloured.

3727	1p. Type **1144**	15	15
3727a	1p. *Arisbe decolour stratos* (yellow ground)	15	15
3727b	1p. *Arisbe decolour stratos* (orange ground)	15	15
3727c	2p. *Arthopala anthelus impar* (with all over pale pink ground)	15	15
3727d	3p. *Zophoessa dataensis nihirai*	15	15
3727da	3p. *Zophoessa dataensis nihirai* (with all over lemon ground)	15	15
3727e	4p. *Liphyra brassolis justini*	15	15
3727ea	4p. *Liphyra brassolis justini* (with all over pale orange ground)	15	15
3728	5p. *Parantica danatti*	15	15
3728a	5p. *Parantica danatti* (blue ground)	15	15
3728b	5p. *Parantica danatti* (squared azure ground)	15	15
3729	6p. *Hebomoia* (inscr "Hebe-mola") *glaucippe philippensis*	15	15
3730	6p. *Moduza urdaneta*	15	15
3731	6p. *Lexias satrapes hiwaga*	15	15
3732	6p. *CheritaOrpheus*	15	15
3733	6p. *Achillides chikae*	15	15
3734	6p. *Arisbe ideaoides* (inscr "ideaoiedes")	15	15
3735	6p. *Delias schoenigi hermeli*	15	15
3736	6p. *Achillides palinurus daedalus*	15	15
3737	6p. *Delias levicki justini*	15	15
3738	6p. *Troides magellanus*		
3739	7p. *Hebomoia* (inscr "Hebe-moia") *glaucippe philippensis*	15	15
3739a	7p. *Hebomoia* (inscr "Hebe-moia") *glaucippe philippensis* (with all over white ground)		
3740	7p. *Moduza urdaneta*	15	15
3740a	7p. *Moduza urdaneta* (with all over white ground)	15	15
3741	7p. *Lexias satrapes hiwaga*	15	15
3741a	7p. *Lexias satrapes hiwaga* (with all over white ground)	15	15
3742	7p. *Cherita orpheus*	15	15
3742a	7p. *Cherita orpheus* (with all over white ground)	15	15
3743	7p. *Achillides chikae*	15	15
3743a	7p. *Achillides chikae* (with all over white ground)	15	15
3744	7p. *Arisbe ideaoides* (inscr "ideaoiedes")	15	15
3744a	7p. *Arisbe ideaoides* (inscr "ideaoiedes") (with all over white ground)		
3745	7p. *Delias schoenigi hermeli*	15	15
3745a	7p. *Delias schoenigihermeli* (with all over white ground)	15	15
3746	7p. *Achillides palinurus daedalus*	15	15
3746a	7p. *Achillides palinurus daedalus* (with all over white ground and microprint)		
3747	7p. *Delias levicki justini*	15	15
3747a	7p. *Delias levicki justini* (with all over white ground)	15	15
3748	7p. *Troides magellanus*	15	15
3748a	7p. *Troides magellanus* (with all over white ground)	15	15
3748ab	9p. *Lexias satrapes amiana*	20	20
3748ac	9p. *Lexias satrapes amiana* (with all over green)	20	20
3748b	10p. *Tanaecia aruna pallida*	35	35
3748ba	10p. *Tanaecia aruna pallida* (with all over azure)	35	35
3749	17p. *Idea electra*	35	35
3750	17p. *Charaxes bajula adoracion*	35	35
3751	17p. *Tanaecia calliphorus*	35	35
3752	17p. *Trogonoptera trojana*	35	35
3752a	20p. *Idea electra electra*	45	45
3752b	20p. *Charaxes bajula adoracion*	45	45
3752c	20p. *Tanaecia calliphorus calliphorus*	45	45
3752d	20p. *Trogonoptera trojana*	45	45
3753	21p. *Cethosia biblis barangingi*	45	45
3754	21p. *Menelaides* (inscr "Me-nalaides") *polytes ledebouria*	45	45
3755	21p. *Appias nero palawanica*	45	45
3756	21p. *Udara tyotaroi*	45	45
3757	22p. *Parantica noeli*	50	50
3758	22p. *Chilasa osmana osmana*	50	50
3759	22p. *Graphium sandawanum joreli*	50	50
3760	22p. *Papilio xuthus benguetanus*	50	50
3761	24p. *Cethosia biblis baranginigi*	55	55
3761a	24p. *Cethosia biblis baranginigi* (with all over green ground)	55	55
3761ba	24p. *Menalaides polytes ledebouria* (with all over green ground)	55	55
3762	24p. *Menalaides polytes ledebouria*	55	55
3763	24p. *Appias nero palawanica*	55	55
3764	24p. *Trogonoptera trojana*	55	55
3765	26p. *Udara tyotaroi*	55	55
3766	26p. *Chilasa osmana osmana*	55	55
3767	26p. *Graphium sandawanum joreli*	55	55
3768	26p. *Papilio xuthus benguetanus*	55	55
3769	30p. *Appias nero domitia*	65	65
3769a	30p. *Appias nero domitia* (with all over pale orange ground) (39×29 mm)	65	65
3770	100p. *Cepora Aspasia olga*	2·20	2·20
3770a	100p. *Cepora Aspasia olga* (with all over cobalt) (39×29 mm)	2·20	2·20

1145 *Chlamys senatoria*

2005. Shells (1st issue). Multicoloured.

3780 6p. Type **1145** 15 15
3781 6p. *Siphonofusus vicdani* 15 15
3782 6p. *Epitonium scalare* 15 15
3783 6p. *Harpa harpa* 15 15
3784 6p. *Chicoreus saulii* 15 15
3785 6p. *Spondylus varians* 15 15
3786 6p. *Spondylus linquaefelis* 15 15
3787 6p. *Melo broderipii* 15 15
MS3788 131×86 mm. 6p.×4, *Siliquaria armata; Argonauta argo; Perotrochus vicdani; Corculum cardissa* 60 60

See also Nos. 3803/**MS**3811.

1146 Presidents Gloria Macapagal-Arroyo and Hu Jintao

2005. 30th Anniv of Philippines—China Diplomatic Relations. State Visit of President Hu Jintao of People's Republic of China. Multicoloured.

3789 6p. Type **1146** 15 15
3790 17p. As No. 3789 but design reversed 35 35
MS3791 79×108 mm. Nos. 3789/90 50 50

1147 Ernesto dela Cruz Ancestral House

2005. Historic Houses. Multicoloured.

3792 6p. Type **1147** 15 15
3793 6p. Limjoco residence 15 15
3794 6p. Pelaez ancestral house 15 15
3795 6p. Vergara house 15 15
MS3796 94×102 mm. 6p.×4, Gliceria Marella Villavicencio; Lasala-Guarin house; Claparols house; Ilagan ancestral house 60 60

1148 University Church, Iloilo

2005. Centenary of Central Philippine University.

3797 **1148** 6p. multicoloured 15 15

1149 Men carrying House (Bayanihan)

2005. Centenary of Rotary International. Multicoloured.

3798 6p. Type **1149** 15 15
3799 22p. As No. 3798 but design reversed 50 50
MS3800 100×144 mm. No. 3798×6 and 3799×2 65 65

1150 Pope John Paul II

2005. Pope John Paul II Commemoration.

3801 6p. Type **1150** 15 15
3802 22p. Leaning on staff 50 50

2005. Shells (2nd issue). As T 1145. Multicoloured.

3803 6p. *Cochlostyla imperator* (vert) 15 15
3804 6p. *Helicostyla turbinoides* (vert) 15 15
3805 6p. *Helicostyla lignaria* (vert) 15 15
3806 6p. *Amphidromus dubius* (vert) 15 15
3807 6p. *Chrysallis fischeri* (vert) 15 15
3808 6p. *Helicostyla bicolorata* (vert) 15 15
3809 6p. *Helicostyla dobiosa* (vert) 15 15
3810 6p. *Helicostyla portei* (vert) 15 15
MS3811 131×86 mm. 6p.×4, *Calocochlia depressa; Cochlostyla sarcinosa; Calocochliaschadenbergi; Helicostyla pulcherrina* 60 60

1151 Blas Ople

2005. 2nd Death Anniv of Blas Ople (journalist and politician).

3812 **1151** 6p. multicoloured 15 15

1152 San Bartolome Parish Church

2005. 400th Anniv of San Bartolome Parish, Magalang.

3813 **1152** 6p. multicoloured 15 15

1153 "Celebrating the Eucharist with Mary" (Carlos Vincent H. Ruiz)

2005. International Year of the Eucharist. Winning Designs in Painting Competition. Designs on the theme "Celebrating the Eucharist with Mary", artist names given. Multicoloured.

3814 6p. Type **1153** 15 15
3815 6p. Rommer A. Fajardo 15 15
3816 6p. Telly Farolan-Somara 15 15
3817 6p. Allen A. Moran 15 15
3819 6p. Elouiza Athena Tentativa 15 15
3820 6p. Jianina Marishka C. Montealto 15 15
MS3821 114×190 mm. Nos. 3814/20 90 90

2005. 10th Anniv of Filipinas Stamp Collectors Club. No. MS2041 surch 15p FILIPINAS STAMP COLLECTORS CLUB 10TH YEAR 1995–2006. Imperf.

MS3822 15p. on 8p. multicoloured 35 35

1155 Children, Flame and Dove (Rojohn Daniel R. Olivar)

2005. 60th Anniv of United Nations. International Year of Sports' Education. Winning Designs in Children's Painting Competition (3823/5) or Millennium Development Goals (3826). Multicoloured.

3823 6p. Type **1155** 15 15
3824 6p. As No. 3823 but with dove and emblem at left 15 15
3825 6p. Dove and open book (Sarahbeth B. Almeiro) 15 15
3826 10p. Emblem 20 20
MS3827 Two sheets, each 110×78 mm. (a) Nos. 3823, 3825/6. (b) Nos. 3824/6 90 90

1156 Building Facade

2005. Centenary of Bureau of Correction.

3828 **1156** 6p. multicoloured 15 15

1157 Pres. Macapagal-Arroyo taking Oath

2005. Inauguration of President Gloria Macapagal-Arroyo. Multicoloured.

3829 6p. Type **1157** 15 15
3830 22p. Giving inaugural speech 50 50

1158 Church, Pony and Trap

2005. Christmas. Multicoloured.

3831 6p. Type **1158** 15 15
3832 6p. The Nativity enclosed in rock 15 15
3833 6p. Joseph leading donkey carrying Mary 15 15
3834 6p. Thatched buildings and Three Kings 15 15

1159 Boxing

2005. 23rd South East Asian Games. Designs showing Gilas (games mascot) as athlete. Multicoloured.

3835 6p. Type **1159** 15 15
3836 6p. Cycling 15 15
3837 6p. Wushu (martial art) 15 15
3838 6p. Bowling 15 15
3839 6p. Badminton 15 15
3840 6p. Billiards 15 15
MS3841 102×111 mm. 5p. Arnis (hand, foot and stick fighting) (horiz); 6p. Chess (horiz); 6p. Dragonboat (horiz) 35 35

MS3842 111×102 mm. 5p. Shooting; 6p. Archery; 6p. Equestrian sports 35 35

1160 "The Fourth Horseman" (Tequi)

2005. Stamp Collecting Month. Print Makers. Multicoloured.

3843 6p. Type **1160** 15 15
3844 6p. "Bulbs" (M. Parial) 15 15
3845 6p. "Breaking Ground" (R. Olazo) 15 15
3846 6p. "Pinoy Worker Abr'd" (Ben Cab) 15 15
MS3847 99×68 mm. 22p. "Form XV" (Brenda Fajardo) (80×30 mm) 50 50

1161 Shih Tzu

2005. New Year. Year of the Dog. Multicoloured.

3848 6p. Type **1161** 15 15
3849 17p. German shepherd 35 35
MS3850 138×81 mm. Nos. 3848/9, each×2 1·00 1·00

1162 Amputee Runner

2005. 3rd ASEAN Para Games. Multicoloured.

3851 6p. Type **1162** 15 15
3852 17p. Wheelchair racer 15 15

1163 Cape Santiago Lighthouse, Calatagan

2005. Lighthouses. Multicoloured.

3853 6p. Type **1163** 15 15
3854 6p. Bagacay, Liloan 15 15
3855 6p. Malabrigo, Lobo 15 15
3856 6p. Capones, San Antonio 15 15
MS3857 141×85 mm. 6p.×4, Tubbataha, Cagayancillo; Cape Bojeador, Burgos; Cape Bolinao, Bolinao; San Fernando Point, San Fernando 60 60

See also Nos. 3875/**MS**3879.

1164 College Building

2006. Centenary of St. Scholastica's College.

3858 **1164** 6p. multicoloured 15 15

1165 Working in Fields (Allen A. Moran)

2006. Centenary of Filipinos in Hawaii. Winning Designs in Painting Competition. Multicoloured.

3859	6p. Type **1165**	15	15
3860	22p. Skyline, people, globe and flags (Cristanto S. Umali)	50	50
MS3861	90×85 mm. Nos. 3859/60	65	65

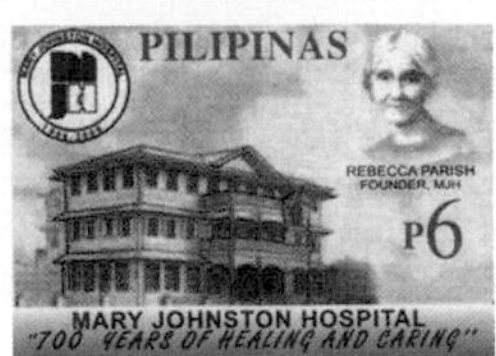

1166 Original Building and Rebecca Parish (founder)

2006. Centenary of Mary Johnston Hospital. Multicoloured.

3862	6p. Type **1166**	15	15
3863	6p. Surgery and modern building	15	15

1167 Cupid

2006. St. Valentine's Day. Multicoloured.

3864	7p. Type **1167**	15	15
3865	7p. Cupid holding envelope	15	15

1168 Archbishop Sin

2006. Cardinal Jaime Lachica Sin (Archbishop of Manila) Commemoration. Multicoloured.

3866	22p. Type **1168**	50	50
3867	22p. Seated	50	50
MS3868	142×86 mm. Nos. 3866/7	1·00	1·00

2006. 1st Death Anniv of Pope John Paul II. Sheet 75×91 mm. No. MS1648 surch 26p.

MS3869	26p. on 7p.50 multicoloured	15	15

No. **MS**3869 was additionally inscribed for the anniversary in the margins.

1170 *Lepidochelys olivacea*

2006. Turtles. Multicoloured.

3870	7p. Type **1170**	15	15
3871	7p. *Eretmochelys imbricate*	15	15
3872	7p. *Caretta caretta*	15	15
3873	7p. *Dermochelys coriacea*	15	15
MS3874	100×70 mm. 26p *Chelonia mydas* (80×30 mm)	55	55

Nos. 3870/3 were issued together, se-tenant, forming a composite design.

2006. Lighthouses. As T 1163. Multicoloured.

3875	7p. Bugui Point Lighthouse, Aroroy, Masbate	15	15
3876	7p. Capul Island, Samar del Norte	15	15
3877	7p. Corregidor Island, Cavite	15	15
3878	7p. Rio Del Pasig, Manila	15	15
MS3879	141×85 mm. 7p.×4, Engano Cape, Cagayan Province; Cabra Point, Lubang; Melville Cape, Balabac Island; Gintotolo Island, Balud	60	60

1171 Badges

2006. 50th Anniv of Xavier School. Multicoloured.

3880	7p. Type **1171**	15	15
3881	7p. School façade	15	15
3882	7p. Paul Hsu Kuangchi (first Christian convert)	15	15
3883	7p. St. Francis Xavier (500th birth anniv)	15	15

1172 Soldier, Wife, Child and Piggy Bank

2006. 50th Anniv of Air Material Wing Savings and Loan Association (AMWSLAI) (Military and Police Association). Multicoloured.

3884	7p. Type **1172**	15	15
3885	7p. Headquarters	15	15

2006. 60th Anniv of Philippines—United Kingdom Diplomatic Relations. No. 1853 surch 60 Years of RP–UK Relations 1946–2006 20p.

3886	26p. on 7p.20 multicoloured	55	55

1174 Family and George Willmann (first Philippine director)

2006. Centenary (2005) of Knights Of Columbus (charitable organization).

3887	**1174** 7p. multicoloured	15	15

1175 Anniversary Emblem and Map

2006. 75th Anniv of Ortigas & Company. Multicoloured.

3888	7p. Type **1175**	15	15
3889	26p. Headquarters and emblem	55	55
MS3890	180×80 mm. Nos. 3888/9, each×2		

1176 Jose Rizal, Snow-covered Mount Fuji and Blossom

2006. 50th Anniv of Philippines—Japan Diplomatic Relations. Multicoloured.

3891	7p. Type **1176**	15	15
3892	20p. J. Rizal, smoking Mount Fuji and blossom	45	45
MS3893	178×80 mm. Nos. 3891/2, each×2		

1177 Roque Ablan, Flag and Coastline

2006. Birth Centenary of Roque B. Ablan (guerrilla leader and war hero).

3894	**1177** 7p. multicoloured	15	15

2006. 10th Anniv of Quezon Philatelic Society. No. 1980 surch and optd 7p.00 Anniversary Quezon Philatelic Society 1996–2006.

3895	7p. on 1p.20 multicoloured	25	25

1179 Emblem

2006. Centenary of Chan-Chu Association. Multicoloured.

3896	7p. Type **1179**	15	15
3897	7p. Seated figure	15	15

1180 Inscr "Himalayan Cat"

2006. Cats. Multicoloured. Phosphorescent markings.

3898	7p. Type **1180**	15	15
3899	7p. Maine Coon	15	15
3900	7p. Red point Siamese	15	15
3901	7p. Persian	15	15
3902	7p. Japanese bobtail	15	15
3903	7p. Ragdoll	15	15
3904	7p. Egyptian mau	15	15
3905	7p. Abyssinian	15	15

1181 "TUMAYO TAYO"

2006. United Nations Month. Multicoloured.

3906	7p. Type **1181**	15	15
3907	26p. "STAND UP"	55	55

1182 Manila Post Office in Ruins (image scaled to 65% of original size)

2006. 110th (2008) Anniv of Philippine Post. Multicoloured.

3908	7p. Type **1182**	15	15
3909	7p. Modern Central Post Office	15	15

Nos. 3908/9 were issued in horizontal *se-tenant* pairs with the sheet.

1183 Lower Slopes (image scaled to 65% of original size)

2006. 1st Philippine Ascent of Mount Everest. Multicoloured.

3910	7p. Type **1183**	15	15
3911	20p. Team members	45	45
3912	26p. Summit	55	55
MS3913	130×90 mm. 7p. As No. 3912; 7p. As No. 3910; 10p. As No. 3911	50	50

1184 Manila Cathedral

2006. Christmas. Multicoloured.

3914	7p. Type **1184**	15	15
3915	20p. St. Augustine Church, Paoay	45	45
3916	24p. Church of Santo Tomas de Villanueva, Miagao	55	55
3917	26p. Barasoain Church	55	55

1185 Pig

2006. New Year. Year of the Pig. Multicoloured.

3918	7p. Type **1185**	15	15
3919	20p. Pig facing left	45	45

1186 Jackfruit

2006. Fruit. Multicoloured.

3920	7p. Type **1186**	15	15
3921	7p. Lanzones	15	15
3922	7p. Coconut	15	15
3923	7p. Bananas	15	15

1187 Graciano Lopez Jaena

2006. Birth Centenary of Graciano Lopez Jaena (journalist and reformer).

3924	**1187** 7p. multicoloured	15	15

1188 Oranges and Grapes

2006. Stamp Collecting Month (November). Pastel Paintings. Multicoloured.

3925	7p. Type **1188**	15	15
3926	7p. Coconut and melon	15	15
3927	7p. Fish and vegetables	15	15
3928	7p. Mother and child (vert)	15	15
MS3929	50×100 mm. 26p. Roses (50×80 mm)	55	55

1189 Fort

2007. 250th Anniv of Ozamiz Cotta.

3930	**1189** 7p. multicoloured	15	15

1190 University Facade

2007. Centenary of Centro Escolar University.

3931	**1190** 7p. multicoloured	25	25

1191 Flag Pole and School Building

2007. Centenary of National School for the Deaf.

3932	**1191** 7p. multicoloured	25	25

1192 Emblem

2007. Centenary of Manulife.

3933	**1192** 7p. multicoloured	25	25

1193 Puente de Isabel II, Cavite

2007. Bridges. Multicoloured.

3934	7p. Type **1193**	25	25
3935	7p. Puente Dampol Dupax, Nueva Viscaya	25	25
3936	7p. Puente de Barit Laoag, Ilocos Norte	25	25
3937	7p. Puente de Blanco Bimondo, Manila	25	25

1194 *Medinilla magnifica*

2007. Flowers. Multicoloured.

3938	7p. Type **1194**	25	25
3939	7p. *Strongylodon elmeri*	25	25
3940	7p. *Amyema imcarnatiflora*	25	25
3941	7p. *Dillenia monatha*	25	25
3942	7p. *Xanthostemon fruticosus*	25	25
3943	7p. *Plumiera acuminate*	25	25
3944	7p. *Paphiopedilum adductum*	25	25
3945	7p. *Rafflesia manillana*	25	25
MS3946	134×60 mm. 26p. *Rafflesia manillana* (120×30 mm)	95	95

1195 Symbols of France

2007. 60th Anniv of Philippines–France Diplomatic Relations. Multicoloured.

3947	7p. Type **1195**	25	25
3948	26p. Symbols of Philippines	95	95
MS3949	52×92 mm. 26p. Symbols of France and Philippines (30×80 mm)	95	95

1196 Inscr 'Diana'

2007. Fish. Multicoloured.

3950	7p. Type **1196**	25	25
3951	7p. Giant trevally	25	25
3952	7p. Skipjack tuna	25	25
3953	7p. Yellowfin tuna	25	25

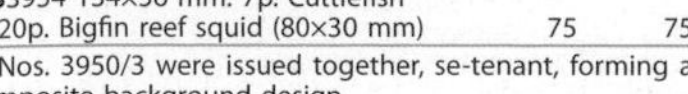

MS3954	134×56 mm. 7p. Cuttlefish 20p. Bigfin reef squid (80×30 mm)	75	75

Nos. 3950/3 were issued together, se-tenant, forming a composite background design.

1197 Emblems

2007. Centenary of Scouting. Multicoloured.

3955	7p. Type **1197**	25	25
3956	7p. Hand and flag	25	25

1198 Tufted Duck

2007. Ducks. Multicoloured.

3957	7p. Type **1198**	25	25
3958	7p. Cotton pygmy goose	25	25
3959	7p. Mallard	25	25
3960	7p. Green-winged teal	25	25
3961	7p. Northern pintail	25	25
3962	7p. Common shelduck	25	25
3963	7p. Northern shoveler	25	25
3964	7p. Greater scaup	25	25

1199 Malacanang Palace, Manila

2007. Architecture. 40th Anniv of ASEAN (Association of South-east Asian Nations). Multicoloured.

3965	7p. Type **1199**	25	25
3966	20p. Secretariat Building, Bandar Seri Begawan, Brunei Darusslam	75	75
3967	20p. National Museum, Cambodia	75	75
3968	20p. Fatahillah Museum, Jakarta	75	75
3969	20p. Traditional house, Laos	75	75
3970	20p. Railway Headquarters Building, Malaysia	75	75
3971	20p. Yangon Post Office, Union of Myanmar	75	75
3972	20p. As Type **1199**	75	75
3973	20p. National Museum, Singapore	75	75
3974	20p. Vimanmek Mansion, Bangkok, Thailand	75	75
3975	20p. Presidential Palace, Hanoi, Vietnam	75	75
MS3976	102×59 mm 20p. Malacanang Palace, Manila (80×30 mm)	75	75

Stamps of a similar design were issued by all member countries.

1200 Ramon Magsaysay

2007. Birth Centenary of Ramon del Fierro Magsaysay (president from 1953–7).

3977	**1200** 7p. multicoloured	25	25

1201 Family

2007. 50th Anniv of Social Security. Multicoloured.

3978	7p. Type **1201**	25	25
3979	7p. President Magsaysay	25	25
3980	7p. President signing Social Security Act	25	25
3981	7p. Social Security building	25	25

No. 3982/3 and Type **1202** have been left for 'Centenary of First Assembly', issued on 16 October 2007, not yet received.

1203 *La Bulakena*

2007. 150th Birth Anniv of Juna Luna (artist). Multicoloured.

3984	7p. Type **1203**	25	25

Nos. 3985/7 have been left for stamps not yet received. See also Nos. **MS**4058 and **MS**4703.

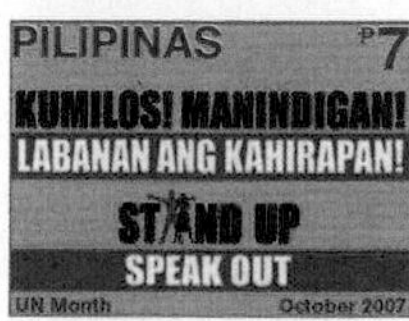

1204 'KUMILOS! MANINDIGAN'

2007. United Nations Month. Multicoloured.

3988	7p. Type **1204**	25	25
3989	26p. STAND UP	1·10	1·10

1205 Asian Fairy Bluebird

2007. Birds. Multicoloured.

399ca	3p. Mountain verditer flycatcher	10	10
2992cb	3p. Mountain verditer flycatcher)	15	15
3990	1p. Black-naped oriole	10	10
3990b	1p. Mugimaki flycatcher	10	10
3991	2p. Type **1205**	10	10
3991da	2p. Narcissus flycatcher (P 13½×14) (11.1.2010) (inscr '2009C')	10	10
3992	3p. Writhed hornbill	10	10
3993	4p. Crimson sunbird	15	15
3993ca	4p. Blue rock thrush	10	10
3993cb	4p. Blue rock thrush	15	15
3994c	5p. Brown shrike (P 13½×14) (11.1.2010) (inscr '2009C')	15	15
3995	7p. Mindanao bleeding heart pigeon	25	25
3996	7p. Nicobar pigeon	25	25
3997	7p. Black chinned fruit dove	25	25
3998	7p. Metallic pigeon	25	25
3999	7p. Pink necked green pigeon	25	25
4000	7p. Amethyst brown dove	25	25
4001	7p. Grey Imperial pigeon	25	25
4002	7p. Red turtle dove	25	25
4003	7p. Pied Imperial pigeon	25	25
4004	7p. Spotted Imperial pigeon	25	25
4005	8p. Hoopoe	25	25
4005ca	8p. Apo myna (2009)	40	40
4006	9p. Short eared owl	30	30
4006ca	9p. Crested serpent eagle	45	45
4006cb	9p. Crested serpent eagle	45	45
4007	10p. Blue winged pitta	30	30
4007ca	10p. Blue-crowned racquet tail	45	45
4007db	17p. Common flameback	50	50
4008	20p. Dwarf kingfisher	35	35
4009	20p. Blue capped wood kingfisher	35	35
4010	20p. White throated kingfisher	35	35
4011	20p. White collared kingfisher	35	35
4012	24p. Inscr 'Green faced parrot finch'	40	40
4012b	24p. Philippine Eagle Owl	1·10	1·10
4012c	24p. Luzon Scops Owl	1·10	1·10
4012d	24p. Philippine Scops Owl	1·10	1·10
4012e	24p. Spotted Wood Owl	1·10	1·10
4012f	24p. Philippine Eagle Owl	1·10	1·10
4012g	24p. Luzon Scops Owl	1·10	1·10
4012h	24p. Philippine Scops Owl	1·10	1·10
4013	24p. Java sparrow	40	40
4014	24p. Yellow breasted bunting	40	40
4015	24p. White cheeked bullfinch	40	40
4016	26p. Great billed parrot	40	40
4017	26p. Philippine cockatoo	40	40
4018	26p. Blue naped parrot	40	40
4019	26p. Blue backed parrot	40	40
4019fa	26p. Philippine tailorbird	1·20	1·20
4019ga	26p. Mountain tailorbird	1·20	1·20
4019ha	26p, Black-headed tailorbird	1·20	1·20
ia4019	26p. Ashy tailorbird (2009) (inscr '2009B')	1·20	1·20

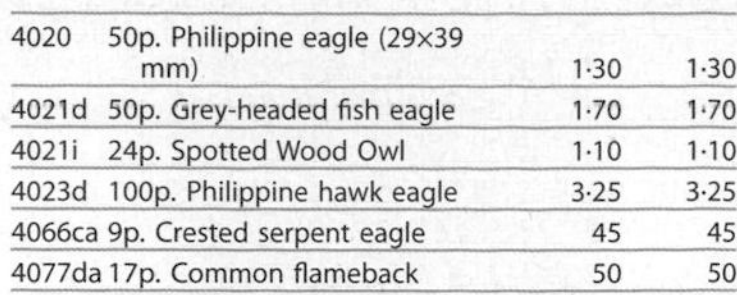

4020	50p. Philippine eagle (29×39 mm)	1·30	1·30
4021d	50p. Grey-headed fish eagle	1·70	1·70
4021i	24p. Spotted Wood Owl	1·10	1·10
4023d	100p. Philippine hawk eagle	3·25	3·25
4066ca	9p. Crested serpent eagle	45	45
4077da	17p. Common flameback	50	50

No. 3990 (1p.) and 3994 (5p.) have been left for stamps not yet received.

Nos. 4021/50 have been left for possible additions to this series.

1206 Manila Central Post Office (1926)

2007. 110th (2008) Anniv of National Postal Service. Multicoloured.

4051	7p. Type **1206**	25	25
4052	20p. Manila Post Office and Juan Marcos de Guzman Arellano (architect) (80×30 mm)	35	35

1207 San Diego de Alcala Cathedral

2007. 425th Anniv of San Diego de Alcala Parish.

4053	**1207** 7p. multicoloured	25	25

1208 Emblem and School Building Façade

2007. 50th Anniv of Sacred Heart School—Hijas de Jesus. Multicoloured.

4054	7p. Type **1208**	25	25
4055	7p. Statue and building	25	25
4056	7p. Mother Superior Eloisa Alonso and arms	25	25
4057	7p. Building and entrance	25	25

2007. National Stamp Collecting Month. 150th Birth Anniv of Juan Luna (2nd issue). Sheet 100×100 mm containing multicoloured designs as T 1203.

MS4058	7p.×4, *Picnic in Normandy* (59×39 mm) (imperf); *El Violinista; Indio Bravo; Old Man with Pipe*	1·10	1·10

1209 Emblem

2007. 60th Anniv of Development Bank of the Philippines. Multicoloured.

4059	7p. Type **1209**	25	25
4060	7p. Street corner building facade	25	25
4061	7p. Multi-storey building and trees	25	25
4062	7p. Six storey building	25	25

1210 Rat

2007. New Year. Year of the Rat. Multicoloured.

4063	7p. Type **1210**	25	25
4064	20p. Rat seated	75	75
MS4065	139×80 mm. Nos. 4063/4, each×2	2·10	2·10

1211 Pres. Ramon Magsaysay and Rev. Bob Pierce (World Vision founder)

2007. 50th Anniv of World Vision. Multicoloured.

4066	7p. Type **1211**	25	25
4067	20p. 50	75	75

1212 Teddy

2007. Christmas. Toys. Multicoloured.

4068	7p. Type **1212**	25	25
4069	20p. Train	75	75
4070	24p. Quad bike	75	75
4071	26p. Angel doll	80	80

2007. 25th Anniv of Cebu Philatelic Society. No. 1981 surch p7. 00and optd Cebu Philatelic Society 25th Anniversary 1982–2007.

4072	7p. on 2p.40 multicoloured	25	25

(1213)

2007. 150th Birth Anniv of Juan Luna (3rd issue). Sheet 125×100 mm containing horiz designs as T 1203. Multicoloured, background colour given.

MS4073	7p.×4, *Parisian Life* (73×48 mm) (imperf); *Parisian Life* (green); *Parisian Life* (red); *Parisian Life* (cerise)	1·10	1·10

1214 St. Dominic de Guzman

2008. 50th Anniv of Dominican School, Manila. Multicoloured.

4074	7p. Type **1214**	30	30
4075	7p. School campus	30	30
4076	7p. School and anniversary emblems	30	30
4077	7p. School building	30	30

1215 Heart filled with Roses

2008. St. Valentine's Day. Multicoloured.

4078	7p. Type **1215**	30	30
4079	7p. Cupid and hearts	30	30

1216 St. Therese, Alfredo Maria Obviar and Anniversary Emblem

2008. 50th Anniv of Missionary Catechists of St. Therese of the Infant Jesus. Multicoloured.

4080	7p. Type **1216**	30	30
4081	7p. MCST emblem	30	30

1217 *Batomys granti* (Luzon furry-tailed rat)

2008. Rats and Mice of Luzon Island. Multicoloured.

4082	7p. Type **1217**	30	30
4083	7p. *Chrotomys whiteheadi* (Luzon striped earth rat)	30	30
4084	7p. *Apomys datae* (Cordillera forest mouse)	30	30
4085	7p. *Archboldomys* (Cordillera shrew mouse)	30	30
MS4086	115×85 mm. 7p. *Pholeomys pallidus* (northern giant cloud rat); 7p. *Carpomys phaeurus* (lesser dwarf cloud rat); 20p. *Crateromys schadenbergi* (bushy-tailed cloud rat) (40×70 mm. Imperf)	1·60	1·60

2008. Taipei 2008–International Stamp Exhibition. Sheet 130×155 mm containing vert stamps as Type 1205. Multicoloured.

MS4087	7p.×10, As Nos. 3995a/4004a but without microprinting; 7p. Philippine eagle perched; 7p. As No. 4017a but without microprinting; 7p. Java sparrow; 7p. Blue-capped wood kingfisher	5·00	5·00

No. **MS**4087 was on sale for 125p.

1218 Emblem

2008. 75th Anniv of National Research Council.

4088	**1218** 7p. multicoloured	30	30

1219 Tents

2008. Centenary of Teachers' Camp, Baguio. Multicoloured.

4089	7p. Type **1219**	30	30
4090	7p. Teachers	30	30

1220 Gasan Bridge, Marinduque

2008. American Colonial Bridges. Multicoloured.

4091	7p. Type **1220**	30	30
4092	7p. Hinigaran Bridge, Negros Occidental	30	30
4093	7p. Wahig Bridge, Dagohoy, Bohol	30	30
4094	7p. Pan-ay Bridge, Capiz	30	30
MS4095	170×60 mm. 7p.×4, Quezon Bridge, Quiapo, Manila; Governor Reynolds Bridge, Guinobatan, Albay; Mauca Railway Bridge, Ragay, Camarines Sur; Balucuan Bridge, Dao, Capiz	1·30	1·30

1221 Manny Pacquiao

2008. Emmanuel 'Pacman' Pacquiao (champion boxer). Sheet 100×100 mm containing T 1221 and similar vert designs showing Manny Pacquiao. Multicoloured.

MS4096	7p.×4, Type **1221**; Wearing robe; Wearing champion's belt; Looking right	1·30	1·30

1222 Building Facade

2008. 50th Anniv Department of Science and Technology (4097) or 50th Anniv of Nuclear Research Institute (4098). Multicoloured.

4097	7p. Type **1222**	30	30
4098	7p. Institute building	30	30

1224 Tai Bei Kong (Most Honored Ancestor)

2008. Centenary of Liong Tek Go Family Association. Multicoloured.

4099	7p. Type **1224**	30	30
4100	7p. Anniversary emblem	30	30

Type **1223** is vacant.

1225 University Seal

2008. Centenary of University of the Philippines. Multicoloured. (a) Size 21×25 mm.

4101	7p. Type **1225**		30
4102	7p. *Carillion* (Juan Nakpil)	30	30
4103	7p. *Oblation* (statue) (Guillermo Tolentino)	30	30
4104	7p. Centenary emblem	30	30

(b) Size 40×30 mm.

4105	7p. As No. 4102	30	30
4106	7p. As No. 4104	30	30
4107	7p. As Type **1225**	30	30
4108	7p. As No. 4103	30	30
MS4109	181×75 mm. 7p.×4, As Nos. 4105/8	1·30	1·30

1226 Fr. Andres de Urdaneta and Monument

2008. 500th Birth Anniv of Fr. Andres (Fray) de Urdaneta. Spanish-Philippine Friendship Day.

4110	**1226** 7p. multicoloured	30	30

1227 Immaculate Conception Chapel

2008. 75th Anniv of Xavier University, Ateneo de Cagayan. Multicoloured

4111	7p. Type **1227**	30	30
4112	7p. St. Francis Xavier (statue)	30	30
4113	7p. Archbishop T. G. Hayes	30	30
4114	7p. Science centre	30	30

1228 College Building

2008. 60th Anniv of Ateneo de Davao University. Multicoloured

4115	7p. Type **1228**	30	30
4116	7p. High School Building	30	30
4117	7p. Preschool and Grade School Building	30	30
4118	7p. *Assumption* (stained glass)	30	30
MS4119	181×75 mm. 7p.×4, As Nos. 4115/18	1·30	1·30

Nos. 4115/18 were printed, *se-tenant*, in blocks of four stamps within the sheet.

The stamps of No. **MS**4119 are arranged in two vertical pairs separated by a large central gutter.

1229 Archery

2008. Olympic Games, Beijing. Designs showing stylized athletes. Multicoloured.

4120	7p. Type **1229**	30	30
4121	20p. Taekwondo	80	80
4122	24p. Equestrian	80	80
4123	26p. Weight lifting	85	85

1230 Pi Kan (Great Ancestor)

2008. Centenary of Se Jo Tong Lim Family Association. T 1230 and similar horiz designs. Multicoloured

4124	7p. Type **1230**		30
4125	7p. Gen. Vicente Lim (WW II Hero) and Senator Roseller Lim	30	30
4126	7p. Binondo Church and Chinese Gate	30	30
4127	7p. Se Jo Tong emblem over symbolic Philippine flag	30	30
MS4128	181×75 mm. 7p.×4, As Nos. 4124/7. Imperf between vertical pairs	1·30	1·30

1231 *Pemphis acidula*

2008. 35th Anniv of Philippine Bonsai Association. Multicoloured.

4129 7p. Type **1231** 30 30
4130 7p. *Ficus microcarpa* 30 30
4131 7p. *Serissa foetida* 30 30
4132 7p. *Pemphis acidula* with wide shallow pot 30 30
4133 7p. *Pemphis acidula* leaning to lower left with deep pot 30 30
4134 7p. *Triphasia trifolia* 30 30
4135 7p. *Pemphis acidula* leaning left with wide pot 30 30
4136 7p. *Bougainville* 30 30
4137 7p. *Murraya* (vert) 30 30
4138 7p. *Pemphis acidula* short upright growth, one large and one smaller branches (vert) 30 30
4139 7p. *Pemphis acidula* single branch on thick bare stem (vert) 30 30
4140 7p. *Pemphis acidula* short twisted growth, single stem with wide base (vert) 30 30
4141 7p. *Pemphis acidula*, two branches, wide base in shallow tray (vert) 30 30
4142 7p. *Antidesma bunius* (vert) 30 30
4143 7p. *Maba buxifolia* (vert) 30 30
4144 7p. *Ficus concina* (vert) 30 30
MS4145 181×75 mm. 7p.×4, *Lagerstroemia indica; Pemphis acidula* hexagonal pot and stand; *Vitex; Ixora chinensis* 1·30 1·30

2008. Jakarta 2008–International Stamp Exhibition. Sheet 140×175 mm containing vert stamps as Type 1205. Multicoloured.

MS4146 7p. Brahminy kite; 7p. Olive-backed sunbird; 7p. Purple-throated sunbird; 7p. Metallic-winged sunbird; 7p. Grey-headed fish eagle; 7p. Plain-throated sunbird; 7p. Lina's sunbird; 7p. Apo sunbird; 7p. Copper-throated sunbird; 7p. Flaming sunbird; 7p. Grey-hooded sunbird; 7p. Lovely sunbird; 7p. Crested serpent eagle; 7p. Philippine hawk eagle; 7p. Blue-crowned racquet tail; 7p. Philippine eagle owl; 7p. Common flameback 5·50 5·50

No. **MS**4087 was on sale for 150p.

1232 Ban Ki-moon

2008. Visit of United Nations Secretary General Ban Ki-moon. Multicoloured.

4147 7p. Type **1232** 30 30
4148 26p. Ban Ki-moon with President Gloria Macapagal 85 85

1233 Boracay Beach, Aklan

2008. 110th Anniv of Postal Service. Tourism. Multicoloured.

4149 7p. Type **1233** 30 30
4150 7p. Intramuros, Manila 30 30
4151 7p. Banaue Rice Terraces, Mountain Province 30 30
4152 7p. Mayon Volcano, Bicol 30 30
4153 20p. Puerto Princesa Underground River, Palawan 80 80
4154 24p. Chocolate Hills, Bohol 80 80
4155 26p. Tuddataila Reef, Palawan 85 85

1234 Mother and Child

2008. Christmas–Mother and Child. Multicoloured.

4156 7p. Type **1234** 30 30
4157 20p. Mother and child (facing left) 80 80
4158 24p. Mother and child holding dove 80 80
4159 26p. Mother carrying child in sling 85 85
MS4160 118×95 mm 7p. Virgin and Child; 26p. Mother and child 1·30 1·30

1235 Joaquin Bordado

2008. National Stamp collecting Month. Comics. T 1235 and similar vert designs showing comic book heroes created by Carlo J. Caparas (Magno Jose J. Caparas). Multicoloured.

4161 7p. Type **1235** 30 30
4162 20p. Totoy Bato 80 80
4163 24p. Gagambino 80 80
4164 26p. Pieta 75 75
MS4165 89×79 mm 7p. Ang Panday; 20p. Panday 1·30 1·30

1236 Benigno Aquino Jr.

2008. 25th Death Anniv of Benigno S. Aquino Jr. (senator, governor of Tarlac and opposition leader to Pres. Ferdinand Marcos. He was assassinated at Manila International Airport). Multicoloured.

4166 7p. Type **1236** 30 30
4167 26p. Pen and ink portrait 85 85

1237 Fernando Bautista

2008. Birth Centenary of Fernando Bautista (founder of University of Baguio).

4168 **1237** 7p. multicoloured 30 30

1238 Ox

2008. Chinese New Year. Year of the Ox. Multicoloured.

4169 7p. Type **1238** 30 30
4170 80p. Ox facing left
MS4171 139×80 mm. Nos. 4169/70, each×2 1·20 1·20

1239 *Carinoplax nana*

2008. Crabs. Multicoloured.

4172 7p. Type **1239** 30 30
4173 7p. *Cyrtomaia largoi* 30 30
4174 7p. *Hirsutodynomene vespertilio* 30 30
4175 7p. *Dicranodromia danielae* 30 30
MS4176 170×110 mm 20p. *Oxypleurodon stimpson*; 20p. *Cyrtomaia ericina* 1·80 1·80

1240 Manuel S. Enverga

2009. Birth Centenary Manuel Sarmiento Enverga (founder Manuel S. Enverga University Foundation, Lucena City).

4177 **1240** 7p. multicoloured 30 30

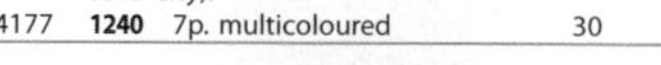

1241 Envelope of Hearts

2009. St. Valentine's Day. Multicoloured.

4178 7p. Type **1241** 30 30
4179 7p. Heart and roses 30 30

1242 'SINING BISWAL' (Visual Arts)

2009. International Arts Festival. Multicoloured.

4180 7p. Type **1242** 30 30
4181 7p. Masks (drama and poetry) 30 30
4182 7p. Dancer (music and dance) 30 30
4183 7p. Building and film credits (architecture and cinema) 30 30·00

1243 Panagbenga Flower Festival, Philippines

2009. 60th Anniv of Philippines–South Korea Diplomatic Relations. Multicoloured.

4184 7p. Type **1243** 30 30
4185 7p. Hangawi Sonori (cow play), Korea 30 30

1244 Quartz

2009. Minerals. Multicoloured.

4186 7p. Type **1244** 30 30
4187 7p. Rhodochrisite 30 30
4188 7p. Malachite 30 30
4189 7p. Nickel 30 30
MS4190 136×80 mm 7p.×4, Cinnabar; Gold; Copper; Magnetite 1·30 1·30

1245 Mother Dionisia Talangpaz and Mother Cecilia Rosa Talangpaz

2009. Augustinian Recollect Sisters.

4191 **1245** 7p. multicoloured 30 30

1246 King's Theatre

2009. Architectural Heritage. Art Deco Theatres and Cinemas. Sheet 100×102 mm containing T 1246 and similar horiz designs. Multicoloured.

MS4192 Type **1246** 30 30
4193 7p. Capitol Theatre 30 30
4194 7p. Joy Theatre 30 30
4195 7p Scala Theatre 30 30
MS4196 7p.×4, Life Theatre; Times Theatre; Bellevue Theatre; Pines Theatre 1·30 1·30

1247 Rodolfo Cornejo

2009. Birth Centenary of Rodolfo S. Cornejo (musician and composer).

4197 **1247** 7p. multicoloured 30 30

1248 City Hall

2009. Taguig–Global City. Multicoloured.

4198 7p. Type **1248** 30 30
4199 7p. Global City 30 30
4200 7p. St. Ana Church 30 30
4201 7p. Blue Mosque 30 30

1249 Tinikling, Philippine Folk Dance

2009. 60th Anniv of Philippines–Thailand Diplomatic Relations. Multicoloured.

4202 7p. Type **1249** 30 30
4203 7p. Ten Krathop Sark, Thailand Folk Dance 30 30

1250 Anniversary Emblem

2009. 150th Anniv of Ateneo de Manila University. Multicoloured

4204 7p. Type **1250** 30 30
4205 7p. Blue Eagle 30 30
4206 7p. Ignatius de Loyola 30 30
4207 7p. Dr. Jose Rizal 30 30
MS4208 192×101 mm. 7p.×4, As Nos. 4204/7 1·30 1·30

1251 Early Church

2009. 400th Anniv of Baler. Multicoloured.

4209	7p. Type **1251**	30	30
4210	7p. New Church	30	30

1252 Chua Tiong (Ancestor)

2009. Centenary of Che Yong Cua and Chua Family Association (1st issue). Multicoloured.

4211	7p. Type **1252**	30	30
4212	7p. Chua Siok To (Grand Ancestor)	30	30
MS4213	167×89 mm. 7p.×4, As Nos. 4124/7,each ×2. Imperf between horizontal pair	1·80	1·80

1253 Pheepoy

2009. Postal Corporation Mascot.

4214	**1253**	7p. multicoloured	30	30

1254 George J. Willmann (founder)

2009. 50th Anniv of Knights of Columbus Fraternal Association of the Philippines.

4215	**1254**	7p. multicoloured	30	30
4216	**1254**	9p. multicoloured	30	30

1255 President Gloria Macapagal-Arroyo and Sultan Haji Hassanal Bolkiah of Brunei

2009. Philippines–Brunei Agricultural Cooperation.

4217	**1255**	7p. multicoloured	30	30

1256 Bamban Bridge, Philippines

1257 Marcelo B. Fernan Bridge, Cebu, Philippines

1258 Cavenagh Bridge, Singapore

1259 Henderson Waves and Alexandra Arch, Singapore

2009. 40th Anniv of Diplomatic Relations between Singapore and the Philippines. Bridges.

4218	**1256**	7p. multicoloured	30	30
4219	**1257**	7p. multicoloured	30	30
4220	**1258**	7p. multicoloured	30	30
4221	**1259**	7p. multicoloured	30	30

Stamps of a similar designs were issued by Singapore.

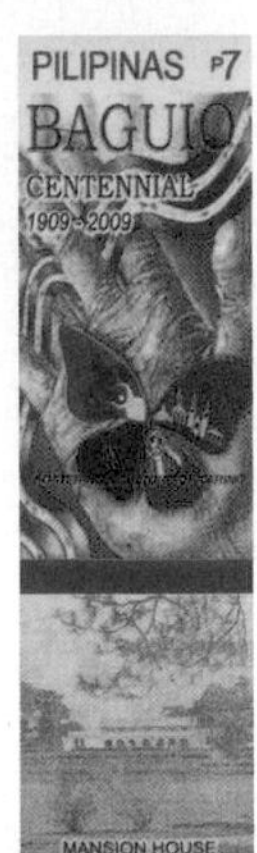

1260 Hand, Emblem and Mansion House

2009. Centenary of Baguio City. Multicoloured.

4222	7p. Type **1260**	30	30
4223	7p. Emblem and Mines View Park	30	30
4224	7p. Emblem, photographs and Baguio Cathedral	30	30
4225	7p. Emblem and Kennon Road	30	30
MS4226	100×100 mm. As Nos. 4222/5	1·30	1·30

1261 Cory Aquino

2009. María Corazón (Cory) Sumúlong Cojuangco Aquino (president 1986–1992) Commemoration. Multicoloured.

4227	7p. Type **1261**	30	30
4228	7p. Facing right	30	30

1262 Pina Barong and Dress

2008. International Year of Natural Fibres. Multicoloured.

4229	7p. Type **1262**	30	30
4230	7p. Abaca bag and hats	30	30
4231	7p. Bank notes made from Abaca	30	30
4232	7p. Abaca rope	30	30

2009. María Corazón (Cory) Sumúlong Cojuangco Aquino (president 1986–1992) Commemoration. As T 1261. Multicoloured.

4233	7p. As Type **1261**	30	30
4234	7p. Facing right	30	30

1263 *Chelarctus aureus*

2009. Lobsters. Multicoloured.

4235	7p. Type **1263**	30	30
4236	7p. *Polycheles coccifer*	30	30
4237	7p. *Metanephrops australiensis*	30	30
4238	7p. *Remiarctus bertholdii*	30	30
MS4239	136×80 mm. 7p.×4, *Metanephrops neptunus; Ibacus ciliatus; Petrarchus brevicomis; Puerulus angulatus*	1·30	1·30

1264 President Manuel L. Quezon and Philippine Flag

2009. 70th Anniv of Quezon City. Multicoloured.

4240	7p. Type **1264**	30	30
4241	7p. Quezon City Hall	30	30
4242	7p. Araneta Center	30	30
4243	7p. Eastwood City	30	30
MS4244	136×80 mm. 7p.×4, Nos. 4240/3	1·30	1·30

2009. Centenary of Che Yong Cua and Chua Family Association (2nd issue).As T 1252.

4245	7p. As Type **1252**	30	30
4246	7p. Cua Lo (Ancestor)	30	30
MS4247	167×89 mm. 7p.×4, As Nos. 4245/6,each ×2. Imperf between horizontal pair	1·30	1·30

1265 70th Anniversary Emblem

2009. 70th Anniv of University of the Philippines Alpha Phi Beta. Multicoloured.

4248	7p. Type **1265**	30	30
4249	7p. Quezon Hall	30	30
4250	7p. Malcolm Hall (UP College of Law)	30	30
4251	7p. Founder members	1·20	1·20

1266 Tumbang Preso

2009. Stamp Colllecting Month. Children's Games. Multicoloured.

4252	7p. Type **1266**	30	30
4253	7p. Luksong Tinik	30	30
4254	7p. Holen	30	30
4255	7p. Sungka	30	30
MS4256	128×102 mm. 7p.×6, Taguan (30×40 mm); Sipa (30×40 mm); Saranggola (30×40 mm); Bangkang papel (30×40 mm); Paluan ng palayok (48×38 mm); Luksong lubid (48×38 mm)	1·80	1·80

1267 Children Caroling

2009. Christmas. Multicoloured.

4257	7p. Type **1267**	30	30
4258	7p. The Nativity	30	30
4259	7p. Three Kings	30	30
4260	7p. Angels	30	30
4261	7p. Christmas decorations	30	30

1268 Cecilia Munoz Palma

2009. Cecilia Munoz Palma (first woman Supreme Court Associate Justice) Commemoration.

4262	**1268**	7p. multicoloured	30	30

1269 Whale Shark (*Rhincodon typus*)

2009. 60th Anniv of Philippines–India Diplomatic Relations. Endangered Marine Life. Multicoloured.

4263	7p. Type **1269**	30	30
4264	7p. Gangetic dolphin (*Platanista gangetica*)	30	30
MS4265	100×80 mm. 7p. As No. 4264; 20p. As Type **1269**	1·30	1·30

1270 Tiger

2009. Chinese New Year. Year of the Tiger. Multicoloured.

4266	7p. Type **1270**	30	30
4267	20p. Tiger facing left	30	30
MS4268	138×81 mm. 7p. As Type **1270**×2; 20p. As No. 4267×2	1·90	1·90

1271 *Hypselodoris apolegma*

2009. Marine Biodiversity. Nudibranchs. Multicoloured.

4269	7p. Type **1271**	30	30
4270	7p. *Glossodoris colemani*	30	30
4271	7p. *Chromodoris sp.*	30	30
4272	7p. *Chromodoris elisabethina*	30	30
MS4273	168×87 mm. 7p.×6, *Jorunna funebris; Chromodoris lochi; Noumea alboannulata ; Chromodoris hintuanesis; Risbechi tryoni; Chromodoris leopardus*	1·80	1·80

1272 Greek Goddess of Flight

2009. 65th Anniv of International Civil Aviation Organization (ICAO). Multicoloured.

4274	7p. Type **1272**	30	30
MS4275	82×106 mm. 7p.×4, As Type **1272**, top left; As Type **1272**, top right; As Type **1272**, bottom left; As Type **1272**, bottom right;	1·20	1·20

1273 Return Ceremony and Seals of Philippines and USA

2009. 50th Anniv of Return of Olongapo to the Philippines. Multicoloured.

4276	7p. Type **1273**	30	30
4277	7p. Parade of Philippine and USA Flags and seals	30	30

2009. Postal Corporation Mascot (Pheepoy).

4278	7p. As Type **1253**	30	30

1274 PCSO Building and Presidents Manuel L. Quezon and Gloria Macapagal Arroyo

2008. 75th Anniv of Charity Sweepstakes Office. Multicoloured.

4279	7p. Type **1274**	30	30
4280	7p. PCSO Building	30	30
4281	7p. PCSO Building and Filipino family	30	30
4282	7p. Building and PCSO employees	30	30
MS4283	135×96 mm. 7p.×4, As Nos. 4279/82	1·20	1·20

1275 Damili (Pottery)

2009. Centenary of San Nicolas, Ilocos Norte.

4284	**1275**	7p. multicoloured	30	30

1276 'Shower the world with LOVE'

2010. St Valentine's Day. Multicoloured.

4285	7p. Type **1276**	35	35
4286	7p. Cupid	35	35

2010. Postal Corporation Mascot (Pheepoy)

4287	7p. As Type **1253**	35	35

1277 Dove

2010. 90th Anniv of Philippine Rotary Club. Multicoloured.

4288	7p. Type **1277**	35	35
4289	7p. Housing project	35	35
4290	7p. Care workers giving child polio vaccine	35	35
4291	7p. Rizal monument and globe	35	35
MS4292	100×86 mm. As Nos. 4288/91. Imperf	1·40	1·40

PILIPINAS P7 2010

Agestra luconica

1278 *Agestra Luconia*

2010. Beetles. Multicoloured.

4293	7p. Type **1278**	35	35
4294	7p. *Glycyphana*	35	35
4295	7p. *Paraplectrone Crassa*	35	35
4296	7p. *Astrea*	35	35
MS4296a	135×80 mm. 7p.×4, *Agestra Semperi Heterorhina Clerota rodriguerzi Agestra antoinei*	1·40	1·40

1279 *Spirobranchus giganteus*

2010. Philippine Marine Biodiversity. Multicoloured.

4297	1p. Type **1279**	10	10
4298	1p. *Hippocampus kuda*	10	10
4299	1p. *Manta birostris*	10	10
4300	2p. *Iossodoris cruentus*	10	10
4301	2p. *Heterocentrotus mammillatus*	10	10
4302	3p. *Siphonogorgia godeffroyi*	10	10
4303	3p. *Heteractis magnifica*	10	10
4304	4p. *Architectonica perspectiva*	20	20
4305	4p. *Linckia laevigata*	20	20
4306	5p. *Cyerce nigrans* (incorrectly inscr 'Sea Hare')	20	20
4307	5p. *Tridacna crocea* (15.6.10)	20	20
4308	5p. *Chelonia mydas*	20	20
4309	5p. *Cyerce nigrans*	20	20
4310	7p. *Pterois volitans*	35	35
4311	7p. *Amphiprion percula*	35	35
4312	8p. *Hymenocera*	35	35
4313	9p. *Centropyge bispinosus*	45	45
4314	9p. *Pomacanthus annularis*	45	45
4315	10p. *Synchiropus splendidsus*	45	45
4316	10p. *Rhinomuraena quaesita*	45	45
4317	15p. *Rhina ancylostoma*	50	50
4318	17p. *Sepioteuthis lessoniana*	55	55
4319	17p. *Taeniura lymma*	55	55
4320	20p. *Rhopalaea crassa*	65	65
4321	20p. *Pseudoceros ferrugineus*	65	65
4322	24p. *Actiniaria* (inscr 'Actineria')	65	65
4323	25p. *Lybia tesselata* (inscr 'Lybia tessellata')	70	70
4324	26p. *Neopetrolisthes maculata*	70	70
4325	30p. *Nautilus pompilius*	80	80
4326	35p. *Cephalopholis miniata* (Cephalopholis miniatus)	80	80
4327	35p. *Gymnothorax Javanicus*	80	80
4328	40p. *Conus textile*	85	85
4329	50p. *Fromia monilis*	90	90
4330	50p. *Cassiopea*	90	90
4331	100p. *Tursiops aduncus*	1·70	1·70
4332	100p. *Hapalochlaena maculosa*	1·70	1·70

Nos. 4333/50 have been left for possible additions to this set.

1280 Anniversary Emblem

2010. 50th Anniv of International Rice Research Institute

4351	7p. Type **1280**	35	35
4352	7p. Institute campus	35	35
4353	7p. Rice field and irrigation canal	35	35
4354	7p. Rice	35	35
MS4355	81×100 mm. Nos. 4351/4	1·40	1·40

1281 Eraño de Guzman Manalo

1282 Eraño de Guzman Manalo

1283 Eraño de Guzman Manalo

1284 Eraño de Guzman Manalo

2010. Eraño de Guzman Manalo (Executive Minister of the Iglesia ni Cristo (Church of Christ), 1963–2009) Commemoration

4356	**1281**	7p. multicoloured	35	35
4357	**1282**	7p. multicoloured	35	35
4358	**1283**	7p. multicoloured	35	35
4359	**1284**	7p. multicoloured	35	35

1285 *Sabungero* (1982)

2010. Birth Centenary of Vicente Manansala (artist)

4360	7p. Type **1285**	35	35
4361	7p. *Bayanishan* (1982) (horiz)	35	35
4362	7p. *Nipa Hut* (1984) (horiz)	35	35
4363	7p. *Fish Vendor* (1982) (horiz)	35	35
4364	7p. *Planting of the First Cross* (1965) (80×30 mm)	95	95
MS4365	132×84 mm. 7p.×4, *Rooster* (1957); *Mamimintakasi* (1954); *I Believe in God* (1948); *Three Carabaos* (1958)	1·40	1·40

1286 Tree and Emblem

2010. Bitaug Tree (*Calophyllum inophyllum*) (oldest tree in Philippines). Multicoloured.

4366	7p. Type **1286**	35	35
4367	9p. As Type **1286** but with design reversed	45	45

1287 University Entrance

2010. 86th Anniv of Bukidnon State University. Multicoloured.

4368	7p. Type **1287**	35	35
4369	7p. Building and lawn	35	35

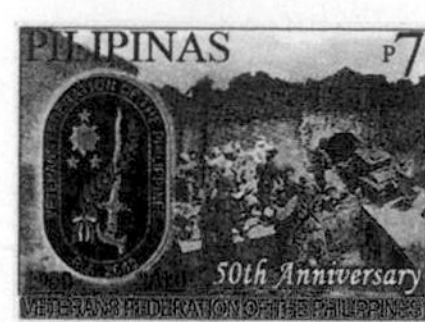

1288 Emblem and Battle Scene

2010. 50th Anniv of Veterans Federation of the Philippines. Multicoloured.

4370	7p. Type **1288**	35	35
4371	7p. Taking prisoners	35	35

1289 Train on Viaduct

2010. 30th Anniv of Light Rail Transit Authority (LRTA). Multicoloured.

4372	7p. Type **1289**	35	35
4373	7p. Electric locomotive	35	35
4374	7p. Electric locomotive, side view and skyline	35	35
4375	7p. LRT Megatren locomotive on viaduct and roadway	35	35
MS4376	170×80 mm. 10p.×4, as Nos 4372/5. Imperf	55	55

1290 Oath Taking

2010. President Benigno Simeon Cojuangco Aquino III's Inauguration

4377	7p. Type **1290**	35	35
4378	40p. Inaugural speech (vert)	1·70	1·70

1291 Emblem and Symbols of TB Control and Treatment

2010. Centenary of Philippine Tuberculosis Society. Multicoloured.

4379	7p. Type **1291**		
4380	9p. As Type **1291** but inscription in English	45	45
MS4381	165×86 mm. 26p. Manuel Quezon birthday seal (1935) (120×30 mm)	1·20	1·20

1292 Our Lady of Peñafrancia (photograph, 1924)

2010. 300 Years of Devotion to Our Lady of Peñafrancia

4382	7p. Type **1292**	35	35
4383	7p. Our Lady of Peñafrancia (2009)	35	35
4384	7p. Our Lady of Peñafrancia shrine (early photograph)	35	35
4385	7p. Basilica Minore of Our Lady of Peñafrancia, Naga City	35	35
MS4386	100×51 mm. 28p. Our Lady of Peñafrancia shrine, Naga City (early photograph) (80×30 mm)	1·30	1·30

1293 Chow Chow

2010. Dogs. Multicoloured.

4387	7p. Type **1293**	35	35
4388	7p. Bull terrier	35	35
4389	7p. Labrador retriever	35	35
4390	7p. Beagle	35	35
MS4391	135×80 mm. 7p.×4, Inscr 'Amerikan Eskimo Dog'; Black and tan coonhound; Afghan hound; Mastiff	1·40	1·40

1294 Hand above Globe above Sea

2010. Protect the Ozone Layer Campaign. Multicoloured.

4392	7p. Type **1294**	35	35
4393	7p. Hands enclosing globe with ozone layer	35	35

1295 CMU Administration Building and Mt. Musuan

2010. Centenary of Central Mindanao University (CMU). Multicoloured.

4303	7p. Type **1295**	35	35
4395	7p. CMU Main Building	35	35

1296 President Macapagal

2010. Birth Centenary of President Diosdado Macapagal

4396	**1296**	7p. multicoloured	35	35

1297 Galleon

1298 Galleon

2010. Dia del Galeon Festival, 2010. Multicoloured.

4397	7p. Type **1297**	35	35
4398	7p. Type **1298**	35	35
MS4399	175×80 mm. As Types **1297** and **1298**	70	70
MS4400	175×80 mm. 7p. As Type **1297**; 40p. As Type **1298**	70	70

1298a Girl holding Plant (Krysten Alarice Tan)

2010. United Nations International Year of Biodiversity. Multicoloured.

4400a	7p. Type **1298a**	35	35
4400b	7p. Girl holding globe and symbols of diversity (Justen Paul Tolentino)	35	35

1298b PhilRice Administrative Building

2010. 25th Anniv of Philippine Rice Institute (PhilRice). Multicoloured.

4401	7p. Type **1298b**	35	35
4402	7p. Test tube	35	35
4403	7p. Field of rice	35	35
4404	7p. Mechanical harvesting	35	35

1299 Pheepoy driving Mail Van

2010. Postal Corporation Mascot (Pheepoy). Multicoloured.

4405	7p. Type **1299**	35	35
MS4406	80×100mm. 7p.×4, As Type **1253**; No. 4278; No. 4287; Type **1299**	1·40	1·40
MS4407	110×70 mm. 7p.×4, As Type **1253**; No. 4278; No. 4287; Type **1299**. Imperf	1·40	1·40

1300 Levi Celerio (Music)

2010. Stamp Collecting Month

4408	7p. Type **1300**	35	35
4409	7p. Leonor Orosa Goquingco (Dance)	35	35
4410	7p. Carlos L. Quirino (Historical Literature)	35	35
4411	7p. Nick Joaquin (Literature)	35	35
MS4412	137×80 mm. Vert. 7p.×3, *Ang Panday Ikatlong Yugto*; *Umpishan Mo Tatapustin Ko*; *Pipeng Kaliwete* (Fernando Poe, Jr. (Film))	1·10	1·10

1301 Oath Taking

2010. Vice President Jejomar Binay's Inauguration

4413	**1301**	7p. multicoloured	35	35

1302 Mary and Joseph in Philippino Costume and Vatican

2010. Christmas. Multicoloured.

4414	7p. Type **1302**	35	35
4415	7p. Holy family	35	35
4416	7p. Holy family in jar	35	35
4417	7p. Holy family and shepherds	35	35

1303 Fernando Poe Jr.

2010. National Stamp Collecting Month (2nd issue). Multicoloured.

4418	7p. Type **1303**	35	35
4419	7p. *Ang Panday Ikatlong Yugto*	35	35
4420	7p. *Umpishan Mo Tatapustin Ko*	35	35
4421	7p. *Pipeng Kaliwete*	35	35

Nos. 4419/21 are as the stamps of **MS**4412.

1304 'Fabilioh!' (official emblem)

2010. Ateneo de Manila Class '60 Re-union. Multicoloured.

4422	7p. Type **1304**	35	35
4423	7p. 'We stand on a hill, between the earth and sky'	35	35
4424	7p. 'Mary for you, for your white and blue'	35	35
4425	7p. 'The Bell Ringers of GESU'	35	35

1305 Rabbit and 'Manigong Bagong Taon'

2010. Chinese New Year. Multicoloured.

MS4428	140×80 mm. 7p.×2, Type **1305**×2; 30p.×2, Rabbit and 'Happy New Year'×2	2·75	2·75

Nos. 4426/7 are left for single stamps, not yet received.

1306 Portrait and As Politician

2010. Birth Centenary of Senator Ambrosio Padilla. Multicoloured.

4429	7p. Type **1306**	35	35
4430	7p. Portrait and as basketball player	35	35

1307 Law Books

2010. 65th Anniv SyCip, Salazar, Hernandez & Gatmaitan Law Firm

4430a	**1307**	7p. multicoloured	35	35

1308 New Building

2010. 60th Anniv of Grace Christian College (GCC). Multicoloured.

4431	7p. Type **1308**	35	35
4432	7p. Anniversary emblem	35	35
4433	7p. Building, 1966	35	35
4434	7p. Founders, Ms. Julia L. Tan, Dr. and Mrs. Edward Spahr	35	35
MS4435	170×80 mm. 7p.×4, Nos. 4431/4	1·40	1·40

OFFICIAL STAMPS

1926. Commemorative issue of 1926 optd OFFICIAL.

O391	**49**	2c. black and green	3·75	1·50
O392	**49**	4c. black and red	3·75	1·80
O393	**49**	18c. black and brown	12·50	6·25
O394	**49**	20c. black and orange	11·00	2·75

1931. Stamps of 1906 optd O.B.

O413	2c. green (No. 337)	25	25
O414	4c. red (No. 338)	25	25
O415	6c. violet (No. 339)	25	25
O416	8c. brown (No. 340)	25	25
O417	10c. blue (No. 341)	35	25
O418	12c. orange (No. 342)	45	25
O419	16c. olive (No. 344)	45	25
O420	20c. orange (No. 345)	45	25
O421	26c. green (No. 346)	55	45
O422	30c. grey (No. 347)	45	45

1935. Nos. 459/68 optd O.B.

O473	2c. red	25	25
O474	4c. green	25	25
O475	6c. brown	25	25
O476	8c. violet	25	25
O477	10c. red	25	25
O478	12c. black	25	25
O479	16c. blue	25	25
O480	20c. bistre	25	25
O481	26c. blue	45	45
O482	30c. red	55	55

1936. Stamps of 1935 Nos. 459/68 optd O. B. COMMONWEALTH (2, 6, 20c.) or O. B. COMMONWEALTH (others).

O538	2c. red	25	25
O539	4c. green	25	25
O540	6c. brown	25	25
O541	8c. violet	25	25
O542	10c. red	25	25
O543	12c. black	25	25
O544	16c. blue	25	25
O545	20c. bistre	45	45
O546	26c. blue	55	55
O547	30c. red	45	45

1941. Nos. 563 and 623 optd O. B.

O565	**104**	2c. green	25	25
O624	-	2c. brown	25	25

1948. Various stamps optd O.B.

O738	**147**	1c. brown	15	10
O668	**125**	2c. green	50	10
O659		4c. brown (No. 629)	15	10
O739	-	5c. red (No. 731)	15	10
O843	-	6c. blue (No. 842)	15	10
O660	**113**	10c. red	20	10
O740	-	10c. blue (No. 732)	20	15
O661	-	16c. grey (No. 632)	2·20	80
O669	-	20c. brown (No. 633)	15	15
O741	-	20c. red (No. 733)	50	15
O670	-	50c. green (No. 634)	75	45

1950. Surch ONE CENTAVO.

O700	**125**	1c. on 2c. green (No. O668)	10	10

1959. No. 810 optd O B.

O811	1c. on 5c. red	15	10

1962. Nos. 898/904 optd G. O.

O908	5s. red	10	10
O909	6s. brown	15	10
O910	6s. blue	15	10
O911	10s. purple	20	15
O912	20s. blue	30	15
O913	30s. red	35	30
O914	50s. violet	45	35

1970. Optd G.O.

O1182	**318**	10s. red	15	10

OFFICIAL SPECIAL DELIVERY STAMP

1931. No. E353b optd O.B.

EO423	**E47**	20c. violet	2·00	90·00

POSTAGE DUE STAMPS

1899. Postage Due stamps of United States of 1894 optd PHILIPPINES.

D268	**D87**	1c. red	9·75	2·30
D269	**D87**	2c. red	9·75	1·80
D270	**D87**	3c. red	27·00	11·00
D271	**D87**	5c. red	23·00	3·75
D272	**D87**	10c. red	30·00	8·50
D273	**D87**	30c. red	£375	£170
D274	**D87**	50c. red	£300	£150

D51 Post Office Clerk

1928

D395	**D51**	4c. red	25	25
D396	**D51**	6c. red	25	45
D397	**D51**	8c. red	25	45
D398	**D51**	10c. red	25	45
D399	**D51**	12c. red	25	45
D400	**D51**	16c. red	35	45
D401	**D51**	20c. red	35	45

1937. Surch 3 CVOS. 3.

D521	**D 51**	3c. on 4c. red	25	25

D118

1947

D644	**D 118**	3c. red	15	15
D645	**D 118**	4c. blue	35	30
D646	**D 118**	6c. green	50	45
D647	**D 118**	10c. orange	80	60

SPECIAL DELIVERY STAMPS

1901. Special Delivery stamp of United States of 1888 optd PHILIPPINES.

E268	**46**	10c. blue (No. E283)	£140	£110

1907. Special Delivery stamp of United States optd PHILIPPINES.

E298	**E 117**	10c. blue	£3250	

E47 Messenger running

1919. Perf (E353), perf or imperf (E353b).

E353	**E 47**	20c. blue	70	35
E353b	**E 47**	20c. violet	70	35

1939. Optd COMMONWEALTH. Perf.

E550		20c. violet	35	35

1945. Optd VICTORY.

E622		20c. violet (No. E550)	1·10	70

E120 Cyclist Messenger and Post Office

1947

E651	**E 120**	20c. purple	60	45

E219 G.P.O., Manila

E891	**E 219**	20c. mauve	35	30

Pt. 1

PITCAIRN ISLANDS

An island group in the Pacific Ocean, nearly midway between Australia and America.

1940. 12 pence = 1 shilling; 20 shillings = 1 pound.
1967. 100 cents = 1 New Zealand dollar.

4 Lt. Bligh and the "Bounty"

1940

1	-	½d. orange and green	55	60
2	-	1d. mauve and magenta	1·00	80
3	-	1½d. grey and red	1·00	50
4	**4**	2d. green and brown	2·25	1·40
5	-	3d. green and blue	1·25	1·40
5b	-	4d. black and green	21·00	11·00
6	-	6d. brown and blue	6·00	1·50
6a	-	8d. green and mauve	24·00	7·00
7	-	1s. violet and grey	5·50	3·50
8	-	2s.6d. green and brown	15·00	4·00

DESIGNS—HORIZ: ½d. Oranges; 1d. Fletcher Christian, crew and Pitcairn Is.; 1½d. John Adams and house; 3d. Map of Pitcairn Is. and Pacific; 4d. Bounty Bible; 6d. H.M.S. "Bounty"; 8d. School, 1949; 1s. Christian and Pitcairn Is.; 2s.6d. Christian, crew and Pitcairn coast.

8a Houses of Parliament, London

1946. Victory.

9	**8a**	2d. brown	70	30
10	**8a**	3d. blue	70	30

8b King George VI and Queen Elizabeth

8c King George VI and Queen Elizabeth

1949. Silver Wedding.

11	**8b**	1½d. red	2·00	1·50
12	**8c**	10s. mauve	40·00	50·00

8d Hermes, Globe and Forms of Transport

8e Hemispheres, Jet-powered Vickers Viking Airliner and Steamer

8f Hermes and Globe

8g U.P.U. Monument

1949. U.P.U.

13	**8d**	2½d. brown	1·25	4·25
14	**8e**	3d. blue	8·00	4·25
15	**8f**	6d. green	4·00	4·25
16	**8g**	1s. purple	4·00	4·25

8h Queen Elizabeth II

1953. Coronation.

17	**8h**	4d. black and green	2·00	3·75

12 Handicrafts: Bird Model

1957

33	-	½d. green and mauve	65	60
19	-	1d. black and green	4·50	1·75
20	-	2d. brown and blue	2·25	60
21	**12**	2½d. brown and orange	50	40
22	-	3d. green and blue	80	40
23	-	4d. red and blue (I)	90	40
23a	-	4d. red and blue (II)	3·50	1·50
24	**12**	6d. buff and blue	3·25	55
25	-	8d. green and red	60	40
26	-	1s. black and brown	2·25	40
27	-	2s. green and orange	11·00	10·00
28	-	2s.6d. blue and red	24·00	11·00

DESIGNS—HORIZ: ½d. "Cordyline terminalis"; 3d. Bounty Bay; 4d. Pitcairn School; 6d. Map of Pacific; 8d. Inland scene; 1s. Model of the "Bounty"; 2s.6d. Launching new whaleboat. VERT: 1d. Map of Pitcairn; 2d. John Adams and "Bounty" Bible; 2s. Island wheelbarrow.

The 4d. Type I is inscr "PITCAIRN SCHOOL"; Type II is inscr "SCHOOL TEACHER'S HOUSE".

20 Pitcairn Island and Simon Young

1961. Cent of Return of Pitcairn Islanders.

29	**20**	3d. black and yellow	50	45
30	-	6d. brown and blue	1·00	75
31	-	1s. orange and green	1·00	75

DESIGNS: 6d. Maps of Norfolk and Pitcairn Islands; 1s. Migrant brigantine "Mary Ann".

20a Protein Foods

1963. Freedom from Hunger.

32	**20a**	2s.6d. blue	4·00	2·00

20b Red Cross Emblem

1963. Cent of Red Cross.

34	**20b**	2d. red and black	1·00	1·00
35	**20b**	2s.6d. red and blue	2·00	4·00

23 Pitcairn Is. Longboat

24 Queen Elizabeth II (after Anthony Buckley)

1964. Multicoloured.. Multicoloured..

36		½d. Type **23**	10	30
37		1d. H.M.S. "Bounty"	30	30
38		2d. "Out from Bounty Bay"	30	30
39		3d. Great frigate bird	75	30
40		4d. White tern	75	30
41		6d. Pitcairn warbler	75	30
42		8d. Red-footed booby	75	30
43		10d. Red-tailed tropic birds	60	30
44		1s. Henderson Island crake	60	30
45		1s.6d. Stephen's lory	2·00	1·25
46		2s.6d. Murphy's petrel	2·00	1·50
47		4s. Henderson Island fruit dove	2·75	1·50
48		8s. Type **24**	1·50	2·00

24a I.T.U. Emblem

1965. Centenary of I.T.U.

49	**24a**	1d. mauve and brown	50	40
50	**24a**	2s.6d. turquoise and blue	2·00	3·00

24b I.C.Y. Emblem

1965. International Co-operation Year.

51	**24b**	1d. purple and turquoise	50	40
52	**24b**	2s.6d. green and lavender	2·00	2·50

24c Sir Winston Churchill and St. Paul's Cathedral in Wartime

1966. Churchill Commemoration.

53	**24c**	2d. blue	1·00	85
54	**24c**	3d. green	1·75	1·00
55	**24c**	6d. brown	2·00	1·75
56	**24c**	1s. violet	2·50	2·50

25 Footballer's Legs, Ball and Jules Rimet Cup

1966. World Cup Football Championship.

57	**25**	4d. multicoloured	75	1·00
58	**25**	2s.6d. multicoloured	1·25	1·75

25a W.H.O. Building.

1966. Inauguration of W.H.O. Headquarters, Geneva.

59	**25a**	8d. black, green and blue	2·00	3·25
60	**25a**	1s.6d. black, purple and ochre	3·50	3·75

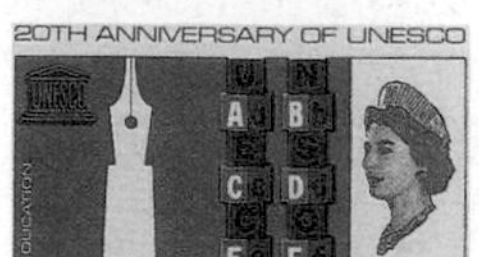

25b "Education"

25c "Science"

25d "Culture"

1966. 20th Anniv of UNESCO.

61	**25b**	½d. multicoloured	20	1·00
62	**25c**	10d. yellow, violet and olive	1·25	1·75
63	**25d**	2s. black, purple and orange	2·50	2·75

36 Mangarevan Canoe, c. 1325

1967. Bicentenary of Discovery of Pitcairn Islands. Multicoloured.

64	½d. Type **36**	10	20
65	1d. P. F. de Quiros and "San Pedro y San Pablo", 1606	20	20
66	8d. "San Pedro y San Pablo" and "Los Tres Reyes", 1606	25	20
67	1s. Carteret and H.M.S. "Swallow", 1767	25	25
68	1s.6d. "Hercules", 1819	25	25

1967. Decimal Currency. Nos. 36/48 surch with "Bounty" anchor and value.

69	**23**	½c. on ½d. multicoloured	10	10
70	-	1c. on 1d. multicoloured	30	1·25
71	-	2c. on 2d. multicoloured	25	1·25
72	-	2½c. on 3d. multicoloured	25	1·25
73	-	3c. on 4d. multicoloured	25	20
74	-	5c. on 6d. multicoloured	30	1·25
75	-	10c. on 8d. multicoloured	50	30
76	-	15c. on 10d. multicoloured	1·50	40
77	-	20c. on 1s. multicoloured	1·50	55
78	-	25c. on 1s.6d. multicoloured	1·50	1·25
79	-	30c. on 2s.6d. multicoloured	1·75	1·25
80	-	40c. on 4s. multicoloured	1·75	1·25
81	**24**	45c. on 8s. multicoloured	1·50	1·50

42 Bligh and "Bounty's" Launch

1967. 150th Death Anniv of Admiral Bligh.

82	**42**	1c. black, ultramarine & blue	10	10
83	-	8c. black, yellow and mauve	25	50
84	-	20c. black, brown and buff	25	55

DESIGNS: 8c. Bligh and followers cast adrift; 20c. Bligh's tomb.

45 Human Rights Emblem

1968. International Human Rights Year.

85	**45**	1c. multicoloured	10	10
86	**45**	2c. multicoloured	10	10
87	**45**	25c. multicoloured	35	35

46 Moro Wood and Flower

1968. Handicrafts (1st series).

88	**46**	5c. multicoloured	20	30
89	-	10c. green, brown and orange	20	40
90	-	15c. violet, brown & salmon	25	40
91	-	20c. multicoloured	25	45

DESIGNS—HORIZ: 10c. flying fish model. VERT: 15c. "Hand" vases; 20c. Woven baskets.

See also Nos. 207/10.

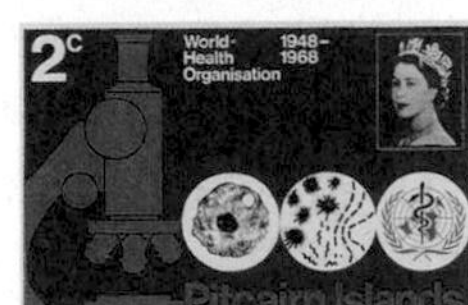

50 Microscope and Slides

1968. 20th Anniv of World Health Organization.

92	**50**	2c. black, turquoise and blue	10	20
93	-	20c. black, orange and purple	40	50

DESIGN: 20c. Hypodermic syringe and jars of tablets.

52 Pitcairn Island

64b Queen Elizabeth II

1969. Multicoloured.. Multicoloured..

94	1c. Type **52**	2·25	2·00
95	2c. Captain Bligh and "Bounty" chronometer	25	15
96	3c. "Bounty" anchor (vert)	25	15
97	4c. Plans and drawing of "Bounty"	2·50	15
98	5c. Breadfruit containers and plant	70	15
99	6c. Bounty Bay	30	20
100	8c. Pitcairn longboat	2·00	20
101	10c. Ship landing point	2·50	85
102	15c. Fletcher Christian's Cave	2·25	1·75
103	20c. Thursday October Christian's house	60	40
104	25c. "Flying fox" cable system (vert)	70	40
105	30c. Radio Station, Taro Ground	55	45
106	40c. "Bounty" Bible	75	60
106a	50c. Pitcairn Coat-of-Arms	2·00	12·00
106b	$1 Type **64b**	5·50	17·00

65 Lantana

1970. Flowers. Multicoloured.

107	1c. Type **65**	15	50
108	2c. "Indian Shot"	20	65
109	5c. Pulau	25	75
110	25c. Wild gladiolus	60	2·00

69 Band-tailed Hind

1970. Fishes. Multicoloured.

111	5c. Type **69**	1·50	1·00
112	10c. High-finned rudderfish	1·50	1·00
113	15c. Elwyn's wrasse	2·00	1·50
114	20c. Yellow wrasse ("Whistling daughter")	2·50	1·50

1971. Royal Visit. No. 101 optd ROYAL VISIT 1971.

115	10c. multicoloured	1·00	1·50

71 Polynesian Rock Carvings

1971. Polynesian Pitcairn. Multicoloured.

116	5c. Type **71**	75	75
117	10c. Polynesian artefacts (horiz)	1·00	1·00
118	15c. Polynesian stone fish-hook (horiz)	1·00	1·00

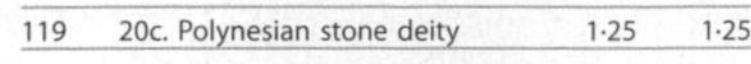

119	20c. Polynesian stone deity	1·25	1·25

72 Commission Flag

1972. 25th Anniv of South Pacific Commission. Multicoloured.

120	4c. Type **72**	40	70
121	8c. Young and elderly (Health)	40	70
122	18c. Junior school (Education)	50	90
123	20c. Goods store (Economy)	60	1·60

73 Red-tailed Tropic Birds and Longboat

1972. Royal Silver Wedding. Multicoloured, background colour given.

124	**73**	4c. green	30	60
125	**73**	20c. blue	45	90

74 Rose-apple

1973. Flowers. Multicoloured.

126	4c. Type **74**	55	55
127	8c. Mountain-apple	65	75
128	15c. "Lata"	80	1·00
129	20c. "Dorcas-flower"	80	1·25
130	35c. Guava	80	1·75

74a Princess Anne and Captain Mark Phillips

1973. Royal Wedding. Multicoloured, background colours given.

131	**74a**	10c. mauve	20	15
132	**74a**	25c. green	25	30

75 Obelisk Vertagus and Episcopal Mitre Shells

1974. Shells. Multicoloured.

147	4c. Type **75**	50	80
148	10c. Turtle dove-shell	60	1·00
149	18c. Indo-Pacific limpet, fringed false limpet and "Siphonaria normalis"	70	1·40
150	50c. "Ctena divergen"	1·00	2·00
MS151	130×121 mm. Nos. 147/50	2·75	14·00

76 Island Post Office

1974. Centenary of U.P.U.

152	**76**	4c. multicoloured	20	35
153	-	20c. purple, brown & black	25	60
154	-	35c. multicoloured	35	70

DESIGNS: 20c. Pre-stamp letter, 1922; 35c. Mailship and Pitcairn longboat.

77 Churchill and Text "Lift up your Hearts ..."

1974. Birth Cent of Sir Winston Churchill.

155	**77**	20c. olive, green and grey	30	65
156	-	35c. brown, green and grey	40	75

DESIGN: 35c. Text "Give us the tools ...".

78 H.M.S. "Seringapatam" (frigate), 1830

1975. Mailboats. Multicoloured.

157	4c. Type **78**	25	50
158	10c. "Pitcairn" (missionary schooner), 1890	30	75
159	18c. "Athenic" (liner), 1904	35	1·10
160	50c. "Gothic" (liner), 1948	60	1·75
MS161	145×110 mm. Nos. 157/60	11·00	16·00

79 "Polistes jadwigae" (wasp)

1975. Pitcairn Insects. Multicoloured.

162	4c. Type **79**	25	45
163	6c. "Euconocephalus sp." (grasshopper)	25	55
164	10c. "Anomis flavia" and "Chasmina tibialis" (moth)	30	70
165	15c. "Pantala flavescens" (skimmer)	40	1·00
166	20c. "Gnathothlibus erotus" (banana moth)	50	1·25

80 Fletcher Christian

1976. Bicent of American Revolution. Mult.

167	5c. Type **80**	20	65
168	10c. H.M.S. "Bounty"	30	80
169	30c. George Washington	25	95
170	50c. "Mayflower", 1620	35	1·50

81 Chair of Homage

1977. Silver Jubilee. Multicoloured.

171	8c. Prince Philip's visit, 1971	10	15
172	20c. Type **81**	20	25
173	50c. Enthronement	40	50

82 The Island's Bell

1977. Multicoloured.. Multicoloured..

174	1c. Type **82**	10	35
175	2c. Building a longboat (horiz)	10	35
176	5c. Landing cargo (horiz)	10	35
177	6c. Sorting supplies (horiz)	10	35
178	9c. Cleaning wahoo (fish)	10	35
179	10c. Cultivation (horiz)	10	35
179a	15c. Sugar Mill (horiz)	50	1·00
180	20c. Grating coconut and bananas (horiz)	15	35
181	35c. The Island church (horiz)	15	50
182	50c. Fetching miro logs, Henderson Is. (horiz)	20	1·00
182b	70c. Burning obsolete stamp issues	50	1·25
183	$1 Prince Philip, Bounty Bay and Royal Yacht "Britannia" (horiz)	40	1·10
184	$2 Queen Elizabeth II (photograph by Reginald Davis)	50	1·25

83 Building a "Bounty" Model

1978. "Bounty" Day. Multicoloured.

185	6c. Type **83**	20	20
186	20c. The model at sea	25	25
187	35c. Burning the model	35	35
MS188	166×122 mm. Nos. 185/7	5·00	9·50

84 Coronation Ceremony

1978. 25th Anniv of Coronation. Sheet 94×78 mm.

MS189	**84** $1.20 multicoloured	80	1·75

85 Harbour before Development

1978. "Operation Pallium" (Harbour Development Project). Multicoloured.

190	15c. Type **85**	25	50
191	20c. Unloading R.F.A. "Sir Geraint"	30	60
192	30c. Work on the jetty	35	70
193	35c. Harbour after development	40	80

86 John Adams and Diary Extract

1979. 150th Death Anniv of John Adams ("Bounty" mutineer). Multicoloured.

194	35c. Type **86**	30	70
195	70c. John Adams' grave and diary extract	45	90

87 Pitcairn's Island sketched from H.M.S. "Amphitrite"

1979. 19th-century Engravings.

196	**87** 6c. black, brown and stone	15	20
197	- 9c. black, violet & lt violet	15	25
198	- 20c. black, green and yellow	15	40
199	- 70c. black, scarlet and red	30	1·00

DESIGNS: 9c. Bounty Bay and Village of Pitcairn; 20c. Lookout Ridge; 70c. Church and School House.

88 Taking Presents to the Square

1979. Christmas. Int Year of the Child. Mult.

200	6c. Type **88**	10	20
201	9c. Decorating trees with presents	10	25
202	20c. Chosen men distributing gifts	15	40
203	35c. Carrying presents home	20	50
MS204	198×73 mm. Nos. 200/3	75	1·40

89 Loading Mail from Supply Ship to Longboats

1980. "London 1980" International Stamp Exhibition. Sheet 120×135 mm containing T 89 and similar horiz designs. Multicoloured.

MS205	35c. Type **89**; 35c. Mail being conveyed by "Flying Fox" (hoisting mechanism) to the Edge; 35c. Tractor transporting mail from the Edge to Adamstown; 35c. Mail being off-loaded at Post Office	75	1·50

90 Queen Elizabeth the Queen Mother at Henley Regatta

1980. 80th Birthday of The Queen Mother.

206	**90** 50c. multicoloured	40	70

1980. Handicrafts (2nd series). As T 46. Multicoloured.

207	9c. Turtles (wood carvings)	10	10
208	20c. Pitcairn wheelbarrow (wood carving)	10	15
209	35c. Gamet (wood carving) (vert)	15	25
210	40c. Woven bonnet and fan (vert)	15	25

91 Part of Adamstown

1981. Landscapes. Multicoloured.

211	6c. Type **91**	10	10
212	9c. Big George	10	15
213	20c. Christian's Cave, Gannets Ridge	15	20
214	35c. Radio Station from Pawala Valley Ridge	20	30
215	70c. Tatrimoa	30	45

92 Islanders preparing for Departure

1981. 125th Anniv of Pitcairn Islanders' Migration to Norfolk Island. Multicoloured.

216	9c. Type **92**	15	30
217	35c. View of Pitcairn Island from "Morayshire"	25	50
218	70c. "Morayshire"	40	90

93 Prince Charles as Colonel-in-Chief, Cheshire Regiment

1981. Royal Wedding. Multicoloured.

219	20c. Wedding bouquet from Pitcairn Islands	20	20
220	35c. Type **93**	25	20
221	$1.20 Prince Charles and Lady Diana Spencer	75	60

94 Lemon

1982. Fruit. Multlcoloured.

222	9c. Type **94**	10	10
223	20c. Pomegranate	15	20
224	35c. Avocado	20	30
225	70c. Pawpaw	40	65

95 Pitcairn Islands Coat of Arms

1982. 21st Birthday of Princess of Wales. Multicoloured.

226	6c. Type **95**	10	20
227	9c. Princess at Royal Opera House, Covent Garden, December 1981	45	20
228	70c. Balcony Kiss	55	60
229	$1.20 Formal portrait	1·00	80

96 Raphael's Angels

1982. Christmas. Raphael's Angels.

230	**96** 15c. black, silver and pink	20	20
231	- 20c. black, silver and yellow	20	20
232	- 50c. brown, silver and stone	30	30
233	- $1 black, silver and blue	40	40

DESIGNS: 20c. to $1 Different details, the 50c. and $1 being vertical.

97 Radio Operator

1983. Commonwealth Day. Multicoloured.

234	6c. Type **97**	10	10
235	9c. Postal clerk	10	10
236	70c. Fisherman	35	65
237	$1.20 Artist	60	1·10

98 "Topaz" sights Smoke on Pitcairn

1983. 175th Anniv of Folger's Discovery of the Settlers. Multicoloured.

238	6c. Type **98**	40	20
239	20c. Three islanders approach the "Topaz"	45	30
240	70c. Capt. Mayhew Folger welcomed by John Adams	70	75
241	$1.20 Folger presented with "Bounty" chronometer	85	1·10

99 Hattie-Tree

1983. Trees of Pitcairn Islands (1st series). Multicoloured.

242	35c. Type **99**	25	55
243	35c. Leaves from Hattie-Tree	25	55
244	70c. Pandanus	40	90
245	70c. Pandanus and basket weaving	40	90

See also Nos. 304/7.

100 Atava wrasse

1984. Fishes. Multicoloured.

246	1c. Type **100**	20	30
247	4c. Black-eared wrasse	30	35
248	6c. Long-finned parrotfish	30	35
249	9c. Yellow-edged lyretail	30	35
250	10c. Black-eared angelfish	30	40
251	15c. Emery's damselfish	40	40
252	20c. Smith's butterflyfish	40	50
253	35c. Crosshatched triggerfish	50	60
254	50c. Yellow damselfish	50	75
255	70c. Pitcairn angelfish	70	95
256	$1 Easter Island soldierfish	70	1·25
257	$1.20 Long-finned anthias	75	2·00
258	$2 White trevally	1·25	2·50
312	90c. As 9c.	4·00	5·00
313	$3 Wakanoura moray	5·50	8·50

101 "Southern Cross"

1984. Night Sky.

259	**101** 15c. blue, lilac and gold	20	20
260	- 20c. blue, green and gold	30	30
261	- 70c. blue, brown and gold	75	75

262	- $1 blue, light blue and gold	1·00	1·00

DESIGNS: 20c. "Southern Fish"; 70c. "Lesser Dog"; $1 "The Virgin".

102 Aluminium Longboat

1984. "Ausipex" International Stamp Exhibition, Melbourne. Sheet 134×86 mm containing T **102** and similar horiz design. Multicoloured.

MS263	50c. Type **102**; $2 Traditional-style wooden longboat	1·50	2·00

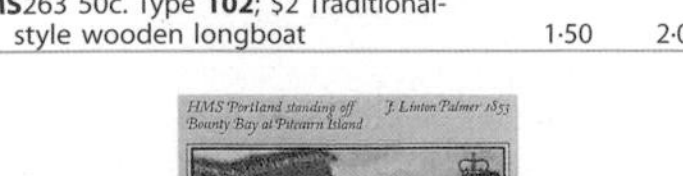

103 "H.M.S. "Portland" standing off Bounty Bay" (J. Linton Palmer)

1985. 19th-century Paintings (1st series). Mult.

264	6c. Type **103**	40	40
265	9c. "Christian's Look Out" (J. Linton Palmer)	40	40
266	35c. "The Golden Age" (J. Linton Palmer)	75	60
267	$2 "A View of the Village, 1825" (William Smyth) (48×31 mm)	1·75	2·25

See also Nos. 308/11.

104 The Queen Mother with the Queen and Princess Margaret, 1980

1985. Life and Times of Queen Elizabeth the Queen Mother. Multicoloured.

268	6c. Receiving the Freedom of Dundee, 1964	10	25
269	35c. Type **104**	30	55
270	70c. The Queen Mother in 1983	50	85
271	$1.20 With Prince Henry at his christening (from photo by Lord Snowdon)	70	1·50
MS272	91×73 mm. $2 In coach at Ascot Races	2·75	2·75

105 "Act 6" (container ship)

1985. Ships (1st issue). Multicoloured.

273	50c. Type **105**	95	1·75
274	50c. "Columbus Louisiana" (container ship)	95	1·75
275	50c. "Essi Gina" (tanker) (48×35 mm)	95	1·75
276	50c. "Stolt Spirit" tanker (48×35 mm)	95	1·75

See also Nos. 296/9.

106 "Madonna and Child" (Raphael)

1985. Christmas. Designs showing "Madonna and Child" paintings. Multicoloured.

277	6c. Type **106**	80	50
278	9c. Krause (after Raphael)	80	50
279	35c. Andreas Mayer	1·50	70
280	$2 Unknown Austrian master	3·00	4·00

107 Green Turtle

1986. Turtles. Multicoloured.

281	9c. Type **107**	75	90
282	20c. Green turtle and Pitcairn Island	1·25	1·25
283	70c. Hawksbill turtle	2·25	3·75
284	$1.20 Hawksbill turtle and Pitcairn Island	2·75	4·25

1986. 60th Birthday of Queen Elizabeth II. As T **246a** of Papua New Guinea.

285	6c. Princess Elizabeth at Royal Lodge, Windsor, 1946	15	20
286	9c. Wedding of Princess Anne, 1973	15	20
287	20c. At Order of St. Michael and St. George service, St. Paul's Cathedral, 1961	25	30
288	$1.20 At Electrical Engineering Concert, Royal Festival Hall, 1971	60	1·25
289	$2 At Crown Agents Head Office, London 1983	75	2·00

107a Prince Andrew and Miss Sarah Ferguson

1986. Royal Wedding. Multicoloured.

290	20c. Type **107a**	50	50
291	$1.20 Prince Andrew aboard "Bluenose II" off Halifax, Canada, 1985	2·25	2·75

108 John I. Tay (pioneer missionary) and First Church

1986. Centenary of Seventh-Day Adventist Church on Pitcairn. Multicoloured.

292	6c. Type **108**	60	60
293	20c. "Pitcairn" (missionary schooner) and second church (1907)	1·50	1·00
294	35c. Baptism at Down Isaac and third church (1945)	1·75	1·50
295	$2 Islanders singing farewell hymn and present church (1954)	4·00	4·75

1987. Ships (2nd series). As T **105**. Multicoloured.

296	50c. "Samoan Reefer" (freighter)	1·10	2·50
297	50c. "Brussel" (container ship)	1·10	2·50
298	50c. "Australian Exporter" (container ship) (48×35 mm)	1·10	2·50
299	50c. "Taupo" (cargo liner) (48×35 mm)	1·10	2·50

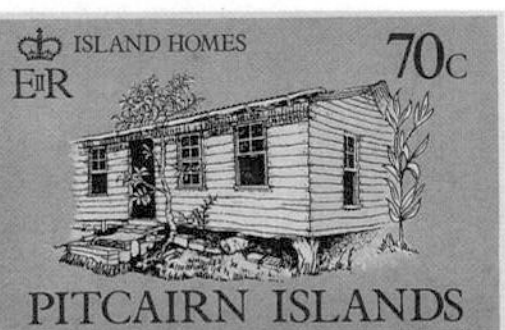

109 Pitcairn Island Home

1987. Pitcairn Island Homes.

300	**109** 70c. black, dp violet & vio	70	60
301	- 70c. black, yellow & brn	70	60
302	- 70c. black, blue & dp blue	70	60
303	- 70c. black, green and deep green	70	60

DESIGNS: Nos. 301/3, different houses.

1987. Trees of Pitcairn Islands (2nd series). As T **99**. Multicoloured.

304	40c. Leaves and flowers from "Erythrina variegata"	1·25	1·75
305	40c. "Erythrina variegata" tree	1·25	1·75
306	$1.80 Leaves from "Aleurites moluccana" and nut torch	2·00	3·00
307	$1.80 "Aleurites moluccana" tree	2·00	3·00

1987. 19th-century Paintings (2nd series). Paintings by Lt. Conway Shipley in 1848. As T **103**. Multicoloured.

308	20c. "House and Tomb of John Adams"	75	60
309	40c. "Bounty Bay"	1·25	85
310	90c. "School House and Chapel"	2·00	2·00
311	$1.80 "Pitcairn Island" (48×31 mm)	3·00	5·50

110 *Bounty* (replica)

1988. Bicentenary of Australian Settlement. Sheet 112×76 mm.

MS314	**110** $3 multicoloured	6·00	3·00

111 H.M.S. "Swallow" (survey ship), 1767

1988. Ships. Multicoloured.

315	5c. Type **111**	50	80
316	10c. H.M.S. "Pandora" (frigate), 1791	50	80
317	15c. H.M.S. "Briton" and H.M.S. "Tagus" (frigates), 1814	55	90
318	20c. H.M.S. "Blossom" (survey ship), 1825	60	85
319	30c. "Lucy Anne" (barque), 1831	70	90
320	35c. "Charles Doggett" (whaling brig), 1831	70	90
321	40c. H.M.S. "Fly" (sloop), 1838	75	95
322	60c. "Camden" (missionary brig.), 1840	1·00	1·40
323	90c. H.M.S. "Virago" (paddle-sloop), 1853	1·00	1·75
324	$1.20 "Rakaia" (screw-steamer), 1867	1·25	2·00
325	$1.80 H.M.S. "Sappho" (screw-sloop), 1882	1·50	2·50
326	$5 H.M.S. "Champion" (corvette), 1893	3·00	5·50

112 Raising the Union Jack, 1838

1988. 150th Anniv of Pitcairn Island Constitution. Each showing different extract from original Constitution. Multicoloured.

327	20c. Type **112**	40	40
328	40c. Signing Constitution on board H.M.S. "Fly", 1838	60	60
329	$1.05 Voters at modern polling station	75	90
330	$1.80 Modern classroom	1·25	1·40

113 Angel

1988. Christmas. Multicoloured.

331	90c. Type **113**	65	70
332	90c. Holy Family	65	70
333	90c. Two Polynesian Wise Men	65	70
334	90c. Polynesian Wise Man and shepherd	65	70

114 Loading Stores, Deptford

1989. Bicentenary of Pitcairn Island Settlement (1st issue). Multicoloured.

335	20c. Type **114**	1·75	1·75
336	20c. H.M.S. "Bounty" leaving Spithead	1·75	1·75
337	20c. H.M.S. "Bounty" at Cape Horn	1·75	1·75
338	20c. Anchored in Adventure Bay, Tasmania	1·75	1·75
339	20c. Crew collecting breadfruit	1·75	1·75
340	20c. Breadfruit in cabin	1·75	1·75

See also Nos. 341/7, 356/61 and 389/94.

1989. Bicentenary of Pitcairn Island Settlement (2nd issue). As T **114**. Multicoloured.

341	90c. H.M.S. "Bounty' leaving Tahiti	3·25	3·25
342	90c. Bligh awoken by mutineers	3·25	3·25
343	90c. Bligh before Fletcher Christian	3·25	3·25
344	90c. Provisioning "Bounty's" launch	3·25	3·25
345	90c. "Mutineers casting Bligh adrift" (Robert Dodd)	3·25	3·25
346	90c. Mutineers discarding breadfruit plants	3·25	3·25
MS347	110×85 mm. 90c. No. 345; 90c. Isle of Man 1989 35p. Mutiny stamp; 90c. Norfolk Island 39c. Mutiny stamp	3·75	4·50

115 R.N.Z.A.F. Lockheed Orion making Mail Drop, 1985

1989. Aircraft. Multicoloured.

348	20c. Type **115**	1·50	60
349	80c. Beech 80 Queen Air on photo-mission, 1983	2·75	1·25
350	$1.05 Boeing-Vertol Chinook helicopter landing diesel fuel from U.S.S. "Breton", 1969	3·00	1·50
351	$1.30 R.N.Z.A.F. Lockheed Hercules dropping bulldozer, 1983	3·00	1·75

116 Ducie Island

1989. Islands of Pitcairn Group. Mult.

352	15c. Type **116**	75	70
353	90c. Henderson Island	2·00	1·50
354	$1.05 Oeno Island	2·25	2·50
355	$1.30 Pitcairn Island	2·25	2·50

1990. Bicentenary of Pitcairn Island Settlement (3rd issue). As T **114**. Multicoloured.

356	40c. Mutineers sighting Pitcairn Island	1·75	1·75
357	40c. Ship's boat approaching landing	1·75	1·75
358	40c. Exploring island	1·75	1·75
359	40c. Ferrying goods ashore	1·75	1·75
360	40c. Burning of H.M.S. "Bounty"	1·75	1·75

361	40c. Pitcairn Island village	1·75	1·75

117 Ennerdale, Cumbria, and Peter Heywood

1990. "Stamp World London '90" International Stamp Exhibition, London. Designs showing English landmarks and "Bounty" crew members. Multicoloured.

362	80c. Type **117**	75	80
363	90c. St. Augustine's Tower, Hackney, and John Adams	85	90
364	$1.05 Citadel Gateway, Plymouth, and William Bligh	1·00	1·25
365	$1.30 Moorland Close, Cockermouth, and Fletcher Christian	1·25	1·40

117a Queen Elizabeth, 1937

1990. 90th Birthday of Queen Elizabeth the Queen Mother.

378	**117a**	40c. multicoloured	75	85
379	-	$3 black and red	3·00	3·75

DESIGN—29×37 mm: $3 King George VI and Queen Elizabeth on way to Silver Wedding Service, 1948.

118 "Bounty" Chronometer and 1940 1d. Definitive

1990. 50th Anniv of Pitcairn Islands Stamps. Multicoloured.

380	20c. Type **118**	80	80
381	80c. "Bounty" Bible and 1958 4d. definitive	1·60	1·75
382	90c. "Bounty" Bell and 1969 30c. definitive	1·75	1·90
383	$1.05 Mutiny on the "Bounty" and 1977 $1 definitive	2·00	2·50
384	$1.30 Penny Black and 1988 15c. definitive	2·25	2·75

119 Stephen's Lory ("Redbreast")

1990. "Birdpex '90" International Stamp Exhibition, Christchurch, New Zealand. Multicoloured.

385	20c. Type **119**	75	75
386	90c. Henderson Island fruit dove ("Wood Pigeon")	1·50	1·60
387	$1.30 Pitcairn warbler ("Sparrow")	1·75	2·75
388	$1.80 Henderson Island crake ("Chicken Bird")	2·00	3·00

1991. Bicentenary of Pitcairn Island Settlement (4th issue). Celebrations. As T **114**. Multicoloured.

389	80c. Re-enacting landing of mutineers	3·25	3·50
390	80c. Commemorative plaque	3·25	3·50
391	80c. Memorial church service	3·25	3·50
392	80c. Cricket match	3·25	3·50
393	80c. Burning model of "Bounty"	3·25	3·50
394	80c. Firework display	3·25	3·50

120 "Europa"

1991. Cruise Liners. Multicoloured.

395	15c. Type **120**	1·25	60
396	80c. "Royal Viking Star"	2·00	1·75
397	$1.30 "World Discoverer"	2·50	2·75
398	$1.80 "Sagafjord"	3·00	3·50

120a Queen in robes of the Order of St. George (vert)

1991. 65th Birthday of Queen Elizabeth II and 70th Birthday of Prince Philip.

399	20c. Prince Philip (vert)	75	30
400	$1.30 Type **120a**	1·50	1·25

121 Bulldozer

1991. Island Transport. Multicoloured.

401	20c. Type **121**	40	30
402	80c. Two-wheeled motorcycle	1·25	1·00
403	$1.30 Tractor	1·25	1·40
404	$1.80 Three-wheeled motorcycle	2·00	2·25

122 The Annunciation

1991. Christmas. Multicoloured.

405	20c. Type **122**	30	30
406	80c. Shepherds and lamb	90	90
407	$1.30 Holy Family	1·25	1·25
408	$1.80 Three Wise Men	1·75	1·75

122c Bounty Bay

1992. 40th Anniv of Queen Elizabeth II's Accession. Multicoloured.

409	20c. Type **122c**	25	25
410	60c. Sunset over Pitcairn	70	70
411	90c. Pitcairn coastline	90	90
412	$1 Three portraits of Queen Elizabeth	95	95
413	$1.80 Queen Elizabeth II	1·60	1·60

123 Insular Shark

1992. Sharks. Multicoloured.

414	20c. Type **123**	80	50
415	$1 Sand tiger	2·00	1·50
416	$1.50 Black-finned reef shark	2·25	2·00
417	$1.80 Grey reef shark	2·50	2·00

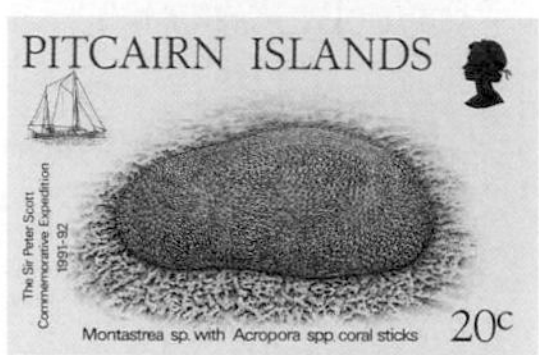

124 "Montastrea sp." and "Acropora spp." (corals)

1992. The Sir Peter Scott Memorial Expedition to Henderson Island. Multicoloured.

418	20c. Type **124**	80	60
419	$1 Henderson sandalwood	1·75	1·50
420	$1.50 Murphy's petrel	3·00	3·25
421	$1.80 Henderson hawkmoth	3·00	3·50

125 Bligh's Birthplace at St. Tudy, Cornwall

1992. 175th Death Anniv of William Bligh. Multicoloured.

422	20c. Type **125**	50	60
423	$1 Bligh on "Bounty"	1·50	1·50
424	$1.50 Voyage in "Bounty's" launch	2·00	2·75
425	$1.80 "William Bligh" (R. Combe) and epitaph	2·25	3·00

126 H.M.S. "Chichester" (frigate)

1993. Modern Royal Navy Vessels. Mult.

426	15c. Type **126**	75	50
427	20c. H.M.S. "Jaguar" (frigate)	75	50
428	$1.80 H.M.S. "Andrew" (submarine)	3·25	3·25
429	$3 H.M.S. "Warrior" (aircraft carrier) and Westland Dragonfly helicopter	5·75	5·50

127 Queen Elizabeth II in Coronation Robes

1993. 40th Anniv of Coronation.

430	**127**	$5 multicoloured	6·00	8·00

128 Pawala Valley Ridge

1993. Island Views. Multicoloured.

431	10c. Type **128**	20	20
432	90c. St. Pauls	90	90
433	$1.20 Matt's Rocks from Water Valley	1·25	1·50
434	$1.50 Ridge Rope to St. Paul's Pool	1·50	1·75
435	$1.80 Ship Landing Point	1·75	2·25

129 Indo-Pacific Tree Gecko

1993. Lizards. Multicoloured.

436	20c. Type **129**	90	50
437	45c. Stump-toed gecko	1·00	1·25
438	45c. Mourning gecko	1·00	1·25
439	$1 Moth skink	2·00	1·50
440	$1.50 Snake-eyed skink	2·50	2·75
441	$1.50 White-bellied skink	2·50	2·75

1994. "Hong Kong '94" International Stamp Exhibition. Nos. 437/8 and 440/1 optd HONG KONG '94 and emblem.

442	45c. Stump-toed gecko	80	90
443	45c. Mourning gecko	80	90
444	$1.50 Snake-eyed skink	2·25	2·75
445	$1.50 White-bellied skink	2·25	2·75

130 Friday October Christian

1994. Early Pitcairners. Multicoloured.

446	5c. Type **130**	20	30
447	20c. Moses Young	50	40
448	$1.80 James Russell McCoy	2·25	2·75
449	$3 Rosalind Amelia Young	3·75	5·00

131 Landing Stores from Wreck of "Wildwave", Oeno Island, 1858

1994. Shipwrecks. Multicoloured.

450	20c. Type **131**	65	60
451	90c. Longboat trying to reach "Cornwallis", Pitcairn Island, 1875	1·75	1·75
452	$1.80 "Acadia" aground, Ducie Island, 1881	3·00	3·50
453	$3 Rescuing survivors from "Oregon", Oeno Island, 1883	4·25	4·50

132 Fire Coral

1994. Corals. Multicoloured.

454	20c. Type **132**	80	70
455	90c. Cauliflower coral and arc-eyed hawkfish (horiz)	2·00	2·00
456	$1 Lobe coral and high-finned rudderfish	2·00	2·00
MS457	100×70 mm. $3 Coral garden and mailed butterflyfish	4·00	5·00

133 Angel and "Ipomoea acuminata"

1994. Christmas. Flowers. Multicoloured.

458	20c. Type **133**	35	35
459	90c. Shepherds and "Hibiscus rosa-sinensis" (vert)	1·25	1·40
460	$1 Star and "Plumeria rubra"	1·25	1·40

461	$3 Holy Family and "Alpinia speciosa" (vert)	3·00	3·75

134 White ("Fairy") Tern on Egg

1995. Birds. Multicoloured.

462	5c. Type **134**	30	60
463	10c. Red-tailed tropic bird chick (vert)	30	60
464	15c. Henderson Island crake with chick	40	70
465	20c. Red-footed booby feeding chick (vert)	40	70
466	45c. Blue-grey noddy	60	80
467	50c. Pitcairn ("Henderson Reed") warbler in nest	65	90
468	90c. Common noddy	1·00	1·00
469	$1 Blue-faced ("Masked") booby and chick (vert)	1·10	1·10
470	$1.80 Henderson Island fruit dove	1·50	1·75
471	$2 Murphy's petrel	1·75	2·25
472	$3 Christmas Island shearwater	2·25	3·00
473	$5 Red-tailed tropic bird juvenile	3·50	4·50

135 Islanders in Longboats

1995. Oeno Island Holiday. Multicoloured.

474	20c. Type **135**	50	60
475	90c. Playing volleyball on beach	1·25	1·25
476	$1.80 Preparing picnic	2·25	3·25
477	$3 Singsong	3·50	5·00

136 Queen Elizabeth the Queen Mother

1995. 95th Birthday of Queen Elizabeth the Queen Mother. Sheet 75×90 mm.

MS478	**136** $5 multicoloured	5·50	6·00

137 Guglielmo Marconi and Early Wireless, 1901

1995. Centenary of First Radio Transmission. Multicoloured.

479	20c. Type **137**	40	60
480	$1 Pitcairn radio transmitter, c. 1938	1·10	1·25
481	$1.50 Satellite Earth Station equipment, 1994	1·75	2·75
482	$3 Communications satellite in orbit, 1992	3·25	5·00

137a United Nations Float, Lord Mayor's Show

1995. 50th Anniv of United Nations. Multicoloured.

483	20c. Type **137a**	30	30
484	$1 R.F.A. "Brambleleaf" (tanker)	1·40	1·25
485	$1.50 U.N. Ambulance	2·00	2·25
486	$3 R.A.F. Lockheed L-1011 TriStar	3·50	3·75

138 Early Morning at the Jetty

1996. Supply Ship Day. Multicoloured.

487	20c. Type **138**	25	30
488	40c. Longboat meeting "America Star" (freighter)	45	55
489	90c. Loading supplies into longboats	1·00	1·10
490	$1 Landing supplies on jetty	1·10	1·25
491	$1.50 Sorting supplies at the Co-op	1·75	2·25
492	$1.80 Tractor towing supplies	1·90	2·25

1996. 70th Birthday of Queen Elizabeth II. As T 55 of Tokelau, each incorporating a different photograph of the Queen. Multicoloured.

493	20c. Bounty Bay	45	45
494	90c. Jetty and landing point, Bounty Bay	1·40	1·40
495	$1.80 Matt's Rocks	2·25	2·50
496	$3 St. Pauls	4·00	4·50

139 Chinese junk

1996. "CHINA '96" 9th Asian International Stamp Exhibition, Peking. Multicoloured.

497	$1.80 Type **139**	2·25	2·50
498	$1.80 H.M.S. "Bounty"	2·25	2·50
MS499	80×79 mm. 90c. China 1984 8f. Year of the Rat stamp; 90c. Polynesian rat eating banana	2·00	2·00

140 Island Profile and Radio Call Signs

1996. Amateur Radio Operations from Pitcairn Islands. Multicoloured.

500	20c. Type **140**	45	45
501	$1.50 Radio operator calling for medical assistance	2·00	2·50
502	$1.50 Doctors giving medical advice by radio	2·00	2·50
503	$2.50 Andrew Young (first radio operator), 1938	2·75	3·00

141 Pitcairn Warbler ("Henderson Island Reed Warbler")

1996. Endangered Species. Local Birds. Mult.

504	5c. Type **141**	30	30
505	10c. Stephen's lory ("Stephen's Lorikeet")	30	30
506	20c. Henderson Island crake ("Henderson Island Rail")	50	50
507	90c. Henderson Island fruit dove	1·25	1·25
508	$2 White tern (horiz)	2·00	2·50
509	$2 Blue-faced booby ("Masked Booby") (horiz)	2·00	2·50

142 Coat of Arms

1997. "HONG KONG '97" International Stamp Exhibition. Chinese New Year ("Year of the Ox"). Sheet 82×87 mm.

MS510	**142** $5 multicoloured	5·00	5·50

143 "David Barker" (supply ship)

1997. 50th Anniv of South Pacific Commission. Sheet 115×56 mm, containing T **143** and similar horiz design. Multicoloured.

MS511	$2.50 Type **143**; $2.50 "McLachlan" (fishing boat)	9·50	9·50

144 Health Centre

1997. Island Health Care. Multicoloured.

512	20c. Type **144**	30	25
513	$1 Nurse treating patient	1·00	1·00
514	$1.70 Dentist treating woman	1·75	2·00
515	$3 Evacuating patient by longboat	3·00	3·75

1997. Golden Wedding of Queen Elizabeth and Prince Philip. As T **188a** of Norfolk Island. Multicoloured.

516	20c. Prince Philip driving carriage	30	40
517	20c. Queen Elizabeth	30	40
518	$1 Prince Philip at Royal Windsor Horse Show, 1996	1·00	1·25
519	$1 Queen Elizabeth with horse	1·00	1·25
520	$1.70 Queen Elizabeth and Prince Philip at the Derby, 1991	1·50	1·75
521	$1.70 Prince Charles hunting, 1995	1·50	1·75

Nos. 516/17, 518/19 and 520/21 respectively were printed together, se-tenant, with the backgrounds forming composite designs.

145 Island and Star

1997. Christmas. Multicoloured.

522	20c. Type **145**	50	40
523	80c. Hand ringing bell	1·25	80
524	$1.20 Presents in baskets	1·40	1·75
525	$3 Families outside church	3·00	3·50

146 Christian's Cave

1997. Christian's Cave. Multicoloured.

526	5c. Type **146**	15	20
527	20c. View from the beach	35	35
528	35c. Cave entrance (vert)	50	50
529	$5 Pathway through forest (vert)	3·75	5·00

147 H.M.S. "Bounty" (Bligh), 1790

1998. Millennium Commemoration (1st issue). Sailing Ships. Multicoloured.

530	20c. Type **147**	1·00	75
531	90c. H.M.S. "Swallow" (Carteret), 1767	1·75	1·10
532	$1.80 H.M.S. "Briton" and H.M.S. "Tagus" (frigates), 1814	2·50	2·25
533	$3 H.M.S. "Fly" (sloop), 1838	3·75	4·00

See also Nos. 549/52 and 577/80.

1998. Diana, Princess of Wales Commemoration. Sheet, 145×70 mm, containing vert designs as T 194a of Norfolk Island. Multicoloured.

MS534	90c. Wearing pearl choker and red evening dress; 90c. Wearing white hat and pearl necklace; 90c. Carrying bouquet; 90c. Wearing white dress and hat (*sold at $3.60+40c. charity premium*)	3·50	3·75

148 "Bidens mathewsii"

1998. Flowers. Multicoloured.

535	20c. Type **148**	1·25	1·00
536	90c. "Hibiscus" sp.	2·25	1·75
537	$1.80 "Osteomeles anthyllidifolia"	3·75	4·25
538	$3 "Ipomoea littoralis"	5·00	6·00

149 Fishing

1998. International Year of the Ocean. Multicoloured.

539	20c. Type **149**	1·40	1·00
540	90c. Diver at wreck of "Cornwallis" (vert)	2·50	1·75
541	$1.80 Reef fish	4·00	4·25
542	$3 Murphy's petrel and great frigate bird (vert)	5·50	6·50
MS543	86×86 mm. Nos. 539/42	13·00	13·00

150 George Nobbs and Class, 1838

1999. Development of Local Education. Mult.

544	20c. Type **150**	1·00	80
545	90c. Children outside thatched school, 1893	1·90	1·60
546	$1.80 Boy in wheelbarrow outside wooden school, 1932	3·25	3·50
547	$3 Modern classroom with computer	4·50	5·00

151 H.M.S. "Bounty" and Anchor

1999. "Australia '99" World Stamp Exhibition, Melbourne. Pitcairn Archaeology Project. Sheet, 190×80 mm, containing T **151** and similar diamond-shaped designs. Multicoloured.

MS548	50c. Type **151**; $1 "Bounty" approaching Pitcairn and cannon; $1.50, "Bounty" on fire and chronometer; $2 "Bounty" sinking and metal bucket	9·50	9·50

152 John Adams (survivor of "Bounty" crew) and Bounty Bay

1999. Millennium Commemoration (2nd issue). Multicoloured.

549 20c. Type **152** 1·00 75
550 90c. "Topaz" (sealer), 1808 2·25 1·40
551 $1.80 George Hunn Nobbs and Norfolk Island 3·00 3·50
552 $3 H.M.S "Champion" (corvette), 1893 5·50 6·50

153 Prince Edward and Miss Sophie Rhys-Jones

1999. Royal Wedding. Multicoloured.

553 $2.50 Type **153** 3·75 4·25
554 $2.50 Engagement photograph 3·75 4·25

154 Bee-keepers at Work

1999. Bee-keeping. Multicoloured. Self-adhesive.

555 20c. Type **154** 1·00 1·00
556 $1 Bee on passion flower 2·25 2·25
557 $1.80 Bees in honeycomb 3·50 4·00
558 $3 Bee on flower and jar of "Mutineer's Dream" honey 5·00 6·00
MS559 74×100 mm. No. 556 5·00 6·00

No. **MS**559 includes the "China '99" International Stamp Exhibition emblem on the sheet margin.

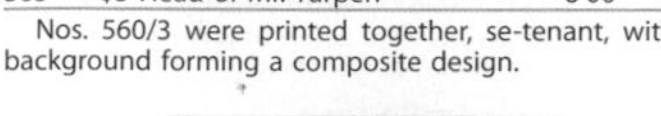

155 Arrival of "Yankee" (schooner), 1937

2000. Protection of "Mr. Turpen" (Galapagos Tortoise on Pitcairn). Multicoloured.

560 5c. Type **155** 2·00 2·50
561 20c. Off-loading Mr. Turpen at Bounty Bay 2·75 3·25
562 35c. Mr. Turpen 3·25 3·75
563 $5 Head of Mr. Turpen 6·00 7·00

Nos. 560/3 were printed together, se-tenant, with the background forming a composite design.

156 *Guettarda speciosa* (flower)

2000. Flowers of Pitcairn Islands. Multicoloured.

564 10c. Type **156** 45 60
565 15c. *Hibiscus tiliaceus* 55 60
566 20c. *Selenicereus grandiflorus* 60 60
567 30c. *Metrosideros collina* 70 70
568 50c. *Alpinia zerumbet* 90 90
569 $1 *Syzygium jambos* 1·50 1·50
570 $1.50 *Commelina diffusa* 2·50 2·50
571 $1.80 *Canna indica* 2·75 2·75
572 $2 *Allamanda cathartica* 3·00 3·25
573 $3 *Calophyllum inophyllum* 4·00 4·50
574 $5 *Ipomea indica* 6·00 7·00
575 $10 *Bauhinia monandra* (40×40 mm) 10·00 12·00

2000. "The Stamp Show 2000" International Stamp Exhibition, London. Sheet, 120×80 mm, containing Nos. 570 and 572.

MS576 $1.50 Commelina diffusa; $2 Allamanda cathartica 7·50 8·50

157 Longboat

2000. Millennium Commemoration (3rd issue). Communications. Multicoloured.

577 20c. Type **157** 1·00 90
578 90c. Landing and Longboat House 2·25 1·40
579 $1.80 Honda quad with trailer of watermelons 3·75 4·00
580 $3 Woman with printer at Satellite Station 5·50 6·50

158 Surveyor and Helicopter

2000. "EXPO 2000" World Stamp Exhibition, Anaheim, U.S.A. Anglo-American Joint Satellite Recovery Survey Mission, Henderson Island, 1966. Sheet, 120×180 mm, containing T **158** and similar vert design. Multicoloured.

MS581 $2.50 Type **158**; $2.50 Survey team and U.S.S. *Sunnyvale* (satellite recovery vessel) 14·00 14·00

No. **MS**581 was issued folded in half horizontally with the issue title, "CLASSIFIED INFORMATION" and seal printed on the gum of the top panel. Details of the survey appear on the other side of this section.

159 Queen Elizabeth the Queen Mother

2000. Queen Elizabeth the Queen Mother's 100th Birthday. Sheet, 127×95 mm (oval-shaped), containing T **159** and similar vert design. Multicoloured.

MS582 $2 Type **159**; $3 Queen Mother wearing plum outfit 5·00 6·00

160 Wrapping Presents

2000. Christmas. Multicoloured.

583 20c. Type **160** 1·00 1·00
584 80c. Ringing island bell 2·25 2·25
585 $1.50 Making decorations 3·75 4·00
586 $3 Opening presents 5·50 6·50

161 *Europa* (liner)

2001. Cruise Ships. Multicoloured.

587 $1.50 Type **161** 3·75 4·50
588 $1.50 *Rotterdam VI* 3·75 4·50
589 $1.50 *Saga Rose* 3·75 4·50
590 $1.50 *Bremen* 3·75 4·50

162 Coconut

2001. Tropical Fruits. Multicoloured.

591 20c. Type **162** 65 65
592 80c. Pomegranate 1·25 1·25
593 $1 Passion fruit 1·50 1·50
594 $3 Pineapple 4·25 5·00
MS595 103×70 mm. Nos. 592 and 594 4·50 5·00

163 Keyboard

2001. Introduction of Pitcairn Islands Internet Domain Name. Multicoloured. Self-adhesive.

596 20c. Type **163** 70 55
597 50c. Circuit board 1·25 80
598 $1 Microchip 1·75 1·25
599 $5 Mouse 5·50 7·50

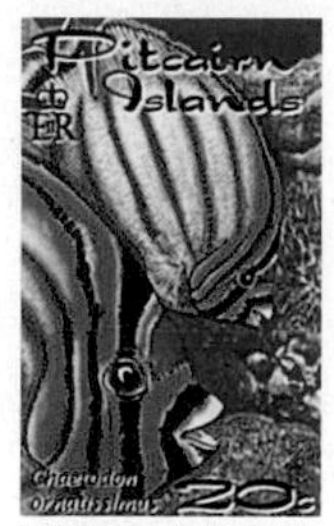

164 Ornate Butterflyfish (*Chaetodon ornatissimus*)

2001. Reef Fish. Multicoloured.

600 20c. Type **164** 1·00 1·00
601 80c. Mailed butterflyfish (*Chaetodon reticulatus*) 2·25 1·40
602 $1.50 Racoon butterflyfish (*Chaetodon lunula*) 3·00 3·50
603 $2 *Henochus chrysostomus* 4·00 4·75
MS604 87×120 mm. Nos. 600 and 603 4·25 4·75

No. **MS**604 has the paper around the outlines of fish along the upper edge of the sheet cut away.

165 Man carrying Driftwood

2001. Woodcarving. Multicoloured.

605 20c. Type **165** 1·00 1·25
606 50c. Carver at work 1·50 2·00
607 $1.50 Working on wood lathe 2·00 2·50
608 $3 Taking carvings to *World Discoverer* (cruise liner) for sale 3·00 3·50

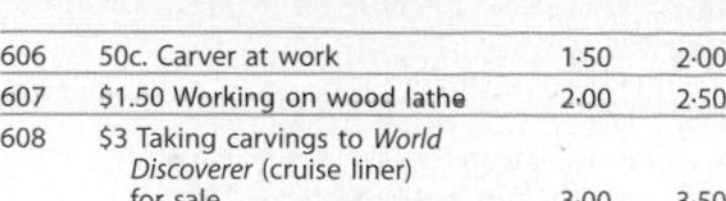

Nos. 605/8 were printed together, se-tenant, with the backgrounds forming a composite design.

166 *Cypraea argus* Shell

2001. Cowrie Shells. Multicoloured.

609 20c. Type **166** 90 75
610 80c. *Cypraea isabella* 1·40 1·10
611 $1 *Cypraea mappa* 1·60 1·50
612 $3 *Cypraea mauritiana* 3·50 5·00

2002. Golden Jubilee. Sheet, 162×95 mm, containing designs as T 153 of Nauru.

MS613 50c. black, violet and gold; $1 multicoloured; $1.20 black, violet and gold; $1.50 multicoloured; $2 multicoloured 8·00 8·50

DESIGNS—HORIZ: 50c. Queen Elizabeth with Princesses Elizabeth and Margaret; $1 Queen Elizabeth in evening dress; $1.20 Princess Elizabeth in evening dress; $1.50 Queen Elizabeth in blue hat and coat. VERT (38×51 mm)—$2 Queen Elizabeth after Annigoni.

167 James McCoy (President of Island Council)

2002. Pitcairn Islands Celebrities. Multicoloured.

614 $1.50 Type **167** 2·75 3·00
615 $1.50 Admiral Sir Fairfax Moresby 2·75 3·00
616 $1.50 Gerald DeLeo Bliss (postmaster, Cristobal, Panama Canal Zone) 2·75 3·00
617 $1.50 Captain Arthur Jones of Shaw Savill Line 2·75 3·00

168 "Simba Christian" (cat)

2002. Pitcairn Cats. Multicoloured.

618 20c. Type **168** 70 50
619 $1 "Miti Christian" 1·50 80
620 $1.50 "Nala Brown" 2·00 2·25
621 $3 "Alicat Palau" 3·25 3·75
MS622 92×86 mm. Nos. 618 and 621 4·75 5·25

2002. Queen Elizabeth the Queen Mother Commemoration. As T 156 of Nauru.

623 40c. black, gold and purple 1·00 65
624 $1 brown, gold and purple 1·75 1·10
625 $1.50 multicoloured 2·25 2·50
626 $2 multicoloured 2·75 3·25
MS627 145×70 mm. Nos. 624 and 626 5·50 6·00

DESIGNS: 40c. Lady Elizabeth Bowes-Lyon, 1910; $1 Lady Elizabeth Bowes-Lyon, 1923; $1.50, Queen Mother at Leatherhead, 1970; $2 Queen Mother at Scrabster. Designs as Nos. 624 and 626 in No. **MS**627 omit the "1900-2002" inscription and the coloured frame.

169 Woman cutting Palm Fronds and Fan

2002. Weaving. Multicoloured.
628 40c. Type **169** 1·75 2·00
629 80c. Woman preparing leaves and woven bag 2·50 2·75
630 $1.50 Millie Christian weaving basket 3·50 4·00
631 $2.50 Thelma Brown at basket stall in the Square 4·50 5·00
Nos. 628/31 were printed together, se-tenant, with the backgrounds forming a composite design.

170 Dudwi Nut Tree (*Aleurites moluccana*)

2002. Trees. Multicoloured.
632 40c. Type **170** 80 60
633 $1 Toa (*Cordia subcordata*) 1·50 1·00
634 $1.50 Miro (*Thespesia populnea*) 2·00 2·00
635 $3 Hulianda (*Cerbera manghas*) 3·50 4·00

171 *America Star* (container ship) and Island Longboat

2003. 21 Years of Blue Star Line Service to Pitcairn Islands. Sheet 158×75 mm.
MS636 **171** $5 multicoloured 11·00 12·00

172 *Conus geographus* Shell

2003. Conus Shells. Multicoloured.
637 40c. Type **172** 1·00 65
638 80c. *Conus textile* 1·40 85
639 $1 *Conus striatus* 1·75 1·25
640 $1.20 *Conus marmoreus* 1·75 1·60
641 $3 *Conus litoglyphus* 4·00 4·75

2003. 50th Anniv of Coronation. As T 115 of Kiribati. Multicoloured.
642 40c. Queen Elizabeth II wearing tiara 80 55
643 80c. Coronation Coach drawn by eight horses 1·25 75
644 $1.50 Queen wearing tiara and white gown 2·00 2·00
645 $3 Queen with bishops and Maids of Honour 3·75 4·75
MS646 95×115 mm. 40c. As No. 642; $3 As No. 645 4·25 4·50

173 Women Storing Leaves in Earthenware Jars and *Bauhinia monandra*

2003. Art of Pitcairn (3rd series). Painted Leaves. Multicoloured.
647 40c. Type **173** 1·25 1·50
648 80c. Woman washing soaked leaves and *Bauhinia monandra* 2·00 2·25
649 $1.50 Bernice Christian with dried leaf and paints and *Sapindrus saponaria* plant 3·50 4·00
650 $3 Charlotte Christian painting leaf, Bauhinia leaf and *Bounty* 5·50 6·50
Nos. 647/50 were printed together, se-tenant with the backgrounds forming a composite design.

174 Diadem Squirrel Fish

2003. Squirrel Fish. Multicoloured.
651 40c. Type **174** 1·00 75
652 80c. Scarlet-finned squirrel fish 1·50 1·25
653 $1.50 Silver-spotted squirrel fish 2·75 2·75
654 $3 Bloodspot squirrel fish 4·50 5·50
MS655 100×80 mm. No. 654 8·00 8·50

175 "Holy Virgin in a Wreath of Flowers" (detail) (Rubens and Jan Brueghel)

2003. Christmas. Multicoloured.
656 40c. Type **175** 90 60
657 $1 "Madonna della Rosa" (detail) (Raphael) 1·50 90
658 $1.50 "Stuppacher Madonna" (detail) (Matthias Grunewald) 2·50 2·00
659 $3 "Madonna with Cherries" (detail) (Titian) 4·25 5·50

176 *Terebra maculate*

2004. Terebra Shells. Multicoloured.
660 40c. Type **176** 85 65
661 80c. *Terebra subulata* 1·40 85
662 $1.20 *Terebra crenulata* 1·90 1·75
663 $3 *Terebra dimidiatai* 4·25 5·50

177 Bounty Bay and Hill of Difficulty

2004. Scenic Views. Multicoloured.
664 50c. Type **177** 1·40 1·00
665 $1 Christian's Cave on rock face (horiz) 2·50 2·00
666 $1.50 St. Paul's Pool 3·75 3·75
667 $2.50 Ridge Rope towards St. Paul's Point (horiz) 5·50 6·50

178 HMS *Pitcairn*

2004. 60th Anniv of Commission of HMS *Pitcairn*. Sheet 135×80 mm.
MS668 **178** $5.50 multicoloured. 11·00 13·00

179 HMAV *Bounty* Replica

2004. HMAV Bounty Replica (three masted ship). Multicoloured.
669 60c. Type **179** 1·75 1·10
670 80c. Stern of ship 2·00 1·40
671 $1 Figurehead 2·50 2·00
672 $3.50 Ropes and HMAV *Bounty* replica sailing 7·00 9·00
MS673 103×72 mm. $3.50 As No. 672 12·00 13·00

180 Murphy's Petrels

2004. Murphy's Petrel. Multicoloured.
674 40c. Type **180** 1·00 70
675 50c. Murphy's petrel and young in nest 1·10 1·00
676 $1 Murphy's petrel from side (vert) 1·75 1·50
677 $2 Head of Murphy's petrel (vert) 2·75 3·25
678 $2.50 Murphy's petrel in flight 3·00 3·75
MS679 154×86 mm. Nos. 674/8 13·00 14·00

181 Beach, Ducie Island

2005. Scenery (1st issue). Ducie and Oeno Islands. Photographs by Dr. Michael Brooke, Cambridge, and Brian Bell, Blenheim. Multicoloured.
680 50c. Type **181** 1·10 80
681 60c. Coral reef, Ducie Island 1·25 1·00
682 80c. Low sun, Ducie Island 1·60 1·25
683 $1 Boat moored off beach, Oeno 1·90 1·75
684 $1.50 Palm trees on beach, Oeno 2·75 3·25
685 $2.50 View of Oeno from sea 4·75 5·50
See also Nos. 704/9.

182 Corona

2005. Solar Eclipse, Oeno. Sheet 144×48 mm containing T **182** and similar circular designs. Multicoloured.
MS686 $1 Type **182**; $2 Chromosphere; $3 Photosphere 10·00 13·00

183 *Hypolimnas bolina* (male)

2005. Blue Moon Butterfly. Sheet 135×51 mm containing T **183** and similar square design. Multicoloured.
MS687 $1.50 Type **183**; $4 *Hypolimnas bolina* (female) 14·00 15·00

184 Prince Charles and Mrs. Camilla Parker-Bowles

2005. Royal Wedding.
688 **184** $5 multicoloured 15·00 15·00

185 HMS *Bounty* (Replica)

2005. HMS *Bounty* (Replica). Multicoloured.
689 40c. Type **185** 1·25 75
690 $1 Port side of ship 2·25 1·75
691 $1.20 Sailing off coast 2·50 2·25
692 $3 Bowsprit and in full sail 6·50 7·50
MS693 122×87 mm. $3 As No. 692 7·00 8·00

186 Bristle-thighed Curlews

2005. Bristle-thighed Curlew (Numenius tahitiensis). Multicoloured.
694 60c. Type **186** 1·75 1·10
695 $1 Back of bird 2·25 1·50
696 $1.50 Beak open (vert) 3·00 3·00
697 $1.80 Beak closed (vert) 3·50 3·75
698 $2 Perched on rock 4·00 4·50
MS699 156×86 mm. Nos. 694/8 13·00 14·00

187 Hibiscus Flower in Bauble

2005. Christmas. Designs showing baubles. Multicoloured.
700 40c. Type **187** 1·25 70
701 80c. Red-tailed tropic bird 2·25 1·40
702 $1.80 Arms 3·25 3·75
703 $2.50 Sailing ship 4·75 6·00

2005. Scenery (2nd issue). Henderson Island. As T **181** showing coastal views and line drawings of fauna. Multicoloured.
704 50c. Flying insects and misty shoreline 1·25 70
705 60c. Parrots and sandy beach 1·75 1·25
706 $1 Tropic birds and sandy bay 2·50 1·75
707 $1.20 Lobsters and shore with overhanging rock ledge 2·50 2·50
708 $1.50 Octopus and cliffs 3·00 3·50
709 $2 Turtles and sandy beach 3·50 4·00

188 Capt William Driver at Ship's Wheel and Old Glory Flag

2006. 175th Anniv of Voyage of Charles Doggett flying Old Glory (Stars and Stripes) Flag. Sheet 133×80 mm.
MS710 **188** $5 multicoloured 7·50 8·50
No. **MS**710 also commemorates the 175th anniversary of the return of the Pitcairn Islanders from Tahiti.

189 Princess Elizabeth

2006. 80th Birthday of Queen Elizabeth II. Multicoloured.
711 40c. Type **189** 80 55
712 80c. Queen wearing tiara, c. 1952 1·25 90
713 $1.80 Wearing yellow dress 2·00 2·50

714	$3.50 Wearing red hat and jacket	4·50	5·50
MS715	143×72 mm. $1.80 As No. 712; $3.50 As No. 713	7·50	8·50

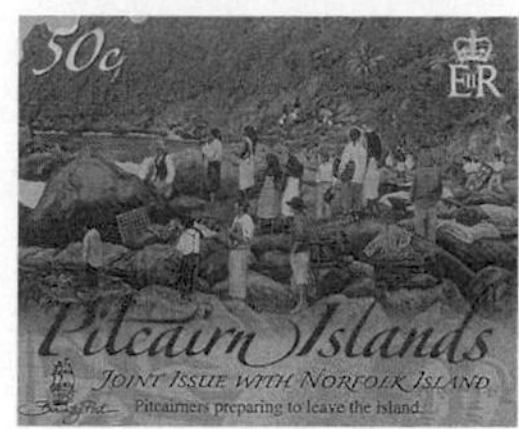

190 Pitcairn Islanders waiting to leave

2006. 150th Anniv of Migration of Pitcairn Islanders to Norfolk Island. Multicoloured.

716	50c. Type **190**	1·50	1·75
717	$1 Emigrant ship *Morayshire* leaving Pitcairn Island	2·25	2·50
718	$1.50 *Morayshire* anchored in Kingston Bay, Norfolk Island	3·00	3·50
719	$3 Arrival of Pitcairn Islanders at Kingston, Norfolk Island	5·00	6·00

Nos. 716/19 are inscribed "JOINT ISSUE WITH NORFOLK ISLAND". The Norfolk Island stamps issued on the same day have different designs.

191 Fisherman with Catch

2006. Early Civilisation (1st series). Cave Dwellers of Henderson Island. Sheet 195×82 mm containing T **191** and similar multicoloured designs.

MS720	60c. Type **191**; $1.20 Child with captive seabird; $2 Man making fish hooks; $2.50 Two women at cave entrance	7·50	8·00

The stamps and margins of No. **MS**720 form a composite design showing cave dwellers on shore of Henderson Island.

See also No. **MS**733.

192 Humpback Whale and Calf

2006. Humpback Whales (*Megaptera novaeangliae*). Multicoloured.

721	$1.50 Type **192**	3·00	3·00
722	$3.50 Tail of humpback whale	5·50	6·00
MS723	125×88 mm. Nos. 721/2	7·50	8·00

193 Sooty Tern

2007. Endangered Species. Terns and Noddies of the Pitcairn Islands. Multicoloured.

724	50c. Type **193**	1·50	1·75
725	60c. Blue-grey ternlet	1·50	1·75
726	$2 Brown noddy	3·00	3·50
727	$3 Black noddy	4·00	4·50
MS728	180×105 mm. Nos. 724/7, each ×2	16·00	18·00

194 Diver searching Seabed for Wreckage from HMS *Bounty*

2007. 50th Anniv of the Raising of the Bounty Anchor. Multicoloured.

729	60c. Type **194**	1·75	2·00
730	$1 Two divers with *Bounty* anchor	2·50	3·00
731	$1.20 Capt. Johnson on board brigantine *Yankee* winching up *Bounty* anchor	2·75	3·25
732	$2.50 *Bounty* anchor on shore	4·50	5·00

2007. Early Civilisation (2nd series). Rock Carvers of Pitcairn. Sheet 195×82 mm containing multicoloured designs as T **191**.

MS733	60c. Man carving petroglyphs into rock; $1.20 Two men carving stone god (horiz); $2 Tool-maker (horiz); $2.50 Man making stone adze	9·00	10·00

The stamps and margins of No. **MS**733 form a composite design showing rock carvers and tool-makers on shore of Pitcairn Island.

195 Salt and Pepper Moth

2007. Salt and Pepper Moth (Utetheisa pulchelloides). Multicoloured.

734	$2 Type **195**	4·00	4·00
735	$4 In flight	6·00	7·00
MS736	135×60 mm. Nos. 734/5	10·00	11·00

196 Crows' Nest

2007. Detail from HMS Bounty Replica. Multicoloured.

737	10c. Type **196**	10	10
738	20c. Ropes and pulleys	25	25
739	40c. Guns	50	50
740	50c. Compass	60	60
741	80c. Wheel	1·00	1·00
742	$1 Figurehead	1·20	1·20
743	$1.50 Mast	1·90	1·90
744	$2 Sail	2·25	2·25
745	$3.50 Sextant	3·00	3·00
746	$4 Lantern and stern of *Bounty*	50	3·50
747	$5 Bell	4·00	4·00
748	$10 Chronometer	8·75	8·75

197 *Gymnosarda unicolor* (dog tooth tuna)

2007. Ocean Fish. Multicoloured.

749	$1 Type **197**	2·50	2·50
750	$1 *Acanthocybium solandri* (wahoo)	2·50	2·50
751	$1 *Coryphaena hippurus* (dorado)	2·50	2·50
752	$1 *Thunnus albacares* (yellow fin tuna)	2·50	2·50
753	$1 *Caranx ignobilis* (giant trevally)	2·50	2·50
754	$1 *Sarda chiliensis lineolata* (bonito)	2·50	2·50

Nos. 749/54 were printed together, se-tenant, forming a composite background design.

198 Oeno Island

2008. Pitcairn Islands from DigitalGlobe Space Satellite. Multicoloured. Self-adhesive.

755	60c. Type **198**	1·50	1·50
756	$1 Pitcairn Island	2·25	2·25
757	$2 Henderson Island	4·00	4·50
758	$2.50 Ducie Island	4·50	5·00

199 Timber-framed Longboat under Construction

2008. Pitcairn's Longboat History. Multicoloured.

759	50c. Type **199**	1·75	2·00
760	$1 Last wooden rowing longboat, launched 1983	2·50	2·75
761	$1.50 Diesel-powered aluminium longboat, arrived 1995	3·50	3·75
762	$3.50 Longboats ashore, Oeno Island at sunset	5·00	5·50

200 Bee on Yellow Guava (*Psidium guajava*) Flower

2008. Flowers and Bees. Designs showing the Italian honey bees (Apis mellifera ligustica) introduced to Pitcairn on island flowers. Multicoloured.

763	$1 Type **200**	2·25	1·50
764	$1.20 Bee on portulaca (*Portulaca oleracea*)	2·75	2·25
765	$1.50 Bee approaching sunflower	3·25	3·00
766	$3 Bee on mountain chestnut tree (*Metrosideros collina*) flower	5·00	6·50
MS767	120×80 mm. Nos. 765/6	8·75	10·00

201 Sunset

2008. Pitcairn Island Sunsets. Multicoloured.

768	50c. Type **201**	1·00	1·00
769	60c. Sunset over sea, tree branches in foreground	1·10	1·10
770	80c. Setting sun reflected in ocean	1·40	1·40
771	$1 Sunset and headland	1·60	1·60
772	$2 Sunset, coast and offshore rocks	3·25	3·75
773	$2.50 Deep red sunset over coast with trees	4·00	4·50

202 Captain Mayhew Folger

2008. Bicentenary of 'the Discovery of a Community' (meeting of Capt Folger of US Topaz and surviving Bounty mutineer John Adams).

MS774	134×80 mm. **202** $5 multicoloured	6·50	7·00

203 Green Turtle

2008. Green Turtles (Chelonia mydas) of Henderson Island. Sheet 192×83 mm containing T **203** and similar multicoloured designs.

MS775	60c. Type **203**; $1 Turtle swimming; $2 Turtle coming ashore; $2.50 Turtle hatchlings	8·00	8·50

The stamps within **MS**775 form a composite design showing turtles coming ashore and hatchlings on a Henderson Island beach.

204 Coconut Crab

2009. Coconut Crab (Birgus latro). Multicoloured.

776	$2.80 Type **204**	5·00	5·50
777	$4 Coconut crab (side view)	7·00	8·00
MS778	109×84 mm. Nos. 776/7	11·00	13·00

205 Departing Pitcairners leaving Kingston Jetty on Norfolk Island

2009. 150th Anniv of the Return of the Pitcairn Islanders from Norfolk Island.Multicoloured.

779	60c. Type **205**	1·75	2·00
780	$1 Pitcairners rowing out to sailing ship *Mary Ann*, 2 December 1858	2·50	3·00
781	$2 Passengers on board *Mary Ann*, approaching PItcairn Island	3·75	4·00
782	$3.50 Newly arrived Pitcairners climbing The Hill of Difficulty, 17 January 1859	5·00	5·50

Nos. 779/82 and the central stamp-size label form a composite design.

206 Giant Panda

2009. 23rd Asian International Stamp Exhibition, Hong Kong. Sheet 135×95 mm containing T **206** and T **262** of Vanuatu. Multicoloured.

MS783	$2.50 Type **206**; 150v. Type **262** of Vanuatu (sold at $5)	11·00	12·00

No. **MS**783 is identical to **MS**1054 of Vanuatu.

207 Charles Darwin and HMS *Bounty*

2009. Birth Bicentenary of Charles Darwin (naturalist and evolutionary theorist). Multicoloured.

784 50c. Type **207** 1·75 1·25
785 $1.50 Darwin, Galapagos giant tortoise and land iguana 3·50 3·50
786 $2 Darwin and Galapagos finches showing beak variations 4·00 4·50
787 $3.50 Darwin, *The Origin of Species* and gorilla 6·00 6·00

208 Wandering Glider Dragonfly

2009. Wandering Glider Dragonfly (Pantala flavescens). Multicoloured.

788 $2.50 Type **208** 4·50 5·00
789 $4 Perched on edge of flower 6·50 7·50
MS790 140×85 mm. Nos. 788/9 11·00 11·50

209 Walrus Amphibious Biplane, August 1937

2009. Visiting Aircraft. Multicoloured.

791 $1 Type **209** 2·50 1·75
792 $1.50 Alouette III helicopter from French cruiser *Jeanne d'Arc*, December 1971 3·75 3·25
793 $1.80 Dassault VP BMS Falcon 900, August 2002 3·75 3·75
794 $2.50 Piper Comanche 260C, March 2007 5·00 6·00

210 HMS *Actaeon*, 1837

2009. Royal Navy Visitors. Sheet 140×103 mm containing T **210** and similar horiz designs. Multicoloured.

MS795 80c. Type **210**; 80c. HMS *Calypso*, 1860; 80c. HMS *Juno*, 1855; $2 HMS *Sutlej*, 1864; $2 HMS *Shah*, 1878; $2 HMS *Pelican*, 1886 15·00 16·00

211 Flatland (Bradley Christian)

2010. Children's Art. Multicoloured.

796 50c. Type **211** 80 80
797 60c. Tedside (Torika Warren-Peu) 90 90
798 $1 St. Pauls (Jayden Warren-Peu) 1·50 1·50
799 $1.80 Beehives in Isaac's Valley (Kimiora Warren-Peu) 2·75 2·75
800 $2 Garnets Ridge (Ralph Warren-Peu) 3·00 3·00
801 $2.50 Ship Landing Point (Ariel Brown) 3·50 3·50

212 Tank

2010. ANZAC Day. T **212** and similar horiz designs, inscribed with the names of Pitcairn Islanders who fought in the World Wars. Multicoloured.

802 50c. Type **212** (Arthur Ray Lacy Young, Floyd Hasting McCoy, Colin Bruce Warren, Walma Laury Warren) 1·50 2·00
803 $1 Fighter aircraft (Boyd Christian, Clement Freeman Coffin, Ralph Chester Young, Ernest Wilfred Warren) 2·00 2·50
804 $1.80 Troopship leaving dock-side (Robert Lowry Young, Edison Percy Young, Vincent Young, Burnell Young) 2·50 3·00
805 $4 Deck of warship with guns (Vivian Joe Christian, Sterling Warren, Andy Rolland Warren) 6·00 7·00

Nos. 802/3 and 804/5 were each printed together, se-tenant, each pair forming a composite design.

2010. London 2010 Festival of Stamps. HMAV Bounty. Sheet 148×90 mm containing Nos. 741/2 and 745

MS806 80c. Wheel; $1 Figurehead; $3.50 Sextant 7·75 7·75

213 Centropyge flavissima

2010. Endangered Species. Reef Fish of the Pitcairn Islands. Multicoloured.

807 60c. Type **213** 80 80
808 $1 *Chaetodon smithi* 1·50 1·50
809 $2 *Centropyge loricula* 3·00 3·00
810 $2.50 *Chaetodon lineolatus* 3·50 3·50
MS811 180×105 mm. Nos. 807/10, each ×2 18·00 18·00

214 Reseach Vessel L'Atalante

2010. Hotspots (submarine volcanoes). Multicoloured.

812 80c. Type **214** 1·10 1·10
813 $1.20 Submersible *Nautile* 1·90 1·90
814 $1.50 Photographing lava tube 2·75 2·75
815 $3 *Nautile* approaching Adams Volcano 4·00 4·00

Nos. 812/15 and the central stamp-size label form a composite design.

215 Orobophana solidula

2010. Endemic Snails. Multicoloured.

816 80c. Type **215** 1·10 1·10
817 $1 *Philonesia filiceti* (dark and light brown shell) 1·90 1·90
818 $1.80 *Orobophana solidula* (orange shell) 2·75 2·75
819 $2.50 *Philonesia filiceti* (striped shell) 3·75 3·75

2010. Royal Navy Visitors (2nd series). Sheet 140×103 mm containing horiz designs as T **210**. Multicoloured.

MS820 $1 HMS *Royalist*, 1898; $1 *Cambrian & Flora*, 1906; $1 HMS *Algerine*, 1911; $1.80 HMS *Leander*, 1937; $1.80 HMS *Monmouth*, 1995; HMS *Sutherland*, 2001 9·75 9·75

216 Yellow Fautu

2011. Endagered Species. Yellow Fautu. Multicoloured.

821 $2.50 Type **216** 3·50 3·50
822 $3 Yellow fautu flower and three buds 4·50 4·50

2011. Indipex 2011 International Stamp Exhibition, New Delhi. Sheet 137×93 mm containing No. 822

MS823 Yellow fautu flower and three buds 4·50 4·50

217 Pink Peony

2011. Peony Flowers. Multicoloured.

824 $1 Type **217** 1·90 1·90
825 $1 White peony with red markings 1·90 1·90

Nos. 824/5 were printed together, *se-tenant*, as horizontal pairs, each pair forming a composite design.

Pt. 5

POLAND

A country lying between Russia and Germany, originally independent, but divided between Prussia, Austria and Russia in 1772/95. An independent republic since 1918. Occupied by Germany from 1939 to 1945.

1860. 100 kopeks = 1 rouble.
1918. 100 pfennig = 1 mark.
1918. 100 halerzy = 1 korona. 100 fenigow = 1 marka.
1924. 100 groszy = 1 złoty.

1 Russian Arms

1860

1b	**1**	10k. blue and red	£675	80·00

2 Sigismund III Vasa Column, Warsaw

1918. Surch POCZTA POLSKA and value in fen. as in T 2.

2	**2**	5f. on 2g. brown	45	70
3	-	10f. on 6g. green	45	65
4	-	25f. on 10g. red	1·60	1·40
5	-	50f. on 20g. blue	3·50	4·00

DESIGNS: 6g. Arms of Warsaw; 10g. Polish eagle; 20g. Jan III Sobieski Monument, Warsaw.

1918. Stamps of German Occupation of Poland optd Poczta Polska or surch also.

6B	**10**	3pf. brown	10·00	7·00
7A	**10**	5pf. green	50	35
8A	**24**	5 on 2½pf. grey	30	20
9A	**10**	5 on 3pf. brown	1·75	1·25
10B	**10**	10pf. red	20	20
11A	**24**	15pf. violet	25	25
12A	**10**	20pf. blue	25	25
13A	**24**	25 on 7½pf. orange	30	20
14A	**10**	30pf. black & orange on buff	20	20
15A	**10**	40pf. black and red	1·00	50
16B	**10**	60pf. mauve	35	35

1918. Stamps of Austro-Hungarian Military Post (Nos. 69/71) optd POLSKA POCZTA and Polish eagle.

17	10h. green	4·75	6·25
18	20h. red	4·75	6·25
19	45h. blue	4·75	6·25

1918. As stamps of Austro-Hungarian Military Post of 1917 optd POLSKA POCZTA and Polish eagle or surch also.

20b	3h. on 3h. olive	19·00	13·00
21	3h. on 15h. red	3·50	2·25
22	10h. on 30h. green	3·75	2·75
23	25h. on 40h. olive	5·00	2·75
24	45h. on 60h. red	3·50	3·50
25	45h. on 80h. blue	6·00	5·00
26	50h. on 60h. red	3·50	4·00
28	50h. green	28·00	21·00
29	90h. violet	4·75	3·50

1919. Stamps of Austria optd POCZTA POLSKA, No. 49 also surch 25.

30	**49**	3h. violet	£200	£190
31	**49**	5h. green	£200	£190
32	**49**	6h. orange	15·00	16·00
33	**49**	10h. purple	£200	£190
34	**49**	12h. blue	18·00	21·00
35	**60**	15h. red	10·00	6·75
36	**60**	20h. green	80·00	70·00
37	**60**	25h. blue	£650	£600
49	**51**	25 on 80h. brown	2·25	3·00
38	**60**	30h. violet	£140	£110
39	**51**	40h. green	13·50	10·00
40	**51**	50h. green	4·50	5·25
41	**51**	60h. blue	2·75	5·75
42	**51**	80h. brown	3·75	5·00
43	**51**	90h. purple	£550	£600
44	**51**	1k. red on yellow	6·75	10·50
45	**52**	2k. blue	4·25	4·75
46	**52**	3k. red	45·00	60·00
47	**52**	4k. green	75·00	85·00
48a	**52**	10k. violet	£3500	£3750

11

1919. Imperf. Re-issued without gum.

50	**11**	2h. grey	35	60
51	**11**	3h. violet	35	60
52	**11**	5h. green	15	35
53	**11**	6h. orange	12·50	22·00
54	**11**	10h. red	15	35
55	**11**	15h. brown	15	15
56	**11**	20h. olive	35	55
57	**11**	25h. red	15	15
58	**11**	50h. blue	25	35
59	**11**	70h. blue	35	60
60	**11**	1k. red and grey	60	85

15

16

17 Agriculture

18 Ploughing in peace

19 Polish Uhlan

1919. For Southern Poland. Value in halerzy or korony. Imperf or perf.

68	**15**	3h. brown	10	10
69	**15**	5h. green	10	10
70	**15**	10h. orange	10	10
71	**15**	15h. red	10	10
72	**16**	20h. brown	10	10
85	**16**	25h. blue	10	10
86	**16**	50h. brown	10	10
75	**17**	1k. green	20	10
88	**17**	1k.50 brown	70	10
89	**17**	2k. blue	90	10
90	**18**	2k.50 purple	90	35
91	**19**	5k. blue	1·40	45

1919. For Northern Poland. Value in fenigow or marki. Imperf or perf.

104	**15**	3f. brown	10	10
105	**15**	5f. green	10	10
179	**15**	5f. blue	30	60
106	**15**	10f. purple	10	10
129	**15**	10f. brown	10	10
107	**15**	15f. red	10	10
108	**16**	20f. blue	10	10
181	**16**	20f. red	30	60
109	**16**	25f. green	10	10
110	**16**	50f. green	10	10
183	**16**	50f. orange	30	60
137	**17**	1m. violet	20	10
112	**17**	1m.50 green	50	25
138	**17**	2m. brown	20	10
114	**18**	2m.50 brown	90	55
139	**18**	3m. brown	30	10
140	**19**	5m. purple	10	10
141	**19**	6m. red	10	10
142	**19**	10m. red	25	15
143	**19**	20m. green	60	35

1919. 1st Polish Philatelic Exhibition and Polish White Cross Fund. Surch I POLSKA WYSTAWA MAREK, cross and new value. Imperf or perf.

116b	**15**	5+5f. green	20	20
117b	**15**	10+5f. purple	50	20
118b	**15**	15+5f. red	20	20
119b	**16**	25+5f. olive	30	20
120	**16**	50+5f. green	75	55

20

21 Prime Minster Paderewski

22 A. Trampezynski

23 Eagle and Sailing Ship

1919. 1st Session of Parliament in Liberated Poland. Dated "1919".

121	**20**	10f. mauve	25	15
122	**21**	15f. red	25	15
123	**22**	20f. brown (21×25 mm)	65	30
124	**22**	20f. brown (17×20 mm)	1·25	1·25
125	-	25f. green	40	15
126	**23**	50f. blue	40	25
127	-	1m. violet	65	55

DESIGN—As Type **21**: 25f. Gen. Pilsudski. As Type **23**: 1m. Griffin and fasces.

24

1920

146	**24**	40f. violet	10	10
182	**24**	40f. brown	30	60
184	**24**	75f. green	30	60

1920. As T 15, but value in marks ("Mk").

147	**15**	1m. red	10	10
148	**15**	2m. green	10	10
149	**15**	3m. blue	10	10
150	**15**	4m. red	10	10
151	**15**	5m. purple	10	10
152	**15**	8m. brown	65	20

1921. Surch 3 Mk and bars.

153	**24**	3m. on 40f. violet	20	10

1921. Red Cross Fund. Surch with cross and 30MK.

154	**19**	5m.+30m. purple	3·50	7·50
155	**19**	6m.+30m. red	3·50	7·50
156	**19**	10m.+30m. red	7·00	15·00
157	**19**	20m.+30m. green	28·00	70·00

28 Sun of Peace

29 Agriculture

1921. New Constitution.

158	**28**	2m. green	1·10	1·90
159	**28**	3m. blue	1·10	1·90
160	**28**	4m. red	55	55
161	**29**	6m. red	55	65
162	**29**	10m. green	90	65
163	-	25m. violet	2·40	2·00
164	-	50m. green and buff	1·60	1·00

DESIGN: 25, 50m. "Peace" (Seated women).

31 Sower

1921. Peace Treaty with Russia.

165	**31**	10m. blue	10	10
166	**31**	15m. brown	10	10
167	**31**	20m. red	10	10

32

1921

170	**32**	25m. violet and buff	10	10
171	**32**	50m. red and buff	10	10
172	**32**	100m. brown and orange	10	10
173	**32**	200m. pink and black	10	10
174	**32**	300m. green	10	10
175	**32**	400m. brown	10	10
176	**32**	500m. purple	10	10
177	**32**	1000m. orange	10	10
178	**32**	2000m. violet	10	10

33 Silesian Miner

1922

185	**33**	1m. black	30	60
186	**33**	1m.25 green	30	60
187	**33**	2m. red	30	60
188	**33**	3m. green	30	60
189	**33**	4m. blue	30	60
190	**33**	5m. brown	30	60
191	**33**	6m. orange	30	1·50
192	**33**	10m. brown	30	60
193	**33**	20m. purple	30	60
194	**33**	50m. olive	30	3·75
195	**33**	80m. red	95	4·50
196	**33**	100m. violet	95	4·50
197	**33**	200m. orange	1·90	7·50
198	**33**	300m. blue	5·00	15·00

34 Copernicus

1923. 450th Birth Anniv of Copernicus (astronomer) and 150th Death Anniv of Konarski (educationist).

199	**34**	1,000m. slate	55	45
200	-	3,000m. brown	25	45
201	**34**	5,000m. red	55	55

DESIGN: 3,000m. Konarski.

1923. Surch.

202	**32**	10 TYSIECY (=10000) on 25m. violet and buff	10	10
206	**15**	20,000m. on 2m. green (No. 148)	35	40
204	**31**	25,000m. on 20m. red	10	10
205	**31**	50,000m. on 10m. blue	20	20
207	**15**	100,000m. on 5m. purple (No. 151)	10	10

39

1924

208	**39**	10,000m. purple	30	30
209	**39**	20,000m. green	10	25
210	**39**	30,000m. red	70	35
211	**39**	50,000m. green	70	35
212	**39**	100,000m. brown	55	30
213	**39**	200,000m. blue	55	25
214	**39**	300,000m. mauve	55	45
215	**39**	500,000m. brown	55	1·90
216	**39**	1,000,000m. pink	55	5·25
217	**39**	2,000,000m. green	90	23·00

40

41 President Wojciechowski

1924. New Currency.

218	**40**	1g. brown	45	40
219	**40**	2g. brown	45	10
220	**40**	3g. orange	55	10
221	**40**	5g. green	70	10
222	**40**	10g. green	70	10
223	**40**	15g. red	70	10
224	**40**	20g. blue	2·75	10
225	**40**	25g. red	3·50	10
226	**40**	30g. violet	17·50	20
227	**40**	40g. blue	4·00	30
228	**40**	50g. purple	2·75	25
229	**41**	1z. red	22·00	2·40

42

1925. National Fund.

230	**42**	1g.+50g. brown	15·00	22·00
231	**42**	2g.+50g. brown	15·00	22·00
232	**42**	3g.+50g. orange	15·00	22·00
233	**42**	5g.+50g. green	15·00	22·00
234	**42**	10g.+50g. green	15·00	22·00
235	**42**	15g.+50g. red	15·00	22·00
236	**42**	20g.+50g. blue	15·00	22·00
237	**42**	25g.+50g. red	15·00	22·00
238	**42**	30g.+50g. violet	15·00	22·00
239	**42**	40g.+50g. blue	15·00	22·00
240	**42**	50g.+50g. purple	15·00	22·00

43 Holy Gate, Vilna **44** Town Hall, Pozan **48** Galleon

1925

241	**43**	1g. brown	30	10
242	-	2g. olive	45	35
243a	-	3g. blue	1·40	10
244a	**44**	5g. green	1·10	10
245a	-	10g. violet	1·10	10
246	-	15g. red	1·10	10
247	**48**	20g. red	6·50	10
248	**43**	24g. blue	7·00	70
249	-	30g. blue	3·75	10
250	-	40g. blue	3·00	10
251	**48**	45g. mauve	13·00	1·10

DESIGNS—As Type **43**: VERT: 2, 30g. Jan III Sobieski Statue, Lwow. As Type **44**: 3, 10g. King Sigismund Vasa Column, Warsaw. HORIZ: 15, 40g. Wawel Castle, Cracow.

49 LVG Schneider Biplane

1925. Air.

252	**49**	1g. blue	45	4·75
253	**49**	2g. orange	45	4·75
254	**49**	3g. brown	45	4·75
255	**49**	5g. brown	45	55
256	**49**	10g. green	1·40	65
257	**49**	15g. mauve	1·60	75
258	**49**	20g. olive	12·50	4·75
259	**49**	30g. red	6·50	1·75
260	**49**	45g. lilac	8·50	3·50

50 Chopin

1927

261	**50**	40g. blue	12·00	2·40

51 Marshal Pilsudski

1927

262	**51**	20g. red	2·00	25
262a	**51**	25g. brown	2·00	25

52 Pres. Moscicki

1927

263	**52**	20g. red	6·00	70

53

1927. Educational Funds.

264	**53**	10g.+5g. purple on green	7·50	10·00
265	**53**	20g.+5g. blue on yellow	7·50	10·00

54 Dr. Karl Kaczkowki

1927. 4th Int Military Medical Congress, Warsaw.

266	**54**	10g. green	2·75	2·10
267	**54**	25g. red	5·25	4·00
268	**54**	40g. blue	7·00	3·00

55 J. Slowacki (poet)

1927. Transfer of Slowacki's remains to Cracow.

269	**55**	20g. red	4·50	75

1928. Warsaw Philatelic Exhibition. Sheet 117×88 mm. T 56/7 in deep sepia.

MS270	50g. and 1z. (+1z.50)	£325	£250

See also Nos. 272/3, 328 and **MS**332a/c.

56 Marshal Pilsudski **57** Pres. Moscicki

1928

272	**56**	50g. grey	2·75	20
272a	**56**	50g. green	6·50	25
273	**57**	1z. black on cream	8·50	20

58 Gen. Joseph Bem

1928

271	**58**	25g. red	2·25	25

59 H. Sienkiewicz

1928. Henryk Sienkiewicz (author).

274	**59**	15g. blue	1·75	25

60 Slav God, "Swiatowit"

1929. National Exhibition, Poznan.

275	**60**	25g. brown	1·75	25

61

1929

276	**61**	5g. violet	20	20
277	**61**	10g. green	55	20
278	**61**	25g. brown	35	25

62 King Jan III Sobieski

1930. Birth Tercentenary of Jan III Sobieski.

279	**62**	75g. purple	5·00	25

63

1930. Centenary of "November Rising" (29 November 1830).

280	**63**	5g. purple	55	20
281	**63**	15g. blue	2·40	35
282	**63**	25g. lake	1·50	20
283	**63**	30g. red	8·00	3·50

64 Kosciusko, Washington and Pulaski

1932. Birth Bicentenary of George Washington.

284	**64**	30g. brown on cream	2·25	35

65

1932

284a	**65**	5g. violet	20	20
285	**65**	10g. green	20	20
285a	**65**	15g. red	20	20
286	**65**	20g. grey	45	20
287	**65**	25g. bistre	45	20
288	**65**	30g. red	1·90	20
289	**65**	60g. blue	20·00	20

67 Town Hall, Torun

1933. 700th Anniv of Torun.

290	**67**	60g. blue on cream	28·00	1·10

68 Franciszek Zwirko (airman) and Stanislaw Wigura (aircraft designer)

1933. Victory in Flight round Europe Air Race, 1932.

292	**68**	30g. green	16·00	1·75

1933. Torun Philatelic Exhibition.

293	**67**	60g. red on cream	18·00	15·00

69 Altar-piece, St. Mary's Church, Cracow

1933. 4th Death Centenary of Veit Stoss (sculptor).

294	**69**	80g. brown on cream	14·00	2·00

70 "Liberation of Vienna" by J. Matejko

1933. 250th Anniv of Relief of Vienna.

295	**70**	1z.20 blue on cream	35·00	12·50

71 Cross of Independence

1933. 15th Anniv of Proclamation of Republic.

296	**71**	30g. red	8·00	40

1934. Katowice Philatelic Exhibition. Optd Wyst. Filat. 1934 Katowice.

297	**65**	20g. grey	35·00	29·00
298	**65**	30g. red	35·00	29·00

73 Marshal Pilsudski and Legion of Fusiliers Badge

1934. 20th Anniv of Formation of Polish Legion.

299	**73**	25g. blue	70	35
300	**73**	30g. brown	2·00	40

1934. Int Air Tournament. Optd Challenge 1934.

301	**49**	20g. olive	12·00	10·00
302	**68**	30g. green	7·50	2·50

1934. Surch in figures.

303	**69**	25g. on 80g. brown on cream	5·00	60
304	**65**	55g. on 60g. blue	4·50	35
305	**70**	1z. on 1z.20 blue on cream	18·00	4·75

77 Marshal Pilsudski

1935. Mourning Issue.

306	**77**	5g. black	75	25
307	**77**	15g. black	75	30
308	**77**	25g. black	1·25	25
309	**77**	45g. black	4·00	2·00
310	**77**	1z. black	7·00	4·25

1935. Optd Kopiec Marszalka Pilsudskiego.

311	**65**	15g. red	80	65
312	**73**	25g. blue	2·75	2·00

79 Pieskowa Skala (Dog's Rock) **80** Pres. Moscicki

1935

313	**79**	5g. blue	50	10
317	-	5g. violet	25	10
314	-	10g. green	50	10
318	-	10g. green	65	10
315	-	15g. blue	2·75	10
319	-	15g. lake	35	10
316	-	20g. black	1·00	10
320	-	20g. orange	55	10
321a	-	25g. green	80	10
322	-	30g. red	1·75	10
323a	-	45g. mauve	1·60	10
324a	-	50g. black	2·50	10
325	-	55g. blue	6·25	40
326	-	1z. brown	3·50	70
327	**80**	3z. brown	2·50	3·50

DESIGNS: 5g. (No. 317) Monastery of Jasna Gora, Czestochowa; 10g. (314) Lake Morskie Oko; 10g. (318) "Batory" (liner) at sea passenger terminal, Gdynia; 15g. (315) "Pilsudski" (liner); 15g. (319) University, Lwow; 20g. (316) Pieniny-Czorsztyn; 20g. (320) Administrative Buildings, Katowice; 25g. Belvedere Palace, Warsaw; 30g. Castle at Mir; 45g. Castle at Podhorce; 50g. Cloth Hall, Cracow; 55g. Raczynski Library, Poznan; 1z. Vilna Cathedral.

1936. 10th Anniv of Moscicki Presidency. As T 57 but inscr "1926. 3. VI. 1936" below design.

328	**57**	1z. blue	5·00	6·00

1936. Gordon-Bennett Balloon Race. Optd GORDON-BENNETT 30. VIII. 1936.

329	30g. red (No. 322)	11·00	5·75
330	55g. blue (No. 325)	11·00	5·75

82 Marshal Smigly-Rydz

1937

331	**82**	25g. blue	35	10
332	**82**	55g. blue	50	10

1937. Visit of King of Rumania. Three sheets each 102×125 mm each containing a block of four of earlier types in new colours.

MS332a **82** 25g. sepia	21·00	32·00
MS332b **56** 50g. blue	21·00	32·00
MS332c **57** 1z. black	21·00	32·00

83 Pres. Moscicki

1938. President's 70th Birthday.

333	**83**	15g. grey	40	10
334	**83**	30g. purple	60	10

84 Kosciuszko, Paine and Washington

1938. 150th Anniv of U.S. Constitution.

335	**84**	1z. blue	1·10	1·40

84a Postal Coach

1938. 5th Philatelic Exhibition, Warsaw. Sheet 130×103 mm.

MS335a **84a** 45g. (×2) green; 55g. (×2) blue	£110	85·00

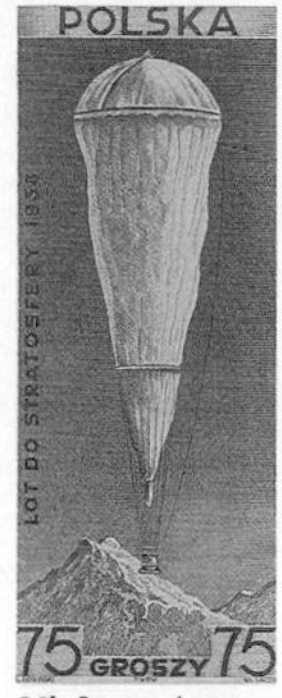

84b Stratosphere Balloon

1938. Proposed Polish Stratosphere Flight. Sheet 75×125 mm.

MS335b **84b** 75g. (+1z.25) violet	90·00	70·00

85a

86 Marshal Pilsudski

1938. 20th Anniv of Independence. (a) As T **85a** and **86**.

336	-	5g. orange	10	10
337	-	10g. green	10	10
338	**85a**	15g. brown (A)	15	15
357	**85a**	15g. brown (B)	35	25
339	-	20g. blue	40	10
340	-	25g. purple	10	10
341	-	30g. red	50	10
342	-	45g. black	90	65
343	-	50g. mauve	1·75	10
344	-	55g. blue	50	10
345	-	75g. green	2·25	1·90
346	-	1z. orange	2·25	1·90
347	-	2z. red	8·50	11·00
348	**86**	3z. blue	8·50	14·00

(b) 102×105 mm, containing four portraits as T 83 but with value and inscr transposed, all in purple.

MS348a 25g. Marshal Pilsudski; 25g. Pres. Narutowicz; 25g. Pres. Moscicki; 25g. Marshal Smigly-Rydz	12·00	20·00

DESIGNS—VERT: 5g. Boleslaw the Brave; 10g. Casimir the Great; 20g. Casimir Jagiellon; 25g. Sigismund August; 30g. Stefan Batory; 45g. Chodkiewicz and Zolkiewski; 50g. Jan III Sobieski; 55g. Symbol of Constitution of May 3rd, 1791; 75g. Kosciuszko, Poniatowski and Dabrowski; 1z. November Uprising 1830–31; 2z. Romuald Traugutt.

(A) Type **85a**. (B) as Type **85a** but crossed swords omitted.

87 Teschen comes to Poland

1938. Acquisition of Teschen.

349	**87**	25g. purple	1·50	35

88 "Warmth"

1938. Winter Relief Fund.

350	**88**	5g.+5g. orange	40	1·40
351	**88**	25g.+10g. purple	85	3·25
352	**88**	55g.+15g. blue	1·40	3·50

89 Tatra Mountaineer

1939. International Ski Championship, Zakopane.

353	**89**	15g. brown	1·10	80
354	**89**	25g. purple	1·40	1·10
355	**89**	30g. red	1·90	1·50

356	**89**	55g. blue	7·50	5·00

90 Pilsudski and Polish Legionaries

1939. 25th Anniv of 1st Battles of Polish Legions.

358	**90**	25g. purple	1·10	45

MS358a 103×125 mm. 25g. T **90**; 25g. T **77**; 25g. T **82**	24·00	32·00

1939–1945. GERMAN OCCUPATION.

1939. T 94 of Germany surch Deutsche Post OSTEN and value.

359	**94**	6g. on 3pf. brown	20	55
360	**94**	8g. on 4pf. blue	20	55
361	**94**	12g. on 6pf. green	20	55
362	**94**	16g. on 8pf. red	65	1·40
363	**94**	20g. on 10pf. brown	20	55
364	**94**	24g. on 12pf. red	20	40
365	**94**	30g. on 15pf. purple	65	1·40
366	**94**	40g. on 20pf. blue	65	55
367	**94**	50g. on 25pf. blue	65	1·10
368	**94**	60g. on 30pf. green	65	55
369	**94**	80g. on 40pf. mauve	65	1·10
370	**94**	1z. on 50pf. black & green	1·50	1·60
371	**94**	2z. on 100pf. black & yell	3·00	3·25

1940. Surch General-Gouvernement, Nazi emblem and value.

372	2g. on 5g. orge (No. 336)	20	40
373	4g. on 5g. orge (No. 336)	20	40
374	6g. on 10g. grn (No. 337)	20	40
375	8g. on 10g. grn (No. 337)	20	40
376	10g. on 10g. green (No. 337)	20	40
377	12g. on 15g. brown (No. 338)	20	40
378	16g. on 15g. brown (No. 338)	20	40
379	24g. on 25g. blue (331)	1·50	3·25
380	24g. on 25g. purple (No. 340)	20	40
382	30g. on 5g.+5g. orange (350)	30	75
381	30g. on 30g. red (No. 341)	20	40
383	40g. on 30g. purple (334)	40	1·10
384	40g. on 25g.+10g. purple (351)	30	75
386a	50g. on 20g. green	1·50	3·25
386b	50g. on 25g. green	6·25	17·00
386c	50g. on 30g. green	19·00	37·00
385	50g. on 50g. mauve (No. 343)	20	75
386d	50g. on 50g. green	1·10	2·10
386	50g. on 55g. blue (332)	30	75
386e	50g. on 1z. green	2·10	4·25
387	60g. on 55g. blue (No. 344)	8·50	19·00
388	80g. on 75g. green (No. 345)	8·50	19·00
388a	1z. on 55g.+15g. blue (352)	4·75	11·50
389	1z. on 1z. orge (No. 346)	9·00	19·00
390	2z. on 2z. red (No. 347)	3·25	7·50
391	3z. on 3z. blue (348)	4·25	10·50

Nos. 386a/e are postage stamps.

93 Copernicus Memorial, Cracow

1940

392	-	6g. brown	30	85
393	-	8g. brown	30	85
394	-	8g. black	70	75
395	-	10g. green	20	30
396	**93**	12g. green	2·75	75
397	**93**	12g. violet	35	40
398	-	20g. brown	20	20
399	-	24g. red	20	20
400	-	30g. violet	20	20
401	-	30g. purple	35	75
402	-	40g. black	20	20
403	-	48g. brown	80	1·30
404	-	50g. blue	20	20
405	-	60g. green	25	30
406	-	80g. violet	55	55
407	-	1z. purple	2·75	85
408	-	1z. green	70	1·30

DESIGNS: 6g. Florian gate, Cracow; 8g. Castle Keep, Cracow; 10g. Cracow Gate, Lublin; 20g. Church of the Dominicans, Cracow; 24g. Wawel Castle, Cracow; 30g. Old Church in Lublin; 40g. Arcade, Cloth Hall, Cracow; 48g. Town Hall, Sandomir; 50g. Town Hall, Cracow; 60g. Courtyard of Wawel Castle, Cracow; 80g. St. Mary's Church, Cracow; 1z. Bruhl Palace, Warsaw.

1940. Red Cross Fund. As last, new colours, surch with Cross and premium in figures.

409	12g.+8g. green	1·90	3·25
410	24g.+16g. green	1·90	3·25
411	50g.+50g. green	2·75	5·25
412	80g.+80g. green	2·75	7·50

95

1940. 1st Anniv of German Occupation.

413	**95**	12g.+38g. green on yellow	1·50	3·50
414	-	24g.+26g. red on yellow	1·50	3·50
415	-	30g.+20g. violet on yellow	2·40	5·75

DESIGNS: 24g. Woman with scarf; 30g. Fur-capped peasant as Type **96**.

96

1940. Winter Relief Fund.

416	**96**	12g.+8g. green	70	2·10
417	**96**	24g.+16g. red	70	2·10
418	**96**	30g.+30g. brown	1·60	3·25
419	**96**	50g.+50g. blue	1·60	3·25

97 Cracow

1941

420	**97**	10z. grey and red	1·30	3·25

98 The Barbican, Cracow

1941

421	**98**	2z. blue	80	1·10
422	-	4z. green	80	1·60

DESIGN: 4z. Tyniec Monastery.

See also Nos. 465/8.

99 Adolf Hitler

1941

423	**99**	2g. grey	15	30
424	**99**	6g. brown	15	30
425	**99**	8g. blue	15	30
426	**99**	10g. green	15	30
427	**99**	12g. violet	15	30
428	**99**	16g. orange	1·60	2·10
429	**99**	20g. brown	15	30
430	**99**	24g. red	15	30
431	**99**	30g. purple	15	30
432	**99**	32g. green	25	55
433	**99**	40g. blue	15	30
434	**99**	48g. brown	1·30	95
435	**99**	50g. blue	20	75
436	**99**	60g. green	20	75
437	**99**	80g. purple	20	75
441	**99**	1z. green	55	1·10
442	**99**	1z.20 brown	55	1·10
443	**99**	1z.60 blue	55	1·60

1942. Hitler's 53rd Birthday. As T 99, but premium inserted in design.

444	30g.+1z. purple on yellow	35	1·90
445	50g.+1z. blue on yellow	35	1·90
446	1z.20+1z. brown on yellow	35	1·90

100 Modern Lublin

1942. 600th Anniv of Lublin.

447	-	12g.+8g. purple	20	85
448	**100**	24g.+6g. brown	20	85
449	-	50g.+50g. blue	20	1·60
450	**100**	1z.+1z. green	40	1·60

DESIGN: 12, 50g. Lublin, after an ancient engraving.

101 Copernicus

1942. 3rd Anniv of German Occupation.

451	-	12g.+18g. violet	15	55
452	-	24g.+26g. red	15	55
453	-	30g.+30g. purple	15	55
454	-	50g.+50g. blue	15	85
455	**101**	1z.+1z. green	20	1·10

DESIGNS: 12g. Veit Stoss (Vit Stvosz); 24g. Hans Durer; 30g. J. Schuch; 50g. J. Elsner.

102 Adolf Hitler

1943. Hitler's 54th Birthday.

456	**102**	12g.+1z. violet	30	1·80
457	**102**	24g.+1z. red	30	1·80
458	**102**	84g.+1z. green	30	1·80

1943. 400th Death Anniv of Nicolas Copernicus (astronomer). As No. 455, colour changed, optd 24. MAI 1543 24. MAI 1943.

459	**101**	1z.+1z. purple	30	2·10

103 Cracow Gate, Lublin

1943. 3rd Anniv of Nazi Party in German-occupied Poland.

460	**103**	12g.+38g. green	15	55
461	-	24g.+76g. red	15	55
462	-	30g.+70g. purple	15	65
463	-	50g.+1z. blue	15	55
464	-	1z.+2z. grey	15	65

DESIGNS: 24g. Cloth Hall, Cracow; 30g. Administrative Building, Radom; 50g. Bruhl Palace, Warsaw; 1z. Town Hall, Lwow.

103a Lwow

1943

465		2z. green	15	30
466		4z. violet	55	1·20
467	**103a**	6z. brown	30	85
468	-	10z. grey and brown	30	85

DESIGNS: 2z. The Barbican, Cracow; 4z. Tyniec Monastery; 10z. Cracow.

104 Adolf Hitler

1944. Hitler's 55th Birthday.

469	**104**	12z.+1z. green	20	1·30
470	**104**	24z.+1z. brown	20	1·30
471	**104**	84z.+1z. violet	20	1·30

105 Konrad Celtis

1944. Culture Funds.

472	**105**	12g.+18g. green	15	1·30
473	-	24g.+26g. red	15	1·30
474	-	30g.+30g. purple	15	1·60
475	-	50g.+50g. blue	15	1·60
476	-	1z.+1z. brown	15	1·60

PORTRAITS: 24g. Andreas Schluter; 30g. Hans Boner; 50g. Augustus the Strong; 1z. Gottlieb Pusch.

105a Cracow Castle

1944. 5th Anniv of German Occupation.

477a	**105a**	10z.+10z. black and red	7·50	55·00

1941-1945 ISSUES OF EXILED GOVERNMENT IN LONDON

For correspondence on Polish sea-going vessels and, on certain days, from Polish Military camps in Great Britain.

106 Ruins of Ministry of Finance, Warsaw

107 Vickers-Armstrong Wellington and Hawker Hurricanes used by Poles in Great Britain

1941

478	-	5g. violet	1·00	1·40
479	**106**	10g. green	1·50	1·50
480	-	25g. grey	1·75	2·00
481	-	55g. blue	2·25	2·00
482	-	75g. olive	5·75	6·50
483	-	80g. red	5·75	6·50
484	**107**	1z. blue	5·75	6·50
485	-	1z.50 brown	5·75	6·50

DESIGNS—VERT: 5g. Ruins of U.S. Embassy, Warsaw; 25g. Destruction of Mickiewicz Monument, Cracow; 1z.50, Polish submarine "Orzel". HORIZ: 55g. Ruins of Warsaw; 75g. Polish machine-gunners in Great Britain; 80g. Polish tank in Great Britain.

POLSKA MARYNARKA HANDLOWA
POCZTA POLSKA GR10

108 Vickers-Armstrong Wellington and U-boat

109 Merchant Navy

1943

486	**108**	5g. red	85	1·10
487	**109**	10g. green	1·10	1·40
488	-	25g. violet	1·10	1·40
489	-	55g. blue	1·50	1·90
490	-	75g. brown	3·00	3·25
491	-	80g. red	3·00	3·25
492	-	1z. olive	3·00	3·25
493	-	1z.50 black	3·75	6·75

DESIGNS—VERT: 25g. Anti-tank gun in France; 55g. Poles at Narvik; 1z. Saboteurs damaging railway line. HORIZ: 75g. The Tobruk road; 80g. Gen. Sikorski visiting Polish troops in Middle East; 1z.50, Underground newspaper office.

1944. Capture of Monte Casino. Nos. 482/5 surch MONTE CASSINO 18 V 1944 and value and bars.

494		45g. on 75g. olive	13·00	16·00
495		55g. on 80g. red	13·00	16·00
496	**107**	80g. on 1z. blue	13·00	16·00
497	-	1z.20 on 1z.50 brown	13·00	16·00

111 Polish Partisans

1945. Relief Fund for Survivors of Warsaw Rising.

498	**111**	1z.+2z. green	7·00	9·25

1944. INDEPENDENT REPUBLIC.

112 Romuald Traugutt

1944. National Heroes.

499	**112**	25g. red	48·00	65·00
500	-	50g. green	48·00	65·00
501	-	1z. blue	48·00	80·00

PORTRAITS: 50g. Kosciuszko; 1z. H. Dabrowski.

113 White Eagle

114 Grunwald Memorial, Cracow

1944

502	**113**	25g. red	1·40	1·10
503	**114**	50g. green	1·40	75

1944. No. 502 surch with value 31.XII., 1943 or 1944 and K.R.N., P.K.W.N. or R.T.R.P.

504	**113**	1z. on 25g. red	2·50	3·50
505	**113**	2z. on 25g. red	2·50	3·50
506	**113**	3z. on 25g. red	2·50	3·50

1945. 82nd Anniv of 1863 Revolt against Russia. Surch with value and 22.I.1863.

507	**112**	5z. on 25g. brown	42·00	65·00

1945. Liberation. No. 502 surch 3zl, with town names and dates as indicated.

508	3z. on 25g. Bydgoszcz 23.1.1945	5·75	9·75
509	3z. on 25g. Czestochowa 17.1.1945	5·75	9·75
510	3z. on 25g. Gniezno 22.1.1945	5·75	9·75
511	3z. on 25g. Kalisz 24.1.1945	5·75	9·75
512	3z. on 25g. Kielce 15.1.1945	5·75	9·75
513	3z. on 25g. Krakow 19.1.1945	5·75	9·75
514	3z. on 25g. Lodz 19.1.1945	5·75	9·75
515	3z. on 25g. Radom 16.1.1945	5·75	9·75
516	3z. on 25g. Warszawa 17.1.1945	14·50	20·00
517	3z. on 25g. Zakopane 29.1.1945	8·00	13·50

120 Flag-bearer and War Victim

1945. Liberation of Warsaw.

518	**120**	5z. red	2·25	2·25

121 Lodz Factories

1945. Liberation of Lodz.

519	**121**	1z. blue	80	40

1945. 151st Anniv of Kosciuszko's Oath of Allegiance. No. 500 surch 5zl. 24.III.1794.

520		5z. on 50g. green	11·50	17·00

123 Grunwald Memorial, Cracow

1945. Cracow Monuments. Inscr "19.1.1945".

521	**123**	50g. purple	25	15
522	-	1z. brown	30	15
523	-	2z. blue	1·10	15
524	-	3z. violet	95	40
525	-	5z. green	6·00	6·75

DESIGNS—VERT: 1z. Kosciuszko Statue; 3z. Copernicus Memorial. HORIZ: 2z. Cloth Hall; 5z. Wawel Castle.

125 H.M.S. "Dragon" (cruiser)

1945. 25th Anniv of Polish Maritime League.

526	**125**	50g.+2z. orange	7·00	10·50
527	-	1z.+3z. blue	4·00	7·50
528	-	2z.+4z. red	2·75	7·00
529	-	3z.+5z. olive	2·75	7·00

DESIGNS—VERT: 1z. "Dar Pomorza" (full-rigged cadet ship); 2z. Naval ensigns. HORIZ: 3z. Crane and tower, Gdansk.

126 Town Hall, Poznan

1945. Postal Employees Congress.

530	**126**	1z.+5z. green	19·00	32·00

127 Kosciuszko Memorial, Lodz

1945

531	**127**	3z. purple	70	25

128 Grunwald, 1410

1945. 535th Anniv of Battle of Grunwald.

532	**128**	5z. blue	6·75	6·25

129 Eagle and Manifesto

1945. 1st Anniv of Liberation.

533	**129**	3z. red	10·00	16·00

130 Westerplatte

1945. 6th Anniv of Defence of Westerplatte.

534	**130**	1z.+9z. slate	21·00	27·00

1945. Surch with new value and heavy bars.

535	**114**	1z. on 50g. green	55	30
536a	**113**	1z.50 on 25g. red	55	30

133 Crane Tower, Gdansk

1945. Liberation of Gdansk (Danzig). Perf or imperf.

537	**133**	1z. olive	20	20
538	-	2z. blue	30	20
539	-	3z. purple	90	20

DESIGNS—VERT: 2z. Stock Exchange, Gdansk. HORIZ: 3z. High Gate, Gdansk.

135 St. John's Cathedral

1945. "Warsaw, 1939–1945". Warsaw before and after destruction. Imperf.

540		1z.50 red	20	10
541	**135**	3z. blue	20	10
542	-	3z.50 green	1·25	45
543	-	6z. grey	25	20
544	-	8z. brown	2·75	55
545	-	10z. purple	55	55

DESIGNS: 1z.50, Royal Castle; 3z.50, City Hall; 6z. G.P.O.; 8z. War Ministry; 10z. Church of the Holy Cross.

136 United Workers

1945. Trades' Union Congress.

546	**136**	1z.50+8z.50 grey	6·75	8·75

137 Soldiers of 1830 and Jan III Sobieski Statue

1945. 115th Anniv of 1830 Revolt against Russia.

547	**137**	10z. grey	8·50	12·50

1946. 1st Anniv of Warsaw Liberation. Nos. 540/5 optd WARSZAWA WOLNA 17 Styczen 1945–1946. Imperf.

548	1z.50 red	1·90	4·25
549	3z. blue	1·90	4·25
550	3z.50 green	1·90	4·25
551	6z. grey	1·90	4·25
552	8z. brown	1·90	4·25
553	10z. purple	1·90	4·25

139 Insurgent

1946. 83rd Anniv of 1863 Revolt.

554	**139**	6z. blue	7·50	10·50

140 Lisunov Li-2 over Ruins of Warsaw

1946. Air.

555	**140**	5z. grey	35	10
556	**140**	10z. purple	45	25
557	**140**	15z. blue	2·75	25
558	**140**	20z. purple	1·10	25
559	**140**	25z. green	2·10	35
560	**140**	30z. red	3·50	50

141 Fighting in Spain

1946. Polish Legion in the Spanish Civil War.

561	**141**	3z.+5z. red	6·00	8·75

142 Bydgoszcz

1946. 600th Anniv of City of Bydgoszcz.

562	**142**	3z.+2z. grey	7·25	13·00

143 "Death" over Majdanek Concentration Camp

1946. Majdanek Concentration Camp.

563	**143**	3z.+5z. green	2·75	4·00

144 Shield and Soldiers

1946. Uprisings in Upper Silesia (1919–23) and Silesian Campaign against the Germans (1939–45).

564	**144**	3z.+7z. brown	95	1·10

145 Infantry

1946. 1st Anniv of Peace.

565	**145**	3z. brown	45	35

146 Polish Coastline

1946. Maritime Festival.

566	**146**	3z.+7z. blue	2·50	3·75

147 Pres. Bierut, Premier O. Morawski and Marshal Zymierski

1946. 2nd Anniv of Polish Committee of National Liberation Manifesto.

567	**147**	3z. violet	3·50	6·00

148 Bedzin Castle

1946. Imperf (5z., 10z.) or perf (6z.).

568	**148**	5z. olive	15	10
568a	**148**	5z. brown	25	15
569	-	6z. black	45	15
570	-	10z. blue	80	25

DESIGNS—VERT: 6z. Tombstone of Henry IV. HORIZ: 10z. Castle at Lanckorona.

149 Crane, Monument and Crane Tower, Gdansk

1946. The Fallen in Gdansk.

571	**149**	3z.+12z. grey	2·25	3·00

150 Schoolchildren at Desk

1946. Polish Work for Education and Fund for International Bureau of Education.

571a	**150**	3z.+22z. red	30·00	55·00
571b	-	6z.+24z. blue	30·00	55·00
571c	-	11z.+19z. green	30·00	55·00
MS571d		128×80 mm. Nos. 571a/c colours slightly changed (sold at 25+75z.)	£450	£900

DESIGNS: 6z. Court of Jagiellonian University, Cracow; 11z. Gregory Piramowicz (1735–1801), founder of the Education Commission.

152 Stojalowski, Bojko, Stapinski and Witos

1946. 50th Anniv of Peasant Movement and Relief Fund.

572	**152**	5z.+10z. green	2·25	3·00
573	**152**	5z.+10z. blue	2·25	3·00
574	**152**	5z.+10z. olive	2·25	3·00

1947. Opening of Polish Parliament. Surch+7 SEJM USTAWODAWCZY 19.1.1947.

575	**147**	3z.+7z. violet	7·50	12·00

1947. 22nd National Ski Championships, Zakopane. Surch 5+15 zl XXII MISTRZOSTWA NARCIARSKIE POLSKI 1947.

576	**113**	5+15z. on 25g. red	3·25	5·00

1947. No. 569 surch 5 ZL in outlined figure and capital letters between stars.

577	5z. on 6z. black	65	25

156 Home of Emil Zegadlowicz

1947. Emil Zegadlowicz Commemoration.

578	**156**	5z.+15z. green	2·25	3·25

157 Frederic Chopin (musician)

158 Boguslawski, Modrzejewska and Jaracz (actors)

1947. Polish Culture. Imperf or perf.

579	-	1z. blue	20	25
580	-	1z. grey	20	10
581	-	2z. brown	25	10
582	-	2z. orange	15	10
583a	**157**	3z. green	60	25
584	**157**	3z. olive	1·90	25
585	**158**	5z. black	60	10
586	**158**	5z. brown	20	10
587	-	6z. grey	1·00	10
588	-	6z. red	35	10
589	-	10z. grey	1·25	10
590	-	10z. blue	1·50	30
591	-	15z. violet	1·60	30
592	-	15z. brown	35	70
593	-	20z. black	2·50	50
594	-	20z. purple	1·10	50
MS594a		210×128 mm in shades similar to second issue of colours listed above (sold at 62+438z.)	£190	£250

PORTRAITS—HORIZ: 1z. Matejko, Malczewski and Chelmonski (painters); 6z. Swietochowski, Zeromski and Prus (writers); 15z. Wyspianski, Slowacki and Kasprowicz (poets). VERT: 2z. Brother Albert of Cracow; 10z. Marie Curie (scientist); 20z. Mickiewicz (poet).

159 Wounded Soldier, Nurse and Child

1947. Red Cross Fund.

595	**159**	5z.+5z. grey and red	3·00	5·00

161 Steelworker

1947. Occupations.

596	**161**	5z. lake	1·40	35
597	-	10z. green	45	20
598	-	15z. blue	90	30
599	-	20z. black	1·40	30

DESIGNS: 10z. Harvester; 15z. Fisherman; 20z. Miner.

1947. Air. Surch LOTNICZA, bars and value.

600	**114**	40z. on 50g. green	2·10	65
602	**113**	50z. on 25g. red	3·25	1·60

1947. Winter Relief Fund.

603	**163**	2z.+18z. violet	1·25	4·50

164 Sagittarius

1948. Air.

604	**164**	15z. violet	1·60	25
605	**164**	25z. blue	1·10	20
606	**164**	30z. brown	1·10	45
607	**164**	50z. green	2·25	45
608	**164**	75z. black	2·25	55
609	**164**	100z. orange	2·25	55

165 Chainbreaker

1948. Revolution Centenaries.

610	**165**	15z. brown	45	10
611	-	30z. brown	1·50	25
612	-	35z. green	3·25	55
613	-	60z. red	1·75	65

PORTRAITS—HORIZ: 30z. Generals H. Dembinski and J. Bem; 35z. S. Worcell, P. Sciegienny and E. Dembowski; 60z. F. Engels and K. Marx.

167 Insurgents

1948. 5th Anniv of Warsaw Ghetto Revolt.

614	**167**	15z. black	2·00	3·50

168 Wheel and Streamers

1948. Warsaw–Prague Cycle Race.

615	**168**	15z. red and blue	3·25	45

169 Cycle Race

1948. 7th Circuit of Poland Cycle Race.

616	**169**	3z. black	1·75	4·00
617	**169**	6z. brown	1·75	4·25
618	**169**	15z. green	2·50	5·50

170 "Oliwa" under Construction

1948. Merchant Marine.

619	**170**	6z. violet	1·40	2·00
620	-	15z. red	1·75	3·00
621	-	35z. grey	2·00	5·00

DESIGNS—HORIZ: 15z. Freighter at wharf; 35z. "General M. Zaruski" (cadet ketch).

173 Firework Display

1948. Wroclaw Exhibition.

622	**173**	6z. blue	55	30
623	**173**	15z. red	90	25
624	**173**	18z. red	1·40	45
625	**173**	35z. brown	1·40	45

174 "Youth"

1948. International Youth Conf, Warsaw.

626	**174**	15z. blue	65	25

175 Roadway, St. Anne's Church and Palace

1948. Warsaw Reconstruction Fund.

627	**175**	15z.+5z. green	25	25

176 Torun Ramparts and Mail Coach

1948. Philatelic Congress, Torun.

628	**176**	15z. brown	1·00	25

177 Streamlined Steam Locomotive No. Pm36-1 (1936), Clock and Winged Wheel

1948. European Railway Conference.

629	**177**	18z. blue	6·00	18·00

178 President Bierut

1948

629a	**178**	2z. orange	15	10
629b	**178**	3z. green	15	10
630	**178**	5z. brown	15	10
631	**178**	6z. black	95	10
631a	**178**	10z. violet	25	10
632	**178**	15z. red	80	10
633	**178**	18z. green	1·10	10
634	**178**	30z. blue	1·90	25
635	**178**	35z. purple	3·00	50

179 Workers and Flag

1948. Workers' Class Unity Congress. (a) Dated "8 XII 1948".

636	**179**	5z. red	85	65
637	-	15z. violet	85	65
638	-	25z. brown	85	65

(b) Dated "XII 1948".

639	**179**	5z. plum	2·00	1·60
640	-	15z. blue	2·00	1·60
641	-	25z. green	2·75	2·25

DESIGNS: 15z. Flags and portraits of Engels, Marx, Lenin and Stalin; 25z. Workers marching and portrait of L. Warynski.

180 Baby

1948. Anti-tuberculosis Fund. Portraits of babies as T 180.

642	**180**	3z.+2z. green	4·00	4·75
643a	-	5z.+5z. brown	3·25	2·75
644a	-	6z.+4z. purple	2·25	4·25
645	-	15z.+10z. red	2·00	3·00

180a Pres. Franklin D. Roosevelt

1948. Air. Honouring Presidents Roosevelt, Pulaski and Kosciuszko.

645a	**180a**	80z. violet	21·00	21·00
645b	-	100z. purple (Pulaski)	21·00	21·00
645c	-	120z. blue (Kosciuszko)	21·00	21·00
MS645d		160×95 mm. Nos. 645a/c 300+200z. colours changed	£250	£375

181 Workers

1949. Trades' Union Congress, Warsaw.

646	**181**	3z. red	1·10	1·25
647	-	5z. blue	1·10	1·25
648	-	15z. green	1·50	1·50

DESIGNS: 5z. inscr "PRACA" (Labour), Labourer and tractor; 15z. inscr "POKOJ" (Peace), Three labourers.

182 Banks of R. Vistula **183** Pres. Bierut

1949. 5th Anniv of National Liberation Committee.

649	**182**	10z. black	2·10	2·00
650	**183**	15z. mauve	2·10	2·00
651	-	35z. blue	2·10	2·00

DESIGN—VERT: 35z. Radio station, Rasyn.

184 Mail Coach and Map

1949. 75th Anniv of U.P.U.

652	**184**	6z. violet	1·25	2·00
653	-	30z. blue (liner)	2·25	2·00
654	-	80z. green (airplane)	4·25	4·75

185 Worker and Tractor

1949. Congress of Peasant Movement.

655	**185**	5z. red	95	25
656	**185**	10z. red	25	10
657	**185**	15z. green	25	10
658	**185**	35z. brown	1·25	1·25

186 Frederic Chopin

1949. National Celebrities.

659	-	10z. purple	2·40	2·10
660	**186**	15z. red	3·25	2·40
661	-	35z. blue	2·40	2·40

PORTRAITS: 10z. Adam Mickiewicz; 35z. Julius Slowacki.

187 Mickiewicz and Pushkin

1949. Polish–Russian Friendship Month.

662	**187**	15z. violet	3·50	4·25

188 Postman

1950. 3rd Congress of Postal Workers.

663	**188**	15z. purple	2·10	2·75

189 Mechanic, Hangar and Aeroplane

1950. Air.

664	**189**	500z. lake	4·50	6·50

190

1950. (a) With frame.

665	**190**	15z. red	60	10

195a

(b) Without frame. Values in "zloty".

673	**195a**	5z. green	15	10
674	**195a**	10z. red	15	10
675	**195a**	15z. blue	95	50
676	**195a**	20z. violet	45	35
677	**195a**	25z. brown	45	35
678	**195a**	30z. red	65	40
679	**195a**	40z. brown	80	50
680	**195a**	50z. olive	1·60	1·00

For values in "groszy" see Nos. 687/94.

191 J. Marchlewski

1950. 25th Death Anniv of Julian Marchlewski (patriot).

666	**191**	15z. black	70	35

192 Workers

1950. Reconstruction of Warsaw.

667	**192**	5z. brown	15	15

See also No. 695.

193 Worker and Flag

1950. 60th Anniv of May Day Manifesto.

668	**193**	10z. mauve	1·75	40
669	-	15z. olive	1·75	25

DESIGN—VERT: 15z. Three workers and flag.

194 Statue

1950. 23rd International Fair, Poznan.

670	**194**	15z. brown	35	10

195 Dove and Globe

1950. International Peace Conference.

671	**195**	10z. green	85	25
672	**195**	15z. brown	35	15

196 Industrial and Agricultural Workers

1950. Six Year Reconstruction Plan.

681	**196**	15z. blue	25	10

See also Nos. 696/e.

197 Hibner, Kniewski and Rutkowski

1950. 25th Anniv of Revolutionaries' Execution.

682	**197**	15z. grey	2·50	65

198 Worker and Dove

1950. 1st Polish Peace Congress.

683	**198**	15z. green	50	25

REVALUATION SURCHARGES. Following a revaluation of the Polish currency, a large number of definitive and commemorative stamps were locally overprinted "Groszy" or "gr". There are 37 known types of overprint and various colours of overprint. We do not list them as they had only local use, but the following is a list of the stamps which were duly authorised for overprinting: Nos. 579/94, 596/615 and 619/58. Overprints on other stamps are not authorized.

Currency Revalued: 100 old zlotys = 1 new zloty.

199 Dove (after Picasso)

1950. 2nd World Peace Congress, Warsaw.

684	**199**	40g. blue	1·75	35
685	**199**	45g. red	35	15

200 General Bem and Battle of Piski

1950. Death Centenary of General Bem.

686	**200**	45g. blue	2·50	2·00

1950. As T 195a. Values in "groszy".

687	**195a**	5g. violet	10	10
688	**195a**	10g. green	10	10
689	**195a**	15g. olive	10	10
690	**195a**	25g. red	10	10
691	**195a**	30g. red	15	10
692	**195a**	40g. orange	15	10
693	**195a**	45g. blue	1·25	10
694	**195a**	75g. brown	70	10

1950. As No. 667 but value in "groszy".

695	**192**	15g. green	10	10

1950. As No. 681 but values in "groszy" or "zlotys".

696	**196**	45g. blue	15	10
696b	**196**	75g. brown	30	10
696d	**196**	1z.15 green	95	10
696e	**196**	1z.20 red	70	10

201 Woman and Doves

1951. Women's League Congress.

697	**201**	45g. red	45	35

202 Battle Scene and J. Dabrowski

1951. 80th Anniv of Paris Commune.

698	**202**	45g. green	30	10

1951. Surch 45 gr.

699	**199**	45g. on 15z. red	55	15

204 Worker with Flag

1951. Labour Day.

700	**204**	45g. red	45	15

205 Smelting Works

1951

701	**205**	40g. blue	25	10
702	**205**	45g. black	25	10
702a	**205**	60g. brown	25	10
702c	**205**	90g. lake	85	10

206 Pioneer and Badge

1951. Int Children's Day. Inscr "I-VI-51".

703	**206**	30g. olive	1·10	65
704	-	45g. blue (Boy, girl and map)	6·25	65

207 St. Staszic

1951. 1st Polish Scientific Congress. Inscr "KONGRES NAUKI POLSKIEJ".

705	**207**	25g. red	3·75	2·75
706	-	40g. blue	60	20
707	-	45g. violet	8·00	1·60
708	-	60g. green	60	20
709	-	1z.15 purple	1·00	55
710	-	1z.20 grey	1·75	20

DESIGNS—As Type **207**: 40g. Marie Curie; 60g. M. Nencki; 1z.15, Copernicus; 1z.20, Dove and book. HORIZ—36×21 mm: 45g. Z. Wroblewski and Olszewski.

209 F. Dzerzhinsky

1951. 25th Death Anniv of Dzerzhinsky (Russian politician).

711	**209**	45g. brown	30	25

210 Pres. Bierut, Industry and Agriculture

1951. 7th Anniv of People's Republic.

712	**210**	45g. red	1·10	15
713	**210**	60g. green	16·00	5·25
714	**210**	90g. blue	3·50	65

211 Young People and Globe

1951. 3rd World Youth Festival, Berlin.

715	**211**	40g. blue	1·10	25

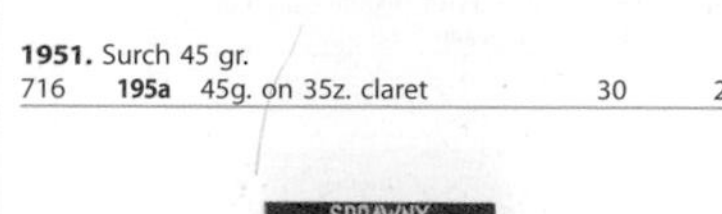

1951. Surch 45 gr.

716	**195a**	45g. on 35z. claret	30	25

213 Sports Badge

1951. Spartacist Games.

717	**213**	45g. green	1·25	1·10

214 Stalin

1951. Polish–Soviet Friendship.

718	**214**	45g. red	20	15
719	**214**	90g. black	45	25

215 Chopin and Moniuszko

1951. Polish Musical Festival.

720	**215**	45g. black	40	20
721	**215**	90g. red	1·50	55

1951. Warsaw Stamp Day. Sheet 90×120 mm comprising Nos. 696a/e printed in brown.

MS721a **196**	Sold at 5z.	13·50	13·50

216 Mining Machinery

1951. Six Year Plan (Mining).

722	**216**	90g. brown	30	15
723	**216**	1z.20 blue	30	15
724	**216**	1z.20+15g. orange	45	20

217 Building Modern Flats

1951. Six Year Plan (Reconstruction).

725	**217**	30g. green	10	10
726	**217**	30g.+15g. red	25	10
727	**217**	1z.15 purple	25	10

218 Installing Electric Cables

1951. Six Year Plan (Electrification).

728	**218**	30g. black	10	10
729	**218**	45g. red	20	10
730	**218**	45g.+15g. brown	55	10

219 M. Nowotko

1952. 10th Anniv of Polish Workers' Coalition.

731	**219**	45g.+15g. lake	20	10
732	-	90g. brown	45	30
733	-	1z.15 orange	45	65

PORTRAITS: 90g. P. Finder; 1z.15, M. Fornalska.

220 Women and Banner

1952. International Women's Day.

734	**220**	45g.+15g. brown	45	10
735	**220**	1z.20 red	50	35

221 Gen. Swierczewski

1952. 5th Death Anniv of Gen. Swierczewski.

736	**221**	45g.+15g. brown	45	10
737	**221**	90g. blue	50	30

222 Ilyushin Il-12 over Farm

1952. Air. Aeroplanes and views.

738	-	55g. blue (Tug and freighters)	35	30
739	**222**	90g. green	35	30
740	-	1z.40 purple (Warsaw)	45	45
741	-	5z. black (Steelworks)	1·40	55

223 President Bierut

1952. Pres. Bierut's 60th Birthday.

742	**223**	45g.+15g. red	45	35
743	**223**	90g. green	80	80
744	**223**	1z.20+15g. blue	1·00	35

224 Cyclists and City Arms

1952. 5th Warsaw–Berlin–Prague Peace Cycle Race.

745	**224**	40g. blue	1·50	90

225 Workers and Banner

1952. Labour Day.

746	**225**	45g.+15g. red	20	15
747	**225**	75g. green	55	35

226 Kraszewski

1952. 140th Birth Anniv of Jozef Ignacy Kraszewski (writer).

748	**226**	25g. purple	50	25

227 Maria Konopnicka

1952. 110th Birth Anniv of Maria Konopnicka (poet).

749	**227**	30g.+15g. green	50	15
750	**227**	1z.15 brown	80	55

228 H. Kollataj

1952. 140th Death Anniv of Hugo Kollataj (educationist and politician).

751	**228**	45g.+15g. brown	35	15
752	**228**	1z. green	50	35

229 Leonardo da Vinci

1952. 500th Birth Anniv of Leonardo da Vinci (artist).

753	**229**	30g.+15g. blue	70	50

230 President Bierut and Children

1952. International Children's Day.

754	**230**	45g.+15g. blue	2·50	70

231 N. V. Gogol

1952. Death Centenary of Nikolai Gogol (Russian writer).

755	**231**	25g. green	85	60

232 Cement Works

1952. Construction of Concrete Works, Wierzbica.

756	**232**	3z. black	2·10	35
757	**232**	10z. red	2·50	35

233 Swimmers

1952. Sports Day.

758	**233**	30g.+15g. blue	4·25	1·10
759	-	45g.+15g. violet	1·50	20
760	-	1z.15 green	1·40	1·50
761	-	1z.20 red	80	80

DESIGNS: 45g. Footballers; 1z.15, Runners; 1z.20, High jumper.

234 Yachts

1952. Shipbuilders' Day.

762	**234**	30g.+15g. green	3·25	70
763	-	45g.+15g. blue	70	25
764	-	90g. plum	70	1·25

DESIGNS—VERT: 45g. Full-rigged cadet ship "Dar Pomorza"; 90g. "Brygada Makowskiego" (freighter) under construction.

235 Young Workers

1952. Youth Festival, Warsaw.

765	**235**	30g.+15g. green	40	25
766	-	45g.+15g. red	70	15
767	-	90g. brown	40	35

DESIGNS—HORIZ: 45g. Girl and boy students; 90g. Boy bugler.

236 "New Constitution"

1952. Adoption of New Constitution.

768	**236**	45g.+15g. green & brown	1·10	15
769	**236**	3z. violet and brown	40	35

237 L. Warynski

1952. 70th Anniv of Party "Proletariat".

770	**237**	30g.+15g. red	55	15
771	**237**	45g.+15g. brown	55	15

238 Jaworzno Power Station

1952. Electricity Power Station, Jaworzno.

772	**238**	45g.+15g. red	70	10
773	**238**	1z. black	65	50
774	**238**	1z.50 green	65	20

239 Frydman

1952. Pleniny Mountain Resorts.

775	**239**	45g.+15g. purple	55	10
776	-	60g. green (Grywald)	35	45
777	-	1z. red (Niedzica)	1·00	15

240 Pilot and Glider

1952. Aviation Day.

778	**240**	30g.+15g. green	1·25	10
779	-	45g.+15g. red	2·00	70
780	-	90g. blue	35	35

DESIGNS: 45g. Pilot and Yakovlev Yak-18U; 90g. Parachutists descending.

241 Avicenna

1952. Birth Millenary of Avicenna (Arab physician).

781	**241**	75g. red	35	25

242 Victor Hugo

1952. 150th Birth Anniv of Victor Hugo (French author).

782	**242**	90g. brown	35	25

243 Shipbuilding

1952. Gdansk Shipyards.

783	**243**	5g. green	15	10
784	**243**	15g. red	15	10

244 H. Sienkiewicz (author)

1952

785	**244**	45g.+15g. brown	35	15

245 Assault on Winter Palace, Petrograd

1952. 35th Anniv of Russian Revolution. Perf or Imperf.

786	**245**	45g.+15g. red	90	20
787	**245**	60g. brown	35	30

246 Lenin

1952. Polish–Soviet Friendship Month.

788	**246**	30g.+15g. purple	35	15
789	**246**	45g.+15g. brown	70	30

247 Miner

1952. Miners' Day.

790	**247**	45g.+15g. black	20	10
791	**247**	1z.20+15g. brown	70	35

248 H. Wieniawski (violinist)

1952. 2nd Wieniawski Int Violin Competition.

792	**248**	30g.+15g. green	1·00	60
793	**248**	45g.+15g. violet	2·75	55

249 Car Factory, Zeran

1952

794	**249**	45g.+15g. green	20	10
795	**249**	1z.15 brown	70	35
800	-	30g.+15g. blue	30	10
801	-	60g.+20g. purple	30	10

DESIGN: 30, 60g. Lorry factory, Lublin.

250 Dove of Peace

1952. Peace Congress, Vienna.

796	**250**	30g. green	75	30
797	**250**	60g. blue	1·40	45

251 Soldier and Flag

1952. 10th Anniv of Battle of Stalingrad.

798	**251**	60g. red and green	5·00	1·60
799	**251**	80g. red and grey	65	50

253 Karl Marx

1953. 70th Death Anniv of Marx.

802	**253**	60g. blue	20·00	11·50
803	**253**	80g. brown	1·10	45

254 Globe and Flag

1953. Labour Day.

804	**254**	60g. red	5·75	3·75
805	**254**	80g. red	45	15

255 Cyclists and Arms of Warsaw

1953. 6th International Peace Cycle Race.

806	-	80g. green	85	40
807	**255**	80g. brown	85	40
808	-	80g. red	13·50	9·25

DESIGNS: As Type **255**, but Arms of Berlin (No. 806) or Prague (No. 808).

256 Boxer

1953. European Boxing Championship, Warsaw. Inscr "17-24. V. 1953".

809	**256**	40g. lake	1·00	45
810	**256**	80g. orange	10·00	4·75
811	-	95g. purple	85	60

DESIGN: 95g. Boxers in ring.

257 Copernicus (after Matejko)

1953. 480th Birth Anniv of Copernicus (astronomer).

812	**257**	20g. brown	1·75	40
813	-	80g. blue	13·50	13·50

DESIGN—VERT: 80g. Copernicus and diagram.

258 "Dalmor" (trawler)

1953. Merchant Navy Day.

814	**258**	80g. green	1·60	10
815	-	1z.35 blue	1·60	3·25

DESIGN: 1z.35, "Czech" (freighter).

259 Warsaw Market-place

1953. Polish National Day.

816	**259**	20g. lake	25	20
817	**259**	2z.35 blue	4·25	3·25

260 Students' Badge

1953. 3rd World Students' Congress, Warsaw. Inscr "III SWIATOWY KONGRESS STUDENTOW". (a) Postage. Perf.

818	-	40g. brown	15	15
819	**260**	1z.35 green	70	15
820	-	1z.50 blue	2·50	2·75

(b) Air. Imperf.

821	**260**	55g. plum	1·75	60
822	**260**	75g. red	90	1·60

DESIGNS—HORIZ: 40g. Students and globe. VERT: 1z.50, Woman and dove.

261 Nurse Feeding Baby

1953. Social Health Service.

823	**261**	80g. red	8·75	5·25
824	-	1z.75 green	40	40

DESIGN: 1z.75, Nurse, mother and baby.

262 M. Kalinowski

1953. 10th Anniv of Polish People's Army.

825	**262**	45g. brown	3·75	3·00
826	-	80g. red	80	10
827	-	1z.75 olive	80	10

DESIGNS—HORIZ: 80g. Russian and Polish soldiers. VERT: 1z.75, R. Pazinski.

263 Jan Kochanowski (poet)

1953. "Renaissance" Commemoration. Inscr "ROK ODRODZENIA".

828	**263**	20g. brown	15	10
829	-	80g. purple	60	10
830	-	1z.35 blue	2·75	1·75

DESIGNS—HORIZ: 80g. Wawel Castle. VERT: 1z.35, Mikolaj Rej (writer).

264 Palace of Science and Culture

1953. Reconstruction of Warsaw. Inscr "WARSZAWA".

831	**264**	80g. red	9·75	1·50
832	-	1z.75 blue	1·90	45
833	-	2z. purple	5·00	3·50

DESIGNS: 1z.75, Constitution Square; 2z. Old City Market, Warsaw.

265 Dunajec Canyon, Pieniny Mountains

1953. Tourist Series.

834		20g. lake and blue	10	10
835		80g. lilac and green	3·25	1·50
836	**265**	1z.75 green and brown	70	10
837	-	2z. black and red	1·10	10

DESIGNS—HORIZ: 20g. Krynica Spa; 2z. Clechocinek Spa. VERT: 80g. Morskie Oko Lake, Tatra Mountains.

266 Skiing

1953. Winter Sports.

838		80g. blue	1·50	40
839	**266**	95g. green	1·25	40
840	-	2z.85 red	4·00	2·10

DESIGNS—VERT: 80g. Ice-skating; 2z.85, Ice-hockey.

267 Infants playing

1953. Children's Education.

841	**267**	10g. violet	60	15
842	-	80g. red	90	30
843	-	1z.50 green	6·00	2·25

DESIGNS: 80g. Girls and school; 1z.50, Two Schoolgirls writing.

268 Class EP 02 Electric Locomotive

1954. Electrification of Railways.

844		60g. blue	8·00	4·75
845	**268**	80g. brown	90	25

DESIGN: 60g. Class EW54 electric commuter train.

269 Mill Girl

1954. International Women's Day.

846	**269**	20g. green	2·45	1·50
847	-	40g. blue	60	10
848	-	80g. brown	60	10

DESIGNS: 40g. Postwoman; 80g. Woman driving tractor.

270 Flags and Mayflowers

1954. Labour Day.

849	**270**	40g. brown	70	40
850	**270**	60g. blue	70	25
851	**270**	80g. red	70	25

271 "Warsaw–Berlin–Prague"

1954. 7th International Peace Cycle Race. Inscr "2-17 MAJ 1954".

852	**271**	80g. brown	80	25
853	-	80g. blue (Dove and cycle wheel)	80	25

272 Symbols of Labour

1954. 3rd Trades' Union Congress, Warsaw.

854	**272**	25g. blue	1·25	1·10
855	**272**	80g. lake	40	25

272a Postal Coach and Plane

1954. Air. 3rd Polish Philatelic Society Congress. Sheet 57×76 mm.

MS855a	272a	5z.+(2z.50) green	26·00	21·00

273 Glider and Flags

1954. International Gliding Competition.

856	-	45g. green	65	15
857	273	60g. violet	1·90	70
858	273	60g. brown	1·25	15
859a	-	1z.35 blue	2·00	25

DESIGNS: 45g. Glider and clouds in frame; 1z.35, Glider and sky.

274 Paczkow

1954. Air. Inscr "POCZTA LOTNICZA".

860	274	60g. green	25	10
861	-	80g. red	35	10
862	-	1z.15 black	1·75	1·60
863	-	1z.50 red	80	10
864	-	1z.55 blue	80	10
865	-	1z.95 brown	1·00	10

DESIGNS—Ilyushin Il-12 airplane over: 80g. Market-place, Kazimierz Dolny; 1z.15, Wawel Castle, Cracow; 1z.50, Town Hall, Wroclaw; 1z.55, Lazienki Palace, Warsaw; 1z.95, Cracow Tower, Lublin.

275 Fencing

1954. 2nd Spartacist Games (1st issue). Inscr "II OGOLNOPOLSKA SPARTAKIADA".

866	275	25g. purple	1·25	50
867	-	60g. turquoise	1·25	35
868	-	1z. blue	2·40	70

DESIGNS—VERT: 60g. Gymnastics. HORIZ: 1z. Running.

276 Spartacist Games Badge

1954. 2nd Spartacist Games (2nd issue).

869	276	60g. brown	1·10	35
870	276	1z.55 grey	1·10	60

277 Battlefield

1954. 10th Anniv of Liberation and Battle of Studzianki.

871	277	60g. green	1·60	40
872	-	1z. blue	5·50	3·00

DESIGN—HORIZ: 1z. Soldier, airman and tank.

278 Steel Works

1954. 10th Anniv of Second Republic.

873		10g. sepia and brown	65	10
874		20g. green and red	35	10
876	278	25g. black and buff	1·00	45
877	-	40g. brown and yellow	45	15
878	-	45g. purple and mauve	45	15
880	-	60g. purple and green	40	25
881	-	1z.15 black and turquoise	6·00	15
882	-	1z.40 brown and orange	12·50	2·50
883	-	1z.55 blue and indigo	2·50	65
884	-	2z.10 blue and cobalt	3·50	1·25

DESIGNS: 10g. Coal mine; 20g. Soldier and flag; 40g. Worker on holiday; 45g. House-builders; 60g. Tractor and binder; 1z.15, Lublin Castle; 1z.40, Customers in bookshop; 1z.55, "Soldek" (freighter) alongside wharf; 2z.10, Battle of Lenino.

279 Steam Train and Signal

1954. Railway Workers' Day.

885	279	40g. blue	3·00	60
886	-	60g. black	2·50	75

DESIGN: 60g. Steam night express.

280 Picking Apples

1954. Polish–Russian Friendship.

887	280	40g. violet	1·60	1·10
888	280	60g. black	70	25

281 Elblag

1954. 500th Anniv of Return of Pomerania to Poland.

889	281	20g. red on blue	1·40	70
890	-	45g. brown on yellow	15	10
891	-	60g. green on yellow	20	10
892	-	1z.40 blue on pink	50	10
893	-	1z.55 brown on cream	70	10

VIEWS: 45g. Gdansk; 60g. Torun; 1z.40, Malbork; 1z.55, Olsztyn.

282 Chopin and Grand Piano

1954. 5th International Chopin Piano Competition, Warsaw (1st issue).

894	282	45g. brown	25	10
895	282	60g. green	60	10
896	282	1z. blue	1·75	80

See also Nos. 906/7.

283 Battle Scene

1954. 160th Anniv of Kosciuszko's Insurrection.

897	283	40g. olive	45	10
898	-	60g. brown	60	10
899	-	1z.40 black	1·50	95

DESIGNS: 60g. Kosciuszko on horseback, with insurgents; 1z.40, Street battle.

284 European Bison

1954. Protected Animals.

900	284	45g. brown and green	35	10
901	-	60g. brown and green	35	10
902	-	1z.90 brown and blue	70	10
903	-	3z. brown and turquoise	1·10	55

ANIMALS: 60g. Elk; 1z.90, Chamois; 3z. Eurasian beaver.

285 "The Liberator"

1955. 10th Anniv of Liberation of Warsaw.

904	285	40g. brown	1·60	70
905	-	60g. blue	1·60	45

DESIGN: 60g. "Spirit of Poland".

286 Bust of Chopin (after L. Isler)

1955. 5th International Chopin Piano Competition (2nd issue).

906	286	40g. brown	55	25
907	286	60g. blue	1·60	80

287 Mickiewicz Monument

1955. Warsaw Monuments.

908	-	5g. green on yellow	20	10
909	-	10g. purple on yellow	20	10
910	-	15g. black on green	20	10
911	-	20g. blue on pink	20	10
912	-	40g. violet on lilac	60	10
913	-	45g. brown on orange	1·25	25
914	287	60g. blue on grey	20	10
915	-	1z.55 green on grey	1·90	25

MONUMENTS: 5g. "Siren"; 10g. Dzerzhinski Statue; 15g. King Sigismund III Statue; 20g. "Brotherhood in Arms"; 40g. Copernicus; 45g. Marie Curie Statue; 1z.55, Kilinski Statue.

288 Flags and Tower

1955. 10th Anniv of Russo-Polish Treaty of Friendship.

916	288	40g. red	35	10
917	288	40g. brown	85	55
918	-	60g. brown	35	10
919	-	60g. turquoise	35	10

DESIGN: 60g. Statue of "Friendship".

289

1955. 8th International Peace Cycle Race.

920	289	40g. brown	45	25
921	-	60g. blue	25	10

DESIGN: 60g. "VIII" and doves.

290 Town Hall, Poznan

1955. 24th International Fair, Poznan.

922	290	40g. blue	25	25
923	290	60g. red	10	10

291 Festival Emblem

1955. Cracow Festival.

924	291	20g. multicoloured	35	10
925	-	40g. multicoloured	10	10
926	291	60g. multicoloured	70	25

No. 925 is as T **291** but horiz and inscr "FESTIWAL SZTUKI", etc.

1955. 6th Polish Philatelic Exhibition, Poznan. Two sheets 50×70 mm as T 290.

MS926a	2z.+(1z.) black and green	4·25	2·40
MS926b	3z.+(1z.50) black and red	21·00	12·50

292 "Peace"

1955. 5th International Youth Festival, Warsaw.

927	-	25g. brown, pink & yellow	25	10
928	-	40g. grey and blue	25	10
929	-	45g. red, mauve and yellow	45	10
930	292	60g. ultramarine and blue	35	10
931	-	60g. black and orange	35	10
932	292	1z. purple and blue	80	80

DESIGNS: 25, 45g. Pansies and dove; 40, 60g. (No. 931) Dove and tower.

293 Motor Cyclists

1955. 13th International Tatra Mountains Motor Cycle Race.

933	293	40g. brown	25	25
934	293	60g. green	10	10

294 Stalin Palace of Culture and Science, Warsaw

1955. Polish National Day.

935	294	60g. blue	10	10
936	294	60g. grey	10	10

937	294	75g. green	55	25
938	294	75g. brown	55	25

295 Athletes

1955. 2nd International Games. Imperf or perf.

939	295	20g. brown	10	10
940	-	40g. purple	15	10
941	-	60g. blue	25	10
942	-	1z. red	45	10
943	-	1z.35 lilac	55	10
944	-	1z.55 green	1·10	80

DESIGNS—VERT: 40g. Throwing the hammer; 1z. Netball; 1z.35, Sculling; 1z.55, Swimming. HORIZ: 60g. Stadium.

1955. International Philatelic Exhibition, Warsaw. Two sheets 61×84 mm. Imperf.

MS944a	1z.+(1z.) As No. 929	4·50	3·25
MS944b	2z.+(1z.) As No. 932	23·00	20·00

296 Szczecin

1955. 10th Anniv of Return of Western Territories.

945	296	25g. green	10	10
946	-	40g. red (Wroclaw)	25	10
947	-	60g. blue (Zielona Gora)	55	10
948	-	95g. black (Opole)	1·50	60

297 Peasants and Flag

1955. 50th Anniv of 1905 Revolution.

949	297	40g. brown	55	45
950	297	60g. red	25	25

298 Mickiewicz **299** Statue

1955. Death Cent of Adam Mickiewicz (poet).

951	298	20g. brown	20	10
952	299	40g. brown and orange	20	10
953	-	60g. brown and green	25	10
954	-	95g. black and red	1·40	45

DESIGNS—As Type **299**: 60g. Sculptured head; 95g. Statue.

300 Teacher and Pupil

1955. 50th Anniv of Polish Teachers' Union.

955	300	40g. brown	1·60	35
956	-	60g. blue	2·75	80

DESIGN: 60g. Open book and lamp.

301 Rook and Hands

1956. 1st World Chess Championship for the Deaf and Dumb, Zakopane.

957	301	40g. red	2·25	80
958	-	60g. blue	1·40	10

DESIGN: 60g. Knight and hands.

302 Ice Skates

1956. 11th World Students' Winter Sports Championship.

959	302	20g. black and blue	3·25	1·60
960	-	40g. blue and green	80	10
961	-	60g. red and mauve	80	10

DESIGNS: 40g. Ice-hockey sticks and puck; 60g. Skis and ski sticks.

303 Officer and "Kilinski" (freighter)

1956. Merchant Navy.

962	303	5g. green	15	10
963	-	10g. red	20	10
964	-	20g. blue	25	10
965	-	45g. brown	90	55
966	-	60g. blue	55	10

DESIGNS: 10g. Tug and barges; 20g. "Pokoj" (freighter) in dock; 45g. Building "Marceii Nowatka" (freighter); 60g. "Fryderyk Chopin" (freighter) and "Radunia" (trawler).

304 Racing Cyclist

1956. 9th International Peace Cycle Race.

967	304	40g. blue	1·10	70
968	304	60g. green	20	10

305 Lodge, Tatra Mountains

1956. Tourist Propaganda.

969	305	30g. green	10	10
970	-	40g. brown	10	10
971	-	60g. blue	1·60	60
972	-	1z.15 purple	55	10

DESIGNS: 40g. Compass, rucksack and map; 60g. Canoe and map; 1z.15, Skis and mountains.

1956. No. 829 surch.

973	10g. on 80g. purple	70	35
974	40g. on 80g. purple	45	10
975	60g. on 80g. purple	45	10
976	1z.35 on 80g. purple	2·25	1·00

307 Ghetto Heroes' Monument

1956. Warsaw Monuments.

977	307	30g. black	10	10
978	-	40g. brown on green	70	35
979	-	1z.55 purple on pink	55	10

STATUES: 40g. Statue of King Jan III Sobieski; 1z.55, Statue of Prince Joseph Poniatowski.

308 "Economic Co-operation"

1956. Russo-Polish Friendship Month.

980		40g. brown and pink	45	35
981	308	60g. red and bistre	25	10

DESIGN: 40g. Polish and Russian dancers.

309 Ludwika Wawrzynska (teacher)

1956. Ludwika Wawrzynska Commemoration.

982	309	40g. brown	95	1·50
983	309	60g. blue	35	10

310 "Lady with a Weasel" (Leonardo da Vinci)

1956. International Campaign for Museums.

984	-	40g. green	2·25	1·40
985	-	60g. violet	95	10
986	310	1z.55 brown	1·90	25

DESIGNS: 40g. Niobe (bust); 60g. Madonna (Vit Stvosz).

310a Music Quotation and Profiles of Chopin and Liszt

1956. Stamp Day. Sheet 55×75 mm.

MS986a	**310a** 4z. (+2z.) green	18·00	18·00

311 Honey Bee and Hive

1956. 50th Death Anniv of Jan Dzierzon (apiarist).

987	311	40g. brown on yellow	1·10	25
988	-	60g. brown on yellow	25	10

DESIGN: 60g. Dr. J. Dzierzon.

312 Fencing

1956. Olympic Games. Inscr "MELBOURNE 1956".

989	312	10g. brown and grey	20	10
990	-	20g. lilac and brown	25	10
991	-	25g. black and blue	70	25
992	-	40g. brown and green	35	10
993	-	60g. brown and red	60	10
994	-	1z.55 brown and violet	2·75	1·10
995	-	1z.55 brown and orange	1·25	35

DESIGNS: No. 990, Boxing; 991, Rowing; 992, Steeplechase; 993, Javelin throwing; 994, Gymnastics; 995, Long jumping (Elizabeth Dunska-krzesinska's gold medal).

313 15th-century Postman

1956. Re-opening of Postal Museum, Wroclaw.

996	313	60g. black on blue	3·00	2·75

314 Snow Crystals and Skier of 1907

1957. 50 Years of Skiing in Poland.

997	314	40g. blue	20	10
998	-	60g. green	20	10
999	-	1z. purple	45	35

DESIGNS (with snow crystals)—VERT: 60g. Skier jumping. HORIZ: 1z. Skier standing.

315 Apple Tree and Globe

1957. U.N.O. Commemoration.

1000	315	5g. red and turquoise	25	10
1001	-	15g. blue and grey	45	10
1002	-	40g. green and grey	80	60
MS1002a		55×70 mm. 1z.50 blue and green	15·00	15·00

DESIGNS—VERT: 15g. U.N.O. emblem; 40g. 1z.50, U.N.O. Headquarters, New York.

316 Skier

1957. 12th Death Annivs of Bronislaw Czech and Hanna Marusarzowna (skiers).

1003	316	60g. brown	90	35
1004	316	60g. blue	45	10

317 Winged Letter

1957. Air. 7th Polish National Philatelic Exhibition, Warsaw.

1005	317	4z.+2z. blue	3·00	3·00
MS1005a		55×75 mm. 4z.+2z. blue (T **317**)	7·00	6·25

318 Foil, Sword and Sabre on Map

1957. World Youth Fencing Championships, Warsaw.

1006	318	40g. purple	45	10
1007	-	60g. red	20	10
1008	-	60g. blue	20	10

DESIGNS: Nos. 1007/8 are arranged in se-tenant pairs in the sheet and together show two fencers duelling.

319 Dr. S. Petrycy (philosopher)

1957. Polish Doctors.

1009	319	10g. brown and blue	10	10
1010	-	20g. lake and green	10	10
1011	-	40g. black and red	10	10
1012	-	60g. purple and blue	45	25
1013	-	1z. blue and yellow	20	10
1014	-	1z.35 brown and green	15	10
1015	-	2z.50 violet and red	35	10
1016	-	3z. brown and violet	45	10

PORTRAITS: 20g. Dr. W. Oczko; 40g. Dr. J. Sniadecki; 60g. Dr. T. Chalubinski; 1z. Dr. W. Bieganski; 1z.35, Dr. J. Dietl; 2z.50, Dr. B. Dybowski; 3z. Dr. H. Jordan.

320 Cycle Wheel and Flower

1957. 10th International Peace Cycle Race.

1017	**320**	60g. blue	25	10
1018	-	1z.50 red (Cyclist)	45	25

321 Fair Emblem

1957. 26th International Fair, Poznan.

1019	**321**	60g. blue	25	25
1020	**321**	2z.50 green	25	25

322 Carline Thistle

1957. Wild Flowers.

1021	**322**	60g. yellow, green & grey	35	10
1022	-	60g. green and blue	35	10
1023	-	60g. olive and grey	35	10
1024	-	60g. purple and green	60	35
1025	-	60g. purple and green	35	10

FLOWERS—VERT: No. 1022, Sea holly; 1023, Edelweiss; 1024, Lady's slipper orchid; 1025, Turk's cap lily.

323 Fireman

1957. International Fire Brigades Conference, Warsaw. Inscr "KONGRES C.T.I.F. WARSZAWA 1957".

1026	**323**	40g. black and red	10	10
1027	-	60g. green and red	10	10
1028	-	2z.50 violet and red	25	10

DESIGNS: 60g. Flames enveloping child; 2z.50, Ear of corn in flames.

324 Town Hall, Leipzig

1957. 4th Int Trade Union Congress, Leipzig.

1029	**324**	60g. violet	25	10

325 "The Letter" (after Fragonard)

1957. Stamp Day.

1030	**325**	2z.50 green	60	10

326 Red Banner

1957. 40th Anniv of Russian Revolution.

1031	**326**	60g. red and blue	10	10
1032	-	2z.50 brown and black	25	10

DESIGN: 2z.50, Lenin Monument, Poronin.

327 Karol Libelt (founder)

1957. Centenary of Poznan Scientific Society.

1033	**327**	60g. red	25	10

328 H. Wieniawski (violinist)

1957. 3rd Wieniawski Int Violin Competition.

1034	**328**	2z.50 blue	35	15

329 Ilyushin Il-14P over Steel Works

1957. Air.

1035	**329**	90g. black and pink	15	10
1036	-	1z.50 brown and salmon	15	10
1037	-	3z.40 sepia and buff	45	10
1038	-	3z.90 brown and yellow	90	60
1039	-	4z. blue and green	45	10
1039a	-	5z. lake and lavender	55	10
1039b	-	10z. brown and turquoise	90	35
1040	-	15z. violet and blue	1·50	45
1040a	-	20z. violet and yellow	1·60	80
1040b	-	30z. olive and buff	2·75	1·10
1040c	-	50z. blue and drab	8·25	1·10

DESIGNS—Ilyushin Il-14P over: 1z.50, Castle Square, Warsaw; 3z.40, Market, Cracow; 3z.90, Szczecin; 4z. Karkonosze Mountains; 5z. Old Market, Gdansk; 10z. Liw Castle; 15z. Lublin; 20z. Cable railway, Kasprowy Wierch; 30z. Porabka Dam; 50z. "Batory" (liner).

For stamp as No. 1039b, but printed in purple only, see No. 1095.

330a J. A. Komensky (Comenius)

1957. 300th Anniv of Publication of Komensky's "Opera Didactica Omnia".

1041	**330a**	2z.50 red	35	10

331 A. Strug

1957. 20th Death Anniv of Andrzej Strug (writer).

1042	**331**	2z.50 brown	35	10

332 Joseph Conrad and Full-rigged Sailing Ship "Torrens"

1957. Birth Centenary of Joseph Conrad (Korzeniowski) (author).

1043	**332**	60g. brown on green	10	10
1044	**332**	2z.50 blue on pink	50	10

333 Postman of 1558

1958. 400th Anniv of Polish Postal Service (1st issue).

1045	**333**	2z.50 purple and blue	35	10

For similar stamps see Nos. 1063/7.

334 Town Hall, Biecz

1958. Ancient Polish Town Halls.

1046	**334**	20g. green	10	10
1047	-	40g. brown (Wroclaw)	10	10
1048	-	60g. blue (Tarnow) (horiz)	10	10
1049	-	2z.10 lake (Gdansk)	15	10
1050	-	2z.50 violet (Zamosc)	55	35

335 Zander

1958. Fishes.

1051	**335**	40g. yellow, black & blue	15	10
1052	-	60g. blue, indigo & green	25	10
1053	-	2z.10 multicoloured	45	10
1054	-	2z.50 green, black & violet	1·50	45
1055	-	6z.40 multicoloured	45	45

DESIGNS—VERT: 60g. Atlantic salmon; 2z.10, Northern pike; 2z.50, Brown trout. HORIZ 6z.40, European grayling.

336 Warsaw University

1958. 140th Anniv of Warsaw University.

1056	**336**	2z.50 blue	35	10

337 Fair Emblem

1958. 27th International Fair, Poznan.

1057	**337**	2z.50 red and black	35	10

338

1958. 7th International Gliding Championships.

1058	**338**	60g. black and blue	10	10
1059	-	2z.50 black and grey	25	10

DESIGN: 2z.50, As Type **338** but design in reverse.

339 Armed Postman

1958. 19th Anniv of Defence of Gdansk Post Office.

1060	**339**	60g. blue	10	10

340 Polar Bear on Iceberg

1958. I.G.Y. Inscr as in T 340.

1061	**340**	60g. black	15	10
1062	-	2z.50 blue	70	10

DESIGN: 2z.50, Sputnik and track of rocket.

341 Tomb of Prosper Prowano (First Polish Postmaster)

1958. 400th Anniv of Polish Postal Service (2nd issue).

1063	**341**	40g. purple and blue	55	10
1064	-	60g. black and lilac	15	10
1065	-	95g. violet and yellow	15	10
1066	-	2z.10 blue and grey	80	45
1067	-	3z.40 brown & turquoise	55	35

DESIGNS: 60g. Mail coach and Church of Our Lady, Cracow; 95g. Mail coach (rear view); 2z.10, 16th-century postman; 3z.40, Kogge.

Nos. 1064/7 show various forms of modern transport in clear silhouette in the background.

342 Envelope, Quill and Postmark

1958. Stamp Day.

1068	**342**	60g. green, red and black	55	55

343 Partisans' Cross

1958. 15th Anniv of Polish People's Army. Polish decorations.

1069	**343**	40g. buff, black and green	15	10
1070	-	60g. multicoloured	15	10
1071	-	2z.50 multicoloured	55	25

DESIGNS: 60g. Virtuti Military Cross; 2z.50, Grunwald Cross.

344 "Mail Coach in the Kielce District" (after painting by A. Kedzierskiego)

1958. Polish Postal Service 400th Anniv Exhibition.

1072	**344**	2z.50 black on buff	90	1·10

345 Galleon

1958. 350th Anniv of Polish Emigration to America.

1073	**345**	60g. green	25	10
1074	-	2z.50 red (Polish emigrants)	45	55

346 UNESCO Headquarters, Paris

1958. Inauguration of UNESCO Headquarters Building, Paris.

1075	**346**	2z.50 black and green	70	55

347 S. Wyspianski (dramatist and painter)

1958. Famous Poles.

1076	**347**	60g. violet	10	10
1077	-	2z.50 green	25	35

PORTRAIT: 2z.50, S. Moniuszko (composer).

348 "Human Rights"

1958. 10th Anniv of Declaration of Human Rights.

1078	**348**	2z.50 lake and brown	60	10

348a Coach and Horses (after A. Kedzierski)

1958. 400th Anniv of Polish Postal Service. Sheet 86×76 mm.

MS1078a	**348a**	50z. blue	18·00	20·00

349 Party Flag

1958. 40th Anniv of Polish Communist Party.

1079	**349**	60g. red and purple	10	10

350 Yacht

1959. Sports.

1080	**350**	40g. ultramarine and blue	35	10
1081	-	60g. purple and salmon	35	10
1082	-	95g. purple and green	70	25
1083	-	2z. blue and green	35	10

DESIGNS: 60g. Archer; 95g. Footballers; 2z. Horseman.

351 The "Guiding Hand"

1959. 3rd Polish United Workers' Party Congress.

1084	**351**	40g. black, brown and red	10	10
1085	-	60g. multicoloured	10	10
1086	-	1z.55 multicoloured	45	25

DESIGNS—HORIZ: 60g. Hammer and ears of corn. VERT: 1z.55, Nowa Huta foundry.

352 Death Cap

1959. Mushrooms.

1087	**352**	20g. yellow, brown & green	2·25	10
1088	-	30g. multicoloured	25	10
1089	-	40g. multicoloured	55	10
1090	-	60g. multicoloured	55	10
1091	-	1z. multicoloured	80	10
1092	-	2z.50 brown, green & bl	1·10	25
1093	-	3z.40 multicoloured	1·25	35
1094	-	5z.60 brown, grn & yell	3·50	1·10

MUSHROOMS: 30g. Butter mushroom; 40g. Cep; 60g. Saffron milk cap; 1z. Chanterelle; 2z.50, Field mushroom; 3z.40, Fly agaric; 5z.60, Brown beech bolete.

1959. Air. 65 Years of Philately in Poland and 6th Polish Philatelic Assn Congress, Warsaw. As No. 1039b but in one colour only.

1095		10z. purple	3·25	3·75

353 "Storks" (after Chelmonski)

1959. Polish Paintings.

1096	**353**	40g. green	15	10
1097	-	60g. purple	35	10
1098	-	1z. black	35	10
1099	-	1z.50 brown	70	25
1100	-	6z.40 blue	3·25	1·10

PAINTINGS—VERT: 60g. "Motherhood" (Wyspianski); 1z. "Madame de Romanet" (Roda-kowski); 1z.50, "Death" (Maiczewski). HORIZ: 6z.40, "The Sandmen" (Gierymski).

354 Miner

1959. 3rd Int Miners' Congress, Katowice.

1101	**354**	2z.50 multicoloured	60	25

355 Sheaf of Wheat ("Agriculture")

1959. 15th Anniv of People's Republic.

1102	**355**	40g. green and black	10	10
1103	-	60g. red and black	10	10
1104	-	1z.50 blue and black	20	10

DESIGNS: 60g. Crane ("Building"); 1z.50, Corinthian column, and book ("Culture and Science").

356 Dr. L. Zamenhof

1959. International Esperanto Congress, Warsaw and Birth Centenary of Dr. Ludwig Zamenhof (inventor of Esperanto).

1105	**356**	60g. black & green on green	15	10
1106	-	1z.50 green, red and violet on grey	80	35

DESIGN: 1z.50, Esperanto Star and globe.

357 "Flowering Pink" (Map of Austria)

1959. 7th World Youth Festival, Vienna.

1107	**357**	60g. multicoloured	10	10
1108	**357**	2z.50 multicoloured	45	45

358

1959. 30th Anniv of Polish Airlines "LOT".

1109	**358**	60g. blue, violet and black	15	10

359 Parliament House, Warsaw

1959. 48th Inter-Parliamentary Union Conf, Warsaw.

1110	**359**	60g. green, red and black	10	10
1111	**359**	2z.50 purple, red & black	55	35

1959. Baltic States' International Philatelic Exhibition, Gdansk. No. 890 optd BALPEX I - GDANSK 1959.

1112		45g. brown on lemon	70	70

361 Dove and Globe

1959. 10th Anniv of World Peace Movement.

1113	**361**	60g. grey and blue	20	10

362 Nurse with Bag

1959. 40th Anniv of Polish Red Cross. Cross in red.

1114	**362**	40g. black and green	20	10
1115	-	60g. brown	20	10
1116	-	2z.50 black and red	90	45

DESIGNS—VERT: 60g. Nurse with bottle and bandages. SQUARE—23×23 mm: 2z.50, J. H. Dunant.

363 Emblem of Polish–Chinese Friendship Society

1959. Polish–Chinese Friendship.

1117	**363**	60g. multicoloured	45	10
1118	**363**	2z.50 multicoloured	25	10

364

1959. Stamp Day.

1119	**364**	60g. red, green & turq	15	10
1120	**364**	2z.50 blue, green and red	25	10

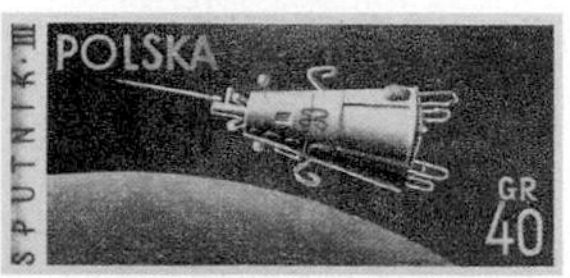

365 Sputnik "3"

1959. Cosmic Flights.

1121	**365**	40g. black and blue	15	10
1122	-	60g. black and lake	25	10
1123	-	2z.50 blue and green	1·10	60

DESIGNS: 60g. Rocket "Mieczta" encircling Sun; 2z.50, Moon rocket "Lunik 2".

366 Schoolgirl

1959. "1000 Schools for Polish Millennium". Inscr as in T 366.

1124	**366**	40g. brown and green	15	10
1125	-	60g. red, black and blue	15	10

DESIGN: 60g. Children going to school.

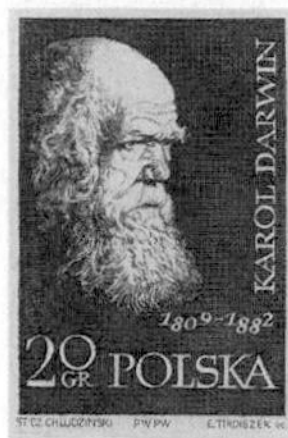

367 Darwin

1959. Famous Scientists.

1126	**367**	20g. blue	10	10
1127	-	40g. olive (Mendeleev)	10	10
1128	-	60g. purple (Einstein)	15	10
1129	-	1z.50 brown (Pasteur)	25	10
1130	-	1z.55 green (Newton)	55	10
1131	-	2z.50 violet (Copernicus)	90	70

368 Costumes of Rzeszow **369** Costumes of Rzeszow

1959. Provincial Costumes (1st series).

1132	**368**	20g. black and green	10	10
1133	**369**	20g. black and green	10	10
1134	-	60g. brown and pink	15	10
1135	-	60g. brown and pink	15	10
1136	-	1z. red and blue	15	10
1137	-	1z. red and blue	15	10

1138	-	2z.50 green and grey	35	10
1139	-	2z.50 green and grey	35	10
1140	-	5z.60 blue and yellow	1·40	55
1141	-	5z.60 blue and yellow	1·40	55

DESIGNS—Male and female costumes of: Nos. 1134/5, Kurpic; 1136/7, Silesia; 1138/9, Mountain regions; 1140/1, Szamotuly.

See also Nos. 1150/9.

370 Piano

1960. 150th Birth Anniv of Chopin and Chopin Music Competition, Warsaw.

1142	**370**	60g. black and violet	45	10
1143	-	1z.50 black, red and blue	70	10
1144	-	2z.50 brown	2·25	1·50

DESIGNS—As Type **370**: 1z.50, Portion of Chopin's music. 25×39½ mm: 2z.50, Portrait of Chopin.

371 Polish 10k. Stamp of 1860 and Postmark

1960. Stamp Centenary.

1145	**371**	40g. red, blue and black	15	10
1146	-	60g. blue, black and violet	25	10
1147	-	1z.35 blue, red and grey	70	45
1148	-	1z.55 red, black & green	80	35
1149	-	2z.50 green, black & ol	1·40	70

DESIGNS: 1z.35, Emblem inscr "1860 1960". Reproductions of Polish stamps: 60g. No. 356; 1z.55, No. 533; 2z.50, No. 1030. With appropriate postmarks.

1960. Provincial Costumes (2nd series). As T **368/69**.

1150	40g. red and blue	10	10
1151	40g. red and blue	10	10
1152	2z. blue and yellow	15	10
1153	2z. blue and yellow	15	10
1154	3z.10 turquoise and green	25	10
1155	3z.10 turquoise and green	25	10
1156	3z.40 brown and turquoise	35	25
1157	3z.40 brown and turquoise	35	25
1158	6z.50 violet and green	1·10	45
1159	6z.50 violet and green	1·10	45

DESIGNS—Male and female costumes of: Nos. 1150/1, Cracow; 1152/3, Lowicz; 1154/5, Kujawy; 1156/7, Lublin; 1158/9, Lubusz.

372 Throwing the Discus

1960. Olympic Games, Rome. Rings and inscr in black.

1160	60g. blue (T **372**)	15	10
1161	60g. mauve (Running)	15	10
1162	60g. violet (Cycling)	15	10
1163	60g. turq (Show jumping)	15	10
1164	2z.50 blue (Trumpeters)	70	35
1165	2z.50 brown (Boxing)	70	35
1166	2z.50 red (Olympic flame)	70	35
1167	2z.50 green (Long jump)	70	35

Stamps of the same value were issued together, se-tenant, forming composite designs illustrating a complete circuit of the stadium track.

373 King Wladislaw Jagiello's Tomb, Wawel Castle

1960. 550th Anniv of Battle of Grunwald.

1168	**373**	60g. brown	25	10
1169	-	90g. green	60	35
1170	-	2z.50 black	2·75	1·50

DESIGNS—As Type **373**: 90g. Proposed Grunwald Monument. HORIZ: 78×35½ mm: 2z.50, "Battle of Grunwald" (after Jan Matejko).

374 1860 Stamp and Postmark

1960. International Philatelic Exn, Warsaw.

1171	**374**	10z.+10z. red, black and blue	6·25	8·00

375 Lukasiewicz (inventor of petrol lamp)

1960. Lukasiewicz Commemoration and 5th Pharmaceutical Congress. Poznan.

1172	**375**	60g. black and yellow	15	10

376 "The Annunciation"

1960. Altar Wood Carvings of St. Mary's Church, Cracow, by Veit Stoss.

1173	**376**	20g. blue	25	10
1174	-	30g. brown	15	10
1175	-	40g. violet	25	10
1176	-	60g. green	25	10
1177	-	2z.50 red	1·10	25
1178	-	5z.60 brown	4·25	4·75
MS1178a		86×107 mm. 10z. black	8·00	6·50

DESIGNS: 30g. "The Nativity"; 40g. "Homage of the Three Kings"; 60g. "The Resurrection"; 2z.50, "The Ascension"; 5z.60, "The Descent of the Holy Ghost". VERT: (72×95 mm). 10z. The Assumption of the Virgin.

377 Paderewski

1960. Birth Centenary of Paderewski.

1179	**377**	2z.50 black	35	35

1960. Stamp Day. Optd DZIEN ZNACZKA 1960.

1180	**371**	40g. red, blue and black	1·25	70

379 Gniezno

1960. Old Polish Towns as T 379.

1181	5g. brown	10	10
1182	10g. green	10	10
1183	20g. brown	10	10
1184	40g. red	10	10
1185	50g. violet	10	10
1186	60g. lilac	10	10
1187	60g. blue	10	10
1188	80g. blue	15	10
1189	90g. brown	15	10
1190	95g. green	35	10
1191	1z. red and lilac	15	10
1192	1z.15 green and orange	35	10
1193	1z.35 mauve and green	15	10
1194	1z.50 brown and blue	35	10
1195	1z.55 lilac and yellow	35	10
1196	2z. blue and lilac	20	10
1197	2z.10 brown and yellow	20	10
1198	2z.50 violet and green	25	10
1199	3z.10 red and grey	35	35
1200	5z.60 grey and green	60	35

TOWNS: 10g. Cracow; 20g. Warsaw; 40g. Poznan; 50g. Plock; 60g. mauve, Kalisz; 60g. blue, Tczew; 80g. Frombork; 90g. Torum; 95g. Puck; 1z. Slupsk; 1z.15, Gdansk; 1z.35, Wroclaw; 1z.50, Szczecin; 1z.55, Opole; 2z. Kolobrzeg; 2z.10, Legnica; 2z.50, Katowice; 3z.10, Lodz; 5z.60, Walbrzych.

380 Great Bustard

1960. Birds. Multicoloured.

1201	10g. Type **380**	15	10
1202	20g. Common Raven	15	10
1203	30g. Great cormorant	15	10
1204	40g. Black stork	25	10
1205	50g. Eagle owl	55	10
1206	60g. White-tailed sea eagle	55	10
1207	75g. Golden eagle	55	10
1208	90g. Short-toed eagle	60	35
1209	2z.50 Rock thrush	3·25	1·60
1210	4z. River kingfisher	2·75	1·10
1211	5z.60 Wallcreeper	4·50	1·25
1212	6z.50 European roller	6·50	3·00

381 Front page of Newspaper "Proletaryat" (1883)

1961. 300th Anniv of Polish Newspaper Press.

1213	-	40g. green, blue and black	55	25
1214	**381**	60g. yellow, red and black	55	25
1215	-	2z.50 blue, violet & black	3·25	2·75

DESIGNS—Newspaper front page: 40g. "Mercuriusz" (first issue, 1661); 2z.50, "Rzeczpospolita" (1944).

382 Ice Hockey

1961. 1st Winter Military Spartakiad.

1216	**382**	40g. black, yellow & lilac	35	10
1217	-	60g. multicoloured	95	15
1218	-	1z. multicoloured	5·25	2·75
1219	-	1z.50 black, yell & turq	90	35

DESIGNS: 60g. Ski jumping; 1z. Rifle-shooting; 1z.50, Slalom.

383 Congress Emblem

1961. 4th Polish Engineers' Conference.

1220	**383**	60g. black and red	15	10

384 Yuri Gagarin

1961. World's 1st Manned Space Flight.

1221	**384**	40g. black, red and brown	60	10
1222	-	60g. red, black and blue	60	35

DESIGN: 60g. Globe and star.

385 Fair Emblem

1961. 30th International Fair, Poznan.

1223	**385**	40g. black, red and blue	10	10
1224	**385**	1z.50 black, blue and red	25	10

See also No. **MS**1245a.

386 King Mieszko I

1961. Famous Poles (1st issue).

1225	**386**	60g. black and blue	10	10
1226	-	60g. black and red	10	10
1227	-	60g. black and green	10	10
1228	-	60g. black and violet	80	25
1229	-	60g. black and brown	10	10
1230	-	60g. black and olive	10	10

PORTRAITS: No. 1226, King Casimire the Great; 1227, King Casmir Jagiellon; 1228, Copernicus; 1229, A. F. Modrzewski; 1230, Kosciuszko.

See also Nos. 1301/6 and 1398/1401.

387 "Leskov" (trawler support ship)

1961. Shipbuilding Industry. Multicoloured.

1231	60g. Type **387**	25	10
1232	1z.55 "Severodvinsk" (depot ship)	35	10
1233	2z.50 "Rambutan" (coaster)	60	35
1234	3z.40 "Krynica" (freighter)	90	45
1235	4z. "B 54" freighter	1·25	70
1236	5z.60 "Bavsk" (tanker)	4·25	1·90

SIZES: 2z.50, As Type **387**; 5z.60, 108×21 mm; Rest, 81×21 mm.

388 Posthorn and Telephone Dial

1961. Communications Ministers' Conference, Warsaw.

1237	**388**	40g. red, green and blue	10	10
1238	-	60g. violet, yellow & purple	15	10
1239	-	2z.50 ultram, blue & bis	55	10
MS1239a		108×66 mm. Nos. 1237/9 (sold at 5z.)	5·25	3·25

DESIGNS: 60g. Posthorn and radar screen; 2z.50, Posthorn and conference emblem.

389 Opole Seal

1961. Polish Western Provinces.

No.	Description	Unused	Used
1240	40g. brown on buff	15	10
1241	40g. brown on buff	15	10
1242	60g. violet on pink	15	10
1243	60g. violet on pink	15	10
1243a	95g. green on blue	25	25
1243b	95g. green on blue	25	25
1244	2z.50 sage on green	45	25
1245	2z.50 sage on green	45	25

DESIGNS—VERT: No. 1240, Type **389**; 1242, Henry IV's tomb; 1243a, Seal of Conrad II; 1244, Prince Barnim's seal. HORIZ: No. 1241, Opole cement works; 1243, Wroclaw apartment-house; 1243b, Factory interior, Zielona Gora; 1245, Szczecin harbour.

See also Nos. 1308/13.

1961. "Intermess II" Stamp Exhibition. Sheet 121×51 mm containing pair of No. 1224 but imperf.

No.	Description	Unused	Used
MS1245a	1z.50 (×2) (sold at 4z.50+2z.50)	5·50	3·50

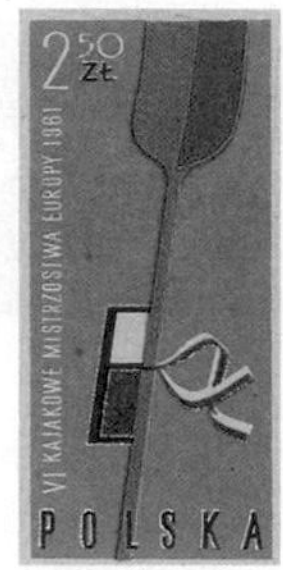

390 Beribboned Paddle

1961. 6th European Canoeing Championships. Multicoloured.

No.	Description	Unused	Used
1246	40g. Two canoes within letter "E" (horiz)	15	10
1247	60g. Two four-seater canoes at finishing post (horiz)	15	10
1248	2z.50 Type **390**	1·25	60

391 Titov and Orbit within Star

1961. 2nd Russian Manned Space Flight.

No.	Type	Description	Unused	Used
1249	391	40g. black, red and pink	45	10
1250	-	60g. blue and black	45	10

DESIGN: 60g. Dove and spaceman's orbit around globe.

392 Monument

1961. 40th Anniv of 3rd Silesian Uprising.

No.	Type	Description	Unused	Used
1251	392	60g. grey and green	10	10
1252	-	1z.55 grey and blue	25	10

DESIGN: 1z.55, Cross of Silesian uprisers.

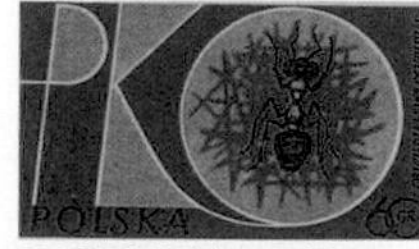

393 P.K.O. Emblem and Ant

1961. Savings Month.

No.	Type	Description	Unused	Used
1253		40g. red, yellow and black	15	10
1254	393	60g. brown, yellow & black	15	10
1255	-	60g. blue, violet and pink	15	10
1256	-	60g. green, red and black	15	10
1257	-	2z.50 mauve, grey & black	2·25	1·25

DESIGNS: No. 1253, Savings Bank motif; 1255, Bee; 1256, Squirrel; 1257, Savings Bank book.

394 "Mail Cart" (after J. Chelmonski)

1961. Stamp Day and 40th Anniv of Postal Museum.

No.	Type	Description	Unused	Used
1258	394	60g. brown	25	10
1259	394	60g. green	25	10

395 Congress Emblem

1961. 5th W.F.T.U. Congress, Moscow.

No.	Type	Description	Unused	Used
1260	395	60g. black	15	10

396 Emblem of Kopasyni Mining Family, 1284

1961. Millenary of Polish Mining Industry.

No.	Type	Description	Unused	Used
1261	396	40g. purple and orange	15	10
1262	-	60g. grey and blue	15	10
1263	-	2z.50 green and black	55	25

DESIGNS: 60g. 14th-century seal of Bytom; 2z.50, Emblem of Int Mine Constructors' Congress, Warsaw, 1958.

397 Child and Syringe

1961. 15th Anniv of UNICEF.

No.	Type	Description	Unused	Used
1264	397	40g. black and blue	10	10
1265	-	60g. black and orange	10	10
1266	-	2z.50 black and turquoise	60	25

DESIGNS—HORIZ: 60g. Children of three races. VERT: 2z.50, Mother and child, and feeding bottle.

398 Cogwheel and Wheat

1961. 15th Economic Co-operative Council Meeting, Warsaw.

No.	Type	Description	Unused	Used
1267	398	40g. red, yellow and blue	15	10
1268	-	60g. red, blue & ultram	15	10

DESIGN: 60g. Oil pipeline map, E. Europe.

399 Caterpillar-hunter

1961. Insects. Multicoloured.

No.	Description	Unused	Used
1269	20g. Type **399**	15	10
1270	30g. Violet ground beetle	15	10
1271	40g. Alpine longhorn beetle	15	10
1272	50g. "Cerambyx cerdo" (long-horn beetle)	15	10
1273	60g. "Carabus auronitens" (ground beetle)	15	10
1274	80g. Stag beetle	25	10
1275	1z.15 Clouded apollo (butterfly)	55	10
1276	1z.35 Death's-head hawk moth	35	10
1277	1z.50 Scarce swallowtail (butterfly)	60	10
1278	1z.55 Apollo (butterfly)	60	10
1279	2z.50 Red wood ant	1·10	45
1280	5z.60 White-tailed bumble bee	5·75	3·50

Nos. 1275/80 are square, 36½×36½ mm.

400 Worker with Flag and Dove

1962. 20th Anniv of Polish Workers' Coalition.

No.	Type	Description	Unused	Used
1281	400	60g. brown, black and red	10	10
1282	-	60g. bistre, black and red	10	10
1283	-	60g. blue, black and red	10	10
1284	-	60g. grey, black and red	10	10
1285	-	60g. blue, black and red	10	10

DESIGNS: No. 1282, Steersman; 1283, Worker with hammer; 1284, Soldier with weapon; 1285, Worker with trowel and rifle.

401 Two Skiers Racing

1962. F.I.S. Int Ski Championships, Zakopane.

No.	Type	Description	Unused	Used
1286	401	40g. blue, grey and red	10	10
1287	401	40g. blue, brown and red	90	25
1288	-	60g. blue, grey and red	20	10
1289	-	60g. blue, brown and red	1·10	60
1290	-	1z.50 blue, grey and red	35	10
1291	-	1z.50 violet, grey and red	1·75	60
MS1291a		67×80 mm. 10z. (+5z.) blue, grey and red	4·25	4·00

DESIGNS—HORIZ: 60g. Skier racing. VERT: 1z.50, Ski jumper; 10z. F.I.S. emblem.

402 Majdanek Monument

1962. Concentration Camp Monuments.

No.	Type	Description	Unused	Used
1292		40g. blue	10	10
1293	402	60g. black	25	10
1294	-	1z.50 violet	35	15

DESIGNS—VERT: (20×31 mm): 40g. Broken carnations and portion of prison clothing (Auschwitz camp); 1z.50, Treblinka monument.

403 Racing Cyclist

1962. 15th International Peace Cycle Race.

No.	Type	Description	Unused	Used
1295	403	60g. black and blue	25	10
1296	-	2z.50 black and yellow	55	10
1297	-	3z.40 black and violet	90	45

DESIGNS—74½×22 mm: 2z.50, Cyclists & "XV". As Type **403**: 3z.40, Arms of Berlin, Prague and Warsaw, and cycle wheel.

405 Lenin Walking

1962. 50th Anniv of Lenin's Sojourn in Poland.

No.	Type	Description	Unused	Used
1298	405	40g. green and light green	45	10
1299	-	60g. lake and pink	15	10
1300	-	2z.50 brown and yellow	45	10

DESIGNS: 60g. Lenin; 2z.50, Lenin wearing cap, and St. Mary's Church, Cracow.

1962. Famous Poles (2nd issue). As T 386.

No.	Description	Unused	Used
1301	60g. black and green	10	10
1302	60g. black and brown	10	10
1303	60g. black and blue	40	10
1304	60g. black and bistre	10	10
1305	60g. black and purple	10	10
1306	60g. black and turquoise	10	10

PORTRAITS: No. 1301, A. Mickiewicz (poet); 1302, J. Slowacki (poet); 1303, F. Chopin (composer); 1304, R. Traugutt (patriot); 1305, J. Dabrowski (revolutionary); 1306, Maria Konopnicka (poet).

406 Gen. K. Swierczewski-Walter (monument)

1962. 15th Death Anniv of Gen. K. Swierczewski-Walter (patriot).

No.	Type	Description	Unused	Used
1307	406	60g. black	15	10

1962. Polish Northern Provinces. As T 389.

No.	Description	Unused	Used
1308	60g. blue and grey	10	10
1309	60g. blue and grey	10	10
1310	1z.55 brown and yellow	20	10
1311	1z.55 brown and yellow	20	10
1312	2z.50 slate and grey	55	35
1313	2z.50 slate and grey	55	35

DESIGNS—VERT: No. 1308, Princess Elizabeth's seal; 1310, Gdansk Governor's seal; 1312, Frombork Cathedral. HORIZ: No. 1309, Insulators factory, Szczecinek; 1311, Gdansk shipyard; 1313, Laboratory of Agricultural College, Kortowo.

407 "Crocus scepusiensis" (Borb)

1962. Polish Protected Plants. Plants in natural colours.

No.	Type	Description	Unused	Used
1314	407	60g. yellow	15	10
1315	A	60g. brown	70	35
1316	B	60g. pink	15	10
1317	C	90g. green	25	10
1318	D	90g. olive	25	10
1319	E	90g. green	25	10
1320	F	1z.50 blue	35	10
1321	G	1z.50 green	45	10
1322	H	1z.50 turquoise	35	10
1323	I	2z.50 green	80	55
1324	J	2z.50 turquoise	80	55
1325	K	2z.50 blue	1·10	55

PLANTS: A, "Platanthera bifolia" (Rich); B, "Aconitum callibotryon" (Rchb.); C, "Gentiana clusii" (Perr. et Song); D, "Dictamnus albus" (L.); E, "Nymphaca alba" (L.); F, "Daphne mezereum" (L.); G, "Pulsatilla vulgaris" (Mill.); H, "Anemone silvestris" (L.); I, "Trollius europaeus" (L.); J, "Galanthus nivalis" (L.); K, "Adonis vernalis" (L.).

408 "The Poison Well", after J. Malczewski

1962. F.I.P. Day ("Federation Internationale de Philatelie").

1326	**408**	60g. black on cream	25	25

409 Pole Vault

1962. 7th European Athletic Championships, Belgrade. Multicoloured.

1327	40g. Type **409**	10	10
1328	60g. 400 m relay	10	10
1329	90g. Throwing the javelin	10	10
1330	1z. Hurdling	10	10
1331	1z.50 High-jumping	10	10
1332	1z.55 Throwing the discus	10	10
1333	2z.50 100 m final	45	10
1334	3z.40 Throwing the hammer	95	35

410 "Anopheles sp."

1962. Malaria Eradication.

1335	**410**	60g. brown and turquoise	10	10
1336	-	1z.50 multicoloured	15	10
1337	-	2z.50 multicoloured	60	25
MS1337a		60×81 mm. 3z. multicoloured	1·25	45

DESIGNS: 1z.50, Malaria parasites in blood; 2z.50, Cinchona plant; 3z. Anopheles mosquito.

411 Cosmonauts "in flight"

1962. 1st "Team" Manned Space Flight.

1338	**411**	60g. green, black & violet	15	10
1339	-	2z.50 red, black and turquoise	45	25
MS1339a		70×94 mm. 10z. red, black and blue	2·75	2·00

DESIGN: 2z.50, Two stars (representing space-ships) in orbit.

412 "A Moment of Determination" (after painting by A. Kamienski)

1962. Stamp Day.

1340	**412**	60g. black	10	10
1341	**412**	2z.50 brown	55	20

413 Mazovian Princes' Mansion, Warsaw

1962. 25th Anniv of Polish Democratic Party.

1342	**413**	60g. black on red	15	10

414 Cruiser "Aurora"

1962. 45th Anniv of Russian Revolution.

1343	**414**	60g. blue and red	15	10

415 J. Korczak (bust after Dunikowski)

1962. 20th Death Anniv of Janusz Korczak (child educator).

1344	**415**	40g. sepia, bistre & brn	15	10
1345	-	60g. multicoloured	35	10
1346	-	90g. multicoloured	35	10
1347	-	1z. multicoloured	35	10
1348	-	2z.50 multicoloured	70	10
1349	-	5z.60 multicoloured	2·40	90

DESIGNS: 60g. to 5z.60, Illustrations from Korczak's children's books.

416 Old Town, Warsaw

1962. 5th T.U. Congress, Warsaw.

1350	**416**	3z.40 multicoloured	70	25

417 Master Buncombe

1962. Maria Konopnicka's Fairy Tale "The Dwarfs and Orphan Mary". Multicoloured.

1351	40g. Type **417**	45	10
1352	60g. Lardie the Fox and Master Buncombe	1·40	1·00
1353	1z.50 Bluey the Frog making music	55	10
1354	1z.55 Peter's kitchen	55	25
1355	2z.50 Saraband's concert in Nightingale Valley	70	70
1356	3z.40 Orphan Mary and Subearthy	2·25	1·60

418 R. Traugutt (insurgent leader)

1963. Centenary of January (1863) Rising.

1357	**418**	60g. black, pink & turq	15	10

419 Tractor and Wheat

1963. Freedom from Hunger. Multicoloured.

1358	40g. Type **419**	15	10
1359	60g. Millet and hoeing	80	25
1360	2z.50 Rice and mechanical harvester	70	35

420 Cocker Spaniel

1963. Dogs.

1361	**420**	20g. red, black and lilac	10	10
1362	-	30g. black and red	10	10
1363	-	40g. ochre, black and lilac	25	10
1364	-	50g. ochre, black and blue	25	10
1365	-	60g. black and blue	25	10
1366	-	1z. black and green	70	25
1367	-	2z.50 brown, yell & blk	1·10	45
1368	-	3z.40 black and red	2·50	1·25
1369	-	6z.50 black and yellow	3·00	4·25

DOGS—HORIZ: 30g. Sheep-dog; 40g. Boxer; 2z.50, Gundog "Ogar"; 6z.50, Great Dane. VERT: 50g. Airedale terrier; 60g. French bulldog; 1z. French poodle; 3z.40, Podhale sheep-dog.

421 Egyptian Galley (15th century B.C.)

1963. Sailing Ships (1st series).

1370	**421**	5g. brown on bistre	10	10
1371	-	10g. turquoise on green	10	10
1372	-	20g. blue on grey	10	10
1373	-	30g. black on olive	10	10
1374	-	40g. blue on blue	10	10
1375	-	60g. purple on brown	15	10
1376	-	1z. black on blue	15	10
1377	-	1z.15 green on pink	30	10

SHIPS: 10g. Phoenician merchantman (15th cent B.C.); 20g. Greek trireme (5th cent B.C.); 30g. Roman merchantman (3rd cent A.D.); 40g. "Mora" (Norman ship, 1066); 60g. Hanse kogge (14th cent); 1z. Hulk (16th cent); 1z.15, Carrack (15th cent).

See also Nos. 1451/66.

422 Insurgent

1963. 20th Anniv of Warsaw Ghetto Uprising.

1378	**422**	2z.50 brown and blue	30	10

423 Centenary Emblem

1963. Red Cross Centenary.

1379	**423**	2z.50 red, blue and yellow	65	20

424 Lizard

1963. Protected Reptiles and Amphibians. Reptiles in natural colours: inscr in black: background colours given.

1380	**424**	30g. green	10	10
1381	-	40g. olive	10	10
1382	-	50g. brown	10	10
1383	-	60g. grey	10	10
1384	-	90g. green	10	10
1385	-	1z.15 grey	10	10
1386	-	1z.35 blue	10	10
1387	-	1z.50 turquoise	30	15
1388	-	1z.55 pale blue	30	10
1389	-	2z.50 lavender	30	20
1390	-	3z. green	75	20
1391	-	3z.40 purple	1·90	1·90

DESIGNS: 40g. Copperhead (snake); 50g. Marsh tortoise; 60g. Grass snake; 90g. Blindworm; 1z.15, Tree toad; 1z.35, Mountain newt; 1z.50, Crested newt; 1z.55, Green toad; 2z.50, "Bombina" toad; 3z. Salamander; 3z.40, "Natterjack" (toad).

425 Epee, Foil, Sabre and Knight's Helmet

1963. World Fencing Championships, Gdansk.

1392	**425**	20g. yellow and brown	10	10
1393	-	40g. light blue and blue	10	10
1394	-	60g. vermilion and red	10	10
1395	-	1z.15 light green & green	10	10
1396	-	1z.55 red and violet	35	10
1397	-	6z.50 yellow, pur & bis	1·25	60
MS1397a		110×93 mm. Nos. 1393/6	30·00	30·00

DESIGNS—HORIZ: Fencers with background of: 40g. Knights jousting; 60g. Dragoons in sword-fight; 1z.15, 18th-century duellists; 1z.55, Old Gdansk. VERT: 6z.50, Inscription and Arms of Gdansk.

1963. Famous Poles (3rd issue). As T 386.

1398	60g. black and brown	10	10
1399	60g. black and brown	10	10
1400	60g. black and turquoise	10	10
1401	60g. black and green	10	10

PORTRAITS: No. 1398, L. Warynski (patriot); 1399, L. Krzywicki (economist); 1400, M. Sklodowska-Curie (scientist); 1401, K. Swierczewski (patriot).

426 Bykovsky and "Vostok 5"

1963. 2nd "Team" Manned Space Flights.

1402	**426**	40g. black, green and blue	10	10
1403	-	60g. black, blue and green	10	10
1404	-	6z.50 multicoloured	90	30

DESIGNS: 60g. Tereshkova and "Vostok 6"; 6z.50, "Vostoks 5 and 6" in orbit.

427 Basketball

1963. 13th European (Men's) Basketball Championships, Wroclaw.

1405	**427**	40g. multicoloured	10	10
1406	-	50g. green, black and pink	10	10
1407	-	60g. black, green and red	10	10
1408	-	90g. multicoloured	10	10
1409	-	2z.50 multicoloured	20	10

1410	-	5z.60 multicoloured	1·50	40

MS1410a 76×86 mm. 10z. (+5z.) multicoloured 2·25 1·10

DESIGNS: 50g. to 2z.50, As Type **427** but with ball, players and hands in various positions; 5z.60, Hands placing ball in net; 10z. Town Hall, People's Hall and Arms of Wroclaw.

428 Missile

1963. 20th Anniv of Polish People's Army. Multicoloured.

1411		20g. Type **428**	10	10
1412		40g. "Blyskawica" (destroyer)	10	10
1413		60g. PZL-106 Kruk (airplane)	10	10
1414		1z.15 Radar scanner	10	10
1415		1z.35 Tank	10	10
1416		1z.55 Missile carrier	10	10
1417		2z.50 Amphibious troop carrier	10	10
1418		3z. Ancient warrior, modern soldier and two swords	30	20

429 "A Love Letter" (after Czachorski)

1963. Stamp Day.

1419	**429**	60g. brown	20	10

1963. Visit of Soviet Cosmonauts to Poland. Nos. 1402/4 optd 23-28. X. 1963 and w Polsce together with Cosmonauts' names.

1420	**426**	40g. black, green and blue	20	10
1421	-	60g. black, blue and green	30	10
1422	-	6z.50 multicoloured	1·40	75

431 Tsiolkovsky's Rocket and Formula

1963. "The Conquest of Space". Inscr in black.

1423	**431**	30g. turquoise	10	10
1424	-	40g. olive	10	10
1425	-	50g. violet	10	10
1426	-	60g. brown	10	10
1427	-	1z. turquoise	10	10
1428	-	1z.50 red	10	10
1429	-	1z.55 blue	10	10
1430	-	2z.50 purple	10	10
1431	-	5z.60 green	65	30
1432	-	6z.50 turquoise	1·10	30

MS1432a 78×106 mm. Nos. 1431/2 (two of each) 30·00 30·00

DESIGNS: 40g. "Sputnik 1"; 50g. "Explorer 1"; 60g. Banner carried by "Lunik 2"; 1z. "Lunik 3"; 1z.50, "Vostok 1"; 1z.55, "Friendship 7"; 2z.50, "Vostoks 3 and 4"; 5z.60, "Mariner 2"; 6z.50, "Mars 1".

432 Mazurian Horses

1963. Polish Horse-breeding. Multicoloured.

1433		20g. Arab stallion "Comet"	15	10
1434		30g. Wild horses	15	10
1435		40g. Sokolski horse	20	10
1436		50g. Arab mares and foals	20	10
1437		60g. Type **432**	20	10
1438		90g. Steeplechasers	45	10
1439		1z.55 Arab stallion "Witez II"	80	10
1440		2z.50 Head of Arab horse (facing right)	1·50	10
1441		4z. Mixed breeds	3·75	60
1442		6z.50 Head of Arab horse (facing left)	5·25	2·40

SIZES—TRIANGULAR (55×27½ mm): 20, 30, 40g. HORIZ: (75×26 mm): 50, 90g., 4z. VERT: as Type **432**: 1z.55, 2z.50, 6z.50.

433 Ice Hockey

1964. Winter Olympic Games, Innsbruck. Mult.

1443		20g. Type **433**	10	10
1444		30g. Slalom	10	10
1445		40g. Downhill skiing	10	10
1446		60g. Speed skating	10	10
1447		1z. Ski-jumping	10	10
1448		2z.50 Tobogganing	10	10
1449		5z.60 Cross-country skiing	75	60
1450		6z.50 Pairs, figure skating	1·50	80

MS1450a 110×94 mm. Nos. 1448 and 1450 (two of each) 23·00 23·00

1964. Sailing Ships (2nd series). As T 421 but without coloured backgrounds. Some new designs.

1451	**421**	5g. brown	10	10
1452	-	10g. green	10	10
1453	-	20g. blue	10	10
1454	-	30g. bronze	10	10
1455	-	40g. blue	10	10
1456	-	60g. purple	10	10
1457	-	1z. brown	15	10
1458	-	1z.15 brown	15	10
1459	-	1z.35 blue	15	10
1460	-	1z.50 purple	15	10
1461	-	1z.55 black	15	10
1462	-	2z. violet	15	10
1463	-	2z.10 green	15	10
1464	-	2z.50 mauve	20	10
1465	-	3z. olive	30	10
1466	-	3z.40 brown	30	10

SHIPS—HORIZ: 10g. to 1z.15, As Nos. 1370/7; 1z.50, "Ark Royal" (English galleon, 1587); 2z.10, Ship of the line (18th cent); 2z.50, Sail frigate (19th cent); 3z. "Flying Cloud" (clipper, 19th cent). VERT: 1z.35, Columbus's "Santa Maria"; 1z.55, "Wodnik" (Polish warship, 17th cent); 2z. Dutch fleute (17th cent); 3z.40, "Dar Pomorza" (cadet ship).

434 "Flourishing Tree"

1964. 20th Anniv of People's Republic (1st issue).

1467	**434**	60g. multicoloured	10	10
1468		60g. black, yellow and red	10	10

DESIGN: No. 1468, Emblem composed of symbols of agriculture and industry.

See also Nos. 1497/1506.

435 European Cat

1964. Domestic Cats. As T 435.

1469		30g. black and yellow	15	10
1470		40g. multicoloured	15	10
1471		50g. black, turquoise & yellow	15	10
1472		60g. multicoloured	35	10
1473		90g. multicoloured	30	10
1474		1z.35 multicoloured	30	10
1475		1z.55 multicoloured	50	10
1476		2z.50 yellow, black and violet	80	45
1477		3z.40 multicoloured	1·90	80
1478		6z.50 multicoloured	3·75	1·90

CATS—European: 30, 40, 60g., 1z.55, 2z.50, 6z.50. Siamese: 50g. Persian: 90g., 1z.35, 3z.40.

Nos. 1472/5 are horiz.

436 Casimir the Great (founder)

1964. 600th Anniv of Jagiellonian University, Cracow.

1479	**436**	40g. purple	10	10
1480	-	40g. green	10	10
1481	-	60g. violet	10	10
1482	-	60g. blue	10	10
1483	-	2z.50 sepia	65	10

PORTRAITS: No. 1480, Hugo Kollataj (educationist and politician); 1481, Jan Dlugosz (geographer and historian); 1482, Copernicus (astronomer); 1483 (36×37 mm), King Wladislaw Jagiello and Queen Jadwiga.

437 Northern Lapwing

1964. Birds. Multicoloured.

1484		30g. Type **437**	15	10
1485		40g. Bluethroat	15	10
1486		50g. Black-tailed godwit	15	10
1487		60g. Osprey (vert)	20	10
1488		90g. Grey heron (vert)	30	10
1489		1z.35 Little gull (vert)	45	10
1490		1z.55 Common shoveler	45	10
1491		5z.60 Black-throated diver	95	30
1492		6z.50 Great crested grebe	1·40	65

438 Red Flag on Brick Wall

1964. 4th Polish United Workers' Party Congress, Warsaw. Inscr "PZPR". Multicoloured.

1493		60g. Type **438**	10	10
1494		60g. Beribboned hammer	10	10
1495		60g. Hands reaching for Red Flag	10	10
1496		60g. Hammer and corn emblems	10	10

439 Factory and Cogwheel

440 Gdansk Shipyard

1964. 20th Anniv of People's Republic (2nd issue).

1497	**439**	60g. black and blue	10	10
1498	-	60g. black and green	10	10
1499	-	60g. red and orange	10	10
1500	-	60g. blue and grey	10	10
1501	**440**	60g. blue and green	10	10
1502	-	60g. violet and mauve	10	10
1503	-	60g. brown and violet	10	10
1504	-	60g. bronze and green	10	10
1505	-	60g. purple and red	10	10
1506	-	60g. brown and yellow	10	10

DESIGNS—As Type **439**: No. 1498, Tractor and ear of wheat; 1499, Mask and symbols of the arts; 1500, Atomic symbol and book. As Type **440**: No. 1502, Lenin Foundry, Nowa Huta; 1503, Cement Works, Chelm; 1504, Turoszow power station; 1505, Petro-chemical plant, Plock; 1506, Tarnobrzeg sulphur mine.

441 Battle Scene

1964. 20th Anniv of Warsaw Insurrection.

1507	**441**	60g. multicoloured	10	10

442 Relay-racing

1964. Olympic Games, Tokyo. Multicoloured.

1508		20g. Triple-jumping	10	10
1509		40g. Rowing	10	10
1510		60g. Weightlifting	10	10
1511		90g. Type **442**	10	10
1512		1z. Boxing	10	10
1513		2z.50 Football	30	10
1514		5z.60 High jumping (women)	90	30
1515		6z.50 High-diving	1·40	45

MS1515a 83×111 mm. Nos. 1514/15 (two of each) 30·00 23·00

MS1515b 79×106 mm. 2z.50 Rifle-shooting, 2z.50 Canoeing, 5z. Fencing, 5z. Basketball 3·50 1·50

SIZES: DIAMOND—20g. to 60g. SQUARE—90g. to 2z.50. VERT: (23½×36 mm)—5z.60, 6z.50.

443 Congress Emblem

1964. 15th Int Astronautical Congress, Warsaw.

1516	**443**	2z.50 black and violet	35	10

444 Hand holding Hammer

1964. 3rd Congress of Fighters for Freedom and Democracy Association, Warsaw.

1517	**444**	60g. red, black and green	10	10

445 S. Zeromski

1964. Birth Cent of Stefan Zeromski (writer).

1518	**445**	60g. brown	10	10

446 Globe and Red Flag

1964. Centenary of "First International".

1519	**446**	60g. black and red	10	10

447 18th-century Stage Coach (after Brodowski)

1964. Stamp Day.

1520	**447**	60g. green	20	10
1521	**447**	60g. brown	20	10

448 Eleanor Roosevelt

1964. 80th Birth Anniv of Eleanor Roosevelt.

1522	**448**	2z.50 brown	20	10

449 Battle of Studzianki (after S. Zoltowski)

1964. "Poland's Struggle" (World War II) (1st issue).

1523	-	40g. black	10	10
1524	-	40g. violet	10	10
1525	-	60g. blue	10	10
1526	-	60g. green	10	10
1527	**449**	60g. bronze	10	10

DESIGNS—VERT: No. 1523, Virtuti Militari Cross; 1524, Westerplatte Memorial, Gdansk; 1525, Bydogoszez Memorial. HORIZ: No. 1526, Soldiers crossing the Oder (after S. Zoltowski).

See also Nos. 1610/12.

449a W. Komarov

1964. Russian Three-manned Space Flight. Sheet 114×63 mm depicting crew.

MS1527a	60g. black and red (T **449a**); 60g. black and green (Feoktistov); 60g. black and blue (Yegorov)	95	50

450 Cyclamen

1964. Garden Flowers. Multicoloured.

1528	20g. Type **450**	10	10
1529	30g. Freesia	10	10
1530	40g. Rose	10	10
1531	50g. Peony	10	10
1532	60g. Lily	10	10
1533	90g. Poppy	10	10
1534	1z.35 Tulip	10	10
1535	1z.50 Narcissus	65	30
1536	1z.55 Begonia	20	10
1537	2z.50 Carnation	45	10
1538	3z.40 Iris	75	30
1539	5z.60 Japanese camelia	1·25	60

Nos. 1534/9 are smaller, 26½×37 mm.

451 Spacecraft of the Future

1964. Space Research. Multicoloured.

1540	20g. Type **451**	10	10
1541	30g. Launching rocket	10	10
1542	40g. Dog "Laika" and rocket	10	10
1543	60g. "Lunik 3" and Moon	10	10
1544	1z.55 Satelite	10	10
1545	2z.50 "Elektron 2"	35	10
1546	5z.60 "Mars 1"	50	10
1547	6z.50+2z. Gagarin seated in capsule	3·50	30

452 "Siren of Warsaw"

1965. 20th Anniv of Liberation of Warsaw.

1548	**452**	60g. green	10	10

453 Edaphosaurus

1965. Prehistoric Animals (1st series). Mult.

1549	20g. Type **453**	10	10
1550	30g. Cryptocleidus (vert)	10	10
1551	40g. Brontosaurus	10	10
1552	60g. Mesosaurus (vert)	10	10
1553	90g. Stegosaurus	10	10
1554	1z.15 Brachiosaurus (vert)	10	10
1555	1z.35 Styracosaurus	20	10
1556	3z.40 Corythosaurus (vert)	50	10
1557	5z.60 Rhamphorhynchus (vert)	1·40	45
1558	6z.50 Tyrannosaurus	1·90	1·10

See also Nos. 1639/47.

454 Petro-chemical Works, Plock, and Polish and Soviet Flags

1965. 20th Anniv of Polish–Soviet Friendship Treaty. Multicoloured.

1559	60g. Seal (vert, 27×38½ mm)	10	10
1560	60g. Type **454**	10	10

455 Polish Eagle and Civic Arms

1965. 20th Anniv of Return of Western and Northern Territories to Poland.

1561	**455**	60g. red	10	10

456 Dove of Peace

1965. 20th Anniv of Victory.

1562	**456**	60g. red and black	10	10

457 I.T.U. Emblem

1965. Centenary of I.T.U.

1563	**457**	2z.50 black, violet & blue	45	10

458 Clover-leaf Emblem and "The Friend of the People" (journal)

1965. 70th Anniv of Peasant Movement. Mult.

1564	40g. Type **458**	10	10
1565	60g. Ears of corn and industrial plant (horiz)	10	10

459 "Dragon" Dinghies

1965. World Finn Sailing Championships, Gdynia. Multicoloured.

1566	30g. Type **459**	10	10
1567	40g. "5.5 m." dinghies	10	10
1568	50g. "Finn" dinghies (horiz)	10	10
1569	60g. "V" dinghies	10	10
1570	1z.35 "Cadet" dinghies (horiz)	20	10
1571	4z. "Star" yachts (horiz)	65	35
1572	5z.60 "Flying Dutchman" dinghies	1·25	60
1573	6z.50 "Amethyst" dinghies (horiz)	1·90	65
MS1573a	79×59 mm. 15z. Finn dinghies	1·75	1·10

460 Marx and Lenin

1965. Postal Ministers' Congress, Peking.

1574	**460**	60g. black on red	10	10

461 17th-cent Arms of Warsaw

1965. 700th Anniv of Warsaw.

1575	**461**	5g. red	10	10
1576	-	10g. green	10	10
1577	-	20g. blue	10	10
1578	-	40g. brown	10	10
1579	-	60g. orange	10	10
1580	-	1z.50 black	10	10
1581	-	1z.55 blue	10	10
1582	-	2z.50 purple	10	10
MS1583		51×62 mm. 3z.40 black and bistre	75	50

DESIGNS—VERT: 10g. 13th-cent antiquities. HORIZ: 20g. Tombstone of last Masovian dukes; 40g. Old Town Hall; 60g. Barbican; 1z.50, Arsenal; 1z.55, National Theatre; 2z.50, Staszic Palace; 3z.40, T **462**.

463 I.Q.S.Y. Emblem

1965. International Quiet Sun Year. Multicoloured. Background colours given.

1584	**463**	60g. blue	10	10
1585	**463**	60g. violet	10	10
1586	-	2z.50 red	30	10
1587	-	2z.50 brown	30	10
1588	-	3z.40 orange	45	10
1589	-	3z.40 olive	45	10

DESIGNS: 2z.50, Solar scanner; 3z.40, Solar System.

464 "Odontoglossum grande"

1965. Orchids. Multicoloured.

1590	20g. Type **464**	10	10
1591	30g. "Cypripedium hibridum"	10	10
1592	40g. "Lycaste skinneri"	10	10
1593	50g. "Cattleya warzewicza"	10	10
1594	60g. "Vanda sanderiana"	10	10
1595	1z.35 "Cypripedium hibridum" (different)	30	10
1596	4z. "Sobralia"	45	30
1597	5z.60 "Disa grandiflora"	1·25	45
1598	6z.50 "Cattleya labiata"	1·90	50

465 Weightlifting

1965. Olympic Games, Tokyo. Polish Medal Winners. Multicoloured.

1599	30g. Type **465**	10	10
1600	40g. Boxing	10	10
1601	50g. Relay-racing	10	10
1602	60g. Fencing	10	10
1603	90g. Hurdling (women's 80 m)	10	10
1604	3z.40 Relay-racing (women's)	45	10
1605	6z.50 "Hop, step and jump"	90	60
1606	7z.10 Volleyball (women's)	1·25	45

466 "The Post Coach" (after P. Michalowski)

1965. Stamp Day.

1607	**466**	60g. brown	20	10
1608	-	2z.50 green	30	10

DESIGN: 2z.50, "Coach about to leave" (after P. Michalowski).

467 U.N. Emblem

1965. 20th Anniv of U.N.O.

1609	**467**	2z.50 blue	30	10

468 Memorial, Holy Cross Mountains

1965. "Poland's Struggle" (World War II) (2nd issue).

1610	**468**	60g. brown	10	10
1611	-	60g. green	10	10
1612	-	60g. brown	10	10

DESIGNS—VERT: No. 1611, Memorial Plaszow. HORIZ: No. 1612, Memorial, Chelm-on-Ner.

469 Wolf

1965. Forest Animals. Multicoloured.

1613		20g. Type **469**	10	10
1614		30g. Lynx	10	10
1615		40g. Red fox	10	10
1616		50g. Eurasian badger	10	10
1617		60g. Brown bear	10	10
1618		1z.50 Wild boar	35	10
1619		2z.50 Red deer	35	10
1620		5z.60 European bison	90	30
1621		7z.10 Elk	1·50	50

470 Gig

1965. Horse-drawn Carriages in Lancut Museum. Multicoloured.

1622		20g. Type **470**	10	10
1623		40g. Coupe	10	10
1624		50g. Ladies' "basket" (trap)	10	10
1625		60g. "Vis-a-vis"	10	10
1626		90g. Cab	10	10
1627		1z.15 Berlinka	15	10
1628		2z.50 Hunting brake	45	10
1629		6z.50 Barouche	1·25	30
1630		7z.10 English brake	1·75	50

Nos. 1627/9 are 77×22 mm and No. 1630 is 104×22 mm.

471 Congress Emblem and Industrial Products

1966. 5th Polish Technicians' Congress, Katowice.

1631	**471**	60g. multicoloured	10	10

1966. 20th Anniv of Industrial Nationalization. Designs similar to T 471. Multicoloured.

1632		60g. Pithead gear (vert)	10	10
1633		60g. "Henryk Jedza" (freighter)	10	10
1634		60g. Petro-chemical works, Plock	10	10
1635		60g. Combine-harvester	10	10
1636		60g. Class EN 57 electric train	10	10
1637		60g. Exhibition Hall, 35th Poznan Fair	10	10
1638		60g. Crane (vert)	10	10

1966. Prehistoric Animals (2nd series). As T 453. Multicoloured.

1639		20g. Terror fish	10	10
1640		30g. Lobefin	10	10
1641		40g. Ichthyostega	10	10
1642		50g. Mastodonsaurus	10	10
1643		60g. Cynognathus	10	10
1644		2z.50 Archaeopteryx (vert)	10	10
1645		3z.40 Brontotherium	60	10
1646		6z.50 Machairodus	90	45
1647		7z.10 Mammuthus	2·10	50

472 H. Sienkiewicz (novelist)

1966. 50th Death Anniv of Henryk Sienkiewicz.

1648	**472**	60g. black on buff	10	10

473 Footballers (Montevideo, 1930)

1966. World Cup Football Championship. (a) Football scenes representing World Cup finals.

1649		20g. Type **473**	10	10
1650		40g. Rome, 1934	10	10
1651		60g. Paris, 1938	10	10
1652		90g. Rio de Janeiro, 1950	10	10
1653		1z.50 Berne, 1954	60	10
1654		3z.40 Stockholm, 1958	60	10
1655		6z.50 Santiago, 1962	1·25	10
1656		7z.10 "London", 1966 (elimination match, Glasgow, 1965)	1·75	35

(b) 61×81 mm.

MS1657	**474**	13z.50+1z.50	2·40	1·40

475 Soldier with Flag, and Dove of Peace

1966. 21st Anniv of Victory Day.

1658	**475**	60g. red and black on silver	10	10

476 Women's Relay-racing

477

1966. 8th European Athletic Championships, Budapest. Multicoloured.

1659		20g. Runner starting race (vert)	10	10
1660		40g. Type **476**	10	10
1661		60g. Throwing the javelin (vert)	10	10
1662		90g. Women's hurdles	10	10
1663		1z.35 Throwing the discus (vert)	10	10
1664		3z.40 Finish of race	45	10
1665		6z.50 Throwing the hammer (vert)	75	35
1666		7z.10 High-jumping	1·10	60
MS1667	**477**	110×66 mm. 5z. Imperf	2·40	1·25

478 White Eagle

1966. Polish Millenary (1st issue). Each red and black on gold.

1668		60g. Type **478**	10	10
1669		60g. Polish flag	10	10
1670		2z.50 Type **478**	10	10
1671		2z.50 Polish flag	10	10

See also Nos. 1717/18.

479 Flowers and Produce

1966. Harvest Festival. Multicoloured.

1672		40g. Type **479**	20	10
1673		60g. Woman and loaf	20	10
1674		3z.40 Festival bouquet	50	35

The 3z.40 is 49×48 mm.

480 Chrysanthemum

1966. Flowers. Multicoloured.

1675		10g. Type **480**	10	10
1676		20g. Poinsettia	10	10
1677		30g. Centaury	10	10
1678		40g. Rose	10	10
1679		60g. Zinnia	10	10
1680		90g. Nasturtium	10	10
1681		5z.60 Dahlia	90	30
1682		6z.50 Sunflower	80	45
1683		7z.10 Magnolia	1·90	50

481 Tourist Map

1966. Tourism.

1684	**481**	10g. red	10	10
1685	-	20g. olive	10	10
1686	-	40g. blue	10	10
1687	-	60g. brown	10	10
1688	-	60g. black	10	10
1689	-	1z.15 green	15	10
1690	-	1z.35 red	10	10
1691	-	1z.55 violet	10	10
1692	-	2z. green	40	10

DESIGNS: 20g. Hela Lighthouse; 40g. Yacht; 60g. (No. 1687), Poniatowski Bridge, Warsaw; 60g. (No. 1688), Mining Academy, Kielee; 1z.15, Dunajee Gorge; 1z.35, Old oaks, Rogalin; 1z.55, Silesian Planetarium; 2z. "Batory" (liner).

482 Roman Capital

1966. Polish Culture Congress.

1693	**482**	60g. red and brown	10	10

483 Stable-man with Percherons

1966. Stamp Day.

1694	**483**	60g. brown	10	10
1695	-	2z.50 green	10	10

DESIGN: 2z.50, Stablemen with horses and dogs.

484 Soldier in Action

1966. 30th Anniv of Jaroslav Dabrowski Brigade.

1696	**484**	60g. black, green and red	10	10

485 Woodland Birds

1966. Woodland Birds. Multicoloured.

1697		10g. Type **485**	15	10
1698		20g. Green woodpecker	15	10
1699		30g. Jay	20	10
1700		40g. Golden oriole	20	10
1701		60g. Hoopoe	20	10
1702		2z.50 Common redstart	45	35
1703		4z. Spruce siskin	1·50	35
1704		6z.50 Chaffinch	1·50	60
1705		7z.10 Great tit	1·50	60

486 Ram (ritual statuette)

1966. Polish Archaeological Research.

1706	**486**	60g. blue	10	10
1707	-	60g. green	10	10
1708	-	60g. brown	10	10

DESIGNS—VERT: No. 1707, Plan of Biskupin settlement. HORIZ: No. 1708, Brass implements and ornaments.

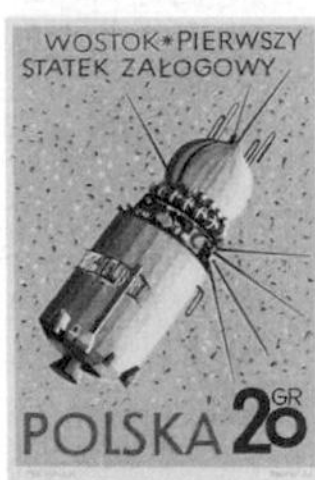

487 "Vostok 1"

1966. Space Research. Multicoloured.

1709	20g. Type **487**	10	10
1710	40g. "Gemini"	10	10
1711	60g. "Ariel 2"	10	10
1712	1z.35 "Proton 1"	10	10
1713	1z.50 "FR 1"	20	10
1714	3z.40 "Alouette"	35	10
1715	6z.50 "San Marco 1"	1·25	10
1716	7z.10 "Luna 9"	1·50	30

488 Polish Eagle and Hammer

1966. Polish Millenary (2nd issue).

1717	**488**	40g. purple, lilac and red	10	10
1718	-	60g. purple, green and red	10	10

DESIGN: 60g. Polish eagle and agricultural and industrial symbols.

489 Dressage

1967. 150th Anniv of Racehorse Breeding in Poland. Multicoloured.

1719	10g. Type **489**	15	10
1720	20g. Cross-country racing	15	10
1721	40g. Horse-jumping	15	10
1722	60g. Jumping fence in open country	30	10
1723	90g. Horse-trotting	30	10
1724	5z.90 Playing polo	90	10
1725	6z.60 Stallion "Ofir"	1·40	45
1726	7z. Stallion "Skowrenek"	2·10	45

490 Black-wedged Butterflyfish

1967. Exotic Fishes. Multicoloured.

1727	5g. Type **490**	10	10
1728	10g. Emperor angelfish	10	10
1729	40g. Racoon butterflyfish	10	10
1730	60g. Clown triggerfish	10	10
1731	90g. Undulate triggerfish	10	10
1732	1z.50 Picasso triggerfish	20	10
1733	4z.50 Black-finned melon butterflyfish	75	10
1734	6z.60 Semicircle angelfish	95	45
1735	7z. Saddle butterflyfish	1·25	75

491 Auschwitz Memorial

1967. Polish Martyrdom and Resistance, 1939–45.

1736	**491**	40g. brown	10	10
1737	-	40g. black	10	10
1738	-	40g. violet	10	10

DESIGNS—VERT: No. 1737, Auschwitz-Monowitz Memorial; 1738, Memorial guide's emblem.

See also Nos. 1770/2, 1798/9 and 1865/9.

492 Cyclists

1967. 20th International Peace Cycle Race.

1739	**492**	60g. multicoloured	10	10

493 Running

1967. Olympic Games (1968). Multicoloured.

1740	20g. Type **493**	10	10
1741	40g. Horse-jumping	10	10
1742	60g. Relay-running	10	10
1743	90g. Weight-lifting	10	10
1744	1z.35 Hurdling	10	10
1745	3z.40 Gymnastics	45	15
1746	6z.60 High-jumping	60	35
1747	7z. Boxing	1·10	65
MS1748	65×86 mm. 10z.+5z. multicoloured	1·90	1·25

DESIGN: (30×30 mm.)—10z. Kusocinski winning 10,000 meters race at Olympic Games, Los Angeles, 1932.

494 Socialist Symbols

1967. Polish Trade Unions Congress, Warsaw.

1749	**494**	60g. multicoloured	10	10

495 "Arnica montana"

1967. Protected Plants. Multicoloured.

1750	40g. Type **495**	10	10
1751	60g. "Aquilegia vulgaris"	10	10
1752	3z.40 "Gentiana punctata"	35	10
1753	4z.50 "Lycopodium clavatum"	35	10
1754	5z. "Iris sibirica"	60	10
1755	10z. "Azalea pontica"	1·10	30

496 Katowice Memorial

1967. Inauguration of Katowice Memorial.

1756	**496**	60g. multicoloured	10	10

497 Marie Curie

1967. Birth Centenary of Marie Curie.

1757	**497**	60g. lake	10	10
1758	-	60g. brown	10	10
1759	-	60g. violet	10	10

DESIGNS: No. 1758, Marie Curie's Nobel Prize diploma; 1759, Statue of Marie Curie, Warsaw.

498 "Fifth Congress of the Deaf" (sign language)

1967. 5th World Federation of the Deaf Congress, Warsaw.

1760	**498**	60g. black and blue	10	10

499 Bouquet

1967. "Flowers of the Meadow". Multicoloured.

1761	20g. Type **499**	10	10
1762	40g. Red poppy	10	10
1763	60g. Field bindweed	10	10
1764	90g. Wild pansy	10	10
1765	1z.15 Tansy	10	10
1766	2z.50 Corn cockle	20	10
1767	3z.40 Field scabious	45	30
1768	4z.50 Scarlet pimpernel	1·40	35
1769	7z.90 Chicory	1·50	30

1967. Polish Martyrdom and Resistance, 1939–45 (2nd series). As T 491.

1770	40g. blue	10	10
1771	40g. green	10	10
1772	40g. black	10	10

DESIGNS—HORIZ: No. 1770, Stutthof Memorial. VERT: No. 1771, Walez Memorial; 1772, Lodz-Radogoszez Memorial.

500 "Wilanow Palace" (from painting by W. Kasprzycki)

1967. Stamp Day.

1773	**500**	60g. brown and blue	10	10

501 Cruiser "Aurora"

1967. 50th Anniv of October Revolution. Each black, grey and red.

1774	60g. Type **501**	10	10
1775	60g. Lenin	10	10
1776	60g. "Luna 10"	10	10

502 Peacock

1967. Butterflies. Multicoloured.

1777	10g. Type **502**	10	10
1778	20g. Swallowtail	10	10
1779	40g. Small tortoiseshell	10	10
1780	60g. Camberwell beauty	15	10
1781	2z. Purple emperor	30	10
1782	2z.50 Red admiral	35	10
1783	3z.40 Pale clouded yellow	35	10
1784	4z.50 Marbled white	1·75	80
1785	7z.90 Large blue	1·90	80

503 Kosciuszko

1967. 150th Death Anniv of Tadeusz Kosciuszko (national hero).

1786	**503**	60g. chocolate and brown	10	10
1787	**503**	2z.50 green and red	20	10

504 "The Lobster" (Jean de Heem)

1967. Famous Paintings.

1788	-	20g. multicoloured	20	10
1789	-	40g. multicoloured	10	10
1790	-	60g. multicoloured	10	10
1791	-	2z. multicoloured	30	20
1792	-	2z.50 multicolured	30	20
1793	-	3z.40 multicoloured	60	20
1794	**504**	4z.50 multicoloured	1·10	60
1795	-	6z.60 multicoloured	1·40	75

DESIGNS (Paintings from the National Museums, Warsaw and Cracow). VERT: 20g. "Lady with a Weasel" (Leonardo da Vinci); 40g. "The Polish Lady" (Watteau); 60g. "Dog fighting Heron" (A. Hondius); 2z. "Fowler tuning Guitar" (J. B. Greuze); 2z.50, "The Tax Collectors" (M. van Reymerswaele); 3z.40, "Daria Fiodorowna" (F. S. Rokotov). HORIZ: 6z.60, "Parable of the Good Samaritan" (landscape, Rembrandt).

505 W. S. Reymont

1967. Birth Centenary of W. S. Reymont (novelist).

1796	**505**	60g. brown, red and ochre	10	10

506 J. M. Ossolinski (medallion), Book and Flag

1967. 150th Anniv of Ossolineum Foundation.

1797	**506**	60g. brown, red and blue	10	10

1967. Polish Martyrdom and Resistance, 1939–45 (3rd series). As T 491.

1798	40g. red	10	10
1799	40g. brown	10	10

DESIGNS—VERT: No. 1798, Zagan Memorial. HORIZ: No. 1799, Lambinowice Memorial.

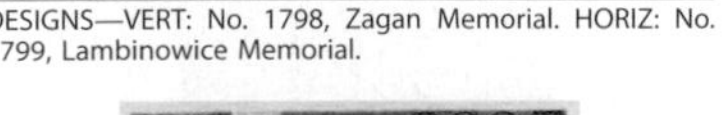

507 Ice Hockey

1968. Winter Olympic Games, Grenoble. Mult.

1800	40g. Type **507**	10	10
1801	60g. Downhill	10	10
1802	90g. Slalom	10	10
1803	1z.35 Speed-skating	10	10
1804	1z.55 Ski-walking	10	10
1805	2z. Tobogganing	20	20
1806	7z. Rifle-shooting on skis	50	45
1807	7z.90 Ski-jumping (different)	95	60

508 "Puss in Boots"

1968. Fairy Tales. Multicoloured.

1808	20g. Type **508**	10	10
1809	40g. "The Raven and the Fox"	10	10
1810	60g. "Mr. Twardowski"	10	10
1811	2z. "The Fisherman and the Fish"	20	10
1812	2z.50 "Little Red Riding Hood"	30	10
1813	3z.40 "Cinderella"	45	10
1814	5z.50 "The Waif"	1·25	45
1815	7z. "Snow White"	1·50	60

509 "Passiflora quadrangularis"

1968. Flowers. Multicoloured.

1816	10g. "Clianthus dampieri"	10	10
1817	20g. Type **509**	10	10
1818	30g. "Strelitzia reginae"	10	10
1819	40g. "Coryphanta vivipara"	10	10
1820	60g. "Odontonia"	10	10
1821	90g. "Protea cyneroides"	10	10
1822	4z.+2z. "Abutilon"	20	10
1823	8z.+4z. "Rosa polyantha"	1·90	30

510 "Peace" (poster by H. Tomaszewski)

1968. 2nd Int Poster Biennale, Warsaw. Mult.

1824	60g. Type **510**	10	10
1825	2z.50 Gounod's "Faust" (poster by Jan Lenica)	10	10

511 Zephyr Glider

1968. 11th World Gliding Championships, Leszno. Gliders. Multicoloured.

1826	60g. Type **511**	10	10
1827	90g. Stork	10	10
1828	1z.50 Swallow	15	10
1829	3z.40 Fly	35	20
1830	4z. Seal	80	30
1831	5z.50 Pirate	95	30

512 Child with "Stamp"

1968. "75 years of Polish Philately". Multicoloured.

1832	60g. Type **512**	10	10
1833	60g. Balloon over Poznan	10	10

513 Part of Monument

1968. Silesian Insurrection Monument, Sosnowiec.

1834	**513**	60g. black and purple	10	10

514 Relay-racing

1968. Olympic Games, Mexico. Multicoloured.

1835	30g. Type **514**	10	10
1836	40g. Boxing	10	10
1837	60g. Basketball	10	10
1838	90g. Long-jumping	10	10
1839	2z.50 Throwing the javelin	15	10
1840	3z.40 Gymnastics	30	10
1841	4z. Cycling	35	10
1842	7z.90 Fencing	65	10
1843	10z.+5z. Torch runner and Aztec bas-relief (56×45 mm)	1·75	30

515 "Knight on a Bay Horse" (P. Michalowski)

1968. Polish Paintings. Multicoloured.

1844	40g. Type **515**	10	10
1845	60g. "Fisherman" (L. Wyczolkowski)	10	10
1846	1z.15 "Jewish Woman with Lemons" (A. Gierymski)	10	10
1847	1z.35 "Eliza Parenska" (S. Wyspianski)	15	10
1848	1z.50 "Manifesto" (W. Weiss)	50	10
1849	4z.50 "Stanczyk" (Jan Matejko) (horiz)	50	10
1850	5z. "Children's Band" (T. Makowski) (horiz)	80	10
1851	7z. "Feast II" (Z. Waliszewski) (horiz)	90	35

516 "September, 1939" (Bylina)

1968. 25th Anniv of Polish People's Army. Designs show paintings.

1852	40g. violet and olive on yellow	10	10
1853	40g. blue and violet on lilac	10	10
1854	40g. green and blue on grey	10	10
1855	40g. black and brown on orange	10	10
1856	40g. purple & green on green	10	10
1857	60g. brown & ultram on bl	10	10
1858	60g. purple & green on green	10	10
1859	60g. olive and red on pink	10	10
1860	60g. green and brown on red	20	10
1861	60g. blue & turquoise on blue	30	10

PAINTINGS AND PAINTERS: No. 1852, Type **516**; 1853, "Partisans" (Maciag); 1854, "Lenino" (Bylina); 1855, "Monte Cassino" (Boratynski); 1856, "Tanks before Warsaw" (Garwatowski); 1857, "Neisse River" (Bylina); 1858, "On the Oder" (Mackiewicz); 1859, "In Berlin" (Bylina); 1860, "Blyskawica" (destroyer) (Mokwa); 1861, "Pursuit" (Mikoyan Gurevich MiG-17 aircraft) (Kulisiewicz).

517 "Party Members" (F. Kowarski)

1968. 5th Polish United Workers' Party Congress, Warsaw. Multicoloured designs showing paintings.

1862	60g. Type **517**	10	10
1863	60g. "Strike" (S. Lentz) (vert)	10	10
1864	60g. "Manifesto" (W. Weiss) (vert)	10	10

1968. Polish Martyrdom and Resistance, 1939–45 (4th series). As T 491.

1865	40g. grey	10	10
1866	40g. brown	10	10
1867	40g. brown	10	10
1868	40g. blue	10	10
1869	40g. brown	10	10

DESIGNS—HORIZ: No. 1865, Tomb of Unknown Soldier, Warsaw; 1866, Guerillas' Monument, Kartuzy. VERT: No. 1867, Insurgents' Monument, Poznan; 1868, People's Guard Insurgents' Monument, Polichno; 1869, Rotunda, Zamosc.

518 "Start of Hunt" (W. Kossak)

1968. Paintings. Hunting Scenes. Multicoloured.

1870	20g. Type **518**	10	10
1871	40g. "Hunting with Falcon" (J. Kossak)	10	10
1872	60g. "Wolves' Raid" (A. Wierusz-Kowalski)	10	10
1873	1z.50 "Home-coming with a Bear" (J. Falat)	30	10
1874	2z.50 "The Fox-hunt" (T. Sutherland)	20	10
1875	3z.40 "The Boar-hunt" (F. Snyders)	30	10
1876	4z.50 "Hunters' Rest" (W. G. Pierow)	1·25	45
1877	8z.50 "Hunting a Lion in Morocco" (Delacroix)	1·25	90

519 Maltese Terrier

1969. Pedigree Dogs. Multicoloured.

1878	20g. Type **519**	10	10
1879	40g. Wire-haired fox-terrier (vert)	20	10
1880	60g. Afghan hound	20	20
1881	1z.50 Rough-haired terrier	20	10
1882	2z.50 English setter	45	10
1883	3z.40 Pekinese	50	20
1884	4z.50 Alsatian (vert)	1·10	30
1885	8z.50 Pointer (vert)	2·25	65

520 House Sign

1969. 9th Polish Democratic Party Congress.

1886	**520**	60g. red, black and grey	10	10

521 "Dove" and Wheat-ears

1969. 5th Congress of United Peasant's Party.

1887	**521**	60g. multicoloured	10	10

522 Running

1969. 75th Anniv of International Olympic Committee and 50th Anniv of Polish Olympic Committee. Multicoloured.

1888	10g. Type **522**	10	10
1889	20g. Gymnastics	10	10
1890	40g. Weightlifting	10	10
1891	60g. Throwing the javelin	10	10
1892	2z.50+50g. Throwing the discus	10	10
1893	3z.40+1z. Running	20	10
1894	4z.+1z.50 Wrestling	60	30
1895	7z.+2z. Fencing	1·10	35

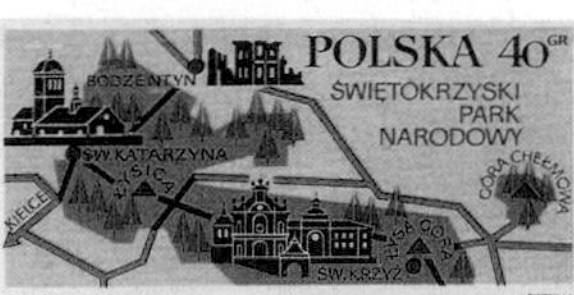

523 Pictorial Map of Swietokrzyski National Park

1969. Tourism (1st series). Multicoloured.

1896	40g. Type **523**	10	10
1897	60g. Niedzica Castle (vert)	10	10
1898	1z.35 Kolobrzeg Lighthouse and yacht	20	10
1899	1z.50 Szczecin Castle and Harbour	20	10
1900	2z.50 Torun and Vistula River	15	10
1901	3z.40 Klodzko, Silesia (vert)	20	20
1902	4z. Sulejow	35	30
1903	4z.50 Kazimierz Dolny market-place (vert)	35	30

See also Nos. 1981/5.

524 Route Map and "Opty"

1969. Leonid Teliga's World Voyage in Yacht "Opty".

1904	**524**	60g. multicoloured	10	10

525 Copernicus (after woodcut by T. Stimer) and Inscription

1969. 500th Birth Anniv (1973) of Copernicus (1st issue).

1905	**525**	40g. brown, red & yellow	10	10
1906	-	60g. blue, red and green	10	10
1907	-	2z.50 olive, red & purple	35	30

DESIGNS: 60g. Copernicus (after J. Falck) and 15th-century globe; 2z.50, Copernicus (after painting by J. Matejko) and diagram of heliocentric system.

See also Nos. 1995/7, 2069/72, 2167/70, 2213/14 and 2217/21.

526 "Memory" Flame and Badge

1969. 5th National Alert of Polish Boy Scout Association.

1908	**526**	60g. black, red and blue	10	10
1909	-	60g. red, black and green	10	10
1910	-	60g. black, green and red	10	10

DESIGN: No. 1909, "Defence" eagle and badge; 1910, "Labour" map and badge.

528 Coal-miner

1969. 25th Anniv of Polish People's Republic. Multicoloured.

1911	60g. Frontier guard and arms	10	10
1912	60g. Plock petro-chemical plant	10	10
1913	60g. Combine-harvester	10	10
1914	60g. Grand Theatre, Warsaw	10	10
1915	60g. Curie statue and University, Lublin	10	10
1916	60g. Type **528**	10	10
1917	60g. Sulphur-worker	10	10
1918	60g. Steel-worker	10	10
1919	60g. Shipbuilder	10	10

Nos. 1911/5 are vert and have white arms embossed in the top portion of the stamps.

529 Astronauts and Module on Moon

1969. 1st Man on the Moon.

1920	**529**	2z.50 multicoloured	60	45

530 "Motherhood" (S. Wyspianski)

1969. Polish Paintings. Multicoloured.

1921	20g. Type **530**	10	10
1922	40g. "Hamlet" (J. Malczewski)	10	10
1923	60g. "Indian Summer" (J. Chelmonski)	10	10
1924	2z. "Two Girls" (Olga Bonznanska) (vert)	20	10
1925	2z.50 "The Sun of May" (J. Mehoffer) (vert)	10	10
1926	3z.40 "Woman combing her Hair" (W. Slewinski)	30	30
1927	5z.50 "Still Life" (J. Pankiewicz)	60	30
1928	7z. "Abduction of the King's Daughter" (W. Wojtkiewicz)	1·25	45

531 "Nike" statue

1969. 4th Congress of Fighters for Freedom and Democracy Association.

1929	**531**	60g. red, black and brown	10	10

532 Majdanek Memorial

1969. Inauguration of Majdanek Memorial.

1930	**532**	40g. black and mauve	10	10

533 Krzczonow (Lublin) Costumes

1969. Provincial Costumes. Multicoloured.

1931	40g. Type **533**	10	10
1932	60g. Lowicz (Lodz)	10	10
1933	1z.15 Rozbasrk (Katowice)	10	10
1934	1z.35 Lower Silesia (Wroclaw)	10	10
1935	1z.50 Opoczno (Lodz)	30	10
1936	4z.50 Sacz (Cracow)	60	15
1937	5z. Highlanders, Cracow	45	30
1938	7z. Kurple (Warsaw)	65	35

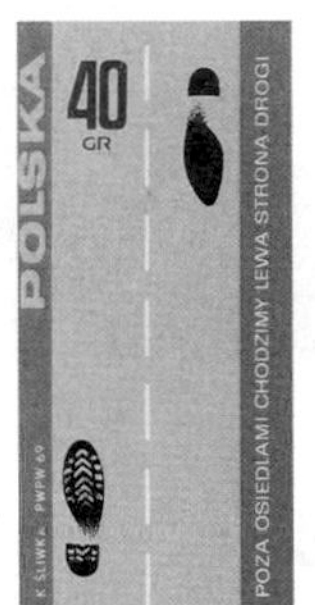

534 "Pedestrians Keep Left"

1969. Road Safety. Multicoloured.

1939	40g. Type **534**	10	10
1940	60g. "Drive Carefully" (horses on road)	10	10
1941	2z.50 "Do Not Dazzle" (cars on road at night)	15	10

535 "Welding" and I.L.O. Emblem

1969. 50th Anniv of I.L.O.

1942	**535**	2z.50 blue and gold	20	10

536 "The Bell-founder"

1969. Miniatures from Behem's Code of 1505. Multicoloured.

1943	40g. Type **536**	10	10
1944	60g. "The Painter"	10	10
1945	1z.35 "The Woodcarver"	10	10
1946	1z.55 "The Shoemaker"	20	10
1947	2z.50 "The Cooper"	20	10
1948	3z.40 "The Baker"	20	20
1949	4z.50 "The Tailor"	60	30
1950	7z. "The Bowyer"	1·00	60

537 "Angel" (19th-century)

1969. Polish Folk Sculpture. Multicoloured.

1951	20g. Type **537**	10	10
1952	40g. "Sorrowful Christ" (19th-century)	10	10
1953	60g. "Sorrowful Christ" (19th-cent) (different)	10	10
1954	2z. "Weeping Woman" (19th-century)	20	10
1955	2z.50 "Adam and Eve" (F. Czajkowski)	20	10
1956	3z.40 "Girl with Birds" (L. Kudla)	30	10
1957	5z.50+1z.50 "Choir" (A. Zegadlo)	75	35
1958	7z.+1z. "Organ-grinder" (Z. Skretowicz)	80	50

Nos. 1957/8 are larger, size 25×35 mm.

538 Leopold Staff

1969. Modern Polish Writers.

1959	**538**	40g. black, olive & green	10	10
1960	-	60g. black, red and pink	10	10
1961	-	1z.35 black, deep blue and blue	10	10
1962	-	1z.50 black, violet & lilac	10	10
1963	-	1z.55 black, deep green and green	10	10
1964	-	2z.50 black, deep blue and blue	20	10
1965	-	3z.40 black, brn & flesh	30	25

DESIGNS: 60g. Wladyslaw Broniewski; 1z.35, Leon Kruczkowski; 1z.50, Julian Tuwim; 1z.55, Konstanty Ildefons Galczynski; 2z.50, Maria Dabrowska; 3z.40, Zofia Nalkowska.

539 Nike Monument

1970. 25th Anniv of Liberation of Warsaw.

1966	**539**	60g. multicoloured	20	10

540 Early Printing Works and Colour Dots

1970. Centenary of Printers' Trade Union.

1967	**540**	60g. multicoloured	10	10

541 Mallard

1970. Game Birds. Multicoloured.

1968	40g. Type **541**	10	10
1969	60g. Common pheasant	30	10
1970	1z.15 Eurasian woodcock	20	10
1971	1z.35 Ruff	30	10
1972	1z.50 Wood pigeon	30	10
1973	3z.40 Black grouse	35	10
1974	7z. Grey partridge	1·90	45
1975	8z.50 Western capercaillie	2·75	50

542 Lenin at Desk

1970. Birth Centenary of Lenin.

1976	**542**	40g. grey and red	10	10
1977	-	60g. brown and red	10	10
1978	-	2z.50 black and red	10	10
MS1979		134×81 mm. No. 1977 ×4	2·10	45

DESIGNS: 60g. Lenin addressing meeting; 2z.50, Lenin at Party conference.

543 Polish and Russian Soldiers in Berlin

1970. 25th Anniv of Liberation.

1980	**543**	60g. multicoloured	10	10

1970. Tourism (2nd series). As T **523**, but with imprint "PWPW 70". Multicoloured.

1981	60g. Town Hall, Wroclaw (vert)	10	10
1982	60g. View of Opol	10	10
1983	60g. Legnica Castle	10	10
1984	60g. Bolkow Castle	10	10
1985	60g. Town Hall, Brzeg	10	10

544 Polish "Flower"

1970. 25th Anniv of Return of Western Territories.

1986	**544**	60g. red, silver and green	10	10

545 Movement Flag

1970. 75th Anniv of Peasant Movement.

1987	**545**	60g. multicoloured	10	10

546 U.P.U. Emblem and New Headquarters

1970. New U.P.U. Headquarters Building, Berne.

1988	**546**	2z.50 blue and turquoise	20	10

547 Footballers

1970. Gornik Zabrze v. Manchester City, Final of European Cup-winners Cup Championship.

1989	**547**	60g. multicoloured	20	10

548 Hand with "Lamp of Learning"

1970. 150th Anniv of Plock Scientific Society.

1990	**548**	60g. olive, red and black	10	10

549 "Olympic Runners" (from Greek amphora)

1970. 10th Session of Int Olympic Academy.

1991	**549**	60g. red, yellow and black	10	10
1992	-	60g. violet, blue and black	10	10
1993	-	60g. multicoloured	10	10
MS1994		71×101 mm. 10z.+5z. multi-coloured	1·90	1·00

DESIGNS: No. 1992, "The Archer"; 1993, Modern runners; **MS**1994, "Horse of Fame" emblem of Polish Olympic Committee.

550 Copernicus (after miniature by Bacciarelli) and Bologna

1970. 500th Birth Anniv (1973) of Copernicus (2nd issue).

1995	**550**	40g. green, orange & lilac	10	10
1996	-	60g. lilac, green & yellow	10	10
1997	-	2z.50 brown, blue & green	35	10

DESIGNS: 60g. Copernicus (after miniature by Lesseur) and Padua; 2z.50, Copernicus (by N. Zinck, after lost Goluchowska portrait) and Ferrara.

551 "Aleksander Orlowski" (self-portrait)

1970. Polish Miniatures. Multicoloured.

1998		20g. Type **551**	10	10
1999		40g. "Jan Matejko" (self-portrait)	10	10
2000		60g. "Stefan Batory" (unknown artist)	10	10
2001		2z. "Maria Leszczynska" (unknown artist)	10	10
2002		2z.50 "Maria Walewska" (Marie-Victorie Jacquetot)	20	10
2003		3z.40 "Tadeusz Kosciuszko" (Jan Rustem)	20	10
2004		5z.50 "Samuel Linde" (G. Landolfi)	65	40
2005		7z. "Michal Oginski" (Nanette Windisch)	1·40	20

552 U.N. Emblem within "Eye"

1970. 25th Anniv of United Nations.

2006	**552**	2z.50 multicoloured	20	10

553 Piano Keyboard and Chopin's Signature

1970. 8th International Chopin Piano Competition.

2007	**553**	2z.50 black and violet	20	10

554 Population Pictograph

1970. National Census. Multicoloured.

2008		40g. Type **554**	10	10
2009		60g. Family in "house"	10	10

555 Destroyer "Piorun" (image scaled to 61% of original size)

1970. Polish Warships, World War II.

2010	**555**	40g. brown	10	10
2011	-	60g. black	10	10
2012	-	2z.50 brown	35	10

DESIGNS: 60g. "Orzel" (submarine); 2z.50, H.M.S. "Garland" (destroyer loaned to Polish Navy).

556 "Expressions" (Maria Jarema)

1970. Stamp Day. Contemporary Polish Paintings. Multicoloured.

2013		20g. "The Violin-cellist" (J. Nowosielski) (vert)	10	10
2014		40g. "View of Lodz" (B. Liberski) (vert)	10	10
2015		60g. "Studio Concert" (W. Taranczewski) (vert)	10	10
2016		1z.50 "Still Life" (Z. Pronaszko) (vert)	10	10
2017		2z. "Hanging-up Washing" (A. Wroblewski) (vert)	10	10
2018		3z.40 Type **556**	20	10
2019		4z. "Canal in the Forest" (P. Potworowski)	45	10
2020		8z.50 "The Sun" (W. Strzeminski)	95	10

557 "Luna 16" landing on Moon

1970. Moon Landing of "Luna 16".

2021	**557**	2z.50 multicoloured	30	10

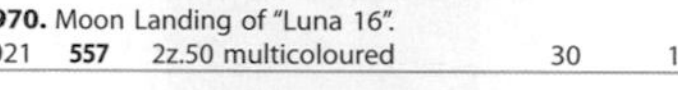

558 "Stag" (detail from "Daniel" tapestry)

1970. Tapestries in Wawel Castle. Multicoloured.

2022		60g. Type **558**	10	10
2023		1z.15 "White Stork" (detail)	30	10
2024		1z.35 "Panther fighting Dragon"	10	10
2025		2z. "Man's Head" (detail, "Deluge" tapestry)	20	10
2026		2z.50 "Child with Bird" (detail, "Adam Tilling the Soil" tapestry)	25	10
2027		4z. "God, Adam and Eve" (detail, "Happiness in Paradise" tapestry)	45	30
2028		4z.50 Royal Monogram tapestry	75	30
MS2029		Two sheets, each 62×89 mm. (a) 5z.50 Polish coat-of-arms; (b) 7z.+3z. Monogram and satyrs. Imperf. Set of 2 sheets	2·10	1·25

559 Cadet ship "Dar Pomorza"

1971. Polish Ships. Multicoloured.

2030		40g. Type **559**	10	10
2031		60g. Liner "Stefan Batory"	10	10
2032		1z.15 Ice-breaker "Perkun"	15	10
2033		1z.35 Lifeboat "R-1"	20	10
2034		1z.50 Bulk carrier "Ziemia Szczecinska"	30	10
2035		2z.50 Tanker "Beskidy"	30	10
2036		5z. Freighter "Hel"	65	20
2037		8z.50 Ferry "Gryf"	1·40	50

560 Checiny Castle

1971. Polish Castles. Multicoloured.

2038		20g. Type **560**	10	10
2039		40g. Wisnicz	10	10
2040		60g. Bedzin	10	10
2041		2z. Ogrodzieniec	15	10
2042		2z.50 Niedzica	15	10
2043		3z.40 Kwidzyn	35	10
2044		4z. Pieskowa Skala	35	10
2045		8z.50 Lidzbark Warminski	90	30

561 Battle of Pouilly, J. Dabrowski and W. Wroblewski

1971. Centenary of Paris Commune.

2046	**561**	60g. brown, blue and red	10	10

562 Plantation

1971. Forestry Management. Multicoloured.

2047		40g. Type **562**	10	10
2048		60g. Forest (27×47 mm)	10	10
2049		1z.50 Tree-felling	20	10

563 "Bishop Marianos"

1971. Fresco. Discoveries made by Polish Expedition at Faras, Nubia. Multicoloured.

2050		40g. Type **563**	10	10
2051		60g. "St. Anne"	10	10
2052		1z.15 "Archangel Michael"	10	10
2053		1z.35 "The Hermit, Anamon"	10	10
2054		1z.50 "Head of Archangel Michael"	10	10
2055		4z.50 "Evangelists' Cross"	35	10
2056		5z. "Christ protecting a nobleman"	60	20
2057		7z. "Archangel Michael" (half-length)	75	45

564 Revolutionaries

1971. 50th Anniv of Silesian Insurrection.

2058	**564**	60g. brown and gold	10	10
MS2059		108×106 mm. No. 2058 ×3	2·10	95

565 "Soldiers"

1971. 25th Anniv of UNICEF Children's Drawings. Multicoloured.

2060		20g. "Peacock" (vert)	10	10
2061		40g. Type **565**	10	10
2062		60g. "Lady Spring" (vert)	10	10
2063		2z. "Cat and Ball"	10	10
2064		2z.50 "Flowers in Jug" (vert)	20	10
2065		3z.40 "Friendship"	30	10
2066		5z.50 "Clown" (vert)	70	30
2067		7z. "Strange Planet"	80	35

566 Fair Emblem

1971. 40th International Fair, Poznan.

2068	**566**	60g. multicoloured	10	10

567 Copernicus's House, Torun

1971. 500th Birth Anniv (1973) of Copernicus (3rd issue). Multicoloured.

2069	40g. Type **567**	10	10
2070	60g. Collegium Naius, Jagiellonian University, Cracow (horiz)	10	10
2071	2z.50 Olsztyn Castle (horiz)	20	10
2072	4z. Frombork Cathedral	70	20

568 Folk Art Pattern

1971. Folk Art. "Paper Cut-outs" showing various patterns.

2073	**568**	20g. black, green and blue	10	10
2074	-	40g. blue, green & cream	10	10
2075	-	60g. brown, blue and grey	10	10
2076	-	1z.15 purple, brn & buff	10	10
2077	-	1z.35 green, red & yellow	10	10

569 "Head of Worker" (X. Dunikowski)

1971. Modern Polish Sculpture. Multicoloured.

2078	40g. Type **569**	10	10
2079	40g. "Foundryman" (X. Dunikowski)	10	10
2080	60g. "Miners" (M. Wiecek)	10	10
2081	60g. "Harvester" (S. Horno-Poplawski)	10	10
MS2082	158×85 mm. Nos. 2078/81	2·40	1·25

570 Congress Emblem and Computer Tapes

1971. 6th Polish Technical Congress, Warsaw.

2083	**570**	60g. violet and red	10	10

571 "Angel" (J. Mehoffer)

1971. Stained Glass Windows. Multicoloured.

2084	20g. Type **571**	10	10
2085	40g. "Lillies" (S. Wyspianski)	10	10
2086	60g. "Iris" (S. Wyspianski)	10	10
2087	1z.35 "Apollo" (S. Wyspianski)	10	10
2088	1z.55 "Two Wise Men" (14th-century)	10	10
2089	3z.40 "The Flight into Egypt" (14th-century)	30	10
2090	5z.50 "Jacob" (14th-century)	50	10
2091	8z.50+4z. "Madonna" (15th-century)	80	10

572 "Mrs. Fedorowicz" (W. Pruszkowski)

1971. Contemporary Art from National Museum, Cracow. Multicoloured.

2092	40g. Type **572**	10	10
2093	50g. "Woman with Book" (T. Czyzeski)	10	10
2094	60g. "Girl with Chrysanthemums" (O. Boznanska)	10	10
2095	2z.50 "Girl in Red Dress" (J. Pankiewicz) (horiz)	10	10
2096	3z.40 "Reclining Nude" (L. Chwistek) (horiz)	20	10
2097	4z.50 "Strange Garden" (J. Mehoffer)	35	10
2098	5z. "Wife in White Hat" (Z. Pronaszko)	45	10
2099	7z.+1z. "Seated Nude" (W. Weiss)	65	45

573 PZL P-11C Fighters

1971. Polish Aircraft of World War II. Mult.

2100	90g. Type **573**	10	10
2101	1z.50 PZL 23A Karas fighters	20	10
2102	3z.40 PZL P-37 Los bomber	30	20

574 Royal Castle, Warsaw (pre-1939)

1971. Reconstruction of Royal Castle, Warsaw.

2103	**574**	60g. black, red and gold	10	10

575 Astronauts in Moon Rover

1971. Moon Flight of "Apollo 15".

2104	**575**	2z.50 multicoloured	45	10
MS2105		122×157 mm. No. 2104 ×6 plus 2 stamp-size se-tenant labels, showing Space scenes	3·75	2·75

576 "Lunokhod 1"

1971. Moon Flight of "Lunik 17" and "Lunokhod 1".

2106	**576**	2z.50 multicoloured	45	10
MS2107		158×118 mm. No. 2106 ×6 plus 2 stamp-size se-tenant labels, showing Space scenes	3·75	1·90

577 Worker at Wheel

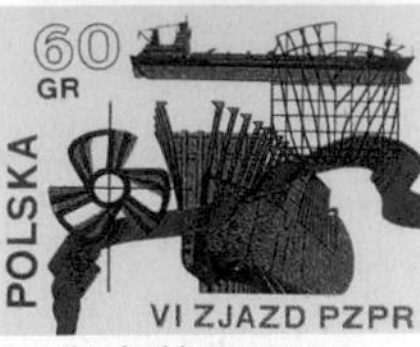
578 Ship-building

1971. 6th Polish United Workers' Party Congress. (a) Party Posters.

2108	**577**	60g. red, blue and grey	10	10
2109	**577**	60g. red and grey (Worker's head)	10	10

(b) Industrial Development. Each in gold and red.

2110	60g. Type **578**	10	10
2111	60g. Building construction	10	10
2112	60g. Combine-harvester	10	10
2113	60g. Motor-car production	10	10
2114	60g. Pit-head	10	10
2115	60g. Petro-chemical plant	10	10
MS2116	102×115 mm. Nos. 2110/15	1·10	80

579 "Prunus cerasus"

1971. Flowers of Trees and Shrubs. Multicoloured.

2117	10g. Type **579**	10	10
2118	20g. "Malusniedzwetzskyana"	10	10
2119	40g. "Pyrus L."	10	10
2120	60g. "Prunus persica"	10	10
2121	1z.15 "Magnolia kobus"	10	10
2122	1z.35 "Crategus oxyacantha"	10	10
2123	2z.50 "Malus M."	10	10
2124	3z.40 "Aesculus carnea"	20	10
2125	5z. "Robinia pseudacacia"	75	20
2126	8z.50 "Prunus avium"	1·40	50

580 "Worker" (sculpture, J. Januszkiewicz)

1972. 30th Anniv of Polish Workers' Coalition.

2127	**580**	60g. black and red	10	10

581 Luge

1972. Winter Olympic Games, Sapporo, Japan. Multicoloured.

2128	40g. Type **581**	10	10
2129	60g. Slalom (vert)	10	10
2130	1z.65 Biathlon (vert)	20	10
2131	2z.50 Ski jumping	35	25
MS2132	85×68 mm. 10z.+5z. Downhill skiing	2·10	1·25

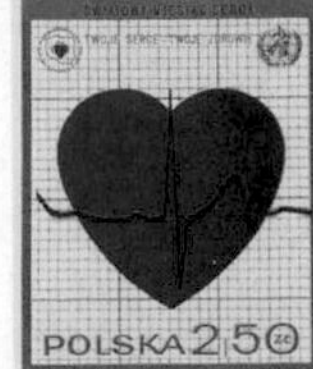
582 "Heart" and Cardiogram Trace

1972. World Heart Month.

2133	**582**	2z.50 multicoloured	20	10

583 Running

1972. Olympic Games, Munich. Multicoloured.

2134	20g. Type **583**	10	10
2135	30g. Archery	10	10
2136	40g. Boxing	10	10
2137	60g. Fencing	10	10
2138	2z.50 Wrestling	10	10
2139	3z.40 Weightlifting	10	10
2140	5z. Cycling	60	10
2141	8z.50 Shooting	95	20
MS2142	70×80 mm. 10z.+5z. As 30g.	1·40	75

584 Cyclists

1972. 25th International Peace Cycle Race.

2143	**584**	60g. multicoloured	10	10

585 Polish War Memorial, Berlin

1972. "Victory Day, 1945".

2144	**585**	60g. green	10	10

586 "Rodlo" Emblem

1972. 50th Anniv of Polish Posts in Germany.

2145	**586**	60g. ochre, red and green	10	10

587 Polish Knight of 972 A.D.

1972. Millenary of Battle of Cedynia.

2146	**587**	60g. multicoloured	10	10

588 Cheetah

1972. Zoo Animals. Multicoloured.

2147	20g. Type **588**	10	10
2148	40g. Giraffe (vert)	20	10
2149	60g. Toco toucan	30	10
2150	1z.35 Chimpanzee	20	10
2151	1z.65 Common gibbon	30	10
2152	3z.40 Crocodile	35	10
2153	4z. Red kangaroo	65	10
2154	4z.50 Tiger (vert)	2·75	60
2155	7z. Mountain zebra	3·00	1·25

589 L. Warynski. (founder)

1972. 90th Anniv of Proletarian Party.

2156	**589**	60g. multicoloured	10	10

590 F. Dzerzhinsky

1972. 95th Birth Anniv of Feliks Dzerzhinsky (Russian politician).

2157	**590**	60g. black and red	10	10

591 Global Emblem

1972. 25th Int Co-operative Federation Congress.

2158	**591**	60g. multicoloured	10	10

592 Scene from "In Barracks" (ballet)

1972. Death Centenary of Stanislaus Moniuszko (composer). Scenes from Works.

2159		10g. violet and gold	10	10
2160		20g. black and gold	10	10
2161		40g. green and gold	10	10
2162		60g. blue and gold	10	10
2163	-	1z.15 blue and gold	10	10
2164		1z.35 blue and gold	10	10
2165		1z.55 green and gold	20	10
2166		2z.50 brown and gold	20	10

DESIGNS: 10g. Type **592**; 20g. "The Countess" (opera); 40g. "The Haunted Manor" (opera); 60g. "Halka" (opera); 1z.15, "New Don Quixote" (ballet); 1z.35, "Verbum Nobile"; 1z.55, "Ideal" (operetta); 2z.50, "Pariah" (opera).

593 "Copernicus the Astronomer"

1972. 500th Birth Anniv (1973) of Nicolas Copernicus. (4th issue).

2167	**593**	40g. black and blue	10	10
2168	-	60g. black and orange	10	10
2169	-	2z.50 black and red	10	10
2170	-	3z.40 black and green	15	10
MS2171		62×102 mm. 10z.+5z. multicoloured	2·75	1·40

DESIGNS: 60g. Copernicus and Polish eagle; 2z.50, Copernicus and Medal; 3z.40, Copernicus and page of book; VERT: (29×48 mm)—10z.+5z. Copernicus charting the planets.

594 "The Amazon" (P. Michalowski)

1972. Stamp Day. Polish Paintings. Multicoloured.

2172	30g. Type **594**	10	10
2173	40g. "Ostafi Laskiewicz" (J. Metejko)	10	10
2174	60g. "Summer Idyll" (W. Gerson)	10	10
2175	2z. "The Neapolitan Woman" (A. Kotsis)	10	10
2176	2z.50 "Girl Bathing" (P. Szyndler)	10	10
2177	3z.40 "The Princess of Thum" (A. Grottger)	10	10
2178	4z. "Rhapsody" (S. Wyspianski)	15	30
2179	8z.50+4z. "Young Woman" (J. Malczewski) (horiz)	35	35

1972. Nos. 1578/9 surch.

2180	50g. on 40g. brown	10	10
2181	90g. on 40g. brown	10	10
2182	1z. on 40g. brown	10	10
2183	1z.50 on 60g. orange	10	10
2184	2z.70 on 40g. brown	15	10
2185	4z. on 60g. orange	30	10
2186	4z.50 on 60g. orange	30	10
2187	4z.90 on 60g. orange	45	10

596 "The Little Soldier" (E. Piwowarski)

1972. Children's Health Centre.

2188	**596**	60g. black and pink	10	10

597 "Royal Castle, Warsaw". (E. J. Dahlberg, 1656)

1972. Restoration of Royal Castle, Warsaw.

2189	**597**	60g. black, violet and blue	10	10

598 Chalet, Chocholowska Valley

1972. Tourism. Mountain Chalets. Multicoloured.

2190	40g. Type **598**	10	10
2191	60g. Hala Ornak (horiz)	10	10
2192	1z.55 Hala Gasienicowa	10	10
2193	1z.65 Valley of Five Lakes (horiz)	15	10
2194	2z.50 Morskie Oko	30	10

599 Trade Union Banners

1972. 7th Polish Trade Union Congresses.

2195	**599**	60g. multicoloured	10	10

600 Congress Emblem

1972. 5th Socialist Youth Union Congress.

2196	**600**	60g. multicoloured	10	10

601 Japanese Azalea

1972. Flowering Shrubs. Multicoloured.

2197	40g. Type **601**	10	10
2198	50g. Alpine rose	10	10
2199	60g. Pomeranian honeysuckle	10	10
2200	1z.65 Chinese quince	10	10
2201	2z.50 Korean cranberry	25	10
2202	3z.40 Pontic azalea	35	10
2203	4z. Delavay's white syringa	75	20
2204	8z.50 Common lilac ("Massena")	1·60	65

602 Piast Knight (10th-century)

1972. Polish Cavalry Through the Ages. Mult.

2205	20g. Type **602**	10	10
2206	40g. 13th-century knight	10	10
2207	60g. Knight of Wladyslaw Jagiello's Army (15th-century) (horiz)	10	10
2208	1z.35 17th-century hussar	10	10
2209	4z. Lancer of National Guard (18th-century)	50	10
2210	4z.50 "Congress Kingdom" cavalry officer	50	10
2211	5z. Trooper of Light Cavalry (1939) (horiz)	1·10	10
2212	7z. Trooper of People's Army (1945)	1·10	60

603 Copernicus

1972. 500th Birth Anniv (1973) of Copernicus (5th issue).

2213	**603**	1z. brown	15	10
2214	**603**	1z.50 ochre	20	10

604 Couple with Hammer and Sickle

1972. 50th Anniv of U.S.S.R. Multicoloured.

2215	40g. Type **604**	10	10
2216	60g. Red star and globe	10	10

605 "Copernicus as Young Man" (Bacciarelli)

1973. 500th Birth Anniv of Copernicus (6th issue). Multicoloured.

2217	1z. Type **605**	10	10
2218	1z.50 "Copernicus" (anon)	10	10
2219	2z.70 "Copernicus" (Zinck Nor)	20	10
2220	4z. "Copernicus" (from Strasbourg clock)	45	30
2221	4z.90 "Copernicus" (Jan Matejko) (horiz)	60	30

606 Coronation Sword

1973. Polish Art. Multicoloured.

2222	50g. Type **606**	10	10
2223	1z. Kruzlowa Madonna (detail)	10	10

2224	1z. Armour of hussar	10	10
2225	1z.50 Carved head from Wavel Castle	10	10
2226	1z.50 Silver cockerel	10	10
2227	2z.70 Armorial eagle	30	10
2228	4z.90 Skarbimierz Madonna	60	35
2229	8z.50 "Portrait of Tenczynski" (anon)	95	60

607 Statue of Lenin

1973. Unveiling of Lenin's Statue, Nowa Huta.

2230	**607**	1z. multicoloured	10	10

608 Coded Letter

1973. Introduction of Postal Codes.

2231	**608**	1z. multicoloured	10	10

609 Wolf

1973. International Hunting Council Congress and 50th Anniv of Polish Hunting Association. Multicoloured.

2232	50g. Type **609**	10	10
2233	1z. Mouflon	10	10
2234	1z.50 Elk	10	10
2235	2z.70 Western capercaillie	10	10
2236	3z. Roe deer	10	10
2237	4z.50 Lynx	55	10
2238	4z.90 Red deer	1·10	35
2239	5z. Wild boar	1·25	45

610 "Salyut"

1973. Cosmic Research. Multicoloured.

2240	4z.90 Type **610**	35	30
2241	4z.90 "Copernicus" (U.S. satellite)	35	30

611 Open Book and Flame

1973. 2nd Polish Science Congress, Warsaw.

2242	**611**	1z.50 multicoloured	10	10

612 Ancient Seal of Poznan

1973. "Polska 73" Philatelic Exhibition, Poznan. Multicoloured.

2243	1z. Type **612**	10	10
2244	1z.50 Tombstone of N. Tomicki	10	10
2245	2z.70 Kalisz paten	20	10
2246	4z. Bronze gates, Gniezno Cathedral (horiz)	30	10
MS2247	91×66 mm. 10z.+5z. purple and olive	1·50	95
MS2248	91×66 mm. 10z.+5z. purple and lilac	6·00	1·10

613 M. Nowotko

1973. 80th Birth Anniv of Marceli Nowotko (party leader).

2249	**613**	1z.50 black and red	10	10

614 Cherry Blossom

1973. Protection of the Environment. Mult.

2250	50g. Type **614**	10	10
2251	90g. Cattle in meadow	10	10
2252	1z. White stork on nest	30	10
2253	1z.50 Pond life	10	10
2254	2z.70 Meadow flora	15	10
2255	4z.90 Ocean fauna	35	10
2256	5z. Forest life	1·90	30
2257	6z.50 Agricultural produce	1·25	50

615 Motor-cyclist

1973. World Speedway Race Championships, Chorzow.

2258	**615**	1z.50 multicoloured	10	10

616 "Copernicus" (M. Bacciarelli)

1973. Stamp Day.

2259	**616**	4z.+2z. multicoloured	45	30

617 Tank

1973. 30th Anniv of Polish People's Army. Mult.

2260	1z. Type **617**	10	10
2261	1z. Mikoyan Gurevich MiG-21D airplane	10	10
2262	1z.50 Guided missile	10	10
2263	1z.50 "Puck" (missile boat)	15	10

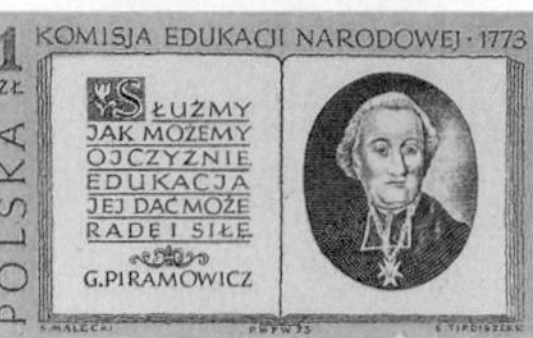

618 G. Piramowicz and Title Page

1973. Bicent of Nat Educational Commission.

2264	**618**	1z. brown and yellow	10	10
2265	-	1z.50 green, & light green	10	10

DESIGN: 1z.50, J. Sniadecki, H. Kollataj and J. U. Niemcewicz.

619 Pawel Strzelecki (explorer) and Red Kangaroo

1973. Polish Scientists. Multicoloured.

2266	1z. Type **619**	10	10
2267	1z. Henryk Arctowski (Polar explorer) and Adelie penguins	20	10
2268	1z.50 Stefan Rogozinkski (explorer) and "Lucy-Margaret" (schooner)	15	10
2269	1z.50 Benedykt Dybowski (zoologist) and sable, Lake Baikal	10	10
2270	2z. Bronislaw Malinowski (anthropologist) and New Guinea dancers	10	10
2271	2z.70 Stefan Drzewiecki (oceanographer) and submarine	20	10
2272	3z. Edward Strasburger (botanist) and classified plants	20	10
2273	8z. Ignacy Domeyko (geologist) and Chilean desert landscape	80	30

620 Polish Flag

1973. 25th Anniv of Polish United Workers' Party.

2274	**620**	1z.40 red, blue and gold	10	10

621 Jelcz-Berliet Coach

1973. Polish Motor Vehicles. Multicoloured.

2275	50g. Type **621**	10	10
2276	90g. Jelcz "316" truck	10	10
2277	1z. Polski-Fiat "126p" saloon	10	10
2278	1z.50 Polski-Fiat "125p" saloon and mileage records	10	10
2279	4z. Nysa "M-521" utility van	30	25
2280	4z.50 Star "660" truck	60	30

622 Iris

1974. Flowers. Drawings by S. Wyspianski.

2281	**622**	50g. purple	10	10
2282	-	1z. green	10	10
2283	-	1z.50 red	10	10
2284	-	3z. violet	30	10
2285	-	4z. blue	30	10
2286	-	4z.50 green	45	10

FLOWERS: 1z. Dandelion; 1z.50, Rose; 3z. Thistle; 4z. Cornflower; 4z.50, Clover.

623 Cottage, Kurpie

1974. Wooden Architecture. Multicoloured.

2287	1z. Type **623**	10	10
2288	1z.50 Church, Sekowa	10	10
2289	4z. Town Hall, Sulmierzycc	20	10
2290	4z.50 Church, Lachowice	30	10
2291	4z.90 Windmill, Sobienie Jeziory	45	20
2292	5z. Orthodox Church, Ulucz	50	20

624 19th-century Mail Coach

1974. Centenary of Universal Postal Union.

2293	**624**	1z.50 multicoloured	10	10

625 Cracow Motif

1974. "SOCPHILEX IV" Int Stamp Exn, Katowice. Regional Floral Embroideries. Multicoloured.

2294	50g. Type **625**	10	10
2295	1z.50 Lowicz motif	10	10
2296	4z. Silesian motif	20	10
MS2297	69×71 mm. No. 2296 ×3	1·10	30

626 Association Emblem

1974. 5th Congress of Fighters for Freedom and Democracy Association, Warsaw.

2298	**626**	1z.50 red	10	10

627 Soldier and Dove

1974. 29th Anniv of Victory over Fascism in Second World War.

2299	**627**	1z.50 multicoloured	10	10

628 "Comecon" Headquarters, Moscow

1974. 25th Anniv of Council for Mutual Economic Aid.

2300	**628**	1z.50 brown, red & blue	10	10

629 World Cup Emblem

1974. World Cup Football Championship, West Germany. Multicoloured.

2301	4z.90 Type **629**	25	15
2302	4z.90 Players and Olympic Gold Medal of 1972	25	15
MS2303	116×83 mm. Nos. 2301/2	10·50	9·00

See also No. **MS**2315.

630 Model of 16th- century Galleon

1974. Sailing Ships. Multicoloured.

2304	1z. Type **630**	10	10
2305	1z.50 Sloop "Dal" (1934)	10	10
2306	2z.70 Yacht "Opty" (Teliga's circumnavigation, 1969)	10	10
2307	4z. Cadet ship "Dar Pomorza", 1972	40	10
2308	4z.90 Yacht "Polonez" (Baranowski's circumnavigation, 1973)	55	25

631 Title page of "Chess" by J. Kochanowski

1974. 10th Inter-Chess Festival, Lublin. Mult.

2309	1z. Type **631**	10	15
2310	1z.50 "Education" (18th-century engraving, D. Chodowiecki)	20	15

632 Lazienkowska Road Junction

1974. Opening of Lazienkowska Flyover.

2311	**632**	1z.50 multicoloured	15	15

633 Face and Map of Poland

1974. 30th Anniv of Polish People's Republic.

2312	**633**	1z.50 black, gold and red	15	10

2313	-	1z.50 multicoloured (silver background)	15	10
2314	-	1z.50 multicoloured (red background)	15	10

DESIGN—31×43 mm: Nos. 2313/14, Polish "Eagle".

1974. Poland–Third Place in World Cup Football Championship. Sheet 107×121 mm containing four stamps as No. 2301, but with inscr in silver instead of black, and two labels.

MS2315	**629**	4z.90 ×4 multicoloured	3·00	1·90

634 Strawberries

1974. 19th International Horticultural Congress, Warsaw. Fruits, Vegetables and Flowers. Mult.

2316	50g. Type **634**	10	10
2317	90g. Blackcurrants	10	10
2318	1z. Apples	10	10
2319	1z.50 Cucumbers	20	10
2320	2z.70 Tomatoes	30	10
2321	4z.50 Green peas	75	10
2322	4z.90 Pansies	1·10	20
2323	5z. Nasturtiums	1·50	30

635 Civic Militia and Security Service Emblem

1974. 30th Anniv of Polish Civic Militia and Security Service.

2324	**635**	1z.50 multicoloured	10	10

636 "Child in Polish Costume" (L. Orlowski)

1974. Stamp Day. Paintings. Multicoloured.

2325	50g. Type **636**	10	10
2326	90g. "Girl with Pigeon" (anon)	10	10
2327	1z. "Portrait of a Girl" (S. Wyspianski)	10	10
2328	1z.50 "The Orphan from Poronin" (W. Slewinski)	10	10
2329	3z. "Peasant Boy" (K. Sichulski)	20	10
2330	4z.50 "Florence Page" (A. Gierymski)	35	10
2331	4z.90 "Tadeusz and Dog" (P. Michalowski)	45	30
2332	6z.50 "Boy with Doe" (A. Kotsis)	60	35

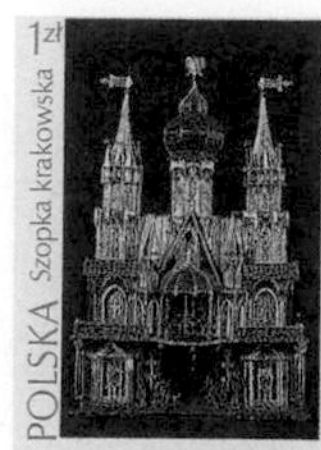

637 "The Crib", Cracow

1974. Polish Art. Multicoloured.

2333	1z. Type **637**	10	10
2334	1z.50 "The Flight to Egypt" (15th-century polyptych)	10	10
2335	2z. "King Sigismund III Vasa" (16th-century miniature)	20	10
2336	4z. "King Jan Olbracht" (16th-century title-page)	75	30

638 Angler and Fish

1974. Polish Folklore. 16th-century Woodcuts (1st series).

2337	1z. black	10	10
2338	1z.50 blue	10	10

DESIGN: 1z. Type **638**; 1z.50, Hunter and wild animals.
See also Nos. 2525/6.

639 "Pablo Neruda" (O. Guayasamin)

1974. 70th Birth Anniv of Pablo Neruda (Chilean poet).

2339	**639**	1z.50 multicoloured	10	10

640 "Nike" Memorial and National Opera House

1975. 30th Anniv of Warsaw Liberation.

2340	**640**	1z.50 multicoloured	10	10

641 Male Lesser Kestrel

1975. Birds of Prey. Multicoloured.

2341	1z. Type **641**	25	10
2342	1z. Lesser kestrel (female)	25	10
2343	1z.50 Western red-footed falcon (male)	25	10
2344	1z.50 Western red-footed falcon (female)	25	10
2345	2z. Northern hobby	30	10
2346	3z. Common kestrel	55	10
2347	4z. Merlin	1·40	75
2348	8z. Peregrine falcon	2·10	1·50

642 Broken Barbed Wire

1975. 30th Anniv of Auschwitz Concentration Camp Liberation.

2349	**642**	1z.50 black and red	10	10

643 Hurdling

1975. 6th European Indoor Athletic Championships, Katowice. Multicoloured.

2350	1z. Type **643**	10	10
2351	1z.50 Pole vault	10	10
2352	4z. Triple jump	30	10
2353	4z.90 Running	30	10
MS2354	72×63 mm. 10z.+5z. green and silver (Montreal Olympics emblem) (26×31 mm)	1·90	90

644 "St. Anne" (Veit Stoss)

1975. "Arphila 1975" International Stamp Exhibition, Paris.

2355	**644**	1z.50 multicoloured	10	10

645 Globe and "Radio Waves"

1975. International Amateur Radio Union Conference, Warsaw.

2356	**645**	1z.50 multicoloured	10	10

646 Stone, Pine and Tatra Mountains

1975. Centenary of Mountain Guides' Association. Multicoloured.

2357	1z. Type **646**	10	10
2358	1z. Gentians and Tatra Mountains	10	10
2359	1z.50 Sudety Mountains (horiz)	10	10
2360	1z.50 Branch of yew (horiz)	10	10
2361	4z. Beskidy Mountains	30	15
2362	4z. Arnica blossoms	30	10

647 Hands holding Tulips and Rifle

1975. 30th Anniv of Victory over Fascism.

2363	**647**	1z.50 multicoloured	10	10

648 Flags of Member Countries

1975. 20th Anniv of Warsaw Treaty Organization.

2364	**648**	1z.50 multicoloured	10	10

649 Hens

1975. 26th European Zoo-technical Federation Congress, Warsaw. Multicoloured.

2365	50g. Type **649**		10	10
2366	1z. Geese		10	10
2367	1z.50 Cattle		10	10
2368	2z. Cow		10	10
2369	3z. Wielkopolska horse		30	20
2370	4z. Pure-bred Arab horses		30	20
2371	4z.50 Pigs		1·10	80
2372	5z. Sheep		1·75	1·10

650 "Apollo" and "Soyuz" Spacecraft linked

1975. "Apollo–Soyuz" Space Project. Mult.

2373	1z.50 Type **650**		10	10
2374	4z.90 "Apollo" spacecraft		45	10
2375	4z.90 "Soyuz" spacecraft		45	25
MS2376	119×156 mm. Nos. 2373 ×2, 2374 ×2 and 2375 ×2		5·25	3·25

651 Organization Emblem

1975. National Health Protection Fund.

2377	**651**	1z.50 blue, black & silver	10	10

652 U.N. Emblem

1975. 30th Anniv of U.N.O.

2378	**652**	4z. multicoloured	30	10

653 Polish Flag within "E" for Europe

1975. European Security and Co-operation Conference, Helsinki.

2379	**653**	4z. red, blue and black	30	25

654 "Bolek and Lolek"

1975. Children's Television Characters. Mult.

2380	50g. Type **654**		10	15
2381	1z. "Jacek" and "Agatka"		10	15
2382	1z.50 "Reksio" (dog)		10	15
2383	4z. "Telesfor" (dragon)		45	15

655 Institute Emblem

1975. 40th Session of International Statistics Institute.

2384	**655**	1z.50 multicoloured	10	10

656 Women's Faces

1975. International Women's Year.

2385	**656**	1z.50 multicoloured	10	10

657 Albatros Biplane

1975. 50th Anniv of First Polish Airmail Stamps. Multicoloured.

2386	2z.40 Type **657**		15	15
2387	4z.90 Ilyushin Il-62 airplane		40	15

658 "Mary and Margaret" and Polish Settlers

1975. Bicentenary of American Revolution. Poles in American Life. Multicoloured.

2388	1z. Type **658**		15	10
2389	1z.50 Polish glass-works, Jamestown		10	10
2390	2z.70 Helena Modrzejewska (actress)		10	10
2391	4z. K. Pulaski (soldier)		25	10
2392	6z.40 T. Kosciuzko (soldier)		60	30
MS2393	117×102 mm. 4z.90 Washington; 4z.90 Kosciuszko; 4z.90 Pulaski		1·10	70

659 Frederic Chopin

1975. 9th International Chopin Piano Competition.

2394	**659**	1z.50 black, lilac & gold	10	20

660 "Self-portrait"

1975. Stamp Day. Birth Centenary of Xawery Dunikowski (sculptor). Multicoloured.

2395	50g. Type **660**		10	10
2396	1z. "Breath"		10	10
2397	1z.50 "Maternity"		15	10
2398	8z.+4z. "Silesian Insurrectionists"		90	35

661 Market Place, Kazimierz Dolny

1975. European Architectural Heritage Year.

2399	**661**	1z. green	10	10
2400	-	1z.50 brown	10	10

DESIGN—VERT: 1z.50, Town Hall, Zamosc.

662 "Lodz" (W. Strzeminski)

1975. "Lodz 75" National Stamp Exhibition.

2401	**662**	4z.50 multicoloured	30	20
MS2402	80×101 mm. No. 2401		95	65

663 Henry IV's Eagle Gravestone Head (14th-century)

1975. Piast Dynasty of Silesia.

2403	**663**	1z. green	10	10
2404	-	1z.50 brown	10	10
2405	-	4z. violet	25	10

DESIGNS: 1z.50, Seal of Prince Boleslaw of Legnica; 4z. Coin of last Prince, Jerzy Wilhelm.

664 Symbolized Figure "7"

1975. 7th Congress of Polish United Workers Party.

2406	**664**	1z. multicoloured	10	10
2407	-	1z.50 red, blue and silver	10	10

DESIGN: 1z.50, Party initials "PZPR".

665 Ski Jumping

1976. Winter Olympic Games, Innsbruck. Mult.

2408	50g. Type **665**		10	10
2409	1z. Ice hockey		10	10
2410	1z.50 Skiing		10	10
2411	2z. Skating		10	10
2412	4z. Tobogganing		30	10
2413	6z.40 Biathlon		40	30

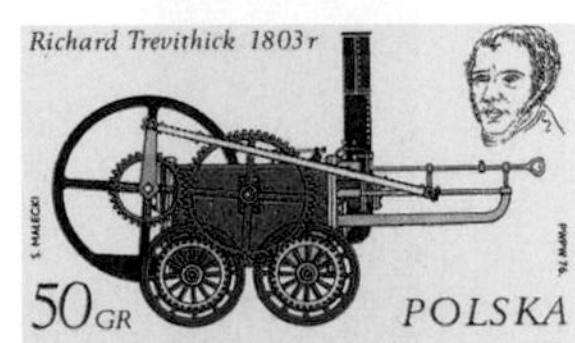

666 Richard Trevithick and his Locomotive, 1803

1976. History of the Railway Locomotive. Mult.

2414	50g. Type **666**		10	10
2415	1z. Murray and Blenkinsop's steam locomotive and carriage, 1810		10	10
2416	1z.50 George Stephenson and his locomotive "Rocket", 1829		10	10
2417	1z.50 Polish "Universal" electric locomotive No. ET22-001, 1969		10	10
2418	2z.70 Robert Stephenson and his locomotive "North Star", 1837		10	10
2419	3z. Joseph Harrison and his locomotive, 1840		15	10
2420	4z.50 Locomotive "Thomas Rogers", 1855, U.S.A.		75	45
2421	4z.90 A. Xiezopolski and Series Ok22 steam locomotive, 1922		75	45

667 Flags of Member Countries

1976. 20th Anniv of Institute for Nuclear Research (C.M.E.A.).

2422	**667**	1z.50 multicoloured	10	10

668 Early Telephone, Satellite and Radar

1976. Telephone Centenary.

2423	**668**	1z.50 multicoloured	10	10

669 Jantar Glider

1976. Air. Contemporary Aviation.

2424	**669**	5z. blue	35	10
2425	-	10z. brown	75	10
2425a	-	20z. olive	1·50	10
2425b	-	50z. lake	3·50	60

DESIGN: 10z. Mil Mi-6 helicopter; 20z. PZL-106A agricultural airplane; 50z. PZL-Mielec TS-11 Iskra jet trainer over Warsaw Castle.

670 Player

1976. World Ice Hockey Championships, Katowice. Multicoloured.

2426	1z. Type **670**		10	10
2427	1z.50 Player (different)		10	10

671 Polish U.N. Soldier

1976. Polish Troops in U.N. Sinai Force.

2428	**671**	1z.50 multicoloured	10	10

672 "Glory to the Sappers" (S. Kulon)

1976. War Memorials. Multicoloured.

2429 1z. Type **672** 10 10
2430 1z. 1st Polish Army Monument, Sandau, Laba (B. Koniuszy) 10 10

673 "Interphil 76"

1976. "Interphil '76" Int Stamp Exn, Philadelphia.

2431 **673** 8z.40 multicoloured 55 30

674 Wielkopolski Park and Tawny Owl

1976. National Parks. Multicoloured.

2432 90g. Type **674** 30 10
2433 1z. Wolinski Park and white-tailed sea eagle 30 10
2434 1z.50 Slowinski Park and seagull 35 10
2435 4z.50 Bieszezadzki Park and lynx 30 10
2436 5z. Ojcowski Park and bat 30 20
2437 6z. Kampinoski Park and elk 35 30

675 Peace Dove within Globe

1976. 25th Anniv of U.N. Postal Administration.

2438 **675** 8z.40 multicoloured 60 25

676 Fencing

1976. Olympic Games, Montreal. Multicoloured.

2439 50g. Type **676** 10 10
2440 1z. Cycling 10 10
2441 1z.50 Football 10 10
2442 4z.20 Boxing 30 10
2443 6z.90 Weightlifting 55 15
2444 8z.40 Athletics 60 25
MS2445 78×94 mm. 10z.+5z. black and red (Volleyball) (23×29 mm) 1·50 85

677 National Theatre

1976. Cent of National Theatre, Poznan.

2446 **677** 1z.50 green and orange 15 15

678 Aleksander Czekanowski and Baikal Landscape

1976. Death Centenary of Aleksander Czekanowski (geologist).

2447 **678** 1z.50 multicoloured 15 15

679 "Sphinx"

1976. Stamp Day. Corinthian Vase Paintings (7th century B.C.). Multicoloured.

2448 1z. Type **679** 10 10
2449 1z.50 "Siren" (horiz) 10 10
2450 2z. "Lion" (horiz) 15 10
2451 4z.20 "Bull" (horiz) 30 10
2452 4z.50 "Goat" (horiz) 30 25
2453 8z.+4z. "Sphinx" (different) 1·00 45

680 Warszawa "M 20"

1976. 25th Anniv of Zeran Motor-car Factory, Warsaw. Multicoloured.

2454 1z. Type **680** 10 10
2455 1z.50 Warszawa "223" 10 10
2456 2z. Syrena "104" 15 10
2457 4z.90 Polski - Fiat "125P" 40 15
MS2458 137×109 mm. Nos. 2454/7 1·90 1·10

681 Molten Steel Ladle

1976. Huta Katowice Steel Works.

2459 **681** 1z.50 multicoloured 15 15

682 Congress Emblem

1976. 8th Polish Trade Unions Congress.

2460 **682** 1z.50 orange, bistre and brown 15 15

683 "Wirzbieto Epitaph" (painting on wood, 1425)

1976. Polish Art. Multicoloured.

2461 1z. Type **683** 10 15
2462 6z. "Madonna and Child" (painted carving, c.1410) 40 15

684 Tanker "Zawrat" at Oil Terminal, Gdansk

1976. Polish Ports. Multicoloured.

2463 1z. Type **684** 10 10
2464 1z. Ferry "Gryf" at Gdansk 10 10
2465 1z.50 Loading container ship "General Bem", Gdynia 20 10
2466 1z.50 Liner "Stefan Batory" leaving Gdynia 20 10
2467 2z. Bulk carrier "Ziemia Szczecinska" loading at Szczecin 25 10
2468 4z.20 Loading coal, Swinoujscie 30 10
2469 6z.90 Pleasure craft, Kolobrzeg 40 30
2470 8z.40 Coastal map 60 30

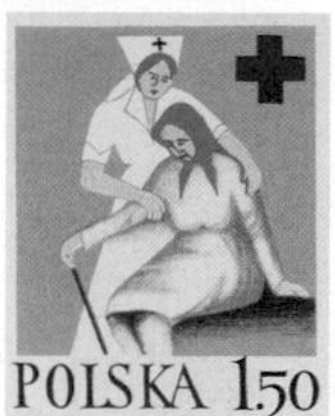

685 Nurse and Patient

1977. Polish Red Cross.

2471 **685** 1z.50 multicoloured 10 10

686 Order of Civil Defence Service

1977. Polish Civil Defence.

2472 **686** 1z.50 multicoloured 10 10

687 Ball in Road

1977. Child Road Safety Campaign.

2473 **687** 1z.50 multicoloured 10 10

688 Dewberries

1977. Wild Fruits. Multicoloured.

2474 50g. Type **688** 10 10
2475 90g. Cowberries 10 10
2476 1z. Wild strawberries 10 10
2477 1z.50 Bilberries 15 10
2478 2z. Raspberries 15 10
2479 4z.50 Sloes 30 10
2480 6z. Rose hips 40 10
2481 6z.90 Hazelnuts 45 30

689 Computer Tape

1977. 30th Anniv of Russian–Polish Technical Co-operation.

2482 **689** 1z.50 multicoloured 10 10

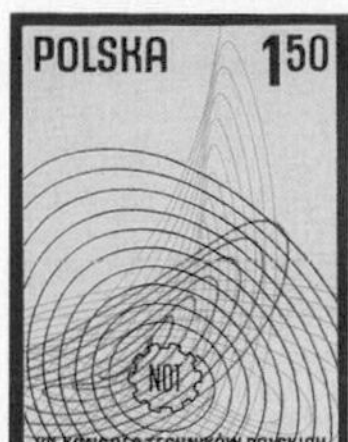

690 Pendulum Traces and Emblem

1977. 7th Polish Congress of Technology.

2483 **690** 1z.50 multicoloured 10 10

691 "Toilet of Venus"

1977. 400th Birth Anniv of Peter Paul Rubens. Multicoloured.

2484 1z. Type **691** 10 10
2485 1z.50 "Bathsheba at the Fountain" 10 10
2486 5z. "Helena Fourment with Fur Coat" 30 10
2487 6z. "Self-portrait" 45 30
MS2488 76×62 mm. 8z.+4z. sepia ("The Stoning of St. Stephan") (21×26 mm) 1·40 85

692 Dove

1977. World Council of Peace Congress.

2489 **692** 1z.50 blue, yellow & black 10 10

693 Cyclist

1977. 30th International Peace Cycle Race.

2490 **693** 1z.50 multicoloured 10 10

694 Wolf

1977. Endangered Animals. Multicoloured.

2491 1z. Type **694** 10 10
2492 1z.50 Great bustard 30 15
2493 1z.50 Common kestrel 30 15
2494 6z. European otter 40 25

695 "The Violinist" (J. Toorenvliet)

1977. "Amphilex 77" Stamp Exhibition, Amsterdam.

2495 **695** 6z. multicoloured 40 30

696 Midsummer's Day Bonfire

1977. Folk Customs. 19th-century Wood Engravings. Multicoloured.

2496	90g. Type **696**		10	10
2497	1z. Easter cock (vert)		10	10
2498	1z.50 "Smigus" (dousing of women on Easter Monday, Miechow district) (vert)		10	10
2499	3z. Harvest Festival, Sandomierz district (vert)		25	10
2500	6z. Children with Christmas crib (vert)		40	10
2501	8z.40 Mountain wedding dance		55	25

697 H. Wieniawski and Music Clef

1977. Wieniawski International Music Competitions, Poznan.

2502	**697**	1z.50 black, red and gold	25	10

698 Apollo ("Parnassius apollo")

1977. Butterflies. Multicoloured.

2503	1z. Type **698**		30	10
2504	1z. Large tortoiseshell ("Nymphalis polychloros")		30	10
2505	1z.50 Camberwell beauty ("Nymphalis antiopa")		40	10
2506	1z.50 Swallowtail ("Papilio machaon")		40	10
2507	5z. High brown fritillary		1·10	10
2508	6z.90 Silver-washed fritillary		1·90	45

699 Keyboard and Arms of Slupsk

1977. Piano Festival, Slupsk.

2509	**699**	1z.50 mauve, blk & grn	15	10

700 Feliks Dzerzhinsky

1977. Birth Centenary of Feliks Dzerzhinsky (Russian politician).

2510	**700**	1z.50 brown and ochre	15	15

701 "Sputnik" circling Earth

1977. 60th Anniv of Russian Revolution and 20th Anniv of 1st Artificial Satellite (1st issue).

2511	**701**	1z.50 red and blue	15	15
MS2512		99×125 mm. No. 2511 ×3 plus three labels	75	75

See also No. 2527.

702 Silver Dinar (11th century)

1977. Stamp Day. Polish Coins. Multicoloured.

2513	50g. Type **702**		10	10
2514	1z. Cracow grosz, 14th-century		10	10
2515	1z.50 Legnica thaler, 17th-century		10	10
2516	4z.20 Gdansk guilder, 18th-century		30	10
2517	4z.50 Silver 5z. coin, 1936		30	10
2518	6z. Millenary 100z. coin, 1966		55	25

703 Wolin Gate, Kamien Pomorski

1977. Architectural Monuments. Multicoloured.

2519	1z. Type **703**		10	10
2520	1z. Larch church, Debno		10	10
2521	1z.50 Monastery, Przasnysz (horiz)		10	10
2522	1z.50 Plock cathedral (horiz)		10	10
2523	6z. Kornik castle (horiz)		45	10
2524	6z.90 Palace and garden, Wilanow (horiz)		55	30

1977. Polish Folklore. 16th-century woodcuts (2nd series). As T 638.

2525	4z. sepia		25	10
2526	4z.50 brown		30	10

DESIGNS: 4z. Bird snaring; 4z.50, Bee-keeper and hives.

704 "Sputnik 1" and "Mercury" Capsule

1977. 20th Anniv of 1st Space Satellite (2nd issue).

2527	**704**	6z.90 multicoloured	45	40

705 DN Category Iceboats

1978. 6th World Ice Sailing Championships.

2528	**705**	1z.50 black, grey & blue	15	10
2529	-	1z.50 black, grey & blue	25	10

DESIGN: No. 2529, Close-up of DN iceboat.

706 Electric Locomotive and Katowice Station

1978. Railway Engines. Multicoloured.

2530	50g. Type **706**		10	10
2531	1z. Steam locomotive No. Py27 and tender No. 721, Znin-Gasawa railway		10	10
2532	1z. Streamlined steam locomotive No. Pm36-1 (1936) and Cegielski's factory, Poznan		10	10
2533	1z.50 Electric locomotive and Otwock station		10	10
2534	1z.50 Steam locomotive No. 17 KDM and Warsaw Stalowa station		10	10
2535	4z.50 Steam locomotive No. Ty51 and Gdynia station		30	10
2536	5z. Steam locomotive No. Tr21 and locomotive works, Chrzanow		40	10
2537	6z. Cockerill steam locomotive and Vienna station		55	30

707 Czeslaw Tanski and Glider

1978. Aviation History and 50th Anniv of Polish Aero Club. Multicoloured.

2538	50g. Type **707**		10	10
2539	1z. Franciszek Zwirko and Stanislaw Wigura with RWD-6 aircraft (vert)		10	10
2540	1z.50 Stanislaw Skarzynski and RWD-5 bis monoplane (vert)		10	10
2541	4z.20 Mil Mi-2 helicopter (vert)		25	10
2542	6z.90 PZL-104 Wilga 35 monoplane		75	25
2543	8z.40 SZD-45 Ogar powered glider		60	25

708 Tackle

1978. World Cup Football Championship, Argentina. Multicoloured.

2544	1z.50 Type **708**		10	10
2545	6z.90 Ball on field (horiz)		45	30

709 Biennale Emblem

1978. 7th International Poster Biennale, Warsaw.

2546	**709**	1z.50 mauve, yell & vio	15	15

710 Kazimierz Stanislaw Gzowski (bridge engineer)

1978. "Capex 78" International Stamp Exhibition, Toronto. Sheet 68×79 mm.

MS2547	**710**	8z.40+4z. multicoloured	1·10	70

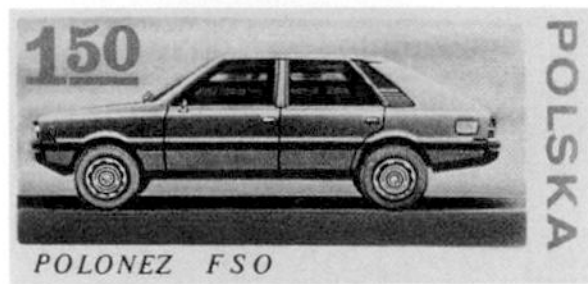

711 Polonez Saloon Car

1978. Car Production.

2548	**711**	1z.50 multicoloured	10	10

712 Fair Emblem

1978. 50th International Fair, Poznan.

2549	**712**	1z.50 multicoloured	10	10

713 Miroslaw Hermaszewski

1978. 1st Pole in Space. Multicoloured. With or without date.

2550	1z.50 Type **713**		10	10
2551	6z.90 M. Hermaszewski and globe		55	25

714 Globe containing Face

1978. 11th World Youth and Students Festival, Havana.

2552	**714**	1z.50 multicoloured	10	10

715 Flowers

1978. 30th Anniv Polish Youth Union. Sheet 69×79 mm.

MS2553	**715**	1z.50 multicoloured	40	40

716 Mosquito and Malaria Organisms

1978. 4th International Congress of Parasitologists, Warsaw and Cracow. Multicoloured.

2554	1z.50 Type **716**		10	10
2555	6z. Tsetse fly and sleeping sickness organism		40	40

717 Pedunculate Oak

1978. Environment Protection. Trees. Mult.

2556	50g. Norway Maple		10	10
2557	1z. Type **717**		10	10
2558	1z.50 White Poplar		10	10
2559	4z.20 Scots Pine		25	10
2560	4z.50 White Willow		25	10
2561	6z. Birch		40	15

718

1978. "PRAGA 1978" International Stamp Exhibition. Sheet 69×79 mm.

MS2562	718	6z. multicoloured	1·10	60

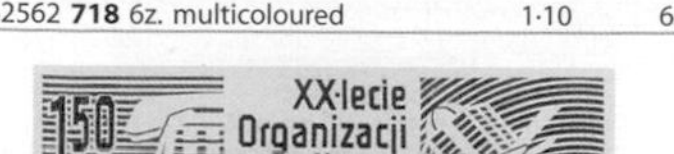

719 Communications

1978. 20th Anniv of Socialist Countries Communications Organization.

2563	719	1z.50 red, lt blue & blue	10	10

720 "Peace" (Andre Le Brun)

1978

2564	720	1z. violet	10	10
2565	720	1z.50 turquoise	10	10
2565a	720	2z. brown	10	10
2565b	720	2z.50 blue	25	10

721 Polish Unit of U.N. Middle East Force

1978. 35th Anniv of Polish People's Army. Mult.

2566		1z.50 Colour party of Tadeusz Kosciuszko 1st Warsaw Infantry Division	10	10
2567		1z.50 Mechanized Unit colour party	10	10
2568		1z.50 Type **721**	10	10

722 "Portrait of a Young Man" (Raphael)

1978. Stamp Day.

2569	722	6z. multicoloured	40	30

723 Janusz Korczak with Children

1978. Birth Centenary of Janusz Korczak (pioneer of children's education).

2570	723	1z.50 multicoloured	25	10

724 Wojciech Boguslawski

1978. Polish Dramatists. Multicoloured.

2571		50g. Type **724**	10	10
2572		1z. Aleksander Fredro	10	10
2573		1z.50 Juliusz Slowacki	10	10
2574		2z. Adam Mickiewicz	10	10
2575		4z.50 Stanislaw Wyspianski	30	10
2576		6z. Gabriela Zapolska	45	25

725 Polish Combatants' Monument and Eiffel Tower

1978. Monument to Polish Combatants in France, Paris.

2577	725	1z.50 brown, blue & red	20	10

726 Przewalski Horses

1978. 50th Anniv of Warsaw Zoo. Multicoloured.

2578		50g. Type **726**	10	10
2579		1z. Polar bears	10	10
2580		1z.50 Indian elephants	25	10
2581		2z. Jaguars	30	10
2582		4z.20 Grey seals	30	10
2583		4z.50 Hartebeests	30	10
2584		6z. Mandrills	45	30

727 Party Flag

1978. 30th Anniv of Polish Workers' United Party.

2585	727	1z.50 red, gold and black	10	10

728 Stanislaw Dubois

1978. Leaders of Polish Workers' Movement.

2586	728	1z.50 blue and red	10	10
2587	-	1z.50 lilac and red	10	10
2588	-	1z.50 olive and red	10	10
2589	-	1z.50 brown and red	10	10

DESIGNS: No. 2587, Aleksander Zawadzki; 2588, Julian Lenski; 2589, Aldolf Warski.

729 Ilyushin Il-62M and Fokker F. VIIb/3m

1979. 50th Anniv of LOT Polish Airlines.

2590	729	6z.90 multicoloured	55	25

730 Steam Train

1979. International Year of the Child. Children's Paintings. Multicoloured.

2591		50g. Type **730**	10	10
2592		1z. "Mother with Children"	10	10
2593		1z.50 Children playing	10	10
2594		6z. Family Group	40	25

731 "Portrait of Artist's Wife with Foxgloves" (Karol Mondrala)

1979. Contemporary Graphics.

2595	-	50g. lilac	10	10
2596	731	1z. green	10	10
2597	-	1z.50 blue	10	10
2598	-	4z.50 brown	30	10

DESIGNS—HORIZ: 50g. "Lightning" (Edmund Bartlomiejezyk). VERT: 1z.50, "The Musicians" (Tadeusz Kulisiewicz); 4z.50, "Head of a Young Man" (Wladyslaw Skoczylas).

732 A. Frycz Modrzewski (political writer), King Stefan Batory and Jan Zamoyski (chancellor)

1979. 400th Anniv (1978) of Royal Tribunal in Piotrkow Trybunalski.

2599	732	1z.50 brown and deep brown	10	10

733 Pole Vaulting

1979. 60th Anniv of Polish Olympic Committee.

2600	733	1z. Lilac, brown and red	10	10
2601	-	1z.50 lilac, brown and red	10	10
2602	-	6z. lilac, brown and red	40	10
2603	-	8z.40 lilac, brown and red	60	25
MS2604		102×61 mm. 10z.+5z. brown	90	75

DESIGNS: 1z.50, High jump; 6z. Skiing; 8z.40, Horse riding; 10z. Olympic rings.

734 European Flounder

1979. Centenary of Polish Angling. Multicoloured.

2605		50g. Type **734**	10	10
2606		90g. Eurasian perch	10	10
2607		1z. European grayling	10	10
2608		1z.50 Atlantic salmon	10	10
2609		2z. Brown trout	15	10
2610		4z.50 Northern pike	30	10
2611		5z. Common carp	45	10
2612		6z. Wels	45	20

735 "30 Years of RWPG"

1979. 30th Anniv of Council of Mutual Economic Aid.

2613	735	1z.50 red, ultram & blue	10	10

736 Soldier, Civilian and Congress Emblem

1979. 6th Congress of Association of Fighters for Liberty and Democracy.

2614	736	1z.50 red and black	10	10

737 St. George's Church, Sofia

1979. "Philaserdica 79" International Stamp Exhibition, Sofia, Bulgaria.

2615	737	1z.50 orange, brn & red	10	10

738 Pope and Auschwitz Concentration Camp Memorial

1979. Visit of Pope John Paul II. Multicoloured.

2616		1z.50 Pope and St. Mary's Church, Cracow	25	10
2617		8z.40 Type **738**	70	30
MS2618		68×79 mm. 50z. Framed portrait of Pope (26×35 mm)	7·00	5·25

739 River Paddle-steamer "Ksiaze Ksawery" and Old Warsaw

1979. 150th Anniv of Vistula River Navigation. Multicoloured.

2619		1z. Type **739**	10	10
2620		1z.50 River paddle-steamer "General Swierczewski" and Gdansk	10	10
2621		4z.50 River tug "Zubr" and Plock	25	10
2622		6z. Passenger launch "Syrena" and modern Warsaw	45	25

740 Statue of Tadeusz Kosciuszko (Marian Konieczny)

1979. Monument to Tadeusz Kosciuszko in Philadelphia.

2623	740	8z.40 multicoloured	40	25

741 Mining Machinery

1979. Wieliczka Salt Mine.

2624	741	1z. brown and black	10	10
2625	-	1z.50 turquoise and black	10	10

DESIGN: 1z.50, Salt crystals.

742 Heraldic Eagle

1979. 35th Anniv of Polish People's Republic.

2626		1z.50 red, silver and black	15	10
2627	**742**	1z.50 red, silver and blue	15	10
MS2628		120×84 mm. Nos. 2626/7 plus label	40	45

DESIGN: No. 2626, Girl and stylized flag.

743 Rowland Hill and 1860 Stamp

1979. Death Centenary of Sir Rowland Hill.

2629	**743**	6z. blue, black and orange	40	10

744 "The Rape of Europa" (Bernardo Stozzi)

1979. International Stamp Exhibition. Sheet 86×63 mm.

MS2630	**744**	10z. multicoloured	75	60

745 Wojciech Jastrzebowski

1979. 7th Congress of International Ergonomic Association, Warsaw.

2631	**745**	1z.50 multicoloured	15	10

746 Monument (Wincenty Kucma)

1979. Unveiling of Monument to Defenders of Polish Post, Gdansk, and 40th Anniv of German Occupation.

2632	**746**	1z.50 grey, sepia and red	15	10
MS2633		79×69 mm. **746** 10z.+5z. grey, sepia and red. Imperf	1·00	85

747 Radio Mast and Telecommunications Emblem

1979. 50th Anniv of International Radio Communication Advisory Committee.

2634	**747**	1z.50 multicoloured	15	10

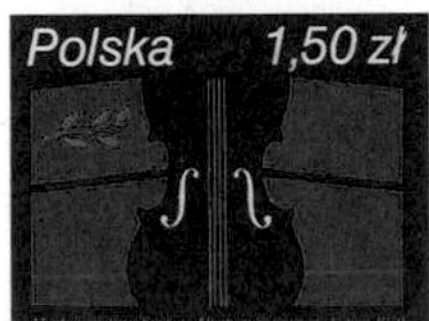

748 Violin

1979. Wieniawski Young Violinists' Competition, Lublin.

2635	**748**	1z.50 blue, orange & green	15	10

749 Statue of Kazimierz Pulaski, Buffalo (K. Danilewicz)

1979. Death Bicentenary of Kazimierz Pulaski (American Revolution Hero).

2636	**749**	8z.40 multicoloured	60	30

750 Franciszek Jozwiak (first Commander)

1979. 35th Anniv of Civic Militia and Security Force.

2637	**750**	1z.50 blue and gold	15	10

751 Post Office in Rural Area

1979. Stamp Day. Multicoloured.

2638	1z. Type **751**	10	10
2639	1z.50 Parcel sorting machinery	10	10
2640	4z.50 Loading containers on train	45	10
2641	6z. Mobile post office	60	25

752 "The Holy Family" (Ewelina Peksowa)

1979. Polish Folk Art. Glass Paintings. Mult.

2642	2z. Type **752**	10	10
2643	6z.90 "The Nativity" (Zdzislaw Walczak)	45	25

753 "Soyuz 30-Salyut 6" Complex and Crystal

1979. Space Achievements. Multicoloured.

2644	1z. Type **753** (1st anniv of 1st Pole in space)	10	10
2645	1z.50 "Kopernik" and "Copernicus" satellites	10	10
2646	2z. "Lunik 2" and "Ranger 7" spacecraft (20th anniv of 1st unmanned Moon landing)	10	10
2647	4z.50 Yuri Gagarin and "Vostok 1"	10	10
2648	6z.90 Neil Armstrong, lunar module and "Apollo 11" (10th anniv of first man on Moon)	25	30
MS2649	120×103 mm. Nos. 2644/8 plus label (sold at 20z.90)	1·25	1·25

754 Coach and Four

1980. 150th Anniv of Sierakow Stud Farm. Mult.

2650	1z. Type **754**	10	10
2651	2z. Horse and groom	10	10
2652	2z.50 Sulky racing	10	10
2653	3z. Hunting	25	10
2654	4z. Horse-drawn sledge	30	10
2655	6z. Haywain	45	10
2656	6z.50 Grooms exercising horses	55	25
2657	6z.90 Show jumping	60	30

755 Slogan on Map of Poland

1980. 8th Polish United Workers' Party Congress. Multicoloured.

2658	2z.50 Type **755**	25	10
2659	2z.50 Janusz Stann (26×46 mm)	25	10

756 Horse Jumping

1980. Olympic Games, Moscow, and Winter Olympic Games, Lake Placid. Multicoloured.

2660	2z. Type **756**	10	10
2661	2z.50 Archery	25	10
2662	6z.50 Skiing	45	10
2663	8z.40 Volleyball	60	30

757 Town Plan and Old Town Hall

1980. 400th Anniv of Zamosc.

2665	**757**	2z.50 buff, green & brn	15	10

758 Satellite orbiting Earth

1980. "Intercosmos" Space Programme. Sheet 63×79 mm.

MS2666	**758**	6z.90+3z. multicoloured	60	70

759 Seals of Poland and Russia

1980. 35th Anniv of Soviet–Polish Friendship Treaty.

2667	**759**	2z.50 multicoloured	25	10

760 "Lenin in Cracow" (Zbigniew Pronaszko)

1980. 110th Birth Anniv of Lenin.

2668	**760**	2z.50 multicoloured	25	10

761 Workers with Red Flag

1980. 75th Anniv of Revolution of 1905.

2669	**761**	2z.50 red, black & yellow	25	10

762 Dove

1980. 35th Anniv of Liberation.

2670	**762**	2z.50 multicoloured	25	10

763 Shield with Crests of Member Nations

1980. 25th Anniv of Warsaw Pact.

2671	**763**	2z. grey and red	25	10

764 Speleological Expedition, Cuba

1980. Polish Scientific Expeditions. Multicoloured.

2672	2z. Type **764**	10	10
2673	2z. Antarctic	30	10
2674	2z.50 Archaeology, Syria	25	10
2675	2z.50 Ethnology, Mongolia	25	10
2676	6z.50 Mountaineering, Nepal	40	10
2677	8z.40 Paleontology, Mongolia	55	25

765 School and Arms

1980. 800th Anniv of Malachowski School, Plock.

2678	**765**	2z. green and black	15	10

766 "Clathrus ruber"

1980. Fungi. Multicoloured.

2679		2z. Type **766**	20	10
2680		2z. "Xerocomus parasiticus"	20	10
2681		2z.50 Old man of the woods ("Strobilomyces floccopus")	25	10
2682		2z.50 "Phallus hadriani"	25	10
2683		8z. Cauliflower fungus	40	20
2684		10z.50 Giant puff-ball	40	45

767 T. Ziolowski and "Lwow"

1980. Polish Merchant Navy School. Cadet Ships and their Captains.

2685		2z. black, mauve and violet	20	10
2686		2z.50 black, light blue and blue	25	10
2687		6z. black, pale green and green	30	10
2688		6z.50 black, yellow and grey	40	10
2689		6z.90 black, grey and green	45	25
2690		8z.40 black, blue and green	55	25

DESIGNS: 2z.50, A. Garnuszewski and "Antoni Garnuszewski"; 6z. A. Ledochowski and "Zenit"; 6z.50, K. Porebski and "Jan Turleski"; 6z.90, G. Kanski and "Horyzont"; 8z.40, Maciejewicz and "Dar Pomorza".

768 Town Hall

1980. Millenary of Sandomir.

2691	**768**	2z.50 brown and black	15	10

769 "Atropa belladonna"

1980. Medicinal Plants. Multicoloured.

2692		2z. Type **769**	15	10
2693		2z.50 "Datura innoxia"	20	10
2694		3z.40 "Valeriana officinalis"	25	10
2695		5z. "Menta piperita"	30	10
2696		6z.50 "Calendula officinalis"	40	25
2697		8z. "Salvia officinalis"	55	30

770 Jan Kochanowski

1980. 450th Birth Anniv of Jan Kochanowski (poet).

2698	**770**	2z.50 multicoloured	25	15

771 U.N. General Assembly

1980. 35th Anniv of U.N.O.

2703	**771**	8z.40 brown, blue & red	60	30

772 Chopin and Trees

1980. 10th International Chopin Piano Competition, Warsaw.

2704	**772**	6z.90 multicoloured	45	30

773 Postman emptying Post Box

1980. Stamp Day. Multicoloured.

2705		2z. Type **773**	20	10
2706		2z.50 Mail sorting	20	10
2707		6z. Loading mail onto aircraft	45	10
2708		6z.50 Letter boxes	55	25
MS2709		12×94 mm. Nos. 2705/8	3·50	1·75

774 Child embracing Dove

1980. United Nations Declaration on the Preparation of Societies for Life in Peace.

2710	**774**	8z.40 multicoloured	60	30

775 "Battle of Olszynka Grochowska" (Wojciech Kossak)

1980. 150th Anniv of Battle of Olszynka Grochowska.

2711	**775**	2z.50 multicoloured	25	15

776 Fire Engine

1980. Warsaw Horse-drawn Vehicles. Mult.

2712		2z. Type **776**	15	10
2713		2z.50 Omnibus	20	10
2714		3z. Brewery dray	25	10
2715		5z. Sledge-cab	30	10
2716		6z. Horse tram	40	30
2717		6z.50 Droshky cab	50	45

777 "Honour to the Silesian Rebels" (statue by Jan Borowczak)

1981. 60th Anniv of Silesian Rising.

2718	**777**	2z.50 green	15	10

778 Picasso

1981. Birth Centenary of Pablo Picasso (artist).

2719	**778**	8z.40 multicoloured	60	30
MS2720		95×130 mm. No. 2719 ×2 plus labels (sold at 20z.80)	2·50	1·40

779 Balloon of Pilatre de Rozier and Romain, 1785

1981. Balloons. Multicoloured.

2721		2z. Type **779**	20	10
2722		2z. Balloon of J. Blanchard and J. Jeffries, 1785	20	10
2723		2z.50 Eugene Godard's quiintuple "acrobatic" balloon, 1850	25	10
2724		3z. F. Hynek and Z. Burzynski's "Kosciuszko", 1933	25	10
2725		6z. Z. Burzynski and N. Wyescki's "Polonia II", 1935	45	25
2726		6z.50 Ben Abruzzo, Max Anderson and Larry Newman's "Double Eagle II", 1978	45	25
MS2727		59×98 mm. 10z.50 Balloon SP-BCU *L.O.P.P.* and Gordon Bennett statuette	80	95

780 "Iphigenia" (Anton Maulbertsch)

1981. "WIPA 1981" International Stamp Exhibition, Vienna.

2728	**780**	10z.50 multicoloured	85	30

781 Wroclaw, 1493

1981. Towns.

2729	-	4z. violet	30	15
2730	-	5z. green	55	15
2731	-	6z. orange	60	15
2732	**781**	6z.50 brown	55	25
2733	-	8z. blue	70	30

DESIGNS—VERT: 4z. Gdansk, 1652; 5z. Cracow, 1493. HORIZ: 6z. Legnica, 1744; 8z. Warsaw, 1618.

782 Sikorski

1981. Birth Centenary of General Wladyslaw Sikorski (statesman).

2744	**782**	6z.50 multicoloured	55	25

783 Faience Vase

1981. Pottery. Multicoloured.

2745		1z. Type **783**	15	10
2746		2z. Porcelain cup and saucer in "Baranowka" design	25	10
2747		2z.50 Porcelain jug, Korzec manufacture	25	10
2748		5z. Faience plate with portrait of King Jan III Sobieski by Thiele	45	25
2749		6z.50 Faience "Secession" vase	60	25
2750		8z.40 Porcelain dish, Cmielow manufacture	75	30

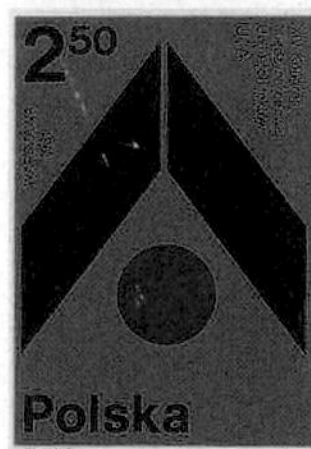

784 Congress Emblem

1981. 14th International Architects' Union Congress, Warsaw.

2751	**784**	2z. yellow, black and red	25	10

785 Wild Boar, Rifle and Oak Leaves

1981. Game Shooting. Multicoloured.

2752		2z. Type **785**	15	10
2753		2z. Elk, rifle and fir twigs	15	10
2754		2z.50 Red fox, shotgun, cartridges and fir branches	25	10
2755		2z.50 Roe deer, feeding rack, rifle and fir branches	25	10
2756		6z.50 Mallard, shotgun, basket and reeds	70	55
2757		6z.50 Barnacle goose, shotgun and reeds (horiz)	70	55

786 European Bison

1981. Protection of European Bison. Mult.

2758		6z.50 Type **786**	70	30
2759		6z.50 Two bison, one grazing	70	30
2760		6z.50 Bison with calf	70	30
2761		6z.50 Calf Feeding	70	30

2762		6z.50 Two bison, both looking towards right	70	30

787 Tennis Player

1981. 60th Anniv of Polish Tennis Federation.

2763	**787**	6z.50 multicoloured	55	30

788 Boy with Model Airplane

1981. Model Making. Multicoloured.

2764	1z. Type **788**	15	10
2765	2z. Model of "Atlas 2" tug	30	10
2766	2z.50 Cars	30	10
2767	4z.20 Man with gliders	30	10
2768	6z.50 Racing cars	60	20
2769	8z. Boy with yacht	70	20

789 Disabled Pictogram

1981. International Year of Disabled Persons.

2770	**789**	8z.40 green, light green and black	70	30

790 17th-cent Flint-lock Pistol

1981. Stamp Day. Antique Weapons. Mult.

2771	2z.50 Type **790**	25	10
2772	8z.40 17th-century gala sabre (vert)	70	25

791 H. Wieniawski and Violin Head

1981. Wieniawski Young Violinists' Competition.

2773	**791**	2z.50 multicoloured	25	15

792 Bronislaw Wesolowski

1981. Activists of Polish Workers' Movement.

2774	**792**	50g. green and black	10	10
2775	-	2z. blue and black	15	10
2776	-	2z.50 brown and black	20	10
2777	-	6z.50 mauve and black	70	25

DESIGNS: 2z. Malgorzata Fornalska; 2z.50, Maria Koszutska; 6z.50, Marcin Kasprzak.

793 F.A.O. Emblem and Globe

1981. World Food Day.

2778	**793**	6z.90 brown, orange & yellow	55	25

794 Helena Modrzejewska (actress)

1981. Bicentenary of Cracow Old Theatre.

2779	**794**	2z. purple, grey and violet	15	10
2780	-	2z.50 blue, stone & brn	25	10
2781	-	6z.50 violet, blue & grn	55	25
2782	-	8z. brown, green and red	85	25

DESIGNS: 2z.50, Stanislaw Kozmian (politician, writer and theatre director); 6z.50, Konrad Swinarski (stage manager and scenographer); 8z. Old Theatre building.

795 Cracow and Vistula River

1981. Vistula River Project. Sheet 62×51 mm.

MS2783	**795**	10z.50 multicoloured	1·25	1·10

796 Gdansk Memorial

1981. Memorials to the Victims of the 1970 Uprisings.

2784	**796**	2z.50+1z. grey, black and red	30	10
2785	-	6z.50+1z. grey, black and blue	75	30

DESIGN: 6z.50, Gdynia Memorial (26×37 mm).

797 "Epiphyllopsis gaertneri"

1981. Succulent Plants. Multicoloured.

2786	90g. Type **797**	15	10
2787	1z. "Cereus tonduzii"	15	10
2788	2z. "Cylindropuntia leptocaulis"	15	10
2789	2z.50 "Cylindropuntia fulgida"	25	10
2790	2z.50 "Coralluma lugardi"	25	10
2791	6z.50 "Nopalea cochenillifera"	1·60	30
2792	6z.50 "Lithops helmutii"	60	30
2793	10z.50 "Cylindropuntia spinosior"	1·00	40

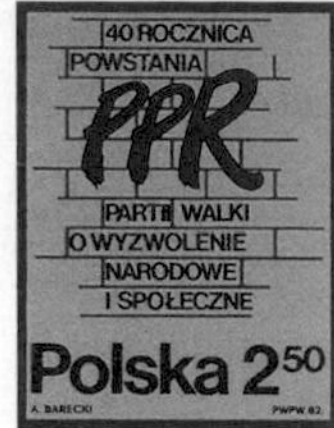

798 Writing on Wall

1982. 40th Anniv of Polish Workers' Coalition.

2794	**798**	2z.50 pink, red and black	25	15

799 Faience Plate

1982. Polish Ceramics. Multicoloured.

2795	1z. Type **799**	15	15
2796	2z. Porcelain cup and saucer, Korzec	25	15
2797	2z.50 Porcelain tureen and sauce-boat, Barnowka	25	15
2798	6z. Porcelain inkpot, Horodnica	55	30
2799	8z. Faience "Hunter's Tumbler", Lubartow	65	30
2800	10z.50 Faience figurine of nobleman, Biala Podlaska	1·10	45

800 Ignacy Lukasiewicz and Lamp

1982. Death Centenary of Ignacy Lukasiewicz (inventor of petroleum lamp).

2801	**800**	1z. multicoloured	15	10
2802	-	2z. multicoloured	25	10
2803	-	2z.50 multicoloured	30	10
2804	-	3z.50 multicoloured	30	10
2805	-	9z. multicoloured	85	30
2806	-	10z. multicoloured	90	35

DESIGNS: 2z. to 10z. Different designs showing lamps.

801 Karol Szymanowski

1982. Birth Centenary of Karol Szymanowski (composer).

2807	**801**	2z.50 brown and gold	25	25

802 RWD 6, 1932

1982. 50th Anniv of Polish Victory in Tourist Aircraft Challenge Competition. Multicoloured.

2808	27z. Type **802**	75	25
2809	31z. RWD 9 (winner of 1934 Challenge)	1·00	30
MS2810	89×101 mm. Nos. 2808/9	2·25	1·60

803 Henryk Sienkiewicz (literature, 1905)

1982. Polish Nobel Prize Winners.

2811	**803**	3z. green and black	10	10
2812	-	15z. brown and black	40	15
2813	-	25z. blue	90	25
2814	-	31z. grey and black	75	45

DESIGNS: 15z. Wladyslaw Reymont (literature, 1924); 25z. Marie Curie (physics, 1903, and chemistry, 1911); 31z. Czeslaw Milosz (literature, 1980).

804 Football as Globe

1982. World Cup Football Championship, Spain. Multicoloured.

2815	25z. Type **804**	75	30
2816	27z. Bull and football (35×28 mm)	85	55

805 "Maria kazimiera Sobieska"

1982. "Philexfrance 82" International Stamp Exhibition, Paris. Sheet 69×86 mm.

MS2817	**805**	65z. multicoloured	2·40	2·40

806 Stanislaw Sierakowski and Boleslaw Domanski (former Association presidents)

1982. 60th Anniv of Association of Poles in Germany.

2818	**806**	4z.50 red and green	40	15

807 Text around Globe

1982. 2nd U.N. Conference on the Exploration and Peaceful Uses of Outer Space, Vienna.

2819	**807**	31z. multicoloured	75	40

1982. No. 2732 surch 10 ^{oo}.

2820	10z. on 6z.50 brown	30	10

809 Father Augustyn Kordecki (prior)

1982. 600th Anniv of "Black Madonna" (icon) of Jasna Gora. Multicoloured.

2821		2z.50 Type **809**	10	10
2822		25z. "Siege of Jasna Gora by Swedes, 1655" (detail) (horiz)	40	10
2823		65z. "Black Madonna"	1·10	45
MS2824		122×108 mm. No. 2823 ×2 (sold at 140z.)	10·50	12·50

The premium on No. **MS**2824 was for the benefit of the Polish Philatelic Federation.

810 Marchers with Banner

1982. Centenary of Proletarian Party.

2825	**810**	6z. multicoloured	30	15

811 Norbert Barlicki

1982. Activists of Polish Workers' Movement.

2826	**811**	5z. light blue, blue and black	10	15
2827	-	6z. deep green, green and black	10	15
2828	-	15z. pink, red and black	25	15
2829	-	20z. mauve, violet and black	40	15
2830	-	29z. light brown, brown and black	45	15

DESIGNS: 6z. Pawel Finder; 15z. Marian Buczek; 20z. Cezaryna Wojnarowska; 29z. Ignacy Daszynski.

812 Dr. Robert Koch

1982. Centenary of Discovery of Tubercle Bacillus. Multicoloured.

2831		10z. Type **812**	25	15
2832		25z. Dr. Odo Bujwid	85	30

813 Carved Head of Woman

813a Head of Ruler

1982. Carved Heads from Wawel Castle.

2835	**813a**	3z.50 brown	15	10
2836	-	5z. green	15	10
2837	-	5z. red	10	10
2838	-	10z. blue	15	10
2839	-	15z. brown	15	10
2840	-	20z. grey	45	10
2841	**813a**	20z. blue	15	10
2842	-	40z. brown	75	10
2843	-	60z. green	15	10
2833	**813**	60z. orange and brown	1·25	25
2834	-	100z. ochre and brown	2·75	40
2843a	-	200z. black	2·25	30

DESIGNS—As T **813**: 100z. Man. As T **813a**: 5z. (2836), Warrior; 5z. (2837), 15z. Woman wearing chaplet; 10z. Man in cap; 20z. (2840), Thinker; 40z. Man in beret; 60z. Young man; 200z. Man.

814 Maximilian Kolbe (after M. Koscielniak)

1982. Sanctification of Maximilian Kolbe (Franciscan concentration camp victim).

2844	**814**	27z. multicoloured	1·00	40

815 Polar Research Station

1982. 50th Anniv of Polish Polar Research.

2845	**815**	27z. multicoloured	1·10	40

816 "Log Floats on Vistula River" (drawing by J. Telakowski)

1982. Views of the Vistula River.

2846	**816**	12z. blue	25	10
2847	-	17z. blue	30	10
2848	-	25z. blue	40	25

DESIGNS: 17z. "Kazimierz Dolny" (engraving by Andriollo); 25z. "Danzig" (18th-cent engraving).

817 Stanislaw Zaremba

1982. Mathematicians.

2849	**817**	5z. lilac, blue and black	25	15
2850	-	6z. orange, violet and black	25	15
2851	-	12z. blue, brown and black	40	15
2852	-	15z. yellow, brown and black	60	25

DESIGNS: 6z. Waclaw Sierpinski; 12z. Zygmunt Janiszewski; 15z. Stefan Banach.

818 Military Council Medal

1982. 1st Anniv of Military Council.

2853	**818**	2z.50 multicoloured	25	15

819 Deanery Gate

1982. Renovation of Cracow Monuments (1st series).

2854	**819**	15z. black, olive & green	45	15
2855	-	25z. black, purple & mauve	55	25
MS2856		75×93 mm. 65z. green, purple and sepia (22×27 mm)	1·25	90

DESIGNS: 25z. Gateway of Collegium Iuridicum; 65z. Street plan of Old Cracow.

See also Nos. 2904/5, 2968/9; 3029/3, 3116 and 3153.

820 Bernard Wapowski Map, 1526

1982. Polish Maps.

2857	**820**	5z. multicoloured	10	10
2858	-	6z. brown, black and red	15	10
2859	-	8z. multicoloured	20	10
2860	-	25z. multicoloured	55	30

DESIGNS: 6z. Map of Prague, 1839; 8z. Map of Poland from Eugen Romer's Atlas, 1908; 25z. Plan of Cracow by A. Buchowiecki, 1703, and Astrolabe.

821 "The Last of the Resistance" (Artur Grottger)

1983. 120th Anniv of January Uprising.

2861	**821**	6z. brown	15	10

822 "Grand Theatre, Warsaw, 1838" (Maciej Zaleski)

1983. 150th Anniv of Grand Theatre, Warsaw.

2862	**822**	6z. multicoloured	15	10

823 Wild Flowers

1983. Environmental Protection. Multicoloured.

2863		5z. Type **823**	15	10
2864		6z. Mute swan and river fishes	30	15
2865		17z. Hoopoe and trees	90	35
2866		30z. Sea fishes	90	45
2867		31z. European bison and roe deer	90	45
2868		38z. Fruit	90	60

824 Karol Kurpinski (composer)

1983. Celebrities.

2869	**824**	5z. light brown and brown	25	10
2870	-	6z. purple and violet	25	10
2871	-	17z. light green and green	60	30
2872	-	25z. light brown and brown	65	30
2873	-	27z. light blue and blue	75	30
2874	-	31z. lilac and violet	85	30

DESIGNS: 6z. Maria Jasnorzewska Pawlikowska (poetess); 17z. Stanislaw Szober (linguist); 25z. Tadeusz Banachiewicz (astronomer and mathematician); 27z. Jaroslaw Iwaskiewicz (writer); 31z. Wladyslaw Tatarkiewicz (philosopher and historian).

825 3000 Metres Steeplechase

1983. Sports Achievements.

2875	**825**	5z. pink and violet	25	15
2876	-	6z. pink, brown and black	25	15
2877	-	15z. yellow and green	45	15
2878	-	27z.+5z. light blue, blue and black	1·00	30

DESIGNS: 6z. Show jumping; 1z. Football; 27z.+5z. Pole vault.

826 Ghetto Heroes Monument (Natan Rappaport)

1983. 40th Anniv of Warsaw Ghetto Uprising.

2879	**826**	6z. light brown & brown	25	15

827 Customs Officer and Suitcases

1983. 30th Anniv of Customs Co-operation Council.

2880	**827**	5z. multicoloured	15	15

828 John Paul II and Jasna Gora Sanctuary

1983. Papal Visit. Multicoloured.

2881		31z. Type **828**	85	40
2882		65z. Niepokalanow Church and John Paul holding crucifix	1·90	75
MS2883		107×81 mm. No. 2882	1·90	1·90

829 Dragoons

1983. 300th Anniv of Polish Relief of Vienna (1st issue). Troops of King Jan III Sobieski. Mult.

2884	5z. Type **829**	15	10
2885	5z. Armoured cavalryman	15	10
2886	6z. Infantry non-commissioned officer and musketeer	25	10
2887	15z. Light cavalry lieutenant	30	30
2888	27z. "Winged" hussar and trooper with carbine	90	45

See also Nos. 2893/6.

830 Arrow piercing "E"

1983. 50th Anniv of Deciphering "Enigma" Machine Codes.

2889	**830**	5z. red, grey and black	15	15

831 Torun

1983. 750th Anniv of Torun.

2890	**831**	6z. multicoloured	25	15
MS2891		142×116 mm. No. 2890 ×4	2·75	2·75

832 Child's Painting

1983. "Order of the Smile" (Politeness Publicity Campaign).

2892	**832**	6z. multicoloured	25	15

833 King Jan III Sobieski

1983. 300th Anniv of Relief of Vienna (2nd issue). Multicoloured.

2893	5z. Type **833**	25	15
2894	6z. King Jan III Sobieski (different)	25	15
2895	6z. "King Jan III Sobieski on Horseback" (Francesco Trevisani)	25	15
2896	25z. "King Jan III Sobieski" (Jerzy Eleuter)	90	30
MS2897	97×75 mm. 65z. +10z. "King Jan III Sobieski at Vienna" (Jan Matejko). Imperf	1·90	1·60

834 Wanda Wasilewska

1983. 40th Anniv of Polish People's Army. Multicoloured.

2898	**834**	5z. multicoloured	10	10
2899	-	5z. deep green, green and black	10	10
2900	-	6z. multicoloured	25	10
2901	-	6z. multicoloured	25	10

DESIGNS—VERT: No. 2899, General Zygmunt Berling; 2900, "The Frontier Post" (S. Poznanski). HORIZ: No. 2901, "Taking the Oath" (S. Poznanski).

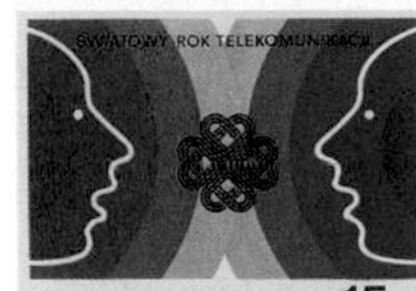

835 Profiles and W.C.Y. Emblem

1983. World Communications Year.

2902	**835**	15z. multicoloured	45	25

836 Boxing

1983. 60th Anniv of Polish Boxing Federation.

2903	**836**	6z. multicoloured	25	15

1983. Renovation of Cracow Monuments (2nd series). As T 819.

2904	5z. brown, purple and black	15	10
2905	6z. black, green and blue	15	15

DESIGNS—HORIZ: 5z. Cloth Hall. VERT: 6z. Town Hall tower.

837 Biskupiec Costume

1983. Women's Folk Costumes. Multicoloured.

2906	5z. Type **837**	15	10
2907	5z. Rozbark	15	10
2908	6z. Warmia & Mazuria	25	10
2909	6z. Cieszyn	25	10
2910	25z. Kurpie	90	30
2911	38z. Lubusk	1·25	55

838 Hand with Sword (poster by Zakrzewski and Krolikowski, 1945)

1983. 40th Anniv of National People's Council.

2912	**838**	6z. multicoloured	25	10

839 Badge of "General Bem" Brigade

1983. 40th Anniv of People's Army.

2913	**839**	5z. multicoloured	25	10

840 Dulcimer

1984. Musical Instruments (1st series). Mult.

2914	5z. Type **840**	15	10
2915	6z. Kettle drum and tambourine	25	15
2916	10z. Accordion	40	30
2917	15z. Double bass	45	40
2918	17z. Bagpipe	55	45
2919	29z. Country band (wood carvings by Tadeusz Zak)	90	65

841 Wincenty Witos

1984. 110th Birth Anniv of Wincenty Witos (leader of Peasants' Movement).

2920	**841**	6z. brown and green	25	10

842 "Clematis lanuginosa"

1984. Clematis. Multicoloured.

2921	5z. Type **842**	20	10
2922	6z. "C. tangutica"	25	10
2923	10z. "C. texensis"	30	10
2924	17z. "C. alpina"	45	15
2925	25z. "C. vitalba"	90	30
2926	27z. "C. montana"	1·00	45

843 "The Ecstasy of St. Francis" (El Greco)

1984. "Espana 84" International Stamp Exhibition, Madrid.

2927	**843**	27z. multicoloured	90	40

844 Handball

1984. Olympic Games, Los Angeles, and Winter Olympics, Sarajevo. Multicoloured.

2928	5z. Type **844**	10	10
2929	6z. Fencing	15	10
2930	15z. Cycling	45	25
2931	16z. Janusz Kusocinski winning 10,000 m race, 1932 Olympics, Los Angeles	60	30
2932	17z. Stanislawa Walasiewiczowna winning 100 m race, 1932 Olympics, Los Angeles	60	30
2933	31z. Women's slalom (Winter Olympics)	1·00	45
MS2934	129×78 mm. Nos. 2931/2	1·25	1·10

The 10z. premium on **MS**2934 was for the benefit of the Polish Olympic Committee.

845 Monte Cassino Memorial Cross and Monastery

1984. 40th Anniv of Battle of Monte Cassino.

2935	**845**	15z. olive and red	55	25

846 "German Princess" (Lucas Cranach)

1984. 19th U.P.U. Congress, Hamburg.

2936	**846**	27z.+10z. multicoloured	55	1·90

847 "Warsaw from the Praga Bank" (Canaletto)

1984. Paintings of Vistula River. Multicoloured.

2937	5z. Type **847**	25	25
2938	6z. "Trumpet Festivity" (A. Gierymski)	25	25
2939	25z. "The Vistula near Bielany District" (J. Rapacki)	90	65
2940	27z. "Steamship Harbour in the Powisle District" (F. Kostrzewski)	1·00	75

848 Order of Grunwald Cross

1984. 40th Anniv of Polish People's Republic. Multicoloured.

2941	5z. Type **848**	25	10
2942	6z. Order of Revival of Poland	25	10
2943	10z. Order of Banner of Labour, First Class	30	10
2944	16z. Order of Builders of People's Poland	60	30
MS2945	156×101 mm. Nos. 2941/4	4·25	6·00

849 Group of Insurgents

1984. 40th Anniv of Warsaw Uprising. Mult.

2946	4z. Type **849**	25	10
2947	5z. Insurgent on postal duty	25	10
2948	6z. Insurgents fighting	25	10
2949	25z. Tending wounded	95	30

850 Defence of Oksywie Holm and Col. Stanislaw Dabek

1984. 45th Anniv of German Invasion. Mult.

2950	5z. Type **850**	25	10
2951	6z. Battle of Bzura River and Gen. Tadeusz Kutrzeba	25	10

See also Nos. 3004/5, 3062, 3126/8, 3172/4 and 3240/3.

851 "Broken Heart" (monument, Lodz Concentration Camp)

1984. Child Martyrs.

2952	851	16z. brown, blue and deep brown	45	25

852 Militiaman and Ruins

1984. 40th Anniv of Security Force and Civil Militia. Multicoloured.

2953	5z. Type **852**	15	10
2954	6z. Militiaman in control centre	25	10

853 First Balloon Flight, 1784 (after Chostovski)

1984. Polish Aviation.

2955	**853**	5z. black, green & mauve	25	10
2956	-	5z. multicoloured	25	10
2957	-	6z. multicoloured	25	10
2958	-	10z. multicoloured	30	10
2959	-	16z. multicoloured	40	15
2960	-	27z. multicoloured	90	30
2961	-	31z. multicoloured	1·10	50

DESIGNS: No. 2956, Michal Scipio del Campo and biplane (1st flight over Warsaw, 1911); 2957, Balloon "Polonez" (winner, Gordon Bennett Cup, 1983); 2958, PWS 101 and Jantar gliders (Lilienthal Medal winners); 2959, PZL-104 Wilga airplane (world precise flight champion, 1983); 2960, Jan Nagorski and Farman M.F.7 floatplane (Arctic zone flights, 1914); 2961, PZL P-37 Los and PZL P-7 aircraft.

854 Weasel

1984. Fur-bearing Animals. Multicoloured.

2962	4z. Type **854**	15	10
2963	5z. Stoat	15	10
2964	5z. Beech marten	25	10
2965	10z. Eurasian beaver	25	10
2966	10z. Eurasian otter	25	10
2967	65z. Alpine marmot	1·90	60

1984. Renovation of Cracow Monuments (3rd series). As T 819.

2968	5z. brown, black and green	15	10
2969	15z. blue, brown and black	30	15

DESIGNS—VERT: 5z. Wawel cathedral. HORIZ: 15z. Wawel castle (royal residence).

855 Protestant Church, Warsaw

1984. Religious Architecture. Multicoloured.

2970	5z. Type **855**	10	10
2971	10z. Saint Andrew's Roman Catholic church, Krakow	25	10
2972	15z. Greek Catholic church, Rychwald	40	10
2973	20z. St. Maria Magdalena Orthodox church, Warsaw	55	10
2974	25z. Tykocin synagogue, Kaczorow (horiz)	60	30
2975	31z. Tatar mosque, Kruszyiany (horiz)	75	30

856 Steam Fire Hose (late 19th century)

1985. Fire Engines. Multicoloured.

2976	4z. Type **856**	10	10
2977	10z. "Polski Fiat", 1930s	25	10
2978	12z. "Jelcz 315" fire engine	30	10
2979	15z. Manual fire hose, 1899	40	10
2980	20z. "Magirus" fire ladder on "Jelcz" chassis	55	30
2981	30z. Manual fire hose (early 18th century)	85	40

857 "Battle of Raclawice" (Jan Styka and Wojciech Kossak)

1985

2982	**857**	27z. multicoloured	60	30

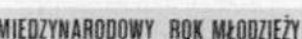

858 Wincenty Rzymowski

1985. 35th Death Anniv of Wincenty Rzymowski (founder of Polish Democratic Party).

2983	**858**	10z. violet and red	30	15

859 Badge on Denim

1985. International Youth Year.

2984	**859**	15z. multicoloured	40	15

860 Boleslaw III, the Wry-mouthed, and Map

1985. 40th Anniv of Return of Western and Northern Territories to Poland. Multicoloured.

2985	5z. Type **860**	10	10
2986	10z. Wladyslaw Gomulka (vice-president of first postwar government) and map	30	15
2987	20z. Piotr Zaremba (Governor of Szczecin) and map	60	25

861 "Victory, Berlin 1945" (Joesf Mlynarski)

1985. 40th Anniv of Victory over Fascism.

2988	**861**	5z. multicoloured	15	15

862 Warsaw Arms and Flags of Member Countries

1985. 30th Anniv of Warsaw Pact.

2989	**862**	5z. multicoloured	15	15

863 Wolves in Winter

1985. Protected Animals. The Wolf. Mult.

2990	5z. Type **863**	15	10
2991	10z. She-wolf with cubs	30	25
2992	10z. Close-up of wolf	30	25
2993	20z. Wolves in summer	60	45

1985. Musical Instruments (2nd series). As T 840. Multicoloured.

2994	5z. Rattle and tarapata	15	10
2995	10z. Stick rattle and berlo	30	10
2996	12z. Clay whistles	40	10
2997	20z. Stringed instruments	60	25
2998	25z. Cow bells	85	25
2999	31z. Wind instruments	1·00	30

864 Cadet Ship "Iskra"

1985. 40th Anniv of Polish Navy.

3000	**864**	5z. blue and yellow	15	10

865 Tomasz Nocznicki

1985. Leaders of Peasants' Movement.

3001	**865**	10z. green	25	10
3002	-	20z. brown	45	25

DESIGN: 20z. Maciej Rataj.

866 Hockey Players

1985. 60th Anniv (1986) of Polish Field Hockey Association.

3003	**866**	5z. multicoloured	15	10

1985. 46th Anniv of German Invasion. As T 850. Multicoloured.

3004	5z. Defence of Wizna and Capt. Wladyslaw Raginis	15	10
3005	10z. Battle of Mlawa and Col. Wilhelm Liszka-Lawicz	30	10

867 Type 20k Goods Wagon

1985. PAFAWAG Railway Rolling Stock. Mult.

3006	5z. Type **867**	15	10
3007	10z. Electric locomotive No. ET22-001, 1969	25	10
3008	17z. Type OMMK wagon	40	25
3009	20z. Type 111A passenger carriage	55	30

868 "Madonna with Child St. John and Angel" (Sandro Botticelli)

1985. "Italia '85" International Stamp Exhibition, Rome. Sheet 81×108 mm.

MS3010	**868** 65z.+15z. multicoloured	1·90	1·90

869 Green-winged Teal

1985. Wild Ducks. Multicoloured.

3011	5z. Type **869**	15	10
3012	5z. Garganey	15	10
3013	10z. Tufted duck	30	10
3014	15z. Common goldeneye	40	10
3015	25z. Eider	65	30

3016 29z. Red-crested pochard 1·00 30

870 U.N. Emblem and "Flags"

1985. 40th Anniv of U.N.O.

3017 **870** 27z. multicoloured 60 30

871 Ballerina

1985. Bicentenary of Polish Ballet.

3018 **871** 5z. green, orange and red 15 10

3019 - 15z. brown, violet & orange 45 10

DESIGN: 15z. Male dancer.

872 "Marysia and Burek in Ceylon"

1985. Birth Centenary of Stanislaw Ignacy Witkiewicz (artist). Multicoloured.

3020 5z. Type **872** 15 10

3021 10z. "Woman with Fox" (horiz) 30 10

3022 10z. "Self-portrait" 30 10

3023 20z. "Compositions (1917–20)" 55 30

3024 25z. "Nena Stachurska" 65 30

873 Oliwa Church Organ and Bach

1985. 300th Birth Anniv of Johann Sebastian Bach (composer). Sheet 67×79 mm.

MS3025 **873** 65z. multicoloured 1·50 1·25

874 Human Profile

1986. Congress of Intellectuals for Defence of Peaceful Future of the World, Warsaw.

3026 **874** 10z. ultramarine, violet and blue 30 10

875 Michal Kamienski and Planetary and Comet's Orbits

1985. Appearance of Halley's Comet.

3027 **875** 25z. blue and brown 60 30

3028 - 25z. deep blue, blue and brown 60 30

DESIGN: No. 3028, "Vega", "Planet A", "Giotto" and "Ice" space probes and comet.

1986. Renovation of Cracow Monuments (4th series). As T 819.

3029 5z. dp brown, brown & black 10 10

3030 10z. green, brown and black 25 10

DESIGNS: 5z. Collegium Maius (Jagiellonian University Museum); 10z. Kazimierz Town Hall.

876 Sun

1986. International Peace Year.

3031 **876** 25z. yellow, light blue and blue 45 25

877 Grey Partridge

1986. Game. Multicoloured.

3032 5z. Type **877** 30 30

3033 5z. Common rabbit 10 10

3034 10z. Common pheasants (horiz) 55 55

3035 10z. Fallow deer (horiz) 15 10

3036 20z. Hare 30 30

3037 40z. Argali 65 65

878 Kulczynski

1986. 10th Death Anniv (1985) of Stanislaw Kulczynski (politician).

3038 **878** 10z. light brown and brown 25 10

879 "Warsaw Fire Brigade, 1871" (detail, Jozef Brodowski)

1986. 150th Anniv of Warsaw Fire Brigade.

3039 **879** 10z. dp brown & brown 25 10

880 Paderewski (composer)

1986. "Ameripex '86" International Stamp Exhibition, Chicago.

3040 **880** 65z. blue, black and grey 1·40 45

881 Footballers

1986. World Cup Football Championship, Mexico.

3041 **881** 25z. multicoloured 45 30

882 "Wilanow"

1986. Passenger Ferries. Multicoloured.

3042 10z. Type **882** 25 15

3043 10z. "Wawel" 25 15

3044 15z. "Pomerania" 30 15

3045 25z. "Rogalin" 55 25

MS3046 Two sheets, each 116×98 mm. (a) Nos. 3042/3 (sold at 30z.); (b) Nos. 3044/5 (sold at 55z.) 6·00 2·40

883 A. B. Dobrowolski, Map and Research Vessel "Kopernik"

1986. 25th Anniv of Antarctic Agreement.

3047 **883** 5z. green, black and red 10 15

3048 - 40z. lavender, violet and orange 1·90 30

DESIGN: 40z. H. Arctowski, map and research vessel "Profesor Siedlecki".

884 Workers and Emblem

1986. 10th Polish United Workers' Party Congress, Warsaw.

3049 **884** 10z. blue and red 25 10

885 "The Paulinite Church on Skalka in Cracow" (detail), 1627

1986. Treasures of Jasna Gora Monastery. Mult.

3050 5z. Type **885** 15 10

3051 5z. "Tree of Jesse", 17th-century 15 10

3052 20z. Chalice, 18th-century 40 25

3053 40z. "Virgin Mary" (detail, chasuble column), 15th-century 1·10 30

886 Precision Flying (Waclaw Nycz)

1986. 1985 Polish World Championship Successes. Multicoloured.

3054 5z. Type **886** 15 10

3055 10z. Windsurfing (Malgorzata Palasz-Piasecka) 40 10

3056 10z. Glider areobatics (Jerzy Makula) 30 10

3057 15z. Wrestling (Bogdan Daras) 30 10

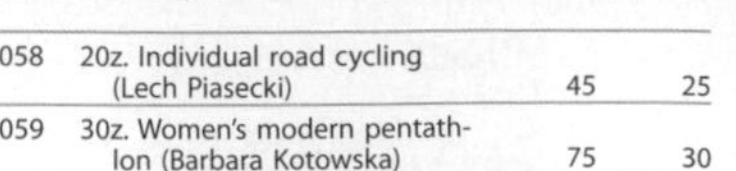

3058 20z. Individual road cycling (Lech Piasecki) 45 25

3059 30z. Women's modern pentathlon (Barbara Kotowska) 75 30

887 "Bird" in National Costume carrying Stamp

1986. "Stockholmia '86" International Stamp Exhibition.

3060 **887** 65z. multicoloured 1·40 45

MS3061 94×80 mm. No. 3060 1·60 1·60

1986. 47th Anniv of German Invasion. As T 850. Multicoloured.

3062 10z. Battle of Jordanow and Col. Stanislaw Maczek 25 10

888 Schweitzer

1986. 10th Death Anniv (1985) of Albert Schweitzer (medical missionary).

3063 **888** 5z. brown, lt brown & blue 15 10

889 Airliner and Postal Messenger

1986. World Post Day.

3064 **889** 40z. brown, blue and red 75 30

MS3065 81×81 mm. No. 3064 ×2 (sold at 120z.) 10·50 9·00

890 Basilisk

1986. Folk Tales. Multicoloured.

3066 5z. Type **890** 15 15

3067 5z. Duke Popiel (vert) 15 15

3068 10z. Golden Duck 25 15

3069 10z. Boruta the Devil (vert) 25 15

3070 20z. Janosik the Robber (vert) 40 15

3071 50z. Lajkonik (vert) 1·10 40

891 Kotarbinski

892 20th-century Windmill, Zygmuntow

1986. Birth Centenary of Tadeusz Kotarbinski (philosopher).

3072 **891** 10z. deep brown and brown 25 30

1986. Wooden Architecture. Multicoloured.

3073 5z. Type **892** 15 10

3074 5z. 17th-century church, Baczal Dolny 15 10

3075 10z. 19th-century Oravian cottage, Zubrzyca Gorna 25 10

3076 15z. 18th-century Kashubian arcade cottage, Wdzydze 25 15

3077 25z. 19th-century barn, Grzawa 55 25

3078 30z. 19th-century watermill, Siolkowice Stare 75 30

893 Mieszko (Mieczyslaw) I

1986. Polish Rulers (1st series). Drawings by Jan Matejko.

3079	**893**	10z. brown and green	30	30
3080	-	25z. black and purple	75	45

DESIGN: 25z. Queen Dobrawa (wife of Mieszko I).

See also Nos. 3144/5, 3193/4, 3251/2, 3341/2, 3351/2, 3387/8, 3461/4, 3511/12, 3548/51, 3641/4, 3705/8, 3732/5, 3819/22 and 3887/91.

894 Star

1986. New Year.

3081	**894**	25z. multicoloured	45	30

895 Trip to Bielany, 1887

1986. Centenary of Warsaw Cyclists' Society.

3082	**895**	5z. multicoloured	10	15
3083	-	5z. brown, light brown and black	10	15
3084	-	10z. multicoloured	25	15
3085	-	10z. multicoloured	25	15
3086	-	30z. multicoloured	60	30
3087	-	50z. multicoloured	1·10	45

DESIGNS — VERT: No. 3083, Jan Stanislaw Skrodaki (1895 touring record holder); 3084, Dynasy (Society's headquarters, 1892–1937); 3085, Mieczyslaw Baranski (1896 Kingdom of Poland road cycling champion); 3086, Karolina Kociecka; 3087, Henryk Weiss (Race champion).

896 Lelewel

1986. Birth Bicentenary of Joachim Lelewel (historian).

3088	**896**	10z.+5z. multicoloured	30	15

897 Krill and "Antoni Garnuszewski" (cadet freighter)

1987. 10th Anniv of Henryk Arctowski Antarctic Station, King George Island, South Shetlands. Multicoloured.

3089	5z. Type **897**	10	10
3090	5z. Antarctic toothfish, marbled rockfish and "Zulawy" (supply ship)	10	10
3091	10z. Southern fulmar and "Pogoria" (cadet brigantine)	30	10
3092	10z. Adelie penguin and "Gedania" (yacht)	30	10
3093	30z. Fur seal and "Dziunia" (research vessel)	40	10
3094	40z. Leopard seals and "Kapitan Ledochowski" (research vessel)	45	30

898 "Portrait of a Woman"

1987. 50th Death Anniv (1986) of Leon Wyczolkowski (artist). Multicoloured.

3095	5z. "Cineraria Flowers" (horiz)	10	10
3096	10z. Type **898**	15	10
3097	10z. "Wooden Church" (horiz)	15	10
3098	25z. "Beetroot Lifting"	40	10
3099	30z. "Wading Fishermen" (horiz)	45	15
3100	40z. "Self-portrait" (horiz)	60	40

899 "Ravage" (from "War Cycle") and Artur Grottger

1987. 150th Birth Anniv of Artur Grottger (artist).

3101	**899**	15z. brown and stone	25	10

900 Swierczewski

1987. 90th Birth Anniv of General Karol Swierczewski.

3102	**900**	15z. green and olive	25	10

901 Strzelecki

1987. 190th Birth Anniv of Pawel Edmund Strzelecki (scientist and explorer of Tasmania).

3103	**901**	65z. green	60	30

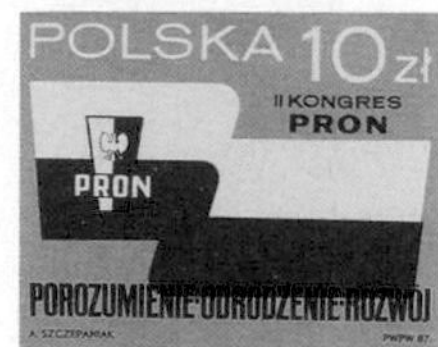
902 Emblem and Banner

1987. 2nd Patriotic Movement for National Revival Congress.

3104	**902**	10z. red, blue and brown	15	10

903 CWS "T-1" Motor Car, 1928

1987. Polish Motor Vehicles. Multicoloured.

3105	10z. Type **903**	10	10
3106	10z. Saurer-Zawrat bus, 1936	10	10
3107	15z. Ursus-A lorry, 1928	25	10
3108	15z. Lux-Sport motor car, 1936	25	10
3109	25z. Podkowa "100" motor cycle, 1939	30	10
3110	45z. Sokol "600 RT" motor cycle, 1935	55	55

904 Royal Palace, Warsaw

1987

3111	**904**	50z. multicoloured	60	30

905 Pope John Paul II

1987. 3rd Papal Visit. Multicoloured.

3112	15z. Type **905**	25	15
3113	45z. Pope and signature	45	30
MS3114	77×66 mm. 50z. Profile of Pope (21×27 mm)	60	60

906 Polish Settler at Kasubia, Ontario

1987. "Capex '87" International Stamp Exhibition, Toronto.

3115	**906**	50z.+20z. multicoloured	75	40

1987. Renovation of Cracow Monuments (5th series). As T 819.

3116	10z. lilac, black and green	15	10

DESIGN: 10z. Barbican.

907 Ludwig Zamenhof (inventor) and Star

1987. Cent of Esperanto (invented language).

3117	**907**	5z. brown, green & black	60	25

908 "Poznan Town Hall" (Stanislaw Wyspianski)

1987. "Poznan 87" National Stamp Exhibition.

3118	**908**	15z. brown and orange	25	15

909 Queen Bee

1987. "Apimondia 87" International Bee Keeping Congress, Warsaw. Multicoloured.

3119	10z. Type **909**	15	10
3120	10z. Worker bee	15	10
3121	15z. Drone	25	10
3122	15z. Hive in orchard	25	10
3123	40z. Worker bee on clover flower	60	25
3124	50z. Forest bee keeper collecting honey	75	30

910 1984 Olympic Stamp and Laurel Wreath

1987. "Olymphilex '87" Olympic Stamps Exhibition, Rome. Sheet 83×57 mm.

MS3125	**910**	45z.+10z. multicoloured	75	85

The premium was for the benefit of the Polish Olympic Committee's fund.

1987. 48th Anniv of German Invasion. As T 850. Multicoloured.

3126	10z. Battle of Mokra and Col. Julian Filipowicz	15	10
3127	10z. Fighting at Oleszyce and Brig.-Gen. Jozef Rudolf Kustron	15	10
3128	15z. PZL P-7 aircraft over Warsaw and Col. Stefan Pawlikowski	30	10

911 Hevelius and Sextant

1987. 300th Death Anniv of Jan Hevelius (astronomer). Multicoloured.

3129	15z. Type **911**	25	10
3130	40z. Hevelius and map of constellations (horiz)	55	25

912 High Jump (World Acrobatics Championships, France)

1987. 1986 Polish World Championship Successes. Multicoloured.

3131	10z. Type **912**	15	10
3132	15z. Two-man canoe (World Canoeing Championships, Canada)	25	10
3133	20z. Marksman (Free pistol event, World Marksmanship Championships, East Germany)	30	15
3134	25z. Wrestlers (World Wrestling Championships, Hungary)	45	15

913 "Stacionar 4" Telecommunications Satellite

1987. 30th Anniv of launch of "Sputnik 1" (first artificial satellite). Sheet 67×82 mm.

MS3135	**913**	40z. multicoloured	55	60

914 Warsaw Post Office and Ignacy Franciszek Przebendowski (Postmaster General)

1987. World Post Day.

3136	**914**	15z. green and red	25	10

915 "The Little Mermaid"

1987. "Hafnia 87" International Stamp Exhibition, Copenhagen. Hans Christain Andersen's Fairy Tales. Multicoloured.

3137	10z. Type **915**	15	10
3138	10z. "The Nightingale"	15	10
3139	20z. "The Wild Swans"	25	15
3140	20z. "The Little Match Girl"	25	15
3141	30z. "The Snow Queen"	40	30
3142	40z. "The Tin Soldier"	55	15

916 Col. Stanislaw Wieckowski (founder)

1987. 50th Anniv of Democratic Clubs.

3143	**916**	15z. black and blue	25	10

1987. Polish Rulers (2nd series). As T 893. Drawings by Jan Matejko.

3144	10z. green and blue	15	15
3145	15z. blue and ultramarine	40	30

DESIGNS: 10z. Boleslaw I, the Brave; 15z. Mieszko (Mieczyslaw) II.

917 Santa Claus with Christmas Trees

1987. New Year.

3146	**917**	15z. multicoloured	15	15

918 Emperor Dragonfly

1988. Dragonflies. Multicoloured.

3147	10z. Type **918**	15	10
3148	15z. Four-spotted libellula ("Libellula quadrimaculata") (vert)	30	10
3149	15z. Banded agrion ("Calopteryx splendens")	30	10
3150	20z. "Condulegaster annulatus" (vert)	30	10
3151	30z. "Sympetrum pedemontanum"	40	25
3152	50z. "Aeschna viridis" (vert)	65	30

1988. Renovation of Cracow Monuments (6th series). As T 819.

3153	15z. yellow, brown and black	15	10

DESIGN: 15z. Florianska Gate.

919 Composition

1988. International Year of Graphic Design.

3154	**919**	40z. multicoloured	40	40

920 17th-century Friesian Wall Clock with Bracket Case

1988. Clocks and Watches. Multicoloured.

3155	10z. Type **920**	15	10
3156	10z. 20th-century annual clock (horiz)	15	10
3157	15z. 18th-century carriage clock	15	10
3158	15z. 18th-century French rococo bracket clock	15	10
3159	20z. 19th-century pocket watch (horiz)	25	10
3160	40z. 17th-cent tile-case clock from Gdansk by Benjamin Zoll (horiz)	40	15

921 Atlantic Salmon and Reindeer

1988. "Finlandia 88" International Stamp Exhibition, Helsinki.

3161	**921**	45z.+30z. multicoloured	60	30

922 Triple Jump

1988. Olympic Games, Seoul. Multicoloured.

3162	15z. Type **922**	25	10
3163	20z. Wrestling	25	10
3164	20z. Canoeing	25	10
3165	25z. Judo	25	10
3166	40z. Shooting	40	15
3167	55z. Swimming	55	30

923 Kukuczka

1988. Award of Special Olympic Silver Medal to Jerzy Kukuczka for Mountaineering Achievements. Sheet 84×66 mm.

MS3168	**923**	70z.+10z. multicoloured	75	75

924 Wheat as Graph on VDU

1988. 16th European Conference of Food and Agriculture Organization, Cracow. Multicoloured.

3169	15z. Type **924**	15	10
3170	40z. Factory in forest	30	10

925 PZL P-37 Los Bomber

1988. 70th Anniv of Polish Republic (1st issue). 60th Anniv of Polish State Aircraft Works.

3171	**925**	45z. multicoloured	30	10

See also Nos. 3175, 3177, 3181/88 and 3190/2.

1988. 49th Anniv of German Invasion. As T 850. Multicoloured.

3172	15z. Battle of Modlin and Brig.-Gen. Wiktor Thommee	25	10
3173	20z. Battle of Warsaw and Brig.-Gen. Walerian Czuma	25	10
3174	20z. Battle of Tomaszow Lubelski and Brig.-Gen. Antoni Szylling	25	10

1988. 70th Anniv of Polish Republic (2nd issue). 50th Anniv of Stalowa Wola Ironworks. As T 925. Multicoloured.

3175	15z. View of plant	15	10

926 Postal Emblem and Tomasz Arciszewski (Postal Minister, 1918–19)

1988. World Post Day.

3176	**926**	20z. multicoloured	15	10

1988. 70th Anniv of Polish Republic (3rd issue). 60th Anniv of Military Institute for Aviation Medicine. As T 925. Multicoloured.

3177	20z. Hanriot XIV hospital aircraft (38×28 mm)	15	10

927 On the Field of Glory Medal

1988. Polish People's Army Battle Medals (1st series). Multicoloured.

3178	20z. Type **927**	15	10
3179	20z. Battle of Lenino Cross	15	10

See also Nos. 3249/50.

928 "Stanislaw Malachowski" and "Kazimierz Nestor Sapieha"

1988. Bicentenary of Four Years Diet (political and social reforms). Paintings of Diet Presidents by Jozef Peszko.

3180	**928**	20z. multicoloured	15	10

929 Ignacy Daszynski (politician)

1988. 70th Anniv of Polish Republic (4th issue). Personalities.

3181	**929**	15z. green, red and black	10	10
3182	-	15z. green, red and black	10	10
3183	-	20z. brown, red and black	15	10
3184	-	20z. brown, red and black	15	10
3185	-	20z. brown, red and black	15	10
3186	-	200z. purple, red & black	1·40	55
3187	-	200z. purple, red & black	1·40	55
3188	-	200z. purple, red & black	1·40	55
MS3189		102×60 mm. Nos. 3186/8	13·50	13·50

DESIGNS: No. 3182, Wincenty Witos (politician); 3183, Julian Marchlewski (trade unionist and economist); 3184, Stanislaw Wojciechowski (politician); 3185, Wojciech Korfanty (politician); 3186, Ignacy Paderewski (musician and politician); 3187; Marshal Jozef Pilsudski; 3188, Gabriel Narutowicz (President, 1922).

1988. 70th Anniv of Polish Republic (5th issue). As T 925. Multicoloured.

3190	15z. Coal wharf, Gdynia Port (65th anniv) (38×28 mm)	10	10
3191	20z. Hipolit Cegielski (founder) and steam locomotive (142nd anniv of H. Cegielski Metal Works, Poznan) (38×28 mm)	15	10
3192	40z. Upper Silesia Tower (main entrance) (60th anniv of International Poznan Fair)	30	10

1988. Polish Rulers (3rd series). Drawings by Jan Matejko. As T 893.

3193	10z. deep brown and brown	30	10
3194	15z. deep brown and brown	45	10

DESIGNS: 10z. Queen Rycheza; 15z. Kazimierz (Karol Odnowiciel) I.

930 Snowman

1988. New Year.

3195	**930**	20z. multicoloured	15	10

931 Flag

1988. 40th Anniv of Polish United Workers' Party.

3196	**931**	20z. red and black	15	10

932 "Blysk"

1988. Fire Boats. Multicoloured.

3197	10z. Type **932**	10	10
3198	15z. "Plomien"	10	10
3199	15z. "Zar"	10	10
3200	20z. "Strazak II"	25	10
3201	20z. "Strazak 4"	25	10
3202	45z. "Strazak 25"	40	30

933 Ardennes

1989. Horses. Multicoloured.

3203	15z. Lippizaner (horiz)	10	10
3204	15z. Type **933**	10	10
3205	20z. English thoroughbred (horiz)	25	10
3206	20z. Arab	25	10
3207	30z. Great Poland race-horse (horiz)	40	10
3208	70z. Polish horse	75	30

934 Wire-haired Dachshund

1989. Hunting Dogs. Multicoloured.

3209	15z. Type **934**	10	10
3210	15z. Cocker spaniel	10	10
3211	20z. Czech fousek pointer	10	10
3212	20z. Welsh terrier	10	10
3213	25z. English setter	15	10
3214	45z. Pointer	30	30

935 Gen. Wladyslaw Anders and Plan of Battle

1989. 45th Anniv of Battle of Monte Cassino.

3215	**935**	80z. multicoloured	40	30

See also Nos. 3227, 3247, 3287 and 3327.

936 Marianne

1989. Bicentenary of French Revolution.

3216	**936**	100z. black, red and blue	40	25
MS3217		93×118 mm. No. 3216 ×2 plus two labels (sold at 270z.)	90	1·10

937 Polonia House

1989. Opening of Polonia House (cultural centre), Pultusk.

3218	**937**	100z. multicoloured	45	25

938 Monument (Bohdan Chmielewski)

1989. 45th Anniv of Civic Militia and Security Force.

3219	**938**	35z. blue and brown	25	15

939 Xaweri Dunikowski (artist)

1989. Recipients of Order of Builders of the Republic of Poland. Multicoloured.

3220	35z. Type **939**	15	10
3221	35z. Stanislaw Mazur (farmer)	15	10
3222	35z. Natalia Gasiorowska (historian)	15	10
3223	35z. Wincenti Pstrowski (initiator of worker performance contests)	15	10

940 Astronaut

1989. 20th Anniv of First Manned Landing on Moon.

3224	**940**	100z. multicoloured	45	25
MS3225		85×85 mm. No. 3224	2·10	1·40

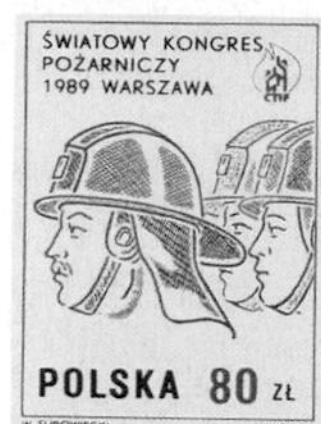

941 Firemen

1989. World Fire Fighting Congress, Warsaw.

3226	**941**	80z. multicoloured	30	10

1989. 45th Anniv of Battle of Falaise. As T 935. Multicoloured.

3227	165z. Plan of battle and Gen. Stanislaw Maczek (horiz)	60	30

942 Daisy

1989. Plants. (a) Perf.

3229	**942**	40z. green	15	10
3230	-	60z. violet	15	10
3231	**942**	150z. red	30	10
3232	-	500z. mauve	30	10
3233	-	700z. green	15	10
3234	-	1000z. blue	90	30

(b) Self-adhesive. Imperf.

3297	2000z. green	40	25
3298	5000z. violet	85	40

DESIGNS: 60z. Juniper; 500z. Wild rose; 700z. Lily of the valley; 1000z. Blue cornflower; 2000z. Water lily; 5000z. Iris.

1989. 50th Anniv of German Invasion. As T 850.

3240	25z. grey, orange and black	25	10
3241	25z. multicoloured	25	10
3242	35z. multicoloured	45	30
3243	35z. multicoloured	45	30

DESIGNS: No. 3240, Defence of Westerplatte and Captain Franciszek Dabrowski; 3241, Defence of Hel and Captain B. Przybyszewski; 3242, Battle of Kock and Brig.-Gen. Franciszek Kleeberg; 3243, Defence of Lwow and Brig.-Gen. Wladyslaw Langner.

943 Museum Emblem

1989. Caricature Museum.

3244	**943**	40z. multicoloured	15	10

944 Rafal Czerwiakowski (founder of first university Surgery Department)

1989. Polish Surgeons' Society Centenary Congress, Cracow.

3245	**944**	40z. blue and black	25	10
3246	-	60z. green and black	25	10

DESIGN: 60z. Ludwik Rydygier (founder of Polish Surgeons' Society).

1989. 45th Anniv of Landing at Arnhem. As T 935. Multicoloured.

3247	210z. Gen. Stanislaw Sosabowski and plan of battle	75	45

945 Emil Kalinski (Postal Minister, 1933–39)

1989. World Post Day.

3248	**945**	60z. multicoloured	25	25

1989. Polish People's Army Battle Medals (2nd series). As T 927. Multicoloured.

3249	60z. "For Participation in the Struggle for the Rule of the People"	25	15
3250	60z. Warsaw 1939–45 Medal	25	15

1989. Polish Rulers (4th series). As T 893. Drawings by Jan Matejko.

3251	20z. black and grey	30	10
3252	30z. sepia and brown	30	30

DESIGNS: 20z. Boleslaw II, the Bold; 30z. Wladyslaw I Herman.

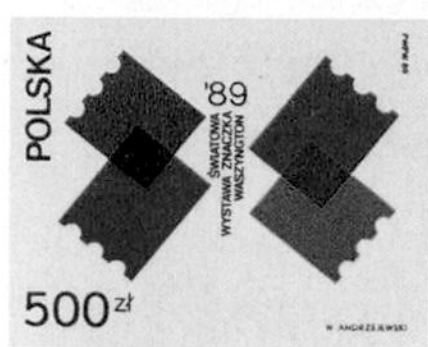

946 Stamps

1989. "World Stamp Expo '89" International Stamp Exhibition, Washington D.C.

3253	**946**	500z. multicoloured	1·10	65

947 Cross and Twig

1989. 70th Anniv of Polish Red Cross.

3254	**947**	200z. red, green and black	45	25

948 Ignacy Paderewski and Roman Dmowski (Polish signatories)

1989. 70th Anniv of Treaty of Versailles.

3255	**948**	350z. multicoloured	60	60

949 Photographer and Medal depicting Maksymilian Strasz

1989. 150th Anniv of Photography. Multicoloured.

3256	40z. Type **949**	15	10
3257	60z. Lens shutter as pupil of eye (horiz)	15	10

1989. No. 2729 surch 500.

3258	500z. on 4z. violet	90	45

951 Painting by Jan Ciaglinski

1989. Flower Paintings by Artists Named. Mult.

3259	25z. Type **951**	10	10
3260	30z. Wojciech Weiss	10	10
3261	35z. Antoni Kolasinski	15	10
3262	50z. Stefan Nacht-Samborski	15	10
3263	60z. Jozef Pankiewicz	15	10
3264	85z. Henryka Beyer	25	25
3265	110z. Wladyslaw Slewinski	30	30
3266	190z. Czeslaw Wdowiszewski	40	40

952 Christ

1989. Icons (1st series). Multicoloured.

3267	50z. Type **952**	15	10
3268	60z. Two saints with books	15	10
3269	90z. Three saints with books	25	15
3270	150z. Displaying scriptures (vert)	40	40
3271	200z. Madonna and child (vert)	45	45
3272	350z. Christ with saints and angels (vert)	45	45

See also Nos. 3345/50.

1990. No. 2839 surch 350 zl.

3273	350z. on 15z. brown	60	30

954 Krystyna Jamroz

1990. Singers. Multicoloured.

3274	100z. Type **954**	25	25
3275	150z. Wanda Werminska	25	25
3276	350z. Ada Sari	40	40
3277	500z. Jan Kiepura	45	45

955 High Jumping

1990. Sports. Multicoloured.

3278	100z. Yachting	15	25
3279	200z. Rugby	15	30
3280	400z. Type **955**	15	30
3281	500z. Ice skating	15	40
3282	500z. Diving	15	45
3283	1000z. Gymnastics	25	30

956 Kozlowski

1990. Birth Centenary (1989) of Roman Kozlowski (palaeontologist).

3284	**956**	500z. brown and red	15	25

957 John Paul II

1990. 70th Birthday of Pope John Paul II.
3285 **957** 1000z. multicoloured 30 30

958 1860 10k. Stamp and Anniversary Stamp

1990. 130th Anniv of First Polish Postage Stamp. Sheet 65×68 mm.
MS3286 **958** 1000z. orange and blue 60 30

1990. 50th Anniv of Battle of Narvik. As T 935. Multicoloured.
3287 1500z. Gen. Zygmunt Bohusz-Szyszko and plan of battle 30 25

959 Ball and Colosseum

1990. World Cup Football Championship, Italy.
3288 **959** 1000z. multicoloured 15 25

1990. No. 3230 surch 700 zl.
3289 700z. on 60z. violet 15 15

961 Memorial

1990. 34th Anniv of 1956 Poznan Uprising.
3290 **961** 1500z. multicoloured 25 15

962 People and "ZUS"

1990. 70th Anniv of Social Insurance.
3291 **962** 1500z. blue, mauve & yellow 30 25

963 Stagnant Pond Snail

1990. Shells. No value expressed.
3292 - B (500z.) lilac 25 10
3293 **963** A (700z.) green 45 10
DESIGN: B, River snail.

964 Cross

1990. 50th Anniv of Katyn Massacre.
3294 **964** 1500z. black and red 25 10

965 Weather Balloon

1990. Polish Hydrology and Meteorology Service. Multicoloured.
3295 500z. Type **965** 10 10
3296 700z. Water-height gauge 25 10

966 Women's Kayak Pairs

1990. 23rd World Canoeing Championships. Mult.
3305 700z. Type **966** 25 10
3306 1000z. Men's kayak singles 30 30

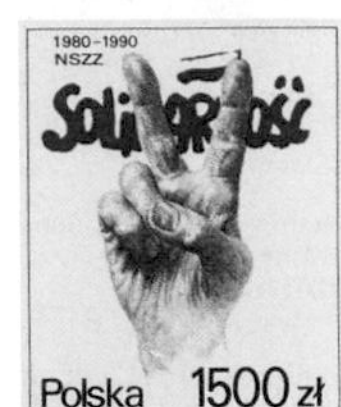

967 Victory Sign

1990. 10th Anniv of Solidarity Trade Union.
3307 **967** 1500z. grey, black and red 25 30

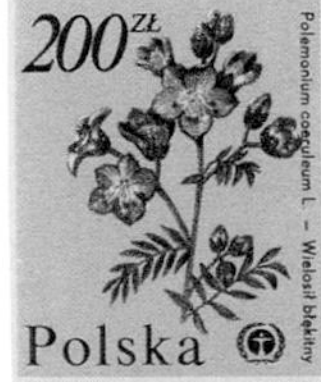

968 Jacob's Ladder

1990. Flowers. Multicoloured.
3308 200z. Type **968** 10 10
3309 700z. Floating heart water fringe ("Nymphoides peltata") 15 10
3310 700z. Dragonhead ("Dracocephalum ruyschiana") 15 10
3311 1000z. "Helleborus purpurascens" 25 10
3312 1500z. Daphne cneorum 45 40
3313 1700z. Campion 65 45

969 Serving Dish, 1870–87

1990. Bicentenary of Cmieow Porcelain Works. Multicoloured.
3314 700z. Type **969** 15 10
3315 800z. Plate, 1887–90 (vert) 25 10
3316 1000z. Cup and saucer, 1887 30 10
3317 1000z. Figurine of dancer, 1941–44 (vert) 30 10
3318 1500z. Chocolate box, 1930–90 55 25
3319 2000z. Vase, 1979 (vert) 60 40

970 Little Owl

1990. Owls. Multicoloured.
3320 200z. Type **970** 10 10
3321 500z. Tawny owl (value at left) 25 10
3322 500z. Tawny owl (value at right) 25 10
3323 1000z. Short-eared owl 40 25
3324 1500z. Long-eared owl 60 30
3325 2000z. Barn owl 85 40

971 Walesa

1990. Lech Walesa, 1984 Nobel Peace Prize Winner and new President.
3326 **971** 1700z. multicoloured 40 25

1990. 50th Anniv of Battle of Britain. As T 935. Multicoloured.
3327 1500z. Emblem of 303 Squadron, Polish Fighter Wing R.A.F. and Hawker Hurricane 45 45

972 Collegiate Church, Tum (12th century)

1990. Historic Architecture. Multicoloured.
3328 700z. Type **972** 25 20
3329 800z. Reszel Castle (11th century) 25 25
3330 1500z. Chelmno Town Hall (16th century) 60 60
3331 1700z. Church of the Nuns of the Visitation, Warsaw (18th century) 60 60

973 "King Zygmunt II August" (anon)

1991. Paintings. Multicoloured.
3332 500z. Type **973** 15 10
3333 700z. "Adoration of the Magi" (Pultusk Codex) 25 10
3334 1000z. "St Matthew" (Pultusk Codex) 30 10
3335 1500z. "Expelling of Merchants from Temple" (Nikolai Haberschrack) 45 30
3336 1700z. "The Annunciation" (miniature) 55 30
3337 2000z. "Three Marys" (Nikolai Haberschrack) 60 40

974 Silver Fir

1991. Cones. Multicoloured.
3338 700z. Type **974** 15 10
3339 1500z. Weymouth pine 25 25
See also Nos. 3483/4.

975 Radziwill Palace

1991. Admission of Poland into European Postal and Telecommunications Conference.
3340 **975** 1500z. multicoloured 30 25

1991. Polish Rulers (5th series). Drawings by Jan Matejko. As T 893 but surch.
3341 1000z. on 40z. black & green 40 25
3342 1500z. on 50z. black and red 55 30
DESIGNS: 1000z. Boleslaw III, the Wry Mouthed; 1500z. Wladyslaw II, the Exile.
Nos. 3341/2 were not issued unsurcharged.

977 Chmielowski

1991. 75th Death Anniv of Adam Chmielowski ("Brother Albert") (founder of Albertine Sisters).
3343 **977** 2000z. multicoloured 40 25

978 Battle (detail of miniature, Schlackenwerth Codex, 1350)

1991. 750th Anniv of Battle of Legnica.
3344 **978** 1500z. multicoloured 30 25

1991. Icons (2nd series). As T 952. Mult.
3345 500z. "Madonna of Nazareth" 10 10
3346 700z. "Christ the Acheirophyte" 15 10
3347 1000z. "Madonna of Vladimir" 25 10
3348 1500z. "Madonna of Kazan" 40 15
3349 2000z. "St. John the Baptist" 55 25
3350 2200z. "Christ the Pentocrator" 85 30

1991. Polish Rulers (6th series). Drawings by Jan Matejko. As T 893.
3351 1000z. black and red 30 25
3352 1500z. black and blue 45 25
DESIGNS: 1000z. Boleslaw IV, the Curly; 1500z. Mieszko (Mieczyslaw) III, the Old.

979 Title Page of Constitution

1991. Bicentenary of 3rd May Constitution.
3353 **979** 2000z. brown, buff & red 40 30
3354 - 2500z. brown, stone & red 55 40
MS3355 85×85 mm. 3000z. multicoloured 75 75
DESIGNS: 2500z. "Administration of Oath by Gustav Taubert" (detail, Johann Friedrich Bolt); 3000z. "Constitution, 3 May 1791" (Jan Matejko).

980 Satellite in Earth Orbit

1991. Europa. Europe in Space.
3356 **980** 1000z. multicoloured 25 25

981 Map and Battle Scene

1991. 50th Anniv of Participation of "Piorun" (destroyer) in Operation against "Bismarck" (German battleship).
3357 **981** 2000z. multicoloured 45 30

982 Arms of Cracow

1991. European Security and Co-operation Conference Cultural Heritage Symposium, Cracow.
3358 **982** 2000z. purple and blue 40 30

983 Pope John Paul II

1991. Papal Visit. Multicoloured.
3359 1000z. Type **983** 25 10
3360 2000z. Pope in white robes 40 30

984 Bearded Penguin

1991. 30th Anniv of Antarctic Treaty.
3361 **984** 2000z. multicoloured 40 30

985 Making Paper

1991. 500th Anniv of Paper Making in Poland.
3362 **985** 2500z. blue and red 40 30

986 Prisoner

1991. Commemoration of Victims of Stalin's Purges.
3363 **986** 2500z. red and black 40 30

987 Pope John Paul II

1991. 6th World Youth Day, Czestochowa. Sheet 70×87 mm.
MS3364 **987** 3500z. multicoloured 75 85

988 Ball and Basket

1991. Centenary of Basketball.
3365 **988** 2500z. multicoloured 55 30

989 "Self-portrait" (Leon Wyczolkowski)

1991. "Bydgoszcz '91" National Stamp Exn.
3366 **989** 3000z. green and brown 55 40
MS3367 155×92 mm. No. 3366 ×4 2·25 2·40

990 Twardowski

1991. 125th Birth Anniv of Kazimierz Twardowski (philosopher).
3368 **990** 2500z. black and grey 60 40

991 Swallowtail

1991. Butterflies and Moths. Multicoloured.
3369 1000z. Type **991** 25 25
3370 1000z. Dark crimson underwing ("Mormonia sponsa") 25 25
3371 1500z. Painted lady ("Vanessa cardui") 30 25
3372 1500z. Scarce swallowtail ("Iphiclides podalirius") 30 25
3373 2500z. Scarlet tiger moth ("Panaxia dominula") 55 40
3374 2500z. Peacock ("Nymphalis io") 55 40
MS3375 127×63 mm. 15000z. Black-veined white (*Aporia crataegi*) (46×33 mm) plus label for "Phila Nippon '91" International Stamp Exhibition 1·90 2·25

992 "The Shepherd's Bow" (Francesco Solimena)

1991. Christmas.
3376 **992** 1000z. multicoloured 30 25

993 Gen. Stanislaw Kopanski and Battle Map

1991. 50th Anniv of Participation of Polish Troops in Battle of Tobruk.
3377 **993** 2000z. multicoloured 40 45

994 Brig.-Gen. Michal Tokarzewski-Karaszewicz

1991. World War II Polish Underground Army Commanders.
3378 **994** 2000z. black and red 40 25
3379 - 2500z. red and violet 45 30
3380 - 3000z. violet and mauve 55 40
3381 - 5000z. brown and green 90 60
3382 - 6500z. dp brown & brn 1·10 75

DESIGNS: 2500z. Gen. Broni Kazimierz Sosnkowski; 3000z. Lt.-Gen. Stefan Rowecki; 5000z. Lt.-Gen. Tadeusz Komorowski; 6500z. Brig.-Gen. Leopold Okulicki.

995 Lord Baden-Powell (founder)

1991. 80th Anniv of Scout Movement in Poland.
3383 **995** 1500z. yellow and green 30 10
3384 - 2000z. blue and yellow 45 30
3385 - 2500z. violet and yellow 55 30
3386 - 3500z. brown and yellow 65 45

DESIGNS: 2000z. Andrzej Malkowski (Polish founder); 2500z. "Watch on the Vistula" (Wojciech Kossak); 3500z. Polish scout in Warsaw Uprising, 1944.

1992. Polish Rulers (7th series). As T 893.
3387 1500z. brown and green 40 25
3388 2000z. black and blue 55 40

DESIGNS: 1500z. Kazimierz II, the Just; 2000z. Leszek I, the White.

996 Sebastien Bourdon

1992. Self-portraits. Multicoloured.
3389 700z. Type **996** 15 10
3390 1000z. Sir Joshua Reynolds 25 10

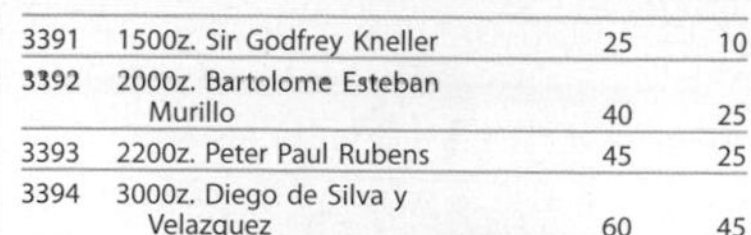

3391 1500z. Sir Godfrey Kneller 25 10
3392 2000z. Bartolome Esteban Murillo 40 25
3393 2200z. Peter Paul Rubens 45 25
3394 3000z. Diego de Silva y Velazquez 60 45

997 Skiing

1992. Winter Olympic Games, Albertville. Mult.
3395 1500z. Type **997** 25 25
3396 2500z. Ice hockey 45 30

998 Manteuffel

1992. 90th Birth Anniv of Tadeusz Manteuffel (historian).
3397 **998** 2500z. brown 45 30

999 Nicolas Copernicus (astronomer)

1992. Famous Poles. Multicoloured.
3398 1500z. Type **999** 25 10
3399 2000z. Frederic Chopin (composer) 40 25
3400 2500z. Henryk Sienkiewicz (writer) 45 25
3401 3500z. Marie Curie (physicist) 60 30
MS3402 80×81 mm. 5000z. Kazimierz Funk (biochemist) 75 75

1000 Columbus and Left-hand Detail of Map

1992. Europa. 500th Anniv of Discovery of America by Columbus. Multicoloured.
3403 1500z. Type **1000** 25 25
3404 3000z. "Santa Maria" and right-hand detail of Juan de la Costa map, 1500 55 45

Nos. 3403/4 were issued together, se-tenant, forming a composite design.

1001 River Czarna Wiselka

1992. Environmental Protection. River Cascades. Multicoloured.
3405 2000z. Type **1001** 40 15
3406 2500z. River Swider 45 40
3407 3000z. River Tanew 60 30
3408 3500z. Mickiewicz waterfall 60 40

1002 Prince Jozef Poniatowski

1992. Bicentenary of Order of Military Virtue. Multicoloured.

3409 1500z. Type **1002** 25 25
3410 3000z. Marshal Jozef Pilsudski 40 30
MS3411 108×93 mm. 20000z. "Virgin Mary of Czestochowa" (icon) (36×57 mm) 3·00 3·50

1003 Family and Heart

1992. Children's Drawings. Multicoloured.

3412 1500z. Type **1003** 25 10
3413 3000z. Butterfly, sun, bird and dog 60 30

1004 Fencing

1992. Olympic Games, Barcelona. Multicoloured.

3414 1500z. Type **1004** 25 10
3415 2000z. Boxing 40 30
3416 2500z. Running 45 30
3417 3000z. Cycling 55 40

1005 Runners

1992. "Olymphilex '92" Olympic Stamps Exhibition, Barcelona. Sheet 86×81 mm.

MS3418 **1005** 20000z. multicoloured 3·50 3·25

1006 Statue of Korczak

1992. 50th Death Anniv of Janusz Korczak (educationist).

3419 **1006** 1500z. black, brown & yellow 30 30

1007 Flag and "V"

1992. 5th Polish Veterans World Meeting.

3420 **1007** 3000z. multicoloured 55 45

1008 Wyszinski

1992. 11th Death Anniv of Stefan Wyszinski (Primate of Poland) (3421) and 1st Anniv of World Youth Day (3422). Multicoloured.

3421 1500z. Type **1008** 30 15
3422 3000z. Pope John Paul II embracing youth 60 45

1009 National Colours encircling World Map

1992. World Meeting of Expatriate Poles, Cracow.

3423 **1009** 3000z. multicoloured 60 45

1010 Polish Museum, Adampol

1992. 150th Anniv of Polish Settlement at Adampol, Turkey.

3424 **1010** 3500z. multicoloured 60 45

1011 18th-century Post Office Sign, Slonim

1992. World Post Day.

3425 **1011** 3500z. multicoloured 60 45

1012 "Dedication" (self-portrait)

1992. Birth Centenary of Bruno Schulz (writer and artist).

3426 **1012** 3000z. multicoloured 55 45

1013 "Seated Girl" (Henryk Wicinski)

1992. Polish Sculptures. Multicoloured.

3427 2000z. Type **1013** 40 15
3428 2500z. "Portrait of Tytus Czyzewski" (Zbigniew Pronaszko) 45 30
3429 3000z. "Polish Nike" (Edward Wittig) 60 45
3430 3500z. "The Nude" (August Zamoyski) 60 45
MS3431 107×90 mm. Nos. 3427/30 1·60 1·60

1014 "10th Theatrical Summer in Zamosc" (Jan Mlodozeniec)

1992. Poster Art (1st series). Multicoloured.

3432 1500z. Type **1014** 25 10
3433 2000z. "Red Art" (Franciszek Starowieyski) 45 30
3434 2500z. "Circus" (Waldemar Swierzy) 50 45
3435 3500z. "Mannequins" (Henryk Tomaszewski) 65 55

See also Nos. 3502/3, 3523/4, 3585/6 and 3712/15.

1015 Girl skipping with Snake

1992. "Polska '93" International Stamp Exn, Poznan (1st issue). Multicoloured.

3436 1500z. Type **1015** 25 10
3437 2000z. Boy on rocking horse with upside-down runners 45 25
3438 2500z. Boy firing bird from bow 45 30
3439 3500z. Girl placing ladder against clockwork giraffe 65 55

See also Nos. 3452, 3453/6 and 3466/9.

1016 Medal and Soldiers

1992. 50th Anniv of Formation of Polish Underground Army. Multicoloured.

3440 1500z. Type **1016** 25 25
3441 3500z. Soldiers 60 55
MS3442 75×95 mm. 20000z.+500z. "WP AK" (26×32 mm) 3·00 3·00

1017 Church and Star

1992. Christmas.

3443 **1017** 1000z. multicoloured 15 10

1018 Wheat

1992. International Nutrition Conference, Rome. Multicoloured.

3444 1500z. Type **1018** 25 10
3445 3500z. Glass, bread, vegetables and jug on table 55 45

1019 Arms of Sovereign Military Order

1992. Postal Agreement with Sovereign Military Order of Malta.

3446 **1019** 3000z. multicoloured 55 45

1020 Arms, 1295

1992. History of the White Eagle (Poland's arms). Each black, red and yellow.

3447 2000z. Type **1020** 40 10
3448 2500z. 15th-century arms 45 30
3449 3000z. 18th-century arms 60 30
3450 3500z. Arms, 1919 65 40
3451 5000z. Arms, 1990 90 55

1021 Exhibition Emblem and Stylized Stamp

1992. Centenary of Polish Philately and "Polska '93" International Stamp Exhibition, Poznan (2nd issue).

3452 **1021** 1500z. multicoloured 25 10

1022 Amber

1993. "Polska '93" International Stamp Exhibition, Poznan (3rd issue). Amber. Multicoloured.

3453 1500z. Type **1022** 25 10
3454 2000z. Pinkish amber 40 25
3455 2500z. Amber in stone 45 45
3456 3000z. Amber containing wasp 60 55
MS3457 82×88 mm. 20000z. Detail of map with necklace representing amber route (44×29 mm) 2·40 2·75

1023 Downhill Skier

1993. Winter University Games, Zakopane.

3458 **1023** 3000z. multicoloured 45 45

1024 Flower-filled Heart

1993. St. Valentine's Day. Multicoloured.

3459	1500z. Type **1024**	25	25
3460	3000z. Heart in envelope	55	45

1993. Polish Rulers (8th series). As T 983 showing drawings by Jan Matejko.

3461	1500z. brown and green	30	25
3462	2000z. black and mauve	55	30
3463	2500z. black and green	65	40
3464	3000z. deep brown and brown	85	55

DESIGNS: 1500z. Wladyslaw Laskonogi; 2000z. Henryk I; 2500z. Konrad I of Masovia; 3000z. Boleslaw V, the Chaste.

1025 Arsenal

1993. 50th Anniv of Attack by Szare Szeregi (formation of Polish Scouts in the resistance forces) on Warsaw Arsenal.

3465	**1025**	1500z. multicoloured	30	30

1026 Jousters with Lances

1993. "Polska '93" International Stamp Exhibition, Poznan (4th issue). Jousting at Golub Dobrzyn. Designs showing a modern and a medieval jouster. Multicoloured.

3466	1500z. Type **1026**	25	10
3467	2000z. Jousters	30	30
3468	2500z. Jousters with swords	75	40
3469	3500z. Officials	65	40

1027 Szczecin

1993. 750th Anniv of Granting of Town Charter to Szczecin.

3470	**1027**	1500z. multicoloured	30	30

1028 Jew and Ruins

1993. 50th Anniv of Warsaw Ghetto Uprising.

3471	**1028**	4000z. black, yellow & blue	90	60

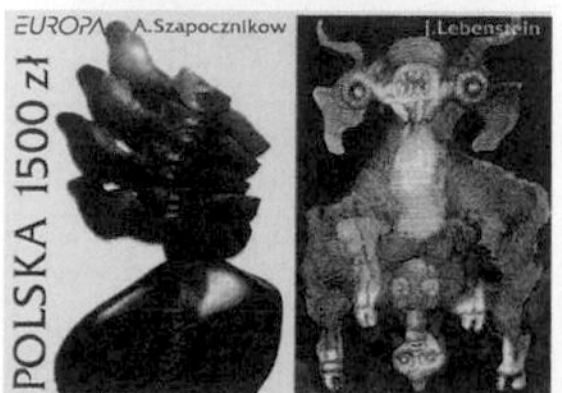

1029 Works by A. Szapocznikow and J. Lebenstein

1993. Europa. Contemporary Art. Multicoloured.

3472	1500z. Type **1029**	25	25
3473	4000z. "CXCIX" (S. Gierawski) and "Red Head" (B. Linke)	65	55

1030 "King Alexander Jagiellonczyk in the Sejm" (Jan Laski, 1505)

1993. 500th Anniv of Parliament.

3474	**1030**	2000z. multicoloured	30	30

1031 Nullo

1993. 130th Death Anniv of Francesco Nullo (Italian volunteer in January 1863 Rising).

3475	**1031**	2500z. multicoloured	45	45

1032 Lech's Encounter with the White Eagle after Battle of Gniezno

1993. "Polska'93" International Stamp Exhibition, Poznan (5th issue). Sheet 103×86 mm.

MS3476 **1032**	50000z. brown	6·75	6·75

1033 Cap

1993. 3rd World Congress of Cadets of the Second Republic.

3477	**1033**	2000z. multicoloured	30	30

1034 Copernicus and Solar System

1993. 450th Death Anniv of Nicolas Copernicus (astronomer).

3478	**1034**	2000z. multicoloured	40	40

1035 Fiki Miki and Lion

1993. 40th Death Anniv of Kornel Makuszynski (writer of children's books). Multicoloured.

3479	1500z. Type **1035**	30	25
3480	2000z. Billy goat	45	30
3481	3000z. Fiki Miki	60	45
3482	5000z. Billy goat riding ostrich	1·00	60

1993. Cones. As T 974. Multicoloured.

3483	10000z. Arolla pine	1·40	85
3484	20000z. Scots pine	3·00	1·50

1036 Eurasian Tree Sparrow

1993. Birds. Multicoloured.

3485	1500z. Type **1036**	30	15
3486	2000z. Pied wagtail	40	25
3487	3000z. Syrian woodpecker	60	45
3488	4000z. Eurasian goldfinch	85	65
3489	5000z. Common starling	90	85
3490	6000z. Northern bullfinch	1·25	90

1037 Soldiers Marching

1993. Bicentenary of Dabrowski's "Mazurka" (national anthem) (1st issue).

3491	**1037**	1500z. multicoloured	30	30

See also Nos. 3526, 3575, 3639 and 3700.

1038 "Madonna and Child" (St. Mary's Basilica, Lesna Podlaska)

1993. Sanctuaries to St. Mary. Multicoloured.

3492	1500z. Type **1038**	25	25
3493	2000z. "Madonna and Child" (St. Mary's Church, Swieta Lipka)	40	30

1039 Handley Page Halifax and Parachutes

1993. The Polish Rangers (Second World War air troop).

3494	**1039**	1500z. multicoloured	30	30

1040 Trumpet Player

1993. "Jazz Jamboree '93" International Jazz Festival, Warsaw.

3495	**1040**	2000z. multicoloured	40	30

1041 Postman

1993. World Post Day.

3496	**1041**	2500z. brown, grey and blue	40	40

1042 St. Jadwiga (miniature, Schlackenwerther Codex)

1993. 750th Death Anniv of St. Jadwiga of Silesia.

3497	**1042**	2500z. multicoloured	45	45

1043 Pope John Paul II

1993. 15th Anniv of Pope John Paul II. Sheet 70×92 mm.

MS3498 **1043**	20000z. multicoloured	3·00	3·00

1044 Golden Eagle and Crown

1993. 75th Anniv of Republic. Multicoloured.

3499	4000z. Type **1044**	65	55
MS3500	66×89 mm. 20000z. Silhouette and shadow of flying eagle (31×38 mm)	3·75	3·75

1045 St. Nicholas

1993. Christmas.

3501	**1045**	1500z. multicoloured	30	30

1993. Poster Art (2nd series). As T 1014. Mult.

3502	2000z. "Come and see Polish Mountains" (M. Urbaniec)	30	30
3503	5000z. Production of Alban Berg's "Wozzeck" (J. Lenica)	75	60

1046 Daisy shedding Petals

1994. Greetings Stamp.

3504	**1046**	1500z. multicoloured	40	40

1047 Cross-country Skiing

1994. Winter Olympic Games, Lillehammer, Norway. Multicoloured.

3505	2500z. Type **1047**	45	45
3506	5000z. Ski jumping	85	75
MS3507	81×80 mm. 10000z. Downhill skiing	1·00	1·60

1048 Bem and Cannon

1994. Birth Bicentenary of General Jozef Bem.
3508 **1048** 5000z. multicoloured 75 75

1049 Jan Zamojski (founder)

1994. 400th Anniv of Zamojski Academy, Zamosc.
3509 **1049** 5000z. grey, black and brown 75 60

1050 Cracow Battalion Flag and Scythes

1994. Bicentenary of Tadeusz Kosciuszko's Insurrection.
3510 **1050** 2000z. multicoloured 40 40

1994. Polish Rulers (9th series). Drawings by Jan Matejko. As T 893.
3511 2500z. black and blue 45 25
3512 5000z. black, deep violet and violet 85 90
DESIGN: 2500z. Leszek II, the Black; 5000a. Przemysl II.

1051 Oil Lamp, Open Book and Spectacles

1994. Europa. Inventions and Discoveries. Mult.
3513 2500z. Type **1051** (invention of modern oil lamp by Ignacy Lukasiewicz) 45 40
3514 6000z. Illuminated filament forming "man in the moon" (astronomy) 1·10 85

1052 "Madonna and Child"

1994. St. Mary's Sanctuary, Kalwaria Zebrzydowska.
3515 **1052** 4000z. multicoloured 60 45

1053 Abbey Ruins and Poppies

1994. 50th Anniv of Battle of Monte Cassino.
3516 **1053** 6000z. multicoloured 75 60

1054 Mazurka

1994. Traditional Dances. Multicoloured.
3517 3000z. Type **1054** 30 30
3518 4000z. Coralski 40 40
3519 9000z. Krakowiak 85 75

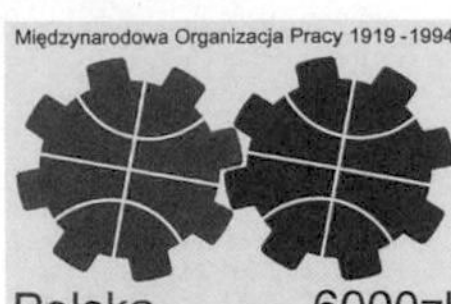

1055 Cogwheels

1994. 75th Anniv of International Labour Organization.
3520 **1055** 6000z. deep blue, blue and black 60 55

1056 Optic Fibre Cable

1994. 75th Anniv of Polish Electricians Association.
3521 **1056** 4000z. multicoloured 55 40

1057 Map of Americas on Football

1994. World Cup Football Championship, U.S.A.
3522 **1057** 6000z. multicoloured 75 75

1994. Poster Art (3rd series). As T 1014. Mult.
3523 4000z. "Monsieur Fabre" (Wiktor Gorka) 45 55
3524 6000z. "8th OISTAT Congress" (Hurbert Hilscher) (horiz) 75 75

1058 Znaniecki

1994. 36th Death Anniv of Professor Florian Znaniecki.
3525 **1058** 9000z. green, bistre & yellow 1·25 85

1994. Bicentenary of Dabrowski's Mazurka (2nd issue). As T 1037. Multicoloured.
3526 2500z. Troops preparing to charge 45 40

1059 Polish Eagle and Ribbon

1994. 50th Anniv of Warsaw Uprising.
3527 **1059** 2500z. multicoloured 45 35

1060 "Stamp" protruding from Pocket

1994. "Philakorea 1994" International Stamp Exhibition, Seoul.
3528 **1060** 4000z. multicoloured 60 45

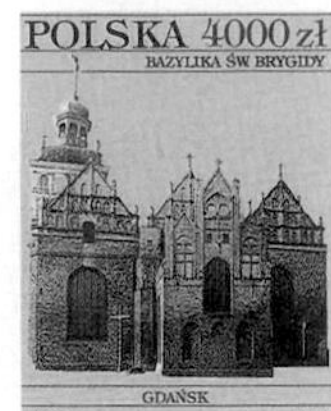

1061 Basilica of St. Brigida, Gdansk

1994. Sanctuaries.
3529 **1061** 4000z. multicoloured 60 40

1062 "Nike" (goddess of Victory)

1994. Centenary of International Olympic Committee.
3530 **1062** 4000z. multicoloured 60 40

1063 Komeda and Piano Keys

1994. 25th Death Anniv of Krzysztof Komeda (jazz musician).
3531 **1063** 6000z. multicoloured 60 50

1064 Long-finned Bristle-mouthed Catfish

1994. Fishes. Multicoloured.
3532 4000z. Type **1064** 60 45
3533 4000z. Freshwater angelfish ("Pterophyllum scalare") 60 45
3534 4000z. Red swordtail ("Xiphophorus helleri"), neon tetra ("Paracheirodon innesi") and Berlin platy 60 45
3535 4000z. Neon tetra ("Poecilia reticulata") and guppies 60 45
Nos. 3532/5 were issued together, se-tenant, forming a composite design.

1065 Arms of Polish Post, 1858

1994. World Post Day.
3536 **1065** 4000z. multicoloured 45 40

1066 Kolbe

1994. Maximilian Kolbe (concentration camp victim) Year.
3537 **1066** 2500z. multicoloured 45 40

1067 Pigeon

1994. Pigeons. Multicoloured.
3538 4000z. Type **1067** 25 30
3539 4000z. Friar pigeon 25 30
3540 6000z. Silver magpie pigeon 40 50
3541 6000z. Danzig pigeon (black) 40 50
MS3542 79×94 mm. 10000z. Short-tail pigeon 1·25 1·40

1068 Musicians playing Carols

1994. Christmas.
3543 **1068** 2500z. multicoloured 35 30

1069 Landscape and E.U. Flag

1994. Application by Poland for Membership of European Union.
3544 **1069** 6000z. multicoloured 90 70

1070 "I Love You" on Pierced Heart

1995. Greetings Stamp.
3545 **1070** 35g. red and blue 25 30

1071 Rain, Sun and Water

1995. 75th Anniv of Hydrological-Meteorological Service.
3546 **1071** 60g. multicoloured 50 40

1072 Flag and Sea

1995. 75th Anniv of Poland's "Marriage to the Sea" (symbolic ceremony commemorating renewal of access to sea).
3547 **1072** 45g. multicoloured 40 30

1995. Polish Rulers (10th series). As T 893 showing drawings by Jan Matejko.
3548 35g. deep brown, brown and light brown 25 25
3549 45g. olive, deep green and green 35 30

3550 60g. brown and ochre 45 40
3551 80g. black and blue 60 60

DESIGNS: 35g. Waclaw II; 45g. Wladyslaw I; 60g. Kazimierz III, the Great; 80g. Ludwik Wegierski.

1073 St. John

1995. 500th Birth Anniv of St. John of God (founder of Order of Hospitallers).
3552 **1073** 60g. multicoloured 45 30

1074 Eggs

1995. Easter. Decorated Easter eggs. Mult, background colours given.
3553 **1074** 35g. red 25 25
3554 - 35g. lilac 25 25
3555 - 45g. blue 35 40
3556 - 45g. green 35 40

1995. Cones. As T 974. Multicoloured.
3557 45g. European larch 30 35
3558 80g. Mountain pine 60 60

1075 Polish Officer's Button and Leaf

1995. Katyn Commemoration Year.
3559 **1075** 80g. multicoloured 60 50

1076 Rose and Barbed Wire

1995. Europa. Peace and Freedom. Multicoloured.
3560 35g. Type **1076** (liberation of concentration camps) 30 35
3561 80g. Flowers in helmet 60 55

1077 Common Cranes

1995. 50th Anniv of Return of Western Territories.
3562 **1077** 45g. multicoloured 60 40

1078 Pope and Wadowice Church Font

1995. 75th Birthday of Pope John Paul II.
3563 **1078** 80g. multicoloured 40 45

1079 Puppets under Spotlight ("Miromagia")

1995. 50th Anniv of Groteska Fairy Tale Theatre. Multicoloured.
3564 35g. Type **1079** 30 25
3565 35g. Puppets in scene from play 30 25
3566 45g. Puppet leaning on barrel ("Thomas Fingerchen") (vert) 40 30
3567 45g. Clown ("Bumstara Circus") 40 30

1080 Cockerill Steam Locomotive and Train, 1845, Warsaw–Vienna

1995. 150th Anniv of Polish Railways. Mult.
3568 35g. Type **1080** 30 20
3569 60g. "Lux-Torpedo" diesel railcar, 1927 50 35
3570 80g. Electric freight train 70 45
3571 1z. Eurocity "Sobieski" express, 1992, Warsaw–Vienna 85 55

1081 Symbols of Nations

1995. 50th Anniv of U.N.O.
3572 **1081** 80g. multicoloured 60 50

1082 Bank

1995. 125th Anniv of Warsaw Commercial Bank.
3573 **1082** 45g. multicoloured 40 40

1083 Loaf and Four-leaved Clover

1995. Centenary of Peasant Movement.
3574 **1083** 45g. multicoloured 40 40

1995. Bicentenary of Dabrowski's "Mazurka" (3rd issue). As T 1037. Multicoloured.
3575 35g. Mounted troops 30 40

1084 Rowan Berries

1995. Fruits of Trees. No value expressed. Mult.
3576 A (35g.) Type **1084** 30 25
3577 B (45g.) Acorns and sessile oak leaves 30 35

1085 Madonna and Child

1995. Basilica of the Holy Trinity, Lezajsk.
3578 **1085** 45g. multicoloured 40 35

1086 Marshal Josef Pilsudski

1995. 75th Anniv of Defence of Warsaw and of Riga Peace Conference.
3579 **1086** 45g. multicoloured 40 40

1087 Dressage

1995. World Carriage Driving Championships, Poznan. Multicoloured.
3580 60g. Type **1087** 40 40
3581 80g. Cross-country event 55 55

1088 Warsaw Technical University

1995. "Warsaw '95" National Stamp Exhibition. Multicoloured.
3582 35g. Type **1088** 30 40
MS3583 94×71 mm. 1z. Castle Place, Warsaw (horiz) 75 85

1089 Russian Space Station and U.S. Spacecraft

1995. 11th World Cosmonauts Congress, Warsaw.
3584 **1089** 80g. multicoloured 60 50

1995. Poster Art (4th series). As T 1014. Mult.
3585 35g. "The Crazy Locomotive" (Jan Sawka) 25 25
3586 45g. "The Wedding" (Eugeniusz Get Stankiewicz) 40 40

1090 Bar from Polonaise (Frederic Chopin)

1995. 13th International Chopin Piano Competition.
3587 **1090** 80g. multicoloured 60 50

1091 Postman

1995. Post Day. Multicoloured.
3588 45g. Type **1091** 40 25
3589 80g. Feather fixed to envelope by seal 60 55

1092 Acrobatic Pyramid

1995. World Acrobatic Sports Championships, Wroclaw.
3590 **1092** 45g. multicoloured 40 40

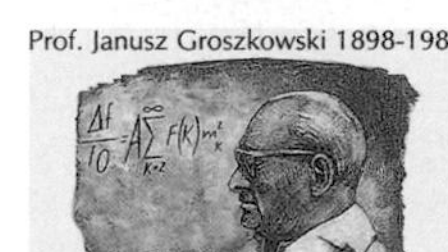

1093 Groszkowski and Formula

1995. 11th Death Anniv of Professor Janusz Groszkowski (radio-electronic scientist).
3591 **1093** 45g. multicoloured 40 40

1094 Crib

1995. Christmas. Multicoloured.
3592 35g. Type **1094** 40 25
3593 45g. Wise men, Christmas tree and star of Bethlehem 40 25

Nos. 3592/3 were issued together, se-tenant, forming a composite design.

1095 Blue Tit

1995. Song Birds. Multicoloured.
3594 35g. Type **1095** 25 20
3595 45g. Long-tailed tit 35 25
3596 60g. Great grey shrike 45 35
3597 80g. Hawfinch 60 45

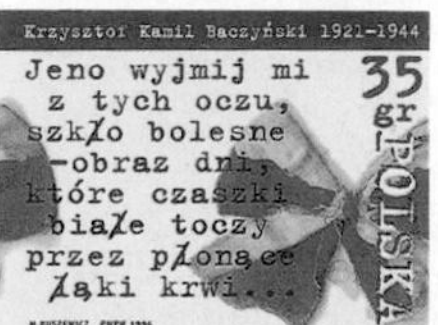

1096 Extract from Poem and Bow

1996. 75th Birth Anniv of Krzysztof Kamil Baczynski (poet).
3598 **1096** 35g. multicoloured 30 40

1097 Cherries and "I love you"

1996. Greetings Stamp.

3599	**1097** 40g. multicoloured	40	20

1098 Romanesque-style Inowlodz Church

1996. Architectural Styles. Multicoloured.

3600	40g. Type **1098**	40	30
3601	55g. Gothic-style St. Mary the Virgin's Church, Cracow	45	35
3602	70g. Renaissance-style St. Sigismund's Chapel, Wawel Castle	60	50
3603	1z. Baroque-style Church of the Order of the Holy Sacrament, Warsaw	90	75

1099 "Oceania"

1996. Sailing Ships. Multicoloured.

3604	40g. Type **1099**	30	30
3605	55g. "Zawisza Czarny" (cadet schooner)	45	40
3606	70g. "General Zaruski" (cadet ketch)	55	55
3607	75g. "Fryderyk Chopin" (cadet brig)	60	55

1100 16th-century Warsaw

1996. 400th Anniv of Warsaw.

3608	**1100** 55g. multicoloured	45	35

1101 Bull (Taurus)

1996. Signs of the Zodiac. Multicoloured.

3609	5g. Workman in water (Aquarius)	15	15
3610	10g. "Fish-person" holding fish (Pisces)	15	15
3611	20g. Type **1101**	10	10
3612	25g. Twins looking through keyhole (Gemini)	15	15
3613	30g. Crab smoking pipe (Cancer)	15	15
3614	40g. Maid and cogwheels (Virgo)	25	25
3615	50g. Lion in military uniform (Leo)	30	25
3616	55g. Couple with head and shoulders as scales (Libra)	30	30
3617	70g. Ram with ram-head (Aries)	45	25
3618	1z. Woman with scorpion's tail hat (Scorpio)	70	35
3619	2z. Archer on motor cycle (Sagittarius)	1·40	70
3620	5z. Office worker shielding face with paper mask (Capricorn)	3·25	1·60

1102 Hanka Ordonowna (singer)

1996. Europa. Famous Women. Multicoloured.

3621	40g. Type **1102**	30	25
3622	1z. Pola Negri (actress)	70	65

1103 Flag of Osiek and Old Photographs forming "1921"

1996. 75th Anniv of Silesian Uprising.

3623	**1103** 55g. red, green and black	40	40

1104 "On Bergamuty Islands"

1996. 50th Anniv of UNICEF. Scenes from Fairy Tales by Jan Brzechwa. Multicoloured.

3624	40g. Type **1104**	35	30
3625	40g. Waiters carrying trays of apples (nursery rhyme)	35	30
3626	55g. Vegetable characters ("At the Market Stall")	55	40
3627	55g. Chef holding duck ("Wacky Duck")	55	40
3628	70g. Woman and birdchild ("The Fibber")	60	60
3629	70g. Red fox ("The Impishness of Witalis Fox")	60	60

1105 "City Walls and Building"

1996. Paintings by Stanislaw Noakowski. Mult.

3630	40g. Type **1105**	30	25
3631	55g. "Renaissance Bedroom"	40	35
3632	70g. "Rural Gothic Church"	50	50
3633	1z. "Renaissance Library"	70	65

1106 Discus on Ribbon

1996. Olympic Games, Atlanta, and Centenary of Modern Olympic Games. Multicoloured.

3634	40g. Type **1106** (gold medal, Halina Konopacka, 1928)	25	25
3635	55g. Tennis ball (horiz)	40	35
3636	70g. Polish Olympic Committee emblem (horiz)	50	45
3637	1z. Bicycle wheel	70	50

1107 Tweezers holding Stamp showing Emblem

1996. "Olymphilex '96" International Sports Stamp Exhibition, Atlanta.

3638	**1107** 1z. multicoloured	70	65

1996. Bicentenary of Dabrowski's Mazurka (4th issue). As T 1037. Multicoloured.

3639	40g. Charge of Polish cavalry at Somosierra	45	30

1108 St. Mary of Przeczycka

1996. St. Mary's Church, Przeczycka.

3640	**1108** 40g. multicoloured	45	35

1996. Polish Rulers (11th series). As T 893.

3641	40g. brown and bistre	30	25
3642	55g. lilac and mauve	45	35
3643	70g. deep grey and grey	55	50
3644	1z. deep green, green and yellow	80	65

DESIGNS: 40g. Queen Jadwiga (wife of Wladyslaw II); 55g. Wladyslaw II Jagiello; 70g. Wladyslaw III Warnenczyk; 1z. Kazimierz IV Jagiellonczyk.

1109 Mt. Giewont and Edelweiss

1996. The Tatra Mountains. Multicoloured.

3645	40g. Type **1109**	30	20
3646	40g. Mt. Krzesanica and spring gentian	30	20
3647	55g. Mt. Koscielec and leopard's bane	45	25
3648	55g. Mt. Swinica and clusius gentian	45	25
3649	70g. Mt. Rysy and ragwort	55	30
3650	70g. Mieguszowieckie peaks and pine trees	55	30

1110 Seifert

1996. 50th Birth Anniv of Zbigniew Seifert (jazz musician).

3651	**1110** 70g. multicoloured	75	45

1111 "Changing of Horses at Post Station" (detail, Mieczyslaw Watorski)

1996. World Post Day. 75th Anniv of Post and Telecommunications Museum, Wroclaw. Paintings. Multicoloured.

3652	40g. Type **1111**	30	25
MS3653	102×81 mm. 1z.+20g. "Mail Coach at Jagniatkowo with View over Karkonosze" (Professor Tager) (42×30 mm)	90	85

1112 Father Christmas on Horse-drawn Sleigh

1996. Christmas. Multicoloured.

3654	40g. Type **1112**	25	10
3655	55g. Carol singers with star lantern	35	25

1113 Head of Male Bison

1996. The European Bison. Multicoloured.

3656	55g. Type **1113**	40	40
3657	55g. Head of female	40	40
3658	55g. Pair of bison	40	40
3659	55g. Male	40	40

1114 Wislawa Szymborska

1996. Award of Nobel Prize for Literature to Wislawa Szymborska (poet).

3660	**1114** 1z. multicoloured	75	65

1115 "I Love You" on King of Hearts Playing Card

1997. Greetings Stamps. Multicoloured.

3661	B (40g.) Type **1115**	30	25
3662	A (55g.) Queen of hearts playing card	45	1·00

Nos. 3661/2 were issued together, se-tenant, forming a composite design.

No. 3661 was sold at the rate for postcards and No. 3662 for letters up to 20 grams.

1116 Blessing the Palms

1997. Easter. Traditional Customs. Multicoloured.

3663	50g. Type **1116**	30	25
3664	60g. Woman and child painting Easter eggs	40	35
3665	80g. Priest blessing the food	55	45
3666	1z.10 Man throwing water over woman's skirts on Easter Monday	65	45

1117 Long Market and Town Hall (after Mateusz Deisch)

1997. Millenary of Gdansk. Each brown, cinnamon and red.

3667	50g. Type **1117**	60	40

MS3668 94×71 mm. 1z.10 St. Mary's Church and Hall of the Main Town (after Mateusz Merian) (horiz) 75 85

1118 St. Adalbert and Monks addressing Pagans

1997. Death Millenary of St. Adalbert (Bishop of Prague).
3669 **1118** 50g. brown 30 25
3670 - 60g. green 40 35
3671 - 1z.10 lilac 70 40
DESIGNS—VERT: 60g. St. Adalbert and anniversary emblem; 1z.10, St. Adalbert.

1119 Mansion House, Lopuszna

1997. Polish Manor Houses. Multicoloured.
3671a 10g Lipkowie, Warsaw 10 10
3672 50g. Type **1119** 20 10
3673 55g. Henryk Sienkewicz Museum, Oblegorek 35 20
3674 60g. Zyrzyn 50 20
3675 65g. Stanislaw Wyspianski Museum, Bronowice, near Cracow 60 20
3675a 70g. Modlnica 65 35
3675b 80g. Grabonog, Gostyn 75 35
3676 90g. Obory, near Warsaw 90 60
3676a 1z. Krzelawice 95 45
3677 1z.10 Ozarow 1·00 35
3678 1z.20 Jozef Krasnewski Museum, Biala 65 35
3678a 1z.40 Winna Gora 75 80
3678b 1z.50 Sulejowku, Warsaw 45 15
3678c 1z.55 Zelazowa Wola 80 80
3678d 1z.60 Potok Zloty 80 95
3678e 1z.65 Sucha, Wegrow 90 95
3679 1z.70 Tulowice 95 1·00
3679a 1z.85 Kasna Dolna 90 80
3679b 1z.90 Petrykozach Mszczonowa 60 20
3680 2z.20 Kuznocin 1·10 95
3681 2z.65 Liwia, Wegrow 1·50 1·10
3682 3z. Janowcu, Pulaw 90 30
3683 10z. Koszuty 5·50 4·00

See also Nos. 3727/8.

1120 The Crock of Gold

1997. Europa. Tales and Legends. Multicoloured.
3685 50g. Type **1120** 30 35
3686 1z.10 Wars, Sawa and mermaid-siren 70 80

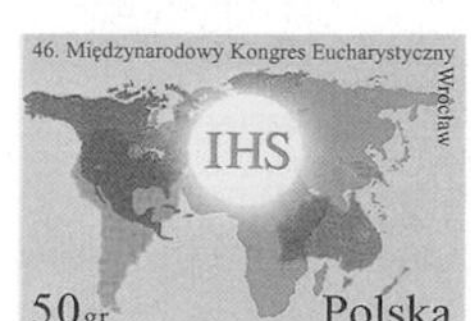

1121 World Map and Emblem

1997. 46th International Eucharistic Congress, Wroclaw.
3687 **1121** 50g. multicoloured 30 35

1122 San Francisco–Oakland Bay Bridge

1997. "Pacific 97" International Stamp Exhibition, San Francisco.
3688 **1122** 1z.30 multicoloured 75 75

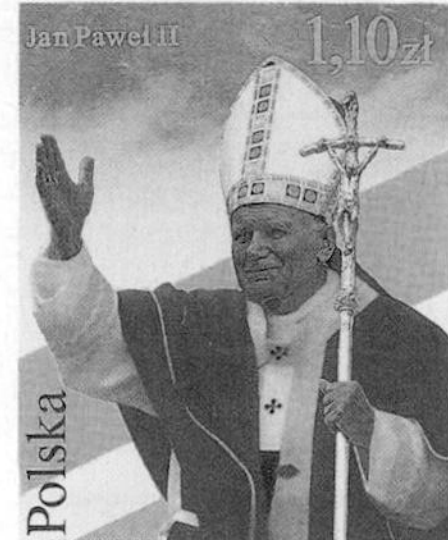

1123 Pope John Paul II

1997. 5th Papal Visit. Sheet 76×90 mm.
MS3689 **1123** 1z.10 multicoloured 75 85

1124 European Long-eared Bat

1997. Bats. Multicoloured.
3690 50g. Type **1124** 30 20
3691 60g. Common noctule 40 25
3692 80g. Brown bat 50 35
3693 1z.30 Red bat 85 55

1125 "Founding of the Main School" (Jan Matejko)

1997. 600th Anniv of Faculty of Theology, Jagiellonian University, Cracow.
3694 **1125** 80g. multicoloured 60 55

1126 Map highlighting Settled Area

1997. Centenary of Polish Migration to Argentina.
3695 **1126** 1z.40 multicoloured 80 75

1127 "Return from War to the Village"

1997. Paintings by Juliusz Kossak. Multicoloured.
3696 50g. Type **1127** 30 25
3697 60g. "Cracowian Wedding" 35 35
3698 80g. "In the Stable" 50 45
3699 1z.10 "Stablehand with Pair of Horses" 65 60

1997. Bicentenary of Dabrowski's "Mazurka" (5th issue). As T 1037.
3700 50g. Dabrowski and Wybicki's arrival in Poznan, 1806 35 35
MS3701 85×77 mm. 1z.10 Manuscript of lyrics and Jozef Wybicki (composer) 75 65

1128 Strzelecki and Route Map around Australia

1997. Birth Bicentenary of Pawel Strzelecki (explorer).
3702 **1128** 1z.50 multicoloured 90 90

1129 Flooded Houses

1997. Flood Relief Fund.
3703 **1129** 60g.+30g. multicoloured 75 65

1130 "Holy Mother of Consolation" (icon)

1997. Church of the Holy Mother of Consolation and St. Michael the Archangel, Gorka Duchowa.
3704 **1130** 50g. multicoloured 30 40

1997. Polish Rulers (12th series). As T 893.
3705 50g. agate, brown and bistre 35 30
3706 60g. purple and blue 45 40
3707 80g. green, deep green and olive 60 50
3708 1z.10 purple and lilac 80 65
DESIGNS: 50g. Jan I Olbracht; 60g. Aleksander Jagiellonczyk; 80g. Zygmunt I, the Old; 1z.10, Zygmunt II August.

1131 Kosz

1997. 24th Death Anniv of Mieczyslaw Kosz (jazz musician).
3709 **1131** 80g. multicoloured 60 50

1132 Globe and posthorn

1997. World Post Day.
3710 **1132** 50g. multicoloured 35 35

1133 St. Basil's Cathedral, Moscow

1997. "Moskva 97" International Stamp Exhibition, Moscow.
3711 **1133** 80g. multicoloured 60 70

1997. Poster Art (5th series). As T 1014.
3712 50g. multicoloured 35 25
3713 50g. black 35 25
3714 60g. multicoloured 40 45
3715 60g. multicoloured 40 45
POSTERS—HORIZ: No. 3712, Advertisement for Radion washing powder (Tadeusz Gronowski). VERT: No. 3713, Production of Stanislaw Witkiewicz's play "Shoemakers" (Roman Cieslewicz); 3714, Production of Aleksander Fredro's play "A Husband and a Wife" (Andrzej Pagowski); 3715, Production of ballet "Goya" (Wiktor Sadowski).

1134 Nativity

1997. Christmas. Multicoloured.
3716 50g. Type **1134** 25 20
3717 60g. Christmas Eve feast (horiz) 35 25
3718 80g. Family going to church for Midnight Mass (horiz) 45 30
3719 1z.10 Waits (carol singers representing animals) 60 40

1135 Common Shelducks

1997. Praecocial Chicks. Multicoloured.
3720 50g. Type **1135** 35 35
3721 50g. Goosanders ("Mergus merganser") 35 35
3722 50g. Common snipes ("Gallinago gallinago") 35 35
3723 50g. Moorhens ("Gallinula chloropus") 35 35

1136 Ski Jumping

1998. Winter Olympic Games, Nagano, Japan.
3724 **1136** 1z.40 multicoloured 80 75

1137 Dog wearing Cat T-shirt inscr "I Love You"

1998. Greetings Stamps. No value expressed. Multicoloured.
3725 B (55g.) Type **1137** 35 25
3726 A (65g.) Cat wearing dog T-shirt 35 35

1998. Polish Manor Houses. No value expressed. As T 1119. Multicoloured.
3727 B (55g.) Gluchy 35 25
3728 A (65g.) Jan Kochanwoski Museum, Czarnolas 35 35

1138 Paschal Lamb

1998. Easter. Multicoloured.
3729 55g. Type **1138** 35 20
3730 65g. The Resurrected Christ 35 20

1139 Polish National Guard and Civilians at Lvov Barricades

1998. 150th Anniv of 1848 Revolutions.
3731 **1139** 55g. brown 45 25

1998. Polish Rulers (13th series). As T 893.
3732 55g. brown and light brown 35 20
3733 65g. purple, deep purple and mauve 40 35
3734 80g. deep green and green 50 45
3735 90g. lilac, purple and mauve 60 45
DESIGNS: 55g. Henryk Walezy; 65g. Queen Anna Jagiellonka (wife of Stefan I); 80g. Stefan I Batory; 90g. Zygmunt III Wasa.

1140 Grey Seal

1998. Protection of Baltic Sea. Marine Life. Mult.
3736 65g. Type **1140** 45 35
3737 65g. "Patoschistus microps" (fish), jellyfish and shells 45 35
3738 65g. Twaite shad ("Alosa fallax") and pipefish ("Syngnathus typhle") 45 35
3739 65g. Common sturgeon ("Acipenser sturio") 45 35
3740 65g. Atlantic salmon ("Salmo salar") 45 35
3741 65g. Common porpoise 45 35
MS3742 76×70 mm. 1z.20 Grey seal 1·60 1·40
Nos. 3736/41 were issued together, se-tenant, forming a composite design.

1141 Exhibition Emblem and 1948 Israeli 500 m. Stamp

1998. "Israel '98" International Stamp Exhibition, Tel Aviv.
3743 **1141** 90g. multicoloured 75 80

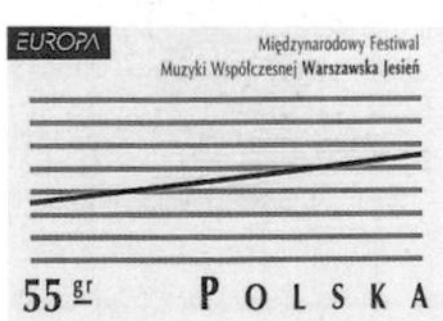

1142 Festival Emblem

1998. Europa. National Festivals.
3744 **1142** 55g. multicoloured 55 50
3745 - 1z.20 black, red and blue 90 95
DESIGNS: 55g. Type **1142** ("Warsaw Autumn" International Festival of Music); 1z.20, State flag and opening bars of "Welcome the May Dawn" (3rd of May Constitution Day).

1144 "Longing Holy Mother"

1998. Coronation of "Longing Holy Mother" (icon in Powsin Church).
3752 **1144** 55g. multicoloured 45 75

1145 "Triple Self-portrait"

1998. 30th Death Anniv of Nikifor (Epifan Drowniak) (artist). Multicoloured.
3753 55g. Type **1145** 35 40
3754 65g. "Cracow Office" 40 50
3755 1z.20 "Orthodox Church" 75 80
3756 2z.35 "Ucrybow Station" 1·50 1·60

1146 Anniversary Inscription

1998. 80th Anniv of Main Board of Statistics.
3757 **1146** 55g. multicoloured 45 40

1147 "Madonna and Child"

1998. Basilica of the Visitation of St. Mary the Virgin, Sejny.
3758 **1147** 55g. multicoloured 45 40

1148 Jesus (stained glass window)

1998. Bicentenary of Diocese of Warsaw.
3759 **1148** 65g. multicoloured 45 50

1998. 17th Congress of Polish Union of Stamp Collectors. Sheet 114×77 mm containing T 1141 and similar horiz design. Each blue and cream.
MS3760 65g. ×2 Composite design showing 17th-century engraving of Szczecin from Descriptio Urbis Stettinensis by Paul Feideborn 85 95

1150 Pierre and Marie Curie (physicists)

1998. Centenary of Discovery of Polonium and Radium.
3761 **1150** 1z.20 multicoloured 70 80

1151 Mazowsze Dancers

1998. 50th Anniv of Mazowsze Song and Dance Group. Multicoloured.
3762 65g. Type **1151** 40 50
3763 65g. Dancers (different) 40 50
Nos. 3762/3 were issued together, se-tenant, forming a composite design.

1152 Mniszchow Palace

1998. Belgium Embassy, Warsaw.
3764 **1152** 1z.20 multicoloured 70 75

1153 "King Sigismund" (Studio of Rubens)

1998. 400th Anniv of Battle of Stangebro.
3765 **1153** 1z.20 brown 70 1·00

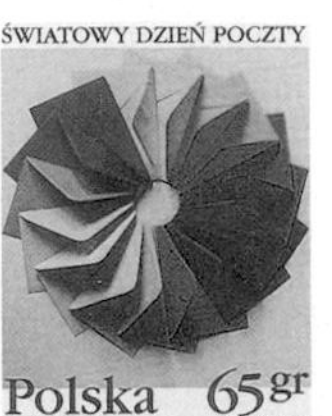

1154 Coloured Envelopes

1998. World Post Day.
3766 **1154** 65g. multicoloured 45 50

1155 Pope John Paul II and People of Different Races

1998. 20th Anniv of Selection of Karol Wojtyla to Papacy.
3767 **1155** 65g. multicoloured 45 50

1156 State Flags and 1919 Seal

1998. 80th Anniv of Independence.
3768 **1156** 65g. black, red and gold 45 50

1157 "Nativity"

1998. Christmas. Polyptych, Grudziadz. Mult.
3769 55g. Type **1157** 40 40
3770 65g. "Adoration of the Wise Men" 40 50

1158 Anniversary Emblem

1998. 50th Anniv of Universal Declaration of Human Rights.
3771 **1158** 1z.20 blue and ultramarine 75 80

1159 Maryla Wereszczakowna and Moonlit Night

1998. Birth Bicentenary of Adam Mickiewicz (poet). Multicoloured.
3772 55g. Type **1159** 30 35
3773 65g. Cranes flying over tomb of Maria Potocka 40 45
3774 90g. Burning candles and cross 45 60
3775 1z.20 House, field of flowers and uhlan's shako 60 75
MS3776 61×76 mm. 2z.45 Mickiewicz (bust by Jean David d'Angers) (30×38 mm) 1·60 2·00

1160 "Piorun" (destroyer), 1942–46

1999. 80th Anniv (1998) of Polish Navy. Mult.
3777 55g. Type **1160** 40 35
3778 55g. "Piorun" (missile corvette), 1994 40 35

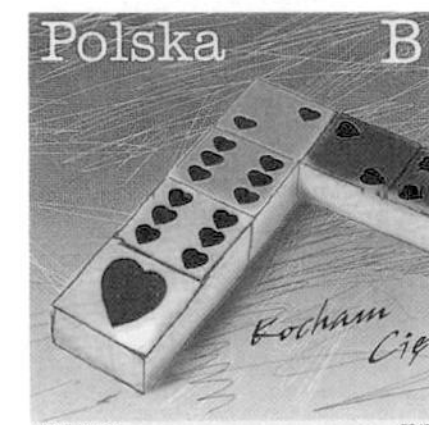

1161 Dominoes

1999. Greetings stamps. Value expressed by letter. Multicoloured.
3779 B (60g.) Type **1161** 40 35
3780 A (65g.) Dominoes (different) 40 45

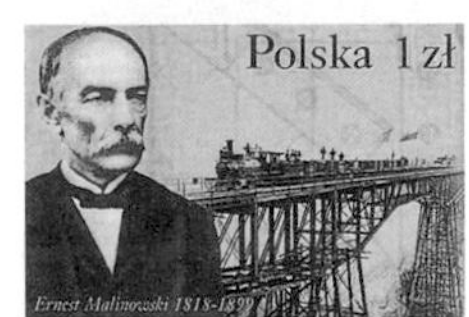

1162 Ernest Malinowski and Railway Bridge over Varrugas Canyon

1999. Polish Engineers. Multicoloured.
3781 1z. Type **1162** (death cent) 55 60
3782 1z.60 Rudolf Modrzejewski and Benjamin Franklin Bridge over Delaware River, Philadelphia 85 95

1163 "Prayer in Ogrojec"

1999. Easter. Multicoloured.
3783 60g. Type **1163** 30 35
3784 65g. "Carrying the Cross" 30 35
3785 1z. "Pieta" 50 55
3786 1z.40 "Resurrection" 75 70
Nos. 3783/4 and 3786 show details of the Grudzic polyptych.

1164 Chinese Ideograms

1999. "China '99" International Stamp Exhibition, Peking. Sheet 80×96 mm.

MS3787	**1164** 1z.70 multicoloured	90	1·10

1165 "Victorious St. Mary of Kozielsk" (sculpture)

1999. Images of Virgin Mary made by Polish Prisoners of War. Multicoloured.

3788	60g. Type **1165**	30	35
3789	70g. "St. Mary of Katyn" (bas-relief, Stanislaw Balos)	40	35

1166 Jan Skrzetuski passing Zbara Fortress ("With Fire and Sword")

1999. "Heroes of the Trilogy " (novels) by Henryk Sienkiewicz. Multicoloured.

3790	70g. Type **1166**	35	35
3791	70g. Onufry Zagloba and 17th-century map of Poland (all three parts)	35	35
3792	70g. Longinus Podbipieta defending Zbara and three Tartars ("With Fire and Sword")	35	35
3793	70g. Bohun with Helena Kunce-wiczowna on way to Czarci Jar ("With Fire and Sword")	35	35
3794	70g. Andrzej Kmicic and cannon at Jasna Gora Monastery ("The Deluge")	35	35
3795	70g. Michal Jerzy Wolodyjowski and Basia Jeziorkowska fencing ("Pan Michael")	35	35

1167 Polish Flag and N.A.T.O. Emblem

1999. 50th Anniv of North Atlantic Treaty Organization and Accession of Poland.

3796	**1167** 70g. multicoloured	45	35

1168 Anniversary Emblem and Headquarters, Strasbourg

1999. 50th Anniv of Council of Europe.

3797	**1168** 1z. multicoloured	55	60

1169 Three-toed Woodpecker

1999. Europa. Parks and Gardens. Bialowieski National Park.

3798	**1169** 1z.40 multicoloured	75	90

1170 Mountain Biking

1999. Youth Sports. Multicoloured.

3799	60g. Type **1170**	40	35
3800	70g. Snowboarding	40	50
3801	1z. Skateboarding	60	60
3802	1z.40 Rollerblading	85	1·00

1171 St. Mary's Church, Cracow, Pope John Paul II and Crowd

1999. 6th Papal Visit to Poland. Multicoloured.

3803	60g. Type **1171**	35	30
3804	70g. Pope and crowd with crosses	40	40
3805	1z. Pope and cheering teenagers	60	50
3806	1z.40 Eiffel Tower (Paris), "Christ the Saviour" (statue, Rio de Janeiro), Pope and church at Fatima, Portugal	80	65

1172 Ignacy Paderewski and Roman Dmowski (signatories)

1999. 80th Anniv of Treaty of Versailles.

3807	**1172** 1z.40 multicoloured	85	1·00

1173 "St. Mary Carefully Listening" (icon)

1999. St. Mary's Sanctuaries. Multicoloured.

3808	60g. Type **1173** (church of St. Mary Queen of Poland, Rokitno)	40	40
3809	70g. "Mary" (statue, Ms. Jazlowiecka), Convent of Order of the Immaculate Conception, Szymanow	40	50

1174 Great Diving Beetle ("Dytiscus marginalis")

1999. Insects. Multicoloured.

3810	60g. Type **1174**	30	35
3811	60g. "Corixa punctata"	30	35
3812	70g. "Limnophilus"	40	45
3813	70g. "Perla marginata"	40	45
3814	1z.40 Emperor dragonfly ("Anax imperator")	80	95

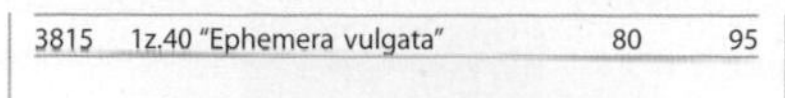

3815	1z.40 "Ephemera vulgata"	80	95

1175 Ksiaz Castle

1999. "Walbrzych '99" 18th National Stamp Exhibition. Sheet 74×105 mm.

MS3816	**1175** 1z. blue	75	85

1176 Red Deer

1999. Eastern Carpathian Mountains International Biosphere Reserve (covering Polish, Ukrainian and Slovakian National Parks). Multicoloured.

3817	1z.40 Type **1176**	70	90
3818	1z.40 Wild cat	70	90

1999. Polish Rulers (14th series). As T 893.

3819	60g. black and green	35	20
3820	70g. brown and light brown	40	35
3821	1z. black and blue	60	40
3822	1z.40 deep purple and purple	80	45

DESIGNS: 60g. Wladyslaw IV Waza; 70g. Jan II Kazimierz; 1z. Michal Korybut Wisniowiecki; 1z.40, Jan III Sobieski.

1177 U.P.U. Emblem

1999. 125th Anniv of Universal Postal Union.

3823	**1177** 1z.40 multicoloured	70	85

1178 Chopin and Academy of Fine Arts, Warsaw

1999. 150th Death Anniv of Frederic Chopin (composer).

3824	**1178** 1z.40 green	70	85

1179 Popieluszko

1999. 15th Death Anniv of Father Jerzy Popieluszko.

3825	**1179** 70g. multicoloured	40	50

1180 Barbed Wire

1999. Homage to 20th-century Heroes of Poland. Sheet 93×70 mm.

MS3826	**1180** 1z. multicoloured	60	70

1181 Angel ("Silent Night")

1999. Christmas. Inscr in Polish with the opening lines of carols. Multicoloured.

3827	60g. Type **1181**	35	25
3828	70g. Angel ("Sleep, Jesus Baby")	40	25
3829	1z. Angel ("Let's Go Everybody to the Stable")	55	40
3830	1z.40 Angel ("The God is Born")	80	60

1182 Polish Museum, Rapperswil Castle, Switzerland

1999. Polish Overseas Cultural Buildings. Mult.

3831	1z. Type **1182**	60	40
3832	1z.40 Marian Priests' Museum, Fawley Court, England	80	60
3833	1z.60 Polish Library, Paris, France	95	65
3834	1z.80 Polish Institute and Gen. Sikorski Museum, London, England	1·10	75

1183 "Proportions of Man" (Da Vinci)

2000. New Year 2000.

3835	**1183** A (70g.) multicoloured	55	50

1184 Bronislaw Malinowski (sociologist)

2000. Polish Personalities. Multicoloured.

3836	1z.55 Type **1184**	75	75
3837	1z.95 Jozef Zwierzycki (geologist)	1·10	1·00

1185 Otto III granting Crown to Boleslaw I

2000. 1000th Anniv of the Gniezno Summit and the Catholic Church in Poland. Multicoloured.

3838	70g. Type **1185**	45	45
3839	80g. Archbishop of Gnesna, and Bishops of Cracovina, Wratislavia and Colberga	45	45
MS3840	77×65 mm. 1z.55 Provincial representatives presenting gifts to Otto III as Roman Emperor (horiz)	90	80

1186 Jesus in Tomb

2000. Easter. Multicoloured.

3841		70g. Type **1186**	45	45
3842		80g. Resurrected Christ	45	45

1187 Saurolophus

2000. Prehistoric Animals. Multicoloured.

3843		70g. Type **1187**	40	45
3844		70g. Gallimimus	40	45
3845		80g. Saichania	45	50
3846		80g. Protoceratops	45	50
3847		1z.55 Prenocephale	85	1·00
3848		1z.55 Velociraptor	85	1·00

1188 Wajda

2000. Presentation of American Film Academy Award to Andrzej Wajda (film director).

3849	**1188**	1z.10 black	60	95

1189 Pope John Paul kneeling, St. Peter's Basilica, Rome

2000. Holy Year 2000 Opening of Holy Door, St. Peter's Basilica, Rome.

3850	**1189**	80g. multicoloured	45	45

1190 Artist and Model, Poster for *Wesele* (play), and Building

2000. Crakow, European City of Culture.

3851	**1190**	70g. multicoloured	40	45
3852	-	1z.55 multicoloured	95	90
MS3853		110×77 mm. 1z.75 blue (39×30 mm)	95	90

DESIGNS: No. 3852, Jagiellonian University, Pope John Paul II, Queen Jadwiga and Krzysztof Penderecki (composer). 38×30 mm—**MS**3853, View of Crakow (wood carving), 1489.

1191 Dying Rose

2000. "Stop Drug Addiction" Campaign.

3854	**1191**	70g. multicoloured	40	45

1192 "Building Europe"

2000. Europa.

3855	**1192**	1z.55 multicoloured	90	75

1193 Pope John Paul II

2000. 80th Birthday of Pope John Paul II.

3856	**1193**	80g. violet	45	45
3857	-	1z.10 multicoloured	60	60
3858	-	1z.55 green	75	90

DESIGNS: No. 3857, Holy Mother, Czestochowa; 3858, Pastoral Staff.

1194 Woman's Face and Fan

2000. "Espana 2000" International Stamp Exhibition, Madrid.

3859	**1194**	1z.55 multicoloured	90	85

1195 Family

2000. Parenthood.

3860	**1195**	70g. multicoloured	40	45

1196 Cathedral, Façade

2000. Millenary of Wroclaw. Sheet 70×90 mm.

MS3861	**1196**	1z.55 multicoloured	85	55

1197 Karol Marcinkowski

2000. Personalities. Multicoloured.

3862		70g. Type **1197** (founder of Scientific Assistance Association)	40	20
3863		80g. Josemaria Escriva de Balaguer (founder of Priests' Association of St. Cross, 1943)	50	30

1198 Gerwazy and the Count

2000. Pan Tadeusz (poem by Adam Mickiewicz). Illustrations by Michal Elwiro Andriolli from the 1882 edition.

3864	**1198**	70g. brown	30	20
3865	-	70g. brown	30	20
3866	-	80g. green	40	25
3867	-	80g. green	40	25
3868	-	1z.10 purple	55	30
3869	-	1z.10 purple	55	30

DESIGNS: No. 3865, Telimenta reclining and the Judge; 3866, Father Robak, Judge and Gerwazy; 3867, Gathering in forest; 3868, Jankiel playing musical instrument; 3869, Zosia and Tadeusz.

1199 Pope John Paul II and St. Peter's Basilica, Rome

2000. National Pilgrimage to Rome. Multicoloured.

3870		80g. Type **1199**	45	25
3871		1z.55 Cross and Colosseum	85	50

1200 "Self-portrait"

2000. Birth Bicentenary of Piotr Michalowski (artist). Multicoloured.

3872		70g. Type **1200**	35	20
3873		80g. "Portrait of a Boy in a Hat"	40	25
3874		1z.10 "Stable-boy Bridling Percherons" (horiz)	60	30
3875		1z.55 "Horses with Cart" (horiz)	80	50

1201 Mary and Jesus (painting), Rozanystok

2000. St. Mary's Sanctuaries. Multicoloured.

3876		70g. Type **1201**	25	10
3877		1z.55 Mary with crown supported by angels, Lichen	55	20

1202 John Bosco (founder of movement)

2000. Salesian Society (religious educational institution) in Poland.

3878	**1202**	80g. multicoloured	45	30

1203 Victory Sign

2000. 20th Anniv of Solidarity Trade Union. Sheet 60×78 mm.

MS3879	**1203**	1z.65 multicoloured	95	60

1204 Running

2000. Olympic Games, Sydney. Multicoloured.

3880		70g. Type **1204**	35	25
3881		80g. Diving, wind-surfing, sailing and kayaking	40	30
3882		1z.10 Weight lifting, high jumping and fencing	55	40
3883		1z.55 Athletics, basketball and judo	80	55

1205 Postman (Tomasz Wistuba)

2000. World Post Day. Winning Entries in Children's Painting Competition. Multicoloured.

3884		70g. Type **1205**	40	30
3885		80g. Customers and flying stork in Post Office (Katarzyna Chrzanowska) (horiz)	45	30
3886		1z.10 Post Office on "stamp" (Joanna Zbik) (horiz)	60	40
3887		1z.55 Woman at Post Office counter (Katarzyna Lonak) (horiz)	85	55

1206 Man with Postage Stamp Wings

2000. 50th Anniv of Polish Philatelic Union. Sheet 75×60 mm.

MS3888	**1206**	1z.55 multicoloured	90	50

2000. Polish Rulers (15th series). As T 893.

3889		70g. black, green and olive	40	30
3890		80g. black and purple	45	30
3891		1z.10 black, blue and cobalt	60	40
3892		1z.55 black and brown	85	55

DESIGNS; 70g. August II; 80g. Stanislaw Leszczynski; 1z.10, August III; 1z.55, Stanislaw August Poniatowski.

1207 Priest and Cross

2000. 60th Anniv of Katyn Massacre. Mult.

3893		70g. Type **1207**	35	20
3894		80g. Pope John Paul II kneeling at monument, Muranow	40	30

1208 Nativity

2000. Christmas. Multicoloured.

3895	70g. Type **1208**	35	30
3896	80g. Wedding at Cana	40	35
3897	1z.10 The Last Supper	55	45
3898	1z.55 The Ascension	80	85

1209 Building Facade

2000. Centenary of Warsaw Art Gallery.

3899	**1209**	70g. multicoloured	45	40

1210 Privately Issued Stamp

2000. Underground Post during Martial Law, 1982–89.

3900	**1210**	80g. multicoloured	45	35

1211 Pope John Paul II, Emblem and Crowd

2001. End of Holy Year 2000. Value expressed by letter.

3901	**1211**	A (1z.10) mult	40	15

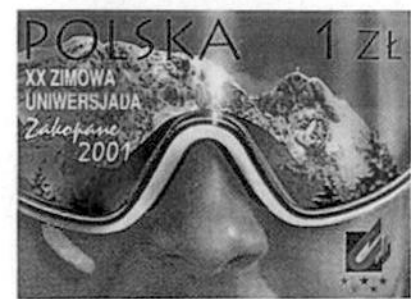

1212 Mountains reflected in Ski Goggles

2001. 20th University Games, Zakopane.

3902	**1212**	1z. multicoloured	35	10

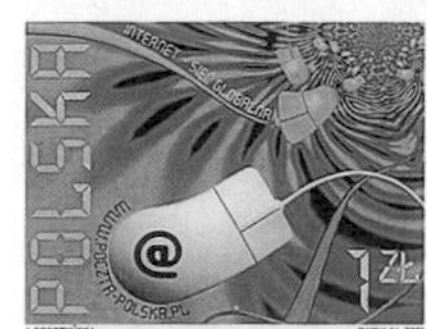

1213 Computer Mouse

2001. The Internet.

3903	**1213**	1z. multicoloured	35	10

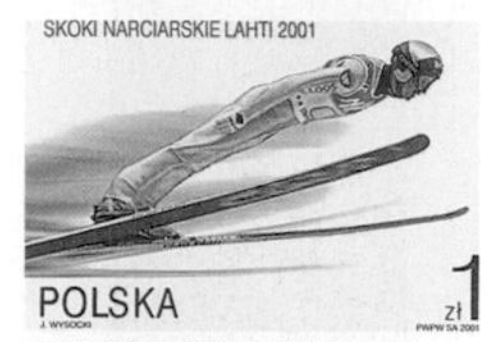

1214 Adam Malysz (ski jumper)

2001. World Classic Seniors Championships. Multicoloured.

3904	1z. Type **1214**	35	10
3905	1z. As Type **1214** but additionally inscribed "Adam Malysz"	35	10
3906	1z. As No. 3905 but additionally inscribed "Mistrzem Swiata"	35	10

1215 Tomb of the Resurrected Christ

2001. Easter. Multicoloured.

3907	1z. Type **1215**	35	10
3908	1z.90 Resurrected Christ and Apostles	35	10

1216 Emblem and Basketball Players

2001. 12th Salesian Youth World Championships, Warsaw.

3909	**1216**	1z. multicoloured	35	10

1217 Water Droplet

2001. Europa. Water Resources.

3910	**1217**	1z.90 multicoloured	65	20

1218 Man and Mermaid on Beach ("Holiday Greetings")

2001. Greetings Stamps. Multicoloured.

3911	1z. Type **1218**	35	10
3912	1z. Man presenting bouquet to woman ("Best Wishes")	35	10

1219 "Christ Blessing Children of Wrzesnia" (Marian Turwid) (stained-glass window), Parish Church, Wrzesnia

2001. Centenary of Support of Wrzesnia Schoolchildren for the Language.

3913	**1219**	1z. multicoloured	35	10

1220 Polish Scientific Institute and Wanda Stachiewicz Library,Montreal, Canada

2001. Polish Institutions Abroad. Multicoloured.

3914	1z. Type **1220**	35	10
3915	1z.90 Bust of Josef Pilsudski, Josef Pilsudski Institute, New York	65	20
3916	2z.10 Polonia Museum, Archives and Library, Orchard Lake, Michigan	75	25
3917	2z.20 Polish Museum, Chicago	75	25

1221 Snowdrop (*Galanthus nivalis*) and European Lynx (*Lynx lynx*)

2001. Convention on International Trade of Wild Animals and Plants Threatened with Extinction (C.I.T.E.S.). Multicoloured.

3918	1z. Type **1221**	35	10
3919	1z. Apollo butterfly (*Parnassius apollo*) and orchid (*Orchis sambucina*)	35	10
3920	1z. Northern eagle owl (*Bubo bubo*) and *Adonis vernalis* (plant)	35	10
3921	1z.90 Lady's slipper orchid (*Cypripedium calceolus*) and brown bear (*Ursus arctos*)	65	20
3922	1z.90 Peregrine falcon (*Falco peregrinus*) and *Orchis pallens*	65	20
3923	1z.90 Wide leaf orchid (*Orchis latifolia*) and European otter (*Lutra lutra*)	65	20
MS3924	90×70 mm. 2z. World map and emblem (35×28 mm)	1·25	80

1222 Cardinal Wyszynski and Text

2001. Birth Centenary of Cardinal Stefan Wyszynski (Primate of Poland, 1948–81).

3925	**1222**	1z. multicoloured	35	10

1223 Father Kolbe and Handwriting

2001. 60th Death Anniv of Maksymilian Maria Kolbe (founder of Knighthood of the Immaculate, and concentration camp victim).

3926	**1223**	1z. multicoloured	35	10

1224 "St. Mary of the Beautiful Love" (icon)

2001. St. Mary's Sanctuaries. Multicoloured.

3927	1z. Type **1224** (Cathedral of St. Martin and St. Nicolas, Bydgoszcz)	35	10
3928	1z. St. Mary of Ludzmierz, Basilica of the Assumption of St. Mary, Ludzmierz	35	10
3929	1z.90 St. Mary the Winner, Church of St. Mary in Piasek, Wroclaw	65	20

1225 Model of Sanctuary

2001. Completion of Section of God's Mercy Sanctuary at Cracow-Lagiewniki.

3930	**1225**	1z. multicoloured	35	10

1226 Ligia, Vinius and Petrinius

2001. *Quo Vadis* (film directed by Jerzy Kawalerowicz). Depicting scenes from the film. Multicoloured.

3931	1z. Type **1226**	35	10
3932	1z. Nero singing at feast	35	10
3933	1z. St. Peter in the catacombs and the baptism of Chilon Chilonides	35	10
3934	1z. Chilon Chilonides and crowd fleeing	35	10
3935	1z. Liga tied to the back of a bull and in the arms of Ursus	35	10
3936	1z. St. Peter blessing Vincius and Liga	35	10

1227 Copper Furnace

2001. "Euro Cuprum 2001" European Stamp Exhibition, Lubin. Multicoloured.

3937	1z. Type **1227**	35	10
3938	1z.90 Engraver at work and men dressing copper sheets	65	20
3939	2z. Inking plates and engraving press	70	20
MS3940	88×76 mm. 3z. 18th-century engraving of Lubin and burin (50×39 mm)	90	30

1228 "Battle of Chocim" (detail, Stanislaw Batowski-Kaczor) and Breast-plate of Stanislaw Skorkowski's Armour

2001. "One Century Passes it Over to Another Century" Exhibition, Polish Military Museum, Warsaw.

3941	**1228**	1z. multicoloured	35	10

1229 Steam and Electric Locomotives

2001. 75th Anniv of Polish State Railways.

3942	**1229**	1z. multicoloured	35	10

1230 Street Scene (Marcin Kuron)

2001. Winners of "Poland in 21st Century" (children's painting competition). Multicoloured.

3943	1z. Type **1230**	35	10
3944	1z.90 Rockets behind girl and boy (Agata Grzyb)	65	20
3945	2z. Futuristic car and house on wheels (Joanna Sadrakula)	70	25

1231 Football and Players

2001. Qualification of Poland for World Cup Football Championship, Japan and South Korea.

3946	**1231**	1z. multicoloured	35	10

1232 Children encircling Globe

2001. World Post Day. United Nations Year of Dialogue among Civilizations.

3947	**1232**	1z.90 multicoloured	65	20

1233 "100 Years Ago" (detail, Wlodzimierz Kugler)

2001. 80th Anniv of Post and Telecommunication Museum, Wroclaw. Sheet 87×70 mm.

MS3948	**1233**	3z.+75g. multicoloured	1·10	35

1234 Violin Peg Box and Scroll

2001. 12th Henryk Wieniawski International Violin Competition, Poznan.

3949	**1234**	1z. multicoloured	35	10

1235 Pope John Paul II

2001. Papal Day.

3950	**1235**	1z. multicoloured	35	10

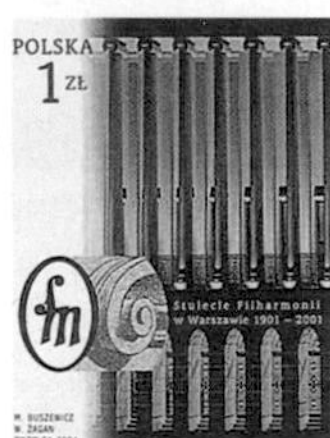

1236 Building Facade

2001. Centenary of National Philharmonic Orchestra.

3951	**1236**	1z. multicoloured	35	10

1237 Pope John Paul II

2001. New Millennium. Multicoloured.

3952	1z. Type **1237**	35	10
3953	1z. President Lech Walesa and cover of 1791 constitution	35	10
3954	1z. Covers of *Glos Wolny Wolnosc Ubespieczaiacy, Kultura, Zniewolony umysl* and *O skutecznym rad sposobie* (magazines)	35	10
3955	1z. Wojciech Boguslawski (actor and dramatist) and Jerzy Grotowski (director)	35	10
3956	1z. General Jozef Pilsudski (soldier and President 1918–22) and posters (1989)	35	10
3957	1z. N.A.T.O. emblem and General Kazimierz Pulaski (soldier)	35	10
3958	1z. Nicolaus Copernicus and Aleksander Wolszczan (astronomers)	35	10
3959	1z. Jan of Glogow (wood engraving) (mathematician and astronomer) and Tadeusz Kotarbinski (physicist)	35	10
3960	1z. "Do Broni" (poster, 1920) and "Bitwa pod Grunwaldem" (detail) (painting, Jan Matejko)	35	10
3961	1z. Leaders of November Uprising, 1830	35	10
3962	1z. Head of John the Apostle (detail) (wooden altarpiece, Wit Stwosz) and sculpture by Magdalena Abakanowicz	35	10
3963	1z. Frederik Chopin, Krzysztof Penderecki (composers) and score of *Mazurka No. 10* by Karol Szymanowski	35	10
3964	1z. Royal Castle, Warsaw and view of Cracow (wood engraving)	35	10
3965	1z. Jan III Sobieski (painting) and emblem of European Union	35	10
3966	1z. Wislawa Szymborska (Nobel Prizewinner for Literature) and Mikolaj Rej (poet)	35	10
3967	1z. Janusz Kusocinski and Robert Korzeniowski (athletes)	35	10

1238 Lower Silesian Crib

2001. Christmas. Multicoloured.

3968	1z. Type **1238**	35	10
3969	1z.90 Lower Silesian Crib (different)	35	10

1239 Radio Station Building and Virgin Mary (statue)

2001. 10th Anniv of "Radio Maryia" (religious broadcasting station). Multicoloured.

3970	1z. Type **MS**1239	30	10
MS3971	176×78 mm. 1z. Virgin Mary (statue) and crowd; 1z. Type **1239**; 1z. Crowd and crowned Virgin Mary (statue)	90	30

1240 Pear and Apple

2002. Valentine's Day.

3972	**1240**	1z.10 multicoloured	25	10

1241 Downhill, Biathlon, Ice-skating, and Ski Jumping

2002. Winter Olympic Games, Salt Lake City, U.S.A.

3973	**1241**	1z.10 multicoloured	25	10

1242 Jan Czerski

2002. Explorers. Multicoloured.

3974	2z. Type **1242**	50	15
3975	2z. Bronislaw Pilsudski	50	15

1243 Gniezno

2002. Polish Cities.

3975a	-	5g. multicoloured	10	10
3975b	-	20g. multicoloured	10	10
3975c	-	30g. multicoloured	10	10
3975d	-	1z.20 multicoloured	25	10
3975e	-	1z.25 multicoloured	25	10
3975ea	-	1z.30 multicoloured	25	10
3975eb	-	1z.35 multicoloured	1·50	55
3975ec	-	1z.35 multicoloured	60	10
3975h	-	1z.80 multicoloured	40	10
3975i	-	1z.90 multicoloured	50	15
3976	**1243**	2z. multicoloured	50	15
3977	-	2z.10 multicoloured	50	15
3977a	-	2z.20 multicoloured	80	25
3977b	-	2z.40 multicoloured	55	20
3977c	-	2z.60 multicoloured	60	20
3977d	-	2z.80 multicoloured	1·00	35
3978	-	3z.20 multicoloured	75	25
3978a	-	3z.40 multicoloured	80	30
3978b	-	3z.45 multicoloured	80	30
3978ba	-	3z.50 green and deep green	1·20	40
3978bc	-	3z.55 multicoloured	3·75	1·40
3978bd	-	3z.65 multicoloured	3·75	1·40

DESIGNS: No. 3975a, Sandomierz (horiz); 3975b, Sieradz; 3975c, Katowice (horiz); 3975d, Torun; 3975e, Gdansk; 3975ea, Poznan (horiz); 3975eb, Gorzow Wielkopolski; 3975ec, Raciborz; 3975h, Kalisz (horiz); 3975i, Lodz (horiz); 3977, Krakow; 3977a, Sopot (horiz); 3977b, Czestochowa (horiz); 3977c, Pfock (horiz); 3977d, Szczecin (horiz); 3978, Warsaw; 3978a, Kazimierz Dolny; 3978b, Lublin (horiz); 3978ba, (Przemysl); 3978bc, Chorow; 3978bd, Jeleria Gora.

1244 Flowers

2002. Easter. Multicoloured.

3979	1z.10 Type **1244**	25	10
3980	2z. Chicks	50	15

1245 Labrador Retriever and Puppies

2002. Domestic and Wild Animals. Multicoloured.

3981	1z.10 Type **1245**	25	10
3982	1z.10 Cat and kittens	25	10
3983	1z.10 Wolf and cubs	25	10
3984	1z.10 Lynx and kittens	25	10

1246 Soldiers marching

2002. 60th Anniv of Evacuation of General Wladislaw Ander's Army from U.S.S.R.

3985	**1246**	1z.10 multicoloured	25	10

1247 Trees (Amanda Zejmis)

2002. Paintings. Multicoloured.

3986	1z.10 Type **1257**	25	10
3987	1z.10 Vase and ornaments (Henryk Paraszczuk)	25	10
3988	2z. Landscape (Lucjan Matula) (horiz)	50	15
3989	3z.20 Basket of flowers (Jozefa Laciak) (horiz)	75	25

1248 Stylized Figures

2002. National Census.

3990	**1248**	1z.10 multicoloured	25	10

1249 Radio Microphone

2002. 50th Anniv of "Radio Free Europe".

3991	**1249**	2z. multicoloured	50	15

1250 Fireman

2002. 10th Anniv of State Fire Brigade.

3992	**1250**	1z.10 multicoloured	25	10

1251 Circus Artist

2002. Europa. Circus.

3993	**1251**	2z. multicoloured	50	15

1252 "Madonna with the Child, St. John the Baptist and the Angel" (Sandro Botticelli)

2002. 140th Anniv of the National Gallery, Warsaw.

3994	**1252**	1z.10 multicoloured	25	10

1253 Maria Konopnicka

2002. 160th Birth Anniv of Maria Konopnicka (poet and writer).

3995	**1253**	1z.10 brown, ochre and green	25	10

1254 Scooter

2002. Children's Games. Multicoloured.

3996	1z.10 Type **1254**	25	10
3997	1z.10 Flying kite	25	10
3998	1z.10 Badminton	25	10

1255 Football and Globe

2002. World Cup Football Championship, Japan and South Korea. Multicoloured.

3999	1z.10 Type **1255**	25	10
4000	2z. Player chasing ball	50	15

1256 Domeyko and Santiago University, Chile

2002. Birth Bicentenary of Ignacego Domeyki (scientist).

4015	**1256**	2z.60 multicoloured	60	20

1257 Hibiscus and Tulips

2002. "Philakorea 2002" International Philatelic Exhibition, Seoul and "Amphilex 2002" International Philatelic Exhibition, Amsterdam.

4016	**1257**	2z. multicoloured	50	15

1258 Pope John Paul II and Basilica of Virgin Mary of the Angel, Kalwaria Zebrzydowska

2002. 7th Papal Visit To Poland (1st issue). Multicoloured.

4017	1z.10 Type **1258**	25	10
4018	1z.80 Pope John Paul II and Sanctuary of God's Mercy, Sisters of Virgin Mary's Convent, Lagiewniki	40	10

See also No. **MS**4022.

1259 "Holy Lady of Assistance"

2002. St. Mary's Sanctuaries. Multicoloured.

4019	1z.10 Type **1259** (Church of the Holy Lady of Assistance, Jaworzno)	25	10
4020	1z.10 "Holy Virgin of Opole" (Cathedral of Holy Cross, Opole)	25	10
4021	2z. "Holy Virgin of Trabki" (Church of the Assumption of the Holy Lady, Trabki Wielkie)	50	15

1260 Pope John Paul II and Wawel Castle, Cracow

2002. 7th Papal Visit To Poland (2nd issue). Sheet 73×57 mm.

MS4022	**1260** 3z.20 black	75	75

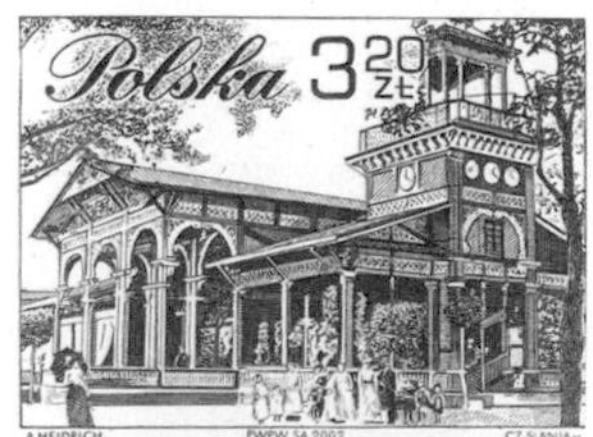
1261 Spa Building, Ciechocinku

2002. 18th Polish Philatelic Association Convention, Ciechocinku. Sheet 74×105 mm.

MS4023	**1261** 3z.20 brown	75	75

1262 Czesnik Raptusiewicz and Dyndalski

2002. "Zemsta" (Revenge) (film directed by Andrzej Wajda). Sheet 177×137 mm containing T 1262, Showing scenes from the film. Multicoloured.

MS4024	1z.10 Type **1262**; 1z.10 Klara and Waclaw; 1z.10 Papkin; 1z.10 Regent Milczek and Papkin; 1z.10 Regent Milczek and Czesnik Raptusiewicz; 1z.10 Podstolina and Klara	1·60	1·60

1263 Schwarzkopf Okl-359

2002. Steam Locomotives, Showing locomotives from Wolsztyn Railway Museum. Multicoloured.

4025	1z.10 Type **1263**	25	10
4026	1z.10 Fablok 0149-7	25	10
4027	2z. Krolewiec Tki3-87	50	15
4028	2z. Express locomotive Pm 36-2	50	15

1264 Hands holding Pens

2002. World Post Day.

4029	**1264**	2z. multicoloured	50	15

1265 Emblem

2002. Anti-Cancer Campaign.

4030	**1265**	1z.10 multicoloured	25	10

1266 Emblem

2002. 50th Anniv of Polish Television. Sheet 185×115 mm containing T 1266 Showing emblems of television programmes. Multicoloured.

MS4031	1z.10 Type **1266** (TV News); 1z.10 TV Theatre; 1z.10 "Pegaz" (cultural programme); 1z.10 "Teleranek" (children's programme)	1·00	1·00

1267 St. Stanislaw

2002. Saints. Sheet 136×165 mm containing T 1267 and similar vert designs. Multicoloured.

MS4032	1z.10 Type **1267**; 1z.10 St. Kazimierz; 1z.10 St. Faustyna Kowalska; 1z.10 St. Benedict; 1z.10 St. Cyril and St. Methody; 1z.10 St. Catherine of Siena	1·60	1·60

1268 Christmas Tree Baubles

2002. Christmas. Multicoloured.

4033	1z.10 Type **1268**	25	10
4034	2z. Small purple and large yellow baubles	50	15

1269 "POLSKA" superimposed on "EUROPA"

2003. Poland's Accession to European Union (1st issue). Negotiations.

4035	**1269**	1z.20 multicoloured	35	10

See also No. 4067, 4069 and 4120.

1270 Pope John Paul II

2003. 25th Anniv of the Pontificate of Pope John Paul II (1st issue). Multicoloured.

4036	1z.20 Type **1270**	35	10
4037	1z.20 Celebrating mass, Victory Square, Warsaw, 1979	35	10
4038	1z.20 Addressing young people, Parc des Princes Stadium, Paris, 1980	35	10
4039	1z.20 Assassination attempt, St. Peter Square, 1981	35	10
4040	1z.20 Giving homily surrounded by flowers, Portugal, 1982	35	10
4041	1z.20 Kneeling in front of Holy Doors, start of Holy Year of Redemption, 1983	35	10
4042	1z.20 Meeting Sandro Pertini, Pres. of Italy, 1984	35	10
4043	1z.20 International Youth Day, Rome, 1985	35	10
4044	1z.20 First visit of Pope to Synagogue, 1986	35	10
4045	1z.20 Inaugurating Year of Mary, 1987	35	10
4046	1z.20 Visiting European Parliament, Strasbourg, 1988	35	10
4047	1z.20 Meeting Mikhail Gorbachev, Pres. Soviet Union, 1989	35	10
4048	1z.20 Visiting lepers in Guinea-Bissau, 1990	35	10
4049	1z20 Addressing Bishop's Synod, 1991	35	10
4050	1z.20 Pronouncing the Catechism, 1992	35	10
4051	1z.20 Enthroned, Assissi, 1993	35	10
4052	1z.20 Celebrating Mass in the Sistine Chapel, 1994	35	10
4053	1z.20 Addressing the United Nations, 1995	35	10
4054	1z.20 Walking through the Brandenburg Gate with Chancellor Helmut Kohl, 1996	35	10
4055	1z.20 Celebrating Mass in Sarajevo, 1997	35	10
4056	1z.20 With Fidel Castro, Cuba, 1998	35	10
4057	1z.20 Opening door, Christmas, 1999	35	10
4058	1z.20 With young people, World Youth Day, Rome, 2000	35	10
4059	1z.20 Closing door of St. Peter's Basilica, 2001	35	10
4060	1z.20 Visiting the Italian Parliament, 2002	35	10

1271 Pope John Paul II on Balcony of St. Peter's Basilica, 1978

2003. 25th Anniv of the Pontificate of Pope John Paul II (2nd issue).

4061	**1271**	10z. silver	3·00	90

1272 Andrzej Modrzewski

2003. 500th Birth Anniv of Andrzej Frycz Modrzewski (writer).

4062	**1272**	1z.20 black	35	10

1273 "Christ Anxious"

2003. Easter. Folk Sculpture. Multicoloured.

4063	1z.20 Type **1273**	35	10
4064	2z.10 "Christ Vanquisher"	60	15

1274 Poznan Ancient and Modern

2003. 750th Anniv of Poznan.

4065	**1274** 1z.20 multicoloured	35	10
MS4066	95×72 mm 3z.40 cinnamon and black (40×31 mm)	1·00	1·00

DESIGN: 3z.40 Ancient view of city and city arms.

1275 Portico and Clouds

2003. Poland's Accession to European Union (2nd issue).

4067	**1275** 1z.20 multicoloured	35	10

1276 Poster for "Vanitas" Exhibition (Wieslaw Walkuski)

2003. Europa. Poster Art.

4068	**1276** 2z.10 multicoloured	60	15

1277 "POLSKA" superimposed on "EUROPA"

2003. Poland's Accession to European Union (3rd issue). Referendum.

4069	**1277** 1z.20 multicoloured	35	10

1278 Island Palace (south view)

2003. Royal Baths, Lazienki Park, Warsaw. Multicoloured.

4070	1z.20 Type **1278**	35	10
4071	1z.80 Island Palace (north view)	55	15
4072	2z.10 Myslewicki Palace	60	15
4073	2z.60 Amphitheatre	75	20

1279 Pyramids and Camel (Anna Golebiewska)

2003. Children's Paintings. Stamp Design Competition Winners. Designs on theme "My Dream Vacation". Multicoloured.

4074	1z.20 Type **1279**	35	10
4075	1z.80 Girl windsurfing (Marlena Krejpcio) (vert)	55	15
4076	2z.10 Wind-surfer and fish (Michal Korzen)	60	15
4077	2z.60 Girl and hens (Ewa Zadjdler)	75	20

1280 "Krak" (anonymous)

2003. Fairy Tales. Multicoloured.

4078	1z.20 Type **1280**	35	10
4079	1z.80 "Stupid Mateo" (Josef Kraszewski)	55	15
4080	2z.10 "Frog Princess" (Antoni Glinski)	60	15
4081	2z.60 "Crock of Gold" (Josef Kraszewski)	75	20

1281 Katowice Cathedral

2003. Katowice 2003 National Stamp Exhibition. Sheet 94×71 mm.

MS4082	**1281** 3z.40 black, brown and ochre	1·00	1·00

No. **MS**4082 also exists imperforate.

1282 "Self Portrait"

2003. Birth Centenary of Julian Falat (artist). Multicoloured.

4083	1z.20 Type **1282**	40	10
4084	1z.80 "Spear Men"	60	20
4085	2z.10 "Winter Landscape with River and Bird" (horiz)	70	20
4086	2z.60 "Aboard Ship-Merchants of Ceylon" (horiz)	85	25

1283 Post Horn

2003. World Post Day.

4087	**1283** 2z.20 multicoloured	75	25

1284 "Holy Virgin of Czestochowa"

2003. St. Mary's Sanctuaries. Multicoloured.

4088	1z.20 Type **1284** (Church of the Holy Redeemer, Warsaw)	40	10
4089	1z.80 "Holy Mother Benevolent" (Basilica of Assumption of Holy Virgin, Krzeszowice)	60	20
4090	2z.10 "Holy Virgin" (Church of the Holy Virgin, Zieleniec)	70	20

1285 Motor Cycle (1903)

2003. Centenary of Motor Cycle Racing in Poland. Multicoloured.

4091	1z.20 Type **1285**	40	20
4092	1z.20 Rudge (c. 1930)	40	10
4093	1z.20 NSU (c. 1940)	40	10

1286 Dancers wearing Traditional Costume

2003. 50th Anniv of Folk Dance Troup "Slask". Multicoloured.

4094	1z.20 Type **1286**	40	10
4095	1z.20 Dancers (different)	40	10

Nos. 4094/5 were issued together, se-tenant, forming a composite design.

1287 Perching Adult holding Fish

2003. Endangered Species. Osprey (Pandion haliaetus). Multicoloured.

4096	1z.20 Type **1287**	40	10
4097	1z.20 Adult and chicks on nest	40	10
4098	1z.20 Adult catching fish (one wing visible)	40	10
4099	1z.20 Adult carrying fish (both wings visible)	40	10

Nos. 4096/9 were issued together, se-tenant, forming a composite design.

1288 Two White Storks

2003. www.poland.gov.pl (Poland on the internet).

4100	**1288** 2z.10 multicoloured	70	20

1289 The Nativity

2003. Christmas. Multicoloured.

4101	1z.20 Type **1289**	40	10
4102	1z.80 Three Kings	60	20
4103	2z.10 Angel appearing to Mary (vert)	70	20
4104	2z.60 Holy Family (vert)	85	25

1290 Wislawa Szymborska

2003. Polish Influence Abroad (1st series). Showing designs from other countries' stamps.

4105	**1290** 1z.20 purple, green and black	40	10
4106	- 1z.80 ultramarine, blue and black (horiz)	60	20
4107	- 2z.10 purple, azure and black	70	20
4108	- 2z.60 slate and black (horiz)	85	25

DESIGNS: 1z.20, Wislawa Szymborska (writer) (as Sweden No. 2120); 1z.80, Marie Sklodowska-Curie (physicist) (as France No. 1765); 2z.10, Czeslaw Milosz (writer) (as Sweden No. 1299); 2z.60, "Holy Virgin of Czestochowa" (as Vatican City No. 481).

See also Nos. 4112/13.

1291 Heart

2004. Orchestra of Holy Day Assistance (fund raising charity).

4109	**1291** 1z.25 multicoloured	40	10

1292 Airliner

2004. 75th Anniv of LOT (Polish airlines).

4110	**1292** 1z.25 multicoloured	40	10

1293 Boy and Girl with Heart-shaped Balloon

2003. St. Valentine.

4111	**1293** 1z.25 multicoloured	40	10

1294 Helena Paderewska

2004. Polish Influence Abroad (2nd series). Multicoloured.

4112	2z.10 Type **1294** co-founder of USA Polish White Cross (humanitarian organization)	70	20
4113	2z.10 Lucjan Bojnowski (New Britain, USA church pioneer)	70	20

1295 Chocolate Rabbit

2004. Easter. Multicoloured.

4114	1z.25 Type **1295**	40	10
4115	2z.10 Ceramic lamb	70	20

1296 Beaver and Frog

2004. Fauna. Multicoloured.

4116	1z.25 Type **1296**	40	10
4117	1z.25 Kingfisher, crayfish, roach and water beetle	40	10
4118	1z.25 Grayling, leech and water snail	40	10
4119	1z.25 Pike, grebe and roach	40	10

Nos. 4116/19 were issued together, se-tenant, forming a composite design.

1297 Map of Europe and New Members' Flags

2004. Poland's Accession to European Union (4th issue).

4120	**1297**	2z.10 multicoloured	70	20

1298 Rucksack as Landscape

2004. Europa. Holidays.

4121	**1298**	2z.10 multicoloured	70	20

1299 Figure (sculpture, St. Mariacki Square, Krakow)

2004. 10th Government Postage Stamp Printers' Conference, Krakow.

4122	**1299**	3z.45 multicoloured	1·10	35

1300 Pope John Paul II

2004. Pope John Paul II visits to Poland, 1970–2002. Two sheets, each 115×185 mm containing T 1300 and similar vert designs. Multicoloured.

MS4123 (a) 1z.25 ×4, Type **1300** (1979); At prayer (1983); Holding reliquary (1987); Resting head against staff (1991). (b) 1z.25 ×4, Holding staff (1991); With raised hand (1997); Seated facing right (1999); Seated facing left (2002). Set of 2 sheets 3·50 3·50

1301 Crimson Rosella (*Platycercus elegans*)

2004. Birds. Multicoloured.

4124	1z.25 Type **1301**	40	10
4125	1z.25 Cockatiel (*Nymphicus hollandicus*)	40	10
4126	1z.25 Budgerigar (*Melopsittacus undulates*)	40	10
4127	1z.25 Spotted-side finch (*Poephila guttata*), Gouldian finch (*Chloebia gouldiae*) and Java sparrow (*Padda oryzivora*)	40	10

1302 "Self-portrait wearing White"

2004. 150th Birth Anniv of Jacek Malczewski (artist). Multicoloured.

4128	1z.25 Type **1302**	40	10
4129	1z.90 "Ellenai"	65	20
4130	2z.10 "Tobias with Harpy" (horiz)	70	20
4131	2z.60 "The Unknown Note" (horiz)	85	25

1303 Sun Wu-Kung (monkey king)

2004. Singapore International Stamp Exhibition. Sheet 90×70 mm.

MS4132 3z.45 multicoloured 1·10 1·10

1304 Boxer

2004. Olympic Games, Athens. Sheet 198×117 mm containing T 1304 and similar horiz designs. Multicoloured.

MS4133 1z.25 ×4, Type **1304**; Hurdler; Show jumper; Wrestler 1·60 1·60

The stamps and margin of **MS**4133 form a composite design.

1305 Witold Gombrowicz

2004. Birth Centenary of Witold Gombrowicz (writer).

4134	**1305**	1z.25 ultramarine	40	10

1306 "Holy Mother of Miedzna"

2004. St. Mary's Sanctuaries. Multlcoloured.

4135	1z.25 Type **1306** (Church of the Annunciation of Our Lady of Miedzna)	40	10
4136	1z.25 "Holy Mary and Family" (John the Baptist Basilica, Studiazianna)	40	10
4137	1z.25 "Holy Virgin of Sianow" (Church of the Nativity of Our Lady of Sianow)	40	10
4138	1z.25 "Holy Mary of Rywald" (St. Sebastian and Nativity of Our Lady, Rywald)	40	10
4139	1z.25 "Holy Mary of Piekary" (Name of Our Lady and St. Bartholome Basilica,Piekary Slaskie)	40	10
4140	1z.25 "Holy Mary of Ruda" (Assumption of Our Lady Church, Ruda)	40	10
4141	1z.25 "Holy Mary of Lomza" (Archangel St. Michael Cathedral, Lomza)	40	10
4142	1z.25 "Holy Mary of Perpetual Assistance" (Barefoot Carmelite Convent,Niedzwiady)	40	10
4143	1z.25 "Holy Mary of Rychwald" (St. Nicholas and Our Lady of Scapular, Rychwald)	40	10
4144	1z.25 "Crying Holy Mary" (St. John the Baptist and Evangelist, Lublin)	40	10
4145	1z.25 "Holy Mary of Dzikow" (Assumption of Our Lady Convent, Tarnobrzeg)	40	10
4146	1z.25 "Holy Mary of Rzeszow" (Assumption of Our Lady Church, Rzeszow)	40	10
4147	1z.25 "Gracious Holy Mary" (St. Stanislaw, St. Peter and St. Paul, Lubaczow)	40	10
4148	1z.25 "Holy Mother of Fatima" (Immaculate Heart of Our Lady of Fatima,Szczecin)	40	10
4149	1z.25 "Pieta of Skrzatusz" (Assumption of Our lady Church, Skrzatusz)	40	10
4150	1z.25 "Pieta of Obory" (Visitation of Our Lady Church, Obory)	40	10
4151	1z.25 "Holy Mary of Jasnagora" (Queen of Poland Sanctuary, Jasnagora)	40	10

1307 Czeslaw Niemen

2004. Czeslaw Wydrzycki (Niemen) (musician) Commemoration.

4152	**1307**	1z.25 black	40	10

1308 Raft on River Dunajec

2004. Raft Men working on River Dunajec (bordering Slovakia and Poland).

4153	**1308**	2z.10 multicoloured	70	20

A stamp of the same design was issued by Slovakia.

1309 Motor Cyclists

2004. Motor Sports. Multicoloured.

4154	1z.25 Type **1309**	40	10
4155	1z.25 Race car	40	10
4156	1z.25 Kart racing	40	10
4157	1z.25 Motor cyclist (2004 International Six Day's Enduro)	40	10

Nos. 4154/7 were issued together, se-tenant, forming a composite design.

1310 Binary Codes forming Postman

2004. World Post Day.

4158	**1310**	2z.10 multicoloured	70	20

1311 Holy Mary Church, Krakow

2004. World Heritage Sites. Multicoloured.

4159	1z.25 Type **1311**	40	10
4160	1z.25 Tower, St. John the Baptist and Evangelist Cathedral, Torun	40	10
4161	1z.25 Town Hall, Zamosc	40	10
4162	1z.25 Riverside, Warsaw (horiz)	40	10
4163	1z.25 Castle, Malbork (horiz)	40	10

1312 People entering Church

2004. Christmas. Multicoloured.

4164	1z.25 Type **1312**	40	10
4165	1z.25 Decorated window (horiz)	40	10

1313 Protoplanet circling Sun

2004. History of Earth. Multicoloured.

4166	1z.25 Type **1313**	40	10
4167	1z.25 Asteroids bombarding earth	40	10
4168	1z.25 Dinosaurs	40	10
4169	1z.25 International space station in orbit	40	10

1314 "13"

2005. Orchestra of Holy Day Assistance (fund raising charity).

4170	**1314**	1z.30 multicoloured	45	15

1315 Konstanty Galczynski

2005. Birth Centenary of Konstanty Ildefons Galczynski (writer).

4171	**1315**	1z.30 multicoloured	45	15

1316 Mikolaj Rej

2005. 500th Birth Anniv of Mikolaj Rej (writer).

4172	**1316**	1z.30 black and vermilion	45	15

1317 Masked Swordsman and Carved Heart on Tree

2005. Greetings Stamp.

4173	**1317**	1z.30 multicoloured	45	15

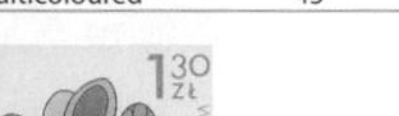

1318 Rabbit

2005. Easter. Multicoloured.

4174	1z.30 Type **1318**	45	15
4175	2z.30 Chick	80	25

1319 "The Little Mermaid"

2005. Birth Bicentenary of Hans Christian Andersen (writer). Multicoloured.

4176	1z.30 Type **1319**	45	15
4177	1z.30 "The Snow Queen"	45	15

1320 Pope John Paul II

2005. Pope John Paul II Commemoration (1st issue).

4178	**1320**	1z.30 multicoloured	45	15

See also No. **MS**4184.

1321 Sky Diving

2005. Extreme Sports. Multicoloured.

4179	1z.30 Type **1321**	45	15
4180	1z.30 Bungee jumping	45	15
4181	1z.30 Rock climbing	45	15
4182	1z.30 White water rafting	45	15

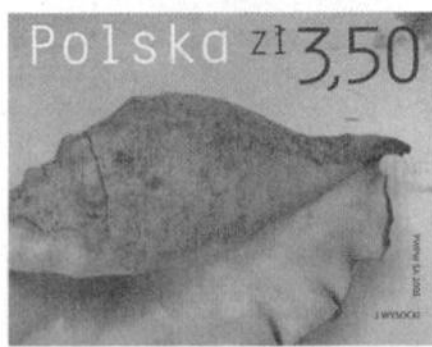
1322 Shell

2005. Pacific Explorer International Stamp Exhibition, Sydney. Sheet 90×70 mm. Perf or imperf.

MS4183 **1322** 3z.50 multicoloured 1·20 1·20

1323 Pope John Paul II

2005. Pope John Paul II Commemoration (2nd issue). Sheet 70×83 mm.

MS4184 **1323** 1z.30 multicoloured 45 15

1324 Bread

2005. Europa. Gastronomy.

4185	**1324**	2z.20 multicoloured	80	25

1325 Rubble

2005. 60th Anniv of End of World War II.

4186	**1325**	1z.30 black and vermilion	45	15

1326 "The Hour of the Crimson Rose" (M. Kruger)

2005. Stories. Sheet 124×124 mm containing T 1326 and similar square designs. Multicoloured.

MS4187 1z.30 Type **1326**; 2z. "The Little Prince" (Antoine de Saint-Exupery); 2z.20 "2000 Leagues under the Sea" (Jules Verne); 2z.80 "In the Desert and the Forest" (H. Sienkiewicz) 3·00 3·00

1327 "Stanislaw Kostka Potocki" (Jacques-Louis David)

2005. Bicentenary of National Museum, Wilanow. Sheet 95×130 mm containing T 1327 and similar vert designs. Multicoloured.

MS4188 1z.30 Type **1327**; 2z.17th-century Nautilus wine cup; 2z.20 Flower girl (18th-century porcelain); 2z.80 19th-century clock 3·00 3·00

1328 Embroidered Rose (Podhale)

2005. Embroidery. Designs showing embroidered roses. Multicoloured.

4189	1z.30 Type **1328**	45	15
4190	2z. Rose (Lowicz)	70	20
4191	2z.20 Rose (Podhale) (different)	80	25
4192	2z.80 Rose (Lowicz) (different)	1·00	35

1329 Hurdling

2005. International Athletics Championship, Helsinki. Sheet 200×115 mm containing T 1329 and similar horiz designs. Multicoloured.

MS4193 1z.30 Type **1329**; 1z.30 Shot put; 2z. Triple jump; 2z. Pole vault 2·30 2·30

1330 Jozef Pilsudski (Commander in Chief)

2005. 85th Anniv of Battle of Warsaw ("Miracle on the Vistula"). Sheet 70×90 mm.

MS4194 **1330** 3z.50 multicoloured 1·20 40

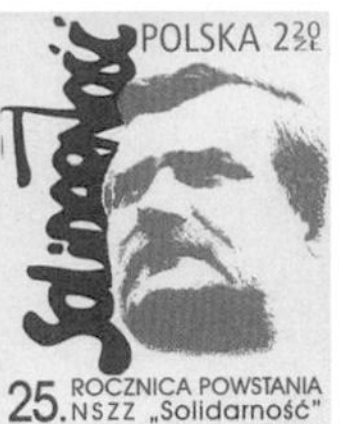
1331 Lech Walesa (founder)

2005. 25th Anniv of Solidarity (trade union).

4195	**1331**	2z.20 vermilion, grey and black	80	25

1332 "80"

2005. 80th Anniv of Radio.

4196	**1332**	1z.30 rosine and black	45	15

1333 Music Score and Frederick Chopin

2005. Frederick Chopin International Piano Competition.

4197	**1333**	2z.20 green, vermilion and black	80	25

1334 Lemur (Opole)

2005. Zoological Gardens. Each black.

4198	1z.30 Type **1334**	45	15
4199	2z. Siberian tiger (*Panthera tigris altaica*) (Wroclaw)	70	20
4200	2z.20 White rhinoceros (*Ceratotherium simum*) (Poznan)	80	25
4201	2z.80 Anteater (Warsaw)	1·00	35

1335 Post Office Building, Cracow

2005. Post Day. Architecture.

4202	**1335**	1z.30 multicoloured	45	15

1336 Gingerbread Men

2005. 60th Anniv of United Nations.

4203	**1336**	2z.20 multicoloured	80	25

1337 St. Maciej's Church and St. Stefan's Statue, Budapest

2005. European Capitals. Multicoloured.

4204	1z.30 Type **1337**	45	15
4205	1z.30 Vilnius Cathedral	45	15
4206	2z.20 Arc de Triomphe, Paris	80	25
4207	2z.20 Monument to the Discoverers Belem, Lisbon	80	25
4208	2z.80 Government building, Dublin	1·00	40

1338 "Ploughing in the Ukraine" (L. J. Wyczolkowski)

2005. Art. Polish Impressionists. Sheet 94×130 mm containing T 1338 and similar horiz designs. Multicoloured.

MS4209 1z.30×2, Type **1338**; "Still Life" (J. Panekiewicz); 2z.×2, "Flower Sellers" (O. Boznanska); "The Garden" (W. Podkowinski) 2·30 2·30

1339 Stethoscope in Pocket

2005. Bicentenary of Doctors' Association.

4210	**1339**	1z.30 multicoloured	45	15

1340 Trees and Angel

2005. Christmas. Multicoloured.

4211	1z.30 Type **1340**	45	15
4212	2z.20 Angel facing right	80	25

1346 *Pedicularis sudetica*

2006. Endangered Species. Flowers. Multicoloured.
4218 1z.30 Type **1346** 1·40 85
4219 2z.40 *Trapa antans* 2·60 85

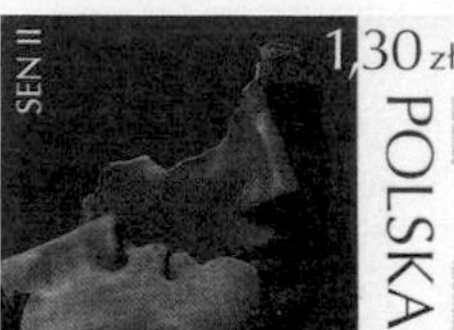

1347 "Dream II"

2006. Contemporary Sculpture. Igor Mitoraj. Multicoloured.
4220 1z.30 Type **1347** 2·25 80
4221 1z.30 "Lips of Eros" 2·25 80

1348 Floral Procession, Palm Sunday

2006. Easter. Multicoloured.
4222 1z.30 Type **1348** 1·40 45
4223 2z.40 Smigus-dynus (dousing with water), Easter Monday 2·60 85

1349 Tree, Man and Stars

2006. Europa. Integration.
4224 **1349** 2z.40 multicoloured 1·40 45

1350 "2006 WASHINGTON"

2006. Washington 2006 International Stamp Exhibition. Sheet 115×77 mm.
MS4225 **1350** 2z.40 blue and vermilion 2·75 2·75

1351 Pope Benedict XVI

2006. Visit of Pope Benedict XVI.
4226 **1351** 1z.30 multicoloured 1·50 50

1352 Stilo

2006. Lighthouses. Multicoloured.
4227 2z.40 Type **1352** 2·75 90
4228 2z.40 Krynica Morska 2·75 90
4229 2z.40 Gaski 2·75 90
4230 2z.40 Niechorze 2·75 90

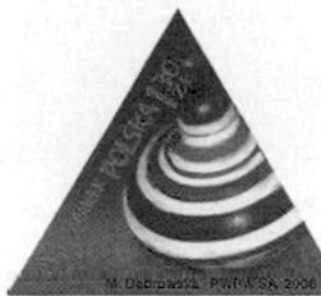
1353 Spinning Top

2006. Toys. Multicoloured.
4231 1z.30 Type **1353** 1·50 50
4232 1z.30 Windmill 1·50 50

1354 Baroque Tankard

2006. Gold and Silver Ware. Multicoloured.
4233 1z.30 Type **1354** 1·50 50
4234 1z.30 Empire Lasting Forever Gold Cup 1·50 50
Stamps of the same design were issued by China.

1355 Workers Procession, Poznan

2006. 50th Anniv of Workers' Revolt, Poznan (MS4235a) and 30th Anniv of Workers' Revolt, Radom (MS4235b). Two sheets, each 90×70 mm containing T 1355 and similar horiz design.
MS4235 (a) 3z.50 blue and black. (28.6)
(b) 3z.50 grey and slate 4·00 4·00
DESIGNS: (a) Type **1355**. (b) Workers on lorry, Radom.

1356 Jerzy Giedroyc

2006. Birth Centenary of Jerzy Giedroyc (journalist).
4236 **1356** 1z.30 black 1·50 50

1357 Edward Szczeklik

2006. Centenary of Internal Medicine Society. Multicoloured.
4237 1z.30 Type **1357** 2·10 70
4238 1z.30 Witold Eugeniusz Orlowskil 2·10 70
4239 1z.30 Antoni Wladyslaw Gluzinski 2·10 70

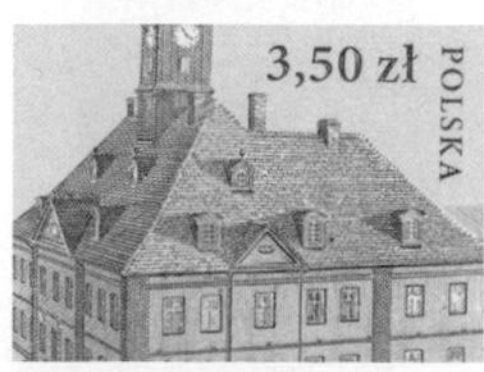

1358 Lubin Town Hall

2006. 19th Convention of Polish Philatelic Association. Sheet 90×70 mm.
MS4240 **1358** 3z.50 multicoloured 4·00 4·00

1363 The Nativity

2006. Christmas. Multicoloured.
4253 1z.30 Type **1363** 1·40 45
4254 2z.40 "Christmas" 2·60 85

1364 Coal bleeding

2006. 25th Anniv of End of Miners' Strike for Solidarity.
4255 **1364** 1z.30 multicoloured 1·40 45

1365 Heart as Planet

2007. Orchestra of Holy Day Assistance (fund raising charity).
4256 **1365** 1z.35 multicoloured 1·40 45

1366 Ice Dancers

2007. European Figure Skating Championships, Warsaw.
4257 **1366** 2z.40 multicoloured 2·50 85

1367 Hearts as Butterflies

2007. St. Valentine's Day.
4258 **1367** 1z.35 multicoloured 1·40 45

1368 Straw Lamb

2007. Easter. Multicoloured.
4259 1z.35 Type **1368** 1·40 45
4260 2z.40 Easter egg chicken 2·60 85

1369 Flags

2007. 50th Anniv of Treaty of Europe.
4261 **1369** 3z.55 multicoloured 3·75 1·40

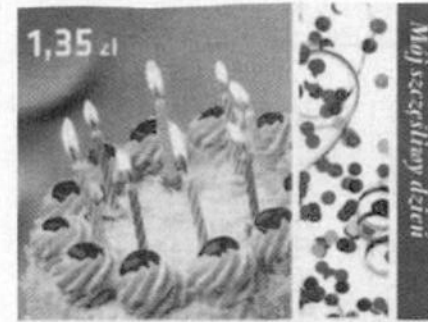

1370 Cake

2007. Greetings Stamps. Multicoloured.
4262 1z.35 Type **1370** 1·40 45
4263 1z.35 Grapes, wine and bread 1·40 45
4264 1z.35 Wedding rings 1·40 45

1371 Recycle Emblem

2007. Earth Day.
4265 **1371** 1z.35 multicoloured 1·40 45

1372 Postal Wagon Type 5G c.1956

2007. Railways. Multicoloured.
4266 1z.35 Type **1372** 1·40 45
4267 1z.35 Carriage Type Cd21b c.1924 1·40 45
4268 2z.40 Carriage Type C3Pr07 c.1909 2·60 85
4269 2z.40 Carriage Type Ci29 c.1929 2·60 85

1373 Scout

2007. Europa. Centenary of Scouting.
4270 **1373** 3z. multicoloured 3·25 1·10

1374 'Little Helen with Vase of Flowers'

2007. Death Centenary of Stanislaw Wyspianski (artist and writer).
4271 **1374** 1z.35 multicoloured 1·40 45

1375 Karol Szymanowski

2007. 125th Birth and 70th Death Anniv of Karol Szymanowski (composer and writer).
4272 **1375** 1z.35 multicoloured 1·40 45

1376 Centre of Cracow, Locating Document and City Arms

2007. 750th Anniv of Cracow.
4273 **1376** 2z.40 multicoloured 3·75 1·30

1377 St. Catherine of Alexandria Church, St. Petersburg

2007. Saint Petersburg 2007 International Philatelic Exhibition. Sheet 90×70 mm.

MS4274	3z. multicoloured	4·25	4·25

1378 Gdansk

2007. Lighthouses. Sheet 90×125 mm containing T 1378 and similar vert designs. Multicoloured.

MS4275	1z.35 Type **1378**; 2z.40 Rozewie; 3z. Kolobrzeg; 3z.55 Hel	11·00	11·00

1379 Virgin Mary and Child

2007. 300th Anniv of Lesniow Monastery.

4276	**1379**	1z.35 multicoloured	1·40	45

1380 Bay

2007. Arab Horses. Multicoloured.

4277	1z.35 Type **1380**	1·30	45
4278	3z. Grey with pink snip	2·75	90
4279	3z.55 Bright bay with long forelock	3·75	1·40
4280	3z.55 Dappled grey	3·75	1·40

1381 *Saguinus imperator* (emperor tamarin)

2007. Polish Zoos. Showing animals. Multicoloured.

4281	1z.35 Type **1381**	1·30	45
4282	3z. *Loxodonta africana* (African elephant)	2·75	90
4283	3z.55 *Ciconia nigra* (black stork)	3·75	1·40
4284	3z.55 *Uncia uncia* (snow leopard)	3·75	1·40

1382 Visual Interpretation of Electronic Sound as City Skyline

2007. Warsaw Autumn 2007–50th Anniv of Festival of Contemporary Music.

4285	**1382**	3z. multicoloured	3·25	1·10

1383 Performers

2007. Centenary of Theatre of Silesia, Katowice

4286	1z.35 muulticolourd	1·30	45

1384 Postmarks

2007. World Post Day

4287	**1384**	1z.35 multicoloured	1·30	45

1385 Dragon's Bridge, Ljubljana, Slovenia

2007. Capital Cities of European Union States. Multicoloured.

4288	1z.35 Type **1385**	1·30	45
4289	1z.35 Roland Monument, Riga, Latvia	1·30	45
4290	3z. Philharmonic Hall, Luxembourg	2·20	70
4291	3z. Plaza de Cibeles, Madrid, Spain	2·20	70
4292	3z.55 Tower Bridge, London, UK	3·00	1·10

1386 Pope John Paul II

2007. 25th Anniv of Pope John Paul II Foundation

4293	**1386**	1z.35 multicoloured	1·30	45

Type

2007. Jerzy Duda-Gracz (artist) Commemoration

4294	**1387**	1z.35 multicoloured	1·30	45

1388 Teddy and Tree

2007. Christmas. Multicoloured.

1z.35 Type **1388**	1·30	45
3z. *Adoration of the Magi* (Mikolaj Haberschrack)	3·25	1·10

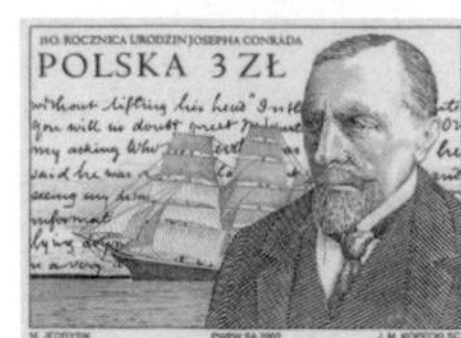

1389 Script, *Otago* and Joseph Conrad

2007. 150th Birth Anniv of Jozef Teodor Konrad Korzeniowski (Joseph Conrad) (writer and sailor).

4297	**1389**	3z. black	3·25	1·10

1390 Envelope and Quill

2008. PostEurop (Association of European Public Postal Operators) Plenary Assembly, Krakow. Sheet 70×90 mm.

MS4298	3z. multicoloured	3·25	3·25

1391 Heart as Open Door

2008. St Valentine's Day.

4299	**1391**	1z.35 multicoloured	1·40	45

1392 Self Portrait, 1858

2008. History of Polish Photography. 190th Birth Anniv of Karol Beyer. Multicoloured.

4300	1z.35 Type **1392**	1·40	45
4301	1z.35 Street scene, Wilanow, 1866	1·40	45
4302	1z.35 Street scene, Warsaw, 1858	1·40	45
4303	1z.35 Russian army tents, 1861	1·40	45

1393 Easter Eggs

2008. Easter. Multicoloured.

4304	1z.35 Type **1393**	1·40	45
4305	2z.40 Eggs (different)	1·40	45

1394 Emblem

2008. 80th Anniv of Straz Graniczna (border guard).

4306	**1394**	2z.10 scarlet and black	1·70	55

1395 TS-11 ISKRA

2008. Polish Airforce. Multicoloured.

4307	3z. Type **1395**	2·20	70
4308	3z.55 F-16 JASTRZAB	2·50	80

1396 Sand Storm

2008. Weather Phenomena. Multicoloured.

4309	1z.35 Type **1396**	1·20	40
4310	1z.35 Lightning	1·20	40
4311	2z.40 Rainbow	1·90	60
4312	2z.40 Tornado	1·90	60

1397 Envelope as Plate

2008. Europa. The Letter.

4313	**1397**	3z. black and silver	2·20	70
MS4313a		90×70 mm. As No. **MS**4313. Imperf	2·40	2·40

1398 Emblem

2008. Euro 2008 European Football Championships, Austria and Switzerland.

4314	**1398**	1z.35 multicoloured	1·20	40

1399 Magnifier and Emblem

2008. EUROSAI Congress, Krakow.

4315	**1399**	3z.55 multicoloured	2·50	80

1400 Toy Train

2008. National Children's Day. Toys. Multicoloured.

4316	1z.35 Type **1400**	1·20	40
4317	3z. Xylophone	2·20	70

1401 Child and Rug

2008. Child Refugees to Esfahan, Iran during World War II.

4318	**1401**	2z.40 multicoloured	1·90	60

1402 Envelope enclosing Romanian Athenaeum Building

2008. EFIRO 2008 International Stamp Exhibition, Bucharest. Sheet 90×70 mm.

MS4319 multicoloured	2·20	70

1403 Madonna and Child

2008. St. Mary's Sanctuaries. St. Mary of the Snow.

4320	**1403**	1z.35 multicoloured	1·20	40

1404 Swimming

2008. Olympic Games, Beijing. Multicoloured.

4321	10g. Type **1404**	25	10
4322	10g. Volleyball	25	10
4323	1z.45 Pole vault	1·30	50
4324	1z.45 Fencing	1·30	50
MS4325	202×116 mm. Nos. 4321/4	3·25	3·25

1405 Siekierkowski Bridge, Warsaw

2008. Bridges. Multicoloured.

4326	1z.45 Type **1405**	1·20	40
4327	1z.45 Pontiatowski Bridge, Warsaw	2·20	70
4328	3z. Bridge, Maurzyce	2·20	70
4329	3z. Ernest Malinowski Bridge, Torun	2·20	70

1406 Prosper Prowana

2008. 450th Anniv of Polish Postal Service. Sheet 120×80 mm containing T 1406 and similar multicoloured designs.

MS4330 1z.45×3, Type **1406**; King Zygmunt August (51×31 mm); Sebastian Montelupi	3·75	3·75

The stamps and margins of **MS**4330 form a composite design.

1407 Wladyslaw Raczkiewicz

2008. Presidents of Government in Exile. Sheet 129×125 mm containing T 1407 and similar horiz designs. Multicoloured.

MS4331 1z.45×6, Type **1407**; Edward Raczynski; August Zaleski; Kazimierz Sabbat; Stanislaw Ostrowski; Ryszard Kaczorowski	7·50	7·50

The central stamps of **MS**4331 form a composite design.

1408 Sports Men and Women

2008. Centenary of Lodz Sports Club.

4332	**1408**	1z.45 vermilion and silver	1·20	40

1409 Native American, Settler and Map

2008. 400th Anniv of Polish Settlers in America.

4333	**1409**	3z. multicoloured	1·20	40

1410 Pigeon Post

2008. World Post Day.

4334	**1410**	2z.10 multicoloured	1·70	60

1411 Mieczyslaw Karlowicz

2008. Composers. Multicoloured.

4335	1z.45 Type **1411**	1·20	40
4336	1z.45 Wojciech Kilar	1·20	40
4337	1z.45 Henryk Mikolaj Gorecki	1·20	40
4338	1z.45 Witold Lutoslawski	1·20	40

1412 Rijksmuseum, Amsterdam

2007. Capital Cities of European Union States. Multicoloured.

4339	1z.45 Type **1412**	1·20	40
4340	1z.45 Royal Library, Copenhagen	1·20	40
4341	3z. Charles Bridge, Prague	2·20	70
4342	3z. Acropolis, Athens	2·20	70
4343	3z.65 Parliament, Vienna	2·75	90

1413 J. Przybora and J. Wasowski

2008. 50th Anniv of Kabaret Starszych Panów (comedy series).

4344	**1413**	1z.45 multicoloured	1·20	40

1414 Maria Konopnicka

2008. Centenary of Rota (the Oath (poem)) by Maria Konopnicka.

4345	**1414**	3z.65 multicoloured	2·75	90

1415 National Arms

2008. Centenary of Independence Day.

4346	**1415**	1z.45 carmine	1·20	40

1416 Stars

2008. Christmas. Multicoloured.

4347	1z.45 Type **1416**	1·20	40
4348	3z. Stars (different)	2·20	70

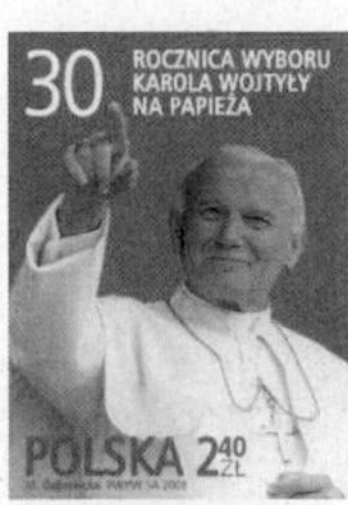

1417 Pope John Paul II

2008. 30th Anniv of Election of Karol Wojtyla as Pope John Paul II.

4349	**1417**	2z.40 multicoloured	3·75	1·20

1418 Zbigniew Herbert

2008. Tenth Death Anniv of Zbigniew Herbert (writer).

4350	**1418**	2z.10 multicoloured	1·70	60

1419 Emblem

2008. United Nations Conference on Climate Change, Poznan.

4351	**1419**	2z.40 multicoloured	3·75	1·20

1420 Postal Messenger (Image scaled to 46% of original size)

2008. 450th Anniv of Polish Postal Service (2nd issue). Sheet 106×75 mm. Self-adhesive.

MS4352 multicoloured	11·00	11·00

No. **MS**4352 was screen printed on silk.

See also **MS**4330.

1421 Louis Braille

2009. Birth Bicentenary of Louis Braille (inventor of Braille writing for the blind).

4353	**1421**	1z.45 multicoloured	1·30	45

No. 4353 was printed with a *se-tenant* stamp size label with embossed Braille letters attached at right.

1422 Witold Pilecki (historian)

2009. Camp Survivors. Multicoloured.

4354	1z.45 Type **1422**	1·30	45
4355	2z.10 Wladyslaw Wolski	1·80	65
4356	2z.40 Ignacy Ludwik Jez	2·00	70
4357	3z. Stanislawa Maria Sawicka	2·30	75

1423 Heart in Four-leafed Clover

2009. St Valentine's Day.

4358	**1423**	1z.45 multicoloured	1·30	45

1424 *Zwiastowanie*

2009. Contemporary Polish Sculpture. 10th Death Anniv of Wladyslaw Hasior. Multicoloured.

4359	1z.45 Type **1424**	1·30	45
4360	1z.45 *Mucha*	1·30	45
4361	2z.10 *Sztandar Zielonej Poetki*	1·80	65
4362	2z.40 *Sztandar Rozbieranie do snu*	2·00	70
MS4363	90×125 mm. Nos. 4359/62	6·50	6·50

1425 *Chrystus Zmartwychwstały*

2009. Easter. Paintings by Szymon Czechowicz. Multicoloured.

4364	1z.55 Type **1425**	1·40	50
4365	3z. *Zlozenie do grobu* (vert)	2·30	75

1426 Fish

2009. China 2009 International Stamp Exhibition, Luoyang. Sheet 90×70 mm.

MS4366	multicoloured	2·30	2·30

1427 *Berek Joselewicz* (Juliusz Kossak)

2009. Polish Year in Israel. Sheet 90×70 mm.

MS4367	multicoloured	2·30	2·30

1428 Cheetahs

2009. African Animals. Sheet 124×90 mm containing T 1428 and similar horiz designs. Each black.

MS4368	1z.55 Type **1428**; 1z.95 Zebras; 2z.40 Gnu and crocodile; 3z. Elephants	7·50	7·50

1429 Numbers as Starburst

2009. Europa. Astronomy.

4369	**1429**	3z. deep turquoise-blue and new blue	2·30	75

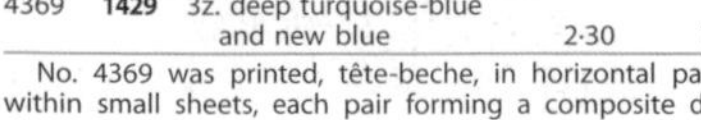

No. 4369 was printed, tête-beche, in horizontal pairs within small sheets, each pair forming a composite design.

1430 Grazyna Bacewicz

2009. Birth Centenary of Grazyna Bacewicz (composer and violinist)

4370	**1430**	1z.55 multicoloured	1·40	50

1431 Tytus de Zoo

2009. 50th (2007) Anniv of Tytus, Romek and A'Tomek (comic created by Henryk Jerzy Chmielewski (Papcio Chmiel)). Multicoloured.

4371	1z.55 Type **1431**	1·40	50
4372	1z.55 Romek	1·40	50
4373	1z.55 A'Tomek	1·40	50

Nos. 4371-4373 were printed, *se-tenant,* in horizontal strips of three stamps within the sheet.

1432 Lech Walesa (leader Trade Union Solidarnosc)

2009. 20th Anniv of Opposition Electoral Success. Sheet 90×70 mm.

MS4374	**1432**	3z.75 multicoloured	3·00	3·00

1433 Saint Bruno

2009. Death Millennary of Saint Bruno of Querfurt (missionary and martyr).

4375	**1433**	3z. multicoloured	2·30	75

1434 *Dar Mlodziezy*(frigate of Naval Academy of Gdynia, built,1982)

2009. Tall Ships' Races–Gdynia 2009. Sheet 90×70 mm.

MS4376	**1434**	3z.75 multicoloured	3·00	3·00

1435 *Phocoena phocoena* (porpoise)

2009. Mammals of the Baltic Sea. Multicoloured.

4377	1z.55 Type **1435**	1·40	50
4378	1z.55 *Halichoreus grypus* (grey seal)	1·40	50
4379	1z.55 *Phoca vitulina* (harbour seal)	1·40	50
4380	1z.55 *Phoca hispida* (ringed seal)	1·40	50

Nos. 4377-4380 were printed, se-tenant, forming a composite design.

1436 Building on Fire

2009. 65th Anniv of Warsaw Uprising against German Occupation. Sheet 90×70 mm.

MS4381	**1436**	3z.75 black and rosine	3·00	3·00

1437 Cerasus avium (*Prunus avium*) (cherry)

2009. Fruit and Flowers. Multicoloured.

4382	1z.95 Type **1437**	1·70	70
4383	3z.75 *Calendula officinalis* (pot marigold)	3·00	1·10

1438 Jan Czochralski (specialist in metallurgy and inventor of Czochralski process)

2009. Poles in Exile. Multicoloured.

4384	1z.55 Type **1438**	1·40	50
4385	1z.55 Antoni Norbert Patek (watchmaker)	1·40	50
4386	1z.95 Ludwik Hirszfeld (micro-biologist and serologist)	1·70	70
4387	1z.95 Marian Rejewski, Henryk Zygalski and Jerzy Rózycki (mathematicians and cryptologists who created replica of Enigma, German encrypting machine)	1·70	1·70

1439 Juliusz Slowacki

2009. Birth Bicentenary of Juliusz Slowacki (poet, playwright and philosopher).

4388	**1439**	1z.55 multicoloured	1·40	50

1440 Attack on Wegierska Górka (village in Zywiec County which held out for three days)

2009. Defensive War 1939. Each black and scarlet-vermilion.

4389	1z.55 Type **1440**	1·40	50
4390	2z.40 Wielun (first town to come under attack)	2·00	70

1441 Ball and Hoop

2009. EuroBasket 2009–European Men's Basketball Championship, Poland.

4391	**1441**	3z. multicoloured	3·00	1·10

1442 Tadeusz Mazowiecki (first premier)

2009. 20th Anniv of First Non-Communist Government following Elections in June, 1989.

4392	**1442**	1z.55 multicoloured	1·40	50

1443 Player in Motion

2009. Women's European Volleyball Championship–2009, Poland.

4393	**1443**	3z. multicoloured	3·00	1·10

2009. Capital Cities of European Union States. As T 1412. Multicoloured.

4394	1z.55 Castle, Bratislava	1·40	50
4395	1z.55 Famagusta Gate, Nicosia	1·40	50
4396	3z. Town Hall, Brussels	3·00	1·10
4397	3z. Courtyard, Warsaw	3·00	1·10
4398	3z.75 National Museum	3·50	1·30

1444 Envelope as Kite

2009. World Post Day.

4399	**1444**	3z. multicoloured	3·00	1·10

1445 Jerzy Popieluszko

2009. 25th Death Anniv of Jerzy Popieluszko (priest and solidarity martyr).

4400	**1445**	1z.55 multicoloured	1·40	50

1446 Volunteer

2009. Centenary of Voluntary Tatra Mountains Rescue Service.

4401	**1446**	1z.55 multicoloured	1·40	50

1447 Pawel Jasienica

2009. Birth Centenary of Leon Lech Beynar (Pawel Jasienica) (writer and historian).

4402	**1447**	1z.55 multicoloured	1·40	50

1448 Jerzy Franciszek Kulczycki

2009. Polish Influence in Europe. Jerzy Franciszek Kulczycki (hero of Battle of Vienna and opened first coffee house in Vienna) Commemoration.

4403	**1448**	1z.55 multicoloured	1·40	50

No. 4403 was printed, *se-tenant* with a stamp size label attached at top, the whole forming a composite design.

1449 Bookplate 'Exlibris Willibald Pirkheimer' (Albrecht Durer)

2009. Lost Treasures. Art. Multicoloured.

4404	1z.55 Type **1449**	1·40	50
4405	1z.55 *Christ falls beneath the Cross* (Peter Paul Rubens)	1·40	50
4406	1z.55 *Joseph recounts his Dream* (Rembrandt)	1·40	50

1450 Choir

2009. Christmas. Multicoloured

4407	1z.55 Type **1450**	1·40	50
4408	2z.40 Holy Family	2·00	70

1451 Letter from Kalwaria to Warsaw, franked with 1860 10k. Stamp (As Type 1)

2010. 150th Anniv of Polish Stamps

MS4409 **1451**	4z.15 multicoloured	4·50	4·50

1452 Skiers

2010. Winter Olympic Games, Vancouver

4410	**1452**	3z. multicoloured	3·00	1·10

1453 British Shorthair

2010. Cats. Multicoloured.

MS4411	1z.55 Type **1453**; 1z.55 Siamese; 1z.95 Somali; 1z.95 Maine Coon; 3z. Persian; 3z. Tortoiseshell and white exotic	13·00	13·00

1454 Frederic Chopin

2010. Birth Bicentenary of Frederic Chopin (composer)

MS4412 **1454**	4z.15 multicoloured	4·50	4·50
MS4412a	4z.15 As Type **1454**. Imperf	4·50	5·00

1455 Lamb

2010. Easter. Multicoloured.

4413	1z.55 Type **1455**	1·40	50
4414	2z.40 Basket of eggs	2·00	70

1456 Warsaw, 1920

2010. History of Polish Photography. Multicoloured.

4415	1z.95 Type **1456**	1·70	60
4416	1z.95 Doorway, Krakow, 1921	1·70	60
4417	1z.95 Old Town Hall, Warsaw, 1920	1·70	60
4418	1z.95 Kasimir side altar, Vilnius Cathedral, 1912	1·70	60

1457 Anniversary Emblem

2010. 20th Anniv of Special Services

4419	**1457**	1z.55 scarlet-vermilion, indigo and silver	1·50	50

1458 Cross of Polish Badges

2010. 60th Anniv of Katyn Massacre

MS4420	multicoloured	3·00	3·00

1459 Tower of Belém, Lisbon

2010. Portugal 2010 International Stamp Exhibition, Lisbon

MS4421 **1459**	3z. multicoloured	3·00	3·00

1460 Boy reading

2010. Europa

4422	**1460**	3z. multicoloured	3·00	3·00

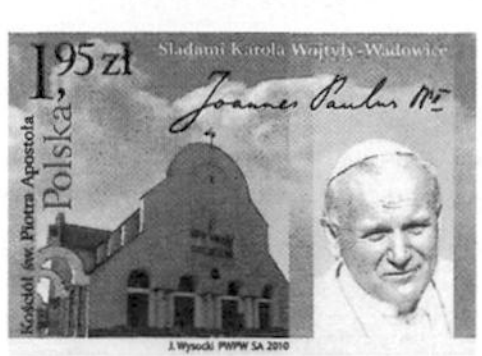
1461 Pope John Paul II and Church of Peter the Apostle, Wadowice

2010. Pope John Paul II (Karol Józef Wojtyła) Commemoration

4423	**1461**	1z.95 multicoloured	1·70	60

1462 Bridge over the Vistula

2010. 750th Anniv of Tczew

4424	**1462**	1z.55 multicoloured	1·40	50

1463 Jerzy Popieluszko

2010. Beatification of Jerzy Popiełuszko (priest and solidarity martyr)

4425	**1463**	1z.95 multicoloured	1·70	60

1464 Convent and Statue of Christ

2010. 750th Anniv of Dominican Ursuline Sisters Convent, Sieradtz

4426	**1464**	1z.55 multicoloured	1·40	50

1465 Battle Scene (Jan Matejko)

2010. 600th Anniv of Battle of Grunvald (First Battle of Tannenberg), during the Polish–Lithuanian–Teutonic War

MS4427 **1465**	8z.30 multicoloured	7·50	7·50

1466 Scouts signalling Semaphore Message, 'STO LAT' (100 YEARS)

2010. Centenary of Polish Scouts' Association

4428	**1466**	1z.95 multicoloured	1·70	60

1467 Forget-me-Not

2010. Flowers

4429	**1467**	4z.15 multicoloured	3·75	1·20

1468 Lech Walesa

2010. 30th Anniv of NSZZ 'Solidarnosc' (Solidarity)

4430	**1468**	3z.75 black, silver and red	3·75	1·20

1469 Sphalerite

2010. Minerals. Multicoloured.

4431	1z.55 Type **1469**	1·40	50
4432	1z.95 Gypsum	1·70	60
4433	2z.40 Agate	2·00	70
4434	3z. Chrysoprase	3·00	1·10

1469a Tower of Postmen

2010. World Post Day

4434	**1469a**	1z.95 multicoloured	1·70	70

1470 Sofia

2010. Capital Cities of European Union States. Magdalena Blazkow.

4436		1z.95 Type **1470**	1·70	70
4437		3z. Bucharest	3·00	1·10

No. 4438 and Type **1471** are left for 'A' stamp issued on 29 October 2010, not yet received.

1472 Players

2010. Centenary of Widzew Lodz Football Club

4439	**1472**	1z.55 multicoloured	1·40	50

1473 Ignacy Paderewski

2010. 150th Birth Anniv of Ignacy Jan Paderewski (composer and Prime Minister (1919))

4440	**1473**	3z. multicoloured	3·00	1·10

1474 Shooting Star, Trail and Christmas Tree

2010. Christmas. Multicoloured.

4441		1z.55 Type **1474**	1·40	50
4442		2z.40 Shooting star, trail and night sky	2·00	70

1475 'Kocham Cie'

2010. Greeting Stamps

4443	**1475**	A multicoloured	1·40	50

MILITARY POST

I. Polish Corps in Russia, 1918.

1918. Stamps of Russia optd POCZTA Pol. Korp. and eagle. Perf or imperf. (70k.).

M1	**22**	3k. red	65·00	65·00
M2	**23**	4k. red	65·00	65·00
M3	**22**	5k. red	22·00	18·00
M4	**23**	10k. blue	22·00	18·00
M5	**22**	10k. on 7k. blue (No. 151)	£550	£650
M6	**10**	15k. blue and purple	4·50	4·50
M7	**14**	20k. red and blue	8·75	7·00
M8	**10**	25k. mauve and green	£110	90·00
M9	**10**	35k. green and purple	4·50	4·50
M10	**14**	40k. green and purple	12·50	8·75
M11	**10**	70k. orge & brn (No. 166)	£325	£275

1918. Stamps of Russia surch Pol. Korp., eagle and value. (a) Perf on Nos. 92/4.

M12A	**22**	10k. on 3k. red	4·50	4·50
M13A	**22**	35k. on 1k. orange	65·00	65·00
M14A	**22**	50k. on 2k. green	4·50	4·50
M15A	**22**	1r. on 3k. red	90·00	80·00

(b) Imperf on Nos. 155/7.

M12B	10k. on 3k. red	2·00	2·00
M13B	35k. on 1k. orange	1·00	1·00
M14B	50k. on 2k. green	2·00	2·00
M15B	1r. on 3k. red	4·00	3·00

II. Polish Army in Russia, 1942

M3 "We Shall Return"

1942

M16	**M3**	50k. brown	£225	£550

NEWSPAPER STAMPS

1919. Newspaper stamps of Austria optd POCZTA POLSKA. Imperf.

N50	**N53**	2h. brown	8·75	10·50
N51	**N53**	4h. green	1·75	2·25
N52	**N53**	6h. blue	1·75	2·25
N53	**N53**	10h. orange	35·00	42·00
N54	**N53**	30h. red	3·75	5·50

OFFICIAL STAMPS

O24

1920

O128	**O24**	3f. red	10	25
O129	**O24**	5f. red	10	10
O130	**O24**	10f. red	10	10
O131	**O24**	15f. red	10	10
O132	**O24**	25f. red	10	10
O133	**O24**	50f. red	10	10
O134	**O24**	100f. red	25	25
O135	**O24**	150f. red	30	30
O136	**O24**	200f. red	30	35
O137	**O24**	300f. red	30	35
O138	**O24**	600f. red	40	50

O70

1933. (a) Inscr "ZWYCZAJNA".

O295	**O70**	(No value) mauve	15	15
O306	**O70**	(No value) blue	20	20

(b) Inscr "POLECONA".

O307	(No value) red	20	20

O93

1940. (a) Size 31×23 mm.

O392	**O93**	6g. brown	80	2·75
O393	**O93**	8g. grey	80	2·75
O394	**O93**	10g. green	80	2·75
O395	**O93**	12g. green	80	2·10
O396	**O93**	20g. brown	80	3·25
O397	**O93**	24g. red	13·00	2·10
O398	**O93**	30g. red	1·10	3·25
O399	**O93**	40g. violet	1·10	5·75
O400	**O93**	48g. green	3·75	5·75
O401	**O93**	50g. blue	1·10	3·25
O402	**O93**	60g. green	80	2·10
O403	**O93**	80g. purple	80	2·75

(b) Size 35×26 mm.

O404	1z. purple and grey	2·10	5·75
O405	3z. brown and grey	2·10	5·75
O406	5z. orange and grey	3·25	6·25

(c) Size 21×16 mm.

O407	6g. brown	80	1·30
O408	8g. grey	80	1·90
O409	10g. green	1·10	2·10
O410	12g. green	80	1·90
O411	20g. brown	80	1·30
O412	24g. red	80	1·30
O413	30g. red	1·10	2·10
O414	40g. violet	1·10	1·70
O415	50g. blue	1·10	2·10

O102

1943

O456	**O102**	6g. brown	20	75
O457	**O102**	8g. blue	20	75
O458	**O102**	10g. green	20	75
O459	**O102**	12g. violet	20	75
O460	**O102**	16g. orange	20	75
O461	**O102**	20g. green	20	75
O462	**O102**	24g. red	20	75
O463	**O102**	30g. purple	20	75
O464	**O102**	40g. blue	20	75
O465	**O102**	60g. green	20	75
O466	**O102**	80g. purple	20	75
O467	**O102**	100g. grey	25	1·30

O128

1945. No value. (a) With control number below design. Perf or imperf.

O534	**O128**	(5z.) blue	45	25
O535	**O128**	(10z.) red	45	25

(b) Without control number below design. Perf.

O748	(60g.) pale blue	35	25
O805	(60g.) indigo	55	25
O806	(1.55z.) red	55	25

The blue and indigo stamps are inscr "ZWYKLA" (Ordinary) and the red stamps "POLECONA" (Registered).

O277

1954. No value.

O871	**O277**	(60g.) blue	20	15
O872	**O277**	(1.55z.) red ("POLECONA")	40	15

POSTAGE DUE STAMPS

1919. Postage Due Stamps of Austria optd POCZTA POLSKA.

D50	**D55**	5h. red	5·50	5·00
D51	**D55**	10h. red	£1750	£2750
D52	**D55**	15h. red	3·25	2·50
D53	**D55**	20h. red	£550	£550
D54	**D55**	25h. red	19·00	17·00
D55	**D55**	30h. red	£950	£950
D56	**D55**	40h. red	£220	£220
D57	**D56**	1k. blue	£2000	£2500
D58	**D56**	5k. blue	£2000	£2500
D59	**D56**	10k. blue	£9750	£9000

1919. Postage Due Provisionals of Austria optd POCZTA POLSKA.

D60	**50**	15 on 36h. (No. D287)	£300	£325
D61	**50**	50 on 42h. (No. D289)	30·00	25·00

D20

1919. Sold in halerzy or fenigow.

D92	**D20**	2h. blue	10	10
D93	**D20**	4h. blue	10	10
D94	**D20**	5h. blue	10	10
D95	**D20**	10h. blue	10	10
D96	**D20**	20h. blue	10	10
D97	**D20**	30h. blue	10	10
D98	**D20**	50h. blue	10	10
D145	**D20**	100h. blue	20	10
D146	**D20**	200f. blue	75	10
D147	**D20**	500h. blue	75	10

The 20, 100 and 500 values were sold in both currencies.

1919. Sold in fenigow.

D128	2f. red	10	10
D129	4f. red	10	10
D130	5f. red	10	10
D131	10f. red	10	10
D132	20f. red	10	10
D133	30f. red	10	10
D134	50f. red	30	30
D135	100f. red	10	10
D136	500f. red	10	10

1921. Stamps of 1919 surch with new value and doplata. Imperf.

D154	**11**	6m. on 15h. brown	70	90
D155	**11**	6m. on 25h. red	50	55
D156	**11**	20m. on 10h. red	1·90	2·10
D157	**11**	20m. on 50h. blue	1·00	1·75
D158	**11**	35m. on 70h. blue	8·75	12·50

D28

1921. Value in marks. (a) Size 17×22 mm.

D159	**D28**	1m. blue	20	10
D160	**D28**	2m. blue	20	10
D161	**D28**	4m. blue	20	10
D162	**D28**	6m. blue	20	10
D163	**D28**	8m. blue	20	10
D164	**D28**	20m. blue	20	10
D165	**D28**	50m. blue	20	10
D166	**D28**	100m. blue	20	10

(b) Size 19×24 mm.

D199	50m. blue	10	10
D200	100m. blue	10	10
D201	200m. blue	10	10
D202	500m. blue	10	10
D203	1000m. blue	10	10
D204	2000m. blue	10	10
D205	10,000m. blue	10	10
D206	20,000m. blue	10	10
D207	30,000m. blue	10	10
D208	50,000m. blue	10	10
D209	100,000m. blue	10	10
D210	200,000m. blue	10	10
D211	300,000m. blue	30	20
D212	500,000m. blue	40	40
D213	1,000,000m. blue	75	55
D214	2,000,000m. blue	1·10	90
D215	3,000,000m. blue	1·40	1·10

1923. Surch.

D216	10,000 on 8m. blue	10	15
D217	20,000 on 20m. blue	10	35
D218	50,000 on 2m. blue	1·25	60

1924. As Type D 28 but value in "groszy" or "zloty". (a) Size 20×25½ mm.

D229	1g. brown	10	10
D230	2g. brown	20	10
D231	4g. brown	20	10
D232	6g. brown	20	10
D233	10g. brown	3·25	10
D234	15g. brown	3·25	10
D235	20g. brown	6·75	10
D236	25g. brown	4·75	10
D237	30g. brown	95	10
D238	40g. brown	1·40	10
D239	50g. brown	1·40	10
D240	1z. brown	90	10
D241	2z. brown	90	25
D242	3z. brown	1·40	45
D243	5z. brown	1·40	30

(b) Size 19×24 mm.

D290	1g. brown	20	10
D291	2g. brown	20	10
D292	10g. brown	90	10
D293	15g. brown	1·40	10
D294	20g. brown	3·25	10
D295	25g. brown	30·00	10

D63

1930

D280	**D63**	5g. brown	35	20

1934. Nos. D79/84 surch.

D301	**D28**	10g. on 2z. brown	20	15
D302	**D28**	15g. on 2z. brown	20	15
D303	**D28**	20g. on 1z. brown	20	15
D304	**D28**	20g. on 5z. brown	1·75	35
D305	**D28**	25g. on 40g. brown	60	35
D306	**D28**	30g. on 40g. brown	65	45
D307	**D28**	50g. on 40g. brown	65	45
D308	**D28**	50g. on 3z. brown	2·10	60

1934. No. 273 surch DOPLATA and value.

D309	10g. on 1z. black on cream	70	20
D310	20g. on 1z. black on cream	1·50	55
D311	25g. on 1z. black on cream	70	20

D88

1938

D350	**D88**	5g. green	15	10
D351	**D88**	10g. green	15	10
D352	**D88**	15g. green	15	10
D353	**D88**	20g. green	40	10
D354	**D88**	25g. green	10	10
D355	**D88**	30g. green	10	10
D356	**D88**	50g. green	45	50
D357	**D88**	1z. green	2·25	1·75

D97

1940. German Occupation.

D420	**D97**	10g. orange	40	1·30
D421	**D97**	20g. orange	40	1·30
D422	**D97**	30g. orange	40	1·30
D423	**D97**	50g. orange	1·30	2·10

D126

1945. Size 26×19½ mm. Perf.

D530	**D126**	1z. brown	10	10
D531	**D126**	2z. brown	20	10
D532	**D126**	3z. brown	25	20
D533	**D126**	5z. brown	40	25

1946. Size 29×21½ mm. Perf or imperf.

D646	1z. brown	10	10
D647	2z. brown	10	10
D572	3z. brown	10	10
D573	5z. brown	10	10
D574	6z. brown	10	10
D575	10z. brown	10	10
D649	15z. brown	10	10
D577	25z. brown	50	20
D651	100z. brown	55	35
D652	150z. brown	80	45

D190

1950

D665	**D190**	5z. red	15	15
D666	**D190**	10z. red	15	15
D667	**D190**	15z. red	15	15
D668	**D190**	20z. red	15	15
D669	**D190**	25z. red	30	15
D670	**D190**	50z. red	45	15
D671	**D190**	100z. red	55	30

1951. Value in "groszy" or "zloty".

D701	5g. red	10	10
D702	10g. red	10	10
D703	15g. red	10	10
D704	20g. red	10	10
D705	25g. red	10	10
D706	30g. red	10	10
D707	50g. red	10	10
D708	60g. red	10	10
D709	90g. red	25	10
D710	1z. red	25	10
D711	2z. red	45	25
D712	5z. purple	95	30

1953. As last but with larger figures of value and no imprint below design.

D804	5g. brown	10	10
D805	10g. brown	10	10
D806	15g. brown	10	10
D807	20g. brown	10	10
D808	25g. brown	10	10
D809	30g. brown	10	10
D810	50g. brown	10	10
D811	60g. brown	10	10
D812	90g. brown	25	10
D813	1z. brown	25	10
D814	2z. brown	45	10

1980. As Type D 190 but redrawn without imprint.

D2699	1z. red	10	10
D2700	2z. drab	10	10
D2701	3z. violet	30	10
D2702	5z. brown	50	30

D1143

1998

D3746	**D1143**	5g. blue, vio & yell	10	10
D3747	**D1143**	10g. blue, turq & yell	10	10
D3748	**D1143**	20g. bl, grn & yell	10	10
D3749	**D1143**	50g. black & yell	15	10
D3750	**D1143**	80g. bl, orge & yell	25	10
D3751	**D1143**	1z. blue, red & yell	35	15

Pt. 5

POLISH POST IN DANZIG

For Polish post in Danzig, the port through which Poland had access to the sea between the two Great Wars.

100 groszy = 1 zloty

Stamps of Poland optd PORT GDANSK.

1925. Issue of 1924.

R1	**40**	1g. brown	55	3·25
R2	**40**	2g. brown	55	7·50
R3	**40**	3g. orange	20	2·10
R4	**40**	5g. green	16·00	10·50
R5	**40**	10g. green	5·25	4·25
R6	**40**	15g. red	30·00	10·50
R7	**40**	20g. blue	1·60	2·10
R8	**40**	25g. red	1·60	2·10
R9	**40**	30g. violet	1·60	2·10
R10	**40**	40g. blue	1·60	2·10
R11	**40**	50g. purple	5·25	3·25

1926. Issues of 1925–28.

R14	**44**	5g. green	1·60	2·75
R15	-	10g. violet (No. 245a)	1·60	2·75
R16	-	15g. red (No. 246)	4·75	5·25
R17	**48**	20g. red	3·25	2·75
R18	**51**	25g. brown	5·25	6·25
R19	**57**	1z. black and cream	30·00	48·00

1929. Issues of 1928/9.

R21	**61**	5g. violet	1·60	3·25
R22	**61**	10g. green	1·60	2·75
R23	**59**	15g. blue	4·25	8·00
R24	**61**	25g. brown	3·25	2·75

1933. Stamp of 1928 with vert opt.

R25	**57**	1z. black on cream	80·00	£170

1934. Issue of 1932.

R26	**65**	5g. violet	3·75	8·50
R27	**65**	10g. green	37·00	£140
R28	**65**	15g. red	3·75	8·50

1936. Issue of 1935.

R29	**79**	5g. blue (No. 313)	3·25	10·50
R31	-	5g. violet (No. 317)	1·20	9·50
R30	-	15g. blue (No. 315)	3·25	12·50
R32	-	15g. lake (No. 319)	1·20	9·50
R33	-	25g. green (No. 321a)	3·25	8·50

R6 Port of Danzig

1938. 20th Anniv of Polish Independence.

R34	**R6**	5g. orange	55	12·50
R35	**R6**	15g. brown	55	12·50
R36	**R6**	25g. purple	55	12·50
R37	**R6**	55g. blue	1·60	26·00

Pt. 5

POLISH POST OFFICE IN TURKEY

Stamps used for a short period for franking correspondance handed in at the Polish Consulate, Constantinople.

100 fenigow = 1 marka

1919. Stamps of Poland of 1919 optd LEVANT. Perf.

1	**15**	3f. brown	42·00	70·00
2	**15**	5f. green	42·00	70·00
3	**15**	10f. purple	42·00	70·00
4	**15**	15f. red	42·00	70·00
5	**15**	20f. blue	42·00	70·00
6	**15**	25f. olive	42·00	70·00
7	**15**	50f. green	42·00	70·00
8	**17**	1m. violet	42·00	70·00
9	**17**	1m.50 green	42·00	70·00
10	**17**	2m. brown	42·00	70·00
11	**18**	2m.50 brown	42·00	70·00
12	**19**	5m. purple	42·00	70·00

Pt. 9

PONTA DELGADO

A district of the Azores, whose stamps were used from 1868, and again after 1905.

1000 reis = 1 milreis.

1892. As T 26 of Portugal but inscr "PONTA DELGADA".

6	5r. yellow	3·75	2·50
7	10r. mauve	3·75	2·50
8	15r. brown	5·00	3·50
9	20r. lilac	5·00	3·50
3	25r. green	11·00	2·50
12	50r. blue	11·00	5·25
25	75r. pink	10·50	8·75
14	80r. green	15·00	14·50
15	100r. brown on yellow	15·00	8·75
28	150r. red on pink	85·00	49·00
16	200r. blue on blue	85·00	70·00
17	300r. blue on brown	85·00	70·00

1897. "King Carlos" key-types inscr "PONTA DELGADA".

29	**S**	2½r. grey	80	50
30	**S**	5r. orange	80	50
31	**S**	10r. green	80	50
32	**S**	15r. brown	11·00	9·75
45	**S**	15r. green	2·75	1·70
33	**S**	20r. lilac	2·75	1·80
34	**S**	25r. green	4·00	1·80
46	**S**	25r. red	2·30	60
35	**S**	50r. blue	4·00	1·80
48	**S**	65r. blue	1·70	75
36	**S**	75r. pink	8·75	1·80
49	**S**	75r. brown on yellow	18·00	9·75
37	**S**	80r. mauve	2·30	1·80
38	**S**	100r. blue on blue	5·25	1·80
50	**S**	115r. brown on pink	4·50	2·00
51	**S**	130r. brown on cream	2·75	2·00
39	**S**	150r. brown on yellow	2·75	2·20
52	**S**	180r. grey on pink	2·75	2·00
40	**S**	200r. purple on pink	9·50	8·50
41	**S**	300r. blue on pink	9·50	8·50
42	**S**	500r. black on blue	20·00	16·00

Pt. 1

POONCH

A state in Kashmir, India. Now uses Indian stamps.

12 pies = 1 anna; 16 annas = 1 rupee

1

1876. Imperf.

1	**1**	6p. red	£16000	£190
2	**1**	½a. red		£5500

4

1880. Imperf.

53	**1**	1p. red	3·50	3·50
12	**4**	½a. red	4·25	4·25
50	**4**	1a. red	4·50	4·75
52	**4**	2a. red (22×22 mm)	5·00	5·50
31	**4**	4a. red (28×27 mm)	7·50	6·50

These stamps were printed on various coloured papers.

OFFICIAL STAMPS

1888. Imperf.

O1		1p. black	4·00	4·00
O7	**4**	½a. black	3·50	4·50
O3	**4**	1a. black	4·00	4·25
O4	**4**	2a. black	8·00	8·00
O5	**4**	4a. black	11·00	15·00

Pt. 6

PORT LAGOS

French Post Office in the Turkish Empire. Closed in 1898.

25 centimes = 1 piastre.

1893. Stamps of France optd Port-Lagos and the three higher values surch also in figures and words.

75	**10**	5c. green	14·00	11·00
76	**10**	10c. black on lilac	48·00	28·00
77	**10**	15c. blue	50·00	65·00
78	**10**	1p. on 25c. black on pink	32·00	29·00
79	**10**	2p. on 50c. red	90·00	85·00
80	**10**	4p. on 1f. green	60·00	85·00

Pt. 6

PORT SAID

French Post Office in Egypt. Closed 1931.

1902. 100 centimes = 1 franc.
1921. 10 milliemes = 1 piastre.

1899. Stamps of France optd PORT SAID.

101		1c. black on blue	1·30	1·70
102		2c. brown on buff	1·20	2·50
103		3c. grey	1·10	2·50
104		4c. brown on grey	90	3·25
105		5c. green	2·30	4·00
107		10c. black on lilac	5·00	7·25
109		15c. blue	6·50	11·00
110		20c. red on green	5·00	17·00
111		25c. black on pink	4·25	90
112		30c. brown	10·00	14·00
113		40c. red on yellow	12·00	16·00
115		50c. red	17·00	14·00
116		1f. green	30·00	23·00
117		2f. brown on blue	65·00	80·00
118		5f. mauve on lilac	70·00	£120

1899. No. 107 surch. (a) 25c VINGT-CINQ.

119		25c. on 10c. black on lilac	£375	£140

(b) VINGT-CINQ only.

121		25c. on 10c. black on lilac	£140	30·00

1902. "Blanc", "Mouchon" and "Merson" key-types inscr "PORT SAID".

122	A	1c. grey	45	85
123	A	2c. purple	35	2·00
124	A	3c. red	50	3·00
125	A	4c. brown	55	2·30
126a	A	5c. green	1·90	2·30
127	B	10c. red	1·60	45
128	B	15c. red	2·50	3·50
128a	B	15c. orange	8·25	9·25
129	B	20c. brown	2·50	4·00
130	B	25c. blue	1·10	45
131	B	30c. mauve	4·25	3·25
132	C	40c. red and blue	3·25	5·50
133	C	50c. brown and lilac	4·00	3·25
134	C	1f. red and green	8·50	12·00
135	C	2f. lilac and buff	11·00	18·00
136	C	5f. blue and buff	32·00	60·00

1915. Red Cross. Surch 5c and red cross.

137	B	10c.+5c. red	1·00	4·25

1921. Surch with value in figures and words (without bars).

151a	A	1m. on 1c. grey	4·00	6·75
152	A	2m. on 5c. green	3·50	6·50
153	B	4m. on 10c. red	2·50	5·00
166a	A	5m. on 1c. grey	11·00	21·00
167	A	5m. on 2c. purple	24·00	38·00
154	A	5m. on 3c. red	12·00	21·00
141	A	5m. on 4c. brown	12·00	28·00
155	B	6m. on 15c. orange	2·75	8·75
156	B	6m. on 15c. red	29·00	36·00
157	B	8m. on 20c. brown	3·25	6·50
168	A	10m. on 2c. purple	12·00	36·00
142	A	10m. on 4c. brown	40·00	55·00
158	B	10m. on 25c. blue	3·50	2·75
159	B	10m. on 30c. mauve	6·25	13·00
144	B	12m. on 30c. mauve	50·00	75·00
145	A	15m. on 4c. brown	15·00	20·00
169	B	15m. on 15c. red	50·00	80·00
170	B	15m. on 20c. brown	60·00	85·00
146	C	15m. on 40c. red and blue	70·00	£100
160	C	15m. on 50c. brown and lilac	5·50	9·25
161	B	15m. on 50c. blue	7·75	5·00
171	C	30m. on 50c. brown & lilac	£250	£250
162	B	30m. on 1f. red and green	4·50	10·00
172	C	60m. on 50c. brown and lilac	£275	£275
149	C	60m. on 2f. lilac and buff	£110	£120
164	C	60m. on 2f. red and green	7·50	24·00
173	C	150m. on 50c. brown and lilac	£300	£300
165	C	150m. on 5f. blue and buff	10·00	24·00

1925. Surch with value in figures and words and bars over old value.

174	A	1m. on 1c. grey	75	5·00
175	A	2m. on 5c. green	2·50	5·00
176	B	4m. on 10c. red	1·20	5·00
177	A	5m. on 3c. red	1·40	3·75
178	B	6m. on 15c. orange	2·30	5·75
179	B	8m. on 20c. brown	2·20	7·25
180	B	10m. on 25c. blue	2·30	3·00
181	B	15m. on 50c. blue	2·75	3·00
182	C	30m. on 1f. red and green	2·20	4·00
183	C	60m. on 2f. red and green	2·50	5·75
184	C	150m. on 5f. blue and buff	4·00	7·50

1927. Altered key-types. Inscr "Mm" below value.

185	A	3m. orange	3·75	8·50
186	B	15m. blue	2·75	4·25
187	B	20m. mauve	3·00	8·75
188	C	50m. red and green	5·00	10·50
189	C	100m. blue and yellow	3·75	14·50
190	C	250m. green and red	12·00	24·00

1927. "French Sinking Fund" issue. As No. 186 (colour changed) surch +5 Mm Caisse d'Amortissement.

191	B	15m.+5m. orange	2·10	11·50
192	B	15m.+5m. mauve	3·00	11·50
193	B	15m.+5m. brown	2·75	11·50
194	B	15m.+5m. lilac	6·50	17·00

POSTAGE DUE STAMPS

1921. Postage Due stamps of France surch in figures and words.

D174	D 11	2m. on 5c. blue	60·00	70·00
D175	D 11	4m. on 10c. brown	75·00	75·00
D176	D 11	10m. on 30c. red	75·00	75·00
D166	D 11	12m. on 10c. brown	60·00	70·00
D167	D 11	15m. on 5c. blue	60·00	85·00
D177	D 11	15m. on 50c. purple	85·00	85·00
D168	D 11	30m. on 20c. olive	75·00	90·00
D169	D 11	30m. on 50c. purple	£2750	£3000

For 1928 issues, see Alexandria.

Pt. 9

PORTUGAL

A country on the S.W. coast of Europe, a kingdom until 1910, when it became a republic.

1853. 1000 reis = 1 milreis.
1912. 100 centavos = 1 escudo.
2002. 100 cents = 1 euro.

1 Queen Maria II

1853. Various frames. Imperf.

1	1	5r. brown	£4500	£1300
4	1	25r. blue	£1400	29·00
6	1	50r. green	£5500	£1500
8	1	100r. lilac	£47000	£3000

5 King Pedro V

1855. Various frames. Imperf.

18a	5	5r. brown	£650	£120
21	5	25r. blue	£600	22·00
22	5	25r. pink	£450	8·75
13	5	50r. green	£750	£110
15	5	100r. lilac	£1200	£150

9 King Luis

1862. Various frames. Imperf.

24	9	5r. brown	£200	39·00
28	9	10r. yellow	£225	70·00
30	9	25r. pink	£160	7·00
32	9	50r. green	£1100	£120
34	9	100r. lilac	£1300	£140

14 King Luis

1866. With curved value labels. Imperf.

35	14	5r. black	£170	14·50
36	14	10r. yellow	£350	£225
38	14	20r. bistre	£275	£100
39	14	25r. pink	£350	12·00
41	14	50r. green	£375	£110
43	14	80r. orange	£375	£110
45	14	100r. purple	£450	£170
46	14	120r. blue	£475	£110

1867. With curved value labels. Perf.

52		5r. black	£180	65·00
54		10r. yellow	£375	£160
56		20r. bistre	£450	£170
57		25r. pink	£100	11·50
60		50r. green	£375	£160
61		80r. orange	£550	£160
62		100r. lilac	£375	£160
64		120r. blue	£450	£110
67		240r. lilac	£1500	£700

15

1870. With straight value labels. Perf.

69	15	5r. black	80·00	8·25
70	15	10r. yellow	£110	43·00
158	15	10r. green	£200	55·00
74	15	15r. brown	£150	43·00
76	15	20r. bistre	£110	38·00
143	15	20r. red	£500	85·00
80	15	25r. red	43·00	5·50
115	15	50r. green	£225	60·00
117	15	50r. blue	£475	80·00
148	15	80r. orange	£180	28·00
153	15	100r. mauve	£100	16·00
93	15	120r. blue	£425	£110
95	15	150r. blue	£500	£180
155	15	150r. yellow	£190	22·00
99	15	240r. lilac	£2250	£1600
156	15	300r. mauve	£180	45·00
128	15	1000r. black	£450	£140

16 King Luis

17

1880. Various frames for T 16.

185	16	5r. black	43·00	6·00
180	17	25r. grey	£475	44·00
188	16	25r. grey	44·00	5·50
190	16	25r. brown	44·00	5·50
184	16	50r. blue	£475	22·00

19 King Luis

1882. Various frames.

229	19	5r. black	19·00	1·70
231	19	10r. green	55·00	6·00
232	19	20r. red	65·00	26·00
212	19	25r. brown	42·00	3·75
234	19	25r. mauve	44·00	4·50
236	19	50r. blue	65·00	4·50
216	19	500r. black	£650	£425
217	19	500r. mauve	£400	85·00

26 King Carlos

1892

271	26	5r. orange	18·00	3·00
239	26	10r. mauve	42·00	8·25
256	26	15r. brown	42·00	6·00
242	26	20r. lilac	50·00	13·50
275	26	25r. green	60·00	4·25
244	26	50r. blue	50·00	14·50
245	26	75r. red	£100	12·00
262	26	80r. green	£130	80·00
248	26	100r. brown on buff	95·00	9·50
265	26	150r. red on pink	£250	80·00
252	26	200r. blue on blue	£250	65·00
267	26	300r. blue on brown	£275	£110

1892. Optd PROVISORIO.

284	19	5r. black	21·00	10·50
283	19	10r. green	24·00	13·50
297	15	15r. brown	27·00	24·00
290	19	20r. red	60·00	34·00
291	19	25r. mauve	21·00	8·25
292	19	50r. blue	£120	95·00
293	15	80r. orange	£150	£140

1893. Optd 1893 PROVISORIO or surch also.

302	19	5r. black	35·00	32·00
303	19	10r. green	33·00	29·00
304	19	20r. red	55·00	47·00
309	19	20r. on 25r. mauve	75·00	65·00
305	19	25r. mauve	£150	£150
306	19	50r. blue	£150	£150
310	15	50r. on 80r. orange	£180	£150
312	15	75r. on 80r. orange	£100	£100
308	15	80r. orange	£150	£140

32 Prince Henry in his Caravel and Family Motto

1894. 500th Birth Anniv of Prince Henry the Navigator.

314	32	5r. orange	5·50	1·20
315	32	10r. red	5·50	1·20
316	32	15r. brown	14·50	4·50
317	32	20r. lilac	14·50	5·25
318	-	25r. green	13·50	1·70
319	-	50r. blue	43·00	9·00
320	-	75r. red	85·00	19·00
321	-	80r. green	85·00	22·00
322	-	100r. brown on buff	65·00	18·00
323	-	150r. red	£190	44·00
324	-	300r. blue on buff	£225	60·00
325	-	500r. purple	£500	£120
326	-	1000r. black on buff	£850	£180

DESIGNS: 25r. to 100r. Prince Henry directing movements of his fleet; 150r. to 1000r. Prince Henry's studies.

35 St. Anthony's Vision

37 St. Anthony ascending into Heaven

1895. 700th Birth Anniv of St. Anthony (Patron Saint). With a prayer in Latin printed on back.

327	35	2½r. black	6·00	2·00
328	-	5r. orange	6·00	2·00
329	-	10r. mauve	17·00	11·00
330	-	15r. brown	20·00	11·00
331	-	20r. lilac	20·00	12·00
332	-	25r. purple and green	17·00	2·00
333	37	50r. brown and blue	42·00	31·00
334	37	75r. brown and red	70·00	55·00
335	37	80r. brown and green	85·00	80·00
336	37	100r. black and brown	75·00	43·00
337	-	150r. red and bistre	£250	£150
338	-	200r. blue and bistre	£225	£160
339	-	300r. grey and bistre	£325	£225
340	-	500r. brown and green	£650	£475
341	-	1000r. lilac and green	£1100	£600

DESIGNS—HORIZ: 5r. to 25r. St. Anthony preaching to fishes. VERT: 150r. to 1000r. St. Anthony from picture in Academy of Fine Arts, Paris.

39 King Carlos

1895. Numerals of value in red (Nos. 354 and 363) or black (others).

342	39	2½r. grey	50	20
343	39	5r. orange	50	20
344	39	10r. green	70	25
345	39	15r. green	70·00	4·00
346	39	15r. brown	£140	5·50
347	39	20r. lilac	90	55
348	39	25r. green	£100	35
349	39	25r. red	55	20
351	39	50r. blue	75	35
352	39	65r. blue	80	45
353	39	75r. red	£170	6·75
354	39	75r. brown on yellow	2·20	1·00
355	39	80r. mauve	2·75	1·60
356	39	100r. blue on blue	1·30	60

357	39	115r. brown on pink	6·50	4·50
358	39	130r. brown on cream	4·50	2·20
359	39	150r. brown on yellow	£225	34·00
360	39	180r. grey on pink	29·00	13·50
361	39	200r. puple on pink	27·00	3·75
362	39	300r. blue on pink	5·00	3·00
363	39	500r. black on blue	12·50	6·75

40 Departure of Fleet

43 Muse of History

44 Da Gama and Camoens and "Sao Gabriel" (flagship)

1898. 4th Centenary of Discovery of Route to India by Vasco da Gama.

378	40	2½r. green	1·90	55
379	-	5r. red	1·90	55
380	-	10r. purple	12·00	2·30
381	43	25r. green	8·25	65
382	44	50r. blue	17·00	4·25
383	-	75r. brown	65·00	17·00
384	-	100r. brown	50·00	17·00
385	-	150r. brown	£110	44·00

DESIGNS—HORIZ: 5r. Arrival at Calicut; 10r. Embarkation at Rastello; 100r. Flagship "Sao Gabriel"; 150r. Vasco da Gama. VERT: 75r. Archangel Gabriel, Patron Saint of the Expedition.

48 King Manoel II

49

1910

390	48	2½r. lilac	40	35
391	48	5r. black	40	35
392	48	10r. green	70	40
393	48	15r. brown	3·75	2·50
394	48	20r. red	1·40	1·10
395	48	25r. brown	85	25
396	48	50r. blue	2·30	95
397	48	75r. brown	14·00	7·75
398	48	80r. grey	4·25	3·25
399	48	100r. brown on green	16·00	4·00
400	48	200r. green on orange	9·00	6·50
401	48	300r. black on blue	11·50	7·25
402	49	500r. brown and green	21·00	18·00
403	49	1000r. black and blue	48·00	38·00

1910. Optd REPUBLICA.

404	48	2½r. lilac	45	30
405	48	5r. black	45	30
406	48	10r. green	4·50	1·50
407	48	15r. brown	1·60	1·20
408	48	20r. red	6·25	2·75
409	48	25r. brown	1·20	45
410	48	50r. blue	8·75	3·25
411	48	75r. brown	15·00	6·75
412	48	80r. grey	4·50	3·50
413	48	100r. brown on green	2·75	1·40
414	48	200r. green on orange	3·25	3·00
415	48	300r. black on blue	5·75	5·00
416	49	500r. brown and green	16·00	13·50
417	49	1000r. black and blue	40·00	30·00

1911. Optd REPUBLICA or surch also.

441	40	2½r. green	75	30
442	D48	5r. black	1·70	75
443	D48	10r. mauve	2·10	1·20
444	-	15r. on 5r. red (No. 379)	1·30	60
445	D48	20r. orange	7·75	5·00
446	43	25r. green	90	45
447	44	50r. blue	4·50	2·10
448	-	75r. brown (No. 383)	65·00	47·00
449	-	80r. on 150r. (No. 385)	8·00	6·25
450	-	100r. brown (No. 384)	8·00	3·75
451	D48	200r. brown on buff	£180	£110
452	D48	300r. on 50r. grey	£130	65·00
453	D48	500r. on 100r. red on pink	70·00	36·00
454	-	1000r. on 10r. (No. 380)	90·00	55·00

1911. Vasco da Gama stamps of Madeira optd REPUBLICA or surch also.

455		2½r. green	17·00	13·50
456		15r. on 5r. red	3·75	3·75
457		25r. green	7·50	7·25
458		50r. blue	17·00	13·50
459		75r. brown	17·00	8·25
460		80r. on 150r. brown	18·00	16·00
461		100r. brown	60·00	13·50
462		1000r. on 10r. purple	60·00	38·00

56 Ceres

1912

484	56	¼c. brown	95	30
485	56	½c. black	1·00	30
486	56	1c. green	1·90	55
515	56	1c. brown	35	30
488	56	1½c. brown	10·50	4·50
516	56	1½c. green	45	30
490	56	2c. red	10·50	3·75
517	56	2c. yellow	1·80	40
702	56	2c. brown	20	20
492	56	2½c. lilac	90	30
521	56	3c. red	55	40
703	56	3c. blue	20	20
495	56	3½c. green	55	30
523	56	4c. green	35	30
704	56	4c. orange	20	20
497	56	5c. blue	10·50	1·00
705	56	5c. brown	20	20
527	56	6c. purple	1·40	65
706	56	6c. brown	20	20
815	56	6c. red	50	40
500	56	7½c. brown	19·00	3·75
529	56	7½c. blue	55	30
530	56	8c. grey	65	65
531	56	8c. green	1·10	70
532	56	8c. orange	1·20	65
503	56	10c. brown	25·00	1·60
707	56	10c. red	20	20
504	56	12c. blue	2·20	1·20
534	56	12c. green	85	55
535	56	13½c. blue	2·20	1·60
481	56	14c. blue on yellow	3·50	2·40
536	56	14c. purple	1·00	85
505	56	15c. brown	3·25	1·30
708	56	15c. black	45	20
709	56	16c. blue	45	20
474	56	20c. brown on green	26·00	2·75
475	56	20c. brown on buff	27·00	7·25
539	56	20c. brown	1·00	70
540	56	20c. green	85	55
541	56	20c. grey	1·20	65
542	56	24c. blue	1·00	65
543	56	25c. pink	85	45
710	56	25c. grey	45	20
819	56	25c. green	95	45
476	56	30c. brown on pink	£190	18·00
477	56	30c. brown on yellow	18·00	3·50
545	56	30c. brown	85	50
820	56	32c. green	95	45
548	56	36c. red	3·00	65
549	56	40c. blue	2·10	1·10
550	56	40c. brown	1·40	55
478	56	50c. orange on orange	26·00	2·20
712	56	40c. green	80	20
713	56	48c. pink	2·00	1·40
553	56	50c. yellow	3·00	1·10
824	56	50c. red	3·50	1·20
554	56	60c. blue	2·75	1·10
715	56	64c. blue	3·25	3·00
826	56	75c. red	3·00	1·30
510	56	80c. pink	2·75	1·70
558	56	80c. lilac	2·40	90
827	56	80c. green	3·00	1·30
559	56	90c. blue	3·00	1·10
717	56	96c. red	4·25	1·90
480	56	1e. green on blue	29·00	2·20
561	56	1e. lilac	6·75	3·50
565	56	1e. blue	7·50	2·20
566	56	1e. purple	7·00	2·50
829	56	1e. red	8·25	1·30
562	56	1e.10 brown	6·75	3·25
563	56	1e.20 green	3·75	2·10
830	56	1e.20 brown	6·00	1·40
831	56	1e.25 blue	5·50	1·40
568	56	1e.50 lilac	30·00	7·75
720	56	1e.60 blue	4·50	75
721	56	2e. green	28·00	1·60
833	56	2e. mauve	36·00	10·50
572	56	2e.40 green	£425	£250
573	56	3e. pink	£425	£225
722	56	3e.20 green	12·00	1·60
723	56	4e.50 yellow	12·00	1·60
575	56	5e. green	90·00	16·00
724	56	5e. brown	£150	5·75
725	56	10e. red	17·00	3·25
577	56	20e. blue	£700	£300

60 Presidents of Portugal and Brazil and Admiral Gago Coutinho, Sacadura Cabral and Fairey IIID

1923. Portugal–Brazil Trans-Atlantic Flight.

578	60	1c. brown	20	1·10
579	60	2c. orange	20	1·10
580	60	3c. blue	20	1·10
581	60	4c. green	20	1·10
582	60	5c. brown	20	1·10
583	60	10c. brown	20	1·10
584	60	15c. black	20	1·10
585	60	20c. green	20	1·10
586	60	25c. red	20	1·10
587	60	30c. brown	1·00	2·75
588	60	40c. brown	70	1·10
589	60	50c. yellow	60	1·30
590	60	75c. purple	60	1·40
591	60	1e. blue	60	2·75
592	60	1e.50 grey	1·10	3·50
593	60	2e. green	1·30	8·75

62 Camoens at Ceuta

63 Saving the "Lusiad"

1924. 400th Birth Anniv of Camoens (poet). Value in black.

600	62	2c. blue	35	35
601	62	3c. orange	35	35
602	62	4c. grey	35	35
603	62	5c. green	35	35
604	62	6c. red	35	35
605	63	8c. brown	35	35
606	63	10c. violet	35	35
607	63	15c. green	35	35
608	63	16c. purple	40	40
609	63	20c. orange	50	40
610	-	25c. violet	50	40
611	-	30c. brown	50	40
612	-	32c. green	1·40	1·40
613	-	40c. blue	50	45
614	-	48c. red	2·10	2·30
615	-	50c. red	2·50	1·50
616	-	64c. green	2·50	1·50
617	-	75c. lilac	2·75	1·50
618	-	80c. brown	1·90	1·50
619	-	96c. red	1·90	1·50
620	-	1e. turquoise	1·60	1·20
621	-	1e.20 brown	9·25	6·75
622	-	1e.50 red	2·50	1·50
623	-	1e.60 blue	2·50	1·50
624	-	2e. green	9·25	6·25
625	-	2e.40 green on green	8·00	4·25
626	-	3e. blue on blue	2·75	1·40
627	-	3e.20 black on turquoise	2·75	1·30
628	-	4e.50 black on yellow	8·50	5·50
629	-	10e. brown on pink	15·00	11·00
630	-	20e. violet on mauve	18·00	11·00

DESIGNS—VERT: 25c. to 48c. Luis de Camoens; 50c. to 96c. 1st Edition of "Lusiad"; 20e. Monument to Camoens. HORIZ: 1e. to 2e. Death of Camoens; 2e.40 to 10e. Tomb of Camoens.

65 Branco's House at S. Miguel de Seide

67 Camilo Castelo Branco

1925. Birth Centenary of Camilo Castelo Branco (novelist). Value in black.

631	65	2c. orange	40	25
632	65	3c. green	40	25
633	65	4c. blue	40	25
634	65	5c. red	40	25
635	65	6c. purple	40	25
636	65	8c. brown	40	25
637	A	10c. blue	40	25
638	67	15c. green	45	35
639	A	16c. orange	55	50
640	A	20c. violet	55	50
641	67	25c. red	55	50
642	A	30c. bistre	55	50
643	A	32c. green	1·70	1·50
644	67	40c. black and green	1·20	95
645	A	48c. red	4·50	5·00
646	B	50c. green	1·20	95
647	B	64c. brown	4·75	5·00
648	B	75c. grey	1·40	1·00
649	67	80c. brown	1·40	1·10
650	B	96c. red	2·40	2·30
651	B	1e. lilac	2·20	2·30
652	B	1e.20 green	2·50	2·30
653	C	1e.50 blue on blue	46·00	22·00
654	67	1e.60 blue	9·00	5·75
655	C	2e. green on green	10·50	6·25
656	C	2e.40 red on orange	£100	50·00
657	C	3e. red on blue	£130	65·00
658	C	3e.20 black on green	60·00	50·00
659	67	4e.50 black and red	25·00	5·75
660	C	10e. brown on buff	26·00	6·00
661	D	20e. black on orange	27·00	6·00

DESIGNS—HORIZ: A, Branco's study. VERT: B, Teresa de Albuquerque; C, Mariana and Joao da Cruz; D, Simao de Botelho. Types B/D shows characters from Branco's "Amor de Peredicao".

76 Afonso I, first King of Portugal, 1140

77 Battle of Aljubarrota

1926. 1st Independence issue. Dated 1926. Centres in black.

671	76	2c. orange	40	40
672	-	3c. blue	40	40
673	76	4c. green	40	40
674	-	5c. brown	40	40
675	76	6c. orange	40	40
676	-	15c. green	40	40
677	76	16c. blue	1·40	1·10
678	77	20c. violet	1·40	1·10
679	-	25c. red	1·40	1·10
680	77	32c. green	1·50	1·30
681	-	40c. brown	1·00	75
682	-	46c. red	6·50	5·00
683	-	50c. bistre	6·50	5·00
684	-	64c. green	9·00	6·50
685	-	75c. brown	9·00	6·25
686	-	96c. red	13·50	10·50
687	-	1e. violet	13·50	11·00
688	77	1e.60 blue	18·00	15·00
689	-	3e. purple	50·00	43·00
690	-	4e.50 green	70·00	55·00
691	77	10e. red	£110	85·00

DESIGNS—VERT: 25, 40, 50, 75c. Philippa de Vilhena arms her sons; 64c., 1e. Don Joao IV, 1640; 96c., 3e., 4e.50, Independence Monument, Lisbon. HORIZ: 3, 5, 15, 46c. Monastery of D. Joao I.

1926. 1st Independence issue surch. Centres in black.

692	2c. on 5c. brown	2·00	1·80
693	2c. on 46c. red	2·00	1·80
694	2c. on 64c. green	2·30	2·10
695	3c. on 75c. brown	2·30	2·10
696	3c. on 96c. red	3·50	2·75
697	3c. on 1e. violet	3·00	2·50
698	4c. on 1e.60 blue	23·00	17·00
699	4c. on 3e. purple	8·50	7·00
700	6c. on 4e.50 green	8·50	7·00
701	6c. on 10e. red	8·75	7·00

80 Goncalo Mendes da Maia

1927. 2nd Independence issue. Dated 1927. Centres in black.

726	**80**	2c. brown	40	20
727	-	3c. blue	40	20
728	**80**	4c. orange	40	20
729	-	5c. brown	40	20
730	-	6c. brown	40	20
731	-	15c. brown	90	65
732	-	16c. blue	1·90	80
733	**80**	25c. grey	2·10	1·50
734	-	32c. green	4·75	2·40
735	-	40c. green	1·30	95
736	**80**	48c. red	20·00	16·00
737	-	80c. violet	14·50	11·00
738	-	96c. red	30·00	22·00
739	-	1e.60 blue	31·00	23·00
740	-	4e.50 brown	44·00	34·00

DESIGNS—HORIZ: 3, 15, 80c. Gulmaraes Castle; 6, 32c. Battle of Montijo. VERT: 5, 16c., 1e.50, Joao das Regras; 40, 96c. Brites de Aimelda; 4e.50, J. P. Ribeiro.

1928. Surch.

742	**56**	4c. on 8c. orange	85	50
743	**56**	4c. on 30c. brown	85	50
744	**56**	10c. on ¼c. brown	85	50
745	**56**	10c. on ½c. black	1·10	65
746	**56**	10c. on 1c. brown	1·10	65
747	**56**	10c. on 4c. green	85	55
748	**56**	10c. on 4c. orange	85	55
749	**56**	10c. on 5c. brown	85	55
751	**56**	15c. on 16c. blue	2·10	1·20
752	**56**	15c. on 20c. brown	65·00	50·00
753	**56**	15c. on 20c. grey	85	50
754	**56**	15c. on 24c. blue	4·00	2·50
755	**56**	15c. on 25c. pink	85	50
756	**56**	15c. on 25c. grey	85	50
757	**56**	16c. on 32c. green	1·60	1·20
758	**56**	40c. on 2c. yellow	85	50
760	**56**	40c. on 2c. brown	85	50
761	**56**	40c. on 3c. blue	85	55
762	**56**	40c. on 50c. yellow	85	50
763	**56**	40c. on 60c. blue	1·60	1·10
764	**56**	40c. on 64c. blue	1·60	1·20
765	**56**	40c. on 75c. pink	1·70	1·40
766	**56**	40c. on 80c. lilac	1·20	80
767	**56**	40c. on 90c. blue	8·25	5·00
768	**56**	40c. on 1e. grey	1·60	1·20
769	**56**	40c. on 1e.10 brown	1·60	1·20
770	**56**	80c. on 6c. purple	1·60	1·10
771	**56**	80c. on 6c. brown	1·60	1·10
772	**56**	80c. on 48c. pink	2·30	1·70
773	**56**	80c. on 1e.50 lilac	3·50	1·90
774	**56**	96c. on 1e.20 green	7·00	4·00
775	**56**	96c. on 1e.20 buff	6·75	4·50
777	**56**	1e.60 on 2e. green	75·00	50·00
778	**56**	1e.60 on 3e.20 green	19·00	11·50
779	**56**	1e.60 on 20e. blue	27·00	15·00

84 Storming of Santarem

1928. 3rd Independence issue. Dated 1928. Centres in black.

780	-	2c. blue	60	35
781	**84**	3c. green	60	35
782	-	4c. red	60	35
783	-	5c. green	60	35
784	-	6c. brown	60	35
785	**84**	15c. grey	1·20	1·10
786	-	16c. purple	1·20	1·10
787	-	25c. blue	1·20	1·10
788	-	32c. green	6·25	5·75
789	-	40c. brown	1·20	1·10
790	-	50c. red	18·00	8·50
791	**84**	80c. grey	18·00	11·00
792	-	96c. red	35·00	23·00
793	-	1e. mauve	60·00	44·00
794	-	1e.60 blue	23·00	17·00
795	-	4e.50 yellow	24·00	22·00

DESIGNS—VERT: 2, 25c., 1e.60, G. Paes; 6, 32, 96c. Joana de Gouveia; 4e.50, Matias de Albuquerque. HORIZ: 4, 16, 50c. Battle of Rolica; 5, 40c., 1e. Battle of Atoleiros.

1929. Optd Revalidado.

805	**56**	10c. red	85	50
806	**56**	15c. black	85	50
807	**56**	40c. brown	1·20	90
808	**56**	40c. green	1·10	65
810	**56**	96c. red	10·50	6·75
811	**56**	1e.60 blue	43·00	27·00

1929. Telegraph stamp surch CORREIO 1$60 and bars.

812	1e.60 on 5c. brown	27·00	17·00

88 Camoens' Poem "Lusiad"

1931

835	**88**	4c. brown	45	20
836	**88**	5c. brown	45	20
837	**88**	6c. grey	45	20
838	**88**	10c. mauve	45	30
839	**88**	15c. black	45	30
840	**88**	16c. blue	2·30	1·00
841	**88**	25c. green	5·75	55
841a	**88**	25c. blue	6·75	65
841b	**88**	30c. green	3·50	65
842	**88**	40c. red	11·50	20
843	**88**	48c. brown	2·30	1·60
844	**88**	50c. brown	55	20
845	**88**	75c. red	9·75	1·80
846	**88**	80c. green	80	25
846a	**88**	95c. red	31·00	10·00
847	**88**	1e. purple	60·00	25
848	**88**	1e.20 green	4·00	1·60
849	**88**	1e.25 blue	3·75	35
849a	**88**	1e.60 blue	60·00	6·75
849b	**88**	1e.75 blue	1·20	35
850	**88**	2e. mauve	1·40	35
851	**88**	4e.50 orange	3·00	40
852	**88**	5e. green	3·00	40

89 St. Anthony's Birthplace

1931. 700th Death Anniv of St. Anthony.

853	**89**	15c. purple	1·60	45
854	-	25c. myrtle and green	1·80	45
855	-	40c. brown and buff	1·60	45
856	-	75c. pink	55·00	22·00
857	-	1e.25 grey and blue	£100	46·00
858	-	4e.50 purple and mauve	55·00	5·50

DESIGNS—VERT: 25c. Saint's baptismal font; 40c. Lisbon Cathedral; 75c. St. Anthony; 1e.25, Santa Cruz Cathedral, Coimbra. HORIZ: 4e.50, Saint's tomb, Padua.

90 Don Nuno Alvares Pereira

1931. 5th Death Centenary of Pereira.

859	**90**	15c. black	1·90	1·70
860	**90**	25c. green and black	10·00	1·70
861	**90**	40c. orange	5·25	95
862	**90**	75c. red	44·00	38·00
863	**90**	1e.25 light blue and blue	50·00	33·00
864	**90**	4e.50 green and brown	£275	85·00

1933. Pereira issue of 1931 surch.

865	15c. on 40c. orange	1·30	75
866	40c. on 15c. black	6·25	3·50
867	40c. on 25c. green & black	1·60	1·20
868	40c. on 75c. red	13·50	8·00
869	40c. on 1e.25 light blue and blue	13·50	6·00
870	40c. on 4e.50 green and brown	13·50	6·00

1933. St. Anthony issue of 1931 surch.

871	-	15c. on 40c. brown and buff	1·70	75
872	**89**	40c. on 15c. purple	3·50	1·60
873	-	40c. on 25c. myrtle and green	3·00	75
874	-	40c. on 75c. pink	13·50	8·00
875	-	40c. on 1e.25 grey and blue	13·50	8·00
876	-	40c. on 4e.50 purple and mauve	13·50	8·00

94 President Carmona

1934

877	**94**	40c. violet	35·00	50

95

1934. Colonial Exhibition.

878	**95**	25c. brown	7·50	1·90
879	**95**	40c. red	36·00	60
880	**95**	1e.60 blue	75·00	20·00

96 Queen Maria

1935. 1st Portuguese Philatelic Exhibition.

881	**96**	40c. red	2·40	40

97 Temple of Diana at Evora

98 Prince Henry the Navigator

99 "All for the Nation"

100 Coimbra Cathedral

1935

882	**97**	4c. black	85	30
883	**97**	5c. blue	90	30
884	**97**	6c. brown	1·40	50
885	**98**	10c. green	13·50	30
886	**98**	15c. red	55	30
887	**99**	25c. blue	12·50	65
888	**99**	40c. brown	4·25	20
889	**99**	1e. red	20·00	75
890	**100**	1e.75 blue	£140	1·90
890a	**99**	10e. grey	46·00	4·50
890b	**99**	20e. blue	60·00	3·25

102 Shield and Propeller

1937. Air.

891	**102**	1e.50 blue	1·40	45
892	**102**	1e.75 red	2·10	50
893	**102**	2e.50 red	2·20	50
893a	**102**	3e. blue	31·00	17·00
893b	**102**	4e. green	40·00	25·00
894	**102**	5e. red	3·50	1·70
895	**102**	10e. purple	6·50	1·80
895a	**102**	15e. orange	30·00	11·00
896	**102**	20e. brown	17·00	4·00
896a	**102**	50e. purple	£325	£120

103 Symbol of Medicine

1937. Centenary of Medical and Surgical Colleges at Lisbon and Oporto.

897	**103**	25c. blue	19·00	1·40

104 Gil Vicente

1937. 400th Death Anniv of Gil Vicente (poet).

898	**104**	40c. brown	36·00	30
899	**104**	1e. red	4·50	30

106 Grapes

1938. Wine and Raisin Congress.

900	**106**	15c. violet	2·50	95
901	**106**	25c. brown	5·00	2·40
902	**106**	40c. mauve	17·00	50
903	**106**	1e.75 blue	55·00	40·00

107 Cross of Avis

1940. Portuguese Legion.

904	**107**	5c. buff	80	35
905	**107**	10c. violet	80	35
906	**107**	15c. blue	80	35
907	**107**	25c. brown	44·00	1·50
908	**107**	40c. green	70·00	60
909	**107**	80c. green	3·75	1·00
910	**107**	1e. red	£100	5·75
911	**107**	1e.75 blue	17·00	4·00
MS911a		155×170 mm. Nos. 904/11 (sold at 5e.50)	£700	£1200

109 Portuguese World Exhibition

1940. Portuguese Centenaries.

912	**109**	10c. purple	45	35
913	-	15c. blue	45	35
914	-	25c. green	2·20	45
915	-	35c. green	2·00	60
916	-	40c. brown	4·75	30
917	**109**	80c. purple	9·75	55
918	-	1e. red	23·00	2·40
919	-	1e.75 blue	13·50	4·00
MS919a		160×229 mm. Nos. 912/9 (sold at 10e.)	£325	£500

DESIGNS—VERT: 15, 35c. Statue of King Joao IV; 25c., 1e. Monument of Discoveries, Belem; 40c., 1e.75, King Afonso Henriques.

113 Sir Rowland Hill

1940. Centenary of First Adhesive Postage Stamps.

920	**113**	15c. purple	50	25
921	**113**	25c. red	50	25
922	**113**	35c. green	50	25
923	**113**	40c. purple	90	25
924	**113**	50c. green	36·00	6·25
925	**113**	80c. blue	3·50	1·80
926	**113**	1e. red	43·00	5·75
927	**113**	1e.75 blue	9·75	5·50
MS928 160×152 mm. Nos. 920/7 (sold at 10e.)			£150	£300

114 Fish-woman of Nazare

1941. Costumes.

932	**114**	4c. green	40	30
933	-	5c. brown	40	30
934	-	10c. purple	5·50	1·70
935	-	15c. green	40	40
936	-	25c. purple	4·50	90
937	-	40c. green	40	30
938	-	80c. blue	7·25	3·25
939	-	1e. red	21·00	2·50
940	-	1e.75 blue	22·00	7·25
941	-	2e. orange	85·00	38·00
MS941a 163×146 mm. Nos. 932/41 (sold at 10e.)			£250	£250

DESIGNS: 5c. Woman from Coimbra; 10c. Vine-grower of Saloio; 15c. Fish-woman of Lisbon; 25c. Woman of Olhao; 40c. Woman of Aveiro; 80c. Shepherdess of Madeira; 1e. Spinner of Viana do Castelo; 1e.75, Horsebreeder of Ribatejo; 2e. Reaper of Alentejo.

115 Caravel

1943

942	**115**	5c. black	35	20
943	**115**	10c. brown	35	20
944	**115**	15c. grey	35	20
945	**115**	20c. violet	35	20
946	**115**	30c. purple	35	20
947	**115**	35c. green	40	20
948	**115**	50c. purple	40	20
948a	**115**	80c. green	6·75	60
949	**115**	1e. red	14·00	20
949a	**115**	1e. lilac	4·25	35
949b	**115**	1e.20 red	6·75	45
949c	**115**	1e.50 green	55·00	55
950	**115**	1e.75 blue	40·00	20
950a	**115**	1e.80 orange	60·00	5·25
951	**115**	2e. brown	3·00	20
951a	**115**	2e. blue	8·75	65
952	**115**	2e.50 red	4·75	20
953	**115**	3e.50 blue	20·00	70
953a	**115**	4e. orange	90·00	3·75
954	**115**	5e. red	2·75	35
954a	**115**	6e. green	£170	6·00
954b	**115**	7e.50 green	60·00	5·50
955	**115**	10e. grey	5·00	35
956	**115**	15e. green	55·00	1·60
957	**115**	20e. green	£200	95
958	**115**	50e. red	£550	1·50

116 Labourer

1943. 1st Agricultural Science Congress.

959	**116**	10c. blue	1·50	50
960	**116**	50c. red	2·40	55

117 Mounted Postal Courier

1944. 3rd National Philatelic Exhibition, Lisbon.

961	**117**	10c. brown	50	25
962	**117**	50c. violet	50	25
963	**117**	1e. red	6·00	1·10
964	**117**	1e.75 blue	6·00	2·50
MS964a 82×121 mm. Nos. 961/4 (sold at 7e.50)			70·00	£350

118 Felix Avellar Brotero

1944. Birth Bicentenary of Avellar Brotero (botanist).

965	**118**	10c. brown	45	25
966	-	50c. green	2·20	25
967	-	1e. red	14·50	2·20
968	**118**	1e.75 blue	11·00	4·50
MS968a 144×195 mm. Nos. 965/8 (sold at 7e.50)			85·00	£200

DESIGN: 50c., 1e. Brotero's statue, Coimbra.

120 Vasco da Gama

1945. Portuguese Navigators.

969	-	10c. brown	45	25
970	-	30c. orange	45	25
971	-	35c. green	95	40
972	**120**	50c. green	2·75	45
973	-	1e. red	7·25	1·10
974	-	1e.75 blue	9·25	3·25
975	-	2e. black	11·00	3·75
976	-	3e.50 red	22·00	6·50
MS976a 167×173 mm. Nos. 969/76 (sold at 15e.)			75·00	£200

PORTRAITS: 10c. Gil Eanes; 30c. Joao Goncalves Zarco; 35c. Bartolomeu Dias; 1e. Pedro Alvares Cabral; 1e.75, Fernao de Magalhaes (Magellan); 2e. Frey Goncalo Velho; 3e.50, Diogo Cao.

121 President Carmona

1945

977	**121**	10c. violet	60	35
978	**121**	30c. brown	60	35
979	**121**	35c. green	55	35
980	**121**	50c. green	1·20	35
981	**121**	1e. red	24·00	2·20
982	**121**	1e.75 blue	20·00	6·00
983	**121**	2e. purple	£120	8·00
984	**121**	3e.50 grey	80·00	12·00
MS984a 136×98 mm. Nos. 977/84 (sold at 15e.)			£325	£350

122

1945. Naval School Centenary.

985	**122**	10c. brown	65	25
986	**122**	50c. green	85	25
987	**122**	1e. red	7·25	1·40
988	**122**	1e.75 blue	7·75	4·00
MS988a 115×134 mm. Nos. 985/8 (sold at 7e.50)			75·00	£200

123 Almourol Castle

1946. Portuguese Castles.

989	-	10c. purple	40	35
990	-	30c. brown	65	35
991	-	35c. green	90	35
992	-	50c. grey	1·50	35
993	**123**	1e. red	50·00	1·90
994	-	1e.75 blue	32·00	3·75
995	-	2e. green	£100	6·50
996	-	3e.50 brown	46·00	8·50
MS996a 135×102 mm. 1e.75 grey-blue on buff (block of 4) (sold at 12e.50)			£275	£450

DESIGNS: Castles at Silves (10c.); Leiria (30c.); Feira (35c.); Guimaraes (50c.); Lisbon (1e.75); Braganza (2e.) and Ourem (3e.50).

124 "Decree Founding National Bank"

1946. Centenary of Bank of Portugal.

997	**124**	50c. blue	1·20	40
MS997a 156×144 mm. No. 997 (block of four) (sold at 7e.50)			£250	£350

125 Madonna and Child

1946. Tercentenary of Proclamation of St. Mary of Castile as Patron Saint of Portugal.

998	**125**	30c. grey	75	35
999	**125**	50c. green	50	35
1000	**125**	1e. red	5·00	1·70
1001	**125**	1e.75 blue	8·00	3·25
MS1001a 108×158 mm. Nos. 998/1001 on grey paper (sold at 7e.50)			90·00	£200

126 Caramulo Shepherdess

1947. Regional Costumes.

1002	**126**	10c. mauve	40	25
1003	-	30c. red	40	25
1004	-	35c. green	80	25
1005	-	50c. brown	1·30	25
1006	-	1e. red	29·00	1·00
1007	-	1e.75 blue	31·00	6·25
1008	-	2e. blue	£110	7·25
1009	-	3e.50 green	75·00	12·00
MS1009a 135×98 mm. Nos. 1002/9 (sold at 15e.)			£325	£400

COSTUMES: 30c. Malpique timbrel player; 35c. Monsanto flautist; 50c. Woman of Avintes; 1e. Maia field labourer; 1e.75, Woman of Algarve; 2e. Miranda do Douro bastonet player; 3e.50, Woman of the Azores.

127 Surrender of the Keys of Lisbon

1947. 800th Anniv of Recapture of Lisbon from the Moors.

1010	**127**	5c. green	40	30
1011	**127**	20c. red	65	30
1012	**127**	50c. violet	95	30
1013	**127**	1e.75 blue	11·50	7·50
1014	**127**	2e.50 brown	16·00	9·50
1015	**127**	3e.50 black	31·00	20·00

128 St. Joao de Brito

1948. Birth Tercentenary of St. Joao de Brito.

1016	**128**	30c. green	40	35
1017	-	50c. brown	40	35
1018	**128**	1e. red	16·00	2·50
1019	-	1e.75 blue	20·00	4·25

DESIGN: 50c., 1e.75, St. Joao de Brito (different).

130 "Architecture and Engineering"

1948. Exhibition of Public Works and National Congress of Engineering and Architecture.

1020	**130**	50c. purple	1·60	45

131 King Joao I

1949. Portraits.

1021	**131**	10c. violet and buff	75	35
1022	-	30c. green and buff	75	35
1023	-	35c. green and olive	1·50	35
1024	-	50c. blue and light blue	2·40	35
1025	-	1e. lake and red	2·50	35
1026	-	1e.75 black and grey	45·00	18·00
1027	-	2e. blue and light blue	28·00	3·00
1028	-	3e.50 chocolate & brown	90·00	33·00
MS1028a 136×98 mm. Nos. 1021/8 (sold for 15e.)			£100	£120

PORTRAITS: 30c. Queen Philippa; 35c. Prince Fernando; 50c. Prince Henry the Navigator; 1e. Nun Alvares; 1e.75, Joao da Regras; 2e. Fernao Lopes; 3e.50, Afonso Domingues.

132 Statue of Angel

1949. 16th Congress of the History of Art.

1029	**132**	1e. red	18·00	30
1030	**132**	5e. brown	4·75	55

133 Hands and Letter

1949. 75th Anniv of U.P.U.

1031	**133**	1e. lilac	55	25
1032	**133**	2e. blue	1·60	35
1033	**133**	2e.50 green	9·25	1·60
1034	**133**	4e. brown	25·00	6·00

134 Our Lady of Fatima

1950. Holy Year.

1035	**134**	50c. green	1·10	40
1036	**134**	1e. brown	5·00	45
1037	**134**	2e. blue	10·50	3·25
1038	**134**	5e. lilac	£160	44·00

135 Saint and Invalid

1950. 400th Death Anniv of San Juan de Dios.

1039	**135**	20c. violet	75	35
1040	**135**	50c. red	1·20	45
1041	**135**	1e. green	2·75	60
1042	**135**	1e.50 orange	35·00	5·25
1043	**135**	2e. blue	28·00	4·00
1044	**135**	4e. brown	80·00	12·50

136 G. Junqueiro

1951. Birth Centenary of Junqueiro (poet).

1045	**136**	50c. brown	9·00	55
1046	**136**	1e. blue	2·75	50

137 Fisherman with Meagre

1951. Fisheries Congress.

1047	**137**	50c. green on buff	8·50	85
1048	**137**	1e. purple on buff	2·00	20

138 Dove and Olive Branch

1951. Termination of Holy Year.

1049	**138**	20c. brown and buff	85	40
1050	**138**	90c. green and yellow	20·00	2·75
1051	-	1e. purple and pink	18·00	45
1052	-	2e.30 green and blue	22·00	3·25

PORTRAIT: 1e., 2e.30, Pope Pius XII.

139 15th century Colonists

1951. 500th Anniv of Colonization of Terceira, Azores.

1053	**139**	50c. blue on flesh	5·50	75
1054	**139**	1e. brown on buff	2·75	70

140 Revolutionaries

1951. 25th Anniv of National Revolution.

1055	**140**	1e. brown	15·00	40
1056	**140**	2e.30 blue	11·50	2·00

141 Coach of King Joao VI

1952. National Coach Museum.

1057	-	10c. purple	40	30
1058	**141**	20c. green	40	30
1059	-	50c. green	1·20	30
1060	-	90c. green	4·75	2·40
1061	-	1e. orange	2·10	35
1062	-	1e.40 pink	11·00	6·50
1063	**141**	1e.50 brown	9·75	3·50
1064	-	2e.30 blue	6·25	3·25

DESIGNS (coaches of): 10, 90c. King Felippe II; 50c., 1e.40, Papal Nuncio to Joao V; 1e., 2e.30, King Jose.

142 "N.A.T.O."

1952. 3rd Anniv of N.A.T.O.

1065	**142**	1e. green and deep green	16·00	65
1066	**142**	3e.50 grey and blue	£500	34·00

143 Hockey Players

1952. 8th World Roller-skating Hockey Championship.

1067	**143**	1e. black and blue	6·00	35
1068	**143**	3e.50 black and brown	10·50	3·50

144 Teixeira

1952. Birth Centenary of Prof. Gomes Teixeira (mathematician).

1069	**144**	1e. mauve and pink	1·50	35
1070	**144**	2e.30 deep blue and blue	11·50	6·50

145 Marshal Carmona Bridge

1952. Centenary of Ministry of Public Works.

1071	**145**	1e. brown on stone	1·20	40
1072	-	1e.40 lilac on stone	20·00	7·25
1073	-	2e. green on stone	12·50	4·50
1074	-	3e.50 blue on stone	21·00	6·25

DESIGNS: 1e.40, 28th May Stadium, Braga; 2e. Coimbra University; 3e.50, Salazar Barrage.

146 St. Francis Xavier

1952. 4th Death Centenary of St. Francis Xavier.

1075	**146**	1e. blue	1·00	40
1076	**146**	2e. purple	2·75	80
1077	**146**	3e.50 blue	38·00	18·00
1078	**146**	5e. lilac	75·00	6·50

147 Medieval Knight

1953

1079	**147**	5c. green on yellow	40	20
1080	**147**	10c. grey on pink	40	20
1081	**147**	20c. orange on yellow	40	20
1081a	**147**	30c. purple on buff	50	20
1082	**147**	50c. black	40	20
1083	**147**	90c. green on yellow	29·00	1·10
1084	**147**	1e. brown on pink	70	20
1085	**147**	1e.40 red	29·00	1·60
1086	**147**	1e.50 red on yellow	90	20
1087	**147**	2e. black	1·40	20
1088	**147**	2e.30 blue	45·00	1·30
1089	**147**	2e.50 black on pink	2·50	25
1089a	**147**	2e.50 green on yellow	2·50	25
1090	**147**	5e. purple on yellow	2·50	25
1091	**147**	10e. blue on yellow	11·00	35
1092	**147**	20e. brown on yellow	22·00	50
1093	**147**	50e. lilac	15·00	70

148 St. Martin of Dume

1953. 14th Centenary of Landing of St. Martin of Dume on Iberian Peninsula.

1094	**148**	1e. black and grey	2·50	35
1095	**148**	3e.50 brown and yellow	20·00	8·25

149 G. Gomes Fernandes

1953. Birth Centenary of Fernandes (fire-brigade chief).

1096	**149**	1e. purple and cream	1·50	35
1097	**149**	2e.30 blue and cream	20·00	8·75

150 Club Emblems, 1903 and 1953

1953. 50th Anniv of Portuguese Automobile Club.

1098	**150**	1e. deep green and green	1·20	40
1099	**150**	3e.50 brown and buff	21·00	8·50

151 Princess St. Joan

1953. 5th Centenary of Birth of Princess St. Joan.

1100	**151**	1e. black and green	2·75	35
1101	**151**	3e.50 deep blue and blue	21·00	10·00

152 Queen Maria II

1953. Centenary of First Portuguese Stamps. Bottom panel in gold.

1102	**152**	50c. red	40	35
1103	**152**	1e. brown	40	35
1104	**152**	1e.40 purple	4·00	1·40
1105	**152**	2e.30 blue	7·50	3·25
1106	**152**	3e.50 blue	7·50	3·25
1107	**152**	4e.50 green	13·00	2·40
1108	**152**	5e. green	15·00	2·10
1109	**152**	20e. violet	£110	12·50

153

1954. 150th Anniv of Trade Secretariat.

1110	**153**	1e. blue and light blue	1·10	25
1111	**153**	1e.50 brown and buff	4·75	1·00

154

1954. People's Education Plan.

1112	**154**	50c. blue and light blue	60	25
1113	**154**	1e. red and pink	60	25
1114	**154**	2e. deep green and green	55·00	1·70
1115	**154**	2e.50 brown and light brown	47·00	2·40

155 Cadet and College Banner

1954. 150th Anniv of Military College.

1116	**155**	1e. brown and green	2·50	35
1117	**155**	3e.50 blue and green	11·00	4·25

156 Father Manuel da Nobrega

1954. 400th Anniv of Sao Paulo.

1118	**156**	1e. brown	1·20	40
1119	**156**	2e.30 blue	95·00	37·00
1120	**156**	3e.50 green	25·00	4·50
1121	**156**	5e. green	80·00	7·25

157 King Sancho I, 1154–1211

1955. Portuguese Kings.

No.	Type	Description	Unused	Used
1122	-	10c. purple	45	35
1123	157	20c. green	45	35
1124	-	50c. blue	55	35
1125	-	90c. green	8·00	2·20
1126	-	1e. brown	2·10	40
1127	-	1e.40 red	16·00	5·50
1128	-	1e.50 green	5·25	1·70
1129	-	2e. red	18·00	4·50
1130	-	2e.30 blue	14·50	4·25

KINGS: 10c. Afonso I; 50c. Afonso II; 90c. Sancho II; 1e. Afonso III; 1e.40, Diniz; 1e.50, Afonso IV; 2e. Pedro I; 2e.30, Fernando.

158 Telegraph Poles

1955. Centenary of Electric Telegraph System in Portugal.

No.	Type	Description	Unused	Used
1131	158	1e. red and brown	1·10	35
1132	158	2e.30 blue and green	42·00	6·25
1133	158	3e.50 green and yellow	41·00	4·75

159 A. J. Ferreira da Silva

1956. Birth Centenary of Ferreira da Silva (teacher).

No.	Type	Description	Unused	Used
1134	159	1e. deep blue, blue and azure	95	35
1135	159	2e.30 deep green, emerald and green	25·00	7·75

160 Steam Locomotive, 1856

1956. Centenary of Portuguese Railways.

No.	Type	Description	Unused	Used
1136	160	1e. olive and green	85	35
1137	-	1e.50 blue and green	19·00	80
1138	-	2e. brown and bistre	50·00	2·20
1139	160	2e.50 brown and deep brown	70·00	3·00

DESIGN: 1e.50, 2e. Class 2500 electric locomotive, 1956.

161 Madonna and Child

1956. Mothers' Day.

No.	Type	Description	Unused	Used
1140	161	1e. sage and green	85	20
1141	161	1e.50 lt brown and brown	2·10	40

162 Almeida Garrett (after Barata Feyo)

1957. Almeida Garrett (writer) Commem.

No.	Type	Description	Unused	Used
1142	162	1e. brown	1·20	35
1143	162	2e.30 lilac	70·00	17·00
1144	162	3e.50 green	24·00	1·80
1145	162	5e. red	£130	16·00

163 Cesario Verde

1957. Cesario Verde (poet) Commem.

No.	Type	Description	Unused	Used
1146	163	1e. brown, buff and green	65	25
1147	163	3e.30 black, olive and green	3·25	1·80

164 Exhibition Emblem

1958. Brussels International Exhibition.

No.	Type	Description	Unused	Used
1148	164	1e. multicoloured	55	25
1149	164	3e.30 multicoloured	2·75	2·00

165 St. Elizabeth

1958. St. Elizabeth and St. Teotonio Commem.

No.	Type	Description	Unused	Used
1150	165	1e. red and cream	45	30
1151	-	2e. green and cream	85	60
1152	165	2e.50 violet and cream	7·25	1·30
1153	-	5e. brown and cream	12·00	1·60

PORTRAIT: 2, 5e. St. Teotonio.

166 Institute of Tropical Medicine, Lisbon

1958. 6th Int Congress of Tropical Medicine.

No.	Type	Description	Unused	Used
1154	166	1e. green and grey	3·25	40
1155	166	2e.50 blue and grey	13·00	2·20

167 Liner

1958. 2nd National Merchant Navy Congress.

No.	Type	Description	Unused	Used
1156	167	1e. brown, ochre & sepia	7·50	40
1157	167	4e.50 violet, lilac and blue	10·50	3·50

168 Queen Leonora

1958. 500th Birth Anniv of Queen Leonora. Frames and ornaments in bistre, inscriptions and value tablet in black.

No.	Type	Description	Unused	Used
1158	168	1e. blue and brown	45	25
1159	168	1e.50 turquoise and blue	6·50	1·00
1160	168	2e.30 blue and green	5·75	2·10
1161	168	4e.10 blue and grey	5·75	2·10

169 Arms of Aveiro

1959. Millenary of Aveiro.

No.	Type	Description	Unused	Used
1162	169	1e. multicoloured	2·10	40
1163	169	5e. multicoloured	22·00	3·00

170

1960. 10th Anniv of N.A.T.O.

No.	Type	Description	Unused	Used
1164	170	1e. black and lilac	55	35
1165	170	3e.50 green and grey	5·25	2·75

171 "Doorway to Peace"

1960. World Refugee Year. Symbol in black.

No.	Type	Description	Unused	Used
1166	171	20c. yellow, lemon & brn	25	20
1167	171	1e. yellow, green and blue	80	20
1168	171	1e.80 yellow and green	1·70	1·40

172 Glider

1960. 50th Anniv of Portuguese Aero Club. Multicoloured.

No.	Description	Unused	Used
1169	1e. Type **172**	40	35
1170	1e.50 Light monoplane	1·30	45
1171	2e. Airplane and parachutes	2·10	1·10
1172	2e.50 Model glider	3·75	1·60

173 Padre Cruz (after M. Barata)

1960. Death Centenary of Padre Cruz.

No.	Type	Description	Unused	Used
1173	173	1e. brown	70	35
1174	173	4e.30 blue	13·50	10·00

174 University Seal

1960. 400th Anniv of Evora University.

No.	Type	Description	Unused	Used
1175	174	50c. blue	40	25
1176	174	1e. brown and yellow	60	25
1177	174	1e.40 purple	4·25	2·40

175 Prince Henry's Arms

1960. 5th Death Centenary of Prince Henry the Navigator. Multicoloured.

No.	Description	Unused	Used
1178	1e. Type **175**	55	35
1179	2e.50 Caravel	4·75	55
1180	3e.50 Prince Henry the Navigator	6·00	2·10
1181	5e. Motto	15·00	1·20
1182	8e. Barketta	6·25	1·20
1183	10e. Map showing Sagres	21·00	3·00

175a Conference Emblem

1960. Europa.

No.	Type	Description	Unused	Used
1184	175a	1e. light blue and blue	45	35
1185	175a	3e.50 red and lake	5·25	3·00

176 Emblems of Prince Henry and Lisbon

1960. 5th National Philatelic Exhibition, Lisbon.

No.	Type	Description	Unused	Used
1186	176	1e. blue, black and green	60	35
1187	176	3e.30 blue, black and light blue	8·75	5·50

177 Portuguese Flag

1960. 50th Anniv of Republic.

No.	Type	Description	Unused	Used
1188	177	1e. multicoloured	50	15

178 King Pedro V

1961. Cent of Lisbon University Faculty of Letters.

No.	Type	Description	Unused	Used
1189	178	1e. green and brown	75	30
1190	178	6e.50 brown and blue	5·00	1·40

179 Arms of Setubal

1961. Centenary of Setubal City.

No.	Type	Description	Unused	Used
1191	179	1e. multicoloured	80	30
1192	179	4e.30 multicoloured	29·00	9·00

180

1961. Europa.

No.	Type	Description	Unused	Used
1193	180	1e. light blue, blue and deep blue	35	35
1194	180	1e.50 light green, green and deep green	2·00	1·80
1195	180	3e.50 pink, red and lake	2·30	2·10

181 Tomar Gateway

1961. 800th Anniv of Tomar.

No.	Type	Description	Unused	Used
1196	-	1e. multicoloured	35	25
1197	181	3e.50 multicoloured	2·10	1·70

DESIGN: 1e. As Type **181** but without ornamental background.

182 National Guardsman

1962. 50th Anniv of National Republican Guard.

1198	**182**	1e. multicoloured	35	25
1199	**182**	2e. multicoloured	3·50	1·20
1200	**182**	2e.50 multicoloured	3·25	1·00

183 St. Gabriel (Patron Saint of Telecommunications)

1962. St. Gabriel Commemoration.

1201	**183**	1e. brown, green and olive	1·00	30
1202	**183**	3e.50 green, brown & ol	1·10	60

184 Scout Badge and Tents

1962. 18th International Scout Conference (1961).

1203	**184**	20c. multicoloured	35	25
1204	**184**	50c. multicoloured	40	25
1205	**184**	1e. multicoloured	85	30
1206	**184**	2e.50 multicoloured	5·75	75
1207	**184**	3e.50 mulitcoloured	2·75	75
1208	**184**	6e.50 multicoloured	1·70	1·30

185 Children with Ball

1962. 10th International Paediatrics Congress, Lisbon. Centres in black.

1209	-	50c. yellow and green	35	25
1210	-	1e. yellow and grey	1·30	25
1211	**185**	2e.80 yellow and brown	4·25	2·10
1212	-	3e.50 yellow and purple	7·75	2·75

DESIGNS: 50c. Children with book; 1e. Inoculating child; 3e.50, Weighing baby.

186 Europa "Honeycomb"

1962. Europa. "EUROPA" in gold.

1213	**186**	1e. ultramarine, light blue and blue	40	35
1214	**186**	1e.50 deep green, light green and green	2·00	1·30
1215	**186**	3e.50 purple, pink and claret	2·30	2·00

187 St. Zenon (the Courier)

1962. Stamp Day. Saint in yellow and pink.

1216	**187**	1e. black and purple	35	30
1217	**187**	2e. black and green	1·60	1·10
1218	**187**	2e.80 black and bistre	2·75	2·75

188 Benfica Emblem and European Cup

1963. Benfica Club's Double Victory in European Football Cup Championship (1961–62).

1219	**188**	1e. multicoloured	1·20	30
1220	**188**	4e.30 multicoloured	2·10	1·90

189 Campaign Emblem

1963. Freedom from Hunger.

1221	**189**	1e. multicoloured	35	30
1222	**189**	3e.30 multicoloured	2·00	1·60
1223	**189**	3e.50 multicoloured	2·20	1·60

190 Mail Coach

1963. Centenary of Paris Postal Conference.

1224	**190**	1e. blue, light blue and grey	35	20
1225	**190**	1e.50 multicoloured	3·00	75
1226	**190**	5e. brown, lilac & lt brown	1·30	60

191 St. Vincent de Paul

1963. 300th Death Anniv of St. Vincent de Paul. Inscr in gold.

1227	**191**	20c. ultramarine and blue	35	35
1228	**191**	1e. blue and grey	55	35
1229	**191**	2e.80 black and green	6·50	2·75
1230	**191**	5e. grey and mauve	5·75	2·00

192 Medieval Knight

1963. 800th Anniv of Military Order of Avis.

1231	**192**	1e. multicoloured	35	25
1232	**192**	1e.50 multicoloured	1·00	40
1233	**192**	2e.50 mulitcoloured	2·00	1·40

193 Europa "Dove"

1963. Europa.

1234	**193**	1e. grey, blue and black	50	35
1235	**193**	1e.50 grey, green & black	4·25	2·00
1236	**193**	3e.50 grey, red and black	6·25	3·00

194 Supersonic Flight

1963. 10th Anniv of T.A.P. Airline.

1237	**194**	1e. blue and deep blue	30	25
1238	**194**	2e.50 light green & green	2·10	1·00
1239	**194**	3e.50 orange and red	2·50	1·80

195 Pharmacist's Jar

1964. 400th Anniv of Publication of "Coloquios dos Simples" (Dissertation on Indian herbs and drugs) by Dr. G. d'Orta.

1240	**195**	50c. brown, black & bis	80	35
1241	**195**	1e. purple, black and red	55	35
1242	**195**	4e.30 blue, black & grey	7·00	5·75

196 Bank Emblem

1964. Centenary of National Overseas Bank.

1243	**196**	1e. yellow, green and blue	35	30
1244	**196**	2e.50 yellow, olive & grn	4·00	1·60
1245	**196**	3e.50 yellow, green & brn	3·50	1·70

197 Sameiro Shrine (Braga)

1964. Centenary of Sameiro Shrine.

1246	**197**	1e. yellow, brown and red	35	25
1247	**197**	2e. yellow, light brown and brown	3·00	1·10
1248	**197**	5e. yellow, green and blue	3·50	1·70

198 Europa "Flower"

1964. Europa.

1249	**198**	1e. deep blue, light blue and blue	1·00	35
1250	**198**	3e.50 brown, light brown and purple	8·00	2·50
1251	**198**	4e.30 deep green, light green and green	9·50	4·75

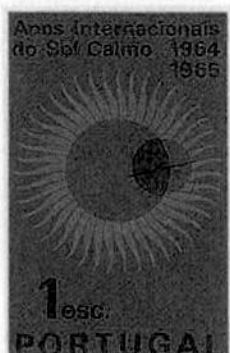

199 Sun and Globe

1964. International Quiet Sun Years.

1252	**199**	1e. mulitcoloured	45	25
1253	**199**	8e. multicoloured	2·20	1·60

200 Olympic "Rings"

1964. Olympic Games, Tokyo.

1254	**200**	20c. multicoloured	35	30
1255	**200**	1e. multicoloured	45	35
1256	**200**	1e.50 multicoloured	2·50	1·60
1257	**200**	6e.50 multicoloured	4·50	3·00

201 E. Coelho (founder)

1964. Centenary of "Diario de Noticias" (newspaper).

1258	**201**	1e. multicoloured	95	20
1259	**201**	5e. multicoloured	11·50	1·60

202 Traffic Signals

1965. 1st National Traffic Congress Lisbon.

1260	**202**	1e. yellow, red and green	40	35
1261	**202**	3e.30 green, red & yellow	10·00	5·25
1262	**202**	3e.50 red, yellow & green	6·50	2·50

203 Dom Fernando (second Duke of Braganza)

1965. 500th Anniv of Braganza.

1263	**203**	1e. red and black	40	25
1264	**203**	10e. green and black	4·50	1·20

204 Angel and Gateway

1965. 900th Anniv of Capture of Coimbra from the Moors.

1265	**204**	1e. multicoloured	35	35
1266	**204**	2e.50 multicoloured	3·00	2·40
1267	**204**	5e. multicoloured	3·75	3·00

205 I.T.U. Emblem

1965. Centenary of I.T.U.

1268	**205**	1e. green and brown	35	35
1269	**205**	3e.50 purple and green	2·40	2·00
1270	**205**	6e.50 blue and green	2·75	1·80

206 C. Gulbenkian

1965. 10th Death Anniv of Calouste Gulbenkian (oil industry pioneer and philanthropist).

1271	**206**	1e. multicoloured	1·00	20
1272	**206**	8e. multicoloured	1·10	75

207 Red Cross Emblem

1965. Centenary of Portuguese Red Cross.

1273	**207**	1e. red, green and black	40	35
1274	**207**	4e. red, green and black	6·50	3·25
1275	**207**	4e.30 red, light red & black	18·00	11·50

208 Europa "Sprig"

1965. Europa.

1276	**208**	1e. lt blue, black and blue	55	35
1277	**208**	3e.50 flesh, brown & red	13·50	2·40
1278	**208**	4e.30 light green, black and green	24·00	11·50

209 North American F-86 Sabre Jet Fighter

1965. 50th Anniv of Portuguese Air Force.

1279	**209**	1e. red, green and olive	45	25
1280	**209**	2e. red, green and brown	2·20	1·00
1281	**209**	5e. red, green and blue	4·50	2·75

210

1965. 500th Birth Anniv of Gil Vicente (poet and dramatist). Designs depicting characters from Vicente's poems.

1282	**210**	20c. multicoloured	25	20
1283	-	1e. multicoloured	70	20
1284	-	2e.50 multicoloured	4·75	80
1285	-	6e.50 multicoloured	2·30	1·10

211 Monogram of Christ

1966. International Committee for the Defence of Christian Civilisation Congress, Lisbon.

1286	**211**	1e. violet, gold and bistre	40	20
1287	**211**	3e.30 black, gold & pur	10·00	5·50
1288	**211**	5e. black, gold and red	7·50	3·00

212 Emblems of Agriculture, Construction and Industry

1966. 40th Anniv of National Revolution.

1289	**212**	1e. black, blue and grey	45	35
1290	**212**	3e.50 brown, light brown and bistre	4·50	2·10
1291	**212**	4e. purple, red and pink	4·50	1·70

213 Giraldo the "Fearless"

1966. 800th Anniv of Reconquest of Evora.

1292	**213**	1e. multicoloured	55	25
1293	**213**	8e. multicoloured	1·80	1·00

214 Salazar Bridge

1966. Inauguration of Salazar Bridge, Lisbon.

1294	**214**	1e. red and gold	45	25
1295	**214**	2e.50 blue and gold	2·50	1·40
1296	-	2e.80 blue and silver	3·25	2·50
1297	-	4e.30 green and silver	3·50	2·50

DESIGN—VERT: 2e.80, 4e.30, Salazar Bridge (different view).

215 Europa "Ship"

1966. Europa.

1298	**215**	1e. multicoloured	60	35
1299	**215**	3e.50 multicoloured	19·00	3·00
1300	**215**	4e.50 multicoloured	19·00	4·75

216 C. Pestana (bacteriologist)

1966. Portuguese Scientists. Portraits in brown and bistre; background colours given.

1301	**216**	20c. green	25	15
1302	-	50c. orange	25	15
1303	-	1e. yellow	35	15
1304	-	1e.50 brown	50	15
1305	-	2e. brown	2·75	25
1306	-	2e.50 green	3·00	70
1307	-	2e.80 orange	4·75	2·50
1308	-	4e.30 blue	6·25	4·75

SCIENTISTS: 50c. E. Moniz (neurologist); 1e. E. A. P. Coutinho (botanist); 1e.50, J. C. da Serra (botanist); 2e. R. Jorge (hygienist and anthropologist); 2e.50, J. L. de Vasconcelos (ethnologist); 2e.80, M. Lemos (medical historian); 4e.30, J. A. Serrano (anatomist).

217 Bocage

1966. Birth Bicentenary (1965) of Manuel M. B. du Bocage (poet).

1309	**217**	1e. black, green and bistre	25	15
1310	**217**	2e. black, green & brown	1·60	70
1311	**217**	6e. black, green and grey	2·10	1·30

218 Cogwheels

1967. Europa.

1312	**218**	1e. blue, black & lt blue	60	35
1313	**218**	3e.50 brown, black and orange	15·00	1·90
1314	**218**	4e.30 green, black and light green	21·00	3·75

219 Adoration of the Virgin

1967. 50th Anniv of Fatima Apparitions. Mult.

1315	1e. Type **219**	20	15
1316	2e.80 Fatima Church	95	90
1317	3e.50 Virgin of Fatima	60	45
1318	4e. Chapel of the Apparitions	70	55

220 Roman Senators

1967. New Civil Law Code.

1319	**220**	1e. red and gold	20	15
1320	**220**	2e.50 blue and gold	3·25	1·80
1321	**220**	4e.30 green and gold	2·75	1·80

221 Lisnave Shipyard

1967. Inauguration of Lisnave Shipyard, Lisbon.

1322	**221**	1e. multicoloured	20	20
1323	-	2e.80 multicoloured	4·00	1·90
1324	**221**	3e.50 multicoloured	3·00	1·80
1325	-	4e.30 multicoloured	3·75	2·00

DESIGN: 2e.80, 4e.30, Section of ship's hull and location map.

222 Serpent Symbol

1967. 6th European Rheumatological Congress, Lisbon.

1326	**222**	1e. multicoloured	20	20
1327	**222**	2e. multicoloured	1·90	1·00
1328	**222**	5e. multicoloured	3·00	2·00

223 Flags of EFTA Countries

1967. European Free Trade Association.

1329	**223**	1e. multicoloured	35	35
1330	**223**	3e.50 multicoloured	2·40	2·00
1331	**223**	4e.30 multicoloured	4·75	4·50

224 Tombstones

1967. Centenary of Abolition of Death Penalty in Portugal.

1332	**224**	1e. green	20	20
1333	**224**	2e. brown	2·10	1·30
1334	**224**	5e. green	3·75	3·00

225 Bento de Goes

1968. Bento de Goes Commemoration.

1335	**225**	1e. blue, brown and green	95	20
1336	**225**	8e. purple, green & brown	2·50	1·00

226 Europa "Key"

1968. Europa.

1337	**226**	1e. multicoloured	60	35
1338	**226**	3e.50 multicoloured	16·00	2·75
1339	**226**	4e.30 multicoloured	24·00	5·00

227 "Maternal Love"

1968. 30th Anniv of Organization of Mothers for National Education (O.M.E.N.).

1340	**227**	1e. black, orange and grey	35	25
1341	**227**	2e. black, orange and pink	2·75	1·00
1342	**227**	5e. black, orange and blue	5·25	2·75

228 "Victory over Disease"

1968. 20th Anniv of W.H.O.

1343	**228**	1e. multicoloured	35	35
1344	**228**	3e.50 multicoloured	2·20	1·10
1345	**228**	4e.30 multicoloured	12·00	8·50

229 Vineyard, Girao

1968. "Lubrapex 1968" Stamp Exhibition. Madeira—"Pearl of the Atlantic". Multicoloured.

1346	50c. Type **229**	25	20
1347	1e. Firework display	30	15
1348	1e.50 Landscape	60	20
1349	2e.80 J. Fernandes Vieira (liberator of Pernambuco) (vert)	3·50	2·50
1350	3e.50 Embroidery (vert)	2·75	1·60
1351	4e.30 J. Goncalves Zarco (navigator) (vert)	12·00	11·50
1352	20e. "Muschia aurea" (vert)	7·75	2·20

230 Pedro Alvares Cabral (from medallion)

1969. 500th Birth Anniv of Pedro Alvares Cabral (explorer).

1353	**230**	1e. blue	40	20
1354	-	3e.50 purple	6·25	3·50
1355	-	6e.50 multicoloured	4·50	3·50

DESIGNS—VERT: 3e.50, Cabral's arms. HORIZ: 6e.50, Cabral's fleet (from contemporary docu-ments).

231 Colonnade

1969. Europa.

1356	**231**	1e. multicoloured	60	35
1357	**231**	3e.50 multicoloured	17·00	3·50
1358	**231**	4e.30 multicoloured	26·00	5·75

232 King Joseph I

1969. Centenary of National Press.

1359	**232**	1e. multicoloured	20	20
1360	**232**	2e. multicoloured	1·70	95
1361	**232**	8e. multicoloured	1·60	1·30

233 I.L.O. Emblem

1969. 50th Anniv of I.L.O.

1362	**233**	1e. multicoloured	25	20
1363	**233**	3e.50 multicoloured	3·00	1·00
1364	**233**	4e.30 multicoloured	4·00	3·25

234 J. R. Cabrilho (navigator and colonizer)

1969. Bicentenary of San Diego, California.

1365	**234**	1e. dp green, yellow & grn	20	20
1366	**234**	2e.50 brown, light brown and blue	2·50	1·00
1367	**234**	6e.50 deep brown, green and brown	3·25	1·90

235 Vianna da Motta (from painting by C. B. Pinheiro)

1969. Birth Centenary (1968) of Jose Vianna da Motta (concert pianist).

1368	**235**	1e. multicoloured	1·20	20
1369	**235**	9e. multicoloured	1·70	1·30

236 Coutinho and Fairey IIID Seaplane

1969. Birth Centenary of Gago Coutinho (aviator). Multicoloured.

1370	1e. Type **236**	35	15
1371	2e.80 Coutinho and sextant	3·75	2·10
1372	3e.30 Type **236**	3·50	3·00
1373	4e.30 As No. 1371	3·50	3·00

237 Vasco da Gama

1969. 500th Birth Anniv of Vasco da Gama. Multicoloured.

1374	1e. Type **237**	35	25
1375	2e.50 Arms of Vasco da Gama	4·75	3·75
1376	3e.50 Route map (horiz)	3·50	1·70
1377	4e. Vasca da Gama's fleet (horiz)	3·25	1·40

238 "Flaming Sun"

1970. Europa.

1378	**238**	1e. cream and blue	60	25
1379	**238**	3e.50 cream and brown	16·00	2·10
1380	**238**	4e.30 cream and green	23·00	6·25

239 Distillation Plant and Pipelines

1970. Inauguration of Porto Oil Refinery.

1381	**239**	1e. blue and light blue	25	20
1382	-	2e.80 black and green	3·50	2·75
1383	**239**	3e.30 green and olive	2·75	2·20
1384	-	6e. brown and light brown	2·50	1·90

DESIGN: 2e.80, 6e. Catalytic cracking plant and pipelines.

240 Marshal Carmona (from sculpture by L. de Almeida)

1970. Birth Centenary of Marshal Carmona.

1385	**240**	1e. green and black	25	10
1386	**240**	2e.50 blue, red and black	2·20	90
1387	**240**	7e. blue and black	2·50	1·70

241 Station Badge

1970. 25th Anniv of Plant-breeding Station.

1388	**241**	1e. multicoloured	30	10
1389	**241**	2e.50 multicoloured	1·80	70
1390	**241**	5e. multicoloured	2·20	90

242 Emblem within Cultural Symbol

1970. Expo 70. Multicoloured.

1391	1e. Compass (postage)	25	15
1392	5e. Christian symbol	2·00	1·70
1393	6e.50 Symbolic initials	4·75	4·00
1394	3e.50 Type **242** (air)	90	45

243 Wheel and Star

1970. Centenaries of Covilha (Nos. 1395/6) and Santarem (Nos. 1397/8). Multicoloured.

1395	1e. Type **243**	30	20
1396	2e.80 Ram and weaving frame	3·50	3·00
1397	1e. Castle	20	15
1398	4e. Two knights	2·30	1·30

244 "Great Eastern" laying Cable

1970. Centenary of Portugal–England Submarine Telegraph Cable.

1399	**244**	1e. black, blue and green	30	15
1400	**244**	2e.50 black, green & buff	2·50	70
1401	-	2e.80 multicoloured	4·00	3·25
1402	-	4e. multicoloured	2·50	1·30

DESIGN: 2e.80, 4e. Cable cross-section.

245 Harvesting Grapes

1970. Port Wine Industry. Multicoloured.

1403	50c. Type **245**	15	10
1404	1e. Harvester and jug	25	10
1405	3e.50 Wine-glass and wine barge	95	25
1406	7e. Wine-bottle and casks	1·60	80

246 Mountain Windmill, Bussaco Hills

1971. Portuguese Windmills.

1407	**246**	20c. brown, black & sepia	15	10
1408	-	50c. brown, black & blue	20	10
1409	-	1e. purple, black and grey	30	10
1410	-	2e. red, black and mauve	1·00	35
1411	-	3e.30 chocolate, black and brown	3·50	2·50
1412	-	5e. brown, black & green	3·25	1·20

WINDMILLS: 50c. Beira Litoral Province; 1e. "Saloio" type Estremadura Province; 2e. St. Miguel Azores; 3e.30, Porto Santo, Madeira; 5e. Pico, Azores.

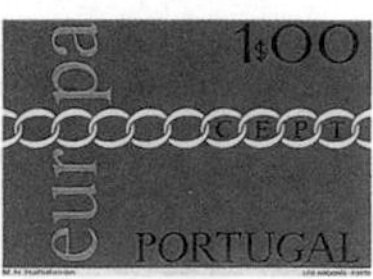
247 Europa Chain

1971. Europa.

1413	**247**	1e. green, blue and black	45	30
1414	**247**	3e.50 yellow, brn & blk	12·00	1·10
1415	**247**	7e.50 brown, green & blk	17·00	2·75

248 F. Franco

1971. Portuguese Sculptors.

1416	**248**	20c. black	15	10
1417	-	1e. red	35	10
1418	-	1e.50 brown	85	60
1419a	-	2e.50 blue	1·20	55
1420	-	3e.50 mauve	1·50	90
1421	-	4e. green	4·00	2·50

DESIGNS: 1e. A. Lopes; 1e.50, A. de Costa Mota; 2e.50, R. Gameiro; 3e.50, J. Simoes de Almeida (the Younger); 4e. F. dos Santos.

249 Pres. Salazar

1971. Pres. Antonio Salazar Commemoration.

1422	**249**	1e. brown, green & orge	25	10
1423	**249**	5e. brown, purple & orge	2·30	80
1424	**249**	10e. brown, blue & orge	3·50	1·60

250 Wolframite

1971. 1st Spanish–Portuguese–American Congress of Economic Geology. Multicoloured.

1425	1e. Type **250**	15	10
1426	2e.50 Arsenopyrite	2·50	60
1427	3e.50 Beryllium	90	55
1428	6e.50 Chalcopyrite	1·70	80

251 Town Gate

1971. Bicentenary of Castelo Branco. Mult.

1429	1e. Type **251**	15	15
1430	3e. Town square and monument	1·80	90
1431	12e.50 Arms of Castelo Branco (horiz)	1·60	90

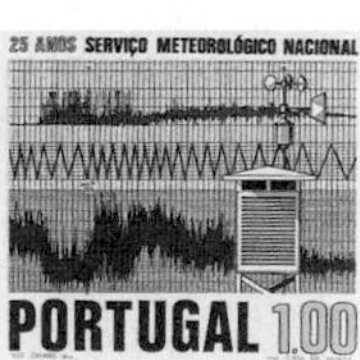
252 Weather Equipment

1971. 25th Anniv of Portuguese Meteorological Service. Multicoloured.

1432	1e. Type **252**	20	10
1433	4e. Weather balloon	3·00	1·40
1434	6e.50 Weather satellite	2·00	1·00

253 Drowning Missionaries

1971. 400th Anniv of Martyrdom of Brazil Missionaries.

1435	**253**	1e. black, blue and grey	15	10
1436	**253**	3e.30 black, purple & brn	2·75	1·90
1437	**253**	4e.80 black, grn & olive	2·75	1·90

254 Man and his Habitat

1971. Nature Conservation. Multicoloured.

1438	1e. Type **254**	15	10
1439	3e.30 Horses and trees ("Earth")	90	60
1440	3e.50 Birds ("The Atmosphere")	90	55
1441	4e.50 Fishes ("Water")	3·50	2·10

255 Clerigos Tower, Oporto

1972. Buildings and Views.

1442	-	5c. grey, black and green	30	15
1443	-	10c. black, green & blue	20	15
1444	-	30c. sepia, brown & yell	20	15
1445p	-	50c. blue, orange & blk	55	10
1446	**255**	1e. black, brown & grn	1·20	10
1447a	-	1e.50 brown, blue & blk	75	10
1448	-	2e. black, brown & pur	3·25	10
1449p	-	2e.50 brown, light brown and grey	55	10
1450p	-	3e. yellow, black & brn	90	10
1451p	-	3e.50 green, orge & brn	55	10
1452	-	4e. black, yellow & blue	1·00	10
1453	-	4e.50 black, brn & grn	1·50	10
1454	-	5e. green, brown & black	9·25	10
1455	-	6e. bistre, green & black	3·75	25
1456	-	7e.50 black, orge & grn	2·10	20
1457	-	8e. bistre, black & green	2·75	15
1458	-	10e. multicoloured	1·30	15
1459	-	20e. multicoloured	8·75	55
1460	-	50e. multicoloured	9·25	40
1461	-	100e. multicoloured	10·00	95

DESIGNS—As T **255**: 5c. Aguas Livres aqueduct, Lisbon; 10c. Lima Bridge; 30c. Monastery interior, Alcobaca; 50c. Coimbra University; 1e.50, Belem Tower, Lisbon; 2e. Domus Municipalis, Braganza; 2e.50, Castle, Vila de Feira; 3e. Misericord House, Viana do Castelo; 3e.50, Window, Tomar Convent; 4e. Gateway, Braga; 4e.50, Dolmen of Carrazeda; 5e. Roman Temple, Evora; 6e. Monastery, Leca do Balio; 7e.50, Almourol Castle; 8e. Ducal Palace, Guimaraes. 31×22 mm: 10e. Cape Girao, Madeira; 20e. Episcopal Garden, Castelo Branco; 50e. Town Hall, Sintra; 100e. Seven Cities' Lake, Sao Miguel, Azores.

256 Arms of Pinhel

1972. Bicentenary of Pinhel's Status as a City. Multicoloured.

1464	1e. Type **256**	25	10
1465	2e.50 Balustrade (vert)	2·30	55
1466	7e.50 Lantern on pedestal (vert)	1·80	80

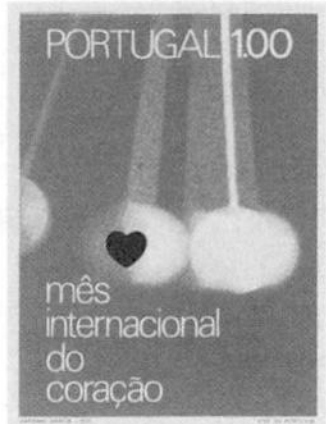

257 Heart and Pendulum

1972. World Heart Month.

1467	**257**	1e. red and lilac	25	15
1468	-	4e. red and green	3·50	1·60
1469	-	9e. red and brown	2·40	1·00

DESIGNS: 4e. Heart in spiral; 9e. Heart and cardiogram trace.

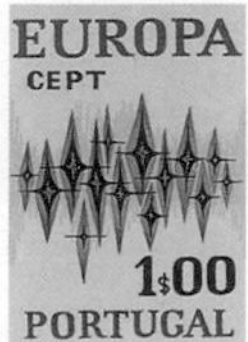

258 "Communications"

1972. Europa.

1470	**258**	1e. multicoloured	50	20
1471	**258**	3e.50 multicoloured	9·75	65
1472	**258**	6e. multicoloured	16·00	2·30

259 Container Truck

1972. 13th International Road Transport Union Congress, Estoril. Multicoloured.

1473	1e. Type **259**	25	20
1474	4e.50 Roof of taxi-cab	2·50	1·50
1475	8e. Motor-coach	2·30	1·30

260 Football

1972. Olympic Games, Munich. Multicoloured.

1476	50c. Type **260**	15	10
1477	1e. Running	20	10
1478	1e.50 Show jumping	55	25
1479	3e.50 Swimming	1·20	50
1480	4e.50 Yachting	1·80	1·40
1481	5e. Gymnastics	3·50	1·50

261 Marquis de Pombal

1972. Pombaline University Reforms. Multicoloured.

1482	1e. Type **261**	20	10
1483	2e.50 "The Sciences" (emblems)	2·10	1·20
1484	8e. Arms of Coimbra University.	2·20	1·60

262 Tome de Sousa

1972. 150th Anniv of Brazilian Independence. Mult.

1485	1e. Type **262**	20	15
1486	2e.50 Jose Bonifacio	1·10	40
1487	3e.50 Dom Pedro IV	1·10	45
1488	6e. Dove and globe	2·10	1·00

263 Sacadura, Cabral, Gago, Coutinho and Fairey III D Seaplane

1972. 50th Anniv of 1st Lisbon–Rio de Janeiro Flight. Multicoloured.

1489	1e. Type **263**	15	10
1490	2e.50 Route map	1·20	70
1491	2e.80 Type **263**	1·50	1·10
1492	3e.80 As 2e.50	1·90	1·60

264 Camoens

1972. 400th Anniv of Camoens' "Lusiads" (epic poem).

1493	**264**	1e. yellow, brown & black	25	15
1494	-	3e. blue, green and black	1·60	95
1495	-	10e. brown, purple & blk	2·30	1·10

DESIGNS: 3e. "Saved from the Sea"; 10e. "Encounter with Adamastor".

265 Graph and Computer Tapes

1973. Portuguese Productivity Conference, Lisbon. Multicoloured.

1496	1e. Type **265**	20	10
1497	4e. Computer scale	1·60	85
1498	9e. Graphs	1·60	80

266 Europa "Posthorn"

1973. Europa.

1499	**266**	1e. multicoloured	75	30
1500	**266**	4e. multicoloured	18·00	1·40
1501	**266**	6e. multicoloured	20·00	2·40

267 Pres. Medici and Arms

1973. Visit of Pres. Medici of Brazil. Mult.

1502	1e. Type **267**	20	15
1503	2e.80 Pres. Medici and globe	1·00	85
1504	3e.50 Type **267**	1·10	80
1505	4e.80 As No. 1503	1·10	85

268 Child Running

1973. "For the Child".

1506	**268**	1e. dp blue, blue & brown	20	10
1507	-	4e. purple, mauve & brn	1·90	85
1508	-	7e.50 orange, ochre and brown	2·30	1·50

DESIGNS: 4e. Child running (to right); 7e.50, Child jumping.

269 Transport and Weather Map

1973. 25th Anniv of Ministry of Communications. Multicoloured.

1509	1e. Type **269**	15	10
1510	3e.80 "Telecommunications"	65	40
1511	6e. "Postal Services"	1·50	90

270 Child and Written Text

1973. Bicentenary of Primary State School Education. Multicoloured.

1512	1e. Type **270**	25	10
1513	4e.50 Page of children's primer	2·10	65
1514	5e.30 "Schooldays" (child's drawing) (horiz)	1·80	95
1515	8e. "Teacher and children" (horiz)	4·75	2·00

271 Electric Tramcar

1973. Centenary of Oporto's Public Transport System. Multicoloured.

1516	1e. Horse tram	30	10
1517	3e.50 Modern bus	2·75	1·90
1518	7e.50 Type **271**	3·00	1·60

Nos. 1516/17 are 31½×31½ mm.

272 League Badge

1973. 50th Anniv of Servicemen's League. Multicoloured.

1519	1e. Type **272**	20	15
1520	2e.50 Servicemen	3·00	85
1521	11e. Awards and medals	2·10	90

273 Death of Nuno Goncalves

1973. 600th Anniv of Defence of Faria Castle by the Alcaide, Nuno Goncalves.

1522	**273**	1e. green and yellow	30	15
1523	**273**	10e. purple and yellow	2·75	1·50

274 Damiao de Gois (after Durer)

1974. 400th Death Anniv of Damiao de Gois (scholar and diplomat). Multicoloured.

1524	1e. Type **274**	20	10
1525	4e.50 Title-page of "Chronicles of Prince Dom Joao"	3·00	80
1526	7e.50 Lute and "Dodecahordon" score	1·80	80

275 "The Exile" (A. Soares dos Reis)

1974. Europa.

1527	**275**	1e. green, blue and olive	90	30
1528	**275**	4e. green, red and yellow	21·00	1·40
1529	**275**	6e. dp green, green & blue	25·00	1·80

276 Light Emission

1974. Inauguration of Satellite Communications Station Network.

1530	**276**	1e.50 green	25	20
1531	-	4e.50 blue	1·80	90
1532	-	5e.30 purple	2·50	1·30

DESIGNS: 4e.50, Spiral Waves; 5e.30, Satellite and Earth.

277 "Diffusion of Hertzian Radio Waves"

1974. Birth Centenary of Guglielmo Marconi (radio pioneer). Multicoloured.

1533	1e.50 Type **277**	20	10
1534	3e.30 "Radio waves across Space"	2·50	1·10
1535	10e. "Radio waves for Navigation"	1·90	80

278 Early Post-boy and Modern Mail Van

1974. Centenary of U.P.U. Multicoloured.

1536	1e.50 Type **278**	15	10
1537	2e. Hand with letters	90	15
1538	3e.30 Sailing packet and modern liner	70	25
1539	4e.50 Dove and airliner	1·40	65
1540	5e.30 Hand with letter	1·40	75
1541	20e. Steam and electric locomotives	3·00	1·60
MS1542	106×147 mm. Nos. 1536/41 (sold at 50e.)	8·75	7·50

279 Luisa Todi

1974. Portuguese Musicians.

1543	**279**	1e.50 purple	20	15
1544	-	2e. red	1·40	35
1545	-	2e.50 brown	1·00	25
1546	-	3e. blue	1·50	50
1547	-	5e.30 green	1·20	80
1548	-	11e. red	1·30	80

PORTRAITS: 2e. Joao Domingos Bomtempo; 2e.50,Carlos Seixas; 3e. Duarte Lobo; 5e.30, Joaode Sousa Carvalho; 11e. Marcos Portugal.

280 Arms of Beja

1974. Bimillenary of Beja. Multicoloured.

1549	1e.50 Type **280**	25	10
1550	3e.50 Beja's inhabitants through the ages	3·00	1·50
1551	7e. Moorish arches	3·25	1·70

281 "The Annunciation"

1974. Christmas. Multicoloured.

1552	1e.50 Type **281**	20	10
1553	4e.50 "The Nativity"	4·00	80
1554	10e. "The Flight into Egypt"	3·50	1·10

282 Rainbow and Dove

1974. Portuguese Armed Forces Movement of 25 April.

1555	**282**	1e.50 multicoloured	15	15
1556	**282**	3e.50 multicoloured	4·00	1·90
1557	**282**	5e. multicoloured	3·00	1·10

283 Egas Moniz

1974. Birth Centenary of Professor Egas Moniz (brain surgeon).

1558	**283**	1e.50 brown and orange	35	15
1559	-	3e.30 orange and brown	3·00	80
1560	-	10e. grey and blue	6·00	1·00

DESIGNS: 3e.30, Nobel Medicine and Physiology Prize medal, 1949; 10e. Cerebral angiograph, 1927.

284 Farmer and Soldier

1975. Portuguese Cultural Progress and Citizens' Guidance Campaign.

1561	**284**	1e.50 multicoloured	25	10
1562	**284**	3e. multicoloured	2·50	85
1563	**284**	4e.50 multicoloured	3·50	1·40

285 Hands and Dove of Peace

1975. 1st Anniv of Portuguese Revolution. Multicoloured.

1564	1e.50 Type **285**	20	10
1565	4e.50 Hands and peace dove	3·50	90
1566	10e. Peace dove and emblem	4·25	1·50

286 "The Hand of God"

1975. Holy Year. Multicoloured.

1567	1e.50 Type **286**	20	15
1568	4e.50 Hand with cross	4·25	1·30
1569	10e. Peace dove	5·75	1·50

287 "The Horseman of the Apocalypse" (detail of 12th-cent manuscript)

1975. Europa. Multicoloured.

1570	1e.50 Type **287**	1·20	15
1571	10e. "Fernando Pessoa" (poet) (A. Negreiros)	55·00	1·90

288 Assembly Building

1975. Opening of Portuguese Constituent Assembly.

1572	**288**	2e. black, red and yellow	45	10
1573	**288**	20e. black, green & yellow	7·50	1·80

289 Hiking

1975. 36th International Camping and Caravanning Federation Rally. Multicoloured.

1574	2e. Type **289**	1·10	15
1575	4e.50 Boating and swimming	3·25	1·40
1576	5e.30 Caravanning	2·40	1·40

290 Planting Tree

1975. 30th Anniv of U.N.O. Multicoloured.

1577	2e. Type **290**	55	10
1578	4e.50 Releasing peace dove	1·80	80
1579	20c. Harvesting corn	4·75	1·60

291 Lilienthal Glider and Modern Space Rocket

1975. 26th International Astronautical Federation Congress, Lisbon. Multicoloured.

1580	2e. Type **291**	70	15
1581	4e.50 "Apollo"–"Soyuz" space link	2·30	1·10
1582	5e.30 R. H. Goddard, R. E. Pelterie, H. Oberth and K. E. Tsiolkovsky (space pioneers)	1·50	1·10
1583	10e. Astronaut and spaceships (70×32 mm)	5·75	1·60

292 Surveying the Land

1975. Centenary of National Geographical Society, Lisbon. Multicoloured.

1584	2e. Type **292**	35	10
1585	8e. Surveying the sea	2·30	90
1586	10e. Globe and people	3·50	1·50

293 Symbolic Arch

1975. European Architectural Heritage Year.

1587	**293**	2e. grey, blue & deep blue	35	25
1588	-	8e. grey and red	4·00	1·10
1589	-	10e. multicoloured	4·50	1·40

DESIGNS: 8e. Stylized building plan; 10e. Historical building being protected from development.

294 Nurse in Hospital Ward

1975. International Women's Year. Multicoloured.

1590	50c. Type **294**	30	15
1591	2e. Woman farm worker	1·10	40
1592	3e.50 Woman office worker	1·40	90
1593	8e. Woman factory worker	2·10	1·50
MS1594	104×115 mm. Nos. 1590/3 (sold at 25e.)	5·50	4·50

295 Pen-nib as Plough Blade

1976. 50th Anniv of National Writers Society.

1595	**295**	3e. blue and red	50	10
1596	**295**	20e. red and blue	5·25	1·60

296 First Telephone Set

1976. Telephone Centenary.

1597	**296**	3e. black, green & dp grn	1·10	15
1598	-	10e.50 black, red and pink	4·25	1·20

DESIGNS: 10e.50, Alexander Graham Bell.

297 "Industrial Progress"

1976. National Production Campaign.

1599	**297**	50c. red	35	10
1600	-	1e. green	55	20

DESIGN: 1e. Consumer goods.

298 Carved Olive-wood Spoons

1976. Europa. Multicoloured.

1601	3e. Type **298**	3·75	50
1602	20e. Gold ornaments	75·00	7·25

299 Stamp Designing

1976. "Interphil 76" International Stamp Exhibition, Philadelphia. Multicoloured.

1603	3e. Type **299**	35	10
1604	7e.50 Stamp being hand-cancelled	1·30	85
1605	10e. Stamp printing	2·20	90

300 King Fernando promulgating Law

1976. 600th Anniv of Law of "Sesmarias" (uncultivated land). Multicoloured.

1606	3e. Type **300**	25	15
1607	5e. Plough and farmers repelling hunters	1·90	60
1608	10e. Corn harvesting	2·75	1·00
MS1609	230×150 mm. Nos. 1606/8 (sold at 30e.)	6·00	£100

301 Athlete with Olympic Torch

1976. Olympic Games, Montreal. Multicoloured.

1610		3e. Type **301**	35	15
1611		7e. Women's relay	1·90	1·50
1612		10e.50 Olympic flame	2·50	1·40

302 "Speaking in the Country"

1976. Literacy Campaign. Multicoloured.

1613		3e. Type **302**	65	15
1614		3e. "Speaking at Sea"	65	15
1615		3e. "Speaking in Town"	65	15
1616a		3e. "Speaking at Work"	85	25
MS1617		145×104 mm. Nos. 1613/16 (sold at 25e.)	18·00	16·00

303 Azure-winged Magpie

1976. "Portucale 77" Thematic Stamp Exhibition, Oporto (1st issue). Flora and Fauna. Mult.

1618		3e. Type **303**	35	10
1619		5e. Lynx	1·50	50
1620		7e. Portuguese laurel cherry and blue tit	1·60	1·10
1621		10e.50 Little wild carnation and lizard	1·80	1·30

See also Nos 1673/8.

304 "Lubrapex" Emblem and Exhibition Hall

1976. "Lubrapex 1976" Luso-Brazilian Stamp Exhibition. Multicoloured.

1622		3e. Type **304**	45	15
1623		20e. "Lubrapex" emblem and "stamp"	3·00	2·00
MS1624		180×142 mm. Nos. 1622/3 (sold at 30e.)	5·00	5·00

305 Bank Emblem

1976. Centenary of National Trust Fund Bank.

1625	**305**	3e. multicoloured	15	10
1626	**305**	7e. multicoloured	2·75	1·20
1627	**305**	15e. multicoloured	4·00	1·40

306 Sheep Grazing

1976. Water Conservation. Protection of Humid Zones. Multicoloured.

1628		1e. Type **306**	55	10
1629		3e. Marshland	1·10	40
1630		5e. Sea trout	3·00	55
1631		10e. Mallards	4·25	1·10

307 "Liberty"

1976. Consolidation of Democratic Institutions.

1632	**307**	3e. grey, green and red	90	25

308 Examining Child's Eyes

1976. World Health Day. Detection and Prevention of Blindness. Multicoloured.

1633		3e. Type **308**	35	15
1634		5e. Welder wearing protective goggles	2·40	35
1635		10e.50 Blind person reading Braille	2·50	1·50

309 Hydro-electric Power

1976. Uses of Natural Energy. Multicoloured.

1636		1e. Type **309**	30	20
1637		4e. Fossil fuel (oil)	60	25
1638		5e. Geo-thermic sources	1·00	35
1639		10e. Wind power	1·70	1·00
1640		15e. Solar energy	3·75	1·70

310 Map of Member Countries

1977. Admission of Portugal to the Council of Europe.

1641	**310**	8e.50 multicoloured	1·60	1·60
1642	**310**	10e. multicoloured	1·80	1·70

311 Bottle inside Human Body

1977. 10th Anniv of Portuguese Anti-Alcoholic Society. Multicoloured.

1643		3e. Type **311**	30	10
1644		5e. Broken body and bottle	1·10	55
1645		15e. Sun behind prison bars and bottle	3·00	1·60

312 Forest

1977. Natural Resources. Forests. Multicoloured.

1646		1e. Type **312**	30	20
1647		4e. Cork oaks	95	35
1648		7e. Logs and trees	2·00	1·60
1649		15e. Trees by the sea	2·00	1·70

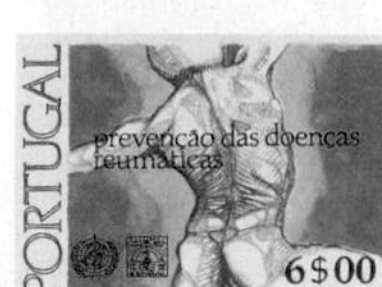

313 Exercising

1977. International Rheumatism Year.

1650	-	4e. orange, brown & blk	35	15
1651	**313**	6e. ultramarine, blue and black	1·50	1·10
1652	-	10e. red, mauve and black	1·40	95

DESIGNS: 4e. Rheumatism victim; 10e. Group exercising.

314 Southern Plains

1977. Europa. Multicoloured.

1653		4e. Type **314**	70	15
1654		8e.50 Northern terraced mountains	4·50	1·00
MS1655		148×95 mm. Nos. 1653/4 each ×3	55·00	33·00

315 John XXI Enthroned

1977. 7th Death Centenary of Pope John XXI. Multicoloured.

1656		4e. Type **315**	30	20
1657		15e. Pope as doctor	80	65

316 Compass

1977. Camoes Day.

1658	**316**	4e. multicoloured	35	20
1659	**316**	8e.50 multicoloured	1·50	1·40

317 Child and Computer

1977. Permanent Education. Multicoloured.

1660		4e. Type **317**	55	20
1661		4e. Flautist and dancers	55	20
1662		4e. Farmer and tractor	55	20
1663		4e. Students and atomic construction	55	20
MS1664		148×96 mm. Nos. 1660/3 (sold at 20e.)	7·50	8·25

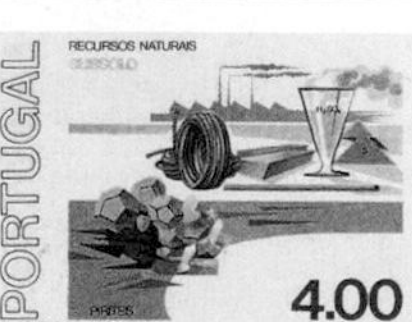

318 Pyrite

1977. Natural Resources. The Subsoil. Mult.

1665		4e. Type **318**	35	15
1666		5e. Marble	1·10	45
1667		10e. Iron ore	1·20	60
1668		20e. Uranium	3·25	1·60

319 Alexandre Herculano

1977. Death Centenary of Alexandre Herculano (writer and politician).

1669	**319**	4e. multicoloured	40	15
1670	**319**	15e. multicoloured	2·00	70

320 Early Steam Locomotive and Peasant Cart (ceramic panel, J. Colaco)

1977. Centenary of Railway Bridge over River Douro. Multicoloured.

1671		4e. Type **320**	40	20
1672		10e. Maria Pia bridge (Eiffel)	3·00	2·20

321 Poviero (Northern coast)

1977. "Portucale 77" Thematic Stamp Exhibition, Oporto (2nd issue). Coastal Fishing Boats. Multicoloured.

1673		2e. Type **321**	55	15
1674		3e. Sea-going rowing boat, Furadouro	40	15
1675		4e. Rowing boat from Nazare	40	20
1676		7e. Caicque from Algarve	60	35
1677		10e. Tunny fishing boat, Algarve	1·20	75
1678		15e. Boat from Buarcos	1·60	1·10
MS1679		148×104 mm. Nos. 1673/8 (sold at 60e.)	6·00	5·00

322 "The Adoration" (Maria do Sameiro A. Santos)

1977. Christmas. Children's Paintings. Mult.

1680		4e. Type **322**	40	15
1681		7e. "Star over Bethlehem" (Paula Maria L. David)	1·40	50
1682		10e. "The Holy Family" (Carla Maria M. Cruz) (vert)	1·60	75
1683		20e. "Children following the Star" (Rosa Maria M. Cardoso) (vert)	3·50	1·60

323 Medical Equipment and Operating Theatre

1978. (a) Size 22×17 mm.

1684	**323**	50c. green, black and red	15	10
1685	-	1e. blue, orange and black	15	10
1686	-	2e. blue, green & brown	15	10
1687	-	3e. brown, green and black	15	10
1688	-	4e. green, blue & brown	20	15
1689	-	5e. blue, green & brown	20	15
1690	-	5e.50 brown, buff and green	25	15
1691	-	6e. brown, yellow & grn	25	15
1692	-	6e.50 blue, deep blue and green	25	15
1693	-	7e. black, grey and blue	25	15
1694	-	8e. ochre, brown and grey	25	15
1694a	-	8e.50 brn, blk & lt brn	40	15
1695	-	9e. yellow, brown & blk	35	15
1696	-	10e. brown, black & grn	35	15
1697	-	12e.50 blue, red and black	45	15
1698	-	16e. brown, black and violet	2·75	45

(b) Size 30×21 mm.

1699		20e. multicoloured	70	15
1700a		30e. multicoloured	1·00	50
1701		40e. multicoloured	90	40
1702		50e. multicoloured	1·30	30
1703		100e. multicoloured	2·20	65
1703a		250e. multicoloured	5·75	1·00

DESIGNS: 1e. Old and modern kitchen equipment; 2e. Telegraph key and masts, microwaves and dish aerial; 3e. Dressmaking and ready-to-wear clothes; 4e. Writing desk and computer; 5e. Tunny fishing boats and modern trawler; 5e.50, Manual and mechanical weaver's looms; 6e. Plough and tractor; 6e.50, Monoplane and B.A.C. One Eleven airliner; 7e. Hand press and modern printing press; 8e. Carpenter's hand tools and mechanical tool; 8e.50, Potter's wheel and modern ceramic machinery; 9e. Old cameras and modern cine and photo cameras; 10e. Axe, saw and mechanical saw; 12e.50, Navigation and radar instruments; 16e. Manual and automatic mail sorting; 20e. Hand tools and building site; 30e. Hammer, anvil, bellows and industrial complex; 40e. Peasant cart and lorry; 50e. Alembic, retorts and modern chemical plant; 100e. Carpenter's shipyard, modern shipyard and tanker; 250e. Survey instruments.

324 Mediterranean Soil

1978. Natural Resources. The Soil. Mult.

1704	4e. Type **324**	40	20
1705	5e. Rock formation	60	25
1706	10e. Alluvial soil	1·60	90
1707	20e. Black soil	3·25	1·30

325 Pedestrian on Zebra Crossing

1978. Road Safety.

1708	**325**	1e. blue, black and orange	20	20
1709	-	2e. blue, black and green	45	20
1710	-	2e.50 blue, black & lt bl	75	20
1711	-	5e. blue, black and red	1·60	25
1712	-	9e. blue, black & ultram	3·75	85
1713	-	12e.50 blue and black	4·50	2·20

DESIGNS: 2e. Motor cyclist; 2e.50, Children in back of car; 5e. Driver in car; 9e. View of road from driver's seat; 12e.50, Road victim ("Don't drink and drive").

326 Roman Tower of Centum Cellas, Belmonte

1978. Europa. Multicoloured.

1714	10e. Type **326**	1·50	35
1715	40e. Belem Monastery, Lisbon	6·00	1·80
MS1716	111×96 mm. Nos. 1714/15 each ×2 (sold at 120e.)	27·00	16·00

327 Roman Bridge, Chaves

1978. 19th Century of Chaves (Aquae Flaviae). Multicoloured.

1717	5e. Type **327**	55	20
1718	20e. Inscribed tablet from bridge	3·25	1·40

328 Running

1978. Sport for All. Multicoloured.

1719	5e. Type **328**	25	15
1720	10e. Cycling	55	35
1721	12e.50 Swimming	1·10	95
1722	15e. Football	1·10	1·10

329 Pedro Nunes

1978. 400th Death Anniv of Pedro Nunes (cosmographer). Multicoloured.

1723	5e. Type **329**	30	10
1724	20e. Nonio (navigation instrument) and diagram	1·70	55

330 Trawler, Crates of Fish and Lorry

1978. Natural Resources. Fishes. Multicoloured.

1725	5e. Type **330**	35	15
1726	9e. Trawler and dockside cranes	90	25
1727	12e.50 Trawler, radar and lecture	1·40	1·10
1728	15e. Trawler with echo-sounding equipment and laboratory	2·50	1·60

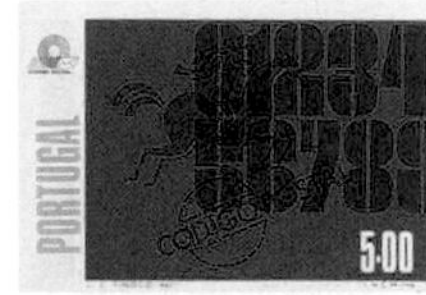

331 Post Rider

1978. Introduction of Post Code. Multicoloured.

1729	5e. Type **331**	45	20
1730	5e. Pigeon with letter	45	20
1731	5e. Sorting letters	45	20
1732	5e. Pen nib and post codes	45	20

332 Symbolic Figure

1978. 30th Anniv of Declaration of Human Rights. Multicoloured.

1733	14e. Type **332**	70	50
1734	40e. Similar symbolic figure, but facing right	2·50	1·40
MS1735	120×100 mm. Nos. 1733/4 each ×2	7·75	5·25

333 Sebastiao Magalhaes Lima

1978. 50th Death Anniv of Magalhaes Lima (journalist and pacifist).

1736	**333**	5e. multicoloured	45	20

334 Portable Post Boxes and Letter Balance

1978. Centenary of Post Museum. Multicoloured.

1737	4e. Type **334**	65	15
1738	5e. Morse equipment	45	20
1739	10e. Printing press and Portuguese stamps of 1853 (125th anniv)	1·60	30
1740	14e. Books, bookcase and entrance to Postal Library (centenary)	2·75	1·90
MS1741	120×99 mm. Nos. 1737/40 (sold at 40e.)	7·00	5·75

335 Emigrant at Railway Station

1979. Portuguese Emigrants. Multicoloured.

1742	5e. Type **335**	25	10
1743	14e. Emigrants at airport	85	65
1744	17e. Man greeting child at railway station	1·60	1·40

336 Traffic

1979. Fight Against Noise. Multicoloured.

1745	4e. Type **336**	60	25
1746	5e. Pneumatic drill	90	20
1747	14e. Loud hailer	1·70	75

337 N.A.T.O. Emblem

1979. 30th Anniv of N.A.T.O.

1748	**337**	5e. blue, red and brown	45	10
1749	**337**	50e. blue, yellow and red	3·75	3·00
MS1750		120×100 mm. Nos. 1748/9 each ×2	8·25	5·25

338 Door-to-door Delivery

1979. Europa. Multicoloured.

1751	14e. Postal messenger delivering letter in cleft stick	1·10	50
1752	40e. Type **338**	2·20	1·10
MS1753	119×103 mm. Nos. 1751/2 each ×2	16·00	8·25

339 Children playing Ball

1979. International Year of the Child. Multicoloured.

1754	5e.50 Type **339**	45	35
1755	6e.50 Mother, baby and dove	45	10
1756	10e. Child eating	55	50
1757	14e. Children of different races	1·10	1·00
MS1758	110×104 mm. Nos. 1754/7 (sold at 40e.)	5·00	4·00

340 Saluting the Flag

1979. Camoes Day.

1759	**340**	6e.50 multicoloured	50	20
MS1760		148×125 mm. No. 1759 ×9	5·50	4·00

341 Pregnant Woman

1979. The Mentally Handicapped. Multicoloured.

1761	6e.50 Type **341**	45	10
1762	17e. Boy sitting in cage	1·00	65
1763	20e. Face, and hands holding hammer and chisel	1·50	1·00

342 Children reading Book

1979. 50th Anniv of International Bureau of Education. Multicoloured.

1764	6e.50 Type **342**	45	10
1765	17e. Teaching a deaf child	2·40	1·30

343 Water Cart, Caldas de Monchique

1979. "Brasiliana 79" International Stamp Exhibition. Portuguese Country Carts. Mult.

1766	2e.50 Type **343**	25	25
1767	5e.50 Wine sledge, Madeira	25	25
1768	6e.50 Wine cart, Upper Douro	40	20
1769	16e. Covered cart, Alentejo	1·10	95
1770	19e. Cart, Mogadouro	1·60	1·30
1771	20e. Sand cart, Murtosa	1·70	55

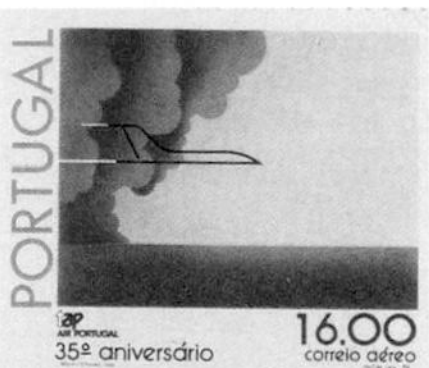

344 Aircraft flying through Storm Cloud

1979. 35th Anniv of TAP National Airline. Multicoloured.

1772	16e. Type **344**	1·40	65
1773	19e. Aircraft and sunset	1·60	1·10

345 Antonio Jose de Almeida

1979. Republican Personalities (1st series).

1774	**345**	5e.50 mauve, grey and red	45	15
1775	-	6e.50 red, grey and carmine	45	10
1776	-	10e. brown, grey and red	65	10
1777	-	16e. blue, grey and red	1·40	75
1778	-	19e.50 green, grey and red	1·80	1·30
1779	-	20e. purple, grey and red	2·00	65

DESIGNS: 6e. Afonso Costa; 10e. Teofilo Braga; 16e. Bernardino Machado; 19e.50, Joao Chagas; 20e. Elias Garcia.

See also Nos. 1787/92.

346 Family Group

1979. Towards a National Health Service. Mult.

1780	6e.50 Type **346**	45	10
1781	20e. Doctor examining patient	1·80	65

347 "The Holy Family"

1979. Christmas. Tile Pictures. Multicoloured.

1782	5e.50 Type **347**	50	35
1783	6e.50 "Adoration of the Shepherds"	50	30
1784	16e. "Flight into Egypt"	1·50	1·10

348 Rotary Emblem and Globe

1980. 75th Anniv of Rotary International. Mult.

1785	16e. Type **348**	1·60	90
1786	50e. Rotary emblem and torch	3·50	2·40

349 Jaime Cortesao

1980. Republican Personalities (2nd series).

1787	-	3e.50 orange and brown	35	15
1788	-	5e.50 green, olive and deep olive	45	25
1789	-	6e.50 lilac and violet	45	25
1790	**349**	11e. multicoloured	2·20	1·30
1791	-	16e. ochre and brown	1·20	80
1792	-	20e. green, blue & lt blue	1·20	55

DESIGNS: 3e.50, Alvaro de Castro; 5e.50, Antonio Sergio; 6e.50, Norton de Matos; 16e. Teixeira Gomes; 20e. Jose Domingues dos Santos.

350 Serpa Pinto

1980. Europa. Multicoloured.

1793	16e. Type **350**	1·10	55
1794	60e. Vasco da Gama	2·75	1·30
MS1795	107×110 mm. Nos. 1793/4 each ×2	9·25	3·25

351 Barn Owl

1980. Protection of Species. Animals in Lisbon Zoo. Multicoloured.

1796	6e.50 Type **351**	30	10
1797	16e. Red fox	1·20	80
1798	19e.50 Wolf	1·50	85
1799	20e. Golden eagle	1·50	80
MS1800	109×107 mm. Nos. 1796/9	5·00	4·00

352 Luis Vaz de Camoes

1980. 400th Death Anniv of Luis Vaz de Camoes (poet).

1801	**352**	6e.50 multicoloured	55	15
1802	**352**	20e. multicoloured	1·40	65

353 Pinto in Japan

1980. 400th Anniv of Fernao Mendes Pinto's "A Peregrinacao" (The Pilgrimage). Multicoloured.

1803	6e.50 Type **353**	45	10
1804	10e. Sea battle	1·30	75

354 Lisbon and Statue of St. Vincent (Jeronimos Monastery)

1980. World Tourism Conference, Manila, Philippines. Multicoloured.

1805	6e.50 Type **354**	45	20
1806	8e. Lantern Tower, Evora Cathedral	65	35
1807	11e. Mountain village and "Jesus with Top-hat" (Mirando do Douro Cathedral)	1·40	75
1808	16e. Canicada dam and "Lady of the Milk" (Braga Cathedral)	1·90	1·00
1809	19e.50 Aveiro River and pulpit from Santa Cruz Monastery, Coimbra	2·20	1·10
1810	20e. Rocha beach and ornamental chimney, Algarve	1·70	80

355 Caravel

1980. "Lubrapex 80" Portuguese–Brazilian Stamp Exhibition, Lisbon. Multicoloured.

1811	6e.50 Type **355**	45	10
1812	8e. Nau	1·20	60
1813	16e. Galleon	1·70	80
1814	19e.50 Early paddle-steamer with sails	2·20	85
MS1815	132×88 mm. Nos. 1811/14 (sold at 60e.)	8·75	7·50

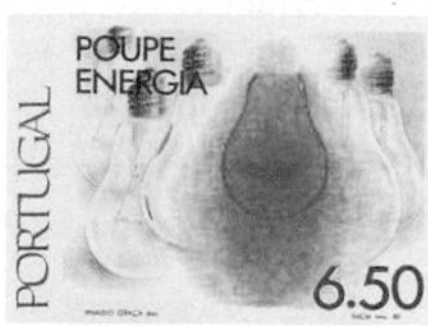

356 Lightbulbs

1980. Energy Conservation. Multicoloured.

1816	6e.50 Type **356**	45	10
1817	16e. Speeding car	2·50	90

357 Duke of Braganza and Open Book

1980. Bicentenary of Academy of Sciences, Lisbon. Multicoloured.

1818	6e.50 Type **357**	40	10
1819	19e.50 Uniformed academician, Academy and sextant	1·90	90

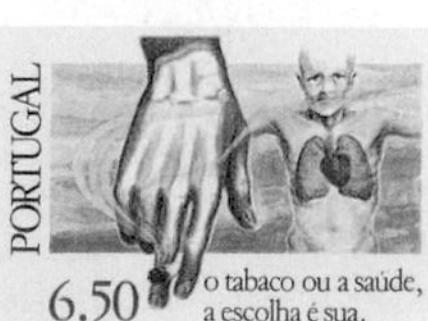

358 Cigarette contaminating Lungs

1980. Anti-Smoking Campaign. Multicoloured.

1820	6e.50 Type **358**	40	10
1821	19e.50 Healthy figure pushing away hand with cigarette	2·40	1·40

359 Head and Computer Punch-card

1981. National Census. Multicoloured.

1822	6e.50 Type **359**	45	25
1823	16e. Houses and punch-card	1·70	1·30

360 Fragata, River Tejo

1981. River Boats. Multicoloured.

1824	8e. Type **360**	40	30
1825	8e.50 Rabelo, River Douro	40	25
1826	10e. Moliceiro, Aveiro River	55	30
1827	16e. Barco, River Lima	95	60
1828	19e.50 Carocho, River Minho	1·00	60
1829	20e. Varino, River Tejo	1·00	55

361 "Rajola" Tile from Setubal Peninsula (15th century)

1981. Tiles (1st series).

1830	**361**	8e.50 multicoloured	95	15
MS1831		146×102 mm. No. 1830 ×6	6·50	80

See also Nos. 1483/**MS**1844, 1847/**MS**1848, 1862/**MS**1864, 1871/**MS**1872, 1885/**MS**1886, 1893/**MS**1894, 1902/**MS**1904, 1914/**MS**1915, 1926/**MS**1927, 1935/**MS**1936, 1941/**MS**1943, 1952/**MS**1953, 1970/**MS**1971, 1972/**MS**1973, 1976/**MS**1978, 1983/**MS**1984, 1993/**MS**1994, 2020/**MS**2021 and 2031/**MS**2033.

362 Agua Dog

1981. 50th Anniv of Kennel Club of Portugal. Multicoloured.

1832	7e. Type **362**	55	30
1833	8e.50 Serra de Aires	55	30
1834	15e. Perdigueiro	1·00	30
1835	22e. Podengo	1·90	80
1836	25e.50 Castro Laboreiro	2·40	1·40
1837	33e.50 Serra de Estrela	2·75	1·00

363 "Agriculture"

1981. May Day. Multicoloured.

1838	8e.50 Type **363**	45	10
1839	25e.50 "Industry"	1·80	1·20

364 Dancer and Tapestry

1981. Europa. Multicoloured.

1840	22e. Type **364**	1·60	65
1841	48e. Painted boat prow, painted plate and shipwright with model boat	3·25	1·70
MS1842	108×109 mm. Nos. 1840/1 each ×2	13·00	6·50

1981. Tiles (2nd series). Horiz design as T 361.

1843	8e.50 multicoloured	95	15
MS1844	146×102 mm. No. 1843 ×6	6·25	5·00

DESIGN: 8e.50, Tracery-pattern tile from Seville (16th century).

365 St. Anthony Writing

1981. 750th Death Anniv of St. Anthony of Lisbon. Multicoloured.

1845	8e.50 Type **365**	55	15
1846	70e. St. Anthony giving blessing	4·75	2·50

1981. Tiles (3rd series). As T 361. Mult.

1847	8e.50 Arms of Jaime, Duke of Braganca (Seville, 1510)	95	15
MS1848	146×102 mm. No. 1847 ×6	6·00	5·00

366 King Joao II and Caravels

1981. 500th Anniv of King Joao II's Accession. Multicoloured.

1849	8e.50 Type **366**	55	15
1850	27e. King Joao II on horseback	3·25	1·10

367 "Dom Luiz", 1862

1981. 125th Anniv of Portuguese Railways. Multicoloured.

1851	8e.50 Type **367**	90	25
1852	19e. Pacific steam locomotive, 1925	2·75	1·30
1853	27e. Alco 1500 diesel locomotive, 1948	2·75	1·40
1854	33e.50 Alsthom BB 2600 electric locomotive, 1974	3·25	1·20

368 "Perrier" Pump, 1856

1981. Portuguese Fire Engines. Multicoloured.

1855	7e. Type **368**	95	25
1856	8e.50 Ford fire engine, 1927	85	25
1857	27e. Renault fire pump, 1914	2·40	1·30
1858	33e.50 Ford "Snorkel" combined hoist and pump, 1978	3·75	1·40

369 "Virgin and Child"

1981. Christmas. Crib Figures. Multicoloured.

1859	7e. Type **369**	1·20	40
1860	8e.50 "Nativity"	95	40
1861	27e. "Flight into Egypt"	2·50	1·50

1981. Tiles (4th series). As T 361. Multicoloured.

1862	8e.50 "Pisana" tile, Lisbon (16th century)	95	20
MS1863	146×102 mm. No. 1862 ×6	6·00	5·00
MS1864	120×102 mm. Nos. 1830, 1843, 1847 and 1862	6·75	5·75

370 St. Francis with Animals

1982. 800th Birth Anniv of St. Francis of Assisi. Multicoloured.

1865	8e.50 Type **370**	50	30
1866	27e. St. Francis helping to build church	2·75	1·90

371 Flags of E.E.C. Members

1982. 25th Anniv of European Economic Community.

1867 **371**	27e. multicoloured	1·70	1·00
MS1868	155×88 mm. No. 1867 ×4	6·75	5·75

372 Fort St. Catherina, Lighthouse and Memorial Column

1982. Centenary of Figueira da Foz City. Mult.

1869	10e. Type **372**	60	10
1870	19e. Tagus Bridge, shipbuilding yard and trawler	2·30	1·20

1982. Tiles (5th series). As T 361. Multicoloured.

1871	10e. Italo-Flemish pattern tile (17th century)	95	20
MS1872	146×102 mm. No. 1871 ×6	6·75	5·00

373 "Sagres I" (cadet barque)

1982. Sporting Events. Multicoloured.

1873	27e. Type **373** (Lisbon sailing races)	2·00	1·10
1874	33e.50 Roller hockey (25th World Championship)	2·75	1·80
1875	50e. "470" dinghies (World Championships)	4·00	1·90
1876	75e. Football (World Cup Football Championship, Spain)	6·25	2·20

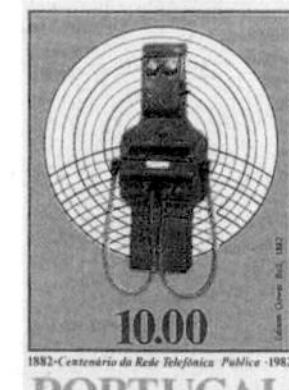

374 Edison Gower Bell Telephone, 1883

1982. Centenary of Public Telephone Service. Multicoloured.

1877	10e. Type **374**	55	10
1878	27e. Consolidated telephone, 1887	1·80	1·40

375 Embassy of King Manuel to Pope Leo X

1982. Europa.

1879 **375**	33e.50 multicoloured	2·75	1·10
MS1880	140×114 mm. No. 1879 ×4	13·00	6·50

376 Pope John Paul II and Shrine of Fatima

1982. Papal Visit. Multicoloured.

1881	10e. Type **376**	55	10
1882	27e. Pope and Sameiro Sanctuary	2·50	1·50
1883	33e.50 Pope and Lisbon Cathedral	3·00	1·50
MS1884	138×78 mm. Nos. 1881/3 each ×2	12·00	5·75

1982. Tiles (6th series). As T 361. Multicoloured.

1885	10e. Altar front panel depicting oriental tapestry (17th century)	95	20
MS1886	146×102 mm. No. 1885 ×6	6·00	5·00

377 Dunlin

1982. "Philexfrance 82" International Stamp Exhibition, Paris. Birds. Multicoloured.

1887	10e. Type **377**	55	15
1888	19e. Red-crested pochard	2·20	80
1889	27e. Greater flamingo	2·50	1·10
1890	33e.50 Black-winged stilt	2·75	1·60

378 Dr. Robert Koch

1982. Centenary of Discovery of Tubercle Bacillus. Multicoloured.

1891	27e. Type **378**	2·00	1·50
1892	33e.50 Lungs	2·30	1·60

1982. Tiles (7th series). As T 361. Multicoloured.

1893	10e. Polychromatic quadrilobate pattern, 1630–40	95	15
MS1894	146×102 mm. No. 1893 ×6	6·00	5·00

379 Wine Glass and Stop Sign

1982. "Don't Drink and Drive".

1895 **379**	10e. multicoloured	70	15

380 Fairey IIID Seaplane "Lusitania"

1982. "Lubrapex 82" Brazilian–Portuguese Stamp Exhibition, Curitiba. Multicoloured.

1896	10e. Type **380**	45	30
1897	19e. Dornier Do-J Wal flying boat "Argus"	2·10	1·00
1898	33e.50 Douglas DC-7C "Seven Seas" airliner	2·50	1·00
1899	50e. Boeing 747-282B jetliner	2·75	1·30
MS1900	155×98 mm. Nos. 1896/9	8·00	6·50

381 Marquis de Pombal

1982. Death Bicentenary of Marquis de Pombal (statesman and reformer).

1901 **381**	10e. multicoloured	70	15

1982. Tiles (8th series). As T 361. Multicoloured.

1902	10e. Monochrome quadrilobate pattern, 1670–90	95	15
MS1903	146×102 mm. No. 1902 ×6	6·00	5·00
MS1904	101×121 mm. Nos. 1871, 1885, 1893 and 1902	6·00	5·00

382 Gallic Cock and Tricolour

1983. Centenary of French Alliance (French language teaching association).

1905 **382**	27e. multicoloured	2·00	1·00

383 Lisnave Shipyard

1983. 75th Anniv of Port of Lisbon Administration.

1906 **383**	10e. multicoloured	70	15

384 Export Campaign Emblem

1983. Export Promotion.

1907 **384**	10e. multicoloured	70	15

385 Midshipman, 1782, and Frigate "Vasco da Gama"

1983. Naval Uniforms. Multicoloured.

1908	12e.50 Type **385**	1·00	15
1909	25e. Seaman and steam corvette "Estefania", 1845	1·70	40
1910	30e. Marine sergeant and cruiser "Adamastor", 1900	2·30	75
1911	37e.50 Midshipman and frigate "Joao Belo", 1982	2·50	90

386 W.C.Y. Emblem

1983. World Cummunications Year. Mult.

1912	10e. Type **386**	55	25
1913	33e.50 W.C.Y. emblem (diff)	2·30	1·40

1983. Tiles (9th series). As T 361. Multicoloured.

1914	12e.50 Hunter killing white bull (tile from Saldanha Palace, Lisbon, 17/18th century)	1·10	20
MS1915	146×102 mm. No. 1914 ×6	7·25	6·25

387 Portuguese Helmet (16th century)

1983. "Expo XVII" Council of Europe Exhibition. Multicoloured.

1916	11e. Type **387**	1·20	35
1917	12e.50 Astrolabe (16th century)	95	35
1918	25e. Portuguese caravels (from 16th-century Flemish tapestry)	2·00	65
1919	30e. Carved capital (12th century)	2·30	70
1920	37e.50 Hour glass (16th century)	2·10	1·20
1921	40e. Detail from Chinese panel painting (16th–17th century)	2·50	1·10
MS1922	115×120 mm. Nos. 1916/21	16·00	9·75

388 Egas Moniz (Nobel Prize winner and brain surgeon)

1983. Europa.

1923 **388**	37e.50 multicoloured	2·75	1·00
MS1924	140×114 mm. No. 1923 ×4	14·50	8·25

389 Passenger in Train

1983. European Ministers of Transport Conference.

1925 **389**	30e. blue, deep blue and silver	3·00	1·00

1983. Tiles (10th series). As T 361. Multicoloured.

1926	12e.50 Tiles depicting birds (18th century)	1·10	20
MS1927	146×102 mm. No. 1926 ×6	7·25	6·25

390 Mediterranean Monk Seal

1983. "Brasiliana 83" International Stamp Exhibition, Rio de Janeiro. Marine Mammals. Multicoloured.

1928	12e.50 Type **390**	1·00	35
1929	30e. Common dolphin	3·75	60
1930	37e.50 Killer whale	3·25	1·60
1931	80e. Humpback whale	5·75	1·50
MS1932	133×81 mm. Nos. 1928/31	14·50	12·50

391 Assassination of Spanish Administrator by Prince John

1983. 600th Anniv of Independence. Mult.

1933	12e.50 Type **391**	1·00	25
1934	30e. Prince John proclaimed King of Portugal	3·50	1·60

1983. Tiles (11th series). As T 361. Multicoloured.

1935	12e.50 Flower pot by Gabriel del Barco (18th century)	1·10	20
MS1936	146×102 mm. No. 1935 ×6	7·00	5·75

392 Bartolomeu de Gusmao and Model Balloon, 1709

1983. Bicentenary of Manned Flight. Mult.

1937	16e. Type **392**	75	15
1938	51e. Montgolfier balloon, 1783	2·75	1·20

393 "Adoration of the Magi"

1983. Christmas. Stained Glass Windows from Monastery of Our Lady of Victory, Batalha. Multicoloured.

1939	12e.50 Type **393**	70	25
1940	30e. "The Flight into Egypt"	3·00	1·20

1983. Tiles (12th series). As T 361. Multicoloured.

1941	12e.50 Turkish horseman (18th century)	1·10	20
MS1942	146×102 mm. No. 1941 ×6	7·00	5·75
MS1943	120×102 mm. Nos. 1914, 1926, 1935 and 1941	6·00	5·00

394 Siberian Tiger

1983. Centenary of Lisbon Zoo. Multicoloured.

1944	16e. Type **394**	1·80	25
1945	16e. Cheetah	1·80	25
1946	16e. Blesbok	1·80	25
1947	16e. White rhino	1·80	25

395 Fighter Pilot and Hawker Hurricane Mk II, 1954

1983. Air Force Uniforms. Multicoloured.

1948	16e. Type **395**	80	10
1949	35e. Pilot in summer uniform and Republic F-84G Thunderjet, 1960	2·50	80
1950	40e. Paratrooper in walking-out uniform and Nord 250ID Noratlas military transport plane, 1966	2·50	85
1951	51e. Pilot in normal uniform and Vought A-70 Corsair II bomber, 1966	3·00	1·20

1984. Tiles (13th series). As T 361. Multicoloured.

1952	16e. Coat of arms of King Jose I (late 18th century)	1·10	20
MS1953	146×102 mm. No. 1952 ×6	7·25	6·25

396 "25" on Crate (25th Lisbon International Fair)

1984. Events.

1954	35e. Type **396**	2·50	85
1955	40e. Wheat rainbow and globe (World Food Day)	2·20	85
1956	51e. Hand holding stylized flower (15th World Congress of International Rehabilitation) (vert)	3·00	1·20

397 National Flag

1984. 10th Anniv of Revolution.

1957	**397**	16e. multicoloured	1·40	20

398 Bridge

1984. Europa.

1958	**398**	51e. multicoloured	3·00	1·50
MS1959		140×114 mm. No. 1958 ×4	14·00	8·25

399 "Panel of St. Vincent"

1984. "Lubrapex 84" Portuguese–Brazilian Stamp Exhibition. Multicoloured.

1960	16e. Type **399**	70	25
1961	40e. "St. James" (altar panel)	3·25	90
1962	51e. "View of Lisbon" (painting)	4·00	1·20
1963	66e. "Head of Youth" (Domingos Sequeira)	4·25	1·60
MS1964	110×111 mm. Nos. 1960/3	12·50	9·75

400 Fencing

1984. Olympic Games, Los Angeles, and 75th Anniv of Portuguese Olympic Committee. Multicoloured.

1965	35e. Type **400**	2·40	70
1966	40e. Gymnastics	2·75	90
1967	51e. Running	3·25	1·30
1968	80e. Pole vaulting	3·50	1·30
MS1969	90×92 mm. 100e. Hurdling	9·75	8·25

1984. Tiles (14th series). As T 361. Multicoloured.

1970	16e. Pictorial tile from Pombal Palace, Lisbon (late 18th century)	1·10	20
MS1971	146×102 mm. No. 1970 ×6	7·25	6·25

1984. Tiles (15th series). As T 361. Multicoloured.

1972	16e. Four art nouveau tiles (late 19th century)	1·10	20
MS1973	146×102 mm. No. 1972 ×6	7·25	6·25

401 Gil Eanes

1984. Anniversaries. Multicoloured.

1974	16e. Type **401** (550th anniv of rounding of Cape Bojador)	55	10
1975	51e. King Pedro IV of Portugal and I of Brazil (150th death anniv)	3·25	1·30

1984. Tiles (16th series). As T 361. Multicoloured.

1976	16e. Grasshoppers and wheat (R. Bordalo Pinheiro, 19th century)	1·10	20
MS1977	146×102 mm. No. 1976 ×6	7·25	6·25
MS1978	120×102 mm. Nos. 1952, 1970, 1972 and 1976	6·00	5·00

402 Infantry Grenadier, 1740, and Regiment in Formation

1985. Army Uniforms. Multicoloured.

1979	20e. Type **402**	80	25
1980	46e. Officer, Fifth Cavalry, 1810, and cavalry charge	3·25	85
1981	60e. Artillery corporal, 1891, and Krupp 9 mm gun and crew	3·25	1·00
1982	100e. Engineer in chemical protection suit, 1985, and bridge-laying armoured car	3·75	1·50

1985. Tiles (17th series). As T 361. Multicoloured.

1983	20e. Detail of panel by Jorge Barrados in Lisbon Faculty of Letters (20th century)	1·10	20
MS1984	146×102 mm. No. 1983 ×6	6·75	5·75

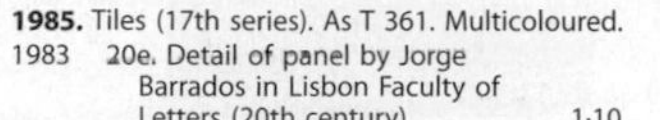

403 Calcada R. dos Santos Kiosk

1985. Lisbon Kiosks. Multicoloured.

1985	20e. Type **403**	1·20	25
1986	20e. Tivoli kiosk, Avenida da Liberdade	1·20	25
1987	20e. Porto de Lisboa kiosk	1·20	25
1988	20e. Rua de Artilharia Um kiosk	1·20	25

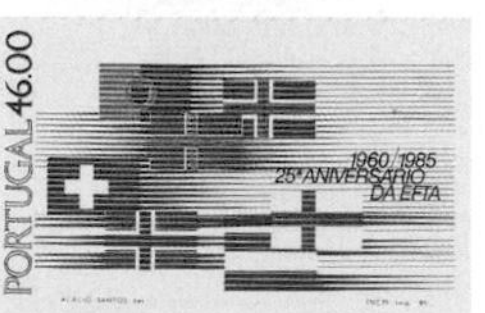

404 Flags of Member Countries

1985. 25th Anniv of European Free Trade Assn.

1989	**404**	46e. multicoloured	1·90	80

405 Profiles

1985. International Youth Year.

1990	**405**	60e. multicoloured	2·40	1·10

406 Woman holding Adufe (tambourine)

1985. Europa.

1991	**406**	60e. multicoloured	4·25	1·70
MS1992		140×114 mm. No. 1991 ×4	18·00	8·25

1985. Tiles (18th series). As T 361. Multicoloured.

1993	20e. Detail of panel by Maria Keil on Avenida Infante Santo (20th century)	1·10	20
MS1994	146×102 mm. No. 1993 ×6	6·75	5·75

407 Knight on Horseback

1985. Anniversaries. Multicoloured.

1995	20e. Type **407** (600th anniv of Battle of Aljubarrota)	90	15
1996	46e. Queen Leonor and hospital (500th anniv of Caldas da Rainha thermal hospital)	2·75	90
1997	60e. Pedro Reinel (500th anniversary of first Portuguese sea-chart)	3·00	1·50

408 Farmhouse, Minho

1985. Architecture.

1998	-	50c. black, bistre and blue	15	15
1999	-	1e. black, yellow & green	15	15
2000	-	1e.50 black, green and emerald	15	15
2001	-	2e.50 brown, orange & bl	15	15
2002	-	10e. black, purple & pink	25	20
2003	**408**	20e. brn, yell & dp yell	40	15
2004	-	22e.50 brown, blue and ochre	40	20
2005	-	25e. brown, yellow & grn	45	15
2006	-	27e. black, grn & yell	65	15
2007	-	29e. black, yellow & orge	65	15
2008	-	30e. black, blue & brown	65	15
2009	-	40e. black, yellow & grn	90	25
2010	-	50e. black, blue & brown	1·00	20
2011	-	55e. black, yellow & grn	1·00	20
2012	-	60e. black, orange & blue	1·30	40
2013	-	70e. black, yellow & orge	1·30	40
2014	-	80e. brown, green and red	1·50	45
2015	-	90e. brown, yellow & grn	1·70	45
2016	-	100e. brown, yellow & bl	2·00	50
2017	-	500e. black, grey and blue	8·50	3·00

DESIGNS: 50e. Saloia house, Estremadura; 1e. Beira inland house; 1e.50, Ribatejo house; 2e.50, Tras-os-montes houses; 10e. Minho and Douro coast house; 22e.50, Alentejo houses; 25e. Sitio house, Algarve; 27e. Beira inland house (different); 29e. Tras-os-montes house; 30e. Algarve house; 40e. Beira inland house (different); 50e. Beira coasthouse; 55e. Tras-os-montes house (different); 60e. Beira coast house (different); 70e. South Estramadura and Alentejo house; 80e. Estremadura house; 90e. Minho house; 100e. Monte house, Alentejo; 500e. Terraced houses, East Algarve.

1985. Tiles (19th series). As T 361. Multicoloured.

2020	20e. Head of woman by Querubim Lapa (20th century)	1·10	20
MS2021	147×101 mm. No. 2020 ×6	6·75	5·75

409 Aquilino Ribeiro (writer)

1985. Anniversaries. Multicoloured.

2022	20e. Type **409** (birth centenary)	95	10
2023	46e. Fernando Pessoa (poet 50th death anniv)	2·40	85

410 Berlenga National Reserve

1985. National Parks and Reserves. Multicoloured.

2024	20e. Type **410**	55	10
2025	40e. Estrela Mountains National Park	2·40	90
2026	46e. Boquilobo Marsh National Reserve	3·00	1·10
2027	80e. Formosa Lagoon National Reserve	3·25	1·20
MS2028	100×68 mm. 100e. Jacinto Dunes National Reserve	7·75	6·50

411 "Nativity"

1985. Christmas. Illustrations from "Book of Hours of King Manoel I". Multicoloured.

2029	20e. Type **411**	60	10
2030	46e. "Adoration of the Three Wise Men"	2·40	90

1985. Tiles (20th series). As T 361. Multicoloured.

2031	20e. Detail of panel by Manuel Cargaleiro (20th century)	1·10	20
MS2032	146×102 mm. No. 2031 ×6	10·50	6·25
MS2033	120×102 mm. Nos. 1983, 1993, 2020 and 2031	6·75	5·75

412 Post Rider

1985. No value expressed.

2034	**412**	(–) green and deep green	1·10	15

413 Map and Flags of Member Countries

1985. Admission of Portugal and Spain to European Economic Community. Multicoloured.

2035	20e. Flags of Portugal and Spain uniting with flags of other members	80	25
2036	57e.50 Type **413**	3·00	1·30

See also No. **MS**2056.

414 Feira Castle

1986. Castles (1st series). Multicoloured.

2037	22e.50 Type **414**	1·20	20
2038	22e.50 Beja Castle	1·20	20

See also Nos. 2040/1, 2054/5, 2065/6, 2073/4, 2086/7 2093/4, 2102/3 and 2108/9.

415 Globe and Dove

1986. International Peace Year.

2039	**415**	75e. multicoloured	3·25	1·40

1986. Castles (2nd series). As T 414. Multicoloured.

2040	22e.50 Braganca Castle	1·20	20
2041	22e.50 Guimaraes Castle	1·20	20

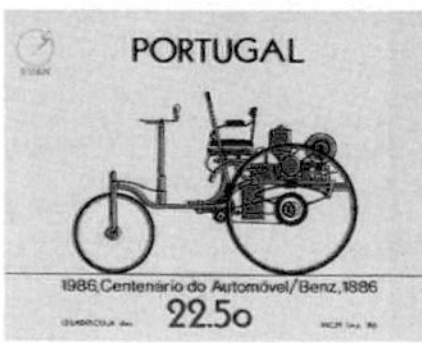

416 Benz Motor Tricycle, 1886

1986. Centenary of Motor Car. Multicoloured.

2042	22e.50 Type **416**	1·50	15
2043	22e.50 Daimler motor car, 1886	1·50	15

417 Allis Shad

1986. Europa.

2044	**417**	68e.50 multicoloured	3·75	1·60
MS2045		140×114 mm. No. 2044 ×4	19·00	9·75

418 Alter

1986. "Ameripex 86" International Stamp Exn, Chicago. Thoroughbred Horses. Multicoloured.

2046	22e.50 Type **418**	80	25
2047	47e.50 Lusitano	2·75	95
2048	52e.50 Garrano	3·00	1·30
2049	68e.50 Sorraia	3·25	1·50

419 Comet

1986. Appearance of Halley's Comet. Sheet 100×68 mm.

MS2050	**419**	100e. multicoloured	15·00	12·50

420 Diogo Cao (navigator) and Monument

1986. Anniversaries. Multicoloured.

2051	22e.50 Type **420** (500th anniv of 2nd expedition to Africa)	80	15
2052	52e.50 Passos Manuel (Director) and capital (150th anniv of National Academy of Fine Arts, Lisbon)	2·10	95
2053	52e.50 Joao Baptista Ribeiro (painter and Oporto Academy Director) and drawing (150th anniv of Portuguese Academy of Fine Arts, Oporto)	2·10	95

1986. Castles (3rd series). As T 414. Multicoloured.

2054	22e.50 Belmonte Castle	1·20	25
2055	22e.50 Montemor-o-Velho Castle	1·20	25

1986. "Europex 86" Stamp Exhibition, Lisbon. Sheet 127×91 mm.

MS2056	Nos. 2035/6 each ×2	8·00	6·50

421 Hand writing on Postcard

1986. Anniversaries. Multicoloured.

2057	22e.50 Type **421** (centenary of first Portuguese postcards)	1·10	20
2058	47e.50 Guardsman and houses (75th anniv of National Republican Guard)	2·00	95
2059	52e.50 Calipers, globe and banner (50th anniv of Order of Engineers)	2·20	1·00

422 Seasonal Mill, Douro

1986. "Luprapex 86" Portuguese–Brazilian Stamp Exhibition, Rio de Janeiro. Multicoloured.

2060	22e.50 Type **422**	80	30
2061	47e.50 Seasonal mill, Coimbra	1·80	1·10
2062	52e.50 Overshot bucket mill, Gerez	2·40	1·20
2063	90e. Permanent stream mill, Braga	3·00	1·10
MS2064	140×114 mm. Nos. 2060/3	12·00	8·25

1987. Castles (4th series). As T 414. Mult.

2065	25e. Silves Castle	1·20	20
2066	25e. Evora-Monte Castle	1·20	20

423 Houses on Stilts, Tocha

1987. 75th Anniv (1986) of Organized Tourism. Multicoloured.

2067	25e. Type **423**	80	25
2068	57e. Fishing boats, Espinho	2·75	1·20
2069	98e. Fountain, Arraiolos	3·50	2·00

424 Hand, Sun and Trees

1987. European Environment Year. Multicoloured.

2070	25e. Type **424**	80	30
2071	57e. Hands and flower on map of Europe	2·00	1·10
2072	74e.50 Hand, sea, purple dye murex shell, moon and rainbow	3·25	1·40

1987. Castles (5th series). As T 414. Multicoloured.

2073	25e. Leiria Castle	1·20	20
2074	25e. Trancoso Castle	1·20	20

425 Bank Borges and Irmao Agency, Vila do Conde (Alvaro Siza)

1987. Europa. Architecture.

2075	**425**	74e.50 multicoloured	3·00	1·60
MS2076		140×114 mm. No. 2075 ×4	15·00	8·25

426 Cape Mondego

1987. "Capex '87" International Stamp Exhibition Toronto. Portuguese Lighthouses. Multicoloured.

2077	25e. Type **426**	1·00	35
2078	25e. Berlenga	1·00	35
2079	25e. Aveiro	1·00	35
2080	25e. Cape St. Vincent	1·00	35

427 Souza-Cardoso (self-portrait)

1987. Birth Centenary of Amadeo de Souza-Cardoso (painter).

2081	**427**	74e.50 multicoloured	2·40	1·10

428 Clipped 400 Reis Silver Coin

1987. 300th Anniv of Portuguese Paper Currency.

2082	**428**	100e. multicoloured	3·25	1·00

429 Dias's Fleet leaving Lisbon

1987. 500th Anniv of Bartolomeu Dias's Voyages (1st issue). Multicoloured.

2083	25e. Type **429**	1·20	20
2084	25e. Ships off coast of Africa	1·20	20

Nos. 2083/4 were printed together, se-tenant, each pair forming a composite design.

See also Nos. 2099/2100.

430 Library

1987. 150th Anniv of Portuguese Royal Library, Rio de Janeiro.

2085	**430**	125e. multicoloured	3·75	1·60

1987. Castles (6th series). As T 414. Multicoloured.

2086	25e. Marvao Castle	1·20	20
2087	25e. St. George's Castle, Lisbon	1·20	20

431 Records and Compact Disc Player

1987. Centenary of Gramophone Record. Sheet 140×114 mm containing T 431 and similar horiz design. Multicoloured.

MS2088	75e. Type **431**; 125e. Early gramophone	12·00	9·75

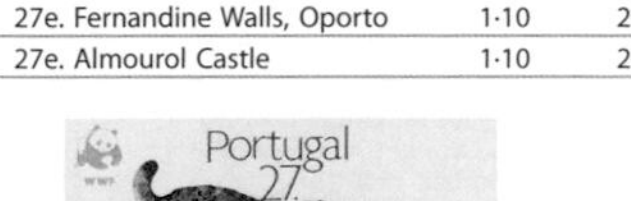

432 Angels around Baby Jesus, Tree and Kings (Jose Manuel Coutinho)

1987. Christmas. Children's Paintings. Mult.

2089	25e. Type **432**	1·10	25
2090	57e. Children dancing around sunburst (Rosa J. Leitao)	2·10	1·00
2091	74e.50 Santa Claus flying on dove (Sonya Alexandra Hilario)	2·30	1·30
MS2092	140×114 mm. Nos. 2089/91	6·75	5·25

1988. Castles (7th series). As T 414. Multicoloured.

2093	27e. Fernandine Walls, Oporto	1·10	20
2094	27e. Almourol Castle	1·10	20

433 Lynx

1988. Iberian Lynx. Multicoloured.

2095	27e. Type **433**	1·40	35
2096	27e. Lynx carrying rabbit	1·40	35
2097	27e. Pair of lynxes	1·40	35
2098	27e. Mother with young	1·40	35

434 King Joao II sending Pero da Covilha on Expedition

1988. 500th Anniv of Voyages of Bartolomeu Dias (2nd issue) (2099/2100) and Pero da Covilha (2101). Multicoloured.

2099	27e. Dias's ships in storm off Cape of Good Hope	1·00	25
2100	27e. Contemporary map	1·00	55
2101	105e. Type **434**	3·25	1·50

Nos. 2099/2100 are as T **429**.

1988. Castles (8th series). As T 414. Multicoloured.

2102	27e. Palmela Castle	1·10	20
2103	27e. Vila Nova da Cerveira Castle	1·10	20

435 19th-century Mail Coach

1988. Europa. Transport and Communications.

2104	**435** 80e. multicoloured	4·25	1·70
MS2105	139×112 mm. As No. 2104 ×4 but with cream background	16·00	9·75

436 Map of Europe and Monnet

1988. Birth Centenary of Jean Monnet (statesman). "Europex 88" Stamp Exhibition.

2106	**436** 60e. multicoloured	1·90	1·10

437 Window reflecting Cordovil House and Fountain

1988. UNESCO World Heritage Site, Evora. "Lubrapex 88" Stamp Exhibition. Sheet 112×139 mm.

MS2107	**437** 150e. multicoloured	10·50	9·25

1988. Castles (9th series). As T 414. Multicoloured.

2108	27e. Chaves Castle	1·10	25
2109	27e. Penedono Castle	1·10	25

438 "Part of a Viola" (Amadeo de Souza-Cardoso)

1988. 20th-century Portuguese Paintings (1st series). Multicoloured.

2110	27e. Type **438**	80	30
2111	60e. "Acrobats" (Almada Negreiros)	2·00	1·00
2112	80e. "Still Life with Viola" (Eduardo Viana)	2·30	1·20
MS2113	138×112 mm. Nos. 2110/12	7·50	6·25

See also Nos. 2121/**MS**2125, 2131/**MS**2134, 2148/**MS**2152, 2166/**MS**2169 and 2206/**MS**2210.

439 Archery

1988. Olympic Games, Seoul. Multicoloured.

2114	27e. Type **439**	1·00	30
2115	55e. Weightlifting	1·90	1·10
2116	60e. Judo	2·00	1·10
2117	80e. Tennis	2·50	1·10
MS2118	114×67 mm. 200e. Yachting (39×30 mm)	12·50	11·50

440 "Winter" (House of the Fountains, Coimbra)

1988. Roman Mosaics of 3rd Century. Mult.

2119	27e. Type **440**	70	30
2120	80e. "Fish" (Baths, Faro)	2·40	1·10

1988. 20th Century Portuguese Paintings (2nd series). As T 438. Multicoloured.

2121	27e. "Internment" (Mario Eloy)	80	20
2122	60e. "Lisbon Houses" (Carlos Botelho)	1·90	80
2123	80e. "Avejao Lirico" (Antonio Pedro)	2·20	1·10
MS2124	140×114 mm. Nos. 2121/3	7·50	6·25
MS2125	139×144 mm. Nos. 2110/12 and 2121/3	13·00	10·50

441 Braga Cathedral

1989. Anniversaries. Multicoloured.

2126	30e. Type **441** (900th anniv)	1·00	40
2127	55e. Caravel, Fischer's lovebird and S. Jorge da Mina Castle (505th anniv)	1·70	80
2128	60e. Sailor using astrolabe (500th anniv of South Atlantic voyages)	2·40	1·30

Nos. 2127/8 also have the "India 89" Stamp Exhibition, New Delhi, emblem.

442 "Greetings"

1989. Greetings Stamps. Multicoloured.

2129	29e. Type **442**	80	20
2130	60e. Airplane distributing envelopes inscribed "with Love"	1·30	70

1989. 20th-Century Portuguese Paintings (3rd series). As T 438. Multicoloured.

2131	29e. "Antithesis of Calm" (Antonio Dacosta)	80	15
2132	60e. "Unskilled Mason's Lunch" (Julio Pomar)	1·90	90
2133	87e. "Simumis" (Vespeira)	2·20	1·20
MS2134	139×111 mm. Nos. 2131/3	7·50	6·25

443 Flags in Ballot Box

1989. 3rd Direct Elections to European Parliament.

2135	**443** 60e. multicoloured	1·90	1·10

444 Boy with Spinning Top

1989. Europa. Children's Games and Toys. Multicoloured.

2136	80e. Type **444**	2·50	1·50
MS2137	138×112 mm. 80e. ×2 Type **444**; 80e. ×2 Spinning tops	8·75	7·25

445 Cable Railway

1989. Lisbon Transport. Multicoloured.

2138	29e. Type **445**	80	25
2139	65e. Electric tramcar	2·30	95
2140	87e. Santa Justa lift	2·40	1·30
2141	100e. Bus	2·75	1·30
MS2142	100×50 mm. 250e. River ferry (39×29 mm)	11·00	10·00

446 Gyratory Mill, Ansiao

1989. Windmills. Multicoloured.

2143	29e. Type **446**	80	25
2144	60e. Stone mill, Santiago do Cacem	2·30	95
2145	87e. Post mill, Afife	2·40	1·20
2146	100e. Wooden mill, Caldas da Rainha	2·75	1·40

447 Drummer Boy

1989. Bicentenary of French Revolution and "Philexfrance 89" International Stamp Exhibition, Paris. Sheet 111×139 mm.

MS2147	**447** 250e. multicoloured	11·00	10·00

1989. 20th-Century Portuguese Paintings (4th series). As T 438.

2148	29e. blue, green and black	75	30
2149	60e. multicoloured	1·90	1·10
2150	87e. multicoloured	2·30	1·40
MS2151	139×111 mm. Nos. 2148/50	7·50	6·25
MS2152	138×144 mm. Nos. 231/3 and 2148/50	13·00	10·50

DESIGNS: 29e. "046-72" (Fernando Lanhas); 60e. "Spirals" (Nadir Afonso); 87e. "Sim" (Carlos Calvet).

448 Luis I (death centenary) and Ajuda Palace, Lisbon

1989. National Palaces (1st series). Multicoloured.

2153	29e. Type **448**	45	20
2154	60e. Queluz Palace	1·80	1·10

See also Nos. 2211/14.

449 "Armeria pseudarmeria"

1989. Wild Flowers. Multicoloured.

2155	29e. Type **449**	70	20
2156	60e. "Santolina impressa"	1·70	80
2157	87e. "Linaria lamarckii"	2·10	1·20
2158	100e. "Limonium multiflorum"	2·50	1·60

450 Blue and White Plate

1990. Portuguese Faience (1st series). Mult.

2159	33e. Type **450**	80	30
2160	33e. Blue and white plate with man in centre	80	30
2161	35e. Vase decorated with flowers	95	35
2162	60e. Fish-shaped jug	1·50	95
2163	60e. Blue and white plate with arms in centre	1·50	95
2164	60e. Blue and white dish with lid	1·50	95
MS2165	112×140 mm. 250e. Plate with crown in centre	7·75	7·00

See also Nos. 2221/**MS**2227 and 2262/**MS**2268.

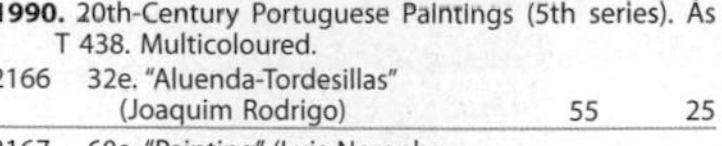

1990. 20th-Century Portuguese Paintings (5th series). As T 438. Multicoloured.

2166	32e. "Aluenda-Tordesillas" (Joaquim Rodrigo)	55	25
2167	60e. "Painting" (Luis Noronha da Costa)	1·70	80
2168	95e. "Painting" (Vasco Costa)	2·30	1·10
MS2169	138×111 mm. Nos. 2166/8	7·50	6·25

451 Joao Goncalves Zarco

1990. Portuguese Navigators.

2170	**451** 2e. red, pink and black	15	15
2171	- 3e. green, blue and black	10	10
2172	- 4e. purple, red and black	10	10
2173	- 5e. brown, grey & black	20	15
2174	- 6e. deep green, green and black	20	15
2175	- 10e. dp red, red & black	15	10
2176	- 32e. green, brown & blk	75	15
2177	- 35e. red, pink and black	70	15
2178	- 38e. blue, lt blue & black	75	25
2179	- 42e. green, grey & black	75	20
2180	- 45e. green, yellow & blk	55	30
2181	- 60e. yellow, purple & blk	1·40	50
2182	- 65e. brown, green & blk	1·30	40
2183	- 70e. violet, mauve & blk	1·20	40
2184	- 75e. olive, green & black	1·00	65
2185	- 80e. orange, brn & blk	1·80	70
2186	- 100e. red, orange & blk	2·40	85
2187	- 200e. green, yellow & blk	3·00	90
2188	- 250e. blue, green & black	4·75	1·90
2189	- 350e. red, pink and black	5·75	2·20

DESIGNS: 3e. Pedro Lopes de Sousa; 4e. Duarto Pacheco Pereira; 5e. Tristao Vaz Teixeira; 6e. Pedro Alvares Cabral; 10e. Joao de Castro; 32e. Bartolomeu Perestrelo; 35e. Gil Eanes: 38e. Vasco da Gama; 42e. Joao de Lisboa; 45e. Joao Rodrigues Cabrilho; 60e. Nuno Tristao; 65e. Joaoda Nova; 70e. Fernao de Magalhaes (Magellan); 75e. Pedro Fernandes de Queiros; 80e. Diogo Gomes; 100e. Diogo de Silves; 200e. Estevao Gomes; 250e. Diogo Cao; 350e. Bartolomeu Dias.

452 Score and Singers

1990. Anniversaries. Multicoloured.

2191	32e. Type **452** (centenary of "A Portuguesa" (national anthem))	60	20
2192	70e. Students and teacher (700th anniv of granting of charter to Lisbon University) (vert)	2·20	1·10

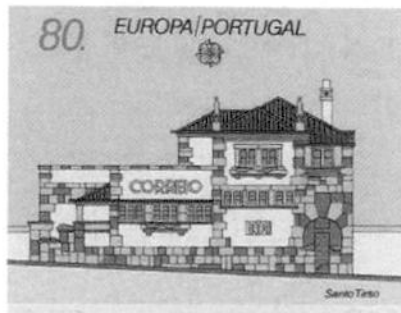

453 Santo Tirso Post Office

1990. Europa. Post Office Buildings. Multicoloured.

2193	80e. Type **453**	2·10	1·10
MS2194	139×111 mm. 80e. ×2 Type **453**; 80e. ×2 19th-century Mail Coach Office	8·25	5·25

454 Stamping Letter

1990. "Stamp World London 90" International Stamp Exhibition and 150th Anniv of the Penny Black. Sheet 111×140 mm.

MS2195	**454** 250e. multicoloured	11·00	9·75

455 Street with Chairs under Trees

1990. Greetings Stamps. Multicoloured.

2196 60e. Type **455** 1·70 90
2197 60e. Hand holding bouquet out of car window 1·70 90
2198 60e. Man with bouquet crossing street 1·70 90
2199 60e. Women with bouquet behind pillar box 1·70 90

456 Camilo Castelo Branco (writer)

1990. Death Anniversaries. Multicoloured.

2200 65e. Type **456** (centenary) 1·30 90
2201 70e. Brother Bartolomeu dos Martires (Bishop of Braga, 400th anniv) 1·90 1·10

457 Barketta

1990. 15th-Century Explorers' Ships. Mult.

2202 32e. Type **457** 55 25
2203 60e. Carvel-built fishing boat 1·60 80
2204 70e. Nau 1·80 1·10
2205 95e. Caravel 2·20 1·40

458 Pena Palace

1990. 20th-Century Portuguese Paintings (6th series). As T 438. Multicoloured.

2206 32e. "Dom Sebastiao" (Costa Pinheiro) 55 30
2207 60e. "Domestic Scene with Green Dog" (Paula Rego) 1·80 1·10
2208 95e. "Homage to Magritte" (Jose de Guimaraes) 2·75 1·30
MS2209 138×112 mm. Nos. 2206/8 4·50 2·40
MS2210 138×145 mm. Nos. 2166/8 and 2206/8 13·00 10·50

1990. National Palaces (2nd series). Mult.

2211 32e. Type **458** 75 25
2212 60e. Vila Palace 1·60 80
2213 70e. Mafra Palace 1·70 1·10
2214 120e. Guimaraes Palace 2·10 1·40

459 Carneiro

1990. 10th Death Anniv of Francisco Sa Carneiro (founder of Popular Democratic Party and Prime Minister, 1980).

2215 **459** 32e. black and brown 70 25

460 Steam Locomotive No. 02, 1887

1990. Centenary of Rossio Railway Station, Lisbon. Multicoloured.

2216 32e. Type **460** 75 25
2217 60e. Steam locomotive No. 010, 1891 1·60 80
2218 70e. Steam locomotive No. 071, 1916 1·70 1·10
2219 95e. Electric train, 1956 2·10 1·40
MS2220 112×80 mm. 200e. Station clock (39×29 mm) 7·50 7·25

1991. Portuguese Faience (2nd series). As T 450. Multicoloured.

2221 35e. Barrel of fish and plate (Rato factory Lisbon) 70 25
2222 35e. Floral vase (Bica do Sapato factory) 70 25
2223 35e. Gargoyle (Costa Briozo factory, Coimbra) 70 25
2224 60e. Dish with leaf pattern (Juncal factory) 1·30 70
2225 60e. Coffee pot (Cavaquinho factory, Oporto) 1·30 70
2226 60e. Mug (Massarelos factory, Oporto) 1·30 70
MS2227 114×140 mm. 250e. Plate with portrait in centre (Miragaia factory, Oporto) 8·25 8·00

461 Greater Flamingoes

1991. European Tourism Year. Multicoloured.

2228 60e. Type **461** 1·20 90
2229 110e. European chameleon 2·30 1·70
MS2230 112×104 mm. 250e. Red deer (39×31 mm) 7·25 7·00

462 "Eutelsat II" Satellite

1991. Europa. Europe in Space. Multicoloured.

2231 80e. Type **462** 2·50 2·00
MS2232 140×112 mm. 80e. ×2, Type **462**; 80e. ×2, "Olympus I" satellite 8·50 5·75

463 Caravel

1991. 16th-Century Explorers' Ships. Mult.

2233 35e. Type **463** 55 30
2234 75e. Port view of nau 1·80 85
2235 80e. Stern view of nau 1·90 1·00
2236 110e. Galleon 2·20 1·10

464 "Isabella of Portugal and Philip the Good" (anon)

1991. "Europhalia 91 Portugal" Festival, Belgium. Sheet 140×112 mm.

MS2237 **464** 300e. multicoloured 10·50 9·50

465 Emerald and Diamond Bow

1991. "Royal Treasures" Exhibition, Ajuda Palace (1st issue). Multicoloured.

2238 35e. Type **465** 55 35
2239 60e. Royal sceptre 1·60 70
2240 70e. Sash of the Grand Cross 1·80 95
2241 80e. Hilt of sabre 1·90 1·00
2242 140e. Crown 2·40 1·20

See also Nos. 2270/4.

466 Antero de Quental (writer)

1991. Anniversaries. Multicoloured.

2243 35e. Type **466** (death centenary) 60 20
2244 110e. Arrival of expedition and baptism of Sonyo prince (500th anniv of first Portuguese missionary expedition to the Congo) 2·40 1·20

467 Faculty of Architecture, Oporto University (Siza Vieira)

1991. Architecture. Multicoloured.

2245 35e. Type **467** 55 20
2246 60e. Torre do Tombo (Arsenio Cordeiro Associates) 1·40 50
2247 80e. Maria Pia bridge over River Douro (Edgar Cardoso) and Donna Maria bridge 1·70 1·00
2248 110e. Setubal–Braga highway 2·10 1·10

468 King Manoel I creating Public Post, 1520

1991. History of Communications in Portugal. Mult.

2249 35e. Type **468** 60 25
2250 60e. Woman posting letter and telegraph operator (merging of posts and telegraph operations, 1881) 1·20 65
2251 80e. Postman, mail van and switchboard operator (creation of Posts and Telecommunications administration, 1911) 1·50 85
MS2252 140×111 mm. 110e. Modern means of communications (introduction of priority mail service, 1991) 2·75 2·30

469 Show Jumping

1991. Olympic Games, Barcelona (1992) (1st issue). Multicoloured.

2253 35e. Type **469** 60 25
2254 60e. Fencing 1·30 55
2255 80e. Shooting 1·60 90
2256 110e. Yachting 2·10 1·10

See also Nos. 2295/8.

470 Peugeot "19", 1899

1991. Caramulo Automobile Museum. Mult.

2257 35e. Type **470** 55 25
2258 60e. Rolls Royce "Silver Ghost", 1911 1·30 55
2259 80e. Bugatti "35B", 1930 1·60 95
2260 110e. Ferrari "1965 Inter", 1950 2·10 1·10
MS2261 140×111 mm. 70e. ×2 Mercedes Benz 380K (1934); 70e ×2 Hispano-Suiza H6b (1924) 6·00 4·50

See also Nos. 2275/**MS**2279.

1992. Portuguese Faience (3rd series). As T 450. Multicoloured.

2262 40e. Jug (Viana do Castelo factory) 65 35
2263 40e. Plate with flower design ("Ratinho" faience, Coimbra) 65 35
2264 40e. Dish with lid (Estremoz factory) 65 35
2265 65e. Decorated violin by Wescislau Cifka (Constancia factory, Lisbon) 1·30 65
2266 65e. Figure of man seated on barrel (Calvaquinho factory, Oporto) 1·30 65
2267 65e. Figure of woman (Fervenca factory, Oporto) 1·30 65
MS2268 112×140 mm. 260e. Political figures by Rafael Bordalo Pinheiro (Caldas da Rainha factory) (44×38 mm) 5·25 5·00

471 Astrolabe (Presidency emblem)

1992. Portuguese Presidency of European Community.

2269 **471** 65e. multicoloured 1·50 1·00

1992. "Royal Treasures" Exhibition, Ajuda Palace (2nd issue). As T 465. Multicoloured.

2270 38e. Coral diadem 55 35
2271 65e. Faberge clock 1·40 75
2272 70e. Gold tobacco box studded with diamonds and emeralds by Jacqumin 1·30 65
2273 85e. Royal sceptre with dragon supporting crown 1·40 90
2274 125e. Necklace of diamond stars by Estevao de Sousa 1·80 1·10

1992. Oeiras Automobile Museum. As T 470. Multicoloured.

2275 38e. Citroen "Torpedo", 1922 55 25
2276 65e. Robert Schneider, 1914 1·40 65
2277 85e. Austin "Seven", 1933 1·60 85
2278 120e. Mercedes Benz armoured "770", 1938 2·00 1·10
MS2279 140×111 mm. 70e. ×2 Renault 10/14 (1911); 70e. ×2 Ford Model T (1927) 6·00 4·50

472 Portuguese Traders

1992. 450th Anniv of First Portuguese Contacts with Japan (1st issue). Details of painting attributed to Kano Domi. Multicoloured.

2280 38e. Type **472** 60 30
2281 120e. Portuguese visitors with gifts 1·90 1·30

See also Nos. 2342/4.

473 Portuguese Pavilion

1992. "Expo '92" World's Fair, Seville.

2282 **473** 65e. multicoloured 1·00 75

474 Cross-staff

1992. Nautical Instruments (1st series). Mult.

2283 60e. Type **474** 95 45
2284 70e. Quadrant 1·30 70
2285 100e. Astrolabe 1·50 90
2286 120e. Compass 1·80 1·10
MS2287 140×112 mm. Nos. 2283/6 6·00 5·00

See also Nos. 2318/21.

475 Royal All Saints Hospital, Lisbon

1992. Anniversaries. Multicoloured.

2288 38e. Type **475** (500th anniv of foundation) 70 40
2289 70e. Lucia, Francisco and Jacinta (75th anniv of apparition of Our Lady at Fatima) 1·20 90
2290 120e. Crane and docks (centenary of Port of Leixoes) 2·00 1·20

476 Columbus with King Joao II

1992. Europa. 500th Anniv of Discovery of America. Multicoloured.

2291 85e. Type **476** 2·40 1·80
MS2292 Six sheets (a) 260e. brown and black (Type **479**); (b) 260e. blue and black (Columbus sighting land); (c) 260e. purple and black (Landing of Columbus); (d) 260e. lilac and black (Columbus welcomed at Barcelona); (e) 260e. black (Columbus presenting natives); (f) 260e. black ("America", Columbus and "Liberty") 41·00 29·00

478 Black-headed Gull flying over contaminated River

1992. 2nd United Nations Conference on Environment and Development, Rio de Janeiro. Multicoloured.

2293 70e. Type **478** 1·10 55
2294 120e. River kingfisher and butterfly beside clean river 1·90 1·10

Nos. 2293/4 were issued together, se-tenant, forming a composite design.

479 Running

1992. Olympic Games, Barcelona (2nd issue). Mult.

2295 38e. Type **479** 55 35
2296 70e. Football 1·30 65
2297 85e. Hurdling 1·50 75
2298 120e. Roller hockey 1·70 1·00
MS2299 140×112 mm. 250e. Basketball 4·50 4·25

480 Bullfighter on Horse

1992. Centenary of Campo Pequeno Bull Ring, Lisbon. Multicoloured.

2300 38e. Type **480** 55 30
2301 65e. Bull charging at horse 1·30 60
2302 70e. Bullfighter attacking bull 1·40 85
2303 155e. Bullfighter flourishing hat 1·90 1·30
MS2304 140×113 mm. 250e. Entrance to ring (35×50 mm) 4·50 4·25

482 Star

1992. European Single Market.

2313 **482** 65e. multicoloured 1·10 75

483 Industrial Safety Equipment

1992. European Year of Health, Hygiene and Safety in the Workplace.

2314 **483** 120e. multicoloured 2·00 1·50

484 Post Office Emblem

1993. No value expressed.

2315 **484** (-) red and black 75 35

No. 2315 was sold at the current first class inland letter rate. This was 42e. at time of issue.

485 Graphic Poem

1993. Birth Centenary of Jose de Almada Negreiros (artist and poet). Multicoloured.

2316 40e. Type **485** 70 35
2317 65e. Trawlers (painting) 1·10 85

486 Sand Clock

1993. Nautical Instruments (2nd series). Mult.

2318 42e. Type **486** 55 25
2319 70e. Nocturlabio 1·10 65
2320 90e. Kamal 1·70 90
2321 130e. Back-staff 2·10 1·00

487 View from Window

1993. Europa. Contemporary Art. Untitled paintings by Jose Escada. Multicoloured.

2322 90e. Type **487** 2·00 1·40
MS2323 140×112 mm. 90e. ×2 Type **487**; 90e. × 2 Body parts 10·00 6·50

488 Rossini and "The Barber of Seville"

1993. Bicentenary of San Carlos National Theatre, Lisbon. Multicoloured.

2324 42e. Type **488** 55 35
2325 70e. Verdi and "Rigoletto" 1·20 65
2326 90e. Wagner and "Tristan and Isolde" 1·50 90
2327 130e. Mozart and "The Magic Flute" 2·30 1·00
MS2328 140×112 mm. 300e. Exterior of theatre (39×29 mm) 5·25 5·00

489 Fireman's Helmet

1993. 125th Anniv of Association of Volunteer Firemen of Lisbon.

2329 **489** 70e. multicoloured 1·30 80

490 Santos-o-Velho, Lisbon

1993. Union of Portuguese-speaking Capital Cities.

2330 **490** 130e. multicoloured 2·10 1·30
MS2331 140×112 mm. No. 2330 ×4 8·50 7·00

491 "Angel of the Annunciation" (from Oporto Cathedral)

1993. Sculptures (1st series). Multicoloured.

2332 42e. Type **491** 55 25
2333 70e. "St Mark" (Cornelius de Holanda) (horiz) 1·30 65
2334 75e. "Madonna and Child" 1·60 70
2335 90e. "Archangel St. Michael" 1·70 75
2336 130e. "Count of Ferreira" (Soares dos Reis) 2·10 1·10
2337 170e. "Construction" (Heldar Batista) 2·40 1·30
MS2338 112×140 mm. 75e. Marble bust of Agrippina the Elder; 75e. "Virgin of the Annunciation" (Master of the Royal Tombs); 75e. "The Widow" (Teixeira Lopes); 75e. "Love Ode" (Canto da Maya) 5·25 4·25

See also Nos. 2380/**MS**2386 and 2466/**MS**2472.

492 Road Tanker and Electric Tanker Train

1993. Int Railways Congress, Lisbon. Mult.

2339 90e. Type **492** 1·20 70
2340 130e. Electric train and traffic jam 2·00 1·10
MS2341 140×112 mm. 300e. Train 4·75 4·50

493 Japanese Man with Musket

1993. 450th Anniv of First Portuguese Visit to Japan (2nd issue). Multicoloured.

2342 42e. Type **493** 55 40
2343 130e. Portuguese missionaries 2·75 1·50
2344 350e. Traders carrying goods 4·50 2·40

494 Peniche Trawler

1993. Trawlers (1st series). Multicoloured.

2345 42e. Type **494** 55 25
2346 70e. Peniche type trawler 1·00 55
2347 90e. "Germano 3" (steam trawler) 1·60 75
2348 130e. "Estrela 1" (steam trawler) 2·00 1·00

See also Nos. 2392/5.

495 Rural Post Bag, 1800

1993. Post Boxes. Multicoloured.

2349 42e. Type **495** 55 30
2350 70e. 19th-century wall-mounted box for railway travelling post office 1·00 55
2351 90e. 19th-century pillar box 1·60 70
2352 130e. Modern multi-function post box 2·00 1·00
MS2353 140×112 mm. 300e. 19th-century box for animal-drawn post wagons 4·75 4·50

496 Imperial Eagle

1993. Endangered Birds of Prey. Multicoloured.

2354 42e. Type **496** 55 30
2355 70e. Eagle owl 1·20 70
2356 130e. Peregrine falcon 2·75 1·10
2357 350e. Hen harrier 4·50 2·40

497 Knot

1993. 40th Anniv of Brazil–Portugal Consultation and Friendship Treaty.

2358 **497** 130e. multicoloured 2·00 1·20

498 Arms

1993. 850th Anniv of Zamora Conference (recognizing Afonso I as King of Portugal). Sheet 106×114 mm.

MS2359 **498** 150e. multicoloured 2·75 2·75

499 Stylized Map of Member Nations

1994. 40th Anniv of Western European Union.

2360 **499** 85e. multicoloured 1·30 85

500 Olympic Rings as Torch Flame

1994. Centenary of Int Olympic Committee. Mult.

2361	100e. Type **500**	2·30	1·10
2362	100e. "100" and rings	2·30	1·10

501 Oliveira Martins (historian)

1994. Centenaries. Multicoloured.

2363	45e. Type **501** (death)	70	30
2364	100e. Florbela Espanca (poet, birth)	1·30	80

502 Map and Prince Henry (image scaled to 65% of original size)

1994. 600th Birth Anniv of Prince Henry the Navigator.

2365	**502**	140e. multicoloured	2·00	1·10

503 Dove

1994. 20th Anniv of Revolution.

2366	**503**	75e. multicoloured	1·00	60

504 Mounted Knight and Explorer with Model Caravel

1994. Europa. Discoveries. Multicoloured.

2367	100e. Type **MS**504	1·60	1·10
MS2368	140×112 mm. 100e. ×2 Type **504**; 100e. ×2 Millet and explorer with model caravel	8·75	6·50

505 Emblem

1994. International Year of the Family.

2369	**505**	45e. red, black and lake	65	25
2370	**505**	140e. red, black and green	1·90	1·10

506 Footballer kicking Ball and World Map

1994. World Cup Football Championship, U.S.A. Multicoloured.

2371	100e. Type **506**	1·40	70
2372	140e. Ball and footballers' legs	2·00	1·00

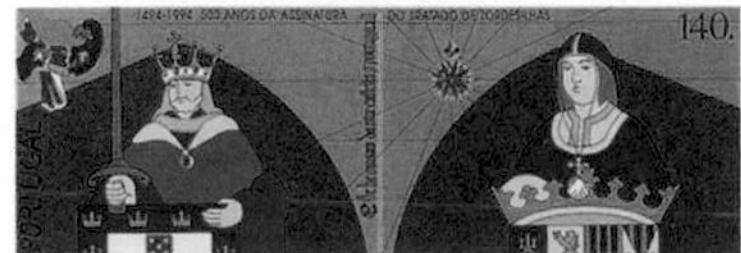

507 King Joao II of Portugal and King Fernando of Spain (image scaled to 65% of original size)

1994. 500th Anniv of Treaty of Tordesillas (defining Portuguese and Spanish spheres of influence).

2373	**507**	140e. multicoloured	2·00	1·10

508 Music

1994. Lisbon, European Capital of Culture. Multicoloured.

2374	45e. Type **508**	50	35
2375	75e. Photography and cinema	1·20	70
2376	100e. Theatre and dance	1·50	1·10
2377	140e. Art	1·90	1·50
MS2378	140×112 mm. Nos. 2374/7	5·75	5·75

509 Emblem

1994. Portuguese Road Safety Year.

2379	**509**	45e. red, green and black	65	30

1994. Sculptures (2nd series). As T 491. Mult.

2380	45e. Carved stonework from Citania de Briteiros (1st century) (horiz)	60	25
2381	75e. Visigothic pilaster (7th century)	80	45
2382	80e. Capital from Amorim Church (horiz)	1·00	60
2383	100e. Laying Christ's body in tomb (attr Joao de Ruao) (Monastery Church of Santa Cruz de Coimbra) (horiz)	1·20	70
2384	140e. Carved wood reliquary (Santa Maria Monastery, Alcobaca) (horiz)	1·80	1·00
2385	180e. Relief of Writers (Leopoldo de Almeida) (Lisbon National Library) (horiz)	2·40	1·20
MS2386	112×140 mm. 75e. Queen Urraca's tomb (Santa Maria Monastery, Alcobaca); 75e. Count of Ourem tomb (Colegiada de Ourem Church); 75e. Joao de Noronha and Isabel de Sousa's tomb (Santa Maria Church, Obidos); 75e. Mausoleum of Admiral Machado dos Santos (Alto de Sao Joao Cemetery, Lisbon)	4·75	4·00

510 Falconer, Peregrine Falcon and Dog

1994. Falconry. Designs showing a peregrine falcon in various hunting scenes. Multicoloured.

2387	45e. Type **510**	50	25
2388	75e. Falcon chasing duck	90	50
2389	100e. Falconer approaching falcon with dead duck	1·20	70
2390	140e. Falcons	1·60	1·00
MS2391	97×121 mm. 250e. Hooded falcon on falconer's arm	3·75	3·75

511 "Maria Arminda"

1994. Trawlers (2nd series). Multicoloured.

2392	45e. Type **511**	50	25
2393	75e. "Bom Pastor"	1·20	50
2394	100e. Aladores trawler with triplex haulers	1·30	70
2395	140e. "Sueste"	1·70	1·00

512 19th-century Horse-drawn Wagon

1994. Postal Transport. Multicoloured.

2396	45e. Type **512**	60	25
2397	75e. Travelling Post Office sorting carriage No. C7, 1910	1·00	50
2398	100e. Mercedes mail van, 1910	1·20	70
2399	140e. Volkswagen mail van, 1950	1·60	95
MS2400	140×112 mm. 250e. Daf truck, 1983A	3·50	3·00

513 Multiple Unit Set, Sintra Suburban Railway (image scaled to 65% of original size)

1994. Modern Electric Locomotives (1st series). Multicoloured.

2401	45e. Type **513**	50	25
2402	75e. Locomotive No. 5611-7 (national network)	95	55
2403	140e. Lisbon Underground train	1·70	95

See also No. 2465.

514 Medal

1994. 150th Anniv of Montepio Geral Savings Bank (45e.) and World Savings Day (100e.). Mult.

2404	45e. Type **514**	65	30
2405	100e. Coins and bee	1·20	65

515 St. Philip's Fort, Setubal

1994. Pousadas (hotels) in Historic Buildings. Multicoloured.

2406	45e. Type **515**	50	25
2407	75e. Obidos Castle	1·20	50
2408	100e. Convent of Loios, Evora	1·30	70
2409	140e. Santa Marinha Monastery, Guimaraes	1·60	95

516 Businessman and Tourist

1994. American Society of Travel Agents World Congress, Lisbon.

2410	**516**	140e. multicoloured	1·80	95

517 Statuette of Missionary, Mozambique

1994. Evangelization by Portuguese Missionaries. Multicoloured.

2411	45e. Type **517**	50	25
2412	75e. "Child Jesus the Good Shepherd" (carving), India	1·20	50
2413	100e. Chalice, Macao	1·30	70
2414	140e. Carving of man in frame, Angola (horiz)	1·60	95

518 Africans greeting Portuguese

1994. 550th Anniv of First Portuguese Landing in Senegal.

2415	**518**	140e. multicoloured	1·80	95

519 Battle Scene (detail of the panel, Hall of Battles, Fronteira Palace, Lisbon)

1994. 350th Anniv of Battle of Montijo. Sheet 63× 83 mm.

MS2416	**519**	150e. multicoloured	2·20	2·20

520 Adoration of the Wise Men

1994. Christmas. Sheet 140×111 mm.

MS2417	**520**	150e. multicoloured	2·20	2·20

521 Great Bustard

1995. European Nature Conservation Year. Multicoloured.

2418	42e. Type **521**	90	55
2419	90e. Osprey	1·50	1·10
2420	130e. Schreiber's green lizard	1·70	1·40
MS2421	140×112 mm. Nos. 2418/20	4·50	5·00

522 St. John and Sick Man

1995. 500th Birth Anniv of St. John of God (founder of Order of Hospitallers).

2422	**522**	45e. multicoloured	65	30

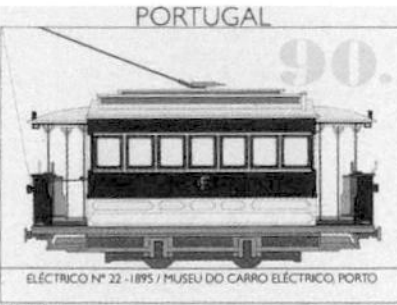

523 Electric Tramcar No. 22, 1895

1995. Centenaries of Trams and Motor Cars in Portugal. Multicoloured.

2423	90e. Type **523**	1·20	55
2424	130e. Panhard and Levassor motor car	1·50	95

524 Bread Seller

1995. 19th-century Itinerant Trades. Multicoloured.

2425	1e. Type **524**	10	10
2426	2e. Laundrywoman	10	10
2427	3e. Broker	10	10
2428	5e. Broom seller	10	10
2429	10e. Fish seller	10	10
2431	20e. Spinning-wheel and spoon seller	20	10
2432	30e. Olive oil and vinegar seller	30	20
2433	40e. Seller of indulgences	40	30
2434	45e. General street trader	50	30
2435	47e. Hot chestnut seller	40	25

2436	49e. Clothes mender	55	40
2437	50e. Fruit seller	70	40
2437a	50e. Pottery seller	65	45
2438	51e. Knife grinder	45	30
2439	75e. Whitewasher	90	60
2440	78e. Cloth seller	90	45
2440b	80e. Carrier/messenger boy	95	55
2440c	85e. Goose seller	1·00	70
2440d	86e. Bread seller	80	55
2440e	95e. Coachman	90	65
2441	100e. Mussels seller	1·30	65
2441a	100e. Milk seller	1·00	70
2442	210e. Basket seller	2·10	1·40
2443	250e. Water seller	2·75	1·60
2444	250e. Pastry seller	2·75	1·60

526 Emblem

1995. 50th Anniv of U.N.O. Multicoloured.

2449	75e. Type **526**	90	55
2450	135e. Clouds and emblem	1·60	1·00
MS2451	140×111 mm. No. 2449/50 each ×2	5·50	5·00

527 Evacuees from Gibraltar arriving at Madeira (image scaled to 64% of original size)

1995. Europa. Peace and Freedom. Portuguese Neutrality during Second World War. Mult.

2452	95e. Type **527**	2·00	1·20
2453	95e. Refugees waiting at Lisbon for transatlantic liner and Aristides de Sousa Mendes (Portuguese Consul in Bordeaux)	2·00	1·20

528 "St. Antony holding Child Jesus" (painting)

1995. 800th Birth Anniv of St. Antony of Padua (Franciscan preacher). Multicoloured.

2454	45e. Type **528**	1·40	35
2455	75e. St. Antony with flowers (vert)	2·50	85
2456	135e. "St. Antony holding Child Jesus" (statue)	4·00	1·60
MS2457	96×110 mm. 250e. "St. Anthony holding Baby Jesus" (18th-century Madeiran statue)	17·00	10·00

529 Carpenters with Axes and Women with Water, 1395

1995. 600th Anniv of Fire Service in Portugal. Multicoloured.

2458	45e. Type **529**	50	25
2459	80e. Fire cart and men carrying barrels of water, 1834	1·00	55
2460	95e. Merryweather steam-powered fire engine, 1867	1·10	70
2461	135e. Zoost fire engine No. 1, 1908	1·50	1·00
MS2462	Two sheets, each 120×100 mm. (a) 4 ×45e. Dutch fire engine, 1701; (b) 4 ×75e. Picota fire engine, 1780 and Portuguese fire cart, 1782	5·25	5·75

530 Coronation

1995. 500th Anniv of Accession of King Manoel I.

2463	530	45e. brown, yellow and red	55	30
MS2464		112×140 mm. No. 2463 ×4	2·50	2·50

1995. Modern Electric Locomotives (2nd series). As T 513.

2465	80e. multicoloured	95	55

DESIGN: 80e. Articulated trams.

1995. Sculptures (3rd series). As T 491. Multicoloured.

2466	45e. "Warrior" (castle statue)	45	25
2467	75e. Double-headed fountain	95	55
2468	80e. "Truth" (monument to Eca de Queiros by Antonio Teixeira Lopes)	95	55
2469	95e. First World War memorial, Abrantes (Ruy Gameiro)	1·10	65
2470	135e. "Fernao Lopes" (Martins Correia)	1·60	1·00
2471	190e. "Fernando Pessoa" (Lagoa Henriques)	2·10	1·30
MS2472	112×140 mm. 75e. "Knight" (from Chapel of the Ferreiros); 75e. "King Jose I" (J. Machado de Castro), Commerce Square, Lisbon; 75e. "King Joao IV" (Francisco Franco), Vila Vicosa; 75e. "Vimara Peres" (Barata Feyo), Oporto Cathedral Square	3·75	3·25

531 "Portugal's Guardian Angel" (sculpture, Diogo Pires)

1995. Art of the Period of Discoveries (15th–16th centuries). Multicoloured.

2473	45e. Type **531**	45	25
2474	75e. Reliquary of Queen Leonor (Master Joao)	95	55
2475	80e. "Don Manuel" (sculpture, Nicolas Chanterenne)	95	55
2476	95e. "St. Anthony" (painting, Nuno Goncalves)	1·10	65
2477	135e. "Adoration of the Three Wise Men" (painting, Grao Vasco)	1·90	1·00
2478	190e. "Christ on the Way to Calvary" (painting, Jorge Afonso)	2·10	1·30
MS2479	140×112 mm. 200e. "St. Vincent" (polyptych, Nuno Goncalves)	2·50	2·00

532 Queiroz

1995. 150th Birth Anniv of Eca de Queiroz (writer).

2480	532	135e. multicoloured	1·50	1·00

533 Archangel Gabriel

1995. Christmas. Multicoloured. (a) With country name at foot.

2481	80e. Type **533**	1·40	1·00
MS2482	112×140 mm. No. 2481×4	6·50	5·00

(b) With country name omitted.

2483	80e. Type **533**	1·30	1·00
MS2484	112×140 mm. No. 2483 ×4	6·25	6·25

534 Airbus Industrie A340/300

1995. 50th Anniv of TAP Air Portugal.

2485	534	135e. multicoloured	1·50	1·00

535 King Carlos I of Portugal (image scaled to 63% of original size)

1996. Centenary of Oceanographic Expeditions. Multicoloured.

2486	95e. Type **535**	1·10	65
2487	135e. Prince Albert I of Monaco	1·60	1·20

536 Books

1996. Anniversaries. Multicoloured.

2488	80e. Type **536** (bicentenary of National Library)	95	55
2489	200e. Hand writing with quill pen (700th anniv of adoption of Portuguese as official language)	2·20	1·40

537 Joao de Deus (poet and author of reading primer)

1996. Writers' Anniversaries. Multicoloured.

2490	78e. Type **537** (death centenary)	95	55
2491	140e. Joao de Barros (historian, philosopher and grammarian, 500th birth)	1·50	1·00

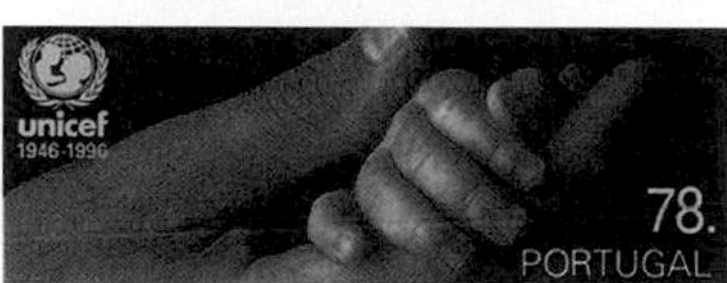

538 Holding Child's Hand (image scaled to 66% of original size)

1996. 50th Anniv of UNICEF. Multicoloured.

2492	78e. Type **538**	1·00	55
2493	140e. Children of different races	1·60	95

539 Helena Vieira da Silva (artist, self-portrait)

1996. Europa. Famous Women.

2494	539	98e. multicoloured	1·70	1·20
MS2495		140×112 mm. No. 2494 ×3	5·50	6·50

540 Match Scene

1996. European Football Championship, England. Multicoloured.

2496	78e. Type **540**	1·00	55
2497	140e. Match scene (different)	1·70	95
MS2498	140×112 mm. Nos. 2496/7	2·75	2·50

541 Caravel and Arms (image scaled to 56% of original size)

1996. 500th Death Anniv of Joao Vaz Corte-Real (explorer). Multicoloured.

2499	140e. Type **541**	1·70	1·00
MS2500	90×127 mm. 315e. Close-up of caravel in Type **541** (39×30 mm)	4·25	4·25

542 Wrestling

1996. Olympic Games, Atlanta. Multicoloured.

2501	47e. Type **542**	50	25
2502	78e. Show jumping	95	55
2503	98e. Boxing	1·10	65
2504	140e. Running	1·50	95
MS2505	96×110 mm. 300e. Athletes at starting blocks	4·00	4·00

543 Hilario and Guitar

1996. Death Centenary of Augusto Hilario (fado singer).

2506	543	80e. multicoloured	95	55

544 Antonio Silva (actor)

1996. Centenary of Motion Pictures. Multicoloured.

2507	47e. Type **544**	50	25
2508	78e. Vasco Santana (actor)	90	55
2509	80e. Laura Alves (actress)	90	55
2510	98e. Auelio Pais dos Reis (director)	1·10	55
2511	100e. Leitao de Barros (director)	1·10	65
2512	140e. Antonio Lopes Ribeiro (director)	1·60	90
MS2513	Two sheets, each 112×140 mm. (a) Nos. 2507/9; (b) Nos. 2510/12	6·50	5·50
MS2514	141×111 mm. Nos. 2507/12	6·50	5·75

545 King Afonso V

1996. 550th Anniv of Alphonsine Collection of Statutes.

2515	545	350e. multicoloured	3·75	2·20

546 Perdigao

1996. Birth Centenary of Jose de Azeredo Perdigao (lawyer and Council of State member).

2516	546	47e. multicoloured	65	40

547 Aveiro

1996. District Arms (1st series). Multicoloured.

2517	47e. Type **547**	55	25
2518	78e. Beja	90	60
2519	80e. Braga	90	60
2520	98e. Braganca	1·10	65
2521	100e. Castelo Branco	1·10	75
2522	140e. Coimbra	1·60	1·00
MS2523	Two sheets, each 140×112 mm. (a) Nos. 2517/19; (b) Nos. 2520/2	7·00	6·50

See also Nos. 2579/**MS**85 and 2648/**MS**54.

548 Henry of Burgundy (governor of Portucale) and his Wife Theresa

1996. 900th Anniv of Foundation of County of Portucale by King Afonso VI of Leon and Castille.

2524	**548**	47e. multicoloured	65	40

549 Rojoes (Pork dish)

1996. Traditional Portuguese Dishes (1st series). Multicoloured.

2525	47e. Type **549**	60	35
2526	78e. Boticas trout	90	50
2527	80e. Oporto tripe	90	50
2528	98e. Baked cod with jacket potatoes	1·10	55
2529	100e. Aveiro eel	1·10	70
2530	140e. Peniche lobster	1·70	90

See also Nos. 2569/74.

550 Lisbon Postman, 1821

1996. 175th Anniv of Home Delivery Postal Service. Multicoloured.

2531	47e. Type **550**	55	25
2532	78e. Postman, 1854	90	65
2533	98e. Rural postman, 1893	1·10	70
2534	100e. Postman, 1939	1·10	80
2535	140e. Modern postman, 1992	1·60	1·00

551 King Manoel I in Shipyard

1996. 500th Anniv (1997) of Discovery of Sea-route to India by Vasco da Gama (1st issue). Multicoloured.

2536	47e. Type **551**	70	35
2537	78e. Departure from Lisbon	1·30	70
2538	98e. Fleet in Atlantic Ocean	1·50	85
2539	140e. Sailing around Cape of Good Hope	1·70	1·00
MS2540	141×113 mm. 315e. "Dream of King Manuel I" (illustration from Poem IV of *The Lusiads* by Luis de Camoes)	4·25	4·25

See also Nos. 2592/**MS**96 and 2665/**MS**80.

552 "Banknote"

1996. 150th Anniv of Bank of Portugal.

2541	**552**	78e. multicoloured	90	55

553 East Timorese Couple

1996. Rights of People of East Timor. Award of 1996 Nobel Peace Prize to Don Carlos Ximenes Belo and Jose Ramos Horton.

2542	**553**	140e. multicoloured	1·50	1·10

554 Clouds forming Map of Europe

1996. Organization for Security and Co-operation in Europe Summit Meeting, Lisbon. Sheet 95×110 mm.

MS2543	**554**	200e. multicoloured	3·00	3·00

555 Portuguese Galleon

1997. Sailing Ships of the India Shipping Line. Multicoloured.

2544	49e. Type **555**	50	35
2545	80e. "Principe da Beira" (nau)	1·20	75
2546	100e. Bow view of "Don Fernando II e Gloria" (sail frigate)	1·20	95
2547	140e. Stern view of "Don Fernando II e Gloria"	1·50	1·10

556 Youth with Flower

1997. "No to Drugs – Yes to Life" (anti-drugs campaign).

2548	**556**	80e. multicoloured	90	60

557 Arms

1997. Bicent of Managing Institute of Public Credit.

2549	**557**	49e. multicoloured	65	40

558 Desman eating Worm

1997. The Pyrenean Desman. Multicoloured.

2550	49e. Type **558**	70	40
2551	49e. Diving	70	40
2552	49e. With wet fur	70	40
2553	49e. Cleaning snout	70	40

559 Moorish Girl guarding Hidden Treasure

1997. Europa. Tales and Legends.

2554	**559**	100e. multicoloured	1·70	1·40
MS2555		140×107 mm. No. 2554 ×3	6·50	6·25

560 Surfing

1997. Adventure Sports. Multicoloured.

2556	49e. Type **560**	55	35
2557	80e. Skateboarding	95	65
2558	100e. In-line skating	1·10	85
2559	140e. Paragliding	1·50	1·10
MS2560	134×113 mm. 150e. B.M.X. cycling; 150e. Hang-gliding	4·00	3·00

561 Night Attack on Santarem Fortress

1997. 850th Anniv of Capture from the Moors of Santarem and Lisbon. Multicoloured.

2561	80e. Type **561**	85	65
2562	80e. Victorious King Afonso riding past Lisbon city walls	85	65
MS2563	140×113 mm. Nos. 2561/2 each ×2	4·25	4·00

562 Frois with Japanese Man

1997. 400th Death Anniv of Father Luis Frois (author of "The History of Japan"). Multicoloured.

2564	80e. Type **562**	1·20	75
2565	140e. Father Frois and church (vert)	1·60	1·10
2566	140e. Father Frois and flowers (vert)	1·60	1·10

563 Indian Children and Jose de Anchieta

1997. Death Anniversaries of Missionaries to Brazil. Multicoloured.

2567	140e. Type **563** (400th)	1·50	1·00
2568	350e. Antonio Vieira in pulpit (300th)	4·00	2·75

1997. Traditional Portuguese Dishes (2nd series). As T 549. Multicoloured.

2569	10e. Scalded kid, Beira Baixa	10	10
2570	49e. Fried shad with bread-pap, Ribatejo	55	35
2571	80e. Lamb stew, Alentejo	90	60
2572	100e. Rich fish chowder, Algarve	1·10	80
2573	140e. Black scabbardfish fillets with maize, Madeira	1·60	1·10
2574	200e. Stewed octopus, Azores	2·20	1·60

564 Centre of Oporto

1997. "Lubrapex 97" Portuguese–Brazilian Stamp Exhibition, Oporto. UNESCO World Heritage Site. Sheet 121×85 mm.

MS2575	**564**	350e. multicoloured	4·25	4·25

565 Couple before Clerk

1997. 700th Anniv of Mutual Assurance in Portugal.

2576	**565**	100e. multicoloured	1·20	80

566 Laboratory, Lisbon

1997. 50th Anniv of National Laboratory of Civil Engineering.

2577	**566**	80e. multicoloured	90	50

567 King Dinis and Arms of Portugal and King Fernando IV and Arms of Castile and Leon

1997. 700th Anniv of Treaty of Alcanices (defining national frontiers).

2578	**567**	80e. multicoloured	90	50

568 Evora

1997. District Arms (2nd series). Multicoloured.

2579	10e. Type **568**	10	10
2580	49e. Faro	55	30
2581	80e. Guarda	80	55
2582	100e. Leiria	1·20	65
2583	140e. Lisbon	1·40	1·00
2584	200e. Portalegre	2·10	1·30
MS2585	Two sheets, each 140×112 mm. (a) Nos. 2579, 2581 and 2583; (b) Nos. 2480, 2582 and 2584	5·00	2·75

569 Chart by Lopo Homem-Reineis, 1519

1997. Portuguese Charts. Multicoloured.

2586	49e. Type **569**	45	25
2587	80e. Chart by Joao Freire, 1546	95	70
2588	100e. Planisphere by Diogo Ribeiro, 1529	1·10	75
2589	140e. Chart showing Tropic of Capricorn (anon), 1630	1·40	95
MS2590	139×112 mm. Nos. 2586/9	4·50	4·50

570 Queen Maria I and Mail Coach

1997. Bicentenary of State Postal Service.

2591	**570**	80e. multicoloured	90	50

571 Erecting Landmark Monument, Quelimane

1997. 500th Anniv of Discovery of Portugal–India Sea Route (2nd issue). Multicoloured.

2592	49e. Type **571**	50	35
2593	80e. Arrival of fleet at Mozambique	90	50
2594	100e. Arrival of fleet in Mombasa	1·10	80
2595	140e. King of Melinde greeting Vasco da Gama	1·50	1·00
MS2596	140×113 mm. 315e. Vasco da Gama on beach at Natal	4·00	4·00

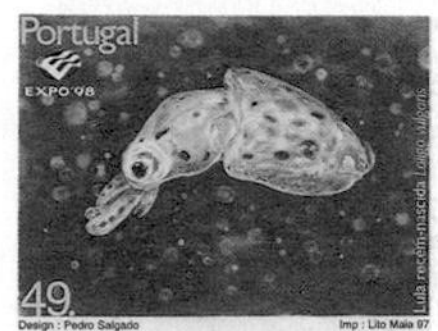

572 Squid

1997. "Expo'98" World Fair, Lisbon. Ocean Life (1st issue). Multicoloured.

2597	49e. Type **572**	50	35
2598	80e. Rock lobster larva	95	65
2599	100e. Adult "Pontellina plumata" (crustacean)	1·10	80
2600	140e. Senegal sole (pastlarva)	1·40	1·20
MS2601	110×150 mm. 100e. *Calcidiscus leptoporus*; 100e. *Tabellaria sp.* colonies	2·50	2·50

See also Nos. 2611/**MS**2615, 2621/**MS**2629 and 2630/41.

573 Sintra

1997. UNESCO World Heritage Site, Sintra. "Indepex 97" International Stamp Exhibition, New Delhi. Sheet 112×140 mm.

MS2602	**573** 350e. multicoloured	4·25	4·25

574 Officer and Plan of Almeida Fortress, 1848

1998. 350th Anniv of Portuguese Military Engineering. Multicoloured.

2603	50e. Type **574**	50	30
2604	80e. Officer and plan of Miranda do Oduro Fortress, 1834	1·10	65
2605	100e. Officer and plan of Moncao Fortress, 1797	1·30	70
2606	140e. Officer and plan of Elvas Fortress, 1806	1·50	1·10

575 Ivens and African Scene

1998. Death Centenary of Roberto Ivens (explorer).

2607	**575**	140e. multicoloured	1·50	1·00

576 Adoration of the Madonna (carving)

1998. 500th Anniv of Holy Houses Misericordia (religious social relief order).

2608	80e. Type **576**	90	50
2609	100e. Attending patient (tile mural)	1·00	85

577 Aqueduct ocer Alcantra

1998. 250th Anniv of Aqueduct of the Free Waters (from Sintra to Lisbon). Sheet 155×110 mm.

MS2610	**577** 350e. multicoloured	4·25	4·25

1998. "Expo '98" World's Fair, Lisbon (2nd issue). Ocean Life. As T 572. Multicoloured.

2611	50e. Crab ("Pilumnus" sp.) larva	50	25
2612	85e. Monkfish ("Lophius piscatonis") larva	1·10	55
2613	100e. Gilthead sea bream ("Sparus aurata") larva	1·20	70
2614	140e. Medusa ("Cladonema radiatum")	1·40	1·00
MS2615	112×140 mm. 110e. Bioluminescent protozoan (*Noctiluca miliaris*); 110e. Dinoflagellate (*Dinophysis acuta*)	2·50	2·50

578 Vasco da Gama Bridge

1998. Opening of Vasco da Gama Bridge (from Sacavem to Montijo).

2616	**578** 200e. multicoloured	2·00	1·60
MS2617	125×85 mm. As No. 2616 but with background extended to edges	2·30	2·20

579 Coloured Balls

1998. 150th Anniv of Oporto Industrial Association.

2618	**579**	80e. multicoloured	90	50

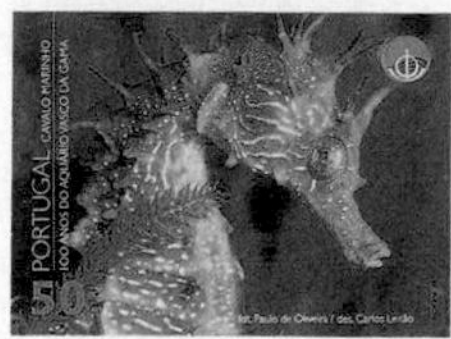

580 Seahorse

1998. International Year of the Ocean. Centenary of Vasco da Gama Aquarium. Multicoloured.

2619	50e. Type **580**	70	35
2620	80e. Angelfish and shoal	95	75

581 Diver and Astrolabe

1998. "Expo '98" World's Fair, Lisbon (3rd issue). (a) The Ocean. Multicoloured.

2621	50e. Type **581**	50	25
2622	50e. Caravel	50	25
2623	85e. Fishes and coral reef (inscr "oceanario")	90	55
2624	85e. Underwater exploration equipment observing fishes	90	55
2625	140e. Mermaid and sea anemones	1·70	1·00
2626	140e. Children with hands on globe	1·70	1·00

(b) Miniature Sheets. Designs as T 581.

MS2627	154×116 mm. 50e. Portuguese Pavilion; 85e. Pavilion of the Future; 85e. Oceanarium; 140e. Knowledge of the Seas Pavilion; 140e. Pavilion of Utopia	6·25	6·25
MS2628	Two sheets, each 147×90 mm. (a) Nos. 2621/6; (b) 80e. Postal mascot; stamps as in No. **MS**2627	7·25	†
MS2629	148×151 mm. Nos. 2597/**MS**2601 and 2611/**MS**2615	14·50	†

(c) As Nos. 2611/14 (but with Latin names removed) and 2621/6. Size 29×23 mm. Self-adhesive.

2630	50e. As No. 2612	85	55
2631	50e. Bioluminescent protozoan	85	55
2632	50e. As No. 2611	85	55
2633	50e. As No. 2613	85	55
2634	50e. Dinoflagellate	85	55
2635	50e. As No. 2614	85	55
2636	85e. Type **581**	1·50	90
2637	85e. As No. 2624	1·50	90
2638	85e. As No. 2626	1·50	90
2639	85e. As No. 2622	1·50	90
2640	85e. As No. 2623 but inscr "Portugal e os Oceanos"	1·50	90
2641	85e. As No. 2625	1·50	90

The designers' names and printer's imprints have been removed from Nos. 2630/41.

582 Revellers before Statues of St. Antony of Padua, St. John and St. Peter

1998. Europa. National Festivals.

2642	**582** 100e. multicoloured	1·50	1·20
MS2643	140×108 mm. No. 2642 ×3	5·00	5·75

583 Marie Curie

1998. Centenary of Discovery of Radium.

2644	**583**	140e. multicoloured	1·40	90

584 Ferreira de Castro and Illustration to "The Jungle"

1998. Birth Centenary of Jose Ferreira de Castro (writer).

2645	**584**	50e. multicoloured	60	35

585 Untitled Painting

1998. Death Centenary of Bernardo Marques (artist).

2646	**585**	85e. multicoloured	90	65

586 Adam (Michelangelo) (detail from Sistine Chapel ceiling)

1998. "Juvalex '98" Stamp Exhibition. 50th Anniv of Universal Declaration of Human Rights. Sheet 90×55 mm.

MS2647	**586** 315e. multicoloured	3·50	3·50

1998. District Arms (3rd series). As T 568. Multicoloured.

2648	50e. Vila Real	50	35
2649	85e. Setubal	1·30	80
2650	85e. Viana do Castelo (150th anniv of elevation to city)	1·30	80
2651	100e. Santarem	1·40	80
2652	100e. Viseu	1·40	80
2653	200e. Oporto	2·00	1·20
MS2654	Two sheets, each 140×113 mm. (a) Nos. 2648, 2650 and 2653; (b) Nos. 2649 and 2651/2	8·25	9·00

587 Glass Production

1998. 250th Anniv of Glass Production in Marinha Grande. Multicoloured.

2655	50e. Type **587**	50	25
2656	80e. Heating glass and finished product	95	65
2657	100e. Bottles and factory	1·00	70
2658	140e. Blue bottles and glass-maker	1·90	1·00

588 "Sagres II" (cadet barque), Portugal

1998. Vasco da Gama Regatta. Multicoloured.

2659	50e. Type **588**	50	30
2660	85e. "Asgard II" (Irish cadet brigantine)	1·20	60
2661	85e. "Rose" (American replica)	1·20	60
2662	100e. "Amerigo Vespucci" (Italian cadet ship)	1·30	80
2663	100e. "Kruzenshtern" (Russian cadet barque)	1·30	80
2664	140e. "Creoula" (Portuguese cadet schooner)	2·00	1·10

589 Da Gama with Pilot Ibn Madjid

1998. 500th Anniv (1997) of Discovery of Sea-route to India by Vasco da Gama (3rd issue). Mult.

2665	50e. Type **551**	75	45
2666	50e. As No. 2537	75	45
2667	50e. As No. 2538	75	45
2668	50e. As No. 2539	75	45
2669	50e. Type **571**	75	45
2670	50e. As No. 2593	75	45
2671	50e. As No. 2594	75	45
2672	50e. As No. 2595	75	45

2673	50e. Type **589**	95	60
2674	50e. "Sao Gabriel" (flagship) in storm	75	45
2675	50e. Fleet arriving at Calicut	75	45
2676	50e. Audience with the Samorin of Calicut	75	45
2677	80e. As No. 2674	1·00	70
2678	100e. As No. 2675	1·10	75
2679	140e. As No. 2676	1·40	90
MS2680	140×112 mm. 315e. King of Melinde listening to Vasco da Gama	4·00	4·00

590 Modern Mail Van

1998. Bicentenaries of Inauguration of Lisbon–Coimbra Mail Coach Service and of Re-organ-ization of Maritime Mail Service to Brazil. Mult.

2681	50e. Type **590**	50	35
2682	140e. Mail coach and "Postilhao da America" (brigantine)	1·80	1·10

591 Globe and Flags of participating Countries

1998. 8th Iberian-American Summit of State Leaders and Govenors, Oporto. Sheet 90×55 mm.

MS2683	**591** 140e. multicoloured	1·70	1·60

592 Cave paintings

1998. Archeological Park, Coa Valley. Sheet 140×113 mm.

MS2684	**592** 350e. multicoloured	4·25	4·25

593 Male and Female Figures

1998. Health Awareness.

2685	**593**	100e. multicoloured	1·20	80

594 Saramago

1998. Jose Saramago (winner of Nobel prize for Literature, 1998). Sheet 140×114 mm.

MS2686	**594** 200e. multicoloured	2·40	2·40

DENOMINATION. From No. 2687 Portugal stamps are denominated both in escudos and in euros. As no cash for this latter is in circulation, the catalogue continues to use the escudo value.

595 Knife Grinder

1999. 19th-Century Itinerant Trades. Multicoloured. Self-adhesive.

2687	51e. Type **595**	50	35
2688	95e. Coachman	1·20	80

596 Flags of European Union Members and Euro Emblem

1999. Introduction of the Euro (European currency).

2696	**596**	95e. multicoloured	1·20	95

597 Galleon and Aborigines

1999. "Australia 99" International Stamp Exhibition, Melbourne. The Portuguese in Australia. Multicoloured.

2697	140e. Kangaroos and galleon	1·40	90
2698	140e. Type **597**	1·40	90
MS2699	137×104 mm. 350e. Motifs of Nos. 2697/8 (79×30 mm)	4·25	4·00

Nos. 2697/8 were issued together, se-tenant, forming a composite design.

598 Norton de Matos

1999. 50th Anniv of Candidature of General Jose Norton de Matos to Presidency of the Republic.

2700	**598**	80e. multicoloured	1·10	70

599 Almeida Garrett

1999. Birth Bicentenary of Joao Baptista Almeida Garrett (writer).

2701	**599**	95e. multicoloured	1·20	75
MS2702	130×105 mm. **599** 210e. multicoloured		2·50	2·40

600 Breguet Bre 16 Bri 2 *Patria*

1999. 25th Anniv of Sarmento de Beires and Brito Pais's Portugal–Macao Flight. Multicoloured.

2703	140e. Type **600**	1·60	1·00
2704	140e. Airco de Havilland D.H.9 biplane	1·60	1·00
MS2705	137×104 mm. Nos. 2703/4	3·25	3·25

601 Carnation

1999. 25th Anniv of Revolution. Multicoloured.

2706	51e. Type **601**	50	30
2707	80e. National Assembly building (78×29 mm)	90	60
MS2708	140×108 mm. Nos. 2706/7	1·60	1·60

602 Council Emblem

1999. 50th Anniv of Council of Europe.

2709	**602**	100e. multicoloured	1·40	1·10

603 Wolf and Iris (Peneda-Geres National Park)

1999. Europa. Parks and Gardens.

2710	**603**	100e. multicoloured	1·40	1·20
MS2711	154×109 mm. No. 2710×3		5·25	6·50

604 Marquis de Pombal

1993. 300th Birth Anniv of Marquis de Pombal (statesman and reformer). Multicoloured.

2712	80e. Type **604**	90	70
MS2713	170×135 mm. 80e. Head of Marquis and part of statue; 210e. Hand holding quill	3·50	2·75

605 Harbour

1999. "Meeting of Cultures". Return of Macao to China. Multicoloured.

2714	51e. Type **605**	50	30
2715	80e. Dancers	90	55
2716	95e. Procession of the Madonna	95	80
2717	100e. Ruins of St. Paul's Baslllca	1·20	80
2718	140e. Garden with bust of Luis Camoes (horiz)	1·60	95

606 de Havilland D.H.82A Tiger Moth

1999. 75th Anniv of Military Aeronautics. Multicoloured.

2719	51e. Type **606**	50	30
2720	51e. Supermarine Spitfire V6 fighter	50	30
2721	85e. Breguet Bre XIV-A2	1·20	65
2722	85e. SPAD VII-C1	1·20	65
2723	95e. Caudron G-3	1·40	75
2724	95e. Junkers Ju 52/3m	1·40	75
MS2725	150×117 mm. Nos. 2719/24	6·25	6·50

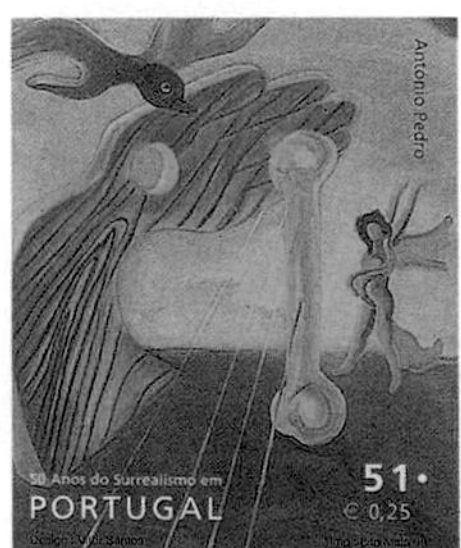

607 Portion by Antonio Pedro

1999. 50th Anniv of Surrealism (modern art movement) in Portugal. Designs showing details by artist named of collective painting "Cadavre Exquis". Multicoloured.

2726	51e. Type **607**	45	30
2727	80e. Vespeira	90	65
2728	95e. Moniz Pereira	95	70
2729	100e. Fernando de Azevedo	1·00	70
2730	140e. Antonio Domingues	1·50	1·00
MS2731	175×153 mm. Nos. 2726/30 forming a composite design of complete picture	4·75	5·25

608 Passenger Train on Bridge

1999. Inauguration of Railway Section of the 25th of April Bridge over River Tagus, Lisbon. Mult.

2732	51e. Type **608**	50	30
2733	95e. Passenger train on bridge (different)	1·20	75
MS2734	Two sheets, each 140×110 mm. (a) 350e. Close-up of part of Type **608** (79×30 mm); (b) 350e. Close-up of part of No. 2733 (79×30 mm)	8·25	8·00

609 Heinrich von Stephan (founder)

1999. 125th Anniv of Universal Postal Union. Multicoloured.

2735	95e. Type **609**	95	70
2736	140e. Globe, letter and keyboard	1·40	90
MS2737	140×98 mm. 315e. Combination of motifs in Nos. 2735/6 (79×29 mm)	3·75	3·50

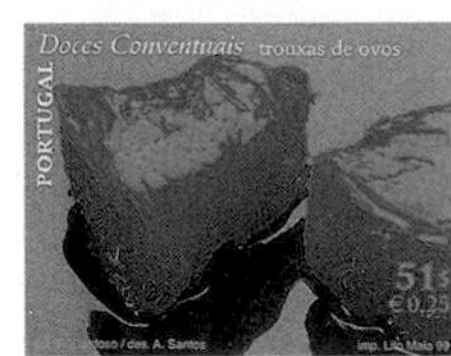

610 Egg Packs

1999. Convent Sweets (1st series). Multicoloured.

2738	51e. Type **610**	50	30
2739	80e. Egg pudding	85	50
2740	95e. Angel's purses	95	65
2741	100e. Abrantes straw	1·60	70
2742	140e. Viseu chestnuts	1·80	1·10
2743	210e. Honey cake	2·20	1·60

See also Nos. 2785/90.

611 Portuguese Troops and Moslem Ships

1999. 750th Anniv of King Afonso III's Conquest of the Algarve.

2744	**611**	100e. multicoloured	1·20	75

612 Camara Pestana (bacteriologist)

1999. Medical Anniversaries. Multicoloured.

2745	51e. Type **612** (death centenary)	50	30
2746	51e. Ricardo Jorge (founder of National Health Institute, 60th death anniv)	50	30
2747	80e. Francisco Gentil (oncologist, 35th death anniv)	85	65
2748	80e. Egas Moniz (neurosurgeon, 125th birth anniv)	85	65
2749	95e. Joao Cid dos Santos (surgeon, 23rd death anniv)	1·00	70
2750	95e. Reynaldo dos Santos (arteriography researcher, 30th death anniv (2000))	1·00	70

613 Jose Diogo de Mascarenhas Neto (first General Mail Lieutenant)

1999. Bicentenary of the Provisional Mail Rules (re-organization of postal system).

2751	**613** 80e. multicoloured	90	55

614 Barata, Stamps and Mural

1999. Birth Centenary of Jaime Martins Barata (artist and stamp designer).

2752	**614** 80e. multicoloured	90	55

615 Wise Men following Star (Maria Goncalves)

1999. Christmas. National Association of Art and Creativity for and by Handicapped Persons. Designs with artists name in brackets. Multicoloured.

2753	51e. Type **615**	45	30
2754	95e. Father Christmas delivering presents (Marta Silva)	95	65
2755	140e. Father Christmas (Luis Farinha)	2·00	95
2756	210e. The Nativity (Maria Goncalves)	2·40	1·30

616 Macanese Architecture

1999. Portuguese–Chinese Cultural Mix in Macao. Sheet 138×90 mm.

MS2757	**616** 140e. black and red	1·80	1·80

618 "Madonna and Child" (Alvaro Pires of Evora) Maia, Oporto)

2000. 2000th Birth Anniv of Jesus Christ.

2759	**618** 52e. multicoloured	80	40

619 Astronaut and Space Craft

2000. The Twentieth Century. Conquest of Space.

2760	**619** 86e. multicoloured	1·10	65

620 Golden Eagle

2000. Birds. (1st series). Multicoloured. (a) Ordinary gum. Size 30×27 mm.

2761	52e. Type **620**	50	35
2762	85e. Great crested grebe	90	65
2763	90e. Greater flamingo	90	70
2764	100e. Northern gannet	1·60	80
2765	215e. Green-winged teal	2·75	1·60

(b) Self-adhesive gum. Size 28×25 mm.

2766	52e. As No. 2761	55	35
2767	100e. As No. 2764	1·00	80

See also Nos. 2832/9.

621 Crowd and Suffragetts

2000. The Twentieth Century (2nd issue). Three sheets, each 190×220 mm, containing T 621 and similar multicoloured designs.

MS2768 (a) 52e. Type **621** (human Rights); 52e. Fashion through the century (59×29 mm); 52e. Windmills, electricity pylon and birds (ecology) (59×39 mm); 52e. Early airplanes, car, stylised steamlined high speed train and ship (transport); 52e. As No. 2760; 52e. Space shuttle on launch pad (conquest of Space). (b) 52e. Marcel Proust and Thomas Marin (novelists), James Joyce (writer), Franz Kafka (novelist), Fernando Pessoa (poet), Jorge Luis Borges and Samuel Beckett (writers) (literature) (49×29 mm); 52e. Achille-Claude Debussy, Igor Stravinsky, Arnold Schoenberg, Bela Bartok, George Gershwin (composers), Charlie Parker (saxophonist) and William (Bill) Evans (pianist) (music) (49×29 mm); 52e. Performers (theatre); 52e. Auditorium and performers (theatre) (59×29 mm); 52e. Sculptures and paintings (art) (49×29 mm); 52e. Abstract art (29×29 mm); 52e. Charlie Chaplin on left (cinema) (49×29 mm); 52e. Woody Allen on left (cinema and television) (29×29 mm); 52e. Old and modern buildings (architecture); 52e. Modern buildings (architecture); 52e. Front and aerial views of modern buildings (architecture). (c) 52e. Edmund Husser, Ludwig Wittgenstein and Martin Heidegger (philosophy); 52e. Jules Poincare, Kurt Godel and Andrei Kolmogorov (mathematics); 52e. Max Planck, Albert Einstein and Niels Bohr (physics) (49×29 mm); 52e. Franz Boas (anthropologist), Levi Strauss (clothing manufacturer) and Margaret Mead (anthropologist) (social science and medicine); 52e. Sigmund Freud (neurologist) and Alexander Fleming (bacteriologist) (social science and medicine) (29×29 mm); 52e. Christiaan Barnard performing operation (organ transplant surgeon) (medicine); 52e. Office workers, Joseph Schumpeter and John Keynes (economics); 52e. Circuit boards (technology); 52e. Fibre optics (technology) (29×29 mm); 52e. Binary code, Alan Tuning (mathematician) and John von Neuman (mathematician) (information technology and telecommunications); 52e. Guglielmo Marconi (physicist) and satellite aerials (information technology and telecommunications); 52e. Binary code and satellite (information technology and telecommunications) (29×29 mm) 22·00 20·00

622 Members' Flags forming Stars

2000. Portuguese Presidency of European Union Council.

2769	**622** 100e. multicoloured	1·50	1·20

623 Native Indians

2000. 500th Anniv of Discovery of Brazil. Multicoloured.

2770	52e. Type **623**	60	40
2771	85e. Native Indians watching Pedro Alvares Cabral's fleet	1·10	75
2772	100e. Ship's crew and sails	1·60	95
2773	140e. Native Indians and Portuguese sailors meeting	1·80	1·30
MS2774	140×140 mm. Nos. 2770/3	5·00	3·50

624 "Building Europe"

2000. Europa.

2775	**624** 100e. multicoloured	2·00	1·70
MS2776	154×109 mm. No. 2775 ×3	6·25	7·75

625 Pope John Paul II and Children

2000. Papal Visit to Portugal. Beatification of Jacinta and Francisco Marto (Children of Fatima).

2777	**625** 52e. multicoloured	75	45

626 Draisienne Bicycle, 1817

2000. "The Stamp Show 2000" International Stamp Exhibition, London. Centenary of International Cycling Union. Bicycles. Mult.

2778	52e. Type **626**	55	40
2779	85e. Michaux, 1868	1·60	75
2780	100e. Ariel, 1871	1·20	95
2781	140e. Rover, 1888	1·90	1·30
2782	215e. BTX, 2000	3·00	1·90
2783	350e. GT, 2000	4·50	3·25
MS2784	140×112 mm. Nos. 2778/83	12·50	12·00

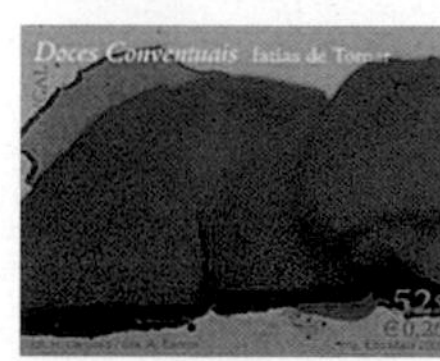
627 Slices of Tomar

2000. Convent Sweets (2nd series). Multicoloured.

2785	52e. Type **627**	55	40
2786	85e. Rodrigo's present	1·60	75
2787	100e. Sericaia	1·20	95
2788	140e. Lo bread	1·90	1·30
2789	215e. Grated bread	3·00	1·90
2790	350e. Royal paraiso cake	4·50	3·25

628 Fishing Boat and Fishes

2000. Fishermen's Day.

2791	**628** 52e. multicoloured	75	45

629 Portuguese Landscapes (image scaled to 55% of original size)

2000. "EXPO 2000" World's Fair, Hanover, Germany. Humanity–Nature–Technology. Mult.

2792	100e. Type **629**	1·20	90
MS2793	140×113 mm. 350e. Portuguese Pavilion, Hanover (39×30 mm)	4·00	4·00

630 Statue and Assembly Hall

2000. 25th Anniv of Constituent Assembly.

2794	**630** 85e. multicoloured	1·10	75

631 Fishermen and Boat

2000. Cod Fishing. Multicoloured.

2795	52e. Type **631**	55	40
2796	85e. Fishing barquentine and fisherman at ship's wheel	1·10	75
2797	100e. Three fishermen and boat	1·20	90
2798	100e. Fisherman and dories on fishing schooner	1·20	90
2799	140e. Fisherman rowing and fishing barquentine	1·90	1·20
2800	215e. Fisherman and fishing schooner	2·75	1·90
MS2801	140×112 mm. Nos. 2795/2800	9·50	9·75

632 De Queiroz

2000. Death Centenary of Eca de Queiroz (author).

2802	**632** 85e. multicoloured	1·10	75

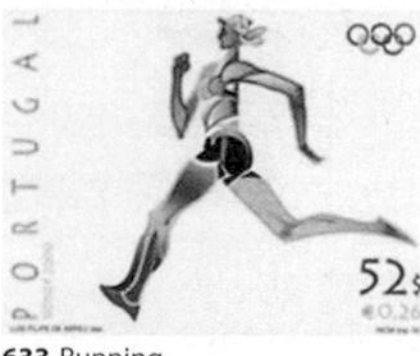

633 Running

2000. Olympic Games, Sydney. Multicoloured.

2803	52e. Type **633**	55	40
2804	85e. Show jumping	1·10	75
2805	100e. Dinghy racing	1·20	90
2806	140e. Diving	1·70	1·20
MS2807	140×112 mm. 85e. Fencing; 215e. Beach volleyball	4·50	4·25

Nos. 2803/6 are wrongly inscribed "Sidney".

634 Airbus A310 and Runway

2000. Inauguration of Madeira Airport Second Runway Extension.

2808	**634** 140e. multicoloured	1·90	1·30
MS2809	110×80 mm. 140e. multicoloured	1·90	2·00

635 Writing Letter on Computer

2000. 50th Anniv of Snoopy (cartoon character created by Charles Schulz). Postal Service. Mult.

2810 52e. Type **635** 55 40

2811 52e. Posting letter 55 40

2812 85e. Driving post van 1·10 75

2813 100e. Sorting post 1·40 90

2814 140e. Delivering post 1·90 1·20

2815 215e. Reading letter 2·40 1·90

MS2816 140×112 mm. Nos. 2810/15 9·25 9·75

636 Drawing, Telescope and Sextant

2000. 125th Anniv of Lisbon Geographic Society. Multicoloured.

2817 85e. Type **636** 1·10 75

2818 100e. Sextant and drawing 1·40 1·00

Nos. 2817/18 were issued together, se-tenant, forming a composite design.

637 Carolina Michaelis de Vasconcellos (teacher)

2001. The Twentieth Century. History and Culture. Multicoloured.

2819 85e. Type **637** 1·00 80

2820 85e. Miguel Bombarda (doctor and politician) 1·00 80

2821 85e. Bernardino Machado (politician) 1·00 80

2822 85e. Tomas Alcaide (lyricist) 1·00 80

2823 85e. Jose Regio (writer) 1·00 80

2824 85e. Jose Rodrigues Migueis (writer) 1·00 80

2825 85e. Vitorino Nemesio (scholar) 1·00 80

2826 85e. Bento de Jesus Caraca (scholar) 1·00 80

638 Athletics

2001. World Indoor Athletics Championship, Lisbon. Multicoloured.

2827 85e. Type **638** 1·10 85

2828 90e. Pole vault 1·10 90

2829 105e. Shot put 1·40 95

2830 250e. High jump 3·25 2·20

MS2831 122×100 mm. 350e. hurdles 4·75 4·75

2001. Birds (2nd series). As T 620. Multicoloured. (a) Ordinary gum. Size 27×25 mm.

2832 53e. Little bustard 60 45

2833 85e. Purple swamphen 95 75

2834 105e. Collared Pratincole 1·20 90

2835 140e. Black-shouldered kite 1·60 1·30

2836 225e. Egyptian vulture 2·75 2·10

(b) Self-adhesive gum. (i) Size 25×21 mm.

2837 53e. As No. 2832 75 45

2838 105e. As No. 2834 1·30 1·00

(ii) Size 48×22 mm.

2839 85e. Purple swamphen 1·30 85

No. 2839 is inscribed "CorreioAzul".

639 Decorated Dish

2001. Arab Artefacts. Multicoloured.

2840 53e. Type **639** 60 40

2841 90e. Painted tile 1·10 80

2842 105e. Carved stone tablet and fortress 1·40 95

2843 140e. Coin 2·40 1·30

2844 225e. Carved container 3·00 2·00

2845 350e. Jug 4·25 3·25

640 Coastal Environment (Angela M. Lopes)

2001. "Stampin' the Future". Winning Entries in Children's International Painting Competition. Multicoloured.

2846 85e. Type **640** 1·00 75

2847 90e. Earth, Sun and watering can (Maria G. Silva) (vert) 1·10 80

2848 105e. Marine life (Joao A. Ferreira) 1·20 95

641 Statue, Building Facade and Stained Glass Window

2001. Centenary of National Fine Arts Society.

2849 85e. Type **641** 1·00 75

2850 105e. Painting and woman 1·20 1·00

MS2851 105×80 mm. 350e. "Hen with Chicks" (detail) (Girao) 4·75 4·75

642 Congress in Session

2001. 25th Anniv of Portuguese Republic Constitution.

2852 **642** 85e. multicoloured 1·10 80

643 Fishes

2001. Europa. Water Resources.

2853 **643** 105e. multicoloured 1·70 1·40

MS2854 140×110 mm. No. 2853 ×3 5·50 6·50

644 Couple and Heart

2001. Greetings Stamps. Multicoloured.

2855 85e. Type **644** 1·10 85

2856 85e. Birthday cake 1·10 85

2857 85e. Glasses 1·10 85

2858 85e. Bunch of flowers 1·10 85

MS2859 91×110 mm. Nos. 2855/8 4·25 4·00

645 Open Book

2001. Porto, European City of Culture. Multicoloured.

2860 53e. Type **645** 60 45

2861 85e. Bridge and Globe 1·10 70

2862 105e. Grand piano 1·20 95

2863 140e. Stage curtain 1·60 1·30

2864 225e. Picture frame 2·75 2·10

2865 350e. Firework display 4·00 3·25

MS2866 140×110 mm. Nos. 2861/6 12·00 11·00

646 Campaign Cannon, 1773

2001. 150th Anniv of Military Museum, Lisbon. Multicoloured.

2867 85e. Type **646** 1·10 80

2868 105e. 16th-century armour 1·40 1·10

MS2869 140×112 mm. 53e. Pistol of King Jose I, 1757; 53e. Cannon on carriage, 1797; 140e. Cannon "Tigre", 1533; 140e. 15th-century helmet 5·00 4·50

647 Brown Bear

2001. Lisbon Zoo. Multicoloured.

2870 53e. Type **647** 55 40

2871 85e. Emperor tamarin 1·00 75

2872 90e. Green iguana 1·00 85

2873 105e. Humboldt penguin 1·30 1·00

2874 225e. Toco toucan 2·75 2·10

2875 350e. Giraffe 4·00 3·25

MS2876 140×112 mm. 85e. Indian elephant (29×38 mm); 85e. Grevy's zebra (29×39 mm); Lion (29×38 mm); White rhinoceros (29×38 mm) 8·00 6·50

648 Emblem

2001. 47th Lion's European Forum, Oporto.

2877 **648** 85e. multicoloured 1·10 75

649 Azinhoso Pillory

2001. Pillories. Multicoloured.

2878 53e. Type **649** 60 45

2879 53e. Soajo 60 45

2880 53e. Braganca 60 45

2881 53e. Linhares 60 45

2882 53e. Arcos de Valdevez 60 45

2883 53e. Vila de Rua 60 45

2884 53e. Sernancelhe 60 45

2885 53e. Frechas 60 45

650 Faces

2001. United Nations Year of Dialogue among Civilizations.

2886 **650** 140e. multicoloured 1·60 1·20

651 Disney

2001. Birth Centenary of Walt Disney (artist and film producer).

2887 53e. Type **651** 65 50

MS2888 160×132 mm. 53e. Huey, Dewey and Louie, and 15th-century Mudejares tiles; 53e. Mickey Mouse and 16th-century tiles forming coat of arms; 53e. Minnie Mouse and 17th-century religious allegory tiles; 53e. Goofy and 18th-century tiles of birds; 53e. Type **651**; 53e. Pluto and 19th-century tile design by Rafael Bordalo Pinheiro; 53e. Donald Duck and 19th-century tiles; 53e. Scrooge McDuck and 20th-century "Querubim Lapa" tiles; 53e. Daisy Duck and 20th-century tile designs by Manuel Cargaleiro 8·00 7·00

652 Royal Police Guard, 1801

2001. Bicentenary of National Guard. Multicoloured.

2889 53e. Type **652** 60 50

2890 85e. Lisbon Municipal Guard bandsman, 1834 1·00 75

2891 90e. Infantry helmet, 1911 and modern guardsman 1·00 80

2892 105e. Mounted division helmet of 1911 and modern guardsmen 1·20 95

2893 140e. Guardsmen with motor-cycle and car 1·60 1·20

2894 350e. Customs and Excise officer and boat 4·25 3·00

MS2895 117×90 mm. 225e. Mounted division helmet and guardsman of 1911 3·00 3·00

653 Chinese Junk

2001. Ships. Multicoloured.

2896 53e. Type **653** 65 50

2897 53e. Portuguese caravel 65 50

654 1c. Coin

2002. New Currency. Multicoloured.

2898 1c. Type **654** 10 10

2899 2c. 2c. coin 10 10

2900 5c. 5c. coin 15 10

2901 10c. 10c. coin 20 15

2902 20c. 20c. coin 45 35

2903 50c. 50c. coin 1·10 90

2904 €1 €1 coin 2·50 1·80

2905 €2 €2 coin 4·75 3·50

655 Horse-rider

2002. No value expressed.

2906 **655** A (28c.) multicoloured 65 50

No. 2906 was sold at the current first class inland letter rate.

657 European Bee-eater

2002. Birds (1st series). Multicoloured. (i) Ordinary gum. Size 30×26 mm.

2914	2c. Type **657**	10	10
2915	28c. Little tern	70	50
2916	43c. Eagle owl	1·00	80
2917	54c. Pin-tailed sandgrouse	1·30	95
2918	60c. Red-necked nightjar	1·40	1·10
2919	70c. Greater spotted cuckoo	1·70	1·30

(ii) Self-adhesive gum. Size 49×23 mm.

2920	43c. Little tern (different)	1·30	85

(iii) Self-adhesive gum. Size 29×24 mm.

2921	28c. As No. 2919	75	55
2922	54c. As No. 2916	1·30	1·00

(iiii) Self-adhesive gum. Size 27×23 mm.

2923	28c. As No. 2919	1·00	70
2924	54c. As No. 2916	1·70	1·10

See also Nos. 2988/92.

658 De Gois (image scaled to 61% of original size)

2002. 500th Birth Anniv of Damiao de Gois (writer).

2925	**658**	45c. multicoloured	1·10	80

659 Loxodromic Curve, Ship and Globe

2002. 500th Birth Anniv of Pedro Nunes (mathematician). Multicoloured.

2926	28c. Type **659**	65	50
2927	28c. Nonius (navigational instrument)	65	50
2928	€1.15 Portrait of Nunes	2·75	2·10
MS2929	140×105 mm Nos. 2926/8	4·25	4·00

660 Children and Flower

2002. America. Youth, Education and Literacy. Multicoloured.

2930	70c. Type **660**	1·60	1·30
2931	70c. Children, book and letters	1·60	1·30
2932	70c. Children and pencil	1·60	1·30

661 Refracting Telescope and Polytechnic School Observatory, Lisbon

2002. Astronomy. Multicoloured.

2933	28c. Type **661**	65	50
2934	28c. 16th-century astrolabe and Colegio dos Nobres, Lisbon	65	50
2935	43c. Quadrant and Solar Observatory, Coimbra	1·00	80
2936	45c. Terrestrial telescope and King Pedro V	1·00	80
2937	45c. Cassegrain telescope and King Luis	1·00	80
2938	54c. Earth, refracting telescope and Observatory, Ajuda	1·30	1·00
2939	€1.15 Cassegrain telescope and Saturn	2·75	2·10
2940	€1.75 Zeiss projector and planets	4·00	3·25
MS2941	140×111 mm. 70c. 18th-century armillary sphere; 70c. 19th-century theodolite	3·75	3·75

662 Square and Compass

2002. Bicentenary of Grande Oriente Lusitano (Masonic Grand Lodge).

2942	**662**	43c. multicoloured	1·10	80

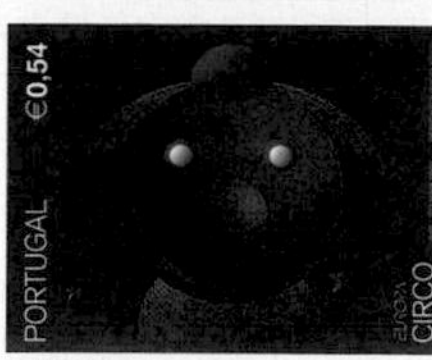

663 Clown

2002. Europa. Circus.

2943	**663** 54c. multicoloured	2·00	1·60
MS2944	140×110 mm No. 2943×3	6·25	7·75

664 *Scabiosa nitens*

2002. Flowers of Azores. Multicoloured.

2945	28c. Type **664**	65	50
2946	45c. *Viburnum tinus subcordatum*	1·00	75
2947	54c. *Euphorbia azorica*	1·20	95
2948	70c. *Lysimachia nemorum azorica*	1·60	1·30
2949	€1.15 *Bellis azorica*	2·75	2·10
2950	€1.75 *Spergularia azorica*	4·00	3·25
MS2951	120×121 mm €1.15 *Azorina vidalli*; €1.75 *Senecio malvifolius*	6·75	6·50

665 Lockheed Martin (General Dynamics) F-16 Fighting Falcon

2002. 50th Anniv of Portuguese Air Force. Multicoloured.

2952	28c. Type **665**	65	50
2953	43c. Sud Aviation SA300 Puma helicopter	1·00	80
2954	54c. Dassault Dornier Alphajet A	1·20	95
2955	70c. Lockheed C-130 Hercules transport aircraft	1·60	1·30
2956	€1.25 Lockheed P-3P Orion reconnaissance aircraft	2·75	2·20
2957	€1.75 Fiat G-91 fighter aircraft	4·00	3·00
MS2958	140×112 mm €1.15 Four Cessna T-37; €1.75 Aerospatiale TB30 Epsilon and Cessna T-37	7·25	7·00

666 Gymnastics

2002. Sports and Sports Anniversaries. Multicoloured.

2959	28c. Type **666** (50th anniv of Portuguese Gymnastic Federation)	60	50
2960	28c. Walking race	60	50
2961	45c. Basketball	1·00	80
2962	45c. Handball	1·00	80
2963	54c. Roller hockey (sixth Women's World Roller Hockey Championship, Pacos de Ferriera)	1·20	95
2964	54c. Fencing (World Fencing Championship, Lisbon)	1·20	95
2965	€1.75 Footballers (World Cup Football Championship, Japan and South Korea)	3·75	3·00
2966	€1.75 Golf	3·75	3·00
MS2967	140×110 mm. €1 Footballer and part of football; €2 Torsos and legs of two players	7·00	5·75

Nos. **MS**2967 was inscribed for "PHILAKOREA 2002" International Stamp Exhibition, Seoul, in the margin.

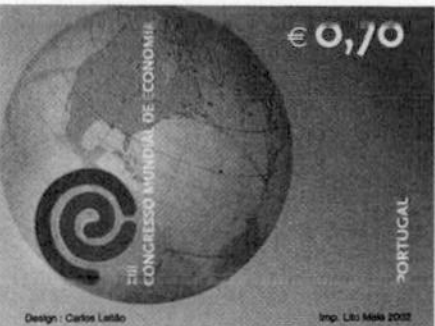

667 Globe and Emblem

2002. 13th World International Economic Association Congress.

2968	**667**	70c. multicoloured	1·60	1·20

668 Anniversary Emblem

2002. 150th Anniv of Ministry of Public Works, Transport and Housing. Multicoloured.

2969	43c. Type **668**	1·00	75
MS2970	144×123 mm. 43c. ×6, Ship and oil terminal; Locomotive; Stylised Boeing 737; Bridge and city skyline; Factories; Houses	6·50	5·00

669 Portrait and Symbols of Industry and Agriculture

2002. 150th Anniv of Technical Education.

2971	**669**	43c. multicoloured	1·00	75

670 Virgin and Child (statue) and Window, Alcobaca Monastery

2002. UNESCO World Heritage Sites. Multicoloured.

2972	28c. Type **670**	60	50
2973	28c. Lion (statue) and embossed ceiling, Jeronimos Monastery	60	50
2974	43c. Column capitals, Guimaraes	95	75
2975	43c. Cherub (statue) and vineyards, Alto Douro	95	75
2976	54c. Corbel, lake and vineyards, Alto Douro (horiz) (80×30 mm)	1·20	95
2977	54c. Houses and statues, Guimaraes (horiz) (80×30 mm)	1·20	95
2978	70c. Carved arch and statue, Jeronimos Monastery (horiz) (80×30 mm)	1·60	1·20
2979	70c. Nave and tomb, Alcobaca Monastery (horiz) (80×30 mm)	1·60	1·20
MS2980	Four sheets, each 141×114 mm. (a) €1.25 Door and statue, Alcobaca Monastery; (b) €1.25 Double doors, Jeronimos Monastery; (c) €1.25 Arches, Guimaraes; (d) €1.25 Grapes, Alto Douro	12·00	9·75

671 1870 Dress Uniform

2003. Bicentenary of Military College, Luz. Multicoloured.

2981	20c. Type **671**	40	35
2982	30c. 1806 uniform	65	50
2983	43c. 1837 parade uniform	95	75
2984	55c. 1861 uniform (rear view)	1·20	95
2985	70c. 1866 dress uniform	1·60	1·30
2986	€2 1912 cavalry cadet uniform	4·50	3·50
MS2987	141×114 mm. €1 1802 uniform; €1 1948 Porta Guiao dress uniform	4·75	4·00

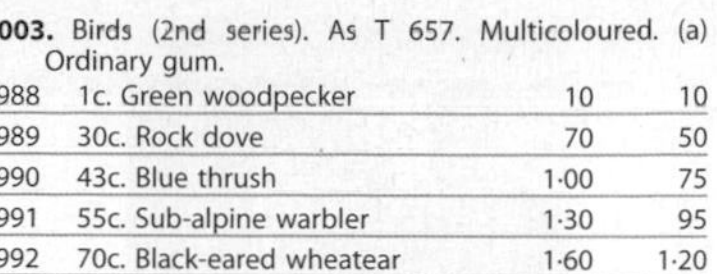

2003. Birds (2nd series). As T 657. Multicoloured. (a) Ordinary gum.

2988	1c. Green woodpecker	10	10
2989	30c. Rock dove	70	50
2990	43c. Blue thrush	1·00	75
2991	55c. Sub-alpine warbler	1·30	95
2992	70c. Black-eared wheatear	1·60	1·20

(b) Self-adhesive gum. Size 27×23 mm.

2992a	30c. No. 2989	75	50
2992b	43c. No. 2990 (50×23 mm)	1·00	80
2992c	55c. No. 2991	1·80	1·20

No. 2992b is inscribed "CorreioAzul".

672 People forming Mobility Symbol

2003. European Year of the Disabled. Multicoloured.

2993	30c. Type **672**	75	50
2994	55c. People forming head shape	1·30	95
2995	70c. As No. 2994 but with eyes, ears and mouth pink	1·60	1·20

673 1853 5r. Stamp and Queen Donna Maria II

2003. 150th Anniv of First Postage Stamp (1st issue). Designs showing 1853 stamps. Multicoloured.

2996	30c. Type **673**	65	50
2997	43c. 25r. stamp and coin	95	75
2998	55c. 50r. stamp and portrait	1·20	95
2999	70c. 100r. stamp and arms	1·60	1·20

See also Nos. 3011 and **MS**3047.

674 *Orchis italica*

2003. Orchids. Multicoloured.

3000	46c. *Aceras anthropophorum*	1·00	80
3001	46c. *Dactylorhiza maculate*	1·00	80
MS3002	Two sheets, each 113×140 mm. (a) 30c. Type **674**; 30c. *Ophrys tenthredinifera*; 30c. *Ophrys fusca fusca*; 30c. *Orchis papilionacea*; 30c. *Barlia robertiana*; 30c. *Ophrys lutea*; 30c. *Ophrys fusca*; 30c. *Ophrys apifera*; 30c. *Dactylorhiza ericetorum*. (b) 30c. *Orchis champagneuxii*; 30c. *Orchis morio*; 30c. *Serapias cordigera*; 30c. *Orchis coriophora*; 30c. *Ophrys bombyliflora*; 30c. *Ophrys vernixia*; 30c. *Ophrys speculum*; 30c. *Ophrys scoplopax*; 30c. *Anacamptis pyramidalis*	14·00	11·00

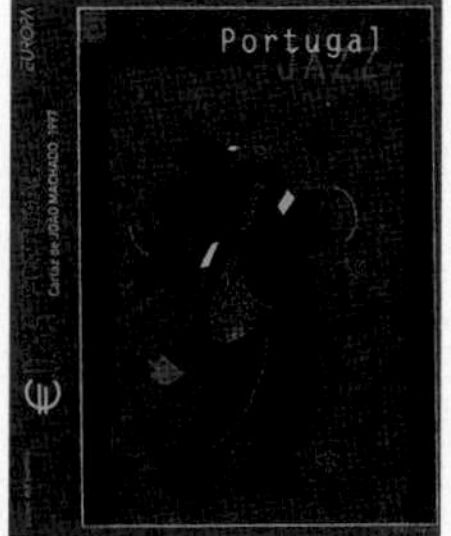

675 Jazz Festival (Joao Machado)

2003. Europa. Poster Art. Multicoloured.

3003	55c. Type **675**	1·60	1·20
3004	55c. Woman wearing swimsuit ("Espimho") (Fred Kradolfer)	1·60	1·20
MS3005	140×113 mm. Nos. 3004/5	3·25	3·50

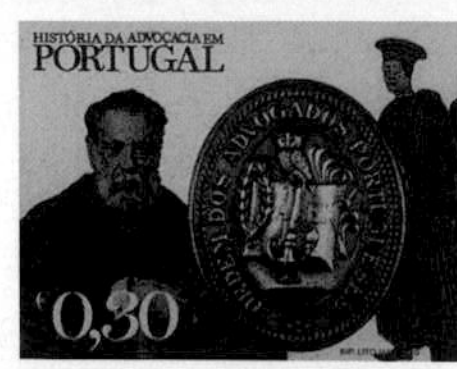
676 Lawyer and Union Seal

2003. International Lawyer's Congress, Lisbon. Multicoloured.

3006	30c. Type **676**	65	50
3007	43c. Lawyers, arms and Court building	95	75
3008	55c. Medieval lawyer, Bishop and legal document	1·20	95
3009	70c. Lawyer's union presidential medal and female lawyer	1·60	1·20
MS3010	140×113 mm. €1 Lawyer wearing red robe and seal; €2 Seal, painted plaque and bishop	7·00	5·50

677 "150" and Stamp (Viseu)

2003. 150th Anniv of Portuguese First Stamp (2nd issue). Itinerant Exhibition.

3011	**677**	30c. multicoloured	80	50
3012	**677**	30c. multicoloured	80	50
3013	**677**	30c. multicoloured	80	50

678 Championship Emblem

2003. Euro 2004 Football Championship, Portugal (1st issue).

3014	**678**	30c. multicoloured	70	50
3015	**678**	43c. multicoloured	1·00	75
3016	**678**	47c. multicoloured	1·10	85
3017	**678**	55c. multicoloured	1·30	95
3018	**678**	70c. multicoloured	1·60	1·20
MS3019		(a) 140×109 mm. 55c. ×4, Parts of championship emblem. (b) 190×200 mm. Nos. 3014/18 and **MS**3019a	5·25	4·25

See also Nos. **MS**3072, 3073/4, 3084/**MS**88, 3110/17, 3119/28 and **MS**3147.

679 Open-topped Car

2003. Centenary of Portuguese Automobile Club. Multicoloured.

3020	30c. Type **679**	65	50
3021	43c. Club engineer riding motorcycle	95	75
3022	€2 Racing cars	4·50	3·50

680 Ricardo do Espirito Santo Silva

2003. 50th Anniv of Ricardo do Espirito Santo Silva Foundation. Multicoloured.

3023	30c. Type **680**	60	50
3024	30c. 18th-century inlaid chess table	60	50
3025	43c. Cutlery box, 1720–1750	95	75
3026	43c. 15th-century silver tray	95	75
3027	55c. 18th-century wooden container	1·20	95
3028	55c. Ming dynasty ceramic box	1·20	95
MS3029	140×112 mm. €1 17th-century cupboard; €1 18th-century tapestry	7·00	5·50

681 "Bay of Funchal" (W. G. James) (1839)

2003. Museums of Madeira. Black (No. MS3034) or multicoloured (others).

3030	30c. Type **681**	60	50
3031	43c. Nativity (straw sculpture, Manuel Orlando Noronha Gois)	1·00	75
3032	55c. "O Largo da Fonte" (Andrew Picken) (1840)	1·30	95
3033	70c. "Le Depart" (Martha Teles) (1983)	1·50	1·20
MS3034	140×112 mm. €1 Vicente Gomes da Silva (photograph); €2 Jorge Bettencourt (photograph)	6·75	5·25

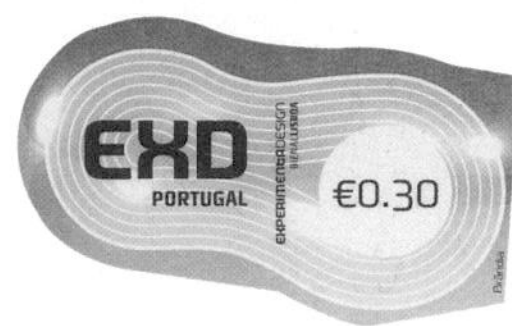
682 Curved Shape containing "EXD"

2003. ExperimentaDesign2003 (design exhibition). Sheet containing T 682 and similar curved designs. Either black (30c.) or black and red (others). Self-adhesive.

3035	30c. Type **682**	65	50
3036	30c. "EXD" centrally	65	50
3037	30c. "EXD" bottom	65	50
3038	30c. "EXD" left	65	50
3039	43c. As No. 3038 but design reversed	95	75
3040	43c. As No. 3037 but design reversed	95	75
3041	43c. As No. 3036 but design reversed	95	75
3042	43c. As No. 3035 but design reversed	95	75
3043	55c. As No. 3035	1·20	90
3044	55c. As No. 3036	1·20	90
3045	55c. As No. 3037	1·20	90
3046	55c. As No. 3038	1·20	90

683 Queen Maria II

2003. 150th Anniv of First Portuguese Stamp (3rd issue). Four sheets, each 140×112 mm containing T 683 and similar multicoloured designs.

MS3047	(a) 30c. Type **683**; 30c. ×4 No. 2996 ×4 (25.9); (b) €1 Queen Maria II and euro coins (90×40 mm) (12.12); (c) €2.50 Seal and postal marks (80×30 mm) (23.9); (d) €3 King Pedro V, 1853 25r. stamp and Queen Maria II (80×30 mm)	18·00	15·00

684 St. John's Well, Vila Real

2003. America. Fountains. Multicoloured.

3048	30c. Type **684**	60	50
3049	43c. Fountain of Virtues, Porto	95	75
3050	55c. Fountain, Giraldo Square, Evora	1·20	95
3051	70c. Senora da Saude fountain, St. Marcos de Tavira	1·50	1·20
3052	€1 Town fountain, Castelo de Vide	2·20	1·70
3053	€2 St. Andreas fountain, Guarda	4·25	2·40

685 Jose I engraved Glass Tumbler (18th-century)

2003. Glass Production. Multicoloured.

3054	30c. Type **685**	60	50
3055	55c. Maria II engraved tumbler (19th-century)	1·20	95
3056	70c. Blue glass vase (Carmo Valente) (20th-century)	1·50	1·20
3057	€2 Bulbous vase (Helena Matos) (20th-century)	4·25	3·50
MS3058	140×112 mm. €1.50 Stained glass window (detail) (Fernando Santos) (19th-century)	3·50	2·75

686 Persian Medicine Jar and Roman Dropper

2003. Medicine and Pharmacy. Multicoloured.

3059	30c. Type **686**	60	50
3060	43c. Ceramic bottle and jar	95	75
3061	55c. Pestle and mortar	1·20	95
3062	70c. Still and glass bottle	1·50	1·20

687 Drawing Board and Chair (Jose Epinho)

2003. Contemporary Design. Multicoloured.

3063	43c. Type **687**	95	75
3064	43c. Telephone point (Pedro Silva Dias) (vert)	95	75
3065	43c. Tea trolley (Cruz de Carvlho)	95	75
3066	43c. Tap (Carlos Aguiar)	95	75
3067	43c. Desk (Daciano da Costa)	95	75
3068	43c. Knives (Eduardo Afonso Dias)	95	75
3069	43c. Stacking chairs (Leonor and Antonio Sena da Silva)	95	75
3070	43c. Flask (Carlos Rocha) (vert)	95	75
3071	43c. Chair (Antonio Garcia) (vert)	95	75

688 Championship Emblem

2003. Euro 2004 Football Championship, Portugal (2nd issue). Stadiums (2nd issue). Sheet 150×165 mm containing T 688 and similar horiz designs. Multicoloured.

MS3072	30c.×10 Type **688**; Municipal stadium, Aveiro; Dr. Magalhaes Pessoa stadium, Leiria; Luz stadium, Lisbon; D. Afonso Henriques stadium, Guimaraes; Municipal stadium, Coimbra; Bessa stadium, Porto; Dragao stadium, Porto; Algarve stadium, Faro-Loule; Jose Alvalade stadium, Lisbon	12·00	6·00

689 Kinas

2004. European Football Championship 2004, Portugal (3rd series). Mascot. Multicoloured. Self-adhesive.

3073	45c. Type **689** (postage)	95	80
3074	€1.75 Kinas and football (air)	3·75	3·00

No. 3073 was inscribed "CorreioAzul". No. 3074 was inscribed "Airmail Priority".

690 King Joao IV and Vila Vicosa

2004. 400th Birth Anniv of King Joao IV. Multicoloured.

3075	45c. Type **690**	95	80
3076	€1 King Joao standing	2·20	1·80

Nos. 3075/6 were issued together, se-tenant, forming a composite design.

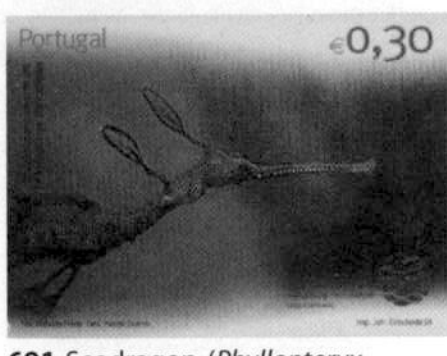
691 Seadragon (*Phyllopteryx taeniolatus*)

2004. Lisbon Oceanarium. Multicoloured.

3077	30c. Type **691**	60	50
3078	45c. Magellanic penguin (*Spheniscus magellanicus*)	95	75
3079	56c. *Hypsypops rubicundus*	1·20	95
3080	72c. Sea otter (*Enhydra lutris*)	1·60	1·30
3081	€1 Grey nurse shark (*Carcharias Taurus*)	2·10	1·70
3082	€2 Atlantic puffin (*Fratercula artica*)	4·25	3·50
MS3083	140×112 mm. €1.50 Macaroni penguin (*Eudyptes Chrysolophus*) (80×30 mm)	3·50	2·75

692 Foot kicking Ball

2004. European Football Championship 2004, Portugal (4th series). Official Match Ball. Multicoloured. Self-adhesive.

3084	10c. Type **692**	25	15
3085	20c. Ball right	45	35
3086	30c. Ball and line	70	50
3087	50c. Ball and goal post	1·10	85
MS3088	105×105 mm. Nos. 3084/7.	4·25	2·30

MS3088 is ordinary gum.

693 Portugal

2004. European Football Championship 2004, Portugal (5th series). Participating Teams. Designs showing Kinas (mascot) and country flags. Multicoloured.

3089	30c. Type **693**	70	55
3090	30c. France	70	55
3091	30c. Sweden	70	55
3092	30c. Czech Republic	70	55
3093	30c. Greece	70	55
3094	30c. UK	70	55
3095	30c. Bulgaria	70	55
3096	30c. Latvia	70	55
3097	30c. Spain	70	55
3098	30c. Switzerland	70	55
3099	30c. Denmark	70	55
3100	30c. Germany	70	55
3101	30c. Russia	70	55
3102	30c. Croatia	70	55
3103	30c. Italy	70	55
3104	30c. Netherlands	70	55

2004. Birds (3rd series). As T 657. Multicoloured.

3105	30c. Red crossbill	60	50
3106	45c. Red-rumped swallow	95	75
3107	55c. Golden oriole	1·20	95
3108	58c. Crested lark	1·30	1·00
3109	72c. Crested tit	1·60	1·30
3109a	30c. As No. 3105 (28×23 mm)	60	50
3109b	45c. As No. 3106 (50×23 mm)	95	75
3109c	56c. As No. 3107 (28×23 mm)	1·20	95

Nos. 3105a/7a all self-adhesive.

694 "Moliceiros" Boat (Aveiro)

2004. European Football Championship 2004, Portugal (6th series). Host Cities. Multicoloured.

3110	30c. Type **694**	65	55
3111	30c. University tower (Coimbra)	65	55
3112	30c. Don Afonso Henriques (statue) (Guimaraes)	65	55
3113	30c. Castle (Leiria)	65	55
3114	30c. Tower (Faro/Loule)	65	55
3115	30c. Bom Jesus (Braga)	65	55
3116	30c. Torre di Belem (Lisbon)	65	55
3117	30c. D. Luís I Bridge (Porto)	65	55

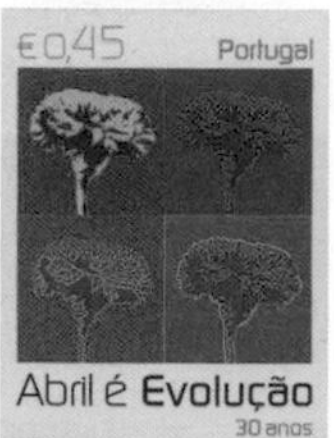

695 Carnations

2004. 30th Anniv of 25 April (Carnation revolution).

3118	**695**	45c. multicoloured	1·00	80

696 Dr. Magalhaes Pessoa Stadium, Leiria

2004. European Football Championship 2004, Portugal (7th series). Stadiums (2nd issue). Multicoloured.

3119	30c. Type **696**	65	55
3120	30c. Municipal stadium, Coimbra	65	55
3121	30c. Municipal stadium, Braga	65	55
3122	30c. Bessa stadium, Porto	65	55
3123	30c. Luz stadium, Lisbon	65	55
3124	30c. D. Afonso Henriques stadium, Guimaraes	65	55
3125	30c. Algarve stadium, Faro-Loule	65	55
3126	30c. Jose Alvalade stadium, Lisbon	65	55
3127	30c. Dragao stadium, Porto	65	55
3128	30c. Municipal stadium, Aveiro	65	55

697 Stylized Figures

2004. European Union. Multicoloured.

3129	30c. Type **697** (EU parliamentary elections)	70	50
3130	56c. EU emblem and new members' flags (80×30 mm) (new members)	1·20	90
MS3131	140×111 mm×2 Original members' flags (80 30 mm)	4·75	4·00

698 Picture Gallery

2004. Europa. Holidays. Multicoloured.

3132	56c. Type **698**	1·50	1·20
3133	56c. Beach	1·50	1·20
MS3134	141×112 mm. Nos. 3132/3	4·50	3·50

699 Bells of Early Telephone

2004. Centenary of Telephone Line from Porto to Lisbon. Multicoloured.

3135	30c. Type **699**	60	50
3136	45c. Insulator	95	75
3137	56c. Fibre optic cable	1·20	95
3138	72c. Video telephone	1·60	1·30
MS3139	140×112 mm. €1. ×2, No. 3135; No. 3138	6·75	4·00

700 Flower (illustration, Maimonides' Mishneh Torah)

2004. Jewish Heritage. Multicoloured.

3140	30c. Type **700**	60	50
3141	45c. Star of David (illustration, Cervera Bible)	95	75
3142	56c. Menorah (illustration, Cervera Bible)	1·20	95
3143	72c. Menorah (carved tablet)	1·60	1·30
3144	€1 Illustration, Abravanel Bible	2·10	1·70
3145	€2 Prophet (statue, de Cristo Convent, Tomar)	4·25	3·50
MS3146	140×112 mm. €1.50 Shaare Tikva Synagogue (centenary)	3·50	2·75

701 Henri Delaunay Trophy

2004. European Football Championship 2004, Portugal (8th series). Sheet 140×112 mm. Multicoloured.

MS3147	**701**	€1 multicoloured	2·40	2·00

702 Stamps

2004. 50th Anniv of Portuguese Philatelic Federation. Multicoloured.

3148	30c. Type **702**	75	50
MS3149	111×79 mm €1.50 Seal	3·50	2·75

703 Footballers Past and Present (image scaled to 55% of original size)

2004. 50th Anniv of Union of European Football Associations (UEFA). Sheet 141×85 mm.

MS3150	€1 multicoloured	2·40	1·90

704 Hurdler

2004. Olympic Games, Athens 2004. Multicoloured.

3151	30c. Type **704**	65	50
3152	45c. High jump	1·10	75

705 Swimmer

2004. Paralymic Games, Athens 2004. Multicoloured.

3153	30c. Type **705**	60	50
3154	45c. Wheelchair racer	95	75
3155	56c. Cyclist	1·20	95
3156	72c. Runner	1·50	1·30

706 Pedro Homem de Melo

2004. Birth Centenary of Pedro Homem de Melo (folklorist). Sheet 140×112 mm.

MS3157	€2 multicoloured	4·75	4·00

707 Museum Facade (image scaled to 55% of original size)

2004. Inauguration of Belem Palace Museum (President of the Republic's Museum). Multicoloured.

3158	45c. Type **708**	1·00	75
MS3159	140×112 mm. €1 Museum interior	2·40	1·90

708 Quim and Manecas (Jose Stuart Carvalhais)

2004. Comic Strips. Multicoloured.

3160	30c. Type **708**	60	50
3161	45c. Guarda Abila (Julio Pinto and Nuno Saraiva)	95	75
3162	56c. Simao Infante (Raul Correia and Eduardo Teixeira Coelho)	1·20	95
3163	72c. APior Banda du Mondo (Jose Carlos Fernandes)	1·50	1·30
MS3164	141×111 mm. 50c.×4, Oespiao Acacio (Relvas); Jim del Monaco (Louro and Simoes); Tomahawk Tom (Vitor Peon); Pitanga (Arlndo Fagundes)	4·75	4·00

709 Third-century Sarcophagus and Mosaic

2004. Viticulture. Multicoloured.

3165	30c. Type **709**	70	50
3166	45c. Mosaic and 12th-century tapestry	1·10	75
3167	56c. Man carrying grapes (14th-century missal) and grape harvesting (15th-century Book of Hours)	1·30	95
3168	72c. Grape harvesting and "Grupo de Leao" (Columbano Bordalo Pine)	1·70	1·30
3169	€1 "Grupo de Leo" and 20th-century stained glass window	2·30	1·70
MS3170	140×115 mm. 50c. ×4, Fields, grapes and mechanical harvester; Harvester and amphora; Barrels in cellar, steel vats and barrels; Barrels, bottling and glass of wine	4·50	4·00

Nos. 3165/6 were issued together, se-tenant, forming a composite design.

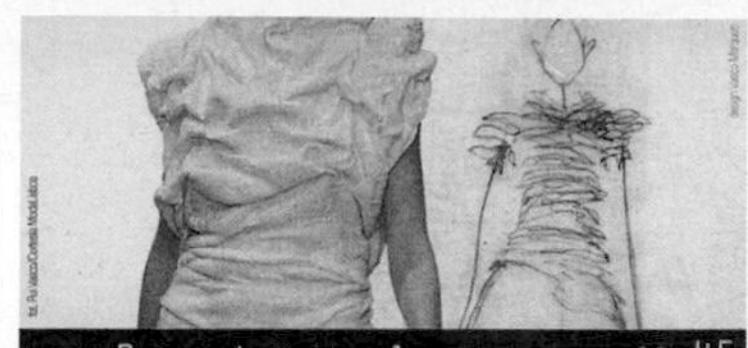

710 Ruched Dress (Alexandra Moura) (image scaled to 61% of original size)

2004. Fashion. Sheet 190×200 mm containing T 710 and similar horiz designs. Multicoloured.

MS3171	45c. ×10, Type **710**; Poncho (Ana Salazar); Boned and laced dress (Filipe Faisca); Ribboned skirt (J. Branco and L. Sanchez); Wrap-over dress Antonio Tenente); Frilled front (Luis Buchinho); White top and skirted pants (Osvaldo Martins); Magenta dress with red attachments (Dino Alves); Silk-edged coat (Alves and Goncalves); Sequinned halter necked dress (Fatima Lopes)	11·00	8·50

711 "Adoration of the Magi" (Jorge Afonso)

2004. Christmas. Multicoloured.

3172	30c. Type **711**	60	50
3173	45c. "Adoration of the Magi" (16th-century Flamenga school)	95	75
3174	56c. "Escape into Egypt" (Francisco Vieira)	1·20	95
3175	72c. "Nativity" (Portuguese school)	1·50	1·30
MS3176	140×112 mm. €3 "Nativity" (detail) (Josefa de Obidos) (50×35 mm)	6·75	5·50

712 "Entrudo", Lazarim, Lamego

2005. Masks. Multicoloured. (a) Ordinary gum.

3177	10c. Type **712**	20	15
3178	30c. "Festa dos Rapazes", Salsas, Braganca	60	50
3179	45c. "Festa do Chocalheiro" Mougadouro, Braganca	90	75
3180	57c. "Cardador", Vale de Ilhavo	1·20	1·00
3181	74c. "Festa dos Rapazes", Avelada, Braganca	1·60	1·30

(b) Self-adhesive gum.

3182	30c. As No. 3178 (29×24 mm)	1·10	50
3183	45c. As No. 3179 (48×23 mm)	1·60	80
3184	57c. As No. 3180 (29×24 mm)	2·10	1·00

No. 3183 is inscribed "Correio Azul".

See also No. 3319/21.

713 Subway Train and Tram

2005. Public Transport. Multicoloured.

3185	30c. Type **713**	60	50
3186	50c. Locomotive and tram	1·00	85
3187	57c. Hovercraft	1·20	1·00
3188	€1 Coach	2·10	1·70
3189	€2 Train	4·25	3·50

Nos. 3185/9 were issued together, se-tenant, forming a composite design.

714 Sortelha

2005. Historic Villages (1st issue). Multicoloured.

3190	30c. Type **714**	65	50
3191	30c. Idanha-a-Velha	65	50
3192	30c. Castelo Novo	65	50
3193	30c. Castelo Rodrigo	65	50
3194	30c. Piodao	65	50
3195	30c. Linhares	65	50
3196	30c. Transcoso	65	50
3197	30c. Monsanto	65	50
3198	30c. Almeida	65	50
3199	30c. Belmonte	65	50
3200	30c. Marialva	65	50
3201	30c. Castelo Mendo	65	50
3202	30c. Buildings and coast, Linhares	65	50
3203	30c. Roof tops, Transcoso	65	50
3204	30c. Church, Marialva	65	50
3205	30c. Castle and houses, Castelo Rodrigo	65	50
3206	30c. Buildings and terrace, Almeida	65	50
3207	30c. Houses, Castelo Mendo	65	50
3208	30c. Rooftops, Sortelha	65	50
3209	30c. Balcony, Belmonte	65	50
3210	30c. Rooftops, Monsanto	65	50
3211	30c. Ruins, Idanha-a-Velha	65	50
3212	30c. Tower, Castelo Novo	65	50
3213	30c. Rooftops, Piodao	65	50
3214	57c. Castle, Linhares	1·30	1·00
3215	57c. Castle walls, Transcoso	1·30	1·00
3216	57c. Bells, Mariavla	1·30	1·00
3217	57c. Church, Castelo Rodrigo	1·30	1·00
3218	57c. Walls, Almeida	1·30	1·00
3219	57c. Rooftops, Castelo Mendo	1·30	1·00
3220	57c. Column, Sortelha	1·30	1·00
3221	57c. Castle walls, Belmonte	1·30	1·00
3222	57c. Tower, Monsanto	1·30	1·00
3223	57c. Doorway, Idanha-a-Velha	1·30	1·00
3224	57c. Rooftops, Castelo Novo	1·30	1·00
3225	57c. Building facade, Piodao	1·30	1·00

See also No. **MS**3247.

715 "A Beira-Mar"

2005. 150th Birth Anniv of Jose Malhoa (artist). Multicoloured.

3226	30c. Type **715**	60	50
3227	45c. "As Promessas"	95	80
MS3228	93×117 mm. €1.77 "Conversa com o Vizinho"	3·75	2·75

716 Cozido a Portuguesa (stew)

2005. Europa. Gastronomy. Multicoloured.

3229	57c. Type **716**	1·50	1·20
MS3230	125×95 mm. 57c.×2, Bacalhau assado com batatas a murro (cod and potatoes)×2	6·50	5·25

717 Paul Harris (founder)

2005. Centenary of Rotary International.

3231	**717** 74c. Multicoloured	1·50	1·30
MS3232	125×95 mm. **717** €1.75 multicoloured	3·75	3·00

718 19th-century Open Carriage (Carrinho de Passeio)

2005. Centenary of National Coach Museum, Lisbon. Multicoloured.

3233	30c. Type **718**	60	50
3234	30c. 19th-century closed carriage (Carruagem de Porto Covo)	60	50
3235	45c. 17th-century carriage (Coche Francisca Saboia)	95	80
3236	45c. 18th-century small carriage ("Das Plumas")	95	80
3237	57c. 18th-century sedan chair	1·20	1·00
3238	74c. 18th-century coach (Coches dos oceanos)	1·60	1·30
MS3239	125×100 mm. €1.75 Queen Amelia	3·75	3·00

719 Pegoes Aqueduct, Tomar

2005. Cultural Heritage. Multicoloured.

3240	5c. Type **719**	10	10
3241	30c. Chalice (1581)	60	50
3242	45c. Stained glass, De Christo convent, Tomar	95	80
3243	57c. Turret, Angra, Azores	1·20	1·00
3244	€1 Ship	2·10	1·70
3245	€2 St. Vincente de Fora church, Lisbon	4·25	3·50
MS3246	112×140 mm. €1.20 Crucifix, Tesauro da Se, Lisbon	3·00	2·75

2005. Historic Villages (2nd issue). 12 sheets, each 60×150 mm containing horiz designs as T 714.

MS3247	(a) Nos. 3202 and 3214 (b) Nos. 3203 and 3215 (c) Nos. 3204 and 3216 (d) Nos. 3205 and 3217 (e) Nos. 3206 and 3218 (f) Nos. 3207 and 3219 (g) Nos. 3208 and 3220 (h) Nos. 3209 and 3221 (i) Nos. 3210 and 3222 (j) Nos. 3211 and 3223 (k) Nos. 3212 and 3224 (l) Nos. 3213 and 3225	19·00	14·00

720 Man and Cat (Raphael Bordallo Pinheiro)

2005. Caricaturists. Multicoloured.

3248	30c. Type **720**	75	50
3249	30c. Bearded man (Sebastiao Sanhudo)	75	50
3250	30c. Soldier (Celso Herminio)	75	50
3251	30c. Man wearing glasses (Leal da Camara)	75	50
3252	30c. Man holding broken pencil (Francisco Valenca)	75	50
3253	30c. Man smoking (Stuart Carvalhais)	75	50
3254	30c. Guarda Ricardo (Sam (Samuel Torres de Carvalho))	75	50
3255	30c. Almada Negreios (Joao Abel Manta)	75	50
3256	30c. Man tie (Augusto Cid)	75	50
3257	30c. Head and pencil (Antonio Atunes)	75	50
3258	30c. Ze Povinho (Raphael Bordallo Pinheiro)	75	50

721 Conductor's Hands

2005. Faro—National Cultural Capital 2005. Multicoloured.

3259	30c. Type **721**	60	50
3260	45c. Ancient pot	95	80
3261	57c. Shell	1·20	1·00
3262	74c. Hands	1·60	1·30

722 Coastline and Bell

2005. Tourism. Multicoloured. (a) Lisbon.

3263	45c. Type **722**	95	75
3264	48c. Monument and tram	1·00	85
3265	57c. Tram, rooftops and cupola	1·40	1·20

(b) Porto e Norte.

3266	45c. Ceramic rooster, valley and church	95	75
3267	48c. Church, bay and wine glass	1·00	85
3268	57c. Wine glass, seafront and yachts	1·40	1·00

Nos. 3263/5 and 3266/8, respectively were printed together, se-tenant, each forming a composite design.

723 Harvesting Bark from protected Cork Trees

2005. Environmental Protection. Multicoloured.

3269	30c. Type **723**	60	50
3270	45c. Fire prevention officers	90	75
3271	57c. Bucaco Forest	1·20	1·00
MS3272	95×95 mm. €2 Chestnut trees (Serra de S. Mamede)	4·00	3·25

724 "50" and UN Emblem

2005. 50th Anniv of United Nations Membership. Multicoloured.

3273	30c. Type **724**	60	50
3274	45c. Dove (International Day of Peace)	90	75
3275	57c. Child (UNESCO—Children at Risk)	1·20	1·00
3276	74c. Albert Einstein (International Year of Physics)	1·50	1·30

725 Sundial, St John the Baptist Church, Sao Joao das Lampas

2005. Annular Solar Eclipse—3rd October. Multicoloured.

3277	45c. Type **725**	95	75
3278	€1 Portable sundial, 1770	2·00	1·70
MS3279	125×135 mm. €1.20×3, Partial eclipse, Lisbon; Annulus, Braganca; Partial eclipse, Faro	7·50	6·00

726 Pen Nib

2005. Communications. Multicoloured.

3280	30c. Type **726**	60	50
3281	45c. Radio microphone	90	75
3282	57c. Television camera	1·20	1·00
3283	74c. Globe and @ (internet)	1·50	1·30
MS3284	Two sheets, each 125×90 mm. (a) €1.10 Newspaper; €1.55 Radio studio. (b) €1.10 Television studio; €1.55 "http://www" (internet)	10·50	10·00

727 Fisherman and Boats, Aldeia da Carrasqueira

2005. Fishing Villages. Multicoloured.

3285	30c. Type **727**	60	50
3286	30c. Moorings and pier, Aldeia da Carrasqueira	60	50
3287	30c. Boat, Tai O, Hong Kong	60	50
3288	30c. Wrapped fish, Tai O	60	50

Nos. 3285/6 and 3287/8 respectively were issued together, se-tenant, forming a composite design.

Stamps of the same design were issued by Hong Kong.

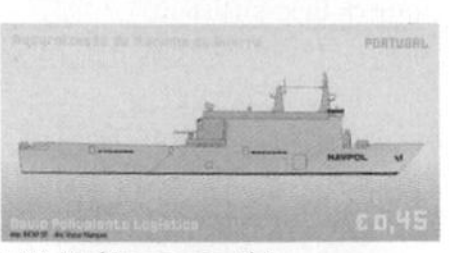
728 Multipurpose Ship

2005. Modernisation of the Navy. Black.

3289	45c. Type **728**	90	75
3290	57c. Hydro-oceanographic ship	1·20	1·00
3291	74c. Patrol vessel	1·50	1·30
3292	€2 Submarine	4·00	3·25

729 Alvaro Cunhal, Women and Children

2005. Alvaro Barreirinhas Cunhal (politician and writer) Commemoration. Multicoloured.

3293	30c. Type **729**	1·00	50
MS3294	112×104 mm. €1 Alvaro Cunhal and girl	1·80	1·80

730 Building

2005. Serralves Foundation. Multicoloured.

3295	30c. Type **730**	60	50
3296	45c. "Projected Shadow of Adami" (Lourdes de Castro)	90	75
3297	48c. Building facade	1·00	85
3298	57c. Trowel (Claes Oldenburg Cooseje van Bruggen)	1·20	95
3299	74c. Hand and painting	1·50	1·30
3300	€1 Path, hedges and lawn	2·00	1·70
MS3301	Two sheets, each 125×150 mm. (a) 30c. As No. 3297 (horiz); 45c. Path; 45c. Columns and balustrade; 45c. Tower; 45c. Canal and evergreens (b) €1 Museum building (80×30 mm); €1 Museum displays (80×30 mm); €1 Parkland	10·50	8·25

731 Futebol Clube do Porto Emblem and Player (1993)

2005. Football Clubs' Centenaries. Showing emblem and player. Multicoloured.

3302	N (30c.) Type **731**	60	50
3303	N (30c.) Sport Lisboa e Benefica (2004)	60	50
3304	N (30c.) Sporting Clube de Portugal (2006)	60	50
MS3305	Three sheets, each 125×96 mm. (a) €1 Porto Football Club emblem and trophy; (b) €1 Sport Lisboa e Benefica emblem, player, stadium and trophy; (c) €1 Anniversary emblem	6·75	1·70

Nos. 3302/4 were for use on letters weighing 20 grams or less.

732 Scenes of Devastation (image scaled to 55% of original size)

2005. 250th Anniv of Earthquake—31 October 1755. Multicoloured.

3306	45c. Type **732**	90	75
3307	€2 Aftermath	4·00	3·25
MS3308	80×80 mm. €2.65 Survivors (40×30 mm)	5·25	4·25

733 Children's Party

2006. Greetings Stamps. Multicoloured. (a) Sheet stamps.

3309	N. Type **733**	60	50
3310	N. Girl and couples	60	50
3311	N. Mother, father and baby	60	50
3312	N. Conductor	60	50
3313	N. Couple about to kiss	60	50

(b) Size 40×29 mm.

3314	N. As No. 3309	60	50
3315	N. As No. 3310	60	50
3316	N. As No. 3311	60	50
3317	N. As No. 3312	60	50
3318	N. As No. 3313	60	50

Nos. 3314/18 were issued together, se-tenant, forming a composite design.

2006. Masks (2nd series). As T 712. Multicoloured. Self-adhesive gum.

3319	N. "Festa dos Rapazes", Salsas, Bragança (29×24 mm)	60	50
3320	A. Lazarim carnival, Bragança (29×24 mm)	90	75
3321	E. "Dia de Ano Novo", Mogadouro, Bragança (29×24 mm)	1·20	1·00

No. 3320 is inscribed "Correio Azul".

No. 3319 was for use on normal domestic mail, up to 20 grams, 3320 was for domestic first class (blue) mail and 3321 was for European mail.

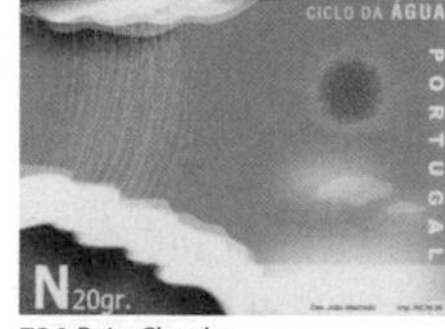

734 Rain Clouds

2006. Water. Multicoloured.

3322	N. Type **734**	60	50
3323	N. Glass of water	60	50
3324	A. Water from tap	90	75
3325	A. Water turbines	90	75
3326	E. Yacht	1·20	1·00
3327	E. Flower	1·20	1·00

Nos. 3322/3 was for use on normal domestic mail, up to 20 grams, 3324/5 was for domestic first class (blue) mail and, 3326/7 was for European mail.

735 Baptising

2006. 500th Birth Anniv of Saint Francis Xavier. Multicoloured.

3328	45c. Type **735**	95	75
3329	€1 Preaching	2·00	1·70
MS3330	85×125 mm. €2.75 Saint Francis Xavier (painting)	4·50	3·25

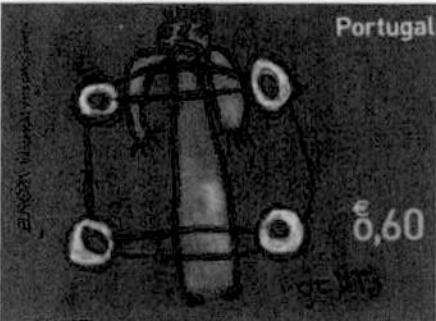

736 Enclosed Figure (Bento Luz)

2006. Europa. Integration. Winning Entries in ANACED (association for art and creativity by and for people with disabilities) Painting Competition. Multicoloured.

3331	60c. Type **736**	1·30	1·00
MS3332	125×95 mm. 60c.×2, Figure in wheelchair (David Fernandes); Aliens and humans from many nations (Ana Sofia, Renarto, Jose Luis and Alcidia)	2·50	2·00

737 Romulo de Carvalho (science writer)

2006. Birth Centenaries. Multicoloured.

3333	€1 Type **737**	2·00	1·70
3334	€1 Agostinho da Silva (philosopher)	2·00	1·70
3335	€1 Thomaz de Mello (artist)	2·00	1·70
3336	€1 Humberto Delgado (politician)	2·00	1·70
3337	€1 Lopes-Graca (composer and musician)	2·00	1·70

738 Players' Legs

2006. UEFA Under-21 Football Championship, Portugal. Sheet 125×65 mm.

MS3338	**738** €2.75 multicoloured	5·50	4·50

739 Players

2006. World Cup Football Championship, Germany. Multicoloured.

3339	45c. Type **739**	90	4·75
3340	€1 Players (different)	2·00	1·70
MS3341	125×85 mm. €2.40 Emblem and trophy	5·00	4·00

739a Mozart (etching)

2006. 250th Birth Anniv of Wolfgang Amadeus Mozart (composer). Etchings by Giovanni Antonio Sasso. Multicoloured.

3341a	60c. Type **739a**	1·20	1·00
MS3341b	90×115 mm. €2.75 Mozart facing right	5·50	4·50

740 Dunes

2006. International Year of Deserts and Desertification. Multicoloured.

3342	30c. Type **740**	60	50
3343	60c. Dead and live trees	1·20	1·00

741 Oceanus (mosaic)

2006. Roman Heritage. Multicoloured.

3344	30c. Type **741**	60	50
3345	45c. Temple, Evora	90	75
3346	50c. Patera de Lameira Larga	1·00	85
3347	60c. Two headed statue ("Herma Bifronte")	1·20	1·00
MS3348	125×95 mm. €2.40 Seahorse (mosaic)	5·00	4·00

2006. Masks (3rd series). As T 712. Multicoloured. Ordinary gum.

3349	3c. Owl (Lazarim carnival, Bragança)	10	10
3350	5c. Scarecrow, "Festa dos Rapazes", Bacal, Braganca	10	10
3351	30c. As No. 3319 ("Festa dos Rapazes", Salsas, Braganca)	60	50
3352	45c. As No. 3320 (Lazarim carnival, Bragança)	90	75
3353	60c. As No. 3321 ("Dia de Ano Novo", Mogadouro, Braganca)	1·20	1·00
3354	75c. Devil ("Dia dos Diabos", Vinhais, Braganca)	1·50	1·30

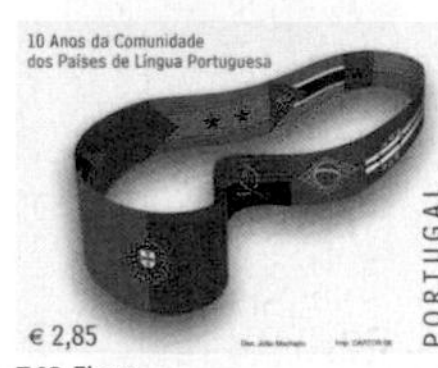

743 Flags

2006. 10th Anniv of Community of Portuguese Speaking Countries (CPLP). Sheet 125×65 mm.

MS3357	**743** €2.85 multicoloured	6·00	4·75

744 "Picture of a Young Woman" (Domenico Ghirlandaio)

2006. 50th Anniv of Calouste Gulbenkian Foundation. Multicoloured.

3358	30c. Type **744**	60	50
3359	45c. Brooch (Rene Lalique)	90	75
3360	60c. Tiles (Turkish c.1573)	1·20	1·00
3361	75c. "Flora" (sculpture) (Jean Baptiste Carpeaux) and Roman medallion	1·50	1·30
3362	€1 Jade jar	2·00	1·70
3363	€2 "Calouste Gulbenkian" (C. J. Watelet)	4·00	3·25
MS3364	125×95 mm. 30c.×4, Statues (art); Books (education); Spectroscope (science); Mother and child (charity)	2·50	2·00

Nos. 3358/63 when laid together form a composite design. The stamps of **MS**3364 form a composite design.

745 Jose Gomes Ferreira School, Lisbon (Raul Hestnes Ferreira)

2006. Contemporary Architecture. Multicoloured.

3365	30c. Type **745**	60	50
3366	30c. Borges & Irmao Bank, Vila do Conde (Alvaro Siza)	60	50
3367	30c. Matosinhos City Council (Alcino Soutinho)	60	50
3368	30c. Casa das Artes, Porto (Eduardo Souto Moura)	60	50
3369	30c. University campus, Santiago (Nuno Portas/CEFAUP)	60	50
3370	30c. Escola Superior de Comunicao Social (ESCS), Lisbon (Carrilho da Graca)	60	50
3371	30c. Plan for Alto do Restelo, Lisbon (Teotonio Pereira, Nuno Portas, Pedro Botelho and Joao Paciencia)	60	50
3372	30c. Order of architects, Lisbon (Manuel Graca Dias and Egas JoseVierira)	60	50
3373	30c. St. Mary's church, Forno, Marco de Canaveses (Alvaro Siza)	60	50
3374	30c. Bairro da Bouca, SAAL, Porto (Alvaro Siza)	60	50

746 Early Camera and Crew

2006. 50th Anniv of First Television Broadcast in Portugal. Multicoloured.

3375	30c. Type **746**	60	50
3376	60c. Modern camera	1·20	1·00

747 Ponte de Alcantara (image scaled to 61% of original size)

2006. Bridges. Multicoloured.

3377	30c. Type **747**	60	50
3378	52c. Ponte de Vila Real de Sto. Antonio	1·10	90

Stamps of similar design were issued by Spain.

748 Grapes and Terraces (image scaled to 56% of original size)

2006. 250th Anniv of Douro Wine Demarcated Region. Sheet 125×95 mm.

MS3379	**748** €2.40 multicoloured	5·00	4·00

749 *Capros aper*

2006. Fish. Multicoloured.

3380	30c. Type **749**	60	50
3381	45c. *Anthias anthias*	90	75
3382	60c. *Lepadogaster lepadogaster*	1·20	1·00
3383	75c. *Gobiusculus flavescens*	1·50	1·30
3384	€1 *Coris julis*	2·00	1·70
3385	€2 *Calliomymus lyra*	4·00	3·25
MS3386	Two sheets, each 125×115 mm. (a) 80c.×2, *Macroramphosus scolopax; Echiichthys vipera*. (b) 80c.×2, *Thalassoma pavo; Blennius ocellaris*	7·00	5·50

750 "a"

2006. School Correspondence. Multicoloured.

3387	N Type **750**	60	50
3388	N "c, g, d"	60	50

751 Flecha de Prata (Silver Arrow)

2006. 150th Anniv of National Railways. Multicoloured.

3389	30c. Type **751**	60	50
3390	45c. Sud-Express	90	75
3391	60c. Foguette	1·20	1·00
3392	€2 Alfa Pendular	4·00	3·25
MS3393	125×95 mm. €1.60 Blessing first train (80×30 mm)	3·25	2·50

752 "A Cidade de Gale"

2006. 500th Anniv of Portuguese in Ceylon. Multicoloured.

3394	30c. Type **752**	60	50
3395	75c. "O Livro das Plantas e Todas as Fortalezas"	1·50	1·30
MS3396	125×95 mm. €2.40 As No. 3394	5·00	4·00

753 16th-century Tiles

2007. In Search of Arab Lisbon. Multicoloured.

3397	30c. Type **753**	60	50
3398	45c. 9th-century limestone carving	90	75
3399	52c. Neo-Arab door	1·00	90
3400	61c. Neo-Arab interior, National Film Library	1·20	1·00
3401	75c. Casa Alentejo	1·50	1·20
3402	€1 Palacete Ribeiro da Cunha	2·00	1·60
MS3403	130×95 mm. €2.95 11th-century Islamic jug	6·00	4·75

754 Laundress wearing Scarves ("Lavadeira") (Minho)

2007. Regional Costume. Multicoloured.

3404	30c. Type **754**	60	50
3405	30c. Bride wearing gold chains ("Noiva") (Minho)	30	50
3406	30c. Cape ("Capa de Honras") (Tras-os-Montes)	60	50
3407	30c. Embroidered tunic ("Pauliteiro") (Tras-os-Montes)	60	50
3408	30c. Fisherman's jersey ("Camisola de Pescador") (Douro Litoral)	60	50
3409	30c. Straw cape ("Coroça") (Beiras/Tras-os-Montes)	60	50
3410	30c. Embroidered apron and skirts ("Saias de Nazare") (Estremadura)	60	50
3411	30c. Horseman wearing red waistcoat ("Campino") (Ribatejo)	60	50
3412	30c. Floral apron and skirt ("Camponesa") (Algarve)	60	50
3413	30c. Cape with fur collar ("Capote") (Alentejo)	60	50
3414	30c. Hooded cloak ("Capote e Capelo") (Azores)	60	50
3415	30c. Short jacket, white shirt and red sash ("Campones") (Beira Litoral)	60	50
3416	30c. Striped dress and red cape ("Viloa") (Madeira)	60	50
3417	30c. Smoked blouse, apron and embroidered cloak ("Camponesa") (Ribatejo)	60	50

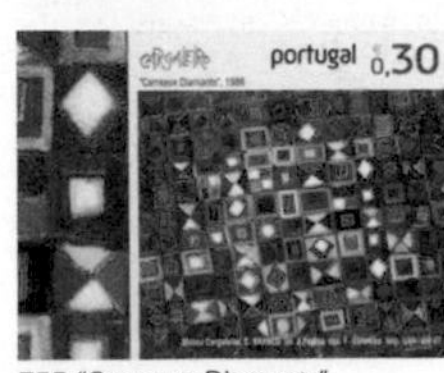

755 "Carreaux Diamants"

2007. Manuel Cargaleiro (artist and ceramist). Multicoloured.

3418	30c. Type **755**	60	50
3419	45c. "Composizione Floreale"	90	75
3420	52c. "Decorcao Mural"	1·20	1·00

756 "D. Joao i Reforca a Casa dos Contos" (painting by Jaime Martins Barata)

2007. Bicentenary of European Court of Auditors. Multicoloured.

3421	30c. Type **756**	60	50
3422	61c. Creation of Court of Auditors (painting by Almada Negreiros)	1·20	1·20
3423	€2 Headquarters of the Court, 1954–1989	4·00	3·25
MS3424	95×125 mm. €2.95 "The Auditor" (tapestry)	6·00	4·75

757 Pen, Flag and Stars

2007. 50th Anniv of Treaty of Rome.

3425	**757** 61c. multicoloured	1·20	1·00

758 Ox-drawn Carriage

2007. Public Transport. Multicoloured. (a) Ordinary gum.

3425a	1c. Articulated bus (8.3.10)	10	10
3425b	6c. Electric car (1927)	10	30
3425c	20c. Bus (1957)	40	30
3426	30c. Type **758**	65	35
3426a	31c. Oldsmobile taxi (1928)	60	45
3426b	32c. Triple unit electric car (1957)	65	50
3426c	32c. Articulated electric car (1995) (8.3.10)	65	50
3427	45c. Horse-drawn tram facing right ("Americano") (1872)	90	70
3427a	47c. Tram (1926)	1·00	60
3427b	47c. Carruagem ML7 (1959)	1·10	35
3427c	47c. Carruagem ML7 (1959)	1·10	35
3427d	47c. Comboio ML79 (1984) (Lisbon metro) (8.3.10)	1·00	60
3428	50c. Horse-drawn tram facing left ("Americano") (1873)	1·00	80
3429	61c. Electric tram (Eletrico No. 22) (1895)	1·20	95
3429a	67c. Coach (1944)	1·40	70
3429b	68c. Bus No. 207 (1960)	1·70	85
3429c	68c. Bus No. 207 (1960)	1·30	1·30
3429d	68c. *Madragoa* (1981) (ferry) (8.3.10)	1·30	1·30
3430	75c. Electric tram (Eletrico No. 283) (1901)	1·50	1·20
3430a	80c. Electric car (1911)	1·60	75
3430b	80c. Trolley bus (1961)	1·60	1·20
3430c	80c. Trolley bus (1961)	1·80	90
3430d	80c. Quadruple unit electric car (1992) (8.3.10)	1·60	70

No. 3436b was for use on normal domestic mail, up to 20 grams, No. 3437b was for domestic first class (blue) mail and No. 3438b was for European mail

(b) Size 30×22 mm. Self-adhesive gum.

3436	N As No. 3427	60	50
3436a	N Oldsmobile taxi (1928)	60	45
3436b	N (32c.) Triple electric car (1957) (As. No. 3426b)	65	50
3436c	N (32c.) Articulated electric car (1995) (inscribed Crreio Azul) (As No. 3426c) (8.3.10)	60	45
3437	A Tram with driver (Eletrico No. 22) (1895)	90	75
3437a	A Tram (1928) inaugeration of electrical tractors company, Estopil	90	70
3437b	A (47c.) Carruagem ML7 (1959) (As. No. 3427b)	1·00	75
3437c	A (47c.) Comboio ML79 (1984) (Lisbon metro) (As No. 3427c) (8.3.10)	90	70
3438	E Tram with driver (Eletrico No. 283) (1901)	1·40	70
3438a	E Coach (1944) ingeration of coach company, Carris	1·40	70
3438b	E (67c.) Bus No. 207 (1960) (As No. 3429b)	1·40	70
3438c	E (67c.) *Madragoa* (1981) (ferry) (As No. 3429c) (8.3.10)	1·40	70

No. 3436 was for use on normal domestic mail, up to 20 grams, No. 3437 was for domestic first class (blue) mail and No. 3438 was for European mail.

759 Castelo do Bode Dam

2007. Dams. Multicoloured. (a) Size 40×30 mm.

3445	30c. Type **759**	60	50

(b) Size 80×30 mm.

3446	30c. Aguieira	60	50
3447	61c. Valeira	1·20	1·00
3448	75c. Alto Lindoso	1·50	1·20
3449	€1 Castelo do Bode extended	2·00	1·60

760 Robert Baden Powell (founder)

2007. Europa. Centenary of Scouting Multicoloured.

3450	61c. Type **760**	1·30	1·00
MS3451	125×95 mm. 61c.×2, Compass; Scouts reading map	2·50	2·00

The stamps of **MS**3451 form a composite design.

2007. Contemporary Architecture. As T 745. Multicoloured.

3452	30c. ESAD, Caldas da Rainha (Vitor Figueiredo)	60	50
3453	30c. Pavilion, Lisbon (Alvaro Siza)	60	50
3454	30c. VTS Tower, Lisbon Port (Goncalo Byrne)	60	50
3455	30c. Casa dos 24, Porto (Fernando Tavora)	60	50
3456	30c. Jose Saramago Library, Loures (Fernando Martins)	60	50
3457	30c. Documentation and Information Centre of President of the Republic, Lisbon (Carrilho da Graca)	60	50
3458	30c. Art Centre, Sines (Aires Mateus)	60	50
3459	30c. Municipal building, Braga (Eduardo Souto Moura)	60	50
3460	30c. Centre for Visual Arts, Coimbra (Joao Mendes Ribeiro)	60	50
3461	30c. Maritime Museum, Ilhavo (ARX Portugal)	60	50
MS3462	125×95 mm. €1.85 Pavilion, Lisbon (Alvaro Siza) (different) (Lisbon Architecture Triennale 2007)	3·75	3·00

The stamps and margins of **MS**3462 form a composite design.

761 Catamarans

2007. ISAF World Sailing Championships. Showing stylized craft. Multicoloured.

3463	61c. Type **761**	1·20	1·00
3464	61c. Two yachts, sail nos. '23' and '105'	1·20	1·00
3465	75c. Yacht, sail no. '75'	1·30	1·10
3466	75c. Two yachts, sail nos. '34' and '16'	1·30	1·10
MS3467	125×95 mm. €2.95 As No. 3465	6·00	4·75

The stamp and margin of **MS**3467 form a composite design.

762 Castelo de Guimaraes

2007. Seven Marvels of Portugal. Multicoloured.

3468	30c. Type **762**	60	50
3469	30c. Palacio de Mateus, Vila Real	60	50
3470	30c. Sao Francisco church, Porto	60	50
3471	30c. Torre dos Clerigos church, Porto	60	50
3472	30c. Clock tower, University of Coimbra	60	50
3473	30c. Ruins, Conimbriga, Condeixa-a-Nova	60	50
3474	30c. Batalha monastery	60	50
3475	30c. Convent of Christ, Tomar	60	50
3476	30c. Almourol castle, Vila Nova da Barquinha	60	50
3477	30c. Alcobaca monastery	60	50
3478	30c. Obidos castle	60	50
3479	30c. Basilica and convent of Mafra	60	50
3480	30c. Marvao castle	60	50
3481	30c. Blockhouses, Monsaraz	60	50
3482	30c. Vila Vicosa Ducal palace	60	50
3483	30c. Roman temple, Evora	60	50
3484	30c. Palacio Nacional da Pena, Sintra	60	50
3485	30c. Palacio Nacional da Queluz, Sintra	60	50
3486	30c. Mosteiro dos Jeronimos, Lisbon	60	50
3487	30c. Torre de Belem, Lisbon	60	50
3488	30c. Sagres fortress, Vila do Bispo	60	50

763 *Ponte* (Amadeo de Souza Cardoso)

2007. Exhibits from Berado Museum Collection. Multicoloured.

3489	45c. Type **763**	90	75
3490	61c. *Les Baigneuses* (Niki de Saint Phalle) (vert)	1·20	1·00
3491	61c. *Interior with Restful Paintings* (Roy Lichtenstein) (vert)	1·20	1·00
3492	61c. *Femme dans un Fauteuil* (Pablo Picasso) (vert)	1·20	1·00
3493	61c. *Le Couple* (Oacar Dominguez) (vert)	1·20	1·00
3494	61c. *Cafe Man Ray* (Man Ray) (vert)	1·20	1·00
3495	61c. *Nectar* (Joana Vasconcelos) (vert)	2·00	1·60
3496	61c. *Head* (Jackson Pollack) (vert)	4·00	3·25

764 Building and Stars

2007. Portugal–Presidency of European Union. Multicoloured.

3497	61c. Type **764**	1·20	1·00
MS3498	125×95 mm. €2.45 As No. **3497** but direction of stars reversed	4·50	4·50

765 SMC Nacional 500cc., 1935

2007. Motorcycles. Multicoloured.

3499	30c. Type **765**	60	50
3500	52c. Famel Fougete, 1959	1·00	90
3501	61c. Vilar Cucciolo, 1955	1·20	1·00
3502	€1 Casal Carina, 1969	2·00	1·60
MS3503	125×95 mm. 61c.×4, Qimera Alma, 1952; Cinal Pachancho, 1958; SIS Sachs V5, 1965; Casal K287, 1985	5·00	4·00

The stamps of **MS**3467 form a composite background design.

766 Globe

2007. Declaration of Winning Entries in New Seven Wonders of the World Competition–Lisbon 2007. Sheet 125×95 mm.

MS3504 €2.95 multicoloured		6·00	4·75

The stamp and margin of **MS**3467 form a composite design.

767 Raul Maria Pereira and Postal Building, Peru

2007. 130th Birth Anniv of Raul Maria Pereira (artist and architect).

3505	**767**	75c. multicoloured	1·50	1·20

Stamp of a similar design was issued by Peru.

768 Jose Valentim Fialho de Almeida

2007. Personalities. Multicoloured.

3506	45c. Type **768** (writer) (150th birth anniv)	90	75
3507	45c. Columbano Bordalo Pinheiro (Columbano) (artist) (150th birth anniv)	90	75
3508	45c. Adolfo Correia da Rocha (Miguel Torga) (writer) (birth centenary)	90	75

769 Hands clasping Ball

2007. Rugby World Cup, France. Sheet 125×95 mm.

MS3509 €1.85 multicoloured		3·75	3·00

The stamp and margin of **MS**3509 form a composite design.

770 *Horus*, 1953

2007. Portuguese Artists. Nadir Afonso. Mult.

3510	30c. Type **770**	60	50
3511	45c. *Veneza*, 1956	90	75
3512	61c. *Procissao em Veneza*, 2002	1·20	1·00

771 Jacaranda

2007. Plants and Animals from the Americas. Multicoloured.

3513	30c. Type **771**	60	50
3514	30c. Potatoes	60	50
3515	30c. Maize	60	50
3516	45c. Cocoa	90	75
3517	61c. Turkeys (inscr 'Peru')	1·20	1·00
3518	75c. Passion fruit	1·50	1·20
MS3519 125×95 mm. €1.85 Humming bird and passion fruit (horiz)		3·75	3·00

The stamp and margin of **MS**3519 form a composite design.

772 Torre de Menagem, Arzila

2007. Architecture. Multicoloured.

3520	30c. Type **772**	60	50
3521	75c. Castelo de Silves, Portugal	1·50	1·20

Stamps of a similar design were issued by Morocco.

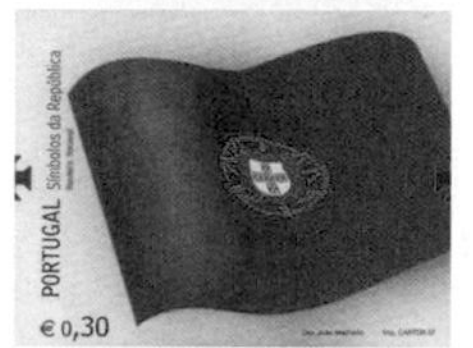

773 National Flag

2007. Symbols of the Republic. Flags. Mult.

3522	30c. Type **773**	60	50
MS3523 95×125 mm. 30c.×5, As Type **773**; President of the Republic; National Assembly; Azores; Madeira		3·00	2·50

The stamps and margins of **MS**3523 form a composite background design.

774 Children and Globe (Sofia Fiteire Passeira)

2007. School Correspondence. Children's Paintings. Multicoloured.

3524	N Type **774**	60	50
3525	N Girls and flowers (Ines Filipa Navrat)	60	50
3526	N Globe enclosed in hands (Maria Correira Borges)	60	50

Nos. 3524/6 were for use on domestic mail weighing 20 grams or less.

775 Fallow Deer (*Cervus dama*)

2007. Mafra National Park. Multicoloured.

3527	30c. Type **775**	60	50
3528	45c. Wild boar (*Sus scrofa*)	90	75
3529	61c. Fox (*Vulpes vulpes*)	1·20	1·00
3530	75c. Red deer (*Cervus elaphus*)	1·50	1·20
3531	€1 Eurasian eagle owl (*Bubo bubo*)	2·00	1·25
3532	€2 Bonelli's eagle (*Hieraaetus fasciatus*)	4·00	2·50

No. **MS**3533 has been left for miniature sheet not yet received.

776 Courtyard, Centro Ismali, Lisbon

2007. 50th Anniv of Ismaili Community in Portugal. Multicoloured.

3533	N Type **776**	60	50
3534	I Aerial view of courtyard	1·50	1·20

777 Cork Tree

2007. Cork Production. Self-adhesive.

3535	**777**	€1 multicoloured	2·00	1·25

No. 3535 was made of cork applied to a paper backing.

780 Family

2008. Infertility Awareness Campaign.

3539	**780**	30c. multicoloured	60	45

781 Woodland

2008. International Year of Planet Earth. Multicoloured. each vert side).

3540	30c. Type **781**	60	45
3541	45c. Clouds	90	70
3542	61c. Volcano erupting	1·20	95
3543	75c. Under water	1·50	1·20

782 Throw

2008. Sporting Events (1st issue). European Judo Championships. Multicoloured.

3544	30c. Type **782**	60	45
3545	61c. Throw (different)	1·20	95
MS3546 125×95 mm. 45c. As Type **782** but including competition emblem; €2 As No. 3545 but including competition emblem		3·00	2·00

See also Nos. 353/6 and 3559.

783 Father Antonio Vieira

2008. Personalities. Multicoloured.

3547	30c. Type **783** (Jesuit and writer) (400th birth anniv)	60	45
3548	30c. Jose Maria Mascarenhas Relvas (politician) (150th birth anniv)	60	45
3549	30c. Aureliano de Mira Fernandes (mathematician) (50th death anniv)	60	45
3550	30c Ricardo Jorge (physician and humanist) (150th birth anniv)	60	45
3551	30c. Maria Elena Vieira da Silva (artist) (birth centenary)	60	45
3552	30c. Manoel Candido Pinto de Oliveira (film director) (birth centenary)	60	45

784 Runners

2008. Sporting Events (2nd issue). Olympic Games, Beijing. Multicoloured.

3553	30c. Type **784**	60	45
3554	30c. Cyclists	60	45
3555	75c. Long jumper	1·50	1·20
MS3556 125×95 mm. 75c.×4, Show jumper; Rower; Marksman; Gymnast		6·00	4·50

The stamps and margins of **MS**3556 form a composite design.

785 Envelope Rider

2008. Europa. The Letter. Multicoloured.

3557	61c. Type **785**	1·20	95
MS3558 125×95 mm. 61c.×2, As Type **785**; Postvan, envelope and bull		2·40	1·90

The stamps of **MS**3558 form a composite design.

786 Athletes (image scaled to 56% of original size)

2008. Sporting Events (3rd issue). European Triathlon Championship, Lisbon.

3559	**786**	€2 multicoloured	4·00	3·00

787 Mother, Child and Teacher

2008. The Rights of the Child. Right to Education. Multicoloured.

3560	30c. Type **787**	60	45
3561	45c. Teacher and pupils	90	70
3562	61c. Children reading	1·20	95
3563	75c. Child reading with parents	1·50	1·20
MS3564 95×125 mm. €2.95 Boy hugging '4'		6·00	4·50

788 Players

2008. Euro 2008–European Football Championships, Austria and Switzerland. Multicoloured.

3565	30c. Type **788**	60	45
3566	61c. Goal keeper catching ball and player	1·20	95
MS3567 125×95 mm. €1.20 Players heading ball; €1.66 Players tackling		5·75	4·50

789 Esposende

2008. Lighthouses. Multicoloured.

3568	30c. Type **789**	60	50
3569	30c. Penedo da Saudade	60	50
3570	30c. Cabo Sardao (horiz)	60	50
3571	30c. Cabo da Roca (horiz)	60	50
3572	30c. Torre do Bugio (horiz)	60	50
3573	30c. Leca	60	50
3574	30c. Montedor	60	50
3575	30c. Santa Marta	60	50
3576	30c. Cabo de Sao Vincente (horiz)	60	50
3577	30c. Cabo Espichel	60	50

790 *Calidris alba* (sanderling)

2008. International Polar Year. Multicoloured.

3578	30c. Type **790**	60	45
3579	52c. *Alca torda* (razorbill)	1·00	85
3580	61c. *Oceanites oceanicus* (Wilson's storm-petrel)	1·20	95
3581	€1 *Sterna paradisea* (arctic tern)	2·00	1·60
MS3582	125×95 mm. €2.95 *Phoca hispida* (ringed seal) and *Ursus maritimus* (polar bear) (80×30 mm)	6·00	4·50

791 Vanwall 57 VW5 driven by Stirling Moss, 1958

2008. 50th Anniv of Formula I Grand Prix in Portugal. Multicoloured.

3583	31c. Type **791**	60	45
3584	67c. Cooper T53 driven by Jack Brabham, 1960	1·40	1·10
3585	80c. Cooper driven by Mark Haywood, 2005	1·60	1·20
3586	€2 McLaren M26 driven by Bobby Vernon Roe	4·00	3·00
MS3587	125×95 mm. €2.45 Fl Grand Prix, 1960 (80×30 mm)	5·00	3·75

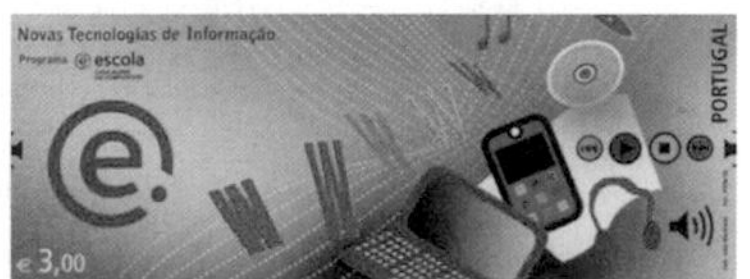

792 Symbols of Information Technology (image scaled to 61% of original size)

2008. Information Technology 'E-School' Programme. Sheet 125×95 mm.

MS3588	multicoloured	6·00	4·75

793 Metal Work

2008. Centenary of Group CUF. Multicoloured.

3589	31c. Type **793**	60	45
3590	67c. Textiles	1·40	1·10
3591	€1 Naval construction	2·00	1·60
3592	€2 Chemicals	4·00	3·00
MS3593	125×95 mm. €2.45 Alfredo da Silva (founder) (vert)	5·00	4·00

794 Vases (17th century)

2008. Pharmaceutical Ceramics. Multicoloured.

3594	31c. Type **794**	60	45
3595	47c. Bottle (18th century)	1·00	80
3596	67c. Vases (17th–18th century)	1·40	1·10
3597	80c. Vases (19th century)	1·60	1·20
MS3598	125×95 mm. €2.45 Pharmacy (17th–18th century)	5·00	4·00

795 Vineyard, Dao Region

2008. Centenary of Demarcated Wine Regions. Multicoloured.

3599	31c. Type **795**	60	45
3600	31c. Barrels, Dao	60	45
3601	31c. Vineyard, Vinhos Verdes	60	45
3602	31c. Terraces, Vinhos Verdes	60	45
3603	31c. Vines, Colares	60	45
3604	31c. Barrels, Colares	60	45
3605	31c. Vineyard, Bucelas	60	45
3606	31c. Barrels, Bucelas	60	45
3607	31c. Barrels, Moscatel de Setubal	60	45
3608	31c. Vineyard, Moscatel de Setubal	60	45

Nos. 3599/600, 3601/2, 3605/6 were printed together, se-tenant, forming a composite design.

796 Centenary of First 'Executivo Republicano Camarario', Lisbon

2008. Republican Ideas. Multicoloured.

3609	31c. Type **796**	60	45
3610	31c. Republican school	60	45
3611	47c. Industrialization	1·00	80
3612	47c. Housing	1·00	80
3613	57c. State modernization	1·20	95
3614	67c. Civil register	1·30	1·00
3615	67c. Public health	1·40	1·10
3616	80c. Civic participation	1·50	1·20
MS3617	125×95 mm. €2.95 Rail–road link project over River Tejo (80×30 mm)	6·00	4·75

797 Olive Grove

2008. Olive Oil Production. Multicoloured.

3618	31c. Type **797**	60	45
3619	47c. Early harvesters	1·00	80
3620	57c. Early milling	1·20	95
3621	67c. Mill stones	1·40	1·10
3622	80c. Oil storage	1·60	1·20
3623	€2 Ready for consumption	4·00	3·00
MS3624	125×95 mm. €1.85 Hands holding olives	3·75	3·00

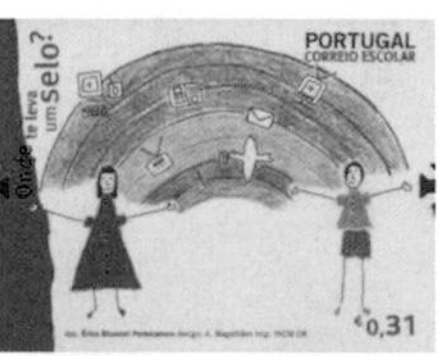

798 Rainbow and Symbols of Communication (Erica Bluemel Potocarrero)

2008. School Correspondence. Childrens Drawings. Multicoloured.

3625	31c. Type **798**	60	45
3626	47c. Girl and symbols of communication (Eloisa Pereira)	1·00	80
3627	67c. Postman (Joao Mario Martins Branco)	1·40	1·10

799 Ponte 25 de Abril, Lisbon

2008. Bridges. Bridges. Multicoloured.

3628	31c. Type **799**	60	45
3629	47c. Arrabida, Porto	1·00	80
3630	57c. Arade, Portimao	1·20	95
3631	67c. Mosteiro, Cinfaes	1·40	1·10
3632	80c. Amizade, Vila Nova de Cerveira	1·60	1·20
3633	€1 St Clara, Coimbra	2·00	1·60
MS3634	125×95 mm. €1.85 Ponte 25 de Abril (80×30 mm)	3·75	3·00

800 Mesoamerican Bas Relief and Ceramic Plate

2008. European Year of Intercultural Dialogue. Multicoloured.

3635	31c. Type **800**	60	45
3636	47c. Asian mask and Greek head	1·00	80
3637	67c. Moorish window and feathered headdress	1·40	1·10
3638	80c. African mask and Chinese lion headdress	1·60	1·20

801 *Waiting for Success* (Henrique Cesar de Araujo Pousao)

2009. Personalities. Multicoloured.

3639	32c. Type **801** (artist) (150th birth anniv)	65	50
3640	32c. Soeiro Pereira Gomes (writer) (birth centenary) (horiz)	65	50

802 Euro Coins

2009. Tenth Anniv of Euro. Multicoloured.

3641	47c. Type **802**	1·00	75
3642	€1 €	2·00	1·50

803 Finches

2009. Birth Bicentenary of Charles Darwin (naturalist and evolutionary theorist). Multicoloured.

3643	32c. Type **803**	65	50
3644	32c. Iguana	65	50
3645	68c. Orchid	1·40	1·00
3646	68c. Diana monkey	1·40	1·00
3647	80c. Platypus	1·60	1·20
3648	80c. Skull and fossils	1·60	1·20
MS3649	125×95 mm. €2.50 *Charles Darwin* (George Richmond) (vert)	5·50	3·75

803b Guitarist (ceramic statue)

2009. African Heritage in Portugal. Multicoloured.

3649a	32c. Type **803b**	65	50
3649b	47c. Trumpeter (altarpiece, St Auta (detail))	1·00	75
3649c	57c. Three children (Conrado Roza)	1·10	75
3649d	68c. Woman	1·40	1·00
3649e	80c. Woman's head (ceramic)	1·60	1·20
3649f	€2 Three musicians (painted wood)	4·25	3·00
MS3649g	125×95 mm. €2.50 Musicians (Joaquim Marques)	4·50	3·00

Type **803a** is vacant.

804 CotA-lacase Enzyme (Nuno Micaêlo)

2009. Aquihaselo. Winning Designs in Painting Competition. Multicoloured.

3650	32c. Type **804**	65	50
3651	32c. Multiplication (Sa de Miranda School pupils)	65	50

805 St. Francis and Dog

2009. 800th Anniv of Franciscan Order. Multicoloured.

3652	32c. Type **805**	65	50
MS3653	125×95 mm. Size 31×40 mm. 50c. St. Francis kneeling; €2 Pope Innocent III giving blessing (vert)	5·50	4·00

806 Álvares Pereira

2009. Canonization of Nuno De Santa Maria (AÁlvares Pereira).

3654	**806** 32c. multicoloured	65	50

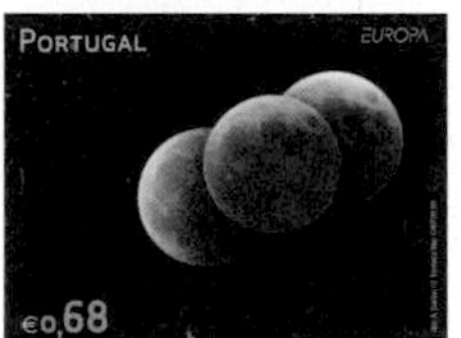

807 Eclipse of the Moon (3rd March 2007) Sequence

2009. Europa. Astronomy. Multicoloured.

3655	68c. Type **807**	1·40	1·00
MS3656	125×95 mm. 68c.×2, European Southern Observatory's 'Very Large Telescope', Chile; As Type **807**	2·75	2·10

The stamps and margins of **MS**3657 form a composite design.

808 Iznik Mosque Lamp (Turkey)

2009. Ceramics. Multicoloured.

3657	32c. Type **808**	65	50
3658	68c. Ceramic Jar (Portugal)	1·40	1·00

Stamps of a similar design were issued by Turkey.

809 Sanctuary

2009. 50th Anniv of Cristo Rei Sanctuary, South Bank of the River Tagus, near Lisbon. Multicoloured.

3659 32c. Type **809** 65 50
3660 68c. Christ (statue) 1·40 1·00
MS3661 125×95 mm. €2.48 Head of Christ, bridge and Lisbon (80×31 mm) 5·00 3·75

810 Bebinca das Sete Colinas (layered pudding) (India)

2009. Flavours of Lusophone (Portuguese speaking countries). Multicoloured.

3662 32c. Type **810** 65 50
3663 32c. Leitoa num ar de Sarapatel (meat dish) (Brazil) 65 50
3664 68c. Caldeirada de cabrito (goat stew) (Angola) 1·40 1·00
3665 68c. Balcalhau, pao, vinho e azeite (cooked dried cod, bread, wine and olive oil) 1·40 1·00
3666 80c. No caldeiro a tempura (stew and tempura) (Asia) 1·60 1·20
3667 80c. Do cozido a Cachupa (slow boiled stew of corn, beans, vegetables, spices and marinated pork or tuna) (Cape Verde Islands) 1·60 1·20
MS3668 125×95 mm. €1.85 Balcalhau, pao, vinho e azeite (detail) (vert) 3·75 2·75

811 'Ensino' (training)

2009. The Lusitanian Horse. Multicoloured.

3669 32c. Type **811** 65 50
3670 32c. Equitacao de Trabalho 65 50
3671 57c. Toureio 1·20 90
3672 68c. Alta Escola 1·40 1·00
3673 80c. Atrelagem de Competicao 1·60 1·20
MS3674 125×95 mm. €2.50 'Alter-Real' 5·00 3·75

812 Alfonso Henriques (statue)

2009. 900th Birth Anniv of Alfonso Henriques (Afonso I, first king of Portugal). Multicoloured.

3675 32c. Type **812** 65 50
MS3676 95×125 mm. €3.07 On horseback 6·00 4·50

813 Trumpeter (Cascais Jazz)

2009. Jazz in Portugal. Multicoloured.

3677 32c. Type **813** 65 50
3678 47c. Trees and musicians as keyboard (Estoril Jazz Festival–Jazz On A Summer Day) 1·00 75
3679 57c. Saxophonist walking in street on instruments (Jazz in August, Calouste Gulbenkian Foundation) 1·20 90
3680 68c. Saxophonist (European Jazz Festival, Oporto) 1·40 1·00
3681 80c. Trumpeter (different) (Guimaraes Jazz Festival) 1·60 1·20
3682 €1 Fish playing saxophone (Seixal Jazz Festival) 2·00 1·50
MS3683 125×95 mm. €3.16 Hot Club of Portugal quartet 6·25 4·75

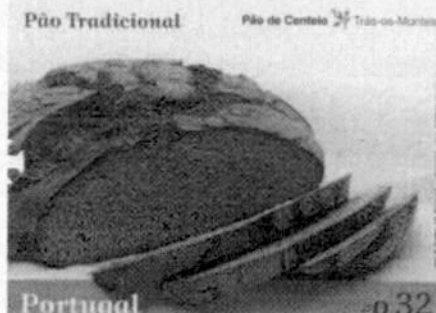

814 Pao de Centeio (rye bread)

2009. Bread. Showing loaves of bread. Multicoloured.

3684 32c. Type **814** 65 50
3685 32c. Quartos (quartered) 65 50
3686 47c. Regueifa (Arabic bread) 1·00 75
3687 68c. Chouriço (bread with sausage) 1·40 1·00
3688 68c. Testa ('brow' bread) 1·40 1·00
3689 80c. Mealhada (bread from Mealhada) 1·60 1·20

Nos. 3690/1 are vacant.

815 Antonio Pedro

2009. Birth Centenary of António Pedro da Costa (actor, writer and painter). Multicoloured.

3692 32c. Type **815** 65 50
MS3693 125×95 mm. €3.16 Facing right 6·25 4·75

816 Building Façade, 1841

2009. Belem Palace. T. Multicoloured.

3694 32c. Type **816** 65 50
3695 47c. Pintura das Sobreporta (painting over doorway) 1·00 75
3696 57c. Copper and silver writing equipment 1·20 90
3697 68c. Satyrs (bas relief) 1·40 1·00
3698 80c. Gold Room, detail of the ceiling molding 1·60 1·20
3699 €1 Floral allegory 2·00 1·50
MS3700 125×95 mm. €2.50 Salas das Bicas (fountain room) 5·50 3·75

817 *Pandion haliaetus* (osprey)

2009. Raptors. Multicoloured.

3701 32c. Type **817** 65 50
3702 80c. *Haliaeetus albicilla* (white-tailed eagle) 1·60 1·20

Stamps of a similar design were issued by Iran.

818 Coffee (smell)

2009. Stamps and the Senses. Birth Bicentenary of Louis Braille (inventor of Braille writing for the blind). Multicoloured.

3703 32c. Type **818** 65 50
3704 68c. Ice lolly (taste) 1·40 1·00
3705 80c. Glasses (vision) 1·60 1·20
3706 €1 Paint (touch) 2·00 1·50
3707 €2 File (Hearing) 4·00 3·00
MS3708 135×105 mm. €2.50 Louis Braille 5·00 3·75

No. **MS**3708 is embossed with Braille letters.

819 Adelaide Cabete

2009. Women of the Republic. Multicoloured.

3709 32c. Type **819** 65 50
3710 32c. Maria Veleda 65 50
3711 57c. Ana de Castro Osorio 1·20 90
3712 68c. Angelina Vidal 1·40 1·00
3713 80c. Carolina Beatriz Angelo 1·60 1·20
3714 €1 Carolina Michaelis 2·00 1·50
MS3715 125×95 mm. €1.15×2, Virginia Quaresma; Emilia de Sousa Costa 4·50 3·50

820 Children (Martina Marques Teixeira Santos)

2009. School Correspondence. Children's Drawings. Multicoloured.

3716 32c. Type **820** 65 50
3717 47c. Lets recycle to improve the world 1·00 75
3718 68c. Post boxes and recycle bins (Manuel Pedro A. B. Paiva Martins) 1·40 1·00

821 Santa and Hearts

2009. Christmas. Multicoloured.

3719 32c. Type **821** 65 50
3720 47c. Santa delivering letter through window 1·00 75
3721 68c. Christmas tree and Santa 1·30 1·00
3722 80c. Santa and reindeer 1·60 1·20
MS3723 125×95 mm. 50c. Santa riding reindeer on rocker; €1 Stocking containing Santa and parcels 3·00 2·20

822 Variato, the Lusitanian (Carlos Santos)

2010. Aqui Há Selo (your own stamp). Multicoloured.

3724 32c. Type **822** 90 70
3725 32c. Dog in a cage (animal abandonment awareness campaign) (Pedro Trindade) 90 70

823 Frédéric François Chopin

2010. Multicoloured

3726 Type **823** 2·00 1·40
3727 68c. Robert Alexander Schumann 2·00 1·40
MS3728 126×95 mm. €2 Frédéric Chopin 6·00 4·50
MS3729 126×95 mm. €2 Robert Schumann 6·00 4·50

No. 3730 is vacant.

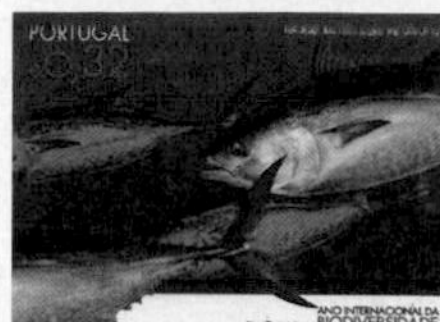

824 Thunnus thynnus (Atlantic bluefin tuna)

2010. International Year of Biodiversity. Multicoloured.

3731 32c. Type **824** 95 70
3732 47c. *Centrophorus granulosus* (gulper shark) 1·30 95
3733 68c. *Ailuropoda melanoleuca* (panda) 2·10 1·60
3734 80c. Hummingbird (Atlantic forest) 2·40 1·80
MS3735 126×95 mm. €2.50 Golden lion tamarin (Atlantic forest) 7·50 7·50

825 Floral Pin

2010. Precious Stones in Portuguese Sacred Art. Multicoloured.

3736 32c. Type **825** 95 70
3737 68c. 18th-century bodice trim 2·10 1·60
3738 €1 Processional cross of Sancho I (detail) 3·00 2·20
MS3739 126×95 mm. €2.50 Crown of Sr. de Fatima (detail) 6·75 5·00

826 Broa

2010. Bread. Multicoloured.

3742 68c. Broa de Avintes (bread from Avintes) 2·10 1·60
3740 32c. Type **826** 95 70
3741 47c. Padas 1·30 95
3743 80c. Pão Alentejano (bread from Alentejano) 2·40 1·80
MS3744 126×95 mm. 80c. Caraça; €1 Pão de Mafra (bread from Mafra) 5·50 4·00

827 Francisco Keli do Amaral (architect) (birth centenary)

2010. Historical and Cultural Personalities. Multicoloured.

3745 32c. Type **827** 95 70
3746 32c. Gomez Eanes de Azuara (writer) (600th birth anniv) 95 70
3747 32c. Fernão Mendes Pinto (explorer) (500th birth anniv) 95 70
3748 32 Alexandre Herculano (novelist and historian) (birth bicentenary) 95 70

828 Monkey

2010. Europa. Multicoloured.

3749 68c. Type **828** 2·00 1·50
MS3750 125×95 mm. 68c.×2, As Type **828**; Man with razor and monkey's tail 4·00 3·00

The stamps and margins of **MS**3750 form a composite design.

829 Pope Benedict XVI

2010. Visit of Pope Benedict XVI to Portugal

3751	68c. Type **829**	2·00	1·50
MS3752	125×95 mm. 80c.×3, Pope Paul VI; Pope John Paul II; Pope Benedict XVI	7·00	5·25

830 Santa Justa, Lisbon

2010. Multicoloured

3753	32c. Type **830**	90	70
3754	47c. Gloria, Lisbon	1·10	80
3755	57c. Guindos funicular, Porto	1·20	90
3756	68c. Bom Jesús do Monte Sanctuary, Braga	1·70	1·30
3757	80c. Santa Luzia, Viana do Castello	2·20	1·70
3758	€1 Nazare	3·50	2·50
MS3759	95×125 mm. €1.25×2, Bica, Lisbon; Lavra, Lisbon	7·00	5·25

831 Exotic Football

2010. World Cup Football Championships, South Africa

(a) Self-adhesive.

3760	80c. Type **831**	2·30	1·70

(b) Ordinary gum

MS3761	105×105 mm (circular). €2.50 Player and cheetah (80×30 mm)	7·25	5·50

832 Estrangeiros e Vilhalpandos

2010. Theatre. Multicoloured.

3762	32c. Type **832**	95	70
3763	32c. Auto da Barca do Inferno	95	70
3764	57c. A Castro	1·20	90
3765	68c. O Fidalgo Aprendiz	1·80	1·40
3766	668c. El-Rei Seleuco	1·80	1·40
3767	80c. Guerras de Alecrim e Manjerona	2·75	2·10

833 'Republic' (Júlio Pomar)

2010. Portugal 2010–World Philatelic Exhibition. Multicoloured.

MS3768	32c. Type **833**; 32c. Francisco dos Santos; 32c. Costa Pinheiro; 32c. Bento Condado; 32c. Luis Maciera; 68c. João Abel Manta; 68c. João Machado; 80c. André Carrilho	10·00	10·00

834 Rabaçal

2010. Cheese. Multicoloured.

3769	32c. Type **834**	95	70
3770	32c. Sierra de Estrela	95	70
3771	47c. Azeitão	1·30	1·00
3772	68c. Cabra Transmontana	2·10	1·60
3773	80c. São Jorge	2·40	1·80
MS3774	95×125 mm. €2.50 Sierra de Estrela (different)	7·00	5·50

835 AzulejoTile with Seated Musician (National Museum, Lisbon)

2010. 130th Anniv of Portugal–Romania Diplomatic Relations. Multicoloured.

3775	68c. Type **835**	1·90	1·40
3776	80c. Blue tile (Peasant Life Museum, Bucharest)	2·10	1·60

Stamps of a similar design were issued by Romania.

836 Synagogue of Tomar

2010. Jewish Quarters in Portugal. Multicoloured.

3777	32c. Type **836**	90	70
3778	57c. Rua Nova de Lamego	1·30	95
3779	68c. Jewish quarter, Castelo de Vide	2·10	1·60
MS3780	125×95 mm. €2.50 Jewish construction (medieval manuscript)	7·00	5·50

837 Rui Veluso (ar de rock)

2010. Portuguese Rock Bands. Multicoloured.

3781	32c. Type **837**	85	65
3782	47c. Herois do Mar (*Herois do Mar*)	1·10	80
3783	57c. GNR (*Pscicopatria*)	1·30	95
3784	68c. UHF (*À flor da pele*)	2·00	1·50
3785	80c. Xutos & Pontapés (*88*)	2·20	1·60
3786	€1 Moonspell (*Wolfheart*)	3·00	2·20
MS3787	125×95 mm. €2.50 Quarteto 1111 (*A Lenda de El-Rei D. Sebastião*)	7·00	5·25

838 Battle of Vimeiro

2010. Bicentenary of Peninsular War. Multiicoloured.

3788	32c. Type **838**	95	70
3789	68c. Battle of Buçaco	2·10	1·60
MS3790	125×95 mm. €2.50 Battle of Pombal (80×30 mm)	7·25	5·50

839 Chamber

2010. Centenary of the Republic. Multicoloured.

3791	32c. Type **839**	1·70	1·30
3792	68c. Senate Chamber	3·50	2·75
MS3793	125×95 mm. €2 Assembly Building, Lisbon	5·75	4·25

840 Research Ship

2010. 50th Anniv of Hydrographic Institute. Multicoloured.

3794	32c. Type **840**	1·10	70
3795	68c. Research ship, Scientist and equipment array	1·90	1·40

Nos. 3794/5 were printed, *se-tenant*, forming a composite design.

841 Clown

2010. Chapito Circus School, Lisbon. Multicoloured.

3796	32c. Type **841**	1·10	70
3797	47c. Clown riding unicycle	1·20	90
3798	68c. Female juggler with hoops	1·90	1·40
3799	80c. Clown wearing stilts and juggling clubs	2·40	1·80
MS3800	125×95 mm. €2.50 Acrobats (30×80 mm)	7·25	5·50

842 Ceres

2010. Centenary of the Republic

3801	**842**	80c. reddish brown and yellow-ochre	2·25	1·70

843 Establishment of Republic, 1910

2010. History of Freedom. Multicoloured.

3802	32c. Type **843**	90	70
3803	32c. Female figure, symbolizing the Republic	90	70
3804	47c. Soldier with machine gun and civilian with rifle	1·20	90
3805	68c. Female symbol of French revolution and revolutionary	1·90	1·50
3806	80c. Male symbol of American revolution driving off British soldiers	2·40	1·80
3807	€1 Medieval cleric, king and peasant ('in the middle ages nobility, clergy and people had different rights and duties and the king's decisions were obeyed without question')	3·25	2·50

CHARITY TAX STAMPS

Used on certain days of the year as an additional postal tax on internal letters. Other values in some of the types were for use on telegrams only. The proceeds were devoted to public charities. If one was not affixed in addition to the ordinary postage, postage due stamps were used to collect the deficiency and the fine.

1911. Optd ASSISTENCIA.

C455	**48**	10r. green (No. 406)	13·00	3·50
C484	**56**	1c. green (No. 486)	9·50	3·00

C57 "Lisbon"

1913. Lisbon Festival.

C485	**C57**	1c. green	1·80	1·30

C58 "Charity"

1915. For the Poor.

C486	**C58**	1c. red	50	45
C669	**C58**	15c. red	95	95

1924. Surch 15 ctvs.

C594	15c. on 1c. red	2·50	1·10

C71 Muse of History

1925. Portuguese Army in Flanders, 1484 and 1918.

C662	**C71**	10c. red	1·80	1·60
C663	**C71**	10c. green	1·80	1·60
C664	**C71**	10c. blue	1·80	1·60
C665	**C71**	10c. brown	1·80	1·60

C73 Monument to De Pombal

C75 Marquis de Pombal

1925. Marquis de Pombal Commemoration.

C666	**C73**	15c. blue and black	1·80	1·10
C667	-	15c. blue and black	1·80	1·10
C668	**C 75**	15c. blue and black	65	55

DESIGN: No. C677, Planning reconstruction of Lisbon.

C81 Hurdler

1928. Olympic Games.

C741	**C81**	15c. black and red	6·00	3·50

NEWSPAPER STAMPS

N16

N17

1876

N180	**N16**	2r. black	33·00	21·00
N178	**N 17**	2½r. green	22·00	2·00
N187	**N 17**	2½r. brown	19·00	1·70

OFFICIAL STAMPS

1938. Optd OFICIAL.

O900	**99**	40c. brown	90	20

O144

1952. No value.

O1069	**O144**	(1e.) black and stone	90	15
O1070	**O144**	(1e.) black and stone	1·00	35

On No. O1069 "CORREIO DE PORTUGAL" is in stone on a black background, on No. O1070 it is in black on the stone background.

PARCEL POST STAMPS

P59

1920

P578	**P59**	1c. brown	55	45
P579	**P59**	2c. orange	55	45
P580	**P59**	5c. brown	55	45
P581	**P59**	10c. brown	55	45
P582	**P59**	20c. blue	75	45
P583	**P59**	40c. red	75	45
P584	**P59**	50c. black	1·10	80
P585	**P59**	60c. blue	1·00	80
P586	**P59**	70c. brown	6·25	3·00
P587	**P59**	80c. blue	6·50	4·75
P588	**P59**	90c. violet	6·75	3·50
P589	**P59**	1e. green	7·00	4·25
P591	**P59**	2e. lilac	20·00	5·25
P592	**P59**	3e. green	37·00	6·00
P593	**P59**	4e. blue	80·00	10·50
P594	**P59**	5e. lilac	£110	7·00
P595	**P59**	10e. brown	£170	12·50

P101

1936

P891	**P101**	50c. grey	1·10	95
P892	**P101**	1e. brown	1·10	95
P893	**P101**	1e.50 violet	1·10	95
P894	**P101**	2e. purple	4·75	1·00
P895	**P101**	2e.50 green	4·75	1·00
P896	**P101**	4e.50 purple	12·50	1·00
P897	**P101**	5e. violet	18·00	1·20
P898	**P101**	10e. orange	23·00	2·50

POSTAGE DUE STAMPS

D48 Da Gama received by the Zamorin of Calicut

1898

D386	**D48**	5r. black	5·00	3·50
D387	**D48**	10r. mauve	6·25	4·00
D388	**D48**	20r. orange	10·50	4·50
D389	**D48**	50r. grey	80·00	9·00
D390	**D48**	100r. red on pink	£120	65·00
D391	**D48**	200r. brown on buff	£130	90·00

D49

1904

D392	**D49**	5r. brown	85	80
D393	**D49**	10r. orange	4·25	1·30
D394	**D49**	20r. mauve	12·00	5·75
D395	**D49**	30r. green	8·50	4·25
D396	**D49**	40r. lilac	9·75	4·25
D397	**D49**	50r. red	65·00	7·25
D398	**D49**	100r. blue	14·50	9·50

1911. Optd REPUBLICA.

D418	5r. brown	80	70
D419	10r. orange	80	70
D420	20r. mauve	2·10	1·80
D421	30r. green	2·00	70
D422	40r. lilac	2·10	70
D423	50r. red	8·75	6·75
D424	100r. blue	9·25	7·25

1915. As Type D 49 but value in centavos.

D491	½c. brown	90	85
D498	1c. orange	1·10	1·00
D493	2c. purple	90	85
D499	3c. green	1·10	1·00
D500	4c. lilac	1·10	1·00
D501	5c. red	1·10	1·00
D497	10c. blue	1·10	1·00

1921

D578	½c. green	80	55
D579	4c. green	80	55
D580	8c. green	80	55
D581	10c. green	80	55
D582	12c. green	90	65
D583	16c. green	90	65
D584	20c. green	90	65
D585	24c. green	90	65
D586	32c. green	1·40	90
D587	36c. green	2·50	1·80
D588	40c. green	2·50	1·80
D589	48c. green	1·60	1·00
D590	50c. green	1·60	1·00
D591	60c. green	1·60	1·00
D592	72c. green	1·60	1·00
D593	80c. green	12·00	10·50
D594	1e.20 green	5·50	5·50

D72

1925. Portuguese Army in Flanders, 1484 and 1918.

D662	**D72**	20c. brown	95	75

1925. De Pombal types optd MULTA.

D663	**C73**	30c. blue	1·90	1·60
D664	-	30c. blue	1·90	1·60
D665	**C75**	30c. blue	1·90	1·60

D82

1928. Olympic Games.

D741	**D82**	30e. black and red	3·00	2·75

D91

1932

D865	**D91**	5e. buff	1·20	90
D866	**D91**	10e. blue	1·20	90
D867	**D91**	20e. pink	2·50	1·30
D868	**D91**	30e. blue	2·75	1·30
D869	**D91**	40e. green	2·75	1·30
D870	**D91**	50e. grey	3·75	1·30
D871	**D91**	60e. pink	7·50	3·50
D872	**D91**	80e. purple	14·00	7·25
D873	**D91**	1e.20 green	23·00	18·00

D108

1940

D912	**D108**	5c. brown	95	60
D922	**D108**	5e. orange	20·00	14·00
D923	**D108**	10c. lilac	50	25
D924	**D108**	20c. red	50	25
D925	**D108**	30c. violet	50	25
D926	**D108**	40c. mauve	50	25
D927	**D108**	50c. blue	50	25
D928	**D108**	60c. green	50	25
D929	**D108**	80c. red	50	25
D930	**D108**	1e. brown	50	25
D931	**D108**	2e. mauve	70	60

D218

1967

D1312	**D218**	10c. brown, yellow and orange	15	10
D1313	**D218**	20e. purple, yellow and brown	15	10
D1314	**D218**	30e. brown, light yellow and yellow	15	10
D1315	**D218**	40e. purple, yellow and bistre	15	10
D1316	**D218**	50e. indigo, blue and light blue	20	10
D1317	**D218**	60e. olive, blue and turquoise	20	10
D1318	**D218**	80e. indigo, blue and light blue	20	10
D1319	**D218**	1e. indigo, bl & ultram	20	10
D1320	**D218**	2e. olive, light green and green	20	15
D1321	**D218**	3e. deep green, light green and green	45	15
D1322	**D218**	4e. deep green, green and turquoise	45	20
D1323	**D218**	5e. brown, mauve and purple	35	20
D1324	**D218**	9e. deep lilac, lilac and violet	45	25
D1325	**D218**	10e. deep purple, grey and purple	45	25
D1326	**D218**	20e. maroon, grey and purple	1·30	35
D1327	**D218**	40e. lilac, grey and mauve	3·00	1·40
D1328	**D218**	50e. maroon, grey and purple	3·75	1·60

D481

1992. Inscr "CORREIOS DE PORTUGAL".

D2305	**D481**	1e. blue, deep blue and black	10	10
D2306	**D481**	2e. light green, green and black	10	10
D2307	**D481**	5e. yellow, brown and black	10	10
D2308	**D481**	10e. red, orange and black	20	10
D2309	**D481**	20e. green, violet and black	35	10
D2310	**D481**	50e. yellow, green and black	80	45
D2311	**D481**	100e. orange, red and black	1·50	1·00
D2312	**D481**	200e. mauve, violet and black	3·00	1·90

1995. Inscr "CTT CORREIOS".

D2445	3e. multicoloured	20	10
D2446	4e. multicoloured	20	10
D2446a	5e. multicoloured	10	10
D2447	9e. multicoloured	45	10
D2447a	10e. red, orange and black	15	10
D2447b	20e. multicoloured	25	20
D2448	40e. multicoloured	80	65
D2449	50e. multicoloured	90	60
D2450	100e. orange, red and black	1·30	90

D656 "0.01"

2002. Multicoloured.. Multicoloured..

D2907	1c. Type D **656**	10	10
D2908	2c. "0.02"	10	10
D2909	5c. "0.05"	15	10
D2910	10c. "0.10"	30	25
D2911	25c. "0.25"	60	50
D2912	50c. "0.50"	1·30	95
D2913	€1 "1"	2·50	2·00

Pt. 9

PORTUGUESE COLONIES

General issues for the Portuguese possessions in Africa: Angola, Cape Verde Islands, Guinea, Lourenco Marques, Mozambique, Congo, St. Thomas and Prince Islands, and Zambezia.

1898. 1000 reis = 1 milreis.
1919. 100 centavos = 1 escudo.

1898. 400th Anniv of Vasco da Gama's Discovery of Route to India. As Nos. 378/85 of Portugal but inscr "AFRICA".

1	2½r. green	1·20	1·00
2	5r. red	1·20	1·00
3	10r. purple	1·20	1·00
4	25r. green	1·20	1·00
5	50r. blue	1·20	1·00
6	75r. brown	10·50	9·00
7	100r. brown	10·50	7·00
8	150r. brown	15·00	7·00

CHARITY TAX STAMPS

C1

1919. Fiscal stamps optd TAXA DE GUERRA.

C1	**C1**	1c. black and green	1·40	1·40
C2	**C1**	5c. black and green	1·40	1·40

POSTAGE DUE STAMPS

D1

1945. Value in black.

D1	**D1**	10c. purple	55	55
D2	**D1**	20c. purple	55	55
D3	**D1**	30c. blue	55	55
D4	**D1**	40c. brown	55	55
D5	**D1**	50c. lilac	55	55
D6	**D1**	1e. brown	2·50	2·50
D7	**D1**	2e. green	4·25	4·25
D8	**D1**	3e. red	7·00	7·00
D9	**D1**	5e. yellow	10·50	10·50

Pt. 9

PORTUGUESE CONGO

The area known as Portuguese Congo, now called Cabinda, was the part of Angola north of the River Congo. It issued its own stamps from 1894 until 1920.

1894. 1000 reis = 1 milreis.
1913. 100 centavos = 1 escudo.

1894. "Figures" key-type inscr " CONGO".

8	**R**	5r. orange	1·70	1·60
9	**R**	10r. mauve	2·50	1·70
10	**R**	15r. brown	4·25	3·50
12	**R**	20r. lilac	4·25	3·50
13	**R**	25r. green	2·75	1·00
22	**R**	50r. blue	4·75	3·00
5	**R**	75r. pink	9·00	5·50
6	**R**	80r. green	11·50	8·00
7	**R**	100r. brown on yellow	10·00	6·75
17	**R**	150r. red on pink	19·00	16·00
18	**R**	200r. blue on blue	19·00	16·00
19	**R**	300r. blue on brown	24·00	20·00

1898. "King Carlos" key-type inscr "CONGO".

24	**S**	2½r. grey	55	45
25	**S**	5r. red	55	45
26	**S**	10r. green	75	45
27	**S**	15r. brown	2·10	1·80
66	**S**	15r. green	1·30	25
28	**S**	20r. lilac	1·40	95
29	**S**	25r. green	2·00	1·30
67	**S**	25r. red	1·30	25
30	**S**	50r. blue	2·30	1·80
68	**S**	50r. brown	3·75	2·75
69	**S**	65r. blue	11·50	9·75
31	**S**	75r. pink	5·75	3·25
70	**S**	75r. purple	4·50	4·00
32	**S**	80r. mauve	4·25	3·50
33	**S**	100r. blue on blue	3·50	2·50
71	**S**	115r. brown on pink	10·50	8·25
72	**S**	130r. brown on yellow	14·00	12·00
34	**S**	150r. brown on yellow	5·75	4·00
35	**S**	200r. purple on pink	7·00	4·25
36	**S**	300r. blue on pink	8·50	4·75
73	**S**	400r. blue on cream	13·50	11·50
37	**S**	500r. black on blue	21·00	15·00
38	**S**	700r. mauve on yellow	36·00	27·00

1902. Surch.

74	S	50r. on 65r. blue	7·00	4·50
40	R	65r. on 15r. brown	6·50	5·00
41	R	65r. on 20r. lilac	6·50	5·00
44	R	65r. on 25r. green	6·50	5·00
46	R	65r. on 300r. blue on brn	8·25	7·75
50	V	115r. on 2½r. brown	6·50	5·00
47	R	115r. on 10r. mauve	6·50	4·75
48	R	115r. on 50r. blue	6·25	4·75
53	R	130r. on 5r. orange	6·50	5·25
54	R	130r. on 75r. pink	6·50	5·00
57	R	130r. on 100r. brn on yell	6·50	5·25
58	R	400r. on 80r. green	2·75	2·20
60	R	400r. on 150r. red on pink	4·00	3·25
61	R	400r. on 200r. blue on blue	4·00	3·25

1902. "King Carlos" key-type of Portuguese Congo optd PROVISORIO.

62	15r. brown	3·00	2·10
63	25r. green	3·00	2·10
64	50r. blue	3·00	2·10
65	75r. pink	7·00	5·00

1911. "King Carlos" key-type of Angola, optd REPUBLICA and CONGO with bar (200r. also surch).

75	2½r. grey	2·20	1·40
76	5r. red	3·00	2·20
77	10r. green	3·00	2·20
78	15r. green	3·00	2·20
79	25r. on 200r. purple on pink	3·25	2·30

1911. "King Carlos" key-type of Portuguese Congo optd REPUBLICA.

80	2½r. grey	45	30
81	5r. orange	65	45
82	10r. green	65	45
83	15r. green	65	45
84	20r. lilac	65	45
85	25r. red	65	45
86	50r. brown	75	45
87	75r. purple	1·30	85
88	100r. blue on blue	1·50	85
89	115r. brown on pink	2·20	1·40
90	130r. brown on yellow	2·20	1·40
143	200r. purple on pink	6·75	5·75
92	400r. blue on cream	7·50	5·75
93	500r. black on blue	7·50	6·00
94	700r. mauve on yellow	10·50	6·75

1913. Surch REPUBLICA CONGO and value on "Vasco da Gama" stamps of (a) Portuguese Colonies.

95	¼c. on 2½r. green	1·80	1·50
96	½c. on 5r. red	1·80	1·50
97	1c. on 10r. purple	1·80	1·50
98	2½c. on 25r. green	1·80	1·50
99	5c. on 50r. blue	2·20	2·10
100	7½c. on 75r. brown	3·75	3·50
101	10c. on 100r. brown	2·75	2·10
102	15c. on 150r. brown	2·00	2·10

(b) Macao.

103	¼c. on ½a. green	2·40	2·30
104	½c. on 1a. red	2·40	2·30
105	1c. on 2a. purple	2·40	2·30
106	2½c. on 4a. green	2·40	2·30
107	5c. on 8a. blue	2·40	2·30
108	7½c. on 12a. brown	4·75	3·25
109	10c. on 16a. brown	3·00	2·30
110	15c. on 24a. brown	3·00	2·30

(c) Portuguese Timor.

111	¼c. on ½a. green	2·40	2·30
112	½c. on 1a. red	2·40	2·30
113	1c. on 2a. purple	2·40	2·30
114	2½c. on 4a. green	2·40	2·30
115	5c. on 8a. blue	2·40	2·30
116	7½c. on 12a. brown	4·75	3·25
117	10c. on 16a. brown	3·00	2·30
118	15c. on 24a. brown	3·00	2·30

1914. "Ceres" key-type inscr "CONGO".

135	U	¼c. green	85	75
120	U	½c. black	1·10	70
121	U	1c. green	3·75	2·75
134	U	1c. green on blue	7·25	5·25
122	U	1½c. brown	2·40	1·50
136	U	2c. red	85	75
124	U	2½c. violet	75	70
125	U	5c. blue	1·10	1·10
126	U	7½c. brown	2·20	1·50
127	U	8c. grey	2·30	2·00
128	U	10c. red	2·30	2·00
129	U	15c. purple	2·40	2·00
130	U	20c. green	2·40	2·00
131	U	30c. brown on green	4·75	3·25
132	U	40c. brown on pink	4·75	3·50
133	U	50c. orange on orange	5·75	3·50

1914. "King Carlos" key-type of Portuguese Congo optd PROVISORIO and REPUBLICA.

146	S	15r. brown (No. 62)	1·60	1·10
147	S	50r. blue (No. 64)	1·60	1·10
140	S	75r. pink (No. 65)	2·20	2·00

1914. Provisional stamps of 1902 optd REPUBLICA.

148		50r. on 65r. blue	1·60	1·10
150	V	115r. on 2½r. brown	1·10	55
151	R	115r. on 10r. mauve	1·00	75
154	R	115r. on 50r. blue	2·50	1·60
156	R	130r. on 5r. orange	1·60	1·10
157	R	130r. on 75r. pink	2·50	1·90
160	R	130r. on 100r. brown on yellow	1·20	75

NEWSPAPER STAMPS

1894. "Newspaper" key-type inscr "CONGO".

N24	V	2½r. brown	95	80

Pt. 9

PORTUGUESE GUINEA

A former Portuguese territory, on the west coast of Africa, with adjacent islands. Used stamps of Cape Verde Islands from 1877 until 1881. In September 1974 the territory became independent and was renamed Guinea-Bissau.

1881. 1000 reis = 1 milreis.
1913. 100 centavos = 1 escudo.

1881. "Crown" key-type inscr "CABO VERDE" and optd GUINE.

19	P	5r. black	7·50	5·75
20	P	10r. yellow	£300	£300
31	P	10r. green	13·00	8·75
21	P	20r. bistre	6·25	4·25
32	P	20r. red	13·00	9·50
13	P	25r. pink	4·50	3·25
28	P	25r. lilac	5·75	3·50
23	P	40r. blue	£325	£225
29	P	40r. yellow	3·50	3·00
24	P	50r. green	£325	£225
30	P	50r. blue	10·50	5·00
16	P	100r. lilac	15·00	11·50
17	P	200r. orange	22·00	15·00
18	P	300r. brown	26·00	20·00

3

1886

35	3	5r. black	11·50	10·50
36	3	10r. green	14·00	7·50
37	3	20r. red	20·00	7·50
38	3	25r. purple	20·00	11·50
46	3	40r. brown	16·00	11·50
40	3	50r. blue	33·00	11·50
47	3	80r. grey	30·00	21·00
48	3	100r. brown	30·00	21·00
43	3	200r. lilac	70·00	42·00
44	3	300r. orange	90·00	65·00

1893. "Figures" key-type inscr "GUINE".

50	R	5r. yellow	3·50	2·10
51	R	10r. mauve	3·50	2·10
52	R	15r. brown	4·50	3·00
53	R	20r. lilac	4·50	3·00
54	R	25r. green	4·50	3·00
55	R	50r. blue	8·00	4·25
57	R	75r. pink	21·00	13·50
58	R	80r. green	21·00	13·50
59	R	100r. brown on buff	21·00	13·50
60	R	150r. red on pink	21·00	13·50
61	R	200r. blue on blue	36·00	28·00
62	R	300r. blue on brown	34·00	28·00

1898. "King Carlos" key-type inscr "GUINE".

65	S	2½r. grey	70	55
66	S	5r. red	70	55
67	S	10r. green	70	55
68	S	15r. brown	5·75	4·25
114	S	15r. green	3·50	1·80
69	S	20r. lilac	2·75	1·80
70	S	25r. green	3·25	2·10
115	S	25r. red	1·80	1·10
71	S	50r. blue	4·25	2·20
116	S	50r. brown	4·50	3·50
117	S	65r. blue	14·50	11·00
72	S	75r. pink	23·00	16·00
118	S	75r. purple	6·25	5·50
73	S	80r. mauve	5·75	3·50
74	S	100r. blue on blue	5·25	3·50
119	S	115r. brown on pink	16·00	11·50
120	S	130r. brown on yellow	17·00	11·50
75	S	150r. brown on yellow	17·00	7·25
76	S	200r. purple on pink	17·00	7·25
77	S	300r. blue on pink	15·00	8·75
121	S	400r. blue on yellow	18·00	12·00
78	S	500r. black on blue	23·00	13·50
79	S	700r. mauve on yellow	33·00	23·00

1902. Surch.

122	S	50r. on 65r. blue	8·75	5·75
81	3	65r. on 10r. green	12·50	7·00
84	R	65r. on 10r. mauve	10·50	5·50
85	R	65r. on 15r. brown	10·50	5·50
82	3	65r. on 20r. red	12·50	7·00
86	R	65r. on 20r. lilac	10·50	5·50
83	3	65r. on 25r. purple	12·50	7·00
88	R	65r. on 50r. blue	5·50	4·75
97	V	115r. on 2½r. brown	7·50	5·25
93	R	115r. on 5r. yellow	10·00	5·25
95	R	115r. on 25r. green	11·50	5·75
89	3	115r. on 40r. brown	11·00	6·75
91	3	115r. on 50r. blue	11·00	6·75
92	3	115r. on 300r. orange	14·00	8·75
98	3	130r. on 80r. grey	14·00	10·00
100	3	130r. on 100r. brown	14·50	10·00
102	R	130r. on 150r. red on pink	11·50	5·75
103	R	130r. on 200r. blue on blue	12·50	6·75
104	R	130r. on 300r. blue on brn	12·50	7·25
105	3	400r. on 5r. black	65·00	60·00
107	R	400r. on 75r. pink	8·25	7·25
108	R	400r. on 80r. green	5·50	3·25
109	R	400r. on 100r. brn on buff	7·00	3·25
106	3	400r. on 200r. lilac	24·00	13·50

1902. "King Carlos" key-type of Portuguese Guinea optd PROVISORIO.

110	15r. brown	4·50	3·00
111	25r. green	4·50	3·00
112	50r. blue	5·50	3·25
113	75r. pink	11·00	9·00

1911. "King Carlos" key-type of Portuguese Guinea optd REPUBLICA.

123	2½r. grey	90	65
124	5r. red	1·10	65
125	10r. green	1·20	65
126	15r. green	1·20	95
127	20r. lilac	1·20	95
128	25r. red	1·20	95
129	50r. brown	1·20	95
130	75r. purple	1·20	95
131	100r. blue on blue	3·00	1·10
132	115r. brown on pink	3·00	1·30
133	130r. brown on yellow	3·00	1·30
134	200r. purple on pink	13·00	5·25
135	400r. blue on yellow	4·25	3·25
136	500r. black on blue	4·25	3·25
137	700r. mauve on yellow	6·75	5·00

1913. Surch REPUBLICA GUINE and value on "Vasco da Gama" stamps. (a) Portuguese Colonies.

138	¼c. on 2½r. green	3·00	2·50
139	½c. on 5r. red	3·00	2·50
140	1c. on 10r. purple	3·00	2·50
141	2½c. on 25r. green	3·00	2·50
142	5c. on 50r. blue	3·00	2·50
143	7½c. on 75r. brown	6·50	5·00
144	10c. on 100r. brown	3·00	2·00
145	15c. on 150r. brown	8·00	6·75

(b) Macao.

146	¼c. on ½a. green	3·25	2·50
147	½c. on 1a. red	3·25	2·50
148	1c. on 2a. purple	3·25	2·50
149	2½c. on 4a. green	3·25	2·50
150	5c. on 8a. blue	3·25	2·50
151	7½c. on 12a. brown	5·75	4·00
152	10c. on 16a. brown	5·00	4·00
153	15c. on 24a. brown	6·25	4·25

(c) Portuguese Timor.

154	¼c. on ½a. green	3·25	2·50
155	½c. on 1a. red	3·25	2·50
156	1c. on 2a. purple	3·25	2·50
157	2½c. on 4a. green	3·25	2·50
158	5c. on 8a. blue	3·25	2·50
159	7½c. on 12a. brown	5·75	4·00
160	10c. on 16a. brown	5·00	4·00
161	15c. on 24a. brown	6·25	4·25

1913. "King Carlos" key-type of Portuguese Guinea optd PROVISORIO and REPUBLICA.

184	15r. brown	2·00	1·80
185	50r. blue	2·00	1·80
164	75r. pink	25·00	16·00

1914. "Ceres" key-type inscr "GUINE". Name and value in black.

204	U	¼c. green	1·40	95
209	U	½c. black	55	50
210	U	1c. green	55	50
211	U	1½c. brown	55	50
212	U	2c. red	55	50
213	U	2c. grey	55	50
214	U	2½c. violet	55	50
215	U	3c. orange	55	50
216	U	4c. red	55	50
217	U	4½c. grey	55	50
218	U	5c. blue	55	50
219	U	6c. mauve	55	50
220	U	7c. blue	75	45
221	U	7½c. brown	55	50
222	U	8c. grey	55	50
223	U	10c. red	55	50
224	U	12c. green	1·30	75
225	U	15c. red	55	50
226	U	20c. green	60	55
227	U	24c. blue	3·25	2·20
228	U	25c. brown	3·75	2·75
180	U	30c. brown on green	10·00	6·50
229	U	30c. green	1·60	75
181	U	40c. brown on pink	6·50	1·30
230	U	40c. turquoise	1·60	85
182	U	50c. orange on orange	6·50	1·30
231	U	50c. mauve	3·75	2·10
232	U	60c. blue	2·75	2·30
233	U	60c. red	3·75	1·60
234	U	80c. red	4·25	2·75
183	U	1e. green on blue	8·75	4·25
235	U	1e. blue	5·75	3·25
236	U	1e. pink	5·50	2·40
237	U	2e. purple	5·50	3·00
238	U	5e. bistre	32·00	16·00
239	U	10e. pink	46·00	17·00
240	U	20e. green	£130	65·00

1915. Provisional stamps of 1902 optd REPUBLICA.

186	S	50r. on 65r. blue	2·00	1·80
187	V	115r. on 2½r. brown	3·25	1·90
190	R	115r. on 5r. yellow	2·20	1·40
191	R	115r. on 25r. green	2·00	1·80
192	3	115r. on 40r. brown	1·90	1·80
194	3	115r. on 50r. blue	1·90	1·80
196	3	130r. on 80r. grey	6·00	3·75
197	3	130r. on 100r. brown	5·00	4·25
199	R	130r. on 150r. red on pink	2·00	1·80
200	R	130r. on 200r. blue on blue	2·00	1·80
201	R	130r. on 300r. blue on brn	2·00	1·80

1920. Surch.

241	U	4c. on ¼c. green	7·50	5·00
242	U	6c. on ½c. black	7·50	5·00
243	S	12c. on 115r. brown on pink (No. 132)	19·00	11·50

1925. Stamps of 1902 (Nos. 107/9) surch Republica and new value.

244	R	40c. on 400r. on 75r. pink	1·90	1·50
245	R	40c. on 400r. on 80r. green	1·90	1·50
246	R	40c. on 400r. on 100r. brown on buff	1·90	1·50

1931. "Ceres" key-type of Portuguese Guinea surch.

247	U	50c. on 60c. red	4·00	3·00
248	U	70c. on 80c. red	4·25	4·00
249	U	1e.40 on 2e. purple	9·75	7·00

24 Ceres

1933

251	24	1c. brown	30	25
252	24	5c. brown	30	25
253	24	10c. mauve	30	25
254	24	15c. black	65	55
255	24	20c. grey	65	55
256	24	30c. green	65	55
257	24	40c. red	1·50	65
258	24	45c. turquoise	1·50	65
259	24	50c. brown	1·50	65
260	24	60c. green	1·50	95
261	24	70c. brown	1·50	95
262	24	80c. green	2·75	1·10
263	24	85c. red	4·75	2·20
264	24	1e. purple	2·30	1·50
265	24	1e.40 blue	8·00	5·00
266	24	2e. mauve	4·50	2·50
267	24	5e. green	15·00	9·00
268	24	10e. brown	27·00	12·00
269	24	20e. orange	85·00	41·00

27 Vasco da Gama

28 Mousinho de Albuquerque

1938

270	**27**	1c. green (postage)	25	25
271	**27**	5c. brown	25	25
272	**27**	10c. red	35	30
273	**27**	15c. purple	35	30
274	**27**	20c. grey	85	35
275	-	30c. purple	85	60
276	-	35c. green	85	65
277	-	40c. brown	85	65
278	-	50c. mauve	85	65
279	-	60c. black	85	65
280	-	70c. violet	85	65
281	-	80c. orange	1·50	75
282	-	1e. red	2·10	75
283	-	1e.75 blue	2·75	1·60
284	-	2e. red	6·75	2·40
285	-	5e. green	9·75	4·75
286	-	10e. blue	13·50	6·00
287	-	20e. brown	46·00	9·50
288	**28**	10c. red (air)	1·50	1·10
289	**28**	20c. violet	1·50	1·10
290	**28**	50c. orange	1·50	1·10
291	**28**	1e. blue	1·50	1·10
292	**28**	2e. red	13·00	6·50
293	**28**	3e. green	4·25	2·10
294	**28**	5e. brown	9·00	2·75
295	**28**	9e. red	13·00	7·00
296	**28**	10e. mauve	23·00	7·75

DESIGNS (postage): 30c. to 50c. Mousinho de Albuquerque; 60c. to 1e. Dam; 1e.75 to 5e. Prince Henry the Navigator; 10, 20e. Afonso de Albuquerque.

31 Cacheu Castle

1946. 500th Anniv of Discovery of Portuguese Guinea.

297	**31**	30c. black and grey	1·50	1·10
298	-	50c. green and light green	75	75
299	-	50c. purple and claret	75	75
300	-	1e.75 blue and light blue	5·00	1·90
301	-	3e.50 red and pink	8·00	3·00
302	-	5e. brown and chocolate	23·00	9·75
303	-	20e. violet and mauve	41·00	16·00

MS303a 175×221 mm. Nos. 297/303 (sold at 40e.) £130 £130

DESIGNS—VERT: 50c. Nuno Tristao; 1e.75, President Grant; 3e.50, Teixeiro Pinto; 5e. Honorio Barreto. HORIZ: 20e. Church at Bissau.

32 Native Huts

1948

304	**32**	5c. brown	25	20
305	-	10c. purple	4·75	2·75
306	-	20c. mauve	1·20	80
307	-	35c. green	1·50	80
308	-	50c. red	75	25
309	-	70c. blue	1·20	75
310	-	80c. green	1·80	75
311	-	1e. red	1·80	75
312	-	1e.75 blue	21·00	9·00
313	-	2e. blue	23·00	2·75
314	-	3e.50 brown	5·00	2·50
315	-	5e. grey	8·25	4·75
316	-	20e. violet	38·00	12·00

MS316a 176×158 mm. Nos. 304/16 (sold at 40e.) £160 £160

DESIGNS: 10c. Crowned crane; 20c., 3e.50, Youth; 35c., 5e. Woman; 50c. Musician; 70c. Man; 80c., 20e. Girl; 1, 2e. Drummer; 1e.75, Bushbuck.

33 Our Lady of Fatima

1948. Statue of Our Lady of Fatima.

317	**33**	50c. green	7·25	6·25

34 Letter and Globe

1949. 75th Anniv of U.P.U.

318	**34**	2e. orange	9·00	4·25

1950. Holy Year. As Nos. 425/6 of Macao.

319	1e. purple	3·50	2·10
320	3e. green	5·50	3·00

36 Our Lady of Fatima

1951. Termination of Holy Year.

321	**36**	1e. brown and buff	1·70	90

37 Doctor examining Patient

1952. 1st Tropical Medicine Congress, Lisbon.

322	**37**	50c. brown and purple	70	70

39 Exhibition Entrance

1953. Missionary Art Exhibition.

323	**39**	10c. red and green	20	20
324	**39**	50c. blue and brown	1·60	60
325	**39**	3e. black and orange	3·75	1·80

40 "Analeptes Trifasciata" (longhorn beetle)

1953. Bugs and Beetles. Multicoloured.

326	5c. Type **40**	20	15
327	10c. "Callidea panaethiopica kirk" (shieldbug)	20	20
328	30c. "Craspedophorus brevicollis" (ground beetle)	20	15
329	50c. "Anthia nimrod" (ground beetle)	30	15
330	70c. "Platypria luctuosa" (leaf beetle)	75	35
331	1e. "Acanthophorus maculatus" (longhorn beetle)	70	20
332	2e. "Cordylomera nitidipennis" (longhorn beetle)	1·60	30
333	3e. "Lycus latissimus" (powder-post beetle)	3·50	55
334	5e. "Cicindeia brunet" (tiger beetle)	3·75	1·40
335	10e. "Colliurus dimidiata" (ground beetle)	9·25	4·25

41 Portuguese Stamp of 1853 and Arms of Portuguese Overseas Provinces

1953. Portuguese Stamp Centenary.

336	**41**	50c. multicoloured	1·60	1·30

42 Father M. de Nobrega and View of Sao Paulo

1954. 4th Centenary of Sao Paulo.

337	**42**	1e. multicoloured	55	30

43 Arms of Cape Verde Islands and Portuguese Guinea

1955. Presidential Visit.

338	**43**	1e. multicoloured	55	30
339	**43**	2e.50 mulitcoloured	95	65

44 Exhibition Emblem Globe and Arms

1958. Brussels International Exhibition.

340	**44**	2e.50 green	1·10	75

45 "Matenus stenegalenis"

1958. 6th Int Congress of Tropical Medicine.

341	**45**	5e. multicoloured	4·75	2·10

46 Statue of Barreto at Bissau

1959. Death Centenary of Honorio Barreto (statesman).

342	**46**	2e.50 multicoloured	55	45

47 Astrolabe

1960. 500th Death Anniv of Prince Henry the Navigator.

343	**47**	2e.50 multicoloured	60	50

48 "Medical Service"

1960. 10th Anniv of African Technical Co-operation Commission.

344	**48**	1e.50 multicoloured	55	45

49 Motor Racing

1962. Sports. Multicoloured.

345	50c. Type **49**	60	15
346	1e. Tennis	95	45
347	1e.50 Putting the shot	70	45
348	2e.50 Wrestling	85	50
349	3e.50 Shooting	95	50
350	15e. Volleyball	2·50	1·30

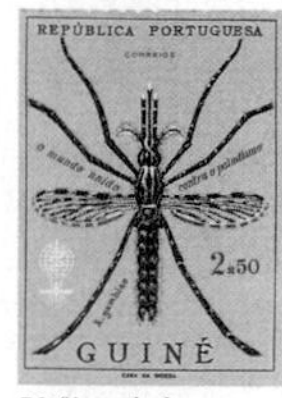

50 "Anopheles gambiae"

1962. Malaria Eradication.

351	**50**	2e.50 multicoloured	95	60

51 Common Spitting Cobra

1963. Snakes. Multicoloured.

352	20c. Type **51**	25	20
353	35c. African rock python	25	20
354	70c. Boomslang	85	50
355	80c. West African mamba	80	35
356	1e.50 Symthe's watersnake	80	25
357	2e. Common night adder	35	20
358	2e.50 Green swampsnake	3·25	50
359	3e.50 Brown house snake	60	30
360	4e. Spotted wolfsnake	75	30
361	5e. Common puff adder	90	50
362	15e. Striped beauty snake	2·20	1·50
363	20e. African egg-eating snake	3·00	2·30

The 2e. and 20e. are horiz.

52 Map of Africa, Boeing 707 and Lockheed L.1049G Super Constellation

1963. 10th Anniv of Transportes Aereos Portugueses (airline).

364	**52**	2e.50 multicoloured	1·10	55

53 J. de A. Corvo

1964. Centenary of National Overseas Bank.

365	**53**	2e.50 multicoloured	1·20	65

54 I.T.U. Emblem and St. Gabriel

1965. Centenary of I.T.U.

366	**54**	2e.50 multicoloured	2·75	1·10

55 Soldier, 1548

1966. Portuguese Military Uniforms. Multicoloured.

367	25c. Type **55**	25	15
368	40c. Arquebusier, 1578	35	15
369	60c. Arquebusier, 1640	50	20
370	1e. Grenadier, 1721	60	20
371	2e.50 Captain of Fusiliers, 1740	1·10	20
372	4e.50 Infantryman, 1740	2·50	45
373	7e.50 Sergeant-major, 1762	5·00	2·10
374	10e. Engineers' officer, 1806	5·00	2·10

56 B. C. Lopes School and Bissau Hospital

1966. 40th Anniv of Portuguese National Revolution.

375	**56**	2e.50 multicoloured	90	65

57 O. Muzanty and Cruiser "Republica"

1967. Centenary of Military Naval Assn. Mult.

376	50c. Type **57**	45	25
377	1e. A. de Cerqueira and destroyer "Guadiana"	1·40	60

58 Chapel of the Apparitions and Monument of the Holy Spirit

1967. 50th Anniv of Fatima Apparitions.

378	**58**	50c. multicoloured	30	15

63 Pres. Tomas

1968. Visit of President Tomas of Portugal.

396	**63**	1e. multicoloured	35	20

64 Cabral's Arms

1968. 500th Birth Anniv of Pedro Cabral (explorer).

397	**64**	2e.50 multicoloured	85	30

66 Admiral Coutinho's Astrolabe

1969. Birth Centenary of Admiral Gago Coutinho.

409	**66**	1e. multicoloured	45	20

67 Arms of Vasco da Gama

1969. 500th Birth Anniv of Vasco da Gama (explorer).

410	**67**	2e.50 multicoloured	50	15

68 L. A. Rebello da Silva

1969. Centenary of Overseas Administrative Reforms.

411	**68**	50c. multicoloured	35	15

69 Arms of King Manoel I

1969. 500th Birth Anniv of Manuel I.

412	**69**	2e. multicoloured	50	15

70 Ulysses Grant and Square, Bolama

1970. Centenary of Arbitral Judgment on Sovereignty of Bolama.

413	**70**	2e.50 multicoloured	60	30

71 Marshal Carmona

1970. Birth Centenary of Marshal Carmona.

414	**71**	1e.50 multicoloured	50	20

73 Camoens

1972. 400th Anniv of Camoens' "The Lusiads" (epic poem).

422	**73**	50c. multicoloured	55	30

74 Weightlifting and Hammer-throwing

1972. Olympic Games, Munich.

423	**74**	2e.50 multicoloured	75	20

75 Fairey IIID Seaplane "Lusitania" taking-off from Lisbon

1972. 50th Anniv of 1st Lisbon–Rio de Janeiro Flight.

424	**75**	1e. multicoloured	30	20

76 W.M.O. Emblem

1973. Centenary of I.M.O./W.M.O.

425	**76**	2e. multicoloured	50	30

CHARITY TAX STAMPS

The notes under this heading in Portugal also apply here.

C16

1919. Fiscal stamp optd REPUBLICA TAXA DE GUERRA.

C241	**C16**	10r. brown, buff & blk	7·50	5·00

1925. Marquis de Pombal Commem stamps of Portugal but inscr "GUINE".

C247	**C73**	15c. black and red	1·20	95
C248	**-**	15c. black and red	1·20	95
C249	**C75**	15c. black and red	1·20	95

C26

1934

C270	**C26**	50c. purple and green	17·00	9·75

C29a Arms

1938

C297	**C29a**	50c. yellow	16·00	8·00
C298	**C29a**	50c. brown and green	16·00	8·00

1942. As Type C 29a but smaller, 20½×25 mm.

C299	50c. black and brown	30	30
C300	50c. black and yellow	4·00	2·20
C301	50c. brown and yellow	6·50	4·00
C302	2e.50 black and blue	55	55
C303	5e. black and green	85	85
C304	10e. black and blue	1·70	1·70

Nos. C302/4 were used at several small post offices as ordinary postage stamps during a temporary shortage.

C59

1967. National Defence. No gum.

C379	**C59**	50c. red, pink and black	20	20
C380	**C59**	1e. red, green and black	35	35
C381	**C59**	5e. red, grey and black	1·10	1·10
C382	**C59**	10e. red, blue and black	3·25	3·25

A 50e. in the same design was for fiscal use only.

C60

1967. National Defence. No gum.

C383	**C60**	50c. red, pink and black	1·30	1·30
C384	**C60**	1e. red, green and black	1·60	1·10
C385	**C60**	5e. red, grey and black	3·25	2·10
C386	**C60**	10e. red, blue and black	5·25	4·25

C61 Carved Statuette of Woman

1967. Guinean Artifacts from Bissau Museum. Multicoloured.

C387	50c. Type C **61**	45	25
C388	1e. "Tree of life"(carving) (horiz)	45	25
C389	2e. Cow-headed statuette	45	25
C390	2e.50 "The Magistrate" (statuette)	65	45
C391	5e. "Kneeling Servant" (statuette)	85	55
C392	10e. Stylized pelican (carving)	1·60	1·30
MSC393	149×199 mm. Nos. C387/92. Imperf. No gold (sold at 25e.)	16·00	16·00

1968. No. C389 but inscr "TOCADOR DE BOMBOLON" surch.

C394	50c. on 2e. multicoloured	45	45
C395	1e. on 2e. multicoloured	45	45

C65 Hands grasping Sword

1969. National Defence.

C398	C65	50c. multicoloured	45	45
C399	C65	1e. multicoloured	45	45
C400	C65	2e. multicoloured	45	45
C401	C65	2e.50 multicoloured	45	45
C402	C65	3e. multicoloured	45	45
C403	C65	4e. multicoloured	55	45
C404	C65	5e. multicoloured	65	55
C405	C65	8e. multicoloured	1·10	1·10
C406	C65	9e. multicoloured	1·30	1·30
C407	C65	10e. multicoloured	1·10	1·10
C408	C65	15e. multicoloured	1·60	1·60

NOTE—30, 50 and 100e. stamps in the same design were for fiscal use only.

C72 Mother and Children

1971

C415	C72	50c. multicoloured	30	25
C416	C72	1e. multicoloured	30	25
C417	C72	2e. multicoloured	30	25
C418	C72	3e. multicoloured	30	25
C419	C72	4e. multicoloured	30	25
C420	C72	5e. multicoloured	55	30
C421	C72	10e. multicoloured	1·10	65

Higher values were intended for fiscal use.

NEWSPAPER STAMP

1983. "Newspaper" key-type inscr "GUINE".

N50	V	2½r. brown	2·40	1·50

POSTAGE DUE STAMPS

1904. "Due" key-type inscr "GUINE". Name and value in black.

D122	W	5r. green	1·60	90
D123	W	10r. grey	1·60	90
D124	W	20r. brown	1·60	90
D125	W	30r. orange	2·50	2·10
D126	W	50r. brown	2·50	2·10
D127	W	60r. brown	7·00	5·25
D128	W	100r. mauve	7·00	5·25
D129	W	130r. blue	7·00	5·25
D130	W	200r. red	11·00	10·00
D131	W	500r. lilac	26·00	10·00

1911. "Due" key-type of Portuguese Guinea optd REPUBLICA.

D138	5r. green	35	25
D139	10r. grey	45	35
D140	20r. brown	70	45
D141	30r. orange	70	45
D142	50r. brown	90	45
D143	60r. brown	2·10	1·60
D208	100r. mauve	3·75	3·25
D145	130r. blue	4·25	3·25
D146	200r. red	4·25	3·25
D147	500r. lilac	3·25	2·50

1921. "Due" key-type of Portuguese Guinea. Currency changed.

D244	½c. green	50	45
D245	1c. grey	50	45
D246	2c. brown	50	45
D247	3c. orange	50	45
D248	5c. brown	50	45
D249	6c. brown	1·30	1·20
D250	10c. mauve	1·30	1·20
D251	13c. blue	1·30	1·20
D252	20c. red	1·30	1·20
D253	50c. grey	1·30	1·20

1925. Marquis de Pombal stamps, as Nos. C247/9 optd MULTA.

D254	C73	30c. black and red	1·20	1·10
D255	-	30c. black and red	1·20	1·10
D256	C75	30c. black and red	1·20	1·10

1952. As Type D 70 of Macao, but inscr "GUINE PORTUGUESA". Numerals in red, name in black (except 2e. in blue).

D323	10c. green and pink	25	25
D324	30c. violet and grey	25	25
D325	50c. green and lemon	25	25
D326	1e. blue and grey	25	25
D327	2e. black and olive	35	35
D328	5e. brown and orange	90	90

Pt. 9

PORTUGUESE INDIA

Portuguese territories on the west coast of India, consisting of Goa, Damao and Diu. Became part of India in December 1961.

1871. 1000 reis = 1 milreis.
1882. 12 reis = 1 tanga; 16 tangas = 1 rupia
1959. 100 centavos = 1 escudo.

1

1871. Perf.

35	1	10r. black	9·00	6·75
33a	1	15r. pink	20·00	13·50
26	1	20r. red	25·00	16·00
21	1	40r. blue	£120	90·00
22	1	100r. green	£100	65·00
23	1	200r. yellow	£300	£250
27	1	300r. purple	£200	£140
28	1	600r. purple	£250	£160
29	1	900r. purple	£250	£160

9

1877. Star above value. Imperf (241/3) or perf (others).

241	9	1½r. black	2·50	1·80
242	9	4½r. green	25·00	20·00
243	9	6r. green	20·00	15·00
48	9	10r. black	48·00	41·00
49	9	15r. pink	50·00	45·00
50	9	20r. red	14·50	13·50
51	9	40r. blue	29·00	26·00
52	9	100r. green	£120	95·00
53	9	200r. yellow	£120	£120
54	9	300r. purple	£170	£140
55	9	600r. purple	£170	£140
56	9	900r. purple	£170	£140

1877. "Crown" key-type inscr "INDIA PORTU-GUEZA". Perf.

65	P	5r. black	8·75	6·00
58	P	10r. buff	14·50	12·50
78	P	10r. green	18·00	14·50
67	P	20r. bistre	12·50	9·25
68	P	25r. pink	14·50	12·50
79	P	25r. grey	65·00	47·00
80	P	25r. purple	47·00	35·00
69	P	40r. blue	25·00	14·50
81	P	40r. yellow	55·00	44·00
70b	P	50r. green	44·00	29·00
82	P	50r. blue	29·00	27·00
71	P	100r. lilac	20·00	18·00
64	P	200r. orange	39·00	29·00
73	P	300r. brown	42·00	39·00

See also Nos. 204/10.

1881. Surch in figures.

213	1	1½ on 10r. black		£475
215	9	1½ on 10r. black	†	£500
90	1	1½ on 20r. red	£120	£110
91	9	1½ on 20r. red	£275	£200
217	1	4½ on 40r. blue	50·00	50·00
223	1	4½ on 100r. green	38·00	32·00
96	1	5 on 10r. black	12·50	9·75
98	9	5 on 10r. black	70·00	44·00
101	1	5 on 15r. pink	2·75	2·75
106	1	5 on 20r. red	4·00	4·00
108	9	5 on 20r. red	4·00	4·00
224	1	6 on 20r. red		
228	1	6 on 100r. green	£475	£450
231	1	6 on 200r. yellow		£225
233	9	6 on 200r. yellow	£650	£650

1881. "Crown" key-type of Portuguese India surch in figures.

199	P	1½ on 4½ on 5r. black	£120	£100
109	P	1½ on 5r. black	2·50	1·60
200	P	1½ on 6 on 10r. green	£170	£150
110	P	1½ on 10r. green	2·50	2·10
111	P	1½ on 20r. bistre	28·00	21·00
157	P	1½ on 25r. grey	65·00	50·00
158	P	1½ on 100r. lilac	£100	90·00
200a	P	1½ on 1t. on 20r. bistre		£150
201	P	2 on 4t. on 50r. green	£425	£350
114	P	4½ on 5r. black	13·00	13·00
115	P	4½ on 10r. green	£275	£275
116	P	4½ on 20r. bistre	5·75	5·25
162	P	4½ on 25r. purple	26·00	21·00
118	P	4½ on 100r. lilac	£190	£190
119a	P	6 on 10r. buff	£100	95·00
120	P	6 on 10r. green	21·00	16·00
121	P	6 on 20r. bistre	29·00	21·00
167	P	6 on 25r. grey	65·00	38·00
168	P	6 on 25r. purple	5·00	3·75
169	P	6 on 40r. blue	£130	95·00
170	P	6 on 40r. yellow	14·50	80·00
171	P	6 on 50r. green	90·00	80·00
127	P	6 on 50r. blue	£110	95·00
202	P	6 on 1t. on 10r. green	£160	
128	P	1t. on 10r. green	£225	£200
129	P	1t. on 20r. bistre	90·00	70·00
175	P	1t. on 25r. grey	60·00	48·00
176	P	1t. on 25r. purple	26·00	19·00
132	P	1t. on 40r. blue	32·00	26·00
134	P	1t. on 50r. blue	48·00	32·00
178	P	1t. on 50r. green	£100	90·00
136	P	1t. on 100r. lilac	38·00	24·00
137	P	1t. on 200r. orange	70·00	60·00
139	P	2t. on 25r. purple	26·00	17·00
182	P	2t. on 25r. grey	65·00	50·00
184	P	2t. on 40r. blue	60·00	50·00
141	P	2t. on 40r. yellow	60·00	48·00
142a	P	2t. on 50r. green	45·00	36·00
143	P	2t. on 50r. blue	£150	£130
144	P	2t. on 100r. lilac	21·00	17·00
188	P	2t. on 200r. orange	70·00	50·00
189	P	2t. on 300r. brown	65·00	60·00
190	P	4t. on 10r. green	19·00	16·00
191	P	4t. on 50r. green	19·00	16·00
148	P	4t. on 200r. orange	85·00	60·00
193	P	8t. on 20r. bistre	80·00	60·00
194	P	8t. on 25r. pink	£375	£325
151	P	8t. on 40r. blue	80·00	65·00
196	P	8t. on 100r. lilac	70·00	60·00
197	P	8t. on 200r. orange	60·00	50·00
198	P	8t. on 300r. brown	70·00	55·00

1882. "Crown" key-type of Portuguese India.

204	1½r. black	1·60	1·10
205	4½r. green	1·60	1·10
206	6r. green	1·60	1·10
207	1t. pink	1·60	95
208	2t. blue	1·60	95
209	4t. purple	1·60	1·30
210	8t. orange	5·75	5·00

1886. "Embossed" key-type Inscr "INDIA PORTUGUEZA".

244	Q	1½r. black	3·75	2·00
245	Q	4½r. olive	4·50	2·20
246	Q	6r. green	5·00	2·75
247	Q	1t. red	7·75	4·50
248	Q	2t. blue	14·50	7·00
249	Q	4t. lilac	14·50	7·00
257	Q	8t. orange	13·00	7·00

1895. "Figures" key-type inscr "INDIA".

271	R	1½r. black	1·90	1·00
259	R	4½r. orange	1·90	1·20
273	R	6r. green	1·90	1·00
274	R	9r. lilac	7·75	5·50
260	R	1t. blue	2·50	1·80
261	R	2t. red	2·50	1·20
262	R	4t. blue	3·25	1·80
270	R	8t. lilac	5·75	3·50

1898. As Vasco da Gama stamps of Portugal T 40 etc, but inscr "INDIA".

275	1½r. green	1·60	70
276	4½r. red	1·60	70
277	6r. purple	1·60	1·00
278	9r. green	2·30	1·00
279	1t. blue	3·25	2·30
280	2t. brown	3·75	2·30
281	4t. brown	3·75	3·00
282	8t. brown	8·00	4·75

DESIGNS—HORIZ: 1½r. Departure of fleet; 4½r. Arrival at Calicut; 6r. Embarkation at Rastello; 4t. Flagship "Sao Gabriel"; 8t. Vasco da Gama. VERT: 9r. Muse of History; 1t. Flagship "Sao Gabriel" and portraits of Da Gama and Camoens; 2t. Archangel Gabriel, patron saint of the expedition.

1898. "King Carlos" key-type inscr "INDIA". Value in red (No. 292) or black (others).

323	S	1r. grey	55	45
283	S	1½r. orange	55	35
324	S	1½r. grey	70	35
325	S	2r. orange	55	35
326	S	2½r. brown	70	35
327	S	3r. blue	70	35
284	S	4½r. green	1·60	1·00
285	S	6r. brown	1·60	1·00
328	S	6r. green	70	35
286	S	9r. lilac	1·60	1·00
287	S	1t. green	1·60	70
329	S	1t. red	80	35
288	S	2t. blue	1·90	70
330	S	2t. brown	3·25	1·50
331	S	2½t. blue	11·50	6·00
289	S	4t. blue on blue	3·75	1·80
332	S	5t. brown on yellow	3·75	2·20
290	S	8t. purple on pink	3·75	2·00
291	S	12t. blue on pink	5·75	3·50
334	S	12t. green on pink	7·50	3·50
292	S	1rp. black on blue	11·50	5·00
335	S	1rp. blue on yellow	16·00	15·00
293	S	2rp. mauve on yellow	16·00	9·75
336	S	2rp. black on yellow	31·00	31·00

1900. No. 288 surch 1½ Reis.

295	1½r. on 2t. blue	3·25	1·80

1902. Surch.

299	R	1r. on 6r. green	95	60
298	Q	1r. on 2t. blue	1·10	70
300	Q	2r. on 4½r. olive	75	60
301	R	2r. on 8t. lilac	95	60
302	Q	2½r. on 6r. green	95	60
303	R	2½r. on 9r. lilac	95	60
305	R	3r. on 4½r. orange	2·10	1·50
304	Q	3r. on 1t. red	75	60
306	R	3r. on 1t. blue	1·90	1·80
337	S	2t. on 2½t. blue and black	3·50	3·00
307	Q	2½t. on 1½r. black	2·50	2·00
310	R	2½t. on 1½r. black	2·50	1·80
309	Q	2½t. on 4t. lilac	2·50	1·80
315	R	5t. on 2t. red	2·50	1·80
317	R	5t. on 4t. blue	2·50	1·80
314	Q	5t. on 8t. orange	1·60	1·00

1902. 1898 "King Carlos" stamps optd PROVISORIO.

319	6r. brown and black	2·75	1·80
320	1t. green and black	2·75	1·80
321	2t. blue and black	2·75	1·80

1911. 1898 "King Carlos" stamps optd REPUBLICA. Value in black.

338	1r. grey	45	30
339	1½r. grey	45	30
340	2r. orange	45	30
341	2½r. brown	70	30
342	3r. blue	70	30
343	4½r. green	70	30
344	6r. green	55	30
345	9r. lilac	70	30
346	1t. red	1·00	30
347	2t. brown	1·10	30
348	4t. blue on blue	2·10	1·70
349	5t. brown on yellow	2·50	1·70
350	8t. purple on pink	7·50	4·25
402	12t. green on pink	9·00	7·25
352	1rp. blue on yellow	11·50	10·00
404	2rp. mauve on yellow	22·00	16·00
405	2rp. black on yellow	22·00	16·00

Both unused and used prices for the following issue (Nos. 371 etc.) are for entire stamps showing both halves.

1911. Various stamps bisected by vertical perforation, and each half surch. (a) On 1898 "King Carlos" key-type.

371	1r. on 2r. orange and black	65	60
372	1r. on 1t. red and black	65	60
378	1r. on 5t. brown and black on yellow	4·25	3·50
374	1½r. on 2½r. brown and black	1·10	90
354	1½r. on 4½r. green and black	23·00	11·00
355	1½r. on 9r. lilac and black	95	70
356	1½r. on 4t. blue and black on blue	95	70
375	2r. on 2½r. brown and black	95	70
357	2r. on 4t. blue and black on blue	1·60	90
376	3r. on 2½r. brown and black	95	70
377	3r. on 2t. brown and black	1·10	90
358	6r. on 4½r. green and black	1·30	1·00
359d	6r. on 9r. lilac and black	1·30	1·00
379	6r. on 8t. purple and black on pink	3·25	2·75

(b) On 1902 Provisional issue.

360	R	1r. on 5t. on 2t. red	11·50	9·50
361	R	1r. on 5t. on 4t. blue	9·50	7·00
363	Q	1r. on 5t. on 8t. orange	4·25	3·00
364	Q	2r. on 2½r. on 6r. green	3·75	3·50
365	R	2r. on 2½r. on 9r. lilac	27·00	21·00
366	R	3r. on 5t. on 2t. red	11·50	7·00
367	R	3r. on 5t. on 4t. blue	11·50	7·00
370	Q	3r. on 5t. on 8t. orange	3·25	2·20

(c) On 1911 issue (optd REPUBLICA).

380	S	1r. on 1r. grey and black	60	55
381	S	1r. on 2r. orange and black	60	55
382	S	1r. on 1t. red and black	60	55
383	S	1r. on 5t. brown and black on yellow	60	55
384	S	1½r. on 4½r. green and black	95	55
386	S	6r. on 9r. lilac and black	95	55
419	S	3r. on 2t. brown and black	9·00	6·25
420	S	6r. on 4½r. green and black	8·00	6·25
422	S	6r. on 8t. purple and black on pink	11·00	9·00

1913. Nos. 275/82 optd REPUBLICA.

389	1½r. green	60	40
390	4½r. red	60	40
391	6r. purple	70	55
392	9r. green	80	55
393	1t. blue	1·50	55
394	2t. brown	2·10	2·20
395	4t. brown	1·80	55
396	8t. brown	3·00	1·30

1914. Stamps of 1902 optd REPUBLICA.

406	**R**	2r. on 8t. lilac	13·50	9·00
407	**Q**	2½r. on 6r. green	1·80	1·40
408	**R**	5t. on 2t. red	9·00	7·25
410	**R**	5t. on 4t. blue	9·00	5·50
415	**S**	1t. green and black (No. 320)	22·00	12·50
458	**S**	2t. blue and black (No. 321)	1·80	1·70
459	**S**	2t. on 2½t. blue and black	2·30	1·70
460	**Q**	5t. on 8t. orange	2·75	2·00

1914. "King Carlos" key-type of Portuguese India optd REPUBLICA and surch.

423	**S**	1½r. on 4½r. green and black	75	70
424	**S**	1½r. on 9r. lilac and black	75	70
425	**S**	1½r. on 12t. green and black on pink	1·30	1·20
426	**S**	3r. on 1t. red and black	85	70
427	**S**	3r. on 2t. brown and black	7·25	6·25
428	**S**	3r. on 8t. purple and black on pink	9·00	7·25
429	**S**	3r. on 1rp. blue and black on yellow	1·20	75
430	**S**	3r. on 2rp. black on yellow	1·40	1·10

1914. Nos. 390 and 392/6 surch.

433	1½ on 4½r. red	75	60
434	1½r. on 9r. green	75	60
435	3r. on 1t. blue	75	60
436	3r. on 2t. brown	3·75	3·25
437	3r. on 4t. brown	75	60
438	3r. on 8t. brown	3·50	1·80

1914. "Ceres" key-type inscr "INDIA". Name and value in black.

439	**U**	1r. green	70	60
440	**U**	1½r. green	70	60
441	**U**	2r. black	1·00	65
442	**U**	2½r. green	1·00	65
443	**U**	3r. lilac	1·20	65
474	**U**	4r. blue	2·00	1·40
444	**U**	4½r. red	1·20	65
445	**U**	5r. green	1·20	65
446	**U**	6r. brown	1·20	65
447	**U**	9r. blue	1·30	70
448	**U**	10r. red	1·60	90
449	**U**	1t. violet	2·50	90
481	**U**	1½t. green	2·00	90
450	**U**	2t. blue	2·75	1·20
483	**U**	2½t. turquoise	2·00	90
451	**U**	3t. brown	3·75	1·50
484	**U**	3t. 4 brown	7·00	3·25
452	**U**	4t. grey	2·75	1·80
453	**U**	8t. purple	7·75	6·50
454	**U**	12t. brown on green	7·00	5·50
455	**U**	1rp. brown on pink	32·00	18·00
487	**U**	1rp. brown	26·00	20·00
456	**U**	2rp. orange on orange	19·00	15·00
488	**U**	2rp. yellow	27·00	20·00
457	**U**	3rp. green on blue	22·00	15·00
489	**U**	3rp. green	41·00	33·00
490	**U**	5rp. red	47·00	37·00

1922. "Ceres" key-type of Portuguese India surch with new value.

492	1½r. on 2r. black	1·50	1·40
496	1½r. on 8t. purple and black	4·00	2·75
497	2½t. on 3t. 4 brown and black	70·00	60·00

34 Vasco da Gama and Flagship "Sao Gabriel"

1925. 400th Death Anniv of Vasco da Gama. No gum.

493	**34**	6r. brown	7·00	4·25
494	**34**	1t. purple	9·50	4·75

36 The Signature of Francis

1931. St. Francis Xavier Exhibition.

498	-	1r. green	1·10	1·00
499	**36**	2r. brown	1·20	1·00
500	-	6r. purple	2·30	1·10
501	-	1½t. brown	8·00	5·50
502	-	2t. blue	13·50	7·75
503	-	2½t. red	19·00	8·00

DESIGNS—VERT: 1r. Monument to St. Francis; 6r. St. Francis in surplice and cassock; 1½t. St. Francis and Cross; 2½t. St. Francis's Tomb. HORIZ: 2t. Bom Jesus Church, Goa.

40 "Portugal" and Galeasse

1933

504	**40**	1r. brown	30	25
505	**40**	2r. brown	30	25
506	**40**	4r. mauve	30	25
507	**40**	6r. green	30	25
508	**40**	8r. black	65	50
509	**40**	1t. grey	65	50
510	**40**	1½t. red	65	50
511	**40**	2t. brown	65	50
512	**40**	2½t. blue	2·00	80
513	**40**	3t. turquoise	2·40	80
514	**40**	5t. red	3·50	80
515	**40**	1rp. green	8·50	3·25
516	**40**	2rp. purple	17·00	8·50
517	**40**	3rp. orange	23·00	13·00
518	**40**	5rp. green	48·00	31·00

1938. As T 27 and 28 of Portuguese Guinea, but inscr "ESTADO DA INDIA".

519	**27**	1r. green (postage)	30	25
520	**27**	2r. brown	30	25
521	**27**	3r. violet	30	25
522	**27**	6r. green	30	25
523	-	10r. red	65	40
524	-	1t. mauve	65	40
525	-	1½t. red	65	40
526	-	2t. orange	65	40
527	-	2½t. blue	65	40
528	-	3t. grey	1·40	50
529	-	5t. purple	2·50	65
530	-	1rp. red	6·50	1·30
531	-	2rp. green	10·00	3·75
532	-	3rp. blue	19·00	8·75
533	-	5rp. brown	38·00	10·50

DESIGNS: 10r. to 1½t. Mousinho de Albuquerque; 2t. to 3t. Prince Henry the Navigator; 5t. to 2rp. Dam; 3, 5rp. Afonso de Albuquerque.

534	**28**	1t. red (air)	2·00	95
535	**28**	2½t. violet	2·00	95
536	**28**	3½t. orange	2·00	95
537	**28**	4½t. blue	2·00	95
538	**28**	7t. red	2·40	95
539	**28**	7½t. green	2·75	95
540	**28**	9t. brown	9·25	2·75
541	**28**	11t. mauve	10·00	2·75

1942. Surch.

549	**40**	1r. on 8r. black	1·30	1·00
546	**40**	1r. on 5t. red	1·30	1·00
550	**40**	2r. on 8r. black	1·30	1·00
547	**40**	3r. on 1½t. red	1·30	1·10
551	**40**	3r. on 2t. brown	1·30	1·10
552	**40**	3r. on 3rp. orange	3·25	2·50
553	**40**	6r. on 2½t. blue	3·25	2·50
554	**40**	6r. on 3t. turquoise	3·25	2·50
542	**40**	1t. on 1½t. red	3·75	3·00
548	**40**	1t. on 2t. brown	3·25	2·50
543	**40**	1t. on 1rp. green	3·75	3·00
544	**40**	1t. on 2rp. purple	3·75	3·00
545	**40**	1t. on 5rp. green	3·75	3·00

48 St. Francis Xavier

1946. Portraits and View.

555	**48**	1r. black and grey	75	40
556	-	2r. purple and pink	75	40
557	-	6r. bistre and buff	75	40
558	-	7r. violet and mauve	3·25	1·30
559	-	9r. brown and buff	3·25	1·30
560	-	1t. green and light green	3·25	1·30
561	-	3½t. blue and light blue	3·50	1·80
562	-	1rp. purple and bistre	8·00	2·20

MS563 169×280 mm. Nos. 555/62 (sold at 1½rp.) 47·00 42·00

DESIGNS: 2r. Luis de Camoens; 6r. Garcia de Orta; 7r. Beato Joao Brito; 9r. Vice-regal Archway; 1t. Afonso de Albuquerque; 3½t. Vasco da Gama; 1rp. D. Francisco de Almeida.

50 D. Joao de Castro

1948. Portraits.

564	**50**	3r. blue and light blue	1·80	90
565	-	1t. green and light green	2·00	1·10
566	-	1½t. purple and mauve	3·00	2·10
567	-	2½t. red and orange	4·00	2·50
568	-	7½t. purple and brown	6·00	3·50

MS569 108×149 mm. Nos. 564/8 (sold at 1rp.) 49·00 44·00

PORTRAITS: 1t. St. Francis Xavier; 1½t. P. Jose Vaz; 2½t. D. Luis de Ataide; 7½t. Duarte Pacheco Pereira.

1948. Statue of Our Lady of Fatima. As T 33 of Portuguese Guinea.

570	1t. green	6·00	4·75

53 Our Lady of Fatima

1949. Statue of Our Lady of Fatima.

571	**53**	1r. light blue and blue	1·50	1·10
572	**53**	3r. yellow, orange and lemon	1·50	1·10
573	**53**	9r. red and mauve	2·20	1·30
574	**53**	2t. green and light green	8·00	2·20
575	**53**	9t. red and vermilion	7·00	3·25
576	**53**	2rp. brown and purple	13·50	4·25
577	**53**	5rp. black and green	26·00	11·00
578	**53**	8rp. blue and violet	55·00	19·00

1949. 75th Anniv of U.P.U. As T 34 of Portuguese Guinea.

579	2½t. red	7·25	3·00

1950. Holy Year. As Nos. 425/6 of Macao.

580	**65**	1r. bistre	1·70	65
588	**65**	1r. red	65	40
589	**65**	2r. green	65	40
590	-	3r. brown	65	40
591	**65**	6r. grey	65	40
592	-	9r. mauve	1·70	1·10
593	**65**	1t. blue	1·70	1·10
581	-	2t. green	2·20	1·00
594	-	2t. yellow	1·70	1·10
595	**65**	4t. brown	1·70	1·10

1950. Nos. 523 and 527 surch.

582	1real on 10r. red	65	55
583	1real on 2½t. blue	65	55
584	2reis on 10r. red	65	55
585	3reis on 2½t. blue	65	55
586	6reis on 2½t. blue	65	55
587	1tanga on 2½t. blue	65	55

1951. Termination of Holy Year. As T 36 of Portuguese Guinea.

596	1rp. blue and grey	2·40	1·70

59 Father Jose Vaz

1951. 300th Birth Anniv of Jose Vaz.

597	**59**	1r. grey and slate	25	15
598	-	2r. orange and brown	25	15
599	**59**	3r. grey and black	85	40
600	-	1t. blue and indigo	40	35
601	**59**	2t. purple and maroon	40	35
602	-	3t. green and black	70	40
603	**59**	9t. violet and blue	70	40
604	-	10t. violet and mauve	1·80	95
605	-	12t. brown and black	3·25	1·30

DESIGNS: 2r., 1, 3, 10t. Sancoale Church Ruins; 12t. Veneravel Altar.

60 Goa Medical School

1952. 1st Tropical Medicine Congress, Lisbon.

606	**60**	4½t. turquoise and black	7·00	3·00

1952. 4th Death Cent of St. Francis Xavier. As Nos. 452/4 of Macao but without lined background.

607	6r. multicoloured	45	35
608	2t. multicoloured	3·00	75
609	5t. green, silver and mauve	6·00	1·70

MS610 76×65 mm. 4t. green, silver and ochre (as No. 609 but smaller); 8t. slate (T **62**) 24·00 21·00

MS611 90×100 mm. 9t. sepia and brown (T **62**) 24·00 21·00

62 St. Francis Xavier

63 Stamp of 1871

3 TANGAS

1952. Philatelic Exhibition, Goa.

612	**63**	3t. black	19·00	16·00
613	**62**	5t. black and lilac	19·00	16·00

64 The Virgin

1953. Missionary Art Exhibition.

614	**64**	6r. black and blue	30	20
615	**64**	1t. brown and buff	1·30	1·00
616	**64**	3t. lilac and yellow	4·00	2·00

1953. Portuguese Postage Stamp Centenary. As T 41 of Portuguese Guinea.

617	1t. multicoloured	1·80	1·20

66 Dr. Gama Pinto

1954. Birth Centenary of Dr. Gama Pinto.

618	**66**	3r. green and grey	40	20
619	**66**	2t. black and blue	90	50

1954. 4th Centenary of Sao Paulo. As T 42 of Portuguese Guinea.

620	2t. multicoloured	1·00	55

67 Academy Buildings

1954. Centenary of Afonso de Albuquerque National Academy.

621	**67**	9t. multicoloured	2·50	75

68 Mgr. Dalgado

1955. Birth Centenary of Mgr. Dalgado.

622	**68**	1r. multicoloured	50	20
623	**68**	1t. multicoloured	90	35

71 M. A. de Sousa

72 F. de Almeida

73 Map of Bacaim

1956. 450th Anniv of Portuguese Settlements in India. Multicoloured. (a) Famous Men. As T 71.

624	6r. Type **71**	45	35
625	1½t. F. N. Xavier	45	35
626	4t. A. V. Lourenco	45	40
627	8t. Father Jose Vaz	1·10	55
628	9t. M. G. de Heredia	1·10	55
629	2rp. A. C. Pacheco	4·50	2·75

(b) Viceroys. As T 72.

630	3r. Type **72**	45	35
631	9r. A. de Albuquerque	45	35
632	1t. Vasco da Gama	65	45
633	3t. N. da Cunha	95	45
634	10t. J. de Castro	1·30	45
635	3rp. C. de Braganca	6·25	3·00

(c) Settlements. As T 73.

636	2t. Type **73**	5·25	3·00
637	2½t. Mombaim	2·40	1·70
638	3½t. Damao	2·40	1·70
639	5t. Diu	1·10	75
640	12t. Cochim	1·80	1·40
641	1rp. Goa	4·25	2·50

74 Map of Damao. Dadra and Nagar Aveli Districts

1957. Centres multicoloured.

642	**74**	3r. grey	25	20
643	**74**	6r. green	25	20
644	**74**	3t. pink	40	30
645	**74**	6t. blue	40	30
646	**74**	11t. bistre	1·30	55
647	**74**	2rp. lilac	2·20	1·20
648	**74**	3rp. yellow	3·25	2·50
649	**74**	5rp. red	5·25	3·25

75 Arms of Vasco da Gama

1958. Heraldic Arms of Famous Men. Multicoloured.

650	2r. Type **75**	40	30
651	6r. Lopo Soares de Albergaria	40	30
652	9r. D. Francisco de Almeida	40	30
653	1t. Garcia de Noronha	45	35
654	4t. D. Afonso de Albuquerque	45	40
655	5t. D. Joao de Castro	90	40
656	11t. D. Luis de Ataide	1·50	1·20
657	1rp. Nuno da Cunha	2·30	1·30

1958. 6th International Congress of Tropical Medicine. As T 45 of Portuguese Guinea.

658	5t. multicoloured	1·50	1·00

DESIGN: 5t. "Holarrhena antidysenterica" (plant).

1958. Brussels Int Exn. As T 44 of Portuguese Guinea.

659	1rp. multicoloured	1·00	85

1959. Surch in new currency.

660	-	5c. on 2r. (No. 650)	45	40
661	**74**	10c. on 3r. grey	45	40
662	-	15c. on 6r. (No. 651)	45	40
663	-	20c. on 9r. (No. 652)	45	40
664	-	30c. on 1t. (No. 653)	45	40
681	-	40c. on 1½t. (No. 566)	45	40
682	-	40c. on 1½t. (No. 625)	45	40
683	-	40c. on 2t. (No. 620)	45	40
665	**73**	40c. on 2t.30	45	40
666	-	40c. on 2½t. (No. 637)	1·00	75
667	-	40c. on 3½t. (No. 638)	45	40
668	**74**	50c. on 3t. pink	45	40
669	-	80c. on 3t. (No. 633)	1·70	75
684	**64**	80c. on 3t. lilac and yellow	45	40
685	-	80c. on 3½t. (No. 561)	45	40
686	-	80c. on 5t. (No. 658)	1·80	55
670	-	80c. on 10t. (No. 634)	1·00	75
687	-	80c. on 1rp. (No. 659)	3·50	1·90
671	-	80c. on 3rp. (No. 635)	1·70	75
672	-	1e. on 4t. (No. 654)	45	40
673	-	1e.50 on 5t. (No. 655)	75	40
674	**74**	2e. on 6t. blue	45	40
675	**74**	2e.50 on 11t. bistre	1·00	40
676	-	4e. on 11t. (No. 656)	1·30	75
677	-	4e.50 on 1rp. (No. 657)	1·80	1·10
678	**74**	5e. on 2rp. lilac	1·70	75
679	**74**	10e. on 3rp. yellow	2·50	1·90
680	**74**	30e. on 5rp. red	7·50	1·90

78 Coin of Manoel I

1959. Portuguese Indian Coins. Designs showing both sides of coins of various rulers. Multicoloured.

688	**74**	5c. Type **78**	25	20
689	**74**	10c. Joao III	25	20
690	**74**	15c. Sebastiao	25	20
691	**74**	30c. Filipe I	45	40
692	**74**	40c. Filipe II	45	40
693	**74**	50c. Filipe III	55	20
694	**74**	60c. Joao IV	55	20
695	**74**	80c. Afonso VI	55	20
696	**74**	1e. Pedro II	55	20
697	**74**	1e.50 Joao V	55	20
698	**74**	2e. Jose I	85	50
699	**74**	2e.50 Maria I	90	40
700	**74**	3e. Prince Regent Joao	90	50
701	**74**	4e. Pedro IV	90	55
702	**74**	4e.40 Miguel	1·20	75
703	**74**	5e. Maria II	1·20	75
704	**74**	10e. Pedro V	1·80	1·60
705	**74**	20e. Luis	4·00	3·25
706	**74**	30e. Carlos	6·00	4·00
707	**74**	50e. Portuguese Republic	9·50	5·25

79 Prince Henry's Arms

1960. 500th Death Anniv of Prince Henry the Navigator.

708	**79**	3e. multicoloured	2·40	1·00

The 1962 sports set and malaria eradication stamp similar to those for the other territories were ready for issue when Portuguese India was occupied, but they were not put on sale there.

CHARITY TAX STAMPS

The notes under this heading in Portugal also apply here.

1919. Fiscal stamp. Type C 1 of Portuguese Africa optd TAXA DE GUERRA.

C491	Rps. 0:00:05, 48 green	3·50	2·75
C492	Rps. 0:02:03, 43 green	7·50	4·75

1925. Marquis de Pombal Commem stamps of Portugal, but inscr "INDIA".

C495	**C73**	6r. pink	70	65
C496	-	6r. pink	70	65
C497	**C75**	6r. pink	70	65

C52 Mother and Child

1948. (a) Inscr "ASSISTENCIA PUBLICA".

C571	**C52**	6r. green	5·50	3·25
C572	**C52**	6r. yellow	3·75	2·50
C573	**C52**	1t. red	5·50	3·25
C574	**C52**	1t. orange	3·75	2·50
C575	**C52**	1t. green	6·00	3·50

(b) Inscr "PROVEDORIA DE ASSISTENCIA PUBLICA".

C607	1t. grey	6·50	3·50

1951. Surch 1 tanga.

C606	1t. on 6r. red	5·25	2·75

1953. Optd "Revalidado" P. A. P. and dotted line.

C617	1t. red	15·00	7·75

C69 Mother and Child

1953. Surch as in Type C 69.

C624	**C69**	1t. on 4t. blue	19·00	12·00

C70 Mother and Child

1956

C625	**C70**	1t. black, green and red	1·30	65
C626	**C70**	1t. blue, orange & grn	1·10	65

1957. Surch 6 reis.

C650	6r. on 1t. black, green and red	1·80	95

1959. Surch.

C688	20c. on 1t. blue, orange and green	85	65
C689	40c. on 1t. blue, orange and green	85	65

C80 Arms and People

1960

C709	**C80**	20e. brown and red	85	65

POSTAGE DUE STAMPS

1904. "Due" key-type inscr "INDIA".

D337	**W**	2r. green	55	55
D338	**W**	3r. green	55	50
D339	**W**	4r. orange	55	50
D340	**W**	5r. grey	55	50
D341	**W**	6r. grey	55	50
D342	**W**	9r. brown	80	75
D343	**W**	1t. red	80	75
D344	**W**	2t. brown	1·50	90
D345	**W**	5t. blue	4·00	3·25
D346	**W**	10t. red	4·00	3·75
D347	**W**	1rp. lilac	18·00	8·50

1911. Nos. D337/47 optd REPUBLICA.

D354	2r. green	35	25
D355	3r. green	35	25
D356	4r. orange	35	25
D357	5r. grey	35	25
D358	6r. grey	45	25
D359	9r. brown	60	25
D360	1t. red	60	25
D361	2t. brown	1·00	55
D362	5t. blue	2·20	1·80
D363	10t. red	6·50	4·00
D364	1rp. lilac	6·50	4·00

1925. Marquis de Pombal stamps, as Nos. C495/7 optd MULTA.

D495	**C73**	1t. pink	55	55
D496	-	1t. pink	55	55
D497	**C75**	1t. pink	55	55

1943. Stamps of 1933 surch Porteado and new value.

D549	**40**	3r. on 2½t. blue	65	55
D550	**40**	6r. on 3t. turquoise	1·50	85
D551	**40**	1t. on 5t. red	2·75	2·30

1945. As Type D 1 of Portuguese Colonies, but optd ESTADO DA INDIA.

D555	2r. black and red	1·20	1·10
D556	3r. black and blue	1·20	1·10
D557	4r. black and yellow	1·20	1·10
D558	6r. black and green	1·20	1·10
D559	1t. black and brown	1·50	1·30
D560	2t. black and brown	1·50	1·30

1951. Surch Porteado and new value and bar.

D588	2rs. on 7r. (No. 558)	70	65
D589	3rs. on 7r. (No. 558)	70	65
D590	1t. on 1rp. (No. 562)	70	65
D591	2t. on 1rp. (No. 562)	70	65

1952. As Type D 70 of Macao, but inscr "INDIA PORTUGUESA". Numerals in red, name in black.

D606	2r. olive and brown	30	20
D607	3r. black and green	30	20
D608	6r. blue and turquoise	40	20
D609	1t. red and grey	45	35
D610	2t. orange, green and grey	1·10	75
D611	10t. blue, green and yellow	4·00	3·50

1959. Nos. D606/8 and D610/11 surch in new currency.

D688	5c. on 2r. multicoloured	40	30
D689	10c. on 3r. multicoloured	40	30
D690	15c. on 6r. multicoloured	55	45
D691	60c. on 2t. multicoloured	1·70	1·40
D692	60c. on 10t. multicoloured	5·00	4·00

Pt. 9

PORTUGUESE TIMOR

The eastern part of Timor in the Indonesian Archipelago. Administered as part of Macao until 1896, then as a separate Portuguese Overseas Province until 1975.

Following a civil war and the intervention of Indonesian forces the territory was incorporated into Indonesia on 17 July 1976.

1885. 1000 reis = 1 milreis.
1894. 100 avos = 1 pataca.
1960. 100 centavos = 1 escudo.

1885. "Crown" key-type inscr "MACAU" optd TIMOR.

1	**P**	5r. black	2·40	2·10
12	**P**	10r. green	6·00	4·75
3	**P**	20r. red	11·00	6·25
4	**P**	25r. lilac	2·20	1·30
5	**P**	40r. yellow	5·25	4·00
6	**P**	50r. blue	2·40	1·70
7	**P**	80r. grey	6·75	4·00
8	**P**	100r. purple	2·40	2·10
19	**P**	200r. orange	5·00	4·00
20	**P**	300r. brown	5·00	4·00

1887. "Embossed" key-type inscr "CORREIO DE TIMOR".

21	**Q**	5r. black	3·75	2·30
22	**Q**	10r. green	4·25	3·00
23	**Q**	20r. red	6·00	3·00
24	**Q**	25r. mauve	7·75	3·75
25	**Q**	40r. brown	13·50	5·50
26	**Q**	50r. blue	13·50	5·50
27	**Q**	80r. grey	15·00	6·25
28	**Q**	100r. brown	17·00	7·75
29	**Q**	200r. lilac	35·00	16·00
30	**Q**	300r. orange	40·00	20·00

1892. "Embossed" key-type inscr "PROVINCIA DE MACAU" surch TIMOR 30 30. No gum.

32		30 on 300r. orange	6·75	5·00

1894. "Figures" key-type inscr "TIMOR".

33	**R**	5r. orange	2·40	1·30
34	**R**	10r. mauve	2·40	1·30
35	**R**	15r. brown	3·50	1·30
36	**R**	20r. lilac	3·50	1·30
37	**R**	25r. green	3·75	2·10
38	**R**	50r. blue	5·50	4·00
39	**R**	75r. pink	7·25	5·50
40	**R**	80r. green	7·25	5·50
41	**R**	100r. brown on buff	5·75	4·75
42	**R**	150r. red on pink	24·00	11·50
43	**R**	200r. blue on blue	24·00	12·50
44	**R**	300r. blue on brown	29·00	13·50

1894. Nos. 21/30 surch PROVISORIO and value in European and Chinese. No gum.

46	**Q**	1a. on 5r. black	2·50	1·50
47	**Q**	2a. on 10r. green	2·75	2·30
48	**Q**	3a. on 20r. red	4·00	2·30
49	**Q**	4a. on 25r. purple	4·00	2·30
50	**Q**	6a. on 40r. brown	6·75	3·00
51	**Q**	8a. on 50r. blue	8·25	4·50
52	**Q**	13a. on 80r. grey	15·00	14·50
53	**Q**	16a. on 100r. brown	15·00	14·50
54	**Q**	31a. on 200r. lilac	41·00	31·00
55	**Q**	47a. on 300r. orange	46·00	36·00

1895. No. 32 further surch 5 avos PROVISORIO and Chinese characters with bars over the original surch.

56		5a. on 30 on 300r. orange	9·00	5·50

1898. 400th Anniv of Vasco da Gama's Discovery of Route to India. As Nos. 1/8 of Portuguese Colonies, but inscr "TIMOR" and value in local currency.

58		½a. green	2·75	2·00
59		1a. red	2·75	2·00
60		2a. purple	2·75	2·00
61		4a. green	2·75	2·00
62		8a. blue	4·25	2·50
63		12a. brown	5·75	3·50
64		16a. brown	5·75	4·25
65		24a. brown	8·75	6·00

1898. "King Carlos" key-type inscr "TIMOR". Name and value in red (78a.) or black (others). With or without gum.

68	**S**	½a. grey	75	65
69	**S**	1a. red	75	65
70	**S**	2a. green	75	65
71	**S**	2½a. brown	2·20	1·60
72	**S**	3a. lilac	2·20	1·60
112	**S**	3a. green	3·50	2·00
73	**S**	4a. green	2·20	1·60
113	**S**	5a. red	2·75	2·00
114	**S**	6a. brown	2·75	2·00
74	**S**	8a. blue	2·20	1·60
115	**S**	9a. brown	2·75	2·00
75	**S**	10a. blue	2·20	1·60
116	**S**	10a. brown	2·75	2·00
76	**S**	12a. pink	6·00	5·25
117	**S**	12a. blue	15·00	12·50
118	**S**	13a. mauve	4·00	2·30
119	**S**	15a. lilac	6·75	4·00
78	**S**	16a. blue on blue	6·00	5·25
79	**S**	20a. brown on yellow	6·00	5·25
120	**S**	22a. brown on pink	6·75	5·00
80	**S**	24a. brown on buff	6·00	5·25
81	**S**	31a. purple on pink	6·00	5·25
121	**S**	31a. brown on cream	6·75	5·00
82	**S**	47a. blue on pink	11·50	8·25
122	**S**	47a. purple on pink	7·00	5·00
83	**S**	78a. black on blue	16·00	10·50
123	**S**	78a. blue on yellow	15·00	10·50

1899. Nos. 78 and 81 surch PROVISORIO and value in figures and bars.

84		10 on 16a. blue on blue	4·25	3·75
85		20 on 31a. purple on pink	4·25	3·75

1902. Surch.

88	**R**	5a. on 5r. orange	2·20	1·60
86	**Q**	5a. on 25r. mauve	3·75	2·10
89	**R**	5a. on 25r. green	2·20	1·60
90	**R**	5a. on 50r. blue	2·40	2·10
87	**Q**	5a. on 200r. lilac	5·75	3·50
95	**V**	6a. on 2½r. brown	1·40	1·20
92	**Q**	6a. on 10r. green	£250	£190
94	**R**	6a. on 20r. lilac	2·40	2·10
93	**Q**	6a. on 300r. orange	5·50	5·00
100	**R**	9a. on 15r. brown	2·40	2·10
98	**Q**	9a. on 40r. brown	6·75	5·00
101	**R**	9a. on 75r. pink	2·40	2·10
99	**Q**	9a. on 100r. brown	6·75	5·00
124	**S**	10a. on 12a. blue	4·25	3·50
104	**R**	15a. on 10r. mauve	4·00	3·00
102	**Q**	15a. on 20r. red	6·75	5·00
103	**Q**	15a. on 50r. blue	£200	£170
105	**R**	15a. on 100r. brn on buff	4·00	3·00
106	**R**	15a. on 300r. blue on brn	4·00	3·00
107	**Q**	22a. on 80r. grey	13·50	10·00
108	**R**	22a. on 80r. green	6·75	5·50
109	**R**	22a. on 200r. blue on blue	6·75	5·50

1902. Nos. 72 and 76 optd PROVISORIO.

110		3a. lilac	3·00	2·10
111		12a. pink	7·25	5·50

1911. Nos. 68, etc, optd REPUBLICA.

125		½a. grey	75	60
126		1a. red	75	60
127		2a. green	75	60
128		3a. green	75	60
129		5a. red	1·40	75
130		6a. brown	1·40	75
131		9a. brown	1·40	75
132		10a. brown	2·20	1·70
133		13a. purple	2·20	1·70
134		15a. lilac	2·20	1·70
135		22a. brown on pink	2·20	1·70
136		31a. brown on cream	2·20	1·70
163		31a. purple on pink	4·50	3·25
137		47a. purple on pink	4·50	3·50
165		47a. blue on pink	7·00	5·50
167		78a. blue on yelow	9·00	7·75
168		78a. black on blue	9·00	5·75

1911. No. 112 and provisional stamps of 1902 optd Republica.

139		3a. green	5·75	4·00
140	**R**	5a. on 5r. orange	2·20	1·90
141	**R**	5a. on 25r. green	2·20	1·90
142	**R**	5a. on 50r. blue	5·00	4·00
144	**V**	6a. on 2½r. brown	4·50	2·50
146	**R**	6a. on 20r. lilac	2·50	1·90
147	**R**	9a. on 15r. brown	2·50	1·90
148	**S**	10a. on 12a. blue	2·50	1·90
149	**R**	15a. on 100r. brown on buff	3·00	2·75
150	**R**	22a. on 80r. green	5·75	3·25
151	**R**	22a. on 200r. blue on blue	5·75	3·25

1913. Provisional stamps of 1902 optd REPUBLICA.

192	**S**	3a. lilac (No. 110)	1·10	80
194	**R**	5a. on 5r. orange	1·10	75
195	**R**	5a. on 25r. green	1·10	75
196	**R**	5a. on 50r. blue	1·10	75
200	**V**	6a. on 2½r. brown	1·10	75
201	**R**	6a. on 20r. lilac	1·10	75
202	**R**	9a. on 15r. brown	1·10	75
203	**R**	9a. on 75r. pink	1·30	75
193	**S**	10a. on 10a. blue	1·10	80
204	**R**	15a. on 10r. mauve	1·30	75
205	**R**	15a. on 100r. brown on buff	1·40	75
206	**R**	15a. on 300r. blue on brn	1·40	75
207	**R**	22a. on 80r. green	3·75	2·30
208	**R**	22a. on 200r. blue on blue	5·75	4·00

1913. Vasco da Gama stamps of Timor optd REPUBLICA or surch also.

169		½a. green	85	65
170		1a. red	85	65
171		2a. purple	95	75
172		4a. green	95	75
173		8a. blue	2·00	1·30
174		10a. on 12a. brown	3·50	2·75
175		16a. brown	2·50	2·00
176		24a. brown	4·00	3·25

1914. "Ceres" key-type inscr "TIMOR". Name and value in black.

211	**U**	½a. green	1·40	1·30
212	**U**	1a. black	1·20	1·10
213	**U**	1½a. green	1·40	1·30
214	**U**	2a. green	3·75	2·75
180	**U**	3a. brown	1·40	1·00
181	**U**	4a. red	1·40	1·00
182	**U**	6a. violet	1·70	1·00
216	**U**	7a. green	2·00	1·20
217	**U**	7½a. blue	2·00	1·20
218	**U**	9a. blue	2·00	1·20
183	**U**	10a. blue	1·70	1·00
219	**U**	11a. grey	3·00	2·50
184	**U**	12a. brown	2·50	1·70
221	**U**	15a. mauve	10·00	5·75
185	**U**	16a. grey	2·50	1·70
222	**U**	18a. blue	10·00	5·75
223	**U**	19a. green	10·00	5·75
186	**U**	20a. red	24·00	6·75
224	**U**	36a. turquoise	10·00	5·75
187	**U**	40a. purple	13·50	6·75
225	**U**	54a. brown	10·00	5·75
188	**U**	58a. brown on green	13·50	6·25
226	**U**	72a. red	20·00	11·50
189	**U**	76a. brown on pink	13·50	10·00
190	**U**	1p. orange on orange	22·00	15·00
191	**U**	3p. green on blue	50·00	26·00
227	**U**	5p. red	80·00	37·00

1920. No. 196 surch ½ Avo P. P. n.°68 19-3-1920 and bars.

229	**R**	½a. on 5a. on 50r. blue	26·00	25·00

1932. Nos. 226 and 221 surch with new value and bars.

230	**U**	6a. on 72a. red	2·00	1·50
231	**U**	12a. on 15a. mauve	2·00	1·50

25a "Portugal" and Galeasse

1935

232	**25a**	½a. brown	45	30
233	**25a**	1a. brown	45	30
234	**25a**	2a. green	45	30
235	**25a**	3a. mauve	45	30
236	**25a**	4a. black	80	50
237	**25a**	5a. grey	80	50
238	**25a**	6a. brown	80	50
239	**25a**	7a. red	80	50
240	**25a**	8a. turquoise	1·30	70
241	**25a**	10a. red	1·30	70
242	**25a**	12a. blue	1·30	70
243	**25a**	14a. green	1·30	70
244	**25a**	15a. purple	1·30	70
245	**25a**	20a. orange	1·30	70
246	**25a**	30a. green	1·60	70
247	**25a**	40a. violet	5·25	2·50
248	**25a**	50a. brown	5·25	2·50
249	**25a**	1p. blue	12·50	7·50
250	**25a**	2p. brown	32·00	11·00
251	**25a**	3p. green	46·00	15·00
252	**25a**	5p. mauve	60·00	31·00

26a Vasco da Gama

26b Airplane over globe

1938

253	**26a**	1a. green (postage)	45	40
254	**26a**	2a. brown	45	40
255	**26a**	3a. violet	45	40
256	**26a**	4a. green	55	40
257	-	5a. red	55	45
258	-	6a. grey	55	45
259	-	8a. purple	55	45
260	-	10a. mauve	55	45
261	-	12a. red	80	55
262	-	15a. orange	1·30	90
263	-	20a. blue	1·30	90
264	-	40a. black	2·00	1·20
265	-	50a. brown	3·00	1·80
266	-	1p. red	10·00	5·75
267	-	2p. olive	27·00	6·75
268	-	3p. blue	30·00	14·50
269	-	5p. brown	60·00	30·00
270	**26b**	1a. red (air)	1·10	1·00
271	**26b**	2a. violet	1·20	80
272	**26b**	3a. orange	1·20	80
273	**26b**	5a. blue	1·30	1·10
274	**26b**	10a. red	1·60	1·30
275	**26b**	20a. green	4·00	1·80
276	**26b**	50a. brown	8·00	5·50
277	**26b**	70a. red	9·50	7·00
278	**26b**	1p. mauve	19·00	10·00

DESIGNS—POSTAGE: 5a. to 8a. Mousinho de Albuquerque; 10a. to 15a. Prince Henry the Navigator; 20a. to 50a. Dam; 1p. to 5p. Afonso de Albuquerque.

1946. Stamps as above but inscr "MOCAMBIQUE" surch TIMOR and new value.

279	**26a**	1a. on 15c. purple (post)	7·25	5·25
280	-	4a. on 35c. green	7·25	5·25
281	-	8a. on 50c. mauve	7·25	5·25
282	-	10a. on 70c. violet	7·25	5·25
283	-	12a. on 1e. red	7·25	5·25
284	-	20a. on 1e.75 blue	7·25	5·25
285	**26b**	8a. on 50c. orange (air)	7·75	5·75
286	**26b**	12a. on 1e. blue	7·75	5·75
287	**26b**	40a. on 3e. green	7·75	5·75
288	**26b**	50a. on 5e. brown	7·75	5·75
289	**26b**	1p. on 10e. mauve	7·75	5·75

1947. Nos. 253/64 and 270/78 optd LIBERTACAO.

290	**26a**	1a. green (postage)	21·00	11·50
291	**26a**	2a. brown	45·00	24·00
292	**26a**	3a. violet	19·00	7·25
293	**26a**	4a. green	19·00	7·25
294	-	5a. red	8·25	2·75
295	-	8a. purple	2·10	90
296	-	10a. mauve	7·75	3·25
297	-	12a. red	7·75	3·25
298	-	15a. orange	7·75	3·25
299	-	20a. blue	£100	50·00
300	-	40a. black	22·00	13·50
301	**26b**	1a. red (air)	32·00	8·00
302	**26b**	2a. violet	32·00	8·00
303	**26b**	3a. orange	32·00	8·00
304	**26b**	5a. blue	32·00	8·00
305	**26b**	10a. red	7·50	2·75
306	**26b**	20a. green	7·50	2·75
307	**26b**	50a. brown	7·50	2·75
308	**26b**	70a. red	19·00	8·00
309	**26b**	1p. mauve	13·50	2·75

30 Girl with Gong

1948

310	-	1a. brown and turquoise	1·30	60
311	**30**	3a. brown and grey	2·75	1·20
312	-	4a. green and mauve	3·75	2·75
313	-	8a. grey and red	2·10	70
314	-	10a. green and brown	2·10	70
315	-	20a. ultramarine and blue	2·10	1·20
316	-	1p. blue and orange	39·00	9·00
317	-	3p. brown and violet	42·00	15·00
MS317a		130×99 mm. Nos. 310/17 (sold at 5p.)	£150	£120

DESIGNS: 1a. Native woman; 4a. Girl with baskets; 8a. Chief of Aleixo de Ainaro; 10a. Timor chief; 20a. Warrior and horse; 1, 3p. Tribal chieftains.

1948. Honouring the Statue of Our Lady of Fatima. As T 33 of Portuguese Guinea.

318		8a. grey	12·50	11·50

1949. 75th Anniv of U.P.U. As T 34 of Portuguese Guinea.

319		16a. brown	30·00	16·00

31 Pottery-making

1950

320	**31**	20a. blue	1·40	1·30
321	-	50a. brown (Young girl)	4·25	1·70

1950. Holy Year. As Nos. 425/6 of Macao.

322		40a. green	3·00	1·90
323		70a. brown	4·75	2·75

32 "Belamcanda chinensis"

1950

324	32	1a. red, green and grey	1·00	60
325	-	3a. yellow, green and brown	4·50	3·25
326	-	10a. pink, green and blue	5·25	3·50
327	-	16a. multicoloured	10·00	4·75
328	-	20a. yellow, green and turquoise	4·50	3·25
329	-	30a. yellow, green and blue	5·25	3·50
330	-	70a. multicoloured	6·75	4·00
331	-	1p. red, yellow and green	11·50	7·00
332	-	2p. green, yellow and red	17·00	12·00
333	-	5p. pink, green and black	27·00	22·00

FLOWERS: 3a. "Caesalpinia pulcherrima"; 10a. "Calotropis gigantea"; 16a. "Delonix regia"; 20a. "Plumeria rubra"; 30a. "Allamanda cathartica"; 70a. "Haemanthus multiflorus"; 1p. "Bauhinia"; 2p. "Eurycles amboiniensis"; 5p. "Crinum longiflorum".

1951. Termination of Holy Year. As T 36 of Portuguese Guinea.

334		86a. blue and turquoise	3·25	2·50

1952. 1st Tropical Medicine Congress, Lisbon. As T 37 of Portuguese Guinea.

335		10a. brown and green	1·70	1·30

DESIGN: Nurse weighing baby.

1952. 400th Death Anniv of St. Francis Xavier. Designs as No. 452/4 of Macao.

336		1a. black and grey	35	20
337		16a. brown and buff	1·60	75
338		1p. red and grey	6·00	2·50

34 Statue of The Virgin

1953. Missionary Art Exhibition.

339	34	3a. brown and light brown	35	20
340	34	16a. brown and stone	1·50	95
341	34	50a. blue and brown	3·00	2·20

1954. Portuguese Stamp Centenary. As T 41 of Portuguese Guinea.

342		10a. multicoloured	2·10	1·70

1954. 400th Anniv of Sao Paulo. As T 42 of Portuguese Guinea.

343		16a. multicoloured	1·50	1·00

35 Map of Timor

1956

344	35	1a. multicoloured	30	15
345	35	3a. multicoloured	30	15
346	35	8a. multicoloured	65	45
347	35	24a. multicoloured	70	45
348	35	32a. multicoloured	85	50
349	35	40a. multicoloured	1·30	65
350	35	1p. multicoloured	4·00	85
351	35	3p. multicoloured	10·00	5·00

1958. 6th International Congress of Tropical Medicine. As T 45 of Portuguese Guinea.

352		32a. multicoloured	5·25	3·75

DESIGN: 32a. "Calophyllum inophyllum" (plant).

1958. Brussels International Exhibition. As T 44 of Portuguese Guinea.

353		40a. multicoloured	1·00	55

1960. New currency. Nos. 344/51 surch thus: $05 and bars.

354		5c. on 1a. multicoloured	30	15
355		10c. on 3a. multicoloured	30	15
356		20c. on 8a. multicoloured	30	15
357		30c. on 24a. multicoloured	30	15
358		50c. on 32s. multicoloured	30	15
359		1e. on 40a. multicoloured	40	35
360		2e. on 40a. multicoloured	65	40
361		5e. on 1p. multicoloured	1·30	90
362		10e. on 3p. multicoloured	4·25	2·00
363		15e. on 3p. multicoloured	4·25	2·75

1960. 500th Death Anniv of Prince Henry the Navigator. As T 47 of Portuguese Guinea. Multicoloured.

364		4e.50 Prince Henry's motto (horiz)	1·00	60

38 Elephant Jar

1962. Timor Art. Multicoloured.

365		5c. Type **38**	30	15
366		10c. House on stilts	30	15
367		20c. Idol	40	25
368		30c. Rosary	60	45
369		50c. Model of outrigger canoe (horiz)	80	50
370		1e. Casket	1·00	50
371		2e.50 Archer	1·10	50
372		4e. Elephant	1·50	50
373		5e. Native climbing palm tree	2·10	50
374		10e. Statuette of woman	5·00	1·50
375		20e. Model of cockfight (horiz)	12·50	3·75
376		50e. House, bird and cat	14·50	4·50

1962. Sports. As T 49 of Portuguese Guinea. Multicoloured.

377		50c. Game shooting	40	15
378		1e. Horse-riding	1·40	45
379		1e.50 Swimming	1·30	60
380		2e. Athletes	1·50	70
381		2e.50 Football	1·80	95
382		15e. Big-game hunting	3·50	2·20

1962. Malaria Eradication. Mosquito design as T 50 of Portuguese Guinea. Multicoloured.

383		2e.50 "Anopheles sundaicus"	1·80	1·00

1964. Centenary of National Overseas Bank. As T 53 of Portuguese Guinea, but portrait of M. P. Chagas.

384		2e.50 multicoloured	1·20	1·00

1965. I.T.U. Centenary. As T 54 of Portuguese Guinea.

385		1e.50 multicoloured	1·80	1·10

1966. 40th Anniv of National Revolution. As T 56 of Portuguese Guinea, but showing different buildings. Multicoloured.

386		4e.50 Dr V. Machado's College and Health Centre, Dili	1·50	1·00

1967. Centenary of Military Naval Assn. As T 57 of Portuguese Guinea. Multicoloured.

387		10c. Gago Coutinho and gunboat "Patria"	40	30
388		4e.50 Sacadura Cabral and Fairey IIID seaplane "Lusitania"	2·75	1·50

39 Sepoy Officer, 1792

1967. Portuguese Military Uniforms. Mult.

389		35c. Type **39**	25	20
390		1e. Infantry officer, 1815	2·30	60
391		1e.50 Infantryman 1879	40	35
392		2e. Infantryman, 1890	40	35
393		2e.50 Infantry officer, 1903	60	35
394		3e. Sapper, 1918	1·00	55
395		4e.50 Commando, 1964	1·70	55
396		10e. Parachutist, 1964	2·40	1·30

1967. 50th Anniv of Fatima Apparitions. As T 58 of Portuguese Guinea.

397		3e. Virgin of the Pilgrims	80	40

1968. 500th Birth Anniv of Pedro Cabral (explorer). As T 64 of Portuguese Guinea. Mult.

398		4e.50 Lopo Homen-Reineis' map, 1519 (horiz)	1·50	80

1969. Birth Centenary of Admiral Gago Coutinho. As T 66 of Portuguese Guinea. Mult.

399		4e.50 Frigate "Almirante Gago Coutinho" (horiz)	1·80	1·20

40 Pictorial Map of 1834, and Arms

1969. Bicentenary of Dili (capital of Timor).

400	40	1e. multicoloured	70	50

1969. 500th Anniv of Vasco da Gama (explorer). As T 67 of Portuguese Guinea. Mult.

401		5e. Convert Medallion	70	50

1969. Centenary of Overseas Administrative Reforms. As T 68 of Portuguese Guinea.

402		5e. multicoloured	80	50

1969. 500th Birth Anniv of King Manoel I. As T 69 of Portuguese Guinea. Multicoloured.

403		4e. Emblem of Manoel I in Jeronimos Monastery	60	40

41 Map, Sir Ross Smith, and Arms of Britain, Timor and Australia

1969. 50th Anniv of 1st England–Australia Flight.

404	41	2e. multicoloured	90	70

1970. Birth Centenary of Marshal Carmona. As T 71 of Portuguese Guinea. Multicoloured.

414		1e. Portrait in civilian dress	50	30

1972. 400th Anniv of Camoens' "The Lusiads" (epic poem). As T 73 of Portuguese Guinea. Multicoloured.

415		1e. Missionaries, natives and galleon	60	40

1972. Olympic Games, Munich. As T 74 of Portuguese Guinea. Multicoloured.

416		4e.50 Football	80	50

1972. 50th Anniv of 1st Flight from Lisbon to Rio de Janeiro. As T 75 of Portuguese Guinea. Multicoloured.

417		1e. Aviators Gago Coutinho and Sacadura Cabral in Fairey IIID seaplane	80	70

1973. W.M.O. Centenary. As T 76 of Portuguese Guinea.

418		20e. multicoloured	2·75	2·10

CHARITY TAX STAMPS

The notes under this heading in Portugal also apply here.

1919. No. 211 surch 2 AVOS TAXA DA GUERRA. With or without gum.

C228	U	2a. on ½a. green	8·50	3·75

1919. No. 196 surch 2 TAXA DE GUERRA and bars.

C230	R	2 on 5a. on 50r. blue	75·00	60·00

1925. Marquis de Pombal Commem. As Nos. 666/8 of Portugal, but inscr "TIMOR".

C231	C73	2a. red	70	50
C232	-	2a. red	70	50
C233	C 75	2a. red	70	50

1934. Educational Tax. Fiscal stamps as Type C 1 of Portuguese Colonies, with values in black, optd Instrucao D. L. n.°7 de 3-2-1934 or surch also. With or without gum.

C234		2a. green	4·75	3·25
C235		5a. green	7·25	3·75
C236		7a. on ½a. pink	7·75	4·50

1936. Fiscal stamps as Type C 1 of Portuguese Colonies, with value in black, optd Assistencia D. L. n.°72. With or without gum.

C253		10a. pink	45	40
C254		10a. green	45	40

C29

1948. No gum.

C310	C29	10a. blue	3·75	1·90
C311	C29	20a. green	4·75	3·25

The 20a. has a different emblem.

1960. Similar design. New currency. No gum.

C364		70c. blue	1·40	1·30
C400		1e.30 green	2·75	2·50

C42 Woman and Star

1969

C405	C42	30c. blue and light blue	55	50
C406	C42	50c. purple and orange	55	50
C407	C42	1e. brown and yellow	55	50

1970. Nos. C364 and C400 surch D. L. n.° 776 and value.

C408		30c. on 70c. blue	13·50	13·00
C409		30c. on 1e.30 green	13·50	13·00
C410		50c. on 70c. blue	31·00	28·00
C411		50c. on 1e.30 green	13·50	13·00
C412		1e. on 70c. blue	18·00	15·00
C413		1e. on 1e.30 green	13·50	13·00

NEWSPAPER STAMPS

1892. "Embossed" key-type inscr "PROVINCIA DE MACAU" surch JORNAES TIMOR 2½ 2½. No gum.

N31	Q	2½ on 20r. red	2·75	1·90
N32	Q	2½ on 40r. brown	2·75	1·90
N33	Q	2½ on 80r. grey	2·75	1·90

1893. "Newspaper" key-type inscr "TIMOR".

N36	V	2½r. brown	1·30	1·00

1894. No. N36 surch ½ avo PROVISORIO and Chinese characters.

N58		½a. on 2½r. brown	90	80

POSTAGE DUE STAMPS

1904. "Due" key-type inscr "TIMOR". Name and value in black. With or without gum (1, 2a.), no gum (others).

D124	W	1a. green	75	65
D125	W	2a. grey	75	65
D126	W	5a. brown	1·70	1·30
D127	W	6a. orange	1·70	1·30
D128	W	10a. brown	2·20	1·30
D129	W	15a. brown	3·75	3·00
D130	W	24a. blue	10·50	6·25
D131	W	40a. red	11·00	6·50
D132	W	50a. orange	14·50	7·00
D133	W	1p. lilac	31·00	17·00

1911. "Due" key-type of Timor optd REPUBLICA.

D139		1a. green	40	35
D140		2a. grey	40	35
D141		5a. brown	65	60
D142		6a. orange	95	75
D143		10a. brown	1·50	1·00
D144		15a. brown	1·90	1·20
D145		24a. blue	3·25	2·30
D146		40a. red	4·25	3·00
D147		50a. orange	5·75	3·25
D178		1p. lilac	14·50	7·00

1925. Marquis de Pombal tax stamps. As Nos. C231/3 of Timor, optd MULTA.

D231	C73	4a. red	70	55
D232	-	4a. red	70	55
D233	C 75	4a. red	70	55

1952. As Type D 70 of Macao, but inscr "TIMOR PORTUGUES". Numerals in red; name in black.

D336		1a. sepia and brown	25	20
D337		3a. brown and orange	25	20
D338		5a. green and turquoise	25	20
D339		10a. green and light green	30	20
D340		30a. violet and light violet	30	20
D341		1p. red and orange	1·30	75

For subsequent issues see **EAST TIMOR**.

Pt. 1

PRINCE EDWARD ISLAND

An island off the East coast of Canada, now a province of that Dominion, whose stamps it uses.

1861. 12 pence = 1 shilling.
1872. 100 cents = 1 dollar.

1

1861. Queen's portrait in various frames. Values in pence.

9	1	1d. orange	48·00	65·00
28	1	2d. red	9·00	15·00
30	1	3d. blue	11·00	19·00
31	1	4d. black	5·50	35·00
18	1	6d. green	£140	£120
20	1	9d. mauve	£100	95·00

7

1870

32	7	4½d. (3d. stg.) brown	65·00	75·00

8

1872. Queen's portrait in various frames. Values in cents.

44	8	1c. orange	9·00	27·00
38	8	2c. blue	26·00	60·00
37	8	3c. red	27·00	38·00
40	8	4c. green	10·00	26·00
41	8	6c. black	6·50	27·00
42	8	12c. mauve	8·00	55·00

Pt. 7

PRUSSIA

Formerly a kingdom in the N. of Germany. In 1867 it became part of the North German Confederation.

1850. 12 pfennig = 1 silbergroschen;
30 silbergroschen = 1 thaler.
1867. 60 kreuzer = 1 gulden.

1 Friedrich Wilhelm IV

1850. Imperf.

14	1	4pf. green	95·00	48·00
4	1	6pf. red	£120	70·00
22	1	½sgr. (=6pf.) red	£250	£200
5	1	1sgr. black on pink	£110	16·00
16	1	1sgr. pink	42·00	5·25
6	1	2sgr. black on blue	£150	21·00
18	1	2sgr. blue	£150	23·00
8	1	3sgr. black on yellow	£150	21·00
21	1	3sgr. yellow	£130	21·00

3

4

1861. Roul.

24	3	3pf. lilac	36·00	60·00
26	3	4pf. green	16·00	16·00
28	3	6pf. orange	16·00	19·00
31	4	1sgr. pink	4·25	2·10
35	4	2sgr. blue	16·00	2·10
36	4	3sgr. yellow	11·50	2·75

5

1866. Printed in reverse on back of specially treated transparent paper. Roul.

38	5	10sgr. pink	£130	£140
39	-	30sgr. blue	£150	£300

The 30 sgr. has the value in a square.

7

1867. Roul.

40	7	1k. green	32·00	60·00
42	7	2k. orange	55·00	£130
43	7	3k. pink	26·00	37·00
45	7	6k. blue	26·00	60·00
46	7	9k. bistre	32·00	65·00

Pt. 9, Pt. 22

PUERTO RICO

A West Indian island ceded by Spain to the United States after the war of 1898. Until 1873 stamps of Cuba were in use. Now uses stamps of the U.S.A.

1873. 100 centimos = 1 peseta.
1881. 1000 milesimas = 100 centavos = 1 peso.
1898. 100 cents = 1 dollar.

A. SPANISH OCCUPATION

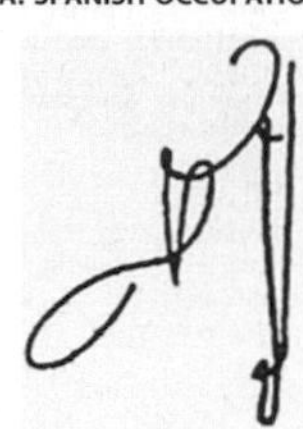

(2)

1873. Nos. 53/5 of Cuba optd with T 2.

1	25c. de p. lilac	55·00	1·60
3	50c. de p. brown	£160	7·75
4	1p. brown	£350	32·00

1874. No. 57 of Cuba with opt similar to T 2 (two separate characters).

5	25c. de p. blue	55·00	3·50

1875. Nos. 61/3 of Cuba with opt similar to T 2 (two separate characters).

6	25c. de p. blue	35·00	4·25
7	50c. de p. green	50·00	5·25
8	1p. brown	£190	28·00

1876. Nos. 65a and 67 of Cuba with opt similar to T 2 (two separate characters).

9	25c. de p. lilac	5·00	3·25
10	50c. de p. blue	12·50	5·25
11	1p. black	70·00	23·00

1876. Nos. 65a and 67 of Cuba with opt as last, but characters joined.

12	25c. de p. lilac	50·00	2·10
13	1p. black	£110	30·00

1877. As T 9 of Philippines, but inscr "PTO-RICO 1877".

14	5c. brown	9·75	4·00
15	10c. red	33·00	4·50
16	15c. green	49·00	22·00
17	25c. blue	19·00	3·25
18	50c. bistre	33·00	7·75

1878. As T 9 of Philippines, but inscr "PTO-RICO 1878".

19	5c. grey	19·00	19·00
20	10c. brown	£300	£120
21	25c. green	2·50	1·40
22	50c. blue	7·50	3·00
23a	1p. bistre	16·00	7·25

1879. As T 9 of Philippines, but inscr "PTO-RICO 1879".

24	5c. red	18·00	9·50
25	10c. brown	18·00	9·50
26	15c. grey	18·00	9·50
27	25c. blue	6·25	2·75
28	50c. green	18·00	9·50
29	1p. lilac	85·00	42·00

1880. "Alfonso XII" key-type inscr "PUERTO-RICO 1880".

30	X	¼c. green	34·00	27·00
31	X	½c. red	8·50	3·50
32	X	1c. purple	16·00	15·00
33	X	2c. grey	8·50	6·25
34	X	3c. buff	8·50	6·25
35	X	4c. black	8·50	6·25
36	X	5c. green	4·00	2·75
37	X	10c. red	4·75	3·00
38	X	15c. brown	8·50	4·75
39	X	25c. lilac	4·00	2·20
40	X	40c. grey	17·00	2·20
41	X	50c. brown	36·00	23·00
42	X	1p. bistre	£130	29·00

1881. "Alfonso XIII" key-type inscr "PUERTO-RICO 1881".

43	½m. red	30	20
45	1m. violet	30	20
46	2m. red	30	20
47	4m. green	30	20
48	6m. purple	30	20
49	8m. blue	30	20
50	1c. green	4·50	1·70
51	2c. red	5·75	4·75
52	3c. brown	13·50	8·00
53	5c. lilac	4·25	45
54	8c. brown	4·25	2·20
55	10c. grey	65·00	13·50
56	20c. bistre	70·00	25·00

1882. "Alfonso XII" key-type inscr "PUERTO-RICO".

57	½m. red	30	20
74	1m. red	25	20
75	1m. orange	25	20
59	2m. mauve	30	20
60	4m. purple	30	20
61	6m. brown	60	20
62	8m. green	60	20
63	1c. green	30	20
64	2c. red	1·80	20
65	3c. yellow	5·75	3·50
76	3c. brown	3·50	75
77	5c. lilac	18·00	2·50
67	8c. brown	5·25	20
68	10c. green	5·25	45
69	20c. grey	8·75	45
70	40c. blue	70·00	24·00
71	80c. bistre	95·00	35·00

1890. "Baby" key-type inscr "PUERTO-RICO".

80	Y	½m. black	25	20
95	Y	½m. grey	20	20
111	Y	½m. brown	20	20
124	Y	½m. purple	25	20
81	Y	1m. green	35	20
96	Y	1m. purple	20	20
112	Y	1m. blue	20	20
125	Y	1m. brown	25	20
82	Y	2m. red	25	20
97	Y	2m. purple	20	20
126	Y	2m. green	25	20
83	Y	4m. black	17·00	9·50
98	Y	4m. blue	20	20
114	Y	4m. brown	20	20
127	Y	4m. green	1·50	50
84	Y	6m. brown	60·00	25·00
99	Y	6m. red	20	20
85	Y	8m. bistre	44·00	37·00
100	Y	8m. green	20	20
86	Y	1c. brown	25	20
101	Y	1c. green	85	20
115	Y	1c. purple	11·50	65
128	Y	1c. red	95	20
87	Y	2c. purple	1·50	1·40
102	Y	2c. pink	1·40	20
116	Y	2c. lilac	4·25	65
129	Y	2c. brown	95	20
88	Y	3c. blue	11·50	1·70
103	Y	3c. orange	1·40	20
117	Y	3c. grey	11·50	65
131	Y	3c. brown	30	20
118	Y	4c. blue	3·00	65
132	Y	4c. brown	1·00	20
89	Y	5c. purple	18·00	65
104	Y	5c. green	1·40	20
133	Y	5c. blue	30	20
120	Y	6c. orange	70	20
134	Y	6c. lilac	30	20
90	Y	8c. blue	24·00	3·00
105	Y	8c. brown	20	20
121	Y	8c. purple	27·00	7·50
135	Y	8c. red	4·50	2·10
106	Y	10c. red	1·90	55
122	Y	20c. red	3·25	65
107	Y	20c. lilac	3·50	75
136	Y	20c. grey	11·00	2·10
93	Y	40c. orange	£250	85·00
108	Y	40c. blue	8·75	6·50
137	Y	40c. red	11·00	2·10
94	Y	80c. green	£700	£275
109	Y	80c. red	23·00	19·00
138	Y	80c. black	46·00	35·00

13 Landing of Columbus

1893. 400th Anniv of Discovery of America by Columbus.

110	13	3c. green	£300	70·00

1898. "Curly Head" key-type inscr "PTO RICO 1898 y 99".

139	Z	1m. brown	25	20
140	Z	2m. brown	25	20
141	Z	3m. brown	25	20
142	Z	4m. brown	3·25	80
143	Z	5m. brown	25	20
144	Z	1c. purple	25	20
145	Z	2c. green	25	20
146	Z	3c. brown	25	20
147	Z	4c. orange	3·25	1·50
148	Z	5c. pink	25	20
149	Z	6c. blue	25	20
150	Z	8c. brown	25	20
151	Z	10c. red	25	20
152	Z	15c. grey	25	20
153	Z	20c. purple	3·50	80
154	Z	40c. lilac	2·50	2·20
155	Z	60c. black	2·50	2·20
156	Z	80c. brown	10·00	8·25
157	Z	1p. green	25·00	18·00
158	Z	2p. blue	55·00	23·00

1898. "Baby" key-type inscr "PUERTO RICO" and optd Habilitado PARA 1898 y '99.

159	Y	½m. purple	23·00	13·50
160	Y	1m. brown	1·80	1·80
161	Y	2m. green	55	55
162	Y	4m. green	55	55
163	Y	1c. purple	4·50	4·50
164	Y	2c. brown	80	1·20
165	Y	3c. blue	50·00	22·00
166	Y	3c. brown	4·25	4·25
167	Y	4c. brown	1·00	1·00
168	Y	4c. blue	29·00	20·00
169	Y	5c. blue	1·00	1·00
170	Y	5c. green	13·50	11·00
172	Y	6c. lilac	1·00	65
173a	Y	8c. red	1·70	1·30
174	Y	20c. grey	1·70	1·70
175	Y	40c. red	4·25	4·25
176	Y	80c. black	50·00	32·00

WAR TAX STAMPS

1898. 1890 and 1898 stamps optd IMPUESTO DE GUERRA or surch also.

W177	1m. blue	3·50	2·30
W178	1m. brown	9·00	6·50
W179	2m. red	17·00	11·00
W180	2m. green	9·00	6·50
W181	4m. green	9·75	9·75
W182a	1c. brown	9·00	5·50
W183	1c. purple	15·00	14·00
W184	2c. purple	1·20	1·20
W185	2c. pink	55	35
W186	2c. lilac	55	35
W187	2c. brown	50	45
W192	2c. on 2m. red	55	35
W193c	2c. on 5c. green	3·50	2·20
W188	3c. orange	17·00	14·00
W194	3c. on 10c. red	3·00	2·20
W195	4c. on 20c. red	17·00	13·00
W189	5c. green	2·30	2·30
W196a	5c. on ½m. brown	3·75	3·75
W197	5c. on 1m. purple	35	35
W198	5c. on 1m. blue	9·00	6·50
W199 Z	5c. on 1m. brown	9·00	6·50
W200 Y	5c. on 5c. green	9·00	5·75
W191	8c. purple	26·00	22·00

B. UNITED STATES OCCUPATION

1899. 1894 stamps of United States (No. 267 etc) optd PORTO RICO.

202	1c. green	5·75	1·60
203	2c. red	5·00	1·40
204	5c. blue	11·50	2·75
205	8c. brown	34·00	20·00
206	10c. brown	23·00	6·75

1900. 1894 stamps of United States (No. 267 etc) optd PUERTO RICO.

210	1c. green	7·50	1·70
212	2c. red	6·25	2·30

POSTAGE DUE STAMPS

1899. Postage Due stamps of United States of 1894 optd PORTO RICO.

D207	D87	1c. red	26·00	6·25
D208	D87	2c. red	23·00	6·75
D209	D87	10c. red	£200	70·00

Pt. 1, Pt. 19

QATAR

An independent Arab Shaikhdom with British postal administration until 23 May 1963. The stamps of Muscat were formerly used at Doha and Urm Said. Later issues by the Qatar Post Department.

1966. 100 dirhams = 1 riyal.
1967. 100 naye paise = 1 rupee.

Stamps of Great Britain surcharged QATAR and value in Indian currency.

1957. Queen Elizabeth II and pictorials.

1	157	1n.p. on 5d. brown	10	10
2	154	3n.p. on ½d. orange	15	20
3	154	6n.p. on 1d. blue	15	20
4	154	9n.p. on 1½d. green	15	15
5	154	12n.p. on 2d. brown	20	3·25
6	155	15n.p. on 2½d. red	15	10
7	155	20n.p. on 3d. lilac	15	10

8	**155**	25n.p. on 4d. blue	40	2·25
9	**157**	40n.p. on 6d. purple	15	25
10	**158**	50n.p. on 9d. olive	40	2·50
11	**159**	75n.p. on 1s.3d. green	50	4·50
12	**159**	1r. on 1s.6d. blue	12·00	10
13	**166**	2r. on 2s.6d. brown	3·50	5·00
14	-	5r. on 5s. red	5·50	7·50
15	-	10r. on 10s. blue	5·50	16·00

1957. World Scout Jubilee Jamboree.

16	**170**	15n.p. on 2½d. red	35	35
17	**171**	25n.p. on 4d. blue	35	35
18	-	75n.p. on 1s.3d. green	40	40

8 Shaikh Ahmad bin All al Thani

9 Peregrine Falcon

11 Oil Derrick

1961

27	**8**	5n.p. red	15	15
28	**8**	15n.p. black	30	15
29	**8**	20n.p. purple	30	15
30	**8**	30n.p. green	35	30
31	**9**	40n.p. red	2·40	30
32	**9**	50n.p. brown	3·25	30
33	-	75n.p. blue	1·60	3·25
34	**11**	1r. red	3·50	35
35	**11**	2r. blue	3·50	2·25
36	-	5r. green	27·00	7·50
37	-	10r. black	60·00	13·00

DESIGNS—As Type **9**: 75n.p. Dhow. As Type **11**: 5r., 10r. Mosque.

1964. Olympic Games, Tokyo. Optd 1964, Olympic rings and Arabic inscr or surch also.

38	**9**	50n.p. brown	3·00	2·40
39	-	75n.p. blue (No. 33)	4·50	3·75
40	-	1r. on 10r. black (No. 37)	6·00	1·90
41	**11**	2r. blue	12·00	3·75
42	**11**	5r. green (No. 36)	31·00	9·75

1964. Pres. Kennedy Commem. Optd John F Kennedy 1917–1963 in English and Arabic or surch also.

43	**9**	50n.p. brown	3·00	1·30
44	-	75n.p. blue (No. 33)	4·50	1·70
45	-	1r. on 10r. black (No. 37)	6·00	2·10
46	**11**	2r. blue	13·00	6·00
47	-	5r. green (No. 36)	32·00	12·00

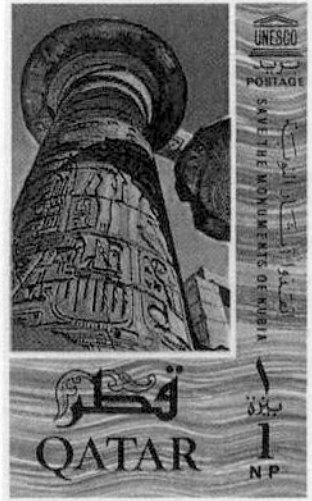

15 Colonnade, Temple of Isis

1965. Nubian Monuments Preservation. Mult.

48	1n.p. Type **15**	2·10	55
49	2n.p. Temple of Isis, Philac	2·40	65
50	3n.p. Trajan's Kiosk, Philac	2·75	70
51	1r. As 3n.p.	4·50	2·00
52	1r.50 As 2n.p.	9·00	2·75
53	2r. Type **15**	2·75	2·50

16 Scouts on Parade

1965. Qatar Scouts.

54	-	1n.p. brown and green	55	45
55	-	2n.p. blue and brown	55	45
56	-	3n.p. blue and green	55	45
57	-	4n.p. brown and blue	55	45
58	-	5n.p. blue and turquoise	55	45
59	**16**	30n.p. multicoloured	5·25	3·50
60	**16**	40n.p. multicoloured	8·00	5·25
61	**16**	1r. multicoloured	16·00	10·50
MS61a		108×76 mm. Nos. 59/61	32·00	19·00

DESIGNS—TRIANGULAR (60×30 mm): 1, 4n.p. Qatar Scout badge; 2, 3, 5n.p. Ruler, badge, palms and camp.

17 "Telstar" and Eiffel Tower

1965. I.T.U. Centenary.

62	**17**	1n.p. brown and blue	55	15
63	-	2n.p. brown and blue	55	15
64	-	3n.p. violet and green	55	15
65	-	4n.p. blue and brown	55	15
66	**17**	5n.p. brown and violet	55	15
67	-	40n.p. black and red	6·50	1·50
68	-	50n.p. brown and green	10·00	1·80
69	-	1r. red and green	13·00	2·75
MS69a		89×89 mm. Nos. 68/9	32·00	13·00

DESIGNS: 2n.p., 1r. "Syncom 3" and pagoda; 3, 40n.p. "Relay" and radar scanner; 4, 50n.p. Post Office Tower (London), globe and satellites.

18 Jigsaw Triggerfish

1965. Fish of the Arabian Gulf. Multicoloured.

70	1n.p. Type **18**	45	30
71	2n.p. Harlequin sweetlips	45	30
72	3n.p. Saddle butterflyfish	45	30
73	4n.p. Thread-finned butterflyfish	45	30
74	5n.p. Masked unicornfish	45	30
75	15n.p. Paradise fish	45	30
76	20n.p. White-spotted surgeonfish	55	45
77	30n.p. Rio Grande cichlid	95	55
78	40n.p. Convict cichlid	1·30	95
79	50n.p. As 2n.p	1·90	1·30
80	75n.p. Type **18**	2·75	1·60
81	1r. As 30n.p.	4·00	1·90
82	2r. As 20n.p.	8·00	5·25
83	3r. As 15n.p.	15·00	6·50
84	4r. As 5n.p.	19·00	8·00
85	5r. As 4n.p.	28·00	9·00
86	10r. As 3n.p.	48·00	12·00

19 Basketball

1966. Pan-Arab Games, Cairo (1965).

87	**19**	1r. black, grey and red	4·25	2·10
88	-	1r. brown and green	4·25	2·10
89	-	1r. red and blue	4·25	2·10
90	-	1r. green and blue	4·25	2·10
91	-	1r. blue and brown	4·25	2·10

SPORTS: No. 88, Horse-jumping; No. 89, Running; No. 90, Football; No. 91, Weightlifting.

1966. Space Rendezvous. Nos. 62/9 optd with two space capsules and SPACE RENDEZVOUS 15th. DECEMBER 1965 in English and Arabic.

92	**17**	1n.p. brown and blue	95	10
93	-	2n.p. brown and blue	95	10
94	-	3n.p. violet and green	95	10
95	-	4n.p. blue and brown	95	10
96	**17**	5n.p. brown and violet	95	10
97	-	40n.p. black and red	6·75	45
98	-	50n.p. brown and green	7·00	55
99	-	1r. red and green	14·00	95
MS100		89×89 mm. Nos. 98/9	43·00	21·00

21 Shaikh Ahmed

1966. Gold and Silver Coinage. Circular designs embossed on gold (G) or silver (S) foil, backed with "Walsall Security Paper" inscr in English and Arabic. Imperf. (a) Diameter 42 mm.

101	**21**	1n.p. bistre and purple (S)	45	15
102	-	3n.p. black and orange (S)	45	15
103	**21**	4n.p. violet and red (G)	45	15
104	-	5n.p. green and mauve (G)	45	15

(b) Diameter 55 mm.

105	**21**	10n.p. brown and violet (S)	85	20
106	-	40n.p. red and blue (S)	2·10	55
107	**21**	70n.p. blue & ultram (G)	3·25	1·30
108	-	80n.p. mauve and green (G)	3·50	1·40

(c) Diameter 64 mm.

109	**21**	1r. mauve and black (S)	6·50	1·50
110	-	2r. green and purple (S)	12·00	3·25
111	**21**	5r. purple and orange (G)	27·00	7·00
112	-	10r. blue and red (G)	55·00	17·00

The 1, 4, 10, 70n.p. and 1 and 5r. each show the obverse side of the coins as Type **21**. The remainder show the reverse side of the coins (Shaikh's seal).

22 I.C.Y. and U.N. Emblem

1966. International Co-operation Year.

113	**22**	40n.p. brown, violet & bl	4·00	2·50
114	**A**	40n.p. violet, brn & turq	4·00	2·50
115	**B**	40n.p. blue, brown & vio	4·00	2·50
116	**C**	40n.p. turquoise, vio & bl	4·00	2·50
MS117		140×87½ mm. Nos. 113/16. Imperf	55·00	43·00

DESIGNS: A, Pres. Kennedy, I.C.Y. emblem and U.N. Headquarters; B, Dag Hammarskjold and U.N. General Assembly; C, Nehru and dove.

Nos. 113/16 were issued together in blocks of four, each sheet containing four blocks separated by gutter margins. Subsequently the sheets were reissued perf and imperf with the opt **U.N. 20TH ANNIVERSARY** on the stamps. The gutter margins were also printed in various designs, face values and overprints.

23 Pres. Kennedy and New York Skyline

1966. Pres. Kennedy Commemoration. Multicoloured.

118	10n.p. Type **23**	45	30
119	30n.p. Pres. Kennedy and Cape Kennedy	75	45
120	60n.p. Pres. Kennedy and Statue of Liberty	1·30	75
121	70n.p. Type **23**	1·60	1·20
122	80n.p. As 30n.p.	1·90	1·30
123	1r. As 60n.p.	2·75	1·90
MS124	105×70 mm. 50n.p. (As 60n.p.). Imperf	32·00	30·00

24 Horse-jumping

1966. Olympic Games Preparation (Mexico). Multicoloured.

125	1n.p. Type **24**	30	25
126	4n.p. Running	30	25
127	5n.p. Throwing the javelin	30	25
128	70n.p. Type **24**	2·40	1·30
129	80n.p. Running	2·50	1·40
130	90n.p. Throwing the javelin	2·75	1·90
MS131	105×70 mm. 50n.p. (As Type **24**)	32·00	27·00

25 J. A. Lovell and Capsule

1966. American Astronauts. Each design showing spacecraft and astronaut. Multicoloured.

132	5n.p. Type **25**	30	25
133	10n.p. T. P. Stafford	30	25
134	15n.p. A. B. Shepard	30	25
135	20n.p. J. H. Glenn	55	30
136	30n.p. M. Scott Carpenter	85	55
137	40n.p. W. M. Schirra	95	65
138	50n.p. V. I. Grissom	1·30	95
139	60n.p. L. G. Cooper	1·90	1·50
MS140	116×75 mm. **26** 50n.p. multicoloured. Imperf	43·00	34·00

Nos. 132/4 are diamond-shaped as Type **25**, the remainder are horiz designs (56×25 mm).

1966. Various stamps with currency names changed to dirhams and riyals by overprinting in English and Arabic. (i) Nos. 27/37 (Definitives).

141	**8**	5d. on 5n.p. red	10·50	7·00
142	**8**	15d. on 15n.p. black	10·50	7·00
143	**8**	20d. on 20n.p. purple	10·50	7·00
144	**8**	30d. on 30n.p. green	38·00	14·00
145	**9**	40d. on 40n.p. red	75·00	28·00
146	**9**	50d. on 50n.p. brown	85·00	33·00
147	-	75d. on 75n.p. blue	£120	39·00
148	**11**	1r. on 1r. red	£140	47·00
149	**11**	2r. on 2r. blue	£160	£110
150	-	5r. on 5r. green	£190	£140
151	-	10r. on 10r. black	£300	£225

(ii) Nos. 70/86 (Fish). Multicoloured.

152	1d. on 1n.p.	2·10	1·70
153	2d. on 2n.p.	2·10	1·70
154	3d. on 3n.p.	2·10	1·70
155	4d. on 4n.p.	2·10	1·70
156	5d. on 5n.p.	2·10	1·70
157	15d. on 15n.p.	2·40	1·70
158	20d. on 20n.p.	2·50	1·70
159	30d. on 30n.p.	2·75	1·70
160	40d. on 40n.p.	3·25	4·25
161	50d. on 50n.p.	4·25	6·50
162	75d. on 75n.p.	5·25	21·00
163	1r. on 1r.	49·00	34·00
164	2r. on 2r.	75·00	43·00
165	3r. on 3r.	85·00	55·00
166	4r. on 4r.	£140	75·00
167	5r. on 5r.	£150	95·00
168	10r. on 10r.	£190	13·00

27 National Library, Doha

1966. Education Day. Multicoloured.

169	2n.p. Type **27**	6·00	55
170	3n.p. School and playing field	6·00	55
171	5n.p. School and gardens	6·00	55
172	1r. Type **27**	14·00	4·25
173	2r. As 3n.p	24·00	9·75
174	3r. As 5n.p	32·00	14·00

28 Palace, Doha

1966. Currency expressed in naye paise and rupees. Multicoloured.

175	2n.p. Type **28**	45	25
176	3n.p. Gulf Street, Shahra Al-Khalij	45	25
177	10n.p. Doha airport	1·70	30
178	15n.p. Garden, Rayan	1·20	30
179	20n.p. Head Post Office, Doha	1·50	30
180	30n.p. Mosque Doha (vert)	2·50	45
181	40n.p. Shaikh Ahmad	4·75	65
182	50n.p. Type **28**	5·25	1·10
183	60n.p. As 3n.p.	8·50	1·60
184	70n.p. As 10n.p.	12·00	2·50
185	80n.p. As 15n.p.	12·50	2·75
186	90n.p. As 20n.p.	14·00	4·75
187	1r. As 30n.p. (vert)	15·00	5·00
188	2r. As 40n.p.	30·00	13·00

29 Hands holding Jules Rimet Trophy

1966. World Cup Football Championship, England.

189	**29**	60n.p. mult (postage)	1·70	1·30
190	-	70n.p. multicoloured	2·00	1·50
191	-	80n.p. multicoloured	2·75	1·90
192	-	90n.p. multicoloured	3·00	2·10
193	-	1n.p. blue (air)	20	20
194	-	2n.p. blue	30	20
195	-	3n.p. blue	45	30
196	-	4n.p. blue	55	45

MS197 Four sheets each 105×70 mm. Each sheet contains one design as Nos. 189/192 with face value of 25n.p. Imperf £110 55·00

DESIGNS: No. 190, Jules Rimet Trophy and "football" globe; No. 191, Footballers and globe; No. 192, Wembley stadium; Nos. 193/6, Jules Rimet Trophy.

30 A.P.U. Emblem

1967. Admission of Qatar to Arab Postal Union.

198	**30**	70d. brown and violet	3·75	1·90
199	**30**	80d. brown and blue	4·75	1·90

31 Astronauts on Moon

1967. U.S. "Apollo" Space Missions. Mult.

200	5d. Type **31**	20	10
201	10d. "Apollo" spacecraft	20	10
202	20d. Landing module on Moon	45	20
203	30d. Blast-off from Moon	85	45
204	40d. "Saturn 5" rocket	1·30	65
205	70d. Type **31**	2·75	1·70
206	80d. As 10d.	3·25	2·40
207	1r. As 20d.	3·50	2·75
208	1r.20 As 30d.	4·25	3·25
209	2r. As 40d.	5·25	4·25
MS210	100×70 mm. No. 209. Imperf	16·00	13·00

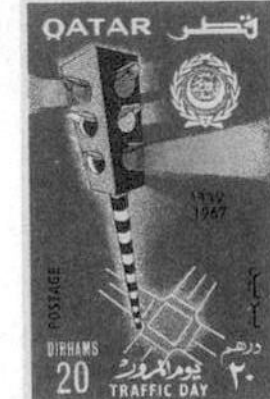

32 Traffic Lights

1967. Traffic Day.

211	**32**	20d. multicoloured	75	30
212	**32**	30d. multicoloured	1·40	65
213	**32**	50d. multicoloured	2·10	1·10
214	**32**	1r. multicoloured	4·25	2·30

33 Brownsea Island and Jamboree Camp, Idaho

1967. Diamond Jubilee of Scout Movement and World Scout Jamboree, Idaho. Multicoloured.

215	1d. Type **33**	45	10
216	2d. Lord Baden-Powell	45	10
217	3d. Pony-trekking	45	10
218	5d. Canoeing	75	15
219	15d. Swimming	2·10	55
220	75d. Rock-climbing	4·75	1·70
221	2r. World Jamboree emblem	13·00	6·00

34 Norman Ship (from Bayeux Tapestry)

1967. Famous Navigators' Ships. Multicoloured.

222	1d. Type **34**	55	10
223	2d. "Santa Maria" (Columbus)	65	10
224	3d. "Sao Gabriel" (Vasco da Gama)	95	10
225	75d. "Vitoria" (Magellan)	5·25	1·90
226	1r. "Golden Hind" (Drake)	7·50	2·75
227	2r. "Gipsy Moth IV" (Chichester)	12·00	3·75

35 Arab Scribe

1968. 10th Anniv of Qatar Postage Stamps. Multicoloured.

228	1d. Type **35**	55	10
229	2d. Pigeon post (vert)	65	15
230	3d. Mounted postman	75	20
231	60d. Rowing boat postman (vert)	4·25	1·80
232	1r.25 Camel postman	8·00	3·00
233	2r. Letter-writing and Qatar 1n.p. stamp of 1957	14·00	4·25

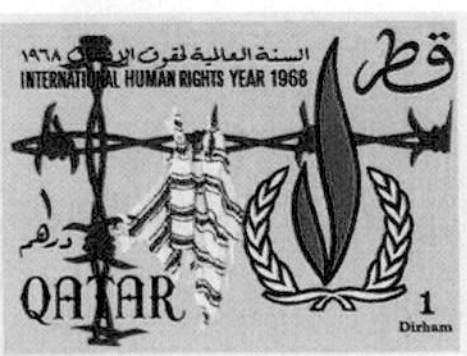

36 Human Rights Emblem and Barbed Wire

1968. Human Rights Year. Multicoloured designs embodying Human Rights emblem.

234	1d. Type **36**	45	15
235	2d. Arab refugees	45	15
236	3d. Scales of justice	65	20
237	60d. Opening doors	3·75	2·10
238	1r.25 Family (vert)	5·25	4·75
239	2r. Human figures	10·50	6·50

37 Shaikh Ahmad

38 Dhow

39 Shaikh Ahmad

1968

240	**37**	5d. green and blue	20	10
241	**37**	10d. brown and blue	55	10
242	**37**	20d. red and black	85	10
243	**37**	25d. green and purple	2·10	20
244	**38**	35d. green, blue and pink	3·50	20
245	-	40d. purple, blue & orange	4·75	30
246	-	60d. brown, blue and violet	6·00	75
247	-	70d. black, blue and green	6·50	95
248	-	1r. blue, yellow and green	8·00	1·20
249	-	1r.25 blue, pink and light blue	9·00	1·40
250	-	1r.50 green, blue & purple	10·50	1·80
251	**39**	2r. blue, brown and cinnamon	15·00	2·40
252	**39**	5r. purple, green and light green	27·00	4·75
253	**39**	10r. brown, ultram & blue	55·00	9·75

DESIGNS—As Type **38**: 40d. Water purification plant; 60d. Oil jetty; 70d. Qatar mosque; 1r. Palace Doha; 1r.25, Doha fort; 1r.50, Peregrine falcon.

41 Maternity Ward

1968. 20th Anniv of W.H.O. Multicoloured.

258	1d. Type **41**	65	10
259	2d. Operating theatre	65	10
260	3d. Dental surgery	65	10
261	60d. X-ray examination table	3·50	70
262	1r.25 Laboratory	8·50	1·90
263	2r. State Hospital Qatar	13·00	3·00

42 Throwing the Discus

1968. Olympic Games, Mexico. Multicoloured.

264	1d. Type **42**	55	25
265	2d. Olympic Flame and runner	55	25
266	3d. "68", rings and gymnast	85	30
267	60d. Weightlifting and Flame	4·00	1·70
268	1r.25 "Flame" in mosaic pattern (vert)	8·00	2·75
269	2r. "Cock" emblem	13·00	3·75

43 U.N. Emblem and Flags

1968. United Nations Day. Multicoloured.

270	1d. Type **43**	20	10
271	4d. Dove of Peace and world map	65	15
272	5d. U.N. Headquarters and flags	65	15
273	60d. Teacher and class	4·50	1·30
274	1r.50 Agricultural workers	7·50	2·00
275	2r. U. Thant and U.N. Assembly	8·50	2·30

44 Trawler "Ross Rayyan"

1969. Progress in Qatar. Multicoloured.

276	1d. Type **44**	20	10
277	4d. Primary school	20	10
278	5d. Doha International Airport	65	15
279	60d. Cement factory and road-making	3·50	95
280	1r.50 Power station and pylon	8·50	2·30
281	2r. Housing estate	12·00	2·75

45 Armoured Cars

1969. Qatar Security Forces. Multicoloured.

282	1d. Type **45**	65	10
283	2d. Traffic control	65	10
284	3d. Military helicopter	75	35
285	60d. Section of military band	4·25	1·50
286	1r.25 Field gun	8·00	2·00
287	2r. Mounted police	14·00	4·00

46 Tanker "Sivella" at Mooring

1969. Qatar's Oil Industry. Multicoloured.

288	1d. Type **46**	55	10
289	2d. Training school	55	10
290	3d. "Sea Shell" (oil rig) and "Shell Dolphin" (supply vessel)	85	25
291	60d. Storage tanks, Halul	3·75	1·40
292	1r.50 Topping plant	10·50	3·00
293	2r. Various tankers, 1890–1968	16·00	4·00

47 "Guest-house" and Dhow-building

1969. 10th Scout Jamboree, Qatar. Multicoloured.

294	1d. Type **47**	30	10
295	2d. Scouts at work	30	10
296	3d. Review and March Past	55	25
297	60d. Interior gateway	5·25	1·50
298	1r.25 Camp entrance	8·50	2·10
299	2r. Hoisting flag, and Shaikh Ahmad	12·00	3·00
MS300	128×110m. Nos. 294/7. Imperf	32·00	15·00

48 Neil Armstrong

1969. 1st Man on the Moon. Multicoloured.

301	1d. Type **48**	30	25
302	2d. Edward Aldrin	30	25
303	3d. Michael Collins	40	30
304	60d. Astronaut on Moon	3·00	1·20
305	1r.25 Take-off from Moon	6·00	3·00
306	2r. Splashdown (horiz)	12·00	4·75

49 Douglas DC-8 and Mail Van

1970. Admission to U.P.U. Multicoloured.

307	1d. Type **49**	30	30
308	2d. Liner "Oriental Empress"	30	30
309	3d. Loading mail-van	55	35
310	60d. G.P.O., Doha	3·25	1·50
311	1r.25 U.P.U. Building, Berne	6·50	2·30
312	2r. U.P.U. Monument, Berne	10·50	3·00

50 League Emblem, Flag and Map

1970. Silver Jubilee of Arab League.

313	**50**	35d. multicoloured	2·10	80
314	**50**	60d. multicoloured	3·75	1·40
315	**50**	1r.25 multicoloured	7·00	2·30
316	**50**	1r.50 multicoloured	9·00	4·00

51 Vickers VC-10 on Runway

1970. 1st Gulf Aviation Vickers VC-10 Flight, Doha–London. Multicoloured.

317	1d. Type **51**	30	25
318	2d. Peregrine falcon and VC-10	75	35
319	3d. Tail view of VC-10	75	35
320	60d. Gulf Aviation emblem on map	4·75	1·30
321	1r.25 VC-10 over Doha	9·75	2·00
322	2r. Tail assembly of VC-10	16·00	3·25

52 "Space Achievements"

1970. International Education Year.

323	**52**	35d. multicoloured	3·00	1·30
324	**52**	60d. multicoloured	6·00	2·40

53 Freesias

1970. Qatar Flowers. Multicoloured.

325	1d. Type **53**	30	15
326	2d. Azalieas	30	15
327	3d. Ixias	30	15
328	60d. Amaryllises	5·25	1·30
329	1r.25 Cinerarias	9·00	2·75
330	2r. Roses	12·00	4·00

54 Toyahama Fishermen with Giant "Fish"

1970. "EXPO 70" World Fair, Osaka. Multicoloured.

331	1d. Type **54**	30	10
332	2d. Expo emblem and map of Japan	40	15
333	3d. Fisherman on Shikoku beach	75	25
334	60d. Expo emblem and Mt. Fuji	4·00	1·30
335	1r.50 Gateway to Shinto Shrine	9·00	2·40
336	2r. Expo Tower and Mt. Fuji	13·00	4·00
MS336a	126×111 mm. Nos. 331/4. Imperf	32·00	15·00

Nos. 333, 334 and 336 are vert.

55 Globe, "25" and U.N. Emblem

1970. 25th Anniv of U.N.O. Multicoloured.

337	1d. Type **55**	55	25
338	2d. Flowers in gun-barrel	55	25
339	3d. Anniversary cake	95	35
340	35d. "The U.N. Agencies"	3·25	1·00
341	1r.50 "Trumpet fanfare"	7·50	2·40
342	2r. "World friendship"	9·75	4·00

56 Al Jahiz (philosopher) and Ancient Globe

1971. Famous Men of Islam. Multicoloured.

343	1d. Type **56**	55	35
344	2d. Saladin (soldier), palace and weapons	55	35
345	3d. Al Farabi (philosopher and musician), felucca and instruments	95	45
346	35d. Ibn Al Haithum (scientist), palace and emblems	4·25	95
347	1r.50 Al Motanabbi (poet), symbols and desert	17·00	3·75
348	2r. Ibn Sina (Avicenna) (physician and philosopher), medical instruments and ancient globe	21·00	5·00

57 Great Cormorant and Water Plants

1971. Qatar Fauna and Flora. Multicoloured.

349	1d. Type **57**	2·00	45
350	2d. Lizard and prickly pear	2·00	45
351	3d. Greater flamingos and palms	2·00	45
352	60d. Arabian oryx and yucca	9·75	2·00
353	1r.25 Mountain gazelle and desert dandelion	20·00	5·25
354	2r. Dromedary, palm and bronzed chenopod	27·00	7·50

58 Satellite Earth Station, Goonhilly

1971. World Telecommunications Day. Mult.

355	1d. Type **58**	30	10
356	2d. Cable ship "Ariel"	30	10
357	3d. Post Office Tower and T.V. control-room	30	10
358	4d. Modern telephones	30	10
359	5d. Video-phone equipment	30	10
360	35d. As 3d.	3·00	95
361	75d. As 5d.	4·25	1·40
362	3r. Telex machine	17·00	3·50

59 Arab Child reading Book

1971. 10th Anniv of Education Day.

363	**59**	35d. multicoloured	1·50	45
364	**59**	55d. multicoloured	3·00	95
365	**59**	75d. multicoloured	5·75	1·60

60 A.P.U. Emblem

1971. 25th Anniv of Arab Postal Union.

366	**60**	35d. multicoloured	1·30	35
367	**60**	55d. multicoloured	2·10	80
368	**60**	75d. multicoloured	2·75	1·30
369	**60**	1r.25 multicoloured	4·00	2·00

61 "Hammering Racism"

1971. Racial Equality Year. Multicoloured.

370	1d. Type **61**	40	10
371	2d. "Pushing back racism"	40	10
372	3d. War-wounded	40	10
373	4d. Working together (vert)	40	10
374	5d. Playing together (vert)	40	10
375	35d. Racial "tidal-wave"	3·00	95
376	75d. Type **61**	6·75	1·60
377	3r. As 2d.	14·50	3·25

62 Nurse and Child

1971. 25th Anniv of UNICEF. Multicoloured.

378	1d. Mother and child (vert)	40	10
379	2d. Child's face	40	10
380	3d. Child with book (vert)	40	10
381	4d. Type **62**	40	10
382	5d. Mother and baby	40	10
383	35d. Child with daffodil (vert)	2·20	60
384	75d. As 3d.	6·75	1·60
385	3r. As 1d.	15·00	3·00

63 Shaikh Ahmad, and Flags of Arab League and Qatar

1971. Independence.

386	**63**	35d. multicoloured	1·30	35
387	-	75d. multicoloured	2·75	80
388	-	1r.25 black, pink & brown	4·00	1·20
389	-	3r. multicoloured	12·50	3·00
MS390		80×128 mm. No. 389. Imperf	37·00	21·00

DESIGNS—HORIZ: 75d. As Type **63**, but with U.N. flag in place of Arab League flag. VERT: 1r.25, Shaikh Ahmad; 3r. Handclasp.

64 European Roller

1972. Birds. Multicoloured.

391	1d. Type **64**	1·30	55
392	2d. River kingfisher	1·30	55
393	3d. Rock thrush	1·30	55
394	4d. Caspian tern	1·50	65
395	5d. Hoopoe	1·50	65
396	35d. European bee eater	6·75	85
397	75d. Golden oriole	13·50	2·75
398	3r. Peregrine falcon	40·00	11·50

1972. Nos. 328/30 surch with value in English and Arabic.

399	10d. on 60d. multicoloured	2·75	65
400	1r. on 1r.25 multicoloured	12·50	3·25
401	5r. on 2r. multicoloured	55·00	12·50

66 Shaikh Khalifa bin Hamad al-Thani

1972

402	**66**	5d. blue and violet	65	25
403	**66**	10d. red and brown	65	65
404	**66**	35d. green and orange	1·70	80
405	**66**	55d. mauve and green	3·25	1·60
406	**66**	75d. mauve and blue	5·25	2·40
407	-	1r. black and brown	7·25	2·50
408	-	1r.25 black and green	8·25	3·25
409	-	5r. black and blue	29·00	10·50
410	-	10r. black and red	55·00	24·00

The rupee values are larger, 27×32 mm.

For similar design but with Shaikh's head turned slightly to right, see Nos. 444a/b.

67 Book Year Emblem

1972. International Book Year.

411	**67**	35d. black and blue	1·90	40
412	**67**	55d. black and brown	3·25	65
413	**67**	75d. black and green	4·75	95
414	**67**	1r.25 black and lilac	7·75	1·60

68 Football

1972. Olympic Games, Munich. Designs depicting sportsmen's hands or feet. Multicoloured.

415	1d. Type **68**	35	25
416	2d. Running (foot on starting block)	35	25
417	3d. Cycling (hand)	35	25
418	4d. Gymnastics (hand)	35	25
419	5d. Basketball (hand)	80	40
420	35d. Discus (hand)	1·90	65
421	75d. Type **68**	3·75	1·10
422	3r. As 2d.	14·50	4·00
MS423	150×108 mm. Nos. 415/20. Imperf	28·00	17·00

69 Underwater Pipeline Construction

1972. "Oil from the Sea". Multicoloured.

424	1d. Drilling (vert)	55	40
425	4d. Type **69**	55	40
426	5d. Offshore rig "Sea Shell"	55	40
427	35d. Underwater "prospecting" for oil	2·50	55
428	75d. As 1d.	5·00	1·20
429	3r. As 5d.	25·00	6·00

70 Administrative Building

1972. Independence Day. Multicoloured.

430	10d. Type **70**	1·30	25
431	35d. Handclasp and Arab League flag	3·25	55
432	75d. Handclasp and U.N. flag	6·75	1·30
433	1r.25 Shaikh Khalifa	11·00	2·00
MS434	129×103 mm. No. 433. Imperf	28·00	17·00

71 Dish Aerial, Satellite and Telephone (I.T.U.)

1972. United Nations Day. Multicoloured.

435	1d. Type **71**	65	55
436	2d. Archaeological team (UNESCO)	65	55
437	3d. Tractor, produce and helicopter (F.A.O.)	65	55
438	4d. Children with books (UNICEF)	65	55
439	5d. Weather satellite (W.M.O.)	75	65
440	25d. Construction workers (I.L.O.)	3·25	1·90
441	55d. Child care (W.H.O.)	6·25	4·00
442	1r. Airliner and van (U.P.U.)	19·00	7·25

72 Emblem and Flags

1972. 10th Session of Arab States Civil Aviation Council, Qatar.

443	**72**	25d. multicoloured	3·50	1·10
444	**72**	30d. multicoloured	5·25	1·60

72a Shaikh Khalifa

1972

444a	**72a**	10d. red and brown	£200	
444b	**72a**	25d. green and purple	£200	

73 Shaikh Khalifa **74** Clock Tower, Doha

1973

445	**73**	5d. multicoloured	1·00	40
446	**73**	10d. multicoloured	1·60	40
447	**73**	20d. multicoloured	2·00	40
448	**73**	25d. multicoloured	2·50	40
449	**73**	35d. multicoloured	3·25	65
450	**73**	55d. multicoloured	5·25	1·10
451	**74**	75d. purple, green and blue	7·75	2·00
452	**73**	1r. multicoloured	17·00	4·75
453	**73**	5r. multicoloured	65·00	23·00
454	**73**	10r. multicoloured	£150	55·00

Nos. 452/4 are larger, 27×32 mm.

75 Housing Development

1973. 1st Anniv of Shaikh Khalifa's Accession. Multicoloured.

455	2d. Road construction	35	25
456	3d. Type **75**	35	25
457	4d. Hospital operating theatre	35	25
458	5d. Telephone exchange	35	25
459	15d. School classroom	1·60	25
460	20d. Television studio	2·00	40
461	35d. Shaikh Khalifa	3·00	65
462	55d. Gulf Hotel, Doha	3·50	1·10
463	1r. Industrial plant	4·75	1·30
464	1r.35 Flour mills	6·25	2·00

76 Aerial Crop-spraying

1973. 25th Anniv of W.H.O. Multicoloured.

465	2d. Type **76**	80	55
466	3d. Drugs and syringe	80	55
467	4d. Woman in wheelchair (Prevention of polio)	80	55
468	5d. Mosquito (Malaria control)	1·60	65
469	55d. Mental patient (Mental Health Research)	12·50	1·90
470	1r. Dead trees (Anti-pollution)	25·00	3·75

77 Weather Ship

1973. Centenary of World Meteorological Organization. Multicoloured.

471	2d. Type **77**	55	40
472	3d. Launching radio-sonde balloon	55	40
473	4d. Hawker Siddeley H.S.125 weather plane	55	40
474	5d. Meteorological station	55	40
475	10d. Met airplane taking-off	1·80	55
476	1r. "Nimbus 1"	13·50	1·70
477	1r.55 Rocket on launch-pad	19·00	3·25

78 Handclasp

1973. Independence Day. Multicoloured.

478	15d. Type **78**	35	15
479	35d. Agriculture	65	25
480	55d. Government building	1·80	65
481	1r.35 View of Doha	4·00	1·50
482	1r.55 Illuminated fountain	4·50	1·70

79 Child planting Sapling (UNESCO)

1973. United Nations Day. Multicoloured.

483	2d. Type **79**	55	15
484	4d. U.N. Headquarters, New York, and flags	55	15
485	5d. Building construction (I.L.O.)	55	15
486	35d. Nurses in dispensary (W.H.O.)	1·50	55
487	1r.35 Radar control (I.T.U.)	5·50	1·60
488	3r. Inspection of wheat and cattle (F.A.O.)	14·50	5·00

80 "Open Gates"

1973. 25th Anniv of Declaration of Human Rights. Multicoloured.

489	2d. Type **80**	35	35
490	4d. Freedom marchers	35	35
491	5d. "Equality of Man"	65	35
492	35d. Primary education	2·00	65
493	1r.35 General Assembly, U.N.	6·75	2·10
494	3r. Flame emblem (vert)	12·50	3·25

81 New Flyover, Doha

1974. 2nd Anniv of Shaikh Khalifa's Accession. Mult.

495	2d. Type **81**	35	25
496	3d. Education symbol	35	25
497	5d. Gas plant	35	25
498	35d. Gulf Hotel, Doha	1·90	65
499	1r.55 Space communications station	8·25	3·25
500	2r.25 Shaikh Khalifa	11·00	4·25

82 Camel Caravan and Articulated Mail Van

1974. Centenary of U.P.U. Multicoloured.

501	2d. Type **82**	55	25
502	3d. Early mail wagon and Japanese "Hikari" express train	55	25
503	10d. "Hindoostan" (paddle-steamer) and "Iberia" (liner)	2·00	65
504	35d. Early (Handley Page H.P.42) and modern (Vickers VC-10) mail planes	3·50	95
505	75d. Manual and mechanized mail-sorting	4·00	1·30
506	1r.25 Early and modern P.O. sales counters	6·75	2·40

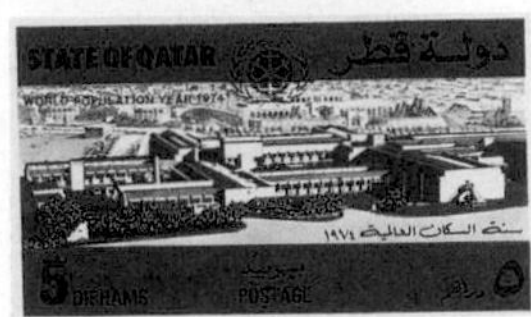

83 Doha Hospital

1974. World Population Year. Multicoloured.

507	5d. Type **83**	20	20
508	10d. W.P.Y. emblem	55	20
509	15d. Emblem within wreath	55	20
510	35d. World population map	1·60	95
511	1r.75 New-born infants and clock ("a birth every minute")	5·50	3·00
512	2r.25 "Ideal Family" group	8·25	4·75

84 Television Station

1974. Independence Day. Multicoloured.

513	5d. Type **84**	45	25
514	10d. Doha palace	90	25
515	15d. Teachers' College	1·30	40
516	75d. Clock tower and mosque	3·50	55
517	1r.55 Roundabout and surroundings	6·75	1·10
518	2r.25 Shaikh Khalifa	10·00	1·60

85 Operating Theatre (W.H.O.)

1974. United Nations Day.

519	**85**	5d. orange, purple & black	55	25
520	-	10d. orange, red and black	1·10	25
521	-	20d. blue, green and black	2·20	40
522	-	25d. blue, brown and black	3·25	55
523	-	1r.75 blue, mauve & black	12·50	1·70
524	-	2r. blue, orange and black	14·50	2·00

DESIGNS: 10d. Satellite earth station (I.T.U.); 20d. Tractor (F.A.O.); 25d. Classroom (UNESCO); 1r.75, African open-air court (Human Rights); 2r. U.P.U. and U.N. emblems (U.P.U.).

86 Vickers VC-10 Airliner

1974. Arab Civil Aviation Day.

525	**86**	20d. multicoloured	2·50	55
526	-	25d. blue, green and yellow	3·50	60
527	-	30d. multicoloured	5·00	65
528	-	50d. red, green and purple	6·25	95

DESIGNS: 25d. Doha airport; 30, 50d. Flags of Qatar and the Arab League.

87 Clock Tower, Doha

1974. Tourism. Multicoloured.

529	5d. Type **87**	1·10	15
530	10d. White-cheeked terns, hoopoes and Shara'o Island (horiz)	1·50	20
531	15d. Fort Zubara (horiz)	1·80	25
532	35d. Dinghies and Gulf Hotel (horiz)	3·00	40
533	55d. Qatar by night (horiz)	3·50	65
534	75d. Arabian oryx (horiz)	5·50	1·10
535	1r.25 Khor-al-Udeid (horiz)	7·75	1·50
536	1r.75 Ruins Wakrah (horiz)	11·00	1·70

88 Traffic Roundabout, Doha

1975. 3rd Anniv of Shaikh Khalifa's Accession. Multicoloured.

537	10d. Type **88**	1·10	15
538	35d. Oil pipelines	1·90	40
539	55d. Laying offshore pipelines	3·00	95
540	1r. Oil refinery	6·25	1·50
541	1r.35 Shaikh Khalifa (vert)	7·75	2·10
542	1r.55 As 1r.35	9·50	3·00

89 Flintlock Pistol

1975. Opening of National Museum. Multicoloured.

543	2d. Type **89**	55	15
544	3d. Arabesque-pattern mosaic	1·00	25
545	35d. Museum buildings	2·50	40
546	75d. Museum archway (vert)	5·25	80
547	1r.25 Flint tools	8·25	1·60
548	3r. Gold necklace and pendant (vert)	18·00	3·00

90 Policeman and Road Signs

1975. Traffic Week. Multicoloured.

549	5d. Type **90**	1·50	25
550	15d. Traffic arrows and signal lights	4·00	65
551	35d. Type **90**	6·25	95
552	55d. As 15d.	10·00	1·50

91 Flag and Emblem

1975. 10th Anniv of Arab Labour Charter.

553	**91**	10d. multicoloured	1·10	25
554	**91**	35d. multicoloured	2·75	55
555	**91**	1r. multicoloured	7·75	1·60

92 Government Building, Doha

1975. 4th Anniv of Independence. Multicoloured.

556	5d. Type **92**	1·10	15
557	15d. Museum and clock tower, Doha	2·00	20
558	35d. Constitution – Arabic text (vert)	2·50	40
559	55d. Ruler and flag (vert)	4·00	55
560	75d. Constitution – English text (vert)	5·00	95
561	1r.25 As 55d.	7·75	1·60

93 Telecommunications Satellite (I.T.U.)

1975. 30th Anniv of U.N.O. Multicoloured.

562	5d. Type **93**	35	15
563	15d. U.N. Headquarters, New York	55	20
564	35d. U.P.U. emblem and map	1·50	40
565	1r. Doctors tending child (UNICEF)	3·50	1·50
566	1r.25 Bulldozer (I.L.O.)	6·75	2·30
567	2r. Students in class (UNESCO)	10·00	3·00

94 Fertilizer Plant

1975. Qatar Industry. Multicoloured.

568	5d. Type **94**	80	15
569	10d. Flour mills (vert)	1·30	20
570	35d. Natural gas plant	2·50	55
571	75d. Oil refinery	6·25	1·90
572	1r.25 Cement works	7·25	2·75
573	1r.55 Steel mills	11·00	3·50

95 Modern Building, Doha

1976. 4th Anniv of Shaikh Khalifa's Accession.

574	**95**	5d. multicoloured	45	40
575	-	10d. multicoloured	55	45
576	-	35d. multicoloured	2·20	55
577	-	55d. multicoloured	3·50	95
578	-	75d. multicoloured	4·50	1·50
579	-	1r.55 multicoloured	11·00	3·75

DESIGNS: Nos. 575/6 and 579 show public buildings; Nos. 577/8 show Shaikh Khalifa with flag.

96 Tracking Aerial

1976. Opening of Satellite Earth Station. Mult.

580	35d. Type **96**	2·50	80
581	55d. "Intelsat" satellite	3·25	1·30
582	75d. Type **96**	4·50	1·90
583	1r. As 55d.	6·75	2·40

97 Early and Modern Telephones

1976. Telephone Centenary.

584	**97**	1r. multicoloured	5·00	2·30
585	**97**	1r.35 multicoloured	6·25	3·00

98 Tournament Emblem

1976. 4th Arabian Gulf Football Cup Tournament. Multicoloured.

586	5d. Type **98**	35	25
587	10d. Qatar Stadium	65	35
588	35d. Type **98**	3·25	40
589	55d. Two players with ball	5·00	95
590	75d. Player with ball	5·50	1·50
591	1r.25 As 10d.	7·75	2·00

99 Qatar Dhow

1976. Dhows.

592	**99**	10d. multicoloured	2·10	25
593	-	35d. multicoloured	4·25	40
594	-	80d. multicoloured	8·25	1·20
595	-	1r.25 multicoloured	11·00	2·00
596	-	1r.50 multicoloured	12·50	2·50
597	-	2r. multicoloured	18·00	4·00

DESIGNS: 35d. to 2r. Various craft.

100 Football

1976. Olympic Games, Montreal. Multicoloured.

598	5d. Type **100**	45	15
599	10d. Yachting	1·10	20
600	35d. Show jumping	2·75	40
601	80d. Boxing	4·50	1·10
602	1r.25 Weightlifting	6·25	1·70
603	1r.50 Basketball	8·25	2·75

101 Urban Housing Development

1976. United Nations Conference on Human Settlements. Multicoloured.

604	10d. Type **101**	45	40
605	35d. U.N. and conference emblems	1·30	55
606	80d. Communal housing development	3·25	80
607	1r.25 Shaikh Khalifa	6·75	2·00

102 Kentish Plover

1976. Birds. Multicoloured.

608	5d. Type **102**	1·30	40
609	10d. Great cormorant	2·75	55
610	35d. Osprey	8·25	95
611	80d. Greater flamingo (vert)	17·00	2·00
612	1r.25 Rock thrush (vert)	26·00	3·00
613	2r. Saker falcon (vert)	30·00	4·00

103 Shaikh Khalifa and Flag

1976. 5th Anniv of Independence. Multicoloured.

614	5d. Type **103**	35	15
615	10d. Type **103**	1·10	40
616	40d. Doha buildings (horiz)	2·00	55
617	80d. As 40d.	2·75	1·10
618	1r.25 "Dana" (oil rig) (horiz)	4·50	1·50
619	1r.50 United Nations and Qatar emblems (horiz)	6·25	1·70

104 U.N. Emblem

1976. United Nations Day.

620	**104**	2r. multicoloured	5·50	1·60
621	**104**	3r. multicoloured	7·75	2·40

105 Shaikh Khalifa

1977. 5th Anniv of Amir's Accession.

622	**105**	20d. multicoloured	1·70	55
623	**105**	1r.80 multicoloured	9·50	2·40

106 Shaikh Khalifa

1977

624	**106**	5d. multicoloured	45	15
625	**106**	10d. multicoloured	65	20
626	**106**	35d. multicoloured	1·10	40
627	**106**	80d. multicoloured	2·20	55
628	**106**	1r. multicoloured	4·50	80
629	**106**	5r. multicoloured	13·50	3·25
630	**106**	10r. multicoloured	33·00	6·50

Nos. 628/30 are larger, size 25×31 mm.

107 Envelope and A.P.U. Emblem

1977. 25th Anniv of Arab Postal Union.

631	**107**	35d. multicoloured	1·60	55
632	**107**	1r.35 multicoloured	5·25	1·90

108 Shaikh Khalifa and Sound Waves

1977. International Telecommunications Day.

633	**108**	35d. multicoloured	1·00	40
634	**108**	1r.80 multicoloured	6·25	2·50

108a Shaikh Khalifa

1977

634a	**108a**	5d. multicoloured	45	45
634c	**108a**	10d. multicoloured	65	65
634d	**108a**	35d. multicoloured	90	90
634e	**108a**	80d. multicoloured	2·20	2·20

109 Parliament Building, Doha

1977. 6th Anniv of Independence. Multicoloured.

635	80d. Type **109**	4·00	1·50
636	80d. Main business district, Doha	4·00	1·50
637	80d. Motorway, Doha	4·00	1·50

110 U.N. Emblem

1977. United Nations Day.

638	**110**	20d. multicoloured	1·10	55
639	**110**	1r. multicoloured	5·50	2·10

111 Steel Mill

1978. 6th Anniv of Amir's Accession. Mult.

640	20d. Type **111**	1·30	25
641	80d. Operating theatre	2·75	55
642	1r. Children's classroom	4·75	80
643	5r. Shaikh Khalifa	13·50	2·50

112 Oil Refinery

1978. 7th Anniv of Independence. Multicoloured.

644	35d. Type **112**	1·00	40
645	80d. Apartment buildings	2·00	80
646	1r.35 Town centre, Doha	3·75	1·50
647	1r.80 Shaikh Khalifa	5·00	1·70

113 Man reading Alphabet

1978. International Literacy Day.

648	**113**	35d. multicoloured	1·70	65
649	**113**	80d. multicoloured	5·00	1·30

114 U.N. Emblem and Qatar Flag

1978. United Nations Day.

650	**114**	35d. multicoloured	1·30	65
651	**114**	80d. multicoloured	4·25	1·30

115 "Human Rights Flame"

1978. 30th Anniv of Declaration of Human Rights. Multicoloured.

652	35d. Type **115**	90	40
653	80d. Type **115**	2·20	1·10
654	1r.25 Flame and scales of justice	3·25	1·60
655	1r.80 As 1r.25	5·00	2·30

116 I.Y.C. Emblem

1979. International Year of the Child.

656	**116**	35d. mauve, blue and black	1·30	1·10
657	**116**	1r.80 green, blue & black	4·25	4·00

117 Shaikh Khalifa

1979

658	**117**	5d. multicoloured	20	15
659	**117**	10d. multicoloured	35	15
660	**117**	20d. multicoloured	80	20
661	**117**	25d. multicoloured	1·00	25
662	**117**	35d. multicoloured	1·50	55
663	**117**	60d. multicoloured	1·90	65
664	**117**	80d. multicoloured	2·50	80
665	**117**	1r. multicoloured	2·75	1·10
666	**117**	1r.25 multicoloured	3·00	1·20
667	**117**	1r.35 multicoloured	3·25	1·50
668	**117**	1r.80 multicoloured	5·00	1·70
669	**117**	5r. multicoloured	11·00	3·25
670	**117**	10r. multicoloured	22·00	6·75

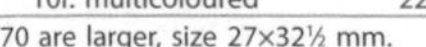

Nos. 665/70 are larger, size 27×32½ mm.

118 Shaikh Khalifa and Laurel Wreath

1979. 7th Anniv of Amir's Accession.

671	**118**	35d. multicoloured	1·10	40
672	**118**	80d. multicoloured	1·60	55
673	**118**	1r. multicoloured	1·80	65
674	**118**	1r.25 multicoloured	2·20	80

119 Wave Pattern and Television Screen

1979. World Telecommunications Day.

675	**119**	2r. multicoloured	4·50	2·00
676	**119**	2r.80 multicoloured	5·50	3·00

120 Two Children supporting Globe

1979. 50th Anniv of Int Bureau of Education.

677	**120**	35d. multicoloured	90	25
678	**120**	80d. multicoloured	3·50	1·10

121 Rolling Mill

1979. 8th Anniv of Independence. Multicoloured.

679	5d. Type **121**	80	15
680	10d. Aerial view of Doha	1·10	25
681	1r.25 Qatar flag	3·75	1·20
682	2r. Shaikh Khalifa	5·50	1·50

122 U.N. Emblem and Flag of Qatar

1979. United Nations Day.

683	**122**	1r.25 multicoloured	4·00	1·10
684	**122**	2r. multicoloured	6·25	1·60

123 Mosque Minaret and Crescent Moon

1979. 3rd World Conference on the Prophet's Seera and Sunna.

685	**123**	35d. multicoloured	3·00	80
686	**123**	1r.80 multicoloured	8·25	1·90

124 Shaikh Khalifa

1980. 8th Anniv of Amir's Accession.

687	**124**	20d. multicoloured	1·10	25
688	**124**	60d. multicoloured	2·75	65
689	**124**	1r.25 multicoloured	4·50	1·20
690	**124**	2r. multicoloured	9·00	2·10

125 Emblem

1980. 6th Congress of Arab Towns Organization, Doha.

691	**125**	2r.35 multicoloured	6·75	1·60
692	**125**	2r.80 multicoloured	10·00	2·10

126 Oil Refinery

1980. 9th Anniv of Independence. Multicoloured.

693	10d. Type **126**	65	15
694	35d. Doha	2·20	55
695	2r. Oil Rig	9·00	2·75
696	2r.35 Hospital	11·00	3·25

127 Figures supporting O.P.E.C. Emblem

1980. 20th Anniv of Organization of Petroleum Exporting Countries.

697	**127**	1r.35 multicoloured	3·25	1·20
698	**127**	2r. multicoloured	5·50	1·90

128 U.N.Emblem

1980. United Nations Day.

699	**128**	1r.35 blue, light blue and purple	2·75	1·30
700	**128**	1r.80 turquoise, green and black	4·00	1·60

129 Mosque and Kaaba, Mecca

1980. 1400th Anniv of Hegira.

701	129	10d. multicoloured	45	25
702	129	35d. multicoloured	1·10	65
703	129	1r.25 multicoloured	2·20	1·30
704	129	2r.80 multicoloured	5·50	3·75

130 I.Y.D.P. Emblem

1981. International Year of Disabled Persons.

705	130	2r. multicoloured	4·50	2·75
706	130	3r. multicoloured	6·75	3·25

131 Student

1981. 20th Anniv of Education Day.

707	131	2r. multicoloured	5·00	2·00
708	131	3r. multicoloured	6·25	2·75

132 Shaikh Khalifa

1981. 9th Anniv of Amir's Accession.

709	132	10d. multicoloured	55	15
710	132	35d. multicoloured	1·30	25
711	132	80d. multicoloured	2·50	65
712	132	5r. multicoloured	13·50	3·75

133 I.T.U. and W.H.O. Emblems and Ribbons forming Caduceus

1981. World Telecommunications Day.

713	133	2r. multicoloured	4·50	1·60
714	133	2r.80 multicoloured	6·75	2·40

134 Torch

1981. 30th International Military Football Championship.

715	134	1r.25 multicoloured	5·00	1·60
716	134	2r.80 multicoloured	8·25	3·00

135 Qatar Flag

1981. 10th Anniv of Independence.

717	135	5d. multicoloured	65	15
718	135	60d. multicoloured	2·10	65
719	135	80d. multicoloured	2·75	80
720	135	5r. multicoloured	17·00	5·00

136 Tractor gathering Crops

1981. World Food Day.

721	136	2r. multicoloured	5·50	3·25
722	136	2r.80 multicoloured	7·75	4·00

137 Red Crescent

1982. Qatar Red Crescent.

723	137	20d. multicoloured	1·10	25
724	137	2r.80 multicoloured	7·75	3·00

138 Shaikh Khalifa

1982. 10th Anniv of Amir's Accession.

725	138	10d. multicoloured	90	15
726	138	20d. multicoloured	1·70	25
727	138	1r.25 multicoloured	6·25	1·30
728	138	2r.80 multicoloured	14·50	3·00

139 Hamad General Hospital

1982. Hamad General Hospital.

729	139	10d. multicoloured	65	25
730	139	2r.35 multicoloured	6·25	3·00

140 Shaikh Khalifa

1982

731	140	5d. multicoloured	35	15
732	140	10d. multicoloured	40	15
733	140	15d. multicoloured	45	15
734	140	20d. multicoloured	50	20
735	140	25d. multicoloured	65	25
736	140	35d. multicoloured	90	35
737	140	60d. multicoloured	1·30	40
738	140	80d. multicoloured	1·70	45
739	-	1r. multicoloured	2·20	65
740	-	1r.25 multicoloured	2·75	80
741	-	2r. multicoloured	4·50	2·00
742	-	5r. multicoloured	11·00	4·75
743	-	10r. multicoloured	22·00	9·50
744	-	15r. multicoloured	31·00	14·50

DESIGNS—25×32 mm: 1r. to 2r. Oil refinery; 5r. to 15r. Doha clock tower.

142 "Bar'zan" Container Ship

1982. 6th Anniv of United Arab Shipping Company.

745	142	20d. multicoloured	1·10	25
746	142	2r.35 multicoloured	10·00	3·00

143 A.P.U. Emblem

1982. 30th Anniv of Arab Postal Union.

747	143	35d. multicoloured	1·10	40
748	143	2r.80 multicoloured	7·75	2·30

144 National Flag

1982. 11th Anniv of Independence.

749	144	10d. multicoloured	80	25
750	144	80d. multicoloured	1·90	55
751	144	1r.25 multicoloured	3·75	1·60
752	144	2r.80 multicoloured	7·25	2·30

145 W.C.Y. Emblem

1983. World Communications Year.

753	145	35d. multicoloured	1·10	55
754	145	2r.80 multicoloured	6·25	2·40

146 Conference Emblem

1983. 2nd Gulf Postal Organization Conference.

755	146	1r. multicoloured	2·50	1·30
756	146	1r.35 multicoloured	4·25	2·00

147 Arabic Script

1983. 12th Anniv of Independence.

757	147	10d. multicoloured	45	25
758	147	35d. multicoloured	80	55
759	147	80d. multicoloured	1·70	80
760	147	2r.80 multicoloured	6·25	2·40

148 Council Emblem

1983. 4th Session of Gulf Co-operation Council Supreme Council.

761	148	35d. multicoloured	1·70	55
762	148	2r.80 multicoloured	7·25	2·40

149 Globe and Human Rights Emblem

1983. 35th Anniv of Declaration of Human Rights. Multicoloured.

763	1r.25 Type **149**	3·25	1·60
764	2r.80 Globe and emblem in balance	7·75	2·40

150 Harbour

151 Shaikh Khalifa

1984

765	150	15d. multicoloured	45	15
765a	151	25d. mult (22×27 mm)	1·00	40
766	150	40d. multicoloured	1·10	60
767	150	50d. multicoloured	1·10	65
767a	151	75d. mult (22×27 mm)	2·50	1·50
768	151	1r. multicoloured	2·75	1·60
769	151	1r.50 multicoloured	3·25	1·70
769a	151	2r. multicoloured	7·25	5·00
770	151	2r.50 multicoloured	5·50	3·00
771	151	3r. multicoloured	7·25	3·25
772	151	5r. multicoloured	13·50	6·00
773	151	10r. multicoloured	22·00	11·50

152 Flag and Shaikh Khalifa

1984. 13th Anniv of Independence.

774	**152**	15d. multicoloured	80	25
775	**152**	1r. multicoloured	2·50	95
776	**152**	2r.50 multicoloured	5·50	2·40
777	**152**	3r.50 multicoloured	7·75	3·00

153 Teacher and Blackboard

1984. International Literacy Day. Multicoloured, background colour behind board given.

778	**153**	1r. mauve	4·50	1·10
779	**153**	1r. orange	4·50	1·10

154 I.C.A.O. Emblem

1984. 40th Anniv of I.C.A.O.

780	**154**	20d. multicoloured	65	25
781	**154**	3r.50 multicoloured	8·25	3·00

155 I.Y.Y. Emblem

1985. International Youth Year.

782	**155**	50d. multicoloured	1·70	65
783	**155**	1r. multicoloured	4·00	1·30

156 Crossing the Road

1985. Traffic Week. Multicoloured, frame colour given.

784	**156**	1r. red	3·25	1·20
785	**156**	1r. blue	3·25	1·20

157 Emblem

1985. 40th Anniv of League of Arab States.

786	**157**	50d. multicoloured	1·60	40
787	**157**	4r. multicoloured	7·75	3·00

158 Doha

1985. 14th Anniv of Independence. Multicoloured.

788		40d. Type **158**	1·00	25
789		50d. Dish aerials and micro-wave tower	1·30	55
790		1r.50 Oil refinery	4·50	1·20
791		4r. Cement works	10·00	4·00

159 O.P.E.C. Emblem in "25"

1985. 25th Anniv of Organization of Petroleum Exporting Countries. Multicoloured, background colours given.

792	**159**	1r. red	4·50	1·30
793	**159**	1r. green	4·50	1·30

160 U.N. Emblem

1985. 40th Anniv of U.N.O.

794	**160**	1r. multicoloured	1·30	1·30
795	**160**	3r. multicoloured	4·25	3·75

161 Emblem

1986. Population and Housing Census.

796	**161**	1r. multicoloured	2·20	1·30
797	**161**	3r. multicoloured	6·75	4·00

162 "Qatari ibn al-Fuja'a" (container ship)

1986. 10th Anniv of United Arab Shipping Company. Multicoloured.

798		1r.50 Type **162**	2·75	2·75
799		4r. "Al Wajda" (container ship)	8·25	6·00

163 Flag and Shaikh Khalifa

1986. 15th Anniv of Independence.

800	**163**	40d. multicoloured	65	55
801	**163**	50d. multicoloured	90	65
802	**163**	1r. multicoloured	1·90	1·30
803	**163**	4r. multicoloured	6·75	4·75

164 Shaikh Khalifa

1987

804	**164**	15r. multicoloured	17·00	12·00
805	**164**	20r. multicoloured	22·00	16·00
806	**164**	30r. multicoloured	39·00	25·00

165 Palace

1987. 15th Anniv of Amir's Accession.

807	**165**	50d. multicoloured	90	55
808	**165**	1r. multicoloured	2·00	1·10
809	**165**	1r.50 multicoloured	2·50	1·30
810	**165**	4r. multicoloured	6·25	4·75

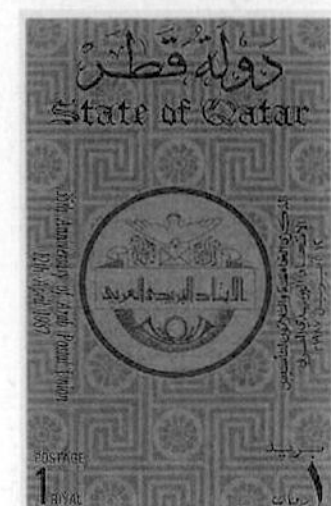

166 Emblem

1987. 35th Anniv of Arab Postal Union.

811	**166**	1r. yellow, green and black	2·75	1·30
812	**166**	1r.50 multicoloured	4·00	2·00

167 Emblem

1987. Gulf Environment Day.

813	**167**	1r. multicoloured	1·90	1·30
814	**167**	4r. multicoloured	7·25	5·25

168 Modern Complex

1987. 16th Anniv of Independence.

815		25d. Type **168**	90	40
816		75d. Aerial view of city	2·50	95
817		2r. Modern building	4·50	2·00
818		4r. Oil refinery	9·00	4·75

169 Pens in Fist

1987. International Literacy Day.

819	**169**	1r.50 multicoloured	2·20	1·30
820	**169**	4r. multicoloured	4·50	4·00

170 Anniversary Emblem

1988. 40th Anniv of W.H.O.

821	**170**	1r.50 yellow, black and blue	2·75	2·50
822	**170**	2r. yellow, black and pink	4·00	3·75

171 State Arms, Shaikh Khalifa and Flag

1988. 17th Anniv of Independence.

823	**171**	50d. multicoloured	1·10	65
824	**171**	75d. multicoloured	1·70	95
825	**171**	1r.50 multicoloured	2·75	2·00
826	**171**	2r. multicoloured	3·50	2·40

172 Post Office

1988. Opening of New Doha General Post Office.

827	**172**	1r.50 multicoloured	2·00	2·00
828	**172**	4r. multicoloured	4·75	4·75

173 Housing Development

1988. Arab Housing Day.

829	**173**	1r.50 multicoloured	2·20	1·60
830	**173**	4r. multicoloured	6·75	3·75

174 Hands shielding Flame

1988. 40th Anniv of Declaration of Human Rights.

831	**174**	1r.50 multicoloured	2·75	2·50
832	**174**	2r. multicoloured	4·00	3·75

175 Dish Aerials and Arrows

1989. World Telecommunications Day.

833	**175**	2r. multicoloured	2·20	2·30
834	**175**	4r. multicoloured	4·50	4·00

176 Headquarters

1989. 10th Anniv of Qatar Red Crescent Society.

835	**176**	4r. multicoloured	9·00	4·75

177 Palace

1989. 18th Anniv of Independence.

836	**177**	75d. multicoloured	1·10	80
837	**177**	1r. multicoloured	2·00	1·90
838	**177**	1r.50 multicoloured	2·50	2·10
839	**177**	2r. multicoloured	3·50	2·40

178 Anniversary Emblem

1990. 40th Anniv of Gulf Air.

840	**178**	50d. multicoloured	1·10	55
841	**178**	75d. multicoloured	1·70	95
842	**178**	4r. multicoloured	8·25	4·00

179 Map and Rising Sun

1990. 19th Anniv of Independence. Multicoloured.

843	50d. Type **179**	1·10	55
844	75d. Map and sunburst	1·70	80
845	1r.50 Musicians and sword dancer	3·25	1·60
846	2r. As No. 845	5·00	2·75

180 Anniversary Emblem

1990. 30th Anniv of Organization of Petroleum Exporting Countries. Multicoloured.

847	50d. Type **180**	1·50	55
848	1r.50 Flags of member nations	4·25	1·60

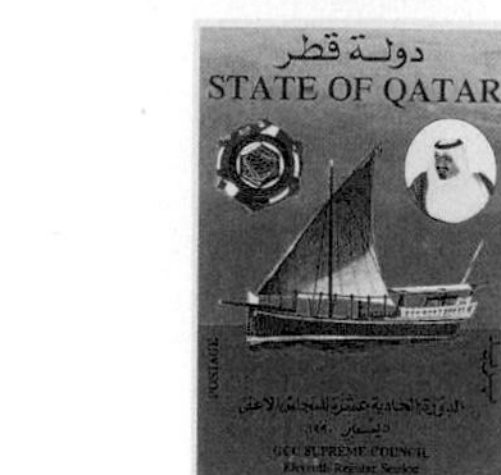

181 Emblem and Dhow

1990. 11th Session of Supreme Council of Gulf Co-operation Council. Multicoloured.

849	50d. Type **181**	1·50	55
850	1r. Council heads of state and emblem	2·50	1·10
851	1r.50 State flag and Council emblem	3·50	1·70
852	2r. State and Council emblems	4·50	2·10

182 "Glossonema edule"

1991. Plants. Multicoloured.

853	10d. Type **182**	95	40
854	25d. "Lycium shawii"	1·10	45
855	50d. "Acacia tortilis"	1·20	1·10
856	75d. "Acacia ehrenbergiana"	1·80	1·20
857	1r. "Capparis spinosa"	2·40	2·40
858	4r. "Cymbopogon parkeri"	11·00	9·50

No. 858 is wrongly inscribed "Cymhopogon".

183 Emblem

1991. 20th Anniv of Independence. Multicoloured.

859	25d. Type **183**	95	40
860	75d. As Type **183** but different Arabic inscription	1·40	65
861	1r. View of Doha (35×32 mm)	1·90	1·10
862	1r.50 Palace (35×32 mm)	3·00	1·90

184 Seabream

1991. Fishes. Multicoloured.

863	10d. Type **184**	70	40
864	15d. Pennant coralfish	80	45
865	25d. Scarlet-finned squirrelfish	1·40	80
866	50d. Smooth houndshark	2·75	1·60
867	75d. Seabream	3·75	2·40
868	1r. Golden trevally	4·50	3·75
869	1r.50 Rabbitfish	7·75	6·00
870	2r. Yellow-banded angelfish	9·00	7·25

185 Shaikh Khalifa

1992. Multicoloured. (a) Size 22×28 or 28×22 mm.

871	10d. Type **185**	10	10
872	25d. North Field gas project	35	15
873	50d. Map of Qatar	60	55
874	75d. Petrochemical factory (horiz)	95	60
875	1r. Oil refinery (horiz)	1·20	80

(b) Size 25×32 or 32×25 mm.

876	1r.50 As No. 872	1·60	1·30
877	2r. As No. 873	1·90	1·60
878	3r. As No. 874	4·25	3·00
879	4r. As No. 875	4·75	3·25
880	5r. As No. 873	5·50	4·00
881	10r. As No. 875	12·00	7·25
882	15r. Shaikh Khalifa (different frame)	16·00	12·00
883	20r. As No. 882	27·00	14·50
884	30r. As No. 882	30·00	24·00

186 Shaikh Khalifa and Gateway

1992. 20th Anniv of Amir's Accession. Mult.

885	25d. Type **186**	60	40
886	50d. Type **186**	1·20	55
887	75d. Archway and "20"	1·80	80
888	1r.50 As No 887	3·50	1·70

187 Heart in Centre of Flower

1992. World Health Day. "Heartbeat, the Rhythm of Health". Multicoloured.

889	50d. Type **187**	95	65
890	1r.50 Heart on clockface and cardiograph (horiz)	2·75	2·00

188 Women dancing

1992. Children's Paintings. Multicoloured.

891	25d. Type **188**	70	15
892	50d. Children's playground	1·60	55
893	75d. Boat race	3·00	65
894	1r.50 Fishing fleet	4·75	1·10
MS895	122×102 mm. Nos. 891/4	£300	£300

189 Runner and Emblems

1992. Olympic Games, Barcelona. Multicoloured.

896	50d. Type **189**	1·40	40
897	1r.50 Footballer and emblems	3·50	1·20

190 Shaikh Khalifa and Script

1992. 21st Anniv of Independence. Multicoloured.

898	50d. Type **190**	85	55
899	50d. Shaikh Kalifa and "21" in English and Arabic	85	55
900	1r. Oil well, pen and dhow (42×42 mm)	1·60	1·20
901	1r. Dhow in harbour (42×42 mm)	1·60	1·20

191 Ball, Flag and Emblem

1992. 11th Arabian Gulf Football Championship. Multicoloured.

902	50d. Type **191**	1·20	65
903	1r. Ball bursting goal net (vert)	2·40	1·30

192 Emblems and Globe

1992. International Nutrition Conference, Rome. Multicoloured.

904	50d. Type **192**	1·80	40
905	1r. Cornucopia (horiz)	3·00	65

193 Mosque

1993. Old Mosques. Each sepia, yellow and brown.

906	1r. Type **193**	1·20	95
907	1r. Mosque (minaret without balcony)	1·20	95
908	1r. Mosque (minaret with wide balcony)	1·20	95
909	1r. Mosque (minaret with narrow balcony)	1·20	95

194 Presenter and Dish Aerial

1993. 25th Anniv of Qatar Broadcasting. Mult.

910	25d. Type **194**	95	15
911	50d. Rocket and satellite	2·20	80
912	75d. Broadcasting House	2·75	1·10
913	1r. Journalists	4·25	1·30
MS914	123×114 mm. Nos. 910/13 forming a composite design	£180	£180

195 Oil Refinery and Sea

1993. 22nd Anniv of Independence. Multicoloured.

915	25d. Type **195**	35	25
916	50d. Flag and clock tower, Doha	70	65
917	75d. "22" in English and Arabic	1·20	1·10
918	1r.50 Flag and fort	2·75	2·30

196 Scroll, Quill and Paper

1993. International Literacy Day. Multicoloured.

919	25d. Type **196**	35	20
920	50d. Fountain pen and flags spelling "Qatar"	70	60
921	75d. Fountain pen and Arabic characters	1·20	95
922	1r.50 Arabic text on scroll and fountain pen	2·75	2·30

197 Girls playing

1993. Children's Games. Multicoloured.

923	25d. Type **197**	85	15
924	50d. Boys playing with propeller (vert)	1·60	55
925	75d. Wheel and stick race (vert)	2·40	80
926	1r.50 Skipping	4·75	1·90
MS927	Two sheets (a) 114×93 mm. Nos. 923 ×2 and 926 ×2; (b) 93×114 mm. Nos. 924 ×2 and 925 ×2	70·00	70·00

198 Lanner Falcon

1993. Falcons. Multicoloured.

928	25d. Type **198**	60	40
929	50d. Saker falcon	1·20	55
930	75d. Barbary falcon	1·80	80
931	1r.50 Peregrine falcon	3·50	1·90
MS932	122×104 mm. Nos. 928/31	£140	£140

199 Headquarters

1994. 30th Anniv of Qatar Insurance Company. Multicoloured.

933	50d. Type **199**	1·20	40
934	1r.50 Company emblem and international landmarks	3·50	1·60

200 Hands catching Drops from Tap

1994. World Water Day. Mulicoloured.

935	25d. Type **200**	1·20	40
936	1r. Hands catching raindrop, water tower, crops and United Nations emblem	2·40	1·60

201 Gavel, Scales and National Flag

1994. Qatar International Law Conference. Multicoloured.

937	75d. Type **201**	95	80
938	2r. Gavel and scales suspended from flag	2·75	2·50

202 Society Emblem

1994. Qatar Society for Welfare and Rehabilitation of the Handicapped. Multicoloured.

939	25d. Type **202**	95	55
940	75d. Handicapped symbol and hands	2·75	1·10

203 Anniversary Emblem

1994. 75th Anniv of I.L.O. Multicoloured.

941	25d. Type **203**	60	40
942	2r. Anniversary emblem and cogwheel	4·25	1·60

204 Family and Emblem

1994. International Year of the Family.

943	**204**	25d. blue and black	85	65
944	-	1r. multicoloured	2·75	1·30

DESIGN: 1r. I.Y.F. emblem and stylized family standing on U.N. emblem.

205 Scroll

1994. 23rd Anniv of Independence. Multicoloured.

945	25d. Type **205**	50	40
946	75d. Oasis	1·20	80
947	1r. Industry	1·80	1·10
948	2r. Scroll (different)	4·25	2·40

206 Map, Airplane and Emblem

1994. 50th Anniv of I.C.A.O. Multicoloured.

949	25d. Type **206**	1·20	40
950	75d. Anniversary emblem	3·50	95

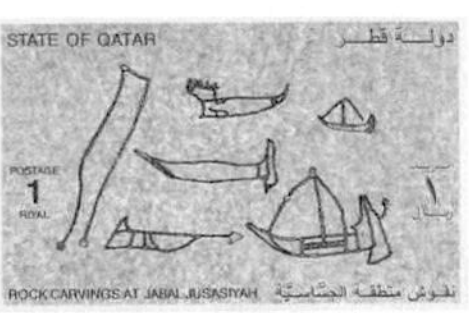

207 Ship-like Carvings

1995. Rock Carvings, Jabal Jusasiyah. Multicoloured.

951	1r. Type **207**	1·10	80
952	1r. Circular and geometric patterns	1·10	80
953	1r. Six irregular-shaped carvings	1·10	80
954	1r. Carvings including three multi-limbed creatures	1·10	80
955	1r. Nine multi-limbed creatures	1·10	80
956	1r. Fishes	1·10	80

208 Precious Wentletrap ("Epitonium scalare")

1995. Gulf Environment Day. Sea Shells. Multicoloured.

957	75d. Type **208**	1·20	95
958	75d. Feathered cone ("Conus pennaceus")	1·20	95
959	75d. "Cerithidea cingulata"	1·20	95
960	75d. "Hexaplex kuesterianus"	1·20	95
961	1r. Giant spider conch ("Lambis truncata sebae")	1·40	1·30
962	1r. Woodcock murex ("Murex scolopax")	1·40	1·30
963	1r. "Thais mutabilis"	1·40	1·30
964	1r. Spindle shell ("Fusinus arabicus")	1·40	1·30

209 Nursing Patient

1995. International Nursing Day. Multicoloured.

965	1r. Type **209**	1·90	1·10
966	1r.50 Vaccinating child	3·00	1·60

210 Schoolchildren

1995. 24th Anniv of Independence. Multicoloured.

967	1r. Type **210**	95	80
968	1r. Palm trees	95	80
969	1r.50 Port	1·60	1·50
970	1r.50 Doha	1·60	1·50

Nos. 967/70 were issued together, se-tenant, forming a composite design.

211 Anniversary Emblem

1995. 50th Anniv of U.N.O.

971	**211**	1r.50 multicoloured	2·40	1·30

212 Addra Gazelle

1996. Mammals. Multicoloured.

972	25d. Type **212**	10	10
973	50d. Beira antelope	50	35
974	75d. "Gazella dorcas pelzelni"	85	65
975	1r. Dorcas gazelle	95	80
976	1r.50 Speke's gazelle	1·80	1·50
977	2r. Soemerring's gazelle	2·40	2·40
MS978	121×81 mm. 3r. Speke's gazelle, *Gazella dorcas pelzelni* and Soemmering's gazelle. Imperf	48·00	44·00

213 Syringes through Skull

1996. International Day against Drug Abuse. Multicoloured.

979	50d. Type **213**	85	55
980	1r. "No entry" sign over syringes in hand	1·60	80

214 Map of Qatar and Games Emblem

1996. Olympic Games, Atlanta. Multicoloured.

981	10d. Type **214**	30	25
982	15d. Rifle shooting	30	25
983	25d. Bowling	30	25
984	50d. Table tennis	85	55
985	1r. Running	1·70	1·60
986	1r.50 Yachting	2·75	2·40

Nos. 981/6 were issued together, se-tenant, forming a composite design.

215 Map, National Flag and Shaikh Hamad

1996. 25th Anniv of Independence.

987	**215**	1r.50 multicoloured	2·10	1·30
988	**215**	2r. multicoloured	2·75	1·70

216 Shaikh Hamad

217 Shaikh Hamad

1996

990	**216**	25d. multicoloured	10	10
991	**216**	50d. multicoloured	50	40
992	**216**	75d. multicoloured	85	55
993	**216**	1r. multicoloured	95	65
994	**217**	1r.50 multicoloured	1·60	1·10
995	**217**	2r. multicoloured	2·10	1·30
997	**217**	4r. multicoloured	4·00	2·75
998	**217**	5r. multicoloured	4·75	5·25
999	**217**	10r. multicoloured	9·75	7·25
1001	**217**	20r. multicoloured	19·00	14·50
1002	**217**	30r. multicoloured	29·00	21·00

218 Doha Clock Tower, Dove and Heads of State

1996. 17th Session of Gulf Co-operation Council Supreme Council, Doha. Multicoloured.

1004	1r. Type **218**	1·30	80
1005	1r.50 Council emblem, dove and national flag	2·40	1·60

219 Children and UNICEF Emblem

1996. 50th Anniv of UNICEF. Multicoloured.

1006	75d. Type **219**	95	65

1007	75d. Children and emblem	95	65

220 Al-Wajbah

1997. Forts. Multicoloured.

1008	25d. Type **220**	50	25
1009	75d. Al-Zubarah (horiz)	1·10	95
1010	1r. Al-Kout Fort, Doha (horiz)	1·30	1·20
1011	3r. Umm Salal Mohammed (horiz)	4·50	4·25

221 World Map and Liquid Gas Containers (½-size illustration) (image scaled to 63% of original size)

1997. Inauguration of Ras Laffan Port.

1012	**221**	3r. multicoloured	4·75	2·75

222 Palomino

1997. Arab Horses. Multicoloured.

1013	25d. Type **222**	50	25
1014	75d. Black horse	1·30	95
1015	1r. Grey	1·80	1·20
1016	1r.50 Bay	2·40	1·90
MS1017	121×81 mm. 3r. Mares and foals	£120	50·00

223 Arabic Script within Wreath, Flag and Shaikh Hamad

1997. 26th Anniv of Independence. Multicoloured.

1018	1r. Type **223**	95	80
1019	1r.50 Amir, oil refinery and Government Palace	1·40	1·20

224 Graph

1997. Middle East and Northern Africa Economic Conference, Doha.

1020	**224**	2r. multicoloured	1·60	1·30

225 Nubian Flower Bee

1998. Insects. Multicoloured.

1021	2r. Type **225**	1·60	1·10
1022	2r. Domino beetle	1·60	1·10
1023	2r. Seven-spotted ladybird	1·60	1·10
1024	2r. Desert giant ant	1·60	1·10
1025	2r. Eastern death's-head hawk moth	1·60	1·10
1026	2r. Arabian darkling beetle	1·60	1·10
1027	2r. Yellow digger	1·60	1·10
1028	2r. Mole cricket	1·60	1·10
1029	2r. Migratory locust	1·60	1·10
1030	2r. Elegant rhinoceros beetle	1·60	1·10
1031	2r. Oleander hawk moth	1·60	1·10
1032	2r. American cockroach	1·60	1·10
1033	2r. Girdled skimmer	1·60	1·10
1034	2r. Sabre-toothed beetle	1·60	1·10
1035	2r. Arabian cicada	1·60	1·10
1036	2r. Pin-striped ground weevil	1·60	1·10
1037	2r. Praying mantis	1·60	1·10
1038	2r. Rufous bombardier beetle	1·60	1·10
1039	2r. Diadem	1·60	1·10
1040	2r. Shore earwig (inscr "Earwing")	1·60	1·10
MS1041	Two sheets, each 91×59 mm. (a) No. 1029; (b) No. 1039	36·00	27·00

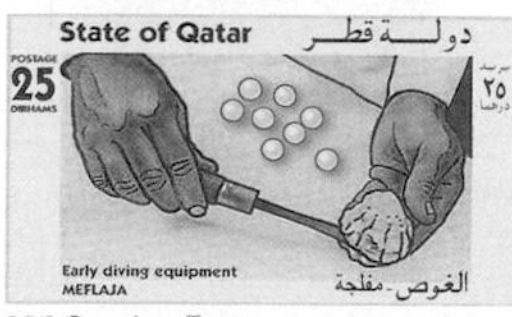

226 Opening Oysters

1998. Early Pearl-diving Equipment. Multicoloured.

1042	25d. Type **226**	50	25
1043	75d. Opened oyster with pearl	1·10	80
1044	1r. Scales for weighing pearls	1·30	1·10
1045	1r.50 Basket for keeping oysters (vert)	2·20	2·00
MS1046	106×83 mm. 2r. Pearl diver	12·00	8·75

227 Shaikh Hamad

1998. 27th Anniv of Independence. Multicoloured.

1047	1r. Type **227**	85	65
1048	1r.50 Shaikh Hamad (horiz)	1·60	1·30

228 Anniversary Emblem

1998. 25th Anniv of University of Qatar.

1049	**228**	1r. multicoloured	85	65
1050	**228**	1r.50 multicoloured	1·60	1·30

229 Dromedaries

1999. Dromedaries. Multicoloured.

1051	25d. Type **229**	35	25
1052	75d. One dromedary	1·10	95
1053	1r. Three dromedaries	1·30	1·20
1054	1r.50 Four young dromedaries with herd	2·20	1·90
MS1055	106×83 mm. 2r. Adult and young	19·00	14·50

230 Emblem

1999. General Assembly of International Equestrian Federation, Doha.

1056	**230**	1r.50 multicoloured	2·40	2·00

231 Umayyad Dirham

1999. Coins. Multicoloured.

1057	1r. Type **231**	85	55
1058	1r. Umayyad dirham (four small circles around edge of right-hand coin)	85	55
1059	1r. Abbasid dirham (three lines of inscr on left-hand coin)	85	55
1060	1r. Abbasid dirham (six lines of inscr on left-hand coin)	85	55
1061	1r. Umayyad dirham (five small circles around edge of right-hand coin)	85	55
1062	2r. Abbasid dirham (three lines on inscr on left-hand coin)	1·60	1·30
1063	2r. Umayyad dinar	1·60	1·30
1064	2r. Abbasid dinar (five lines of inscr on left-hand coin)	1·60	1·30
1065	2r. Murabitid dinar	1·60	1·30
1066	2r. Fatimid dinar	1·60	1·30
MS1067	Two sheets, each 112×70 mm. (a) 2r. Arab Sasanian dirham; (b) 3r. Umayyad dirham	24·00	19·00

232 Shaikh Hamad

1999. 28th Anniv of Independence.

1068	**232**	1r. multicoloured	85	65
1069	**232**	1r.50 multicoloured	1·60	1·10

233 Tree of Letters

1999. 125th Anniv of Universal Postal Union. Multicoloured.

1070	1r. Type **233**	85	65
1071	1r.50 General Post Office, Doha (horiz)	1·60	1·10

234 Postal Emblems on "Stamps"

1999. 5th Arab Gulf Countries Stamp Exhibition, Doha. Multicoloured.

1072	1r. Type **234**	85	65
1073	1r.50 Exhibition emblem (horiz)	1·60	1·10

235 Flower and Emblem

1999. National Committee for Children with Special Needs.

1074	**235**	1r.50 multicoloured	1·80	1·30

236 Clock Tower

2000. New Millennium.

1075	**236**	1r.50 gold and red	1·40	1·30
1076	**236**	2r. gold and blue	2·20	2·00

237 Emir Cup and Court

2000. New Millennium Open Tennis Championships, Qatar. Multicoloured.

1077	1r. Type **237**	1·20	1·10
1078	1r.50 Emir Cup and racquet	1·80	1·60

238 Map and Water Droplet

2000. Gulf Co-operation Council Water Week. Mult.

1079	1r. Type **238**	1·20	1·10
1080	1r.50 Dried earth and water droplet	1·80	1·60

239 Bat and Ball

2000. 15th Asian Table Tennis Championship, Doha.

1081	**239**	1r.50 multicoloured	1·80	1·30

240 Shaikh Hamad, Fort and Emblem

2000. 29th Anniv of Independence. Multicoloured.

1082	1r. Type **240**	1·20	1·20
1083	1r.50 Shaikh Hamad, city and oil drilling platform	1·80	1·80

241 Emblem and Dove carrying Letter

2000. 50th Anniv of Qatar Post Office. Multicoloured.

1084	1r.50 Type **241**	1·80	1·80
1085	2r. Emblem, magnifying glass and building facade	2·40	2·40

242 Emblem

2000. 9th Islamic Summit Conference, Doha. Multicoloured.

1086	1r. Type **242**	1·20	1·20
1087	1r.50 Emblem and olive branch (47×30 mm)	1·80	1·80

243 Gas Terminal

2001. "Clean Environment". Multicoloured.

1088	1r. Type **243**	1·20	1·10
1089	1r.50 Oryx and gas installation	1·70	1·60
1090	2r. Flamingoes and Ras Laffan city skyline	2·75	2·40
1091	3r. Earth viewed from space	3·50	3·25

244 Castle, Koran and Ship

2001. 30th Anniv of Independence.

1092	**244** 1r. multicoloured	1·20	1·20
1093	**244** 1r.50 multicoloured	1·80	1·80

245 Children encircling Globe

2001. United Nations Year of Dialogue among Civilizations. Multicoloured.

1094	1r.50 Type **245**	1·80	1·80
1095	2r. Leaves	2·75	2·75

246 Building and Emblem

2001. 4th World Trade Organization Ministerial Conference, Doho, Qatar.

1096	**246** 1r. multicoloured	1·40	95
1097	**246** 1r.50 multicoloured	2·20	1·40

247 Door

2001. Traditional Wooden Doors. Multicoloured.

1098	25d. Type **247**	35	35
1099	75d. Small door in left-hand panel and large bolt at right	85	85
1100	1r.50 Plain doors	1·80	1·80
1101	2r. Knocker at left and smaller door in right-hand panel	2·40	2·40
MS1102	100×70 mm. 3r. As No. 1101	16·00	16·00

248 Uruguay, 1930

2002. World Cup Football Championship, Japan and South Korea. Multicoloured.

1103	2r. Type **248**	2·10	2·10
1104	2r. Italy, 1934	2·10	2·10
1105	2r. France, 1938	2·10	2·10
1106	2r. Brasil, 1950	2·10	2·10
1107	2r. Switzerland, 1954	2·10	2·10
1108	2r. Sweden, 1958	2·10	2·10
1109	2r. Chile, 1962	2·10	2·10
1110	2r. England, 1966	2·10	2·10
1111	2r. Mexico, 1970	2·10	2·10
1112	2r. West Germany, 1974	2·10	2·10
1113	2r. Argentina, 1978	2·10	2·10
1114	2r. Spain, 1982	2·10	2·10
1115	2r. Mexico, 1986	2·10	2·10
1116	2r. Italy, 1990	2·10	2·10
1117	2r. USA, 1994	2·10	2·10
1118	2r. France, 1998	2·10	2·10
1119	2r. 2002 Championship emblem	2·10	2·10
1120	2r. World Cup trophy	2·10	2·10
MS1121	133×78 mm. Nos. 2019/20	5·75	5·75

249 Championship Emblem

2002. 14th Asian Games, Busan. Sheet 133×73 mm containing T 249 and similar vert design. Multicoloured.

MS1122	1r. Type **249**; 1r. 15th (2006) Asian Games championship emblem	5·75	5·75

250 Emblem

2002. 1st Anniv of Global Post Code. Multicoloured.

1123	**250** 1r. multicoloured	1·20	1·00
1124	**250** 3r. multicoloured	3·50	3·25

251 Runner, Heart and No-Smoking Sign

2003. World No-Smoking Day.

1125	**251** 1r.50 multicoloured	1·50	1·50

No. 1125 was printed using thermochromatic (heat sensitive) ink. When the image is pressed parts of the design disappear leaving only the runner visible.

252 Boy and Crescent

2003. 25th Anniv of Qatar Red Crescent (humanitarian organization). Multicoloured.

1126	75d. Type **252**	1·20	80
1127	75d. Building facade	1·20	80

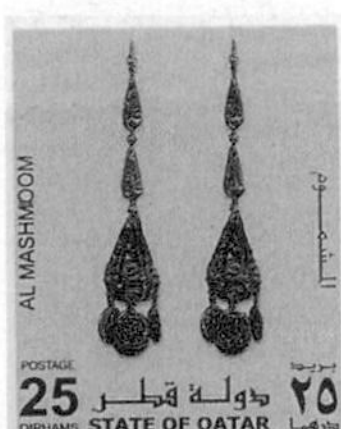

253 Al Mashmoom (earrings)

2003. Jewellery. Multicoloured.

1128	25d. Type **253**	35	25
1129	25d. Al Mertash (necklace)	35	25
1130	50d. Khatim (ring)	60	45
1131	50d. Ishqab (earrings)	60	45
1132	1r.50 Shmailat (bangle)	2·00	1·60
1133	1r.50 Tassa (headdress)	2·00	1·60

254 *Wright Flyer*

2003. Centenary of Powered Flight. Sheet 110×76 mm containing T 254 and similar horiz designs. Multicoloured. P 14½.

MS1134	50d. ×4 Type **254**; Otto Lilienthal's glider; Qatar Airways Boeing A330; Airplane	2·00	2·00

255 Family and Emblems

2004. 10th Anniv of International Year of the Family.

1135	**255** 2r.50 blue and light blue	2·30	2·30

256 FIFA Emblem

2004. Centenary of FIFA (Federation Internationale de Football Association).

1136	**256** 50d. multicoloured	45	45

257 Flag, Shaikh Hamad and Book

2004. Establishment of Permanent Constitution.

1137	**257** 75d. multicoloured	70	70

258 Athens 2004 and Olympic Emblems

2004. Olympic Games, Athens 2004. Sheet 72×72 mm containing T 258 and similar vert design. Multicoloured.

MS1138	3r. ×2, Type **258**; As Type **258** but with colours and face value reversed	5·75	5·75

259 Motorcyclist

2004. MotoGP 2004 Grand Prix, Qatar. Sheet 100×131 mm containing T 259 and similar horiz design. Multicoloured.

MS1139	3r. ×2, Type **259** ×2; 3r.50 ×2, Two motorcyclists	6·50	6·50

260 Emblem

2004

1140	**260** 50d. olive	45	45
1141	**260** 50d. green	45	45
1142	**260** 50d. brown	45	45
1143	**260** 50d. purple	45	45
1144	**260** 50d. blue	45	45

261 Hand holding Olive Branch

2004. National Human Rights Committee.

1145	**261** 50d. multicoloured	45	45

262 Al Sadd Sports Club

2004. 17th Arabian Gulf Cup. Sheet 100×100 mm containing T 262 and similar multicoloured designs.

MS1146	1r.50 ×5, Type **262**; Ball and player's legs (vert); Games emblem (35×35 mm); Goalkeeper (vert); Sudaifi (games mascot)	4·50	4·50

263 Orry

2004. 15th Asian Games, 2006, Doha. Official Mascot. Showing Orry (official mascot). Multicoloured. (a) Ordinary gum.

1147	50d. Type **263**	30	30
1148	1r. Sitting in dhow (horiz)	55	55
1149	1r.50 Marking off calender (horiz)	90	90
1150	2r. Carrying flaming torch	1·20	1·20
1151	3r. Lighting flame	1·80	1·80
1152	3r.50 Waving flag at Khalifa stadium	2·00	2·00

(b) Self-adhesive.

1153	50d. Type **263**	30	30
1154	1r. No. 1148 (horiz)	55	55
1155	1r.50 No. 1149 (horiz)	90	90
1156	2r. No. 1150	1·20	1·20
1157	3r. No. 1151	1·80	1·80
1158	3r.50 No. 1152	2·00	2·00

264 De Soto (1950)

2005. Classic Cars. Sheet 110×130 mm containing T 264 and similar horiz designs. Multicoloured.

MS1159	50d. ×8, Type **264**; Chevrolet (1958); Dodge Sedan (1938); Chrysler (1947); Dodge Power Wagon; Orange Chevrolet truck; Green Dodge truck; Two-tone Dodge truck	2·40	2·40

265 *Team Daedalus* Catamaran

2005. Oryx Quest 2005 (round the world sail race). Catamarans. Multicoloured.

1160	50d. Type **265**	30	30
1161	50d. With Qatar flag as sail	30	30
1162	50d. *Team Cheyenne* (vert)	30	30
1163	50d. *Team Geronimo* (vert)	30	30

266 Kiccoro and Morizo (exhibition mascots)

2005. Expo 2005 World Exposition, Aichi. Multicoloured.

1164	50d. Type **266**	30	30
1165	50d. Qatar flag	30	30

267 Emblem

2005. Doha Development Forum. Sheet 95×75 mm containing T 267 and similar horiz design. Multicoloured.

MS1166	6r.×2, Type **267**; Emblem (different)	6·50	6·50

268 Sheikh Hamad bin Khalifa al Thani

2005. 10th Anniv of Accession of Emir Sheikh Hamad bin Khalifa al Thani. Sheet 160×53 mm.

MS1167	**268** 2r.50 multicoloured	1·60	1·60

269 Sarajevo and Doha

2005

1168	**269**	2r.50 multicoloured	1·60	1·60

270 Flag

2005. Self-adhesive.

1169	**270**	50d. purple	30	30
1170	**270**	1r. purple	55	55
1171	**270**	1r.50 purple	90	90
1172	**270**	2r.50 purple	1·50	1·50
1173	**270**	3r. purple	1·80	1·80
1174	**270**	3r.50 purple	2·00	2·00

271 Children

2005. Al Jazeera Children's Channel. Sheet 144×75 mm. Multicoloured.

MS1175	50d.×4, Type **271**; Air balloon; Runners; Family	1·20	1·20

The stamps and margins of **MS**1175 form a composite design.

272 Gold Emblem

2005. National Philatelic and Numismatic Club. Sheet 99×77 mm. Multicoloured.

MS1176	1r.×2, Type **272**; Silver emblem	1·30	1·30

273 Emblem

2005. Gulf Co-operation Council Stamp Exhibition, Doha. Multicoloured.

1177	1r. Type **273**	80	80
1178	1r. Envelope and stamp as figures	80	80

274 Fireman and Appliance

2006. International Civil Defence Day. Multicoloured.

1179	50d. Type **274**	30	30
1180	2r.50 Recuers on rope ladder and appliance	1·60	1·60
MS1181	130×146 mm. Nos. 1179/80, each×4	7·75	7·75

275 Flag

2006. 25th Anniv of Gulf Co-operation Council. Multicoloured.

1182	50d. Type **275**	30	30
MS1183	165×105 mm. 5r. Flags of member states. Imperf	3·25	3·25

Stamps of similar designs were issued by Kuwait, Oman, United Arab Emirates, Saudi Arabia and Bahrain.

276 Emblem

2006. World Cup Football Championship, Germany.

1184	**276**	2r. multicoloured	1·40	1·40

277 Torches

2006. Torch Relay. Dohar (2006).

1185	**277**	50d. multicoloured	30	30

278 Young Man and Child

2006. Volunteers. Dohar (2006).

1186	**278**	75d. multicoloured	50	50

279 Athletes Village

2006. Venues. Dohar 2006. Multicoloured.

1187	1r.50 Type **279**	95	95
1188	1r.50 Khalifa Stadium	95	95
1189	1r.50 Aspire facility	95	95
1190	1r.50 Al-dana Club	95	95
MS1191	126×179 mm. 5r. As Nos. 1187/90. Imperf	3·25	3·25

279a Runner

2006. Sports. Dohar 2006 (1st issue). Multicoloured.

1192	50d. Type **279a**	30	30
1193	50d. Judo combatants	30	30
1194	50d. Tennis player	30	30
1195	50d. Swimmer about to dive	30	30
1196	50d. Cyclist	30	30

280 Footballer and Ball

2006. Sports. Dohar 2006 (2nd issue). Mult.

1197	50d. Type **280**	30	30
1198	50d. Orry cycling	30	30
1199	50d. Handball	30	30
1200	50d. Table tennis	30	30
1201	50d. Orry playing football	30	30

281 Racecourse

2007. Exceptional Meeting of General Assembly of Pan-Arab Equestrian Federation. Multicoloured.

1202	2d.50 Type **281**	1·60	1·60
MS1203	85×70 mm. 5d. Shelkh Hamad Bin Khalifa Al-Thani (vert)	3·25	3·25

282 Girl Athlete

2007. Doha 2016–Olympic and Paralympic Games Bid. Sheet 210×148 mm containing T 282 and similar square designs. Multicoloured.

MS1204	50d.×4, Type **282**; Boy crouched: Children with arms raised; Children with arms raised side view	1·40	1·40

283 Emblem and Flags of Member States

2007. Session of the Gulf Cooperation Council Supreme Council, Doha, 2007.

1205	**283**	50d. multicoloured	30	30

284 Symbol of Sheikh Jassim Bin Mohammad Bin Thani

2007. Rulers of Qatar. Sheet 140×120 mm containing T 284 and similar multicoloured designs.

MS1206	2r.50×7, Type **284**; Sheikh Hamad bin Khalifa Al-Thani (38×55 mm); As Type **284**; Sheikh Ali Bin Abdullah Al-Thani; Sheikh Abdullah Bin Qassim Al-Thani; Sheikh Khalifa bin Hamad Al-Thani; Sheikh Ahmed Bin Ali Bin Abdullah Al-Thani	9·75	9·75

285 Green Dome, Al-Masjid al-Nabawi (Mosque of the Prophet), Medina

2007. Islamic Holy Places. Multicoloured.

1207	2r.50 Type **285**	1·60	1·60
1208	2r.50 Ka'ba and Black Stone, Mecca	1·60	1·60
1209	2r.50 Dome of the Rock (Qubbat as-Sakhrah), Jerusalem	1·60	1·60
MS1210	95×60 mm. 5r. Composite image of Dome of the Rock, Ka'ba, Black Stone and Green Dome. Imperf	3·25	3·25

286 Emblem

2008. Arab Philatelic Exhibition, Doha. Mult.

1211	50d. Type **286**	30	30
MS1212	90×115 mm. 5r. Emblem. Imperf	3·25	3·25

287 Al Marash

2008. Traditional Perfume. Sheet 181×84 mm containing T 287 and similar vert designs. Multicoloured.

MS1213	1r.50×4, Type **287**; Oud perfume oil; Agar wood; Al Moghass	3·75	3·75

The stamps and margins of **MS**1213 form a composite design and, when rubbed, release perfume .

288 Emblem

2008. Zaragoza 2008 International Water and Sustainable Development Exhibition. Sheet 210×148 mm containing T 288 and similar square designs. Multicoloured.

MS1214	50d.×4, Type **288**; As Type **288**; Fluvi (mascot); Fluvi enclosed in water droplet	1·30	1·30

289 Pigeon (image scaled to 69% of original size)

2008. Arab Post Day. Sheet 170×60 mm containing T 289 and similar horiz designs. Multicoloured.

MS1215 5r.×2, Type **289**; Camels		6·50	6·50

290 Emblem

2008. Olympic Games, Beijing. Sheet 136×95 mm containing T 290 and similar multicoloured designs.

MS1216 50d.×2, Type **290**; As Type **290**; 3r. Emblem and athletes (70×36 mm)	2·50	2·50

291 Emblem

2008. 14th GCC Stamp Exhibition, Doha.

1217	**291**	50d. multicoloured	30	30

292 Emblem

2008. Police Day.

1218	**292**	50d. multicoloured (bistre)	30	30
1219	**292**	50d. multicoloured (white)	30	30

293 Museum Building

2008. Museum of Modern Art.

1220	**293**	50d. multicoloured	30	30
MS1221 100×75 mm 5r. As Type **293**			3·25	3·25

294 Waquif Souk

2008. Waquif Souk. Multicoloured.

1222	1r.50 Type **294**	1·10	1·10
1223	1r.50 Women	1·10	1·10
1224	1r.50 Man and shops	1·10	1·10
1225	1r.50 Man and tower	1·10	1·10

295 City Skyline

2009. Towards a Responsible Media.

1226	**295**	50d. multicoloured	40	40

296 Tears

2009. Tears for Gaza. Multicoloured.

1227	1r. Type **296**	70	70
MS1228 115×57 mm. 10r. Tears and wire. Imperf		7·25	7·25

297 Emblem

2009. 10th Anniv of Democratic Elections.

1229	**297**	50d. multicoloured	40	40

298 Emblem

2009. al-Quds—2009 Capital of Arab Culture.

1230	**298**	1r. multicoloured	85	85

299 Woodchat Shrike

2009. Birds. Multicoloured.

1231	50d. Type **299**	30	30
1232	50d. Chiffchaf	30	30
1233	50d. Yellow wagtail	30	30
1234	50d. Orphean warbler	30	30
1235	50d. Isabelline shrike	30	30
1236	50d. Lesser grey shrike	30	30
1237	50d. Orphean warbler (head)	30	30
1238	50d. Woodchat shrike (head)	30	30
1239	50d. Isabelline shrike (head)	30	30
1240	50d. Lesser grey shrike (head)	30	30
1241	50d. Chiffchaf (head)	30	30
1242	50d. Yellow wagtail (head)	30	30
MS1243 98×60 mm. 5r. Cream-coloured courser		2·75	2·75

POSTAGE DUE STAMPS

D40

1968

D254	**D40**	5d. blue	38·00	38·00
D255	**D40**	10d. red	43·00	43·00
D256	**D40**	20d. green	55·00	55·00
D257	**D40**	30d. lilac	60·00	60·00

Pt. 1

QU'AITI STATE IN HADHRAMAUT

The stamps of Aden were used in Qu'aiti State in Hadhramaut from 22 April 1937 until 1942.

1937. 16 annas = 1 rupee.
1951. 100 cents = 1 shilling.
1966. 1000 fils = 1 dinar.

(I) Issues inscribed "SHIHR and MUKALLA"

1 Sultan of Shihr and Mukalla **2** Mukalla Harbour

1942

1	**1**	½a. green	1·50	50
2	**1**	¾a. brown	2·25	30
3	**1**	1a. blue	1·00	1·00
4	**2**	1½a. red	2·00	50
5	-	2a. brown	2·00	1·75
6	-	2½a. blue	50	30
7	-	3a. brown and red	1·25	1·00
8	-	8a. red	1·00	40
9	-	1r. green	7·00	4·00
10	-	2r. blue and purple	16·00	10·00
11	-	5r. brown and green	32·00	15·00

DESIGNS—VERT: 2a. Gateway of Shihr; 3a. Outpost of Mukalla; 1r. Du'an. HORIZ: 2½a. Shibam; 8a. 'Einat; 2r. Mosque in Hureidha; 5r. Meshhed.

1946. Victory. Optd VICTORY ISSUE 8TH JUNE 1946.

12	**2**	1½a. red	15	1·00
13	-	2½a. blue	15	15

1949. Royal Silver Wedding. As T 4b/c of Pitcairn Islands.

14	1½a. red	50	4·50
15	5r. green	17·00	11·00

1949. U.P.U. As T 4d/g of Pitcairn Islands surch.

16	2½a. on 20c. blue	15	30
17	3a. on 30c. red	1·50	1·25
18	8a. on 50c. orange	25	1·50
19	1r. on 1s. blue	30	50

1951. Stamps of 1942 surch in cents or shillings.

20	5c. on 1a. blue	15	20
21	10c. on 2a. sepia	15	20
22	15c. on 2½a. blue	15	20
23	20c. on 3a. sepia and red	30	75
24	50c. on 8a. red	50	2·50
25	1s. on 1r. green	2·25	55
26	2s. on 2r. blue and purple	8·50	28·00
27	5s. on 5r. brown and green	17·00	40·00

1953. Coronation. As T 4h of Pitcairn Islands.

28	15c. black and blue	1·00	55

(II) Issues inscribed "HADHRAMAUT"

11 Metal Work

1955. Occupations. Portrait as in T 11.

29	**11**	5c. blue	70	10
30	-	10c. black (Mat-making)	1·00	10
31a	-	15c. green (Weaving)	50	40
32	-	25c. red (Pottery)	40	10
33	-	35c. blue (Building)	70	10
34a	-	50c. orange (Date cultivation)	50	30
35	-	90c. brown (Agriculture)	50	15
36	-	1s. black and orange (Fisheries) (horiz)	50	10
37	-	1s.25 black and orange (Lime-burning) (horiz)	75	55
38	-	2s. black and blue (Dhow building) (horiz)	4·00	60
39	-	5s. black and green (Agriculture) (horiz)	5·00	2·00
40	-	10s. black and red (as No. 37) (horiz)	10·00	7·50

22 Metal Work

1963. Occupations. As Nos. 29/40 but with inset portrait of Sultan Awadh bin Saleh el Qu'aiti, as in T 22.

41	**22**	5c. blue	10	1·75
42	-	10c. black	10	1·50
43	-	15c. green	10	1·75
44	-	25c. red	15	75
45	-	35c. blue	15	2·00
46	-	50c. orange	15	1·00
47	-	70c. brown (As No. 35)	20	75
48	-	1s. black and lilac	25	30
49	-	1s.25 black and orange	60	4·75
50	-	2s. black and blue	3·25	1·75
51	-	5s. black and green	13·00	28·00
52	-	10s. black and red	25·00	28·00

1966. Nos. 41/52 surch SOUTH ARABIA in English and Arabic, with value and bar.

53	**5**	5f. on 5c.	10	60
54	-	5f. on 10c.	1·00	1·00
55	-	10f. on 15c.	10	30
56	-	15f. on 25c.	10	80
57	-	20f. on 35c.	10	2·00
58	-	25f. on 50c.	10	70
59	-	35f. on 70c.	10	70
60	-	50f. on 1s.	65	30
61	-	65f. on 1s.25	1·50	30
62	-	100f. on 2s.	4·00	1·25
63	-	250f. on 5s.	2·25	1·50
64	-	500f. on 10s.	26·00	3·00

1966. Churchill Commemoration. Nos. 54/6 optd 1874–1965 WINSTON CHURCHILL.

65	5f. on 10c.	7·00	15·00
66	10f. on 15c.	8·00	16·00
67	15f. on 25c.	9·00	17·00

1966. President Kennedy Commemoration. Nos. 57/9 optd 1917–63 JOHN F. KENNEDY.

68	20f. on 35c.	1·25	6·00
69	25f. on 50c.	1·25	6·50
70	35f. on 70c.	1·25	7·50

25 World Cup Emblem

1966. World Cup Football Championship.

71	**25**	5f. purple and orange	2·25	25
72	-	10f. violet and green	2·50	25
73	-	15f. purple and orange	2·75	30
74	-	20f. violet and green	3·00	30
75	**25**	25f. green and red	3·25	30
76	-	35f. blue and yellow	3·75	35
77	-	50f. green and red	4·25	40
78	**25**	65f. blue and yellow	5·00	40
MS78a 110×110 mm. Nos. 77/8			40·00	7·50

DESIGNS: 10, 35f. Wembley Stadium; 15, 50f. Footballers; 20f. Jules Rimet Cup and football.

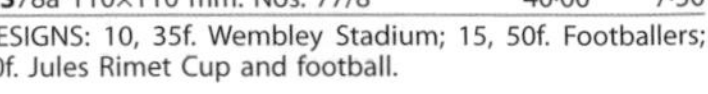

29 Mexican Hat and Basket

1966. Pre-Olympic Games, Mexico (1968).

79	29	75f. sepia and green	1·25	75

30 Telecommunications Satellite

1966. International Co-operation Year.

80	30	5f. mauve, purple and green	2·75	35
81	-	10f. multicoloured	3·00	35
82	-	15f. purple, blue and red	3·25	40
83	30	20f. blue, purple and red	3·50	45
84	-	25f. multicoloured	3·50	45
85	30	35f. purple, red and blue	4·00	50
86	-	50f. purple, green and red	4·75	55
87	30	65f. brown, violet and red	5·50	55

DESIGNS: 10f. Olympic runner (inscr "ROME 1960"); 15f. Fishes; 25f. Olympic runner (inscr "TOKIO 1964"); 50f. Tobacco plant.

APPENDIX

The following stamps have either been issued in excess of postal needs or have not been made available to the public in reasonable quantities at face value.

1967

Stampex, London. Postage 5, 10, 15, 20, 25f.; Air 50, 65f.
Amphilex International Stamp Exhibition, Amsterdam. Air 75f.
Olympic Games, Mexico (1968). 75f.
Paintings. Postage 5, 10, 15, 20, 25f.; Air 50, 65f.
Scout Jamboree, Idaho. Air 35f.
Space Research. Postage 10, 25, 35, 50, 75f.; Air 100, 250f.

The National Liberation Front is said to have taken control of Qu'aiti State in Hadhramaut on 17 September 1967.

Pt. 1

QUEENSLAND

The north eastern state of the Commonwealth of Australia whose stamps it now uses.

12 pence = 1 shilling; 20 shillings = 1 pound.

1

1860. Imperf.

1	1	1d. red	£4250	£800
2	1	2d. blue	£10000	£1700
3	1	6d. green	£7500	£800

1860. Perf.

94		1d. red	55·00	5·50
99		2d. blue	50·00	1·75
65		3d. green	£110	6·00
101		3d. brown	90·00	9·50
103		4d. yellow	£850	30·00
54		4d. grey	£275	22·00
55		4d. lilac	£250	18·00
27		6d. green	£120	12·00
29		1s. grey	£225	22·00
108		1s. purple	70·00	9·00
119		2s. blue	£110	50·00
121		2s.6d. red	£180	65·00
58		5s. red	£550	£110
123		5s. yellow	£250	£100
125		10s. brown	£475	£180
127		20s. red	£1100	£225

7

1879

134	7	1d. brown	65·00	7·50
135	7	1d. orange	45·00	7·50
136	7	1d. red	42·00	5·50
138	7	2d. blue	65·00	2·25
141	7	4d. yellow	£200	12·00
142	7	6d. green	£120	6·00
145	7	1s. mauve	£110	10·00

1880. Nos. 136 surch Half-penny.

151		½d. on 1d. brown	£250	£150

9

1882

152	9	2s. blue	£180	50·00
158	9	2s.6d. orange	45·00	26·00
159	9	5s. red	42·00	40·00
160	9	10s. brown	£110	50·00
161	9	£1 green	£275	80·00

13 **12** **14**

1882. Shaded background around head.

185	13	½d. green	9·00	2·00
206	12	1d. orange	2·50	1·50
204	12	2d. blue	5·50	60
191	14	2½d. red	14·00	2·25
192	12	3d. brown	9·00	3·75
193	12	4d. yellow	13·00	3·00
196	12	6d. green	11·00	2·00
173	12	1s. mauve	16·00	4·50
197	12	2s. brown	42·00	35·00

15

16

17

1895. Head on white background.

208	15	½d. green	2·75	1·25
210	16	1d. red	3·50	50
212	16	2d. blue	26·00	50
213	17	2½d. red	20·00	5·00
215	17	5d. brown	24·00	4·50

19

1896

229	19	1d. red	15·00	70

21

1897. Same designs, but figures in all four corners, as T 21.

286		½d. green	1·75	3·75
232		1d. red	2·50	40
234		2d. blue	4·50	40
236		2½d. red	17·00	26·00
238		2½d. purple on blue	9·50	3·00
241		3d. brown	8·00	3·00
244		4d. yellow	10·00	3·00
294		4d. black	23·00	5·00
246		5d. brown	8·50	3·00
250		6d. green	7·00	3·25
298		1s. mauve	18·00	3·00
254		2s. green	30·00	32·00

26

1899

262a	26	½d. green	2·50	2·50

27

1900. S. African War Charity. Inscr "PATRIOTIC FUND 1900".

264a	27	1d. (1s.) mauve	£120	£110
264b	-	2d. (2s.) violet (horiz)	£300	£275

28

1903

266	28	9d. brown and blue	30·00	5·00

REGISTRATION STAMP

1861. Inscr "REGISTERED".

20	1	(No value) yellow	85·00	40·00

Pt. 9

QUELIMANE

A district of Portuguese E. Africa, now part of Mozambique, whose stamps it now uses.

100 centavos = 1 escudo.

1913. Surch REPUBLICA QUELIMANE and new value on "Vasco da Gama" stamps of (a) Portuguese Colonies.

1	¼c. on 2½r. green	2·75	2·00
2	½c. on 5r. red	2·75	2·00
3	1c. on 10r. purple	2·75	2·00
4	2½c. on 25r. green	2·75	2·00
5	5c. on 50r. blue	2·75	2·00
6	7½c. on 75r. brown	4·75	2·75
7	10c. on 100r. brown	3·00	1·50
8	15c. on 150r. brown	3·00	1·50

(b) Macao.

9	¼c. on ½a. green	2·75	2·00
10	½c. on 1a. red	2·75	2·00
11	1c. on 2a. purple	2·75	2·00
12	2½c. on 4a. green	2·75	2·00
13	5c. on 8a. blue	2·75	2·00
14	7½c. on 12a. brown	4·75	2·75
15	10c. on 16a. brown	3·00	1·50
16	15c. on 24a. brown	3·00	1·50

(c) Portuguese Timor.

17	¼c. on ½a. green	2·75	2·00
18	½c. on 1a. red	2·75	2·00
19	1c. on 2a. purple	2·75	2·00
20	2½c. on 2a. green	2·75	2·00
21	5c. on 8a. blue	2·75	2·00
22	7½c. on 12a. brown	4·75	2·75
23	10c. on 16a. brown	3·00	1·50
24	15c. on 24a. brown	3·00	1·50

1914. "Ceres" key-type inscr "QUELIMANE".

25	U	¼c. green	1·20	1·10
26	U	½c. black	2·30	1·50
42	U	1c. green	2·10	1·60
28	U	1½c. brown	3·00	1·90
29	U	2c. red	3·00	2·30
30	U	2¼c. violet	1·20	85
31	U	5c. blue	2·10	1·60
43	U	7½c. brown	2·10	1·60
33	U	8c. grey	2·50	1·90
44	U	10c. red	2·10	1·60
35	U	15c. purple	3·50	3·00
45	U	20c. green	2·10	1·60
37	U	30c. brown on green	5·25	4·00
38	U	40c. brown on pink	5·75	4·00
39	U	50c. orange on orange	5·75	4·00
40	U	1e. green on blue	6·50	4·50

Pt. 1

RAJASTHAN

Formed in 1948 from states in Rajputana, India, which included Bundi, Jaipur and Kishangarh whose separate posts functioned until 1 April 1950. Now uses Indian stamps.

12 pies = 1 anna; 16 annas = 1 rupee.

BUNDI

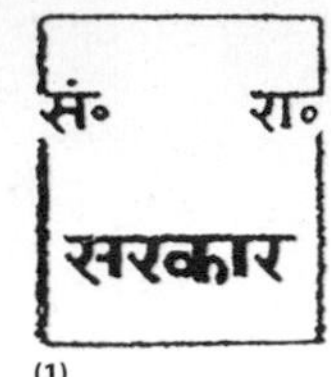

(1)

1949. Nos. 86/92 of Bundi or optd with T 1.

1A	21	¼a. green	7·00	£120
2B	21	½a. violet	7·50	65·00
3A	21	1a. green	6·00	60·00
11	-	2a. red	15·00	90·00
12	-	4a. orange	5·00	90·00
6A	-	8a. blue	12·00	
14	-	1r. brown	7·50	

Nos. 1, 2, 3 and 6 used are worth about six times the unused prices.

JAIPUR

राजस्थान

RAJASTHAN

(2)

1949. Stamps of Jaipur optd with T 2.

15	7	¼a. black and purple	10·00	26·00
16	7	½a. black and violet	9·00	27·00
17	7	¾a. black and orange	10·00	32·00
18	7	1a. black and blue	9·00	60·00
19	7	2a. black and orange	9·50	80·00
20	7	2½a. black and red	9·50	38·00
21	7	3a. black and green	11·00	90·00
22	7	4a. black and green	9·50	£100
23	7	6a. black and blue	9·50	£150
24	7	8a. black and brown	16·00	£200
25	7	1r. black and bistre	23·00	£325

KISHANGARH

1949. Stamps of Kishangarh handstamped with T 1. (a) On stamps of 1899.

26a	2	¼a. pink		£325
27	2	½a. blue	£900	
29	2	1a. lilac	17·00	50·00
30	2	4a. brown	£100	£140
31	2	1r. green	£375	£400
31a	2	2r. red	£425	
32	2	5r. mauve	£425	£425

(b) On stamps of 1904.

33	13	½a. brown		£300
33a	13	1a. blue		£350
34	13	4a. brown	13·00	
35	2	8a. grey	£140	£225
36	13	8a. violet	11·00	
37	13	1r. green	12·00	
38	13	2r. yellow	19·00	
39	13	5r. brown	30·00	

(c) On stamps of 1912.

40	14	½a. green	£550	£325
41	14	1a. red		£375
43	14	2a. purple	£305	11·00
44	14	4a. blue		£800
45	14	8a. brown	5·00	
46	14	1r. mauve	10·00	
47	14	2r. green	10·00	
48	14	5r. brown	£500	

(d) On stamps of 1928.

56	16	¼a. blue	65·00	65·00
57	16	½a. green	38·00	40·00
58	-	1a. red	£140	£120
59	-	2a. purple	£325	£325
61	16	4a. brown	3·50	11·00
51	16	8a. violet	6·50	75·00
63	16	1r. green	6·50	
53	16	2r. yellow	16·00	
54	16	5r. red	16·00	

Pt. 1

RAJPIPLA

A state of Bombay, India. Now uses Indian stamps.

12 pies = 1 anna; 12 annas = 1 rupee.

1 (1 pice)

2 (2a.)

1880

1	1	1p. blue	5·50	45·00
2	2	2a. green	30·00	£140
3	2	4a. red	16·00	85·00

Pt. 19

RAS AL KHAIMA

Arab Shaikhdom in the Arabian Gulf. Ras al Khaima joined the United Arab Emirates in February 1972 and U.A.E. stamps were used in the shaikhdom from 1 January 1973.

1964. 100 naye paise = 1 rupee.
1966. 100 dirhams = 1 riyal.

1 Shaikh Saqr bin Mohamed al-Qasimi

3 Dhow

1964

1	1	5n.p. brown and black	10	10
2	1	15n.p. blue and black	20	20
3	-	30n.p. brown and black	35	35
4	-	40n.p. blue and black	55	45
5	-	75n.p. red and black	1·30	90
6	3	1r. brown and green	1·90	1·30
7	3	2r. brown and violet	4·00	2·75
8	3	5r. brown and blue	12·50	8·25

DESIGNS—As Type **1**: 30n.p. to 75n.p. Seven palms.

3a Pres. Kennedy inspecting "Friendship 7"

1965. Pres. Kennedy Commemoration.

9	3a	2r. blue and brown	1·30	1·30
10	-	3r. blue and brown	2·20	2·20
11	-	4r. blue and brown	3·25	3·25
MS11a		Three sheets 140×108 or 108×140 mm. 1r. stamps in block of four as Nos. 9/11	14·50	13·50

DESIGNS—HORIZ: 3r. Kennedy and wife. VERT: 4r. Kennedy and flame of remembrance.

4 Sir Winston Churchill and Houses of Parliament

1965. Churchill Commemoration.

12	4	2r. blue and brown	1·30	1·30
13	-	3r. blue and brown	2·20	2·20
14	-	4r. blue and brown	3·25	3·25
MS14a		Three sheets 140×108 or 108×140 mm. 1r. stamps in blocks of four as Nos. 12/14	12·50	6·75

DESIGNS—HORIZ: 3r. Churchill and Pres. Roosevelt; 4r. Churchill, and Heads of State at his funeral.

1965. Olympic Games, Tokyo (1964). Optd OLYMPIC TOKYO 1964 in English and Arabic and Olympic "rings".

15	3	1r. brown and green	80	80
16	3	2r. brown and violet	1·70	1·70
17	3	5r. brown and blue	4·25	4·25

1965. Death Centenary of Abraham Lincoln. Optd ABRAHAM LINCOLN 1809-1865 in English and Arabic.

18		1r. brown and green	80	80
19		2r. brown and violet	1·70	1·70
20		5r. brown and blue	4·25	4·25

1965. 20th Death Anniv of Pres. Roosevelt. Optd FRANKLIN D. ROOSEVELT 1882-1945 in English and Arabic.

21		1r. brown and green	80	80
22		2r. brown and violet	1·70	1·70
23		5r. brown and blue	4·25	4·25

8 Satellite and Tracking Station

1966. I.T.U. Centenary. Multicoloured.

24		15n.p. Type **8**	35	20
25		50n.p. Post Office Tower, London, "Telstar" and tracking gantry	55	35
26		85n.p. Rocket on launching-pad and "Relay"	1·20	45
27		1r. Type **8**	1·50	55
28		2r. As 50n.p.	2·50	65
29		3r. As 85n.p.	3·00	1·30
MS30		110×80 mm. 5r. Globe and satellites (53×33 mm). Imperf	5·50	3·25

9 Swimming

1966. Pan-Arab Games, Cairo (1965).

31	A	1n.p. brown, pink and green	10	10
32	B	2n.p. black, grey and green	10	10
33	C	3n.p. brown, pink and green	10	10
34	D	4n.p. brown, pink and purple	10	10
35	A	5n.p. black, grey and orange	15	10
36	9	10n.p. brown, pink and blue	20	15
37	B	25n.p. brown, pink and cinnamon	55	20
38	C	50n.p. black, grey and violet	1·10	55
39	D	75n.p. black, grey and blue	1·80	80
40	9	1r. black, grey and green	2·50	1·00
MS41		D 100×85 mm. 5r. violet, blue and yellow. Imperf	7·25	6·75

DESIGNS: A, Running; B, Boxing; C, Football; D, Fencing.

10 Carpenter

1966. American Astronauts.

42	10	25n.p. black, gold and purple	20	10
43	-	50n.p. black, silver & brown	35	20
44	-	75n.p. black, silver and blue	55	30
45	-	1r. black, silver and bistre	80	35
46	-	2r. black, silver and mauve	1·70	90
47	-	3r. black, gold and green	2·50	1·20
48	-	4r. black, gold and red	3·25	1·80
49	-	5r. black, gold and blue	4·00	2·10
MS50		Two sheets each 156×106 mm containing stamps as Nos. 42/5 and 46/9 but without face values. Imperf (sold at 4e. each)	9·50	4·00

ASTRONAUTS: 50n.p. Glenn; 75n.p. Shepard; 1r. Cooper; 2r. Grissom; 3r. Schirra; 4r. Stafford; 5r. Lovell.

11 Shaikh Sabah of Kuwait and Shaikh Saqr of Ras al Khaima

1966. International Co-operation Year.

51	11	1r. black and red	90	45
52	A	1r. black and lilac	90	45
53	B	1r. black and pink	90	45
54	C	1r. black and green	90	45
55	D	1r. black and green	90	45
56	E	1r. black and yellow	90	45
57	F	1r. black and orange	90	45
58	G	1r. black and blue	90	45
MS59		Two sheets each 127×115 mm. Nos. 51/4 and 55/8. Imperf	8·25	4·25

SHAIKH SAQR AND WORLD LEADERS: A, Shaikh Ahmad of Qatar; B, Pres. Nasser; C, King Hussein; D, Pres. Johnson; E, Pres. De Gaulle; F, Pope Paul VI; G, Prime Minister Harold Wilson.

NEW CURRENCY SURCHARGES. During the latter half of 1966 various issues appeared surcharged in dirhams and riyals. The 1964 definitives with this surcharge are listed below as there is considerable evidence of their postal use. Nos. 24/58 also exist with these surcharges.

In August 1966 Nos. 1/14, 24/9 and 51/8 appeared surcharged in fils and rupees. As Ras Al Khaima did not adopt this currency their status is uncertain.

1966. Nos. 1/8 with currency names changed to dirhams and riyals by overprinting in English and Arabic.

60	1	5d. on 5n.p. brown and black	10	10
60a	-	5d. on 75n.p. red and black	45	35
64b	3	5d. on 5r. brown and blue	45	35
61	1	15d. on 15n.p. blue & black	45	40
62	-	30d. on 30n.p. brown and black	90	80
63	-	40d. on 40n.p. blue & black	1·20	1·10
64	-	75d. on 75n.p. red and black	2·20	2·10
65	3	1r. on 1r. brown and green	1·80	1·70
66	3	2r. on 2r. brown and violet	3·75	3·25
67	3	5r. on 5r. brown and blue	7·25	6·25

15 W.H.O. Building and Flowers

1966. Inauguration of W.H.O. Headquarters, Geneva.

68	15	15d. multicoloured (postage)	35	15
69	-	35d. multicoloured	1·00	20
70	15	50d. multicoloured (air)	1·10	45
71	-	3r. multicoloured	3·25	1·10
MS72		79×72 mm. No. 71. Imperf	5·00	2·20

DESIGN: 35d., 3r. As Type **15** but with red instead of yellow flowers at left.

16 Queen Elizabeth II presenting Jules Rimet Cup to Bobby Moore, Captain of England Team

1966. Air. England's Victory in World Cup Football Championship. Multicoloured.

73		1r. Wembley Stadium	1·10	45
74		2r. Goalkeeper saving ball	1·90	90
75		3r. Footballers with ball	2·75	1·30
76		4r. Type **16**	3·75	2·50
MS77		Two sheets each 90×80 mm. Nos. 73 and 76. Imperf	10·00	7·75

17 Shaikh Saqr

18 Oil Rig

1971

78	17	5d. multicoloured		
79	18	20d. multicoloured		
80	17	30d. multicoloured		

For later issues see **UNITED ARAB EMIRATES**.

APPENDIX

The following stamps have either been issued in excess of postal needs or have not been available to the public in reasonable quantities at face value. Such stamps may later be given full listing if there is evidence of regular postal use.

1967

"The Arabian Nights". Paintings. Air 30, 70d., 1, 2, 3r.
Cats. Postage 1, 2, 3, 4, 5d.: Air 3r.
Arab Paintings. 1, 2, 3, 4, 10, 20, 30d.
European Paintings. Air 60, 70d., 1, 2, 3, 5, 10r.
50th Birth Anniv of Pres. John F. Kennedy. Optd on 1965 Pres. Kennedy Commem. 2, 3, 4r.
World Scout Jamboree, Idaho. Postage 1, 2, 3, 4d.; Air 35, 75d., 1r.
U.S. "Apollo" Disaster. Optd on 1966 American Astronauts issue. 25d. on 25n.p., 50d. on 50n.p., 75d. on 75n.p., 1, 2, 3, 4, 5r.
Summer Olympics Preparation, Mexico 1968. Postage 10, 20, 30, 40d.; Air 1, 2r.
Winter Olympics Preparation, Grenoble 1968. Postage 1, 2, 3, 4, 5d.; Air 85d., 2, 3r.

1968

Mothers' Day. Paintings. Postage 20, 30, 40, 50d.; Air 1, 2, 3, 4r.
International Human Rights Year. 2r.×3.
International Museum Campaign. Paintings. 15, 15, 20, 25, 35, 40, 45, 60, 70, 80, 90d.; 1, 1r.25, 1r.50, 2r.50, 2r.75.
Winter Olympic Medal Winners, Grenoble. 50d., 1, 1r.50, 2, 2r.50, 3r.
Olympic Games, Mexico. Air 1, 2, 2, 3, 3, 4r. 5th Death Anniv of Pres. John F. Kennedy. Air. 2, 3r.
Christmas. Religious Paintings. Postage 20, 30, 40, 50, 60d., 1r.; Air 2, 3, 4r.

1969

Famous Composers (1st series). Paintings. 25, 50, 75d., 1r.50, 2r.50.
Famous Operas. 20, 40, 60, 80d., 1, 2r.
Famous Men. Postage 20, 30, 50d.; Air 1r.50, 2, 3, 4, 5r.
International Philatelic Exhibition, Mexico 1968 (EFIMEX). Postage 10, 10, 25, 35, 40, 50, 60, 70d.; Air 1, 2, 3, 5, 5r.
Int Co-operation in Olympics. 1, 2, 3, 4r.
International Co-operation in Space. Air 1r.50, 2r.50, 3r.50, 4r.50.
Birth Bicentenary of Napoleon. Paintings. Postage 1r.75, 2r.75, 3r.75; Air 75d.
"Apollo" Moon Missions. Air 2, 2r.50, 3, 3r.50, 4, 4r.50, 5, 5r.50.
"Apollo 11" Astronauts. Air 2r.25, 3r.25, 4r.25, 5r.25.
"Apollo 12" Astronauts. Air 60d., 2r.60, 3r.60, 4r.60, 5r.60.

1970

Christmas 1969. Religious Paintings. Postage 50d.; Air 3, 3r.50.
World Cup, Mexico. Air 1, 2, 3, 4, 5, 6r.
Easter. Religious Paintings. Postage 50d.; Air 3, 3r.50.
Paintings by Titian and Tiepolo. Postage 50, 50d.; Air 3, 3, 3r.50, 3r.50.
Winter Olympics, Sapporo 1972. Air 1, 2, 3, 4, 5, 6r.
Olympic Games, Munich 1972. Air 1, 2, 3, 4, 5, 6r.
Paul Gauguin's Paintings. Postage 50d.; Air 3, 3r.50.
Christmas. Religious Paintings. Postage 50d.; Air 3, 3r.50.
"World Cup Champions, Brazil". Optd on Mexico World Cup issue. Air 1, 2, 3, 4, 5, 6r.
"EXPO 70" World Fair, Osaka, Japan (1st issue). Postage 40, 45, 50, 55, 60, 65, 70, 75d.; Air 80, 85, 90, 95d., 1r.60, 1r.65, 1r.85, 2r.
"EXPO 70" World Fair, Osaka, Japan (2nd issue). Postage 55, 65, 75d.; Air 25, 85, 95d., 1r.50, 1r.75.
Space Programmes. Air 1r.×6, 2r.×6, 4r.×6.
Famous Frenchmen. Air 1r.×4, 2r.×4, 2r.50×2, 3r.×2, 4r.×4, 5r.50×2.
Int Philatelic Exn (Philympia '70). Air 1r.×4, 1r.50×4, 2r.50×4, 3r.×4, 4r.×4.
Events in the Life of Christ. Religious Paintings. 5, 10, 25, 50d., 1, 2, 5r.
"Stages of the Cross". Religious Paintings. 10, 20, 30, 40, 50, 60, 70, 80d., 1, 1r.50, 2, 2r.50, 3, 3r.50.
The Life of Mary. Religious Paintings. 10, 15, 30, 60, 75d., 3, 4r.

1971

Easter. "Stages of the Cross" (1970) but with additional inscr "EASTER". 10, 20, 30, 40, 50, 60, 70, 80d., 1, 1r.50, 2, 2r.50, 3, 3r.50.
Charles de Gaulle Memorial. Postage 50d.; Air 1, 1r.50, 2, 3, 4r.
Safe Return of "Apollo 14". Postage 50d.; Air 1, 1r.50, 2, 3, 4r.
U.S.A.–Japan Baseball Friendship. Postage 10, 25, 30, 80d.; Air 50, 70d., 1, 1r.50.
Munich Olympics, 1972. Postage 50d.; Air 1, 1r.50, 2, 3, 4r.
Cats. 35, 60, 65, 110, 120, 160d.
13th World Jamboree, Japan. Postage 30, 50, 60, 75d.; Air 1, 1r.50, 3, 4r.
Sapporo Olympic Gold Medal Winners. Optd on 1970 Winter Olympics, Sapporo 1972, issue. Air 1, 2, 3, 4, 5, 6r.
Munich Olympic Medal Winners, Optd on 1970 Summer Olympics, Munich 1972, issue. Air 1, 2, 3, 4, 5, 6r.
Japanese Locomotives. Postage 30, 35, 75d.; Air 90d., 1, 1r.75.
"Soyuz 11" Russian Cosmonauts Memorial. Air 1, 2, 3, 4r.
"Apollo 15". Postage 50d.; Air 1, 1r.50, 2, 3, 4r.
Dogs. 5, 20, 75, 85, 185, 200d.
Durer's Paintings. Postage 50d.; Air 1, 1r.50 2, 3, 4r.
Famous Composers (2nd series). Postage 50d.; Air 1, 1r.50, 2, 3, 4r.
"Soyuz 11" and "Salyut" Space Projects. Postage 50 d,; Air 1, 1r.50, 2, 3, 4r.
Butterflies. Postage 15, 20, 70d.; Air 1r.25, 1r.50, 1r.70.
Wild Animals. 10, 40, 80 d,; 1r.15, 1r.30, 1r.65.
Fishes. 30, 50, 60, 90d., 1r.45, 1r.55.
Ludwig van Beethoven. Portraits. Postage 50d.; Air 1, 1r.50, 2, 3, 4r.

1972

Birds. 50, 55, 80, 100, 105, 190d.
Winter Olympics, Sapporo (1st issue). Postage 20, 30, 50d., Air 70, 90d., 2r.50
Winter Olympics, Sapporo (2nd issue). Postage 5, 60, 80, 90d.; Air 1r.10, 1r.75
Mozart. Portraits. Postage 50d.; Air 1, 1r.50, 2, 3, 4r.
Olympic Games, Munich. Postage 50d.; Air 1, 1r.50, 2, 3, 4r.
"In Memory of Charles de Gaulle". Optd on 1971 Charles de Gaulle memorial issue. Postage 50d.; Air 1, 1r.50, 2, 3, 4r.
Winter Olympics, Sapporo (3rd issue). Postage 15, 45d.; Air 65, 75d., 1r.20, 1r.25.
Horses. Postage 10, 25, 30d.; Air 1r.40, 1r.80, 1r.95.
Parrots. 40, 45, 70, 95d., 1r.35, 1r.75.
"Apollo 16". Postage 50d.; Air 1, 1r.50, 2, 3, 4r.
European Footballers. Postage 50d.; Air 1, 1r.50, 2, 3, 4r.

A number of issues on gold or silver foil also exist, but it is understood that these were mainly for presentation purposes, although valid for postage.

In common with the other states of the United Arab Emirates the Ras al Khaima stamp contract was terminated on 1st August 1972, and any further new issues released after that date were unauthorized.

Pt. 1

REDONDA

A dependency of Antigua.

The following stamps were issued in anticipation of commercial and tourist development, philatelic mail being handled by a bureau in Antigua. Since at the present time the island is uninhabited, we do not list or stock these items. It is understood that the stamps are valid for the prepayment of postage in Antigua. Miniature sheets, imperforate stamps etc, are excluded from this section.

1979

Antigua 1976 definitive issue optd **REDONDA**. 3, 5, 10, 25, 35, 50, 75c., $1, $2.50, $5, $10.
Antigua Coronation Anniversary issue optd **REDONDA**. 10, 30, 50, 90c., $2.50.
Antigua World Cup Football Championship issue optd **REDONDA**. 10, 15c., $3.
Death Centenary of Sir Rowland Hill. 50, 90c., $2.50, $3.
International Year of the Child 25, 50c., $1, $2.
Christmas. Paintings. 8, 50, 90c., $3.

1980

Marine Life. 8, 25, 50c., $4.
75th Anniv of Rotary International. 25, 50c., $1, $2.
Birds of Redonda. 8, 10, 15, 25, 30, 50c., $1, $2, $5.
Olympic Medal Winners, Lake Placid and Moscow. 8, 25, 50c., $3.
80th Birthday of Queen Elizabeth the Queen Mother. 10c., $2.50.
Christmas Paintings. 8, 25, 50c., $4.

1981

Royal Wedding. 25, 55c., $4.
Christmas. Walt Disney Cartoon Characters. 1/2, 1, 2, 3, 4, 5, 10c., $2.50, $3.
World Cup Football Championship, Spain (1982). 30c.×2, 50c.×2, $1×2, $2×2.

1982

Boy Scout Annivs. 8, 25, 50c., $3, $5.
Butterflies. 8, 30, 50c., $2.
21st Birthday of Princess of Wales. $2, $4.
Birth of Prince William of Wales. Optd on Princess of Wales 21st Birthday issue. $2, $4.
Christmas. Walt Disney's "One Hundred and One Dalmatians". 1/2, 1, 2, 3, 4, 5, 10c., $2.50, $3.

1983

Easter. 500th Birth Anniv of Raphael. 10, 50, 90c., $5.
Bicent of Manned Flight. 10, 50, 90c., $2.50.
Christmas. Walt Disney Cartoon Characters. "Deck the Halls". 1/2, 1, 2, 3, 4, 5, 10c., $2.50, $3.

1984

Easter. Walt Disney Cartoon Characters. 1/2, 1, 2, 3, 4, 5, 10c., $2, $4.
Olympic Games, Los Angeles. 10, 50, 90c., $2.50.
Christmas. 50th Birthday of Donald Duck. 45, 60, 90c., $2, $4.

1985

Birth Bicentenary of John J. Audubon (ornithologist) (1st issue). 60, 90c., $1, $3.
Life and Times of Queen Elizabeth the Queen Mother. $1, $1.50, $2.50.
Royal Visit. 45c., $1, $4.
150th Birth Anniv of Mark Twain (author). 25, 50c., $1.50, $3.
Birth Bicentenaries of Grimm Brothers (folklorists). Walt Disney cartoon characters. 30, 60, 70c., $4.

1986

Birth Bicentenary of John J. Audubon (ornith-ologist) (2nd issue). 90c., $1, $1.50, $3.
Appearance of Halley's Comet. 5, 15, 55c., $4.
Centenary of Statue of Liberty (1st issue). 20, 25, 30c., $4.
60th Birthday of Queen Elizabeth II. 50, 60c., $4.
Royal Wedding. 60c., $1, $4.
Christmas (1st issue). Disney characters in Hans Andersen Stories. 30, 60, 70c., $4.
Christmas (2nd issue). "Wind in the Willows" (by Kenneth Grahame). 25, 50c., $1.50, $3.

1987

"Capex '87" International Stamp Exhibition, Toronto. Disney characters illustrating Art of Animation. 25, 30, 50, 60, 70c., $1.50, $3, $4.
Birth Centenary of Marc Chagall (artist). 10, 30, 40, 60, 90c., $1, $3, $4.
Centenary of Statue of Liberty (2nd issue). 10, 15, 25, 30, 40, 60, 70, 90c., $1, $2, $3, $4.
250th Death Anniv of Sir Isaac Newton (scientist). 20c., $2.50.
750th Anniv of Berlin. $1, $4.
Bicentenary of U.S. Constitution. 30c., $3.
16th World Scout Jamboree, Australia. 10c., $4.

1988

500th Anniv (1992) of Discovery of America by Columbus. 15, 30, 45, 60, 90c., $1, $2, $3.
"Finlandia '88" International Stamp Exhibition, Helsinki. Disney characters in Finnish scenes. 1, 2, 3, 4, 5, 6c., $5, $6.
Olympic Games, Seoul. 25, 60c., $1.25, $3.
500th Birth Anniv of Titian. 10, 25, 40, 70, 90c., $2, $3, $4.

1989

20th Anniv of First Manned Landing on Moon. Disney characters on Moon. 1/2, 1, 2, 3, 4, 5c., $5, $6.
500th Anniv (1992) of Discovery of America by Columbus (2nd issue). Pre-Columbian Societies. 15, 45, 45, 50c., $2, $2, $3, $3.
Christmas. Disney Characters and Cars of 1950s. 25, 35, 45, 60c., $1, $2, $3, $4.

1990

Christmas. Disney Characters and Hollywood cars. 25, 35, 40, 60c., $2, $3, $4, $5.

1991

Nobel Prize Winners. 5, 15, 25, 40, 50c., $1, $2, $4.

Pt. 6

RÉUNION

An island in the Indian Ocean, E. of Madagascar now an overseas department of France.

100 centimes = 1 franc.

1

1852. Imperf. No gum.

1	1	15c. black on blue	£35000	£23000
2	1	30c. black on blue	£33000	£22000

1885. Stamps of French Colonies surch R and value in figures. Imperf.

5	D	5c. on 30c. brown	55·00	50·00
7	H	5c. on 30c. brown	4·50	7·25
3	A	5c. on 40c. orange	£300	£275
6	F	5c. on 40c. orange	60·00	65·00
8	H	5c. on 40c. red on yellow	65·00	£120
9	H	10c. on 40c. red on yellow	11·00	4·50
10	H	20c. on 30c. brown	70·00	65·00
4	A	25c. on 40c. orange	60·00	55·00

1891. Stamps of French Colonies optd REUNION. Imperf (Types F and H) or perf (Type J).

17A	J	1c. black on blue	90	2·50
18B	J	2c. brown on buff	65	75
19A	J	4c. brown on grey	3·00	4·25
20A	J	5c. green on green	5·00	1·30
21A	J	10c. black on lilac	30·00	2·30
22A	J	15c. blue on blue	60·00	1·60
23A	J	20c. red on green	14·50	16·00
24A	J	25c. black on pink	60·00	1·40
13A	H	30c. brown	55·00	65·00
25Aa	J	35c. black on yellow	16·00	23·00
11B	F	40c. orange	£425	£425
14A	H	40c. red on yellow	34·00	21·00
26A	J	40c. red on buff	£100	95·00
15A	H	75c. red	£325	£325
27A	J	75c. red on pink	£500	£425
12B	F	80c. pink	80·00	70·00
16A	H	1f. green	70·00	60·00
28B	J	1f. green	£425	£375

1891. Stamps of French Colonies surch REUNION and new value.

29	02c. on 20c. red on green	4·00	6·25
31	2 on 20c. red on green	3·00	3·25
30	15c. on 20c. red on green	11·00	3·75

1892. "Tablet" key-type inscr "REUNION".

34	D	1c. black and red on blue	20	20
35	D	2c. brown and blue on buff	1·30	35
36	D	4c. brown and blue on grey	2·30	20
37	D	5c. green	1·10	20
38	D	10c. black and blue on lilac	5·75	1·20
51	D	10c. red and blue	3·25	20
39	D	15c. blue and red	55·00	45
52	D	15c. grey and red	11·00	10
40	D	20c. red and blue on green	19·00	10·00
41	D	25c. black and red on pink	23·00	2·00
53	D	25c. blue and red	25·00	38·00
42	D	30c. brown and blue on drab	27·00	11·00
43	D	40c. red and blue on yellow	55·00	14·50
44	D	50c. red and blue on pink	£100	17·00
54	D	50c. brown and red on blue	65·00	70·00
55	D	50c. brown and blue on blue	65·00	70·00
45	D	75c. brown and red on orange	65·00	65·00
46	D	1f. green and red	65·00	65·00

1893. Stamp of French Colonies, "Commerce" type, surch 2 c.

47	J	2c. on 20c. red on green	2·50	2·50

1901. "Tablet" key-type surch in figures.

56	D	5c. on 40c. red and blue on yellow	3·25	8·50
57	D	5c. on 50c. red and blue on pink	5·25	6·00
58	D	15c. on 75c. brown and red on orange	25·00	29·00
59	D	15c. on 1f. green and red	16·00	9·00

16 Map of Reunion

17 View of Saint-Denis and Arms of the Colony

18 View of St. Pierre and Crater Dolomieu

1907

60	16	1c. red and lilac	35	35
61	16	2c. blue and brown	55	1·00
62	16	4c. red and green	90	1·60
63	16	5c. red and green	2·75	35
92	16	5c. violet and yellow	70	35
64	16	10c. green and red	7·75	30
93	16	10c. turquoise and green	55	35
94	16	10c. red and lake on blue	1·00	45
65	16	15c. blue and black	3·75	1·60
95	16	15c. turquoise and green	85	50
96	16	15c. red and blue	3·50	1·80
66	17	20c. green and olive	3·50	1·80
67	17	25c. brown and blue	7·75	90
97	17	25c. blue and brown	1·50	35
68	17	30c. green and brown	1·30	1·00
98	17	30c. pink and red	3·25	4·50
99	17	30c. red and grey	1·80	1·70
100	17	30c. light green and green	3·50	5·25
69	17	35c. blue and brown	3·50	1·60
101	17	40c. brown and green	2·10	30
70	17	45c. pink and violet	2·75	4·75
102	17	45c. red and purple	2·00	4·25
103	17	45c. red and mauve	4·50	10·00
71	17	50c. blue and brown	3·00	2·30
104	17	50c. ultramarine and blue	2·30	2·50
105	17	50c. violet and yellow	2·00	35
106	17	60c. brown and blue	2·30	6·75
107	17	65c. blue and violet	4·50	4·25
72	17	75c. pink and red	2·50	1·00
108	17	75c. purple and brown	4·50	5·25
109	17	90c. pink and red	11·50	21·00
73	18	1f. blue and brown	4·00	2·75
110	18	1f. blue	3·25	2·20
111	18	1f. lilac and brown	4·75	1·80
112	18	1f.10 mauve and brown	4·25	4·75
113	18	1f.50 lt blue & blue on bl	24·00	28·00
74	18	2f. green and red	7·00	1·70
114	18	3f. mauve on pink	13·00	14·50
75	18	5f. brown and pink	11·00	9·25

1912. "Tablet" key-type surch.

76A	D	05 on 2c. brown and red on buff	60	35
77A	D	05 on 15c. grey and red	45	35
78A	D	05 on 20c. red and blue on green	3·50	7·25
79A	D	05 on 25c. black and red on pink	1·80	5·50
80A	D	05 on 30c. brown and blue on drab	35	2·00
81A	D	10 on 40c. red and blue on yellow	1·00	3·75
82A	D	10 on 50c. brown and blue on blue	2·30	3·75
83A	D	10 on 75c. brown and red on orange	1·90	16·00

1915. Red Cross Surch 5c and red cross.

90	16	10c.+5c. green and red	1·20	5·75

1917. Surch 0,01.

91	0,01 on 4c. chestnut and brown	4·75	3·50

1922. Surch in figures only.

115	17	40 on 20c. yellow and green	75	1·30
116	17	50 on 45c. red and purple	4·50	1·80
117	17	50 on 45c. red and mauve	£250	£250
118	17	50 on 65c. blue and violet	5·25	3·75
119	17	60 on 75c. carmine and red	85	55
120	16	65 on 15c. blue and black	3·00	8·50
121	16	85 on 15c. blue and black	2·50	8·25
122	17	85 on 75c. pink and red	2·30	8·75
123	17	90 on 75c. pink and red	3·25	3·25

1924. Surch in cents and francs.

124	18	25c. on 5f. brown and pink	1·80	8·00
125	18	1f.25 on 1f. blue	1·70	2·50
126	18	1f.50 on 1f. light blue and blue on blue	1·50	65
127	18	3f. on 5f. blue and red	4·75	3·50
128	18	10f. on 5f. red and green	23·00	44·00
129	18	20f. on 5f. pink and brown	26·00	46·00

1931. "Colonial Exhibition" key-types inscr "REUNION".

130	E	40c. green and black	5·50	6·00
131	F	50c. mauve and black	5·75	4·50
132	G	90c. red and black	4·50	6·75
133	H	1f.50 blue and black	8·50	9·00

30 Cascade, Salazie

31 Anchain Peak, Salazie

32 Leon Dierx Museum

1933

134 **30** 1c. purple 30 2·50
135 **30** 2c. brown 10 1·90
136 **30** 3c. mauve 75 5·50
137 **30** 4c. olive 20 3·50
138 **30** 5c. orange 35 40
139 **30** 10c. blue 40 70
140 **30** 15c. black 20 50
141 **30** 20c. blue 40 2·75
142 **30** 25c. brown 70 75
143 **30** 30c. green 80 1·00
144 **31** 35c. green 1·70 6·50
145 **31** 40c. blue 2·50 1·80
146 **31** 40c. brown 65 6·50
147 **31** 45c. mauve 1·60 7·25
148 **31** 45c. green 1·70 6·75
149 **31** 50c. red 65 10
150 **31** 55c. orange 3·00 4·50
151 **31** 60c. blue 90 6·75
152 **31** 65c. olive 4·25 2·50
153 **31** 70c. olive 3·50 7·25
154 **31** 75c. brown 7·25 12·50
155 **31** 80c. black 1·80 7·00
156 **31** 90c. red 5·50 5·25
157 **31** 90c. purple 1·70 2·00
158 **31** 1f. green 5·50 45
159 **31** 1f. red 3·00 5·50
160 **31** 1f. black 1·30 6·75
161 **32** 1f.25 brown 1·20 6·25
162 **32** 1f.25 red 3·00 7·50
163 **30** 1f.40 blue 3·00 7·25
164 **32** 1f.50 blue 65 35
165 **30** 1f.60 red 3·00 6·50
166 **32** 1f.75 olive 3·00 90
167 **30** 1f.75 blue 2·75 7·50
168 **32** 2f. red 90 2·10
169 **30** 2f.25 blue 5·25 8·75
170 **30** 2f.50 brown 2·50 3·00
171 **32** 3f. violet 1·40 1·80
172 **32** 5f. mauve 1·40 6·25
173 **32** 10f. blue 2·10 7·00
174 **32** 20f. brown 2·75 8·50

1937. Air. Pioneer Flight from Reunion to France by Laurent, Lenier and Touge. Optd REUNION – FRANCE par avion "ROLAND GARROS".

174a **31** 50c. red £275 £250

1937. International Exhibition, Paris. As Nos. 168/73 of St.-Pierre et Miquelon.

175 20c. violet 1·60 7·50
176 30c. green 1·50 7·50
177 40c. red 90 6·00
178 50c. brown and agate 1·10 3·25
179 90c. red 1·40 4·25
180 1f.50 blue 1·80 7·50

34 Caudron C-600 "Aiglon"

1938. Air.

181 **34** 3f.65 blue and red 1·10 1·00
182 **34** 6f.65 brown and red 1·60 5·50
183 **34** 9f.65 red and blue 1·00 7·50
184 **34** 12f.65 brown and green 1·60 8·25

1938. International Anti-cancer Fund. As T 17a of Oceanic Settlements.

185 1f.75+50c. blue 6·75 36·00

1939. New York World's Fair. As T 17b of Oceanic Settlements.

186 1f.25 red 2·10 7·75
187 2f.25 blue 1·70 7·75

1939. 150th Anniv of French Revolution. As T 17c of Oceanic Settlements.

188 45c.+25c. green and black (postage) 10·50 24·00
189 70c.+30c. brown and black 10·50 24·00
190 90c.+35c. orange and black 10·50 24·00
191 1f.25+1f. red and black 10·50 24·00
192 2f.25+2f. blue and black 10·50 24·00
193 3f.65+4f. blk & orge (air) 17·00 42·00

1943. Surch 1f.

194 **31** 1f. on 65c. green 2·50 1·30

1943. Optd France Libre.

198 **30** 1c. purple (postage) 75 8·00
199 **30** 2c. brown 80 6·25
200 **30** 3c. purple 75 7·75
195 **16** 4c. red and green 1·80 11·50
201 **30** 4c. green 55 8·00
202 **30** 5c. red 1·20 8·00
203 **30** 10c. blue 35 3·75
204 **30** 15c. black 45 7·75
205 **30** 20c. blue 1·10 7·75
206 **30** 25c. brown 1·20 6·00
207 **30** 30c. green 85 5·00
208 **31** 35c. green 55 7·00
209 **31** 40c. blue 55 5·50
210 **31** 40c. brown 85 5·00
211 **31** 45c. mauve 55 7·00
212 **31** 45c. green 65 5·25
213 **31** 50c. red 70 3·75
214 **31** 55c. orange 55 6·75
215 **31** 60c. blue 2·30 7·75
216 **31** 65c. green 1·00 7·00
217 **31** 70c. green 1·50 7·50
196 **17** 75c. pink and red 85 7·75
218 **31** 75c. brown 2·75 10·50
219 **31** 80c. black 35 7·00
220 **31** 90c. purple 45 5·75
221 **31** 1f. green 1·10 6·25
222 **31** 1f. red 55 3·00
223 **31** 1f. black 1·40 8·75
240 **31** 1f. on 65c. green (No. 194) 75 2·50
224 **32** 1f.25 brown 75 8·00
225 **32** 1f.25 red 2·10 7·00
238 - 1f.25 red (No. 186) 90 9·50
226 **30** 1f.40 blue 1·40 7·50
227 **32** 1f.50 blue 90 6·75
228 **30** 1f.60 red 1·20 6·75
229 **32** 1f.75 green 85 7·00
230 **30** 1f.75 blue 2·30 12·00
231 **32** 2f. red 1·20 4·00
232 **30** 2f.25 blue 90 7·50
239 - 2f.25 blue (No. 187) 1·20 9·50
233 **30** 2f.50 brown 2·00 12·00
234 **32** 3f. violet 70 5·50
241 **34** 3f.65 blue and red (air) 2·75 12·00
197 **18** 5f. brown and pink 50·00 75·00
235 **32** 5f. mauve 1·20 2·50
242 **34** 6f.65 brown and red 2·75 12·00
243 **34** 9f.65 red and blue 2·75 12·00
236 **32** 10f. blue 2·10 16·00
244 **34** 12f.65 brown and green 2·75 12·00
237 **32** 20f. brown 5·25 21·00

37 Chief Products

1943. Free French Issue.

245 **37** 5c. brown 10 3·25
246a **37** 10c. blue 1·10 2·30
247 **37** 25c. green 35 5·25
248 **37** 30c. red 70 5·00
249 **37** 40c. green 35 5·25
250 **37** 80c. mauve 85 3·75
251 **37** 1f. purple 80 35
252 **37** 1f.50 red 1·10 90
253 **37** 2f. black 55 2·10
254 **37** 2f.50 blue 1·10 4·75
255 **37** 4f. violet 1·30 1·00
256 **37** 5f. yellow 1·00 30
257 **37** 10f. brown 1·20 75
258 **37** 20f. green 1·50 1·40

1944. Air. Free French Administration. As T 19a of Oceanic Settlements.

259 1f. orange 85 55
260 1f.50 red 55 75
261 5f. purple 70 1·30
262 10f. black 1·40 4·75
263 25f. blue 2·00 4·25
264 50f. green 1·90 1·50
265 100f. red 2·30 3·25

1944. Mutual Air and Red Cross Funds. As T 19b of Oceanic Settlements.

266 5f.+20f. black 1·00 8·75

1945. Eboue. As T 20a of Oceanic Settlements.

267 2f. black 35 80
268 25f. green 65 6·50

1945. Surch.

269 50c. on 5c. brown 1·00 5·50
270 60c. on 5c. brown 1·10 6·75
271 70c. on 5c. brown 55 6·75
272 1f.20 on 5c. brown 1·00 6·00
273 2f.40 on 25c. green 1·40 4·75
274 3f. on 25c. green 1·00 2·30
275 4f.50 on 25c. green 1·00 2·50
276 15f. on 2f.50 blue 75 75

1946. Air. Victory. As T 20b of Oceanic Settlements.

277 8f. grey 65 2·30

1946. Air. From Chad to the Rhine. As T 20c of Oceanic Settlements.

278 5f. red 1·40 7·75
279 10f. violet 1·00 7·00
280 15f. black 1·20 7·25
281 20f. red 1·40 5·00
282 25f. blue 1·50 6·00
283 50f. green 1·70 8·75

39 Cliffs

40 Banana Tree and Cliff

41 Mountain Landscape

42 Shadow of Airplane over Coast

1947

284 **39** 10c. orange & grn (postage) 20 4·25
285 **39** 30c. orange and blue 35 5·50
286 **39** 40c. orange and brown 35 6·50
287 - 50c. brown and green 35 3·75
288 - 60c. brown and blue 20 7·00
289 - 80c. green and brown 35 7·00
290 - 1f. purple and blue 45 35
291 - 1f.20 grey and green 1·00 6·50
292 - 1f.50 purple and orange 80 7·25
293 **40** 2f. blue and green 85 50
294 **40** 3f. purple and green 1·40 2·50
295 **40** 3f.60 pink and red 1·20 7·75
296 **40** 4f. blue and brown 1·80 2·30
297 **41** 5f. mauve and brown 2·30 1·10
298 **41** 6f. blue and brown 1·70 1·50
299 **41** 10f. orange and blue 2·10 3·00
300 - 15f. purple and blue 2·50 8·25
301 - 20f. blue and orange 3·25 14·00
302 - 25f. brown and mauve 2·75 5·25
303 **42** 50f. green and grey (air) 7·50 23·00
304 - 100f. orange and brown 13·00 36·00
305 - 200f. blue and orange 10·00 46·00

DESIGNS—20×37 mm: 50c. to 80c. Cutting sugar cane; 1f. to 1f.50, Cascade. 28×50 mm: 100f. Douglas DC-4 airplane over Reunion. 37×20 mm: 15f. to 25f. "Ville de Strasbourg" (liner) approaching Reunion. 50×28 mm: 200f. Reunion from the air.

1949. Stamps of France surch CFA and value. (a) Postage. (i) Ceres.

306 **218** 50c. on 1f. red 10 1·60
307 **218** 60c. on 2f. green 85 10·00

(ii) Nos. 972/3 (Arms).

308 10c. on 30c. black, red and yellow (Alsace) 35 5·25
309 30c. on 50c. brown, yellow and red (Lorraine) 20 7·50

(iii) Nos. 981, 979 and 982/a (Views).

310 5f. on 20f. blue (Finistere) 1·40 90
311 7f. on 12f. red (Luxembourg Palace) 1·00 3·75
312 8f. on 25f. blue (Nancy) 3·00 90
313 10f. on 25f. brown (Nancy) 1·00 45

(iv) Marianne.

314 **219** 1f. on 3f. mauve 80 10
315 **219** 2f. on 4f. green 50 35
316 **219** 2f. on 5f. green 2·75 14·50
317 **219** 2f. on 5f. violet 1·40 20
318 **219** 2f.50 on 5f. blue 2·75 40·00
319 **219** 3f. on 6f. red 1·10 35
320 **219** 3f. on 6f. green 55 45
321 **219** 4f. on 10f. violet 1·10 35
322 **219** 6f. on 12f. blue 1·80 70
323 **219** 6f. on 12f. orange 1·80 85
324 **219** 9f. on 18f. red 1·30 8·75

(v) Conques Abbey.

325 **263** 11f. on 18f. blue 90 2·50

(b) Air. (i) Nos. 967/70 (Mythology).

326 - 20f. on 40f. green 1·60 55
327 **236** 25f. on 50f. pink 2·00 30
328 **237** 50f. on 100f. blue 2·75 1·30
329 - 100f. on 200f. red 11·50 10·00

(ii) Nos. 1056 and 1058/9 (Cities).

330 100f. on 200f. green (Bordeaux) 40·00 36·00
331 200f. on 500f. red (Marseilles) 40·00 48·00
332 500f. on 1000f. purple and black on blue (Paris) 95·00 £160

1950. Stamps of France surch CFA and value. (a) Nos. 1050 and 1052 (Arms).

342 10c. on 50c. yellow, red and blue (Guyenne) 10 3·75
343 1f. on 2f. red, yellow and green (Auvergne) 1·10 9·25

(b) On Nos. 1067/8 and 1068b (Views).

344 - 5f. on 20f. red (Comminges) 1·10 50
345 **284** 8f. on 25f. blue (Wandrille) 70 35
346 - 15f. on 30f. blue (Arbois) 60 50

1951. Nos. 1123/4 of France (Arms) surch CFA and value.

347 50c. on 1f. red, yellow and blue (Bearn) 20 75
348 1f. on 2f. yellow, blue and red (Touraine) 10 20

1952. Nos. 1138 and 1144 of France surch CFA and value.

349 **323** 5f. on 20f. violet (Chambord) 55 35
350 **317** 8f. on 40f. violet (Bigorre) 90 35

1953. Stamps of France surch CFA and value. (a) Nos. 1162, 1168 and 1170 (Literary Figures and National Industries).

351 3f. on 6f. lake and red (Gargantua) 45 35
352 8f. on 40f. brown and chocolate (Porcelain) 55 10
353 20f. on 75f. red and carmine (Flowers) 1·80 80

(b) Nos. 1181/2 (Arms).

354 50c. on 1f. yellow, red and black (Poitou) 35 65
355 1f. on 2f. yellow, blue and brown (Champagne) 35 7·75

1954. Stamps of France surch CFA and value. (a) Postage. (i) Nos. 1188 and 1190 (Sports).

356 8f. on 40f. blue and brown (Canoeing) 2·75 2·30
357 20f. on 75f. red and orange (Horse jumping) 11·00 55·00

(ii) Nos. 1205/8 and 1210/11 (Views).

358 2f. on 6f. indigo, blue and green (Lourdes) 85 1·30
359 3f. on 8f. green and blue (Andelys) 90 7·50
360 4f. on 10f. brown and blue (Royan) 1·20 65
361 6f. on 12f. lilac and violet (Quimper) 1·50 75
362 9f. on 18f. indigo, blue and green (Cheverny) 1·70 12·00
363 10f. on 20f. brown, chestnut and blue (Ajaccio) 2·75 2·50

(iii) No. 1229 (Arms).

364 1f. on 2f. yellow, red and black (Angoumois) 10 10

(b) Air. Nos. 1194/7 (Aircraft).

365 50f. on 100f. brown and blue (Mystere IV) 2·50 90
366 100f. on 200f. purple and blue (Noratlas) 2·30 2·50
367 200f. on 500f. red and orange (Magister) 17·00 34·00
368 500f. on 1000f. indigo, purple and blue (Provence) 10·00 30·00

1955. Stamps of France surch CFA and value. (a) Nos. 1262/5, 1266, 1268 and 1268b (Views).

369 2f. on 6f. red (Bordeaux) 60 1·10
370 3f. on 8f. blue (Marseilles) 90 65
371 4f. on 10f. blue (Nice) 1·10 1·00
372 5f. on 12f. brown and grey (Cahors) 55 35
373 6f. on 18f. blue and green (Uzerche) 35 35
374 10f. on 25f. brown and chestnut (Brouage) 35 35
375 17f. on 70f. black and green (Cahors) 1·30 9·50

(b) No. 1273 (Arms).

376 50c. on 1f. yellow, red and blue (Comtat Venaissin) 10 35

1956. Nos. 1297/1300 of France (Sports) surch CFA and value.

377 8f. on 30f. black and grey (Basketball) 55 20
378 9f. on 40f. purple and brown (Pelota) 55 90
379 15f. on 50f. violet and purple (Rugby) 1·20 2·00

380 20f. on 75f. green, black and blue (Climbing) 65 1·70

1957. Stamps of France surch CFA and value. (a) Postage. (i) Harvester.
381 **344** 2f. on 6f. brown 40 10
382 **344** 4f. on 12f. purple 75 55
383 **344** 5f. on 10f. green 65 40

(ii) France.
384 **362** 10f. on 20f. blue 35 10
385 **362** 12f. on 25f. red 65 35

(iii) No. 1335 (Le Quesnoy).
386 7f. on 15f. black and green 60 35

(iv) Nos. 1351, 1352/3, 1354/5 and 1356a (Tourist Publicity).
387 3f. on 10f. chocolate and brown (Elysee) 40 40
388 6f. on 18f. brown and blue (Beynac) 65 1·50
389 9f. on 25f. brown and grey (Valencay) 60 4·50
390 17f. on 35f. mauve and red (Rouen) 80 3·25
391 20f. on 50f. brown and green (St. Remy) 45 35
392 25f. on 85f. purple (Evian-les-Bains) 1·10 60

(b) Air. Nos. 1319/20 (Aircraft).
393 200f. on 500f. black and blue (Caravelle) 6·00 10·00
394 500f. on 1000f. black, violet and brown (Alouette II) 9·25 34·00

1960. Nos. 1461, 1464 and 1467 of France (Tourist Publicity) surch CFA and value.
395 7f. on 15c. indigo and blue (Laon) 1·40 40
396 20f. on 50c. purple and green (Tlemcen) 7·75 1·40
397 50f. on 1f. violet, green and blue (Cilaos) 80 50

1961. Harvester and Sower stamps of France (in new currency) surch CFA and value.
398 **344** 5f. on 10c. green 65 90
400 **453** 10f. on 20c. red and turquoise 65 20

1961. "Marianne" stamp of France surch 12f. CFA.
401 **463** 12f. on 25c. grey & purple 45 20

1961. Nos. 1457, 1457b and 1459/60 of France (Aircraft) surch CFA and value.
402 100f. on 2f. purple and blue (Noratlas) 4·50 1·90
403 100f. on 2f. indigo and blue (Mystere Falcon 20) 1·20 1·30
404 200f. on 5f. black and blue (Caravelle) 4·50 5·00
405 500f. on 10f. black, violet and brown (Alouette II) 14·00 9·25

1962. Red Cross stamps of France (Nos. 1593/4) surch CFA and value.
409 10f.+5f. on 20c.+10c. 1·30 5·00
410 12f.+5f. on 25c.+10c. 1·50 8·25

1962. Satellite Link stamps of France surch CFA and value.
411 12f. on 25c. (No. 1587) 90 2·75
412 25f. on 50c. (No. 1588) 50 5·25

1963. Nos. 1541 and 1545 of France (Tourist Publicity) surch CFA and value.
413 7f. on 15c. grey, purple and blue (Saint-Paul) 1·20 3·00
414 20f. on 45c. brown, green and blue (Sully) 80 90

1963. Nos. 1498b/9b and 1499e/f of France (Arms) surch CFA and value.
415 1f. on 2c. yellow, green and blue (Gueret) 35 20
416 2f. on 5c. mult (Oran) 65 35
417 2f. on 5c. red, yellow and blue (Armiens) 75 20
418 5f. on 10c. blue, yellow and red (Troyes) 1·10 20
419 6f. on 18c. multicoloured (St. Denis) 35 50
420 15f. on 30c. red and blue (Paris) 1·00 20

1963. Red Cross stamps of France Nos. 1627/8 surch CFA and value.
421 10f.+5f. on 20c.+10c. 2·00 10·50
422 12f.+5f. on 25c.+10c. 1·70 10·50

1964. 'PHILATEC 1964' International Stamp Exhibition stamp of France surch CFA and value.
423 12f. on 25c. (No. 1629) 1·10 45

1964. Nos. 1654/5 of France (Tourist Publicity) surch CFA and value.
431 20f. on 40c. chocolate, green and brown (Ronchamp) 85 3·00
432 35f. on 70c. purple, green and blue (Provins) 1·10 1·70

1964. Red Cross stamps of France Nos. 1665/6 surch CFA and value.
433 10f.+5f. on 20c.+10c. 1·70 4·25
434 12f.+5f. on 25c.+10c. 1·60 5·75

1965. No. 1621 of France (Saint Flour) surch 3F CFA.
435 30f. on 60c. red, green & blue 1·00 1·70

1965. Nos 1684/5 and 1688 of France (Tourist Publicity) surch CFA and value.
436 25f. on 50c. blue, green and bistre (St. Marie) 1·50 2·00
437 30f. on 60c. brown and blue (Aix les Bains) 1·20 2·00
438 50f. on 1f. grey, green and brown (Carnac) 2·00 1·40

1965. Tercent of Colonization of Reunion. As No. 1692 of France, but additionally inscr 'CFA'.
439 15f. blue and red 1·50 40

1965. Red Cross stamps of France Nos. 1698/9 surch CFA and value.
440 12f.+5f. on 25c.+10c. 2·00 6·75
441 15f.+5f. on 30c.+10c. 2·00 6·75

1966. "Marianne" stamp of France surch 10f CFA.
442 **476** 10f. on 20c. red and blue 2·10 4·00

1966. Launching of 1st French Satellite. Nos. 1696/7 (plus se-tenant label) of France surch CFA and value.
443 15f. on 30c. blue, turquoise and light blue 1·10 3·75
444 30f. on 60c. blue, turquoise and light blue 2·20 3·75

1966. Red Cross stamps of France Nos. 1733/4 surch CFA and value.
445 12f.+5f. on 25c.+10c. 1·50 6·00
446 15f.+5f. on 30c.+10c. 1·50 6·00

1967. World Fair Montreal. No. 1747 of France surch CFA and value.
447 30f. on 60c. 95 4·75

1967. No. 1700 of France (Arms of Auch) surch 2fCFA.
448 2f. on 5c. red and blue 1·10 4·25

1967. 50th Anniv of Lions Int. No. 1766 of France surch CFA and value.
449 20f. on 40c. 1·40 4·00

1967. Red Cross. Nos. 1772/3 of France surch CFA and value.
450 12f.+5f. on 25c.+10c. 2·30 11·00
451 15f.+5f. on 30c.+10c. 2·30 11·00

1968. French Polar Exploration. No. 1806 of France surch CFA and value.
452 20f. on 40c. 2·30 5·50

1968. Red Cross stamps of France Nos. 1812/13 surch CFA and value.
453 12f.+5f. on 25c.+10c. 2·10 7·00
454 15f.+5f. on 30c.+10c. 2·10 7·00

1969. Stamp Day. No. 1824 of France surch CFA and value.
455 15f.+5f. on 30c.+10c. 2·00 6·25

1969. "Republique" stamps of France surch CFA and value.
456 **604** 15f. on 30c. green 1·60 3·50
457 **604** 20f. on 40c. mauve 1·30 80

1969. No. 1735 of France (Arms of Saint-Lo) surch 10F CFA.
458 10f. on 20c. multicoloured 2·10 3·25

1969. Birth Bicent of Napoleon Bonaparte. No. 1845 of France surch CFA and value.
459 35f. on 70c. green, violet & bl 2·75 5·50

1969. Red Cross stamps of France Nos. 1853/4 surch CFA and value.
460 20f.+7f. on 40c.+15c. 2·30 6·75
461 20f.+7f. on 40c.+15c. 2·10 6·75

1970. Stamp Day. No. 1866 of France surch CFA and value.
462 20f.+5f. on 40c.+10c. 2·10 5·00

1970. Red Cross. Nos. 1902/3 of France surch CFA and value.
463 20f.+7f. on 40c.+15c. 4·00 7·25
464 20f.+7f. on 40c.+15c. 4·00 7·25

1971. "Marianne" stamp of France surch 25f CFA.
465 **668** 25f. on 50c. mauve 1·30 65

1971. Stamp Day. No. 1919 of France surch CFA and value.
466 25f.+5f. on 50c.+10c. 1·40 5·50

1971. "Antoinette". No. 1920 of France surch CFA and value.
467 40f. on 80c. 2·10 6·25

1971. No. 1928 of France (Rural Aid) surch CFA and value.
468 **678** 15f. on 40c. 1·80 3·50

1971. Nos. 1931/2 of France (Tourist Publicity) surch CFA and value.
469 45f. on 90c. brown, green and ochre (Riquewihr) 1·60 3·25
470 50f. on 1f.10 brown, blue and green (Sedan) 1·70 2·00

1971. 40th Anniv of 1st Meeting of Crafts Guilds Association. No. 1935 of France surch CFA and value.
471 **680** 45c. on 90c. purple & red 1·70 4·50

63 Reunion Chameleon

1971. Nature Protection.
472 **63** 25f. green, brown & yellow 2·30 2·00

64 De Gaulle in Uniform (June 1940)

1971. De Gaulle Commemoration.
473 **64** 25f. black 2·50 4·00
474 - 25f. blue 2·50 4·00
475 - 25f. red 2·50 4·00
476 - 25f. black 2·50 4·00

DESIGNS: No. 473, De Gaulle in uniform (June, 1940); No. 474, De Gaulle at Brazzaville, 1944; No. 475, De Gaulle in Paris, 1944; No. 476, De Gaulle as President of the French Republic, 1970 (T **64**).

1971. Nos. 1942/3 of France (Red Cross Fund) surch CFA and value.
477 15f.+5f. on 30c.+10c. 2·50 6·50
478 25f.+5f. on 50c.+10c. 3·25 6·50

65 King Penguin, Map and Exploration Ships

1972. Bicentenary of Discovery of Crozet Islands and Kerguelen (French Southern and Antarctic Territories).
479 **65** 45f. black, blue and brown 7·75 14·50

1972. No. 1956 of France surch CFA and value.
480 **688** 25f.+5f. on 50c+10c. blue, drab and yellow 2·50 6·00

1972. No. 1966 of France (Blood Donors) surch CFA and value.
481 **692** 15f. on 40c. red 2·30 3·50

1972. Air. No 1890 of France (Daurat and Vanier) surch CFA and value.
482 **662** 200f. on 5f. brn, grn & bl 4·50 4·50

1972. Postal Codes. Nos. 1969/70 of France surch CFA and value.
483 **695** 15f. on 30c. red, black and green 2·00 5·25
484 **695** 25f. on 50c. yell, blk & red 1·60 1·80

1972. Red Cross Fund. Nos. 1979/80 of France surch CFA and value.
485 **701** 15f.+5f. on 30c.+10c. 2·10 5·25
486 **701** 25f.+5f. on 50c.+10c. 2·50 5·25

1973. Stamp Day. No. 1996 of France surch CFA and value.
487 **707** 25f.+5f. on 50c.+10c. 4·25 6·50

1973. No. 2011 of France surch CFA and value.
488 **714** 45f. on 90c. green, violet and blue 2·75 5·50

1973. No. 2008 of France surch CFA and value.
489 50f. on 1f. green, brown & bl 2·50 2·00

1973. No. 1960 of France surch CFA and value.
490 100f. on 2f. purple and green 2·75 4·75

1973. No. 2021/2 of France surch CFA and value.
491 **721** 15f.+5f. on 30c.+10c. green and red 3·25 6·75
492 **721** 25f.+5f. on 50c.+10c. red and black 3·25 5·00

1973. No. 2026 of France surch CFA and value.
494 **725** 25f. on 50c. brown, blue and purple 3·00 3·25

1974. Stamp Day. No. 2031 surch FCFA and value.
495 **727** 25f.+5f. on 50c.+10c. 2·75 5·25

1974. French Art. No. 2033/6 surch FCFA and value.
496 100f. on 2f. multicoloured 2·75 5·75
497 100f. on 2f. multicoloured 2·00 8·00
498 100f. on 2f. brown and blue 3·00 7·00
499 100f. on 2f. multicoloured 2·30 8·00

1974. French Lifeboat Service. No. 2040 surch FCFA and value.
500 **731** 45f. on 90c. blue, red and brown 2·50 6·50

1974. Centenary of Universal Postal Union. No. 2057 surch FCFA and value.
501 **741** 60f. on 1f.20 green, red and blue 2·30 6·75

1974. "Marianne" stamps of France surch FCFA and value.
502 **668** 30f. on 60c. green 2·30 7·25
503 **668** 40f. on 80c. red 2·50 7·50

From 1 January 1975 the CFA franc was replaced by the French Metropolitan franc, and Reunion subsequently used unsurcharged stamps of France.

1974. Red Cross Fund. "The Seasons". Nos. 2059/60 surch FCFA and value.
504 **743** 30f.+7f. on 60c.+15c. 3·50 6·75
505 - 40f.+7f. on 80c.+15c. 3·50 7·00

PARCEL POST STAMPS

P5

1890
P11 **P5** 10c. black on yellow (black frame) £300 £200
P13 **P5** 10c. black on yellow (blue frame) 42·00 38·00

From 1 January 1975 the CFA franc was replaced by the French Metropolitan franc, and Reunion subsequently used unsurcharged stamps of France.

P20

1907. Receipt stamps surch as in Type P 20.
P76 **P20** 10c. brown and black 44·00 34·00
P77 **P20** 10c. brown and red 44·00 34·00

POSTAGE DUE STAMPS

D4

1889. Imperf.
D11A **D4** 5c. black 36·00 7·25
D12A **D4** 10c. black 12·00 6·50
D13B **D4** 15c. black 60·00 29·00
D14A **D4** 20c. black 70·00 5·50
D15A **D4** 30c. black 75·00 6·75

D19

1907
D76 **D19** 5c. red on yellow 20 35
D77 **D19** 10c. blue on blue 60 1·30
D78 **D19** 15c. black on grey 1·30 3·75
D79 **D19** 20c. pink 1·80 1·00
D80 **D19** 30c. green on green 65 5·25

D81	D19	50c. red on green	1·40	1·80
D82	D19	60c. pink on blue	1·60	5·75
D83	D19	1f. lilac	1·80	5·00

1927. Surch.

D130	2f. on 1f. red	5·00	26·00
D131	3f. on 1f. brown	5·75	26·00

D33 Arms of Reunion

1933

D175	D33	5c. purple	20	4·50
D176	D33	10c. green	20	5·50
D177	D33	15c. brown	20	4·50
D178	D33	20c. orange	35	5·50
D179	D33	30c. olive	35	6·50
D180	D33	50c. blue	35	7·50
D181	D33	60c. brown	70	7·50
D182	D33	1f. violet	1·00	7·50
D183	D33	2f. blue	80	7·50
D184	D33	3f. red	1·00	7·50

D43

1947

D306	D43	10c. mauve	10	5·75
D307	D43	30c. brown	10	5·50
D308	D43	50c. green	35	6·00
D309	D43	1f. brown	1·30	7·25
D310	D43	2f. red	2·75	7·00
D311	D43	3f. brown	1·70	7·50
D312	D43	4f. blue	1·60	8·25
D313	D43	5f. red	1·60	8·25
D314	D43	10f. green	1·50	8·00
D315	D43	20f. blue	2·75	8·50

1949. As Type D 250 of France, but inscr "TIMBRE TAXE" surch CFA and value.

D333	10c. on 1f. blue	10	7·00
D334	50c. on 2f. blue	10	5·50
D335	1f. on 3f. red	40	6·00
D336	2f. on 4f. violet	80	6·75
D337	3f. on 5f. pink	1·50	8·00
D338	5f. on 10f. red	1·40	8·00
D339	10f. on 20f. brown	1·20	8·50
D340	20f. on 50f. green	3·50	17·00
D341	50f. on 100f. green	8·75	55·00

1962. Wheat Sheaves Type of France surch CFA and value.

D406	D457	1f. on 5c. mauve	1·30	6·25
D407	D457	10f. on 20c. brown	2·50	7·75
D408	D457	20f. on 50c. green	16·00	36·00

1964. Nos. D1650/4 and D1656/7 of France surch CFA and value.

D424	-	1f. on 5c.	35	4·50
D425	-	5f. on 10c.	35	4·50
D426	D 539	7f. on 15c.	40	4·75
D427	-	10f. on 20c.	2·10	5·50
D428	-	15f. on 30c.	75	5·00
D429	-	20f. on 50c.	40	5·00
D430	-	50f. on 1f.	90	6·00

Pt. 1

RHODESIA

A British territory in central Africa, formerly administered by the British South Africa Co. In 1924 divided into the territories of Northern and Southern Rhodesia which issued their own stamps (q.v.). In 1964 Southern Rhodesia was renamed Rhodesia; on becoming independent in 1980 it was renamed Zimbabwe.

1890. 12 pence = 1 shilling; 20 shillings = 1 pound.
1970. 100 cents = 1 dollar.

1 Arms of the Company

1890. The pound values are larger.

18	1	½d. blue and red	3·00	4·50
1	1	1d. black	14·00	3·25
20	1	2d. green and red	19·00	5·50
21	1	3d. black and green	19·00	3·75
22	1	4d. brown and black	35·00	4·25
3	1	6d. blue	40·00	3·75
23	1	8d. red and blue	18·00	19·00
4	1	1s. brown	50·00	13·00
5	1	2s. orange	65·00	32·00
6	1	2s.6d. purple	40·00	50·00
25	1	3s. brown and green	£170	90·00
26	1	4s. black and red	40·00	50·00
8	1	5s. yellow	80·00	60·00
9	1	10s. green	£100	£100
10	-	£1 blue	£250	£150
11	-	£2 red	£500	£170
12	-	£5 green	£1600	£450
13	-	£10 brown	£2750	£700

1891. Surch in figures.

14	½d. on 6d. blue	£140	£475
15	2d. on 6d. blue	£170	£650
16	4d. on 6d. blue	£190	£750
17	8d. on 1s. brown	£200	£850

5

1896. The ends of ribbons containing motto cross the animals' legs.

41	5	½d. grey and mauve	4·50	3·25
42	5	1d. red and green	8·50	4·50
43	5	2d. brown and mauve	19·00	7·00
31	5	3d. brown and blue	9·50	2·00
44a	5	4d. blue and mauve	17·00	50
46	5	6d. mauve and red	14·00	75
34	5	8d. green and mauve on buff	13·00	60
35	5	1s. green and blue	18·00	2·75
47	5	2s. blue and green on buff	40·00	10·00
48	5	2s.6d. brown & pur on yell	85·00	55·00
36	5	3s. green and mauve on blue	75·00	42·00
37	5	4s. red and blue on green	55·00	2·75
49	5	5s. brown and green	55·00	10·00
50	5	10s. grey and red on rose	£120	65·00

1896. Surch in words.

51	1	1d. on 3d. black and green	£600	£750
52	1	1d. on 4s. black and red	£300	£325
53	1	3d. on 5s. yellow	£190	£225

1896. Cape of Good Hope stamps optd BRITISH SOUTH AFRICA COMPANY.

58	6	½d. black (No. 48)	15·00	22·00
59	17	1d. red (No. 58a)	16·00	23·00
60	6	2d. brown (No. 60)	22·00	13·00
61	6	3d. red (No. 40)	55·00	75·00
62	6	4d. blue (No. 51)	26·00	24·00
63	4	6d. purple (No. 52a)	65·00	75·00
64	6	1s. yellow (No. 65)	£140	£140

9

1897. The ends of motto ribbons do not cross the animals' legs.

66	9	½d. grey and mauve	5·00	8·00
67	9	1d. red and green	5·50	7·50
68	9	2d. brown and mauve	15·00	3·50
69	9	3d. brown and blue	5·50	50
70	9	4d. blue and mauve	18·00	3·75
71	9	6d. mauve and red	12·00	3·50
72	9	8d. green and mauve on buff	19·00	50
73	9	£1 black and brown on green	£375	£225

10

11

1898. Nos. 90/93a are larger (24×28½ mm).

75a	10	½d. green	4·25	2·75
77	10	1d. red	9·00	50
79	10	2d. brown	6·00	1·50
80	10	2½d. blue	13·00	1·50
81	10	3d. red	11·00	80
82	10	4d. olive	9·50	30
83	10	6d. purple	18·00	2·50
84	11	1s. brown	25·00	3·75
85	11	2s.6d. grey	60·00	1·75
86	11	3s. violet	27·00	3·25
87	11	5s. orange	55·00	17·00
88	11	7s.6d. black	90·00	27·00
89	11	10s. green	50·00	1·50
90	-	£1 purple	£375	£140
91	-	£2 brown	£120	6·50
92	-	£5 blue	£3250	£2500
93	-	£10 lilac	£3250	£2250
93a	-	£20 brown	£15000	

13 Victoria Falls

1905. Visit of British Assn. and Opening of Victoria Falls Bridge across Zambesi.

94	13	1d. red	7·00	8·00
95	13	2½d. blue	15·00	9·50
96	13	5d. red	30·00	55·00
97	13	1s. green	35·00	50·00
98	13	2s.6d. black	£110	£150
99	13	5s. violet	£100	40·00

1909. Optd RHODESIA. or surch also.

100	10	½d. green	3·75	2·25
101	10	1d. red	7·50	1·25
102	10	2d. brown	3·00	6·00
103	10	2½d. blue	1·75	80
104	10	3d. red	2·25	1·75
105	10	4d. olive	8·50	3·00
114	10	5d. on 6d. purple	9·50	17·00
106	10	6d. purple	6·00	7·50
116	11	7½d. on 2s.6d. grey	4·00	3·75
117a	11	10d. on 2s. violet	5·50	3·75
107c	11	1s. brown	11·00	7·50
118	11	2s. on 5s. orange	12·00	7·50
108	11	2s.6d. grey	26·00	11·00
109	11	3s. violet	21·00	11·00
110	11	5s. orange	42·00	60·00
111	11	7s.6d. black	£100	26·00
112	11	10s. green	60·00	19·00
113	-	£1 purple	£190	95·00
113d	-	£2 brown	£3250	£275
113e	-	£5 blue	£7500	£4250

17

1910

119	17	½d. green	13·00	1·75
123	17	1d. red	29·00	3·75
128	17	2d. black and grey	65·00	7·50
131a	17	2½d. blue	24·00	8·50
135	17	3d. purple and yellow	50·00	15·00
140	17	4d. black and orange	50·00	23·00
141	17	5d. purple and olive	40·00	55·00
145	17	6d. purple and mauve	50·00	21·00
148	17	8d. black and purple	£170	£100
149	17	10d. red and purple	48·00	50·00
152	17	1s. black and green	65·00	20·00
153	17	2s. black and blue	£100	75·00
157	17	2s.6d. black and red	£325	£375
158	17	3s. green and violet	£225	£190
160a	17	5s. red and green	£275	£200
160b	17	7s.6d. red and blue	£650	£425
164	17	10s. green and orange	£425	£500
166	17	£1 red and black	£1300	£375

18

1913

187	18	½d. green	8·00	2·25
192	18	1d. red	4·00	3·00
198	18	1½d. brown	5·50	2·25
291	18	2d. black and grey	11·00	7·50
200	18	2½d. blue	7·00	38·00
259	18	3d. black and yellow	14·00	3·50
261	18	4d. black and orange	19·00	9·50
212	18	5d. black and green	6·00	18·00
295	18	6d. black and mauve	6·00	6·50
230	18	8d. violet and green	16·00	75·00
247	18	10d. blue and red	14·00	42·00
272	18	1s. black and blue	9·00	11·00
273	18	2s. black and brown	18·00	18·00
236	18	2s.6d. blue and brown	70·00	50·00
304	18	3s. brown and blue	£110	£150
239	18	5s. blue and green	80·00	85·00
252	18	7s.6d. mauve and grey	£150	£275
309	18	10s. red and green	£200	£250
242	18	£1 black and purple	£425	£600

1917. Surch Half Penny (without hyphen or full stop).

280	½d. on 1s. red	2·50	9·50

1917. Surch Half-Penny. (with hyphen and full stop).

281	½d. on 1d. red	1·75	8·50

RHODESIA

The following stamps are for the former Southern Rhodesia, renamed Rhodesia.

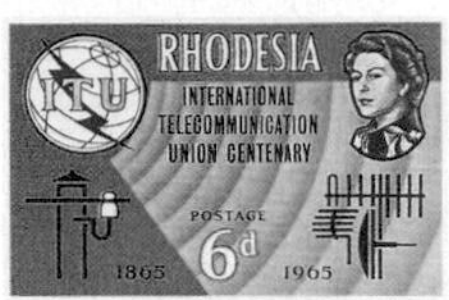

59 "Telecommunications"

1965. Centenary of I.T.U.

351	59	6d. violet and olive	1·50	40
352	59	1s.3d. violet and lilac	1·50	40
353	59	2s.6d. violet and brown	3·50	4·50

60 Bangala Dam

1965. Water Conservation. Multicoloured.

354	3d. Type **60**	30	10
355	4d. Irrigation canal	1·25	1·25
356	2s.6d. Cutting sugar cane	2·25	3·50

63 Sir Winston Churchill, Quill, Sword and Houses of Parliament

1965. Churchill Commemoration.

357	63	1s.3d. black and blue	70	35

64 Coat of Arms

1965. "Independence".

358	64	2s.6d. multicoloured	15	15

1966. Optd INDEPENDENCE 11th November 1965. (a) On Nos. 92/105 of Southern Rhodesia.

359	45	½d. yellow, green and blue	10	10
360	-	1d. violet and ochre	10	10
361	-	2d. yellow and violet	10	10
362	-	3d. brown and blue	10	10
363	-	4d. orange and green	15	10
364	50	6d. red, yellow and green	15	10
365	-	9d. brown, yellow and green	30	10
366	-	1s. green and ochre	40	10
367	-	1s.3d. red, violet and green	50	50
368	-	2s. blue and ochre	60	3·25
369	-	2s.6d. blue and red	60	1·00
370	56	5s. multicoloured	2·00	5·50
371	-	10s. multicoloured	5·00	2·25
372	-	£1 multicoloured	1·25	2·25

(b) Surch on No. 357.

No.	Type	Description	Mint	Used
373	**63**	5s. on 1s.3d. black and blue	5·00	12·00

67 Emeralds

1966. As Nos. 92/105 of Southern Rhodesia, but inscr "RHODESIA" as in T 67. Some designs and colours changed.

No.	Type	Description	Mint	Used
374	-	1d. violet and ochre	10	10
375	-	2d. orange & grn (As No. 96)	10	10
376	-	3d. brown and blue	10	10
377	**67**	4d. green and brown	1·75	10
378	**50**	6d. red, yellow and green	15	10
379	-	9d. yellow & vio (As No. 94)	60	20
380	**45**	1s. yellow, green and blue	15	10
381	-	1s.3d. bl & ochre (As No. 101)	25	15
382	-	1s.6d. brn, yell & grn (As No. 98)	2·25	25
383	-	2s. red, vio & grn (As No. 100)	60	80
384	-	2s.6d. blue, red & turquoise	1·50	20
385	**56**	5s. multicoloured	1·00	90
386	-	10s. multicoloured	4·25	3·50
387	-	£1 multicoloured	3·25	7·00

Nos. 379/80 are in larger format as Type **50** of Southern Rhodesia.

Stamps in these designs were later printed locally. These vary only slightly from the above in details and shade.

For Nos. 376, 380 and 382/4 in dual currency see Nos. 408/12.

68 Zeederberg Coach, c. 1895

1966. 28th Congress of Southern Africa Philatelic Federation ("Rhopex").

No.	Type	Description	Mint	Used
388	**68**	3d. multicoloured	15	10
389	-	9d. multicoloured	15	20
390	-	1s.6d. blue and black	25	30
391	-	2s.6d. pink, green and black	30	55
MS392		126×84 mm. Nos. 388/91	5·00	11·00

DESIGNS: 9d. Sir Rowland Hill; 1s.6d. The Penny Black; 2s.6d. Rhodesian stamp of 1892 (No. 12).

69 De Havilland Dragon Rapide (1946)

1966. 20th Anniv of Central African Airways.

No.	Type	Description	Mint	Used
393	**69**	6d. multicoloured	1·00	35
394	-	1s.3d. multicoloured	1·00	40
395	-	2s.6d. multicoloured	1·50	1·50
396	-	5s. black and blue	2·00	4·50

AIRCRAFT: 1s.3d. Douglas DC-3 (1953); 2s.6d. Vickers Viscount 748 "Matopos" (1956); 5s. B.A.C. One Eleven.

70 Kudu

1967. Dual Currency Issue. As Nos. 376, 380 and 382/4. but value in dual currency as T 70.

No.	Type	Description	Mint	Used
408	**70**	3d./2½c. brown and blue	50	15
409	-	1s./10c. yellow, green and blue (No. 380)	50	25
410	-	1s.6d./15c. brown, yellow and green (No. 382)	4·75	70
411	-	2s./20c. red, violet and green (No. 383)	3·25	4·00
412	-	2s.6d./25c. ultramarine, red and blue (No. 384)	20·00	26·00

71 Dr. Jameson (administrator)

1967. Famous Rhodesians (1st series) and 50th Death Anniv of Dr. Jameson.

No.	Type	Description	Mint	Used
413	**71**	1s.6d. multicoloured	20	35

See also Nos. 426, 430, 457, 458, 469, 480, 488 and 513.

72 Soapstone Sculpture (Joram Mariga)

1967. 10th Anniv of Opening of Rhodes National Gallery.

No.	Type	Description	Mint	Used
414	**72**	3d. brown, green and black	10	10
415	-	9d. blue, brown and black	20	20
416	-	1s.3d. multicoloured	20	25
417	-	2s.6d. multicoloured	25	60

DESIGNS: 9d. "The Burgher of Calais" (detail, Rodin); 1s.3d. "The Knight" (stamp design wrongly inscr) (Roberto Crippa); 2s.6d. "John the Baptist" (Mossini).

73 Baobab Tree

1967. Nature Conservation.

No.	Type	Description	Mint	Used
418	**73**	4d. brown and black	10	20
419	-	4d. green and black	25	20
420	-	4d. grey and black	25	20
421	-	4d. orange and black	10	20

DESIGNS—HORIZ: No. 419, White rhinoceros; No. 420, African elephants. VERT: No. 421, Wild gladiolus.

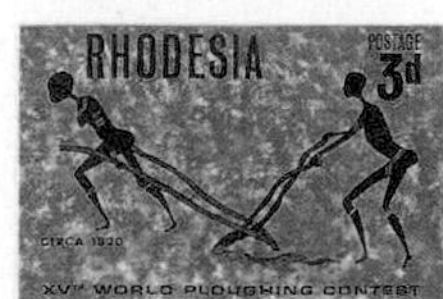

74 Wooden Hand Plough

1968. 15th World Ploughing Contest, Norton, Rhodesia.

No.	Type	Description	Mint	Used
422	**74**	3d. orange, red and brown	10	10
423	-	9d. multicoloured	15	20
424	-	1s.6d. multicoloured	20	55
425	-	2s.6d. multicoloured	20	75

DESIGNS: 9d. Early wheel plough; 1s.6d. Steam powered tractor, and ploughs; 2s.6d. Modern tractor, and plough.

75 Alfred Beit (national benefactor)

1968. Famous Rhodesians (2nd issue).

No.	Type	Description	Mint	Used
426	**75**	1s.6d. orange, black & brn	20	30

76 Raising the Flag, Bulawayo, 1893

1968. 75th Anniv of Matabeleland.

No.	Type	Description	Mint	Used
427	**76**	3d. orange, red and black	15	10
428	-	9d. multicoloured	15	20
429	-	1s.6d. green, emerald & blk	20	60

DESIGNS: 9d. View and coat of arms of Bulawayo; 1s.6d. Allan Wilson (combatant in the Matabele War).

77 Sir William Henry Milton (administrator)

1969. Famous Rhodesians (3rd issue).

No.	Type	Description	Mint	Used
430	**77**	1s.6d. multicoloured	40	55

78 2ft. Gauge Locomotive No. 15, 1897

1969. 70th Anniv of Opening of Beira–Salisbury Railway. Multicoloured.

No.	Type	Description	Mint	Used
431		3d. Type **78**	30	10
432		9d. 7th Class steam locomotive No. 43, 1903	50	40
433		1s.6d. Beyer, Peacock 15th Class steam locomotive No. 413, 1951	60	75
434		2s.6d. Class DE2 diesel-electric locomotive No. 1203, 1955	1·00	3·00

79 Low Level Bridge

1969. Bridges of Rhodesia. Multicoloured.

No.	Type	Description	Mint	Used
435		3d. Type **79**	20	10
436		9d. Mpudzi bridge	40	20
437		1s.6d. Umniati bridge	60	60
438		2s.6d. Birchenough bridge	80	1·25

80 Harvesting Wheat

81 Devil's Cataract, Victoria Falls

1970. Decimal Currency.

No.	Type	Description	Mint	Used
439	**80**	1c. multicoloured	10	10
440	-	2c. multicoloured	10	10
441	-	2½c. multicoloured	10	10
441c	-	3c. multicoloured	1·25	10
442	-	3½c. multicoloured	10	10
442b	-	4c. multicoloured	1·75	1·00
443	-	5c. multicoloured	15	10
443b	-	6c. multicoloured	4·00	3·75
443c	**81**	7½c. multicoloured	7·00	60
444	**81**	8c. multicoloured	75	20
445	-	10c. multicoloured	60	10
446	-	12½c. multicoloured	1·50	10
446a	-	14c. multicoloured	12·00	70
447	-	15c. multicoloured	1·25	15
448	-	20c. multicoloured	1·00	15
449	-	25c. multicoloured	4·00	60
450	-	50c. turquoise and blue	1·25	55
451	-	$1 multicoloured	4·75	2·00
452	-	$2 multicoloured	8·50	15·00

DESIGNS—As Type **80**: 2c. Pouring molten metal; 2½c. Zimbabwe Ruins; 3c. Articulated lorry; 3½c., 4c. Statue of Cecil Rhodes; 5c. Mine headgear; 6c. Hydrofoil "Seaflight". As Type **81**: 10c. Yachting on Lake Mcllwaine; 12½c. Hippopotamus in river; 14c., 15c. Kariba Dam; 20c. Irrigation canal. 31×26 mm: 25c. Bateleurs; 50c. Radar antenna and Vickers Viscount 810; $1 "Air Rescue"; $2 Rhodesian flag.

82 Despatch Rider, c. 1890

1970. Inauguration of Posts and Telecommunications Corporation. Multicoloured.

No.	Type	Description	Mint	Used
453		2½c. Type **82**	30	10
454		3½c. Loading mail at Salisbury airport	40	50
455		15c. Constructing telegraph line, c. 1890	45	1·25
456		25c. Telephone and modern telecommunications equipment	50	2·00

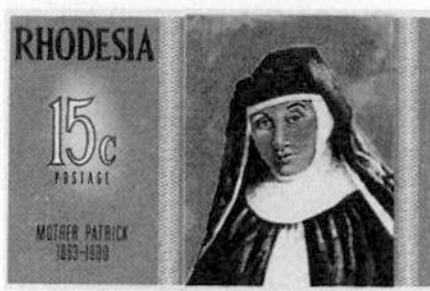

83 Mother Patrick (Dominican nurse and teacher)

1970. Famous Rhodesians (4th issue).

No.	Type	Description	Mint	Used
457	**83**	15c. multicoloured	60	50

84 Fredrick Courteney Selous (big-game hunter, explorer and pioneer)

1971. Famous Rhodesians (5th issue).

No.	Type	Description	Mint	Used
458	**84**	15c. multicoloured	40	70

85 Hoopoe

1971. Birds of Rhodesia (1st series). Multicoloured.

No.	Type	Description	Mint	Used
459		2c. Type **85**	50	20
460		2½c. Half-collared kingfisher (horiz)	50	10
461		5c. Golden-breasted bunting	70	20
462		7½c. Carmine bee eater	80	20
463		8c. Red-eyed bulbul	80	30
464		25c. Senegal wattled plover (horiz)	1·50	1·50

See also Nos. 537/42.

86 Porphyritic Granite

1971. "Granite 71" Geological Symposium. Multicoloured.

No.	Type	Description	Mint	Used
465		2½c. Type **86**	35	10
466		7½c. Muscovite mica seen through microscope	50	20
467		15c. Granite seen through microscope	90	55
468		25c. Geological map of Rhodesia	90	1·50

87 Dr. Robert Moffat (missionary)

1972. Famous Rhodesians (6th issue).

No.	Type	Description	Mint	Used
469	**87**	13c. multicoloured	50	75

88 Bird ("Be Airwise")

1972. "Prevent Pollution". Multicoloured.

No.	Type	Description	Mint	Used
470		2½c. Type **88**	15	10
471		3½c. Antelope ("Be Countrywise")	15	20
472		7c. Fish ("Be Waterwise")	15	30
473		13c. City ("Be Citywise")	20	55

1972. "Rhophil '72". Nos. 439, 441 and 442 with commemorative inscr in margins.

MS474	1c. multicoloured	1·10	2·00
MS474/6	Set of 3 sheets	3·00	5·50
MS475	2½c. multicoloured	1·10	2·00
MS476	3½c. multicoloured	1·10	2·00

89 "The Three Kings"

1972. Christmas.

477	**89**	2c. multicoloured	10	10
478	**89**	5c. multicoloured	15	20
479	**89**	13c. multicoloured	30	55

90 Dr. David Livingstone

1973. Famous Rhodesians (7th issue).

480	**90**	14c. multicoloured	50	75

91 W.M.O. Emblem

1973. Centenary of I.M.O./W.M.O.

481	**91**	3c. multicoloured	10	10
482	**91**	14c. multicoloured	30	15
483	**91**	25c. multicoloured	40	75

92 Arms of Rhodesia

1973. 50th Anniv of Responsible Government.

484	**92**	2½c. multicoloured	10	10
485	**92**	4c. multicoloured	15	15
486	**92**	7½c. multicoloured	20	25
487	**92**	14c. multicoloured	35	1·25

93 George Pauling (construction engineer)

1974. Famous Rhodesians (8th issue).

488	**93**	14c. multicoloured	50	1·25

94 Greater Kudu

1974. Multicoloured. (a) Antelopes.

489	1c. Type **94**	10	10
490	2½c. Eland	75	10
491	3c. Roan antelope	10	10
492	4c. Reedbuck	20	10
493	5c. Bushbuck	20	60

95 Thunbergia

(b) Wild Flowers.

494	6c. Type **95**	20	10
495	7½c. Flame lily	50	20
496	8c. As 7½c.	20	10
497	10c. Devil thorn	20	10
498	12c. Hibiscus	40	2·00
499	12½c. Pink sabi star	1·00	35
500	14c. Wild pimpernel	1·00	35
501	15c. As 12½c.	40	75
502	16c. As 14c.	40	30

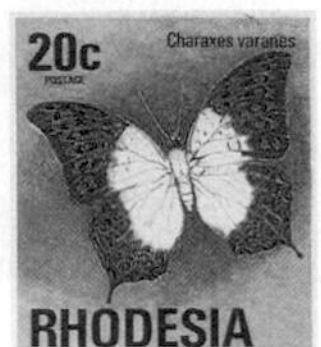
96 "Charaxes varanes"

(c) Butterflies.

503	20c. Type **96**	1·00	35
504	24c. "Precis hierta" (sp. "cebrene")	40	40
505	25c. As 24c.	1·50	1·50
506	50c. "Colotis regina"	40	60
507	$1 "Graphium antheus"	40	60
508	$2 "Hamanumida daedalus"	40	75

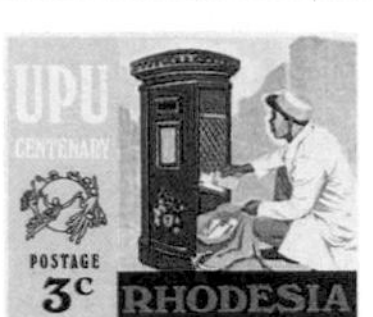
97 Collecting Mail

1974. Centenary of U.P.U. Multicoloured.

509	3c. Type **97**	15	10
510	4c. Sorting mail	15	10
511	7½c. Mail delivery	20	20
512	14c. Weighing parcel	30	90

98 Thomas Baines (artist)

1975. Famous Rhodesians (9th issue).

513	**98**	14c. multicoloured	50	60

99 "Euphorbia confinalis"

1975. Int Succulent Congress, Salisbury ("Aloe '75"). Multicoloured.

514	2½c. Type **99**	10	10
515	3c. "Aloe excelsa"	10	10
516	4c. "Hoodia lugardii"	10	10
517	7½c. "Aloe ortholopha"	15	10
518	14c. "Aloe musapana"	30	10
519	25c. "Aloe saponaria"	50	2·00

100 Prevention of Head Injuries

1975. Occupational Safety. Multicoloured.

520	2½c. Type **100**	10	10
521	4c. Bandaged hand and gloved hand	15	10
522	7½c. Broken glass and eye	15	15
523	14c. Blind man and welder with protective mask	20	55

101 Telephones, 1876 and 1976

1976. Telephone Centenary.

524	**101**	3c. grey and blue	10	10
525	-	14c. black and brown	20	55

DESIGN: 14c. Alexander Graham Bell.

1976. Nos. 495, 500 and 505 surch.

526	8c. on 7½c. multicoloured	15	15
527	16c. on 14c. multicoloured	15	15
528	24c. on 25c. multicoloured	20	60

103 Roan Antelope

1976. Vulnerable Wildlife. Multicoloured.

529	4c. Type **103**	10	10
530	6c. Brown hyena	15	60
531	8c. Hunting dog	15	10
532	16c. Cheetah	20	35

104 Msasa

1976. Trees of Rhodesia. Multicoloured.

533	4c. Type **104**	10	10
534	6c. Red mahogany	10	10
535	8c. Mukwa	15	10
536	16c. Rhodesian teak	20	55

105 Garden Bulbul ("Blackeyed-Bulbul")

1977. Birds of Rhodesia (2nd series). Mult.

537	3c. Type **105**	15	10
538	4c. Yellow-mantled whydah ("Yellow-mantled Wydah")	15	10
539	6c. Cape longclaw ("Orange throated longclaw")	20	60
540	8c. Magpie shrike ("Eastern Long-tailed Shrike")	20	35
541	16c. Lesser blue-eared glossy starling ("Lesser Blue-eared Starling")	25	60
542	24c. Green wood hoopoe ("Red-billed Wood hoopee")	30	1·10

106 "Lake Kyle" (Joan Evans)

1977. Landscape Paintings. Multicoloured.

543	3c. Type **106**	10	10
544	4c. "Chimanimani Mountains" (Joan Evans)	10	10
545	6c. "Rocks near Bonsor Reef" (Alice Balfour)	10	30
546	8c. "A Dwala near Devil's Pass" (Alice Balfour)	10	10
547	16c. "Zimbabwe" (Alice Balfour)	15	30
548	24c. "Victoria Falls" (Thomas Baines)	25	60

107 Virgin and Child

1977. Christmas.

549	**107**	3c. multicoloured	10	10
550	**107**	6c. multicoloured	10	20
551	**107**	8c. multicoloured	10	10
552	**107**	16c. multicoloured	15	30

108 Fair Spire

1978. Trade Fair Rhodesia, Bulawayo. Multicoloured.

553	4c. Type **108**	10	10
554	8c. Fair Spire (different)	15	25

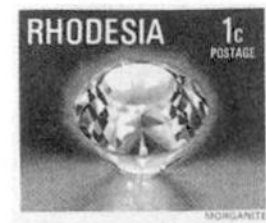
109 Morganite

1978. Gemstones, Wild Animals and Waterfalls. Multicoloured.

555	1c. Type **109**	10	10
556	3c. Amethyst	10	10
557	4c. Garnet	10	10
558	5c. Citrine	10	10
559	7c. Blue topaz	10	10
560	9c. White rhinoceros	15	10
561	11c. Lion	10	20
562	13c. Warthog	10	1·25
563	15c. Giraffe	15	30
564	17c. Common zebra	15	10
565	21c. Odzani Falls	15	40
566	25c. Goba Falls	15	15
567	30c. Inyangombi Falls	15	15
568	$1 Bridal Veil Falls	20	35
569	$2 Victoria Falls	30	60

Nos. 560/4 are 26×23 mm, and Nos. 565/9 32×27 mm.

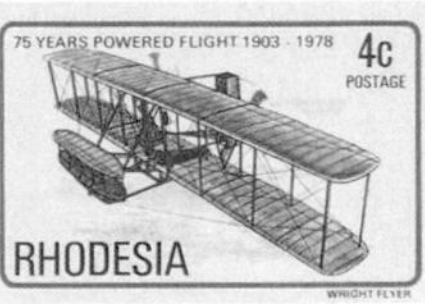
112 Wright Flyer I

1978. 75th Anniv of Powered Flight. Mult.

570	4c. Type **112**	10	10
571	5c. Bleriot XI	10	10
572	7c. Vickers Vimy "Silver Queen II"	10	10
573	9c. Armstrong Whitworth A.W.15 Atalanta	10	10
574	17c. Vickers Viking 1B "Zambezi"	10	10
575	25c. Boeing 720B	15	50

POSTAGE DUE STAMPS

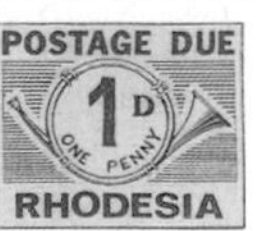
D2

1965. Roul.

D8	**D2**	1d. red	50	12·00
D9	**D2**	2d. blue	40	8·00
D10	**D2**	4d. green	50	8·00
D11	**D2**	6d. plum	50	6·00

D3 Zimbabwe Bird (soapstone sculpture)

1966

D12	**D3**	1d. red	60	3·25
D13	**D3**	2d. blue	75	1·75
D14	**D3**	4d. green	75	4·00
D15	**D3**	6d. violet	75	1·50
D16	**D3**	1s. brown	75	1·50
D17	**D3**	2s. black	1·00	5·00

1970. Decimal Currency. As Type D 3 but larger (26×22½ mm).

D18		1c. green	75	1·25
D19		2c. blue	75	60
D20		5c. violet	1·25	1·75
D21		6c. yellow	6·00	4·00
D22		10c. red	1·25	4·00

Pt. 1

RHODESIA AND NYASALAND

Stamps for the Central African Federation of Northern and Southern Rhodesia and Nysaland Protectorate. The stamps of the Federation were withdrawn on 19 February 1964 when all three constituent territories had resumed issuing their own stamps.

12 pence = 1 shilling; 20 shillings = 1 pound.

1 Queen Elizabeth II

2 Queen Elizabeth II

1954

1	**1**	½d. orange	15	10
2	**1**	1d. blue	15	10
3	**1**	2d. green	15	10
3a	**1**	2½d. ochre	6·50	10
4	**1**	3d. red	20	10
5	**1**	4d. brown	60	20
6	**1**	4½d. green	30	1·50
7	**1**	6d. purple	2·25	10
8	**1**	9d. violet	2·50	1·00
9	**1**	1s. grey	2·50	10
10	**2**	1s.3d. red and blue	4·75	40
11	**2**	2s. blue and brown	8·50	6·00
12	**2**	2s.6d. black and red	8·00	2·25
13	**2**	5s. violet and olive	22·00	7·50
14	-	10s. turquoise and orange	22·00	9·50
15	-	£1 olive and lake	38·00	30·00

The 10s. and £1 are as Type **2** but larger (31×17 mm) and have the name at top and foliage on either side of portrait.

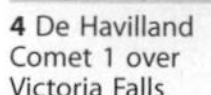
4 De Havilland Comet 1 over Victoria Falls

5 Livingstone and Victoria Falls

1955. Cent of Discovery of Victoria Falls.

16	**4**	3d. blue and turquoise	1·00	30
17	**5**	1s. purple and blue	55	70

6 Tea Picking

11 Lake Bangweulu

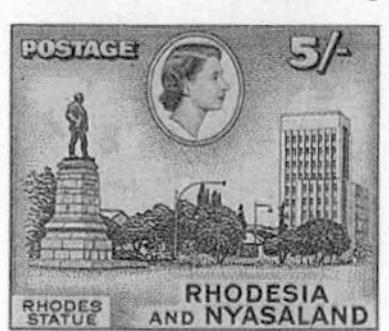
17 Rhodes Statue

1959

18	**6**	½d. black and green	1·25	2·00
19	-	1d. red and black	30	10
20	-	2d. violet and brown	2·50	50
21	-	2½d. purple and blue	2·00	2·00
22	-	3d. black and blue	1·00	10
23	**11**	4d. purple and green	1·50	10
24	-	6d. blue and green	2·75	10
24a	-	9d. brown and violet	9·00	3·00
25	-	1s. green and blue	1·25	10
26	-	1s.3d. green and brown	3·00	10
27	-	2s. green and red	4·00	60
28	-	2s.6d. blue and brown	7·00	65
29	**17**	5s. brown and green	15·00	2·50
30	-	10s. brown and red	28·00	25·00
31	-	£1 black and violet	48·00	65·00

DESIGNS—VERT (as Type **6**): 1d. V.H.F. mast; 2d. Copper mining; 2½d. Fairbridge Memorial. (As Type **11**): 6d. Eastern Cataract, Victoria Falls. HORIZ (as Type **6**): 3d. Rhodes's grave. (As Type **11**): 9d. Rhodesian railway trains; 1s. Tobacco; 1s.3d. Lake Nyasa; 2s. Chirundu Bridge; 2s.6d. Salisbury Airport. (As Type **17**): 10s. Mlanje; £1 Federal Coat of Arms.

20 Kariba Gorge, 1955

1960. Opening of Kariba Hydro-electric Scheme.

32	**20**	3d. green and orange	70	10
33	-	6d. brown and bistre	70	20
34	-	1s. blue and green	2·50	4·00
35	-	1s.3d. blue and brown	2·50	3·25
36	-	2s.6d. purple and red	3·50	8·50
37	-	5s. violet and turquoise	9·00	11·00

DESIGNS: 6d. 330 k.V. power lines; 1s. Barrage wall; 1s.3d. Barrage and lake; 2s.6d. Interior of power station; 5s. Queen Mother and barrage wall (inscr "ROYAL OPENING").

26 Miner drilling

1961. 7th Commonwealth Mining and Metallurgical Congress.

38	**26**	6d. green and brown	65	20
39	-	1s.3d. black and blue	65	80

DESIGN: 1s.3d. Surface installations, Nchanga Mine.

28 De Havilland Hercules "City of Basra" on Rhodesian Airstrip

1962. 30th Anniv of 1st London–Rhodesian Airmail Service.

40	**28**	6d. green and red	1·50	75
41	-	1s.3d. blue, black and yellow	1·75	50
42	-	2s.6d. red and violet	4·00	6·50

DESIGNS: 1s.3d. Short S.23 flying boat "Canopus" taking off from Zambesi; 2s.6d. Hawker Siddeley Comet 4 at Salisbury Airport.

31 Tobacco Plant

1963. World Tobacco Congress, Salisbury.

43	**31**	3d. green and olive	30	10
44	-	6d. green, brown and blue	40	35
45	-	1s.3d. brown and blue	1·25	45
46	-	2s.6d. yellow and brown	1·50	3·25

DESIGNS: 6d. Tobacco field; 1s.3d. Auction floor; 2s.6d. Cured tobacco.

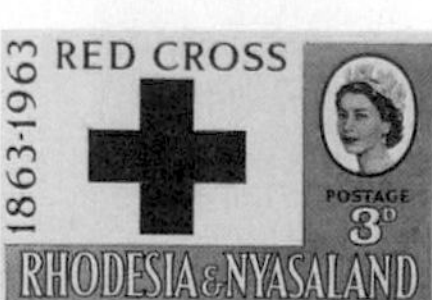
35

1963. Centenary of Red Cross.

47	**35**	3d. red	1·25	10

36 African "Round Table" Emblem

1963. World Council of Young Men's Service Clubs, Salisbury.

48	**36**	6d. black, gold and green	75	1·50
49	**36**	1s.3d. multicoloured	1·00	1·25

POSTAGE DUE STAMPS

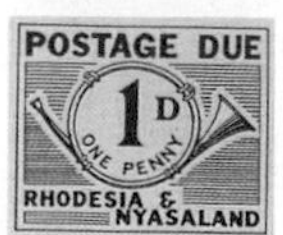
D1

1961

D1	**D1**	1d. red	3·75	5·50
D2	**D1**	2d. blue	3·00	3·00
D3	**D1**	4d. green	3·50	9·50
D4	**D1**	6d. purple	4·50	7·50

Pt. 21

RIAU-LINGGA ARCHIPELAGO

A group of islands E. of Sumatra and S. of Singapore. Part of Indonesia.

100 cents or sen = 1 rupiah.

1954. Optd RIAU. (a) On stamps of Indonesia.

1	**96**	5s. red	28·00	19·00
2	**96**	7½s. green	20	35
3	**96**	10s. blue	32·00	40·00
4	**96**	15s. violet	80	80
5	**96**	20s. red	95	1·10
6	**96**	25s. green	65·00	22·00
7	**97**	30s. red	2·40	1·60
8	**97**	35s. violet	20	35
9	**97**	40s. green	20	35
10	**97**	45s. purple	25	35
11	**97**	50s. brown	£190	32·00
12	**98**	60s. brown	20	35
13	**98**	70s. grey	60	65
14	**98**	75s. blue	3·25	1·60
15	**98**	80s. purple	50	1·90
16	**98**	90s. green	50	1·10

(b) On Netherlands Indies Nos. 566/71.

17		1r. violet	6·25	1·60
18		2r. green	65	1·90
19		3r. purple	95	1·90
20		5r. brown	95	1·90
21		10r. black	1·25	2·40
22		25r. brown	1·25	2·40

1958. Stamps of Indonesia optd RIAU.

26	**115**	5s. blue	20	35
27	**115**	10s. brown (No. 714)	40	35
28	**115**	15s. purple (No. 715)	40	1·50
29	-	20s. green (No. 716)	40	35
30	-	25s. brown (No. 717)	40	35
31	-	30s. orange (No. 718)	40	35
32	-	50s. brown (No. 722)	40	35

1960. Stamps of Indonesia optd RIAU.

33	**99**	1r.25 orange	95	3·25
34	**99**	1r.50 brown	95	3·25
35	**99**	2r.50 brown	1·25	4·75
36	**99**	4r. green	25	4·75
37	**99**	6r. mauve	25	4·75
38	**99**	15r. stone	25	4·75
39	**99**	20r. purple	25	6·25
40	**99**	40r. green	25	7·00
41	**99**	50r. violet	35	7·50

Pt. 9

RIO DE ORO

A Spanish territory on the West Coast of North Africa, renamed Spanish Sahara in 1924.

100 centimos = 1 peseta.

1905. "Curly Head" key-type inscr "COLONIA DE RIO DE ORO".

1	**Z**	1c. green	4·75	4·50
2	**Z**	2c. red	4·75	4·50
3	**Z**	3c. black	4·75	4·50
4	**Z**	4c. brown	4·75	4·50
5	**Z**	5c. red	4·75	4·50
6	**Z**	10c. brown	4·75	4·50
7	**Z**	15c. brown	4·75	4·50
8	**Z**	25c. blue	£120	55·00
9	**Z**	50c. green	60·00	23·00
10	**Z**	75c. violet	60·00	31·00
11	**Z**	1p. brown	41·00	12·50
12	**Z**	2p. orange	£140	85·00
13	**Z**	3p. lilac	90·00	31·00
14	**Z**	4p. green	90·00	31·00
15	**Z**	5p. blue	£120	65·00
16	**Z**	10p. red	£275	£200

1906. "Curly Head" key-type surch HABILITADO PARA 15 CENTS in circle.

17		15c. on 25c. blue	£300	£190

3

11

7

1907

18	**3**	1c. purple	4·25	3·75
19	**3**	2c. black	4·25	3·75
20	**3**	3c. brown	4·25	3·75
21	**3**	4c. red	4·25	3·75
22	**3**	5c. brown	4·25	3·75
23	**3**	10c. brown	4·25	3·75
24	**3**	15c. blue	4·25	3·75
25	**3**	25c. green	19·00	3·75
26	**3**	50c. purple	19·00	3·75
27	**3**	75c. brown	19·00	3·75
28	**3**	1p. buff	28·00	3·75
29	**3**	2p. lilac	7·00	3·75
30	**3**	3p. green	7·00	3·75
31	**3**	4p. blue	12·00	7·50
32	**3**	5p. red	12·00	7·50
33	**3**	10p. green	12·00	19·00

1907. Nos. 9/10 surch 1907 10 Cens.

34	**Z**	10c. on 50c. green	£160	41·00
35	**Z**	10c. on 75c. violet	£120	41·00

1908. Nos. 12 and 26 surch 1908 and value.

36		2c. on 2p. orange	95·00	41·00
37	**3**	10c. on 50c. purple	32·00	6·25

1908. Surch HABILITADO PARA 15 CENTS in circle.

38		15c. on 25c. green	38·00	6·75
39		15c. on 75c. brown	50·00	13·00
40		15c. on 1p. buff	50·00	13·00
71		15c. on 3p. green	£250	36·00
72		15c. on 5p. red	16·00	15·00

1908. Large Fiscal stamp inscr "TERRITORIOS ESPANOLES DEL AFRICA OCCIDENTAL" surch HABILITADO PARA CORREOS RIO DE ORO 5 CENS. Imperf.

45		5c. on 50c. green	£110	47·00

1909

47	**7**	1c. orange	95	65
48	**7**	2c. orange	95	65
49	**7**	5c. green	95	65
50	**7**	10c. red	95	65
51	**7**	15c. green	95	65
52	**7**	20c. purple	2·50	1·10
53	**7**	25c. blue	2·50	1·10
54	**7**	30c. red	2·50	1·10
55	**7**	40c. brown	2·50	1·10
56	**7**	50c. purple	4·50	1·10
57	**7**	1p. brown	6·25	5·25
58	**7**	4p. red	7·50	8·00
59	**7**	10p. purple	17·00	14·00

1910. Nos. 13/16 surch 1910 and value.

60	**Z**	10c. on 5p. blue	22·00	14·00
62	**Z**	10c. on 10p. red	21·00	12·50
65	**Z**	15c. on 3p. lilac	21·00	12·50
66	**Z**	15c. on 4p. green	21·00	12·50

1911. Surch with value in figures and words.

67	**3**	2c. on 4p. blue	16·00	13·00
68	**3**	5c. on 10p. green	41·00	13·00
69	**3**	10c. on 2p. lilac	20·00	14·00
70	**3**	10c. on 3p. green	£250	80·00

1912

73	**11**	1c. pink	35	20
74	**11**	2c. lilac	35	20
75	**11**	5c. green	35	20
76	**11**	10c. red	35	20
77	**11**	15c. brown	35	20
78	**11**	20c. brown	35	20
79	**11**	25c. blue	35	20
80	**11**	30c. lilac	35	20
81	**11**	40c. green	35	20
82	**11**	50c. purple	35	20
83	**11**	1p. red	7·75	1·40
84	**11**	4p. red	8·50	7·50
85	**11**	10p. brown	13·50	12·50

12

14

15

1914

86	12	1c. brown	40	20
87	12	2c. purple	40	20
88	12	5c. green	40	20
89	12	10c. red	40	20
90	12	15c. red	40	20
91	12	20c. red	40	20
92	12	25c. blue	40	20
93	12	30c. green	40	20
94	12	40c. orange	40	20
95	12	50c. brown	40	20
96	12	1p. lilac	9·50	3·75
97	12	4p. red	12·50	3·75
98	12	10p. violet	12·50	11·50

1917. Nos. 73/85 optd 1917.

99	11	1c. pink	18·00	1·70
100	11	2c. lilac	18·00	1·70
101	11	5c. green	3·25	1·70
102	11	10c. red	3·25	1·70
103	11	15c. brown	3·25	1·70
104	11	20c. brown	3·25	1·70
105	11	25c. blue	3·25	1·70
106	11	30c. lilac	3·25	1·70
107	11	40c. green	3·25	1·70
108	11	50c. purple	3·25	1·70
109	11	1p. red	18·00	11·00
110	11	4p. red	31·00	14·50
111	11	10p. brown	55·00	24·00

1919

112	14	1c. brown	1·00	70
113	14	2c. purple	1·00	70
114	14	5c. green	1·00	70
115	14	10c. red	1·00	70
116	14	15c. red	1·00	70
117	14	20c. orange	1·00	70
118	14	25c. blue	1·00	70
119	14	30c. green	1·00	70
120	14	40c. orange	1·00	70
121	14	50c. brown	1·00	70
122	14	1p. lilac	7·50	7·25
123	14	4p. red	12·50	14·00
124	14	10p. violet	18·00	24·00

1920

125	15	1c. purple	90	65
126	15	2c. pink	90	65
127	15	5c. red	90	65
128	15	10c. purple	90	65
129	15	15c. brown	90	65
130	15	20c. green	90	65
131	15	25c. orange	90	65
132	15	30c. blue	5·75	6·25
133	15	40c. orange	3·25	3·00
134	15	50c. purple	3·25	3·00
135	15	1p. green	50·00	3·00
136	15	4p. red	9·50	7·00
137	15	10p. brown	24·00	20·00

1921. As Nos. 14/26 of La Aguera but inscr "RIO DE ORO".

138	1c. yellow	90	60
139	2c. brown	90	60
140	5c. green	90	60
141	10c. red	90	60
142	15c. green	90	60
143	20c. blue	90	60
144	25c. blue	90	60
145	30c. pink	1·70	1·70
146	40c. violet	1·70	1·70
147	50c. orange	1·70	1·70
148	1p. mauve	5·75	2·75
149	4p. purple	16·00	11·00
150	10p. brown	24·00	25·00

For later issues see **SPANISH SAHARA**.

Pt. 9

RIO MUNI

A coastal settlement between Cameroun and Gabon, formerly using the stamps of Spanish Guinea. On 12 October 1968 it became independent and joined Fernando Poo to become Equatorial Guinea.

100 centimos = 1 peseta.

1 Native Boy reading Book

1960

1	1	25c. grey	30	25
2	1	50c. brown	30	25
3	1	75c. purple	30	25
4	1	1p. red	30	25
5	1	1p.50 green	30	25
6	1	2p. purple	30	25
7	1	3p. blue	55	35
8	1	5p. brown	1·30	45
9	1	10p. green	2·30	70

2 Cactus

1960. Child Welfare Fund.

10	2	10c.+5c. purple	55	55
11	-	15c.+5c. brown	55	55
12	-	35c. green	55	55
13	2	80c. green	65	65

DESIGNS: 15c. Sprig with berries; 35c. Star-shaped flowers.

3 Bishop Juan de Ribera

1960. Stamp Day.

14	3	10c.+5c. red	55	55
15	-	20c.+5c. green	55	55
16	-	30c.+10c. brown	55	55
17	3	50c.+20c. brown	65	65

DESIGNS: 20c. Portrait of man (after Velazquez); 30c. Statue.

4 Mandrill with Banana

1961. Child Welfare. Inscr "PRO-INFANCIA 1961".

18	4	10c.+5c. red	55	55
19	-	25c.+10c. violet	55	55
20	4	80c.+20c. green	65	65

DESIGN—VERT: 25c. African elephant.

5

1961. 25th Anniv of Gen. Franco as Head of State.

21	-	25c. grey	55	55
22	5	50c. brown	55	55
23	-	70c. green	55	55
24	5	1p. red	65	65

DESIGNS: 25c. Map; 70c. Government building.

6 Statuette

1961. Stamp Day. Inscr "DIA DEL SELLO 1961".

25	6	10c.+5c. red	55	55
26	-	25c.+10c. purple	55	55
27	6	30c.+10c. brown	55	55
28	-	1p.+10c. orange	65	65

DESIGN: 25c., 1p. Figure holding offering.

7 Girl wearing Headdress

1962. Child Welfare. Inscr "PRO-INFANCIA 1962".

29	7	25c. violet	55	55
30	-	50c. green	55	55
31	7	1p. brown	65	65

DESIGN: 50c. Native mask.

8 African Buffalo

1962. Stamp Day. Inscr "DIA DEL SELLO 1962".

32	8	15c. green	55	55
33	-	35c. purple	55	55
34	8	1p. red	65	65

DESIGN—VERT: 35c. Gorilla.

9 Statuette

1963. Seville Flood Relief.

35	9	50c. green	55	55
36	9	1p. brown	65	65

10 "Blessing"

1963. Child Welfare. Inscr "PRO-INFANCIA 1963".

37	-	25c. violet	55	55
38	10	50c. green	55	55
39	-	1p. red	65	65

DESIGN: 25c., 1p. Priest.

11 Child at Prayer

1963. "For Barcelona".

40	11	50c. green	55	55
41	11	1p. brown	65	65

12 Copal Flower

1964. Stamp Day. Inscr "DIA DEL SELLO 1963".

42	12	25c. violet	55	55
43	-	50c. turquoise	55	55
44	12	1p. red	65	65

FLOWER—HORIZ: 50c. Cinchona blossom.

13 Giant Ground Pangolin

1964. Child Welfare. Inscr "PRO-INFANCIA 1964".

45	13	25c. violet	55	55
46	-	50c. green (Chameleon)	55	55
47	13	1p. brown	65	65

1964. Wild Life. As T 13 but without "PRO INFANCIA" inscription.

48	15c. brown	20	20
49	25c. violet	20	20
50	50c. green	20	20
51	70c. green	20	20
52	1p. brown	95	20
53	1p.50 green	95	20
54	3p. blue	1·90	30
55	5p. brown	4·75	45
56	10p. green	8·50	1·20

ANIMALS: 15, 70c., 3p. Crocodile; 25c., 1, 5p. Leopard; 50c., 1p.50, 10p. Black rhinoceros.

14 "Goliath" Frog

1964. Stamp Day.

57	14	50c. green	55	55
58	-	1p. red	55	55
59	14	1p.50 green	65	65

DESIGN—VERT: 1p. Helmeted guineafowl.

15 Woman

1965. 25th Anniv of End of Spanish Civil War.

60	15	50c. green	55	55
61	-	1p. red	55	55
62	-	1p.50 turquoise	65	65

DESIGNS: 1p. Nurse; 1p.50, Logging.

16 Goliath Beetle

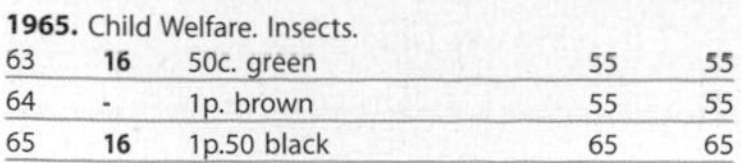

1965. Child Welfare. Insects.

63	**16**	50c. green	55	55
64	-	1p. brown	55	55
65	**16**	1p.50 black	65	65

DESIGN: 1p. "Acridoxena hewaniana".

17 Leopard and Arms of Rio Muni

1965. Stamp Day.

66	-	50c. grey	55	55
67	**17**	1p. brown	55	55
68	-	2p.50 violet	2·10	2·10

DESIGN—VERT: 50c., 2p.50, Common pheasant.

18 African Elephant and Grey Parrot

1966. Child Welfare.

69	**18**	50c. brown	55	55
70	**18**	1p. lilac	55	55
71	-	1p.50 blue	65	65

DESIGN: 1p.50, African and lion.

19 Water Chevrotain

1966. Stamp Day.

72	**19**	10c. brown and ochre	55	55
73	-	40c. brown and yellow	55	55
74	**19**	1p.50 violet and red	55	55
75	-	4p. blue and green	65	65

DESIGN—VERT: 40c., 4p. Giant ground pangolin.

20 Floss Flowers

1967. Child Welfare.

76	**20**	10c. yellow, olive and green	55	55
77	-	40c. green, black and mauve	55	55
78	**20**	1p.50 red and blue	55	55
79	-	4p. black and green	65	65

DESIGNS: 40c., 4p. Ylang-ylang (flower).

21 Bush Pig

1967. Stamp Day.

80	**21**	1p. chestnut and brown	55	55
81	-	1p.50 brown and green	55	55
82	-	3p.50 brown and green	1·10	1·10

DESIGNS—VERT: 1p.50, Potto. HORIZ: 3p.50, African golden cat.

1968. Child Welfare. Signs of the Zodiac. As T 56a of Spanish Sahara.

83	1p. mauve on yellow	55	55
84	1p.50 brown on pink	55	55
85	2p.50 violet on yellow	95	95

DESIGNS: 1p. Cancer (crab); 1p.50, Taurus (bull); 2p.50, Gemini (twins).

Pt. 8

ROMAGNA

One of the Papal states, now part of Italy. Stamps issued prior to union with Sardinia in 1860.

100 bajocchi = 1 scudo.

1

1859. Imperf.

2	**1**	½b. black on buff	43·00	£375
3	**1**	1b. black on grey	43·00	£190
4	**1**	2b. black on buff	60·00	£200
5	**1**	3b. black on green	70·00	£375
6	**1**	4b. black on brown	£800	£190
7	**1**	5b. black on lilac	85·00	£450
8	**1**	6b. black on green	£475	£9500
9	**1**	8b. black on pink	£275	£2250
10	**1**	20b. black on green	£275	£3250

Pt. 3

ROMANIA

A republic in S.E. Europe bordering on the Black Sea, originally a kingdom formed by the union of Moldavia and Wallachia.

1858. 40 parale = 1 piastre.
1867. 100 bani = 1 leu.
2005. 10000 leu (l.) = 1 new leu (l.)

MOLDAVIA

1

1858. Imperf.

No.	Type	Description	Unused	Used
1		27p. black on red	£42000	£16000
2		54p. blue on green	£21000	£6500
3		81p. blue on blue	£40000	£44000
4		108p. blue on pink	£30000	£14000

2

1858. Imperf.

No.	Type	Description	Unused	Used
12	2	5p. black	£200	
13	2	40p. blue	£200	£225
14	2	80p. red	£650	£400

ROMANIA

4

1862. Imperf.

No.	Type	Description	Unused	Used
29	4	3p. yellow	£120	£325
30	4	6p. red	£100	£300
31	4	30p. blue	75·00	85·00

5 Prince Alexander Cuza

1865. Imperf.

No.	Type	Description	Unused	Used
49a	5	2p. orange	75·00	£325
46	5	5p. blue	50·00	£325
48	5	20p. red	42·00	50·00

6 Prince Carol

1866. Imperf.

No.	Type	Description	Unused	Used
60	6	2p. black on yellow	42·00	£120
61	6	5p. black on blue	75·00	£900
62	6	20p. black on red	37·00	31·00

7 Prince Carol

1868. Imperf.

No.	Type	Description	Unused	Used
71	7	2b. orange	50·00	42·00
72	7	3b. mauve	65·00	47·00
66c	7	4b. blue	80·00	75·00
67	7	18b. red	£250	37·00

8

1869. Without beard. Imperf.

No.	Type	Description	Unused	Used
74	8	5b. orange	90·00	50·00
75	8	10b. blue	47·00	42·00
76	8	15b. red	47·00	42·00
77c	8	25b. blue and orange	45·00	31·00
78	8	50b. red and blue	£190	60·00

9

1871. With beard. Imperf.

No.	Type	Description	Unused	Used
83	9	5b. red	50·00	42·00
84	9	10b. orange	75·00	47·00
99	9	10b. blue	50·00	65·00
86	9	15b. red	£275	£250
87	9	25b. brown	65·00	60·00
100	9	50b. red and blue	£225	£250

1872. Perf.

No.	Type	Description	Unused	Used
93	9	5b. red	85·00	50·00
94	9	10b. blue	85·00	50·00
95	9	25b. brown	60·00	50·00

10

1872. Perf.

No.	Type	Description	Unused	Used
124	10	1¼b. black	7·75	3·25
112	10	1½b. green	7·75	5·25
105	10	3b. green	47·00	7·25
125	10	3b. olive	21·00	16·00
106	10	5b. bistre	26·00	5·75
126	10	5b. green	8·25	4·25
107	10	10b. blue	26·00	6·25
127c	10	10b. red	16·00	3·25
115	10	15b. brown	90·00	11·50
128a	10	15b. red	42·00	12·50
110	10	25b. orange	£180	23·00
130	10	25b. blue	£170	31·00
116	10	30b. red	£225	65·00
111	10	50b. red	£200	50·00
131	10	50b. bistre	£150	42·00

11 King Carol

1880

No.	Type	Description	Unused	Used
146a	11	15b. brown	14·50	3·25
147	11	25b. blue	29·00	4·25

12 King Carol

1885. On white or coloured papers.

No.	Type	Description	Unused	Used
161	12	1½b. black	4·25	2·10
163	12	3b. green	6·25	2·10
165a	12	3b. violet	6·25	2·10
166	12	5b. green	6·25	2·10
168	12	10b. red	6·25	3·25
169	12	15b. brown	18·00	3·25
171	12	25b. blue	21·00	7·25
186	12	50b. brown	95·00	26·00

14 King Carol

1890

No.	Type	Description	Unused	Used
271	14	1½b. lake	2·10	1·60
272a	14	3b. mauve	2·50	2·50
273	14	5b. green	4·25	2·10
274	14	10b. red	26·00	2·10
255	14	15b. brown	26·00	4·75
306	14	25b. blue	17·00	7·75
307	14	50b. orange	33·00	16·00

15

1891. 25th Anniv of Reign.

No.	Type	Description	Unused	Used
300	15	1½b. lake	7·25	8·25
293	15	3b. mauve	7·25	8·25
294	15	5b. green	9·50	10·50
295	15	10b. red	9·50	10·50
303	15	15b. brown	9·50	8·25

17

19

1893. Various frames as T 17 and 19.

No.	Type	Description	Unused	Used
316		1 BANI brown	1·60	1·00
426		1 BAN brown	2·10	1·60
317		1½b. black	1·60	90
533		3b. brown	1·00	40
319		5b. blue	2·50	1·30
534		5b. green	2·10	50
320		10b. green	4·50	1·30
535		10b. red	2·10	50
332		15b. pink	6·25	1·60
400		15b. black	3·25	1·00
430		15b. brown	3·50	1·30
545		15b. violet	2·50	50
322		25b. mauve	5·25	1·60
701		25b. blue	1·00	30
421		40b. green	12·50	1·90
324		50b. orange	21·00	2·50
325		1l. pink and brown	37·00	2·50
326		2l. brown and orange	42·00	4·25

See also Nos. 532 etc.

25 Four-in-hand Postal Coach
26 New Post Office, Bucharest

1903. Opening of New Post Office in 1901.

No.	Type	Description	Unused	Used
464	25	1b. brown	2·10	1·80
465	25	3b. red	4·25	2·10
466	25	5b. green	7·75	3·25
467	25	10b. red	6·25	3·25
468	25	15b. black	6·25	4·25
472	26	15b. black	5·25	4·25
469	25	25b. blue	21·00	12·50
473	26	25b. blue	12·50	7·75
470	25	40b. green	31·00	16·00
474	26	40b. green	21·00	10·50
471	25	50b. orange	38·00	21·00
475	26	50b. orange	23·00	12·50
476	26	1l. brown	18·00	10·50
477	26	2l. red	£160	80·00
478	26	5l. lilac	£190	£130

See also No. 1275.

1905. Various frames as T 17 and 19.

No.	Type	Description	Unused	Used
532		1 ban black	40	30
625b		1½b. yellow	3·25	2·50
703		40b. brown	1·80	1·00
697		50b. pink	2·10	1·00
432		1l. black and green	42·00	3·75
706		1l. green	2·40	95
433		2l. black and brown	31·00	4·75
707		2l. orange	3·25	1·00

27 Queen of Romania spinning

1906. Welfare Fund. Motto: "God guide our Hand".

No.	Type	Description	Unused	Used
481	27	3b.(+7) brown	7·75	5·25

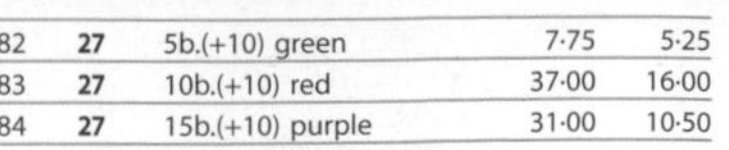

No.	Type	Description	Unused	Used
482	27	5b.(+10) green	7·75	5·25
483	27	10b.(+10) red	37·00	16·00
484	27	15b.(+10) purple	31·00	10·50

28 Queen of Romania weaving

1906. Welfare Fund. Motto: "Woman weaves the Future of the Country".

No.	Type	Description	Unused	Used
485	28	3b.(+7) brown	7·75	5·25
486	28	5b.(+10) green	7·75	5·25
487	28	10b.(+10) red	42·00	16·00
488	28	15b.(+10) lilac	26·00	10·50

29 Queen of Romania nursing wounded Soldier

1906. Welfare Fund. Motto: "The Wounds dressed and the Tears wiped away".

No.	Type	Description	Unused	Used
489	29	3b.(+7) brown	7·75	5·25
490	29	5b.(+10) green	7·75	5·25
491	29	10b.(+10) red	42·00	16·00
492	29	15b.(+10) purple	26·00	10·50

30

1906. 25th Anniv of Kingdom.

No.	Type	Description	Unused	Used
493	30	1b. black and bistre	1·00	50
494	30	3b. black and brown	2·50	1·00
495	30	5b. black and green	1·60	75
496	30	10b. black and red	1·60	75
497	30	15b. black and violet	1·60	75
498	30	25b. black and blue	14·50	7·75
499	30	40b. black and brown	6·25	1·60
500	30	50b. black and brown	6·25	1·60
501	30	1l. black and red	6·25	1·60
502	30	2l. black and orange	6·25	1·60

31 Prince Carol at Battle of Calafat

1906. 40 Years' Rule of Prince and King. Dated "1906".

No.	Type	Description	Unused	Used
503	-	1b. black and bistre	75	50
504	-	3b. black and brown	1·60	50
505	31	5b. black and green	1·80	50
506	-	10b. black and red	1·30	50
507	-	15b. black and violet	1·30	50
508	-	25b. black and blue	7·75	6·25
508a	-	25b. black and green	9·25	6·25
509	-	40b. black and brown	2·10	1·60
510	-	50b. black and brown	2·30	1·60
511	-	1l. black and red	2·30	1·80
512	-	2l. black and orange	2·50	2·50

DESIGNS—HORIZ: 1b. Prince Carol taking oath of allegiance in 1866; 3b. Prince in carriage; 10b. Meeting of Prince and Osman Pasha, 1878; 15b. Carol when Prince in 1866 and King in 1906; 25b. Romanian Army crossing Danube, 1877; 40b. Triumphal entry into Bucharest, 1878; 50b. Prince at head of Army in 1877; 1l. King Carol at Cathedral in 1896; 2l. King at shrine of S. Nicholas, 1904.

32

1906. Welfare Fund. Motto: "But Glory, Honour and Peace to All that do Good".

513	**32**	3b.(+7) brown, bistre and blue	4·25	2·10
514	**32**	5b.(+10) green, red and bistre	4·25	2·10
515	**32**	10b.(+10) red, bistre and blue	6·25	4·25
516	**32**	15b.(+10) violet, bistre and blue	17·00	5·25

33 Peasant ploughing and Angel

1906. Jubilee Exhibition, Bucharest.

517	**33**	5b. black and green	5·25	1·60
518	**33**	10b. black and red	5·25	1·60
519	-	15b. black and violet	7·75	2·50
520	-	25b. black and blue	7·75	2·50
521	-	30b. brown and red	10·50	2·50
522	-	40b. brown and green	11·50	3·25
523	-	50b. black and orange	10·50	3·75
524	-	75b. sepia and brown	9·50	3·75
525	-	1l.50 brown and mauve	£120	50·00
526	-	2l.50 brown and yellow	42·00	31·00
527	-	3l. brown and orange	31·00	31·00

DESIGNS—HORIZ: 15, 25b. Exhibition Building. VERT: 30, 40b. Farmhouse; 50, 75b. (different), Royal Family pavilion; 1l.50, 2l.50, King Carol on horseback; 3l. Queen Elizabeth (Carmen Sylva).

34 Princess Maria and her Children receiving Poor Family conducted by an Angel

1907. Welfare Fund.

528	**34**	3b.(+7) brown	5·25	2·10
529	**34**	5b.(+10) brown and green	5·25	2·10
530	**34**	10b.(+10) brown and red	5·25	2·10
531	**34**	15b.(+10) brown and blue	5·25	2·10

35

1908

575	**35**	5b. green	3·25	30
562	**35**	10b. red	50	20
577	**35**	15b. violet	6·25	2·40
564	**35**	25b. blue	2·10	20
579	**35**	40b. green	75	20
702	**35**	40b. brown	5·75	2·50
566	**35**	50b. orange	75	20
705	**35**	50b. red	1·80	1·00
581	**35**	1l. brown	2·30	50
582	**35**	2l. red	9·50	2·50

37

1908

583	**37**	1b. black	50	10
590	**37**	3b. brown	1·00	10
585	**37**	5b. green	50	10
592	**37**	10b. red	50	10
594	**37**	15b. olive	1·00	10
599	**37**	15b. violet	11·50	10·50
692	**37**	15b. brown	1·00	50

38

39 Troops crossing Danube

1913. Acquisition of Southern Dobruja.

626	-	1b. black	1·00	50
627	**38**	3b. brown and grey	2·50	1·00
628	**39**	5b. black and green	2·10	50
629	-	10b. black and orange	1·00	50
630	-	15b. violet and brown	2·50	1·00
631	-	25b. brown and blue	3·75	1·60
632	**39**	40b. red and brown	7·25	6·25
633	**38**	50b. blue and yellow	16·00	8·25
634	**38**	1l. brown and blue	29·00	19·00
635	**38**	2l. red and red	42·00	26·00

DESIGNS—VERT (As Type **38**): 1b. "Dobruja" holding flag. HORIZ (As Type **39**): 10b. Town of Constanza; 25b. Church and School in Dobruja. (24×16 mm): 15b. Mircea the Great and King Carol.

1918. Surch 25. BANI.

657	**37**	25b. on 1b. black	2·10	1·00

1918. Optd 1918.

662	5b. green	75	50
663	10b. red	75	50

TRANSYLVANIA

The Eastern portion of Hungary. Union with Romania proclaimed in December 1918 and the final frontiers settled by the Treaty of Trianon on 4 June 1920.

The following issues for Transylvania (Nos. 747/858) were valid throughout Romania.

(The "F" stands for King Ferdinand and "P.T.T." for Posts Telegraphs and Telephones).

The values "BANI", "LEU" or "LEI" appear above or below the monogram.

A. Issues for Cluj (Kolozsvar or Klausenburg)

BANI

(42)

1919. Various stamps of Hungary optd as T 42. (a) Flood Relief Charity stamps of 1913.

747	**7**	1l. on 1f. grey	21·00	18·00
748	**7**	1l. on 2f. yellow	£120	85·00
749	**7**	1l. on 3f. orange	50·00	42·00
750	**7**	1l. on 5f. green	2·50	1·60
751	**7**	1l. on 10f. red	2·50	1·60
752	**7**	1l. on 12f. lilac on yellow	9·00	5·75
753	**7**	1l. on 16f. green	4·75	3·25
754	**7**	1l. on 25f. blue	50·00	42·00
755	**7**	1l. on 35f. purple	5·25	3·25
756	**8**	1l. on 1k. red	65·00	50·00

(b) War Charity stamps of 1916.

757	**20**	10(+2) b. red	30	20
758	-	15(+2) b. violet	30	20
759	**22**	40(+2) b. lake	40	30

(c) Harvesters and Parliament Types.

760	**18**	2b. brown	20	20
761	**18**	3b. red	30	20
762	**18**	5b. green	30	20
763	**18**	6b. blue	30	20
764	**18**	10b. red	£140	£100
765	**18**	15b. violet (No. 244)	5·00	3·75
766	**18**	15b. violet	20	10
767	**18**	25b. blue	20	10
768	**18**	35b. brown	20	10
769	**18**	40b. olive	20	10
770	**19**	50b. purple	30	20
771	**19**	75b. blue	40	30
772	**19**	80b. green	40	30
773	**19**	1l. lake	40	30
774	**19**	2l. brown	55	40
775	**19**	3l. grey and violet	3·50	2·50
776	**19**	5l. brown	2·75	2·10
777	**19**	10l. lilac and brown	3·50	2·50

(d) Charles and Zita stamps.

778	**27**	10b. red	30·00	21·00
779	**27**	15b. violet	11·50	7·75
780	**27**	20b. brown	50	30
781	**27**	25b. blue	85	50
782	**28**	40b. green	50	30

B. Issues for Oradea (Nagyvarad or Grosswardein)

Bani

(43)

1919. Various stamps of Hungary optd as T 43. (a) "Turul" Type.

794	**7**	2b. yellow	5·25	4·75
795	**7**	3b. orange	9·75	8·50
796	**7**	6b. drab	95	50
797	**7**	16b. green	21·00	12·50
798	**7**	50b. lake on blue	1·30	1·00
799	**7**	70b. brown and green	20·00	18·00

(b) Flood Relief Charity stamps of 1913.

800	**7**	1l. on 1f. grey	1·20	1·10
801		1l. on 2f. yellow	4·75	4·50
802		1l. on 3f. orange	1·60	1·30
803		1l. on 5l. green	30	20
804		1l. on 6f. drab	1·20	1·10
805		1l. on 10f. red	30	20
806		1l. on 12f. lilac on yellow	50·00	46·00
807		1l. on 16f. green	1·50	1·30
808		1l. on 20f. brown	6·50	6·25
809		1l. on 25f. blue	4·50	3·25
810		1l. on 35f. purple	4·50	3·25

(c) War Charity stamp of 1915.

811	5+2b. green (No. 173)	11·50	11·50

(d) War Charity stamps of 1916.

812	**20**	10(+2) b. red	70	70
813	-	15(+2) b. violet	30	20
814	**22**	40(+2) b. lake	30	30

(e) Harvesters and Parliament Types.

815	**18**	2b. brown	20	20
816	**18**	3b. red	20	20
817	**18**	5b. green	30	20
818	**18**	6b. blue	90	65
819	**18**	10b. red	1·60	1·00
820	**18**	15b. violet (No. 244)	£130	£100
821	**18**	15b. violet	15	10
822	**18**	20b. brown	15·00	9·50
823	**18**	25b. blue	30	20
824	**18**	35b. brown	35	20
825	**18**	40b. olive	30	20
826	**19**	50b. purple	40	30
827	**19**	75b. blue	20	20
828	**19**	80b. green	30	30
829	**19**	1l. lake	55	40
830	**19**	2l. brown	20	20
831	**19**	3l. grey and violet	4·50	4·25
832	**19**	5l. brown	2·75	2·50
833	**19**	10l. lilac and brown	1·60	1·50

(f) Charles and Zita stamps.

834	**27**	10b. red	2·75	2·10
835	**27**	20b. brown	20	20
836	**27**	25b. blue	45	30
837	**27**	40b. green	70	50

(g) Harvesters and Parliament Types.

838	**18**	2b. brown	2·10	1·30
839	**18**	3b. red	40	30
840	**18**	4b. grey	30	20
841	**18**	5b. green	40	30
842	**18**	6b. blue	2·30	1·60
843	**18**	10b. red	21·00	17·00
844	**18**	20b. brown	1·90	1·30
845	**18**	40b. olive	40	30
846	**19**	1l. lake	30	20
847	**19**	3l. grey and violet	1·20	85
848	**19**	5l. brown	4·75	3·75

(h) Charles and Zita stamps.

849	**27**	10b. red	£130	£130
850	**27**	20b. brown	2·75	2·10
851	**27**	25b. blue	70	40
852	**28**	50b. purple	30	20

(k) Harvesters and Parliament Types inscr "MAGYAR POSTA".

853	**18**	5b. green	20	20
854	**18**	20b. red	20	20
855	**18**	20b. brown	25	20
856	**18**	25b. blue	1·00	50
857	**18**	40b. olive	1·00	75
858	**19**	5l. brown	8·75	6·50

(44) King Ferdinand's Monogram

1919. Optd with T 44.

873	**37**	1b. black	30	20
874	**37**	5b. green	40	50
878a	**37**	10b. red	20	20

45 King Ferdinand

1920

891	**45**	1b. black	20	15
892	**45**	5b. green	20	15
893	**45**	10b. red	20	15
882	**45**	15b. brown	75	30
895	**45**	25b. blue	30	30
896	**45**	25b. brown	30	30
910	**45**	40b. brown	65	20
898	**45**	50b. pink	85	20
887	**45**	1l. green	1·60	30
900	**45**	1l. red	40	30
889	**45**	2l. orange	2·10	50
902	**45**	2l. blue	1·00	35
903	**45**	2l. red	3·25	2·10

46 King Ferdinand

1922

923	**46**	3b. black	20	10
924	**46**	5b. black	10	10
925	**46**	10b. green	20	10
926	**46**	25b. brown	20	10
927	**46**	25b. red	30	10
928	**46**	30b. violet	30	10
929	**46**	50b. yellow	50	30
930	**46**	60b. green	1·50	75
931	**46**	1l. violet	40	10
932	**46**	2l. red	2·10	20
933a	**46**	2l. green	65	20
934	**46**	3l. blue	3·25	1·00
935a	**46**	3l. brown	3·25	1·00
936a	**46**	3l. pink	37·00	10·50
937	**46**	3l. red	1·20	10
938	**46**	5l. green	2·75	1·00
939b	**46**	5l. brown	1·00	10
940	**46**	6l. blue	4·50	1·60
941	**46**	6l. red	8·25	4·25
942	**46**	6l. olive	4·50	1·00
943	**46**	7l.50 blue	4·25	50
944	**46**	10l. blue	4·25	50

47 Cathedral of Alba Julia

48 King Ferdinand

49 State Arms

51 Michael the Brave and King Ferdinand

1922. Coronation.

1032	**47**	5b. black	50	30
1033	**48**	25b. brown	1·30	50
1034	**49**	50b. green	1·30	75
1035	-	1l. olive	1·60	1·00
1036	**51**	2l. red	1·60	1·00
1037	-	3l. blue	3·25	1·60
1050	-	6l. violet	8·75	7·00

DESIGNS—As Type **48**: 1l. Queen Marie as a nurse; 3l. Portrait of King but rectangular frame. Larger (21×33 mm): 6l. Queen Marie in coronation robes.

54 King Ferdinand

1926. King's 60th Birthday. Imperf or perf.

1051	**54**	10b. green	75	50
1052	**54**	25b. orange	75	50
1053	**54**	50b. brown	75	50
1054	**54**	1l. violet	75	50
1055	**54**	2l. green	75	50
1056	**54**	3l. red	75	1·00
1057	**54**	5l. brown	75	1·00
1058	**54**	6l. olive	75	1·00
1059	**54**	9l. grey	75	1·00
1060	**54**	10l. blue	75	1·00

55 Map of Romania

1927. 50th Anniv of Romanian Geographical Society.

1061	**55**	1+9l. violet	5·25	2·10
1062	-	2+8l. green	5·25	2·10
1063	-	3+7l. red	5·25	2·10
1064	-	5+5l. blue	5·25	2·10
1065	-	6+4l. olive	7·75	3·25

DESIGNS: 2l. Stephen the Great; 3l. Michael the Brave; 5l. Carol and Ferdinand; 6l. Adam Clisi Monument.

60 King Carol and King Ferdinand

1927. 50th Anniv of Independence.

1066	**60**	25b. red	1·00	20
1067	-	30b. black	1·00	30
1068	-	50b. green	1·00	30
1069	**60**	1l. blue	1·00	30
1070	-	2l. green	1·00	40
1071	-	3l. purple	1·00	50
1072	-	4l. brown	1·00	65
1073	-	4l.50 brown	3·25	2·10
1074	-	5l. brown	1·00	50
1075	-	6l. red	2·10	1·20
1076	**60**	7l.50 blue	1·00	50
1077	**60**	10l. blue	3·25	1·00

DESIGNS—HORIZ: 30b., 2, 3, 5l. King Ferdinand. VERT: 50b., 4l., 4l.50, 6l. King Ferdinand as in Type **60**.

63 King Michael

1928

1080	**63**	25b. black	50	20
1081	**63**	30b. pink	1·00	20
1082	**63**	50b. olive	50	20

64 King Michael

1928. (a) Size 18½×24½ mm.

1083	**64**	1l. purple	1·00	20
1084	**64**	2l. green	1·30	20
1085	**64**	3l. red	1·60	20
1086	**64**	5l. brown	2·50	20
1087	**64**	7l.50 blue	11·50	1·30
1088	**64**	10l. blue	9·50	50

(b) Size 18×23 mm.

1129		1l. purple	1·00	20
1130		2l. green	1·60	20
1131		3l. red	3·25	20
1132		7l.50 blue	6·25	1·60
1133		10l. blue	21·00	10·50

65 Bessarabian Parliament House

1928. 10th Anniv of Annexation of Bessarabia.

1092	**65**	1l. green	2·30	1·00
1093	**65**	2l. brown	2·30	1·00
1094	-	3l. sepia	2·30	1·00
1095	-	5l. lake	2·75	1·30
1096	-	7l.50 blue	2·75	1·30
1097	-	10l. blue	7·25	3·25
1098	-	20l. violet	9·50	4·25

DESIGNS: 3, 5, 20l. Hotin Fortress; 7l.50, 10l. Fortress Cetatea Alba.

66 Bleriot SPAD 33 Biplane

1928. Air.

1099	**66**	1l. brown	7·75	5·25
1100	**66**	2l. blue	7·75	5·25
1101	**66**	5l. red	7·75	5·25

67 King Carol and King Michael

1928. 50th Anniv of Acquisition of Northern Dobruja.

1102	**67**	1l. green	1·80	65
1103	-	2l. brown	1·80	65
1104	**67**	3l. grey	2·50	65
1105	-	5l. mauve	3·25	75
1106	-	7l.50 blue	3·75	85
1107	-	10l. blue	5·25	2·10
1108	-	20l. red	9·00	2·50

DESIGNS: 2l. Constanza Harbour and Carol Lighthouse; 5l., 7l.50, Adam Clisi Monument; 10, 20l. Saligny Bridge over River Danube, Cernavoda.

68

69 The Union

1929. 10th Anniv of Union of Romania and Transylvania.

1109	**68**	1l. purple	4·25	2·10
1110	**69**	2l. green	4·25	2·10
1111	-	3l. brown	4·75	2·10
1112	-	4l. red	4·75	2·50
1113	-	5l. orange	6·25	2·50
1114	-	10l. blue	7·75	5·25

DESIGNS—HORIZ: 1l. Ferdinand I, Stephen the Great, Michael the Brave, Hunyadi and Brancoveanu; 10l. Ferdinand I. VERT: 2l. Union; 3l. Avram Jancu; 4l. King Michael the Brave; 5l. Bran Castle.

1930. Stamps of King Michael optd 8 IUNIE 1930 (Accession of Carol II).

1134	**63**	25b. black (postage)	50	20
1135	**63**	30b. pink	1·00	20
1136	**63**	50b. olive	1·00	20
1142	**64**	1l. purple (No. 1129)	50	20
1147	**66**	1l. brown (air)	21·00	10·50
1143	**64**	2l. green (No. 1130)	50	20
1148	**66**	2l. blue	21·00	10·50
1144	**64**	3l. red (No. 1131)	65	20
1137	**64**	5l. brown	2·10	20
1149	**66**	5l. red	21·00	10·50
1140	**64**	7l.50 blue (No. 1087)	5·25	1·00
1145	**64**	7l.50 blue (No. 1132)	4·25	85
1138	**64**	10l. blue (No. 1088)	4·25	1·00
1146	**64**	10l. blue (No. 1133)	3·50	80

72 King Carol II

73 King Carol II

1930

1172	**72**	25b. black	50	10
1173	**72**	50b. brown	1·30	65
1174	**72**	1l. violet	50	10
1175	**72**	2l. green	1·00	10
1176	**73**	3l. red	2·00	10
1177	**73**	4l. orange	2·30	10
1178	**73**	6l. red	2·75	10
1179	**73**	7l.50 blue	3·25	30
1180	-	10l. blue	7·75	10
1181	-	16l. green	18·00	30
1182	-	20l. yellow	21·00	85

DESIGN: 10l. to 20l. Portrait as Type **72**, but in plain circle, with "ROMANIA" at top.

76 King Carol II

1930. Air.

1183	**76**	1l. violet on blue	3·25	5·00
1184	**76**	2l. green on blue	4·00	5·25
1185	**76**	5l. brown on blue	7·25	5·25
1186	**76**	10l. blue on blue	15·00	6·75

77 Map of Romania

78 Woman with Census Paper

1930. National Census.

1187	**77**	1l. violet	1·80	50
1188	**78**	2l. green	3·00	60
1189	**78**	4l. orange	3·50	40
1190	**78**	6l. red	8·25	65

79 King Carol II

1931

1191	**79**	30l. blue and olive	1·40	75
1192	**79**	50l. blue and red	2·75	1·30
1193	**79**	100l. blue and green	5·75	2·75

80 King Carol II

81 King Carol I

82 Kings Carol II, Ferdinand I and Carol I

1931. 50th Anniv of Romanian Monarchy.

1200	**80**	1l. violet	3·75	1·90
1201	**81**	2l. green	5·75	1·90
1202	-	6l. red	13·00	3·00
1203	**82**	10l. blue	19·00	5·75
1204	-	20l. orange	23·00	7·50

DESIGNS—As Type **80**: 6l. King Carol II, facing right. As Type **81**: 20l. King Ferdinand I.

83 Naval Cadet Ship "Mircea"

1931. 50th Anniv of Romanian Navy.

1205	**83**	6l. red	6·75	4·25
1206	-	10l. blue	9·00	4·50
1207	-	12l. green	38·00	5·00
1208	-	20l. orange	17·00	9·00

DESIGNS: 10l. Monitors "Lascar Catargiu" and "Mihail Kogalniceaunu"; 16l. Monitor "Ardeal"; 20l. Destroyer "Regele Ferdinand".

84 Bayonet Attack

87 King Carol I

88 Infantry Attack

89 King Ferdinand I

1931. Centenary of Romanian Army.

1209	**84**	25b. black	2·30	1·10
1210	-	50b. brown	3·00	1·50
1211	-	1l. violet	3·75	1·90
1212	**87**	2l. green	6·00	2·30
1213	**88**	3l. red	13·00	6·75
1214	**89**	7l.50 blue	17·00	15·00
1215	-	16l. green	20·00	6·75

DESIGNS: 50b. Infantryman, 1870, 20×33 mm: 1l. Infantry and drummer, 1830, 23×36 mm: 16l. King Carol II in uniform with plumed helmet, 21×34 mm.

91 Scouts' Encampment

1931. Romanian Boy Scouts' Exhibition Fund.

1221	**91**	1l.+1l. red	5·75	3·75
1222	-	2l.+2l. green	7·50	4·50
1223	-	3l.+3l. blue	9·00	5·75
1224	-	4l.+4l. brown	11·50	7·50
1225	-	6l.+6l. brown	15·00	7·50

DESIGNS—VERT: As Type **91**: 3l. Recruiting, 22×37½ mm; 2l. Rescue work, 22×41½ mm; 4l. Prince Nicholas; 6l. King Carol II in scoutmaster's uniform.

92a Farman F.121 Jaribu

1931. Air.

1226	**92a**	2l. green	1·90	1·00
1227	-	3l. red	3·00	1·30
1228	-	5l. brown	3·75	1·70
1229	-	10l. blue	9·00	3·75
1230	-	20l. violet	23·00	5·25

DESIGNS—As T **92a**: 3l. Farman F.300 and biplane; 5l. Farman F.60 Goliath; 10l. Fokker F.XII. 34×20 mm: 20l. Three aircraft flying in formation.

95 Kings Carol II, Ferdinand I and Carol I

1931

1231	**95**	16l. green	15·00	90

96 Alexander the Good

1932. 500th Death Centenary of Alexander I, Prince of Moldavia.

1232	**96**	6l. red	17·00	11·50

97 King Carol II

1932

1248	**97**	10l. blue	17·00	75

98 Semaphore Signaller

1932. Boy Scouts' Jamboree Fund.

1256	-	25b.+25b. green	4·50	1·90
1257	**98**	50b.+50b. blue	5·75	3·75
1258	-	1l.+1l. green	6·50	5·75
1259	-	2l.+2l. red	11·50	7·50
1260	-	3l.+3l. blue	27·00	15·00
1261	-	6l.+6l. brown	30·00	23·00

DESIGNS—VERT: As Type **98**: 25b. Scouts in camp; 1l. On the trail; 3l. King Carol II; 6l. King Carol and King Michael when a Prince. HORIZ: 20×15 mm: 2l. Camp fire.

99 Cantacuzino and Gregory Chika

1932. 9th International Medical Congress.

1262	**99**	1l. red	9·75	7·50
1263	-	6l. orange	24·00	11·50
1264	-	10l. blue	42·00	19·00

DESIGNS: 6l. Congress in session; 10l. Hygeia and Aesculapius.

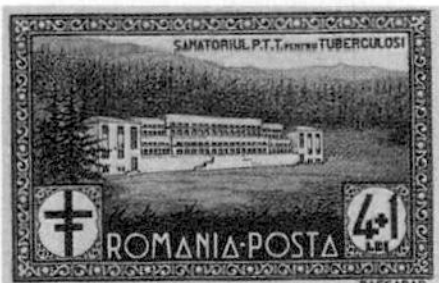

100 Tuberculosis Sanatorium

1932. Postal Employees' Fund.

1265	**100**	4l.+1l. green	9·00	4·50
1266	-	6l.+1l. brown	10·00	5·50
1267	-	10l.+1l. blue	18·00	9·00

DESIGNS—VERT: 6l. War Memorial tablet. HORIZ: 10l. Convalescent home.

101 King Carol II

1932. International Philatelic Exhibition, Bucharest (EFIRO). Sheet 100×125 mm.

MS1267a	6l.+5l. olive	85·00	70·00

102 "Bull's head" **103** Dolphins **104** Arms

1932. 75th Anniv of First Moldavian Stamps. Imperf.

1268	**102**	25b. black	2·40	45
1269	-	1l. purple	4·00	95
1270	**103**	2l. green	4·25	1·10
1271	-	3l. red	4·75	1·40
1272	**104**	6l. red	5·75	1·60
1273	-	7l.50 blue	7·25	2·30
1274	-	10l. blue	9·75	3·75

DESIGNS—As Type **103**: 1l. Lion rampant and bridge; 3l. Eagle and castles; 7l.50, Eagle; 10l. Bull's head.

1932. 30th Anniv of Opening of G.P.O., Bucharest. As T 25 but smaller.

1275		16l. green	21·00	9·25

105 Ruins of Trajan's Bridge, Arms of Turnu-Severin and Towers of Severus

1933. Centenary of Founding of Turnu-Severin.

1279	**105**	25b. green	1·50	40
1280	-	50b. blue	1·90	60
1281	-	1l. brown	3·50	95
1282	-	2l. green	4·75	1·50

DESIGNS: 50b. Trajan at the completion of bridge over the Danube; 1l. Arrival of Prince Carol at Turnu-Severin; 2l. Trajan's Bridge.

107 Carmen Sylva and Carol I

1933. 50th Anniv of Construction of Pelesch Castle, Sinaia.

1283	**107**	1l. violet	3·50	2·40
1284	-	3l. brown	4·00	3·50
1285	-	6l. red	4·75	4·00

DESIGNS: 3l. Eagle and medallion portraits of Kings Carol I, Ferdinand I and Carol II; 6l. Pelesch Castle.

108 Wayside Shrine

1934. Romanian Women's Exhibition. Inscr "L.N.F.R. MUNCA NOASTRA ROMANEASCA".

1286	**108**	1l.+1l. brown	3·50	2·40
1287	-	2l.+1l. blue	4·75	3·00
1288	-	3l.+1l. green	6·25	4·25

DESIGNS—HORIZ: 2l. Weaver. VERT: 3l. Spinner.

1934. Mamaia Jamboree Fund. Nos. 1256/61 optd MAMAIA 1934 and Arms of Constanza.

1289		26b.+25b. green	7·25	4·75
1290	**98**	50b.+50b. blue	9·75	5·75
1291	-	1l.+1l. green	11·50	9·25
1292	-	2l.+2l. red	14·50	10·50
1293	-	3l.+3l. blue	31·00	18·00
1294	-	6l.+6l. brown	35·00	24·00

110 King Carol II

1934

1295		50b. brown	1·90	60
1296	**110**	2l. green	3·50	60
1297	**110**	4l. orange	5·75	60
1298	-	6l. lake	14·50	60

DESIGNS: 50b. Profile portrait of King Carol II in civilian clothes; 6l. King Carol in plumed helmet.

112 "Grapes for Health"

1934. Bucharest Fruit Exhibition.

1299	**112**	1l. green	7·25	4·00
1300	-	2l. brown	7·25	4·00

DESIGN: 2l. Woman with fruit.

113 Crisan, Horia and Closca

1935. 150th Anniv of Death of Three Romanian Martyrs. Portraits inscr "MARTIR AL NEAMULUI 1785".

1301	**113**	1l. violet	1·20	70
1302	-	2l. green (Crisan)	1·60	95
1303	-	6l. brown (Closca)	4·25	1·60
1304	-	10l. blue (Horia)	7·25	3·50

114 Boy Scouts

1935. 5th Anniv of Accession of Carol II.

1305		25b. black	5·75	4·00
1306		1l. violet	9·75	6·75
1307	**114**	2l. green	11·50	9·75
1308	-	6l.+1l. brown	14·50	11·50
1309	-	10l.+2l. blue	31·00	29·00

DESIGNS—VERT: 25b. Scout saluting; 1l. Bugler; 6l. King Carol II. HORIZ: 10l. Colour party.

1935. Portraits as T 110 but additionally inscr "POSTA".

1310		25b. black	20	10
1311		50b. brown	20	10
1312		1l. violet	50	10
1313	**110**	2l. green	95	10
1315	-	3l. red	1·50	10
1316	-	3l. blue	1·90	30
1317	**110**	4l. orange	3·00	10
1318	-	5l. red	2·40	70
1319	-	6l. lake	3·00	10
1320	-	7l.50 blue	3·50	70
1321	-	8l. purple	3·50	70
1322	**110**	9l. blue	4·75	80
1323	-	10l. blue	1·90	30
1324	-	12l. blue	3·00	1·30
1325	-	15l. brown	3·00	95
1326	-	16l. green	4·00	60
1327	-	20l. orange	2·40	80
1328	-	24l. red	4·75	95

PORTRAITS—IN PROFILE: 25b., 15l. In naval uniform; 50b., 3, 8, 10l. In civilian clothes. THREE-QUARTER FACE: 1, 5, 7l.50, In civilian clothes. FULL FACE: 6, 12, 16, 20, 24l. In plumed helmet.

118 King Carol II

1936. Bucharest Exhibition and 70th Anniv of Hohenzollern-Sigmaringen Dynasty.

1329	**118**	6l.+1l. red	2·40	1·20

119 Oltenia Peasant Girl

1936. 6th Anniv of Accession of Carol II Inscr "O.E.T.R. 8 IUNIE 1936".

1330	**119**	50b.+50b. brown	1·90	95
1331	-	1l.+1l. violet	1·50	95
1332	-	2l.+1l. green	1·60	1·20
1333	-	3l.+1l. red	2·40	1·50
1334	-	4l.+2l. red	3·00	1·50
1335	-	6l.+3l. grey	4·00	1·90
1336	-	10l.+5l. blue	6·25	4·00

DESIGNS (costumes of following districts)—VERT: 1l. Banat; 4l. Gori; 6l. Neamz. HORIZ: 2l. Saliste; 3l. Hateg; 10l. Suceava (Bukovina).

120 Brasov Jamboree Badge

1936. National Scout Jamboree, Brasov.

1337		1l.+1l. blue	9·75	8·25
1338		3l.+3l. grey	14·50	8·25
1339	**120**	6l.+6l. red	19·00	8·25

DESIGNS: 1l. National Scout Badge; 3l. Tenderfoot Badge.

121 Liner "Transylvania"

1936. 1st Marine Exhibition, Bucharest.

1343	-	1l.+1l. violet	11·50	5·25
1344	-	3l.+2l. blue	9·75	5·75
1345	**121**	6l.+3l. red	12·50	8·25

DESIGNS: 1l. Submarine "Delfinul"; 3l. Naval cadet ship "Mircea".

1936. 18th Anniv of Annexation of Transylvania and 16th Anniv of Foundation of "Little Entente" Nos. 1320 and 1323 optd CEHOSLOVACIA YUGOSLAVIA 1920-1936.

1346	7l.50 blue	7·25	5·75
1347	10l. blue	7·25	5·75

123 Creanga's Birthplace

1937. Birth Centenary of Ion Creanga (poet).

1348	**123**	2l. green	1·90	95
1349	-	3l. red	2·40	1·10
1350	**123**	4l. violet	3·00	1·40
1351	-	6l. brown	7·25	3·00

DESIGN: 3, 6l. Portrait of Creanga, 37×22 mm.

124 Footballers

1937. 7th Anniv of Accession of Carol II.

1352	**124**	25b.+25b. olive	1·90	30
1353	-	50b.+50b. brown	1·90	50
1354	-	1l.+50b. violet	2·40	70
1355	-	2l.+1l. green	3·00	80
1356	-	3l.+1l. red	4·75	95
1357	-	4l.+1l. red	7·75	1·10
1358	-	6l.+2l. brown	9·75	1·60
1359	-	10l.+4l. blue	11·50	2·40

DESIGNS—HORIZ: 50b. Swimmer; 3 1. King Carol II hunting; 10l. U.F.S.R. Inaugural Meeting. VERT: 1l. Javelin thrower; 2l. Skier; 4l. Rowing; 6l. Steeplechaser.

Premium in aid of the Federation of Romanian Sports Clubs (U.F.S.R.).

127 Curtea de Arges Cathedral

1937. "Little Entente".

1360	**127**	7l.50 blue	3·00	1·50
1361	**127**	10l. blue	4·00	95

128 Hurdling

1937. 8th Balkan Games, Bucharest. Inscr as in T 115.

1362	-	1l.+1l. violet	1·90	1·20
1363	-	2l.+1l. green	2·40	1·60
1364	**128**	4l.+1l. red	3·00	2·10
1365	-	6l.+1l. brown	3·50	2·40
1366	-	10l.+1l. blue	10·50	4·25

DESIGNS: 1l. Sprinting; 2l. Throwing the javelin; 6l. Breasting the tape; 10l. High jumping.

1937. 16th Birthday of Crown Prince Michael and his promotion to Rank of Sub-lieutenant. Sheet 125×152 mm containing four stamps of 1935–40 surch.

MS1367 2l. on 20l. (No. 1327); 6l. on 10l. (No. 1323); 10l. on 6l. (No. 1319); 20l. on 2l. (No. 1313)	14·50	16·00

129 Arms of Romania, Greece, Turkey and Yugoslavia

1938. Balkan Entente.

1368	**129**	7l.50 blue	2·40	1·30
1369	**129**	10l. blue	3·50	1·10

130 King Carol II

1938. New Constitution. Profile portraits of King inscr "27 FEBRUARIE 1938". 6l. shows Arms also.

1370	**130**	3l. red	1·50	80
1371	-	6l. brown	2·40	80
1372	-	10l. blue	3·50	1·60

131 King Carol II and Provincial Arms

1938. Fund for Bucharest Exhibition celebrating 20th Anniv of Union of Provinces.

1373	**131**	6l.+1l. mauve	1·90	95

132 Dimitrie Cantemir

1938. Boy Scouts' Fund. 8th Anniv of Accession of Carol II. Inscr "STRAJA TARII 8 IUNIE 1938".

1374	**132**	25b.+25b. olive	95	60
1375	-	50b.+50b. brown	1·50	60
1376	-	1l.+1l. violet	1·50	60
1377	-	2l.+2l. green	1·60	60
1378	-	3l.+2l. mauve	1·60	60
1379	-	4l.+2l. red	1·60	60
1380	-	6l.+2l. brown	1·90	70
1381	-	7l.50 blue	2·40	95
1382	-	10l. blue	3·00	95
1383	-	16l. green	4·00	3·00
1384	-	20l. red	5·75	3·00

PORTRAITS: 50b. Maria Doamna; 1l. Mircea the Great; 2l. Constantin Brancoveanu; 3l. Stephen the Great; 4l. Prince Cuza; 6l. Michael the Brave; 7l.50, Queen Elisabeth; 10l. King Carol II; 16l. King Ferdinand I; 20l. King Carol I.

134 "The Spring"

1938. Birth Centenary of Nicholas Grigorescu (painter).

1385	**134**	1l.+1l. blue	3·00	95
1386	-	2l.+1l. green	3·00	1·90
1387	-	4l.+1l. red	3·00	1·90
1388	-	6l.+1l. red	4·00	3·00
1389	-	10l.+1l. blue	8·75	4·00

DESIGNS—HORIZ: 2l. "Escorting Prisoners" (Russo-Turkish War 1877–78); 4l. "Returning from Market". VERT: 6l. "Rodica, the Water Carrier"; 10l. Self-portrait.

135 Prince Carol in Royal Carriage

1939. Birth Centenary of King Carol I.

1390	**135**	25b. black	20	10
1391	-	50b. brown	20	10
1392	-	1l. violet	50	10
1393	-	1l.50 green	20	10
1394	-	2l. blue	20	10
1395	-	3l. red	20	10
1396	-	4l. red	20	10
1397	-	5l. black	20	10
1398	-	7l. black	20	10
1399	-	8l. blue	50	30
1400	-	10l. mauve	95	30
1401	-	12l. blue	95	30
1402	-	15l. blue	1·90	30
1403	-	16l. green	1·90	80

DESIGNS—HORIZ: 50b. Prince Carol at Battle of Calafat; 1l.50, Sigmaringen and Pelesch Castles; 15l. Carol I, Queen Elizabeth and Arms of Romania. VERT: 1l. Examining plans for restoring Curtea de Arges Monastery; 2l. Carol I and Queen Elizabeth; 3l. Carol I at age of 8; 4l. In 1866; 5l. In 1877; 7l. Equestrian statue; 8l. Leading troops in 1878; 10l. In General's uniform; 12l. Bust; 16l. Restored Monastery of Curtea de Arges.

1939. As last but in miniature sheet form. Perf or Imperf.

MS1404 141×116 mm. Nos. 1390/1 and 1393 (sold at 20l.)	4·75	14·50
MS1405 126×146 mm. Nos. 1394 and 1398/1400	4·75	14·50
MS1406 126×146 mm. Nos. 1395/6 and 1401 (sold at 50l.)	4·75	14·50

136 Romanian Pavilion N.Y. World's Fair

1939. New York World's Fair.

1407	**136**	6l. lake	1·50	80
1408	-	12l. blue	1·50	80

DESIGN: 12l. Another view of Pavilion.

137 Michael Eminescu, after painting by Joano Basarab

1939. 50th Death Anniv of Michael Eminescu (poet).

1409	**137**	5l. black	1·50	80
1410	-	7l. red	1·50	80

DESIGN: 7l. Eminescu in later years.

138 St. George and Dragon

1939. 9th Anniv of Accession of Carol II and Boy Scouts' Fund.

1411	**138**	25b.+25b. grey	95	70
1412	**138**	50b.+50b. brown	95	70
1413	**138**	1l.+1l. blue	1·10	70
1414	**138**	2l.+2l. green	1·20	70
1415	**138**	3l.+2l. purple	1·50	70
1416	**138**	4l.+2l. orange	1·90	95
1417	**138**	6l.+2l. red	2·10	95
1418	**138**	8l. grey	2·40	95
1419	**138**	10l. blue	2·50	1·20
1420	**138**	12l. blue	3·00	1·90
1421	**138**	16l. green	4·00	2·40

139 Diesel Railcar, Class 142 Steam Locomotive (1936) and Locomotive "Calugareni" (1869)

1939. 70th Anniv of Romanian Railways.

1422	**139**	1l. violet	2·10	80
1423	-	4l. red	2·10	80
1424	-	5l. grey	2·10	80
1425	-	7l. mauve	2·10	80
1426	-	12l. blue	4·00	2·10
1427	-	15l. green	4·25	3·00

DESIGNS—HORIZ: 4l. Class 142 steam train crossing bridge, 1936; 15l. Railway Headquarters, Budapest. VERT: 5, 7l. Locomotive "Calugareni" (1869) leaving station; 12l. Diesel-mechanical twin set (1937) crossing bridge.

1940. Balkan Entente. As T 103 of Yugoslavia, but with Arms rearranged.

1428		12l. blue	1·50	95
1429		16l. blue	1·50	95

141 King Carol II

1940. Aviation Fund.

1430	**141**	1l.+50b. green	40	30
1431	**141**	2l.50+50b. green	60	50
1432	**141**	3l.+1l. red	80	60
1433	**141**	3l.50+50b. brown	85	70
1434	**141**	4l.+1l. orange	1·10	80
1435	**141**	6l.+1l. blue	1·60	50
1436	**141**	9l.+1l. blue	1·90	1·50
1437	**141**	14l.+1l. green	2·30	1·90

142 King Carol II

1940. 10th Anniv of Accession and Aviation Fund. Portraits of King Carol II.

1438	**142**	1l.+50b. purple	1·50	50
1439	**142**	4l.+1l. brown	1·50	70
1440	-	6l.+1l. blue	1·50	95
1441	-	8l. red	1·90	1·20
1442	-	16l. blue	2·40	1·50
1443	-	32l. brown	3·50	2·40

PORTRAITS: 6, 16l. In steel helmet; 8l. In military uniform; 32l. In flying helmet.

144 The Iron Gates of the Danube

1940. Charity. 10th Anniv of Accession of Carol II and Boy Scouts' Fund. Inscr "STRAJA TARII 8 IUNIE 1940".

1444	**144**	1l.+1l. violet	95	70
1445	-	2l.+1l. brown	1·10	80
1446	-	3l.+1l. green	1·20	95
1447	-	4l.+1l. black	1·30	1·10
1448	-	5l.+1l. orange	1·50	1·20
1449	-	8l.+1l. red	1·90	1·30
1450	-	12l.+2l. blue	2·40	1·50
1451	-	16l.+2l. grey	4·25	3·00

DESIGNS—HORIZ: 3l. Hotin Fortress; 4l. Hurez Monastery. VERT: 2l. Greco-Roman ruins; 5l. Church in Suceava; 8l. Alba Julia Cathedral; 12l. Village Church, Transylvania; 16l. Triumphal Arch, Bucharest.

1940. Armaments Fund. Nos. MS1404/6 optd PRO PATRIA 1940. Perf or Imperf.

MS1452 on No. **MS**1404	24·00	29·00
MS1453 on No. **MS**1405	29·00	48·00
MS1454 on No. **MS**1406	39·00	75·00

145 King Michael

1940

1455	**145**	25b. green	10	10
1456	**145**	50b. olive	10	10
1457	**145**	1l. violet	10	10
1458	**145**	2l. orange	10	10
1608	**145**	3l. brown	10	10
1609	**145**	3l.50 brown	10	10
1459	**145**	4l. grey	10	10
1611	**145**	4l.50 brown	10	10
1460	**145**	5l. pink	10	10
1613	**145**	6l.50 violet	10	10
1461	**145**	7l. blue	10	10
1615	**145**	10l. mauve	10	10
1616	**145**	11l. blue	10	10
1463	**145**	12l. blue	10	10
1464	**145**	13l. purple	10	10
1618	**145**	15l. blue	20	10
1619	**145**	16l. blue	10	10
1620	**145**	20l. brown	20	10
1621	**145**	29l. blue	1·60	1·30
1467	**145**	30l. green	30	10
1468	**145**	50l. brown	30	10
1469	**145**	100l. brown	95	10

146 King Michael

1940. Aviation Fund.

1470	**146**	1l.+50b. green	10	10
1471	**146**	2l.+50b. green	10	10
1472	**146**	2l.50+50b. green	10	10
1473	**146**	3l.+1l. violet	10	10
1474	**146**	3l.50+50b. pink	20	20
1475	**146**	4l.+50b. red	20	10
1476	**146**	4l.+1l. brown	10	10
1477	**146**	5l.+1l. red	1·50	50
1478	**146**	6l.+1l. blue	10	10
1479	**146**	7l.+1l. green	50	20
1480	**146**	8l.+1l. violet	30	10
1481	**146**	12l.+1l. brown	50	30
1482	**146**	14l.+1l. blue	50	10
1483	**146**	19l.+1l. mauve	1·20	50

147 Codreanu (founder)

148 Codreanu (founder)

1940. "Iron Guard" Fund.

1484	**147**	7l.+30l. grn (postage)	8·25	7·75
1485	**148**	20l.+5l. green (air)	4·75	5·75

149 Ion Mota

1941. Marin and Mota (legionaries killed in Spain).

1486	-	7l.+7l. red	4·75	4·75
1487	**149**	15l.+15l. blue	6·75	6·75
MS1487a 89×35 mm. As Nos. 1486/7 both in green. Imperf. (sold at 300l.)			£120	£150

DESIGN: 7l. Vasile Marin.

150 Library

1941. Carol I Endowment Fund. Inscr "1891 1941".

1488	-	1l.50+43l.50 violet	2·40	2·40
1489	150	2l.+43l. red	2·40	2·40
1490	-	7l.+38l. red	2·40	2·40
1491	-	10l.+35l. green	2·75	2·75
1492	-	16l.+29l. brown	3·00	3·00

DESIGNS: 1l.50, Ex-libris; 7l. Foundation building and equestrian statue; 10l. Foundation stone; 16l. King Michael and Carol I.

1941. Occupation of Cernauti. Nos. 1488/92 optd CERNAUTI 5 Iulie 1941.

1493		1l.50+43l.50 violet	4·75	4·75
1494	150	2l.+43l. red	4·75	4·75
1495	-	7l.+38l. red	4·75	4·75
1496	-	10l.+35l. green	4·75	4·75
1497	-	16l.+29l. brown	5·00	5·00

1941. Occupation of Chisinau. Nos. 1488/92 optd CHISINAU 16 Iulie 1941.

1498		1l.50+43l.50 violet	4·75	4·75
1499	150	2l.+43l. red	4·75	4·75
1500	-	7l.+38l. red	4·75	4·75
1501	-	10l.+35l. green	4·75	4·75
1502	-	16l.+29l. brown	5·00	5·00

153 "Charity"

1941. Red Cross Fund. Cross in red.

1503	153	1l.50+38l.50 violet	1·90	1·20
1504	153	2l.+38l. red	1·90	1·20
1505	153	5l.+35l. olive	1·90	1·20
1506	153	7l.+33l. brown	1·90	1·20
1507	153	10l.+30l. blue	2·40	2·20
MS1508 105×73 mm. Nos. 1506/7. Imperf. (sold at 200l.)			29·00	31·00

154 Prince Voda

1941. Conquest of Transdniestria.

1572	154	3l. orange	50	1·00
1509	154	6l. brown	50	50
1510	154	12l. violet	95	1·00
1511	154	24l. blue	1·50	1·60

155 King Michael and Stephen the Great

1941. Anti-Bolshevik Crusade. Inscr "RAZBOIUL SFANT CONTRA BOLSEVISMULUI".

1512	155	10l.+30l. blue	3·00	4·75
1513	-	12l.+28l. red	3·00	4·75
1514	-	16l.+24l. brown	4·00	5·25
1515	-	20l.+20l. violet	4·00	5·25
MS1516 105×73 mm. 16l. blue (emblems and angel with sword); 20l. red (helmeted soldiers and eagle). No gum. (sold at 200l.)			14·50	21·00

DESIGNS: 12l. Hotin and Akkerman Fortresses; 16l. Arms and helmeted soldiers; 20l. Bayonet charge and Arms of Romania.

1941. Fall of Odessa. Nos. 1512/15 optd ODESA 16 Oct. 1941.

1517	155	10l.+30l. blue	3·00	4·75
1518	-	12l.+28l. red	3·00	4·75
1519	-	16l.+24l. brown	4·00	5·25
1520	-	20l.+20l. violet	4·00	5·25
MS1521 (No. **MS**1516)			24·00	26·00

157 Hotin

1941. Restoration of Bessarabia and Bukovina (Suceava). Inscr "BASARABIA" or "BUCOVINA".

1522		25b. red	10	10
1523	157	50b. brown	10	10
1524	-	1l. violet	10	10
1525	-	1l.50 green	10	10
1526	-	2l. brown	10	10
1527	-	3l. olive	30	10
1528	-	5l. olive	50	20
1529	-	5l.50 brown	50	20
1530	-	6l.50 mauve	1·20	75
1531	157	9l.50 grey	1·20	75
1532	-	10l. purple	80	20
1533	-	13l. blue	85	40
1534	-	17l. brown	1·10	30
1535	-	26l. green	1·30	65
1536	-	39l. blue	2·30	85
1537	-	130l. yellow	7·25	5·25

VIEWS—VERT: 25b., 5l. Paraclis Hotin; 3l. Dragomirna; 13l. Milisauti. HORIZ: 1, 17l. Sucevita; 1l.50, Soroca; 2, 5l.50, Tighina; 6l.50, Cetatea Alba; 10, 130l. Putna; 26l. St. Nicolae, Suceava; 39l. Monastery. Rughi.

1941. Winter Relief Fund. Inscr "BASARABIA" or "BUCOVINA".

1538		3l.+50b. red	60	30
1539		5l.50+50b. orange	95	85
1540		5l.50+1l. black	95	85
1541		6l.50+1l. brown	1·20	1·20
1542		8l.+1l. blue	95	50
1543		9l.50+1l. blue	1·20	1·00
1544		10l.50+1l. blue	1·30	50
1545		16l.+1l. mauve	1·50	1·20
1546	157	25l.+1l. grey	1·60	1·30

VIEWS—HORIZ: 3l. Sucevita; 5l.50, (1539), Monastery, Rughi; 5l.50, (1540), Tighina; 6l.50, Soroca; 8l. St. Nicolae, Suceava; 10l.50, Putna; 16l. Cetatea Alba. VERT: 8l.50, Milisauti.

158 Titu Maiorescu

1942. Prisoners of War Relief Fund through International Education Office, Geneva.

1549	158	9l.+11l. violet	95	1·30
1550	158	20l.+20l. brown	2·40	3·25
1551	158	20l.+30l. blue	2·75	3·50
MS1552 128×81 mm. Nos. 1549/51. Imperf. No gum. (sold at 200l.)			11·50	13·50

159 Coat-of-Arms of Bukovina

1942. 1st Anniv of Liberation of Bukovina.

1553	159	9l.+4l. red	4·00	5·25
1554	-	18l.+32l. blue	4·00	5·25
1555	-	20l.+30l. red	4·00	5·25

ARMORIAL DESIGNS: 18l. Castle; 20l. Mounds and crosses.

160 Map of Bessarabia, King Michael, Antonescu, Hitler and Mussolini

1942. 1st Anniv of Liberation of Bessarabia.

1556	160	9l.+41l. brown	4·00	5·25
1557	-	18l.+32l. olive	4·00	5·25
1558	-	20l.+30l. blue	4·00	5·25

DESIGNS—VERT: 18l. King Michael and Marshal Antonescu below miniature of King Stephen. HORIZ: 20l. Marching soldiers and miniature of Marshal Antonescu.

161 Statue of Miron Costin

1942. 1st Anniv of Incorporation of Transdniestria.

1559	161	6l.+44l. brown	2·40	4·25
1560	161	12l.+38l. violet	2·40	4·25
1561	161	24l.+26l. blue	2·40	4·25

162 Andrei Muresanu

1942. 80th Death Anniv of A. Muresanu (novelist).

1562	162	5l.+5l. violet	1·50	1·60

163 Statue of Avram Iancu

1943. Fund for Statue of Iancu (national hero).

1563	163	16l.+4l. brown	1·50	1·70

164 Nurse and wounded Soldier

1943. Red Cross Charity. Cross in red.

1564	164	12l.+88l. red	1·20	1·30
1565	164	16l.+84l. blue	1·20	1·30
1566	164	20l.+80l. olive	1·20	1·30
MS1567 100×60 mm. Nos. 1565/6 (different shades). Imperf. No gum. (sold at 500l.)			9·75	12·50

165 Sword and Shield

1943. Charity. 2nd Year of War. Inscr "22 JUNIE 1941 22 JUNIE 1943".

1568	165	36l.+164l. brown	4·00	5·25
1569	-	62l.+138l. blue	4·00	5·25
1570	-	76l.+124l. red	4·00	5·25
MS1571 90×65 mm. Nos. 1569/70 (different shades). Imperf. No gum. (sold at 600l.)			24·00	26·00

DESIGNS—VERT: 62l. Sword severing chain; 76l. Angel protecting soldier and family.

167 P. Maior

1943. Transylvanian Refugees' Fund (1st issue).

1576	167	16l.+134l. red	95	1·00
1577	-	32l.+118l. blue	95	1·00
1578	-	36l.+114l. purple	95	1·00
1579	-	62l.+138l. red	95	1·00
1580	-	91l.+109l. brown	95	1·00

PORTRAITS—VERT: 32l. G. Sincai; 36l. T. Cipariu; 91l. G. Cosbuc. HORIZ: 62l. Horia, Closca and Crisan.

See also Nos. 1584/8.

169 King Michael and Marshal Antonescu

1943. 3rd Anniv of King Michael's Reign.

1581	169	16l.+24l. blue	3·50	3·75

170 Sports Shield

1943. Charity. Sports Week.

1582	170	16l.+24l. blue	1·30	1·00
1583	170	16l.+24l. brown	1·30	1·00

1943. Transylvanian Refugees' Fund (2nd issue) Portraits as T 167.

1584		16l.+134l. mauve	1·00	1·00
1585		51l.+99l. orange	1·00	1·00
1586		56l.+144l. red	1·00	1·00
1587		76l.+124l. blue	1·00	1·00
1588		77l.+123l. brown	1·00	1·00

PORTRAITS—VERT: 16l. S. Micu; 51l. G. Lazar; 56l. O. Goga; 76l. S. Barnutiu; 77l. A. Saguna.

171 Calafat, 1877

1943. Centenary of National Artillery.

1596	171	1l.+1l. brown	50	50
1597	-	2l.+2l. violet	50	50
1598	-	3l.50+3l.50 blue	50	50
1599	-	4l.+4l. mauve	50	50
1600	-	5l.+5l. orange	1·50	1·60
1601	-	6l.50+6l.50 blue	1·50	1·60
1602	-	7l.+7l. purple	1·90	2·10
1603	-	20l.+20l. red	3·00	3·25

DESIGNS—HORIZ: (1l. to 7l. inscr battle scenes): 2l. "1916–1918"; 3l.50, Stalingrad; 4l. Crossing R. Tlsza; 5l. Odessa; 6l.50, Caucasus; 7l. Sevastopol; 20l. Bibescu and King Michael.

172 Association Insignia

1943. 25th Anniv of National Engineers' Assn.

1624	172	21l.+29l. brown	1·50	1·60

173 Motor-cycle and Delivery Van

1944. Postal Employees' Relief Fund and Bicentenary of National Postal Service. (a) Without opt.

1625	173	1l.+49l. red	3·00	3·25
1626	-	2l.+48l. mauve	3·00	3·25
1627	-	4l.+46l. blue	3·00	3·25
1628	-	10l.+40l. purple	3·00	3·25
MS1629 143×86 mm. Nos. 1625/7 but in red (sold at 200l.)			9·75	10·50
MS1630 As last but in violet and imperf			9·75	10·50

(b) Optd 1744 1944.

1631	173	1l.+49l. red	6·25	6·75
1632	-	2l.+48l. mauve	6·25	6·75
1633	-	4l.+46l. blue	6·25	6·75
1634	-	10l.+40l. purple	6·25	6·75
MS1635 (No. **MS**1629)			24·00	31·00
MS1636 (No. **MS**1630)			24·00	31·00

DESIGNS—HORIZ: 2l. Post motorcycle, post van and eight horses; 4l. Chariot. VERT: Horseman and globe.

174 Dr. Cretzulescu

1944. Cent of Medical Teaching in Romania.

1637	**174**	35l.+65l. blue	1·50	1·60

175 Rugby Player

1944. 30th Anniv of Foundation of National Rugby Football Association.

1638	**175**	16l.+184l. red	6·25	6·75

176 Stefan Tomsa Church, Radaseni **177** Fruit Pickers

1944. Cultural Fund. Town of Radaseni. Inscr "RADASENI".

1639	**176**	5l.+145l. blue	1·30	1·30
1640	-	12l.+138l. red	1·30	1·30
1641	**177**	15l.+135l. orange	1·30	1·30
1642	-	32l.+118l. brown	1·30	1·30

DESIGNS—HORIZ: 12l. Agricultural Institution; 32l. School.

178 Queen Helen

1945. Red Cross Relief Fund. Portrait in black on yellow and Cross in red.

1643	**178**	4l.50+5l.50 violet	50	50
1644	**178**	10l.+40l. brown	70	75
1645	**178**	15l.+75l. blue	95	1·00
1646	**178**	20l.+80l. red	1·50	1·60

179 King Michael and Carol I Foundation, Bucharest

1945. King Carol I Foundation Fund.

1647	**179**	20l.+180l. orange	70	75
1648	**179**	25l.+175l. slate	70	75
1649	**179**	35l.+165l. brown	70	75
1650	**179**	76l.+125l. violet	70	75
MS1651		74×60 mm. 200l.+1000l. blue (as T **179** but portrait of King Carol I) Imperf. No gum	9·75	9·75

180 A. Saguna **181** A. Muresanu

1945. Liberation of Northern Transylvania. Inscr "1944".

1652	**180**	25b. red	95	1·00
1653	**181**	50b. orange	50	1·00
1654	-	4l.50 brown	50	1·00
1655	-	11l. blue	50	1·00
1656	-	15l. green	50	1·00
1657	-	31l. violet	50	1·00
1658	-	35l. grey	50	1·00
1659	-	41l. olive	50	1·00
1660	-	55l. brown	50	1·00
1661	-	61l. mauve	50	1·00
1662	-	75l.+75l. brown	50	1·00

DESIGNS—HORIZ: 4l.50, Samuel Micu; 31l. George Lazar; 55l. Horia, Closca and Crisan; 61l. Petru Maior; 75l. King Ferdinand and King Michael. VERT: 11l. George Sincai; 15l. Michael the Brave; 35l. Avram Iancu; 41l. Simeon Barnutiu.

182 King Michael **183** King Michael **184** King Michael

185 King Michael

1945

1663	**182**	50b. grey	10	10
1664	**183**	1l. brown	10	10
1665	**183**	2l. violet	10	10
1666	**182**	2l. brown	10	10
1667	**183**	4l. green	10	10
1668	**184**	5l. mauve	10	10
1669	**182**	10l. blue	10	10
1670	**182**	10l. brown	10	10
1671	**183**	10l. brown	10	10
1672	**182**	15l. mauve	10	10
1673	**182**	20l. blue	10	10
1674	**182**	20l. lilac	10	10
1675	**184**	20l. purple	10	10
1676	**184**	25l. red	10	10
1677	**184**	35l. brown	10	10
1678	**184**	40l. red	30	10
1679	**183**	50l. blue	10	10
1680	**183**	55l. red	30	10
1681	**184**	75l. green	50	10
1682	**185**	80l. orange	50	10
1683	**185**	80l. blue	10	10
1684	**182**	80l. blue	10	10
1685	**185**	100l. brown	10	10
1686	**182**	137l. green	50	10
1687	**185**	160l. green	10	10
1688	**185**	160l. violet	50	10
1689	**185**	200l. green	50	10
1690	**185**	200l. red	10	10
1691	**183**	200l. red	10	10
1692	**185**	300l. blue	10	10
1693	**185**	360l. brown	50	10
1694	**185**	400l. violet	10	10
1695	**183**	400l. red	10	10
1696	**185**	480l. brown	50	10
1697	**182**	500l. mauve	50	10
1698	**185**	600l. green	10	10
1699	**184**	860l. brown	80	20
1700	**185**	1000l. green	50	10
1701	**182**	1500l. green	50	10
1702	**185**	2400l. lilac	95	10
1703	**183**	2500l. blue	50	10
1704	**185**	3700l. blue	95	10
1705	**182**	5000l. grey	40	10
1706	**182**	8000l. green	95	20
1707	**185**	10000l. brown	1·20	30

186 N. Jorga

1945. War Victims' Relief Fund.

1708	-	12l.+188l. blue	95	1·00
1709	-	16l.+184l. brown	95	1·00
1710	**186**	20l.+180l. brown	95	1·00
1711	-	32l.+168l. red	95	1·00
1712	-	35l.+165l. blue	95	1·00
1713	-	36l.+164l. violet	95	1·00
MS1714		76×60 mm. Nos. 1711/12 but mauve. Imperf. (sold at 1000l.)	29·00	31·00

PORTRAITS: 12l. Ian Gheorghe Duca (Prime Minister, 1933); 16l. Virgil Madgearu (politician); 32l. Ilie Pintilie (communist); 35l. Bernath Andrei (communist); 36l. Filimon Sarbu (saboteur).

187 Books and Torch

1945. Charity. 1st Romanian–Soviet Congress Fund. Inscr "ARLUS".

1715	**187**	20l.+80l. olive	60	65
1716	-	35l.+165l. red	60	65
1717	-	75l.+225l. blue	60	65
1718	-	80l.+420l. brown	60	65
MS1719		60×75 mm. As Nos. 1716/17 but in red. Imperf. (sold at 900l.)	11·50	12·50

DESIGNS: 35l. Soviet and Romanian flags; 75l. Drawn curtain revealing Kremlin; 80l. T. Vladimirescu and A. Nevsky.

188 Karl Marx

1945. Trade Union Congress, Bucharest. Perf or imperf.

1720	**188**	75l.+425l. red	4·00	4·25
1723	**188**	75l.+425l. blue	11·50	12·50
1721	-	120l.+380l. blue	4·00	4·25
1724	-	120l.+380l. brown	11·50	12·50
1722	-	155l.+445l. brown	4·00	4·25
1725	-	155l.+445l. red	11·50	12·50

PORTRAITS: 120l. Engels; 155l. Lenin.

189 Postman

1945. Postal Employees. Inscr "MUNCA P.T.T.".

1726	**189**	100l. brown	95	1·00
1727	**189**	100l. olive	95	1·00
1728	-	150l. brown	1·50	1·60
1729	-	150l. red	1·50	1·60
1730	-	250l. olive	2·40	2·50
1731	-	250l. blue	2·40	2·50
1732	-	500l. mauve	19·00	21·00

DESIGNS: 150l. Telegraphist; 250l. Lineman; 500l. Post Office, Bucharest.

190 Throwing the Discus

1945. Charity. With shield inscr "O.S.P.". Perf or imperf.

1733	**190**	12l.+188l. olive (post)	3·50	3·75
1738	-	12l.+188l. orange	3·50	3·75
1734	-	16l.+184l. blue	3·50	3·75
1739	-	16l.+184l. purple	3·50	3·75
1735	-	20l.+180l. green	3·50	3·75
1740	-	20l.+180l. violet	3·50	3·75
1736	-	32l.+168l. mauve	3·50	3·75
1741	-	32l.+168l. green	3·50	3·75
1737	-	35l.+165l. blue	3·50	3·75
1742	-	35l.+165l. olive	3·50	3·75
1743	-	200l.+1000l. bl (air)	29·00	31·00

DESIGNS—As T **190**: 16l. Diving; 20l. Skiing; 32l. Volleyball; 35l. "Sport and work". 36×50 mm: 200l. Airplane and bird.

192 Agricultural and Industrial Workers

1945. 1st Anniv of Romanian Armistice with Russia.

1744	**192**	100l.+400l. red	1·20	1·30
1745	-	200l.+800l. blue	1·20	1·30

DESIGN: 200l. King Michael, "Agriculture" and "Industry".

193 T. Vladimirescu

1945. Charity. Patriotic Defence Fund. Inscr "APARAREA PATRIOTICA".

1746		20l.+580l. brown	8·75	11·50
1747		20l.+580l. mauve	8·75	11·50
1748		40l.+560l. blue	8·75	11·50
1749		40l.+560l. green	8·75	11·50
1750		55l.+545l. red	8·75	11·50
1751		55l.+545l. brown	8·75	11·50
1752	**193**	60l.+540l. blue	8·75	11·50
1753	**193**	60l.+540l. brown	8·75	11·50
1754	-	80l.+520l. red	8·75	11·50
1755	-	80l.+520l. mauve	8·75	11·50
1756	-	100l.+500l. green	8·75	11·50
1757	-	100l.+500l. brown	8·75	11·50

DESIGNS—HORIZ: 20l. "Political Amnesty"; 40l. "Military Amnesty"; 55l. "Agrarian Amnesty"; 100l. King Michael and "Recontruction". VERT: 80l. Nicholas Horia.

194 Destitute Children

1945. Child Welfare Fund.

1758	**194**	40l. blue	95	50

195 I. Ionescu, G. Titeica, A. G. Idachimescu and V. Cristescu

1945. 50th Anniv of Founding of Journal of Mathematics.

1759	**195**	2l. brown	20	10
1760	-	80l. blue	70	75

DESIGN: 80l. Allegory of Learning.

196 Saligny Bridge

1945. 50th Anniv of Saligny Bridge over River Danube, Cernavoda.

1761	**196**	80l. black	95	50

197 Class E.18 Electric Locomotive, 1935, Germany

198

1945. Charity. 16th Congress of Romanian Engineers. Perf or imperf. (a) Postage.

1762	**197**	10l.+490l. olive	95	1·00
1767	**197**	10l.+490l. blue	95	1·00
1763	-	20l.+480l. brown	95	1·00
1768	-	20l.+480l. violet	95	1·00
1764	-	25l.+475l. purple	95	1·00
1769	-	25l.+475l. green	95	1·00
1765	-	55l.+445l. blue	95	1·00
1770	-	55l.+445l. grey	95	1·00
1766	-	100l.+400l. brown	95	1·00
1771	-	100l.+400l. mauve	95	1·00

(b) Air. Symbolical design as T 198. Imperf.

1772	**198**	80l.+420l. grey	2·40	2·50
1773	-	200l.+800l. blue	2·40	2·50
MS1774		75×55 mm. 80l. purple (as 1772)	14·50	19·00
MS1775		75×55 mm. 80l. green (as 1773)	24·00	27·00

DESIGNS—As Type **197**: 20l. Coats of Arms; 25l. Arterial road; 55l. Oil wells; 100l. "Agriculture". As T **198**: 200l. Icarus and Lockheed 14 Super Electra airplane.

199 Globe and Clasped Hands

1945. Charity. World Trade Union Congress, Paris. Symbolical designs inscr "CONFERINTA MONDIAL LA SINDICALA DIN PARIS 25 SEPTEMVRE 1945".

1776	**199**	80l.+920l. mauve	24·00	26·00
1777	-	160l.+1840l. brown	24·00	26·00
1778	-	320l.+1680l. violet	24·00	26·00
1779	-	440l.+2560l. green	24·00	26·00

DESIGNS: 160l. Globe and Dove of Peace; 320l. Hand and hammer; 440l. Scaffolding and flags.

1946. Nos 1444/5 surch in figures.

1780	10l.+90l. on 100l.+400l.	1·90	2·10
1781	10l.+90l. on 200l.+800l.	1·90	2·10
1782	20l.+80l. on 100l.+400l.	1·90	2·10
1783	20l.+80l. on 200l.+800l.	1·90	2·10
1784	80l.+120l. on 100l.+400l.	1·90	2·10
1785	80l.+120l. on 200l.+800l.	1·90	2·10
1786	100l.+150l. on 100l.+400l.	1·90	2·10
1787	100l.+150l. on 200l.+800l.	1·90	2·10

200 Sower

201 Distribution of Title Deeds

1946. Agrarian Reform. Inscr "REFORMA AGRARA".

1788	-	80l. blue	60	65
1789	**200**	50l.+450l. red	60	65
1790	**201**	100l.+900l. purple	60	65
1791	-	200l.+800l. orange	60	65
1792	-	400l.+1600l. green	60	65
MS1793		75×60 mm. 80l. blue (as No. 1789 but larger) (sold at 100l.) (air)	19·00	21·00

DESIGNS—VERT: 80l Blacksmith and ploughman. HORIZ: 200l. Ox-drawn farm wagon; 400l. Plough and tractor.

202

1946. 25th Anniv of Bucharest Philharmonic Orchestra.

1794	**202**	10l. blue	20	10
1795	-	20l. brown	20	10
1796	-	55l. green	20	10
1797	-	80l. violet	20	10
1798	-	160l. orange	20	10
1799	**202**	200l.+800l. red	1·50	1·60
1800	-	350l.+1650l. blue	1·90	2·10
MS1801		No. 1799×12+4 labels	60·00	65·00
MS1802		No. 1800×12+4 labels	60·00	65·00

DESIGNS: 20l., 55l., 160l. "XXV" and musical score; 80l., 350l. G. Enescu.

203 Building Worker

1946. Labour Day. Designs of workers inscr "ZIUA MUNCII".

1803	**203**	10l. red	20	10
1804	**203**	10l. green	95	1·00
1805	**203**	20l. blue	95	1·00
1806	**203**	20l. brown	20	10
1807	**203**	200l. red	50	50

204 Sky-writing

1946. Air. Labour Day. Sheet 70×63 mm.

MS1808 200l. blue and vermilion (sold at 10,000l.)	19·00	21·00

205 Sower

1946. Youth Issue.

1809	**205**	10l.+100l. red & brn	50	50
1810	-	10l.+200l. pur & blue	50	50
1811	-	80l.+200l. brn & pur	50	50
1812	-	80l.+300l. mve & brn	50	50
1813	-	200l.+400l. red & grn	50	50

DESIGNS: No. 1810, Hurdling; 1811, Student; 1812, Worker and factory; 1813, Marching with flag.

206 Aviator and Aircraft

1946. Air. Youth Issue.

1814		200l. blue and green	4·75	5·25
1815	**206**	500l. blue and orange	4·75	5·25

DESIGN: 200l. Airplane on ground.

207 Football

1946. Sports, designs inscr "O.S.P." Perf or imperf.

1816	**207**	10l. blue (postage)	50	50
1817	-	20l. red	50	50
1818	-	50l. violet	50	50
1819	-	80l. brown	50	50
1820	-	160l.+1340l. green	50	50
1821	-	300l. red (air)	1·90	2·50
1822	-	300l.+1200l. blue	1·90	2·50
MS1823		58×64 mm. 300l. crimson (as No. 1821 but larger). Imperf. (sold at 1300l.)	21·00	23·00

DESIGNS: 20l. Diving; 50l. Running; 80l. Mountaineering; 160l. Ski jumping; 300l. (both) Flying.

208 "Traditional Ties"

1946. Romanian–Soviet Friendship Pact.

1824	**208**	80l. brown	50	50
1825	-	100l. blue	50	50
1826	-	300l. grey	50	50
1827	-	300l.+1200l. red	95	1·00
MS1828		70×65 mm. 1000l. scarlet (as No. 1827) (sold at 6000l.)	9·75	10·50

DESIGNS: 100l. "Cultural ties"; 300l. "Economic ties"; 300l.+1200l. Dove.

No. 1827 also exists imperf.

209 Banat Girl holding Distaff

1946. Charity. Women's Democratic Federation.

1829		80l. olive	40	40
1830	**209**	80l.+320l. red	40	40
1831	-	140l.+360l. orange	40	40
1832	-	300l.+450l. green	40	40
1833	-	600l.+900l. blue	40	40
MS1834		80×65 mm. 500l.+9500l. vermilion and chocolate (air)	9·75	10·50

DESIGNS: 80l. Girl and handloom; 140l. Wallachian girl and wheatsheaf; 300l. Transylvanian horsewoman; 600l. Moldavian girl carrying water.

211 King Michael and Food Transport

1947. Social Relief Fund.

1845		300l. olive	50	50
1846	**211**	600l. mauve	50	50
1847	-	1500l.+3500l. orange	50	50
1848	-	3700l.+5300l. violet	50	50
MS1849		52×36 mm. **212** 5000l.+5000l. ultramarine. Imperf. No gum	9·75	10·50

DESIGNS—VERT: 300l. Loaf of bread and hungry child; 1500l. Angel bringing food and clothing to destitute people; 3700l. Loaf of bread and starving family.

213 King Michael and Chariot

1947. Peace.

1850	**213**	300l. purple	50	50
1851	-	600l. brown	50	50
1852	-	3000l. blue	50	50
1853	-	7200l. green	50	50

DESIGNS—VERT: 600l. Winged figure of Peace; 300l. Flags of four Allied Nations; 7200l. Dove of Peace.

214 Symbols of Labour and Clasped Hands

1947. Trades Union Congress.

1854	**214**	200l. blue (postage)	70	75
1855	**214**	300l. orange	70	75
1856	**214**	600l. red	70	75
1857	-	1100l. blue (air)	95	1·00

DESIGN—22×37 mm: 1100l. As Type **214** with Lockheed Super Electra airplane at top.

216 Worker and Torch

1947. Air. Trades Union Congress. Imperf.

1858	**216**	3000l.+7000l. brown	95	1·00

218 Symbolical of "Learning"

1947. Charity. People's Culture.

1859	-	200l.+200l. blue	20	30
1860	-	300l.+300l. brown	20	30
1861	-	600l.+600l. green	20	30
1862	-	1200l.+1200l. blue	20	30
1863	**218**	1500l.+1500l. red	20	30
MS1864		64×80 mm. 3700l.+3700l. blue and brown (as T **218**). Imperf	3·00	3·75

DESIGNS—HORIZ: 200l. Boys' reading class; 300l. Girls' school; 600l. Engineering classroom; 1200l. School building.

219 King Michael

1947

1865	**219**	1000l. blue	20	20
1869	**219**	3000l. blue	30	30
1866	**219**	5500l. green	30	30
1870	**219**	7200l. mauve	30	30
1871	**219**	15000l. blue	50	30
1867	**219**	20000l. brown	70	40
1872	**219**	21000l. mauve	50	30
1873	**219**	36000l. violet	95	85
1868	**219**	50000l. orange	1·30	65

Nos. 1865/8 are size 18×21½ mm and Nos. 1869/73 are 25×30 mm.

220 N. Grigorescu

221 Lisunov Li-2 Airliner

1947. Charity. Institute of Romanian–Soviet Studies.

1874	-	1500l.+150l. purple (postage)	40	40
1875	-	1500l.+1500l. orange	40	40
1876	-	1500l.+1500l. green	40	40
1877	**220**	1500l.+1500l. blue	40	40
1878	-	1500l.+1500l. blue	40	40
1879	-	1500l.+1500l. lake	40	40
1880	-	1500l.+1500l. red	40	40
1881	-	1500l.+1500l. brown	40	40
1882	**221**	15000l.+15000l. green (air)	95	1·00

PORTRAITS: No. 1874, Petru Movila; 1875, V. Babes; 1876, M. Eminescu; 1878, P. Tchaikovsky; 1879, M. Lomonosov; 1880, A. Pushkin; 1881, I. Y. Repin.

No. 1882 is imperf.

222 Miner

1947. Charity. Labour Day.

1883	**222**	1000l.+1000l. olive	40	40
1884	-	1500l.+1500l. brown	40	40
1885	-	2000l.+2000l. blue	40	40
1886	-	2500l.+2500l. mauve	40	40
1887	-	3000l.+3000l. red	40	40

DESIGNS: 1500l. Peasant; 2000l. Peasant woman; 2500l. Intellectual; 3000l. Factory worker.

224 Douglas DC-4 Airliner over Black Sea

1947. Air. Labour Day.

1888		3000l. red	50	50
1889		3000l. green	50	50
1890		3000l. brown	50	50
1891	**224**	3000l.+12,000l. blue	95	1·00

DESIGNS—24½×30 mm: No. 1888, Four parachutes; 1889, Air Force Monument; 1890, Douglas DC-4 over landscape.

225 King Michael and Timber Barges

1947. Designs with medallion portrait of King Michael.

1892	-	50b. orange	20	10
1893	**225**	1l. brown	20	10
1894	-	2l. blue	20	10
1895	-	3l. red	50	20
1896	-	5l. blue	50	20
1897	-	10l. blue	70	30
1898	-	12l. violet	95	30
1899	-	15l. blue	1·50	30
1900	-	20l. brown	2·40	50
1901	-	32l. brown	6·25	2·50
1902	-	36l. lake	6·25	2·50

DESIGNS: 50b. Harvesting; 2l. River Danube; 3l. Reshitza Industries; 5l. Curtea de Arges Cathedral; 10l. Royal Palace, Bucharest; 12, 36l. Saligny Bridge, Cernavoda; 15, 32l. Liner "Transylvania" in Port of Constantza; 20l. Oil Wells, Prahova.

1947. Balkan Games. Surch 2+3 LEI C.B.A. 1947 and bar.

1903	**219**	2+3l. on 36,000l. violet	1·50	1·60

227

1947. 17th Congress of General Assn of Romanian Engineers. With monogram as in T 227.

1904	**227**	1l.+1l. red (postage)	20	10
1905	-	2l.+2l. brown	20	10
1906	-	3l.+3l. violet	20	10
1907	-	4l.+4l. olive	30	30
1908	-	5l.+5l. blue (air)	1·10	1·20

DESIGNS: 2l. Sawmill; 3l. Refinery; 4l. Steel mill; 5l. Gliders over mountains.

1947. Charity. Soviet–Romanian Amity. As No. 1896 surch ARLUS 1-7-XI. 1947 +5. Imperf.

1909		5l.+5l. blue	95	75

229 Beehive

1947. Savings Day.

1910	**229**	12l. red	95	50

230 Food Convoy

1947. Patriotic Defence.

1911	**230**	1l.+1l. blue	50	50
1912	-	2l.+2l. brown	50	50
1913	-	3l.+3l. red	50	50
1914	-	4l.+4l. blue	50	50
1915	-	5l.+5l. red	50	50

SYMBOLIC DESIGNS—HORIZ: 2l. Soldiers' parcels ("Everything for the front"); 3l. Modern hospital ("Heal the wounded"); 4l. Hungry children ("Help famine-stricken regions"). VERT: 5l. Manacled wrist and flag.

231 Allegory of work

1947. Charity. Trades Union Congress, Bucharest. Inscr "C.G.M. 1947".

1916		2l.+10l. red (postage)	50	50
1917	**231**	7l.+10l. black	50	50
1918	-	11l. red and blue (air)	95	1·00

DESIGNS—As T **231**: 2l. Industrial and agricultural workers. 23×18 mm: 11l. Lisunov Li-2 airliner over demonstration.

233 Map of Romania

1948. Census of 1948.

1925	**233**	12l. blue	95	30

234 Printing Works and Press

1948. 75th Anniv of Romanian State Stamp Printing Works.

1926	**234**	6l. red	2·40	1·60
1927	**234**	7l.50 green	1·50	20

235 Discus Thrower

1948. Balkan Games, 1947. Inscr as in T 235. Imperf or perf.

1928	**235**	1l.+1l. brown (postage)	70	85
1929	-	2l.+2l. red	95	1·30
1930	-	5l.+5l. blue	1·50	2·10
1931	-	7l.+7l. violet (air)	2·40	2·10
1932	-	10l.+10l. green	3·50	4·25

DESIGNS: 2l. Runner; 5l. Heads of two young athletes; 7, 10l. Airplane over running track.

1948. Nos. 1892/1902 optd R.P.R. (Republica Populara Romana).

1933	50b. orange	50	30
1934	1l. brown	50	20
1935	2l. blue	1·20	30
1936	3l. red	1·20	30
1937	5l. blue	1·90	40
1938	10l. blue	2·40	50
1939	12l. violet	3·00	50
1940	15l. blue	3·00	65
1941	20l. brown	4·00	75
1942	32l. brown	9·75	4·25
1943	36l. lake	9·75	4·25

237 Industrial Worker

1948. Young Workers' Union. Imperf or perf.

1954	**237**	2l.+2l. blue (postage)	50	1·00
1955	-	3l.+3l. green	60	1·00
1956	-	5l.+5l. brown	70	1·00
1957	-	8l.+8l. red	85	1·00
1958	-	12l.+12l. blue (air)	2·10	3·25

DESIGNS—As Type **237**: 3l. Peasant girl and wheatsheaf; 5l. Student and book. TRIANGULAR: 8l. Youths bearing Filimon Sarbu banner. 36×23 mm: 12l. Airplane and barn swallows.

240 "Friendship"

1948. Romanian–Bulgarian Amity.

1959	**240**	32l. brown	1·90	1·00

241 "New Constitution"

1948. New Constitution.

1960	**241**	1l. red	70	50
1961	**241**	2l. orange	95	75
1962	**241**	12l. blue	3·00	1·30

242 Globe and Banner

243 Aviator and Heinkel He 116A

1948. Labour Day.

1963	**242**	8l.+8l. red (postage)	2·40	3·75
1964	-	10l.+10l. green	3·50	5·25
1965	-	12l.+12l. brown	4·75	6·25
1966	**243**	20l.+20l. blue (air)	8·25	10·50

DESIGNS—HORIZ: 10l. Peasants and mountains. VERT: 12l. Worker and factory.

244 Barbed Wire Entanglement

1948. Army Day.

1967	-	1l.50+1l.50 red (postage)	60	65
1968	**244**	2l.+2l. purple	60	65
1969	-	4l.+4l. brown	1·10	1·20
1970	-	7l.50+7l.50 black	1·90	2·10
1971	-	8l.+8l. violet	2·10	2·30
1972	-	3l.+3l. blue (air)	9·75	10·50
1973	-	5l.+5l. blue	14·50	16·00

DESIGNS—VERT: 1l.50, Infantry; 3l. Ilyushin Stormovik fighter planes; 5l. Petlyakov Pe-2 dive bomber Il-2M3. HORIZ: 4l. Artillery; 7l.50, Tank; 8l. Destroyer.

245 Five Portraits

246 Proclamation of Islaz

1948. Cent of 1848 Revolution. Dated "1848 1948".

1974		2l.+2l. purple	60	95
1975	**245**	5l.+5l. violet	80	95
1976	**246**	11l. red	1·20	1·90
1977	-	10l.+10l. green	1·10	95
1978	-	36l.+18l. blue	2·50	4·00

DESIGNS—22×38 mm. HORIZ: 10l. Balcescu, Petofi, Iancu, Barnutiu Baritiu and Murcu. VERT: 2l. Nicolas Balcescu; 36l. Balcescu, Kogalniceanu, Alecsandri and Cuza.

247 Emblem of Republic

1948

1980	**247**	0.50l. red	50	20
2023	**247**	50b. red	50	30
1981	**247**	1l. brown	50	10
1982	**247**	2l. green	50	10
1983	**247**	3l. grey	70	20
1984	**247**	4l. brown	70	20
1985	**247**	5l. blue	70	20
2028	**247**	5l. violet	95	10
1986	**247**	10l. blue	1·90	20

No. 2023 is inscribed "BANI 0.50" (= ½ bani) and in No. 1980 this was corrected to "LEI 0.50".

248 Monimoa Gliders

249 Yachts

1948. Air Force and Navy Day. (a) Air Force (vert).

1987	**248**	2l.+2l. blue	1·90	1·90
1988	-	5l.+5l. violet	1·90	1·90
1989	-	8l.+8l. red	3·00	3·00
1990	-	10l.+10l. brown	4·00	4·00

(b) Navy (horiz).

1991	**249**	2l.+2l. green	1·90	1·90
1992	-	5l.+5l. grey	1·90	1·90
1993	-	8l.+8l. blue	3·00	3·00
1994	-	10l.+10l. red	4·00	4·00

DESIGNS—AIR FORCE: 5l. Aurel Vlaicu's No. 1 "Crazy Fly" airplane; 8l. Lisunov Li-2 airliner and tractor; 10l. Lisunov Li-2 airliner. NAVY: 5l. "Mircea" (cadet ship), 1882; 8l. "Romana Mare" (Danube river steamer); 10l. "Transylvania" (liner).

1948. Surch.

1995	**240**	31l. on 32l. brown	1·50	50

251 Newspapers and Torch

1948. Press Week. Imperf or perf.

1996	**251**	5l.+5l. red	50	10
1997	**251**	10l. brown	95	95
1998	-	10l.+10l. violet	1·50	1·50
1999	-	15l.+15l. blue	1·90	1·90

DESIGNS—HORIZ: 10l. (No. 1998), Flag, torch and ink-well. VERT: 15l. Alex Sahia (journalist).

252 Soviet Soldiers' Monument

1948. Romanian–Russian Amity.

2000	**252**	10l. red (postage)	95	95
2001	-	10l.+10l. green	4·00	4·75
2002	-	15l.+15l. blue	4·75	7·25
2003	-	20l.+20l. blue (air)	14·50	19·00

DESIGNS—VERT: 10l. (No. 2001), Badge of Arlus; 15l. Kremlin. HORIZ: 20l. Lisunov Li-2 airplane.

255 Emblem of Republic

1948. Air. Designs showing aircraft.

2004	**255**	30l. red	95	20
2005	-	50l. green	1·50	70
2006	-	100l. blue	4·75	1·90

DESIGNS: 50l. Workers in a field; 100l. Steam train, airplane and liner.

256 Lorry

1948. Work on Communications.

2007		1l.+1l. black and green	95	1·90
2008	**256**	3l.+3l. black & brown	1·30	1·90
2009	-	11l.+11l. black & blue	5·25	4·75
2010	-	15l.+15l. black and red	6·75	7·75

MS2011 110×85 mm. Nos. 2007/10 but in red, blue and red respectively. Imperf. No gum 34·00 39·00

DESIGNS: 1l. Dockers loading freighter; 11l. Lisunov Li-2 airliner on ground and in the air; 15l. Steam train.

257 Nicolas Balcescu

1948

2012	**257**	20l. red	1·50	50

258 Hands Breaking Chain

1948. 1st Anniv of People's Republic.

2013	**258**	5l. red	95	50

259 Runners

1948. National Sports Organization. Imperf or perf.

2014	**259**	5l.+5l. green (postage)	4·75	4·75
2017	**259**	5l.+5l. brown	4·75	4·75
2015	-	10l.+10l. violet	7·25	7·25
2018	-	10l.+10l. red	7·25	7·25
2016	-	20l.+20l. blue (air)	24·00	24·00
2019	-	20l.+20l. green	24·00	24·00

DESIGNS—HORIZ: 10l. Parade of athletes with flags. VERT: 20l. Boy flying model airplane.

260 Lenin

1949. 25th Death Anniv of Lenin. Perf or imperf.

2020	**260**	20l. black	95	50

261 Dancers

1949. 90th Anniv of Union of Romanian Principalities.

2021	**261**	10l. blue	95	50

262 I. C. Frimu and Revolutionaries

1949. 30th Death Anniv of Ion Frimu (union leader and journalist). Perf or imperf.

2022	**262**	20l. red	95	50

263 Pushkin

1949. 150th Birth Anniv of A. S. Pushkin (Russian poet).

2030	**263**	11l. red	1·50	85
2031	**263**	30l. green	1·90	95

264 Globe and Posthorn

265 Forms of Transport

1949. 75th Anniv of U.P.U.

2032	**264**	20l. brown	2·40	1·50
2033	**265**	30l. blue	4·75	2·40

266 Russians entering Bucharest

1949. 5th Anniv of Russian Army's Entry into Bucharest. Perf or imperf.

2034	**266**	50l. brown on green	1·20	1·20

267 "Romanian–Soviet Amity"

1949. Romanian–Soviet Friendship Week. Perf or imperf.

2035	**267**	20l. red	95	50

268 Forms of Transport

1949. International Congress of Transport Unions. Perf or imperf.

2036	**268**	11l. blue	1·20	1·20
2037	**268**	20l. red	1·70	1·70

269 Stalin

1949. Stalin's 70th Birthday. Perf or imperf.

2038	**269**	31l. green	95	50

1950. Philatelic Exhibition, Bucharest. Sheet 110×80 mm comprising T 1 and 247. Imperf. No gum.

MS2039 81 (p) blue and deep blue; 10l. carmine and rose (sold at 50l.) 7·25 4·75

270 "The Third Letter" **271** Michael Eminescu

1950. Birth Centenary of Eminescu (poet).

2040	**270**	11l. green	1·50	50
2041	-	11l. brown	2·40	95
2042	-	11l. mauve	1·50	50
2043	-	11l. violet	1·50	50
2044	**271**	11l. blue	1·50	50

DESIGNS (Scenes representing poems): No. 2041, "Angel and Demon"; 2042, "Ruler and Proletariat"; 2043, "Life".

272 "Dragaica Fair"

1950. Birth Centenary of Ion Andreescu (painter). (a) Perf.

2045	**272**	5l. olive	1·50	95
2047	-	20l. brown	3·00	1·90

(b) Perf or imperf.

2046	11l. blue	2·40	95

DESIGNS—VERT: 11l. Andreescu. HORIZ: 20l. "The Village Well".

273 Factory and Graph

1950. State Plan, 1950 Inscr "PLANUL DU STAT 1950".

2048	**273**	11l. red	60	30
2049	-	31l. violet	1·50	70

DESIGN: 31l. Tractor and factories.
No. 2048 exists imperf.

274 Worker and Flag

1950. Labour Day. Perf or imperf.

2050	**274**	31l. orange	80	10

275 Emblem of Republic

1950

2051	**275**	50b. black	30	20
2052	**275**	1l. red	20	10
2053	**275**	2l. grey	20	10
2054	**275**	3l. purple	30	10
2055	**275**	4l. mauve	20	10
2056	**275**	5l. brown	30	10
2057	**275**	6l. green	30	10
2058	**275**	7l. brown	30	10
2059	**275**	7l.50 blue	50	10
2060	**275**	10l. brown	80	10
2061	**275**	11l. red	80	10
2062	**275**	15l. blue	60	10
2063	**275**	20l. green	60	10
2064	**275**	31l. green	95	10
2065	**275**	36l. brown	1·90	80

For stamps as Type **275** but with inscriptions in white, see Nos. 2240, etc, and Nos. 2277/8.

276 Trumpeter and Drummer

1950. 1st Anniv of Romanian Pioneers Organization.

2074	**276**	8l. blue	1·90	95
2075	-	11l. purple	2·40	1·50
2076	-	31l. red	4·25	3·00

DESIGNS: 11l. Children reading; 31l. Youth parade.

277 Engineer

1950. Industrial Nationalization.

2077	**277**	11l. red	70	50
2078	**277**	11l. blue	1·20	50
2079	**277**	11l. brown	1·20	50
2080	**277**	11l. olive	70	30

278 Aurel Vlaicu and his Airplane No. 1 "Crazy Fly"

1950. 40th Anniv of 1st Flight by A. Vlaicu.

2081	**278**	3l. green	50	20
2082	**278**	6l. blue	85	30
2083	**278**	8l. blue	95	50

279 Mother and Child

1950. Peace Congress, Bucharest.

2084	**279**	11l. red	50	30
2085	-	20l. brown	60	30

DESIGN: 20l. Lathe operator and graph.

280 Statue and Flags

1950. Romanian–Soviet Amity.

2086	**280**	30l. brown	95	50

1950. Romanian–Hungarian Amity. Optd TRAIASCA PRIETENIA ROMANO-MAGHIARAI.

2087	**275**	15l. blue	1·60	50

282 Young People and Badge

1950. GMA Complex Sports Facilities. Designs incorporating badge.

2088	-	3l. red	1·90	1·90
2089	**282**	5l. brown	1·50	1·50
2090	**282**	5l. blue	1·50	1·50
2091	-	11l. green	1·50	1·50
2092	-	31l. olive	3·50	3·50

DESIGNS: 3l. Agriculture and Industry; 11l. Runners; 31l. Gymnasts.

283

1950. 3rd Congress of "ARLUS".

2093	**283**	11l. orange on orange	70	50
2094	**283**	11l. blue on blue	70	50

284 Ski-jumper

1951. Winter Sports.

2095	**284**	4l. brown	1·90	1·90
2096	-	5l. red	1·50	1·50
2097	-	11l. blue	1·50	1·50
2098	-	20l. brown	1·50	1·50
2099	-	31l. green	3·50	3·50

DESIGNS: 5l. Skater; 11l. Skier; 20l. Ice hockey; 31l. Tobogganing.

286 Peasant and Tractor

1951. Agricultural and Industrial Exhibition.

2100		11l. brown	50	50
2101	**286**	31l. blue	95	50

DESIGN—VERT: 11l. Worker and machine.

287 Star of the Republic, Class I-II

1951. Orders and Medals. Perf or imperf.

2102	-	2l. green	30	30
2103	-	4l. blue	50	50
2104	-	11l. red	80	80
2105	**287**	35l. brown	1·10	1·10

DESIGNS: 2l. Medal of Work; 4l. Star of the Republic, Class III–V; 11l. Order of Work.

288 Youth Camp

1951. 2nd Anniv of Romanian Pioneers Organization.

2106	**288**	1l. green	1·50	90
2107	-	11l. blue	1·50	90
2108	-	35l. red	1·90	1·30

DESIGNS—VERT: 11l. Children meeting Stalin. HORIZ: 35l. Decorating boy on parade.

289 Woman and Flags

1951. International Women's Day. Perf or imperf.

2109	**289**	11l. brown	95	45

290 Ion Negulici

1951. Death Centenary of Negulici (painter).

2110	**290**	35l. red	4·75	3·00

291 Cyclists

1951. Romanian Cycle Race.

2111	**291**	11l. brown	3·00	1·30

292 F. Sarbu

1951. 10th Death Anniv of Sarbu (patriot).

2112	**292**	11l. brown	95	45

293 "Revolutionary Romania"

1951. Death Centenary of C. D. Rosenthal (painter).

2113	**293**	11l. green	2·40	90
2114	**293**	11l. orange	2·40	90
2115	-	11l. brown	2·40	90
2116	-	11l. violet	2·40	90

DESIGN—VERT: Nos. 2115/16, "Rumania calls to the Masses".

294 Students

1951. 3rd World Youth Festival, Berlin.

2117	**294**	1l. red	95	60
2118	-	5l. blue	1·90	60
2119	-	11l. purple	3·00	1·30

DESIGNS: 5l. Girl, boy and flag; 11l. Young people around globe.

295 "Scanteia" Building

1951. 20th Anniv of "Scanteia" (Communist newspaper).

2120	**295**	11l. blue	95	45

296 Soldier and Pithead

1951. Miners' Day.

2121	**296**	5l. blue	80	35
2122	-	11l. mauve	1·10	45

DESIGN: 11l. Miner and pithead.

297 Order of Defence

1951. Liberation Day.

2123	**297**	10l. red	70	45

298 Oil Refinery

1951. Five-Year Plan. Dated "1951 1955".

2124	**298**	1l. olive (postage)	95	20
2125	-	2l. red	50	20
2126	-	3l. red	95	55
2127	-	4l. brown	70	20
2128	-	5l. green	70	20
2129	-	6l. blue	2·40	1·30
2130	-	7l. green	1·50	55
2131	-	8l. brown	1·20	45
2132	-	11l. blue	1·20	35
2133	-	35l. violet	1·50	90
2134	-	30l. green (air)	4·00	2·75
2135	-	50l. brown	5·75	3·75

DESIGNS: 2l. Miner and pithead; 3l. Soldier and pylons; 4l. Steel furnace; 5l. Combine-harvester; 6l. Canal construction; 7l. Threshing machine; 8l. Sanatorium; 11l. Dam and pylons; 30l. Potato planting; 35l. Factory; 50l. Liner, steam locomotive and Lisunov Li-2 airliner.

299 Orchestra and Dancers

1951. Music Festival.

2136	**299**	11l. brown	70	45
2137	-	11l. blue (Mixed choir)	95	60
2138	-	11l. mauve (Lyre and dove) (vert)	70	45

300 Soldier and Arms

1951. Army Day.

2139	**300**	11l. blue	95	45

301 Arms of U.S.S.R. and Romania

1951. Romanian–Soviet Friendship.

2140	**301**	4l. brown on buff	50	45
2141	**301**	35l. orange	95	90

302 P. Tcancenco

1951. 25th Death Anniv of Tcancenco (revolutionary).

2142	**302**	10l. olive	95	90

303 Open Book "1907"

304 I. L. Caragiale

1952. Birth Centenary of Ion Caragiale (dramatist). (a) Unissued values surch.

2143	**303**	20b. on 11l. red	1·60	70
2144	-	55b. on 11l. green	2·10	1·00
2145	**304**	75b. on 11l. blue	3·75	1·20

(b) Without surch.

2146	**303**	55b. red	4·00	60
2147	-	55b. green	4·00	60
2148	**304**	55b. blue	4·00	60
2149	-	1l. brown	5·75	2·20

DESIGNS—HORIZ: Nos. 2144, 2147, Profile of Caragiale; 1l. Caragiale addressing assembly.

1952. Currency revalued. Surch.

2174	**275**	3b. on 1l. red	3·00	1·30
2175	**275**	3b. on 2l. grey	3·00	1·30
2176	**275**	3b. on 4l. mauve	3·00	1·30
2177	**275**	3b. on 5l. red	3·00	1·30
2178	**275**	3b. on 7l.50 blue	3·00	1·30
2179	**275**	3b. on 10l. brown	3·00	1·30
2157a	**255**	3b. on 30l. red	5·25	3·50
2158	-	3b. on 50l. (No. 2005)	2·10	1·00
2159	-	3b. on 100l. (No. 2006)	3·00	1·30
2191	**278**	10b. on 3l. green	4·00	1·30
2218	**301**	10b. on 4l. brown on buff	3·00	1·40
2192	**278**	10b. on 6l. blue	4·00	1·30
2193	**278**	10b. on 8l. blue	4·00	1·30
2220	**302**	10b. on 10l. olive	3·00	1·40
2160	**263**	10b. on 11l. red	5·25	2·00
2164	**270**	10b. on 11l. green	4·00	2·30
2165	-	10b. on 11l. (No. 2041)	4·00	2·30
2166	-	10b. on 11l. (No. 2042)	4·00	2·30
2167	-	10b. on 11l. (No. 2043)	4·00	2·30
2168	**271**	10b. on 11l. blue	4·00	2·30
2161	**263**	10b. on 30l. green	5·25	2·00
2219	**301**	10b. on 35l. orange	3·00	1·40
2199	-	20b. on 2l. (No. 2102)	6·25	2·75
2200	-	20b. on 4l. (No. 2103)	6·25	2·75
2171	**273**	20b. on 11l. red	4·75	1·50

2201	-	20b. on 11l. (No. 2104)	6·25	2·75
2194	-	20b. on 20l. (No. 2085)	4·75	2·20
2172	-	20b. on 31l. (No. 2049)	4·75	1·50
2202	**287**	20b. on 35l. brown	6·25	2·75
2206	**298**	35b. on 1l. olive	3·00	1·30
2207	-	35b. on 2l. (No. 2125)	3·00	1·30
2208	-	35b. on 3l. (No. 2126)	5·75	2·75
2209	-	35b. on 4l. (No. 2127)	6·75	3·00
2210	-	35b. on 5l. (No. 2128)	5·75	4·50
2151	**241**	50b. on 12l. blue	5·25	1·50
2180	**275**	55b. on 50b. black	8·75	2·20
2181	**275**	55b. on 3l. purple	8·75	2·20
2195	-	55b. on 3l. (No. 2088)	29·00	18·00
2169	**272**	55b. on 5l. olive	12·50	4·00
2204	**295**	55b. on 5l. blue	7·25	3·25
2182	**275**	55b. on 6l. green	8·75	2·20
2183	**275**	55b. on 7l. brown	8·75	2·20
2188	**276**	55b. on 8l. blue	11·50	5·25
2205	**297**	55b. on 10l. red	7·25	3·25
2170	-	55b. on 11l. (No. 2046)	12·50	4·00
2189	-	55b. on 11l. (No. 2075)	11·50	5·25
2150	**233**	55b. on 12l. blue	4·00	2·30
2184	**275**	55b. on 15l. blue	11·50	2·20
2185	**275**	55b. on 20l. green	8·75	2·20
2196	-	55b. on 20l. (No. 2098)	44·00	18·00
2186	**275**	55b. on 31l. green	8·75	2·20
2173	**274**	55b. on 31l. orange	6·25	4·00
2190	-	55b. on 31l. (No. 2076)	11·50	5·25
2197	-	55b. on 31l. (No. 2099)	44·00	18·00
2198	**286**	55b. on 31l. blue	7·25	4·50
2203	-	55b. on 35l. (No. 2108)	10·50	5·75
2187	**275**	55b. on 36l. brown	11·50	2·20
2211	-	1l. on 6l. (No. 2129)	7·75	6·25
2212	-	1l. on 7l. (No. 2130)	7·75	3·00
2213	-	1l. on 8l. (No. 2131)	7·75	6·25
2214	-	1l. on 11l. (No. 2132)	7·75	3·50
2216	-	1l. on 30l. (No. 2134)	12·50	2·75
2215	-	1l. on 35l. (No. 2133)	10·50	3·00
2217	-	1l. on 50l. (No. 2135)	12·50	2·75
2152	-	1l.75 on 2l.+2l. purple (No. 1974)	19·00	5·75
2153	**245**	1l.75 on 5l.+5l. violet	19·00	5·75
2154	**246**	1l.75 on 11l. red	19·00	5·75
2155	-	1l.75 on 10l.+10l. (No. 1977)	19·00	5·75
2156	-	1l.75 on 36l.+18l. (No. 1978)	19·00	5·75

1952. Air. Surch with airplane, AERIANA and value.

2162	**264**	3l. on 20l. brown	29·00	23·00
2163	**265**	5l. on 30l. blue	44·00	31·00

307 Railwayman

1952. Railway Day.

2229	**307**	55b. brown	4·00	45

308 Gogol and character from "Taras Bulba"

1952. Death Centenary of Nikolai Gogol (Russian writer).

2230	**308**	55b. blue	3·00	45
2231	-	1l.75 green	4·75	60

DESIGN—VERT: 1l.75, Gogol and open book.

309 Maternity Medal

1952. International Women's Day.

2232	**309**	20b. blue and purple	1·20	20
2233	-	55b. brown and chestnut	2·40	55
2234	-	1l.75 brown and red	5·75	75

MEDALS: 55b. "Glory of Maternity" medal; 1l.75, "Mother Heroine" medal.

310 I. P. Pavlov

1952. Romanian–Soviet Medical Congress.

2235	**310**	11l. red	4·00	45

311 Hammer and Sickle Medal

1952. Labour Day.

2236	**311**	55b. brown	3·50	45

312 Boy and Girl Pioneers

1952. 3rd Anniv of Romanian Pioneers Organization.

2237	**312**	20b. brown	1·90	20
2238	-	55b. green	4·75	30
2239	-	1l.75 blue	9·75	65

DESIGNS—VERT: 55b. Pioneer nature-study group. HORIZ: 1l.75, Worker and pioneers.

1952. As T 275 but with figures and inscriptions in white. Bani values size 20¼×24¼ mm, lei values size 24½×29½ mm.

2240	**275**	3b. orange	70	30
2241	**275**	5b. red	95	20
2242	**275**	7b. green	1·20	30
2243	**275**	10b. brown	1·50	20
2244	**275**	20b. blue	1·90	20
2245	**275**	35b. brown	3·50	20
2246	**275**	50b. green	4·00	20
2247	**275**	55b. violet	8·75	20
2248	**275**	1l.10 brown	7·75	45
2249	**275**	1l.75 violet	31·00	65
2250	**275**	2l. olive	8·25	75
2251	**275**	2l.35 brown	9·75	65
2252	**275**	2l.55 orange	11·50	65
2253	**275**	3l. green	12·50	65
2254	**275**	5l. red	16·00	1·10

For similar stamps with star added at top of emblem, see Nos. 2277/8.

314 "Smirdan" (after Grigorescu)

1952. 75th Anniv of Independence.

2255	**314**	50b. lake	1·50	10
2256	-	1l.10 blue	2·40	55

DESIGN—HORIZ: 1l.10, Romanian and Russian soldiers.

315 Leonardo da Vinci

1952. 500th Anniv of Birth of Leonardo da Vinci.

2257	**315**	55b. violet	6·75	65

316 Miner

1952. Miners' Day.

2258	**316**	20b. red	3·00	55
2259	**316**	55b. violet	3·00	55

317 Students' Union Badge

1952. Int Students' Union Council, Bucharest.

2260	**317**	10b. blue	70	10
2261	-	20b. orange	4·00	45
2262	-	55b. green	4·00	65
2263	-	1l.75 red	7·25	1·40

DESIGNS—HORIZ: 20b. Student in laboratory (35½×22 mm); 1l.75, Six students dancing (30×24 mm). VERT: 55b. Students playing football (24×30 mm).

318 Soldier, Sailor and Airman

1952. Army Day.

2264	**318**	55b. blue	2·40	45

319 Statue and Flags

320 Workers and Views of Russia and Romania (after N. Parlius)

1952. Romanian–Soviet Friendship.

2265	**319**	55b. red	1·60	10
2266	**320**	1l.75 brown	4·00	65

321 Rowing

1952. Physical Culture.

2267	**321**	20b. blue	7·75	45
2268	-	1l.75 red (Athletes)	16·00	1·20

322 N. Balcescu (after C. Tattarescu)

1952. Death Centenary of Balcescu (revolutionary).

2269	**322**	55b. grey	4·75	20
2270	**322**	1l.75 olive	11·50	1·20

323 Emblem and Flags

1952. New Constitution.

2271	**323**	55b. green	4·00	45

324

1952. 5th Anniv of People's Republic.

2272	**324**	55b. multicoloured	4·75	65

325 Millo, Caragiale and Mme. Romanescu

1953. Centenary of Caragiale National Theatre.

2273	**325**	55b. blue	4·75	45

326 Foundry Worker

1953. 3rd Industrial and Agricultural Congress.

2274	**326**	55b. green	1·50	20
2275	-	55b. orange	1·50	20
2276	-	55b. brown	1·90	65

DESIGNS—HORIZ: No. 2275, Farm workers and tractor; 2276, Workman, refinery and oil wells.

1953. As Nos. 2240, etc, but with star added at top of emblem.

2277	**275**	5b. red	95	20
2278	**275**	55b. purple	1·60	30

327 "The Strikers of Grivitsa" (after Nazarev)

1953. 20th Anniv of Grivitsa Strike.

2279	**327**	55b. brown	4·00	45

328

1953. 5th Anniv of Treaty of Friendship with Russia.

2280	**328**	55b. brown on blue	4·00	45

329 Table Tennis Badge

1953. 20th World Table Tennis Championship, Bucharest.
2281 **329** 55b. green 9·75 1·60
2282 **329** 55b. brown 9·75 1·60

330 Oltenian Carpet

1953. Romanian Art.
2283 - 10b. green 1·90 10
2284 - 20b. brown 3·00 10
2285 - 35b. violet 3·50 20
2286 - 55b. blue 6·25 20
2287 **330** 1l. purple 11·50 45
DESIGNS—VERT: 10b. Pottery; 20b. Campulung peasant girl; 55b. Apuseni Mountains peasant girl. HORIZ: 35b. National dance.

331 Karl Marx

1953. 70th Death Anniv of Karl Marx.
2288 **331** 1l.55 brown 4·75 55

332 Pioneers planting Tree

1953. 4th Anniv of Romanian Pioneers Organization.
2289 **332** 35b. green 2·40 30
2290 - 55b. blue 3·00 35
2291 - 1l.75 brown 6·75 85
DESIGNS—VERT: 55b. Boy and girl flying model gliders. HORIZ: 1l.75, Pioneers and instructor.

333 Women and Flags

1953. 3rd World Congress of Women.
2292 **333** 55b. brown 3·00 45

334

1953. 4th World Youth Festival.
2293 **334** 20b. orange 1·50 45
2294 - 55b. blue 2·40 95
2295 - 65b. red 3·50 1·40
2296 - 1l.75 purple 9·75 2·75
DESIGNS—VERT: 55b. Students releasing dove over globe. HORIZ: 65b. Girl presenting bouquet; 1l.75, Folk dancers.

335 Cornfield and Forest

1953. Forestry Month.
2297 20b. blue 1·60 20
2298 **335** 38b. green 4·75 1·40
2299 - 55b. brown 5·75 45
DESIGNS—VERT: 20b. Waterfall and trees; 55b. Forestry worker.

336 V. V. Mayakovsky

1953. 60th Birth Anniv of Vladimir Mayakovsky (Russian poet).
2300 **336** 55b. brown 3·50 65

337 Miner

1953. Miners' Day.
2301 **337** 1l.55 black 5·25 45

338 Telephonist, G.P.O. and P.O. Worker

1953. 50th Anniv of Construction of G.P.O.
2302 **338** 20b. brown 50 10
2303 - 55b. olive 95 10
2304 - 1l. blue 2·40 30
2305 - 1l.55 lake 3·50 75
DESIGNS: 55b. Postwoman and G.P.O.; 1l. G.P.O. radio transmitter and map; 1l.55, Telegraphist, G.P.O. and teletypist.

339

1953. 9th Anniv of Liberation.
2306 **339** 55b. brown 2·40 45

340 Soldier and Flag

1953. Army Day.
2307 **340** 55b. olive 2·40 45

341 Girl and Model Glider

1953. Aerial Sports.
2308 **341** 10b. green and orange 4·25 55
2309 - 20b. olive and brown 8·75 30
2310 - 55b. purple and red 16·00 95
2311 - 1l.75 brown and purple 19·00 1·40
DESIGNS: 20b. Parachutists; 55b. Glider and pilot; 1l.75, Zlin Z-22 monoplane.

342 Workman, Girl and Flags

1953. Romanian–Soviet Friendship.
2312 **342** 55b. brown 1·30 20
2313 - 1l.55 lake 3·00 55
DESIGN: 1l.55, Spassky Tower (Moscow Kremlin) and Volga–Don canal.

343 "Unity"

1953. 3rd World Trades' Union Congress.
2314 **343** 55b. olive 1·20 30
2315 - 1l.25 red 3·00 95
DESIGN—VERT: 1l.25, Workers, flags and globe.

344 C. Porumbescu

1953. Birth Centenary of Porumbescu (composer).
2316 **344** 55b. lilac 11·50 45

345 Agricultural Machinery

1953. Agricultural designs.
2317 **345** 10b. olive 50 10
2318 - 35b. green 70 10
2319 - 2l.55 brown 5·75 1·20
DESIGNS: 35b. Tractor drawing disc harrows; 2l.55, Cows grazing.

346 Vlaicu and his Airplane No. 1 "Crazy Fly"

1953. 40th Death Anniv of Vlaicu (pioneer aviator).
2320 **346** 50b. blue 2·50 45

347 Lenin

1954. 30th Death Anniv of Lenin.
2321 **347** 55b. brown 3·00 45

348 Red Deer Stag

1954. Forestry Month.
2322 **348** 20b. brown on yellow 4·75 55
2323 - 55b. violet on yellow 4·00 55
2324 - 1l.75 blue on yellow 5·75 1·10
DESIGNS: 55b. Pioneers planting tree; 1l.75, Forest.

349 Calimanesti

1954. Workers' Rest Homes.
2325 **349** 5b. black on yellow 70 20
2326 - 1l.55 black on blue 3·00 30
2327 - 2l. green on pink 4·75 45
2328 - 2l.35 brown on green 4·50 1·40
2329 - 2l.55 brown on green 6·25 1·90
DESIGNS: 1l.55, Siniai; 2l. Predeal; 2l.35, Tusnad; 2l.55, Govora.

350 O. Bancila

1954. 10th Death Anniv of Bancila (painter).
2330 **350** 55b. green and brown 5·75 2·75

351 Child and Dove of Peace

1954. International Children's Day.
2331 **351** 55b. brown 2·40 45

352 Girl Pioneer feeding Calf

1954. 5th Anniv of Romanian Pioneer Organization.
2332 **352** 20b. black 70 20
2333 - 55b. blue 1·20 45
2334 - 1l.75 red 4·00 95
DESIGNS: 55b. Girl Pioneers harvesting; 1l.75, Young Pioneers examining globe.

353 Stephen the Great

1954. 450th Death Anniv of Stephen the Great.
2335 **353** 55b. brown 4·00 55

354 Miner operating Coal-cutter

1954. Miners' Day.
2336 **354** 1l.75 black 4·00 85

355 Dr. V. Babes

1954. Birth Centenary of Babes (pathologist).
2337 **355** 55b. red 3·00 45

356 Sailor, Flag and Destroyer "Regele Ferdinand"

1954. Navy Day.

2338	**356**	55b. blue	2·40	45

357 Dedication Tablet

1954. 5th Anniv of Mutual Aid Organization.

2339	-	20b. violet	70	20
2340	**357**	55b. brown	1·20	45

DESIGN: 20b. Man receiving money from counter clerk.

358 Liberation Monument

1954. 10th Anniv of Liberation.

2341	**358**	55b. violet and red	1·90	45

359 Recreation Centre

1954. Liberation Anniv Celebrations.

2342	**359**	20b. blue	70	10
2343	-	38b. violet	1·20	45
2344	-	55b. purple	1·50	30
2345	-	1l.55 brown	3·50	55

DESIGNS—38×22 mm: 55b. "Scanteia" offices. 24½×29½ mm: 38b. Opera House, Bucharest; 1l.55, Radio Station.

360 Pilot and Mikoyan Gurevich MiG-15 Jet Fighters

1954. Aviation Day.

2346	**360**	55b. blue	4·00	45

361 Chemical Plant and Oil Derricks

1954. International Chemical and Petroleum Workers Conference, Bucharest.

2347	**361**	55b. black	3·50	65

362 Dragon Pillar, Peking

1954. Chinese Culture Week.

2348	**362**	55b. black on yellow	3·50	65

363 T. Neculuta

1954. 50th Death Anniv of Dumitru Theodor Neculuta (poet).

2349	**363**	55b. violet	3·00	45

364 ARLUS Badge **365** Friendship

1954. 10th Anniv of "ARLUS" and Romanian–Russian Friendship.

2350	**364**	55b. red	95	30
2351	**365**	65b. purple	1·50	45

366 G. Tattarescu

1954. 60th Death Anniv of Gheorghe Tattarescu (painter).

2352	**366**	55b. red	3·50	45

367 B. Iscovescu

1954. Death Centenary of Barbu Iscovescu (painter).

2353	**367**	1l.75 brown	4·75	95

368 Teleprinter

1954. Cent of Telecommunications in Romania.

2354	**368**	50b. lilac	2·40	45

369 Wild Boar

1955. Forestry Month. Inscr "LUNA PADURII 1955".

2355	**369**	35b. brown	2·10	20
2356	-	65b. blue	2·50	45
2357	-	1l.20 red	5·75	95

DESIGNS: 65b. Tree planting; 1l.20, Logging.

370 Airman

1955. Occupations.

2358		3b. blue	50	10
2359		5b. violet	30	10
2360	**370**	10b. brown	50	10
2361	-	20b. mauve	70	10
2362	-	30b. blue	1·20	30
2363	-	35b. turquoise	95	10
2364	-	40b. blue	1·90	30
2365	-	55b. olive	1·90	10
2366	-	1l. violet	2·40	10
2367	-	1l.55 lake	4·00	10
2368	-	2l.35 buff	5·25	95
2369	-	2l.55 green	7·75	65

DESIGNS: 3b. Scientist; 5b. Foundryman; 20b. Miner; 30b. Tractor driver; 35b. Schoolboy; 40b. Girl student; 55b. Bricklayer; 1l. Sailor; 1l.55, Mill girl; 2l.35, Soldier; 2l.55, Telegraph linesman.

371 Clasped Hands

1955. International Conference of Postal Municipal Workers, Vienna.

2370	**371**	25b. red	95	45

372 Lenin

1955. 85th Birth Anniv of Lenin. Portraits of Lenin.

2371	**372**	20b. brown and bistre	95	30
2372	-	55b. brown (full face)	1·90	45
2373	-	1l. lake and red (half length)	3·00	55

373 Dove and Globe

1955. Peace Congress, Helsinki.

2374	**373**	55b. blue	2·40	45

374 War Memorial, Berlin

1955. 10th Anniv of Victory over Germany.

2375	**374**	55b. blue	1·90	45

375 Children and Dove

1955. International Children's Day.

2376	**375**	55b. brown	2·10	45

376 "Service"

1955. European Volleyball Championships.

2377	-	55b. mauve and pink	7·25	1·40
2378	**376**	1l.75 mauve and yellow	16·00	1·40

DESIGN: 55b. Volleyball players.

377 People's Art Museum

1955. Bucharest Museums.

2379	-	20b. mauve	50	20
2380	-	55b. brown	95	20
2381	**377**	1l.20 black	2·40	95
2382	-	1l.75 green	4·00	95
2383	-	2l.55 purple	6·75	1·10

MUSEUMS—30×24½ mm: 20b. Theodor Aman; 2l.55, Simu. 34×23 mm: 55b. Lenin-Stalin; 1l.75, Republican Art.

378 Mother and Child

1955. 1st World Mothers' Congress, Lausanne.

2384	**378**	55b. blue	2·40	45

379 "Nature Study"

1955. 5th Anniv of Pioneer Headquarters, Bucharest.

2385	-	10b. blue	95	10
2386	**379**	20b. green	1·90	10
2387	-	55b. purple	4·25	45

DESIGNS: 10b. Model railway; 55b. Headquarters building.

380 Coxed Four

1955. Women's European Rowing Championships, Snagov.

2388	**380**	55b. green	11·50	1·10
2389	-	1l. blue (Woman sculler)	19·00	1·50

381 Anton Pann (folklorist)

1955. Romanian Writers.

2390		55b. blue	1·90	45
2391		55b. grey	1·90	45
2392	381	55b. olive	1·90	45
2393	-	55b. violet	1·90	45
2394	-	55b. purple	1·90	45

PORTRAITS—No. 2390, Dimitrie Cantemir (historian); 2391, Metropolitan Dosoftei (religious writer); 2393, Constantin Cantacuzino (historian); 2394, Ienachita Vacarescu (poet, grammarian and historian).

382 Marksman

1955. European Sharpshooting Championships, Bucharest.

2395	382	1l. brown and light brown	8·75	95

383 Fire Engine

1955. Firemen's Day.

2396	383	55b. red	2·50	65

384

1955. 10th Anniv of W.F.T.U.

2397	384	55b. olive	70	20
2398	-	1l. blue	1·20	45

DESIGN: 1l. Workers and flag.

385 Spraying Fruit Trees

1955. Fruit and Vegetable Cultivation.

2399	385	10b. green	1·30	20
2400	-	20b. red	1·50	45
2401	-	55b. blue	4·00	45
2402	-	1l. lake	5·25	1·40

DESIGNS: 20b. Fruit picking; 55b. Harvesting grapes; 1l. Gathering vegetables.

386

1955. 4th ARLUS Congress.

2403	386	20b. blue and buff	1·50	45

387 Michurin

1955. Birth Cent of Ivan Michurin (Russian botanist).

2404	387	55b. blue	2·40	45

388 Cotton

1955

2405	-	10b. purple (Sugar beet)	85	30
2406	388	20b. grey	1·20	30
2407	-	55b. blue (Linseed)	3·00	85
2408	-	1l.55 brown (Sunflower)	5·75	1·50

389 Sheep and Shepherd blowing Bucium

1955

2409	389	5b. brown and green	1·20	20
2410	-	10b. violet and bistre	1·60	30
2411	-	35b. brown and salmon	3·50	75
2412	-	55b. brown and bistre	5·75	1·00

DESIGNS: 10b. Pigs and farm girl; 35b. Cows and dairy maid; 55b. Horses and groom.

390 Johann von Schiller (novelist)

1955. Literary Anniversaries.

2413		20b. blue	70	10
2414		55b. blue	1·60	35
2415	390	1l. grey	3·00	45
2416		1l.55 brown	5·25	1·40
2417	-	1l.75 violet	6·25	1·40
2418	-	2l. lake	7·25	2·30

DESIGNS: 20b. Hans Christian Andersen (children's writer, 150th birth anniv); 55b. Adam Mickiewicz (poet, death centenary); 1l. Type **390** (150th death anniv); 1l.55, Baron de Montesquieu (philosopher, death bicentenary); 1l.75, Walt Whitman (centenary of publication of "Leaves of Grass"; 2l. Miguel de Cervantes (350th anniv of publication of "Don Quixote").

391 Bank and Book

1955. Savings Bank.

2419	391	55b. blue	3·00	45
2420	391	55b. violet	9·75	5·50

392 Family

1956. National Census.

2421	-	55b. orange	70	20
2422	392	1l.75 brown and green	3·00	95

DESIGNS: 55b. "21 FEBRUARIE 1956" in circle.

393 Brown Hare

1956. Wild Life.

2423	393	20b. black and green	3·00	95
2424	-	20b. black and olive	3·00	95
2425	-	35b. black and blue	3·00	95
2426	-	50b. brown and blue	3·00	95
2427	-	55b. green and bistre	3·00	95
2428	-	55b. brown and turquoise	3·00	95
2429	-	1l. lake and green	6·25	1·90
2430	-	1l.55 lake and blue	6·25	1·90
2431	-	1l.75 brown and green	6·25	1·90
2432	-	2l. brown and blue	29·00	23·00
2433	-	3l.25 black and green	29·00	23·00
2434	-	4l.25 brown and salmon	29·00	23·00

DESIGNS—VERT: No. 2424, Great bustard; 35b. Brown trout; 1l.55, Eurasian red squirrel; 1l.75, Western capercaillie; 4l.25, Red deer. HORIZ: 50b. Wild boar; No. 2427, Common pheasant; No. 2428, Brown bear; 1l. Lynx; 2l. Chamois; 3l.25, Pintail.

See also Nos. 2474/85.

394 Insurgents

1956. 85th Anniv of Paris Commune.

2435	394	55b. red	2·40	65

395 Boy and Globe

1956. International Children's Day.

2436	395	55b. violet	3·50	45

396 Red Cross Nurse

1956. 2nd Romanian Red Cross Congress.

2437	396	55b. olive and red	4·00	45

397 Tree

1956. Forestry Month.

2438	397	20b. grey on green	1·90	30
2439	-	55b. black on green	5·75	45

DESIGN: 55b. Lumber train.

398 Woman Speaking

1956. International Women's Congress, Bucharest.

2440	398	55b. green	2·40	45

399 Academy Buildings

1956. 90th Anniv of Romanian People's Academy.

2441	399	55b. green and buff	2·40	45

400 Vuia, Biplane, Vuia No. 1 and Yakovlev Yak-25 Fighters

1956. 50th Anniv of 1st Flight by Traian Vuia (pioneer airman).

2442	400	55b. brown and olive	3·00	45

401 Georgescu and Statues

1956. Birth Centenary of Ion Georgescu (sculptor).

2443	401	55b. brown and green	4·00	45

402 Farm Girl

1956. Collective Farming. (a) Inscr "1951–1956".

2444	402	55b. plum	11·50	11·00

(b) Inscr "1949–56".

2445		55b. plum	2·10	45

403 Black-veined White

1956. Insect Pests.

2446	403	10b. cream, black and violet	4·75	55
2447	-	55b. orange and brown	7·25	75
2448	-	1l.75 lake and olive	19·00	14·00
2449	-	1l.75 brown and olive	16·00	1·60

PESTS: 55b. Colorado potato beetle; 1l.75 (2), May beetle.

404 Striker

1956. 50th Anniv of Dockers' Strike at Galatz.

2450	404	55b. brown on pink	2·40	45

405

1956. 25th Anniv of "Scanteia" (Communist newspaper).

2451	405	55b. blue	1·90	45

406 Gorky

1956. 20th Death Anniv of Maksim Gorky.

2452	406	55b. brown	2·40	45

407 T. Aman

1956. 125th Birth Anniv of Aman (painter).

2453	**407**	55b. grey	4·00	95

408 Snowdrops and Polyanthus

1956. Flowers. Designs multicoloured. Colours of backgrounds given.

2454	**408**	5b. blue	95	45
2455	-	55b. black	3·50	85
2456	-	1l.75 blue	7·75	1·10
2457	-	3l. green	11·50	1·80

FLOWERS: 55b. Daffodil and violets; 1l.75, Antirrhinums and campanulas; 3l. Poppies and lilies of the valley.

409 Janos Hunyadi

1956. 500th Death Anniv of Hunyadi.

2458	**409**	55b. violet	2·40	55

410 Olympic Flame

1956. Olympic Games.

2459	**410**	20b. red	95	35
2460	-	55b. blue	1·50	40
2461	-	1l. mauve	3·00	55
2462	-	1l.55 turquoise	4·00	65
2463	-	1l.75 violet	5·25	95

DESIGNS: 55b. Water-polo; 1l. Ice-skating; 1l.55, Canoeing; 1l.75, High-jumping.

411 George Bernard Shaw (dramatist)

1956. Cultural Anniversaries.

2464		20b. blue	60	20
2465		35b. red	80	20
2466	**411**	40b. brown	85	20
2467	-	50b. brown	1·10	20
2468	-	55b. olive	1·20	20
2469	-	1l. turquoise	2·10	30
2470	-	1l.55 violet	3·00	30
2471	-	1l.75 blue	4·00	30
2472	-	2l.55 purple	5·25	45
2473	-	3l.25 blue	5·75	1·10

DESIGNS: 20b. Benjamin Franklin (U.S. statesman and journalist, 250th birth anniv); 35b. Toyo Oda (painter, 450th death anniv); 40b. Type **411** (birth centenary); 50b. Ivan Franco (writer, birth centenary); 55b. Pierre Curie (physicist, 50th death anniv); 1l. Henrik Ibsen (dramatist, 50th death anniv); 1l.55, Fyodor Dostoevsky (novelist, 75th death anniv); 1l.75, Heinrich Heine (poet, death centenary); 2l.55, Wolfgang Amadeus Mozart (composer, birth bicentenary); 3l.25, Rembrandt (artist, 350th birth anniv).

1956. Wild Life. As Nos. 2423/34 but colours changed. Imperf.

2474	20b. brown and green	6·75	6·50
2475	20b. black and blue	6·75	6·50
2476	35b. black and blue	6·75	6·50
2477	50b. black and brown	6·75	6·50
2478	55b. black and violet	6·75	6·50
2479	55b. brown and green	6·75	6·50
2480	1l. brown and blue	6·75	6·50
2481	1l.55 brown and bistre	6·75	6·50
2482	1l.75 purple and green	6·75	6·50
2483	2l. black and blue	6·75	6·50
2484	3l.25 brown and green	6·75	6·50
2485	4l.25 brown and violet	6·75	6·50

412 Ilyushin Il-18 Airliner over City

1956. Air. Multicoloured.

2486	20b. Type **412**	95	65
2487	55b. Ilyushin Il-18 over mountains	1·50	95
2488	1l.75 Ilyushin Il-18 over cornfield	4·25	1·40
2489	2l.55 Ilyushin Il-18 over seashore	6·25	2·30

413 Georgi Enescu

1956. 75th Birth Anniv of Enescu (musician).

2490	-	55b. blue	1·90	45
2491	**413**	1l.75 purple	4·00	65

DESIGN: 55b. Enescu when a child, holding violin.

414 "Rebels" (after Octav Bancila)

1957. 50th Anniv of Peasant Revolt.

2492	**414**	55b. grey	2·40	45

415 Stephen the Great

1957. 500th Anniv of Accession of Stephen the Great.

2493	**415**	55b. brown	1·90	55
2494	**415**	55b. olive	1·50	95

416 Gheorghe Marinescu (neurologist) and Institute of Medicine

1957. National Congress of Medical Sciences, Bucharest, and Centenary of Medical and Pharmaceutical Teaching in Bucharest (11.75).

2495	**416**	20b. green	70	30
2496	-	35b. brown	95	45
2497	-	55b. purple	1·60	65
2498	-	1l.75 red and blue	6·25	2·30

DESIGNS: As T **416**: 35b. Ioan Cantacuzino (bacteriologist) and Cantacuzino Institute; 55b. Victor Babes (pathologist and bacteriologist) and Babes Institute. 66×23 mm: 1l.75, Nicolae Kretzulescu and Carol Dairla (physicians) and Faculty of Medicine, Bucharest.

417 Gymnast and Spectator

1957. 1st European Women's Gymnastic Championships, Bucharest.

2499	**417**	20b. green	95	20
2500	-	35b. red	1·50	30
2501	-	55b. blue	3·00	45
2502	-	1l.75 purple	8·25	1·10

DESIGNS—HORIZ: 35b. On asymmetric bars; 55b. Vaulting over horse. VERT: 1l.75, On beam.

418 Emblems of Atomic Energy

1957. 2nd A.S.I.T. Congress.

2503	**418**	55b. brown	1·90	30
2504	**418**	55b. blue	2·40	45

419 Dove and Handlebars

1957. 10th International Cycle Race.

2505	**419**	20b. blue	70	20
2506	-	55b. brown	1·90	45

DESIGN: 55b. Racing cyclist.

420 Rhododendron

1957. Flowers of the Carpathian Mountains.

2513	**420**	5b. red and grey	50	10
2514	-	10b. green and grey	70	20
2515	-	20b. orange and grey	80	20
2516	-	35b. olive and grey	1·50	30
2517	-	55b. blue and grey	1·60	30
2518	-	1l. red and grey	3·75	1·00
2519	-	1l.55 yellow and grey	4·00	55
2520	-	1l.75 violet and grey	7·25	65

FLOWERS: 10b. Daphne; 20b. Lily; 35b. Edelweiss; 55b. Gentian; 1l. Dianthus; 1l.55, Primula; 1l.75, Anemone.

421 N. Grigorescu

1957. 50th Death Anniv of Nicolae Grigorescu (painter).

2521		20b. green	95	20
2522	**421**	55b. brown	2·40	30
2523	-	1l.75 blue	8·75	1·10

DESIGNS—HORIZ: 20b. "Ox-cart"; 1l.75, "Attack on Smirdan".

422 Festival Visitors

423 Festival Emblem

1957. 6th World Youth Festival, Moscow.

2524	**422**	20b. purple	30	10
2525	-	55b. green	80	20
2526	**423**	1l. orange	1·60	65
2527	-	1l.75 blue	3·00	45

DESIGNS: 55b. Girl with flags (22×38 mm); 1l.75, Dancers (49×20 mm).

424 Destroyer "Stalingrad"

1957. Navy Day.

2528	**424**	1l.75 blue	2·40	45

425 "The Trumpeter" (after N. Grigorescu)

1957. 80th Anniv of War of Independence.

2529	**425**	20b. violet	2·40	45

426 Soldiers Advancing

1957. 40th Anniv of Battle of Marasesti.

2530	**426**	1l.75 brown	3·00	45

427 Child with Dove

1957. Red Cross.

2531	**427**	55b. green and red	2·40	45

428 Sprinter and Bird

1957. Int Athletic Championships, Bucharest.

2532	**428**	20b. black and blue	70	10
2533	-	55b. black and yellow	2·10	30
2534	-	1l.75 black and red	5·75	75

DESIGNS: 55b. Javelin-thrower and bull; 1l.75, Runner and stag.

429 Ovid

1957. Birth Bimillenary of Ovid (Latin poet).

2535	**429**	1l.75 blue	4·25	95

430 Congress Emblem

1957. 4th W.F.T.U. Congress, Leipzig.

2536	**430**	55b. blue	1·50	45

431 Oil Refinery, 1957

1957. Centenary of Romanian Petroleum Industry.

2537	**431**	20b. brown	70	10
2538	**431**	20b. blue	70	10
2539	-	55b. purple	1·50	65

DESIGN: 55b. Oil production, 1857 (horse-operated borer).

432 Lenin, Youth and Girl

1957. 40th Anniv of Russian Revolution.

2540	**432**	10b. red	50	10
2541	-	35b. purple	95	20
2542	-	55b. brown	1·50	55

DESIGNS—HORIZ: 35b. Lenin and flags; 55b. Statue of Lenin.

433 Artificial Satellite encircling Globe

1957. Air. Launching of Artificial Satellite by Russia.

2543	**433**	25b. blue	70	20
2544	-	3l.75 green	4·00	75
2545	**433**	25b. blue	70	20
2546	-	3l.75 blue	4·00	75

DESIGN: 3l.75 (2), Satellite's orbit around Globe.

See also Nos. 2593/6.

434 Peasant Soldiers

1957. 520th Anniv of Bobilna Revolution.

2547	**434**	50b. purple	60	20
2548	-	55b. grey	80	45

DESIGN—VERT: 55b. Bobilna Memorial.

435 Endre Ady

1957. 80th Birth Anniv of Endre Ady (Hungarian poet).

2549	**435**	55b. olive	1·90	45

436 Laika and "Sputnik 2"

1957. Space Flight of Laika (dog).

2550	**436**	1l.20 blue and brown	4·75	95
2551	**436**	1l.20 blue and brown	4·75	95

437 Black-winged Stilt

1957. Fauna of the Danube Delta.

2552	**437**	5b. grey & brown (postage)	30	10
2553	-	10b. orange and green	40	10
2554	-	20b. orange and red	50	10
2555	-	50b. orange and green	95	10
2556	-	55b. blue and purple	1·50	20
2557	-	1l.30 orange and violet	2·40	20
2558	-	3l.30 grey and blue (air)	4·75	1·10
2559	-	5l. orange and red	7·25	1·60

DESIGNS—VERT: 10b. Great egret; 20b. White spoonbill; 50b. Stellate sturgeon. HORIZ: 55b. Stoat; 1l.30, Eastern white pelican; 3l.30, Black-headed gull; 5l. White-tailed sea eagle.

438 Emblem of Republic and Flags

1957. 10th Anniv of People's Republic.

2560	**438**	25b. buff, red and blue	50	20
2561	-	55b. yellow	95	30
2562	-	1l.20 red	1·90	65

DESIGNS: 55b. Emblem, Industry and Agriculture; 1l.20, Emblem, the Arts and Sports.

439 Republican Flag

1958. 25th Anniv of Strike at Grivitsa.

2563	**439**	1l. red and brown on buff	1·50	45
2564	**439**	1l. red and blue on buff	1·50	45

440 "Telecommunications"

1958. Socialist Countries' Postal Ministers Conference, Moscow.

2565	**440**	55b. violet	70	35
2566	-	1l.75 purple	1·60	45

DESIGN: 1l.75, Telegraph pole and pylons carrying lines.

441 Nicolae Balcescu (historian)

1958. Romanian Writers.

2567	**441**	5b. blue	60	20
2568	-	10b. black	70	30
2569	-	35b. blue	80	35
2570	-	55b. brown	1·10	45
2571	-	1l.75 black	2·75	65
2572	-	2l. green	4·00	75

DESIGNS: 10b. Ion Creanga (folklorist); 35b. Alexandru Vlahuta (poet); 55b. Mihail Eminescu (poet); 1l.75, Vasile Alecsandri (poet and dramatist); 2l. Barbu Delavrancea (short-story writer and dramatist).

442 Fencer

1958. World Youth Fencing Championships, Bucharest.

2573	**442**	1l.75 mauve	3·00	45

443 Symbols of Medicine and Sport

1958. 25th Anniv of Sports Doctors' Service.

2574	**443**	1l.20 red and green	3·00	45

444

1958. 4th Int Congress of Democratic Women.

2575	**444**	55b. blue	1·60	45

445 Linnaeus (botanist)

1958. Cultural Anniversaries (1957).

2576	**445**	10b. blue	30	20
2577	-	20b. brown	60	20
2578	-	40b. mauve	95	30
2579	-	55b. blue	1·50	20
2580	-	1l. mauve	1·90	30
2581	-	1l.75 blue	2·40	55
2582	-	2l. brown	4·25	65

DESIGNS: 10b. Type **445** (250th birth anniv); 20b. Auguste Comte (philosopher, death centenary); 40b. William Blake (poet and artist, birth bicentenary); 55b. Mikhail Glinka (composer, death centenary); 1l. Henry Longfellow (poet, 150th birth anniv); 1l.75, Carlo Goldoni (dramatist, 250th birth anniv); 2l. John Komensky, Comenius (educationist, 300th death anniv).

446 Parasol Mushroom

1958. Mushrooms. As T 446.

2583	**446**	5b. brown, lt brn & blue	30	20
2584	-	10b. brown, buff and bronze	30	20
2585	-	20b. red, yellow and grey	70	20
2586	-	30b. brown, orge & green	95	30
2587	-	35b. brown, lt brn & bl	1·10	20
2588	-	55b. brown, red and green	1·50	20
2589	-	1l. brown, buff and green	2·40	30
2590	-	1l.55 pink, drab and grey	3·50	45
2591	-	1l.75 brown, buff and green	4·00	55
2592	-	2l. yellow, brown and green	5·75	65

MUSHROOMS: 10b. "Clavaria aurea"; 20b. Caesar's mushroom; 30b. Saffron milk cap; 35b. Honey fungus; 55b. Shaggy ink cap; 1l. "Morchella conica"; 1l.55, Field mushroom; 1l.75, Cep; 2l. Chanterelle.

1958. Brussels International Exhibition. Nos. 2543/4 and 2545/6 optd EXPOZITIA UNIVERSALA BRUXELLES 1958 and star or with star only.

2593	**433**	25b. green	4·75	1·90
2595	**433**	25b. blue	4·75	1·90
2594	-	3l.75 green	24·00	14·00
2596	-	3l.75 blue	24·00	14·00

448 Racovita and "Belgica" (Gerlache expedition, 1897)

1958. 10th Death Anniv (1957) of Emil Racovita (naturalist and explorer).

2597	**448**	55b. indigo and blue	1·60	35
2598	-	1l.20 violet and olive	4·00	45

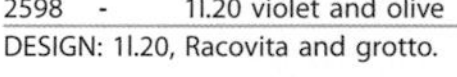

DESIGN: 1l.20, Racovita and grotto.

449 Sputnik encircling Globe

1958. Air. Launching of Third Artificial Satellite by Russia.

2599	**449**	3l.25 buff and blue	7·25	1·90

450 Servicemen's Statue

1958. Army Day.

2600	**450**	55b. brown (postage)	50	20
2601	-	75b. purple	70	20
2602	-	1l.75 blue	1·60	30
2603	-	3l.30 violet (air)	3·00	75

DESIGNS: 75b. Soldier guarding industrial plant; 1l.75, Sailor hoisting flag, and "Royal Ferdinand" destroyer; 3l.30, Pilot and Mikoyan Gurevich MiG-17 jet fighters.

451 Costume of Oltenia

452 Costume of Oltenia

1958. Provincial Costumes.

No.	Type	Description	Unused	Used
2604	**451**	35b. red, black and yellow (female)	50	30
2605	**452**	35b. red, black and yellow (male)	50	30
2606	-	40b. red, brown and light brown (female)	60	35
2607	-	40b. red, brown and light brown (male)	60	35
2608	-	50b. brown, red and lilac (female)	70	30
2609	-	50b. brown, red and lilac (male)	70	30
2610	-	55b. red, brown and drab (female)	95	35
2611	-	55b. red, brown and drab (male)	95	35
2612	-	1l. carmine, brown and red (female)	1·90	45
2613	-	1l. carmine, brown and red (male)	1·90	45
2614	-	1l.75 red, brown and blue (female)	2·50	65
2615	-	1l.75 red, brown and blue (male)	2·50	65

PROVINCES: Nos. 2606/7, Tara Oasului; 2608/9, Transylvania; 2610/11, Muntenia; 2612/3, Banat; 2614/5, Moldova.

453 Stamp Printer

1958. Romanian Stamp Centenary. Inscr "1858 1958".

No.	Type	Description	Unused	Used
2617	**453**	35b. blue	60	20
2618	-	55b. brown	85	20
2619	-	1l.20 blue	1·50	40
2620	-	1l.30 plum	1·90	45
2621	-	1l.55 brown	2·40	30
2622	-	1l.75 red	2·50	35
2623	-	2l. violet	3·00	65
2624	-	3l.30 brown	4·00	95
MS2625		80×89 mm. 10l. blue on pale blue	60·00	55·00
MS2626		80×89 mm. 10l. red. Imperf	80·00	75·00

DESIGNS: 55b. Scissors and Moldavian stamps of 1858; 1l.20, Driver with whip and mail coach; 1l.30, Postman with horn and mounted courier; 1l.55 to 3l.30, Moldavian stamps of 1858 (Nos. 1/4).

454 Runner

1958. 3rd Youth Spartacist Games.

No.	Type	Description	Unused	Used
2627	**454**	1l. brown	1·90	45

455 Revolutionary Emblem

1958. 40th Anniv of Workers' Revolution.

No.	Type	Description	Unused	Used
2628	**455**	55b. red	1·20	45

456 Boy Bugler

1958. 10th Anniv of Education Reform.

No.	Type	Description	Unused	Used
2629	**456**	55b. red	1·20	45

457 Alexandru Cuza

1959. Centenary of Union of Romanian Provinces.

No.	Type	Description	Unused	Used
2630	**457**	1l.75 blue	2·40	45

458 First Cosmic Rocket

1959. Air. Launching of 1st Cosmic Rocket.

No.	Type	Description	Unused	Used
2631	**458**	3l.25 blue on salmon	16·00	2·30

1959. Air. 10th Anniv of State Philatelic Services. No. MS2625 optd 10 ANI DE COMERT FILATELIC DE STAT 1949–1959 in red.

No.	Type	Description	Unused	Used
MS2632		10l. blue on pale blue	£225	£200

459 Charles Darwin (naturalist)

1959. Cultural Anniversaries.

No.	Type	Description	Unused	Used
2633	**459**	55b. black (postage)	95	20
2634	-	55b. blue	95	20
2635	-	55b. red	95	20
2636	-	55b. purple	95	20
2637	-	55b. brown	95	20
2638	-	3l.25 blue (air)	4·75	95

DESIGNS—No. 2633, Type **459** (150th birth anniv); 2634, Robert Burns (poet, birth bicentenary); 2635, Aleksandr Popov (radio pioneer, birth centenary); 2636, Sholem Aleichem (writer, birth centenary); 2637, Frederick Handel (composer, death bicentenary); 2638, Frederic Joliot-Curie (nuclear physicist, 10th anniv of World Peace Council).

460 Maize

1959. 10th Anniv of Collective Farming in Romania.

No.	Type	Description	Unused	Used
2639	**460**	55b. green	60	30
2640	-	55b. orange	60	30
2641	-	55b. purple	60	30
2642	-	55b. olive	60	30
2643	-	55b. brown	60	30
2644	-	55b. bistre	60	30
2645	-	55b. blue	60	30
2646	-	55b. bistre	60	30
2647	-	5l. red	4·75	1·00

DESIGNS—VERT: No. 2640, Sunflower with bee; 2641, Sugar beet. HORIZ: No. 2642, Sheep; 2643, Cattle; 2644, Rooster and hens; 2645, Farm tractor; 2646, Farm wagon and horses; 2647 (38×26½ mm), Farmer and wife, and wheatfield within figure "10".

461 Rock Thrush

1959. Air. Birds in natural colours. Inscriptions in grey. Colours of value tablets and backgrounds given.

No.	Type	Description	Unused	Used
2648	**461**	10b. grey on buff	30	20
2649	-	20b. grey on grey	30	20
2650	-	35b. grey on deep grey	40	20
2651	-	40b. red on pink	50	20
2652	-	55b. grey on green	70	20
2653	-	55b. grey on cream	70	20
2654	-	55b. green on azure	70	20
2655	-	1l. red on yellow	2·40	30
2656	-	1l.55 red on pink	3·00	30
2657	-	5l. grey on green	7·75	2·75

BIRDS—HORIZ: No. 2649, Golden oriole; 2656, Long-tailed tit; 2657, Wallcreeper. VERT: No. 2650, Northern lapwing; 2651, Barn swallow; 2652, Great spotted woodpecker; 2653, Eurasian goldfinch; 2654, Great tit; 2655, Northern bullfinch.

462 Young Couple

1959. 7th World Youth Festival, Vienna. Inscr "26 VII-4 VIII 1959".

No.	Type	Description	Unused	Used
2658	**462**	1l. blue	1·20	30
2659	-	1l.60 red	1·60	35

DESIGN: 1l.60, Folk-dancer in national costume.

463 Workers and Banners

464

1959. 15th Anniv of Liberation.

No.	Type	Description	Unused	Used
2660	**463**	55b. multicoloured	95	45
MS2661		1l.20 multicoloured (39×72 mm). Imperf. No gum	3·00	1·40

1959. Air. Landing of Russian Rocket on the Moon. Surch h. 00.02.24" 14-IX-1959 PRIMA RACHETA COSMICA IN LUNA 5 LEI and bars.

No.	Type	Description	Unused	Used
2662	**458**	5l. on 3l.25 blue on salmon	14·50	4·25

(466)

1959. 8th Balkan Games. Optd with T 466 in silver.

No.	Type	Description	Unused	Used
2663	**454**	1l. brown	16·00	16·00

467 Prince Vlad Tepes and Charter

1959. 500th Anniv of Bucharest.

No.	Type	Description	Unused	Used
2664	**467**	20b. black and blue	95	35
2665	-	40b. black and brown	1·80	35
2666	-	55b. black and bistre	3·00	55
2667	-	55b. black and purple	3·50	55
2668	-	1l.55 black and lilac	5·75	1·50
2669	-	1l.75 black and turquoise	6·25	2·00

DESIGNS—HORIZ: 40b. Peace Buildings, Bucharest; 55b. (No. 2666), Atheneum; 55b. (No 2667), "Scanteia" Printing House; 1l.55, Opera House; 1l.75, "23 August" Stadium.

468 Football

1959. International Sport. Multicoloured.

No.	Description	Unused	Used
2671	20b. Type **468** (postage)	50	20
2672	35b. Motor-cycle racing (horiz)	60	20
2673	40b. Ice-hockey (horiz)	80	30
2674	55b. Handball	95	20
2675	1l. Horse-jumping	1·50	20
2676	1l.50 Boxing	3·00	30
2677	1l.55 Rugby football (horiz)	3·00	20
2678	1l.60 Tennis (horiz)	3·50	45
2679	2l.80 Hydroplaning (horiz) (air)	4·25	1·20

STAMP DAY ISSUES. The annual issues for Stamp Day in November together with the stamp issued on 30 March 1963 for the Romanian Philatelists' Conference are now the only stamps which carry a premium which is expressed on se-tenant labels. This was for the Association of Romanian Philatelists. These labels were at first seperated by a vertical perforation but in the issues from 1963 to 1971 the label is an integral part of the stamp.

469 "Lenin"

1959. Launching of Atomic Ice-breaker "Lenin".

No.	Type	Description	Unused	Used
2680	**469**	1l.75 violet	3·50	65

470 Stamp Album and Magnifier

1959. Stamp Day.

No.	Type	Description	Unused	Used
2681	**470**	1l.60(+40b.) blue	95	45

471 Foxglove

1959. Medicinal Flowers. Multicoloured.

No.	Description	Unused	Used
2682	20b. Type **471**	30	10
2683	40b. Peppermint	60	30
2684	55b. False camomile	80	20
2685	55b. Cornflower	1·10	20
2686	1l. Meadow saffron	1·50	30
2687	1l.20 Monkshood	1·60	30
2688	1l.55 Common poppy	2·40	45
2689	1l.60 Silver lime	2·40	55
2690	1l.75 Dog rose	2·50	55
2691	3l.20 Yellow pheasant's-eye	4·00	75

472 Cuza University

1959. Centenary of Cuza University, Jassy.

No.	Type	Description	Unused	Used
2692	**472**	55b. brown	95	45

473 Rocket, Dog and Rabbit

1959. Air. Cosmic Rocket Flight.

2693	**473**	1l.55 blue	4·75	45
2694	-	1l.60 blue on cream	5·25	75
2695	-	1l.75 blue	5·25	75

DESIGNS—HORIZ: (52×29½ mm): 1l.60, Picture of "invisible" side of the Moon, with lists of place-names in Romanian and Russian. VERT—(As Type **473**): 1l.75, Lunik 3's trajectory around the Moon.

474 G. Cosbuc

1960. Romanian Authors.

2696	**474**	20b. blue	50	35
2697	-	40b. purple	95	35
2698	-	50b. brown	1·20	35
2699	-	55b. purple	1·20	35
2700	-	1l. violet	2·10	45
2701	-	1l.55 blue	3·50	55

PORTRAITS: 40b. I. L. Caragiale; 50b. G. Alexandrescu; 55b. A. Donici; 1l. C. Negruzzi; 1l.55, D. Bolintineanu.

475 Huchen

1960. Romanian Fauna.

2702	**475**	20b. blue (postage)	50	20
2703	-	55b. brown (Tortoise)	95	20
2704	-	1l.20 lilac (Common shelduck)	2·10	65
2705	-	1l.30 blue (Golden eagle) (air)	2·40	65
2706	-	1l.75 green (Black grouse)	2·40	65
2707	-	2l. red (Lammergeier)	2·50	95

476 Woman and Dove

1960. 50th Anniv of International Women's Day.

2708	**476**	55b. blue	1·50	65

477 Lenin (after painting by M. A. Gerasimov)

1960. 90th Birth Anniv of Lenin.

2709	**477**	40b. purple	80	30
2710	-	55b. blue	1·10	30
MS2711		65×75 mm. 1l.55 red	5·75	3·75

DESIGNS: 55b. Statue of Lenin by Boris Carogea; 1l.50 Lenin (sculpture by C. Baraschi).

478 "Victory"

1960. 15th Anniv of Victory.

2712	**478**	40b. blue	70	30
2714	**478**	40b. purple	3·50	3·75
2713	-	55b. blue	70	30
2715	-	55b. purple	3·50	3·75

DESIGN: 55b. Statue of soldier with flag.

479 Rocket Flight

1960. Air. Launching of Soviet Rocket.

2716	**479**	55b. blue	4·75	65

480 Diving

1960. Olympic Games, Rome (1st issue). Mult.

2717		40b. Type **480**	2·40	2·30
2718		55b. Gymnastics	2·40	2·30
2719		1l.20 High jumping	2·40	2·30
2720		1l.60 Boxing	2·40	2·30
2721		2l.45 Canoeing	2·40	2·30
2722		3l.70 Canoeing	6·25	6·75

Nos. 2717/9 and 2720/1 are arranged together in "brickwork" fashion, se-tenant, in sheets forming complete overall patterns of the Olympic rings.

No. 2722 is imperf.

481 Gymnastics

1960. Olympic Games, Rome (2nd issue).

2723	-	20b. blue	20	10
2724	**481**	40b. purple	60	20
2725	-	55b. blue	85	10
2726	-	1l. red	1·20	20
2727	-	1l.60 purple	1·60	30
2728	-	2l. lilac	2·50	55
MS2729		90×69 mm. 5l. ultramarine	19·00	19·00
MS2730		90×69 mm. 6l. red. Imperf	34·00	33·00

DESIGNS: 20b. Diving; 55b. High-jumping; 1l. Boxing; 1l.60, Canoeing; 2l. Football; 5, 6l. Olympic flame and stadium.

482 Industrial Scholars

1960

2731	**482**	3b. mauve (postage)	10	10
2732	-	5b. brown	10	10
2733	-	10b. purple	20	10
2734	-	20b. blue	20	10
2735	-	30b. red	30	10
2736	-	35b. red	30	10
2737	-	40b. bistre	30	10
2738	-	50b. violet	30	10
2739	-	55b. blue	40	10
2740	-	60b. green	40	10
2741	-	75b. olive	50	10
2742	-	1l. red	70	10
2743	-	1l.20 black	60	10
2744	-	1l.50 purple	1·50	10
2745	-	1l.55 turquoise	80	10
2746	-	1l.60 blue	95	10
2747	-	1l.75 brown	1·20	10
2748	-	2l. brown	1·50	30
2749	-	2l.40 violet	1·60	20
2750	-	3l. blue	1·90	30
2751	-	3l.20 blue (air)	3·00	10

DESIGNS—VERT: 5b. Diesel train; 10b. Dam; 20b. Miner; 30b. Doctor; 35b. Textile worker; 50b. Children at play; 55b. Timber tractor; 1l. Atomic reactor; 1l.20, Petroleum refinery; 1l.50, Iron-works; 1l.75, Mason; 2l. Road-roller; 2l.40, Chemist; 3l. Radio communications and television. HORIZ: 40b. Grand piano and books; 60b. Combine harvester; 75b. Cattle-shed; 1l.55, Dock scene; 1l.60, Runner; 3l.20, Baneasa Airport, Bucharest.

483 Vlaicu and his Airplane No. 1 "Crazy Fly"

484 I.A.R. 817 Flying Ambulance

485 Pilot and Mikoyan Gurevich MiG-17 Jet Fighters

1960. 50th Anniv of 1st Flight by A. Vlaicu and Aviation Day.

2752	**483**	10b. brown and yellow	20	10
2753	-	20b. brown and orange	30	10
2754	**484**	35b. red	50	10
2755	-	40b. violet	70	10
2756	**485**	55b. blue	95	10
2757	-	1l.60 multicoloured	2·40	45
2758	-	1l.75 multicoloured	3·00	65

DESIGNS—As T **483**: 20b. Vlaicu in flying helmet and his No. 2 airplane; 40b. Antonov An-2 biplane spraying crops. 59×22 mm: 1l.60, Ilyushin Il-18 airliner and Baneasa airport control tower; 1l.75, Parachute descents.

486 Worker and Emblem

1960. 3rd Workers' Party Congress.

2759	**486**	55b. orange and red	1·50	45

487 Leo Tolstoy (writer)

1960. Cultural Anniversaries.

2760	**487**	10b. purple	20	10
2761	-	20b. brown	40	10
2762	-	35b. blue	50	10
2763	-	40b. green	60	20
2764	-	55b. brown	95	20
2765	-	1l. green	1·50	45
2766	-	1l.20 purple	1·60	20
2767	-	1l.55 grey	1·90	30
2768	-	1l.75 brown	3·00	55

DESIGNS: 10b. Type **487** (50th death anniv); 20b. Mark Twain (writer, 50th death anniv); 35b. Katsushika Hokusai (painter, birth bicentenary); 40b. Alfred de Musset (poet, 150th birth anniv); 55b. Daniel Defoe (writer, 300th birth anniv); 1l. Janos Bolyai (mathematician, death centenary); 1l,20, Anton Chekhov (writer, birth centenary); 1l.55, Robert Koch (bacteriologist, 50th death anniv); 1l.75, Frederic Chopin (composer, 150th birth anniv).

488 Tomis (Constantza)

1960. Black Sea Resorts. Multicoloured.

2769		20b. Type **488** (postage)	50	10
2770		35b. Constantza	70	10
2771		40b. Vasile Roaita	70	20
2772		55b. Mangalia	95	20
2773		1l. Eforie	1·50	45
2774		1l.60 Eforie (different)	2·40	30
2775		2l. Mamaia (air)	3·00	95

489 Globe and Flags

1960. International Puppet Theatre Festival, Bucharest. Designs (24×28½ mm, except 20b.) show puppets. Multicoloured.

2776		20b. Type **489**	30	10
2777		40b. Petrushka	50	10
2778		55b. Punch	60	10
2779		1l. Kaspar	1·10	20
2780		1l.20 Tindarica	1·30	20
2781		1l.75 Vasilache	1·90	30

490 Viennese Emperor Moth

1960. Air. Butterflies and Moths. Multicoloured.

2782		10b. Type **490**	30	10
2783		20b. Poplar admiral	30	10
2784		40b. Scarce copper	50	10
2785		55b. Swallowtail	95	20
2786		1l.60 Death's-head hawk moth	3·00	45
2787		1l.75 Purple emperor	4·00	55

SIZES: TRIANGULAR—36½×21½ mm: 20, 40b. VERT—23½×34 mm: 55b., 1l.60. HORIZ—34×23½ mm: 1l.75.

491 Children tobogganing

1960. Village Children's Games. Multicoloured.

2788		20b. Type **491**	20	10
2789		35b. "Oina" (ball-game) (horiz)	30	10
2790		55b. Ice-skating (horiz)	60	10
2791		1l. Running	1·20	20
2792		1l.75 Swimming (horiz)	2·50	30

492 Striker and Flag

1960. 40th Anniv of General Strike.

2793	**492**	55b. red and lake	95	45

493 Compass Points and Ilyushin Il-18 Airliner

1960. Air. Stamp Day.

2794	**493**	55b.(+45b.) blue	95	45

494 "XV", Globe and "Peace" Banner

1960. 15th Anniv of World Democratic Youth Federation.

2795	**494**	55b. yellow and blue	95	45

495 Black Sea Herrings

1960. Fishes.

2796	-	10b. brown, yell & grn	20	10
2797	-	20b. multicoloured	50	10
2798	-	40b. brn, lt brn & yell	70	10
2799	**495**	55b. grey, blue & orge	95	10
2800	-	1l. multicoloured	1·60	20
2801	-	1l.20 multicoloured	2·40	30
2802	-	1l.60 multicoloured	3·00	45

FISHES: 10b. Common carp; 20b. Zander; 40b. Black Sea turbot; 1l. Wels; 1l.20, Sterlet; 1l.60, Beluga.

496 Woman tending Vine (Cotnari)

1960. Romanian Vineyards. Multicoloured.

2803	20b. Dragasani	20	10
2804	30b. Dealul Mare (horiz)	50	10
2805	40b. Odobesti (horiz)	70	10
2806	55b. Type **496**	95	20
2807	75b. Tirnave	1·60	30
2808	1l. Minis	2·40	45
2809	1l.20 Murfatlar	3·00	75
MS2810	95×115 mm. 5l. Antique wine jug. Imperf. No gum	5·75	3·75

497 "Furnaceman" (after I. Irimescu)

1961. Romanian Sculptures.

2811	**497**	5b. red	10	10
2812	-	10b. violet	20	10
2813	-	20b. black	30	10
2814	-	40b. bistre	70	10
2815	-	50b. brown	80	10
2816	-	55b. red	1·10	10
2817	-	1l. purple	1·50	20
2818	-	1l.55 blue	2·40	30
2819	-	1l.75 green	3·00	30

SCULPTURES—VERT: 10b. "Gh. Doja" (I. Vlad); 20b. "Reunion" (B. Caragea); 40b. "Enescu" (G. Anghel); 50b. "Eminescu" (C. Baraschi); 1l. "Peace" (I. Jalea); 1l.55, "Construction Socialism" (C. Medrea); 1l.75, "Birth of an Idea" (A. Szobotka). HORIZ: 55b. "Peasant Uprising, 1907" (M. Constantinescu).

498 Slalom Racer

1961. Air. 50th Anniv of Romanian Winter Sports. (a) Perf.

2820		10b. olive and grey	30	10
2821	**498**	20b. red and grey	40	10
2822	-	25b. turquoise and grey	70	10
2823	-	40b. violet and grey	80	10
2824	-	55b. blue and grey	95	20
2825	-	1l. red and grey	1·40	30
2826	-	1l.55 brown and grey	2·10	35
		(b) Imperf.		
2827		10b. blue and grey	20	10
2828	**498**	20b. brown and grey	50	30
2829	-	25b. olive and grey	70	45
2830	-	40b. red and grey	80	75
2831	-	55b. turquoise and grey	95	95
2832	-	1l. violet and grey	1·50	1·40
2833	-	1l.55 red and grey	2·10	2·00

DESIGNS—HORIZ: Skier: racing (10b.), jumping (55b.), walking (1l.55). VERT: 25b. Skiers climbing slope; 40b. Toboggan; 1l. Rock-climber.

499 Petru Poni (chemist)

1961. Romanian Scientists. Inscr "1961". Portraits in sepia.

2834	**499**	10b. brown and pink	10	20
2835	-	20b. purple and yellow	30	20
2836	-	55b. red and blue	70	20
2837	-	1l.55 violet and orange	2·40	55

PORTRAITS: 20b. Anghel Saligny (engineer) and Saligny Bridge, Cernavoda; 55b. Constantin Budeanu (electrical engineer); 1l.55, Gheorghe Titeica (mathematician).

500 Yuri Gagarin in Capsule

1961. Air. World's First Manned Space Flight. Inscr "12 IV 1961". (a) Perf.

2838		1l.35 blue	1·40	35
2839	**500**	3l.20 blue	3·50	1·00
		(b) Imperf.		
2840		3l.20 red	11·50	4·25

DESIGN—VERT: 1l.35, Yuri Gagarin.

501 Freighter "Galati"

1961. Merchant Navy. Multicoloured.

2841	20b. Type **501**	50	10
2842	40b. "Oltenita" (Danube passenger vessel)	50	10
2843	55b. "Tomis" (hydrofoil)	70	10
2844	1l. "Arad" (freighter)	1·50	20
2845	1l.55 "N. Cristea" (tug)	2·40	30
2846	1l.75 "Dobrogea" (freighter)	3·00	45

502 Red Flag with Marx, Engels and Lenin

1961. 40th Anniv of Romanian Communist Party.

2847	**502**	35b. multicoloured	95	30
2848	-	55b. multicoloured	1·50	30
MS2849		114×80 mm. 1l. multicoloured. Imperf. No gum	3·50	1·60

DESIGNS: 55b. Two bill-posters; 1l. "Industry and Agriculture" and party emblem.

503 Eclipse over Scanteia Building and Observatory

1961. Air. Solar Eclipse.

2850		1l.60 blue	2·10	30
2851	**503**	1l.75 blue	2·50	30

DESIGN: 1l.60, Eclipse over Palace Square, Bucharest.

504 Roe Deer

1961. Forest Animals. Inscr "1961". Multicoloured.

2852	10b. Type **504**	20	20
2853	20b. Lynx (horiz)	50	20
2854	35b. Wild boar (horiz)	70	30
2855	40b. Brown bear (horiz)	1·20	30
2856	55b. Red deer	1·50	30
2857	75b. Red fox (horiz)	1·60	30
2858	1l. Chamois	1·90	30
2859	1l.55 Brown hare	2·40	45
2860	1l.75 Eurasian badger	3·00	55
2861	2l. Roe deer	3·50	95

505 George Enescu

1961. 2nd International George Enescu Festival.

2862	**505**	3l. lavender and brown	3·00	65

506 Yuri Gagarin and German Titov

1961. Air. 2nd Soviet Space Flight.

2863	-	55b. blue	95	10
2864	-	1l.35 violet	1·50	30
2865	**506**	1l.75 red	2·40	45

DESIGNS—VERT: 55b. "Vostok 2" in flight; 1l.35, G. S. Titov.

507 Iris

1961. Centenary of Bucharest Botanical Gardens. Flowers in natural colours. Background and inscription colours given. Perf or imperf.

2866	-	10b. yellow and brown	10	10
2867	-	20b. green and red	20	10
2868	-	25b. blue, green and red	30	10
2869	-	35b. lilac and grey	50	10
2870	**507**	40b. yellow and violet	70	10
2871	-	55b. blue and ultramarine	95	10
2872	-	1l. orange and blue	1·60	20
2873	-	1l.20 blue and brown	1·90	20
2874	-	1l.55 brown and lake	2·40	20
MS2875		125×92 mm. 1l.75 black, green and carmine	7·25	4·25

FLOWERS—HORIZ: 10b. Primula; 35b. Opuntia; 1l. Hepatica. VERT: 20b. Dianthus; 25b. Peony; 55b. Ranunculus; 1l.20, Poppy; 1l.55, Gentian; C. Davila, D. Brindza and Botanical Gardens buildings.

508 Cobza Player

1961. Musicians. Multicoloured.

2876	10b. Pan piper	10	10
2877	20b. Alpenhorn player (horiz)	20	10
2878	40b. Flautist	50	10
2879	55b. Type **508**	1·10	10
2880	60b. Bagpiper	1·30	20
2881	1l. Cembalo player	1·70	45

509 Heraclitus (Greek philosopher)

1961. Cultural Anniversaries.

2882	**509**	10b. purple	70	30
2883	-	20b. brown	70	30
2884	-	40b. green	70	30
2885	-	55b. mauve	1·20	30
2886	-	1l.35 blue	1·50	30
2887	-	1l.75 violet	1·90	30

DESIGNS: 20b. Sir Francis Bacon (philosopher and statesman, 400th birth anniv); 40b. Rabindranath Tagore (poet and philosopher, birth centenary); 55b. Domingo Sarmiento (writer, 150th birth anniv; 1l.35, Heinrich von Kleist (dramatist, 150th death anniv); 1l.75, Mikhail Lomonosov (writer, 250th birth anniv).

510 Olympic Flame

1961. Olympic Games 1960. Gold Medal Awards. Inscr "MELBOURNE 1956" or "ROMA 1960". Perf or imperf.

2888		10b. turquoise and ochre	20	15
2889	**510**	20b. red	20	15
2890	-	20b. grey	20	15
2891	-	35b. brown and ochre	50	15
2892	-	40b. purple and ochre	60	15
2893	-	55b. blue	70	20
2894	-	55b. blue	70	20
2895	-	55b. red and ochre	70	20
2896	-	1l.35 blue and ochre	2·40	30
2897	-	1l.75 red and ochre	3·50	40
MS2898		109×86 mm. 4l. multicoloured. Imperf. No gum	14·50	11·00

DESIGNS (Medals)—DIAMOND: 10b. Boxing; 35b. Pistol-shooting; 40b. Rifle-shooting; 55b. (No. 2895), Wrestling; 1l.35, High-jumping. VERT: as Type **510**: 20b. (No. 2890), Diving; 55b. (No. 2893), Water-polo; 55b. (No. 2894), Women's high-jumping. HORIZ—45×33 mm: 1l.75, Canoeing. Larger — 4l. Gold medals of Melbourne and Rome.

511 "Stamps Round the World"

1961. Air. Stamp Day.

2899	**511**	55b.(+45b.) blue, brown and red	1·50	65

512 Tower Building, Republic Palace Square, Bucharest

1961. Air. Modern Romanian Architecture. Mult.

2900		20b. Type **512**	30	10
2901		40b. Constantza Railway Station (horiz)	50	20
2902		55b. Congress Hall, Republic Palace, Bucharest (horiz)	60	20
2903		75b. Rolling mill, Hunedoara (horiz)	70	20
2904		1l. Apartment blocks, Bucharest (horiz)	95	20
2905		1l.20 Circus Building, Bucharest (horiz)	1·20	45
2906		1l.75 Workers' Club, Mangalia (horiz)	1·90	30

513 U.N. Emblem

1961. 15th Anniv of U.N.O. Perf or imperf.

2907	-	20b. multicoloured	30	10
2908	-	40b. multicoloured	70	20
2909	**513**	55b. multicoloured	1·20	30

DESIGNS (bearing U.N. emblem): 20b. Peace dove over Eastern Europe; 40b. Peace dove and youths of three races.

514 Workers with Flags

1961. 5th W.F.T.U. Congress, Moscow.

2910	**514**	55b. red	1·20	45

515 Cock and Savings Book

1962. Savings Day. Inscr "1962". Multicoloured.

2911		40b. Type **515**	50	30
2912		55b. Savings Bank book, bee and "honeycombs" of agriculture, housing and industry	70	30

516 Footballer

1962. European Junior Football Competition, Bucharest.

2913	**516**	55b. brown and green	1·90	45

517 Ear of Corn, Map and Tractor

1962. Completion of Agricultural Collectivisation Project. Inscr "1962".

2914	**517**	40b. red and orange	30	10
2915	-	55b. lake and yellow	50	10
2916	-	1l.55 yellow, red and blue	1·20	45

DESIGNS: 55b. Commemorative medal; 1l.55, Wheatsheaf, and hammer and sickle emblem.

518 Handball Player

1962. Women's World Handball Championships, Bucharest.

2917	**518**	55b. violet and yellow	1·90	45

519 Canoe Race

1962. Boating and Sailing. Inscr "1962". (a) Perf.

2918	**519**	10b. blue and mauve	30	10
2919	-	20b. blue and brown	40	10
2920	-	40b. blue and brown	60	10
2921	-	55b. blue and ultramarine	70	20
2922	-	1l. blue and red	1·40	20
2923	-	1l.20 blue and purple	1·60	20
2924	-	1l.55 blue and red	1·90	20
2925	-	3l. blue and violet	3·00	55

(b) Imperf. Colours changed.

2926	**519**	10b. blue and ultramarine	30	30
2927	-	20b. blue and mauve	50	30
2928	-	40b. blue and red	80	55
2929	-	55b. blue and brown	95	75
2930	-	1l. blue and brown	1·60	95
2931	-	1l.20 blue and violet	1·80	1·00
2932	-	1l.55 blue and red	2·10	1·10
2933	-	3l. blue and purple	4·00	1·90

DESIGNS: 20b. Kayak; 40b. Racing "eight"; 55b. Sculling; 1l. "Star" yachts; 1l.20, Power boats; 1l.55, "Flying Dutchman" dinghy; 3l. Canoe slalom.

520 Jean Jacques Rousseau

1962. Cultural Anniversaries (writers).

2934	**520**	40b. green	40	20
2935	-	55b. purple	50	30
2936	-	1l.75 blue	1·10	20
MS2937		91×122 mm. 3l.30 brown	7·25	5·50

DESIGNS: 40b. T **520** (250th birth anniv); 55b. Ion Caragiale (dramatist, 50th death anniv); 1l.75, Aleksandr Herzen (150th birth anniv). 32×55 mm—3l.30 Caragiale (full-length portrait).

521 Flags and Globes

1962. World Youth Festival, Helsinki.

2938	**521**	55b. multicoloured	1·50	45

522 Traian Vuia (aviator)

1962. Romanian Celebrities.

2939	**522**	15b. brown	20	20
2940	-	20b. red	30	20
2941	-	35b. purple	50	20
2942	-	40b. blue	60	20
2943	-	55b. blue	70	20
2944	-	1l. blue	1·20	20
2945	-	1l.20 red	1·50	30
2946	-	1l.35 turquoise	1·60	30
2947	-	1l.55 violet	1·90	20

PORTRAITS: 20b. Alexandru Davila (writer); 35b. Vasile Pirvan (archaeologist); 40b. Ion Negulici (painter); 55b. Grigore Cobilcescu (geologist); 1l. Dr. Gheorghe Marinescu (neurologist); 1l.20, Dr. Ion Cantacuzino (bacteriologist); 1l.35, Dr. Victor Babes (bacteriologist and pathologist; 1l.55, Dr. Constantin Levaditi (medical researcher).

523 Anglers by Pond

1962. Fishing Sport. Multicoloured.

2948		10b. Rod-fishing in fishing punts	10	10
2949		25b. Line-fishing in mountain pool	20	10
2950		40b. Type **523**	50	15
2951		55b. Anglers on beach	60	15
2952		75b. Line-fishing in mountain stream	95	15
2953		1l. Shore-fishing	1·10	20
2954		1l.75 Freshwater-fishing	1·70	20
2955		3l.25 Fishing in Danube delta	3·00	25

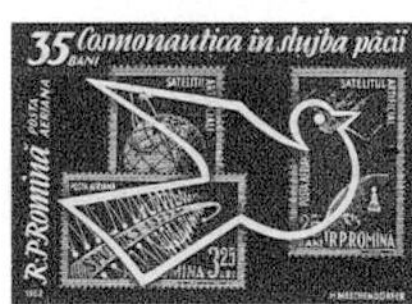

524 Dove and "Space" Stamps of 1957/58

1962. Air. Cosmic Flights.

2956	**524**	35b. brown	20	10
2957	-	55b. green	50	20
2958	-	1l.35 blue	1·20	30
2959	-	1l.75 red	1·90	35
MS2960		107×79 mm. Nos. 2956/9, but imperf and colours changed: 35b. blue, 55b. brown; 1l.35 red; 1l.75 green	5·25	1·90

DESIGNS—Dove and: 55b. "Space" stamps of 1959; 1l.35, "Space" stamps of 1957 ("Laika"), 1959 and 1960; 1l.75, "Spacemen" stamps of 1961.

1962. Romanian Victory in European Junior Football Competition, Bucharest. Surch 1962. Campioana Europeana 2 lei.

2961	**516**	2l. on 55b. brown & grn	4·00	3·75

1962. Romanian Victory in Women's World Handball Championships, Bucharest. Surch Campioana Mondiala 5 lei.

2962	**518**	5l. on 55b. vio & yell	7·25	4·75

527 "Vostok 3" and "4" in Orbit

1962. Air. 1st "Team" Manned Space Flight.

2963	-	55b. violet	50	20
2964	**527**	1l.60 blue	1·50	40
2965	-	1l.75 purple	1·90	45

DESIGNS: 55b. Andrian Nikolaev (cosmonaut); 1l.75, Pavel Popovich (cosmonaut).

528 Child and Butterfly

1962. Children.

2966	**528**	20b. blue, brown and red	30	10
2967	-	30b. yellow, blue and red	35	10
2968	-	40b. blue, red & turquoise	40	10
2969	-	55b. olive, blue and red	70	10
2970	-	1l.20 red, brown & blue	1·90	25
2971	-	1l.55 ochre, blue and red	3·00	30

DESIGNS—VERT: 30b. Girl feeding dove; 40b. Boy with model yacht; 1l.20, Boy violinist and girl pianist. HORIZ: 55b. Girl teaching boy to write; 1l.55, Pioneers around camp-fire.

529 Pottery

1962. 4th Sample Fair, Bucharest. Inscr "AL IV-LEA PAVILION DE MOSTRE BUCURESTI 1962". Multicoloured.

2972		5b. Type **529** (postage)	60	15
2973		10b. Preserved foodstuffs	70	15
2974		20b. Chemical products	80	15
2975		40b. Ceramics	85	10
2976		55b. Leather goods	1·10	10
2977		75b. Textiles	1·30	10
2978		1l. Furniture and fabrics	1·50	10
2979		1l.20 Office equipment	1·90	10
2980		1l.55 Needlework	2·50	10
2981		1l.60 Fair pavilion (horiz) (air)	3·00	30

530 Lenin and Red Flag

1962. 45th Anniv of Russian Revolution.

2982	**530**	55b. brown, red and blue	1·50	45

531 "The Coachmen" (after Szatmay)

1962. Air. Stamp Day and Centenary of 1st Romanian Stamps.

2983	**531**	55b.(+45b.) black and blue	1·90	55

532 Lamb

1962. Prime Farm Stock.

2984	**532**	20b. black and blue	20	10
2985	-	40b. brown, yellow & blue	30	10
2986	-	55b. green, buff and orange	50	10
2987	-	1l. brown, buff and grey	80	10
2988	-	1l.35 brown, black & green	1·20	20
2989	-	1l.55 brown, black & red	1·30	30
2990	-	1l.75 brown, cream & blue	1·90	65

DESIGNS—HORIZ: 40b. Ram; 1l.55, Heifer; 1l.75, Sows. VERT: 55b. Bull; 1l. Pig; 1l.35, Cow.

533 Arms, Industry and Agriculture

1962. 15th Anniv of People's Republic.

2991	**533**	1l.55 multicoloured	1·90	45

534 Strikers

1963. 30th Anniv of Grivitsa Strike.

2992	**534**	1l.75 multicoloured	1·90	45

535 Tractor-driver

1963. Freedom from Hunger.

2993	**535**	40b. blue	30	10
2994	-	55b. brown	60	10
2995	-	1l.55 red	1·50	20
2996	-	1l.75 green	1·60	30

DESIGNS (each with F.A.O. emblem): 55b. Girl harvester; 1l.55, Child with beaker of milk; 1l.75, Girl vintager.

1963. Air. Romanian Philatelists' Conference, Bucharest. No. 2983 optd A.F.R. surrounded by CONFERINTA PE TARA BUCURESTI 30-III-1963 in diamond shape.

2997	**531**	55b.(+45b.) blk & bl	6·25	6·00

The opt is applied in the middle of the se-tenant pair—stamp and 45b. label.

537 Sighisoara Glass Factory

1963. Air. "Socialist Achievements".

2998	**537**	30b. blue and red	30	10
2999	-	40b. green and violet	50	15
3000	-	55b. red and blue	70	15
3001	-	1l. violet and brown	1·10	20
3002	-	1l.55 red and blue	1·30	25
3003	-	1l.75 blue and purple	1·50	30

DESIGNS: 40b. Govora soda works; 55b. Tirgul-Jiu wood factory; 1l. Savinesti chemical works; 1l.55, Hunedoara metal works; 1l.75, Brazi thermic power station.

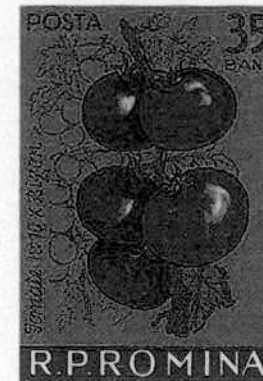

538 Tomatoes

1963. Vegetable Culture. Multicoloured.

3004	35b. Type **538**	30	10
3005	40b. Hot peppers	60	10
3006	55b. Radishes	70	15
3007	75b. Aubergines	95	20
3008	1l.20 Mild peppers	1·50	30
3009	3l.25 Cucumbers (horiz)	3·00	45

539 Moon Rocket "Luna 4"

1963. Air. Launching of Soviet Moon Rocket "Luna 4". The 1l.75 is imperf.

3010	**539**	55b. red and blue	60	30
3011	**539**	1l.75 red and violet	1·90	30

540 Chick

1963. Domestic Poultry.

3012	**540**	20b. yellow and blue	30	10
3013	-	30b. red, blue and brown	50	10
3014	-	40b. blue, orange & brn	60	10
3015	-	55b. multicoloured	70	10
3016	-	70b. blue, red and purple	80	10
3017	-	1l. red, grey and blue	95	15
3018	-	1l.35 red, blue and ochre	1·10	20
3019	-	3l.20 multicoloured	2·10	35

POULTRY: 30b. Cockerel; 40b. Duck; 55b. White Leghorn; 70b. Goose; 1l. Rooster; 1l.35, Turkey (cock); 3l.20, Turkey (hen).

541 Diving

1963. Swimming. Bodies in drab.

3020	**541**	25b. green and brown	20	10
3021	-	30b. yellow and olive	30	10
3022	-	55b. red and turquoise	50	10
3023	-	1l. red and green	80	15
3024	-	1l.35 mauve and blue	95	15
3025	-	1l.55 orange and violet	1·70	20
3026	-	2l. yellow and mauve	1·70	45

DESIGNS—HORIZ: 30b. Crawl; 55b. Butterfly; 1l. Back stroke; 1l.35, Breast stroke. VERT: 1l.55, Swallow diving; 2l. Water polo.

542 Congress Emblem

1963. International Women's Congress, Moscow.

3027	**542**	55b. blue	95	45

543 Valery Bykovsky and Globe

1963. Air. 2nd "Team" Manned Space Flights.

3028	**543**	55b. blue	70	20
3029	-	1l.75 red	2·40	45
MS3030		118×80 mm. 1l.20, 1l.60 blue	4·75	2·30

DESIGNS: 1l.75 Valentina Tereshkova and globe; 25×41 mm—1l.20 Bykovsky; 1l.60 Tereshkova.

The stamps in No. **MS**3030 form a composite design.

544 Class 142 Steam Locomotive, 1936

1963. Air. Transport. Multicoloured.

3031	40b. Type **544**	60	20
3032	55b. Class 060-DA diesel-electric locomotive, 1959	70	20
3033	75b. Trolley bus	95	30
3034	1l.35 "Oltenita" (Danube passenger vessel)	2·10	35
3035	1l.75 Ilyushin Il-18 airplane	3·00	45

545 William Thackeray (novelist)

1963. Cultural Anniversaries. Inscr "MARILE ANNIVERSARI CULTURALE 1963".

3036	**545**	40b. black and lilac	30	15
3037	-	50b. black and brown	60	15
3038	-	55b. black and olive	80	15
3039	-	1l.55 black and red	1·60	15
3040	-	1l.75 black and blue	1·90	30

PORTRAITS: 40b. Type **545** (death centenary); 50b. Eugene Delacroix (painter, death centenary); 55b. Gheorghe Marinescu (neurologist, birth centenary); 1l.55, Giuseppe Verdi (composer, 150th birth anniv); 1l.75, Konstantin Stanislavsky (actor and stage director, birth centenary).

546 Walnuts

1963. Fruits and Nuts. Multicoloured.

3041	10b. Type **546**	50	10
3042	20b. Plums	50	10
3043	40b. Peaches	80	10
3044	55b. Strawberries	1·10	10
3045	1l. Grapes	1·20	15
3046	1l.55 Apples	1·60	20
3047	1l.60 Cherries	2·10	30
3048	1l.75 Pears	2·50	30

1963. Air. 50th Death Anniv of Aurel Vlaicu (aviation pioneer). No. 2752 surch 1913–1963 50 ani de la moarte 1,75 lei.

3049	**483**	1l.75 on 10b. brn & yell	4·75	1·90

549 Romanian 1l.55 "Centenary" Stamp of 1958

1963. Air. Stamp Day and 15th U.P.U. Congress. Inscr "AL XV-LEA CONGRESS", etc.

3055	**549**	20b. brown and blue	20	10
3056	-	40b. blue and mauve	25	10
3057	-	55b. mauve and blue	30	10
3058	-	1l.20 violet and buff	70	15
3059	-	1l.55 green and red	1·10	20
3060	-	1l.60+50b. mult	2·10	45

DESIGNS (Romanian stamps): 40b. (1l.20) "Laika", 1957 (blue); 55b. (3l.20) "Gagarin", 1961; 1l.20, (55b.) "Nikolaev" and (1l.75) "Popovich", 1962; 1l.55, (55b.) "Postwoman", 1953; 1l.60, U.P.U. Monument, Berne, globe, map of Romania and aircraft (76×27 mm).

551 Ski Jumping

1963. Winter Olympic Games, Innsbruck, 1964. (a) Perf.

3061	**551**	10b. blue and red	50	20
3062	-	20b. brown and blue	70	20
3063	-	40b. brown and green	85	10
3064	-	55b. brown and violet	1·10	20
3065	-	60b. blue and brown	1·20	30
3066	-	75b. blue and mauve	1·50	45
3067	-	1l. blue and ochre	1·90	45
3068	-	1l.20 blue and turquoise	2·40	65

(b) Imperf. Colours changed.

3069	**551**	10b. brown and green	1·50	95
3070	-	20b. brown and violet	1·50	95
3071	-	40b. blue and red	1·50	95
3072	-	55b. brown and blue	1·50	95
3073	-	60b. blue and turquoise	1·50	95
3074	-	75b. blue and ochre	1·50	95
3075	-	1l. blue and mauve	1·50	95
3076	-	1l.20 blue and brown	1·50	95
MS3077		120×80 mm. 1l.50 ultramarine and red	11·50	9·25

DESIGNS: 20b. Speed skating; 40b. Ice hockey; 55b. Figure skating; 60b. Slalom; 75b. Biathlon; 1l. Bobsleighing; 1l.20 Cross-country skiing. HORIZ: 1l.55 Stadium, Innsbruck.

552 Cone, Fern and Conifer

1963. 18th Anniv of Reafforestation Campaign.

3078	**552**	55b. green	30	20
3079	-	1l.75 blue	1·20	30

DESIGN: 1l.75, Chestnut trees.

553 Silkworm Moth

1963. Bee-keeping and Silkworm-breeding. Mult.

3080	10b. Type **553**	50	10
3081	20b. Moth emerging from chrysalis	70	10
3082	40b. Silkworm	85	15
3083	55b. Honey bee (horiz)	95	20
3084	60b. Honey bee on flower	1·20	30
3085	1l.20 Honey bee approaching orange flowers (horiz)	1·60	45
3086	1l.35 Honey bee approaching pink flowers (horiz)	2·10	55
3087	1l.60 Honey bee and sunflowers (horiz)	2·40	65

548 Volleyball

1963. European Volleyball Championships.

3050	**548**	5b. mauve and grey	50	10
3051	-	40b. blue and grey	70	10
3052	-	55b. turquoise and grey	95	15
3053	-	1l.75 brown and grey	1·90	30
3054	-	3l.20 violet and grey	3·00	45

DESIGNS: 40b. to 1l.75, Various scenes of play at net; 3l.20, European Cup.

554 Carved Pillar

1963. Village Museum, Bucharest.

3088	**554**	20b. purple	30	10
3089	-	40b. blue (horiz)	50	10
3090	-	55b. violet (horiz)	60	10
3091	-	75b. green	80	10
3092	-	1l. red and brown	1·20	10
3093	-	1l.20 green	1·50	15
3094	-	1l.75 blue and brown	2·40	15

DESIGNS: Various Romanian peasant houses.

555 Yuri Gagarin

1964. Air. "Space Navigation". Soviet flag, red and yellow; U.S. flag, red and blue; backgrounds, light blue; portrait and inscription colours below. (a) Perf.

3095	**555**	5b. blue	30	10
3096	-	10b. violet	50	10
3097	-	20b. bronze	60	10
3098	-	35b. grey	65	10
3099	-	40b. violet	70	15
3100	-	55b. violet	85	20
3101	-	60b. brown	95	30
3102	-	75b. blue	1·20	35
3103	-	1l. purple	1·60	45
3104	-	1l.40 purple	1·90	95

(b) Imperf. Colours changed.

3105	**555**	5b. violet	10	10
3106	-	10b. blue	10	10
3107	-	20b. grey	40	15
3108	-	35b. bronze	85	45
3109	-	40b. purple	1·20	55
3110	-	55b. purple	1·60	65
3111	-	60b. blue	1·60	95
3112	-	75b. brown	2·10	1·30
3113	-	1l. violet	2·50	1·60
3114	-	1l.40 violet	3·25	2·40
MS3115		120×80 mm. 2l. multicoloured	11·50	9·25

PORTRAITS (with flags of their countries)—As Type **555**: 10b. German Titov; 20b. John Glenn; 35b. Scott Carpenter; 60b. Walter Schirra; 75b. Gordon Cooper. 35½×33½ mm: 40b. Andrian Nikolaev; 55b. Pavel Popovich; 1l. Valery Bykovsky; 1l.40, Valentina Tereshkova. 59×43 mm—2l. Globe, orbits, laurel sprigs and commemorative dates.

556 George Stephanescu (composer)

1964. Romanian Opera Singers and their stage roles. Portraits in brown.

3116	**556**	10b. olive	50	10
3117	-	20b. blue	60	10
3118	-	35b. green	70	10
3119	-	40b. light blue	80	10
3120	-	55b. mauve	95	10
3121	-	75b. violet	1·10	10
3122	-	1l. blue	1·20	20
3123	-	1l.35 violet	1·50	20
3124	-	1l.55 red	2·40	30

DESIGNS: 20b. Elena Teodorini in "Carmen"; 35b. Ion Bajenaru in "Petru Rares"; 40b. Dimitrie Popovici-Bayreuth as Alberich in "Ring of the Nibelung"; 55b. Haricled Dardee in "Tosca"; 75b. George Folescu in "Boris Godunov"; 1l. Jean Athanasiu in "Rigoletto"; 1l.35, Traian Grosarescu as Duke in "Rigoletto"; 1l.55, Nicolae Leonard as Hoffmann in "Tales of Hoffmann".

557 Prof. G. M. Murgoci

1964. 8th International Soil Congress, Bucharest.

3125	**557**	1l.60 indigo, ochre and blue	1·20	45

558 "Ascalaphus macaronius" (owl-fly)

1964. Insects. Multicoloured.

3126	5b. Type **558**	20	10
3127	10b. "Ammophila sabulosa" (digger wasp)	30	10
3128	35b. "Scolia maculata" (dagger wasp)	50	10
3129	40b. Swamp tiger moth	60	10
3130	55b. Gypsy moth	70	15
3131	1l.20 Great banded grayling	1·10	20
3132	1l.55 "Carabus fabricii malachiticus" (ground beetle)	1·60	20
3133	1l.75 "Procerus gigas" (ground beetle)	2·10	30

559 "Nicotiana alata"

1964. Romanian Flowers. Multicoloured.

3134	10b. Type **559**	30	15
3135	20b. "Pelargonium"	50	15
3136	40b. "Fuchsia gracilis"	60	15
3137	55b. "Chrysanthemum indicum"	70	15
3138	75b. "Dahlia hybrida"	80	15
3139	1l. "Lilium croceum"	1·50	20
3140	1l.25 "Hosta ovata"	1·60	30
3141	1l.55 "Tagetes erectus"	1·90	30

560 Cross Country

1964. Horsemanship.

3142	-	40b. multicoloured	50	10
3143	**560**	55b. brown, red and lilac	70	20
3144	-	1l.35 brown, red & green	1·60	30
3145	-	1l.55 mauve, blue & bis	2·40	45

DESIGNS—HORIZ: 40b. Dressage; 1l.55, Horse race. VERT: 1l.35, Show jumping.

561 Brown Scorpionfish

1964. Constantza Aquarium. Fish designs. Mult.

3146	5b. Type **561**	10	10
3147	10b. Peacock blenny	10	10
3148	20b. Black Sea horse-mackerel	20	10
3149	40b. Russian sturgeon	50	10
3150	50b. Short-snouted seahorse	60	20
3151	55b. Tub gurnard	70	20
3152	1l. Beluga	1·20	20

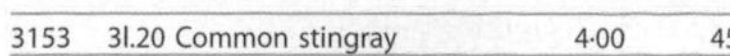

3153	3l.20 Common stingray	4·00	45

562 M. Eminescu (poet)

1964. Cultural Anniversaries. Portraits in brown.

3154	**562**	5b. green	20	10
3155	-	20b. red	20	10
3156	-	35b. red	50	10
3157	-	55b. bistre	70	10
3158	-	1l.20 blue	1·50	20
3159	-	1l.75 violet	1·90	45

DESIGNS: Type **562** (75th death anniv); 20b. Ion Creanga (folklorist, 75th death anniv); 35b. Emil Girleanu (writer, 50th death anniv); 55b. Michelangelo (artist, 400th death anniv); 1l.20, Galileo Galilei (astronomer, 400th birth anniv); 1l.75, William Shakespeare (dramatist, 400th birth anniv).

563 Cheile Bicazului (gorge)

1964. Mountain Resorts.

3160	**563**	40b. lake	50	10
3161	-	55b. blue	70	10
3162	-	1l. purple	95	10
3163	-	1l.35 brown	1·20	15
3164	-	1l.75 green	1·90	20

DESIGNS—VERT: 55b. Cabin on Lake Bilea; 1l. Poiana Brasov ski-lift; 1l.75, Alpine Hotel. HORIZ: 1l.35, Lake Bicaz.

564 High Jumping

1964. Balkan Games. Multicoloured.

3165	30b. Type **564**	30	10
3166	40b. Throwing the javelin	30	10
3167	55b. Running	60	10
3168	1l. Throwing the discus	1·20	15
3169	1l.20 Hurdling	1·20	15
3170	1l.55 Flags of competing countries (24×44 mm)	1·40	20

565 Arms and Flag

1964. 20th Anniv of Liberation. Multicoloured.

3171	55b. Type **565**	40	10
3172	60b. Industrial plant (horiz)	50	15
3173	75b. Harvest scene (horiz)	60	20
3174	1l.20 Apartment houses (horiz)	1·10	30
MS3175	131×94 mm. 2l. "Agriculture and Industry". Imperf. No gum	4·25	2·75

566 High Jumping

1964. Olympic Games, Tokyo. Multicoloured. (a) Perf.

3176	20b. Type **566**	30	10
3177	30b. Wrestling	50	10
3178	35b. Volleyball	60	15
3179	40b. Canoeing	70	20
3180	55b. Fencing	95	20
3181	1l.20 Gymnastics	1·10	30
3182	1l.35 Football	1·50	45
3183	1l.55 Rifle-shooting	1·90	55

(b) Imperf. Colours changed and new values.

3184	20b. Type **566**	40	10
3185	30b. Wrestling	50	10
3186	35b. Volleyball	80	15
3187	40b. Canoeing	85	20
3188	55b. Fencing	1·70	55
3189	1l.60 Gymnastics	3·50	1·50
3190	2l. Football	3·75	1·90
3191	2l.40 Rifle-shooting	4·50	2·75
MS3192	80×110 mm. 3l.25 Runner (no gum)	11·50	7·00

567 George Enescu

1964. 3rd International George Enescu Festival.

3193	**567**	10b. green	20	10
3194	-	55b. purple	60	20
3195	-	1l.60 purple	1·60	65
3196	-	1l.75 blue	2·10	45

DESIGNS (Portraits of Enescu): 55b. At piano; 1l.60, Medallion; 1l.75, When an old man.

568 Python

1964. Bucharest Zoo. Multicoloured.

3197	5b. Type **568**	10	10
3198	10b. Black swans	40	10
3199	35b. Ostriches	50	10
3200	40b. Crowned cranes	70	20
3201	55b. Tigers	80	20
3202	1l. Lions	1·40	20
3203	1l.55 Grevy's zebras	2·10	20
3204	2l. Bactrian camels	3·00	45

569 Brincoveanu, Cantacuzino, Lazar and Academy

1964. Anniversaries. Multicoloured.

3205	20b. Type **569**	10	10
3206	40b. Cuza and seal	20	10
3207	55b. Emblems and the Arts (vert)	30	15
3208	75b. Laboratory workers and class	50	20
3209	1l. Savings Bank building	80	45

EVENTS, etc—HORIZ: 20b. 270th Anniv of Domneasca Academy; 40b., 75b. Bucharest University centenary; 1l. Savings Bank centenary. VERT: 55b. "Fine Arts" centenary (emblems are masks, curtain, piano keyboard, harp, palette and brushes).

570 Soldier

1964. Centenary of Army Day.

3210	570	55b. blue and light blue	80	45

571 Post Office of 19th and 20th Centuries

1964. Air. Stamp Day.

3211	571	1l.60+40b. blue, red and yellow	1·90	95

No. 3211 is a two-part design, the two parts being arranged vert, imperf between.

572 Canoeing Medal (1956)

1964. Olympic Games—Romanian Gold Medal Awards. Medals in brown and bistre (Nos. 3218/19 and 3226/7 in sepia and gold). (a) Perf.

3212	572	20b. red and blue	50	10
3213	-	30b. green and blue	60	15
3214	-	35b. turquoise and blue	70	20
3215	-	40b. lilac and blue	95	25
3216	-	55b. orange and blue	1·20	30
3217	-	1l.20 green and blue	1·50	35
3218	-	1l.35 brown and blue	1·90	45
3219	-	1l.55 mauve and blue	2·40	45

(b) Imperf. Colours changed and new values.

3220	572	20b. orange and blue	20	20
3221	-	30b. turquoise and blue	50	35
3222	-	35b. green and blue	50	35
3223	-	40b. green and blue	80	55
3224	-	55b. red and blue	80	55
3225	-	1l.60 lilac and blue	2·40	1·90
3226	-	2l. mauve and blue	3·00	2·40
3227	-	2l.40 brown and blue	4·00	3·25
MS3228		140×110 mm. 10l. gold, blue and blue (no gum)	14·50	11·00

MEDALS: 30b. Boxing (1956); 35b. Pistol-shooting (1956); 40b. High-jumping (1960); 55b. Wrestling (1960); 1l.20, 1l.60, Rifle-shooting (1960); 1l.35, 2l. High-jumping (1964); 1l.55, 2l.40, Throwing the javelin (1964). HORIZ: 10l. Tokyo gold medal and world map.

573 Strawberries

1964. Forest Fruits. Multicoloured.

3229	5b. Type **573**	20	10
3230	35b. Blackberries	30	10
3231	40b. Raspberries	50	15
3232	55b. Rosehips	60	15
3233	1l.20 Blueberries	1·20	20
3234	1l.35 Cornelian cherries	1·50	20
3235	1l.55 Hazel nuts	1·60	20
3236	2l.55 Cherries	2·10	30

574 "Syncom 3"

1965. Space Navigation. Multicoloured.

3237	30b. Type **574**	30	10
3238	40b. "Syncom 3" (different)	50	10
3239	55b. "Ranger 7" (horiz)	80	15
3240	1l. "Ranger 7" (different) (horiz)	95	20
3241	1l.20 "Voskhod 1" (horiz)	1·50	20
3242	5l. Konstantin Feoktistov, Vladimir Komarov and Boris Yegorov (cosmonauts) and "Voskhod 1" (52×29 mm)	3·50	1·20

575 U.N. Headquarters, New York

1965. 20th Anniv of U.N.O.

3243	575	55b. gold, blue and red	70	20
3244	-	1l.60 multicoloured	1·20	45

DESIGN: 1l.60, Arms and U.N. emblem on Romanian flag.

576 Spur-thighed Tortoise

1965. Reptiles. Multicoloured.

3245	5b. Type **576**	15	10
3246	10b. Crimean lizard	20	10
3247	20b. Three-lined lizard	20	10
3248	40b. Snake-eyed skink	40	10
3249	55b. Slow worm	50	10
3250	60b. Sand viper	70	10
3251	1l. Arguta	85	20
3252	1l.20 Orsini's viper	95	20
3253	1l.35 European whip snake	1·50	20
3254	3l.25 Four-lined rat snake	3·00	45

577 Tabby Cat

1965. Domestic Cats. Multicoloured.

3255	5b. Type **577**	20	10
3256	10b. Ginger tomcat	30	10
3257	40b. White Persians (vert)	50	20
3258	55b. Kittens with shoe (vert)	70	10
3259	60b. Kitten with ball of wool (vert)	1·10	10
3260	75b. Cat and two kittens (vert)	1·50	15
3261	1l.35 Siamese (vert)	1·90	30
3262	3l.25 Heads of three cats (62×29 mm)	3·50	95

1965. Space Flight of "Ranger 9" (24.3.65). No. 3240 surch RANGER 9 24-3-1965 5 Lei and floral emblem over old value.

3263	5l. on 1l. multicoloured	29·00	29·00

579 Ion Bianu (philologist)

1965. Cultural Anniversaries. Portraits in sepia.

3264	579	40l. blue	40	10
3265	-	55b. ochre	40	10
3266	-	60b. purple	50	10
3267	-	1l. red	70	15
3268	-	1l.35 olive	95	20
3269	-	1l.75 red	1·60	45

PORTRAITS, etc: 40b. Type **579** (30th death anniv); 55b. Anton Bacalbasa (writer, birth cent); 60b. Vasile Conta (philosopher, 120th birth anniv); 1l. Jean Sibelius (composer, birth cent); 1l.35, Horace (Roman poet, birth bimillenary); 1l.75, Dante Alighieri (poet, 700th birth anniv).

580 I.T.U. Emblem and Symbols

1965. Centenary of I.T.U.

3270	580	1l.75 blue	1·60	45

581 Derdap Gorge (The Iron Gate)

1965. Inaug of Derdap Hydro-electric Project.

3271	581	30b. (25d.) green and grey	30	20
3272	-	55b. (50d.) red and grey	50	30
MS3273		103×80 mm. 80b., 1l.20, 100d., 150d. multicoloured (sold at 4l. or 500d.)	4·75	4·75

DESIGNS: 55b. Derap Dam; **MS**3273, Arms of Romania and Yugoslavia on alternate stamps with outline of dam superimposed over the four stamps.

582 Rifleman

1965. European Shooting Championships, Bucharest. Multicoloured. (a) Perf.

3274	20b. Type **582**	20	10
3275	40b. Prone rifleman	30	15
3276	55b. Pistol shooting	50	10
3277	1l. "Free" pistol shooting	95	20
3278	1l.60 Standing rifleman	1·50	20
3279	2l. Various marksmen	1·90	65

(b) Imperf. Colours changed and new values.

3280	40b. Prone rifleman	20	10
3281	55b. Pistol shooting	30	20
3282	1l. "Free" pistol shooting	70	30
3283	1l.60 Standing rifleman	1·10	45
3284	3l.25 Type **582**	1·90	95
3285	5l. Various marksmen	3·50	1·60

Apart from Type **582** the designs are horiz, the 2l. and 5l. being larger, 51½×28½ mm.

583 "Fat-Frumos and the Beast"

1965. Romanian Fairy Tales. Multicoloured.

3286	20b. Type **583**	40	10
3287	40b. "Fat-Frumos and Ileana Cosinzeana"	40	10
3288	55b. "Harap Alb" (horseman and bear)	50	10
3289	1l. "The Moralist Wolf"	95	10
3290	1l.35 "The Ox and the Calf"	1·50	20
3291	2l. "The Bear and the Wolf" (drawing a sledge)	1·90	35

584 Honey Bee on Flowers

1965. 20th International Bee-keeping Association Federation ("Apimondia") Congress, Bucharest.

3292	584	55b. black, red and yellow	70	20
3293	-	1l.60 multicoloured	1·70	30

DESIGN—HORIZ: 1l.60, Congress Hall.

585 Pavel Belyaev, Aleksei Leonov, "Voskhod 2" and Leonov in Space

1965. Space Achievements. Multicoloured.

3294	5b. "Proton 1"	30	15
3295	10b. "Sonda 3" (horiz)	40	30
3296	15b. "Molnia 1"	50	35
3297	1l.75 Type **585**	1·60	20
3298	2l.40 "Early Bird" satellite	2·40	30
3299	3l.20 "Gemini 3" and astronauts in capsule	4·00	45
3300	3l.25 "Mariner 4"	4·25	65
3301	5l. "Gemini 5" (horiz)	4·75	1·90

586 Marx and Lenin

1965. Socialist Countries' Postal Ministers' Congress, Peking.

3302	586	55b. multicoloured	95	45

587 Common Quail

1965. Migratory Birds. Multicoloured.

3303	5b. Type **587**	20	10
3304	10b. Eurasian woodcock	30	10
3305	20b. Common snipe	40	10
3306	40b. Turtle dove	50	10
3307	55b. Mallard	60	10
3308	60b. White fronted goose	70	15
3309	1l. Common crane	95	20
3310	1l.20 Glossy ibis	1·20	20
3311	1l.35 Mute swan	1·50	30
3312	3l.25 Eastern white pelican (32×73 mm)	3·00	95

588 V. Alecsandri

1965. 75th Death Anniv of Vasile Alecsandri (poet).

3313	**588**	55b. multicoloured	95	45

589 Zanzibar Water-lily

1965. Cluj Botanical Gardens. Multicoloured.

3314	5b. Bird-of-paradise flower (vert)	15	10
3315	10b. "Stanhopea tigrina" (orchid) (vert)	20	10
3316	20b. "Paphiopedilum insigne" (orchid) (vert)	25	10
3317	30b. Type **589**	30	10
3318	40b. "Ferocactus glaucescens" (cactus)	50	10
3319	55b. Tree-cotton	70	15
3320	1l. "Hibiscus rosa sinensis"	95	20
3321	1l.35 "Gloxinia hibrida" (vert)	1·50	20
3322	1l.75 Amazon water-lily	2·40	25
3323	2l.30 Hibiscus, water-lily, bird-of-paradise flower and botanical building (52×30 mm)	3·00	65

590 Running

1965. Spartacist Games. Multicoloured.

3324	55b. Type **590**	50	20
3325	1l.55 Football	1·20	30
3326	1l.75 Diving	1·40	35
3327	2l. Mountaineering (inscr "TURISM")	1·50	45
3328	5l. Canoeing (inscr "CAMPIONATELLE EUROPENE 1965") (horiz)	2·50	95

591 Pigeon and Horseman

592 Pigeon on TV Aerial

1965. Stamp Day.

3329	**591**	55b.+45b. blue & mve	70	10
3330	**592**	1l. brown and green	80	30
3331	-	1l.75 brown and green	1·90	45

DESIGN: As Type **592**: 1l.75, Pigeon in flight.

593 Chamois

1965. "Hunting Trophies".

3332	**593**	55b. brown, yell & mve	50	10
3333	-	1l. brown, green and red	95	20
3334	-	1l.60 brown, blue & orange	1·60	30
3335	-	1l.75 brown, red & green	1·90	35
3336	-	3l.20 multicoloured	2·40	85

DESIGNS—37×23 mm: 1l. Brown bear; 1l.60, Red deer stag; 1l.75, Wild boar. 49×37½ mm: 3l.20, Trophy and antlers of red deer.

594 Dachshund

1965. Hunting Dogs. Multicoloured.

3337	5b. Type **594**	10	10
3338	10b. Spaniel	20	10
3339	40b. Retriever with eurasian woodcock	40	10
3340	55b. Fox terrier	60	10
3341	60b. Red setter	95	20
3342	75b. White setter	1·50	20
3343	1l.55 Pointers	2·40	45
3344	3l.25 Duck-shooting with retriever	3·50	1·60

SIZES: DIAMOND—47½×47½ mm: 10b. to 75b. HORIZ—43½×29 mm: 1l.55, 3l.25.

595 Pawn and Globe

1966. World Chess Championships, Cuba. Mult.

3345	20b. Type **595**	50	10
3346	40b. Jester and bishop	60	10
3347	55b. Knight and rook	85	15
3348	1l. As No. 3347	1·50	20
3349	1l.60 Type **595**	2·40	30
3350	3l.25 As No. 3346	4·00	1·90

596 Tractor, Corn and Sun

1966. Co-operative Farming Union Congress.

3351	**596**	55b. green and yellow	70	45

597 G. Gheorghiu-Dej

1966. 1st Death Anniv of Gheorghe Gheorghiu-Dej (President 1961–65).

3352	**597**	55b. black and gold	70	45
MS3353		90×100 mm. 5l. Portrait as in Type **597**	5·75	5·75

598 Congress Emblem

1966. Communist Youth Union Congress.

3354	**598**	55b. red and yellow	70	45

599 Dance of Moldova

1966. Romanian Folk-dancing.

3355	**599**	30b. black and purple	50	10
3356	-	40b. black and red	70	35
3357	-	55b. black and turquoise	95	10
3358	-	1l. black and lake	1·30	10
3359	-	1l.60 black and blue	1·90	30
3360	-	2l. black and green	4·25	2·30

DANCES OF: 40b. Oltenia; 55b. Maramures; 1l. Muntenia; 1l.60, Banat; 2l. Transylvania.

600 Footballers

1966. World Cup Football Championship, England.

3361	**600**	5b. multicoloured	30	10
3362	-	10b. multicoloured	40	10
3363	-	15b. multicoloured	60	15
3364	-	55b. multicoloured	1·10	20
3365	-	1l.75 multicoloured	2·50	45
3366	-	4l. multicoloured	4·50	4·50
MS3367		85×100 mm. 10l. gold, black and blue	11·50	11·50

DESIGNS: 10b. to 1l.75, Various footballing scenes; 4l. Jules Rimet Cup. 33×46 mm—10l. As No. 3366.

601 "Agriculture and Industry"

1966. Trade Union Congress, Bucharest.

3368	**601**	55b. multicoloured	70	45

602 Red-breasted Flycatcher

1966. Song Birds. Multicoloured.

3369	5b. Type **602**	30	10
3370	10b. Red crossbill	50	10
3371	15b. Great reed warbler	70	10
3372	20b. Common redstart	80	15
3373	55b. European robin	1·30	15
3374	1l.20 Bluethroat	1·60	20
3375	1l.55 Yellow wagtail	2·40	35
3376	3l.20 Penduline tit	4·25	2·75

603 "Venus 3"

1966. Space Achievements. Multicoloured.

3377	10b. Type **603**	50	10
3378	20b. "FR 1" satellite	60	20
3379	1l.60 "Luna 9"	3·50	30
3380	5l. "Gemini 6" and "7"	5·75	2·30

604 Urechia Nestor (historian)

1966. Cultural Anniversaries.

3381	-	5b. blue, black and green	10	10
3382	-	10b. green, black and red	10	10
3383	**604**	20b. purple, black & green	10	10
3384	-	40b. brown, black & blue	30	10
3385	-	55b. green, black & brn	40	10
3386	-	1l. violet, black and bistre	85	20
3387	-	1l.35 olive, black & blue	1·20	30
3388	-	1l.60 purple, blk & green	1·90	55
3389	-	1l.75 purple, blk & orge	1·20	30
3390	-	3l.25 lake, black and blue	1·90	55

PORTRAITS: 5b. George Cosbuc (poet, birth cent); 10b. Gheorghe Sincai (historian, 150th death anniv); 20b. Type **604** (birth cent); 40b. Aron Pumnul (linguist, death cent); 55b. Stefan Luchian (painter, 50th death anniv); 1l. Sun Yat-sen (Chinese statesman, birth cent); 1l.35, Gottfried Leibnitz (philosopher, 250th death anniv); 1l.60, Romain Rolland (writer, birth cent); 1l.75, Ion Ghica (revolutionary and diplomat, 150th birth anniv); 3l.25, Constantin Cantacuzino (historian, 250th death anniv).

605 "House" (after Petrascu)

1966. Paintings in National Gallery, Bucharest. Multicoloured.

3391	5b. Type **605**	15	15
3392	10b. "Peasant Girl" (Grigorescu) (vert)	20	15
3393	20b. "Midday Rest" (Rescu)	50	20
3394	55b. "Portrait of a Man" (Van Eyck) (vert)	1·20	30
3395	1l.55 "The 2nd Class Compartment" (Daumier)	4·75	55
3396	3l.25 "The Blessing" (El Greco) (vert)	6·75	6·00

606 "Hottonia palustris"

1966. Aquatic Flora. Multicoloured.

3397	5b. Type **606**	20	10
3398	10b. "Ceratophyllum submersum"	30	10
3399	20b. "Aldrovanda vesiculosa"	40	10
3400	40b. "Callitriche verna"	60	10
3401	55b. "Vallisneria spiralis"	70	15
3402	1l. "Elodea canadensis"	1·50	20
3403	1l.55 "Hippuris vulgaris"	2·10	35
3404	3l.25 "Myriophyllum spicatum" (28×49½ mm)	4·00	2·30

607 Diagram showing one metre in relation to quadrant of Earth

1966. Centenary of Metric System in Romania.

3405	**607**	55b. blue and brown	50	10
3406	-	1l. violet and green	80	35

DESIGN: 1l. Metric abbreviations and globe.

608 Putna Monastery

1966. 500th Anniv of Putna Monastery.

3407	**608**	2l. multicoloured	1·60	55

609 "Medicine"

1966. Centenary of Romanian Academy.

3408	**609**	40b. multicoloured	20	10
3409	-	55b. multicoloured	30	15
3410	-	1l. brown, gold and blue	60	20
3411	-	3l. brown, gold & yellow	2·10	1·40

DESIGNS—As Type **609**: 55b. "Science" (formula). 22½×33½ mm: 1l. Gold medal. 67×27 mm: 3l. Ion Radulescu (writer), Mihail Kogalniceanu (historian) and Traian Savulescu (biologist).

610 Crayfish

1966. Crustaceans and Molluscs. Mult.

3412	5b. Type **610**	20	10
3413	10b. Netted nassa (vert)	30	10
3414	20b. Marbled rock crab	40	10
3415	40b. "Campylaea trizona" (snail)	50	15
3416	55b. Lucorum helix	70	20
3417	1l.35 Mediterranean blue mussel	1·70	30
3418	1l.75 Stagnant pond snail	2·10	35
3419	3l.25 Swan mussel	3·50	2·30

611 Bucharest and Mail Coach

1966. Stamp Day.

3420	**611**	55b.+45b. mult	1·50	75

No. 3420 is a two-part design arranged horiz, imperf between.

612 "Ursus spelaeus"

1966. Prehistoric Animals.

3421	**612**	5b. blue, brown and green	30	10
3422	-	10b. violet, bistre & green	40	10
3423	-	15b. brown, purple & green	50	15
3424	-	55b. violet, bistre & green	95	20
3425	-	1l.55 blue, brown & grn	2·50	30
3426	-	4l. mauve, bistre & green	4·75	2·30

ANIMALS: 10b. "Mamuthus trogontherii"; 15b. "Bison priscus"; 55b. "Archidiscodon"; 1l.55, "Megaceros eurycerus". (43×27 mm): 4l. "Deinotherium gigantissimum".

613 "Sputnik 1" orbiting Globe

1967. 10 Years of Space Achievements. Mult.

3427	10b. Type **613** (postage)	20	10
3428	20b. Yuri Gagarin and "Vostok 1"	30	10
3429	25b. Valentina Tereshkova ("Vostok 6")	40	10
3430	40b. Andrian Nikolaev and Pavel Popovich ("Vostok 3" and "4")	60	10
3431	55b. Aleksei Leonov in space ("Voskhod 2")	85	15
3432	1l.20 "Early Bird" (air)	1·20	30
3433	1l.55 Photo transmission ("Mariner 4")	1·50	30
3434	3l.25 Space rendezvous ("Gemini 6" and "7")	1·90	75
3435	5l. Space link up ("Gemini 8")	3·00	2·75

614 Barn Owl

1967. Birds of Prey. Multicoloured.

3442	10b. Type **614**	50	10
3443	20b. Eagle owl	60	10
3444	40b. Saker falcon	60	10
3445	55b. Egyptian vulture	70	10
3446	75b. Osprey	80	20
3447	1l. Griffon vulture	1·60	20
3448	1l.20 Lammergeier	1·90	45
3449	1l.75 Cinereous	2·40	1·90

615 "Washerwoman" (after I. Steriadi)

1967. Paintings.

3450	-	10b. blue, gold and red	20	10
3451	**615**	20b. green, gold & ochre	30	20
3452	-	40b. red, gold and blue	60	20
3453	-	1l.55 purple, gold & blue	1·20	45
3454	-	3l.20 brown, gold & brn	3·00	65
3455	-	5l. brown, gold & orange	4·25	3·00

PAINTINGS—VERT: 10b. "Model in Fancy Dress" (I. Andreescu); 40b. "Peasants Weaving" (S. Dimitrescu); 1l.55, "Venus and Cupid" (L. Cranach); 5l. "Haman beseeching Esther" (Rembrandt). HORIZ: 3l.20, "Hercules and the Lion" (Rubens).

616 Woman's Head

1967. 10th Anniv of C. Brancusi (sculptor). Sculptures.

3456	**616**	5b. brown, yellow and red	10	10
3457	-	10b. black, green & violet	20	10
3458	-	20b. black, green and red	25	10
3459	-	40b. black, red & green	30	20
3460	-	55b. black, olive and blue	70	30
3461	-	1l.20 brown, violet and orange	1·60	35
3462	-	3l.25 black, green and mauve	3·00	1·40

DESIGNS—HORIZ: 10b. Sleeping muse; 40b. "The Kiss"; 3l.25, Gate of Kisses, Targujiu. VERT: 20b. "The Endless Column"; 55b. Seated woman; 1l.20, "Miss Pogany".

617 Copper and Silver Coins of 1867

1967. Centenary of Romanian Monetary System.

3463	**617**	55b. multicoloured	50	45
3464	-	1l.20 multicoloured	1·10	1·00

DESIGN: 1l.20, Obverse and reverse of modern silver coin (1966).

618 "Infantryman" (Nicolae Grigorescu)

1967. 90th Anniv of Independence.

3465	**618**	55b. multicoloured	1·60	1·60

619 Peasants attacking (after Octav Bancila)

1967. 60th Anniv of Peasant Rising.

3466	**619**	40b. multicoloured	70	65
3467	-	1l.55 multicoloured	1·60	1·60

DESIGN—HORIZ: 1l.55, Peasants marching (after S. Luchian).

620 "Centaurca pinnatifida"

1967. Carpathian Flora. Multicoloured.

3468	20b. Type **620**	20	20
3469	40b. "Erysimum transsilvanicum"	30	20
3470	55b. "Aquilegia transsilvanica"	50	20
3471	1l.20 Alpine violet	1·50	10
3472	1l.75 Bellflower	1·70	20
3473	4l. Mountain avens (horiz)	4·00	2·30

621 Towers, Sibiu

1967. Historic Monuments and International Tourist Year. Multicoloured.

3474	20b. Type **621**	50	20
3475	40b. Castle at Cris	70	20
3476	55b. Wooden church, Plopis	95	20
3477	1l.60 Ruins, Neamtului	1·60	30
3478	1l.75 Mogosoaia Palace, Bucharest	1·90	35
3479	2l.25 Church, Voronet	3·00	1·90
MS3480	101×89 mm. **662** 5l. blue, black and light blue. Imperf	4·75	4·75

No. 3479 is horiz, 48½×36 mm.

623 "Battle of Marasesti" (E. Stoica)

1967. 50th Anniv of Battles of Marasesti, Marasti and Oituz.

3481	**623**	55b. brown, blue and grey	95	65

624 Dinu Lipatti (composer and pianist)

1967. Cultural Anniversaries.

3482	**624**	10b. violet, blue and black	10	10
3483	-	20b. blue, brown & black	15	10
3484	-	40b. brown, turq & blk	20	10
3485	-	55b. brown, red and black	30	10
3486	-	1l.20 brown, olive & black	50	30
3487	-	1l.75 green, blue & black	1·10	85

DESIGNS: 10b. Type **624** (50th birth anniv); 20b. Alexandru Orascu (architect, 150th birth anniv); 40b. Grigore Antipa (biologist, birth cent); 55b. Mihail Kogalniceanu (politician and historian, 150th birth anniv); 1l.20, Jonathan Swift (satirist, 300th birth anniv); 1l.75, Marie Curie (physicist, birth cent).

625 Wrestling

1967. World Wrestling Championships, Bucharest. Designs showing wrestlers and globes.

3488	**625**	10b. multicoloured	10	10
3489	-	20b. mult (horiz)	20	10
3490	-	55b. multicoloured	30	10
3491	-	1l.20 multicoloured	95	20
3492	-	2l. multicoloured (horiz)	1·60	1·00

626 Inscription on Globe

1967. International Linguists' Congress, Bucharest.

3493	**626**	1l.60 ultramarine, red and blue	1·50	45

627 Academy

1967. Centenary of Book Academy, Bucharest.

3494	**627**	55b. grey, brown and blue	1·50	45

628 Dancing on Ice

1967. Winter Olympic Games, Grenoble. Mult.

3495		20b. Type **628**	10	10
3496		40b. Skiing	20	10
3497		55b. Bobsleighing	30	10
3498		1l. Downhill skiing	70	20
3499		1l.55 Ice hockey	95	30
3500		2l. Games emblem	1·50	45
3501		2l.30 Ski jumping	1·90	1·10
MS3502		80×100 mm. 5l. Bobsleighing. Imperf	6·25	6·00

629 Curtea de Arges Monastery

1967. 450th Anniv of Curtea de Arges Monastery.

3503	**629**	55b. multicoloured	95	45

630 Karl Marx and Title Page

1967. Centenary of Karl Marx's "Das Kapital".

3504	**630**	40b. black, yellow and red	70	45

631 Lenin

1967. 50th Anniv of October Revolution.

3505	**631**	1l.20 black, gold and red	1·20	45

632 Arms of Romania

633 Telephone Dial and Map

1967. (a) T 632.

3506	**632**	40b. blue	50	10
3507	**632**	55b. yellow	70	20
3508	**632**	1l.60 red	1·60	30

(b) T 633 and similar designs.

3509	-	5b. green	10	10
3510	-	10b. red	10	10
3511	-	20b. grey	10	10
3512	-	35b. blue	10	10
3513	-	40b. blue	20	10
3514	-	50b. orange	20	10
3515	-	55b. red	30	10
3516	-	60b. brown	30	10
3517	-	1l. green	40	10
3518	-	1l.20 violet	50	10
3519	-	1l.35 blue	60	10
3520	-	1l.50 red	70	10
3521	-	1l.55 brown	80	10
3522	-	1l.75 green	85	10
3523	-	2l. yellow	95	10
3524	-	2l.40 blue	1·10	10
3525	**633**	3l. turquoise	1·20	20
3526	-	3l.20 ochre	1·40	20
3527	-	3l.25 blue	1·60	20
3528	-	4l. mauve	1·60	20
3529	-	5l. violet	1·90	20

DESIGNS—23×17 mm: 5b. "Carpati" lorry; 20b. Railway Travelling Post Office coach; 35b. Zlin Z-226A Akrobat plane; 60b. Electric parcels truck. As Type **633**: 1l.20, Motorcoach; 1l.35, Mil Mi-4 helicopter; 1l.75, Lakeside highway; 2l. Postal van; 3l.20, Ilyushin Il-18 airliner; 4l. Electric train; 5l. Telex instrument and world map. 17×23 mm: 10b. Posthorn and telephone emblem; 40b. Power pylons; 50b. Telephone handset; 55b. Dam. As T **633** but vert: 1l. Diesel-electric train; 1l.50, Trolley-bus; 1l.55, Radio station; 2l.40, T.V. relay station; 3l.25, Liner "Transylvania".

No. 3525 also commemorates the 40th anniv of the automatic telephone service.

See also Nos. 3842/57.

634 "Crossing the River Buzau" (lithograph by Raffet) (image scaled to 52% of original size)

1967. Stamp Day.

3530	**634**	55b.+45b. blue and ochre	1·50	65

635 Monorail Train and Globe

1967. World Fair, Montreal. Multicoloured.

3531		55b. Type **635**	20	10
3532		1l. Expo emblem within atomic symbol	50	10
3533		1l.60 Gold cup and world map	70	20
3534		2l. Expo emblem	1·30	75

636 Arms and Industrial Scene

1967. 20th Anniv of Republic. Multicoloured.

3535		40b. Type **636**	20	10
3536		55b. Arms of Romania	30	10
3537		1l.60 Romanian flag (34×48 mm)	95	30
3538		1l.75 Arms and cultural emblems	1·80	1·20

637 I.A.R. 817 Flying Ambulance

1968. Air. Romanian Aviation.

3539	-	40b. multicoloured	20	10
3540	**637**	55b. multicoloured	30	10
3541	-	1l. multicoloured	50	10
3542	-	2l.40 multicoloured	1·60	65

DESIGNS—VERT: 40b. Antonov An-2 biplane spraying crops; 1l. "Aviasan" emblem and airliner; 2l.40, Mircea Zorileanu (pioneer aviator) and biplane.

638 "Angelica and Medor" (S. Ricci)

1968. Paintings in Romanian Galleries. Mult.

3543	40b. "Young Woman" (Misu Pop) (vert)	50	20
3544	55b. "Little Girl in Red Scarf" (N. Grigorescu) (vert)	70	30
3545	1l. "Old Nicholas, the Cobza-player" (S. Luchian) (vert)	1·20	45
3546	1l.60 "Man with Skull" (Dierick Bouts) (vert)	1·50	45
3547	2l.40 Type **638**	1·90	65
3548	3l.20 "Ecce Homo" (Titian) (vert)	4·00	5·00
MS3549	75×90 mm. 5l. As 3l.20. Imperf	11·50	11·50

See also Nos. 353/8, 3631/**MS**37, 3658/**MS**64, 3756/**MS**62 and 3779/**MS**85.

639 "Anemones" (Luchian)

1968. Birth Centenary of Stefan Luchian (painter). Sheet 90×100 mm. Imperf.

MS3550	10l. multicoloured	11·50	11·50

640 Human Rights Emblem

1968. Human Rights Year.

3551	**640**	1l. multicoloured	1·20	45

641 W.H.O. Emblem

1968. 20th Anniv of W.H.O.

3552	**641**	1l.60 multicoloured	1·60	45

642 "The Hunter" (after N. Grigorescu)

1968. Hunting Congress, Mamaia.

3553	**642**	1l.60 multicoloured	1·60	45

643 Pioneers and Liberation Monument

1968. Young Pioneers. Multicoloured.

3554	5b. Type **643**	20	10
3555	40b. Receiving scarves	25	10
3556	55b. With models	30	10
3557	1l. Operating radio sets	60	10
3558	1l.60 Folk-dancing	95	30
3559	2l.40 In camp	1·30	75

644 Prince Mircea

1968. 550th Death Anniv of Prince Mircea (the Old).

3560	**644**	1l.60 multicoloured	1·60	45

645 Ion Ionescu de la Brad (scholar)

1968. Cultural Anniversaries.

3561	**645**	40b. multicoloured	30	20
3562	-	55b. multicoloured	60	30

PORTRAITS AND ANNIVS: 40b. Type **645** (150th birth anniv); 55b. Emil Racovita (scientist, birth cent).

646 "Pelargonium zonale"

1968. Garden Geraniums. Multicoloured.

3563	10b. Type **646**	10	10
3564	20b. "Pelargonium zonale" (orange)	15	10
3565	40b. "Pelargonium zonale" (red)	20	10
3566	55b. "Pelargonium zonale" (pink)	30	10
3567	60b. "Pelargonium grandiflorum" (red)	50	10
3568	1l.20 "Pelargonium peltatum" (red)	70	20
3569	1l.35 "Pelargonium peltatum" (pink)	95	20
3570	1l.60 "Pelargonium grandiflorum" (pink)	1·50	95

647 "Nicolae Balcescu" (Gheorghe Tattarescu)

1968. 120th Anniv of 1848 Revolution. Paintings. Multicoloured.

3571	55b. Type **647**	60	10
3572	1l.20 "Avram Iancu" (B. Iscovescu)	1·10	20
3573	1l.60 "Vasile Alecsandri" (N. Livaditti)	2·10	95

648 Throwing the Javelin

1968. Olympic Games, Mexico. Multicoloured.

3574		10b. Type **648**	10	10
3575		20b. Diving	10	10
3576		40b. Volleyball	20	15
3577		55b. Boxing	40	15
3578		60b. Wrestling	60	15
3579		1l.20 Fencing	70	20
3580		1l.35 Punting	95	30
3581		1l.60 Football	1·60	45
MS3582		77×90 mm. 5l. running. Imperf	5·75	5·75

1968. Paintings in the Fine Arts Museum, Bucarest. Multicoloured.

3583		10b. "The Awakening of Romania" (G. Tattarescu) (28×49 mm)	10	10
3584		20b. "Composition" (Teodorescu Sionion)	20	10
3585		35b. "The Judgement of Paris" (H. van Balen)	30	10
3586		60b. "The Mystical Betrothal of St. Catherine" (L. Sustris)	60	20
3587		1l.75 "Mary with the Child Jesus" (J. van Bylert)	1·90	45
3588		3l. "The Summer" (J. Jordaens)	4·25	2·30

649 F.I.A.P. Emblem within "Lens"

1968. 20th Anniv of International Federation of Photographic Art (F.I.A.P.).

3589	**649**	1l.60 multicoloured	1·50	45

650 Academy and Harp

1968. Centenary of Georgi Enescu Philharmonic Academy.

3590	**650**	55b. multicoloured	80	45

651 Triumph of Trajan (Roman metope)

1968. Historic Monuments.

3591	**651**	10b. green, blue and red	20	10
3592	-	40b. blue, brown and red	30	10
3593	-	55b. violet, brown & green	50	10
3594	-	1l.20 purple, grey and ochre	95	20
3595	-	1l.55 blue, green & pur	1·50	30
3596	-	1l.75 brown, bistre and orange	1·90	95

DESIGNS—HORIZ: 40b. Monastery Church, Moldovita; 55b. Monastery. Church, Cozia; 1l.20, Tower and Church, Tirgoviste; 1l.55, Palace of Culture, Jassy; 1l.75, Corvinus Castle, Hunedoara.

652 Old Bucharest (18th-cent painting) (image scaled to 63% of original size)

1968. Stamp Day.

3597	**652**	55b.+45b. multicoloured	1·70	95

653 Mute Swan

1968. Fauna of Nature Reservations. Multicoloured.

3598		10b. Type **653**	10	10
3599		20b. Black-winged stilt	20	10
3600		40b. Common shelduck	30	10
3601		55b. Great egret	50	10
3602		60b. Golden eagle	70	10
3603		1l.20 Great bustard	95	30
3604		1l.35 Chamois	1·20	30
3605		1l.60 European bison	1·90	65

654 "Entry of Michael the Brave into Alba Julia" (E. Stoica)

1968. 50th Anniv of Union of Transylvania with Romania. Multicoloured.

3606		55b. Type **654**	40	20
3607		1l. "Union Dance" (T. Aman)	80	20
3608		1l.75 "Alba Julia Assembly"	1·50	55
MS3609		121×111 mm. Nos. 3606/8. Imperf. (Sold at 4l.)	4·00	4·00

655 Neamtz Costume (female)

1968. Provincial Costumes (1st series). Mult.

3610		5b. Type **655**	10	10
3611		40b. Neamtz (male)	30	10
3612		55b. Hunedoara (female)	70	15
3613		1l. Hunedoara (male)	95	20
3614		1l.60 Brasov (female)	1·50	30
3615		2l.40 Brasov (male)	2·10	1·40

See also Nos. 3617/22.

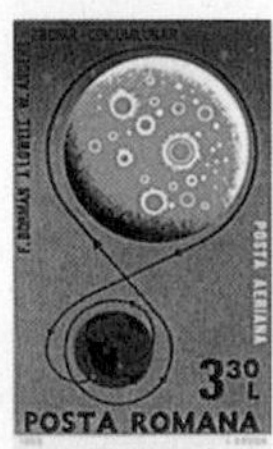

656 Earth, Moon and Orbital Track of "Apollo 8"

1969. Air. Flight of "Apollo 8" around the Moon.

3616	**656**	3l.30 black, silver & blue	2·40	2·30

1969. Provincial Costumes (2nd series). As T 655. Multicoloured.

3617		5b. Doli (female)	10	10
3618		40b. Doli (male)	30	10
3619		55b. Arges (female)	70	15
3620		1l. Arges (male)	95	20
3621		1l.60 Timisoara (female)	1·50	30
3622		2l.40 Timisoara (male)	2·10	1·40

657 Fencing

1969. Sports.

3623	**657**	10b. grey, black & brown	10	10
3624	-	20b. grey, black and violet	10	10
3625	-	40b. grey, black and blue	15	10
3626	-	55b. grey, black and red	20	10
3627	-	1l. grey, black and green	40	10
3628	-	1l.20 grey, black and blue	50	15
3629	-	1l.60 grey, black and red	80	30
3630	-	2l.40 grey, black & green	1·50	95

DESIGNS: 20b. Throwing the javelin; 40b. Canoeing; 55b. Boxing; 1l. Volleyball; 1l.20, Swimming; 1l.60, Wrestling; 2l.40, Football.

1969. Nude Paintings in the National Gallery. As T 638. Multicoloured.

3631		10b. "Nude" (C. Tattarescu)	10	10
3632		20b. "Nude" (T. Pallady)	10	10
3633		35b. "Nude" (N. Tonitza)	20	10
3634		60b. "Venus and Cupid" (Flemish School)	50	20
3635		1l.75 "Diana and Endymion" (M. Liberi)	1·90	95
3636		3l. "The Three Graces" (J. H. von Achen)	4·00	2·30
MS3637		73×91 mm. 5l. Designs as 1l.75	5·50	5·50

SIZES—36×49 mm: 10b., 35b., 60b., 1l.75. 27×49 mm: 3l. 49×36 mm: 20b.

658 "Soyuz 4" and "Soyuz 5"

1969. Air. Space Link-up of "Soyuz 4" and "Soyuz 5".

3638	**658**	3l.30 multicoloured	2·40	2·30

659 I.L.O. Emblem

1969. 50th Anniv of International Labour Office.

3639	**659**	55b. multicoloured	95	45

660 Stylized Head

1969. Inter-European Cultural Economic Co-operation.

3640	**660**	55b. multicoloured	50	45
3641	**660**	1l.50 multicoloured	1·90	1·90

661 Posthorn

1969. Postal Ministers' Conference, Bucharest.

3642	**661**	55b. deep blue and blue	70	45

662 Referee introducing Boxers

1969. European Boxing Championships, Bucharest. Multicoloured.

3643		35b. Type **662**	20	10
3644		40b. Sparring	30	10
3645		55b. Leading with punch	50	10
3646		1l.75 Declaring the winner	1·50	95

663 "Apollo 9" and Module over Earth

1969. Air. "Apollo" Moon Flights. Multicoloured.

3647		60b. Type **663**	30	10
3648		2l.40 "Apollo 10" and module approaching Moon (vert)	1·90	35

664 Lesser Purple Emperor

1969. Butterflies and Moths. Multicoloured.

3649		5b. Type **664**	10	10
3650		10b. Willow-herb hawk moth	10	10
3651		20b. Eastern pale clouded yellow	10	10
3652		40b. Large tiger moth	20	10
3653		55b. Pallas's fritillary	50	10
3654		1l. Jersey tiger moth	60	10
3655		1l.20 Orange-tip	95	30
3656		2l.40 Meleager's blue	2·40	1·60

665 Astronaut and Module on Moon

1969. Air. First Man on the Moon.

3657	**665**	3l.30 multicoloured	2·40	2·30

1969. Paintings in the National Gallery, Bucharest. Multicoloured. As T 638.

3658		10b. "Venetian Senator" (School of Tintoretto)	10	10
3659		20b. "Sofia Kretzulescu" (G. Tattarescu)	10	10
3660		35b. "Philip IV" (Velasquez)	30	10
3661		35b. "Man Reading" (Memling)	70	15
3662		1l.75 "Lady D'Aguesseau" (Vigee-Lebrun)	1·50	30
3663		3l. "Portrait of a Woman" (Rembrandt)	3·50	1·90
MS3664		91×78 mm. 5l. "Return of the Prodigal Son" (Licino). Imperf	4·75	4·75

666 Communist Flag

1969. 10th Romanian Communist Party Congress.

3665	**666**	55b. multicoloured	80	45

667 Symbols of Learning

1969. National "Economic Achievements" Exhibition, Bucharest. Multicoloured.

3666	35b. Type **667**	20	10
3667	40b. Symbols of Agriculture and Science	30	10
3668	1l.75 Symbols of Industry	1·50	35

668 Liberation Emblem

1969. 25th Anniv of Liberation. Multicoloured.

3669	10b. Type **668**	20	10
3670	55b. Crane and trowel	30	15
3671	60b. Flags on scaffolding	50	20

669 Juggling on Trick-cycle

1969. Romanian State Circus. Multicoloured.

3672	10b. Type **669**	10	10
3673	20b. Clown	10	10
3674	35b. Trapeze artists	30	10
3675	60b. Equestrian act	50	10
3676	1l.75 High-wire act	95	20
3677	3l. Performing tiger	1·90	1·10

670 Forces' Memorial

1969. Army Day and 25th Anniv of People's Army.

3678	**670**	55b. black, gold and red	70	45

671 Electric Train (1965) and Steam Locomotive "Calugareni" (1869)

1969. Centenary of Romanian Railways.

3679	**671**	55b. multicoloured	80	45

672 "Courtyard" (M. Bouquet) (⅔-size illustration) (image scaled to 72% of original size)

1969. Stamp Day.

3680	**672**	55b.+45b. multicoloured	1·50	95

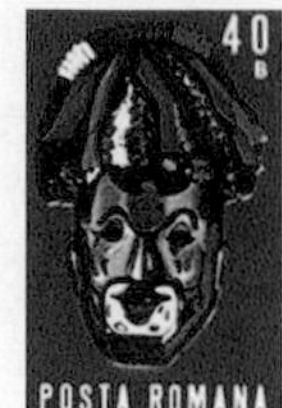

673 Branesti Mask

1969. Folklore Masks. Multicoloured.

3681	40b. Type **673**	30	10
3682	55b. Tudora mask	40	10
3683	1l.55 Birsesti mask	95	30
3684	1l.75 Rudaria mask	1·30	75

674 "Apollo 12" above Moon

1969. Moon Landing of "Apollo 12".

3685	**674**	1l.50 multicoloured	1·50	1·40

675 "Three Kings" (Voronet Monastery)

1969. Frescoes from Northern Moldavian Monasteries (1st series). Multicoloured.

3686	10b. Type **675**	10	10
3687	20b. "Three Kings" (Sucevita)	20	10
3688	35b. "Holy Child in Manger" (Voronet)	30	10
3689	60b. "Ship" (Sucevita) (vert)	60	15
3690	1l.75 "Walled City" (Moldovita)	1·70	35
3691	3l. "Pastoral Scene" (Voronet) (vert)	3·50	1·90

See also Nos. 3736/42 and 3872/8.

676 "Old Mother Goose", Capra

1969. New Year. Children's Celebrations. Mult.

3692	40b. Type **676**	20	10
3693	55b. Decorated tree, Sorcova	30	10
3694	1l.50 Drummers, Buhaiul	1·20	20
3695	2l.40 Singer and bellringer, Plugusurol	1·50	75

677 Players and Emblem

1970. World Ice Hockey Championships (Groups B and C), Bucharest. Multicoloured.

3696	20b. Type **677**	10	10
3697	55b. Goalkeeper	30	10
3698	1l.20 Two players	85	15
3699	2l.40 Goalmouth melee	1·60	95

678 Small Pasque Flower

1970. Flowers. Multicoloured.

3700	5b. Type **678**	10	10
3701	10b. Yellow pheasant's-eye	10	10
3702	20b. Musk thistle	10	10
3703	40b. Dwarf almond	10	10
3704	55b. Dwarf bearded iris	10	10
3705	1l. Flax	50	10
3706	1l.20 Sage	70	10
3707	2l.40 Peony	3·00	1·10

679 Japanese Woodcut

1970. World Fair, Osaka, Japan. Expo 70. Mult.

3714	20b. Type **679**	20	20
3715	1l. Japanese pagoda (29×92 mm)	1·20	65
MS3716	182×120 mm. 5l. As design of 1l.	5·75	5·75

The design on 1l. and 5l. is vert, 29×92 mm. On No. **MS**3716 the face value appears on the sheet and not the stamp.

680 B.A.C. One Eleven Series 475 Jetliner and Silhouettes of Aircraft

1970. 50th Anniv of Romanian Civil Aviation. Multicoloured.

3717	60b. Type **680**	50	20
3718	2l. Tail of B.A.C. One Eleven Series 475 and control tower at Otopeni Airport, Bucharest	1·20	55

681 Lenin

1970. Birth Centenary of Lenin.

3719	**681**	40b. multicoloured	70	45

682 "Camille" (Monet) and Maximum Card

1970. Maximafila Franco–Romanian Philatelic Exn, Bucharest.

3720	**682**	1l.50 multicoloured	1·90	5·50

683 "Prince Alexander Cuza" (Szathmary)

1970. 150th Birth Anniv of Prince Alexandru Cuza.

3721	**683**	55b. multicoloured	1·10	45

684 "Co-operation" Map

1970. Inter-European Cultural and Economic Co-operation.

3722	**684**	40b. green, brown & black	50	45
3723	**684**	1l.50 blue, brown & blk	95	95

685 Victory Monument, Bucharest

1970. 25th Anniv of Liberation.

3724	**685**	55b. multicoloured	95	45

686 Greek Silver Drachma, 5th cent B.C.

1970. Ancient Coins.

3725	**686**	10b. black and blue	10	10
3726	-	20b. black and red	20	10
3727	-	35b. bronze and green	30	10
3728	-	60b. black and brown	50	10
3729	-	1l.75 black and blue	1·20	10
3730	-	3l. black and red	2·40	1·10

DESIGNS—HORIZ: 20b. Getic-Dacian silver didrachm, 2nd—1st-cent B.C.; 35b. Copper sestertius of Trajan, 106 A.D.; 60b. Mircea ducat, 1400; 1l.75, Silver groschen of Stephen the Great, 1460. VERT: 3l. Brasov klippe-thaler, 1601.

687 Footballers and Ball

1970. World Cup Football Championship, Mexico.

3731	**687**	40b. multicoloured	20	10
3732	-	55b. multicoloured	30	10
3733	-	1l.75 multicoloured	1·20	35
3734	-	3l.30 multicoloured	2·10	1·00
MS3735		110×110 mm. 6l. Four designs with face values 1l.20, 1l.50, 1l.55 and 1l.75	4·75	4·75

DESIGNS: Nos. 3732/4, various football scenes as Type **687**.

1970. Frescoes from Northern Moldavian Monasteries (2nd series). As T 675. Mult.

3736	10b. "Prince Petru Rares and Family" (Moldovita)	10	10
3737	20b. "Metropolitan Grigore Rosca" (Voronet) (28×48 mm)	20	10
3738	40b. "Alexander the Good and Family" (Sucevita)	30	10
3739	55b. "The Last Judgement" (Voronet) (vert)	50	10

3740		1l.75 "The Last Judgement" (Voronet) (different)	1·20	30
3741		3l. "St. Anthony" (Voronet)	2·50	1·60
MS3742		90×77 mm. 5l. "Byzantine Manor" (Arbore)	4·75	4·75

688 "Apollo 13" Spashdown

1970. Air. Space Flight of "Apollo 13".

3743	**688**	1l.50 multicoloured	95	95

689 Engels

1970. 150th Birth Anniv of Friedrich Engels.

3744	**689**	1l.50 multicoloured	1·50	45

690 Exhibition Hall

1970. National Events. Multicoloured.

3745		35b. "Iron Gates" Dam	20	10
3746		55b. Freighter and flag	30	10
3747		1l.50 Type **690**	1·10	20

EVENTS: 35b. Danube navigation projects; 55b. 75th anniv of Romanian Merchant Marine; 1l.50, 1st International Fair, Bucharest.

691 New Headquarters Building

1970. New U.P.U. Headquarters Building, Berne.

3748	**691**	1l.50 blue and ultramarine	1·60	45

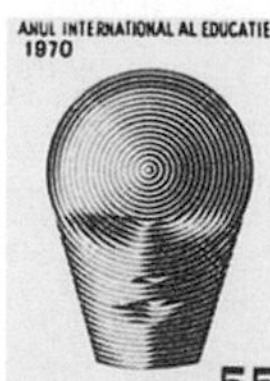

692 Education Year Emblem

1970. International Education Year.

3749	**692**	55b. plum, black and red	95	45

693 "Iceberg"

1970. Roses. Multicoloured.

3750		20b. Type **693**	10	10
3751		35b. "Wiener Charme"	10	10
3752		55b. "Pink Lustre"	20	10
3753		1l. "Piccadilly"	95	15
3754		1l.50 "Orange Delbard"	1·20	20
3755		2l.40 "Sibelius"	2·10	1·40

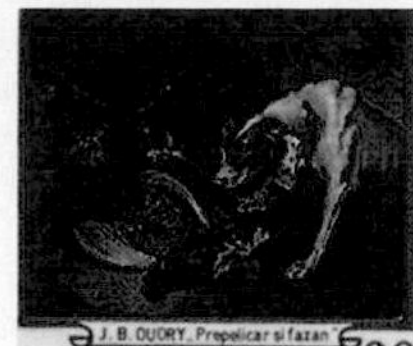

694 "Spaniel and Pheasant" (J. B. Oudry)

1970. Paintings in Romanian Galleries. Mult.

3756		10b. "The Hunt" (D. Brandi) (38×50 mm)	10	10
3757		20b. Type **694**	10	10
3758		35b. "The Hunt" (Jan Fyt) (38×50 mm)	20	10
3759		60b. "After the Chase" (Jordaens) (As T **694**)	50	10
3760		1l.75 "The Game Dealer" (F. Snyders) (50×38 mm)	1·20	30
3761		3l. "The Hunt" (A. de Gryeff) (As T **694**)	2·10	95
MS3762		90×78 mm. 5l. Design as 1l.75	4·75	4·75

695 Refugee Woman and Child

1970. Danube Flood Victims (1st issue).

3763	**695**	55b. black, blue and green (postage)	20	10
3764	-	1l.50 multicoloured	80	30
3765	-	1l.75 multicoloured	1·50	75
3766	-	60b. black, drab and blue (air)	40	10

DESIGNS: 60b. Helicopter rescue; 1l.50, Red Cross post; 1l.75, Building reconstruction.

See also No. 3777.

696 U.N. Emblem

1970. 25th Anniv of United Nations.

3767	**696**	1l.50 multicoloured	1·50	45

697 Arab Horse

1970. Horses. Multicoloured.

3768		20b. Type **697**	10	10
3769		35b. American trotter	10	10
3770		55b. Ghidran	40	10
3771		1l. Hutul	95	10
3772		1l.50 Thoroughbred	1·50	30
3773		2l.40 Lippizaner	4·00	1·90

698 Beethoven

1970. Birth Bicentenary of Ludwig van Beethoven (composer).

3774	**698**	55b. multicoloured	1·60	45

699 "Mail-cart in the Snow" (E. Volkers) (image scaled to 64% of original size)

1970. Stamp Day.

3775	**699**	55b.+45b. mult	1·60	1·10

700 Henri Coanda's Model Airplane

1970. Air. 60th Anniv of First Experimental Turbine-powered Airplane.

3776	**700**	60b. multicoloured	1·60	45

701 "The Flood" (abstract, Joan Miro)

1970. Danube Flood Victims (2nd issue).

3777	**701**	3l. multicoloured	3·00	2·75
MS3778		79×95 mm. **701** 5l. multicoloured. Imperf	7·25	7·25

702 "Sight" (G. Coques)

1970. Paintings from the Bruckenthal Museum, Sibiu. Multicoloured.

3779		10b. Type **702**	10	10
3780		20b. "Hearing"	10	10
3781		35b. "Smell"	20	10
3782		60b. "Taste"	50	10
3783		1l.75 "Touch"	95	20
3784		3l. Bruckenthal Museum	2·40	1·10
MS3785		90×78 mm. 5l. "View of Sibiu, 1808" (lithograph) (horiz)	5·75	5·75

Nos. 3779/83 show a series of pictures by Coques entitled "The Five Senses".

703 Vladimirescu (after Theodor Aman)

1971. 150th Death Anniv of Tudor Vladimirescu (Wallachian revolutionary).

3786	**703**	1l.50 multicoloured	1·60	45

704 "Three Races"

1971. Racial Equality Year.

3787	**704**	1l.50 multicoloured	1·60	45

705 Alsatian

1971. Dogs. Multicoloured.

3788		20b. Type **705**	10	10
3789		35b. Bulldog	10	10
3790		55b. Fox terrier	20	10
3791		1l. Setter	95	10
3792		1l.50 Cocker spaniel	1·50	45
3793		2l.40 Poodle	4·25	2·40

706 "Luna 16" leaving Moon

1971. Air. Moon Missions of "Luna 16" and "Luna 17". Multicoloured.

3794		3l.30 Type **706**	2·40	2·30
3795		3l.30 "Lunokhod 1" on Moon	2·40	2·30

707 Proclamation of the Commune

1971. Centenary of Paris Commune.

3796	**707**	40b. multicoloured	95	45

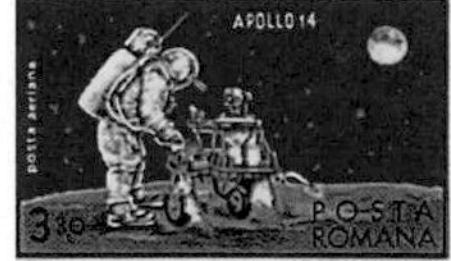

708 Astronaut and Moon Trolley

1971. Air. Moon Mission of "Apollo 14".

3797	**708**	3l.30 multicoloured	2·40	2·30

709 "Three Fists" Emblem and Flags

1971. Trade Union Congress, Bucharest.

3798	**709**	55b. multicoloured	95	45

710 "Toadstool" Rocks, Babele

1971. Tourism. Multicoloured.

3799		10b. Gorge, Cheile Bicazului (vert)	10	10
3800		40b. Type **710**	10	10
3801		55b. Winter resort, Poiana Brasov	20	10
3802		1l. Fishing punt and tourist launch, Danube delta	80	10
3803		1l.50 Hotel, Baile Sovata	1·40	20
3804		2l.40 Venus, Jupiter and Neptune Hotels, Black Sea (77×29 mm)	1·90	1·10

711 "Arrows"

1971. Inter-European Cultural Economic Co-operation. Multicoloured.

3805	55b. Type **711**	95	95
3806	1l.75 Stylized map of Europe	1·90	1·90

712 Museum Building

1971. Historical Museum, Bucharest.

3807	**712**	55b. multicoloured	70	45

713 "The Secret Printing-press" (S. Szonyi)

1971. 50th Anniv of Romanian Communist Party. Multicoloured.

3808	35b. Type **713**	20	10
3809	40b. Emblem and red flags (horiz)	20	10
3810	55b. "The Builders" (A. Anastasiu)	40	10

714 "Motra Tone" (Kole Idromeno)

1971. "Balkanfila III". International Stamp Exhibition, Bucharest. Multicoloured.

3811	1l.20+60b. Type **714**	1·20	1·10
3812	1l.20+60b. "Maid" (Vladimir Dimitrov-Maistora)	1·20	1·10
3813	1l.20+60b. "Rosa Botzaris" (Joseph Stieler)	1·20	1·10
3814	1l.20+60b. "Portrait of a Lady" (Katarina Ivanovic)	1·20	1·10
3815	1l.20+60b. "Agreseanca" (C. Popp de Szathmary)	1·20	1·10
3816	1l.20+60b. "Woman in Modern Dress" (Calli Ibrahim)	1·20	1·10
MS3817	90×79 mm. 5l. "Dancing the Hora" (Theodor Aman) (horiz)	4·75	4·75

Each stamp has a premium-carrying "tab" as shown in Type **714**.

715 Pomegranate

1971. Flowers. Multicoloured.

3818	20b. Type **715**	10	10
3819	35b. "Calceolus speciosum"	10	10
3820	55b. "Life jagra"	20	10
3821	1l. Blood-drop emlets	60	20
3822	1l.50 Dwarf morning glory	95	35
3823	2l.40 "Phyllocactus phyllanthoides" (horiz)	1·90	55

716 "Nude" (J. Iser)

1971. Paintings of Nudes. Multicoloured.

3824	10b. Type **716**	10	10
3825	20b. "Nude" (C. Ressu) (29×50 mm)	10	10
3826	35b. "Nude" (N. Grigorescu)	10	10
3827	60b. "Odalisque" (Delacroix) (horiz)	20	10
3828	1l.75 "Nude in a Landscape" (Renoir)	1·20	30
3829	3l. "Venus and Cupid" (Il Vecchio) (horiz)	2·10	95
MS3830	90×78 mm. 5l. "Venus and Amour" (Il Bronzino) (horiz)	7·25	7·25

717 Cosmonauts Patsaev, Dobrovolsky and Volkov (B5)

1971. Air. "Soyuz 11" Commemoration. Sheet 101×81 mm.

MS3831	6l. black and blue	11·50	11·50

718 Astronauts and Lunar Rover on Moon

1971. Air. Moon Flight of "Apollo 15".

3833	**718**	1l.50 multicoloured (blue background)	2·40	2·30

No. 3833 also exists imperforate, with background colour changed to green, from a restricted printing.

719 "Fishing Boats" (M. W. Arnold)

1971. Marine Paintings. Multicoloured.

3835	10b. "Coastal Storm" (B. Peters)	10	10
3836	20b. "Seascape" (I. Backhuysen)	10	10
3837	35b. "Boat in Stormy Seas" (A. van de Eertvelt)	30	10
3838	60b. Type **719**	50	10
3839	1l.75 "Seascape" (I. K. Aivazovsky)	1·20	35
3840	3l. "Fishing boats, Braila" (J. A. Steriadi)	2·50	75
MS3841	78×90 mm. 5l. "Venetian Fishing-boats" (N. Darascu) (vert)	5·75	5·75

1971. As Nos. 3517/29 and three new designs but in smaller format, 17×23 or 23×17 mm.

3842	1l. green	40	20
3843	1l.20 violet	50	20
3844	1l.35 blue	60	20
3845	1l.50 red	65	20
3846	1l.55 brown	70	20
3847	1l.75 green	80	20
3848	2l. yellow	85	20
3849	2l.40 blue	1·10	20
3850	3l. blue	1·30	20
3851	3l.20 brown	1·40	20
3852	3l.25 blue	1·50	20
3853	3l.60 blue	1·60	20
3854	4l. mauve	1·70	20
3855	4l.80 blue	1·90	20
3856	5l. violet	2·10	20
3857	6l. mauve	2·50	20

NEW DESIGNS—VERT: 3l.60, Clearing letter box; 4l.80, Postman on round; 6l. Postal Ministry, Bucharest.

720 "Neagoe Basarab" (fresco, Curtea de Arges)

1971. 450th Death Anniv of Prince Neagoe Basarab, Regent of Wallachia.

3858	**720**	60b. multicoloured	80	45

721 "T. Pallady" (self-portrait)

1971. Artists' Anniversaries.

3859	**721**	40b. multicoloured	10	10
3860	-	55b. black, stone and gold	20	10
3861	-	1l.50 black, stone & gold	70	10
3862	-	2l.40 multicoloured	1·60	45

DESIGNS (self-portraits: 40b. Type **721** (birth centenary); 55b. Benevenuto Cellini (400th death anniv); 1l.50, Jean Watteau (250th death anniv); 2l.40, Albrecht Durer (500th birth anniv).

722 Persian Text and Seal

1971. 2500th Anniv of Persian Empire.

3863	**722**	55b. multicoloured	95	45

723 Figure Skating

1971. Winter Olympic Games, Sapporo, Japan (1972). Multicoloured.

3864	10b. Type **723**	10	10
3865	20b. Ice-hockey	10	10
3866	40b. Biathlon	10	10
3867	55b. Bobsleighing	20	10
3868	1l.75 Downhill skiing	1·20	30
3869	3l. Games emblem	4·00	1·40
MS3870	78×90 mm. 5l. Symbolic flame (38×50 mm). Imperf	4·75	4·75

724 "Lady with Letter" (Sava Hentia)

1971. Stamp Day.

3871	**724**	1l.10+90b. mult	1·90	1·10

1971. Frescoes from Northern Moldavian Monasteries (3rd series). As T 675. Multicoloured.

3872	10b. "St. George and The Dragon" (Moldovita) (vert)	10	10
3873	20b. "Three Kings and Angel" (Moldovita) (vert)	10	10
3874	40b. "The Crucifixion" (Moldovita) (vert)	10	10
3875	55b. "Trial" (Voronet) (vert)	20	10
3876	1l.75 "Death of a Martyr" (Voronet) (vert)	1·50	30
3877	3l. "King and Court" (Arborea)	3·00	1·90
MS3878	78×90 mm. 5l. Wall of frescoes, Voronet (vert)	4·75	4·75

725 Matei Millo (dramatist, 75th death anniv)

1971. Famous Romanians. Multicoloured.

3879	55b. Type **725**	30	20
3880	1l. Nicolae Iorga (historian, birth cent)	70	30

726 Magellan and Ships (450th death anniv)

1971. Scientific Anniversaries.

3881	**726**	40b. mauve, blue & green	20	10
3882	-	55b. blue, green and lilac	20	10
3883	-	1l. multicoloured	60	10
3884	-	1l.50 green, blue & brn	85	30

DESIGNS AND ANNIVERSARIES: 55b. Kepler and observatory (400th birth anniv); 1l. Gagarin, rocket and Globe (10th anniv of first manned space flight); 1l.50, Lord Rutherford and atomic symbol (birth cent).

727 Lynx Cubs

1972. Young Wild Animals. Multicoloured.
3885 20b. Type **727** 10 10
3886 35b. Red fox cubs 10 10
3887 55b. Roe deer fawns 20 10
3888 1l. Wild piglets 60 20
3889 1l.50 Wolf cubs 95 20
3890 2l.40 Brown bear cubs 3·00 1·60

728 U.T.C. Emblem

1972. 50th Anniv of Communist Youth Union (U.T.C.).
3891 **728** 55b. multicoloured 70 45

729 Wrestling

1972. Olympic Games, Munich (1st issue). Mult.
3892 10b. Type **729** 10 10
3893 20b. Canoeing 20 10
3894 55b. Football 30 10
3895 1l.55 High-jumping 80 15
3896 2l.90 Boxing 1·60 20
3897 6l.70 Volleyball 4·00 2·30
MS3898 100×81 mm. 6l. Runner with Olympic Torch (air) 16·00 16·00
See also Nos. 3914/**MS**3920 and 3926.

730 Stylized Map of Europe

1972. Inter-European Cultural and Economic Co-operation.
3899 **730** 1l.75 gold, black & mve 1·50 1·40
3900 - 2l.90 gold, black & green 1·90 1·90
DESIGN: 2l.90, "Crossed arrows" symbol.

731 Astronauts in Lunar Rover

1972. Air. Moon Flight of "Apollo 16".
3901 **731** 3l. blue, green and pink 1·90 1·90

732 Modern Trains and Symbols

1972. 50th Anniv of International Railway Union.
3902 **732** 55b. multicoloured 1·50 45

733 "Summer" (P. Brueghel)

1972. "Belgica 72" Stamp Exhibition, Brussels. Sheet 89×76 mm.
MS3903 6l. multicoloured 5·75 5·75

734 "Paeonia romanica"

1972. Scarce Romanian Flowers.
3904 **734** 20b. multicoloured 10 10
3905 - 40b. purple, green & brown 20 10
3906 - 55b. brown and blue 30 10
3907 - 60b. red, green and light green 50 15
3908 - 1l.35 multicoloured 95 20
3909 - 2l.90 multicoloured 2·10 65
DESIGNS: 40b. "Dianthus callizonus"; 55b. Edelweiss; 60b. Vanilla orchid; 1l.35, "Narcissus stellaris"; 2l.90, Lady's slipper.

735 Saligny Bridge, Cernavoda

1972. Danube Bridges. Multicoloured.
3910 1l.35 Type **735** 60 10
3911 1l.75 Giurgeni Bridge, Vadul Oii 95 20
3912 2l.75 Friendship Bridge, Giurgiu–Ruse (Bulgaria) 1·90 45

736 North Railway Station, Bucharest, 1872

1972. Cent of North Railway Station, Bucharest.
3913 **736** 55b. multicoloured 1·20 45

737 Water-polo

1972. Olympic Games, Munich (2nd issue). Mult.
3914 10b. Type **737** 10 10
3915 20b. Pistol-shooting 20 10
3916 55b. Throwing the discus 30 10
3917 1l.55 Gymnastics 85 20
3918 2l.75 Canoeing 1·90 30
3919 6l.40 Fencing 3·50 1·90
MS3920 90×78 mm. 6l. Football (air) 14·50 14·50

738 Rotary Stamp- printing Press

1972. Centenary of State Stamp-printing Works.
3921 **738** 55b. multicoloured 95 45

739 "E. Stoenescu" (Stefan Popescu)

1972. Romanian Art. Portraits. Multicoloured.
3922 55b. Type **739** 10 10
3923 1l.75 Self-portrait (Octav Bancila) 50 10
3924 2l.90 Self-portrait (Gheorghe Petrascu) 1·10 20
3925 6l.50 Self-portrait (Ion Andreescu) 2·10 65

740 Runner with Torch

1972. Olympic Games, Munich (3rd issue). Olympic Flame.
3926 **740** 55b. purple & blue on silver 1·50 45

741 Aurel Vlaicu, his Airplane No. 1 "Crazy Fly" and Silhouette of Boeing 707 Jetliner

1972. Air. Romanian Aviation Pioneers. Mult.
3927 60b. Type **741** 20 10
3928 3l. Traian Vuia, Vuia No. 1 and silhouette of Boeing 707 jetliner 1·90 95

742 Cluj Cathedral

1972
3929 **742** 1l.85 violet (postage) 25 10
3930 - 2l.75 grey 50 10
3931 - 3l.35 red 70 10
3932 - 3l.45 green 70 10
3933 - 5l.15 blue 95 10
3934 - 5l.60 blue 1·10 10
3935 - 6l.20 mauve 1·20 10
3936 - 6l.40 brown 1·30 10
3937 - 6l.80 red 1·40 10
3938 - 7l.05 black 1·50 10
3939 - 8l.45 red 1·60 10
3940 - 9l.05 green 1·60 10
3941 - 9l.10 blue 1·60 10
3942 - 9l.85 green 1·90 10
3943 - 10l. brown 2·00 10
3944 - 11l.90 blue 2·10 20
3945 - 12l.75 violet 2·20 20
3946 - 13l.30 red 2·40 20
3947 - 16l.20 green 3·00 20
3948 - 14l.60 blue (air) 2·50 55
DESIGNS—HORIZ: (As Type **742**): 2l.75, Sphinx Rock, Mt. Bucegi; 3l.45, Sinaia Castle; 5l.15, Hydro-electric power station, Arges; 6l.40, Hunidoara Castle; 6l.80, Bucharest Polytechnic complex; 9l.05, Coliseum, Sarmisegtetuza; 9l.10, Hydro-electric power station, Iron Gates. (29×21 mm): 11l.90, Palace of the Republic, Bucharest; 13l.30, City Gate, Alba Julia; 14l.60, Otopeni Airport, Bucharest. VERT: (As Type **742**): 3l.35, Heroes' Monument, Bucharest; 5l.60, Iasi-Biserica; 6l.20, Bran Castle; 7l.05, Black Church, Brasova; 8l.45, Atheneum, Bucharest; 9l.85, Decebal's statue, Cetatea Deva. (20×30 mm): 10l. City Hall Tower, Sibiu; 12l.75, T.V. Building, Bucharest; 16l.20, Clock Tower, Sighisoara.

743 Satu Mare

1972. Millenium of Satu Mare.
3949 **743** 55b. multicoloured 95 45

744 Davis Cup on Racquet

1972. Final of Davis Cup Men's Team Tennis Championship, Bucharest.
3950 **744** 2l.75 multicoloured 2·40 65

745 "Venice" (Gheorghe Petrascu)

1972. UNESCO "Save Venice" Campaign. Paintings of Venice. Multicoloured.
3951 10b. Type **745** 10 10
3952 20b. Gondolas (N. Darascu) 10 10
3953 55b. Palace (Petrascu) 20 10
3954 1l.55 Bridge (Marius Bunescu) 50 10
3955 2l.75 Palace (Darascu) (vert) 1·20 20
3956 6l.40 Canal (Bunesca) 2·50 1·20
MS3957 91×79 mm. 6l. Old houses (Petrascu) 5·75 5·75

746 Fencing and Bronze Medal

1972. Munich Olympic Games Medals. Mult.
3958 10b. Type **746** 10 10
3959 20b. Handball and Bronze Medal 20 10
3960 35b. Boxing and Silver Medal 30 10
3961 1l.45 Hurdling and Silver Medal 85 10
3962 2l.75 Shooting, Silver and Bronze Medals 1·80 20
3963 6l.20 Wrestling and two Gold Medals 4·25 2·30
MS3964 90×80 mm. 6l. Gold and Silver medals (horiz) (air) 14·50 14·50

747 "Travelling Romanies" (E. Volkers) (image scaled to 71% of original size)

1972. Stamp Day.
3965 **747** 1l.10+90b. mult 1·70 95

748 Flags and "25"

1972. 25th Anniv of Proclamation of Republic. Multicoloured.

3966 55b. Type **748** 30 10
3967 1l.20 Arms and "25" 70 20
3968 1l.75 Industrial scene and "25" 1·10 30

749 "Apollo 1", "2" and "3"

1972. "Apollo" Moon Flights. Multicoloured.

3969 10b. Type **749** 10 10
3970 35b. Grissom, Chaffee and White 10 10
3971 40b. "Apollo 4, 5, 6" 10 10
3972 55b. "Apollo 7, 8" 30 10
3973 1l. "Apollo 9, 10" 50 10
3974 1l.20 "Apollo 11, 12" 75 10
3975 1l.85 "Apollo 13, 14" 1·00 15
3976 2l.75 "Apollo 15, 16" 1·80 20
3977 3l.60 "Apollo 17" 3·25 1·50
MS3978 89×77 mm. 6l. Astronauts and Lunar Rover on Moon (horiz) (air) 18·00 18·00

750 European Bee Eater

1973. Protection of Nature. Multicoloured. (a) Birds.

3979 1l.40 Type **750** 50 10
3980 1l.85 Red-breasted goose 75 20
3981 2l.75 Peduline tit 1·30 50

(b) Flowers.

3982 1l.40 Globe flower 50 10
3983 1l.85 Martagon lily 75 20
3984 2l.75 Gentian 1·30 50

751 Copernicus

1973. 500th Birth Anniv of Copernicus (astronomer).

3985 **751** 2l.75 multicoloured 1·30 50

752 Suceava Costume (female)

1973. Regional Costumes. Multicoloured.

3986 10b. Type **752** 10 10
3987 40b. Suceava (male) 10 10
3988 55b. Harghila (female) 20 10
3989 1l.75 Harghila (male) 85 10
3990 2l.75 Gorj (female) 1·30 30
3991 6l.40 Gorj (male) 2·50 1·50

753 Dimitrie Paciurea (sculptor)

1973. Anniversaries. Multicoloured.

3992 10b. Type **753** (birth centenary) 10 10
3993 40b. Ioan Slavici (writer, 125th birth anniv) 10 10
3994 55b. Gheorghe Lazar (educationist, death cent) 30 10
3995 6l.40 Alexandru Flechtenmacher (composer, birth cent) 3·25 1·50

754 Map of Europe

1973. Inter-European Cultural and Economic Co-operation.

3996 **754** 3l.35 gold, blue & purple 1·00 1·00
3997 - 3l.60 gold and purple 2·10 2·00

DESIGN: 3l.60, Emblem.

755 "The Rape of Proserpine" (Hans von Achen)

1973. "IBRA 73" Stamp Exhibition, Munich. Sheet 90×78 mm.

MS3998 12l. multicoloured 12·50 12·50

756 Hand with Hammer and Sickle

1973. Anniversaries. Multicoloured.

3999 40b. Type **756** 65 30
4000 55b. Flags and bayonets 75 40
4001 1l.75 Prince Cuza 1·60 50

EVENTS: 40b. 25th anniv of Romanian Workers and Peasant Party; 55b. 40th anniv of National Anti-Fascist Committee; 1l.75, Death cent of Prince Alexandru Cuza.

757 W.M.O. Emblem and Weather Satellite

1973. Centenary of W.M.O.

4002 **757** 2l. multicoloured 1·60 50

758 "Dimitri Ralet" (anon)

1973. "Socfilex III" Stamp Exhibition, Bucharest. Portrait Paintings. Multicoloured.

4003 40b. Type **758** 10 10
4004 60b. "Enacheta Vacarescu" (A. Chladek) 20 10
4005 1l.55 "Dimitri Aman" (C. Lecca) 65 10
4006 4l.+2l. "Barbat at his Desk" (B. Iscovescu) 2·50 1·50
MS4007 78×89 mm. 6l.+2l. "The Poet Alecsandri and his Family" (N. Livaditti) (38×51 mm) 6·25 6·25

759 Prince Dimitri Cantemir

1973. 300th Birth Anniv of Dimitri Cantemir, Prince of Moldavia (writer). Multicoloured.

4008 **759** 1l.75 multicoloured 1·60 50
MS4009 77×90 mm. 6l. multicoloured 6·25 6·25

DESIGNS: (38×51 mm)—6l. Miniature of Cantemir.

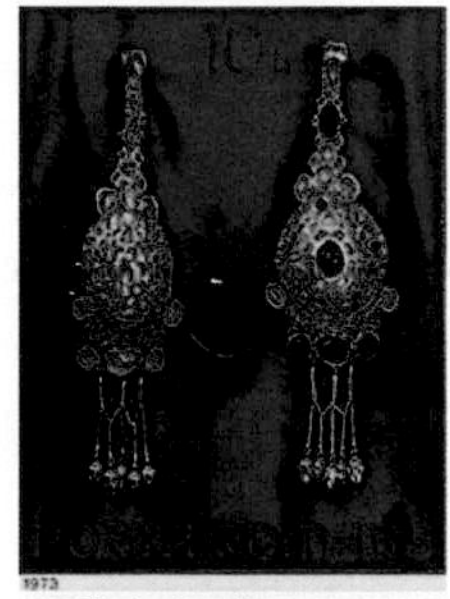
760 Fibular Brooches

1973. Treasures of Pietroasa. Multicoloured.

4010 10b. Type **760** 10 10
4011 20b. Golden figurine and bowl (horiz) 10 10
4012 55b. Gold oil flask 20 10
4013 1l.55 Brooch and bracelets (horiz) 85 10
4014 2l.75 Gold platter 1·30 20
4015 6l.80 Filgree cup holder (horiz) 2·50 1·50
MS4016 78×91 mm. 12l. Jewelled breast-plate 6·25 6·25

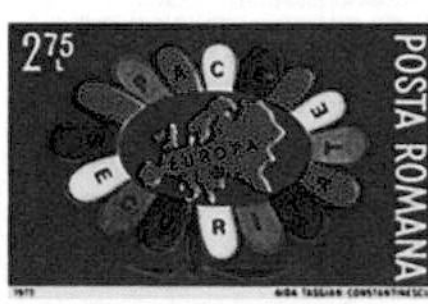

761 Map with Flower

1973. European Security and Co-operation Conference, Helsinki. Sheet 152×81 mm containing T 761 and similar horiz design. Multicoloured.

MS4017 2l.75 ×2 Type **761**; 5l. ×2 Europe "Tree" 4·25 4·25

762 Oboga Jar

1973. Romanian Ceramics. Multicoloured.

4018 10b. Type **762** 10 10
4019 20b. Vama dish and jug 10 10
4020 55b. Maginea bowl 10 10
4021 1l.55 Sibiu Saschiz jug and dish 85 15
4022 2l.75 Pisc pot and dish 1·30 20
4023 6l.80 Oboga "bird" vessel 2·50 70

763 "Postilion" (A. Verona)

1973. Stamp Day.

4024 **763** 1l.10+90b. mult 1·00 1·00

764 "Textile Workers" (G. Saru)

1973. Paintings showing Workers. Multicoloured.

4025 10b. Type **764** 10 10
4026 20b. "Construction Site" (M. Bunescu) (horiz) 10 10
4027 55b. "Shipyard Workers" (H. Catargi) (horiz) 20 10
4028 1l.55 "Working Man" (H. Catargi) 50 15
4029 2l.75 "Miners" (A. Phoebus) 1·00 20
4030 6l.80 "The Spinner" (N. Grigorescu) 2·50 80
MS4031 90×77 mm. 12l. "Harvest Meal" (S. Popescu) (horiz) 6·25 6·25

765 Town Hall, Craiova

1974. (a) Buildings.

4032 **765** 5b. red 10 10
4033 - 10b. blue 10 10
4034 - 20b. orange 10 10
4035 - 35b. green 10 10
4036 - 40b. violet 10 10
4037 - 50b. blue 10 10
4038 - 55b. brown 20 10
4039 - 60b. red 20 10
4040 - 1l. blue 30 10
4041 - 1l.20 green 30 20

(b) Ships.

4042 1l.35 black 30 10
4043 1l.45 blue 30 10
4044 1l.50 red 30 10
4045 1l.55 blue 40 10
4046 1l.75 green 40 10
4047 2l.20 blue 50 10
4048 3l.65 lilac 95 20
4049 4l.70 purple 1·40 30

DESIGNS—VERT: 10b. "Column of Infinity", Tirgu Jiu; 40b. Romanesque church, Densus; 50b. Reformed Church, Dej; 1l. Curtea de Arges Monastery. HORIZ: 20b. Heroes' Monument, Marasesti; 35b. Citadel, Risnov; 55b. Castle, Maldarasti; 60b. National Theatre, Jassy; 1l.20, Fortress and church, Tirgu Mures; 1l.35, Danube Tug "Impingator"; 1l.45, Freighter "Dimbovita"; 1l.50, Danube passenger vessel "Muntenia"; 1l.55, Cadet barque "Mircea"; 1l.75, Liner "Transylvania"; 2l.20, Bulk carrier "Oltul"; 3l.65, Trawler "Mures"; 4l.70, Tanker "Arges".

767 "Boats at Honfleur" (Monet)

1974. Impressionist Paintings. Multicoloured.

4056	20b. Type **767**	10	10
4057	40b. "Moret Church" (Sisley) (vert)	10	10
4058	55b. "Orchard in Blossom" (Pissarro)	20	10
4059	1l.75 "Jeanne" (Pissarro) (vert)	75	10
4060	2l.75 "Landscape" (Renoir)	1·30	30
4061	3l.60 "Portrait of a Girl" (Cezanne) (vert)	2·30	60
MS4062	78×84 mm. 10l. "Women Bathing" (Renoir) (vert)	6·25	6·25

768 Trotting with Sulky

1974. Cent of Horse-racing in Romania. Mult.

4063	40b. Type **768**	10	10
4064	55b. Three horses racing	20	10
4065	60b. Horse galloping	30	15
4066	1l.55 Two trotters racing	65	20
4067	2l.75 Three trotters racing	1·60	30
4068	3l.45 Two horses racing	2·30	60

769 Nicolas Titulescu (Romanian League of Nations Delegate)

1974. Interparliamentary Congress Session, Bucharest.

4069	**769**	1l.75 multicoloured	1·00	50

770 Roman Monument

1974. 1850th Anniv of Cluj (Napoca). Sheet 78×91 mm.

MS4070	10l. black and brown	6·25	6·25

771 "Anniversary Parade" (Pepene Cornelia)

1974. 25th Anniv of Romanian Pioneers Organization.

4071	**771**	55b. multicoloured	1·00	50

772 "Europe"

1974. Inter-European Cultural and Economic Co-operation. Multicoloured.

4072	2l.20 Type **772**	1·00	1·00
4073	3l.45 Satellite over Europe	2·10	2·00

1974. Romania's Victory in World Handball Championships. No. 3959 surch ROMANIA CAMPIOANA MONDIALA 1974 175L.

4074	1l.75 on 20b. multicoloured	5·25	5·00

774 Postal Motor Boat

1974. U.P.U. Centenary. Multicoloured.

4075	20b. Type **774**	10	10
4076	40b. Loading mail train	10	10
4077	55b. Loading Ilyushin Il-62M mail plane	20	15
4078	1l.75 Rural postman delivering letter	95	20
4079	2l.75 Town postman delivering letter	1·20	30
4080	3l.60 Young stamp collectors	1·80	50
MS4081	90×78 mm. 4l. Postman clearing postbox; 6l. Letters and GPO, Bucharest (each 28×22 mm)	6·25	6·25

775 Footballers

1974. World Cup Football Championship, West Germany.

4082	**775**	20b. multicoloured	10	10
4083	-	40b. multicoloured	10	10
4084	-	55b. multicoloured	20	10
4085	-	1l.75 multicoloured	50	20
4086	-	2l.75 multicoloured	1·00	30
4087	-	3l.60 multicoloured	1·60	50
MS4088		90×78 mm. 10l. Three footballers (horiz, 50×38 mm)	6·25	6·25

DESIGNS: Nos. 4083/7, Football scenes similar to Type **775**.

776 Anniversary Emblem

1974. 25th Anniv of Council for Mutual Economic Aid.

4089	**776**	55b. multicoloured	85	50

777 U.N. and World Population Emblems

1974. World Population Year Conference, Bucharest.

4090	**777**	2l. multicoloured	1·30	50

778 Emblem on Map of Europe

1974. "Euromax 1974" International Stamp Exhibition, Bucharest.

4091	**778**	4l.+3l. yellow, bl & red	3·25	70

779 Hand drawing Peace Dove

1974. 25th Anniv of World Peace Movement.

4092	**779**	2l. multicoloured	1·30	50

780 Prince John of Wallachia (400th birth anniv)

1974. Anniversaries.

4093	**780**	20b. blue	10	10
4094	-	55b. red	20	10
4095	-	1l. blue	30	10
4096	-	1l.10 brown	40	10
4097	-	1l.30 purple	65	10
4098	-	1l.40 violet	75	20

DESIGNS AND ANNIVERSARIES—VERT: 1l. Iron and Steel Works, Hunedoara (220th anniv); 1l.10, Avram Iancu (revolutionary, 150th anniv); 1l.30, Dr. C. I. Parhon (birth cent); 1l.40, Dosoftel (metropolitan) (350th birth anniv). HORIZ: 55b. Soldier guarding industrial installations (Romanian People's Army, 30th anniv).

781 Romanian and Soviet Flags as "XXX"

1974. 30th Anniv of Liberation. Multicoloured.

4099	40b. Type **781**	20	10
4100	55b. Citizens and flags (horiz)	30	20

782 View of Stockholm

1974. "Stockholmia 1974" International Stamp Exhibition. Sheet 91×78 mm.

MS4101	10l. multicoloured	6·25	6·25

783 "Centaurea nervosa"

1974. Nature Conservation. Wild Flowers. Mult.

4102	20b. Type **783**	10	10
4103	40b. "Fritillaria montana"	10	10
4104	55b. Yew	20	15
4105	1l.75 "Rhododendron kotschyi"	75	20
4106	2l.75 Alpine forget-me-not	1·00	30
4107	3l.60 Pink	1·60	50

784 Bust of Isis

1974. Romanian Archaeological Finds. Sculpture. Multicoloured.

4108	20b. Type **784**	10	10
4109	40b. Glykon serpent	20	10
4110	55b. Head of Emperor Decius	30	15
4111	1l.75 Romanian Woman	65	20
4112	2l.75 Mithras	1·00	30
4113	3l.60 Roman senator	1·70	50

785 Sibiu Market Place

1974. Stamp Day.

4114	**785**	2l.10+1l.90 mult	2·30	60

1974. "Nationala 74" Stamp Exhibition. No. 4114 optd EXPOZITIA FILATELICA "NATIONALA '74" 15–24 noiembrie Bucuresti.

4115	**786**	2l.10+1l.90 mult	4·25	4·25

787 Party Emblem

1974. 11th Romanian Communist Party Congress, Bucharest.

4116	**787**	55b. multicoloured	20	10
4117	-	1l. multicoloured	50	30

DESIGN: 1l. Similar to Type **787**, showing party emblem and curtain.

788 "The Discus-thrower" (Myron)

1974. 60th Anniv of Romanian Olympic Committee.

4118	**788**	2l. multicoloured	1·60	50

789 "Skylab"

1974. "Skylab" Space Laboratory Project.

4119	**789**	2l.50 multicoloured	1·60	1·50

790 Dr. Albert Schweitzer

1974. Birth Centenary of Dr. Albert Schweitzer (Nobel Peace Prize-winner).

4120 **790** 40b. brown 50 50

791 Handball

1975. World Universities Handball Championships, Romania.

4121 **791** 55b. multicoloured 20 10
4122 - 1l.75 multicoloured (vert) 65 20
4123 - 2l.20 multicoloured 95 30

DESIGNS: 1l.75, 2l.20, similar designs to Type **791**.

792 "Rocks and Birches"

1975. Paintings by Ion Andreescu. Multicoloured.

4124 20b. Type **792** 10 10
4125 40b. "Peasant Woman with Green Kerchief" 10 10
4126 55b. "Winter in the Forest" 20 15
4127 1l.75 "Winter in Barbizon" (horiz) 50 20
4128 2l.75 Self-portrait 1·00 50
4129 3l.50 "Main Road" (horiz) 1·60 80

793 Torch and Inscription

1975. 10th Anniv of Romanian Socialist Republic.

4130 **793** 40b. multicoloured 50 30

794 "Battle of the High Bridge" (O. Obedeanu)

1975. 500th Anniv of Victory over the Ottomans at High Bridge.

4131 **794** 55b. multicoloured 65 30

795 "Peasant Woman Spinning" (Nicolae Grigorescu)

1975. International Women's Year.

4132 **795** 55b. multicoloured 65 30

796 "Self-portrait"

1975. 500th Birth Anniv of Michelangelo.

4133 **796** 5l. multicoloured 2·50 50

797 Escorial Palace, Madrid

1975. "Espana 1975" International Stamp Exhibition, Madrid. Sheet 90×78 mm.

MS4134 10l. multicoloured 5·25 5·25

798 Mitsui Children's Science Pavilion, Okinawa

1975. International Exposition, Okinawa.

4135 **798** 4l. multicoloured 2·30 60

799 "Peonies" (Nicolae Tonitza)

1975. Inter-European Cultural and Economic Co-operation. Multicoloured.

4136 2l.20 Type **799** 1·00 1·00
4137 3l.45 "Chrysanthemums" (Stefan Luchian) 1·60 1·50

800 Dove with Coded Letter

1975. Introduction of Postal Coding.

4138 **800** 55b. multicoloured 65 30

801 Convention Emblem on "Globe"

1975. Centenary of International Metre Convention.

4139 **801** 1l.85 multicoloured 1·30 50

802 Mihail Eminescu and Museum

1975. 125th Birth Anniv of Mihail Eminescu (poet).

4140 **802** 55b. multicoloured 65 30

803 Roman Coins and Stone Inscription

1975. Bimillenary of Alba Julia.

4141 **803** 55b. multicoloured 65 30

804 "On the Banks of the Seine" (TH. Pallady)

1975. "Arphila 1975" International Stamp Exhibition, Paris. Sheet 76×90 mm.

MS4142 10l. multicoloured 5·25 5·25

805 Ana Ipatescu

1975. Death Cent of Ana Ipatescu (revolutionary).

4143 **805** 55b. mauve 65 30

806 Turnu-Severin

1975. European Architectural Heritage Year. Roman Antiquities.

4144 - 55b. black and brown 20 10
4145 - 1l.20 black, lt bl & bl 30 20
4146 - 1l.55 black and green 50 30
4147 - 1l.75 black and red 75 40
4148 **806** 2l. black and ochre 85 50
4149 - 2l.25 black and blue 1·60 80
MS4150 79×91 mm. 10l. multicoloured 3·25 3·25

DESIGNS—VERT: 55b. Emperor Trajan; 1l.20, Trajan's Column, Rome; 1l.55, Decebalus (sculpture); 10l. Roman remains, Gradiste. HORIZ: 1l.75, Imperial monument, Adam Clissi; 2l.25, Trajan's Bridge.

807 "Apollo" and "Soyuz" Spacecraft

1975. Air. "Apollo"–"Soyuz" Space Link. Mult.

4151 1l.75 Type **807** 1·60 1·50
4152 3l.25 "Apollo" and "Soyuz" linked together 2·10 2·00

808 "Michael the Brave" (Aegidius Sadeler)

1975. 375th Anniv of First Political Union of Romanian States. Multicoloured.

4153 55b. Type **808** 20 10
4154 1l.20 "Ottoman Envoys bringing gifts to Michael the Brave" (T. Aman) (horiz) 50 10
4155 2l.75 "Michael the Brave at Calugareni" (T. Aman) 1·20 30

809 Map of Europe

1975. European Security and Co-operation Conference, Helsinki. Sheet 111×81 mm containing T 809 and similar horiz designs. Multicoloured.

MS4156 2l.75 Type **809**; 5l. Open book; 5l. Children playing Postage; 2l.75 Peace doves (air) 2·50 2·50

810 Larkspur

1975. Flowers. Multicoloured.

4157 20b. Type **810** 10 10
4158 40b. Long-headed poppy 10 10
4159 55b. Common immortelle 20 10
4160 1l.75 Common rock-rose 65 20
4161 2l.75 Meadow clary 1·30 30
4162 3l.60 Chicory 1·60 50

1975. International Philatelic Fair, Riccione (Italy). Optd Tîrg international de mărci postale Riccione – Italia 23-25 august 1975.

4163 **796** 5l. multicoloured 5·25 5·00

812 Policeman using Walkie-talkie

1975. Road Safety.

4164 **812** 55b. blue 65 30

813 Text on Map of Pelendava

1975. 1750th Anniv of First Documentary Attestations of Daco-Getian Settlements of Pelendava and 500th Anniv of Craiova. Multicoloured.

4165 20b. Type **813** 15 10
4166 55b. Map of Pelendava showing location of Craiova (82×33 mm) 20 10
4167 1l. Text on map of Pelendava 40 15

Nos. 4165/7 were issued together, se-tenant, forming a composite design.

814 Muntenia Carpet

1975. Romanian Traditional Carpets. Mult.

4168 20b. Type **814** 10 10
4169 40b. Banat 10 10
4170 55b. Oltenia 20 10
4171 1l.75 Moldova 85 20
4172 2l.75 Oltenia (different) 1·20 30
4173 3l.60 Maramures 1·50 50

815 T.V. "12M" Minibus

1975. Romanian Motor Vehicles. Multicoloured.

4174 20b. Type **815** 10 10
4175 40b. L.K.W. "19 A.L.P." Oil tanker 10 10
4176 55b. A.R.O. "240" Field car 20 10
4177 1l.75 L.K.W. "R 8135 F" Truck 85 20
4178 2l.75 P.K.W. "Dacia 1300" Saloon car 1·20 30
4179 3l.60 L.K.W. "R 19215 D.F.K." Tipper truck 1·50 50

816 Postal Transit Centre, Bucharest

1975. Stamp Day. Multicoloured.

4180 1l.50+1l.50 Type **816** 2·10 1·00
4181 2l.10+1l.90 Aerial view of P.T.C. 3·75 1·50

817 "Winter" (Peter Brueghel)

1975. "Themabelga 1975" International Stamp Exhibition, Brussels. Sheet 90×78 mm.

MS4182 10l. multicoloured 5·75 5·75

818 Tobogganing

1976. Winter Olympics Games, Innsbruck. Mult.

4183 20b. Type **818** 10 10
4184 40b. Rifle-shooting (biathlon) (vert) 20 15
4185 55b. Downhill skiing (slalom) 40 20
4186 1l.75 Ski jumping 75 30
4187 2l.75 Figure skating (women's) 1·40 50
4188 3l.60 Ice hockey 1·50 1·10
MS4189 91×78 mm. 10l. Bobsleighing 9·00 9·00

819 "Washington at Valley Forge" (W. Trego)

1976. Bicent of American Revolution. Mult.

4190 20b. Type **819** 10 10
4191 40b. "Washington at Trenton" (Trumbull) (vert) 10 10
4192 55b. "Washington crossing the Delaware" (Leutze) 20 10
4193 1l.75 "Capture of the Hessians" (Trumbull) 50 20
4194 2l.75 "Jefferson" (Sully) (vert) 1·00 30
4195 3l.60 "Surrender of Cornwallis at Yorktown" (Trumbull) 1·30 40
MS4196 91×78 mm. 10l. "Signing of Declaration of Independence" (J. Trumbull) 5·25 5·25

820 "Prayer"

1976. Birth Centenary of Constantin Brancusi (sculptor). Multicoloured.

4197 55b. Type **820** 20 10
4198 1l.75 Architectural Assembly, Tg. Jiu 50 30
4199 3l.60 C. Brancusi 1·80 50

821 Anton Davidoglu (mathematician) (birth cent)

1976. Anniversaries. Multicoloured.

4200 40b. Type **821** 20 10
4201 55b. Prince Vlad Tepes (500th death anniv) 20 10
4202 1l.20 Costache Negri (patriot—death centenary) 40 10
4203 1l.75 Gallery, Archives Museum (50th anniv) 65 20

822 Inscribed Tablets, Tibiscum (Banat)

1976. Daco-Roman Archaeological Finds. Mult.

4204 **822** 20b. multicoloured 10 10
4205 - 40b. black, grey and red 20 10
4206 - 55b. multicoloured 30 15
4207 - 1l.75 multicoloured 85 20
4208 - 2l.75 black, grey and red 1·00 30
4209 - 3l.60 black, grey & green 1·70 70
MS4210 78×91 mm. 10l. multicoloured 6·25 6·25

DESIGNS: 40b. Sculptures (Banat); 55b. Inscribed tablet, coins and cup (Crisana); 1l.75, Pottery (Crisana); 2l.75, Altar and spears, Maramures (Banat); 3l.60, Vase and spears, Maramures.

823 Dr. Carol Davila

1976. Centenary of Romanian Red Cross. Mult.

4211 55b. Type **823** (postage) 20 10
4212 1l.75 Nurse and patient 50 10
4213 2l.20 First aid 75 10
4214 3l.35 Blood donors (air) 1·30 20

824 King Decebalus Vase

1976. Inter-European Cultural and Economic Co-operation. Vases from Cluj-Napoca porcelain factory. Multicoloured.

4215 2l.20 Type **824** 50 50
4216 3l.45 Vase with portrait of King Michael the Brave 1·20 1·00

825 Romanian Arms

1976

4217 **825** 1l.75 multicoloured 1·30 50

826 De Havilland D.H.9C

1976. Air. 50th Anniv of Romanian Airline. Mult.

4218 20b. Type **826** 10 10
4219 40b. I.C.A.R. Comercial 15 10
4220 60b. Douglas DC-3 20 10
4221 1l.75 Antonov An-24 75 15
4222 2l.75 Ilyushin Il-62 jetliner 1·00 30
4223 3l.60 Boeing 707 jetliner 1·60 50

827 Gymnastics

1976. Olympic Games, Montreal. Multicoloured.

4224 20b. Type **827** 10 10
4225 40b. Boxing 20 10
4226 55b. Handball 40 10
4227 1l.75 Rowing (horiz) 75 20
4228 2l.75 Gymnastics (different) (horiz) 1·00 30
4229 3l.60 Canoeing (horiz) 1·60 40
MS4230 91×78 mm. 10l. Gymnastics (55×42 mm) 6·25 6·25

828 Spiru Haret

1976. 125th Birth Anniv of Spiru Haret (mathematician).

4231 **828** 20b. multicoloured 50 30

829 Daco-Getian Sculpture on Map of Buzau

1976. 1600th Anniv of Buzau State.

4232 **829** 55b. multicoloured 65 30

1976. Philatelic Exhibition, Bucharest. No. 4199 surch EXPOZITIA FILATELICA BUCURESTI 12–19 IX 1976 1,80+.

4233 3l.60+1l.80 multicoloured 7·75 7·75

831 Red Deer

1976. Endangered Animals. Multicoloured.

4234 20b. Type **831** 10 10
4235 40b. Brown bear 20 10
4236 55b. Chamois 30 10
4237 1l.75 Wild boar 50 15
4238 2l.75 Red fox 1·00 30
4239 3l.60 Lynx 1·60 50

832 Cathedral, Milan

1976. "Italia '76" International Philatelic Exhibition, Milan.

4240 **832** 4l.75 multicoloured 1·80 50

833 D. Grecu (gymnast) and Bronze Medal

1976. Olympic Games, Montreal. Romanian Medal Winners. Multicoloured.

4241 20b. Type **833** 10 10
4242 40b. Fencing (Bronze Medal) 10 10
4243 55b. Javelin (Bronze Medal) 20 10
4244 1l.75 Handball (Silver Medal) 40 15
4245 2l.75 Boxing (Silver and Bronze Medals) (horiz) 85 20
4246 3l.60 Wrestling (Silver and Bronze Medals) (horiz) 1·30 50
4247 5l.70 Nadia Comaneci (gymnastics – 3 Gold, 1 Silver and 1 Bronze Medals) (27×42 mm) 3·75 1·80
MS4248 90×78 mm. 10l. D. Vasile (canoeist) and gold and silver medals (42×54 mm) 6·25 6·25

834 "Carnations and Oranges"

1976. Floral Paintings by Stefan Luchian. Mult.

4249 20b. Type **834** 10 10
4250 40b. "Flower Arrangement" 10 10
4251 55b. "Immortelles" 10 10
4252 1l.75 "Roses in Vase" 50 15

4253 2l.75 "Cornflowers" 75 20
4254 3l.60 "Carnations in Vase" 1·40 30

835 "Elena Cuza" (T. Aman)

1976. Stamp Day.
4255 **835** 2l.10+1l.90 mult 2·30 1·70

836 Arms of Alba

1976. Romanian Districts' Coats of Arms (1st series). Multicoloured.

4256	55b. Type **836**	30	10
4257	55b. Arad	30	10
4258	55b. Arges	30	10
4259	55b. Bacau	30	10
4260	55b. Bihor	30	10
4261	55b. Bistrita Nasaud	30	10
4262	55b. Botosani	30	10
4263	55b. Brasov	30	10
4264	55b. Braila	30	10
4265	55b. Buzau	30	10
4266	55b. Caras-Severin	30	10
4267	55b. Cluj	30	10
4268	55b. Constanta	30	10
4269	55b. Covasna	30	10
4270	55b. Dimbovita	30	10

See also Nos. 4307/31, 4496/520 and 4542/63.

837 "Ox Cart"

1977. Paintings by Nicolae Grigorescu. Mult.

4271	55b. Type **837**	20	10
4272	1l. "Self-portrait" (vert)	30	10
4273	1l.50 "Shepherdess"	40	10
4274	2l.15 "Girl with Distaff"	85	15
4275	3l.40 "Shepherd" (vert)	1·00	30
4276	4l.80 "Halt at the Well"	1·60	50

838 Telecommunications Station, Cheia

1977
4277 **838** 55b. multicoloured 50 30

839 I.C.A.R.1

1977. Air. Romanian Gliders. Multicoloured.

4278	20b. Type **839**	10	10
4279	40b. IS-3d	10	10
4280	55b. RG-5	20	10
4281	1l.50 IS-11	50	15
4282	3l. IS-29D	1·00	30
4283	3l.40 IS-28B	1·80	50

840 Red Deer

1977. Protected Animals. Multicoloured.

4284	55b. Type **840**	20	10
4285	1l. Mute swan	30	10
4286	1l.50 Egyptian vulture	50	10
4287	2l.15 European bison	75	15
4288	3l.40 White-headed duck	1·30	30
4289	4l.80 River kingfisher	1·60	50

841 "The Infantryman" (Oscar Obedeanu)

1977. Cent of Independence. Paintings. Mult.

4290	55b. Type **841**	20	10
4291	1l. "Artillery Battery at Calafat" (S. Hentia) (horiz)	40	10
4292	1l.50 "Soldiers Attacking" (Stefan Luchian)	50	10
4293	2l.15 "Battle of Plevna" (horiz)	95	15
4294	3l.40 "The Artillerymen" (Nicolae Grigorescu) (horiz)	1·30	30
4295	4l.80+2l. "Battle of Rahova" (horiz)	2·75	1·20
MS4296	90×78 mm. 10l. "Battle of Grivitza"	5·25	5·25

842 Sinaia, Carpathians

1977. Inter-European Cultural and Economic Co-operation. Views. Multicoloured.
4297 2l. Type **842** 65 30
4298 2l.40 Auroa, Black Sea 85 50

843 Petru Rares, Prince of Moldavia

1977. Anniversaries. Multicoloured.
4299 40b. Type **843** (450th anniv of accession) 50 30
4300 55b. Ion Caragiale (dramatist, 125th birth anniv) 50 30

844 Nurse with Children and Emblems

1977. 23rd Int Red Cross Conference, Bucharest.
4301 **844** 1l.50 multicoloured 75 50

845 Triumphal Arch, Bucharest

1977. 60th Anniv of Battles of Marasti, Marasesti and Oituz.
4302 **845** 2l.15 multicoloured 1·40 50

846 Boeing 707 Jetliner over Bucharest Airport

1977. European Security and Co-operation Conference, Belgrade. Sheet 80×70 mm.
MS4303 10l. yellow, carmine and blue 2·50 2·50

847 Postwoman and Letters

1977. Air.
4304 20l. Type **847** 5·25 1·50
4305 30l. Douglas DC-10 jetliner and mail 7·75 2·50

848 Mount Titano Castle, San Marino

1977. Centenary of San Marino Postage Stamps.
4306 **848** 4l. multicoloured 2·30 50

1977. Romanian District Coats of Arms (2nd series). As T 836. Multicoloured.

4307	55b. Dolj	30	10
4308	55b. Galati	30	10
4309	55b. Gorj	30	10
4310	55b. Harghita	30	10
4311	55b. Hunedoara	30	10
4312	55b. Ialomita	30	10
4313	55b. Iasi	30	10
4314	55b. Ilfov	30	10
4315	55b. Maramures	30	10
4316	55b. Mehedinti	30	10
4317	55b. Mures	30	10
4318	55b. Neamt	30	10
4319	55b. Olt	30	10
4320	55b. Prahova	30	10
4321	55b. Salaj	30	10
4322	55b. Satu Mare	30	10
4323	55b. Sibiu	30	10
4324	55b. Suceava	30	10
4325	55b. Teleorman	30	10
4326	55b. Timis	30	10
4327	55b. Tulcea	30	10
4328	55b. Vaslui	30	10
4329	55b. Vilcea	30	10
4330	55b. Vrancea	30	10
4331	55b. Romanian postal emblem	30	10

849 Gymnast on Vaulting Horse

1977. Gymnastics. Multicoloured.

4332	20b. Type **849**	10	10
4333	40b. Floor exercise	10	10
4334	55b. Gymnast on parallel bars	20	10
4335	1l. Somersault on bar	40	15
4336	2l.15 Gymnast on rings	85	30
4337	4l.80 Gymnastic exercise	2·50	1·00

850 Dispatch Rider and Army Officer

1977. Stamp Day.
4338 **850** 2l.10+1l.90 mult 2·10 2·00

851 Two Dancers with Sticks

1977. Calusarii Folk Dance. Multicoloured.

4339	20b. Type **851**	10	10
4340	40b. Leaping dancer with stick	10	10
4341	55b. Two dancers	20	10
4342	1l. Dancer with stick	40	15
4343	2l.15 Leaping dancers	85	30
4344	4l.80 Leaping dancer	2·50	1·00
MS4345	81×71 mm. 10l. Two children in costume	5·25	5·25

852 "Carpati" at Cazane

1977. European Navigation on the Danube. Mult.

4346	55b. Type **852**	20	10
4347	1l. "Mircesti" near Orsova	25	10
4348	1l.50 "Oltenita" near Calafat	35	20
4349	2l.15 Hydrofoil at Giurgiu port	50	30
4350	3l. "Herculani" at Tulcea	85	40
4351	3l.40 "Muntenia" at Sulina	1·00	50
4352	4l.80 Map of Danube delta	2·10	1·00
MS4353	81×71 mm. 10l. River god Danubius (relief from Trajan's Column) (vert)	3·25	3·25

853 Arms and Flag of Romania

1977. 30th Anniv of Romanian Republic. Mult.
4354 55b. Type **853** 20 15
4355 1l.20 Romanian-built computers 55 20

4356	1l.75 National Theatre, Craiova	1·10	40

854 Firiza Dam

1978. Romanian Dams and Hydro-electric Installations. Multicoloured.

4357	20b. Type **854**	10	10
4358	40b. Negovanu dam	10	10
4359	55b. Piatra Neamt power station	20	10
4360	1l. Izvorul Montelui Bicaz dam	35	10
4361	2l.15 Vidraru dam	65	20
4362	4l.80 Danube barrage and navigation system, Iron Gates	1·70	50

855 LZ-1 over Lake Constance

1978. Air. Airships. Multicoloured.

4363	60b. Type **855**	20	10
4364	1l. Santos Dumont's "Ballon No. 6" over Paris	35	10
4365	1l.50 Beardmore R-34 over Manhattan Island	55	10
4366	2l.15 N.4 "Italia" at North Pole	80	15
4367	3l.40 "Graf Zeppelin" over Brasov	1·30	30
4368	4l.80 "Graf Zeppelin" over Sibiu	2·20	65
MS4369	80×70 mm. 10l. "Graf Zeppelin" over Bucharest (50×38 mm)	5·50	5·50

856 Footballers and Emblem

1978. World Cup Football Championship, Argentina.

4370	**856**	55b. blue	20	10
4371	-	1l. orange	20	10
4372	-	1l.50 yellow	35	10
4373	-	2l.15 red	65	10
4374	-	3l.40 green	1·20	20
4375	-	4l.80 mauve	2·20	30
MS4376		80×70 mm. 10l. blue (38×50 mm)	5·50	5·50

DESIGNS: 1l.50 to 10l., Footballers and emblem, similar to Type **856**.

857 King Decebalus of Dacia

1978. Inter-European Cultural and Economic Co-operation. Multicoloured.

4377	1l.30 Type **857**	55	50
4378	3l.40 Prince Mircea the Elder	1·70	1·60

858 Worker and Factory

1978. 30th Anniv of Nationalization of Industry.

4379	**858**	55b. multicoloured	55	30

859 Spindle and Fork Handle, Transylvania

1978. Wood-carving. Multicoloured.

4380	20b. Type **859**	10	10
4381	40b. Cheese mould, Muntenia	20	10
4382	55b. Spoons, Oltenia	35	10
4383	1l. Barrel, Moldavia	45	15
4384	2l.15 Ladle and mug, Transylvania	80	20
4385	4l.80 Water bucket, Oltenia	1·70	65

860 Danube Delta

1978. Tourism. Multicoloured.

4386	55b. Type **860**	10	10
4387	1l. Bran Castle (vert)	20	10
4388	1l.50 Moldavian village	45	10
4389	2l.15 Muierii caves	65	15
4390	3l.40 Cable car at Boiana Brasov	1·10	20
4391	4l.80 Mangalia (Black Sea resort)	1·90	40
MS4392	80×70 mm. 10l. Strehaia Fortress and Monastery (37×49 mm)	6·75	6·75

861 MC-6 Electron Microscope

1978. Romanian Industry. Multicoloured.

4393	20b. Type **861**	10	10
4394	40b. Hydraulic excavator	10	10
4395	55b. Power station control room	35	10
4396	1l.50 Oil drillheads	55	15
4397	3l. C-12 combine harvester (horiz)	90	20
4398	3l.40 Petro-chemical combine, Pitesti	1·10	30

862 Polovraci Cave

1978. Caves and Caverns. Multicoloured.

4399	55b. Type **862**	10	10
4400	1l. Topolnita	20	10
4401	1l.50 Ponoare	45	10
4402	2l.15 Ratei	65	15
4403	3l.40 Closani	1·20	20
4404	4l.80 Epuran	1·90	50

863 Gymnastics

1978. "Daciada" Romanian Games. Multicoloured.

4405	55b. Type **863**	10	10
4406	1l. Running	20	10
4407	1l.50 Skiing	45	10
4408	2l.15 Horse jumping	65	15
4409	3l.40 Football	1·20	20
4410	4l.80 Handball	1·90	40

864 Zoomorphic Gold Plate

1978. Daco-Roman Archaeology. Multicoloured.

4411	20b. Type **864**	10	10
4412	40b. Gold torque	20	10
4413	55b. Gold cameo ring	35	10
4414	1l. Silver bowl	55	15
4415	2l.15 Bronze eagle (vert)	90	20
4416	4l.80 Silver armband	1·20	50
MS4417	74×89 mm. 10l. Gold helmet (38×50 mm). Imperf	19·00	19·00

865 Symbols of Equality

1978. International Anti-Apartheid Year.

4418	**865**	3l.40 black, yellow & red	1·30	1·00

866 Romulus, Remus and Wolf

1978. International Stamp Exhibition, Essen. Sheet 75×90 mm.

MS4419	10l. multicoloured	14·50	16·00

867 Ptolemaic Map of Dacia (2000th anniv of first record of Ziridava)

1978. Anniversaries in the History of Arad. Mult.

4420	40b. Type **867**	10	10
4421	55b. Meeting place of National Council (60th anniv of unified Romania)	10	10
4422	1l.75 Ceramic pots (950th anniv of first documentary evidence of Arad)	55	30

868 Dacian Warrior

1978. Stamp Day.

4423	**868**	6l.+3l. multicoloured	1·70	1·00

No. 4423 was issued se-tenant with a premium- carrying tab as shown in Type **868**.

869 Assembly at Alba Julia

1979. 60th Anniv of National Unity. Mult.

4424	55b. Type **869**	20	10
4425	1l. Open book, flag and sculpture	35	20

870 Wright Brothers and Wright Type A

1979. Air. Pioneers of Aviation. Multicoloured.

4426	55b. Type **870**	10	10
4427	1l. Louis Bleriot and Bleriot XI monoplane	20	10
4428	1l.50 Anthony Fokker and Fokker F.VIIa/3m "Josephine Ford"	45	10
4429	2l.15 Andrei Tupolev and Tupolev ANT-25	65	15
4430	3l. Otto Lilienthal and Lilienthal monoplane glider	80	20
4431	3l.40 Traian Vuia and Vuia No. 1	90	25
4432	4l.80 Aurel Vlaicu and No. 1 "Crazy Fly"	1·00	30
MS4433	79×70 mm. 10l. Henri Coanda and turbine-powered model airplane	5·50	5·50

871 Dacian Warrior

1979. 2050th Anniv of Independent Centralized Dacic State. Details from Trajan's Column. Multicoloured.

4434	5b. Type **871**	20	10
4435	1l.50 Dacian warrior on horseback	55	30

872 "The Heroes from Vaslui"

1979. International Year of the Child (1st issue). Children's Paintings. Multicoloured.

4436	55b. Type **872**	10	10
4437	1l. "Tica's Folk Music Band"	20	10
4438	1l.50 "Buildingsite"	45	10

4439 2l.15 "Industrial Landscape" (horiz) 55 15
4440 3l.40 "Winter Holiday" (horiz) 1·00 20
4441 4l.80 "Pioneers' Celebration" (horiz) 1·30 30

See also Nos. 4453/6.

873 Championship Emblem

1979. European Junior Ice Hockey Championship, Miercurea-Ciuc, and World Championship, Galati. Multicoloured.

4442 1l.30 Type **873** 35 10
4443 3l.40 Championship emblem (different) 1·00 30

874 Dog's tooth Violet

1979. Protected Flowers. Multicoloured.

4444 55b. Type **874** 10 10
4445 1l. Alpine violet 20 10
4446 1l.50 "Linum borzaeanum" 45 10
4447 2l.15 "Convolvulus persicus" 55 15
4448 3l.40 Auricula 1·00 20
4449 4l.80 "Aquilegia transsylvanica" 1·30 30

875 Street with Mail Coach and Post-rider

1979. Inter-European Cultural and Economic Co-operation.

4450 1l.30 Type **875** (postage) 55 30
4451 3l.40 Boeing 707 and motorcycle postman (air) 90 50

876 Oil Derrick

1979. International Petroleum Congress, Bucharest.

4452 **876** 3l.40 multicoloured 1·00 50

877 Children with Flowers

1979. International Year of the Child (2nd issue). Multicoloured.

4453 40b. Type **877** 10 10
4454 1l. Children at creative play 35 10
4455 2l. Children with hare 55 20
4456 4l.60 Young pioneers 1·50 30

878 Young Pioneer

1979. 30th Anniv of Romanian Young Pioneers.

4457 **878** 55b. multicoloured 55 30

879 "Woman in Garden"

1979. Paintings by Gh. Tattarescu. Multicoloured.

4458 20b. Type **879** 10 10
4459 40b. "Muntenian Woman" 10 10
4460 55b. "Muntenian Man" 10 10
4461 1l. "General G. Magheru" 45 15
4462 2l.15 "The Artist's Daughter" 80 20
4463 4l.80 "Self-portrait" 1·70 50

880 Brasov University

1979. Contemporary Architecture. Multicoloured.

4464 20b. State Theatre, Tirgu Mures 10 10
4465 40b. Type **880** 10 10
4466 55b. Administration Centre, Baia Mare 10 10
4467 1l. Stefan Gheorghiu Academy, Bucharest 35 15
4468 2l.15 Adminstration Centre, Botosani 65 20
4469 4l.80 House of Culture, Tirgoviste 1·50 50

881 Stefan Gheorghiu

1979. Anniversaries. Multicoloured.

4470 40b. Type **881** (birth cent) 45 20
4471 55b. Statue of Gheorghe Lazar (poet) (birth bicent) 55 30
4472 2l.15 Fallen Workers monument (Strike at Lupeni, 50th anniv) 65 40

882 Moldavian and Wallachian Women and Monuments to Union

1979. 120th Anniv of Union of Moldavia and Wallachia.

4473 **882** 4l.60 multicoloured 1·70 50

883 Party and National Flags

1979. 25th Anniv of Liberation. Multicoloured.

4474 55b. Type **883** 20 10
4475 1l. "Workers' Militia" (L. Suhar) (horiz) 45 20

884 Freighter "Galati"

1979. Ships. Multicoloured.

4476 55b. Type **884** 10 10
4477 1l. Freighter "Bucuresti" 35 10
4478 1l.50 Bulk carrier "Resita" 45 10
4479 2l.15 Bulk carrier "Tomis" 65 15
4480 3l.40 Tanker "Dacia" 1·00 20
4481 4l.80 Tanker "Independenta" 1·50 30

885 "Snapdragons"

1979. "Socfilex 79" Stamp Exhibition, Bucharest. Flower Paintings by Stefan Luchian. Mult.

4482 40b. Type **885** 10 10
4483 60b. "Carnations" 20 10
4484 1l.55 "Flowers on a Stairway" 45 10
4485 4l.+2l. "Flowers of the Field" 1·90 1·00
MS4486 79×70 mm. 10l.+5l. "Roses" 6·75 6·75

886 Gymnast

1979. 4th European Sports Conference, Berchtesgaden. Sheet 90×75 mm.

MS4487 10l. multicoloured 17·00 17·00

887 Party and National Flags

1979. 12th Romanian Communist Party Congress. Sheet 70×80 mm.

MS4488 5l. multicoloured 4·50 4·50

888 Olympic Stadium, Melbourne (1956 Games)

1979. Olympic Games, Moscow (1980). Olympic Stadia. Multicoloured.

4489 55b. Type **888** 10 10
4490 1l. Rome (1960) 35 10
4491 1l.50 Tokyo (1964) 45 10
4492 2l.15 Mexico City (1968) 65 15
4493 3l.40 Munich (1972) 1·00 20
4494 4l.80 Montreal (1978) 1·50 30
MS4495 79×69 mm. 10l. Moscow (1980) 6·75 6·50

1979. Municipal Coats of Arms. As T 836. Mult.

4496 1l.20 Alba Julia 35 10
4497 1l.20 Arad 35 10
4498 1l.20 Bacau 35 10
4499 1l.20 Baia Mare 35 10
4500 1l.20 Birlad 35 10
4501 1l.20 Botosani 35 10
4502 1l.20 Brasov 35 10
4503 1l.20 Braila 35 10
4504 1l.20 Buzau 35 10
4505 1l.20 Calarasi 35 10
4506 1l.20 Cluj 35 10
4507 1l.20 Constanta 35 10
4508 1l.20 Craiova 35 10
4509 1l.20 Dej 35 10
4510 1l.20 Deva 35 10
4511 1l.20 Drobeta Turnu Severin 35 10
4512 1l.20 Focsani 35 10
4513 1l.20 Galati 35 10
4514 1l.20 Gheorghe Gheorghiu Dej 35 10
4515 1l.20 Giurgiu 35 10
4516 1l.20 Hunedoara 35 10
4517 1l.20 Iasi 35 10
4518 1l.20 Lugoj 35 10
4519 1l.20 Medias 35 10
4520 1l.20 Odorheiu Secuiesc 35 10

889 Costumes of Maramures (female)

1979. Costumes. Multicoloured.

4521 20b. Type **889** 10 10
4522 40b. Maramures (male) 10 10
4523 55b. Vrancea (female) 10 10
4524 1l.50 Vrancea (male) 45 10
4525 3l. Padureni (female) 90 30
4526 3l.40 Padureni (male) 1·00 40

890 Post Coding Desks

1979. Stamp Day.

4527 **890** 2l.10+1l.90 mult 1·20 50

891 Figure Skating

1979. Winter Olympic Games, Lake Placid (1980). Multicoloured.

4528 55b. Type **891** 10 10
4529 1l. Downhill skiing 35 10
4530 1l.50 Biathlon 45 10
4531 2l.15 Bobsleighing 65 15
4532 3l.40 Speed skating 1·00 20
4533 4l.80 Ice hockey 1·50 30
MS4534 70×78 mm. 10l. Ice hockey (different) (37×49 mm) 5·50 5·50

892 Locomotive "Calugareni", 1869

1979. International Transport Exhibition, Hamburg. Multicoloured.

4535	55b. Type **892**	10	10
4536	1l. Steam locomotive "Orleans"	35	10
4537	1l.50 Steam locomotive No. 1059	45	10
4538	2l.15 Steam locomotive No. 150211	65	15
4539	3l.40 Steam locomotive No. 231085	1·00	20
4540	4l.80 Class 060-EA electric locomotive	1·50	30
MS4541	80×70 mm. 10l. Diesel locomotive (50×38 mm)	6·75	6·75

1980. Arms (4th series). As T 836. Multicoloured.

4542	1l.20 Oradea	35	10
4543	1l.20 Petrosani	35	10
4544	1l.20 Piatra Neamt	35	10
4545	1l.20 Pitesti	35	10
4546	1l.20 Ploiesti	35	10
4547	1l.20 Resita	35	10
4548	1l.20 Rimnicu Vilcea	35	10
4549	1l.20 Roman	35	10
4550	1l.20 Satu Mare	35	10
4551	1l.20 Sibiu	35	10
4552	1l.20 Sighetu Marmatiei	35	10
4553	1l.20 Sighisoara	35	10
4554	1l.20 Suceava	35	10
4555	1l.20 Tecuci	35	10
4556	1l.20 Timisoara	35	10
4557	1l.20 Tirgoviste	35	10
4558	1l.20 Tirgu Jiu	35	10
4559	1l.20 Tirgu-Mures	35	10
4560	1l.20 Tulcea	35	10
4561	1l.20 Turda	35	10
4562	1l.20 Turnu Magurele	35	10
4563	1l.20 Bucharest	35	10

893 Dacian Warrior

1980. 2050th Anniv of Independent Centralized Dacian State under Burebista.

4564	55b. Type **893**	10	10
4565	1l.50 Dacian fighters with flag	45	20

894 River Kingfisher

1980. European Nature Protection Year. Mult.

4566	55b. Type **894**	25	10
4567	1l. Great egret (vert)	35	10
4568	1l.50 Red-breasted goose	40	10
4569	2l.15 Red deer (vert)	50	15
4570	3l.40 Roe deer fawn	60	20
4571	4l.80 European bison (vert)	1·20	30
MS4572	90×78 mm. 10l. Eastern white pelicans ("Pelecanus onocrotallus") (38×50 mm)	3·00	3·00

895 Scarborough Lily

1980. Exotic Flowers from Bucharest Botanical Gardens. Multicoloured.

4573	55b. Type **895**	10	10
4574	1l. Floating water hyacinth	35	10
4575	1l.50 Jacobean lily	50	10
4576	2l.15 Rose of Sharon	70	15
4577	3l.40 Camellia	1·10	20
4578	4l.80 Lotus	1·60	35

896 Tudor Vladimirescu

1980. Anniversaries. Multicoloured.

4579	40b. Type **896** (revolutionary leader) (birth bicent)	10	10
4580	55b. Mihail Sadoveanu (writer) (birth cent)	10	10
4581	1l.50 Battle of Posada (650th anniv)	50	15
4582	2l.15 Tudor Arghezi (poet) (birth cent)	70	20
4583	3l. Horea (leader, Transylvanian uprising) (250th birth anniv)	95	35

897 George Enescu playing Violin

1980. Inter-European Cultural and Economic Co-operation. Two sheets, each 107×81 mm containing horiz designs as T 897.

MS4584 (a) 1l.30 ×4 emerald (Type **897**); red (Enescu conducting); violet (Enescu at piano); blue (Enescu composing). (b) 3l.40 ×4 emerald (Beethoven at piano); red (Beethoven conducting); violet (Beethoven at piano (different); blue (Beethoven composing) Set of 2 sheets 8·50 8·50

898 Dacian Fruit Dish

1980. Bimillenary of Dacian Fortress, Petrodava (now Piatra Neamt).

4585	898	1l. multicoloured	60	35

899 Throwing the Javelin

1980. Olympic Games, Moscow. Multicoloured.

4586	55b. Type **899**	10	10
4587	1l. Fencing	35	10
4588	1l.50 Pistol shooting	50	10
4589	2l.15 Single kayak	70	15
4590	3l.40 Wrestling	1·10	20
4591	4l.80 Single skiff	1·60	35
MS4592	90×78 mm. 10l. Handball (38×50 mm)	4·75	4·75

900 Postman handing Letter to Woman

1980. 2050th Anniv of Independent Centralized Dacic State National Stamp Exhibition. Sheet 78×90 mm.

MS4593	5l.+5l. multicoloured	4·75	4·75

901 Congress Emblem

1980. 15th International Congress of Historical Sciences.

4594	901	55b. deep blue and blue	60	35

902 Fireman carrying Child

1980. Firemen's Day.

4595	902	55b. multicoloured	60	35

903 Chinese and Romanian Stamp Collectors

1980. Romanian–Chinese Stamp Exhibition, Bucharest.

4596	903	1l. multicoloured	95	55

904 National Assembly Building, Bucharest

1980. European Security and Co-operation Conference, Madrid. Sheet 78×90 mm.

MS4597	10l. multicoloured	3·00	3·00

905 Rooks and Chessboard

1980. 24th Chess Olympiad, Malta. Multicoloured.

4598	55b. Knights and chessboard	10	10
4599	1l. Type **905**	35	10
4600	2l.15 Male head and chessboard	70	15
4601	4l.80 Female head and chessboard	1·60	35

906 Dacian Warrior

1980. Military Uniforms. Multicoloured.

4602	20b. Type **906**	10	10
4603	40b. Moldavian soldier (15th century)	10	10
4604	55b. Wallachian horseman (17th century)	10	10
4605	1l. Standard bearer (19th century)	35	10
4606	1l.50 Infantryman (19th century)	50	15
4607	2l.15 Lancer (19th century)	70	20
4608	4l.80 Hussar (19th century)	1·60	45

907 Burebista (sculpture, P. Mercea)

1980. Stamp Day and 2050th Anniv of Independent Centralized Dacic State.

4609	907	2l. multicoloured	60	35

908 George Oprescu

1981. Celebrities' Birth Anniversaries. Mult.

4610	1l.50 Type **908** (historian and art critic, centenary)	50	10
4611	2l.15 Marius Bunescu (painter, centenary)	70	15
4612	3l.40 Ion Georgescu (sculptor, 125th anniv)	1·20	20

909 St. Bernard

1981. Dogs. Multicoloured.

4613	40b. Mountain sheepdog (horiz)	10	10
4614	55b. Type **909**	10	10
4615	1l. Fox terrier (horiz)	35	10
4616	1l.50 Alsatian (horiz)	50	15
4617	2l.15 Boxer (horiz)	70	20
4618	3l.40 Dalmatian (horiz)	1·20	35
4619	4l.80 Poodle	1·80	55

910 Paddle-steamer "Stefan cel Mare"

1981. 125th Anniv of European Danube Commission. Multicoloured.

4620	55b. Type **910**	25	10
4621	1l. "Prince Ferdinand de Roumanie" steam launch	30	20
4622	1l.50 Paddle-steamer "Tudor Vladimirescu"	35	30
4623	2l.15 Dredger "Sulina"	50	35
4624	3l.40 Paddle-steamer "Republica Populara Romana"	60	45
4625	4l.80 Freighter in Sulina Channel	1·20	90
MS4626	90×78 mm. 10l. "Moldova" (tourist ship) sailing past Galati (49×38 mm)	3·00	3·00

911 Bare-neck Pigeon

1981. Pigeons. Multicoloured.

4627	40b. Type **911**	10	10
4628	55b. Orbetan pigeon	20	10
4629	1l. Craiova chestnut pigeon	35	10
4630	1l.50 Timisoara pigeon	50	15
4631	2l.15 Homing pigeon	70	20
4632	3l.40 Salonta giant pigeon	1·20	35

912 Party Flag and Oak Leaves

1981. 60th Anniv of Romanian Communist Party.

4633	**912**	1l. multicoloured	60	35

913 "Invirtita" Dance, Oas-Maramured

1981. Inter-European Cultural and Economic Co-operation. Two sheets, each 107×81 mm containing horiz designs as T 913. Multicoloured.

MS4634	(a) 2l.50 ×4 Type **913**; "Hora" dance, Dobrogea; "Briuletul" dance, Oltenia; "Arderleana" dance, Crisana. (b) 2l.50 ×4 "Taraneasca" dance, Moldovia; "Invirtita Sibiana" dance, Transylvania; "Jocul de 2" dance, Banat; "Calusul" dance, Muntenia Set of 2 sheets	4·75	4·75

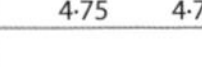

914 "Soyuz 40"

1981. Air. Soviet–Romanian Space Flight. Mult.

4635	55b. Type **914**	10	10
4636	3l.40 "Soyuz"–"Salyut" link-up	1·20	45
MS4637	78×90 mm. 10l. Cosmonauts and space complex (49×38 mm)	4·75	4·75

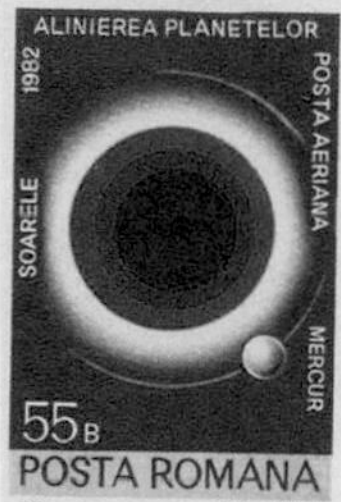

915 Sun and Mercury

1981. Air. The Planets. Multicoloured.

4638	55b. Type **915**	10	10
4639	1l. Venus, Earth and Mars	25	20
4640	1l.50 Jupiter	50	45
4641	2l.15 Saturn	60	55
4642	3l.40 Uranus	1·10	1·00
4643	4l.80 Neptune and Pluto	1·60	1·50
MS4644	90×77 mm. 10l. Earth seen from the Moon (38×49 mm)	4·75	4·75

916 Industrial Symbols

1981. "Singing Romania" National Festival. Mult.

4645	55b. Type **916**	25	10
4646	1l.50 Technological symbols	60	15
4647	2l.15 Agricultural symbols	85	20
4648	3l.40 Cultural symbols	1·20	55

917 Book and Flag

1981. "Universiada" Games, Bucharest. Mult.

4649	1l. Type **917**	25	10
4650	2l.15 Games emblem	60	35
4651	4l.80 Stadium (horiz)	1·40	1·10

918 "Woman in an Interior"

1981. 150th Birth Anniv of Theodor Aman (painter). Multicoloured.

4652	40b. "Self-portrait"	10	10
4653	55b. "Battle of Giurgiu" (horiz)	10	10
4654	1l. "Family Picnic" (horiz)	25	10
4655	1l.50 "The Painter's Studio" (horiz)	60	15
4656	2l.15 Type **918**	70	20
4657	3l.10 Aman Museum, Bucharest (horiz)	1·20	30

919 "The Thinker of Cernavoda" (polished stone sculpture)

1981. 16th International Congress of Historical Sciences.

4658	**919**	3l.40 multicoloured	1·20	1·10

920 Blood Donation

1981. Blood Donor Campaign.

4659	**920**	55b. multicoloured	60	35

921 Central Military Hospital

1981. 150th Anniv of Central Military Hospital, Bucharest.

4660	**921**	55b. multicoloured	60	35

922 Paul Constantinescu

1981. Romanian Musicians and Composers. Mult.

4661	40b. George Enescu	10	10
4662	55b. Type **922**	10	10
4663	1l. Dinu Lipatti	35	10
4664	1l.50 Ionel Perlea	50	15
4665	2l.15 Ciprian Porumbescu	70	20
4666	3l.40 Mihail Jora	1·20	45

923 Children at Stamp Exhibition

1981. Stamp Day.

4667	**923**	2l. multicoloured	60	35

924 Hopscotch

1981. Children's Games and Activities. Mult.

4668	40b. Type **924** (postage)	10	10
4669	55b. Football	10	10
4670	1l. Children with balloons and hobby horse	25	15
4671	1l.50 Fishing	35	20
4672	2l.15 Dog looking through school window at child	60	35
4673	3l. Child on stilts	85	55
4674	4l. Child tending sick dog	1·20	90
4675	4l.80 Children with model gliders (air)	1·40	1·10

Nos. 4671/15 are from illustrations by Norman Rockwell.

925 Football Players

1981. World Cup Football Championship, Spain (1982). Multicoloured.

4676	55b. Type **925**	10	10
4677	1l. Goalkeeper saving ball	25	10
4678	1l.50 Player heading ball	35	20
4679	2l.15 Player kicking ball over head	60	35
4680	3l.40 Goalkeeper catching ball	85	55
4681	4l.80 Player kicking ball	1·20	90
MS4682	90×78 mm. 10l. Goalkeeper catching ball headed by player (38×50 mm)	4·75	4·75

926 Alexander the Good, Prince of Moldavia

1982. Anniversaries. Multicoloured.

4683	1l. Type **926** (550th death anniv)	35	15
4684	1l.50 Bodgan P. Hasdeu (historian, 75th death anniv)	50	20
4685	2l.15 Nicolae Titulescu (diplomat and politician, birth centenary)	85	35

927 Entrance to Union Square Station

1982. Inauguration of Bucharest Underground Railway. Multicoloured.

4686	60b. Type **927**	25	10
4687	2l.40 Platforms and train at Heroes' Square station	85	35

928 Dog rescuing Child from Sea

1982. Dog, Friend of Mankind. Multicoloured.

4688	55b. Type **928**	10	10
4689	1l. Shepherd and sheepdog (vert)	35	15
4690	3l. Gundog (vert)	95	20
4691	3l.40 Huskies	1·10	20
4692	4l. Dog carrying woman's basket (vert)	1·20	35
4693	4l.80 Dog guiding blind person (vert)	1·40	35
4694	5l. Dalmatian and child with doll	1·60	45
4695	6l. St. Bernard	1·80	45

929 Dove, Banner and Crowd

1982. 60th Anniv of Communist Youth Union. Mult.

4696	1l. Type **929**	25	15
4697	1l.20 Construction worker	25	15
4698	1l.50 Farm workers	35	15
4699	2l. Laboratory worker and students	60	20
4700	2l.50 Labourers	85	30
4701	3l. Choir, musicians and dancers	95	35

930 Bran

1982. Inter-European Cultural and Economic Co-operation. Two sheets, each 108×80 mm containing horiz designs as T 930. Multicoloured.
MS4702 2l.50 ×4 Type **930**; Hunedoara; Sinaia; Lasi. (b) 2l.50 ×4 Neuschwanstein; Stolzenfeis; Katz-Loreley; Linderhof Set of 2 sheets 7·25 7·25

931 Constantin Brancusi (sculptor)

1982. "Philexfrance '82" International Stamp Exhibition, Paris. Sheet 71×81 mm.
MS4703 10l. multicoloured 4·75 4·75

932 Harvesting Wheat

1982. 20th Anniv of Agricultural Co-operatives. Multicoloured.

4704	50b. Type **932** (postage)	10	10
4705	1l. Cows and milking equipment	25	10
4706	1l.50 Watering apple trees	35	15
4707	2l.50 Cultivator in vineyard	70	30
4708	3l. Watering vegetables	95	35
4709	4l. Helicopter spraying cereal crop (air)	1·20	45
MS4710	68×80 mm. 10l. Aerial view of new village (50×37 mm)	4·75	4·75

933 Vladimir Nicolae's Standard 1 Hang-glider

1982. Air. Hang-gliders. Multicoloured.

4711	50b. Type **933**	10	10
4712	1l. Excelsior D	25	10
4713	1l.50 Dedal-1	35	20
4714	2l.50 Entuziast	85	35
4715	4l. AK-22	1·20	55
4716	5l. Grifrom	1·60	65

934 Baile Felix

1982. Spas and Health Resorts. Multicoloured.

4717	50b. Type **934**	10	10
4718	1l. Predeal (horiz)	25	10
4719	1l.50 Baile Herculane	50	15
4720	2l.50 Eforie Nord (horiz)	70	30
4721	3l. Olimp (horiz)	85	35
4722	5l. Neptun (horiz)	1·60	55

935 "Legend"

1982. Paintings by Sabin Balasa. Multicoloured.

4723	1l. Type **935**	35	15
4724	1l.50 "Contrasts"	50	20
4725	2l.50 "Peace Relay"	1·30	55
4726	4l. "Genesis of the Romanian People" (vert)	1·40	65

936 Vlaicu Monument, Banesti-Prahova

1982. Air. Birth Centenary of Aurel Vlaicu (aviation pioneer). Multicoloured.

4727	50b. Vlaicu's glider, 1909 (horiz)	10	10
4728	1l. Type **936**	35	20
4729	2l.50 Air Heroes' Monument	95	55
4730	3l. Vlaicu's No. 1 airplane "Crazy Fly", 1910 (horiz)	1·10	65

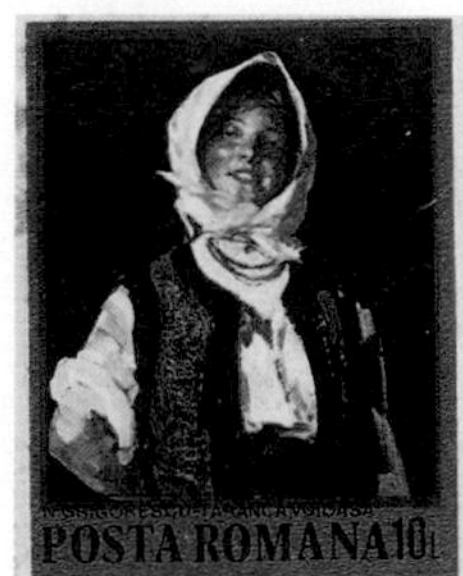

937 "Cheerful Peasant Woman"

1982. 75th Death Anniv Nicolae Grigorescu (artist). Sheet 70×80 mm.
MS4731 10l. multicoloured 4·75 4·75

938 Central Exhibition Pavilion

1982. "Tib '82" International Fair, Bucharest.
4732 **938** 2l. multicoloured 70 35

939 Young Pioneer with Savings Book and Books

1982. Savings Week. Multicoloured.

4733	1l. Type **939**	35	15
4734	2l. Savings Bank advertisement (Calin Popovici)	70	20

940 Postwoman delivering Letters

1982. Stamp Day. Multicoloured.

4735	1l. Type **940**	35	15
4736	2l. Postman	70	20

941 "Brave Young Man and the Golden Apples" (Petre Ispirescu)

1982. Fairy Tales. Multicoloured.

4737	50b. Type **941**	10	10
4738	1l. "Bear tricked by the Fox" (Ion Creanga)	25	10
4739	1l.50 Warrior fighting bird ("Prince of Tears" (Mihai Eminescu))	50	15
4740	2l.50 Hen with bag ("Bag with Two Coins" (Ion Creanga))	70	20
4741	3l. Rider fighting three-headed dragon ("Ileana Simziana" (Petre Ispirescu))	85	35
4742	5l. Man riding devil ("Danila Prepeleac" (Ion Creanga))	1·60	55

942 Symbols of Industry, Party Emblem and Programme

1982. Romanian Communist Party National Conference, Bucharest. Multicoloured.

4743	1l. Type **942**	35	15
4744	2l. Wheat symbols of industry and Party emblem and open programme	70	20

943 Wooden Canteen from Suceava

1982. Household Utensils.

4745	**943**	50b. red	10	10
4746	-	1l. blue	35	10
4747	-	1l.50 orange	60	10
4748	-	2l. blue	70	10
4749	-	3l. green	1·10	10
4750	-	3l.50 green	1·30	10
4751	-	4l. brown	1·60	10
4752	-	5l. blue	1·90	10
4753	-	6l. blue	2·30	10
4754	-	7l. purple	2·75	10
4755	-	7l.50 mauve	2·75	10
4756	-	8l. green	3·00	10
4757	-	10l. red	3·00	10
4758	-	20l. violet	4·25	20
4759	-	30l. blue	7·25	35
4760	-	50l. brown	12·00	45

DESIGNS: As T **943**—VERT: 1l. Ceramic plates from Radauti; 2l. Jug and plate from Vama-Maramures; 3l. Wooden churn and pail from North Moldavia; 4l. Wooden spoons and ceramic plate from Cluj; 5l. Ceramic bowl and pot from Marginea-Suceava. HORIZ: 1l.50, Wooden dipper from Valea Mare; 3l.50, Ceramic plates from Leheceni-Crisana. 29×23 mm: 10l. Wooden tubs from Hunedoara and Suceava; 30l. Wooden spoons from Alba. 23×29 mm: 6l. Ceramic pot and jug from Bihor; 7l. Distaff and spindle from Transylvania; 7l.50, Double wooden pail from Suceava; 8l. Pitcher and ceramic plate from Oboga and Horezu; 20l. Wooden canteen and six glasses from Horezu; 50l. Ceramic plates from Horezu.

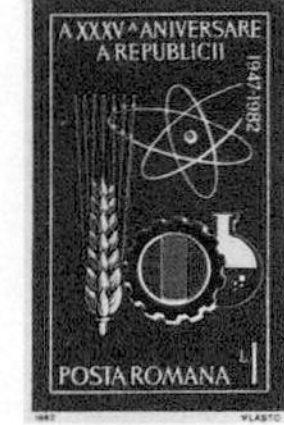

944 Wheat, Cogwheel, Flask and Electricity Emblem

1982. 35th Anniv of People's Republic. Mult.

4767	1l. Type **944**	35	15
4768	2l. National flag and oak leaves	70	35

945 H. Coanda and Diagram of Jet Engine

1983. Air. 25 Years of Space Exploration. Mult.

4769	50b. Type **945**	10	10
4770	1l. H. Oberth and diagram of rocket	35	10
4771	1l.50 "Sputnik 1", 1957 (first artificial satellite)	60	15
4772	2l.50 "Vostok 1", (first manned flight)	85	20
4773	4l. "Apollo 11, 1969 (first Moon landing)	1·40	35
4774	5l. Space shuttle "Columbia"	1·80	55
MS4775	93×80 mm. 10l. Earth (41×53 mm)	7·25	7·25

946 Rombac One Eleven 500 Jetliner

1983. Air. First Romanian-built Jetliner.
4776 **946** 11l. blue 4·25 80

947 Matei Millo in "The Discontented" by Vasile Alecsandri

1983. Romanian Actors.

4777	**947**	50b. red and black	10	10
4778	-	1l. green and black	35	10
4779	-	1l.50 violet and black	60	10
4780	-	2l. brown and black	70	10
4781	-	2l.50 green and black	95	15
4782	-	3l. blue and black	1·20	20
4783	-	4l. green and black	1·40	35
4784	-	5l. lilac and black	1·80	45

DESIGNS: 1l. Mihail Pascaly in "Director Millo" by Vasile Alecsandri; 1l.50, Aristizza Romanescu in "The Dogs" by H. Lecca; 2l. C. I. Nottara in "Blizzard" by B. S. Delavrancea; 2l.50, Grigore Manolescu in "Hamlet" by William Shakespeare; 3l. Agatha Birsescu in "Medea" by Lebouvet; 4l. Ion Brezeanu in "The Lost Letter" by I. L. Caragiale; 5l. Aristide Demetriad in "The Despotic Prince" by Vasile Alecsandri.

948 Hugo Grotius

1983. 400th Birth Anniv of Hugo Grotius (Dutch jurist).

4785	**948**	2l. brown	95	55

949 Aro "10"

1983. Romanian-built Vehicles. Multicoloured.

4786	50b. Type **949**	25	10
4787	1l. Dacia "1300" Break	50	10
4788	1l.50 Aro "242"	70	15
4789	2l.50 Aro "244"	1·20	20
4790	4l. Dacia "1310"	1·90	35
4791	5l. Oltcit "Club"	2·40	55

950 Johannes Kepler (astronomer)

1983. Inter-European Cultural and Economic Co-operation. Two sheets, each 110×80 mm containing horiz designs as T 950. Multicoloured.

MS4792 (a) 3l. ×4 Type **950**; Alexander von Humboldt (explorer) and "Pizarro" J.W. von Goethe (writer); Richard Wagner (composer). (b) 3l. ×4 Ion Andreescu (artist); George Constantinescu (engineer); Tudor Arghezi (writer); C. I. Parhon (physician) Set of 2 sheets 7·25 7·25

951 National and Communist Party Flags

1983. 50th Anniv of 1933 Workers' Revolution.

4793	**951**	2l. multicoloured	95	55

952 Loading Mail into Boeing 707

1983. Air. World Communications Year.

4794	**952**	2l. multicoloured	95	55

953 Bluethroat

1983. Birds of the Danube Delta. Multicoloured.

4795	50b. Type **953**	25	10
4796	1l. Rose-coloured starling	50	10
4797	1l.50 European roller	70	15
4798	2l.50 European bee eater	1·20	20
4799	4l. Reed bunting	1·90	35
4800	5l. Lesser grey shrike	2·40	45

954 Kayak

1983. Water Sports. Multicoloured.

4801	50b. Type **954**	25	10
4802	1l. Water polo	50	10
4803	1l.50 Canoeing	70	15
4804	2l.50 Diving	1·20	20
4805	4l. Rowing	1·90	35
4806	5l. Swimming (start of race)	2·40	45

955 Postman on Bicycle

1983. Stamp Day. Multicoloured.

4807	1l. Type **955**	35	15
4808	3l.50(+3l.) National flag as stamp	1·40	1·10

MS4809 90×79 mm. 10l. Unloading mail from Rombac One Eleven 500 at Bucharest airport (38×50 mm) (air) 7·25 7·25

No. 4808 was issued se-tenant with a premium-carrying tab showing the Philatelic Association emblem.

956 "Geum reptans"

1983. European Flora and Fauna. Multicoloured.

4810	1l. Type **956**	70	45
4811	1l. Long-headed poppy	70	45
4812	1l. Stemless carline thistle	70	45
4813	1l. "Paeonia peregrina"	70	45
4814	1l. "Gentiana excisa"	70	45
4815	1l. Eurasian red squirrel	70	45
4816	1l. "Grammia quenselii" (butterfly)	70	45
4817	1l. Middle-spotted woodpecker	70	45
4818	1l. Lynx	70	45
4819	1l. Wallcreeper	70	45

957 "Girl with Feather"

1983. Paintings by Corneliu Baba. Multicoloured.

4820	1l. Type **957**	50	15
4821	2l. "Congregation"	95	20
4822	3l. "Farm Workers"	1·40	35
4823	4l. "Rest in the Fields" (horiz)	1·90	45

958 Flag and Oak Leaves

1983. 65th Anniv of Union of Transylvania and Romania. Multicoloured.

4824	1l. Type **958**	50	20
4825	2l. National and Communist Party Flags and Parliament building, Bucharest	95	35

959 Postman and Post Office

1983. "Balkanfila IX '83" Stamp Exhibition, Bucharest. Multicoloured.

4826	1l. Type **959**	50	20
4827	2l. Postwoman and Athenaeum Concert Hall	95	35

MS4828 90×78 mm. 10l. Balkan flags and Athenaeum Concert Hall (37×50 mm) 4·75 4·75

960 "Orient Express" at Bucharest, 1883

1983. Centenary of "Orient Express". Sheet 90×78 mm.

MS4829 10l. multicoloured 7·25 7·25

961 Cross-country Skiing

1984. Winter Olympic Games, Sarajevo. Mult.

4830	50b. Type **961**	10	10
4831	1l. Biathlon	35	15
4832	1l.50 Ice skating	50	20
4833	2l. Speed skating	70	35
4834	3l. Ice hockey	95	45
4835	3l.50 Bobsleighing	1·20	55
4836	4l. Luge	1·40	65
4837	5l. Downhill skiing	1·80	85

962 Prince Cuza and Arms

1984. 125th Anniv of Union of Moldova and Wallachia. Sheet 90×78 mm.

MS4838 10l. multicoloured 4·75 4·75

963 Palace of Udriste Nasturel (Chancery official)

1984. Anniversaries.

4839	50b. green, pink and silver	25	10
4840	1l. violet, green and silver	50	10
4841	1l.50 multicoloured	70	15
4842	2l. brown, blue and silver	95	20
4843	3l.50 multicoloured	1·70	40
4844	4l. multicoloured	1·90	45

DESIGNS: 50b. Type **963** (325th death anniv); 1l. Miron Costin (poet, 350th birth anniv); 1l.50, Crisan (Giurgiu Marcu) (leader of peasant revolt, 250th birth anniv); 2l. Simion Barnutiu (scientist, 175th birth anniv); 3l.50, Diuliu Zamfirescu (writer, 125th birth anniv); 4l. Nicolae Milescu at Great Wall of China (explorer, 275th death anniv).

964 Chess Game

1984. 15th Balkan Chess Championships, Baile Herculane. Sheet 107×80 mm containing T 964 and similar horiz designs. Multicoloured.

MS4845 3l. ×4 various chess games 7·25 7·25

965 Orsova Bridge

1984. Inter-European Cultural and Economic Co-operation. Two sheets each 108×81 mm containing horiz designs as T 965. Multicoloured.

MS4846 (a) 3l. ×4 Type **965**; Arges Bridge, Basarabi Bridge; Ohaba Bridge all in Rumania. (b) 3l. ×4 Kohlbrand Bridge, Hamburg; Bosphorus Bridge, Istanbul; Europa Bridge, Innsbruck; Tower Bridge, London Set of 2 sheets 7·25 7·25

966 Sunflower

1984. Protection of Environment. Multicoloured.

4847	1l. Type **966**	50	10
4848	2l. Red deer	95	20
4849	3l. Carp	1·40	45
4850	4l. Jay	1·90	55

967 Flowering Rush

1984. Flowers of the Danube. Multicoloured.

4851	50b. Arrowhead	25	10
4852	1l. Yellow iris	50	10
4853	1l.50 Type **967**	70	15
4854	3l. White water lily	1·40	30
4855	4l. Fringed water lily (horiz)	1·90	35
4856	5l. Yellow water lily (horiz)	2·40	55

968 Crowd with Banners

1984. 45th Anniv of Anti-Fascist Demonstration.

4857	**968**	2l. multicoloured	1·20	55

969 High Jumping

1984. Olympic Games, Los Angeles (1st issue). Multicoloured.

4858	50b. Type **969**	10	10
4859	1l. Swimming	35	15
4860	1l.50 Running	50	20
4861	3l. Handball	1·10	50
4862	4l. Rowing	1·30	60
4863	5l. Canoeing	1·90	90

See also Nos. 4866/73.

970 Congress Emblem

1984. 25th Ear, Nose and Throat Association Congress, Bucharest.

4864	**970**	2l. multicoloured	95	55

971 Footballers and Romanian Flag

1984. European Cup Football Championship. Two sheets, each 109×81 mm containing horiz designs as T 971 showing footballers and national flag. Multicoloured.

MS4865 (a) 3l. ×Type **971**; West Germany; Portugal; Spain. (b) 3l. ×4 France; Belgium; Yugoslavia; Denmark Set of 2 sheets 12·00 12·00

1984. Olympic Games, Los Angeles (2nd issue). As T 969. Multicoloured.

4866	50b. Boxing	10	10
4867	1l. Rowing	25	10
4868	1l. Handball	40	15
4869	2l. Judo	50	20
4870	3l. Wrestling	85	40
4871	3l.50 Fencing	95	45
4872	4l. Kayak	1·10	50
4873	5l. Swimming	1·40	65

972 Mihai Ciuca (bacteriologist, cent)

1984. Birth Anniversaries. Dated "1983".

4874	**972**	1l. purple, blue and silver	35	15
4875	-	2l. brown and silver	70	20
4876	-	3l. green, brown and silver	1·10	45
4877	-	4l. violet, green and silver	1·40	55

DESIGNS: 2l. Petre S. Aurelian (agronomist, 150th anniv); 3l. Alexandru Vlahuta (writer, 125th anniv); 4l. Dimitrie Leonida (engineer, centenary).

973 Lockhead 14 Super Electra

1984. Air. 40th Anniv of International Civil Aviation Organization. Multicoloured.

4878	50b. Type **973**	25	10
4879	1l.50 Britten Norman Islander	70	20
4880	3l. Rombac One Eleven 500 jetliner	1·40	45
4881	6l. Boeing 707 jetliner	3·00	55

974 Flags, Flame and Power Station

1984. 40th Anniv of Liberation.

4882	**974**	2l. multicoloured	1·20	55

975 Lippizaner

1984. Horses. Multicoloured.

4883	50b. Type **975**	25	10
4884	1l. Hutul	50	10
4885	1l.50 Bukovina	70	15
4886	2l.50 Nonius	1·20	20
4887	4l. Arab	1·90	35
4888	5l. Romanian halfbreed	2·40	45

976 V. Racila (woman's singles sculls, gold)

1984. Romanian Olympic Games Medal Winners. Two sheets, each 125×129 mm containing four designs as T 976. Multicoloured.

MS4889 (a) 3l. ×6 Type **976**; P. Becheru and N. Vlad (weightlifting, gold); D. Melinte (800m.) and M. Puica (3000m. women's running, gold); Men's canoeing (Canadian pairs, gold); Fencing (silver); Women's modern rhythmic gymnastics (silver). (b) 3l. ×6, Women's team gymnastics (gold); Women's kayak fours (gold); A. Stanciu (women's long jump, gold); I. Draica and V. Andrei (wrestling, gold); Judo (bronze); Pistol shooting (silver) Set of 2 sheets 18·00 18·00

977 Memorial, Alba Julia

1984. Bicentenary of Horea, Closa and Crisan Uprisings.

4890	**977**	2l. multicoloured	70	45

978 "Portrait of a Child" (TH. Aman)

1984. Paintings of Children. Multicoloured.

4891	50b. Type **978**	10	10
4892	1l. "The Little Shepherd" (N. Grigorescu)	35	10
4893	2l. "Lica with an Orange" (St. Luchian)	70	15
4894	3l. "Portrait of a Child" (N. Tonitza)	1·10	20
4895	4l. "Portrait of a Boy" (S. Popp)	1·60	35
4896	5l. "Portrait of Young Girl" (I. Tuculescu)	2·00	45

979 Stage Coach and Romanian Philatelic Association Emblem

1984. Stamp Day.

4897	**979**	2l.(+1l.) multicoloured	95	55

No. 4897 was issued with premium-carrying label as shown in T **979**.

980 Flags and Party Emblem

1984. 13th Romanian Communist Party Congress, Bucharest. Sheet 90×78 mm.

MS4898 10l. multicoloured 8·50 8·50

981 Dalmatian Pelicans

1984. Protected Animals. Dalmatian Pelicans. Mult.

4899	50b. Type **981**	25	15
4900	1l. Pelican on nest	60	35
4901	1l. Pelicans on lake	60	35
4902	2l. Pelicans roosting	95	55

982 Dr. Petru Groza (former President)

1984. Anniversaries. Multicoloured.

4903	50b. Type **982** (birth centenary)	10	10
4904	1l. Alexandru Odobescu (writer) (150th birth anniv)	35	10
4905	2l. Dr. Carol Davila (physician) (death centenary)	60	15
4906	3l. Dr. Nicolae Gh. Lupu (physician) (birth centenary)	1·10	20
4907	4l. Dr. Daniel Danielopolu (physician) (birth centenary)	1·30	35
4908	5l. Panait Istrati (writer) (birth centenary)	1·80	45

983 Generator

1984. Centenary of Power Station and Electric Street Lighting in Timisoara. Multicoloured.

4909	1l. Type **983**	35	20
4910	2l. Street lamp	70	35

984 Gounod and Paris Opera House

1985. Inter-European Cultural and Economic Co-operation. Composers. Two sheets, each 110×80 mm containing horiz designs as T 984.

MS4911 (a) 3l. ×4 green and violet (Type **984**); red and blue (Strauss and Munich Opera House); violet and green (Mozart and Vienna Opera House); blue and red (Verdi and La Scala, Milan). (b) 3l. ×4 violet and green (Tchaikovsky and Bolshoi Theatre, Moscow); blue and red (Enescu and Bucharest Opera House); green and violet (Wagner and Dresden Opera House); red and blue (Moniuszko and Warsaw Opera House) Set of 2 sheets 7·25 7·25

985 August Treboniu Laurian (linguist and historian)

1985. Anniversaries. Multicoloured.

4912	50b. Type **985** (175th birth anniv)	10	10
4913	1l. Grigore Alexandrescu (writer) (death centenary)	25	10
4914	1l.50 Gheorghe Pop de Basesti (politician) (150th birth anniv)	50	15
4915	2l. Mateiu Caragiale (writer) (birth centenary)	70	20
4916	3l. Gheorghe Ionescu-Sisesti (scientist) (birth centenary)	95	35
4917	4l. Liviu Rebreanu (writer) (birth centenary)	1·40	55

986 Students in Science Laboratory

1985. International Youth Year. Multicoloured.

4918	1l. Type **986**	35	20
4919	2l. Students on construction site	70	35

MS4920 91×79 mm. 10l. Students with banner and dove (53×41 mm) 4·75 4·75

987 Racoon Dog

1985. Protected Animals. Multicoloured.

4921	50b. Type **987**	25	10

4922	1l. Grey partridge	50	10
4923	1l.50 Snowy owl	70	10
4924	2l. Pine marten	95	15
4925	3l. Eurasian badger	1·30	20
4926	3l.50 Eurasian otter	1·40	30
4927	4l. Western Capercaillie	1·70	35
4928	5l. Great bustard	2·00	45

988 Flags and Victory Monument, Bucharest

1985. 40th Anniv of Victory in Europe Day.

4929	**988**	2l. multicoloured	1·20	55

989 Union Emblem

1985. Communist Youth Union Congress.

4930	**989**	2l. multicoloured	70	55

990 Route Map and Canal

1985. Danube–Black Sea Canal. Multicoloured.

4931	1l. Type **990**	50	10
4932	2l. Canal and bridge, Cernavoda	95	15
4933	3l. Road over Canal, Medgidia	1·40	20
4934	4l. Canal control tower, Agigea	1·80	35
MS4935	90×79 mm. 10l. Opening ceremony (53×39 mm)	9·00	9·00

991 Brown Pelican

1985. Birth Bicentenary of John J. Audubon (ornithologist). Multicoloured.

4936	50b. American robin (horiz)	25	10
4937	1l. Type **991**	50	10
4938	1l.50 Yellow-crowned night heron	70	15
4939	2l. Northern oriole	95	20
4940	3l. Red-necked grebe	1·40	35
4941	4l. Mallard (horiz)	1·90	45

992 "Fire"

1985. Paintings by Ion Tuculescu. Multicoloured.

4942	1l. Type **992**	25	10
4943	2l. "Circulation"	60	20
4944	3l. "Interior of Peasant's Home" (horiz)	85	35
4945	4l. "Sunset" (horiz)	1·20	55

993 Peacock

1985. Butterflies and Moths. Multicoloured.

4946	50b. Type **993**	10	10
4947	1l. Swallowtail	35	10
4948	2l. Red admiral	70	15
4949	3l. Emperor moth	1·20	20
4950	4l. Hebe tiger moth	1·60	35
4951	5l. Eyed hawk moth	1·90	45

994 Transfagarasan Mountain Road

1985. 20th Anniv of Election of General Secretary Nicolae Ceausescu and 9th Communist Party Congress. Multicoloured.

4952	1l. Type **994**	60	20
4953	2l. Danube–Black Sea Canal	1·20	35
4954	3l. Bucharest underground railway	1·80	55
4955	4l. Irrigating fields	2·40	80

995 Romanian Crest, Symbols of Agriculture and "XX"

1985. 20th Anniv of Romanian Socialist Republic. Multicoloured.

4956	1l. Type **995**	60	25
4957	2l. Crest, symbols of industry and "XX"	1·20	35

996 Daimlers' Motor Cycle, 1885

1985. Centenary of Motor Cycle. Sheet 91×79 mm.

MS4958	10l. multicoloured	4·75	4·75

997 "Senecio glaberrimus"

1985. 50th Anniv of Retezat National Park. Mult.

4959	50b. Type **997**	25	10
4960	1l. Chamois	50	15
4961	2l. "Centaurea retezatensis"	95	20
4962	3l. Violet	1·20	25
4963	4l. Alpine marmot	1·70	35
4964	5l. Golden eagle	2·00	55
MS4965	91×80 mm. 10l. Lynx ("Lynx lynx")	6·00	6·00

998 Universal "530 DTC"

1985. Romanian Tractors. Multicoloured.

4966	50b. Type **998**	10	10
4967	1l. Universal "550 M HC"	35	15
4968	1l.50 Universal "650 Super"	50	20
4969	2l. Universal "850"	70	25
4970	3l. Universal "S 1801 IF" tracked front loader	1·20	35
4971	4l. Universal "A 3602 IF" front loader	1·80	55

999 Costume of Muscel (female)

1985. Costumes (1st series). Multicoloured.

4972	50b. Type **999**	10	10
4973	50b. Muscel (male)	10	10
4974	1l.50 Bistrita-Nasaud (female)	50	20
4975	1l.50 Bistrita-Nasaud (male)	50	20
4976	2l. Vrancea (female)	70	35
4977	2l. Vrancea (male)	70	35
4978	3l. Vilcea (female)	95	45
4979	3l. Vilcea (male)	95	45

See also Nos. 5143/5150.

1000 Footballer attacking Goal

1985. World Cup Football Championship, Mexico (1986) (1st issue). Multicoloured.

4980	50b. Type **1000**	10	10
4981	1l. Player capturing ball	35	15
4982	1l.50 Player heading ball	50	20
4983	2l. Player about to tackle	70	25
4984	3l. Player heading ball and goalkeeper	1·20	35
4985	4l. Player kicking ball over-head	1·80	55

See also Nos. 5038/43.

1001 U.N. Emblem and "40"

1985. 40th Anniv of U.N.O. (4986) and 30th Anniv of Romanian Membership (4987).

4986	2l. Type **1001**	60	45
4987	2l. U.N. building, New York, U.N. emblem and Romanian crest	60	45

1002 Copper

1985. Minerals. Multicoloured.

4988	50b. Quartz and calcite	10	10
4989	1l. Type **1002**	25	15
4990	2l. Gypsum	70	20
4991	3l. Quartz	95	25
4992	4l. Stibium	1·30	35
4993	5l. Tetrahedrite	1·80	55

1003 Posthorn

1985. Stamp Day.

4994	**1003**	2l.(+1l.) multicoloured	1·20	1·10

1004 Goofy as Hank waking to find himself at Camelot

1985. 150th Birth of Mark Twain (writer). Scenes from "A Connecticut Yankee in King Arthur's Court" (film). Multicoloured.

4995	50b. Type **1004**	3·00	2·20
4996	50b. Hank at the stake and Merlin (Mickey Mouse)	3·00	2·20
4997	50b. Hank being hoisted onto horseback in full armour	3·00	2·20
4998	50b. Pete as Sir Sagramoor on horseback	3·00	2·20
MS4999	122×96 mm. 5l. Hank at the tournament against Sir Sagramor	24·00	24·00

1985. Birth Bicentenaries of Grimm Brothers (folklorists). Scenes from "The Three Brothers". As T 1004. Multicoloured.

5000	1l. Father (Donald Duck) bidding farewell to the brothers (Huey, Louie and Dewey)	7·25	6·75
5001	1l. Louie as fencing master brother	7·25	6·75
5002	1l. Louie keeping rain off his father with sword	7·25	6·75
5003	1l. Huey as blacksmith brother shoeing galloping horse	7·25	6·75
5004	1l. Dewey as barber brother shaving Brer Rabbit on the run	7·25	6·75
MS5005	120×95 mm. 5l. Brothers playing music	24·00	24·00

1005 Wright Brothers (aviation pioneers) and Wright Flyer 1

1985. Explorers and Pioneers. Multicoloured.

5006	1l. Type **1005**	35	10
5007	1l.50 Jacques Yves Cousteau (undersea explorer) and "Calypso"	50	10
5008	2l. Amelia Earhart (first woman trans-Atlantic flyer) and Fokker F.VIIb/3m seaplane "Friendship"	70	15
5009	3l. Charles Lindbergh (first solo trans-Atlantic flyer) and Ryan NYP Special "Spirit of St. Louis"	1·10	20
5010	3l.50 Sir Edmund Hillary (first man to reach summit of Everest)	1·20	25
5011	4l. Robert Peary and Emil Racovita (polar explorers)	1·40	30

5012 5l. Richard Byrd (polar explorer and aviator) and polar supply ship 1·80 40
5013 6l. Neil Armstrong (first man on Moon) and Moon 1·90 45

1006 Edmond Halley and Comet

1986. Air. Appearance of Halley's Comet.
5014 2l. Type **1006** 70 25
5015 4l. Comet, orbit and space probes 1·70 45

No. 5014 is wrongly inscr "Edmund".

1007 "Nina in Green"

1986. Paintings by Nicolae Tonitza. Multicoloured.
5016 1l. Type **1007** 35 10
5017 2l. "Irina" 70 20
5018 3l. "Forester's Daughter" 1·10 35
5019 4l. "Woman on Veranda" 1·40 55

1008 Wild Cat ("Felis silvestris")

1986. Inter-European Cultural and Economic Co-operation. Two sheets, each 110×81 mm containing horiz designs as T 1008. Multicoloured.
MS5020 (a) 3l. ×4 Type **1008**; Stoat ("Mustela erminea"); Capercaillie ("Tetrao urogallus"); Brown bear ("Ursus arctos"). (b) 3l. ×4 "Dianthus callizonus"; Arolla pine ("Pinus cembra"); Willow ("Salix" sp.); "Rosa pendulina" Set of 2 sheets 7·25 7·25

1009 Goofy playing Clarinet

1986. 50th Anniv of Colour Animation. Scenes from "Band Concert" (cartoon film). Mult.
5021 50b. Type **1009** 3·00 2·20
5022 50b. Clarabelle playing flute 3·00 2·20
5023 50b. Mickey Mouse conducting 3·00 2·20
5024 50b. Paddy and Peter Pig playing euphonium and trumpet 3·00 2·20
5025 1l. Conductor Mickey and flautist Donald Duck 7·25 6·75
5026 1l. Donald caught in trombone slide 7·25 6·75
5027 1l. Horace playing drums 7·25 6·75
5028 1l. Donald selling ice cream 7·25 6·75
5029 1l. Mickey and euphonium caught in tornado 7·25 6·75
MS5030 120×95 mm. 5l. Instruments and musicians in tree 24·00 24·00

1010 Hotel Diana, Baile Herculane

1986. Spa Hotels. Multicoloured.
5031 50b. Type **1010** 10 10
5032 1l. Hotel Termal, Baile Felix 25 15
5033 2l. Hotels Delfin, Meduza and Steaua de Mare, North Eforie 60 20
5034 3l. Hotel Caciulata, Calimanesti-Caciulata 95 25
5035 4l. Villa Palas, Slanic Moldova 1·30 35
5036 5l. Hotel Bradet, Sovata 1·90 55

1011 Ceausescu and Red Flag

1986. 65th Anniv of Romanian Communist Party.
5037 **1011** 2l. multicoloured 1·90 1·10

1012 Italy v. Bulgaria

1986. World Cup Football Championship, Mexico (2nd issue). Multicoloured.
5038 50b. Type **1012** 10 10
5039 1l. Mexico v. Belgium 25 15
5040 2l. Canada v. France 60 20
5041 3l. Brazil v. Spain 85 25
5042 4l. Uruguay v. W. Germany 1·40 35
5043 5l. Morocco v. Poland 1·90 55

1013 Alexandru Papanas' Bucker Bu 133 Jungmesister Biplane (Aerobatics Champion, 1936)

1986. Air. "Ameripex" '86 International Stamp Exhibition, Chicago. Sheet 120×95 mm.
MS5044 10l. multicoloured 4·75 4·75

1014 "Tulipa gesneriana"

1986. Garden Flowers. Multicoloured.
5045 50b. Type **1014** 10 10
5046 1l. "Iris hispanica" 35 15
5047 2l. "Rosa hybrida" 70 20
5048 3l. "Anemone coronaria" 1·10 25
5049 4l. "Freesia refracta" 1·40 35
5050 5l. "Chrysanthemum indicum" 1·90 55

1015 Mircea the Great and Horsemen

1986. 600th Anniv of Mircea the Great's Accession.
5051 **1015** 2l. multicoloured 70 45

1016 Thatched House with Veranda, Alba

1986. 50th Anniv of Museum of Historic Dwellings, Bucharest. Multicoloured.
5052 50b. Type **1016** 10 10
5053 1l. Stone-built house, Arges 35 15
5054 2l. House with veranda, Constanta 70 20
5055 3l. House with tiled roof and steps, Timis 1·10 25
5056 4l. House with ramp to veranda, Neamt 1·60 35
5057 5l. Two storey house with first floor veranda, Gorj 1·90 55

1017 Julius Popper (Tierra del Fuego, 1886–93)

1986. Polar Research. Multicoloured.
5058 50b. Type **1017** 10 10
5059 1l. Bazil Gh. Assan (Spitzbergen, 1896) 35 15
5060 2l. Emil Racovita and "Belgica" (barque) (Antarctic, 1897–99) 70 20
5061 3l. Constantin Dumbrava (Greenland, 1927–28) 1·10 25
5062 4l. Romanian participation in 17th Soviet Antarctic Expedition, 1971–72 1·60 35
5063 5l. 1977 "Sinoe" and 1979–80 "Tirnava" krill fishing expeditions 1·90 55

1018 Dove and map on Globe

1986. International Peace Year. Sheet 89×77 mm.
MS5064 5l. multicoloured 3·50 3·50

1019 The Blusher

1986. Fungi. Multicoloured.
5065 50b. Type **1019** 10 10
5066 1l. Oak mushroom 35 15
5067 2l. Peppery milk cap 70 20
5068 3l. Shield fungus 1·10 25
5069 4l. The charcoal burner 1·60 35
5070 5l. "Tremiscus helvelloides" 1·90 55

1020 Group of Cyclists

1986. Cycle Tour of Romania. Multicoloured.
5071 1l. Type **1020** 35 15
5072 2l. Motor cycle following cyclist 70 20
5073 3l. Jeep following cyclists 1·10 35
5074 4l. Winner 1·40 45
MS5075 90×78 mm. 10l. Cyclist (38×51 mm) 4·75 4·75

1021 Emblem

1986. 40th Anniv of UNESCO and 30th Anniv of Romanian Membership.
5076 **1021** 4l. multicoloured 1·30 55

1022 Petru Maior (historian) (225th birth anniv)

1986. Birth Anniversaries.
5077 **1022** 50b. purple, gold and green 10 10
5078 - 1b. green, gold and mauve 25 10
5079 - 2l. red, gold and blue 70 10
5080 - 3l. blue, gold and brown 1·20 20

DESIGNS: 1l. George Topirceanu (writer, centenary); 2l. Henri Coanda (engineer, centenary); 3l. Constantin Budeanu (engineer, centenary).

1023 Coach and Horses (image scaled to 61% of original size)

1986. Stamp Day.
5081 **1023** 2l.(+1l.) multicoloured 1·20 1·10

No. 5081 includes the se-tenant premium-carrying tab shown in Type **1023**.

1024 F 300 Oil Drilling Rigs

1986. Industry. Multicoloured.
5082 50b. Type **1024** 10 10
5083 1l. "Promex" excavator (horiz) 35 15

5084	2l. Petrochemical refinery, Pitesti	70	20
5085	3l. Tipper "110 t" (horiz)	1·10	25
5086	4l. "Coral" computer	1·60	35
5087	5l. 350 m.w. turbine (horiz)	1·90	55

1025 "Goat"

1986. New Year Folk Customs. Multicoloured.

5088	50b. Type **1025**	10	10
5089	1l. Sorcova	35	15
5090	2l. Plugusorul	70	20
5091	3l. Buhaiul	1·10	25
5092	4l. Caiutii	1·60	35
5093	5l. Uratorii	1·90	55

1026 Tin Can and Motor Car ("Re-cycle metals")

1986. "Save Waste Materials".

5094	**1026**	1l. red and orange	35	20
5095	-	2l. light green and green	85	35

DESIGN: 2l. Trees and hand with newspaper ("Re-cycle waste paper").

1027 Flags and Young People

1987. 65th Anniv of Communist Youth Union. Multicoloured.

5096	1l. Type **1027**	35	10
5097	2l. Anniversary emblem	85	35
5098	3l. Flags and young people (different)	1·10	55

1028 Anniversary Emblem

1987. 25th Anniv of Agricultural Co-operatives.

5099	**1028**	2l. multicoloured	70	55

1029 Administrative Building, Satu Mare

1987. Inter-European Cultural and Economic Co-operation. Two sheets, each 110×80 mm containing horiz designs as T 1029. Multicoloured.

MS5100 3l. ×4 (a) Type **1029**; House of Toung Pioneers, Bucharest; Valahia Hotel, Tirgoviste; Caciulata Hotel, Caciulata. (b) 3l. ×4 Exhibition Pavilion, Bucharest; Intercontinental Hotel, Bucharest; Europa Hotel, Eforie Nord; Polytechnic Institute, Bucharest Set of 2 sheets 8·50 8·50

1030 "Birch Trees by Lake" (Ion Andreescu)

1987. Paintings. Multicoloured.

5101	50b. Type **1030**	10	10
5102	1l. "Young Peasant Girls spinning" (N. Grigorescu)	35	15
5103	2l. "Washerwoman" (St. Luchian)	70	20
5104	3l. "Interior" (St. Dimitrescu)	1·10	25
5105	4l. "Winter Landscape" (Al. Ciucurencu)	1·60	35
5106	5l. "Winter in Bucharest" (N. Tonitza) (vert)	1·90	55

1031 "1907" and Peasants

1987. 80th Anniv of Peasant Uprising.

5107	**1031**	2l. multicoloured	70	55

1032 Players

1987. 10th Students World Men's Handball Championship.

5108	**1032**	50b. multicoloured	10	10
5109	-	1l. multicoloured (horiz)	35	15
5110	-	2l. multicoloured	70	20
5111	-	3l. multicoloured (horiz)	1·10	25
5112	-	4l. multicoloured	1·60	35
5113	-	5l. multicoloured (horiz)	1·90	55

DESIGNS: 1l. to 5l. Various match scenes.

1033 1 Leu Coin

1987. Currency. Multicoloured.

5114	1l. Type **1033**	60	35
MS5115	90×78 mm. 10l. 10lei banknote (53×41 mm)	4·75	4·75

1034 Eastern White Pelicans in the Danube Delta

1987. Tourism. Multicoloured.

5116	50b. Type **1034**	10	10
5117	1l. Cable car above Transfagarasan mountain road	35	15
5118	2l. Cheile Bicazului	70	20
5119	3l. Ceahlau mountains	1·10	30
5120	4l. Lake Capra, Fagaras mountains	1·60	35
5121	5l. Borsa orchards	1·90	55

1035 Henri August's Glider, 1909

1987. Air. Aircraft. Multicoloured.

5122	50b. Type **1035**	10	10
5123	1l. Sky diver jumping from IS-28 B2 glider	35	15
5124	2l. IS-29 D2 glider	70	20
5125	3l. IS-32 glider	1·10	30
5126	4l. I.A.R.35 light airplane	1·60	35
5127	5l. IS-28 M2 aircraft	1·90	55

1036 Youth on Winged Horse

1987. Fairy Tales by Petre Ispirescu. Multicoloured.

5128	50b. Type **1036**	10	10
5129	1l. King and princesses ("Salt in the Food")	35	15
5130	2l. Girl on horse fighting lion ("Ileana Simziana")	70	20
5131	3l. Youth with bow and arrow aiming at bird ("The Youth and the Golden Apples")	1·10	30
5132	4l. George and dead dragon ("George the Brave")	1·60	35
5133	5l. Girl looking at sleeping youth ("The Enchanted Pig")	1·90	55
MS5134	90×79 mm. 10l. Youth holding sun and moon ("Greuceanu") (41×53 mm)	4·75	4·75

1037 Class L 45H Diesel Shunter

1987. Railway Locomotives. Multicoloured.

5135	50b. Type **1037**	10	10
5136	1l. Class LDE 125 diesel goods locomotive	35	15
5137	2l. Class LDH 70 diesel goods locomotive	70	20
5138	3l. Class LDE 2100 diesel locomotive	1·10	30
5139	4l. Class LDE 3000 diesel locomotive	1·60	35
5140	5l. Class LE 5100 electric locomotive	1·90	55

1038 Alpine Columbine ("Aquelegia alpine")

1987. Nature Reserves in Europe. Two sheets, each 150×135 mm containing horiz designs as T 1038. Multicoloured.

MS5141 Two sheets (a) 1l. ×12 Type **1038**; Pasque flower ("Pulsatilla vernalis"); Alpine aster ("Aster alpinus"); "Soldanell pusilla"; Ornage lily ("Lilium bulbiferum"); Alpine bearberry ("Arctostaphylos uva-ursi"); "Crocus vernus"; Golden hawksbeard ("Crepis aurea"); Lady's slipper ("Cypripedium calceolus"); "Centaurea nervosa"; Mountain avens ("Dryas octopetala"); "Gentiana excisa". (b) 1l. ×12 Pine martern ("Martes Martes"); Lynx ("Felis lynx"); Polar bear ("Ursus maritimus"); European otter ("Lutra lutra"); European bison ("Bison bonasus"); Red-breasted goose ("Branta ruficollis"); Greater flamingo ("Phoenicopterus rubber"); Great bustard ("Otis tarda"); Black grouse ("Lyrurus tetrix"); Lammergeier ("Gypaetus barbatus"); Marbled polecat ("Vormela peregusna"); White-headed duck ("Oxyura leucocephala") Set of 2 sheets 16·00 16·00

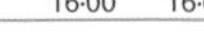

1039 Bucharest Municipal Arms

1987. "Philatelia '87" International Stamp Fair, Cologne. Sheet 79×109 mm containing T 1039 and similar design. Multicoloured.

MS5142 3l. Type **1039**; 3l. Cologne arms 4·75 4·75

1987. Costumes (2nd series). As T 999. Mult.

5143	1l. Tirnave (female)	35	15
5144	1l. Tirnave (male)	35	15
5145	2l. Buzau (female)	70	20
5146	2l. Buzau (male)	70	20
5147	3l. Dobrogea (female)	1·10	30
5148	3l. Dobrogea (male)	1·10	30
5149	4l. Ilfov (female)	1·40	35
5150	4l. Ilfov (male)	1·40	35

1040 Postal Services (image scaled to 61% of original size)

1987. Stamp Day.

5151	**1040**	2l.(+1l.) multicoloured	1·20	1·10

No. 5151 includes the se-tenant premium-carrying tab shown in Type **1040**, the stamp and tab forming a composite design.

1041 Honey Bee on Flower

1987. Bee-keeping. Multicoloured.

5152	1l. Type **1041**	35	15
5153	2l. Honey bee, sunflowers and hives	85	20
5154	3l. Hives in Danube delta	1·20	35
5155	4l. Apiculture Complex, Bucharest	1·70	45

1042 Car behind Boy on Bicycle

1987. Road Safety. Multicoloured.

5156	50b. Type **1042**	10	10

5157	1l. Children using school crossing	35	15
5158	2l. Driver carelessly opening car door	70	20
5159	3l. Hand holding crossing sign and children using zebra crossing	1·10	30
5160	4l. Speedometer and crashed car	1·60	35
5161	5l. Child's face and speeding car	1·90	55

1043 Red Flag and Lenin

1987. 70th Anniv of Russian Revolution.

5162	**1043** 2l. multicoloured		1·20	55

1044 Biathlon

1987. Winter Olympic Games, Calgary (1988). Multicoloured.

5163	50b. Type **1044**	10	10
5164	1l. Slalom	25	10
5165	1l.50 Ice hockey	35	10
5166	2l. Luge	50	15
5167	3l. Speed skating	85	20
5168	3l.50 Figure skating	95	35
5169	4l. Downhill skiing	1·20	40
5170	5l. Two-man bobsleigh	1·40	55

1045 Crest and National Colours

1987. 40th Anniv of People's Republic.

5171	**1045** 2l. multicoloured	95	55

1046 Pres. Ceausescu and Flags

1988. 70th Birthday and 55 Years of Revolutionary Activity of Pres. Ceausescu.

5172	**1046** 2l. multicoloured	1·40	80

1047 Wide-necked Pot, Marginea

1988. Pottery. Multicoloured.

5173	50b. Type **1047**	10	10
5174	1l. Flask, Oboga	35	15
5175	2l. Jug and saucer, Horezu	70	20
5176	3l. Narrow-necked pot, Curtea de Arges	1·10	30
5177	4l. Jug, Birsa	1·60	35
5178	5l. Jug and plate, Vama	1·90	55

1048 "Santa Maria"

1988. Inter-European Cultural and Economic Co-operation. Two sheets, each 110×80 mm containing horiz designs as T 1048. Multicoloured.

MS5179 Two sheets (a) 3l. ×4 Type **1048**; Dish aerials, Cheia earth station; Bucharest underground train; Airbus Industrie A320 jetliner. (b) 3l. ×4 Mail coach and horses; "ECS" satellite; Oltcit motor car; "ICE" express train Set of 2 sheets	8·50	8·50

1049 Ceramic Clock

1988. Clocks in Ploiesti Museum. Multicoloured.

5180	50b. Type **1049**	10	10
5181	1l.50 Gilt clock with sun at base	35	15
5182	2l. Clock with pastoral figure	70	20
5183	3l. Gilt clock surmounted by figure	95	30
5184	4l. Vase-shaped clock	1·60	35
5185	5l. Clock surmounted by porcelain figures	1·90	55

1050 West German Flag and Player kicking Ball into Net

1988. European Football Championship, West Germany. Two sheets each 110× 80 mm containing horiz designs as T 1050. Multicoloured.

MS5186 3l. ×4 Type **1050**; Goalkeeper diving to save ball and Spanish flag; Italian flag and player; Players and Danish flag. (b) 3l. ×4 English flag, referee and player; Players and Netherlands flag; Irish flag and players; Players and flag of U.S.S.R. Set of 2 sheets	12·00	12·00

1051 Constantin Brincoveanu

1988. 300th Anniv of Election of Constantin Brincoveanu as Ruler of Wallachia.

5187	**1051** 2l. multicoloured	70	55

1052 Gymnastics

1988. Olympic Games, Seoul (1st issue). Mult.

5188	50b. Type **1052**	10	10
5189	1l.50 Boxing	35	15
5190	2l. Lawn tennis	70	20
5191	3l. Judo	95	30
5192	4l. Running	1·60	35
5193	5l. Rowing	1·90	55

See also Nos. 5197/5204.

1053 Postal Emblems and Roses

1988. Romanian–Chinese Stamp Exhibition, Bucharest.

5194	**1053** 2l. multicoloured	70	55

1054 Player and Wimbledon Centre Court

1988. "Grand Slam" Tennis Championships. Two sheets each 110×80 mm containing horiz designs as T 1054. Multicoloured.

MS5195 (a) 3l. ×4 Type **1054**; Wimbledon match; Flushing Meadows match; Flushing Meadows centre courts, New York. (b) 3l. ×4 Melbourne centre court; Melbourne match; Roland Garros match; Roland Garros centre court, Paris Set of 2 sheets	12·00	12·00

1055 "Bowl of Flowers" (Stefan Luchian)

1988. "Praga '88" International Stamp Exhibition. Sheet 90×78 mm.

MS5196 5l. multicoloured	3·50	3·50

1056 Running

1988. Olympic Games, Seoul (2nd issue). Mult.

5197	50b. Type **1056**	10	10
5198	1l. Canoeing	25	10
5199	1l.50 Gymnastics	35	10
5200	2l. Double kayak	50	15
5201	3l. Weightlifting	85	20
5202	3l.50 Swimming	95	35
5203	4l. Fencing	1·20	40
5204	5l. Double sculls	1·40	45

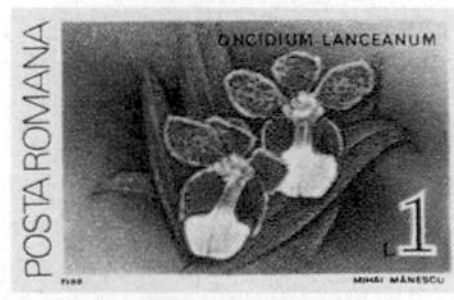

1057 "Oncidum lanceanum"

1988. Orchids. Two sheets, each 150×137 mm containing horiz designs as T 1057. Multicoloured.

MS5205 (a) 1l. ×2 Type **1057**; "Cattleya trianae"; "Sophronitis cernua"; "Bulbophyllum lobbii"; "Lycaste cruenta"; "Mormolyce ringens"; "Phragmipedium schlimii"; "Angraecum atropurpurea"; "Dendrobium nobile"; "Oncidium splendidum". (b) 1l. ×12 "Brassavola perrinii"; "Paphiopedilum maudiae"; "Sophronitis coccinea"; "Vandopsis lissochiloides"; "Phalaenopsis lueddemanniana"; "Chysis bractescens"; "Cochleanthes discolor"; "Phalaenopsis amabilis"; "Pleione pricei"; "Sobralia macrantha"; "Aspasia lunata"; "Cattleya citrina" Set of 2 sheets	14·50	14·00

1058 Past and Present Postal Services (image scaled to 60% of original size)

1988. Stamp Day.

5206	**1058** 2l.(+1l.) multicoloured	95	90

No. 5206 includes the se-tenant premium-carrying tab shown in T **1058**.

1059 Gymnastics and Three Gold Medals

1988. Seoul Olympic Games Romanian Medal Winners. Two sheets, each 110×80 mm containing horiz designs as T 1059. Multicoloured.

MS5207 (a) 3l. ×4 Type **1059**; Pistol shooting and gold medal; Weightlifting and silver medal; Boxing and silver medal. (b) 3l. ×4 Athletics and silver medals; Swimming and silver medal; Wrestling and gold medal; Rowing and gold medal Set of 2 sheets	12·00	12·00

1060 State Arms

1988. 70th Anniv of Union of Transylvania and Romania.

5208	**1060** 2l. multicoloured	1·20	1·10

1061 Athenaeum Concert Hall, Bucharest (centenary)

1988. Romanian History. Multicoloured.

5209	50b. Type **1061**	10	10
5210	1l.50 Roman coin showing Drobeta Bridge	35	15
5211	2l. Ruins (600th anniv of Suceava as capital of Moldavian feudal state)	70	20
5212	3l. Scroll, arms and town (600th anniv of first documentary reference to Pitesti)	95	30
5213	4l. Dacian warriors from Trajan's Column	1·60	35
5214	5l. Thracian gold helmet from Cotofenesti-Prahova	1·90	55

1062 Zapodeni, 17th century

1989. Traditional House Architecture. Mult.

5215	50b. Type **1062**	10	10
5216	1l.50 Berbesti, 18th century	35	15
5217	2l. Voitinel, 18th century	70	20
5218	3l. Chiojdu Mic, 18th century	95	30
5219	4l. Cimpanii de Sus, 19th century	1·60	35
5220	5l. Naruja, 19th century	1·90	55

1063 Red Cross Worker

1989. Life-saving Services. Multicoloured.

5221	50b. Type **1063**	10	10
5222	1l. Red Cross orderlies giving first aid to girl (horiz)	35	10
5223	1l.50 Fireman carrying child	60	10
5224	2l. Rescuing child from earthquake damaged building	70	15
5225	3l. Mountain rescue team transporting casualty on sledge (horiz)	1·10	20
5226	3l.50 Rescuing climber from cliff face	1·20	30
5227	4l. Rescuing child from river	1·30	35
5228	5l. Lifeguard in rowing boat and children playing in sea (horiz)	1·60	45

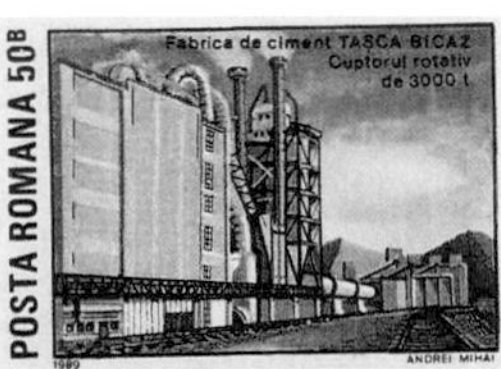

1064 Tasca Bicaz Cement Factory

1989. Industrial Achievements. Multicoloured.

5229	50b. Type **1064**	10	10
5230	1l.50 New railway bridge, Cernavoda	50	15
5231	2l. Synchronous motor, Resita	70	20
5232	3l. Bucharest underground	95	30
5233	4l. Mangalia–Constanta train ferry	1·30	35
5234	5l. "Gloria" (oil drilling platform)	1·60	55

1065 Flags and Symbols of Industry and Agriculture

1988. 50th Anniv of Anti-Fascist Demonstration.

5235	2l. Type **1065**	1·20	55
MS5236	90×78 mm. 10l. Flag and demonstrators	7·75	7·75

1066 Roses

1989. "Bulgaria '89" International Stamp Exhibition, Sofia. Sheet 90×78 mm.

MS5237	10l. multicoloured	4·75	4·75

1067 Girls playing with Dolls

1989. Inter-European Cultural and Economic Co-operation. Children. Two sheets, each 110×80 mm containing horiz designs as T 1067.

MS5238 (a) 3l. ×4 Type **1067**; Playing football; On beach; Playing with toy cars. (b) 3l. ×4 Playing in sea; On slides; At playground; Flying kites Set of 2 sheets 8·50 8·50

1068 Ion Creanga (writer, death centenary)

1989. Anniversaries. Multicoloured.

5239	1l. Type **1068**	35	10
5240	2l. Mihai Eminescu (poet, death centenary)	85	35
5241	3l. Nicolae Teclu (scientist, 150th birth anniv)	1·20	55

1069 State and Communist Party Flags and Symbols of Industry and Agriculture

1989. 45th Anniv of Liberation.

5242	**1069**	2l. multicoloured	1·20	55

1070 "Pin-Pin"

1989. Romanian Cartoon Films. Multicoloured.

5243	50b. Type **1070**	10	10
5244	1l. "Maria"	35	10
5245	1l.50 "Gore and Grigore"	60	15
5246	2l. "Pisoiul, Balanel, Manole, Monk"	70	20
5247	3l. "Gruia lui Novac"	1·10	30
5248	3l.50 "Mihaela"	1·20	35
5249	4l. "Harap Alb"	1·30	40
5250	5l. "Homo Sapiens"	1·60	45

1071 Globe, Letter and Houses (image scaled to 69% of original size)

1989. Stamp Day.

5251	**1071**	2l.(+1l.) multicoloured	1·20	1·10

No. 5251 includes the se-tenant premium-carrying tab as illustrated in T **1071**.

1072 Storming of the Bastille

1989. Bicentenary of French Revolution. Mult.

5252	50b. Type **1072**	10	10
5253	1l.50 Street boy and Marianne	60	15
5254	2l. Maximilien de Robespierre	70	20
5255	3l. Rouget de Lisle singing the "Marseillaise"	1·10	30
5256	4l. Denis Diderot (encyclopaedist)	1·40	45
5257	5l. Crowd with banner	1·80	55
MS5258	90×78 mm. 10l. "Philexfrance '89" International Stamp Exhibition emblem and Eiffel Tower (50×39 mm)	6·00	6·00

1073 Conrad Haas and Diagram

1989. Air. Space Pioneers. Multicoloured.

5259	50b. Type **1073**	10	10
5260	1l.50 Konstantin Tsiolkovski and diagram	60	15
5261	2l. Hermann Oberth and equation	70	20
5262	3l. Robert Goddard and diagram	1·10	35
5263	4l. Sergei Pavlovich Korolev, Earth and satellite	1·40	45
5264	5l. Wernher von Braun and landing module	1·80	55

1074 Horse-drawn Mail Coach

1989. Air. "World Stamp Expo '89" International Stamp Exhibition, Washington D.C. Sheet 90×77 mm.

MS5265	5l. multicoloured	3·75	3·75

1075 State and Party Flags and Emblem

1989. 14th Communist Party Congress, Bucharest.

5266	**1075**	2l. multicoloured	1·20	55
MS5267		77×89 mm. 10l. multicoloured	7·25	7·25

DESIGNS: 10l. Party emblem and "XIV".

1076 Date, Flag, Victory Sign and Candles

1990. Popular Uprising (1st issue).

5268	**1076**	2l. multicoloured	85	55

See also Nos. 5294/5301.

1077 Flags and Footballers

1990. World Cup Football Championship, Italy (1st issue).

5269	**1077**	50b. multicoloured	10	10
5270	-	1l.50 multicoloured	60	15
5271	-	2l. multicoloured	70	20
5272	-	3l. multicoloured	1·10	35
5273	-	4l. multicoloured	1·40	45
5274	-	5l. multicoloured	1·80	55

DESIGNS: 1l.50 to 5l. Showing flags and footballers.

See also Nos. 5276/83.

1078 Penny Black and Moldavian 27p. Stamp

1990. "Stamp World London '90" International Stamp Exhibition. Sheet 90×78 mm.

MS5275	10l. multicoloured	4·75	4·75

1079 Footballers

1990. World Cup Football Championship, Italy (2nd issue).

5276	**1079**	50b. multicoloured	10	10
5277	-	1l. multicoloured	35	10
5278	-	1l.50 multicoloured	60	15
5279	-	2l. multicoloured	70	20
5280	-	3l. multicoloured	1·10	30
5281	-	3l.50 multicoloured	1·20	35
5282	-	4l. multicoloured	1·30	40
5283	-	5l. multicoloured	1·60	45

DESIGNS: 1l. to 5l. Different football scenes.

1080 German Shepherds

1990. International Dog Show, Brno. Mult.

5284	50b. Type **1080**	10	10
5285	1l. English setter	35	10
5286	1l.50 Boxers	60	10
5287	2l. Beagles	70	15
5288	3l. Dobermann pinschers	1·20	20
5289	3l.50 Great Danes	1·40	30
5290	4l. Afghan hounds	1·60	35
5291	5l. Yorkshire terriers	2·00	40

1081 Fountain, Brunnen

1990. "Riccione 90" International Stamp Fair.

5292	**1081**	2l. multicoloured	90	60

1082 Athenaeum Concert Hall, Bucharest, and Chinese Temple

1990. Romanian–Chinese Stamp Exhibition, Bucharest.

5293	**1082**	2l. multicoloured	90	60

1083 Soldiers and Crowd at Television Headquarters, Bucharest

1990. Popular Uprising (2nd issue). Multicoloured.

5294		50b.+50b. Republic Palace ablaze, Bucharest (horiz)	25	10
5295		1l.+1l. Crowd in Opera Square, Timisoara	65	15
5296		1l.50+1l. Soldiers joining crowd in Town Hall Square, Tirgu Mures (horiz)	90	20
5297		2l.+1l. Type **1083**	1·00	25
5298		3l.+1l. Mourners at funeral, Timisoara (horiz)	1·30	30
5299		3l.50+1l. Crowd celebrating, Brasov	1·50	35
5300		4l.+1l. Crowd with banners, Sibiu (horiz)	1·70	35
5301		5l.+2l. Cemetery, Bucharest (horiz)	2·20	40
MS5302		90×78 mm. 5l.+2l. Foreign aid (53×41 mm)	3·75	3·75

1084 "Nicolae Cobzarul" (Stefan Luchian)

1990. Paintings damaged during the Uprising. Mult.

5303		50b. Type **1084**	15	10
5304		1l.50 "Woman in White" (Ion Andreescu)	40	10
5305		2l. "Florist" (Luchian)	65	15
5306		3l. "Vase of Flowers" (Jan Brueghel, the elder)	90	25
5307		4l. "Spring" (Pieter Brueghel, the elder) (horiz)	1·30	35
5308		5l. "Madonna and Child" (G. B. Paggi)	1·50	50

1085 Flag Stamps encircling Globe (image scaled to 70% of original size)

1990. Stamp Day.

5309	**1085**	2l.(+1l.) multicoloured	1·30	1·20

No. 5309 includes the se-tenant premium-carrying tab as shown in Type **1085**.

1086 Constantin Cantacuzino (historian, 350th birth anniv)

1990. Anniversaries.

5310	**1086**	50b. brown and blue	15	10
5311	-	1l.50 green and mauve	40	10
5312	-	2l. red and blue	65	15
5313	-	3l. blue and brown	90	25
5314	-	4l. brown and blue	1·30	35
5315	-	5l. violet and green	1·50	50

DESIGNS: 1l.50, Ienachita Vacarescu (writer, 250th birth anniv); 2l. Titu Maiorescu (politician, 150th birth anniv); 3l. Nicolae Iorga (historian, 50th death anniv); 4l. Martha Bibescu (writer, birth centenary); 5l. Stefan Procupiu (scientist, birth centenary).

1087 Column of Infinity

1990. National Day.

5316	**1087**	2l. multicoloured	75	60

1990. 1st Anniv of Popular Uprising. No. 5268 surch L4 UN AN DE LA VICTORIA REVOLUTIEI.

5317	**1076**	4l. on 2l. multicoloured	1·50	60

1089 "Irises"

1991. Death Centenary of Vincent van Gogh (painter). Multicoloured.

5318		50b. Type **1089**	15	10
5319		2l. "The Artist's Room"	25	10
5320		3l. "Illuminated Coffee Terrace" (vert)	50	15
5321		3l.50 "Orchard in Blossom"	65	20
5322		5l. "Sunflowers" (vert)	90	25

1090 Greater Black- backed Gull

1991. Water Birds.

5323	**1090**	50b. blue	10	10
5324	-	1l. green	15	10
5325	-	1l.50 bistre	20	10
5326	-	2l. blue	25	10
5327	-	3l. green	40	10
5328	-	3l.50 green	50	10
5329	-	4l. violet	65	10
5330	-	5l. brown	75	10
5331	-	6l. brown	1·40	10
5332	-	7l. blue	1·50	25

DESIGNS: 1l. Common tern; 1l.50, Pied avocet; 2l. Pomarine skua; 3l. Northern lapwings; 3l.50, Red-breasted merganser; 4l. Little egret; 5l. Dunlin; 6l. Black- tailed godwit; 7l. Whiskered tern.

1091 Crucifixion

1991. Easter.

5333	**1091**	4l. multicoloured	65	60

1092 "Eutelsat 1" Communications Satellite

1991. Europa. Europe in Space.

5334	**1092**	4l.50 multicoloured	5·00	1·20

1093 Posthorn

1991

5335	**1093**	4l.50 blue	75	60

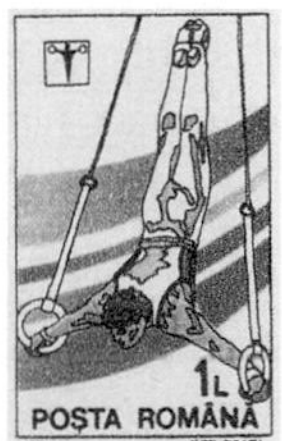

1094 Rings Exercise

1991. Gymnastics. Multicoloured.

5336		1l. Type **1094**	15	10
5337		1l. Parallel bars	15	10
5338		4l.50 Vaulting	50	10
5339		4l.50 Asymmetric bars	50	10
5340		8l. Floor exercises	90	15
5341		9l. Beam	1·20	20

For similar design to No. 5341, surcharged 90l. on 5l., see No. 5431.

1095 Curtea de Arges Monastery

1991. Monasteries. Multicoloured.

5342		1l. Type **1095**	15	10
5343		1l. Putna	15	10
5344		4l.50 Varatec	50	10
5345		4l.50 Agapia (horiz)	50	10
5346		8l. Golia (horiz)	90	10
5347		9l. Sucevita (horiz)	1·20	10

1096 Hotel Continental, Timisoara

1991. Hotels.

5349	**1096**	1l. blue	15	10
5350	-	2l. green	15	10
5351	-	4l. red	25	10
5352	-	5l. violet	50	10
5353	-	6l. brown	25	25
5354	-	8l. brown	25	25
5355	-	9l. red	1·20	35
5356	-	10l. green	1·00	35
5357	-	18l. red	1·30	35
5358	-	20l. orange	1·40	35
5359	-	25l. blue	1·70	60
5360	-	30l. purple	2·20	70
5361	-	45l. blue	1·90	50
5362	-	60l. brown	2·50	85
5363	-	80l. violet	3·25	95
5364b	-	120l. blue and grey	3·75	25
5365	-	160l. red and pink	5·00	35
5366	-	250l. blue and grey	6·50	50
5367	-	400l. brown and ochre	8·25	60
5368	-	500l. deep green & green	9·50	70
5369	-	800l. mauve and pink	11·50	95

DESIGNS—As T **1096**: HORIZ: 2l. Valea Caprei Chalet, Mt. Fagaras; 5l. Hotel Lebada, Crisan; 6l. Muntele Rosu Chalet, Mt. Ciucas; 8l. Trans-silvania Hotel, Cluj-Napoca; 9l. Hotel Orizont, Predeal; 20l. Alpin Hotel, Poiana Brasov; 25l. Constanta Casino; 30l. Miorita Chalet, Mt. Bucegi; 45l. Sura Dacilor Chalet, Poiana Brasov; 60l. Valea Draganului Tourist Complex; 80l. Hotel Florica, Venus. VERT: 4l. Intercontinental Hotel, Bucharest; 10l. Hotel Roman, Baile Herculcane; 18l. Rarau Chalet, Mt. Rarau. 26×40 mm: 120l. International Complex, Baile Felix; 160l. Hotel Egreta, Tulcea. 40×26 mm: 250l. Valea de Pesti Motel, Jiului Valley; 400l. Baisoara Tourist Complex; 500l. Bradul Hotel, Covasna; 800l. Gorj Hotel, Jiu.

Nos. 5362/9 have no frame.

1097 Gull and Sea Shore

1991. "Riccione 91" Stamp Exhibition, Riccione, Italy.

5381	**1097**	4l. multicoloured	65	60

1098 Vase decorated with Scarlet and Military Macaws

1991. Romanian–Chinese Stamp Exhibition. Mult.

5382		5l. Type **1098**	50	35
5383		5l. Vase with peony decoration	50	35

1099 Academy Emblem

1991. 125th Anniv of Romanian Academy.

5384	**1099**	1l. blue	65	60

1100 "Flowers" (Nicu Enea)

1991. "Balcanfila '91" Stamp Exhibition, Bacau. Multicoloured.

5385		4l. Type **1100**	65	25
5386		5l.(+2l.) "Peasant Girl of Vlasca" (Georghe Tattarescu)	75	35
MS5387		90×77 mm. 20l. Exhibition venue (53×41 mm)	2·50	2·50

1101 Red-Billed Blue Magpie ("Casa erythorhynchai")

1991. Birds. Two sheets, each 136×150 mm containing vert designs as T 1101. Multicoloured.

MS5388 (a) 2l. ×12 Type **1101**; Grey-headed bush shrike ("Malaconotus blanchoti"); Eastern bluebird ("Sialia sialis"); Western meadowlark ("Sturnella neglecta"); Malabar trogon ("Harpactes fasciatus"); Hoopoe ("Upupa epops"); Blue wren ("Malurus cyaneus"); Scaly ground roller ("Brachypteryus squamigera"); Blue vanga ("Leptopterus madagascariensis"); White-headed wood hoopoe ("Phoeniculus bollei"); Red-headed woodpecker ("Melanerpes erythrocephalus"); Scarlet minivet ("Pericrocotus flammeus"). (b) 2l. ×12 Golden-backed honeyeater ("Melithreptus laetior"); Kagu ("Rhynochetos jubata"); American robin ("Turdus migratorius"); Magpie robin ("Copsychus saularis"); Rock thrush ("Monticola saxatilis"); Yellow-headed blackbird ("Xanthocephalus xanthocephalus"); Pel's fishing owl ("Scotopelia peli"); Long-tailed silky flycatcher ("Ptilogonys caudatus"); Puerto Rican tody ("Todus mexicanus"); White-rumped shama ("Copsychus malabaricus"); Mangrove red-headed honeyeater ("Myzomela erythrocephala"); Montezuma oropendola ("Gymnostinops montezuma") Set of 2 sheets		9·25	9·25

1102 Map with House and People

1991. Population and Housing Census.

5389	**1102**	5l. multicoloured	65	60

1103 Bridge

1991. "Phila Nippon '91" International Stamp Exhibition, Tokyo.

5390	**1103**	10l. ochre, brown & red	1·30	35
5391	-	10l. multicoloured	1·30	35

DESIGN: No. 5391, Junk.

1104 Isabel ("Graellsia isabellae")

1991. Butterflies and Moths. Two sheets, each 155×36 mm containing horiz designs as T 1104. Multicoloured.

MS5392 (a) 3l. ×12 Type **1104**; Orange-tip ("Antocharis cardamines"); Hebe tiger moth ("Ammobiota festiva"); Comma ("Polygonia c-album"); "Catocala promisa"; Purple tiger moth ("Phyparia purpurata"); "Arctica villica"; "Polyommatus daphnis"; Southern festoon ("Zerynthia polyxena"); Oleander hawk moth ("Daphnis nerii"); "Licaena dispar rutila"; "Parage roxelana". (b) 3l. ×12 Paradise birdwing ("Ornithoptera paradisea"); Bhutan glory ("Bhutanitis lidderdalii"); "Morpho Helena"; "Ornithoptera croesus"; Red-splashed sulphur ("Phoebis avellaneda"); Queen Victoria's birdwing ("Ornithoptera victoriae"); Kaiser-i-hind ("Teinopalpus imperialis"); "Hypolimnas dexithea"; "Dabasa payeni"; "Morpho achilleana"; "Heliconius melpomene"; "Agrias claudina sardanapalus" Set of 2 sheets	13·00	13·00

1105 Running

1991. World Athletics Championships, Tokyo. Multicoloured.

5393	1l. Type **1105**	25	10
5394	4l. Long jumping	50	10
5395	5l. High jumping	65	10
5396	5l. Athlete in starting blocks	65	10
5397	9l. Hurdling	1·20	20
5398	10l. Throwing the javelin	1·30	20

1106 Mihail Kogalniceanu (policitian and historian, death cent)

1991. Anniversaries.

5399	**1106**	1l. brown, blue & dp blue	25	10
5400	-	4l. green, lilac and violet	50	10
5401	-	5l. brown, blue & ultramarine	65	10
5402	-	5l. blue, brown and red	65	10
5403	-	9l. red, blue & deep blue	1·20	20
5404	-	10l. black, lt brn & brn	1·30	20

DESIGNS: No. 5400, Nicolae Titulescu (politician and diplomat, 50th death anniv); 5401, Andrei Mureseanu (poet, 175th birth anniv); 5402, Aron Pumnul (writer, 125th death anniv); 5403, George Bacovia (writer, 110th birth anniv); 5404, Perpessicius (literature critic, birth centenary).

1107 Library Building

1991. Centenary of Central University Library.

5405	**1107**	8l. brown	1·00	60

1108 Coach and Horses (image scaled to 70% of original size)

1991. Stamp Day.

5406	**1108**	8l.(+2l.) multicoloured	1·30	1·20

No. 5406 includes the se-tenant premium-carrying label shown in Type **1108**.

1109 "Nativity" (17th-century icon)

1991. Christmas.

5407	**1109**	8l. multicoloured	1·00	60

1110 Biathlon

1992. Winter Olympic Games, Albertville. Mult.

5408	4l. Type **1110** (postage)	15	10
5409	5l. Downhill skiing	20	10
5410	8l. Cross-country skiing	25	10
5411	10l. Two-man luge	40	10
5412	20l. Speed skating	75	10
5413	25l. Ski-jumping	90	20
5414	30l. Ice hockey	1·20	20
5415	45l. Men's figure skating	1·50	30
MS5416	95×78 mm. 75l. Women's figure skating (37×52 mm) (air)	4·00	4·00

1112 Jug, Plate, Tray and Bowl

1992. Romanian Porcelain from Cluj Napoca. Multicoloured.

5419	4l. Type **1112**	15	10
5420	5l. Tea set	15	10
5421	8l. Jug and goblet (vert)	20	10
5422	30l. Tea set (different)	1·00	20
5423	45l. Vase (vert)	1·50	35

1113 Atlantic Mackerels

1992. Fishes. Multicoloured.

5424	4l. Type **1113**	15	10
5425	5l. Tench	15	10
5426	8l. Brook charr	20	10
5427	10l. Romanian bullhead perch	25	10
5428	30l. Nase	90	25
5429	45l. Black Sea red mullet	1·40	40

1114 Vase decorated with Scarlet and Military Macaws

1992. Apollo Art Gallery. Unissued stamp surch.

5430	**1114**	90l. on 5l. multicoloured	3·25	60

1115 Gymnast on Beam

1992. Individual Gymnastic Championships, Paris. Unissued stamp surch.

5431	**1115**	90l. on 5l. multicoloured	3·25	60

For similar 9l. value, see No. 5341.

1116 Dressage

1992. Horses. Multicoloured.

5432	6l. Type **1116**	15	10
5433	7l. Racing (horiz)	15	10
5434	10l. Rearing	25	10
5435	25l. Jumping gate	75	15
5436	30l. Stamping foot (horiz)	1·00	20
5437	50l. Winged horse	1·50	25

1117 Columbus and "Santa Maria"

1992. Europa. 500th Anniv of Discovery of America by Columbus. Sheet 130×88 mm containing T 1117 and similar horiz designs. Multicoloured.

MS5438 35l. Type **1117**; 35l. Columbus (hatless) and "Nina" at sea; 35l. Columbus (in hat) and "Pinta"; 35l. Columbus, "Santa Maria" and island	38·00	38·00

1118 "Descent into Hell" (icon)

1992. Easter.

5439	**1118**	10l. multicoloured	65	50

1119 Emblem

1992. "Granada '92" International Thematic Stamp Exhibition. Sheet 122×72 mm containing T 1119 and similar vert designs.

MS5440 10l. red, emerald and black; 25l. multicoloured; 30l. multicoloured	2·50	2·50

DESIGNS: 25l. Spanish 1850 6c. and Moldavian 1858 27p. stamps; 30l. Courtyard, Alhambra.

1120 Tower and Hand Pump

1992. Centenary of Bucharest Fire Tower.

5441	**1120**	10l. multicoloured	65	50

1121 Filipino Vinta and Rook

1992. 30th Chess Olympiad, Manila, Philippines. Multicoloured.

5442	10l. Type **1121**	40	25
5443	10l. Exterior of venue and chessmen	40	25
MS5444	91×79 mm. 75l. Chessboard on beach (41×53 mm)	3·25	3·25

1122 Post Rider approaching Town

1992. Stamp Day.

5445	**1122**	10l.+4l. pink, violet and blue	65	50

1123 Pistol shooting

1992. Olympic Games, Barcelona. Multicoloured.

5446	6l. Type **1123**	10	10
5447	7l. Weightlifting	10	10
5448	9l. Two-man kayak (horiz)	15	10
5449	10l. Handball	25	10
5450	25l. Wrestling (horiz)	40	10
5451	30l. Fencing (horiz)	50	15
5452	50l. Running	90	25
5453	55l. Boxing (horiz)	1·00	30
MS5454	90×79 mm. 100l. Rowing (50×39 mm)	2·50	2·50

1124 Ion Bratianu

1992. 130th Anniv of Foreign Ministry. Designs showing former Ministers.

5455	**1124**	10l. violet, green and deep green	10	10
5456	-	25l. purple, blue & dp blue	25	10
5457	-	30l. blue, purple & brn	30	10

DESIGNS: 25l. Ion Duca; 30l. Grigore Gafencu.

1125 "The Thinker of Cernavoda" (sculpture)

1992. "Expo 92" World's Fair, Seville. "Era of Discovery". Multicoloured.

5458	6l. Type **1125**	10	10
5459	7l. Trajan's bridge, Turnu-Severin	10	10
5460	10l. House on stilts	10	10
5461	25l. Saligny Bridge, Cernavoda	25	10
5462	30l. Traian Vuia's No. 1 airplane	40	10
5463	55l. Hermann Oberth's rocket	65	20
MS5464	79×91 mm. 100l. "Kneeling Figure" (sculpture, Constantin Brancusi) (41×49 mm)	1·30	1·30

1126 Doves posting Letters in Globe

1992. World Post Day.

5465	**1126**	10l. multicoloured	65	50

1127 "Santa Maria" and Bust of Columbus

1992. 500th Anniv of Discovery of America by Columbus. Multicoloured.

5466	6l. Type **1127**	15	10
5467	10l. "Nina"	15	10
5468	25l. "Pinta"	50	15
5469	55l. Columbus claiming New World	90	25
MS5470	91×79 mm. 100l. Columbus and "Santa Maria" (38×51 mm)	2·50	2·50

1128 Post Office Emblem

1992. 1st Anniv of Establishment of R.A. Posta Romana (postal organization).

5471	**1128**	10l. multicoloured	65	50

1129 Jacob Negruzzi (writer, 150th birth anniv)

1992. Anniversaries.

5472	**1129**	6l. green and violet	10	10
5473	-	7l. mauve, purple and green	10	10
5474	-	9l. blue and mauve	10	10
5475	-	10l. light brown, brown and blue	10	10
5476	-	25l. blue and brown	25	10
5477	-	30l. green and blue	50	10

DESIGNS: 7l. Grigore Antipa (biologist, 125th birth anniv); 9l. Alexe Mateevici (poet, 75th death anniv); 10l. Cezar Petrescu (writer, birth centenary); 25l. Octav Onicescu (mathematician, birth centenary); 30l. Ecaterina Teodoroiu (First World War fighter, 75th death anniv).

1130 American Bald Eagle

1992. Animals. Multicoloured.

5478	6l. Type **1130**	10	10
5479	7l. Spotted owl	10	10
5480	9l. Brown bear	15	10
5481	10l. American black oystercatcher (horiz)	15	10
5482	25l. Wolf (horiz)	25	10
5483	30l. White-tailed deer (horiz)	40	10
5484	55l. Elk (horiz)	90	25
MS5485	91×80 mm. 100l. Killer whale ("Orcinus orca") (horiz)	1·90	1·90

1131 Arms

1992. New State Arms.

5486	**1131**	15l. multicoloured	65	50

1132 Buildings and Street, Mogosoaiei

1992. Anniversaries. Multicoloured.

5487	7l. Type **1132** (300th anniv)	10	10
5488	9l. College building and statue, Roman (600th anniv)	10	10
5489	10l. Prince Basarab, monastery and Princess Despina (475th anniv of Curtea de Arges Monastery)	10	10
5490	25l. Bucharest School of Architecture (80th anniv)	20	10

1133 Nativity

1992. Christmas.

5491	**1133**	15l. multicoloured	65	50

1134 Globe and Key-pad on Telephone

1992. New Telephone Number System.

5492	**1134**	15l. black, red and blue	65	50

1135 Woman's Gymnastics (two gold medals)

1992. Romanian Medals at Olympic Games, Barcelona. Two sheets, each 110×80 mm containing horiz designs as T 1135. Multicoloured.

MS5493	(a) 35l. ×4 Type **1135**; Rowing (two gold medals); Fencing and bronze medal; High jumping and silver medal. (b) 35l. ×4 Shooting and bronze medal; Bronze medal and wrestling; Weightlifting and bronze medal; Bronze medal and boxing. Set of 2 sheets	3·75	3·75

1136 Mihai Voda Monastery

1993. Destroyed Bucharest Buildings. Mult.

5494	10l. Type **1136**	10	10
5495	15l. Vacaresti Monastery	10	10
5496	25l. Unirii Hall	20	10
5497	30l. Mina Minovici Medico-legal Institute	50	10

1137 Parseval Sigsfeld Kite-type Observation Balloon "Draken"

1993. Air. Balloons. Multicoloured.

5498	30l. Type **1137**	25	15
5499	90l. Caquot observation balloon, 1917	1·70	35

1138 Crucifixion

1993. Easter.

5500	**1138**	15l. multicoloured	65	50

1139 Hawthorn

1993. Medicinal Plants. Multicoloured.

5501	10l. Type **1139**	10	10
5502	15l. Gentian	10	10
5503	25l. Sea buckthorn	45	10
5504	30l. Billberry	50	10
5505	50l. Arnica	1·00	20
5506	90l. Dog rose	1·90	25

1140 Stanescu

1993. 60th Birth Anniv of Nichita Stanescu (poet).

5507	**1140**	15l. multicoloured	65	50

1141 Mounted Courier

1993. Stamp Day.

5508	**1141**	15l.+10l. multicoloured	65	50

1142 Exhibition Venue

1993. "Polska '93" International Stamp Exhibition, Poznan. Sheet 90×78 mm.

MS5509	200l. multicoloured	2·50	2·50

1143 Black-billed Magpie

1993. Birds.

5510	**1143**	5l. black and green	15	10
5511	-	10l. black and red	15	10
5512	-	15l. black and red	15	10
5513	-	20l. black and brown	25	10
5514	-	25l. black and red	25	10
5515	-	50l. black and yellow	40	10
5516	-	65l. black and red	50	10
5517	-	90l. black and red	75	10
5518	-	160l. black and blue	1·30	15
5519	-	250l. black and mauve	1·70	25

DESIGNS—HORIZ: 10l. Golden eagle. VERT: 15l. Northern bullfinch; 20l. Hoopoe; 25l. Great spotted woodpecker; 50l. Golden oriole; 65l. White winged crossbill; 90l. Barn swallows; 160l. Azure tit; 250l. Rose-coloured starling.

1144 Long-hair

1993. Cats. Multicoloured.

5520	10l. Type **1144**	25	20
5521	15l. Tabby-point long-hair	25	20
5522	30l. Red long-hair	40	20
5523	90l. Blue Persian	90	20
5524	135l. Tabby	1·20	20
5525	160l. Long-haired white Persian	1·50	25

1145 "Lola Artists' Sister" (Pablo Picasso)

1993. Europa. Contemporary Art. Sheet 75×105 mm containing T 1145 and similar vert designs. Multicoloured.

MS5526	280l. Type **1145**; 280l. "World Inception" (sculpture, Constantin Brancusi); 280l. "Girl with Idol" (sculpture, Ion Irimescu); 280l. "Woman in Grey" (Alexandru Ciucurencu)	6·50	6·50

1146 Adder

1993. Protected Animals. Multicoloured.

5527	10l. Type **1146**	25	15
5528	15l. Lynx (vert)	25	15
5529	25l. Common shelduck	40	15
5530	75l. Huchen	90	15
5531	105l. Poplar admiral	1·20	20
5532	280l. Alpine longhorn beetle	1·50	35

1147 Pine Marten

1993. Mammals.

5533	**1147**	10l. black and yellow	25	10
5534	-	15l. black and brown	25	10
5535	-	20l. red and black	25	10
5536	-	25l. black and brown	40	10
5537	-	30l. black and red	40	10
5538	-	40l. black and red	40	10
5539	-	75l. black and yellow	65	10
5540	-	105l. black and brown	1·00	10
5541	-	150l. black and orange	1·20	15
5542	-	280l. black and yellow	2·50	25

DESIGNS—HORIZ: 15l. Common rabbit; 30l. Red fox; 150l. Stoat; 280l. Egyptian mongoose. VERT: 20l. Eurasian red squirrel; 25l. Chamois; 40l. Argali; 75l. Small spotted genet; 105l. Garden dormouse.

1148 Brontosaurus

1993. Prehistoric Animals. Multicoloured.

5543	29l. Type **1148**	15	15
5544	46l. Plesiosaurus	50	15
5545	85l. Triceratops	75	15
5546	171l. Stegosaurus	1·70	20
5547	216l. Tyannosaurus	1·90	25
5548	319l. Archaeopteryx	2·50	35

1149 "Woman selling Eggs" (Marcel Iancul)

1993. "Telafila 93" Israel–Romanian Stamp Exhibition, Tel Aviv. Sheet 90×78 mm.

MS5549	535l. multicoloured	3·25	3·25

1150 St. Stefan the Great, Prince of Moldavia

1993. Icons. Multicoloured.

5550	75l. Type **1150**	25	10
5551	171l. Prince Costantin Brancoveanu of Wallachia with his sons Constantin, Stefan, Radu and Matei and Adviser Ianache Vacarescu	65	15
5552	216l. St. Antim Ivireanul, Metropolitan of Wallachia	1·50	25

1151 Mounted Officers

1993. Centenary of Rural Gendarmeric Law.

5553	**1151**	29l. multicoloured	65	50

1993. "Riccione 93" International Stamp Fair. No. 5292 surch Riccione '93 3-5 septembrie 171L.

5554	**1081**	171l. on 2l. multicoloured	1·30	60

1153 Temple Roof

1993. "Bangkok 1993" International Stamp Exhibition. Sheet 79×90 mm.

MS5555	535l. multicoloured	3·25	3·25

1154 George Baritiu

1993. Anniversaries.

5556	**1154**	29l. flesh, black and lilac	10	10
5557	-	46l. flesh, black and blue	15	10
5558	-	85l. flesh, black & green	40	10
5559	-	171l. flesh, black & purple	75	15
5560	-	216l. flesh, black & blue	90	20
5561	-	319l. flesh, black and grey	1·50	25

DESIGNS: 29l. Type **1154** (politician and journalist, death centenary); 46l. Horia Creanga (architect, 50th death anniv); 85l. Armand Calinescu (leader of Peasant National Party, birth centenary); 171l. Dr. Dumitru Bagdasar (neuro-surgeon, birth centenary); 216l. Constantin Brailoiu (musician, birth centenary); 319l. Iuliu Maniu (Prime Minister, 1927–30 and 1932–33, 40th death anniv).

1993. 35th Annivs of Romanian Philatelic Association and Romanian Philatelic Federation. No. 5445 surch 35 ANI DE ACTIVITATE AFR-FFR 1958–1993 70L+45L.

5562	**1122**	70l.+45l. on 10l.+4l. pink, violet and blue	65	50

1156 Map, National Flag and Council Emblem

1993. Admission to Council of Europe. Sheet 90×78 mm.

MS5563	1590l. multicoloured	7·75	7·75

1157 Iancu Flondor (Bukovinan politician)

1993. 75th Anniv of Union of Bessarabia, Bukovina and Transylvania with Romania.

5564	**1157**	115l. brown, blue and black	65	25
5565	-	245l. violet, yellow and green	1·30	30
5566	-	255l. multicoloured	1·40	30
5567	-	325l. brown, pink and deep brown	1·90	35
MS5568		90×78 mm. 1060l. multicoloured (map in several shades of brown) (41×53 mm)	15·00	15·00

DESIGNS: 245l. Ionel Bratianu (Prime Minister 1918–19, 1922–26 and 1027; 255l. Iuliu Maniu (Prime Minister, 1927–30 and 1932–33); 325l. Pantelemon Halippa (Bessarabian politician); 1060l, King Ferdinand I and map.

1158 Emblem

1993. Anniversaries. Multicoloured.

5569	115l. Type **1158** (75th anniv of General Association of Romanian Engineers)	65	25
5570	245l. Statue of Johannes Honterus (450th anniv of Romanian Humanist School)	1·30	30
5571	255l. Bridge, arms on book spine and seal (625th anniv of first documentary reference to Slatina)	1·40	30
5572	325l. Map and town arms (625th anniv of first documentary reference to Braila)	1·50	35

1159 "Nativity" (17th-century icon)

1993. Christmas.

5573	**1159**	45l. multicoloured	65	50

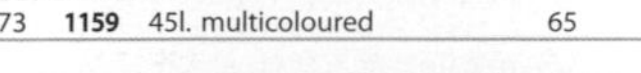

1160 "Clivina subterranea"

1993. Movile Cave Animals. Multicoloured.

5574	29l. Type **1160**	10	10
5575	46l. "Nepa anophthalma"	15	10
5576	85l. "Haemopis caeca"	50	15
5577	171l. "Lascona cristiani"	90	25
5578	216l. "Semisalsa dobrogica"	1·30	30
5579	319l. "Armadilidium tabacarui"	1·90	35
MS5580	90×78 mm. 535l. Diver exploring cave (41×53 mm)	2·50	2·50

1161 Prince Alexandru Ioan Cuza and Seal

1994. 130th Anniv of Court of Accounts.

5581	**1161**	45l. multicoloured	65	50

1162 Opera House

1994. Destroyed Buildings of Bucharest. Mult.

5582	115l. Type **1162**	40	15
5583	245l. Church of Vacaresti Monastery (vert)	90	25
5584	255l. St. Vineri's Church	1·30	35
5585	325l. Cloisters of Vacaresti Monastery	1·40	40

1164 Speed Skating

1994. Winter Olympic Games, Lillehammer, Norway. Multicoloured.

5588	70l. Type **1164**	10	10
5589	115l. Skiing	50	10
5590	125l. Bobsleighing	65	10
5591	245l. Cross-country skiing	90	15
5592	255l. Ski jumping	1·00	20
5593	325l. Figure skating	1·40	25
MS5594	90×78 mm. 1590l. Single luge (41×53 mm) (air)	5·75	5·75

1165 Sarichioi Windmill, Tulcea

1994. Mills. Multicoloured.

5595	70l. Type **1165**	10	10
5596	115l. Nucarilor Valley windmill, Tulcea	25	10
5597	125l. Caraorman windmill, Tulcea	40	10
5598	245l. Romanii de Jos watermill, Valcea	75	15
5599	255l. Enisala windmill, Tulcea (horiz)	90	20
5600	325l. Nistoresti watermill, Vrancea	1·30	25

1166 Calin the Backward

1994. Fairy Tales. Multicoloured.

5601	70l. Type **1166**	25	10
5602	115l. Ileana Cosanzeana flying	60	10
5603	125l. Ileana Cosanzeana seated	65	10
5604	245l. Ileana Cosanzeana and castle	1·00	15
5605	255l. Agheran the Brave	1·20	20
5606	325l. The Enchanted Wolf carrying Ileana Cosanzeana	1·50	25

1167 "Resurrection of Christ" (17th-century icon)

1994. Easter.

5607	**1167**	60l. multicoloured	65	50

1168 "Struthiosaurus transylvanicus"

1994. Prehistoric Animals. Multicoloured.

5608	90l. Type **1168**	25	10
5609	130l. Megalosaurus	40	10
5610	150l. Parasaurolophus	65	15
5611	280l. Stenonychosaurus	1·00	20
5612	500l. Camarasaurus	1·30	25
5613	635l. Gallimimus	1·50	30

1169 Hermann Oberth (rocket designer)

1994. Europa. Inventions. Sheet 109×78 mm containing T 1169 and similar horiz design.

MS5614	240l. blue, indigo and black; 2100l. blue and black	6·50	6·50

DESIGN: 2100l. Henri Coanda (airplane designer).

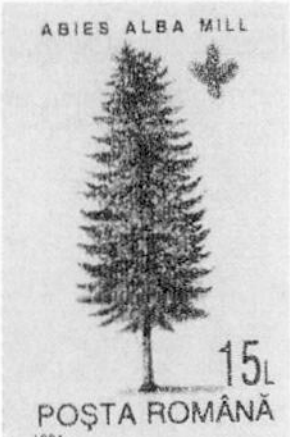

1170 Silver Fir

1994. Trees. Each green and black.

5615	15l. Type **1170**	10	10
5616	35l. Scots pine	10	10
5617	45l. White poplar	15	10
5618	60l. Pedunculate oak	20	10
5619	70l. European larch	25	10
5620	125l. Beech	50	10
5621	350l. Sycamore	1·00	10
5622	940l. Ash	3·25	35
5623	1440l. Norway spruce	4·50	50
5624	3095l. Large-leaved lime	9·00	60

1171 Players and Flags of U.S.A., Switzerland, Colombia and Romania

1994. World Cup Football Championship, U.S.A. Designs showing various footballing scenes and flags of participating countries. Multicoloured.

5625	90l. Type **1171**	10	10
5626	130l. Brazil, Russia, Cameroun and Sweden (Group B)	40	10
5627	150l. Germany, Bolivia, Spain and South Korea (Group C)	65	10
5628	280l. Argentina, Greece, Nigeria and Bulgaria (Group D)	1·00	20
5629	500l. Italy, Ireland, Norway and Mexico (Group E)	1·30	25
5630	635l. Belgium, Morocco, Netherlands and Saudi Arabia (Group F)	1·50	35
MS5631	91×78 mm. 2075l. Goalkeeper stopping goal attempt (53×41 mm)	5·00	5·00

1172 Torch-bearer and Centenary Emblem

1994. Centenary of International Olympic Committee. Ancient Greek Athletes. Mult.

5632	150l. Type **1172**	40	10
5633	280l. Discus-thrower and International Sports Year emblem	90	25
5634	500l. Wrestlers and Olympic Peace emblem	1·30	30
5635	635l. Arbitrator and "Paris 1994" centenary congress emblem	2·50	35
MS5636	90×78 mm. 2075l. Athletes, National Olympic Committee emblem and wreath (80th anniv of Romanian membership of Olympic movement) (53×41 mm)	5·00	5·00

1173 National History Museum (former Postal Headquarters, Bucharest)

1994. Stamp Day.

5637	**1173**	90l.+60l. multicoloured	65	50

1174 Death Trumpet ("Craterellus cormucopoiodes")

1994. Edible (MS5638a) and Poisonous (MS5638b) Fungi. Two sheets, each 155×72 mm containing vert designs as T 1174. Multicoloured.

MS5638	(a) 30l. Type **1174**; 60l. Wood blewit ("Lepista nuda"); 150l. Cep ("Boletus edulis"); 940l. Common puff-ball ("Lycoperdon perlatum"). (b) 90l. Satan's mushroom ("Boletus satanus"); 280l. Death cap ("Amanita phalloides"); 350l. Red-staining inocybe ("Inocybe patouillardii, wrongly inscr "patonillardi"); 500l. Fly agaric ("Amanita muscaria") Set of 2 sheets	6·50	6·50

1175 Traian Vuia's Airplane No. 1, 1906

1994. Air. 50th Anniv of I.C.A.O.

5639	**1175**	110l. brown, black & blue	25	25
5640	-	350l. multicoloured	1·30	25
5641	-	500l. multicoloured	1·90	30
5642	-	635l. black, ultramarine and blue	2·50	30

DESIGNS: 350l. Rombac One Eleven; 500l. Boeing 737-300; 635l. Airbus Industrie A310.

1176 Turning Fork

1994. "Philakorea 1994" International Stamp Exhibition, Seoul.

5643	**1176**	60l. black, orange and mauve	65	50
MS5644		78×91 mm. 2075l. multicoloured	4·50	4·50

DESIGN—38×52 mm. No. 5644, Korean drummer.

1177 Beluga

1994. Environmental Protection of Danube Delta. Multicoloured.

5645	150l. Type **1177**	50	10
5646	280l. Orsini's viper	90	15

5647	500l. White-tailed sea eagle	1·50	20
5648	635l. European mink	1·70	25

MS5649 90×78 mm. 2075l. "Periploca gracca" (plant) (50×38 mm) 5·00 5·00

1994. Victory of Romanian Team in European Gymnastics Championships, Stockholm. Nos. 5338/9 surch Echipa Romaniei Compioana Europeana Stockholm 1994 and value.

5650	150l. on 4l.50 multicoloured	65	35
5651	525l. on 4l.50 multicoloured	1·90	50

1179 Elephant

1994. The Circus. Multicoloured.

5652	90l. Type **1179**	25	10
5653	130l. Balancing bear (vert)	40	10
5654	150l. Cycling monkeys	65	15
5655	280l. Tiger jumping through hoop	1·30	20
5656	500l. Clown on tightrope balancing dogs	1·70	25
5657	635l. Clown on horseback	2·20	35

1994. World Post Day. No. 5465 surch 150LEI 1994 Posta - cea mai buna alegere.

5658	**1126**	150l. on 10l. mult	65	50

1181 Emblem

1994. 20th International Fair, Bucharest.

5659	**1181**	525l. multicoloured	1·90	60

1182 Sterlet

1994. Sturgeons.

5660	150l. Type **1182**	65	10
5661	280l. Russian sturgeon	1·30	15
5662	500l. Stellate sturgeon	1·90	20
5663	635l. Common sturgeon	2·50	25

1183 Snake

1994. Romanian–Chinese Stamp Exhibition, Timisoara and Cluj-Napoca. Multicoloured.

5664	150l. Type **1183**	65	25
5665	1135l. Dragon	4·50	50

1184 Early Steam Train, Bucharest–Giurgii Line

1994. 125th Anniv of Romanian Railway Administration.

5666	**1184**	90l. multicoloured	65	50

1185 Alexandru Orascu (architect and mathematician)

1994. Anniversaries. Multicoloured.

5667	30l. Type **1185** (death centenary)	25	15
5668	60l. Gheorghe Polizu (physician, 175th birth anniv)	40	15
5669	150l. Iulia Hasdeu (writer, 125th birth anniv)	65	15
5670	280l. S. Mehedinti (scientist, 125th birth anniv)	75	15
5671	350l. Camil Petrescu (writer, birth centenary)	1·20	25
5672	500l. N. Paulescu (physician, 125th birth anniv)	1·30	35
5673	940l. L. Grigorescu (painter, birth centenary)	3·25	50

See also No. 5684.

1186 Nativity

1994. Christmas.

5674	**1186**	60l. multicoloured	65	50

1187 St. Mary's Church, Cleveland, U.S.A.

1994

5675	**1187**	610l. multicoloured	1·90	60

1188 Anniversary Emblem

1994. 20th Anniv of World Tourism Organization.

5676	**1188**	525l. blue, orange & black	1·90	60

1189 Military Aviation Medal, 1938

1994. Military Decorations. Sheet 73×104 mm containing T 1189 and similar vert designs. Multicoloured.

MS5677 30l. Type **1189**; 60l. "For Valour" Cross, Third Class, 1916; 150l. Military Medal, First Class, 1880; 940l. Rumanian Star, 1877 3·25 3·25

1190 Kittens

1994. Young Domestic Animals. Multicoloured.

5678	90l. Type **1190**	15	25
5679	130l. Puppies	25	25
5680	150l. Kid	40	25
5681	280l. Foal	75	25
5682	500l. Rabbit kittens	1·50	35
5683	635l. Lambs	1·90	50

1994. Death Centenary of Gheorghe Tattarescu (painter). As T 1185. Multicoloured.

5684	90l. Tattarescu	65	50

1191 Emblem

1995. Save the Children Fund.

5685	**1191**	60l. blue	65	50

1192 Tanar

1995. Brasov Youth. Neighbourhood Group Leaders. Multicoloured.

5686	40l. Type **1192**	15	25
5687	60l. Batran	25	25
5688	150l. Curcan	40	25
5689	280l. Dorobant	75	25
5690	350l. Brasovechean	1·30	25
5691	500l. Rosior	1·50	35
5692	635l. Albior	1·90	50

1193 Hand and Barbed Wire

1995. 50th Anniv of Liberation of Concentration Camps.

5693	**1193**	960l. black and red	1·30	60

1194 Emblems of French and Romanian State Airlines

1995. Air. 75th Anniv of Founding of Franco-Romanian Air Company.

5694	**1194**	60l. blue and red	25	10
5695	-	960l. blue and black	1·70	35

DESIGN: 960l. Potez IX biplane and Paris–Bucharest route map.

1195 Ear of Wheat

1995. 50th Anniversaries. Multicoloured.

5696	675l. Type **1195** (F.A.O.)	1·30	25
5697	960l. Anniversary emblem (U.N.O.)	1·90	35
5698	1615l. Hand holding pen showing members' flags (signing of U.N. Charter)	2·50	55

1196 "Resurrection" (icon)

1995. Easter.

5699	**1196**	60l. multicoloured	65	50

1197 "Youth without Age and Life without Death"

1995. Fairy Tales. Multicoloured.

5700	90l. Type **1197**	15	20
5701	130l. "The Old Man's Servant and the Old Woman's Servant" (vert)	20	20
5702	150l. "The Prince with the Golden Hair"	25	20
5703	280l. "Son of the Red King"	90	20
5704	500l. "Praslea the Brave and the Golden Apples" (vert)	1·70	20
5705	635l. "King Dafin" (drawn by golden horses)	2·50	25

1198 Enescu

1995. 40th Death Anniv of George Enescu (composer).

5706	**1198**	960l. orange and black	1·40	60

1199 Dove with Section of Rainbow

1995. Europa. Peace and Freedom. Multicoloured.

5707	150l. Type **1199**	15	10
5708	4370l. Dove wings forming "EUROPA" around rainbow	9·50	9·00

1200 Blaga

1995. Birth Centenary of Lucian Blaga (poet).

5709	**1200**	150l. multicoloured	65	50

See also Nos. 5745/9.

1201 Bucharest Underground Railway, 1979

1995. Transport.

5712	**1201**	470l. yellow and black (postage)	65	10
5713	-	630l. red and blue	90	10
5714	-	675l. red and black	90	10
5715	-	755l. blue and black	1·00	10
5716	-	1615l. green and black	1·90	50
5717	-	2300l. green and black	3·00	25
5718	-	2550l. black and red	3·25	25
5719	-	285l. green and black (air)	25	10
5720	-	715l. red and blue	90	10
5721	-	965l. black and blue	3·00	10
5722	-	1575l. green and black	2·30	35
5723	-	3410l. blue and black	4·50	60

DESIGNS—HORIZ: 285l. I.A.R. 80 aircraft (70th anniv of Romanian aeronautical industry); 630l. "Masagerul" (post boat); 715l. I.A.R. 316 Red Cross helicopter; 755l. "Razboieni" (container ship); 965l. Sud Aviation SA 330 Puma helicopter; 1575l. I.A.R. 818H seaplane; 2300l. Trolleybus, 1904; 2550l. Steam train, 1869; 3410l. Boeing 737-300 (75th anniv of Romanian air transport). VERT: 675l. Cable-car, Brasov; 1615l. Electric tram, 1894.

1202 "Dacia" (liner)

1995. Centenary of Romanian Maritime Service. Multicoloured.

5735	90l. Type **1202**	25	20
5736	130l. "Imparatul Traian" (Danube river steamer) (horiz)	25	20
5737	150l. "Romania" (Danube river steamer) (horiz)	25	20
5738	280l. "Costinesti" (tanker) (horiz)	40	20
5739	960l. "Caransebes" (container ship) (horiz)	1·30	25
5740	3410l. "Tutova" (car ferry) (horiz)	4·50	85

1203 Fallow Deer

1995. European Nature Conservation Year. Mult.

5741	150l. Type **1203**	25	25
5742	280l. Great bustard	40	25
5743	960l. Lady's slipper	1·90	60
5744	1615l. Stalagmites	2·50	1·20

1995. Anniversaries. As T 1200. Multicoloured.

5745	90l. D. Rosca (birth centenary)	25	25
5746	130l. Vasile Conta (150th birth anniv)	25	25
5747	280l. Ion Barbu (birth centenary)	25	25
5748	960l. Iuliu Hatieganu (110th birth anniv)	1·20	30
5749	1650l. Dimitrie Brandza (botanist) (death centenary)	2·00	40

1204 Youths and Torch-bearer

1995. European Youth Olympic Days.

5750	**1204**	1650l. multicoloured	2·50	60

1205 Post Wagon (image scaled to 46% of original size)

1995. Stamp Day. Centenary of Upper Rhine Local Post.

5751	**1205**	960l. (+715l.) mult	2·50	60

No. 5751 includes the se-tenant premium-carrying tab shown in Type **1205**.

1206 Saligny Bridge

1995. Centenary of Saligny Bridge, Cernavoda.

5752	**1206**	675l. multicoloured	1·30	60

1207 Mallard

1995. Domestic Birds. Multicoloured.

5753	90l. Type **1207**	25	20
5754	130l. Red junglefowl (hen)	25	20
5755	150l. Helmeted guineafowl	25	20
5756	280l. Common turkey	65	20
5757	960l. Greylag goose	1·50	25
5758	1650l. Red junglefowl (cock)	2·30	35

1208 General Dr. Victor Anastasiu

1995. 75th Anniv of Institute of Aeronautics Medicine.

5759	**1208**	960l. ultramarine, blue and red	1·90	60

1209 Battle Scene

1995. 400th Anniv of Battle of Calugareni.

5760	**1209**	100l. multicoloured	65	50

1210 Giurgiu Castle

1995. Anniversaries. Multicoloured.

5761	250l. Type **1210** (600th anniv)	40	15
5762	500l. Neamtului Castle (600th anniv) (vert)	65	15
5763	960l. Sebes-Alba Mill (700th anniv)	1·30	20
5764	1615l. Dorohoi Church (500th anniv) (vert)	1·90	30
5765	1650l. Military observatory, Bucharest (centenary) (vert)	2·30	35

1211 Moldovita Monastery

1995. UNESCO World Heritage Sites. Mult.

5766	675l. Type **1211**	65	25
5767	960l. Hurez Monastery	1·30	35
5768	1615l. Biertan Castle (horiz)	1·90	50

1212 Racket

1995. 5th Open Tennis Championships, Bucharest.

5769	**1212**	1020l. multicoloured	1·90	60

1213 Ion Ionescu (editor)

1995. Centenary of Mathematics Gazette.

5770	**1213**	100l. pink and brown	65	50

1214 "Albizzia julibrissin"

1995. Plants from Bucharest Botanical Garden. Multicoloured.

5771	50l. Type **1214**	15	10
5772	100l. Yew	15	10
5773	150l. "Paulownia tomentosa"	15	10
5774	500l. Bird of Paradise flower	75	10
5775	960l. Amazon water-lily	1·50	35
5776	2300l. Azalea	2·75	50

1215 St. John's Church

1995. 600th Anniv of First Documentary Reference to Piatra-Neamt.

5777	**1215**	250l. multicoloured	1·30	1·20

1216 George Apostu (sculptor, 10th death (1996))

1995. Anniversaries.

5778	**1216**	150l. green and black	25	20
5779	-	250l. blue and black	50	20
5780	-	500l. light brown, brown and black	75	20
5781	-	960l. rose, purple and black	1·50	25
5782	-	1650l. brown and black	2·30	50

DESIGNS: 250l. Emil Cioran (philosopher, death in 1995); 500l. Eugen Ionescu (writer, 1st death anniv); 960l. Elena Vacarescu (poetess, 130th birth (1996)); 1650l. Mircea Eliade (philosopher, 10th death (1996)).

1217 Running

1995. Olympic Games, Atlanta (1996) (1st issue). Multicoloured.

5783	50l. Type **1217**	15	15
5784	100l. Gymnastics	15	15
5785	150l. Canoeing	15	15
5786	500l. Fencing	90	15
5787	960l. Rowing	1·50	25
5788	2300l. Boxing	3·50	60
MS5789	78×92 mm. 2610l. Gymnastics (different) (41×53 mm)	3·75	3·75

See also Nos. 5829/**MS**5834.

1218 Nativity

1995. Christmas.

5790	**1218**	100l. multicoloured	65	50

1219 Masked Person

1996. Folk Masks of Maramures (250l.) and Moldavia (others).

5791	**1219**	250l. multicoloured	65	25
5792	-	500l. multicoloured	1·00	25
5793	-	960l. mult (vert)	1·70	35
5794	-	1650l. mult (vert)	2·50	50

DESIGNS: 500l. to 1650l. Different masks.

1220 Tristan Tzara

1996. Writers' Birth Anniversaries. Multicoloured.
5795 150l. Type **1220** (centenary) 25 10
5796 1500l. Anton Pann (bicentenary) 2·30 35

1221 "Resurrection" (icon)

1996. Easter.
5797 **1221** 150l. multicoloured 65 50

1222 National History Museum

1996. "Romfilex '96" Romanian–Israeli Stamp Exhibition. Sheet 124×73 mm containing T 1222 and similar vert designs.
MS5798 150l. brown and black; 370l. multicoloured; 1500l. multicoloured 10·00 10·00
DESIGNS: 370l. "On The Terrace at Sinaia" (Theodor Aman); 1500l. "Old Jerusalem" (Reuven Rubin).

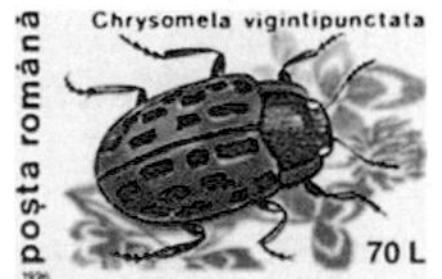

1223 "Chrysomela vigintipunctata" (leaf beetle)

1996. Beetles.
5799 **1223** 70l. yellow and black 20 10
5800 - 220l. red and black 20 10
5801 - 370l. brown and black 40 10
5802 - 650l. black, red & grey 65 10
5803 - 700l. red, black and green 75 10
5804 - 740l. black and yellow 90 10
5805 - 960l. black and red 1·20 10
5806 - 1000l. yellow and black 1·20 10
5807 - 1500l. black and brown 1·90 25
5808 - 2500l. red, black & green 2·50 50
DESIGNS: 220l. "Cerambyx cerdo" (longhorn beetle); 370l. "Entomoscelis adonidis"; 650l. Ladybird; 700l. Caterpillar-hunter; 740l. "Hedobia imperialis"; 960l. European rhinoceros beetle; 1000l. Bee chafer; 1500l. "Purpuricenus kaehleri" (longhorn beetle); 2500l. "Anthaxia salicis".

1224 Dumitru Prunariu (first Romanian cosmonaut)

1996. "Espamer" Spanish–Latin American and "Aviation and Space" Stamp Exhibitions, Seville, Spain. Sheet 91×78 mm.
MS5809 2720l. multicoloured 2·50 2·50

1225 Arbore Church

1996. UNESCO World Heritage Sites. Mult.
5810 150l. Type **1225** 25 25
5811 1500l. Voronet Monastery 1·70 35
5812 2550l. Humor Monastery 3·25 60

1226 Ana Aslan (doctor)

1996. Europa. Famous Women. Multicoloured.
5813 370l. Type **1226** 40 35
5814 4140l. Lucia Bulandra (actress) 6·25 5·75

1227 "Mother and Children" (Oana Negoita)

1996. 50th Anniv of UNICEF. Prize-winning Children's Paintings. Multicoloured.
5815 370l. Type **1227** 40 35
5816 740l. "Winter Scene" (Badea Cosmin) 90 35
5817 1500l. "Children and Sun over House" (Nicoleta Georgescu) 1·50 50
5818 2550l. "House on Stilts" (Biborka Bartha) (vert) 2·30 70

1228 Goalkeeper with Ball

1996. European Football Championship, England. Multicoloured.
5819 220l. Type **1228** 10 10
5820 370l. Player with ball 25 10
5821 740l. Two players with ball 65 15
5822 1500l. Three players with ball 1·40 25
5823 2550l. Player dribbling ball 2·40 50
MS5824 90×78 mm. 4050l. Balls and two players (41×53 mm) 3·75 3·75
Nos. 5819/23 were issued together, se-tenant, forming a composite design of the pitch and stadium.

1229 Metropolitan Toronto Convention Centre (venue)

1996. "Capex '96" International Stamp Exhibition, Toronto, Canada. Multicoloured.
5825 150l. Type **1229** 65 50
MS5826 78×90 mm. 4050l. View of City (41×52 mm) 3·75 3·75

1230 Factory

1996. 225th Anniv of Resita Works.
5827 **1230** 150l. brown 65 50

1996. 5th Anniv of Establishment of R.A. Posta Romana (postal organization). No. 5471 surch 1996 - 5 ANI DE LA INFIINTARE L150.
5828 **1128** 150l. on 10l. multicoloured 65 60

1232 Boxing

1996. Centenary of Modern Olympic Games and Olympic Games, Atlanta (2nd issue). Mult.
5829 220l. Type **1232** 25 10
5830 370l. Running 40 10
5831 740l. Rowing 90 15
5832 1500l. Judo 1·70 35
5833 2550l. Gymnastics (asymmetrical bars) 2·75 50
MS5834 90×78 mm. 4050l. Gymnastics (beam) (53×41 mm) (air) 3·75 3·75
No. **MS**5834 also commemorates "Olymphilex '96" sports stamp exhibition, Atlanta.

1233 Postman, Keyboard and Stamp under Magnifying Glass (image scaled to 71% of original size)

1996. Stamp Day.
5835 **1233** 1500l. (+650l.) mult 1·90 60
No. 5835 includes the se-tenant premium-carrying tab shown in Type **1233**.

1234 White Spruce

1996. Coniferous Trees. Multicoloured.
5836 70l. Type **1234** 15 10
5837 150l. Serbian spruce 15 10
5838 220l. Blue Colorado spruce 15 10
5839 740l. Sitka spruce 90 10
5840 1500l. Scots pine 1·70 25
5841 3500l. Maritime pine 3·75 60

1235 Grass Snake

1996. Animals. Multicoloured.
5842 70l. Type **1235** 15 10
5843 150l. Hermann's tortoise 15 10
5844 220l. Eurasian sky lark (horiz) 15 10
5845 740l. Red fox (horiz) 90 10
5846 1500l. Common porpoise 1·70 25
5847 3500l. Golden eagle (horiz) 3·75 60

1236 Madonna and Child

1996. Christmas.
5848 **1236** 150l. multicoloured 65 50

1237 Stan Golestan (composer, 40th)

1996. Death Anniversaries.
5849 **1237** 100l. pink and black 25 25
5850 - 150l. purple and black 40 35
5851 - 370l. orange and black 65 60
5852 - 1500l. red and black 2·00 1·90
DESIGNS: 150l. Corneliu Coposu (politician, 1st); 370l. Horia Vintila (writer, 4th); 1500l. Alexandru Papana (test pilot, 50th).

1238 Ford "Spider", 1930

1996. Motor Cars. Two sheets containing horiz designs as T 1238. Multicoloured.
MS5853 (a) 110×78 mm 70l. Type **1238**; 150l. Citroen (1932); 220l. Rolls Royce (1936); 280l. Mercedes Benz (1933). (b) 113×80 mm. 120l. Jaguar SS 100 (1937); 2500l. Bugatti Type 59 (1934); 2550l. Mercedes Benz 500K Roadster (1936); 2550l. Alfa Romeo 8C (1931) Set of 2 sheets 10·00 10·00

1239 Deng Xiaoping and Margaret Thatcher

1997. "Hong Kong '97" Stamp Exhibition. Sheet 92×78 mm.
MS5854 1500l. multicoloured 1·90 1·90

1240 Stoat

1997. Fur-bearing Mammals. Multicoloured.
5855 70l. Type **1240** 25 25
5856 150l. Arctic fox 25 25
5857 220l. Racoon-dog 25 25
5858 740l. European otter 40 30
5859 1500l. Muskrat 75 35
5860 3500l. Pine marten 1·90 60

1241 Bow

1997. 26th Anniv of Greenpeace (environmental organization). The "Rainbow Warrior" (campaign ship). Multicoloured.

5861	150l. Type **1241**	25	25
5862	370l. Ship and ice	25	25
5863	1940l. Ship cruising past beach	1·00	35
5864	2500l. Rainbow and ship	1·70	35
MS5865	90×77 mm. 4050l. Ship carrying banner (49×38 mm)	3·25	3·25

1242 Thomas Edison (inventor)

1997. Birth Anniversaries. Multicoloured.

5866	200l. Type **1242** (150th anniv)	25	25
5867	400l. Franz Schubert (composer, bicentenary)	40	30
5868	3600l. Miguel de Cervantes Saavedra (writer, 450th anniv)	2·50	60

1243 Emblem

1997. Inauguration of Mobile Telephone Network in Romania.

5869	**1243**	400l. multicoloured	65	50

1244 Surdesti

1997. Churches. Each brown, agate and green.

5870	200l. Type **1244**	25	20
5871	400l. Plopis	25	20
5872	450l. Bogdan Voda	25	20
5873	850l. Rogoz	50	25
5874	3600l. Calinesti	1·70	30
5875	6000l. Birsana	2·75	50

1245 Al. Demetrescu Dan in "Hamlet", 1916

1997. 2nd Shakespeare Festival, Craiova. Mult.

5876	200l. Type **1245**	15	10
5877	400l. Constantin Serghie in "Othello", 1855	15	10
5878	2400l. Gheorghe Cozorici in "Hamlet", 1957	1·30	1·20
5879	3600l. Ion Manolescu in "Hamlet", 1924	1·90	1·80

1246 Vlad Tepes Dracula (Voivode of Wallachia)

1997. Europa. Tales and Legends. Dracula. Mult.

5880	400l. Type **1246**	25	10
5881	4250l. Dracula the myth	3·00	2·40

1247 "Dolichothele uberiformis"

1997. Cacti. Multicoloured.

5882	100l. Type **1247**	25	25
5883	250l. "Rebutia"	25	25
5884	450l. "Echinofossulocactus lamellosus"	25	25
5885	500l. "Ferocactus glaucescens"	25	25
5886	650l. "Thelocactus"	25	25
5887	6150l. "Echinofossulocactus albatus"	5·00	1·20

1248 National Theatre, Cathedral and Statue of Mihai Viteazul

1997. "Balcanmax'97" Maximum Cards Exhibition, Cluj-Napoca.

5888	**1248**	450l. multicoloured	65	60

1249 19th-century Postal Transport (image scaled to 61% of original size)

1997. Stamp Day.

5889	**1249**	3600l. (+1500l.) multicoloured	3·25	1·80

No. 5889 includes the se-tenant premium-carrying tab shown in Type **1249**.

1997. Nos. 5349/55 and 5357 surch.

5890	250l. on 1l. blue	25	25
5891	250l. on 2l. green	25	25
5892	250l. on 4l. red	25	25
5893	450l. on 5l. violet	25	25
5894	450l. on 6l. brown	25	25
5895	450l. on 18l. red	25	25
5896	950l. on 9l. red	40	25
5897	3600l. on 8l. brown	1·90	35

1251 Archway of Vlad Tepes Dracula's House

1997. Sighisoara. Multicoloured.

5898	250l. Type **1251**	25	15
5899	650l. Town Hall clocktower	40	15
5900	3700l. Steps leading to fortress and clocktower	2·00	1·20

1252 Tourism Monument

1997. Rusca Montana, Banat.

5901	**1252**	950l. multicoloured	40	25

1253 Printing Works

1997. 125th Anniv of Stamp Printing Works.

5902	**1253**	450l. red, brown and blue	65	40

1254 Emil Racovita (biologist) and "Belgica" (polar barque)

1997. Centenary of Belgian Antarctic Expedition.

5903	**1254**	450l. blue, grey and black	25	10
5904	-	650l. red, yellow and black	25	10
5905	-	1600l. green, pink and black	75	15
5906	-	3700l. brown, yellow and black	2·50	1·60

DESIGNS: 650l. Frederick Cook (anthropologist and photographer) and "Belgica" at sea; 1600l. Roald Amundsen and "Belgica" in port; 3700l. Adrien de Gerlache (expedition commander) and "Belgica" ice-bound.

1997. "Aeromfila '97" Stamp Exhibition, Brasov. No. 5334 surch 1050 L. AEROMFILA'97 Brasov and airplane.

5907	**1292**	1050l. on 4l.50 mult	65	40

1256 Campsite

1997. Romanian Scout Association. Multicoloured.

5908	300l. Type **1256**	15	10
5909	700l. Romanian Scout Association emblem	25	15
5910	1050l. Joined hands	50	30
5911	1750l. Carvings	75	45
5912	3700l. Scouts around campfire	1·80	1·10

Nos. 5908/12 were issued together, se-tenant, forming a composite design.

1997. 9th Romanian–Chinese Stamp Exhibition, Bucharest. No. 5293 surch A IX-a editie a expozitiei filatelice romano-chineza 1997 500 L.

5913	**1082**	500l. on 2l. mult	65	40

1258 Ion Mihalache (politician)

1997. Anniversaries. Multicoloured.

5914	500l. Type **1258** (34th death anniv)	25	15
5915	1050l. King Carol I (131st anniv of accession) (black inscriptions and face value)	65	40
5916	1050l. As No. 5915 but mauve inscriptions and face value	65	40
5917	1050l. As No. 5915 but blue inscriptions and face value	65	40
5918	1050l. As No. 5915 but brown inscriptions and face value	65	40

1259 Rugby

1997. Sports. Multicoloured.

5919	500l. Type **1259**	25	15
5920	700l. American football (vert)	40	25
5921	1750l. Oina (Romanian bat and ball game)	75	45
5922	3700l. Mountaineering (vert)	2·50	1·60

1260 New Building

1998. 130th Anniv of Bucharest Chamber of Commerce and Industry.

5923	**1260**	700l. multicoloured	65	40

1261 Biathlon

1998. Winter Olympic Games, Nagano, Japan. Mult.

5924	900l. Type **1261**	60	40
5925	3900l. Figure skating	2·30	1·60

1262 "Romania breaking the Chains on Libertatii Plain" (C. D. Rosenthal)

1998. National Tricolour Flag Day. Sheet 78×90 mm.

MS5926	900l. multicoloured	1·20	1·20

1263 Four-leaved Clover (Good luck and Success)

1998. Europa. National Festivals.

5927	**1263**	900l. green and red	1·20	80

5928 - 3900l. red, orange and green 28·00 19·00

DESIGN: 3900l. Butterfly (youth and suaveness).

1264 Alfred Nobel

1998. The 20th-century (1st series). Multicoloured.
5929 700l. Type **1264** (establishment of Nobel Foundation, 1901) 45 30
5930 900l. Guglielmo Marconi (first radio-telegraphic trans-Atlantic link, 1901) 60 40
5931 1500l. Albert Einstein (elaboration of Theory of Relativity, 1905) 70 45
5932 3900l. Traian Vuia (his first flight, 1906) 2·30 1·60

See also Nos. 5991/5, 6056/9, 6060/3, 6128/31, 6133/6, 6205/8 and 6230/3.

1265 Shrine, Cluj

1998. Roadside Shrines. Multicoloured.
5933 700l. Type **1265** 35 25
5934 900l. Crucifixion, Prahovac 45 30
5935 1500l. Shrine, Arges 1·20 80

1998. "Israel '98" International Stamp Exhibition, Tel Aviv. No. MS5798 with each stamp surch ISRAEL '98 and the old value cancelled by Menora emblem.
MS5936 700l. on 150l. brown and black; 900l. on 370l. multicoloured; 3900l. on 1500l. multicoloured 3·50 3·50

1267 Dr. Thoma Ionescu (founder) and Coltea Hospital, Bucharest

1998. Centenary of Romanian Surgery Society.
5937 **1267** 1050l. grey, brown and red 60 40

1998. Nos. 5350/1, 5353/4 and 5357 surch, the old value cancelled by a clover leaf.
5938 50l. on 2l. green 45 30
5939 100l. on 8l. brown 45 30
5940 200l. on 4l. red 45 30
5941 400l. on 6l. brown 45 30
5942 500l. on 18l. red 45 30

1269 Player

1998. World Cup Football Championship, France. Sheet 74×104 mm containing T 1269 and similar vert designs. Each ultramarine, brown and green.
MS5943 800l. Type **1269**; 1050l. Player in air; 1850l. Player bouncing ball on knee; 4150l. Player preparing to kick ball 4·75 4·75

1998. Nos. 5615/17 and 5620 surch, the old value cancelled by a hare.
5944 - 700l. on 125l. green and black 60 40
5945 - 800l. on 35l. green and black 60 40
5946 - 1050l. on 45l. green and black 60 40
5947 **1170** 4150l. on 15l. green and black 60 40

1998. Nos. 5352 and 5355 surch, the old value cancelled by a heart.
5948 1000l. on 9l. red 60 40
5949 1500l. on 5l. violet 60 40

1272 Brown Kiwi

1998. Nocturnal Birds. Multicoloured.
5950 700l. Type **1272** 45 30
5951 1500l. Barn owl 60 40
5952 1850l. Water rail 70 45
5953 2450l. European nightjar 1·70 1·20

1998. No. 5361 surch, the old value cancelled by a sign of the zodiac.
5954 250l. on 45l. blue (Aries) 60 40
5955 350l. on 45l. blue (Taurus) 60 40
5956 400l. on 45l. blue (Gemini) 60 40
5957 450l. on 45l. blue (Cancer) 60 40
5958 850l. on 45l. blue (Leo) 60 40
5959 900l. on 45l. blue (Aquarius) 60 40
5960 1000l. on 45l. blue (Libra) 60 40
5961 1600l. on 45l. blue (Scorpio) 1·20 80
5962 2500l. on 45l. blue (Sagittarius) 4·75 3·50

1274 81p. Stamp and Waslui Cancellation

1998. 140th Anniv of Bull's Head Issue of Moldavia. Multicoloured.
5963 700l. Type **1274** 60 40
5964 1050l. 27p. stamp and Jassy cancellation 70 45
MS5965 130×80 mm. 4150l.+850l. 54 and 108p. stamps and Galatz cancellation (53×41 mm) 3·50 3·50

1275 Soldiers and Revolutionaries fighting

1998. 150th Anniv of the 1848 Revolutions.
5966 **1275** 1050l. black, yellow and red 60 40

1276 Nikolaus Lenau (poet)

1998. German Personalities of Banat.
5967 **1276** 800l. orange, black and pink 45 35
5968 - 1850l. orange, black and green 80 65
5969 - 4150l. orange, black and blue 1·70 1·40

DESIGNS: 1850l. Stefan Jager (artist); 4150l. Adam Muller-Guttenbrunn (writer).

1277 Diver and Marine Life

1998. International Year of the Ocean.
5970 **1277** 1100l. multicoloured 60 45

1998. Nos. 5336/7 surch, the old value cancelled by a sporting emblem.
5971 **1094** 50l. on 1l. multicoloured (Figure skater) 60 45
5972 - 50l. on 1l. multicoloured (Trophy) 60 45

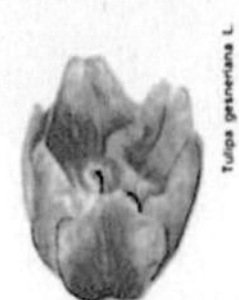

1279 "Tulipa gesneriana"

1998. Flowers. Multicoloured.
5973 350l. Type **1279** 25 20
5974 850l. "Dahlia variabilis" "Rubin" 45 35
5975 1100l. Martagon lily 60 45
5976 4450l. "Rosa centifolia" 2·30 1·90

No. 5975 commemorates the 50th anniv of the Horticulture Institute, Bucharest.

1998. Various stamps surch. (a) Nos. 5399/5404, the old value cancelled by a transport emblem.
5977 **1106** 50l. on 1l. brown, blue and deep blue (Car) 25 20
5978 - 50l. on 4l. green, lilac and violet (Steam locomotive) 25 20
5979 - 50l. on 5l. brown, blue and ultramarine (Lorry) 25 20
5980 - 50l. on 5l. blue, brown and red (Helicopter) 25 20
5981 - 50l. on 9l. red, blue and deep blue (Airplane) 25 20
5982 - 50l. on 10l. black, light brown and brown (Ship) 25 20

(b) Nos. 5472/5 and 5477, the old value cancelled by a bird.
5983 **1129** 50l. on 6l. green and violet (Cockerel) 25 20
5984 - 50l. on 7l. mauve, purple and green (Duck) 25 20
5985 - 50l. on 9l. blue and mauve (Swan) 25 20
5986 - 50l. on 10l. light brown, brown and blue (Dove) 25 20
5987 - 50l. on 30l. green and blue (Swallow) 25 20

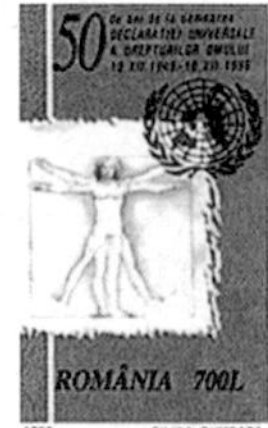

1281 "Proportions of Man" (Leonardo da Vinci)

1998. 50th Anniv of Universal Declaration of Human Rights.
5988 **1281** 700l. multicoloured 60 45

1282 Paciurea

1998. 125th Birth Anniv of Dimitrie Paciurea (sculptor).
5989 **1282** 850l. multicoloured 60 45

1283 Eclipse

1998. Total Eclipse of the Sun (1999) (1st issue).
5990 **1283** 1100l. multicoloured 60 45

See also No. 6050.

1284 Sinking of "Titanic" (liner), 1912

1998. The 20th century (2nd series).
5991 **1284** 350l. black, bl & red 25 20
5992 - 1100l. multicoloured 45 35
5993 - 1600l. multicoloured 60 45
5994 - 2000l. multicoloured 70 55
5995 - 2600l. blk, grey & red 1·40 1·10

DESIGNS: 1100l. Henri Coanda and his turbine-powered model airplane, 1910; 1600l. Louis Bleriot and his "Bleriot XI" airplane (first powered flight across English Channel, 1909); 2000l. Freighter in locks and map of American sea routes (opening of Panama Canal, 1914); 2600l. Prisoners in courtyard (Russian October revolution, 1917).

1998. Christmas. Nos. 5491 and 5674 surch with the old value cancelled by a Christmas emblem.
5996 **1133** 2000l. on 15l. multicoloured (Christmas tree) 95 75
5997 **1186** 2600l. on 60l. multicoloured (Father Christmas) 95 75

1286 Gonovez Lighthouse

1998. Lighthouses. Multicoloured.
5998 900l. Type **1286** 25 20
5999 1000l. Constanta 35 30
6000 1100l. Sfantu Gheorghe 45 35
6001 2600l. Sulina 1·60 1·30

1287 Arnota Monastery

1999. Monasteries. Multicoloured.
6002 500l. Type **1287** 25 20
6003 700l. Bistrita 35 30
6004 1100l. Dintr'un Lemn 45 35
6005 2100l. Govora 60 45
6006 4850l. Tismana 1·70 1·40

1999. No. 5492 surch with the old value cancelled by various fungi.
6007 **1134** 50l. on 15l. black, red and blue 25 20
6009 **1134** 400l. on 15l. black, red and blue 25 20
6010 **1134** 2300l. on 15l. black, red and blue 60 45
6011 **1134** 3200l. on 15l. black, red and blue 1·20 95

1999. No. 5384 surch with the old value cancelled by a musical instrument.
6012 **1099** 100l. on 1l. blue (guitar) 25 20
6013 **1099** 250l. on 1l. blue (saxophone) 35 30

1290 "Magnolia soulangiana"

1999. Shrubs. Multicoloured.
6014 350l. Type **1290** 10 10
6015 1000l. "Stewartia malacodendron" 25 20
6016 1100l. "Hibiscus rosa- sinensis" 35 30
6017 5350l. "Clematis patens" 2·30 1·90

1292 Easter Eggs

1999. Easter.
6023 **1292** 1100l. multicoloured 60 45

1999. No. 5799 surch with the old value cancelled by a dinosaur emblem.
6024 **1223** 100l. on 70l. yellow and black (Brontosaurus) 25 20
6025 **1223** 200l. on 70l. yellow and black (Iguanodon) 25 20
6026 **1223** 200l. on 70l. yellow and black (Allosaurus) 25 20
6027 **1223** 1500l. on 70l. yellow and black (Diplodocus) 30 25
6028 **1223** 1600l. on 70l. yellow and black (Tyrannosaurus) 35 30
6029 **1223** 3200l. on 70l. yellow and black (Stegosaurus) 80 65
6030 **1223** 6000l. on 70l. yellow and black (Plateosaurus) 1·50 1·20

1294 Girdle of Keys (Padureni)

1999. Jewellery. Multicoloured.
6031 1200l. Type **1294** 25 20
6032 2100l. Pendant of keys (Ilia, Hunedoara) 45 35
6033 2600l. Jewelled bib (Maramures) 60 45
6034 3200l. Necklace (Banat) (horiz) 1·70 1·40

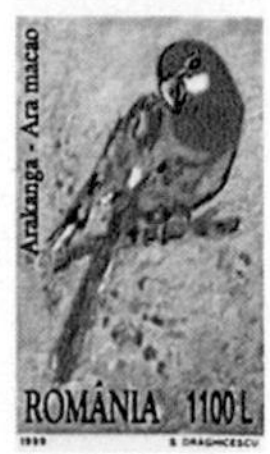

1295 Scarlet Macaw

1999. Birds. Multicoloured.
6035 1100l. Type **1295** 25 20
6036 2700l. White peafowl 60 45
6037 3700l. Common peafowl 80 65
6038 5700l. Sulphur-crested cockatoo 1·30 1·00

1296 Council Flag and Headquarters, Strasbourg

1999. 50th Anniv of Council of Europe.
6039 **1296** 2300l. multicoloured 1·20 95

1297 St. Peter's Cathedral, Rome

1999. Papal Visit.
6040 **1297** 1300l. mauve and black 95 75
6041 - 1600l. mauve and black 1·00 85
6042 - 2300l. multicoloured 1·20 95
6043 - 6300l. multicoloured 1·30 1·00
DESIGNS: 1600l. Patriarchal Cathedral, Bucharest; 2300l. Father Teoctist (patriarch of Romanian Orthodox church); 6300l. Pope John Paul II (after Dina Bellotti).

1298 Northern Shoveler

1999. Europa. Parks and Gardens: the Danube Delta Nature Reserve. Multicoloured.
6044 1100l. Type **1298** 60 45
6045 5700l. Black stork 1·70 1·40

1299 Gheorghe Cartan (historian, 150th birth anniv)

1999. Anniversaries.
6046 **1299** 600l. green, black & red 10 10
6047 - 1100l. purple, blk & red 25 20
6048 - 2600l. blue, black & red 45 35
6049 - 7300l. brown, blk & red 2·00 1·60
DESIGNS: 1100l. George Calinescu (critic and novelist, birth centenary); 2600l. Johann Wolfgang von Goethe (dramatist, 250th birth anniv); 7300l. Honore de Balzac (novelist, birth bicentenary).

1300 Moon eclipsing Sun

1999. Total Eclipse of the Sun (2nd issue).
6050 **1300** 1100l. multicoloured 60 45

1301 Cigarette and Man with Arms Crossed

1999. Public Health Awareness Campaign. Mult.
6051 400l. Type **1301** (anti-smoking) 10 10
6052 800l. Bottles and man cradling glass and bottle (alcohol abuse) 25 20
6053 1300l. Cannabis leaf, pills and man injecting arm (drugs) 35 30
6054 2500l. Profiles and man on intravenous drip (HIV) 45 35

1302 Eclipse and Pavarotti (opera singer)

1999. Luciano Pavarotti's Concert on Day of Eclipse, Bucharest.
6055 **1302** 8100l. multicoloured 3·00 2·30

1303 Alexander Fleming (bacteriologist)

1999. The 20th century (3rd series). Multicoloured.
6056 800l. Type **1303** (discovery of penicillin, 1928) 25 20
6057 3000l. "Swords into Ploughshares" (sculpture) and map of Europe, Africa and Asia (foundation of League of Nations, 1920) 60 45
6058 7300l. Harold Clayton Urey (chemist) (discovery of heavy water, 1932) 1·50 1·20
6059 17000l. Deep sea drilling (first oil platform, Beaumont, Texas, 1934) 4·00 3·25

1304 Karl Landsteiner (pathologist)

1999. The 20th-century (4th series).
6060 **1304** 1500l. orange, black and yellow 25 20
6061 - 3000l. ochre, black and brown 60 45
6062 - 7300l. multicoloured 1·50 1·20
6063 - 17000l. multicoloured 4·00 3·25
DESIGNS: 1500l. Type **1304** (discovery of blood groups, 1900–02); 3000l. Nicolae Paulescu (biochemist) (discovery of insulin, 1921); 7300l. Otto Hahn (radiochemist) (discovery of nuclear fission, 1938); 17000l. Ernst Ruska (electrical engineer) (designer of first electron microscope, 1931).

1305 Posthorn in Envelope and Berne

1999. 125th Anniv of Universal Postal Union.
6064 **1305** 3100l. multicoloured 1·70 1·40

1306 Grigore Vasiliu Birlic

1999. Comic Actors. Each purple, black and red.
6065 900l. Type **1306** 25 20
6066 1500l. Toma Caragiu 35 30
6067 3100l. Constantin Tanase 60 45
6068 7950l. Charlie Chaplin 1·70 1·40
6069 8850l. Stan Laurel and Oliver Hardy (horiz) 2·30 1·90

1307 Monastery

1999. 275th Anniv of Stavropoleos Church.
6070 **1307** 2100l. brown, stone and black 60 45

1308 Snowboarding

1999. New Olympic Sports. Multicoloured.
6071 1600l. Type **1308** 50 40
6072 1700l. Softball 60 45
6073 7950l. Taekwondo 1·70 1·40

1309 Christmas Tree and Bell

1999. Christmas. Multicoloured.
6074 1500l. Type **1309** 35 30
6075 3100l. Father Christmas with presents 60 45

1310 Child as Flower (Antonela Vieriu)

1999. 10th Anniv of U.N. Convention on the Rights of the Child. Multicoloured.
6076 900l. Type **1310** 25 20
6077 3400l. Girl writing numbers (Ana-Maria Bulete) (vert) 60 45
6078 8850l. Group of people (Maria-Luiza Rogojeanu) 2·10 1·70

1311 Diana, Princess of Wales

1999. Diana, Princess of Wales Commemoration.
6079 **1311** 6000l. multicoloured 1·70 1·40

1312 Ferrari 365 GTB/4, 1968

1999. Birth Centenary (1998) of Enzo Ferrari (car designer). Multicoloured.
6080 1500l. Type **1312** 25 20
6081 1600l. Dino 246 GT, 1970 35 30
6082 1700l. 365 GT/4BB, 1973 60 45
6083 7950l. Mondial 3.2, 1985 1·70 1·40
6084 8850l. F 355, 1994 1·90 1·50
6085 14500l. 456 MGT, 1998 3·50 2·75

1313 Child with Romanian Flag

1999. 10th Anniv of Popular Uprising.
6086 **1313** 2100l. multicoloured 60 45

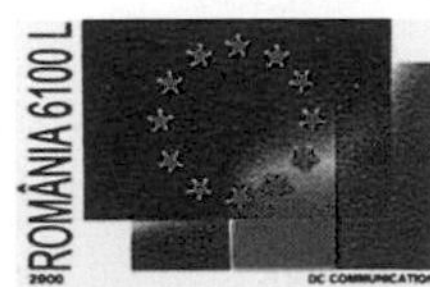

1314 European Union Flag

2000. European Union Membership Negotiations.
6087 **1314** 6100l. multicoloured 1·70 1·40

1315 Eminescu

2000. 150th Birth Anniv of Mihail Eminescu (poet). Sheet 120×92 mm containing T 1315 and similar horiz designs. Each grey, agate and black.
MS6088 3400l. Type **1315**; 3400l. Eminescu and people seated at table; 3400l. Eminescu and star shining over woman; 3400l. Eminescu and three men 4·75 4·75

1316 Cupid

2000. St. Valentine's Day. Multicoloured.
6089 1500l. Type **1316** 60 45
6090 7950l. Couple 1·70 1·40

1317 Easter Eggs

2000. Easter.
6091 **1317** 1700l. blue, green and orange 60 45

2000. Nos. 5855 and 5842 surch, the old value cancelled by a different emblem.
6092 1700l. on 70l. multicoloured (crown) 60 45
6093 1700l. on 70l. multicoloured (snake) 60 45

1319 Greater Bird of Paradise

2000. Birds of Paradise. Multicoloured.
6094 1700l. Type **1319** 60 45
6095 2400l. Magnificent bird of paradise 1·20 95
6096 9050l. Superb bird of paradise 1·70 1·40
6097 10050l. King bird of paradise 2·30 1·90

2000. Nos. 5342/3 surch.
6098 1900l. on 1l. multicoloured 60 45
6099 2000l. on 1l. multicoloured 60 45

2000. Nos. 5310/14 surch, the old value cancelled by various book and quill emblems.
6100 1700l. on 50b. brown and black 45 35
6101 1700l. on 1l.50 green and mauve 45 35
6102 1700l. on 2l. red and blue 45 35
6103 1700l. on 3l. blue and brown 45 35
6104 1700l. on 4l. brown and blue 45 35

1322 Cineraria

2000. Flowers. Multicoloured.
6105 1700l. Type **1322** 25 20
6106 3100l. Indoor lily 45 35
6107 5800l. Plumeria 1·40 1·10
6108 10050l. Fuchsia 2·10 1·70

2000. Nos. 5303/7 surch, the old value cancelled by an easel with palette emblem.
6109 1700l. on 50b. multicoloured 45 35
6110 1700l. on 1l.50 multicoloured 45 35
6111 1700l. on 2l. multicoloured 45 35
6112 1700l. on 3l. multicoloured 45 35
6113 1700l. on 4l. multicoloured 45 35

1324 "Building Europe"

2000. Europa.
6114 **1324** 10150l. multicoloured 3·50 2·75

2000. Death Centenary of Vincent van Gogh (artist). Nos. 5318 and 5321 surch, the old value cancelled by paint palette emblem.
6115 1700l. on 50b. multicoloured 60 45
6116 1700l. on 3l.50 multicoloured 60 45

2000. No. 5642 surch, the old value cancelled by an airship.
6117 1700l. on 635l. black, ultramarine and blue 60 45
6118 2000l. on 635l. black, ultramarine and blue 1·20 95
6119 3900l. on 635l. black, ultramarine and blue 1·20 95
6120 9050l. on 635l. black, ultramarine and blue 1·20 95

1327 Mihai the Brave and Soldiers

2000. Anniversaries. Multicoloured.
6121 3800l. Type **1327** (400th anniv of first union of the Romanian provinces (Wallachia, Transylvania and Moldavia)) 95 75
6122 9050l. Printing press (550th anniv of the 42 line Bible (first Bible printed in Latin)) (36×23 mm) 2·00 1·60

2000. No. 5801 surch, the old value cancelled by a flower.
6123 10000l. on 370l. brown and black 1·70 1·40
6124 19000l. on 370l. brown and black 3·50 2·75
6125 34000l. on 370l. brown and black 6·50 5·00

1329 Arnhem, Players and Flags of Romania and Portugal

2000. European Football Championship, The Netherlands and Belgium. Sheet 82×121 mm containing T 1329 and similar vert designs, each showing a map of Europe pinpointing the named town. Multicoloured.
MS6126 3800l. Type **1329**; 3800l. Players, Charleroi and English and Romanian flags; 10150l. Players, Liege and Romanian and German flags; 10150l. Goalkeeper and Rotterdam 5·75 5·75

1330 Ferdinand von Zeppelin and Airship

2000. Centenary of First Zeppelin Flight.
6127 **1330** 2100l. multicoloured 60 45

1331 Enrico Fermi (physicist) and Mathematical Equation

2000. The 20th Century (5th series).
6128 **1331** 2100l. black, grey and red 45 35
6129 - 2200l. black and grey 75 60
6130 - 2400l. red and black 80 65
6131 - 6000l. multicoloured 85 70
DESIGNS: 2100l. Type **1331** (construction of first nuclear reactor, 1942); 2200l. United Nations Charter (signing of charter, 1945); 2400l. Edith Piaf (singer) (release of *La Vie en Rose* (song), 1947); 6000l. Sir Edmund Percival Hillary (mountaineer) (conquest of Mt. Everest, 1953).

2000. No. 5365 surch, the old value cancelled by a bird.
6132 1700l. on 160l. red and pink 60 45

1333 Globe and "Sputnik 1" Satellite

2000. The Twentieth Century (6th series).
6133 **1333** 1700l. multicoloured 35 30
6134 - 3900l. multicoloured 1·40 1·10
6135 - 6400l. black and red 1·50 1·20
6136 - 11300l. multicoloured 1·60 1·30
DESIGNS: 1700l. Type **1333** (launch of first man-made satellite, 1957); 3900l. Yuri Gagarin (first manned space flight, 1961); 6400l. Surgeons operating (first heart transplant operation, 1967); 11300l. Edwin E. Aldrin and Moon (first manned landing on Moon, 1969).

1334 Boxing

2000. Olympic Games, Sydney. Multicoloured.
6137 1700l. Type **1334** 45 35
6138 2200l. High jump 50 40
6139 3900l. Weight lifting 60 45
6140 6200l. Gymnastics 1·50 1·20
MS6141 89×78 mm. 11300l. Athletics (41×53 mm) 3·00 3·00

1335 Gabriela Szabo (athlete) and Emblem

2000. "Olymphilex 2000" International Olympic Stamp Exhibition, Sydney. Sheet 81×60 mm.
MS6142 14100l. multicoloured 3·50 3·50

1336 Palace of Agriculture Ministry

2000. Bucharest Palaces.
6143 **1336** 1700l. black and grey 45 35
6144 - 2200l. black and stone (horiz) 50 40
6145 - 2400l. black and green (horiz) 60 45
6146 - 3900l. black and brown (horiz) 70 55
DESIGNS: 2200l. Cantacuzino Palace (now George Enescu Museum); 2400l. Grigore Ghica Palace; 3900l. Stirbei Palace (now Museum of Ceramics and Glass).

2000. No. 5836 surch, the old value cancelled by a house.
6147 300l. on 70l. multicoloured 60 45

2000. No. 5349 surch.
6148 300l. on 1l. blue 60 45

2000. Air. No. 5695 surch.
6149 2000l. on 960l. blue & black 25 20
6150 4200l. on 960l. blue & black 60 45
6151 4600l. on 960l. blue & black 95 75
6152 6500l. on 960l. blue & black 1·20 95

1340 Ilie Ilascu (political prisoner)

2000. 50th Anniv of United Nations Convention on Human Rights.
6153 **1340** 11300l. multicoloured 3·00 2·30

2000. No. 5700 surch, the old value cancelled by an inkwell and quill emblem.
6154 2000l. on 90l. multicoloured 60 45

2000. No. 5556 surch.
6155 2000l. on 29l. flesh, blk & lil 60 45

1343 Leopard

2000. Big Cats.
6156 **1343** 1200l. multicoloured 10 10
6157 - 2000l. blue and black 25 20
6158 - 2200l. multicoloured 30 25
6159 - 2300l. multicoloured 35 30
6160 - 4200l. brown, bl & blk 60 45
6161 - 6500l. multicoloured 1·70 1·40
MS6162 90×78 mm. 14100l. multicoloured 3·50 3·50
DESIGNS: 2000l. Snow Leopard; 2200l. Lion; 2300l. Bobcat; 4200l Mountain lion; 6500l Tiger; 53×41 mm—14100l. Lions.

1344 Camil Ressu

2000. Self-portraits. Multicoloured.
6163 2000l. Type **1344** 25 20
6164 2400l. Jean Al Steriadi 35 30
6165 4400l. Nicolae Tonitza 60 45
6166 15000l. Nicolae Grigorescu 3·00 2·30

1345 Christmas Tree

2000. Christmas.
6167 **1345** 4400l. multicoloured 60 45

1346 Jesus Christ and Angel

2000. Birth Bimillenary of Jesus Christ. Mult.
6168 2000l. Type **1346** 25 20
6169 7000l. Jesus Christ and dove (22×38 mm) 1·50 1·20

2000. No. 5624 surch, the previous value cancelled by different animals.
6170 7000l. on 3095l. Large-leaved lime (Pig) 2·00 1·60
6171 10000l. on 3095l. Large-leaved lime (Bear) 2·00 1·60
6172 11500l. on 3095l. Large-leaved lime (Cow) 2·00 1·60

1349 Globe and Fireworks

2001. New Millennium.
6176 **1349** 11500l. multicoloured 2·30 1·90

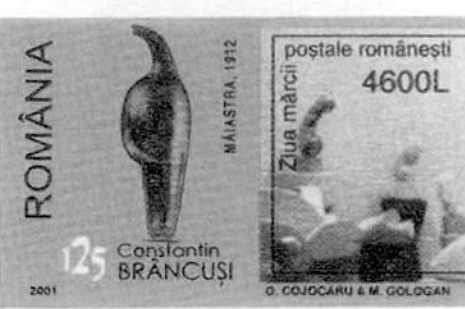

1350 Sculpture

2001. 125th Birth Anniv of Constantin Brancusi (sculptor). Multicoloured.
6177 4600l. Type **1350** 70 55
6178 7200l. Display of sculptures 1·00 85
Nos. 6177/8 were issued together, se-tenant, forming a composite design.

2001. No. 5542 surch, the previous value cancelled by different snakes.
6179 7400l. on 280l. black & yell 1·20 95
6180 13000l. on 280l. black & yell 2·30 1·90

1352 Ribbons forming Heart

2001. St. Valentine's Day. Each red and grey.
6181 2200l. Type **1352** 25 20
6182 11500l. Pierced heart 1·60 1·30

2001. Nos. 5595/6 and 5598 surch, the previous value cancelled by an ear of corn.
6183 1300l. on 245l. mult 25 20
6184 2200l. on 115l. mult 35 30
6185 5000l. on 115l. mult 70 55
6186 16500l. on 70l. mult 3·00 2·30

1354 Hortensia Papadat-Bengescu

2001. Birth Anniversaries. Multicoloured.
6187 1300l. Type **1354** 25 20
6188 2200l. Eugen Lovinescu (writer, 120th anniv) 30 25
6189 2400l. Ion Minulescu (poet, 120th anniv) 35 30
6190 4600l. Andre Malraux (writer, centenary) 60 45
6191 7200l. George H. Gallup (opinion pollster and journalist, centenary) 1·50 1·20
6192 35000l. Walt Disney (artist and film producer, centenary) 6·50 5·50

1355 Chick inside Egg

2001. Easter.
6193 **1355** 2200l. multicoloured 60 45

1356 Sloe (*Prunus spinosa*)

2001. Berries. Multicoloured.
6194 2200l. Type **1356** 25 20
6195 4600l. Red currant (*Ribes rubrum L.*) 60 45
6196 7400l. Gooseberry (*Ribes uva-crispa*) 1·70 1·40
6197 11500l. Mountain cranberry (*Vaccinium vitis-idaea L.*) 2·10 1·70

1357 Hagi

2001. Retirement of George Hagi (footballer).
6198 **1357** 2200l. multicoloured 60 45

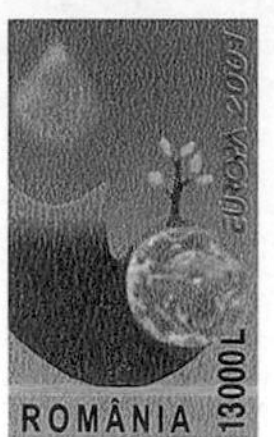

1358 Water Droplet and Globe surmounted by Tree

2001. Europa. Water Resources.
6199 **1358** 13000l. multicoloured 2·30 1·90

1359 Collie

2001. Dogs. Multicoloured.
6200 1300l. Type **1359** 25 20
6201 5000l. Basset hound 80 65
6202 8000l. Siberian husky 1·20 95
6203 13500l. Ciobanesc mioritic 2·00 1·60

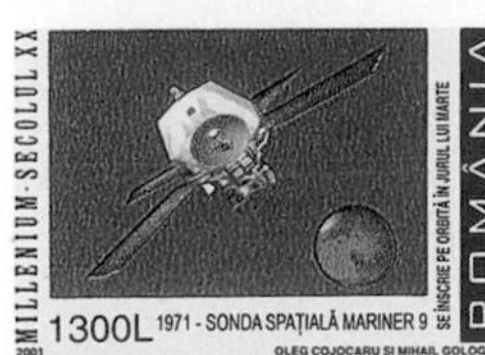

1360 Goddess Europa

2001. Romanian Presidency of Organization for Security and Co-operation in Europe.
6204 **1360** 11500l. multicoloured 2·30 1·90

1361 Mariner 9 (spacecraft) and Mars

2001. The 20th Century (7th series). Multicoloured.
6205 1300l. Type **1361** (first orbit of Mars, 1979) 25 20
6206 2400l. Bull (discovery of Paleolithic cave paintings, Ardeche, 1994) 60 45
6207 5000l. Nadia Comaneci (gymnast) (first "10" for gymnastics, Olympic Games, Montreal, 1976) 95 75
6208 8000l. Wall (fall of the Berlin wall, 1989) 1·20 95

1362 George Palade (Nobel Prize winner for medicine, 1974)

2001. 50th Anniv of United Nations High Commissioner for Refugees.
6209 **1362** 13500l. multicoloured 2·30 1·90

2001. Various stamps surch the previous values cancelled by various emblems as stated.
6210 **1100** 300l. on 4l. multicoloured (candlestick) 25 20
6211 **1110** 300l. on 4l. multicoloured (biathlon) 25 20
6212 **1132** 300l. on 7l. multicoloured (harp) 25 20
6213 - 300l. on 9l. multicoloured (No. 5488) (lyre) 25 20
6214 **1168** 300l. on 90l. multicoloured (lizard) 25 20
6215 **1190** 300l. on 90l. multicoloured (computer mouse) 25 20
6216 **1202** 300l. on 90l. multicoloured (fish) 25 20
6217 - 300l. on 90l. multicoloured (No. 5745) (chess knight) 25 20
6218 **1207** 300l. on 90l. multicoloured (fungi) 25 20
6219 **1157** 300l. on 115l. brown, blue and black (scroll) 25 20
6220 **1158** 300l. on 115l. multicoloured (train) 25 20
6222 - 300l. on 115l. multicoloured (No. 5602) (kite) 25 20
6229a **1162** 300l. on 115l. multicoloured (rectangle) 25 20

2001. Nos. 5715/16 and 5720 surch, the previous values cancelled by a sign of the zodiac.
6223 2500l. on 755l. blue and black (Pisces) (postage) 35 30
6224 2500l. on 1615l. green and black (Capricorn) 35 30
6225 2500l. on 715l. red and blue (Aquarius) (air) 35 30

1365 Trap Racing

2001. Equestrian Competitive Events. Mult.
6226 1500l. Type **1365** 35 30
6227 2500l. Dressage 45 35
6228 5300l. Show jumping 70 55
6229 8300l. Flat racing 1·40 1·10

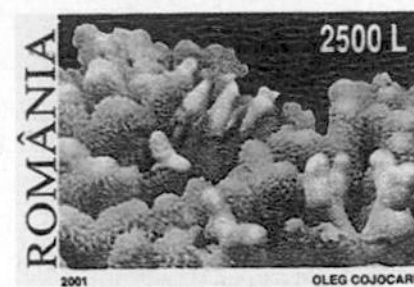

1366 Augustin Maior and Drawing

2001. The 20th Century (8th series). Multicoloured.
6230 1500l. Type **1366** (invention of multiple telephony, 1906) 35 30
6231 5300l. Pioneer 10 (satellite) (launched, 1972) 80 65
6232 13500l. Microchip (introduction of first microprocessor, 1971) 1·70 1·40
6233 15500l. Hubble space telescope (launched, 1990) 2·30 1·90

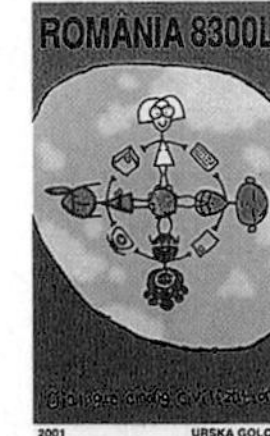

1367 Finger Coral (*Porites porites*)

2001. Corals and Sea Anemones (1st series). Multicoloured.
6234 2500l. Type **1367** 25 20
6235 8300l. Giant sea anemone (*Condylactis gigantia*) 95 75
6236 13500l. Northern red anemone (*Anemonia telia*) 1·70 1·40
6237 37500l. Common sea fan (*Gorgonia ventalina*) 4·75 4·00
See also No. **MS**6260.

1368 Children encircling Globe

2001. United Nations Year of Dialogue among Civilizations.
6238 **1368** 8300l. multicoloured 1·20 95

1369 King, Bear and Cat

2001. Comics. Multicoloured.
6239 13500l. Type **1369** 1·50 1·20
6240 13500l. Fox beating drum and kicking cat 1·50 1·20
6241 13500l. King sleeping and fox beating drum 1·50 1·20
6242 13500l. Cat giving fox drum 1·50 1·20
6243 13500l. Drum exploding 1·50 1·20

1370 Top of Wreath with Baubles

2001. Christmas. Multicoloured.
6244 2500l. Type **1370** 60 45
6245 2500l. Bottom of wreath with stars 60 45
Nos. 6244/5 were issued together, se-tenant, forming a composite design of a wreath.

1371 Scorpio

2001. Signs of the Zodiac (1st series). Multicoloured.
6246 1500l. Type **1371** 25 20
6247 2500l. Libra 35 30
6248 5500l. Capricorn 60 45
6249 9000l. Pisces 1·20 95
6250 13500l. Aquarius 1·70 1·40
6251 16500l. Sagittarius 2·30 1·90
See also Nos. 6254/9.

1372 Building

2001. Centenary of Central Post Headquarters, Bucharest. Multicoloured.
6252 5500l. Type **1372** 70 55
6253 5500l. Obverse of medal showing building, 1901 (vert) 70 55

2002. Signs of the Zodiac (2nd series). As T 1371. Multicoloured.

6254	1500l. Aries	25	20
6255	2500l. Taurus	35	30
6256	5500l. Gemini	60	45
6257	8700l. Cancer	1·00	85
6258	9000l. Leo	1·10	90
6259	23500l. Virgo	2·75	2·20

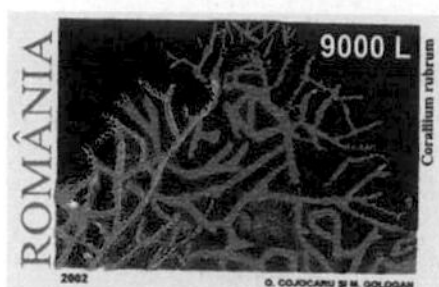

1373 Red Coral (*Corallum rubrum*)

2002. Corals and Sea Anemones (2nd series). Sheet 106×77 mm containing T 1373 and similar horiz designs. Multicoloured.

MS6260 9000l. Type **1373**; 9000l. Elkhorn coral (*Acropora palmate*); 16500l. Beadlet anemone (*Actinia equine*); 16500l. Pulmose anemone (*Metridium senile*) 6·50 6·50

1374 Emanuil Gojdu

2002. Birth Bicentenary of Emanuil Gojdu (nationalist).

6261	**1374**	2500l. black, blue and deep blue	60	45

1375 Mice

2002. St. Valentine's Day. Multicoloured.

6262	5500l. Type **1375**	70	55
6263	43500l. Elephants	5·25	4·75

1376 Ion Mincu

2002. Birth Anniversaries.

6267	**1376**	1500l. green and black	25	20
6268	-	2500l. multicoloured	35	30
6269	-	5500l. multicoloured	70	55
6270	-	9000l. multicoloured	1·00	85
6271	-	16500l. multicoloured	2·00	1·60
6272	-	34000l. multicoloured	4·00	3·50

DESIGNS: Type **1376** (architect) (150th); 2500l. Costin Nenitescu (chemist) (centenary); 5500l. Alexander Dumas (writer) (bicentenary); 9000l. Serban Cioculescu (literary historian) (centenary); 16500l. Leonardo da Vinci (artist) (550th); 34000l. Victor Hugo (writer) (bicentenary).

1377 Flag and Statue of Liberty

2002. "United We Stand". Multicoloured.

6273	25500l. Type **1377**	3·00	2·30
6274	25500l. Flags and monument	3·00	2·30

Nos. 6273/4 were issued together, se-tenant, forming a composite design.

1378 Fortified Church and Tower, Saschiz

2002. Germanic Fortresses and Churches in Translyvania. Multicoloured.

6275	1500l. Type **1378**	25	20
6276	2500l. Church staircase, Darjiu	35	30
6277	6500l. Fortress, Viscri (horiz)	70	55
6278	10500l. Fortified church, Vorumloc (horiz)	1·20	95
6279	13500l. Tower gate, Calnic	1·60	1·30
6280	17500l. Fortified church, Prejmer	2·00	1·60

1379 Crucifixion

2002. Easter. Showing miniatures by Picu Patrut. Multicoloured.

6281	2500l. Type **1379**	35	30
6282	10500l. Resurrection	1·40	1·10

1380 Clown

2002. Europa. Circus. Multicoloured.

6283	17500l. Type **1380**	2·30	1·90
6284	25500l. Clown (different)	3·50	2·75

1381 "Dorobantul" (Nicolae Grigorescu)

2002. 125th Anniv of Independence. Sheet 77×91 mm.

MS6285 **1381** 25500l. multicoloured 4·75 4·75

1382 Post Mark

2002. 50th Anniv of International Federation Stamp Dealers' Association (IFSDA). Sheet 105×75 mm containing T 1382 and similar horiz designs. Multicoloured.

MS6286 10000l. Type **1382**; 10000l. IFSDA emblem; 27500l. World Trade Centre, Bucharest; 27500l. Philatelic shop, Bucharest 8·75 8·75

1383 Mountains

2002. Year of Mountains (2000l.) and Year of Eco-tourism (3000l.). Multicoloured.

6287	2000l. Type **1383**	25	20
6288	3000l. Landscape and recycling symbol (32×24 mm)	35	30

1384 Cricket

2002. Sport. Multicoloured.

6289	7000l. Type **1384**	80	65
6290	11000l. Polo	1·30	1·00
6291	15500l. Golf	1·70	1·40
6292	19500l. Baseball	2·20	1·80

1385 Ion Luca Caragiale

2002. Anniversaries. Multicoloured.

6293	10000l. Type **1385** (playwright) (150th birth anniv)	1·20	95
6294	10000l. National Theatre, Bucharest (150th anniv)	1·20	95

Nos. 6293/4 were issued together, se-tenant, forming a composite design within the sheet.

1386 Financial Postal Service Emblem

2002. Postal Services.

6295	**1386**	2000l. multicoloured	25	20
6296	-	3000l. red, yellow and blue	35	30
6297	-	8000l. multicoloured	95	75
6298	-	10000l. purple and brown	1·20	95
6299	-	13000l. red, grey and black	1·40	1·10
6300	-	15500l. multicoloured	1·70	1·40
6301	-	20500l. mauve, blue and black	2·30	1·90
6302	-	27500l. multicoloured	3·25	2·50

DESIGNS: 2000l. Type **1386**; 3000l. Romania Post emblem; 8000l. Direct mailing centre emblem; 10000l. Post building (130th anniv); 13000l. Direct marketing emblem; 15500l. Rapid post emblem; 20500l. Priority post emblem; 27500l. Globe and stamp album (Romafilatelia).

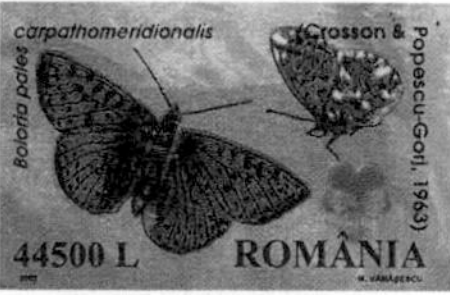

1387 *Boloria pales carpathomeridionalis*

2002. Butterflies. Sheet 101×71 mm containing T 1387 and similar horiz designs. Multicoloured.

MS6310 44500l. Type **1387**; 44500l. *Erebia pharte romaniae*; 44500l. *Peridea korbl herculana*; 44500l. *Tomares nogelii dobrogensis* 19·00 19·00

1388 Locomotive 50115 (1930)

2002. Steam Locomotives. 130th Anniv of First Locomotive made at Machine Factory, Resita (MS6317). Multicoloured.

6311	4500l. Type **1388**	45	35
6312	6500l. 50025 (1921)	70	55
6313	7000l. 230128 (1933)	80	65
6314	11000l. 764493 (1956)	1·20	95
6315	19500l. 142072 (1939)	2·10	1·70
6316	44500l. 704209 (1909)	4·75	4·25

MS6317 75×90 mm. 72500l. Steam locomotive (1872) (42×54 mm) 8·25 8·25

1389 Knight and Bishop

2002. 35th Chess Olympiad, Bled, Slovenia. Sheet 102×62 mm containing T 1389 and similar vert designs. Multicoloured.

MS6318 20500l. Type **1389**; 20500l. King and knight; 20500l. Queen and rook 7·00 7·00

1390 Quince (*Cydonia oblonga*)

2002. Fruit. Multicoloured.

6319	15500l. Type **1390**	1·70	1·40
6320	20500l. Apricot (*Armeniaca vulgaris*)	2·30	1·90
6321	44500l. Cherries (*Cerasus vulgaris*)	4·75	4·25
6322	73500l. Mulberry (*Morus nigra*)	8·25	7·50

1391 Father Christmas carrying Parcels

2002. Christmas. Multicoloured.

6323	3000l. Type **1391**	35	30
6324	15500l. Father Christmas and computer	1·70	1·40

1392 Eagle (Romanian emblem), Flags and NATO Emblem

2002. Romania Invitation to join North Atlantic Treaty Organization (NATO). Sheet 168×106 mm containing T 1392.

MS6325 131000l. ×2, Type **1392** ×2 29·00 29·00

No. **MS**6325 contains a central label showing NATO emblem.

1393 "Braila Harbour" (Jean-Alexandru Steriadi)

2003. Art. Multicoloured.

6326	4500l. Type **1393**	45	35
6327	6500l. "Balcic" (Nicolae Darascu)	70	55
6328	30500l. "Conversation" (Nicolae Vermont)	3·25	2·75

6329 34000l. "Dalmatia" (Nicolae Darascu) 3·75 3·25

6330 46500l. "Fishing Boats" (Jean-Alexandru Steriadi) 5·25 4·75

6331 53000l. "Nude" (Bogdan Pietris) 5·75 5·25

MS6332 75×91 mm. 83500l. "Woman on Seashore" (Nicolae Grigorescu) (42×54 mm) 9·25 9·25

1394 Building Facade

2003. 80th Anniv of National Military Palace, Bucharest.

6333 **1394** 5000l. multicoloured 60 45

1395 Ladybird

2003. March Amulet (good luck). Multicoloured.

6334 3000l. Type **395** 45 35

6335 5000l. Chimney sweep (vert) 70 55

1396 "10"

2003. 10th Anniv of Romania signing European Agreement (precursor to joining EU).

6336 **1396** 142000l. multicoloured 14·00 14·00

1397 Ion Irimescu

2003. Birth Anniversaries. Multicoloured.

6337 6000l. Type **1397** (sculptor) (centenary) 60 45

6338 18000l. Hector Berlioz (composer) (bicentenary) 1·70 1·40

6339 20000l. Vincent van Gogh (artist) (150th) 2·00 1·60

6340 36000l. Groeges de Bellio (doctor and art collector) (175th) 3·50 3·00

1398 Post Palace

2003. Architecture. Multicoloured.

6341 4500l. Type **1398** 45 35

6342 5500l. Central Savings House 55 45

6343 10000l. National Bank (horiz) 85 75

6344 15500l. Stock Exchange 1·40 1·20

6345 20500l. Carol I University 1·80 1·60

6346 46500l. Athenium 4·00 3·50

MS6347 76×91 mm. 73500l. Palace of Justice (42×54 mm) 6·50 6·50

1399 Map (detail) (upper left quadrant)

2003. Pieter van den Keere (Petrus Kærius Cælavit) (cartographer) Commemoration. Two sheets containing T 1399 and similar multicoloured designs.

MS6348 (a) 120×90 mm. 30500l. ×4 "Vetus description Daciarum" (description of Dacia); (b) 76×91 mm. 46500l. National Map and Book Museum (42×54 mm) 15·00 15·00

1400 Rabbit carrying Egg and Envelope

2003. Easter.

6349 **1400** 3000l. multicoloured 55 45

1401 Eurasian Scops Owl (*Otus scops*)

2003. Owls. Multicoloured.

6350 5000l. Type **1401** 45 35

6351 8000l. Ural owl (*Strix uralensis*) 65 55

6352 10000l. Eurasian pygmy owl (*Glaucidium passerinum*) 85 75

6353 13000l. Short-eared owl (*Asio flammeus*) 1·10 95

6354 15500l. Long-eared owl (*Asio otus*) 1·30 1·10

6355 20500l. Tengmalm's owl (*Aegolius funereus*) 2·20 1·90

1402 Butterfly emerging from Cocoon

2003. Europa. Poster Art. Multicoloured.

6356 20500l. Type **1402** 2·20 1·90

6357 73500l. Figure holding Painting 6·50 5·50

1403 Dumltru Staniloae

2003. Birth Centenaries. Multicoloured.

6358 4500l. Type **1403** (theologian) 45 35

6359 8000l. Alexandru Ciucurencu (artist) 65 55

6360 30500l. Ilarie Voronca (poet) 2·50 2·20

6361 46500l. Victor Brauner (artist) 4·00 3·50

1404 "Fantastic Animals"

2003. Birth Centenary of Victor Brauner (artist). Sheet 175×129 mm containing T 1404 and similar multicoloured designs showing paintings.

MS6362 10000l. ×12. Type **1404**; "Self Portrait" ×3 (24×33 mm); "Heron of Alexandria" (24×33 mm); "Surrealist Composition"; "Drobegea Landscape"; "Nude" (24×33 mm); "Drobegea Landscape" (different); "Courteous Passivity"; "Ion Minulescu Portrait" (abstract) (24×33 mm); "Dragon" 11·00 11·00

1405 Nostradamus and Astrolabe

2003. 500th Birth Anniv of Nostradamus (prophet). Multicoloured.

6363 73500l. Type **1405** 6·00 5·00

6364 73500l. Astrolabe, diagram and Nostradamus 6·00 5·00

1406 Magnifying Glass, Building and Emblem

2003. Post Day. Centenary of Timisoara Philatelic Association.

6365 **1406** 5000l. multicoloured 55 45

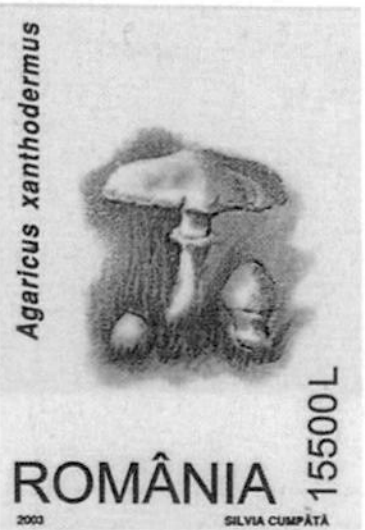

1407 Yellow Stainer (*Agaricus xanthodermus*)

2003. Fungi. Two sheets each 126×75 mm containing T 1407 and similar vert designs. Multicoloured.

MS6366 (a) 15500l. ×3 Type **1407**; Basket fungus (*Clathrus rubber*); Panther cap (*Amanita pantherina*); (b) 20500l. ×3 Red-capped scaber stalk (*Leccinum aurantiacum*); Chicken mushroom (*Laetiporus sulphurous*); *Russula xerampelina* 11·00 11·00

1408 Skydiving

2003. Extreme Sports. Multicoloured.

6367 5000l. Type **1408** 45 35

6368 8000l. Windsurfing (horiz) 65 55

6369 10000l. Motor cycle racing (horiz) 85 75

6370 30500l. Skiing 2·50 2·20

1409 Green Lizard
Lacerta viridis

2003. Amphibians. Sheet 125×105 mm containing T 1409 and similar vert designs.

MS6371 18000l. ×4 Type **1409**; Green tree frog (*Hyla arborea*); Snake-eyed skink (*Ablepharus kitaibelii*); Common frog (*Rana temporaria*) 7·50 7·50

1410 Cobza (stringed instrument)

2003. Traditional Instruments (1st series). Multicoloured.

6372 1000l. Type **1410** 10 10

6373 4000l. Bucium (wind) 35 30

6374 6000l. Vioara cu Goarna (violin with horn) 55 45

1411 Map and Statue

2003. 125th Anniv of Berlin Treaty returning Dobrudja to Romania.

6375 **1411** 16000l. multicoloured 1·30 1·10

1412 Pope John Paul II and Teoctist, Romanian Patriarch

2003. 25th Anniv of Pontificate of Pope John Paul II. Multicoloured.

6376 16000l. Type **1412** 1·30 1·10

6377 16000l. Pope John Paul II and Teoctist (different) 1·30 1·10

1413 Father Christmas

2003. Christmas.

6378 **1413** 4000l. black, rosine and orange 45 40

6379 - 4000l. black and orange 45 40

DESIGN: No. 6379. Snowman.

Nos. 6378/9 were issued, together, se-tenant, forming a composite design.

1414 Woman wearing Suit and Cloche Hat (1921–1930)

2003. 20th-century Women's Fashion. Multicoloured.

6380 4000l. Type **1414** 45 40
6381 4000l. Wearing coat with fur collar (1931–1940) 45 40
6382 21000l. Wearing hat and carrying muff (1901–1910) 1·70 1·40
6383 21000l. Wearing caped coat and hat (1911–1920) 1·70 1·40

1415 Early Woman Footballer

2003. Centenary of FIFA (Federation Internationale de Football Association). Multicoloured.

6384 3000l. Type **1415** 25 20
6385 4000l. Players and film camera 35 30
6386 6000l. Heads and newsprint 50 40
6387 10000l. Boots, pad and ball 85 70
6388 34000l. Rule book and pitch 3·00 2·40

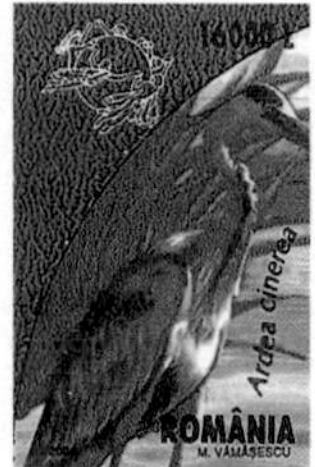

1416 Grey Heron (*Ardea cinerea*)

2004. Water Birds. Sheet 94×96 mm containing T 1416 and similar vert designs. Multicoloured.

MS6389 16000l. ×4 Type **1416**; Mallard (*Anas platyrhynchos*); Great crested grebe (*Podiceps cristatus*); Eastern white pelican (*Pelecanus onocrotalus*) 5·25 5·25

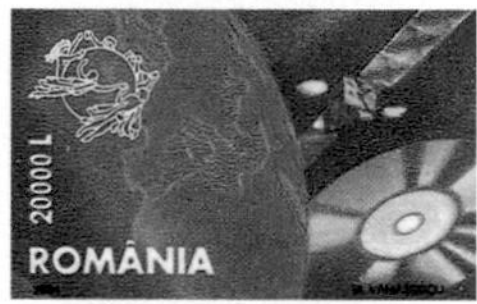

1417 Globe, Satellite and Disc

2004. Information Technology. Sheet 93×69 mm containing T 1417 and similar horiz design. Multicoloured.

MS6390 20000l. ×4 Type **1417**; Computer screen; Satellite dish; Computer keyboard 6·50 6·50

1418 Amerigo Vespucci

2004. 550th Birth Anniv of Amerigo Vespucci (explorer). Multicoloured.

6391 16000l. Type **1418** 1·30 1·10
6392 31000l. Sailing ship 2·75 2·20

1420 UPU Emblem

1421 Easter Egg and Rabbit holding Envelope

1422 Bullet Locomotive, Japan

1423 NATO Headquarters

1424 Pierre de Coubertin

1419 Couple

2004. St. Valentine.

6393 **1419** 21000l. multicoloured 1·80 1·50

2004. Universal Postal Union Congress, Bucharest (1st. issues). Multicoloured.

6394 31000l. Type **1420** 2·40 2·00
6395 31000l. Bird holding envelope 2·40 2·00

Nos. 6394/5 were issued together, se-tenant, forming a composite design.

See also Nos. 6445/50.

2004. Easter.

6396 **1421** 4000l. multicoloured 60 50

2004. Modern Locomotives. Multicoloured.

6397 4000l. Type **1422** 40 35
6398 6000l. TGV, France 55 45
6399 10000l. KTX, South Korea 90 75
6400 16000l. AVE, Spain 1·40 1·20
6401 47000l. ICE, Germany 4·00 3·25
6402 56000l. Eurostar, UK and France 5·00 4·25

MS6403 92×77 mm. 77000l. *Blue Arrow* (Sageti Albastre), Romania (54×42 mm) 6·50 6·50

2004. Romania's Accession to NATO.

6404 **1423** 40000l. multicoloured 1·00 85

2004. 90th Anniv of Romanian Olympic Committee. Sheet 120×86 mm containing T 1423 and similar multicoloured designs.

MS6405 16000l.+5000l. ×3, Type **1424** (founder of modern Olympics); Olympic stadium, Athens, 1896 (54×42 mm); George Bibescu (founder member) 5·00 5·00

2004. 20th-century Women's Fashion. Vert designs as T 1414 showing women's clothes. Mult.

6406 4000l. Calf length suit and hat (1941–1950) 50 40
6407 4000l. Knee length coat (1951–1960) 50 40
6408 21000l. Dress and jacket (1981–1990) 1·90 1·60
6409 21000l. Sleeveless dress (1991–2000) 1·90 1·60
6410 31000l. Mini skirted coat (1961–1970) 2·75 2·20
6411 31000l. Trouser suit (1971–1980) 2·75 2·20

Nos. 6406/7, 6408/9 and 6410/11, respectively, were issued together, se-tenant, each pair forming a composite design.

1425 Marksman

2004. 51st International Council for Game and Wildlife Conservation General Assembly. Multicoloured.

6412 16000l. Type **1425** 1·30 1·10
6413 16000l. Dog's head and pheasant 1·30 1·10
6414 16000l. Stag 1·30 1·10
6415 16000l. Ibex 1·30 1·10
6416 16000l. Bear 1·30 1·10

MS6417 99×87 mm. 16000l. Stag (54×42 mm) 1·30 1·30

Nos. 6412/16 were issued, together, se-tenant strips of five stamps, each strip forming a composite design.

1426 Sun and Shoreline

2004. Europa. Holidays. Multicoloured.

6418 21000l. Type **1426** 1·80 1·50
6419 77000l. Sun and snowy mountains 6·25 5·25

1427 Mihai Viteazul (Michael the Brave) (statue)

2004

6420 **1427** 3000l. multicoloured 1·00 85

1428 Facade

2004. National Philatelic Museum.

6421 **1428** 4000l. multicoloured 1·00 85

1429 Bram Stoker

2004. "Dracula" (novel by Bram Stoker). Sheet 142×84 mm containing T 1429 and similar vert designs. Multicoloured.

MS6422 31000l. ×4, Type **1429**; Dracula and cross; Dracula carrying woman; Dracula in coffin 10·00 10·00

1430 Anghel Saligny

2004. Anniversaries. Multicoloured.

6423 4000l. Type **1430** (engineer) (150th birth) 25 25
6424 16000l. Gheorgi Anghel (sculptor) (birth centenary) 1·00 95
6425 21000l. George Sand (Aurore Dupin) (writer) (birth bicentenary) 1·30 1·20
6426 31000l. Oscar Wilde (writer) (150th birth) 1·90 1·70

1431 Romainian Atheneum Bucharest

2004

6427 **1431** 10000l. olive and green 1·00 95

1432 Johnny Weissmuller

2004. Birth Centenary of Johnny Weissmuller (athlete and actor).

6428 **1432** 21000l. multicoloured 1·20 1·10

1433 Aircraft and Emblem

2004. 50th Anniv of TAROM Air Transport.

6429 **1433** 16000l. multicoloured 1·30 1·20

1434 Footballs and Anniversary Emblem

2004. Centenary of FIFA (Federation Internationale de Football Association).

6430 **1434** 31000l. multicoloured 2·30 2·10

1435 Stefan III (fresco), Dobrovat Monastery

2004. 500th Death Anniv of Stefan III (Stefan cel Mare) (Moldavian ruler). Two sheets, each 173×62 mm, containing T 1435 and similar horiz designs. Multicoloured.

MS6431 (a) 10000l. ×3, Type **1435**; Ruins of Sucevei; Stefan III (embroidered panel). (b) 16000l. pale brown; 16000l. multicoloured; 16000l. pale brown 5·75 5·75

DESIGN: **MS**6431b. 16000l. ×3, Putna monastery; Stefan III (painting); Neamt fortress.

1436 Alexandru Macedonski

2004. Anniversaries. Multicoloured.

6432	2000l. Type **1436** (writer) (150th birth)	20	20
6433	3000l. Victor Babes (scientist) (150th birth)	35	30
6434	6000l. Arthur Rimbaud (writer) (150th birth)	45	40
6435	56000l. Salvador Dali (artist) (birth centenary)	4·50	4·00

1437 King Ferdinand and First Stamp Exhibition Poster

2004. Post Day. 80th Anniv of First National Stamp Exhibition.

6436	**1437**	21000l. + 10000l. ×4 multicoloured	2·20	2·00

1438 Zeppelin LZ-127 and Buildings

2004. 75th Anniv of Zeppelin LZ-127's Flight over Brasov.

6437	**1438**	31000l. multicoloured	2·30	2·10

1439 Bank Building

2004. 140th Anniv of National Savings Bank (Casa de Economii si Consemnatiuni).

6438	**1439**	5000l. multicoloured	1·00	90

1440 Firemen and Engine

2004. 24th International CTIF (International Fire-fighters Association) Symposium, Brasov. Multicoloured.

6439	12000l. Type **1440**	85	75
6440	12000l. Firemen fighting fire	85	75

1441 Woman Rower

2004. Olympic Games, Athens. Multicoloured.

6441	7000l. Type **1441**	55	50
6442	12000l. Fencers	1·00	90
6443	21000l. Swimmer	1·80	1·60
6444	31000l.+9000l. Gymnast	3·25	2·75

1442 23rd Conference Emblem and 2004 Romania Stamp

2004. Universal Postal Union Congress, Bucharest (2nd issue). Showing emblem and stamps commemorating congresses. Multicoloured.

6445	8000l. Type **1442**	60	55
6446	10000l. 1974 Switzerland	75	65
6447	19000l. 1994 South Korea	1·70	1·50
6448	31000l. 1990 China	2·50	2·20
6449	47000l. 1989 USA	4·00	3·50
6450	77000l. 1979 Brasil	6·25	5·50

1443 "L'appel"

2004. 10th Death Anniv of Idel Ianchelevici (sculptor). Statues. Multicoloured.

6451	21000l. Type **1443**	1·60	1·40
6452	31000l. "Perennis perdurat poeta"	2·20	2·00

Stamps of the same design were issued by Belgium.

1444 Bronze Age Cucuteni Pot

2004. Cultural Heritage. Multicoloured.

6453	5000l. Type **1444**	50	45
6454	5000l. Drum supported by phoenixes and tigers	50	45

Stamps of the same design were issued by China.

1445 Gerard Kremer (Geradus Mercator) and Jodocus Hondius

2004. European Anniversaries. Sheet 158×144 mm containing T 1445 and similar horiz designs. Multicoloured.

MS6455	118000l.×3, Type **1445** (cartographers) (450th anniv of Mercator's map of Europe and 400th anniv of Hondius—Mercator atlas); UPU monument, Berne (23rd UPU congress, Bucharest); Amerigo Vespucci (explorer) (550th birth anniv)	26·00	26·00

1446 Roman Riders and Foot Soldiers

2004. Fragments of Trajan's Column (Roman monument) (1st issue).

6456	**1446**	7000l. grey and ultramarine	55	50
6457	-	12000l. brown and ultramarine	1·00	90
6458	-	19000l. orange and ultramarine	1·60	1·40
6459	-	56000l. carmine and ultramarine	4·50	4·00

DESIGNS: Type **1446**; 12000l. Neptune and soldiers embarking on ships; 19000l. Fortress and soldier holding cauldron in stream; 56000l. Chariot in moat and soldiers attacking fortress.

See also Nos. 6468/70.

1447 "Simfonia" (Symphony) Rose

2004. Roses. Multicoloured.

6460	8000l. Type **1447**	65	60
6461	15000l. "Foc de Tabara" (Camp fire)	1·20	1·10
6462	25000l. "Golden Elegance"	2·00	1·80
6463	36000l. "Doamna in mov" (Lady in mauve)	3·00	2·50
MS6464	120×90 mm. Nos. 6460/3	6·50	6·50

1448 Ilie Nastase

2004. Ilie Nastase (tennis player). Multicoloured.

6465	10000l. Type **1448**	1·00	90
MS6466	Two sheets. (a) 110×200 mm. 72000l. Ilie Nastase (42×52 mm). (b) 91×110 mm. As No. **MS**6466a. Imperf	10·00	9·00

1449 Father Christmas

2004. Christmas.

6467	**1449**	5000l. multicoloured	1·00	90

2004. Fragments of Trajan's Column (Roman monument) (2nd issue). As T 1446.

6468	21000l. green and ultramarine	1·70	1·50
6469	31000l. black and ultramarine	2·50	2·20
6470	145000l. vermilion and ultramarine	12·00	10·50

DESIGNS: 21000l. Ritual sacrifice; 31000l. Soldiers, trees, water and heads on posts; 145000l. Stone encampment.

1450 Scouts Emblem

2004. International Organizations. Showing emblems. Multicoloured.

6471	12000l. Type **1450**	1·00	90
6472	16000l. Lions International	1·30	1·20
6473	19000l. Red Cross and Red Crescent	1·60	1·40
MS6474	90×78 mm. 87000l. Dimitrie Cantemir (writer and linguist) (Freemasonry) (42×52 mm)	6·50	6·50

1451 Iolanda Balas-Soter

2004. Olympic Games, Athens. Women Athletes. Each black and gold.

6475	5000l. Type **1451** (high jump)	55	50
6476	33000l. Elsabeta Lipa (rowing)	3·25	2·75
6477	77000l. Ivan Patzaichin (kayaking)	6·50	5·75

1452 "Tristan Tzara" (M. H. Maxy)

2004. Modern Art. Two sheets, each 129×78 mm containing T 1452 and similar vert designs. Multicoloured.

MS6478	(a) 7000l.×3, Type **1452**; "Baroneasa" (Merica Ramniceanu); "Portret de Femeie" (Jean David). (b) 12000l.×3, "Compozitie" (Marcel Iancu); "Femele care viseaza II" (Victor Brauner); "Compozitie" (Hans Mattis-Teutsch)	4·50	4·50

1453 Gheorghe Magheru

2005. Anniversaries (1st issue). Multicoloured.

6479	15000l. Type **1453** (revolutionary leader) (125th death anniv)	1·20	1·10
6480	25000l. Christian Dior (dress designer) (birth centenary)	2·00	1·80
6481	35000l. Henry Fonda (actor) (birth centenary)	3·00	2·50
6482	72000l. Greta Garbo (actress) (birth centenary)	5·50	5·00
6483	77000l. George Valentin Bibescu (aviation pioneer) (125th birth anniv)	6·25	5·50

See also Nos. 6512/16.

1454 Emblem

2005. Centenary of Rotary International (charitable organization.).

6484	**1454**	21000l. multicoloured	7·00	6·25

1455 Wedding Pitcher (Oboga-Olt)

2005. Pottery (1st issue). Multicoloured.

6485	3000l. Type **1455**	35	20
6486	5000l. Jugs and pitchers (Sacel-Maramures)	45	30
6487	12000l. Pitcher (Horezu-Valcea)	1·10	90
6488	16000l. Wedding pitcher (Corund-Harghita)	1·30	1·10

See also Nos. 6498/6500, 6591/7, 6605/6, 6639/42, 6650/3, 6684/7 6781/4, 6794/7, 6817/24 and 6824/5.

1456 Elopteryx nopcsai

2005. Dinosaurs. Multicoloured.

6489	21000l. Type **1456**	2·00	1·90
6490	31000l. Telmatosaurus transylvanicus (inscr "transsylvanicus")	3·00	2·75
6491	35000l. Struthiosaurus transilvanicus	3·25	3·00

6492	47000l. Hatzegopteryx thambema	4·25	4·00
MS6493	125×120 mm. Nos. 6489/92	11·50	11·50

1457 *Carassius auratus*

2005. Fish. Multicoloured.

6494	21000l. Type **1457**	2·00	1·90
6495	31000l. *Symphysodon discus*	3·00	2·75
6496	36000l. *Labidochromis*	3·25	3·00
6497	47000l. *Betta splendens*	4·25	4·00
MS6497a	120×103 mm. Nos. 6494/7	12·00	12·00

2005. Pottery (2nd issue). As T 1455. Multicoloured.

6498	7000l. Wedding pitchers (Romana-Olt)	65	60
6499	8000l. Jug (Vadul Crisului-Bihor)	80	75
6500	10000l. Jug (Tara Barsei-Brasov)	90	85

1458 "Castle of the Carpathians"

2005. Death Centenary of Jules Verne (writer). Multicoloured.

6501	19000l. Type **1458**	1·70	1·60
6502	21000l. "The Danube Pilot"	2·00	1·90
6503	47000l. "Claudius Bombarnac"	4·25	4·00
6504	56000l. "The Stubborn Keraban"	5·25	5·00
MS6505	120×116 mm. Nos. 6501/4	12·00	12·00

1459 Last Supper (icon) (Matei Purcariu)

2005. Easter. Multicoloured.

6506	5000l. Type **1459**	40	35
6507	5000l. Crucifixion	40	35
6508	5000l. Resurrection	40	35

1460 Pope John Paul II and Stylized Dove

2005. Pope John Paul II Commemoration. Multicoloured.

6509	5000l. Type **1460**	40	35
6510	21000l. Vatican	2·00	1·90
MS6511	106×78 mm Nos. 6509/10 each×2	4·50	4·50

2005. Anniversaries (2nd issue). As T 1453. Multicoloured.

6512	3000l. Hans Christian Anderson (writer) (birth bicentenary)	25	25
6513	5000l. Jules Verne (writer) (death centenary)	55	50
6514	12000l. Albert Einstein (physicist) (50th death anniv)	1·10	1·00
6515	21000l. Dimitrie Gusti (sociologist and philosopher) (50th death anniv)	2·00	1·90
6516	22000l. George Enescu (musician) (50th death anniv)	2·10	2·00

1461 Map of Romania and European Stars

2005. Signing of Treaty of Accession to European Union. Multicoloured.

6517	5000l. Type **1461**	50	50
6518	5000l. As No. 6516 but map and vertical band silver	50	50

(1461a)

2005. No. 5623 surch as T 1461a.

6519	1500l. on 1440l.	55	50

1462 Archer on Horseback and Casserole

2005. Europa. Gastronomy. Multicoloured.

6520	21000l. Type **1462**	1·80	1·70
6521	77000l. Retriever, fowl, vegetables and wine glass	6·50	6·25
MS6522	120×90 mm. Nos. 6520/1, each×2	17·00	17·00

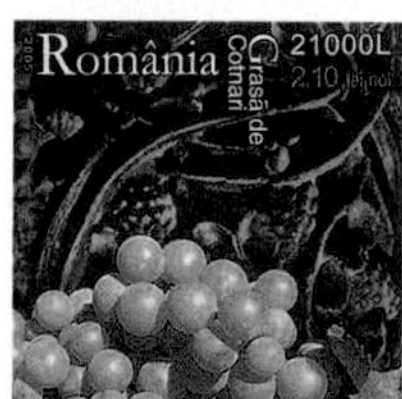

1463 Grasa de Cotnari Grapes

2005. Viticulture. Showing grape varieties. Multicoloured.

6523	21000l. Type **1463**	1·70	1·60
6524	21000l. Feteasca neagra	1·70	1·60
6525	21000l. Feteasca alba	1·70	1·60
6526	21000l. Victoria	1·70	1·60

1464 Fire Supervision

2005. Romania Scouts. Multicoloured.

6527	22000l. Type **1464**	1·80	1·70
6528	22000l. Orienteering	1·80	1·70
6529	22000l. Trail marking	1·80	1·70
6530	22000l. Rock climbing	1·80	1·70

On 1 July 2005 the currency of Romania was simplified so that now 1 new leu equals 10000 old leu.

1465 1 bani Coin

2005. New Currency. Designs showing old and new currency. Multicoloured.

6531	30b. Type **1465**	35	30
6532	30b. As No. 6531 but design reversed	35	30
6533	50b. 1 leu bank note	55	50
6534	50b. As No. 6533 but design reversed	55	50
6535	70b. 5 bani coin	65	60
6536	70b. As No. 6535 but design reversed	65	60
6537	80b. 5 lei note	75	70
6538	80b. As No. 6537 but design reversed	75	70
6539	1l. 10 lei note	1·00	90
6540	1l. As No. 6539 but design reversed	1·00	90
6541	1l.20 50 lei note	1·10	1·00
6542	1l.20 As No. 6541 but design reversed	1·10	1·00
6543	1l.60 100 lei note	1·40	1·30
6544	1l.60 As No. 6543 but design reversed	1·40	1·30
6545	2l.10 10 bani	1·80	1·70
6546	2l.10 As No. 6545 but design reversed	1·80	1·70
6547	2l.20 500 lei note	2·10	1·90
6548	2l.20 As No. 6547 but design reversed	2·10	1·90
6549	3l.10 50 bani coin	3·00	2·75
6550	3l.10 As No. 6549 but design reversed	3·00	2·75

1466 *Constanta* (teaching ship)

2005. Stamp Day. Ships. Multicoloured.

6551	2l.20 Type **1466**	1·80	1·70
6552	2l.20 *Counter Admiral Horia Macellariu* (corvette)	1·80	1·70
6553	2l.20 *Mihail Kogalniceanu*	1·80	1·70
6554	2l.20 *Marasesti* (frigate)	1·80	1·70

1467 Rainbow and Sphinx

2005. Floods—July 2005 (1st issue).

6555	**1467** 50b. multicoloured	1·00	90

See also Nos. 6563/6.

1468 Cardinal Joseph Ratzinger

2005. Enthronement of Pontificate of Benedict XVI. Multicoloured.

6556	1l.20 Type **1468**	1·00	90
6557	2l.10 Pope Benedict XVI	1·70	1·60
MS6558	122×98 mm. Nos. 6556/7	2·75	2·75

1469 Christopher Columbus

2005. 50th Anniv of Europa Stamps. 500th Death Anniv of Christopher Columbus (2006). Multicoloured.

6559	4l.70 Type **1469**	3·75	3·50
6560	4l.70 *Santa Maria* at left and Columbus	3·75	3·50
6561	4l.70 *Santa Maria* at right and Columbus	3·75	3·50
6562	4l.70 Christopher Columbus wearing wig and hat	3·75	3·50

1470 "The Forest Mailman" (Bianca Paul)

2005. Floods—July 2005 (2nd issue). Winning Entries in Children's Design a Stamp Competition. Multicoloured.

6563	30b. Type **1470**	25	25
6564	40b. "The Road to You" (Daniel Ciornei)	35	30
6565	60b. "A Messenger of Peace" (Stefan Ghiliman) (horiz)	65	60
6566	1l. "Good News for Everybody" (Adina Elena Mocanu) (horiz)	85	80

11,80L
(1471)

2005. International Philatelic Exhibition, Bucharest. No. MS6455 optd as T 1471.

MS6567	11l.80×3 on 118000l.×3, multicoloured	30·00	30·00

1472 Jagd Terrier

2005. Hunting Dogs. Multicoloured.

6568	2l.20 Type **1472**	1·80	1·70
6569	2l.20 Rhodesian ridgeback	1·80	1·70
6570	2l.20 Munsterlander	1·80	1·70
6571	2l.20 Bloodhound	1·80	1·70
6572	2l.20 Copoi ardelenesc (Transylvanian hound)	1·80	1·70
6573	2l.20 Pointer	1·80	1·70

1473 Bull's Head

2005. 1st Anniv of National Philatelic Museum.

6574	**1473** 40b. multicoloured	1·00	90

1474 Emblem

2005. World Information Society Summit, Tunis.

6575	**1474** 5l.60 multicoloured	4·00	3·75

1475 Members Flags, Dove and UN Emblem (50th anniv of Romania's membership)

2005. United Nations Anniversaries. Multicoloured.

6576	40b. Type **1475**	55	50
6577	1l.50 Council chamber (Romania's membership of Security Council, 2004—5 and Presidency, October 2005)	1·40	1·30

6578 2l.20 UN building and dove (60th anniv of UN) 2·00 1·80
MS6579 164×76 mm. Nos. 6576/8 3·50 3·50

1476 Birthplace and Society Emblem (image scaled to 68% of original size)

2005. 160th Birth Anniv of Dimitrie Butculescu (1st president of Romanian Philatelic Society). Multicoloured.
6580 50b. Type **1476** 50 45
6581 50b. Romanian Philatelic Society gazette and Dimitrie Butculescu 50 45
MS6582 114×82 mm. 9l. Dimitrie Butculescu. Imperf 7·50 7·50

1477 Library Building

2005. 110th Anniv of Central University Library (formerly Carol I University Foundation). Multicoloured.
6583 60b. Type **1477** 50 45
6584 60b. Horse and rider (statue) (21×30 mm) 50 45
MS6585 137×96 mm. Nos. 6583/4 1·00 1·00

1478 Gusat Englez (English Pouter)

2005. Domestic Pigeons. Multicoloured.
6586 2l.50 Type **1478** 2·10 1·90
6587 2l.50 Jucator pestrit (Parlour roller) 2·10 1·90
6588 2l.50 Calator tip standard (Standard carrier) 2·10 1·90
6589 2l.50 Zburator de Andaluzia (Andalusian) 2·10 1·90

1479 "Thinker of Hamangia"

2005. 60th Anniv of UNESCO.
6590 **1479** 2l.10 multicoloured 1·80 1·70

2005. Pottery (3rd issue). As T 1455. Multicoloured.
6591 30b. Jug (Leheceni, Bihor) 35 30
6592 50b. Pitcher (Vladesti, Valcea) 55 50
6593 1l. Pitcher (Curtea de Arges, Arges) 85 80
6594 1l.20 Jug (Vama, Satu Mare) 1·10 1·00
6595 2l.20 Jug (Barsa, Arad) 1·80 1·70
6596 2l.50 Wide-necked pitcher (Corund, Harghita) 2·20 2·00
6597 14l.50 Wide-necked pitcher (Valea Izei, Maramures) 11·50 10·50

1480 The Annunciation

2005. Christmas. Designs showing icons. Mult.
6598 50b. Type **1480** 40 35
6599 50b. The Nativity (48×83 mm) 40 35
6600 50b. Madonna and Child 40 35

1481 "Inscripti" (Virgil Preda)

2005. Contemporary Romanian Art. Multicoloured.
6601 1l.50 Type **1481** 1·20 1·10
6602 1l.50 "Gradina suspendata" (Alin Gheorghiu) (horiz) 1·20 1·10
6603 1l.50 "Still Life" (Constantin Ceraceanu) (horiz) 1·20 1·10
6604 1l.50 "Monstru 1" (Cristian Paleologu) 1·20 1·10

2005. Pottery (4th issue). As T 1455. Multicoloured.
6605 4l.70 Jug (Targu Neamt) 4·00 3·75
6606 5l.60 Jug and lidded jug (Poiana Deleni) 4·75 4·25

1482 Norwegian Forest Cat

2006. Cats. Multicoloured.
6607 30b. Type **1482** 25 25
6608 50b. Turkish Van 50 45
6609 70b. Siamese 60 60
6610 80b. Ragdoll 75 70
6611 1l.20 Persian 1·10 1·00
6612 1l.60 Birman (Inscr "Sacred cat of Burma") 1·50 1·40
MS6613 144×108 mm. As Nos. 6607/12. Imperf 4·25 4·25

1483 Wolfgang Amadeus Mozart (composer) (250th birth anniv)

2006. Anniversaries. Multicoloured.
6614 50b. Type **1483** 50 45
6615 1l.20 Ion Bratianu (politician) (185th birth anniv) 1·10 1·00
6616 2l.10 Grigore Moisii (mathematician) (birth centenary) 2·00 1·90

1484 Ice Dance

2006. Winter Olympic Games, Turin. Sheet 123×92 mm containing T 1484 and similar square designs. Multicoloured.
MS6617 1l.60×4, Type **1484**; 1l.60 Downhill skiing; Bobsleigh; Biathlon 6·25 6·25

No. **MS**6617 has an enlarged illustrated central gutter showing Elisabeta Lipa holding the Olympic torch.

Nos. 6618/20 are vacant.

1485 1868 Charles I 20lei

2006. Gold Coins. Multicoloured.
6621 30b. Type **1485** 25 25
6622 50b. 1906 Charles I 50lei 50 45
6623 70b. 1906 Charles I 100lei 60 60
6624 1l. 1922 Ferdinand I 50lei 1·00 95
6625 1l.20 1939 Charles II 100lei 1·10 1·00
6626 2l.20 1940 Charles II 100lei 2·10 2·00

1486 Crucifixion

2006. Easter. Icons. Multicoloured.
6627 50b. Type **1486** 50 45
6628 50b. Mary grieving 50 45
6629 50b. Mary grieving (different) 50 45
6630 50b. Removing Christ from the Cross 50 45
6631 50b. Ascension to heaven 50 45
MS6632 132×132 mm. Nos. 6627/31 2·50 2·50

1487 Traian Vuia and Drawing

2006. Centenary of Traian Vuia's First Powered Flight. Multicoloured.
6633 70b. Type **1487** 60 60
6634 80b. *Vuia I* 75 70
6635 1l.60 *Vuia II* 1·50 1·40
MS6636 114×91 mm. Nos. 6633/5 2·50 2·50
MS6637 116×84 mm. 4l.70 Traian Vuia seated on *Vuia I* (42×52 mm) 4·00 4·00

1488 Leopold Senghor

2006. Birth Centenary of Leopold Sedar Senghor (writer and president of Senegal 1960–1980).
6638 **1488** 2l.10 multicoloured 1·80 1·70

2006. Pottery (5th issue). Wedding Pots. As T 1455. Multicoloured.
6639 60b. Jug with animal spout (Poienita Arges) 50 45
6640 70b. Complex pot with storks (Oboga Olt) 60 60
6641 80b. Jug with raised decoration (Oboga Olt) 75 70
6642 1l.60 Figure as jug (Romana Olt) 1·40 1·30

1489 "Turkestanica"

2006. Tulips. Multicoloured.
6643 30b. Type **1489** 25 25
6644 50b. "Ice Follies" 35 35
6645 1l. "Cardinal" 75 70
6646 1l.50 "Yellow Empress" (47×33 mm) 1·10 1·00
6647 2l.10 "Donna Bella" 1·70 1·60
6648 3l.60 "Don Quixot" (47×33 mm) 3·00 2·75
MS6649 112×122 mm. As Nos. 6643/8 7·50 7·50

2006. Pottery (6th issue). As T 1455. Multicoloured.
6650 30b. Jug with snakes and frog (Oboga Olt) 35 35
6651 40b. Jug with pig's head spout (Radauti Suceava) 50 45
6652 2l.50 Jar with handle and raised decoration (Vladesti Valcea) 2·40 2·20
6653 3l.10 Jar with four handles (Jupanesti, Timis) 2·50 2·40

1490 House and Children

2006. Europa. Integration. Multicoloured.
6654 2l.10 Type **1490** 1·90 1·70
6655 3l.10 Adult and child approaching house 2·40 2·20

1491 1866 Carol I 2p. Stamp (As Type **6**)

2006. 140th Anniv of Romanian Dynasty. 125th Anniv of Proclamation of Romanian Kingdom.
6656 30b. Type **1491** 35 35
6657 1l. 1920 Ferdinand I 1b. stamp (As No. 879) 85 80
6658 2l.10 1930 Carol II 7l.50 (As No. 1179) 1·90 1·70
6659 2l.50 1940 Michael I 20l. stamp (As No. 1466) 2·40 2·20
MS6660 140×145 mm. Nos. 6656/9 5·25 5·25
MS6661 125×90 mm. 4l.70 1906 Carol I 15b. stamp (As No. 507) (horiz) 4·00 4·00

1492 Christopher Columbus (500th death anniv)

2006. Anniversaries. Multicoloured.
6662 50b. Type **1492** 45 40
6663 1l. Paul Cezanne (death centenary) 95 85
6664 1l.20 Henrik Ibsen (composer) (death centenary) 1·20 1·10

1493 Opening Ceremony

2006. Dimitrie Gusti National Village Museum.
6665 **1493** 2l.20 multicoloured 1·90 1·70

2006. 25th Anniv of First Romanian Astronaut. No. MS5809 surch.
MS6666 2l.10 on 2720l. mult 1·80 1·70

The margins of **MS**6666 were additionally overprinted for the anniversary.

1495 Main Entrance, Charles I Park

2006. Centenary of General Expo and Charles I Park, Bucharest. Multicoloured.
6667 30b. Type **1495** 30 30
6668 50b. Tepes Castle 45 40
6669 1l. Post Office pavilion 85 80
6670 1l.20 Danube European Commission pavilion 1·10 1·00
6671 1l.60 Palace of Industry 1·50 1·40

6672	2l.20 Roman arenas	2·10	2·00
MS6673	160×130 mm. Nos. 6667/72	5·75	5·75
MS6674	115×85 mm. 2l.20 Palace of Art	1·90	1·90

1496 Bela Bartok

2006. Composers' 125th Birth Anniversaries. Multicoloured.

6675	1l.20 Type **1496**	95	85
6676	1l.20 George Inescu	95	85
MS6677	95×82 mm. Nos. 6675/6	2·00	2·00

Stamps of a similar design were issued by Hungary.

1497 Trophy

2006. World Cup Football Championship, Germany. Multicoloured.

6678	30b. Type **1497**	35	30
6679	50b. Ball in net	45	40
6680	1l. Player	90	85
6681	1l.20 Hands holding trophy	1·10	1·00
MS6682	93×93 mm. Nos. 6678/81	2·50	2·50

1498 Young People

2006. International Day against Drug Abuse and Illegal Drug Trafficking.

6683	**1498**	2l.20 multicoloured	1·90	1·80

2006. Pottery (7th issue). As T 1455. Multicoloured.

6684	30b. Jar with handle and central decoration (Golesti-Arges)	35	30
6685	70b. Jug with spout and raised decoration (Romana-Olt)	65	65
6686	1l. Ornate jug with bird's head spout and circular base of birds (Oboga-Olt)	90	85
6687	2l.20 White bodied jar with handle and floral decoration (Vama-Satu Mare)	1·90	1·80

1499 Woman and Accoutrements

2006. Stamp Day. 1900th Death Anniv of Decebalus (Decebal), King of Dacia. Multicoloured.

6688	30b. Type **1499**	35	30
6689	50b. Man, facing left	55	50
6690	1l.20 Helmet (c. 150 AD)	1·10	1·00
6691	3l.10 Man standing	2·75	2·50
MS6692	116×87 mm. Nos. 6688/91	4·50	4·50

1500 Fluorite

2006. Minerals. Multicoloured.

6693	30b. Type **1500**	35	30
6694	50b. Quartz	45	40
6695	1l. Agate	90	85
6696	1l.20 Zinc blende (sphalerite)	1·10	1·00
6697	1l.50 Amethyst	1·50	1·40
6698	2l.20 Stibnite	2·00	1·90
MS6699	168×85 mm. Nos. 6693/8	5·75	5·75

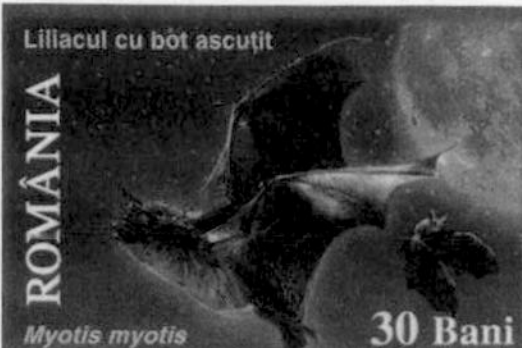

1501 *Myotis myotis*

2006. Bats. Multicoloured.

6700	30b. Type **1501**	35	30
6701	50b. *Rhinolophus hipposideros*	45	40
6702	1l. *Plecotus auritus*	90	85
6703	1l.20 *Pipistrellus pipistrellus*	1·10	1·00
6704	1l.60 *Nycatalus lasiopterus*	1·50	1·40
6705	2l.20 *Barbastella barbastella*	2·00	1·90
MS6706	116×140 mm. Nos. 6700/5	5·75	5·75

The stamps and margins of **MS**6706 form a composite design.

1502 Wartberg Type 1B-n2 (1854)

2006. 150th Anniv of First Railway Line from Oravita—Bazias. Multicoloured.

6707	30b. Type **1502**	35	30
6708	50b. Ovidiu Type C-n2 (1860)	45	40
6709	1l. Curierulu Type 1B-n2 (1869)	90	85
6710	1l.20 Berlad Type 1A1-n2 (1869)	1·10	1·00
6711	1l.50 Unirea Type 1B-n2 (1877)	1·30	1·30
6712	1l.60 Fulger King Charles I Pullman Express (1933)	1·50	1·40
MS6713	138×108 mm. 2l.20 Steyerdorf Type CB-2nf (72×33 mm)	2·00	2·00

1503 1858 27p. Stamp (As Type **1**)

2006. EFIRO 2008, International Stamp Exhibition, Bucharest. Showing first Romanian Stamps. Multicoloured.

6714	30b. Type **1503**	35	30
6715	50b. As No. 2	45	40
6716	1l.20 As No. 3	1·10	1·00
6717	1l.60 As No. 4	1·50	1·40
MS6718	100×123 mm. 2l.20 Bull's head (42×52 mm)	1·90	1·90

1504 Goddess of Fortune

2006. Centenary of National Lottery.

6719	**1504**	1l. multicoloured	1·00	95

(1505)

2006. Gymnastics. No. MS5834 surch as T 1505.

6720	5l.60 on 4050l. multicoloured	4·75	4·75

1506 "Muse endormie"

2006. 130th Birth Anniv of Constantin Brancusi (sculptor). Multicoloured.

6721	2l.10 Type **1506**	1·80	1·70
6722	3l.10 "Le sommeil"	2·75	2·50
MS6723	130×94 mm. Nos. 6721/2	4·50	4·50

Stamps of a similar design were issued by France.

1507 "Thinker of Hamangia" (Neolithic sculpture)

2006. 11th La Francaphone (French speaking countries and organizations) Meeting, Bucharest.

6724	**1507**	1l.20 multicoloured	1·00	95
MS6725	90×95 mm. **1507** (42×52 mm) 5l.60 multicoloured		4·75	4·75

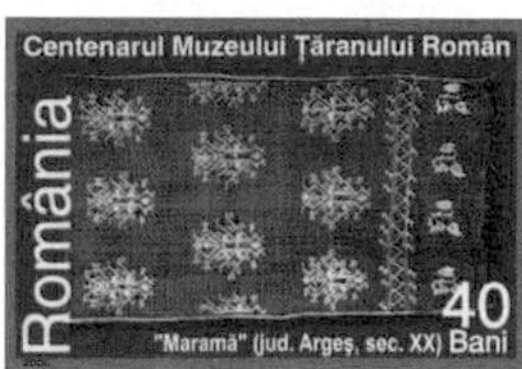

1508 Head Covering (Arges)

2006. Centenary of Peasant Museum. Multicoloured.

6726	40b. Type **1508**	35	30
6727	70b. Necklace (Dobruja)	65	65
6728	1l.60 Coin necklace (Bucovina)	1·50	1·40
6729	3l.10 Alexandru Tzigara-Samurcas (founder)	3·00	2·75

1509 Alexandru Ioan Cuza (ruler at time of founding of National Police force)

2006. 10th Anniv of Romanian Membership of International Police Association. Sheet 95×95 mm.

MS6730	**1509**	8l.70 multicoloured	7·25	7·25

1510 Adult and Chicks

2006. Endangered Species. Eurasian Spoonbill (Platalea leucorodia). Multicoloured.

6731	80b. Type **1510**	80	75
6732	80b. Two adults feeding	80	75
6733	80b. In flight	80	75
6734	80b. Two heads facing right	80	75
MS6735	170×120 mm. Nos. 6731/4	2·75	2·75

1511 Loyal Service

2006. National Orders. Multicoloured.

6736	30b. Type **1511**	20	20
6737	80b. Romanian Star	65	65
6738	2l.20 For Merit	1·90	1·80
6739	2l.50 First Class Sports Merit	2·10	2·00

1512 Radu Beligan

2006. Actors. Multicoloured.

6740	40b. Type **1512**	35	30
6741	1l. Carmen Stanescu	90	85
6742	1l.50 Dina Cocea	1·30	1·30
6743	2l.20 Colea Rautu	2·10	2·00

1513 Holy Virgin Empress

2006. Christmas. Icons. Multicoloured.

6744	50b. Type **1513**	50	45
6745	50b. Holy Virgin with Baby Jesus on the Throne	50	45
6746	50b. Worship of the Magi	50	45

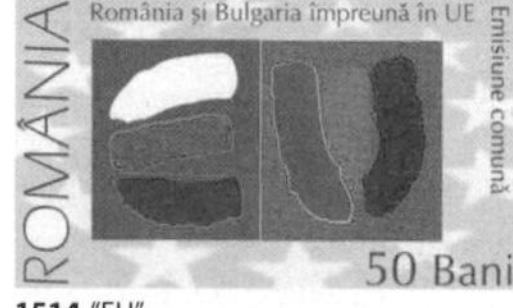

1514 "EU"

2006. Romania and Bulgaria's Membership of European Union. Multicoloured.

6747	50b. Type **1514**	45	40
6748	2l.10 Ballot box and flags	1·80	1·70

Stamps of a similar design were issued by Bulgaria.

1515 "AD PERPETUAM REI MEMORIAM" (For the eternal remembrance) (image scaled to 71% of original size)

2006. Contemporary Art. Works by Ciprian Paleologu. Multicoloured.

6749	30b. Type **1515**	35	30
6750	1l.50 "CUI BONO?" (Whose interest?)	1·30	1·30
6751	3l.60 "USQVE AD FINEM" (All the way)	3·25	3·25

1516 Obverse of 200 leu Banknote

2006. New Banknote. Multicoloured.

6752	50b. Type **1516**	45	40
6753	1l.20 Reverse of 200l. banknote	1·00	95

1517 Children

2006. 60th Anniv of UNICEF.
6754 **1517** 3l.10 multicoloured 2·75 2·50

1518 Sphinx, Bucegi

2007. Romania's Accession to European Union.
6755 **1518** 2l.20 multicoloured 1·90 1·80

No. 6755 has an attached label showing map of Romania and EU stars.

1519 Altar Rock Cave, Bihorului Mountains

2007. Centenary of Publication "Essay on Biospeleological Problems" (study of cave living organisms) by Emil Racovita (Romanian scientific pioneer). Multicoloured.

6756	40b. Type **1519**	35	30
6757	1l.60 Emil Racovita	1·30	1·30
6758	7l.20 *Ursus spelaeus*	6·25	5·75
6759	8l.70 Microscope and *Typhlocirolana moraguesi*	7·25	6·75
MS6760	131×112 mm. Nos. 6756/9	13·50	13·50

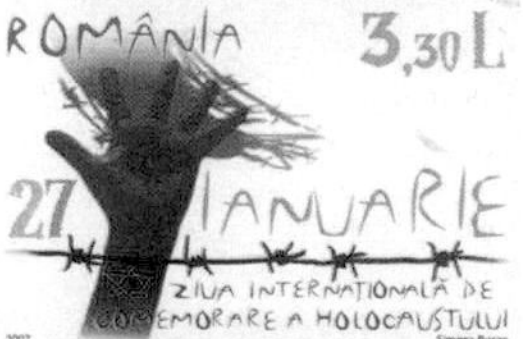

1520 Hand and Wire

2007. International Holocaust Remembrance Day.
6761 **1520** 3l.30 multicoloured 2·75 2·50

1521 *Hippocampus hippocampus* (Inscr "Hypocampus hypocampus")

2007. Black Sea Fauna. Multicoloured.

6762	70b. Type **1521**	65	65
6763	1l.50 *Delphinus delphis*	1·50	1·40
6764	3l.10 *Caretta caretta*	3·25	3·00
6765	7l.70 *Trigla lucerna*	6·75	6·25
MS6766	190×121 mm. Nos. 6762/5	11·00	11·00

1522 Gustave Eiffel (construction engineer)

2007. Personalities. Multicoloured.

6767	60b. Type **1522**	55	50
6768	80b. Maria Cutarida (first woman doctor)	80	75
6769	2l.10 Virginia Woolf (writer)	2·00	1·90
6770	3l.50 Nicolae Titulescu (politician)	3·25	3·00

1523 Decorated Egg, Olt

2007. Easter. Multicoloured.

6771	50b. Type **1523**	40	35
6772	50b. The Risen Christ (icon)	40	35
6773	50b. Decorated Egg, Bucovina	40	35

1524 *Cephalanthera rubra*

2007. Orchids. Multicoloured.

6774	30b. Type **1524**	35	30
6775	1l.20 *Epipactis palustris*	1·10	1·00
6776	1l.60 *Dactylorhiza maculate*	1·50	1·40
6777	2l.50 *Anacamptis pyramidalis*	2·20	2·10
6778	2l.70 *Limodorum abortivum*	2·50	2·30
6779	6l. *Ophrys scolopax*	5·50	5·00
MS6780	148×113 mm. 30b. Type **1524**; 1l,20 *Epipactis palustris*; 1l.60 *Dactylorhiza maculata*; 2l.50 *Anacamptis pyramidalis*; 2l.70 *Limodorum abortivum*; 6l. *Ophrys scolopax*	12·00	12·00

2007. Pottery (8th issue). As T 1455. Multicoloured.

6781	70b. Brown plate with central rooster (Obaga-Olt)	70	65
6782	1l. Mottled plate inscr "1898" (Vama-Satu Mare)	95	90
6783	2l.10 Cream plate with central soldier (Valea Izea-Maramures)	2·20	2·00
6784	2l.20 Cream bodied plate with overall decoration (Fragaras-Brasov)	2·30	2·10

1525 *Accipiter nisus* (sparrow hawk)

2007. Raptors. Multicoloured.

6785	50b. Type **1525**	55	50
6786	80b. *Circus aeruginosus* (marsh harrier)	80	75
6787	1l.60 *Aquila pomarina* (lesser spotted eagle)	1·60	1·50
6788	2l.50 *Buteo buteo* (common buzzard)	2·50	2·40
6789	3l.10 *Athene noctua* (little owl)	3·25	3·00
MS6790	65×90 mm. 4l.70 *Falco subbuteo* (hobby) (42×52 mm)	4·25	4·25

1526 Scouts

2007. Europa. Centenary of Scouting. Sheet 87×117 mm containing T 1526 and similar vert designs. Multicoloured.

6791	2l.10 Type **1526**	1·80	1·70
6792	7l.70 Robert Baden Powell (founder)	6·00	5·75

1527 Curtea Veche (Principal Court) (image scaled to 68% of original size)

2007. Old Bucharest. Multicoloured.

6792a	30b. Type **1527**	25	25
6792b	50b. Sturdza Palace	55	50
6792c	70b. National Military Circle	70	65
6792d	1l.60 National Theatre	1·50	1·40
6792e	3l.10 I. C. Bratianu Square	3·00	2·75
6792f	4l.70 Senate Square	4·75	4·50
MS6793	(a) 87×117 mm. 30b. As Type **1527**; 50b. As No. 6792b; 70b. As No. 6792c; 1l.60 As No. 6792d; 3l.10 As No. 6792e; 4l.70 As No. 6792f. (b) 131×111 mm. 5l.60 Romanian Athenaeum (52×42 mm)	12·00	12·00

2007. Pottery (9th issue). As T 1455. Multicoloured.

6794	70b. Cream plate with central spiral design (Vladesti-Vdlcea)	70	65
6795	80b. Cream bodied plate with green overall decoration (Vistea-Brasov)	80	75
6796	1l.60 Brown plate with geometric design (Tansa-lasi)	1·50	1·40
6797	3l.10 Green decorated plate (Romdana-Olt)	3·00	2·75

1528 Emblem and Medal

2007. 60th Anniv of Steaua Sports Club.
6798 **1528** 7l.70 multicoloured 7·00 6·75

1529 Palace Facade

2007. 110th Anniv of National Savings Bank Palace. Sheet 145×160 mm. Multicoloured.

6799	4l.70 Type **1529**	4·25	4·00
MS6800	5l.60 multicoloured	5·00	5·00

1530 Altemberger House (image scaled to 70% of original size)

2007. Sibiu–European Capital of Culture–2007. Multicoloured.

6801	30b. Type **1530**	25	25
6802	50b. Liars' Bridge and Council Tower	55	50
6803	60b. Parochial Evangelical Church	60	60
6804	70b. Grand Square c. 1780	70	65
6805	2l.10 Brukenthal Palace and St. Nepomuk Statue c. 1935	2·00	1·90
6806	5l.60 Panorama c. 1790 (painting) (F. Neuhauser)	5·50	5·00
MS6807	(a) 190×160 mm. 30b. As Type **1530**; 50b. As No. 6802; 60b. As No. 6803; 70b. As No. 6804; 2l.10 As No. 6805; 5l.60 As No. 6806. (b) 127×102 mm. 4l.70 Sibiu Fortress c. 1650 (52×42 mm)	13·50	13·50

The stamp and margin of **MS**6807 form a composite design of Sibiu Fortress.

1530a *Anser erthyropus* (lesser white-fronted goose)

2007. Ducks and Geese. Multicoloured.

6808	40b. Type **1530a**	40	40
6809	60b. *Branta ruficollis* (red-breasted goose)	70	65
6810	1l.60 *Anas acuta* (northern pintail)	1·50	1·40
6811	2l.10 *Anser albifrons* (white-fronted goose)	2·00	1·90
6812	3l.60 *Netta rufina* (red-crested pochard)	3·75	3·50
6813	4l.70 *Anas querquedula* (garganey)	4·50	4·25
MS6814	(a) 173×124 mm. 40b. As Type **1530a**; 60b. As No. 6809; 1l.60 As No. 6810; 2l.10 As No. 6811; 3l.60 As No. 6812; 4l.70 As No. 6813. (b) 120×95 mm. 5l.60 *Anas clypeata* (northern shoveler) (52×42 mm). Imperf	16·00	16·00

1530b Bisra Local 6 Heller Stamp and Early Carriage (image scaled to 71% of original size)

2007. Stamp Day. Centenary of Bisra Local Post. Multicoloured.

6815	50b. Type **1530b**	45	45
6816	2l.10 Bisra Local 2 Heller Stamp and early postman	1·90	2·40

2007. Pottery (10th and 11th issue). As T 1455. Multicoloured.

6817	60b. Fawn plate with all over decoration (Lapus-Maramures)	70	65
6818	80b. Brown dish with yellow scrafiti designs (Luncavita-Tulcea)	80	75
6819	1l.10 Cream dish with star-shaped central decoration (Luncavita-Tulcea)	1·10	1·00
6820	1l.40 Brown bodied jar with handle and cream and green decoration (Horezu-Valcea)	1·40	1·30
6821	1l.60 Cream plate with central green and yellow flowers and border decoration (Radauti-Suceava)	1·50	1·40
6822	1l.80 Large green bodied cup with brown and white decoration (Baia Mare-Maramures)	1·80	1·70
6823	2l.90 Cream bodied cup with dark brown orange decoration (Oboga-Olt)	2·75	2·50
6824	7l.70 Wide bodied cup with brown and white dotted decoration (Baia Mare-Maramures)	7·25	7·00

1530c Father Teoctist

2007. Father Teoctist (Toader Arapasu) (Patriarch of Romanian Orthodox Church) Commemoration.
6825 **1530c** 80b. multicoloured 1·00 95

1530d 1858 5 Parale Stamp (As Type **2**)

2007. EFIRO 2008, International Stamp Exhibition, Bucharest (2nd issue). Multicoloured.

6826	1l.10 Type **1530d**	1·10	1·00
6827	2l.10 1858 40 parale stamp (As Type **3**)	2·00	1·90
6828	3l.30 1858 80 parale stamp (As No. 10)	3·25	3·00
MS6829	120×100 mm. 5l.60 Bull's Head emblem	5·50	5·50

1531 Johannes Honterus (1498–1549) (cartographer)

2007. German Personalities in Romania. Mult.

6830	1l.90 Type **1531**	1·90	1·80
6831	2l.10 Herman Oberth (1894–1989) (space travel theorist)	2·00	1·90
6832	3l.90 Stephan Ludwig Roth (1796–1849) (educationalist)	3·75	3·50

1532 Luxembourg House, Sibiu

2007. Sibiu Joint European Capital of Culture—2007. Multicoloured.

6833	3l.60 Type **1532**	3·50	3·25
MS6834	123×95 mm. 4l.30 Luxembourg House, Sibiu (52×42 mm)	4·00	4·00

Stamps of a similar design were issued by Luxembourg.

1533 Obverse and Reverse of 1867 1 ban Coin (Image scaled to 68% of original size)

2007. 40th Anniv of Modern Currency. Multicoloured.

6835	3l.90 Type **1533**	3·75	3·50
MS6836	184×108 mm. 5l.60 1870 1 leu silver coin (30×30 mm circular)	5·50	5·50

No. 6835 is perforated around the design of the obverse of the 1 ban coin and partially perforated in the centre of the stamp.

1534 Tackle

2007. Rugby World Cup Championships, France. Multicoloured.

6837	1l.80 Type **1534**	2·00	1·90
6838	3l.10 Scrum	3·50	3·25

1535 *Sputnik* (first man made satellite)

2007. 50th Anniv of Space Exploration. Multicoloured.

6839	3l.10 Type **1535**	3·50	3·25
MS6840	85×70 mm. 5l.60 1870 1 *Sputnik* (52×42 mm)	6·25	6·25

The stamp and margin of **MS**6840 form a composite design of *Sputnik* over the Earth.

1536 *Birth of Jesus Christ* (icon)

2007. Christmas.

6841	**1536**	80b. multicoloured	1·00	95

2007. Pottery (12th issue). As T 1455. Mult.

6842	2l.10 Cream jug with green and brown garlands (Transylvania)	2·30	2·20
6843	3l.10 Cream jug with central border and green base (Horezu-Valcea)	3·50	3·25
6844	7l.20 Brown cup with blue, green and white decoration (Obarsa-Hunedoara)	8·25	7·75
6845	8l.70 Brown cup with white medallion containing flower (Baia Mare-Maramures)	9·50	9·00

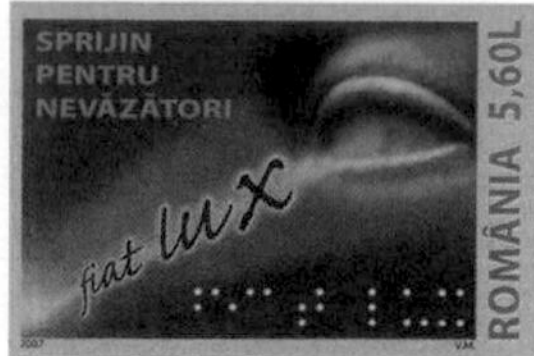
1537 Eye

2007. Support for the Blind.

6846	**1537**	5l.60 multicoloured	6·25	6·00

1538 *Orsova* (Romania)

2007. Danube Ports and Ships. Multicoloured.

6847	1l. Orsova port	1·10	1·00
6848	1l.10 Novi Sad port	1·20	1·20
MS6849	187×107 mm. 2l.10×2, Type **1538**; *Sirona* (Serbia)	5·50	5·50

No. **MS**6847 also contains two stamp size labels, showing arms of Romania and Serbia, which, with the margins, form a composite background design.

Stamps of a similar design were issued by Serbia.

1539 *Ursus maritimus* (polar bear)

2007. Polar Fauna. Multicoloured.

6850	30b. Type **1539**	30	25
6851	50b. *Pagophilus groenlandicus* (harp seal) (vert)	55	55
6852	1l.90 *Alopex lagopus* (Arctic fox) (vert)	2·20	2·00
6853	3l.30 *Aptenodytes forsteri* (emperor penguin)	4·25	4·00
6854	3l.60 *Balaenoptera musculus* (blue whale)	4·50	4·25
6855	4l.30 *Odobenus rosmarus* (walrus) (vert)	5·50	5·25

1540 *Lepiota rhacodes*

2008. Fungi. Multicoloured.

6856	1l.20 Type **1540**	1·30	1·20
6857	1l.40 *Lactarius deliciosus*	1·40	1·40
6858	2l. *Morchella esculenta*	2·20	2·00
6859	2l.40 *Paxillus involutus*	2·50	2·40
6860	3l. *Gyromitra esculenta*	3·25	3·00
6861	4l.50 *Russula emetica*	5·00	4·75
MS6862	130×116 mm. Nos. 6856/61	16·00	16·00

1541 *Voison-Farman I* and Henri Farman

2008. Centenary of First 1000m Closed Circuit Flight in One Minute.

6863	**1541**	5l. multicoloured	5·50	5·25

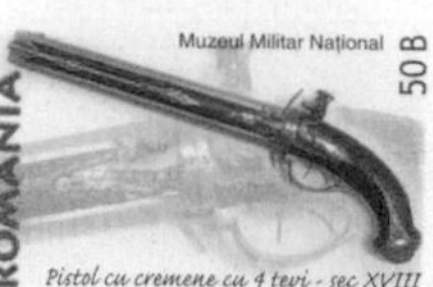
1542 18th-Century European Flint Pistol

2008. Pistols from the Collection of National Military Museum. Multicoloured.

6864	50b. Type **1542**	55	55
6865	1l. 18th-century flint pistol, Liege	1·10	1·10
6866	2l.40 7.65 mm. Mannlicher carbine pistol, 1903	2·50	2·40
6867	5l. 8 mm. Revolver, 1915	5·50	5·25
MS6868	118×75 mm. Nos. 6864/7	9·50	9·50

1543 *Explorer 1*

2008. 50th Anniv (2007) of Space Exploration. Multicoloured.

6869	1l. Type **1543**	1·10	1·10
6870	2l.40 *Sputnik 3*	2·50	2·40
6871	3l.10 *Jupiter AM-13*	3·25	3·00

1544 Resurrected Christ (iconostasis), Scaune Church, Bucharest

2008. Easter.

6872	**1544**	1l. multicoloured	1·10	1·10

2008. Pottery (13th issue). As T 1455. Multicolored.

6873	2l. Brown mug with yellow and lower white decoration (Cosesti, Arges)	2·20	2·00
6874	2l.40 Cream bodied jug with pictorial decoration (Radauti, Suceava)	2·50	2·40
6875	6l. Brown bodied jug with central decoration (Baia Mare, Maramures)	6·50	6·00
6876	7l.60 Cream lidded pot with handles (Vladesti, Valcea)	8·25	7·75

1545 Angel and Emblems

2008. NATO Summit, Bucharest. Multicoloured.

6877	6l. Type **1545**	6·50	6·00
6878	6l. As No. 6877 but with silver emblem	6·50	6·00
6879	6l. As No. 6877 but with gold emblem	6·50	6·00

1546 *Helarctos malayanus* (sun bear)

2008. Bears. Multicoloured.

6880	60b. Type **1546**	70	70
6881	1l.20 *Ursus americanus* (American black bear) (horiz)	1·30	1·20
6882	1l.60 *Ailuropoda melanoleuca* (giant panda) (horiz)	1·90	1·80
6883	3l. *Melursus ursinus* (sloth bear) (horiz)	3·25	3·00
6884	5l. *Tremarctos ornatus* (spectacled bear)	5·50	5·25
MS6885	77×85 mm. 9l.10 *Ursus arctos* (brown bear) (42×51 mm)	9·75	9·75

1547 Athletics

2008. Olympic Games, Beijing. Sheet 78×142 mm containing T 1547 and similar horiz designs. Multicoloured.

MS6886	1l.×4, Type **1547**; Gymnastics; Swimming; Rowing	5·00	5·00

1548 Map and Outline of Envelope

2008. Europa. The Letter. Multicoloured.

6887	1l.60 Type **1548**	1·90	1·80
6888	8l.10 A 'Priority' envelope and European stars	8·50	8·50
MS6889	122×92 mm. Nos. 6887/8, each×2	22·00	22·00

1549 Fauna

2008. Centenary of Grigore Antipa National Natural History Museum.Multicoloured.

6890	2l.40 Type **1549**	2·50	2·40
6891	3l. Grigore Antipa (founder)	3·25	3·00

1550 Building, Stars and '€'

2008. 10th Anniv of European Central Bank.

6892	**1550**	3l.10 multicoloured	3·50	3·25

1551 1859 5p. Stamp (As Type **2**) and Emblems (image scaled to 68% of original size)

2008. EFIRO 2008, International Stamp Exhibition, Bucharest (3rd issue). Designs showing early stamps and exhibition emblems. Multicoloured.

6893	50b. Type **1551**	55	55
6894	1l. 1862 6p. stamp (As No. 24)	1·10	1·10
6895	2l.40 1865 2p. stamp (As Type **5**)	2·50	2·40
6896	3l.10 1891 1½p. stamp (As Type **15**)	3·50	3·25
6897	4l.50 1903 1b. stamp (As No. 464)	5·00	4·75
6898	6l. 1932 6l. stamp (As Type **96**)	6·50	6·00
MS6899	152×122 mm. 8l.10 Exhibition emblem (30×30 mm)	8·50	8·50

MS6899a	192×162 mm. Nos. 6893/8	17·00	17·00

1552 Weaving (Romania) (image scaled to 68% of original size)

2008. 45th Anniv of Romania—Kuwait Diplomatic Relations. Multicoloured.

6900	2l. Type **1552**	2·20	2·00
6901	2l. Model boat builder (Kuwait)	2·20	2·00
MS6902	112×83 mm. 3l.30 Romanian fire appliance	3·50	3·50

Stamps of a similar design were issued by Kuwait.

1553 Scene from *7 Arts* (winning animated film)

2008. 50th Anniv of Ion Popescu-Gopo's Grand Prix at Film Festival, Tours. Multicoloured.

6903	1l.40 Type **1553**	1·40	1·40
6904	4l.70 Ion Popescu-Gopo and trophy	5·25	5·00
MS6905	100×125 mm. Nos. 6903/4	6·50	6·50

1554 St Gheorghe Church, Voronet Monastery (Romania)

2008. UNESCO World Heritage Sites in Romania and Russia. Multicoloured.

6906	3l. Type **1554**	3·25	3·00
6907	4l.30 St Dimitrie Church, Vladimir (Russia)	4·50	4·25
MS6908	130×105 mm. Nos. 6906/7	8·50	8·50

Stamps of a similar design were issued by Russia.

1555 Fagaras Castle

2008. Castles. Multicoloured.

6909	1l. Type **1555**	1·10	1·10
6910	2l.10 Peles	2·30	2·20
6911	3l. Huniad	3·25	3·00
6912	5l. Bethlen-Cris	5·50	5·25
MS6913	135×118 mm. Nos. 6909/12	12·00	12·00

1556 Page from Missal

2008. 500th Anniv of Printing of Macarie's Missal (first book printed in Romania). Multicoloured.

6914	4l.30 Type **1556**	5·50	5·25
MS6915	97×83 mm. 9l. 10 Two pages from missal (52×42 mm)	10·00	10·00

1557 Church of the Three Holy Hierachs

2008. 600th Anniv of Iasi City Documentary Accreditation. Multicoloured.

6916	1l. Type **1557**	1·10	1·10
6917	1l.60 Metropolitan Cathedral	1·90	1·80
6918	2l.10 Vasile Alecsandri National Theatre	2·30	2·20
6919	3l.10 Museum of Unification	3·50	3·25
MS6920	133×100 mm. 9l. 10 Palace of Culture (42×52 mm)	10·00	10·00
MS6921	182×98 mm. nos. 6916/19	8·75	8·75

1558 Queen Marie

2008. Stamp Day. 70th Death Anniv of Queen Marie of Romania. Multicoloured.

6922	1l. Type **1558**	1·10	1·10
6923	3l. Older facing left	3·25	3·00
MS6924	102×68 mm. Nos. 6921/2	4·50	4·50

1559 Moldova

2008. Heraldry. Designs showing arms. Multicoloured.

6925	60b. Type **1559**	70	70
6926	1l. Wallachia	1·10	1·10
6927	3l. Transylvania	3·25	3·00
6928	3l.10 Bucharest	3·50	3·25
MS6929	126×92 mm. Nos. 6925/8	8·50	8·50
MS6930	119×147 mm. 6l. Seal (42×52 mm)	6·50	6·50

1560 Power Station (image scaled to 68% of original size)

2008. Tenth Anniv of Nuclearelectrica.

6931	**1560** 2l.10 multicoloured	2·30	2·20

1561 Stylized Airwaves

2008. 80th Anniv of National Radio Broadcasting Society.

6932	**1561** 2l.40 multicoloured	2·50	2·40

1562 The Nativity

2008. Christmas. Multicoloured.

6933	1l. Type **1562**	1·10	1·10
MS6933a	As Type **1562**	1·10	1·10

1563 *Nymphaea lotus*

2008. Petea Creek Natural Reservation. Multicoloured.

6934	1l.40 Type **1563**	1·40	1·40
6935	1l.60 *Scardinius racovitzai*	1·90	1·80
6936	3l.10 *Melanopsis parreyssi*	3·50	3·25
MS6937	140×100 mm. Nos. 6934/6	6·75	6·75

The stamps and margins of **MS**6937 form a composite design.

1564 Early Coat of Arms

2009. 150th Anniv of Union. Multicoloured.

6938	2l.40 Type **1564**	2·50	2·40
MS6939	162×118 mm. 9l.10 Arms (different)	10·00	10·00

1565 '10'

2009. Tenth Anniv of Euro Currency. Multicoloured.

6940	3l. Type **1565**	3·25	3·00
6941	3l. As Type **1565**	3·25	3·00

No. 6941 has the '10' stamped in gold foil.

1566 *Crucifixion*

2009. Easter. Scenes from Iconostasis, Metropolitan Cathedral, Iasi. Multicoloured.

6942	1l. Type **1566**	1·10	1·10
6943	1l. *Resurrection*	1·10	1·10
6944	1l. *Ascension*	1·10	1·10

1567 *Alcedo atthis*

2009. Birds of Danube Delta. Multicoloured.

6945	50b. Type **1567** (kingfisher)	55	50
6946	1l.60 *Himantopus himantopus* (black-winged stilt) (48×33 mm)	1·90	1·80
6947	2l.10 *Egretta alba*(great egret) (48×33 mm)	2·30	2·20
6948	3l.10 *Falco cherrug* (Danube falcon)	3·50	3·25
MS6949	174×50 mm. Nos. 6945/8	8·25	8·25
MS6950	80×105 mm. 8l.10 *Halaeetus albicilla* (white-tailed eagle) (36×36 mm) (diamond)	8·75	8·75

1568 Penguin and Teardrop

2009. Preserve Polar Regions and Glaciers. Multicoloured.

6951	1l.60 Type **1568**	1·90	1·80
6952	8l.10 Melting Polar ice cap	8·75	8·50
MS6953	130×100 mm. Nos. 6951/2	10·00	10·00

It is reported that No. **MS**6953 also exists with silver foil printing.

1569 *Leontopodium alpinum* (eidelweiss)

2009. Flowers. Multicoloured.

6954	30b. Type **1569**	35	30
6955	60b. *Aster alpinus* (alpine aster)	70	65
6956	1l. *Dianthus superbus* (large pink)	1·10	1·00
6957	1l.20 *Silene nivalis* (pigeon's gizzard)	1·20	1·10
6958	2l.40 *Campanula persicifolia* (bell flower)	2·50	2·40
6959	3l.10 *Lilium martagon* (Turk's cap lily)	3·50	3·25

1570 Drilling Platform

2009. Centenary of Romgaz.

6960	**1570** 2l.40 multicoloured	2·50	2·40

1571 Galileo Galilei, Telescope and Tower of Pisa

2009. Europa. Astronomy.

6961	2l.40 Type **1571**	2·50	2·40
6962	9l.10 Map of constellations	9·00	8·75
MS6962a	113×91 mm. 2l.40×2, Type **1571**×2; 9l. 10×2, No. 6962×2	23·00	23·00

1572 Palace of Europe, Strasbourg

2009. 60th Anniv of Council of Europe.

6963	**1572** 6l. multicoloured	6·25	2·25

1573 Emblem (Municipal Director General of Police, Bucharest)

2009. European Capitals' Police Agencies Conference, Bucharest. Multicoloured.

6964	1l. Type **1573**	1·10	1·00
6965	1l.60 Police badge	1·70	1·60

1574 Timisoara (first European city with electric street lighting)

2009. Romania–European Source of Energy. Multicoloured.

6966 80b. Type **1574** 75 70
6967 2l.10 Turda (first European town lit with natural gas) 2·00 1·90
6968 3l. Iron Gates I hydroelectric power plant 3·00 2·75
MS6969 184×133 mm. Nos. 6966/8 3·75 3·75

1575 Symbols of First Moon Landing

2009. 40th Anniv of Moon Landing. Multicoloured.

6970 3l. Type **1575** 3·00 2·75
MS6971 128×116 mm. 14l.50 Footprint on the moon 14·00 14·00

1576 The Church on the Hill

2009. Sighisoara–UNESCO World Heritage Site. Multicoloured.

6972 1l. Type **1576** 1·10 1·00
6973 1l.60 Historic town centre 1·70 1·60
6974 6l. Clock tower 6·25 6·00
MS6975 114×100 mm. 7l.60 Old town (52×42 mm) 7·50 7·50
MS6975a 151×140 mm. Nos. 6972/4 9·00 9·00

1577 Anghel Saligny and Bridge at Cernavoda (image scaled to 68% of original size)

2009. 155th Birth Anniv of Anghel Saligny (engineer). Multicoloured.

6976 2l.10 Type **1577** 2·00 1·90
6977 2l.40 Anghel Saligny and span of bridge at Cernavoda 2·50 2·40

1578 First Electric Tram, Frankfurt (1884)

2009. Electric Trams. Showing the first trams and arms of the relevant city. Multicoloured.

6978 80b. Type **1578** 75 70
6979 1l.20 Bucharest (1894) 1·10 1·00
6980 1l.60 Vienna (1897) 1·70 2·60
6981 2l.10 Braila (1899) 2·00 1·90
6982 2l.40 London (1901) 2·50 2·40
MS6983 140×100 mm. 8l.10 Berlin (1881) (48×33 mm) 8·25 8·25

1579 *Aquila chrysaetos* (golden eagle)

2009. Endangered Species. Multicoloured.

6984 30b. Type **1579** 25 20
6985 50b. *Lynx lynx* (lynx) (vert) 45 40
6986 60b. *Cervus elaphus* (red deer) 55 50
6987 1l.40 *Huso huso* (European sturgeon) (vert) 1·50 1·40
6988 3l. *Testudo graeca ibera* (Greek tortoise) 3·25 3·00
6989 6l. *Otis tarda* (great bustard) (vert) 6·50 6·25

1580 Dimtrie Cantemir (twice Prince of Moldavia, philosopher, historian, composer, musicologist, linguist, ethnographer and geographer)

2009. Romania—European Treasure. Sheet 161×137 mm containing T 1580 and similar horiz designs. Multicoloured.

MS6990 3l.×8, Type **1580**; George Enescu (composer, violinist, pianist and conductor); Three Saint Hierarchs Church, Iasi; Black Church and Johannes Honterus (humanist) (statue): *Egreta garzetta*, Retezat National Park; *Rupicapra rupicapra*, Retezat National Park; Cramposa (viticulture); Traditional crafts, Maramures 25·00 25·00

1581 Buna Vestire Church (image scaled to 68% of original size)

2009. 550th Anniv of Bucharest. Multicoloured.

6991 30b. Type **1581** 25 20
6992 80b. Coltea Hospital 75 70
6993 3l. Sutu Palace 3·25 3·00
6994 4l.70 Architecture School 5·75 5·50
MS6995 140×184mm. Nos. 6991/4 10·50 10·50
MS6996 110×120mm. 8l.10 Patriarchal Cathedral, Bucharest (52×42 mm) 8·50 8·50

1582 Dove, Tears and Woman's Face (image scaled to 68% of original size)

2009. International Day of Non-Violence.

6997 **1582** 3l. multicoloured 3·25 3·00

1583 Pipeline

2009. 35th Anniv of Transgaz (international natural gas transit).

6998 **1583** 5l. multicoloured 5·50 5·25

1584 Emblem

2009. 150th Anniv of Armed Forces General Staff.

6999 **1584** 7l.60 multicoloured 7·75 7·50

1585 The Nativity (icon, Buna Vestire Church (St Anthony the Great), Old Court, Bucharest))

2009. Christmas.

7000 **1585** 1l. multicoloured 1·10 1·00

1586 Building Facade and Alexandru Ioan Cuza

2009. 150th Anniv of Faculty of Law, University of Bucharest.

7001 **1586** 9l.10 multicoloured 9·50 9·25

1587 Avram Goldfaden and Stage

2009. Death Centenary of Avram Goldfaden (founder of first Yiddish theatre (1876), Iasi, Romania).

7002 **1587** 3l.10 multicoloured 3·25 2·00

1588 *Mireca* (three masted barque)

2009. Centenary of Constanta Harbour. Multicoloured.

7003 1l. Type **1588** 1·10 1·00
7004 5l. King Carol I lighthouse 5·50 5·00
MS7005 105×145 mm. Nos. 7003/4 6·50 6·50

1589 *Apis mellifera mellifera*

2010. Honey Bees. Multicoloured.

7006 50b. Type **1589** 40 35
7007 2l.10 *Apis mellifera ligustica* 2·00 1·90
7008 3l.10 *Apis mellifera carnica* 3·50 3·25
7009 4l.30 *Apis mellifera caucasica* 5·50 5·25

1590 Skiing

2010. Winter Olympic Games, Vancouver. Multicoloured.

7010 60b. Type **1590** 55 50
7011 80l. Speed skating 75 70
7012 1l. Skeleton bob (horiz) 1·10 1·00
7013 7l.60 Bobsleigh (horiz) 7·50 7·25

1591 *Brachypelma albopilosum*

2010. Tarantulas.

7014 50b. Type **1591** 45 40
7015 80b. *Haplopelma lividum* 75 70
7016 1l.20 *Brachypelma smithi* 1·10 1·00
7017 9l.10 *Grammostola rosea* 9·50 9·25

1592 Constanta Genoese Lighthouse

2010. Lighthouses. Multicoloured.

7018 60b. Type **1592** 55 50
7019 80b. Sulina 75 70
7020 1l.20 Mangalia 1·10 1·00
7021 1l.60 Tuzla 1·50 1·25
7022 8l.10 Constanta North 7·50 7·25

1593 The Resurrection (20th-century icon)

2010. Easter.

7023 **1593** 1l. multicoloured 1·10 1·00

1594 *Vlaicu I*

2010. 65th Anniv of International Civil Aviation Convention (ICAO).

7024 **1594** 8l.10 multicoloured 7·75 £750

1595 Grigore Alexandru Chica (founder) and Gendarmerie

2010. 160th Anniv of Romanian Gendarmerie.

7025 **1595** 9l.10 multicoloured 8·50 8·25

1596 Eugeniu Carada

2010. Death Centenary of Eugeniu Carada (politician).

MS7026 **1596** 9l.10 multicoloured 8·50 8·25

1597 Scene from Little Red Riding Hood

2010. Europa. Multicoloured.

7027	4l.30 Type **1597**	4·75	4·50
7028	7l.60 Boy and dragon reading	8·00	7·75
MS7029	127×108 mm. Nos. 7027/8, each×2	19·00	18·00

1598 Melk Abbey, Austria (image scaled to 68% of original size)

2010. Danube Heraldry (1st issue)

7030	1l.40 Type **1598**	1·10	1·00
7031	2l.40 Bratislava Castle, Slovakia	2·50	2·25
7032	3l.10 Ilok Fortress, Croatia	3·25	3·00
7033	4l.30 Parliament Palace, Budapest, Hungary	4·75	4·50
MS7034	228×220 mm. Nos. 7030/3	11·00	10·00
MS7035	174×167 mm. 14l.50 *Mother Baar* (sculpture) (Adolf Heer) (36×36 mm)	13·00	12·00

1599 Quartz

2010. Minerals. Multicoloured.

7036	50b. Type **1599**	45	
7037	1i.40 Gold ore	1·10	1·00
7038	1l.60 Rhodochrosite	1·50	1·40
7039	2l.40 Calcite	2·50	2·25
7040	7l.60 Red barite	8·00	7·75

1600 Hucul (Carpathian)

2010. Horses

7041	60b. Type **1600**	55	50
7042	1i. Arabian	1·10	1·00
7043	2l. Lipizzaner (vert)	1·90	1·75
7044	2l.10 Furioso North Star	2·00	1·90
7045	5l. Shagya Arabian	5·25	5·00

1601 Emblem and Children

2010. 20th Anniv of Save the Children Romania Organization

7046	**1601** 3l.10 multicoloured	3·25	3·00

1602 Vipera ursinii (meadow viper)

2010. Protected Fauna of the Danube River. Multicoloured.

7047	1l.40 Type **1602**	1·10	1·00
7048	1l.60 *Phalacrocorax pygmaeus* (pygmy cormorant)	1·50	1·40
7049	2l. *Phalacrocorax pygmaeus* (pygmy cormorant)	1·00	1·90
7050	7l.60 *Pelecanus crispus* (Dalmatian pelican)	8·00	7·75
MS7051	140×60 mm. Nos. 7047/50	11·00	10·00

1603 AzulejoTile with Seated Musician (National Museum, Lisbon)

2010. 130th Anniv of Portugal–Romania Diplomatic Relations. Multicoloured.

7052	2l.10 Type **1603**	2·00	1·90
7053	3l.10 Blue tile (Peasant Life Museum, Bucharest)	3·25	3·00

Stamps of a similar design were issued by Portugal.

1604 Arms

2010. Stamp Day

7054	**1604** 6l. multicoloured	6·25	6·00

1605 Clivia miniata

2010. 150th Anniv of Botanic Gardens, Bucharest

7055	1l.60 Type **1605**	1·50	1·40
7056	2l.10 *Magnolia kobus*	2·00	1·90
7057	2l.40 *Strelitzia juncea*	2·50	2·40
7058	3l. *Hepatica transsilvanica*	3·25	3·00
7059	3l.10 *Dicentra spectabilis*	3·25	3·00
MS7060	100×70 mm. 7l.60 Dimitrie Brandza (garden constructor) (36×36 mm)	8·00	7·75

1606 Carpathian Sphinx, Walker with Binoculars and 'Romania'

2010. Tourism. Multicoloured.

7061	1l. Type **1606**	1·10	1·00
7062	1l.60 Carpathian landscape and bearded figure facing left and 'Romania' at right	1·50	1·40
MS7063	108×78 mm. 1l. As Type **1606** (42×26 mm); 1l.60 As No. 7062 (42×26 mm)	1·10	1·00
MS70664	97×78 mm. 9l.10 Mountain landscape (84×26 mm)	9·25	9·00

1607 Games Emblem, Medal and Symbols of Study

2010. Youth Olympic Games, Singapore

MS7065	multicoloured	7·50	7·25

1608 Nahuel Huapi Lake, Argentina

2010. 80th Anniv of Argentina–Romania Diplomatic Relations. Multicoloured.

7066	2l.10 Type **1608**	2·00	1·90
7067	3l.19 Balea Lake, Romania	3·25	3·00

Stamps of a similar design were issued by Argentina.

1609 100l. Banknote

2010. 130th Anniv of National Bank. Multicoloured.

7068	2l.40 Type **1609**	2·50	2·25
7069	4l.30 100l. banknote (different)	4·75	4·50
MS7070	122×120 mm. Nos. 7068/9	7·25	7·00

1610 Steam Locomotive, Salzburg, Austria

2010. Orient Express. Multicoloured.

7071	2l.40 Type **1610**	2·50	2·40
7072	4l.70 Steam locomotive, Sinaia, Romania	7·75	7·50
MS7073	160×95 mm. Nos. 7071/2	9·75	9·50

1611 Children in Landscape (Save the Children) (Ioana Vezeanu)

2010. 20th Anniv of Ratification of UN Convention on Rights of the Child

7074	**1611** 6l. multicoloured	6·50	6·25

2010. Danube Heraldry (2nd issue). Multicoloured.

7075	1l.40 Ram Fortress, Serbia	1·50	1·40
7076	2l.40 Theatre, Ruse, Bulgaria	2·50	2·40
7077	3l.10 'Bogdan Petriceicu Hasdeu', Cahul State University, Moldova	3·25	3·00
7078	4l.30 Assumption of Virgin Mary Church, Izmail, Ukraine	4·75	4·50
MS7079	228×220 mm. Nos. 7075/8	10·00	9·00
MS7080	174×167 mm. 14l.50 Navigation Arch, Galati (designed by Petre Antonescu) (36×36 mm)	13·00	12·00

Multicoloured designs as T **1598**.

1612 Henri Coanda and Coanda Jet Aircraft

2010. Centenary of Henri Coanda's Jet Aircraft

MS7081	multicoloured	13·00	12·00

1613 Arms

2010. 130th Anniv of National Grand Lodge of Romania. Multicoloured.

7082	3l. Type **1613**	3·25	3·00
7083	5l. Square and Compass	5·50	5·00

1614 Wine Barrels

2010. Viticulture. Multicoloured.

7084	2l.10 Type **1614**	2·00	1·90
7085	3l.10 Grapes and decorated ceramic wine jug	3·25	3·00
MS7086	80×60 mm Horiz. 2l.10 As Type **1614**; 3l.10 As No. 7085	5·25	5·00

1615 Birth of Our Lord (icon, Gheorghe Tattarescu) (Metropolitan Cathedral, Iasi)

2010. Christmas. Multicoloured.

7087	1l. Type **1615**	90	85
7088	3l.10 *Birth of Our Lord* (Murillo School)	3·25	3·00

Stamps of the same design were issued by Vatican City.

1616

2010. Romania–World Firsts. Multicoloured.

7089	3l. Type **1616**	3·25	3·00
7090	4l.30 Horizontal mill wheel mill (13th–14th century, precursor of turbine)	4·75	4·50
7091	5l. Fountain pen designed by Petrache Poenaru (Patent no. 3208, 1827)	5·75	5·50
7092	8l.10 Aerodynamic car, invented by Aurel Persu (German patent no. 402683, 1922)	7·50	7·25

1616a *Zamenis longissimus* (Aesculapian snake)

2011. Reptiles. Multicoloured.

7093	60b. Type **1616a**	50	45
7094	2l.40 *Podarcis taurica* (Balkan wall lizard)	2·50	2·40
7095	3l. *Vipera ammodytes ammodytes* (horned viper)	3·25	3·00
7096	9l.10 *Vipera ursinii moldavica* (Moldavian meadow viper)	9·50	9·00

1617 *Mercury* (George Demetrescu Mirea)

2011. Art. Multicoloured.

7097	1l.40 Type **1617**	1·10	1·00
7098	2l.10 *Marine* (Eugeniu Voinescu)	2·00	1·90
7099	3l. *Rodica* (Nicolae Grigorescu)	3·25	3·00
7100	7l.60 *Prometheus* (George Demetrescu Mirea)	7·25	7·00

1618 Ursilor

2011. Caves

30b.	7101 Type **1618**	25	20
7102	50b. Closani	50	45
7103	60b. Muierii	55	50
7104	3l. Meziad (horiz)	3·25	3·00
7105	3l.10 Vantului (horiz)	3·25	3·00
7106	8l.70 Sura Mare (horiz)	7·75	7·50

1619 *Ara illiger* (Illiger's macaw)

2011. Parrots and Parakeets. Multicoloured.

7107	1l.60 Type **1619**	1·50	1·25
7108	2l.10 *Ara macao* (Scarlet macaw)	2·00	1·90
7109	2l.40 *Primolius auricollis* (yellow-collared macaw)	2·25	2·00
7110	4l.70 *Platycercus eximius* (eastern rosella)	5·25	5·00
7111	5l. *Melopsittacus undulatus* (budgerigar)	5·50	5·25
MS7112	80×103 mm. 9l.10 *Nymphicus hollandicus* (cockatiel)		

1620 Globe and Child

2011. World Down Syndrome Day

7113	**1620**	3l. muulticoloured	3·25	3·00

1621 Crucifixion (icon, from Oravita Church)

2011. Easter

7114	**1621**	1l. multicoloured	1·10	1·00

1622 Peony

2011. *Paeonia peregrina* (Romanian Peony). Multicoloured.

7115	1l. Type **1622**	1·10	1·00
MS7116	100×70 mm. 2l. *Paeonia tenufolia* (Romanian Peony)	2·00	1·90

1623 *Parnasssius apollo*

2011. Butterflies and Moth. Multicoloured.

7117	50b. Type **1623**	45	50
7118	60b. *Greta oto* (vert)	55	50
7119	2l.40 *Morpho nestira*	2·50	2·40
7120	3l. *Papilio machaon*	3·35	3·00
7121	4l.50 *Attacus atlas*	4·75	4·50
7122	5l. *Inachis io*	5·00	4·75
MS7122a	105×65 mm. 8l.10 *Iphiclides podalirius*		

1624 Palace of Parliament

2011. Palace of Parliament, Bucharest. Multicoloured.

7123	30b. Type **1624**	25	20
7124	50b. Senate entrance hall	45	40
7125	60b. Senate plenary hall	55	50
7126	3l. Human Rights room	3·25	3·00
7127	4l.30 Plenary hall of the Chamber of Deputies	4·75	4·50
7128	7l.60 Palace of Parliament, gate and entrance	7·75	7·50

1625 Deer in Forest

2011. Europa. Forests. Multicoloured.

7130	2l.40 Type **1625**	2·50	2·40
7131	9l.10 Squirrel on conifer branch	8·75	8·50

1626 Aries

2011. Western Zodiac. Multicoloured.

7132	30b. Type **1626**	25	20
7133	50b. Taurus	50	45
7134	60b. Gemini	55	50
7135	80b. Cancer	70	65
7136	1l.40 Leo	1·10	1·00
7137	14l.50 Virgo	12·00	11·00

1627 Dumitru Dorin Prunariu (first Romanian cosmonaut)

2011. 50th Anniv of First Manned Space Flight, 30th Anniv of First Flight of Romanian Cosmonaut and 50th Anniv of First Session of UN Committee on the Peaceful Use of Outer Space. Multicoloured.

7138	3l. Type **1627**	3·25	3·00
7139	4l.710 Yuri Gagarin (first man in space)	5·50	5·25

EXPRESS LETTER STAMPS

1919. Transylvania. Cluj Issue. No. E245 of Hungary optd as T 42.

E784	**E18**	2b. olive and red	30	45

1919. Transylvania. Oradea Issue. No. E245 of Hungary optd as T 42.

E860	2b. olive and red	40	70

FRANK STAMPS

F38

1913. Silistra Commemoration Committee.

F626	**F38**	(-) brown	7·75	9·50

F108 Mail Coach and Biplane

1933. For free postage on book "75th Anniv of Introduction of Rumanian Postage Stamp".

F1286	**F108**	(-) green	5·75	4·75

1946. For Internees' Mail via Red Cross. Nos. T1589/95 optd SCUTIT DE TAXA POSTALA SERVICIUL PRIZONIERILOR DE RAZBOI and cross.

F1809	**T171**	(-) on 50t. orange	1·50	1·60
F1810	**T171**	(-) on 1l. lilac	1·50	1·60
F1811	**T171**	(-) on 2l. brown	1·50	1·60
F1812	**T171**	(-) on 4l. blue	1·50	1·60
F1813	**T171**	(-) on 5l. violet	1·50	1·60
F1814	**T171**	(-) on 8l. green	1·50	1·60
F1815	**T171**	(-) on 10l. brown	1·50	1·60

F209 Queen Helen

1946. For Internees' Mail via Red Cross. Perf or imperf.

F1829A	**F209**	(-) green and red	70	75
F1830A	**F209**	(-) purple and red	70	75
F1831A	**F209**	(-) red and carmine	70	75

F227 King Michael

F228 Torch and Book

1947. King Michael's Fund. Perf or imperf. (a) Postage.

F1904	**F227**	(-) purple	1·50	1·90
F1905	**F228**	(-) blue	1·50	1·90
F1906	-	(-) brown	1·50	1·90

(b) Air. No. F1904 overprinted "PRIN AVION".

F1907A	**F227**	(-) purple	70	75

DESIGN: As Type 227 but horiz—No. F1906, Man writing and couple reading.

NEWSPAPER STAMPS

1919. Transylvania. Cluj Issue. No. N136 of Hungary optd as T 42.

N783	**N9**	2b. orange	2·50	2·10

1919. Transylvania. Oradea Issue. No. 136 of Hungary optd as T 43.

N859	2b. orange	50	70

OFFICIAL STAMPS

O71 Rumanian Eagle and National Flag

1929

O1115	**O71**	25b. orange	20	10
O1116	**O71**	50b. brown	20	10
O1117	**O71**	1l. violet	20	10
O1118	**O71**	2l. green	20	10
O1119	**O71**	3l. red	30	10
O1120	**O71**	4l. olive	50	15
O1221	**O71**	6l. blue	1·20	20
O1222	**O71**	10l. blue	35	25
O1223	**O71**	25l. red	1·00	60
O1224	**O71**	50l. violet	3·00	1·70

1930. Optd 8 IUNIE 1930.

O1150	25b. orange	50	20
O1151	50b. brown	50	20
O1152	1l. violet	50	20
O1153	2l. green	50	20
O1159	3l. red	50	20
O1154	4l. olive	75	20
O1155	6l. blue	85	40
O1161	10l. blue	1·60	30
O1166	25l. red	50	30
O1157	50l. violet	10·50	3·75

O80

1931

O1243	**O80**	25b. black	20	10
O1195	**O80**	1l. purple	25	25
O1196	**O80**	2l. green	55	40
O1197	**O80**	3l. red	60	40
O1247	**O80**	6l. red	1·90	75

PARCEL POST STAMPS

1895. As Type D 12 but inscr at top "TAXA DE FACTAGIU".

P353	25b. brown	8·25	1·00
P479	25b. red	6·25	2·10

1928. Surch FACTAJ 5 LEI.

P1078	**46**	5l. on 10b. green	2·10	85

POSTAGE DUE STAMPS

A. Ordinary Postage Due Stamps

D12

1881

D152	**D12**	2b. brown	5·25	4·25
D153	**D12**	5b. brown	26·00	6·25
D200	**D12**	10b. brown	10·50	1·00
D201	**D12**	30b. brown	10·50	1·00
D156	**D12**	50b. brown	21·00	7·25
D157	**D12**	60b. brown	26·00	10·50

1887

D448	2b. green	75	20
D449	5b. green	50	20
D450	10b. green	50	20
D451	30b. green	50	20
D371	50b. green	1·90	50
D458	60b. green	5·25	1·40

D38

1911

D617	**D38**	2b. blue on yellow	50	10

D618	**D38**	5b. blue on yellow	50	10
D619	**D38**	10b. blue on yellow	50	10
D604	**D38**	15b. blue on yellow	40	10
D621	**D38**	20b. blue on yellow	50	10
D622	**D38**	30b. blue on yellow	1·00	20
D623	**D38**	50b. blue on yellow	1·60	20
D624	**D38**	60b. blue on yellow	1·80	50
D609	**D38**	2l. blue on yellow	2·10	85

1918. Optd TAXA DE PLATA.

D675	**37**	5b. green	3·00	1·00
D676	**37**	10b. red	3·00	1·00

1918. Re-issue of Type D 38. On greenish or white paper.

D1001	**D38**	5b. black	20	10
D722	**D38**	10b. black	20	10
D995	**D38**	20b. black	20	10
D735	**D38**	30b. black	75	30
D736	**D38**	50b. black	85	85
D998	**D38**	60b. black	20	10
D1007	**D38**	1l. black	40	20
D1010	**D38**	2l. black	75	30
D991	**D38**	3l. black	20	10
D992	**D38**	6l. black	50	10
D1547	**D38**	50l. black	50	20
D1548	**D38**	100l. black	70	30

1919. Transylvania. Cluj Issue. No. D190 etc of Hungary optd as T 42.

D786	**D9**	1b. red and green	£275	£275
D787	**D9**	2b. red and green	55	55
D788	**D9**	5b. red and green	75·00	75·00
D789	**D9**	10b. red and green	30	30
D790	**D9**	15b. red and green	12·50	12·50
D791	**D9**	20b. red and green	25	25
D792	**D9**	30b. red and green	19·00	19·00
D793	**D9**	50b. red and green	13·00	13·00

1919. Transylvania. Oradea Issue. No. D190, etc of Hungary optd as T 43.

D861	1b. red and green	26·00	26·00
D862	2b. red and green	20	20
D863	5b. red and green	5·75	5·75
D864	6b. red and green	3·75	3·75
D865	10b. red and green	30	30
D866	12b. red and green	80	80
D867	15b. red and green	80	80
D868	20b. red and green	20	20
D869	30b. red and green	85	85

1930. Optd 8 IUNIE 1930.

D1168	**D38**	1l. black	40	20
D1169	**D38**	2l. black	40	20
D1170	**D38**	3l. black	50	40
D1171	**D38**	6l. black	1·60	1·00

D98

1932

D1249	**D98**	1l. black	10	10
D1250	**D98**	2l. black	10	10
D1251	**D98**	3l. black	20	10
D1252	**D98**	6l. black	20	10
D1835	**D98**	20l. black	20	10
D1839	**D98**	50l. black	20	15
D1840	**D98**	80l. black	40	20
D1841	**D98**	100l. black	60	30
D1842	**D98**	200l. black	95	65
D1843	**D98**	500l. black	1·50	1·00
D1844	**D98**	5000l. black	2·40	1·60

D233

1947. Type D 233 (without opts) perforated down centre.

D1919	2l. red	50	
D1920	4l. blue	95	
D1921	5l. black	1·50	
D1922	10l. brown	2·40	

The left half of Nos. D1919/22, showing Crown, served as a receipt and was stuck in the postman's book and so does not come postally used.

Prices for Nos. D1919/22 are for unused horizontal pairs.

1948. Nos. D1919/22, optd as in Type D 233.

D1944	2l. red	40	20
D1945	4l. blue	60	30
D1946	5l. black	95	65
D1947	10l. brown	1·90	85

Prices for Nos. D1944 to D4055 are for unused horizontal pairs.

D276 Badge and Postwoman

1950

D2066	**D 276**	2l. red	1·50	1·50
D2067	**D 276**	4l. blue	1·50	1·50
D2068	**D 276**	5l. green	2·40	2·40
D2069	**D 276**	10l. brown	3·00	3·00

1952. Currency revalued. Nos. D2066/9 surch 4 Bani on each half.

D2221	4b. on 2l. red	95	90
D2222	10b. on 4l. blue	95	90
D2223	20b. on 5l. green	2·40	2·20
D2224	50b. on 10l. brown	3·00	2·75

D420 G.P.O., Bucharest and Posthorn

1957

D2507	**D 420**	3b. black	20	10
D2508	**D 420**	5b. orange	20	10
D2509	**D 420**	10b. purple	20	10
D2510	**D 420**	20b. red	20	10
D2511	**D 420**	40b. green	40	20
D2512	**D 420**	1l. blue	95	30

D614

1967

D3436	**D 614**	3b. green	20	10
D3437	**D 614**	5b. blue	20	10
D3438	**D 614**	10b. mauve	20	10
D3439	**D 614**	20b. red	20	10
D3440	**D 614**	40b. brown	70	30
D3441	**D 614**	1l. violet	2·40	45

D766 Postal Emblems and Postman

1974

D4050	**D 766**	5b. blue	20	20
D4051	**D 766**	10b. green	20	20
D4052	-	20b. red	20	20
D4053	-	40b. violet	50	20
D4054	-	50b. brown	50	20
D4055	-	1l. orange	1·00	20

DESIGNS: 20b., 40b. Dove with letter and Hermes with posthorn; 50b., 1l. G.P.O., Bucharest and emblem with mail van.

Prices for Nos. D4050/55 are for unused horizontal pairs.

1982. As Type D 766.

D4761		25b. violet	25	10
D4762	**D 766**	50b. yellow	35	10
D4763	-	1l. red	60	10
D4764	-	2l. green	1·20	15
D4765	**D 766**	3l. brown	1·80	15
D4766	-	4l. blue	3·00	20

DESIGNS: 25b., 1l. Dove with letter and Hermes with posthorn; 2, 4l. G.P.O., Bucharest and emblem with mail van.

D1111

1992

D5417	**D 1111**	4l. red	1·00	35
D5418	**D 1111**	8l. blue	1·30	60

D1163

1994

D5586	**D 1163**	10l. brown	65	50
D5587	**D 1163**	45l. orange	65	50

1999. Nos. D4762/4 and D4766 surch.

D6018	50l. on 50b. yellow	25	20
D6019	50l. on 1l. red	25	20
D6020	100l. on 2l. green	25	20
D6021	700l. on 1l. red	25	20
D6022	1100l. on 4l. blue	25	20

2001. Nos. D5417 and D5587 surch on both stamps in the pair.

D6173	500l. on 4l. red	10	10
D6174	1000l. on 4l. red	25	20
D6175	2000l. on 45l. orange	45	35

B. Postal Tax Due Stamps

1915. Optd TIMBRU DE AJUTOR.

TD643	**D38**	5b. blue on yellow	65	30
TD644	**D38**	10b. blue on yellow	85	50

TD42

1917. Green or white paper.

TD655	**TD42**	5b. brown	75	30
TD738	**TD42**	5b. red	1·00	50
TD654	**TD42**	10b. red	30	30
TD741	**TD42**	10b. brown	1·00	50

1918. Optd TAXA DE PLATA.

TD680	**T40**	5b. black	50	30
TD681	**T40**	10b. brown	50	30

1922. As Type TD 42 but inscr "ASSISTENTA SOCIALA". On green or white paper.

TD1028	10b. brown	20	20
TD1029	20b. brown	20	20
TD1030	25b. brown	30	30
TD1031	50b. brown	30	30

1931. Aviation Fund. Optd TIMBRUL AVIATIEI.

TD1219	**D38**	1l. black	40	25
TD1220	**D38**	2l. black	40	25

TD106

1932

TD1278	**TD106**	3l. black	1·60	95

POSTAL TAX STAMPS

Soldiers' Families Fund

The following stamps were for compulsory use at certain times on inland mail to raise money for various funds. In some instances where the stamps were not applied the appropriate Postal Tax Postage Due stamps were applied.

Other denominations exist but these were purely for revenue purposes and were not applied to postal matter.

1915. Optd TIMBRU DE AJUTOR.

T638	**37**	5b. green	30	10
T639	**37**	10b. red	75	30

T41 The Queen Weaving

1916

T649	**T41**	5b. black	30	30
T710	**T41**	5b. green	1·00	40
T650	**T41**	10b. brown	75	50
T711	**T41**	10b. black	1·00	40

The 50b. and 1, 2, 5 and 50l. in similar designs were only used fiscally.

1918. Optd 1918.

T667		5b. black	1·00	50
T671	**37**	5b. green (No. T638)	47·00	47·00
T668		10b. brown	1·60	1·00
T672	**37**	10b. red (No. T639)	47·00	47·00

T47 "Charity"

1921. Social Welfare.

T978	**T47**	10b. green	20	10
T979	**T47**	25b. black	20	10

Aviation Fund

T91

1931

T1216	**T91**	50b. green	75	30
T1217	**T91**	1l. brown	1·50	30
T1218	**T91**	2l. blue	2·30	30

T98

1932

T1253	**T98**	50b. green	75	30
T1254	**T98**	1l. brown	1·10	30
T1255	**T98**	2l. blue	1·20	30

Stamps as Type **98** but inscr "FONDUL AVIATIEI" were only for fiscal use. Nos. T1253/5 could only be used fiscally after 1937.

T105

1932. Cultural Fund.

T1276	**T105**	2l. blue	1·50	65
T1277	**T105**	2l. brown	1·20	55

These were for compulsory use on postcards.

T121 "Aviation"

1936

T1340	**T121**	50b. green	50	40
T1341	**T121**	1l. brown	95	40
T1342	**T121**	2l. blue	95	40

Other stamps inscr "FONDUL AVIATIEI" were only for fiscal use.

T171 King Michael

1943

T1589	**T171**	50b. orange	40	40
T1590	**T171**	1l. lilac	40	40
T1591	**T171**	2l. brown	40	40
T1592	**T171**	4l. blue	40	40
T1593	**T171**	5l. violet	40	40
T1594	**T171**	8l. green	40	40
T1595	**T171**	10l. brown	40	40

1947. Fiscal stamps (22×18½ mm), perf vert through centre surch IOVR and value.

T1923	1l. on 2l. red	20	20
T1924	5l. on 1l. green	95	1·00

1948. Vert designs (approx 18½×22 mm). Inscr "I.O.V.R.".

T1948	1l. red	30	50
T1949	1l. violet	70	50
T1950	2l. blue	95	75
T1951	5l. yellow	4·75	3·25

SAVINGS BANK STAMPS

1919. Transylvania. Cluj Issue. No. B199 of Hungary optd as T 42.

B785	**B17**	10b. purple	50	75

1919. Transylvania. Oradea Issue. No. B199 of Hungary optd as T 43.

B861	10b. purple	50	70

Pt. 2

ROMANIAN OCCUPATION OF HUNGARY

100 filler = 1 korona.

A. BANAT BACSKA

The following stamps were issued by the Temesvar postal authorities between the period of the Serbian evacuation and the Romanian occupation. This area was later divided, the Western part going to Yugoslavia and the Eastern part going to Romania.

1919. Stamps of Hungary optd Banat Bacska 1919. (a) "Turul" Type.

1	**7**	50f. red on blue	16·00	16·00

(b) War Charity stamps of 1916.

2	**20**	10f.(+2f.) red	1·10	1·10
3	-	15f.(+2f.) violet	1·10	1·10
4	**22**	40f.(+2f.) red	1·10	1·10

(c) Harvesters and Parliament Types.

5	**18**	2f. brown	1·10	1·10
6	**18**	3f. purple	1·10	1·10
7	**18**	5f. green	1·10	1·10
8	**18**	6f. blue	1·10	1·10
9	**18**	15f. purple	1·10	1·10
10	**18**	35f. brown	16·00	16·00
11	**19**	50f. purple	16·00	16·00
12	**19**	75f. blue	1·10	1·10
13	**19**	80f. green	1·10	1·10
14	**19**	1k. red	1·10	1·10
15	**19**	2k. brown	1·10	1·10
16	**19**	2k. grey and violet	27·00	27·00
17	**19**	5k. light brown and brown	1·60	1·60
18	**19**	10k. mauve and brown	2·75	2·75

(d) Charles and Zita stamps.

19	**27**	10f. pink	1·10	1·10
20	**27**	20f. brown	1·10	1·10
21	**27**	25f. blue	1·10	1·10
22	**28**	40f. green	1·10	1·10
23	**28**	50f. violet	1·10	1·10

(e) Harvesters Type inscr "MAGYAR POSTA".

24	**18**	10f. red	16·00	16·00
25	**18**	20f. brown	16·00	16·00
26	**18**	25f. blue	18·00	18·00

(f) Various Types optd KOZTARSASAG.
(i) Harvesters and Parliament Types.

27		4f. grey	1·10	1·10
28		5f. green	1·10	1·10
29		6f. blue	1·10	1·10
30		10f. red	18·00	18·00
31		20f. brown	16·00	16·00
32		40f. green	1·10	1·10
33	**19**	1k. red	1·10	1·10
34	**19**	2k. brown	16·00	16·00
35	**19**	3k. grey and violet	16·00	16·00
36	**19**	5k. light brown and brown	16·00	16·00
37	**19**	10k. mauve and brown	16·00	16·00

(iii) Charles portrait stamps.

38	**27**	15f. purple	16·00	16·00
39	**27**	25f. blue	1·10	1·10

(g) Serbian Occupation of Temesvar stamps.

40	**18**	10f. on 2f. brown	1·10	1·10
41	**20**	45f. on 10f.(+2f.) red	1·10	1·10
42	**18**	1k.50 on 15f. purple	1·10	1·10

EXPRESS LETTER STAMP

1919. No. E245 of Hungary optd Banat Bacska 30 FILLER 1919.

E44	**E18**	30f. on 2f. green and red	1·10	1·10

NEWSPAPER STAMP

1919. No. N136 of Hungary optd Banat Bacska 1919.

N43	**N9**	(2f.) orange	1·10	1·10

POSTAGE DUE STAMPS

1919. Nos. D191 etc optd as above.

D46	**D9**	2f. red and green	1·10	1·10
D47	**D9**	10f. red and green	1·10	1·10
D48	**D9**	15f. red and green	16·00	16·00
D49	**D9**	20f. red and green	1·10	1·10
D50	**D9**	30f. red and green	16·00	16·00
D51	**D9**	50f. black and green	18·00	18·00

SAVINGS BANK STAMP

1919. No. B199 of Hungary surch Banat Bacska 50 FILLER 1919.

B45	**B17**	50f. on 10f. purple	1·10	1·10

B. DEBRECEN

This area was later returned to Hungary.

(1)

1919. Stamps of Hungary optd with T1 or surch in addition. (a) "Turul" Type.

1	**7**	2f. yellow	16·00	16·00
2	**7**	3f. orange	27·00	27·00
3	**7**	6f. brown	4·25	4·25

(b) War Charity stamps of 1915.

4		2f.+2f. yellow (No. 171)	27·00	27·00
5		3f.+2f. orange (No. 172)	27·00	27·00

(c) War Charity stamps of 1916.

6	**20**	10f.(+2f.) red	30	30
7	-	15f.(+2f.) lilac	1·60	1·60
8	**22**	40f.(+2f.) red	1·10	1·10

(d) Harvesters and Parliament Types.

9	**18**	2f. brown	20	20
10	**18**	3f. purple	20	20
11	**18**	5f. green	55	55
12	**18**	6f. blue	20	20
13	**18**	10f. red (No. 243)	43·00	43·00
14	**18**	15f. violet (No. 244)	22·00	22·00
15	**18**	15f. purple	7·00	7·00
16	**18**	20f. brown	16·00	16·00
17	**18**	25f. blue	95	95
18	**18**	35f. brown	11·00	11·00
19	**18**	35f. on 3f. purple	30	30
20	**18**	40f. green	75	75
21	**18**	45f. on 2f. brown	30	30
22	**19**	50f. purple	85	85
23	**19**	75f. blue	30	30
24	**19**	80f. green	55	55
25	**19**	1k. red	55	55
26	**19**	2k. brown	30	30
27	**19**	3k. grey and violet	7·00	7·00
28	**19**	3k. on 75f. blue	2·75	2·75
29	**19**	5k. light brown and brown	2·75	2·75
30	**19**	5k. on 75f. blue	95	95
31	**19**	10k. mauve and brown	22·00	22·00
32	**19**	10k. on 80f. green	1·80	1·80

(e) Charles and Zita stamps.

33	**27**	10f. pink	6·50	6·50
34	**27**	15f. purple	3·75	3·75
35	**27**	20f. brown	3·25	3·25
36	**27**	25f. blue	55	55
37	**28**	40f. green	60·00	60·00
38	**28**	50f. purple	30	30

(f) Harvesters and Parliament Types inscr "MAGAR POSTA".

39	**18**	5f. green	20	20
40	**18**	6f. blue	1·60	1·60
41	**18**	10f. red	20	20
42	**18**	20f. brown	20	20
43	**18**	25f. blue	20	20
44	**18**	45f. orange	1·80	1·80
45	**19**	5k. brown	£1100	

(g) Various Types optd KOZTARSASAG.
(i) Harvesters and Parliament Types.

46	**18**	2f. brown	30	30
47	**18**	3f. purple	8·50	8·50
48	**18**	4f. grey	20	20
49	**18**	5f. green	20	20
50	**18**	10f. red	2·75	2·75
51	**18**	20f. brown	55	55
52	**18**	40f. green	30	30
53	**19**	1k. red	30	30
54	**19**	2k. brown	7·50	7·50
55	**19**	3k. grey and violet	1·80	1·80
56	**19**	5k. light brown and brown	80·00	80·00

(ii) War Charity stamps of 1916.

57	**20**	10f.(+2f.) red	2·75	2·75
58	-	15f.(+2f.) lilac	18·00	18·00
59	**22**	40f.(+2f.) red	2·75	2·75

(iii) Charles and Zita stamps.

60	**27**	10f. pink	2·20	2·20
61	**27**	15f. purple	3·75	3·75
62	**27**	20f. brown	3·25	3·25
63	**27**	25f. blue	55	55
64	**28**	50f. purple	30	30

2

4

1920. Types 2 and 4 and similar design, optd with inscr as T 1 but in circle.

65A	**2**	2f. brown	20	20
66A	**2**	3f. brown	20	20
67A	**2**	4f. violet	20	20
68A	**2**	5f. green	20	20
69A	**2**	6f. grey	20	20
70A	**2**	10f. red	20	20
71A	**2**	15f. violet	20	20
72A	**2**	20f. brown	20	20
73A	-	25f. blue	20	20
74A	-	30f. brown	20	20
75A	-	35f. purple	20	20
76A	-	40f. green	55	55
77A	-	45f. red	20	20
78A	-	50f. mauve	20	20
79A	-	60f. green	20	20
80A	-	75f. blue	20	20
81A	**4**	80f. green	20	20
82A	**4**	1k. red	30	30
83B	**4**	1k.20 orange	8·00	8·00
84A	**4**	2k. brown	55	55
85A	**4**	3k. brown	65	65
86A	**4**	5k. brown	65	65
87A	**4**	10k. purple	75	75

DESIGN: Nos. 73/80, Horseman using lasso.

5

1920. War Charity. Type 5 with circular opt, and "Segely belyeg" at top.

88	**5**	20f. green	1·10	1·10
89	**5**	20f. green on blue	30	30
90	**5**	50f. brown	1·10	1·10
91	**5**	50f. brown on mauve	55	55
92	**5**	1k. green	1·10	1·10
93	**5**	1k. green on green	55	55
94	**5**	2k. green	55	55

EXPRESS LETTER STAMP

1919. No. E245 of Hungary optd with T 1.

E66	**E18**	2f. green and red	45	45

NEWSPAPER STAMP

1919. No. N136 of Hungary optd with T 1.

N65	**N9**	2f. orange	20	20

POSTAGE DUE STAMPS

1919. (a) Nos. D190 etc of Hungary optd with T 1.

D68	**D9**	1f. red and green	6·50	6·50
D69	**D9**	2f. red and green	20	20
D70	**D9**	5f. red and green	80·00	80·00
D71	**D9**	6f. red and green	8·00	8·00
D72	**D9**	10f. red and green	20	20
D73	**D9**	12f. red and green	32·00	32·00
D74	**D9**	15f. red and green	1·60	1·60
D75	**D9**	20f. red and green	1·60	1·60
D76	**D9**	30f. red and green	1·60	1·60

(b) With KOZTARSASAG opt.

D77		2f. red and green	5·50	5·50
D78		3f. red and green	5·50	5·50
D79		10f. red and green	5·50	5·50
D80		20f. red and green	5·50	5·50
D81		40f. red and green	5·50	5·50
D82		50f. red and green	5·50	5·50

D6

1920

D95	**D6**	5f. green	55	55
D96	**D6**	10f. green	55	55
D97	**D6**	20f. green	55	55
D98	**D6**	30f. green	55	55
D99	**D6**	40f. green	55	55

SAVINGS BANK STAMP

1919. No. B199 of Hungary optd with T 1.

B67	**B17**	10f. purple	13·00	13·00

C. TEMESVAR

After being occupied by Serbia this area was then occupied by Romania. It later became part of Romania and was renamed Timisoara.

1919. Stamps of Hungary surch. (a) Harvesters Type.

6	**18**	30 on 2f. brown	30	30
7	**18**	1k. on 4f. grey (optd **KOZTARSASAG**)	30	30
8	**18**	150 on 3f. purple	30	30
9	**18**	150 on 5f. green	30	30

(b) Express Letter Stamp.

10	**E18**	3 KORONA on 2f. green and red	20	20

1919. Charity stamp of Hungary surch PORTO 40.

D11	40 on 15+(2f.) lilac (No. 265)	45	45

POSTAGE DUE STAMPS

(D 8)

1919. Postage Due stamps of Hungary surch with Type D 8.

D12	**D9**	60 on 2f. red and green	9·75	9·75
D13	**D9**	60 on 10f. red and green	85	85

Pt. 16

ROMANIAN POST OFFICES IN THE TURKISH EMPIRE

Romanian P.O.s in the Turkish Empire including Constantinople. Now closed.

I. General Issues
40 paras = 1 piastre.

II. Constantinople
100 bani = 1 leu.

I. GENERAL ISSUES

1896. Stamps of Romania of 1893 surch in "PARAS".

9	10pa. on 5b. blue (No. 319)	20·00	20·00
10	20pa. on 10b. green (No. 320)	20·00	20·00
11	1pi. on 25b. mauve (No. 322)	20·00	20·00

II. CONSTANTINOPLE

(1)

1919. Stamps of Romania of 1893–1908 optd with T 1.

1	**37**	5b. green	29·00	29·00
2	**37**	10b. red	20·00	20·00
3	**37**	15b. brown	20·00	20·00
4	-	25b. blue (No. 701)	35·00	35·00
14	-	40b. brown (No. 703)	29·00	29·00

1919. 1916 Postal Tax stamp of Romania optd with T 1.

16	**T41**	5b. green	29·00	29·00

Pt. 1

ROSS DEPENDENCY

A dependency of New Zealand in the Antarctic on the Ross Sea.

The post office closed on 30 September 1987, but re-opened in November 1994.

1957. 12 pence = 1 shilling; 20 shillings = 1 pound.
1967. 100 cents = 1 dollar.

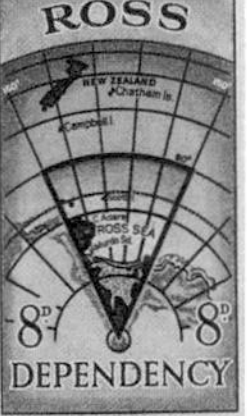

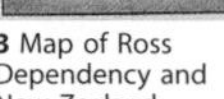

3 Map of Ross Dependency and New Zealand

4 Queen Elizabeth II

1957

1	-	3d. blue	1·00	60
2	-	4d. red	1·00	60
3	**3**	8d. red and blue	1·00	60
4	**4**	1s.6d. purple	1·00	60

DESIGNS—HORIZ (As Type **3**): 3d. H.M.S. "Erebus"; 4d. Shackleton and Scott.

5 H.M.S. "Erebus"

1967. Nos. 1-4 with values inscr in decimal currency as T 5.

5	**5**	2c. blue	9·00	7·50
6	-	3c. red	3·00	4·75
7	**3**	7c. red and blue	3·00	6·00
8	**4**	15c. purple	2·75	9·00

6 South Polar Skua

7 Scott Base

1972

9a	6	3c. black, grey and blue	70	1·60
10a	-	4c. black, blue and violet	15	1·60
11a	-	5c. black, grey and lilac	15	1·60
12a	-	8c. black, grey and brown	15	1·60
13a	7	10c. black, green and grey	15	1·60
14a	-	18c. black, violet and light violet	15	1·60

DESIGNS—As Type **6**: 4c. Lockheed Hercules airplane at Williams Field; 5c. Shackleton's Hut; 8c. Supply ship H.M.N.Z.S. "Endeavour". As Type **7**: 18c. Tabular ice flow.

8 Adelie Penguins and South Polar Skua

1982. Multicoloured.. Multicoloured..

15	5c. Type **8**	1·25	1·60
16	10c. Tracked vehicles	20	1·50
17	20c. Scott Base	20	75
18	30c. Field party	20	40
19	40c. Vanda Station	20	40
20	50c. Scott's hut, Cape Evans	20	40

9 South Polar Skua

1994. Wildlife. Multicoloured.

21	5c. Type **9**	40	40
22	10c. Snow petrel chick	50	50
23	20c. Black-browed albatross	60	60
24	40c. Emperor penguins	2·50	1·75
25	45c. As 40c.	80	80
26	50c. Bearded penguins ("Chin-strap Penguins")	80	80
27	70c. Adelie penguin	90	90
28	80c. Elephant seals	90	90
29	$1 Leopard seal	1·00	1·00
30	$2 Weddell seal	1·50	1·75
31	$3 Crabeater seal pup	2·25	2·75

10 Capt. James Cook with H.M.S. "Resolution" and H.M.S. "Adventure"

1995. Antarctic Explorers. Multicoloured.

32	40c. Type **10**	1·50	1·50
33	80c. James Clark Ross with H.M.S. "Erebus" and H.M.S. "Terror"	1·75	1·75
34	$1 Roald Amundsen and "Fram"	2·00	2·00
35	$1.20 Robert Scott with "Terra Nova"	2·50	2·50
36	$1.50 Ernest Shackleton with "Endurance"	2·75	2·75
37	$1.80 Richard Byrd with Ford 4-AT-B Trimotor "Floyd Bennett" (airplane)	2·75	2·75

11 Inside Ice Cave

1996. Antarctic Landscapes. Multicoloured.

38	40c. Type **11**	60	45
39	80c. Base of glacier	1·00	80
40	$1 Glacier ice fall	1·25	90
41	$1.20 Climbers on crater rim (horiz)	1·50	1·10
42	$1.50 Pressure ridges (horiz)	1·75	2·00
43	$1.80 Fumarole ice tower (horiz)	1·90	2·25

12 Snow Petrel

1997. Antarctic Seabirds. Multicoloured. (a) With "WWF" panda emblem.

44	40c. Type **12**	80	60
45	80c. Pintado petrel ("Cape Petrel")	1·25	90
46	$1.20 Antarctic fulmar	1·60	1·25
47	$1.50 Antarctic petrel	1·60	1·25

(b) Without "WWF" panda emblem.

48	40c. Type **12**	1·50	1·25
49	80c. Pintado petrel ("Cape Petrel")	1·75	1·75
50	$1 Dove prion ("Antarctic Prion")	2·00	1·75
51	$1.20 Antarctic fulmar	2·25	2·00
52	$1.50 Antarctic petrel	2·25	2·00
53	$1.80 Antarctic tern	2·25	2·00

Nos. 48/53 were printed together, se-tenant, with the backgrounds forming a composite design.

13 Sculptured Sea Ice

1997. Ice Formation. Multicoloured.

54	40c. Type **13**	60	40
55	80c. Glacial tongue	80	70
56	$1 Stranded tabular iceberg	1·00	90
57	$1.20 Autumn at Cape Evans	1·10	1·00
58	$1.50 Sea ice in summer thaw	1·40	1·25
59	$1.80 Sunset at tubular icebergs	1·50	1·50

14 Sea Smoke, McMurdo Sound

1999. Night Skies. Multicoloured.

60	40c. Type **14**	1·00	65
61	80c. Alpenglow, Mount Erebus	1·50	90
62	$1.10 Sunset, Black Island	1·60	1·25
63	$1.20 Pressure ridges, Ross Sea	1·90	1·40
64	$1.50 Evening light, Ross Island	2·25	1·60
65	$1.80 Mother of pearl clouds, Ross Island	2·75	1·75

15 R.N.Z.A.F. C130 Hercules

2000. Antarctic Transport. Multicoloured.

66	40c. Type **15**	1·50	60
67	80c. Hagglunds BV206 All Terrain carrier	1·60	85
68	$1.10 Tracked 4×4 motorbike	1·90	1·25
69	$1.20 ASV track truck	1·90	1·25
70	$1.50 Squirrel helicopter	2·25	1·40
71	$1.80 Elan skidoo	2·25	1·40

2001. Penguins. As T 604 of New Zealand. Multicoloured.

72	40c. Two emperor penguins	75	60
73	80c. Two adelie penguins	1·10	1·00
74	90c. Emperor penguin leaving water	1·25	1·00
75	$1.30 Adelie penguin in water	1·60	1·40
76	$1.50 Group of emperor penguins	1·90	1·50
77	$2 Group of adelie penguins	2·25	1·90

16 British Explorers by Sledge

2002. Antarctic Discovery Expedition, 1901–1904. Each black, grey and stone.

78	40c. Type **16**	1·10	70
79	80c. H.M.S. *Discovery*, at anchor	2·00	1·00
80	90c. H.M.S. *Discovery*, trapped in ice	2·00	1·10
81	$1.30 Sledges and tents on the ice	2·25	1·60
82	$1.50 Crew of H.M.S. *Discovery*	2·75	1·75
83	$2 Scott's base at Hut Point	3·00	1·90

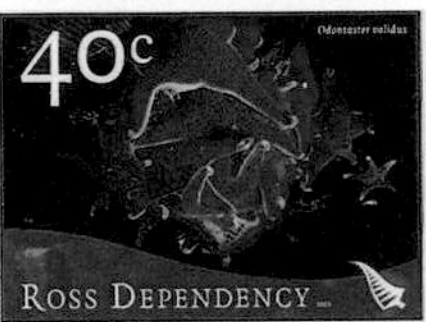

17 *Odontaster validus* (red seastar)

2003. Marine Life. Multicoloured.

84	40c. Type **17**	1·00	65
85	90c. *Beroe cucumis* (comb jelly)	2·00	1·00
86	$1.30 *Macroptychaster accrescens* (giant seastar)	2·50	1·40
87	$1.50 *Sterechinus neumayeri* (sea urchin)	2·75	1·50
88	$2 *Perkinsiana littoralis* (fan worm)	3·00	2·00

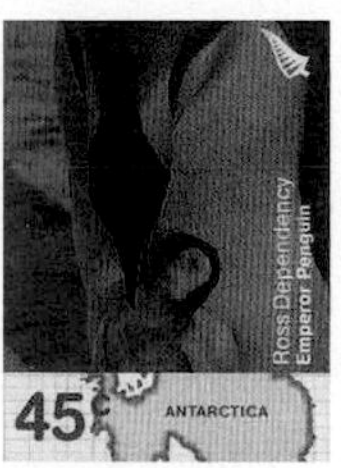

18 Penguin and Chick

2004. Emperor Penguins. Multicoloured.

89	45c. Type **18**	1·40	75
90	90c. Penguin chick	2·50	1·40
91	$1.35 Penguin feeding chick	2·75	1·75
92	$1.50 Two penguins and chick	2·75	2·25
93	$2 Group of penguins	3·00	2·75

19 Dry Valleys (Craig Potton)

2005. Photographs of Antarctica. Multicoloured.

94	45c. Type **19**	1·25	70
95	90c. Emperor penguins (Andris Apse)	2·00	1·50
96	$1.35 Antarctic fur seal (Mark Mitchell)	2·25	2·25
97	$1.50 Hut of Captain Robert F Scott (Colin Monteath)	3·00	2·75
98	$2 Antarctic minke whale (Kim Westerskov)	3·25	3·00

20 Biologist, 1957–8

2006. 50th Anniv of New Zealand Antarctic Programme. Multicoloured.

99	45c. Type **20**	1·25	80
100	90c. Hydrologists, 1979–80	2·25	1·75
101	$1.35 Geologist, 1984–5	2·75	2·75
102	$1.50 Meteorologists, 1994–5	3·00	3·25
103	$2 Marine biologist, 2004–5	3·50	4·00

21 Beaver Aircraft

2007. 50th Anniv of Commonwealth Trans-Antarctic Expedition. Each blue and black.

104	50c. Type **21**	1·25	85
105	$1 Harry Ayres and sledge	1·75	1·25
106	$1.50 Sledge dogs	2·75	2·75
107	$2 TE20 Ferguson tractor	3·00	3·25
108	$2.50 HMNZS *Endeavour*	3·50	4·00
MS109	120×80 mm. Nos. 107/8	7·50	7·50

22 Departure of *Nimrod* from Lyttelton

2008. Centenary of British Antarctic Expedition, 1907–1909. Multicoloured.

110	50c. Type **22**	1·10	75
111	$1 Expedition hut, Cape Royds	1·75	1·40
112	$1.50 Arrol-Johnston car (first vehicle on Antarctica)	2·50	2·50
113	$2 Professor Edgeworth David, Douglas Mawson and Alistair Mackay, first to reach South Magnetic Pole, 16 January 1909	3·00	3·25
114	$2.50 Setting out for first ascent of Mount Erebus, 1908	3·50	4·00

23 Map of Antarctica

2009. 50th Anniv of the Antarctic Treaty. Each showing silhouettes in Antarctic landscape. Multicoloured.

115	50c. Type **23**	90	90
116	$1 Penguins ('Antarctica shall be used for peaceful purposes only')	1·75	1·75
117	$1.80 Scientist ('Freedom of scientific investigation')	3·00	3·00
118	$2.30 Flags ('International co-operation in scientific investigation')	3·25	3·25
119	$2.80 Seal ('Preservation and conservation of living resources')	3·50	3·50

24 Sperm Whale

2010. Whales of the Southern Ocean. Multicoloured.

120	60c. Type **24**	1·10	1·10
121	$1.20 Minke whale	2·25	2·25
122	$1.90 Sei whale	3·25	3·25
123	$2.40 Killer whale	3·50	3·50
124	$2.90 Humpback whale	3·75	3·75
MS125	160×85 mm. Nos. 120/4	14·00	14·00

Pt. 6

ROUAD ISLAND (ARWAD)

An island in the E. Mediterranean off the coast of Syria. A French P.O. was established there during 1916.

25 centimes = 1 piastre.

1916. "Blanc" and "Mouchon" key-types inscr "LEVANT" and optd ILE ROUAD (vert).

1	A	5c. green	£450	£225
2	B	10c. red	£450	£225
3	B	1pi. on 25c. blue	£450	£225

1916. "Blanc" "Mouchon" and "Merson" key-types inscr "LEVANT" and optd ILE ROUAD horiz.

4	A	1c. grey	30	5·25
5	A	2c. purple	35	6·50
6	A	3c. red	70	6·25
7	A	5c. green	1·50	5·00
8	B	10c. red	2·30	8·50
9	B	15c. red	1·70	8·00
10	B	20c. brown	3·75	9·00
11	B	1p. on 25c. blue	5·00	9·50
12	B	30c. lilac	3·00	11·00
13	C	40c. red and blue	4·75	16·00
14	C	2p. on 50c. brown & lav	6·75	17·00
15	C	4p. on 1f. red and yellow	12·00	36·00
16	C	30p. on 5f. blue and yellow	48·00	75·00

Pt. 4

RUANDA-URUNDI

Part of German E. Africa, including Ruanda and Urundi, occupied by Belgian forces during the war of 1914–18 and a Trust Territory administered by Belgium until 1 July 1962. The territory then became two separate independent states, named Rwanda and Burundi.

100 centimes = 1 franc.

1916. Nos. 70/77 of Belgian Congo optd. (a) RUANDA.

1	32	5c. black and green	65·00	
2	33	10c. black and red	55·00	
3	13	15c. black and green	£100	
4	34	25c. black and blue	60·00	
5	14	40c. black and red	65·00	
6	-	50c. black and red	70·00	
7	-	1f. black and brown	£225	
7a	-	5f. black and orange	£3000	

(b) URUNDI.

8	32	5c. black and green	65·00	
9	33	10c. black and red	60·00	
10	13	15c. black and green	£100	
11	34	25c. black and blue	65·00	
12	14	40c. black and red	65·00	
13	-	50c. black and red	70·00	
14	-	1f. black and brown	£225	
14a	-	5f. black and orange	£3000	

1916. Stamps of Belgian Congo of 1915 optd EST AFRICAIN ALLEMAND OCCUPATION BELGE. DUITSCH OOST AFRIKA BELGISCHE BEZETTING.

15	32	5c. black and green	1·70	3·00
16	33	10c. black and red	2·00	3·75
17	13	15c. black and green	65	2·50
18	34	25c. black and blue	4·75	4·00
19	14	40c. black and lake	11·00	12·00
20	-	50c. black and lake	10·00	10·50
21	-	1f. black and olive	2·00	3·25
22	-	5f. black and orange	3·75	8·00

1918. Belgian Congo Red Cross stamps of 1918 optd A. O.

23	32	5c.+10c. blue and green	35	6·75
24	33	10c.+15c. blue and red	1·00	6·75
25	13	15c.+20c. blue and green	1·20	6·75
26	34	25c.+25c. blue	2·30	6·50
27	14	40c.+40c. blue and lake	1·20	7·50
28	-	50c.+50c. blue and lake	1·80	21·00
29	-	1f.+1f. blue and olive	3·00	12·50
30	-	5f.+5f. blue and orange	25·00	34·00
31	-	10f.+10f. blue and green	60·00	£120

1922. Stamps of 1916 surch.

32		5c. on 50c. black and lake	3·75	21·00
33	32	10c. on 5c. black and green	1·70	3·50
34a	14	25c. on 40c. black and lake	7·25	8·00
35	33	30c. on 10c. black and red	40	7·00
36	34	50c. on 25c. black and blue	3·50	6·75

1924. Belgian Congo stamps of 1923 optd RUANDA URUNDI.

37	A	5c. yellow	1·20	1·80
38	B	10c. green	65	1·90
39	C	15c. brown	35	85
40	D	20c. green	35	2·30
41	E	20c. green	40	1·40
42	F	25c. brown	50	15
43	46	30c. pink	60	1·40
44	46	30c. green	35	2·30
45	D	40c. purple	50	2·75
46	G	50c. blue	35	35
47	G	50c. orange	35	2·75
48	E	75c. orange	45	30
49	E	75c. blue	55	30
50	H	1f. brown	35	1·70
51	H	1f. blue	1·40	1·70
52	I	3f. brown	2·50	9·50
53	J	5f. grey	4·00	10·00
54	K	10f. black	14·50	34·00

1925. Stamp of Belgian Congo optd RUANDA-URUNDI. Inscriptions in French or in Flemish.

61	55	25c.+25c. black and red	50	7·00

1925. Native cattle type of Belgian Congo optd RUANDA-URUNDI.

62	56	45c. purple	85	7·50
63	56	60c. red	55	85

1927. Belgian Congo stamps of 1923 optd RUANDA URUNDI in two lines, wide apart.

64	B	10c. green	10	5·75
65	C	15c. brown	3·50	9·50
66	46	35c. green	2·50	3·75
67	46	75c. red	1·50	4·00
68	H	1f. red	3·00	3·75
69	D	1f.25 blue	5·50	8·25
70	D	1f.50 blue	1·30	4·75
71	D	1f.75 blue	3·00	3·00

1927. No. 144 of Belgian Congo optd RUANDA URUNDI.

72		1f.75 on 1f.50 blue	65	6·50

1930. Native Fund stamps of Belgian Congo (Nos. 160/8), optd RUANDA URUNDI.

73		10c.+5c. red	65	7·25
74		20c.+10c. brown	1·70	8·50
75		35c.+15c. green	2·75	10·50
76		60c.+30c. purple	2·30	9·50
77		1f.+50c. red	2·30	13·50
78		1f.75+75c. blue	3·75	17·00
79		3f.50+1f.50 lake	8·75	29·00
80		5f.+2f.50 brown	5·25	24·00
81		10f.+5f. black	5·00	28·00

1931. Nos. 68 and 71 surch.

82	H	1f.25 on 1f. red	6·75	1·20
83	D	2f. on 1f.75 blue	4·00	2·25

10 Mountain Scenery

1931

84	-	5c. red	1·40	3·00
85	10	10c. grey	75	2·30
86	-	15c. red	80	5·00
87	-	25c. purple	1·00	4·00
88	-	40c. green	2·75	6·25
89	-	50c. violet	30	1·80
90	-	60c. red	45	7·00
91	-	75c. black	1·90	5·50
92	-	1f. red	1·90	1·60
93	-	1f.25 brown	55	60
94	-	1f.50 purple	1·90	3·75
95	-	2f. blue	2·00	7·00
96	-	2f.50 blue	2·30	2·00
97	-	3f.25 purple	75	5·00
98	-	4f. red	2·75	3·00
99	-	5f. grey	4·00	3·00
100	-	10f. purple	4·25	8·50
101	-	20f. brown	10·00	19·00

DESIGNS—HORIZ: 15c. Warrior; 25c. Chieftain's kraal; 50c. Head of African buffalo; 1f. Wives of Urundi chiefs; 1f.50, 2f. Wooden pot hewer; 2f.50, 3f.25, Workers making tissues from ficus bark; 4f. Hutu Potter. VERT: 5, 60c., Native porter; 40c. Two cowherds; 75c. Native greeting; 1f.25, Mother and child; 5f. Ruanda dancer; 10f. Warriors; 20f. Native prince of Urundi.

11 King Albert I

1934. King Albert Mourning Stamp.

102	11	1f.50 black	2·00	1·20

11a Queen Astrid and Children

1936. Charity. Queen Astrid Fund.

103	11a	1f.25+5c. brown	2·75	6·25
104	11a	1f.50+10c. red	1·60	7·50
105	11a	2f.50+25c. blue	1·40	9·50

1941. Stamps of Belgian Congo optd RUANDA URUNDI.

106	78	10c. grey	40·00	36·00
107	78	1f.75 orange	9·25	18·00
108	78	2f.75 blue	12·00	17·00

1941. Ruanda-Urundi stamps of 1931 surch.

109		5c. on 40c. green	11·00	26·00
110		60c. on 50c. violet	28·00	34·00
111		2f.50 on 1f.50 purple	5·50	13·50
112		3f.25 on 2f. blue	29·00	38·00

1941. Stamps of Belgian Congo optd RUANDA URUNDI and surch also.

113	-	5c. on 1f.50 black and brown (No. 222)	25	2·30
114	-	75c. on 90c. brown and red (No. 221)	4·50	9·75
115	78	2f.50 on 10f. red	5·25	8·25

14a "Belgium shall rise Again"

1942. War Relief.

116	14a	10f.+40f. red	7·75	19·00
117	14a	10f.+40f. blue	7·25	19·00

On No. 116 the French slogan is above the Flemish, on No. 117 vice versa.

1942. Nos. 107/8 of Ruanda-Urundi surch.

118	78	75c. on 1f.75 orange	18·00	26·00
119	78	2f.50 on 2f.75 blue	25·00	29·00

15a Head of Warrior

1942

120	A	5c. red	10	3·25
121	A	10c. green	35	1·30
122	A	15c. brown	65	2·50
123	A	20c. blue	35	3·50
124	A	25c. purple	90	1·00
125	A	30c. blue	1·50	2·00
126	A	50c. green	95	55
127	A	60c. brown	1·40	1·40
128	15a	75c. black and lilac	2·50	90
129	15a	1f. black and brown	2·50	1·20
130	15a	1f.25 black and red	2·50	1·90
131	B	1f.75 brown	4·50	3·50
132	B	2f. orange	4·25	3·00
133	B	2f.50 red	2·75	15
134	C	3f.50 green	1·70	75
135	C	5f. orange	2·30	85
136	C	6f. blue	2·50	40
137	C	7f. black	1·50	1·20
138	C	10f. brown	2·50	2·50
139	-	20f. black and brown	4·50	5·00
140	-	50f. black and red	11·50	8·25
141	-	100f. black and green	16·00	18·00

DESIGNS—As Type **15a** (various frames): A, Oil palms; C, Askari sentry; 20f. Head of zebra. 35×24 mm: B, Leopard. 29×34 mm: 50f. Askari sentry; 100f. Head of warrior.

1944. Red Cross Fund. Nos. 126, 130, 131 and 134 surch Au profit de la Croix Rouge Ten voordeele van het Roode Kruis (50c., 1f.75) or with Flemish and French reversed (others) and premium.

147		50c.+50f. green	4·25	16·00
148		1f.25+100f. black and red	5·25	20·00
149		1f.75+100f. brown	6·50	16·00
150		3f.50+100f. green	4·00	20·00

17 Seated Figure

1948. Native Carvings.

151	17	10c. orange	35	4·50
152	A	15c. blue	45	5·75
153	B	20c. blue	1·00	3·75
154	C	25c. red	50	50
155	D	40c. purple	1·10	3·25
156	17	50c. brown	1·50	10
157	A	70c. green	1·60	3·00
158	B	75c. purple	2·30	2·75
159	C	1f. purple and orange	1·00	65
160	D	1f.25 red and blue	2·00	2·30
161	E	1f.50 red and green	4·00	3·75
162	17	2f. red and vermilion	80	35
163	A	2f.50 green and brown	2·50	35
164	B	3f.50 green and blue	2·75	1·70
165	C	5f. red and bistre	1·50	35
166	D	6f. green and orange	2·50	45
167	E	10f. brown and violet	3·50	2·75
168	F	20f. brown and red	4·50	4·50
169	E	50f. black and brown	8·25	4·75
170	F	100f. black and red	13·00	8·25

DESIGNS: A, Seated figure (different); B, Kneeling figure; C, Double mask; D, Mask; E, Mask with tassels; F, Mask with horns.

1949. Surch.

171		3f. on 2f.50 (No. 163)	1·20	25
172		4f. on 6f. (No. 166)	2·50	1·40
173		6f.50 on 6f. (No. 166)	3·00	35

18a St. Francis Xavier

1953. 400th Death Anniv of St. Francis Xavier.

174	18a	1f.50 black and blue	1·50	1·90

19 "Dissotis"

1953. Flowers Multicoloured.

175	10c. Type **19**	15	1·30
176	15c. "Protea"	15	3·25
177	20c. "Vellozia"	15	75
178	25c. "Littonia"	75	2·75
179	40c. "Ipomoea"	75	2·75
180	50c. "Angraecum"	1·00	70
181	60c. "Euphorbia"	1·80	3·50
182	75c. "Ochna"	3·00	2·50
183	1f. "Hibiscus"	2·00	70
184	1f.25 "Protea"	4·75	6·25
185	1f.50 "Schizoglossum"	55	1·00
186	2f. "Ansellia"	3·00	2·50
187	3f. "Costus"	1·80	50
188	4f. "Nymphaea"	3·25	2·00
189	5f. "Thunbergia"	3·25	2·00
190	7f. "Gerbera"	1·10	1·30
191	8f. "Gloriosa"	3·50	2·50
192	10f. "Silene"	2·30	1·30
193	20f. "Aristolochia"	9·50	2·75

20 King Baudouin and Mountains

1955

194	20	1f.50 black and red	5·00	3·50
195	-	3f. black and green	5·00	2·50
196	-	4f.50 black and blue	5·00	1·20
197	-	6f.50 black and purple	5·50	90

DESIGNS: 3f. Forest; 4f.50, River; 6f.50, Grassland.

20a Mozart when a Child

1956. Birth Bicentenary of Mozart.

198	**20a**	4f.50+1f.50 violet	3·25	13·00
199	-	6f.50+2f.50 purple	5·75	26·00

DESIGN—52×36 mm: 6f.50, Queen Elizabeth and Mozart sonata.

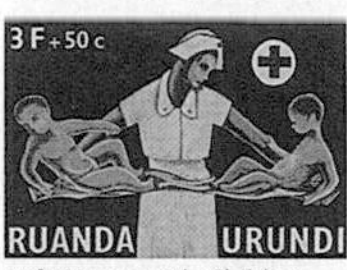

20b Nurse with Children

1957. Red Cross Fund.

200	**20b**	3f.+50c. blue	2·75	9·00
201	-	4f.50+50c. green	2·30	9·00
202	-	6f.50+50c. brown	2·00	10·50

DESIGNS: 4f.50, Doctor inoculating patient; 6f.50, Nurse in tropical kit bandaging patient.

21 Gorilla

1959. Fauna.

203	**21**	10c. black, red and brown	10	25
204	–	20c. black and green	10	20
205	–	40c. black, olive and mauve	35	1·60
206	–	50c. brown, yellow and green	65	1·90
207	–	1f. black, blue and brown	1·40	1·30
208	–	1f.50 black and orange	3·00	2·30
209	–	2f. black, brown and turquoise	1·80	1·30
210	–	3f. black, red and brown	2·75	2·50
211	–	5f. multicoloured	2·30	2·30
212	–	6f.50 brown, yellow and red	85	50
213	–	8f. black, mauve and blue	3·00	2·30
214	–	10f. multicoloured	2·75	2·00

DESIGNS—VERT: 10c., 1f. Type **21**: 40c., 2f. Eastern black and white colobus. HORIZ: 20c.1f.50, African buffaloes; 50c., 6f.50, Impala; 3, 8f. African elephants; 5, 10f. Eland and common zebras.

POSTAGE DUE STAMPS

1924. Postage Due stamps of Belgian Congo optd RUANDA URUNDI.

D55	**D54**	5c. brown	10	50
D56a	**D54**	10c. red	10	1·10
D57	**D54**	15c. violet	35	1·00
D58	**D54**	30c. green	35	4·00
D59a	**D54**	50c. blue	1·10	1·90
D60	**D54**	1f. grey	1·00	4·00

1943. Postage Due stamps of Belgian Congo optd RUANDA URUNDI.

D142	**D86**	10c. olive	80	6·75
D143	**D86**	20c. blue	15	5·50
D144	**D86**	50c. green	1·90	6·75
D145	**D86**	1f. brown	95	7·50
D146	**D86**	2f. orange	30	5·50

1959. Postage Due stamps of Belgian Congo optd RUANDA URUNDI.

D215	**D99**	10c. brown	1·70	7·25
D216	**D99**	20c. purple	1·60	3·00
D217	**D99**	50c. green	3·25	6·00
D218	**D99**	1f. blue	4·75	6·00
D219	**D99**	2f. red	5·00	7·75
D220	**D99**	4f. violet	4·25	9·25
D221	**D99**	6f. blue	4·50	10·00

For later issues see **BURUNDI** and **RWANDA**.

Pt. 10

RUSSIA

A country in the E. of Europe and N. Asia. An empire until 1917 when the Russian Socialist Federal Soviet Republic was formed. In 1923 this became the Union of Soviet Socialist Republics (U.S.S.R.), eventually comprising 15 constituent republics.

In 1991 the U.S.S.R. was dissolved and subsequent issues were used in the Russian Federation only.

100 kopeks = 1 rouble.

1

1858. Imperf.

1	**1**	10k. blue and brown	£8500	£650

1858. Perf.

21		10k. blue and brown	36·00	1·40
22		20k. orange and blue	80·00	15·00
23		30k. green and red	95·00	29·00

5

1863

8	**5**	5k. black and blue	17·00	£225

No. 8 was first issued as a local but was later authorised for general use.

9

1864

18	**9**	1k. black and yellow	5·00	1·30
30	**9**	2k. black and red	13·00	2·50
19b	**9**	3k. black and green	6·00	2·40
20	**9**	5k. black and lilac	13·00	2·50

8

1875

31	**8**	7k. red and grey	10·50	1·70
32	**8**	8k. red and grey	13·50	2·10
33	**8**	10k. blue and brown	30·00	5·50
34	**8**	20k. orange and blue	41·00	4·50

12 No thunderbolts

1883. Posthorns in design without thunderbolts, as T 12.

38A	**9**	1k. orange	4·25	1·00
39A	**9**	2k. green	6·50	1·00
41A	**9**	3k. red	6·50	1·00
42Bb	**9**	5k. purple	6·00	80
43Bb	**9**	7k. blue	5·25	95
44Bb	**10**	14k. red and blue	9·25	65
45A	**10**	35k. green and purple	32·00	5·75
46A	**10**	70k. orange and brown	55·00	5·75
47	**11**	3r.50 grey and black	£550	£475
48	**11**	7r. yellow and black	£600	£550

13 With thunderbolts **14** **15**

1889. Posthorns in design with thunderbolts as T 13. Perf.

50	**9**	1k. orange	55	10
51	**9**	2k. green	55	10
52	**9**	3k. red	60	10
53	**14**	4k. red	60	25
54	**9**	5k. purple	85	10
55	**9**	7k. blue	60	10
56	**14**	10k. blue	85	15
114A	**10**	14k. red and blue	15	10
100	**10**	15k. blue and purple	2·00	45
116A	**14**	20k. red and blue	10	50
102	**10**	25k. violet and green	20	30
103	**10**	35k. green and purple	3·75	75
79	**11**	3r.50 grey and black	13·00	6·00
122A	**11**	3r.50 green and red	25	40
80	**11**	7r. yellow and black	10·50	7·50
124Ab	**11**	7r. pink and green	45	85

For imperf stamps, see Nos. 107B/125aB.

16 Monument to Admiral Kornilov at Sevastopol

1905. War Orphans Fund (Russo-Japanese War).

88	**16**	3 (6) k. brown, red and green	2·50	2·50
82	-	5 (8) k. purple and yellow	2·20	2·10
83	-	7 (10) k. blue, lt blue & pink	3·00	2·10
87	-	10 (13) k. blue, lt bl & yell	2·50	2·50

DESIGNS: 5(8) k. Monument to Minin and Pozharsky, Moscow; 7(10) k. Statue of Peter the Great, St. Petersburg; 10(13) k. Moscow Kremlin.

20 **22** **23**

1906

107A	**22**	1k. orange	35	15
93	**22**	2k. green	45	10
94	**22**	3k. red	40	10
95	**23**	4k. red	20	15
96	**22**	5k. red	1·20	40
97	**22**	7k. blue	60	15
98a	**23**	10k. blue	3·75	1·50
123Aa	**20**	5r. blue and green	50	50
125Aa	**20**	10r. grey, red and yellow	1·30	1·30

For imperf stamps, see Nos. 107B/125aB.

25 Nicholas II **26** Elizabeth

27 The Kremlin

1913. Tercentenary of Romanov Dynasty. Views as T 27 and portraits as T 25/26.

126	1k. orange (Peter I)	30	15
127	2k. green (Alexander II)	40	15
128	3k. red (Alexander III)	45	15
129	4k. red (Peter I)	45	15
130	7k. brown (Type **25**)	50	25
131	10k. blue (Nicholas II)	70	35
132	14k. green (Katherine II)	60	25
133	15k. brown (Nicholas I)	1·10	40
134	20k. olive (Alexander I)	1·60	40
135	25k. red (Alexis)	1·60	75
136	35k. green and violet (Paul I)	1·40	55
137	50k. grey and brown (T **26**)	2·40	75
138	70k. brown and green (Michael I, the first Russian tsar)	2·50	1·30
139	1r. green (Type **27**)	9·50	5·00
140	2r. brown	15·00	6·75
141	3r. violet	31·00	8·50
142	5r. brown	38·00	19·00

DESIGNS—As T **27**: 2r. The Winter Palace; 3r. Romanov House, Moscow (birthplace of first Romanov tsar). 23×29 mm: 5r. Nicholas II.

31 Russian hero, Ilya Murometz

1914. War Charity.

151	**31**	1 (2) k. green & red on yell	85	1·70
144	-	3 (4) k. green and red on red	95	2·50
145	-	7 (8) k. green and brown on buff	95	2·50
161	-	10 (11) k. brown and blue on blue	1·70	2·50

DESIGNS: 3k. Cossack shaking girl's hand; 7k. Symbolical of Russia surrounded by her children; 10k. St. George and Dragon.

1915. As last. Colours changed.

155	**31**	1 (2) k. grey and brown	1·30	2·10
156	-	3 (4) k. black and red	1·30	2·10
158	-	10 (11) k. brown and blue	1·70	2·50

35

1915. Nos. 131, 133 and 134 printed on card with inscriptions on back as T 35. No gum.

165	10k. blue	1·00	4·25
166	15k. brown	1·00	4·25
167	20k. olive	1·30	4·25

1916. Various types surch.

168	-	10k. on 7k. brown (No. 130)	35	35
170	**22**	10k. on 7k. blue	35	25
169	-	20k. on 14k. green (No. 132)	35	35
171	**10**	20k. on 14k. red and blue	35	25

1917. Various earlier types, but imperf.

107B	**22**	1k. orange	50	10
108B	**22**	2k. green	15	10
109B	**22**	3k. red	15	10
110B	**23**	4k. red	50	2·20
111B	**22**	5k. lilac	15	10
113B	**23**	10k. blue	14·50	27·00
115B	**10**	15k. blue & pur (No. 100)	15	10
116B	**14**	20k. red and blue	15	40
117Bd	**10**	25k. vio & grn (No. 102)	1·30	2·50
118B	**10**	35k. grn & pur (No. 103)	15	35
119B	**14**	50k. green and purple	15	35
120B	**10**	70k. orange and brown (No. 120)	15	35
121B	**15**	1r. orange and brown	10	10
122B	**11**	3r.50 green and red	45	60
123Ba	**20**	5r. blue and green	45	60
124B	**11**	7r. pink and green	1·10	1·60
125B	**20**	10r. grey, red and yellow	39·00	36·00

39 **41**

1916. Types of 1913 printed on card with surch on back as T 39 or 41, or optd with figure "1" or "2" in addition on front. No gum.

172	**39**	1k. orange (No. 126)	29·00	42·00
175	**39**	1 on 1k. orange (No. 126)	1·20	4·25
177	**41**	1 on 1k. orange (No. 126)	1·30	6·25
173	**39**	2k. green (No. 127)	44·00	50·00
176	**39**	2 on 2k. green (No. 127)	1·20	4·25
178	**41**	2 on 2k. green (No. 127)	85	3·75
174	**39**	3k. red (No. 128)	1·30	4·25
179	**41**	3k. red (No. 128)	85	3·75

45 Cutting the Fetters

1918

187	**45**	35k. blue	1·30	10·00
188	**45**	70k. brown	1·40	14·00

46 Agriculture and Industry

47 Triumph of Revolution

48 Agriculture **49** Industry

55 Science and Arts **56**

64 Industry

1921. Imperf.

195	**48**	1r. orange	1·70	8·50
196	**48**	2r. brown	1·70	8·50
197	**49**	5r. blue	1·70	8·50
198	**46**	20r. blue	4·25	6·75
199	**47**	40r. blue	3·00	5·50
214	**48**	100r. yellow	15	25
215	**48**	200r. brown	25	35
216	**55**	250r. purple	15	25
217	**48**	300r. green	45	1·00
218	**49**	500r. blue	50	2·10
219	**49**	1000r. red	15	25
256	**64**	5000r. violet	1·00	1·70
257	**46**	7500r. blue	45	60
259	**46**	7500r. blue on buff	60	85
258	**64**	10000r. blue	10·50	11·50
260	**64**	22500r. purple on buff	60	85

1921. 4th Anniv of October Revolution. Imperf.

227	**56**	100r. orange	85	2·50
228	**56**	250r. violet	85	2·50
229	**56**	1000r. purple	85	2·50

57 Famine Relief Work

58

1921. Charity. Volga Famine. Imperf.

230	**57**	2250r. green	5·25	8·50
231	**57**	2250r. red	4·25	8·50
232	**57**	2250r. brown	4·25	12·00
233	**58**	2250r. blue	10·50	15·00

1922. Surch. Imperf.

236	**49**	5000r. on 5r. blue	1·60	2·50
239	**48**	5000r. on 1r. orange	1·60	2·10
240	**48**	5000r. on 2r. brown	1·60	2·10
242	**46**	5000r. on 20r. blue	3·00	3·25
243	**47**	10000r. on 40r. blue	2·20	2·50

Р. С. Ф. С. Р.
ГОЛОДАЮЩИМ
250 р.+250 р.

(62)

1922. Famine Relief. Surch as T 62. Perf.

245	**45**	100r.+100r. on 70k. brown	1·10	1·70
247	**45**	250r.+250r. on 25k. blue	1·10	1·70

(63)

1922. Surch as T 63. Imperf.

250	**55**	7500r. on 250r. purple	25	25
251	**55**	100000r. on 250r. purple	25	35

65

1922. Obligatory Tax. Rostov-on-Don issue. Famine Relief. Various sizes. Without gum. Imperf.

261	**65**	2T. (2000r.) green	39·00	£250
262	-	2T. (2000r.) red	35·00	£250
263	-	4T. (4000r.) red	44·00	£250
264	-	6T. (6000r.) green	39·00	£250

DESIGNS: 2T. red, Worker and family (35×42 mm); 4T. Clasped hands (triangular, 57 mm each side); 6T. Sower (29×59 mm).

РСФСР
Филателия
– детям
19 - 8 - 22

70 "Philately for the children"

1922. Optd with T 70. Perf or imperf.

273	**22**	1k. orange	£500	£400
274	**22**	2k. green	27·00	46·00
275	**22**	3k. red	12·50	25·00
276	**22**	5k. red	11·50	25·00
277	**23**	10k. blue	11·50	25·00

71

1922. 5th Anniv of October Revolution. Imperf.

279	**71**	5r. black and yellow	60	45
280	**71**	10r. black and brown	60	45
281	**71**	25r. black and purple	2·40	1·50
282	**71**	27r. black and red	5·25	4·25
283	**71**	45r. black and blue	3·50	2·50

1922. Air. Optd with airplane. Imperf.

284		45r. black and green	17·00	42·00

73

1922. Famine Relief. Imperf.

285	**73**	20r.+5r. lilac	35	1·70
286	-	20r.+5r. violet	35	1·70
287	-	20r.+5r. blue	35	1·70
288	-	20r.+5r. blue	2·40	11·50

DESIGNS—HORIZ: No. 286, Freighter; No. 287, Steam train. VERT: No. 288, Airplane.

(77)

1922. Surch as T 77. Imperf or perf.

289	**14**	5r. on 20k. red and blue	3·00	34·00
290	**10**	20r. on 15k. blue & purple	3·00	34·00
291	**10**	20r. on 70k. orange and brown	15	25
292a	**14**	30r. on 50k. green & pur	35	35
293	**10**	40r. on 15k. blue & pur	15	25
294	**10**	100r. on 15k. blue & pur	25	25
295	**10**	200r. on 15k. blue & pur	25	25

78 Worker **79** Soldier

1922. Imperf or perf.

303	**78**	10r. blue	60	1·00
304	**79**	50r. brown	45	65
305	**79**	70r. purple	45	65
310	**79**	100r. red	60	40

1 мая
1923 г. Филателия —
Трудящимся,
1 р.+1 р.

(80)

1923. Charity. Surch as T 80. Imperf.

315	**71**	1r.+1r. on 10r. black and brown	35·00	43·00
317	**55**	2r.+2r. on 250r. purple	36·00	42·00
318	**64**	4r.+4r. on 5000r. violet	70·00	75·00

83 Worker **84** Peasant **85** Soldier

1923. Perf.

320	**85**	3r. red	15	15
321	**83**	4r. brown	15	15
322	**84**	5r. blue	15	15
323	**85**	10r. grey	25	25
324	**85**	20r. purple	35	35

86 Reaper

88 Tractor

1923. Agricultural Exn, Moscow. Imperf or perf.

325	**86**	1r. brown and orange	2·20	5·50
326	-	2r. green and light green	2·20	5·50
327	**88**	5r. blue and light blue	2·20	5·50
328	-	7r. rose and pink	2·20	5·50

DESIGNS: As Type **86**: 2r. Sower; 7r. Exhibition buildings.

90 Worker **91** Peasant **92** Soldier **93**

94 **95**

1923. Perf (some values also imperf).

335	**90**	1k. yellow	35	25
359	**91**	2k. green	55	20
360	**92**	3k. brown	65	20
361	**90**	4k. red	55	20
434	**90**	5k. purple	85	40
363	**91**	6k. blue	85	25
364	**92**	7k. brown	85	25
437	**90**	8k. olive	1·30	35
366	**91**	9k. red	1·30	55
341	**92**	10k. blue	90	50
385	**90**	14k. grey	1·70	35
386	**91**	15k. yellow	2·40	1·10
442	**92**	18k. violet	3·00	65
443	**90**	20k. green	3·00	65
444	**91**	30k. violet	2·30	65
445	**92**	40k. grey	4·50	85
343	**91**	50k. brown	4·50	1·20
447	**92**	1r. red and brown	5·75	1·50
375	**93**	2r. green and red	10·00	3·00
449	**94**	3r. green and brown	16·00	4·50
450	**95**	5r. brown and blue	19·00	6·75

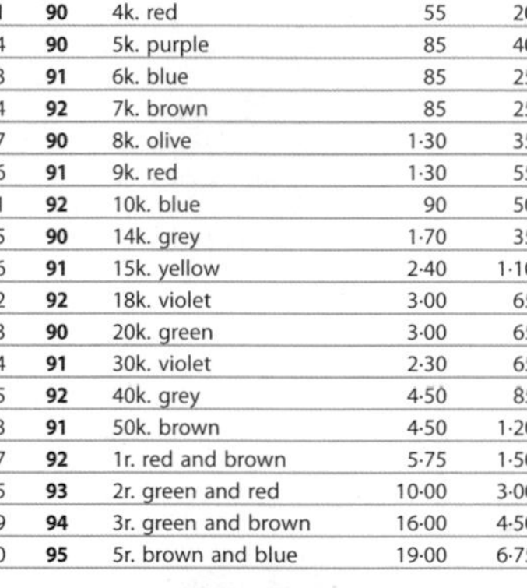

96 Lenin

1924. Lenin Mourning. Imperf or perf.

413	**96**	3k. black and red	4·00	1·80
414	**96**	6k. black and red	3·00	1·40
411	**96**	12k. black and red	4·25	85
412	**96**	20k. black and red	3·50	5·00

97 Fokker F.III Airplane

1924. Air. Surch. Imperf.

417	**97**	5k. on 3r. blue	3·25	1·50
418	**97**	10k. on 5r. green	2·50	1·00
419	**97**	15k. on 1r. brown	3·25	1·50
420	**97**	20k. on 10r. red	3·25	1·50

С. С. С. Р.
пострадавшему
от наводнения
Ленинграду.
3 к. + 10 к.

99 Trans "For the victims of the flood in Leningrad"

1924. Leningrad Flood Relief. Surch as T 99. Imperf.

421	**48**	3+10k. on 100r. yellow	1·90	1·50

422	**48**	7+20k. on 200r. brown	1·90	1·50
423	**48**	14+30k. on 300r. green	2·75	2·30
424	**49**	12+40k. on 500r. blue	2·75	2·30
425	**49**	20+50k. on 1000r. red	2·75	2·30

102 Lenin Mausoleum, Moscow

1925. 1st Death Anniv of Lenin. Imperf or perf.

426A	**102**	7k. blue	3·50	2·30
427A	**102**	14k. olive	8·75	4·25
428A	**102**	20k. red	5·75	3·00
429B	**102**	40k. brown	7·50	2·30

104 Lenin

1925

451	**104**	1r. brown	14·50	5·00
452	**104**	2r. brown	16·00	5·75
850	**104**	3r. green	2·50	1·10
851	**104**	5r. brown	3·25	2·30
852	**104**	10r. blue	7·00	6·25

106 Prof. Lomonosov and Academy of Sciences, Leningrad

1925. Bicentenary of Academy of Sciences.

456b	**106**	3k. brown	4·25	2·50
457	**106**	15k. olive	6·00	3·25

107 A. S. Popov

1925. 30th Anniv of Popov's Radio Discoveries.

458	**107**	7k. blue	2·75	1·30
459	**107**	14k. green	4·50	2·00

110 Moscow Barricade

1925. 20th Anniv of 1905 Rebellion. Imperf or perf.

463b	-	3k. green	7·50	5·00
464c	-	7k. brown	8·75	5·00
465a	**110**	14k. red	7·00	3·00

DESIGNS—VERT: 3k. Postal rioters; 7k. Orator and crowd.

111 "Decembrists in Exiles" (detail, A. Moravov)

112 Senate Square, St. Petersburg, 1825

1925. Centenary of Decembrist Rebellion. Imperf or perf.

466A	**111**	3k. green	5·25	5·00
467A	**112**	7k. brown	5·25	3·25
468A	-	14k. red	7·00	4·25

DESIGN—VERT: 14k. Medallion with heads of Pestel, Ryleev, Bestuzhev-Ryumin, Muravev-Apostol and Kakhovsky.

114

1926. 6th International Proletarian Esperanto Congress.

471	**114**	7k. red and green	5·25	3·25
472	**114**	14k. violet and green	6·00	1·70

115 Waifs

116 Lenin when a Child

1926. Child Welfare.

473B	**115**	10k. brown	85	65
474B	**116**	20k. blue	2·30	1·20

1927. Same type with new inscriptions.

475	**115**	8k.+2k. green	1·00	1·40
476	**116**	18k.+2k. red	2·40	2·00

ПОЧТОВАЯ
МАРКА
КОП. 8 КОП.
(117)

1927. Postage Due stamps surch with T 117.

491A	**D104**	8k. on 1k. red	1·60	2·75
492A	**D104**	8k. on 2k. violet	1·60	2·75
493A	**D104**	8k. on 3k. blue	1·60	2·75
494A	**D104**	8k. on 7k. yellow	1·60	2·75
494Ab	**D104**	8k. on 8k. green	1·60	2·75
494Ad	**D104**	8k. on 10k. blue	1·60	2·75
494Af	**D104**	8k. on 14k. brown	1·60	2·75

1927. Various types of 7k. surch (some values imperf or perf).

496Ba	**92**	8k. on 7k. brown		
523	**107**	8k. on 7k. blue	3·50	3·25
524	-	8k. on 7k. brn (No. 464c)	10·50	7·50
526	**114**	8k. on 7k. red and green	17·00	14·50
527	**112**	8k. on 7k. brown	12·00	10·00

119 Dr. Zamenhof

1927. 40th Anniv of Publication of Zamenhof's "Langue Internationale" (Esperanto).

498B	**119**	14k. green and brown	4·75	2·10

120 Tupolev ANT-3 Biplane and Map

1927. 1st Int Air Post Congress, The Hague.

499	**120**	10k. blue and brown	22·00	6·75
500	**120**	15k. red and olive	26·00	10·00

121 Worker, Soldier and Peasant

124 Sailor and Worker

122 Allegory of Revolution

1927. 10th Anniv of October Revolution.

501	**121**	3k. red	2·75	1·00
502	**122**	5k. brown	6·50	2·50
503	-	7k. green	9·50	4·00
504	**124**	8k. black and brown	3·75	1·80
505	-	14k. red and blue	6·50	1·80
506	-	18k. blue	4·75	1·50
507	-	28k. brown	15·00	11·00

DESIGNS—HORIZ: (As Type **122**): HORIZ: 7k. Smolny Institute; 14k. Map of Russia inscr "C.C.C.P."; 18k. Various Russian races; 28k. Worker, soldier and peasant.

128 Worker

129 Peasant

130 Lenin

1927

508	**128**	1k. orange	1·30	65
509	**129**	2k. green	1·30	25
510	**128**	4k. blue	1·30	25
511	**129**	5k. brown	1·30	25
512	**129**	7k. red	6·50	1·30
513	**128**	8k. green	3·25	35
514	**128**	10k. brown	2·75	35
515	**130**	14k. green	3·25	65
516	**130**	18k. olive	6·50	65
517	**130**	18k. blue	5·75	1·00
518	**129**	20k. olive	3·75	40
519	**128**	40k. red	14·00	2·50
520	**129**	50k. blue	8·25	1·30
521	**128**	70k. olive	14·00	1·70
522	**129**	80k. orange	23·00	3·25

131 Infantryman, Lenin Mausoleum and Kremlin

1928. 10th Anniv of Red Army.

529	**131**	8k. brown	2·40	50
530	-	14k. blue	3·25	65
531	-	18k. red	3·25	1·50
532	-	28k. green	5·00	4·25

DESIGNS: 14k. Sailor and cruiser "Aurora"; 18k. Cavalryman; 28k. Airman.

135 Young Factory Workers

1929. Child Welfare.

536	**135**	10k.+2k. brown & sepia	3·00	1·70
537	-	20k.+2k. blue & brown	5·75	4·25

DESIGN: 20k. Children in harvest field.

See also Nos. 567/8.

137 Trumpeter sounding the Assembly

1929. 1st All-Union Gathering of Pioneers.

538	**137**	10k. brown	26·00	11·50
539	**137**	14k. blue	14·00	5·00

138 Worker (after I. Shadr)

139 Factory Girl

140 Peasant

141 Farm Girl

142 Guardsman

143 Worker, Soldier and Peasant (after I. Smirnov)

144 Lenin

242a Miner

242b Steel foundryman

242c Infantryman

242d Airman

242e Arms of U.S.S.R.

149 Central Telegraph Office, Moscow

150 Lenin Hydro-electric Power Station

743a Farm Girl

743b Architect

744 Furnaceman

1929. Perf, but some values exist imperf.

541	**138**	1k. yellow	1·30	15
542	**139**	2k. green	1·30	15
543	**140**	3k. blue	1·30	15
544	**141**	4k. mauve	1·60	25
545	**142**	5k. brown	2·20	35
847a	**242a**	5k. red	25	15
546	**143**	7k. red	2·50	40
547	**138**	10k. grey	3·25	50
727f	**139**	10k. blue	1·10	25
1214b	**139**	10k. black	70	60
554	**144**	14k. blue	1·70	75
548	**143**	15k. blue	3·50	50
847b	**242b**	15k. blue	1·70	1·10
847c	**242c**	15k. green	50	25
549	**140**	20k. green and blue	4·25	65
727h	**141**	20k. green	85	40
2252a	**743a**	20k. olive	30	15
2252b	**743b**	25k. brown	1·50	80
550	**139**	30k. violet and lilac	6·00	1·00
847d	**242d**	30k. blue	1·00	25
727l	**144**	40k. blue	1·30	60
727m	**141**	50k. brown and buff	1·70	3·25
847f	**242e**	60k. red	1·30	60
2253	**744**	60k. red	90	45
2253a	**744**	60k. blue	1·20	35
552	**142**	70k. red and pink	10·50	2·10
553	**140**	80k. brown and yellow	13·00	2·50
561	**149**	1r. blue	8·75	1·30
562	**150**	3r. brown and green	26·00	8·50

Nos. 727f, 1214b and 550 show the factory girl without factory in background. Nos. 549, 727m, 552, 553 have designs like those shown but with unshaded background.

151 Industry

153 "More metal more machines"

1929. Industrial Loan Propaganda.

563	**151**	5k. brown	2·50	1·50
564	-	10k. olive	6·50	5·00
565	**153**	20k. green	8·75	4·25
566	-	28k. violet	6·00	4·25

DESIGNS—HORIZ: 10k. Tractors. VERT: 28k. Blast furnace and graph of pig-iron output.

1930. Child Welfare.

567	**135**	10k.+2k. olive	3·50	3·25
568	-	20k.+2k. grn (as No. 537)	4·75	4·50

155 Cavalrymen (after M. Grekov)

1930. 10th Anniv of 1st Red Cavalry.

569	**155**	2k. green	8·75	3·00
570	-	5k. brown	8·75	3·00
571	-	10k. olive	19·00	6·75
572	-	14k. blue and red	16·00	4·25

DESIGNS: 5k. Cavalry attack (after Yu. Merkulov); 10k. Cavalry facing left (after M. Grekov); 14k. Cavalry charge (after Yu. Merkulov).

159 Group of Soviet Pupils

1930. Educational Exhibition, Leningrad.

573	**159**	10k. green	3·50	1·30

160

1930. Air. "Graf-Zeppelin" (airship) Flight to Moscow.

574	**160**	40k. blue	44·00	21·00
575	**160**	80k. red	35·00	13·50

162 Battleship "Potemkin"

1930. 25th Anniv of 1905 Rebellion. Imperf or perf.

576B	**162**	3k. red	3·50	1·20
577B	-	5k. blue	6·00	1·80
578B	-	10k. red and green	8·75	3·25

DESIGNS—HORIZ: 5k. Barricade and rebels. VERT: 10k. Red flag at Presnya barricade.

165 From the Tundra (reindeer) to the Steppes (camel)

166 Above Dnieprostroi Dam

1931. Airship Construction Fund. Imperf or perf.

579c	**165**	10k. violet	7·00	5·00
580b	**166**	15k. blue	44·00	18·00
581c	-	20k. red	7·00	6·75
582b	-	50k. brown	10·50	7·50
583c	-	1r. green	13·00	12·50

DESIGNS—As Type **165**. VERT: 20k. Above Lenin's Mausoleum. HORIZ: 1r. Airship construction. As Type **166**: 50k. Above the North Pole.

See also No. E592.

170 "Graf Zeppelin" over Ice breaker "Malygin"

1931. Air. "Graf Zeppelin" (airship) North Pole Flight. Imperf or perf.

584	**170**	30k. purple	31·00	18·00
585b	**170**	35k. green	31·00	21·00
586	**170**	1r. black	39·00	25·00
587	**170**	2r. blue	31·00	18·00

172 Maksim Gorky

1932. 40th Anniv of Publication of "Makar Chadra".

590	**172**	15k. brown	13·00	5·00
591	**172**	35k. blue	39·00	13·50

1932. Airship Construction Fund. Imperf or perf.

592	**166**	15k. black	6·50	2·10

173 Storming the Winter Palace

1932. 15th Anniv of October Revolution.

593	-	3k. violet	3·50	1·70
594	**173**	5k. brown	3·50	1·70
595	-	10k. blue	5·25	3·25
596	-	15k. green	4·25	2·50
597	-	20k. red	8·75	4·25
598	-	30k. grey	27·00	11·00
599	-	35k. brown	£130	£110

DESIGNS—HORIZ: 10k. Dnieper Dam; 15k. Harvesting with combines; 20k. Industrial works, Magnitogorsk; 30k. Siberians listening to Moscow broadcast. VERT: 3k. Lenin's arrival in Petrograd; 35k. People of the World hailing Lenin.

175 "Liberation"

1932. 10th Anniv of International Revolutionaries' Relief Organization.

600	**175**	50k. red	18·00	7·50

176 Museum of Fine Arts

1932. 1st All-Union Philatelic Exn, Moscow.

601	**176**	15k. brown	26·00	14·50
602	**176**	35k. blue	65·00	36·00

177 Trier, Marx's Birthplace

1933. 50th Death Anniv of Marx.

603	**177**	3k. green	7·00	1·30
604	-	10k. brown	10·50	2·50
605	-	35k. purple	25·00	10·00

DESIGNS—VERT: 10k. Marx's grave, Highgate Cemetery; 35k. Marx.

1933. Leningrad Philatelic Exhibition. Surch LENINGRAD 1933 in Russian characters and premium.

606	**176**	15k.+30k. black & brn	95·00	65·00
607	**176**	35k.+70k. blue	£170	75·00

182

183

1933. Ethnographical Issue. Racial types.

608	-	1k. brown (Kazakhs)	7·75	95
609	**183**	2k. blue (Lesgins)	6·50	95
610	-	3k. green (Crimean Tatars)	10·00	1·50
611	-	4k. brown (Jews of Birobidzhan)	7·00	95
612	-	5k. red (Tungusians)	4·75	75
613	-	6k. blue (Buryats)	9·75	1·10
614	-	7k. brown (Chechens)	9·75	1·10
615	-	8k. red (Abkhazians)	9·75	1·10
616	-	9k. blue (Georgians)	10·50	1·40
617	-	10k. brown (Samoyedes)	7·00	1·50
618	-	14k. green (Yakuts)	6·75	90
619	-	15k. purple (Ukrainians)	7·00	1·00
620	-	15k. black (Uzbeks)	6·75	80
621	-	15k. blue (Tadzhiks)	6·75	80
622	-	15k. brown (Transcaucasians)	7·75	1·40
623	-	15k. green (Byelorussians)	7·50	90
624	-	15k. orange (Great Russians)	7·75	90
625	-	15k. red (Turkmens)	7·75	1·00
626	-	20k. blue (Koryaks)	15·00	2·10
627	-	30k. red (Bashkirs)	21·00	2·30
628	**182**	35k. brown (Chuvashes)	38·00	3·00

SIZES: Nos. 608, 610/11, 614/17, 626/7, As T **182**: Nos. 612/13, 618. As T **183**: Nos. 619/24, 48×22 mm. No. 625, 22×48 mm.

186 V. V. Vorovsky

1933. Communist Party Activists. Dated "1933", "1934" or "1935".

629	**186**	1k. green	1·30	65
718b	-	2k. violet	6·50	1·40
630	-	3k. blue	3·00	85
719	-	4k. purple	6·50	4·50
631	-	5k. brown	7·00	2·30
632	-	10k. blue	22·00	7·50
633	-	15k. red	65·00	31·00
720	-	40k. brown	13·00	8·25

DESIGNS: 2k. M. Frunze; 3k. V. M. Volodarsky; 4k. N. E. Bauman; 5k. M. S. Uritsky; 10k. Iacov M. Sverdlov; 15k. Viktor P. Nogin; 40k. S. M. Kirov.

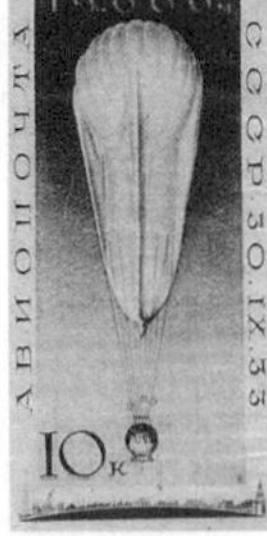

187 Stratosphere Balloon "U.S.S.R.-1" over Moscow

1933. Air. Stratosphere record (19000 m).

634	**187**	5k. blue	£120	30·00
635	**187**	10k. red	65·00	10·00
636	**187**	20k. violet	32·00	6·25

188 Massed Standard Bearers

1933. 15th Anniv of Order of Red Banner.

637	**188**	20k. red, yellow and black	4·25	2·50

189 Commissar Shaumyan

1934. 15th Death Anniv of 26 Baku Commissars.

638	**189**	4k. brown	10·50	1·90
639	-	5k. black	10·50	1·90
640	-	20k. violet	5·75	1·30
641	-	35k. blue	31·00	8·50
642	-	40k. red	15·00	5·50

DESIGNS: 5k. Commissar Dzhaparidze. HORIZ: 20k. The 26 condemned commissars; 35k. Monument in Baku; 40k. Workman, peasant and soldier dipping flags in salute.

190 Tupolev ANT-9 PS9 over Oilfield

1934. Air. 10th Anniv of Soviet Civil Aviation and U.S.S.R. Airmail Service.

643B		5k. blue	16·00	4·75
644B	**190**	10k. green	16·00	4·75
645B	-	20k. red	29·00	6·00
646A	-	50k. blue	55·00	18·00
647B	-	80k. violet	31·00	7·50

DESIGNS: Tupolev ANT-9 PS9 airplane over: 5k. Furnaces at Kuznetsk; 20k. Harvesters; 50k. Volga–Moscow Canal; 80k. Ice breaker "OB" in the Arctic.

191 New Lenin Mausoleum

1934. 10th Death Anniv of Lenin.

648	**191**	5k. brown	4·25	1·20
649	**191**	10k. blue	25·00	5·00
650	**191**	15k. red	9·50	2·50
651	**191**	20k. green	4·75	1·20
652	**191**	35k. brown	20·00	3·75

192 Fyodorov Monument, Moscow, and Hand and Rotary Presses

1934. 350th Death Anniv of Ivan Fyodorov (first Russian printer).

653	**192**	20k. red	13·00	4·50
654	**192**	40k. blue	13·50	4·50

194 Dmitri Mendeleev

1934. Birth Centenary of Dmitri Mendeleev (chemist).

655	-	5k. green	8·75	1·90
656	**194**	10k. brown	33·00	8·50
657	**194**	15k. red	21·00	7·50
658	-	20k. blue	9·00	3·75

DESIGN—VERT: 5k., 20k. Mendeleev seated.

195 A. V. Vasenko and "Osoaviakhim"

1934. Air. Stratosphere Balloon "Osoaviakhim" Disaster Victims.

659A		5k. purple	26·00	6·25
660A	**195**	10k. brown	75·00	8·75
661A	-	20k. violet	50·00	6·25
1042	-	1r. green	8·75	3·25
1043	**195**	1r. green	8·75	3·25
1044	-	1r. blue	8·75	3·25

DESIGNS: 5k., 1r. (No. 1042). I. D. Usyskin; 20k., 1r. (No. 1044), P. F. Fedoseenko.

The 1r. values, issued in 1944, commemorated the 10th anniv of the disaster.

196 Airship "Pravda"

1934. Air. Airship Travel Propaganda.

662	**196**	5k. red	22·00	6·75
663	-	10k. lake	22·00	6·75
664	-	15k. brown	38·00	17·00
665	-	20k. black	44·00	11·50
666	-	30k. blue	85·00	30·00

DESIGNS—HORIZ: 10k. Airship landing; 15k. Airship "Voroshilov"; 30k. Airship "Lenin" and route map. VERT: 20k. Airship's gondolas and mooring mast.

199 Stalin and Marchers inspired by Lenin

1934. "Ten Years without Lenin". Portraits inscr "1924–1934".

667		1k. black and blue	4·25	1·30
668		3k. black and blue	4·25	1·40
669		5k. black and blue	10·50	3·25
670		10k. black and blue	5·50	2·50
671		20k. blue and orange	9·25	3·50
672	**199**	30k. red and orange	50·00	18·00

DESIGN—VERT: 1k. Lenin aged 3; 3k. Lenin as student; 5k. Lenin as man; 10k. Lenin as orator. HORIZ: 20k. Red demonstration, Lenin's Mausoleum.

200 "War Clouds"

1935. Anti-War. Inscr "1914–1934".

673	**200**	5k. black	8·75	3·25
674	-	10k. blue	14·50	6·75
675	-	15k. green	25·00	8·75
676	-	20k. brown	12·00	4·00
677	-	35k. red	55·00	17·00

DESIGNS: 10k. "Flight from a burning village"; 15k. "Before war and afterwards"; 20k. "Ploughing with the sword"; 35k. "Fraternization".

202 Capt. Voronin and Ice-breaker "Chelyuskin"

1935. Air. Rescue of "Chelyuskin" Expedition.

678	**202**	1k. orange	6·25	1·40
679	-	3k. red	6·50	1·70
680	-	5k. green	7·00	1·40
681	-	10k. brown	12·00	2·10
682	-	15k. black	13·50	2·75
683	-	20k. purple	19·00	3·50
684	-	25k. blue	55·00	21·00
685	-	30k. green	70·00	28·00
686	-	40k. violet	39·00	4·00
687	**202**	50k. blue	47·00	14·00

DESIGNS—HORIZ: 3k. Prof. Schmidt and Schmidt Camp; 50k. Schmidt Camp deserted. VERT: 5k. A. V. Lyapidevsky; 10k. S. A. Levanevsky; 15k. M. G. Slepnev; 20k. I. V. Doronin; 25k. M. V. Vodopyanov; 30k. V. S. Molokov; 40k. N. P. Kamanin.

205 Underground Station

1935. Opening of Moscow Underground.

688	-	5k. orange	11·50	3·75
689	-	10k. blue	13·00	3·50
690	**205**	15k. red	95·00	26·00
691	-	20k. green	27·00	9·25

DESIGNS—As Type **205**: 5k. Excavating tunnel; 10k. Section of tunnel, escalator and station. 48½×23 mm: 20k. Train in station.

207 Rowing

1935. Spartacist Games.

692		1k. blue and orange	3·00	1·30
693		2k. blue and black	3·00	1·30
694	**207**	3k. brown and green	6·00	2·75
695	-	4k. blue and red	3·00	1·30
696	-	5k. brown and violet	3·00	1·30
697	-	10k. purple and red	11·50	2·75
698	-	15k. brown and black	32·00	10·50
699	-	20k. blue and brown	16·00	5·50
700	-	35k. brown and blue	30·00	11·50
701	-	40k. red and brown	23·00	6·75

DESIGNS: 1k. Running; 2k. Diving; 4k. Football; 5k. Skiing; 10k. Cycling; 15k. Lawn tennis; 20k. Skating; 35k. Hurdling; 40k. Parade of athletes.

208 Friedrich Engels

1935. 40th Death Anniv of F. Engels.

702	**208**	5k. red	7·25	1·20
703	**208**	10k. green	5·00	2·50
704	**208**	15k. blue	13·00	3·25
705	**208**	20k. black	5·50	3·50

Перелет Москва— Сан-Франциско через Сев. полюс 1935 1 Р.

(209)

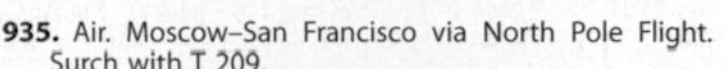

1935. Air. Moscow–San Francisco via North Pole Flight. Surch with T 209.

706		1r. on 10k. brown (No. 681)	£350	£450

210 A "Lion Hunt" from a Sassanian Silver Plate

1935. 3rd International Congress of Persian Art and Archaeology, Leningrad.

707	**210**	5k. orange	9·75	1·40
708	**210**	10k. green	9·75	2·10
709	**210**	15k. purple	12·50	3·25
710	**210**	35k. brown	20·00	5·75

211 M. I. Kalinin

1935. Pres. Kalinin's 60th Birthday. Autographed portraits inscr "1875–1935".

711	-	3k. purple	80	30
712	-	5k. green	1·30	35
713	-	10k. blue	1·40	65
714	**211**	20k. brown	2·20	1·30

DESIGNS: 3k. Kalinin as machine worker; 5k. Harvester; 10k. Orator.

See also No. 1189.

212 Tolstoi

1935. 25th Death Anniv of Tolstoi (writer).

715b	-	3k. violet and black	80	35
716b	**212**	10k. brown and blue	2·00	80
717b	-	20k. brown and green	4·00	2·00

DESIGNS: 3k. Tolstoi in 1860; 20k. Monument in Moscow.

213 Pioneers securing Letter-box

1936. Pioneer Movement.

721b	**213**	1k. green	1·30	50
722	**213**	2k. red	1·00	60
723b	-	3k. blue	1·60	1·50
724b	-	5k. red	1·60	1·10
725b	-	10k. blue	4·25	4·25
726	-	15k. brown	6·50	3·25

DESIGNS: 3, 5k. Pioneer preventing another from throwing stones; 10k. Pioneers disentangling kite line from telegraph wires; 15k. Girl pioneer saluting.

214 N. A. Dobrolyubov

1936. Birth Centenary of N. Dobrolyubov (author and critic).

727b	**214**	10k. purple	9·25	4·75

215 Pushkin (after T. Paita)

1937. Death Centenary of A. S. Pushkin (poet).

728	**215**	10k. brown	60	50
729	**215**	20k. green	60	50
730	**215**	40k. red	1·60	65
731	-	50k. blue	3·25	1·30
732a	-	80k. red	5·00	1·70
733a	-	1r. green	11·00	3·00

DESIGN: 50k. to 1r. Pushkin's Monument, Moscow (A. Opekushin).

216 Pushkin Monument, Moscow (A. Operkushin)

1937. Pushkin Exn, Moscow. Sheet 105×89 mm.

MS733c		**215** 10k. brown; **216** 50k. brown	10·50	£120

217 Meyerhold Theatre

1937. 1st Soviet Architectural Congress.

734A	**217**	3k. red	1·30	85
735A	-	5k. lake	1·50	65
736A	**217**	10k. brown	1·90	50
737A	-	15k. black	3·25	95
738A	-	20k. olive	1·50	60
739A	-	30k. black	1·80	85
740A	-	40k. violet	2·50	1·30
741A	-	50k. brown	4·25	1·40
MS741aB		120×93 mm. 40k.×4 violet (as No. 740). Imperf	35·00	£100

DESIGNS—As T **217**: 5, 15k. G.P.O.; 20, 50k. Red Army Theatre. 45×27 mm: 30k. Hotel Moscow; 40k. Palace of Soviets.

218 F. E. Dzerzhinsky

1937. 10th Death Anniv of Feliks Dzerzhinsky.

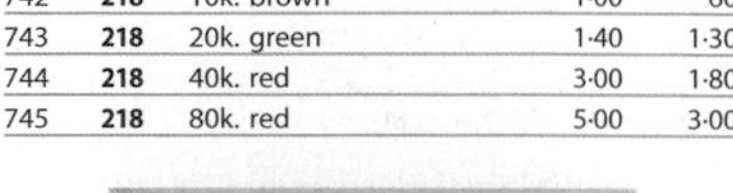

742	**218**	10k. brown	1·00	60
743	**218**	20k. green	1·40	1·30
744	**218**	40k. red	3·00	1·80
745	**218**	80k. red	5·00	3·00

219 Yakovlev Ya-7 Air 7

1937. Air. Air Force Exhibition.

746	**219**	10k. black and brown	2·50	60
747	-	20k. black and green	2·50	60
748	-	30k. black and brown	4·25	65
749	-	40k. black and purple	8·75	1·30
750	-	50k. black and violet	10·50	3·00
751	-	80k. brown and blue	13·00	3·00
752	-	1r. black, orange & brown	26·00	5·50
MS752b		165×90 mm. No. 752×4. Imperf	£120	£275

DESIGNS—As T **219**: 20k. Tupolev ANT-9; 30k. Tupolev ANT-6 bomber; 40k. O.S.G.A. 101 flying boat; 50k. Tupolev ANT-4 TB-1 bomber. 60×26 mm: 80k. Tupolev ANT-20 "Maksim Gorki"; 1r. Tupolev ANT-14 "Pravda".

220 Arms of Ukraine

221 Arms of U.S.S.R.

1937. New U.S.S.R. Constitution. Arms of Constituent Republics.

753	-	20k. blue (Armenia)	2·75	90
754	-	20k. purple (Azerbaijan)	2·75	90
755	-	20k. brown (Byelorussia)	2·75	90
756	-	20k. red (Georgia)	2·75	90
757	-	20k. green (Kazakhstan)	2·75	90
758	-	20k. red (Kirghizia)	2·75	90
759	-	20k. red (Tadzhikistan)	2·75	90
760	-	20k. red (Turkmenistan)	2·75	90
761	**220**	20k. red (Ukraine)	2·75	90
762	-	20k. orange (Uzbekistan)	2·75	90
763	-	20k. blue (R.S.F.S.R.)	2·75	90
764	**221**	40k. red (U.S.S.R.)	7·75	3·25

222 "Worker and Collective Farmer" (sculpture, Vera Mukhina)

223 Russian Pavilion, Paris Exhibition

1938. Paris International Exhibition.

765	**222**	5k. red	1·30	50
766	**223**	20k. red	1·70	50
767	**222**	50k. blue	3·50	1·30

224 Shota Rustaveli

1938. 750th Anniv of Poem "Knight in Tiger Skin".

768	**224**	20k. green	1·70	60

225 Route of North Pole Flight

1938. North Pole Flight.

769	**225**	10k. black and brown	1·70	35
770	**225**	20k. black and grey	3·50	65
771	-	40k. red and green	7·75	2·30
772	-	80k. red and deep red	2·50	1·40

DESIGN: 40k., 80k. Soviet Flag at North Pole.

227 Infantryman

1938. 20th Anniv of Red Army.

773	**227**	10k. black and red	65	35
774	-	20k. black and red	85	35
775	-	30k. black, red and blue	1·50	40
776	-	40k. black, red and blue	2·20	1·00
777	-	50k. black and red	2·75	1·00
778a	-	80k. black and red	5·00	1·30
779	-	1r. black and red	3·25	2·20

DESIGNS—VERT: 20k. Tank driver; 30k. Sailor; 40k. Airman; 50k. Artilleryman. HORIZ: 80k. Stalin reviewing cavalry; 1r. Machine gunners.

229 G. Baidukov, V. Chkalov and A. Belyakov

1938. 1st Flight over North Pole.

780	**229**	10k. red and black	2·20	60
781	**229**	20k. red and black	2·20	60
782	**229**	40k. red and brown	4·00	1·80
783	**229**	50k. red and purple	7·50	3·25

230 M. Gromov, A. Yumashov and S. Danilin

1938. 2nd Flight over North Pole.

784	**230**	10k. purple	4·00	60
785	**230**	20k. black	4·00	1·30
786	**230**	50k. purple	7·00	1·70

231 Ice-breaker "Murman" approaching Survivors

1938. Rescue of Papanin's North Pole Meteorological Party.

787	**231**	10k. purple	4·25	65
788	**231**	20k. blue	4·25	95
789	-	30k. brown	7·75	1·30
790	-	50k. blue	8·75	2·50

DESIGNS—VERT: 30, 50k. Papanin survivors.

233 Nurse weighing Baby

234 Children visiting Statue of Lenin

1938. Soviet Union Children.

791	**233**	10k. blue	1·50	40
792	**234**	15k. blue	1·50	50
793	-	20k. purple	2·00	55
794	-	30k. red	2·40	85
795	-	40k. brown	2·75	1·10
796	-	50k. blue	5·75	1·80
797	-	80k. green	7·50	2·10

DESIGNS—HORIZ: 20, 40k. Biology class; 30k. Health camp; 50, 80k. Young inventors at play.

235 Crimean landscape

1938. Views of Crimea and Caucasus.

798	**235**	5k. black	1·30	65
799	**A**	5k. brown	1·30	65
800	**B**	10k. green	2·50	85
801	**C**	10k. brown	2·50	1·00
802	**D**	15k. black	5·00	1·20
803	**A**	15k. black	5·00	1·20
804	**E**	20k. brown	4·25	1·40
805	**C**	30k. black	5·25	1·60
806	**F**	40k. brown	5·25	1·60
807	**G**	50k. green	5·75	2·30
808	**H**	80k. brown	6·50	2·40
809	**I**	1r. green	11·00	6·25

DESIGNS—HORIZ: A, Yalta (two views); B, Georgian military road; E, Crimean resthouse; F, Alupka; H, Crimea; I, Swallows' Nest Castle. VERT: C, Crimea (two views); D, Swallows' Nest Castle; G, Gurzuf Park.

236 Schoolchildren and Model Tupolev ANT-6 Bomber

1938. Aviation.

810	**236**	5k. purple	2·00	85
811	-	10k. brown	2·00	85
812	-	15k. red	2·50	1·00
813	-	20k. blue	2·50	1·00
814	-	30k. red	4·25	1·80
815	-	40k. blue	7·25	2·00
816	-	50k. green	13·00	2·30
817	-	80k. brown	8·25	3·25
818	-	1r. green	14·00	3·50

DESIGNS—HORIZ: 10k. Glider in flight; 40k. Yakovlev VT-2 seaplane; 1r. Tupolev ANT-6 bomber. VERT: 15k. Captive observation balloon; 20k. Airship "Osoaviakhim" over Kremlin; 30k. Parachutists; 30k. Balloon in flight; 80k. Stratosphere balloon.

237 Underground Railway

1938. Moscow Underground Railway Extension.

819		10k. violet	2·30	85
820		15k. brown	2·50	1·00
821		20k. black	3·50	1·10
822		30k. violet	4·75	1·50
823	**237**	40k. black	5·25	1·90
824	-	50k. brown	5·75	2·75

DESIGNS—VERT: 10k. Mayakovskaya station; 15k. Sokol station; 20k. Kievsskaya station. HORIZ: 30k. Dynamo station; 50k. Revolutskaya station.

238 Miner and Pneumatic Drill

1938. 20th Anniv of Federation of Young Lenin Communists.

825		20k. blue	1·20	40
826	**238**	30k. purple	1·50	50
827	-	40k. purple	1·90	55
828	-	50k. red	2·50	1·00
829	-	80k. blue	6·75	1·40

DESIGNS—VERT: 20k. Girl parachutist; 50k. Students and university. HORIZ: 40k. Harvesting; 80k. Airman, sailor and battleship "Marat".

239 Diving

1938. Soviet Sports.

830	**239**	5k. red	2·00	40
831	-	10k. black	2·75	75
832	-	15k. brown	4·50	85
833	-	20k. green	4·50	1·10
834	-	30k. purple	9·25	1·40
835	-	40k. green	10·00	1·60
836	-	50k. blue	9·25	2·50
837	-	80k. blue	9·25	3·75

DESIGNS: 10k. Discus throwing; 15k. Tennis; 20k. Motor cycling; 30k. Skiing; 40k. Sprinting; 50k. Football; 80k. Athletic parade.

241 Council of People's Commissars Headquarters and Hotel Moscow

1939. New Moscow. Architectural designs as T 241.

838		10k. brown	1·00	65
839	**241**	20k. green	1·70	85
840	-	30k. purple	2·20	1·00
841	-	40k. blue	3·00	1·30
842	-	50k. red	4·25	1·50
843	-	80k. olive	7·00	2·30
844	-	1r. blue	7·75	3·00

DESIGNS—HORIZ: 10k. Gorky Avenue; 30k. Lenin Library; 40k. Crimea suspension and 50k. Arched bridges over River Moskva; 80k. Khimki river station. VERT: 1r. Dynamo underground station.

242 Paulina Osipenko

1939. Women's Moscow–Far East Flight.

845	**242**	15k. green	1·50	85
846	-	30k. purple	1·50	1·10
847	-	60k. red	3·00	1·70

PORTRAITS: 30k. Marina Raskova; 60k. Valentina Grisodubova.

243 Russian Pavilion, N.Y. World's Fair

1939. New York World's Fair.

848		30k. red and black	2·50	60
849	**243**	50k. brown and blue	4·25	1·10

DESIGN—VERT: (26×41½ mm): 30k. Statue over Russian pavilion.

244 T. G. Shevchenko in early Manhood

1939. 125th Birth Anniv of Shevchenko (Ukrainian poet and painter).

853	**244**	15k. black and brown	2·00	65
854	-	30k. black and red	3·00	1·00
855	-	60k. brown and green	5·25	2·10

DESIGNS: 30k. Last portrait of Shevchenko; 60k. Monument to Shevchenko, Kharkov.

245 Milkmaid

1939. All Union Agricultural Fair.

856	**245**	10k. red	70	15
857	-	15k. red	70	35
858a	-	20k. grey	1·30	40
859	-	30k. orange	95	25
860	-	30k. violet	95	25
861	-	45k. green	1·70	35
862	-	50k. brown	1·20	40
863a	-	60k. violet	3·50	1·70
864	-	80k. violet	1·20	90
865	-	1r. blue	2·50	1·20

DESIGNS—HORIZ: 15k. Harvesting; 20k. Sheep farming; 30k. (No. 860) Agricultural Fair Pavilion. VERT: 30k. (No. 859) Agricultural Fair Emblem; 45k. Gathering cotton; 50k. Thoroughbred horses; 60k. "Agricultural Wealth"; 80k. Girl with sugar beet; 1r. Trapper.

18 АВГУСТА
ДЕНЬ АВИАЦИИ СССР
(247)

1939. Aviation Day. As Nos. 811, 814/16 and 818 (colours changed) optd with T 247.

866		10k. red	1·20	65
867		30k. blue	2·00	65
868		40k. green	2·50	90
869		50k. violet	3·25	1·10
870		1r. brown	7·00	3·75

1939. Surch.

871	141	30k. on 4k. mauve	19·00	12·00

249 Saltykov-Shchedrin

1939. 50th Death Anniv of M. E. Saltykov-Shchedrin (writer and satirist).

872	249	15k. red	65	25
873	-	30k. green	85	40
874	249	45k. brown	1·00	55
875	-	60k. blue	1·60	80

DESIGN: 30, 60k. Saltykov-Shchedrin in later years.

250 Kislovodsk Sanatorium

1939. Caucasian Health Resorts.

876	250	5k. brown	50	15
877	-	10k. red	50	25
878	-	15k. green	55	35
879	-	20k. green	60	45
880	-	30k. blue	75	55
881	-	50k. black	2·20	1·00
882	-	60k. purple	2·50	1·20
883	-	80k. red	3·50	1·60

DESIGNS: 10, 15, 30, 50, 80k. Sochi Convalescent Homes; 20k. Abkhazia Sanatorium, Novyi Afon; 60k. Sukumi Rest Home.

251 M. I. Lermontov

1939. 125th Birth Anniv of Lermontov (poet and novelist).

884	251	15k. brown and blue	1·50	50
885	-	30k. black and green	3·00	85
886	-	45k. blue and red	3·25	2·10

252 N. G. Chernyshevsky

1939. 50th Death Anniv of N. G. Chernyshevsky (writer and politician).

887B	252	15k. green	1·00	35
888A	252	30k. violet	1·70	55
889A	252	60k. green	2·20	1·00

253 A. P. Chekhov

1940. 80th Birth Anniv of Chekhov (writer).

890	253	10k. green	60	20
891	253	15k. blue	65	20
892	-	20k. violet	1·10	35
893	-	30k. brown	2·10	65

DESIGN: 20, 30k. Chekhov with hat on.

254 Welcoming Soviet Troops

1940. Occupation of Eastern Poland.

893a	254	10k. red	1·10	40
894	-	30k. green	1·30	55
895	-	50k. black	1·70	1·10
896	-	60k. blue	2·20	1·20
897	-	1r. red	5·00	2·00

DESIGNS: 30k. Villagers welcoming tank crew; 50, 60k. Soldier distributing newspapers to crowd; 1r. People waving to column of tanks.

255 Ice-breaker "Georgy Sedov" and Badigin and Trofimov

1940. Polar Research.

898		15k. green	2·20	60
899	255	30k. violet	4·00	80
900	-	50k. brown	5·25	1·90
901	-	1r. blue	9·50	2·50

DESIGNS: 15k. Ice-breaker "Iosif Stalin" and portraits of Papanin and Belousov; 50k. Badgin and Papanin meeting. LARGER. (46×26 mm): 1r. Route of drift of "Georgy Sedov".

256 V. Mayakovsky

1940. 10th Death Anniv of Mayakovsky (poet).

902	256	15k. red	35	20
903	256	30k. brown	65	25
904	-	60k. violet	1·30	65
905	-	80k. blue	1·10	65

DESIGN—VERT: 60, 80k. Mayakovsky in profile wearing a cap.

257 Timiryazev

1940. 20th Death Anniv of K. A. Timiryazev (scientist).

906		10k. blue	70	40
907		15k. violet	70	40
908	257	30k. brown	1·30	65
909	-	60k. green	3·00	1·30

DESIGNS—HORIZ: 10k. Miniature of Timiryazev and Academy of Agricultural Sciences, Moscow; 15k. Timiryazev in laboratory. VERT: 60k. Timiryazev's statue (by S. Merkurov), Moscow.

258 Relay Runner

1940. 2nd All Union Physical Culture Festival.

910	258	15k. red	1·30	40
911a	-	30k. purple	2·20	40
912a	-	50k. blue	5·25	2·10
913	-	60k. blue	4·25	1·70
914	-	1r. green	7·00	2·50

DESIGNS—HORIZ: 30k. Girls parade; 60k. Skiing; 1r. Grenade throwing. VERT: 50k. Children and sports badges.

259 Tchaikovsky and Passage from his "Fourth Symphony"

1940. Birth Cent of Tchaikovsky (composer).

915		15k. green	1·60	40
916	259	20k. brown	1·70	55
917	259	30k. blue	1·90	75
918	-	50k. red	2·75	90
919	-	60k. red	3·00	1·30

DESIGNS: 15, 50k. Tchaikovsky's house at Klin; 60k. Tchaikovsky and excerpt from "Eugene Onegin".

260 Central Regions Pavilion

ПАВИЛЬОН «ПОВОЛЖЬЕ»
No. 920

ПАВИЛЬОН «ДАЛЬНИЙ ВОСТОК»
No. 921

[illegible]
No. 922

ПАВИЛЬОН МОСКОВСКОЙ, РЯЗАНСКОЙ И ТУЛЬСКОЙ ОБЛ.
No. 923

ПАВИЛЬОН УКРАИНСКОЙ ССР
No. 924

ПАВИЛЬОН БЕЛОРУССКОЙ ССР
No. 925

ПАВИЛЬОН АЗЕРБАЙДЖАНСКОЙ ССР
No. 926

ПАВИЛЬОН ГРУЗИНСКОЙ ССР
No. 927

ПАВИЛЬОН АРМЯНСКОЙ ССР
No. 928

[illegible]
No. 929

ПАВИЛЬОН ТУРКМЕНСКОЙ ССР
No. 930

ПАВИЛЬОН ТАДЖИКСКОЙ ССР
No. 931

ПАВИЛЬОН КИРГИЗСКОЙ ССР
No. 932

ПАВИЛЬОН КАРЕЛО-ФИНСКОЙ ССР
No. 933

ПАВИЛЬОН КАЗАХСКОЙ ССР
No. 934

ГЛАВНЫЙ ПАВИЛЬОН
No. 935

ПАВИЛЬОН МЕХАНИЗАЦИИ
No. 936

1940. All Union Agricultural Fair, Coloured reproductions of Soviet Pavilions in green frames as T 260. Inscriptions at foot as illustrated.

920	10k. Volga provinces (RSFSR) (horiz)	2·50	1·70
921	15k. Far East	1·90	1·30
922	30k. Leningrad and North East RSFSR	2·20	1·30
923	30k. Three Central Regions (RSFSR)	2·20	1·30
924	30k. Ukrainian SSR	2·20	1·30
925	30k. Byelorussian SSR	2·20	1·30
926	30k. Azerbaijan SSR	2·20	1·30
927	30k. Georgian SSR (horiz)	2·20	1·30
928	30k. Armenian SSR	2·20	1·30
929	30k. Uzbek SSR	2·20	1·30
930	30k. Turkmen SSR (horiz)	2·20	1·30
931	30k. Tadzhik SSR	2·20	1·30
932	30k. Kirgiz SSR	2·20	1·30
933	30k. Karelo-Finnish SSR	2·20	1·30
934	30k. Kazakh SSR	2·20	1·30
935	50k. Main Pavilion	3·50	2·50
936	60k. Mechanization Pavilion and the statue of Stalin	4·25	3·25

261 Grenade Thrower

1940. 20th Anniv of Wrangel's Defeat at Perekop (Crimea). Perf or imperf.

937A	-	10k. green	1·10	35
938A	261	15k. red	65	35
939A	-	30k. brown and red	1·40	85
940A	-	50k. purple	1·30	75
941A	-	60k. blue	1·30	75
942A	-	1r. black	2·50	1·50

DESIGNS—VERT: 10k. Red Army Heroes Monument; 30k. Map of Perekop and portrait of M. V. Frunze; 1r. Victorious soldier. HORIZ: 50k. Soldiers crossing R. Sivash; 60k. Army H.Q. at Stroganovka.

262 Railway Bridge and Moscow–Volga Canal, Khimka

1941. Industrial and Agricultural Records.

943		10k. blue	60	40
944		15k. mauve	60	40
945	262	20k. blue	1·70	85
946	-	30k. brown	2·20	85
947	-	50k. brown	85	40
948	-	60k. brown	1·70	85
949	-	1r. green	3·50	2·10

DESIGNS—VERT: 10k. Coal-miners and pithead; 15k. Blast furnace; 1r. Derricks and petroleum refinery. HORIZ: 30k. Steam locomotives; 50k. Harvesting; 60k. Ball-bearing vehicles.

263 Red Army Ski Corps

1941. 23rd Anniv of Red Army. Designs with Hammer, Sickle and Star Symbol.

950a	263	5k. violet	1·30	40
951	-	10k. blue	1·00	35
952	-	15k. green	50	35
953a	-	20k. red	80	25
954a	-	30k. brown	70	25
955a	-	45k. green	2·50	85
956	-	50k. blue	85	85
957	-	1r. green	1·20	1·00
957b	-	3r. green	7·00	3·25

DESIGNS—VERT: 10k. Sailor; 20k. Cavalry; 30k. Automatic Rifle Squad; 50k. Airman; 1, 3r. Marshal's star. HORIZ: 15k. Artillery; 45k. Clearing a hurdle.

264 N. E. Zhukovsky and Air Force Academy

1941. 20th Death Anniv of Zhukovsky (scientist).

958		15k. blue	70	25
959	264	30k. red	1·50	40
960	-	50k. red	2·20	60

DESIGNS—VERT: 15k. Zhukovsky; 50k. Zhukovsky lecturing.

265 Thoroughbred Horses

1941. 15th Anniv of Kirghiz S.S.R.

961	**265**	15k. brown	3·00	60
962a	-	30k. violet	4·25	1·10

DESIGN: 30k. Coal miner and colliery.

266 Arms of Karelo-Finnish S.S.R.

1941. 1st Anniv of Karelo-Finnish Republic.

963	**266**	30k. red	1·00	65
964	**266**	45k. green	1·00	85

267 Marshal Suvorov

1941. 150th Anniv of Battle of Izmail.

965	-	10k. green	85	40
966	-	15k. red	85	45
967	**267**	30k. blue	2·20	60
968	**267**	1r. brown	3·00	1·90

DESIGN: 10, 15k. Storming of Izmail.

268 Spassky Tower, Kremlin

1941

970	**268**	1r. red	2·20	65
971	-	2r. brown	4·75	1·40

DESIGN—HORIZ: 2r. Kremlin Palace.

269 "Razin on the Volga"

1941. 25th Death Anniv of Surikov (artist).

972		20k. black	3·50	1·80
973	**269**	30k. red	5·75	1·80
974	-	50k. purple	11·00	5·50
975	**269**	1r. green	14·50	9·00
976	-	2r. brown	33·00	10·50

DESIGNS—VERT: 20, 50k. "Suvorov's march through Alps, 1799"; 2r. Surikov.

270 Lenin Museum (interior)

1941. 5th Anniv of Lenin Museum.

977	**270**	15k. red	3·50	2·50
978	-	30k. violet on mauve	24·00	17·00
979	**270**	45k. green	8·75	6·75
980	-	1r. red on rose	21·00	17·00

DESIGN: 30k., 1r. Exterior of Lenin Museum.

271 M. Yu. Lermontov

1941. Death Centenary of M. Yu. Lermontov (poet and novelist).

981	**271**	15k. grey	11·50	7·50
982	**271**	30k. violet	17·00	12·50

272 Poster by L. Lisitsky

1941. Mobilization.

983a	**272**	30k. red	22·00	25·00

273 Mass Enlistment

1941. National Defence.

984	**273**	30k. blue	85·00	65·00

274 Alishir Navoi

1942. 5th Centenary of Uzbek poet Mir Ali Shir (Alishir Navoi).

985	**274**	30k. brown	35·00	14·50
986	**274**	1r. purple	17·00	21·00

275 Lt. Talalikhin ramming Enemy Bomber

289a Five Heroes

1942. Russian Heroes (1st issue).

987	**275**	20k. blue	60	35
988	**A**	30k. grey	70	40
989	**B**	30k. black	70	40
990	**C**	30k. black	70	40
991	**D**	30k. black	70	40
992	**C**	1r. green	6·00	4·00
993	**D**	2r. green	11·50	6·75
1048c	**275**	30k. green	1·30	60
1048d	**A**	30k. blue	1·30	60
1048e	**C**	30k. green	1·30	60
1048f	**D**	30k. purple	1·30	60
1048g	**289a**	30k. blue	1·30	60

DESIGNS: A, Capt. Gastello and burning fighter plane diving into enemy petrol tanks; B, Maj-Gen. Dovator and Cossack cavalry in action; C, Shura Chekalin guerrilla fighting; D, Zoya Kosmodemyanskaya being led to death.

See also Nos. 1072/6.

276 Anti-tank Gun

1942. War Episodes (1st series).

994	**276**	20k. brown	2·20	1·00
995	-	30k. blue	2·20	1·00
996	-	30k. green	2·20	1·00
997	-	30k. red	2·20	1·00
998	-	60k. grey	5·25	3·25
999	-	1r. brown	6·00	5·00

DESIGNS—HORIZ: 30k. (No. 996), Guerrillas attacking train; 30k. (No. 997), Munition worker; 1r. Machine gunners. VERT: 30k. (No. 995), Signallers; 60k. Defenders of Leningrad.

277 Distributing Gifts to Soldiers

1942. War Episodes (2nd series).

1000	**277**	20k. blue	1·90	1·00
1001	-	20k. purple	1·90	1·00
1002	-	30k. purple	2·40	1·50
1003	-	45k. red	7·75	3·00
1004	-	45k. blue	6·00	4·25

DESIGNS—VERT: No. 1001, Bomber destroying tank; No. 1002, Food packers; No. 1003, Woman sewing; No. 1004, Anti-aircraft gun.

See also Nos. 1013/17.

278 Munition Worker

1943. 25th Anniv of Russian Revolution.

1005	**278**	5k. brown	60	35
1006	-	10k. brown	85	25
1007	-	15k. blue	70	25
1008	-	20k. blue	70	25
1009	-	30k. brown	1·00	40
1010	-	60k. brown	1·70	85
1011	-	1r. red	2·50	1·50
1012	-	2r. brown	5·25	2·50

DESIGNS: 10k. Lorry convoy; 15k. Troops supporting Lenin's banner; 20k. Leningrad seen through an archway; 30k. Spassky Tower, Lenin and Stalin; 60k. Tank parade; 1r. Lenin speaking; 2r. Star of Order of Lenin.

279 Nurses and Wounded Soldier

1943. War Episodes (3rd series).

1013	**279**	30k. green	1·60	1·20
1014	-	30k. green (Scouts)	1·60	1·20
1015	-	30k. brown (Mine-thrower)	1·60	1·20
1016	-	60k. green (Anti-tank troops)	2·50	1·40
1017	-	60k. blue (Sniper)	2·50	1·40

280 Routes of Bering's Voyages

1943. Death Bicent of Vitus Bering (explorer).

1018		30k. blue	1·70	40
1019	**280**	60k. grey	3·00	85
1020	-	1r. green	9·50	2·20
1021	**280**	2r. brown	16·00	4·50

DESIGN: 30k., 1r. Mt. St. Ilya.

281 Gorky

1943. 75th Birth Anniv of Maksim Gorky (novelist).

1022	**281**	30k. green	1·10	35
1023	**281**	60k. blue	1·50	40

282 Order of the Great Patriotic War

(a) Order of Suvorov

1943. War Orders and Medals (1st series), Medals with ribbon attached.

1024	**282**	1r. black	3·50	2·50
1025	**a**	10r. olive	10·50	9·25

See also Nos. 1051/8, 1089/94, 1097/99a, 1172/86, 1197/1204 and 1776/80a.

283 Karl Marx

1943. 125th Birth Anniv of Marx.

1026	**283**	30k. blue	1·70	85
1027	**283**	60k. green	3·50	1·70

284 Naval Landing Party

1943. 25th Anniv of Red Army and Navy.

1028	**284**	20k. brown	35	25
1029	-	30k. green	45	20
1030	-	60k. green	1·30	50
1031	**284**	3r. blue	3·00	90

DESIGNS: 30k. Sailors and anti-aircraft gun; 60k. Tanks and infantry.

285 Ivan Turgenev

1943. 125th Birth Anniv of Ivan Turgenev (novelist).

1032	**285**	30k. green	16·00	15·00
1032a	**285**	60k. violet	22·00	18·00

286 Loading a Gun

1943. 25th Anniv of Young Communist League.

1033	**286**	15k. blue	65	20
1034	-	20k. orange	65	25
1035	-	30k. brown and red	80	20
1036a	-	1r. green	1·30	40
1037	-	2r. green	2·40	85

DESIGNS—As T **286**: 20k. Tank and banner; 1r. Infantrymen; 2r. Grenade thrower. 22½×28½ mm: 30k. Bayonet fighter and flag.

287 V. V. Mayakovsky

1943. 50th Birth Anniv of Mayakovsky (poet).

1038	**287**	30k. orange	1·00	60
1039	**287**	60k. blue	1·10	65

288 Memorial Tablet and Allied Flags

1943. Teheran Three Power Conference and 26th Anniv of Revolution.

1040	**288**	30k. black	1·10	50
1041	**288**	3r. blue	4·25	1·30

289 Defence of Odessa

1944. Liberation of Russian Towns.

1045	-	30k. brown and red	70	30
1046	-	30k. blue	70	30
1047	-	30k. green	70	30
1048	289	30k. green	70	30

MS1048b 139×105 mm. No. 1047×4. Imperf 22·00 17·00

DESIGNS: No. 1045, Stalingrad; No. 1046, Sevastopol; No. 1047, Leningrad.

АВИАПОЧТА
1944 г.
1 РУБЛЬ
(290)

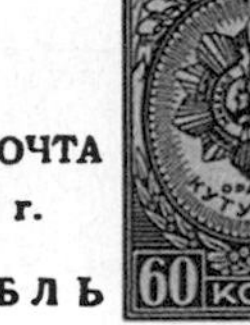

291 Order of Kutusov

(b) Order of Patriotic War

(c) Order of Aleksandr Nevsky **(d)** Order of Suvorov **(e)** Order of Kutusov

1944. Air. Surch with T 290.

1049	275	1r. on 30k. grey	2·20	65
1050	A	1r. on 30k. blue (No. 1048d)	2·20	65

1944. War Orders and Medals (2nd series). Various Stars without ribbons showing as Types b to e. Perf or imperf. (a) Frames as T 291.

1051B	b	15k. red	45	25
1052B	c	20k. blue	45	25
1053A	d	30k. green	1·00	50
1054A	e	60k. red	1·70	85

(b) Frames as T 282.

1055B	b	1r. black	85	40
1056B	c	3r. blue	3·25	1·00
1057B	e	5r. green	4·25	1·70
1058B	d	10r. red	4·75	3·25

293 Lenin Mausoleum and Red Square, Moscow

1944. "Twenty Years without Lenin". As Nos. 667/72, but inscr "1924–1944", and T 293.

1059	-	30k. black and blue	50	40
1060	199	30k. red and orange	50	40
1061	-	45k. black and blue	60	40
1062	-	50k. black and blue	85	50
1063	-	60k. black and blue	1·80	60
1064	293	1r. brown and blue	2·20	1·30
1065	199	3r. black and orange	4·25	3·00

DESIGNS—VERT: Lenin at 3 years of age (No. 1059): at school (45k.); as man (50k.); as orator (60k.).

294 Allied Flags

1944. 14 June (Allied Nations' Day).

1066	294	60k. black, red and blue	1·70	60
1067	294	3r. blue and red	6·25	2·10

295 Rimsky-Korsakov and Bolshoi Theatre

1944. Birth Centenary of Rimsky-Korsakov (composer). Imperf or perf.

1068A	295	30k. grey	45	15
1069A	295	60k. green	60	15
1070A	295	1r. green	1·30	25
1071A	295	3r. violet	2·50	65

296 Nuradilov and Machine-gun

297 Polivanova and Kovshova

1944. War Heroes (3rd issue).

1072	296	30k. green	50	40
1073	-	60k. violet	1·00	50
1074	-	60k. blue	1·00	50
1075	297	60k. green	1·60	50
1076	-	60k. black	1·60	50

DESIGNS—HORIZ: No. 1073, Matrosov defending a snow-trench; 1074, Luzak hurling a hand grenade. VERT: No. 1076, B. Safonev, medals and aerial battle over the sea.

298 S. A. Chaplygin

1944. 75th Birth Anniv of S. A. Chaplygin (scientist).

1077	298	30k. grey	35	25
1078	298	1r. brown	1·40	1·20

299 V. I. Chapaev

1944. Heroes of 1918 Civil War.

1079	299	30k. green	1·00	40
1080	-	30k. black (N. Shchors)	1·00	40
1081	-	30k. green (S. Lazo)	1·00	40

For 40k. stamp as Type **299**, see No. 1531.
See also Nos. 1349/51.

300 Repin (self-portrait) **301** "Reply of the Cossacks to Sultan Mahmoud IV"

1944. Birth Centenary of Ilya Refimovich Repin (artist). Imperf or perf.

1082A	300	30k. green	1·20	35
1083A	301	50k. green	1·20	35
1084A	301	60k. blue	1·20	35
1085A	300	1r. brown	1·80	50
1086A	301	2r. violet	3·25	1·10

302 I. A. Krylov

1944. Death Centenary of Krylov (fabulist).

1087	302	30k. brown	1·10	25
1088	302	1r. blue	1·70	50

(f) Partisans' Medal **(g)** Medal for Bravery **(h)** Order of Bogdan Chmlelnitsky **(j)** Order of Victory

(k) Order of Ushakov **(l)** Order of Nakhimov

1945. War Orders and Medals (3rd series). Frame as T 291 with various centres as Types f to l. Perf or imperf.

1089A	f	15k. black	45	15
1090A	g	30k. blue	85	25
1091A	h	45k. blue	1·50	40
1092A	j	60k. red	2·40	45
1093A	k	1r. blue	3·25	1·00
1094A	l	1r. green	3·25	1·00

303 Griboedov (after P. Karatygin)

1945. 150th Birth Anniv of Aleksander S. Griboedov (author).

1095	303	30k. green	1·50	50
1096	303	60k. brown	2·20	85

1945. War Orders and Medals (4th series). Frames as T 282. Various centres.

1097	g	1r. black	1·70	65
1098	h	2r. black	4·25	1·30
1098a	h	2r. purple	44·00	22·00
1098b	h	2r. olive	10·50	5·00
1099	j	3r. red	5·25	1·50
1099a	j	3r. purple	6·50	2·75

305 Soldier

1945. Relief of Stalingrad.

1100	305	60k. black and red	1·70	1·30
1101	305	3r. black and red	4·25	2·75

MS1101b 103×138 mm. No. 1101×4. Imperf 48·00 42·00

306 Standard Bearer

1945. Red Army Victories.

1102	306	20k. green, red and black	45	25
1103	-	30k. black and red	50	40
1104	-	1r. green and red	2·20	1·60

DESIGN—HORIZ: 30k. Infantry v. Tank; 1r. Infantry charge.

308 Attack

1945. Liberation of Russian Soil.

1105	308	30k. blue	70	60
1106	-	60k. red	1·00	85
1107	-	1r. green	2·40	1·60

DESIGNS: 60k. Welcoming troops; 1r. Grenade thrower.

309 Badge and Guns

1945. Red Guards Commemoration.

1108	309	60k. red	3·00	1·00

310 Barricade

1945. Battle of Moscow.

1109	-	30k. blue	45	35
1110	310	60k. black	85	50
1111	-	1r. black	1·50	90

DESIGNS: 30k. Tanks in Red Square, Moscow. 1r. Aerial battle and searchlights.

311 Prof. Lomonosov and Academy of Sciences, Leningrad

1945. 220th Anniv of Academy of Sciences.

1112		30k. blue	1·10	40
1113	311	2r. black	3·50	1·00

DESIGN—VERT: 30k. Moscow Academy, inscr "1725–1945".

312 Popov

1945. 50th Anniv of Popov's Radio Discoveries.

1114	312	30k. blue	75	35
1115	312	60k. red	1·30	60
1116	-	1r. brown (Popov)	2·10	1·00

314 Motherhood Medal

315 Motherhood Medal

1945. Orders and Medals of Motherhood. Imperf or perf.

1117B	314	20k. brown on blue	50	35
1118B	-	30k. brown on green	70	50
1119B	-	60k. red	1·40	1·20
1120B	315	1r. black on green	1·80	65
1121B	-	2r. blue	2·75	1·40
1122B	-	3r. red on blue	4·00	2·10

DESIGNS: 30k., 2r. Order of Motherhood Glory; 60k., 3r. Order of Heroine-Mother.

317 Ilyushin Il-2M3 Stormovik Fighters

318 Petlyakov Pe-8 TB-7 Bomber

1945. Air. Aviation Day.

1123	**316**	1r. brown	3·50	1·20
1124	**317**	1r. brown	3·50	1·20
1125	-	1r. red	3·50	1·20
1126	-	1r. black	3·50	1·20
1127	-	1r. blue	3·50	1·20
1128	-	1r. green	3·50	1·20
1129	**318**	1r. grey	3·50	1·20
1130	-	1r. brown	3·50	1·20
1131	-	1r. red	3·50	1·20

DESIGNS—As Type **317**: No. 1125, Lavochkin La-7 fighter shooting tail off enemy plane; 1126, Ilyushin Il-4 DB-3 bombers dropping bombs; 1127, Tupolev ANT-60 Tu-2 bombers in flight; 1128, Polikarpov Po-2 biplane. As Type **318**: No. 1130, Yakovlev Yak-3 fighter destroying Messerschmitt BF 109 fighter; 1131, Yakovlev Yak-9 fighter destroying Henschel Hs 129B fighter.

See also Nos. 1163/71.

ПРАЗДНИК
ПОБЕДЫ

9 мая
1945 года

(319)

1945. VE Day. No. 1099 optd with T 319.

1132	**j**	3r. red	4·00	1·50

320 Lenin

321 Lenin

1945. 75th Birth Anniv of Lenin.

1133	**320**	30k. blue	45	25
1134	-	50k. brown	1·00	25
1135	-	60k. red	1·10	35
1136	**321**	1r. black	2·00	50
1137	-	3r. brown	3·75	1·80

DESIGNS—VERT: (inscr "1870–1945"). 50k. Lenin at desk; 60k. Lenin making a speech; 3r. Portrait of Lenin.

322 Kutuzov (after R. Volkov)

1945. Birth Bicentenary of Mikhail Kutuzov (military leader).

1138	**322**	30k. blue	95	35
1139	**322**	60k. brown	1·70	65

323 A. I. Herzen

1945. 75th Death Anniv of Herzen (author and critic).

1140	**323**	30k. brown	85	25
1141	**323**	2r. black	2·50	65

324 I. I. Mechnikov

1945. Birth Centenary of Mechnikov (biologist).

1142	**324**	30k. brown	80	25
1143	**324**	1r. black	1·70	60

325 Friedrich Engels

1945. 125th Birth Anniv of Engels.

1144	**325**	30k. brown	85	40
1145	**325**	60k. green	1·30	75

326 Observer and Guns

327 Heavy Guns

1945. Artillery Day.

1146	**326**	30k. brown	1·80	1·50
1147	**327**	60k. black	4·25	3·00

328 Tank Production

1945. Home Front.

1148	**328**	20k. blue and brown	1·70	50
1149	-	30k. black and brown	2·20	75
1150	-	60k. brown and green	3·50	1·30
1151	-	1r. blue and brown	4·75	1·70

DESIGNS: 30k. Harvesting; 60k. Designing aircraft; 1r. Firework display.

329 Victory Medal

330 Soldier with Victory Flag

1946. Victory Issue.

1152	**329**	30k. violet	35	25
1153	**329**	30k. brown	35	25
1154	**329**	60k. black	60	30
1155	**329**	60k. brown	60	30
1156	**330**	60k. black and red	1·80	90

331 Arms of U.S.S.R.

332 Kremlin, Moscow

1946. Supreme Soviet Elections.

1157	**331**	30k. red	80	35
1158	**332**	45k. red	1·10	40
1159	**331**	60k. green	2·20	85

333 Tank Parade

334 Infantry Parade

1946. 28th Anniv of Red Army and Navy.

1160	**333**	60k. brown	1·30	40
1161	**333**	2r. violet	2·50	1·30
1162	**334**	3r. black and red	5·25	1·80

1946. Air. As Nos. 1123/31.

1163	-	5k. violet (as No. 1130)	60	40
1164	**316**	10k. red	60	40
1165	**317**	15k. red	65	45
1166	**318**	15k. green	65	45
1167	-	20k. black (as No. 1127)	65	45
1168	-	30k. violet (as No. 1127)	1·30	90
1169	-	30k. brown (as No. 1128)	1·30	90
1170	-	50k. blue (as No. 1125)	2·10	1·50
1171	-	60k. blue (as No. 1131)	3·50	1·70

1946. War Orders with Medals (5th series). Frames as T 291 with various centres as Types A to P.

1172	**A**	60k. red	1·70	1·30
1173	**B**	60k. red	1·70	1·30
1174	**C**	60k. green	1·70	1·30
1175	**D**	60k. green	1·70	1·30
1176	**E**	60k. green	1·70	1·30
1177	**F**	60k. blue	1·70	1·30
1178	**G**	60k. blue	1·70	1·30
1179	**H**	60k. violet	1·70	1·30
1180	**J**	60k. purple	1·70	1·30
1181	**K**	60k. brown	1·70	1·30
1182	**L**	60k. brown	1·70	1·30
1183	**M**	60k. purple	1·70	1·30
1184	**N**	60k. red	1·70	1·30
1185	**O**	60k. blue	1·70	1·30
1186	**P**	60k. purple	1·70	1·30

336 P. L. Chebyshev

1946. 125th Birth Anniv of Chebyshev (mathematician).

1187	**336**	30k. brown	60	35
1188	**336**	60k. black	1·10	55

1946. Death of President Kalinin. As T 211, but inscr "3-VI-1946".

1189		20k. black	2·20	1·00

337 Gorky

1946. 10th Death Anniv of Maksim Gorky (novelist).

1190	**337**	30k. brown	65	25
1191	-	60k. green	1·10	60

DESIGN: 60k. Gorky and laurel leaves.

338 Gagry

1946. Health Resorts.

1192		15k. brown	50	20
1193	**338**	30k. green	70	30
1194	-	30k. green	70	30
1195	-	45k. brown	1·00	50

DESIGNS—HORIZ: 15k. Sukumi; 45k. Novy Afon. VERT: 30k. (No. 1194) Sochi.

339 Stalin and Parade of Athletes

1946. Sports Festival.

1196	**339**	30k. green	8·25	4·50

340 Partisan Medal

1946. War Medals (6th series). Frames as T 282 with various centres.

1197	**340**	1r. red	2·20	1·30
1198	**B**	1r. green	2·20	1·30
1199	**C**	1r. brown	2·20	1·30
1200	**D**	1r. blue	2·20	1·30
1201	**G**	1r. grey	2·20	1·30
1202	**H**	1r. red	2·20	1·30
1203	**K**	1r. purple	2·20	1·30
1204	**L**	1r. red	2·20	1·30

341 Moscow Opera House

1946. Moscow Buildings.

1205	-	5k. brown	40	15
1206	**341**	10k. grey	45	15
1207	-	15k. brown	45	25
1208	-	20k. brown	85	35
1209	-	45k. green	1·10	60
1210	-	50k. brown	1·20	85
1211	-	60k. violet	1·60	1·00
1212	-	1r. brown	2·40	1·70

DESIGNS—VERT: 5k. Church of Ivan the Great and Kremlin; 1r. Spassky Tower (larger). HORIZ: 15k. Hotel Moscow; 20k. Theatre and Sverdlov Square; 45k. As 5k. but horiz; 50k. Lenin Museum; 60k. St. Basil's Cathedral and Spassky Tower (larger).

342 Tanks in Red Square

1946. Heroes of Tank Engagements.

1213	**342**	30k. green	2·40	1·90
1214	**342**	60k. brown	4·00	2·75

343 "Iron"

1946. 4th Stalin "Five-Year Reconstruction Plan". Agriculture and Industry.

1215	-	5k. olive	35	15
1216	-	10k. green	45	15
1217	-	15k. brown	50	25
1218	-	20k. violet	85	35
1219	**343**	30k. brown	1·20	50

DESIGNS—HORIZ: 5k. "Agriculture"; 15k. "Coal". VERT: 10k. "Oil"; 20k. "Steel".

344 Soviet Postage Stamps

1946. 25th Anniv of Soviet Postal Services.

1220	-	15k. black and red	2·20	1·10
1221	-	30k. brown and green	3·00	2·00
1222	**344**	60k. black and green	4·75	3·50
MS1222a		138×104 mm. 15k	85·00	65·00
MS1222b		132×104 mm. 30k	85·00	65·00
MS1222c		142×102 mm. 60k	85·00	65·00

DESIGNS: 15k. (48½×23 mm). Stamps on map of U.S.S.R.; 30k. (33×22½ mm). Reproduction of Type **47**.

345 Lenin and Stalin

1946. 29th Anniv of Russian Revolution. Imperf or Perf.

1223b	**345**	30k. orange	3·50	3·00
1224b	**345**	30k. green	3·50	3·00
MS1224c		101×134 mm. No. 1223×4. Imperf	80·00	50·00

346 N. A. Nekrasov

1946. 125th Birth Anniv of Nekrasov (poet).

1225	**346**	30k. black	1·00	40
1226	**346**	60k. brown	1·60	60

347 Stalin Prize Medal

1946. Stalin Prize.

1227	**347**	30k. green	2·75	1·00

348 Dnieperprostroi Dam

1946. Restoration of Dnieperprostroi Hydro-electric Power Station.

1228	**348**	30k. black	1·70	65
1229	**348**	60k. blue	3·00	1·10

349 A. Karpinsky

1947. Birth Centenary of Karpinsky (geologist).

1230	**349**	30k. green	1·40	75
1231	**349**	50k. black	2·75	1·00

350 N. E. Zhukovsky

1947. Birth Centenary of Zhukovsky (scientist).

1232	**350**	30k. black	1·80	60
1233	**350**	60k. blue	2·75	1·10

351 Lenin Mausoleum

352 Lenin

1947. 23rd Death Anniv of Lenin.

1234	**351**	30k. green	1·30	65
1235	**351**	30k. blue	1·30	65
1236	**352**	50k. brown	3·50	1·30

For similar designs inscr "1924/1948" see Nos. 1334/6.

353 Nikolai M. Przhevalsky

1947. Centenary of Soviet Geographical Society.

1237	-	20k. brown	2·00	65
1238	-	20k. blue	2·00	65
1239	**353**	60k. olive	3·50	1·70
1240	-	60k. brown	3·50	1·70

DESIGN: 20k. Miniature portrait of F. P. Litke and full-rigged ship "Senyavin".

354 Arms of R.S.F.S.R.

356 Arms of U.S.S.R.

1947. Supreme Soviet Elections. Arms of Constituent Republics. As T 354.

1241	**354**	30k. red (Russian Federation)	90	65
1242	-	30k. brown (Armenia)	90	65
1243	-	30k. bistre (Azerbaijan)	90	65
1244	-	30k. green (Byelorussia)	90	65
1245	-	30k. grey (Estonia)	90	65
1246	-	30k. brown (Georgia)	90	65
1247	-	30k. purple (Karelo-Finnish S.S.R.)	90	65
1248	-	30k. orange (Kazakhstan)	90	65
1249	-	30k. purple (Kirgizia)	90	65
1250	-	30k. brown (Latvia)	90	65
1251	-	30k. green (Lithuania)	90	65
1252	-	30k. purple (Moldavia)	90	65
1253	-	30k. green (Tadzhikistan)	90	65
1254	-	30k. black (Turkmenistan)	90	65
1255	-	30k. blue (Ukraine)	90	65
1256	-	30k. brown (Uzbekistan)	90	65
1257	**356**	1r. multicoloured	3·00	1·80

A hammer and sickle in the centre of No. 1247 and at the base of No. 1249 should assist identification.

357 Russian Soldier

1947. 29th Anniv of Soviet Army. Perf or imperf.

1258B	**357**	20k. black	70	40
1259B	-	30k. blue	85	50
1260B	-	30k. brown	85	50

DESIGNS—VERT: No. 1259, Military cadet. HORIZ: No. 1260, Soldier, sailor and airman.

359 A. S. Pushkin

1947. 110th Death Anniv of Pushkin (poet).

1261	**359**	30k. black	1·10	65
1262	**359**	50k. green	1·60	1·10

360 Schoolroom

1947. International Women's Day.

1263	**360**	15k. blue	3·75	2·30
1264	-	30k. red	7·00	3·00

DESIGN—26½×39½ mm: 30k. Women students and banner.

362 Moscow Council Building

1947. 30th Anniv of Moscow Soviet. Perf or imperf.

1265b	**362**	30k. red, blue and black	2·30	1·60

363 May Day Procession

1947. May Day.

1266	**363**	30k. red	1·70	1·30
1267	**363**	1r. green	4·00	3·00

364 Yakovlev Yak-9 Fighter and Flag

1947. Air Force Day.

1268	**364**	30k. violet	95	35
1269	**364**	1r. blue	2·40	85

365 Yakhromsky Lock

1947. 10th Anniv of Volga–Moscow Canal.

1270	-	30k. black	75	15
1271	**365**	30k. lake	75	15
1272	-	45k. red	95	35
1273	-	50k. blue	1·30	35
1274	-	60k. red	1·50	50
1275	-	1r. violet	2·50	85

DESIGNS—HORIZ: 30k. (No. 1270), Karamyshevsky Dam; 45k. Yakhromsky Pumping Station; 50k. Khimki Pier; 1r. Lock No. 8. VERT: 60k. Map of Volga–Moscow Canal.

800 лет Москвы
1147—1947 гг.
(366)

1947. 800th Anniv of Moscow (1st issue). Optd as T 366.

1276	20k. brown (No. 1208)	70	35
1277	50k. brown (No. 1210)	1·40	65
1278	60k. violet (No. 1211)	1·90	85
1279	1r. brown (No. 1212)	4·00	2·10

See also Nos. 1286/1300.

367 Izmailovskaya Station

1947. Opening of New Moscow Underground Stations. Inscr "M".

1280	**367**	30k. blue	80	20
1281	-	30k. brown	80	20
1282	-	45k. brown	1·30	40
1283	-	45k. violet	1·30	40
1284	-	60k. green	2·20	60
1285	-	60k. red	2·20	60

DESIGNS—HORIZ: No. 1281, Power plant; No. 1282, Sokol underground station; No. 1283, Stalinskaya underground station; No. 1284, Kievskaya underground station. VERT: No. 1285, Maya Kovskaya underground station.

368 Crimea Bridge, Moscow

1947. 800th Anniv of Moscow (2nd issue).

1286	**368**	5k. brown and blue	45	15
1287	-	10k. black and brown	35	15
1288	-	30k. grey	1·50	40
1289	-	30k. blue	1·50	40
1290	-	30k. brown	1·50	40
1291	-	30k. green	1·50	40
1292	-	30k. green	1·50	40
1293	-	50k. green	1·70	85
1294	-	60k. blue	2·20	65
1295	-	60k. black and brown	2·20	65
1296	-	1r. purple	3·50	1·30

Centre in yellow, red and blue.

1297		1r. blue	5·75	1·90
1298		2r. red	8·75	3·00
1299		3r. blue	14·00	4·25
1300		5r. blue	26·00	8·50
MS1300b		140×175 mm. No. 1299	65·00	42·00

DESIGNS—VERT: 10k. Gorky Street, Moscow; 30k. (No. 1292), Pushkin Place; 60k. (No. 1294), 2r. Kremlin; 1r. (No. 1296), "Old Moscow" after A. M. Vasnetsov; 1r. (No. 1279), St. Basil Cathedral. HORIZ: 30k. (No. 1288), Kiev railway station; 30k. (No. 1289), Kazan railway station; 30k. (No. 1290), Central Telegraph Offices; 30k. (No. 1291), Kaluga Street; 50k. Kremlin; 3r. Kremlin; 5r. Government Buildings. (54½×24½ mm): 60k. (No. 1295), Bridge and Kremlin.

369 "Ritz", Gagry

1947. U.S.S.R. Health Resorts. (a) Vertical.

1301	**369**	30k. green	85	35
1302	-	30k. green (Sukhumi)	85	35

370 "Zapadugol", Sochi

(b) Horizontal.

1303	**370**	30k. black	85	35
1304	-	30k. brown ("New Riviera", Sochi)	85	35
1305	-	30k. purple ("Voroshilov", Sochi)	85	35
1306	-	30k. violet ("Gulripsh", Sukhumi)	85	35
1307	-	30k. blue ("Kemeri", Riga)	85	35
1308	-	30k. brown ("Abkhazia", Novyi Afon)	85	35
1309	-	30k. bistre ("Krestyansky", Livadia)	85	35
1310	-	30k. blue ("Kirov", Kislovodsk)	85	35

371 1917 Revolution

1947. 30th Anniv of Revolution. Perf or imperf.

1311A	**371**	30k. black and red	70	40
1312B	-	50k. blue and red	1·70	60
1313B	**371**	60k. black and red	1·40	75
1314B	-	60k. brown and red	1·40	75
1315B	-	1r. black and red	3·00	1·30
1316B	-	2r. green and red	5·25	3·00

DESIGNS: 50k., 1r. "Industry"; 60k. (No. 1314), 2r. "Agriculture".

372 Metallurgical Works

1947. Post-War Five Year Plan. Horiz industrial designs. All dated "1947" except No. 1324. Perf or imperf.

1317A	**372**	15k. brown	45	25
1318A	-	20k. brown (Foundry)	50	35
1319A	**372**	30k. purple	1·00	40
1320A	-	30k. green (Harvesting machines)	1·00	40
1321A	-	30k. brown (Tractor)	1·00	40
1322A	-	30k. brown (Tractors)	1·00	40
1323A	-	60k. bistre (Harvesting machines)	1·70	85
1324A	-	60k. purple (Builders)	1·70	85
1325A	-	1r. orange (Foundry)	3·00	1·50
1326A	-	1r. red (Tractor)	3·00	1·50
1327A	-	1r. violet (Tractors)	3·00	1·50

373 Spassky Tower, Kremlin

1947

1328	**373**	60k. red	10·50	5·75
1329a	**373**	1r. red	2·00	65

374 Peter I Monument

1948. 4th Anniv of Relief of Leningrad.

1330	-	30k. violet	70	25
1331	**374**	50k. green	1·10	40
1332	-	60k. black	1·70	60
1333	-	1r. violet	2·40	1·30

DESIGNS—HORIZ: 30k. Winter Palace; 60k. Peter and Paul Fortress; 1r. Smolny Institute.

1948. 24th Death Anniv of Lenin. As issue of 1947, but dated "1924 1928".

1334	**351**	30k. red	95	50
1335	**351**	60k. blue	1·90	1·00

1336	**352**	60k. green	2·50	1·30

376 Government Building, Kiev

1948. 30th Anniv of Ukrainian S.S.R. Various designs inscr "XXX" and "1917–1947".

1337	**376**	30k. blue	70	35
1338	-	50k. violet	1·20	60
1339	-	60k. brown	1·40	85
1340	-	1r. brown	3·00	1·90

DESIGNS: 50k. Dnieper hydro-electric power station; 60k. Wheatfield and granary; 1r. Metallurgical works and colliery.

377 Vasily I. Surikov

1948. Birth Centenary of Surikov (artist).

1341	**377**	30k. brown	1·70	65
1342	**377**	60k. green	2·40	1·40

378 Skiing

1948. R.S.F.S.R. Games.

1343	**378**	15k. blue	2·40	40
1344	-	20k. blue	3·50	60

DESIGN—VERT: 20k. Motor cyclist crossing stream.

379 Artillery

380 Bulganin and Military School

1948. 30th Anniv of Founding of Soviet Defence Forces and of Civil War. (a) Various designs with arms and inscr "1918 XXX 1948".

1345	**379**	30k. brown	1·30	50
1346	-	30k. grey	1·30	50
1347	-	30k. blue	1·30	50
1348	**380**	60k. brown	2·50	1·20

DESIGNS—VERT: No. 1346, Navy. HORIZ: No. 1347, Air Force.

(b) Portraits of Civil War Heroes as Nos. 1079/81.

1349	**299**	60k. brown (Chapaev)	1·70	1·30
1350	-	60k. green (Shchors)	1·70	1·30
1351	-	60k. blue (Lazo)	1·70	1·30

381 Karl Marx and Friedrich Engels

1948. Centenary of Publication of "Communist Manifesto".

1352	**381**	30k. black	1·70	85
1353	**381**	50k. brown	2·50	1·70

382 Miner

384b Arms of U.S.S.R.

384d Spassky Tower, Kremlin

1948

1354	**382**	5k. black	1·70	85
1355	-	10k. violet (Sailor)	1·70	85
1356	-	15k. blue (Airman)	5·00	2·10
1361i	**382**	15k. black	1·30	60
1357	-	20k. brown (Farm girl)	5·25	2·50
1361j	-	20k. green (Farm girl)	1·30	85
1361ka	-	25k. blue (Airman)	85	65
1358	**384b**	30k. brown	6·00	4·25
1361l	-	30k. brown (Scientist)	1·60	1·80
1361n	**384b**	40k. red	5·25	1·70
1359	-	45k. violet (Scientist)	10·50	5·50
1361f	**384d**	50k. blue	26·00	17·00
1361	-	60k. green (Soldier)	23·00	11·00

385 Parade of Workers

1948. May Day.

1362	**385**	30k. red	1·20	65
1363	**385**	60k. blue	2·30	1·20

386 Belinsky (after K. Gorbunov)

1948. Death Centenary of Vissarion Grigorievich Belinsky (literary critic and journalist).

1364	**386**	30k. brown	1·20	65
1365	**386**	50k. green	1·50	1·20
1366	**386**	60k. violet	1·90	1·50

387 Ostrovsky

388 Ostrovsky (after V. Perov)

1948. 125th Birth Anniv of Aleksandr Ostrovsky (dramatist).

1367A	**387**	30k. green	1·70	85
1368A	**388**	60k. brown	2·50	1·40
1369A	**388**	1r. violet	4·00	2·10

389 I. I. Shishkin (after I. Kramskoi)

390 "Rye Field"

1948. 50th Death Anniv of Shishkin (landscape painter).

1370	**389**	30k. brown and green	3·25	1·70
1371	**390**	50k. yellow, red and blue	5·50	3·25
1372	-	60k. multicoloured	7·25	3·25

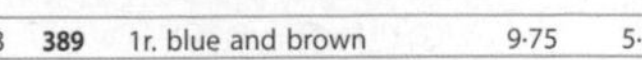

1373	**389**	1r. blue and brown	9·75	5·25

DESIGN—HORIZ: 60k. "Morning in the Forest".

391 Factories

1948. Leningrad Workers' Four-Year Plan.

1374	**391**	15k. brown and red	2·50	1·30
1375	-	30k. black and red	2·20	1·70
1376	**391**	60k. brown and red	6·00	3·25

DESIGN—HORIZ (40×22 mm): 30k. Proclamation to Leningrad workers.

392 Arms and People of the U.S.S.R.

1948. 25th Anniv of U.S.S.R.

1377	**392**	30k. black and red	1·70	1·30
1378	**392**	60k. olive and red	3·25	3·25

393 Caterpillar drawing Seed Drills

1948. Five Year Agricultural Plan.

1379	**393**	30k. red	1·00	50
1380	**393**	30k. green	1·00	50
1381	-	45k. brown	1·60	85
1382	**393**	50k. black	1·80	90
1383	-	60k. green	2·10	1·10
1384	-	60k. green	2·10	1·10
1385	-	1r. violet	4·50	1·90

DESIGNS: 30k. (No. 1380), 1r. Harvesting sugar beet; 45, 60k. (No. 1383), Gathering cotton; 60k. (No. 1384), Harvesting machine.

ИЮЛЬ
1948
года
(394)

1948. Air Force Day. Optd with T 394.

1386	**364**	30k. violet	5·25	3·25
1387	**364**	1r. blue	6·00	5·00

395 Miners

1948. Miners' Day.

1388	**395**	30k. blue	1·20	65
1389	-	60k. violet	2·30	1·30
1390	-	1r. green	4·00	2·10

DESIGNS: 60k. Inside a coal mine; 1r. Miner's emblem.

396 A. Zhdanov

1948. Death of A. A. Zhdanov (statesman).

1391	**396**	40k. blue	3·00	1·30

397 Sailor

1948. Navy Day.

1392	**397**	30k. green	2·20	1·20
1393	**397**	60k. blue	4·00	2·20

398 Football

1948. Sports.

1394	-	15k. violet	1·30	15
1395a	**398**	30k. brown	2·50	25
1396	-	45k. brown	3·00	35
1397a	-	50k. blue	4·00	35

DESIGNS—VERT: 15k. Running; 50k. Diving. HORIZ: 45k. Power boat racing.

399 Tank and Drivers

1948. Tank Drivers' Day.

1398	**399**	30k. black	2·00	1·50
1399	-	1r. red	4·75	3·25

DESIGN: 1r. Parade of tanks.

400 Horses and Groom

1948. Five Year Livestock Development Plan.

1400	**400**	30k. black	2·50	1·70
1401	-	60k. green	4·25	2·50
1402	**400**	1r. brown	7·00	4·25

DESIGN: 60k. Dairy farming.

401 Steam and Electric Locomotives

1948. Five Year Transport Plan.

1403	**401**	30k. brown	5·50	2·50
1404	**401**	50k. green	7·75	4·25
1405	-	60k. blue	13·00	5·00
1406	-	1r. violet	17·00	6·75

DESIGNS: 60k. Road traffic; 1r. Liner "Vyacheslav Molotov".

402 Iron Pipe Manufacture

1948. Five Year Rolled Iron, Steel and Machine-building Plan.

1407		30k. violet	1·80	1·00
1408		30k. purple	1·80	1·00
1409		50k. brown	2·75	1·50
1410		50k. black	2·75	1·50
1411		60k. brown	3·75	2·50
1412	**402**	60k. red	3·75	2·50
1413	**402**	1r. blue	5·75	3·25

DESIGNS—HORIZ: Nos. 1407, 1410, Foundry; No. 1408/9, Pouring molten metal; No. 1411, Group of machines.

403 Abovyan

1948. Death Centenary of Khachatur Abovyan (writer).

1414	**403**	40k. purple	3·00	2·50
1415	**403**	50k. green	4·00	3·25

404 Miner

1948. Five Year Coal Mining and Oil Extraction Plan.

1416	**404**	30k. black	1·70	1·00
1417	**404**	60k. brown	3·50	2·00
1418	-	60k. brown	3·50	2·00
1419	-	1r. green	6·00	4·25

DESIGN: Nos. 1418/19, Oil wells and tanker train.

405 Farkhadsk Power Station

1948. Five Year Electrification Plan.

1420	**405**	30k. green	2·20	1·70
1421	-	60k. red	4·25	3·25
1422	**405**	1r. red	7·50	5·00

DESIGN: 60k. Zuevsk Power Station.

406 Flying Model Aircraft

1948. Government Care of School Children's Summer Vacation.

1423	**406**	30k. green	8·75	3·25
1424	-	45k. red	13·00	4·50
1425	-	45k. violet	10·50	4·25
1426	-	60k. blue	14·00	6·25
1427	-	1r. blue	28·00	11·00

DESIGNS—VERT: No. 1424, Boy and girl saluting; 60k. Boy trumpeter. HORIZ: No. 1425, Children marching; 1r. Children round camp fire.

407 Children in School

408 Flag of U.S.S.R.

1948. 30th Anniv of Lenin's Young Communist League.

1428		20k. purple	4·25	1·30
1429		25k. red	5·25	1·70
1430		40k. brown and red	8·75	2·75
1431	**407**	50k. green	10·50	3·25
1432	**408**	1r. multicoloured	23·00	13·50
1433	-	2r. violet	17·00	10·00

DESIGNS—HORIZ: 20k. Youth parade. VERT: 25k. Peasant girl; 40k. Young people and flag; 2r. Industrial worker.

409 Interior of Theatre

1948. 50th Anniv of Moscow Arts Theatre.

1434	**409**	50k. blue	3·50	2·50
1435	-	1r. purple	6·00	5·00

DESIGN: 1r. Stanislavsky and Dantchenko.

410 Searchlights over Moscow

1948. 31st Anniv of October Revolution.

1436	**410**	40k. red	3·00	2·40
1437	**410**	1r. green	6·50	5·25

411 Artillery Barrage

1948. Artillery Day.

1438	**411**	30k. blue	6·75	3·00
1439	**411**	1r. red	15·00	7·00

412 Trade Union Building (venue)

1948. 16th World Chess Championship, Moscow.

1440	**412**	30k. blue	5·25	1·10
1441	-	40k. violet	7·00	1·40
1442	**412**	50k. brown	9·50	1·80

DESIGN—VERT: 40k. Players' badge showing chessboard and rook.

413 Stasov and Building

1948. Death Centenary of Stasov (architect).

1443	-	40k. brown	1·40	1·30
1444	**413**	1r. black	3·25	3·00

DESIGN—VERT: 40k. Portrait of Stasov.

414 Yakovlev Yak-9 Fighters and Flag

1948. Air Force Day.

1445a	**414**	1r. blue	8·75	2·50

415 Statue of Ya. M. Sverdlov

1948. 225th Anniv of Sverdlovsk City. Imperf or perf.

1446B	**415**	30k. blue	70	15
1447B	-	40k. purple	1·70	40
1448B	**415**	1r. green	2·00	60

DESIGN: 40k. View of Sverdlovsk.

416 Sukhumi

1948. Views of Crimea and Caucasus.

1449	**416**	40k. green	1·00	35
1450	-	40k. violet	1·00	35
1451	-	40k. mauve	1·00	35
1452	-	40k. brown	1·00	35
1453	-	40k. purple	1·00	35
1454	-	40k. green	1·00	35
1455	-	40k. blue	1·00	35
1456	-	40k. green	1·00	35

DESIGNS—VERT: No. 1450, Gardens, Sochi; 1451, Eagle-topped monument, Pyatigorsk; 1452, Cliffs, Crimea. HORIZ: No. 1453, Terraced gardens, Sochi; 1454, Roadside garden, Sochi; 1455, Colonnade, Kislovodsk; 1456, Seascape, Gagry.

417 State Emblem

1949. 30th Anniv of Byelorussian Soviet Republic.

1457	**417**	40k. red	2·20	1·70
1458	**417**	1r. green	4·00	2·50

418 M. V. Lomonosov

1949. Establishment of Lomonosov Museum of Academy of Sciences.

1459	**418**	40k. brown	2·00	1·70
1460	**418**	50k. green	2·40	2·00
1461	-	1r. blue	4·75	4·00

DESIGN—HORIZ: 1r. Museum.

419 Lenin Mausoleum

1949. 25th Death Anniv of Lenin.

1462	**419**	40k. brown and green	7·00	5·75
1463	**419**	1r. brown & deep brown	12·00	11·00
MS1463a		175×132 mm. No. 1463×4	£250	£250

420 Dezhnev's Ship

1949. 300th Anniv of Dezhnev's Exploration of Bering Strait.

1464	-	40k. green	13·00	10·00
1465	**420**	1r. grey	26·00	18·00

DESIGN: 40k. Cape Dezhnev.

421 "Women in Industry"

1949. International Women's Day.

1466	**421**	20k. violet	50	15
1467	-	25k. blue	80	15
1468	-	40k. red	1·00	25
1469	-	50k. grey	1·30	35
1470	-	50k. brown	1·30	35
1471	-	1r. green	3·50	50
1472	-	2r. red	5·25	95

DESIGNS—HORIZ: 25k. Kindergarten; 50k. grey, Woman teacher; 50k. brown, Women in field; 1r. Women sports champions. VERT: 40k., 2r. Woman broadcasting.

422 Admiral S. O. Makarov

1949. Birth Centenary of Admiral S. O. Makarov (naval scientist).

1473	**422**	40k. blue	1·70	1·30
1474	**422**	1r. red	4·25	3·00

423 Soldier

1949. 31st Anniv of Soviet Army.

1475	**423**	40k. red	13·00	10·50

424 Kirov Military Medical Academy

1949. 150th Anniv of Kirov Military Medical Academy.

1476	**424**	40k. red	1·70	1·50
1477	-	50k. blue	2·30	2·00
1478	**424**	1r. green	4·75	4·00

DESIGN: 50k. Professors Botkin, Pirogov and Sechenov and Kirov Academy.

425 V. R. Williams

1949. Agricultural Reform.

1479	**425**	25k. green	3·50	3·25
1480	**425**	50k. brown	6·00	5·50

425a Three Russians with Flag

1949. Labour Day.

1481	**425a**	40k. red	1·70	1·30
1482	**425a**	1r. green	3·50	2·50

426 Newspapers and Books

1949. Press Day. Inscr "5 MAR 1949".

1483	**426**	40k. red	4·25	4·25
1484	-	1r. violet	9·50	7·25

DESIGN: 1r. Man and boy reading newspaper.

427 A. S. Popov and Radio Equipment

1949. Radio Day.

1485	**427**	40k. violet	2·50	2·30
1486	-	50k. brown	3·50	3·25
1487	**427**	1r. green	7·00	5·50

DESIGN—HORIZ: 50k. Popov demonstrating receiver to Admiral Makarov.

428 A. S. Pushkin

429 "Pushkin reading Poems to Southern Society" (Dmitry Kardovsky)

1949. 150th Birth Anniv of Pushkin (poet).

1488	**428**	25k. black and grey	1·40	1·00
1489	-	40k. black and brown	2·30	2·10
1490	**429**	40k. purple and red	2·30	2·10
1491	-	1r. grey and brown	5·75	5·75
1492	**429**	2r. blue and brown	13·00	10·00
MS1492a 110×142 mm. Nos. 1488/9 (two of each). Imperf			70·00	42·00

DESIGNS—VERT: No. 1489, Pushkin portrait after Kiprensky. HORIZ: 1r. Pushkin museum, Boldino.

430 "Boksimi Typlokod" (tug)

1949. Centenary of Krasnoe Sormovo Machine-building and Ship-building Plant, Gorky.

1493	**430**	40k. blue	7·00	5·75
1494	-	1r. brown	13·00	9·00

DESIGN: 1r. Freighter "Bolshaya Volga".

431 I. V. Michurin

1949. Agricultural Reform.

1495	**431**	40k. blue	2·20	1·30
1496	**431**	1r. green	4·25	2·75

432 Yachting

1949. National Sports.

1497	**432**	20k. blue	1·20	15
1498	-	25k. green	1·20	20
1499	-	30k. violet	1·70	25
1500	-	40k. brown	2·40	40
1501	-	40k. green	2·40	40
1502	-	50k. grey	2·50	60
1503	-	1r. red	6·00	1·30
1504	-	2r. black	9·50	2·50

DESIGNS: 25k. Canoeing; 30k. Swimming; 40k. (No. 1500), Cycling; 40k. (No. 1501), Football; 50k. Mountaineering; 1r. Parachuting; 2r. High jumping.

433 V. V. Dokuchaev

1949. Soil Research.

1505	**433**	40k. brown	1·60	40
1506	**433**	1r. green	3·25	85

434 V. I. Bazhenov

1949. 150th Death Anniv of V. I. Bazhenov (architect).

1507	**434**	40k. violet	2·20	50
1508	**434**	1r. brown	4·75	1·30

435 A. N. Radischev

1949. Birth Bicent of A. N. Radischev (writer).

1509	**435**	40k. green	2·10	1·70
1510	**435**	1r. grey	4·25	3·00

436 Green Cape Sanatorium, Makhindzhauri

1949. State Sanatoria. Designs showing various buildings.

1511	**436**	40k. green	85	25
1512	-	40k. green	85	25
1513	-	40k. blue	85	25
1514	-	40k. violet	85	25
1515	-	40k. red	85	25
1516	-	40k. orange	85	25
1517	-	40k. brown	85	25
1518	-	40k. brown	85	25
1519	-	40k. black	85	25
1520	-	40k. black	85	25

DESIGNS—HORIZ: No. 1512, VTsSPS No. 41, Zheleznovodsk; No. 1513, Energetics, Hosta; No. 1514, VTsSPS No. 3, Kislovodsk; No. 1515, VTsSPS No. 3, Hosta; No. 1516, State Theatre, Sochi; No. 1517, Clinical, Tskhaltubo; No. 1518, Frunze, Sochi; No. 1519, VTsSPS No. 1, Kislovodsk; No. 1520, Communication, Hosta.

437 I. P. Pavlov

1949. Birth Centenary of I. P. Pavlov (scientist).

1521	**437**	40k. brown	1·30	40
1522	**437**	1r. black	2·50	85

438 Globe and Letters

1949. 75th Anniv of U.P.U. Perf or imperf.

1523B	**438**	40k. blue and brown	2·20	40
1524B	**438**	50k. violet and blue	2·50	60

439 Tree Planting Machines

440 Map of S. W. Russia

1949. Forestry and Field Conservancy.

1525	**439**	25k. green	7·25	4·25
1526	-	40k. violet	1·80	85
1527	**440**	40k. green and black	1·80	85
1528	-	50k. blue	2·40	1·50
1529	**439**	1r. black	5·25	2·50
1530	-	2r. brown	7·75	5·00

DESIGNS—33×22½ mm: 40k. violet, Harvesters; 50k. River scene. 33×19½ mm: 2r. Old man and children.

1949. 30th Death Anniv of V. I. Chapaev (military strategist).

1531	**299**	40k. orange	11·50	10·00

442 I. S. Nikitin (after P. Borel)

1949. 125th Birth Anniv of Nikitin (poet).

1532	**442**	40k. brown	1·30	40
1533	**442**	1r. blue	2·50	65

443 Malyi Theatre, Moscow

1949. 125th Anniv of Malyi Theatre, Moscow.

1534	**443**	40k. green	1·60	35
1535	**443**	50k. orange	2·10	40
1536	-	1r. brown	4·25	90

DESIGN: 1r. Five portraits and theatre.

444 Crowd with Banner

1949. 32nd Anniv of October Revolution.

1537	**444**	40k. red	3·00	2·50
1538	**444**	1r. green	4·75	4·50

445 Sheep and Cows

1949. Cattle-breeding Collective Farm.

1539	**445**	40k. brown	1·30	65
1540	**445**	1r. violet	3·00	1·30

446 Lenin Hydro-electric Station, Caucasus

447 Ilyushin Il-12 Airliners and Map

1949. Air. Aerial views and map.

1541	**446**	50k. brown on yellow	2·20	1·10
1542	-	60k. brown on buff	3·25	85
1543	-	1r. orange on yellow	4·25	1·90
1544	-	1r. brown on buff	4·25	1·90
1545	-	1r. blue on blue	4·25	1·90
1546	**447**	1r. blue, red and grey	10·50	4·25
1547	-	2r. red on blue	13·00	7·25
1548	-	3r. green on blue	26·00	10·00

DESIGNS—Ilyushin Il-12 airplane over: HORIZ: No. 1542, Farm; 1543, Sochi. VERT: 1544, Leningrad; 1545, Aleppo; 1547, Moscow; 1548, Arctic.

448 Ski Jumping

1949. National Sports.

1549	**448**	20k. green	1·30	25
1550	-	40k. orange	3·50	85
1551	-	50k. blue	3·00	85
1552	-	1r. red	6·00	85
1553	-	2r. violet	10·50	1·70

DESIGNS: 40k. Girl gymnast; 50k. Ice hockey; 1r. Weight-lifting; 2r. Shooting wolves.

449 Diesel-electric Train

1949. Modern Railway Development.

1554		25k. red	2·50	50
1555	**449**	40k. violet	3·00	85
1556	-	50k. brown	4·00	1·10
1557	**449**	1r. green	9·50	2·10

DESIGNS: 25k. Electric tram; 50k. Steam train.

450 Arms of U.S.S.R.

1949. Constitution Day.

1558	**450**	40k. red	7·75	5·75

451 Government Buildings, Dushanbe

1949. 20th Anniv of Republic of Tadzhikstan.

1559	-	20k. blue	80	10
1560	-	25k. green	95	10
1561	**451**	40k. red	1·30	35
1562	-	50k. violet	1·60	35
1563	**451**	1r. black	3·00	90

DESIGNS: 20k. Textile mills; 25k. Irrigation canal; 50k. Medical University.

451a Stalin's Birthplace

1949. Stalin's 70th Birthday. Sheet 177×233 mm. Multicoloured.

MS1563a	40k. Type **451a**; 40k. Lenin and Stalin in Leningrad, 1917; 40k. Lenin and Stalin in Gorky; 40k. Marshal Stalin	£160	£160

452 People with Flag

1949. 10th Anniv of Incorporation of West Ukraine and West Byelorussia in U.S.S.R.

1564	**452**	40k. red	9·50	9·25
1565	-	40k. orange	9·50	9·25

DESIGN—VERT: No. 1565, Ukrainians and flag.

453 Worker and Globe

1949. Peace Propaganda.

1566	**453**	40k. red	95	25
1567	**453**	50k. blue	1·10	40

454 Government Buildings, Tashkent

1950. 25th Anniv of Uzbek S.S.R.

1568	-	20k. blue	50	25
1569	-	25k. black	70	25
1570	**454**	40k. red	1·10	25
1571	-	40k. violet	1·30	25
1572	-	1r. green	2·75	75
1573	-	2r. brown	5·25	1·70

DESIGNS: 20k. Teachers' College; 25k. Opera and Ballet House, Tashkent; 40k. (violet) Navots Street, Tashkent; 1r. Map of Fergana Canal; 2r. Lock, Fergana Canal.

455 Dam

1950. 25th Anniv of Turkmen S.S.R.

1574		25k. black	5·25	4·00
1575	**455**	40k. brown	1·70	1·30
1576	-	50k. green	4·25	3·25
1577	**455**	1r. violet	8·75	5·75

DESIGNS: 25k. Textile factory, Ashkhabad; 50k. Carpet-making.

456 "Lenin at Rozliv" (sculpture, V. Pinchuk)

1950. 26th Death Anniv of Lenin.

1578	**456**	40k. brown and grey	1·00	30
1579	-	50k. red, brown and green	1·50	40
1580	-	1r. buff, green and brown	3·25	90

DESIGNS—HORIZ: 50k. Lenin's Office, Kremlin; 1r. Lenin Museum, Gorky.

457 Film Show

1950. 30th Anniv of Soviet Film Industry.

1581	**457**	25k. brown	17·00	14·50

458 Voter

1950. Supreme Soviet Elections. Inscr "12 МАРТА 1950".

1582	**458**	40k. green on yellow	4·00	3·00
1583	-	1r. red	7·00	5·00

DESIGN: 1r. Kremlin and flags.

459 Monument (I. Rabinovich)

1950. Unveiling of Monument in Moscow to Pavlik Morozov (model Soviet youth).

1584	**459**	40k. black and red	4·25	3·50
1585	**459**	1r. green and red	7·75	5·75

460 Lenin Central Museum

1950. Moscow Museums. Buildings inscr "МОСКВА 1949".

1586	**460**	40k. olive	1·30	35
1587	-	40k. red	1·30	35
1588	-	40k. turquoise	1·30	35
1589	-	40k. brown	1·30	35
1590	-	40k. mauve	1·30	35
1591	-	40k. blue (no tree)	1·30	35
1592	-	40k. brown	1·30	35
1593	-	40k. blue (with tree)	1·30	35
1594	-	40k. red	1·30	35

DESIGNS—HORIZ: (33½×23½ mm): No. 1587, Revolution Museum; 1588, Tretyakov Gallery; 1589, Timiryazev Biological Museum; No. 1591, Polytechnic Museum; 1593, Oriental Museum. (39½×26½ mm): No. 1590, Pushkin Pictorial Arts Museum. VERT: (22½×33½ mm): No. 1592, Historical Museum; 1594, Zoological Museum.

461 Hemispheres and Wireless Mast

1950. International Congress of P.T.T. and Radio Trade Unions, London.

1595	**461**	40k. green on blue	4·00	3·25
1596	**461**	50k. blue on blue	5·25	4·50

462 Three Workers

1950. Labour Day.

1597	**462**	40k. red and black	4·00	3·00
1598	-	1r. red and black	7·00	5·50

DESIGN—HORIZ: 1r. Four Russians and banner.

463 A. S. Shcherbakov

1950. 5th Death Anniv of Shcherbakov (statesman).

1599	**463**	40k. black	1·70	1·30
1600	**463**	1r. green on pink	3·50	3·00

464 Suvorov (after N. Utkin)

1950. 150th Death Anniv of Suvorov.

1601	**464**	40k. blue on pink	4·00	2·10
1602	-	50k. brown on pink	4·75	2·50
1603	-	60k. black on blue	4·75	3·25
1604	**464**	1r. brown on yellow	7·00	5·00
1605	-	2r. green	13·00	8·50

DESIGNS—32½×47 mm: 50k. "Suvorov crossing the Alps" (V. I. Surikov). 24½×39½ mm—60k. Order of Suvorov and military parade (after portrait by N. Smdyak). 19½×33½ mm—2r. "Suvorov in the Alps" (N. Abbakumov).

465 Statue

1950. 5th Anniv of Victory over Germany.

1606	**465**	40k. red and brown	4·25	3·25
1607	-	1r. red	9·50	5·75

DESIGN—22½×33 mm: 1r. Medal for the Victory over Germany (profile of Stalin and Order of Victory).

466 Sowing on Collective Farm

1950. Agricultural Workers.

1608		40k. green on blue	3·50	2·30
1609	**466**	40k. brown on pink	3·50	2·30
1610	**466**	1r. blue on yellow	6·00	4·25

DESIGNS: No. 1608, Collective farmers studying.

467 G. M. Dimitrov

1950. 1st Death Anniv of Bulgarian Premier, Dimitrov.

1611	**467**	40k. black on yellow	2·50	1·70
1612	**467**	1r. black on orange	4·75	3·75

468 State Opera and Ballet House, Baku

1950. 30th Anniv of Azerbaijan S.S.R.

1613	**468**	25k. green on yellow	2·20	1·50
1614	-	40k. brown on red	4·50	3·00
1615	-	1r. black on orange	7·00	5·00

DESIGNS: 40k. Science Academy; 1r. Stalin Avenue, Baku.

469 Lenin Street, Stalingrad

1950. Stalingrad Reconstruction.

1616		20k. blue	1·30	1·10
1617	**469**	40k. green	2·30	1·70
1618	-	50k. orange	4·25	3·25
1619	-	1r. black	6·50	5·00

DESIGNS—VERT: 20k. Pobeda Cinema. HORIZ: 50k. Gorky Theatre; 1r. Pavlov House and Tank Memorial.

470 Kaluzhskaya Station

1950. Underground Railway Stations.

1620	**470**	40k. green on buff	1·70	50
1621	**A**	40k. red	1·70	50
1622	**B**	40k. blue on buff	1·70	50
1623	**C**	1r. brown on yellow	4·25	1·30
1624	**D**	1r. violet on blue	4·25	1·30
1625	**A**	1r. green on yellow	4·25	1·30
1626	**E**	1r. black on orange	4·25	1·30

DESIGNS—HORIZ: (34×22½ mm): A, Culture Park; B, Taganskaya; C, Kurskaya; D, Paveletskaya. (34×18½ mm): E, Taganskaya.

471 National Flags and Civilians

1950. Unconquerable Democracy. Flags in red, blue and yellow.

1627	**471**	40k. black	1·60	25
1628	**471**	50k. brown	1·70	40
1629	**471**	1r. green	2·75	60

472 Trade Union Building

1950. 10th Anniv of Latvian S.S.R.

1630	**472**	25k. brown	1·10	75
1631	-	40k. red	1·60	1·20
1632	-	50k. green	2·50	1·70
1633	-	60k. blue	3·00	2·10
1634	-	1r. violet	5·00	3·50
1635	-	2r. brown	8·25	7·25

DESIGNS—VERT: 40k. Cabinet Council Offices; 50k. Monument to Jan Rainis (poet); 2r. Academy of Sciences. HORIZ: 60k. Theatre, Riga; 1r. State University, Riga.

473 Marite Melnikaite

1950. 10th Anniv of Lithuanian S.S.R.

1636	-	25k. blue	2·40	1·40
1637	**473**	40k. brown	4·75	3·00
1638	-	1r. red	10·50	5·50

DESIGNS—HORIZ: 25k. Academy of Sciences; 1r. Cabinet Council Offices.

474 Stalingrad Square, Tallinn

1950. 10th Anniv of Estonian S.S.R.

1639	**474**	25k. green	1·30	85
1640	-	40k. red	2·20	1·30
1641	-	50k. blue on yellow	2·75	2·10
1642	-	1r. brown on blue	7·50	5·75

DESIGNS—HORIZ: 40k. Government building; 50k. Opera and Ballet Theatre, Tallin. VERT: 1r. Viktor Kingisepp (revolutionary).

475 Signing Peace Appeal

1950. Peace Conference.

1643	**475**	40k. red on pink	2·40	1·60
1644	-	40k. black	2·40	1·60
1645	-	50k. red	4·25	3·25
1646	**475**	1r. brown on pink	6·50	5·25

DESIGNS—VERT: 40k. black, Children and teacher; 50k. Young people with banner.

476 Bellingshausan Lazarev and Globe

1950. 130th Anniv of 1st Antarctic Expedition.

1647	**476**	40k. red on blue	24·00	12·50
1648	-	1r. violet on blue	37·00	25·00

DESIGN—VERT: 1r. "Mirnyi" and "Vostok" (ships) and map of Antarctica.

477 Frunze (after I. Brodsky)

1950. 25th Death Anniv of M.V. Frunze (military strategist).

1649	**477**	40k. blue on pink	4·25	3·25
1650	**477**	1r. brown on blue	10·50	6·75

478 M. I. Kalinin

1950. 75th Birth Anniv of Kalinin (statesman).

1651	**478**	40k. green	1·70	1·00
1652	**478**	1r. brown	3·50	1·90
1653	**478**	5r. violet	8·75	7·50

479 Picking Grapes

1950. 30th Anniv of Armenian S.S.R.

1654	**479**	20k. blue on pink	1·70	1·30
1655	-	40k. orange on blue	2·50	1·90
1656	-	1r. black on yellow	6·25	4·50

DESIGNS—HORIZ: (33×16 mm): 40k. Government Offices. VERT: (21½×33 mm): 1r. G. M. Sundukian (dramatist).

480 Kotelnicheskaya Quay

1950. Moscow Building Projects.

1657	**480**	1r. brown on pink	40·00	28·00
1658	-	1r. black on pink	40·00	28·00
1659	-	1r. brown on blue	40·00	28·00
1660	-	1r. green on yellow	40·00	28·00
1661	-	1r. blue on pink	40·00	28·00
1662	-	1r. black	40·00	28·00
1663	-	1r. orange	40·00	28·00
1664	-	1r. green on blue	40·00	28·00

DESIGNS—HORIZ: No. 1659, Vosstaniya Square; 1660, Smolenskaya Square; 1662, Krasnye Vorota; 1664, Moscow University. VERT: No. 1658, Hotel Ukraine, Dorogomilovskaya Quay; 1661, Hotel Leningrad; 1663, Zaryade.

481 Spassky Tower, Kremlin

1950. 33rd Anniv of October Revolution.

1665	**481**	1r. red, yellow and green	17·00	10·00

482 "Golden Autumn"

1950. 50th Death Anniv of Levitan (painter).

1666	**482**	40k. multicoloured	4·25	85
1667	-	50k. brown	8·75	4·25

DESIGN: 50k. Portrait of Levitan by V. Serov.

483 Aivazovsky (after A. Tyranov)

1950. 50th Death Anniv of Aivazovsky (painter). Multicoloured centres.

1668		40k. brown	3·50	65
1669		50k. brown	4·25	85
1670	**483**	1r. blue	8·75	1·70

PAINTINGS—HORIZ: 40k. "Black Sea"; 50k. "Ninth Wave".

484 Newspapers "Iskra" and "Pravda"

1950. 50th Anniv of Newspaper "Iskra".

1671	-	40k. red and black	17·00	11·50
1672	**484**	1r. red and black	33·00	17·00

DESIGN: 40k. Newspapers and banners.

485 Government Offices

1950. 30th Anniv of Kazakh S.S.R.

1673	**485**	40k. black on blue	5·00	3·25
1674	-	1r. brown on yellow	6·50	5·00

DESIGN: 1r. Opera House, Alma-Ata.

486 Decembrists and "Decembrist Rising in Senate Square, St. Petersburg, 14 December 1825" (K. Kolman)

1950. 125th Anniv of Decembrist Rising.

1675	**486**	1r. brown on yellow	7·75	6·75

487 Govt Offices, Tirana

1951. Friendship with Albania.

1676	**487**	40k. green on blue	22·00	17·00

488 Greeting Soviet Troops

1951. Friendship with Bulgaria.

1677	**488**	25k. black on blue	2·50	2·10
1678	-	40k. orange on pink	6·25	3·50
1679	-	60k. brown on orange	7·00	5·00

DESIGNS: 40k. Lenin Square, Sofia; 60k. Monument to Soviet fighters, Kolarovgrad.

489 Lenin at Razliv

1951. 27th Death Anniv of Lenin. Multicoloured centres.

1680	**489**	40k. green	3·00	85
1681	-	1r. blue	5·75	1·70

DESIGN: 1r. Lenin talking to young Communists.

490 Horses

1951. 25th Anniv of Kirghiz S.S.R.

1682	**490**	25k. brown on blue	5·75	5·00
1683	-	40k. green on blue	8·75	7·50

DESIGN—33×22½ mm: 40k. Government Offices, Frunze.

490a Gathering Lemons

1951. 30th Anniv of Georgia S.S.R.

1683a		20k. green on yellow	2·00	1·30
1683b	**490a**	25k. orange and violet	3·00	2·10
1683c	-	40k. brown on blue	4·75	3·25
1683d	-	1r. green and brown	10·50	6·25

DESIGNS—VERT: 20k. State Opera and Ballet Theatre, Tbilisi. HORIZ: 40k. Rustaveli Avenue, Tbilisi; 1r. Plucking tea.

491 University, Ulan Bator

1951. Friendship with Mongolia.

1684	**491**	25k. violet on orange	1·80	85
1685	-	40k. orange on yellow	2·75	1·30
1686	-	1r. multicoloured	7·50	4·25

DESIGNS—HORIZ: (37×25 mm): 40k. State Theatre, Ulan Bator. VERT: (22×33 mm): 1r. State Emblem and Mongolian Flag.

492 D. A. Furmanov

1951. 25th Death Anniv of D. A. Furmanov (writer).

1687	**492**	40k. brown on blue	5·25	3·25
1688	-	1r. black on orange	7·00	5·00

DESIGN—HORIZ: 1r. Furmanov writing.

493 Soviet Soldiers Memorial, Berlin (E. Buchetich)

1951. Stockholm Peace Appeal.

1689	**493**	40k. green and red	6·00	3·75
1690	**493**	1r. black and red	13·50	8·75

494 Factories

1951. 150th Anniv of Kirov Machine-building Factory, Leningrad.

1691	**494**	40k. brown on yellow	7·00	5·00

495 Bolshoi State Theatre

1951. 175th Anniv of State Theatre.

1692	**495**	40k. multicoloured	4·25	85
1693	-	1r. multicoloured	8·75	2·50

DESIGN: 1r. Theatre and medallions of Glinka, Tchaikovsky, Moussorgsky, Rimsky-Korsakov, Borodin and theatre.

496 National Museum, Budapest

1951. Hungarian Peoples' Republic. Buildings in Budapest.

1694		25k. green	1·70	1·30
1695		40k. blue	1·60	1·30
1696	**496**	60k. black	2·50	2·00
1697	-	1r. black on pink	5·25	3·75

DESIGNS—HORIZ: 25k. Liberty Bridge; 40k. Parliament buildings. VERT: 1r. Liberation Monument.

497 Harvesting

1951. Agricultural Scenes.

1698	**497**	25k. green	1·10	85
1699	-	40k. green on blue	1·70	1·30
1700	-	1r. brown on yellow	3·00	3·00
1701	-	2r. green on pink	5·75	5·00

DESIGNS: 40k. Apiary; 1r. Gathering citrus fruit; 2r. Harvesting cotton.

498 M. I. Kalinin

1951. 5th Death Anniv of Pres. Kalinin.

1702		20k. black, sepia & brown	85	35
1703	**498**	40k. brown, dp grn & grn	1·70	60
1704	-	1r. black, bl & ultram	3·50	1·30

DESIGNS—HORIZ: 20k. Kalinin Museum. VERT: 1r. Statue of Kalinin (G. Alekseev).

499 F. E. Dzerzhinsky

1951. 25th Death Anniv of Dzerzhinsky (founder of Cheka).

1705	**499**	40k. red	3·25	2·20
1706	-	1r. black (Portrait in uniform)	5·25	3·25

500 P. K. Kozlov

1951. Russian Scientists.

1707	**500**	40k. orange	1·70	35
1708	-	40k. orange on pink	1·70	35
1709	-	40k. orange on blue	7·00	2·30
1710	-	40k. brown	1·70	35
1711	-	40k. brown on pink (facing left)	1·70	35
1712	-	40k. brown on pink (facing right)	1·70	35
1713	-	40k. grey	1·70	35
1714	-	40k. grey on pink	1·70	35
1715	-	40k. grey on blue	7·00	2·30
1716	-	40k. green	1·70	35
1717	-	40k. green on pink	1·70	35
1718	-	40k. blue	1·70	35
1719	-	40k. blue on pink	1·70	35
1720	-	40k. blue on blue	1·70	35
1721	-	40k. violet	1·70	35
1722	-	40k. violet on pink	1·70	35

PORTRAITS: No. 1708, N. N. Miklukho-Makai; 1709, A. M. Butlerov; 1710, N. I. Lobachevsky; 1711, K. A. Timiryazev; 1712, N. S. Kurnakov; 1713, P. N. Yablochkov; 1714, A. N. Severtsov; No. 1715, K. E. Tsiolkovsky; 1716, A. N. Lodygin; 1717, A. G. Stoletov; 1718, P. N. Lebedev; 1719, A. O. Kovalesky; 1720, D. I. Mendeleev; 1721, S. P. Krasheninnikov; 1722, S. V. Kovalevskaya.

501 Kalinnikov

1951. Russian Composers.

1723	**501**	40k. grey on pink	10·50	8·50
1724	-	40k. brown on pink	10·50	8·50

PORTRAIT: No. 1724, A. Alyabev (after N. Andreev).

502 Aviation Society Badge

1951. Aviation Developement.

1725	**502**	40k. multicoloured	1·30	15
1726	-	60k. multicoloured	2·40	50
1727	-	1r. multicoloured	3·25	85
1728	-	2r. multicoloured	6·00	1·50

DESIGNS—VERT: 60k. Boys and model gliders; 1r. Parachutists descending. HORIZ: (45×25 mm): 2r. Flight of Yakovlev Yak-18U trainers.

503 Vasnetsov (after I. Kramskoi)

1951. 25th Death Anniv of Vasnetsov (painter).

1729	**503**	40k. brown, buff and blue	4·25	85
1730	-	1r. multicoloured	6·00	1·30

DESIGN (47×33 mm): 1r. "Three Heroes".

504 Lenin, Stalin and Dnieperprostroi Dam

1951. 34th Anniv of October Revolution.

1731	**504**	40k. blue and red	6·00	3·25
1732	-	1r. brown and red	10·50	5·75

DESIGN: 1r. Lenin, Stalin and Spassky Tower.

505 Volga–Don Canal

1951. Construction of Hydro-electric Power Stations.

1733		20k. multicoloured	4·75	3·25
1734	**505**	30k. multicoloured	6·00	5·00
1735	-	40k. multicoloured	7·50	6·75
1736	-	60k. multicoloured	11·50	7·50
1737	-	1r. multicoloured	23·00	11·50

DESIGNS—VERT: (32×47 mm): 20k. Khakhovsky power station. HORIZ: (47×32 mm); 40k. Stalingrad dam; 60k. Excavator and map of Turkmen canal; 1r. Kuibyshev power station.

506 Signing Peace Petition

1951. 3rd U.S.S.R. Peace Conference.

1738	**506**	40k. red and brown	9·50	8·50

507 M. V. Ostrogradsky

1951. 150th Birth Anniv of Ostrogradsky (mathematician).

1739	**507**	40k. brown on pink	8·50	5·75

508 Zhizka Monument, Prague (B. Kafka)

1951. Friendship with Czechoslovakia.

1740	**508**	20k. blue on pink	4·50	1·70
1741	-	25k. red on yellow	7·75	3·25
1742	-	40k. orange on orange	16·00	4·25
1743	-	60k. grey on pink	7·75	3·25
1744	-	1r. grey on cream	8·75	5·75

DESIGNS—VERT: 25k. Soviet Army Monument, Ostrava; 40k. J. Fucik by M. Shvabinsky; 60k. Smetana Museum, Prague. HORIZ: 1r. Soviet Soldiers Monument, Prague.

509 Volkhovsky Hydro-electric Station and Lenin Monument

1951. 25th Anniv of Lenin Volkhovsky Hydro-electric Station.

1745a	**509**	40k. yellow, indigo and blue	1·30	65
1746	**509**	1r. yellow, indigo and violet	4·00	1·70

510 Lenin when a Student (after V. Prager)

1952. 28th Death Anniv of Lenin. Multicoloured centres.

1747	**510**	40k. green	2·20	75
1748	-	60k. blue	2·75	90
1749	-	1r. brown	3·50	1·40

DESIGNS—HORIZ: 60k. Lenin and children (after A. Varlamov); 1r. Lenin talking to peasants (after V. Serov).

511 P. P. Semenov-Tian-Shansky

1952. 125th Birth Anniv of Semenov-Tian-Shansky (scientist).

1750	**511**	1r. brown on blue	4·25	3·25

512 Skaters

1952. Winter Sports.

1751	**512**	40k. multicoloured	2·50	65
1752	-	60k. multicoloured (Skiers)	3·50	1·00

513 V. O. Kovalevsky

1952. Birth Centenary of Kovalevsky (scientist).

1753	**513**	40k. brown on yellow	7·00	6·00

514 Gogol (after F. Moller) and Character from "Taras Bulba"

1952. Death Centenary of Nikolai Gogol (writer).

1754	**514**	40k. black on blue	1·30	35
1755	-	60k. orange and black	1·70	40
1756	-	1r. multicoloured	3·00	1·70

DESIGNS: 60k. Gogol and Belinsky (after B. Lebedev); 1r. Gogol and Ukrainian peasants.

515 G. K. Ordzhonikidze

1952. 15th Death Anniv of Ordzhonikidze (statesman).

1757	**515**	40k. green on pink	7·00	5·00
1758	**515**	1r. black on blue	8·75	6·75

516 Workers and Flag

1952. 15th Anniv of Stalin Constitution.

1759	**516**	40k. red and black on cream	7·00	4·25
1760	-	40k. red and green on green	7·00	4·25
1761	-	40k. red and brown on blue	7·00	4·25
1762	-	40k. red and black	7·00	4·25

DESIGNS—HORIZ: No. 1760, Chess players at recreation centre; 1761, Old people and banners. VERT: No. 1762, Schoolgirl and Spassky Tower, Kremlin.

517 Novikov-Priboy and Battleship "Orel"

1952. 75th Birth Anniv of Novikov-Priboy (writer).

1763	**517**	40k. grey, yellow & green	3·00	1·00

518 Victor Hugo

1952. 150th Birth Anniv of Victor Hugo (French writer).

1764	**518**	40k. black, blue & brown	1·60	50

519 Yulaev (after T. Nechaevoi)

1952. Birth Bicent of Yulaev (Bashkirian hero).

1765	**519**	40k. red on pink	1·70	50

520 G. Ya. Sedov

1952. 75th Birth Anniv of Sedov (Arctic explorer).

1766	**520**	40k. brown, blue & green	10·50	8·00

521 Arms and Flag of Rumania

1952. Friendship with Rumania.

1767	**521**	40k. multicoloured	1·60	85
1768	-	60k. green on pink	2·50	1·70
1769	-	1r. blue	3·75	2·50

DESIGNS—VERT: 60k. Soviet Soldiers' Monument, Bucharest. HORIZ: 1r. University Square, Bucharest.

522 Zhukovsky (after K. Bryullov)

1952. Death Centenary of V. Zhukovsky (poet).

1770	**522**	40k. black on blue	1·10	60

523 Bryullov (after V. Tropilin)

1952. Death Centenary of K. Bryullov (artist).

1771	**523**	40k. green on blue	1·10	60

524 Ogarev (after M. Lemmel)

1952. 75th Death Anniv of Ogarev (revolutionary writer).

1772	**524**	40k. green	65	35

525 Uspensky (after N. Yaroshenko)

1952. 50th Death Anniv of Uspensky (writer).

1773	**525**	40k. brown and blue	2·50	1·00

526 Nakhimov (after V. Timm)

1952. 150th Birth Anniv of Admiral Nakhimov.

1774	**526**	40k. multicoloured	4·00	2·50

527 Tartu University

1952. 150th Anniv of Extension of Tartu University.

1775	**527**	40k. black on salmon	3·00	1·70

1952. War Orders and Medals (7th series). Frame as T 282 with various centres.

1776	**F**	1r. brown	12·00	9·25
1777	**P**	2r. red	2·00	1·30
1778	**J**	3r. violet	1·00	75
1779a	**A**	5r. lake	1·30	85
1780	**E**	10r. red	1·70	1·00

528 Kayum Nasyri

1952. 50th Death Anniv of Nasyri (educationist).

1781	**528**	40k. brown on yellow	3·00	2·30

529 A. N. Radishchev

1952. 150th Death Anniv of Radishchev (writer).

1782	**529**	40k. black and red	2·75	1·70

530 Entrance to Volga–Don Canal

1952. 35th Anniv of Russian Revolution.

1783	**530**	40k. multicoloured	6·50	4·25
1784	-	1r. yellow, red and brown	8·75	5·75

DESIGN: 1r. Lenin, Stalin, Spassky Tower and flags.

531 P. A. Fedotov

1952. Death Centenary of Fedotov (painter).

1785	**531**	40k. brown and lake	2·40	1·20

532 Polenov (after I. Repin)

533 "Moscow Courtyard" (painting)

1952. 25th Death Anniv of Polenov (painter).

1786	**532**	40k. lake and buff	1·70	60
1787	**533**	1r. blue and grey	3·75	1·30

534 Odoevsky (after N. Bestuzhev)

1952. 150th Birth Anniv of A. I. Odoevsky (poet).

1788	**534**	40k. black and red	1·70	50

535 Mamin-Sibiryak

1952. Birth Centenary of D. N. Mamin-Sibiryak (writer).

1789	**535**	40k. green on yellow	1·30	50

536 V. M. Bekhterev

1952. 25th Death Anniv of Bekhterev (psychiatrist).

1790	**536**	40k. black, grey and blue	1·50	60

537 Komsomolskaya Koltsevaya Station (image scaled to 64% of original size)

1952. Underground Stations. Multicoloured centres.

1791	-	40k. violet	2·00	50
1792	-	40k. blue	2·00	50
1793	-	40k. grey	2·00	50
1794	**537**	40k. green	2·00	50

STATIONS: No. 1791, Belorussia Koltsevaya; 1792, Botanical Gardens; 1793, Novoslo-bodskaya.

538 U.S.S.R. Arms and Flags

1952. 30th Anniv of U.S.S.R.

1795	**538**	1r. brown, red and green	5·25	3·50

539 Lenin and Flags (after A. Gerasimov)

1953. 29th Death Anniv of Lenin.
1796 **539** 40k. multicoloured 5·25 4·25

540 Peace Prize Medal

1953. Stalin Peace Prize.
1797 **540** 40k. yellow, blue & brown 5·50 5·00

541 V. V. Kuibyshev

1953. 65th Birth Anniv of Kuibyshev (statesman).
1798 **541** 40k. black and lake 2·00 1·30

542 V. V. Mayakovsky

1953. 60th Birth Anniv of Mayakovsky (poet).
1799 **542** 40k. black and red 3·00 2·30

543 N. G. Chernyshevsky

1953. 125th Birth Anniv of Chernyshevsky (writer).
1800 **543** 40k. brown and buff 3·00 2·50

544 R. Volga Lighthouse

1953. Volga–Don Canal. Multicoloured.

1801	40k. Type **544**	2·00	75
1802	40k. Lock No. 9	2·00	75
1803	40k. Lock No. 13	2·00	75
1804	40k. Lock No. 15	2·00	75
1805	40k. Tsimlyanskaya hydro-electric station	2·00	75
1806	1r. "Iosif Stalin" (river vessel)	3·50	1·70

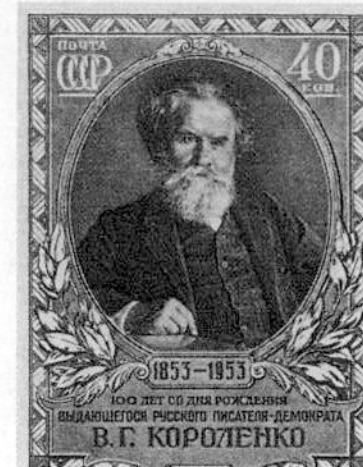

545 V. G. Korolenko

1953. Birth Centenary of Korolenko (writer).
1807 **545** 40k. brown 1·10 25

546 Tolstoi (after N. Ge)

1953. 125th Birth Anniv of Leo Tolstoi (writer).
1808 **546** 1r. brown 7·00 3·75

547 Lomonosov University and Students

1953. 35th Anniv of "Komsomol" (Russian Youth Organization). Multicoloured.

1809	40k. Type **547**	2·40	1·70
1810	1r. Four medals and "Komsomol" badge	5·25	3·50

548 Peoples of the U.S.S.R.

1953. 36th Anniv of Russian Revolution. Mult.

1811	40k. Type **548**	10·50	8·50
1812	60k. Lenin and Stalin in Smolny Institute, 1917	14·00	11·50

549 Lenin Medallion

1953. 50th Anniv of Communist Party.
1813 **549** 40k. multicoloured 4·00 3·00

550 Lenin Statue

551 Peter I Monument

1953. Views of Leningrad as T 550/1.

1814	**550**	40k. black on yellow	2·20	1·30
1815	**550**	40k. brown on pink	1·30	85
1816	-	40k. brown on yellow	2·20	1·30
1817	-	40k. black on buff	1·30	85
1818	**551**	1r. brown on blue	4·00	3·00
1819	**551**	1r. violet on yellow	3·25	2·50
1820	-	1r. green on pink	4·00	3·00
1821	-	1r. brown on blue	3·25	2·50

DESIGNS: As Type **550**: Nos. 1816/17, Admiralty. As Type **551**: 1820/1, Smolny Institute.

552 Lenin and Book "What is to be Done?"

1953. 50th Anniv of 2nd Social Democratic Workers' Party Congress.
1822 **552** 1r. brown and red 7·75 6·75

553 Pioneers and Moscow University Model

1953. Peace Propaganda.
1823 **553** 40k. black, olive and grey 4·00 3·00

554 Griboedov (after I. Kramskoi)

1954. 125th Death Anniv of A. S. Griboedov (author).

1824	**554**	40k. purple on buff	2·00	1·70
1825a	**554**	1r. black on green	5·75	4·25

555 Kremlin

1954. General Election.
1826 **555** 40k. grey and red 3·00 2·20

556 V. P. Chkalov

1954. 50th Birthday of Chkalov (aviator).
1827 **556** 1r. multicoloured 6·00 2·10

557 "Lenin in Smolny Institute" (after I. Brodsky)

1954. 30th Death Anniv of Lenin. Multicoloured.

1828	40k. Lenin (after M. Rundaltsov) (26×38 mm)	3·00	2·20
1829	40k. Type **557**	3·00	2·20
1830	40k. Cottage Museum, Ulyanovsk (after I. Sokolov)	3·00	2·20
1831	40k. "Lenin proclaims Soviet Regime" (V. Serov) (48×35 mm)	3·00	2·20
1832	40k. "Lenin at Kazan University" (A. Pushnin) (48×35 mm)	3·00	2·20

558 Stalin

1954. 1st Death Anniv of Stalin.
1833 **558** 40k. brown 4·00 2·75

559 Supreme Soviet Buildings in Kiev and Moscow

1954. Tercentenary of Reunion of Ukraine with Russia. Multicoloured. (a) Designs as T 559 inscr "1654–1954".

1834	40k. Type **559**	1·30	40
1835	40k. Shevchenko Memorial, Kharkhov (vert)	1·30	40
1836	40k. State Opera House, Kiev	1·30	40
1837	40k. Shevchenko University, Kiev	1·30	40
1838	40k. Academy of Sciences, Kiev	1·70	50
1839	60k. Bogdan Chmielnitsky Memorial, Kiev (vert)	2·20	65
1840	1r. Flags of R.S.F.S.R. and Ukrainian S.S.R. (vert)	4·25	85
1841	1r. Shevchenko Monument, Kanev (vert)	3·00	1·70
1842	1r. Pereyaslavskaya Rada	4·25	85

(b) No. 1098b optd with five lines of Cyrillic characters as inscr at top of T 559.
1843 **h** 2r. green 8·75 2·10

561 Running

1954. Sports. Frames in brown.

1844	**561**	40k. black and stone	1·40	35
1845	-	40k. black and blue	1·40	35
1846	-	40k. brown and buff	1·40	35
1847	-	40k. black and blue	1·40	35
1848	-	40k. black	1·40	35
1849	-	1r. grey and blue	5·25	1·50
1850	-	1r. black and blue	5·25	1·50
1851	-	1r. brown and drab	5·25	1·50

DESIGNS—HORIZ: No. 1845, "Soling" yachts; 1846, Cycling; 1847, Swimming; 1848, Hurdling; 1849, Mountaineering; 1850, Skiing. VERT: No. 1851, Basketball.

562 Cattle

1954. Agriculture.

1852	**562**	40k. blue, brown & cream	2·50	60
1853	-	40k. green, brown & buff	2·50	60

1854	-	40k. black, blue and green	2·50	60

DESIGNS: No. 1853, Potato cultivation; 1854, Collective farm hydro-electric station.

563 A. P. Chekhov

1954. 50th Death Anniv of Chekhov (writer).

1855	**563**	40k. brown and green	1·10	50

564 Bredikhin, Struve, Belopolsky and Observatory

1954. Rebuilding of Pulkov Observatory.

1856	**564**	40k. black, blue and violet	8·75	2·50

565 M. I. Glinka

1954. 150th Birth Anniv of Glinka (composer).

1857	**565**	40k. brown, pink and red	2·50	1·30
1858	-	60k. multicoloured	3·50	1·50

DESIGN—HORIZ: (38×25½ mm): 60k. "Glinka playing piano for Pushkin and Zhukovsky" (V. Artamonov).

566 Exhibition Emblem

1954. Agricultural Exhibition. Multicoloured.

1859	40k. Type **566**	1·10	85
1860	40k. Agricultural Pavilion	1·10	85
1861	40k. Cattle breeding Pavilion	1·10	85
1862	40k. Mechanization Pavilion	1·10	85
1863	1r. Exhibition Entrance	3·50	2·10
1864	1r. Main Pavilion	3·50	2·10

Nos. 1860/3 are horiz, 1860/1 being 41×30½ mm, 1862, 40×30 mm and 1863 41×33 mm. No. 1864 is vert, 29×41 mm.

567 N. A. Ostrovsky

1954. 50th Birth Anniv of Ostrovsky (writer).

1865	**567**	40k. multicoloured	1·70	40

568 Monument

1954. Centenary of Defence of Sevastopol.

1866	**568**	40k. black, brown & grn	1·50	40
1867	-	60k. black, brown & buff	1·70	65
1868	-	1r. multicoloured	3·50	1·00

DESIGNS—HORIZ: 60k. Heroes of Sevastopol (after V. Timm). VERT: 1r. Admiral Nakhimov (after V. Timm).

569 Marx, Engels, Lenin and Stalin

1954. 37th Anniv of October Revolution.

1869	**569**	1r. brown, red and orange	5·75	3·75

570 Kazan University

1954. 150th Anniv of Kazan University.

1870	**570**	40k. blue on blue	1·20	85
1871	**570**	60k. red	2·00	1·30

571 Salomea Neris

1954. 50th Birth Anniv of Salomea Neris (poetess).

1872	**571**	40k. multicoloured	1·30	65

572 Cultivating Vegetables

1954. Agriculture. Multicoloured.

1873	40k. Type **572**	1·60	40
1874	40k. Tractor and plough	1·60	40
1875	40k. Harvesting flax (49×25½ mm)	1·60	40
1876	60k. Harvesting sunflowers (49×25½ mm)	3·00	65

573 Stalin

1954. 75th Birth Anniv of Stalin.

1877	**573**	40k. purple	1·50	50
1878	**573**	1r. blue	3·50	1·40

574 Rubinstein (after I. Repin)

1954. 125th Birth Anniv of Rubinstein (composer).

1879	**574**	40k. black and purple	2·00	85

575 V. M. Garshin

1955. Birth Centenary of Garshin (writer).

1880	**575**	40k. black, brown & grn	1·70	1·30

576 Ilyushin Il-12 over Landscape

1955. Air.

1881	-	1r. multicoloured	1·70	40
1882	**576**	2r. black and green	3·75	60

DESIGN: 1r. Ilyushin Il-12 over coastline.

577 Savitsky (after N. Frandkovsky) and "Construction of Railway"

1955. 50th Death Anniv of K. Savitsky (painter).

1883	**577**	40k. brown	1·70	65
MS1883a		151×119 mm. No. 1883×4	31·00	29·00
MS1883b		Ditto brown inscriptions	39·00	34·00

578 Clasped Hands

1955. International Conference of Postal and Municipal Workers, Vienna.

1884	**578**	50k. multicoloured	1·30	60

579 Pushkin and Mickiewicz

1955. 10th Anniv of Russo-Polish Friendship Agreement.

1885	**579**	40k. multicoloured	2·40	40
1886	-	40k. black	2·40	40
1887	-	1r. multicoloured	5·25	85
1888	-	1r. multicoloured	5·25	85

DESIGNS: No. 1886, "Brotherhood in Arms" Monument, Warsaw (26½×39 mm); No. 1887, Palace of Science, Warsaw (37½×25½ mm); No. 1888, Copernicus and Matejko (39×26½ mm).

580 Lenin at Shushenskoe (after V. Basov)

1955. 85th Birth Anniv of Lenin. Multicoloured centres.

1889	**580**	60k. red	2·30	35
1890	-	1r. red	4·00	60
1891	-	1r. red	4·00	60

DESIGNS: No. 1890, Lenin in secret printing house (after F. Golubkov) (26½×39 mm). As Type **580**: No. 1891, Lenin and Krupskaya at Gorky (after N. Sysoev).

581 Schiller

1955. 150th Death Anniv of Schiller (poet).

1892	**581**	40k. brown	1·70	1·10

582 Ilyushin Il-12 over Globe

1955. Air.

1893	**582**	2r. brown	3·50	1·30
1894	**582**	2r. blue	3·50	1·30

583 V. Mayakovsky

1955. 25th Death Anniv of Mayakovsky (poet).

1895	**583**	40k. multicoloured	1·10	35

584 Tadzhik S.S.R. Pavilion

1955. Agricultural Exhibition. Soviet Pavilion. Multicoloured designs with green frames.

1896	40k. R.S.F.S.R.	85	30
1897	40k. Byelorussian S.S.R.	85	30
1898	40k. Type **584**	85	30
1899	40k. Azerbaijan S.S.R.	85	30
1900	40k. Latvian S.S.R.	85	30
1901	40k. Lithuanian S.S.R.	85	30
1902	40k. Karelo-Finnish S.S.R.	85	30
1903	40k. Estonian S.S.R.	85	30
1904	40k. Armenian S.S.R.	85	30
1905	40k. Ukrainian S.S.R.	85	30
1906	40k. Georgian S.S.R.	85	30
1907	40k. Kazakh S.S.R.	85	30
1908	40k. Turkmen S.S.R.	85	30
1909	40k. Kirgiz S.S.R.	85	30
1910	40k. Uzbek S.S.R.	85	30
1911	40k. Moldavian S.S.R.	85	30
MS1911a	156×104 mm. 40k. R.S.F.S.R	26·00	25·00
MS1911b	156×104 mm. 40k. Byelorussian S.S.R.	26·00	25·00
MS1911c	156×104 mm. 40k. Ukrainian S.S.R.	26·00	25·00

585 M. V. Lomonosov and University

1955. Bicentenary of Lomonosov University. Multicoloured.

1912	40k. Type **585**	1·10	40
1913	1r. Lomonosov University	1·90	75
MS1913b 151×108 mm. 40k. Type **585**		13·00	11·50
MS1913c 151×109 mm. 1r. Lomonosov University		22·00	17·00

586 A. G. Venetsianov (self-portrait) and "The Labours of Spring"

1955. 175th Birth Anniv of Venetsianov (painter). Multicoloured centre.

1914	**586**	1r. black	2·75	65
MS1914a 151×115 mm. No. 1914 (block of four)			22·00	17·00

587 A. Lyadov

1955. Birth Centenary of Lyadov (composer).

1915	**587**	40k. multicoloured	1·60	65

588 A. S. Popov

1955. 60th Anniv of Popov's Radio Discoveries. Multicoloured centres.

1916	**588**	40k. blue	1·50	25
1917	**588**	1r. brown	2·75	50

589 Lenin

590 "Capture of Winter Palace" (detail, P. Sokolov-Skalya)

1955. 38th Anniv of Russian Revolution.

1918	**589**	40k. multicoloured	2·30	1·30
1919	**590**	40k. multicoloured	2·30	1·30
1920	-	1r. multicoloured	5·25	2·50

DESIGN: As T **590**: 1r. Lenin speaking to revolutionaries (after D. Nalbandyan).

„Сев. полюс"
— Москва
1955 г.

(591)

1955. Air. Opening of North Pole Scientific Stations. Nos. 1881/2 optd with T 591.

1921		1r. multicoloured	13·00	8·50
1922	**576**	2r. black and green	18·00	10·00

592 Magnitogorsk

1955. 25th Anniv of Magnitogorsk.

1923	**592**	40k. multicoloured	1·70	40

593 Mil Mi-4 Helicopter over Station

1955. North Pole Scientific Stations.

1924	**593**	40k. multicoloured	3·25	35
1925	**593**	60k. multicoloured	3·50	65
1926	-	1r. multicoloured	5·25	1·00
MS1926a 154×111 mm. No. 1926 (block of four)			39·00	25·00

DESIGN: 1r. Meteorologist taking observations.

594 Shubin (self-portrait)

1955. 150th Death Anniv of Shubin (sculptor).

1927	**594**	40k. multicoloured	1·00	25
1928	**594**	1r. multicoloured	1·70	40

595 A. N. Krylov

1956. 10th Death Anniv of Krylov (scientist).

1929	**595**	40k. multicoloured	1·10	35

596 Racing

1956. International Horse Racing.

1930	**596**	40k. sepia and brown	1·30	35
1931	**596**	60k. blue and green	1·50	50
1932	-	1r. purple and blue	2·75	75

DESIGN—HORIZ: 1r. Trotting.

597 Badge and Stadium

1956. 5th Spartacist Games.

1933	**597**	1r. purple and green	1·80	65

598 Atomic Power Station

1956. Foundation of Atomic Power Station of Russian Academy of Sciences.

1934	**598**	25k. multicoloured	85	25
1935	-	60k. yellow, turq & brn	2·00	40
1936	**598**	1r. yellow, red and blue	2·75	85

DESIGN: 60k. Top of atomic reactor.

599 Statue of Lenin (E. Buchetich)

1956. 20th Communist Party Congress.

1937	**599**	40k. multicoloured	1·00	40
1938	**599**	1r. multicoloured	1·70	60

600 Kh. Abovyan

1956. 150th Birth Anniv of Khatchatur Abovyan (Armenian writer).

1939	**600**	40k. black on blue	1·30	60

601 Revolutionaries (after N. Tereshchenko)

1956. 50th Anniv of 1905 Revolution.

1940	**601**	40k. multicoloured	4·25	1·70

602

ПАВИЛЬОН «УРАЛ»
No. 1941

ПАВИЛЬОН СЕВЕРО-ВОСТОЧНЫХ ОБЛАСТЕЙ
No. 1942

ПАВИЛЬОН ЦЕНТРАЛЬНЫХ ЧЕРНОЗЕМНЫХ ОБЛАСТЕЙ
No. 1943

ПАВИЛЬОН «ЛЕНИНГРАД • СЕВЕРО-ЗАПАД»
No. 1944

ПАВИЛЬОН МОСКОВСКОЙ, ТУЛЬСКОЙ, КАЛУЖСКОЙ, РЯЗАНСКОЙ И БРЯНСКОЙ ОБЛАСТЕЙ
No. 1945

ПАВИЛЬОН БАШКИРСКОЙ АССР
No. 1946

ПАВИЛЬОН ДАЛЬНЕГО ВОСТОКА
No. 1947

ПАВИЛЬОН ТАТАРСКОЙ АССР
No. 1948

ПАВИЛЬОН ЦЕНТРАЛЬНЫХ ОБЛАСТЕЙ
No. 1949

ПАВИЛЬОН ЮНЫХ НАТУРАЛИСТОВ
No. 1950

ПАВИЛЬОН СЕВЕРНОГО КАВКАЗА
No. 1951

ПАВИЛЬОН «СИБИРЬ»
No. 1952

ПАВИЛЬОН «ПОВОЛЖЬЕ»
No. 1953

1956. Agricultural Exhibition. Multicoloured. Views of Pavilions of U.S.S.R. regions as T 602. Inscr "ВСХВ".

1941	1r. Ural	1·50	40
1942	1r. North East	1·50	40
1943	1r. Central Black Soil Region	1·50	40
1944	1r. Leningrad	1·50	40
1945	1r. Moscow-Tula-Kaluga-Ryazan-Bryansk	1·50	40
1946	1r. Bashkir	1·50	40
1947	1r. Far East	1·50	40
1948	1r. Tatar	1·50	40
1949	1r. Central Regions	1·50	40
1950	1r. Young Naturalists	1·50	40
1951	1r. North Caucasus	1·50	40
1952	1r. Siberia	1·50	40
1953	1r. Volga	1·50	40

603 N. A. Kasatkin (painter)

1956. Kasatkin Commemoration.

1954	**603**	40k. red	1·10	50

604 A. E. Arkhipov and Painting "On the Oka River"

1956. Arkhipov Commemoration.

1955	**604**	40k. multicoloured	1·50	25
1956	**604**	1r. multicoloured	2·75	50

605 I. P. Kulibin

1956. 220th Birth Anniv of Kulibin (inventor).

1957	**605**	40k. multicoloured	1·30	50

606 "Fowler" (after Perov)

1956. Perov Commemoration. Inscr "1956". Multicoloured centres.

1958	-	40k. green	1·70	35
1959	**606**	1r. brown	3·50	75
1960	-	1r. brown	3·50	75

DESIGNS—VERT: No. 1958, Self-portrait. HORIZ: No. 1960, "Hunters Resting".

607 Lenin (after P. Vasilev)

1956. 86th Birth Anniv of Lenin.

1961	**607**	40k. multicoloured	9·50	5·50

608 N. I. Lobachevsky (after L. Kryukov)

1956. Death Cent of Lobachevsky (mathematician).

1962	**608**	40k. brown	85	35

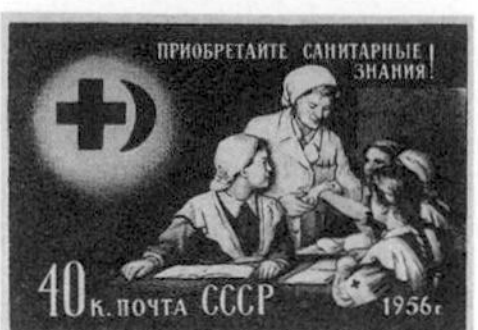

609 Student Nurses

1956. Red Cross.

1963	**609**	40k. red, blue and brown	1·10	40
1964	-	40k. red, olive & turquoise	1·10	40

DESIGN—37½×25½ mm: No. 1964, Nurse and textile factory.

610 Scientific Station

1956. Air. Opening of North Pole Scientific Station No. 6.

1965	**610**	1r. multicoloured	4·75	2·10

611 Sechenov (after I. Repin)

1956. 50th Death Anniv (1995) of I. Sechenov (naturalist).

1966	**611**	40k. multicoloured	1·70	60

612 Arsenev

1956. V. K. Arsenev (writer).

1967	**612**	40k. black, violet & pink	2·20	75

613 I. V. Michurin

1956. Birth Centenary of Michurin (naturalist). Multicoloured centres.

1968	**613**	25k. brown	50	15
1969	-	60k. green	1·10	30
1970	**613**	1r. blue	2·20	50

DESIGN—47½×26½ mm: 60k. Michurin and children.

614 Savrasov (after V. Perov)

1956. 125th Birth Anniv (1955) of A. K. Savrasov (painter).

1971	**614**	1r. brown and yellow	1·70	85

615 N. K. Krupskaya (Lenin's wife)

1956. Krupskaya Commemoration.

1972	**615**	40k. brown, black & blue	1·70	85

616 S. M. Kirov

1956. 70th Birth Anniv of Kirov (statesman).

1973	**616**	40k. multicoloured	85	50

617 A. A. Blok

1956. Blok (poet) Commemoration.

1974	**617**	40k. brown, black & olive	1·10	60

618 N. S. Leskov

1956. 125th Birth Anniv of Leskov (writer).

1975	**618**	40k. multicoloured	85	25
1976	**618**	1r. multicoloured	1·90	50

619 Factory Building

1956. 25th Anniv of Rostov Agricultural Machinery Works.

1977	**619**	40k. multicoloured	1·10	60

620 G. N. Fedotova (actress)

1956. Fedotova Commemoration.

1978	**620**	40k. multicoloured	85	35

For similar stamp see No. 2159.

621 P. M. Tretyakov (after I. Repin) and Art Gallery

1956. Centenary of Tretyakov Art Gallery, Moscow.

1979	**621**	40k. multicoloured	2·20	65
1980	-	40k. multicoloured	2·20	65

DESIGN—VERT: No. 1980, "Rooks have arrived" (painting by Savrasov).

622 Relay-race

1956. Spartacist Games.

1981	**622**	10k. red	35	10
1982	-	25k. brown	45	15
1983	-	25k. multicoloured	45	15
1984	-	25k. blue	45	15
1985	-	40k. blue	80	25
1986	-	40k. green	80	25
1987	-	40k. brown and green	80	25
1988	-	40k. deep brown, brown and green	80	25
1989	-	40k. red, green and light green	80	25
1990	-	40k. brown	80	25
1991	-	40k. multicoloured	80	25
1992	-	60k. violet	2·00	40
1993	-	60k. violet	2·00	40
1994	-	1r. brown	3·50	85

DESIGNS—VERT: No. 1982, Volleyball; 1983, Swimming; 1984, Rowing; 1985, Diving; 1989, Flag and stadium; 1990, Tennis; 1991, Medal; 1993, Boxing. HORIZ: No. 1986, Cycle racing; 1987, Fencing; 1988, Football; 1992, Gymnastics; 1994, Netball.

623 Parachutist Landing

1956. 3rd World Parachute-jumping Competition.

1995	**623**	40k. multicoloured	1·10	35

624 Construction Work

1956. Builders' Day.

1996a	**624**	40k. orange	85	40
1997	-	60k. brown	1·10	50
1998	-	1r. blue	2·50	65

DESIGNS: 60k. Plant construction; 1r. Dam construction.

625 Self-portrait and "Volga River Boatmen"

626 "Reply of the Cossacks to Sultan Mahmoud IV"

1956. 26th Death Anniv of I. E. Repin (artist).

1999	**625**	40k. multicoloured	4·00	1·50
2000	**626**	1r. multicoloured	7·75	2·20

627 Robert Burns

1956. 160th Death Anniv of Burns (Scots poet).

2001	**627**	40k. brown	7·50	5·25
2002	**627**	40k. brown and blue	5·25	3·25

628 Ivan Franko

1956. Birth Cent of Franko (writer) (1st issue).

2003	**628**	40k. purple	95	50
2004	**628**	1r. blue	1·50	65

See also No. 2037.

1956. Lesya Ukrainka Commemoration. As T 615 but portrait of Ukrainka (author).

2005	40k. black, brown and green	95	65

629 M. Aivazov (farmer)

1956. 148th Birthday of Aivazov. (a) Wrongly inscr "Muhamed" (7 characters).

2006	**629**	40k. green	35·00	29·00

(b) Corrected to "Makmud" (6 characters).

2006a	40k. green	17·00	10·00

630 Statue of Nestor (M. Antokol)

1956. 900th Birth Anniv of Nestor (historian).

2007	**630**	40k. multicoloured	1·10	35
2008	**630**	1r. multicoloured	2·20	60

631 Ivanov (after S. Postnikov)

1956. 150th Birth Anniv of A. A. Ivanov (painter).

2009	**631**	40k. brown and grey	95	30

632 Feeding Poultry

1956. Agriculture. Multicoloured.

2010	10k. Type **632**	45	15
2011	10k. Harvesting	45	15
2012	25k. Gathering maize	85	35
2013	40k. Maize field	1·30	35
2014	40k. Tractor station	1·30	35
2015	40k. Cattle grazing	1·30	35
2016	40k. "Agriculture and Industry"	1·30	35

SIZES: Nos. 2010, 2014/15, 37×25½ mm. Nos. 2011/13, 37×28 mm. No. 2016, 37×21 mm.

633 Mozart

1956. Cultural Anniversaries.

2017	40k. blue (Type **633**)	1·60	50
2018	40k. green (Curie)	1·60	50
2019	40k. lilac (Heine)	1·60	50
2020	40k. brown (Ibsen)	1·60	50
2021	40k. green (Dostoevsky)	1·60	50
2022	40k. brown (Franklin)	1·60	50
2023	40k. black (Shaw)	1·60	50
2024	40k. orange (Sessku-Toyo Oda)	1·60	50
2025	40k. black (Rembrandt)	1·60	50

Nos. 2022/5 are larger, 25×38 mm.

634 Mirnyi Base and Supply Ship "Lena"

1956. Soviet Scientific Antarctic Expedition.

2026	**634**	40k. turquoise, red & grey	3·50	1·30

1956. Julia Zhemaite Commemoration. As T 615 but portrait of Zhemaite (author).

2027	40k. green, brown and sepia	1·10	35

635 F. A. Bredikhin

1956. 125th Birth Anniv of Bredikhin (astronomer).

2028	**635**	40k. multicoloured	4·25	1·10

636 G. I. Kotovsky

1956. 75th Birth Anniv of Kotovsky (military leader).

2029a	**636**	40k. mauve	5·25	3·25

637 Shatura Electric Power Station

1956. 30th Anniv of Shatura Electric Power Station.

2030	**637**	40k. multicoloured	85	35

638 Marshal Suvorov (after Utkin)

1956. 225th Birth Anniv of Marshal Suvorov.

2031	**638**	40k. lake and orange	80	35
2032	**638**	1r. brown and olive	1·70	50
2033	**638**	3r. black and brown	4·25	1·30

639 Kryakutni's Ascent (after G. Savitsky)

1956. 225th Anniv of First Balloon Flight by Kryakutni.

2034	**639**	40k. multicoloured	1·90	70

640 Vasnetsov (after S. Malyutin) and "Dawn at the Voskresenski Gate"

1956. 30th Death Anniv of A. M. Vasnetsov (artist).

2035	**640**	40k. multicoloured	1·60	60

641 Y. M. Shokalsky (oceanographer)

1956. Birth Cent of Shokalsky.

2036	**641**	40k. brown and blue	1·90	60

642 Franko (after I. Trush)

1956. Birth Centenary of Franko (writer) (2nd issue).

2037	**642**	40k. green	75	25

643 Indian Temple and Books

1956. Kalidasa (Indian poet) Commemoration.

2038	**643**	40k. red	80	25

644 F. G. Vokov (actor) (after A. Losenko) and State Theatre

1956. Bicentenary of Leningrad State Theatre.

2039	**644**	40k. black, red and yellow	60	25

645 Lomonosov (after L. Miropolsky) at St. Petersburg University

1956. Russian Writers.

2040	**645**	40k. multicoloured	1·20	25
2041	-	40k. multicoloured	1·10	25
2042	-	40k. brown and blue	1·10	25
2043	-	40k. olive, brown & black	1·10	25
2044	-	40k. brown and turquoise	1·10	25
2045	-	40k. purple and brown	1·10	25
2046	-	40k. olive and blue	1·10	25

DESIGNS: No. 2041, Gorky (after V. Efanov) and scene from "Mother" (novel); 2042, Pushkin and statue of Peter the Great, Leningrad (illustrating poem "Bronze Horseman"); 2043, Rustavely and episode from "The Knight in the Tiger Skin" (poem); 2044, Tolstoy and scene from "War and Peace" (novel); 2045, V. G. Belinsky and titles of literary works; 2046, M. Y. Lermontov and Daryal Pass.

See also Nos. 2076, 2089/90, 2256, 2316/22 and 2458.

646 Vitus Bering and Routes of his Voyages

1956. 275th Birth Anniv of Bering (explorer).

2047	**646**	40k. multicoloured	1·90	1·30

647 Mendeleev

1957. 50th Death Anniv of Dmitri Mendeleev (chemist).

2048	**647**	40k. brown, grey & black	2·50	1·40

648 M. I. Glinka

1957. Death Centenary of Glinka (composer). Mult.

2049a	40k. Type **648**	95	45
2050a	1r. Scene from "Ivan Susanin"	2·10	85

649 Youth Festival Emblem

1957. All Union Festival of Soviet Youth.

2051	**649**	40k. multicoloured	50	25

650 Ice Hockey Player

1957. 23rd World and 35th European Ice Hockey Championships, Moscow.

2052a	-	25k. violet	75	15
2053a	**650**	40k. blue	95	15
2054a	-	60k. green	1·20	25

DESIGNS: 25k. Championship emblem; 60k. Goalkeeper.

651 Youth Festival Emblem and Pigeon

1957. 6th World Youth Festival, Moscow (1st issue). Perf or imperf.

2055	**651**	40k. multicoloured	60	15
2056	**651**	60k. multicoloured	1·20	35

See also Nos. 2084/7 and 2108/11.

652 Factory Plant

1957. Cent of "Red Proletariat" Plant. Moscow.

2057	**652**	40k. multicoloured	1·10	35

653 Sika Deer

1957. Russian Wildlife. Multicoloured.

2057a	10k. Grey partridge	90	25
2058	15k. Black grouse	90	15
2058a	15k. Polar bear	70	35
2059	20k. Type **653**	75	15
2059a	20k. Brown hare	70	35
2059b	25k. Tiger	80	60
2059c	25k. Wild horse	80	60
2060	30k. Mallard	1·50	25
2061	30k. European bison	1·50	25
2062	40k. Elk	1·80	35
2063	40k. Sable	1·80	35
2063a	40k. Eurasian red squirrel	95	25
2063b	40k. Yellow-throated marten	95	25
2063c	60k. Hazel grouse	2·40	1·00
2063d	1r. Mute swan	3·50	1·70

Nos. 2058/a, 2059a/62, 2063a/b and 2063d are horiz.

See also Nos. 2534/6.

654 Vologda Lace-making

1957. Regional Handicrafts. Multicoloured.

2064	40k. Moscow wood-carving	1·70	40
2065	40k. Woman engraving vase	1·70	40
2066	40k. Type **654**	1·70	40
2067	40k. Northern bone-carving	1·70	40
2067a	40k. Wood-block engraving	1·20	45
2067b	40k. Turkmen carpet-weaving	1·20	45

655 G. V. Plekhanov

1957. Birth Centenary of Plekhanov (politician).

2068	**655**	40k. plum	80	35

656 A. N. Bakh

1957. Birth Centenary of Bakh (biochemist).

2069a	**656**	40k. multicoloured	1·30	35

657 L. Euler

1957. 250th Birth Anniv of Euler (mathematician).

2070a	**657**	40k. black and purple	5·75	6·00

658 Lenin in Meditation

1957. 87th Birth Anniv of Lenin. Multicoloured.

2071	40k. Type **658**	1·10	25
2072	40k. Lenin carrying pole	1·10	25
2073	40k. Talking with soldier and sailor	1·10	25

659 Dr. William Harvey

1957. 300th Death Anniv of Dr. William Harvey (discoverer of circulation of blood).

2074	**659**	40k. brown	80	25

660 M. A. Balakirev

1957. 120th Birth Anniv of Balakirev (composer).

2075	**660**	40k. black	1·20	35

661 12th-century Narrator

1957. "The Tale of the Host of Igor".

2076	**661**	40k. multicoloured	80	35

662 Agricultural Medal

1957. Cultivation of Virgin Soil.

2077	**662**	40k. multicoloured	1·20	35

663 A. I. Herzen (after N. Ge) and N. P. Ogarev (after M. Lemmel) (founders)

1957. Centenary of Publication of Magazine "Kolokol".

2078	**663**	40k. brown, black & blue	95	35

664 Monument

250 лет
Ленинграда
(665)

1957. 250th Anniv of Leningrad. Vert designs as T 664 and stamps as Nos. 1818 and 1820 optd as T 665.

2079	**664**	40k. green	60	25
2080	-	40k. violet	60	25
2081	-	40k. brown	60	25
2082	**551**	1r. brown on green	1·40	35
2083	-	1r. green on salmon	1·40	35

DESIGNS: No. 2080, Nevsky Prospect, Leningrad; No. 2081, Lenin Statue.

666 Youths with Banner

1957. 6th World Youth Festival, Moscow (2nd issue). Multicoloured. Perf or imperf.

2084A	10k. Type **666**	25	10
2084Aa	20k. Sculptor with statue	50	25
2085A	25k. Type **666**	50	15
2086A	40k. Dancers	60	15
2087A	1r. Festival emblem and fireworks over Moscow State University	1·60	50

667 A. M. Lyapunov

1957. Birth Centenary of Lyapunov (mathematician).

2088	**667**	40k. brown	6·25	3·75

668 T. G. Shevchenko (after I. Repin) and Scene from "Katharina"

1957. 19th-Century Writers. Multicoloured.

2089	40k. Type **668**	90	35
2090	40k. N. G. Chernyshevsky and scene from "What is to be Done?"	90	35

669 Henry Fielding

1957. 250th Birth Anniv of Fielding (novelist).

2091	**669**	40k. multicoloured	60	25

670 Racing Cyclists

1957. 10th International Cycle Race.

2092	**670**	40k. multicoloured	1·30	35

671 Interior of Observatory

1957. International Geophysical Year (1st issue).

2093	**671**	40k. brown, yellow and blue	1·70	50
2094	-	40k. indigo, yellow and blue	2·40	50
2095	-	40k. violet and lavender	2·20	70
2095a	-	40k. blue	2·20	35
2095b	-	40k. green	2·20	35
2095c	-	40k. yellow and blue	2·20	35

DESIGNS—As T **671**: No. 2094, Meteor in sky; 2095a, Malakhit radar scanner and balloon (meteorology); 2095b, "Zarya" (non-magnetic research schooner) (geo-magnetism); 2095c, Northern Lights and C-180 camera. 15×21 mm: No. 2095, Rocket.

See also Nos. 2371/3a.

672 Gymnast

1957. 3rd International Youth Games.

2096	**672**	20k. brown and blue	30	15
2097	-	25k. red and green	40	15
2098	-	40k. violet and red	70	30
2099	-	40k. olive, red and green	70	30
2100	-	60k. brown and blue	1·50	50

DESIGNS—As Type **672**: No. 2097, Wrestlers; 2098, Young athletes; 2099, Moscow Stadium; 2100, Throwing the javelin.

673 Football

1957. Russian Successes at Olympic Games, Melbourne.

2101		20k. brown, blue & black	35	15
2102		20k. red and green	35	15
2103		25k. blue and orange	40	20
2104	**673**	40k. multicoloured	70	25
2105	-	40k. brown and purple	70	25
2106	-	60k. brown and violet	1·00	50

DESIGNS—VERT: No. 2101, Throwing the javelin; 2102, Running; 2103, Gymnastics; 2105, Boxing; 2106, Weight-lifting.

674 Yanka Kupala

1957. 75th Birth Anniv of Kupala (poet).

2107	**674**	40k. brown	4·50	2·75

675 Moscow State University

1957. 6th World Youth Festival (3rd issue). Moscow Views.

2108	-	40k. black and brown	60	15
2109	-	40k. black and purple	60	15
2110	-	1r. black and blue	1·30	30
2111	**675**	1r. black and red	1·30	30

DESIGNS—HORIZ: No. 2108, Kremlin; 2109, Stadium; 2110, Bolshoi State Theatre.

676 Lenin Library

1957. Int Philatelic Exn, Moscow. Perf or imperf.

2112	**676**	40k. turquoise	80	25

MS2112c 144×101 mm. **676** 40k.×2 blue. Imperf — 39·00 50·00

677 Dove of Peace encircling Globe

1957. "Defence of Peace".

2113	**677**	40k. multicoloured	1·30	50
2114	**677**	1r. multicoloured	2·40	1·00

1957. Birth Centenary of Clara Zetkin (German revolutionary). As T 615 but portrait of Zetkin.

2115	40k. multicoloured	1·20	35

678 P. Beranger

1957. Death Centenary of Beranger (French poet).

2116	**678**	40k. green	1·20	30

679 Krengholm Factory, Narva

1957. Centenary of Krengholm Textile Factory, Narva, Estonia.

2117	**679**	40k. brown	1·90	60

680 Factory Plant and Statue of Lenin (M. Kharlamev)

1957. Centenary of Krasny Vyborzhetz Plant, Leningrad.

2118	**680**	40k. blue	70	35

681 Stasov (after I. Repin)

1957. 50th Death Anniv of Stasov (art critic).

2119	**681**	40k. brown	60	15
2120	**681**	1r. blue	1·50	35

682 Pigeon with Letter

1957. International Correspondence Week.

2121	**682**	40k. blue	50	20
2122	**682**	60k. purple	80	25

683 K. E. Tsiolkovsky

1957. Birth Centenary of Tsiolkovsky (scientist).

2123	**683**	40k. multicoloured	6·25	1·10

684 Congress Emblem

1957. 4th World T.U.C., Leipzig.

2124	**684**	40k. blue on blue	70	35

685 Students

1957. 40th Anniv of Russian Revolution. (a) 1st issue. As T 685. Multicoloured. Perf or Imperf.

2125A	10k. Type **685**	20	10
2126A	40k. Railway worker (horiz)	50	20
2127A	40k. Portrait of Lenin on banner	50	15
2128A	40k. Lenin and workers with banners	50	15
2129A	60k. Harvester (horiz)	1·30	60

686 Workers and Emblem (Ukraine)

1957. 40th Anniv of Russian Revolution (2nd issue). Multicoloured.

2130	40k. Type **686**	90	35
2131	40k. Estonia	90	35
2132	40k. Uzbekistan	90	35
2133	40k. R.S.F.S.R. (horiz)	90	35
2134	40k. Belorussia (horiz)	90	35
2135	40k. Lithuania (horiz)	90	35
2136	40k. Armenia (horiz)	90	35
2137	40k. Azerbaijan (horiz)	90	35
2138	40k. Georgia (horiz)	90	35
2139	40k. Kirghizia (horiz)	90	35
2140	40k. Turkmenistan (horiz)	90	35
2141	40k. Tadzhikistan (horiz)	90	35
2142	40k. Kazakhstan (horiz)	90	35
2143	40k. Latvia (horiz)	90	35
2144	40k. Moldavia (horiz)	90	35

687 Lenin (after G. Goldstein)

1957. 40th Anniv of Russian Revolution (3rd issue). As T 687.

2145	**687**	40k. blue	1·90	70
2146	-	60k. red	2·40	1·00

DESIGN—HORIZ: 60k. Lenin at desk.

1957. 40th Anniv of Russian Revolution (4th issue). Imperf.

MS2146a 145×99 mm. Nos. 2079/80 and 1816	10·50	5·25
MS2146b 144×101 mm. Nos. 2126/7 and 2129	10·50	5·25

688 Satellite encircling Globe

1957. Launching of 1st Artifical Satellite.

2147	**688**	40k. indigo on blue	3·50	85
2148	**688**	40k. blue	3·50	85

689 Meteor Falling

1957. Sikhote-Alin Meteor.

2149	**689**	40k. multicoloured	2·75	1·10

690 Kuibyshev Power Station Turbine

1957. All Union Industrial Exhibition (1st issue).

2150	**690**	40k. brown	95	25

See also Nos. 2168.

4/X-57 г. Первый в мире искусств. спутник Земли

(691)

1957. 1st Artificial Satellite of the World. Optd with T 691.

2151	**683**	40k. multicoloured	44·00	26·00

692 Soviet War Memorial, Berlin (after Ye. Bunchetich)

1957. Bicentenary of Academy of Arts, Moscow.

2152	-	40k. black on salmon	60	15
2153	**692**	60k. black	95	15
2154	-	1r. black on pink	1·70	35

DESIGNS—25½×37½ mm: 40k. Academy and portraits of K. Bryullov, I. Repin and V. Surikov (after I. Repin). 21½×32 mm: 1r. "Worker and Collective Farmer", Moscow (sculpture, Vera Mukhina).

693 Arms of Ukraine

1957. 40th Anniv of Ukraine S.S.R.

2155	**693**	40k. multicoloured	95	25

694 Garibaldi

1957. 150th Birth Anniv of Garibaldi.

2156	**694**	40k. purple, maroon and green	80	25

695 Edvard Grieg

1957. 50th Death Anniv of Grieg (composer).

2157	**695**	40k. black on salmon	1·50	35

696 Borovikovsky (after I. Bugaevsky-Blagodarny)

1957. Birth Bicent of Borovikovsky (painter).

2158	**696**	40k. brown	95	25

1967. M. N. Ermolova (actress) Commemoration. As T 620 but portrait of Ermolova.

2159	40k. brown and violet	1·10	40

698 Kolas

1957. 75th Birth Anniv of Yakyb Kolas (poet).

2160	**698**	40k. black	4·00	3·00

699 Mitskyavichyus-Kapsukas

1957. 22nd Death Anniv of V. S. Mitskyavichyus-Kapsukas (Communist Party leader).

2161	**699**	40k. brown	4·00	2·50

700 G. Z. Bashindzhagian

1957. Bashindzhagian (artist) Commemoration.

2162	**700**	40k. brown	4·00	2·50

701 Kuibyshev Hydro- electric Station

1957. 40th Anniv of Kuibyshev Hydro-electric Station.

2163	**701**	40k. blue on flesh	1·10	25

702 "To the Stars" (Ye. Buchetich)

1957. Launching of 2nd Artificial Satellite.

2164	**702**	20k. red and black	95	10
2165	**702**	40k. green and black	1·50	15
2166	**702**	60k. brown and black	2·00	25
2167	**702**	1r. blue and black	3·00	60

703 Allegory of Industry

1958. All Union Industrial Exn (2nd issue).

2168	**703**	60k. red, black & lavender	1·10	30

1958. Rosa Luxemburg Commemoration. As T 615 but portrait of Luxemburg (German revolutionary).

2169	40k. brown and blue	1·10	35

704 Tsi Bai-shi

1958. Tsi Bai-shi (Chinese artist) Commem.

2170	**704**	40k. violet	60	25

705 Linnaeus (Carl von Linne)

1958. 250th Birth Anniv of Linnaeus.

2171	**705**	40k. brown	4·25	3·00

706 Tolstoi

1958. 75th Birth Anniv of A. N. Tolstoi (writer).

2172	**706**	40k. bistre	70	25

707 Soldier, Sailor and Airman

1958. 40th Anniv of Red Army. Multicoloured.

2173	25k. Battle of Narva, 1918	40	15
2174	40k. Type **707**	60	20
2175	40k. Soldier and blast-furnace-man (vert)	60	20
2176	40k. Soldier and sailor (vert)	60	20

2177 60k. Storming the Reichstag, 1945 1·50 60

708 E. Charents

1958. Charents (Armenian poet) Commemoration.
2178 **708** 40k. brown 3·25 2·50

709 Henry W. Longfellow

1958. 150th Birth Anniv of Longfellow.
2179 **709** 40k. black 3·25 2·50

710 Blake

1958. Birth Bicentenary of William Blake (poet).
2180 **710** 40k. black 3·25 2·50

711 Tchaikovsky

1958. Tchaikovsky International Music Competition, Moscow.
2181A **711** 40k. multicoloured 1·30 35
2182A - 40k. multicoloured 1·30 35
2183Aa - 1r. purple and green 3·75 85
DESIGNS—HORIZ: No. 2182A, Scene from "Swan Lake" ballet. VERT: No. 2183Aa, Pianist, violinist and inset portrait of Tchaikovsky.

712 Admiral Rudnev and Cruiser "Varyag"

1958. 45th Death Anniv of Admiral Rudnev.
2184 **712** 40k. multicoloured 1·90 50

713 Gorky (after I. Brodsky)

1958. 90th Death Anniv of Maksim Gorky (writer).
2185 **713** 40k. multicoloured 1·10 25

714 Congress Emblem and Spassky Tower, Kremlin

1958. 13th Young Communists' League Congress, Moscow.
2186 **714** 40k. violet on pink 70 15
2187 **714** 60k. red on flesh 1·10 25

715 Russian Pavilion

1958. Brussels Int Exhibition. Perf or imperf.
2188 **715** 10k. multicoloured 20 10
2189 **715** 40k. multicoloured 70 15

716 J. A. Komensky ("Comenius")

1958. Komensky Commem.
2190 **716** 40k. green 4·00 3·00

717 Lenin

1958. Lenin Commemoration.
2191 **717** 40k. blue 60 10
2192 **717** 60k. red 90 15
2193 **717** 1r. brown 1·60 40

**200 лет Академии
художеств СССР. 1957**

(718)

1958. Bicentenary of Russian Academy of Artists. Optd with T 718.
2194 **557** 40k. multicoloured 6·75 1·80

719 C. Goldoni

1958. 250th Birth Anniv of C. Goldoni (Italian dramatist).
2195 **719** 40k. brown and blue 1·10 25

720 Lenin Prize Medal

1958. Lenin Prize Medal.
2196 **720** 40k. red, yellow & brown 80 25

721 Karl Marx

1958. Karl Marx Commemoration.
2197 **721** 40k. brown 85 15
2198 **721** 60k. blue 1·20 25
2199 **721** 1r. red 2·10 45

722 Federation Emblem

1958. 4th International Women's Federation Congress.
2200 **722** 40k. blue and black 70 15
2201 **722** 60k. blue and black 1·10 25

723 Radio Beacon, Airliner and Freighter

1958. Radio Day.
2202 **723** 40k. green and red 2·40 35

724 Chavchavadze (after G. Gabashvili)

1958. Chavchavadze (Georgian poet) Commem.
2203 **724** 40k. black and blue 80 25

725 Flags of Communist Countries

1958. Socialist Countries' Postal Ministers Conference, Moscow.
2204 **725** 40k. multicoloured (A) 18·00 7·00
2205 **725** 40k. multicoloured (B) 11·50 5·75
Central flag to left of inscription is in red, white and mauve. (A) has red at top and white at foot, (B) is vice versa.

726 Camp Bugler

1958. "Pioneers" Day. Inscr "1958".
2206 **726** 10k. multicoloured 40 15
2207 - 25k. multicoloured 50 20
DESIGN: 25k. Pioneer with model airplane.

727 Negro, European and Chinese Children

1958. International Children's Day. Inscr "1958".
2208 **727** 40k. multicoloured 70 20
2209 - 40k. multicoloured 70 20
DESIGN: No. 2209, Child with toys, and atomic bomb.

728 Fooballers and Globe

1958. World Cup Football Championship, Sweden. Perf or imperf.
2210 **728** 40k. multicoloured 90 20
2211 **728** 60k. multicoloured 1·50 45

729 Rimsky-Korsakov

1958. Rimsky-Korsakov (composer) Commem.
2212 **729** 40k. brown and blue 1·60 35

730 Athlete

1958. 14th World Gymnastic Championships, Moscow. Inscr "XIV". Multicoloured.
2213 40k. Type **730** 70 15
2214 40k. Gymnast 70 15

731 Young Construction Workers

1958. Russian Youth Day.
2215 **731** 40k. orange and blue 60 15
2216 **731** 60k. orange and green 80 20

732 Atomic Bomb, Globe, Sputniks, Atomic Symbol and "Lenin" (atomic ice-breaker)

1958. International Disarmament Conf, Stockholm.
2217 **732** 60k. black, orange & blue 3·50 70

733 Kiev Arsenal Uprising, 1918

1958. 40th Anniv of Ukrainian Communist Party.
2218 **733** 40k. violet and red 1·10 25

734 Silhouette of Moscow State University

1958. 5th Int Architects Union Congress, Moscow.

2219	**734**	40k. blue and red	95	15
2220	-	60k. multicoloured	1·40	25

MS2220a 105×143 mm. Nos. 2219/20. Imperf 14·50 10·50

DESIGN—VERT: 60k. "U.I.A. Moscow 1958" in square panel of bricks and "V" in background.

735 Sadruddin Aini

1958. 80th Birth Anniv of Sadruddin Aini (Tadzhik writer).

2221	**735**	40k. red, black and buff	70	25

736 Third Artificial Satellite

1958. Launching of 3rd Artificial Satellite.

2222a	**736**	40k. red, blue and green	1·60	50

737 Conference Emblem

1958. 1st World T.U. Young Workers' Conf, Prague.

2223	**737**	40k. blue and purple	50	35

738 Tupolev Tu-110 Jetliner

1958. Civil Aviation. Perf or imperf.

2224A	-	20k. black, red and blue	50	10
2225A	-	40k. black, red and green	80	15
2226A	-	40k. black, red and blue	80	15
2227A	-	60k. red, buff and blue	90	20
2228A	**738**	60k. black and red	90	20
2229A	-	1r. black, red and orange	2·00	45
2230A	-	2r. black, red and purple	3·00	60

DESIGNS—Russian aircraft flying across globe: No. 2224A, Ilyushin Il-14M; 2225A, Tupolev Tu-104; 2226A, Tupolev Tu-114 Rossiya; 2229A, Antonov An-10 Ukraina; 2230A, Ilyushin Il-18B; No. 2227A, Global air routes.

739 L. A. Kulik (scientist)

1958. 50th Anniv of Tunguz Meteor.

2231	**739**	40k. multicoloured	2·20	50

740 Crimea Observatory

1958. 10th International Astronomical Union Congress, Moscow.

2232	**740**	40k. turquoise and brown	1·30	20
2233	-	60k. yellow, violet & blue	1·40	30
2234	-	1r. brown and blue	2·40	50

DESIGNS—HORIZ: 60k. Moscow University. VERT: 1r. Telescope of Moscow Observatory.

741 15th-century Scribe

1958. Centenary of 1st Russian Postage Stamp.

2235	**741**	10k. multicoloured	20	10
2236	-	10k. multicoloured	20	10
2237	-	25k. blue, black and green	50	15
2238	-	25k. black and blue	50	15
2239	-	40k. brown, purple & sep	90	35
2240	-	40k. lake and brown	90	35
2241	-	40k. black, orange and red	90	35
2242	-	60k. turquoise, blk & vio	1·50	45
2243	-	60k. black, turquoise and purple	1·50	45
2244	-	1r. multicoloured	2·30	80
2245	-	1r. purple, black and orange	2·30	80

MS2245a Nos. 2235/8 and 2240. Imperf 9·75 6·00

MS2245b Nos. 2239 and 2242/3. Imperf 19·00 8·75

DESIGNS—HORIZ: No. 2236, 16th-century courier; 2237, Ordin-Nashchokin (17th-century postal administrator) (after Kh. Gusikov) and postal sleigh coach; 2238, 18th-century mail coach; 2239, Reproduction of Lenin portrait stamp of 1947; 2240, 19th-century postal troika (three-horse sleigh); 2241, Tupolev Tu-104 jetliner; 2242, Parcel post train; 2243, V. N. Podbelsky (postal administrator, 1918–20) and postal scenes; 2244, Parcel post Tupolev Tu-104; 2245, Globe and modern forms of mail transport.

741a Facade of Exhibition Building

1958. Stamp Cent Philatelic Exhibition, Leningrad.

2246	**741a**	40k. brown & lt brown	70	25

742 Vladimir Gateway

1958. 850th Anniv of Town of Vladimir. Mult.

2247	40k. Type **742**	60	15
2248	60k. Street scene in Vladimir	95	25

743 Chigorin

1958. 50th Death Anniv of Mikhail Ivanovich Chigorin (chess player).

2249	**743**	40k. green and black	1·80	35

745 Red Cross Nurse and Patient

1958. 40th Anniv of Red Cross and Crescent Societies.

2254	**745**	40k. multicoloured	80	25
2255	-	40k. red, yellow and brown	80	25

DESIGN: No. 2255, Convalescent home.

746 Saltykov-Shchedrin (after I. Kramskoi) and Scene from his Works

1958. 69th Death Anniv of Mikhail Saltykov-Shchedrin (writer).

2256	**746**	40k. black and purple	80	25

For similar stamps see Nos. 2316/22 and 2458.

747 V. Kapnist (after A. Osipov)

1958. Birth Bicentenary of V. Kapnist (poet).

2257	**747**	40k. black and blue	1·10	25

748 Yerevan, Armenia

1958. Republican Capitals.

2258	40k. brown (T **748**)	70	45
2259	40k. violet (Baku, Azerbaijan)	70	45
2260	40k. brown (Minsk, Byelorussia)	70	45
2261	40k. blue (Tbilisi, Georgia)	70	45
2262	40k. green (Tallin, Estonia)	70	45
2263	40k. green (Alma-Ata, Kazakhstan)	70	45
2264	40k. blue (Frunze, Kirgizia)	70	45
2265	40k. brown (Riga, Latvia)	70	45
2266	40k. red (Vilnius, Lithuania)	70	45
2267	40k. bistre (Kishinev, Moldavia)	70	45
2268	40k. violet (Moscow, R.S.F.S.R.)	70	45
2269	40k. blue (Stalinabad, Tadzhikistan)	70	45
2270	40k. green (Ashkhabad, Turkmenistan)	70	45
2271	40k. mauve (Kiev, Ukraine)	70	45
2272	40k. black (Tashkent, Uzbekistan)	70	45

See also No. 2940.

749 Open Book, Torch, Lyre and Flowers

1958. Asian-African Writers' Conference, Tashkent.

2273	**749**	40k. orange, black and olive	1·10	20

750 Rudaki

1958. 1100th Birth Anniv of Rudaki (Tadzhik poet and musician).

2274	**750**	40k. multicoloured	70	15

751 Statue of Founder Vakhtang I Gorgasal (E. Amashukeli)

1958. 1500th Anniv of Founding of Tbilisi (Georgian capital).

2275	**751**	40k. multicoloured	1·30	35

752 Chelyabinsk Tractor Plant

1958. 25th Anniv of Industrial Plants.

2276	**752**	40k. green and yellow	60	25
2277	-	40k. blue and light blue	60	25
2278	-	40k. lake and light orange	60	25

DESIGNS: No. 2277, Ural machine construction plant; No. 2278, Zaporozhe foundry plant.

753 Young Revolutionary

1958. 40th Anniv of Young Communists League. Multicoloured.

2279	10k. Type **753**	25	15
2280	20k. Riveters	40	15
2281	25k. Soldier	50	20
2282	40k. Harvester	90	25
2283	60k. Builder	1·30	35
2284	1r. Students	2·40	85

754 Marx and Lenin (bas-relief)

1958. 41st Anniv of October Revolution.

2285	**754**	40k. black, yellow and red	95	25
2286	-	1r. multicoloured	1·40	45

DESIGN—HORIZ: 1r. Lenin (after N. Andreev) with student, peasant and miner.

755 "Human Rights"

1958. 10th Anniv of Declaration of Human Rights.

2287	**755**	60k. blue, black and buff	75	25

756 Yesenin

1958. 30th Death Anniv of Sergei Yesenin (poet).

2288	**756**	40k. multicoloured	60	25

757 Kuan Han-ching

1958. Kuan Han-ching (Chinese playwright) Commemoration.

2289	**757**	40k. black and blue	60	25

758 Ordzhonikidze

1958. 21st Death Anniv of G. K. Ordzhonikidze (statesman).
2290 **758** 40k. multicoloured 75 25

759 John Milton

1958. 350th Birth Anniv of John Milton (poet).
2291 **759** 40k. brown 1·20 25

760 Lenin's Statue, Minsk (M. Manizer)

1958. 40th Anniv of Byelorussian Republic.
2292 **760** 40k. brown, grey and red 80 25

761 Fuzuli

1958. Fuzuli (Azerbaijan poet) Commemoration.
2293 **761** 40k. bistre and turquoise 1·20 25

762 Census Emblem

1958. All Union Census, 1959. Multicoloured.
2294 40k. Type **762** 40 15
2295 40k. Census official with worker's family 40 15

763 Eleonora Duse

1958. Birth Centenary of Eleonora Duse (Italian actress).
2296 **763** 40k. black, grey and green 1·10 25

764 Rule

1958. Death Centenary of K. F. Rule (naturalist).
2297 **764** 40k. black and blue 1·20 35

765 Atomic Ice-breaker "Lenin"

1958. All-Union Industrial Exhibition. Mult.
2298 40k. Type **765** 2·50 1·20
2299 60k. Class TE 3 diesel-electric frieght locomotive 4·75 1·70

766 Moon Rocket and Sputniks

1959. 21st Communist Party Congress, Moscow.
2300 - 40k. multicoloured 60 25
2301 - 60k. multicoloured 80 45
2302 **766** 1r. multicoloured 3·00 1·20
DESIGNS: 40k. Lenin (after N. Andreev), Red Banner and Kremlin view; 60k. Workers beside Lenin hydro-electric plant, Volga River.

767 E. Torricelli

1959. 350th Birth Anniv of Torricelli (physicist).
2303 **767** 40k. black and green 1·10 25

768 Ice Skater

1959. Women's World Ice Skating Championships, Sverdlovsk.
2304 **768** 25k. multicoloured 60 15
2305 **768** 40k. black, blue and grey 90 25

769 Charles Darwin

1959. 150th Birth Anniv of Charles Darwin (naturalist).
2306 **769** 40k. brown and blue 1·20 25

770 N. Gamaleya

1959. Birth Centenary of Gamaleya (microbiologist).
2307 **770** 40k. black and red 1·20 35

771 Sholem Aleichem

1959. Birth Centenary of Aleichem (Jewish writer).
2308 **771** 40k. brown 95 25

Победа баскетбольной команды СССР. Чили 1959 г.
(772)

1959. Russian (Unofficial) Victory in World Basketball Championships, Chile. No. 1851 optd with T 772.
2309 1r. brown and drab 10·50 8·75

1959. Birth Bicent of Robert Burns. Optd 1759 1959.
2310 **627** 40k. brown and blue 23·00 19·00

774 Selma Lagerlof

1959. Birth Centenary of Selma Lagerlof (Swedish writer).
2311 **774** 40k. black, brown and cream 1·10 25

775 P. Cvirka

1959. 50th Birth Anniv of Cvirka (Lithuanian poet).
2312 **775** 40k. black and red on yellow 70 25

776 F. Joliot-Curie (scientist)

1959. Joliot-Curie Commemoration.
2313 **776** 40k. black and turquoise 1·50 45

777 Popov and Polar Rescue by Ice-breaker "Ermak"

1959. Birth Centenary of A. S. Popov (radio pioneer).
2314 **777** 40k. brown, black & blue 1·20 45
2315 - 60k. multicoloured 1·70 65
DESIGN: 60k. Popov and radio tower.

1959. Writers as T 746. Inscr "1959".
2316 40k. grey, black and red 1·70 95
2317 40k. brown, sepia and yellow 1·70 95
2318 40k. brown and violet 1·70 95
2319 40k. multicoloured 1·70 95
2320 40k. black, olive and yellow 1·70 95
2321 40k. multicoloured 1·70 95
2322 40k. slate and violet 1·70 95
PORTRAITS (with scene from works): No. 2316, Anton Chekhov; 2317, Ivan Krylov (after K. Bryullov); 2318, Aleksandr Ostrovsky; 2319, Aleksandr Griboedov (after I. Kramskoi); 2320, Nikolai Gogol (after F. Moller); 2321, Sergei Aksakov (after I. Kramskoi); 2322, Aleksei Koltsov (after K. Gorbunov).

778 Saadi (Persian poet)

1959. Saadi Commemoration.
2323 **778** 40k. black and blue 70 20

779 Orbeliani (Georgian writer)

1959. Orbeliani Commemoration.
2324 **779** 40k. black and red 70 15

780 "Hero riding Dolphin"

1959. Birth Tercentenary of Ogata Korin (Japanese artist).
2325 **780** 40k. multicoloured 2·75 2·20

781 "Rossiya" on Odessa-Batum Service

1959. Russian Liners. Multicoloured.
2326 10k. "Sovetsky Soyuz" on Vladi-vostok–Kamchatka service 40 20
2327 20k. "Feliks Dzerzhinsky" on Odessa–Latakia service 60 20
2328 40k. Type **781** 95 25
2329 40k. "Kooperatsiya" on Mur-mansk–Tyksi service 95 25
2330 60k. "Mikhail Kalinin" leaving Leningrad 1·20 35
2331 1r. "Baltika" on Leningrad–London service 1·70 60

782 Trajectory of Moon Rocket

1959. Launching of Moon Rocket. Inscr "2-1-1959".
2332 **782** 40k. brown and pink 1·20 45
2333 - 40k. blue and light blue 1·20 45
DESIGN: No. 2333, Preliminary route of moon rocket after launching.

783 Lenin

1959. 89th Birth Anniv of Lenin.
2334 **783** 40k. brown 1·20 45

784 M. Cachin

1959. 90th Birth Anniv of Marcel Cachin (French communist leader).
2335 **784** 60k. brown 1·10 35

785 Youths with Banner

1959. 10th Anniv of World Peace Movement.
2336 **785** 40k. multicoloured 80 35

786 A. von Humboldt

1959. Death Centenary of Alexander von Humboldt (German naturalist).
2337 **786** 40k. brown and violet 1·20 35

787 Haydn

1959. 150th Death Anniv of Haydn (Austrian composer).
2338 **787** 40k. brown and blue 1·20 25

788 Mountain Climbing

1959. Tourist Publicity. Multicoloured.
2339 40k. Type **788** 95 35
2340 40k. Map reading 95 35
2341 40k. Cross country skiing 95 35
2342 40k. Canoeing (horiz) 95 35

789 Exhibition Emblem and New York Coliseum

1959. Russian Scientific, Technological and Cultural Exhibition, New York.
2343 **789** 20k. multicoloured 50 20
2344 **789** 40k. multicoloured 80 25
MS2344a 61×76 mm. As No. 2344 but larger. Imperf 6·75 4·75

790 Statue of I. Repin (painter), Moscow (M. Manizer)

1959. Cultural Celebrities. Inscr "1959". Statues in black.
2345 **790** 10k. ochre 20 10
2346 - 10k. red 20 10
2347 - 20k. lilac 40 10
2348 - 25k. turquoise 70 20
2349 - 60k. green 95 25
2350 - 1r. blue 1·50 50
STATUES: 10k. (No. 2346), Lenin, Ulanovsk (M. Manizer); 80k. V. Mayakosky (poet), Moscow (A. Kibalnikov); 25k Aleksandr Pushkin (writer), Leningrad, (M. Anikushin); 60k. Maksim Gorky (writer), Moscow (Vera Mukhina); 1r. Tchaikovsky (composer), Moscow (Vera Mukhina).

791 Russian Sturgeon

1959. Fisheries Protection.
2350a 20k. black and blue 45 10
2350b 25k. brown and lilac 55 15
2351 **791** 40k. black and turquoise 75 20
2351a - 40k. purple and mauve 95 25
2352 - 60k. black and blue 1·50 45
DESIGNS: 20k. Zander; 25k. Northern fur seals; 40k. (No. 2351a), Common whitefish; 60k. Chum salmon and map.

792 Louis Braille

1959. 150th Birth Anniv of Braille (inventor of Braille).
2353 **792** 60k. brown, yell & turq 80 25

793 Musa Djalil (Tatar poet)

1959. Djalil Commemoration.
2354 **793** 40k. black and violet 80 25

794 Vaulting

1959. 2nd Russian Spartakiad. Inscr "1959".
2355 **794** 15k. grey and purple 30 10
2356 - 25k. grey, brown & green 60 10
2357 - 30k. olive and red 70 15
2358 - 60k. grey, blue and yellow 1·10 35
DESIGNS—HORIZ: 25k. Running; 60k. Water polo. VERT: 30k. Athletes supporting Spartakiad emblem.

795

1959. 2nd International T.U. Conference, Leipzig.
2359 **795** 40k. red, blue and yellow 80 25

796 Steel Worker

1959. Seven Year Plan.
2360 - 10k. red, blue and violet 20 10
2361 - 10k. lt red, dp red & yell 20 10
2362 - 15k. red, yellow & brn 25 10
2363 - 15k. brown, green & bis 25 10
2364 - 20k. red, yellow & green 30 10
2365 - 20k. multicoloured 30 10
2366 - 30k. red, flesh & purple 50 15
2366a - 30k. multicoloured 50 15
2367 **796** 40k. orange, yellow & bl 60 20
2368 - 40k. red, pink and blue 60 20
2369 - 60k. red, blue and yellow 1·00 35
2370 - 60k. red, buff and blue 1·00 35
DESIGNS: 2360, Chemist; 2361, Spassky Tower, hammer and sickle; 2362, Builder's labourer; 2363, Farm girl; 2364, Machine minder; No. 2365, Tractor driver; 2366, Oil technician; 2366a, Cloth production; . 2368, Coal miner; 2369, Iron moulder; 2370, Power station.

797 Glaciologist

1959. International Geophysical Year (2nd issue).
2371 **797** 10k. turquoise 60 15
2372 - 25k. red and blue 1·30 25
2373 - 40k. red and blue 1·50 30
2373a - 1r. blue and yellow 2·75 80
DESIGNS: 25k. Oceanographic survey ship "Vityaz"; 40k. Antarctic map, camp and emperor penguin; 1r. Observatory and rocket.

798 Novgorod

1959. 11th Centenary of Novgorod.
2374 **798** 40k. red, brown and blue 70 25

799 Schoolboys in Workshop

1959. Industrial Training Scheme for School-leavers. Inscr "1959".
2375 **799** 40k. violet 50 15
2376 - 1r. blue 1·10 35
DESIGN: 1r. Children at night-school.

800 Exhibition Emblem

1959. All Union Exhibition.
2377 **800** 40k. multicoloured 60 35

801 Russian and Chinese Students

1959. 10th Anniv of Chinese Peoples' Republic.
2378 **801** 20k. multicoloured 30 15
2379 - 40k. multicoloured 70 25
DESIGN: 40k. Russian miner and Chinese foundryman.

802 Postwoman

1959. International Correspondence Week.
2380 **802** 40k. multicoloured 60 15
2381 **802** 60k. multicoloured 80 25

803 Mahtumkuli (after A. Khadzhiev)

1959. 225th Birth Anniv of Mahtumkuli (Turkestan writer).
2382 **803** 40k. brown 70 25

804 Arms and Workers of the German Democratic Republic

1959. 10th Anniv of German Democratic Republic.
2383 **804** 40k. multicoloured 50 15
2384 - 60k. purple and cream 70 25
DESIGN—VERT: 60k. Town Hall, East Berlin.

805 Lunik 3's Trajectory around the Moon

1959. Launching of "Lunik 3" Rocket.
2385 **805** 40k. violet 1·90 35

806 Republican Arms and Emblem

1959. 30th Anniv of Tadzhikistan Republic.
2386 **806** 40k. multicoloured 1·30 25

807 Red Square, Moscow

1959. 42nd Anniv of October Revolution.
2387 **807** 40k. red 70 25

808 Capitol, Washington and Kremlin, Moscow

1959. Visit of Russian Prime Minister to U.S.A.
2388 **808** 60k. blue and yellow 1·10 35

809 Mil Mi-1 Helicopter

1959. Military Sports.

2389	**809**	10k. red and violet	30	10
2390	-	25k. brown and blue	55	10
2391	-	40k. blue and brown	60	15
2392	-	60k. bistre and blue	90	25

DESIGNS: 25k. Skin diver; 40k. Racing motor cyclist; 60k. Parachutist.

810 Track of Moon Rocket

1959. Landing of Russian Rocket on Moon. Inscr "14. IX.1959". Multicoloured.

2393	40k. Type **810**	1·10	25
2394	40k. Diagram of flight trajectory	1·10	25

811 Liberty Monument (Zs. Kisfaludy-Strobl), Budapest

1959. 15th Anniv of Hungarian Republic. Mult.

2395	20k. Sandor Petofi (Hungarian poet) (horiz)	35	15
2396	40k. Type **811**	70	20

812 Manolis Glezos (Greek Communist)

1959. Glezos Commemoration.

2397	**812**	40k. brown and blue	14·50	9·50

813 A. Voskresensky (chemist)

1959. Voskresensky Commemoration.

2398	**813**	40k. brown and blue	80	25

814 River Chusovaya

1959. Tourist Publicity. Inscr "1959".

2399	**814**	10k. violet	20	10
2400	-	10k. mauve	20	10
2401	-	25k. blue	30	15
2402	-	25k. red	30	15
2403	-	25k. olive	30	15
2404	-	40k. red	55	25
2405	-	60k. turquoise	70	25
2406	-	1r. green	1·40	70
2407	-	1r. orange	1·40	70

DESIGNS: No. 2400, Riza Lake, Caucasus; 2401, River Lena; 2402, Iskanderkuly Lake; 2403, Coastal region; 2404, Lake Baikal; . 2405, Beluha Mountains, Altay; 2406, Khibinsky Mountains; 2407, Gursuff region, Crimea.

815 "The Trumpeters of the First Horse Army" (M. Grekov)

1959. 40th Anniv of Russian Cavalry.

2408	**815**	40k. multicoloured	1·20	85

816 A. P. Chekhov and Moscow Residence

1960. Birth Centenary of Chekhov (writer).

2409	**816**	20k. red, brown & vio	40	15
2410	-	40k. brown, blue & sepia	80	25

DESIGN: 40k. Chekhov and Yalta residence.

817 M. V. Frunze

1960. 75th Birth Anniv of M. V. Frunze (military leader).

2411	**817**	40k. brown	70	35

818 G. N. Gabrichevsky

1960. Birth Centenary of G. N. Gabrichevsky (microbiologist).

2412	**818**	40k. brown and violet	1·10	35

819 Vera Komissarzhevskaya

1960. 50th Death Anniv of V. F. Komissarzhevskaya (actress).

2413	**819**	40k. brown	70	25

820 Free-skating

1960. Winter Olympic Games.

2414	-	10k. blue and orange	50	10
2415	-	25k. multicoloured	70	10
2416	-	40k. orange, blue & pur	90	15
2417	**820**	60k. violet, brown & grn	1·50	25
2418	-	1r. blue, red and green	2·30	50

DESIGNS: 10k. Ice hockey; 25k. Ice skating; 40k. Skiing; 1r. Ski jumping.

821 Timur Frunze (fighter pilot) and Air Battle

1960. War Heroes. Multicoloured.

2419	40k. Type **821**	4·00	2·50
2420	1r. Gen. Chernyakhovksy and battle scene	1·50	80

822 Mil Mi-4 Helicopter over Kremlin

1960. Air.

2421	**822**	60k. blue	1·30	25

823 Women of Various Races

1960. 50th Anniv of International Women's Day.

2422	**823**	40k. multicoloured	95	25

824 "Swords into Ploughshares" (Ye. Buchetich)

1960. Presentation of Statue by Russia to U.N.

2423	**824**	40k. yellow, bistre and blue	70	25
MS2423a		78×115 mm. No. 2423	2·40	1·00

15 лет
освобождения
Венгрии

(825)

1960. 15th Anniv of Liberation of Hungary. Optd with T 825.

2424	**811**	40k. multicoloured	6·25	4·75

826 Lenin when a Child

1960. 90th Birth Anniv of Lenin. Portraits of Lenin. Multicoloured.

2425	**826**	10k. multicoloured	20	10
2426	-	20k. multicoloured	40	10
2427	-	30k. multicoloured	50	15
2428	-	40k. multicoloured	70	25
2429	-	60k. multicoloured	1·40	35
2430	-	1r. brown, blue and red	1·80	50

DESIGNS: Lenin: 20k. holding child (after N. Zkukov); 30k. and revolutionary scenes; 40k. with party banners; 60k. and industrial scenes; 1r. with globe and rejoicing people (after A. Seral).

827 "Lunik 3" photographing Moon

1960. Flight of "Lunik 3". Inscr "7.X.1959".

2431	**827**	40k. yellow and blue	1·30	45
2432	-	60k. yellow, blue & indigo	1·50	45

DESIGN: 60k. Lunar map.

828 Government House, Baku

1960. 40th Anniv of Azerbaijan Republic.

2433	**828**	40k. brown, bistre & yell	70	25

829 "Fraternization" (K. Pokorny)

1960. 15th Anniv of Czechoslovak Republic.

2434	**829**	40k. black and blue	60	15
2435	-	60k. brown and yellow	95	25

DESIGN: 60k. Charles Bridge, Prague.

830 Furnaceman

1960. Completion of First Year of Seven Year Plan.

2436	**830**	40k. brown and red	60	25

831 Popov Museum, Leningrad

1960. Radio Day.

2437	**831**	40k. multicoloured	1·10	35

832 Robert Schumann

1960. 150th Birth Anniv of Schumann (composer).

2438	**832**	40k. black and blue	1·10	35

833 Sverdlov

1960. 75th Birth Anniv of Ya. M. Sverdlov (statesman).

2439	**833**	40k. sepia and brown	1·70	50

834 Magnifier and Stamp

1960. Philatelists' Day.

2440	**834**	60k. multicoloured	1·30	50

835 Petrozavodsk (Karelian Republic)

1960. Capitals of Autonomous Republic (1st issue).

2441	**835**	40k. turquoise	1·10	70
2442	-	40k. blue	1·10	70
2443	-	40k. green	1·10	70
2444	-	40k. purple	1·10	70
2445	-	40k. red	1·10	70
2446	-	40k. blue	95	35
2447	-	40k. brown	95	35
2448	-	40k. brown	95	35
2449	-	40k. red	95	35
2450	-	40k. brown	95	35

CAPITALS: Nos. 2442, Batumi (Adzharian); 2443, Izhevsk (Udmurt); 2444, Grozny (Chechen-Ingush); 2445, Cheboksary (Chuvash); 2446, Yakutsk (Yakut); 2447, Ordzhonikidze (North Ossetian); 2448, Nukus (Kara-Kalpak); 2449, Makhachkala (Daghestan); 2450, Yoshkar-Ola (Mari).

See also Nos. 2586/92 and 2703/5.

836 Children of Different Races

1960. International Children's Day. Multicoloured.

2451	10k. Type **836**	20	10
2452	20k. Children on farm (vert)	40	15
2453	25k. Children with snowman	50	15
2454	40k. Children in zoo gardens	90	25

1960. 40th Anniv of Karelian Autonomous Republic. Optd 40 лет КАССР 8.VI.1960.

2455	**835**	40k. turquoise	3·75	2·50

838 Rocket

1960. Launching of Cosmic Rocket "Spacecraft 1" (first "Vostok" type spacecraft).

2456	**838**	40k. red and blue	1·90	60

839 I.F.A.C. Emblem

1960. 1st International Automation Control Federation Congress, Moscow.

2457	**839**	60k. brown and yellow	1·90	45

1960. Birth Centenary (1959) of Kosta Khetagurov (poet). As T 746. Inscr "1960".

2458	40k. brown and blue	95	25

DESIGN: 40k. Portrait of Khetagurov and scene from his works.

840 Cement Works, Belgorod

1960. 1st Plant Construction of Seven Year Plan.

2459	**840**	25k. black and blue	30	10
2460	-	40k. black and red	50	15

DESIGN. 40k. Metal works, Novokrivorog.

841 Capstans and Cogwheel

1960. Industrial Mass-Production Plant.

2461	**841**	40k. turquoise	80	15
2462	-	40k. purple (Factory plant)	80	15

842 Vilnius (Lithuania)

1960. 20th Anniv of Soviet Baltic Republics. Multicoloured.

2463	40k. Type **842**	70	15
2464	40k. Riga (Latvia)	70	15
2465	40k. Tallin (Estonia)	70	15

843 Running

1960. Olympic Games. Inscr "1960". Multicoloured.

2466	5k. Type **843**	20	10
2467	10k. Wrestling	25	10
2468	15k. Basketball	40	10
2469	20k. Weightlifting	40	10
2470	25k. Boxing	40	10
2471	40k. High diving	60	15
2472	40k. Fencing	60	15
2473	40k. Gymnastics	60	15
2474	60k. Canoeing	90	25
2475	1r. Horse jumping	2·20	60

1960. 20th Anniv of Moldavian Republic. As T 842.

2476	40k. multicoloured	70	15

DESIGN: 40k. Kishinev (capital).

Международная ярмарка в Риччоне

(844)

1960. International Exhibition, Riccione. No. 2471 optd with T 844.

2477	40k. multicoloured	19·00	13·00

845 "Agriculture and Industry"

1960. 15th Anniv of Vietnam Democratic Republic.

2478	40k. Type **845**	60	15
2479	60k. Book Museum, Hanoi (vert)	90	15

846 G. H. Minkh

1960. 125th Birth Anniv of G. H. Minkh (epidemiologist).

2480	**846**	60k. brown and bistre	80	25

847 "March" (after I. Levitan)

1960. Birth Centenary of I. Levitan (painter).

2481	**847**	40k. black and olive	1·10	25

848 "Forest" (after Shishkin)

1960. 5th World Forestry Congress, Seattle.

2482	**848**	1r. brown	2·40	70

849 Addressing Letter

1960. International Correspondence Week.

2483	**849**	40k. multicoloured	50	15
2484	**849**	60k. multicoloured	80	35

850 Kremlin, Dogs "Belka" and "Strelka" and Rocket Trajectory

1960. 2nd Cosmic Rocket Flight.

2485	**850**	40k. purple and yellow	1·20	25
2486	**850**	1r. blue and orange	1·90	35

851 Globes

1960. 15th Anniv of W.F.T.U.

2487	**851**	60k. blue, drab and lilac	90	25

852 People of Kazakhstan

1960. 40th Anniv of Kazakh Soviet Republic.

2488	**852**	40k. multicoloured	90	25

853 "Karl Marx"

1960. River Boats. Multicoloured.

2489	25k. Type **853**	50	10
2490	40k. "Lenin"	80	15
2491	60k. "Raketa" (hydrofoil)	1·50	35

854 A. N. Voronikhin and Leningrad Cathedral

1960. Birth Bicentenary of A. N. Voronikhin (architect).

2492	**854**	40k. black and grey	80	25

855 Motor Coach

1960. Russian Motor Industry.

2493	-	25k. black and blue	50	10
2494	-	40k. blue and olive	60	15
2495	-	60k. red and turquoise	1·20	20
2496	**855**	1r. multicoloured	1·90	45

DESIGNS: 25k. Lorry; 40k. "Volga" car; 60k. "Moskvich" car.

856 J. S. Gogebashvily

1960. 120th Birth Anniv of J. S. Gogebashvily (Georgian teacher).

2497	**856**	40k. black and lake	80	25

857 Industrial Plant and Power Plant

1960. 43rd Anniv of October Revolution.

2498	**857**	40k. multicoloured	80	25

858 Federation Emblem

1960. 15th Anniv of International Federation of Democratic Women.

2499	**858**	60k. red and grey	95	25

859 Youth of Three Races

1960. 15th Anniv of World Democratic Youth Federation.

2500	**859**	60k. multicoloured	95	25

40 лет Удмуртской АССР 4/XI 1960.

(860)

1960. 40th Anniv of Udmurt Autonomous Republic. No. 2443 optd with T 860.

2501	40k. green	3·00	1·70

861 Tolstoi and his Moscow Residence

1960. 50th Death Anniv of Leo Tolstoi (writer).

2502	**861**	20k. multicoloured	40	15
2503	-	40k. brown, sepia & blue	70	15
2504	-	60k. multicoloured	1·30	35

DESIGNS—HORIZ: 40k. Tolstoi and his country estate. VERT: 60k. Full face portrait.

862 Government House, Yerevan

1960. 40th Anniv of Armenian Republic.

2505	**862**	40k. multicoloured	70	25

863 Students and University

1960. Opening of Friendship University, Moscow.

2506	**863**	40k. purple	70	25

864 Tulip

1960. Russian Flowers. Multicoloured.

2507	20k. Type **864**	30	10
2508	20k. Autumn crocus	30	10
2509	25k. Marsh marigold	40	10
2510	40k. Tulip	50	15
2511	40k. Panax	50	15
2512	60k. Hypericum	95	25
2513	60k. Iris	95	25
2514	1r. Wild rose	1·70	45

865 Engels

1960. 140th Birth Anniv of Engels.

2515	**865**	60k. grey	1·50	35

866 Mark Twain

1960. 125th Birth Anniv of Mark Twain.

2516	**866**	40k. bistre and orange	3·00	2·00

867 N. Pirogov

1960. 150th Birth Anniv of N. Pirogov (surgeon).

2517	**867**	40k. brown and green	70	25

868 Chopin (after Eugene Delacroix)

1960. 150th Birth Anniv of Chopin.

2518	**868**	40k. bistre and buff	1·70	25

869 North Korean Flag and Emblem

1960. 15th Anniv of Korean Liberation.

2519	**869**	40k. multicoloured	1·10	25

870 Lithuanian Costumes

1960. Provincial Costumes (1st issue). Inscr "1960". Multicoloured.

2520	10k. Type **870**	40	15
2521	60k. Uzbek costumes	1·50	45

See also Nos. 2537/45, 2796 and 2835/8.

871 A. Tseretely

1960. 120th Birth Anniv of A. Tseretely (Georgian poet).

2522	**871**	40k. purple and lilac	1·30	25

872 Worker

1961. Inscr "1961".

2523	**872**	1k. bistre	30	10
2524	-	2k. green	30	10
2525	-	3k. violet	1·90	15
2526	-	4k. red	75	15
2526a	-	4k. brown	9·75	7·00
2527	-	6k. red	5·75	65
2528	-	6k. claret	1·50	15
2529	-	10k. orange	3·00	15
2530	-	16k. blue	5·00	95
2533a	-	12k. purple	5·25	3·50

DESIGNS: 2k. Combine harvester; 3k. Cosmic rocket; 4k. Soviet Arms and Flag; 6k. Spassky Tower and Kremlin; 10k. "Worker and Collective Farmer" (sculpture, Vera Mukhina); 12k. Monument to F. Minin and D. Pozharsky and Spassky Tower; 16k. Airliner over power station.

1961. Russian Wild Life. As T 653 but inscr "1961". Centres in natural colours. Frame colours given.

2534	1k. sepia (Brown bear)	50	25
2535	6k. black (Eurasian beaver)	1·20	80
2536	10k. black (Roe deer)	1·50	95

The 1k. is vert and the rest horiz.

1961. Provincial Costumes (2nd issue). As T 870 but inscr "1961".

2537	2k. red, brown and stone	30	10
2538	2k. multicoloured	30	10
2539	3k. multicoloured	50	15
2540	3k. multicoloured	50	15
2541	3k. multicoloured	50	15
2542	4k. multicoloured	60	20
2543	6k. multicoloured	70	25
2544	10k. multicoloured	1·50	35
2545	12k. multicoloured	2·20	45

COSTUMES: No. 2337, Moldavia; 2538, Georgia; 2539, Ukraine; 2540, Byelorussia; 2541, Kazakhs; 2542, Koryaks; 2543, Russia; 2544, Armenia; 2545, Estonia.

873 "Ruslan and Lyudmila" (Pushkin)

1961. Scenes from Russian Fairy Tales. Mult.

2546	1k. "Geese Swans"	50	10
2547	3k. "The Fox, the Hare and the Cock"	60	15
2548	4k. "The Little Humpbacked Horse"	80	15
2549	6k. "The Muzhik and the Bear"	1·30	25
2550	10k. Type **873**	1·50	45

874 Lenin, Map and Power Station

1961. 40th Anniv of State Electricity Plan.

2551	**874**	4k. brown, yellow & blue	70	25
2552	**874**	10k. black, purple and salmon	1·30	35

875 Tractor

1961. Soviet Agricultural Achievements. Inscr "1961".

2553	-	3k. mauve and blue	50	15
2554	**875**	4k. black and green	70	15
2555	-	6k. brown and blue	80	25
2556	-	10k. purple and olive	1·20	35

DESIGNS: 3k. Dairy herd; 6k. Agricultural machinery; 10k. Fruit picking.

876 Dobrolyubov (after P. Borel)

1961. 125th Birth Anniv of N. A. Dobrolyubov (writer).

2557	**876**	4k. buff, black and blue	65	25

877 N. D. Zelinsky

1961. Birth Centenary of N. D. Zelinsky (chemist).

2558	**877**	4k. purple and mauve	65	25

878 Georgian Republic Flag

1961. 40th Anniv of Georgian Republic.

2559	**878**	4k. multicoloured	40	15

879 Sgt. Miroshnichenko and Battle

1961. War Hero.

2560	**879**	4k. blue and purple	70	25

See also Nos. 2664/5.

880 Self-portrait and Birthplace

1961. Death Centenary of T. G. Shevchenko (Ukrainian poet and painter).

2561	**880**	3k. brown and violet	40	15
2562	-	6k. purple and green	70	25

DESIGN: 6k. Shevchenko in old age (after I. Kramskoi), pen, book and candle.

See also Nos. 2956/62.

881 A. Rublev

1961. 600th Birth Anniv of Rublev (painter).

2563	**881**	4k. multicoloured	70	25

882 Statue of Shevchenko (poet), Kharkov (M. Manizer)

1961. Cultural Celebrities.

2564	-	2k. brown and blue	30	15
2565	**882**	4k. brown and black	35	20
2566	-	4k. brown and purple	40	20

DESIGNS: 2k. Shchors Monument, Kiev (M. Lysenko); 4k. (No. 2566), Kotovsky Monument, Kishinev (L. Dubinovsky).

883 N. V. Sklifosovsky

1961. 125th Birth Anniv of N. Y. Sklifosovsky (surgeon).

2567	**883**	4k. black and blue	50	15

884 Robert Koch

1961. 50th Death Anniv of Robert Koch (German microbiologist).

2568	**884**	6k. brown	70	25

885 Zither-player and Folk Dancers

1961. 50th Anniv of Russian National Choir.

2569	**885**	4k. multicoloured	45	15

886 "Popular Science"

1961. Cent of "Vokrug Sveta" (science magazine).

2570	**886**	6k. brown, blue and deep blue	1·20	80

887 Venus Rocket

1961. Launching of Venus Rocket.

2571	**887**	6k. orange and blue	1·50	25

2572	-	10k. blue and yellow	2·00	45

DESIGN: 10k. Capsule and flight route.

4 коп. имени Патриса Лумумбы 1961 г. 

(888)

1961. Patrice Lumumba (Congolese politician) Commemoration (1st issue). Surch with T 888.

2573	863	4k. on 40k. purple	1·40	1·00

See also No. 2593.

889 African breaking Chains

1961. Africa Freedom Day. Inscr "1961".

2574	889	4k. multicoloured	30	15
2575	-	6k. purple, orange and blue	50	25

DESIGN: 6k. Hands clasping Torch of Freedom, and map.

891 Yuri Gagarin

1961. World's First Manned Space Flight. Inscr "12-IV-1961". Perf or imperf.

2576A	891	3k. blue	60	15
2577A	-	6k. blue, violet and red	80	35
2578A	-	10k. red, green & brown	1·30	50

DESIGNS—37×26 mm: 6k. Rocket and Spassky Tower; 10k. Rocket, Gagarin and Kremlin.

892 Lenin

1961. 91st Birth Anniv of Lenin.

2579	892	4k. blk, salmon and red	40	15

893 Rabindranath Tagore

1961. Birth Centenary of Tagore (Indian writer).

2580	893	6k. black, bistre and red	60	25

894 Garibaldi

1961. International Labour Exhibition, Turin.

2581	-	4k. salmon and red	50	10
2582	894	6k. salmon and lilac	60	15

DESIGN: 4k. "To the Stars" (statue, G. Postnikov).

895 Lenin

1961

2583	895	20k. green and brown	1·50	1·10
2584	-	30k. blue and brown	2·40	1·70
2585	-	50k. red and brown	4·75	3·50

PORTRAITS (Lenin): 30k. In cap; 50k. Profile.

1961. Capitals of Autonomous Republics (2nd issue). As T 835.

2586	4k. deep violet	50	25
2587	4k. blue	50	25
2588	4k. orange	50	25
2589	4k. black	50	25
2590	4k. lake	50	25
2591	4k. green	50	25
2592	4k. deep purple	50	25

CAPITALS: No. 2586, Nalchik (Kabardino-Balkar); 2587, Ulan-Ude (Buryat); 2588, Sukhumi (Abkhazia); 2589, Syktyvkar (Komi); 2590, Nakhichevan (Nakhichevan); 2591, Rodina Cinema, Elista (Kalmyk); 2592, Ufa (Bashkir).

896 Patrice Lumumba

1961. Lumumba Commemoration (2nd issue).

2593	896	2k. multicoloured	40	15

897 Kindergarten

1961. International Children's Day.

2594	897	2k. blue and orange	25	10
2595	-	3k. violet and ochre	35	15
2596	-	4k. drab and red	50	20

DESIGNS—HORIZ: 3k. Children in Pioneer camp. VERT: 4k. Children with toys and pets.

898 Chernushka and Rocket

1961. 4th and 5th "Spacecraft" Flights.

2597		2k. black, blue and violet	40	15
2598	898	4k. turquoise and blue	70	25

DESIGN—HORIZ: 2k. Dog "Zvezdochka", rocket and controller (inscr "25.III.1961").

899 Belinsky (after I. Astafev)

1961. 150th Birth Anniv of Vissarion Grigorievich Belinsky (literary critic and journalist).

2599	899	4k. black and red	50	15

900

1961. 40th Anniv of Soviet Hydro-meteorological Service.

2600	900	6k. multicoloured	95	35

901 D. M. Karbyshev

1961. Lieut-Gen. Karbyshev (war hero).

2601	901	4k. black, red and yellow	40	15

902 Glider

1961. Soviet Spartakiad.

2602	902	4k. red and grey	40	15
2603	-	6k. red and grey	60	25
2604	-	10k. red and grey	95	45

DESIGNS: 6k. Inflatable motor boat; 10k. Motor cyclists.

903 Sukhe Bator Monument and Govt. Buildings, Ulan Bator

1961. 40th Anniv of Revolution in Mongolia.

2605	903	4k. multicoloured	70	25

904 S. I. Vavilov

1961. 70th Birthday of Vavilov (scientist).

2606	904	4k. brown, bistre & green	40	15

905 V. Pshavela

1961. Birth Cent of Pshavela (Georgian poet).

2607	905	4k. brown and cream	50	25

906 "Youth Activities"

1961. World Youth Forum.

2608	-	2k. brown and orange	40	15
2609	-	4k. green and lilac	50	25
2610	906	6k. blue and ochre	70	25

DESIGNS—HORIZ: 2k. Youths pushing tank into river. VERT: 4k. "Youths and progress".

907

1961. 5th Int Biochemical Congress, Moscow.

2611	907	6k. multicoloured	70	25

908

1961. Centenary of "Kalevipoeg" (Estonian Saga).

2612	908	4k. yellow, turq & blk	40	15

909 Javelin Thrower

1961. 7th Soviet Trade Union Sports.

2613	909	6k. red	60	25

910 A.D. Zakharov (after S. Shchukin)

1961. Birth Bicentenary of Zakharov (architect).

2614	910	buff, brown and blue	70	25

911 Counter-attack (after P. Krivonogov)

1961. War of 1941–45 (1st issue). Inscr "1961".

2615	911	4k. multicoloured	60	25
2616	-	4k. multicoloured	60	25
2617	-	4k. indigo and brown	60	25

DESIGNS: No. 2616, Sailor with bayonet; No. 2617, Soldier with tommy gun.

See also Nos. 2717 and 2851/5.

912 Union Emblem

1961. 15th Anniv of International Union of Students.

2617a	912	6k. violet and red	50	15

913 Stamps commemorating Industry

1961. 40th Anniv of First Soviet Stamp. Centres multicoloured.

2618	913	2k. ochre and brown	40	15
2619	-	4k. blue and indigo	50	25
2620	-	6k. green and olive	95	35
2621	-	10k. buff and brown	1·40	60

DESIGNS (stamps commemorating): 4k. Electrification; 8k. Peace; 10k. Atomic energy.

914 Titov and "Vostok 2"

1961. 2nd Manned Space Flight. Perf or imperf.

2622A		4k. blue and purple	80	25
2623A	914	6k. orange, green & brn	1·10	35

DESIGN: 4k. Space pilot and globe.

915 Angara River Bridge

1961. Tercentenary of Irkutsk, Siberia.

2624	915	4k. black, lilac and bistre	60	20

916 Letters and Mail Transport

1961. International Correspondence Week.

2625	916	4k. black and mauve	80	25

917 Workers and Banners

1961. 22nd Communist Party Congress (1st issue).

2626	917	2k. brown, yellow and red	20	15
2627	-	3k. blue and orange	1·10	25
2628	-	4k. red, buff and purple	40	25
2629	-	4k. orange, black & mve	40	25
2630	-	4k. sepia, brown and red	40	25

DESIGNS: No. 2627, Moscow University and obelisk; 2628, Combine harvester; 2629, Workmen and machinery; 2630, Worker and slogan.

See also No. 2636.

918 Soviet Monument, Berlin

1961. 10th Anniv of International Federation of Resistance Fighters.

2631	918	4k. grey and red	40	15

919 Adult Education

1961. Communist Labour Teams.

2632	-	2k. purple & red on buff	20	10
2633	919	3k. brown & red on buff	30	15
2634	-	4k. blue and red on cream	40	25

DESIGNS: 2k. Worker at machine; 4k. Workers around piano.

920 Rocket and Globes

1961. Cosmic Flights. Aluminium-surfaced paper.

2635	920	1r. red and black on silver	34·00	31·00

XXII съезд КПСС

(921)

1961. 22nd Communist Party Congress (2nd issue). Optd with T 921.

2636	1r. red and black on silver	34·00	35·00

922 Imanov (after A. Kasteev)

1961. 42nd Death Anniv of Amangeldy Imanov (Kazakh Leader).

2637	922	4k. sepia, brown & green	40	15

923 Liszt, Piano and Music

1961. 150th Birth Anniv of Liszt.

2638	923	4k. brown, purple & yell	90	25

924 Flags, Rocket and Skyline

1961. 44th Anniv of October Revolution.

2639	924	4k. red, purple and yellow	75	15

925 Congress Emblem

1961. 5th W.F.T.U. Congress, Moscow. Inscr "MOCKBA 1961".

2640	925	2k. red and bistre	25	10
2641	-	2k. violet and grey	25	10
2642	-	4k. brown, purple & blue	50	15
2643	-	4k. red, blue and violet	50	15
2644	925	6k. red, bistre and green	70	25
2645	-	6k. blue, purple and bistre	70	25

DESIGNS—HORIZ: Nos. 2641, 2645, Negro breaking chains. VERT: No. 2642, Hand holding hammer; 2643, Hands holding globe.

926 Statue of Lomonosov (N. Tomsky) and Lomonosov University

1961. 250th Birth Anniv of Mikhail Lomonosov (scientist).

2646	926	4k. brown, green and blue	50	15
2647	-	6k. blue, buff and green	70	25
2648	-	10k. brown, blue & pur	1·40	45

DESIGNS—VERT: 6k. Lomonosov at desk (after M. Shreier). HORIZ: 10k. Lomonosov (after L. Miropolsky), his birthplace, and Leningrad Academy of Science.

927 Power Workers

1961. Young Builders of Seven Year Plan. Inscr "1961".

2649	927	3k. grey, brown and red	50	15
2650	-	4k. brown, blue and red	45	15
2651	-	6k. grey, brown and red	70	20

DESIGNS: 4k. Welders; 6k. Engineer with theodolite.

928 Scene from "Romeo and Juliet" (Prokotiev)

1961. Russian Ballet (1st issue). Multicoloured.

2652	6k. Type **928**	95	25
2653	10k. Scene from "Swan Lake" (Tchaikovsky)	1·30	45

See also Nos. 2666/7.

929 Hammer and Sickle

1961. 25th Anniv of Soviet Constitution.

2654	929	4k. lake, yellow and red	50	20

930 A. Pumpur

1961. 120th Birth Anniv of Pumpur (Lettish poet).

2655	930	4k. purple and grey	30	15

1961. Air. Surch 1961 r. 6 kon. and wavy lines.

2656	822	6k. on 60k. blue	95	25

932 "Bulgarian Achievements"

1961. 15th Anniv of Bulgarian Republic.

2657	932	4k. multicoloured	40	15

933 Nansen and "Fram"

1961. Birth Centenary of Nansen (explorer).

2658	933	6k. brown, blue and black	1·90	60

934 M. Dolivo-Dobrovolsky

1962. Birth Centenary of Dolivo-Dobrovolsky (electrical engineer).

2659	934	4k. blue and bistre	50	25

935 A. S. Pushkin (after O. Kiprensky)

1962. 125th Death Anniv of Pushkin (poet).

2660	935	4k. black, red and buff	50	25

936 Soviet Woman

1962. Soviet Women.

2661	936	4k. black, bistre & orange	40	15

937 People's Dancers

1962. 25th Anniv of Soviet People's Dance Ensemble.

2662	937	4k. brown and red	40	15

938 Skaters

1962. Ice Skating Championships, Moscow.

2663	938	4k. blue and orange	50	15

1962. War Heroes. As T 879 but inscr "1962".

2664	4k. brown and blue	95	35
2665	6k. turquoise and brown	1·30	45

DESIGNS: 4k. Lieut. Shalandin, tanks and Yakovlev Yak-9T fighters; 6k. Capt. Gadzhiev, "K-3" submarine and sinking ship.

1962. Russian Ballet (2nd issue). As T 928 but inscr "1962".

2666	2k. multicoloured	50	20
2667	3k. multicoloured	50	20

DESIGNS: Scenes from—2k. "Red Flower" (Glier); 3k. "Paris Flame" (Asafev).

СОВЕТСКИЕ КОНЬКОБЕЖЦЫ— ЧЕМПИОНЫ МИРА

(939)

1962. Soviet Victory in Ice Skating Championships. Optd with T 939.

2668	4k. blue and orange	4·00	2·50

940 Skiing

1962. 1st People's Winter Games, Sverdlovsk.

2669	940	4k. violet and red	50	20
2670	-	6k. turquoise and purple	70	25
2671	-	10k. red, black and blue	1·30	45

DESIGN: 6k. Ice Hockey; 10k. Figure skating.

941 A. I. Herzen (after N. Ge)

1962. 150th Birth Anniv of A. I. Herzen (writer).

2672	941	4k. flesh, black and blue	40	15

942 Lenin on Banner

1962. 14th Leninist Young Communist League Congress. Inscr "1962".

2673	**942**	4k. red, yellow and purple	30	10
2674	-	6k. purple, orange & blue	40	15

DESIGN—HORIZ: 6k. Lenin (after A. Mylnikov) on flag.

943 Rocket and Globe

1962. 1st Anniv of World's First Manned Space Flight. Perf or imperf.

2675	**943**	10k. multicoloured	1·20	45

944 Tchaikovsky (after sculpture by Z. M. Vilensky)

1962. 2nd Int Tchaikovsky Music Competition.

2676	**944**	4k. drab, black and blue	60	15

945 Youth of Three Races

1962. International Day of "Solidarity of Youth against Colonialism".

2677	**945**	6k. multicoloured	50	15

946 The Ulyanov (Lenin's) Family

1962. 92nd Birth Anniv of Lenin.

2678	**946**	4k. brown, grey and red	50	15
2679	-	10k. purple, red and black	1·10	35

DESIGN: 10k. Bust of Lenin (N. Sokolov).

947 "Cosmos 3"

1962. Cosmic Research.

2680	**947**	6k. black, violet and blue	80	25

948 Charles Dickens

1962. 150th Birth Anniv of Charles Dickens.

2681	**948**	6k. purple, turq & brn	80	25

949 J. J. Rousseau

1962. 250th Birth Anniv of Rousseau.

2682	**949**	6k. bistre, purple and grey	70	25

950 Karl Marx Monument, Moscow (L. Kerbel)

1962. Karl Marx Commemoration.

2683	**950**	4k. grey and blue	50	15

951 Lenin reading "Pravda"

1962. 50th Anniv of "Pravda" Newspaper.

2684	**951**	4k. purple, red and buff	40	25
2685	-	4k. multicoloured	40	25
2686	-	4k. multicoloured	40	25

DESIGNS—25×38 mm: No. 2685, Statuary and front page of first issue of "Pravda"; No. 2686, Lenin (after A. Mylnikov) and modern front page of "Pravda".

952 Mosquito and Campaign Emblem

1962. Malaria Eradication. Perf (6k. also imperf).

2687	**952**	4k. black, turquoise & red	50	15
2688	**952**	6k. black, green and red	80	35

953 Model Rocket Construction

1962. 40th Anniv of All Union Lenin Pioneer Organization. Designs embody Pioneer badge. Multicoloured.

2689	2k. Lenin and Pioneers giving Oath	30	10
2690	3k. Lenya Golikov and Valya Kotik (pioneer heroes)	30	15
2691	4k. Type **953**	50	15
2692	4k. Hygiene education	50	20
2693	6k. Pioneers marching	95	30

1962. 25th Anniv of First Soviet Polar Drifting Station. No. MS1926a optd "1962" in red on each stamp and with commemorative inscription optd in margin below stamps.

MS2693a 154×111 mm. No. 1926×4	£120	£110

954 M. Mashtotz

1962. 1600th Birth Anniv of Mesrop Mashtotz (author of Armenian Alphabet).

2694	**954**	4k. brown and yellow	50	15

955 Ski Jumping

1962. F.I.S. International Ski Championships, Zakopane (Poland).

2695	**955**	2k. red, brown and blue	30	10
2696	-	10k. blue, black and red	95	45

DESIGN—VERT: 10k. Skier.

956 I. Goncharov (after I. Kramskoi)

1962. 150th Birth Anniv of I. Goncharov (writer).

2697	**956**	4k. brown and grey	40	15

957 Cycle Racing

1962. Summer Sports Championships.

2698	**957**	2k. black, red and brown	40	10
2699	-	4k. black, yellow & brn	75	20
2700	-	10k. black, lemon & blue	90	30
2701	-	12k. brown, yellow & bl	95	40
2702	-	16k. multicoloured	1·50	50

DESIGN—VERT: 4k. Volleyball; 10k. Rowing; 16k. Horse jumping. HORIZ: 12k. Football (goal keeper).

1962. Capitals of Autonomous Republics. 3rd issue. As T 835.

2703	4k. black	60	25
2704	4k. purple	60	25
2705	4k. green	60	25

CAPITALS: No. 2703, Kazan (Tatar); No. 2704, Kyzyl (Tuva); No. 2705, Saransk (Mordovian).

958 Lenin Library, 1862

1962. Centenary of Lenin Library.

2706	**958**	4k. black and grey	40	20
2707	-	4k. black and grey	40	20

DESIGN: No. 2707, Modern library building.

959 Fur Bourse, Leningrad and Ermine

1962. Fur Bourse Commemoration.

2708	**959**	6k. multicoloured	80	45

960 Pasteur

1962. Centenary of Pasteur's Sterilization Process.

2709	**960**	6k. brown and black	70	35

961 Youth and Girl with Book

1962. Communist Party Programme. Mult.

2710	2k. Type **961**	30	15
2711	4k. Workers of three races and dove	40	15

962 Hands breaking Bomb

1962. World Peace Congress, Moscow.

2712	**962**	6k. bistre, black and blue	40	15

963 Ya. Kupala and Ya. Kolas

1962. Byelorussian Poets Commemoration.

2713	**963**	4k. brown and yellow	40	15

964 Sabir

1962. Birth Centenary of Sabir (Azerbaijan poet).

2714	**964**	4k. brown, buff and blue	40	15

965 Congress Emblem

1962. 8th Anti-cancer Congress, Moscow.

2715	**965**	6k. red, black and blue	50	25

966 N. N. Zinin

1962. 150th Birth Anniv of N. N. Zinin (chemist).

2716	**966**	4k. brown and violet	40	15

1962. War of 1941–45 (2nd issue). As T 911 inscr "1962".

2717	4k. multicoloured	80	45

DESIGN: Sailor throwing petrol bomb (Defence of Sevastopol, after A. Deinekin).

967 M. V. Nesterov (painter) (after P. Korin)

1962. Russian Artists Commemoration.

2718	**967**	4k. multicoloured	50	15
2719	-	4k. brown, purple & grey	50	15
2720	-	4k. black and brown	50	15

PORTRAITS—VERT: No. 2719, I. N. Kramskoi (painter) (after N. Yovoshenko). HORIZ: No. 2220, I. D. Shadr (sculptor).

968 "Vostok-2"

1962. 1st Anniv of Titov's Space Flight. Perf or imperf.

2721A	**968**	10k. purple, black & blue	1·20	45
2722A	**968**	10k. orange, black & blue	1·20	45

969 Nikolaev and "Vostok 3"

1962. 1st "Team" Manned Space Flight. Perf or imperf.

2723A	**969**	4k. brown, red and blue	95	25
2724A	-	4k. brown, red and blue	95	25
2725A	-	6k. multicoloured	1·60	35

DESIGNS: No. 2724A, As Type **969** but with Popovich and "Vostok-4"; No. 2725A (47×28½ mm), Cosmonauts in flight.

970 House of Friendship

1962. People's House of Friendship, Moscow.

2726	**970**	6k. grey and blue	40	15

971 Lomonosov University and Atomic Symbols

1962. "Atoms for Peace".

2727	**971**	4k. multicoloured	50	25
2728	-	6k. multicoloured	80	35

DESIGN: 6k. Map of Russia, Atomic symbol and "Peace" in ten languages.

972 Common Carp and Bream

1962. Fish Preservation Campaign.

2729	**972**	4k. yellow, violet and blue	60	15
2730	-	6k. blue, black and orange	80	25

DESIGN: 6k. Atlantic salmon.

973 F. E. Dzerzhinsky

1962. Birth Anniv of Feliks Dzerzhinsky (founder of Cheka).

2731	**973**	4k. blue and green	30	15

974 O. Henry

1962. Birth Cent of O. Henry (American writer).

2732	**974**	6k. black, brown & yell	60	25

975 Field Marshals Barclay de Tolly, Kutuzov and Bagration

1962. 150th Anniv of Patriotic War of 1812.

2733	**975**	3k. brown	40	10
2734	-	4k. blue	60	15
2735	-	6k. slate	70	20
2736	-	10k. violet	95	25

DESIGNS: 4k. D. V. Davydov and partisans; 6k. Battle of Borodino; 10k. Partisan Vasilisa Kozhina escorting French prisoners of war.

976 Lenin Street, Vinnitsa

1962. 600th Anniv of Vinnitsa.

2737	**976**	4k. black and bistre	40	15

977 Transport, "Stamp" and "Postmark"

1962. International Correspondence Week.

2738	**977**	4k. black, purple & turq	40	15

978 Cedar

1962. 150th Anniv of Nikitsky Botanical Gardens. Multicoloured.

2739	3k. Type **978**	40	10
2740	4k. "Vostok-2" canna (plant)	50	15
2741	6k. Strawberry tree (arbutus)	60	20
2742	10k. "Road to the Stars" (chrysanthemum)	90	25

979 Builder

1962. "The Russian People". Multicoloured.

2743	4k. Type **979**	40	15
2744	4k. Textile worker	40	15
2745	4k. Surgeon	40	15
2746	4k. Farm girl	40	15
2747	4k. P. T. instructor	40	15
2748	4k. Housewife	40	15
2749	4k. Rambler	40	15

980 "Sputnik 1"

1962. 5th Anniv of Launching of "Sputnik 1".

2750	**980**	10k. multicoloured	1·20	50

981 Akhundov (after N. Ismailov)

1962. 150th Birth Anniv of Mirza Akhundov (poet).

2751	**981**	4k. brown and green	40	15

982 Harvester

1962. "Settlers on Virgin Lands". Multicoloured.

2752	4k. Type **982**	60	25
2753	4k. Surveyors, tractors and map	60	25
2754	4k. Pioneers with flag	60	25

983 N. N. Burdenko

1962. Soviet Scientists. Inscr "1962". Multicoloured.

2755	4k. Type **983**	40	15
2756	4k. V. P. Filatov (wearing beret)	40	15

984 Lenin Mausoleum

1962. 92nd Birth Anniv of Lenin.

2757	**984**	4k. multicoloured	40	15

985 Worker with Banner

1962. 45th Anniv of October Revolution.

2758	**985**	4k. multicoloured	40	15

986 "Into Space" (sculpture, G. Postnikov)

1962. Space Flights Commem. Perf or imperf.

2759A	**986**	6k. black, brown and blue	70	25
2760A	**986**	10k. ultram, bis & vio	1·10	45

(987)

1962. Launching of Rocket to Mars (1st issue). Optd with T 987.

2761		10k. blue, bistre and violet	5·75	3·50

See also No. 2765.

988 T. Moldo (Kirghiz poet)

1962. Poets' Anniversaries.

2762	**988**	4k. black and red	60	25
2763	-	4k. black and blue	60	25

DESIGN: No. 2763, Sayat-Nova (Armenian poet) with musical instrument (after G. Ruthkyan).

989 Hammer and Sickle

1962. 40th Anniv of U.S.S.R.

2764	**989**	4k. yellow, red and crimson	50	25

990 Mars Rocket in Space (image scaled to 64% of original size)

1962. Launching of Rocket to Mars (2nd issue).

2765	**990**	10k. violet and red	1·20	50

991 Chemical Industry and Statistics

1962. 22nd Communist Party Congress. "Achievements of the People". Multicoloured.

2766	4k. Type **991**	60	25
2767	4k. Engineering (machinery and atomic symbol)	60	25
2768	4k. Hydro-electric power	60	25
2769	4k. Agriculture (harvester)	60	25
2770	4k. Engineering (surveyor and welder)	60	25
2771	4k. Communications (telephone installation)	60	25
2772	4k. Heavy industry (furnace)	60	25
2773	4k. Transport (signalman, etc)	60	25
2774	4k. Dairy farming (milkmaid, etc)	60	25

All the designs show production targets relating to 1980.

992 Chessmen

1962. 30th Soviet Chess Championships, Yerevan.

2775	**992**	4k. black and ochre	95	45

993 Four Soviet Cosmonauts (image scaled to 33% of original size)

1962. Soviet Cosmonauts Commem. Perf or imperf.

2776	**993**	1r. black and blue	8·75	8·75

994 V. K. Blucher (military commander)

1962. V. K. Blucher Commemoration.

2777	**994**	4k. multicoloured	50	15

995 V. N. Podbelsky

1962. 75th Birth Anniv of V. N. Podbelsky (postal administrator, 1918–20).

2778	**995**	4k. violet and brown	40	15

996 A. Gaidar

1962. Soviet Writers.

2779	**996**	4k. buff, black and blue	40	15
2780	-	4k. multicoloured	40	15

DESIGN: No. 2780, A. S. Makharenko.

997 Dove and Christmas Tree

1962. New Year. Perf or imperf.

2781	**997**	4k. multicoloured	40	25

998 D. N. Pryanishnikov (agricultural chemist)

1962. D. N. Pryanishnikov Commemoration.

2782	**998**	4k. multicoloured	40	15

999 Rose-coloured Starlings

1962. Birds.

2783	**999**	3k. black, red and green	50	10
2784	-	4k. black, brown & orge	60	15
2785	-	6k. blue, black and red	70	15
2786	-	10k. blue, black and red	1·20	35
2787	-	16k. red, blue and black	1·70	60

BIRDS: 4k. Red-breasted geese; 6k. Snow geese; 10k. Great white cranes; 16k. Greater flamingos.

1000 F.I.R. Emblem and Handclasp

1962. 4th International Federation of Resistance Heroes Congress.

2788	**1000**	4k. violet and red	40	15
2789	**1000**	6k. turquoise and red	60	25

1001 Badge and Yakovlev Yak-9 Fighters

1962. 20th Anniv of French Air Force "Normandy-Niemen" Unit.

2790	**1001**	6k. red, green and buff	80	25

1002 Map and Savings Book

1962. 40th Anniv of Soviet Banks.

2791	**1002**	4k. multicoloured	30	15
2792	-	6k. multicoloured	50	20

DESIGN: 6k. Savings book and map containing savers.

1003 Fertilizer Plant, Rustavi, Georgia

1962. Heavy Industries.

2793	**1003**	4k. black, lt blue & blue	40	15
2794	-	4k. black, turquoise & grn	40	15
2795	-	4k. black, blue and grey	40	15

DESIGNS: No. 2794, Construction of Bratsk hydro- electric station; 2795, Volzhskaya hydro-electric station, Volgograd.

1962. Provincial Costumes (3rd issue). As T 870. Inscr "1962".

2796		3k. red, brown and drab	50	25

COSTUME: 3k. Latvia.

1004 K. S. Stanislavsky

1963. Russian Stage Celebrities.

2797	**1004**	4k. green on pale green	50	15
2798	-	4k. brown	50	15
2799	-	4k. brown	50	15

PORTRAITS AND ANNIVERSARIES: No. 2797, Type **1004** (actor, birth cent); 2798, M. S. Shchepkin (actor, death cent); 2799, V. D. Durov (animal trainer and circus artiste, birth cent).

1005 A. S. Serafimovich

1963. Russian Writers and Poets.

2800	**1005**	4k. brown, sepia & mve	50	15
2801	-	4k. brown and purple	50	15
2802	-	4k. brown, red and buff	50	15
2803	-	4k. brown and green	50	15
2804	-	4k. brown, sepia & mve	50	15
2805	-	4k. multicoloured	50	15

PORTRAITS AND ANNIVERSARIES: 2800, (birth cent); 2801, Demyan Bednyi (80th birth anniv); 2802, G. I. Uspensky (120th birth anniv); 2803, N. P. Ogarev (150th birth anniv); 2804, V. Ya. Bryusov (90th birth anniv); 2805, F. V. Gladkov (80th birth anniv).

1006 Children in Nursery

1963. Child Welfare.

2806	**1006**	4k. black and orange	45	25
2807	-	4k. purple, blue & orge	45	25
2808	-	4k. bistre, red and green	45	25
2809	-	4k. purple, red & orange	45	25

DESIGNS: No. 2807, Children with nurse; 2808, Young pioneers; 2809, Students at desk and trainee at lathe.

1007 Dolls and Toys

1963. Decorative Arts. Multicoloured.

2810	4k. Type **1007**	40	15
2811	6k. Pottery	50	25
2812	10k. Books	80	35
2813	12k. Porcelain	1·10	35

1008 Ilyushin Il-62 Jetliner

1962. 40th Anniv of "Aeroflot" Airline.

2814	**1008**	10k. black, brown & red	95	45
2815	-	12k. multicoloured	1·20	50
2816	-	16k. red, black and blue	1·50	80

DESIGNS: 12k. "Aeroflot" emblem; 16k. Tupolev Tu-124 airliner.

1009 M. N. Tukhachevsky

1963. 45th Anniv of Red Army and War Heroes.

2817	**1009**	4k. green and turquoise	40	15
2818	-	4k. black and brown	40	15
2819	-	4k. brown and blue	40	15
2820	-	4k. black and red	40	15
2821	-	4k. violet and mauve	40	15

DESIGNS (Army heroes and battle scenes): 2817, Type **1009** (70th birth anniv); 2818, U. M. Avetisyan; 2819, A. M. Matrosov; 2820, I. V. Panfilov; 2821, Ya. F. Fabricius.

1010 M. A. Pavlov (scientist)

1963. Academy of Sciences Members.

2822	**1010**	4k. blue, grey and brown	40	15
2823	-	4k. brown and green	40	15
2824	-	4k. multicoloured	40	15
2825	-	4k. brown, red and blue	40	15
2826	-	4k. multicoloured	40	15

PORTRAITS: No. 2823, I. V. Kurchatov; No. 2824, V. I. Vernadsky. LARGER (23½×30 mm): No. 2825, A. Krylov; No. 2826, V. Obruchev. All commemorate birth centenaries except No. 2823 (60th anniv of birth).

1011 Games Emblem

1963. 5th Soviet T.U. Winter Sports.

2827	**1011**	4k. orange, black & blue	40	15

Советские
хоккеисты-
чемпионы
мира
и Европы.
Стокгольм.
1963 г.

(1012)

1963. Soviet Victory in Swedish Ice Hockey Championships. No. 2670 optd with T 1012.

2828	6k. turquoise and purple	2·10	85

1013 V. Kingisepp

1963. 75th Birth Anniv of Victor Kingisepp (Estonian Communist Party Leader).

2829	**1013**	4k. brown and blue	40	15

1014 R. M. Blauman

1963. Birth Centenary of Rudolf Blauman (Latvian writer).

2830	**1014**	4k. purple and blue	40	15

1015 Globe and Flowers

1963. "World without Arms and Wars". Perf or imperf.

2831	**1015**	4k. green, blue and red	40	10
2832	-	6k. lilac, green and red	60	15
2833	-	10k. violet, blue and red	1·10	35

DESIGNS: 6k. Atomic emblem and pylon; 10k. Sun and rocket.

1016 Lenin (after I. Brodsky)

1963. 93rd Birth Anniv of Lenin.

2834	**1016**	4k. brown and red	4·75	2·75

1963. Provincial Costumes (4th issue). As T 870. Inscr "1963". Multicoloured.

2835	3k. Tadzhikistan	45	20
2836	4k. Azerbaijan	60	25
2837	4k. Kirgizia	60	25
2838	4k. Turkmenistan	60	25

1017 "Luna 4" Rocket

1963. Launching of "Luna 4" Space Rocket. Perf or imperf.
2839 **1017** 6k. red, black and blue 80 35

See also No. 3250.

1018 Woman and Lido

1963. 5th Anniv of World Health Day. Mult.
2840 2k. Type **1018** 30 10
2841 4k. Man and stadium 40 15
2842 10k. Child and school 95 35

1019 Sputniks and Globe

1963. Cosmonautics Day.
2843 **1019** 10k. blue, black and purple (white figures of value) 90 35
2843b **1019** 10k. blue, black and purple (blue figures) 90 35
2844 - 10k. purple, black and blue (white figures) 90 35
2844a - 10k. purple, black and blue (purple figures) 90 35
2845 - 10k. red, black and yellow (white figures) 90 35
2845a - 10k. red, black and yellow (yellow figures) 90 35

DESIGNS: Nos. 2844/a, "Vostok 1" and Moon; Nos. 2845/a, Space rocket and Sun.

1021 Cuban Horsemen with Flag

1963. Cuban-Soviet Friendship.
2846 **1021** 4k. black, red and blue 50 10
2847 - 6k. black, blue and red 60 15
2848 - 10k. blue, red and black 80 35

DESIGNS: 6k. Hands, weapon, book and flag; 10k. Crane, hoisting tractor and flags.

1022 J. Hasek

1963. 40th Death Anniv of Jaroslav Hasek (writer).
2849 **1022** 4k. black 50 15

1023 Karl Marx

1963. 80th Death Anniv of Karl Marx.
2850 **1023** 4k. black and brown 40 15

1963. War of 1941–45 (3rd issue). As T 911 inscr "1963".
2851 4k. multicoloured 50 15
2852 4k. multicoloured 50 15
2853 4k. multicoloured 50 15
2854 4k. sepia and red 50 15
2855 6k. olive, black and red 80 35

DESIGNS: No. 2851, Woman making shells (Defence of Leningrad, 1942); 2852, Soldier in winter kit with tommy gun (20th anniv of Battle of the Volga); 2853, Soldiers attacking (Liberation of Kiev, 1943); 2854, Tanks and map indicating Battle of Kursk, 1943; 2855, Tank commander and tanks.

1024 International P.O. Building

1963. Opening of Int Post Office, Moscow.
2856 **1024** 6k. brown and blue 70 25

1025 Medal and Chessmen

1963. World Chess Championship, Moscow. Perf or imperf.
2857A **1025** 4k. multicoloured 60 15
2858A - 6k. blue, mauve and ultramarine 70 20
2859A - 16k. black, mauve & pur 1·50 50

DESIGNS: 6k. Chessboard and pieces; 16k. Venue and pieces.

1026 Wagner

1963. 150th Birth Anniv of Wagner and Verdi (composers).
2860 **1026** 4k. black and red 60 25
2861 - 4k. purple and red 60 25

DESIGN: No. 2861, Verdi.

1027 Boxers on "Glove"

1963. 15th European Boxing Championships, Moscow. Multicoloured.
2862 4k. Type **1027** 40 15
2863 6k. Referee and winning boxer on "glove" 60 25

1028 Bykovsky and "Vostok 5"

1963. Second "Team" Manned Space Flights (1st issue). Perf or imperf.
2864A **1028** 6k. brown and purple 60 25
2865A - 6k. red and green 60 25
2866A - 10k. red and blue 1·10 35

DESIGNS: No. 2865, Tereshkova and "Vostok 6"; No. 2866, Allegory—"Man and Woman in Space".

See also Nos. 2875/7.

**Всемирный
конгресс
женщин.**
(1029)

1963. International Women's Congress, Moscow. Optd with T 1029.
2867 **1015** 4k. green, blue and red 60 35

1030 Cycling

1963. 3rd People's Spartakiad. Multicoloured. Perf or imperf.
2868B 3k. Type **1030** 30 10
2869A 4k. Athletics 35 30
2870B 6k. Swimming (horiz) 50 15
2871B 12k. Basketball 90 35
2872B 16k. Football 1·30 50
MS2872aA 152×105 mm. As Nos. 2868/9 and 2871/2 but colours changed. Imperf 4·00 1·70

1031 Globe, Film and Camera

1963. International Film Festival, Moscow.
2873 **1031** 4k. blue, black & brown 40 15

1032 V. V. Mayakovsky

1963. 70th Birth Anniv of Mayakovsky (poet).
2874 **1032** 4k. brown 50 25

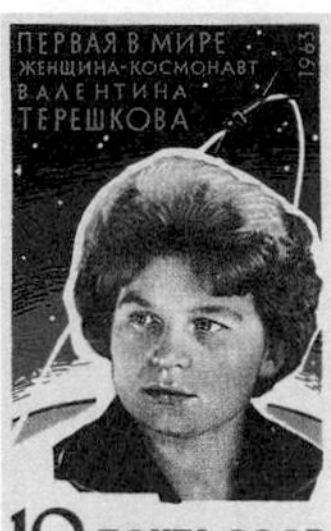

1033 Tereshkova

1963. 2nd "Team" Manned Space Flights (2nd issue). Multicoloured.
2875 4k. Bykovsky (horiz) 60 15
2876 4k. Tereshkova (horiz) 60 15
2877 10k. Type **1033** 1·80 50

1034 Ice Hockey Player

1963. Russian Ice Hockey Championships.
2878 **1034** 6k. blue and red 90 25

1035 Lenin

1963. 60th Anniv of 2nd Socialist Party Congress.
2879 **1035** 4k. black and red 40 15

1036 Freighter and Crate

1963. Red Cross Centenary.
2880 **1036** 6k. red and green 75 20
2881 - 12k. red and blue 1·50 35

DESIGN: 12k. Centenary emblem.

1037 Guibozo (polo)

1963. Regional Sports.
2882 3k. multicoloured 40 10
2883 **1037** 4k. black, red and ochre 50 15
2884 - 6k. red, brown & yellow 70 25
2885 - 10k. black, brn & olive 95 35

DESIGNS—HORIZ: 3k. Lapp reindeer racing; 6k. Buryat archery. VERT: 10k. Armenian wrestling.

1038 Aleksandr Mozhaisky and his Monoplane

1963. Aviation Celebrities.
2886 **1038** 6k. black and blue 60 15
2887 - 10k. black and blue 90 35
2888 - 16k. black and blue 1·50 60

DESIGNS: 10k. Pyotr Nesterov and "looping the loop"; 16k. N. E. Zhukovsky and "aerodynamics".

1039 S. S. Gulak-Artemovsky (composer, 150th birth anniv)

1040 Olga Kobilyanska (writer) (birth centenary)

1963. Celebrities.
2889 **1039** 4k. black and red 50 20
2890 - 4k. brown and purple 50 20
2891 - 4k. brown and violet 50 20
2892 **1040** 4k. mauve and brown 50 20
2893 - 4k. mauve and green 50 20

DESIGNS AND ANNIVERSARIES: As Type **1039**: No. 2893, M. I. Petraskas (Lithuanian composer) and scene from one of his works (90th birth anniv). As Type **1040**: No. 2890, G. D. Eristavi (writer, death cent, 1964); No. 2891, A. S. Dargomizhsky (composer, 150th birth anniv).

1041 Antarctic Map and Supply Ship "Ob"

1963. Arctic and Antarctic Research. Mult.
2894 3k. Type **1041** 50 30
2895 4k. Convoy of snow tractors and map 60 30
2896 6k. Globe and aircraft at polar base 95 45
2897 12k. "Sovetskaya Ukraina" (whale factory ship), whale catcher and whale 1·90 85

1042 Letters and Transport

1963. International Correspondence Week.

2898	**1042**	4k. violet, orange & blk	40	15

1043 E. O. Paton

1963. 10th Death Anniv of Paton (engineer).

2899	**1043**	4k. black, red and blue	40	15

1045 D. Diderot

1963. 250th Birth Anniv of Denis Diderot (French philosopher).

2900	**1045**	4k. brown, blue & bistre	60	25

1046 "Peace"

1963. "Peace—Brotherhood—Liberty—Labour". All black, red and lake.

2901	4k. Type **1046**	50	20
2902	4k. Worker at desk and couple consulting plan ("Labour")	50	20
2903	4k. Artist and couple ("Liberty")	50	20
2904	4k. Voters ("Equality")	50	20
2905	4k. Man shaking hands with couple with banner ("Brotherhood")	50	20
2906	4k. Family group ("Happiness")	50	20

1047 Academy of Sciences, Frunze

1963. Centenary of Union of Kirgizia and Russia.

2907	**1047**	4k. blue, yellow and red	40	15

1049 Lenin and Congress Building

1963. 13th Soviet Trade Unions' Congress, Moscow.

2908	**1049**	4k. red and black	30	10
2909	-	4k. red and black	30	10

DESIGN: No. 2909, Lenin with man and woman workers.

1050 Ilya Mechnikov

1963. 75th Anniv of Pasteur Institute, Paris.

2910	**1050**	4k. green and bistre	50	15
2911	-	6k. violet and bistre	70	25
2912	-	12k. blue and bistre	1·50	45

PORTRAITS: 6k. Pasteur; 12k. Calmette.

1051 Cruiser "Aurora" and Rockets

1963. 46th Anniv of October Revolution.

2913	**1051**	4k. black, orange & lake	50	15
2914	**1051**	4k. black, red and lake	70	35

1052 Gur Emi Mausoleum

1963. Ancient Samarkand Buildings. Mult.

2915	4k. Type **1052**	60	15
2916	4k. Shachi-Zinda Mosque	60	15
2917	6k. Registan Square (55×28½ mm)	75	25

1053 Inscription, Globe and Kremlin

1963. Signing of Nuclear Test-ban Treaty, Moscow.

2918	**1053**	6k. violet and pale blue	70	25

1054 Pushkin Monument, Kiev (A. Kovalev)

1963

2919	**1054**	4k. brown	40	15

1056 Shukhov and Radio Tower, Moscow

1963. 110th Birth Anniv of V. G. Shukhov (engineer).

2920	**1056**	4k. black and green	50	15

1057 Ya. Steklov and "Izvestia"

1963. 90th Birth Anniv of Ya. M. Steklov (first editor of "Izvestia").

2921	**1057**	4k. black and mauve	50	15

1058 Buildings and Emblems of Moscow (and U.S.S.R.) and Prague (and Czechoslovakia)

1963. 20th Anniv of Soviet-Czech Friendship Treaty.

2922	**1058**	6k. red, bistre and blue	50	10

1059 F. A. Poletaev (soldier) and Medals

1963. Poletaev Commemoration.

2923	**1059**	4k. multicoloured	40	10

1062 J. Grimau (Spanish Communist)

1963. Grimau Commemoration.

2924	**1062**	6k. violet, red and cream	50	25

1063 Rockets

1963. New Year (1st issue).

2925	**1063**	6k. multicoloured	60	25

1064 "Happy New Year"

1963. New Year (2nd issue).

2926	**1064**	4k. red, blue and green	40	10
2927	**1064**	6k. red, blue and green	60	25

1067 Topaz

1963. "Precious Stones of the Urals". Multicoloured.

2928	2k. Type **1067**	30	15
2929	4k. Jasper	50	35
2930	6k. Amethyst	70	45
2931	10k. Emerald	90	60
2932	12k. Ruby	1·10	85
2933	16k. Malachite	1·50	1·00

1068 Sputnik 7

1963. "First in Space". Gold, vermilion and grey.

2934	10k. Type **1068**	95	35
2935	10k. Moon landing	95	35
2936	10k. Back of Moon	95	35
2937	10k. Vostok 7	95	35
2938	10k. Twin flight	95	35
2939	10k. Seagull (first woman in space)	95	35

1069 Dushanbe Putovsky Square

1963. Dushanbe, Capital of Tadzhikistan.

2940	**1069**	4k. blue	50	15

1071 Flame and Rainbow

1963. 15th Anniv of Declaration of Human Rights.

2941	**1071**	6k. multicoloured	50	15

1072 F. A, Sergeev ("Artem")

1963. 80th Birth Anniv of Sergeev (revolutionary).

2942	**1072**	4k. brown and red	40	10

1073 Sun and Globe

1964. International Quiet Sun Year.

2943	-	4k. black, orange & mve	40	10
2944	**1073**	6k. blue, yellow and red	50	15
2945	-	10k. violet, red and blue	70	25

DESIGNS—HORIZ: 4k. Giant telescope and sun; 10k. Globe and Sun.

1074 K. Donelaitis

1964. 250th Birth Anniv of K. Donelaitis (Lithuanian poet).

2946	**1074**	4k. black and myrtle	40	10

1075 Speed Skating

1964. Winter Olympic Games, Innsbruck.

2947B	**1075**	2k. black, mauve & bl	30	10
2948B	-	4k. black, blue & mve	40	15
2949B	-	6k. red, black and blue	60	20

2950B	-	10k. black, mve & grn	90	35
2951B	-	12k. black, grn & mve	95	45

DESIGNS: 4k. Skiing; 6k. Games emblem; 10k. Rifle shooting (biathlon); 12k. Figure skating (pairs).

See also Nos. 2969/73.

1076 Golubkina (after N. Ulyanov) and Statue, Tolstoi

1964. Birth Cent of A. S. Golubkina (sculptress).

2952	**1076**	4k. sepia and grey	40	10

1077 "Agriculture"

1964. Heavy Chemical Industries. Multicoloured.

2953	4k. Type **1077**	50	10
2954	4k. "Textiles"	50	10
2955	4k. "Tyre Production"	50	10

150 років з дня народження. 1964 р.

(1078)

1079 Shevchenko's Statue, Kiev (M. Manizer)

1964. 150th Birth Anniv of T. G. Shevchenko (Ukrainian poet and painter). No. 2561 optd with T 1078 and designs as T 1079.

2956	**880**	3k. brown and violet	4·75	3·50
2959	**1079**	4k. green	30	10
2960	**1079**	4k. red	30	10
2961	-	6k. blue	50	15
2962	-	6k. brown	50	15
2957	-	10k. violet and brown	1·10	25
2958	-	10k. brown and bistre	1·10	25

DESIGNS: Nos. 2957/8, Portrait of Shevchenko by I. Repin; Nos. 2961/2, Self-portrait.

1080 K. S. Zaslonov

1964. War Heroes.

2963	**1080**	4k. sepia and brown	50	15
2964	-	4k. purple and blue	50	15
2965	-	4k. blue and red	50	15
2966	-	4k. brown and blue	50	15

PORTRAITS: No. 2964, N. A. Vilkov; 2965, Yu. V. Smirnov; 2966, V. Z. Khoruzhaya.

1081 Fyodorov printing the first Russian book, "Apostle"

1964. 400th Anniv of First Russian Printed Book. Multicoloured.

2967	4k. Type **1081**	40	10
2968	6k. Statue of Ivan Fyodorov, Moscow (S. Volnukin), books and newspapers	50	25

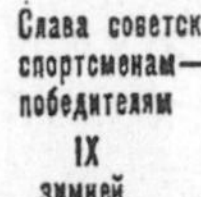
Слава советским спортсменам— победителям IX зимней Олимпиады!

(1082)

1964. Winter Olympic Games, Soviet Medal Winners. (a) Nos. 2947/51 optd with T 1082 or similarly.

2969	2k. black, mauve and blue	30	10
2970	4k. black, blue and mauve	40	15
2971	6k. red, black and blue	50	25
2972	10k. black, mauve and green	90	35
2973	12k. black, green and mauve	1·10	45

1083 Ice Hockey Player

(b) New designs.

2974	**1083**	3k. red, black & turquoise	50	15
2975	-	16k. orange and brown	1·50	70

DESIGN: 16k. Gold medal and inscr "Triumph of Soviet Sport–11 Gold, 8 Silver, 6 Bronze medals".

1084 Militiaman and Factory Guard

1964. "Public Security".

2976	**1084**	4k. blue, red and black	40	15

1085 Lighthouse, Odessa and Sailor

1964. 20th Anniv of Liberation of Odessa and Leningrad. Multicoloured.

2977	4k. Type **1085**	40	15
2978	4k. Lenin Statue, Leningrad	40	15

1086 Sputniks

1964. "The Way to the Stars". Imperf or perf. (a) Cosmonautics. As T 1086.

2979B	4k. green, black and red	50	15
2980A	6k. black, blue and red	70	60
2981A	12k. turquoise, brown & black	1·40	1·20

DESIGNS: 6k. "Mars I" space station; 12k. Gagarin and space capsule.

1087 N. I. Kibalchich

(b) Rocket Construction Pioneers. As T 1087.

2982B	10k. black, green and violet	1·30	45
2983B	10k. black, turquoise and red	1·30	45
2984B	10k. black, turquoise and red	1·30	45
2985B	10k. black and blue	1·30	45

DESIGNS: No. 2982B, Type **1087**; 2983B, F. A. Zander; 2984B, K. E. Tsiolkovsky; 2985B, Pioneers' medallion and Saransk memorial.

1088 Lenin

1964. 94th Birth Anniv of Lenin.

2986a	**1088**	4k. black, blue & mve	4·00	3·00

1089 Shakespeare (400th Birth Anniv)

1964. Cultural Anniversaries.

2987	-	6k. yellow, brn & sepia	1·10	45
2988	**1089**	10k. brown and olive	1·30	60
2989	-	12k. green and brown	2·10	80

DESIGNS AND ANNIVERSARIES: 6k. Michelangelo (400th death anniv); 12k. Galileo (400th birth anniv).

1090 Crop-watering Machine and Produce

1964. "Irrigation".

2990	**1090**	4k. multicoloured	40	10

1091 Gamarnik

1964. 70th Birth Anniv of Ya. B. Gamarnik (Soviet Army commander).

2991	**1091**	4k. brown, blue & black	40	10

1092 D. I. Gulia (Abhazian poet)

1964. Cultural Anniversaries.

2992	**1092**	4k. black, green and light green	40	15
2993	-	4k. black, verm & red	40	15
2994	-	4k. black, brown & bis	40	15
2995	-	4k. black, yellow & brn	40	15
2996	-	4k. multicoloured	40	15
2997	-	4k. black, yellow & brn	40	15

DESIGNS: No. 2993, Nijazi (Uzbek writer, composer and painter); 2994, S. Seifullin (Kazakh poet); 2995, M. M. Kotsyubinsky (writer); 2996, S. Nazaryan (Armenian writer); 2997, T. Satylganov (Kirghiz poet).

1093 A. Gaidar

1964. 60th Birth Annivs of Writers A. P. Gaidar and N. A. Ostrovsky.

2998	**1093**	4k. red and blue	40	10
2999	-	4k. green and red	40	10

DESIGN: No. 2999, N. Ostrovsky and battle scene.

1094 Indian Elephant

1964. Centenary of Moscow Zoo. Multicoloured. Imperf or perf.

3000A	1k. Type **1094**	10	10
3001A	2k. Giant panda	20	10
3002A	4k. Polar bear	50	10
3003A	6k. Elk	60	15
3004A	10k. Eastern white pelican	95	25
3005A	12k. Tiger	1·10	35
3006A	16k. Lammergeier	1·50	50

The 2k. and 12k. are horiz; the 4k. and 10k. are "square", approx 26½×28 mm.

150 лет вхождения в состав России 1964

4 коп.

(1095)

1964. 150th Anniv of Union of Azerbaijan and Russia. Surch with T 1095.

3007	**328**	4k. on 40k. brown, bistre and yellow	6·25	3·50

1096 Rumanian Woman and Emblems on Map

1964. 20th. Anniv of Rumanian–Soviet Friendship Treaty.

3008	**1096**	6k. multicoloured	60	25

1097 Maize

1964. Agricultural Crops. Multicoloured. Imperf or perf.

3009B	2k. Type **1097**	20	10
3010B	3k. Wheat	25	10
3011B	4k. Potatoes	30	15
3012B	6k. Peas	50	15
3013B	10k. Sugar beet	80	35
3014B	12k. Cotton	1·10	45
3015B	16k. Flax	1·50	50

1098 Flag and Obelisk

1964. 20th Anniv of Liberation of Byelorussia.

3016	**1098**	4k. multicoloured	40	10

1099 Leningrad G.P.O.

1964. 250th Anniv of Leningrad's Postal Service.

3017	**1099**	4k. black, bistre and red	40	10

1100 Map of Poland and Emblems

1964. 20th Anniv of Polish People's Republic.
3018 **1100** 6k. multicoloured 50 25

1101 Horse-jumping

1964. Olympic Games, Tokyo. Imperf or perf.
3019B **1101** 3k. multicoloured 20 10
3020B - 4k. red, black & yellow 30 10
3021B - 6k. red, black and blue 40 15
3022B - 10k. red, black & turq 70 25
3023B - 12k. black and grey 80 30
3024B - 16k. violet, red and blue 1·20 35
MS3024aB 90×71 mm. 1r. green background £250 £250
MS3024bB 90×71 mm. 1r. red background 9·75 4·25
DESIGNS: 4k. Weightlifting; 6k. Pole vaulting; 10k. Canoeing; 12k Gymnastics; 16k. Fencing; 1r. Gymnast and stadium.

1102 M. Thorez (French Communist leader)

1964. Maurice Thorez Commemoration.
3025 **1102** 4k. black and red 1·30 50

1103 Three Races

1964. International Anthropologists and Ethnographers Congress, Moscow.
3026 **1103** 6k. black and yellow 50 25

1104 Jawaharlal Nehru

1964. Nehru Commemoration.
3027 **1104** 4k. brown and grey 50 15

1104a

1964. World Orbit Flights. Sheet of six multicoloured stamps as T **1104a** making up composite design showing Earth, Moon, spacecraft etc.
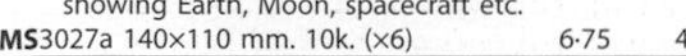
MS3027a 140×110 mm. 10k. (×6) 6·75 4·75

1105 Globe and Banner

1964. Centenary of "First International".
3028 **1105** 4k. red, bistre and blue 40 15
3029 - 4k. red, olive and black 40 15
3030 - 4k. drab, red and lake 40 15
3031 - 4k. red, black and blue 40 15
3032 - 4k. multicoloured 40 15
DESIGNS: No. 3029, Communist Party manifesto; 3030, Marx and Engels; 3031, Chain breaker; 3032, Lenin.

1106 A. V. Vishnevsky (surgeon)

1964. "Outstanding Soviet Physicians".
3033 **1106** 4k. brown and purple 40 10
3034 - 4k. brown, red & yellow 40 10
3035 - 4k. brown, blue & bistre 40 10
DESIGNS: No. 3034, N. A. Semashko (public health pioneer). Both are 90th birth anniversaries. No. 3035, D. I. Ivanovsky and siphon (25×32 mm).

1107 Bulgarian Flag, Rose and Emblems

1964. 20th Anniv of Bulgarian People's Republic.
3036 **1107** 6k. red, green and drab 60 25

1108 P. Togliatti (Italian Communist leader)

1964. Togliatti Commemoration.
3037 **1108** 4k. black and red 40 10

1110 Globe and Letters

1964. International Correspondence Week.
3038 **1110** 4k. mauve, blue & brn 40 10

1111 Soviet and Yugoslav Soldiers

1964. 20th Anniv of Liberation of Belgrade.
3039 **1111** 6k. multicoloured 50 25

1112 East German Arms, Industrial Plants, Freighter "Havel" and Electric Goods Train

1964. 15th Anniv of German Democratic Republic.
3040 **1112** 6k. multicoloured 60 25

1113 Woman holding Bowl of Produce (Moldavian Republic)

1964. 40th Anniv of Soviet Republic. (a) As T **1113**.
3041 **1113** 4k. brown, green and red 50 15
3042 - 4k. multicoloured 50 15
3043 - 4k. red, purple & yellow 50 15

40 лет Советскому Таджикистану
1964 год
(1115)

(b) Optd with T **1115**.
3044 **1069** 4k. blue 1·30 60
DESIGNS—VERT: No. 3042, Woman holding Arms (Turkmenistan); 3043, Man and woman holding produce (Uzbekistan); 3044, commemorates the Tadzhikistan Republic.

1116 Yegorov

1964. Three-manned Space Flight. (a) Portraits in black, orange and turquoise.
3045 4k. Type **1116** 50 15
3046 4k. Feoktistov 50 15
3047 4k. Komarov 50 15
These can be identified by the close proximation of the Russian names on the stamps to the English versions.

(b) Designs 73½×22½ mm.
3048 6k. purple and violet 80 20
3049 10k. violet and blue 1·30 45
MS3049a 120×56 mm. 50k. violet, red and grey. Imperf 7·25 3·50
DESIGNS: 6k. The three cosmonauts; 10k. Space ship "Voskhod 1".

1117 Soldier and Flags

1964. 20th Anniv of Liberation of Ukraine.
3050 **1117** 4k. multicoloured 40 10

1119 Lermontov's Birthplace

1964. 150th Birth Anniv of M. Lermontov (poet).
3051 **1119** 4k. violet 40 15
3052 - 6k. black 60 25
3053 - 10k. brown and flesh 95 45
DESIGNS: 6k. Lermontov (after K. Gorbunov); 10k. Lermontov talking with V. Belinsky.

1120 Hammer and Sickle

1964. 47th Anniv of October Revolution.
3054 **1120** 4k. multicoloured 40 10

1964. 94th Birth Anniv of Lenin. Sheet 144×101 mm, comprising pair of No. 2679.
MS3054a 10k. purple, lake and black 3·00 1·70

1121 N. K. Krupskaya (Lenin's wife)

1964. Birth Anniversaries.
3055 **1121** 4k. multicoloured 40 10
3056 - 4k. multicoloured 40 10
DESIGNS: 3055 (95th anniv); 3056, A. I. Yelizarova-Ulyanova (Lenin's sister) (cent).

1122 Mongolian Woman and Lamb

1964. 40th Anniv of Mongolian People's Republic.
3057 **1122** 4k. multicoloured 50 25

1124 Butter Mushroom

1964. Mushrooms. Multicoloured.
3058A 2k. Type **1124** 30 10
3059A 4k. Chanterelle 50 15
3060A 6k. Ceps 65 25
3061A 10k. Red-capped sacker stalk 1·10 45
3062A 12k. Saffron milk cap 1·40 50

1125 A. P. Dovzhenko

1964. 70th Birth Anniv of Dovzhenko (film producer).
3063 **1125** 4k. blue and grey 40 10

1126 Christmas Tree, Star and Globe

1964. New Year.
3064 **1126** 4k. multicoloured 75 25

1127 Struve

1964. Death Centenary of V. Ya. Struve (scientist).
3065 **1127** 4k. brown and blue 60 15

1128 Ivanov (after O. Braz) and "March of the Moscovites. 16th Century"

1964. Birth Centenary of S. V. Ivanov (painter).

3066	**1128**	4k. brown and black	70	25

1129 Scene from Film

1964. 30th Anniv of Film "Chapaev".

3067	**1129**	6k. black and green	60	25

1130 Test-tubes, Jar and Agricultural Scenes

1964. Chemistry for the National Economy.

3068	**1130**	4k. purple and olive	30	10
3069	-	6k. black and blue	50	25

DESIGN: 6k. Chemical plant.

1131 Cranberries

1964. Woodland Fruits. Multicoloured.

3070	1k. Type **1131**	15	10
3071	3k. Bilberries	20	10
3072	4k. Rowanberries	30	15
3073	10k. Blackberries	70	25
3074	16k. Red bilberries	1·10	50

1132 Library

1964. 250th Anniv of Academy of Sciences Library, Leningrad.

3075	**1132**	4k. black, green and red	50	15

1133 Congress Palace and Spassky Tower

1964

3076	**1133**	1r. blue	6·75	1·70

1134 Mt Khan-Tengri

1964. Mountaineering. Multicoloured.

3077	4k. Type **1134**	30	10
3078	6k. Mt Kazbek (horiz)	50	15
3079	12k. Mt Ushba	90	35

1136 Bowl

1964. Kremlin Treasures. Multicoloured.

3080	4k. Helmet	50	15
3081	6k. Quiver	70	25
3082	10k. Coronation headgear	1·00	35
3083	12k. Ladle	1·40	45
3084	16k. Type **1136**	1·80	85

1137 I. M. Sivko

1965. War Heroes.

3085	**1137**	4k. black and violet	40	15
3086	-	4k. brown and blue	40	15

DESIGN: No. 3086, General I. S. Polbin.

1138 Dante

1965. 700th Birth Anniv of Dante.

3087	**1138**	4k. black, bistre and purple	70	25

1139 Blood Donor

1965. Blood Donors. Multicoloured.

3088	4k. Type **1139**	40	15
3089	4k. Hand holding red carnation	40	15

1140 N. P. Kravkov

1965. Birth Cent of N. Kravkov (pharmacologist).

3090	**1140**	4k. multicoloured	40	10

1141 Figure Skaters

1965. European Figure Skating Championships, Moscow.

3091	**1141**	6k. red, black and green	60	25

See also No. 3108.

1965. World Ice Hockey Championships, Moscow. Designs similar to T 1141 but depicting ice hockey players.

3092	4k. red, blue and bistre	50	15

1142 Alsatian

1965. Hunting and Service Dogs.

3093	-	1k. black, yellow and red	20	10
3097	-	2k. brown, blue & black	20	10
3098	**1142**	3k. black, red and yellow	20	10
3099	-	4k. black, brown & grn	30	15
3100	-	4k. black, orange & grn	30	15
3101	-	6k. black, brown & blue	50	25
3102	-	6k. black, red and blue	50	25
3094	-	10k. multicoloured	80	45
3095	-	12k. black, brown & vio	95	50
3096	-	16k. multicoloured	1·50	70

DESIGNS—HORIZ: 1k. Hound; 2k. Setter; 4k. (3099) (value in green) Fox terrier; 4k. (3100) (value in orange) Pointer; 6k. (3101) Borzoi; 12k. Husky. VERT: 6k. (3102) Sheepdog; 10k. Collie; 16k. Caucasian sheepdog.

1143 R. Sorge

1965. Richard Sorge (Soviet secret agent) Commem.

3103	**1143**	4k. black and red	60	25

1144 I.T.U. Emblem and Telecommunications Symbol

1965. Centenary of I.T.U.

3104	**1144**	6k. violet and blue	70	25

1145 Leonov in Space (image scaled to 66% of original size)

1965. Space Flight of "Voskhod 2" (1st issue). Imperf or perf.

3105	**1145**	10k. orange, black & bl	95	35
MS3106		1r. black, red and blue	1·60	85

See also Nos. 3138/9.

1965. Ice Hockey Championships. Optd ТАМПЕРЕ 1965 г.

3107	**1034**	6k. blue and red	7·75	3·00

Советские фигуристы— чемпионы мира в парном катании

(1147)

1965. Soviet Victory in European Figure Skating Championships. Optd with T 1147.

3108	**1141**	6k. red, black and green	3·00	2·50

1148 Soldier and Woman

1965. 20th Anniversaries.

3109	**1148**	6k. multicoloured	50	15
3110	-	6k. multicoloured	50	15
3111	-	6k. ochre and red	50	15
3112	-	6k. multicoloured	50	15
3113	-	6k. multicoloured	50	15

DESIGNS: No. 3109, Type **1148** (Czech Liberation); 3110, Statue and emblems of development (Friendship with Hungary); 3111, Polish and Soviet arms (Polish–Soviet Friendship Treaty); 3112, Viennese buildings and Russian soldier (Freeing of Vienna); 3113, Liberation medal, Polish flag and building reconstruction (Freeing of Warsaw).

See also Nos. 3182 and 3232.

1149 Statue Rockets and Globe

1150 Rockets and Radio-telescope

1965. National Cosmonautics Day. Nos. 3117/18 on aluminium-surfaced paper.

3114	**1149**	4k. green, black and red	30	15
3115	-	12k. purple, red and blue	80	35
3116	-	16k. multicoloured	1·10	45
3117	**1150**	20k. red, black and green on silver	7·25	5·25
3118	-	20k. red, black and blue on silver	7·25	5·25

DESIGNS: 12k. Statue and Globe; 16k. Rockets and Globe; No. 3118, Globe, satellite and cosomonauts.

1151 Lenin (after bas-relief by V. Sayapin)

1965. Lenin's 95th Birth Anniv.

3119	**1151**	10k. blue, black & brn	95	45

1152 Poppies

1965. Flowers.

3120	**1152**	1k. red, lake and green	10	10
3121	-	3k. yellow, brown & grn	30	10
3122	-	4k. lilac, black and green	40	15
3123	-	6k. red, deep green and green	60	20
3124	-	10k. yellow, pur & grn	1·10	25

FLOWERS: 3k. Marguerite; 4k. Peony; 6k. Carnation; 10k. Tulips.

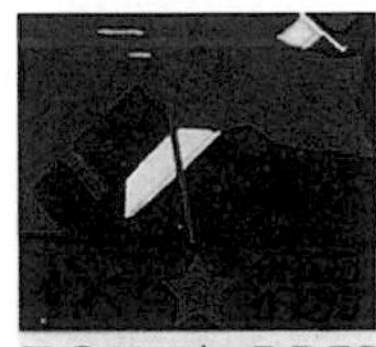

1153 Red Flag, Reichstag Building and Broken Swastika

1965. 20th Anniv of Victory.

3125	**1153**	1k. black, gold and red	20	10
3126	-	2k. red, black and gold	30	15
3127	-	3k. blue and gold	50	15
3128	-	4k. violet and gold	60	15
3129	-	4k. green and gold	60	15
3130	-	6k. purple, green & gold	1·20	25
3131	-	10k. purple, brn & gold	1·60	30
3132	-	12k. black, red and gold	1·90	35
3133	-	16k. red and gold	2·40	45
3134	-	20k. black, red and gold	3·00	70

DESIGNS: 2k. Soviet mother holding manifesto (poster by I. Toidze); 3k. "The Battle for Moscow" (V. Bogatkin); 4k. (No. 3128), "Partisan Mother" (from S. Gerasimov's film); 4k. (No. 3129), "Red Army Soldiers and Partisans" (from Yu. Neprintsev's film); 6k. Soldiers and flag (poster by V. Ivanov); 10k. "Mourning the Fallen Hero" (from F. Bogorodsky's film); 12k. Soldier and worker holding bomb (poster by V. Korestsky); 16k. Victory celebrations, Red Square, Moscow (from K. Yuon's film); 20k. Soldier and machines of war.

1153a Popov's Radio Invention

1965. 70th Anniv of A. S. Popov's Radio Discoveries. Sheet 144×100 mm comprising six stamps without face value.

MS3135	1r. multicoloured	6·25	3·50

DESIGNS: T **1153a**: Transistor radio; TV screen; Radar; Radiotelescope; Telecommunications satellite. The value is printed on the sheet.

1154 Marx and Lenin

1965. Marxism and Leninism.

3136	**1154**	6k. black and red	60	15

No. 3136 is similar in design to those issued by China and Hungary for the Postal Ministers' Congress, Peking, but this event is not mentioned on the stamp or in the Soviet philatelic bulletins.

1155 Bolshoi Theatre

1965. International Theatre Day.

3137	**1155**	6k. ochre, black & turq	60	15

1156 Leonov

1965. "Voskhod 2" Space Flight (2nd issue).

3138	**1156**	6k. violet and silver	50	15
3139	-	6k. purple and silver	50	15

DESIGN: No. 3139, Belyaev.

1157 Yakov Sverdlov (revolutionary)

1965. 80th Birth Anniversaries.

3140	**1157**	4k. black and brown	45	10
3141	-	4k. black and violet	45	10

PORTRAIT: No. 3141, J. Akhunbabaev (statesman).

1158 Otto Grotewohl (1st death anniv)

1965. Annivs of Grotewohl and Thorez (Communist leaders).

3142	**1158**	4k. black and purple	45	10
3143	-	6k. brown and red	60	15

DESIGN: 6k. Maurice Thorez (65th birth anniv).

1159 Telecommunications Satellite

1965. International Co-operation Year. Mult.

3144	3k. Type **1159**	30	10
3145	6k. Star and sputnik	55	15
3146	6k. Foundry ladle, iron works and map of India	55	15

No. 3145 signifies peaceful uses of atomic energy and No. 3146 co-operation with India.

1160 Congress Emblem, Chemical Plant and Symbols

1965. 20th International Congress of Pure and Applied Chemistry, Moscow.

3147	**1160**	4k. red, black and blue	40	10

1161 V. A. Serov (after I. Repin)

1965. Birth Centenary of V. A. Serov (painter).

3148	**1161**	4k. black, brn & stone	1·10	25
3149	-	6k. black and drab	1·60	35

DESIGN: 6k. Full length portrait of Chaliapin (singer) by Serov.

1162 Vsevolod Ivanov and Armoured Train

1965. Famous Writers.

3150	**1162**	4k. black and purple	45	15
3151	-	4k. black and violet	45	15
3152	-	4k. black and blue	45	15
3153	-	4k. black and grey	45	15
3154	-	4k. black, red and green	45	15
3155	-	4k. black and brown	45	15

WRITERS AND ANNIVERSARIES: No. 3150, (70th birth anniv); 3151, A. Kunanbaev and military parade; 3152, J. Rainis (Lettish poet: 90th birth anniv); 3153, E. J. Vilde (Estonian author): 90th birth anniv); 3154, M. Ch. Abegjan (Armenian writer and critic: 90th birth anniv); 3155, M. L. Kropivnitsky and scene from play (Ukrainian playwright).

1163 Festival Emblem

1965. Film Festival, Moscow.

3156	**1163**	6k. black, gold and blue	60	15

1164 Concert Arena, Tallin

1965. 25th Anniv of Incorporation of Estonia, Lithuania and Latvia in the U.S.S.R.

3157	**1164**	4k. multicoloured	40	10
3158	-	4k. brown and red	40	10
3159	-	4k. brown, red and blue	40	10

DESIGNS—VERT: No. 3158, Lithuanian girl and Arms. HORIZ: No. 3159, Latvian Flag and Arms.

1165 Hand holding "Peace Flower"

1965. Peace Issue.

3160	**1165**	6k. yellow, black & blue	60	25

1167 "Potemkin" Sailors Monument (V. Bogdanov), Odessa

1965. 60th Anniv of 1905 Rebellion.

3161	**1167**	4k. blue and red	40	15
3162	-	4k. green, black and red	40	15
3163	-	4k. green, black and red	40	15
3164	-	4k. brown, black and red	40	15

DESIGNS: No. 3162, Demonstrator up lamp post; 3163, Defeated rebels; 3164, Troops at street barricade.

1168 G. Gheorgi-Dej (Rumanian Communist)

1965. G. Gheorgi-Dej Commemoration.

3165	**1168**	4k. black and red	40	10

1169 Power Station

1965. Industrial Progress.

3166	**1169**	1k. multicoloured	10	10
3167	-	2k. black, orange & yell	20	10
3168	-	3k. violet, yell & ochre	20	10
3169	-	4k. deep blue, blue and red	35	10
3170	-	6k. blue and bistre	50	20
3171	-	10k. brown, yellow and orange	80	25
3172	-	12k. turquoise and red	1·10	35
3173	-	16k. purple, blue & blk	1·40	45

DESIGNS: 2k. Steel works; 3k. Chemical works and formula; 4k. Machine tools production; 6k. Building construction; 10k. Agriculture; 12k. Communications and transport; 16k. Scientific research.

1170 Relay Racing

1965. Trade Unions Spartakiad. Multicoloured.

3174	4k. Type **1170**	40	15
3175	4k. Gymnastics	40	15
3176	4k. Cycling	40	15

1171 Gymnastics

1965. Schoolchildren's Spartakiad.

3177	**1171**	4k. red and blue	30	10
3178	-	6k. red, brown & turq	50	15

DESIGN: 6k. Cycle racing.

1172 Throwing the Javelin and Running

1965. American–Soviet Athletic Meeting, Kiev.

3179	**1172**	4k. red, brown and lilac	30	10
3180	-	6k. red, brown and green	50	15
3181	-	10k. red, brown and grey	60	35

DESIGNS: 6k. High jumping and putting the shot; 10k. Throwing the hammer and hurdling.

1173 Star, Palms and Lotus

1965. 20th Anniv of North Vietnamese People's Republic.

3182	**1173**	6k. multicoloured	50	15

1174 Worker with Hammer (World T.U. Federation)

1965. 20th Anniv of International Organizations.

3183	**1174**	6k. drab and plum	40	15
3184	-	6k. brown, red and blue	40	15
3185	-	6k. lt brown & turquoise	40	15

DESIGNS: No. 3184, Torch and heads of three races (World Democratic Youth Federation); No. 3185, Woman holding dove (International Democratic Women's Federation).

1176 P. K. Sternberg (astonomer: birth cent)

1965. Scientists' Anniversaries.

3186	**1176**	4k. brown and blue	50	15
3187	-	4k. black and purple	50	15
3188	-	4k. black, purple & yell	50	15

PORTRAITS: No. 3187, Ch. Valikhanov (scientific writer: death cent); 3188, V. A. Kistyakovsky (scientist: birth cent).

1177 "Battleship 'Potemkin'" (dir. Sergei Eisenshtein)

1965. Soviet Cinema Art. Designs showing scenes from films. Multicoloured.

No.	Type	Description	Mint	Used
3189		4k. Type **1177**	40	10
3190		6k. "Young Guard" (dir. S. Coesinov)	50	20
3191		12k. "A Soldier's Ballad" (dir. G. Chuthrai)	1·10	35

1178 Mounted Postman and Map

1965. History of the Russian Post Office.

No.	Type	Description	Mint	Used
3192	**1178**	1k. green, brown & vio	35	20
3193	-	1k. brown, ochre & grey	35	20
3194	-	2k. brown, blue and lilac	40	15
3195	-	4k. black, ochre & pur	50	15
3196	-	6k. black, green & brn	70	20
3197	-	12k. sepia, brown & blue	1·30	35
3198	-	16k. plum, red and grey	1·50	50

DESIGNS: No. 3193, Mail coach and map; 2k. Early steam train and medieval kogge; 4k. Mail lorry and map; 6k. Diesel-electric train and various transport; 12k. Moscow Post Office electronic facing sorting and cancelling machines; 16k. Airports and Lenin.

1179 "Vostok" and "Mirnyi" (Antarctic exploration vessels)

1965. Polar Research Annivs.

No.	Type	Description	Mint	Used
3199		4k. black, orange & blue	70	15
3200		4k. black, orange & blue	70	15
3201		6k. sepia and violet	80	30
3202	**1179**	10k. black, drab and red	1·30	45
3203	-	16k. black, violet & brn	1·50	70

DESIGNS—HORIZ: 37½×25½ mm: No. 3199, Ice breakers "Taimyr" and "Vaigach" in Arctic (50th anniv); 3200, Atomic ice breaker "Lenin"; 3201, Dikson settlement (50th anniv); 3203, Vostok Antarctic station. SQUARE. No. 3202, (145th anniv of Lazarev–Bellingshausen Expedition).

Nos. 3199/200 were issued together, se-tenant, forming a composite design.

1180 Basketball Players and Map of Europe

1965. European Basketball Championships, Moscow. Sheet 65×90 mm.

No.	Type	Description	Mint	Used
MS3204		1r. multicoloured	6·75	3·50

1181 Agricultural Academy

1965. Centenary of Academy of Agricultural Sciences, Moscow.

No.	Type	Description	Mint	Used
3205	**1181**	4k. violet, red and drab	30	15

1182 Lenin (after P. Vasilev)

1965. 48th Anniv of October Revolution. Sheet 64×95 mm.

No.	Type	Description	Mint	Used
MS3206		10k. black, red and silver	3·50	2·40

1183 N. Poussin (self-portrait)

1965. 300th Death Anniv of Nicolas Poussin (French painter).

No.	Type	Description	Mint	Used
3207	**1183**	4k. multicoloured	50	25

1184 Kremlin

1965. New Year.

No.	Type	Description	Mint	Used
3208	**1184**	4k. red, silver and black	50	15

1185 M. I. Kalinin

1966. 90th Birth Anniv of Kalinin (statesman).

No.	Type	Description	Mint	Used
3209	**1185**	4k. lake and red	40	10

1186 Klyuchevski Volcano

1965. Soviet Volcanoes. Multicoloured.

No.	Type	Description	Mint	Used
3210		4k. Type **1186**	40	15
3211		12k. Karumski Volcano (vert)	1·00	35
3212		16k. Koryaski Volcano	1·40	50

1187 Oktyabrskaya Station, Moscow

1965. Soviet Metro Stations.

No.	Type	Description	Mint	Used
3213	**1187**	6k. blue	50	15
3214	-	6k. brown	50	15
3215	-	6k. brown	50	15
3216	-	6k. green	50	15

STATIONS: No. 3214, Leninksy Prospekt, Moscow; 3215, Moscow Gate, Leningrad; 3216, Bolshevik Factory, Kiev.

1188 Common Buzzard

1965. Birds of Prey. Birds in black.

No.	Type	Description	Mint	Used
3217	**1188**	1k. grey	20	10
3218	-	2k. brown	30	10
3219	-	3k. olive	50	10
3220	-	4k. drab	60	15
3221	-	10k. brown	1·20	35
3222	-	12k. blue	1·50	45
3223	-	14k. blue	1·70	50
3224	-	16k. purple	1·90	50

BIRDS—VERT: 2k. Common kestrel; 3k. Tawny eagle; 4k. Red kite; 10k. Peregrine falcon; 16k. Gyr falcon. HORIZ: 12k. Golden eagle; 14k. Lammergeier.

1189 "Red Star" (medal) and Scenes of Odessa

1965. Heroic Soviet Towns. Multicoloured.

No.	Type	Description	Mint	Used
3225		10k. Type **1189**	60	30
3226		10k. Leningrad	60	30
3227		10k. Kiev	60	30
3228		10k. Moscow	60	30
3229		10k. Brest-Litovsk	60	30
3230		10k. Volgograd	60	30
3231		10k. Sevastopol	60	30

1190 Flag, Map and Parliament Building, Belgrade

1965. 20th Anniv of Yugoslavia Republic.

No.	Type	Description	Mint	Used
3232	**1190**	6k. multicoloured	80	20

1191 Tupolev Tu-134 Jetliner

1965. Soviet Civil Aviation. Multicoloured.

No.	Type	Description	Mint	Used
3233		6k. Type **1191**	70	15
3234		10k. Antonov An-24	95	25
3235		12k. Mil Mi-10 helicopter	1·20	35
3236		16k. Beriev Be-10 flying boat	1·60	45
3237		20k. Antonov An-22 Anteus	1·90	50

1192 "The Proposal of Marriage" (P. Fedotov, 150th birth anniv)

1965. Soviet Painters' Annivs.

No.	Type	Description	Mint	Used
3238	-	12k. black and red	1·70	45
3239	**1192**	16k. blue and red	2·75	60

DESIGN—VERT: 12k. "A Collective Farm Watchman" (S. Gerasimov, 80th birth anniv).

1193 Crystallography Congress Emblem

1966. International Congresses, Moscow.

No.	Type	Description	Mint	Used
3240	**1193**	6k. black, blue and bistre	40	15
3241	-	6k. black, red and blue	40	15
3242	-	6k. purple, grey & black	40	15
3243	-	6k. black and blue	40	15
3244	-	6k. black, red and yellow	40	15

CONGRESS EMBLEMS: No. 3241, Microbiology; 3242, Poultry-raising; 3243, Oceanography; 3244, Mathematics.

1194 Postman and Milkmaid (19th-century statuettes, des A. Venetsianov)

1966. Bicentenary of Dmitrov Ceramic Works. Multicoloured.

No.	Type	Description	Mint	Used
3245		6k. Type **1194**	40	15
3246		10k. Modern tea set	70	35

1195 Rolland (after A. Yar-Kravchenko)

1966. Birth Centenary of Romain Rolland (French writer) and 150th Birth Anniv of Eugene Potier (French poet).

No.	Type	Description	Mint	Used
3247	**1195**	4k. brown and blue	40	15
3248	-	4k. brown, red and black	40	15

DESIGN: No. 3248, Potier and revolutionary scene.

1196 Mongol Horseman

1966. 20th Anniv of Soviet–Mongolian Treaty.

No.	Type	Description	Mint	Used
3249	**1196**	4k. multicoloured	40	15

„ЛУНА-9"—НА ЛУНЕ!
3.2.1966

(1197)

1966. Landing of "Luna 9" Rocket on Moon. Optd with T 1197.

No.	Type	Description	Mint	Used
3250	**1017**	6k. red, black and blue	6·25	6·00

1198 Supply Ship "Ob"

1966. 10th Anniv of Soviet Antarctic Expedition.

No.	Type	Description	Mint	Used
3251	**1198**	10k. lake and silver	3·00	1·70
3252	-	10k. lake, silver and blue	3·00	1·70
3253	-	10k. lake, silver and blue	3·00	1·70

DESIGNS—TRIANGULAR: No. 3252, Snow vehicle. DIAMOND: No. 3253, Antarctic map. This stamp is partly perf across the centre.

1199 Mussa Dyalil and Scene from Poem

1966. Writers.

No.	Type	Description	Mint	Used
3254	**1199**	4k. black and brown	40	10
3255	-	4k. black and green	40	10
3256	-	4k. black and green	40	10

WRITERS: No. 3254 (Azerbaijan writer: 60th birth anniv); 3255, Akob Akopyan (Armenian poet: birth cent); 3256, Djalil Mamedkulizade (Azerbaijan writer: birth cent).

1200 Lenin (after bust by Kibalnikov)

1966. Lenin's 96th Birth Anniv.

3257	**1200**	10k. gold and green	1·30	50
3258	**1200**	10k. silver and red	1·30	50

1201 N. Ilin

1966. War Heroes.

3259	**1201**	4k. violet and red	30	15
3260	-	4k. lilac and blue	30	15
3261	-	4k. brown and green	30	15

PORTRAITS: No. 3260, G. P. Kravchenko; 3261, A. Uglovsky.

1202 Scene from "Alive and Dead" (dir. A. Stolper)

1966. Soviet Cinema Art.

3262	**1202**	4k. black, green and red	30	10
3263	-	10k. black and blue	65	25

DESIGN: 10k. Scene from "Hamlet" (dir. G. Kozintsev).

1203 Kremlin and Inscription

1966. 23rd Soviet Comunist Party Congress, Moscow (1st issue).

3264	**1203**	4k. gold, red and blue	40	10

See also Nos. 3337/41.

Учредительная конференция Всесоюзного общества филателистов. 1966

(1204)

1966. Philatelists All-Union Society Conference. No. 3198 optd with T 1204.

3265	16k. plum, red and grey	4·75	2·30

1205 Ice Skating

1966. 2nd People's Winter Spartakiad.

3266	**1205**	4k. blue, red and olive	40	10
3267	-	6k. red, lake and lilac	50	25
3268	-	10k. lake, red and blue	80	35

DESIGNS: Inscription emblem and 6k. Ice hockey; 10k. Skiing.

Nos. 3266/8 are each perf across the centre.

1206 Liner "Aleksandr Pushkin"

1966. Soviet Transport.

3269		4k. multicoloured	60	15
3270		6k. multicoloured	70	15
3271		10k. multicoloured	95	25
3272	**1206**	12k. multicoloured	1·10	30
3273	-	16k. multicoloured	1·20	35

DESIGNS—HORIZ: 4k. Electric train; 6k. Map of Lenin Volga–Baltic canal system; 16k. Silhouette of liner "Aleksandr Pushkin" on globe. VERT: 10k. Canal lock (Volga–Baltic canal).

Nos. 3271/3 commemorate the inauguration of Leningrad–Montreal Sea Service.

1207 Government Building, Frunze

1966. 40th Anniv of Kirgizia.

3274	**1207**	4k. red	40	10

1208 S. M. Kirov (80th Birth Anniv)

1966. Soviet Personalities.

3275	**1208**	4k. brown	40	10
3276	-	4k. green	40	10
3277	-	4k. violet	40	10

PORTRAITS: No. 3276, G. I. Ordzhonikidze (80th birth anniv); 3277, Ion Yakir (military commander, 70th birth anniv).

1209 Lenin

1966. 23rd Soviet Communist Party Congress, Moscow (2nd issue). Sheet 119×80 mm.

MS3278	50k. red, silver and lake	4·00	1·30

1210 A. Fersman (mineralogist)

1966. Soviet Scientists. Multicoloured. Colours of name panels below.

3279	**1210**	4k. blue	60	20
3280	-	4k. brown	60	20
3281	-	4k. violet	60	20
3282	-	4k. brown and blue	60	20

PORTRAITS: No. 3280, D. K. Zabolotnyi (micro-biologist); 3281, M. A. Shatelen (electrical engineer); 3282, O. Yu. Shmidt (arctic explorer).

„Луна-10"—XXIII съезду КПСС

(1211)

1966. Launching of "Luna 10". As No. 3284, but imperf, optd with T 1211.

3283	**1212**	10k. multicoloured	4·00	3·00

1212 Arrowheads, "Luna 9" and Orbit

1966. Cosmonautics Day. Multicoloured.

3284	10k. Type **1212**	60	25
3285	12k. Rocket launching and different orbit	65	30

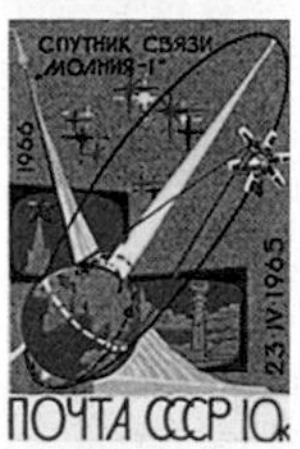

1213 "Molniya I" in Orbit

1966. Launching of "Molniya I" Telecommunications Satellite.

3286	**1213**	10k. multicoloured	80	35

1214 Ernst Thalmann (80th birth anniv)

1966. Prominent Leaders.

3287	**1214**	6k. red	60	15
3288	-	6k. violet	60	15
3289	-	6k. brown	60	15

PORTRAITS: No. 3288, Wilhelm Pieck (90th birth anniv); 3289, Sun Yat-sen (birth cent).

1216 Spaceman and Soldier

1966. 15th Young Communist League Congress.

3290	**1216**	4k. black and red	40	10

1217 Ice Hockey Player

1966. Soviet Victory in World Ice Hockey Championships.

3291	**1217**	10k. multicoloured	70	25

1218 N. I. Kuznetsov

1966. War Heroes. Guerrilla Fighters.

3292	**1218**	4k. black and green	30	10
3293	-	4k. black and yellow	30	10
3294	-	4k. black and blue	30	10
3295	-	4k. black and purple	30	10
3296	-	4k. black and violet	30	10

PORTRAITS: No. 3293, I. Y. Sudmalis; 3294, A. A. Morozova; No. 3295, F. E. Strelets; 3296, T. P. Bumazhkov.

1219 Tchaikovsky

1966. 3rd International Tchaikovsky Music Competition, Moscow.

3297		4k. black, red and yellow	50	10
3298	**1219**	6k. black, red and yellow	60	10
3299	-	16k. black, red and blue	1·40	45

DESIGNS: 4k. Moscow State Conservatoire of Music; 16k. Tchaikovsky's house and museum, Klin.

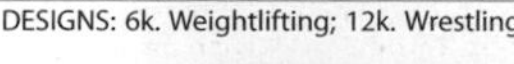

1220 Running

1966. Sports Events.

3300	**1220**	4k. brown, olive & green	30	20
3301	-	6k. black, bistre & orge	50	30
3302	-	12k. black, bistre & blue	70	40

DESIGNS: 6k. Weightlifting; 12k. Wrestling.

1222 Gold Medal and Chess Pieces

1966. World Chess Championship, Moscow.

3303	**1222**	6k. multicoloured	1·90	80

1223 Jules Rimet Cup and Football

1966. World Cup Football Championship (England) and World Fencing Championships (Moscow).

3304	**1223**	4k. black, gold and red	30	10
3305	-	6k. multicoloured	40	15
3306	-	12k. multicoloured	70	25
3307	-	16k. multicoloured	1·10	45

DESIGNS: 6k. Footballers; 12k. Fencers; 16k. Fencer and fencing emblems.

1224 Sable, Lake Baikal and Animals (image scaled to 60% of original size)

1966. Barguzin Nature Reserve.

3308	**1224**	4k. black and blue	80	35
3309	-	6k. black and purple	1·10	45

DESIGN: 6k. Map of reserve, and brown bear.

1225 Lotus Plants

1966. 125th Anniv of Sukhumi Botanical Gardens.

3310	**1225**	3k. red, yellow and green	30	10
3311	-	6k. bistre, brown & blue	50	15
3312	-	12k. red, green & turq	80	35

DESIGNS: 6k. Palms and cypresses; 12k. Water lilies.

1226 "Venus 3" Medal, Globe and Flight Trajectory

1966. Space Achievements.

3313	**1226**	6k. black, silver and red	60	25
3314	-	6k. deep blue, blue and brown	60	25
3315	-	6k. ochre and blue	60	25
3316	-	6k. multicoloured	60	25
3317	-	6k. pink, mauve & black	60	25

DESIGNS: No. 3314, Spacedogs, Ugolek and Veterok; 3315, "Luna 10"; 3316, "Molniya I"; 3317, "Luna 2's" pennant, Earth and Moon.

1227 Itkol

1966. Tourist Resorts. Multicoloured.

3318	1k. Type **1227**	10	10
3319	4k. Cruise ship on the Volga	30	10
3320	6k. Archway, Leningrad (27½×28 mm)	50	15
3321	10k. Castle, Kislovodsk	70	25
3322	12k. Ismail Samani Mausoleum, Bokhara	90	35
3323	16k. Kavkaz Hotel, Sochi (Black Sea)	1·30	45

1229 Fencing

1966. World Sports Championships of 1966. Sheet 155×155 mm comprising four 10k. stamps as T 1229.

MS3324	4×10k. multicoloured	8·75	3·50

DESIGNS: Type **1229**: Jules Rimet Cup (football); Chessmen; Ice Hockey.

1230 Congress Emblem

1966. 7th Consumers' Co-operative Societies Congress, Moscow.

3325	**1230**	4k. yellow and brown	50	15

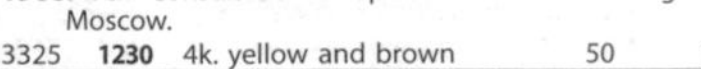

1231 Peace Dove and Japanese Crane

1966. Soviet–Japanese Meeting, Khabarovsk.

3326	**1231**	6k. black and red	60	25

1232 "Avtandil at a Mountain Spring", after engraving by S. Kabulazde

1233

1966. 800th Birth Anniv of Shota Rustaveli (Georgian poet).

3327	-	3k. black on green	40	10
3328	-	4k. brown on yellow	50	10
3329	**1232**	6k. black on blue	60	15
MS3330	98×68 mm. **1233**	50k. green and bistre	5·75	2·00

DESIGNS: 3k. Scene from poem "The Knight in the Tiger's Skin" (after I. Toidze); 4k. Rustaveli, (after bas-relief by Ya. Nikoladze).

1234 Arms, Moscow Skyline and Fireworks

1966. 49th Anniv of October Revolution.

3331	**1234**	4k. multicoloured	40	10

1235 Trawler, Net and Map of Lake Baikal

1966. Fish Resources of Lake Baikal. Mult.

3332	2k. Baikal grayling (horiz)	30	10
3333	4k. Baikal sturgeon (horiz)	30	20
3334	6k. Type **1235**	40	35
3335	10k. Omul (horiz)	70	50
3336	12k. Baikal whitefish (horiz)	90	60

1236 "Agriculture and Industry"

1966. 23rd Soviet Communist Party Congress, Moscow (3rd issue).

3337	**1236**	4k. silver and brown	30	15
3338	-	4k. silver and blue	30	15
3339	-	4k. silver and red	30	15
3340	-	4k. silver and red	30	15
3341	-	4k. silver and green	30	15

DESIGN (Map as Type **1236** with symbols of): No. 3338, "Communications and Transport"; 3339, "Education and Technology"; 3340, "Increased Productivity"; 3341, "Power Resources".

1237 Government Buildings, Kishinev

1966. 500th Anniv of Kishinev (Moldavian Republic).

3342	**1237**	4k. multicoloured	40	10

1238 Clouds, Rain and Decade Emblem

1966. International Hydrological Decade.

3343	**1238**	6k. multicoloured	50	25

1239 Nikitin Monument (S. Orlov and A. Zavalor), Kalinin

1966. 50th Anniv of Afanasy Nikitin's Voyage to India.

3344	**1239**	4k. black, green & yell	40	10

1240 Scene from "Nargiz" (Muslim Magomaev)

1966. Azerbaijan Operas.

3345	**1240**	4k. ochre and black	50	20
3346	-	4k. green and black	50	20

DESIGN: No. 3346, Scene from "Kehzoglu" (Uzeir Gadzhibekov).

1241 "Luna 9" and Moon

1242 Agricultural and Chemical Symbols

1966

3347		1k. brown	10	10
3348	**1241**	2k. violet	10	10
3349	-	3k. purple	20	10
3350	-	4k. red	20	10
3351	-	6k. blue	40	10
3563	-	10k. olive	1·10	45
3353	-	12k. brown	60	15
3354	-	16k. blue	80	25
3355	-	20k. red, blue and drab	95	35
3566	-	20k. red	1·80	80
3356	**1242**	30k. green	1·50	45
3357	-	50k. ultram, blue & grey	2·40	60
3568	-	50k. blue	6·00	1·40
3358	-	1r. black and red	5·00	1·50
3569	-	1r. brown and black	9·50	2·30

DESIGNS—As Type **1241**: 1k. Palace of Congresses, Kremlin; 3k. Youth, girl and Lenin emblem; 4k. Arms and hammer and sickle emblem; 6k. "Communications" (Antonov An-10A Ukrainia airplane and sputnik); 10k. Soldier and star emblem; 12k. Furnaceman; 16k. Girl with dove. As Type **1242**: 20k. Workers' demonstration and flower; 50k. "Postal communications"; 1r. Lenin and industrial emblems.

1243 "Presenting Arms"

1966. 25th Anniv of People's Voluntary Corps.

3359	**1243**	4k. brown and red	40	10

1245 Campaign Meeting

1966. "Hands off Vietnam".

3360	**1245**	6k. multicoloured	40	10

1246 Servicemen

1966. 30th Anniv of Spanish Civil War.

3361	**1246**	6k. black, red and ochre	50	10

1247 Ostankino TV Tower, "Molniya I" (satellite) and "1967"

1966. New Year and "50th Year of October Revolution".

3362	**1247**	4k. multicoloured	50	20

НОВЫЙ ЭТАП КОСМИЧЕСКОЙ ЭРЫ

1248 Flight Diagram (image scaled to 64% of original size)

1966. Space Flight and Moon Landing of "Luna 9".

3363	**1248**	10k. black and silver	80	35
3364	-	10k. red and silver	80	35
3365	-	10k. black and silver	80	35

DESIGNS—SQUARE (25×25 mm): No. 3364, Arms of Russia and lunar pennant. HORIZ: No. 3365, "Lunar 9" on Moon's surface.

1249 Statue, Tank and Medal

1966. 25th Anniv of Battle of Moscow.

3366		4k. brown	30	10
3367	**1249**	6k. ochre and sepia	40	15
3368	-	10k. yellow and brown	70	35

DESIGNS—HORIZ: (60×28 mm): 4k. Soviet troops advancing; 10k. "Moscow at peace"– Kremlin, Sun and "Defence of Moscow" medal.

1250 Cervantes and Don Quixote

1966. 350th Death Anniv of Cervantes.

3369	**1250**	6k. brown, green and deep green	50	15

1252 Bering's Ship "Sv. Pyotr" and Map of Komandor Islands

1966. Soviet Far Eastern Territories. Mult.

3370	1k. Type **1252**	30	10
3371	2k. Medny Island and map	40	15
3372	4k. Petropavlovsk Harbour, Kamchatka	60	25
3373	6k. Geyser, Kamchatka (vert)	70	35
3374	10k. Avatchinskaya Bay, Kamchatka	90	50
3375	12k. Northern fur seals, Bering Is	1·10	70
3376	16k. Common guillemot colony, Kurile Islands	2·40	85

1254 "The Lute Player" (Caravaggio)

1966. Art Treasures of the Hermitage Museum, Leningrad.

3377	-	4k. black on yellow	30	10
3378	-	6k. black on grey	50	15
3379	-	10k. black on lilac	70	25
3380	-	12k. black on green	95	25
3381	**1254**	16k. black on buff	1·20	40

DESIGNS—HORIZ: 4k. "Golden Stag" (from Scythian battle shield (6th cent B.C.). VERT: 6k. Persian silver jug (5th cent A.D.; 10k. Statue of Voltaire (Houdon, 1781); 12k. Malachite vase (Urals, 1840).

1255 Sea-water Distilling Apparatus

1967. World Fair, Montreal.

3382	**1255**	4k. black, silver & green	25	15
3383	-	6k. multicoloured	40	25
3384	-	10k. multicoloured	70	35
MS3385		127×76 mm. 30k. multicoloured	3·50	1·70

DESIGNS—VERT: 6k. "Atomic Energy" (explosion and symbol). HORIZ: 10k. Space station "Proton 1"; 30k. Soviet pavilion.

1256 Lieut. B. I. Sizov

1967. War Heroes.

3386	**1256**	4k. brown on yellow	50	15
3387	-	4k. brown on drab	50	15

DESIGN: No. 3387, Private V. V. Khodyrev.

1257 Woman's Face and Pavlov Shawl

1967. International Women's Day.

3388	**1257**	4k. red, violet and green	40	10

1258 Cine-camera and Film "Flower"

1967. 5th International Film Festival, Moscow.

3389	**1258**	6k. multicoloured	50	10

1259 Factory Ship "Cheryashevsky"

1967. Soviet Fishing Industry. Multicoloured.

3390	6k. Type **1259**	60	45
3391	6k. Refrigerated trawler	60	45
3392	6k. Crab canning ship	60	45
3393	6k. Trawler	60	45
3394	6k. Seine-fishing boat, Black Sea	60	45

1260 Newspaper Cuttings, Hammer and Sickle

1967. 50th Anniv of Newspaper "Izvestiya".

3395	**1260**	4k. multicoloured	40	10

1261 I.S.O. Congress Emblem

1967. Moscow Congresses.

3396	6k. turquoise, black and blue	40	10
3397	6k. red, black and blue	40	10

DESIGNS: No. 3396, Type **1261** (7th Congress of Int Standards Assn "I.S.O."); 3397, "V" emblem of 5th Int Mining Congress.

1262 I.T.Y. Emblem (image scaled to 74% of original size)

1967. International Tourist Year.

3398	**1262**	4k. black, silver and blue	40	10

Вена - 1967

(1263)

1967. Victory in World Ice Hockey Championship. No. 3291 optd with T 1263.

3399	**1217**	10k. multicoloured	3·00	1·90

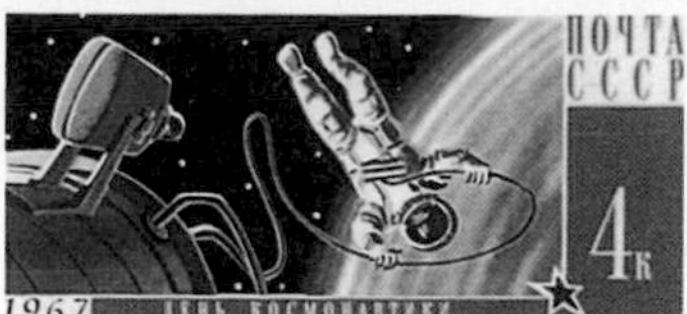

1264 A. A. Leonov in Space

1967. Cosmonautics Day. Multicoloured.

3400	4k. Type **1264**	40	10
3401	10k. Rocket and Earth	80	25
3402	16k. "Luna 10" over Moon	1·10	50

1265 "Lenin as Schoolboy" (V. Tsigal)

1967. Lenin's 97th Birth Anniv.

3403	**1265**	2k. brown, yellow & grn	30	10
3404	-	3k. brown and lake	50	15
3405	-	4k. green, yellow and olive	65	20
3406	-	6k. silver, black and blue	95	25
3407	-	10k. blue, black & silver	1·90	50
3408	-	10k. black and gold	80	35

SCULPTURES—VERT: 3k. Lenin's monument, Ulyanovsk; 6k. Bust of Lenin (G. and Yu. Neroda); 10k. (both) "Lenin as Leader" (N. Andreev). HORIZ: 4k. "Lenin at Razliv" (V. Pinchuk).

1266 M. F. Shmyrev

1967. War Heroes.

3409	**1266**	4k. sepia and brown	25	10
3410	-	4k. brown and blue	25	10
3411	-	4k. brown and violet	25	10

DESIGNS: No. 3410, Major-General S. V. Rudnev; 3411, First Lieut. M. S. Kharchenko.

1267 Transport crossing Ice on Lake Ladoga

1967. Siege of Leningrad, 1941–42.

3412	**1267**	4k. grey, red and cream	40	10

1268 Marshal Biryuzov

1967. Biryuzov Commemoration.

3413	**1268**	4k. green and yellow	40	10

1269 Minsk Old and New

1967. 900th Anniv of Minsk.

3414	**1269**	4k. green and black	40	10

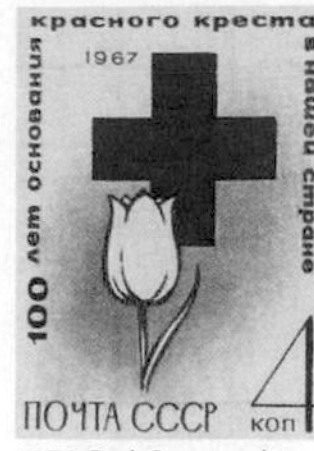

1270 Red Cross and Tulip

1967. Centenary of Russian Red Cross.

3415	**1270**	4k. red and ochre	50	15

1271 Russian Stamps of 1918 and 1967

1967. 50th Anniv of U.S.S.R. Philatelic Exn, Moscow.

3416	**1271**	20k. green and blue	1·60	70
MS3417		92×75 mm. **1271** 20k. green (pair). Imperf	5·75	1·70

1272 Komsomolsk-on-Amur and Map

1967. 35th Anniv of Komsomolsk-on-Amur.

3418	**1272**	4k. brown and red	60	15

1273 Motor Cyclist (International Motor Rally, Moscow)

1967. Sports and Pastimes. International Events.

3419	-	1k. brown, bistre & grn	25	10
3420	-	2k. brown	25	10
3421	-	3k. blue	25	10
3422	-	4k. turquoise	25	10
3423	-	6k. purple and bistre	40	10
3424	**1273**	10k. purple and lilac	90	35

DESIGNS AND EVENTS: 1k. Draughts board and players (World Draughts Championships); 2k. Throwing the javelin; 3k. Running; 4k. Long jumping (all preliminary events for Europa Cup Games); 6k. Gymnast (World Gymnastics Championships).

1274 "Sputnik 1" orbiting Globe (image scaled to 66% of original size)

1967. 10th Anniv of First Earth Satellite. Sheet 105×132 mm.

MS3425	30k. multicoloured	4·50	2·20

1275 G. D. Gai (soldier)

1967. Commander G. D. Gai Commemoration.

3426	**1275**	4k. black and red	40	10

1276 Games Emblem and Cup

1967. All Union Schoolchildren's Spartakiad.

3427	**1276**	4k. red, black and silver	30	10

1277 Spartakiad Emblem and Cup

1967. 4th People's Spartakiad.

3428	4k. black, red and silver	35	15
3429	4k. black, red and silver	35	15
3430	4k. black, red and silver	35	15
3431	4k. black, red and silver	35	15

DESIGNS: Each with Cup. No. 3428, Type **1277**; No. 3429, Gymnastics; 3430, Diving; 3431, Cycling.

1278 V. G. Klochkov (Soviet hero)

1967. Klochkov Commemoration.

3432	**1278**	4k. black and red	35	15

1279 Crest, Flag and Capital of Moldavia

АРМЯНСКАЯ ССР
ՀԱՅԿԱԿԱՆ ՍՍՀ

No. 3433

АЗЕРБАЙДЖАНСКАЯ ССР
АЗӘРБАЈҸАН ССР

No. 3434

БЕЛОРУССКАЯ ССР
БЕЛАРУСКАЯ ССР

No. 3435

ЭСТОНСКАЯ ССР
EESTI NSV

No. 3436

ГРУЗИНСКАЯ ССР
საქართველოს სსრ

No. 3437

КАЗАХСКАЯ ССР
ҚАЗАҚ ССР

No. 3438

КИРГИЗСКАЯ ССР
КЫРГЫЗ ССР

No. 3439

ЛАТВИЙСКАЯ ССР
LATVIJAS PSR

No. 3440

ЛИТОВСКАЯ ССР
LIETUVOS TSR

No. 3441

МОЛДАВСКАЯ ССР
РСС МОЛДОВЕНЯСКЭ

No. 3442

РОССИЙСКАЯ СОВЕТСКАЯ ФЕДЕРАТИВНАЯ СОЦИАЛИСТИЧЕСКАЯ РЕСПУБЛИКА

No. 3443

ТАДЖИКСКАЯ ССР
РСС ТОҶИКИСТОН

No. 3444

ТУРКМЕНСКАЯ ССР
ТYРКМЕНИСТАН ССР

No. 3445

No. 3446

УЗБЕКСКАЯ ССР
ЎЗБЕКИСТОН ССР

No. 3447

1967. 50th Anniv of October Revolution (1st issue). Designs showing crests, flags and capitals of the Soviet Republics. Multicoloured.

3433	4k. Armenia	25	15
3434	4k. Azerbaijan	25	15
3435	4k. Belorussia	25	15
3436	4k. Estonia	25	15
3437	4k. Georgia	25	15
3438	4k. Kazakhstan	25	15
3439	4k. Kirgizia	25	15
3440	4k. Latvia	25	15
3441	4k. Lithuania	25	15
3442	4k. Type **1279**	25	15
3443	4k. Russia	25	15
3444	4k. Tadjikistan	25	15
3445	4k. Turkmenistan	25	15
3446	4k. Ukraine	25	15
3447	4k. Uzbekistan	25	15
3448	4k. Soviet Arms	25	15

No. 3448 is size 47×32 mm.
See also Nos. 3473/82.

1280 Telecommunications Symbols

1967. "Progress of Communism".

3449	**1280**	4k. red, purple and silver	3·50	2·00

1281 Manchurian Crane and Dove

1967. Soviet–Japanese Friendship.

3450	**1281**	16k. brown, black & red	1·10	45

1282 Karl Marx and Title Page

1967. Centenary of Karl Marx's "Das Kapital".

3451	**1282**	4k. brown and red	40	10

1283 Arctic Fox

1967. Fur-bearing Animals.

3452	**1283**	2k. blue, black & brown	20	10
3453	-	4k. blue, black and drab	30	10
3454	-	6k. ochre, black & green	50	15
3455	-	10k. brown, black & grn	60	25
3456	-	12k. black, ochre & vio	80	35
3457	-	16k. brown, black & yell	95	45
3458	-	20k. brown, black & turq	1·30	60

DESIGNS—VERT: 4k. Red fox; 12k. Stoat; 16k. Sable. HORIZ: 6k. Red fox; 10k. Muskrat; 20k. European mink.

1284 Ice Skating

1967. Winter Olympic Games, Grenoble (1968). Multicoloured.

3459	2k. Type **1284**	20	10
3460	3k. Ski jumping	30	10
3461	4k. Games emblem (vert)	35	10
3462	10k. Ice hockey	70	25
3463	12k. Skiing	95	45

1285 Krasnodon Memorial

1967. 25th Anniv of Krasnodon Defence.

3464	**1285**	4k. black, yellow & pur	30	10

1285a Map and Snow Leopard (image scaled to 59% of original size)

1967. Cedar Valley Nature Reserve.

3465	**1285a**	10k. black and bistre	80	35

1286 Badge and Yakovlev Yak-9 Fighters

1967. 25th Anniv of French "Normandie-Niemen" Fighter Squadron.

3466	**1286**	6k. red, blue and gold	40	15

1287 Militiaman and Soviet Crest

1967. 50th Anniv of Soviet Militia.

3467	**1287**	4k. red and blue	40	10

1288 Cosmonauts in Space

1967. Space Fantasies. Multicoloured.

3468	4k. Type **1288**	30	10
3469	6k. Men on the Moon (horiz)	40	15
3470	10k. Cosmic vehicle	70	20
3471	12k. Planetary landscape (horiz)	80	30
3472	16k. Imaginary spacecraft	1·10	45

1289 Red Star and Soviet Crest (image scaled to 69% of original size)

1967. 50th Anniv of October Revolution (2nd issue). "50 Heroic Years". Designs showing paintings and Soviet Arms. Multicoloured.

3473	4k. Type **1289**	30	15
3474	4k. "Lenin addressing Congress" (Serov—1955)	30	15
3475	4k. "Lenin explaining the GOELRO map" (Schmatko—1957)	30	15
3476	4k. "The First Cavalry" (Grekov—1924)	30	15
3477	4k. "Students" (Yoganson—1928)	30	15
3478	4k. "People's Friendship" (Karpov—1924)	30	15
3479	4k. "Dawn of the Five Year Plan" (construction work, Romas—1934)	30	15
3480	4k. "Farmers' Holiday" (Gerasimov—1937)	30	15
3481	4k. "Victory in World War II" (Korolev—1965)	30	15
3482	4k. "Builders of Communism" (Merpert and Skripkov—1965)	30	15
MS3483	93×141 mm. 40k. (2) in designs of Nos. 3474, 3482, but smaller (60×28 mm) and colours changed	5·75	2·50

1290 S. Katayama

1967. Katayama (founder of Japanese Communist Party) Commemoration.

3484	**1290**	6k. green	30	10

1291 Hammer, Sickle and First Earth Satellite

1967. 50th Anniv of October Revolution (3rd issue). "Conquest of Space". Sheet 129×80 mm.

MS3485	1r. lake	7·75	3·50

1292 T.V. Tower, Moscow

1967. Opening of Ostankino T.V. Tower, Moscow.

3486	**1292**	16k. black, silver & orge	1·10	35

1293 Narva-Joesuu (Estonia)

1967. Baltic Health Resorts. Multicoloured.

3487	4k. Yurmala (Latvia)	20	10
3488	6k. Type **1293**	30	15
3489	10k. Druskininkai (Lithuania)	60	20
3490	12k. Zelenogradsk (Kaliningrad) (vert)	75	25
3491	16k. Svetlogorsk (Kaliningrad) (vert)	1·10	45

1294 K.G.B. Emblem

1967. 50th Anniv of State Security Commission (K.G.B.).

3492	**1294**	4k. red, silver and blue	40	10

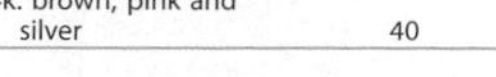

1295 Moscow View

1967. New Year.

3493	**1295**	4k. brown, pink and silver	40	10

1296 Revolutionaries at Kharkov, and Monument

1967. 50th Anniv of Ukraine Republic.

3494	**1296**	4k. multicoloured	30	10
3495	-	6k. multicoloured	50	15
3496	-	10k. multicoloured	70	20

DESIGNS: 6k. Hammer and sickle and industrial and agricultural scenes; 10k. Unknown Soldier's monument, Kiev, and young Ukrainians with welcoming bread and salt.

1297 Armoury, Commandant and Trinity Towers

1967. Kremlin Buildings.

3497	**1297**	4k. brown, purple & grn	25	10
3498	-	6k. brown, green & yell	35	15
3499	-	10k. brown and grey	60	20
3500	-	12k. green, violet and cream	85	35
3501	-	16k. brown, red and light brown	95	35

DESIGNS—HORIZ: 6k. Cathedral of the Annunciation. VERT: 10k. Konstantino-Yelenin, Alarm and Spassky Towers; 12k. Ivan the Great's bell tower; 16k. Kutafya and Trinity Towers.

1298 Moscow Badge, Lenin's Tomb and Rockets

1967. "50 Years of Communist Development".

3502	**1298**	4k. lake	40	25
3503	-	4k. brown	40	25
3504	-	4k. green	40	25
3505	-	4k. blue	40	25
3506	-	4k. blue	40	25

DESIGNS—HORIZ: No. 3503, Computer-tape cogwheel and industrial scene; 3504, Ear of wheat and grain silo; 3505, Microscope, radar antennae and Moscow University. VERT: No. 3506, T.V. Tower, "Aleksandr Pushkin" (liner), railway bridge and jet airliner.

1299 Unknown Soldier's Tomb, Kremlin

1967. "Unknown Soldier" Commemoration.

3507	**1299**	4k. red	40	10

1300 "The Interrogation of Communists" (B. Ioganson)

1967. Paintings in the Tretyakov Gallery, Moscow. Multicoloured.

3508		3k. Type **1300**	20	10
3509		4k. "The Sea-shore" (I. Aivazovsky)	30	10
3510		4k. "The Lace Maker" (V. Tropinin) (vert)	30	10
3511		6k. "The Bakery" (T. Yablonskaya) (60×34 mm)	50	15
3512		6k. "Aleksandr Nevsky" (part of triptych by P. Korin) (34×60 mm)	50	15
3513		6k. "Boyarynya Morozova" (V. Surikov) (60×34 mm)	50	15
3514		10k. "The Swan Maiden" (M. Vrubel) (vert)	1·00	35
3515		10k. "The Arrest of a Propagandist" (I. Repin)	1·00	35
3516		16k. "Moscow Suburb in February" (G. Nissky)	2·00	55

1301 Congress Emblem

1968. 14th Soviet Trade Unions Congress, Moscow.

3517	**1301**	6k. red and green	40	10

1302 Lieut. S. G. Baikov

1968. War Heroes.

3518	**1302**	4k. black and blue	30	10
3519	-	4k. blue and green	30	10
3520	-	4k. black and red	30	10

PORTRAITS: No. 3519, Lieut. P. L. Guchenko; No. 3520, A. A. Pokaltchuk.

1303 Racehorses

1968. Soviet Horse Breeding.

3521	**1303**	4k. black, purple & blue	30	25
3522	-	6k. black, blue and red	40	35
3523	-	10k. black, brn & turq	70	55
3524	-	12k. black, green & brn	80	65
3525	-	16k. black, red and green	1·10	90

DESIGNS (each with horse's head and horses "in the field"). VERT: 6k. Show horses; 12k. Show jumpers. HORIZ: 10k. Trotters; 16k. Hunters.

1304 M. Ulyanova

1968. 90th Birth Anniv of M. I. Ulyanova (Lenin's sister).

3526	**1304**	4k. blue and green	40	10

1305 Red Star and Forces' Flags

1968. 50th Anniv of Soviet Armed Forces. Multicoloured.

3527		4k. Type **1305**	35	15
3528		4k. Lenin addressing recruits (horiz)	35	15
3529		4k. Recruiting poster (D. Moor) and volunteers (horiz)	35	15
3530		4k. Red Army entering Vladivostok, 1922, and monument (L. Shervud) (horiz)	35	15
3531		4k. Dnieper Dam and statue "On Guard" (horiz)	35	15
3532		4k. "Liberators" poster (V. Ivanov) and tanks in the Ukraine (horiz)	35	15
3533		4k. "To the East" poster and retreating Germans fording river (horiz)	35	15
3534		4k. Stalingrad battle monument and German prisoners-of-war	35	15
3535		4k. Victory parade, Red Square, Moscow, and monument, Treptow (Berlin) (horiz)	35	15
3536		4k. Rockets, tank, warships and Red Flag	35	15
MS3537		73×100 mm. 1r. Design as No. 3536 but smaller. Imperf	6·00	3·25

1306 Gorky (after Serov)

1968. Birth Centenary of Maksim Gorky (writer).

3538	**1306**	4k. brown and drab	40	10

1307 Fireman and Appliances

1968. 50th Anniv of Soviet Fire Services.

3539	**1307**	4k. black and red	35	10

1308 Linked Satellites

1968. Space Link of "Cosmos" Satellites.

3540	**1308**	6k. black, gold & purple	40	10

1309 N. N. Popudrenko

1968. War Heroes.

3541	**1309**	4k. black and green	30	10
3542	-	4k. black and lilac	30	10

DESIGN: No. 3542, P. P. Vershigora.

1310 Protective Hand

1968. "Solidarity with Vietnam".

3543	**1310**	6k. multicoloured	45	20

1311 Leonov filming in Space

1968. Cosmonautics Day. Multicoloured.

3544		4k. Type **1311**	50	25
3545		6k. "Kosmos 186" and "Kosmos 188" linking in space	70	35
3546		10k. "Venera 4" space probe	1·10	65

1312 Lenin

1968. Lenin's 98th Birth Anniv.

3547	**1312**	4k. multicoloured	1·00	35
3548	-	4k. black, red and gold	1·00	35
3549	-	4k. brown, red and gold	1·00	35

DESIGNS: No. 3548, Lenin speaking in Red Square; No. 3549, Lenin in peaked cap speaking from lorry during parade.

1313 Navoi (after V. Kaidalov)

1968. 525th Birth Anniv of Alisher Navoi (Uzbek poet).

3550	**1313**	4k. brown	40	10

1314 Karl Marx

1968. 150th Birth Anniv of Karl Marx.

3551	**1314**	4k. black and red	45	10

1315 Frontier Guard

1968. 50th Anniv of Soviet Frontier Guards. Multicoloured.

3552		4k. Type **1315**	35	10
3553		6k. Jubilee badge	50	15

1316 Gem and Congress Emblem

1968. "International Congresses and Assemblies".

3554	**1316**	6k. deep blue, blue and green	40	20
3555	-	6k. gold, orange & brn	40	20
3556	-	6k. gold, black and red	40	20
3557	-	6k. orange, black & mve	40	20

DESIGNS: No. 3554, Type **1316** (8th Enriched Minerals Congress); 3555, Power stations, pylon and emblem (7th World Power Conference); 3556, "Carabus schaenherri" (ground beetle) and emblem (13th Entomological Congress); 3557, Roses and emblem (4th Congress on Volatile Oils).

1317 S. Aini

1968. 90th Birth Anniv of Sadriddin Aini (Tadzhik writer).

3570	**1317**	4k. purple and bistre	40	10

1318 Congress Emblem and Postrider

1968. Meeting of U.P.U. Consultative Commission, Moscow.

3571	**1318**	6k. red and grey	45	25
3572	-	6k. red and yellow	45	25

DESIGN: No. 3572, Emblem and transport.

1319 "Kiev Uprising" (after V. Boroday)

1968. 50th Anniv of Ukraine Communist Party.

3573	**1319**	4k. red, purple and gold	30	10

1320 Athletes and "50"

1968. Young Communist League's 50th Anniv Games.

3574	**1320**	4k. red, drab and yellow	35	10

1321 Handball

1968. Various Sports Events.

3575	**1321**	2k. multicoloured	20	10
3576	-	4k. multicoloured	30	15
3577	-	6k. multicoloured	45	25
3578	-	10k. red, black & bistre	60	30
3579	-	12k. multicoloured	90	40

DESIGNS AND EVENTS—VERT: Type **1321** (World Handball Games, Moscow); 6k. Yachting (20th Baltic Regatta); 10k. Football (70th anniv of Russian soccer). HORIZ: 4k. Table tennis (All European Juvenile Competitions); 12k. Underwater swimming (European Underwater Sports Championships, Alushta, Ukraine).

1322 Girl Gymnasts

1968. Olympic Games, Mexico. Backgrounds in gold.

3580	**1322**	4k. turquoise and blue	20	10
3581	-	6k. violet and red	30	15
3582	-	10k. green and turquoise	60	25
3583	-	12k. brown and orange	75	30
3584	-	16k. blue and pink	1·00	40
MS3585		90×65 mm. 40k. multicoloured	2·50	1·50

DESIGNS: 6k. Weightlifting; 10k. Rowing; 12k. Women's hurdles; 16k. Fencing match; 40k. Running.

1323 Gediminas Tower, Vilnius (Vilna)

1968. 50th Anniv of Soviet Lithuania.

3586	**1323**	4k. red, drab and purple	40	10

1324 Tbilisi University

1968. 50th Anniv of Tbilisi University.

3587	**1324**	4k. beige and green	35	10

1325 "Death of Laocoon and his Sons" (from sculpture by Agesandre, Polidor and Asinodor)

1968. "Promote Solidarity with the Greek Democrats".

3588	**1325**	6k. drab, purple & brn	5·50	4·50

1326 Cavalryman

1968. 50th Anniv of Leninist Young Communist League (Komsomol) (1st issue). Multicoloured.

3589		2k. Type **1326**	10	10
3590		3k. Young workers	20	10
3591		4k. Army officer	25	15
3592		6k. Construction workers	30	20
3593		10k. Agricultural workers	50	25
MS3594		78×101 mm. 50k. Type **1326**. Imperf	4·00	1·80

See also No. 3654.

1327 Institute and Molecular Structure

1968. 50th Anniv of N. S. Kurnakov Institute of Chemistry.

3595	**1327**	4k. purple, black and blue	30	10

1328 Letter

1968. Int Correspondence Week and Stamp Day.

3596	**1328**	4k. brown, red and lake	25	10
3597	-	4k. blue, ochre and deep blue	25	10

DESIGN: No. 3597, Russian stamps.

1329 "The 26 Baku Commissars" (statue, S. Merkurov)

1968. 50th Anniv of Execution of 26 Baku Commissars.

3598	**1329**	4k. multicoloured	30	10

1330 T. Antikainen

1968. 70th Birthday of Toivo Antikainen (Finnish Communist leader).

3599	**1330**	6k. brown and grey	35	10

1331 Liner "Ivan Franko"

1968. Soviet Merchant Marine.

3600	**1331**	6k. red, dp blue & blue	40	10

1332 Order of the October Revolution

1968. 51st Anniv of October Revolution.

3601	**1332**	4k. multicoloured	30	10

1333 P. P. Postyshev (1887–1940)

1968. Soviet Personalities.

3602	**1333**	4k. black	35	10
3603	-	4k. black	35	10
3604	-	4k. black	35	10

DESIGNS: No. 3603, S. G. Shaumian (1878–1918); 3604, A. Ikramov (1898–1938).

1334 Statuette of Warrior and Ararat Mountains

1968. 2,750th Anniv of Yerevan (Armenian capital).

3605	**1334**	4k. blk & brn on grey	30	10
3606	-	12k. brn & sepia on yell	70	35

DESIGN: 12k. David Sasunsky Monument (Ye. Kochar).

1335 I. S. Turgenev

1968. 150th Birth Anniv of Ivan Turgenev (writer).

3607	**1335**	4k. green	30	10

1336 American Bison and Common Zebra

1968. Fauna. Soviet Wildlife Reservations. Mult.

3608		4k. Type **1336**	50	10
3609		4k. Purple swamphen and lotus	50	10
3610		6k. Great egrets (vert)	60	20
3611		6k. Ostrich and golden pheasant (vert)	60	20
3612		10k. Eland and guanaco	90	35
3613		10k. Glossy ibis and white spoonbill	90	35

1337 Building and Equipment

1968. 50th Anniv of Lenin Radio-laboratory, Gorky.

3614	**1337**	4k. blue and ochre	30	10

1338 Prospecting for Minerals

1968. Geology Day. Multicoloured.

3615		4k. Type **1338**	40	15
3616		6k. "Tracking down" metals	40	25
3617		10k. Oil derrick	85	25

1339 Djety-Oguz Kirgizia

1968. Central Asian Spas. Multicoloured.

3618		4k. Type **1339**	30	15
3619		4k. Borovoe, Kazakhstan (horiz)	30	15
3620		6k. Issyk-kul, Kirgizia (horiz)	40	20
3621		6k. Borovoe, Kazakhstan	40	20

1340 Silver Medal, "Philatec", Paris 1964

1968. Awards to Soviet Post Office at Foreign Stamp Exhibitions.

3622		4k. black, silver and purple	30	10
3623		6k. black, gold and blue	50	15
3624		10k. black, gold and blue	60	25
3625		12k. black, silver & turquoise	80	30
3626		16k. black, gold and red	90	45
3627		20k. black, gold and blue	1·00	55
3628		30k. black, gold and brown	1·30	80

DESIGNS: 4k. Type **1340**; 6k. Plaque, "Debria", Berlin, 1959; 10k. Cup and medals, Riccione, 1952, 1968; 12k. Diploma and medal, "Thematic Biennale", Buenos Aires, 1965; 16k. Trophies and medals, Rome, 1952, 1954; 20k. Medals and plaques, "Wipa", Vienna, 1966; 30k. Glass trophies, Prague, 1950, 1955, 1962.

1341 V. K. Lebedinsky

1968. Birth Centenary of Lebedinsky (physicist).

3629	**1341**	4k. multicoloured	40	10

1342 Soldier with Flag

1968. 50th Anniv of Estonian Workers' Commune.

3630	**1342**	4k. black and red	30	10

1343 TV Satellite and Receiving Stations

1968. Satellite TV Transmissions. T 1343 and similar square designs. Multicoloured.

MS3631		96×76 mm. 16k.×3 (a) Type **1343**; (b) TV satellite; (c) Receiving station	6·00	2·30

1344 Moscow Buildings and Fir Branch

1968. New Year.

3632	**1344**	4k. multicoloured	45	15

1345 G. Beregovoi (cosmonaut)

1968. Flight of "Soyuz 3".

3633	**1345**	10k. black, red and blue	70	35

1346 Electric Train, Map and Emblem

1968. Soviet Railways.

3634	**1346**	4k. orange and mauve	30	15
3635	-	10k. brown and green	80	35

DESIGN: 10k. Track-laying train.

1347 Red Flag, Newspapers and Monument at Minsk

1968. 50th Anniv of Byelorussian Communist Party.

3636	**1347**	4k. black, brown and red	30	10

1348 "The Reapers" (A. Venetsianov)

1968. Paintings in State Museum, Leningrad. Mult.

3637		1k. Type **1348**	20	10
3638		2k. "The Last Days of Pompeii" (K. Bryullov) (61×28 mm)	40	10
3639		3k. "A Knight at the Crossroads" (V. Vasentsov) (61×28 mm)	50	15
3640		4k. "Conquering a Town in Winter" (V. Surikov) (61×28 mm)	70	20
3641		6k. "The Lake" (I. Levitan) (61×28 mm)	85	25
3642		10k. "The Year 1919: Alarm" (K. Petrov-Vodkin)	1·00	25
3643		16k. "The Defence of Sevastopol" (A. Deineka) (61×28 mm)	1·30	30
3644		20k. "Homer's Bust (G. Korzhev)	1·50	35
3645		30k. "The Celebration in Uritsky Square" (B. Kustodiev) (61×28 mm)	2·00	55
3646		50k. "The Duel between Peresvet and Chelumbei" (M. Avilov) (61×28 mm)	3·50	90

1349 House, Onega Region

1968. Soviet Architecture.

3647	**1349**	3k. brown on buff	30	10
3648	-	4k. green on yellow	40	20
3649	-	6k. violet on grey	70	25
3650	-	10k. blue on green	1·00	35
3651	-	12k. red on drab	1·30	65
3652	-	16k. black on yellow	1·50	90

DESIGNS: 4k. Farmhouse door, Gorky region; 6k. Wooden church, Kishi; 10k. Citadel, Rostov-Yaroslavl; 12k. Entrance gate, Tsaritzino; 16k. Master-builder Rossi's Street, Leningrad.

1968. 50th Death Anniv of N. G. Markin (1893–1918) (revolutionary). As T 1333.

3653		4k. black	30	10

1350 Flags and Order of October Revolution

1968. 50th Anniv of Leninist Young Communist League (Komsomol) (2nd issue).

3654	**1350**	12k. multicoloured	60	25

1351 "Declaration of Republic"

1969. 50th Anniv of Belorussian Republic. Mult.

3655		2k. Type **1351**	15	10
3656		4k. Partisans at war, 1941–45	30	20
3657		6k. Reconstruction workers	40	25

1352 Red Guard in Riga (statue)

1969. 50th Anniv of Soviet Revolution in Latvia.

3658	**1352**	4k. red and orange	30	10

1353 Cosmonauts Shatalov, Volynov, Yeliseev and Khtunov

1969. Space Flights of "Soyuz 4" and "Soyuz 5". Sheet 95×68 mm.

MS3659		50k. brown and ochre	6·00	3·25

1354 University Buildings

1969. 150th Anniv of Leningrad University.

3660	**1354**	10k. black and lake	60	25

1355 Krylov (after K. Bryullov)

1969. Birth Bicent of Ivan Krylov (fabulist).

3661	**1355**	4k. multicoloured	30	10

1356 N. D. Filchenkov

1969. War Heroes.

3662	**1356**	4k. brown and red	30	10
3663	-	4k. brown and green	30	10

DESIGN: No. 3663, A. A. Kosmodemiansky.

1357 "The Wheel Turns Round Again" (sculpture, Zs. Kisfaludi-Strobl)

1969. 50th Anniv of 1st Hungarian Soviet Republic.

3664	**1357**	6k. black, red and green	30	10

1358 Crest and Symbols of Petro-chemical Industry

1969. 50th Anniv of Bashkir Autonomous Soviet Socialist Republic.

3665	**1358**	4k. multicoloured	25	10

1359 "Vostok 1" on Launching-pad

1969. Cosmonautics Day. Multicoloured.

3666		10k. Type **1359**	70	25
3667		10k. "Zond 5" in Lunar orbit (horiz)	70	25
3668		10k. Sergei Pavlovich Korolev (space scientist) (horiz)	70	25
MS3669		92×68 mm. 80k. "Soyuz 3" (horiz)	5·00	2·50

1360 Lenin University, Kazan

1969. Buildings connected with Lenin. Mult.

3670		4k. Type **1360**	30	15
3671		4k. Lenin Museum, Kuibyshev	30	15
3672		4k. Lenin Museum, Pskov	30	15
3673		4k. Lenin Museum, Shushenskaya	30	15
3674		4k. "Hay Hut", Razliv	30	15
3675		4k. Lenin Museum, Gorky Park, Leningrad	30	15
3676		4k. Smolny Institute, Leningrad	30	15
3677		4k. Lenin's Office, Kremlin	30	15
3678		4k. Library, Ulyanovsk (wrongly inscr "Lenin Museum")	30	15
3679		4k. Lenin Museum, Ulyanovsk	30	15

1361 Telephone and Radio Set

1969. 50th Anniv of VEF Electrical Works, Riga.

3680	**1361**	10k. brown and red	60	25

1362 I.L.O. Emblem

1969. 50th Anniv of Int Labour Organization.

3681	**1362**	6k. gold and red	30	10

1363 Otakar Jaros

1969. Otakar Jaros (Czech war hero) Commem.

3682	**1363**	4k. black and blue	40	10

1364 P. E. Dybenko

1969. Soviet Personalities. 80th Birth Annivs.

3683	**1364**	4k. red	30	10
3684	-	4k. blue	30	10

DESIGN: No. 3684, S. V. Kosior (1889–1939).

1365 Suleiman Stalsky

1969. Birth Centenary of Suleiman Stalsky (Dagestan poet).

3685	**1365**	4k. green and brown	40	10

1366 Rose "Clear Glade"

1969. Academy of Sciences Botanical Gardens, Moscow. Multicoloured.

3686	2k. Type **1366**	20	10
3687	4k. Lily "Slender"	30	15
3688	10k. "Cattleya hybr" (orchid)	60	20
3689	12k. Dahlia "Leaves Fall"	70	25
3690	14k. Gladiolus "Ural Girl"	1·00	45

1367 Scientific Centre

1969. 50th Anniv of Ukraine Academy of Sciences, Kiev.

3691	**1367**	4k. purple and yellow	35	10

1368 Gold Medal within Film "Flower"

1969. Cine and Ballet Events, Moscow. Mult.

3692	6k. Type **1368** (6th Int Cinema Festival)	35	10
3693	6k. Ballet dancers (1st Int Ballet Competitions)	35	10

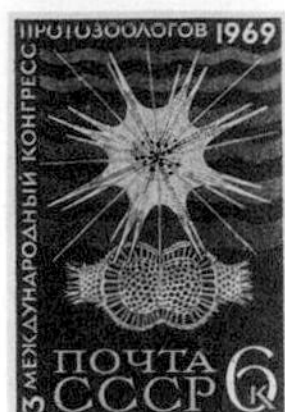

1369 Congress Emblem

1969. 3rd Int Protozoologists Congress, Leningrad.

3694	**1369**	6k. multicoloured	80	25

1370 Estonian Singer

1969. Centenary of Estonian Choir Festival.

3695	**1370**	4k. red and ochre	40	10

1371 Mendeleev (after N. Yarashenko) and Formula

1969. Centenary of Mendeleev's Periodic Law of Elements.

3696	**1371**	6k. brown and red	60	25
MS3697		76×104 mm. 30k. carmine	4·50	2·00

DESIGN: 30×41 mm. 30k. Dimtir Mendeleev (chemist).

1372 Peace Banner and World Landmarks

1969. 20th Anniv of World Peace Movement.

3698	**1372**	10k. multicoloured	40	25

1373 Rocket on Laser Beam, and Moon

1969. "50 Years of Soviet Inventions".

3699	**1373**	4k. red, black and silver	30	10

1374 Kotlyarevsky

1969. Birth Bicentenary of Ivan Kotlyarevsky (Ukrainian writer).

3700	**1374**	4k. black, brown & grn	30	10

Стокгольм. 1969

(1375)

1969. Soviet Ice Hockey Victory in World Championships, Stockholm. No. 2828 further optd with 1375.

3701	6k. turquoise and purple	4·00	2·75

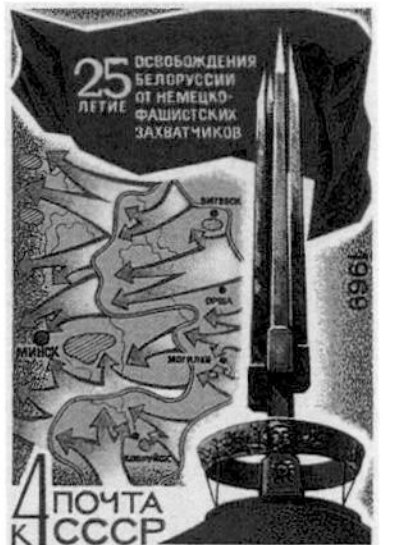

1376 War Memorial in Minsk (A. Bembel) and Campaign Map

1969. 25th Anniv of Belorussian Liberation.

3702	**1376**	4k. red, purple and olive	30	10

1377 Hands holding Torch, and Bulgarian Arms

1969. 25th Anniv of Bulgarian and Polish Peoples' Republics.

3703	**1377**	6k. multicoloured	35	10
3704	-	6k. red and ochre	35	10

DESIGN: No. 3704, Polish map, flag and arms.

1378 Registan Square, Samarkand

1969. 2,500th Anniv of Samarkand. Mult.

3705	4k. Type **1378**	40	10
3706	6k. Intourist Hotel, Samarkand	50	20

1379 Liberation Monument, Nikolaev

1969. 25th Anniv of Liberation of Nikolaev.

3707	**1379**	4k. red, violet and black	35	10

1380 Volleyball (European Junior Championships)

1969. International Sporting Events.

3708	**1380**	4k. red, brown & orange	30	10
3709	-	6k. multicoloured	45	10

DESIGN: 6k. Canoeing (European Championships).

1381 M. Munkacsy and detail of painting, "Peasant Woman churning Butter"

1969. 125th Birth Anniv of Mihaly Munkacsy (Hungarian painter).

3710	**1381**	6k. black, orange & brn	40	10

1382 Miners' Statue, Donetsk

1969. Centenary of Donetsk.

3711	**1382**	4k. mauve and grey	30	10

1383 "Horse-drawn Machine-guns" (M. Grekov)

1969. 50th Anniv of 1st Cavalry Army.

3712	**1383**	4k. brown and red	45	15

1384 Ilya Repin (self-portrait)

1969. 125th Birth Anniv of Ilya Repin (painter). Multicoloured.

3713	4k. "Barge-haulers on the Volga"	30	10
3714	6k. "Unexpected"	40	10
3715	10k. Type **1384**	60	20
3716	12k. "The Refusal of Confession"	80	25
3717	16k. "Dnieper Cossacks"	1·00	35

1385 Running

1969. 9th Trade Unions' Games, Moscow.

3718	1385	4k. black, green and red	20	10
3719	-	10k. black, blue & green	40	10
MS3720 70×95 mm. **1385** 20k. black, bistre and red. Imperf			2·00	90

DESIGN: 10k. Gymnastics.

1386 V. L. Komarov

1969. Birth Cent of V. L. Komarov (botanist).

3721	1386	4k. brown and olive	30	10

1387 O. Tumanyan and Landscape

1969. Birth Cent of O. Tumanyan (Armenian poet).

3722	1387	10k. black and blue	60	25

1388 Turkoman Drinking- horn (2nd-cent B.C.)

1969. Oriental Art Treasures, State Museum of Oriental Art, Moscow. Multicoloured.

3723	4k. Type **1388**	30	10
3724	6k. Simurg vessel, Persia (13th-century)	40	15
3725	12k. Statuette, Korea (8th-century)	60	20
3726	16k. Bodhisatva statuette, Tibet (7th-century)	80	35
3727	20k. Ebisu statuette, Japan (17th-century)	1·10	55

1389 Mahatma Gandhi

1969. Birth Centenary of Mahatma Gandhi.

3728	1389	6k. brown	60	20

1390 Black Stork at Nest

1969. Belovezhaskaya Pushcha Nature Reserve. Multicoloured.

3729	4k. Type **1390**	40	10
3730	6k. Red deer and fawn	50	20
3731	10k. European bison fighting	70	25
3732	12k. Lynx and cubs	80	35
3733	16k. Wild boar and young	1·00	45

No. 3731 is larger, 76×24 mm.

1391 "Komitas" and Rural Scene

1969. Birth Cent of "Komitas" (S. Sogomonyan, Armenian composer).

3734	1391	6k. black, flesh and grey	40	15

1392 Sergei Gritsevets (fighter-pilot)

1969. Soviet War Heroes.

3735	1392	4k. black and green	30	10
3736	-	4k. brown, red & yellow	30	10
3737	-	4k. brown and green	30	10

DESIGNS: As Type **1392**. No. 3737, Lisa Chaikina (partisan). (35½×24 mm); No. 3736, A. Cheponis, Y. Alexonis and G. Boris (Kaunas resistance fighters).

1393 I. Pavlov (after portrait by A. Yar-Kravchenko)

1969. 120th Birth Anniv of Ivan P. Pavlov (physiologist).

3738	1393	4k. multicoloured	30	10

1394 D.D.R. Arms and Berlin Landmarks

1969. 20th Anniv of German Democratic Republic.

3739	1394	6k. multicoloured	50	20

1395 A. V. Koltsov (from portrait by A. Yar-Kravchenko)

1969. 160th Birth Anniv of A. V. Koltsov (poet).

3740	1395	4k. brown and blue	30	10

1396 Arms of Ukraine and Memorial

1969. 25th Anniv of Ukraine Liberation.

3741	1396	4k. red and gold	40	15

1397 Kremlin, and Hammer and Sickle

1969. 52nd Anniv of October Revolution.

3742	1397	4k. multicoloured	30	10
MS3743 99×61 mm. 50k. gold, pink and red (40×30 mm)			3·50	1·50

1398 G. Shonin and V. Kubasov ("Soyuz 6")

1969. Triple Space Flights.

3744	1398	10k. green and gold	60	35
3745	-	10k. green and gold	60	35
3746	-	10k. green and gold	60	35

DESIGNS: No. 3745, A. Filipchenko, V. Volkov and V. Gorbatko ("Soyuz 7"); No. 3746, V. Shatalov and A. Yeliseev ("Soyuz 8").

1399 Lenin when a Youth (after V. Tsigal) and Emblems

1969. U.S.S.R. Youth Philatelic Exhibition to commemorate Lenin's Birth Centenary, Kiev.

3747	1399	4k. lake and pink	40	20

1400 Corps Emblem on Red Star

1969. 50th Anniv of Red Army Communications Corps.

3748	1400	4k. red, brown & bistre	30	15

1401 "Worker and Collective Farmer" (sculpture, Vera Mukhina) and Title-page

1969. 3rd Soviet Collective Farmers' Congress, Moscow.

3749	1401	4k. brown and gold	30	10

1402 "Vasilisa, the Beauty" (folk tale)

1969. Russian Fairy Tales. Multicoloured.

3750	4k. Type **1402**	40	30
3751	10k. "Maria Morevna" (folk tale)	90	65
3752	16k. "The Golden Cockerel" (Pushkin) (horiz)	1·30	70
3753	20k. "Finist, the Fine Fellow" (folk tale)	1·50	1·00
3754	50k. "Tale of the Tsar Saltan" (Pushkin)	3·00	2·00

1403 Venus Plaque and Radio-telescope

1969. Space Exploration.

3755	1403	4k. red, brown and black	40	10
3756	-	6k. purple, grey & black	50	20
3757	-	10k. multicoloured	80	45
MS3758 117×80 mm. 50k. (2) multicoloured. Imperf			6·00	3·25

DESIGNS: 6k. "Zond 7". Smaller (27×40 mm) 50k. (a) As 10k. (b) Close-up of Moon's surface taken by "Zond 6".

1404 Soviet and Afghan Flags

1969. 50th Anniv of U.S.S.R.–Afghanistan Diplomatic Relations.

3759	1404	6k. red, black and green	40	10

1405 Red Star and Arms

1969. Coil Stamp.

3760	1405	4k. red	2·00	1·50

1406 Mikoyan Gurevich MiG-3 and MiG-23 Fighters

1969. "30 Years of MiG Aircraft".

3761	1406	6k. black, grey and red	80	25

1407 Lenin

1969. New Year.

3762	1407	4k. multicoloured	30	10

1408 Tupolev ANT-2

1969. Development of Soviet Civil Aviation.

3763	1408	2k. multicoloured	20	10
3764	-	3k. multicoloured	25	10
3765	-	4k. multicoloured	25	10
3766	-	6k. black, red and purple	30	20
3767	-	10k. multicoloured	60	25
3768	-	12k. multicoloured	70	35
3769	-	16k. multicoloured	90	45
3770	-	20k. multicoloured	1·10	55
MS3771 92×66 mm. 50k. multicoloured			4·00	2·00

AIRCRAFT: 3k. Polikarpov Po-2; 4k. Tupolev ANT-9; 6k. TsA-GI 1-EA helicopter; 10k. Tupolev ANT-20 "Maksim Gorky"; 12k. Tupolev Tu-104; 16k. Mil Mi-10 helicopter; 20k. Ilyushin Il-62; 50k. Tupolev Tu-144.

1409 Model Gliders

1969. Technical Sports.
3772	**1409**	3k. purple	20	10
3773	-	4k. green	25	10
3774	-	6k. brown	35	10

DESIGNS: 4k. Speed boat racing; 6k. Parachuting.

1410 Rumanian Arms and Soviet Memorial, Bucharest

1969. 25th Anniv of Rumanian Liberation.
3775	**1410**	6k. red and brown	40	25

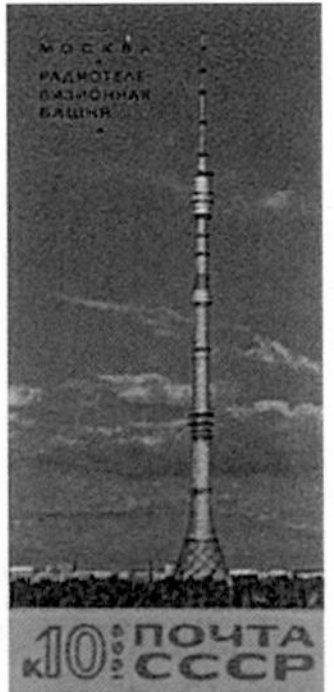

1411 TV Tower, Ostankino

1969. Television Tower, Ostankino, Moscow.
3776	**1411**	10k. multicoloured	50	25

1412 "Lenin" (after N. Andreev)

1970. Birth Centenary of V. I. Lenin (1st issue). Multicoloured.
3777	4k. Type **1412**	30	15
3778	4k. "Marxist Meeting, Petrograd" (A. Moravov)	30	15
3779	4k. "Second RSDRP Congress" (Yu. Vinogradov)	30	15
3780	4k. "First Day of Soviet Power" (N. Babasyak)	30	15
3781	4k. "Visiting Lenin" (F. Modorov)	30	15
3782	4k. "Conversation with Ilich" (A. Shirokov)	30	15
3783	4k. "May Day 1920" (I. Brodsky)	30	15
3784	4k. "With Lenin" (V. Serov)	30	15
3785	4k. "Conquerors of the Cosmos" (A. Deyineka)	30	15
3786	4k. "Communism Builders" (A. Korentsov, Ye. Merkulov, V. Burakov)	30	15

See also Nos. 3812/21.

1413 F. V. Sychkov and Painting "Tobogganing"

1970. Birth Centenary of F. V. Sychkov (artist).
3787	**1413**	4k. blue and brown	40	15

1414 "Vostok", "Mirnyi" and Antarctic Map

1970. 150th Anniv of Antarctic Expedition by Bellinghausen and Lazarev.
3788	**1414**	4k. turquoise, mauve & bl	75	25
3789	-	16k. red, green & purple	1·50	55

DESIGN: 16k. Modern polar-station and map.

1415 V. I. Peshekhonov

1970. Soviet War Heroes.
3790	**1415**	4k. purple and black	20	10
3791	-	4k. brown and olive	20	10

DESIGN: No. 3791, V. B. Borsoev (1906–1945).

1416 Geographical Society Emblem

1970. 125th Anniv of Russian Geographical Society.
3792	**1416**	6k. multicoloured	40	10

1417 "The Torch of Peace" (A. Dumpe)

1970. 60th Anniv of Int Women's Solidarity Day.
3793	**1417**	6k. drab and turquoise	40	10

1418 Ivan Bazhov (folk hero) and Crafts

1970. World Fair "Expo 70", Osaka, Japan.
3794	**1418**	4k. black, red and green	20	10
3795	-	6k. silver, red and black	35	15
3796	-	10k. multicoloured	50	25
MS3797		72×97 mm. 50k. red	3·50	1·80

DESIGNS: 6k. U.S.S.R. Pavilion; 10k. Boy and model toys; 50k. Lenin in cap.

1419 Lenin

1970. Lenin Birth Centenary. All-Union Philatelic Exhibition, Moscow.
3798	**1419**	4k. black, gold and red	30	10
MS3799		73×92 mm. **1419** 20k. gold, red and black. Imperf	£130	70·00

1420 Friendship Tree

1970. Friendship Tree, Sochi.
3800	**1420**	10k. multicoloured	60	35

1421 Ice Hockey Players

1970. World Ice Hockey Championships, Stockholm, Sweden.
3801	**1421**	6k. green and blue	60	20

1422 Hammer, Sickle and Azerbaijan Emblems

1970. 50th Anniv of Soviet Republics.
3802	**1422**	4k. red and gold	30	10
3803	-	4k. brown and silver	30	10
3804	-	4k. purple and gold	30	10

DESIGNS: No. 3803, Woman and motifs of Armenia; 3804, Woman and emblem of Kazakh Republic.

1423 Worker and Book

1970. UNESCO "Lenin Centenary" Symposium.
3805	**1423**	6k. ochre and lake	50	25

1424 D. N. Medvedev

1970. Partisan War Heroes.
3806	**1424**	4k. brown	30	10
3807	-	4k. brown	30	10

PORTRAIT: No. 3807, K. P. Orlovsky.

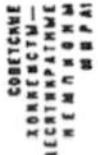
(1425)

1970. Russian Victory in World Ice Hockey Championships, Stockholm. No. 3801 optd with T 1425.
3808	**1421**	6k. green and blue	80	35

1426 Hungarian Arms and Budapest View

1970. 25th Anniv of Hungarian and Czech Liberation. Multicoloured.
3809	6k. Type **1426**	30	10
3810	6k. Czech Arms and Prague view	30	10

1427 Cosmonauts' Emblem

1970. Cosmonautics Day.
3811	**1427**	6k. multicoloured	30	10

1428 Lenin, 1891

1970. Birth Centenary of Lenin (2nd issue).
3812	**1428**	2k. green	10	10
3813	-	2k. olive	10	10
3814	-	4k. blue	20	10
3815	-	4k. lake	20	10
3816	-	6k. brown	40	10
3817	-	6k. lake	40	10
3818	-	10k. purple	55	25
3819	-	10k. brown	55	25
3820	-	12k. black and silver	60	30
3821	-	12k. red and gold	60	30
MS3822		66×102 mm. 20k. black and silver	4·00	1·80

PORTRAITS OF LENIN: No. 3813, In 1900; 3814, In 1914; 3815, In 1916; 3816, 3817, 3818, In 1918; 3819, In 1920; 3820, **MS**3822, Sculptured head by Yu. Kolesnikov; 3821, Sculptured head by N. Andreev.

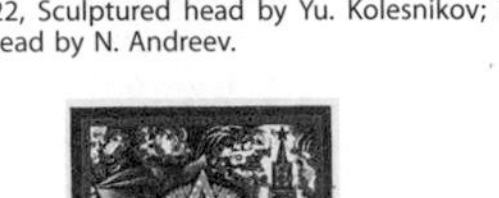

1429 Order of Victory

1970. 25th Anniv of Victory in Second World War.
3823	**1429**	1k. gold, grey and purple	10	10
3824	-	2k. purple, brn & gold	10	10
3825	-	3k. red, black and gold	20	10
3826	-	4k. red, brown and gold	25	10
3827	-	10k. gold, red & purple	60	30
MS3828		67×97 mm. **1429** 30k. gold, grey and red. Imperf	2·75	1·20

DESIGNS: 2k. Eternal Flame; 3k. Treptow Monument, Berlin; 4k. Home Defence Order; 10k. Hero of the Soviet Union and Hero of Socialist Labour medals.

1430 Komsomol Badge

1970. 16th Congress of Leninist Young Communist League (Komsomol).
3829	**1430**	4k. multicoloured	30	10

1431 Lenin (sculpture, Yu. Kolesnikov)

1970. World Youth Meeting for Lenin Birth Centenary.
3830	**1431**	6k. red	30	10

1432 "Young Workers" and Federation Emblem

1970. 25th Anniv of World Democratic Youth Federation.

3831	**1432**	6k. black and blue	40	10

1433 Arms and Government Building, Kazan

1970. 50th Anniv of Russian Federation Autonomous Soviet Socialist Republics.

3832	**1433**	4k. blue	40	15
3833	-	4k. green	40	15
3834	-	4k. red	40	15
3835	-	4k. brown	40	15
3836	-	4k. green	40	15
3837	-	4k. brown	40	15

DESIGNS: Arms and Government Buildings. No. 3832, (Tatar Republic); 3833, Petrozavodzk (Karelian Republic); 3834, Cheboksary (Chuvash Republic); 3835, Elista (Kalmyk Republic); 3836, Izhevsk (Udmurt Republic); 3837, Ioshkar-Ola (Mari Republic).

See also Nos. 3903/7, 4052/3, 4175, 4253, 4298, 4367 and 4955.

1434 Gymnast on Bar (World Championships, Yugoslavia)

1970. International Sporting Events.

3838	**1434**	10k. red and drab	55	25
3839	-	16k. brown and green	80	40

DESIGN: 16k. Three footballers (World Cup Championship, Mexico).

1435 "Swords into Ploughshares" (sculpture by E. Vuchetich)

1970. 25th Anniv of United Nations.

3840	**1435**	12k. purple and green	60	25

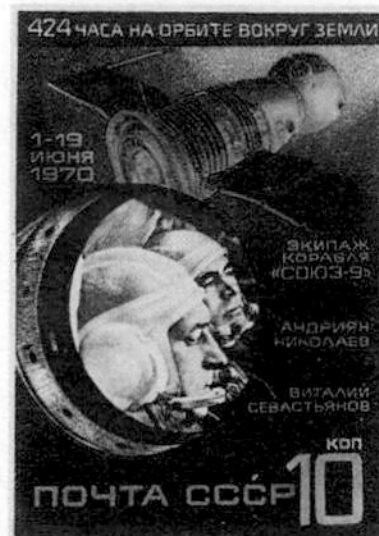

1436 Cosmonauts and "Soyuz 9"

1970. Space Flight by "Soyuz 9".

3841	**1436**	10k. black, red & purple	60	25

1437 Engels

1970. 150th Birth Anniv of Friedrich Engels.

3842	**1437**	4k. brown and red	30	15

1438 Cruiser "Aurora"

1970. Soviet Warships.

3843	**1438**	3k. pink, lilac and black	30	20
3844	-	4k. black and yellow	35	20
3845	-	10k. blue and mauve	85	45
3846	-	12k. brown and buff	1·10	55
3847	-	20k. purple, blue & turq	1·60	70

DESIGNS: 4k. Missile cruiser "Groznyi"; 10k. Cruiser "Oktyabrskaya Revolyutsiya"; 12k. Missile cruiser "Varyag"; 20k. Nuclear submarine "Leninsky Komsomol".

1439 Soviet and Polish Workers

1970. 25th Anniv of Soviet-Polish Friendship Treaty.

3848	**1439**	6k. red and blue	30	10

1440 Allegory of the Sciences

1970. 13th Int Historical Sciences Congress, Moscow.

3849	**1440**	4k. multicoloured	30	10

1441 Mandarins

1970. Fauna of Sikhote-Alin Nature Reserve. Multicoloured.

3850	4k. Type **1441**	40	20
3851	6k. Yellow-throated marten	40	20
3852	10k. Asiatic black bear (vert)	60	35
3853	16k. Red deer	1·00	55
3854	20k. Tiger	1·30	70

1442 Magnifying Glass, "Stamp" and Covers

1970. 2nd U.S.S.R. Philatelic Society Congress, Moscow.

3855	**1442**	4k. silver and red	30	10

1443 V. I. Kikvidze

1970. 75th Birth Anniv of V. J. Kikvidze (Civil War hero).

3856	**1443**	4k. brown	30	10

1444 University Building

1970. 50th Anniv of Yerevan University.

3857	**1444**	4k. red and blue	30	10

1445 Pioneer Badge

1970. Pioneer Organization.

3858	**1445**	1k. gold, red and grey	10	10
3859	-	2k. grey and brown	10	10
3860	-	4k. multicoloured	20	10

DESIGNS: 2k. "Lenin with Children" (sculpture, N. Scherbakov), 4k. Red Star and scarf.

1446 Library Book-plate (A. Kuchas)

1970. 400th Anniv of Vilnius (Vilna) University Library (Lithuania).

3861	**1446**	4k. black, grey and silver	30	10

1447 Woman with Bouquet

1970. 25th Anniv of International Democratic Women's Federation.

3862	**1447**	6k. brown and blue	30	10

1448 Milkmaid and Cows ("Livestock")

1970. Soviet Agriculture. Multicoloured.

3863	4k. Type **1448**	30	10
3864	4k. Driver, tractor and harvester ("Mechanization")	30	10
3865	4k. Lock-operator and canal ("Irrigation and Chemical Research")	30	10

1449 Lenin addressing Meeting

1970. 53rd Anniv of October Revolution.

3866	**1449**	4k. gold and red	30	10
MS3867		107×82 mm. **1449** 30k. gold and red	3·00	1·20

50 лет
ленинскому плану
ГОЭЛРО • 1970
(1450)

1970. 50th Anniv of GOELRO Electrification Plan. No. 3475 optd with T 1450.

3868	4k. multicoloured	1·00	55

1451 Spassky Tower, Kremlin

1970. New Year.

3869	**1451**	6k. multicoloured	30	10

1452 A. A. Baikov

1970. Birth Centenary of A. A. Baikov (metallurgic scientist).

3870	**1452**	4k. black and brown	30	10

1453 Tsyurupa (after A. Yar-Kravchenkol)

1970. Birth Centenary of A. D. Tsyurupa (Vice-Chairman of Soviet People's Commissars).

3871	**1453**	4k. brown and yellow	30	10

1454 St. Basil's Cathedral, Red Square, Moscow

1970. Tourism.

3872	**1454**	4k. multicoloured	20	10
3873	-	6k. blue, indigo & brown	40	10
3874	-	10k. brown and green	50	15
3875	-	12k. multicoloured	60	20
3876	-	14k. blue, red and brown	75	25
3877	-	16k. multicoloured	80	30

DESIGNS: 6k. Scene from ballet "Swan Lake" (Tchaikovsky); 10k. Sika deer; 12k. Souvenir handicrafts; 14k. "Swords into Ploughshares" (sculpture by Ye. Vuchetich); 16k. Tourist and camera.

1455 Camomile

1970. Flowers. Multicoloured.

3878		4k. Type **1455**	20	10
3879		6k. Dahlia	30	10
3880		10k. Phlox	50	15
3881		12k. Aster	70	25
3882		16k. Clematis	1·00	35

1456 African Woman and Child

1970. 10th Anniv of U.N. Declaration on Colonial Independence.

3883	**1456**	10k. brown and blue	60	25

1457 Beethoven

1970. Birth Bicentenary of Beethoven (composer).

3884	**1457**	10k. purple and pink	1·60	90

1458 "Luna 16" in Flight

1970. Flight of "Luna 16".

3885	**1458**	10k. green	50	20
3886	-	10k. purple	50	20
3887	-	10k. green	50	20

MS3888 100×76 mm. 20k.×3 as Nos. 3885/7 but change of colours 5·00 2·30

DESIGNS: No. 3886, "Luna 16" on Moon's surface; 3887, Parachute descent.

1459 Speed Skating

1970. Trade Unions' Winter Games (1971).

3889	**1459**	4k. blue, red and grey	20	10
3890	-	10k. green, brn & grey	60	25

DESIGN: 10k. Cross-country skiing.

1460 "The Conestabile Madonna" (Raphael)

1970. Foreign Paintings in Soviet Galleries. Mult.

3891		3k. Type **1460**	20	10
3892		4k. "Saints Peter and Paul" (El Greco)	30	10
3893		10k. "Perseus and Andromeda" (Rubens) (horiz)	50	20
3894		12k. "The Return of the Prodigal Son" (Rembrandt)	60	25
3895		16k. "Family Portrait" (Van Dyck)	85	25
3896		20k. "The Actress Jeanne Samary" (Renoir)	1·00	35
3897		30k. "Woman with Fruit" (Gauguin)	1·40	70

MS3898 73×101 mm. 50k. "Madonna Litte" (Leonardo da Vinci). Imperf 5·50 2·75

1461 Harry Pollitt and Freighter "Jolly George"

1970. 80th Birth Anniv of H. Pollitt (British Communist).

3899	**1461**	10k. brown and purple	40	20

1462 "75" Emblem

1970. 75th Anniv of Int Co-operative Alliance.

3900	**1462**	12k. red and green	60	25

1463 Sculptured Head of Lenin (A. Belostotsky and E. Fridman)

1971. 24th Soviet Union Communist Party Congress.

3901	**1463**	4k. red and gold	30	10

1464 "50", State Emblem and Flag

1971. 50th Anniv of Georgian Soviet Republic.

3902	**1464**	4k. multicoloured	30	10

1971. 50th Anniv of Autonomous Soviet Socialist Republics. Similar designs to T 1433, but dated "1971".

3903		4k. turquoise	40	15
3904		4k. red	40	15
3905		4k. red	40	15
3906		4k. blue	40	15
3907		4k. green	40	15

DESIGNS: No. 3903, Russian Federation Arms and Supreme Soviet building (Dagestan Republic); 3904, National emblem and symbols of agriculture and industry (Abkhazian Republic); 3905, Arms, produce and industry (Adjarian Republic); 3906, Arms and State building (Kabardino-Balkar Republic); 3907, Arms, industrial products and Government building (Komi Republic).

1465 Genua Fortress and Cranes

1971. 2500th Anniv of Feodosia (Crimean city).

3908	**1465**	10k. multicoloured	60	20

1466 Palace of Culture, Kiev

1971. 24th Ukraine Communist Party Congress, Kiev.

3909	**1466**	4k. multicoloured	30	10

1467 "Features of National Economy"

1971. 50th Anniv of Soviet State Planning Organization.

3910	**1467**	6k. red and brown	40	10

1468 N. Gubin, I. Chernykh and S. Kosinov (dive-bomber crew)

1971. Soviet Air Force Heroes.

3911	**1468**	4k. brown and green	30	10

1469 Gipsy Dance

1971. State Folk Dance Ensemble. Multicoloured.

3912		10k. Type **1469**	60	25
3913		10k. Russian "Summer" dance (women in circle)	60	25
3914		10k. Ukraine "Gopak" dance (dancer leaping)	60	25
3915		10k. Adjar "Khorumi" dance (with drummer)	60	25
3916		10k. "On the Ice" (ballet)	60	25

1470 L. Ukrainka

1971. Birth Centenary of Lesya Ukrainka (Ukrainian writer).

3917	**1470**	4k. red and brown	30	10

1471 "Luna 17" Module on Moon

1971. Soviet Moon Exploration.

3918	**1471**	10k. brown and violet	50	25
3919	-	12k. brown and blue	80	35
3920	-	12k. brown and blue	80	35
3921	-	16k. brown and violet	1·00	45

MS3922 91×69 mm. As Nos. 3918/21 but smaller 32½×21½ mm 4·00 1·80

DESIGNS: No. 3919, Control room and radio telescope; 3920, Moon trench; 3921, "Lunokhod 1" Moon-vehicle.

1472 Fighting at the Barricades

1971. Centenary of Paris Commune.

3923	**1472**	6k. black, brown and red	30	10

1473 Hammer, Sickle and Development Emblems

1971. 24th Soviet Communist Party Congress, Moscow.

3924	**1473**	6k. red, bistre & brown	30	10

1474 Gagarin Medal, Spaceships and Planets

1971. 10th Anniv of First Manned Space Flight (1st issue) and Cosmonautics Day.

3925	**1474**	10k. olive, yellow & brn	50	20
3926	-	12k. purple, blue & grey	60	25

DESIGN: 12k. Spaceship over Globe and economic symbols.

See also No. 3974.

1475 E. Birznieks-Upitis

1971. Birth Centenary of E. Birznieks-Upitis (Lithuanian writer).

3927	**1475**	4k. red and green	30	10

1476 Honey Bee on Flower

1971. 23rd Int Bee-keeping Congress, Moscow.

3928	**1476**	6k. multicoloured	40	20

1477 "Vostok 1"

1971. 10th Anniv of First Manned Space Flight (2nd issue). Sheet 94×77 mm containing horiz designs as T 1477.

MS3929	10k. purple, 12k. (2) green, 16k. purple	4·50	1·80

1478 Memorial Building

1971. Lenin Memorial Building, Ulyanovsk.

3930	**1478**	4k. olive and red	30	10

1479 Lieut-Col. N. I. Vlasov

1971. 26th Anniv of Victory in 2nd World War.

3931	**1479**	4k. brown and green	30	10

1480 Khafiz Shirazi

1971. 650th Birth Anniv of Khafiz Shirazi (Tadzhik writer).

3932	**1480**	4k. multicoloured	30	10

1481 "GAZ-66" Truck

1971. Soviet Motor Vehicles.

3933	**1481**	2k. multicoloured	20	10
3934	-	3k. multicoloured	20	10
3935	-	4k. blue, black and lilac	25	10
3936	-	4k. green, purple & drab	25	10
3937	-	10k. red, black and lilac	60	20

DESIGNS: 3k. "BelAZ-540" tipper truck; 4k. (3935) "Moskvitch-412" 4-door saloon; 4k. (3936) "Zaporozhets ZAZ-968" 2-door saloon; 10k. "Volga GAZ-24" saloon.

1482 Bogomolets (after A. Yar-Kravchenko)

1971. 90th Birth Anniv of A. A. Bogomolets (medical scientist).

3938	**1482**	4k. black, pink & orange	30	10

1483 Commemorative Scroll

1971. International Moscow Congresses.

3939	**1483**	6k. brown and green	35	10
3940	-	6k. multicoloured	35	10
3941	-	6k. multicoloured	35	10

DESIGNS AND EVENTS—HORIZ: No. 3939, (13th Science History Congress); 3940, Oil derrick and symbols (8th World Oil Congress). VERT: No. 3941, Satellite over globe (15th General Assembly of Geodesics and Geophysics Union).

1484 Sukhe Bator Statue, Ulan Bator

1971. 50th Anniv of Revolution in Mongolia.

3942	**1484**	6k. grey, gold and red	30	10

1485 Defence Monument (E. Guirbulis)

1971. 30th Anniv of Defence of Liepaja, Latvia.

3943	**1485**	4k. brown, black & grey	30	10

1486 Treaty Emblem

1971. 10th Anniv of Antarctic Treaty and 50th Anniv of Soviet Hydrometeorological Service.

3944	**1486**	6k. deep blue, black and blue	80	35
3945	-	10k. violet, black & red	1·10	45

DESIGN: 10k. Hydrometeorological map.

1487 "Motherland" (sculpture, Yu. Vuchetich)

1971. 20th Anniv of "Federation Internationale des Resistants".

3946	**1487**	6k. green and red	30	10

1488 Throwing the Discus

1971. 5th Summer Spartakiad.

3947	**1488**	3k. blue on pink	15	10
3948	-	4k. green on flesh	20	10
3949	-	6k. brown on green	30	15
3950	-	10k. purple on blue	60	25
3951	-	12k. brown on yellow	65	30

DESIGNS: 4k. Archery; 6k. Horse-riding (dressage); 10k. Basketball; 12k. Wrestling.

1489 "Benois Madonna" (Leonardo da Vinci)

1971. Foreign Paintings in Russian Museums. Multicoloured.

3952	2k. Type **1489**	10	10
3953	4k. "Mary Magdalene confesses her Sins" (Titian)	20	15
3954	10k. "The Washerwoman" (Chardin) (horiz)	50	25
3955	12k. "Young Man with Glove" (Hals)	60	35
3956	14k. "Tancred and Erminia" (Poussin) (horiz)	70	35
3957	16k. "Girl Fruit-seller" (Murillo)	80	45
3958	20k. "Child on Ball" (Picasso)	1·30	65

1490 Lenin Badge and Kazakh Flag

1971. 50th Anniv of Kazakh Communist Youth Assn.

3959	**1490**	4k. brown, red and blue	30	10

1491 Posthorn within Star

1971. International Correspondence Week.

3960	**1491**	4k. black, blue and green	30	10

1492 A. Spendiarov (Armenian composer) (after M. Saryan)

1971. Birth Anniversaries. Multicoloured.

3961	4k. Type **1492** (cent)	30	10
3962	4k. Nikolai Nekrasov (after I. Kramskoi) (poet, 150th anniv)	30	10
3963	10k. Fyodor Dostoevsky (after V. Perov) (writer, 150th anniv)	70	35

1493 Z. Paliashvili

1971. Birth Centenary of Z. Paliashvili (Georgian composer).

3964	**1493**	4k. brown	30	10

1494 Emblem, Gorky Kremlin and Hydrofoil

1971. 750th Anniv of Gorky (formerly Nizhnii-Novgorod) (1st issue).

3965	**1494**	16k. multicoloured	70	30

See also No. 3974.

1495 Students and Globe

1971. 25th Anniv of Int Students Federation.

3966	**1495**	6k. blue, red and brown	30	10

1496 Atlantic White-sided Dolphins

1971. Marine Fauna. Multicoloured.

3967	4k. Type **1496**	30	15
3968	6k. Sea otter	50	25
3969	10k. Narwhals	70	45
3970	12k. Walrus	80	55
3971	14k. Ribbon seals	1·30	70

1497 Star and Miners' Order

1971. 250th Anniv of Coal Discovery in Donetz Basin.

3972	**1497**	4k. red, brown and black	30	10

1498 Lord Rutherford and Atomic Formula

1971. Birth Cent of Lord Rutherford (physicist).

3973	**1498**	6k. brown and purple	40	15

1499 Statue of Maksim Gorky (Vera Mukhina) and View

1971. 750th Anniv of Gorky (formerly Nizhni-Novgorod) (2nd issue).

3974	**1499**	4k. multicoloured	30	10

1500 Santa Claus in Troika

1971. New Year.

3975	**1500**	10k. red, gold and black	50	25

1501 Workers and Marx Books ("International Socialist Solidarity") (image scaled to 68% of original size)

1971. 24th Soviet Union Communist Party Congress Resolutions.

3976	**1501**	4k. blue, ultram & red	30	15
3977	-	4k. red, yellow & brown	30	15
3978	-	4k. lilac, black and red	30	15
3979	-	4k. bistre, brown and red	30	15
3980	-	4k. red, green and yellow	30	15
MS3981		90×66 mm. 20k. vermilion, purple and green	2·50	90

DESIGNS: No. 3977, Farmworkers and wheatfield ("Agricultural Production"); 3978, Factory production line ("Increased Productivity"); 3979, Heavy industry ("Industrial Expansion"); 3980, Family in department store ("National Welfare"); (40×22 mm) 20k. Workers' demonstration.

1502 "Meeting" (V. Makovsky)

1971. Russian Paintings. Multicoloured.

3982	2k. Type **1502**	20	10
3983	4k. "Girl Student" (N. Yaroshenko)	30	10
3984	6k. "Woman Miner" (N. Kasatkin)	40	15
3985	10k. "Harvesters" (G. Myasoedov) (horiz)	60	20
3986	16k. "Country Road" (A. Savrasov)	90	35
3987	20k. "Pine Forest" (I. Shishkin) (horiz)	1·30	55
MS3988	94×68 mm. 50k. "Self-portrait" (I. Kramskoi) (31×43 mm)	3·00	1·40

See also Nos. 4064/70.

1503 V. V. Vorovsky

1971. Birth Centenary of V. V. Vorovsky (diplomat).

3989	**1503**	4k. brown	30	10

1504 Dobrovolsky, Volkov and Patsaev

1971. "Soyuz 11" Cosmonauts Commemoration.

3990	**1504**	4k. black, purple & orge	30	10

1505 Order of the Revolution and Building Construction

1971. 54th Anniv of October Revolution.

3991	**1505**	4k. multicoloured	25	10

1506 E. Vakhtangov (founder) and characters from "Princess Turandot"

1971. 50th Anniv of Vakhtangov Theatre, Moscow.

3992	**1506**	10k. red and lake	50	25
3993	-	10k. yellow and brown	50	25
3994	-	10k. orange and brown	50	25

DESIGNS—HORIZ: No. 3993, B. Shchukin (actor) and scene from "The Man with the Rifle"; 3994, R. Simonov (director) and scene from "Cyrano de Bergerac".

1507 "Dzhambul Dzhabaiev" (A. Yar-Kravchenko)

1971. 125th Anniv of Dzhambul Dzhabaiev (Kazakh poet).

3995	**1507**	4k. brown, yell & orge	30	10

1508 Pskov Kremlin

1971. Historical Buildings. Multicoloured.

3996	3k. Type **1508**	15	10
3997	4k. Novgorod kremlin	20	10
3998	6k. Smolensk fortress and Liberation Monument	25	10
3999	10k. Kolomna kremlin	40	15
MS4000	67×88 mm. 50k. Kremlin, Red Square, Moscow (22×32 mm)	3·00	1·20

1509 William Foster

1971. 90th Birth Anniv of Foster (American communist).

4001	**1509**	10k. black and brown	20·00	20·00
4002	**1509**	10k. black and brown	60	25

No. 4001 shows the incorrect date of death "1964"; 4002 shows the correct date, "1961".

1510 Fadeev and Scene from "The Rout" (novel)

1971. 70th Birth Anniv of Aleksandr Fadeev (writer).

4003	**1510**	4k. orange and blue	30	10

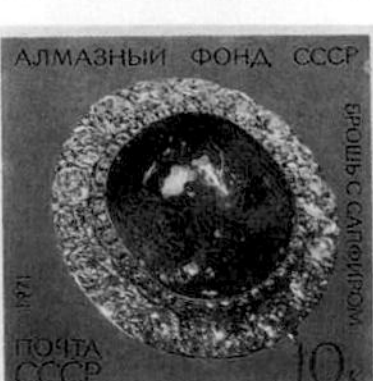

1511 Sapphire Brooch

1971. Diamonds and Jewels. Multicoloured.

4004	10k. Type **1511**	60	20
4005	10k. "Shah" diamond	60	20
4006	10k. "Narcissi" diamond brooch	60	20
4007	20k. Amethyst pendant	1·00	45
4008	20k. "Rose" platinum and diamond brooch	1·00	45
4009	30k. Pearl and diamond pendant	1·50	65

1512 Vanda Orchid

1971. Tropical Flowers. Multicoloured.

4010	1k. Type **1512**	15	10
4011	2k. "Anthurium scherzerianum"	20	10
4012	4k. "Cactus epiphyllum"	30	15
4013	12k. Amaryllis	60	35
4014	14k. "Medinilla magnifica"	80	45
MS4015	81×97 mm. 10k.×4 Designs as Nos. 4010 and 4012/14 but smaller (19×26 mm) and with white backgrounds	2·50	90

1513 Peter the Great's Imperial Barge, 1723

1971. History of the Russian Navy (1st series). Multicoloured.

4016	1k. Type **1513**	20	10
4017	4k. Galleon "Orel", 1668 (vert)	40	25
4018	10k. Ship of the line "Poltava", 1712 (vert)	1·00	70
4019	12k. Ship of the line "Ingermanland", 1715 (vert)	1·20	90
4020	16k. Steam frigate "Vladimir", 1848	1·60	1·20

See also Nos. 4117/21, 4209/13 and 4303/6.

1514 Ice Hockey Players

1971. 25th Anniv of Soviet Ice Hockey.

4021	**1514**	6k. multicoloured	60	25

1515 Baku Oil Installations

1971. Baku Oil Industry.

4022	**1515**	4k. black, red and blue	40	10

1516 G. M. Krzhizhanovsky

1972. Birth Centenary of G. M. Krzhizhanovsky (scientist).

4023	**1516**	4k. brown	30	10

1517 Scriabin

1972. Birth Centenary of Aleksandr Scriabin (composer).

4024	**1517**	4k. blue and green	40	10

1518 Red-faced Cormorant

1972. Sea Birds. Multicoloured.

4025	4k. Type **1518**	30	10
4026	6k. Ross's gull (horiz)	45	25
4027	10k. Pair of barnacle geese	60	45
4028	12k. Pair of spectacled eiders (horiz)	80	55
4029	16k. Mediterranean gull	1·00	70

1519 Speed Skating

1972. Winter Olympic Games, Sapporo, Japan. Multicoloured.

4030	4k. Type **1519**	15	10
4031	6k. Figure skating	20	10
4032	10k. Ice hockey	50	20
4033	12k. Ski jumping	70	25
4034	16k. Cross-country skiing	80	35
MS4035	67½×92 mm. 50k. "Sapporo" emblem and Olympic rings	2·50	90

1520 Heart Emblem

1972. World Heart Month.

4036	**1520**	4k. red and green	30	10

1521 Fair Emblem

1973. 50th Anniv of Soviet Participation in Leipzig Fair.

4037	**1521**	16k. gold and red	90	45

1522 Labour Emblems

1972. 15th Soviet Trade Unions Congress, Moscow.

4038	**1522**	4k. brown, red and pink	30	10

1523 "Aloe arborescens"

1972. Medicinal Plants. Multicoloured.

4039	1k. Type **1523**	10	10
4040	2k. Yellow horned poppy	10	10
4041	4k. Groundsel	20	10
4042	6k. Nephrite tea	30	15
4043	10k. Kangaroo apple	60	25

1524 Alexandra Kollontai (diplomat) (birth cent)

1972. Birth Anniversaries.

4044	**1524**	4k. brown	30	10
4045	-	4k. lake	30	10
4046	-	4k. bistre	30	10

CELEBRITIES: No. 4045, G. Chicherin (Foreign Affairs Commissar) (birth cent); 4046, "Kamo" (S. A. Ter-Petrosyan—revolutionary) (90th birth anniv).

СОВЕТСКИЕ СПОРТСМЕНЫ
ЗАВОЕВАЛИ
8 ЗОЛОТЫХ
МЕДАЛЕЙ,
5 СЕРЕБРЯНЫХ,
3 БРОНЗОВЫХ.

(1525)

1972. Soviet Medals at Winter Olympic Games, Sapporo. No. MS4035 optd with T 1525 on the sheet.

MS4047	50k. multicoloured	7·00	4·50

1526 "Salyut" Space-station and "Soyuz" Spacecraft

1972. Cosmonautics Day. Multicoloured.

4048	6k. Type **1526**	40	25
4049	6k. "Mars 2" approaching Mars	40	25
4050	16k. Capsule, "Mars 3"	80	40

1527 Factory and Products

1972. 250th Anniv of Izhora Factory.

4051	**1527**	4k. purple and silver	30	10

1972. 50th Anniv of Russian Federation Autonomous Soviet Socialist Republics. Designs similar to T 1433, but dated "1972".

4052	4k. blue	30	10
4053	4k. mauve	30	10

DESIGNS: No. 4052, Arms, natural resources and industry (Yakut Republic); 4053, Arms, agriculture and industry (Checheno-Ingush Republic).

1528 L. Sobinov and scene from "Eugene Onegin"

1972. Birth Centenary of L. Sobinov (singer).

4054	**1528**	10k. brown	50	20

1529 Symbol of Knowledge and Children reading Books

1972. International Book Year.

4055	**1529**	6k. multicoloured	40	10

1530 Pavlik Morosov Monument (I. Rabinovich) and Pioneers Saluting

1972. 50th Anniv of Pioneer Organization.

4056	**1530**	1k. multicoloured	10	10
4057	-	2k. purple, red and green	15	10
4058	-	3k. blue, red and brown	20	10
4059	-	4k. red, blue and green	20	10
MS4060		103×82 mm. 30k. multicoloured	2·50	1·10

DESIGNS: Horiz 2k. Girl laboratory worker and Pioneers with book; 3k. Pioneer Place, Chukotka, and Pioneers at work; 4k. Pioneer parade. Vert (25×37 mm) 30k. Colour party (similar to 4k.).

1531 Pioneer Trumpeter

1972. "50th Anniv of Pioneer Organization" Youth Stamp Exhibition, Minsk.

4061	**1531**	4k. purple, red & yellow	30	10

1532 "World Security"

1972. European Security Conference, Brussels.

4062	**1532**	6k. blue, turquoise & gold	1·50	1·20

1533 M. S. Ordubady

1972. Birth Centenary of M. S. Ordubady (Azerbaijan writer).

4063	**1533**	4k. purple and orange	30	10

1972. Russian Paintings. As T 1502, but dated "1972". Multicoloured.

4064	2k. "Cossack Hetman" (I. Nikitin)	10	10
4065	4k. "F. Volkov" (A. Lossenko)	20	10
4066	6k. "V. Majkov" (F. Rokotov)	30	15
4067	10k. "N. Novikov" (D. Levitsky)	50	25
4068	12k. "G. Derzhavin" (V. Borovikovsky)	60	35
4069	16k. "Peasants' Dinner" (M. Shibanov) (horiz)	80	45
4070	20k. "Moscow View" (F. Alexeiev) (horiz)	1·30	55

1534 G. Dimitrov

1972. 90th Birth Anniv of Georgi Dimitrov (Bulgarian statesman).

4071	**1534**	6k. brown and bistre	30	10

1535 Congress Building and Emblem

1972. 9th Int Gerontology Congress, Kiev.

4072	**1535**	6k. brown and blue	35	10

1536 Fencing

1972. Olympic Games, Munich.

4073	**1536**	4k. purple and gold	35	10
4074	-	6k. green and gold	40	10
4075	-	10k. blue and gold	50	15
4076	-	14k. blue and gold	70	35
4077	-	16k. red and gold	90	45
MS4078		67×87 mm. 50k. scarlet, gold and green	2·50	1·10

DESIGNS: 6k. Gymnastics; 10k. Canoeing; 14k. Boxing; 16k. Running; 50k. Weightlifting.

1537 Amundsen, Airship N.1 "Norge" and Northern Lights

1972. Birth Centenary of Roald Amundsen (Polar explorer).

4079	**1537**	6k. blue and brown	1·50	90

1538 Market-place, Lvov (Lemberg)

1972. Ukraine's Architectural Monuments. Mult.

4080	4k. Type **1538**	20	10
4081	6k. 17th-century house, Tchernigov (horiz)	30	15
4082	10k. Kovnirovsky building, Kiev (horiz)	50	20
4083	16k. Kamenetz-Podolsk Castle	80	40

1539 Indian Flag and Asokan Capital

1972. 25th Anniv of India's Independence.

4084	**1539**	6k. red, blue and green	40	20

1540 Liberation Monument, Vladivostok, and Cavalry

1972. 50th Anniv of Liberation of Far Eastern Territories.

4085	**1540**	3k. grey, orange and red	15	10
4086	-	4k. grey, yellow & ochre	20	10
4087	-	6k. grey, pink and red	30	15

DESIGNS: 4k. Labour Heroes Monument, Khabarovsk, and industrial scene; 6k. Naval statue, Vladivostok, "Vladivostok" (cruiser) and jet fighters.

1541 Miners' Day Emblem

1972. 25th Anniv of Miners' Day.

4088	**1541**	4k. red, black and violet	30	10

1542 "Boy with Dog" (Murillo)

1972. Paintings by Foreign Artists in Hermitage Gallery, Leningrad. Multicoloured.

4089	4k. "Breakfast" (Velazquez) (horiz)	20	10
4090	6k. "The Milk Seller's Family" (Le Nain) (horiz)	30	15
4091	10k. Type **1542**	60	35
4092	10k. "The Capricious Girl" (Watteau)	90	55
4093	20k. "Moroccan with Horse" (Delacroix)	1·10	65
MS4094	75×100 mm. 50k. Van Dyck (self-portrait)	3·75	1·60

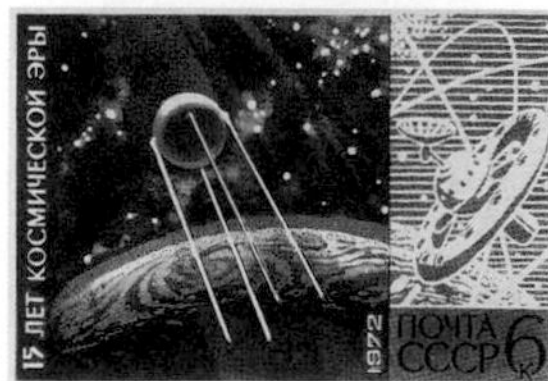

1543 "Sputnik I"

1972. 15th Anniv of "Cosmic Era". Multicoloured.

4095	6k. Type **1543**	40	20
4096	6k. Launch of "Vostok I"	40	20
4097	6k. "Lunokhod" vehicle on Moon	40	20
4098	6k. Man in space	40	20
4099	6k. "Mars 3" module on Mars	40	20
4100	6k. Touch down of "Venera 7" on Venus	40	20

1544 Konstantin Mardzhanishvili

1972. Birth Centenary of K. Mardzhanishvili (Georgian actor).

4101	**1544**	4k. green	30	10

1545 Museum Emblem

1972. Centenary of Popov Central Communications Museum.

4102	**1545**	4k. blue, purple & green	30	10

1546 Exhibition Labels

1972. "50th Anniv of U.S.S.R." Philatelic Exhibition.

4103	**1546**	4k. red & black on yell	30	10

1547 Lenin

1972. 55th Anniv of October Revolution.

4104	**1547**	4k. red and gold	30	10

1548 Militia Badge and Soviet Flag

1972. 55th Anniv of Soviet Militia.

4105	**1548**	4k. gold, red and brown	30	10

1549 Arms of U.S.S.R.

1972. 50th Anniv of U.S.S.R.

4106	**1549**	4k. gold, purple and red	20	10
4107	-	4k. gold, red and brown	20	10
4108	-	4k. gold, purple & green	20	10
4109	-	4k. gold, purple and grey	20	10
4110	-	4k. gold, purple and grey	20	10
MS4111		127×102 mm. 30k. red and gold	2·20	90

DESIGNS: No. 4107, Lenin and banner; No. 4108, Arms and Kremlin; No. 4109, Arms and industrial scenes; No. 4110, Arms, worker and open book "U.S.S.R. Constitutions"; **MS**4111, Arms and Spassky Tower.

1550 Emblem of U.S.S.R.

СЛАВА
СОВЕТСКИМ ОЛИМПИЙЦАМ,
ЗАВОЕВАВШИМ
50 ЗОЛОТЫХ, 27 СЕРЕБРЯНЫХ
И 22 БРОНЗОВЫЕ НАГРАДЫ!

(1551)

1972. U.S.S.R. Victories in Olympic Games, Munich. Multicoloured.

4112	20k. Type **1550**	1·00	35
4113	30k. Olympic medals	1·50	65
MS4114	Sheet No. **MS**4078 optd with T **1551** in red on margin	3·75	2·50

1552 Savings Book

1972. "50 Years of Soviet Savings Bank".

4115	**1552**	4k. blue and purple	30	10

1553 Kremlin and Snowflakes

1972. New Year.

4116	**1553**	6k. multicoloured	30	10

1554 Battleship "Pyotr Veliky"

1972. History of the Russian Navy (2nd series). Multicoloured.

4117	2k. Type **1554**	20	10
4118	3k. Cruiser "Varyag"	20	10
4119	4k. Battleship "Potemkin"	40	15
4120	6k. Cruiser "Ochakov"	50	20
4121	10k. Minelayer "Amur"	90	35

1555 Skovoroda (after P. Meshcheryakov)

1972. 250th Birth Anniv of Grigory S. Skovoroda.

4122	**1555**	4k. blue	30	10

1556 "Pioneer Girl with Books" (N. A. Kasatkin)

1972. "History of Russian Painting". Mult.

4123	2k. "Meeting of Village Party Members" (E. M. Cheptsov) (horiz)	15	10
4124	4k. Type **1556**	20	15
4125	6k. "Party Delegate" (G. G. Ryazhsky)	30	20
4126	10k. "End of Winter—Midday" (K. F. Yuon) (horiz)	40	25
4127	16k. "Partisan Lunev" (N. I. Strunnikov)	70	40
4128	20k. "Self-portrait in Fur Coat" (I. E. Grabar)	90	50
MS4129	90×70 mm. 50k. "In Blue Space" (A. A. Rylov) (horiz)	4·50	1·40

1557 Child reading Safety Code

1972. Road Safety Campaign.

4130	**1557**	4k. black, blue and red	30	10

1558 Emblem of Technology

1972. Cent of Polytechnic Museum, Moscow.

4131	**1558**	4k. red, yellow and green	30	10

1559 "Venus 8" and Parachute

1972. Space Research.

4132	**1559**	6k. blue, black and purple	35	10
MS4133		90×70 mm. 50k.×2 brown	21·00	14·50

DESIGNS—(40×20 mm): **MS**4133. (a) "Venera 8". (b) "Mars 3".

1560 Solidarity Emblem

1973. 15th Anniv of Asian and African People's Solidarity Organization.

4134	**1560**	10k. blue, red and brown	45	25

1561 Town and Gediminas Tower

1973. 650th Anniv of Vilnius (Vilna).

4135	**1561**	10k. red, black and green	40	20

1562 I. V. Babushkin

1973. Birth Cent of I. V. Babushkin (revolutionary).

4136	**1562**	4k. black	40	10

1563 Tupolev Tu-154 Jetliner

1973. 50th Anniv of Soviet Civil Aviation.

4137	**1563**	6k. multicoloured	60	25

1564 "30" and Admiralty Spire, Leningrad

1973. 30th Anniv of Relief of Leningrad.

4138	**1564**	4k. black, orange & brn	30	10

1565 Portrait and Masks (Mayakovsky Theatre)

1973. 50th Anniv of Moscow Theatres.

4139	**1565**	10k. multicoloured	40	10
4140	-	10k. red and blue	40	10

DESIGN: No. 4140, Commemorative panel (Mossoviet Theatre).

1566 Prishvin (after A. Kirillov)

1973. Birth Centenary of Mikhail Prishvin (writer).

4141	**1566**	4k. multicoloured	40	10

1567 Heroes' Square, Volgograd

1973. 30th Anniv of Stalingrad Victory. Detail from Heroes' Memorial.

4142	-	3k. black, yellow & orge	20	10
4143	**1567**	4k. yellow and black	20	10
4144	-	10k. multicoloured	40	15
4145	-	12k. black, light red and red	60	20
MS4146		93×73 mm. 20k.×2 multi-coloured	2·75	1·20

DESIGNS—VERT (28×59 mm): 3k. Soldier and Allegory; 12k. Hand with torch; (18×40 mm)—Allegory, Mamai Barrow. HORIZ (59×28 mm)—Mourning mother; (40×18 mm) 20k. Mamai Barrow.

1568 Copernicus and Planetary Chart

1973. 500th Birth Anniv of Copernicus (astronomer).

4147	**1568**	10k. brown and blue	60	25

1569 Chaliapin (after K. Korovin)

1973. Birth Centenary of Fyodor Chaliapin (opera singer).
4148 **1569** 10k. multicoloured 50 20

1570 Ice Hockey Players

1973. World Ice Hockey Championships, Moscow.
4149 **1570** 10k. brown, blue & gold 70 30
MS4150 64×85 mm. 50k. sepia, green and gold (players) (21×32 mm) 2·50 1·20

1571 Athletes

1973. 50th Anniv of Central Red Army Sports Club.
4151 **1571** 4k. multicoloured 20 10

1572 Red Star, Tank, and Map

1973. 30th Anniv of Battle of Kursk.
4152 **1572** 4k. black, red and grey 30 20

1573 N. E. Bauman

1973. Birth Centenary of Nikolai Bauman (revolutionary).
4153 **1573** 4k. brown 40 10

1574 Red Cross and Red Crescent

1973. International Co-operation.
4154 **1574** 4k. red, black and green 20 10
4155 - 6k. light blue, red and blue 30 15
4156 - 16k. green, red and mauve 80 30

DESIGNS AND EVENTS: 4k. (50th anniv of Soviet Red Cross and Red Crescent Societies Union); 6k. Mask, emblem and theatre curtain (15th Int Theatre Institution Congress); 16k. Floral emblem (10th World Festival of Youth, Berlin).

1575 Ostrovsky (after V. Perov)

1973. 150th Birth Anniv of Aleksandr Ostrovsky (writer).
4157 **1575** 4k. multicoloured 30 10

1576 Satellites

1973. Cosmonautics Day. Multicoloured.
4158 6k. Type **1576** 30 10
4159 6k. "Lunokhod 2" 30 10
MS4160 75×100 mm. 20k.×3, each 51×21 mm in lake, plum and gold 3·25 1·50
MS4161 As No. **MS**4160 but in green, purple and gold 3·25 1·50

1577 "Guitarist" (V. Tropinin)

1973. "History of Russian Painting". Mult.
4162 2k. Type **1577** 15 10
4163 4k. "The Young Widow" (P. Fedotov) 20 10
4164 6k. "Self-portrait" (O. Kiprensky) 30 20
4165 10k. "An Afternoon in Italy" (K. Bryullov) 45 25
4166 12k. "That's My Father's Dinner!" (boy with dog) (A. Venetsianov) 55 30
4167 16k. "Lower Gallery of Albano" (A. Ivanov) (horiz) 75 35
4168 20k. "Yermak conquering Siberia" (V. Surikov) (horiz) 1·00 50

1578 Athlete and Emblems

1973. 50th Anniv of Dynamo Sports Club.
4169 **1578** 4k. multicoloured 30 10

СОВЕТСКИЕ ХОККЕИСТЫ – ЧЕМПИОНЫ МИРА И ЕВРОПЫ 1973 ГОДА

(1579) (image scaled to 72% of original size)

1973. U.S.S.R.'s Victory in World Ice-Hockey Championships. No. MS4150 optd with T 1579 and frame at foot in green.
MS4170 67×86 mm. 50k. sepia, green and gold 7·75 5·25

1580 Liner "Mikhail Lermontov"

1973. Inauguration of Leningrad–New York Trans-Atlantic Service.
4171 **1580** 16k. multicoloured 80 35

1581 E. T. Krenkel and Polar Scenes

1973. 70th Birth Anniv of E. T. Krenkel (Polar explorer).
4172 **1581** 4k. brown and blue 1·30 90

1582 Sports

1973. "Sport for Everyone".
4173 **1582** 4k. multicoloured 30 10

1583 Girls' Choir

1973. Centenary of Latvian Singing Festival.
4174 **1583** 10k. multicoloured 40 20

1973. 50th Anniv of Russian Federation Autonomous Soviet Socialist Republics. Design similar to T 1433, but dated "1973".
4175 4k. blue 30 10

DESIGN: No. 4175, Arms and industries of Buryat Republic.

1584 Throwing the Hammer

1973. Universiade Games, Moscow. Mult.
4176 2k. Type **1584** 10 10
4177 3k. Gymnastics 10 10
4178 4k. Swimming 20 15
4179 16k. Fencing 85 35
MS4180 70×88 mm. 50k. Throwing the javelin 2·50 1·10

1585 Tereshkova

1973. 10th Anniv of Woman's First Space Flight by Valentina Nikolaieva-Tereshkova. Sheet 89×70 mm containing horiz designs as T 1585. Multicoloured.
MS4181 20k.×3 (a) Type **1585**; (b) Tereshkova with Indian and African women; (c) Holding her baby 3·25 1·50

1586 European Bison

1973. Caucasus and Voronezh Nature Reserves. Multicoloured.
4182 1k. Type **1586** 10 10
4183 3k. Ibex 15 10
4184 4k. Caucasian snowcocks 25 20
4185 6k. Eurasian beaver with young 40 25
4186 10k. Red deer with fawns 60 45

1587 Lenin, Banner and Membership Card

1973. 70th Anniv of 2nd Soviet Social Democratic Workers Party Congress.
4187 **1587** 4k. multicoloured 30 10

1588 A. R. al-Biruni (after M. Nabiev)

1973. Millennium of Abu Reihan al-Biruni (astronomer and mathematician).
4188 **1588** 6k. brown 30 15

1589 Schaumberg Palace, Bonn, and Spassky Tower, Moscow

1973. General Secretary Leonid Brezhnev's Visits to West Germany, France and U.S.A. Multicoloured.
4189 **1589** 10k. mauve, brn & buff 40 15
4190 - 10k. brown, ochre and yellow 40 15
4191 - 10k. red, grey and brown 40 15
MS4192 134×139 mm. 4k.×3 as Nos. 4189/91, each crimson, flesh and deep olive 4·75 3·25

DESIGNS: No. 4189, Type **1589**; Eiffel Tower, Paris and Spassky Tower; 4191, White House, Washington and Spassky Tower.

See also Nos. 4245 and 4257.

1590 "Portrait of the Sculptor S. T. Konenkov" (P. Korin)

1973. "History of Russian Paintings". Mult.
4193 2k. Type **1590** 10 10
4194 4k. "Farm-workers' Supper" (A. Plastov) 15 10
4195 6k. "Letter from the Battle-front" (A. Laktionov) 25 15
4196 10k. "Mountain Landscape" (M. Saryan) 45 25
4197 16k. "Wedding on Tomorrow's Street" (Yu. Pimenov) 75 35
4198 20k. "Ice Hockey" (mosaic, A. Deineka) 1·00 45
MS4199 72×92 mm. 50k. "Lenin making Speech" (B. Johanson) 2·75 1·10

1591 Lenin Museum

1973. Inaug of Lenin Museum, Tashkent.

4200	**1591**	4k. multicoloured	30	10

1592 Steklov

1973. Birth Centenary of Y. Steklov (statesman).

4201	**1592**	4k. brown, red and pink	30	10

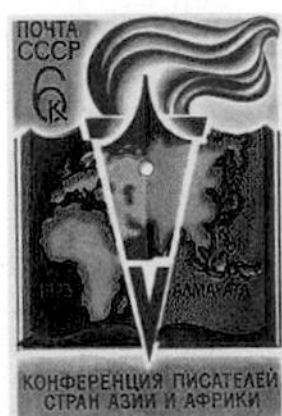

1593 "The Eternal Pen"

1973. Afro-Asian Writers' Conference, Alma-Ata.

4202	**1593**	6k. multicoloured	35	15

1594 "Oplopanax elatum"

1973. Medicinal Plants. Multicoloured.

4203	1k. Type **1594**	10	10
4204	2k. Ginseng	15	10
4205	4k. Spotted orchid	20	10
4206	10k. Arnica	40	25
4207	12k. Lily of the valley	55	35

1595 I. Nasimi (after M. Abdullaev)

1973. 600th Birth Anniv of Imadeddin Nasimi (Azerbaijan poet).

4208	**1595**	4k. brown	40	15

1596 Cruiser "Kirov"

1973. History of Russian Navy (3rd series). Multicoloured.

4209	3k. Type **1596**	20	10
4210	4k. Battleship "Oktyabrskaya Revolyutsiya"	25	10
4211	6k. Submarine "Krasnogvar-deets"	30	20
4212	10k. Destroyer "Soobrazitelnyi"	60	25
4213	16k. Cruiser "Krasnyi Kavkaz"	1·00	45

1597 Pugachev and Battle Scene

1973. Bicentenary of Peasant War.

4214	**1597**	4k. multicoloured	30	10

1598 Red Flag encircling Globe

1973. 15th Anniv of Magazine "Problems of Peace and Socialism".

4215	**1598**	6k. red, gold and green	40	15

1599 Leningrad Mining Institute

1973. Bicentenary of Leningrad Mining Institute.

4216	**1599**	4k. multicoloured	30	10

1600 Laurel and Hemispheres

1973. World Congress of "Peaceful Forces", Moscow.

4217	**1600**	6k. multicoloured	40	15

1601 Elena Stasova

1973. Birth Centenary of Yelena Stasova (party official).

4218	**1601**	4k. mauve	30	10

1602 Order of People's Friendship

1973. Foundation of Order of People's Friendship.

4219	**1602**	4k. multicoloured	30	10

1603 Marshal Malinovsky

1973. 75th Birth Anniv of Marshal R. Malinovsky.

4220	**1603**	4k. grey	30	10

1604 Workers and Red Guard

1973. 250th Anniv of Sverdlovsk.

4221	**1604**	4k. black, gold and red	30	10

1605 D. Cantemir

1973. 300th Birth Anniv of Dmitri Cantemir (Moldavian scientist and encyclopaedist).

4222	**1605**	4k. red	30	10

1606 Pres. Allende of Chile

1973. Allende Commemoration.

4223	**1606**	6k. black and brown	40	15

1607 Kremlin

1973. New Year.

4224	**1607**	6k. multicoloured	30	10

1608 N. Narimanov

1973. Birth Centenary (1970) of Nariman Narimanov (Azerbaijan politician).

4225	**1608**	4k. green	30	10

1609 "Russobalt" Touring Car (1909)

1973. History of Soviet Motor Industry (1st series). Multicoloured.

4226	2k. Type **1609**	15	10
4227	3k. "AMO-F15" lorry (1924)	15	10
4228	4k. Spartak "NAMI-1" tourer (1927)	20	10
4229	12k. Yaroslavsky "Ya-6" bus (1929)	60	25
4230	16k. Gorkovsky "GAZ-A" tourer (1932)	90	45

See also Nos. 4293/7, 4397/401 and 4512/16.

1610 "Game and Lobster" (Sneiders)

1973. Foreign Paintings in Soviet Galleries. Mult.

4231	4k. Type **1610**	15	10
4232	6k. "Young Woman with Ear-rings" (Rembrandt) (vert)	20	10
4233	10k. "Sick Woman and Physi-cian" (Steen) (vert)	40	15
4234	12k. "Attributes of Art" (Chardin)	45	20
4235	14k. "Lady in a Garden" (Monet)	50	25
4236	16k. "Village Lovers" (Bastien-Lepage) (vert)	60	30
4237	20k. "Girl with Fan" (Renoir) (vert)	70	40
MS4238	78×103 mm. 50k. "Flora" (Rembrandt) (vert)	2·50	1·50

1611 Great Sea Gate, Tallin

1973. Historical Buildings of Estonia, Latvia and Lithuania.

4239	**1611**	4k. black, red and green	20	10
4240	-	4k. brown, red and green	20	10
4241	-	4k. multicoloured	20	10
4242	-	10k. multicoloured	50	25

DESIGNS: No. 4240, Organ pipes and Dome Cathedral, Riga; 4241, Traku Castle, Lithuania; 4242, Town Hall and weather-vane, Tallin.

1612 Picasso

1973. Pablo Picasso Commemoration.

4243	**1612**	6k. green, red and gold	50	20

1613 Petrovsky

1973. I. G. Petrovsky (mathematician and Rector of Moscow University) Commemoration.

4244	**1613**	4k. multicoloured	30	10

1973. Brezhnev's Visit to India. As T 1589, but showing Kremlin, Red Fort, Delhi and flags.

4245	4k. multicoloured	40	20

1614 Soviet Soldier and Title Page

1974. 50th Anniv of "Red Star" Newspaper.

4246 **1614** 4k. black, red and gold 30 10

1615 Siege Monument and Peter the Great Statue, Leningrad

1974. 30th Anniv of Soviet Victory in Battle for Leningrad.

4247 **1615** 4k. multicoloured 40 15

1616 Oil Workers

1974. 10th Anniv of Tyumen Oil fields.

4248 **1616** 4k. black, red and blue 40 15

1617 "Comecon" Headquarters, Moscow

1974. 25th Anniv of Council for Mutual Economic Aid.

4249 **1617** 16k. green, red & brown 70 35

1618 Skaters and Stadium

1974. European Women's Ice Skating Championships, Medeo, Alma-Ata.

4250 **1618** 6k. red, blue and slate 30 10

1619 Kunstkammer Museum, Leningrad, Text and Academy

1974. 250th Anniv of Russian Academy of Sciences.

4251 **1619** 10k. multicoloured 35 15

1620 L. A. Artsimovich

1974. 1st Death Anniv of Academician L. A. Artsimovich (physicist).

4252 **1620** 4k. brown and green 30 10

1974. 50th Anniv of Autonomous Soviet Socialist Republics. Design similar to T 1433, but dated "1974".

4253 4k. brown 30 10

DESIGN: No. 4253, Arms and industries of Nakhichevan ASSR (Azerbaijan).

1621 K. D. Ushinsky

1974. 150th Birth Anniv of K. D. Ushinsky (educationalist).

4254 **1621** 4k. brown and green 30 10

1622 M. D. Millionshchikov

1974. 1st Death Anniv of M. D. Millionshchikov (scientist).

4255 **1622** 4k. brown, pink & green 30 10

1623 Spartakiad Emblem

1974. 3rd Winter Spartakiad Games.

4256 **1623** 10k. multicoloured 40 15

1974. General Secretary Leonid Brezhnev's Visit to Cuba. As T 1589 but showing Kremlin, Revolution Square, Havana and Flags.

4257 4k. multicoloured 40 20

1624 Young Workers and Emblem

1974. Scientific and Technical Youth Work Review.

4258 **1624** 4k. multicoloured 30 10

1625 Theatre Facade

1974. Cent of Azerbaijan Drama Theatre, Baku.

4259 **1625** 6k. brown, red & orange 30 10

1626 Globe and Meteorological Activities

1974. Cosmonautics Day.

4260 **1626** 6k. blue, red and violet 30 10

4261 - 10k. brown, red and blue 40 25

4262 - 10k. black, red & yellow 40 25

DESIGNS: No. 4261, V. G. Lazarev and O. G. Makarov, and launch of "Soyuz 12"; 4262, P. I. Klimuk and V. V. Lebedev, and "Soyuz 13".

1627 "Odessa by Moonlight" (Aivazovsky)

1974. Marine Paintings by Ivan Aivazovsky. Mult.

4263 2k. Type **1627** 10 10

4264 4k. "Battle of Chesme" (vert) 15 10

4265 6k. "St. George's Monastery" 20 10

4266 10k. "Storm at Sea" 40 15

4267 12k. "Rainbow" 65 20

4268 16k. "Shipwreck" 85 35

MS4269 68×91 mm. 50k. "Ivan Aivazovsky" (I. Kramskoi) (vert) 2·30 90

1628 Young Communists

1974. 17th Leninist Young Communist League (Komsomol) Congress (4270) and 50th Anniv of Naming League after Lenin (4271). Multicoloured.

4270 4k. Type **1628** 20 10

4271 4k. "Lenin" (from sculpture by V. Tsigal) 20 10

1629 "Lenin at the Telegraph" (I. E. Grabar)

1974. 104th Birth Anniv of Lenin. Sheet 108×82 mm.

MS4272 50k. multicoloured 2·30 90

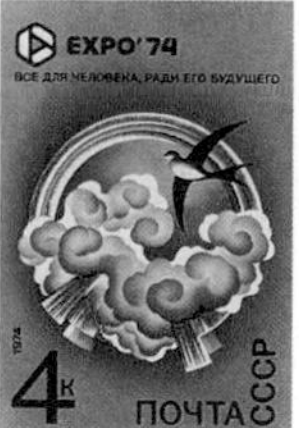

1630 Swallow ("Atmosphere")

1974. "EXPO 74" World Fair, Spokane, U.S.A. "Preserve the Environment".

4273 **1630** 4k. black, red and lilac 15 10

4274 - 6k. yellow, black & blue 20 10

4275 - 10k. black, violet and red 45 15

4276 - 16k. blue, green & black 65 25

4277 - 20k. black, brn & orge 90 45

MS4278 73×93 mm. 50k. multicoloured 2·30 90

DESIGNS: 6k. Fish and globe ("The Sea"); 10k. Crystals ("The Earth"); 16k. Rose bush ("Flora"); 20k. Young red deer ("Fauna"); (30×42 mm) 50k. Child and Sun ("Protect the Environment").

1632 Congress Emblem within Lucerne Grass

1974. 12th International Congress of Meadow Cultivation, Moscow.

4280 **1632** 4k. red, green & dp green 30 10

1633 Saiga

1974. 1st International Theriological Congress, Moscow. Fauna. Multicoloured.

4281 1k. Type **1633** 15 10

4282 3k. Asiatic wild ass 30 15

4283 4k. Russian desman 35 20

4284 6k. Northern fur seal 50 30

4285 10k. Bowhead whale 90 40

1634 Tchaikovsky and Competition Emblem

1974. 5th Int Tchaikovsky Music Competition.

4286 **1634** 6k. black, violet & green 40 10

1635 "Puskin" (O. A. Kipernsky)

1974. 175th Birth Anniv of Aleksandr Pushkin (writer). Sheet 101×81 mm.

MS4287 50k. multicoloured 2·30 90

1636 Marshal F. I. Tolbukhin

1974. 80th Birth Anniv of Marshal F. I. Tolbukhin.

4288 **1636** 4k. green 30 10

1631 "Cobble-stone, Proletarian Weapon" (sculpture, I. Shadr)

1974. 50th Anniv of Central Museum of the Revolution.

4279 **1631** 4k. green, red and gold 30 10

1637 K. Stanislavsky, V. Nemirovich-Danchenko and Theatre Curtain

1974. 75th Anniv of Moscow Arts Festival.

4289 **1637** 10k. multicoloured 40 15

1638 Runner and Emblem

1974. 13th Soviet Schools Spartakiad, Alma Ata.
4290 **1638** 4k. multicoloured 30 10

1639 Modern Passenger Coach

1974. Centenary of Yegorov Railway Wagon Works, Leningrad.
4291 **1639** 4k. multicoloured 40 25

1640 Shield and Monument on Battle Map

1974. 30th Anniv of Liberation of Belorussia.
4292 **1640** 4k. multicoloured 30 10
See also No. 4301.

1974. History of Soviet Motor Industry (2nd series). As T 1609. Multicoloured.

4293	2k. Gorkovsky "GAZ-AA" lorry (1932)	15	10
4294	3k. Gorkovsky "GAZ-03-30" bus (1933)	15	10
4295	4k. Moscow Auto Works "ZIS-5" lorry (1933)	20	10
4296	14k. Moscow Auto Works "ZIS-8" bus (1934)	70	25
4297	16k. Moscow Auto Works "ZIS-101" saloon car (1936)	80	35

1974. 50th Anniv of Soviet Republics. As T 1433, dated "1974".
4298 4k. red 30 15
DESIGN: 4k. Arms and industries of North Ossetian Republic.
No. 4298 also commemorates the 200th anniv of Ossetia's merger with Russia.

1641 Liberation Monument (E. Kuntsevich) and Skyline

1974. 800th Anniv of Poltava.
4299 **1641** 4k. red and brown 30 10

1642 Flag and "Nike" Memorial, Warsaw

1974. 30th Anniv of Polish People's Republic.
4300 **1642** 6k. brown and red 40 15

1974. 30th Anniv of Liberation of Ukraine. As T 1640, but background details and colours changed.
4301 4k. multicoloured 30 10

1644 Admiral Isakov

1974. 80th Birth Anniv of Admiral I. S. Isakov.
4302 **1644** 4k. blue 30 10

1645 Minesweeper

1974. History of the Russian Navy (4th series). Modern Warships. Multicoloured.

4303	3k. Type **1645**	20	10
4304	4k. Aligator II tank landing ship	25	10
4305	6k. "Moskova" helicopter carrier	50	25
4306	16k. Destroyer "Otvazhny"	1·00	50

1646 Pentathlon Sports

1974. World Modern Pentathlon Championships, Moscow.
4307 **1646** 16k. brown, gold & blue 70 30

1647 D. Ulyanov

1974. Birth Centenary of D. Ulyanov (Lenin's brother).
4308 **1647** 4k. green 30 10

1648 V. Menzhinsky

1974. Birth Cent of V. Menzhinsky (statesman).
4309 **1648** 4k. maroon 30 10

1649 "Lilac" (P. P. Konchalovsky)

1974. Soviet Paintings. Multicoloured.

4310	4k. Type **1649**	15	10
4311	6k. "Towards the Wind" (sailing) (E. Kalnins)	25	15
4312	10k. "Spring" (young woman) (O. Zardaryan)	45	25
4313	16k. "Northern Harbour" (G. Nissky)	75	30
4314	20k. "Daughter of Soviet Kirgiz" (S. Chuikov) (vert)	90	35

1650 S. M. Budennyi

1974. Marshal S. M. Budennyi Commemoration.
4315 **1650** 4k. green 30 10

1651 Page of First Russian Dictionary

1974. 400th Anniv of First Russian Primer.
4316 **1651** 4k. red, black and gold 30 10

1652 Flags and Soviet War Memorial, (K. Baraski), Bucharest

1974. 30th Anniv of Rumanian Liberation.
4317 **1652** 6k. blue, yellow and red 30 10

1653 Vitebsk

1974. Millenary of Vitebsk.
4318 **1653** 4k. red and green 30 10

1654 Kirgizia

1974. 50th Anniv of Soviet Republics. Flags, Agricultural and Industrial Emblems. Mult. Background colours given.

4319	**1654**	4k. blue	20	10
4320	-	4k. purple	20	10
4321	-	4k. blue	20	10
4322	-	4k. yellow	20	10
4323	-	4k. green	20	10

DESIGNS: No. 4320, Moldavia; 4321, Tadzhikistan; 4322, Turkmenistan; 4323, Uzbekistan.

1655 Bulgarian Crest and Flags

1974. 30th Anniv of Bulgarian Revolution.
4324 **1655** 6k. multicoloured 30 10

1656 G.D.R. Crest and Soviet War Memorial, Treptow, Berlin

1974. 25th Anniv of German Democratic Republic.
4325 **1656** 6k. multicoloured 30 10

1657 Text and Stamp

1974. 3rd Soviet Philatelic Society Congress, Moscow. Sheet 111×71 mm.
MS4326 50k. bistre, black and claret 14·00 8·00

1658 Theatre and Laurel Wreath

1974. 150th Anniv of Maly State Theatre, Moscow.
4327 **1658** 4k. gold, red and black 30 10

1659 "Guests from Overseas"

1974. Birth Centenary of Nikolai K. Rorich (painter).
4328 **1659** 6k. multicoloured 35 10

1660 Soviet Crest and U.P.U. Monument, Berne

1974. Centenary of U.P.U. Multicoloured.

4329	10k. Type **1660**	50	20
4330	10k. Ukraine crest, U.P.U. Emblem and U.P.U. H.Q., Berne	50	20
4331	10k. Byelorussia crest, U.P.U. emblem and mail transport	50	20
MS4332	122×77 mm. 30k. Ilyushin Il-62M jetliner and U.P.U. emblem; 30k. Mail coach and U.P.U. emblem; 40k. U.P.U. emblem (each 31×43 mm)	14·00	9·00

1661 Order of Labour Glory

1974. 57th Anniv of October Revolution. Mult.

4333	4k. Type **1661**	20	10
4334	4k. Kamaz truck (vert)	20	10
4335	4k. Hydro-electric power station, Nurek (vert)	20	10

1662 Soviet "Space Stations" over Mars

1974. Soviet Space Exploration. Multicoloured.

No.	Type	Description	Mint	Used
4336		6k. Type **1662**	30	10
4337		10k. P. R. Popovich and Yu. P. Artyukhin ("Soyuz 14" cosomonauts)	50	25
4338		10k. I. V. Sarafanov and L. S. Demin ("Soyuz 15" cosmonauts)	50	25

SIZES—VERT: No. 4337, 28×40 mm. HORIZ: No. 4338, 40×28 mm.

1663 Mongolian Crest Flag

1974. 50th Anniv of Mongolian People's Republic.

No.	Type	Description	Mint	Used
4339	**1663**	6k. multicoloured	30	10

1664 Commemorative Inscription

1974. 30th Anniv of Estonian Liberation.

No.	Type	Description	Mint	Used
4340	**1664**	4k. multicoloured	30	10

1665 Liner "Aleksandr Pushkin", Freighter and Tanker

1974. 50th Anniv of Soviet Merchant Navy.

No.	Type	Description	Mint	Used
4341	**1665**	4k. multicoloured	30	10

1666 Spassky Clock-tower, Kremlin, Moscow

1974. New Year.

No.	Type	Description	Mint	Used
4342	**1666**	4k. multicoloured	30	10

1667 "The Market Place" (Beuckelaar)

1974. Foreign Paintings in Soviet Galleries. Mult.

No.	Type	Description	Mint	Used
4343		4k. Type **1667**	15	10
4344		6k. "Woman selling Fish" (Pieters) (vert)	25	10
4345		10k. "A Goblet of Lemonade" (Terborsh) (vert)	35	15
4346		14k. "Girl at Work" (Metsu) (vert)	50	30
4347		16k. "Saying Grace" (Chardin) (vert)	55	35
4348		20k. "The Spoilt Child" (Greuze) (vert)	80	45
MS4349		77×104 mm. 50k. "Self-portrait" (David) (vert)	2·50	90

1668 "Ostrowskia magnifica"

1974. Flowers. Multicoloured.

No.	Type	Description	Mint	Used
4350		1k. Type **1668**	10	10
4351		2k. "Paeonia intermedia"	10	10
4352		4k. "Roemeria refracta"	20	10
4353		10k. "Tulipia dasystemon"	45	25
4354		12k. "Dianthus versicolor"	55	30

1669 Nikitin (after P. Borel)

1974. 150th Birth Anniv of I. S. Nikitin (poet).

No.	Type	Description	Mint	Used
4355	**1669**	4k. black, green & olive	30	10

1670 Leningrad Mint Building

1974. 250th Anniv of Leningrad Mint.

No.	Type	Description	Mint	Used
4356	**1670**	6k. multicoloured	30	10

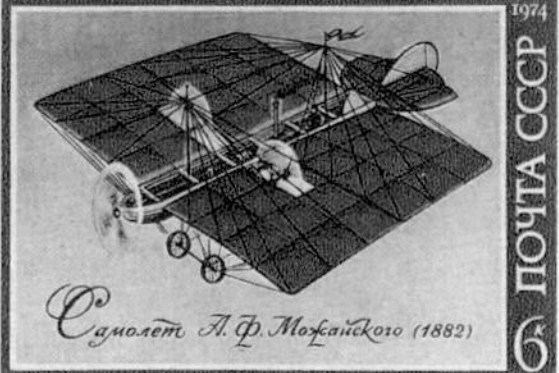

1671 Mozhaisky's Monoplane, 1884

1974. Early Russian Aircraft (1st series). Mult.

No.	Type	Description	Mint	Used
4357		6k. Type **1671**	40	25
4358		6k. Grizidubov No. 2 biplane, 1910	40	25
4359		6k. Sikorsky "Russia A", 1910	40	25
4360		6k. Sikorsky Russky Vityaz, 1913	40	25
4361		6k. Grigorovich M-5 flying boat, 1914	40	25

See also Nos. 4580/4, 4661/6 and 4791/6.

1672 Gymnastics and Army Sports Palace, Moscow

1974. Sports Buildings for Olympic Games, Moscow. Sheet 95×74 mm containing T 1672 and similar horiz designs in vermilion, brown and green.

MS4362 10k. Type **1672**; 10k. Running and Znamemsky Brothers' Athletics Hall, Sokolniki; 10k. Football and Lenin Central Stadium; 10k. Canoeing and Rowing Canal, Moscow 3·50 1·50

1673 Komsomol Emblem and Rotary Press ("Komsomolskaya Pravda")

1975. 50th Anniv of Children's Newspapers.

No.	Type	Description	Mint	Used
4363	**1673**	4k. red, black and blue	30	10
4364	-	4k. red, black and silver	30	10

DESIGN—VERT: No. 4364, Pioneer emblem and newspaper sheet ("Pioneerskaya Pravda").

1674 Emblem and Skiers (8th Trade Unions' Games)

1975. Winter Spartakiads.

No.	Type	Description	Mint	Used
4365	**1674**	4k. orange, black & blue	30	10
4366	-	16k. bistre, black & blue	60	30

DESIGN—HORIZ: 16k. Emblem, ice hockey player and skier (5th Friendly Forces Military Games).

1975. "50th Anniv of Automomous Soviet Socialist Republics. Designs similar to T 1433, but dated "1975".

No.	Type	Description	Mint	Used
4367		4k. green	30	15

DESIGN: No. 4367, Arms, industries and produce of Kara-kalpak ASSR (Uzbekistan).

1675 "David"

1975. 500th Birth Anniv of Michelangelo.

No.	Type	Description	Mint	Used
4368	**1675**	4k. deep green and green	20	20
4369	-	6k. brown and ochre	25	20
4370	-	10k. deep green & green	40	30
4371	-	14k. brown and ochre	50	30
4372	-	20k. deep green & green	1·00	40
4373	-	30k. brown and ochre	1·50	65
MS4374		166×74 mm. 50k. multicoloured	3·25	1·50

DESIGNS—HORIZ: 6k. "Crouching Boy"; 10k. "Rebellious Slave"; 14k. "Creation of Adam" (detail, Sistine Chapel ceiling); 20k. Staircase of Laurentiana Library, Florence; 30k. Christ and the Virgins (detail of "The Last Judgement", Sistine Chapel). VERT: 50k. Self-portrait.

1676 Mozhaisky, his Monoplane (1884) and Tupolev Tu-144 Jetliner

1975. 150th Birth Anniv of Aleksandr Mozhaisky (aircraft designer).

No.	Type	Description	Mint	Used
4375	**1676**	6k. brown and blue	40	15

1677 Convention Emblem

1975. Cent of International Metre Convention.

No.	Type	Description	Mint	Used
4376	**1677**	6k. multicoloured	30	10

1678 Games Emblem

1975. 6th Summer Spartakiad.

No.	Type	Description	Mint	Used
4377	**1678**	6k. multicoloured	30	10

1679 Towers of Charles Bridge, Prague (Czechoslovakia)

1975. 30th Anniv of Liberation. Multicoloured.

No.	Type	Description	Mint	Used
4378		6k. Type **1679**	20	10
4379		6k. Liberation Monument and Parliament Buildings, Budapest (Hungary)	20	10

1680 French and Soviet Flags

1975. 50th Anniv of Franco-Soviet Diplomatic Relations.

No.	Type	Description	Mint	Used
4380	**1680**	6k. multicoloured	30	10

1681 Yuri Gagarin (bust by L. Kerbel)

1975. Cosmonautics Day.

No.	Type	Description	Mint	Used
4381	**1681**	6k. red, silver and blue	30	10
4382	-	10k. red, black and blue	40	20
4383	-	16k. multicoloured	55	25

DESIGNS—HORIZ: 10k. A. A. Gubarev, G. M. Grechko ("Soyuz 17") and "Salyut 4"; 16k. A. V. Filipchenko, N. N. Rukavishnikov and "Soyuz 16".

1682 Treaty Emblem

1975. 20th Anniv of Warsaw Treaty.

No.	Type	Description	Mint	Used
4384	**1682**	6k. multicoloured	20	10

1683 Emblem and Exhibition Hall, Sokolniki, Moscow

1975. "Communication 75" International Exhibition, Moscow.

No.	Type	Description	Mint	Used
4385	**1683**	6k. red, silver and blue	30	10

1684 Lenin

1975. 30th Anniv of Victory in Second World War. Multicoloured.

4386	4k. Type **1684**	20	10
4387	4k. Eternal flame and Guard of Honour	20	10
4388	4k. Woman in ammunition factory	20	10
4389	4k. Partisans	20	10
4390	4k. "Destruction of the enemy"	20	10
4391	4k. Soviet forces	20	10
MS4392	111×57 mm. 50k. Order of the Patriotic War (33×49 mm). Imperf	7·00	4·50

1685 "Lenin" (V. G. Tsyplakov)

1975. 105th Birth Anniv of Lenin.

4393	**1685**	4k. multicoloured	30	10

1686 Victory Emblems

1975. "Sozfilex 75" International Stamp Exhibition.

4394	**1686**	6k. multicoloured	30	10
4395	**1686**	6k. multicoloured	30	10
MS4395a		69×95 mm. **1686** 50k. multicoloured	2·00	90

1687 "Apollo"–"Soyuz" Space Link

1975. "Apollo"–"Soyuz" Space Project.

4396	**1687**	20k. multicoloured	80	45

1975. History of Soviet Motor Industry (3rd series). As T 1609.

4397	2k. black, orange and blue	15	10
4398	3k. black, brown and green	15	10
4399	4k. black, blue and green	20	10
4400	12k. black, buff and purple	50	25
4401	16k. black, green and olive	70	30

DESIGNS: 2k. Gorkovsky "GAZ-M1" saloon, 1936; 3k. Yaroslavsky "YAG-6" truck, 1936; 4k. Moscow Auto Works "ZIS-16" bus, 1938; 12k. Moscow KIM Works "KIM-10" saloon, 1940; 16k. Gorkovsky "GAZ-67B" field car, 1943.

1688 Irrigation Canal and Emblem

1975. 9th Int Irrigation Congress, Moscow.

4402	**1688**	6k. multicoloured	30	10

1689 Flags and Crests of Poland and Soviet Union

1975. 30th Anniv of Soviet–Polish Friendship.

4403	**1689**	6k. multicoloured	30	10

1690 A. A. Leonov in Space

1975. 10th Anniv of First Space Walk by A. A. Leonov.

4404	**1690**	6k. multicoloured	35	10

1691 Ya. M. Sverdlov

1975. 90th Birth Anniv of Ya. M. Sverdlov (statesman).

4405	**1691**	4k. brown, buff & silver	25	10

1692 Congress Emblem

1975. 8th Int Plant Conservation Congress, Moscow.

4406	**1692**	6k. multicoloured	30	10

1693 Emblem and Plants

1975. 12th Int Botanical Congress, Leningrad.

4407	**1693**	6k. multicoloured	60	15

1694 U.N.O. Emblem

1975. 30th Anniv of United Nations Organization. Sheet 67×78 mm.

MS4408	50k. gold, blue and light blue	2·50	1·10

1695 Festival Emblem

1975. 9th International Film Festival, Moscow.

4409	**1695**	6k. multicoloured	30	10

1696 Crews of "Apollo" and "Soyuz"

1975. "Apollo"–"Soyuz" Space Link. Mult.

4410	10k. Type **1696**	40	10
4411	12k. "Apollo" and "Soyuz 19" in docking procedure	60	25
4412	12k. "Apollo" and "Soyuz 19" linked together	60	25
4413	16k. Launch of "Soyuz 19" (vert)	70	30
MS4414	83×120 mm. 50k. Mission Control Centre, Moscow (55×26 mm)	2·00	1·10

1697 Russian Sturgeon

1975. Int Exposition, Okinawa. Marine Life.

4415	**1697**	3k. bistre, black and blue	20	10
4416	-	4k. lilac, black and blue	25	10
4417	-	6k. purple, black & green	30	10
4418	-	10k. brown, black & bl	40	20
4419	-	16k. green, black & purple	60	25
4420	-	20k. blue, pur & stone	80	30
MS4421		83×120 mm. 30k. black, lilac and blue; 30k. black, lilac and blue	2·50	1·00

DESIGNS:—SQUARE: 4k. Thomas rapa whelk; 6k. European eel; 10k. Long-tailed duck; 16k. Crab; 20k. Grey damselfish. HORIZ: (56×26 mm)—30k. (2) Common dolphin (different).

1698 "Parade in Red Square, Moscow" (K. F. Yuon)

1975. Birth Centenaries of Soviet Painters. Mult.

4422	1k. Type **1698**	10	10
4423	2k. "Winter Morning in Industrial Moscow" (K. P. Yuon)	15	10
4424	6k. "Soldiers with Captured Guns" (E. E. Lansere)	30	10
4425	10k. "Excavating the Metro Tunnel" (E. E. Lansere)	50	25
4426	16k. "A. A. Pushkin and N. N. Pushkina at Palace Ball" (N. P. Ulyanov) (vert)	70	35
4427	20k. "Lauriston at Kutuzov's Headquarters" (N. P. Ulyanov)	90	45

1699 Conference Emblem

1975. European Security and Co-operation Conf, Helsinki.

4428	**1699**	6k. black, gold and blue	1·00	55

1700 Isaakjan (after M. Sargan)

1975. Birth Centenary of Avetic Isaakjan (Armenian poet).

4429	**1700**	4k. multicoloured	30	10

1701 M. K. Ciurlionis

1975. Birth Centenary of M. K. Ciurlionis (Lithuanian composer).

4430	**1701**	4k. gold, green & yellow	30	10

1702 J. Duclos

1975. Jacques Duclos (French communist leader) Commemoration.

4431	**1702**	6k. purple and silver	30	10

1703 Al Farabi (after L. Leontev)

1975. 1100th Birth Anniv of Al Farabi (Persian philosopher).

4432	**1703**	6k. multicoloured	30	10

1704 Ruffs

1975. 50th Anniv of Berezinsky and Stolby Nature Reserves. Multicoloured.

4433	1k. Type **1704**	20	10
4434	4k. Siberian musk deer	25	15
4435	6k. Sable	30	25
4436	10k. Western capercaillie	50	35
4437	16k. Eurasian badger	70	55

1705 Korean Crest with Soviet and Korean Flags

1975. 30th Anniversaries. Multicoloured.

4438	6k. Type **1705** (Korean liberation)	30	10
4439	6k. Vietnamese crest, Soviet and Vietnamese flags (Vietnam Democratic Republic)	30	10

1706 Cosmonauts, "Soyuz 18" and "Salyut 4" Linked

1975. Space Flight of "Soyuz 18–Salyut 4" by Cosmonauts P. Klimuk and V. Sevastyanov.
4440 **1706** 10k. black, red and blue 40 15

1707 Yesenin

1975. 80th Birth Anniv of Yesenin (poet).
4441 **1707** 6k. brown, yell & grey 30 10

1708 Standardization Emblems

1975. 50th Anniv of Soviet Communications Standardization Committee.
4442 **1708** 4k. multicoloured 20 10

1709 Astrakhan Lamb

1975. 3rd International Astrakhan Lamb Breeding Symposium, Samarkand.
4443 **1709** 6k. black, green & stone 30 10

1710 M. P. Konchalovsky

1975. Birth Centenary of M. P. Konchalovsky (therapeutist).
4444 **1710** 4k. brown and red 20 10

1711 Exhibition Emblem

1975. 3rd All-Union Philatelic Exhibition, Yerevan.
4445 **1711** 4k. red, brown and blue 20 10

1712 I.W.Y. Emblem and Rose

1975. International Women's Year.
4446 **1712** 6k. red, blue & turquoise 30 10

1713 Parliament Buildings, Belgrade

1975. 30th Anniv of Yugoslav Republic.
4447 **1713** 6k. blue, red and gold 30 10

1714 Title-page of 1938 Edition

1975. 175th Anniv of Publication of "Tale of the Host of Igor".
4448 **1714** 4k. red, grey and bistre 20 10

1715 M. I. Kalinin (statesman)

1975. Celebrities' Birth Centenaries.
4449 **1715** 4k. brown 20 10
4450 - 4k. brown 20 10
DESIGN: No. 4450, A. V. Lunacharsky (politician).

1716 Torch and Inscription

1975. 70th Anniv of Russian 1905 Revolution.
4451 **1716** 4k. red and brown 20 10

1717 Track-laying Machine and Baikal-Amur Railway

1975. 58th Anniv of October Revolution. Mult.
4452 4k. Type **1717** 25 10
4453 4k. Rolling mill, Novolipetsk steel plant (vert) 25 10
4454 4k. Formula and ammonia plant, Nevynomyssk chemical works (vert) 25 10

1718 "Decembrists in Senate Square" (D. N. Kardovsky) (image scaled to 72% of original size)

1975. 150th Anniv of Decembrist Rising.
4455 **1718** 4k. multicoloured 25 10

1719 Star of Spassky Tower

1975. New Year.
4456 **1719** 4k. multicoloured 20 10

1720 "Village Street"

1975. 125th Birth Anniv of F. A. Vasilev (painter). Multicoloured.
4457 2k. Type **1720** 10 10
4458 4k. "Forest Path" 15 10
4459 6k. "After the Thunderstorm" 25 10
4460 10k. "Forest Marsh" (horiz) 40 20
4461 12k. "In the Crimean Mountains" 50 25
4462 16k. "Wet Meadow" (horiz) 80 35
MS4463 63×94 mm. 50k. Vasilev (after I. Kramskoi) 2·30 90

1721 "Venus" Spacecraft

1975. Space Flights of "Venus 9" and "Venus 10".
4464 **1721** 10k. multicoloured 40 20

1722 G. Sundukyan

1975. 150th Birth Anniv of G. Sundukyan (Armenian playwright).
4465 **1722** 4k. multicoloured 20 10

1723 Iceland Poppy

1975. Flowers (1st series). Multicoloured.
4466 4k. Type **1723** 10 10
4467 6k. Globe flower 20 10
4468 10k. Yellow anemone 35 20
4469 12k. Snowdrop windflower 45 25
4470 16k. "Eminium lehemannii" 60 30
See also Nos. 4585/9.

1724 A. L. Mints

1975. A. L. Mints (scientist) Commemoration.
4471 **1724** 4k. brown and gold 20 10

1725 "Demon" (A. Kochupalov)

1975. Miniatures from Palekh Art Museum (1st series). Multicoloured.
4472 4k. Type **1725** 20 10
4473 6k. "Vasilisa the Beautiful" (I. Vakurov) 30 15
4474 10k. "The Snow Maiden" (T. Zubkova) 50 25
4475 16k. "Summer" (K. Kukulieva) 70 45
4476 20k. "Fisherman and Goldfish" (I. Vakurov) (horiz) 90 55
See also Nos. 4561/5.

1726 Pieck

1976. Birth Centenary of Wilhelm Pieck (President of German Democratic Republic).
4477 **1726** 6k. black 30 10

1727 Saltykov-Shchedrin (after I. Kramskoi)

1976. 150th Birth Anniv of M. Saltykov-Shchedrin (writer).
4478 **1727** 4k. multicoloured 20 10

1728 Congress Emblem

1976. 25th Communist Party Congress, Moscow (1st issue).
4479 **1728** 4k. gold, brown and red 20 10
MS4480 106×74 mm. **1728** 50k. gold, lake and vermilion (27×37 mm) 2·30 90
See also Nos. 4489 and 4556/60.

1729 Lenin (statue, S. Merkurov), Kiev

1976. 25th Ukraine Communist Party Congress, Kiev.
4481 **1729** 4k. black, red and blue 20 10

1730 Ice Hockey

1976. Winter Olympic Games, Innsbruck (1st series). Multicoloured.

4482	2k. Type **1730**	15	10
4483	4k. Skiing	20	10
4484	6k. Figure skating	30	15
4485	10k. Speed skating	40	25
4486	20k. Tobogganing	75	40
MS4487	90×80 mm. 50k. red, yellow and blue (Games emblem) (vert)	2·30	90

See also No. **MS**4492.

1731 Marshal C. E. Voroshilov

1976. 95th Birth Anniv of Marshal C. E. Voroshilov.

4488	**1731**	4k. green	20	10

1732 Congress Hall and Red Banner

1976. 25th Communist Party Congress, Moscow (2nd issue).

4489	**1732**	20k. orange, red & green	4·00	3·00

1733 "Lenin on Red Square" (P. Vasilev)

1976. 106th Birth Anniv of Lenin.

4490	**1733**	4k. multicoloured	25	10

1734 Atomic Symbol and Institute Emblem

1976. 20th Anniv of Joint Institute of Nuclear Research, Dubna.

4491	**1734**	6k. multicoloured	25	10

СЛАВА
СОВЕТСКОМУ
СПОРТУ!
(1735a)

СПОРТСМЕНЫ СССР
ЗАВОЕВАЛИ
13 ЗОЛОТЫХ,
6 СЕРЕБРЯНЫХ,
8 БРОНЗОВЫХ
МЕДАЛЕЙ!
(1735b)

1976. Winter Olympic Games, Innsbruck (2nd issue). Dedicated to Soviet Medal Winners. No. MS4487 optd with Types 1735a and 1735b in red.

MS4492	90×80 mm. 50k. red, yellow and blue	9·00	7·25

1736 Bolshoi Theatre

1976. Bicentenary of Bolshoi Theatre.

4493	**1736**	10k. blue, brn & ochre	50	20

1737 "Back from the Fair"

1976. Birth Centenary of P. P. Konchalovsky (painter). Multicoloured.

4494	1k. Type **1737**	10	10
4495	2k. "The Green Glass"	10	10
4496	6k. "Peaches"	30	20
4497	16k. "Meat, Game and Vegetables by the Window"	70	30
4498	20k. Self-portrait (vert)	1·00	45

1738 "Vostok", "Salyut" and "Soyuz" Spacecraft

1976. 15th Anniv of First Manned Space Flight by Yuri Gagarin.

4499	4k. Type **1738**	20	10
4500	6k. "Meteor" and "Molniya" satellites	30	15
4501	10k. Cosmonauts on board "Salyut" space-station	50	20
4502	12k. "Interkosmos" satellite and "Apollo"–"Soyuz" space link	60	25
MS4503	65×100 mm. 50k. black (Yuri Gagarin) (37×52 mm)	15·00	10·00

1739 I. A. Dzhavakhishvili

1976. Birth Centenary of I. A. Dzhavakhishvili (scientist).

4504	**1739**	4k. black, stone and green	20	10

1740 S. Vurgun

1976. 70th Birth Anniv of Samed Vurgun (Azerbaijan poet).

4505	**1740**	4k. black, brown & green	20	10

1741 Festival Emblem

1976. 1st All-Union Amateur Art Festival.

4506	**1741**	4k. multicoloured	20	10

1742 F. I. P. Emblem

1976. 50th Anniv of International Philatelic Federation.

4507	**1742**	6k. red and blue	25	10

1744 Dnepropetrovsk Crest

1976. Bicentenary of Dnepropetrovsk.

4509	**1744**	4k. multicoloured	20	10

1745 N. N. Burdenko

1976. Birth Centenary of N. N. Burdenko (neurologist).

4510	**1745**	4k. brown and red	20	10

1746 K. A. Trenev

1976. Birth Centenary of K. A. Trenev (playwright).

4511	**1746**	4k. multicoloured	20	10

1976. History of Soviet Motor Industry (4th series). As T 1609.

4512	2k. black, red and green	10	10
4513	3k. black, orange and bistre	15	10
4514	4k. black, buff and blue	20	15
4515	12k. black, green and brown	50	25
4516	16k. black, red and yellow	75	35

DESIGNS: 2k. Moscow Auto Works "ZIS-110" saloon, 1945; 3k. Gorkovsky "GAZ-51" truck, 1946; 4k. Gorkovsky "GAZ-M20 (Pobeda)" saloon, 1946; 12k. Moscow Auto Works "ZIS-150" truck, 1947; 16k. Moscow Auto Works "ZIS-154" bus, 1947.

1747 Canoeing

1976. Olympic Games, Montreal. Multicoloured.

4517	4k. Type **1747**	10	10
4518	6k. Basketball (vert)	20	10
4519	10k. Graeco-Roman wrestling	30	15
4520	14k. Discus throwing (vert)	50	20
4521	16k. Rifle-shooting	60	25
MS4522	67×88 mm. 50k. Obverse and reverse of Gold medal	2·75	1·20

See also No. **MS**4552.

1748 Electric Railway Train

1976. 50th Anniv of Soviet Railway Electrification.

4523	**1748**	4k. black, red and green	35	10

1749 L. M. Pavlichenko

1976. 60th Birth Anniv of L. M. Pavlichenko (war heroine).

4524	**1749**	4k. brown, yellow and silver	20	10

1750 L. E. Rekabarren

1976. Birth Centenary of Luis Rekabarren (founder of Chilean Communist Party).

4525	**1750**	6k. black, red and gold	20	10

1751 "Fresh Partner"

1976. Russian Art. Paintings by P. A. Fedotov. Multicoloured.

4526	2k. Type **1751**	10	10
4527	4k. "Fastidious Fiancee" (horiz)	15	10
4528	6k. "Aristocrat's Breakfast"	20	15
4529	10k. "The Gamblers" (horiz)	50	25
4530	16k. "The Outing"	70	30
MS4531	70×90 mm. 50k. Self-portrait	2·00	90

1752 S. S. Nemetkin

1976. Birth Centenary of Sergei S. Nemetkin (chemist).

4532	**1752**	4k. black, yellow & blue	20	10

1753 Soviet Armed Forces Order

1976. (a) As T 1753. Size 14×21½ mm.

4533	1k. olive	15	10
4534	2k. magenta	20	10
4535	3k. scarlet	25	10
4536	4k. red	35	10
4537	6k. blue	45	10
4538	10k. green	60	10
4539	12k. ultramarine	80	25
4540	16k. green	1·00	35

1754 Marx and Lenin (sculpture, Ye. Belostotsky and E. Fridman)

(b) As T 1754.

4541	20k. lake	1·40	45
4542	30k. vermillion	2·30	65

4543		50k. brown	3·50	70
4544		1r. blue	5·50	1·50

DESIGNS: 2k. Gold Star (military) and Hammer and Sickle (labour) decorations; 3k. "Worker and Collective Farmer" (sculpture, Vera Mukhina); 4k. Soviet crest; 6k. Globe and Tupolev Tu-154 jetliner (Soviet postal communications); 10k. Soviet Reputation for Work order; 12k. Yury Gagarin and rocket (space exploration); 16k. International Lenin Prize medal (international peace and security); 30k. Council for Mutual Economic Aid building; 50k. Lenin (after P. Zhukov); 1r. Satellites orbiting globe.

See also Nos. 4669/82.

1755 Cattle Egret

1976. Water Birds. Multicoloured.

4545		1k. Type **1755**	20	10
4546		3k. Black-throated diver	30	20
4547		4k. Black coot	40	25
4548		6k. Atlantic puffin	80	45
4549		10k. Slender-billed gull	1·30	70

1756 Peace Dove with Laurel

1976. 2nd Stockholm World Peace Appeal.

4550	**1756**	4k. blue, yellow and gold	20	10

1757 Federation Emblem

1976. 25th Anniv of International Resistance Movement Federation.

4551	**1757**	6k. black, gold and blue	20	10

СПОРТСМЕНЫ
СССР
ЗАВОЕВАЛИ
47 ЗОЛОТЫХ,
43 СЕРЕБРЯНЫХ
И 35 БРОНЗОВЫХ
МЕДАЛЕЙ!

СОВЕТСКОМУ
СПОРТУ
СЛАВА!

(1758)

1976. Olympic Games, Montreal (2nd issue). Dedicated to Soviet Medal Winners. No. MS4522 optd with T 1758.

MS4552 67×88 mm. 50k. Obverse and reverse of Gold Medal		8·25	5·50

1759 Soviet and Indian Flags

1976. Soviet–Indian Friendship.

4553	**1759**	4k. multicoloured	20	10

1760 B. V. Volynov and V. M. Zholobov

1976. Space Flight of "Soyuz 21".

4554	**1760**	10k. black, blue & brn	40	20

1761 UNESCO Emblem

1976. 30th Anniv of UNESCO.

4555	**1761**	16k. brown, bistre & blue	60	40

1762 "Industry"

1976. 25th Communist Party Congress (3rd issue).

4556	**1762**	4k. brown, red & yellow	20	10
4557	-	4k. green, red & orange	20	10
4558	-	4k. violet, red and pink	20	10
4559	-	4k. deep red, red and grey	20	10
4560	-	4k. violet, red and blue	20	10

DESIGNS: No. 4557, "Agriculture"; 4558, "Science and Technology"; 4559, "Transport and Communications"; 4560, "International Co-operation".

1763 "The Ploughman" (I. Golikov)

1976. Minatures from Palekh Art Museum (2nd series). Multicoloured.

4561		2k. Type **1763**	10	10
4562		4k. "The Search" (I. Markichev) (vert)	20	15
4563		12k. "The Firebird" (A. Kotukhin)	65	45
4564		14k. "Folk Festival" (A. Vatagin) (vert)	75	45
4565		20k. "Victory" (I. Vakurov) (vert)	1·00	70

1764 Shostakovich and Part of 7th Symphony

1976. 70th Birth Anniv of Dmitri Shostakovich (composer).

4566	**1764**	6k. blue	40	10

1765 G. K. Zhukov

1976. 80th Birth Anniversaries of Soviet Marshals.

4567	**1765**	4k. green	20	10
4568	-	4k. brown	20	10

DESIGN: No. 4568, K. K. Rokossovsky.

1766 "Interkosmos 14" Satellite

1976. International Co-operation in Space Research.

4569	**1766**	6k. blue, gold and black	20	10
4570	-	10k. violet, gold & black	30	10
4571	-	12k. purple, gold & black	40	20
4572	-	16k. green, gold & black	50	30
4573	-	20k. mauve, gold & black	90	35

DESIGNS: 10k. "Aryabhata" (Indian satellite); 12k. "Apollo"–"Soyuz" space link; 16k. "Aureole" (French satellite); 20k. Globe and spacecraft.

1767 V. I. Dal

1976. 175th Birth Anniv of V. I. Dal (scholar).

4574	**1767**	4k. green	20	10

1768 Electric Power Station

1976. 59th Anniv of October Revolution. Mult.

4575		4k. Type **1768**	20	10
4576		4k. Balashovo fabrics factory	20	10
4577		4k. Irrigation ditch construction	20	10

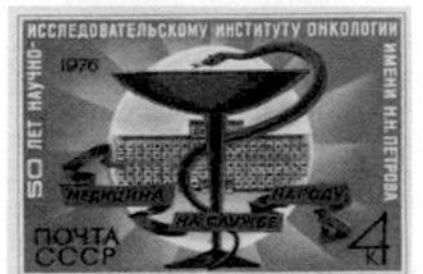

1769 Medicine Emblem

1976. 50th Anniv of Petrov Institute of Cancer Research.

4578	**1769**	4k. lilac, gold and blue	25	10

1770 M. A. Novinsky (oncologist)

1976. Centenary of Cancer Research.

4579	**1770**	4k. brown, blue and buff	25	10

1771 Hakkel VII Biplane, 1911

1976. Early Russian Aircraft (2nd series). Mult.

4580		3k. Type **1771**	10	10
4581		6k. Hakkel IX monoplane, 1912	20	15
4582		12k. Steglau No. 2, 1912	40	20
4583		14k. Dybovsky Dolphin, 1913	55	25
4584		16k. Sikorsky Ilya Mourometz, 1914	60	35

See also Nos. 4661/6 and 4791/6.

1976. Flowers (2nd series). As T 1723. Mult.

4585		1k. Safflower	10	10
4586		2k. Anemone	10	10
4587		3k. Gentian	10	10
4588		4k. Columbine	20	10

4589		6k. Fitillaria	30	15

1772 New Year Greeting

1976. New Year.

4590	**1772**	4k. multicoloured	20	10

1773 "Parable of the Vineyard"

1976. 370th Birth Anniv of Rembrandt. Mult.

4591		4k. Type **1773**	20	10
4592		6k. "Danae"	25	15
4593		10k. "David and Jonathan" (vert)	50	20
4594		14k. "The Holy Family" (vert)	65	25
4595		20k. "Andrian" (vert)	90	45
MS4596		125×66 mm. 50k. "Artaxeres, Hamann and Esther"	12·00	8·50

1774 "Luna 24" and Emblem

1976. "Luna 24" Unmanned Space Flight to Moon.

4597	**1774**	10k. brown, yellow & blue	40	20

1775 "Pailot"

1976. Russian Ice-breakers (1st series). Mult.

4598		4k. Type **1775**	40	10
4599		6k. "Ermak" (vert)	50	15
4600		10k. "Fyodor Litke"	70	20
4601		16k. "Vladmir Ilich" (vert)	1·00	45
4602		20k. "Krassin"	1·30	55

See also Nos. 4654/60, 4843/8 and 5147.

1776 "Raduga" Experiment and Cosmonauts

1976. "Soyuz 22" Space Flight by V. F. Bykovsky and V. V. Aksenov.

4603	**1776**	10k. green, blue and red	40	20

1777 Olympic Torch

1976. Olympic Games, Moscow (1980).

4604	**1777**	4k.+2k. black, red and blue	35	20
4605	-	10k.+5k. black, blue and red	60	30
4606	-	16k.+6k. black, mauve and yellow	1·20	45
MS4607		63×83 mm. 60k.+30k. black, gold and red	8·75	5·00

DESIGNS: 30×42 mm—10, 16k. Games Emblem. 27×38 mm—6k. Kemlin.

1778 Society Emblem and "Red Star"

1977. 50th Anniv of Red Banner Forces Voluntary Society.

4608	**1778**	4k. multicoloured	20	10

1779 S. P. Korolev Memorial Medallion

1977. 70th Birth Anniv of S. P. Korolev (scientist and rocket pioneer).

4609	**1779**	4k. gold, black and blue	20	10

1780 Congress Emblem

1977. World Peace Congress, Moscow.

4610	**1780**	4k. gold, ultramarine and blue	20	10

1781 Sedov and "Sv. Foka"

1977. Birth Cent of G. Y. Sedov (polar explorer).

4611	**1781**	4k. multicoloured	50	20

1782 Working Class Monument, Red Flag and Newspaper Cover

1977. 60th Anniv of Newspaper "Izvestiya".

4612	**1782**	4k. black, red and silver	20	10

1783 Ship on Globe

1977. 24th International Navigation Congress, Leningrad.

4613	**1783**	6k. blue, black and gold	25	10

1784 Kremlin Palace of Congresses, Moscow

1977. 16th Soviet Trade Unions Congress.

4614	**1784**	4k. gold, black and red	20	10

1785 L. A. Govorov

1977. 80th Birth Anniv of Marshal L. A. Govorov.

4615	**1785**	4k. brown	20	10

1786 Academy Emblem, Text and Building

1977. 150th Anniv of Grechko Naval Academy, Leningrad.

4616	**1786**	6k. multicoloured	20	10

1787 J. Labourbe

1977. Birth Centenary of Jeanne Labourbe (French communist).

4617	**1787**	4k. black, blue and red	20	10

1788 Chess Pieces

1977. 6th European Chess Team Championship, Moscow.

4618	**1788**	6k. multicoloured	50	30

1789 "Soyuz 23" and Cosmonauts

1977. "Soyuz 23" Space Flight by V. D. Zudov and V. I. Rozhdestvensky.

4619	**1789**	10k. red, black & brown	40	20

1790 Novikov-Priboi

1977. Birth Centenary of Aleksei Novikov-Priboi (writer).

4620	**1790**	4k. black, orange & blue	20	10

1791 "Welcome" (N. M. Soloninkin)

1977. Folk Paintings from Fedoskino Village. Multicoloured.

4621	4k. Type **1791**	20	10
4622	6k. "Along the Street" (V. D. Antonov) (horiz)	25	10
4623	10k. "Northern Song" (J. V. Karapaev)	50	15
4624	12k. "Fairy Tale about Tzar Sultan" (A. I. Kozlov)	55	20
4625	14k. "Summer Troika" (V. A. Nalimov) (horiz)	60	25
4626	16k. "Red Flower" (V. D. Lipitsky)	70	35

1792 Congress Emblem

1977. World Electronics Congress, Moscow.

4627	**1792**	6k. red, grey and blue	20	10

1793 "In Red Square" (K. V. Filatov)

1977. 107th Birth Anniv of Lenin.

4628	**1793**	4k. multicoloured	20	10

1794 Yuri Gagarin and Spacecraft

1977. Cosmonautics Day.

4629	**1794**	6k. blue, lilac and purple	30	15

1795 N. I. Vavilov

1977. 90th Birth Anniv of N. I. Vavilov (biologist).

4630	**1795**	4k. black and brown	20	10

1796 F. E. Dzerzhinsky

1977. Birth Centenary of Feliks Dzerzhinsky (founder of Cheka).

4631	**1796**	4k. black	20	10

1797 Mountain Saxifrage

1977. Flowers. Multicoloured.

4632	2k. Type **1797**	10	10
4633	3k. Pinks	10	10
4634	4k. "Novosieversia glacialis"	20	15
4635	6k. "Cerastium maximum"	30	25
4636	16k. "Rhododendron aureum"	70	45

1798 V. V. Gorbatko and Yu. N. Glazkov (cosmonauts)

1977. "Soyuz 24–Salyut 5" Space Project.

4637	**1798**	10k. black, red and blue	45	20

1799 I. S. Konev

1977. 80th Birth Anniv of Soviet Marshals.

4638	**1799**	4k. green	30	15
4639	-	4k. black	30	15
4640	-	4k. brown	30	15

DESIGNS: No. 4639, V. D. Sokolovsky; 4640, K. A. Meretskov.

1800 Festival Emblem

1977. 10th International Film Festival, Moscow.

4641	**1800**	6k. gold, red and lake	20	10

1801 Greco-Roman Wrestling

1977. Olympic Sports (1st series).

4642	**1801**	4k.+2k. black, ochre and gold	20	10
4643	-	6k.+3k. black, green and gold	30	10
4644	-	10k.+5k. black, mauve and gold	50	20
4645	-	16k.+6k. black, blue and gold	70	35
4646	-	20k.+10k. black, brown and gold	1·60	55

DESIGNS: 6k. Free-style wrestling; 10k. Judo; 16k. Boxing; 29k. Weightlifting.

See also Nos. 4684/9, 4749/53, 4820/4, 4870/4, 4896/4900, 4962/6 and 4973/7.

1802 "Portrait of a Chambermaid"

1977. 400th Birth Anniv of Rubens. Multicoloured.

4647	4k. Type **1802**	20	10
4648	6k. "The Lion Hunt" (horiz)	25	15
4649	10k. "Stone Carriers" (horiz)	40	20
4650	12k. "Water and Earth Alliance"	60	25
4651	20k. "Landscape with Rainbow" (horiz)	95	45

MS4652 104×74 mm. 50k. Rubens" (detail from "Portrait of Rubens and his Son") 2·30 90

1803 "Judith" (detail)

1977. 500th Birth Anniv of Giorgione. Sheet 77×104 mm.
MS4653 50k. multicoloured 2·30 90

1977. Soviet Ice-breakers (2nd series). As T 1775. Multicoloured.

4654	4k. "Aleksandr Sibiryakov"	25	10
4655	6k. "Georgy Sedov"	30	15
4656	10k. "Sadko"	55	35
4657	12k. "Dezhnev"	65	45
4658	14k. "Sibur"	75	55
4659	16k. "Lena"	90	65
4660	20k. "Amguema"	1·10	70

1977. Air. Early Soviet Aircraft (3rd series). As T 1771 but dated 1977.

4661	4k. black, brown and blue	20	10
4662	6k. black, orange and green	25	15
4663	10k. black, mauve and blue	30	25
4664	12k. black, blue and red	40	35
4665	16k. multicoloured	50	45
4666	20k. black, green and blue	70	55

DESIGNS: 4k. Porokhovshchikov P-IV bis biplane trainer, 1917; 6k. Kalinin AK-1, 1924; 10k. Tupolev ANT-3 R-3, 1925; 12k. Tupolev ANT-4 TB-1 bomber, 1929; 16k. Polikarpov R-5 biplane, 1929; 20k. Shavrov Sh-2 flying boat, 1930.

1804 Stamps and Emblem

1977. "60th Anniv of October Revolution" Philatelic Exhibition, Moscow.

4667	1804	4k. red, blue and brown	20	10

1805 Buildings and Arms, Stavropol

1977. Bicentenary of Stavropol.

4668	1805	6k. gold, red and green	25	10

1976. As Nos. 4533/44 and new value. (a) As T 1753.

4669	1k. olive	10	10
4670	2k. mauve	10	10
4671	3k. red	10	10
4672	4k. red	15	10
4673	6k. blue	30	10
4674	10k. green	40	10
4675	12k. blue	50	20
4676	15k. blue	65	25
4677	16k. green	60	20

(b) As T 1754.

4678	20k. red	70	35
4679	30k. red	90	40
4680	32k. blue	1·60	50
4681	50k. brown	1·30	55
4682	1r. blue	3·00	1·10

DESIGNS: 2k. Gold Star (military) and Hammer and Sickle (labour) decorations; 3k. "Worker and Collective Farmer" (sculpture, Vera Mukhina); 4k. Soviet crest; 6k. Globe and Tupolev Tu-154 jetliner (Soviet postal communications); 10k. Soviet Reputation for Work Order; 12k. Yuri Gagarin and rocket (space exploration); 15k. Ostankino T.V. tower and globe; 16k. International Lenin Prize medal (international peace and security); 30k. Council for Mutual Economic Aid building; 32k. Ilyushin Il-76 airplane and compass rose; 50k. Lenin (after P. Zhukov); 1r. Satellites orbiting globe.

The 6 and 32k. are airmail stamps.

1806 "Arktika"

1977. Journey to North Pole of "Arktika" (atomic ice-breaker). Sheet 107×80 mm.
MS4683 50k. multicoloured 12·50 6·00

1977. Olympic Sports (2nd series). As T 1801.

4684	4k.+2k. black, gold and red	20	10
4685	6k.+3k. black, gold & blue	50	20
4686	10k.+5k. black, gold & grn	75	25
4687	16k.+6k. black, gold & olive	1·00	35
4688	20k.+10k. black, gold & pur	1·80	65

MS4689 92×72 mm. 50k.+25k. black, gold and blue 9·50 6·75

DESIGNS—HORIZ: 4k. Cycling; 10k. Rifle-shooting; 16k. Horse-jumping; 20k. Fencing; 50k. horse-jumping and fencing (Modern pentathlon). VERT: 6k. Archery.

1807 Yuri Gagarin and "Vostok" Spacecraft

1977. 20th Anniv of Space Exploration.

4690	1807	10k. red, blue and brown	40	20
4691	-	10k. brown, blue & violet	40	20
4692	-	10k. red, purple & green	40	20
4693	-	20k. green, brown & red	60	25
4694	-	20k. purple, red and blue	60	25
4695	-	20k. red, blue and green	60	25

MS4696 66×86 mm. 50k. gold and lake (22×32 mm) 15·00 9·00

DESIGNS: No. 4691, Space walking; 4692, "Soyuz" spacecraft and "Salyut" space station linked; 4693, "Proton 4" satellite; 4694, "Luna Venus" and "Mars" space stations; 4695, "Intercosmos 10" satellite and "Apollo" and "Soyuz" spacecraft linked; MS4696, "Sputnik 1" satellite.

1808 Carving from St. Dmitri's Cathedral, Vladimir (12th-cent)

1977. Russian Art. Multicoloured.

4697	4k. Type **1808**	20	10
4698	6k. Bracelet, Ryazan (12th cent)	20	15
4699	10k. Detail of Golden Gate from Nativity Cathedral, Suzdal (13th-cent)	30	15
4700	12k. Detail from "Arch-angel Michael" (icon) (A. Rublev) (15th-cent)	40	20
4701	16k. Gold and marble chalice made by I. Fomin (15th-cent)	60	25
4702	20k. St. Basil's Cathedral, Moscow (16th-cent)	70	30

1809 "Snowflake and Fir Twig"

1977. New Year.

4703	1809	4k. multicoloured	20	10

1810 Cruiser "Aurora"

1977. 60th Anniv of October Revolution.

4704	1810	4k. multicoloured	20	10
4705	-	4k. black, red and gold	20	10
4706	-	4k. black, red and gold	20	10
4707	-	4k. multicoloured	20	10

MS4708 106×71 mm. 30k. black, vermilion and gold 1·30 55

DESIGNS: No. 4705, Statue of Lenin; 4706, Page of "Izvestiya", book by Brezhnev and crowd; 4707, Kremlin spire, star and fireworks. 26×38 mm—30k. Lenin medal.

1811 First Clause of U.S.S.R. Constitution

1977. New Constitution.

4709	1811	4k. yellow, red & brown	20	10
4710	-	4k. multicoloured	20	10

MS4711 112×82 mm. 50k. multicoloured 2·00 1·00

DESIGNS: 47×32 mm—No. 4710 People of U.S.S.R. welcoming new constitution. 69×47 mm—50k. Constitution as open book, and laurel branch.

1812 Leonid Brezhnev

1977. New Constitution (2nd issue). Sheet 143×74 mm.
MS4712 50k. multicoloured 2·30 1·50

1813 Postwoman and Post Code

1977. Postal Communications. Multicoloured.

4713	4k. Type **1813**	20	10
4714	4k. Letter collection	20	10
4715	4k. "Map-O" automatic sorting machine	20	10
4716	4k. Mail transport	20	10
4717	4k. Delivering the mail	20	10

1814 Red Fort, Delhi and Asokan Capital

1977. 30th Anniv of Indian Independence.

4718	1814	6k. gold, purple and red	30	10

1815 Monument, Kharkov

1977. 60th Anniv of Establishment of Soviet Power in the Ukraine.

4719	1815	6k. multicoloured	20	10

1816 Adder

1977. Snakes and Protected Animals. Mult.

4720	1k. Type **1816**	10	10
4721	4k. Levantine viper	15	15
4722	6k. Saw-scaled viper	20	20
4723	10k. Central Asian viper	35	25
4724	12k. Central Asian cobra	45	35
4725	16k. Polar bear and cub	55	45
4726	20k. Walrus and young	75	65
4727	30k. Tiger and cub	1·00	80

1817 Olympic Emblem and Arms of Vladimir

1977. 1980 Olympics. "Tourism around the Golden Ring" (1st issue). Multicoloured.

4728	1r.+50k. Type **1817**	4·50	2·75
4729	1r.+50k. Vladimir Hotel	4·50	2·75
4730	1r.+50k. Arms of Suzdal	4·50	2·75
4731	1r.+50k. Pozharsky monument	4·50	2·75
4732	1r.+50k. Arms of Ivanovo and Frunze monument	4·50	2·75
4733	1r.+50k. Monument to Revolutionary Fighters	4·50	2·75

See also Nos. 4828/31, 4850/3, 4914/17, 4928/9, 4968/9, 4981/2 and 4990/5.

1818 Combine Harvester

1978. 50th Anniv of "Gigant" Collective Farm, Rostov.

4734	1818	4k. brown, red & yellow	20	10

1819 Kremlin Palace of Congresses

1978. 18th Leninist Young Communist League (Komsomol) Congress.

4735	1819	4k. multicoloured	20	10

1820 Globe, Obelisk and Emblem

1978. 8th International Federation of Resistance Fighters Congress, Minsk.

4736	**1820**	6k. red, blue and black	20	10

1821 Red Army Detachment and Modern Sailor, Airman and Soldier

1978. 60th Anniv of Soviet Military Forces. Mult.

4737	4k. Type **1821**	20	10
4738	4k. Defenders of Moscow monument (detail), Lenin banner and Order of Patriotic War	20	10
4739	4k. Soviet soldier	20	10

1822 "Celebration in a Village" (image scaled to 68% of original size)

1978. Birth Centenary of Boris M. Kustodiev (artist). Multicoloured.

4740	4k. Type **1822**	20	10
4741	6k. "Shrovetide"	25	10
4742	10k. "Morning" (50×36 mm)	40	20
4743	12k. "Merchant's Wife drinking Tea" (50×36 mm)	50	25
4744	20k. "Bolshevik" (50×36 mm)	70	40
MS4745	92×72 mm. 50k. "Self-portrait" (36×50 mm)	2·00	90

1823 Gubarev and Remek at Launch Pad

1978. Soviet–Czech Space Flight. Multicoloured.

4746	6k. Type **1823**	20	10
4747	15k. "Soyuz-28" docking with "Salyut-6" space station	50	20
4748	32k. Splashdown	1·00	40

1978. Olympic Sports (3rd series). As T 1801. Multicoloured.

4749	4k.+2k. Swimmer at start	20	10
4750	6k.+3k. Diving (vert)	40	25
4751	10k.+5k. Water polo	70	45
4752	10k.+6k. Canoeist	1·00	65
4753	20k.+10k. Single sculls	1·50	90
MS4754	92×71 mm. 50k.+25k. grey, black and green (Double sculls)	9·00	6·00

1824 "Soyuz" Capsules linked to "Salyut" Space Station

1978. Cosmonautics Day.

4755	**1824**	6k. gold, blue and deep blue	20	10

1825 Shield and Laurel Wreath

1978. 9th World Congress of Trade Unions.

4756	**1825**	6k. multicoloured	20	10

1826 E. A. and M. E. Cherepanov and their Locomotive, 1833

1978. Russian Locomotives (1st series). Mult.

4757	1k. Type **1826**	20	10
4758	2k. Series D locomotive, 1845	20	10
4759	3k. Series V locomotive (first passenger train, 1845)	20	20
4760	16k. Series Gv locomotive, 1863–67	95	70
4761	20k. Series Bv locomotive, 1863–67	1·20	80

Nos. 4758/61 are horizontal designs.
See also Nos. 4861/5.

1827 Lenin (after V. A. Servo)

1978. 108th Birth Anniv of Lenin. Sheet 73×96 mm.

MS4762	50k. multicoloured	2·00	1·00

1828 "XI" and Laurel Branch

1978. 11th World Youth and Students Festival, Havana.

4763	**1828**	4k. multicoloured	20	10

1829 Tulip "Bolshoi Theatre"

1978. Moscow Flowers. Multicoloured.

4764	1k. Type **1829**	10	10
4765	2k. Rose "Moscow Morning"	10	10
4766	4k. Dahlia "Red Star"	15	10
4767	10k. Gladiolus "Moscovite"	40	20
4768	12k. Iris "To Il'ich's Anniversary"	45	25

1830 I.M.C.O. Emblem

1978. 20th Anniv of Intergovernment Maritime Consultative Organization, and World Maritime Day.

4769	**1830**	6k. multicoloured	20	10

1831 "Salyut-6" Space Station performing Survey Work

1978. "Salyut-6" Space Station. Multicoloured.

4770	15k. Type **1831**	50	30
4771	15k. Yu. V. Romanenko and G. M. Grechko	50	30

Nos. 4770/1 were issued in se-tenant pairs forming a composite design.

1832 "Space Meteorology"

1978. Space Research. Multicoloured.

4772	10k. Type **1832**	35	20
4773	10k. "Soyuz" orbiting globe ("Natural resources")	35	20
4774	10k. Radio waves, ground station and "Molniya" satellite ("Communication")	35	20
4775	10k. Human figure, "Vostok" orbiting Earth ("Medicine and biology")	35	20
MS4776	102×77 mm. "Prognoz" satellite ("Physics") (36×51 mm)	2·00	90

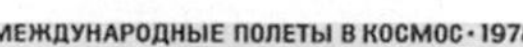

1833 Transporting Rocket to Launch Site

1978. Soviet–Polish Space Flight. Multicoloured.

4777	6k. Type **1833**	20	10
4778	15k. Crystal (Sirena experiment)	50	25
4779	32k. Space station, map and scientific research ship "Kosmonavt Vladimir Komarov"	1·20	55

1834 Komsomol Awards

1978. 60th Anniv of Leninist Young Communist League (Komsomol). Multicoloured.

4780	4k. Type **1834**	20	10
4781	4k. Products of agriculture and industry	20	10

1835 M. V. Zakharov

1978. 80th Birth Anniv of Marshal M. V. Zakharov.

4782	**1835**	4k. brown	20	10

1836 N. G. Chernyshevsky

1978. 150th Birth Anniv of Nikolai G. Chernyshevsky (revolutionary).

4783	**1836**	4k. brown and yellow	20	10

1837 Snow Petrel

1978. Antarctic Fauna. Multicoloured.

4784	1k. Snares Island penguin (horiz)	40	15
4785	3k. Type **1837**	55	15
4786	4k. Emperor penguin	70	15
4787	6k. Antarctic icefish	90	20
4788	10k. Southern elephant-seal (horiz)	1·00	25

1838 Torch and Flags

1978. Construction of Orenburg–U.S.S.R. Western Frontier Gas Pipe-line.

4789	**1838**	4k. multicoloured	20	10

1839 William Harvey

1978. 400th Birth Anniv of William Harvey (discoverer of blood circulation).

4790	**1839**	6k. green, black and blue	25	10

1978. Air. Early Russian Aircraft (3rd series). As T 1771.

4791	4k. green, brown and black	15	10
4792	6k. multicoloured	25	20
4793	10k. yellow, blue and black	45	25
4794	12k. orange, blue and black	55	35
4795	16k. blue, deep blue and black	70	45
4796	20k. multicoloured	95	55

DESIGNS: 4k. Polikarpov Po-2 biplane, 1928; 6k. Kalinin K-5, 1929; 10k. Tupolev ANT-6 TB-3 bomber, 1930; 12k. Putilov Stal-2, 1931; 16k. Beriev Be-2 MBR-2 reconnaissance seaplane, 1932; 20k. Polikarpov I-16 fighter, 1934.

1840 "Bathing of Red Horse"

1978. Birth Centenary of K. S. Petrov-Vodkin (painter). Multicoloured.

4797	4k. Type **1840**	10	10
4798	6k. "Petrograd, 1918"	20	10
4799	10k. "Commissar's Death"	40	20
4800	12k. "Rose Still Life"	50	20
4801	16k. "Morning Still Life"	65	25
MS4802	92×72 mm. 50k. "Self-portrait" (vert)	1·70	90

1841 Assembling "Soyuz 31"

1978. Soviet–East German Space Flight. Mult.

4803	6k. Type **1841**	20	10
4804	15k. Space photograph of Pamir mountains	70	25
4805	32k. Undocking from space station	1·40	45

1842 "Molniya 1" Satellite, "Orbita" Ground Station and Tupolev Tu-134 Jetliner

1978. "PRAGA 78" International Stamp Exhibition.

4806	**1842**	6k. multicoloured	30	20

1843 Tolstoi

1978. 150th Birth Anniv of Leo Tolstoi (novelist).

4807	**1843**	4k. green	1·60	1·20

1844 Union Emblem

1978. 14th General Assembly of International Union for the Protection of Nature and Natural Resources, Ashkhabad.

4808	**1844**	4k. multicoloured	20	10

1845 Bronze Figure, Erebuni Fortress

1978. Armenian Architecture. Multicoloured.

4809	4k. Type **1845**	15	10
4810	6k. Echmiadzin Cathedral	20	10
4811	10k. Khachkary (carved stones)	30	10
4812	12k. Matenadaran building (repository of manuscripts) (horiz)	40	20
4813	16k. Lenin Square, Yerevan (horiz)	50	25

1846 Monument (P. Kufferge)

1978. 70th Anniv of Russian Aid to Messina Earthquake Victims.

4814	**1846**	6k. multicoloured	25	10

1847 Emblem, Ostankino TV Tower and Hammer and Sickle

1978. 20th Anniv of Organization for Communications Co-operation.

4815	**1847**	4k. multicoloured	20	10

1978. "60th Anniv of Komsomol" Philatelic Exhibition. Optd with T 1848.

4816	**1834**	4k. multicoloured	1·50	1·20

1849 "Diana" (detail)

1978. 450th Birth Anniv of Paolo Veronese (artist). Sheet 76×115 mm.

MS4817	50k. multicoloured	1·80	1·00

1850 Kremlin

1978. 1st Anniv of New Constitution. Sheet 160×85 mm.

MS4818	30k. multicoloured	1·30	90

1851 Shaumyan

1978. Birth Centenary of Stephan Georgievich Shaumyan (Commissar).

4819	**1851**	4k. green	20	10

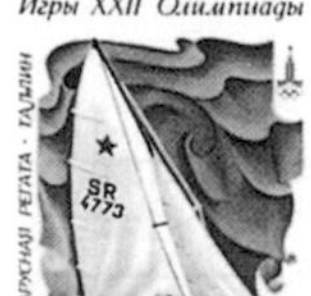

1852 "Star" Yacht

1978. Olympic Sports (4th series). Sailing Regatta, Tallin. Multicoloured.

4820	4k.+2k. Type **1852**	20	10
4821	6k.+3k. "Soling" yacht	30	15
4822	10k.+5k. "470" dinghy	50	35
4823	16k.+6k. "Finn" dinghy	80	55
4824	20k.+10k. "Flying Dutchman" dinghy	1·20	70
MS4825	71×94 mm. 50k.+25k. "Tornado" class catamaran (horiz)	9·00	5·50

1853 Industrial Structures and Flags

1978. 61st Anniv of October Revolution.

4826	**1853**	4k. multicoloured	20	10

1854 Black Sea Ferry

1978. Inauguration of Ilichevsk–Varna, Bulgaria, Ferry Service.

4827	**1854**	6k. multicoloured	20	10

1855 Zagorsk

1978. 1980 Olympics. "Tourism around the Golden Ring" (2nd issue). Multicoloured.

4828	1r.+50k. Type **1855**	4·00	2·50
4829	1r.+50k. Palace of Culture, Zagorsk	4·00	2·50
4830	1r.+50k. Kremlin, Rostov- Veliki	4·00	2·50
4831	1r.+50k. View of Rostov- Veliki	4·00	2·50

1856 Church of the Intercession on River Nerl

1978. "Masterpieces of Old Russian Culture". Mult.

4832	6k. Golden crater (horiz)	20	10
4833	10k. Type **1856**	40	15
4834	12k. "St. George and the Dragon" (15th-century icon)	50	20
4835	16k. Tsar Cannon (horiz)	60	25

1857 Cup with Snake and Institute

1978. 75th Anniv of Herzen Oncology Research Institute, Moscow.

4836	**1857**	4k. gold, purple & black	20	10

1858 Nestor Pechersky and "Chronicle of Past Days"

1978. History of the Russian Posts. Multicoloured.

4837	4k. Type **1858**	15	10
4838	6k. Birch-bark letter	20	10
4839	10k. Messenger with trumpet	35	20
4840	12k. Mail sledges	40	20
4841	16k. Interior of Prikaz Post Office	50	25

1859 Spassky Tower, Kremlin

1978. New Year.

4842	**1859**	4k. multicoloured	30	20

1978. Soviet Ice breakers (3rd series). As T 1775. Multicoloured.

4843	4k. "Vasily Pronchishchev"	20	10
4844	6k. "Kapitan Belousov" (vert)	30	20

4845	10k. "Moskva"	40	25
4846	12k. "Admiral Makarov"	50	35
4847	16k. "Lenin" atomic ice- breaker (vert)	70	40
4848	20k. "Arktika" atomic ice-breaker	80	45

1860 V. Kovalenok and A. Ivanchenkov

1978. "140 Days in Space".

4849	**1860**	10k. multicoloured	40	25

1978. 1980 Olympics "Tourism around the Golden Ring" (3rd issue). As T 1855. Multicoloured.

4850	1r.+50k. Alexander Nevsky Monument, Pereslavl-Zalessky	4·00	2·50
4851	1r.+50k. Peter I Monument, Pereslavl-Zalessky	4·00	2·50
4852	1r.+50k. Monastery of the Transfiguration, Yaroslavl	4·00	2·50
4853	1r.+50k. Ferry terminal and Eternal Glory Monument, Yaroslavl	4·00	2·50

1861 Globe and Newspaper Titles

1978. 60th Anniv of "Soyuzpechati" State Newspaper Distribution Service. Sheet 106×82 mm.

MS4854	30k. multicoloured	1·30	70

1862 Cuban Flags

1979. 20th Anniv of Cuban Revolution.

4855	**1862**	6k. multicoloured	20	10

1863 Government Building, Minsk

1979. 60th Anniv of Byelorussian Soviet Socialist Republic and Communist Party.

4856	**1863**	4k. multicoloured	20	10

1864 Flags and Reunion Monument

1979. 325th Anniv of Reunion of Ukraine with Russia.

4857	**1864**	4k. multicoloured	20	10

1865 Old and New University Buildings

1979. 400th Anniv of Vilnius University.

4858	**1865**	4k. black and pink	20	10

1866 Exhibition Hall and First Bulgarian Stamp

1979. "Philaserdica 79" International Stamp Exhibition, Sofia.

4859	**1866**	15k. multicoloured	60	25

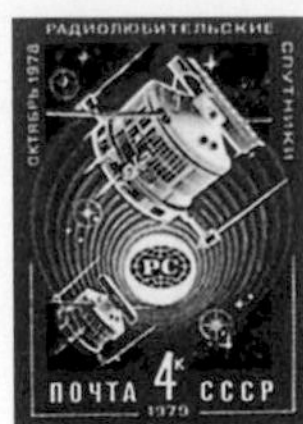

1867 Satellites "Radio 1" and "Radio 2"

1979. Launching of "Radio" Satellites.

4860	**1867**	4k. multicoloured	45	20

1868 Series A Locomotive, 1878

1979. Railway Locomotives (2nd series). Mult.

4861	2k. Type **1868**	15	10
4862	3k. Class Shch steam locomotive, 1912	15	10
4863	4k. Class Lp steam locomotive, 1915	25	15
4864	6k. Class Su steam locomotive, 1925	45	25
4865	15k. Class L steam locomotive, 1947	1·10	70

1869 Medal and Komsomol Pass

1979. 25th Anniv of Development of Virgin and Disused Land. Sheet 99×67 mm.

MS4866	50k. multicoloured	1·90	70

1870 "Venera 12" over Venus

1979. "Venera" Flights to Venus.

4867	**1870**	10k. red, lilac and purple	45	20

1871 Albert Einstein

1979. Birth Centenary of Albert Einstein (physicist).

4868	**1871**	6k. multicoloured	35	15

1872 Congress Emblem

1979. 21st World Veterinary Congress, Moscow.

4869	**1872**	6k. multicoloured	20	10

1873 Free Exercise

1979. Olympic Sports (5th series). Gymnastics.

4870	**1873**	4k.+2k. brown, stone and orange	15	10
4871	-	6k.+3k. blue, grey and violet	20	15
4872	-	10k.+5k. red, stone and brown	40	25
4873	-	16k.+6k. mauve, grey and purple	70	40
4874	-	20k.+10k. red, stone and brown	1·30	65
MS4875		91×71 mm. 50k.+25k. brown, stone and light brown	7·00	4·50

DESIGNS:—VERT: 6k. Parallel bars; 10k. Horizontal bar; 16k. Beam; 20k. Asymmetric bars. HORIZ: 50k. Rings.

1874 "To Arms" (poster by R. Beren)

1979. 60th Anniv of First Hungarian Socialist Republic.

4876	**1874**	4k. multicoloured	20	10

1875 Cosmonauts at Yuri Gagarin Training Centre

1979. Soviet–Bulgarian Space Flight. Mult.

4877	6k. Type **1875**	20	10
4878	32k. Landing of cosmonauts	95	40

1876 "Intercosmos" (image scaled to 75% of original size)

1979. Cosmonautics Day.

4879	**1876**	15k. multicoloured	60	30

1877 Ice Hockey

1979. World and European Ice Hockey Championship, Moscow. Sheet 85×65 mm.

MS4880	50k. red, blue and maroon	2·00	90

See also **MS**4888.

1878 Exhibition Emblem

1979. U.S.S.R. Exhibition, London.

4881	**1878**	15k. multicoloured	40	20

1879 Lenin

1979. 109th Birth Anniv of Lenin. Sheet 89×71 mm.

MS4882	50k. multicoloured	2·00	90

1880 Antonov An-28

1979. Air. Soviet Aircraft. Multicoloured.

4883	2k. Type **1880**	10	10
4884	3k. Yakovlev Yak-42	20	15
4885	10k. Tupolev Tu-154	50	25
4886	15k. Ilyushin Il-76	75	30
4887	32k. Ilyushin Il-86	1·40	65

СОВЕТСКИЕ ХОККЕИСТЫ—
ЧЕМПИОНЫ МИРА
И ЕВРОПЫ
(1881)

1979. Soviet Victory in European Ice Hockey Championship. No. MS4880 optd in margin with T 1881.

MS4888	50k. red, blue and maroon	4·75	2·50

1882 "Tent" Monument, Mining Institute, Pushkin Theatre and Blast Furnace

1979. 50th Anniv of Magnitogorsk City.

4889	**1882**	4k. multicoloured	20	10

1883 Child and Apple Blossom

1979. International Year of the Child (1st issue).

4890	**1883**	4k. multicoloured	20	10

See also Nos. 4918/21.

1884 Bogorodsk Wood-carvings

1979. Folk Crafts. Multicoloured.

4891	2k. Type **1884**	10	10
4892	3k. Khokhloma painted dish and jars	10	10
4893	4k. Zhostovo painted tray	15	10
4894	6k. Kholmogory bone-carvings	25	15
4895	15k. Vologda lace	50	35

1885 Football

1979. Olympic Sports (6th series). Multicoloured.

4896	**1885**	4k.+2k. blue, grey and orange	25	10
4897	-	6k.+3k. yellow, orange and blue	35	10
4898	-	10k.+5k. green, red and mauve	45	15
4899	-	16k.+6k. purple, blue and green	55	25
4900	-	20k.+10k. yellow, red and green	1·00	60

DESIGNS—VERT: 6k. Basketball; 10k. Volleyball. HORIZ: 16k. Handball; 20k. Hockey.

1886 Lenin Square Underground Station

1979. Tashkent Underground Railway.

4901	**1886**	4k. multicoloured	30	15

1887 V. A. Dzhanibekov and O. G. Makarov

1979. "Soyuz 27"–"Salyut 6"–"Soyuz 26" Orbital Complex.

4902	**1887**	4k. multicoloured	30	15

1888 Council Building and Flags of Member Countries

1979. 30th Anniv of Council of Mutual Economic Aid.

4903	**1888**	16k. multicoloured	60	25

1889 Scene from "Battleship Potemkin"

1979. 60th Anniv of Soviet Films (1st issue) and 11th International Film Festival, Moscow.

4904	**1889**	15k. multicoloured	60	25

See also No. 4907.

1979. 50th Anniv of First Five Year Plan. Sheet 66×87 mm.

MS4905	30k. multicoloured	1·20	55

1891 U.S.S.R. Philatelic Society Emblem

1979. 4th U.S.S.R. Philatelic Society Congress. Sheet 92×66 mm.

MS4906	50k. rose and green	1·80	70

1892 Exhibition Hall and Film Still

1979. 60th Anniv of Soviet Films (2nd issue).

4907	**1892**	4k. multicoloured	20	10

1893 "Lilac" (K. A. Korovin)

1979. Flower Paintings. Multicoloured.

4908	1k. "Flowers and Fruits" (I. F. Khrutsky) (horiz)	10	10
4909	2k. "Phloxes" (I. N. Kramskoi)	15	10
4910	3k. Type **1893**	20	10
4911	15k. "Bluebells" (S. V. Gerasimov)	50	25
4912	32k. "Roses" (P. P. Konchalovsky) (horiz)	90	45

1894 John McClean

1979. Birth Centenary of John McClean (first Soviet consul for Scotland).

4913	**1894**	4k. black and red	20	10

1979. 1980 Olympics. "Tourism around the Golden Ring" (4th issue). As T 1855. Multicoloured.

4914	1r.+50k. Narikaly Fortress, Tbilisi	4·00	2·75
4915	1r.+50k. Georgian Philharmonic Society Concert Hall and "Muse" (sculpture), Tbilisi	4·00	2·75
4916	1r.+50k. Chir-Dor Mosque, Samarkand	4·00	2·75
4917	1r.+50k. People's Friendship Museum and "Courage" monument, Tashkent	4·00	2·75

1895 "Friendship" (Lena Liberda)

1979. International Year of the Child (2nd issue). Children's Paintings. Multicoloured.

4918	2k. Type **1895**	10	10
4919	3k. "After Rain" (Daniya Akhmetshina)	10	10
4920	4k. "Dance of Friendship" (Liliya Elistratova)	20	10
4921	15k. "On the Excursion" (Vika Smalyuk)	40	20

1896 Golden Oriole

1979. Birds. Multicoloured.

4922	2k. Type **1896**	20	10
4923	3k. Lesser spotted woodpecker	25	10
4924	4k. Crested tit	35	10
4925	10k. Barn owl	80	25
4926	15k. European nightjar	1·00	40

1897 Soviet Circus Emblem

1979. 60th Anniv of Soviet Circus.

4927	**1897**	4k. multicoloured	20	10

1979. 1980 Olympics. "Tourism around the Golden Ring" (5th issue). As T 1855. Multicoloured.

4928	1r.+50k. Relics of Yerevan's origin	4·00	2·75
4929	1r.+50k. Armenian State Opera and Ballet Theatre, Yerevan	4·00	2·75

1898 Marx, Engels, Lenin and View of Berlin

1979. 30th Anniv of German Democratic Republic.

4930	**1898**	6k. multicoloured	30	20

1899 V. A. Lyakhov, V. V. Ryumin and "Salyut 6"

1979. Lyakhov and Ryumin's 175 Days in Space. Multicoloured.

4931	15k. Type **1899**	45	25
4932	15k. Radio telescope mounted on "Salyut 6"	45	25

Nos. 4931/2 were issued together, se-tenant, forming a composite design.

1900 Hammer and Sickle

1979. 62nd Anniv of October Revolution.

4933	**1900**	4k. multicoloured	20	10

1901 Communications Equipment and Signal Corps Emblem

1979. 60th Anniv of Signal Corps.

4934	**1901**	4k. multicoloured	20	10

1902 "Katherine" (T. G. Shevchenko)

1979. Ukrainian Paintings. Multicoloured.

4935	2k. Type **1902**	10	10
4936	3k. "Into Service" (K. K. Kostandi)	15	10
4937	4k. "To Petrograd" (A. M. Lopukhov)	25	10
4938	10k. "Return" (V. N. Kostetsky)	30	15
4939	15k. "Working Morning" (M. G. Belsky)	40	25

1903 Shabolovka Radio Mast, Moscow

1979. 50th Anniv of Radio Moscow.

4940	**1903**	32k. multicoloured	1·20	55

1904 Misha (Olympic mascot)

1979. New Year.

4941	**1904**	4k. multicoloured	30	15

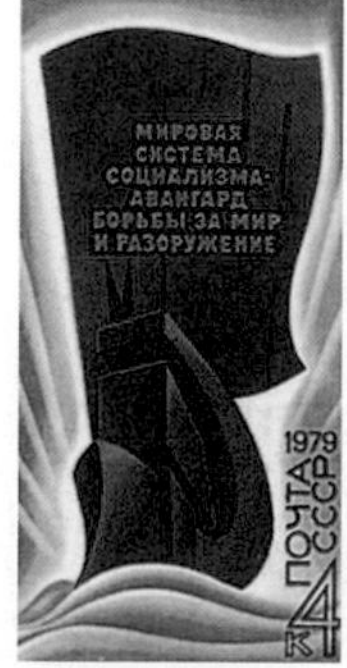

1905 "Peace" and Hammer and Sickle

1979. "Peace Programme in Action". Mult.

4942	4k. Type **1905**	20	10

4943	4k. Hand holding demand for peace	20	10
4944	4k. Hands supporting emblem of peace	20	10

1906 Traffic Policeman

1979. Road Safety. Multicoloured.

4945	3k. Type **1906**	10	10
4946	4k. Child playing in road	20	10
4947	6k. Speeding car out of control	25	10

1907 "Vulkanolog"

1979. Soviet Scientific Research Ships. Mult.

4948	1k. Type **1907**	10	10
4949	2k. "Professor Bogorov"	10	10
4950	4k. "Ernst Krenkel"	15	10
4951	6k. "Kosmonavt Vladislav Volkov"	25	15
4952	10k. "Kosmonavt Yuri Gagarin"	40	20
4953	15k. "Akademik Kurchatov"	65	30

1908 Skiers at North Pole

1979. Ski Expedition to North Pole. Sheet 66×85 mm.

MS4954	50k. multicoloured	2·00	90

1909 Industrial Landscape

1980. 50th Anniv of Mordovian ASSR of Russian Federation.

4955	**1909**	4k. red	20	10

1910 Speed Skating

1980. Winter Olympic Games, Lake Placid.

4956	**1910**	4k. blue, lt blue & orange	20	10
4957	-	6k. violet, blue & orange	20	10
4958	-	10k. red, blue and gold	30	20
4959	-	15k. brown, blue & turquoise	40	25
4960	-	20k. turquoise, blue and red	50	30
MS4961		60×90 mm. 50k. multicoloured	2·00	1·50

DESIGNS—HORIZ: 6k. Figure skating (pairs); 10k. Ice hockey; 15k. Downhill skiing. VERT: 20k. Luge; 50k. Cross-country skiing.

1911 Running

1980. Olympic Sports (7th series). Athletics. Mult.

4962	4k.+2k. Type **1911**	20	10
4963	6k.+3k. Hurdling	25	10
4964	10k.+5k. Walking (vert)	50	35
4965	16k.+6k. High jumping	75	45
4966	20k.+10k. Long jumping	1·10	65

1912 N. I. Podvoisky

1980. Birth Centenary of Nikolai Ilich Podvoisky (revolutionary).

4967	**1912**	4k. brown	20	10

1980. 1980 Olympics. "Tourism around the Golden Ring" (6th issue). Moscow. As T 1855. Mult.

4968	1r.+50k. Kremlin	4·00	3·00
4969	1r.+50k. Kalinin Prospect	4·00	3·00

1913 "Rainbow" (A. K. Savrasov) (image scaled to 66% of original size)

1980. Birth Annivs of Soviet Artists. Mult.

4970	6k. "Harvest Summer" (A. G. Venetsianov (bicent)) (vert)	25	10
4971	6k. Type **1913** (150th anniv)	25	10
4972	6k. "Old Yerevan" (M. S. Saryan) (centenary)	25	10

1980. Olympic Sports (8th series). Athletics. As T 1911. Multicoloured.

4973	4k.+2k. Pole vaulting	20	10
4974	6k.+3k. Discus throwing	25	15
4975	10k.+5k. Javelin throwing	50	25
4976	16k.+6k. Hammer throwing	75	45
4977	20k.+10k. Putting the shot	1·10	60
MS4978	92×72 mm. 50k.+25k. Relay racing	7·00	5·50

1914 Aleksei Leonov

1980. 15th Anniv of First Space Walk in Space. Sheet 111×73 mm.

MS4979	50k. multicoloured	2·00	1·20

1915 Georg Ots

1980. 60th Birth Anniv of Georg K. Ots (artist).

4980	**1915**	4k. blue	20	10

1980. 1980 Olympics. "Tourism around the Golden Ring" (7th issue). As T 1855. Multicoloured.

4981	1r.+50k. St. Isaac's Cathedral, Leningrad	4·00	3·00
4982	1r.+50k. Monument to the Defenders of Leningrad	4·00	3·00

1916 Order of Lenin

1980. 50th Anniv of Order of Lenin.

4983	**1916**	4k. multicoloured	20	10

1917 Cosmonauts, "Salyut", "Soyuz" Complex and Emblem

1980. Intercosmos Space Programme. Sheet 117×81 mm.

MS4984	50k. multicoloured	2·00	1·50

1918 Lenin (after G. Nerod)

1980. 110th Birth Anniv of Lenin. Sheet 91×79 mm.

MS4985	30k. brown, gold and vermilion	1·20	90

1919 "Motherland" (detail of Heroes Monument, Volgograd)

1980. 35th Anniv of World War II Victory. Mult.

4986	4k. Type **1919**	20	10
4987	4k. Victory Monument, Treptow Park, Berlin	20	10
4988	4k. Victory Parade, Red Square, Moscow	20	10

1920 Government House, Arms and Flag of Azerbaijan

1980. 60th Anniv of Azerbaijan Soviet Republic.

4989	**1920**	4k. multicoloured	20	10

1980. 1980 Olympics. "Tourism around the Golden Ring" (8th issue). As T 1855. Multicoloured.

4990	1r.+50k. Bogdan Khmelnitsky Monument and St. Sophia Monastery, Kiev	4·00	3·00
4991	1r.+50k. Underground bridge over River Dnieper, Kiev	4·00	3·00
4992	1r.+50k. Sports Palace and War Memorial, Minsk	4·00	3·00
4993	1r.+50k. House of Cinematography, Minsk	4·00	3·00
4994	1r.+50k. Old City, Tallin	4·00	3·00
4995	1r.+50k. Hotel Viru, Tallin	4·00	3·00

1921 Monument, Ivanovo

1980. 75th Anniv of First Soviet of Workers Deputies, Ivanovo.

4996	**1921**	4k. multicoloured	20	10

1922 Shield and Industrial Complexes

1980. 25th Anniv of Warsaw Treaty.

4997	**1922**	32k. multicoloured	1·30	70

1923 Yakovlev Yak-24 Helicopter, 1953

1980. Helicopters. Multicoloured.

4998	1k. Type **1923**	10	10
4999	2k. Mil Mi-8, 1962	10	10
5000	3k. Kamov Ka-26, 1965	20	10
5001	6k. Mil Mi-6, 1957	30	20
5002	15k. Mil Mi-10K, 1965	80	55
5003	32k. Mil Mi-V12, 1969	1·90	1·10

1924 Title Page of Book

1980. 1500th Birth Anniv of David Anacht (Armenian philosopher).

5004	**1924**	4k. multicoloured	20	10

1925 Medical Check-up of Cosmonauts

1980. Soviet–Hungarian Space Flight. Mult.

5005	6k. Type **1925**	20	10
5006	15k. Crew meeting on "Salyut-6" space station	45	25
5007	32k. Press conference	1·00	65

1926 Red Fox

1980. Fur-bearing Animals. Multicoloured.

5008		2k. Type **1926**	10	10
5009		4k. Artic fox (horiz)	20	10
5010		6k. European mink	30	25
5011		10k. Coypu	50	35
5012		15k. Sable (horiz)	70	55

1927 Kazan

1980. 60th Anniv of Tatar Republic.

5013	**1927**	4k. multicoloured	20	10

1928 College and Emblem

1980. 150th Anniv of Bauman Technical College, Moscow.

5014	**1928**	4k. multicoloured	20	10

1929 Ho Chi Minh

1980. 90th Birth Anniv of Ho Chi Minh (Vietnamese leader).

5015	**1929**	6k. multicoloured	25	10

1930 Arms, Monument and Modern Buildings

1980. 40th Anniv of Soviet Socialist Republics of Lithuania, Latvia and Estonia. Multicoloured.

5016	**1930**	4k. Lithuania	20	10
5017	-	4k. Latvia	20	10
5018	-	4k. Estonia	20	10

1933 Crew of "Soyuz 27" at Launching Site

1980. Soviet–Vietnamese Space Flight. Mult.

5019		6k. Type **1933**	30	25
5020		15k. Cosmonauts at work in space	60	55
5021		32k. Cosmonauts returning to Earth	1·50	1·00

1934 Avicenna (after E. Sokdov and M. Gerasimov)

1980. Birth Millenary of Avicenna (Arab philosopher and physician).

5022	**1934**	4k. multicoloured	20	10

1935 "Khadi-7" Gas turbine Car

1980. Racing cars designed by Kharkov Automobile and Road-building Institute. Mult.

5023		2k. Type **1935**	10	10
5024		6k. "Khadi-10" piston engined car	25	20
5025		15k. "Khadi-11 E" electric car	70	35
5026		32k. "Khadi-13 E" electric car	1·30	65

1936 Arms, Flags, Government House and Industrial Complex

1980. 60th Anniv of Kazakh Soviet Socialist Republic.

5027	**1936**	4k. multicoloured	20	10

1937 "Self-portrait" and "The Spring"

1980. Birth Bicent of Jean Ingres (French painter).

5028	**1937**	32k. multicoloured	1·10	75

1938 "Morning on Kulikovo Field" (A. Bubnov)

1980. 600th Anniv of Battle of Kulikovo.

5029	**1938**	4k. multicoloured	20	10

1939 Town Hall

1980. 950th Anniv of Tartu, Estonia.

5030	**1939**	4k. multicoloured	20	10

1940 Yuri V. Malyshev and Valdimir V. Aksenov

1980. "Soyuz T-2" Space Flight.

5031	**1940**	10k. multicoloured	40	30

1941 Theoretical Training

1980. 20th Anniv of Gagarin Cosmonaut Training Centre. Multicoloured.

5032		6k. Type **1941**	20	10
5033		15k. Practical training	40	30
5034		32k. Physical endurance tests	95	50

1942 Crew Training

1980. Soviet–Cuban Space Flight. Multicoloured.

5035		6k. Type **1942**	20	10
5036		15k. Physical exercise on board space complex	40	20
5037		32k. Returned cosmonauts and space capsule	95	50

1943 "Bargaining" (Nevrev) (image scaled to 50% of original size)

1980. 150th Birth Anniv of N. V. Nevrev and K. D. Flavitsky (painters). Multicoloured.

5038		6k. Type **1943**	25	10
5039		6k. "Princess Tarakanova" (Flavitsky)	25	10

1944 Vasilevsky

1980. 85th Birth Anniv of Marshal A. M. Vasilevsky.

5040	**1944**	4k. green	20	10

1945 Banner

1980. 63rd Anniv of October Revolution.

5041	**1945**	4k. red, gold and purple	20	10

1946 Guramishvili

1980. 275th Birth Anniv of David Guramishvili (Georgian poet).

5042	**1946**	4k. green, silver and black	20	10

1947 Ioffe

1980. Birth Centenary of A. F. Ioffe (physicist).

5043	**1947**	4k. brown and buff	20	10

1948 Siberian Cedar

1980. Trees. Multicoloured.

5044		2k. Type **1948**	10	10
5045		4k. Pedunculate oak	15	10
5046		6k. Lime (vert)	20	10
5047		10k. Sea buckthorn	35	20
5048		15k. Ash	50	30

1949 Misha the Bear (Olympic mascot)

1980. Completion of Olympic Games, Moscow. Sheet 93×73 mm.

MS5049	**1949**	1r. multicoloured	12·00	9·00

1950 Suvorov (after N. Utkin)

1980. 250th Birth Anniv of Field Marshal A. V. Suvorov.

5050	**1950**	4k. blue	20	10

1951 State Emblem and Republican Government House

1980. 60th Anniv of Armenian Soviet Socialist Republic.

5051	**1951**	4k. multicoloured	20	10

1952 Blok (after K. Somov)

1980. Birth Cent of Aleksandr Aleksandrovich Blok (poet).

5052	**1952**	4k. multicoloured	20	10

1980. Soviet Scientific Research Ships (2nd series). As T 1907. Multicoloured.

5053	2k. "Ayu-Dag"	10	10
5054	3k. "Valerian Uryvaev"	10	10
5055	4k. "Mikhail Somov"	20	10
5056	6k. "Akademik Sergei Korolev"	25	15
5057	10k. "Otto Schmidt"	50	40
5058	15k. "Akademik Mstislav Keldysh"	70	50

1953 Spassky Tower and Kremlin Palace of Congresses

1980. New Year.

5059	**1953**	4k. multicoloured	20	10

1955 Sable in Cedar

1980. Perf or imperf (2r.), perf (others).

5060	-	3k. orange	10	10
5061	-	5k. blue	20	10
5063	**1955**	35k. olive	1·20	75
5064	-	45k. brown	2·00	1·20
5066	-	50k. green	2·00	1·50
5067a	-	2r. black	75	55
5068	-	3r. black	8·75	6·50
5069	-	3r. green	2·50	1·90
5071	-	5r. blue	4·50	2·75

DESIGNS—14×22 mm: 3k. State flag; 5k. Forms of transport. 22×33 mm: 45k. Spassky Tower; 50k. Vodovzodny Tower and Grand Palace, Moscow Kremlin; 2r. "Arklika" atomic ice-breaker; 3r. Globe, child and olive branch; 5r. Globe and feather ("Peace").

1957 Institute Building

1980. 50th Anniv of Institute for Advanced Training of Doctors.

5075	**1957**	4k. multicoloured	20	10

1958 Lenin Monument, Leningrad, and Dneproges Hydro-electric Station

1980. 60th Anniv of GOELRO (electrification plan).

5076	**1958**	4k. multicoloured	20	10

1959 Nesmeyanov

1980. Academician A. N. Nesmeyanov (organic chemist) Commemoration.

5077	**1959**	4k. multicoloured	20	10

1960 Nagatinsky Bridge

1980. Moscow Bridges. Multicoloured.

5078	4k. Type **1960**	20	10
5079	6k. Luzhniki underground railway bridge	40	15
5080	15k. Kalininsky bridge	50	40

1961 Timoshenko

1980. 10th Death Anniv of Marshal S. K. Timoshenko.

5081	**1961**	4k. purple	20	10

1962 Indian and Russian Flags with Government House, New Delhi

1980. President Brezhnev's Visit to India.

5082	**1962**	4k. multicoloured	30	20

1963 Antarctic Research Station

1981. Antarctic Exploration. Multicoloured.

5083	4k. Type **1963**	20	10
5084	6k. Antennae, rocket, weather balloon and tracked vehicle (Meteorological research)	50	30
5085	15k. Map of Soviet bases and supply ship "Ob"	1·50	65

1964 Arms and Symbols of Agriculture and Industry

1981. 60th Anniv of Dagestan Autonomous Soviet Socialist Republic.

5086	**1964**	4k. multicoloured	30	20

1965 Hockey Players and Emblem

1981. 12th World Hockey Championships, Khabarovsk.

5087	**1965**	6k. multicoloured	30	20

1966 Banner and Star

1981. 26th Soviet Communist Party Congress. Multicoloured.

5088	4k. Type **1966**	20	10
5089	20k. Kremlin Palace of Congresses and Lenin (51×36 mm)	1·50	1·10

1967 Lenin and Congress Building

1981. 26th Ukraine Communist Party Congress.

5090	**1967**	4k. multicoloured	30	20

1968 Keldysh

1981. 70th Birth Anniv of Academician Mtislav Vsevolodovich Keldysh (mathematician).

5091	**1968**	4k. multicoloured	30	20

1969 Banner and Kremlin Palace of Congress

1981. 26th Soviet Communist Party Congress (2nd issue). Sheet 97×74 mm.

MS5092	**1969**	50k. multicoloured	2·30	1·60

1970 Baikal–Amur Railway

1981. Construction Projects of the 10th Five Year Plan. Multicoloured.

5093	4k. Type **1970**	20	10
5094	4k. Urengoi gas field	20	10
5095	4k. Sayano-Shushenakaya hydro-electric dam	20	10
5096	4k. Atommash Volga–Don atomic reactor	20	10
5097	4k. Syktyvkar paper mill	20	10
5098	4k. Giant excavator, Ekibastuz	20	10

1971 Freighter and Russian and Indian Flags

1981. 25th Anniv of Soviet–Indian Shipping Line.

5099	**1971**	15k. multicoloured	80	55

1972 Arms, Monument and Building

1981. 60th Anniv of Georgian Soviet Socialist Republic.

5100	**1972**	4k. multicoloured	30	20

1973 Arms and Abkhazian Scenes

1981. 60th Anniv of Abkhazian Autonomous Soviet Socialist Republic.

5101	**1973**	4k. multicoloured	20	20

1974 Institute Building

1981. 60th Anniv of Moscow Electrotechnical Institute of Communications.

5102	**1974**	4k. multicoloured	30	20

1975 Communications Equipment and Satellite

1981. 30th All-Union Amateur Radio Exhibition.

5103	**1975**	4k. multicoloured	30	20

1976 L. I. Popov and V. V. Ryumin

1981. 185 Days in Space of Cosmonauts Popov and Ryumin. Multicoloured.

5104	15k. Type **1976**	60	45
5105	15k. "Salyut 6"–"Soyuz" complex	60	45

1977 O. G. Makarov, L. D. Kizim and G. M. Strekalov

1981. "Soyuz T-3" Space Flight.
5106 **1977** 10k. multicoloured 50 30

1978 Rocket Launch

1981. Soviet–Mongolian Space Flight. Mult.
5107 6k. Type **1978** 30 20
5108 15k. Mongolians watching space flight on television 50 30
5109 32k. Re-entry stages 1·00 70

1979 Bering

1981. 300th Birth Anniv of Vitus Bering (navigator).
5110 **1979** 4k. blue 35 20

1980 Yuri Gagarin and Globe

1981. 20th Anniv of First Manned Space Flight. Multicoloured.
5111 6k. Type **1980** 25 10
5112 15k. S. P. Korolev (spaceship designer) 60 40
5113 32k. Statue of Gagarin and "Interkosmos" emblem 1·20 70
MS5114 102×62 mm. 50k. Head of Gagarin (51×36 mm) 8·00 5·25

1981 "Salyut" Orbital Space Station

1981. 10th Anniv of First Manned Space Station.
5115 **1981** 32k. multicoloured 1·50 95

1982 Lenin (after P. V. Vasilev)

1981. 111th Birth Anniv of Lenin. Sheet 93×91 mm.
MS5116 **1982** 50k. multicoloured 1·80 1·20

1983 Prokofiev

1981. 90th Birth Anniv of S. S. Prokofiev (composer).
5117 **1983** 4k. lilac 30 10

1984 New Hofburg Palace, Vienna

1981. "WIPA 1981" International Stamp Exhibition, Vienna.
5118 **1984** 15k. multicoloured 80 45

1985 Arms, Industrial Complex and Docks

1981. 60th Anniv of Adzharskian Autonomous Soviet Socialist Republic.
5119 **1985** 4k. multicoloured 20 10

1986 N. N. Benardos

1981. Centenary of Invention of Welding.
5120 **1986** 6k. multicoloured 20 10

1987 Congress Emblem

1981. 14th Congress of International Union of Architects, Warsaw.
5121 **1987** 15k. multicoloured 80 45

1988 "Albanian Girl in Doorway" (A. A. Ivanov)

1981. Paintings. Multicoloured.
5122 10k. Type **1988** 50 25
5123 10k. "Sunset over Sea at Livorno" (N. N. Ge) (horiz) 50 25
5124 10k. "Demon" (M. A. Vrubel) (horiz) 50 25
5125 10k. "Horseman" (F. A. Rubo) 50 25

1989 Flight Simulator

1981. Soviet–Rumanian Space Flight. Mult.
5126 6k. Type **1989** 20 10
5127 15k. "Salyut"–"Soyuz" space complex 50 25
5128 32k. Cosmonauts greeting journalists after return 1·00 55

1990 "Primula minima"

1981. Flowers of the Carpathians. Multicoloured.
5129 4k. Type **1990** 20 10
5130 6k. "Carlina acaulis" 25 15
5131 10k. "Parageum montanum" 35 25
5132 15k. "Atragene alpina" 60 30
5133 32k. "Rhododendron kotschyi" 1·20 55

1991 Gyandzhevi

1981. 840th Birth Anniv of Nizami Gyandzhevi (poet and philosopher).
5134 **1991** 4k. brown, yellow & green 20 10

1992 Longo

1981. Luigi Longo (Italian politician). Commem.
5135 **1992** 6k. multicoloured 20 10

1993 Running

1981. Sports. Multicoloured.
5136 4k. Type **1993** 20 10
5137 6k. Football 20 15
5138 10k. Throwing the discus 35 25
5139 15k. Boxing 50 30
5140 32k. Swimmer on block 1·20 55

1994 Flag and Arms of Mongolia

1981. 60th Anniv of Revolution in Mongolia.
5141 **1994** 6k. multicoloured 20 10

1995 Spassky Tower and Film encircling Globe

1981. 12th International Film Festival, Moscow.
5142 **1995** 15k. multicoloured 80 40

1996 "Lenin"

1981. River Ships. Multicoloured.
5143 4k. Type **1996** 25 15
5144 6k. "Kosmonavt Gagarin" (tourist ship) 30 20
5145 15k. "Valerian Kuibyshev" (tourist ship) 70 45
5146 32k. "Baltysky" (freighter) 1·60 95

1981. Russian Ice-breakers (4th issue). As T 1775. Multicoloured.
5147 15k. "Malygin" 1·00 65

1997 Industry

1981. Resolutions of the 26th Party Congress. Multicoloured.
5148 4k. Type **1997** 20 10
5149 4k. Agriculture 20 10
5150 4k. Energy 20 10
5151 4k. Transport and communications 20 10
5152 4k. Arts and science 20 10
5153 4k. International co-operation 20 10

1998 Ulyanov

1981. 150th Birth Anniv of I. N. Ulyanov (Lenin's father).
5154 **1998** 4k. brown, black & green 20 10

1999 Facade of Theatre (image scaled to 73% of original size)

1981. 225th Anniv of Pushkin Drama Theatre, Leningrad.
5155 **1999** 6k. multicoloured 25 10

2000 Brushes, Palette and Gerasimov

1981. Birth Centenary of A. M. Gerasimov (artist).
5156 **2000** 4k. multicoloured 20 10

2001 Institute Building

1981. 50th Anniv of Institute of Physical Chemistry, Academy of Sciences, Moscow.
5157 **2001** 4k. multicoloured 20 10

2002 Severtzov's Tit Warbler

1981. Song Birds. Multicoloured.

5158	6k. Type **2002**	30	20
5159	10k. Asiatic paradise flycatcher (vert)	45	30
5160	15k. Jankowski's bunting	70	45
5161	20k. Vinous-throated parrotbill (vert)	85	55
5162	32k. Hodgson's bushchat (vert)	1·30	85

2003 Arms and Industrial Scenes

1981. 60th Anniv of Komi A.S.S.R.
5163 **2003** 4k. multicoloured 35 15

2004 Orbiting Satellite and Exhibition Emblem

1981. "Svyaz 81" Communications Exhibition.
5164 **2004** 4k. multicoloured 20 10

2005 Buildings, Arms and Monument

1981. 60th Anniv of Kabardino-Balkar A.S.S.R.
5165 **2005** 4k. multicoloured 20 10

2006 Soviet Soldier (monument, Treptow Park, Berlin)

1981. 25th Anniv of Soviet War Veterans Committee.
5166 **2006** 4k. multicoloured 20 10

2007 Four-masted Barque "Tovarishch"

1981. Cadet Sailing Ships. Multicoloured.

5167	4k. Type **2007**	20	10
5168	6k. Barquentine "Vega"	25	15
5169	10k. Schooner "Kodor" (vert)	40	25
5170	15k. Three-masted barque "Tovarishch"	55	40
5171	20k. Four-masted barque "Kruzenshtern"	90	55
5172	32k. Four-masted barque "Sedov" (vert)	1·30	85

2008 Russian and Kazakh Citizens with Flags

1981. 250th Anniv of Unification of Russia and Kazakhstan.
5173 **2008** 4k. multicoloured 20 10

2009 Lavrentev

1981. Academician Mikhail Alekseevich Lavrentev (mathematician) Commemoration.
5174 **2009** 4k. multicoloured 20 10

2010 Kremlin Palace of Congresses, Moscow, and Arch of the General Staff, Leningrad

1981. 64th Anniv of October Revolution.
5175 **2010** 4k. multicoloured 20 10

2011 Transmitter, Dish Aerial and "Ekran" Satellite

1981. "Ekran" Television Satellite.
5176 **2011** 4k. multicoloured 25 10

2012 V. V. Kovalyonok and V. P. Savinykh

1981. "Soyuz T-4"–"Salyut 6" Space Complex. Multicoloured.

5177	10k. Type **2012**	35	25
5178	10k. Microscope slide, crystal and text	35	25

2013 Picasso

1981. Birth Centenary of Pablo Picasso (artist). Sheet 101×71 mm.
MS5179 50k. olive, sepia and blue 4·00 2·75

2014 Merkurov

1981. Birth Centenary of Sergei Dmitrievich Merkurov (sculptor).
5180 **2014** 4k. brown, green & bis 20 10

2015 "Autumn" (Nino A. Piromanashvili)

1981. Paintings by Georgian Artists. Multicoloured.

5181	4k. Type **2015**	20	10
5182	6k. "Gurian Woman" (Sh. G. Kikodze)	20	10
5183	10k. "Travelling Companions" (U. M. Dzhaparidze) (horiz)	40	30
5184	15k. "Shota Rustaveli" (S. S. Kobuladze)	65	40
5185	32k. "Tea Pickers" (V. D. Gudiashvili" (horiz))	1·30	95

2016 Arms and Saviour Tower, Moscow

1981. New Year.
5186 **2016** 4k. multicoloured 20 10

2017 Horse-drawn Sleigh (19th century)

1981. Moscow Municipal Transport.

5187	**2017**	4k. brown and silver	20	10
5188	-	6k. green and silver	25	10
5189	-	10k. lilac and silver	30	20
5190	-	15k. black and silver	50	30
5191	-	20k. brown and silver	70	45
5192	-	32k. red and silver	1·30	75

DESIGNS: 6k. Horse tram (19th century); 10k. Horse-drawn cab (19th century); 15k. Taxi, 1926; 20k. British Leyland bus, 1926; 32k. Electric tram, 1912.

2018 Saviour Tower, Moscow and Rashtrapati Bhavan Palace, New Delhi

1981. Inauguration of Tropospheric Communications Link between U.S.S.R. and India. Sheet 123×67 mm.
MS5193 50k. multicoloured 2·00 1·30

2019 Modern Kiev

1982. 1500th Anniv of Kiev.
5194 **2019** 10k. multicoloured 45 25

2020 S. P. Korolev

1982. 75th Birth Anniv of Academician S. P. Korolev (spaceship designer).
5195 **2020** 4k. multicoloured 20 10

2021 Arms and Industrial Complex

1982. 60th Anniv of Checheno-Ingush A.S.S.R.
5196 **2021** 4k. multicoloured 25 10

2022 Arms and Construction Sites

1982. 60th Anniv of Yakut A.S.S.R.
5197 **2022** 4k. multicoloured 25 10

2023 Hikmet

1982. 80th Birth Anniv of Nazim Hikmet (Turkish poet).
5198 **2023** 6k. multicoloured 20 10

2024 "The Oaks"

1982. 150th Birth Anniv of I. I. Shishkin (artist).

5199	**2024**	6k. multicoloured	30	20

2025 Trade Unionists and World Map

1982. 10th World Trade Unions Congress, Havana.

5200	**2025**	15k. multicoloured	55	40

2026 Kremlin Palace of Congresses and Flag

1982. 17th Soviet Trade Unions Congress.

5201	**2026**	4k. multicoloured	20	10

2027 "Self-portrait"

1982. 150th Birth Anniv of Edouard Manet (artist).

5202	**2027**	32k. multicoloured	1·30	70

2028 Show Jumping

1982. Soviet Horse breeding. Multicoloured.

5203		4k. Type **2028**	20	10
5204		6k. Dressage	30	20
5205		15k. Racing	60	40

2029 Tito

1982. President Tito of Yugoslavia Commemoration.

5206	**2029**	6k. brown and black	20	10

2030 University, Book and Monument

1982. 350th Anniv of University of Tartu.

5207	**2030**	4k. multicoloured	20	10

2031 Heart on Globe

1982. 9th Int Cardiologists Conference, Moscow.

5208	**2031**	15k. multicoloured	50	30

2032 Shooting and Skating

1982. 5th Winter Spartakiad. Sheet 93×66 mm.

MS5209	50k. multicoloured	2·00	1·20

2033 Blackberry

1982. Wild Berries. Multicoloured.

5210	4k. Type **2033**	20	10
5211	6k. Blueberries	25	10
5212	10k. Cranberry	40	20
5213	15k. Cherry	70	40
5214	32k. Strawberry	1·30	75

2034 "Venera 13" and "14"

1982. "Venera" Space Flights to Venus.

5215	**2034**	10k. multicoloured	40	25

2035 "M. I. Lopukhina" (V. L. Borovikovsky)

1982. Paintings. Multicoloured.

5216	6k. Type **2035**	25	15
5217	6k. "E. V. Davydov" (O. A. Kiprensky)	25	15
5218	6k. "The Unequal Marriage" (V. V. Pukirev)	25	15

2036 Chukovsky

1982. Birth Cent of K. I. Chukovsky (author).

5219	**2036**	4k. black and grey	20	10

2037 Rocket, "Soyuz" Spaceship, Globe and Space Station

1982. Cosmonautics Day.

5220	**2037**	6k. multicoloured	30	15

2038 Lenin (sculpture, N. V. Tomsky)

1982. 112th Birth Anniv of Lenin. Sheet 68×87 mm.

MS5221	50k. multicoloured	2·00	1·20

2039 Solovev-Sedoi

1982. 75th Birth Anniv of V. P. Solovev-Sedoi (composer).

5222	**2039**	4k. brown	25	10

2040 Dimitrov

1982. Birth Centenary of Georgi Dimitrov (Bulgarian statesman).

5223	**2040**	6k. green	25	10

2041 Masthead

1982. 70th Anniv of "Pravda" (Communist Party Newspaper).

5224	**2041**	4k. multicoloured	20	10

2042 Congress Emblem and Ribbons

1982. 19th Congress of Leninist Young Communist League (Komsomol).

5225	**2042**	4k. multicoloured	20	10

2043 Globe and Hands holding Seedling

1982. 10th Anniv of U.N. Environment Programme.

5226	**2043**	6k. multicoloured	25	10

2044 Pioneers

1982. 60th Anniv of Pioneer Organization.

5227	**2044**	4k. multicoloured	20	10

2045 I.T.U. Emblem, Satellite and Receiving Station

1982. I.T.U. Delegates' Conference, Nairobi.

5228	**2045**	15k. multicoloured	60	40

2046 Class VL-80t Electric Locomotive

1982. Locomotives. Multicoloured.

5229	4k. Type **2046**	25	10
5230	6k. Class TEP-75 diesel	30	15
5231	10k. Class TEM-7 diesel	60	40
5232	15k. Class VL-82m electric	1·00	65
5233	32k. Class EP-200 electric	1·80	95

2047 Players with Trophy and Football

1982. World Cup Football Championship, Spain.

5234	**2047**	20k. lilac, yellow and brown	70	45

2048 Hooded Crane

1982. 18th International Ornithological Congress, Moscow. Multicoloured.

5235	2k. Type **2048**	10	10
5236	4k. Steller's sea eagle	20	15
5237	6k. Spoon-billed sandpiper	30	20
5238	10k. Bar-headed goose	70	30
5239	15k. Sociable plover	1·00	40
5240	32k. White stork	2·00	85

2049 Buildings and Workers with Picks

1982. 50th Anniv of Komsomolsk-on-Amur.

5241	**2049**	4k. multicoloured	20	10

2050 "The Cart"

1982. Birth Centenary of M. B. Grekov (artist).

5242	**2050**	6k. multicoloured	40	20

2051 U.N. Flag

1982. Second U.N. Conference on the Exploration and Peaceful Uses of Outer Space, Vienna.

5243	**2051**	15k. multicoloured	60	40

2052 Scientific Research in Space

1982. Soviet–French Space Flight. Multicoloured.

5244	6k. Type **2052**	20	10
5245	20k. Rocket and trajectory	70	45
5246	45k. Satellites and globe	1·50	90
MS5247	96×68 mm. 50k. Flags, space station and emblems (41×29 mm)	2·00	1·20

2053 "Legend of the Golden Cockerel" (P. I. Sosin)

1982. Lacquerware Paintings. Multicoloured.

5248	6k. Type **2053**	25	15
5249	10k. "Minin's Appeal to Count Pozharsky" (I. A. Fomichev)	30	25
5250	15k. "Two Peasants" (A. F. Kotyagin)	50	40
5251	20k. "The Fisherman" (N. P. Klykov)	70	45

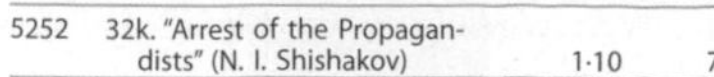

5252	32k. "Arrest of the Propagandists" (N. I. Shishakov)	1·10	75

2054 Early Telephone, Moscow, Leningrad, Odessa and Riga

1982. Telephone Centenary.

5253	**2054**	4k. multicoloured	20	10

2055 P. Schilling (inventor)

1982. 150th Anniv of Electro-magnetic Telegraph in Russia.

5254	**2055**	6k. multicoloured	25	10

2056 Gymnast and Television Screen

1982. Intervision Cup Gymnastics Contest.

5255	**2056**	15k. multicoloured	50	30

2057 Mastyazhart Glider, 1923

1982. Gliders (1st series). Multicoloured.

5256	4k. Type **2057**	20	10
5257	6k. Red Star, 1930	25	20
5258	10k. TsAGI-2, 1934	50	40
5259	20k. Stakhanovets, 1939 (60×27 mm)	1·00	55
5260	32k. GR-29, 1941 (60×27 mm)	1·50	95

See also Nos. 5301/5.

2058 Garibaldi

1982. 175th Birth Anniv of Giuseppe Garibaldi.

5261	**2058**	6k. multicoloured	20	10

2059 Emblem

1982. 25th Anniv of International Atomic Energy Agency.

5262	**2059**	20k. multicoloured	70	45

2060 F.I.D.E. Emblem, Chess Symbol for Queen and Equestrian Statue

1982. World Chess Championship Interzone Tournaments for Women (Tbilisi) and Men (Moscow). Multicoloured.

5263	6k. Type **2060**	40	20
5264	6k. F.I.D.E. emblem, chess symbol for King and Kremlin tower	40	20

2061 Shaposhnikov

1982. Birth Cent of Marshal B. M. Shaposhnikov.

5265	**2061**	4k. brown	20	10

2062 Clenched Fist

1982. 70th Anniv of African National Congress.

5266	**2062**	6k. multicoloured	25	15

2063 Botkin

1982. 150th Birth Anniv of S. P. Botkin (therapeutist).

5267	**2063**	4k. green	20	10

2064 "Sputnik 1"

1982. 25th Anniv of First Artificial Satellite. Sheet 92×62 mm.

MS5268	50k. multicoloured	2·50	1·40

А. КАРПОВ —
обладатель восьми
„Шахматных Оскаров"

(2065)

1982. Anatoly Karpov's Victory in World Chess Championship. No. 5264 optd with T 2065.

5269	6k. multicoloured	60	40

2066 Submarine "S-56"

1982. Soviet Naval Ships. Multicoloured.

5270	4k. Type **2066**	20	10
5271	6k. Minelayer "Gremyashchy"	25	15
5272	15k. Minesweeper "Gafel"	50	40
5273	20k. Cruiser "Krasnyi Krim"	80	55
5274	45k. Battleship "Sevastopol"	1·80	1·00

2067 Flag and Arms

1982. 65th Anniv of October Revolution.

5275	**2067**	4k. multicoloured	20	10

2068 House of the Soviets, Moscow

1982. 60th Anniv of U.S.S.R. Multicoloured.

5276	10k. Type **2068**	35	25
5277	10k. Dneiper Dam and statue	35	25
5278	10k. Soviet war memorial and resistance poster	35	25
5279	10k. Newspaper, worker holding peace text, and sun illuminating city	35	25
5280	10k. Workers' Monument, Moscow, rocket, Ilyushin Il-86 jetliner and factories	35	25
5281	10k. Soviet arms and Kremlin tower	35	25

See also No. **MS**5290.

Всесоюзная
филателистическая
выставка

(2069)

1982. All-Union Stamp Exhibition, Moscow. No. 5280 optd with T 2069.

5282	10k. multicoloured	80	50

2070 "Portrait of an Actor" (Domenico Fetti)

1982. Italian Paintings in the Hermitage Museum, Leningrad. Multicoloured.

5283	4k. Type **2070**	20	10
5284	10k. "St. Sebastian" (Pietro Perugino)	40	30
5285	20k. "Danae" (Titian) (horiz)	70	45
5286	45k. "Portrait of a Woman" (Correggio)	1·40	75
5287	50k. "Portrait of a Young Man" (Capriolo)	1·60	95
MS5288	46×81 mm. 50k.×2 "Portrait of a Young Woman" (Francesco Melzi)	5·50	2·75

2072 Hammer and Sickle, Clock and Date

1982. New Year.

5289	**2072**	4k. multicoloured	20	10

2073 Lenin

1982. 60th Anniv of U.S.S.R. (2nd issue). Sheet 85×96 mm.

MS5290	2073	50k. green and gold	2·00	1·10

2074 Camp and Route to Summit of Mt. Everest

1982. Soviet Ascent of Mount Everest. Sheet 66×86 mm.

MS5291	2074	50k. multicoloured	2·50	1·30

2075 Kherson Lighthouse, Black Sea

1982. Lighthouses (1st series). Multicoloured.

5292	6k. Type **2075**	40	20
5293	6k. Vorontsov lighthouse, Odessa, Black Sea	40	20
5294	6k. Temryuk lighthouse, Sea of Azov	40	20
5295	6k. Novorossiisk lighthouse, Black Sea	40	20
5296	6k. Dneiper harbour light	40	20

See also Nos. 5362/6 and 5449/53.

2076 F. P. Tolstoi

1983. Birth Bicentenary of Fyodor Petrovich Tolstoi (artist).

5297	2076	4k. multicoloured	20	10

2077 Masthead of "Iskra"

1983. 80th Anniv of 2nd Social Democratic Workers' Congress.

5298	2077	4k. multicoloured	20	10

2078 Army Star and Flag

1983. 65th Anniv of U.S.S.R. Armed Forces.

5299	2078	4k. multicoloured	15	10

2079 Ilyushin Il-86 Jetliner over Globe

1983. 60th Anniv of Aeroflot (state airline). Sheet 73×99 mm.

MS5300	50k. multicoloured	2·00	1·10

1983. Gliders (2nd series). As T 2057. Mult.

5301	2k. Antonov A-9, 1948	10	10
5302	4k. Sumonov KAU-12, 1957	20	15
5303	6k. Antonov A-15, 1960	30	20
5304	20k. SA-7, 1970	90	75
5305	45k. LAK-12, 1979	1·90	1·30

2080 "The Holy Family"

1983. 500th Birth Anniv of Raphael (artist).

5306	2080	50k. multicoloured	1·60	95

2081 B. N. Petrov

1983. 70th Birth Anniv of Academician B. N. Petrov (chairman of Interkosmos).

5307	2081	4k. multicoloured	20	10

2082 Tashkent Buildings

1983. 2000th Anniv of Tashkent.

5308	2082	4k. multicoloured	30	20

2083 Popov, Serebrov and Savitskaya

1983. "Soyuz T-7"–"Salyut 7"–"Soyuz T-5" Space Flight.

5309	2083	10k. multicoloured	50	30

2084 Globe within Posthorn

1983. World Communications Year. Sheet 72×107 mm.

MS5310	2084	50k. multicoloured	2·30	1·40

2085 Aleksandrov and Bars of Music

1983. Birth Centenary of A. V. Aleksandrov (composer).

5311	2085	4k. multicoloured	25	10

2086 "Portrait of an Old Woman"

1983. Rembrandt Paintings in Hermitage Museum, Leningrad. Multicoloured.

5312	4k. Type **2086**	20	10
5313	10k. "Portrait of a Learned Man"	40	25
5314	20k. "Old Warrior"	80	45
5315	45k. "Portrait of Mrs B. Martens Doomer"	1·50	95
5316	50k. "Sacrifice of Abraham"	1·80	1·10
MS5317	144×81 mm. 50k.×2 "Portrait of an Old Man in Red"	6·00	3·25

2087 Space Complex

1983. Cosmonautics Day. Sheet 61×91 mm.

MS5318	2987	50k. multicoloured	2·50	1·20

2088 "Revolution is a Storm" (N. N. Zhukov)

1983. 113th Birth Aniv of Lenin. Sheet 73×91 mm.

MS5319	2088	50k. brown	1·70	95

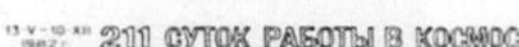

2089 A. N. Berezovoi and V. V. Lebedev

1983. 211 Days in Space of Berezovoi and Lebedev. Multicoloured.

5320	10k. Type **2089**	50	30
5321	10k. "Salyut 7"–"Soyuz T" space complex	50	30

2090 Marx

1983. Death Centenary of Karl Marx.

5322	2090	4k. multicoloured	20	10

2091 Memorial, Building and Hydrofoil

1983. Rostov-on-Don.

5323	2091	4k. multicoloured	20	10

2092 Kirov Theatre

1983. Bicentenary of Kirov Opera and Ballet Theatre, Leningrad.

5324	2092	4k. black, blue and gold	25	10

2093 Arms, Communications and Industrial Complex

1983. 60th Anniv of Buryat A.S.S.R.

5325	2093	4k. multicoloured	25	10

2094 Sports Vignettes

1983. 8th Summer Spartakiad.

5326	2094	6k. multicoloured	20	10

2095 Khachaturyan

1983. 80th Birth Anniv of Aram I. Khachaturyan (composer).

5327	2095	4k. brown	30	10

2096 Tractor and Factory

1983. 50th Anniv of Lenin Tractor Factory, Chelyabinsk.

5328	2096	4k. multicoloured	20	10

2097 Simon Bolivar

1983. Birth Bicentenary of Simon Bolivar.

5329	**2097**	6k. deep brown, brown and black	25	10

2098 18th-century Warship and modern Missile Cruiser "Groznyi"

1983. Bicentenary of Sevastopol.

5330	**2098**	5k. multicoloured	35	15

2099 Snowdrops

1983. Spring Flowers. Multicoloured.

5331	4k. Type **2099**	20	10
5332	6k. Siberian squills	25	15
5333	10k. "Anemone hepatica"	50	30
5334	15k. Cyclamen	60	40
5335	20k. Yellow star of Bethlehem	1·10	65

2100 "Vostok 6" and Tereshkova

1983. 20th Anniv of First Woman Cosmonaut Valentina V. Tereshkova's Space Flight.

5336	**2100**	10k. multicoloured	45	30

2101 P. N. Pospelov

1983. 85th Birth Anniv of Pyotr Nicolaievich Pospelov (scientist).

5337	**2101**	4k. multicoloured	25	15

2102 Congress Emblem

1983. 10th European Rheumatologists' Congress, Moscow.

5338	**2102**	4k. multicoloured	20	10

2103 Film around Globe and Festival Emblem

1983. 13th International Film Festival, Moscow.

5339	**2103**	20k. multicoloured	65	40

2104 Vakhtangov

1983. Birth Centenary of Ye. B. Vakhtangov (producer and actor).

5340	**2104**	5k. multicoloured	30	15

2106 "U.S.S.R.-1"

1983. Fishing Vessels. Multicoloured.

5341	4k. Type **2105**	20	10
5342	6k. Refrigerated trawler	25	10
5343	10k. "Pulkovsky Meridian" (deep-sea trawler)	45	20
5344	15k. Refrigerated freighter	50	35
5345	20k. "50 Let SSR" (factory ship)	1·00	65

1983. 50th Anniv of Stratosphere Balloon's Record Altitude Flight.

5346	**2106**	20k. multicoloured	1·00	65

2107 Sockeye Salmon

1983. Fishes. Multicoloured.

5347	4k. Type **2107**	20	10
5348	6k. Zerro	30	20
5349	15k. Spotted wolffish	60	30
5350	20k. Round goby	90	55
5351	45k. Starry flounder	1·80	1·20

2108 Exhibition Emblem

1983. "Sozphilex 83" Stamp Exhibition, Moscow.

5352	**2108**	6k. multicoloured	25	10
MS5353	90×69 mm. 50k. green		2·30	1·20

DESIGN: 36×22 mm—50k. Moskva River.

2109 Posthorns

1983. 125th Anniv of First Russian Postage Stamp. Sheet 78×65 mm.

MS5354	**2109**	50k. stone and black	1·80	1·20

2110 S.W.A.P.O. Flag and Emblem

1983. Namibia Day.

5355	**2110**	5k. multicoloured	20	10

2111 Palestinian with Flag

1983. Palestinian Solidarity.

5356	**2111**	5k. multicoloured	25	10

2112 Emblem and Ostankino TV Tower, Moscow

1983. 1st European Radio-telegraphy Championship, Moscow.

5357	**2112**	6k. multicoloured	20	10

2113 Council Session Emblem

1983. 4th UNESCO International Communications Development Programme Council Session, Tashkent.

5358	**2113**	10k. blue, mauve & black	40	20

2114 Mohammed al-Khorezmi

1983. 1200th Birth Anniv of Mohammed al-Khorezmi (astonomer and mathematician).

5359	**2114**	4k. multicoloured	20	10

2115 Yegorov

1983. Birth Centenary of Marshal A. I. Yegorov.

5360	**2115**	4k. purple	20	10

2116 Treaty

1983. Bicentenary of First Russian–Georgian Friendship Treaty.

5361	**2116**	6k. multicoloured	25	10

1983. Lighthouses (2nd series). As Type 2075. Multicoloured.

5362	1k. Kipu lighthouse, Baltic Sea	10	10
5363	5k. Keri lighthouse, Gulf of Finland	30	15
5364	10k. Stirsudden lighthouse, Gulf of Finland	45	30
5365	12k. Takhkun lighthouse, Baltic Sea	65	40
5366	20k. Tallin lighthouse, Gulf of Finland	1·00	65

2117 "Wife's Portrait with Flowers" (I. F. Khrutsky)

1983. Byelorussian Paintings. Multicoloured.

5367	4k. Type **2117**	20	10
5368	6k. "Early spring" (V. K. Byalynitsky-Birulya)	25	15
5369	15k. "Young Partisan" (E. A. Zaitsev) (vert)	50	40
5370	20k. "Partisan Madonna" (M. A. Savitsky) (vert)	80	55
5371	45k. "Corn Harvest" (V. K. Tsvirko)	1·60	95

2118 Steel Mill

1983. Centenary of Hammer and Sickle Steel Mill.

5372	**2118**	4k. multicoloured	20	10

2119 Grain Production

1983. Food Programme. Multicoloured.

5373	5k. Type **2119**	30	20
5374	5k. Cattle breeding	30	20
5375	5k. Fruit and vegetable production	30	20

2120 Banner and Symbols of Economic Growth

1983. 66th Anniv of October Revolution.

5376 **2120** 4k. multicoloured 20 10

2121 Ivan Fyodorov

1983. 400th Death Anniv of Ivan Fyodorov (printer) and 420th Anniv of Publication of "The Apostle" (first Russian printed book).

5377 **2121** 4k. black 20 10

2122 Pipeline Construction

1983. Inaug of Urengoi–Uzhgorod Gas Pipeline.

5378 **2122** 5k. multicoloured 25 15

2123 Sidorenko

1983. Academician A. V. Sidorenko (geologist) Commemoration.

5379 **2123** 4k. multicoloured 25 15

2124 Marchers pushing Nuclear Weapons off Globe

1983. Nuclear Disarmament.

5380 **2124** 5k. multicoloured 25 10

2125 Makhtumkuli

1983. 250th Birth Anniv of Makhtumkuli (Turkmen poet).

5381 **2125** 5k. multicoloured 25 15

2126 "Madonna and Child under Apple Tree" (Cranach the Elder)

1983. German Paintings in the Hermitage Museum. Multicoloured.

5382 4k. Type **2126** 20 10

5383 10k. "Self-portrait" (Anton Raphael Mengs) 40 20

5384 20k. "Self-portrait" (Jurgens Ovens) 70 45

5385 45k. "On Board a Sailing Vessel" (Caspar David Friedrich) 1·40 75

5386 50k. "Rape of the Sabine Women" (Johann Schonfeld) (horiz) 1·60 1·00

MS5387 144×79 mm. 50k.×2 "Portrait of a Young Man" (Holbein) 5·75 2·75

2127 Sukhe Bator

1983. 90th Birth Anniv of Sukhe Bator (Mongolian statesman).

5388 **2127** 5k. multicoloured 25 15

2128 Globe and Hand holding Baby

1983. International Association of Physicians against Nuclear War.

5389 **2128** 5k. multicoloured 20 10

2129 Moscow Kremlin Tower Star

1983. New Year.

5390 **2129** 5k. multicoloured 20 10

2130 Children's Music Theatre

1983. New Buildings in Moscow.

5391 **2130** 3k. green 10 10

5392 - 4k. blue 20 10

5393 - 6k. brown 25 15

5394 - 20k. green 70 45

5395 - 45k. green 1·50 85

DESIGNS—VERT: 4k. Hotel and Tourist Centre. HORIZ: 6k. Russian Federation Soviet (parliament building); 20k. Hotel Izmailovo; 45k. Novosti News and Press Agency.

2131 Mother and Child with Flowers

1983. Environmental Protection and Peace. Sheet 81×65 mm.

MS5396 **2131** 50k. multicoloured 3·50 1·40

2132 Cuban Flag

1984. 25th Anniv of Cuban Revolution.

5397 **2132** 5k. multicoloured 25 15

2133 Broadcasting Station

1984. 50th Anniv of Moscow Broadcasting Network.

5398 **2133** 4k. multicoloured 25 15

2134 Speed Skating

1984. Women's European Skating Championship, Alma-Ata.

5399 **2134** 5k. multicoloured 25 10

2135 "T-34" Medium Tank

1984. World War II Armoured Vehicles. Mult.

5400 10k. Type **2135** 50 30

5401 10k. "KV" heavy tank 50 30

5402 10k. "IS-2" heavy tank 50 30

5403 10k. "SU-100" self-propelled gun 50 30

5404 10k. "ISU-152" heavy self-propelled gun 50 30

2136 Biathlon

1984. Winter Olympic Games, Sarajevo. Mult.

5405 5k. Type **2136** 20 10

5406 10k. Speed skating 40 20

5407 20k. Ice hockey 70 40

5408 45k. Figure skating 1·30 85

2137 Mandrill

1984. 120th Anniv of Moscow Zoo. Multicoloured.

5409 2k. Type **2137** 10 10

5410 3k. Blesbok 10 10

5411 4k. Snow leopard 20 10

5412 5k. South African crowned crane 30 20

5413 20k. Blue and yellow macaw 1·00 75

2138 Gagarin

1984. 50th Birth Anniv of Yuri Alekseevich Gagarin (first man in Space).

5414 **2138** 15k. blue 50 30

2139 Young Farmers

1984. 30th Anniv of Development of Unused Land. Sheet 67×86 mm.

MS5415 **2139** 50k. multicoloured 2·00 95

2140 "E. K. Vorontsova" (George Hayter)

1984. English Paintings in Hermitage Museum, Leningrad. Multicoloured.

5416 4k. Type **2140** 20 10

5417 10k. "Portrait of Mrs. Harriet Greer" (George Romney) 40 20

5418 20k. "Approaching Storm" (George Morland) (horiz) 70 40

5419 45k. "Portrait of an Unknown Man" (Marcus Gheeraerts, the younger) 1·50 95

5420 50k. "Cupid untying the Robe of Venus" (Joshua Reynolds) 1·80 1·10

MS5421 144×80 mm. 50k.×2 "Portrait of a Lady in Blue" (Thomas Gainsborough) 5·75 2·30

2141 Ilyushin

1984. 90th Birth Anniv of Academician S. V. Ilyushin (aircraft designer).

5422 **2141** 5k. light brown, brown and black 25 15

2142 Bubnov

1984. Birth Centenary of Andrei Sergeevich Bubnov (Communist Party Leader).

5423	2142	5k. light brown, brown and black	25	15

2143 Launching Site of "M-100" Meteorological Station

1984. Soviet–Indian Space Co-operation. Mult.

5424		5k. Type **2143**	25	15
5425		20k. Satellite and observatory (space geodesy)	60	40
5426		45k. Rocket, satellites and dish aerials (Soviet–Indian space flight)	1·50	75
MS5427		66×86 mm. 50k. Cosmonauts abroad "Salyut 7" space station (25×36 mm)	2·00	95

2144 Globe and Cosmonaut

1984. Cosmonautics Day.

5428	2144	10k. multicoloured	40	20

2145 "Chelyuskin" (ice-breaker) and Route Map

1984. 50th Anniv of Murmansk–Vladivostok Voyage of "Chelyuskin". Multicoloured.

5429		6k. Type **2145**	30	20
5430		15k. Evacuation of sinking ship	70	40
5431		45k. Air rescue of crew	1·80	95

2146 Order of Hero of the Soviet Union

1984. 50th Anniv of Order of Hero of the Soviet Union. Sheet 105×70 mm.

MS5432	2146	50k. multicoloured	2·00	95

2147 Lenin (after Ye. N. Shirokov)

1984. 114th Birth Anniv of Lenin. Sheet 100×78 mm.

MS5433	2147	50k. multicoloured	2·00	95

2148 Lotus

1984. Aquatic Flowers. Multicoloured.

5434		1k. Type **2148**	10	10
5435		2k. Euriala	10	10
5436		3k. Yellow water lilies (horiz)	15	10
5437		10k. White water lilies (horiz)	45	30
5438		20k. Marshflowers (horiz)	85	55

2149 Globe and Peace March (left)

1984. Peace.

5439	2149	5k. multicoloured	25	15
5440	-	5k. red, gold and black	25	15
5441	-	5k. multicoloured	25	15

DESIGNS: No. 5440, Hammer and sickle and text; 5441, Globe and peace march (right).

2150 Welder

1984. 50th Anniv of E. O. Paton Institute of Electric Welding, Kiev.

5442	2150	10k. multicoloured	30	20

2151 Communications Emblem

1984. 25th Conference of Community for Mutual Economic Aid Electrical and Postal Communi-cations Standing Committee, Cracow.

5443	2151	10k. multicoloured	30	20

2152 Emblem and Symbols of Match Venues

1984. European Youth Football Championship.

5444	2152	15k. multicoloured	50	30

2153 Maurice Bishop

1984. 40th Birth Anniv of Maurice Bishop (former Prime Minister of Grenada).

5445	2153	5k. brown	25	10

2154 Lenin and Museum

1984. 60th Anniv of Lenin Central Museum, Moscow.

5446	2154	5k. multicoloured	20	10

2155 Freighter, Monument and Aurora Borealis

1984. 400th Anniv of Archangel.

5447	2155	5k. multicoloured	20	10

2156 Headquarters and Spassky Tower, Moscow

1984. Council of Mutual Economic Aid Conference, Moscow.

5448	2156	5k. blue, red and black	25	15

1984. Lighthouses (3rd series). As T 2075. Mult.

5449		1k. Petropavlovsk lighthouse, Kamchatka	10	10
5450		2k. Tokarev lighthouse, Sea of Japan	10	10
5451		4k. Basargin lighthouse, Sea of Japan	20	10
5452		5k. Kronotsky lighthouse, Kamchatka	25	15
5453		10k. Marekan lighthouse, Sea of Okhotsk	40	20

2157 Vladimir A. Lyakhov and Aleksandr Aleksandrov

1984. 150 Days in Space of "Salyut 7"–"Soyuz T-9" Cosmonauts.

5454	2157	15k. multicoloured	50	30

2158 Liner

1984. 60th Anniv of Morflot (Soviet merchant fleet).

5455	2158	10k. multicoloured	40	20

2159 Komsomol Badge and Banner

1984. 60th Anniv of Naming of Young Communist League (Komsomol) after Lenin.

5456	2159	5k. multicoloured	25	10

2160 Memorial, Minsk

1984. 40th Anniv of Byelorussian Liberation.

5457	2160	5k. multicoloured	25	10

2161 Congress Emblem

1984. 27th International Geological Congress, Moscow.

5458	2161	5k. blue, gold and deep blue	25	10

2162 Polish Arms and Flag

1984. 40th Anniv of Republic of Poland.

5459	2162	5k. multicoloured	25	10

2163 Asafev

1984. Birth Centenary of Boris Vladimirovich Asafev (composer).

5460	2163	5k. green	25	10

2164 Russian and Mexican Flags and Scroll

1984. 60th Anniv of U.S.S.R.–Mexico Diplomatic Relations.

5461	**2164**	5k. multicoloured	25	10

2165 Title Page of "The Princess-Frog"

1984. Folk Tales. Illustration by I. Bilibin. Mult.

5462	5k. Type **2165**	40	20
5463	5k. Hunter and frog in marshland	40	20
5464	5k. Old man and hunter in forest	40	20
5465	5k. Crowd and mute swans	40	20
5466	5k. Title page of "Ivan the Tsarevich, the Fire-bird and the Grey Wolf"	40	20
5467	5k. Ivan and the Fire-bird	40	20
5468	5k. Grave and Ivan on horse	40	20
5469	5k. Ivan and princess	40	20
5470	5k. Title page of "Vasilisa the Beautiful"	40	20
5471	5k. Knight on horse	40	20
5472	5k. Tree-man in forest	40	20
5473	5k. Vasilisa and skulls	40	20

2166 Basketball

1984. "Friendship 84" Sports Meetings. Mult.

5474	1k. Type **2166**	10	10
5475	5k. Gymnastics (vert)	20	10
5476	10k. Weightlifting	30	15
5477	15k. Wrestling	55	30
5478	20k. High jumping	80	45

2167 Flag and Soviet Soldiers' Monument, Bucharest

1984. 40th Anniv of Rumania's Liberation.

5479	**2167**	5k. multicoloured	25	10

2168 Emblem, Chess Symbol for Queen and Motherland Statue

1984. World Chess Championship Finals for Women (Volgograd) and Men (Moscow).

5480	**2168**	15k. gold, red and black	80	40
5481	-	15k. multicoloured	80	40

DESIGN: No. 5481, Emblem, chess symbol for king and Spassky tower, Moscow Kremlin.

2169 Party House and Soviet Army Monument, Sofia, and State Emblem

1984. 40th Anniv of Bulgarian Revolution.

5482	**2169**	5k. multicoloured	25	10

2170 Arms and Flag

1984. 10th Anniv of Ethiopian Revolution.

5483	**2170**	5k. multicoloured	25	10

2171 Excavator

1984. 50th Anniv of Lenin Machine-building Plant, Novokramatorsk.

5484	**2171**	5k. multicoloured	25	10

2172 Arms and Symbols of Industry and Agriculture

1984. 60th Anniv of Nakhichevan A.S.S.R.

5485	**2172**	5k. multicoloured	25	10

V СЪЕЗД ВОФ. МОСКВА. ОКТЯБРЬ 1984 г.

(2173) (image scaled to 74% of original size)

1984. 5th Philatelic Congress, Moscow. No. MS5354 optd with T 2173.

MS5486	50k. stone and black	2·30	1·40

2174 "Luna 3" photographing Moon

1984. 25th Anniv of Photography in Space. Mult.

5487	5k. Type **2174**	25	10
5488	20k. "Venera-9" and control centre	70	35
5489	45k. "Meteor" meteorological satellite and Earth	1·40	85
MS5490	60×81 mm. 50k. V. Lyakhov installing solar battery on "Salyut 7" space station (21×32 mm)	2·00	95

2175 Arms and Flag

1984. 35th Anniv of German Democratic Republic.

5491	**2175**	5k. multicoloured	25	10

2176 Arms and Motherland Statue, Kiev

1984. 40th Anniv of Liberation of the Ukraine.

5492	**2176**	5k. multicoloured	40	15

2177 Town, Arms and Countryside

1984. 60th Anniv of Moldavian Soviet Socialist Republic.

5493	**2177**	5k. multicoloured	25	10

2178 Arms, Power Station and Mountains

1984. 60th Anniv of Kirgizia Soviet Socialist Republic.

5494	**2178**	5k. multicoloured	25	10

2179 Arms and Symbols of Industry and Agriculture

1984. 60th Anniv of Tadzhikistan Soviet Socialist Republic.

5495	**2179**	5k. multicoloured	25	10

2180 Flags and Spassky Tower

1984. 67th Anniv of October Revolution.

5496	**2180**	5k. multicoloured	25	10

2181 Arms, State Building and Dam

1984. 60th Anniv of Uzbekistan Soviet Socialist Republic.

5497	**2181**	5k. multicoloured	25	10

2182 Arms, Flag and State Building

1984. 60th Anniv of Turkmenistan Soviet Socialist Republic.

5498	**2182**	5k. multicoloured	25	10

2183 Medal, Workers, Diesel Train and Route Map

1984. Completion of Baikal–Amur Railway.

5499	**2183**	5k. multicoloured	30	15

2184 Ilyushin Il-86 Jetliner, Rocket, "Soyuz"–"Salyut" Complex and Museum

1984. 60th Anniv of M. V. Frunze Central House of Aviation and Cosmonautics, Moscow.

5500	**2184**	5k. multicoloured	20	10

2185 "Girl in Hat" (Jean-Louis Voile)

1984. French Paintings in Hermitage Museum, Leningrad. Multicoloured.

5501	4k. Type **2185**	20	10
5502	10k. "The Stolen Kiss" (Jean-Honore Fragonard) (horiz)	40	20
5503	20k. "Woman at her Toilette" (Edgar Degas)	80	45
5504	45k. "Pygmalion and Galatea" (Francois Boucher) (horiz)	1·60	75
5505	50k. "Landscape with Polyphemus" (Nicolas Poussin) (horiz)	1·80	1·00
MS5506	144×79 mm. 50k.×2 "Child with Whip" (Pierre-Auguste Renoir)	5·50	2·75

2186 Mongolian Arms and Flag

1984. 60th Anniv of Mongolian People's Republic.

5507	**2186**	5k. multicoloured	25	10

2187 Spassky Tower and Snowflakes

1984. New Year.

5508	**2187**	5k. multicoloured	25	20

2188 Leaf and Urban Landscape

1984. Environmental Protection. Sheet 90×65 mm.

MS5509	**2188**	5k. multicoloured	2·50	1·40

2189 Horse-drawn Crew Wagon (19th-century)

1984. Fire Engines (1st series). Multicoloured.

5510	3k. Type **2189**	15	10
5511	5k. 19th-century horse-drawn steam pump	25	15
5512	10k. "Freze" fire engine, 1904	50	30
5513	15k. "Lessner" fire engine, 1904	80	40
5514	20k. "Russo-Balt" fire engine, 1913	1·10	55

See also Nos. 5608/12.

2190 Space Observatory and Flight Trajectory

1984. International Venus–Halley's Comet Space Project (1st issue).

5515	**2190**	15k. multicoloured	60	40

See also Nos. 5562 and 5630.

2191 Indira Gandhi

1984. Indira Gandhi (Indian Prime Minister) Commemoration.

5516	**2191**	5k. light brown & brown	35	20

2192 Heroes of December Revolution Monument, Moscow

1985. 80th Anniv of 1905 Revolution.

5517	**2192**	5k. multicoloured	25	10

УНИВЕРСИТЕТУ ДРУЖБЫ НАРОДОВ ИМЕНИ ПАТРИСА ЛУМУМБЫ

ПОЧТА·5к·СССР

2193 Jubilee Emblem

1985. 25th Anniv of Patrice Lumumba University, Moscow.

5518	**2193**	5k. multicoloured	30	20

2194 Frunze

1985. Birth Centenary of Mikhail Vasilievich Frunze (military strategist).

5519	**2194**	5k. stone, black and blue	30	20

2195 Arms and Industrial Landscape

1985. 60th Anniv of Karakalpak A.S.S.R.

5520	**2195**	5k. multicoloured	20	10

2196 Ice Hockey Player

1985. 10th Friendly Armies Winter Spartakiad.

5521	**2196**	5k. multicoloured	30	20

2197 Dulcimer Player and Title Page

1985. 150th Anniv of "Kalevala" (Karelian poems collected by Elino Lonnrot).

5522	**2197**	5k. brown, blue & black	40	20

2198 Pioneer Badge

1985. 60th Anniv of "Pionerskaya Pravda" (children's newspaper).

5523	**2198**	5k. multicoloured	40	20

2199 Maria Aleksandrovna Ulyanova

1985. 150th Birth Anniv of Maria Aleksandrovna Ulyanova (Lenin's mother).

5524	**2199**	5k. black	25	10

2200 "Young Madonna Praying" (Francisco de Zurbaran)

1985. Spanish Paintings in Hermitage Museum, Leningrad. Multicoloured.

5525	4k. Type **2200**	20	10
5526	10k. "Still Life" (Antonio Pereda) (horiz)	35	20
5527	20k. "The Immaculate Conception" (Bartolome Esteban Murillo)	70	45
5528	45k. "The Grinder" (Antonio Puga) (horiz)	1·60	85
5529	50k. "Count Olivares" (Diego Velazquez)	1·80	1·00
MS5530	145×80 mm. 50k.×2 "Antonia Zarate" (Francisco de Goya)	6·00	2·75

2201 Cosmonauts and Globe

1985. "Expo 85" World's Fair, Tsukuba, Japan. Multicoloured.

5531	5k. Type **2201**	20	10
5532	10k. "Molniya-I" communications satellite	30	20
5533	20k. Energy sources of the future	70	45
5534	45k. Futuristic city	1·50	75
MS5535	64×85 mm. 50k. Soviet exhibition emblem, globe and tree (36×47 mm)	2·00	95

2202 Bach (after Hausman)

1985. 300th Birth Anniv of Johann Sebastian Bach (composer). Sheet 65×91 mm.

MS5536	**2201**	50k. black	2·30	1·10

2203 Hungarian Arms and Budapest

1985. 40th Anniv of Hungary's Liberation.

5537	**2203**	5k. multicoloured	30	15

2204 Emblem and Text

1985. 60th Anniv of Union of Soviet Societies of Friendship and Cultural Relations with Foreign Countries.

5538	**2204**	15k. multicoloured	50	35

2205 Cosmonauts, "Soyuz T" Training Model and Gagarin

1985. Cosmonautics Day. 25th Anniv of Yuri A. Gagarin Cosmonauts Training Centre.

5539	**2205**	15k. multicoloured	50	35

2206 Young People of Different Races

1985. 12th World Youth and Students' Festival, Moscow. Multicoloured.

5540	1k. Type **2206**	10	10
5541	3k. Girl with festival emblem in hair	15	10
5542	5k. Rainbow and girl	20	10
5543	20k. Youth holding camera	70	45
5544	45k. Festival emblem	1·50	75

2207 Soviet Memorial, Berlin-Treptow

1985. 40th Anniv of Victory in Second World War (1st issue). Multicoloured.

5545	5k. Type **2207**	25	20
5546	5k. Partisans	25	20
5547	5k. Lenin, soldier and Moscow Kremlin	25	20
5548	5k. Soldiers and military equipment	25	20
5549	5k. Woman worker, tank, tractor and assembly of Ilyushin Il-2M3 Stormovik fighter	25	20
MS5550	90×65 mm. 50k. Order of Patriotic War, Second Class (27×39 mm)	2·00	95

2208 Lenin and Paris Flat

1985. 115th Birth Anniv of Lenin. Multicoloured.

5551	5k. Type **2208**	25	20
5552	5k. Lenin and Lenin Museum, Tampere, Finland	25	20
MS5553	65×89 mm. 30k. Lenin (26×38 mm)	1·30	75

See also No. 5555.

Всесоюзная филателистическая выставка

„40 лет Великой Победы"

(2209)

1985. "Second World War Victory" Philatelic Exhibition. No. 5545 optd with T 2209.

5554	**2207**	5k. multicoloured	40	30

2210 Victory Order (image scaled to 69% of original size)

1985. 40th Anniv of Victory in Second World War (2nd issue).

5555	**2210**	20k. multicoloured	70	45

2211 Czechoslovakian Arms and Prague Buildings

1985. 40th Anniv of Czechoslovakia's Liberation.

5556	**2211**	5k. multicoloured	30	15

2212 Members' Flags on Shield

1985. 30th Anniv of Warsaw Pact Organization.

5557	**2212**	5k. multicoloured	25	10

2213 Sholokhov and Books

1985. 80th Birth Anniv of Mikhail Aleksandrovich Sholokhov (writer).

5558	**2213**	5k. multicoloured	25	15
5559	-	5k. multicoloured	25	15
5560	-	5k. black, gold and brown	25	15

DESIGNS—As T **2213**. No. 5559, Sholokhov and books (different). 36×51 mm: No. 5560, Sholokhov.

2214 Sverdlov

1985. Birth Centenary of Ya. M. Sverdlov (Communist Party Leader).

5561	**2214**	5k. brown and red	25	10

1985. International Venus–Halley's Comet Space Project (2nd issue). As T 2190. Multicoloured.

5562	15k. "Vega" space probe and Venus	60	40

2215 Battleship "Potemkin"

1985. 80th Anniv of Mutiny on Battleship "Potemkin".

5563	**2215**	5k. black, red and gold	25	10

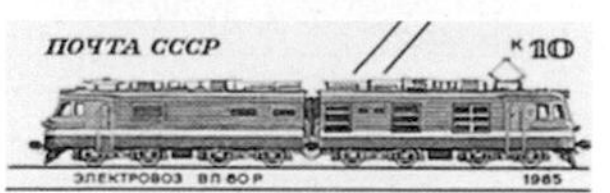

2216 Class VL-80R Electric Locomotive

1985. Locomotives and Rolling Stock.

5564	**2216**	10k. green	60	30
5565	-	10k. brown	60	30
5566	-	10k. blue	60	30
5567	-	10k. brown	60	30
5568	-	10k. blue	60	30
5569	-	10k. blue	60	30
5570	-	10k. brown	60	30
5571	-	10k. green	60	30

DESIGNS: No. 5565, Coal wagon; 5566, Oil tanker wagon; 5567, Goods wagon; 5568, Refrigerated wagon; 5569, Class TEM-2 diesel locomotive; 5570, Type SV passenger carriage; 5571, Mail van.

2217 Camp and Pioneer Badge

1985. 60th Anniv of Artek Pioneer Camp.

5572	**2217**	4k. multicoloured	30	15

2218 Leonid Kizim, Vladimir Solovyov and Oleg Atkov

1985. "237 Days in Space".

5573	**2218**	15k. multicoloured	60	30

2219 Youths of different Races

1985. International Youth Year.

5574	**2219**	10k. multicoloured	40	20

2220 "Beating Swords into Ploughshares" (sculpture) and U.N. Emblem

1985. 40th Anniv of U.N.O. (1st issue).

5575	**2220**	45k. blue and gold	1·80	95

See also No. 5601.

2221 Festival Emblem

1985. 12th World Youth and Students' Festival, Moscow (2nd issue). Sheet 64×90 mm.

MS5576	30k. multicoloured	1·30	75

2222 Larkspur

1985. Plants of Siberia. Multicoloured.

5577	2k. Type **2222**	10	10
5578	3k. "Thermopsis lanceolata"	10	10
5579	5k. Rose	20	10
5580	20k. Cornflower	70	40
5581	45k. Bergenia	1·40	85

2223 V. A. Dzhanibekov, S. E. Savitskaya and I. P. Volk

1985. 1st Anniv of First Space-walk by Woman Cosmonaut.

5582	**2223**	10k. multicoloured	40	20

2224 Cecilienhof Palace and Flags

1985. 40th Anniv of Potsdam Conference.

5583	**2224**	15k. multicoloured	50	30

2225 Finland Palace

1985. 10th Anniv of European Security and Co-operation Conference, Helsinki.

5584	**2225**	20k. multicoloured	80	50

2226 Russian and N. Korean Flags and Monument

1985. 40th Anniv of Liberation of Korea.

5585	**2226**	5k. multicoloured	25	10

2227 Pamir Shrew

1985. Protected Animals. Multicoloured.

5586	2k. Type **2227**	10	10
5587	3k. Satunin's jerboa (horiz)	10	10
5588	5k. Desert dormouse	20	10
5589	20k. Caracal (47×32 mm)	70	40
5590	45k. Goitred gazelle (47×32 mm)	1·50	90
MS5591	90×65 mm. 50k. Leopard (horiz)	2·50	1·40

2228 A. G. Stakhanov and Industrial Scenes

1985. 50th Anniv of Stakhanov Movement (for high labour productivity).

5592	**2228**	5k. yellow, red and black	25	10

2229 Cup, Football, F.I.F.A. Emblem and Kremlin Tower

1985. World Junior Football Championship, Moscow.

5593	**2229**	5k. multicoloured	25	10

2230 Chess Pieces

1985. World Chess Championship Final between Anatoly Karpov and Gary Kasparov.

5594	**2230**	10k. multicoloured	60	30

2231 Vietnam State Emblem

1985. 40th Anniv of Vietnamese Independence.

5595	**2231**	5k. multicoloured	30	15

2232 Immortality Monument and Buildings

1985. Millenary of Bryansk.

5596	**2232**	5k. multicoloured	30	15

2233 Title Page

1985. 800th Anniv of "Song of Igor's Campaigns".

5597	**2233**	10k. multicoloured	40	20

2234 Lutsk Castle

1985. 900th Anniv of Lutsk.

5598	**2234**	5k. multicoloured	30	15

2235 Gerasimov

1985. Birth Centenary of Sergei Vasilievich Gerasimov (artist).

5599	**2235**	5k. multicoloured	25	10

2236 Globe, Cruiser "Aurora" and 1917

1985. 68th Anniv of October Revolution.

5600	**2236**	5k. multicoloured	20	10

2237 Headquarters, New York, and Flag

1985. 40th Anniv of U.N.O. (2nd issue).

5601	**2237**	15k. green, blue and black	60	30

2238 Krisjanis Barons

1985. 150th Birth Anniv of Krisjanis Barons (writer).

5602	**2238**	5k. black and brown	25	10

2239 Lenin and Worker breaking Chains

1985. 90th Anniv of Petersburg Union of Struggle for Liberating the Working Class.

5603	**2239**	5k. multicoloured	20	10

2240 Telescope

1985. 10th Anniv of World's Largest Telescope.

5604	**2240**	10k. blue	40	20

2241 Angolan Arms and Flag

1985. 10th Anniv of Independence of Angola.

5605	**2241**	5k. multicoloured	25	10

2242 Yugoslav Arms, Flag and Parliament Building

1985. 40th Anniv of Federal People's Republic of Yugoslavia.

5606	**2242**	5k. multicoloured	25	10

2243 Troitsky Tower and Palace of Congresses

1985. New Year.

5607	**2243**	5k. multicoloured	20	10

1985. Fire Engines (2nd series). As T 2189. Mult.

5608	3k. "AMO-F15", 1926	15	10
5609	5k. "PMZ-1", 1933	25	15
5610	10k. "ATs-40", 1977	45	20
5611	20k. "AL-30" with automatic ladder, 1970	80	40
5612	45k. "AA-60", 1978	1·60	75

2244 Samantha Smith

1985. Samantha Smith (American schoolgirl peace campaigner) Commemoration.

5613	**2244**	5k. brown, blue and red	40	20

2245 N. M. Emanuel

1985. Academician N. M. Emanuel (chemist) Commemoration.

5614	**2245**	5k. multicoloured	25	10

2246 Family and Places of Entertainment

1985. Anti-alcoholism Campaign. Multicoloured.

5615	5k. Type **2246**	25	10
5616	5k. Sports centre and family	25	10

2247 Emblem

1986. International Peace Year.

5617	**2247**	20k. blue, green & silver	60	30

2248 Banners and Kremlin Palace of Congresses

1986. 27th Soviet Communist Party Congress.

5618	**2248**	5k. multicoloured	20	10
5619	-	20k. multicoloured	65	40
MS5620		95×65 mm. 50k. red, gold and black	1·80	95

DESIGNS—36×51 mm: 20k. Palace of Congresses, Spassky Tower and Lenin. 27×39 mm—50k. Lenin (after sculpture by N. Andreev).

2249 1896 Olympics Medal

1986. 90th Anniv of First Modern Olympic Games.

5621	**2249**	15k. multicoloured	50	30

2250 Tulips

1986. Plants of Russian Steppes. Multicoloured.

5622	4k. Type **2250**	20	10
5623	5k. Grass (horiz)	25	10
5624	10k. Iris	40	25
5625	15k. Violets	60	35
5626	20k. Cornflower	75	50

2251 Voronezh and Arms

1986. 400th Anniv of Voronezh.

5627	**2251**	5k. multicoloured	20	10

2252 Bela Kun

1986. Birth Centenary of Bela Kun (Hungarian Communist Party leader).

5628	**2252**	10k. blue	30	20

2253 Pozela

1986. 90th Birth Anniv of Karolis Pozela (founder of Lithuanian Communist Party).

5629	**2253**	5k. grey	25	10

2254 "Vega 1" and Halley's Comet

1986. International Venus–Halley's Comet Space Project (3rd issue). As T 2190. Multicoloured.

5630	15k. "Vega 1" and Halley's Comet	60	30
MS5631	65×91 mm. 50k. Type **2254** (different)	2·00	95

2255 Crimson-spotted Moth

1986. Butterflies and Moths listed in U.S.S.R. Red Book (1st series). Multicoloured.

5632	4k. Type **2255**	20	10
5633	5k. Eastern festoon	25	10
5634	10k. Sooty orange-tip	50	30
5635	15k. Dark crimson underwing	75	40
5636	20k. "Satyrus bischoffi"	1·00	55

See also Nos. 5726/30.

2256 Globe and Model of Space Complex

1986. "Expo '86" World's Fair, Vancouver.

5637	**2256**	20k. multicoloured	70	45

2257 Kirov

1986. Birth Centenary of S. M. Kirov (Communist Party Secretary).

5638	**2257**	5k. black	25	10

2258 Tsiolkovsky

1986. Cosmonautics Day. Multicoloured.

5639	5k. Type **2258**	20	10
5640	10k. Sergei Pavlovich Korolev (rocket designer) and "Vostok" rocket (vert)	35	25
5641	15k. Yuri Gagarin, "Vega", sputnik and globe (25th anniv of first man in space)	60	40

2259 Ice Hockey Player

1986. World Ice Hockey Championship, Moscow.

5642	**2259**	15k. multicoloured	60	30

2260 Thalmann

1986. Birth Centenary of Ernst Thalmann (German politician).

5643	**2260**	10k. deep brown	40	25
5644	**2260**	10k. lake-brown	40	25

2261 Lenin Museum, Leipzig

1986. 116th Birth Anniv of Lenin.

5645	**2261**	5k. multicoloured	25	10
5646	-	5k. olive, brown & black	25	10
5647	-	5k. multicoloured	25	10

DESIGNS: No. 5646, Lenin (after P. Belousov) and Lenin Museum, Prague; 5647, Lenin Museum, Poronine, Poland.

2262 Tambov and Arms

1986. 350th Anniv of Tambov.

5648	**2262**	5k. multicoloured	25	10

2263 Dove with Olive Branch and Globe

1986. 25th Anniv of Soviet Peace Fund.

5649	**2263**	10k. multicoloured	40	30

2264 Emblem and Cyclists

1986. 39th Peace Cycle Race.

5650	**2264**	10k. multicoloured	35	25

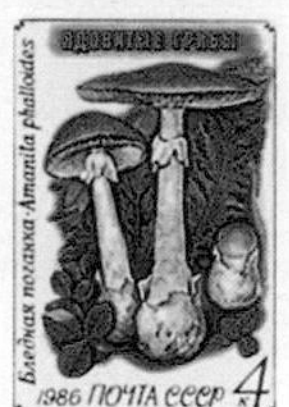

2265 Death Cap

1986. Fungi. Multicoloured.

5651	4k. Type **2265**	20	10
5652	5k. Fly agaric	30	10
5653	10k. Panther cap	50	20
5654	15k. Bitter bolete	80	40
5655	20k. Clustered woodlover	1·00	45

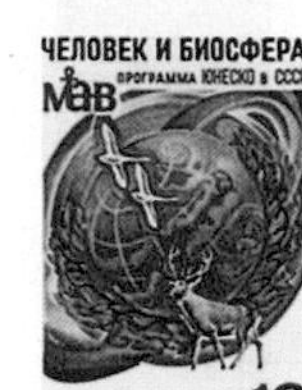

2266 Globe and Wildlife

1986. UNESCO Man and Biosphere Programme.

5656	**2266**	10k. multicoloured	45	30

2267 Torch and Runner

1986. 9th People's Spartakiad.

5657	**2267**	10k. multicoloured	40	25

2268 Kuibyshev

1986. 400th Anniv of Kuibyshev (formerly Samara).

5658	**2268**	5k. multicoloured	25	10

No. 5658 depicts the Lenin Museum, Eternal Glory and V. I. Chapaev monuments and Gorky State Theatre.

2269 Ostankino T.V. Tower

1986. "Communication 86" International Exhibition, Moscow.

5659	**2269**	5k. multicoloured	20	10

2270 Footballers

1986. World Cup Football Championship, Mexico. Multicoloured.

5660	5k. Type **2270**	20	10
5661	10k. Footballers (different)	45	25
5662	15k. Championship medal	55	40

2271 "Lane in Albano" (M. I. Lebedev)

1986. Russian Paintings in Tretyakov Gallery, Moscow. Multicoloured.

5663	4k. Type **2271**	20	10
5664	5k. "View of the Kremlin in foul Weather" (A. K. Savrasov) (horiz)	25	10
5665	10k. "Sunlit Pine Trees" (I. I. Shishkin)	35	20
5666	15k. "Journey Back" (A. E. Arkhipov) (69×33 mm)	60	30
5667	45k. "Wedding Procession in Moscow" (A. P. Ryabushkin) (69×33 mm)	1·60	75

2272 Arms and City

1986. 300th Anniv of Irkutsk City Status.

5668	**2272**	5k. multicoloured	25	10

2273 World Map, Stadium and Runners

1986. International Goodwill Games, Moscow.

5669	**2273**	10k. blue, brown & black	40	25
5670	**2273**	10k. blue, sepia & black	40	20

2274 Globe, Punched Tape and Keyboard

1986. UNESCO Programmes in U.S.S.R. Mult.

5671	5k. Type **2274**	20	10
5672	10k. Landscape and geological section (geological correlation)	40	20
5673	15k. Oceanographic research vessel, albatross and ocean (Inter-governmental Oceanographic Commission)	60	35
5674	35k. Fluvial drainage (International Hydrological Programme)	1·00	60

2275 Arms and Town Buildings

1986. 400th Anniv of Tyumen, Siberia.

5675	**2275**	5k. multicoloured	25	10

2276 Olof Palme

1986. Olof Palme (Swedish Prime Minister) Commemoration.

5676	**2276**	10k. blue, black & brn	40	25

2277 Hands, Ball and Basket

1986. 10th Women's Basketball Championship.

5677	**2277**	15k. brown, black & red	50	30

2278 "Ural-375D"

1986. Lorries. Multicoloured.

5678	4k. Type **2278**	20	10
5679	5k. "GAZ-53A"	25	10
5680	10k. "KrAZ-256B"	40	25
5681	15k. "MAZ-515B"	60	35
5682	20k. "ZIL-133GYa"	75	45

2279 Lenin Peak

1986. U.S.S.R. Sports Committee's International Mountaineers' Camps (1st series). Multlcoloured.

5683	4k. Type **2279**	20	10
5684	5k. E. Korzhenevskaya Peak	25	10
5685	10k. Belukha Peak	35	25
5686	15k. Communism Peak	60	30
5687	30k. Elbrus Peak	1·00	65

See also Nos. 5732/5.

2280 Globe and "Red Book"

1986. Environmental Protection. Sheet 60×90 mm.

MS5688	50k. multicoloured	2·50	1·50

2281 Lenin Monument and Drama Theatre

1986. 250th Anniv of Chelyabinsk City.

5689	**2281**	5k. multicoloured	25	10

2282 "Mukran", Maps and Flags

1986. Opening of Mukran (East Germany)–Klaipeda (U.S.S.R.) Railway Ferry.

5690	**2282**	15k. multicoloured	75	40

2283 Victory Monument and Buildings

1986. 750th Anniv of Siauliai, Lithuania.

5691	**2283**	5k. buff, brown and red	25	15

2284 Lenin Monument and Moscow Kremlin

1986. 69th Anniv of October Revolution.

5692	**2284**	5k. multicoloured	30	15

2285 Ice-breaker "Vladivostok", Mil Mi-4 Helicopter, Satellite and Map

1986. Antarctic Drift of "Mikhail Somov" (research vessel). (a) As Type 2285.

5693		5k. blue, black and red	30	20
5694		10k. multicoloured	60	30
MS5695		70×90 mm. 50k. ultramarine and black	2·50	2·00

15.III–26.VII.1985
Дрейф во льдах Антарктики
(2286)

(b) No. 5055 optd with T 2286.

5696		4k. multicoloured	1·00	70

DESIGN—As T **2285**: 10k. Map and "Mikhail Somov". 51×36 mm—"Mikhail Somov" icebound.

Nos. 5693/4 were printed together, se-tenant, forming a composite design.

2287 Class Eu No. 684–37, Slavyansk

1986. Steam Locomotive as Monuments. Mult.

5697		4k. Type **2287**	20	10
5698		5k. Class FD No. 3000, Novosibirsk	25	10
5699		10k. Class Ov No. 5109, Volgograd	45	20
5700		20k. Class SO No. 17-1613, Dnepropetrovsk	80	40
5701		30k. Class FDp No. 20-578, Kiev	1·30	65

2288 G. K. Ordzhonikidze

1986. Birth Centenary of Grigory Konstantinovich Ordzhonikidze (revolutionary).

5702	**2288**	5k. grey	25	15

2289 Novikov and Score

1986. 90th Birth Anniv of Anatoli Novikov (composer).

5703	**2289**	5k. brown	25	15

2290 U.N. and UNESCO Emblem

1986. 40th Anniv of UNESCO.

5704	**2290**	10k. silver and blue	55	40

2291 Sun Yat-sen

1986. 120th Birth Anniv of Sun Yat-sen (first President of Chinese Republic).

5705	**2291**	5k. black and grey	25	15

2292 Lomonosov

1986. 275th Birth Anniv of Mikhail Vasilievich Lomonosov (scientist).

5706	**2292**	5k. brown	25	10

2293 Ya-1, 1927

1986. Sports Aircraft designed by Aleksandr Yakovlev. Multicoloured.

5707		4k. Type **2293**	20	10
5708		5k. VT-2 trainer, 1935	20	10
5709		10k. Yak-18, 1946	40	25
5710		20k. Yak-50, 1972	80	45
5711		30k. Yak-55, 1981	1·30	75

2294 Spassky, Senate and Nikolsky Towers, Kremlin

1986. New Year.

5712	**2294**	5k. multicoloured	20	10

2295 Computer and Terminal

1986. Resolutions of 27th Communist Party Congress. Multicoloured.

5713		5k. Type **2295** (scientific and technical progress)	25	15
5714		5k. Construction engineer and building project	25	15
5715		5k. City (welfare of people)	25	15
5716		5k. Peace demonstration at Council for Mutual Economic Aid building (peace)	25	15
5717		5k. Spassky Tower and Kremlin Palace, Moscow Kremlin (unity of party and people)	25	15

2296 Parkhomenko

1986. Birth Centenary of Aleksandr Parkhomenko (revolutionary).

5718	**2296**	5k. black	25	15

2297 Machel

1986. Samora Moizes Machel (President of Mozambique) Commemoration.

5719	**2297**	5k. brown and black	25	15

2298 Russian State Museum (Mikhailovsky Palace)

1986. Palace Museums of Leningrad.

5720	**2298**	5k. brown and green	25	20
5721	-	10k. green and blue	35	25
5722	-	15k. blue and green	60	30
5723	-	20k. green and brown	70	50
5724	-	50k. brown and blue	1·60	95

DESIGNS: 10k. Hermitage Museum (Winter Palace); 15k. Grand Palace Museum (Petrodvorets); 20k. Catherine Palace Museum (Pushkin); 50k. Palace Museum (Pavlovsk).

2299 Couple and Industrial Landscape

1987. 18th Soviet Trades Union Congress, Moscow.

5725	**2299**	5k. multicoloured	20	10

2300 Chinese Windmill

1987. Butterflies listed in U.S.S.R. Red Book (2nd series). Multicoloured.

5726		4k. Type **2300**	20	10
5727		5k. Swallowtail	20	10
5728		10k. Southern swallowtail	40	20
5729		15k. "Papilio maackii"	60	30
5730		30k. Scare swallowtail	1·00	60

2301 Karlis Miesnieks

1987. Birth Centenary of Karlis Miesnieks (Latvian artist).

5731	**2301**	5k. multicoloured	25	15

1987. U.S.S.R. Sports Committee's International Mountaineers' Camps (2nd series). As T 2279. Multicoloured.

5732		4k. Chimbulak Gorge	20	10
5733		10k. Shavla Gorge	30	20
5734		20k. Donguz-Orun and Nakra-Tau, Caucasus	80	40
5735		35k. Kazbek, Caucasus	1·30	65

2302 Stasys Simkus

1987. Birth Centenary of Stasys Simkus (Lithuanian composer).

5736	**2302**	5k. purple and yellow	25	15

2303 V. I. Chapaev

1987. Birth Cent of Vasily Ivanovich Chapaev (revolutionary).

5737	**2303**	5k. brown	20	10

2304 Lenin

1987. 20th Leninist Young Communist League (Komsomol) Congress, Moscow. Multicoloured.

5738		5k. Type **2304**	20	10
MS5739		60×85 mm. 50k. Emblem, laurel branch, banner and decoration ribbons (23×32 mm)	2·00	95

2305 Heino Eller

1987. Birth Centenary of Heino Eller (Estonian composer).

5740 **2305** 5k. light brown & brown 30 20

2306 Orbeli

1987. Birth Centenary of Academician Iosif Abgarovich Orbeli (first President of Armenian Academy of Sciences).

5741 **2306** 5k. brown and pink 25 15

2307 Bears in and out of Water

1987. Polar Bears. Multicoloured.

5742 5k. Type **2307** 30 20

5743 10k. Mother and cubs 50 35

5744 20k. Mother and cubs (different) 90 45

5745 35k. Bears 1·50 95

2308 "Sputnik 1" and Globe

1987. Cosmonautics Day. Multicoloured.

5746 10k. Type **2308** (30th anniv of launching of first artificial satellite) 40 25

5747 10k. "Vostok-3", Vostok-4" and globe (25th anniv of first group space flight) 40 25

5748 10k. "Mars-1" and globe (25th anniv of launching of automatic interplanetary station) 40 25

2309 Emblem and Headquarters, Bangkok

1987. 40th Anniv of U.N. Economic and Social Commission for Asia and the Pacific Ocean.

5749 **2309** 10k. multicoloured 40 25

2310 "Birthday" (N. A. Sysoev)

1987. 117th Birth Anniv of Lenin. Multicoloured.

5750 5k. Type **2310** 20 10

5751 5k. "V. I. Lenin with Delegates to the Third Congress of the Young Communist League" (P. P. Belousov) 20 10

MS5752 130×67 mm. 10k. "Lenin's Underground Activity" (D. A. Nalnabdyan) (39×27 mm); 20k. "Lenin" (N. Andreev) (39×55 mm); 10k. "We'll Show the Earth a New Way" (A. G. Lysenko) (39×27 mm); 10k. "Before the Assault" (S. P. Viktorov) (39×27 mm); 10k. "Lenin in Smolny, October 1917" (M. G. Sokolov) (39×27 mm) 1·80 95

2311 Gymnast on Rings

1987. European Gymnastics Championships, Moscow.

5753 **2311** 10k. multicoloured 40 25

2312 Cyclists and "40"

1987. 40th Peace Cycle Race.

5754 **2312** 10k. multicoloured 40 25

2313 Menzbir's Marmot

1987. Mammals listed in U.S.S.R. Red Book. Multicoloured.

5755 5k. Type **2313** 25 10

5756 10k. Ratel (horiz) 40 25

5757 15k. Snow leopard (32×47 mm) 75 45

2314 "Maksim Gorky"

1987. River Tourist Ships. Multicoloured.

5758 5k. Type **2314** 25 15

5759 10k. "Aleksandr Pushkin" 45 25

5760 30k. "Sovetsky Soyuz" 1·10 55

2315 "Portrait of a Woman" (Lucas Cranach the Elder)

1987. West European Art in Hermitage Museum, Leningrad. Multicoloured.

5761 4k. Type **2315** 20 10

5762 5k. "St. Sebastian" (Titian) 20 10

5763 10k. "Justice" (drawing, Albrecht Durer) 35 25

5764 30k. "Adoration of the Magi" (Peter Breughel the younger) (horiz) 1·10 55

5765 50k. "Statue of Ceres" (Peter Paul Rubens) 1·80 95

2316 Car Production Line and Lenin Hydro-electric Power Station

1987. 250th Anniv of Togliatti (formerly Stavropol).

5766 **2316** 5k. multicoloured 20 10

2317 Pushkin (after T. Rait)

1987. 150th Death Anniv of Aleksandr S. Pushkin (poet).

5767 **2317** 5k. deep brown, yellow and brown 25 15

2318 Kovpak

1987. Birth Centenary of Major-General Sidor Artemevich Kovpak.

5768 **2318** 5k. black 20 10

2319 Congress Emblem

1987. World Women's Congress, Moscow.

5769 **2319** 10k. multicoloured 40 25

2320 Arms, Kremlin, Docks, Drama Theatre and Yermak Monument

1987. 400th Anniv of Tobolsk, Siberia.

5770 **2320** 5k. multicoloured 25 15

2321 Party Flag and Mozambican

1987. 25th Anniv of Mozambique Liberation Front (FRELIMO) (5771) and 10th Anniv of U.S.S.R.–Mozambique Friendship and Co-operation Treaty (5772). Multicoloured.

5771 5k. Type **2321** 25 15

5772 5k. Mozambique and U.S.S.R. flags 25 15

2322 "Scolopendrium vulgare"

1987. Ferns. Multicoloured.

5773 4k. Type **2322** 20 10

5774 5k. "Ceterach officinarum" 25 10

5775 10k. "Salvinia natans" (horiz) 40 20

5776 15k. "Matteuccia struthiopteris" 60 30

5777 50k. "Adiantum pedatum" 1·60 75

2323 Moscow Kremlin and Indian Coin

1987. Indian Festival in U.S.S.R. (5778) and U.S.S.R. Festival in India (5779). Multicoloured.

5778 5k. Type **2323** 25 15

5779 5k. Hammer, sickle, open book, satellite and Red Fort, Delhi 25 15

2324 Rossiya Hotel (venue), Globe and Film

1987. 15th International Film Festival, Moscow.

5780 **2324** 10k. multicoloured 40 25

2325 Cosmonauts training

1987. Soviet–Syrian Space Flight. Multicoloured.

5781 5k. Type **2325** 25 10

5782 10k. Moscow–Damascus satellite link and cosmonauts watching television screen 40 20

5783 15k. Cosmonauts at Gagarin monument, Zvezdny 60 40

MS5784 90×62 mm. 50k. "Mir" space station (36×25 mm) 2·00 95

2326 Emblem and Vienna Headquarters

1987. 30th Anniv of Int Atomic Energy Agency.

5785 **2326** 20k. multicoloured 80 50

2327 14th–16th Century Messenger

1987. Russian Postal History.

5786	**2327**	4k. black and brown	20	10
5787	-	5k. black and brown	25	15
5788	-	10k. black and brown	40	20
5789	-	30k. black and brown	1·00	55
5790	-	35k. black and brown	1·30	65
MS5791 95×70 mm. 50k. black and yellow			2·00	95

DESIGNS: 5k. 17th–19th century horse-drawn sledge and 17th-century postman; 10k. 16th-century and 18th-century sailing packets; 30k. 19th-century railway mail vans; 35k. 1905 post car and 1926 "AMO-F-15" van; 50k. Mail-vans in front of Moscow Head Post Office.

2328 "V. I. Lenin" (P. V. Vasilev)

1987. 70th Anniv of October Revolution. Mult.

5792	5k. Type **2328**	25	15
5793	5k. "V. I. Lenin proclaims Soviet Power" (V. A. Serov)	25	15
5794	5k. "Long Live the Socialist Revolution!" (V. V. Kuznetsov)	25	15
5795	5k. "Storming the Winter Palace" (V. A. Serov) (69×32 mm)	25	15
5796	5k. "On the Eve of the Storm" (portraying Lenin, Sverdlov and Podvoisky) (V. V. Pimenov) (69×32 mm)	25	15
MS5797 87×73 mm. 30k. (black and gold) "Lenin" (statue, V. V. Kozlov) (vert)		1·30	65

2329 Anniversary Emblem

1987. 175th Anniv of Battle of Borodino. Sheet 111×82 mm.

MS5798 1r. brown, black and blue	3·50	1·90

2330 Postyshev

1987. Birth Centenary of Pavel Petrovich Postyshev (revolutionary).

5799	**2330**	5k. blue	25	15

2331 Yuri Dolgoruky (founder) Monument

1987. 840th Anniv of Moscow.

5800	**2331**	5k. brown, yell & orge	25	15

2332 Ulugh Beg (astronomer and mathematician)

1987. Scientists.

5801	**2332**	5k. multicoloured	25	20
5802	-	5k. black, green and blue	25	20
5803	-	5k. deep brown, brown and blue	25	20

DESIGNS: No. 5801, Type **2332** (550th anniv of "New Astronomical Tables"); 5802, Isaac Newton (300th anniv of "Principia Mathematica"); 5803, Marie Curie (120th birth anniv).

2333 KOSPAS Satellite

1987. 5th Anniv of KOSPAS–SARSAT (international satellite air/sea search system). Sheet 62×80 mm.

MS5804 50k. multicoloured	2·00	1·20

Всесоюзная филателистическая выставка „70 лет Великого Октября"

(2334)

1987. "70th Anniv of October Revolution" All-Union Stamp Exhibition. No. 5795 optd with T 2334.

5805	5k. multicoloured	60	40

2335 "There will be Cities in the Taiga" (A. A. Yakovlev)

1987. Soviet Paintings of the 1980s. Multicoloured.

5806	4k. Type **2335**	20	10
5807	5k. "Mother" (V. V. Shcherbakov)	20	15
5808	10k. "My Quiet Homeland" (V. M. Sidorov) (horiz)	35	20
5809	30k. "In Yakutsk, Land of Pyotr Alekseev" (A. N. Osipov) (horiz)	95	55
5810	35k. "Ivan's Return" (V. I. Yerofeev) (horiz)	1·10	65
MS5811 92×78 mm. 50k. "Sun over Red Square" (P. P. Ossovsky)		2·00	95

2336 Reed

1987. Birth Centenary of John Reed (American journalist and founder of U.S. Communist Party).

5812	**2336**	10k. brown, yell & blk	35	25

2337 Marshak

1987. Birth Centenary of Samuil Yakovlevich Marshak (poet).

5813	**2337**	5k. brown	20	10

2338 Chavchavadze

1987. 150th Anniv of Ilya Grigoryevich Chavchavadze (writer).

5814	**2338**	5k. blue	25	15

2339 Indira Gandhi

1987. 70th Birth Anniv of Indira Gandhi (Indian Prime Minister, 1966–77 and 1980–84).

5815	**2339**	5k. brown and black	30	20

2340 Vadim N. Podbelsky (revolutionary)

1987. Birth Centenaries.

5816	**2340**	5k. black	20	10
5817	-	5k. blue	20	10

DESIGN: No. 5817, Academician Nikolai Ivanovich Vavilov (geneticist).

2341 Tokamak Thermonuclear System

1987. Science.

5818	**2341**	5k. brown and grey	25	15
5819	-	10k. green, blue and black	40	25
5820	-	20k. black, stone and drab	65	40

DESIGNS: 10k. Kola borehole; 20k. "Ratan-600" radio telescope.

2342 Bagramyan

1987. 90th Birth Anniv of Marshal Ivan Khristoforovich Bagramyan.

5821	**2342**	5k. brown	25	15

2343 Moscow Kremlin

1987. New Year.

5822	**2343**	5k. multicoloured	20	10

2344 Flags, Spassky Tower, Moscow, and Capitol, Washington

1987. Soviet–American Intermediate and Short-range Nuclear Weapons Treaty.

5823	**2344**	10k. multicoloured	40	20

2345 Grigori Andreevich Spiridov and "Tri Svyatitelya"

1987. Russian Naval Commanders (1st series).

5824	**2345**	4k. blue and deep blue	20	10
5825	-	5k. purple and blue	25	15
5826	-	10k. purple and blue	40	20
5827	-	25k. blue and deep blue	90	55
5828	-	30k. blue and deep blue	1·00	65

DESIGNS: 5k. Fyodor Fyodorovich Ushakov and "Sv. Pavel"; 10k. Dmitri Nikolaevich Senyavin, Battle of Afon and "Tverdyi" (battleship); 25k. Mikhail Petrovich Lazarev and "Azov"; 30k. Pavel Stepanovich Nakhimov and "Imperatritsa Maria".

See also Nos. 6091/6.

2346 Torch

1987. 30th Anniv of Asia–Africa Solidarity Organization.

5829	**2346**	10k. multicoloured	35	25

2347 Biathlon

1988. Winter Olympic Games, Calgary. Mult.

5830	5k. Type **2347**	25	15
5831	10k. Cross-country skiing	40	20
5832	15k. Slalom	50	30
5833	20k. Figure skating (pairs)	70	40
5834	30k. Ski jumping	1·10	45
MS5835 62×80 mm. 50k. Ice hockey (horiz)		2·00	95

2348 1918 Stamps

1988. 70th Anniv of First Soviet Postage Stamps.

5836	**2348**	10k. blue, brown and gold	40	25
5837	**2348**	10k. brown, blue and gold	40	25

On No. 5836 the lower stamp depicted is the 35k. in blue, on No. 5837 the lower stamp is the 70k. in brown.

2349 Emblem

1988. 40th Anniv of W.H.O.
5838 **2349** 35k. gold, blue and black 1·50 95

2350 Byron

1988. Birth Bicentenary of Lord Byron (English poet).
5839 **2350** 15k. black, green and blue 50 30

2351 Exchange Activities and National Flags

1988. 30th Anniv of Agreement on Cultural, Technical and Educational Exchanges with U.S.A.
5840 **2351** 20k. multicoloured 70 40

2352 Lomov-Oppokov

1988. Birth Centenary of Georgy Ippolitovich Lomov-Oppokov (Communist party official).
5841 **2352** 5k. black and brown 25 15

2353 "Little Humpbacked Horse" (dir. I. Ivanov-Vano, animated L. Milchin)

1988. Soviet Cartoon Films. Multicoloured.
5842 1k. Type **2353** 10 10
5843 3k. "Winnie the Pooh" (dir. F. Khitruk, animated V. Zuikov and E. Nazarov) 10 10
5844 4k. "Gena the Crocodile" (dir. R. Kachanov, animated L. Shartsmann) 20 10
5845 5k. "Just You Wait!" (dir. V. Kotyonochkin, animated S. Rusakov) 30 20
5846 10k. "Hedgehog in a Mist" (dir. Yu. Norshtein, animated F. Yarbusova) 50 30
MS5847 95×75 mm. 30k. Cover and stamps ("The Post" dir. M. Tsekhanovsky) 1·30 75

2354 Bonch-Bruevich

1988. Birth Centenary of Mikhail Alexandrovich Bonch-Bruevich (radio engineer).
5848 **2354** 10k. black and brown 35 25

2355 Nurse and Emblems

1988. 125th Anniv of International Red Cross and Red Crescent.
5849 **2355** 15k. black, blue and red 60 40

2356 Skater

1988. World Speed Skating Championships, Alma-Ata.
5850 **2356** 15k. blue, violet and black 50 35

2357 Makarenko

1988. Birth Centenary of Anton Semenovich Makarenko (educationist and writer).
5851 **2357** 10k. green 40 25

2358 Skorina

1988. 500th Birth Anniv of Frantsisk Skorina (printer).
5852 **2358** 5k. black 25 15

2359 Banners and Globe

1988. Labour Day.
5853 **2359** 5k. multicoloured 20 10

2360 Kingisepp

1988. Birth Centenary of Victor Eduardovich Kingisepp (revolutionary).
5854 **2360** 5k. green 25 15

2361 Track and Athlete

1988. Centenary of Russian Athletics.
5855 **2361** 15k. multicoloured 50 30

2362 M. S. Shaginyan

1988. Birth Centenary of Marietta Sergeevna Shaginyan (writer).
5856 **2362** 10k. brown 35 20

2363 Palace of Congresses, Moscow, Finlandia Hall, Helsinki, and National Flags

1988. 40th Anniv of U.S.S.R.–Finland Friendship Treaty.
5857 **2363** 15k. multicoloured 50 30

2364 "Mir"–"Soyuz TM" Space Complex and "Progress" Spacecraft

1988. Cosmonautics Day.
5858 **2364** 15k. multicoloured 50 30

2365 Sochi

1988. 150th Anniv of Sochi.
5859 **2365** 5k. multicoloured 25 15

2366 "Victory" (P. A. Krivonogov)

1988. V. E. Day.
5860 **2366** 5k. multicoloured 20 10

2367 Lenin Museum, Moscow

1988. 118th Birth Anniv of Lenin. Designs showing branches of Lenin Central Museum.
5861 **2367** 5k. brown, deep brown and gold 20 10
5862 - 5k. red, purple and gold 20 10
5863 - 5k. ochre, brown & gold 20 10
5864 - 5k. yellow, green & gold 20 10
DESIGNS: No. 5862, Kiev; 5863, Leningrad; 5864, Krasnoyarsk.

See also Nos. 5990/2 and 6131/3.

2368 Akulov

1988. Birth Centenary of Ivan Alekseevich Akulov (Communist Party official).
5865 **2368** 5k. blue 25 15

2369 Soviet Display Emblem

1988. "Expo 88" World's Fair, Brisbane.
5866 **2369** 20k. multicoloured 70 40

2370 Marx

1988. 170th Birth Anniv of Karl Marx.
5867 **2370** 5k. brown 20 10

2371 Soldiers and Workers

1988. Perestroika (Reformation).
5868 **2371** 5k. multicoloured 20 10
5869 - 5k. brown, red & orange 20 10
DESIGN: No. 5869, Banner, industrial scenes and worker.

Спортсмены СССР завоевали 11 золотых, 9 серебряных и 9 бронзовых медалей!

(2372)

1988. Winter Olympic Games Soviet Medal Winners. No. MS5835 optd with T 2372.
MS5870 62×80 mm. 50k. multicoloured 2·00 1·50

2373 Shvernik

1988. Birth Centenary of Nikolai Mikhailovich Shvernik (politician).
5871 **2373** 5k. black 25 15

2374 Russian Borzoi

1988. Hunting Dogs. Multicoloured.
5872 5k. Type **2374** 25 10
5873 10k. Kirgiz borzoi 35 20
5874 15k. Russian hound 50 30
5875 20k. Russian spaniel 65 45
5876 35k. East Siberian husky 1·30 75

2375 Flags, Spassky Tower and Handshake

1988. Soviet–American Summit, Moscow.
5877 **2375** 5k. multicoloured 25 15

2376 Kuibyshev

1988. Birth Centenary of Valerian Vladimirovich Kuibyshev (politician).
5878 **2376** 5k. brown 25 15

2377 Flags, "Mir" Space Station and "Soyuz TM" Spacecraft

1988. Soviet–Bulgarian Space Flight.
5879 **2377** 15k. multicoloured 60 35

2378 Crowd and Peace Banners

1988. "For a Nuclear-free World".
5880 **2378** 5k. multicoloured 20 10

2379 Red Flag, Hammer and Sickle and Laurel Branch

1988. 19th Soviet Communist Party Conference, Moscow (1st issue). Multicoloured.
5881 5k. Type **2379** 20 10
5882 5k. Lenin on red flag and interior of Palace of Congresses (35×23 mm) 20 10
MS5883 100×65 mm. 50k. Palace of Congresses and Spassky Tower, Moscow, Kremlin (50×36 mm) 2·00 1·50

See also Nos. 5960/2.

2380 Flags, Skis and Globe

1988. Soviet–Canadian Transarctic Ski Expedition.
5884 **2380** 35k. multicoloured 1·60 95

2381 Hurdling

1988. Olympic Games, Seoul. Multicoloured.
5885 5k. Type **2381** 20 20
5886 10k. Long jumping 30 20
5887 15k. Basketball 50 30
5888 20k. Gymnastics 60 40
5889 30k. Swimming 1·00 65
MS5890 80×65 mm. 50k. Football 2·00 1·40

2382 Giant Bellflower

1988. Deciduous Forest Flowers. Multicoloured.
5891 5k. Type **2382** 20 10
5892 10k. Spring pea (horiz) 30 20
5893 15k. Lungwort 50 30
5894 20k. Turk's cap lily 60 40
5895 35k. "Ficaria verna" 1·50 60

2383 Phobos and "Phobos" Space Probe

1988. Phobos (Mars Moon) International Space Project.
5896 **2383** 10k. multicoloured 40 25

2384 Komsomol Badge

1988. 70th Anniv of Leninist Young Communist League (Komsomol).
5897 **2384** 5k. multicoloured 25 15

2385 Mandela

1988. 70th Birthday of Nelson Mandela (African nationalist).
5898 **2385** 10k. multicoloured 50 40

2386 "Obeyan Serebryanyi, Light Grey Arab Stallion" (N. E. Sverchkov)

1988. Paintings in Moscow Horse Breeding Museum. Multicoloured.
5899 5k. Type **2386** 25 10
5900 10k. "Konvoets" (Kabardin breed) (M. A. Vrubel) (vert) 35 20
5901 15k. "Horsewoman on Orlov-Rastopchin Horse" (N. E. Sverchkov) 50 35
5902 20k. "Letuchy, Grey Stallion of Orlov Trotter Breed" (V. A. Serov) (vert) 80 45
5903 30k. "Sardar, an Akhaltekin Stallion" (A. B. Villevalde) 1·20 65

Филвыставка.
Москва
(2387)

1988. Stamp Exhibition, Moscow. No. 5897 optd with T 2387.
5904 **2384** 5k. multicoloured 50 40

2388 Voikov

1988. Birth Centenary of Pyotr Lazarevich Voikov (diplomat).
5905 **2388** 5k. black 20 10

2389 "Portrait of O. K. Lansere" (Z. E. Serebryakova)

1988. Soviet Culture Fund. Multicoloured.
5906 10k.+5k. Type **2389** 50 35
5907 15k.+7k. "Boyarynya (noblewoman) looking at Embroidery Design" (K. V. Lebedev) (horiz) 70 45
5908 30k.+15k. "Talent" (N. P. Bogdanov-Belsky) 1·50 95
MS5909 70×90 mm. 1r.+50k. "Holy Trinity" (icon, Novgorod School) 5·25 3·50

2390 Envelopes and U.P.U. Emblem

1988. International Correspondence Week.
5910 **2390** 5k. turquoise, blue & black 25 15

2391 "Mir" Space Station and "Soyuz-TM" Spacecraft

1988. Soviet–Afghan Space Flight.
5911 **2391** 15k. green, red and black 60 35

2392 Emblem and Open Book

1988. 30th Anniv of "Problems of Peace and Socialism" (magazine).
5912 **2392** 10k. multicoloured 35 25

2393 Kviring

1988. Birth Centenary of Emmanuil Ionovich Kviring (politician).
5913 **2393** 5k. black 25 15

2394 "Ilya Muromets" (Russia) (R. Smirnov)

1988. Epic Poems of Soviet Union (1st series). Illustrations by artists named. Multicoloured.
5914 10k. Type **2394** 35 20
5915 10k. "Cossack Golota" (Ukraine) (M. Deregus) (horiz) 35 20
5916 10k. "Musician-Magician" (Byelorussia) (N. Poplavskaya) 35 20
5917 10k. "Koblandy Batyr" (Kazakhstan) (I. Isabaev) (horiz) 35 20
5918 10k. "Alpamysh" (Uzbekistan) (R. Khalilov) 35 20

See also Nos. 6017/21 and 6139/43.

2395 "Appeal of the Leader" (detail, I. M. Toidze)

1988. 71st Anniv of October Revolution.
5919 **2395** 5k. multicoloured 20 10

2396 Bolotov

1988. 250th Birth Anniv of Andrei Timofeevich Bolotov (agriculturalist).

5920	**2396**	10k. brown	35	20

2397 Tupolev

1988. Birth Centenary of Academician Andrei Nikolaevich Tupolev (aircraft designer).

5921	**2397**	10k. blue	35	20

2398 Bear

1988. Zoo Relief Fund. Multicoloured.

5922	10k.+5k. Type **2398**	50	30
5923	10k.+5k. Wolf	50	30
5924	10k.+10k. Fox	1·00	55
5925	20k.+10k. Wild boar	1·00	55
5926	20k.+10k. Lynx	1·00	55

2399 "Sibir" (atomic ice-breaker)

1988. Soviet Arctic Expedition.

5927	**2399**	20k. multicoloured	1·10	75

2400 Ustinov

1988. 80th Birth Anniv of Marshal Dmitri Fyodorovich Ustinov.

5928	**2400**	5k. brown	20	10

2401 National Initials

1988. 10th Anniv of U.S.S.R.–Vietnam Friendship Treaty.

5929	**2401**	10k. multicoloured	35	25

2402 Building Facade

1988. 50th Anniv of State House of Broadcasting and Sound Recording.

5930	**2402**	10k. multicoloured	35	25

2403 Emblem

1988. 40th Anniv of Declaration of Human Rights.

5931	**2403**	10k. multicoloured	35	25

2404 Life Guard of Preobrazhensky Regt. with Peter I's New Year Decree

1988. New Year.

5932	**2404**	5k. multicoloured	20	10

2405 Flags and Cosmonauts

1988. Soviet–French Space Flight.

5933	**2405**	15k. multicoloured	60	35

2406 "Skating Rink" (Olya Krutova)

1988. Lenin Soviet Children's Fund. Children's Paintings. Multicoloured.

5934	5k.+2k. Type **2406**	30	20
5935	5k.+2k. "Cock" (Nasta Shcheglova)	30	20
5936	5k.+2k. "May is flying over the Meadows, May is flying over the Fields" (Larisa Gaidash)	30	20

2407 Lacis

1988. Birth Cent of Martins Lacis (revolutionary).

5937	**2407**	5k. green	25	15

★
КОСМИЧЕСКАЯ
ПОЧТА

(2408)

1988. "Space Post". No. 4682 optd with T 2408.

5938	1r. blue	5·50	3·50

СПОРТСМЕНЫ СССР ЗАВОЕВАЛИ
55 ЗОЛОТЫХ, 31 СЕРЕБРЯНУЮ
И 46 БРОНЗОВЫХ МЕДАЛЕЙ
СЕУЛ • 1988

(2409)

1988. Olympic Games Soviet Medal. No. MS5890 optd with T 2409.

MS5939	80×65 mm. 50k. multicoloured	2·00	1·40

2410 Post Messenger

1988

6072	**2410**	1k. brown	10	10
6073	-	2k. brown	10	10
6074	-	3k. green	10	10
6075	-	4k. blue	10	10
6076	-	5k. red	15	10
6077a	-	7k. blue	30	20
6078	-	10k. brown	30	20
6079	-	12k. purple	45	30
6080	-	13k. violet	50	30
6081	-	15k. blue	40	30
6082	-	20k. brown	60	40
6083	-	25k. green	80	45
6084	-	30k. blue	90	55
6085	-	35k. brown	1·00	75
6086	-	50k. blue	1·70	95
6087	-	1r. blue	3·00	1·90

DESIGNS: 2k. Old mail transport (sailing packet, steam train and mail coach); 3k. "Aurora" (cruiser); 4k. Spassky Tower and Lenin's Tomb, Red Square, Moscow; 5k. State emblem and flag; 7k. Modern mail transport (Ilyushin Il-86 jetliner, Mil Mi-2 helicopter, "Aleksandr Pushkin" (liner), train and mail van); 10k. "The Worker and the Collective Farmer" (statue, Vera Mukhina); 12k. Rocket on launch pad; 13k. Satellite; 15k. "Orbit" dish aerial; 20k. Symbols of art and literature; 25k. "The Discus-thrower" (5th-century Greek statue by Miron); 30k. Map of Antarctica and emperor penguins; 35k. "Mercury" (statue, Giovanni da Bologna); 50k. Great white cranes; 1r. Universal Postal Union emblem.

2411 Great Cascade and Samson Fountain

1988. Petrodvorets Fountains. Each green and grey.

5952	5k. Type **2411**	25	15
5953	10k. Adam fountain (D. Bonazza)	35	20
5954	15k. Golden Mountain cascade (Niccolo Michetti and Mikhail Zemtsov)	50	35
5955	30k. Roman fountains (Bartolomeo Rastrelli)	1·10	55
5956	50k. Oaklet trick fountain (Rastrelli)	1·70	1·10

2412 1st-cent B.C. Gold Coin of Tigran the Great

1988. Armenian Earthquake Relief. Armenian History. Multicoloured.

5957	20k.+10k. Type **2412**	1·00	55
5958	30k.+15k. Rispsime Church	1·30	95
5959	50k.+25k. "Madonna and Child" (18th-century fresco, Ovnat Ovnatanyan)	2·30	1·50

2413 Hammer and Sickle

1988. 19th Soviet Communist Party Conference, Moscow (2nd issue). Multicoloured.

5960	5k. Type **2413**	25	15
5961	5k. Hammer and sickle and building girders	25	15
5962	5k. Hammer and sickle and wheat	25	15

2414 "Buran"

1988. Launch of Space Shuttle Buran. Sheet 93×63 mm.

MS5963	50k. multicoloured	2·20	1·10

2415 "Vostok" Rocket, "Lunar 1", Earth and Moon

1989. 30th Anniv of First Russian Moon Flight.

5964	**2415**	15k. multicoloured	60	35

2416 Virtanen

1989. Birth Centenary of Jalmari Virtanen (poet).

5965	**2416**	5k. brown and bistre	25	15

2417 Headquarters Building, Moscow

1989. 40th Anniv of Council for Mutual Economic Aid.

5966	**2417**	10k. multicoloured	35	25

2418 Forest Protection

1989. Nature Conservation. Multicoloured.

5967	5k. Type **2418**	20	10
5968	10k. Arctic preservation	40	25
5969	15k. Anti-desertification campaign	60	40

2419 18th-century Samovar

1989. Russian Samovars in State Museum, Leningrad. Multicoloured.

5970	5k. Type **2419**	25	15
5971	10k. 19th-century barrel samovar by Ivan Lisitsin of Tula	35	20
5972	20k. 1830s Kabachok travelling samovar by Sokolov Brothers factory, Tula	60	40
5973	30k. 1840s samovar by Nikolai Malikov factory, Tula	90	55

2420 Mussorgsky (after Repin) and Scene from "Boris Godunov"

1989. 150th Birth Anniv of Modest Petrovich Mussorgsky (composer).

5974	**2420**	10k. purple and brown	40	25

2421 Dybenko

1989. Birth Centenary of Pavel Dybenko (military leader).

5975	**2421**	5k. black	25	15

2422 Shevchenko

1989. 175th Birth Anniv of Taras Shevchenko (Ukrainian poet and painter).

5976	**2422**	5k. brown, green & black	25	15

2423 "Lilium speciosum"

1989. Lilies. Multicoloured.

5977	5k. Type **2423**	20	10
5978	10k. "African Queen"	40	20
5979	15k. "Eclat du Soir"	50	30
5980	30k. "White Tiger"	1·20	55

2424 Marten

1989. Zoo Relief Fund. Multicoloured.

5981	10k.+5k. Type **2424**	50	30
5982	10k.+5k. Squirrel	50	30
5983	20k.+10k. Hare	1·10	65
5984	20k.+10k. Hedgehog	1·10	65
5985	20k.+10k. Badger	1·10	65

2425 Red Flag, Rainbow and Globe

1989. Centenary of "Second International" Declaration of 1 May as Labour Day. Sheet 105×75 mm.

MS5986	30k. multicoloured	1·20	75

2426 "Victory Banner" (P. Loginov and V. Pamfilov)

1989. Victory Day.

5987	**2426**	5k. multicoloured	25	15

2427 "Mir" Space Station (image scaled to 74% of original size)

1989. Cosmonautics Day.

5988	**2427**	15k. multicoloured	40	35

2428 Emblem and Flags

1989. U.S.–Soviet Bering Bridge Expedition.

5989	**2428**	10k. multicoloured	40	25

1989. 119th Birth Anniv of Lenin. As T 2367. Branches of Lenin Central Museum.

5990	5k. brown, ochre and gold	20	15
5991	5k. deep brown, brn & gold	20	15
5992	5k. multicoloured	20	15

DESIGNS: No. 5990, Frunze; 5991, Kazan; 5992, Kuibyshev.

2429 "Phobos"

1989. Launch of "Phobos" Space Probe to Mars. Sheet 89×65 mm.

MS5993	50k. multicoloured	1·90	95

2430 Statue

1989. 70th Anniv of First Hungarian Soviet Republic.

5994	**2430**	5k. multicoloured	30	20

2431 "Motherland Statue"

1989. 400th Anniv of Volgograd (formerly Tsaritsyn).

5995	**2431**	5k. multicoloured	25	15

2432 Drone

1989. Honey Bees. Multicoloured.

5996	5k. Type **2432**	20	10
5997	10k. Bees, flowers and hive	30	20
5998	20k. Bee on flower	60	35
5999	35k. Feeding queen bee	1·30	65

2433 Negative and Positive Images

1989. 150th Anniv of Photography.

6000	**2433**	5k. multicoloured	25	15

2434 Map above Dove as Galley

1989. "Europe—Our Common Home". Mult.

6001	5k. Type **2434**	20	10
6002	10k. Laying foundations of Peace	40	25
6003	15k. White storks' nest	70	45

2435 Mukhina modelling "God of Northern Wind" (after M. Nesterov)

1989. Birth Centenary of Vera Mukhina (sculptress).

6004	**2435**	5k. blue	25	15

2436 Racine

1989. 150th Birth Anniv of Jean Racine (dramatist).

6005	**2436**	15k. multicoloured	60	40

2437 Rabbit

1989. Lenin Soviet Children's Fund. Children's Paintings. Multicoloured.

6006	5k.+2k. Type **2437**	25	15
6007	5k.+2k. Cat	25	15
6008	5k.+2k. Nurse	25	15

See also Nos. 6162/4.

2438 Kuratov

1989. 150th Birth Anniv of Ivan Kuratov (writer).

6009	**2438**	5k. deep brown & brown	30	20

2439 Emblem

1989. 13th World Youth and Students' Festival, Pyongyang.

6010	**2439**	10k. multicoloured	40	25

2440 Common Shelduck

1989. Ducks (1st series). Multicoloured.

6011	5k. Type **2440**	25	10
6012	15k. Green-winged teal	50	30
6013	20k. Ruddy shelduck	70	45

See also Nos. 6159/61 and 6264/6.

2441 "Storming of Bastille" (Gelman after Monnet)

1989. Bicentenary of French Revolution.

6014	**2441**	5k. multicoloured	20	10
6015	-	15k. blue, black and red	50	30
6016	-	20k. blue, black and red	65	40

DESIGNS: 15k. Jean-Paul Marat, Georges Danton and Maximilien Robespierre; 20k. "Marseillaise" (relief by F. Rude from Arc de Triomphe).

1989. Epic Poems of Soviet Union (2nd series). Illustrations by named artists. As T 2394. Mult.

6017	10k. "Amirani" (Georgia) (V. Oniani)	40	20
6018	10k. "Koroglu" (Azerbaijan) (A. Gadzhiev)	40	20
6019	10k. "Fir, Queen of Grass Snakes" (Lithuania) (A. Makunaite)	40	20
6020	10k. "Mioritsa" (Moldavia) (I. Bogdesko)	40	20
6021	10k. "Lachplesis" (Lettish) (G. Wilks)	40	20

2442 Observatory

1989. 150th Anniv of Pulkovo Observatory.

6022	**2442**	10k. multicoloured	40	25

2443 Hemispheres, Roses in Envelope and Posthorn

1989. International Letter Week.

6023	**2443**	5k. multicoloured	25	15

2444 Lynx

1989. 50th Anniv of Tallin Zoo.

6024	**2444**	10k. multicoloured	35	20

2445 Ships and Peter I

1989. 275th Anniv of Battle of Hango Head. Sheet 95×65 mm.
MS6025 50k. blue, black and brown 1·80 95

2446 Buildings, Container Ship and Bicentenary Emblem

1989. Bicentenary of Nikolaev.
6026 **2446** 5k. multicoloured 25 15

2447 Nkrumah

1989. 80th Birth Anniv of Kwame Nkrumah (first Prime Minister and President of Ghana).
6027 **2447** 10k. multicoloured 40 25

2448 1921 40r. Stamp

1989. 6th All-Union Philatelic Society Congress, Moscow.
6028 **2448** 10k. multicoloured 40 25

2449 Cooper

1989. Birth Bicentenary of James Fenimore Cooper (writer) (1st issue).
6029 **2449** 15k. multicoloured 50 30
See also Nos. 6055/9.

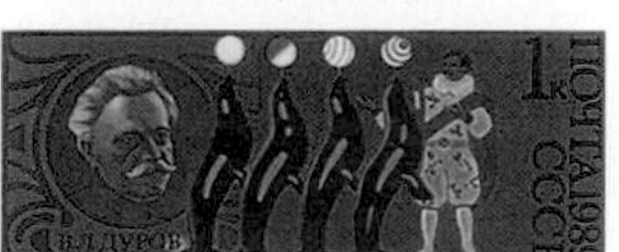
2450 V. L. Durov (trainer) and Sealions

1989. 70th Anniv of Soviet Circus. Multicoloured.
6030 1k. Type **2450** 10 10
6031 3k. M. N. Rumyantsev (clown "Karandash") with donkey 10 10
6032 4k. V. I. Filatov (founder of Bear Circus) and bears on motor cycles 20 10
6033 5k. E. T. Kio (illusionist) and act 30 15
6034 10k. V. E. Lazarenko (clown and acrobat) and act 50 25
MS6035 80×65 mm. 30k. Moscow Circus building, Tsvetnoi Boulevard (33×21½ mm) 1·20 85

2451 Emblem on Glove

1989. International Amateur Boxing Association Championship, Moscow.
6036 **2451** 15k. multicoloured 50 30

2452 Li Dazhao

1989. Birth Centenary of Li Dazhao (co-founder of Chinese Communist Party).
6037 **2452** 5k. brown, stone & black 25 15

2453 Khetagurov

1989. 130th Birth Anniv of Kosta Khetagurov (Ossetian writer).
6038 **2453** 5k. brown 25 15

2454 "October Guardsmen" (M. M. Chepik)

1989. 72nd Anniv of October Revolution.
6039 **2454** 5k. multicoloured 20 10

2455 Russian Spoons, Psaltery, Balalaika, Zhaleika and Accordion

1989. Traditional Musical Instruments (1st series). Multicoloured.
6040 10k. Type **2455** 40 25
6041 10k. Ukrainian bandura, trembita, drymba, svyril (pipes) and dulcimer 40 25
6042 10k. Byelorussian tambourine, bastlya (fiddle), lera and dudka (pipe) 40 25
6043 10k. Uzbek nagors (drums), rubab, zang, karnai and gidzhak 40 25
See also Nos. 6183/6 and 6303/5.

2456 "Demonstration of First Radio Receiver, 1895" (N. A. Sysoev)

1989. 130th Birth Anniv of Aleksandr Stepanovich Popov (radio pioneer).
6044 **2456** 10k. multicoloured 40 25

2457 National Flag and Provincial Arms

1989. 40th Anniv of German Democratic Republic.
6045 **2457** 5k. multicoloured 30 25

2458 Polish National Colours forming "45"

1989. 45th Anniv of Liberation of Poland.
6046 **2458** 5k. multicoloured 25 15

2459 Kosior

1989. Birth Centenary of Stanislav Vikentievich Kosior (vice-chairman of Council of People's Commissars).
6047 **2459** 5k. black 25 15

2460 Nehru

1989. Birth Centenary of Jawaharlal Nehru (Indian statesman).
6048 **2460** 15k. brown 50 30

2461 "Village Market" (A. V. Makovsky)

1989. Soviet Culture Fund. Multicoloured.
6049 4k.+2k. Type **2461** 25 15
6050 5k.+2k. "Lady in Hat" (E. L. Zelenin) 30 20
6051 10k.+5k. "Portrait of the Actress Bazhenova" (A. F. Sofronova) 50 30
6052 20k.+10k. "Two Women" (Hugo Shaiber) 90 75
6053 30k.+15k. 19th-century teapot and plates from Popov porcelain works 1·50 95

2462 Berzin

1989. Birth Centenary of Yan Karlovich Berzin (head of Red Army Intelligence).
6054 **2462** 5k. black 25 15

2463 "The Hunter"

1989. Birth Bicentenary of James Fenimore Cooper (writer) (2nd issue). Illustrations of his novels. Multicoloured.
6055 20k. Type **2463** 70 45
6056 20k. "Last of the Mohicans" 70 45
6057 20k. "The Pathfinder" 70 45
6058 20k. "The Pioneers" 70 45
6059 20k. "The Prairie" 70 45
Nos. 6055/9 were printed together, se-tenant, forming a composite design.

2464 St. Basil's Cathedral and Minin and Pozharsky Statue, Moscow

1989. Historical Monuments (1st series). Mult.
6060 15k. Type **2464** 55 35
6061 15k. Sts. Peter and Paul Cathedral and statue of Peter I, Leningrad 55 35
6062 15k. St. Sophia's Cathedral and statue of Bogdan Chmielnitsky, Kiev 55 35
6063 15k. Khodzha Ahmed Yasavi mausoleum, Turkestan 55 35
6064 15k. Khazret Khyzr Mosque, Samarkand 55 35
See also Nos. 6165/72 and 6231/3.

2465 Dymkovo Toy

1989. New Year.
6065 **2465** 5k. multicoloured 20 10

2466 Soviet Lunar Vehicle

1989. "Expo 89" International Stamp Exhibition, Washington D.C. Multicoloured.
6066 25k. Type **2466** 1·00 65
6067 25k. Astronaut and landing module on Moon 1·00 65
6068 25k. Cosmonauts on Mars 1·00 65
6069 25k. Flag and shield on Mars 1·00 65
MS6070 104×84 mm. Nos. 6066/9 4·25 3·00

2467 Barn Swallow

1989. Nature Preservation. Sheet 65×90 mm.
MS6071 20k.+10k. multicoloured 1·50 1·20

1989. Russian Naval Commanders (2nd series). As T 2345.

6091		5k. blue and brown	20	10
6092		10k. blue and brown	30	20
6093		15k. blue and deep blue	50	30
6094		20k. blue and deep blue	60	45
6095		30k. blue and brown	95	75
6096		35k. blue and brown	1·50	95

DESIGNS: 5k. V. A. Kornilov and "Vladimer" (steam frigate) and "Pervaz-Bakhric" (Turkish) steam frigate); 10k. V. I. Istomin and "Parizh"; 15k. G. I. Nevelskoi and "Baikal"; 20k. G. I. Butakov and iron-clad squadron; 30k. A. A. Popov, "Pyotr Veliky" and "Vitze Admirial Popov"; 35k. S. O. Makarov, "Intibah" (Turkish warship) and "Veliky Khyaz Konstantin".

2468 Acid Rain destroying Rose

1990. Nature Conservation. Multicoloured.

6097		10k. Type **2468**	40	30
6098		15k. Oil-smeared great black-headed gull perching on globe	65	40
6099		20k. Blade sawing down tree	70	45

2469 Ladya Monument and Golden Gates, Kiev (Ukraine)

1990. Republic Capitals. Multicoloured.

6100		5k. Lenin Palace of Culture, Government House and Academy of Sciences, Alma-Ata (Kazakhstan)	20	15
6101		5k. Library, Mollanepes Theatre and War Heroes Monument, Ashkhabad (Turkmenistan)	20	15
6102		5k. Maiden's Tower and Divan-Khane Palace, Baku (Azerbaijan)	20	15
6103		5k. Sadriddin Aini Theatre and Avicenna Monument, Dushanbe (Tadzhikistan)	20	15
6104		5k. Spendyarov Theatre and David Sasunsky Monument, Yerevan (Armenia)	20	15
6105		5k. Satylganov Philharmonic Society building and Manas Memorial, Frunze (Kirgizia)	20	15
6106		5k. Type **2469**	20	15
6107		5k. Cathedral and Victory Arch, Kishinev (Moldavia)	20	15
6108		5k. Government House and Liberation Monument, Minsk (Byelorussia)	20	15
6109		5k. Konstantino-Yeleninsky Tower and Ivan the Great Bell Tower, Moscow (Russian Federation)	20	15
6110		5k. Cathedral, "Three Brothers" building and Freedom Monument, Riga (Latvia)	20	15
6111		5k. Herman the Long, Oliviste Church, Cathedral and Town hall towers and wall turret, Tallin (Estonia)	20	15
6112		5k. Kukeldash Medrese and University, Tashkent (Uzbekistan)	20	15
6113		5k. Metekh Temple and Vakhtang Gorgasal Monument, Tbilisi (Georgia)	20	15
6114		5k. Gediminas Tower and St. Anne's Church, Vilnius (Lithuania)	20	15

2470 Flag and Hanoi Monument

1990. 60th Anniv of Vietnamese Communist Party.

6115	**2470**	5k. multicoloured	25	15

2471 Ho Chi Minh

1990. Birth Cent of Ho Chi Minh (Vietnamese leader).

6116	**2471**	10k. brown and black	40	25

2472 Snowy Owl

1990. Owls. Multicoloured.

6117		10k. Type **2472**	25	20
6118		20k. Eagle owl (vert)	45	30
6119		55k. Long-eared owl	1·10	55

2473 Paddle-steamer, Posthorn and Penny Black

1990. 150th Anniv of the Penny Black.

6120	**2473**	10k. multicoloured	30	20
6121	-	20k. black and gold	60	35
6122	-	20k. black and gold	60	35
6123	-	35k. multicoloured	1·30	95
6124	-	35k. multicoloured	1·30	95
MS6125		87×65 mm. 1r. black and green (36×25 mm)	4·00	2·10

DESIGNS: No. 6121, Anniversary emblem and Penny Black (lettered "T P"); 6122, As No. 6121 but stamp lettered "T F"; 6123, "Stamp World London 90" International Stamp Exhibition emblem and Penny Black (lettered "V K"); 6124, As No. 6123 but stamp lettered "A H" ; 1r. Penny Black and anniversary emblem.

2474 Electric Cables

1990. 125th Anniv of I.T.U.

6126	**2474**	20k. multicoloured	70	45

2475 Flowers

1990. Labour Day.

6127	**2475**	5k. multicoloured	25	15

2476 "Victory, 1945" (A. Lysenko)

1990. 45th Anniv of Victory in Second World War.

6128	**2476**	5k. multicoloured	25	15

2477 "Mir" Space Complex and Cosmonaut

1990. Cosmonautics Day.

6129	**2477**	20k. multicoloured	60	40

2478 Lenin

1990. "Leniniana '90" All-Union Stamp Exhibition.

6130	**2478**	5k. brown	25	15

1990. 120th Birth Anniv of Lenin. Branches of Lenin Central Museum. As T 2367.

6131		5k. red, lake and gold	25	15
6132		5k. pink, purple and gold	25	15
6133		5k. multicoloured	25	15

DESIGNS: No. 6131, Ulyanovsk; 6132, Baku; 6133, Tashkent.

2479 Scene from "Iolanta" (opera) and Tchaikovsky

1990. 150th Birth Anniv of Pyotr Ilich Tchaikovsky (composer).

6134	**2479**	15k. black	70	45

2480 Golden Eagle

1990. Zoo Relief Fund. Multicoloured.

6135		10k.+5k. Type **2480**	50	30
6136		20k.+10k. Saker falcon ("Falco cherrug")	1·00	75
6137		20k.+10k. Common raven ("Corvus corax")	1·00	75

2481 Etching by G. A. Echeistov

1990. 550th Anniv of "Dzhangar" (Kalmuk folk epic).

6138	**2481**	10k. ochre, brown & black	40	25

1990. Epic Poems of Soviet Union (3rd series). Illustrations by named artists. As T 2394. Mult.

6139		10k. "Manas" (Kirgizia) (T. Gertsen) (horiz)	40	25
6140		10k. "Gurugli" (Tadzhikistan) (I. Martynov) (horiz)	40	25
6141		10k. "David Sasunsky" (Armenia) (M. Abegyan)	40	25
6142		10k. "Gerogly" (Turkmenistan) (I. Klychev)	40	25
6143		10k. "Kalevipoeg" (Estonia) (O. Kallis)	40	25

2482 Goalkeeper and Players

1990. World Cup Football Championship, Italy. Multicoloured.

6144		5k. Type **2482**	20	10
6145		10k. Players	40	25
6146		15k. Attempted tackle	50	30
6147		25k. Referee and players	80	45
6148		35k. Goalkeeper saving ball	1·30	65

2483 Globe and Finlandia Hall, Helsinki

1990. 15th Anniv of European Security and Co-operation Conference, Helsinki.

6149	**2483**	15k. multicoloured	60	40

2484 Competitors and Target

1990. 45th World Shooting Championships, Moscow.

6150	**2484**	15k. multicoloured	50	35

2485 Glaciology Research

1990. Soviet–Australian Scientific Co-operation in Antarctica. Multicoloured.

6151		5k. Type **2485**	25	15
6152		50k. Krill (marine biology research)	1·70	1·30
MS6153		84×65 mm. Nos. 6151/2	2·00	1·50

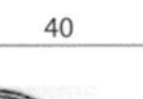

2486 Emblem and Sports Pictograms

1990. Goodwill Games, Seattle.

6154	**2486**	10k. multicoloured	40	25

2487 Troops and Badge of order of Aleksandr Nevsky (B2)

1990. 750th Anniv of Battle of Neva. Sheet 94×65 mm.

MS6155	**2487**	50k. multicoloured	2·00	1·20

2488 Greylag Geese

1990. Poultry. Multicoloured.

6156		5k. Type **2488**	25	10
6157		10k. Adlers (chickens)	35	25
6158		15k. Common turkeys	50	40

2489 Mallards

1990. Ducks (2nd series). Multicoloured.

6159		5k. Type **2489**	15	10
6160		15k. Common goldeneyes	50	40
6161		20k. Red-crested pochards	60	45

1990. Lenin Soviet Children's Fund. Children's Paintings. As T 2437. Multicoloured.

6162		5k.+2k. Clown	25	20
6163		5k.+2k. Ladies in crinolines	25	20
6164		5k.+2k. Children with banner	25	20

1990. Historical Monuments (2nd series). As T 2464. Multicoloured.

6165 15k. St. Nshan's Church, Akhpat (Armenia) 50 30
6166 15k. Shirvanshah Palace, Baku (Azerbaijan) 50 30
6167 15k. Soroki Fortress and statue of Stefan III, Kishinev (Moldavia) 50 30
6168 15k. Spaso-Efrosinevsky Cathedral, Polotsk (Byelorussia) 50 30
6169 15k. St. Peter's Church and 16th-century Riga (Latvia) 50 30
6170 15k. St. Nicholas's Church and carving of city arms, Tallin (Estonia) 50 30
6171 15k. Mtatsminda Pantheon and statue of Nikoloz Baratashvili, Tbilisi (Georgia) 50 30
6172 15k. Cathedral and bell tower, Vilnius (Lithuania) 50 30

2490 Sordes

1990. Prehistoric Animals. Multicoloured.

6173 1k. Type **2490** 10 10
6174 3k. Chalicotherium (vert) 10 10
6175 5k. Indricotherium (vert) 20 10
6176 10k. Saurolophus (vert) 35 30
6177 20k. Cephalaspid ostracoderm 70 45

2491 "St. Basil's Cathedral and Kremlin, Moscow" (Sanjay Adhikari)

1990. Indo–Soviet Friendship. Children's Paintings. Multicoloured.

6178 10k. Type **2491** 40 30
6179 10k. "Life in India" (Tanya Vorontsova) 40 30

2492 Pigeon Post

1990. Letter Writing Week.

6180 **2492** 5k. blue 20 10

2493 Traffic on Urban Roads

1990. Traffic Safety Week.

6181 **2493** 5k. multicoloured 30 20

2494 Grey Heron

1990. Nature Conservation. Sheet 65×90 mm.

MS6182 20k.+10k. multicoloured 1·50 95

1990. Traditional Musical Instruments (2nd series). As T 2455. Multicoloured.

6183 10k. Azerbaijani balalian, shar and caz (stringed instruments), zurna and drum 50 30
6184 10k. Georgian bagpipes, tambourine, flute, pipes and chonguri (stringed instrument) 50 30
6185 10k. Kazakh flute, rattle, daubra and kobyz (stringed instruments) 50 30
6186 10k. Lithuanian bagpipes, horns and kankles 50 30

2495 Killer Whales

1990. Marine Mammals.

6187 25k. Type **2495** 85 50
6188 25k. Northern sealions 85 50
6189 25k. Sea otter 85 50
6190 25k. Common dolphin 85 50

2496 "Lenin among Delegates to Second Congress of Soviets" (S. V. Gerasimov)

1990. 73rd Anniv of October Revolution.

6191 **2496** 5k. multicoloured 25 10

2497 Ivan Bunin (1933)

1990. Nobel Prize Winners for Literature.

6192 **2497** 15k. brown 55 40
6193 - 15k. brown 55 40
6194 - 15k. black 55 40

DESIGNS: No. 6193, Mikhail Sholokhov (1965); 6194, Boris Pasternak.

2498 "Sever 2"

1990. Research Submarines. Multicoloured.

6195 5k. Type **2498** 20 10
6196 10k. "Tinro 2" 35 20
6197 15k. "Argus" 55 30
6198 25k. "Paisis" 80 65
6199 35k. "Mir" 1·20 85

2499 "Motherland" Statue (E. Kocher), Screen and Emblem

1990. "Armenia '90" Stamp Exhibition, Yerevan. (a) Type 2499.

6200 **2499** 10k. multicoloured 40 25

Филателистическая
выставка
„Армения-90"

(2500)

Восстановление,
милосердие,
помощь

(2501)

(b) Nos. 5957/9 optd with T 2500 (20k.) or as T 2501.

6201 **2412** 20k.+10k. mult 95 55
6202 - 30k.+15k. mult 1·50 85
6203 - 50k.+25k. mult 2·50 1·40

2502 S. A. Vaupshasov

1990. Intelligence Agents.

6204 **2502** 5k. dp grn, grn and blk 25 15
6205 - 5k. dp brn, brn and blk 25 15
6206 - 5k. deep blue, blue and black 25 15
6207 - 5k. brown, buff & black 25 15
6208 - 5k. brown, bistre and black 25 15

DESIGNS: No. 6205, R. I. Abel; 6206, Kim Philby; 6207, I. D. Kudrya; 6208, Konon Molodyi (alias Gordon Lonsdale).

2503 Soviet and Japanese Flags above Earth

1990. Soviet–Japanese Space Flight.

6209 **2503** 20k. multicoloured 70 40

2504 Grandfather Frost and Toys

1990. New Year.

6210 **2504** 5k. multicoloured 20 10

2505 "Unkrada"

1990. Soviet Culture Fund. Paintings by N. K. Rerikh. Multicoloured.

6211 10k.+5k. Type **2505** 40 25
6212 20k.+10k. "Pskovo-Pechorsky Monastery" 70 45

2506 "Joys to all those in Need" (detail of icon) and Fund Emblem

1990. Soviet Charity and Health Fund. Sheet 90×70 mm.

MS6213 **2506** 50k.+25k. multicoloured 2·00 1·40

2507 Globe, Eiffel Tower and Flags

1990. "Charter for New Europe". Signing of European Conventional Arms Treaty, Paris.

6214 **2507** 30k. multicoloured 70 55

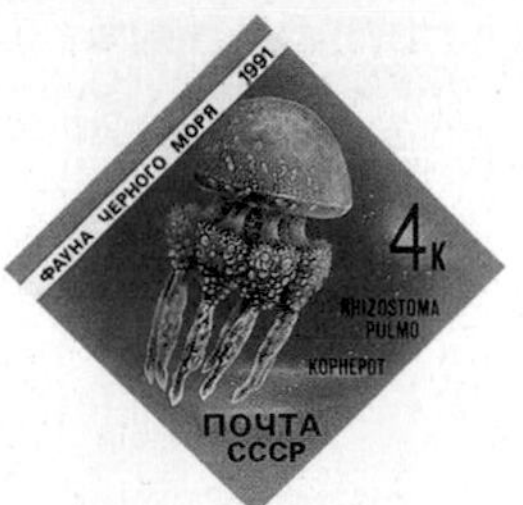

2508 Jellyfish

1991. Marine Animals. Multicoloured.

6215 4k. Type **2508** 10 10
6216 5k. Anemone 20 10
6217 10k. Spurdog 35 15
6218 15k. European anchovy 45 25
6219 20k. Bottle-nosed dolphin 50 30

2509 Keres

1991. 75th Birth Anniv of Paul Keres (chess player).

6220 **2509** 15k. brown 40 25

2510 Radioactive Particles killing Vegetation

1991. 5th Anniv of Chernobyl Nuclear Power Station Disaster.

6221 **2510** 15k. multicoloured 40 25

2511 "Sorrento Coast with View of Capri" (Shchedrin)

1991. Birth Bicentenary of Silvestr Shchedrin and 150th Birth Anniv of Arkhip Kuindzhi (painters). Multicoloured.

6222 10k. Type **2511** 20 15
6223 10k. "New Rome. View of St. Angelo's Castle" (Shchedrin) 20 15
6224 10k. "Evening in the Ukraine" (Kuindzhi) 20 15
6225 10k. "Birch Grove" (Kuindzhi) 20 15

2512 White Stork

1991. Zoo Relief Fund.

6226 **2512** 10k.+5k. mult 45 30

2513 Sturgeon and Bell Tower, Volga

1991. Environmental Protection. Multicoloured.

6227 10k. Type **2513** 25 15
6228 15k. Sable and Lake Baikal 35 30
6229 20k. Saiga and dried bed of Aral Sea 45 35

2514 Swallowtail on Flower

1991. 25th Anniv of All-Union Philatelic Society. Sheet 90×65 mm.

MS6230	20k.+10k. multicoloured	1·10	80

1991. Historical Monuments (3rd series). As T 2464. Multicoloured.

6231	15k. Minaret, Uzgen, Kirgizia	20	15
6232	15k. Mohammed Bashar Mausoleum, Tadzhikistan	20	15
6233	15k. Talkhatan-baba Mosque, Turkmenistan	20	15

2515 G. Shelikhov and Kodiak, 1784

1991. 500th Anniv of Discovery of America by Columbus. Russian Settlements.

6234	2515	20k. blue and black	30	15
6235	-	30k. bistre, brown & blk	50	30
6236	-	50k. orange, brown & blk	80	45

DESIGNS: 30k. Aleksandr Baranov and Sitka, 1804; 50k. I. Kuskov and Fort Ross, California, 1812.

2516 Satellite and Liner

1991. 10th Anniv of United Nations Transport and Communications in Asia and the Pacific Programme.

6237	2516	10k. multicoloured	25	15

2517 Yuri Gagarin in Uniform

1991. Cosmonautics Day. 30th Anniv of First Man in Space. Each brown.

6238	25k. Type **2517**	40	30
6239	25k. Gagarin wearing space suit	40	30
6240	25k. Gagarin in uniform with cap	40	30
6241	25k. Gagarin in civilian dress	40	30
MS6242	85×110 mm. Nos. 6238/41	1·50	75

МЕЖДУНАРОДНАЯ ВЫСТАВКА
«К ЗВЁЗДАМ-91»
КОСМОС НА СЛУЖБЕ МИРА И ПРОГРЕССА

(2518)

1991. "Ad Astra-91" International Stamp Exhibition, Moscow. No. MS6242 optd with T 2518.

MS6243	85×119 mm. 4×25k. brown	2·40	1·70

2519 "May 1945" (A. and S. Tkachev)

1991. Victory Day.

6244	2519	5k. multicoloured	20	10

2520 "Lenin working on Book 'Materialism and Empirical Criticism' in Geneva Library" (P. Belousov)

1991. 121st Birth Anniv of Lenin.

6245	2520	5k. multicoloured	20	10

2521 Prokofiev

1991. Birth Centenary of Sergei Prokofiev (composer).

6246	2521	15k. brown	30	20

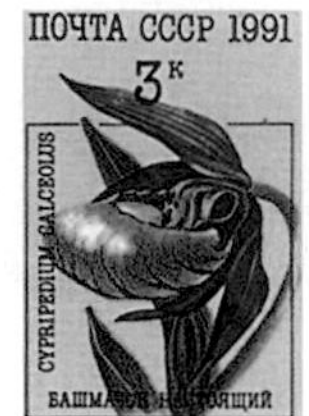

2522 Lady's Slipper

1991. Orchids. Multicoloured.

6247	3k. Type **2522**	10	10
6248	5k. Lady orchid	15	10
6249	10k. Bee orchid	20	15
6250	20k. Calypso	25	15
6251	25k. Marsh helleborine	35	25

2523 Ilya I. Mechnikov (medicine, 1908)

1991. Nobel Prize Winners. Each black.

6252	15k. Type **2523**	25	15
6253	15k. Ivan P. Pavlov (medicine, 1904)	25	15
6254	15k. A. D. Sakharov (peace, 1975)	25	15

2524 Soviet and British Flags in Space

1991. Soviet–British Space Flight.

6255	2524	20k. multicoloured	35	25

2525 Saroyan

1991. 10th Death Anniv of William Saroyan (writer).

6256	2525	1r. multicoloured	1·70	1·30

2526 "The Universe"

1991. Lenin Soviet Children's Fund. Paintings by V. Lukyanets. Multicoloured.

6257	10k.+5k. Type **2526**	20	10
6258	10k.+5k. "Another Planet"	20	10

2527 Miniature from "Ostromirov Gospel" (first book written in Cyrillic), 1056–57

1991. Culture of Medieval Russia. Multicoloured.

6259	10k. Type **2527**	20	15
6260	15k. Page from "Russian Truth" (code of laws), 11th–13th century	25	15
6261	20k. Portrait of Sergy Radonezhsky (embroidered book cover), 1424	30	25
6262	25k. "The Trinity" (icon, Andrei Rublev), 1411	35	25
6263	30k. Illustration from "Book of the Apostles", 1564	50	40

Шилохвость · Anas acuta 1991
ПОЧТА СССР

2528 Pintails

1991. Ducks (3rd series). Multicoloured.

6264	5k. Type **2528**	20	10
6265	15k. Greater scaups	45	25
6266	20k. White-headed ducks	55	35

2529 Emblem

1991. European Conference on Security and Co-operation Session, Moscow.

6267	2529	10k. multicoloured	25	15

2530 Patroness

1991. Soviet Charity and Health Fund.

6268	2530	20k.+10k. mult	35	25

2531 Woman in Traditional Costume

1991. 1st Anniv of Declaration of Ukrainian Sovereignty.

6269	2531	30k. multicoloured	30	20

2532 "Albatros"

1991. Airships. Multicoloured.

6270	1k. Type **2532**	10	10
6271	3k. GA-42	15	10
6272	4k. "Norge" (horiz)	15	10
6273	5k. "Pobeda" (horiz)	20	10
6274	20k. LZ-127 "Graf Zeppelin" (horiz)	55	30

2533 "Sv. Pyotr" and Route Map

1991. 250th Anniv of Vitus Bering's and A. Chirkov's Expedition. Multicoloured.

6275	30k. Type **2533**	40	25
6276	30k. Sighting land	40	25

2534 Girl with Letter

1991. Letter Writing Week.

6277	2534	7k. brown	20	10

2535 Bell and Bell Towers

1991. Soviet Culture Fund.

6278	2535	20k.+10k. mult	30	20

The belfries depicted are from Kuliga-Drakonovo, Church of the Assumption in Pskov, Ivan the Great in Moscow and Cathedral of the Assumption in Rostov.

2536 Kayak Race and "Santa Maria"

1991. Olympic Games, Barcelona (1992) (1st issue). Multicoloured.

6279	10k. Type **2536**	20	10
6280	20k. Running and Church of the Holy Family	25	15
6281	30k. Football and stadium	30	20

See also Nos. 6362/4.

2537 Rainbow, Globe and Flags

1991. Soviet–Austrian Space Flight.

6282	2537	20k. multicoloured	30	25

2538 Ascension Day (Armenia)

1991. Folk Festivals. Multicoloured.

No.	Description	Unused	Used
6283	15k. Type **2538**	20	15
6284	15k. Women carrying dishes of wheat (Novruz holiday, Azerbaijan)	20	15
6285	15k. Throwing garlands in water (Ivan Kupala summer holiday, Belorussia)	20	15
6286	15k. Stick wrestling and dancing round decorated tree (New Year, Estonia) (horiz)	20	15
6287	15k. Masked dancers (Berikaoba spring holiday, Georgia)	20	15
6288	15k. Riders with goat skin (Kazakhstan) (horiz)	20	15
6289	15k. Couple on horses (Kirgizia) (horiz)	20	15
6290	15k. Couple leaping over flames (Ligo (Ivan Kupala) holiday, Latvia) (horiz)	20	15
6291	15k. Family on way to church (Palm Sunday, Lithuania) (horiz)	20	15
6292	15k. Man in beribboned hat and musicians (Plugusorul (New Year) holiday, Moldova)	20	15
6293	15k. Sledge ride (Shrovetide, Russian Federation)	20	15
6294	15k. Musicians on carpet and stilt-walkers (Novruz holiday, Tajikistan)	20	15
6295	15k. Wrestlers (Harvest holiday, Turkmenistan) (horiz)	20	15
6296	15k. Dancers and couple with lute and tambourine (Christmas, Ukraine) (horiz)	20	15
6297	15k. Girls with tulips (Tulip holiday, Uzbekistan)	20	15

2539 Dimitry Komar

1991. Defeat of Attempted Coup. Multicoloured.

No.	Description	Unused	Used
6298	7k. Type **2539**	20	10
6299	7k. Ilya Krichevsky	20	10
6300	7k. Vladimir Usov	20	10
MS6301	90×64 mm. 50k. Barricades around Russian Federation Government House (51×33 mm)	50	40

Nos. 6298/6300 depict victims killed in opposing the attempted coup.

2540 Federation Government House and Flag

1991. Election of Boris Yeltsin as President of the Russian Federation.

No.	Type	Description	Unused	Used
6302	**2540**	7k. blue, gold and red	20	10

1991. Traditional Musical Instruments (3rd series). As T 2455. Multicoloured.

No.	Description	Unused	Used
6303	10k. Kirgiz flutes, komuzes and kyyak (string instruments)	25	15
6304	10k. Latvian ganurags and stabule (wind), tambourine, duga and kokle (string instruments)	25	15
6305	10k. Moldavian flute, bagpipes, nai (pipes), kobza and tsambal (string instruments)	25	15

2541 Decorations and Gifts

1991. New Year.

No.	Type	Description	Unused	Used
6306	**2541**	7k. multicoloured	20	10

2542 Nikolai Mikhailovich Karamzin

1991. Historians' Birth Anniversaries. Mult.

No.	Description	Unused	Used
6307	10k. Type **2542** (225th anniv)	25	15
6308	10k. V. O. Klyuchevsky (150th anniv)	25	15
6309	10k. Sergei M. Solovyov (171st anniv)	25	15
6310	10k. V. N. Tatishchev (after A. Osipov) (305th anniv)	25	15

RUSSIAN FEDERATION

2543 Cross-country Skiing and Ski Jumping

1992. Winter Olympic Games, Albertville, France. Multicoloured.

No.	Description	Unused	Used
6311	14k. Type **2543**	15	10
6312	1r. Aerobatic skiing	30	25
6313	2r. Two and four-man bobsleighing	75	60

2544 Tiger Cubs

1992. Nature Conservation. Sheet 90×65 mm.

No.	Description	Unused	Used
MS6314	3r.+50k. multicoloured	1·50	1·20

2545 Battle Scene

1992. 750th Anniv of Battle of Lake Peipus. Sheet 95×65 mm.

No.	Description	Unused	Used
MS6315	50k. multicoloured	75	60

2546 Golden Gate, Vladimir

1992

No.	Type	Description	Unused	Used
6316	**2546**	10k. orange	15	10
6317	-	15k. brown	15	10
6318	-	20k. red	15	10
6344	-	25k. red	20	15
6319	-	30k. black	15	10
6320	-	50k. blue	15	10
6321	-	55k. turquoise	15	10
6322	-	60k. green	15	10
6323	-	80k. purple	20	10
6324	-	1r. brown	20	10
6325	-	1r.50 green	25	15
6326	-	2r. blue	25	15
6327	-	3r. red	30	20
6328	-	4r. brown	25	15
6329	-	5r. brown	40	25
6330	-	6r. blue	35	25
6331	-	10r. blue	40	25
6332	-	15r. brown	25	10
6333	-	25r. purple	1·10	70
6334	-	45r. black	95	40
6335	-	50r. violet	20	10
6336	-	75r. brown	1·70	85
6337	-	100r. green	2·30	1·10
6338	**2546**	150r. blue	30	25
6339	-	250r. green	45	30
6340	-	300r. red	65	50
6341	-	500r. purple	95	65
6341a	-	750r. green	55	50
6341b	-	1000r. grey	85	55
6342	-	1500r. green	95	80
6342a	-	2500r. bistre	1·60	1·30
6342b	-	5000r. blue	3·25	2·50

DESIGNS: 15k. Pskov kremlin; 20, 50k. St. George killing dragon; 25, 55k. Victory Arch, Moscow; 30, 80k. "Millennium of Russia" monument (M. Mikeshin), Novgorod; 60k., 300r. Statue of K. Minin and D. Pozharsky, Moscow; 1, 4r. Church, Kizhky; 1r.50, 6r. Statue of Peter I, St. Petersburg; 2r. St. Basil's Cathedral, Moscow; 3r. Tretyakov Gallery, Moscow; 5r. Europe House, Moscow; 10r. St. Isaac's Cathedral, St. Petersburg; 15, 45r. "The Horse-tamer" (statue), St. Petersburg; 25, 75r. Statue of Yuri Dolgoruky, Moscow; 50r. Rostov Kremlin; 100r. Moscow Kremlin; 250r. Church, Bogulyubovo; 500r. Moscow University; 750r. State Library, Moscow; 1000r. Peter and Paul Fortress, St. Petersburg; 1500r. Pushkin Museum, Moscow; 2500r. Admiralty, St. Petersburg; 5000r. Bolshoi Theatre, Moscow.

2547 "Victory" (N. Baskakov)

1992. Victory Day.

No.	Type	Description	Unused	Used
6350	**2547**	5k. multicoloured	20	10

2548 Western Capercaillie, Oak and Pine

1992. Prioksko–Terrasnyi Nature Reserve.

No.	Type	Description	Unused	Used
6351	**2548**	50k. multicoloured	20	10

2549 "Mir" Space Station, Flags and Cosmonauts

1992. Russian–German Joint Space Flight.

No.	Type	Description	Unused	Used
6352	**2549**	5r. multicoloured	60	45

2550 "Santa Maria" and Columbus

1992. 500th Anniv of Discovery of America by Columbus (1st issue). Sheet 88×65 mm.

No.	Type	Description	Unused	Used
MS6353	**2550**	3r. multicoloured	70	65

See also No. 6386.

2551 Pinocchio

1992. Characters from Children's Books (1st series). Multicoloured.

No.	Description	Unused	Used
6354	25k. Type **2551**	20	10
6355	30k. Cipollino	20	10
6356	35k. Dunno	20	10
6357	50k. Karlson	20	10

See also Nos. 6391/5.

2552 Russian Cosmonaut and Space Shuttle

1992. International Space Year. Multicoloured.

No.	Description	Unused	Used
6358	25r. Type **2552**	60	40
6359	25r. American astronaut and "Mir" space station	60	40
6360	25r. "Apollo" and "Vostok" spacecraft and sputnik	60	40
6361	25r. "Soyuz", "Mercury" and "Gemini" spacecraft	60	40

Nos. 6358/61 were issued together, se-tenant, forming a composite design.

2553 Handball

1992. Olympic Games, Barcelona (2nd issue).

No.	Type	Description	Unused	Used
6362	**2553**	1r. multicoloured	20	15
6363	-	2r. red, blue and black	25	20
6364	-	3r. red, green and black	50	30

DESIGNS—HORIZ: 2r. Fencing; 3r. Judo.

2554 L. A. Zagoskin and Yukon River, Alaska, 1842–44

1992. Expeditions. Multicoloured.

No.	Description	Unused	Used
6365	55k. Type **2554**	10	10
6366	70k. N. N. Miklukho-Maklai in New Guinea, 1871–74	15	10
6367	1r. G. I. Langsdorf and route map of expedition to Brazil, 1822–28	20	15

2555 Garganeys

1992. Ducks. Multicoloured.

No.	Description	Unused	Used
6368	1r. Type **2555**	20	15
6369	2r. Common pochards	30	25
6370	3r. Falcated teals	50	30

2556 "Taj Mahal Mausoleum in Agra"

1992. 150th Birth Anniv of Vasily Vasilevich Vereshchagin (painter).

No.	Description	Unused	Used
6371	1r.50 Type **2556**	25	20
6372	1r.50 "Don't Touch, Let Me Approach!"	25	20

2557 "The Saviour" (icon, Andrei Rublyov)

1992

6373	**2557**	1r. multicoloured	20	15

2558 Cathedral of the Assumption

1992. Moscow Kremlin Cathedrals. Multicoloured.

6374	1r. Type **2558**	20	15
6375	1r. Cathedral of the Annunciation (15th century)	20	15
6376	1r. Archangel Cathedral (16th century)	20	15

See also Nos. 6415/17 and 6440/2.

2559 Russian "Nutcracker" Puppets

1992. Centenary of First Production of Tchaikovsky's Ballet "Nutcracker". Mult.

6377	10r. Type **2559**	40	25
6378	10r. German "Nutcracker" puppets	40	25
6379	25r. Pas de deux from ballet	75	45
6380	25r. Dance of the toys	75	45

2560 "Meeting of Joachim and Anna"

1992. Icons. Multicoloured.

6381	10r. Type **2560**	50	45
6382	10r. "Madonna and Child"	50	45
6383	10r. "Archangel Gabriel" (head)	50	45
6384	10r. "Saint Nicholas" (½-length portrait)	50	45

2561 Clockface and Festive Symbols

1992. New Year.

6385	**2561**	50k. multicoloured	20	10

2562 "Discovery of America" Monument (Z. Tsereteli)

1992. 500th Anniv of Discovery of America by Columbus.

6386	**2562**	15r. multicoloured	75	60

2563 Petipa and Scene from "Paquita"

1993. 175th Birth Anniv of Marius Petipa (choreographer). Multicoloured.

6387	25r. Type **2563**	40	30
6388	25r. "Sleeping Beauty", 1890	40	30
6389	25r. "Swan Lake", 1895	40	30
6390	25r. "Raimunda", 1898	40	30

2564 Scrub 'n' Rub

1993. Characters from Children's Books (2nd series). Illustrations by Kornei Chukovsky. Mult.

6391	2r. Type **2564**	10	10
6392	3r. Big Cockroach	20	15
6393	10r. The Buzzer Fly	25	20
6394	15r. Doctor Doolittle	50	30
6395	25r. Barmalei	70	40

Nos. 6391/5 were issued together, se-tenant, forming a composite design.

2565 Castle

1993. 700th Anniv of Vyborg.

6396	**2565**	10r. multicoloured	30	25

2566 Part of Diorama in Belgorod Museum

1993. Victory Day. 50th Anniv of Battle of Kursk.

6397	**2566**	10r. multicoloured	30	25

2567 African Violet

1993. Pot Plants. Multicoloured.

6398	10r. Type **2567**	20	10
6399	15r. "Hibiscus rosa-sinensis"	25	10
6400	25r. "Cyclamen persicum"	35	20
6401	50r. "Fuchsia hybrida"	70	35
6402	100r. "Begonia semperflorens"	1·40	70

2568 "Molniya 3"

1993. Communications Satellites. Multicoloured.

6403	25r. Type **2568**	35	20
6404	45r. "Ekran M"	50	30
6405	50r. "Gorizont"	65	40
6406	75r. "Luch"	95	45
6407	100r. "Ekspress"	1·50	75
MS6408	88×66 mm. 250r. Earth receiving station (horiz)	3·00	1·70

2569 Snuff Box (Dmitry Kolesnikov) and Tankard

1993. Silverware. Multicoloured.

6409	15r. Type **2569**	15	10
6410	25r. Teapot	20	10
6411	45r. Vase	30	15
6412	75r. Tray and candlestick	50	35
6413	100r. Cream jug, coffee pot and sugar basin (Aleksandr Kordes)	70	45
MS6414	90×65 mm. 250r. Biscuit and sweet dishes (47×33 mm)	2·50	1·90

1993. Novgorod Kremlin. As T 2558. Mult.

6415	25r. Kukui and Knyazhaya Towers (14th–17th century)	20	15
6416	25r. St. Sophia's Cathedral (11th century)	20	15
6417	25r. St. Sophia belfry (15th–18th century)	20	15
MS6418	70×93 mm. 250r. "Our Lady of the Apparition" (icon) (41×29 mm)	1·80	1·40

2570 Map

1993. Inauguration of Denmark–Russia Submarine Cable and 500th Anniv of Friendship Treaty.

6419	**2570**	90r. green & deep green	40	25

2571 Steller's Eider

1993. Ducks. Multicoloured.

6420	90r. Type **2571**	40	20
6421	100r. Eider	50	30
6422	250r. King eider	1·20	60

2572 Ringed Seal

1993. Marine Animals. Multicoloured.

6423	50r. Type **2572**	20	10
6424	60r. "Paralithodes brevipes" (crab)	30	15
6425	90r. Japanese common squid	55	30
6426	100r. Cherry salmon	75	35
6427	250r. Fulmar	1·10	55

2573 Ceramic Candlestick, Skopino

1993. Traditional Art. Multicoloured.

6428	50r. Type **2573**	25	20
6429	50r. Painted tray with picture "Summer Troika", Zhostovo (horiz)	25	20
6430	100r. Painted box, lid and distaff, Gorodets	45	30
6431	100r. Enamel icon of St. Dmitry of Solun, Rostov	45	30
6432	250r. "The Resurrection" (lacquer miniature), Fedoskino	1·00	60

2574 Banknotes and Coins

1993. 175th Anniv of Goznak (State printing works and mint).

6433	**2574**	100r. multicoloured	40	25

2575 Peter I and "Goto Predestinatsiya"

1993. 300th Anniv of Russian Navy (1st issue). Multicoloured.

6434	100r. Type **2575**	20	15
6435	100r. K. A. Shilder and first all-metal submarine	20	15
6436	100r. I. A. Amosov and "Arkhimed" (frigate)	20	15
6437	100r. I. G. Bubnov and "Bars" (submarine)	20	15
6438	100r. B. M. Malinin and "Dekabrist" (submarine)	20	15
6439	100r. A. I. Maslov and "Kirov" (cruiser)	20	15

See also Nos. 6502/5, 6559/62 and 6612/18.

1993. Moscow Kremlin. As T 2558. Mult.

6440	100r. Faceted Hall (15th century)	20	15
6441	100r. Church of the Deposition of the Virgin's Robe (15th century)	20	15
6442	100r. Grand Palace (17th century)	20	15

2576 Tiger

1993. The Tiger. Multicoloured.

6443	50r. Type **2576**	10	10
6444	100r. Tiger in undergrowth	20	10
6445	250r. Two tiger cubs	50	30
6446	500r. Tiger in snow	1·00	45

2577 Splash of Blood on Figure

1993. Anti-AIDS Campaign.

6447	**2577**	90r. red, black and lilac	30	25

2578 Seasonal Decorations

1993. New Year.

6448	**2578**	25r. multicoloured	20	10

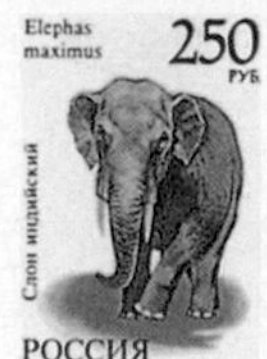

2579 Indian Elephant

1993. Animals. Multicoloured.

6449	250r. Type **2579**	45	30
6450	250r. Japanese white-naped crane	45	30
6451	250r. Giant panda	45	30
6452	250r. American bald eagle	45	30
6453	250r. Dall's porpoise	45	30
6454	250r. Koala	45	30
6455	250r. Hawaiian monk seal	45	30
6456	250r. Grey whale	45	30

2580 Rimsky-Korsakov and Scene from "Sadko"

1994. 150th Birth Anniv of Nikolai Rimsky-Korsakov (composer). Scenes from his operas. Multicoloured.

6457	250r. Type **2580**	50	30
6458	250r. "The Golden Cockerel"	50	30
6459	250r. "The Tsar's Bride"	50	30
6460	250r. "The Snow Maiden"	50	30

2581 "Epiphyllum peacockii"

1994. Cacti. Multicoloured.

6461	50r. Type **2581**	20	10
6462	100r. "Mammillaria swinglei"	30	20
6463	100r. "Lophophora williamsii"	30	20
6464	250r. "Opuntia basilaris"	45	30
6465	250r. "Selenicereus grandiflorus"	45	30

2582 York Minster, Great Britain

1994. Churches. Multicoloured.

6466	150r. Type **2582**	35	25
6467	150r. Small Metropolis church, Athens	35	25
6468	150r. Roskilde Cathedral, Denmark	35	25
6469	150r. Notre Dame Cathedral, Paris	35	25
6470	150r. St. Peter's, Vatican City	35	25
6471	150r. Cologne Cathedral, Germany	35	25
6472	150r. Seville Cathedral, Spain	35	25
6473	150r. St. Basil's Cathedral, Moscow	35	25
6474	150r. St. Patrick's Cathedral, New York	35	25

2583 "Soyuz" entering Earth's Atmosphere and "TsF-18" Centrifuge

1994. Yuri Gagarin Cosmonaut Training Centre. Multicoloured.

6475	100r. Type **2583**	20	10
6476	250r. "Soyuz"–"Mir" space complex and "Mir" simulator	40	20
6477	500r. Cosmonaut on space walk and hydrolaboratory	70	40

2584 Map and Rocket Launchers (Liberation of Russia)

1994. 50th Anniv of Liberation. Multicoloured.

6478	100r. Type **2584**	20	15
6479	100r. Map and airplanes (Ukraine)	20	15
6480	100r. Map, tank and soldiers (Belorussia)	20	15

2585 Beautiful Gate, Moscow

1994. Architects' Birth Anniversaries.

6481	2585	50r. sepia, black and brown	10	10
6482	-	100r. brown, black and flesh	15	10
6483	-	150r. green, black and olive	25	20
6484	-	300r. violet, black and grey	40	25

DESIGNS: 50r. Type **2585** (D. V. Ukhtomsky, 250th anniv); 100r. Academy of Sciences, St. Petersburg (Giacomo Quarenghi, 250th anniv); 150r. Trinity Cathedral, St. Petersburg (V. P. Stasov, 225th anniv); 300r. Church of Christ the Saviour, Moscow (K. A. Ton, bicentenary).

2586 "Christ and the Sinner"

1994. 150th Birth Anniv of Vasily Dmitrievich Polenev (painter). Multicoloured.

6485	150r. Type **2586**	20	15
6486	150r. "Golden Autumn"	20	15

2587 European Wigeon

1994. Ducks. Multicoloured.

6487	150r. Type **2587**	25	15
6488	250r. Tufted duck	40	25
6489	300r. Baikal teal	60	30

2588 Games Emblem and Runners

1994. 3rd Goodwill Games, St. Petersburg.

6490	2588	100r. multicoloured	20	10

2589 Pyotr Leonidovich Kapitsa

1994. Physics Nobel Prize Winners. Each sepia.

6491	150r. Type **2589** (1978)	25	15
6492	150r. Pavel Alekseevich Cherenkov (1958)	25	15

2590 Olympic Flag

1994. Cent of International Olympic Committee.

6493	2590	250r. multicoloured	40	25

2591 Design Motifs of First Russian Stamp

1994. Russian Stamp Day.

6494	2591	125r. multicoloured	15	10

2592 Snuff Box (D. Vinogradov)

1994. 250th Anniv of Imperial (now M. Lomonosov) Porcelain Factory, St. Petersburg. Multicoloured.

6495	50r. Type **2592**	10	10
6496	100r. Candlestick	10	10
6497	150r. "Water-Carrier" (statuette, after S. Pimenov)	20	10
6498	250r. Sphinx vase	30	20
6499	300r. "Lady with Mask" (statuette, after K. Somov)	50	25
MS6500	60×90 mm. 500r. Dinner service (F. Solntsev) (36×36 mm)	90	65

2593 Centre of Asia Obelisk

1994. 50th Anniv of Incorporation of Tuva into Russian Socialist Federal Soviet Republic (R.S.F.S.R.).

6501	2593	125r. mulitcoloured	15	10

2594 Vice-Admiral V. M. Golovnin (Kurile Islands, 1811)

1994. 300th Anniv of Russian Navy (2nd issue). Explorations. Multicoloured.

6502	250r. Type **2594**	30	20
6503	250r. Admiral I. F. Kruzenshtern (first Russain round-the-world expedition, 1803–06)	30	20
6504	250r. Admiral Ferdinand Petrovich Vrangel (Alaska, 1829–35)	30	20
6505	250r. Admiral F. P. Litke (Novaya Zemlya, 1821–24)	30	20

2595 Horses and Grandfather Frost

1994. New Year.

6506	2595	125r. blue, red and black	25	20

2596 Griboedov (after N. I. Utkin)

1995. Birth Bicentenary of Aleksandr Sergeevich Griboedov (dramatist and diplomat).

6507	2596	250r. brown, light brown and black	30	25

2597 "Sheherazade"

1995. 115th Birth Anniv of Mikhail Fokine (choreographer). Scenes from Ballets. Mult.

6508	500r. Type **2597**	40	25
6509	500r. "The Fire Bird"	40	25
6510	500r. "Petrushka"	40	25

2598 Kutuzov (after J. Doe) and Sculptures from Monument, Moscow

1995. 250th Birth Anniv of Field-Marshal Mikhail Ilarionovich Kutuzov, Prince of Smolensk.

6511	2598	300r. multicoloured	30	25

2599 English Yard, Varvarka Street

1995. 850th Anniv (1997) of Moscow (1st issue). Multicoloured.

6512	125r. Type **2599**	10	10
6513	250r. House of Averky Kirillov (scribe), Bersenevskaya Embankment	15	10
6514	300r. Volkov house, Bolshoi Kharitonevsky Lane	20	10

See also Nos. 6600/5, **MS**6649 and 6666/75.

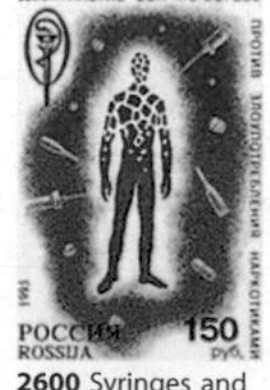

2600 Syringes and Drugs around Addict

1995. U.N. Anti-drugs Decade.

6515	2600	150r. multicoloured	15	10

2601 Shoreline

1995. Endangered Animals. Multicoloured.

6516	250r. Type **2601**	20	15
6517	250r. Ringed seal	20	15
6518	250r. Lynx	20	15

6519	250r. Landscape	20	15

Nos. 6516/19 were issued together, se-tenant, Nos. 6516/17 and 6518/19 respectively forming composite designs.

2602 Tomb of the Unknown Soldier, Moscow

1995. 50th Anniv of End of Second World War. Multicoloured.

6520	250r. Sir Winston Churchill, U.S. Pres. Franklin Roosevelt and Iosif Stalin (Yalta Conference) (horiz)	30	25
6521	250r. Storming of the Reichstag, Berlin (horiz)	30	25
6522	250r. Flags, map of Germany and German banners (Potsdam Conference)	30	25
6523	250r. Bombers (operation against Japanese in Manchuria (horiz))	30	25
6524	250r. Urn with victims' ashes, Auschwitz, and memorial, Sachsenhausen (liberation of concentration camps) (horiz)	30	25
6525	250r. Type **2602**	30	25
6526	500r. Victory Parade, Moscow (36×47 mm)	50	40
MS6527	64×89 mm. No. 6526	1·00	90

2603 Aleksandr Popov (radio pioneer) and Radio-telegraph Equipment

1995. Centenary of Radio.

6528	**2603**	250r. multicoloured	20	10

2604 Spreading Bellflower

1995. Meadow Flowers. Multicoloured.

6529	250r. Type **2604**	20	10
6530	250r. Ox-eye daisy ("Leucanthemum vulgare")	20	10
6531	300r. Red clover ("Trifolium pratense")	25	20
6532	300r. Brown knapweed ("Centaurea jacea")	25	20
6533	500r. Meadow cranesbill	60	40

2605 Eurasian Sky Lark ("Alauda arvensis")

1995. Songbirds. Multicoloured.

6534	250r. Type **2605**	20	10
6535	250r. Song thrush ("Turdus philomelos")	20	10
6536	500r. Eurasian goldfinch ("Carduelis carduelis")	35	20
6537	500r. Bluethroat ("Cyanosylvia svecica")	35	20
6538	750r. Thrush nightingale ("Luscinia luscinia")	50	40

2606 U.S. Space Shuttle "Atlantis"

1995. Russian–American Space Co-operation. Mult.

6539	1500r. Type **2606**	90	45
6540	1500r. "Mir" space station	90	45
6541	1500r. "Apollo" spacecraft	90	45
6542	1500r. "Soyuz" spacecraft	90	45

Nos. 6539/42 were issued together, se-tenant, forming a composite design of the spacecraft over Earth.

2607 Cathedral of the Trinity, Jerusalem

1995. Russian Orthodox Churches Abroad. Mult.

6543	300r. Type **2607**	20	10
6544	300r. Apostles Saints Peter and Paul Cathedral, Karlovy Vary, Czechoslovakia	20	10
6545	500r. St. Nicholas's Cathedral, Vienna	35	25
6546	500r. St. Nicholas's Cathedral, New York	35	25
6547	750r. St. Aleksei's Cathedral, Leipzig	50	30

2608 Kremlin Cathedrals

1995. 900th Anniv of Ryazan.

6548	**2608**	250r. multicoloured	20	15

2609 Easter Egg with Model of "Shtandart" (yacht)

1995. Faberge Exhibits in Moscow Kremlin Museum. Multicoloured.

6549	150r. Type **2609**	10	10
6550	250r. Goblet	20	10
6551	300r. Cross pendant	25	15
6552	500r. Ladle	35	20
6553	750r. Easter egg with model of Alexander III monument	50	30
MS6554	65×90 mm. 1500r. "Moscow Kremlin" easter egg (36×51 mm)	1·00	85

2610 Harlequin Duck

1995. Ducks. Multicoloured.

6555	500r. Type **2610**	30	20
6556	750r. Baer's pochard	50	25
6557	1000r. Goosander	70	40

2611 City Buildings

1995. "Singapore '95" International Stamp Exhibition Sheet 90×65 mm.

MS6558	**2611**	2500r. multicoloured	1·60	1·40

2612 "The Battle of Grengam, July 27, 1720" (F. Perrault)

1995. 300th Anniv of Russian Navy (3rd issue). Paintings. Multicoloured.

6559	250r. Type **2612**	20	10
6560	300r. "Preparations for Attacking the Turkish Fleet in the Bay of Cesme, Night of June 26, 1770" (P. Hackert)	25	15
6561	500r. "The Battle at the Revel Roadstead, May 2, 1790" (A. Bogolyubov)	35	20
6562	750r. "The Kronstadt Roadstead" (I. Aivazovsky)	50	30

2613 State Flag and Arms

1995. Constitution of the Russian Federation.

6563	**2613**	500r. multicoloured	40	30

2614 Emblem and San Francisco Conference, 1945

1995. 50th Anniv of U.N.O.

6564	**2614**	500r. brown, blue and yellow	40	30

2615 White Storks in Nest

1995. Europa. Peace and Freedom. Multicoloured.

6565	1500r. Type **2615**	1·30	65
6566	1500r. Stork flying over landscape	1·30	65

Nos. 6565/6 were issued together, se-tenant, forming a composite design.

2616 "Birth of Christ" (icon, Assumption Cathedral, St. Cyril's Monastery, White Sea)

1995. Christmas.

6567	**2616**	500r. multicoloured	40	30

2617 Yuri Dolgoruky (1090–1157), Kiev and Building of Moscow

1995. History of Russian State (1st series). Mult.

6568	1000r. Type **2617**	60	35
6569	1000r. Aleksandr Nevsky (1220–63), Battle of Lake Peipus and as Grand Duke of Vladimir	60	35
6570	1000r. Mikhail Yaroslavich (1271–1318), Tver and torture by the Golden Horde	60	35
6571	1000r. Dmitry Donskoi (1350–89), Moscow Kremlin and Battle of Kulikovo	60	35
6572	1000r. Ivan III (1440–1505), marriage to Sophia Paleologa and Battle of Ugra River	60	35

See also Nos. 6640/3.

2618 Semyonov

1996. Birth Centenary of Nikolai Semyonov (Nobel Prize winner for chemistry, 1956).

6573	**2618**	750r. grey	40	25

2619 Pansies

1996. Flowers. Multicoloured.

6574	500r. Type **2619**	25	15
6575	750r. Sweet-williams ("Dianthus barbatus")	40	20
6576	750r. Sweet peas ("Lathyrus odoratus")	40	20
6577	1000r. Crown imperial ("Fritillaria imperialis")	50	30
6578	1000r. Snapdragons ("Antirrhinum majus")	50	30

2620 Tabbies

1996. Cats. Multicoloured.

6579	1000r. Type **2620**	50	30
6580	1000r. Russian blue	50	30
6581	1000r. White Persian	50	30
6582	1000r. Sealpoint Siamese	50	30
6583	1000r. Siberian	50	30

2621 Torch Bearer

1996. Centenary of Modern Olympic Games. Sheet 64×85 mm.

MS6584	5000r. multicoloured	2·20	1·60

2622 "Laying down of Banners" (A. Mikhailov)

1996. Victory Day.

6585 **2622** 1000r. multicoloured 50 30

2623 Tula Kremlin and Monument to Peter I

1996. 850th Anniv of Tula.

6586 **2623** 1500r. multicoloured 70 40

2624 Putilovsky Works Tramcar, 1896

1996. Centenary of First Russian Tramway, Nizhny Novgorod. Multicoloured.

6587 500r. Type **2624** 25 15
6588 750r. Sormovo tramcar, 1912 40 20
6589 750r. 1928 Series X tramcar, 1928 40 20
6590 1000r. 1931 Series KM tramcar, 1931 60 40
6591 1000r. Type LM-57 tramcar, 1957 60 40
6592 2500r. Model 71-608K tramcar, 1973 1·20 65
MS6593 80×68 mm. No. 6592 1·80 1·00

2625 Ye. Dashkova (President of Academy of Sciences)

1996. Europa. Famous Women.

6594 **2625** 1500r. green and black 80 45
6595 - 1500r. purple and black 80 45

DESIGN: No. 6594, S. Kovalevskaya (mathematician).

2626 Children walking Hand in Hand

1996. 50th Anniv of UNICEF.

6596 **2626** 1000r. multicoloured 50 30

2627 "Post Troika in Snowstorm" (P. Sokolov)

1996. Post Troikas in Paintings. Muliticoloured.

6597 1500r. Type **2627** 80 45
6598 1500r. "Post Troika in Summer" (P. Sokolov) 80 45
6599 1500r. "Post Troika" (P. Gruzinsky) 80 45

2628 "View of Bridge over Yauza and of Shapkin House in Moscow" (J. Delabarte)

1996. 850th Anniv (1997) of Moscow (2nd issue). Paintings. Multicoloured.

6600 500r. Type **2628** 30 15
6601 500r. "View of Moscow from Balcony of Kremlin Palace" (detail, J. Delabarte) 30 15
6602 750r. "View of Voskresenskie and Nikolskie Gates and Kamenny Bridge" (F. Ya. Alekseev) 40 25
6603 750r. "Moscow Yard near Volkhonka" (anon) 40 25
6604 1000r. "Varvarka Street" (anon) 50 30
6605 1000r. "Sledge Races in Petrovsky Park" 50 30

2629 Traffic Policeman and Pedestrian Crossing

1996. 60th Anniv of Traffic Control Department. Sheet 120×150 mm containing T 2629 and similar horiz designs. Multicoloured.

MS6606 1500r. Type **2629**; 1500r. Children learning road safety; 1500r. Examiner and learner vehicle 2·00 1·40

2630 Basketball

1996. Olympic Games, Atlanta, U.S.A. Mult.

6607 500r. Type **2630** 25 15
6608 1000r. Boxing 50 30
6609 1000r. Swimming 50 30
6610 1500r. Gymnastics 90 45
6611 1500r. Hurdling 90 45

2631 "Yevstafy" (ship of the line), 1762

1996. 300th Anniv of Russian Navy (4th issue). (a) As T 2631.

6612 **2631** 750r. brown and yellow 40 25
6613 - 1000r. deep blue, cobalt and blue 50 30
6614 - 1000r. purple, pink and rose 50 30
6615 - 1500r. multicoloured 75 40
6616 - 1500r. black, grey and stone 75 40

DESIGNS: No. 6613, "Petropavlovsk" (battleship); 6614, "Novik" (destroyer); 6615, "Tashkent" (destroyer); 6616, "S-13" (submarine).

(b) Size 35 x 24 mm. Each blue and black.

6617 1000r. "Principium" (galley) 50 30
6618 1000r. "Admiral Kuznetsov" (aircraft carrier) 50 30

Sheet size 130×65 mm containing as Nos. 6617/18 and similar horiz designs. Multicoloured (blue background).

MS6619 1000r. As No. 6617; 1000r. Nuclear-powered submarine; 1000r. "Azov" (ship of the line); 1000r. As No. 6618 2·00 1·40

2632 Gorsky and Scenes from "Gudula's Daughter" and "Salambo"

1996. 125th Birth Anniv of Aleksandr Gorsky (ballet choreographer). Multicoloured.

6620 750r. Type **2632** 40 25
6621 750r. Scene from "La Bayadere" 40 25
6622 1500r. Scene from "Don Quixote" 75 40
6623 1500r. Scene from "Giselle" 75 40

2633 National Flags

1996. Formation of Community of Sovereign Republics (union of Russian Federation and Belarus).

6624 **2633** 1500r. multicoloured 70 40

2634 Chalice

1996. Objets d'Art. Multicoloured.

6625 1000r. Type **2634** 50 25
6626 1000r. Perfume bottles 50 25
6627 1000r. Double inkwell 50 25
6628 1500r. Coffee pot 75 40
6629 1500r. Pendent scent containers (one ladybird-shaped) 75 40
MS6630 70×90 mm. 5000r. "Our Lady of Kazan" (icon) (36×51 mm) 2·30 1·60

2635 Symbols of Science and Culture on Open Book

1996. 50th Anniv of UNESCO.

6631 **2635** 1000r. black, gold and blue 50 30

2636 "Madonna and Child" (icon), Moscow

1996. Orthodox Religion. Multicoloured.

6632 1500r. Type **2636** 70 40
6633 1500r. Stavrovouni Monastery, Cyprus 70 40
6634 1500r. "St. Nicholas" (icon), Cyprus 70 40
6635 1500r. Voskresenkie ("Resurrection") Gate, Moscow 70 40

2637 Clockface of Spassky Tower, Moscow Kremlin

1996. New Year.

6636 **2637** 1000r. multicoloured 40 25

2638 First Match between U.S.S.R. and Canada, 1972

1996. 50th Anniv of Ice Hockey in Russia. Mult.

6637 1500r. Type **2638** 65 35
6638 1500r. Goalkeeper and players (first match between Moscow and Prague, 1948) 65 35
6639 1500r. Players and referee (Russia versus Sweden) 65 35

1996. History of Russian State (2nd series). As T 2617. Multicoloured.

6640 1500r. Basil III (1479–1533), removal of bell from Pskov and Siege of Smolensk, 1514 75 40
6641 1500r. Ivan IV the Terrible (1530–84), coronation in Cathedral of the Assumption (Moscow Kremlin) and executions by the Oprichnina 75 40
6642 1500r. Fyodor I Ivanovich (1557–98), with Cossacks and Siberian Kings, and election of love (first Russian Patriarch) 75 40
6643 1500r. Boris Godunov (1551–1605), as Tsar in 1598 and food distribution during famine, 1601–03 75 40

2639 Maule's Quince ("Chaenomeles japonica")

1997. Shrubs. Multicoloured.

6644 500r. Type **2639** 25 15
6645 500r. Ornamental almond ("Amygdalus triloba") 25 15
6646 1000r. Broom ("Cytisus scoparius") 50 30
6647 1000r. Burnet rose ("Rosa pimpinellifolia") 50 30
6648 1000r. Mock orange ("Philadelphus coronarius") 50 30

2640 Foundation Festival Emblem

1997. 850th Anniv of Moscow (3rd issue). Sheet 94×71 mm.

MS6649 3000r. multicoloured 1·50 1·20

2641 Dmitri Shostakovich (composer) (from 90th birth anniv (1996) medal)

1997. "Shostakovich and World Musical Culture" International Music Festival.

6650 **2641** 1000r. multicoloured 50 25

2642 Russian Federation Arms

1997. 500th Anniv of Double Eagle as Russian State Emblem. Sheet 94×76 mm.

MS6651	3000r. multicoloured	1·50	95

2643 Post Emblem

1997

6652	**2643**	100r. brown and black	10	10
6653	-	150r. mauve and black	10	10
6654	-	250r. green and black	10	10
6655	-	300r. green and black	10	10
6656	-	500r. blue and black	30	15
6657	-	750r. brown and black	35	20
6658	-	1000r. red and blue	45	25
6659	-	1500r. blue and black	65	40
6660	-	2000r. green and black	75	45
6661	-	2500r. red and black	1·10	60
6662	-	3000r. violet and black	1·30	70
6663	-	5000r. brown and black	2·00	90

DESIGNS: 100r. Combine harvesters in field; 150r. Oil rigs; 250r. White storks; 300r. Radio mast; 750r. St. George killing dragon; 1000r. State flag and arms; 1500r. Electric pylon inside generating machinery; 2000r. Class VL65 electric railway locomotive; 2500r. Moscow Kremlin; 3000r. Space satellite; 5000r. Pianist and theatre.

For these designs in revised currency, see Nos. 6718/35.

2644 Ioan Zlatoust Church, Sofiiski Cathedral and Admiral Barsh's House

1997. 850th Anniv of Vologda.

6664	**2644**	1000r. multicoloured	50	25

2645 "Volga Svyatoslavovich" (I. Bilibin)

1997. Europa. Tales and Legends.

6665	**2645**	1500r. multicoloured	90	45

2646 Jesus Christ the Saviour Cathedral

1997. 850th Anniv of Moscow (3rd issue). Mult.

6666	1000r. Type **2646**	50	30
6667	1000r. Towers and walls of Kremlin	50	30
6668	1000r. Grand Palace and cathedrals, Kremlin	50	30
6669	1000r. St. Basil's Cathedral, Spassky Tower and Trinity Church	50	30
6670	1000r. "St. George killing Dragon" (16th-century icon)	50	30
6671	1000r. First reference to Moscow in Ipatevsky Chronicle, 1147	50	30
6672	1000r. Prince Daniil Alexandrovich and Danilov Monastery	50	30
6673	1000r. "Building Moscow Kremlin, 1366" (16th-century miniature)	50	30
6674	1000r. Kazan cap and "Coronation of Ivan IV" (miniature)	50	30
6675	1000r. 16th-century plan of Moscow	50	30

Nos. 6666/75 were issued together, se-tenant, Nos. 6666/70 forming a composite design of Moscow in late 19th century.

2647 Mil Mi-14 (float)

1997. Helicopters. Multicoloured.

6676	500r. Type **2647**	25	15
6677	1000r. Mil Mi-24 (gunship)	40	20
6678	1500r. Mil Mi-26 (transport)	60	30
6679	2000r. Mil Mi-28 (gunship)	80	40
6680	2500r. Mil Mi-34 (patrol)	1·20	55

2648 "The Priest and Balda"

1997. Birth Bicentenary (1999) of Aleksandr Sergeevich Pushkin (poet) (1st issue). Mult.

6681	500r. Type **2648**	20	10
6682	1000r. "Tsar Saltan"	50	20
6683	1500r. "The Fisherman and the Golden Fish"	70	30
6684	2000r. "The Dead Princess and the Seven Knights"	90	45
6685	3000r. "The Golden Cockerel"	1·30	65

See also Nos. 6762/6 and 6827/9.

2649 Petrodvorets (St. Petersburg) National Flags and Marble Temple, Bangkok

1997. Centenary of Russia–Thailand Diplomatic Relations and of Visit of King Rama V to St. Petersburg.

6686	**2649**	1500r. multicoloured	65	30

2650 Siberian Flying Squirrel

1997. Wildlife. Multicoloured.

6687	500r. Type **2650**	25	15
6688	750r. Lynx	40	20
6689	1000r. Western capercaillie	50	20
6690	2000r. European otter	1·10	45
6691	3000r. Western curlew	1·60	75

2651 Arkhangel Province

1997. Regions of the Russian Federation (1st series). Multicoloured.

6692	1500r. Type **2651**	65	30
6693	1500r. Kaliningrad Province (vert)	65	30
6694	1500r. Kamchatka Province	65	30
6695	1500r. Krasnodar Territory	65	30
6696	1500r. Sakha Republic (Yakutiya) (vert)	65	30

See also Nos. 6784/8, 6831/5, 6920/5, 6980/4, 7062/6, 7153/8, 7229/33 and 7315/20.

2652 Klyopa flying with Balloons

1997. Klyopa (cartoon character). Multicoloured.

6697	500r. Type **2652**	20	15
6698	1000r. Klyopa hang-gliding over Red Square	50	20
6699	1500r. Klyopa in troika (45×33 mm)	65	40

2653 Emblem, Mascot and Russian Federation 1992 and 20k. Stamp

1997. "Moscow 97" International Stamp Exhbition. Multicoloured.

6700	1500r. Russian Empire 1858 10k. and R.S.F.S.R. 1918 35k. stamps, and Spassky Tower, Moscow Kremlin	65	30
6701	1500r. Type **2653**	65	30

2654 Indian Flag and Asokan Capital

1997. 50th Anniv of Independence of India.

6702	**2654**	500r. multicoloured	25	15

2655 Presentation of Standard

1997. 325th Birth Anniv of Tsar Peter I. Mult.

6703	2000r. Type **2655** (creation of regular army and navy)	75	40
6704	2000r. Sea battle (access to Baltic Sea)	75	40
6705	2000r. Peter I reviewing plans (construction of St. Petersburg)	75	40
6706	2000r. Council (administrative reforms)	75	40
6707	2000r. Boy before tutor (cultural and educational reforms)	75	40
MS6708	65×90 mm. 5000r. Peter I	2·00	1·50

2656 Pictograms of Five Events

1997. 50th Anniv of Modern Pentathlon in Russia.

6709	**2656**	1000r. multicoloured	40	20

2657 Match Scenes

1997. Centenary of Football in Russia.

6710	**2657**	2000r. multicoloured	90	45

2658 Radiation and Earth

1997. World Ozone Layer Day. 10th Anniv of Montreal Protocol (on reduction of use of chlorofluorocarbons).

6711	**2658**	1000r. multicoloured	40	20

2659 National Flag and Palace of Europe, Strasbourg

1997. Admission of Russian Federation to European Council.

6712	**2659**	1000r. multicoloured	45	25

2660 "Boris and Gleb" (14th-century icon)

1997. Centenary of Russian State Museum, St. Petersburg (1st issue). Multicoloured.

6713	500r. Type **2660**	20	15
6714	1000r. "Volga Boatmen" (I. Repin) (horiz)	40	20
6715	1500r. "Promenade" (Marc Chagall)	60	30
6716	2000r. "Merchant's Wife taking Tea" (B. Kustodiev)	80	45

See also Nos. 6753/**MS**6757.

2661 Sketch by Puskin of Himself and Onegin

1997. Translation into Hebrew by Abraham Shlonsky of Yevgeny Onegin (poem) by Aleksandr Pushkin. Sheet 76×60 mm.

MS6717	3000r. black, magenta and yellow	1·50	1·20

1998. As Nos. 6652/63 but in reformed currency.

6718	10k. brown and black (as No. 6652)	10	10
6719	15k. mauve and black (as No. 6653)	10	10
6720	25k. green and black (as No. 6654)	10	10
6721	30k. green and black (as No. 6655)	10	10
6723	50k. blue and black (Type **2643**)	20	15
6726	1r. red and blue (as No. 6658)	50	20
6727	1r.50 blue and black (as No. 6659)	70	30
6728	2r. green and black (as No. 6660)	1·00	45
6729	2r.50 red and black (as No. 6661)	1·10	55
6730	3r. violet and black (as No. 6662)	1·40	65
6735	5r. brown and black (as No. 6663)	2·40	1·10

2662 "Menshikov in Beresovo" (detail, Surikov)

1998. 150th Birth Anniversaries of Vasily Ivanovich Surikov and V. M. Vasnetsov (artists). Multicoloured.

6741 1r.50 Type **2662** 80 40
6742 1r.50 "Morozov Boyar's Wife" (Surikov) 80 40
6743 1r.50 "Battle between Slavs and Nomads" (detail, Vasnetsov) (vert) 80 40
6744 1r.50 "Tsarevich Ivan on a Grey Wolf" (Vasnetsov) 80 40

2663 Cross-country Skiing

1998. Winter Olympic Games, Nagano, Japan. Mult.

6745 50k. Type **2663** 20 10
6746 1r. Figure skating (pairs) 45 20
6747 1r.50 Biathlon 65 35

2664 Red-tailed Black Labeo "Epalzeorhynchus bicolor"

1998. Fishes. Multicoloured.

6748 50k. Type **2664** 20 10
6749 50k. Jewel tetra ("Hyphessobrycon callistus") 20 10
6750 1r. Galina's catfish ("Synodontis galinae") 40 20
6751 1r.50 "Botia kristinae" 60 30
6752 1r.50 "Cichlasoma labiatum" 60 30

2665 "The Last Day of Pompeii" (K. P. Bryullov)

1998. Centenary of State Russian Museum, St. Petersburg (2nd issue). Multicoloured.

6753 1r.50 Type **2665** 70 35
6754 1r.50 "The Ninth Wave" (I. K. Aivazovsky) 70 35
6755 1r.50 "Pines for Masts" (I. I. Shishkin) 70 35
6756 1r.50 "Our Lady of Tenderness for Sick Hearts" (K. S. Petrov-Vodkin) 70 35
MS6757 91×70 mm. 3f. "The Milhailovsky Palace" (K.P. Beggrov) (51×36 mm) 1·10 50

2666 Saddleback Dolphins

1998. "Expo '98" World's Fair, Lisbon, Portugal. Sheet 91×71 mm.

MS6758 **2666** 3r. multicoloured 1·10 50

2667 Theatre and Characters

1998. Centenary of Moscow Art Theatre.

6759 **2667** 1r.50 multicoloured 55 30

2668 "End of Winter" (Shrove-tide)

1998. Europa. National Festivals.

6760 **2668** 1r.50 multicoloured 55 30

2669 War Memorial, Venets Hotel, History Museum and Goncharovsky Pavilion

1998. 350th Anniv of Ulyanovsk (formerly Simbirsk).

6761 **2669** 1r. multicoloured 40 15

2670 "The Lyceum"

1998. Birth Bicentenary (1999) of Aleksandr Sergeevich Pushkin (poet) (2nd issue). Drawings by Pushkin.

6762 **2670** 1r.50 black and blue 45 30
6763 - 1r.50 brown, stone & blk 45 30
6764 - 1r.50 brown, stone & blk 45 30
6765 - 1r.50 brown, stone & blk 45 30
6766 - 1r.50 black and blue 45 30

DESIGNS: No. 6763, "A.N. Wolf"; 6764, Self-portrait; 6765, "Tatyana" (from "Vevgeny Onegin"); 6766, Knight in armour (manuscript cover from 1830).

2671 Local History Museum and Peter I Monument

1998. 300th Anniv of Taganrog.

6767 **2671** 1r. multicoloured 40 15

2672 Games Emblem

1998. World Youth Games, Moscow. Sheet 70×90 mm.

MS6768 3r. multicoloured 1·10 50

2673 Tsar Nicholas II

1998. 80th Death Anniv of Tsar Nicholas II.

6769 **2673** 3r. multicoloured 1·00 45

2674 Grapes

1998. Berries. Multicoloured.

6770 50k. Type **2674** 15 10
6771 75k. Raspberry 25 15
6772 1r. Magnolia vine 30 15
6773 1r.50 Cowberrry 55 30
6774 2r. Arctic bramble 70 35

2675 Landmarks

1998. 275th Anniv of Yekaterinburg.

6775 **2675** 1r. multicoloured 40 15

2676 Leontina Cohen

1998. Intelligence Agents.

6776 **2676** 1r. blue, indigo & blk 40 15
6777 - 1r. brown, yellow & blk 40 15
6778 - 1r. green, dp green & blk 40 15
6779 - 1r. purple, brown & blk 40 15

DESIGNS: No. 6777, Morris Cohen; 6778, L. R. Kvasnikov; 6779, A. A. Yatskov.

2677 Order of St. Andrew

1998. Russian Orders (1st series). Multicoloured.

6780 1r. Type **2677** 30 15
6781 1r.50 Order of St. Catherine 45 20
6782 2r. Order of St. Aleksandr Nevsky 60 30
6783 2r.50 Order of St. George 75 35

See also Nos. 6807/11 and 7242/7.

1998. Regions of the Russian Federation (2nd series). As T 2651. Multicoloured.

6784 1r.50 Republic of Buryatiya (vert) 55 30
6785 1r.50 Republic of Kareliya (vert) 55 30
6786 1r.50 Khabarovsk Province 55 30
6787 1r.50 Murmansk Province 55 30
6788 1r.50 Primorsky Province 55 30

2678 Universal Postal Union Emblem

1998. World Post Day.

6789 **2678** 1r. multicoloured 30 15

2679 Anniversary Emblem

1998. 50th Anniv of Universal Declaration of Human Rights.

6790 **2679** 1r.50 multicoloured 70 30

2680 Headquarters, Moscow

1998. 10th Anniv of Menatep Bank.

6791 **2680** 2r. multicoloured 55 30

2681 Aviation

1998. Achievements of the Twentieth Century. Multicoloured.

6792 1r. Type **2681** 40 25
6793 1r. Computers 40 25
6794 1r. Genetics 40 25
6795 1r. Nuclear energy 40 25
6796 1r. Space exploration 40 25
6797 1r. Television 40 25

2682 Koshkin

1998. Birth Centenary of Mikhail Illch Koshkin (tank designer).

6798 **2682** 1r. multicoloured 25 15

2683 Grandfather Frost

1998. New Year.

6799 **2683** 1r. multicoloured 15 10

2684 Telephone and Switchboard Operators

1999. Centenary of First Long-distance Telephone Link in Russia (between Moscow and St. Petersburg).

6800 **2684** 1r. multicoloured 20 15

2685 Western Capercaillie

1999. Hunting. Multicoloured.
6801 1r. Type **2685** 20 15
6802 1r.50 Shooting mallard ducks from rowing boat 25 15
6803 2r. Falconry (Gyr falcon) 35 20
6804 2r.50 Wolves 45 25
6805 3r. Bears 55 30

2686 Russian Ship of the Line off Corfu

1999. Bicentenary of Russian Naval Expedition to Mediterranean under Command of Admiral Fyodor Ushakov. Sheet 90×70 mm.
MS6806 5r. multicoloured 95 50

1999. Russian Orders (2nd series). As T 2677. Multicoloured.
6807 1r. Order of St. Vladimir 15 10
6808 1r.50 Order of St. Anne 25 15
6809 2r. Order of St. John of Jerusalem 30 20
6810 2r.50 Order of the White Eagle 40 30
6811 3r. Order of St. Stanislas 45 35

2687 18th-century Ship of the Line

1999. 300th Anniv of Adoption of St. Andrew's Flag by Tsar Peter I. Sheet 90×70 mm.
MS6812 **2687** 7r. multicoloured 90 85

2688 "Family at Tea" (Sofya Kondrashina)

1999. Russia in the 21st Century. Children's paintings. Multicoloured.
6813 1r.20 Type **2688** 20 15
6814 1r.20 "My Town" (Yuri Lapushkov) 20 15
6815 1r.20 "Fantasy City" (Aleksander Khudyshin) (vert) 20 15

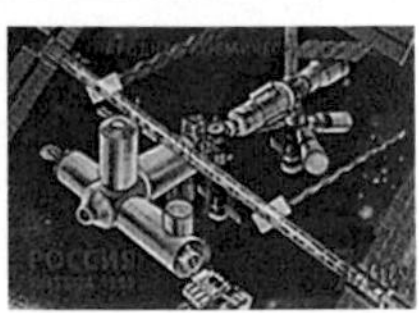
2689 "Alpha" International Space Station

1999. Space Exploration Day. Sheet 120×68 mm.
MS6816 7r. multicoloured 1·00 75

2690 Albrecht Durer's House

1999. "iBRA '99" International Stamp Exhibition, Nuremberg, Germany.
6817 **2690** 3r. multicoloured 50 30

2691 Setting Weighted Lines

1999. Fishing. Multicoloured.
6818 1r. Type **2691** 20 10
6819 2r. Fishing by rod and line from bank and boat 30 20
6820 2r. Fishing by rod and line from kayak 30 20
6821 3r. Fishing through holes in ice 45 25
6822 3r. Underwater fishing 45 25

2692 Council Flag and Headquarters, Strasbourg, and Spassky Tower, Moscow

1999. 50th Anniv of Council of Europe.
6823 **2692** 3r. multicoloured 50 30

2693 Oksky State Natural Biosphere Preserve

1999. Europa. Parks and Gardens.
6824 **2693** 5r. multicoloured 80 45

2694 Stag

1999. Red Deer. Multicoloured.
6825 2r.50 Type **2694** 60 35
6826 2r.50 Doe and fawns 60 35

2695 Pushkin, 1815 (after S. G. Chirikov)

1999. Birth Bicentenary of Aleksandr Sergeevich Pushkin (poet) (3rd issue). Multicoloured.
6827 1r. Type **2695** 15 10
6828 3r. Pushkin, 1826 (after I.-E. Viven) 45 25
6829 5r. Pushkin, 1836 (after Karl Bryullov) 75 45
MS6830 110×70 mm. 7r. Pushkin, 1827 (after V. A. Tropinin) (29×41 mm) 1·00 75

1999. Regions of the Russian Federation (3rd series). As T 2651. Multicoloured.
6831 2r. Republic of North Osetia-Alaniya 35 25
6832 2r. Republic of Bashkortostan (vert) 35 25
6833 2r. Kirov Province 35 25
6834 2r. Evenk Autonomous Region (vert) 35 25
6835 2r. Stavropol Region 35 25

2696 Rose "Carina" ("Happy Birthday")

1999. Greetings stamps. Roses. Multicoloured.
6836 1r.20 Type **2696** 20 10
6837 1r.20 "Gloria Dei" ("From the bottom of my heart") 20 10
6838 2r. "Candia" ("Congratulations") 30 15
6839 3r. "Confidence" ("Be happy") 40 25
6840 4r. "Ave Maria" ("With love") 50 35

1999. No. 6342b surch 1.20.
6841 1r.20 on 5000r. blue 20 15

2698 River Station, City Arms and Nativity of the Virgin Cathedral

1999. 250th Anniv of Rostov-on-Don.
6842 **2698** 1r.20 multicoloured 25 20

2699 Automatic Post Sorting

1999. 125th Anniv of Universal Postal Union.
6843 **2699** 3r. multicoloured 50 30

2700 "Horsewoman"

1999. Birth Bicentenary of Karl Bryullov (painter). Multicoloured.
6844 2r.50 Type **2700** 35 25
6845 2r.50 "Portrait of Yu. P. Samoilova and Amacilia Paccini" 35 25

2701 IZh-1 Motorcycle, 1929

1999. Russian Motor Cycles. Multicoloured.
6846 1r. Type **2701** 10 10
6847 1r.50 L-300, 1930 20 10
6848 2r. M-72, 1941 30 15
6849 2r.50 M-1-A, 1945 40 20
6850 5r. IZ–"Planeta-5", 1987 60 30

2702 Suvorov's Vanguard passing Lake Klontal (after engraving by L. Hess)

1999. Bicentenary of General Aleksandr Suvorov's Crossing of the Alps. Multicoloured.
6851 2r.50 Type **2702** 35 25
6852 2r.50 Schollenen Gorge Monument, Suvorov and soldiers 35 25

2703 Horse Racing

1999. Traditional Sports. Multicoloured.
6853 2r. Type **2703** 30 20
6854 2r. Wrestling 30 20
6855 2r. Gorodki (game with stick and blocks of wood) 30 20
6856 2r. Sleigh and deer team race 30 20
6857 2r. Weightlifting (vert) 30 20

2704 Leonid Utesov

1999. Singers. Multicoloured.
6858 2r. Type **2704** 30 20
6859 2r. Lidiya Ruslanova (in costume) 30 20
6860 2r. Klavdiya Shulzhenko (with hands clasped) 30 20
6861 2r. Mark Bernes (playing accordion) 30 20
6862 2r. Bulat Okudzhava (playing guitar in street scene) 30 20
6863 2r. Vladimir Vysotsky (with guitar and arms out wide) 30 20
6864 2r. Igor Talkov (with arm raised) 30 20
6865 2r. Victor Tsoi (playing guitar) 30 20

2705 Players chasing Ball and Club Badge

1999. Spartak-Alaniya, National Football Champions.
6877 **2705** 2r. multicoloured 30 20

2706 Father Christmas and "2000"

1999. Christmas and New Year. Multicoloured.
6878 1r.20 Type **2706** 25 15
6879 1r.20 "2000", globe as pearl and shell 25 15

2707 "The Raising of the Daughter of Jairus" (V. D. Polenov)

2000. Bimillenary of Christianity. Religious Paintings. Multicoloured.
6880 3r. Type **2707** 50 30
6881 3r. "Christ in the Wilderness" (I. N. Kramskoy) 50 30
6882 3r. "Christ in the House of Mary and Martha" (G. I. Semiradsky) 50 30
6883 3r. "What is Truth?" (N. N. Ge) (vert) 50 30
MS6884 120×96 mm. 7r. "The Appearance of Christ to the People" (A. A. Ivanov) (51×36 mm) 1·00 95

See also Nos. **MS**6883 and **MS**6887.

2708 "The Virgin the Orans" (mosaic, St. Sophie's Cathedral, Kiev, Ukraine)

2000. Bimillenary of Christianity (2nd issue). Sheet 151×100 mm containing T 2708 and similar vert designs. Multicoloured.

MS6885	3r. Type **2708**; 3r. "Christ Pantocrator" (fresco, Spaso-Preobrazhenskaya Church, Polotsk, Belarus); 3r. "The Virgin of Vladimir" (icon, Tretyakov State Museum, Moscow)	1·50	95

2709 Psurtsev and Central Telegraph Office, Moscow

2000. Birth Centenary of Nikolai D. Psurtsev (statesman).

6886	**2709**	2r.50 multicoloured	40	20

2710 Domes of Kremlin Cathedrals, Moscow

2000. Bimillenary of Christianity (3rd issue). Sheet 151×87 mm.

MS6887	10r. multicoloured	2·00	1·20

2711 R. L. Samoilovich

2000. Polar Explorers. Multicoloured.

6888	2r. Type **2711**	40	20
6889	2r. V. Yu Vize and polar station	40	20
6890	2r. M. M. Somov and ship	40	20
6891	2r. P. A. Gordienko and airplane	40	20
6892	2r. A. F. Treshnikov and tracked vehicles	40	20

2712 N. A. Panin-Kolomenkin (first Russian Olympic Ice-skating Champion, 1908)

2000. The Twentieth Century (1st issue). Sport. Multicoloured.

6893	25k. Type **2712**	10	10
6894	30k. Wrestlers (Olympic Games, Stockholm, 1912)	10	10
6895	50k. Athlete crossing finishing line (All-Russian Olympiad, 1913 and 1914)	10	10
6896	1r. Cyclists (All-Union Spartacist Games, 1928)	10	10
6897	1r.35 Emblem and parade of athletes (Sports Association for Labour and Defence, 1931)	15	10
6898	1r.50 Emblem and athletes ("Honoured Master of Sports", 1934)	20	10
6899	2r. Gymnasts and shot-putter (Olympic Games, Helsinki, 1952)	25	10
6900	2r.50 V. P. Kutz and athletes (Olympic Games, Melbourne, 1956)	30	15
6901	3r. Gold Medal, goalkeeper and player (Olympic Football Champion, Melbourne Olympic Games)	35	20
6902	4r. Mikhail Botvinnik (World Chess Champion, 1948–57, 1958–60 and 1961–63)	55	30
6903	5r. Soviet Union–Canada ice hockey match, 1972	70	40
6904	6r. Stadium and emblem (Olympic Games, Moscow, 1980)	85	45

See also Nos. 6926/37, 6950/61 and 6964/76.

2713 Emblem

2000. 50th Anniv of World Meteorological Society. Sheet 90×60 mm.

MS6905	7r. multicoloured	1·20	95

2714 Soldier (L. F. Golovanov)

2000. 55th Anniv of End of Second World War. Posters by named artists. Multicoloured.

6906	1r.50 Type **2714**	25	15
6907	1r.50 Mother and son (N. N. Vatolina)	25	15
6908	1r.50 Soldiers celebrating (V. V. Suryaninov)	25	15
6909	1r.50 Soldier and woman (V. I. Ladyagin)	25	15
6910	5r. Soldier and emblem (V. S. Klimashin)	65	40
MS6911	100×70 mm. No. 6910	80	65

2715 "Apollo"–"Soyuz" Space Link, 1975

2000. International Space Co-operation. Mult.

6912	2r. Type **2715**	30	15
6913	3r. Projected international space station and flags (horiz)	45	25
6914	5r. Rocket taking off from launch pad at sea	70	40

2716 Mother and Child crossing Road and Emblem

2000. World Road Safety Week.

6915	**2716**	1r.75 multicoloured	35	25

2717 Star of David, Doves and "Holocaust"

2000. Holocaust Victims' Commemoration.

6916	**2717**	2r. multicoloured	40	25

2718 Spassky Tower and President's Flag

2000. Election of President Vladimir Putin.

6917	**2718**	1r.75 multicoloured	30	20

2719 "Building Europe"

2000. Europa.

6918	**2719**	7r. multicoloured	1·20	70

2720 Globe, Shell, Cogs, Human Eye and Emblem

2000. "Expo 2000" International Stamp Exhibition, Hanover. Sheet 92×71 mm.

MS6919	10r. multicoloured	1·80	95

2000. Regions of the Russian Federation (4th issue). As T 2651. Multicoloured.

6920	3r. Republic of Kalmyk (vert)	50	25
6921	3r. Mari El Republic (vert)	50	25
6922	3r. Tatarstan Republic (vert)	50	25
6923	3r. Udmurt Republic (vert)	50	25
6924	3r. Chuvash Republic	50	25
6925	3r. Autonomous Republic of Yamalo Nentsky	50	25

2721 V. K. Arkadjev (Observation of Ferromagnetic Resonance, 1913)

2000. The Twentieth Century (2nd issue). Science. Multicoloured.

6926	1r.30 Type **2721** (botanist and plant geneticist)	20	10
6927	1r.30 Nikolai Ivanovich Vavilov (botanist and plant geneticist) and ears of corn (theory on plant divergence)	20	10
6928	1r.30 N. N. Luzin (founder of Moscow Mathematical School, 1920–30)	20	10
6929	1r.75 I. E. Tamm and chemical model (Phenoms Theory, 1929)	25	10
6930	1r.75 P. L. Kapitsa and diagram of experiment (discovery of liquid helium superfluidity, 1938)	25	10
6931	1r.75 Nikolai Nikolayevich Semenov (physical chemist) (chemical chain reactions theory, 1934)	25	10
6932	2r. V. I. Veksler and charged particles in accelerators, 1944–45	30	15
6933	2r. Mayan text (decipherment of Mayan language by Yu V. Knorozov, 1950s)	30	15
6934	2r. A. V. Ivanov (discovery of pogonophora, 1955–57)	30	15
6935	3r. Globe, Moon and Luna 3 (first photograph of Moon's dark side, 1959)	40	20
6936	3r. Scientific equipment (development of quantum electronics, 1960s)	40	20
6937	3r. N. J. Tolstoi (ethnolinguistic dictionary, 1995)	40	20

2722 Chihuahua

2000. Dogs. Multicoloured.

6938	1r. Type **2722**	10	10
6939	1r.50 Terrier	20	10
6940	2r. Poodle	30	15
6941	2r.50 French bulldog	40	20
6942	3r. Japanese chin	50	25

2723 Fencing

2000. Olympic Games, Sydney. Multicoloured.

6943	2r. Type **2723**	30	20
6944	3r. Synchronized swimming	50	30
6945	5r. Volleyball	70	45

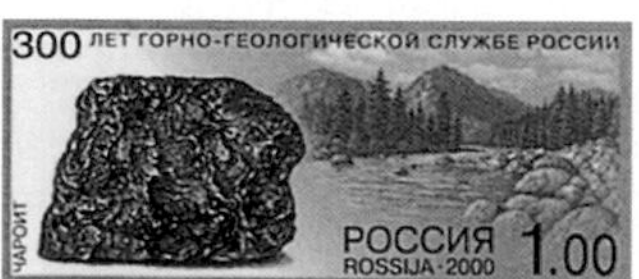

2724 Charoit

2000. Minerals. Multicoloured.

6946	1r. Type **2724**	20	10
6947	2r. Haematite	30	20
6948	3r. Rock crystal	40	30
6949	4r. Gold	60	40

2725 Ballerina and Actors

2000. The Twentieth Century (3rd series). Culture. Multicoloured.

6950	30k. Type **2725** (touring ballet and opera companies, 1908–14)	10	10
6951	50k. "Black Square" (K. S. Malevich)	10	10
6952	1r. Sergi Mikhailovich Eisenstein (director) and scene from *Battleship Potemkin* (film, 1925)	10	10
6953	1r.30 Book and Aleksei Maksimovich Gorky (writer)	15	10
6954	1r.50 Sculptures and red star	20	10
6955	1r.75 Vladimir Vladimirovich Mayakovsky (poet and playwright) and propaganda posters, 1920s	20	10
6956	2r. V. E. Meierkhold and K. S. Stanislavsky (theatre producers)	25	15
6957	2r.50 Dmitri Dmitriyevich Shostakovich (composer) and musicians	30	15
6958	3r. Galina Sergeyevna Ulanova (ballerina) and dancers	40	20
6959	4r. A. T. Tvardovsky (poet)	60	30
6960	5r. Fountain and Great Palace, Petrodvorets (restoration of historical monuments)	70	30
6961	6r. D. S. Likhachev (literary critic)	80	40

2726 Zander (*Stizostedion lucioperca*) and Common Whitefish (*Coregonus lavaretus managenoides*)

2000. Fish of Chudsko-Pskovskoye Lake. Mult.

6962	2r.50 Type **2726**	40	20
6963	2r.50 European smelt (*Osmerus eperlanus spirinchus*) and European cisco (*Coregonus albula*)	40	20

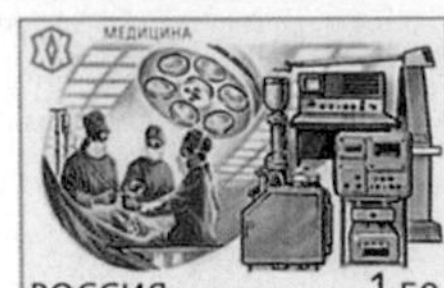

2727 Doctors Operating and Medical Equipment

2000. The Twentieth Century (4th series). Technology. Multicoloured.

6964	1r.50 Type **2727**	20	10
6965	1r.50 City skyline (construction)	20	10
6966	1r.50 Bus, car and truck (transport)	20	10
6967	2r. Dam, electricity pylons and generator (engineering)	30	15
6968	2r. Telephones, televisions and rocket and satellite (communication)	30	15
6969	2r. Space stations and rocket (space technology)	30	15
6970	3r. Civil and military airplanes (aviation)	40	20
6971	3r. Steam, diesel and electric trains (rail transport)	40	20
6972	3r. Container ship, sailing ship and cruise liner (sea transport)	40	20
6973	4r. Furnace (metallurgy)	60	30
6974	4r. Oil refinery and truck (oil-refining industry)	60	30
6975	4r. Truck, conveyor and drill (mineral extraction)	60	30

2728 Moscow Kremlin, Pokrovsky Cathedral and Christmas Tree

2000. New Millennium.

6977	**2728** 2r. multicoloured	25	15

2729 Emblem

2000. 80th Anniv of Foreign Intelligence Service.

6978	**2729** 2r.50 multicoloured	40	20

2730 Navigation School, Moscow and Mathematical Equipment

2001. 300th Anniv of Russian Naval Education. Sheet 110×130 mm containing T 2710 and similar horiz designs. Multicoloured.

MS6979	1r.50 Type **2730**; 2r. Ship, chart of Antarctica and navigation equipment; 8r. St. Petersburg Naval Institute and statue	1·50	95

2001. Regions of the Russian Federation (5th issue). As T 2651. Multicoloured.

6980	3r. Republic of Dagestan	40	25
6981	3r. Republic of Kabardino-Balkaskaya	40	25
6982	3r. Republic of Komi (vert)	40	25
6983	3r. Samara region	40	25
6984	3r. Chita region	40	25

2001. As Nos. 6718/35 but new designs and currency expressed as "P".

6985	10p. mauve and black	1·30	55
6986	25p. brown and black	3·25	1·50
6987	50p. blue and black	6·50	3·00
6988	100p. mauve and black	12·50	6·00

DESIGNS: 10p. Ballet dancer; 25p. Gymnast; 50p. Globe and computer; 100p. Universal Postal Union emblem.

2731 White Tulip ("Happy Birthday")

2001. Greetings Stamps. Tulips. Multicoloured.

7000	2r. Type **2731**	30	20
7001	2r. Deep pink tulips ("With Love")	30	20
7002	2r. Orange tulip ("Good Luck")	30	20
7003	2r. Yellow tulip ("Congratulations")	30	20
7004	2r. Magenta and white tulip ("Be Happy")	30	20

2732 I. A. Galitsin

2001. 300th Birth Anniv of Andrei Matveeich Matveev (artist) (Nos. 7005/6) and 225th Birth Anniv of Vasily Andreevich Tropinin (artist) (Nos. 7007/8). Multicoloured.

7005	3r. Type **2732**	45	30
7006	3r. A. P. Galitsina	45	30
7007	3r. P. A. Bulakhov	45	30
7008	3r. E. I. Karzinkina	45	30

2733 "Senate Square and St. Peter the Great Monument" (B. Patersen)

2001. 300th Anniv of St. Petersburg. Paintings. Multicoloured.

7009	1r. Type **2733**	10	10
7010	2r. "English embankment near Senate" (B. Patersen)	25	15
7011	3r. "Mikhailovsky Castle from Fontanka Embankment" (B. Patersen)	40	20
7012	4r. "River Moika near Stable Department" (A. E. Martynov)	60	30
7013	5r. "Neva from Peter and Paul Fortress" (K. P. Beggrov)	75	40

2734 *Pyrrhosoma numphula* (damselfly)

2001. Damselflies and Dragonflies. Multicoloured.

7014	1r. Type **2734**	10	10
7015	1r.50 *Epitheca bimaculata* (dragonfly)	25	15
7016	2r. Brown aeshna (*Aeschna grandis*)	30	20
7017	3r. *Libellula depressa* (dragonfly)	50	25
7018	5r. *Coenagrion hastulatum* (damselfly)	70	35

2735 Yuri Gagarin, S. P. Korolev (spaceship designer) and Baikonur Launch Site

2001. 40th Anniv of First Manned Space Flight. Multicoloured.

7019	3r. Type **2735**	40	20
7020	3r. Gagarin in uniform	40	20

Nos. 7019/20 were issued together, se-tenant, forming a composite design.

2736 Baikal Lake

2001. Europa. Water Resources.

7021	**2736** 8r. multicoloured	1·00	75

2737 Emblem

2001. 75th Anniv of International Philatelic Federation.

7022	**2737** 2r.50 multicoloured	35	20

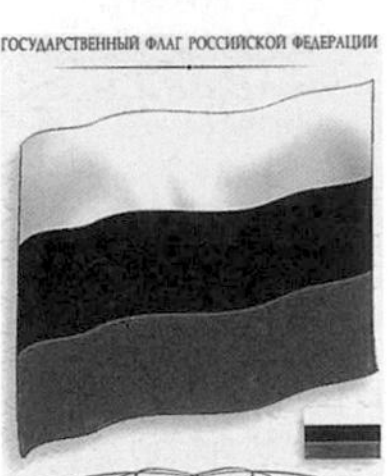

2738 Russian Flag

2001. State Emblems. Multicoloured.

7023	2r.50 Type **2738**	35	20
7024	2r.50 Russian Federation national anthem	35	20
7025	5r. State Arms	75	55
MS7026	Sheet 150×00 mm. 2r.50 Type **2738**; 2r.50 As No. 7024; 100r. State Arms	18·00	17·00

The 100r. stamp in No. **MS**7026 has the arms embossed in gold foil.

2739 Map of Russian Federation and State Arms

2001. 11th Anniv of Declaration of State Sovereignty.

7027	**2739** 5r. multicoloured	1·00	70

2740 Cathedral of the Assumption, Vladimir (1189)

2001. Religious Architecture. Multicoloured.

7028	2r.50 Type **2740**	45	25
7029	2r.50 Cathedral of the Nativity of the Virgin, Zvenigorod (1405)	45	25
7030	2r.50 Cathedral of the Intercession of the Virgin of the Old Belief Community of Rogozhsk, Moscow (1792)	45	25
7031	2r.50 Roman Catholic Church of the Immaculate Conception of the Blessed Virgin Mary, Moscow (1911)	45	25
7032	2r.50 Lutheran Church of St. Peter, St. Petersburg (1838)	45	25
7033	2r.50 Prayer House of the Evangelical Christians (Pentecostal), Lesosibirsk (1999)	45	25
7034	2r.50 Revival Church of Evangelical Christians (Baptist), Bezhitsk, Bryansk (1996)	45	25
7035	2r.50 Church of Seventh Day Adventists, Ryazan (1996)	45	25
7036	2r.50 Armenian Cathedral Surb Khach, Rostov-on-Don (1792) and Monastery of St. Daniel, Moscow (13th-century)	45	25
7037	2r.50 First Mosque, Ufa (1830)	45	25
7038	2r.50 Hay Market Mosque, Kazan (1849)	45	25
7039	2r.50 Choral Synagogue, Moscow (1891)	45	25
7040	2r.50 Large Choral Synagogue, St. Petersburg (1893)	45	25
7041	2r.50 Buddhist Soskshin-Dugan, Ivolginsk Datsan (1976)	45	25

2741 "Sokol" (high speed passenger train)

2001. 150th Anniv of St. Petersburg–Moscow Railway. Sheet 90 ×80 mm.

MS7042	**2741** 12r. multicoloured	1·50	95

2742 G. S. Titov (cosmonaut)

2001. 40th Anniv of First Manned Space Flight.

7043	**2742** 3r. multicoloured	50	25

2743 Faina G. Ranevskaya in Cinderella

2001. Cinema Actors. Showing scenes from their films. Multicoloured.

7044	2r.50 Type **2743**	40	25
7045	2r.50 Mikhail I. Zharov in *Peter I*	40	25
7046	2r.50 Lubov P. Orlova in *Circus*	40	25
7047	2r.50 Nikolai A. Kryuchkov in *Tractor Drivers*	40	25
7048	2r.50 Yury V. Nikulin in *Diamond Arm*	40	25
7049	2r.50 Anatoly D. Papanov in *Alive and Dead*	40	25
7050	2r.50 Evgeny P. Leonov in *Stripy Voyage*	40	25
7051	2r.50 Nikolai N. Rybnikov in *Height*	40	25
7052	2r.50 Andrei A. Mironov in *Twelve Chairs*	40	25

2744 Lazarian and Institute

2001. Death Bicentenary of Horhannes Lazarian (founder of Oriental Languages Institute, Moscow).

7053	**2744** 2r.50 multicoloured	45	30

A stamp in a similar design was issued by Armenia.

2745 Arkadi Raikin

2001. 90th Birth Anniv of Arkadi I. Raikin (actor).

7054	**2745** 2r. agate and black	30	20

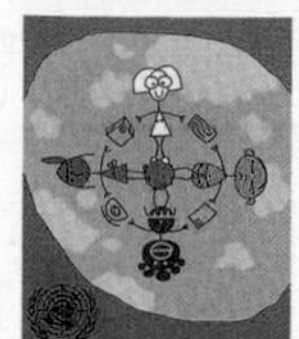

2746 Children encircling Globe

2001. United Nations Year of Dialogue among Civilizations.

7055	**2746**	5r. multicoloured	70	40

2747 Vladimir Dal

2001. Birth Bicentenary of Vladimir I. Dal (writer and lexicographer). Sheet 70×100 mm.

MS7056 **2747**	10r. multicoloured	1·50	95

2748 Court Tower

2001. 10th Anniv of Russian Federation Constitutional Court.

7057	**2748**	3r. multicoloured	50	30

2749 Tsar Nicholas I, St. Petersburg Winter Palace and Coin

2001. 160th Anniv of Savings Bank.

7058	**2749**	2r.20 multicoloured	40	20

2750 Soldiers, Map and Red Square

2001. 60th Anniv of Battle for Moscow. Sheet 100×76 mm.

MS7059 **2750**	10r. multicoloured	1·50	95

2751 Union Emblem

2001. 10th Anniv of Union of Independent States.

7060	**2751**	2r. multicoloured	45	25

2752 Father Christmas driving Troika with Three White Horses

2001. "Happy New Year".

7061	**2752**	2r.50 multicoloured	35	20

2002. Regions of the Russian Federation (6th issue). As T 2651. Multicoloured.

7062	3r. Amur region	40	25
7063	3r. Republic of Karachaevo-Cherkeskaya	40	25
7064	3r. Republic of Altai (vert)	40	25
7065	3r. Sakhalin region	40	25
7066	3r. Republic of Khakassiya	40	25

2753 Skiing

2002. Winter Olympic Games, Salt Lake City. Multicoloured.

7067	3r. Type **2753**	40	25
7068	4r. Figure skating	50	30
7069	5r. Ski-jumping	60	40

2754 Dove, Rainbow and Globe

2002. "World Unity against Terrorism".

7070	**2754**	5r. multicoloured	70	40

2755 Locomotive emerging from Tunnel

2002. Centenary of Trans-Siberian Railway. Sheet 92×73 mm.

MS7071 **2755**	12r. multicoloured	1·80	1·40

2756 "Courtesan" (Hendrick Golzius)

2002. 150th Anniv of New Hermitage Museum, St. Petersburg. Multicoloured.

7072	2r.50 Type **2756**	40	25
7073	2r.50 "Ecco Homo" (Peter Paul Rubens)	40	25
7074	5r. 16th-century Italian Burgonet (helmet)	75	55
7075	5r. The Gonzaga Cameo	75	55
MS7076	76×106 mm. 12r. "New Hermitage" (Luigi Premazzi) (51×48 mm) (horiz)	2·50	2·30

2757 Cinnabar Lily ("Congratulations")

2002. Greetings Stamps. Lilies. Multicoloured.

7077	2r.50 Type **2757**	40	20
7078	2r.50 Orange lily ("Happy Birthday")	40	20
7079	2r.50 Pink lily ("Happiness")	40	20
7080	2r.50 Gilded lily ("From our Hearts")	40	20
7081	2r.50 Regal lily ("Love and Joy")	40	20

2758 Cane-Corso

2002. Dogs. Multicoloured.

7082	1r. Type **2758**	20	10
7083	2r. Shar pei	30	15
7084	3r. Bull mastiff	40	20
7085	4r. Brazilian mastiff (*Fila Brasileiro*)	55	30
7086	5r. Neapolitan mastiff	65	40
MS7087	151×152 mm. Nos. 7082×2, 7083×4 and 7084/6	3·50	2·75

2759 Cathedral of Our Lady of Kazan and Marshal Barclay de Tolli Monument

2002. 300th Anniv of St. Petersburg. Multicoloured.

7088	5r. Type **2759**	75	55
7089	5r. St. Isaak Cathedral	75	55
7090	25r. River Neva, St. Peter and Paul Fortress and gilded angel (vert)	3·50	3·25
7091	25r. Griboedov Canal, Cathedral of the Resurrection and gilded griffin	3·50	3·25
7092	25r. Gilded ship and Admiralty building	3·50	3·25

2760 Artur Artuzov

2002. Intelligence Agents. Sheet 141×91 mm containing T 2760 and similar horiz designs.

MS7093	2r.×6, Type **2760**; Nikolai Demidenko; Jan Olsky; Sergei Putzitsky; Vladimir Styrne; Grigory Syroezhkin	2·00	1·60

2761 Juggler, Trapeze Artist and Clown

2002. Europa. Circus.

7094	**2761**	8r. multicoloured	1·20	55

2762 Pavel Nakhimov

2002. Birth Bicentenary of Pavel S. Nakhimov (naval commander).

7095	**2762**	2r. multicoloured	30	20

2763 Congress Emblem

2002. 5th Eurosai (European Organization of Supreme Audit Institutions) Congress, Moscow.

7096	**2763**	2r. multicoloured	40	25

2764 Geysers

2002. Volcanoes of Kamchatka Region. Multicoloured.

7097	1r. Type **2764**	10	10
7098	2r. Caldera, Uzon volcano	30	15
7099	3r. Karymsky volcano	50	25
7100	5r. Troitsky acid lake, Maly Semyachic volcano	60	30

2765 Russian Carriage (c. 1640)

2002. Horse-drawn Carriages. Multicoloured.

7101	2r.50 Type **2765**	40	30
7102	2r.50 Enclosed sleigh, Moscow (1732)	40	30
7103	5r. Coupe carriage, Berlin (1746)	80	55
7104	5r. English carriage (c. 1770)	80	55
7105	5r. St. Petersburg Berline type carriage (1769)	80	55
MS7106	151×71 mm. 25r.×3 Nos. 7103/5	8·00	7·50

2766 Helicopter KA-10

2002. Birth Centenary of Nikolai Kamov (helicopter designer and manufacturer). Multicoloured.

7107	1r. Type **2766**	10	10
7108	1r.50 KA-22	20	15
7109	2r. KA-26	30	20
7110	2r.50 Navy helicopter KA-27	35	25
7111	5r. Army helicopter KA-50 Black Shark	55	35

2767 Anatoli Sobchak

2002. 65th Birth Anniv of Anatoli Sobchak (reformer and mayor of St. Petersburg).

7112	**2767**	3r.25 multicoloured	50	30

2768 Demoiselle Crane (*Anthropoides virgo*)

2002. Endangered Species. Birds. Multicoloured.

7113	2r.50 Type **2768**	40	20
7114	2r.50 Great black-headed gull (Pallas' Gull) (*Larus ichthyaetus Pallas*)	40	20

Stamps of the same design were issued by Kazakhstan.

2769 City and Emblem

2002. 850th Anniv of Kostroma.

7115	**2769** 2r. multicoloured	35	25

2770 Ministry of Internal Affairs

2002. Bicentenary of Government Ministries. Multicoloured.

7116	3r. Type **2770**	50	30
7117	3r. Palace Square, Alexander column, St. Petersburg and Ministry of Foreign Affairs building, Moscow	50	30
7118	3r. Church, Ministry of Defence building and state emblem (foreground)	50	30
7119	3r. Educational symbols and Moscow State University building	50	30
7120	3r. State emblem (centre) and Ministry of Finance building	50	30
7121	3r. Justice (statue), column, flag and state emblem (right) (Ministry of Justice)	50	30

2771 Census Emblem surrounded by People

2002. National Census. Multicoloured. (a) Self-adhesive.

7122	3r. Type **2771**	30	20

(b) Ordinary gum.

7123	4r. Census emblem	40	30

2772 Russian Millenary Monument, Novgorod

2002. 1140th Anniv of Russian State.

7124	**2772** 3r. multicoloured	40	25

2773 Custom House, Archangelsk (19th-century engraving)

2002. Custom and Excise Service. Sheet 117×137 mm containing T 2773 and similar horiz designs. Multicoloured.

MS7125	2r. Type **2773**; 3r. Custom officers on horseback, St. Petersburg; 5r. Customs warehouse, Kalanchovsky Square	1·50	1·20

2774 The Motherland (statue)

2002. 60th Anniv of Battle for Stalingrad. Sheet 101×75 mm.

MS7126	**2774** 10r. multicoloured	1·20	1·10

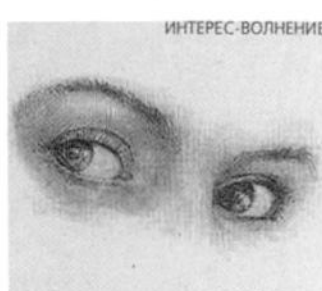

2775 Eyes

2002. Eyes. Sheet 181×107 mm containing T 2775 and similar square designs. Multicoloured.

MS7127	1r.50×10 Ten different stamps showing eyes	2·00	1·60

2776 Emperor Alexander I, Neva River and St. Peter and Paul Cathedral

2002. History of Russian State. Alexander I. Multicoloured.

7128	4r. Type **2776**	50	30
7129	4r. N. M. Karamzin (author, History of State) and Alexander I	50	30
7130	7r. M. Speransky handing plan for Code of Law to Alexander I	75	60
7131	7r. Alexander I entering Paris, 1814	75	60
MS7132	66×91 mm. 10r. Alexander I	1·50	1·20

2777 Saint Daniel Monastery, Moscow (1282)

2002. Monasteries (1st series). Multicoloured.

7133	5r. Type **2777**	65	40
7134	5r. Holy Trinity Monastery, Sergiev Posad (1337)	65	40
7135	5r. Transfiguration of Our Saviour Monastery, Valaam (14th-century)	65	40
7136	5r. Rev. Savva of Storozha Monastery, Zvenigorod (1398)	65	40
7137	5r. Monastery of the Holy Assumption, Pechory (1470)	65	40

See also Nos. 7168/73.

2778 Snowman on Skis

2002. "Happy New Year".

7138	**2778** 3r.50 multicoloured	40	20

2779 *Artemis with Deer* (sculpture) and Palace, Arkhangelkoe

2002. Palaces and Parks. Multicoloured. Self-adhesive.

7138a	1r. Oatankino Palace and Appollo Belvedere statue, Moscow	20	10
7138b	1r.50 Gatchina Palace and Paul II monument, St. Petersburg	25	10
7139	2r. Type **2779**	30	15
7140	2r.50 *Omphala* (sculpture) Chinese Palace, Oranienbaum	40	20
7141	3r. *Gryphon* (sculpture) and mansion, Marfino	50	25
7142	4r. *Erminia* (sculpture) and palace, Pavlovsk	70	30
7143	5r. Scamander river (allegorical sculpture) and palace, Kuskovo	75	35
7144	6r. Peter's Palace and fountain, Peterhoff, St. Petersburg	90	40
7149	10r. Catherine Palace and Aphrodite statue, Tsarskoye, St. Petersburg	70	30

2780 I. V. Kurchatov and Nuclear Reactor

2003. Physicists' Birth Centenaries. Multicoloured.

7150	2r.50 Type **2780**	35	20
7151	2r.50 A. P. Alexandrov, reactor and *Arktica* (nuclear-powered ice-breaker)	35	20

2781 Map, Lake Contours and Ice Cores

2003. International Antarctic Lake Survey. Sheet 90×65 mm containing T 2781 and similar horiz design. Multicoloured.

MS7152	5r. Type **2781**; 5r. Vostok polar station and drilling rig	1·50	1·20

2003. Regions of the Russian Federation (7th issue). As T 2651. Multicoloured.

7153	3r. Kemerovo region	40	25
7154	3r. Kurgan region	40	25
7155	3r. Astrakhan region (vert)	40	25
7156	3r. Magadan region	40	25
7157	3r. Perm region	40	25
7158	3r. Ulijanovsk region	40	25

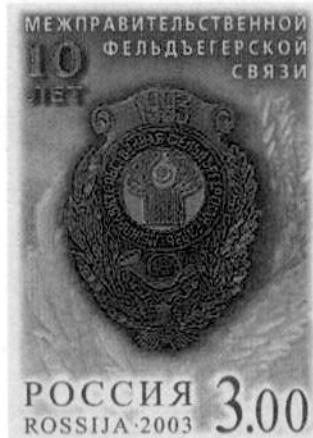

2782 Organization Emblem

2003. 10th Anniv of Intergovernmental Communications Courier Service.

7159	**2782** 3r. multicoloured	45	25

2783 Russian Tennis Fans

2003. Russia, Winner of Davis Cup, 2002. Multicoloured.

7160	4r. Type **2783**	50	30
7161	8r. Flags, net and ball	1·00	45
MS7162	125×91 mm. 50r. Davis Cup	6·50	6·00

2784 Building Yaroslavl Fortress, Yaroslav the Wise and Crowd

2003. History of Russian State. Princes. Multicoloured.

7163	8r. Type **2784**	1·00	55
7164	8r. Entering Kiev, Vladimir Monomach and Vladimir giving "Admonition"	1·00	55
7165	8r. Riding with army, Daniel of Moscow and founding St. Daniel monastery	1·00	55
7166	8r. Inauguration, Ivan Ivanovich of Moscow and Golden Horde	1·00	55

2785 Alexander Nevsky Cathedral, Peter I (statue) and Karelia Postal Building

2003. 300th Anniv of Petrozavodsk City.

7167	**2785** 3r. multicoloured	50	30

2003. Monasteries (2nd series). As T 2777. Multicoloured.

7168	5r. Yuriev Monastery, Novgorod (1030)	70	40
7169	5r. Tolgsky Nunnery (1314)	70	40
7170	5r. Kozelsk Optina Pustyn Monastery (14th–15th century)	70	40
7171	5r. Solovetsky Zosima and Savvatii Monastery, Zvenigorod (14th century)	70	40
7172	5r. Novodevichy Nunnery, Smolensk (1524)	70	40
7173	5r. Seraphim Nunnery, Diveeyevo, Nizhny Novgorod (1780)	70	40

2786 State Theatre, Youth Theatre, Statue and Novosibirsk Science Academy Emblem

2003. Centenary of Novosibirsk City.

7174	**2786** 3r. multicoloured	50	30

2787 "Capture of Swedish Ships Gedan and Astrild, Neva Delta, May 7, 1703" (painting, L. Blinov)

2003. 300th Anniv of Baltic Fleet. Sheet 90×129 mm.

MS7175	**2787** 12r. multicoloured	1·50	1·40

2788 Aram Khachaturyan and *Spartacus* (ballet)

2003. Birth Centenary of Aram I. Katchaturyan (composer).

7176	**2788**	2r.50 multicoloured	30	20

2789 "My first Steps for Einem Biscuits"

2003. Europa. Poster Art.

7177	**2789**	8r. multicoloured	1·20	75

2790 Bells of St. Rumbold's Cathedral, Maline

2003. 150th Anniv of Belgium–Russia Diplomatic Relations. Multicoloured.

7178	5r. Type **2790**	70	40
7179	5r. Bells of St. Peter and Paul's Cathedral, St. Petersburg	70	40

Nos. 7178/9 were issued together, se-tenant, forming a composite design.

Stamps of the same design were issued by Belgium.

2791 Anichkov Bridge over Fontanka River

2003. 300th Anniv of St. Petersburg. Multicoloured.

7180	5r. Type **2791**	80	40
7181	5r. Raised bridge on Neva river	80	40
7182	5r. Central Naval Museum, Vasilievsky Island	80	40
7183	5r. Palace Square	80	40
7184	5r. Winter Palace	80	40
7185	5r. Summer Gardens	80	40
MS7186	3 sheets, each 165×70 mm. (a) 50r. The Bronze Horseman (statue, E. Falkonet) (38×51 mm); (b) 75r. As **MS**7186a (38×51 mm) (23.5); (c) 100r. As **MS**7186a (38×51 mm)	21·00	20·00

2792 Earth, Vostok Flight Paths and Valentina Tereshkova

2003. 40th Anniv of First Female Cosmonaut (Valentina V. Tereshkova).

7187	**2792**	3r. multicoloured	40	30

2793 Globe and Emblem

2003. 2nd International "21st-century without Drugs" Conference, Moscow.

7188	**2793**	3r. multicoloured	50	30

2794 Pskov Kremlin and Mirozhsky Monastery Cathedral

2003. 1100th Anniv of Pskov City.

7189	**2794**	3r. multicoloured	50	30

2795 Town Arms and Andrey Dubensky Monument

2003. 375th Anniv of Krasnoyarsk City.

7190	**2795**	4r. multicoloured	60	35

2796 5r. Coin and Industrial Scene

2003. Transparent Economy Legislation.

7191	**2796**	5r. multicoloured	70	40

2797 Belfry, Prokhorovka and Triumphal Arch, Kursk

2003. 60th Anniv of Battle for Kursk. Sheet 100×75 mm.

MS7192	**2797**	10r. multicoloured	1·20	85

2798 Stone Pillars, Manpupuner Mountains

2003. UNESCO World Heritage Sites. Komi Virgin Forest. Multicoloured.

7193	2r. Type **2798**	30	20
7194	3r. Kozhim river	45	35
7195	5r. Pechora river	55	40

2799 Tsar Peter I receiving Letter from Count Aspraksin, Voronezh

2003. 300th Anniv of St. Petersburg Post. Sheet 103×95 mm.

MS7196	**2799**	12r. multicoloured	1·50	1·40

2800 Stag Beetle (*Lucanus cervus*)

2003. Beetles. Multicoloured.

7197	1r. Type **2800**	20	10
7198	2r. Caterpillar hunter (*Calosoma sycophanta*)	30	20
7199	3r. *Carabus lopatini*	40	30
7200	4r. *Carabus costricticollis*	50	35
7201	5r. *Carabus caucasicus*	60	40

2801 Association Emblem

2003. 10th Anniv of International Association of Science Academies.

7202	**2801**	2r.50 multicoloured	35	25

2802 Archangel Mikhail Church, Transbaikalia Rail Building, Shumovs Palace and Post Building

2003. 350th Anniv of Chita, Eastern Siberia.

7203	**2802**	3r. multicoloured	45	30

2803 Icebergs and Climate Zones Map

2003. World Climate Change Conference, Moscow.

7204	**2803**	4r. multicoloured	60	30

2804 Satan's Bolete (*Boletus satanas*) (poisonous) and Oak Mushroom (*Boletus luridus*) (edible)

2003. Fungi. Edible and poisonous fungi. Multicoloured.

7205	2r. Type **2804**	25	15
7206	2r.50 Death cap (*Amanita phalloides*) (poisonous) and Field mushroom (*Agricus campestris*) (edible)	30	20
7207	3r. The panther (*Amanita pantherina*) (poisonous) and The blusher (*Amanita rubescens*) (edible)	40	30
7208	4r. *Amanita porphyria* (poisonous) and Grisette (*Amanita vaginata*) (edible)	50	35
7209	5r. Bitter bolete (*Tylopilus fellus*) (poisonous) and edible mushroom (*Boletus edulis*) (edible)	60	40

2805 Pineapple

2003. Fruits. Multicoloured.

7210	5r. Type **2805**	70	40
7211	5r. Strawberries	70	40
7212	5r. Apples	70	40
7213	5r. Pear	70	40
7214	5r. Melon	70	40

Nos. 7210/14 were each perforated in a circle within an outer perforated square and impregnated with the scent of the fruit pictured.

2806 Caspian Seal (*Phoca caspia*)

2003. Preservation of the Caspian Sea. Multicoloured.

7215	2r.50 Type **2806**	40	20
7216	2r.50 Beluga (*Huso huso*)	40	20

Stamps of a similar design were issued by Iran.

2807 18th-century Printing Works and *Vedomosti* (newspaper)

2003. 300th Anniv of Russian Journalism. Sheet 90×65 mm.

MS7217	**2807**	10r. multicoloured	1·20	70

2808 Russo-Balt K 12/20 (1911)

2003. Russian Cars. Multicoloured.

7218	3r. Type **2808**	40	20
7219	4r. Nami 1 (1929)	50	30
7220	4r. Gaz M1 (1939)	50	30
7221	5r. Gaz 67b (1946)	60	40
7222	5r. Gaz M20 "Pobeda" (1954)	60	40

2809 Spassky Tower, Constitution Title Page and Kremlin

2003. 10th Anniv of Russian Federation Constitution.

7223	**2809**	3r. multicoloured	40	20

2810 Airship Count Zeppelin, Icebreaker *Malygin*, Call Sign and Ernst Krenkel

2003. Birth Centenary of Ernst Krenkel (polar radio operator and explorer).

7224	**2810**	4r. multicoloured	50	25

2811 "The Battle of Sinop" (A. P. Bogolyubov)

2003. 150th Anniv of Battle of Sinop (Crimea war). Sheet 121×84 mm.

MS7225	**2811**	12r. multicoloured	1·50	95

2812 Grandfather Frost

2003. "Happy New Year".

7226	**2812**	7r. multicoloured	1·20	65

2813 Federation Council Building and Interior

2003. 10th Anniv of Federation Council and State Duma (parliament). Multicoloured.

7227	2r.50 Type **2813**	40	25
7228	2r.50 Stat Duma building and interior	40	25

2004. Regions of the Russian Federation (8th issue). As T 2651. Multicoloured.

7229	5r. Belgorod region	80	40
7230	5r. Ivanov region	80	40
7231	5r. Lipetsk region	80	40
7232	5r. Nenetsky autonomous region	80	40
7233	5r. Nizhny Novogorod region	80	40

2814 Unknown Warrior (statue)

2004. 60th Anniv of World War II Offensive. Sheet 130×95 mm.

MS7234	**2814** 10r. multicoloured	1·20	85

2815 Valery Chkalov

2004. Birth Centenary of Valery Chkalov (test pilot).

7235	**2815** 3r. multicoloured	50	30

2816 The Stone Flower

2004. 125th Birth Anniv of Pavel Bazhov (writer). Showing scenes from his books. Multicoloured.

7236	2r. Type **2816**	30	15
7237	4r. The Malachite Box	50	25
7238	6r. Golden Hair	70	40
MS7239	131×143 mm. Nos. 7236/8, each ×2	3·00	2·30

2817 Yuli Khariton

2004. Birth Centenary of Yuli Khariton (physicist).

7240	**2817** 3r. multicoloured	50	30

2818 Yuri Gagarin

2004. 70th Birth Anniv of Yuri Gagarin (first astronaut).

7241	**2818** 3r. multicoloured	40	20

2004. Monasteries (3rd series). As T 2777. Multicoloured.

7242	8r. St. Panteleimon Monastery, Mount Athos, Greece (11th-century)	1·20	75
7243	8r. Kiev-Pecherskaya Lavra Monastery, Ukraine (1051)	1·20	75
7244	8r. Evfrosinia Convent, Polotsk, Belarus (1128)	1·20	75
7245	8r. Gornensky Convent, Israel (1886)	1·20	75
7246	8r. Pyukhtinsky Convent of the Assumption, Estonia (1891)	1·20	75

2819 S. O. Makarov Monument, Cathedral and Kronshlot Fort (1704)

2004. 300th Anniv of Kronshtadt (town).

7248	**2819** 4r. multicoloured	75	40

2820 Aries

2004. Western Zodiac. Multicoloured.

7249	5r. Type **2820**	75	40
7250	5r. Leo	75	40
7251	5r. Sagittarius	75	40
7252	5r. Pisces	75	40
7253	5r. Cancer	75	40
7254	5r. Scorpio	75	40
7255	5r. Capricorn	75	40
7256	5r. Taurus	75	40
7257	5r. Virgo	75	40
7258	5r. Gemini	75	40
7259	5r. Aquarius	75	40
7260	5r. Libra	75	40

2821 Catherine II in M. V. Lomonosov's Study

2004. 275th Birth Anniv of Empress Catherine II. Multicoloured.

7261	6r. Type **2821** (patronage of arts and sciences)	90	55
7262	7r. Giving alms (support for education and charity) (vert)	1·00	65
7263	8r. Legislative Commission, Kremlin, Moscow (state reform) (vert)	1·10	75
7264	9r. Viewing fleet from Inkermansky Palace, Crimea (border expansion)	1·20	95
MS7265	73×91 mm. 15r. Catherine II (37×52 mm)	2·30	1·40

2822 City and Beach

2004. Europa. Holidays.

7266	**2822** 8r. multicoloured	1·00	55

2823 Port Arthur Medal

2004. Centenary of Battle of Port Arthur (Sino-Russian war, 1905–5). Sheet 75×95 mm.

MS7267	**2823** 10r. multicoloured	1·50	95

2824 Mikhail Glinka

2004. Birth Centenary of Mikhail Glinka (composer). Multicoloured.

7268	4r. Type **2824**	60	35
7269	4r. Scene from *Life for the Tsar* (opera)	60	35
7270	4r. Scene from *Ruslan and Lyudmila*	60	35

2825 Crown (carved relief)

2004. Reopening of Amber Room, Tsarskoe Selo State Museum (2003). Multicoloured.

7271	5r. Type **2825**	75	45
7272	5r. "Moses and Pharaon escaping from Serpents" (cameo) (vert)	75	45
7273	5r. Head surrounded by garland (carved relief)	75	45
MS7274	125×91 mm. 25r. "Touch and Smell" (mosaic) (52×40 mm)	3·50	3·50

2826 National Flags as Heart-shaped Kite

2004. 21st-century German—Russian Youth Forum.

7275	**2826** 8r. multicoloured	1·00	55

A stamp of the same design was issued by Germany.

2827 Vladimir Kokkinaki

2004. Birth Centenary of Vladimir Kokkinaki (test pilot).

7276	**2827** 3r. multicoloured	40	20

2828 "Victory"

2004. Art. Paintings by Sergey Prisekin. Multicoloured.

7277	5r. Type **2828**	70	40
7278	5r. "Whosoever lives by the Sword shall perish by the Sword" (1983) (65×32 mm)	70	40
7279	5r. "Marshal Zhukov" (1980)	70	40
7280	5r. "We have honoured the Oath of Allegiance" (1991) (65×32 mm)	70	40

2829 Riding Habit

2004. Women's Costumes. Multicoloured.

7281	4r. Type **2829**	55	25
7282	4r. Two women, wearing riding habit and hat with brim and wearing walking dress, bonnet and shawl	55	25
7283	4r. Two women, wearing riding habit and hat with veil and wearing open-fronted dress with sash	55	25

2830 Runner

2004. Olympic Games, Athens. Multicoloured.

7284	3r. Type **2830**	50	25
7285	3r. Wrestlers	1·00	55

2831 Launch of Saratov Class Tanker

2004. 300th Anniv of Admiralty Wharfs (shipbuilding company). Sheet 76×96 mm.

MS7286	**2831** 12r. multicoloured	1·50	95

2832 Ducks using Pedestrian Crossing

2004. Children's Road Safety Campaign. Sheet 101×106 mm containing T 2832 and similar horiz designs.

MS7287	4r. ×5, Type **2832**; Crossing at traffic lights; Road closed by garden; Motor cycle stopping suddenly for girl playing ball; Car smash between teddy bears and chicken	2·50	2·30

2833 Wolverine

2004. Wolverine (Gulo gulo). Multicoloured.

7288	8r. Type **2833**	1·10	65
7289	8r. With prey	1·10	65
7290	8r. Standing on branch	1·10	65
7291	8r. Mother and cubs	1·10	65

2834 Buildings

2004. 400th Anniv of Tomsk (town).

7292	**2834** 4r. multicoloured	60	30

2835 Hand holding Globe

2004. Centenary of ITAR TASS (news agency).

7293	**2835** 4r. multicoloured	60	30

2836 N. L. Duhov

2004. Birth Centenaries. Multicoloured.

7294	5r. Type **2836** (military designer)	70	40
7295	5r. B. G. Muzrukov (manufacturer)	70	40

2837 Paul I

2004. 250th Birth Anniv of Emperor Paul I. Multicoloured.

7296	10r. Type **2837**	1·30	65
7297	10r. Wearing crown and robes	1·30	65
MS7298	90×75 mm. 20r. Wearing tri-corn hat	2·75	1·90

2838 Svyatoslav Rerikh

2004. Birth Centenary of Svyatoslav Nikolayevich Rerikh (artist).

7299	**2838**	4r. multicoloured	60	35

2839 Vsevolod the Big Nest

2004. History of Russian State. 850th Birth Anniv of Vsevolod III Yuryevich (Vsevolod the Big Nest).

7300	**2839**	12r. multicoloured	1·60	95

2840 University Building

2004. Bicentenary of Kazan State University.

7301	**2840**	5r. multicoloured	70	40

2841 Bowl (c. 1880—90)

2004. Silverware. Multicoloured.

7302	4r.70 Type **2841**	70	40
7304	4r.70 Ladle (c.1910)	70	40
7305	4r.70 Jug (c. 1900)	70	40
7306	4r.70 Vase (c. 1900—08) (vert)	70	40

2842 Tree

2004. Happy New Year. Self-adhesive.

7307	**2842**	5r. multicoloured	60	35

2843 Belukha Mountain

2004. Altai Mountain Range. Multicoloured.

7308	2r. Type **2843**	25	15
7309	3r. Katun River	45	20
7310	5r. Teletskoye Lake	65	35

2844 R-7 Intercontinental Missile

2004. 50th Anniv of Baikonur Cosmodrome. Multicoloured.

7311	2r.50 Type **2844**	30	20
7312	3r.50 Proton rocket	45	25
7313	4r. Soyuz rocket	55	30
7314	6r. Zenit rocket	70	40

2005. Regions of the Russian Federation (9th issue). As T 2651. Multicoloured.

7315	5r. Koyrak region	70	40
7316	5r. Mordovia Republic	70	40
7317	5r. Smolensk region	70	40
7318	5r. Taimyr autonomous region	70	40
7319	5r. Tver region	70	40
7320	5r. Chukotski autonomous region	70	40

2845 University Building

2005. 250th Anniv of Lomonosov State University, Moscow.

7321	**2845**	5r. multicoloured	60	35

2846 Tree and Emblem

2005. EXPO 2005 World Exposition, Aichi, Japan. Sheet 91×71 mm.

MS7322	**2846** 15r. multicoloured	2·00	1·60

2847 Drinking Horn with Bull-shaped Base

2005. Sarmat (early tribe) Artefacts from Filippov Burial Ground. Multicoloured.

7323	5r. Type **2847**	65	45
7324	5r. Bear-shaped bowl	65	45
7325	7r. Camels on gold hemisphere	95	65
7326	7r. Deer-shaped ornament (vert)	95	65

2848 Type M Submarine VI-bis Series

2005. Submarines. Multicoloured.

7327	2r. Type **2848**	35	20
7328	3r. Type S submarine IX- bis series	45	20
7329	5r. Type Sch submarine X-bis series	65	35
7330	8r. Type K submarine	1·00	55

2849 Suyumbike Tower

2005. Kazan Millenary. Multicoloured.

7331	5r. Type **2849**	65	30
7332	5r. Kul Sharif Mosque	65	30
7333	7r. Cathedral of the Annunciation	90	55
MS7333a	143×133 mm. Nos. 7331/3	2·00	1·50

2850 Alexander with W. Schukowskij

2005. 150th Anniv of Coronation of Emperor Alexander II.

7334	10r. Type **2850**	1·50	95
7335	10r. Coronation in Uspenski Cathedral in the Kremlin	1·50	95
7336	10r. In his study	1·50	95
7337	10r. Mounted during Turkish—Russian war	1·50	95
MS7338	92×77 mm. 25r. Alexander II	3·25	2·50

2851 Russian Soldier signing Column (Berlin, 1945)

2005. 60th Anniv of End of World War II. Multicoloured.

7339	2r. Type **2851**	30	15
7340	2r. Soldiers celebrating (Berlin, 1945)	30	15
7341	3r. Soldier feeding pigeons (Kalinsky front, 1943)	40	20
7342	3r. Soldiers holding flowers (Moscow, 1945)	40	20

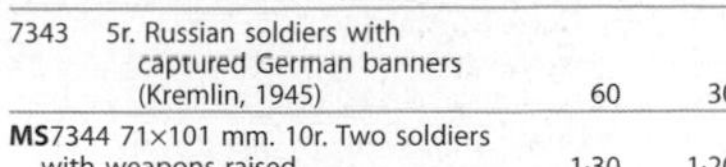

7343	5r. Russian soldiers with captured German banners (Kremlin, 1945)	60	30
MS7344	71×101 mm. 10r. Two soldiers with weapons raised	1·30	1·20

2852 City Hall

2005. 60th Anniv of Liberation of Vienna.

7345	**2852**	6r. multicoloured	1·00	55

2853 Greater Spotted Eagle (*Aquila clanga*)

2005. Fauna. Sheet 133×68 mm containing T 2853 and similar horiz designs. Multicoloured.

MS7346	5r.×4, Type **2853**; *Catocala sponsa*; Beaver (*Castor fiber*); Badger (*Meles meles*)	2·50	2·50

The stamps and margin of No. **MS**7346 form a composite design.

Stamps of the same design were issued by Belarus.

2854 Train and Map of First Route

2005. 70th Anniv of Moscow Metro. Sheet 91×71 mm containing T 2854 and similar horiz design. Multicoloured.

MS7347	5r. Type **2854**; 10r. Modern routes	2·00	1·90

2855 Emblem

2005. Moscow's Bid for Olympic Games—2012.

7348	**2855**	4r. multicoloured	60	40

2856 Blinis, Caviar and Samovar

2005. Europa. Gastronomy.

7349	**2856**	8r. multicoloured	1·00	55

2857 M.A. Sholokhov

2005. Birth Centenary of Mikhail Aleksandrovich Sholokhov (writer).

7350	**2857**	5r. black and brown	75	40

2858 Sable (*Martes zibellina*)

2005. Fauna. Multicoloured.

7351	8r. Type **2858**	1·00	55

7352	8r. Siberian tiger (*Panthera tigris altaica*)	1·00	55

Stamps of a similar design were issued by People's Democratic Republic of Korea.

2859 *Bombus armeniacus*

2005. Bees. Multicoloured.

7353	3r. Type **2859**	45	20
7354	4r. *Bombus fragrans*	70	35
7355	5r. *Bombus anachoreta*	80	40
7356	6r. *Bombus unicus*	90	45
7357	7r. *Bombus czerskii*	1·00	1·60

2860 Monuments, Gate and Towers

2005. 750th Anniv of Kaliningrad (Koenigsberg).

7358	**2860**	5r. multicoloured	80	45

2861 University Facade

2005. 175th Anniv of Moscow Technical University.

7359	**2861**	5r. multicoloured	70	40

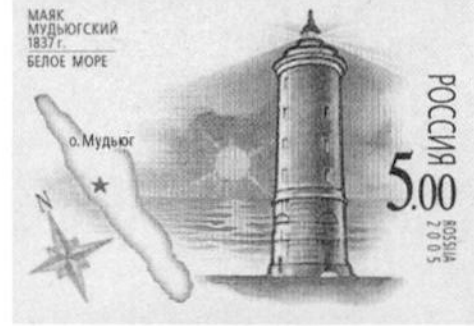

2862 Mudyugsky Lighthouse

2005. Lighthouses. Multicoloured.

7360	5r. Type **2862**	90	45
7361	6r. Solovetsky lighthouse	1·00	50
7362	8r. Svyatonossky lighthouse	1·20	60

2863 MiG-3 Fighter Aircraft

2005. Birth Centenary of Artem Ivanovich Mikoyan (aircraft designer). Multicoloured.

7363	5r. Type **2863**	90	45
7364	5r. MiG-15	90	45
7365	5r. MiG-21	90	45
7366	5r. MiG-25	90	45
7367	5r. MiG-29	90	45

2864 Priest blessing Troops

2005. 625th Anniv of Kulikovo Battle (Russian victory against the Mongols). Sheet 97×65 mm.

MS7368	**2864**	15r. multicoloured	2·00	1·90

2865 Hands

2005. Earth. Sheet 147×105 mm containing T 2865 and similar horiz designs. Multicoloured.

MS7369	3r. Type **2865**; 3r.50 Water droplets on leaf; 3r.50 Surf; 4r. Snow-topped mountain; 4r.50 Waterfall; 5r. Water droplets	2·75	2·50

2866 Alexander Suvorov

2005. 275th Birth Anniv of Alexander Vasilievich Suvorov (military commander).

7370	**2866**	4r. multicoloured	60	40

2867 Early Sea Infantry

2005. 300th Anniv of Sea Infantry. Multicoloured.

7371	2r. Type **2867**	30	20
7372	3r. Fighting in Crimea	40	25
7373	4r. Fighting during World War II	50	30
7374	5r. Modern Sea Infantry	60	40

2868 Ded Moroz (Father Christmas)

2005

7375	**2868**	5r. multicoloured	60	40

2869 Emblem

2005. 60th Anniv of UNESCO.

7376	**2869**	5r.60 multicoloured	70	45

2870 Trees

2005. Christmas and New Year.

7377	**2870**	5r.60 multicoloured	60	40

2871 AH-12

2006. Birth Centenary of Oleg Konstantinovich Antonov (aircraft designer). Multicoloured.

7378	5r.60 Type **2871**	70	45
7379	5r.60 AH-24	70	45
7380	5r.60 AH-124	70	45
7381	5r.60 AH-74	70	45
7382	5r.60 AH-3T	70	45

2872 Speed Skating

2006. Winter Olympic Games, Turin. Multicoloured.

7383	4r. Type **2872**	50	30
7384	4r. Luge	50	30
7385	4r. Snowboarding	50	30

2873 Armenian and Russian Flags and Arms

2006. Year of Armenia in Russia.

7386	**2873**	10r. multicoloured	1·50	1·10

2874 *Ob* (Icebreaker) and Mirnyi Station

2006. 50th Anniv of Antarctic Research. Multicoloured.

7387	7r. Type **2874**	90	55
7388	7r. Plane Il-76 and *Academic Fedorov* (scientific ship)	90	55
7389	7r. Transport and sea researcher	90	55

2875 "Portrait of N. N. Ge" (I. E. Repin)

2006. 175th Birth Anniv of Nikolai Nikolaevich Ge (artist). Multicoloured.

7390	5r.60 Type **2875**	75	45
7391	5r.60 "Peter I interrogating Tsarevich Aleksei" (horiz)	75	45

2876 "Self-portrait"

2006. 150th Birth Anniv of Mikhail Aleksandrovich Vrubel (artist). Multicoloured.

7392	5r.60 Type **2876**	75	45
7393	5r.60 "Tsarevna-Swan"	75	45

2877 Atomic Submarine No. 667A

2006. Centenary of Russian Submarine Navy. Atomic Submarines. Multicoloured.

7394	3r. Type **2877**	40	25
7395	4r. Submarine No. 671	50	30
7396	6r. Submarine No. 941	80	45
7397	7r. Submarine No. 949a	90	55

2878 Ivan Groznyi's Throne

2006. Bicentenary of Kremlin Museums, Moscow. Multicoloured.

7398	5r. Type **2878**	75	55
7399	5r. Tsar Mikhail Fyodorovich's mace	75	55
7400	5r. Tsar Mikhail Fyodorovich's helmet	75	55
7401	5r. State sword and shield	75	55
7401a	20r. Monomakh's cap	5·75	5·50
7401b	20r. As Type **2878**	5·75	5·50
7401c	20r. As No. 7399	5·75	5·50
7401d	20r. As No. 7400	5·75	5·50
7401e	20r. As No. 7401	5·75	5·50
MS7402	122×97 mm. 15r. Monomakh	2·10	2·00

2879 AIR1

2006. Birth Centenary of Alexandr Sergevich Yakovlev (aircraft designer). Multicoloured.

7403	5r. Type **2879**	70	45
7404	5r. YAK-54	70	45
7405	5r. YAK-141	70	45
7406	5r. YAK-42	70	45
7407	5r. YAK-130	70	45

2880 Arms

2006. Centenary of State Duma. Sheet 90×71 mm.

MS7408	**2880**	15r. multicoloured	2·00	1·90

2881 State Arms

2006. State Arms and Flag. Multicoloured.

7409	5r.60 Type **2881**	75	45
7410	5r.60 State flag	75	45

2882 "Trinity" (Andrey Rublev)

2006. 150th Anniv Tretiakov State Picture Gallery. Multicoloured.

7411	5r.60 Type **2882**	80	45
7412	5r.60 "Girl with peaches" (V.A. Serov)	80	45
7413	5r.60 "Above eternal rest" (I. I. Levitan) (horiz)	80	45
7414	5r.60 "Three Bogatyrs" (V. M. Vasnetsov) (horiz)	80	45
MS7415	90×71 mm. 15r. Gallery building (49×37 mm)	2·00	1·90

2883 Emperor Aleksandr III

2006. Emperor Aleksandr III. Multicoloured.
7416 10r. Type **2883** 1·40 1·10
7417 10r. Aleksandr III, flags and ships 1·40 1·10
MS7418 91×76 mm. 15r. Aleksandr III in close up 3·25 3·00

2884 Statue and Towers

2006. 150th Anniv of Blagoveschensk.
7419 **2884** 5r. multicoloured 70 45

2885 Ship in Dry Dock

2006. 150th Anniv of Baltic Plant. Sheet 70×90 mm.
MS7420 **2885** 12r. multicoloured 1·60 1·50

2886 Stadium at Night

2006. 50th Anniv of Luzhniki Olympic Complex, Moscow.
7421 **2886** 6r. multicoloured 80 55

2887 Summer Bouquet

2006. Flowers. Designs showing part of a seasonal bouquet. Multicoloured.
7422 7r. Type **2887** 1·10 75
7423 7r. Autumn 1·10 75
7424 7r. Winter 1·10 75
7425 7r. Spring 1·10 75

Nos. 7422/5 were issued together, se-tenant, forming a composite design.

2888 Deer

2006. 250th Anniv of Altai as Part of Russia.
7426 **2888** 5r. multicoloured 80 55

2006. Regions of the Russian Federation (10th issue). As T 2651. Multicoloured.
7427 6r. Adygeja Republic (vert) 1·10 75
7428 6r. Vladimir region (vert) 1·10 75
7429 6r. Kostroma region 1·10 75
7430 6r. Pskov region 1·10 75
7431 6r. Rjazan region 1·10 75
7432 6r. Tula region 1·10 75

2889 *Kruzenshtern* (four masted training barque)

2006. Kruzenshtern's Circumnavigation of the Globe to celebrate the Bicentenary of Adam Johann Ritter von Krustenstern's Voyage.
7433 **2889** 4r. multicoloured 60 40

2890 Map of Spitzbergen

2006. 75th Anniv of Arcticugol Trust.
7434 **2890** 4r. multicoloured 60 40

2891 Left Wing Facade

2006. 250th Anniv of Tsarskoye Selo (Catherine's Palace). Sheet 166×74 mm containing T 2891 and similar horiz designs. Multicoloured.
MS7435 5r. Type **2891**; 6r. Central facade; 7r. Right wing 3·50 3·25

The stamps and margins of **MS**7435 form a composite design of the Palace facade.

2892 "A. A. Ivanov" (S. P. Postnikov)

2006. Birth Bicentenary of Alexander Andreyevich Ivanov (artist). Multicoloured.
7436 6r. Type **2892** 1·50 1·20
7437 6r. "Branch" (A. A. Ivanov) (horiz) 1·50 1·20

2893 *A. M. Vasnetsov* (N. D. Kuznetsov)

2006. 150th Birth Anniv of Apollinary Mikhailovich Vasnetsov (artist). Multicoloured.
7438 6r. Type **2893** 80 70
7439 6r. *Novodevichy Monastery* (horiz) 80 70

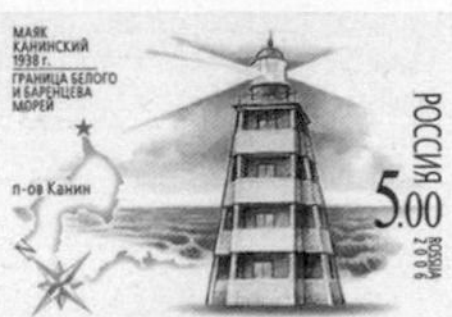

2894 Kanin Peninsula

2006. Lighthouses. Multicoloured.
7440 5r. Type **2894** 90 55
7441 6r. Kildin Island 1·10 75
7442 8r. Rybachiy (vert) 1·30 95

2895 Masks and Auditorium

2006. 250th Anniv of State Theatre. Sheet 91×71 mm.
MS7443 **2895** 15r. multicoloured 2·10 1·90

2896 *Rhodostethia rosea* (Ross's gull)

2006. Fauna of Sakha (Yakutia) Republic. Multicoloured.
7444 3r. Type **2896** 20 10
7445 4r. *Grus leucogeranus* (Siberian crane) 30 20
7446 5r. *Ursus maritimus* (polar bear) 50 30
7447 6r. *Equus caballus* (domestic horse) 70 55
7448 7r. *Rangifer tarandus* (caribou) 95 75

2897 Students

2006. Centre for Russian Language Development.
7449 **2897** 7r. multicoloured 3·50 2·50

2898 D. S. Likhachev

2006. Birth Centenary of Dmitri Sergeyevich Likhachev (writer).
7450 **2898** 5r. brown, grey and black 50 30

2899 Mountain Peak

2006. Natural Heritage, West Caucasus. Multicoloured.
7451 6r. Type **2899** 70 55
7452 7r. River 95 75
7453 8r. Bison 1·20 95

Nos. 7451/3 were issued together, se-tenant, forming a composite design of a mountain scene.

2900 Transmitter

2006. 75th Anniv of Regular Broadcasting.
7454 **2900** 7r. multicoloured 95 75

2901 Handset

2006. 15th Anniv of Mobile Telephony.
7455 **2901** 7r. multicoloured 95 75

2902 N. A. Kristofari (first investor) and Bank Facade

2006. 165th Anniv of National Saving Bank. Multicoloured.
7456 7r. Type **2902** 95 75
MS7457 96×71 mm. 15r. N. A. Kristofari (30×42 mm) 2·10 1·90

2903 Emblem

2006. Russian Membership of Council of Europe.
7458 **2903** 8r. multicoloured 1·20 95

2904 Emblem

2006. 15th Anniv of Regional Commonwealth in Communication.
7459 **2904** 5r. multicoloured 50 30

2905 Snowmen

2006. Ded Moroz.
7460 **2905** 7r. multicoloured 95 75

2906 Atlas (image scaled to 74% of original size)

2006. National Atlas.
7461 **2906** 6r. multicoloured 70 55

2907 Snow-covered Tree

2006. New Year.
7462 **2907** 7r. multicoloured 95 75

2908 V. M. Behterev

2007. 150th Birth Anniv of Vladimir Mikhailovich Behterev (psychologist and neuropathologist).
7463 **2908** 5r. multicoloured 50 30

2909 "I. I. Shishkin" (I. N. Kramskoy)

2007. 175th Birth Anniv of Ivan Ivanovitch Shishkin (artist). Multicoloured.
7464 7r. Type **2909** 95 75
7465 7r. "In the north wild..." (I. I. Shishkin) 95 75

2910 St. George's Cross

2007. Bicentenary of Cross of St. George. Multicoloured.
7466 10r. Type **2910** 1·50 1·20
MS7467 90×126 mm. 50r. St George's Cross (different) (56×56 mm) 7·00 6·50

2911 Academy Facade

2007. Centenary of Russian Economic Academy.
7468 **2911** 5r. multicoloured 50 30

2912 "Self-portrait"

2007. 225th Birth Anniv of Orest Adamovich Kiprensky (artist). Multicoloured.
7469 7r. Type **2912** 95 75
7470 7r. "Bednaja Liza" 95 75

2913 Russian Mail Emblem

2007
7471 **2913** 6r.50 blue 80 65

2914 Research Ship and Station

2007. International Polar Year. Sheet 190×77 mm containing T 2914 and similar horiz designs. Multicoloured.
MS7472 6r. Type **2914**; 7r. Polar ice pack; 8r. Ptarmigan 3·00 2·75
The stamps of **MS**7472 form a composite design.

2915 Arseny Alexandrovich Tarkovsky

2007. Russian Cinema. Sheet 71×90 mm containing T 2915 and similar horiz designs. Multicoloured.
MS7473 8r. Type **2915** (birth centenary); 8r. Andrey Arsenyevich Tarkovsky (75th birth anniv) 2·30 2·20

2916 Sputnik

2007. 50th Anniv of Space Exploration. Sheet 110×110 mm containing T 2916 and similar square designs. Multicoloured.
MS7474 10r. Type **2916**; 20r. Sergey Pavlovich Korolyov (chief rocket designer and engineer) (birth centenary); 20r. Konstantin Eduardovitch Tsiolkovsky ('father of cosmonautics') (150th birth anniv) 7·00 6·00
The stamps and margins of **MS**7474 form a composite design.

2917 Russian and Bashkiria Leaders

2007. 450th Anniv of the Assimilation of Bashkiria into Russia.
7475 **2917** 6r.50 multicoloured 1·00 85

2918 *Pavel Chistyakov* (I. E. Repin)

2007. 175th Birth Anniv of Pavel Petrovich Chistyakov (artist). Multicoloured.
7476 7r. Type **2918** 1·00 85
7477 7r. *Pavel Chistyakov* (V. A. Serov) 1·00 85

2919 *Vladimir Borovikovsky* (I. V. Bugaevsky-Blagodarny)

2007. 250th Birth Anniv of Vladimir Lukich Borovikovsky (artist). Multicoloured.
7478 7r. Type **2919** 1·00 85
7479 7r. *Anna and Varvara Gagarina* 1·00 85

2920 1858 10k. Stamp (As Type 1)

2007. 150th Anniv of First Russian Stamp. Sheet 95×81 mm.
MS7480 **2920** 10r. blue and brown 1·40 1·20
The stamp and margins of **MS**7480 form a composite design.

2921 Early Handset

2007. 125th Anniv of Telephony.
7481 **2921** 5r. multicoloured 1·00 85

2922 Athena (statue), Cupola, Academy of Art

2007. 250th Anniv of Academy of Art. Sheet 92×76 mm.
MS7482 25r. bistre and agate 3·50 3·00
The stamp and margins of **MS**7482 form a composite design.

2923 Exhibition Emblem

2007. St. Petersburg–2007 World Stamp Exhibition.
7483 **2923** 5r. ultramarine, gold and blue 1·00 85

2924 Launch Pad

2007. 50th Anniv of Cosmodrome, Pleseck. Sheet 91×76 mm.
MS7484 12r. multicoloured 1·75 1·50
The stamp and margins of **MS**7484 form a composite design.

2925 Mountains

2007. 300th Anniv of the Assimilation of Hakasia into Russia.
7485 **2925** 6r.50 multicoloured 1·00 85

2926 N. A. Lunin

2007. Submariners' Birth Centenaries. Mult.
7486 7r. Type **2926** 1·00 85
7487 7r. M. I. Gadjiev 1·00 85
Nos. 7486/7 were issued together, horizontal se-tenant strips of two stamps surrounding a central stamp size label, showing a submarine, the whole forming a composite design.

2927 S. P. Botkin

2007. 175th Birth Anniv of Sergei Petrovich Botkin (medical scientist).
7488 **2927** 5r. blue 1·00 85

2007. Regions of the Russian Federation (11th issue). As T 2651. Multicoloured.
7489 7r. Altai region 1·10 95
7490 7r. Vologda region 1·10 95
7491 7r. Irkutsk region 1·10 95
7492 7r. Novosibirsk region 1·10 95
7493 7r. Orlov region 1·10 95
7494 7r. Rostov region 1·10 95

2928 Emblem

2007. 50th Anniv of Biblio-Globus Bookshop. Sheet 91×72 mm.
MS7495 12r. multicoloured 1·60 1·40

2929 Child writing

2007. Year of Russian Language (1st issue). Sheet 92×106 mm.
MS7496 12r. multicoloured 1·60 1·40

2930 *Gladiolus gandavensis*

2007. Flora. Sheet 92×106 mm contiaining T 2930 and similar horiz designs. Multicoloured.
MS7497 6r.×4, Type **2930**; *Iris ensata; Rosa hybrida; Nelumbo nucifera* 3·75 3·25

The stamps and margins of **MS**7497 form a composite design.

2931 *Ciconia boyciana* (oriental stork)

2007. Endangered Species. Multicoloured.

7498	5r. Type **2931**	85	75
7499	6r. *Uncia uncia* (snow leopard)	95	85
7500	7r. *Bison bonasus* (European bison)	1·10	95

2932 AMO-F-15 (1924)

2007. Early Russian Lorries. Multicoloured.

7501	8r. Type **2932**	1·00	85
7502	8r. GAZ-AA (MM) (1932)	1·00	85
7503	8r. ZIS-5V (1942)	1·00	85

2933 Russian House of Science and Culture, Berlin

2007. Year of Russian Language (2nd issue).
7504 **2933** 8r. multicoloured 1·10 95

2934 Vladimirskaya Heavy Type Horse

2007. Domestic Horse Breeds. Multicoloured.

7505	6r. Type **2934**	90	80
7506	7r. Orlovskaya warm blood	1·00	85
7507	7r. Vyatskaya	1·00	85
7508	8r. Donskaya	1·20	1·00
MS7509	132×98 mm. As Nos. 7505/8	3·75	3·25

2935 Snowmen

2007. Happy New Year.
7510 **2935** 8r. multicoloured 1·10 95

2936 Deep-water Device Mir-1

2007. Arktika 2007 (first ever crewed descent to sea floor at North Pole). Multicoloured.

7511	8r. Type **2936**	1·10	95
7512	8r. The North Pole and Russian flag	1·10	95

2937 A. N. Tolstoi

2008. 125th Birth Anniv of Aleksei Nikolaevich Tolstoi (writer).
7513 **2937** 6r. multicoloured 90 80

2938 Mail Troika and Russian Empire Type **1**

2008. 150th Anniv of First Russian Stamp.
7514 **2938** 8r. multicoloured 1·10 95

2939 Lev Davidovich Landau

2008. Birth Centenaries of Nobel Prize Winning Physicists. Multicoloured.

7515	6r. Type **2939** (1962)	90	80
7516	6r. Il'ja Mikhailovich Frank (1958)	90	80

2940 Augustin de Betancourt

2008. 250th Birth Anniv of Augustin de Betancourt y Molina (engineer and architect).
7517 **2940** 9r. multicoloured 1·20 1·10

2941 Park

2008. 450th Anniv of Astrakhan.
7518 **2941** 9r. multicoloured 1·20 1·10

2942 Valentin Glushko

2008. Birth Centenary of Valentin Petrovich Glushko (engineer and spacecraft designer).
7519 **2942** 8r. multicoloured 1·25 1·10

2943 Buckle

2008. Archaeological Heritage. Sheet 145×70 mm containing T 2943 and similar horiz designs. Multicoloured.
MS7520 12r.×3, Type **2943**; Bronze plaque with two oxen ; Deer 5·50 5·50

The stamps and margins of **MS**7520 form a composite design.

2944 Competitors

2008. Olympic Games, Beijing. Multicoloured.

7521	8r. Type **2944**	1·25	1·10
7522	8r. Competitors, fencing and tennis central	1·25	1·10
7523	8r. Competitors, pole vault and archery central	1·25	1·10

Nos. 7521/3 were issued together, se-tenant, forming a composite design.

2945 Flags

2008. 225th Anniv of Black Sea Fleet. Sheet 70×90 mm.
MS7524 **2945** 15r. multicoloured 2·25 2·25

2946 Early and Modern Letters

2008. Europa. The Letter.
7525 **2946** 8r. multicoloured 1·25 1·10

2947 National Flag

2008. Inauguration of Dmitry Anatolyevich Medvedev as President.
7526 **2947** 7r. multicoloured 1·00 90

2008. Regions of the Russian Federation (12th issue). As T 2651. Multicoloured.

7527	8r. Volgograd region	1·25	1·10
7528	8r. Krasnoyarsk region	1·25	1·10
7529	8r. Penza region	1·25	1·10
7530	8r. Sverdlov region	1·25	1·10
7531	8r. Yaroslavl region	1·25	1·10

2948 St Dimitry Church, Vladimir (Russia)

2008. UNESCO World Heritage Sites in Romania and Russia. Multicoloured.

7532	12r. Type **2948**	4·50	4·00
7533	12r. St Gheorghe Church, Voronet Monastery (Romania)	4·50	4·00

Stamps of a similar design were issued by Romania.

2949 Helicopter

2008. 50th Anniversary of Helicopter Sports.
7534 **2949** 5r. multicoloured 3·25 3·00

2950 Pokrovsky Cathedral

2008
7535 **2950** 7r.50 multicoloured 4·50 4·00

2951 Flags and Aircraft Carrier

2008. 75th Anniv of North Fleet. Sheet 70×90 mm.
MS7536 **2951** 15r. multicoloured 9·00 9·00

2952 Emblem

2008. 450th Anniv of Udmurtia's Assimilation into Russia.
7537 **2952** 7r.50 multicoloured 4·50 4·00

2953 Church (1714)

2008. Kizhi–World Heritage Site. Sheet 116×70 mm containing T 2953 and similar vert designs. Multicoloured.
MS7538 10r.×3, Type **2953**; Bell tower (1862); Church (1694–17) 17·00 17·00

The stamps and margins of **MS**7538 form a composite design.

2954 Emperor Nicholas I

2008. Russian History. Sheet 90×78 mm.

MS7539	**2954** 35r. multicoloured	19·00	19·00

2955 *Krasin*

2008. International Polar Year. Sheet 190×77 mm containing T **2955** and similar horiz designs. Multicoloured.

MS7540	6r. Type **2955**; 7r. *Rossija*; 8r. Small icebreaker	11·50	11·50

The stamps and margins of **MS**7540 form a composite design.

2956 Hare

2008. Animals. Multicoloured.

7541	10k. Type **2956**	30	25
7542	15k. As Type **2956**		
7543	25k. As Type **2956**	30	25
7544	30k. Fox	30	25
7545	50k. As No. 7544	30	25
7546	1r. As No. 7544	35	30
7547	1r.50 Lynx	35	30
7548	2r. As No. 7547	1·20	1·10
7549	2r.50 As No. 7547	1·90	1·70
7550	3r. Elk	2·40	2·20
7551	4r. As No. 7550	2·75	2·50
7552	5r. As No. 7550	3·25	3·00
7553	6r. Bear	3·25	3·00
7554	10r. As No. 7553	3·50	3·00
7555	25r. As No. 7553	12·50	12·00

2957 Emblem

2008. 190th Anniv of GOZNAK (banknote and coin producer). Sheet 130×65 mm.

MS7556	**2957** 20r. multicoloured	10·00	10·00

2958 Squirrel and Woodpecker

2008. Fauna and Flora. Multicoloured.

7557	7r. Type **2958**	1·25	1·10
7558	7r. Fawn	1·25	1·10
7559	7r. Fungi	1·25	1·10

Nos. 7557/9 were issued together, se-tenant, the whole forming a composite design of a woodland scene.

2008. Regions of the Russian Federation (13th issue). As T 2651. Multicoloured.

7560	8r. Leningrad region	1·50	1·25

2959 Medal

2008. Russian History. Cossacks. Sheet 114×148 mm containing T **2959** and similar horiz designs. Multicoloured.

MS7561	10r.×3, Type **2959**; Badge; Sabre	5·00	5·00

The stamps and margins of **MS**7561 form a composite design.

2960 Helicopter Kamov Ka–32A

2008. Helicopters. Multicoloured.

7562	7r. Type **2960**	1·25	1·10
7563	7r. Kamov Ka–226	1·25	1·10

No. 7564 is left for miniature sheet, not yet received.

2961 Forest and Mountains in Mist

2008. World Heritage. Central Sikhote–Alin. Multicoloured.

7564	7r. Type **2961**	1·00	90
7565	8r. Forest and mist	1·10	1·00
7566	9r. Forest	1·10	1·00

Nos. 7564/6 plus a stamp size label were printed, se-tenant, forming a composite design of forested valley.

2962 State Flag and Arms

2008. 15th Anniv of Federal Assembly of Russia. Multicoloured.

7567	10r. Type **2962**	1·40	1·40
7568	10r. State flag as map of Russia	1·40	1·40

2963 Bridge over Moscow River

2008. Bridges. Multicoloured.

7569	6r. Type **2963**	1·10	1·00
7570	7r. Bridge over Volga, Kimry	1·20	1·10
7571	8r. Bridge over Ob, Surgut	1·30	1·20
7572	9r. Bridge over Neva, St. Petersburg	1·40	1·30

2964 Swimmer

2008. Centenary of Shuvalov Swimming School.

7573	**2964** 8r. multicoloured	1·10	1·00

2965 Trophy and Player

2008. Russia—World Hockey Champions, 2008.

7574	**2965** 8r. multicoloured	1·10	1·00

2966 Leitner Bicycle (1917)

2008. Bicycles. Multicoloured.

7575	7r. Type **2966**	1·00	90
7576	7r. Racing cycle (1938)	1·00	90
7577	7r. B-22 ladies cycle (1954)	1·00	9·90

Nos. 7578/9 are left for single stamp and miniature sheet, not yet received.

2967 Kremlin Tower and State Symbols

2008. Happy New Year.

7578	**2967** 7r.50 multicoloured	1·00	90

2968 Kerchief with Chain and Pendants

2008. Decorative Art of Dagestan.

7579	7r.50 Type **2968**	90	85
7580	7r.50 Headdress 'Kjukjem'	90	85
7581	7r.50 Pendant from wedding headdress 'Margjal'	90	85
7582	7r.50 Man with dagger in sheath	90	85

2009. Regions of the Russian Federation (14th issue). As T **2651**. Multicoloured.

7583	9r. Voronezh region	1·00	90
7584	9r. Chelyabinsk region	1·00	90
7585	9r. Sararov region	1·00	90

2969 Ernesto 'Che' Guevara and Cuban Flag

2009. 50th Anniv of Cuban Revolution.

7586	**2969** 10r. multicoloured	1·10	1·00

2970 Museum Building

2009. 300th Anniv of Naval Museum.

7587	**2970** 7r. multicoloured	1·00	90

2971 *Self Portrait*, 1851

2009. 175th Birth Anniv of Vasily Grigorevich Perov (artist). Multicoloured.

7588	9r. Type **2971**	1·00	90
7589	9r. *Tea-Party at Mytishchi near Moscow*, 1862	1·00	90

2972 Dmitri Mendeleev

2009. 175th Birth Anniv of Dmitri Ivanovich Mendeleev (chemist and creator of first version of periodic table of elements). Sheet 110×75 mm.

MS7590	**2972** 15r. multicoloured	1·75	1·75

2973 G. Bakhchivandji

2009. Birth Centenary of G.Y. Bakhchivandji (test pilot).

7591	**2973** 10r. multicoloured	1·10	1·00

2974 Yuri Gagarin and Signature

2009. 75th Birth Anniv of Yuri Alekseyevich Gagarin (cosmonaut and first man in space).

7592	**2974** 10r. multicoloured	1·10	1·00

2975 Alexander Popov

2009. 150th Birth Anniv of Alexander Stepanovich Popov (physicist). Sheet 90×70 mm.

MS7593	**2975** 20r. multicoloured	2·30	2·20

2976 Scene from *The Government Inspector*

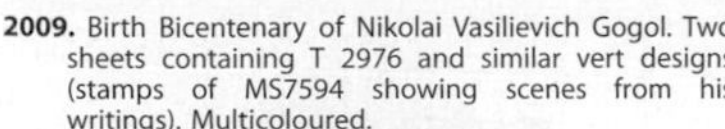

2009. Birth Bicentenary of Nikolai Vasilievich Gogol. Two sheets containing T 2976 and similar vert designs (stamps of MS7594 showing scenes from his writings). Multicoloured.

MS7594	149×125 mm. 6r. Type **2976**; 7r. *Dead Souls*; 8r. *Overcoat*; 9r. *Taras Bulba*	18·00	18·00
MS7595	100×70 mm. 15r. Nikolai Gogol (painting)	2·00	2·00

The stamps and margins of No. **MS**7594 form a composite design.

2977 SVT–40 and AVS–36 Rifles

2009. Weapons. Multicoloured.

7596	7r. Type **2977**	1·10	1·00
7597	8r. Revolver, 1895 and TT pistol, 1933	1·20	1·10
7598	9r. PPS–43 and PPSH–41 submachine guns	1·30	1·20
7599	10r. DP and SG–43 machine guns	1·40	1·30

2978 Symbols of Astronomy

2009. Europa. Astronomy.

7600	**2978**	9r. multicoloured	3·75	3·50

2979 A. Y. Kupfer (academician–physicist instigated meteorological observations in whole territory of Russian Empire) (1779-1865)

2009. 175th Anniv of Hydrometeorologic Service. Multicoloured.

7601	8r. Type **2979**	1·20	1·10
7602	9r. Satellite and weather map	1·30	1·20

2980 Catherine I

2009. 325th Birth Anniv of Catherine I, Empress of Russia. Sheet 90×75 mm.

MS7603	**2980**	35r. multicoloured	19·00	19·00

2981 Emblem

2009. 400th Anniv of Assimilation of Kalmykia into Russian State

7604	**2981**	7r. multicoloured	1·10	1·00

2982 *Lenin*

2009. 50th Anniv of Ice Breaker Fleet. Multicoloured.

7605	7r. Type **2982**	4·00	3·75
7606	8r. *Taimyr*	4·25	4·00
7607	9r. *Yamal*	4·75	5·00
7608	10r. *50 Years of Victory*	5·25	5·00

No. 7609 is vacant

2983 *Peter I at Battle of Poltava* (I. G. Tannauer)

2009. 300th Anniv of Battle of Poltava. Sheet 83×127 mm.

MS7610	**2983**	30r. multicoloured	16·00	16·00

2984 Stylized Figures and Flag

2009. Year of Youth.

7611	**2984**	8r. multicoloured	1·10	1·00

2009. Regions of the Russian Federation (15th Issue). As T **2651**. Multicoloured.

7612	9r. Ingushetiya Republic	1·40	1·30
7613	9r. Tomsk region	1·40	1·30
7614	9r. Chechen Republic	1·40	1·30

2985 Helicopter Mi-1

2009. Birth Centenary of Mikhail Leontyevich Mil (aircraft engineer). Sheet 160×100 mm containing T 2985 and similar horiz designs showing helicopters. Multicoloured.

MS7615	5r. Type **2985**; 6r. Mi-4.; 7r. Mi-8; 8r. Mi-34.; 9r. Mi-28	6·50	6·50

No. **MS**7615 also contains a stamp size label showing M. L. Mil, which with the stamps and margins, form a composite design.

2986 *Self Portrait At the Dressing-Table*

2009. 125th Birth Anniv of Zinaida Yevgenyevna Serebriakova (artist). Multicoloured.

7616	9r. Type **2986**	1·40	1·30
7617	9r. *Field in Autumn*	1·40	1·30

2987 Andrei Gromyko

2009. Andrei Andreyevich Gromyko (Soviet Union Minister for Foreign Affairs (1957–85) and Presidium of the Supreme Soviet Chairman (1985–88).

7618	**2987**	7r. multicoloured	1·50	1·40

2988 17th-Century Monastery Complex

2009. World Heritage Site. Solovetsky Islands. Sheet 110×155 mm containing T 2988 and similar horiz designs. Multicoloured.

MS7619	12r.×4, Type **2988**; 19th-century complex; 15th-century building; Andrei Pervozvannyi church	5·00	5·00

The stamps and margins of **MS**719 form a composite design

2989 Ship on Spire of Admiralty (Symbol of St-Petersburg)

2009. Symbols of Moscow and St Petersburg. Multicoloured.

7620	6r.60 Type **2989**	90	85
7621	9r. St.Georgyi (Symbol of Moscow)	1·40	1·30

2990 Bridge over the Oka, Nizhni Novgorod

2009. Bridges. Multicoloured.

7622	6r. Type **2990**	75	70
7623	7r. Bridge over the Irtysh, Khanty-Mansiysk	90	85
7624	8r. Bridge over the Matseta, Sochi	1·00	95
7625	9r. Bridge over the Don, Rostov on Don	1·10	1·00

2991 Belgorod

2009. Town Emblems. Sheet 125×88 mm containing T 2991 and similar square designs. Multicoloured.

MS7626	10r.×5 Type **2991**; Kursk; Orel; Polyarny; Pzhev	5·25	5·25

2992 Church

2009. 1150th Anniv of the Veliky Novgorod. Sheet 105×77 mm.

MS7627	**2992**	50r. multicoloured	19·00	19·00

2993 Ermak Timofeevich

2009. History of Russian Cossacks. Sheet 160×100 mm containing T 2993 and similar vert designs. Multicoloured.

MS7628	10r.×3, Type **2993**; Semen Ivanovich Dezhnev; Matvei Ivanovich Platov	3·75	3·75

2994 Girls Headdress, Moscow Region

2009. 19th-century Headdresses and Hat. Multicoloured.

7629	9r. Type **2994**	1·00	1·00
7630	9r. Wedding headdress, mid 19th-century Nizhegorodskiy region	1·00	1·00
7631	9r. Woman's headdress, Yaroslavl region	1·00	1·00
7632	9r. Man's hat, Tver region	1·00	1·00

2995 Astrakhan Kremlin

2009. Kremlins. Multicoloured. Self-adhesive.

7633	1r. Type **2995**	35	35
7634	1r.50 Zaraisk	40	40
7635	2r. Kazan	70	70
7636	2r.50 Kolomna	90	90
7637	3r. Rostov	1·00	1·00
7638	4r. Nizhny Novgorod	1·10	1·10
7639	5r. Novgorod	1·20	1·20
7640	6r. Pskov	1·30	1·30
7641	10r. Moscow	1·50	1·50
7642	25r. Ryazan	3·50	3·50
7643	50r. Tobolsk	7·00	7·00
7644	100r. Tula	14·00	14·00

2996 WFP Emblem

2009. United Nations World Food Programme.

7645	**2996**	10r. multicoloured	1·25	1·25

2997 V. I. Istomin

2009. Birth Bicentenary of Vladimir Ivanovich Istomin (rear admiral and hero of Siege of Sevastopol).

7646	**2997**	10r. multicoloured	1·25	1·25

2998 Tyre Tracks over Traffic Sign

2009. Road Safety Campaign.
7647 **2998** 9r. multicoloured 1·00 1·00

2999 Award

2009. 75th Anniv of the Award of the Hero of Soviet Union. Gold Star.
7648 **2999** 9r. multicoloured 1·00 1·00

2999a Departmental Arms

2009. Bicentenary of Department of Transportation of Russia
7648a **2999a** 9r. multicoloured 1·00 1·00

3000 Empress Elizaveta

2009. 300th Birth Anniv of Empress Elizaveta Petrovna. Sheet 90×75 mm.
MS7649 **3000** 40r. multicoloured 5·00 5·00

3001 School Building

2009. Bicentenary of Mikhail Shchepkin Drama School
7649a **3001** 10r. multicoloured 1·25 1·25

3002 Researcher, Weather Equipment and Polar Vehicle

2009. 50th Anniv of Antarctic Treaty
7650 **3002** 15r. multicoloured 2·00 2·00

3003 Kremlin, Moscow enclosed in Snowflake

2009. Happy New Year
7651 **3003** 10r. multicoloured 1·25 1·25

3004 Arms, Transporter and Rocket

2009. 50th Anniv of Strategic Rocket Forces (Strategic Missile Troops) of the Russian Federation
7652 **3004** 9r. multicoloured 1·00 1·00

3005 Verkhnyaya Pyshma

2009. Fountains of Russia

7653	9r. Type **3005**	1·00	1·00
7654	10r. Nizhny Novgorod	1·25	1·25
7655	12r. Novy Urengoy (vert)	1·50	1·50
7656	15r. Yaroslavl	2·00	2·00

3006 Valentina Stepanovna Grizodubova (commander of flight of Rodina (Motherland), ANT-37 airplane, setting international women's record for straight-line distance flight)

2010. Birth Centenaries. Multicoloured.

7657	10r. Type **3006**	1·25	1·25
7658	10r. Anatoly Konstantinovich Serov (biplane fighter ace who took part in Spanish Civil War) and aircraft I-15	1·25	1·25

3007 Lady with Dog

2010. 150th Birth Anniv of Anton Pavlovich Chekhov (writer)

MS7659	127×70 mm. 8r. Type **3007**; 10r. *The Seagull*; 12r. *An Artist's Story* (The House with the Mezzanine)	3·50	3·50
MS7660	73×100 mm. 20r. Anton Chekhov (36×50 mm) (oval)	3·50	3·50

3008

2010. 50th Anniv of Peoples' Friendship University
7661 **3008** 10r. multicoloured 1·40 1·40

2010. Animals. Multicoloured.

7662	10k. As Type **2956** (hare)	10	10
7663	15k As Type **2956**	10	10
7664	25k. As Type **2956**	10	10
7665	30k. As No. 7544 (fox)	10	10
7666	50k. As No. 7544	10	10
7667	1r. As No. 7544	35	35
7668	1r.50 As No. 7547 (lynx)	40	40
7669	2r. As No. 7547	70	70
7670	2r.50 As No. 7547	90	90
7671	3r. As No. 7550 (elk)	1·00	1·00
7672	4r. As No. 7550	1·10	1·10
7673	5r. As No. 7550	1·20	1·20
7674	6r. As No. 7553 (bear)	1·30	1·30
7675	10r. As No. 7553	1·50	1·50
7676	25r. As No. 7553	3·50	3·50

3009 Games Emblem

2010. Winter Olympic Games, Vancouver
7677 **3009** 15r. multicoloured 2·00 2·00

3010 Prince Dmitry Mikhaylovich Golitsyn

2010. 275th Birth Anniv of Fyodor Stepanovich Rokotov (Fedor Rokotov) (artist). Multicoloured.

7678	10r.50 Type **3010**	1·40	1·40
7679	10r.50 *Countess Varvara Alekseyevna Musina–Pushkina*	1·40	1·40

2010. Regions of the Russian Federation (16th issue)

7680	10r.50 Cornfield, lace and dam, Orenburg region	1·50	1·50
7681	10r.50 Yaks and pewter clasp, Tuva Republic	1·50	1·50

Horiz designs as T **2651**.

3011 Polar Researcher, Aircraft, Research Station and Eugeny Feodorov

2010. Birth Centenary of Eugeny Feodorov (geophysicist)
7682 **3011** 12r. multicoloured 1·60 1·60

3012 Malgobek

2010. Town Emblems. Multicoloured.
MS7683 10r.×5 Type **3012**; Elnja; Elets; Voronev; Luga 7·25 7·25

3013 Tank BT-7M

2010. 65th Anniv of Second World War (1st issue). Multicoloured.

7684	9r. Type **3013**	1·10	1·10
7685	10r. Tank T-70	1·40	1·40
7686	11r. T-34-85	1·75	1·75
7687	12r. Tank IS-2	2·00	2·00

3014 Victory Order

2010. 65th Anniv of Second World War (2nd issue)
MS7688 **3014** 50r. multicoloured 7·75 7·75

3015 Boy reading

2010. Europa
7689 **3015** 10r.50 multicoloured 1·50 1·50

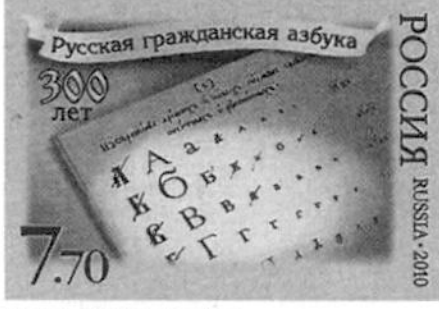

3016 Cyrillic Script

2010. 300th Anniv of Cyrillic Alphabet
7690 **3016** 7r.70 multicoloured 1·25 1·25

3017 Ivan Fyodorov (statue)

2010. 500th Birth Anniv of Ivan Fyodorov (Fedorovych) (Eastern Slavonic printing pioneer)
MS7691 **3017** 50r. multicoloured 7·75 7·75

3018 Wooden Pocket Watch (M.S. Bronnikov and Son) (early 1900)

2010. Science and Technology. Multicoloured.
MS7692 6r. Type **3018**; 9r. Victory wristwatch (1949); 12r. Shturmanskie wristwatch (1949); 15r. Gloriya wristwatch (1990) 6·00 6·00

3019 Self Portrait

2010. 275th Birth Anniv of Dmitry Lewitsky (artist). Multicoloured.

7693	10r.50 Type **3019**	1·50	1·50
7694	10r.50 *G.I. Alymova*	1·50	1·50

3020 Church and Archipelago

2010. Historical and Cultural Heritage, Valaam

MS7695	**3020**	25r. multicoloured	3·75	3·75

3021 Egyptian Gates

2010. 300th Anniv of Tsarskoe Selo (Pushkin)

MS7696 15r.×3, Type **3021**; A. S. Pushkin (statue) (vert); Aleksandrovsky Palace 6·50

3022 Archangel Mikhail (Andrey Rublev) (15th-century)

2010. Icons. Multicoloured.

7697		15r. Type **3022**	2·10	2·10
7698		15r. *Virgin Mary Odigitrija* (14th-century)	2·10	2·10

Stamps of a similar design were issued by Serbia.

3023 Coastline

2010. 150th Anniv of Vladivostok

7699	**3023**	15r. multicoloured	2·25	2·25

EXPRESS STAMPS

E171 Motor Cyclist

1932. Inscr "EXPRES".

E588	**E171**	5k. sepia	11·50	3·75
E589	-	10k. purple	17·00	6·75
E590	-	80k. green	44·00	18·00

DESIGNS—HORIZ: 10k. Express motor van; 80k. Class Ta steam locomotive.

E173 Polar Region and Kalinin K-4 Airplane over Ice-breaker "Taimyr"

1932. Air Express. 2nd Int Polar Year and Franz Joseph's Land to Archangel Flight.

E591	**E173**	50k. red	50·00	21·00
E592	**E173**	1r. green	£170	85·00

POSTAGE DUE STAMPS

Доплата
1 коп.
золотом.
(D96)

1924. Surch as Type D 96.

D401b	**45**	1k. on 35k. blue	70	75
D402b	**45**	3k. on 35k. blue	70	75
D403b	**45**	5k. on 35k. blue	70	75
D404	**45**	8k. on 35k. blue	1·30	75
D405b	**45**	10k. on 35k. blue	1·30	90
D406b	**45**	12k. on 70k. brown	85	75
D407c	**45**	14k. on 35k. blue	1·30	75
D408b	**45**	32k. on 35k. blue	1·30	1·30
D409c	**45**	40k. on 35k. blue	1·30	90

ДОПЛАТА
1 коп.
(D99)

1924. Optd with Type D 99.

D421	**48**	1k. on 100r. yellow	5·25	12·50

D104

1925

D464	**D104**	1k. red	60	1·50
D465	**D104**	2k. mauve	60	1·50
D466	**D104**	3k. blue	65	1·60
D467	**D104**	7k. yellow	70	1·60
D468	**D104**	8k. green	85	1·60
D469	**D104**	10k. blue	90	1·80
D470	**D104**	14k. brown	1·50	3·75

Pt. 17

RUSSIAN POST OFFICES IN CHINA

Russian Post Offices were opened in various towns in Manchuria and China from 1870 onwards.

1899. 100 kopeks = 1 rouble.
1917. 100 cents = 1 dollar (Chinese).

КИТАЙ
(1)

1899. Arms types (with thunderbolts) of Russia optd with T 1.

1	**9**	1k. orange	75	1·00
2	**9**	2k. green	75	1·00
3	**9**	3k. red	75	1·00
9	**14**	4k. red	2·00	2·50
4	**9**	5k. purple	75	1·00
5	**9**	7k. blue	1·50	2·50
6	**14**	10k. blue	1·50	2·50
30	**10**	14k. red and blue	85	75
31	**10**	15k. blue and brown	60	1·10
32	**14**	20k. red and blue	50	75
33	**10**	25k. violet and green	75	1·80
34	**10**	35k. green and purple	65	40
35	**14**	50k. green and purple	30	40
36	**10**	70k. orange and brown	30	55
37	**15**	1r. orange and brown	1·30	2·00
20	**11**	3r.50 grey and black	10·00	13·00
21	**20**	5r. blue and green on green	8·00	10·00
22	**11**	7r. yellow and black	15·00	10·00
23	**20**	10r. grey and red on yellow	75·00	75·00

1910. Arms types of Russia optd with T 1.

24	**22**	1k. orange	50	55
25	**22**	2k. green	50	55
26	**22**	3k. red	40	55
27	**23**	4k. red	50	40
28	**22**	7k. blue	50	55
29	**23**	10k. blue	50	40

1917. Arms types of Russia surch in "cents" and "dollars" diagonally in one line.

42	**22**	1c. on 1k. orange	75	5·50
43	**22**	2c. on 2k. green	75	5·50
44	**22**	3c. on 3k. red	75	5·50
45	**23**	4c. on 4k. red	1·60	4·25
46	**22**	5c. on 5k. lilac	1·60	15·00
47	**23**	10c. on 10k. blue	1·60	15·00
48	**10**	14c. on 14k. red and blue	1·60	10·00
49	**10**	15c. on 15k. blue and purple	1·60	15·00
50	**14**	20c. on 20k. red and blue	1·60	15·00
51	**10**	25c. on 25k. violet and green	1·60	15·00
52	**10**	35c. on 35k. green & purple	1·90	15·00
53	**14**	50c. on 50k. green & purple	1·60	18·00
54	**10**	70c. on 70k. orange & brn	1·60	16·00
55	**15**	1d. on 1r. orge & brn on brn	1·60	16·00
39	**10**	3d.50 on 3r.50 grey & blk	11·50	32·00
40	**20**	5d. on 5r. bl & dp bl on grn	11·50	32·00
41	**11**	7d. on 7r. yellow and black	11·00	32·00
57	**20**	10d. on 10r. grey and red on yellow	16·00	£120

1920. Arms types of Russia surch in "cents" in two lines. Perf or imperf.

65	**22**	1c. on 1k. orange	36·00	30·00
59	**22**	2c. on 2k. green	30·00	32·00
60	**22**	3c. on 3k. red	30·00	32·00
61	**23**	4c. on 4k. red	32·00	35·00
62	**22**	5c. on 5k. lilac	32·00	32·00
63	**23**	10c. on 10k. blue	£200	£150
64	**22**	10c. on 10k. on 7k. blue	£140	£120

Pt. 3

RUSSIAN POST OFFICE IN CRETE

4 metallik = 1 grosion (Turkish piastre)

(RETHYMNON PROVINCE)

The Russian Postal Service operated from 1 May to 29 July 1899.

These issues were optd with circular control marks as shown on Types R **3/4**. Prices are for stamps with these marks, but unused examples without them are known.

R1

R2

1899. Imperf.

R1	**R 1**	1m. blue	55·00	15·00
R2	**R 2**	1m. green	12·00	9·75
R3	**R 2**	2m. red	£250	£150
R4	**R 2**	2m. green	12·00	9·75

R3

1899. Without stars in oval.

R5	**R 3**	1m. pink	60·00	33·00
R6	**R 3**	2m. pink	60·00	33·00
R7	**R 3**	1g. pink	60·00	33·00
R8	**R 3**	1m. blue	60·00	33·00
R9	**R 3**	2m. blue	60·00	33·00
R10	**R 3**	1g. blue	60·00	33·00
R11	**R 3**	1m. green	60·00	33·00
R12	**R 3**	2m. green	60·00	33·00
R13	**R 3**	1g. green	60·00	33·00
R14	**R 3**	1m. red	60·00	33·00
R15	**R 3**	2m. red	60·00	33·00
R16	**R 3**	1g. red	60·00	33·00
R17	**R 3**	1m. orange	60·00	33·00
R18	**R 3**	2m. orange	60·00	33·00
R19	**R 3**	1g. orange	60·00	33·00
R20	**R 3**	1m. yellow	60·00	33·00
R21	**R 3**	2m. yellow	60·00	33·00
R22	**R 3**	1g. yellow	60·00	33·00
R23	**R 3**	1m. black		£600
R24	**R 3**	2m. black		£600
R25	**R 3**	1g. black		£600

R4

1899. Starred at each side.

R26	**R 4**	1m. pink	35·00	20·00
R27	**R 4**	2m. pink	15·00	9·75
R28	**R 4**	1g. pink	11·00	9·75
R29	**R 4**	1m. blue	23·00	13·00
R30	**R 4**	2m. blue	15·00	9·75
R31	**R 4**	1g. blue	11·00	8·50
R32	**R 4**	1m. green	17·00	13·00
R33	**R 4**	2m. green	15·00	9·75
R34	**R 4**	1g. green	11·00	8·50
R35	**R 4**	1m. red	20·00	13·00
R36	**R 4**	2m. red	15·00	9·75
R37	**R 4**	1g. red	11·00	8·50

Pt. 16

RUSSIAN POST OFFICES IN THE TURKISH EMPIRE

General issues for Russian P.O.'s in the Turkish Empire and stamps specially overprinted for use at particular offices.

1863. 100 kopeks = 1 rouble.
1900. 40 paras = 1 piastre.

1 Inscription = "Dispatch under Wrapper to the East"

1863. Imperf.

2a	**1**	6k. blue	£350	£2000

2

3

1865. Imperf.

4	**2**	(10pa.) brown and blue	£800	£650
5	**3**	(2pi.) blue and red	£1300	£800

4

5

1865. Imperf.

6	**4**	(10pa.) red and blue	40·00	65·00
7	**5**	(2pi.) blue and red	95·00	80·00

The values of 4/7 were 10pa. (or 2k.) and 2pi. (or 20k.).

6 Inscription = "Eastern Correspondence"

1868. Perf.

14	**6**	1k. brown	8·25	8·25
11	**6**	3k. green	33·00	24·00
16	**6**	5k. blue	8·25	4·00
17a	**6**	10k. red and green	95·00	10·00

See also Nos. 26/35.

1876. Surch with large figures of value.

24	7k. on 10k. red and green	£130	80·00
22	8k. on 10k. red and green	95·00	80·00

1879

26	1k. black and yellow	4·75	1·60
32	1k. orange	4·00	1·60
27	2k. black and red	8·25	2·40
33	2k. green	8·25	3·25
34	5k. purple	8·25	4·00
28	7k. red and grey	9·75	1·60
35	7k. blue	8·25	2·40

1900. Arms types of Russia surch in "PARA" or "PIASTRES".

37	9	4pa. on 1k. orange	10	10
50	22	5pa. on 1k. orange	10	10
38	9	10pa. on 2k. green	15	15
51	22	10pa. on 2k. green	10	10
201	22	15pa. on 3k. red	10	90
41	14	20pa. on 4k. red	25	15
52	23	20pa. on 4k. red	10	10
42	9	20pa. on 5k. purple	25	30
181	22	20pa. on 5k. purple	10	10
43	14	1pi. on 10k. blue	25	15
53	23	1pi. on 10k. blue	10	10
182	10	1½pi. on 15k. blue & purple	15	15
183	14	2pi. on 20k. red and blue	15	15
184	10	2½pi. on 25k. violet & green	15	15
185	10	3½pi. on 35k. green & pur	25	25
54	14	5pi. on 50k. green and lilac	25	40
55	10	7pi. on 70k. orange & brn	40	60
56	15	10pi. on 1r. orange and brown on brown	60	90
48	11	35pi. on 3r.50 grey & blk	6·50	6·50
202	20	50pi. on 5r. blue on green	4·00	£130
49	11	70pi. on 7r. yellow & black	11·50	11·50
203	20	100pi. on 10r. grey and red on yellow	16·00	£400

12

1909. As T 14, 15, and 11 of Russia, but ship and date in centre as T 12, and surch in "paras" or "piastres".

57	14	5pa. on 1k. orange	40	40
58	14	10pa. on 2k. green	60	60
59	14	20pa. on 4k. red	80	1·30
60	14	1pi. on 10k. blue	1·30	1·60
61	14	5pi. on 50k. green & purple	2·00	4·00
62	14	7pi. on 70k. orange & brn	4·00	6·00
63	15	10pi. on 1r. orange & brown	8·25	9·75
64	11	35pi. on 3r.50 green & pur	13·50	60·00
65	11	70pi. on 7r. pink and green	40·00	90·00

The above stamps exist overprinted for Constantinople, Jaffa, Jerusalem, Kerassunde, Mount Athos, Salonika, Smyrna, Trebizonde, Beyrouth, Dardanelles, Mytilene and Rizeh. For full list see Part 10 (Russia) of the Stanley Gibbons Catalogue.

1913. Nos. 126/42 (Romanov types) of Russia surch.

186	5pa. on 1k. orange	10	10
187	10pa. on 3k. green	10	10
188	15pa. on 3k. red	10	10
189	20pa. on 4k. red	10	10
190	1pi. on 10k. blue	15	15
191	1½pi. on 15k. brown	40	40
192	2pi. on 20k. green	40	40
193	2½pi. on 25k. purple	60	60
194	3½pi. on 35k. green and violet	1·30	1·30
195	5pi. on 50k. grey and brown	1·40	1·40
196	7pi. on 70k. brown and green	8·25	20·00
197	10pi. on 1r. green	9·75	20·00
198	20pi. on 2r. brown	6·00	8·25
199	30pi. on 3r. violet	8·25	£275
200	50pi. on 5r. brown	£130	£650

Pt. 14

RWANDA

An independent republic established in July 1962, formerly part of Ruanda-Urundi.

100 centimes = 1 franc.

1 Pres. Kayibanda and Map

1962. Independence.

1	1	10c. sepia and green	10	10
2	-	40c. sepia and purple	10	10
3	1	1f. sepia and blue	70	35
4	-	1f.50 sepia and brown	10	10
5	1	3f.50 sepia and orange	10	10
6	-	6f.50 sepia and blue	15	10
7	1	10f. sepia and olive	30	15
8	-	20f. sepia and red	60	30

DESIGN: Nos. 2, 4, 6, 8 are as Type **1** but with halo around Rwanda on map in place of "R".

1963. Admission to U.N. No. 204 of Ruanda-Urundi with coloured frame obliterating old inscr (colours below), and surch Admission a l'O.N.U. 18-9-1962 REPUBLIQUE RWANDAISE and new value.

9	3f.50 on 3f. grey	10	10
10	6f.50 on 3f. pink	1·10	90
11	10f. on 3f. blue	25	25
12	20f. on 3f. silver	40	40

1963. Flowers issue of Ruanda-Urundi (Nos. 178 etc) optd REPUBLIQUE RWANDAISE or surch also in various coloured panels over old inscription and values. Flowers in natural colours.

13	25c. orange and green	20	20
14	40c. salmon and green	20	20
15	60c. purple and green	20	20
16	1f.25 blue and green	90	90
17	1f.50 green and violet	90	90
18	2f. on 1f.50 green and violet	1·40	1·10
19	4f. on 1f.50 green and violet	1·40	1·10
20	5f. green and purple	1·40	1·10
21	7f. brown and green	1·40	1·10
22	10f. olive and purple	1·75	1·50

The coloured panels are in various shades of silver except No. 19 which is in blue.

4 Ears of Wheat and Native Implements

1963. Freedom from Hunger.

23	4	2f. brown and green	10	10
24	4	4f. mauve and blue	10	10
25	4	7f. red and grey	20	10
26	4	10f. green and yellow	75	55

5 Coffee

1963. 1st Anniv of Independence.

27	5	10c. brown and blue	10	10
28	-	20c. yellow and blue	10	10
29	-	30c. green and orange	10	10
30	5	40c. brown and turquoise	10	10
31	-	1f. yellow and purple	10	10
32	-	2f. green and blue	80	45
33	5	4f. brown and red	10	10
34	-	7f. yellow and green	20	15
35	-	10f. green and violet	35	30

DESIGNS: 20c., 1, 7f. Bananas; 30c., 2, 10f. Tea.

5a "Post and Telecommunications"

1963. 2nd Anniv of African and Malagasy Posts and Telcommunications Union.

36	5a	14f. multicoloured	1·10	90

6 Postal Services Emblem

1963. Admission of Rwanda to U.P.U.

37	6	50c. blue and pink	10	10
38	6	1f.50 brown and blue	65	45
39	6	3f. purple and grey	10	10
40	6	20f. green and yellow	45	20

7 Emblem

1963. 15th Anniv of Declaration of Human Rights.

41	7	5f. red	15	10
42	7	6f. violet	50	35
43	7	10f. blue	35	15

8 Child Care

1963. Red Cross Centenary.

44	8	10c. multicoloured	10	10
45	-	20c. multicoloured	10	10
46	-	30c. multicoloured	10	10
47	-	40c. brown, red and violet	10	10
48	8	2f. multicoloured	80	60
49	-	7f. multicoloured	15	10
50	-	10f. brown, red and brown	20	15
51	-	20f. brown, red and orange	60	35

DESIGNS—HORIZ: 20c., 7f. Patient having blood test; 40, 20c. Stretcher party. VERT: 30c., 10f. Doctor examining child.

9 Map and Hydraulic Pump

1964. World Meteorological Day.

52	9	3f. sepia, blue and green	10	10
53	9	7f. sepia, blue and red	35	20
54	9	10f. sepia, blue and orange	50	35
MS54a		72×52 mm. 25f. sepia, blue and lilac	3·25	3·25

1964. Stamps of Ruanda-Urundi optd REPUBLIQUE RWANDAISE or surch also in black over coloured metallic panels obliterating old inscription or value.

55	10c. on 20c. (No. 204)	10	10
56	20c. (No. 204)	10	10
57	30c. on 1f.50 (No. 208)	10	10
58	40c. (No. 205)	10	10
59	50c. (No. 206)	10	10
60	1f. (No. 207)	10	10
61	2f. (No. 209)	10	10
62	3f. (No. 210)	10	10
63	4f. on 3f.50 on 3f. (No. 228)	20	10
64	5f. (No. 211)	20	10
65	7f.50 on 6f.50 (No. 212)	45	15
66	8f. (No. 213)	4·50	2·25
67	10f. (No. 214)	65	20
68	20f. (No. 229)	1·10	45
69	50f. (No. 230)	2·10	85

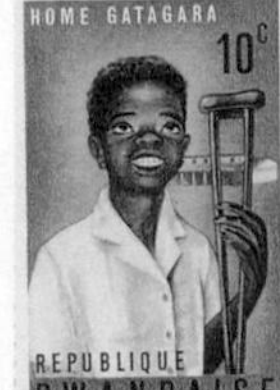

10 Boy with Crutch

1964. Gatagara Re-education Centre.

70	10	10c. sepia and violet	10	10
71	-	40c. sepia and blue	10	10
72	-	4f. sepia and brown	10	10
73	10	7f.50 sepia and green	35	15
74	-	8f. sepia and bistre	1·40	95
75	-	10f. sepia and purple	45	20

DESIGNS—HORIZ: 40c., 8f. Children operating sewing machines. VERT: 4, 10f. Crippled child on crutches.

11 Running

1964. Olympic Games, Tokyo. Sportsmen in slate.

76	11	10c. blue	10	10
77	-	20c. red	10	10
78	-	30c. turquoise	10	10
79	-	40c. brown	10	10
80	11	4f. blue	10	10
81	-	5f. green	1·40	1·25
82	-	20f. purple	35	35
83	-	50f. grey	1·10	90
MS83a		135×100 mm. Designs as Nos. 76/9. 10f. grey; 20f. green; 30f. green; 40f. blue	4·00	4·00

DESIGNS—VERT: 20c., 5f. Basketball; 40c., 50f. Football. HORIZ: 20f. High-jumping.

12 Faculties of "Letters" and "Sciences"

1965. National University. Multicoloured.

84	10c. Type **12**	10	10
85	20c. Student with microscope and building ("Medicine") (horiz)	10	10
86	30c. Scales of Justice, Hand of Law ("Social Sciences" and "Normal High School")	10	10
87	40c. University buildings (horiz)	10	10
88	5f. Type **12**	10	10
89	7f. As 20c.	15	10
90	10f. As 30c.	1·00	85
91	12f. As 40c.	30	15

13 Abraham Lincoln

1965. Death Centenary of Abraham Lincoln.

92	13	10c. green and red	10	10
93	13	20c. brown and blue	10	10
94	13	30c. violet and red	10	10
95	13	40c. blue and brown	10	10
96	13	9f. brown and purple	20	15
97	13	40f. purple and green	1·90	70
MS97a		65×77 mm 50f. purple and red	2·10	2·10

14 Marabou Storks

1965. Kagera National Park. Multicoloured.

98		10c. Type **14**	30	15
99		20c. Common zebras	10	10
100		30c. Impalas	10	10
101		40c. Crowned cranes, hippopotami and cattle egrets	30	15
102		1f. African buffaloes	10	10
103		3f. Hunting dogs	10	10
104		5f. Yellow baboons	4·25	1·10
105		10f. African elephant and map	20	15
106		40f. Reed cormorants and African darters	1·75	50
107		100f. Lions	2·25	50

SIZES—As Type **14**: VERT: 30c., 2, 5f. HORIZ: 20, 40c., 3, 10f. LARGER (45×25½ mm); 40, 100f.

15 "Telstar" Satellite

1965. Centenary of I.T.U. Multicoloured.

108		10c. Type **15**	10	10
109		40c. "Syncom" satellite	10	10
110		4f.50 Type **15**	1·40	50
111		50f. "Syncom" satellite	90	35
MS111a		89×65 mm. 60f. "UIT" on globe	2·25	2·25

16 "Colotis aurigineus"

1965. Rwanda Butterflies. Multicoloured.

112		10c. "Papilio bromius"	15	20
113		15c. "Papilio hesperus"	15	20
114		20c. Type **16**	15	20
115		30c. "Amphicallia pactolicus"	15	20
116		35c. "Lobobunaea phaedusa"	15	20
117		40c. "Papilio jacksoni ruandana"	15	20
118		1f.50 "Papilio dardanus"	15	20
119		3f. "Amaurina elliotti"	4·25	1·25
120		4f. "Colias electo pseudohecate"	2·75	1·00
121		10f. "Bunaea alcinoe"	55	30
122		50f. "Athletes gigas"	1·75	85
123		100f. "Charaxes ansorgei R"	3·50	1·25

The 10, 30, 35c., 3, 4 and 100f. are vert.

17 Cattle and I.C.Y. Emblem

1965. International Co-operation Year.

124	**17**	10c. green and yellow	10	10
125	-	40c. brown, blue and green	10	10
126	-	4f.50 green, brown & yell	1·10	50
127	-	45f. purple and brown	90	40

DESIGNS: 40c. Crater lake and giant plants; 4f.50, Gazelle and candelabra tree; 45f. Mt. Ruwenzori. Each with I.C.Y. emblem.

18 Pres. Kennedy, Globe and Satellites

1965. 2nd Anniv of Pres. Kennedy's Death.

128	**18**	10c. brown and green	10	10
129	**18**	40c. brown and red	10	10
130	**18**	50c. brown and blue	10	10
131	**18**	1f. brown and olive	10	10
132	**18**	8f. brown and violet	1·75	1·10
133	**18**	50f. brown and grey	1·10	90
MS133a		92×100 mm. 40f. sepia and orange; 60f. sepia and blue	7·50	7·50

19 Madonna and Child

1965. Christmas.

134	**19**	10c. green and gold	10	10
135	**19**	40c. brown and gold	10	10
136	**19**	50c. blue and gold	10	10
137	**19**	4f. black and gold	70	65
138	**19**	6f. violet and gold	15	10
139	**19**	30f. brown and gold	65	45

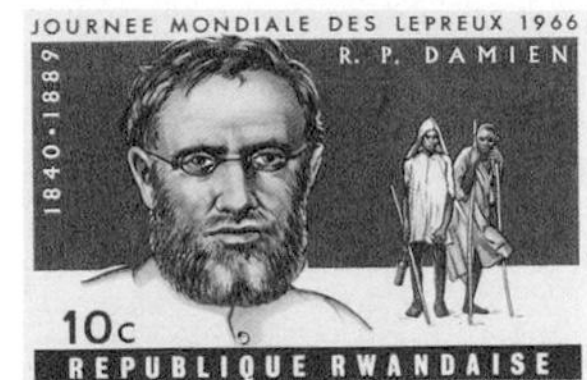

20 Father Damien

1966. World Leprosy Day.

140	**20**	10c. blue and brown	10	10
141	-	40c. red and blue	10	10
142	**20**	4f.50 slate and green	20	15
143	-	45f. brown and red	1·75	1·25

DESIGNS: 40c., 45f. Dr. Schweitzer.

21 Pope Paul, Rome and New York

1966. Pope Paul's Visit to U.N. Organization.

144	**21**	10c. blue and brown	10	10
145	-	40c. indigo and blue	10	10
146	**21**	4f.50 blue and purple	1·60	1·00
147	-	50f. blue and green	1·00	55

DESIGN: 40c., 50f. Pope Paul, Arms and U.N. emblem.

22 "Echinops amplexicaulis" and "E. bequaertii"

1966. Flowers. Multicoloured.

148		10c. Type **22**	10	10
149		20c. "Haemanthus multiflorus" (vert)	10	10
150		30c. "Helichrysum erici-rosenii"	10	10
151		40c. "Carissa edulis" (vert)	10	10
152		1f. "Spathodea campanulata" (vert)	10	10
153		3f. "Habenaria praestans" (vert)	10	10
154		5f. "Aloe lateritia" (vert)	4·50	2·25
155		10f. "Ammocharis tinneana" (vert)	30	20
156		40f. "Erythrina abyssinica"	1·10	75
157		100f. "Capparis tomentosa"	2·75	1·40
MS158		58×60 mm. No. 157	3·75	3·00

23 W.H.O. Building

1966. Inaug of W.H.O. Headquarters, Geneva.

159	**23**	2f. olive	10	10
160	**23**	3f. red	20	20
161	**23**	5f. blue	10	10

24 Football

1966. "Youth and Sports".

162	**24**	10c. black, blue and green	10	10
163	-	20c. black, green and red	10	10
164	-	30c. black, purple and blue	10	10
165	**24**	40c. black, green and bistre	10	10
166	-	9f. black, purple and grey	20	10
167	-	50f. black, blue and purple	1·10	1·00

DESIGNS: 20c., 9f. Basketball; 30c., 50f. Volleyball.

25 Mother and Child within Flames

1966. Nuclear Disarmament.

168	**25**	20c. brown, red and mauve	10	10
169	**25**	30c. brown, red and green	10	10
170	**25**	50c. brown, red and blue	10	10
171	**25**	6f. brown, red and yellow	10	10
172	**25**	15f. brown, red & turquoise	65	30
173	**25**	18f. brown, red and lavender	65	40

26 Football

1966. World Cup Football Championship.

174	**26**	20c. blue and turquoise	10	10
175	**26**	30c. blue and violet	10	10
176	**26**	50c. blue and green	10	10
177	**26**	6f. blue and mauve	20	10
178	**26**	12f. blue and brown	1·10	35
179	**26**	25f. indigo and blue	2·25	60

27 Yellow-crested Helmet Shrike and Mikeno Volcano

1966. Rwanda Scenery.

180	**27**	10c. green	30	10
181	-	40c. lake	10	10

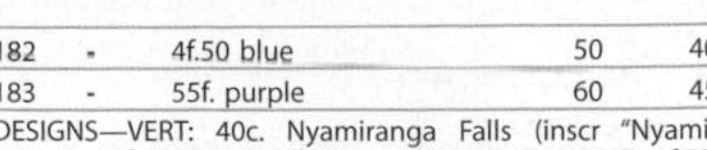

182	-	4f.50 blue	50	40
183	-	55f. purple	60	45

DESIGNS—VERT: 40c. Nyamiranga Falls (inscr "Nyamilanga"); 55f. Rusumo Falls (inscr "Rusumu"). HORIZ: 4f.50, Gahinga and Mahubura Volcanoes, and giant plants.

28 UNESCO and Cultural Emblems

1966. 20th Anniv of UNESCO.

184	**28**	20c. mauve and blue	10	10
185	-	30c. turquoise and black	10	10
186	-	50c. brown and black	10	10
187	-	1f. violet and black	10	10
188	**28**	5f. green and brown	10	10
189	-	10f. brown and black	15	10
190	-	15f. purple and blue	55	35
191	-	50f. blue and black	65	50

DESIGNS: 30c., 10f. "Animal" primer; 50c., 15f. Atomic symbol and drill operator; 1, 50f. Nubian monument partly submerged in the Nile.

29 "Bitis gabonica"

1967. Snakes. Multicoloured.

192		20c. Head of mamba	20	15
193		30c. Python (vert)	20	15
194		50c. Type **29**	20	15
195		1f. "Naja melanoleuca" (vert)	20	15
196		3f. Head of python	20	15
197		5f. "Psammophis sibilans" (vert)	45	15
198		20f. "Dendroaspis jamesoni kaimosae"	1·25	50
199		70f. "Dasypeltis scabra" (vert)	1·50	70

30 Girders and Tea Flower

1967. Ntaruka Hydro-electric Project.

200	**30**	20c. blue and purple	10	10
201	-	30c. brown and black	10	10
202	-	50c. violet and brown	10	10
203	**30**	4f. purple and green	10	10
204	-	25f. green and violet	50	50
205	-	50f. brown and blue	1·00	1·00

DESIGNS: 30c., 25f. Power conductors and pyrethrum flower; 50c., 50f. Barrage and coffee beans.

31 Cogwheel

1967. 7th Europa Stamp Exhibition, Naples. Two sheets each 90×67 mm.

MS206		(a) **31** 100f. brown on cream; (b) **31** 100f. purple on cream. Set of 2 sheets	4·25	4·25

32 Dancers

1967. "Expo 67" World Fair, Montreal (1st issue). Sheet 75×90 mm.

MS207	**32** 180f. violet	3·00	3·00

See also Nos. 222/9.

33 "St. Martin" (Van Dyck)

1967. Paintings.

208	**33**	20c. black, gold and violet	10	10
209	-	40c. black, gold and green	10	10
210	-	60c. black, gold and red	10	10
211	-	80c. black, gold and blue	10	10
212	**33**	9f. black, gold and brown	90	50
213	-	15f. black, gold and red	35	20
214	-	18f. black, gold and bronze	35	20
215	-	26f. black, gold and lake	45	45

PAINTINGS—HORIZ: 40c., 15f. "Rebecca and Eliezer" (Murillo); 80c., 26f. "Job and his Friends" (attributed to Il Calabrese). VERT: 60c., 18f. "St. Christopher" (D. Bouts).

34 Rwanda "Round Table" Emblem and Common Zebra's Head

1967. Rwanda "Round Table" Fund for Charitable Works. Each with "Round Table" Emblem. Mult.

216	20c. Type **34**	10	10
217	40c. African elephant's head	10	10
218	60c. African buffalo's head	10	10
219	80c. Impala's head	10	10
220	18f. Ear of wheat	35	15
221	100f. Palm	1·60	90

35 "Africa Place" and Dancers

1967. World Fair, Montreal.

222	**35**	20c. blue and sepia	10	10
223	-	30c. purple and sepia	10	10
224	-	50c. orange and sepia	10	10
225	-	1f. green and sepia	10	10
226	-	3f. violet and sepia	10	10
227	**35**	15f. green and sepia	15	15
228	-	34f. red and sepia	50	40
229	-	40f. turquoise and sepia	70	55

DESIGNS: "Africa Place" (two different views used alternately in order of value) and 30c., 3f. Drum and handicrafts; 50c., 40f. Dancers leaping; 1f., 34f. Spears, shields and weapons.

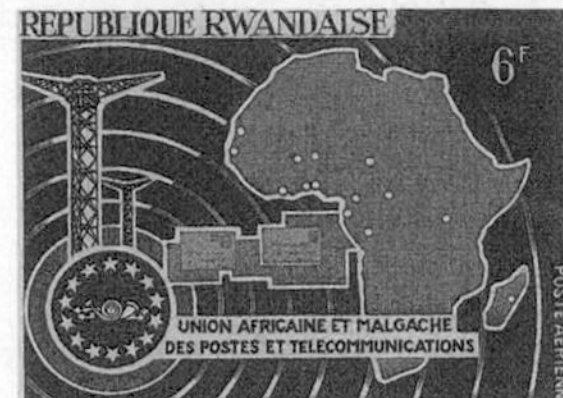

35a Map of Africa, Letters and Pylons

1967. Air. 5th Anniv of U.A.M.P.T.

230	**35a**	6f. slate, brown and lake	20	10
231	**35a**	18f. purple and brown	65	35
232	**35a**	30f. red, green and blue	1·10	65

36 Common Zebra's Head and Lion's Emblem

1967. 50th Anniv of Lions International.

233	**36**	20c. black, blue and violet	10	10
234	**36**	80c. black, blue and green	10	10
235	**36**	1f. black, blue and red	10	10
236	**36**	8f. black, blue and brown	20	10
237	**36**	10f. black, blue and ultramarine	30	20
238	**36**	50f. black, blue and green	1·40	95

37 Red Bishop

1967. Birds of Rwanda. Multicoloured.

239	20c. Type **37**	10	30
240	40c. Woodland kingfisher (horiz)	10	30
241	60c. Red-billed quelea	10	30
242	80c. Double-toothed barbet (horiz)	10	30
243	2f. Pin-tailed whydah	25	30
244	3f. Red-chested cuckoo (horiz)	35	30
245	18f. Green wood hoopoe	1·40	55
246	25f. Cinnamon-chested bee eater (horiz)	2·00	90
247	80f. Regal sunbird	4·50	2·50
248	100f. Fan-tailed whydah (horiz)	6·50	3·00

38 Ice Skating

1968. Winter Olympic Games, Grenoble. T 38 and similar vert designs in sheet 130×90 mm.

MS249	50f. black, blue and emerald (Type **38**); 50f. black, emerald and blue (Ski-jumping)	1·90	1·90

39 Running, and Mexican Antiquities

1968. Olympic Games, Mexico (1st issue). Mult.

250	20c. Type **39**	35	10
251	40c. Hammer-throwing	35	10
252	60c. Hurdling	35	10
253	80c. Javelin-throwing	35	10
254	8f. Football (vert)	45	10
255	10f. Mexican horseman and cacti (vert)	45	10
256	12f. Hockey (vert)	55	10
257	18f. Cathedral (vert)	70	15
258	20f. Boxing (vert)	90	55
259	30f. Mexico City (vert)	1·10	65

The 20c. to 80c. include Mexican antiquities in their designs.

40 Dr. Martin Luther King

1968. Martin Luther King Commemoration. Miniature sheet 81×81 mm.

MS260	**40** 100f. brown	1·90	1·40

41 "Diaphananthe fragrantissima"

1968. Flowers. Multicoloured.

261	20c. Type **41**	10	10
262	40c. "Phaeomeria speciosa"	10	10
263	60c. "Ravenala madagascariensis"	10	10
264	80c. "Costus afer"	10	10
265	2f. Banana flowers	10	10
266	3f. Flowers and young fruit of pawpaw	10	10
267	18f. "Clerodendron sp."	35	15
268	25f. Sweet potato flowers	45	30
269	80f. Baobab flower	1·90	80
270	100f. Passion flower	2·25	1·25

42 Horse-jumping

1966. Olympic Games, Mexico (2nd issue).

271	**42**	20c. brown and orange	10	10
272	-	40c. brown and turquoise	10	10
273	-	60c. brown and purple	10	10
274	-	80c. brown and blue	10	10
275	-	38f. brown and red	50	40
276	-	60f. brown and green	1·10	65

SPORTS: 40c. Judo; 60c. Fencing; 80c. High-jumping; 38f. High-diving; 60f. Weightlifting. Each design also represents the location of previous Olympics as at left in Type **42**.

43 Tuareg (Algeria)

1968. African National Costumes (1st series). Mult.

277	30c. Type **43**	10	10
278	40c. Upper Volta	10	10
279	60c. Senegal	10	10
280	70c. Rwanda	10	10
281	8f. Morocco	10	10
282	20f. Nigeria	35	20
283	40f. Zambia	80	35
284	50f. Kenya	1·10	55

See also Nos. 345/52.

44 "The Nativity" (G. Barbarelli (Giorgione))

1968. Christmas. Miniature sheet 86×86 mm.

MS285	**44** 100f.green	1·90	1·90

For annual Christmas miniature sheets see Nos. **MS**319, **MS**399, **MS**433, **MS**506, **MS**579, **MS**628, **MS**718, **MS**792 and **MS**850.

44a "Alexandre Lenoir" (J. L. David)

1968. Air. "Philexafrique" Stamp Exhibition, Abidjan (Ivory Coast, 1969) (1st issue).

286	**44a**	100f. multicoloured	2·50	1·60

45 Rwanda Scene and Stamp of Ruanda-Urundi (1953)

1969. Air. "Philexafrique" Stamp Exn (2nd issue).

287	**45**	50f. multicoloured	1·90	1·25

46 "The Musical Angels" (Van Eyck)

1969. "Paintings and Music". Multicoloured.

288	20c. Type **46** (postage)	10	10
289	40c. "The Angels' Concert" (M. Grunewald)	10	10
290	60c. "The Singing Boy" (Frans Hals)	10	10
291	80c. "The Lute player" (G. Terborch)	10	10
292	2f. "The Fifer" (Manet)	10	10
293	6f. "Young Girls at the Piano" (Renoir)	15	10
294	50f. "The Music Lesson" (Fragonard) (air)	1·40	85
295	100f. "Angels playing their Musical Instruments" (Memling) (horiz)	2·75	1·60
MS296	Two sheets 90×80 mm. Each 75f. Designs as (a) 60c. and (b) 6f. Pair	4·00	4·00

47 Tuareg Tribesmen

1969. African Headdresses (1st series). Mult.

297	20c. Type **47**	10	10
298	40c. Young Ovambo woman	10	10
299	60c. Ancient Guinean and Middle Congo festival head-dresses	10	10
300	80c. Guinean "Dagger" dancer	10	10
301	8f. Nigerian Muslims	10	10
302	20f. Luba dancer, Kabondo (Congo)	40	20
303	40f. Senegalese and Gambian women	85	45
304	80f. Rwanda dancer	1·25	1·00

See also Nos. 408/15.

48 "The Moneylender and his Wife" (Quentin Metsys)

1969. 5th Anniv of African Development Bank.

305	**48**	30f. multicoloured on silver	55	50
306	-	70f. multicoloured on gold	1·60	1·40

DESIGN: 70f. "The Moneylender and his Wife" (Van Reymerswaele).

49 Astronaut with Camera

1969. 1st Man on the Moon. Miniature sheet 96×110 mm.

MS307 **49** 100f. blue	2·25	2·25

See also No. **MS**417.

50 Pyrethrum

1969. Medicinal Plants. Multicoloured.

308	20c. Type **50**	10	10
309	40c. Aloes	10	10
310	60c. Cola	10	10
311	80c. Coca	10	10
312	3f. Hagenia	10	10
313	75f. Cassia	1·40	80
314	80f. Cinchona	2·25	90
315	100f. Tephrosia	2·50	1·10

51 Revolutionary

1969. 10th Anniv of Revolution.

316	**51**	6f. multicoloured	15	10
317	**51**	18f. multicoloured	50	45
318	**51**	40f. multicoloured	1·00	95

52 "The Holy Night" (Correggio)

1969. Christmas. Miniature sheet 85×85 mm.

MS319 **52** 100f. ultramarine	2·10	2·10

53 "Napoleon on Horseback" (David)

1969. Birth Bicent of Napoleon Bonaparte. Mult. Portraits of Napoleon. Artist's name given.

320	20c. Type **53**	10	10
321	40c. Debret	10	10
322	60c. Gautherot	10	10
323	80c. Ingres	10	10
324	8f. Pajou	20	15
325	20f. Gros	55	40
326	40f. Gros	1·00	55
327	80f. David	2·25	1·25

54 "The Quarryman" (O. Bonnevalle)

1969. 50th Anniv of I.L.O. Multicoloured.

328	20c. Type **54**	10	10
329	40c. "Ploughing" (detail Brueghel's "Descent of Icarus")	10	10
330	60c. "The Fisherman" (C. Meunier)	10	10
331	80c. "Ostend Slipway" (J. van Noten)	10	10
332	8f. "The Cook" (P. Aertsen)	20	10
333	10f. "Vulcan's Blacksmiths" (Velazquez)	35	15
334	50f. "Hiercheuse" (C. Meunier)	1·25	60
335	70f. "The Miner" (P. Paulus)	1·60	80

Nos. 330, 332 and 334/5 are vert.

55 "The Derby at Epsom" (Gericault)

1970. Paintings of Horses. Multicoloured.

336	20c. Type **55**	10	10
337	40c. "Horses leaving the Sea" (Delacroix)	10	10
338	60c. "Charles V at Muhlberg" (Titian) (vert)	10	10
339	80c. "To the Races, Amateur Jockeys" (Degas)	10	10
340	8f. "Horsemen at Rest" (Wouwermans)	20	10
341	20f. "Officer of the Imperial Guard" (Gericault) (vert)	60	30
342	40f. "Horse and Dromedary" (Bonnevalle)	1·50	45
343	80f. "The Prodigal Child" (Rubens)	2·00	80

56 "The Fleet in the Bay of Naples" (Brueghel)

1970. 10th "Europa" Stamp Exhibition, Naples. Miniature sheet 110×96 mm.

MS344 **56** 100f. purple

1970. African National Costumes (2nd series). As T 43. Multicoloured.

345	20c. Tharaka Meru woman	10	10
346	30c. Niger flautist	10	10
347	50c. Tunisian water-carrier	10	10
348	1f. Kano ceremonial (Nigeria)	10	10
349	3f. Mali troubador	10	10
350	5f. Quipongo, Angola women	10	10
351	50f. Mauritanian at prayer	95	55
352	90f. Sinehatiali dancers, Ivory Coast	2·00	1·00

58 Footballer attacking Goal

1970. World Cup Football Championship, Mexico.

353	**58**	20c. multicoloured	10	10
354	-	30c. multicoloured	10	10
355	-	50c. multicoloured	10	10
356	-	1f. multicoloured	10	10
357	-	6f. multicoloured	10	10
358	-	18f. multicoloured	45	30
359	-	30f. multicoloured	85	45
360	-	90f. multicoloured	2·00	95

Nos. 354/60 show footballers in various positions, similar to Type **58**.

59 Flowers and Green Peafowl

1970. "EXPO 70", World Fair, Osaka, Japan. Mult.

361	20c. Type **59**	60	10
362	30c. Torii gate and "Hibiscus" (Yashuda)	10	10
363	50c. Dancer and "Musician" (Katayama)	10	10
364	1f. Sun Tower and "Warrior"	10	10
365	3f. House and "Seated Buddha"	10	10
366	5f. Pagoda and "Head of Girl" (Yamakawa)	10	10
367	20f. Greeting and "Imperial Palace"	55	35
368	70f. Expo emblem and "Horseman"	1·60	90

60 Two Young Gorillas

1970. Gorillas of the Mountains.

369	**60**	20c. black and green	35	35
370	-	40c. black, brown & purple	35	35
371	-	60c. black, blue and brown	35	35
372	-	80c. black, orange & brown	35	35
373	-	1f. black and mauve	35	35
374	-	2f. multicoloured	35	35
375	-	15f. black and sepia	70	45
376	-	100f. black, brown and blue	3·75	2·25

GORILLA—VERT: 40c. Squatting; 80c. Beating chest; 2f. Eating banana; 100f. With young. HORIZ: 60c. Walking; 1f. With family; 15f. Heads.

61 Cinchona Bark

1970. 150th Anniv of Discovery of Quinine. Mult.

377	20c. Type **61**	10	10
378	80c. Pharmaceutical equipment	10	10
379	1f. Anopheles mosquito	10	10
380	3f. Malaria patient and nurse	10	10
381	25f. "Attack" on mosquito	55	35
382	70f. Pelletier and Caventou (discoverers of quinine)	1·50	80

62 Rocket in Flight

1970. Moon Missions. Multicoloured.

383	20c. Type **62**	10	10
384	30c. Separation during orbit	10	10
385	50c. Spaceship above the moon	10	10
386	1f. Module and astonauts on moon	10	10
387	3f. Take-off from the moon	10	10
388	5f. Return journey to earth	15	10
389	10f. Final separation before landing	30	15
390	80f. Splashdown	2·25	1·40

63 F. D. Roosevelt and "Brasscattleya olympia alba"

1970. 25th Death Anniv of F. D. Roosevelt. Portraits and Orchids.

391	**63**	20c. brown, blue and black	10	10
392	-	30c. brown, red and black	10	10
393	-	50c. brown, orange & black	10	10
394	-	1f. brown, green and black	10	10
395	-	2f. green, brown and black	10	10
396	-	6f. green, purple and black	20	15
397	-	30f. green, blue and black	1·25	40
398	-	60f. green, red and black	2·00	70

ORCHIDS: 30c. "Laeliocattleya callistoglossa"; 50c. "Chondrorhyncha chestertoni"; 1f. "Paphiopedilum"; 2f. "Cymbidium hybride"; 6f. "Cattleya labiata"; 30f. "Dendrobium nobile"; 60f. "Laelia gouldiana".

1970. Christmas. Miniature sheet 72×85 mm containing single stamp as T 52 but vert.

MS399 100f. blue DESIGN: "Adoration of the Shepherds" (Juan de Ribera)	2·10	2·10

65 Pope Paul VI

1970. Centenary of 1st Vatican Council.

400	**65**	10c. brown and gold	10	10
401	-	20c. green and gold	10	10
402	-	30c. lake and gold	10	10
403	-	40c. blue and gold	10	10
404	-	1f. violet and gold	10	10
405	-	18f. purple and gold	50	20
406	-	20f. orange and gold	60	20
407	-	60f. brown and gold	1·60	70

POPES: 20c. John XXIII; 30c. Pius XII; 40c. Pius XI; 1f. Benedict XV; 18f. Pius X; 20f. Leo XIII; 60f. Pius IX.

1971. African Headdresses (2nd series). Mult. As T 47.

408	20c. Rendille woman	10	10
409	30c. Chad woman	10	10
410	50c. Bororo man (Niger)	10	10
411	1f. Masai man (Kenya)	10	10
412	5f. Air girl (Niger)	10	10
413	18f. Rwanda woman	35	20
414	25f. Mauritania man	65	35
415	50f. Rwanda girls	1·50	65

66 General de Gaulle

1971. De Gaulle Commemoration. Miniature sheet 70×80 mm.

MS416	**66** 100f. blue	2·75	1·75

1971. Moon Mission of Apollo 14. As No. MS307 but colour changed and additionally inscr "APOLLO 14".

MS417	**49** 100f. brown and red	3·75	3·75

68 "Beethoven" (C. Horneman)

1971. Birth Cent (1970) of Beethoven. Portraits and funeral scene by various artists. Mult.

418	20c. Type **68**	10	10
419	30c. K. Stieler	10	10
420	50c. F. Schimon	10	10
421	3f. H. Best	10	10
422	6f. W. Fassbender	30	10
423	90f. "Beethoven's Burial" (Stober)	2·10	2·00

69 Horse-jumping

1971. Olympic Games, Munich (1972) (1st issue).

424	**69**	20c. gold and black	10	10
425	-	30c. gold and purple	10	10
426	-	50c. gold and violet	10	10
427	-	1f. gold and green	10	10
428	-	8f. gold and red	20	10
429	-	10f. gold and violet	30	15
430	-	20f. gold and brown	50	30
431	-	60f. gold and green	1·40	65

DESIGNS: 30c. Running (start); 50c. Basketball; 1f. High-jumping; 8f. Boxing; 10f. Pole-vaulting; 20f. Wrestling; 60f. Gymnastics.

See also Nos. 490/7.

70 U.A.M.P.T. H.Q. and Rwandaise Woman and Child

1971. Air. 10th Anniv of U.A.M.P.T.

432	**70**	100f. multicoloured	2·10	2·00

1971. Christmas. Miniature sheet 63×84 mm containing single stamp as T 52, but vert.

MS433	100f. blue	2·10	2·10

DESIGN: "The Nativity" (Van Dyck).

72 "Durer" (self-portrait)

1971. 500th Birth Anniv of Durer. Paintings. Multicoloured.

434	20c. "Adam"	10	10
435	30c. "Eve"	10	10
436	50c. "Portrait of H. Holzschuher"	10	10
437	1f. "Mourning the Dead Christ"	10	10
438	3f. "Madonna and Child"	10	10
439	5f. "St. Eustace"	10	10
440	20f. "St. Paul and St. Mark"	45	30
441	70f. Type **72**	1·60	1·00

73 Astronauts in Moon Rover

1972. Moon Mission of "Apollo 15".

442	**73**	600f. gold	95·00	

74 Participation in Sport

1972. National Guard. Multicoloured.

443	4f. Type **74**	10	10
444	6f. Transport of emergency supplies	15	10
445	15f. Helicopter transport for the sick	40	20
446	25f. Participation in health service	65	35
447	50f. Guard, map and emblem (vert)	1·25	1·10

75 Ice Hockey

1972. Winter Olympic Games, Sapporo, Japan. Multicoloured.

448	20c. Type **75**	10	10
449	30c. Speed-skating	10	10
450	50c. Ski-jumping	10	10
451	1f. Figure skating	10	10
452	6f. Cross-country skiing	10	10
453	12f. Slalom	15	15
454	20f. Tobogganing	45	20
455	60f. Downhill skiing	1·40	1·10

76 Savanna Monkey and Impala

1972. Akagera National Park. Multicoloured.

456	20c. Type **76**	15	10
457	30c. African buffalo	15	10
458	50c. Common zebra	15	10
459	1f. White rhinoceros	40	40
460	2f. Warthogs	15	10
461	6f. Hippopotamus	20	10
462	18f. Spotted hyenas	40	20
463	32f. Helmeted guineafowl	2·25	95
464	60f. Waterbucks	2·00	1·10
465	80f. Lion and lioness	2·75	1·75

77 Family supporting Flag

1972. 10th Anniv of Referendum.

466	**77**	6f. multicoloured	10	10
467	**77**	18f. multicoloured	45	35
468	**77**	60f. multicoloured	1·25	1·10

78 Variable Sunbirds

1972. Rwanda Birds. Multicoloured.

469	20c. Common waxbills	10	10
470	30c. Collared sunbird	15	10
471	50c. Type **78**	20	10
472	1f. Greater double-collared sunbird	30	10
473	4f. Ruwenzori puff-back flycatcher	35	15
474	6f. Red-billed fire finch	40	20
475	10f. Scarlet-chested sunbird	70	20
476	18f. Red-headed quelea	1·50	40
477	60f. Black-headed gonolek	4·75	1·50
478	100f. African golden oriole	8·00	2·40

79 King Baudouin and Queen Fabiola with President and Mrs. Kayibanda in Rwanda

1972. "Belgica 72" Stamp Exhibition, Brussels.

479	-	18f. multicoloured	70	70
480	-	22f. multicoloured	90	90
481	**79**	40f. blue, black and gold	1·75	1·75

DESIGNS: 18f. Rwanda village; 22f. View of Bruges. Nos. 479/80 are smaller, size 39×36 mm.

80 Announcement of Independence

1972. 10th Anniv of Independence.

482	**80**	20c. green and gold	10	10
483	-	30c. purple and gold	10	10
484	-	50c. sepia and gold	10	10
485	-	6f. blue and gold	10	10
486	-	10f. purple and gold	15	10
487	-	15f. blue and gold	35	20
488	-	18f. brown and gold	45	30
489	-	50f. green and gold	1·10	70

DESIGNS—HORIZ: 30c. Promotion ceremony, officers of the National Guard; 50c. Pres. Kayibanda, wife and family; 6f. Pres. Kayibanda casting vote in legislative elections; 10f. Pres. and Mrs. Kayibanda at "Festival of Justice"; 15f. President and members of National Assembly; 18f. Investiture of Pres. Kayibanda. VERT: 50f. President Kayibanda.

81 Horse-jumping

1972. Olympic Games, Munich (2nd issue).

490	**81**	20c. green and gold	10	10
491	-	30c. violet and gold	10	10
492	-	50c. green and gold	10	10
493	-	1f. purple and gold	10	10
494	-	6f. black and gold	10	10
495	-	18f. brown and gold	35	30
496	-	30f. violet and gold	80	55
497	-	44f. blue and gold	1·10	65

DESIGNS: 30c. Hockey; 50c. Football; 1f. Long-jumping; 6f. Cycling; 18f. Yachting; 30f. Hurdling; 44f. Gymnastics.

82 Runners

1972. Racial Equality Year. "Working Together". Multicoloured.

498	20c. Type **82**	10	10
499	30c. Musicians	10	10
500	50c. Ballet dancers	10	10
501	1f. Medical team in operating theatre	10	10
502	6f. Weaver and painter	10	10
503	18f. Children in class	35	20
504	24f. Laboratory technicians	55	35
505	50f. U.N. emblem and hands of four races	1·00	65

1972. Christmas. Miniature sheet 91×107 mm containing single stamp as T 52, but vert. Perf or imperf.

MS506	100f. brown	2·10	2·10

DESIGN: "Adoration of the Shepherds" (J. Jordaens).

84 "Phymateus brunneri"

1973. Rwanda Insects. Multicoloured.

507	20c. Type **84**	10	10
508	30c. "Diopsis fumipennis" (vert)	10	10
509	50c. "Kitoko alberti"	10	10
510	1f. "Archibracon fasciatus" (vert)	10	10
511	2f. "Ornithacris cyanea imperialis"	10	10
512	6f. "Clitodaca fenestralis" (vert)	15	10
513	18f. "Senaspis oesacus"	40	20
514	22f. "Phonoctonus grandis" (vert)	55	35
515	70f. "Loba leopardina"	2·25	2·40
516	100f. "Ceratocoris distortus" (vert)	4·00	3·10
MS517	101×80 mm. 80f. "Phymateus brunneri" (size 44×35 mm)	3·50	3·50

85 "Emile Zola" (Manet)

1973. International Book Year. "Readers and Writers". Paintings and portraits. Multicoloured.

518	20c. Type **85**	10	10
519	30c. "Rembrandt's Mother" (Rembrandt)	10	10
520	50c. "St. Jerome removing Thorn from Lion's paw" (Colantonio)	10	10
521	1f. "St. Peter and St. Paul" (El Greco)	10	10
522	2f. "Virgin and Child" (Van der Weyden)	10	10
523	6f. "St. Jerome in his Cell" (Antonella de Messina)	15	10
524	40f. "St. Barbara" (Master of Flemalle)	1·00	60
525	100f. "Don Quixote" (O. Bonnevalle)	2·40	1·90
MS526	70×80 mm. 100f. Pres. Kayibanda	1·90	1·75

86 Longombe

1973. Musical Instruments. Multicoloured.

527	20c. Type **86**	10	10
528	30c. Horn	10	10
529	50c. "Xylophone"	10	10
530	1f. "Harp"	10	10
531	4f. Alur horns	10	10
532	6f. Horn, bells and drum	10	10
533	18f. Drums	40	40
534	90f. Gourds	2·00	1·40

87 "Rubens and Isabelle Brandt" (Rubens)

1973. "IBRA" Stamp Exhibition, Munich. Famous Paintings. Multicoloured.

535	20c. Type **87**	10	10
536	30c. "Portrait of a Lady" (Cranach the Younger)	10	10
537	50c. "Woman peeling Turnips" (Chardin)	10	10
538	1f. "Abduction of the Daughters of Leucippe" (Rubens)	10	10
539	2f. "Virgin and Child" (Lippi)	10	10
540	6f. "Boys eating Fruit" (Murillo)	20	10
541	40f. "The Sickness of Love" (Steen)	90	45
542	100f. "Jesus divested of His Garments" (El Greco)	2·25	1·40
MS543	75×90 mm. 100f. "Oswalt Krel" (Durer)	2·00	1·75

88 Map of Africa and Doves

1973. 10th Anniv of O.A.U. Multicoloured.

544	6f. Type **88**	20	10
545	94f. Map of Africa and hands	2·25	1·90

1973. Pan-African Drought Relief. Nos. 308/13 and 315 optd SECHERESSE SOLIDARITE AFRICAINE and No. 315 additionally surch.

546	**50**	20c. multicoloured	10	10
547	-	40c. multicoloured	10	10
548	-	60c. multicoloured	10	10
549	-	80c. multicoloured	10	10
550	-	3f. multicoloured	10	10
551	-	75f. multicoloured	1·60	1·40
552	-	100f.+50f. multicoloured	5·00	4·00

90 Six-banded Distichodus

1973. Fishes. Multicoloured.

553	20c. Type **90**	10	10
554	30c. Lesser tigerfish	10	10
555	50c. Angel squeaker	10	10
556	1f. Nile mouthbrooder	10	10
557	2f. African lungfish	15	10
558	6f. Mandeville's catfish	35	10
559	40f. Congo tetra	1·90	95
560	150f. Golden julie	6·25	3·50
MS561	90×70 mm **90** 100f.	4·00	4·00

91 Crane with Letter and Telecommunications Emblem

1973. 12th Anniv of U.A.M.P.T.

562	**91**	100f. blue, brown and mauve	2·50	1·90

1973. African Fortnight, Brussels. Nos. 408/15 optd QUINZAINE AFRICAINE BRUXELLES 15/30 SEPT. 1973 and globe.

563	20c. multicoloured	10	10
564	30c. multicoloured	10	10
565	50c. multicoloured	10	10
566	1f. multicoloured	10	10
567	5f. multicoloured	10	10
568	18f. multicoloured	40	20
569	25f. multicoloured	50	45
570	50f. multicoloured	1·40	85

1973. Air. Congress of French-speaking Nations, Liege. No. 432 optd LIEGE ACCUEILLE LES PAYS DE LANGUE FRANCAISE 1973 (No. 562) or congress emblem (No. 563).

571	100f. multicoloured	4·00	2·75
572	100f. multicoloured	4·00	2·75

1973. 13th Europa Stamp Exhibition, Naples. No. MS344 optd NAPLES 1973.

MS573	**56** 100f. purple	2·00	1·90

1973. 25th Anniv of Declaration of Human Rights. Nos. 443/7 optd with Human Rights emblem.

574	**74**	4f. multicoloured	10	10
575	-	6f. multicoloured	10	10
576	-	15f. multicoloured	30	15
577	-	25f. multicoloured	60	40
578	-	50f. multicoloured	1·40	95

1973. Christmas. Miniature sheet 102×87 mm containing single stamp as T 52.

MS579	100f. violet	2·00	1·90

DESIGN: "Adoration of the Shepherds" (Giido Reni)

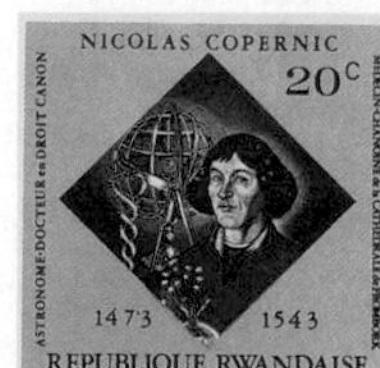

96 Copernicus and Astrolabe

1973. 500th Birth Anniv of Copernicus. Mult.

580	20c. Type **96**	10	10
581	30c. Copernicus	10	10
582	50c. Copernicus and heliocentric system	10	10
583	1f. Type **96**	10	10
584	18f. As 30c.	65	60
585	80f. As 50c.	2·40	2·00
MS586	75×81 mm. 100f. As 30c	2·40	2·25

97 Pres. Habyarimana

1974. "New Regime".

587	**97**	1f. brown, black and buff	10	10
588	**97**	2f. brown, black and blue	10	10
589	**97**	5f. brown, black and red	10	10
590	**97**	6f. brown, black and blue	10	10
591	**97**	26f. brown, black and lilac	55	45
592	**97**	60f. brown, black and green	1·25	1·00

98 "Christ between the Two Thieves" (Rubens)

1974. Easter. Miniature sheet 92×77 mm.

MS593	**98** 100f. sepia	4·50	4·50

99 Yugoslavia v Zaire

1974. World Cup Football Championship, West Germany. Players represent specified teams. Mult.

594	20c. Type **99**	10	10
595	40c. Netherlands v Sweden	10	10
596	60c. West Germany v Australia	10	10
597	80c. Haiti v Argentina	10	10
598	2f. Brazil v Scotland	10	10
599	6f. Bulgaria v Uruguay	10	10
600	40f. Italy v Poland	80	65
601	50f. Chile v East Germany	1·40	1·00

100 Marconi's Steam Yacht "Elettra"

1974. Birth Centenary of Guglielmo Marconi (radio pioneer). Multicoloured.

602	20c. Type **100**	20	10
603	30c. Cruiser "Carlo Alberto"	20	10
604	50c. Marconi's telegraph equipment	10	10
605	4f. "Global Telecommunications"	10	10
606	35f. Early radio receiver	85	45
607	60f. Marconi and Poldhu radio station	1·50	1·10
MS608	95×70 mm. 50f. Type **100**	1·40	1·40

101 "Diane de Poiters" (Fontainebleau School)

1974. International Stamp Exhibitions "Stockholmia" and "Internaba". Paintings from Stockholm and Basle. Multicoloured.

609	20c. Type **101**	10	10
610	30c. "The Flute-player" (J. Leyster)	10	10
611	50c. "Virgin Mary and Child" (G. David)	10	10
612	1f. "The Triumph of Venus" (F. Boucher)	10	10
613	10f. "Harlequin Seated" (P. Picasso)	15	10
614	18f. "Virgin and Child" (15th-century)	35	15
615	20f. "The Beheading of St. John" (H. Fries)	45	35
616	50f. "The Daughter of Andersdotter" (J. Hockert)	1·40	1·00
MS617	Six sheets each 86×73 mm. Each sheet contains two designs as Nos. 609/16 but with face values of 15f. for each stamp. Designs as Nos. 609, 611, 612 and 514 occur twice in the set of six stamps	4·50	4·50
MS618	One sheet 86×117 mm. As Nos. 610, 612, 614 and 616 but each stamp with a face value of 25f	1·80	1·80

102 Monastic Messenger

1974. Centenary of U.P.U. Multicoloured.

619	20c. Type **102**	10	10
620	30c. Inca messenger	10	10
621	50c. Moroccan postman	10	10
622	1f. Indian postman	10	10
623	18f. Polynesian postman	55	40
624	80f. Early Rwanda messenger with horn and drum	2·00	1·40

1974. 15th Anniv of Revolution. Nos. 316/18 optd 1974 15e ANNIVERSAIRE.

625	**51**	6f. multicoloured		
626	**51**	18f. multicoloured		
627	**51**	40f. multicoloured		

1974. Christmas. Miniature sheet 106×90 mm containing single stamp as T 52.

MS628	100f. green	3·25	3·25

DESIGN: "Adoration of the Magi"

1974. 10th Anniv of African Development Bank. Nos. 305/6 optd 1974 10e ANNIVERSAIRE.

629	**48**	30f. multicoloured	85	65
630	-	70f. multicoloured	1·90	1·40

105 Head of Uganda Kob

1975. Antelopes. Multicoloured.

631	20c. Type **105**	15	10
632	30c. Bongo with calf (horiz)	15	10
633	50c. Roan antelope and sable antelope heads	15	10
634	1f. Young sitatungas (horiz)	15	10
635	4f. Great kudu	15	10
636	10f. Impala family (horiz)	80	10
637	34f. Waterbuck head	2·00	70
638	100f. Giant eland (horiz)	5·75	2·50
MS639	Two sheets each 125×90 mm. (a) 40f. Impala; (b) 60f. Great kudu	5·75	5·75

106 "The Deposition" (Raphael)

1975. Easter. Four sheets 130×89 mm each containing single stamps as T 106. Multicoloured.
MS640 (a) 20f. Type **106**; (b) 30f. "Pieta" (Cranach the Elder); (c) 50f. "Oleta" (Van der Weyden); (d) "Pieta" (Lopez) 4·50 4·50

107 "Prince Carlos Balthezar" (Velazquez)

1975. Espana 75 International Stamp Exhibition, Madrid. Four sheets 89×130 mm each containing single stamp as T 107. Multicoloured.
MS641 (a) 20f. Type **107**; (b) 30f. "Princess Margarita of Austria" (Velazquez); (c) 50f. "The Divine Shepherd" (Murillo); (d) 100f. "Francisco Goya" (Lopez) 4·50 4·50

108 Pyrethrum Daisies

1975. Agricultural Labour Year. Multicoloured.
642 20c. Type **108** 10 10
643 30c. Tea plant 10 10
644 50c. Coffee berries 10 10
645 4f. Bananas 10 10
646 10f. Maize 20 10
647 12f. Sorghum 35 15
648 26f. Rice 80 45
649 47f. Coffee cultivation 1·60 90
MS650 Two sheets 56×78 mm. (a) 25f. As 50c.; (b) 75f. As 47f 2·50 2·50

1975. Arphila 75 International Stamp Exhibition, Paris. Two sheets 89×130 mm each containing single stamp as T 107. Multicoloured.
MS651 (a) 75f. "Louis XIV" (Rigaud); (b) 125f. "Hussar Officer on Horseback" (Gericault) 4·50 4·50

1975. Holy Year. Nos. 400/7 optd 1975 ANNEE SAINTE.
652 **65** 10c. brown and gold 10 10
653 - 20c. green and gold 10 10
654 - 30c. lake and gold 10 10
655 - 40c. blue and gold 10 10
656 - 1f. violet and gold 10 10
657 - 18f. purple and gold 40 20
658 - 20f. orange and gold 45 20
659 - 60f. brown and gold 1·90 1·25

110 Eastern White Pelicans

1975. Aquatic Birds. Multicoloured.
660 20c. Type **110** 10 10
661 30c. Malachite kingfisher 10 10
662 50c. Goliath herons 10 10
663 1f. Saddle-bill stork 10 10
664 4f. African jacana 40 15
665 10f. African darter 85 35
666 34f. Sacred ibis 2·40 1·00
667 80f. Hartlaub's duck 6·50 2·75
MS668 Two sheets 131×89 mm each containing single stamp size 35×51 mm (a) 40f. Flamingoes; (b) 60f. Crowned cranes 3·00 3·00

111 Globe and Emblem

1975. World Population Year (1974). Mult.
669 20f. Type **111** 45 30
670 26f. Population graph 65 35
671 34f. Symbolic doorway 95 50

112 "La Toilette" (M. Cassatt)

1975. International Women's Year. Multicoloured.
672 20c. Type **112** 10 10
673 30c. "Mother and Child" (G. Melchers) 10 10
674 50c. "The Milk Jug" (Vermeer) 10 10
675 1f. "The Water-carrier" (Goya) 10 10
676 8f. Coffee picking 20 10
677 12f. Laboratory technician 35 20
678 18f. Rwandaise mother and child 55 20
679 60f. Woman carrying water jug 1·50 1·25
MS680 Two sheets each 89×130 mm. (a) 25f. "Empress Josephine" (Prud'hon); (b) 40f. "Madame Vigee-Lebrun and Daughter" (self-portrait) 4·25 4·25

113 "Arts"

1975. 10th Anniv of National University. The Faculties. Multicoloured.
681 20c. Type **113** 10 10
682 30c. "Medicine" 10 10
683 1f.50 "Jurisprudence" 10 10
684 18f. "Science" 40 20
685 26f. "Commerce" 45 30
686 34f. University Building, Kigali 85 55

1975. 300th Death Anniv of Jan Vermeer (painter). Four sheets 130×89 mm each containing single stamp as T 107. Multicoloured.
MS687 (a) 20f. "Man and Woman drinking Wine" (detail); (b) 30f. "Woman reading letter"; (c) 50f. "The Painter in his Studio" (detail, showing model); (d) 100f. "Young Woman playing Virginals" 4·25 4·25

114 Cattle at Pool, and "Impatiens stuhlmannii"

1975. Protection of Nature. Multicoloured.
688 20c. Type **114** 10 10
689 30c. Euphorbis "candelabra" and savannah bush 10 10
690 50c. Bush fire and "Tapinanthus prunifolius" 10 10
691 5f. Lake Bulera and "Nymphaea lotus" 10 10
692 8f. Soil erosion and "Protea madiensis" 15 10
693 10f. Protected marshland and "Melanthera brownei" 20 15
694 26f. Giant lobelias and groundsel 55 40
695 100f. Sabyinyo volcano and "Polystachya kermesina" 2·50 2·25

1975. Pan-African Drought Relief. Nos. 345/52 optd or surch SECHERESSE SOLIDARITE 1975 (both words share same initial letter).
696 20c. multicoloured 10 10
697 30c. multicoloured 10 10
698 50c. multicoloured 10 10
699 1f. multicoloured 10 10
700 3f. multicoloured 10 10
701 5f. multicoloured 15 10
702 50f.+25f. multicoloured 1·60 1·25
703 90f.+25f. multicoloured 2·40 2·00

116 Loading Douglas DC-8F Jet Trader

1975. Year of Increased Production. Multicoloured.
704 20c. Type **116** 10 10
705 30c. Coffee-picking plant 10 10
706 50c. Lathe operator 10 10
707 10f. Farmer with hoe (vert) 15 10
708 35f. Coffee-picking (vert) 60 55
709 54f. Mechanical plough 1·10 95

117 African Woman with Basket on Head

1975. "Themabelga" Stamp Exhibition, Brussels. African Costumes.
710 **117** 20c. multicoloured 10 10
711 - 30c. multicoloured 10 10
712 - 50c. multicoloured 10 10
713 - 1f. multicoloured 10 10
714 - 5f. multicoloured 10 10
715 - 7f. multicoloured 15 10
716 - 35f. multicoloured 70 60
717 - 51f. multicoloured 1·40 95
DESIGNS: 30c. to 51f. Various Rwanda costumes.

1975. Christmas. Miniature sheet 106×90 mm containing single stamp as T 52.
MS718 100f. mauve 3·00 3·00
DESIGN: "Adoration of the Magi".

118 Dr. Schweitzer, Organ Pipes and Music Score

1976. World Leprosy Day.
719 - 20c. lilac, brown and black 10 10
720 - 30c. lilac, green and black 10 10
721 **118** 50c. lilac, brown and black 10 10
722 - 1f. lilac, purple and black 10 10
723 - 3f. lilac, blue and black 10 10
724 - 5f. lilac, brown and black 10 10
725 **118** 10f. lilac, blue and black 30 10
726 - 80f. lilac, red and black 1·90 1·40
DESIGNS: Dr. Schweitzer and: 20c. Piano keyboard and music; 30c. Lambarene Hospital; 1f. Lambarene residence; 3f. as 20c.; 5f. as 30 c; 80f. as 1f.

119 "Surrender at Yorktown"

1976. Bicentenary of American Revolution. Mult.
727 20c. Type **119** 10 10
728 30c. "The Sergeant-Instructor at Valley Forge" 10 10
729 50c. "Presentation of Captured Yorktown Flags to Congress" 10 10
730 1f. "Washington at Fort Lee" 10 10
731 18f. "Washington boarding a British warship" 45 30
732 26f. "Washington studying Battle plans" 55 40
733 34f. "Washington firing a Cannon" 90 55
734 40f. "Crossing the Delaware" 1·00 85
MS735 108×90 mm. 100f. "Ships "Bonhomme", "Richard" and "Serapis" in Battle" 2·40 2·40

120 Sister Yohana

1976. 75th Anniv of Catholic Church in Rwanda. Multicoloured.
736 20c. Type **120** 10 10
737 30c. Abdon Sabakati 10 10
738 50c. Father Alphonse Brard 10 10
739 4f. Abbe Balthazar Gafuku 10 10
740 10f. Monseigneur Bigirumwami 20 10
741 25f. Save Catholic Church (horiz) 60 45
742 60f. Kabgayi Catholic Cathedral (horiz) 1·25 80

121 Yachting

1976. Olympic Games, Montreal (1st issue).
743 **121** 20c. brown and green 10 10
744 - 30c. blue and green 10 10
745 - 50c. black and green 10 10
746 - 1f. violet and green 10 10
747 - 10f. blue and green 20 10
748 - 18f. brown and green 35 30
749 - 29f. purple and green 80 60
750 - 51f. deep green and green 1·00 80
DESIGNS: 30c. Horse-jumping; 50c. Long jumping; 1f. Hockey; 10f. Swimming; 18f. Football; 29f. Boxing; 51f. Gymnastics.
See also Nos. 767/74.

122 Bell's Experimental Telephone and Manual Switchboard

1976. Telephone Centenary.
751 **122** 20c. brown and blue 10 10
752 - 30c. blue and violet 10 10
753 - 50c. brown and blue 10 10
754 - 1f. orange and blue 10 10
755 - 4f. mauve and blue 10 10
756 - 8f. green and blue 2·50 35
757 - 26f. red and blue 70 55
758 - 60f. lilac and blue 1·40 1·00

DESIGNS: 30c. Early telephone and man making call; 50c. Early telephone and woman making call; 1f. Early telephone and exchange building; 4f. Alexander Graham Bell and "candlestick" telephone; 8f. Rwanda subscriber and dial telephone; 26f. Dish aerial, satellite and modern handset; 60f. Rwanda PTT building, operator and push-button telephone.

1976. Bicentenary of Declaration of American Independence. Nos. 727/34 optd INDEPENDENCE DAY and Bicentennial Emblem.

759	**119**	20c. multicoloured	10	10
760	-	30c. multicoloured	10	10
761	-	50c. multicoloured	10	10
762	-	1f. multicoloured	10	10
763	-	18f. multicoloured	35	20
764	-	26f. multicoloured	65	45
765	-	34f. multicoloured	80	55
766	-	40f. multicoloured	1·10	80

124 Football

1976. Olympic Games, Montreal (2nd issue). Mult.

767		20c. Type **124**	10	10
768		30c. Rifle-shooting	10	10
769		50c. Canoeing	10	10
770		1f. Gymnastics	10	10
771		10f. Weightlifting	15	10
772		12f. Diving	30	20
773		26f. Horse-riding	55	40
774		50f. Throwing the hammer	1·40	90
MS775		190×60 mm containing four stamps in horiz strip: 20f. Start of race; 30f. Running; 40f. leaping hurdle; 60f. Breasting tape (all horiz)	3·25	3·25

125 "Apollo" and "Soyuz" Launches and ASTP Badge

1976. "Apollo"–"Soyuz" Test Project. Mult.

776		20c. Type **125**	10	10
777		30c. "Soyuz" rocket	10	10
778		50c. "Apollo" rocket	10	10
779		1f. "Apollo" after separation	10	10
780		2f. Approach to link-up	10	10
781		12f. Spacecraft docked	35	15
782		30f. Sectional view of interiors	1·10	55
783		54f. "Apollo" splashdown	2·25	1·25

126 "Eulophia cucullata"

1976. Rwandaise Orchids. Multicoloured.

784		20c. Type **126**	10	10
785		30c. "Eulophia streptopetala"	10	10
786		50c. "Disa stairsii"	10	10
787		1f. "Aerangis kotschyana"	10	10
788		10f. "Eulophia abyssinica"	20	10
789		12f. "Bonatea steudneri"	30	15
790		26f. "Ansellia gigantea"	1·10	45
791		50f. "Eulophia angolensis"	2·00	1·25

1976. Christmas. Miniature sheet 109×90 mm containing single stamp as T 52.

MS792	100f. blue	2·75	2·75

DESIGN: "The Nativity" (Francois Boucher).

1977. World Leprosy Day. Nos. 719/26 optd with JOURNEE MONDIALE 1977.

793	-	20c. lilac, brown and black	10	10
794	-	30c. lilac, green and black	10	10
795	**118**	50c. lilac, brown and black	10	10
796	-	1f. lilac, purple and black	10	10
797	-	3f. lilac, blue and black	10	10
798	-	5f. lilac, brown and black	20	10
799	**118**	10f. lilac, brown and black	35	20
800	-	80f. lilac, red and black	1·60	1·60

128 Hands embracing "Cultural Collaboration"

1977. 10th OCAM Summit Meeting, Kigali. Mult.

801		10f. Type **128**	30	10
802		26f. Hands embracing "Technical Collaboration"	70	40
803		64f. Hands embracing "Economic Collaboration"	1·25	90

129 "Christ Crucified" (Rubens)

1977. Easter. Two sheets each 89×129 mm. Multicoloured.

MS804	(a) 25f. Type **129**; (b) 75f. "Christ on the Straw" (Rubens)	2·40	2·40

1977. World Water Conference. Nos. 688/95 optd CONFERENCE MONDIALE DE L'EAU.

805	**114**	20c. multicoloured	10	10
806	-	30c. multicoloured	10	10
807	-	50c. multicoloured	10	10
808	-	5f. multicoloured	15	10
809	-	8f. multicoloured	20	10
810	-	10f. multicoloured	40	15
811	-	26f. multicoloured	1·40	75
812	-	100f. multicoloured	3·50	3·25

131 Roman Signal Post and African Tam-Tam

1977. World Telecommunications Day. Mult.

813		20c. Type **131**	10	10
814		30c. Chappe's semaphore and post-rider	10	10
815		50c. Morse code	10	10
816		1f. "Goliath" laying Channel cable	10	10
817		4f. Telephone, radio and television	10	10
818		18f. "Kingsport" and maritime communications satellite	75	40
819		26f. Telecommunications satellite and aerial	50	40
820		50f. "Mariner 2" satellite	1·40	90

1977. Amphilex 77 International Stamp Exhibition, Amsterdam. Two sheets each 129×99 mm containing vert designs as T 107. Multicoloured.

MS822	(a) 40f. "The Night Watch" (Raphael); (b) 60f. "The Port of Amsterdam" (Willem van der Velde the Junior)	2·25	2·25

132 "The Ascent to Calvary" (detail)

1977. 400th Birth Anniv of Peter Paul Rubens. Multicoloured.

823		20c. Type **132**	10	10
824		30c. "The Judgement of Paris" (horiz)	10	10
825		50c. "Marie de Medici, Queen of France"	10	10
826		1f. "Heads of Negroes" (horiz)	10	10
827		4f. "St. Idelfonse Triptych" (detail)	10	10
828		8f. "Helene Fourment with her Children" (horiz)	15	10
829		26f. "St. Idelfonse Triptych" (different detail)	80	65
830		60f. "Helene Fourment"	2·50	1·75

133 Chateau Sassenage, Grenoble

1977. Air. 10th Anniv of International French Language Council.

831	**133**	50f. multicoloured	1·60	1·10

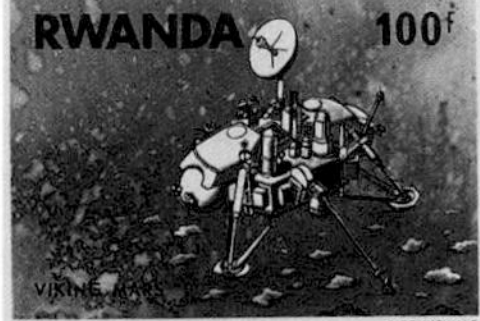

134 "Viking" on Mars

1977. "Viking" Mission to Mars. Miniature sheet 129×90 mm.

MS832	**134**	100f. multicoloured	3·25	3·25

135 Long-crested Eagle

1977. Birds of Prey. Multicoloured.

833		20c. Type **135**	10	10
834		30c. African harrier hawk	10	10
835		50c. African fish eagle	15	10
836		1f. Hooded vulture	15	15
837		3f. Augur buzzard	20	15
838		5f. Black kite	30	15
839		20f. Black-shouldered kite	1·50	70
840		100f. Bateleur	5·75	3·25

1912. Dr. Wernher von Braun Commemoration. Nos. 776/83 optd with in memoriam WERNHER VON BRAUN 1912 - 1977.

841		20c. Type **125**	10	10
842		30c. "Soyuz" rocket	10	10
843		50c. "Apollo" rocket	10	10
844		1f. "Apollo" after separation	10	10
845		2f. Approach to link up	10	10
846		12f. Spacecraft docked	40	20
847		30f. Sectional view of interiors	1·40	50
848		54f. "Apollo" after splashdown	2·50	1·50

1977. Espamer 77 Stamp Exhibition, Barcelona. No. MS641 optd ESPAMER'77.

MS849	Four sheets each 89×130 mm. (a) 20f.; (b) 30f.; (c) 50f.; (d) 100f	4·50	4·50

1977. Christmas. Miniature sheet 88×88 mm containing single stamp as T 52 but square 37×37 mm.

MS850	100f. violet	3·00	3·00

DESIGN: "The Nativity" (Rubens).

138 Scout playing Whistle

1978. 10th Anniv of Rwanda Scout Association. Multicoloured.

851		20c. Type **138**	10	10
852		30c. Camp fire	10	10
853		50c. Scouts constructing a platform	10	10
854		1f. Two scouts	10	10
855		10f. Scouts on look-out	20	10
856		18f. Scouts in canoe	45	35
857		26f. Cooking at camp fire	80	60
858		44f. Lord Baden-Powell	1·50	1·25

139 Chimpanzees

1978. Apes. Multicoloured.

859		20c. Type **139**	10	10
860		30c. Gorilla	10	10
861		50c. Eastern black-and-white colobus	10	10
862		3f. Eastern needle-clawed bushbaby	10	10
863		10f. Mona monkey	30	10
864		26f. Potto	65	65
865		60f. Savanna monkey	1·90	1·90
866		150f. Olive baboon	3·75	3·75

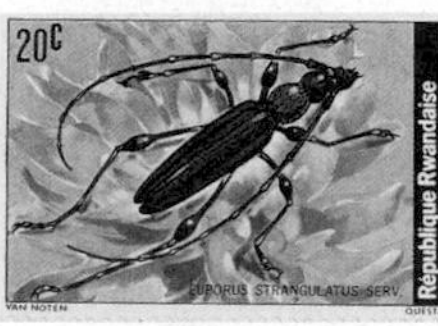

140 "Euporus strangulatus"

1978. Beetles. Multicoloured.

867		20c. Type **140**	10	10
868		30c. "Rhina afzelii" (vert)	10	10
869		50c. "Pentalobus palini"	10	10
870		3f. "Corynodes dejeani" (vert)	10	10
871		10f. "Mecynorhina torquata"	20	10
872		15f. "Mecocerus rhombeus" (vert)	55	10
873		20f. "Macrotoma serripes"	75	20
874		25f. "Neptunides stanleyi" (vert)	90	40
875		26f. "Petrognatha gigas"	90	40
876		100f. "Eudicella gralli" (vert)	3·25	2·50

141 Poling Boat across River of Poverty

1978. National Revolutionary Development Movement. Multicoloured.

877		4f. Type **141**	10	10
878		10f. Poling boat to right	15	10
879		26f. Type **141**	60	40
880		60f. As 10f.	1·10	85

142 Footballers, Cup and Flags of Netherlands and Peru

1978. World Cup Football Championship, Argentina. Multicoloured.

881		20c. Type **142**	10	10
882		30c. Flags of FIFA, Sweden and Spain	10	10
883		50c. Mascot and flags of Scotland and Iran	10	10
884		2f. Emblem and flags of West Germany and Tunisia	10	10
885		3f. Cup and flags of Italy and Hungary	10	10
886		10f. Flags of FIFA, Brazil and Austria	20	10
887		34f. Mascot and flags of Poland and Mexico	85	70
888		100f. Emblem and flags of Argentina and France	2·50	2·00

No. 883 shows the Union Jack.

143 Wright Brothers and Wright Flyer I, 1903

1978. Aviation History. Multicoloured.

889	20c. Type **143**	10	10
890	30c. Alberto Santos-Dumont and biplane "14 bis", 1906	10	10
891	50c. Henri Farman and Farman Voisin No. 1 bis, 1908	10	10
892	1f. Jan Olieslagers and Bleriot XI	10	10
893	3f. General Italo Balbo and Savoia S-17 flying boat, 1919	10	10
894	10f. Charles Lindbergh and "Spirit of St. Louis", 1927	15	10
895	55f. Hugo Junkers and Junkers Ju 52/3m, 1932	1·10	55
896	60f. Igor Sikorsky and Vought-Sikorsky VS-300 helicopter prototype	1·60	85
MS897	78×95 mm. 130f. "Concorde" (46×25 mm)	3·00	3·00

143a Great Spotted Woodpecker and Oldenburg 1852⅓sgr. Stamp

1978. Air. "Philexafrique" Stamp Exhibition, Libreville, Gabon and Int Stamp Fair, Essen, West Germany. Multicoloured.

898	30f. Type **143a**	1·40	90
899	30f. Greater kudu and Rwanda 1967 20c. stamp	1·40	90

144 "Adoration of the Magi" (Durer)

1978. Christmas. Sheet 64×84 mm.

MS900	**144** 200f. sepia	4·00	4·00

1978. 15th Anniv of Organization of African Unity. Nos. 544/5 optd 1963 1978.

901	**88**	6f. multicoloured	30	10
902	-	94f. multicoloured	1·90	1·10

146 Spur-winged Goose and Mallard

1978. Stock Rearing Year. Multicoloured.

903	20c. Type **146**	20	10
904	30c. Goats (horiz)	10	10
905	50c. Chickens	10	10
906	4f. Rabbits (horiz)	20	10
907	5f. Pigs	20	10
908	15f. Common turkey (horiz)	90	30
909	50f. Sheep and cattle	1·50	50
910	75f. Bull (horiz)	1·90	70

147 "Papilio demodocus"

1979. Butterflies. Multicoloured.

911	20c. Type **147**	10	10
912	30c. "Precis octavia"	10	10
913	50c. "Charaxes smaragdalis caerulea"	10	10
914	4f. "Charaxes guderiana"	15	10
915	15f. "Colotis evippe"	20	10
916	30f. "Danaus limniace petiverana"	55	30
917	50f. "Byblia acheloia"	1·50	55
918	150f. "Utetheisa pulchella"	3·75	1·40

148 "Euphorbia grantii" and Women weaving

1979. "Philexafrique" Exhibition, Libreville. Mult.

919	40f. Type **148**	1·40	85
920	60f. Drummers and "Intelsat" satellite	2·25	1·10

149 "Polyscias fulva"

1979. Trees. Multicoloured.

921	20c. Type **149**	10	10
922	30c. "Entandrophragma excelsum" (horiz)	10	10
923	50c. "Ilex mitis"	10	10
924	4f. "Kigelia africana" (horiz)	15	10
925	15f. "Ficus thonningi"	35	10
926	20f. "Acacia senegal" (horiz)	50	20
927	50f. "Symphonia globulifera"	1·25	45
928	110f. "Acacia sieberana" (horiz)	2·50	1·25

150 European Girl

1979. International Year of the Child. Each brown, gold and stone.

929	26f. Type **150**	65	60
930	26f. Asian	65	60
931	26f. Eskimo	65	60
932	26f. Asian boy	65	60
933	26f. African	65	60
934	26f. South American Indian	65	60
935	26f. Polynesian	65	60
936	26f. European girl (different)	65	60
937	42f. European and African (horiz)	2·00	65
MS938	62×76 mm. 100f. Children of different races (29×41 mm)	3·75	3·75

151 Basket Weaving

1979. Handicrafts. Multicoloured.

939	50c. Type **151**	10	10
940	1f.50 Wood-carving (vert)	10	10
941	2f. Metal working	10	10
942	10f. Basket work (vert)	35	10
943	20f. Basket weaving (different)	50	20
944	26f. Mural painting (vert)	65	55
945	40f. Pottery	95	65
946	100f. Smelting (vert)	2·50	1·75

152 Children lighting Christmas Tree Candle

1979. Christmas. Sheet 85×65 mm.

MS947	**152** 200f. ultramarine	4·50	4·50

153 Rowland Hill and 40c. Ruanda Stamp of 1916

1979. Death Centenary of Sir Rowland Hill. Multicoloured.

948	20c. Type **153**	10	10
949	30c. 1916 Occupation stamp	10	10
950	50c. 1918 "A.O." overprint	10	10
951	3f. 1925 overprinted 60c. stamp	10	10
952	10f. 1931 50c. African buffalo stamp	30	10
953	26f. 1942 20f. Common zebra stamp	65	15
954	60f. 1953 25f. Protea stamp	1·40	60
955	100f. 1960 Olympic stamp	2·75	1·10

154 Strange Weaver

1980. Birds. Multicoloured.

956	20c. Type **154**	15	10
957	30c. Regal sunbird (vert)	15	15
958	50c. White-spotted crake	15	15
959	3f. Black-casqued hornbill	30	15
960	10f. Ituri owl (vert)	70	25
961	26f. African emerald cuckoo	1·60	65
962	60f. Black-crowned waxbill (vert)	3·00	1·50
963	100f. Crowned eagle (vert)	5·50	2·50

155 Armstrong's first Step on Moon

1980. 10th Anniv of "Apollo 11" Moon Landing. Multicoloured.

964	50c. Type **155**	10	10
965	1f.50 Aldrin descending to Moon's surface	10	10
966	8f. Planting the American flag	55	10
967	30f. Placing seisometer	95	60
968	50f. Taking samples	1·75	70
969	60f. Setting-up experiment	2·50	90
MS970	70×58 mm. 200f. Armstrong descending to Moon's surface	7·75	7·75

156 Butare Rotary Club Banner, Globe and Chicago Club Emblem of 1905

1980. 75th Anniv of Rotary International. Mult.

971	20c. Type **156**	10	10
972	30c. Kigali Rotary Club banner	10	10
973	50c. Type **156**	10	10
974	4f. As No. 972	15	10
975	15f. Type **156**	35	10
976	20f. As No. 972	45	20
977	50f. Type **156**	95	45
978	60f. As No. 972	1·10	65

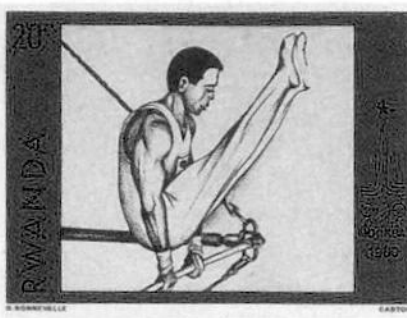

157 Gymnastics

1980. Olympic Games, Moscow.

979	**157**	20c. yellow and black	10	10
980	-	30c. green and black	10	10
981	-	50c. red and black	10	10
982	-	3f. blue and black	15	10
983	-	20f. orange and black	45	20
984	-	26f. purple and black	50	25
985	-	50f. turquoise and black	1·10	45
986	-	100f. brown and black	2·50	1·10

DESIGNS: 30c. Basketball; 50c. Cycling; 3f. Boxing; 20f. Archery; 26f. Weightlifting; 50f. Javelin; 100f. Fencing.

158 "The Amalfi Coast" (Giacinto Gigante)

1980. 20th Europa Stamp Exhibition, Naples. Sheet 117×89 mm.

MS987	**158** 200f. multicoloured	4·50	4·50

159 "Geaster"

1980. Mushrooms. Multicoloured.

988	20c. Type **159**	10	10
989	30c. "Lentinus atrobrunneus"	10	10
990	50c. "Gomphus stereoides"	10	10
991	4f. "Cantharellus cibarius"	30	10
992	10f. "Stilbothamnium dybowskii"	65	20
993	15f. "Xeromphalina tenuipes"	90	20
994	70f. "Podoscypha elegans"	3·75	80
995	100f. "Mycena"	7·50	1·60

160 "At the Theatre" (Toulouse-Lautrec)

1980. Impressionist Paintings. Multicoloured.

996	20c. "Still Life" (horiz) (Renoir)	10	10
997	30c. Type **160**	10	10
998	50c. "Seaside Garden" (Monet) (horiz)	10	10
999	4f. "Mother and Child" (Mary Cassatt)	10	10
1000	5f. "Starry Night" (Van Gogh) (horiz)	20	10
1001	10f. "Three Dancers at thelr Toilette" (Degas)	35	10
1002	50f. "The Card Players" (Cezanne) (horiz)	1·10	45
1003	70f. "Tahitian Girls" (Gauguin)	1·75	65
1004	100f. "La Grande Jatte" (Seurat) (horiz)	2·75	90

MS1005 Four sheets each 137×101 mm. (a) 4f. No. 999, 26f. Type **160**; (b) 10f. As No. 998, 50f.; (c) 5f. No. 1000 75f. As No. 996; (d) 10f. No. 1001, 70f. No. 1003 5·50 5·50

161 "Virgin of the Harpies" (detail, Andrea del Sarto)

1980. Christmas. Sheet 65×84 mm.
MS1006 **161** 200f. black 4·50 4·50

162 Revolutionary Scene

1980. 150th Anniv of Belgian Independence. Scenes of the Independence War from contemporary engravings.

1007	**162**	20c. green and brown	10	10
1008	-	30c. buff and brown	10	10
1009	-	50c. blue and brown	10	10
1010	-	9f. orange and brown	20	10
1011	-	10f. mauve and brown	30	10
1012	-	20f. green and brown	45	20
1013	-	70f. pink and brown	1·50	65
1014	-	90f. yellow and brown	1·90	1·00

163 Draining the Marshes

1980. Soil Protection and Conservation Year. Mult.

1015	20c. Type **163**	25	10
1016	30c. Bullock in pen (mixed farming and land fertilization)	10	10
1017	1f.50 Land irrigation and rice	10	10
1018	8f. Soil erosion and planting trees	20	10
1019	10f. Terrace	30	15
1020	40f. Crop fields	1·00	40
1021	90f. Bean crop	2·10	85
1022	100f. Picking tea	2·25	1·10

164 "Pavetta rwandensis"

1981. Flowers. Multicoloured.

1023	20c. Type **164**	10	10
1024	30c. "Cytrorchis praetermissa"	10	10
1025	50c. "Pavonia urens"	10	10
1026	4f. "Cynorkis kassnerana"	10	10
1027	5f. "Gardenia ternifolia"	15	10
1028	10f. "Leptactina platyphylla"	20	10
1029	20f. "Lobelia petiolata"	50	15
1030	40f. "Tapinanthus brunneus"	1·25	50
1031	70f. "Impatiens niamniamensis"	1·60	95

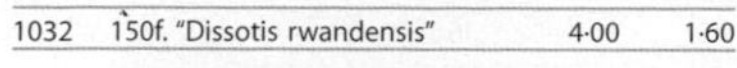

1032	150f. "Dissotis rwandensis"	4·00	1·60

165 Mother and Child

1981. SOS Children's Village. Multicoloured.

1033	20c. Type **165**	10	10
1034	30c. Child with pots	10	10
1035	50c. Children drawing	10	10
1036	1f. Girl sewing	10	10
1037	8f. Children playing	20	10
1038	10f. Girl knitting	20	10
1039	70f. Children making models	1·50	70
1040	150f. Mother and children	3·25	1·60

166 Carol Singers

1981. Paintings by Norman Rockwell. Mult.

1041	20c. Type **166**	10	10
1042	30c. People of different races	10	10
1043	50c. Father Christmas	10	10
1044	1f. Coachman	10	10
1045	8f. Man at piano	15	10
1046	20f. "Springtime"	50	20
1047	50f. Man making donation to girl "nurse"	1·25	70
1048	70f. Clown	1·75	1·10

167 Serval

1981. Carnivorous Animals. Multicoloured.

1049	20c. Type **167**	10	10
1050	30c. Black-backed jackal	10	10
1051	2f. Servaline genet	10	10
1052	2f.50 Banded mongoose	10	10
1053	10f. Zorilla	20	10
1054	15f. Zaire clawless otter	55	10
1055	70f. African golden cat	1·75	1·25
1056	200f. Hunting dog (vert)	5·75	4·25

168 Drummer

1981. Telecommunications and Health. Mult.

1057	20c. Type **168**	10	10
1058	30c. Telephone receiver and world map	10	10
1059	2f. Airliner and radar screen	10	10
1060	2f.50 Satellite and computer tape	10	10
1061	10f. Satellite orbit and dish aerial	20	10
1062	15f. Tanker and radar equipment	35	25
1063	70f. Red Cross helicopter	1·90	70
1064	200f. Satellite	4·25	2·25

169 "St. Benedict leaving His Parents"

1981. 1500th Birth Anniv of St. Benedict. Mult.

1065	20c. Type **169**	10	10
1066	30c. Portrait (10th century) (vert)	10	10
1067	50c. Portrait (detail from "The Virgin of the Misericord" polyptich) (vert)	10	10
1068	4f. "St. Benedict presenting the Rules of His Order"	10	10
1069	5f. "St. Benedict and His Monks at their Meal"	15	10
1070	20f. Portrait (13th century) (vert)	45	40
1071	70f. St. Benedict at prayer (detail from "Our Lady in Glory with Sts. Gregory and Benedict") (vert)	1·75	1·40
1072	100f. "Priest bringing the Easter Meal to St. Benedict" (Jan van Coninxlo)	2·75	1·75

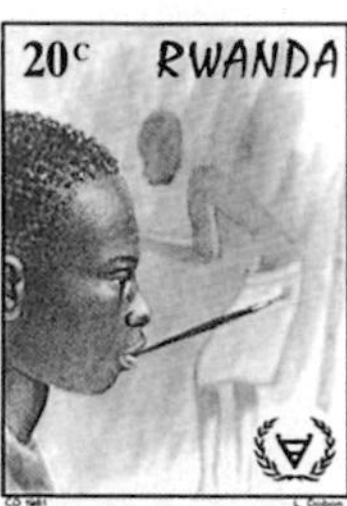

170 Disabled Child painting with Mouth

1981. International Year of Disabled Persons. Mult.

1073	20c. Type **170**	10	10
1074	30c. Boys on crutches playing football	10	10
1075	4f.50 Disabled girl knitting	10	10
1076	5f. Disabled child painting pot	15	10
1077	10f. Boy in wheelchair using saw	20	10
1078	60f. Child using sign language	1·25	60
1079	70f. Child in wheelchair playing with puzzle	1·60	70
1080	100f. Disabled child	2·00	1·10

171 "Adoration of the Magi" (Hugo van der Goes)

1981. Christmas. Sheet 85×85 mm.
MS1081 **171** 200f. lake 3·75 3·75

172 Kob drinking at Pool

1981. Rural Water Supplies. Multicoloured.

1082	20c. Type **172**	10	10
1083	30c. Women collecting water (vert)	10	10
1084	50c. Constructing a pipeline	10	10
1085	10f. Woman collecting water from pipe (vert)	20	10
1086	10f. Man drinking	45	20
1087	70f. Woman collecting water (vert)	1·50	70
1088	100f. Floating pump (vert)	2·50	1·10

173 Cattle

1982. World Food Day. Multicoloured.

1089	20c. Type **173**	10	10
1090	30c. Bee keeping	10	10
1091	50c. Fishes	10	10
1092	1f. Avocado	10	10
1093	8f. Boy eating banana	10	10
1094	20f. Sorghum	45	15
1095	70f. Vegetables	1·50	65
1096	100f. Three generations and balanced diet	3·00	1·10

174 "Hibiscus berberidfolius"

1982. Flowers. Multicoloured.

1097	20c. Type **174**	10	10
1098	30c. "Hypericum lanceolatum" (vert)	10	10
1099	50c. "Canarina eminii"	10	10
1100	4f. "Polygala ruwenzoriensis"	10	10
1101	10f. "Kniphofia grantii" (vert)	15	10
1102	35f. "Euphorbia candelabrum" (vert)	90	60
1103	70f. "Disa erubescens" (vert)	1·75	80
1104	80f. "Gloriosa simplex"	2·40	1·10

175 Pres. Habyarimana and Flags

1982. 20th Anniv of Independence. Multicoloured.

1105	10f. Type **175**	20	10
1106	20f. Hands releasing doves (Peace)	35	20
1107	30f. Clasped hands and flag (Unity)	65	35
1108	50f. Building (Development)	1·00	50

176 Football

1982. World Cup Football Championship, Spain.

1109	**176**	20c. multicoloured	10	10
1110	-	30c. multicoloured	10	10
1111	-	1f.50 multicoloured	10	10
1112	-	8f. multicoloured	15	10
1113	-	10f. multicoloured	20	10
1114	-	20f. multicoloured	40	15
1115	-	70f. multicoloured	1·60	65
1116	-	90f. multicoloured	2·25	85

DESIGNS: 30c. to 90f. Designs show different players.

177 Microscope and Slide

1982. Centenary of Discovery of Tubercle Bacillus. Multicoloured.

1117	10f. Type **177**	15	10
1118	20f. Hand with test tube and slide	40	15
1119	70f. Lungs and slide	1·60	65
1120	100f. Dr. Robert Koch	2·25	95

178 "St. Anne, Virgin and Child and Donor" (detail, Van der Goes)

1982. Belgica 82 and Philexfrance 82 International Stamp Exhibitions. Four sheets each 130×90 mm. Multicoloured.

MS1121	(a) 40f. Type **178**; (b) 40f. "Portrait of Madame Recamier" (David); (c) 60f. "Pygmalion" (P. Delvaux); (d) 60f. "Liberty guiding the People" (E. Delacroix)	4·25	4·25

179 "Virgin and Child" (Murillo)

1982. Christmas. Sheet 85×85 mm.

MS1122	**179** 200f. magenta	4·25	4·25

180 African Elephants

1982. 10th Anniv of United Nations Environment Programme. Multicoloured.

1123	20c. Type **180**	10	10
1124	30c. Lion hunting impala	10	10
1125	50c. Flower	10	10
1126	4f. African buffalo	10	10
1127	5f. Impala	10	10
1128	10f. Flower (different)	20	10
1129	20f. Common zebra	45	15
1130	40f. Crowned cranes	1·50	35
1131	50f. African fish eagle	1·75	55
1132	70f. Woman with basket of fruit	1·60	80

181 Scout tending Injured Kob

1982. 75th Anniv of Scout Movement. Mult.

1133	20c. Type **181**	10	10
1134	30c. Tents and northern doubled-collared sunbird	35	10
1135	1f.50 Campfire	10	10
1136	8f. Scout	15	10
1137	10f. Knot	20	10
1138	20f. Tent and campfire	40	15
1139	70f. Scout cutting stake	1·90	80
1140	90f. Scout salute	2·40	1·00

182 Northern Double-collared Sunbird

1983. Nectar-sucking Birds. Multicoloured.

1141	20c. Type **182**	10	10
1142	30c. Regal sunbird (horiz)	10	10
1143	50c. Red-tufted malachite sunbird	10	10
1144	4f. Bronze sunbird (horiz)	25	10
1145	5f. Collared sunbird	35	10
1146	10f. Blue-headed sunbird (horiz)	70	20
1147	20f. Purple-breasted sunbird	1·40	50
1148	40f. Coppery sunbird (horiz)	3·00	95
1149	50f. Olive-bellied sunbird	3·25	1·25
1150	70f. Red-chested sunbird (horiz)	4·50	2·00

183 Driving Cattle

1983. Campaign Against Soil Erosion. Mult.

1151	20c. Type **183**	10	10
1152	30c. Pineapple plantation	10	10
1153	50c. Interrupted ditches	10	10
1154	9f. Hedged terraces	20	10
1155	10f. Re-afforestation	20	10
1156	20f. Anti-erosion barriers	40	15
1157	30f. Contour planting	65	30
1158	50f. Terraces	1·00	40
1159	60f. River bank protection	1·40	60
1160	70f. Alternate fallow and planted strips	1·60	80

184 Feeding Ducks

1983. Birth Cent of Cardinal Cardijan (founder of Young Catholic Workers Movement). Mult.

1161	20c. Type **184**	10	10
1162	30c. Harvesting bananas	10	10
1163	50c. Carrying melons	10	10
1164	10f. Wood-carving	20	10
1165	19f. Making shoes	35	15
1166	20f. Children in field of millet	45	15
1167	70f. Embroidering	1·40	60
1168	80f. Cardinal Cardijan	1·60	65

185 Young Gorillas

1983. Mountain Gorillas. Multicoloured.

1169	20c. Type **185**	10	10
1170	30c. Gorilla family	10	10
1171	9f.50 Young and adult	45	30
1172	10f. Mother with young	45	30
1173	20f. Heads	65	45
1174	30f. Adult and head	90	50
1175	60f. Adult (vert)	2·00	1·40
1176	70f. Close-up of adult (vert)	2·40	1·50

186 "Madonna del Granduca" (Raphael)

1983. Christmas. Sheet 72×85 mm.

MS1177	**186** 200f. green	4·50	4·50

187 "Hagenia abyssinica"

1984. Trees. Multicoloured.

1178	20c. Type **187**	10	10
1179	30c. "Dracaena steudneri"	10	10
1180	50c. "Phoenix reclinata"	10	10
1181	10f. "Podocarpus milanjianus"	15	10
1182	19f. "Entada abyssinica"	40	15
1183	70f. "Parinari excelsa"	1·60	65
1184	100f. "Newtonia buchananii"	2·00	95
1185	200f. "Acacia gerrardi" (vert)	4·50	1·60

188 "Hikari" Express Train, Japan

1984. World Communications Year. Multicoloured.

1186	20c. Type **188**	20	10
1187	30c. Liner and radar	15	10
1188	4f.50 Radio and transmitter	15	10
1189	10f. Telephone dial and cable	20	10
1190	15f. Letters and newspaper	35	10
1191	50f. Airliner and control tower	1·10	45
1192	70f. Television and antenna	1·60	65
1193	100f. Satellite and computer tape	2·50	90

189 "Le Martial", 1783

1984. Bicentenary of Manned Flight. Mult.

1194	20c. Type **189**	10	10
1195	30c. De Rozier and Marquis d'Arlandes flight, 1783	10	10
1196	50c. Charles and Robert (1783) and Blanchard (1784) flights	10	10
1197	9f. M. and Mme. Blanchard	20	10
1198	10f. Blanchard and Jeffries, 1785	20	10
1199	50f. Demuyter (1937) and Piccard and Kipfer (1931) flights	1·10	40
1200	80f. Modern hot-air balloons	2·75	1·90
1201	200f. Trans-Atlantic flight, 1978	3·50	2·50

190 Equestrian

1984. Olympic Games, Los Angeles. Multicoloured.

1202	20c. Type **190**	10	10
1203	30c. Windsurfing	15	10
1204	50c. Football	10	10
1205	9f. Swimming	20	10
1206	10f. Hockey	20	10
1207	40f. Fencing	1·25	70
1208	80f. Running	2·00	1·75
1209	200f. Boxing	5·00	4·00

191 Mare and Foal

1984. Common Zebras and African Buffaloes. Mult.

1210	20c. Type **191**	10	10
1211	30c. Buffalo and calf (vert)	10	10
1212	50c. Pair of zebras (vert)	10	10
1213	9f. Zebras fighting	20	10
1214	10f. Close-up of buffalo (vert)	30	10
1215	80f. Herd of zebras	1·90	1·40
1216	100f. Close-up of zebras (vert)	2·50	1·75
1217	200f. Buffalo charging	4·75	3·50

192 "Virgin adoring the Child" (Correggio)

1984. Christmas. Sheet 72×85 mm.

MS1218	**192** 200f. emerald	4·75	4·75

193 Gorillas at Water-hole

1985. Gorillas. Multicoloured.

1219	10f. Type **193**	1·90	80
1220	15f. Two gorillas in tree	2·75	85
1221	25f. Gorilla family	3·75	2·10
1222	30f. Three adults	4·75	3·00
MS1223	127×93 mm. 200f. As No. 1219 (35×50 mm)	5·25	5·25

194 Man feeding Fowl

1985. Food Production Year. Multicoloured.

1224	20c. Type **194**	20	10
1225	30c. Men carrying pineapples	15	10
1226	50c. Farm animals	10	10
1227	9f. Men filling sacks with produce	20	10
1228	10f. Agricultural instruction	30	10
1229	50f. Sowing seeds	1·00	45
1230	80f. Storing produce	1·60	65
1231	100f. Working in banana plantation	2·10	80

195 Emblem

1985. 10th Anniv of National Revolutionary Redevelopment Movement.

1232	**195**	10f. multicoloured	20	10
1233	**195**	30f. multicoloured	65	30
1234	**195**	70f. multicoloured	1·60	70

196 U.N. Emblem within "40"

1985. 40th Anniv of U.N.O.

1235	**196**	50f. multicoloured	1·10	90
1236	**196**	100f. multicoloured	2·50	2·10

197 Barn Owls

1985. Birth Bicentenary of John J. Audubon (ornithologist). Multicoloured.

1237	10f. Type **197**	75	30
1238	20f. White-faced scops owls	1·60	60
1239	40f. Ruby-throated humming birds	3·00	1·10
1240	80f. Eastern meadowlarks	6·75	2·40

198 "Participation, Development and Peace"

1985. International Youth Year. Multicoloured.

1241	7f. Type **198**	15	10
1242	9f. Cycling	30	10
1243	44f. Youths carrying articles on head (teamwork)	1·10	45
1244	80f. Education	1·75	80

1985. 75th Anniv of Girl Guide Movement. Nos. 1133/40 optd 1910/1985 and guide emblem.

1245	20c. Type **181**	10	10
1246	30c. Tents	30	10
1247	1f.50 Campfire	10	10
1248	8f. Scout	20	10
1249	10f. Knot	20	10
1250	20f. Tent and campfire	45	10
1251	70f. Scout cutting stake	1·60	65
1252	90f. Scout salute	2·50	90

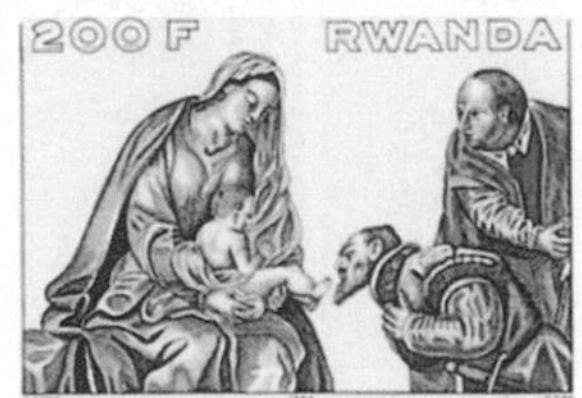

200 "Adoration of the Magi" (Titian)

1985. Christmas. Sheet 72×85 mm.

MS1253	**200**	200f. magenta	4·25	4·25

201 Container Lorry (Transport)

1986. Transport and Communications. Mult.

1254	10f. Type **201**	35	10
1255	30f. Handstamping cover (posts)	80	35
1256	40f. Kigali Earth Station (telecommunication)	1·10	45
1257	80f. Kigali airport (aviation) (48×31 mm)	1·75	1·25

1986. Intensified Agriculture Year. Nos. 1152/60 optd ANNEE 1986 INTENSIFICATION AGRICOLE or surch also.

1258	9f. Hedged terraces	20	10
1259	10f. Re-afforestation	20	10
1260	10f. on 30c. Pineapple plantation	20	10
1261	10f. on 50c. Interrupted ditches	20	10
1262	20f. Anti-erosion barriers	45	20
1263	30f. Contour planning	65	35
1264	50f. Terraces	1·10	50
1265	60f. River bank protection	1·40	55
1266	70f. Alternate fallow and planted strips	1·60	70

203 Morocco v England

1986. World Cup Football Championship, Mexico. Multicoloured.

1267	2f. Type **203**	10	10
1268	4f. Paraguay v Iraq	10	10
1269	5f. Brazil v Spain	10	10
1270	10f. Italy v Argentina	55	35
1271	40f. Mexico v Belgium	1·60	85
1272	45f. France v Russia	1·75	1·00

204 Roan Antelopes

1986. Akagera National Park. Multicoloured.

1273	4f. Type **204**	15	10
1274	7f. Whale-headed storks	45	20
1275	9f. Cape eland	20	10
1276	10f. Giraffe	40	10
1277	80f. African elephant	2·50	85
1278	90f. Crocodile	3·00	1·00
1279	100f. Heuglin's masked weavers	5·00	2·75
1280	100f. Zebras and eastern white pelican	5·00	2·75

205 People of Different Races on Globe

1986. Christmas. International Peace Year. Mult.

1281	10f. Type **205**	35	15
1282	15f. Dove and globe	45	15
1283	30f. Type **205**	80	35
1284	70f. As No. 1282	1·75	1·00

206 Mother breast-feeding Baby

1987. UNICEF Child Survival Campaign. Multicoloured.

1285	4f. Type **206**	15	15
1286	6f. Mother giving oral rehydration therapy to baby	20	15
1287	10f. Nurse immunizing baby	35	25
1288	70f. Nurse weighing baby and graph	1·75	1·60

207 Couple packing Baskets with Food

1987. Food Self-sufficiency Year. Multicoloured.

1289	5f. Type **207**	10	10
1290	7f. Woman and baskets of food	15	10
1291	40f. Man with baskets of fish and fruits	1·75	45
1292	60f. Fruits and vegetables	2·25	80

208 Pres. Habyarimana and Soldiers

1987. 25th Anniv of Independence. Multicoloured.

1293	10f. Type **208**	20	10
1294	40f. President at meeting	90	45
1295	70f. President with Pope John Paul II	2·50	85
1296	100f. Pres. Habyarimana (vert)	2·50	1·10

209 Bananas

1987. Fruits. Multicoloured.

1297	10f. Type **209**	20	10
1298	40f. Pineapples (horiz)	90	45
1299	80f. Papaya (horiz)	2·25	90
1300	90f. Avocados (horiz)	2·50	1·00
1301	100f. Strawberries	2·50	1·10

210 Mother carrying cub

1987. The Leopard. Multicoloured.

1302	50f. Type **210**	2·00	1·10
1303	50f. Leopards fighting	2·00	1·10
1304	50f. Leopards with prey	2·00	1·10
1305	50f. Leopard with prey in tree	2·00	1·10
1306	50f. Leopard leaping from tree	2·00	1·10

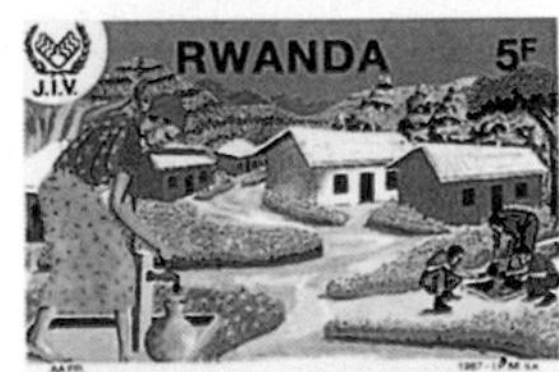

211 Village Activities

1987. International Volunteers Day. Mult.

1307	5f. Type **211**	10	10
1308	12f. Pupils in schoolroom	35	10
1309	20f. View of village	55	30
1310	60f. Woman tending oxen	1·75	85

212 "Virgin and Child" (Fra Angelico)

1987. Christmas. Sheet 65×85 mm.

MS1311	**212**	200f. blue	4·25	4·25

213 Carpenter's Shop

1988. Rural Incomes Protection Year. Mult.

1312	10f. Type **213**	20	10
1313	40f. Dairy farm	95	95
1314	60f. Workers in field	1·50	55
1315	80f. Selling baskets of eggs	2·10	1·50

214 Chimpanzees

1988. Primates of Nyungwe Forest. Multicoloured.

1316	2f. Type **214**	25	15
1317	3f. Black and white colobus	25	15
1318	10f. Lesser bushbabies	85	50
1319	90f. Monkeys	6·00	3·00

215 Boxing

1988. Olympic Games, Seoul. Multicoloured.

1320	5f. Type **215**	10	10
1321	7f. Relay race	15	10
1322	8f. Table tennis	20	10
1323	10f. Running	35	15
1324	90f. Hurdling	2·25	1·00

216 "25" on Map of Africa

1988. 25th Anniv of Organization of African Unity. Multicoloured.

1325	5f. Type **216**	15	10
1326	7f. Hands clasped across map	20	10
1327	8f. Building on map	20	10
1328	90f. Words forming map	2·75	2·25

217 "Virgin of the Soup" (Paul Veronese)

1988. Christmas. Sheet 65×85 mm.

MS1329	**217**	200f. turquoise	4·25	4·25

218 Newspaper Fragment and Refugees in Boat

1988. 125th Anniv of Red Cross Movement. Mult.

1330	10f. Type **218**	20	10
1331	30f. Red Cross workers and patient	80	35

1332	40f. Red Cross worker and elderly lady (vert)	95	40
1333	100f. Red Cross worker and family (vert)	2·75	1·25

219 "Plectranthus barbatus"

1989. Plants. Multicoloured.

1334	5f. Type **219**	15	20
1335	10f. "Tetradenia riparia"	50	20
1336	20f. "Hygrophila auriculata"	1·00	45
1337	40f. "Datura stramonium"	2·10	1·00
1338	50f. "Pavetta ternifolia"	2·75	1·40

220 Emblem, Dates and Sunburst

1989. Centenary of Interparliamentary Union. Mult.

1339	10f. Type **220**	30	10
1340	30f. Lake	85	65
1341	70f. River	1·60	1·40
1342	90f. Sun's rays	2·25	1·75

221 "Adoration of the Magi" (Peter Paul Rubens)

1989. Christmas. Sheet 70×90 mm.

MS1343	**221** 100f. black	2·40	2·40

222 Throwing Clay and Finished Pots

1989. Rural Self-help Year. Multicoloured.

1344	10f. Type **222**	30	10
1345	70f. Carrying baskets of produce (vert)	1·60	1·40
1346	90f. Firing clay pots	2·50	2·00
1347	200f. Clearing roadway	5·00	3·50

223 "Triumph of Marat" (Boilly)

1990. Bicentenary of French Revolution. Mult.

1348	10f. Type **223**	30	10
1349	60f. "Rouget de Lisle singing La Marseillaise" (Pils)	1·60	1·50
1350	70f. "Oath of the Tennis Court" (Jacques Louis David)	2·00	1·75
1351	100f. "Trial of Louis XVI" (Joseph Court)	3·00	2·75

224 Old and New Lifestyles

1990. 30th Anniv of Revolution. Multicoloured.

1352	10f. Type **224**	30	10
1353	60f. Couple holding farming implements (vert)	1·60	1·40
1354	70f. Modernization	1·75	1·40
1355	100f. Flag, map and warrior	2·50	2·50

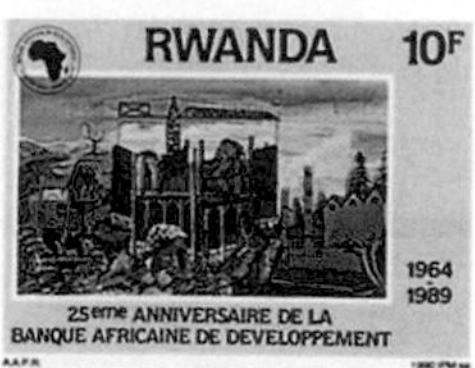

225 Construction

1990. 25th Anniv (1989) of African Development Bank. Multicoloured.

1356	10f. Type **225**	30	10
1357	20f. Tea picking	55	35
1358	40f. Road building	1·10	95
1359	90f. Tea pickers and modern housing	2·50	2·10

226 Penny Black (image scaled to 60% of original size)

1990. Belgica 90 International Stamp Exhibition, Brussels. Multicoloured.

MS1360	Three sheets each 82×42 mm. (a) 100f. Type **226**; (b) 100f. Belgian 1982 10f.+5f. football stamp (World Cup, Italy); (c) 100f. Rwanda 1973 30c. musician stamp	5·75	5·75

1990. World Cup Football Championship, Italy. Nos. 1267/72 optd ITALIA 90.

1361	**203**	2f. multicoloured	35	35
1362	-	4f. multicoloured	35	35
1363	-	5f. multicoloured	40	40
1364	-	10f. multicoloured	65	65
1365	-	40f. multicoloured	2·50	2·50
1366	-	45f. multicoloured	2·75	2·75

228 Pope John Paul II

1990. Papal Visits. Multicoloured.

1367	10f. Type **228**	75	75
1368	70f. Pope giving blessing	8·25	8·25
MS1369	105×110 mm. 100f. Pope praying (35×50 mm)	8·75	8·75

229 Adults learning Alphabet at School

1991. International Literacy Year (1990). Mult.

1370	10f. Type **229**	15	10
1371	20f. Children reading at school	35	20
1372	50f. Lowland villagers learning alphabet in field	90	80
1373	90f. Highland villagers learning alphabet outdoors	1·40	1·10

230 Tool-making

1991. Self-help Organizations. Multicoloured.

1374	10f. Type **230**	15	10
1375	20f. Rearing livestock	35	20
1376	50f. Textile manufacture	1·40	1·10
1377	90f. Construction	2·00	1·50

231 Statue of Madonna

1992. Death Centenary of Cardinal Lavigerie (founder of Orders of White Fathers and Sisters).

1378	**231**	5f. multicoloured	95	1·00
1379	-	15f. multicoloured	2·50	2·50
1380	-	70f. black and mauve	12·00	12·00
1381	-	110f. black and blue	18·00	20·00

DESIGNS—VERT: 15f. White Sister; 110f. Cardinal Lavigerie. HORIZ: 70f. White Fathers in Uganda, 1908.

232 Fisherman

1992. Int Nutrition Conference, Rome. Mult.

1382	15f. Type **232**	80	45
1383	50f. Market fruit stall	1·60	1·40
1384	100f. Man milking cow	3·25	2·75
1385	500f. Woman breastfeeding	17·00	14·50

233 Running

1993. Olympic Games, Barcelona (1992). Mult.

1386	20f. Type **233**	2·50	2·50
1387	30f. Swimming	4·00	4·50
1388	90f. Football	12·00	10·00
MS1389	85×124 mm. Nos. 1386/9	18·00	17·00

234 Toad

1998. Animals. Multicoloured.

1390	15f. Type **234**	20	30
1391	100f. Snail	80	85
1392	150f. Porcupine	1·25	1·25
1393	300f. Chameleon	2·50	2·75
MS1394	95×95 mm. Nos. 1390/3. Imperf	4·75	5·25

235 "Opuntia"

1998. Plants. Multicoloured.

1395	15f. Type **235**	20	30
1396	100f. "Gloriosa superba"	80	85
1397	150f. "Markhamia lutea"	1·25	1·25
1398	300f. "Hagenia abyssinica" (horiz)	2·50	2·75
MS1399	95×113 mm. Nos. 1395/8. Imperf	4·75	4·75

Pt. 18

RYUKYU ISLANDS

Group of islands between Japan and Taiwan, formerly Japanese until occupied by U.S. forces in 1945. After a period of military rule they became semi-autonomous under U.S. administration. The Amami Oshima group reverted to Japan in December 1953. The remaining islands were returned to Japan on 15 May 1972. Japanese stamps are now in use.

1948. 100 sen = 1 yen.
1958. 100 cents = 1 dollar (U.S.).

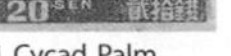
1 Cycad Palm

3 Tribute Junk

1948

1B	1	5s. purple	2·30	2·75
2A	-	10s. green	2·75	3·75
3A	1	20s. green	2·75	3·75
4B	3	30s. red	2·30	2·30
5B	-	40s. purple	2·30	2·30
6A	3	50s. blue	3·50	4·50
7B	-	1y. blue	6·50	6·50

DESIGNS: 10s., 40s. Easter lily; 1y. Farmer with hoe.

1950

8	6	50s. red	45	45
10	-	1y. blue	3·50	2·75
11	-	2y. purple	15·00	7·25
12	-	3y. pink	38·00	11·00
13	-	4y. grey	18·00	11·00
14	-	5y. green	11·00	6·00

DESIGNS: 1y. Shuri woman; 2y. Former Okinawa Palace, Shuri; 3y. Dragon's head; 4y. Okinawa women; 5y. Common spider and strawberry conches and radula scallop.

6 Shi-Shi Roof Tiles

12 Dove over Map of Ryukyus

1950. Air.

15	12	8y. blue	£120	39·00
16	12	12y. green	75·00	29·00
17	12	16y. red	23·00	23·00

14 University and Shuri Castle

1951. Inauguration of Ryukyu University.

19	14	3y. brown	75·00	23·00

15 Pine Tree

1951. Afforestation Week.

20	15	3y. green	70·00	23·00

16 Flying Goddess

1951. Air.

21	16	13y. blue	3·25	1·40
22	16	18y. green	4·50	3·50
23	16	30y. mauve	6·00	2·30
24	16	40y. purple	7·75	4·25
25	16	50y. orange	9·00	7·25

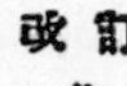

(17)

1952. Surch as T 17.

27	6	10y. on 50s. red	12·00	7·00
29	-	100y. on 2y. purple (No. 11)	£2250	£1300

18 Dove and Bean Seedling

1952. Establishment of Ryukyuan Government.

30	18	3y. red	£170	36·00

19 Madanbashi Bridge

1952

31	19	1y. red	35	25
32	-	2y. green	45	25
33	-	3y. turquoise	70	35
34	-	6y. blue	4·50	3·00
35	-	10y. red	5·50	3·50
36	-	30y. green	13·50	7·25
37	-	50y. purple	17·00	11·00
38	-	100y. purple	23·00	7·25

DESIGNS: 2y. Presence Chamber, Shuri Palace; 3y. Shuri Gate; 6y. Sogenji Temple Wall; 10y. Bensaitendo Temple; 30y. Sonohyamutake Gate; 50y. Tamaudum Mausoleum, Shuri; 100y. Hosho-chai Bridge.

27 Reception at Shuri Castle

28 Perry and American Fleet at Naha Harbour

1953. Centenary of Commodore Perry's Visit to Okinawa.

39	27	3y. purple	16·00	7·25
40	28	6y. blue	2·30	3·50

29 Chofu Ota and Matrix

1953. 3rd Press Week.

41	29	4y. brown	18·00	6·00

30 Wine Flask to fit around Waist

1954

42	30	4y. brown	1·40	70
43	-	15y. red	3·50	3·00
44	-	20y. orange	3·25	3·25

DESIGNS: 15y. Tung Dar Bon (lacquer bowl); 20y. Kasuri (textile pattern).

33 Shigo Toma and Pen-nib

1954. 4th Press Week.

45	33	4y. blue	20·00	7·25

34 Noguni Shrine and Sweet Potatoes

1955. 350th Anniv of Introduction of Sweet Potato Plant.

46	34	4y. blue	16·00	7·25

35 Stylized Trees

1956. Afforestation Week.

47	35	4y. green	12·00	6·00

38 Nidotekito Dance

1956. National Dances.

48	-	5y. purple	1·20	90
49	-	8y. violet	2·30	2·00
50	38	14y. brown	3·50	3·25

DESIGNS: 5y. Willow dance; 8y. Straw-hat dance.

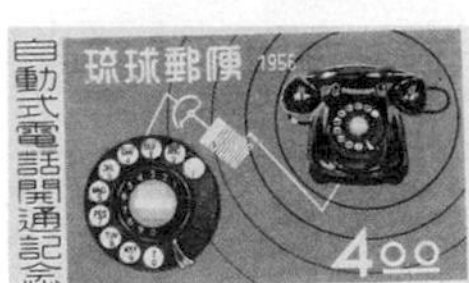
39 Telephone and Dial

1956. Inauguration of Telephone Dialling System.

51	39	4y. violet	22·00	12·00

40 Floral Garland

1956. New Year.

52	40	2y. multicoloured	3·25	1·80

41 Flying Goddess

1957. Air.

53	41	15y. green	8·25	3·50
54	41	20y. red	13·50	7·25
55	41	35y. green	16·00	9·00
56	41	45y. brown	20·00	11·00
57	41	60y. grey	23·00	14·50

42 "Rocket" Pencils

1957. 7th Press Week.

58	42	4y. blue	1·20	90

43 Phoenix

1957. New Year.

59	43	2y. multicoloured	45	25

44 Various Ryukyuan Postage Stamps

1958. 10th Anniv of First Postage Stamps of Ryukyu Islands.

60	44	4y. multicoloured	1·20	90

45 Stylized Dollar Sign over Yen Symbol

1958. With or without gum (Nos. 68/69), no gum (others).

61	45	½c. yellow	80	70
62	45	1c. green	1·30	1·10
63	45	2c. blue	2·00	1·80
64	45	3c. red	1·80	1·60
65	45	4c. green	2·00	1·80
66	45	5c. brown	4·50	3·50
67	45	10c. blue	6·75	4·25
68	45	25c. blue	9·00	7·25
69	45	50c. grey	18·00	11·00
70	45	$1 purple	14·50	7·25

46 Gateway of Courtesy

1958. Restoration of Shuri Gateway.

71	46	3c. multicoloured	1·50	1·10

47 Lion Dance

1958. New Year.

72	47	1½c. multicoloured	55	25

48 Trees

1959. Afforestation Week.

73	**48**	3c. multicoloured	70	65

49 Atlas Moth

1959. Japanese Biological Teachers' Conference, Okinawa.

74	**49**	3c. multicoloured	2·75	1·20

50 Hibiscus

1959. Multicoloured. (a) Inscr as in T 50.

75	½c. Type **50**	35	25
76	3c. Moorish idol	1·40	45
77	8c. Zebra moon, banded bonnet and textile cone (shells)	13·50	6·00
78	13c. Leaf butterfly (value at left)	3·25	2·30
79	17c. Jellyfish	23·00	11·00

(b) Inscr smaller and 13c. with value at right.

87	½c. Type **50**	55	35
88	3c. As No. 76	2·30	45
89	8c. As No. 77	5·75	2·30
90	13c. As No. 78	2·00	1·20
91	17c. As No. 79	15·00	6·00

55 Yakazi (Ryukyuan toy)

1959. New Year.

80	**55**	1½c. multicoloured	70	55

改訂 9¢

(56)

1959. Air. Surch as T 56.

81	**41**	9c. on 15y. green	2·75	1·80
82	**41**	14c. on 20y. red	3·50	3·50
83	**41**	19c. on 35y. green	8·25	6·00
84	**41**	27c. on 45y. brown	17·00	7·75
85	**41**	35c. on 60y. grey	18·00	11·00

57 University Badge

1960. 10th Anniv of University of the Ryukyus.

86	**57**	3c. multicoloured	1·40	70

1960. Air. Surch.

92	**30**	9c. on 4y. brown	4·50	1·50
93	-	14c. on 5y. purple (No. 48)	5·00	2·30
94	-	19c. on 15y. red (No. 43)	4·50	2·75
95	**38**	27c. on 14y. brown	8·75	4·50
96	-	35c. on 20y. orange (No. 44)	10·00	7·25

60 "Munjuru"

1960. Ryukyuan Dances. Mult. (a) Inscr as in T 60.

97	1c. Type **60**	1·80	1·10
98	2½c. "Inohabushi"	3·25	1·50
99	5c. "Hatomabushi"	1·10	1·00
100	10c. "Hanafu"	1·60	1·00

(b) As T 60 but additionally inscr "RYUKYUS".

107	1c. Type **60**	20	20
108	2½c. As No. 98	20	20
109	4c. As No. 98	25	35
110	5c. As No. 99	25	25
111	10c. As No. 100	55	45
112	20c. "Shudun"	3·25	1·30
113	25c. "Haodori"	1·10	90
114	50c. "Nobori Kuduchi"	3·25	1·30
115	$1 "Koteibushi"	6·25	45

65 Start of Race

1960. 8th Kyushu Athletic Meeting.

101	-	3c. red, green and blue	6·75	2·75
102	**65**	8c. green and orange	1·80	1·20

DESIGN: 3c. Torch and coastal scene.

66 Little Egret and Rising Sun

1960. National Census.

103	**66**	3c. brown	6·75	3·25

67 Bull Fight

1960. New Year.

104	**67**	1½c. brown, buff and blue	3·00	1·40

68 Native Pine Tree

1961. Afforestation Week.

105	**68**	3c. deep green, red & green	2·00	1·60

69 Naha, Junk, Liner and City Seal

1961. 40th Anniv of Naha City.

106	**69**	3c. turquoise	2·75	1·80

74 Flying Goddess

1961. Air.

116	**74**	9c. multicoloured	45	20
117	-	14c. multicoloured	70	65
118	-	19c. multicoloured	1·10	80
119	-	27c. multicoloured	3·50	90
120	-	35c. multicoloured	2·30	1·60

DESIGNS: 14c. Flying goddess playing flute; 19c. Wind god; 27c. Wind god (different); 35c. Flying goddess over trees.

79 White Silver Temple

1961. Unification of Itoman District and Takamine, Kanegushiku and Miwa Villages.

121	**79**	3c. brown	2·30	1·80

80 Books and Bird

1961. 10th Anniv of Ryukyu Book Week.

122	**80**	3c. multicoloured	1·40	1·10

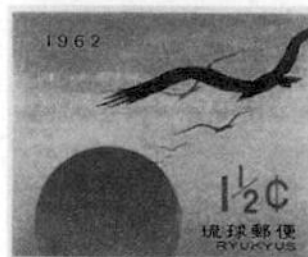

81 Sunrise and Eagles

1961. New Year.

123	**81**	1½c. red, black and gold	3·50	1·80

82 Govt Building, Steps and Trees

1962. 10th Anniv of Ryukyu Government. Mult.

124	1½c. Type **82**	80	70
125	3c. Government building	1·10	90

85 Shuri Gate and Campaign Emblem

1962. Malaria Eradication. Multicoloured.

126	3c. "Anopheles hyrcanus sinensis" (mosquito)	80	70
127	8c. Type **85**	1·40	1·40

86 Windmill, Dolls and Horse

1962. Children's Day.

128	**86**	3c. multicoloured	1·50	1·10

87 "Hibiscus liliaceus"

1962. Ryukyu Flowers. Multicoloured.

129	½c. Type **87**	25	20
130	2c. "Ixora chinensis"	25	25
131	3c. "Erythrina indica"	55	20
132	3c. "Caesalpinia pulcherrima"	25	25
133	8c. "Schima mertensiana"	80	45
134	13c. "Impatiens balsamina"	1·10	65
135	15c. "Hamaomoto" (herb)	1·80	1·00
136	17c. "Alpinia speciosa"	1·40	90
142	1½c. "Etithyllum strictum"	35	25

No. 142 is smaller, 18¾×22½ mm.

95 Akaeware Bowl

1962. Philatelic Week.

137	**95**	3c. multicoloured	5·00	3·00

96 Kendo (Japanese Fencing)

1962. All-Japan Kendo Meeting.

138	**96**	3c. multicoloured	6·00	3·25

97 "Hare and Water" (textile design)

1962. New Year.

139	**97**	1½c. multicoloured	2·30	1·40

98 Reaching Maturity (clay relief)

1963. Adults' Day.

140	**98**	3c. gold, black and blue	1·10	70

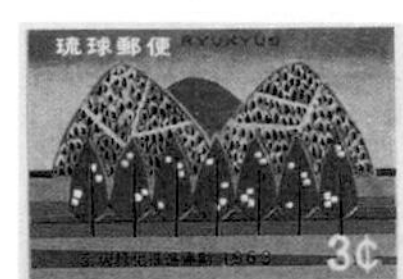

99 Trees and Wooded Hills

1963. Afforestation Week.

141	**99**	3c. multicoloured	1·10	90

101 Okinawa Highway

1963. Opening of Okinawa Highway.

143	**101**	3c. multicoloured	1·50	1·20

102 Black Kites over Islands

1963. Bird Week.

144	**102**	3c. multicoloured	2·30	1·40

104 Lacquerware Bowl

1963. Opening of Shioya Bridge, Okinawa.

145	**103**	3c. multicoloured	1·40	1·20

103 Shioya Bridge

1963. Philatelic Week.

146	**104**	3c. multicoloured	3·50	2·75

105 Convair 880 Jetliner and Shuri Gate

1963. Air.

147	**105**	5½c. multicoloured	35	25
148	-	7c. black, red and blue	45	35

DESIGN: 7c. Convair 880 jetliner over sea.

107 Map and Emblem

1963. Meeting of Junior Int Chamber, Naha.

149	**107**	3c. multicoloured	1·00	90

108 Nakagusuku Castle Ruins

1963. Ancient Buildings Protection Week.

150	**108**	3c. multicoloured	1·40	90

109 Flame

1963. 15th Anniv of Declaration of Human Rights.

151	**109**	3c. multicoloured	90	65

110 Bingata "dragon" (textile design)

1963. New Year.

152	**110**	1½c. multicoloured	90	45

111 Carnation

1964. Mothers' Day.

153	**111**	3c. multicoloured	90	55

112 Pineapples and Sugar-cane

1964. Agricultural Census.

154	**112**	3c. multicoloured	55	40

113 Hand-woven Sash

1964. Philatelic Week.

155	**113**	3c. brown, blue and pink	70	65

114 Girl Scout and Emblem

1964. 10th Anniv of Ryukyu Girl Scouts.

156	**114**	3c. multicoloured	55	35

115 Transmitting Tower

1964. Inauguration of Ryukyu–Jap'an Microwave Link.

157	**115**	3c. green and black	1·10	90
158	-	8c. blue and black	1·50	1·40

DESIGN: 8c. "Bowl" receiving aerial.

Both stamps have "1963" cancelled by bars and "1964" inserted in black.

117 Shuri Gate and Olympic Torch

1964. Passage of Olympic Torch through Okinawa.

159	**117**	3c. multicoloured	45	35

118 "Naihanchi" (Karate stance)

1964. Karate ("self-defence"). Multicoloured.

160	3c. Type **118**	70	55
161	3c. "Makiwara" (karate training)	65	55
162	3c. "Kumite" exercise	55	55

121 "Miyara Dunchi" (old Ryukyuan Residence)

1964. Ancient Buildings Protection Week.

163	**121**	3c. multicoloured	45	35

122 Bingata "snake" (textile design)

1964. New Year.

164	**122**	1½c. multicoloured	55	40

123 Boy Scouts, Badge and Shuri Gate

1965. 10th Anniv of Ryukyuan Boy Scouts.

165	**123**	3c. multicoloured	60	45

124 "Samisen" (musical instrument)

1965. Philatelic Week.

166	**124**	3c. multicoloured	60	45

125 Stadium

1965. Completion of Onoyama Sports Ground.

167	**125**	3c. multicoloured	35	25

126 Kin Power Station

1965. Completion of Kin Power Plant.

168	**126**	3c. multicoloured	45	35

127 I.C.Y. Emblem and "Globe"

1965. International Co-operation Year and 20th Anniv of United Nations.

169	**127**	3c. multicoloured	35	25

128 City Hall, Naha

1965. Completion of Naha City Hall.

170	**128**	3c. multicoloured	35	25

129 Semaruhakogame Turtle

1965. Ryukyuan Turtles. Multicoloured.

171	3c. Type **129**	80	45
172	3c. Taimai or hawksbill turtle	80	45
173	3c. Yamagame or hill tortoise	80	45

132 Bingata "horse" (textile design)

1965. New Year.

174	**132**	1½c. multicoloured	35	25

133 Pryer's Woodpecker

1966. "Natural Monument" (Wildlife). Mult.

175	3c. Type **133**	65	35
176	3c. Sika deer	65	35
177	3c. Dugong	65	35

136 Pacific Swallow

1966. Bird Week.

178	**136**	3c. multicoloured	55	40

137 Lilies and Ruins

1966. Memorial Day (Battle of Okinawa).

179	**137**	3c. multicoloured	35	30

138 University of the Ryukyus

1966. Transfer of University of the Ryukyus to Government Administration.

180	**138**	3c. multicoloured	35	30

139 Lacquer Box

1966. Philatelic Week.

181	**139**	3c. multicoloured	35	30

140 Ryukyuan Tiled House

1966. 20th Anniv of UNESCO.

182	**140**	3c. multicoloured	35	30

141 "GRI" Museum, Shuri

1966. Completion of Government Museum, Shuri.

183	**141**	3c. multicoloured	35	30

142 Nakasone-Tuimya Tomb

1966. Ancient Buildings Protection Week.

184	**142**	3c. multicoloured	35	30

143 Bingata "ram" (textile design)

1966. New Year.

185	**143**	1½c. multicoloured	55	35

144 Tomato Anemonefish

1966. Tropical Fish. Multicoloured.

186	3c. Type **144**	75	45
187	3c. Blue-spotted boxfish	75	45
188	3c. Long-nosed butterflyfish	75	45
189	3c. Clown triggerfish	75	45
190	3c. Saddle butterflyfish	75	45

149 Tsuboya Urn

1967. Philatelic Week.

191	**149**	3c. multicoloured	45	30

150 Episcopal Mitre

1967. Sea Shells. Multicoloured.

192	3c. Type **150**	65	35
193	3c. Venus comb murex ("Murex (Aranea) triremus")	65	35
194	3c. Chiragra spider conch ("Lambis (Harpago) chiragra")	70	45
195	3c. Great green turban ("Turbo (Olearia) marmoratus")	70	45
196	3c. Bubble conch ("Euprotomus bulla")	70	45

155 Roof Tiles and Emblem

1967. International Tourist Year.

197	**155**	3c. multicoloured	35	30

156 Mobile Clinic

1967. 15th Anniv of Anti-T.B. Association.

198	**156**	3c. multicoloured	35	30

157 Hojo Bridge, Enkaku

1967. Ancient Buildings Protection Week.

199	**157**	3c. multicoloured	35	30

158 Bingata "monkey" (textile design)

1967. New Year.

200	**158**	1½c. multicoloured	35	30

159 T.V. Tower and Map

1967. Opening of T.V. Broadcasting Stations in Miyako and Yaeyama.

201	**159**	3c. multicoloured	35	30

160 Dr. Nakachi and Assistant

1968. 120th Anniv of 1st Ryukyu Vaccination (by Dr. Kijin Nakachi).

202	**160**	3c. multicoloured	35	30

161 Medicine Case (after Sokei Dana)

1968. Philatelic Week.

203	**161**	3c. multicoloured	55	35

162 Young Man, Book, Map and Library

1968. Library Week.

204	**162**	3c. multicoloured	50	35

163 Postmen with Ryukyu Stamp of 1948

1968. 20th Anniv of 1st Ryukyu Islands Stamps.

205	**163**	3c. multicoloured	45	35

164 Temple Gate

1968. Restoration of Enkaku Temple Gate.

206	**164**	3c. multicoloured	45	35

165 Old Man Dancing

1968. Old People's Day.

207	**165**	3c. multicoloured	45	35

166 "Mictyris longicarpus"

1968. Crabs. Multicoloured.

208	3c. Type **166**	90	65
209	3c. "Uca dubia"	90	65
210	3c. "Baptozius vinosus"	90	65
211	3c. "Cardisoma carnifex"	90	65
212	3c. "Ocypode ceratophthalma"	90	65

171 Saraswati Pavilion

1968. Ancient Buildings Protection Week.

213	**171**	3c. multicoloured	40	30

172 Player

1968. 35th All-Japan East v West Men's Softball Tennis Tournament, Onoyama.

214	**172**	3c. multicoloured	45	35

173 Bingata "cock" (textile design)

1968. New Year.

215	**173**	1½c. multicoloured	80	35

174 Boxer

1969. 20th All-Japan Boxing Championships.

216	**174**	3c. multicoloured	45	35

175 Inkwell Screen

1969. Philatelic Week.

217	**175**	3c. multicoloured	45	25

176 UHF Antennae and Map

1969. Inauguration of Okinawa–Sakishima U.H.F. Radio Service.

218	**176**	3c. multicoloured	35	25

177 Gate of Courtesy

1969. 22nd All-Japan Formative Education Study Conference, Naha.

219	**177**	3c. multicoloured	35	25

178 "Tug of War" Festival

1969. Traditional Religious Ceremonies. Mult.

220	3c. Type **178**	65	45
221	3c. "Hari" canoe race	65	45
222	3c. "Izaiho" religious ceremony	65	45
223	3c. "Ushideiku" dance	65	45
224	3c. "Sea God" dance	65	45

1969. No. 131 surch.

225	½c. on 3c. multicoloured	70	65

184 Nakamura-Ke

1969. Ancient Buildings Protection Week.

226	**184**	3c. multicoloured	35	25

185 Kyuzo Toyama and Map

1969. 70th Anniv of Toyama's Ryukyu–Hawaii Emigration Project.

227	**185**	3c. multicoloured	45	35

No. 227 has "1970" cancelled by bars and "1969" inserted in black.

186 Bingata "dog and flowers" (textile design)

1969. New Year.

228	**186**	1½c. multicoloured	55	35

187 Sake Flask

1970. Philatelic Week.

229	187	3c. multicoloured	40	25

188 "Shushin-Kaneiri"

189 "Chu-nusudu"

190 "Mekarushi"

191 "Nidotichiuchi"

192 "Kokonomaki"

1970. "Kumi-Odori" Ryukyu Theatre. Mult.

230	188	3c. multicoloured	75	60
231	189	3c. multicoloured	75	60
232	190	3c. multicoloured	75	60
233	191	3c. multicoloured	75	60
234	192	3c. multicoloured	75	60
MS235		94×102 mm. Nos. 230×4	6·00	6·00
MS236		94×102 mm. Nos. 231×4	6·00	6·00
MS237		94×102 mm. Nos. 232×4	6·00	6·00
MS238		94×102 mm. Nos. 233×4	6·00	6·00
MS239		94×102 mm. Nos. 234×4	6·00	6·00

193 Observatory

1970. Completion of Underwater Observatory, Busena-Misaki, Nago.

240	193	3c. multicoloured	80	35

194 Noboru Jahana (politician)

1970. Famous Ryukyuans.

241	194	3c. purple	65	65
242	-	3c. green	80	65
243	-	3c. black	65	65

PORTRAITS: No. 242, Saion Gushichan Bunjaku (statesman); 243, Choho Giwan (Regent).

197 "Population

1970. Population Census.

244	197	3c. multicoloured	35	30

198 "Great Cycad of Une"

1970. Ancient Buildings Protection Week.

245	198	3c. multicoloured	45	30

199 Ryukyu Islands, Flag and Japan Diet

1970. Election of Ryukyu Representatives to the Japanese Diet.

246	199	3c. multicoloured	90	65

200 "Wild Boar" (Bingata textile design)

1970. New Year.

247	200	1½c. multicoloured	55	35

201 "Jibata" (hand-loom)

202 "Filature" (spinning-wheel)

203 Farm-worker wearing "Shurunnu" Coat and "Kubagasa" Hat

204 Woman using "Shiri-Ushi" (rice huller)

205 Fisherman's "Umi-Fujo" (box) and "Yutui" (bailer)

1971. Ryukyu Handicrafts.

248	201	3c. multicoloured	45	35
249	202	3c. multicoloured	45	35
250	203	3c. multicoloured	45	35
251	204	3c. multicoloured	45	35
252	205	3c. multicoloured	45	35

206 "Taku" (container)

1971. Philatelic Week.

253	206	3c. multicoloured	45	30

207 Civic Emblem with Old and New City Views

1971. 50th Anniv of Naha's City Status.

254	207	3c. multicoloured	55	45

208 Restored Battlefield, Okinawa

1971. Government Parks. Multicoloured.

255		3c. Type **208**	35	35
256		3c. Haneji Inland Sea	35	35
257		4c. Yabuchi Island	35	35

211 Deva King, Torinji Temple

1971. Ancient Buildings Protection Week.

258	211	4c. multicoloured	55	45

212 "Rat" (Bingata textile pattern)

1971. New Year.

259	212	2c. multicoloured	70	55

213 Student-nurse and Candle

1971. 25th Anniv of Nurses' Training Scheme.

260	213	4c. multicoloured	55	45

214 Islands and Sunset

1972. Maritime Scenery. Multicoloured.

261		5c. Type **214**	35	70
262		5c. Coral reef (horiz)	35	70
263		5c. Island and short-tailed albatrosse	90	90

217 Dove and Flags of Japan and U.S.A

1972. Ratification of Treaty for Return of Ryukyu Islands to Japan.

264	217	5c. multicoloured	70	1·10

218 "Yushibin" (ceremonial sake container)

1972. Philatelic Week.

265	218	5c. multicoloured	55	1·10

EXPRESS DELIVERY STAMP

E13 Sea-horse

1951

E18	E13	5y. blue	38·00	23·00

Pt. 7

SAAR

A German territory South-east of Luxembourg. Occupied by France under League of Nations control from 1920 to 1935. Following a plebiscite, Saar returned to Germany in 1935 from when German stamps were used until the French occupation in 1945, after which Nos. F1/13 of Germany followed by Nos. 203 etc of Saar were used. The territory was autonomous under French protection until it again returned to Germany at the end of 1956 following a national referendum. Issues from 1957 were authorised by the German Federal Republic pending the adoption of German currency on 6 July 1959, after which West German stamps were used.

1920–May 1921. 100 pfennig = 1 mark.
May 1921–March 1935. 100 centimes = 1 franc.
1935–47. 100 pfennig = 1 reichsmark.
1947. 100 pfennig = 1 Saarmark.
November 1947–July 1959. 100 centimes =1 franc.
From 1959. 100 pfennig = 1 Deutsche mark.

LEAGUE OF NATIONS COMMISSION

1920. German stamps inscr "DEUTSCHES REICH" optd Sarre and bar.

1	24	2pf. grey	1·90	5·75
2c	24	2½pf. grey	2·10	7·50
3	10	3pf. brown	1·40	3·75
4c	10	5pf. green	65	1·30
5	24	7½pf. orange	85	2·30
6	10	10pf. red	75	1·70
7	24	15pf. violet	65	1·40
8	10	20pf. blue	65	1·40
9	10	25pf. black & red on yellow	12·50	26·00
10	10	30pf. black & orange on buff	23·00	48·00
11	24	35pf. brown	75	1·70
12	10	40pf. black and red	75	1·70
13	10	50pf. black & pur on cream	75	1·40
14	10	60pf. purple	75	1·70
15	10	75pf. black and green	65	1·60
16	10	80pf. black and red on red	£250	£350
17b	12	1m. red	37·00	60·00

1920. Bavarian stamps optd Sarre or SARRE (Nos. 30/1) and bars.

18	15	5pf. green	95	2·10
19	15	10pf. red	95	2·10
19a	15	15pf. red	1·30	2·50
21	15	20pf. blue	85	2·10
22	15	25pf. grey	15·00	21·00
23	15	30pf. orange	8·50	15·00
24	15	40pf. green	13·50	21·00
25	15	50pf. brown	2·10	3·75
26	15	60pf. green	4·25	10·50

27	**16**	1m. brown	21·00	42·00
28	**16**	2m. violet	80·00	£180
29	**16**	3m. red	£160	£200
30	-	5m. blue (No. 192)	£1000	£1200
31	-	10m. green (No. 193)	£180	£350

1920. German stamps inscr "DEUTSCHES REICH" optd SAARGEBIET.

32	**10**	5pf. green	30	65
33	**10**	5pf. brown	65	1·10
34	**10**	10pf. red	30	65
35	**10**	10pf. orange	60	65
36	**24**	15pf. violet	30	65
37	**10**	20pf. blue	30	65
38	**10**	20pf. green	95	65
39	**10**	30pf. black & orange on buff	55	65
40	**10**	30pf. blue	75	95
41	**10**	40pf. black and red	40	65
42	**10**	40pf. red	1·40	95
43	**10**	50pf. black & purple on buff	55	65
44	**10**	60pf. purple	85	65
45	**10**	75pf. black and green	95	65
46	**12**	1m.25 green	3·00	1·60
47	**12**	1m.50 brown	2·75	1·60
48	**13**	2m.50 purple	5·25	17·00
49	**10**	4m. red and black	11·50	30·00

1920. No. 45 of Saar surch 20 and No. 102 of Germany surch SAARGEBIET, arms and value.

50		20 on 75pf. black and green	55	1·60
51	**24**	5m. on 15pf. purple	6·50	21·00
52	**24**	10m. on 15pf. purple	7·50	25·00

9 Miner

11 Colliery Shafthead

12 Burbach Steelworks

1921

53	-	5pf. violet and green	40	65
54	**9**	10pf. orange and blue	40	65
55	-	20pf. grey and green	40	1·40
56	-	25pf. blue and brown	55	1·10
57	-	30pf. brown and green	55	95
58	-	40pf. red	55	65
59	-	50pf. black and grey	1·30	5·25
60	-	60pf. brown and red	2·10	4·75
61	-	80pf. blue	95	1·60
62	-	1m. black and red	1·10	2·10
63	**11**	1m.25 green and brown	1·30	2·75
64	-	2m. black and orange	3·25	5·25
65	-	3m. sepia and brown	4·25	12·50
66	-	5m. violet and yellow	12·50	30·00
67	-	10m. brown and green	16·00	32·00
68	**12**	25m. blue, black and red	42·00	95·00

DESIGNS—As Type **11**. HORIZ: 5pf. Mill above Mettlach; 20pf. Pit head at Reden; 25pf. River traffic, Saarbrucken; 30pf. River Saar at Mettlach; 40pf. Slag-heap, Volklingen; 50pf. Signal gantry, Saarbrucken; 80pf. "Old Bridge", Saarbrucken; 1m. Wire-rope Railway; 2m. Town Hall, Saarbrucken; 3m. Pottery, Mettlach; 5m. St. Ludwig's Church; 10m. Chief Magistrate's and Saar Commissioner's Offices. VERT: 60pf. Gothic Chapel, Mettlach.

See also Nos. 84/97.

1921. Nos. 55/68 surch in French currency.

70	3c. on 20pf. grey and green	55	65
71	5c. on 25pf. blue and brown	55	65
72	10c. on 30pf. brown and green	55	65
73	15c. on 40pf. red	65	65
74	20c. on 50pf. black and grey	55	65
75	25c. on 60pf. brown and red	65	65
76	30c. on 80pf. blue	2·10	1·40
77	40c. on 1m. black and red	2·75	65
78	50c. on 1m.25 green & brown	4·25	1·40
79	75c. on 2m. black and orange	5·25	2·75
80	1f. on 3m. black and brown	6·25	3·25
81	2f. on 5m. violet and yellow	16·00	8·50
82	3f. on 10m. brown and green	21·00	34·00
83	5f. on 25m. blue, black and red	23·00	48·00

1922. Larger designs (except 5f.) and value in French currency.

84	3c. green (as No. 62)	55	85
85	5c. black & orange (as No. 54)	55	55
86	10c. green (as No. 61)	55	55
87	15c. brown (as No. 62)	1·60	55
98	15c. orange (as No. 62)	3·25	55
88	20c. blue & yellow (as No. 64)	18·00	55
100	25c. red and yellow (as No. 64)	3·25	55
90	30c. red and yellow (as No. 58)	2·75	2·75
91	40c. brown & yell (as No. 65)	1·30	55
92	50c. blue & yellow (as No. 56)	1·30	55
93	75c. green & yellow (as No. 65)	18·00	32·00
94	1f. brown (as No. 66)	3·25	1·10
95	2f. violet (as No. 63)	4·75	4·25
96	3f. green & orange (as No. 60)	32·00	8·50
97	5f. brown & choc (as No. 68)	32·00	60·00

14 Madonna of Blieskastel

1925

102	**14**	45c. purple	3·75	6·75
103	**14**	10f. brown (31×36 mm)	21·00	32·00

15 Army Medical Service

1926. Welfare Fund.

104	**15**	20c.+20c. green	10·50	26·00
105	-	40c.+40c. brown	10·50	26·00
106	-	50c.+50c. orange	10·50	26·00
107	-	1f.50+1f.50 blue	25·00	65·00

DESIGNS: 40c. Hospital work (nurse and patient); 50c. Child welfare (children at a spring); 1f.50, Maternity nursing service.

18 Tholey Abbey

1926

108		10c. brown	95	65
109		15c. green	55	1·40
110		20c. brown	55	65
111	**18**	25c. blue	95	65
112	-	30c. green	1·30	65
113	-	40c. brown	95	65
114	**18**	50c. red	1·30	65
114a	-	60c. orange	5·25	75
115	-	75c. purple	95	65
116	-	80c. orange	3·25	11·50
116a	-	90c. red	16·00	23·00
117	-	1f. violet	3·25	65
118	-	1f.50 blue	6·25	65
119	-	2f. red	7·50	65
120	-	3f. green	15·00	1·70
121	-	5f. brown	16·00	9·50

DESIGNS—VERT: 10, 30c. Fountain, St. Johann, Saarbrucken. HORIZ: 15, 75c. Saar Valley near Gudingen; 20, 40, 90c. View from Saarlouis fortifications; 60, 80c., 1f. Colliery shafthead; 1f.50, 2, 3, 5f. Burbach Steelworks.

1927. Welfare Fund. Optd 1927–28.

122	**15**	20c.+20c. green	17·00	37·00
123	**15**	40c.+40c. brown	17·00	37·00
124	**15**	50c.+50c. orange	15·00	26·00
125	**15**	1f.50+1f.50 blue	23·00	85·00

19 Breguet 14 Biplane over Saarbrucken

1928. Air.

126	**19**	50c. red	5·25	5·25
127	**19**	1f. violet	8·50	6·25

20 "The Blind Beggar" by Dyckmanns

1928. Christmas Charity.

128	**20**	40c.(+40c.) brown	16·00	95·00
129	**20**	50c.(+50c.) purple	16·00	95·00
130	**20**	1f.(+1f.) violet	16·00	95·00
131	-	1f.50(+1f.50) blue	16·00	95·00
132	-	2f.(+2f.) red	19·00	£140
133	-	3f.(+3f.) green	19·00	£180
134	-	10f.(+10f.) brown	£475	£5500

DESIGNS: 1f.50, 2, 3f. "Almsgiving" by Schiestl; 10f. "Charity" by Raphael (picture in circle).

1929. Christmas Charity. Paintings. As T **20**.

135	40c.(+15c.) green	2·75	7·50
136	50c.(+20c.) red	5·25	12·50
137	1f.(+50c.) purple	5·25	15·00
138	1f.50(+75c.) blue	5·25	15·00
139	2f.(+1f.) red	5·25	15·00
140	3f.(+2f.) green	10·50	34·00
141	10f.(+8f.) brown	65·00	£180

DESIGNS: 40c. to 1f. "Orphaned" by H. Kaulbach; 1f.50, 2, 3f. "St. Ottilia" by M. Feuerstein; 10f. "The Little Madonna" by Ferruzzio.

1930. Nos. 114 and 116 surch.

141a	**18**	40c. on 50c. red	2·10	2·10
142	-	60c. on 80c. orange	2·75	3·25

1931. Christmas Charity (1930 issue). Paintings. As T **20**.

143	40c.(+15c.) brown	10·50	32·00
144	60c.(+20c.) orange	10·50	32·00
145	1f.(+50c.) red	10·50	65·00
146	1f.50(+75c.) blue	16·00	65·00
147	2f.(+1f.) brown	16·00	65·00
148	3f.(+2f.) green	26·00	65·00
149	10f.(+10f.) brown	£130	£375

DESIGNS: 40, 60c., 1f.50, "The Safetyman" (miner and lamp) by F. Zolnhofer; 1, 2, 3f. "The Good Samaritan" by J. Heinemann; 10f. "At the Window" by F. G. Waldmuller.

1931. Christmas Charity. Paintings. As T **20**.

150	40c.(+15c.) brown	17·00	48·00
151	60c.(+20c.) red	17·00	48·00
152	1f.(+50c.) purple	21·00	75·00
153	1f.50(+75c.) blue	25·00	75·00
154	2f.(+1f.) red	30·00	75·00
155	3f.(+2f.) green	37·00	£130
156	5f.(+5f.) brown	£130	£425

DESIGNS: 40c. to 1f. "St. Martin" by F. Boehle; 1f.50, 2f. "Charity" by Ridgeway-Knight; 5f. "The Widow's Mite" by Dubufe.

29 Focke Wulf A-17 Mowe over Saarbrucken Airport

1932. Air.

157	**29**	60c. red	8·50	6·25
158	**29**	5f. brown	60·00	£130

30 Kirkel Castle Ruins

1932. Christmas Charity.

159	**30**	40c.(+15c.) brown	12·50	30·00
160	-	60c.(+20c.) red	12·50	30·00
161	-	1f.(+50c.) purple	19·00	55·00
162	-	1f.50(+75c.) blue	26·00	65·00
163	-	2f.(+1f.) red	26·00	75·00
164	-	3f.(+2f.) green	75·00	£225
165	-	5f.(+5f.) brown	£160	£375

DESIGNS—VERT: 60c. Blieskastel Church; 1f. Ottweiler Church; 1f.50, St. Michael's Church, Saarbrucken; 2f. Cathedral and fountain, St. Wendel; 3f. St. John's Church, Saarbrucken. HORIZ: 5f. Kerpen Castle, Illingen.

32 Scene of the Disaster

1933. Neunkirchen Explosion Disaster.

166	**32**	60c.(+60c.) orange	22·00	26·00
167	**32**	3f.(+3f.) green	48·00	95·00
168	**32**	5f.(+5f.) brown	48·00	95·00

33 "Love"

1934. Christmas Charity.

169	**33**	40c.(+15c.) brown	7·50	21·00
170	-	60c.(+20c.) red	7·50	21·00
171	-	1f.(+50c.) mauve	9·50	26·00
172	-	1f.50(+75c.) blue	19·00	48·00
173	-	2f.(+1f.) red	17·00	48·00
174	-	3f.(+2f.) green	19·00	48·00
175	-	5f.(+5f.) brown	42·00	£120

DESIGNS: 60c. "Solicitude". 1f. "Peace". 1f.50, "Consolation". 2f. "Welfare". 3f. "Truth". 5f. Countess Elizabeth von Nassau.

Nos. 169/74 show statues by C. L. Pozzi in church of St. Louis, Saarbrucken.

1934. Saar Plebiscite. Optd VOLKSABSTIMMUNG 1935. (a) Postage. On Nos. 108/15, 116a/21 and 103.

176		10c. brown	55	75
177		15c. green	55	75
178		20c. brown	85	1·80
179	**18**	25c. blue	85	1·80
180	-	30c. green	55	75
181	-	40c. brown	55	95
182	**18**	50c. red	95	1·80
183	-	60c. orange	55	75
184	-	75c. purple	95	1·80
185	-	90c. red	95	1·90
186	-	1f. violet	95	2·10
187	-	1f.50 blue	1·70	4·25
188	-	2f. red	2·75	6·25
189	-	3f. green	6·25	12·50
190	-	5f. brown	26·00	42·00
191	**14**	10f. brown	32·00	80·00

(b) Air. On Nos. 126/7 and 157/8.

192	**19**	50c. red	5·25	9·50
193	**29**	60c. red	4·25	3·75
194	**19**	1f. violet	9·50	12·50
195	**29**	5f. brown	12·50	19·00

1934. Christmas Charity. Nos. 169/75 optd VOLKSABSTIMMUNG 1935.

196	**33**	40c.(+15c.) brown	4·75	19·00
197	-	60c.(+20c.) red	4·75	19·00
198	-	1f.(+50c.) mauve	15·00	34·00
199	-	1f.50(+75c.) blue	9·50	34·00
200	-	2f.(+1f.) red	15·00	48·00
201	-	3f.(+2f.) green	13·50	42·00
202	-	5f.(+5f.) brown	20·00	55·00

FRENCH OCCUPATION

36 Coal-miner

37 Loop of the Saar

1947. Inscr "SAAR".

203	**36**	2pf. grey	30	55
204	**36**	3pf. orange	30	65
205	**36**	6pf. green	30	55
206	**36**	8pf. red	30	40
207	**36**	10pf. mauve	30	55
208	**36**	12pf. green	30	65
209	-	15pf. brown	30	8·50
210	-	16pf. blue	30	55
211	-	20pf. red	30	55
212	-	24pf. brown	30	55
213	-	25pf. mauve	65	30·00
214	-	30pf. green	30	1·10
215	-	40pf. brown	30	1·60
216	-	45pf. red	75	21·00
217	-	50pf. violet	75	30·00
218	-	60pf. violet	65	30·00
219	-	75pf. blue	30	55
220	-	80pf. orange	30	55

221	-	84pf. brown	30	55
222	37	1m. green	30	65

DESIGNS—As T **36**: 15pf. to 24pf. Steel workers; 25pf. to 50pf. Sugar beet harvesters; 60pf. to 80pf. Mettlach Abbey. As T **37**—VERT: 84pf. Marshal Ney.

1947. As last surch in French currency.

223B	36	10c. on 2pf. grey	30	75
224B	36	60c. on 3pf. orange	30	1·50
225B	36	1f. on 10pf. mauve	30	75
226B	36	2f. on 12pf. green	40	1·90
227B	-	3f. on 15pf. brown	40	1·90
228B	-	4f. on 16pf. blue	40	10·50
229B	-	5f. on 20pf. red	40	1·40
230B	-	6f. on 24pf. brown	40	85
231B	-	9f. on 30pf. green	55	18·00
232B	-	10f. on 50pf. violet	55	26·00
233B	-	14f. on 60pf. violet	85	18·00
234B	-	20f. on 84pf. brown	1·40	27·00
235B	37	50f. on 1m. green	1·90	27·00

42 Clasped Hands

43 Builders

44 Saar Valley

1948. Inscr "SAARPOST".

236	42	10c. red (postage)	95	2·75
237	42	60c. blue	95	2·75
238	42	1f. black	40	40
239	-	2f. red	55	40
240	-	3f. brown	55	40
241	-	4f. red	55	40
242	-	5f. violet	55	40
243	-	6f. red	95	40
244	-	9f. blue	6·25	65
245	-	10f. blue	3·75	1·10
246	-	14f. purple	5·25	1·50
247	43	20f. red	10·50	1·50
248	-	50f. blue	18·00	3·75
249	44	25f. red (air)	6·25	4·25
250	44	50f. blue	3·75	3·25
251	44	200f. red	37·00	48·00

DESIGNS—As Type **42**: 2, 3f. Man's head;. 4, 5f. Woman's head; 6, 9f. Miner's head. As Type **43**: 10f. Blast furnace chimney; 14f. Foundry; 50f. Facade of Mettlach Abbey.

46 Floods in St. Johann, Sarbrucken

1948. Flood Disaster Relief Fund. Flood Scenes.

252	-	5f.+5f. green (postage)	5·75	44·00
253	46	6f.+4f. purple	5·75	42·00
254	-	12f.+8f. red	8·50	55·00
255	-	18f.+12f. blue	10·50	65·00
MS255a 147×104 mm. Nos. 252/5. Imperf			£750	£3500
256	-	25f.+25f. brown (air)	32·00	£300
MS256a 90×60 mm. No. 256			£650	£2500

DESIGNS—VERT: 18f. Flooded street, Saarbrucken. HORIZ: 5f. Flooded industrial area; 12f. Landtag building, Saarbrucken; 25f. Floods at Ensdorf, Saarlouis.

47 Map of Saarland

1948. 1st Anniv of Constitution.

257	47	10f. red	2·75	5·25
258	47	25f. blue	3·75	10·50

48 Hikers and Ludweiler Hostel

1949. Youth Hostels Fund.

259	48	8f.+5f. brown	4·75	£140
260	-	10f.+7f. green	5·75	£140

DESIGN: 10f. Hikers and Weisskirchen hostel.

49 Chemical Research

1949. Saar University.

261	49	15f. red	9·50	65

50 Mare and Foal

1949. Horse Day.

262	50	15f.+5f. red	16·00	42·00
263	-	25f.+15f. blue	21·00	48·00

DESIGN: 25f. Two horses in steeple-chase.

51 Symbolic of Typography

52 Labourer and Foundry

1949

264		10c. purple	40	2·75
265		60c. black	40	2·75
266		1f. red	1·60	40
267		3f. brown	10·50	55
268		5f. violet	2·75	40
269		6f. green	13·50	55
270		8f. green	1·60	85
271	51	10f. orange	6·25	40
272	-	12f. green	19·00	40
273	-	15f. red	9·50	40
274	-	18f. mauve	3·75	6·75
275	52	20f. grey	2·75	40
276	-	25f. blue	26·00	40
277	-	30f. red	23·00	65
278	-	45f. purple	6·25	75
279	-	60f. green	10·50	2·75
280	-	100f. brown	13·50	3·25

DESIGNS—As Type **51**: 10c. Building trade; 60c. Beethoven; 1f. and 3f. Heavy industries; 5f. Slag heap; 6f. and 15f. Colliery; 8f. Posthorn and telephone; 12f. and 18f. Pottery. As Type **52**—VERT: 25f. Blast furnace worker; 60f. Landsweiler; 100f. Wiebelskirchen. HORIZ: 30f. St. Arnual; 45f. "Giant's Boot", Rentrisch.

53 Detail from "Moses Striking the Rock" (Murillo)

1949. National Relief Fund.

281	53	8f.+2f. blue	10·50	55·00
282	-	12f.+3f. green	12·50	65·00
283	-	15f.+5f. purple	19·00	£110
284	-	25f.+10f. blue	32·00	£170
285	-	50f.+20f. purple	48·00	£300

DESIGNS: 12f. "Our Lord healing the Paralytic" (Murillo); 15f. "The Sick Child" (Metsu); 25f. "St. Thomas of Villanueva" (Murillo); 50f. "Madonna of Blieskastel".

54 A. Kolping

1950. Honouring Adolf Kolping (miners' padre).

286	54	15f.+5f. red	34·00	£110

55 P. Wust

1950. 10th Death Anniv of Peter Wust (philosopher).

287	55	15f. red	17·00	9·50

56 Mail Coach

1950. Stamp Day.

288	56	15f.+5f. brown and red	90·00	£150

57 "Food for the Hungry"

1950. Red Cross Fund.

289	57	25f.+10f. lake and red	36·00	85·00

58 St. Peter

1950. Holy Year.

290	58	12f. green	4·25	13·50
291	58	15f. red	6·25	12·50
292	58	25f. blue	10·50	27·00

59 Town Hall, Ottweiler

1950. 400th Anniv of Ottweiler.

293	59	10f. brown	8·00	10·50

61

1950. Saar's Admission to Council of Europe.

294	61	25f. blue (postage)	48·00	16·00
295	-	200f. red (air)	£190	£325

DESIGN: 200f. As T **61** but with dove in flight over book.

62 St. Lutwinus enters Monastery

1950. National Relief Fund. Inscr "VOLKSHILFE".

296	62	8f.+2f. brown	12·50	42·00
297	-	12f.+3f. green	11·50	42·00
298	-	15f.+5f. brown	16·00	70·00
299	-	25f.+10f. blue	17·00	95·00
300	-	50f.+20f. purple	25·00	£160

DESIGNS: 12f. Lutwinus builds Mettlach Abbey; 15f. Lutwinus as Abbot; 25f. Bishop Lutwinus confirming children at Rheims; 50f. Lutwinus helping needy.

63 Orphans

1951. Red Cross Fund.

301	63	25f.+10f. green and red	25·00	85·00

64 Mail-carriers, 1760

1951. Stamp Day.

302	64	15f. purple	11·50	25·00

65 Allegory

1951. Trade Fair.

303	65	15f. green	3·75	8·50

66 Flowers and Building

1951. Horticultural Show, Bexbach.

304	66	15f. green	3·75	2·30

67 Calvin and Luther

1951. 375th Anniv of Reformation in Saar.

305	67	15f.+5f. brown	4·75	9·50

68 "The Good Mother" (Lepicie)

1951. National Relief Fund. Inscr "VOLKSHILFE 1951".

306	**68**	12f.+3f. green	8·50	25·00
307	-	15f.+5f. violet	10·50	25·00
308	-	18f.+7f. red	9·50	25·00
309	-	30f.+10f. blue	16·00	48·00
310	-	50f.+20f. brown	26·00	95·00

PAINTINGS: 18f. "Outside the Theatre" (Kampf); 18f. "Sisters of Charity" (Browne); 30f. "The Good Samaritan" (Bassano); 50f. "St. Martin and the Poor" (Van Dyck).

69 Mounted Postman

1952. Stamp Day.

311	**69**	30f.+10f. blue	16·00	37·00

70 Athlete bearing Olympic Flame

1952. 15th Olympic Games, Helsinki. Inscr "OLYMPISCHE SPIELE 1952".

312	**70**	15f.+5f. green	8·00	16·00
313	-	30f.+5f. blue	8·00	18·00

DESIGN: 30f. Hand, laurels and globe.

71 Globe and Emblem

1952. Saar Fair.

314	**71**	15f. red	3·25	1·80

72 Red Cross and Refugees

1952. Red Cross Week.

315	**72**	15f. red	4·75	1·80

73 G.P.O., Saarbrucken

1952. (A) Without inscr in or below design. (B) With inscr.

316	-	1f. green (B)	30	30
317	-	2f. violet	30	30
318	-	3f. red	30	30
319	**73**	5f. green (A)	6·25	30
320	**73**	5f. green (B)	30	30
321	-	6f. purple	55	30
322	-	10f. brown	55	30
323	**73**	12f. green (B)	95	30
324	-	15f. brown (A)	10·50	30
325	-	15f. brown (B)	4·75	30
326	-	15f. red (B)	40	30
327	-	18f. purple	3·75	6·25
329	-	30f. blue	1·30	1·30
334	-	500f. red	21·00	85·00

DESIGNS—HORIZ: 1, 15f. (3) Colliery shafthead; 2, 10f. Ludwigs High School, Saarbrucken; 3, 18f. Gersweiler Bridge; 6f. Mettlach Bridge; 30f. University Library, Saarbrucken. VERT: 500f. St. Ludwig's Church, Saarbrucken.

74 "Count Stroganov as a Boy" (Greuze)

1952. National Relief Fund. Paintings inscr "VOLKSHILFE 1952".

335	**74**	15f.+5f. brown	4·25	15·00
336	-	18f.+7f. red	6·25	19·00
337	-	30f.+10f. blue	8·50	21·00

PORTRAITS: 18f. "The Holy Shepherd" (Murillo); 30f. "Portrait of a Boy" (Kraus).

75 Fair Symbol

1953. Saar Fair.

338	**75**	15f. blue	2·75	2·10

76 Postilions

1953. Stamp Day.

339	**76**	15f. blue	9·00	17·00

77 Henri Dunant

1953. Red Cross Week and 125th Anniv of Birth of Dunant (founder).

340	**77**	15f.+5f. brown and red	3·75	9·50

78 "Painter's Young Son" (Rubens)

1953. National Relief Fund. Paintings inscr "VOLKSHILFE 1953".

341	-	15f.+5f. violet	4·25	7·50
342	-	18f.+7f. red	4·25	8·00
343	**78**	30f.+10f. green	6·25	12·50

DESIGNS—VERT: 15f. "Clarice Strozzi" (Titian). HORIZ: 18f. "Painter's Children" (Rubens).

79 St. Benedict blessing St. Maurus

1953. Tholey Abbey Fund.

344	**79**	30f.+10f. black	3·50	10·50

80 Saar Fair

1954. Saar Fair.

345	**80**	15f. green	2·75	1·30

81 Postal Motor Coach

1954. Stamp Day.

346	**81**	15f. red	12·50	18·00

82 Red Cross and Child

1954. Red Cross Week.

347	**82**	15f.+5f. brown	4·25	9·50

83 Madonna and Child (Holbein)

1954. Marian Year.

348	**83**	5f. red	3·25	4·25
349	-	10f. green	3·25	4·25
350	-	15f. blue	4·25	7·50

DESIGNS: 10f. "Sistine Madonna" (Raphael); 15f. "Madonna and Child with Pear" (Durer).

84 "Street Urchin with a Melon" (Murillo)

1954. National Relief Fund. Paintings inscr "VOLKSHILFE 1954".

351	**84**	5f.+3f. red	1·30	1·90
352	-	10f.+5f. green	1·30	1·90
353	-	15f.+7f. violet	1·30	2·75

DESIGNS: 10f. "Maria de Medici" (A. Bronzino); 15f. "Baron Emil von Maucler" (J. F. Dietrich).

85 Cyclist and Flag

1955. World Cross-Country Cycle Race.

354	**85**	15f. blue, red and black	55	95

86 Rotary Emblem and Industrial Plant

1955. 50th Anniv of Rotary International.

355	**86**	15f. brown	55	1·10

87 Exhibitors' Flags

1955. Saar Fair.

356	**87**	15f. multicoloured	55	95

88 Nurse and Baby

1955. Red Cross Week.

357	**88**	15f.+5f. black and red	75	1·40

89 Postman

1955. Stamp Day.

358	**89**	15f. purple	2·75	3·25

1955. Referendum. Optd VOLKSBEFRAGUNG 1955.

359		15f. red (No. 326)	65	95
360		18f. purple (No. 327)	65	75
361		30f. blue (No. 329)	85	95

91 "Mother" (Durer)

1955. National Relief Fund. Durer paintings inscr as in T 91.

362	**91**	5f.+3f. green	65	1·70
363	-	10f.+5f. green	1·10	2·10
364	-	15f.+7f. bistre	1·50	2·50

PAINTINGS: 10f. "The Praying Hands"; 15f. "The Old Man from Antwerp".

92

1956. Saar Fair.

365	**92**	15f. green and red	55	1·30

93 Radio Tower

1956. Stamp Day.

366	**93**	15f. green and turquoise	55	1·30

94 Casualty Station

1956. Red Cross Week.

367	**94**	15f.+5f. brown	55	1·30

95

1956. Olympic Games.

368	**95**	12f.+3f. blue and green	75	95
369	**95**	15f.+5f. brown & purple	75	95

96 Winterberg Memorial

1956. Winterberg Memorial Reconstruction Fund.

370	**96**	5f.+2f. green	40	65
371	**96**	12f.+3f. purple	40	65
372	**96**	15f.+5f. brown	40	85

97 "Portrait of Lucrezia Crivelli" (da Vinci)

1956. National Relief Fund. Inscr as in T 97.

373	**97**	5f.+3f. blue	40	40
374	-	10f.+5f. red	40	65
375	-	15f.+7f. green	40	1·10

PAINTINGS: 10f. "Saskia" (Rembrandt); 15f. "Lady Playing Spinet" (Floris).

RETURN TO GERMANY

98 Arms of the Saar

1957. Return of the Saar to Germany.

376	**98**	15f. blue and red	30	55

99 President Heuse

1957. (a) Without "F" after figure of value.

377	**99**	1f. green	30	20
378	**99**	2f. violet	30	20
379	**99**	3f. brown	30	20
380	**99**	4f. mauve	40	1·10
381	**99**	5f. green	30	20
382	**99**	6f. red	30	65
383	**99**	10f. grey	30	40
384	**99**	12f. orange	30	20
385	**99**	15f. green	30	20
386	**99**	18f. red	85	3·25
387	**99**	25f. lilac	65	1·10
388	**99**	30f. purple	65	1·10
389	**99**	45f. green	1·50	3·75
390	**99**	50f. brown	1·50	1·70
391	**99**	60f. red	2·10	4·25
392	**99**	70f. orange	3·75	6·25
393	**99**	80f. green	1·30	4·75
394	**99**	90f. grey	3·75	8·50
395	**99**	100f. red (24×29½ mm)	3·25	10·50
396	**99**	200f. lilac (24×29½ mm)	8·50	34·00

(b) With "F" after figure of value.

406	1f. grey	30	30
407	3f. blue	30	30
408	5f. green	30	30
409	6f. brown	30	65
410	10f. violet	30	30
411	12f. orange	30	30
412	15f. green	55	30
413	18f. grey	2·75	6·25
414	20f. green	1·60	4·25
415	25f. brown	55	55
416	30f. mauve	1·30	55
417	35f. brown	3·25	4·25
418	45f. green	2·75	5·25
419	50f. brown	1·30	2·75
420	70f. green	6·25	7·50
421	80f. blue	3·25	6·75
422	90f. red	7·50	8·50
423	100f. orange (24×29½ mm)	6·25	9·50
424	200f. green (24×29½ mm)	11·50	34·00
425	300f. blue (24 ×29½ mm)	12·50	38·00

100 Iron Foundry

1957. Saar Fair.

397	**100**	15f. red and black	30	55

101 Arms of Merzig and St. Pierre Church

1957. Centenary of Merzig.

398	**101**	15f. blue	30	55

101a "Europa" Tree

1957. Europa.

399	**101a**	20f. orange and yellow	85	1·40
400	**101a**	35f. violet and pink	1·30	1·90

101b Young Miner

1957. Humanitarian Relief Fund.

401	**101b**	6f.+4f. black & brown	30	30
402	-	12f.+6f. black & green	30	40
403	-	15f.+7f. black and red	40	55
404	-	30f.+10f. black & blue	55	95

DESIGNS: 12f. Miner drilling at coalface; 15f. Miner with coal-cutting machine; 30f. Operator at mine lift-shaft.

101c Carrier Pigeons

1957. International Correspondence Week.

405	**101c**	15f. black and red	30	55

101d Max and Moritz (cartoon characters)

1958. 150th Death Anniv of Wilhelm Busch (writer and illustrator).

426	**101d**	12f. green and black	30	30
427	-	15f. red and black	30	55

DESIGN: 15f. Wilhelm Busch.

101e "Prevent Forest Fires"

1958. Forest Fires Prevention Campaign.

428	**101e**	15f. black and red	30	55

101f Diesel and First Oil Engine

1958. Birth Centenary of Rudolf Diesel (engineer).

429	**101f**	12f. green	30	55

101g "The Fox who stole the Goose"

1958. Berlin Students' Fund.

430	**101g**	12f.+6f. red, black and green	20	40
431	-	15f.+7f. brown, green and red	30	55

DESIGN: 15f. "A Hunter from the Palatinate".

102 Saarbrucken Town Hall and Fair Emblem

1958. Saar Fair.

432	**102**	15f. purple	30	55

103 Homburg

1958. 400th Anniv of Homburg.

433	**103**	15f. green	30	55

103a Emblem

1958. 150th Anniv of German Gymnastics.

434	**103a**	12f. black, green and grey	30	55

103b Schulze-Delitzsch

1958. 150th Birth of Schulze-Delitzsch (pioneer of German Co-operative Movement).

435	**103b**	12f. green	30	55

103c "Europa"

1958. Europa.

436	**103c**	12f. blue and green	75	1·30
437	-	30f. red and blue	95	1·90

103d Friedrich Raiffeisen (philanthropist)

1958. Humanitarian Relief and Welfare Funds.

438	**103d**	6f.+4f. brn, lt brn & chest	30	30
439	-	12f.+6f. red, yell & grn	30	30
440	-	15f.+7f. blue, grn & red	65	65
441	-	30f.+10f. yellow, grn & bl	65	85

DESIGNS—Inscr "WOHLFAHRTSMARKE": 12f. Dairymaid; 15f. Vine-dresser 30f. Farm labourer.

103e Fugger

1959. 500th Birth Anniv of Jakob Fugger (merchant prince).

442	**103e**	15f. black and red	30	55

104 Hands holding Crates

1959. Saar Fair.

443	**104**	15f. red	30	55

105 Saarbrucken

1959. 50th Anniv of Greater Saarbrucken.

444	**105**	15f. blue	30	55

105a Humboldt

1959. Death Centenary of Alexander von Humboldt (naturalist).

445	**105a**	15f. blue	55	65

OFFICIAL STAMPS

1922. Nos. 84 to 94 optd DIENSTMARKE.

O98	3c. green	1·30	42·00
O99	5c. black and orange	55	55
O100	10c. green	55	40
O109	15c. orange	3·25	65
O101	15c. brown	55	40
O102	20c. blue and yellow	55	40
O111	25c. red and yellow	3·25	65
O104	30c. red and yellow	55	40
O105	40c. brown and yellow	75	40
O106	50c. blue and yellow	75	40
O112	75c. green and yellow	6·25	3·25
O108a	1f. brown	16·00	3·25

1927. Nos. 108/15, 117 and 119 optd DIENSTMARKE.

O128	10c. brown	2·75	3·25
O129	15c. green	2·75	8·50
O130	20c. brown	2·75	2·10
O131	25c. blue	3·25	8·50
O122	30c. green	7·50	1·10
O133	40c. brown	2·75	40
O134	50c. red	5·25	55
O135	60c. orange	1·60	40
O136	75c. purple	3·25	1·10
O137	1f. violet	3·25	55
O138	2f. red	3·25	55

O51 Arms

1949

O264	**O51**	10c. red	55	25·00
O265	**O51**	30c. black	40	30·00
O266	**O51**	1f. green	40	1·40
O267	**O51**	2f. red	2·10	1·60
O268	**O51**	5f. blue	2·75	1·40
O269	**O51**	10f. black	1·10	1·40
O270	**O51**	12f. mauve	10·50	15·00
O271	**O51**	15f. blue	1·10	1·40
O272	**O51**	20f. green	2·75	1·60
O273	**O51**	30f. mauve	7·50	6·25
O274	**O51**	50f. purple	2·75	5·25
O275	**O51**	100f. brown	95·00	£400

Pt. 1

SABAH

Formerly North Borneo, now part of Malaysia.

100 cents = 1 Malaysian dollar.

1964. Nos. 391/406 of North Borneo optd SABAH.

408	1c. green and red	10	10
409	4c. olive and orange	15	50
410	5c. sepia and violet	30	10
411	6c. black and turquoise	1·25	10
412	10c. green and red	2·25	10
413	12c. brown and myrtle	20	10
414	20c. turquoise and blue	5·50	10
415	25c. black and red	1·00	90
416	30c. sepia and olive	30	10
417	35c. slate and brown	30	20
418	50c. green and bistre	30	10
419	75c. blue and purple	4·50	1·00
420	$1 brown and green	12·00	2·00
421	$2 brown and slate	17·00	3·00
422	$5 green and purple	17·00	14·00
423	$10 red and blue	18·00	35·00

138 "Vanda hookeriana"

1965. As No. 115/21 of Kedah, but with Arms of Sabah inset as T 138.

424	**138**	1c. multicoloured	10	1·25
425	-	2c. multicoloured	10	2·00
426	-	5c. multicoloured	10	10
427	-	6c. multicoloured	30	1·50
428	-	10c. multicoloured	30	10
429	-	15c. multicoloured	3·00	10
430	-	20c. multicoloured	3·00	75

The higher values used in Sabah were Nos. 20/7 of Malaysia.

139 "Hebomoia glaucippe"

1971. Butterflies. As Nos. 124/30 of Kedah, but with Sabah Arms inset as T 139.

432		1c. multicoloured	65	2·50
433		2c. multicoloured	75	2·50
434		5c. multicoloured	80	50
435		6c. multicoloured	1·00	2·00
436	**139**	10c. multicoloured	80	15
437	-	15c. multicoloured	1·00	10
438	-	20c. multicoloured	1·10	1·25

The higher values in use with this issue were Nos. 64/71 of Malaysia.

140 "Hibiscus rosa-sinensis"

1979. As Nos. 135/41 of Kedah, but with Arms of Sabah as T 140.

445	1c. "Rafflesia hasseltii"	10	1·60
446	2c. "Pterocarpus indicus"	10	1·60
447	5c. "Lagerstroemia speciosa"	15	50
448	10c. "Durio zibethinus"	30	10
449	15c. Type **140**	50	10
450	20c. "Rhododendron scortechinii"	30	10
451	25c. "Etlingera elatior" (inscr "Phaeomeria speciosa")	80	20

The higher values in use with this issue were Nos. 190/7 of Malaysia.

141 Coffee

1986. As Nos. 152/8 of Kedah but with Arms of Sabah as in T 141.

459	1c. Type **141**	10	30
460	2c. Coconuts	10	30
461	5c. Cocoa	15	15
462	10c. Black pepper	15	10
463	15c. Rubber	25	10
464	20c. Oil palm	25	10
465	30c. Rice	35	15

142 *Nelumbium nelumbo* (sacred lotus)

2007. Garden Flowers. As Nos. 210/15 of Johore, but with Arms of Sabah as in T 142. Multicoloured.

466	5s. Type **142**	10	10
467	10s. *Hydrangea macrophylla*	15	10
468	20s. *Hippeastrum reticulatum*	25	15
469	30s. *Bougainvillea*	40	20
470	40s. *Ipomoea indica*	50	30
471	50s. *Hibiscus rosa-sinensis*	65	35

Pt. 1

ST CHRISTOPHER

One of the Leeward Is. Stamps superseded in 1890 by Leeward Islands general issue.

12 pence = 1 shilling.

1

1870

11	**1**	½d. green	4·25	2·25
6	**1**	1d. mauve	75·00	7·00
13	**1**	1d. red	2·50	2·25
14	**1**	2½d. brown	£180	60·00
16	**1**	2½d. blue	4·00	1·50
8	**1**	4d. blue	£200	15·00
18	**1**	4d. grey	1·50	1·00
9	**1**	6d. green	55·00	5·00
19	**1**	6d. olive	90·00	£400
20	**1**	1s. mauve	£100	65·00

1885. Surch in words.

23	½d. on half of 1d. red	28·00	42·00
26	1d. on ½d. green	45·00	55·00
28	1d. on 2½d. blue	70·00	70·00
24	1d. on 6d. green	20·00	38·00
22	4d. on 6d. green	65·00	50·00

1886. Surch in figures.

25	4d. on 6d. green	55·00	95·00

Pt. 1

ST HELENA

An island in the South Atlantic Ocean, west of Africa.

1856. 12 pence = 1 shilling; 20 shillings = 1 pound.
1971. 100 pence = 1 pound.

The early stamps of St. Helena, other than the 6d., were formed by printing the 6d., in various colours and surcharging it with new values in words or (in case of the 21/2d.) in figures.

1

1856. Imperf.

3	1d. on 6d. red	£150	£225
5	4d. on 6d. red	£500	£250
1	6d. blue	£500	£180

1861. Perf.

36	½d. on 6d. green	2·50	2·75
37	1d. on 6d. red	4·75	3·75
39	2d. on 6d. yellow	3·00	8·00
40	2½d. on 6d. blue	3·00	5·50
42	3d. on 6d. purple	6·50	5·00
14	4d. on 6d. red	£140	60·00
43c	4d. on 6d. brown	27·00	17·00
25	6d. blue	£450	50·00
44	6d. grey	32·00	5·00
30	1s. on 6d. green	21·00	12·00
20	5s. on 6d. yellow	60·00	70·00

11

1890

46	**11**	½d. green	2·75	6·50
47	**11**	1d. red	19·00	2·00
48	**11**	1½d. brown and green	4·50	9·50
49	**11**	2d. yellow	5·00	12·00
50	**11**	2½d. blue	18·00	12·00
51	**11**	5d. violet	11·00	30·00
52	**11**	10d. brown	24·00	60·00

12

1902. Inscr "POSTAGE POSTAGE".

53	**12**	½d. green	1·50	2·75
54	**12**	1d. red	12·00	70

13 Government House

14 The Wharf

1903

55	**13**	½d. brown and green	2·00	3·25
56	**14**	1d. black and red	1·50	35
57	**13**	2d. black and green	7·50	1·25
58	**14**	8d. black and brown	23·00	32·00
59	**13**	1s. brown and orange	26·00	40·00
60	**14**	2s. black and violet	60·00	90·00

1908. Inscr "POSTAGE & REVENUE".

64	**12**	2½d. blue	2·00	1·50
66a	**12**	4d. black and red on yellow	4·75	18·00
67a	**12**	6d. purple	9·00	14·00
70	**12**	10s. green and red on green	£350	£275

1912. As T 13/14 but with medallion of King George V.

72	**13**	½d. black and green	2·25	10·00
73	**14**	1d. black and red	4·75	1·75
89	**14**	1d. green	2·25	45·00
74	**14**	1½d. black and orange	3·50	9·00
90	**14**	1½d. red	11·00	42·00
75	**13**	2d. black and grey	4·75	1·75
76	**14**	2½d. black and blue	3·50	7·00
77	**13**	3d. black & purple on yellow	3·50	5·00
91	**13**	3d. blue	25·00	80·00
78	**14**	8d. black and purple	7·00	55·00
79	**13**	1s. black on green	9·00	35·00
80	**14**	2s. black and blue on blue	48·00	85·00
81	**14**	3s. black and violet	70·00	£140

18

1912. Inscr "POSTAGE & REVENUE".

83	**18**	4d. black and red on yellow	13·00	25·00
84	**18**	6d. purple	4·00	5·00

1913. Inscr "POSTAGE POSTAGE".

85	4d. black and red on yellow	8·00	2·75
86	6d. purple	14·00	28·00

1916. Surch WAR TAX ONE PENNY.

87	1d.+1d. black and red (No. 73)	3·50	3·25

1919. Surch WAR TAX 1d.

88	1d.+1d. black and red (No. 73)	2·00	4·50

22 Badge of St. Helena

1922

97	**22**	½d. grey and black	4·00	4·00
98	**22**	1d. grey and green	3·00	1·60
99	**22**	1½d. red	2·75	13·00
100	**22**	2d. grey and brown	3·75	2·00
101	**22**	3d. blue	2·00	4·00

92	22	4d. grey and black on yellow	12·00	6·00
103	22	5d. green and red on green	3·50	5·50
104	22	6d. grey and purple	4·50	8·00
105	22	8d. grey and violet	4·00	8·00
106	22	1s. grey and brown	6·50	9·00
107	22	1s.6d. grey & green on grn	15·00	55·00
108	22	2s. purple and blue on blue	21·00	50·00
109	22	2s.6d. grey & red on yellow	16·00	70·00
110	22	5s. grey and green on yellow	38·00	75·00
111	22	7s.6d. grey and orange	£110	£180
112	22	10s. grey and green	£150	£225
113	22	15s. grey and purple on blue	£950	£1900
96	22	£1 grey and purple on red	£450	£600

23 Lot and Lot's Wife

1934. Centenary of British Colonization.

114	**23**	½d. black and purple	1·00	80
115	-	1d. black and green	65	85
116	-	1½d. black and red	2·50	3·25
117	-	2d. black and orange	3·25	1·25
118	-	3d. black and blue	1·40	4·50
119	-	6d. black and blue	3·25	3·00
120	-	1s. black and brown	6·50	18·00
121	-	2s.6d. black and red	45·00	60·00
122	-	5s. black and brown	90·00	90·00
123	-	10s. black and purple	£300	£325

DESIGNS—HORIZ: 1d. The "Plantation"; 1½d. Map of St. Helena; 2d. Quay, Jamestown; 3d. James Valley; 6d. Jamestown; 1s. Munden's Promontory; 5s. High Knoll; 10s. Badge of St. Helena. VERT: 2s.6d. St. Helena.

32a Windsor Castle

1935. Silver Jubilee.

124	**32a**	1½d. blue and red	1·00	5·50
125	**32a**	2d. blue and grey	2·50	90
126	**32a**	6d. green and blue	9·50	3·25
127	**32a**	1s. grey and purple	22·00	24·00

32b King George VI and Queen Elizabeth

1937. Coronation.

128	**32b**	1d. green	40	75
129	**32b**	2d. orange	55	45
130	**32b**	3d. blue	80	50

33 Badge of St. Helena

1938

131	**33**	½d. violet	15	65
132	**33**	1d. green	9·00	2·25
132a	**33**	1d. orange	30	30
149	**33**	1d. black and green	1·25	1·50
133	**33**	1½d. red	30	40
150	**33**	1½d. black and red	1·40	1·50
134	**33**	2d. orange	30	15
151	**33**	2d. black and red	1·40	1·50
135	**33**	3d. blue	80·00	18·00
135a	**33**	3d. grey	30	30
135b	**33**	4d. blue	2·00	2·50
136	**33**	6d. blue	2·00	2·75
136a	**33**	8d. green	3·50	1·00
137	**33**	1s. brown	1·25	1·25
138	**33**	2s.6d. purple	20·00	6·50
139	**33**	5s. brown	20·00	16·00
140	**33**	10s. purple	20·00	19·00

33a Houses of Parliament, London

1946. Victory.

141	**33a**	2d. orange	40	50
142	**33a**	4d. blue	60	30

33b King George VI and Queen Elizabeth

33c King George VI and Queen Elizabeth

1948. Silver Wedding.

143	**33b**	3d. black	30	30
144	**33c**	10s. blue	26·00	42·00

33d Hermes, Globe and Forms of Transport

33e Hemispheres, Jet-powered Vickers Viking Airliner and Steamer

33f Hermes and Globe

33g U.P.U. Monument

1949. U.P.U.

145	**33d**	3d. red	25	1·00
146	**33e**	4d. blue	3·00	1·75
147	**33f**	6d. green	65	3·00
148	**33g**	1s. black	35	1·10

33h Queen Elizabeth II

1953. Coronation.

152	**33h**	3d. black and lilac	1·50	1·50

34 Badge of St. Helena

1953

153	**34**	½d. black and green	30	30
154	-	1d. black and green	15	20
155	-	1½d. black and purple	4·75	1·50
156	-	2d. black and red	50	30
157	-	2½d. black and red	40	30
158	-	3d. black and brown	3·25	30
159	-	4d. black and blue	40	1·00
160	-	6d. black and violet	40	30
161	-	7d. black and grey	80	1·75
162	-	1s. black and red	40	70
163	-	2s.6d. black and violet	20·00	8·00
164	-	5s. black and sepia	24·00	10·00
165	-	10s. black and yellow	35·00	13·00

DESIGNS—HORIZ: 1d. Flax plantation; 2d. Lace-making; 2½d. Drying flax; 3d. St. Helena sand plover; 4d. Flagstaff and The Barn (hills); 6d. Donkeys carrying flax; 7d. Map; 1s. The Castle; 2s.6d. Cutting flax; 5s. Jamestown; 10s. Longwood House. VERT: 1½d. Heart-shaped Waterfall.

45 Stamp of 1856

1956. Cent of First St. Helena Postage Stamp.

166	**45**	3d. blue and red	10	10
167	**45**	4d. blue and brown	10	20
168	**45**	6d. blue and purple	15	25

47 East Indiaman "London" off James Bay

1959. Tercentenary of Settlement.

169	-	3d. black and red	15	15
170	**47**	6d. green and blue	50	75
171	-	1s. black and orange	50	75

DESIGNS—HORIZ: 3d. Arms of East India Company; 1s. Commemoration Stone.

1961. Tristan Relief Fund. Nos. 46 and 49/51 of Tristan da Cunha surch ST. HELENA Tristan Relief and premium.

172	2½c.+3d. black and red	£1500	£600
173	5c.+6d. black and blue	£1600	£650
174	7½c.+9d. black and red	£2250	£900
175	10c.+1s. black and brown	£2250	£1100

50 St. Helena Butterflyfish

63 Queen Elizabeth II with Prince Andrew (after Cecil Beaton)

1961

176	**50**	1d. multicoloured	40	20
177	-	1½d. multicoloured	50	20
178	-	2d. red and grey	15	20
179	-	3d. multicoloured	70	20
180	-	4½d. multicoloured	60	60
181	-	6d. red, sepia and olive	5·50	70
182	-	7d. brown, black and violet	35	70
183	-	10d. purple and blue	35	70
184	-	1s. yellow, green and brown	55	1·25
185	-	1s.6d. grey and blue	11·00	4·75
186	-	2s.6d. red, yellow & turq	2·50	2·50
187	-	5s. yellow, brown and green	14·00	4·25
188	-	10s. red, black and blue	13·00	10·00
189	**63**	£1 brown and blue	20·00	18·00

DESIGNS—VERT (as Type **50**): 1½d. Yellow canary; 3d. Queen Elizabeth II; 4½d. Red-wood flower; 6d. Madagascar red fody; 1s. Gum-wood flower; 1s.6d. White tern; 5s. Night-blooming Cereus. HORIZ (as T **50**): 2d. Brittle starfish; 7d. Trumpetfish; 10d. Feather starfish; 2s.6d. Orange starfish; 10s. Deep-water bullseye.

63a Protein Foods

1963. Freedom from Hunger.

190	**63a**	1s.6d. blue	75	40

63b Red Cross Emblem

1963. Centenary of Red Cross.

191	**63b**	3d. red and black	30	25
192	**63b**	1s.6d. red and blue	70	1·75

1965. First Local Post. Optd FIRST LOCAL POST 4th JANUARY 1965.

193	**50**	1d. multicoloured	10	25
194	-	3d. multicoloured (No. 179)	10	25
195	-	6d. red, sepia and olive (No. 181)	40	30
196	-	1s.6d. grey & blue (No. 185)	60	35

64a I.T.U. Emblem

1965. Centenary of I.T.U.

197	**64a**	3d. blue and brown	25	25
198	**64a**	6d. purple and green	35	25

64b I.C.Y. Emblem

1965. Centenary of I.C.Y.

199	**64b**	1d. purple and turquoise	30	15
200	**64b**	6d. green and lavender	30	15

64c Sir Winston Churchill and St. Paul's Cathedral in Wartime

1966. Churchill Commemoration.

201	**64c**	1d. blue	15	25
202	**64c**	3d. green	25	25
203	**64c**	6d. brown	40	30
204	**64c**	1s.6d. violet	45	85

64d Footballer's Legs, Ball and Jules Rimet Cup

1966. World Cup Football Championship.

205	**64d**	3d. multicoloured	50	35
206	**64d**	6d. multicoloured	75	35

64e W.H.O. Emblem

1966. Inauguration of W.H.O. Headquarters, Geneva.

207	**64e**	3d. black, green and blue	75	20
208	**64e**	1s.6d. black, purple & ochre	2·25	1·00

64f "Education"

64g "Science"

64h "Culture"

1966. 20th Anniv of UNESCO.

209	**64f**	3d. multicoloured	75	20
210	**64g**	6d. yellow, violet and olive	1·25	50
211	**64h**	1s.6d. black, purple & orge	2·00	1·75

65 Badge of St. Helena

1967. New Constitution.

212	**65**	1s. multicoloured	10	10
213	**65**	2s.6d. multicoloured	20	20

66 Fire of London

1967. 300th Anniv of Arrival of Settlers after Great Fire of London.

214	**66**	1d. red and black	15	10
215	-	3d. blue and black	20	10
216	-	6d. violet and black	20	15
217	-	1s.6d. green and black	20	20

DESIGNS: 3d. East Indiaman "Charles"; 6d. Settlers landing at Jamestown; 1s.6d. Settlers clearing scrub.

70 Interlocking Maps of Tristan and St. Helena

1968. 30th Anniv of Tristan da Cunha as a Dependency of St. Helena.

218	**70**	4d. purple and brown	10	10
219	-	8d. olive and brown	10	30
220	**70**	1s.9d. blue and brown	10	40
221	-	2s.3d. blue and brown	15	40

DESIGNS: 8d. and 2s.3d. Interlocking maps of Tristan and St. Helena (different).

72 Queen Elizabeth and Sir Hudson Lowe

1968. 150th Anniv of Abolition of Slavery in St. Helena.

222	**72**	3d. multicoloured	10	15
223	**72**	9d. multicoloured	10	20
224	-	1s.6d. multicoloured	15	30
225	-	2s.6d. multicoloured	25	45

DESIGN: Nos. 224 and 225, Queen Elizabeth and Sir George Bingham.

74 Blue Gum Eucalyptus and Road Construction

1968. Multicoloured.. Multicoloured..

226		½d. Type **74**	10	10
227		1d. Electricity development	10	10
228		1½d. Dental unit	15	10
229		2d. Pest control	15	10
230		3d. Flats in Jamestown	30	10
231		4d. Livestock improvement	20	10
232		6d. Schools broadcasting	50	10
233		8d. Country Cottages	30	10
234		10d. New school buildings	30	10
235		1s. Reafforestation	30	10
236		1s.6d. Heavy lift crane	70	3·00
237		2s.6d. Lady Field Children's Home	70	3·50
238		5s. Agricultural training	70	3·50
239		10s. New General Hospital	2·00	4·50
240		£1 Lifeboat "John Dutton"	8·00	15·00

PLANTS SHOWN: ½, 4d., 1s.6d. Blue gum eucalyptus; 1d., 6d., 2s.6d. Cabbage-tree; 1½d., 8d., 5s. St. Helena redwood; 2, 10d., 10s. Scrubweed; 3d., 1s., £1 Tree-fern.

89 Brig *Perseverance*

1969. Mail Communications. Multicoloured.

241		4d. Type **89**	20	20
242		8d. "Phoebe" (screw steamer)	25	40
243		1s.9d. "Llandovery Castle" (liner)	25	60
244		2s.3d. "Good Hope Castle" (cargo liner)	25	75

93 W.O. and Drummer of the 53rd Foot, 1815

1969. Military Uniforms. Multicoloured.

245		6d. Type **93**	15	25
246		8d. Officer and Surgeon, 20th Foot, 1816	15	25
247		1s.8d. Drum Major, 66th Foot, 1816, and Royal Artillery Officer, 1820	20	45
248		2s.6d. Private, 91st Foot, and 2nd Corporal, Royal Sappers and Miners, 1832	20	55

97 Dickens, Mr. Pickwick and Job Trotter (*Pickwick Papers*)

1970. Death Cent of Charles Dickens. Mult.

249		4d. Type **97**	80	15
250		8d. Mr. Bumble and Oliver ("Oliver Twist")	90	15
251		1s.6d. Sairey Gamp and Mark Tapley ("Martin Chuzzlewit")	1·00	20
252		2s.6d. Jo and Mr. Turveydrop ("Bleak House")	1·00	25

All designs include a portrait of Dickens as Type **97**.

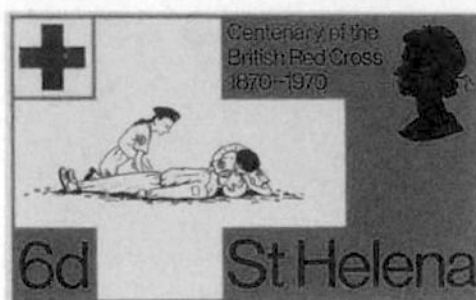

98 "Kiss of Life"

1970. Centenary of British Red Cross.

253	**98**	6d. bistre, red and black	15	15
254	-	9d. green, red and black	15	20
255	-	1s.9d. grey, red and black	20	30
256	-	2s.3d. lilac, red and black	20	45

DESIGNS: 9d. Nurse with girl in wheelchair; 1s.9d. Nurse bandaging child's knee; 2s.3d. Red Cross emblem.

99 Officer's Shako Plate (20th Foot)

1970. Military Equipment (1st issue). Mult.

257		4d. Type **99**	20	20
258		9d. Officer's breast plate (66th Foot)	25	30
259		1s.3d. Officer's Full Dress shako (91st Foot)	25	40
260		2s.11d. Ensign's shako (53rd Foot)	40	60

See also Nos. 281/4, 285/8 and 291/4.

100 Electricity Development

1971. Decimal Currency. Designs as Nos. 227/40, inscr as T 100.

261		½p. multicoloured	10	10
262		1p. multicoloured	10	10
263		1½p. multicoloured	10	10
264		2p. multicoloured	1·75	1·00
265		2½p. multicoloured	10	10
266		3½p. multicoloured	30	10
267		4½p. multicoloured	10	10
268		5p. multicoloured	10	10
269		7½p. multicoloured	40	35
270		10p. multicoloured	30	35
271		12½p. multicoloured	30	50
272		25p. multicoloured	60	1·25
273		50p. multicoloured	1·00	2·00
274		£1 multicoloured	20·00	15·00

101 St. Helena holding the "True Cross"

1971. Easter.

275	**101**	2p. multicoloured	10	10
276	**101**	5p. multicoloured	10	15
277	**101**	7½p. multicoloured	15	20
278	**101**	12½p. multicoloured	20	25

102 Napoleon (after painting by J. L. David) and Tomb on St. Helena

1971. 150th Death Anniv of Napoleon. Mult.

279		2p. Type **102**	20	50
280		34p. "Napoleon at St. Helena" (H. Delaroche)	45	1·00

1971. Military Equipment (2nd issue). As T 99. Multicoloured.

281		1½p. Artillery Private's hanger	20	30
282		4p. Baker rifle and socket bayonet	25	60
283		6p. Infantry Officer's sword	25	80
284		22½p. Baker rifle and sword bayonet	40	1·25

1972. Military Equipment (3rd issue). As T 99. Multicoloured.

285		2p. multicoloured	15	20
286		5p. lilac, blue and black	15	40
287		7½p. multicoloured	20	50
288		12½p. sepia, brown and black	30	60

DESIGNS: 2p. Royal Sappers and Miners breast-plate, post 1823; 5p. Infantry sergeant's spontoon, c. 1830; 7½p. Royal Artillery officer's breast-plate, c. 1830; 12½p. English military pistol, c. 1800.

103 St. Helena Sand Plover and White Tern

1972. Royal Silver Wedding.

289	**103**	2p. green	20	40
290	**103**	16p. brown	30	85

1973. Military Equipment (4th issue). As T 99. Multicoloured.

291		2p. Other Rank's shako, 53rd Foot, 1815	25	55
292		5p. Band and Drums sword, 1830	30	1·00
293		7½p. Royal Sappers and Miners Officer's hat, 1830	40	1·25
294		12½p. General's sword, 1831	45	1·50

103a Princess Anne and Captain Mark Phillips

1973. Royal Wedding. Multicoloured, background colours given.

295	**103a**	2p. blue	15	10
296	**103a**	18p. green	25	20

104 *Westminster* and *Claudine* beached, 1849

1973. Tercentenary of East India Company Charter. Multicoloured.

297		1½p. Type **104**	25	55
298		4p. "True Briton", 1790	35	80
299		6p. "General Goddard" in action, 1795	35	80
300		22½p. "Kent" burning in the Bay of Biscay, 1825	70	2·25

105 U.P.U. Emblem and Ships

1974. Centenary of U.P.U. Multicoloured.

301	5p. Type **105**	20	25
302	25p. U.P.U. emblem and letters	40	55
MS303	89×84 mm. Nos. 301/2	75	1·50

106 Churchill in Sailor Suit and Blenheim Palace

1974. Birth Cent of Sir Winston Churchill.

304	106	5p. multicoloured	20	20
305	-	25p. black, pink and purple	30	60
MS306		108×93 mm. Nos. 304/5	75	2·00

DESIGN: 25p. Churchill and River Thames.

107 Capt. Cook and H.M.S. *Resolution*

1975. Bicentenary of Capt. Cook's Return to St. Helena. Multicoloured.

307	5p. Type **107**	30	20
308	25p. Capt. Cook and Jamestown	40	40

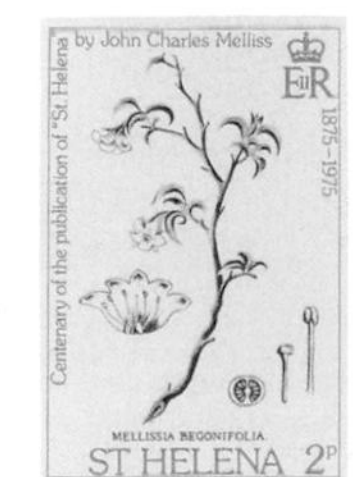

108 *Mellissia begonifolia* (tree)

1975. Centenary of Publication of "St. Helena" by J. C. Melliss. Multicoloured.

310	2p. Type **108**	15	30
311	5p. "Mellissius adumbratus" (beetle)	15	35
312	12p. St. Helena sand plover (bird) (horiz)	50	80
313	25p. Melliss's scorpionfish (horiz)	50	1·00

109 £1 Note

1976. First Issue of Currency Notes. Mult.

314	8p. Type **109**	30	30
315	33p. £5 Note	60	80

110 1d. Stamp of 1863

1976. Festival of Stamps, London.

316	110	5p. brown, black and pink	15	15
317	-	8p. black, green & lt green	20	30
318	-	25p. multicoloured	35	45

DESIGNS—VERT: 8p. 1d. stamp of 1922. HORIZ: 25p. Mail carrier "Good Hope Castle".

111 "High Knoll, 1806" (Capt. Barnett)

1976. Aquatints and Lithographs of St. Helena. Multicoloured.

319B	1p. Type **111**	30	75
320A	3p. "The Friar Rock, 1815" (G. Bellasis)	40	1·25
321A	5p. "The Column Lot, 1815" (G. Bellasis)	30	1·25
322A	6p. "Sandy Bay Valley, 1809" (H. Salt)	30	1·25
323A	8p. "Scene from Castle Terrace, 1815" (G. Bellasis)	40	1·25
324A	9p. "The Briars, 1815"	40	1·25
325A	10p. "Plantation House, 1821" (J. Wathen)	50	60
326A	15p. "Longwood House, 1821" (J. Wathen)	45	55
327A	18p. "St. Paul's Church" (V. Brooks)	45	1·50
328A	26p. "St. James's Valley, 1815" (Capt. Hastings)	45	1·50
329A	40p. "St. Matthew's Church, 1860" (V. Brooks)	70	1·75
330A	£1 "St. Helena, 1815" (G. Bellasis)	1·50	3·75
331B	£2 "Sugar Loaf Hill, 1821" (J. Wathen)	2·00	5·00

Nos. 330A and 331B are larger, 47×34 mm.

The 1 and 10p. and the £2 come with or without date imprint.

112 Duke of Edinburgh paying Homage

1977. Silver Jubilee. Multicoloured.

332	8p. Royal Visit, 1947	10	20
333	15p. Queen's sceptre with dove	20	25
334	26p. Type **112**	30	35

113 Halley's Comet (from Bayeux Tapestry)

1977. Tercentenary of Halley's Visit. Mult.

335	5p. Type **113**	35	30
336	8p. Late 17th-century sextant	50	30
337	27p. Halley and Halley's Mount, St. Helena	1·00	75

114 Sea Lion

1978. 25th Anniv of Coronation.

338	-	25p. agate, red and silver	30	50
339	-	25p. multicoloured	30	50
340	114	25p. agate, red and silver	30	50

DESIGNS: No. 338, Black Dragon of Ulster; No. 339, Queen Elizabeth II.

115 Period Engraving of St. Helena

1978. Wreck of the "Witte Leeuw". Multicoloured.

341	3p. Type **115**	15	15
342	5p. Chinese porcelain	15	20
343	8p. Bronze cannon	15	30
344	9p. Chinese porcelain (different)	15	35
345	15p. Pewter mug and ceramic flasks	20	55
346	20p. Dutch East Indiaman	30	70

116 H.M.S. *Discovery*

1979. Bicentenary of Captain Cook's Voyages, 1768–79. Multicoloured.

347	3p. Type **116**	15	15
348	8p. Cook's portable observatory	15	25
349	12p. "Pharnaceum acidum" (sketch by Joseph Banks)	20	35
350	25p. Flaxman/Wedgwood medallion of Capt. Cook	30	90

117 Sir Rowland Hill

1979. Death Centenary of Sir Rowland Hill.

351	117	5p. multicoloured	10	15
352	-	8p. multicoloured	15	20
353	-	20p. multicoloured	30	40
354	-	32p. black, magenta & mve	40	55

DESIGNS—HORIZ: 8p. 1965 1d. First Local Post stamp; 20p. 1863 1d. on 6d. surcharged stamp; 32p. 1902 1d. stamp.

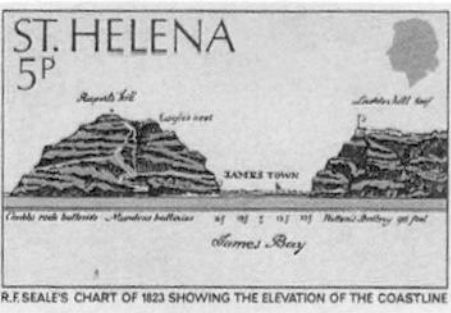

118 R. F. Seal's Chart of 1823 showing the Elevation of the Coastline

1979. 150th Anniv of Inclined Plane.

355	118	5p. black, grey and stone	15	15
356	-	8p. black, grey and stone	15	20
357	-	50p. multicoloured	60	75

DESIGNS—HORIZ: 8p. The Inclined Plane in 1829; VERT: 50p. The Inclined Plane in 1979.

119 Napoleon's Tomb, 1848

1980. Centenary of Empress Eugenie's Visit.

358	119	5p. brown, pink and gold	10	20
359	-	8p. brown, stone and gold	15	25
360	-	62p. brown, flesh and gold	65	80
MS361		180×110 mm. Nos. 358/60	80	1·10

DESIGNS: 8p. Landing at St. Helena; 62p. The Empress at Napoleon's Tomb.

120 East Indiaman

1980. "London 1980" Int Stamp Exhibition. Mult.

362	5p. Type **120**	10	15
363	8p. "Dolphin" postal stone	10	15
364	47p. Postal stone outside Castle entrance, Jamestown	50	60
MS365	111×120 mm. Nos. 362/4	75	80

121 Queen Elizabeth the Queen Mother in 1974

1980. 80th Birthday of the Queen Mother.

366	121	24p. multicoloured	35	50

122 The Briars, 1815

1980. 175th Anniv of Wellington's Visit. Multicoloured.

367	9p. Type **122**	15	15
368	30p. "Wellington" (Goya) (vert)	45	45

123 Redwood

1981. Endemic Plants. Multicoloured.

369	5p. Type **123**	15	20
370	8p. Old father live forever	15	20
371	15p. Gumwood	20	25
372	27p. Black cabbage	35	45

124 Detail from Reinel Portolan Chart, *c* 1530

1981. Early Maps.

373	124	5p. multicoloured	15	15
374	-	8p. black, red and grey	15	20
375	-	20p. multicoloured	30	35
376	-	30p. multicoloured	35	50
MS377		114×83 mm. 24p. black and grey	40	65

DESIGNS: 8p. John Thornton's Map of St. Helena, c. 1700; 20p. Map of St. Helena, 1815; 24p. Part of Gastaldi's map of Africa, 16th-century; 30p. Map of St. Helena, 1817.

125 Prince Charles as Royal Navy Commander

1981. Royal Wedding. Multicoloured.

378	14p. Wedding bouquet from St. Helena	15	20
379	29p. Type **125**	25	30

380 32p. Prince Charles and Lady Diana Spencer 30 35

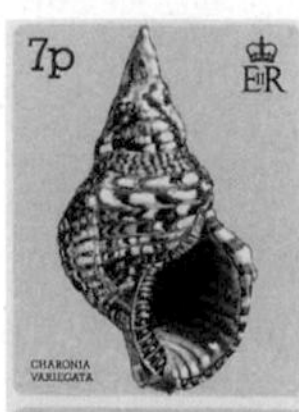

126 Atlantic Trumpet Triton (*Charonia variegata*)

1981. Sea Shells. Multicoloured.

381 7p. Type **126** 15 20
382 10p. St. Helena cowrie 15 20
383 25p. Common purple janthina 30 40
384 53p. Rude pen shell 50 1·00

127 Traffic Duty

1981. 25th Anniv of Duke of Edinburgh Award Scheme. Multicoloured.

385 7p. Type **127** 15 10
386 11p. Signposting 15 15
387 25p. Animal care 30 30
388 50p. Duke of Edinburgh, in Guard's uniform, on horseback 50 60

128 *Sympetrum dilatatum* (dragonfly)

1982. Insects (1st series). Multicoloured.

389 7p. Type **128** 20 20
390 10p. "Aplothorax burchelli" (beetle) 20 20
391 25p. "Ampulex compressa" (wasp) 35 35
392 32p. "Labidura herculeana" (earwig) 35 35

See also Nos. 411/14.

129 Charles Darwin

1982. 150th Anniv of Charles Darwin's Voyage. Multicoloured.

393 7p. Type **129** 20 20
394 14p. Flagstaff Hill and Darwin's hammer 25 35
395 25p. Common pheasant ("Ring-necked Pheasant") and Chukar partridge 50 70
396 29p. H.M.S. "Beagle" off St. Helena 60 80

130 Prince and Princess of Wales at Balmoral, Autumn, 1981

1982. 21st Birthday of Princess of Wales. Multicoloured.

397 7p. St. Helena coat of arms 10 15
398 11p. Type **130** 25 15
399 29p. Bride on Palace balcony 30 35
400 55p. Formal portrait 70 60

1982. Commonwealth Games, Brisbane. Nos. 326 and 328 optd 1st PARTICIPATION COMMONWEALTH GAMES 1982.

401 15p. "Longwood House, 1821" (J. Wathen) 25 25
402 26p. "St. James's Valley, 1815" (Capt. Hastings) 45 45

132 Lord Baden-Powell

1982. 75th Anniv of Boy Scout Movement.

403 **132** 3p. brown, grey and yellow 15 15
404 - 11p. brown, grey and green 20 25
405 - 29p. brown, grey & orange 30 60
406 - 59p. brown, grey and green 60 1·25

DESIGNS—HORIZ: 11p. Boy Scout (drawing by Lord Baden-Powell); 59p. Camping at Thompsons Wood. VERT: 29p. Canon Walcott.

133 King and Queen Rocks

1982. Views of St. Helena by Roland Svensson. Multicoloured.

407 7p. Type **133** 15 20
408 11p. "Turk's Cap" 15 25
409 29p. Coastline from Jamestown (horiz) 35 65
410 59p. "Mundens Point" (horiz) 60 1·40

1983. Insects (2nd series). As T 128. Mult.

411 11p. "Acherontia atropos" (hawk moth) 15 30
412 15p. "Helenasaldula aberrans" (shore-bug) 15 35
413 29p. "Anchastus compositarum" (click beetle) 25 55
414 59p. "Lamprochrus cossonoides" (weevil) 55 1·25

134 *Trametes versicolor* ("*Coriolus versicolor*")

1983. Fungi. Multicoloured.

415 11p. Type **134** 20 25
416 15p. "Pluteus brunneisucus" 20 40
417 29p. "Polyporus induratus" (horiz) 30 60
418 59p. "Coprinus angulatus" 55 1·25

135 Java Sparrow

1983. Birds. Multicoloured.

419 7p. Type **135** 30 20
420 15p. Madagascar red fody 45 35
421 33p. Common waxbill 80 70
422 59p. Yellow canary 1·50 1·40

136 Birth of St. Helena

1983. Christmas. Life of St. Helena (1st series). Multicoloured.

423 10p. Type **136** 20 55
424 15p. St. Helena being taken to convent 20 55

See also Nos. 450/3 and 468/71.

137 1934 Centenary ½d. Stamp

1984. 150th Anniv of St. Helena as a British Colony. Multicoloured.

425 1p. Type **137** 10 20
426 3p. 1934 1d. stamp 10 20
427 6p. 1934 1½d. stamp 10 30
428 7p. 1934 2d. stamp 15 30
429 11p. 1934 3d. stamp 20 40
430 15p. 1934 6d. stamp 25 45
431 29p. 1934 1s. stamp 40 95
432 33p. 1934 5s. stamp 45 1·25
433 59p. 1934 10s. stamp 65 2·00
434 £1 1934 2s.6d. stamp 1·00 3·25
435 £2 St. Helena Coat of Arms 1·75 5·00

138 Prince Andrew and H.M.S. *Invincible* (aircraft carrier)

1984. Visit of Prince Andrew. Multicoloured.

436 11p. Type **138** 25 25
437 60p. Prince Andrew and H.M.S. "Herald" (survey ship) 75 1·40

139 *St. Helena* (schooner)

1984. 250th Anniv of "Lloyd's List" (newspaper). Multicoloured.

438 10p. Type **139** 20 20
439 18p. Solomons Facade (local agent) 25 35
440 25p. Lloyd's Coffee House, London 30 55
441 50p. "Papanui" (freighter) 75 1·00

140 Twopenny Coin and Donkey

1984. New Coinage. Multicoloured.

442 10p. Type **140** 20 35
443 15p. Five pence coin and St. Helena sand plover 20 45
444 29p. Penny coin and yellow-finned tuna 30 75
445 50p. Ten pence coin and arum lily 40 1·25

141 Mrs. Rebecca Fuller (former Corps Secretary)

1984. Centenary of Salvation Army on St. Helena. Multicoloured.

446 7p. Type **141** 15 35
447 11p. Meals-on-wheels service (horiz) 15 45
448 25p. Salvation Army Citadel, Jamestown (horiz) 25 80
449 60p. Salvation Army band at Jamestown Clock Tower 55 2·00

1984. Christmas. Life of St. Helena (2nd series). As T 136. Multicoloured.

450 6p. St. Helena visits prisoners 15 20
451 10p. Betrothal of St. Helena 20 30
452 15p. Marriage of St. Helena to Constantius 25 40
453 33p. Birth of Constantine 50 70

142 Queen Elizabeth the Queen Mother aged Two

1985. Life and Times of Queen Elizabeth the Queen Mother. Multicoloured.

454 11p. Type **142** 20 25
455 15p. At Ascot with the Queen 20 35
456 29p. Attending Gala Ballet at Covent Garden 40 65
457 55p. With Prince Henry at his christening 60 1·00

MS458 91×73 mm. 70p. The Queen Mother with Ford "V8 Pilot" 1·75 1·60

143 Axillary Cardinalfish

1985. Marine Life. Multicoloured.

459 7p. Type **143** 15 25
460 11p. Chub mackerel 15 30
461 15p. Skipjack tuna 20 40
462 33p. Yellow-finned tuna 35 75
463 50p. Stump 50 1·25

144 John J. Audubon

1985. Birth Bicentenary of John J. Audubon (ornithologist).

464 **144** 11p. black and brown 15 25
465 - 15p. multicoloured 30 35
466 - 25p. multicoloured 40 55
467 - 60p. multicoloured 65 1·40

DESIGN—HORIZ (from original Audubon paintings): 15p. Moorhen ("Common Gallinule); 25p. White-tailed tropic bird; 68p. Common noddy.

1985. Christmas. Life of St. Helena (3rd series). As T 136. Multicoloured.

468 7p. St. Helena jouneys to the Holy Land 20 25
469 10p. Zambres slays the bull 20 30
470 15p. The bull restored to life: conversion of St. Helena 25 40
471 60p. Resurrection of the corpse: the True Cross identified 75 1·50

145 Church Provident Society for Women Banner

1986. Friendly Societies' Banners. Mult.

472	10p. Type **145**	15	25
473	11p. Working Men's Christian Association	15	25
474	25p. Church Benefit Society for Children	25	55
475	29p. Mechanics and Friendly Benefit Society	25	65
476	33p. Ancient Order of Foresters	30	70

145a Princess Elizabeth making 21st Birthday Broadcast, South Africa, 1947

1986. 60th Birthday of Queen Elizabeth II. Mult.

477	10p. Type **145a**	15	20
478	15p. Silver Jubilee photograph, 1977	25	30
479	20p. Princess Elizabeth on board H.M.S. "Vanguard", 1947	30	35
480	50p. In the U.S.A., 1976	45	1·00
481	65p. At Crown Agents Head Office, London, 1983	50	1·10

146 Plaque at Site of Halley's Observatory on St. Helena

1986. Appearance of Halley's Comet. Multicoloured.

482	9p. Type **146**	30	35
483	12p. Edmond Halley	35	35
484	20p. Halley's planisphere of the southern stars	65	70
485	65p. "Unity" on passage to St. Helena, 1676	2·00	3·25

146a Prince Andrew and Miss Sarah Ferguson

1986. Royal Wedding. Multicoloured.

486	10p. Type **146a**	20	25
487	40p. Prince Andrew with Governor J. Massingham on St. Helena	80	85

147 James Ross and H.M.S. *Erebus*

1986. Explorers.

488	147	1p. brown and pink	30	1·50
489	-	3p. deep blue and blue	30	1·50
490	-	5p. deep green and green	30	1·50
491	-	9p. brown and red	40	1·50
492	-	10p. deep brown and brown	40	1·50
493	-	12p. green and light green	40	1·50
494	-	15p. brown and pink	50	1·50
495	-	20p. blue and light blue	55	1·50
496	-	25p. sepia and pink	55	1·50
497	-	40p. deep green and green	60	1·75
498	-	60p. deep brown and brown	70	2·00
499	-	£1 deep blue and blue	1·00	3·00
500	-	£2 deep lilac and lilac	1·50	5·00

DESIGNS: 3p. Robert FitzRoy and H.M.S. "Beagle"; 5p. Adam Johann von Krusenstern and "Nadezhda"; 9p. William Bligh and H.M.S. "Resolution"; 10p. Otto von Kotzebue and "Rurik"; 12p. Philip Carteret and H.M.S. "Swallow"; 15p. Thomas Cavendish and "Desire"; 20p. Louis-Antoine de Bougainville and "La Boudeuse"; 25p. Fyedor Petrovich Litke and "Senyavin"; 40p. Louis Isidore Duperrey and "La Coquille"; 60p. John Byron and H.M.S. "Dolphin"; £1 James Cook and H.M.S. "Endeavour"; £2 Jules Dumont d'Urville and "L'Astrolabe".

148 Prince Edward and H.M.S. *Repulse* (battle cruiser), 1925

1987. Royal Visits to St. Helena. Multicoloured.

501	9p. Type **148**	1·75	1·25
502	13p. King George VI and H.M.S. "Vanguard" (battleship), 1947	2·25	1·50
503	38p. Prince Philip and Royal Yacht "Britannia", 1957	4·00	3·50
504	45p. Prince Andrew and H.M.S. "Herald" (survey ship), 1984	4·00	3·50

149 St. Helena Tea Plant

1987. Rare Plants (1st series). Multicoloured.

505	9p. Type **149**	65	60
506	13p. Baby's toes	80	80
507	38p. Salad plant	1·50	2·50
508	45p. Scrubwood	1·75	2·75

See also Nos. 531/4.

150 Lesser Rorqual

1987. Marine Mammals. Multicoloured.

509	9p. Type **150**	1·25	75
510	13p. Risso's dolphin	1·25	1·00
511	45p. Sperm whale	3·00	3·25
512	60p. Euphrosyne dolphin	3·25	3·75
MS513	102×72 mm. 75p. Humpback whale (48×31 mm)	6·50	7·00

1987. Royal Ruby Wedding. Nos. 477/81 optd 40TH WEDDING ANNIVERSARY.

514	10p. Princess Elizabeth making 21st birthday broadcast, South Africa, 1947	20	35
515	15p. Silver Jubilee photograph, 1977	20	40
516	20p. Princess Elizabeth on board H.M.S. "Vanguard", 1947	40	55
517	50p. In the U.S.A., 1976	50	1·10
518	65p. At Crown Agents Head Office, London, 1983	50	1·50

151 *Defence* and Dampier's Signature, 1691

1988. Bicentenary of Australian Settlement. Ships and Signatures. Multicoloured.

519	9p. Type **151**	1·50	90
520	13p. H.M.S. "Resolution" (Cook), 1775	2·00	2·00
521	45p. H.M.S. "Providence" (Bligh), 1792	3·25	4·00
522	60p. H.M.S. "Beagle" (Darwin), 1836	4·25	5·50

152 "The Holy Virgin with the Child"

1988. Christmas. Religious Paintings. Mult.

523	5p. Type **152**	10	30
524	20p. "Madonna"	40	50
525	38p. "The Holy Family with St. John"	75	1·50
526	60p. "The Holy Virgin with the Child"	1·25	2·00

152a Lloyds Under- writing Room, 1886

1988. 300th Anniv of Lloyd's of London.

527	152a	9p. deep brown and brown	40	50
528	-	20p. multicoloured	2·00	1·00
529	-	45p. multicoloured	2·50	1·75
530	-	60p. multicoloured	2·75	2·25

DESIGNS—VERT: 60p. "Spangereid" (full-rigged ship) on fire, St. Helena, 1920. HORIZ: 20p. "Edinburgh Castle" (liner); 45p. "Bosun Bird" (freighter).

153 Ebony

1989. Rare Plants (2nd series). Multicoloured.

531	9p. Type **153**	40	40
532	20p. St. Helena lobelia	70	70
533	45p. Large bellflower	1·40	2·00
534	60p. She cabbage tree	1·60	2·50

1989. Military Uniforms of 1815. Multicoloured.

535	9p. Type **154**	65	90
536	13p. Officer, 53rd Foot	75	1·00
537	20p. Royal Marine	85	1·10
538	45p. Officer, 66th Foot	1·40	1·90
539	60p. Private, 66th Foot	1·60	2·25

154 Private, 53rd Foot

1989. "Philexfrance 89" International Stamp Exhibition, Paris. Nos. 535/9 optd PHILEXFRANCE 89 and emblem.

540	9p. Type **154**	80	1·10
541	13p. Officer, 53rd Foot	90	1·25
542	20p. Royal Marine	1·10	1·40
543	45p. Officer, 66th Foot	1·50	2·00
544	60p. Private, 66th Foot	1·60	2·25

156 Agricultural Studies

1989. New Prince Andrew Central School. Mult.

545	13p. Type **156**	85	85
546	20p. Geography lesson	1·40	1·40
547	25p. Walkway and classroom block	1·50	1·50
548	60p. Aerial view of School	3·00	5·25

157 "The Madonna with the Pear" (Dürer)

1989. Christmas. Religious Paintings. Multicoloured.

549	10p. Type **157**	60	50
550	20p. "The Holy Family under the Appletree" (Rubens)	85	90
551	45p. "The Virgin in the Meadow" (Raphael)	2·00	2·50
552	60p. "The Holy Family with St. John" (Raphael)	2·50	3·50

158 Chevrolet "6" 30 cwt Lorry, 1930

1989. Early Vehicles. Multicoloured.

553	9p. Type **158**	85	80
554	20p. Austin "Seven", 1929	1·50	1·50
555	45p. Morris "Cowley" 11.9h.p., 1929	2·25	2·75
556	60p. Sunbeam 25h.p., 1932	2·75	4·25
MS557	93×74 mm. £1 Ford "Model A Fordor"	8·00	9·00

159 Sheep

1990. Farm Animals. Multicoloured.

558	9p. Type **159**	50	65
559	13p. Pigs	60	80
560	45p. Cow and calf	1·50	2·50
561	60p. Geese	2·00	3·50

160 1840 Twopence Blue

1990. "Stamp World London 90" International Stamp Exhibition, London.

562	160	13p. black and blue	50	50
563	-	20p. multicoloured	75	85
564	-	38p. multicoloured	1·25	2·00
565	-	45p. multicoloured	1·60	2·25

DESIGNS: 20p. 1840 Penny Black and 19th-century St. Helena postmark; 38p. Delivering mail to sub-post office; 45p. Mail van and Post Office, Jamestown.

161 Satellite Dish

1990. Modern Telecommunications Links. Mult.

566	20p. Type **161**	75	1·10
567	20p. Digital telephone exchange	75	1·10
568	20p. Public card phone	75	1·10
569	20p. Facsimile machine	75	1·10

161a Lady Elizabeth Bowes-Lyon, April, 1923

1990. 90th Birthday of Queen Elizabeth the Queen Mother.

570	**161a**	25p. multicoloured	1·00	75
571	-	£1 black and brown	2·75	3·75

DESIGN—29×37 mm: £1 Queen Elizabeth visiting communal kitchen, 1940.

162 *Dane* (mail ship), 1857

1990. Maiden Voyage of "St. Helena II". Multicoloured.

572	13p. Type **162**	1·25	85
573	20p. "St. Helena I" off-loading at St. Helena	1·60	1·40
574	38p. Launch of "St. Helena II"	2·25	2·75
575	45p. The Duke of York launching "St. Helena II"	2·75	3·50
MS576	100×100 mm. £1 "St. Helena II" and outline map of St. Helena	8·50	9·00

163 Baptist Chapel, Sandy Bay

1990. Christmas. Local Churches. Multicoloured.

577	10p. Type **163**	40	40
578	13p. St. Martin in the Hills Church	50	50
579	20p. St. Helena and the Cross Church	75	75
580	38p. St. James Church	1·25	2·25
581	45p. St. Paul's Cathedral	1·50	2·25

164 "Funeral Cortege, Jamestown Wharf" (detail V. Adam)

1990. 150th Anniv of Removal of Napoleon's Body.

582	**164**	13p. black, brown & green	1·75	1·25
583	-	20p. black, brown and blue	2·50	1·75
584	-	38p. black, brown & mauve	4·00	3·75
585	-	45p. multicoloured	4·00	4·00

DESIGNS: 20p. "Coffin being conveyed to the 'Belle Poule' " (detail, V. Adam); 38p. "Transfer of the Coffin to the 'Normandie', Cherbourg" (detail, V. Adam); 45p. "Napoleon's Tomb, St. Helena" (T. Sutherland).

165 Officer, Leicestershire Regiment

1991. Military Uniforms of 1897. Multicoloured.

586	13p. Type **165**	1·25	1·25
587	15p. Officer, York & Lancaster Regiment	1·25	1·25
588	20p. Colour-sergeant, Leicestershire Regiment	1·50	1·50
589	38p. Bandsman, York and Lancaster Regiment	2·50	3·00
590	45p. Lance-corporal, York and Lancaster Regiment	3·00	3·50

165a Queen Elizabeth II

1991. 65th Birthday of Queen Elizabeth II and 70th Birthday of Prince Philip. Multicoloured.

591	25p. Type **165a**	1·00	1·40
592	25p. Prince Philip in naval uniform	1·00	1·40

166 "Madonna and Child" (T. Vecellio)

1991. Christmas. Religious Paintings. Multicoloured.

593	10p. Type **166**	70	55
594	13p. "The Holy Family" (A. Mengs)	80	65
595	20p. "Madonna and Child" (W. Dyce)	1·25	1·00
596	38p. "The Two Trinities" (B. Murillo)	2·00	2·50
597	45p. "The Virgin and Child" (G. Bellini)	2·25	3·00

167 Matchless (346cc) Motorcycle, 1947

1991. "Phila Nippon '91" International Stamp Exn, Tokyo. Motorcycles. Multicoloured.

598	13p. Type **167**	1·00	80
599	20p. Triumph "Tiger 100" (500cc), 1950	1·50	1·10
600	38p. Honda "CD" (175cc), 1967	2·25	2·75
601	45p. Yamaha "DTE 400", 1976	2·50	3·00
MS602	72×49 mm. 65p. Suzuki "RM" (250cc), 1984	7·50	9·00

168 *Eye of the Wind* (cadet brig) and Compass Rose

1992. 500th Anniv of Discovery of America by Columbus and Re-enactment Voyages. Multicoloured.

603	15p. Type **168**	2·00	1·25
604	25p. "Soren Larsen" (cadet brigantine) and map of Re-enactment Voyages	2·75	2·25
605	35p. "Santa Maria", "Nina" and "Pinta"	3·50	3·50
606	50p. Columbus and "Santa Maria"	4·00	4·50

168a Prince Andrew Central School

1992. 40th Anniv of Queen Elizabeth II's Accession. Multicoloured.

607	11p. Type **168a**	40	40
608	15p. Plantation House	55	55
609	25p. Jamestown	85	95
610	35p. Three portraits of Queen Elizabeth	1·10	1·50
611	50p. Queen Elizabeth II	1·40	1·90

169 H.M.S. *Ledbury* (minesweeper)

1992. 10th Anniv of Liberation of Falkland Islands. Ships. Multicoloured.

612	13p. Type **169**	80	80
613	20p. H.M.S. "Brecon" (minesweeper)	1·10	1·10
614	38p. "St. Helena I" (mail ship) off South Georgia	1·75	2·25
615	45p. Launch collecting first mail drop, 1982	2·25	3·00
MS616	116×116 mm. 13p.+3p. Type **169**; 20p.+4p. As No. 613; 38p.+8p. As No. 614; 45p.+9p. As No. 615	5·50	5·50

The premium on No. **MS**616 were for the S.S.A.F.A.

170 Shepherds and Angel Gabriel

1992. Christmas. Children's Nativity Plays. Multicoloured.

617	13p. Type **170**	1·00	85
618	15p. Shepherds and Three Kings	1·10	95
619	20p. Mary and Joseph	1·25	1·00
620	45p. Nativity scene	2·50	4·00

171 Disc Jockey, Radio St. Helena (25th anniv)

1992. Local Anniversaries. Multicoloured.

621	13p. Type **171**	75	75
622	20p. Scout parade (75th anniv of Scouting on St. Helena)	1·25	1·25
623	38p. H.M.S. "Providence" (sloop) and breadfruit (bicent of Capt. Bligh's visit)	2·25	3·25
624	45p. Governor Brooke and Plantation House (bicent)	2·25	3·50

172 Moses in the Bulrush

1993. Flowers (1st series). Multicoloured.

625	9p. Type **172**	1·00	75
626	13p. Periwinkle	1·25	90
627	20p. Everlasting flower	1·60	1·25
628	38p. Cigar plant	2·75	3·25
629	45p. "Lobelia erinus"	2·75	3·25

See also Nos. 676/80.

173 Adult St. Helena Sand Plover and Eggs

1993. Endangered Species. St. Helena Sand Plover ("Wirebird"). Multicoloured.

630	3p. Type **173**	90	90
631	5p. Male attending brooding female	90	90
632	12p. Adult with downy young	1·75	1·75
633	25p. Two birds in immature plumage	2·25	2·25
634	40p. Adult in flight	2·50	2·75
635	60p. Young bird on rocks	2·75	3·50

Nos. 634/5 are without the W.W.F. emblem.

174 Yellow Canary ("Swainson's Canary")

1993. Birds. Multicoloured.

636	1p. Type **174**	40	1·00
637	3p. Rock partridge	55	1·00
638	11p. Feral rock pigeon	70	80
639	12p. Common waxbill	70	80
640	15p. Common mynah	80	80
641	18p. Java sparrow	85	80
642	25p. Red-billed tropic bird (horiz)	1·10	1·00
643	35p. Madeiran storm petrel (horiz)	1·40	1·25
644	75p. Madagascar red fody	2·50	3·25
645	£1 White tern ("Common fairy tern") (horiz)	2·75	3·50
646	£2 Giant petrel (horiz)	4·50	7·00
647	£5 St. Helena sand plover ("Wirebird")	10·00	13·00

175 Football and Teddy Bear

1993. Christmas. Toys. Multicoloured.

648	12p. Type **175**	85	85
649	15p. Yacht and doll	90	90
650	18p. Palette and rocking horse	95	95
651	25p. Model airplane and kite	1·40	1·60
652	60p. Guitar and roller skates	2·50	4·00

176 Arum Lily

1994. Flowers and Children's Art. Multicoloured.

653	12p. Type **176**	40	65
654	12p. "Arum Lily" (Delphia Mittens)	40	65
655	25p. Ebony	75	1·00
656	25p. "Ebony" (Jason Rogers)	75	1·00
657	35p. Shell ginger	95	1·10
658	35p. "Shell Ginger" (Jeremy Moyce)	95	1·10

177 Abyssinian Guinea Pig

1994. "Hong Kong '94" International Stamp Exhibition. Pets. Multicoloured.

659 12p. Type **177** 70 70
660 25p. Common tabby cat 1·40 1·40
661 53p. Plain white and black rabbits 2·25 3·00
662 60p. Golden labrador 2·50 3·25

178 Springer's Blenny

1994. Fishes. Multicoloured.

663 12p. Type **178** 75 75
664 25p. St. Helena damselfish 1·50 1·50
665 53p. Melliss's scorpionfish 2·25 3·25
666 60p. St. Helena wrasse 2·75 3·50

179 *Lampides boeticus*

1994. Butterflies. Multicoloured.

667 12p. Type **179** 75 75
668 25p. "Cynthia cardui" 1·50 1·50
669 53p. "Hypolimnas bolina" 2·25 2·75
670 60p. "Danaus chrysippus" 2·75 3·25

180 "Silent Night!"

1994. Christmas. Carols. Multicoloured.

671 12p. Type **180** 55 45
672 15p. "While Shepherds watched their Flocks by Night" 60 50
673 25p. "Away in a Manger" 1·00 90
674 38p. "We Three Kings" 1·50 2·25
675 60p. "Angels from the Realms of Glory" 2·25 3·75

1994. Flowers (2nd series). As T 172. Multicoloured.

676 12p. Honeysuckle 35 35
677 15p. Gobblegheer 40 40
678 25p. African lily 70 80
679 38p. Prince of Wales feathers 1·00 1·60
680 60p. St. Johns lily 1·75 3·25

181 Fire Engine

1995. Emergency Services. Multicoloured.

681 12p. Type **181** 1·25 75
682 25p. Lifeboat 1·40 90
683 53p. Police car 2·75 3·00
684 60p. Ambulance 3·00 3·50

182 Site Clearance

1995. Construction of Harpers Valley Earth Dam. Multicoloured.

685 25p. Type **182** 80 1·10
686 25p. Earthworks in progress 80 1·10
687 25p. Laying outlet pipes 80 1·10
688 25p. Revetment block protection 80 1·10
689 25p. Completed dam 80 1·10

Nos. 685/9 were printed together, se-tenant, forming a composite design.

182a "Lady Denison Pender" (cable ship)

1995. 50th Anniv of End of Second World War. As T 161 of Ascension. Multicoloured.

690 5p. Type **182a** 1·00 1·40
691 5p. H.M.S. "Dragon" (cruiser) 1·00 1·40
692 12p. R.F.A. "Darkdale" (tanker) 1·75 1·90
693 12p. H.M.S. "Hermes" (aircraft carrier, launched 1919) 1·75 1·90
694 25p. Men of St. Helena Rifles 2·75 3·00
695 25p. Governor Major W. J. Bain Gray taking salute 2·75 3·00
696 53p. 6-inch coastal gun, Ladder Hill 3·25 3·50
697 53p. Flags signalling "VICTORY" 3·25 2·50
MS698 75×85 mm. £1 Reverse of 1939–45 War Medal (vert) 2·50 2·75

The two designs for each value were printed together, se-tenant, forming composite designs.

183 Blushing Snail

1995. Endemic Invertebrates. Multicoloured.

699 12p. Type **183** 1·10 1·10
700 25p. Golden sail spider 1·75 1·75
701 53p. Spiky yellow woodlouse 2·75 3·50
702 60p. St. Helena shore crab 3·00 3·75
MS703 85×83 mm. £1 Giant earwig 5·50 6·50

184 *Epidendrum ibaguense*

1995. "Singapore '95" International Stamp Exhibition. Orchids. Sheet, 122×74 mm, containing T 184 and similar vert design. Multicoloured.

MS704 50p. Type **184**; 50p. "Vanda Miss Joaquim" 6·00 7·00

185 "Santa Claus outside Market" (Jason Alex Rogers)

1995. Christmas. Children's Paintings. Multicoloured.

705 12p. Type **185** 35 35
706 15p. "Santa Claus and band" (Che David Yon) 45 45
707 25p. "Santa Claus outside Community Centre" (Leon Williams) 70 75
708 38p. "Santa Claus in decorated street" (Stacey McDaniel) 1·00 1·40
709 60p. "Make a better World" (Kisha Karla Kacy Thomas) 1·75 3·50

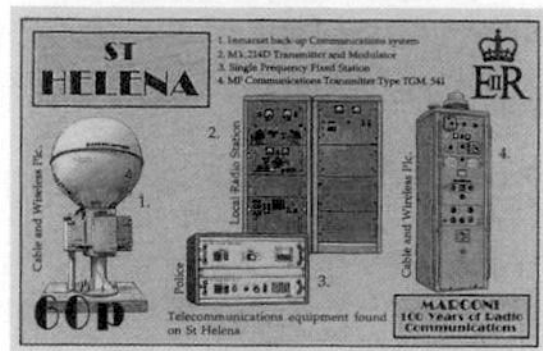

186 *Walmer Castle*, 1915

1996. Union Castle Mail Ships (1st series). Multicoloured.

710 12p. Type **186** 1·25 80
711 25p. "Llangibby Castle", 1934 1·75 1·25
712 53p. "Stirling Castle", 1940 3·00 3·25
713 60p. "Pendennis Castle", 1965 3·00 3·75

See also Nos. 757/60.

187 Early Telecommunications Equipment

1996. Centenary of Radio. Multicoloured.

714 60p. Type **187** 1·50 2·00
715 £1 Guglielmo Marconi and "Elettra" (yacht) 2·50 3·50

1996. 70th Birthday of Queen Elizabeth II. As T 55 of Tokelau, each incorporating a different photograph of the Queen. Multicoloured.

716 15p. Jamestown 50 40
717 25p. Prince Andrew School 75 65
718 53p. Castle entrance 1·50 2·25
719 60p. Plantation House 1·75 2·50
MS720 64×86 mm. £1.50 Queen Elizabeth II 3·25 4·50

188 Helicopter Mail to H.M.S. *Protector* (ice patrol ship), 1964

1996. "CAPEX '96" International Stamp Exhibition, Toronto. Mail Transport. Mult.

721 12p. Type **188** 65 60
722 25p. Postman on motor scooter, 1965 90 80
723 53p. Loading mail plane, Wideawake Airfield, Ascension Island 1·50 2·25
724 60p. "St. Helena II" (mail ship) unloading at St. Helena 1·75 2·50
MS725 98×73 mm. £1 L.M.S. No. 5624 "St. Helena" locomotive (43×27 mm) 2·75 3·75

189 "Mr. Porteous's House"

1996. Napoleonic Sites. Multicoloured.

726 12p. Type **189** 1·50 1·00
727 25p. "The Briars' Pavilion" 2·25 1·60
728 53p. "Longwood House" 3·50 4·00
729 60p. "Napoleon's Tomb" 3·50 4·00

190 Frangipani and Sandy Bay from Diana's Peak

1996. Christmas. Flowers and Views. Multicoloured.

730 12p. Type **190** 40 40
731 15p. Bougainvillaea and Upper Jamestown from Sampsons's Battery 50 50
732 25p. Jacaranda and Jacob's Ladder 75 75
733 £1 Pink periwinkle and Lot's Wife Ponds 2·75 5·00

191 Black Cabbage Tree

1997. Endemic Plants from Diana's Peak National Park. Multicoloured.

734 25p. Type **191** 1·75 2·00
735 25p. Whitewood 1·75 2·00
736 25p. Tree fern 1·75 2·00
737 25p. Dwarf jellico 1·75 2·00
738 25p. Lobelia 1·75 2·00
739 25p. Dogwood 1·75 2·00

Nos. 734/9 were printed together, se-tenant, with the backgrounds forming a composite design.

1997. "HONG KONG '97" International Stamp Exhibition. Sheet 130×90 mm, containing design as No. 644.

MS740 75p. Madagascar red fody 2·25 2·50

192 João da Nova's Lookout sighting St. Helena, 1502

1997. 500th Anniv of the Discovery of St. Helena (1st issue). Multicoloured.

741 20p. Type **192** 1·75 1·40
742 25p. Don Fernando Lopez (first inhabitant) and cockerel, 1515 1·90 1·40
743 30p. Thomas Cavendish and "Desire", 1588 2·00 1·60
744 80p. "Royal Merchant" (English galleon), 1591 4·00 5·25

See also Nos. 762/5, 786/9, 810/13, 828/31 and 857/60.

1997. Return of Hong Kong to China. Sheet 130×90 mm, containing design as No. 647, but changed face value and imprint date. W w 14 (sideways). P 14½×14.

MS745 75p. St. Helena Sand Plover ("Wirebird") 1·75 2·25

192a Royal Family's Visit, 1947

1997. Golden Wedding of Queen Elizabeth and Prince Philip. Multicoloured.

746 10p. Type **192a** 85 90
747 10p. Wedding photograph of Princess Elizabeth and Prince Philip 85 90
748 15p. Princess Elizabeth and Prince Philip, 1947 1·00 1·25
749 15p. Presenting bouquets, Royal Visit, 1947 1·00 1·25
750 50p. Prince Philip on Royal Visit, 1957 1·90 2·50
751 50p. Wedding party on balcony, 1947 1·90 2·50
MS752 111×70 mm. £1.50, Queen Elizabeth and Prince Philip in landau (horiz) 7·00 8·00

193 Flower Arrangement

1997. Christmas. 25th Anniv of the Duke of Edinburgh's Award in St. Helena. Multicoloured.

753 15p. Type **193** 1·00 65
754 20p. Calligraphy 1·25 80
755 40p. Camping 2·50 2·50
756 75p. Table laid for Christmas dinner 3·75 6·00

1998. Union Castle Mail Ships (2nd series). As T 186. Multicoloured.

757 20p. "Avondale Castle", 1900 2·50 1·75
758 25p. "Dunnottar Castle", 1936 2·50 1·75
759 30p. "Llandovery Castle", 1943 2·75 2·00
760 80p. "Good Hope Castle", 1977 5·00 6·50

194 Wearing green and white Hat, 1983

1998. Diana, Princess of Wales Commemoration. Sheet 145×70 mm containing vert designs as T 194.

MS761	30p. Wearing white jacket; 30p. Wearing green jacket, 1996; 30p. In evening dress, 1991 (sold at £1.20 + 20p. charity premium)	2·25	3·25

1998. 500th Anniv of the Discovery of St. Helena (2nd issue). As T 192. Multicoloured.

762	20p. Settlers planting crops, 1659	1·25	90
763	25p. Dutch invasion, 1672	1·40	90
764	30p. Recapture by the English, 1673	1·50	1·25
765	80p. Royal Charter of 1673	3·50	4·75

195 *Desire* (Cavendish), 1588

1998. Maritime Heritage. Multicoloured.

766	10p. Type **195**	1·75	1·75
767	15p. "Witte Leeuw" (Dutch East Indiaman), 1602	2·25	1·75
768	20p. H.M.S. "Swallow" and H.M.S. "Dolphin" (Carteret), 1751	2·50	1·25
769	25p. H.M.S. "Endeavour" (Cook), 1771	3·00	1·50
770	30p. H.M.S. "Providence" (sloop), 1792	2·50	1·25
771	35p. "St. Helena" (East India Company schooner), 1815	2·75	2·00
772	40p. H.M.S. "Northumberland" (ship of the line), 1815	2·75	2·00
773	50p. "Rurik" (Von Kotzebue), 1815	3·00	3·00
774	75p. H.M.S. "Erebus" (Ross), 1826	3·50	4·00
775	80p. "Keying" (junk), 1847	3·50	4·00
776	£2 "La Belle Poule" (French frigate), 1840	7·50	9·00
777	£5 H.M.S "Rattlesnake" (screw corvette), 1861	14·00	18·00

No. 771 is inscribed "H.M.S." in error.

196 Metal Lanterns

1998. Christmas. Island Crafts. Multicoloured.

778	15p. Type **196**	70	60
779	20p. Wood-turned bowls	80	65
780	30p. Inlaid woodwork on jewellery box	1·10	90
781	85p. Hessian and seedwork bag and hat	2·75	4·50

197 H.M.S. *Endeavour* (Cook), 1771

1999. "Australia '99" World Stamp Exhibition, Melbourne. Sheet 120×80 mm.

MS782	**197** £1.50, multicoloured	6·50	7·00

197a Photographs of Prince Edward and Miss Sophie Rhys-Jones

1999. Royal Wedding. Multicoloured.

783	30p. Type **197a**	60	65
784	£1.30 Engagement photograph	2·50	3·25

1999. 500th Anniv of the Discovery of St. Helena (3rd issue). As T 192 but horiz. Multicoloured.

786	20p. Jamestown fortifications	1·50	1·10
787	25p. Roadway up Ladder Hill, 1718	1·60	1·25
788	30p. Governor Skottowe with Captain Cook at St. James Church, 1775	3·50	1·75
789	80p. Presentation of sword of honour to Governor Brooke, 1799	3·75	5·00

199 King and Queen visiting Jamestown

1999. "Queen Elizabeth the Queen Mother's Century". Multicoloured.

790	15p. Type **199**	80	65
791	25p. Viewing bomb damage, Buckingham Palace, 1940	95	75
792	30p. With Prince Andrew, 1997	1·10	90
793	80p. Presenting colour to R.A.F. Central Flying School, and with Red Arrows	2·50	3·75
MS794	145×70 mm. £1.50, Queen Elizabeth, 1937, and Royal Family on balcony after Coronation	4·00	4·50

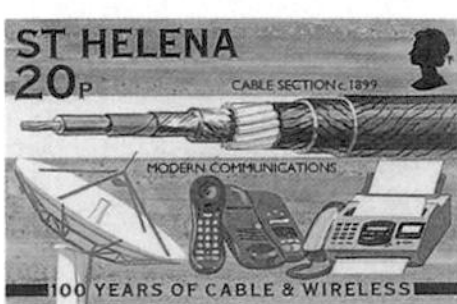

200 Modern Communications Equipment and Section of 1899 Cable

1999. Centenary of Cable & Wireless Communications plc on St. Helena.

795	**200**	20p. multicoloured	1·50	1·25
796	-	25p. black, brown and bistre	2·00	1·50
797	-	30p. black, brown and bistre	2·00	1·75
798	-	80p. multicoloured	2·75	4·50

DESIGNS: 25p. "Seine" (cable ship); 30p. "Anglia" (cable ship); 80p. Cable & Wireless Headquarters, The Briars.

201 *Victoria* (cruise liner) at St. Helena (image scaled to 67% of original size)

1999. Union Castle Line Centenary Voyage. Sheet 88×72 mm.

MS799	**201** £2 multicoloured	15·00	15·00

202 King Edward VI

2000. "Stamp Show 2000" International Stamp Exhibition, London. Kings and Queens of England. Multicoloured.

800	30p. Type **202**	1·90	1·90
801	30p. King James I	1·90	1·90
802	30p. King William III and Queen Mary II	1·90	1·90
803	30p. King George II	1·90	1·90
804	30p. Queen Victoria	1·90	1·90
805	30p. King George VI	1·90	1·90

203 Distillation Plant at Ruperts

2000. Centenary of Second Boer War (1st issue). Multicoloured.

806	15p. Type **203**	1·40	1·25
807	25p. Camp at Broadbottom	2·00	1·60
808	30p. Committee of Boer prisoners	2·25	2·00
809	80p. General Cronje and family at Kent Cottage	5·00	5·75

2000. 500th Anniv of the Discovery of St. Helena (4th issue). As T 192, but horiz. Multicoloured.

810	20p. East India Company flag with crest and Union Jack with colony badge	2·25	2·50
811	25p. Sir Hudson Lowe and Sir George Bingham with broken chains (abolition of slavery, 1832)	2·25	1·50
812	30p. Napoleon, British warship and funeral cortege	2·75	2·00
813	80p. Chief Dinizulu in exile, 1890	5·00	7·00

204 Princess Margaret

2000. Royal Birthdays. Sheet, 145×75 mm, containing T 204 and similar multicoloured designs.

MS814	25p. Type **204**; 25p. Prince William; 25p. Duke of York; 25p. Princess Royal; 50p. Queen Mother (42×56 mm)	25·00	25·00

205 *Beauty and the Beast*

2000. Christmas. Pantomimes. Multicoloured.

815	20p. Type **205**	1·40	1·75
816	20p. *Puss in Boots*	1·40	1·75
817	20p. *Little Red Riding Hood*	1·40	1·75
818	20p. *Jack and the Beanstalk*	1·40	1·75
819	20p. *Snow White and the Seven Dwarfs*	1·14	1·75

206 Chinese White Dolphin

2001. "HONG KONG 2001" Stamp Exhibition. Sheet 150×90 mm, containing T 206 and similar horiz design showing dolphins. Multicoloured.

MS820	30p. Type **206**; 40p. Striped dolphin	7·00	8·00

207 First St. Helena Postage Stamp

2001. Death Centenary of Queen Victoria. Mult.

821	10p. Type **207**	1·10	1·10
822	15p. H.M.S. *Beagle* off St. Helena, 1836	1·75	1·50
823	20p. Jamestown Square (horiz)	1·25	1·25
824	25p. Queen Victoria with Prince Albert and children (horiz)	1·75	1·50
825	30p. Diamond Jubilee procession (horiz)	2·70	4·00
826	50p. Lewis Carroll and characters from *Alice in Wonderland*	9·00	9·50
MS827	105×80 mm. £1.50, Sacks of St. Helena coffee at Great Exhibition	4·00	5·00

2001. 500th Anniv of the Discovery of St. Helena (5th series). As T 192, but horiz. Multicoloured.

828	20p. Men of St. Helena Rifles	2·25	1·75
829	25p. Prince Andrew School and Jamestown Community Centre	2·00	1·75
830	30p. Flax industry	2·00	2·00
831	80p. *St. Helena II* (mail ship)	5·50	6·50

208 H.M.S. *Dunedin* (light cruiser)

2001. Royal Navy Ships of Second World War. Multicoloured.

832	15p. Type **208**	1·75	1·50
833	20p. H.M.S. *Repulse* (battle cruiser)	2·00	2·25
834	25p. H.M.S. *Nelson* (battleship)	2·25	1·60
835	30p. H.M.S. *Exmoor* (destroyer)	2·25	1·75
836	40p. H.M.S. *Eagle* (aircraft carrier, launched 1918)	2·75	2·75
837	50p. H.M.S. *Milford* (sloop)	3·25	3·75

209 Tammy Wynette and "It came upon the Midnight Clear"

2001. Christmas. Carols. Each showing carol title and Tammy Wynette ("First Lady of Country Music"). Multicoloured.

838	10p. Type **209**	60	60
839	15p. "Joy to the World"	70	70
840	20p. "Away in a Manger"	80	80
841	30p. "Silent Night"	95	95
MS842	65×99 mm. £1.50 Tammy Wynette (vert)	3·75	4·50

210 Napoleon as a Young Man

2001. 180th Death Anniv of Napoleon Bonaparte. Multicoloured.

843	20p. Type **210**	1·50	1·00
844	25p. Napoleon at military school	1·75	1·25
845	30p. Napoleon dancing	2·00	1·60
846	80p. Napoleon with children	4·25	5·00

211 Princess Elizabeth and Princess Margaret as Girl Guides

2002. Golden Jubilee.

847	**211**	20p. agate, red and gold	1·25	85
848	-	25p. multicoloured	1·40	1·00
849	-	30p. brown, red and gold	1·50	1·25
850	-	80p. multicoloured	3·50	3·75
MS851		162×95 mm. Nos. 847/50 and 50p. multicoloured	8·50	8·00

DESIGNS—HORIZ: 25p. Queen Elizabeth in evening dress, 1967; 30p. Queen Elizabeth with Prince Charles and Princess Anne, 1952; 80p. Queen Elizabeth on Remembrance Sunday, Durban, 1999. VERT (38×51 mm)— 50p. Queen Elizabeth after Annigoni.

Designs as Nos. 847/50 in No. **MS**851 omit the gold frame around each stamp and the "Golden Jubilee 1952-2002" inscription.

212 Young St. Helena Sand Plover

2002. St. Helena Sand Plover ("Wirebird"). Multicoloured.

852	10p. Type **212**	85	90
853	15p. Chick running (vert)	1·25	1·10
854	30p. Adult bird in flight	1·50	1·40
855	80p. Chick	3·25	4·00
MS856	175×80 mm. 25p. Adult bird (vert) and Nos. 852/5	6·00	6·75

213 Sir William Doveton (Council member) and Jamestown Harbour

2002. 500th Anniv of the Discovery of St. Helena (6th issue). Local Celebrities. All showing Jamestown Harbour. Multicoloured.

857	20p. Type **213**	90	90
858	25p. Canon Lawrence Walcott	1·00	1·00
859	30p. Governor Hudson Janisch	1·25	1·25
860	80p. Dr. Wilberforce Arnold	2·75	4·00

214 H.M.S. *Hermes* (aircraft carrier)

2002. Royal Navy Ships from the Falklands War. Multicoloured.

861	15p. Type **214**	80	80
862	20p. H.M.S. *Leeds Castle* (patrol vessel)	90	90
863	25p. H.M.S. *Intrepid* (assault ship)	1·00	1·00
864	30p. H.M.S. *Glasgow* (destroyer)	1·10	1·10
865	40p. St. Helena I supplying H.M.S. *Brecon* and H.M.S. *Ledbury* (minesweepers)	1·50	1·75
866	50p. H.M.S. *Courageous* (submarine)	1·75	2·25

215 Queen Mother with Prince Andrew, 1960

2002. Queen Elizabeth the Queen Mother Commemoration.

867	**215**	20p. brown, gold and purple	80	80
868	-	25p. multicoloured	90	90
869	-	30p. brown, gold and purple	1·00	1·00
870	-	50p. multicoloured	1·50	2·25
MS871		145×70 mm. 35p. black and gold; £1 multicoloured	4·00	4·50

DESIGNS: 25p. Queen Mother at Cheltenham Races; 30p. Lady Elizabeth Bowes-Lyon, 1923; 35p. Queen Elizabeth, 1945; 50p. Queen Mother at St. Patrick's Day Parade, 1984; £1 Queen Mother at Sandown Races, 1998. Designs in No. **MS**871 omit the "1900–2002" inscription and the coloured frame.

216 Sperm Whale Pod Underwater

2002. Endangered Species. Sperm Whale. Multicoloured.

872	10p. Type **216**	65	70
873	15p. Sperm whale on surface	80	90
874	20p. Two sperm whales underwater	1·00	1·25
875	30p. Tail fin of sperm whale	1·40	1·75

217 The Princess Royal in Blues and Royals' Uniform

2002. Visit of the Princess Royal to St. Helena. Sheet 62×72 mm.

MS876	**217** £2 multicoloured	7·00	8·00

218 Plantation House and Arms

2003. Tourism. Multicoloured.

877	25p. Type **218**	1·25	1·40
878	25p. *St. Helena II* (mail ship) in Jamestown harbour	1·25	1·40
879	25p. *QE2* (cruise liner) off St. Helena	1·25	1·40
880	25p. Napoleon's Tomb and Briars Pavilion	1·25	1·40
881	25p. Ebony Flower and Diana's Peak	1·25	1·40
882	25p. St. Helena sand plover ("Wirebird") and Napoleon's House	1·25	1·40
883	25p. Broadway House	1·25	1·40
884	25p. St. Helena Golf Course	1·25	1·40
885	25p. Yacht and dolphins	1·25	1·40
886	25p. Sport fishing	1·25	1·40
887	25p. Diving	1·25	1·40
888	25p. St. Helena Museum	1·25	1·40

219 Queen Elizabeth II in Coronation Robes (photograph by Cecil Beaton)

2003. 50th Anniv of Coronation. Multicoloured.

889	30p. Type **219**	1·40	1·10
890	50p. Queen and Duke of Edinburgh in Coronation Coach	2·00	2·50
MS891	95×115 mm. 30p. As Type **219**; 50p. As No. 890	2·40	3·35

220 Queen Elizabeth II

2003

892	**220**	£2.50 multicoloured	5·50	5·50

221 *Leonotis nepetifolia*

2003. Wild Flowers. Multicoloured.

893	10p. Type **221**	1·00	1·25
894	15p. *Buddleia madagascariensis*	1·40	1·25
895	20p. *Datura suaveolens*	1·50	1·00
896	25p. *Fuchsia boliviana*	1·50	1·25
897	30p. *Commelina diffusa*	1·75	1·50
898	40p. *Solanum mauritianum*	2·25	2·25
899	50p. *Tecoma stans*	2·50	2·75
900	75p. *Kalanchoe pinnata*	3·50	3·75
901	80p. *Hedychium chrysoleucum*	3·50	3·75
902	£1 *Canna indica*	3·75	4·25
903	£2 *Alpinia nutans*	6·50	7·50
904	£5 *Lantana camara*	14·00	15·00

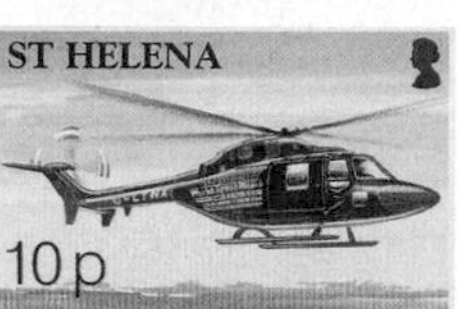

222 Westland WG-13 Lynx Helicopter

2003. Centenary of Powered Flight. Multicoloured.

905	10p. Type **222**	1·00	1·00
906	15p. Douglas C-124 Globemaster	1·10	1·00
907	20p. British Aerospace Nimrod AEW Mk 3	1·25	1·00
908	25p. Lockheed C-130 Hercules	1·40	1·10
909	30p. Lockheed L-1011 TriStar	1·50	1·40
910	50p. *Wright Flyer*	2·25	3·00
MS911	115×65 mm. £1.80 Supermarine *Walrus*	6·00	7·00

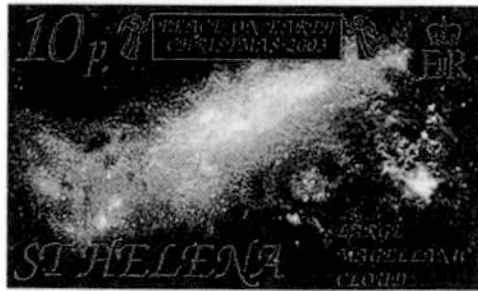

223 Large Magellanic Cloud

2003. Christmas. The Southern Sky. Multicoloured.

912	10p. Type **223**	85	85
913	15p. Small Magellanic cloud	1·00	1·00
914	20p. Omega Centauri globular cluster	1·25	1·25
915	25p. Eta Carinae nebula ("ETA CARRNAE")	1·40	1·40
916	30p. Southern Cross constellation	1·50	1·50

224 Christiaan Barnard (heart transplant pioneer)

2004. Medical Pioneers. Multicoloured.

917	10p. Type **224**	1·25	1·25
918	25p. Marie Curie (developer of X-radiography)	2·00	1·40
919	30p. Louis Pasteur (bacteriologist)	2·00	1·60
920	50p. Sir Alexander Fleming (discoverer of penicillin)	3·00	4·00

225 Freesia

2004. Bicentenary of Royal Horticultural Society. Multicoloured.

921	10p. Type **225**	40	50
922	15p. Bottle Brush	60	60
923	30p. Ebony	1·10	1·10
924	50p. Olive	1·50	2·00
MS925	111×111 mm. £1 Maurandya	2·50	3·00

226 St. Matthew

2004. Christmas. Stained Glass Windows. Multicoloured.

926	10p. Type **226**	45	50
927	15p. St. John	65	55
928	20p. St. Peter	80	65
929	30p. St. James	1·10	1·00
930	50p. St. Paul	2·00	3·00

227 SS *Umtata*

2004. Merchant Ships. Multicoloured.

931	20p. Type **227**	1·50	1·00
932	30p. SS *Umzinto*	2·25	1·40
933	50p. SS *Umtali*	3·25	3·25
934	80p. SS *Umbilo*	5·00	5·50

228 The Friar

2005. Rock Formations. Multicoloured.

935	35p. Type **228**	1·90	2·25
936	40p. Sugar Loaf	2·00	2·75
937	50p. The Turk's Cap	2·00	2·50
938	£1 Lot's Wife	3·00	3·50

229 HMS *Bellerophon, Aigle* and *Monarca*

2005. Bicentenary of the Battle of Trafalgar (1st issue). Multicoloured.

939	10p. Type **229**	1·00	1·00
940	20p. British 18 Pdr Naval Pattern canon	1·50	1·00
941	30p. HMS *Victory*	2·50	1·50
942	50p. First Lieutenant in the Royal Navy, 1805 (vert)	3·25	3·25
943	60p. HMS *Conqueror* (vert)	3·50	4·00
944	80p. Vice-Admiral Sir Horatio Nelson (vert)	4·75	6·00
MS945	120×79 mm. 75p. Admiral Cuthbert Collingwood (vert); 75p. HMS *Royal Sovereign* (vert)	8·00	8·50

Nos. 941 contains traces of powdered wood from HMS *Victory*.

See also Nos. 969/71.

230 HMS *Milford* (sloop)

2005. 60th Anniv of the End of World War II. Multicoloured.

946	20p. Type **230**	1·40	1·60
947	20p. HMS *Nelson* (battleship)	1·40	1·60
948	20p. RFA *Darkdale* (tanker)	1·40	1·60
949	20p. HMS *St Helena* (frigate)	1·40	1·60
950	20p. Atlantic Star medal	1·40	1·60
951	30p. Alan M. Turing (codebreaker) and Enigma code machine	1·60	1·75
952	30p. Captain Johnnie Walker and HMS *Starling* (sloop)	1·60	1·75
953	30p. Winston Churchill	1·60	1·75
954	30p. Churchill infantry tank	1·60	1·75
955	30p. Hawker Hurricanes	1·60	1·75

231 Pope John Paul II

2005. Pope John Paul II Commemoration.

956	**231**	50p. multicoloured	2·50	2·50

232 Sir Francis Drake

2005. Famous Elizabethans. Multicoloured.

957	10p. Type **232**	1·00	1·00
958	10p. *The Golden Hind*	1·00	1·00
959	15p. Sir Walter Raleigh	1·40	1·40
960	15p. *The Ark Royal*	1·40	1·40
961	25p. Queen Elizabeth I	1·75	1·75
962	25p. The Armada	1·75	1·75
963	£1 William Shakespeare	4·50	4·50
964	£1 The Old Globe Theatre	4·50	4·50

233 "The Little Fir Tree"

2005. Christmas and Birth Bicentenary of Hans Christian Andersen (writer). Multicoloured.

965	10p. Type **233**	55	55
966	25p. "The Ugly Duckling"	90	80
967	30p. "The Snow Queen"	1·00	1·00
968	£1 "The Little Mermaid"	3·25	4·25

234 HMS *Victory*

2005. Bicentenary of the Battle of Trafalgar (2nd issue). Multicoloured.

969	50p. Type **234**	2·50	1·75
970	80p. Ships engaged in battle (horiz)	3·75	3·50
971	£1.20 Admiral Lord Nelson	5·50	6·50

235 1961 Tristan Relief Fund stamps and Postcard

2006. 150th Anniv of the First St. Helena Postage Stamp. Treasures of the British Library. Multicoloured.

972	10p. Type **235**	1·00	1·00
973	20p. Cape of Good Hope 1855–63 1s. deep dark green triangular	1·50	1·00
974	25p. USA 1918 24c. inverted Curtiss JN-4 "Jenny" variety	1·60	1·10
975	30p. 1856 6d. blue (first St. Helena stamp)	1·60	1·25
976	80p. 1840 penny black	3·75	3·75
977	£1.20 Mauritius 1847 2d. deep blue	5·50	6·50
MS978	100×60 mm. £2 As 30p	8·00	9·50

236 Europa Stars with EU Flag

2006. 50th Anniv of the First Europa Stamps. Multicoloured.

979	10p. Type **236**	75	75
980	30p. Stars in circle and holding letter	1·25	1·00
981	80p. Stars and ball	2·75	3·00
982	£1.20 Stars in circle and holding stamp	3·75	4·75
MS983	122×77 mm. Nos. 979/82	7·00	8·50

237 Princess Elizabeth

2006. 80th Birthday of Queen Elizabeth II. Multicoloured.

984	10p. Type **237**	1·00	1·00
985	30p. Queen Elizabeth wearing tiara, c. 1952	1·50	1·00
986	80p. Wearing tiara and fur stole	3·75	3·75
987	£1.20 In close-up	5·00	6·00
MS988	144×75 mm. £1 Wearing tiara and pearl drop earrings, c. 1952; £1 Wearing cream sweater	7·00	8·50

238 Orange flowers (Emma-Jane Yon)

2006. St. Helena Arts and Crafts. Designs showing artwork from exhibition at Museum of St. Helena. Multicoloured.

989	30p. Type **238**	1·10	1·25
990	30p. Arum lily (Emma-Jane Yon)	1·10	1·25
991	30p. Hibiscus (Christina Stroud)	1·10	1·25
992	30p. Dolphins off coast (Christina Stroud)	1·10	1·25
993	30p. Pattern of blue flowers (Muriel Gardener)	1·10	1·25
994	30p. Wood turning by Jackie Essex	1·10	1·25
995	30p. Pottery dish by Corinda Essex	1·10	1·25
996	30p. Fish (Laura Lawrence)	1·10	1·25
997	30p. Peeled orange (Emma-Jane Yon)	1·10	1·25
998	30p. Sculptures by Sandy Walters and Johnny Drummond	1·10	1·25
999	30p. Pottery bowl by Serena Thorpe	1·10	1·25
1000	30p. Shells on beach (Christina Stroud)	1·10	1·25
1001	30p. Flower arrangement (Christina Stroud)	1·10	1·25
1002	30p. Succulent (Laura Lawrence)	1·10	1·25
1003	30p. Two fish (Laura Lawrence)	1·10	1·25
1004	30p. Pink fish (Laura Lawrence)	1·10	1·25

239 A Partridge in a Pear Tree

2006. Christmas. "The Twelve Days of Christmas" (carol) (1st issue). Multicoloured.

1005	10p. Type **239**	65	75
1006	15p. Two turtle doves	80	90
1007	25p. Three French hens	1·00	1·10
1008	30p. Four calling birds	1·10	1·25
1009	50p. Five gold rings	1·75	2·50
1010	£1 Six geese a-laying	3·00	4·25

240 Queen Victoria and First Victoria Cross Award Ceremony, 1857

2006. Exploration and Innovation. Anniversaries. Multicoloured.

1011	20p. Type **240**	1·50	1·50
1012	20p. Victoria Cross (150th anniv) and Charge of the Light Brigade	1·50	1·50
1013	25p. Charles Darwin (170th anniv of visit to St. Helena)	1·75	1·75
1014	25p. St. Helena sand plover ("Wirebird") and landscape near Sandy Bay	1·75	1·75
1015	30p. Isambard Kingdom Brunel (birth bicent) and coal railway, Cardiff Docks	2·00	2·00
1016	30p. RMS *St. Helena*, Cardiff Docks	2·00	2·00
1017	£1 Charles Dickens and Dingley Dell cricket match	4·50	4·50
1018	£1 Samuel Pickwick and cricket match (170th anniv of "The Pickwick Papers")	4·50	4·50

Nos. 1011/12, 1013/14, 1015/16 and 1017/18 were each printed together, se-tenant, each pair forming a composite background design.

241 Napoleon II (1811–32)

2007. The Napoleons. Multicoloured.

1019	25p. Type **241**	1·25	80
1020	30p. Napoleon I (1769–1821)	1·40	1·00
1021	£1 Napoleon III (1808–73)	3·25	4·25
MS1022	156×75 mm. Nos. 1019/21	5·50	5·50

242 Princess Elizabeth and Duke of Edinburgh

2007. Diamond Wedding of Queen Elizabeth II and Duke of Edinburgh. Multicoloured.

1023	25p. Type **242**	1·50	90
1024	35p. Princess Elizabeth on her wedding day	1·75	1·25
1025	40p. Wedding photograph	1·75	1·25
1026	£2 Princess Elizabeth getting out of car	8·50	10·00
MS1027	125×85 mm. £2 Wedding photograph (42×56 mm)	8·50	10·00

243 Black Noddy

2007. BirdLife International (2nd series). Seabirds. Multicoloured.

1028	15p. Type **243**	90	75
1029	30p. Madeiran storm petrel	1·25	1·00
1030	50p. Masked booby	2·50	1·75
1031	£2 Sooty tern	7·50	8·50

244 Scout Emblems

2007. Centenary of Scouting. Multicoloured.

1032	15p. Type **244**	90	70
1033	30p. Lord Baden-Powell inspecting scouts, May 1936	1·25	1·00
1034	50p. Lord Baden-Powell and Rev. L. C. Walcott	2·00	2·00
1035	£1 Lord Baden-Powell	3·50	4·50
MS1036	90×65 mm. £1 Badge of 1st Jamestown Scout Group (vert); £1 Lord Baden-Powell (150th birth anniv) (vert)	6·50	8·00

245 'Seven Swans a-Swimming'

2007. Christmas. 'The Twelve Days of Christmas' (carol). Multicoloured.

1037	10p. Type **245**	55	70
1038	15p. Eight Maids a-Milking	80	1·00
1039	25p. Nine Ladies Dancing	1·25	1·40
1040	30p. Ten Lords a-Leaping	1·25	1·40
1041	50p. Eleven Pipers Piping	1·75	2·00
1042	£1 Twelve Drummers Drumming	3·25	3·75

246 SS *Savannah*, (first steamship crossing), 1819

2007. Atlantic Firsts. Multicoloured.

1043	25p. Type **246**	1·25	90
1044	40p. Alcock and Brown's Vickers FB-27 Vimy, 1919 (first aeroplane crossing)	1·75	1·75
1045	45p. Alain Gerbault's sloop *Firecrest*, 1923 (first east-west solo sailing)	1·75	1·75
1046	£1.20 Charles Lindbergh's *Spirit of St. Louis* (first solo flight)	4·75	5·50

247 Airco D.H.9

2008. 90th Anniv of the Royal Air Force. Multicoloured.

1047	15p. Type **247**	1·00	90
1048	25p. Hawker Hurricane	1·40	1·10
1049	35p. Handley Page Hastings	1·75	1·75
1050	40p. English Electric Lightning	1·90	1·90
1051	50p. Harrier GR7	2·25	2·50
MS1052	110×70 mm. £1.50 Berlin Airlift, June 1948–September 1949	6·50	7·70

248 Longwood House, 1821

2008. 150th Anniv of the Purchase of Longwood House and Napoleon's Tomb. Sheet 165×95 mm containing T 248 and similar horiz designs. Multicoloured.

MS1053	90p. Type **248**; £1 Napoleon's Tomb; £1.25 Longwood House, 2008	13·00	15·00

249 Brown Booby

2008. Sea Birds (2nd series). Multicoloured.

1054	15p. Type **249**	1·00	80
1055	35p. Brown noddy	1·60	1·40
1056	40p. Fairy tern	1·75	1·40
1057	£1.25 Red-billed tropicbird	4·50	5·00

250 Deepwater Bullseye (*Cookeolus japonicus*)

2008. Fish. Multicoloured.

No.	Description	Mint	Used
1058	5p. Type **250**	30	40
1059	10p. Five finger (*Abudefduf saxatilis*)	50	60
1060	15p. Deepwater greenfish (*Holanthias fronticinctus*)	80	70
1061	20p. Hardback soldier (*Holocentrus adscensionis*)	1·00	85
1062	25p. Deepwater gurnard (*Scorpaena mellissii*)	1·25	85
1063	35p. Red mullet (*Apogon axillaris*)	1·50	1·25
1064	40p. Softback soldier (*Myripristis jacobus*)	1·60	1·40
1065	50p. Rock bullseye (*Heteropriacanthus cruentatus*)	1·75	1·75
1066	80p. Gurnard (*Scorpaena plumieri*)	2·75	2·75
1067	£1 Cunningfish (*Chaetodon sanctaehelenae*)	3·25	3·25
1068	£2 Hogfish (*Acanthostracion notacanthus*)	6·00	6·00
1069	£5 Marmalade razorfish (*Xyrichtys blanchardi*)	14·00	15·00
MS1070	171×167 mm. Nos. 1058/69	38·00	40·00

251 St. Helena Flag

2008. St. Helena Island Flag. Self-adhesive.

No.	Type	Description	Mint	Used
1071	**251**	35p. multicoloured	2·50	2·50

252 African Lily (*Agapanthus africanus*)

2008. Flowers at Christmas. Multicoloured.

No.	Description	Mint	Used
1072	15p. Type **252**	75	65
1073	25p. Christmas cactus (*Delosperma cooperi*)	1·40	90
1074	35p. Honeysuckle (*Lonicera periclymenem*)	1·40	1·40
1075	40p. St. John's lily (*Lilium longiflorum*)	1·40	1·40
1076	£1 Crucifix orchid (*Epidendrum radicans*)	3·25	3·75

253 Rupert Brooke (1914) and *The Soldier*

2008. 90th Anniv of the End of World War I. Designs showing war poets and extracts from their poems. Multicoloured.

No.	Description	Mint	Used
1077	10p. Type **253**	65	70
1078	15p. Siegfried Sassoon (1919) and *Aftermath*	90	75
1079	25p. Wilfred Owen (1917) and *Anthem for Doomed Youth*	1·25	90
1080	35p. Laurence Binyon (1914) and *For the Fallen*	1·75	1·75
1081	40p. John McCrae (1915) and *In Flanders Fields*	1·90	1·90
1082	50p. Edward Thomas (1915) and *In Memoriam*	2·25	2·25
MS1083	110×70 mm. £2 Cenotaph, St. Helena	7·50	8·50

254 Henry VIII (as young man)

2009. 500th Birth Anniv of King Henry VIII. Multicoloured.

No.	Description	Mint	Used
1084	50p. Type **254**	2·00	2·00
1085	50p. Catherine of Aragon	2·00	2·00
1086	50p. Anne Boleyn	2·00	2·00
1087	50p. Jane Seymour	2·00	2·00
1088	50p. Henry VIII (in middle age)	2·00	2·00
1089	50p. *Mary Rose* (galleon)	2·00	2·00
1090	50p. Anne of Cleves	2·00	2·00
1091	50p. Catherine Howard	2·00	2·00
1092	50p. Katherine Parr	2·00	2·00
1093	50p. Hampton Court	2·00	2·00

255 Westland Sea King Helicopter

2009. Centenary of Naval Aviation. Multicoloured.

No.	Description	Mint	Used
1094	15p. Type **255**	1·40	1·10
1095	35p. Fairey Swordfish	2·25	2·25
1096	40p. BAe Harrier	2·25	2·25
1097	50p. Blackburn Buccaneer	2·50	2·75
MS1098	110×70 mm. £1.50 Pioneer naval aviator Lt. E. L. Gerrard in cockpit of aircraft, Central Flying School, 1913	7·00	7·50

256 The Briars Pavilion, c. 1857

2009. 50th Anniv of Donation of the Briars Pavilion (Emperor Napolean's home 18 October to 10 December 1815) to the French Government. Sheet 95×166 mm containing T 256 and similar horiz designs. Multicoloured. W w 14 (sideways).

No.	Description	Mint	Used
MS1099	90p. Type **256**; £1 Napolean and Betsy Balcombe; £1.25 The Briars Pavilion, 2008	13·00	15·00

257 Deep Space Tracking Station, Ascension Island

2009. International Year of Astronomy. 40th Anniv of First Moon Landing. Multicoloured. W w 18 (sideways). P 13.

No.	Description	Mint	Used
1100	15p. Type **257**	75	60
1101	35p. Early experiment by Dr. Robert Goddard	1·50	1·50
1102	40p. Apollo 11 launch, 1969	1·50	1·50
1103	90p. STS41: *Discovery* Landing, 1984	3·00	3·25
1104	£1.20 Working on International Space Station, 2001	3·75	4·25
MS1105	100×80 mm. £1.20 *Surveyor III, I Presume* (astronauts Pete Conrad and Alan Bean approach Surveyor III) (Alan Bean) (39×59 mm). Wmk upright	4·25	4·50

258 Father Christmas in Street Parade

2009. Christmas. Multicoloured.

No.	Description	Mint	Used
1106	15p. Type **258**	75	60
1107	25p. Nativity play in church	1·00	75
1108	40p. Church lit at night	1·50	1·50
1109	£1 Street at night with Christmas tree and lights	3·25	3·75

259 St. Paul's Cathedral

2009. 150th Anniv of Diocese . Multicoloured.

No.	Description	Mint	Used
1110	15p. Type **259**	75	60
1111	35p. St. Matthew's Church	1·50	1·50
1112	40p. St. James' Church	1·50	1·50
1113	£1 Piers Calveley Claughton	3·25	3·25

260 Charles I

2010. 350th Anniv of the Restoration of King Charles II. 'Revolution to Restoration'. Multicoloured.

No.	Description	Mint	Used
1114	50p. Type **260**	2·00	2·00
1115	50p. Charles II	2·00	2·00
1116	50p. Prince Rupert	2·00	2·00
1117	50p. Oliver Cromwell	2·00	2·00
1118	50p. Richard Cromwell	2·00	2·00
1119	50p. Charles I arrests MPs	2·00	2·00
1120	50p. New Model Army	2·00	2·00
1121	50p. Execution of Charles I	2·00	2·00
1122	50p. Dissolution of Parliament	2·00	2·00
1123	50p. Coronation of Charles II	2·00	2·00

261 Children in Bomb Shelter

2010. 70th Anniv of the Battle of Britain. The Blitz. Multicoloured.

No.	Description	Mint	Used
1124	15p. Type **261**	75	65
1125	25p. Firemen	1·40	1·10
1126	35p. Milkman	1·50	1·40
1127	40p. Wrecked bus	1·75	1·50
1128	90p. Aircraft trails over city	3·25	3·50
1129	£1 Warden with binoculars watching for enemy aircraft	3·50	4·00
MS1130	110×70 mm. £1.50 Sir Douglas Bader	6·00	7·00

262 Great Britain King George V 1912 1d. Stamp

2010. Centenary of Accession of King George V

No.	Description	Mint	Used
MS1131	110×70 mm. **262** £1.50 multicoloured	6·00	7·00

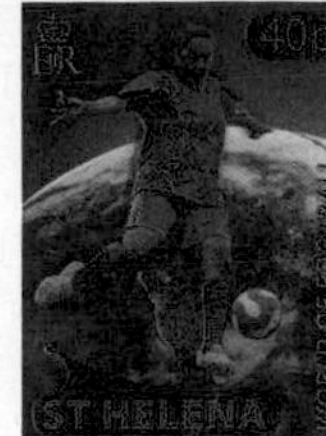

263 Football Player and Globe

2010. World Cup Football Championship, South Africa. Multicoloured.

No.	Description	Mint	Used
1132	40p. Type **263**	1·40	1·40
1133	40p. Globe showing South Africa	1·40	1·40
1134	40p. Two players and globe	1·40	1·40
MS1135	130×100 mm. Nos. 1132/4	4·00	4·25

264 Rainbows

2010. Centenary of Girlguiding. Multicoloured.

No.	Description	Mint	Used
1136	15p. Type **264**	70	75
1137	25p. Brownies	1·25	90
1138	40p. Guides	1·70	1·70
1139	90p. Lord and Lady Baden-Powell	3·35	3·50

265 Crucifix Orchid and Jacob's Ladder

2010. Christmas. Multicoloured.

No.	Description	Mint	Used
1140	15p. Type **265**	75	70
1141	25p. St. John's lily and Diana's Peak	1·25	90
1142	40p. Agapanthus and High Knoll Fort	1·75	1·75
1143	£1 Honeysuckle and Heart Shaped Waterfall	3·25	3·50

266 R.M.S. *St. Helena*, 2010

2010. 20th Anniv of R.M.S. *St. Helena*. Multicoloured.

No.	Description	Mint	Used
1144	15p. Type **266**	75	70
1145	35p. Arrival at St. Helena on her maiden voyage	1·25	90
1146	40p. Launch of R.M.S. *St. Helena*, 1990	1·75	1·75
1147	90p. Captain's table	3·25	5·50

267 Queen Elizabeth II

2011. Queen Elizabeth II and Prince Philip 'A Lifetime of Service'. Multicoloured.

No.	Description	Mint	Used
1148	15p. Type **267**	50	50
1149	25p. Queen Elizabeth II and Prince Philip (wearing tweed jacket), c. 1960	85	85
1150	35p. Queen Elizabeth II and Prince Philip, c. 1955	1·25	1·25
1151	40p. Queen Elizabeth II (wearing yellow) and Prince Philip, 1970s	1·40	1·40
1152	40p. Queen Elizabeth II (wearing turquoise-green jacket and hat) and Prince Philip, 1970s	1·40	1·40

1153	90p. Prince Philip, 1970s	3·00	3·00
MS1154	175×164 mm. Nos. 1148/53 and three stamp-size labels	8·00	8·00
MS1155	110×70 mm. £1.50 Queen Elizabeth II and Prince Philip, c. 2010	5·00	5·00

POSTAGE DUE STAMPS

D1 Outline Map of St. Helena

1986

D1	**D1**	1p. deep brown and brown	10	40
D2	**D1**	2p. brown and orange	15	40
D3	**D1**	5p. brown and red	20	45
D4	**D1**	7p. black and violet	20	50
D5	**D1**	10p. black and blue	25	50
D6	**D1**	25p. black and green	65	1·25

Pt. 1

ST KITTS

On 23 June 1980 separate postal administrations were formed for St. Kitts and for Nevis, although both islands remained part of the State of St. Kitts-Nevis.

100 cents = 1 West Indian dollar.

1980. As Nos. 394/406 of St. Kitts-Nevis optd St Kitts.

29B	5c. multicoloured	10	10
30B	10c. multicoloured	10	10
31A	12c. multicoloured	35	80
32B	15c. multicoloured	10	10
33B	25c. multicoloured	10	10
34B	30c. multicoloured	10	10
35B	40c. multicoloured	10	15
36A	45c. multicoloured	50	15
37A	50c. multicoloured	10	15
38A	55c. multicoloured	15	15
39A	$1 multicoloured	10	25
40A	$5 multicoloured	30	1·00
41A	$10 multicoloured	35	1·75

9 H.M.S. "Vanguard", 1762

1980. Ships. Multicoloured.

42	4c. Type **9**	10	10
43	10c. H.M.S. "Boreas", 1787	10	10
44	30c. H.M.S. "Druid", 1827	15	10
45	55c. H.M.S. "Winchester", 1831	15	15
46	$1.50 Harrison Line "Philosopher", 1857	30	35
47	$2 Harrison Line "Contractor", 1930	35	45

10 Queen Elizabeth the Queen Mother at Royal Variety Performance, 1978

1980. 80th Birthday of The Queen Mother.

48	**10**	$2 multicoloured	25	60

11 The Three Wise Men

1980. Christmas. Multicoloured.

49	5c. Type **11**	10	10
50	15c. The Shepherds	10	10
51	30c. Bethlehem	10	10
52	$4 Nativity scene	50	60

12 Purple-throated Carib **13** Bananaquit

1981. Birds. Multicoloured.

53A	1c. Magnificent frigate bird	15	20
54A	4c. Wied's crested flycatcher	25	20
55A	5c. Type **12**	25	20
56A	6c. Burrowing owl	35	30
57A	8c. Caribbean martin ("Purple Martin")	30	30
58A	10c. Yellow-crowned night heron	25	20
59A	15c. Type **13**	25	20
60A	20c. Scaly-breasted thrasher	30	20
61A	25c. Grey kingbird	30	20
62A	30c. Green-throated carib	30	20
63A	40c. Ruddy turnstone	35	30
64A	45c. Black-faced grassquit	35	30
65A	50c. Cattle egret	40	30
66A	55c. Brown pelican	40	30
67A	$1 Lesser Antillean bullfinch	60	60
68A	$2.50 Zenaida dove	1·25	2·25
69A	$5 American kestrel ("Sparrow Hawk")	2·25	3·50
70A	$10 Antillean crested hummingbird	4·50	6·00

The 1c. to 10c. are vertical as Type **12**. The remainder are horizontal as Type **13**.

14 Battalion Company Sergeant 3rd Regt of Foot ("The Buffs"), c. 1801

1981. Military Uniforms. Multicoloured.

71	5c. Type **14**	10	10
72	30c. Battalion Company Officer, 45th Regt of Foot, 1796–97	15	10
73	55c. Battalion Company Officer, 9th Regt of Foot, 1790	15	10
74	$2.50 Grenadier, 38th Regt of Foot, 1751	45	35

14a "Saudadoes"

14b Prince Charles and Lady Diana Spencer (image scaled to 60% of original size)

1981. Royal Wedding. Royal Yachts. Mult.

75	55c. Type **14a**	10	10
77	$2.50 "Royal George"	25	30
78	$2.50 As No. 76	70	70
79	$4 "Britannia"	35	50
80	$4 As No. 76	75	1·00
MS81	120×109 mm. $5 No. 76	1·00	1·00
82	55c. Type **14b**	15	30

15 Miriam Pickard (first Guide Commissioner)

1981. 50th Anniv of St. Kitts Girl Guide Movement. Multicoloured.

84	5c. Type **15**	10	10
85	30c. Lady Baden-Powell's visit, 1964	15	10
86	55c. Visit of Princess Alice, 1960	25	10
87	$2 Thinking Day parade, 1980's	45	35

16 Stained-glass Windows

1981. Christmas.

88	**16**	5c. multicoloured	10	10
89	-	30c. multicoloured	10	10
90	-	55c. multicoloured	15	10
91	-	$3 multicoloured	50	50

DESIGNS: 30c. to $3, Various designs showing stained-glass windows.

17 Admiral Samuel Hood

1982. Bicentenary of Brimstone Hill Siege.

92	**17**	15c. multicoloured	10	10
93	-	55c. multicoloured	20	10
MS94		96×71 mm.–$5 black, orange and brown	1·10	1·10

DESIGNS: 55c. Marquis De Bouille; $5 Battle scene.

18 Alexandra, Princess of Wales, 1863

1982. 21st Birthday of Princess of Wales. Multicoloured.

95	15c. Type **18**	10	10
96	55c. Coat of arms of Alexandra of Denmark	15	15
97	$6 Diana, Princess of Wales	55	80

1982. Birth of Prince William of Wales. Nos. 95/7 optd ROYAL BABY.

98	15c. Type **18**	10	10
99	55c. Coat of Arms of Alexandra of Denmark	15	15
100	$6 Diana, Princess of Wales	55	80

20 Naturalist Badge

1982. 75th Anniv of Boy Scout Movement. Multicoloured.

101	5c. Type **20**	10	10
102	55c. Rescuer badge	30	15
103	$2 First Aid badge	80	90

21 Santa with Christmas Tree and Gifts

1982. Christmas. Children's Paintings. Multicoloured.

104	5c. Type **21**	10	10
105	55c. The Inn	15	10
106	$1.10 Three Kings	20	15
107	$3 Annunciation	40	40

22 Cruise Ship "Stella Oceanis" at Basseterre

1983. Commonwealth Day. Multicoloured.

108	55c. Type **22**	15	10
109	$2 "Queen Elizabeth 2" at Basseterre	35	40

1983. Military Uniforms (2nd series). As T 14. Multicoloured.

110	15c. Light Company Private, 15th Regt. of Foot, c. 1814	20	10
111	30c. Battalion Company Officer, 15th Regt. of Foot, c. 1780	30	15
112	55c. Light Company Officer, 5th Regt. of Foot, c. 1822	30	20
113	$2.50 Battalion Company Officer, 11th Regt. of Foot, c. 1804	60	1·60

23 Sir William Smith (founder)

1983. Centenary of Boys' Brigade. Multicoloured.

114	10c. Type **23**	25	10
115	45c. B.B. members on steps of Sandy Point Methodist Church	30	10
116	50c. Brigade drummers	30	10
117	$3 Boys' Brigade badge	70	2·25

1983. Nos. 55, 59/63 and 66/70 optd INDEPENDENCE 1983.

118A	5c. Type **12**	15	10
119B	15c. Type **13**	30	10
120B	20c. Scaly-breasted thrasher	35	10
121B	25c. Grey kingbird	40	10
122B	30c. Green-throated carib	45	15
123B	40c. Turnstone	50	20
124B	55c. Brown pelican	55	30
125B	$1 Lesser Antillean bullfinch	1·00	50
126B	$2.50 Zenaida dove	1·75	1·75
127A	$5 American kestrel	2·50	2·75
128B	$10 Antillean crested hummingbird	4·00	5·50

25 Montgolfier Balloon, 1783

1983. Bicentenary of Manned Flight. Multicoloured.

129	10c. Type **25**	10	10
130	45c. Sikorsky "Russkiy Vityaz" biplane (horiz)	15	10
131	50c. Lockhead Tristar 500 (horiz)	15	15

132	$2.50 Bell XS-1 (horiz)	1·00	90
MS133	108×145 mm. Nos. 129/32	1·25	1·25

26 Star over West Indian Town

1983. Christmas. Multicoloured.

134	15c. Type **26**	10	10
135	30c. Shepherds watching Star	10	10
136	55c. Mary and Joseph	10	10
137	$2.50 The Nativity	30	40
MS138	130×130 mm. Nos. 134/7	50	1·10

27 Parrot in Tree

1984. Batik Designs (1st series).

139	**27**	45c. multicoloured	10	10
140	-	50c. multicoloured	10	10
141	-	$1.50 blue, yellow and purple	35	70
142	-	$3 multicoloured	55	1·75

DESIGNS: 50c. Man under coconut tree; $1.50, Women with fruit; $3 Butterflies.

See also Nos. 169/72.

28 Cushion Star

1984. Marine Life. Multicoloured.

143	5c. Type **28**	30	30
144	10c. Rough file shell	35	30
145	15c. Red-lined cleaning shrimp	35	15
146	20c. Bristleworm	35	15
147	25c. Flamingo tongue	40	15
148	30c. Christmas tree worm	40	20
149	40c. Pink-tipped anemone	55	25
150	50c. Smallmouth grunt	55	30
151	60c. Glass-eyed snapper	1·25	75
152	75c. Reef squirrelfish	90	70
153	$1 Sea fans and flamefish (vert)	1·00	60
154	$2.50 Reef butterflyfish (vert)	2·25	3·50
156	$10 Cocoa damselfish (vert)	7·50	14·00
205	$5 Black-barred soldierfish (vert)	6·00	10·00

The 10c., 60c., $5 and $10 come with or without imprint date.

29 Agriculture

1984. 25th Anniv of The 4-H Organisation. Multicoloured.

157	30c. Type **29**	15	10
158	55c. Animal husbandry	20	15
159	$1.10 The 4-H Pledge	35	60
160	$3 On parade	65	1·25

30 Construction of Royal St. Kitts Hotel

1984. 1st Anniv of Independence of St. Kitts-Nevis. Multicoloured.

161	15c. Type **30**	15	10
162	30c. Independence celebrations	20	15
163	$1.10 National Anthem and aerial view (vert)	40	60
164	$3 "Dawn of a New Day" (vert)	1·00	1·40

31 Opening Presents

1984. Christmas. Multicoloured.

165	15c. Type **31**	15	10
166	60c. Singing carols	45	35
167	$1 Nativity play	75	60
168	$2 Leaving church on Christmas Day	1·40	1·10

1985. Batik Designs (2nd series). Horiz designs as T 27.

169	15c. black, green and light green	15	10
170	40c. black, blue and light blue	30	15
171	60c. black, orange and red	45	25
172	$3 black, brown and light brown	1·25	2·25

DESIGNS: 15c. Country bus; 40c. Donkey cart; 60c. Rum shop and man on bicycle; $3 "Polynesia" (cruise schooner).

32 Container Ship "Tropic Jade"

1985. Ships. Multicoloured.

173	40c. Type **32**	1·00	30
174	$1.20 "Atlantic Clipper" (schooner)	2·00	1·50
175	$2 "Mandalay" (schooner)	2·25	2·50
176	$2 "Cunard Countess" (liner)	2·25	2·50

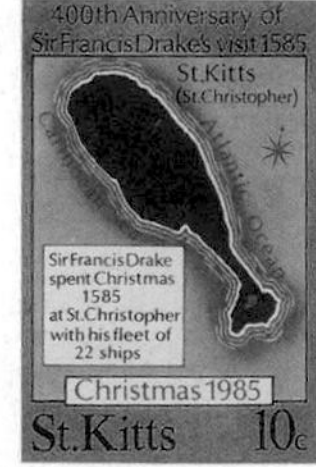

33 James Derrick Cardin (leading Freemason)

1985. 150th Anniv of Mount Olive S. C. Masonic Lodge. Multicoloured.

177	15c. Type **33**	65	30
178	75c. Banner of Mount Olive Lodge	1·40	1·25
179	$1.20 Masonic symbols (horiz)	1·40	3·00
180	$3 Lodge Charter, 1835	1·75	5·00

34 Map of St. Kitts

1985. Christmas. 400th Anniv of Sir Francis Drake's Visit. Multicoloured.

181	10c. Type **34**	30	15
182	40c. "Golden Hind"	60	35
183	60c. Sir Francis Drake	60	50
184	$3 Drake's heraldic shield	75	4·00

35 Queen Elizabeth and Prince Philip on St. Kitts

1986. 60th Birthday of Queen Elizabeth. Multicoloured.

185	10c. Type **35**	15	10
186	20c. Queen Elizabeth on St. Kitts	25	15
187	40c. At Trooping the Colour	50	30
188	$3 In Sweden	2·00	3·00

1986. Royal Wedding. As T 146a of St. Helena. Multicoloured.

189	15c. Prince Andrew and Miss Sarah Ferguson	15	10
190	$2.50 Prince Andrew	1·00	2·00

36 Family on Smallholding

1986. Agriculture Exhibition. Multicoloured.

191	15c. Type **36**	20	10
192	$1.20 Hands holding people, computers and crops	1·25	1·60

1986. 40th Anniv of U.N. Week. Nos. 185/8 optd 40th ANNIVERSARY U.N. WEEK 19-26 OCT.

207	10c. Type **35**	15	15
208	20c. Queen Elizabeth on St. Kitts	25	20
209	40c. At Trooping the Colour	30	30
210	$3 In Sweden	1·00	3·25

38 Adult Green Monkey with Young

1986. Endangered Species. Green Monkeys on St. Kitts. Multicoloured.

211	15c. Type **38**	3·00	50
212	20c. Adult on ground	3·25	50
213	60c. Young monkey in tree	6·50	2·50
214	$1 Adult grooming young monkey	6·50	4·50

39 Frederic Bartholdi (sculptor)

1986. Centenary of Statue of Liberty. Multicoloured.

215	40c. Type **39**	30	30
216	60c. Torch (1876) and head (1878) on exhibition (horiz)	40	60
217	$1.50 "Isere" (French warship) carrying statue (horiz)	1·00	1·75
218	$3 Statue of Liberty, Paris 1884	1·25	3·00
MS219	70×85 mm. $3.50 Head of Statue of Liberty	2·25	3·50

40 Officer, 9th Regt. (East Norfolk), 1792

1987. Military Uniforms (3rd series). Multicoloured.

220	15c. Type **40**	40	30
221	15c. Officer, Regt de Neustrie, 1779	40	30
222	40c. Sergeant, 3rd Regt of Foot ("The Buffs"), 1801	65	45
223	40c. Officer, French Artillery, 1812	65	45
224	$2 Light Company Private, 5th Regt, 1778	1·25	3·00
225	$2 Grenadier of the Line, 1796	1·25	3·00
MS226	121×145 mm. Nos. 220/5	6·75	8·00

41 Sugar Cane Warehouse

1987. Sugar Cane Industry. Multicoloured (colour of panel behind "ST. KITTS" given).

227	**41**	15c. yellow	20	30
228	-	15c. brown	20	30
229	-	15c. lilac	20	30
230	-	15c. blue	20	30
231	-	15c. turquoise	20	30
232	-	75c. light green	25	85
233	-	75c. lilac	25	85
234	-	75c. deep green	25	85
235	-	75c. yellow	25	85
236	-	75c. turquoise	25	85

DESIGNS: Nos. 227/31, Sugar cane factory; Nos. 232/6, Loading sugar train.

Nos. 227/31 and 232/6 were each printed together, se-tenant, forming composite designs.

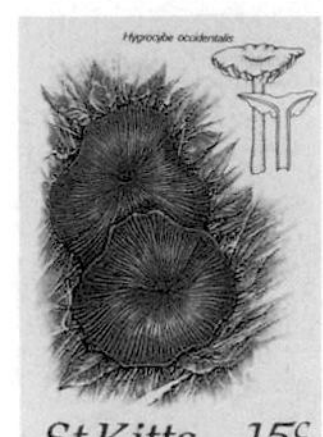

42 B.W.I.A. L-1011 TriStar 500

1987. Aircraft visiting St. Kitts. Multicoloured.

237	40c. Type **42**	75	30
238	60c. L.I.A.T. Hawker Siddeley Super 748	95	60
239	$1.20 W.I.A. De Havilland DHC-6 Twin Otter	1·50	2·75
240	$3 American Eagle Aerospatiale/Aeritalia ATR-42	2·75	4·75

43 "Hygrocybe occidentalis"

1987. Fungi. Multicoloured.

241	15c. Type **43**	80	20
242	40c. "Marasmius haematocephalus"	1·25	40
243	$1.20 "Psilocybe cubensis"	2·75	2·75
244	$2 "Hygrocybe acutoconica"	3·50	3·50
245	$3 "Boletellus cubensis"	4·00	4·50

44 Carnival Clown

1987. Christmas. Different clowns.

246	**44**	15c. multicoloured	25	15
247	-	40c. multicoloured	55	30
248	-	$1 multicoloured	1·25	1·40
249	-	$3 multicoloured	2·50	4·00

See also Nos. 266/9.

45 Ixora

1988. Flowers. Multicoloured.

250	15c. Type **45**	30	15
251	40c. Shrimp plant	55	30
252	$1 Poinsettia	1·00	1·40
253	$3 Honolulu rose	2·50	4·00

46 Fort Thomas Hotel

1988. Tourism (1st series). Hotels. Multicoloured.

254	60c. Type **46**	70	70
255	60c. Fairview Inn	70	70
256	60c. Frigate Bay Beach Hotel	70	70
257	60c. Ocean Terrace Inn	70	70
258	$3 The Golden Lemon	2·25	2·75
259	$3 Royal St. Kitts Casino and Jack Tar Village	2·25	2·75
260	$3 Rawlins Plantation Hotel and Restaurant	2·25	2·75

See also Nos. 270/5.

47 Ball, Wicket and Leeward Islands Cricket Association Emblem

1988. 75th Anniv of Leeward Islands Cricket Tournament. Multicoloured.

261	40c. Type **47**	2·00	30
262	$3 Cricket match at Warner Park	4·25	4·50

48 Flag of St. Kitts-Nevis

1988. 5th Anniv of Independence. Multicoloured.

263	15c. Type **48**	1·00	20
264	60c. Arms of St. Kitts	1·00	80
MS265	61×53 mm. $5 Princess Margaret presenting Constitutional Instrument to Prime Minister Kennedy Simmonds, 1983	4·00	4·25

1988. Christmas. As T 44 showing carnival masqueraders.

266	15c. multicoloured	10	10
267	40c. multicoloured	20	25
268	80c. multicoloured	40	55
269	$3 multicoloured	1·25	2·50

1989. Tourism (2nd series). Colonial Architecture. As T 46. Multicoloured.

270	20c. Georgian house	20	15
271	20c. Colonial-style house	20	15
272	$1 Romney Manor	50	80
273	$1 Lavington Great House	50	80
274	$2 Government House	70	1·60
275	$2 Treasury Building	70	1·60

For a redrawn version of No. 275 in a miniature sheet, see No. **MS**400.

49 Red Cross Nurse with Hospital Patient

1989. 125th Anniv of International Red Cross.

276	**49**	40c. multicoloured	30	30
277	-	$1 multicoloured	65	75
278	-	$3 red and black	1·75	2·75

DESIGNS: $1 Loading patient into ambulance; $3 125th anniversary logo.

50 Battle on the Champ-de-Mars

1989. "Philexfrance 89" International Stamp Exhibition, Paris. Sheet 115×99 mm.

MS279	**50** $5 multicoloured	3·25	3·75

50a Lunar Rover on Moon

1989. 20th Anniv of First Manned Landing on Moon. Multicoloured.

280	10c. Type **50a**	10	10
281	20c. Crew of "Apollo 13" (30×30 mm)	10	10
282	$1 "Apollo 13" emblem (30×30 mm)	45	65
283	$2 "Apollo 13" splashdown, South Pacific	95	1·50
MS284	100×83 mm. $3 Aldrin leaving "Apollo 11" lunar module	3·50	4·00

51 Outline Map of St. Kitts

1989

285	**51**	10c. mauve and black	20	20
286	**51**	15c. red and black	25	10
287	**51**	20c. orange and black	25	10
288	**51**	40c. yellow and black	40	20
289	**51**	60c. blue and black	60	50
290	**51**	$1 green and black	90	1·25

52 "Santa Mariagallante" passing St. Kitts, 1493

1989. 500th Anniv (1992) of Discovery of America by Columbus (1st issue). Multicoloured.

291	15c. Type **52**	2·00	30
292	80c. Arms of Columbus and map of fourth voyage, 1502–04	3·50	1·75
293	$1 Navigation instruments c. 1500	3·50	1·75
294	$5 Columbus and map of second voyage, 1493–96	10·00	11·00

See also Nos. 359/60.

53 Poinciana Tree

1989. "World Stamp Expo '89" International Stamp Exhibition, Washington. Multicoloured.

295	15c. Type **53**	50	10
296	40c. Fort George Citadel, Brimstone Hill	90	30
297	$1 Private, Light Company, 5th Foot, 1778	2·50	1·40
298	$3 St. George's Anglican Church	3·25	5·00

54 "Junonia evarete"

1990. Butterflies. Multicoloured.

299	15c. Type **54**	1·00	40
300	40c. "Anartia jatrophae"	1·75	40
301	60c. "Heliconius charitonia"	1·75	80
302	$3 "Biblis hyperia"	3·75	5·50

1990. "Expo '90" International Garden and Greenery Exhibition, Osaka. Nos. 299/302 optd EXPO 90 and logo.

303	15c. Type **54**	1·25	50
304	40c. "Anartia jatrophae"	2·00	50
305	60c. "Heliconius charitonia"	2·00	85
306	$3 "Biblis hyperia"	4·25	6·00

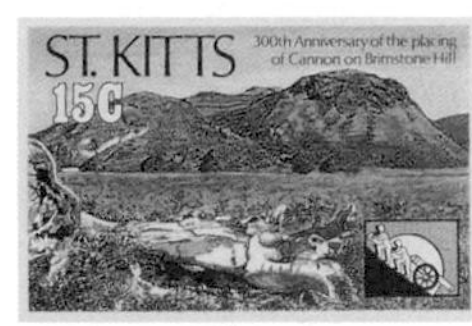

56 Brimstone Hill

1990. 300th Anniv of English Bombardment of Brimstone Hill. Multicoloured.

307	15c. Type **56**	45	20
308	40c. Restored Brimstone Hill fortifications	70	30
309	60c. 17th-century English marine and Fort Charles under attack	1·25	1·60
310	$3 English sailors firing cannon	3·50	4·50

The 309 exists se-tenant, as a horizontal pair, with No. 310. Each pair shows a composite design.

57 Supermarine Spitfire Mk Vb "St. Kitts Nevis I" 71 Squadron

1990. 50th Anniv of Battle of Britain. Sheet 103×76 mm. containing T 57 and similar horiz design. Multicoloured.

MS311	$3 Type **57**; $3 Supermarine Spitfire Mk Vb "St. Kitts Nevis II" 345 Squadron	14·00	14·00

58 "Romney" (freighter)

1990. Ships. Multicoloured.

312	10c. Type **58**	60	20
313	15c. "Baralt" (freighter)	75	20
314	20c. "Wear" (mail steamer)	75	20
315	25c. "Sunmount" (freighter)	75	20
316	40c. "Inanda" (cargo liner)	1·00	25
317	50c. "Alcoa Partner" (freighter)	1·00	30
318	60c. "Dominica" (freighter)	1·10	30
319	80c. "C.G.M Provence" (container ship)	1·25	40
320	$1 "Director" (freighter)	1·25	70
321	$1.20 Barque	1·75	1·75
322	$2 "Chignecto" (packet steamer)	2·50	2·50
323	$3 "Berbice" (mail steamer)	2·75	3·50
324	$5 "Vamos" (freighter)	4·00	5·00
325	$10 "Federal Maple" (freighter)	6·50	8·50

59 Single Fork Game

1990. Christmas. Traditional Games. Multicoloured.

326	10c. Type **59**	15	10
327	15c. Boulder breaking	15	10
328	40c. Double fork	30	30
329	$3 The run up	1·75	3·75

60 White Periwinkle

1991. Flowers. Multicoloured.

330	10c. Type **60**	70	20
331	40c. Pink oleander	1·40	30
332	60c. Pink periwinkle (vert)	1·90	70
333	$2 White oleander (vert)	3·25	4·25

61 Census Logo

1991. National Census.

334	**61**	15c. multicoloured	30	15
335	**61**	$2.40 multicoloured	2·50	3·25

The $2.40 differs from Type **61** by showing "ST. KITTS" in a curved panel.

1991. 65th Birthday of Queen Elizabeth II and 70th Birthday of Prince Philip. As T 165a of St. Helena. Multicoloured.

336	$1.20 Prince Philip	75	1·00
337	$1.80 Queen holding bouquet of flowers	1·75	2·10

62 Nassau Grouper

1991. Fishes. Multicoloured.

338	10c. Type **62**	50	20
339	60c. Hogfish	1·25	50
340	$1 Red hind	2·00	1·50
341	$3 Porkfish	3·50	5·00

63 School of Continuing Studies, St. Kitts and Chancellor Sir Shridath Ramphal

1991. 40th Anniv of University of West Indies. Multicoloured.

342	15c. Type **63**	40	15
343	50c. Administration Building, Barbados	70	40
344	$1 Engineering Building, Trinidad and Tobago	1·25	1·25
345	$3 Mona Campus, Jamaica and Sir Shridath Ramphal	3·00	4·50

64 Whipping The Bull

1991. Christmas. "The Bull" (Carnival play). Multicoloured.

346	10c. Type **64**	40	10
347	15c. Death of The Bull	40	10
348	60c. Cast of characters and musicians	1·25	60
349	$3 The Bull in procession	3·00	4·50

1992. 40th Anniv of Queen Elizabeth II's Accession. As T 168a of St. Helena. Multicoloured.

350	10c. St. Kitts coastline	40	10
351	40c. Warner Park Pavilion	2·00	50
352	60c. Brimstone Hill	75	40
353	$1 Three portraits of Queen Elizabeth	1·00	1·00
354	$3 Queen Elizabeth II	1·90	2·75

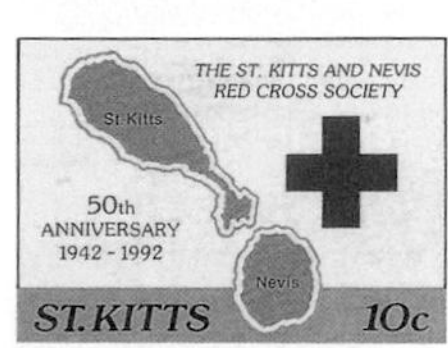

65 Map of St. Kitts-Nevis

1992. 50th Anniv of St. Kitts-Nevis Red Cross Society. Multicoloured.

355	10c. Type **65**	1·50	45
356	20c. St. Kitts-Nevis flag	2·25	45
357	50c. Red Cross House, St. Kitts	1·50	80
358	$2.40 Henri Dunant	3·50	5·00

66 Columbus meeting Amerindians

1992. Organization of East Caribbean States. 500th Anniv of Discovery of America by Columbus (2nd issue). Multicoloured.

359	$1 Type **66**	1·75	1·25
360	$2 Ships approaching island	3·50	4·00

67 Fountain, Independence Square

1992. Local Monuments. Multicoloured.

361	25c. Type **67**	25	20
362	50c. Berkeley Memorial Drinking Fountain	35	35
363	80c. Sir Thomas Warner's Tomb	55	65
364	$2 War Memorial	1·10	2·25

68 Joseph and Mary travelling to Bethlehem

1992. Christmas. Multicoloured.

365	20c. Type **68**	30	20
366	25c. Shepherds and star	30	20
367	80c. Wise Men with gifts	65	55
368	$3 Mary, Joseph and Holy Child	1·75	3·50

68a Short Singapore III

1993. 75th Anniv of Royal Air Force. Aircraft. Multicoloured.

369	25c. Type **68a**	85	20
370	50c. Bristol Beaufort Mk II	1·40	30
371	80c. Westland Whirlwind Series 3 H.A.R. 10 helicopter	3·00	1·50
372	$1.60 English Electric Canberra	3·00	3·50
MS373	110×78 mm. $2 Handley Page 0/400; $2 Fairey Long Range monoplane; $2 Vickers Wellesley; $2 Sepecat Jaguar G.R.1	11·00	11·00

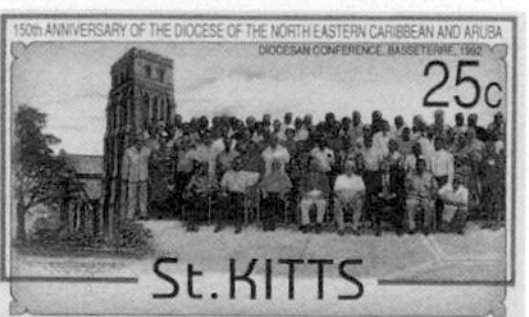

69 Members of Diocesan Conference, Basseterre, 1992

1993. 150th Anniv of Anglican Diocese of North-eastern Caribbean and Aruba. Multicoloured.

374	25c. Type **69**	15	10
375	50c. Cathedral of St. John the Divine (vert)	40	35
376	80c. Coat of arms and motto	70	85
377	$2 The Right Revd. Daniel Davis (first bishop) (vert)	1·50	2·75

70 1953 Coronation 2c. Stamp and Ampulla

1993. 40th Anniv of Coronation. Multicoloured.

378	10c. Type **70**	40	20
379	25c. 1977 Silver Jubilee $1.50 stamp and anointing spoon	50	20
380	80c. 1977 Silver Jubilee 55c. stamp and tassels	1·00	1·25
381	$2 1978 25th anniv of Coronation stamps and sceptre	2·00	3·50

71 Flags of Girls Brigade and St. Kitts-Nevis

1993. Centenary of Girls Brigade. Multicoloured.

382	80c. Type **71**	2·50	1·00
383	$3 Girls Brigade badge and coat of arms	4·00	4·50

72 Aspects of St. Kitts on Flag

1993. 10th Anniv of Independence. Multicoloured.

384	20c. Type **72**	1·00	15
385	80c. Coat of arms and Independence anniversary logo	1·25	80
386	$3 Coat of arms and map	4·25	4·50

73 "Hibiscus sabdariffa"

1993. Christmas. Flowers. Multicoloured.

387	25c. Type **73**	25	10
388	50c. "Euphorbia pulcherrima"	60	45
389	$1.60 "Euphorbia leucocephala"	1·75	2·50

74 Mesosaurus

1994. Prehistoric Aquatic Reptiles. Multicoloured.

390	$1.20 Type **74**	1·40	1·75
391	$1.20 Placodus	1·40	1·75
392	$1.20 Liopleurodon	1·40	1·75
393	$1.20 Hydrotherosaurus	1·40	1·75
394	$1.20 Caretta	1·40	1·75

Nos. 390/4 were printed together, se-tenant, with the background forming a composite design.

1994. "Hong Kong '94" International Stamp Exhibition. Nos. 390/4 optd HONG KONG '94 and emblem.

395	$1.20 Type **74**	1·90	2·25
396	$1.20 Placodus	1·90	2·25
397	$1.20 Liopleurodon	1·90	2·25
398	$1.20 Hydrotherosaurus	1·90	2·25
399	$1.20 Caretta	1·90	2·25

75 Sir Shridath Ramphal

1994. First Recipients of Order of the Caribbean Community. Multicoloured.

401	10c. Type **75**	30	50
402	10c. Star of Order	20	30
403	10c. Derek Walcott	30	50
404	10c. William Demas	30	50
405	$1 Type **75**	1·25	1·40
406	$1 As No. 402	1·00	1·00
407	$1 As No. 403	1·25	1·40
408	$1 As No. 404	1·25	1·40

76 Family singing Carols

1994. Christmas. Int Year of the Family. Mult.

409	25c. Type **76**	15	10
410	25c. Family unwrapping Christmas presents	15	10
411	80c. Preparing for Christmas carnival	60	60
412	$2.50 Nativity	1·90	3·00

77 Green Turtle swimming

1995. Endangered Species. Green Turtle. Multicoloured.

427	10c. Type **77**	40	50
428	40c. Turtle crawling up beach	55	60
429	50c. Burying eggs	60	60
430	$1 Young heading for sea	75	1·00

78 St. Christopher 1d. Stamps of 1870

1995. 125th Anniv of St. Kitts Postage Stamps. Each including the St. Christopher 1870 1d. Multicoloured.

431	25c. Type **78**	15	15
432	80c. St. Kitts-Nevis 1935 Silver Jubilee 1d.	45	50
433	$2.50 St. Kitts-Nevis 1946 Victory 1d.	1·75	2·25
434	$3 St. Christopher Nevis Anguilla 1953 Coronation 2c.	2·00	2·50

1995. 50th Anniv of End of Second World War. As T 182a of St. Helena. Multicoloured.

435	20c. Caribbean Regiment patrol, North Africa	15	15
436	50c. Grumman TBF Avengers (bombers)	35	35
437	$2 Supermarine Spitfire MK Vb (fighter)	1·25	1·50
438	$8 U. S. Navy destroyer escort	5·00	6·50
MS439	75×85 mm. $3 Reverse of 1939–45 War Medal (vert)	1·75	2·00

79 Telecommunication Links between Islands

1995. 10th Anniv of SKANTEL (telecommunications company). Multicoloured.

440	10c. Type **79**	25	10
441	25c. Payphone and computer link	30	15
442	$2 Telecommunications tower and dish aerial	2·25	2·50
443	$3 Silhouette of dish aerial at sunset	2·50	3·50

80 Water Treatment Works

1995. 50th Anniv of United Nations. Multicoloured.

444	40c. Type **80**	35	25
445	50c. Beach	55	30
446	$1.60 Dust cart	1·75	2·25
447	$2.50 Forest	2·75	3·75

81 F.A.O. Emblem and Vegetables

1995. 50th Anniv of F.A.O. Multicoloured.

448	25c. Type **81**	20	10
449	50c. Glazed carrots and West Indian peas with rice	35	30
450	80c. Tania and cassava plants	50	60
451	$1.50 Waterfall, Green Hill Mountain	2·50	2·75

82 Flame Helmet

1996. Sea Shells. Multicoloured.

452	$1.50 Type **82**	95	1·10
453	$1.50 Triton's trumpet	95	1·10
454	$1.50 King helmet	95	1·10
455	$1.50 True tulip	95	1·10
456	$1.50 Queen conch	95	1·10

83 L.M.S. No. 45614 Steam Locomotive "Leeward Islands" in Green Livery

1996. "CAPEX '96" International Stamp Exhibition, Toronto.

457	10c. Type **83**	50	30
MS458	110×80 mm. $10 L.M.S. No. 5614 "Leeward Islands" steam locomotive in red livery (48×31½ mm)	7·50	7·50

84 Athlete and National Flag

1996. Centennial Olympic Games, Atlanta. Multicoloured.

459	10c. Type **84**	15	15
460	25c. High jumper and U.S.A. flag	20	20
461	80c. Athlete and Olympic flag	50	55
462	$3 Poster for 1896 Olympic Games, Athens	1·75	2·50
MS463	70×64 mm. $6 Olympic torch	3·25	3·50

85 Volunteer Rifleman, 1896

1996. Centenary of Defence Force. Multicoloured.

464	10c. Type **85**	15	15
465	50c. Mounted infantryman, 1911	35	35
466	$2 Drummer, 1940–60	1·25	1·75
467	$2.50 Ceremonial uniform, 1996	1·40	2·00

86 "Holy Virgin and Child" (A. Colin)

1996. Christmas. Religious Paintings. Multicoloured.

468	15c. Type **86**	20	10
469	25c. "Holy Family" (after Rubens)	25	10
470	50c. "Madonna with the Goldfinch" (Krause after Raphael)	45	35
471	80c. "Madonna on Throne with Angels" (17th-cent Spanish)	75	1·00

1997. "HONG KONG '97" International Stamp Exhibition. Sheet 130×90 mm, containing No. 323.

MS472	$3 "Berbice" (mail steamer)	1·60	2·00

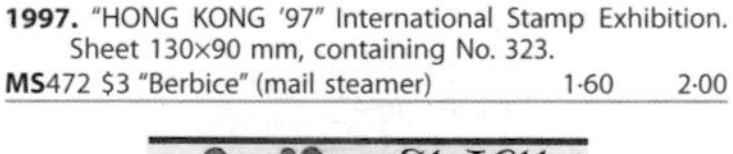

87 Princess Parrotfish

1997. Fishes. Multicoloured.

473	$1 Type **87**	80	80
474	$1 Yellow-bellied hamlet	80	80
475	$1 Coney	80	80
476	$1 Fin-spot wrasse	80	80
477	$1 Doctor fish	80	80
478	$1 Squirrelfish	80	80
479	$1 Queen angelfish	80	80
480	$1 Spanish hogfish	80	80
481	$1 Red hind	80	80
482	$1 Red grouper	80	80
483	$1 Yellow-tailed snapper	80	80
484	$1 Mutton hamlet	80	80

1997. Golden Wedding of Queen Elizabeth and Prince Philip. As T 192a of St. Helena. Multicoloured.

485	10c. Queen Elizabeth in evening dress	70	1·00
486	10c. Prince Philip and Duke of Kent at Trooping the Colour	70	1·00
487	25c. Queen Elizabeth in phaeton at Trooping the Colour	90	1·10
488	25c. Prince Philip in naval uniform	90	1·10
489	$3 Queen Elizabeth and Prince Philip	2·50	2·75
490	$3 Peter Phillips on horseback	2·50	2·75
MS491	110×70 mm. $6 Queen Elizabeth and Prince Philip in landau (horiz).	5·50	6·50

Nos. 485/6, 487/8 and 489/90 respectively were printed together, se-tenant, with the backgrounds forming composite designs.

88 C. A. Paul Southwell (first Chief Minister)

1997. National Heroes Day. Multicoloured.

492	25c. Type **88**	15	25
493	25c. Sir Joseph France (trade union leader)	15	25
494	25c. Robert Bradshaw (first Prime Minister)	15	25
495	$3 Sir Joseph France, Robert Bradshaw and C. A. Paul Southwell (horiz)	1·75	2·50

89 Wesley Methodist Church

1997. Christmas. Churches. Multicoloured.

496	10c. Type **89**	10	10
497	10c. Zion Moravian Church	10	10
498	$1.50 St. George's Anglican Church (vert)	1·00	1·00
499	$15 Co-Cathedral of the Immaculate Conception (vert)	8·50	11·00

90 Common Long-tail Skipper

1997. Butterflies. Multicoloured.

500	10c. Type **90**	15	10
501	15c. White peacock	20	10
502	25c. Caribbean buckeye	25	15
503	30c. The red rim	25	15
504	40c. Cassius blue	30	20
505	50c. The flambeau	35	25
506	60c. Lucas's blue	50	30
507	90c. Cloudless sulphur	70	40
508	$1 The monarch	75	45
509	$1.20 Fiery skipper	85	85
510	$1.60 The zebra	1·10	1·10
511	$3 Southern dagger tail	2·00	2·25
512	$5 Polydamus swallowtail	3·25	3·50
513	$10 Tropical chequered skipper	6·00	6·50

1998. Diana, Princess of Wales Commemoration. As T 62a of Tokelau. Multicoloured.

514	30c. Wearing hat	30	30
MS515	145×70 mm. $1.60, As 30c.; $1.60, Wearing red jacket; $1.60, Wearing white jacket; $1.60, Carrying bouquets. (sold at $6.40 + 90c. charity premium)	3·00	3·50

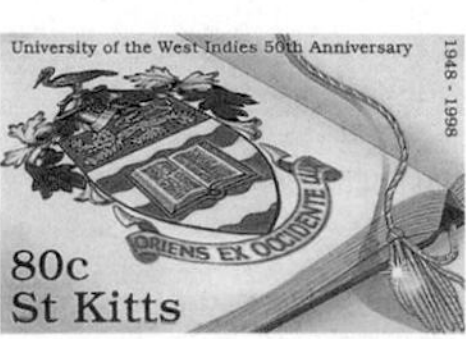

91 University Arms on Book

1998. 50th Anniv of University of West Indies. Multicoloured.

516	80c. Type **91**	45	40
517	$2 University arms and mortarboard	95	1·40

92 Santa at Carnival

1998. Christmas. Multicoloured.

518	80c. Type **92**	45	40
519	$1.20 Santa with two carnival dancers	65	1·00

93 Launching Rowing Boat

1999. 125th Anniv of Universal Postal Union. Multicoloured.

520	30c. Type **93**	25	20
521	90c. Pictorial map of St. Kitts	1·00	80

94 Caribbean Martin

1999. Birds of the Eastern Caribbean. Multicoloured.

522	80c. Type **94**	60	70
523	80c. Spotted sandpiper	60	70
524	80c. Sooty tern	60	70
525	80c. Red-tailed hawk	60	70
526	80c. Brown trembler	60	70
527	80c. Belted kingfisher	60	70
528	80c. Black-billed whistling duck	60	70
529	80c. Yellow warbler	60	70
530	80c. Blue-headed hummingbird	60	70
531	80c. Antillean Euphonia	60	70
532	80c. Fulvous whistling duck	60	70
533	80c. Mangrove cuckoo	60	70
534	80c. Carib grackle	60	70
535	80c. Caribbean elaenia	60	70
536	80c. Scaly-breasted ground dove	60	70
537	80c. Forest thrush	60	70

94a Lift-off

1999. 30th Anniv of First Manned Landing on Moon. Multicoloured.

538	80c. Type **94a**	60	40
539	90c. In Moon orbit	70	65
540	$1 Buzz Aldrin on Moon's surface	80	85
541	$1.20 Heat shields burning during re-entry	90	1·25
MS542	90×80 mm. $10 Earth as seen from Moon (circular, 40 mm diam)	4·75	5·00

95 Local Quartet

1999. Christmas. Musicians. Multicoloured.

543	10c. Type **95**	20	10
544	30c. Trio	30	20
545	80c. Sextet	60	40
546	$2 Quartet in green jerseys	1·10	2·00

96 "Rockets, Saturn and Earth" (A. Taylor)

1999. New Millennium. Children's Paintings. Multicoloured.

547	10c. Type **96**	30	15
548	30c. "Y2K, computer and Earth weeping" (T. Liburd)	45	25
549	50c. "Alien destroying computer" (D. Moses)	55	35
550	$1 "Technology past, present and future" (P. Liburd)	90	1·25

97 Carnival Celebrations

2000. "Carifesta VII" Arts Festival. Multicoloured.

551	30c. Type **97**	30	20
552	90c. Carifesta logo	75	65
553	$1.20 Stylized dancer with streamer (vert)	1·00	1·40

98 Steam Locomotive No. 133, U.S. Military Railroad, 1864

2001. Railways in the American Civil War. Multicoloured (except for Nos. MS578a and c).

554	$1.20 Type **98**	1·10	1·10
555	$1.20 Locomotive *Quigley*, Louisville and Nashville Railroad, 1860	1·10	1·10
556	$1.20 Locomotive *Colonel Holobird*, New Orleans, Opelousas and Great Western Railroad, 1865	1·10	1·10
557	$1.20 Locomotive No. 150, U.S. Military Railroad, 1864	1·10	1·10
558	$1.20 Locomotive *Doctor Thompson*, Atlanta and West Point Railroad, 1860	1·10	1·10
559	$1.20 Locomotive No. 156, U.S. Military Railroad, 1856	1·10	1·10
560	$1.20 Locomotive *Governor Nye*, U.S. Military Railroad, 1863	1·10	1·10
561	$1.20 Locomotive No. 31, Illinois Central Railroad, 1856	1·10	1·10
562	$1.20 Locomotive *C.A. Henry*, Memphis, Clarksville and Louisville Line, 1863	1·10	1·10
563	$1.20 Locomotive No. 152, Illinois Central Railroad, 1856	1·10	1·10
564	$1.20 Locomotive No. 116, U.S. Military Railroad, 1863	1·10	1·10
565	$1.20 Locomotive *Job Terry* (shown as No. 111 of the Wilmington and Weldon Railroad, 1890)	1·10	1·10
566	$1.60 Locomotive *Dover*, U.S. Military Railroad, 1856	1·40	1·40
567	$1.60 Locomotive *Scout*, Richmond to Gordonsville Line, 1861	1·40	1·40
568	$1.60 Baltimore & Ohio Railroad Locomotive, 1861	1·40	1·40
569	$1.60 Locomotive *John. M. Forbes*, Philadelphia, Wilmington and Baltimore Railroad, 1861	1·40	1·40
570	$1.60 Locomotive *Edward Kidder*, Wilmington and Weldon Railroad, 1866	1·40	1·40
571	$1.60 Locomotive *William W. Wright*, U.S. Military Railroad, 1863	1·40	1·40
572	$1.60 Locomotive No. 83, Illinois Central Railroad, 1856	1·40	1·40
573	$1.60 Locomotive *The General*, Western and Atlantic Railroad, 1855	1·40	1·40
574	$1.60 Locomotive No. 38, Louisville and Nashville Railroad, 1860	1·40	1·40
575	$1.60 Locomotive *Texas*, Western and Atlantic Railroad, 1856	1·40	1·40
576	$1.60 Locomotive No. 162, U.S. Military Railroad, 1864	1·40	1·40
577	$1.60 Locomotive *Christopher Adams Jr.*, Memphis and Littlerock Line, 1853	1·40	1·40

MS578 Four sheets, each 99×78 mm. (a) $5 Brigadier-general Herman Haupt (Federal railway chief) (brown and black) (vert). (b) $5 General George B. McClellan (vert). (c) $5 General Ulysses S. Grant (brown, grey and black) (vert). (d) $5 General Robert E. Lee (vert). Set of 4 sheets 18·00 20·00

No. 577 is inscribed "Chritopher" in error.

99 Bananaquit

2001. Caribbean Flora and Fauna. Multicoloured.

No.	Description	Unused	Used
579	$1.20 Type **99**	80	85
580	$1.20 Anthurium (face value in white)	80	85
581	$1.20 Common dolphin	80	85
582	$1.20 Horse mushroom	80	85
583	$1.20 Green anole	80	85
584	$1.20 Monarch butterfly	80	85
585	$1.20 Heliconia	80	85
586	$1.20 Anthurium (black face value)	80	85
587	$1.20 *Oncidium splendidum*	80	85
588	$1.20 Trumpet creeper	80	85
589	$1.20 Bird of paradise	80	85
590	$1.20 Hibiscus	80	85
591	$1.60 Beaugregory	90	95
592	$1.60 Banded butterflyfish	90	95
593	$1.60 Cherubfish	90	95
594	$1.60 Rock beauty	90	95
595	$1.60 Red snapper	90	95
596	$1.60 Leatherback turtle	90	95
597	$1.60 Figure-of-eight butterfly	90	95
598	$1.60 Banded king shoemaker	90	95
599	$1.60 Orange theope	90	95
600	$1.60 Grecian shoemaker	90	95
601	$1.60 Clorinde	90	95
602	$1.60 Small lace-wing	90	95
603	$1.60 Laughing gull	90	95
604	$1.60 Sooty tern	90	95
605	$1.60 Red-billed tropic bird ("White-tailed Tropicbird")	90	95
606	$1.60 Painted bunting	90	95
607	$1.60 Belted kingfisher	90	95
608	$1.60 Yellow-bellied sapsucker	90	95

MS609 Five sheets, each 82×112 mm. (a) $5 Iguana (horiz). (b) $5 *Leochilus carinatus* (orchid). (c) $5 Redband parrotfish (horiz). (d) $5 Common morpho (butterfly) (horiz). (e) $5 Ruby-throated hummingbird (horiz). Set of 5 sheets 15·00 16·00

No. 608 is inscribed "Yello-bellied" in error.

100 Symbolic Family and House

2001. Population and Housing Census. Multicoloured.

No.	Description	Unused	Used
610	30c. Type **100**	30	15
611	$3 People with Census symbol	2·00	2·50

101 Coronation of Queen Victoria

2001. Death Centenary of Queen Victoria. Multicoloured (except No. MS616).

No.	Description	Unused	Used
612	$2 Type **101**	1·50	1·75
613	$2 Wedding of Queen Victoria and Prince Albert	1·50	1·75
614	$2 Royal Family with Crimean War veterans	1·50	1·75
615	$2 Queen Victoria with Prince Albert	1·50	1·75

MS616 88×113 mm. $5 Queen Victoria as Empress of India. (43×52 mm) (black) 3·75 4·00

102 Mao Tse-tung, 1926

2001. 25th Death Anniv of Mao Tse-tung (Chinese leader). Multicoloured.

No.	Description	Unused	Used
617	$2 Type **102**	1·50	1·75
618	$2 Mao Tse-tung, 1945 (face value at top left)	1·50	1·75
619	$2 Mao Tse-tung, 1945 (face value at bottom left)	1·50	1·75

MS620 160×142 mm. $3 Mao Tse-tung in blue jacket 3·75 4·00

103 "On the Coast at Trouville" (Monet)

2001. 75th Death Anniv of Claude-Oscar Monet (French painter). Multicoloured.

No.	Description	Unused	Used
621	$2 Type **103**	2·00	2·00
622	$2 "Vetheuil in Summer"	2·00	2·00
623	$2 "Yellow Iris near Giverny"	2·00	2·00
624	$2 "Coastguard's Cottage at Varengeville"	2·00	2·00

MS625 137×111 mm. $5 "Poplars on Banks of Epte" (vert) 4·25 4·50

104 Queen Elizabeth carrying Bouquet

2001. 75th Birthday of Queen Elizabeth II. Multicoloured.

No.	Description	Unused	Used
626	$2 Type **104**	1·50	1·75
627	$2 Wearing cream floral hat	1·50	1·75
628	$2 Wearing blue coat and hat	1·50	1·75
629	$2 Queen in beige hat and dress	1·50	1·75

MS630 80×109 mm. $5 Queen Elizabeth riding 3·75 4·00

105 French Dragoons from *Sicilian Vespers* (opera)

2001. Death Centenary of Giuseppe Verdi (Italian composer). Designs showing Sicilian (opera). Multicoloured.

No.	Description	Unused	Used
631	$2 Type **105**	1·75	1·75
632	$2 French dragoons, drinking round table	1·75	1·75
633	$2 Original costume design	1·75	1·75
634	$2 Inhabitants of Palermo	1·75	1·75

MS635 80×108 mm. $5 Montserrat Caballe as Elena 4·25 4·25

Nos. 631/2 are inscribed "FREWNCH" and **MS**635 "MOUNTSERRAT", all in error.

106 "Hatsufunedayu as a Tatebina" (Shigenobu)

2001. "Philanippon 01" International Stamp Exhibition, Tokyo. Japanese Woodcuts. Multicoloured.

No.	Description	Unused	Used
636	50c. Type **106**	40	30
637	80c. "Samurai Kodenji as Tsuyu No Mae" (Kiyonobu I)	60	45
638	$1 "Nakamura Senya as Tokonatsu" (Kiyomasu I)	75	55
639	$1.60 "Sunida River" (Shunsho)	1·10	1·25
640	$2 "Kuemon Yoba the Wrestler" (Shune I)	1·50	1·75
641	$3 "Two actors" (Kiyonobu I/ Tori I)	2·00	2·50

MS642 78×78 mm. $5 "Actors with swords" (Shune I) 3·75 4·00

107 Submarine "A1", 1902

2001. Centenary of Royal Navy Submarine Service. Multicoloured.

No.	Description	Unused	Used
643	$1.50 Type **107**	2·00	2·00
644	$1.50 H.M.S. *Dreadnought* (battleship), 1906	2·00	2·00
645	$1.50 H.M.S. *Amethyst* (cruiser), 1903	2·00	2·00
646	$1.50 H.M.S. *Barham* (battleship), 1914	2·00	2·00
647	$1.50 H.M.S. *Exeter* (cruiser), 1929	2·00	2·00
648	$1.50 H.M.S. *Eagle* (aircraft carrier), 1918	2·00	2·00

MS649 129×90 mm. $5 H.M.S. *Dreadnought* (nuclear submarine), 1960 (43×57 mm) 6·00 6·00

Nos. 644 and **MS**649 are inscribed "DREADNAUGHT" and No. 646 "BARNHAM", both in error.

108 *Maxillaria cucullata* (orchid)

2001. . Caribbean Flora and Fauna. Multicoloured.

No.	Description	Unused	Used
650	$1.20 Type **108**	80	85
651	$1.20 *Cattleya dowiana*	80	85
652	$1.20 *Rossioglossum grande*	80	85
653	$1.20 *Aspasia epidendroides*	80	85
654	$1.20 *Lycaste skinneri*	80	85
655	$1.20 *Cattleya percivaliana*	80	85
656	$1.20 Brown trembler ("Trembler")	80	85
657	$1.20 Red-billed tropicbird	80	85
658	$1.20 Red-footed booby	80	85
659	$1.20 Red-legged thrush	80	85
660	$1.20 Painted bunting	80	85
661	$1.20 Bananaquit	80	85
662	$1.60 Killer whale (horiz)	90	95
663	$1.60 Cuvier's beaked whale (horiz)	90	95
664	$1.60 Humpback whale (horiz)	90	95
665	$1.60 Sperm whale (horiz)	90	95
666	$1.60 Blue whale (horiz)	90	95
667	$1.60 Whale shark (horiz)	90	95
668	$1.60 *Pholiota spectabilis*	90	95
669	$1.60 *Flammula penetrans*	90	95
670	$1.60 *Ungulina marginata*	90	95
671	$1.60 *Collybia iocephala*	90	95
672	$1.60 *Amanita muscaria*	90	95
673	$1.60 *Coprinus comatus*	90	95
674	$1.60 Orange-barred sulphur	90	95
675	$1.60 Giant swallowtail	90	95
676	$1.60 Orange theope butterfly	90	95
677	$1.60 Blue night butterfly	90	95
678	$1.60 Grecian shoemaker	90	95
679	$1.60 Cramer's mesene	90	95

MS680 Five sheets, each 99×69 mm (No. **MS**680c) or 69×99 mm (others). (a) $5 *Psychilis atropurpurea* (orchid). (b) $5 Ruby-throated hummingbird. (c) $5 Sei Whale (*horiz*). (d) $5 *Lepiota procera (fungus)*. (e) $5 Figure-of-eight butterfly. Set of 5 sheets 16·00 18·00

No. 672 is inscribed "Aminita" and No. 673 "Corinus", both in error.

109 Christmas Tree and Angel

2001. Christmas and Carnival. Multicoloured.

No.	Description	Unused	Used
681	10c. Type **109**	20	15
682	30c. Fireworks	30	15
683	80c. Christmas wreath	60	35
684	$2 Steel drums	1·50	1·75

110 Coronation Coach

2002. Golden Jubilee (2nd issue). Multicoloured.

No.	Description	Unused	Used
685	$2 Type **110**	1·40	1·50
686	$2 Prince Philip after polo	1·40	1·50
687	$2 Queen Elizabeth and the Queen Mother in evening dress	1·40	1·50
688	$2 Queen Elizabeth in evening dress	1·40	1·50

MS689 76×108 mm. $5 Queen Elizabeth presenting Prince Philip with polo trophy 3·50 3·75

111 Downhill Ski-ing

2002. Winter Olympic Games, Salt Lake City. Multicoloured.

No.	Description	Unused	Used
690	$3 Type **111**	2·00	2·25
691	$3 Cross country ski-ing	2·00	2·25

MS692 82×102 mm. Nos. 690/1 4·00 4·50

112 Xiong Nu Tribesman and Dog

2002. Chinese New Year ("Year of the Horse"). "Wen-Gi's Return to Han" (Chang Yu). Multicoloured.

No.	Description	Unused	Used
693	$1.60 Type **112**	1·00	1·10
694	$1.60 Group of Xiong Nu tribesmen	1·00	1·10
695	$1.60 Wen-Gi (Chinese noblewoman)	1·00	1·10
696	$1.60 Standard bearer	1·00	1·10

ST. KITTS $1.65
ESPAÑA
SPAIN 1982
POSTERS OF PAST WORLD CUPS

113 World Cup Poster, Spain, 1982

2002. World Cup Football Championship, Japan and Korea (2002). Multicoloured.

697	$1.65 Type **113**	1·00	1·10
698	$1.65 Just Fontaine, (France)	1·00	1·10
699	$1.65 American footballer	1·00	1·10
700	$1.65 Swedish footballer	1·00	1·10
701	$6 Daegu Stadium, Korea (56×42 mm)	3·50	4·00
MS702	51×3 mm. $6 Roger Milla (Cameroun), Italy, 1990	3·75	4·00

114 Policeman's Cap, Fireman's Helmet with U.S. and St. Kitts Flags

2002. "United We Stand". Support for Victims of 11 September 2001 Terrorist Attacks.

703	**114**	80c. multicoloured	1·00	1·00

115 Sakura-jima Volcano, Kyushu, Japan

2002. International Year of Mountains. Multicoloured.

704	$2 Type **115**	1·25	1·40
705	$2 Mount Assiniboine, Alberta, Canada	1·25	1·40
706	$2 Mount Asgard, Baffin Island, Canada	1·25	1·40
707	$2 Bugaboo Spire, British Columbia, Canada	1·25	1·40
MS708	75×57 mm. $6 Mount Owen, Wyoming, U.S.A.	3·75	4·00

116 Scout saluting

2002. 20th World Scout Jamboree, Thailand. Multicoloured.

709	$2 Type **116**	1·25	1·40
710	$2 Silver Award 2 badge	1·25	1·40
711	$2 Illinois Scout badge	1·25	1·40
712	$2 Scout with ceremonial sword	1·25	1·40
MS713	78×84 mm. $6 Environmental Merit badge (vert)	3·75	4·00

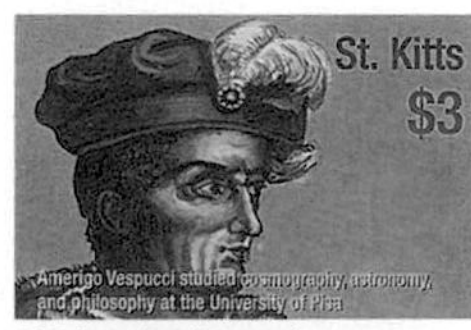

117 Amerigo Vespucci

2002. 500th Anniv of Amerigo Vespucci's Third Voyage. Multicoloured.

714	$3 Type **117**	1·75	1·90
715	$3 Map of the World by Waldseemüller, 1507	1·75	1·90
716	$3 Vespucci with globe	1·75	1·90
MS717	55×76 mm. $6 Vespucci as an old man (vert)	3·75	4·00

118 Kim Collins running

2002. Kim Collins (Commonwealth Games gold medallist) Commemoration. Multicoloured.

718	30c. Type **118**	30	15
719	90c. Collins with World Championship bronze medal	95	85

119 Charles Lindbergh

2002. Famous People of the 20th Century. (a) 75th Anniv of First Solo Transatlantic Flight. Sheet 130×145 mm.

MS720	$1.50 Type **119** (black, violet and red); $1.50 Lindbergh holding propellor of Ryan NYP Special *Spirit of St. Louis* (maroon, violet and red); $1.50 Lindbergh (brown, violet and red); $1.50 Lindbergh and *Spirit of St. Louis* (maroon and red); $1.50 Lindbergh wearing flying helmet (purple, violet and red); $1.50 Lindbergh (claret, violet and red)	6·50	7·00

(b) Life and Times of President John F. Kennedy. Two sheets, each 132×145 mm. Multicoloured.

MS721	$2 John Kennedy in Solomon Islands, 1942; $2 Torpedo boat commander, 1942; Naval ensign, 1941; Receiving medal for gallantry, 1944	2·75	3·25
MS722	$2 President Kennedy forming Peace Corps; $2 Promoting Space Programme; $2 With Civil Rights leaders; $2 Signing Nuclear Disarmament Treaty with Soviet Union	4·50	5·00

(c) 5th Death Anniv of Diana, Princess of Wales. Two sheets, each 132×145 mm. Multicoloured.

MS723	$2 Princess Diana wearing jacket with mauve edged collar; $2 Wearing dress with frilled neckline; $2 Wearing pink dress; $2 Wearing mauve dress	4·50	5·00
MS724	$2 Wearing protective vest; $2 Wearing turquoise jacket; $2 Wearing yellow blouse; $2 Wearing red dress	4·50	5·00

(d) Queen Elizabeth the Queen Mother Commemoration. Sheet 200×143 mm, containing two of each design. Multicoloured.

MS725	$2×2 Duchess of York; $2×2 Queen Mother	4·50	5·00

120 Sour Sop

2002. Christmas. Island Fruits. Multicoloured.

726	10c. Type **120**	25	15
727	80c. Passion fruit	80	35
728	$1 Sugar apple	1·00	65
729	$2 Custard apple	1·75	2·25

121 Ram

2003. Chinese New Year ("Year of the Ram"). Multicoloured.

MS730	110×122 mm. $1×2 Type **121**; $1×2 Brown and white ram with spiral horns; $1×2 Brown ram with long horns	4·00	4·50

122 Pelican and Emblem

2003. 30th Anniv of CARICOM.

731	**122**	30c. multicoloured	80	55

123 Queen Victoria Bear

2003. Centenary of the Teddy Bear. Multicoloured.

MS732	135×156 mm. $2 Type **123**; $2 Teddy Roosevelt bear; $2 George Washington bear; $2 General Patton bear	5·00	5·50
MS733	90×113 mm. $5 Buffalo Bill bear	3·50	4·00

124 Queen Elizabeth II

2003. 50th Anniv of Coronation. Multicoloured.

MS734	156×94 mm. $3 Type **124**; $3 Queen wearing tiara and pink sash; $3 Wearing tiara and blue sash	6·50	7·00
MS735	106×76 mm. $6 Wearing tiara and blue robes	3·75	4·00

125 Prince William as Toddler

2003. 21st Birthday of Prince William. Multicoloured.

MS736	156×86 mm. $3 Type **125**; $3 As schoolboy; $3 As adult	6·50	7·00
MS737	106×76 mm. $5 As young boy, waving from carriage	3·50	3·75

126 Voisin LA5

2003. Centenary of Powered Flight. Multicoloured.

MS738	185×106 mm. $2 Type **126**; $2 Gotha G.V.; $2 Polikarpov I-16; $2 Bell YFM-1	5·50	6·50
MS739	106×76 mm. $5 Bristol Type 142 Blenheim Mk I	3·50	3·75

127 Miguel Indurain (1991–95)

2003. Centenary of Tour de France. Designs showing past winners. Multicoloured.

MS740	166×106 mm. $2 Type **127**; $2 Miguel Indurain (1995); $2 Bjarne Riis (1996); $2 Jan Ullrich (1997)	5·50	6·00
MS741	105×75 mm. $5 Miguel Indurain (1991–5)	3·50	3·75

128 "Child with Wooden Horse (Claude)"

2003. 30th Death Anniv of Pablo Picasso (artist). Multicoloured.

MS742	178×103 mm. $1.60 Type **128**; $1.60 "Child with a Ball (Claude)"; $1.60 "The Butterfly Catcher"; $1.60 "Boy with a Lobster"; $1.60 "Baby wearing Polka-Dot Dress"; $1.60 "El Bobo" (after Murillo)	6·50	7·00
MS743	68×86 mm. $5 Woman with baby (63×80 mm). Imperf	3·50	3·75

129 Scout and Seaman with Globe (1937)

2003. 25th Death Anniv of Norman Rockwell (artist). T 129 and similar vert designs showing illustrations from scout calendars. Multicoloured.

MS744	141×180 mm. $2 Type **129**; $2 Scouts hiking (1937); $2 Boy and dog at window (1968); $2 Scout and statue (1932)	5·50	6·00
MS745	60×83 mm. $5 Scout with cub scout (1950)	3·50	3·75

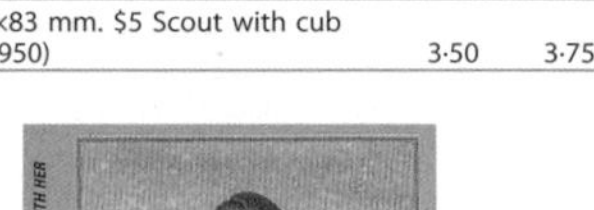

130 "Tokiwa Gozen with her Son in the Snow" (Shunkyokusai Hokumei)

2003. Japanese Art. Multicoloured.

746	90c. Type **130**	70	40
747	$1 "Courtesan and Asahina" (attrib. Eshosai Choki)	75	45
748	$1.50 "Parody of Sugawara no Michizane seated on an Ox" (Utagawa Toyokuni)	1·10	1·10
749	$3 "Visiting a Flower Garden" (detail) (Utagawa Kunisada)	2·00	2·25
MS750	147×147 mm. $2 "Akugenta Yoshihira" holding crossbow; $2 Holding painting; $2 As woman, with hand outstretched; $2 Holding sword	5·50	6·00
MS751	86×115 mm. $6 "The Courtesan Katachino under a Cherry Tree" (Utagawa Toyoharu)	3·75	4·00

No. **MS**750 shows a set of four prints of "Akugenta Yoshihira" by Utagawa Kunisada.

131 "A Family Group" (detail)

2003. Rembrandt (artist) Commemoration. Multicoloured.

752	50c. Type **131**	50	25
753	$1 "Portrait of Cornelis Claesz Anslo and Aeltje Gerritsdr Schouten" (horiz)	75	45

754	$1.60 "Portrait of a Young Woman"	1·25	1·25
755	$3 "Man in Military Costume"	2·00	2·25
MS756	181×172 mm. $2 "An Old Woman Reading"; $2 "Hendrickje Stoffels"; $2 "Rembrandt's Mother"; $2 "Saskia"	5·50	6·00
MS757	152×117 mm. $5 "Judas returning the Thirty Pieces of Silver"	3·50	3·75

132 "White Gibbon" (Giuseppe Castiglione)

2004. Chinese New Year ("Year of the Monkey").

MS758	156×141 mm. **132** $1.60×4 multicoloured	4·00	4·25
MS759	158×92 mm. **132** $3 multicoloured (30×37 mm)	2·00	2·25

133 Jiri Guth Jarkovsky

2004. Olympic Games, Athens. Multicoloured.

760	50c. Type **133**	40	25
761	90c. Olympic poster, Munich (1972)	65	40
762	$1 Medal and Eiffel Tower, Paris (1900)	75	45
763	$3 Wrestling (Greek bronze statue) (horiz)	2·00	2·25

134 12th SP Panzer Division and Map

2004. 60th Anniv of D-Day Landings.

MS764	Two sheets. (a) 178×106 mm. $2 ×4 multicoloured; purple; maroon; purple and deep purple. (b) 100×68 mm. $5 multicoloured Set of 2 sheets	9·50	11·00

DESIGNS: **MS**764 (a) $2 ×4 Type **134**; German heavy tank; Soldier aiming weapon; Soldiers and tank. (b) $5 Allied cemetery, Normandy.

135 Pope John Paul II

2004. 25th Anniv of the Pontificate of Pope John Paul II. Multicoloured.

MS765	147×105 mm. $2 ×4 Type **135**; Walking in gardens; Standing with hands crossed; Holding Pastoral Staff	6·00	6·50

136 Berti Vogts

2004. European Football Championship 2004, Portugal. Commemoration of Match between Germany and Czech Republic (1996). Multicoloured.

MS766	Two sheets (a) 147×86 mm. $2 ×4 Type **136**; Patrik Berger; Oliver Bierhoff; Empire Stadium. (b) 97×86 mm. $5 German team (1996) (51×48 mm) Set of 2 sheets	8·50	9·50

137 Deng Xiaoping

2004. Birth Centenary of Deng Xiaoping (Chinese leader, 1978–89).

MS767	**137** $5 multicoloured	3·50	3·75

138 American Standard 4-4-0

2004. Bicentenary of Steam Trains. Multicoloured.

768	$2 Type **138**	1·60	1·60
769	$2 New South Wales Government Class "79" 4-4-0	1·60	1·60
770	$2 Johnson Midland Single 4-2-2	1·60	1·60
771	$2 Union Pacific FEF-3 Class 4-8-4	1·60	1·60
772	$2 Northumbrian 0-2-2	1·60	1·60
773	$2 Prince Class 2-2-2	1·60	1·60
774	$2 Adler 2-2-2	1·60	1·60
775	$2 London and North Western Railway Webb Compound 2-4-0	1·60	1·60
776	$2 Italian State Railways Class 685 2-6-2	1·60	1·60
777	$2 Swiss Federal Railways 4-6-0	1·60	1·60
778	$2 British Engineering Standards Association Class 4-6-0	1·60	1·60
779	$2 Great Western City Class 4-4-0	1·60	1·60
MS780	Three sheets. (a) 98×68 mm. $5 CN Class U-2 4-8-4. (b) 98×68 mm. $5 Crampton 4-2-0. (c) 68×98 mm. $5 Baldwin 2-8-2	12·00	13·00

139 Demetrio Albertini

2004. Centenary of FIFA (Federation Internationale de Football Association). Multicoloured.

MS781	193×97 mm. $2×4, Type **139**; Romario; Gerd Muller; Danny Blanchflower	5·00	5·50
MS782	107×87 mm. $5 Gianfranco Zola	3·25	3·50

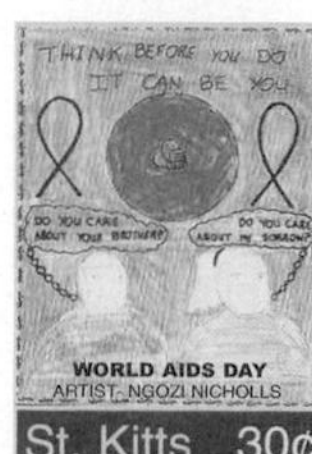

140 Couple with Thought Bubbles and (Ngozi Nicholls) AIDS Ribbons

2004. World AIDS Day. Multicoloured.

783	30c. Type **140**	40	20
784	80c. Man in shackles, fire, top of globe and characters dancing (Travis Liburd)	90	50
785	90c. Flag inscribed with "AIDS or LIFE" (Darren Kelly) (horiz)	1·00	75
786	$1 Red "AIDS", syringe and smiley condom (Shane Berry)	1·25	1·40

141 Hen and Three Chicks

2005. Chinese New Year ("Year of the Rooster"). Multicoloured.

787	$1.60 Type **141**	1·00	1·00
MS788	70×100 mm. $5 As No. 787 but design enlarged	3·25	3·50

142 *Papilio demoleus*

2005. Butterflies. Multicoloured.

MS789	127×151 mm. $2×4, Type **142**; *Ephemeroptera*; *Hamadryas februa*; *Aphylla caraiba*	5·00	5·50
MS790	100×70 mm. $5 *Lycaenidae cupido minimus*	3·25	3·50

143 Bahama ("White-cheeked") Pintail

2005. Ducks. Multicoloured.

791	25c. Type **143**	50	25
792	$1 Fulvous whistling duck	1·10	75
793	$2 White-faced whistling duck	1·75	1·90
794	$3 Red-billed ("Black-bellied") whistling duck	2·40	2·75

144 Ocelot

2005. Wildcats. Multicoloured.

MS795	128×152 mm. $2×4, Type **144**; Bengal leopard; Tiger; Leopard	5·00	5·00
MS796	101×70 mm. $5 Sumatran tiger	4·00	4·25

145 Australian King Parrot

2005. Parrots. Multicoloured.

MS797	128×152 mm. $2×4, Type **145**; Rose-breasted cockatoo; Pale-headed rosella; Eastern rosella	6·00	6·50
MS798	101×70 mm. $5 Two rainbow lorikeets (horiz)	3·25	3·50

146 Triceratops

2005. Prehistoric Animals. Multicoloured.

MS799	Three sheets, each 150×84 mm. (a) $3×3, Type **146**; Deinonychus; Apatosaurus. (b) $3×3, Sabre-toothed tiger; Edmontosaurus; Tyrannosaurus rex. (c) $3×3, Dimetroden; Homalocephale; Stegosaurus	16·00	18·00
MS800	Three sheets, each 100×70 mm. (a) $5 Brontosaurus (vert). (b) $5 Andrewsarchus. (c) $5 Woolly mammoth (vert)	8·00	8·50

147 *Montagne*

2005. Bicentenary of the Battle of Trafalgar. Multicoloured.

801	50c. Type **147**	80	45
802	90c. *San Jose*	1·00	70
803	$2 *Imperieuse*	2·00	2·25
804	$3 *San Nicolas*	2·50	2·75
MS805	69×99 mm. $5 British Navy gun crew aboard HMS *Victory*	5·00	5·50

148 Beijing Rotary

2005. Centenary of Rotary International (Humanitarian organisation). Multicoloured.

806	$3 Type **148**	2·00	2·25
807	$3 Man lying against pillow	2·00	2·25
808	$3 Man in hospital	2·00	2·25

149 US Navy Hudson PBO-1 Patrol Bombers

2005. 60th Anniv of Victory in Europe. Multicoloured.

809	$2 Type **149**	1·75	1·75
810	$2 Soldiers	1·75	1·75
811	$2 General Dwight D. Eisenhower	1·75	1·75
812	$2 German Prisoners of War	1·75	1·75
813	$2 Newspaper headline	1·75	1·75

150 Jules Verne

2005. Death Centenary of Jules Verne (writer).

814	**150**	$2 brown and bistre	1·75	1·75
815	-	$2 blue	1·75	1·75
816	-	$2 multicoloured	1·75	1·75
817	-	$2 multicoloured	1·75	1·75
MS818		99×70 mm. $5 multicoloured	4·75	5·00

DESIGNS: No. 814, Type **150**; 815, Sea monster attack; 816, Rouquayrol (breathing apparatus); 817, Modern aqualung; **MS**818, Atomic submarine.

151 "Hans Christian Andersen Fairy Tales"

2005. Birth Bicentenary of Hans Christian Anderson (artist and children's writer). Multicoloured.

MS819 115×172 mm. $3×3, Type **151**, *The Emperor's New Clothes*; *The Nutcracker* 5·50 6·50

MS820 70×101 mm. $5 Characters and Banner (*The Emperor's New Clothes*) 3·25 3·50

152 USS *Arizona*

2005. 60th Anniv of Victory in Japan. Multicoloured.

821 $2 Type **152** 1·75 1·75
822 $2 Captain Franklin van Valkenburgh 1·75 1·75
823 $2 Hiroshima 1·75 1·75
824 $2 Marker of first atomic bomb loading pit on Tinian Island 1·75 1·75
825 $2 Memorial cenotaph at Hiroshima Peace Park 1·75 1·75

153 Pope John Paul II and Nelson Mandela

2005. Pope John Paul II Commemoration.

826 **153** $3 multicoloured 3·00 3·00

154 Junk

2005. TAIPEI 2005 International Stamp Exhibition. Multicoloured.

827 $2 Type **154** 1·25 1·40
828 $2 Junk with yellow sails 1·25 1·40
829 $2 Junk with dark orange sails 1·25 1·40
830 $2 Junk with white sails 1·25 1·40

155 "Virgin and Child" (detail) (Gerard David)

2005. Christmas. Multicoloured.

831 30c. Type **155** 25 10
832 50c. "Virgin and Child" (detail) (different) (Gerard David) 40 25
833 90c. "Virgin and Child" (detail) (different) (Gerard David) 75 45
834 $2 "Virgin and Child" (detail) (Bartolomeo Suardi Bramentine) 1·40 1·50

MS835 67×97 mm. $5 "The Nativity" (Martin Schongauer) 3·25 3·50

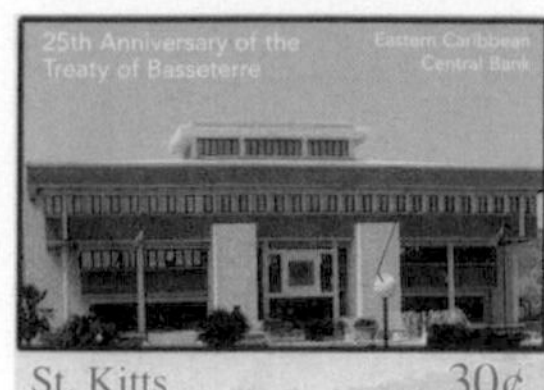

156 Eastern Caribbean Central Bank, Basseterre, St. Kitts

2006. 25th Anniv of the Treaty of Basseterre (established Organisation of Eastern Caribbean States). Multicoloured.

836 30c. Type **156** 30 15
837 90c. Flags of member countries 1·10 75

MS838 100×75 mm. $2.50 Inset portraits of OECS heads of government (vert) 1·00 1·00

157 "Bathsheba with King David's Letter" (detail)

2006. 400th Birth Anniv of Rembrandt Harmenszoon van Rijn (artist). Multicoloured.

839 50c. Type **157** 30 25
840 80c. "Isaac and Rebecca (The Jewish Bride)" (detail of bride) 50 40
841 90c. "Isaac and Rebecca (The Jewish Bride)" (detail of groom) 55 45
842 $1 "Samson threatening his Father-in-Law" (detail of father-in-law) 60 55
843 $1.60 "Samson threatening his Father-in-Law" (detail of Samson) 90 1·00
844 $2 "Equestrian Portrait" (detail) 1·25 1·50

MS845 100×70 mm. $6 "Landscape with a Stone Bridge" (detail). Imperf 3·50 3·75

158 "Mary in Adoration before the Sleeping Infant" (detail)

2006. Christmas. Showing paintings by Peter Paul Rubens. Multicoloured.

846 25c. Type **158** 25 15
847 60c. "The Holy Family under the Apple Tree" (detail, Mary and Jesus) 55 30
848 $1 "The Holy Family under the Apple Tree" (detail, Infant John the Baptist) 60 45
849 $1.20 "St. Francis of Assisi Receives the Infant Jesus from Mary" (detail, Mary and Jesus) 70 60
850 $2 Type **158** 1·25 1·40
851 $2 As No. 847 1·25 1·40
852 $2 As No. 848 1·25 1·40
853 $2 As No. 849 1·25 1·40

159 Queen Elizabeth II

2007. 80th Birthday of Queen Elizabeth II. Multicoloured.

854 $2 Type **159** 1·25 1·40
855 $2 Wearing tiara and Order of the Garter 1·25 1·40
856 $2 At Trooping the Colour 1·25 1·40
857 $2 On throne, wearing crown 1·25 1·40

MS858 120×120 mm. $5 Seated at desk 2·75 3·00

160 Christopher Columbus

2007. 500th Death Anniv (2006) of Christopher Columbus. Sheet 100×70 mm.

MS859 **160** $6 multicoloured 3·25 3·50

161 Dove, Emblem and Ribbon of Flags

2007. Centenary of World Scouting. Multicoloured.

860 $3 Type **161** 1·75 1·90

MS861 110×80 mm. $5 Dove, emblem and ribbon of flags (horiz) 2·75 3·00

162 Pre-Launch Tests at the Kourou Launch Site

2007. Space Anniversaries. Multicoloured. (a) 20th Anniv of Giotto Comet Probe.

862 $1.60 Type **162** 90 1·00
863 $1.60 Halley's Comet (black background) 90 1·00
864 $1.60 Halley's Comet (seen from Earth's surface) 90 1·00
865 $1.60 *Giotto* Comet Probe 90 1·00
866 $1.60 *Giotto* Spacecraft mounted on Rocket Ariane 90 1·00
867 $1.60 Halley's Comet (blue background) 90 1·00

(b) 40th Anniv of Luna 9 Moon Landing.

868 $2 Molniya rocket on launch vehicle (vert) 90 1·00
869 $2 *Luna 9* flight apparatus (vert) 90 1·00
870 $2 *Luna 9* soft lander (vert) 90 1·00
871 $2 Image of "Ocean of Storms" on Moon's surface (vert) 90 1·00

MS872 100×70 mm. $5 Space Station MIR, 1986–2001 2·75 3·00

163 John Kennedy shaking hands with Peace Corps Volunteers

2007. 90th Birth Anniv of John F. Kennedy (American President 1960–3). Multicoloured.

873 $2 Type **163** 1·25 1·40
874 $2 Volunteer Ida Shoatz running school lunch programme in the Peruvian Andes 1·25 1·40
875 $2 R. Sargent Shriver, Director, Peace Corps 1·25 1·40
876 $2 John Kennedy greeting Peace Corps volunteers 1·25 1·40
877 $2 John Kennedy and map showing Guatemala, El Salvador and Honduras 1·25 1·40
878 $2 John Kennedy and South American mother and daughter 1·25 1·40
879 $2 John Kennedy and map showing Colombia 1·25 1·40
880 $2 Map showing Venezuela, Guyana, Suriname and French Guiana 1·25 1·40

Nos. 873/6 (showing Peace Corps volunteers) and 877/80 (showing "Alliance for Progress" for economic co-operation between North and South America).

164 Betty Boop

2007. Betty Boop. Multicoloured, background colours given.

881 $1.60 Type **164** 90 1·00
882 $1.60 With microphone (emerald) 90 1·00
883 $1.60 With hat and cane (white) 90 1·00
884 $1.60 With arms raised (violet) 90 1·00
885 $1.60 With arms outstretched to side (blue) 90 1·00
886 $1.60 Seated, with right leg raised (yellow) 90 1·00

MS887 100×70 mm. $3 Wearing red dress with white flower design (green heart background); $3 With right hand held out (inverted purple heart background) 3·25 3·50

165 Marilyn Monroe

2007. 80th Birth Anniv (2006) of Marilyn Monroe (actress). Multicoloured.

888 $2 Type **165** 1·60 1·60
889 $2 Wearing spectacles, hair wrapped in towel 1·60 1·60
890 $2 Facing forwards, bare shoulders 1·60 1·60
891 $2 Facing left, hand on chin 1·60 1·60

166 Elvis Presley

2007. 30th Death Anniv of Elvis Presley (1st issue). Multicoloured.

892 $2 Type **166** (inscr in blue) 1·60 1·60

893	$2 As Type **166** (inscr in magenta)	1·60	1·60
894	$2 As Type **166** (inscr in black)	1·60	1·60
895	$2 As Type **166** (inscr in lavender)	1·60	1·60
896	$2 Elvis Presley playing guitar and signature	1·60	1·60

See also Nos. 920/5.

167 Two Tiger Sharks

2007. Endangered Species. Tiger Shark (Galeocerdo cuvier). Multicoloured.

897	$1.20 Type **167**	75	75
898	$1.20 Two sharks, foreground shark with mouth open	75	75
899	$1.20 Tiger shark	75	75
900	$1.20 Three tiger sharks, showing spotted markings	75	75
MS901	115×168 mm. Nos. 897/900	3·25	3·25

168 *Rhynchostele cervantesii*

2007. Orchids. T **168** and similar vert designs. Multicoloured.

MS902	131×109 mm. $2×4 Type **168**; *Oerstedella wallisii; Disa uniflora; Pleioneformosana*	6·50	6·50
MS903	70×100 mm. $6 *Dendrobium bracteosum*	4·75	4·75

The stamps and margins of No. **MS**902 form a composite background design of white orchids.

169 Brown Noddy

2007. Seabirds of the World. Multicoloured.

904	$2 Type **169**	1·60	1·60
905	$2 Royal albatross	1·60	1·60
906	$2 Masked booby	1·60	1·60
907	$2 Great cormorant	1·60	1·60
MS908	70×100 mm. $6 Rock cormorant (vert)	4·75	4·75

170 Cherries

2007. Fruit. Multicoloured.

909	10c. Type **170**	10	10
910	15c. Coconut	15	15
911	30c. Watermelon	20	20
912	40c. Pineapple	25	25
913	50c. Guava	30	30
914	60c. Sugar apple	35	35
915	80c. Passion fruit	45	45
916	90c. Star apple	50	50
917	$1 Tangerines	60	60
918	$5 Noni fruit	3·00	3·00
919	$10 Papaya	5·75	5·75

171 Elvis Presley

2007. 30th Death Anniv of Elvis Presley (2nd issue). Multicoloured.

920	$1.60 Type **171**	90	90
921	$1.60 Wearing white jacket with black eagle design	90	90
922	$1.60 Wearing black shirt	90	90
923	$1.60 Wearing blue shirt	90	90
924	$1.60 Wearing white shirt and red waistcoat	90	90
925	$1.60 Wearing white leather jacket	90	90

Nos. 920/5 were printed together, se-tenant, in sheetlets of six stamps with enlarged illustrated right margins.

172 Pope Benedict XVI

2007. 80th Birthday of Pope Benedict XVI.

926	**172**	$1.10 multicoloured	85	85

173 Queen Elizabeth II

2007. Diamond Wedding of Queen Elizabeth II and Prince Philip. Multicoloured.

927	$1.60 Type **173**	90	90
928	$1.60 Princess Elizabeth and Prince Philip on wedding day, 1949	90	90
MS929	100×70 mm. $6 Queen Elizabeth and Prince Philip in recent years	4·75	4·75

174 Concorde in Flight

2007. Concorde. Multicoloured.

930	$1.60 Type **174**	90	90
931	$1.60 Concorde in flight (side view)	90	90
932	$1.60 Concorde over Singapore (panel yellow-olive at left, bright yellow-green at right)	90	90
933	$1.60 Concorde at Melbourne Airport, Australia ('Austria' in panel)	90	90
934	$1.60 As No. 932	90	90
935	$1.60 As No. 933 ('Spain' at left of panel)	90	90
936	$1.60 As No. 932 (bright yellow-green (Italy) in centre of panel)	90	90
937	$1.60 As No. 933 (bright yellow-green at left and yellow-olive (Black Sea) at right of panel)	90	90

175 Diana, Princess of Wales

2007. 10th Death Anniv of Diana, Princess of Wales. Multicoloured.

938	$2 Type **175**	1·60	1·60
939	$2 Diana, Princess of Wales (chestnut background)	1·60	1·60
939a	$2 Wearing pearl necklace	1·60	1·60
940	$2 Wearing white and mauve brimmed hat	1·60	1·60
MS941	70×100 mm. $6 As No. 940	4·75	4·75

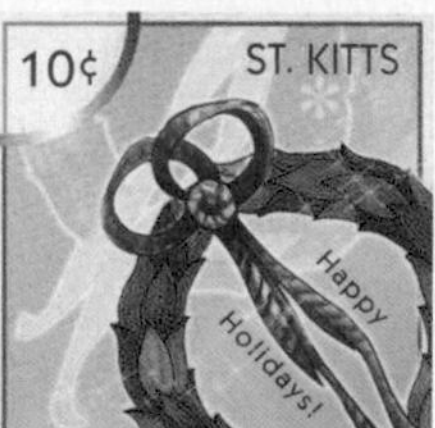

176 Door Wreath with Mauve Ribbons

2007. Christmas. Designs showing Christmas door wreaths. Multicoloured.

942	10c. Type **176**	15	15
943	30c. Wreath with cherries and red bow	20	20
944	60c. Wreath with holly and red ribbon	35	35
945	$1 Holly leaves and berries and yellow ribbon	60	60

177 Paris World's Fair, 1900

2008. Olympic Games, Beijing. Multicoloured.

946	$1.40 Type **177**	85	85
947	$1.40 Poster for Olympic Games, Paris, 1900	85	85
948	$1.40 Charlotte Cooper (Britain), tennis gold medallist, 1900	85	85
949	$1.40 Alvin Kraenzlein (USA), quadruple athletics gold medallist, 1900	85	85

178 Bethel Chapel

2008. 230th Anniv of the Moravian Church in St. Kitts. Multicoloured.

950	10c. Type **178**	15	15
951	$3 Zion Chapel	1·75	1·75
952	$10 Bethesda Chapel (vert)	5·75	5·75

179 University of the West Indies Centre, St. Kitts

2008. 60th Anniv of the University of the West Indies.

953	**179**	30c. multicoloured	25	25
954	–	90c. scarlet, yellow and black	90	90
955	–	$5 scarlet, yellow and black	2·75	2·75

DESIGNS—VERT: 90c. Anniversary emblem. HORIZ—$5 Anniversary emblem.

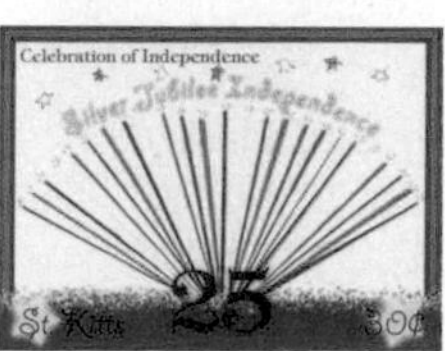

180 Emblem

2008. 25th Anniv of Independence of St. Kitts-Nevis. Multicoloured.

956	30c. Type **180** (Davern Johnson)	25	25
957	$1 Produce of St. Kitts (Yvado Simmonds)	95	95
958	$5 Sailing ship with national flag as sail ('Sailing Towards Our Future') (Richard Browne) (vert)	2·75	2·75
958a	$25 '25' and lifebelt ('Riding the Waves') (Dennis Richards) (vert)	9·50	9·50

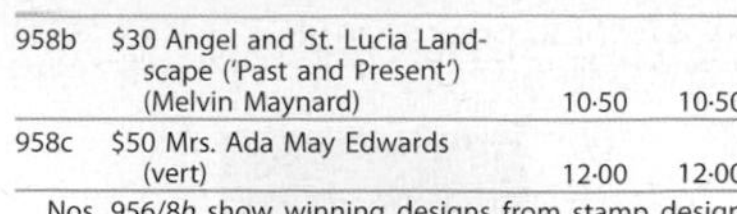

958b	$30 Angel and St. Lucia Landscape ('Past and Present') (Melvin Maynard)	10·50	10·50
958c	$50 Mrs. Ada May Edwards (vert)	12·00	12·00

Nos. 956/8*b* show winning designs from stamp design competition.

181 Elvis Presley

2008. 40th Anniv of Elvis Presley's '68 Special' (TV programme). Multicoloured.

959	$1.60 Type **181**	1·25	1·25
960	$1.60 In profile, wearing black leather jacket	1·25	1·25
961	$1.60 Wearing red shirt and black waistcoat	1·25	1·25
962	$1.60 Wearing blue shirt	1·25	1·25
963	$1.60 Wearing beige shirt	1·25	1·25
964	$1.60 Wearing white shirt and red tie	1·25	1·25

182 Pope Benedict XVI and Statue of Virgin Mary

2008. 150th Anniv of the Apparition of the Virgin Mary to St. Bernadette and Visit of Pope Benedict XVI to Lourdes. Sheet 127×178 mm containing T **182** and similar horiz designs.

MS965	$2×4 multicoloured	7·00	7·00

The four stamps within **MS**965 are as Type **182** but all have slightly different backgrounds of the church building showing in the backgrounds of the stamps.

183 R. L. Bradshaw

2008. 75th Anniv of the St. Kitts Labour Party.

966	**183**	10c. multicoloured	15	15

184 Palm Trees with Christmas Baubles

2008. Christmas. Multicoloured.

967	10c. Type **184**	15	15
968	50c. Palm trees and beach house on stilts	30	30
969	60c. Palm trees and star	35	35
970	$1 Baubles on Christmas tree	95	95

185 Pres. Barack Obama

2009. Inauguration of President Barack Obama. Multicoloured.

MS971	133×100 mm. $3 Type **185**×4	14·00	14·00

MS972 80×110 mm. $10 Pres. Obama (37×37 mm, circular)		10·00	10·00

186 Princess Diana

2009. Princess Diana Commemoration. Sheet 150×100 mm containing T 186 and similar vert designs. Multicoloured. Litho.

MS973 Type **186**; Wearing mauve dress; Wearing white strapless dress; Wearing blue off the shoulder dress with ruffle		7·00	7·00

187 *Freewinds* lit at Night

2009. 20th Anniv of Freewinds (cruise ship) calling at St. Kitts. Multicoloured.

MS974 112×135 mm. 30c. Type **187**; 90c. *Freewinds* and sailing ship at St. Kitts; $3 Bow of *Freewinds* with crew on decks (42×56 mm);		3·00	3·00
MS975 144×100 mm. $2 *Freewinds* with crew on decks (79×59 mm)		1·60	1·60

188 Brimstone Hill Fortress

2009. Tenth Anniv of Inscription of Brimstone Hill Fortress, St. Kitts on UNESCO World Heritage List. Litho.

976	**188**	90c. multicoloured	95	95

189 Michael Jackson

2009. Michael Jackson Commemoration. Multicoloured.

MS977 127×178 mm. $2.50×4 Type **189** (green inscriptions); Wearing blue shirt with white jacket, tie and hat (green inscriptions); As Type **189** (blue inscriptions); Wearing blue shirt with white jacket, tie and hat (blue inscriptions)		5·50	5·50
MS978 178×127 mm. $2.50×4 Wearing red jacket×2; With python×2		5·50	5·50

190 John Kennedy jr. as Child

2009. 10th Death Anniv of John F. Kennedy Jr. Sheet 130×100 mm containing T 190 and similar vert designs. Multicoloured.

MS979 Type **190**; With his parents; With his mother on horseback; As adult		5·50	5·50

191 Saturn 5 Rocket

2009. 40th Anniv of the First Manned Moon Landing. International Year of Astronomy. Multicoloured.

MS980 150×100 mm. $2.50×4 Type **191**; Astronaut's bootprint on Moon; Bald Eagle, Pres. John F. Kennedy and Earth seen from Moon; Apollo 11 Command Module above Moon		5·50	5·50
MS981 100×70 mm. $6 Command Module in space		3·50	3·50

192 St. Kitts & Nevis Flag and 'MERRY CHRISTMAS'

2009. Christmas. Multicoloured.

982	10c. Type **192**	10	10
983	30c. Candy canes	25	25
984	$1.20 Outline map of St. Kitts-Nevis with Christmas trees	95	95
985	$3 St. Kitts & Nevis flag as cake decorated with candles and Christmas tree	1·50	1·50

193 Elvis Presley

2010. 75th Birth Anniv of Elvis Presley. Sheet 120×194 mm containing T 193 and similar vert designs. Multicoloured.

MS986 Type 193; Wearing jacket and tie; Wearing white jacket; Looking to left; Wearing jacket and shirt; Wearing dark zipped jacket		7·50	7·50

194 Scarlet Peacock (*Anartia amathea*)

2010. Butterflies of the Caribbean. Multicoloured.

987	30c. Type **194**	25	25
988	90c. Gulf fritillary (*Agraulis vanillae*)	95	95
989	$3 White peacock (*Anartia jatrophae*)	1·75	1·75
990	$5 Painted lady (*Vanessa virginiensis*)	4·50	4·50
MS991 $2.50×4 Ruddy daggerwing (*Marpesia petreus*); Danaid eggfly (*Hypolimnas misippus*); Mangrove buckeye (*Junonia evarete*); Black swallowtail (*Papilio polyxenes*)		5·50	5·50
MS992 $3 Owl butterfly (*Caligo memnon*); $3 Giant swallowtail (*Papilio cresphontes*)		5·50	5·50

The stamps and margins of Nos. **MS**991/2 form composite designs.

195 Solitary Sandpiper (*Tringa solitaria*)

2010. Birds of the Caribbean. Multicoloured.

993	30c. Type **195**	25	25
994	90c. Piping plover (*Charadrius melodus*)	95	85
995	$3 Prairie warbler (*Dendroica discolor*)	2·50	2·50
996	$5 Western sandpiper (*Calidris* or *Erolia mauri*)	4·50	4·50
MS997 150×100 mm. $2.50×4 Masked booby (*Sula dactylatra*); Sooty tern (*Onychoprion fuscatus*); Brown booby (*Sula leucogaster*); Black noddy (*Anous minutus*)		5·50	5·50
MS998 110×80 mm. $3 Long-billed dowitcher (*Limnodromus scolopaceus*); $3 Willet (*Tringa semipalmata*)		4·75	4·75

196 Statue of Abraham Lincoln

2010. Birth Bicentenary of Abraham Lincoln (US President 1861–5)

MS999 $2.50×4 Type **196**		5·50	5·50

197 Red Lionfish (Pterois volitans)

2010. Reef Fish of the Caribbean. Multicoloured.

1000	30c. Type **197**	20	20
1001	90c. Stoplight parrotfish (*Sparisoma viride*)	90	90
1002	$3 Black Jack (*Caranx lugubris*)	2·10	2·10
1003	$5 Bermuda blue angelfish (*Holacanthus bermudensis*)	4·00	4·00
MS1004 100×140 mm. $2.50×4 Banggai cardinalfish (*Pterapogon kauderni*); Barrier reef anemonefish (*Amphipron akindynos*); Crevelle Jack (*Caranx hippos*); Lookdown fish (*Selene vomer*)		5·00	5·00
MS1005 100×70 mm. $3 Red Sea clownfish (*Amphiprion bicinctus*); $3 Saddleback clownfish (*Amphiprion polymnus*)		8·00	8·00

198 *Alboleptonia stylophora*

2010. Fungi of the Caribbean. Multicoloured.

1006	25c. Type **198**	20	20
1007	80c. *Cantharellus cibarius*	75	75
1008	$1 *Armillaria puiggarii*	90	90
1009	$5 *Battarrea phalliodes*	4·00	4·00
MS1010 106×140 mm. $2×6 *Cantharellus cinnabarinus*; *Collybia aurata*; *Collybia biformis*; *Amanita ocreata*; *Calocybe cyanea*; *Chroogomphus rutilus* (all horiz)		8·00	8·00

No. **MS**1010 was inscr 'ANTVERPIA 2010 09–12/04/2010 NATIONAL & EUROPEAN CHAMPIONSHIP OF PHILATELY' on the top right margin.

BOY SCOUTS OF AMERICA
100TH ANNIVERSARY·1910-2010
$2.50 ST. KITTS

199 Cub Scout and Emblem

2010. Centenary of Boy Scouts of America. Multicoloured.

MS1011 $2.50×4 Type **199**; Scout cooking over campfire and emblem; Varsity scouts playing basketball and emblem; Venture scout kayaking and emblem		5·00	5·00
MS1012 $2.50×4 Scouts of 1910 and 2010 and emblem; Boy using pick-axe and Order of the Arrow emblem; Man painting with roller and Alpha Phi Omega emblem; Eagle scout handing out voting forms and emblem		5·00	5·00

OFFICIAL STAMPS

1980. Nos. 32/41 optd OFFICIAL.

O1A	15c. multicoloured	10	10
O2A	25c. multicoloured	10	10
O3A	30c. multicoloured	10	10
O4A	40c. multicoloured	10	15
O5A	45c. multicoloured	15	15
O6A	50c. multicoloured	15	15
O7A	55c. multicoloured	15	15
O8A	$1 multicoloured	25	25
O9A	$5 multicoloured	80	1·50
O10A	$10 multicoloured	1·00	2·50

1981. Nos. 59/70 optd OFFICIAL.

O11	15c. Bananaquit	20	10
O12	20c. Scaly-breasted thrasher	20	10
O13	25c. Grey kingbird	25	10
O14	30c. Green-throated carib	25	10
O15	40c. Turnstone	35	15
O16	45c. Black-faced grassquit	40	20
O17	50c. Cattle egret	40	20
O18	55c. Brown pelican	50	25
O19	$1 Lesser Antillean bullfinch	75	45
O20	$2.50 Zenaida dove	1·60	1·00
O21	$5 American kestrel	2·75	2·00
O22	$10 Antillean crested hummingbird	5·00	4·25

1983. Nos. 75/80 optd OFFICIAL or surch also.

O23	45c. on $2.50 "Royal George"	15	15
O24	45c. on $2.50 Prince Charles and Lady Diana Spencer	25	25
O25	55c. "Saudadoes"	15	15
O26	55c. Prince Charles and Lady Diana Spencer	30	30
O27	$1.10 on $4 "Britannia"	30	40
O28	$1.10 on $4 Prince Charles and Lady Diana Spencer	60	70

1984. Nos. 145/56 optd OFFICIAL.

O29	15c. Red-lined cleaning shrimp	70	1·25
O30	20c. Bristleworm	80	1·50
O31	25c. Flamingo tongue	80	1·50
O32	30c. Christmas tree worm	90	1·50
O33	40c. Pink-tipped anemone	1·00	1·50
O34	50c. Small-mouthed grunt	1·00	1·50
O35	60c. Glass-eyed snapper	1·25	2·00
O36	75c. Reef squirrelfish	1·50	2·50
O37	$1 Sea fans and flamefish (vert)	2·00	2·50
O38	$2.50 Reef butterflyfish (vert)	3·75	6·00
O39	$5 Black-barred soldierfish (vert)	5·50	3·00
O40	$10 Cocoa damselfish (vert)	8·50	6·00

Pt. 1

ST KITTS-NEVIS

Islands of the Leeward Is., Br. W. Indies. The general issues for Leeward Is, were in concurrent use until 1 July 1956. From 1952 the stamps are inscribed "St. Christopher, Nevis and Anguilla". Achieved Associated Statehood on 27 February 1967. St. Kitts and Nevis had separate postal administrations from 23 June 1980.

1903. 12 pence = 1 shilling; 20 shillings = 1 pound.
1951. 100 cents = 1 West Indian dollar.

1 Christopher Columbus

2 Medicinal Spring

1903

1	1	½d. purple and green	1·75	70
12	1	½d. green	1·00	60
13	2	1d. grey and red	5·00	25
14a	2	1d. red	1·00	20
3	1	2d. purple and brown	2·75	11·00
16	1	2½d. black and blue	23·00	4·00
17	1	2½d. blue	2·50	50
18a	2	3d. green and orange	2·75	2·75
19ab	1	6d. black and purple	8·00	29·00
7	1	1s. green and orange	7·50	11·00
8	1	2s. green and black	12·00	20·00
9	1	2s.6d. black and violet	18·00	42·00
10	2	5s. purple and green	60·00	55·00

1916. Optd WAR TAX.

22a	½d. green	1·00	50

1918. Optd WAR STAMP.

23	1½d. orange	1·00	80

4 **5**

1920

37a	4	½d. green	2·25	80
38	5	1d. red	65	15
39	5	1d. violet	6·50	1·00
26	4	1½d. yellow	1·25	1·75
40	4	1½d. red	5·00	1·50

40a	4	1½d. brown	1·00	30
41	5	2d. grey	50	60
43	4	2½d. brown	3·00	9·50
44	4	2½d. blue	1·50	1·00
45	5	3d. blue	1·00	4·25
45a	5	3d. purple on yellow	75	2·75
46aw	4	6d. purple and mauve	4·00	6·00
31	5	1s. black on green	3·50	4·00
47	4	2s. purple and blue on blue	8·50	27·00
33	5	2s.6d. black and red on blue	5·00	38·00
34	4	5s. green and red on yellow	5·00	40·00
35	5	10s. green and red on green	12·00	48·00
36	4	£1 purple and black on red	£250	£350

6 Old Road Bay and Mount Misery

1923. Tercentenary Commemoration.

48	6	½d. black and green	2·25	7·00
49	6	1d. black and violet	4·50	1·50
50	6	1½d. black and red	4·50	10·00
51	6	2d. black and grey	3·75	1·50
52	6	2½d. black and brown	6·00	32·00
53	6	3d. black and blue	3·75	15·00
54	6	6d. black and purple	9·50	32·00
55	6	1s. black and green	14·00	32·00
56	6	2s. black and blue on blue	50·00	75·00
57	6	2s.6d. black and red on blue	50·00	90·00
59	6	5s. black and red on yellow	90·00	£200
58	6	10s. black and red on green	£300	£475
60	6	£1 black and purple on red	£800	£1600

1935. Silver Jubilee. As T 32a of St. Helena.

61	1d. blue and red	1·00	70
62	1½d. blue and grey	75	75
63	2½d. brown and blue	1·00	1·00
64	1s. grey and purple	10·00	16·00

1937. Coronation. As T 32b of St. Helena.

65	1d. red	30	25
66	1½d. brown	40	10
67	2½d. blue	60	1·60

Nos. 61/7 are inscribed "ST. CHRISTOPHER AND NEVIS".

7 King George VI

8 King George VI and Medicinal Spring

10 King George VI and Anguilla Island

1938

68a	7	½d. green	10	10
69a	7	1d. red	1·75	50
70	7	1½d. orange	20	30
71b	8	2d. red and grey	1·25	1·25
72a	7	2½d. blue	70	30
73g	8	3d. purple and red	10·00	10·00
74	-	6d. green and purple	6·50	3·00
75b	8	1s. black and green	4·00	85
76ab	8	2s.6d. black and red	12·00	4·50
77b	-	5s. green and red	24·00	12·00
77e	10	10s. black and blue	14·00	19·00
77f	10	£1 black and brown	14·00	23·00

The 6d. and 5s. are as Type **8**, but with the Christopher Columbus device as in Type **4**.

1946. Victory. As T 33a of St. Helena.

78	1½d. orange	10	10
79	3d. red	10	30

1949. Silver Wedding. As T 33b/c of St. Helena.

80	2½d. blue	10	50
81	5s. red	9·00	6·50

1949. U.P.U. As T 33d/g of St. Helena.

82	2½d. blue	15	30
83	3d. red	2·10	2·50
84	6d. mauve	20	1·75
85	1s. green	20	40

1950. Tercentary of British Settlement in Anguilla. Optd ANGUILLA TERCENTENARY 1650–1950.

86	7	1d. red	10	20
87	7	1½d. orange	10	50
88	7	2½d. blue	15	20
89	8	3d. purple and red	50	75
90	-	6d. green and purple (No. 74d)	30	20
91	8	1s. black and green	1·25	25

10a Arms of University

10b Princess Alice

1951. Inauguration of B.W.I. University College.

92	10a	3c. black and orange	30	15
93	10b	12c. green and mauve	30	2·00

ST. CHRISTOPHER, NEVIS AND ANGUILLA

13 Bath House and Spa

1952

94	13	1c. green and ochre	15	2·25
95	-	2c. green	1·00	1·00
96	-	3c. red and violet	30	1·25
97	-	4c. red	20	20
98	-	5c. blue and grey	30	10
99	-	6c. blue	30	15
100	-	12c. blue and brown	1·25	10
101	-	24c. black and red	30	10
102	-	48c. olive and brown	2·25	4·00
103	-	60c. ochre and green	2·00	4·25
104	-	$1.20 green and blue	7·00	4·25
105	-	$4.80 green and red	13·00	18·00

DESIGNS—HORIZ: 2c. Warner Park; 4c. Brimstone Hill; 5c. Nevis from the sea, North; 6c. Pinney's Beach, Nevis; 24c. Old Road Bay; 48c. Sea Island cotton, Nevis; 60c. The Treasury; $1.20, Salt pond, Anguilla; $4.80, Sugar factory. VERT: 3c. Map of the islands; 12c. Sir Thomas Warner's tomb.

1953. Coronation. As T 33h of St. Helena.

106	2c. black and green	30	30

1954. As 1952 but with portrait of Queen Elizabeth II.

106a	½c. olive (as $1.20)	30	10
107	1c. green and ochre	20	10
108	2c. green	50	10
109	3c. red and violet	65	10
110	4c. red	15	10
111	5c. blue and grey	15	10
112	6c. blue	70	10
112b	8c. black	3·00	25
113	12c. blue and brown	15	10
114	24c. black and red	15	10
115	48c. olive and brown	1·00	60
116	60c. ochre and green	5·50	7·00
117	$1.20 green and blue	18·00	2·75
117b	$2.40 black and orange	15·00	12·00
118	$4.80 green and red	20·00	11·00

DESIGNS (new values)—VERT: 8c. Sombrero Lighthouse. HORIZ: $2.40, Map of Anguilla and Dependencies.

27 Alexander Hamilton and View of Nevis

1956. Birth Bicent of Alexander Hamilton.

119	27	24c. green and blue	60	25

27a Federation Map

1958. British Caribbean Federation.

120	27a	3c. green	60	15
121	27a	6c. blue	90	2·50
122	27a	12c. red	1·00	35

28 1d. Stamp of 1861

1961. Centenary of Nevis Stamp.

123	28	2c. red and green	20	20
124	28	8c. red and blue	25	10
125	28	12c. lilac and red	30	15
126	28	24c. green and orange	35	15

The 8c., 12c. and 24c. show the original 4d., 6d. and 1s. stamps of Nevis respectively.

1963. Cent of Red Cross. As T 63b of St. Helena.

127	3c. red and black	10	10
128	12c. red and blue	20	40

33 Loading Sugar Cane, St. Kitts

1963. Multicoloured.. Multicoloured..

129	½c. New Lighthouse, Sombrero	10	10
130	1c. Type **33**	10	10
131	2c. Pall Mall Square, Basseterre	10	10
132	3c. Gateway, Brimstone Hill Fort, St. Kitts	10	10
133	4c. Nelson's Spring, Nevis	10	10
134	5c. Grammar School, St. Kitts	3·50	10
135	6c. Crater, Mt. Misery, St. Kitts	10	10
136	10c. Hibiscus	15	10
137	15c. Sea Island cotton, Nevis	70	10
138	20c. Boat-building, Anguilla	30	10
139	25c. White-crowned pigeon	2·25	10
140	50c. St. George's Church Tower, Basseterre	60	25
141	60c. Alexander Hamilton	1·00	30
142	$1 Map of St. Kitts-Nevis	2·50	40
143	$2.50 Map of Anguilla	2·50	2·75
144	$5 Arms of St. Christopher, Nevis and Anguilla	7·00	7·00

The ½, 2, 3, 15, 25, 60c., $1 and $5 are vert, the rest horiz.

1964. Arts Festival. Optd ARTS FESTIVAL ST KITTS 1964.

145	3c. multicoloured (No. 132)	10	15
146	25c. multicoloured (No. 139)	20	15

1965. Cent of I.T.U. As T 64a of St. Helena.

147	2c. bistre and red	10	10
148	50c. blue and olive	40	50

1965. I.C.Y. As T 64b of St. Helena.

149	2c. purple and green	10	20
150	25c. green and violet	50	10

1966. Churchill Commemoration. As T 64c of St. Helena.

151	½c. blue	10	2·75
152	3c. green	35	10
153	15c. brown	80	20
154	25c. violet	85	20

48a Queen Elizabeth and Duke of Edinburgh

1966. Royal Visit.

155	48a	3c. black and blue	25	30
156	48a	25c. black and mauve	55	30

1966. World Cup Football Championship. As T 64d of St. Helena.

157	6c. multicoloured	40	20
158	25c. multicoloured	60	10

49 Festival Emblem

1966. Arts Festival.

159	49	3c. multicoloured	10	10
160	49	25c. multicoloured	20	10

1968. Inauguration of W.H.O. Headquarters, Geneva. As T 64e of St. Helena.

161	3c. black, green and blue	10	10
162	40c. black, purple and brown	30	20

1966. 20th Anniv of UNESCO. As T 64f/h of St. Helena.

163	3c. multicoloured	10	10
164	6c. yellow, violet and olive	10	10
165	40c. black, purple and orange	30	35

50 Government Headquarters, Basseterre

1967. Statehood. Multicoloured.

182	3c. Type **50**	10	10
183	10c. National flag	10	10
184	25c. Coat of arms	15	15

53 John Wesley and Cross

1967. West Indies Methodist Conference.

185	53	3c. black, red and violet	10	10
186	-	25c. black, turquoise & blue	15	10
187	-	40c. black, yellow & orange	15	15

DESIGNS: 25c. Charles Wesley and cross; 40c. Thomas Coke and cross.

56 Handley Page Dart Herald over "Jamaica Producer" (freighter)

1968. Caribbean Free Trade Area.

188	56	25c. multicoloured	40	10
189	56	50c. multicoloured	40	20

57 Dr. Martin Luther King

1968. Martin Luther King Commemoration.

190	57	50c. multicoloured	15	10

58 "Mystical Nativity" (Botticelli)

1968. Christmas.

191	**58**	12c. multicoloured	10	10
192	-	25c. multicoloured	10	10
193	**58**	40c. multicoloured	15	10
194	-	50c. multicoloured	15	10

DESIGN: 25c., 50c. "The Adoration of the Magi" (Rubens).

60 Tarpon Snook

1968. Fishes.

195	**60**	6c. multicoloured	10	10
196	-	12c. black, green and blue	15	10
197	-	40c. multicoloured	25	10
198	-	50c. multicoloured	30	15

FISHES: 12c. Needlefish; 40c. Horse-eyed jack; 50c. Black-finned snapper.

64 The Warner Badge and Islands

1969. Sir Thomas Warner Commem. Multicoloured.

199	20c. Type **64**	10	10
200	25c. Sir Thomas Warner's tomb	10	10
201	40c. Charles I's Commission	15	15

67 "The Adoration of the Kings" (Mostaert)

1969. Christmas. Multicoloured.

202	10c. Type **67**	10	10
203	25c. As 10c.	10	10
204	40c. "The Adoration of the Kings" (Geertgen)	10	10
205	50c. As 40c.	10	10

73 Portuguese Caravels (16th-cent)

1970. Multicoloured. (except ½c.).

206	½c. Pirates and treasure at Frigate Bay (black, orange and green)	10	10
207	1c. English two-decker warship, 1650	30	10
208	2c. Naval flags of colonizing nations	15	10
209	3c. Rapier hilt (17th-century)	15	10
210	4c. Type **73**	20	10
211	5c. Sir Henry Morgan and fire-ships, 1669	60	40
212	6c. L'Ollonois and pirate carrack (16th-century)	30	10
213	10c. 17th-century smugglers' ship	30	10
214	15c. "Piece of Eight"	2·00	40
215	20c. Cannon (17th-century)	35	10
216	25c. Humphrey Cole's astrolabe, 1574	40	10
217	50c. Flintlock pistol (17th-cent)	85	80
218	60c. Dutch flute (17th-cent)	1·50	70
219	$1 Capt. Bartholomew Roberts and his crew's death warrant	1·50	75
220	$2.50 Railing piece (gun) (16th-century)	1·25	4·50
221	$5 Drake, Hawkins and sea battle	1·50	4·50
280	$10 The Apprehension of Blackbeard (Edward Teach)	20·00	13·00

The ½c. to 3c., 15c., 25c., 60c. and $1 are vert designs.

85 Graveyard Scene ("Great Expectations")

1970. Death Cent of Charles Dickens.

222	**85**	4c. brown, gold and green	10	80
223	-	20c. brown, gold and purple	10	20
224	-	25c. brown, gold and green	10	20
225	-	40c. brown, gold and blue	15	35

DESIGNS—HORIZ: 20c. Miss Havisham and Pip ("Great Expectations"). VERT: 25c. Dickens' birthplace; 40c. Charles Dickens.

86 Local Steel Band

1970. Festival of Arts. Multicoloured.

226	20c. Type **86**	10	10
227	25c. Local string band	10	10
228	40c. Scene from "A Midsummer Night's Dream"	15	15

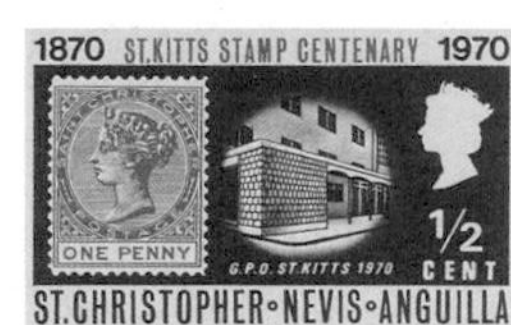

87 1d. Stamp of 1870 and Post Office, 1970

1970. Stamp Centenary.

229	**87**	½c. green and red	10	10
230	-	20c. purple, green and red	10	10
231	-	25c. purple, green and red	10	10
232	-	50c. red, green and black	30	45

DESIGNS: 20c., 25c., 1d. and 6d. stamps of 1870; 50c.6d. stamp of 1870 and early postmark.

88 "Adoration of the Shepherds" (Frans van Floris)

1970. Christmas. Multicoloured.

233	3c. Type **88**	10	10
234	20c. "The Holy Family" (Van Dyck)	10	10
235	25c. As 20c.	10	10
236	40c. Type **88**	15	50

89 Monkey Fiddle

1971. Flowers. Multicoloured.

237	½c. Type **89**	10	50
238	20c. Tropical mountain violet	15	10
239	30c. Trailing morning glory	15	15
240	50c. Fringed epidendrum	30	1·00

90 Royal Poinciana

1971. Philippe de Poincy Commem. Mult.

241	20c. Type **90**	10	10
242	30c. Chateau de Poincy	10	10
243	50c. De Poincy's badge (vert)	20	15

91 The East Yorks

1971. Siege of Brimstone Hill, 1782. Multicoloured.

244	½c. Type **91**	10	10
245	20c. Royal Artillery	20	10
246	30c. French infantry	30	10
247	50c. The Royal Scots	40	20

92 "Crucifixion" (Massys)

1972. Easter.

248	**92**	4c. multicoloured	10	10
249	**92**	20c. multicoloured	10	20
250	**92**	30c. multicoloured	10	25
251	**92**	40c. multicoloured	10	25

93 "Virgin and Child" (Borgognone)

1972. Christmas. Multicoloured.

252	3c. Type **93**	10	10
253	20c. "Adoration of the Kings" (J. Bassano) (horiz)	15	10
254	25c. "Adoration of the Shepherds" (Domenichino)	15	10
255	40c. "Virgin and Child" (Fiorenzo di Lorenzo)	20	10

1972. Royal Silver Wedding. As T 103 of St. Helena, but with brown pelicans in background.

256	20c. red	35	20
257	25c. blue	35	20

95 Landing on St. Christopher, 1623

1973. 300th Anniv of Sir Thomas Warner's Landing on St. Christopher. Multicoloured.

258	4c. Type **95**	15	10
259	25c. Growing tobacco	15	10
260	40c. Building fort at Old Road	20	10
261	$2.50 "Concepcion"	80	1·10

96 "The Last Supper" (Titian)

1973. Easter. Paintings of "The Last Supper" by the artists listed. Multicoloured.

262	4c. Type **96**	10	10
263	25c. Ascribed to Roberti	10	10
264	$2.50 Juan de Juanes (horiz)	70	60

1973. Royal Visit. Nos. 258/61 optd VISIT OF H. R. H. THE PRINCE OF WALES 1973.

265	**95**	4c. multicoloured	10	15
266	-	25c. multicoloured	10	15
267	-	40c. multicoloured	15	15
268	-	$2.50 multicoloured	45	50

99 Harbour Scene and 2d. Stamp of 1903

1973. 70th Anniv of First St. Kitts-Nevis Stamps. Multicoloured.

285	4c. Type **99**	10	10
286	25c. Sugar-mill and 1d. stamp of 1903	15	10
287	40c. Unloading boat and ½d. stamp of 1903	35	10
288	$2.50 Rock-carvings and 3d. stamp of 1903	1·00	1·00
MS289	144×95 mm. Nos. 285/8	1·50	4·50

1973. Royal Wedding. As T 103a of St. Helena. Multicoloured, background colours given.

290	25c. green	15	10
291	40c. brown	15	10

100 "Madonna and Child" (Murillo)

1973. Christmas. Paintings of "The Holy Family" by the artists listed. Multicoloured.

292	4c. Type **100**	10	10
293	40c. Mengs	15	10
294	60c. Sassoferrato	20	15
295	$1 Filippino Lippi (horiz)	25	30

101 "Christ carrying the Cross" (S. del Piombo)

1974. Easter. Multicoloured.

296	4c. Type **101**	10	10
297	25c. "The Crucifixion" (Goya)	15	10
298	40c. "Trinity" (Ribera)	15	10
299	$2.50 "The Deposition" (Fra Bartolomeo) (horiz)	1·00	1·00

102 University Centre, St. Kitts

1974. 25th Anniv of University of West Indies. Multicoloured.

300	10c. Type **102**	10	10
301	$1 As Type **102** but showing different buildings	20	25
MS302	99×95 mm. Nos. 300/1	35	65

103 Hands reaching for Globe

1974. Family Planning.

303	103	4c. brown, blue and black	10	10
304	-	25c. multicoloured	10	10
305	-	40c. multicoloured	10	10
306	-	$2.50 multicoloured	35	55

DESIGNS—HORIZ: 25c. Instruction by nurse; $2.50, Emblem and globe on scales. VERT: 40c. Family group.

104 Churchill as Army Lieutenant

1974. Birth Centenary of Sir Winston Churchill. Multicoloured.

307	4c. Type **104**	10	10
308	25c. Churchill as Prime Minister	15	10
309	40c. Churchill as Knight of the Garter	15	10
310	60c. Churchill's statue, London	25	15
MS311	99×148 mm. Nos. 307/10	75	1·25

105 Aeroplane and Map

1974. Opening of Golden Rock Airport, St. Kitts. Sheets 98×148 mm.

MS312	**105** 40c. multicoloured	20	40
MS313	45c. multicoloured	20	40

106 "The Last Supper" (Dore)

1975. Easter. Paintings by Dore. Multicoloured.

314	4c. Type **106**	10	10
315	25c. "Christ Mocked"	10	10
316	40c. "Jesus falling beneath the Cross"	10	10
317	$1 "The Erection of the Cross"	25	30

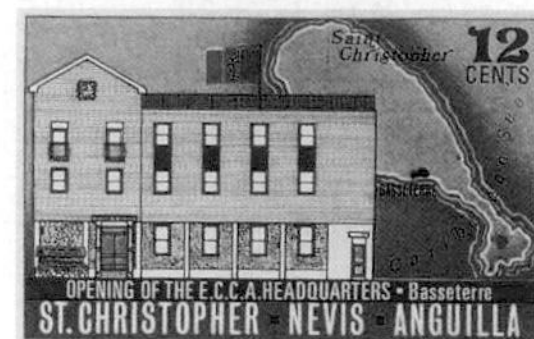

107 E.C.C.A. H.Q. Buildings, Basseterre

1975. Opening of East Caribbean Currency Authority's Headquarters.

318	107	12c. multicoloured	10	10
319	-	25c. multicoloured	10	10
320	-	40c. red, silver and grey	15	10
321	-	45c. multicoloured	15	15

DESIGNS: 25c. Specimen one-dollar banknote; 40c. Half-dollar of 1801 and current 4-dollar coin; 45c. Coins of 1801 and 1960.

108 Evangeline Booth (Salvation Army General)

1975. International Women's Year. Multicoloured.

338	4c. Type **108**	30	10
339	25c. Sylvia Pankhurst	35	10
340	40c. Marie Curie	2·50	80
341	$2.50 Lady Annie Allen (teacher and guider)	1·50	4·25

109 Golfer

1975. Opening of Frigate Bay Golf Course.

342	**109**	4c. black and red	80	10
343	**109**	25c. black and yellow	1·10	10
344	**109**	40c. black and green	1·40	20
345	**109**	$1 black and blue	1·90	2·75

110 "St. Paul" (Pier Francesco Sacchi)

1975. Christmas. Religious Paintings. Multicoloured.

346	25c. Type **110**	25	10
347	40c. "St. James" (Bonifazio di Pitati)	30	10
348	45c. "St. John the Baptist" (Mola)	30	10
349	$1 "St. Mary" (Raphael)	80	2·00

111 "Crucifixion" (detail)

1976. Easter. Stained Glass Window. Multicoloured.

350	4c. Type **111**	10	35
351	4c. Type **111**	10	35
352	4c. Type **111**	10	35
353	25c. "Last Supper"	35	10
354	40c. "Last Supper" (different)	40	10
355	$1 "Baptism of Christ"	70	70

Nos. 350/2 were printed together, se-tenant, forming a composite design, No. 350 being the left-hand stamp.

Nos. 353/5 are size 27×35 mm.

1976. West Indian Victory in World Cricket Cup. As Nos. 559/60 of Barbados.

356	12c. Map of the Caribbean	60	20
357	40c. Prudential Cup	1·40	50
MS358	95×80 mm. Nos. 356/7	4·25	3·75

112 Crispus Attucks and the Boston Massacre

1976. Bicentenary of American Revolution. Mult.

359	20c. Type **112**	20	10
360	40c. Alexander Hamilton and Battle of Yorktown	25	10
361	45c. Jefferson and Declaration of Independence	25	10
362	$1 Washington and the Crossing of the Delaware	45	85

113 "The Nativity" (Sforza Book of Hours)

1976. Christmas. Multicoloured.

363	20c. Type **113**	10	10
364	40c. "Virgin and Child with St. John" (Pintoricchio)	15	10
365	45c. "Our Lady of Good Children" (Ford Maddox-Brown)	15	10
366	$1 "Little Hands Outstretched to Bless" (Margaret Tarrant)	35	50

114 Royal Visit, 1966

1977. Silver Jubilee. Multicoloured.

367	50c. Type **114**	10	10
368	55c. The Sceptre	10	10
369	$1.50 Bishops paying homage	25	50

115 "Christ on the Cross" (Niccolo di Liberatore)

1977. Easter. Paintings from National Gallery, London. Multicoloured.

370	25c. Type **115**	10	10
371	30c. "The Resurrection" (imitator of Mantegna)	10	10
372	50c. "The Resurrection" (Ugolino da Siena) (horiz)	15	10
373	$1 "Christ Rising from the Tomb" (Gaudenzio Ferrari)	25	30

116 Estridge Mission

1977. Bicentenary of Moravian Mission.

374	**116**	4c. black, green and blue	10	10
375	-	20c. black, mauve & violet	10	10
376	-	40c. black, yellow & orge	15	15

DESIGNS: 20c. Mission symbol; 40c. Basseterre Mission.

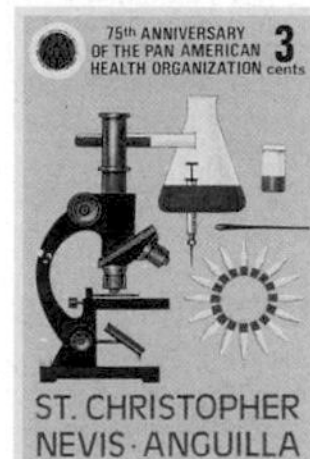

117 Laboratory Instruments

1977. 75th Anniv of Pan-American Health Organization.

377	**117**	3c. multicoloured	20	10
378	-	12c. multicoloured	35	60
379	-	20c. multicoloured	40	10
380	-	$1 brown, orange and black	1·00	1·40

DESIGNS: 12c. Fat cells, blood cells and nerve cells; 20c. "Community participation in health"; $1 Inoculation.

118 "Nativity" (West Window)

1977. Christmas. Stained-glass windows from Chartres Cathedral. Multicoloured.

381	4c. Type **118**	10	10
382	6c. "Three Magi" (west window)	10	10
383	40c. "La Belle Verriere"	35	10
384	$1 "Virgin and Child" (Rose window)	75	45

119 Savanna Monkey with Vervet

1978. The Savanna Monkey.

385	**119**	4c. brown, red and black	10	10

386	-	5c. multicoloured	10	10
387	119	55c. brown, green & black	30	10
388	-	$1.50 multicoloured	75	60

DESIGN: 5c., $1.50, Savanna monkeys on branch.

120 Falcon of Edward III

1978. 25th Anniv of Coronation.

389	**120**	$1 brown and red	15	20
390	-	$1 multicoloured	15	20
391	-	$1 brown and red	15	20

DESIGNS: No. 390, Queen Elizabeth II; No. 391, Brown pelican.

121 Tomatoes

1978. Multicoloured.. Multicoloured..

392		1c. Type **121**	10	20
393		2c. Defence Force band	10	20
394		5c. Radio and T.V. station	10	10
395		10c. Technical college	10	10
396		12c. T.V. assembly plant	10	75
397		15c. Sugar canoe harvesting	15	20
398		25c. Crafthouse (craft centre)	15	10
399		30c. "Europa" (liner)	1·50	1·50
400		40c. Lobster and sea crab	30	10
401		45c. Royal St. Kitts Hotel and golf course	2·75	1·25
402		50c. Pinney's Beach, Nevis	30	10
403		55c. New runway at Golden Rock	1·25	10
404		$1 Cotton picking	35	30
405		$5 Brewery	75	1·25
406		$10 Pineapples and peanuts	1·00	1·75

122 Investiture

1978. 50th Anniv of Boy Scout Movement on St. Kitts and Nevis. Multicoloured.

407		5c. Type **122**	10	30
408		10c. Map reading	10	30
409		25c. Pitching tent	20	30
410		40c. Cooking	35	45
411		50c. First aid	40	55
412		55c. Rev. W. A. Beckett (founder of scouting in St. Kitts)	45	55

123 Wise Man with Gift of Gold

1978. Christmas. Multicoloured.

413		5c. Type **123**	10	10
414		15c. Wise Man with gift of Frankincense	10	10
415		30c. Wise Man with gift of Myrrh	10	10
416		$2.25 Wise Man paying homage to the Infant Jesus	35	50

124 "Canna coccinea"

1979. Local Flowers (1st series). Multicoloured.

417		5c. Type **124**	10	10
418		30c. "Heliconia bihai"	25	20
419		55c. "Ruellia tuberosa"	30	30
420		$1.50 "Gesneria ventricosa"	50	1·60

See also Nos. 430/3.

125 St. Christopher 1870 1d. Stamp and Sir Rowland Hill

1979. Death Centenary of Sir Rowland Hill. Multicoloured.

421		5c. Type **125**	10	10
422		15c. 1970 Stamp Centenary 50c. commemorative	10	10
423		50c. Great Britain 1841 2d. blue	30	35
424		$2.50 St. Kitts-Nevis 1923 300th Anniv of Colony £1 commemorative	70	1·10

126 "The Woodman's Daughter"

1979. Christmas. International Year of the Child. Paintings by Sir John Millais. Multicoloured.

425		5c. Type **126**	10	10
426		25c. "Cherry Ripe"	25	25
427		30c. "The Rescue"	25	25
428		55c. "Bubbles"	30	30

1980. Local Flowers (2nd series). As T 124. Multicoloured.

430		4c. "Clerodendrum aculeatum"	30	10
431		55c. "Inga laurina"	30	20
432		$1.50 "Epidendrum difforme"	1·40	1·75
433		$2 "Salvia serotina"	60	2·25

127 Nevis Lagoon

1980. "London 1980" International Stamp Exhibition. Multicoloured.

434		5c. Type **127**	15	10
435		30c. Fig Tree Church (vert)	25	10
436		55c. Nisbet Plantation	45	25
437		$3 "Nelson" (Fuger) (vert)	1·75	1·60
MS438		107×77 mm. 75c. Detail of "Nelson Falling" (D. Dighton)	1·40	75

OFFICIAL STAMPS

1980. Nos. 396, 398 and 400/6 optd OFFICIAL.

O1		12c. multicoloured	80	1·25
O2		25c. multicoloured	15	20
O3		40c. multicoloured	40	50
O4		45c. multicoloured	2·50	2·00
O5		50c. multicoloured	30	40
O6		55c. multicoloured	1·25	50
O7		$1 multicoloured	70	2·25
O8		$5 multicoloured	80	2·50
O9		$10 multicoloured	1·00	3·50

Pt. 1

ST LUCIA

One of the Windward Islands, British West Indies. Achieved Associated Statehood on 1 March 1967.

1860. 12 pence = 1 shilling; 20 shilllings = 1 pound.
1949. 100 cents = 1 West Indian dollar.

1

1860. No value on stamps.

5ax	1	(1d.) red	70·00	90·00
11a	1	(1d.) black	25·00	12·00
7	1	(4d.) blue	£130	£140
16	1	(4d.) yellow	£120	24·00
8x	1	(6d.) green	£190	£180
17a	1	(6d.) violet	£120	22·00
18a	1	(1s.) orange	£160	16·00

HALFPENNY
(3)

1881. With value added by surch as T 3.

25	1	½d. green	26·00	38·00
26	1	1d. black	38·00	15·00
24	1	2½d. red	50·00	25·00
27	1	4d. yellow	£300	23·00
28	1	6d. violet	40·00	40·00
29	1	1s. orange	£275	£170

5

1882

43	5	½d. green	4·00	1·00
32	5	1d. red	50·00	16·00
46	5	2½d. blue	8·00	1·00
48	5	4d. brown	5·50	2·25
35	5	6d. lilac	£250	£200
36	5	1s. brown	£375	£150

1886

44	5	1d. mauve	6·00	30
45	5	2d. blue and orange	5·50	1·00
47	5	3d. mauve and green	6·50	5·50
41	5	6d. mauve and blue	5·00	14·00
50	5	1s. mauve and red	9·00	5·00
51	5	5s. mauve and orange	50·00	£150
52	5	10s. mauve and black	90·00	£150

1891. Surch in words.

56	5	½d. on 3d. mauve and green	80·00	27·00
55	5	1d. on 4d. brown	6·50	3·75

1891. Surch ½d.

54	5	½d. on half 6d. (No. 41)	28·00	3·25

9

1902

58	9	½d. purple and green	3·00	1·50
65	9	½d. green	1·75	1·00
66	9	1d. purple and red	8·00	1·25
67	9	1d. red	4·25	30
68a	9	2½d. purple and blue	17·00	4·50
69	9	2½d. blue	3·75	1·75
70	9	3d. purple and yellow	11·00	3·00
71	9	3d. purple on yellow	3·00	18·00
72	9	6d. purple and violet	23·00	26·00
73	9	6d. purple	75·00	90·00
62	9	1s. green and black	15·00	42·00
75	9	1s. black on green	4·75	8·00
76	9	5s. green and red	80·00	£190
77	9	5s. green and red on yellow	60·00	70·00

11 The Pitons

1902. 400th Anniv of Discovery by Columbus.

63	**11**	2d. green and brown	11·00	1·75

12

13

14

1912

78	12	½d. green	70	50
79	12	1d. red	1·90	10
93	12	1d. brown	1·40	15
94	14	1½d. red	75	2·50
95	13	2d. grey	75	15
81a	12	2½d. blue	3·75	2·75
97	12	2½d. orange	13·00	55·00
82	12	3d. purple on yellow	1·25	2·25
99a	12	3d. blue	4·50	11·00
83a	14	4d. black and red on yellow	70	1·50
102	12	6d. purple	2·00	4·75
85	12	1s. black on green	4·75	5·00
103	12	1s. brown	4·75	3·25
104	13	2s.6d. black & red on blue	18·00	27·00
88	12	5s. green and red on yellow	25·00	85·00

1916. No. 79 optd WAR TAX in two lines.

89	12	1d. red	13·00	18·00

1916. No. 79 optd WAR TAX in one line.

90	12	1d. red	1·25	30

1935. Silver Jubilee. As T 32a of St. Helena.

109		½d. black and green	30	1·75
110		2d. blue and grey	1·25	1·40
111		2½d. brown and blue	1·60	1·40
112		1s. grey and purple	16·00	18·00

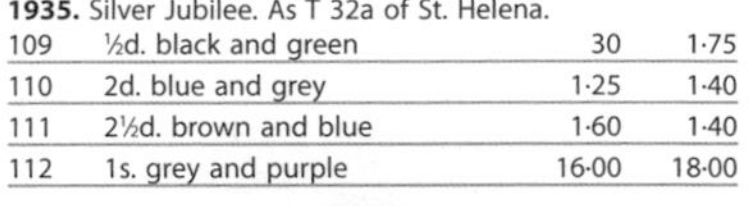

19 Port Castries

1936. King George V.

113	19	½d. black and green	30	50
114	-	1d. black and brown	40	10
115	-	1½d. black and red	55	30
116	19	2d. black and grey	50	20
117	-	2½d. black and blue	50	15
118	-	3d. black and green	1·25	70
119	19	4d. black and brown	1·00	1·00
120	-	6d. black and orange	1·00	1·00
121	-	1s. black and blue	2·75	2·50
122	-	2s.6d. black and blue	13·00	14·00
123	-	5s. black and violet	16·00	20·00
124	-	10s. black and red	55·00	85·00

DESIGNS—HORIZ: 1d., 2½d., 6d. Columbus Square, Castries (inscr "Colombus Square" in error); 1s. Fort Rodney, Pigeon Island; 5s. Government House; 10s. Badge of Colony. VERT: 1½d, 3d. Ventine Falls; 2s.6d. Inniskilling Monument.

1937. Coronation. As T 32b of St. Helena.

125		1d. violet	30	35
126		1½d. red	55	20
127		2½d. blue	55	1·25

26 King George VI

27 Columbus Square

1938. King George VI.

128a	26	½d. green	10	10
129a	26	1d. violet	10	15
129c	26	1d. red	10	10
130a	26	1½d. red	1·50	2·00
131a	26	2d. grey	10	10
132a	26	2½d. blue	40	10
132b	26	2½d. violet	1·00	10
133a	26	3d. orange	20	10
133b	26	3½d. blue	1·00	15
134a	27	6d. red	5·00	35
134c	26	8d. brown	3·50	30
135a	-	1s. brown	75	30
136	-	2s. blue and purple	7·50	1·25
136a	26	3s. purple	8·00	1·75
137	-	5s. black and mauve	16·00	14·00
138	-	10s. black on yellow	15·00	9·00
141	26	£1 sepia	15·00	8·00

DESIGNS—As Type **27**: 1s. Government House; 2s. The Pitons; 5s. "Lady Hawkins" loading bananas. VERT: 10s. Device of St. Lucia as Type **33**.

1946. Victory. As T 33a of St. Helena.

142		1d. violet	10	20
143		3½d. blue	10	20

1948. Silver Wedding. As T 33b/c of St. Helena.

144		1d. red	15	10
145		£1 purple	17·00	35·00

33 Device of St. Lucia

1949. New Currency.

146	**26**	1c. green	25	10
147	**26**	2c. mauve	1·00	10
148	**26**	3c. red	1·75	3·00
149	**26**	4c. grey	1·50	40
150	**26**	5c. violet	1·75	10
151	**26**	6c. orange	1·50	4·00
152	**26**	7c. blue	4·00	3·25
153	**26**	12c. red	5·50	4·50
154	**26**	16c. brown	5·00	50
155	**33**	24c. blue	50	10
156	**33**	48c. olive	1·50	1·25
157	**33**	$1.20 purple	2·50	9·50
158	**33**	$2.40 green	6·00	18·00
159	**33**	$4.80 red	12·00	18·00

1949. U.P.U. As T 33d/g of St. Helena.

160		5c. violet	15	1·00
161		6c. orange	1·60	2·50
162		12c. mauve	20	20
163		24c. green	30	20

1951. Inauguration of B.W.I. University College. As T 10a/b of St. Kitts-Nevis.

164		3c. black and red	45	75
165		12c. black and red	65	75

34 Phoenix rising from Burning Buildings

1951. Reconstruction of Castries.

166	**34**	12c. red and blue	35	1·00

1951. New Constitution. Optd NEW CONSTITUTION 1951.

167	**26**	2c. mauve	20	80
168	**26**	4c. grey	20	60
169	**26**	5c. violet	25	80
170	**26**	12c. red	1·00	60

1953. Coronation. As T 33h of St. Helena.

171		3c. black and red	70	10

1953. As 1949 but portrait of Queen Elizabeth II facing left and new Royal Cypher.

172		1c. green	10	10
173		2c. purple	10	10
174		3c. red	10	10
175		4c. grey	10	10
176		5c. violet	10	10
177		6c. orange	15	1·00
178		8c. red	30	10
179		10c. blue	10	10
180		15c. brown	30	10
181	**33**	25c. blue	30	10
182	**33**	50c. olive	4·50	3·25
183	**33**	$1 green	4·00	5·00
184	**33**	$2.50 red	5·00	6·50

1958. British Caribbean Federation. As T 27a of St. Kitts-Nevis.

185		3c. green	40	50
186		6c. blue	75	1·75
187		12c. red	1·00	80

38 Columbus's "Santa Maria" off the Pitons

1960. New Constitution for the Windward and Leeward Islands.

188	**38**	8c. red	40	45
189	**38**	10c. orange	40	45
190	**38**	25c. blue	60	50

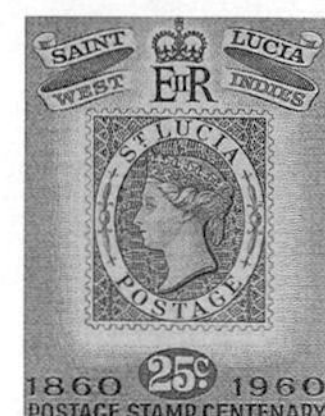

39 Stamp of 1860

1960. Stamp Centenary.

191	**39**	5c. red and blue	25	10
192	**39**	16c. blue and green	45	90
193	**39**	25c. green and red	45	15

1963. Freedom from Hunger. As T 63a of St. Helena.

194		25c. green	30	10

1963. Cent of Red Cross. As T 63b of St. Helena.

195		4c. red and black	20	50
196		25c. red and blue	50	1·75

40 Queen Elizabeth II (after A. C. Davidson-Houston)

41 Queen Elizabeth II (after A. C. Davidson-Houston)

42 Fishing Boats

1964

197	**40**	1c. red	10	10
198	**40**	2c. violet	30	1·00
199	**40**	4c. green	1·00	30
200	**40**	5c. blue	30	10
201	**40**	6c. brown	1·00	2·50
202	**41**	8c. multicoloured	10	10
203	**41**	10c. multicoloured	1·00	10
204	**42**	12c. multicoloured	50	1·50
205	-	15c. multicoloured	20	10
206	-	25c. multicoloured	20	10
207	-	35c. blue and buff	3·00	10
208	-	50c. multicoloured	2·50	10
209	-	$1 multicoloured	1·25	2·50
210	-	$2.50 multicoloured	2·50	2·00

HORIZ (as Type **42**): 15c. Pigeon Island; 25c. Reduit Beach; 35c. Castries Harbour; 50c. The Pitons. VERT (as Type **42**): $1 Vigie Beach. (As Type **41**): $2.50, Head and shoulders portrait of Queen Elizabeth II.

The 35c. and 50c. show a royal Cypher in place of the portrait.

45a Shakespeare and Memorial Theatre, Stratford-upon-Avon

1964. 400th Birth Anniv of Shakespeare.

211	**45a**	10c. green	30	10

1965. Centenary of I.T.U. As T 64a of St. Helena.

212		2c. mauve and purple	10	10
213		50c. lilac and green	70	90

1965. I.C.Y. As T 64b of St. Helena.

214		1c. purple and green	10	10
215		25c. green and violet	20	20

1966. Churchill Commemoration. As T 64c of St. Helena.

216		4c. blue	15	10
217		6c. green	60	3·00
218		25c. brown	75	15
219		35c. violet	75	20

1966. Royal Visit. As T 48a of St. Kitts-Nevis.

220		4c. black and blue	65	25
221		25c. black and mauve	1·25	75

1966. World Cup Football Championship. As T 64d of St. Helena.

222		4c. multicoloured	25	10
223		25c. multicoloured	75	30

1966. Inauguration of W.H.O. Headquarters, Geneva. As T 64e of St. Helena.

224		4c. black, green and blue	15	30
225		25c. black, purple and brown	45	40

1966. 20th Anniv of U.N.E.S.C.O. As T 64f/h of St. Helena.

226		4c. multicoloured	15	10
227		12c. yellow, violet and olive	25	65
228		25c. black, purple and orange	50	35

51 Map of St. Lucia

1967. Statehood. Nos. 198, 202/9 and 257 optd STATEHOOD 1st MARCH 1967.

229	**40**	2c. violet (postage)	20	15
230	**40**	5c. blue	20	10
231	**40**	6c. brown	20	10
232	**41**	8c. multicoloured	30	10
233	**41**	10c. multicoloured	30	10
234	**42**	12c. multicoloured	20	10
235	-	15c. multicoloured	60	1·00
236	-	25c. multicoloured	30	1·00
237	-	35c. blue and buff	1·25	35
238	-	50c. multicoloured	50	1·10
239	-	$1 multicoloured	50	75
240	**51**	15c. blue (air)	10	10

52 "Madonna and Child with the Infant Baptist" (Raphael)

1967. Christmas.

241	**52**	4c. multicoloured	10	10
242	**52**	25c. multicoloured	30	10

53 Batsman and Sir Frederick Clarke (Governor)

1968. M.C.C.'s West Indies Tour.

243	**53**	10c. multicoloured	20	30
244	**53**	35c. multicoloured	45	55

54 "The Crucified Christ with the Virgin Mary, Saints and the Angels" (Raphael)

1968. Easter Commemoration.

245	**54**	10c. multicoloured	10	10
246	-	15c. multicoloured	10	10
247	**54**	25c. multicoloured	15	10
248	-	35c. multicoloured	15	10

DESIGN: 15, 35c. "Noli me tangere" (detail by Titian).

56 Dr. Martin Luther King

1968. Martin Luther King Commemoration.

250	**56**	25c. blue, black and flesh	15	15
251	**56**	35c. blue, black and flesh	15	15

57 "Virgin and Child in Glory" (Murillo)

1968. Christmas.

252	**57**	5c. multicoloured	10	10
253	-	10c. multicoloured	10	10
254	**57**	25c. multicoloured	15	10
255	-	35c. multicoloured	15	10

DESIGN: 10, 35c. "Madonna with Child" (Murillo).

59 Purple-throated Carib

1969. Birds. Multicoloured.

256		10c. Type **59**	35	35
257		15c. St. Lucia amazon	40	40
258		25c. Type **59**	50	45
259		35c. As 15c.	65	50

61 "Head of Christ Crowned with Thorns" (Reni)

1969. Easter. Multicoloured.

260		10c. Type **61**	10	10
261		15c. "Resurrection of Christ" (Sodoma)	10	10
262		25c. Type **61**	15	15
263		35c. As the 15c.	15	15

63 Map showing CARIFTA Countries

1969. 1st Anniv of CARIFTA.

264	**63**	5c. multicoloured	10	15
265	**63**	10c. multicoloured	10	15
266	-	25c. multicoloured	15	15
267	-	35c. multicoloured	15	15

DESIGN: 25, 35c. Handclasp and names of CARIFTA countries.

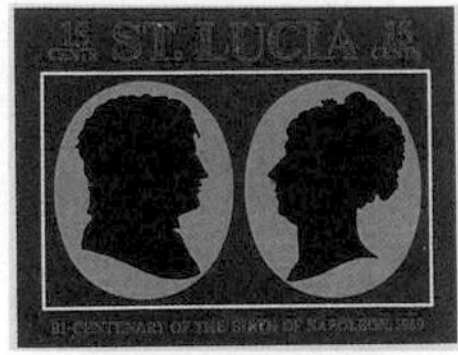

65 Emperor Napoleon and Empress Josephine

1969. Birth Bicent of Napoleon Bonaparte.

268	**65**	15c. multicoloured	10	10
269	**65**	25c. multicoloured	10	10
270	**65**	35c. multicoloured	10	10
271	**65**	50c. multicoloured	15	55

66 "Virgin and Child" (P. Delaroche)

1969. Christmas. Paintings. Multicoloured, background colours given.

272	**66**	5c. gold and purple	10	10
273	-	10c. gold and blue	10	10
274	**66**	25c. gold and red	20	10
275	-	35c. gold and green	20	10

DESIGN: 10c., 35c. "Holy Family" (Rubens).

68 House of Assembly

1970. Multicoloured.. Multicoloured..

276	1c. Type **68**	10	10
277	2c. Roman Catholic Cathedral	15	10
278	4c. The Boulevard, Castries	1·00	10
279	5c. Castries Harbour	1·50	10
280	6c. Sulphur springs	15	10
281	10c. Vigie Airport	2·00	10
282	12c. Reduit Beach	20	10
283	15c. Pigeon Island	30	10
284	25c. The Pitons and yacht	80	10
285	35c. Marigot Bay	40	10
286	50c. Diamond Waterfall	70	80
287	$1 Flag of St. Lucia	40	70
288	£2.50 St. Lucia coat of arms	55	1·75
289	$5 Queen Elizabeth II	1·00	4·00
289a	$10 Map of St. Lucia	5·00	9·00

Nos. 286/9a are vert.

69 "The Sealing of the Tomb" (Hogarth)

1970. Easter. Multicoloured.

290	25c. Type **69**	15	20
291	35c. "The Three Marys at the Tomb" (Hogarth)	15	20
292	$1 "The Ascension" (Hogarth)	30	40

The $1 is larger 39×54 mm.

Nos. 290/2 were issued in a triptych, with the $1 value 10 mm higher than the other values.

72 Charles Dickens and Dickensian Characters

1970. Death Cent of Charles Dickens.

293	**72**	1c. multicoloured	10	10
294	**72**	25c. multicoloured	20	10
295	**72**	35c. multicoloured	25	10
296	**72**	50c. multicoloured	35	1·25

73 Nurse and Emblem

1970. Cent of British Red Cross. Multicoloured.

297	10c. Type **73**	15	15
298	15c. Flags of Great Britain, Red Cross and St. Lucia	25	25
299	25c. Type **73**	35	40
300	35c. As 15c.	40	40

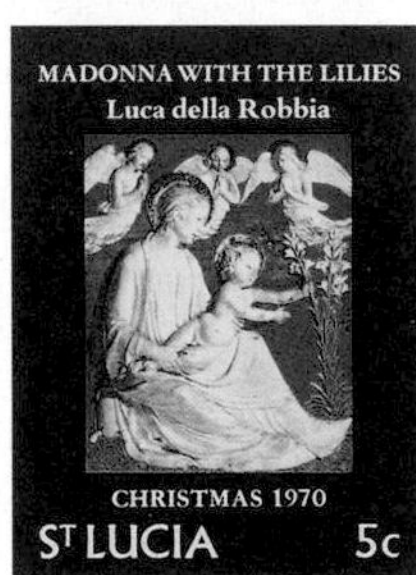

74 "Madonna with the Lilies" (Luca della Robbia)

1970. Christmas.

301	**74**	5c. multicoloured	10	10
302	**74**	10c. multicoloured	15	10
303	**74**	35c. multicoloured	30	10
304	**74**	40c. multicoloured	30	30

75 "Christ on the Cross" (Rubens)

1971. Easter. Multicoloured.

305	10c. Type **75**	10	10
306	15c. "Descent from the Cross" (Rubens)	15	10
307	35c. Type **75**	30	10
308	40c. As 15c.	30	40

76 Moule a Chique Lighthouse

1971. Opening of Beane Field Airport. Mult.

309	5c. Type **76**	50	15
310	25c. Boeing 727-200 landing at Beane Field	50	15

77 Morne Fortune

78 Morne Fortune, Modern View

1971. Old and New Views of St. Lucia. Multicoloured.

311	5c. Type **77**	10	20
312	5c. Type **78**	10	20
313	10c. Castries City (old view)	10	20
314	10c. Castries City (modern view)	10	20
315	25c. Pigeon Island (old view)	15	30
316	25c. Pigeon Island (modern view)	15	30
317	50c. Old view from grounds of Government House	25	75
318	50c. Modern view from grounds of Government House	25	75

The old views are taken from paintings by J. H. Caddy.

79 "Virgin and Child with two Angels" (Verrocchio)

1971. Christmas. Multicoloured.

319	5c. Type **79**	10	10
320	10c. "Virgin and Child, St. John the Baptist and an Angel" (Morando)	10	10
321	35c. "Madonna and Child" (Battista)	15	10
322	40c. Type **79**	20	25

80 "St. Lucia" (Dolci School) and Coat of Arms

1971. National Day.

323	**80**	5c. multicoloured	10	10
324	**80**	10c. multicoloured	15	10
325	**80**	25c. multicoloured	25	10
326	**80**	50c. multicoloured	45	40

81 "The Dead Christ Mourned" (Carracci)

1972. Easter. Multicoloured.

327	10c. Type **81**	10	10
328	25c. "Angels weeping over the dead Christ" (Guercino)	20	10
329	35c. Type **81**	30	10
330	50c. As 25c.	40	40

82 Science Block and Teachers' College

1972. Morne Educational Complex. Mult.

331	5c. Type **82**	10	10
332	15c. University Centre	10	10
333	25c. Secondary School	10	10
334	35c. Technical College	15	10

83 Steamship Stamp and Map

1972. Centenary of First Postal Service by St. Lucia Steam Conveyance Co. Ltd.

335	**83**	5c. multicoloured	15	10
336	-	10c. blue, mauve and black	20	10
337	-	35c. red, blue and black	45	10
338	-	50c. multicoloured	75	1·00

DESIGNS: 10c. Steamship stamp and Castries Harbour; 35c. Steamship stamp and Soufriere; 50c. Steamship stamps.

84 "The Holy Family" (Sebastiano Ricci)

1972. Christmas.

339	**84**	5c. multicoloured	10	10
340	**84**	10c. multicoloured	10	10
341	**84**	35c. multicoloured	20	10
342	**84**	40c. multicoloured	25	15

1972. Royal Silver Wedding. As T 103 of St. Helena, but with Arms and St. Lucia Amazon.

343	15c. red	40	20
344	35c. green	20	40

86 Week-day Headdress

1973. Local Headdresses. Multicoloured.

345	5c. Type **86**	10	10
346	10c. Formal style	10	10
347	25c. Unmarried girl's style	15	10
348	50c. Ceremonial style	25	85

87 Coat of Arms

1973

349A	**87**	5c. green	10	75
350A	**87**	10c. blue	15	75
351A	**87**	25c. brown	15	75
953	**87**	10c. green	75	75

88 H.M.S. "St. Lucia", 1830

1973. Historic Ships. Multicoloured.

352	15c. Type **88**	20	10
353	35c. H.M.S. "Prince of Wales", 1765	30	10
354	50c. "Oliph Blossom", 1605	40	75
355	$1 H.M.S. "Rose", 1757	70	1·00
MS356	122×74 mm. Nos. 352/5	1·00	2·75

89 Plantation and Flower

1973. Banana Industry. Multicoloured.

357	5c. Type **89**	10	10
358	15c. Aerial spraying	15	10
359	35c. Boxing plant	20	10
360	50c. Loading a boat	50	40

90 "The Virgin with Child" (Maratta)

1973. Christmas. Multicoloured.

361	5c. Type **90**	10	10
362	15c. "Madonna in the Meadow" (Raphael)	10	10
363	35c. "The Holy Family" (Bronzino)	20	10
364	50c. "Madonna of the Pear" (Durer)	30	35

1973. Royal Wedding. As T 103a of St. Helena. Multicoloured, background colours given.

365	40c. green	10	10
366	50c. lilac	10	10

91 "The Betrayal"

1974. Easter. Paintings by Ugolino da Siena. Multicoloured.

369	5c. Type **91**	10	10
370	35c. "The Way to Calvary"	15	10
371	80c. "The Deposition"	15	15
372	$1 "The Resurrection"	20	25
MS373	180×140 mm. Nos. 369/72	1·00	2·00

92 3-Escalins Coins, 1798

1974. Coins of Old St. Lucia. Multicoloured.

374	15c. Type **92**	15	10
375	35c. 6-esculins coins, 1798	15	10
376	40c. 2-livres 5-sols coins, 1813	20	10
377	$1 6-livres 15-sols coins, 1813	35	65
MS378	151×115 mm. Nos. 374/7	1·00	2·75

93 Baron de Laborie

1974. Past Governors of St. Lucia. Mult.

379	5c. Type **93**	10	10
380	35c. Sir John Moore	10	10
381	80c. Sir Dudley Hill	15	10
382	$1 Sir Frederick Clarke	25	35

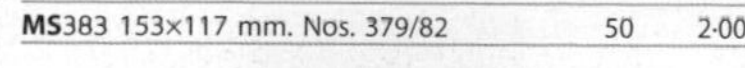

MS383	153×117 mm. Nos. 379/82	50	2·00

94 "Virgin and Child" (Andrea del Verrocchio)

1974. Christmas. Multicoloured.

384	5c. Type **94**	10	10
385	35c. "Virgin and Child" (Andrea della Robbia)	10	10
386	80c. "Madonna and Child" (Luca della Robbia)	15	15
387	$1 "Virgin and Child" (Rossellino)	20	25
MS388	92×140 mm. Nos. 384/7	70	2·00

95 Churchill and Montgomery

1974. Birth Centenary of Sir Winston Churchill.

389	5c. Type **95**	10	10
390	$1 Churchill and Truman	30	35

96 "Christ on the Cross" (School of Van der Weyden)

1975. Easter. Multicoloured.

391	5c. Type **96**	10	10
392	35c. "Noli me tangere" (Romano)	10	10
393	80c. "Calvary" (Gallego)	20	20
394	$1 "Noli me tangere" (Correggio)	30	35

97 "Nativity" (French Book of Hours)

1975. Christmas. Multicoloured.

399	5c. Type **97**	10	10
400	10c. "King" (stained glass window)	10	30
401	10c. "Virgin and Child" (stained glass window)	10	30
402	10c. "King and Cattle" (stained glass window)	10	30
403	40c. "Nativity" (Hastings Book of Hours)	30	10
404	$1 "Virgin and Child with Saints" (Borgognone)	70	90
MS405	105×109 mm. Nos. 399 and 403/4	75	1·00

Nos. 400/2 were printed together, se-tenant, forming a composite design of the Epiphany.

98 America Schooner "Hanna"

1975. Bicent of American Revolution. Ships. Mult.

406	½c. Type **98**	10	30
407	1c. "Prince of Orange" (British sailing packet)	10	30
408	2c. H.M.S. "Edward" (sloop)	15	30
409	5c. "Millern" (British merchantman)	25	10
410	15c. "Surprise" (American lugger)	40	10
411	35c. H.M.S. "Serapis" (frigate)	45	10
412	50c. "Randolph" (American frigate)	50	1·00
413	$1 "Alliance" (American frigate)	50	2·50
MS414	142×116 mm. Nos. 410/13	3·00	4·50

99 Laughing Gull

1976. Birds. Multicoloured.

415	1c. Type **99**	30	2·00
416	2c. Little blue heron	30	2·00
417	4c. Belted kingfisher	35	1·25
418	5c. St. Lucia amazon ("St Lucia Parrot")	1·75	1·25
419	6c. St. Lucia oriole	1·25	2·00
420	8c. Grey trembler ("Trembler")	1·50	2·75
421	10c. American kestrel ("Sparrow Hawk")	1·25	35
422	12c. Red-billed tropic bird	2·00	2·50
423	15c. Moorhen ("Common Gallinule")	1·25	15
424a	25c. Common noddy ("Brown Noddy")	1·00	30
425	35c. Sooty tern	3·25	1·50
426	50c. Osprey	7·00	3·50
427	$1 White-breasted trembler ("White-breasted Thrasher")	4·00	3·50
428	$2.50 St. Lucia black finch	7·50	6·50
429	$5 Red-necked pigeon ("Ramier")	7·50	4·50
430a	$10 Caribbean elaenia	2·25	7·50

99a Caribbean Map

1976. West Indies Victory in World Cricket Cup. Multicoloured.

431	50c. Type **99a**	1·00	1·00
432	$1 Prudential Cup	1·00	2·50
MS433	92×79 mm. Nos. 431/2	3·50	4·50

100 H.M.S. "Ceres"

1976. Royal Navy Crests. Multicoloured.

434	10c. Type **100**	40	10
435	20c. H.M.S. "Pelican"	70	10
436	40c. H.M.S. "Ganges"	90	10
437	$2 H.M.S. "Ariadne"	2·25	2·75

101 "Madonna and Child" (Murillo)

1976. Christmas. Multicoloured.

438	10c. Type **101**	10	10
439	20c. "Madonna and Child with Angels" (Costa)	10	10
440	50c. "Madonna and Child Enthroned" (Isenbrandt)	15	10
441	$2 "Madonna and Child with St. John" (Murillo)	50	65
MS442	105×93 mm. $2.50 As Type **101**	1·00	1·25

102 Queen Elizabeth II

1977. Silver Jubilee.

443	**102** 10c. multicoloured	10	10
444	**102** 20c. multicoloured	10	10
445	**102** 40c. multicoloured	10	15
446	**102** $2 multicoloured	40	90
MS447	128×95 mm. **102** $2.50 multicoloured	45	1·00

103 Scouts from Tapion School

1977. Caribbean Boy Scout Jamboree. Multicoloured.

448	½c. Type **103**	10	10
449	1c. Sea scouts	10	10
450	2c. Scout from Micoud	10	10
451	10c. Two scouts from Tapion School	20	10
452	20c. Venture scout	20	10
453	50c. Scout from Gros Islet	35	45
454	$1 Sea scouts in motor boat	50	1·00
MS455	75×85 mm. $2.50 As $1	1·10	3·00

104 "Nativity" (Giotto)

1977. Christmas. Multicoloured.

456	½c. Type **104**	10	10
457	1c. "Perugia triptych" (Fra Angelico)	10	10
458	2c. "Virgin and Child" (El Greco)	10	10
459	20c. "Madonna of the Rosary" (Caravaggio)	15	10
460	50c. "Adoration of the Magi" (Velazquez)	20	10
461	$1 "Madonna of Carmel" (Tiepolo)	30	35
462	$2.50 "Adoration of the Magi" (Tiepolo)	45	80

105 "Susan Lunden"

1977. 400th Birth Anniv of Rubens. Mult.

463	10c. Type **105**	10	10
464	35c. "The Rape of the Sabine Women" (detail)	15	10
465	50c. "Ludovicus Nonnius"	30	10
466	$2.50 "Minerva protects Pax from Mars" (detail)	85	90
MS467	145×120 mm. Nos. 463/6	1·25	2·25

106 Yeoman of the Guard and Life Guard

1978. 25th Anniv of Coronation. Mult.

468	15c. Type **106**	10	10
469	20c. Groom and postillion	10	10
470	50c. Footman and coachman	10	10
471	$3 State trumpeter and herald	35	90
MS472	114×88 mm. $5 Master of the Horse and Gentleman-at-Arms	60	90

107 Queen Angelfish

1978. Fish. Multicoloured.

473	10c. Type **107**	40	10
474	20c. Four-eyed butterflyfish	60	10
475	50c. French angelfish	90	30
476	$2 Yellow-tailed damselfish	1·10	2·25
MS477	155×89 mm. $2.50 Rock beauty	2·25	1·90

108 French Grenadier and Map of the Battle

1978. Bicent of Battle of Cul-de-Sac. Mult.

478	10c. Type **108**	60	15
479	30c. British Grenadier officer and Map of St. Lucia (Bellin), 1762	1·00	20
480	50c. Coastline from Gros Islet to Cul-de-Sac and British Fleet opposing French landings	1·10	25
481	$2.50 General James Grant, 1798, and Light Infantrymen of 46th Regiment	1·90	2·50

109 The Annunciation

1978. Christmas. Multicoloured.

482	30c. Type **109**	10	10
483	50c. Type **109**	15	10
484	55c. The Nativity	15	10
485	80c. As 55c.	20	20

110 Hewanorra International Air Terminal

1979. Independence. Multicoloured.

486	10c. Type **110**	10	10
487	30c. New coat of arms	10	10
488	50c. Government House and Sir Allen Lewis (first Governor-General)	15	10
489	$2 French, St. Lucia and Union flags on map of St. Lucia	30	45
MS490	127×80 mm. Nos. 486/9	50	1·00

111 Popes Paul VI and John Paul I

1979. Pope Paul VI Commemoration. Mult.

491	10c. Type **111**	10	10
492	30c. Pres. Sadat of Egypt with Pope Paul	20	10
493	50c. Pope Paul with Secretary-General U Thant	35	10
494	55c. Pope Paul and Prince Minister Golda Meir of Israel	40	25
495	$2 Martin Luther King received in audience by Pope Paul	1·00	70

112 Dairy Farming

1979. Agricultural Diversification. Mult.

496	10c. Type **112**	10	10
497	35c. Fruit and vegetables	10	10
498	50c. Water conservation	20	10
499	$3 Copra industry	75	1·10

113 Lindbergh and Sikorsky S-38A Flying Boat

1979. 50th Anniv of Lindbergh's Inaugural Airmail Flight via St. Lucia.

500	**113**	10c. black, red and orange	50	10
501	-	30c. multicoloured	60	10
502	-	50c. multicoloured	60	10
503	-	$2 multicoloured	80	85

DESIGNS: 30c. Sikorsky S-38A flying boat and route map; 50c. Arrival at La Toc, September, 1929; $2 Letters on first flight.

114 "A Prince of Saxony" (Cranach the Elder)

1979. International Year of the Child. Famous Paintings. Multicoloured.

504	10c. Type **114**	10	10
505	50c. "The Infanta Margarita" (Velazquez)	15	10
506	$2 "Girl playing Badminton" (Chardin)	45	40
507	$2.50 "Mary and Francis Wilcox" (Stock)	45	45
MS508	113×94 mm. $5 "Two Children" (Picasso)	1·10	1·25

115 Notice of Introduction of Penny Post

1979. Death Cent of Sir Rowland Hill. Mult.

509	10c. Type **115**	10	10
510	50c. Wyon essay	15	10
511	$2 First St. Lucia stamp	25	50
512	$2.50 G.B. 1840 Penny Black	35	60
MS513	111×85 mm. $5 Sir Rowland Hill	70	90

116 "Madonna and Child" (Bernardino Fungai)

1979. Christmas. International Year of the Child. Paintings of the "Madonna and Child" by artists named. Multicoloured.

514	10c. Type **116**	10	10
515	50c. Carlo Dolci	20	10
516	$2 Titian	50	50
517	$2.50 Giovanni Bellini	60	50
MS518	94×120 mm. Nos. 514/17	1·25	1·60

117 St. Lucia Steam Conveyance Co. Ltd. Cover, 1873

1980. "London 1980" Int Stamp Exhibition. Mult.

519	10c. Type **117**	10	10
520	30c. S.S. "Assistance" 1d. postmark, 1879	10	10
521	50c. Postage due handstamp, 1929	15	10
522	$2 Crowned-circle Paid stamp, 1844	40	55
MS523	86×76 mm. Nos. 519/22	65	90

118 Mickey Mouse astride Rocket

1980. 10th Anniv (1979) of Moon Landing. Disney characters in Space Scenes. Multicoloured.

524	½c. Type **118**	10	10
525	1c. Donald Duck being towed by rocket (horiz)	10	10
526	2c. Minnie Mouse on Moon	10	10
527	3c. Goofy hitching lift to Mars	10	10
528	4c. Goofy and Moondog (horiz)	10	10
529	5c. Pluto burying bone on Moon (horiz)	10	10
530	10c. Donald Duck and love-sick Martian (horiz)	10	10
531	$2 Donald Duck paddling spaceship (horiz)	1·75	1·00
532	$2.50 Mickey Mouse driving moonbuggy (horiz)	1·75	1·10
MS533	102×127 mm. $5 Goofy leaping from space-ship on to Moon	3·25	2·75

119 Queen Elizabeth the Queen Mother

1980. 80th Birthday of The Queen Mother.

534	**119**	10c. multicoloured	15	10
535	**119**	$2.50 multicoloured	35	1·00
MS536		85×65 mm. **119** $3 multicoloured	60	1·50

120 Hawker Siddeley H.S.748

1980. Transport. Multicoloured.

537	5c. Type **120**	30	30
538	10c. Douglas DC-10-30 airliner	65	30
539	15c. Local bus	35	40
540	20c. "Geestcrest" (freighter)	35	40
541	25c. Britten Norman Islander aircraft	65	30
542	30c. "Charles" (pilot boat)	40	50
543	50c. Boeing 727-200 airliner	1·00	60
544	75c. "Cunard Countess" (liner)	65	1·25
545	$1 Lockheed TriStar 500 airliner	85	1·40
546	$2 "Booker Vulcan" (cargo liner)	1·25	2·00
547	$5 Boeing 707-420 airliner	5·00	6·00
548	$10 "Queen Elizabeth 2" (liner)	5·00	8·00

121 Shot-putting

1980. Olympic Games, Moscow. Mult.

549	10c. Type **121**	10	10
550	50c. Swimming	20	10
551	$2 Gymnastics	80	50
552	$2.50 Weightlifting	90	60
MS553	108×83 mm. $5 Athletes with Olympic torch	1·50	1·40

122 Coastal Landscape within Cogwheel

1980. 75th Anniv of Rotary International. Different coastal landscapes within cogwheel.

554	**122**	10c. multicoloured	10	10
555	-	50c. multicoloured	15	10
556	-	$2 black, red and yellow	40	40
557	-	$2.50 multicoloured	50	55
MS558		108×106 mm. $5 multicoloured	1·25	1·75

123 Sir Arthur Lewis

1980. Nobel Prize Winners. Multicoloured.

559	10c. Type **123**	10	10
560	50c. Martin Luther King Jnr	20	15
561	$2 Ralph Bunche	50	60
562	$2.50 Albert Schweitzer	70	80
MS563	115×91 mm. $5 Albert Einstein	2·25	2·00

1980. Hurricane Relief. Nos. 538/9 and 542 surch $1.50 1980 HURRICANE RELIEF.

564	$1.50 on 15c. multicoloured	30	40
565	$1.50 on 20c. multicoloured	30	40
566	$1.50 on 50c. multicoloured	30	40

125 "The Nativity" (Giovanni Battista)

1980. Christmas. Paintings. Multicoloured.

567	10c. Type **125**	10	10
568	30c. "Adoration of the Kings" (Pieter the Elder)	10	10
569	$2 "Adoration of the Shepherds" (ascribed to Murillo)	40	60

MS570	102×88 mm. $1×3, Angel with people of St. Lucia (composite design) (each 30×75 mm)	80	90

126 Brazilian Agouti

1981. Wildlife. Multicoloured.

571	10c. Type **126**	15	10
572	50c. St. Lucia amazon ("St. Lucia Parrot")	1·00	20
573	$2 Purple-throated carib	1·75	80
574	$2.50 Fiddler crab	1·25	1·00
MS575	103×87 mm. $5 "Danaus plexippus" (butterfly)	2·40	2·50

127 Prince Charles at Balmoral

1981. Royal Wedding. Multicoloured.

576	25c. Prince Charles and Lady Diana Spencer	10	10
577	50c. Clarence House	10	10
578	$4 Type **127**	40	55
MS579	96×82 mm. $5 Class Coach and coachman	50	50

128 Lady Diana Spencer

1981. Royal Wedding. Mult. Self-adhesive.

580	50c. Type **128**	25	45
581	$2 Prince Charles	30	60
582	$5 Prince Charles and Lady Diana Spencer	1·50	1·75

129 "The Cock"

1981. Birth Bicentenary of Picasso. Mult.

583	30c. Type **129**	25	10
584	50c. "Man with an Ice-cream"	35	10
585	55c. "Woman dressing her Hair"	35	10
586	$3 "Seated Woman"	95	85
MS587	128×102 mm. $5 "Night Fishing at Antibes"	1·75	1·75

130 "Industry"

1981. 25th Anniv of Duke of Edinburgh Award Scheme. Multicoloured.

588	10c. Type **130**	10	10
589	35c. "Community service"	15	10
590	50c. "Physical recreation"	15	10
591	$2.50 Duke of Edinburgh speaking at Caribbean Conference, 1975	45	70

131 Louis Braille

1981. International Year for Disabled People. Famous Disabled People. Multicoloured.

592	10c. Type **131**	20	10
593	50c. Sarah Bernhardt	20	10
594	$2 Joseph Pulitzer	70	70
595	$2.50 Henri de Toulouse-Lautrec	1·00	85
MS596	115×90 mm. $5 Franklin Delano Roosevelt	1·00	1·25

132 "Portrait of Fanny Travis Cochran" (Cecilia Beaux)

1981. Decade for Women. Paintings. Mult.

597	10c. Type **132**	10	10
598	50c. "Women with Dove" (Marie Laurencin)	25	10
599	$2 "Portrait of a Young Pupil of David" (Aimee Duvivier)	75	70
600	$2.50 "Self-portrait" (Rosalba Carriera)	90	85
MS601	104×78 mm. "Self-portrait" (Elizabeth Vigee-le-Brun)	1·00	1·25

133 "Adoration of the Magi" (Sfoza)

1981. Christmas. Paintings. Multicoloured.

602	10c. Type **133**	10	10
603	30c. "The Adoration of the Kings" (Orcanga)	20	10
604	$1.50 "The Adoration of the Kings" (Gerard)	45	50
605	$2.50 "The Adoration of the Kings" (Foppa)	75	85

134 1860 1d. Stamp

1981. 1st Anniv of U.P.U. Membership. Mult.

606	10c. Type **134**	20	10
607	30c. 1969 First Anniversary of Caribbean Free Trade Area 25c. commemorative	40	10
608	50c. 1979 Independence $2 commemorative	45	50
609	$2 U.P.U. emblem with U.P.U. and St. Lucia flags	1·40	2·25
MS610	128×109 mm. $5 U.P.U. Headquarters, Berne and G.P.O. Building, Castries	1·00	1·50

135 Scene from Football Match

1982. World Cup Football Championship, Spain.

611	135	10c. multicoloured	60	10
612	-	50c. multicoloured	1·25	15
613	-	$2 multicoloured	1·75	90
614	-	$2.50 multicoloured	2·00	1·00
MS615		104×84 mm.–$5 multicoloured	2·50	2·25

DESIGNS: 50c. to $5, Scenes from different matches.

136 Pigeon Island National Park

1982. Bicent of Battle of the Saints. Mult.

616	10c. Type **136**	25	15
617	35c. Battle scene	80	15
618	50c. Rodney (English admiral) and De Grasse (French admiral)	1·10	65
619	$2.50 Map of the Saints, Martinique and St. Lucia	3·75	4·50
MS620	125×75 mm. Nos. 616/19	6·00	7·00

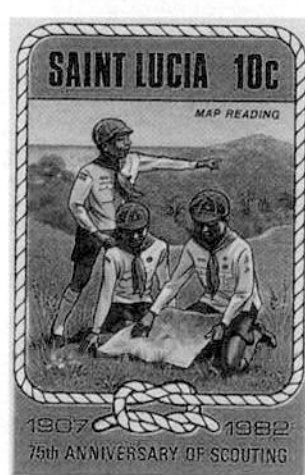
137 Map-reading

1982. 75th Anniv of Boy Scout Movement. Multicoloured.

621	10c. Type **137**	10	10
622	50c. First Aid practice	30	15
623	$1.50 Camping	75	80
624	$2.50 Campfire singsong	1·25	1·50

138 Leeds Castle

1982. 21st Birthday of Princess of Wales. Mult.

625	50c. Type **138**	30	20
626	$2 Princess Diana boarding aircraft	2·25	75
627	$4 Wedding	2·25	1·40
MS628	102×75 mm. $5 Princess of Wales	4·00	2·00

139 "Adoration of the Kings" (detail, Jan Brueghel)

1982. Christmas. Multicoloured.

629	10c. Type **139**	10	10
630	30c. "Nativity" (Lorenzo Costa)	15	10
631	50c. "Virgin and Child" (Fra Filippo Lippi)	25	15
632	80c. "Adoration of the Shepherds" (Nicolas Poussin)	40	55

140 The Pitons

1983. Commonwealth Day. Multicoloured.

633	10c. Type **140**	10	10
634	30c. Tourist beach	15	10
635	50c. Banana harvesting	20	15
636	$2 Flag of St. Lucia	1·50	1·50

141 Crown Agents Headquarters, Millbank, London

1983. 150th Anniv of Crown Agents. Mult.

637	10c. Type **141**	10	10
638	15c. Road construction	10	10
639	50c. Road network map	20	25
640	$2 First St. Lucia stamp	60	1·25

142 Communications at Sea

1983. World Communications Year. Mult.

641	10c. Type **142**	15	10
642	50c. Communications in the air	40	15
643	$1.50 T.V. transmission via satellite	90	75
644	$2.50 Computer communications	1·40	1·25
MS645	107×88 mm. $5 Weather satellite	1·50	1·75

143 Long-jawed Squirrelfish

1983. Coral Reef Fishes. Multicoloured.

646	10c. Type **143**	10	10
647	50c. Banded butterflyfish	20	15
648	$1.50 Black-barred soldierfish	60	1·75
649	$2.50 Yellow-tailed snapper	80	1·60
MS650	122×97 mm. $5 Red hind	2·50	3·25

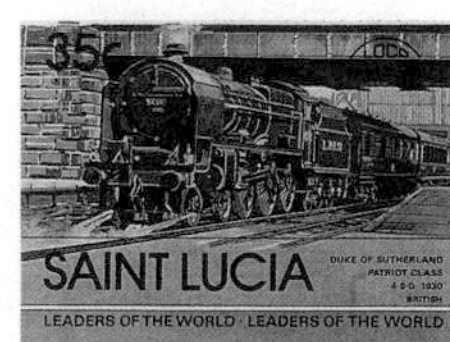
144 "Duke of Sutherland" (1930)

1983. Leaders of the World. Railway Locomotives (1st series).

651	144	35c. multicoloured	15	20
652	-	35c. multicoloured	15	20
653	-	35c. multicoloured	15	20
654	-	35c. multicoloured	15	20
655	-	50c. multicoloured	20	30
656	-	50c. multicoloured	20	30
657	-	50c. multicoloured	20	30
658	-	50c. multicoloured	20	30
659	-	$1 multicoloured	25	50
660	-	$1 multicoloured	25	50
661	-	$1 multicoloured	25	50
662	-	$1 multicoloured	25	50
663	-	$2 multicoloured	30	70
664	-	$2 multicoloured	30	70
665	-	$2 multicoloured	30	70
666	-	$2 multicoloured	30	70

DESIGNS—(The first in each pair shows technical drawings and the second the locomotive at work): Nos. 651/2, "Duke of Sutherland", Great Britain (1930); 653/4, "City of Glasgow", Great Britain (1940); 655/6, "Lord Nelson", Great Britain (1926); 657/8, "Leeds United", Great Britain (1928); 659/60, "Bodmin", Great Britain (1945); 661/2, "Eton", Great Britain (1930); 663/4, "Flying Scotsman", Great Britain (1923); 665/6, "Rocket", Great Britain (1829).

See also Nos. 715/26, 761/76, 824/31 and 858/73.

145 "The Niccolini-Cowper Madonna"

1983. Christmas. 500th Birth Anniv of Raphael. Multicoloured.

667		10c. Type **145**	10	10
668		30c. "The Holy Family with a Palm Tree"	15	10
669		50c. "The Sistine Madonna"	20	30
670		$5 "The Alba Madonna"	70	3·25

146 George III

1984. Leaders of the World. British Monarchs. Multicoloured.

671		5c. Battle of Waterloo	10	15
672		5c. Type **146**	10	15
673		10c. George III at Kew	10	15
674		10c. Kew Palace	10	15
675		35c. Coat of Arms of Elizabeth I	10	20
676		35c. Elizabeth I	10	20
677		60c. Coat of Arms of George III	20	35
678		60c. George III (different)	20	35
679		$1 Elizabeth I at Hatfield	20	40
680		$1 Hatfield Palace	20	40
681		$2.50 Spanish Armada	30	60
682		$2.50 Elizabeth I (different)	30	60

147 Clarke & Co's Drug Store

1984. Historic Buildings. Multicoloured.

683		10c. Type **147**	10	10
684		45c. Colonial architecture (horiz)	30	25
685		65c. Colonial "chattel" house (horiz)	45	35
686		$2.50 Treasury after 1906 earthquake (horiz)	1·75	1·60

148 Logwood

1984. Forestry Resources. Multicoloured.

699		10c. Type **148**	15	10
700		45c. Calabash	40	30
701		65c. Gommier (vert)	35	55
702		$2.50 Raintree	65	2·75

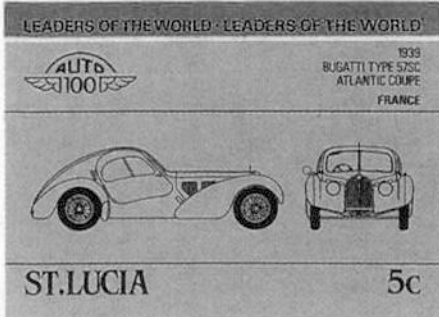

149 Bugatti Type "57SC Atlantic Coupe"

1984. Leaders of the World. Automobiles (1st series). The first in each pair showing technical drawings and the second paintings.

703	**149**	5c. black, lilac and yellow	10	10
704	-	5c. multicoloured	10	10
705	-	10c. black, blue and red	10	10
706	-	10c. multicoloured	10	10
707	-	$1 black, green and brown	15	25
708	-	$1 multicoloured	15	25
709	-	$2.50 black, pink and blue	30	40
710	-	$2.50 multicoloured	30	40

DESIGNS: Nos. 703/4, Bugatti Type "57SC Atlantic Coupe"; 705/6, Chevrolet "Bel Air Convertible"; 707/8, Alfa Romeo "1750 GS (Zagato)"; 709/10, Duesenberg "SJ Roadster".

See also Nos. 745/60, 789/96 and 902/13.

150 Pygmy Gecko

1984. Endangered Wildlife. Multicoloured.

711		10c. Type **150**	20	10
712		45c. Maria Island ground lizard	35	50
713		65c. Green iguana	40	85
714		$2.50 Couresse snake	45	3·50

1984. Leaders of the World. Railway Locomotives (2nd series). As T 144, the first in each pair showing technical drawings and the second the locomotive at work.

715		1c. multicoloured	10	10
716		1c. multicoloured	10	10
717		15c. multicoloured	10	15
718		15c. multicoloured	10	15
719		50c. multicoloured	15	15
720		50c. multicoloured	15	15
721		75c. multicoloured	15	20
722		75c. multicoloured	15	20
723		$1 multicoloured	20	25
724		$1 multicoloured	20	25
725		$2 multicoloured	25	35
726		$2 multicoloured	25	35

DESIGNS: Nos. 715/16, "Taw", Great Britain (1897); 717/18, Class Be 6/8 "Crocodile" electric locomotive, Switzerland (1920); 719/20, "The Countess", Great Britain (1903); 721/2, Class GE 6/6 electric locomotive, Switzerland (1921); 723/4, Class P8, Germany (1906); 725/6, "Adler", Germany (1835).

151 Men's Volleyball

1984. Leaders of the World. Olympic Games, Los Angeles. Multicoloured.

727		5c. Type **151**	10	10
728		5c. Women's volleyball	10	10
729		10c. Women's hurdles	10	10
730		10c. Men's hurdles	10	10
731		65c. Show jumping	15	20
732		65c. Dressage	15	20
733		$2.50 Women's gymnastics	40	50
734		$2.50 Men's gymnastics	40	50

152 Glass of Wine and Flowers

1984. Christmas. Multicoloured.

735		10c. Type **152**	10	10
736		35c. Priest and decorated altar	10	10
737		65c. Nativity scene	15	25
738		$3 Holy Family	50	1·50
MS739		147×77 mm. Nos. 735/8	1·60	4·50

153 Slaves preparing Manioc

1984. 150th Anniv of Abolition of Slavery. Each black and brown.

740		10c. Type **153**	10	10
741		35c. Sifting and cooking cassava flour	10	10
742		55c. Cooking pot, and preparing tobacco	10	20
743		$5 Stripping tobacco leaves for twist tobacco	90	2·50
MS744		154×110 mm. As Nos. 740/3, but without dates and side inscription and with the face values in different positions	1·50	4·50

1984. Leaders of the World. Automobiles (2nd series). As T 149, the first in each pair showing technical drawings and the second paintings.

745		10c. black, green and brown	10	10
746		10c. multicoloured	10	10
747		30c. black, blue and green	15	15
748		30c. multicoloured	15	15
749		55c. black, yellow and brown	15	30
750		55c. multicoloured	15	30
751		65c. black, grey and lilac	15	35
752		65c. multicoloured	15	35
753		75c. black, brown and red	15	35
754		75c. multicoloured	15	35
755		$1 black, brown and blue	15	40
756		$1 multicoloured	15	40
757		$2 black, green and red	20	50
758		$2 multicoloured	20	50
759		$3 black, brown and red	25	60
760		$3 multicoloured	25	60

DESIGNS: Nos. 745/6, Panhard and Levassor; 747/8, N.S.U. "RO-80" Saloon; 749/50, Abarth "Bialbero"; 751/2, TVR "Vixen 2500M"; 753/4, Ford "Mustang" Convertible; 755/6, Ford "Model T"; 757/8, Aston Martin "DB3S"; 759/60, Chrysler "Imperial CG Dual Cowl" Phaeton.

1985. Leaders of the World. Railway Locomotives (3rd series). As T 144, the first in each pair showing technical drawings and the second the locomotive at work.

761		5c. multicoloured	10	20
762		5c. multicoloured	10	20
763		15c. multicoloured	10	20
764		15c. multicoloured	10	20
765		35c. multicoloured	15	20
766		35c. multicoloured	15	20
767		60c. multicoloured	15	25
768		60c. multicoloured	15	25
769		75c. multicoloured	15	30
770		75c. multicoloured	15	30
771		$1 multicoloured	15	30
772		$1 multicoloured	15	30
773		$2 multicoloured	25	45
774		$2 multicoloured	25	45
775		$2.50 multicoloured	30	55
776		$2.50 multicoloured	30	55

DESIGNS: Nos. 761/2, Class C53, Japan (1928); 763/4, Class L No. 39, India (1885); 765/6, Class B18¼, Australia (1926); 767/8, "Owain Glyndwr", Great Britain (1923); 769/70, "Lion", Great Britain (1838); 771/2, LNWR locomotive, Great Britain (1873); 773/4, Class Q6 No. 2238, Great Britain (1921); 775/6, Class H No. 106, Great Britain (1920).

154 Girl Guide Badge in Shield and Crest of St. Lucia

1985. 75th Anniv of Girl Guide Movement and 60th Anniv of Guiding in St. Lucia.

777	**154**	10c. multicoloured	50	10
778	**154**	35c. multicoloured	1·50	15
779	**154**	65c. multicoloured	2·00	75
780	**154**	$3 multicoloured	4·25	7·50

155 "Clossiana selene"

1985. Leaders of the World. Butterflies. Mult.

781		15c. Type **155**	10	10
782		15c. "Inachis io"	10	10
783		40c. "Philaethria dido"	10	15
784		40c. "Callicore sorana"	10	15
785		60c. "Kallima inachus"	15	15
786		60c. "Hypanartia paullus"	15	15
787		$2.25 "Morpho helena"	25	50
788		$2.25 "Ornithoptera meridionalis"	25	50

1985. Leaders of the World. Automobiles (3rd series). As T 149, the first in each pair showing technical drawings and the second paintings.

789		15c. black, blue and red	10	10
790		15c. multicoloured	10	10
791		50c. black, orange and red	15	20
792		50c. multicoloured	15	20
793		$1 black, green and orange	15	20
794		$1 multicoloured	15	20
795		$1.50 black, green and brown	20	35
796		$1.50 multicoloured	20	35

DESIGNS: 789/90, Hudson "Eight" (1940); 791/2, KdF (1937); 793/4, Kissel "Goldbug" (1925); 795/6, Ferrari "246 GTS" (1973).

156 Grenadier, 70th Regiment, c. 1775

1985. Military Uniforms. Multicoloured.

928		5c. Type **156**	30	60
798		10c. Officer, Grenadier Company, 14th Regiment, 1780	40	15
930		15c. Private, Battalion Company, 2nd West India Regiment, 1803	45	35
799		20c. Officer, Battalion Company, 46th Regiment, 1781	60	30
800		25c. Officer, Royal Artillery, c. 1782	60	15
801		30c. Officer, Royal Engineers, 1782	80	30
802		35c. Officer, Battalion Company, 54th Regiment, 1782	70	20
935		45c. Private, Grenadier Company, 14th Regiment, 1782	70	50
936		50c. Gunner, Royal Artillery, 1796	80	60
937		60c. Officer, Battalion Company, 5th Regiment, 1778	90	70
805		65c. Private, Battalion Company, 85th Regiment, c. 1796	90	55
806		75c. Private, Battalion Company, 76th Regiment, c. 1796	90	80
940		80c. Officer, Battalion Company, 27th Regiment, c. 1780	1·25	90
807		90c. Private, Battalion Company, 81st Regiment, c. 1796	1·00	90
808		$1 Sergeant, 74th (Highland) Regiment, 1796	1·10	90
943		$2.50 Private, Light Company, 93rd Regiment, 1803	3·25	4·50
944		$5 Private, Battalion Company, 1st West India Regiment, 1803	4·00	9·00
811		$15 Officer, Royal Artillery, 1850	8·00	20·00
946		$20 Private, Grenadier Company, 46th Regiment, 1778	18·00	27·00

157 Messerschmitt Bf 109E

1985. Leaders of the World. Military Aircraft. The first in each pair shows paintings and the second technical drawings.

812	157	5c. multicoloured	10	15
813	-	5c. black, blue and yellow	10	15
814	-	55c. multicoloured	25	40
815	-	55c. black, blue and yellow	25	40
816	-	60c. multicoloured	25	40
817	-	60c. black, blue and yellow	25	40
818	-	$2 multicoloured	40	75
819	-	$2 black, blue and yellow	40	75

DESIGNS: Nos. 812/13, Messerschmitt Bf 109E; 814/15, Avro Type 683 Lancaster Mk I; 816/17, North American P-51D Mustang; 818/19, Supermarine Spitfire Mk II.

158 Magnificent Frigate Birds ("Frigate Bird"), Frigate Island Bird Sanctuary

1985. Nature Reserves. Multicoloured.

820	10c. Type **158**	35	20
821	35c. Mangrove cuckoo, Scorpion Island, Savannes Bay	65	45
822	65c. Lesser yellowlegs ("Yellow Sandpiper"), Maria Island Reserve	75	85
823	$3 Audubon's shearwaters, Lapins Island Reserve	1·00	5·00

1985. Leaders of the World Railway Locomotives (4th series). As T 144. The first in each pair shows technical drawings and the second the locomotive at work.

824	10c. multicoloured	10	10
825	10c. multicoloured	10	10
826	30c. multicoloured	15	15
827	30c. multicoloured	15	15
828	75c. multicoloured	20	25
829	75c. multicoloured	20	25
830	$2.50 multicoloured	40	70
831	$2.50 multicoloured	40	70

DESIGNS: Nos. 824/5, Tank locomotive No. 28, Great Britain (1897); 826/7, Class M No. 1621, Great Britain (1893); 828/9, Class "Dunalastair", Great Britain (1896); 830/1, "Big Bertha" type No. 2290, Great Britain (1919).

159 Queen Elizabeth the Queen Mother

1985. Leaders of the World. Life and Times of Queen Elizabeth the Queen Mother. Various portraits.

832	159	40c. multicoloured	10	20
833	-	40c. multicoloured	10	20
834	-	75c. multicoloured	15	25
835	-	75c. multicoloured	15	25
836	-	$1.10 multicoloured	15	35
837	-	$1.10 multicoloured	15	35
838	-	$1.75 multicoloured	20	55
839	-	$1.75 multicoloured	20	55
MS840		84×114 mm – $2 multicoloured; $2 multicoloured	60	1·40

Each value was issued in pairs showing a floral pattern across the bottom of the portraits which stops short of the left-hand edge on the first stamp and of the right-hand edge on the second.

160 "Youth playing Banjo" (Wayne Whitfield)

1985. International Youth Year. Paintings by Young St. Lucians.

841	160	10c. black, blue and mauve	20	10
842	-	45c. multicoloured	60	25
843	-	75c. multicoloured	60	50
844	-	$3.50 multicoloured	1·40	3·00
MS845		123×86 mm. – $5 multicoloured	1·25	3·50

DESIGNS—VERT (as T **160**): 45c. "Motor-cyclist" (Mark Maragh); 75c. "Boy and Girl at Pitons" (Bartholomew Eugene); $3.50, "Abstract" (Lyndon Samuel). HORIZ (80×55 mm): $5 Young people and St. Lucia landscapes.

1985. Royal Visit. Nos. 649, 685/6, 702, 713, 778 and 836/7 optd CARIBBEAN ROYAL VISIT 1985.

846	154	35c. multicoloured	5·50	3·00
847	-	65c. mult (No. 685)	1·00	2·75
848	-	65c. mult (No. 713)	5·00	3·75
849	-	$1.10 mult (No. 836)	5·00	8·00
850	-	$1.10 mult (No. 837)	5·00	8·00
851	-	$2.50 mult (No. 649)	7·00	8·00
852	-	$2.50 mult (No. 686)	1·00	3·50
853	-	$2.50 mult (No. 702)	1·00	3·50

161 "Papa Jab"

1985. Christmas. Masqueraders. Mult.

854	10c. Type **161**	30	10
855	45c. "Paille Bananne"	40	30
856	65c. "Cheval Bois"	40	1·50
MS857	70×83 mm. $4 "Madonna and Child" (Dunstan St. Omer)	1·00	1·90

1986. Leaders of the World. Railway Locomotives (5th series). As T 144. The first in each pair shows technical drawings and the second the locomotive at work.

858	5c. multicoloured	10	15
859	5c. multicoloured	10	15
860	15c. multicoloured	15	15
861	15c. multicoloured	15	15
862	30c. multicoloured	20	30
863	30c. multicoloured	20	30
864	60c. multicoloured	25	40
865	60c. multicoloured	25	40
866	75c. multicoloured	30	50
867	75c. multicoloured	30	50
868	$1 multicoloured	35	60
869	$1 multicoloured	35	60
870	$2.25 multicoloured	45	80
871	$2.25 multicoloured	45	80
872	$3 multicoloured	45	80
873	$3 multicoloured	45	80

DESIGNS: Nos. 858/9, Cog locomotive "Tip Top", U.S.A. (1983); 860/1, Electric locomotive "Stephenson", Great Britain (1975); 862/3, Class D No. 737, Great Britain (1901); 864/5, No. 13 Class electric locomotive, Great Britain (1922); 866/7, Electric locomotive "Electra", Great Britain (1954); 868/9, "City of Newcastle", Great Britain (1922); 870/1, Von Kruckenburg propeller-driven railcar, Germany (1930); 872/3, No. 860, Japan (1893).

162 Campfire Cooking Utensils

1986. 75th Annivs of Girl Guide Movement and Boy Scouts of America. Two sheets, each 85×113 mm, containing vert designs as T 162. Multicoloured.

MS874	$4 Type **162**; $4 Scout salute	2·50	4·00
MS875	$6 Wickerwork; $6 Lady Baden-Powell	2·75	4·25

The two stamps in each sheet were printed together, se-tenant, forming a composite design.

Nos. **MS**874/5 exist with plain or decorative margins.

Overprints on these miniature sheets commemorating "Capex '87" International Stamp Exhibition, Toronto, were not authorised by the St. Lucia administration.

162a Queen Elizabeth II

1986. 60th Birthday of Queen Elizabeth II (1st issue). Multicoloured.

876	5c. Type **162a**	10	10
877	$1 Princess Elizabeth	15	30
878	$3.50 Queen Elizabeth II (different)	40	1·10
879	$6 In Canberrra, 1982 (vert)	55	1·60
MS880	85×115 mm. $8 Queen Elizabeth II (different)	3·25	6·00

163 Queen Elizabeth and Marian Home

1986. 60th Birthday of Queen Elizabeth II (2nd issue). Multicoloured.

881	10c. Type **163**	50	15
882	45c. Queen addressing rally, Mindoo Phillip Park, 1985	85	35
883	50c. Queen opening Leon Hess Comprehensive School, 1985	95	50
884	$5 Queen Elizabeth and Government House, Castries	3·25	5·50
MS885	121×85 mm. $7 Queen Elizabeth and Royal Yacht "Britannia", Castries	4·75	7·50

164 Pope John Paul II kissing Ground, Castries Airport

1986. Visit of Pope John Paul II. Multicoloured.

886	55c. Type **164**	1·25	80
887	60c. Pope and St. Joseph's Convent	1·25	90
888	80c. Pope and Castries Catholic Cathedral (vert)	1·75	2·25
MS889	85×123 mm. $6 Pope John Paul II (vert)	8·00	9·00

164a Miss Sarah Ferguson

1986. Royal Wedding (1st issue). Multicoloured.

890	80c. Type **164a**	65	85
891	80c. Prince Andrew	65	85
892	$2 Prince Andrew and Miss Sarah Ferguson (horiz)	90	2·00
893	$2 Prince Andrew with Mrs. Nancy Reagan (horiz)	90	2·00

See also Nos. 897/901.

165 Peace Corps Teacher with Students

1986. 25th Anniv of United States Peace Corps. Multicoloured.

894	80c. Type **165**	30	40
895	$2 President John Kennedy (vert)	90	1·75
896	$3.50 Peace Corps emblem between arms of St. Lucia and U.S.A.	1·25	3·00

166 Prince Andrew in Carriage

1986. Royal Wedding (2nd issue). Mult.

897	50c. Type **166**	40	30
898	80c. Miss Sarah Ferguson in coach	50	50
899	$1 Duke and Duchess of York at altar	55	60
900	$3 Duke and Duchess of York in carriage	1·00	2·75
MS901	115×85 mm. $7 Duke and Duchess of York on Palace balcony after wedding (horiz)	3·75	6·50

1986. Automobiles (4th series). As T 149, the first in each pair showing technical drawings and the second paintings.

902	20c. multicoloured	15	15
903	20c. multicoloured	15	15
904	50c. multicoloured	15	20
905	50c. multicoloured	15	20
906	60c. multicoloured	15	20
907	60c. multicoloured	15	20
908	$1 multicoloured	15	20
909	$1 multicoloured	15	20
910	$1.50 multicoloured	20	20
911	$1.50 multicoloured	20	20
912	$3 multicoloured	30	45
913	$3 multicoloured	30	45

DESIGNS: Nos. 902/3, AMC "AMX" (1969); 904/5, Russo-Baltique (1912); 906/7, Lincoln "K.B" (1932); 908/9, Rolls-Royce "Phantom II Continental" (1933); 910/11, Buick "Century" (1939); 912/13, Chrysler "300 C" (1957).

167 Chak-Chak Band

1986. Tourism (1st series). Multicoloured.

914	15c. Type **167**	15	10
915	45c. Folk dancing	25	15
916	80c. Steel band	40	55
917	$5 Limbo dancing	1·00	3·00
MS918	157×109 mm. $10 Fire-eating	3·75	8·50

See also Nos. 988/92.

168 St. Ann Catholic Church, Mon Repos

1986. Christmas. Multicoloured.

919	10c. Type **168**	15	10
920	40c. St. Joseph the Worker Catholic Church, Gros Islet	30	15
921	80c. Holy Trinity Anglican Church, Castries	45	60
922	$4 Our Lady of the Assumption Catholic Church, Soufriere (vert)	90	3·25
MS923	120×101 mm. $7 St. Lucy Catholic Church, Micoud	2·50	6·50

169 Outline Map of St. Lucia

1987

924B	169	5c. black and brown	20	20
925A	169	10c. black and green	20	20
926A	169	45c. black and orange	50	50
927B	169	50c. black and blue	50	50
927cA	169	$1 black and red	75	75

170 Statue of Liberty and Flags of France and U.S.A.

1987. Cent of Statue of Liberty (1986). Mult.

947	15c. Type **170**	60	10
948	80c. Statue and "Mauretania I" (liner)	1·50	55
949	$1 Statue and Concorde	2·75	1·50
950	$5 Statue and flying boat at sunset	3·00	5·50
MS951	107×88 mm. $6 Statue and Manhattan at night	3·00	4·50

171 First Cadastral Survey Map and Surveying Instruments, 1775

1987. New Cadastral Survey of St. Lucia. Multicoloured.

955	15c. Type **171**	60	15
956	60c. Map and surveying instruments, 1814	1·25	85
957	$1 Map and surveying instruments, 1888	1·50	1·50
958	$2.50 Cadastral survey map and surveying instruments, 1987	2·75	4·25

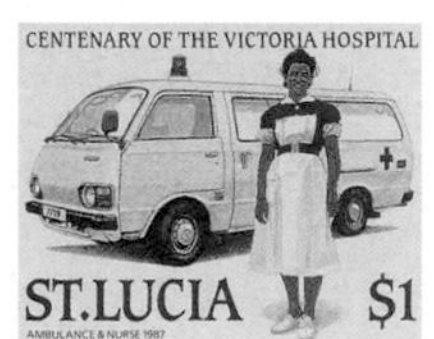

172 Ambulance and Nurse, 1987

1987. Cent of Victoria Hospital, Castries. Mult.

959	**172**	$1 multicoloured	2·25	2·75
960	-	$1 blue	2·25	2·75
961	-	$2 multicoloured	2·75	3·25
962	-	$2 blue	2·75	3·25
MS963		86×68 mm. – $4.50 multicoloured	6·50	8·00

DESIGNS: No. 960, Nurse and carrying hammock, 1913; 961, $2 Victoria Hospital, 1987; 962, Victoria Hospital 1887; $4.50, Hospital gates, 1987.

173 "The Holy Family"

1987. Christmas. Paintings. Multicoloured.

964	15c. Type **173**	30	10
965	50c. "Adoration of the Shepherds"	60	30
966	60c. "Adoration of the Magi"	60	80
967	90c. "Madonna and Child"	85	2·25
MS968	82×67 mm. $6 Type **173**	3·00	5·50

174 St. Lucia Amazon perched on Branch

1987. St. Lucia Amazon. Multicoloured.

969	15c. Type **174**	2·00	40
970	35c. Pair in flight	3·00	55
971	50c. Perched on branch (rear view)	4·00	2·25
972	$1 Emerging from tree	5·50	5·00

175 Carib Clay Zemi

1988. Amerindian Artifacts. Multicoloured.

973	25c. Type **175**	15	10
974	30c. Troumassee cylinder	20	15
975	80c. Three pointer stone	45	45
976	$3.50 Dauphine petroglyph	1·75	3·50

176 East Caribbean Currency

1988. 50th Anniv of St. Lucia Co-operative Bank. Multicoloured.

977	10c. Type **176**	20	10
978	45c. Castries branch	55	35
979	60c. As 45c.	75	95
980	80c. Vieux Fort branch	1·25	1·60

177 Rural Telephone Exchange

1988. 50th Anniv of Cable and Wireless (West Indies) Ltd. Multicoloured.

981	15c. Type **177**	20	15
982	25c. Early and modern telephones	20	15
983	80c. St. Lucia Teleport dish aerial	50	45
984	$2.50 Map showing Eastern Caribbean Microwave System	3·25	2·75

178 Stained Glass Window

1988. Cent of Methodist Church in St. Lucia. Mult.

985	15c. Type **178**	10	10
986	80c. Church interior	40	45
987	$3.50 Methodist Church, Castries	1·50	2·25

179 Garnished Lobsters

1988. Tourism (2nd series). Designs showing local delicacies. Multicoloured.

988	10c. Type **179**	70	1·00
989	30c. Cocktail and tourists at buffet	85	1·10
990	80c. Fresh fruits and roasted breadfruit	1·25	1·60
991	$2.50 Barbecued red snappers (fish)	2·50	2·75
MS992	80×104 mm. $5.50 Fruit stall, Castries market	2·25	3·25

Nos. 988/91 were printed together, se-tenant, forming a composite design of tourists at beach barbecue.

1988. 300th Anniv of Lloyd's of London. As T 152a of St. Helena.

1004	10c. black, lilac and brown	45	15
1005	60c. multicoloured	1·25	75
1006	80c. multicoloured	1·60	1·25
1007	$2.50 multicoloured	3·00	4·50

DESIGNS—VERT: 10c. San Francisco earthquake; $2.50, Castries fire, 1948. HORIZ: 60c. Castries Harbour; 80c. "Lady Nelson" (hospital ship), 1942.

180 Snow on the Mountain

1988. Christmas. Flowers. Multicoloured.

1008	15c. Type **180**	30	10
1009	45c. Christmas candle	55	50
1010	60c. Balisier	70	90
1011	80c. Poinsettia	1·00	1·60
MS1012	79×75 mm. $5.50 Christmas flower arrangement	2·00	3·50

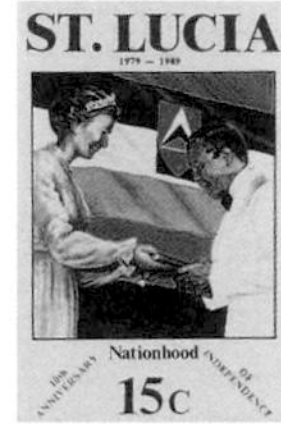

181 Princess Alexandra presenting Constitution

1989. 10th Anniv of Independence. Mult.

1013	15c. Type **181**	40	15
1014	80c. Geothermal well	1·10	60
1015	$1 Sir Arthur Lewis Community College	70	60
1016	$2.50 Pointe Seraphine shopping centre	1·25	2·25
MS1017	47×62 mm. $5 Man with national flag	2·25	3·25

182 "Gerronema citrinum"

1989. Fungi. Multicoloured.

1022	15c. Type **182**	1·25	30
1023	25c. "Lepiota spiculata"	1·50	30
1024	50c. "Calocybe cyanocephala"	2·50	1·10
1025	$5 "Russula puiggarii"	7·00	9·50

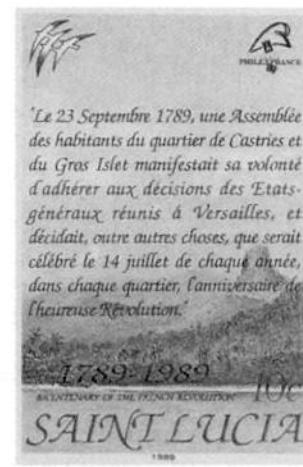

183 Local Revolutionary Declaration, 1789, and View of St. Lucia

1989. Bicentenary of the French Revolution. Designs include the "PHILEXFRANCE". International Stamp Exhibition logo. Mult.

1026	10c. Type **183**	40	15
1027	60c. Hoisting Revolutionary flag, Morne Fortune, 1791 (horiz)	2·50	80
1028	$1 Declaration of Rights of Man and view of St. Lucia	2·50	1·50
1029	$3.50 Arrival of Capt. La Crosse, Gros Islet, 1792 (horiz)	8·50	9·00

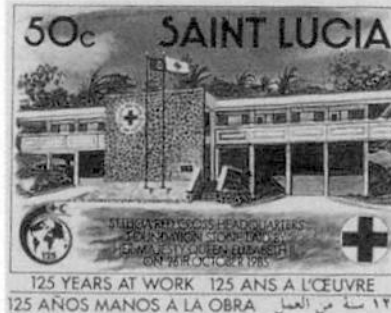

184 Red Cross Headquarters, St. Lucia

1989. 125th Anniv of Int Red Cross. Mult.

1030	50c. Type **184**	1·25	1·25
1031	80c. Red Cross seminar, Castries, 1987	1·75	2·00
1032	$1 Red Cross ambulance	2·00	2·25

185 Christmas Lantern

1989. Christmas.

1033	**185**	10c. multicoloured	25	10
1034	-	50c. multicoloured	65	40
1035	-	90c. multicoloured	1·00	1·25
1036	-	$1 multicoloured	1·25	1·25

DESIGNS: 50c. to $1 various decorative "building" lanterns.

186 Gwi Gwi

1990. Endangered Trees. Multicoloured.

1081	10c. China	50	50
1082	15c. Latanier	50	20
1039	20c. Type **186**	1·00	1·00
1084	25c. L'encens	30	20
1085	50c. Bois lele	30	35
1042	80c. Bois d'amande	1·00	40
1043	95c. Mahot piman grand bois	1·75	1·00
1044	$1 Balata	1·25	75
1045	$1.50 Pencil cedar	2·50	2·50
1046	$2.50 Bois cendre	4·50	4·50
1047	$5 Lowye cannelle	6·50	7·00
1048	$25 Chalantier grand bois	15·00	22·00

187 Father Tapon and Original College Building

1990. International Literacy Year. Centenary of St. Mary's College, Castries. Multicoloured.

1049	30c. Type **187**	15	15
1050	45c. Brother M. C. Collins and St. Mary's College	25	25
1051	75c. Literacy class	45	55
1052	$2 Children approaching "door to knowledge"	1·50	2·25

1990. 90th Birthday of Queen Elizabeth the Queen Mother. As T 161a of St. Helena.

1053	50c. multicoloured	1·00	35
1054	$5 black and blue	3·75	4·75

DESIGNS—(21×36 mm): 50c. Crowning of Queen Consort, 1937. (29×37 mm): $5 Queen Elizabeth arriving at New Theatre, London 1949.

1990. "EXPO 90" International Garden and Greenery Exhibition, Osaka. No. 1047 optd EXPO '90 and emblem.

1055	$5 Lowye cannelle	3·50	4·00

189 "Adoration of the Magi" (Rubens)

1990. Christmas. Religious Paintings. Mult.

1056	10c. Type **189**	50	20
1057	30c. "Adoration of the Shepherds" (Murillo)	1·25	20
1058	80c. "Adoration of the Magi" (Rubens) (different)	1·75	75
1059	$5 "Adoration of the Shepherds" (Philippe de Champaigne)	6·50	8·50

190 "Vistafjord" (liner)

1991. Cruise Ships. Multicoloured.

1060	50c. Type **190**	1·50	40
1061	80c. "Windstar" (schooner)	2·00	1·10
1062	$1 "Unicorn" (brig)	2·25	1·50
1063	$2.50 Game-fishing launch	4·75	7·50
MS1064	82×65 mm. $5 Ships in Castries Harbour	11·00	11·00

191 "Battus polydamas"

1991. Butterflies. Multicoloured.

1065	60c. Type **191**	2·00	65
1066	80c. "Strymon simaethis"	2·25	1·10
1067	$1 "Mestra cana"	2·75	1·25
1068	$2.50 "Allosmaitia piplea"	5·50	7·50

192 Mural, Jacmel Church

1991. Christmas. Paintings by Duncan St. Omer. Multicoloured.

1069	10c. Type **192**	30	10
1070	15c. "Red Madonna" (vert)	40	10
1071	80c. Mural, Monchy Church	1·50	70
1072	$5 "Blue Madonna" (vert)	4·50	7·00

193 Yacht and Map

1991. Atlantic Rally for Cruising Yachts. Multicoloured.

1073	60c. Type **193**	1·50	1·50
1074	80c. Yachts off St. Lucia	1·75	1·75

1992. Organization of East Caribbean States. 500th Anniv of Discovery of America by Columbus. As T 66 of St. Kitts. Multicoloured.

1075	$1 Columbus meeting Amerindians	2·25	1·75
1076	$2 Ships approaching island	3·25	3·50

194 Amerindian Village

1992. Discovery of St. Lucia. Multicoloured.

1077	15c. Type **194**	40	20
1078	40c. Ships of Juan de la Cosa and islands, 1499	2·00	50
1079	50c. Columbus sailing between Martinique and St. Lucia, 1502	2·50	70
1080	$5 Legendary shipwreck of Gimie	7·50	10·00

195 "Virgin and Child" (Delaroche)

1992. Christmas. Religious Paintings. Mult.

1092	10c. Type **195**	65	20
1093	15c. "The Holy Family" (Rubens)	65	20
1094	60c. "Virgin and Child" (Luini)	2·50	1·75
1095	80c. "Virgin and Child" (Sassoferrato)	2·50	2·25

196 "Death" and Gravestone

1993. Anti-drugs Campaign.

1096	**196**	$5 multicoloured	6·00	7·00

197 "Gros Piton from Delcer, Choiseul" (Dunstan St. Omer)

1993. Carib Art. Multicoloured.

1097	20c. Type **197**	20	10
1098	75c. "Reduit Bay" (Derek Walcott)	75	75
1099	$5 "Woman and Child at River" (Nancy Cole Auguste)	4·25	7·00

198 "The Madonna of the Rosary" (Murillo)

1993. Christmas. Religious Paintings. Mult.

1100	15c. Type **198**	20	10
1101	60c. "The Madonna and Child" (Van Dyck)	65	60
1102	95c. "The Annunciation" (Champaigne)	1·10	1·50

199 The Pitons

1994. Bicentenary of the Abolition of Slavery in St. Lucia.

1103	**199**	20c. multicoloured	65	45
MS1104		115×75 mm. $5 multicoloured	4·50	6·00

200 "Euphorbia pulcherrima"

1994. Christmas. Flowers. Multicoloured.

1105	20c. Type **200**	15	10
1106	75c. "Heliconia rostrata"	55	50
1107	95c. "Alpinia purpurata"	75	75
1108	$5.50 "Anthurium andreanum"	3·75	7·00

See also Nos. 1122/5 and 1156/9.

201 18th-century Map of St. Lucia

1995. Bicentenary of Battle of Rabot. Multicoloured.

1109	20c. Type **201**	25	15
1110	75c. Insurgent slaves	60	55
1111	95c. 9th Foot (Royal Norfolk Regiment) attacking	1·10	1·40
MS1112	150×100 mm. $5.50 Plan of battle	3·25	4·00

1995. 50th Anniv of End of Second World War. As T 182a of St. Helena. Multicoloured.

1113	20c. St. Lucian members of the A.T.S.	40	15
1114	75c. German U-boat off St. Lucia	1·25	80
1115	95c. Bren gun-carriers of the Caribbean Regiment, North Africa	1·50	1·25
1116	$1.10 Supermarine Spitfire Mk V "St. Lucia"	1·75	2·00
MS1117	75×85 mm. $5.50 Reverse of 1939–45 War Medal (vert)	2·75	3·50

201a Sud Aviation SE 330 Puma Helicopter, Cambodia, 1991–93

1995. 50th Anniv of United Nations. Multicoloured.

1118	10c. Type **201a**	15	10
1119	65c. Renault lorry, Bosnia, 1995	50	50
1120	$1.35 Transall C-160 aircraft, Cambodia, 1991–93	95	1·40
1121	$5 Douglas DC-3 aircraft, Korea, 1950–54	3·75	6·00

1995. Christmas. Flowers. As T 200, each including Madonna and Child. Multicoloured.

1122	15c. "Eranthemum nervosum"	15	10
1123	70c. Bougainvillea	45	45
1124	$1.10 "Allamanda cathartica"	70	90
1125	$3 "Rosa sinensis"	1·75	3·50

202 Calypso King

1996. Carnival. Multicoloured.

1126	20c. Type **202**	70	10
1127	65c. Carnival dancers	1·50	55
1128	95c. King of the Band float	2·00	85
1129	$3 Carnival Queen	4·00	6·50

203 Dry River Bed

1996. Inaug of New Irrigation Project. Mult.

1130	20c. Type **203**	10	10
1131	65c. People bathing in stream	40	45
1132	$5 New dam	3·00	4·75

204 Produce Market

1996. Tourism. Multicoloured.

1133	65c. Type **204**	45	45
1134	75c. Horse-riding on beach	55	55
1135	95c. Bride and groom	70	75
1136	$5 Jazz band	2·75	4·50

205 Athlete of 1896

1996. Centenary of Modern Olympic Games. Multicoloured.

1137	15c. Type **205**	65	85
1138	15c. Athlete of 1996	65	85
1139	75c. Catamaran and dinghy	1·75	2·00
1140	75c. Sailing dinghies	1·75	2·00

Nos. 1137/8 and 1139/40 respectively were printed together, se-tenant, forming composite designs.

206 Spanish Royal Standard, 1502, and Caravel

1996. Flags and Ships. Multicoloured.

1141	10c. Type **206**	1·00	30
1142	15c. Skull and crossbones, 1550, and pirate carrack	1·75	30
1143	20c. Dutch royal standard, 1650, and galleon	70	20
1144	25c. Union Jack, 1739, and ship of the line	75	25
1145	40c. French royal standard, 1750, and ship of the line	2·00	40
1146	50c. Martinique and St. Lucia flag, 1766, and French brig	1·00	40
1147	55c. White Ensign, 1782, and frigate squadron	1·00	40
1148	65c. Red Ensign, 1782, and frigates in action	1·00	50
1149	75c. Blue Ensign, 1782, and brig	1·25	60
1150	95c. The Tricolour, 1792, and French frigate	1·25	60
1151	$1 Union Jack, 1801, and West Indies Grand Fleet	1·25	70
1152	$2.50 Confederate States of America flag, 1861, and cruiser	2·50	2·00

1153	$5 Canadian flag, 1915–19, and "V" or "W" class destroyer	4·00	4·00
1154	$10 United States flag, 1942–48, and "Fletcher" class destroyer	7·00	8·00
1155	$25 Flag of St. Lucia and "Royal Princess" (cruise liner)	14·00	16·00

The design of the $5 value is incorrect. There were no "V" or "W" class destroyers in the Canadian Navy where ships up to 1965 flew the White Ensign.

1996. Christmas. Flowers. As T 200, each including Madonna and Child. Multicoloured.

1156	20c. "Cordia sebestena"	15	10
1157	75c. "Cryptostegia grandiflora"	50	50
1158	95c. "Hibiscus elatus"	65	65
1159	$5 "Caularthron bicornutum"	4·00	6·00

1997. Golden Wedding of Queen Elizabeth and Prince Philip. As T 192a of St. Helena. Multicoloured.

1160	75c. Queen Elizabeth at Warwick, 1996	1·25	1·40
1161	75c. Prince Philip with carriage horses	1·25	1·40
1162	95c. Prince Philip	1·25	1·40
1163	95c. Queen in phaeton at Trooping the Colour	1·25	1·40
1164	$1 Queen Elizabeth and Prince Philip at Sandringham, 1982	1·25	1·40
1165	$1 Princess Anne show jumping	1·25	1·40
MS1166	110×70 mm. $5 Queen Elizabeth and Prince Philip in landau (horiz)	3·25	4·00

Nos. 1160/1, 1162/3 and 1164/5 respectively were printed together, se-tenant, with the backgrounds forming composite designs.

207 "St. George" capsized, 1935

1997. Marine Disasters. Multicoloured.

1167	20c. Type **207**	1·10	25
1168	55c. Wreck of "Belle of Bath" (freighter)	1·75	30
1169	$1 "Ethelgonda" (freighter) aground on rocks, 1897	2·75	1·50
1170	$2.50 Hurricane, 1817	3·50	6·00

208 Attack on Praslin

1997. Bicentenary of the Brigands' War. Mult.

1171	20c. Type **208**	80	25
1172	55c. British troops at Battle of Dennery	1·40	40
1173	70c. Discussing peace agreement	1·40	1·00
1174	$3 Members of 1st West India Regiment	4·00	6·00

209 "Roseau Church" (detail, Dunstan St. Omer)

1997. Christmas. Paintings by Dunstan St. Omer. Multicoloured.

1175	20c. Type **209**	20	10
1176	60c. Altarpiece, Regional Seminary, Trinidad	45	35
1177	95c. "Our Lady of the Presentation", Trinidad	60	60
1178	$5 "The Four Days of Creation"	2·75	5·00

210 Diana, Princess of Wales

1998. Diana, Princess of Wales Commemoration.

1179	**210** $1 multicoloured	60	65

211 Signatories to CARICOM Treaty, 1973

1998. 25th Anniv of CARICOM. Multicoloured.

1180	20c. Type **211**	15	10
1181	75c. Flags of CARICOM and St. Lucia	85	75

212 St. Lucia Oriole

1998. Wild Life (1st series). Birds. Multicoloured.

1197	70c. Type **212**	1·00	65
1198	75c. Lesser antillean pewee	1·00	70
1199	95c. Bridled quail dove	1·25	95
1200	$1.10 Semper's warbler	2·00	2·00

See also Nos. 1212/15.

213 "Siproeta stelenes" and Chain

1998. 50th Anniv of Universal Declaration of Human Rights. Butterflies. Multicoloured.

1201	20c. Type **213**	90	20
1202	65c. "Pseudolycaena marsyas" and chain	1·50	60
1203	70c. "Heliconius melpomene" and rope	1·50	60
1204	$5 "Phoebis philea" and chain	4·25	6·00

214 "Tabebuia serratifolia"

1998. Christmas. Flowers. Multicoloured.

1205	20c. Type **214**	40	10
1206	50c. "Hibiscus sabdariffa"	75	30
1207	95c. "Euphorbia leucocephala"	1·25	45
1208	$2.50 "Calliandra slaneae"	2·25	3·50

215 "The Black Prometheus" (wall painting)

1998. 50th Anniv of University of West Indies. Multicoloured.

1209	15c. Type **215**	15	10
1210	75c. Sir Arthur Lewis College, St. Lucia	50	40
1211	$5 University arms and the Pitons, St. Lucia	2·75	4·50

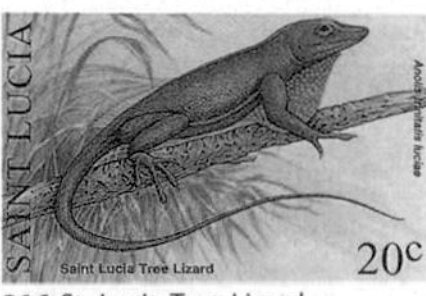

216 St. Lucia Tree Lizard

1999. Wildlife (2nd series). Reptiles. Multicoloured.

1212	20c. Type **216**	25	10
1213	75c. Boa constrictor	70	45
1214	95c. Leatherback turtle	75	50
1215	$5 St. Lucia whiptail	2·75	4·50

217 "Tees" (mail steamer), 1893

1999. 125th Anniv of Universal Postal Union. Multicoloured.

1216	20c. Type **217**	50	20
1217	65c. Sikorsky S.38 (flying boat), 1929	90	45
1218	95c. "Lady Drake" (cargo liner), 1930	1·00	55
1219	$3 DC10 airliner, 1999	2·25	3·25
MS1220	100×84 mm. $5 Heinrich von Stephan (founder of U.P.U.) (30×37 mm)	2·50	3·50

218 The Nativity

1999. Christmas. New Millennium. Multicoloured.

1221	20c. Type **218**	20	10
1222	$1 Cathedral of the Immaculate Conception	80	1·00

219 Original Badge of the Colony

2000. 21st Anniv of Independence. Multicoloured.

1223	20c. Type **219**	15	10
1224	75c. Colonial badge, 1939	50	50
1225	95c. Coat of Arms as Associated State, 1967	65	75
1226	$1 Coat of Arms on Independence, 1979	80	85

220 Sugar Factory, Vieux-Fort

2000. History of St. Lucia. Multicoloured.

1227	20c. Type **220**	20	15
1228	65c. Coaling ship, Port Castries	75	45
1229	$1 Fort Rodney, Pigeon Island	85	65
1230	$5 Ruins of military hospital, Pigeon Island	3·00	4·50

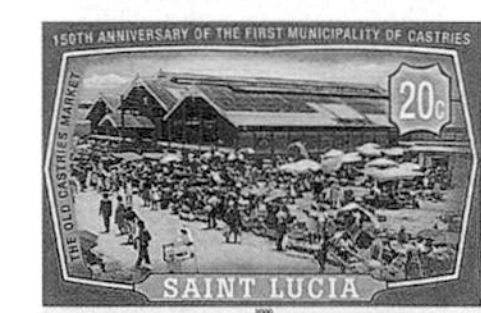

221 The Old Market, Castries

2000. 150th Anniv of Castries Municipality. Mult.

1231	20c. Type **221**	20	15
1232	75c. Central Library	65	45
1233	95c. Harbour	1·00	70
1234	$5 Henry H. Breen (first municipality mayor, 1851) and Joseph Desir (first city mayor, 1967)	2·75	4·50

222 Brownies and Badge

2000. 75th Anniv of Girl Guides in St. Lucia. Multicoloured.

1235	70c. Type **222**	65	40
1236	$1 Girl Guides parade	90	70
1237	$2.50 Brownies in camp and Guides with flag	2·25	3·25

223 Holy Trinity Church, Castries

2000. Christmas. Churches. Multicoloured.

1238	20c. Type **223**	30	15
1239	50c. St. Paul's Church, Vieux-Fort	50	30
1240	95c. Christ Church, Soufriere	80	55
1241	$2.50 Grace Church, River D'Oree	2·00	3·00

224 St. Lucia Black Finch

2001. Endangered Species. Birds of St. Lucia. Multicoloured.

1242	20c. Type **224**	75	65
1243	20c. White-breasted trembler ("White-breasted Thrasher")	75	65
1244	95c. St. Lucia oriole	1·10	1·25
1245	95c. Forest thrush	1·10	1·25

225 Open-air Jazz Concert

2001. 10th Anniv of Jazz Festival. Multicoloured.

1246	20c. Type **225**	30	15
1247	$1 Jazz concert on the beach	1·00	75
1248	$5 Jazz band	4·00	5·00

226 Union Jack, Pitons and Frigate (Arrival of Civil Administrator, 1801)

2001. Bicentenary of Civil Administration. Multicoloured.

1249	20c. Type **226**	40	20
1250	65c. Napoleon, Tricolor and Conseil Superior, 1802	70	40
1251	$1.10 King George III, Union Jack and British fleet (introduction of Privy Council, 1803)	1·25	85
1252	$3 King George IV and island map (Treaty of Paris, 1814)	2·50	3·25

227 Three-panel Stained Glass Window

2001. Christmas. Multicoloured.

1253	20c. Type **227**	40	15
1254	95c. Circular stained glass window	1·25	55
1255	$2.50 Arched stained glass window	3·00	3·50

2002. Golden Jubilee. As T 211 of St. Helena.

1256	25c. brown, blue and gold	50	20
1257	65c. multicoloured	1·00	85
1258	75c. brown, blue and gold	1·10	1·10
1259	95c. multicoloured	1·50	1·50

MS1260	162×95 mm. Nos. 1256/9 and $5 multicoloured	4·75	5·50

DESIGNS—HORIZ: 25c. Princess Elizabeth in June 1927; 65c. Queen Elizabeth wearing striped turban; 75c. Princess Elizabeth in 1947; 95c. Queen Elizabeth arriving at St. Paul's Cathedral, 1996. VERT: (38×51 mm)—$5 Queen Elizabeth after Annigoni.

Designs as Nos. 1256/9 in No. **MS**1260 omit the gold frame around each stamp and the "Golden Jubilee 1952–2002" inscription.

228 H.M.S. *St. Lucia* (brig), 1803

2002. Royal Navy Ships. Multicoloured.

1261	15c. Type **228**	65	25
1262	75c. H.M.S. *Thetis* (frigate), 1781	1·50	70
1263	$1 H.M.S. *Berwick* (cruiser), 1903	1·75	1·10
1264	$5 H.M.S. *Victory* (Nelson), 1805	3·75	5·00

2002. Queen Elizabeth the Queen Mother Commemoration. As T 215 of St. Helena.

1265	50c. brown, gold and purple	70	45
1266	65c. multicoloured	85	65
1267	95c. brown, gold and purple	1·25	1·10
1268	$1 multicoloured	1·40	1·60
MS1269	145×70 mm. $2 black and gold; $2 multicoloured	4·00	4·25

DESIGNS: 50c. Duchess of York with Princess Elizabeth, 1926; 65c. Queen Mother at St. Peter's Church Thurso, 1992; 95c. Queen Elizabeth at Church Army services club London, 1943; $1 Queen Mother at Sandown Races, 1999; $2 (black and gold) Duchess of York, 1920s; $2 (multicoloured) Queen Mother at unveiling of S.O.E. Memorial, 1996. Designs in No. **MS**1269 omit the "1900–2002" inscription and the coloured frame.

229 Derek Walcott

2002. 10th Anniv of Award of Nobel Literature Prize to Derek Walcott. Multicoloured.

1270	20c. Type **229**	45	20
1271	65c. Father Christmas with children (horiz)	80	50
1272	70c. Dancers	85	60
1273	$5 Outboard motor boat (cover illustration from *Omeros*) (horiz)	3·75	5·00

230 William and Catherine Booth

2002. Centenary of Salvation Army on St. Lucia. Multicoloured.

1274	20c. Type **230**	70	35
1275	$1 Early St. Lucia Salvation Army parade	1·75	1·25
1276	$2.50 Salvation Army shield symbol and crest	3·00	3·50

231 "The Adoration of the Shepherds" (Bernardino da Asola)

2003. Christmas. Religious Paintings from The National Gallery, London. Multicoloured.

1277	20c. Type **231**	40	10
1278	50c. "The Adoration of the Kings" (Girolamo da Treviso) (vert)	75	30
1279	75c. "The Adoration of the Kings" (Vincenzo Foppa) (vert)	1·10	40
1280	$5 "The Adoration of the Shepherds" (Le Nain brothers)	4·75	6·50

2003. 50th Anniv of Coronation. As T 219 of St. Helena. Multicoloured.

1281	20c. Queen Elizabeth II wearing Imperial State Crown	45	20
1282	75c. Coronation Coach passing Buckingham Palace gate	1·10	1·00
MS1283	95×115 mm. $2.50 As 75c.; $2.50 As 20c.	4·25	4·50

232 Letters (1803 and 1844) and Fleuron

2003. Bicentenary of Continuous Mail Service. Multicoloured.

1284	20c. Type **232**	35	25
1285	25c. Stamps of 1860	35	25
1286	65c. *Hewanorra* (steam packet), 1920 and map	90	65
1287	75c. Post Offices of 1900 and 2003	1·00	1·00

233 St. Lucia Amazon Date Stamp, 1822

2003. Coil stamps. Multicoloured.

1288	10c. Type **233**	10	10
1289	25c. The Pitons, St. Lucia	15	15

234 Sikorsky S-38 (flying boat)

2003. Centenary of Powered Flight. Multicoloured.

1290	20c. Type **234**	45	20
1291	70c. Consolidated PBY-5A Catalina (amphibian)	75	45
1292	$1 Lockheed Lodestar	1·10	75
1293	$5 Supermarine Spitfire Mk V *St. Lucia*	4·25	5·00

235 Sorrel Flowers and Ginger Root

2003. Christmas. Multicoloured.

1294	20c. Type **235**	45	15
1295	75c. Sorrel drink and ginger ale	90	40
1296	95c. Masqueraders	1·25	85
1297	$1 People making Christmas lanterns	1·25	85

236 Raising St. Lucia Flag

2004. 25th Anniv of Independence. Multicoloured.

1298	20c. Type **236**	40	15
1299	95c. Sailing ship, aircraft, cargo ship and bananas	1·00	55
1300	$1.10 Anniversary emblem (horiz)	1·00	80
1301	$5 Cruise ships, Castries harbour (horiz)	3·50	4·50

237 Antillean Crested Hummingbird

2004. Birds of the Caribbean. Multicoloured.

1302	$1 Type **237**	85	1·00
1303	$1 Lesser Antillian pewee ("Saint Lucia Pewee")	85	1·00
1304	$1 Purple-throated carib	85	1·00
1305	$1 Grey trembler	85	1·00
1306	$1 Rufous-throated solitaire	85	1·00
1307	$1 Adelaide's warbler ("Saint Lucia Warbler")	85	1·00
1308	$1 Antillean euphonia	85	1·00
1309	$1 Semper's warbler	85	1·00

Nos. 1302/9 were printed together with the backgrounds forming composite designs.

238 Sailing

2004. Tourism. Multicoloured.

1310	45c. Type **238**	50	30
1311	65c. Horse-riding	70	55
1312	70c. Scuba diving	75	70
1313	$1.10 Walking near waterfall	1·00	1·10

239 Hypodermic Needle and Couple ("Prevent")

2004. World AIDS Awareness Day. Multicoloured.

1314	30c. Type **239**	50	50
1315	30c. Two children ("Educate us") and woman	50	50

240 "The Adoration of the Kings" (Dosso)

2004. Christmas. Religious Paintings. Multicoloured.

1316	30c. Type **240**	25	15
1317	75c. "The Adoration of the Shepherds" (Poussin) (vert)	65	40
1318	95c. "The Adoration of the Kings" (Joos) (vert)	80	70
1319	$1 "The Adoration of the Shepherds" (Fabritius)	85	75

241 Convent Schoolgirls

2005. 150th Anniv of St. Joseph's Convent. Multicoloured.

1320	30c. Type **241**	35	15
1321	95c. St. Joseph's Convent	1·00	55
1322	$2.50 Street scene	2·50	3·00

2005. Bicentenary of the Battle of Trafalgar. Multicoloured. As T 229 of St. Helena.

1323	30c. HMS *Thunderer*	55	25
1324	75c. HMS *Britannia* and *Bucentaure*	1·10	65
1325	95c. Vice-Admiral Sir Horatio Nelson (vert)	1·40	75
1326	$5 HMS *Victory*	4·75	5·50
MS1327	120×79 mm. $10 HMS *Thunderer* (44×44 mm)	9·50	10·50

No. 1326 contains traces of powdered wood from HMS *Victory*.

2005. Pope John Paul II Commemoration. As T 231 of St. Helena.

1328	$2 multicoloured	2·00	2·00

242 Church of the Purification of the Blessed Virgin, Laborie

2005. Christmas. Multicoloured.

1329	30c. Type **242**	30	15
1330	$5 The Minor Basilica of the Immaculate Conception, Castries	3·25	3·50

243 Akee

2005. Flowering Fruits. Multicoloured.

1331	15c. Type **243**	20	15
1332	20c. Belogen	20	15
1333	25c. Mago	20	15
1334	30c. Wezin	25	15
1335	50c. Papai	45	30
1336	55c. Pwin	45	30
1337	65c. Z'icaque	55	40
1338	70c. Chataigne	60	50
1339	75c. Cashima	65	50
1340	95c. Gwiav	85	70
1341	$1 Macabou	85	70
1342	$2.50 Zapoti	1·75	1·90
1343	$5 Cashew	3·25	3·50
1344	$25 Zabwico	15·00	16·00

244 Axe Head

2006. Environment Fragile. Designs showing works of art by Llewellyn Xavier. Multicoloured.

1345	20c. Type **244**	30	15
1346	30c. Stylized turtle	35	15
1347	$2.50 Pre-Columbian vase	2·00	2·25
1348	$5 Pre-Columbian zemi	3·50	4·00

245 Two Players

2006. World Cup Football Championship, Germany. Multicoloured. .

1349	95c. Type **245**	90	75
1350	$2 Two players (different)	1·75	2·00
MS1351	110×70 mm. Nos. 1349/50	2·50	2·75

246 LIAT Aircraft in Flight

2006. 50th Anniv of LIAT (Leeward Islands Air Transport) Airline. Multicoloured.

1352	30c. Type **246**	40	20
1353	75c. LIAT aircraft on ground	85	90

247 Sesenne Descartes and Choir

2006. Christmas. Folk Songs. Multicoloured.

1354	95c. Type **247**	85	60

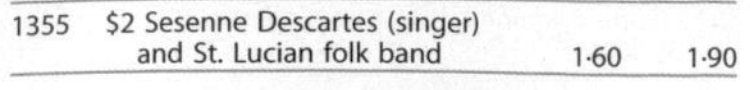

1355	$2 Sesenne Descartes (singer) and St. Lucian folk band	1·60	1·90

248 Mindoo Phillip (cricketer)

2007. Cricket in St. Lucia. Multicoloured.

1356	30c. Type **248**	35	15
1357	75c. Outline map of St. Lucia	75	65
1358	95c. Beausejour Cricket Grounds (horiz)	90	90
MS1359	116×90 mm. $5 Beausejour Cricket Grounds (56×42 mm)	3·50	4·00

249 Scouts Inspection, Queen's Birthday Parade, 1954

2007. Centenary of Scouting. Multicoloured.

1360	30c. Type **249**	25	25
1361	$5 Cub scout laying wreath, Remembrance Day Parade, 2005	3·00	3·00
MS1362	90×65 mm. $2.50 St. Lucia Scout Association membership badge (vert); $2.50 Lord Baden-Powell (founder) (vert)	3·00	3·00

250 Lantern Parade

2007. Christmas. Multicoloured.

1363	30c. Type **250**	25	25
1364	$10 Nativity scene	6·00	6·00

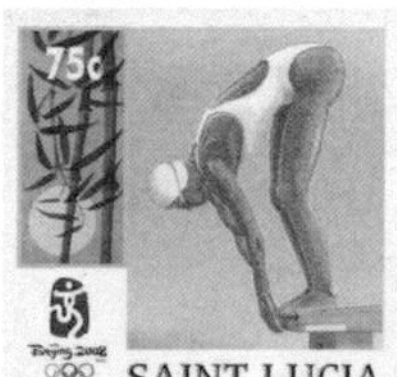

251 Swimmer

2008. Olympic Games, Beijing. Multicoloured.

1365	75c. Type **251**	55	55
1366	95c. Distance runner	65	65
1367	$1 Sprinter	75	75
1368	$2.50 High jumper	1·50	1·50

252 Scroll

2008. 60th Anniv of the University of the West Indies.

1369	**252**	$5 multicoloured	4·00	4·00

253 Male Whiptail Lizard

2008. Endangered Species. St. Lucia Whiptail Lizard (Cnemidophorus vanzoi). Multicoloured.

1370	75c. Type **253**	1·00	1·00
1371	$2.50 Female lizard	1·75	1·75
1372	$5 Two male lizards	3·50	3·50
1373	$10 Male and female lizards	6·75	6·75

254 Christmas Wreath, Gift and Bell

2008. Christmas. Multicoloured.

1374	95c. Type **254**	1·25	1·25
1375	$5 Candle and nativity scene	3·50	3·50

255 Castries Waterfront

2009. 30th Anniv of Independence. Multicoloured.

1376	30c. Type **255**	35	35
1377	$2.50 Roseau Dam	2·00	2·00
1378	$5 Rodney Bay Marina	3·00	3·00
1379	$10 Sir John Compton and St. Lucia flag	6·00	6·00

256 Lobelia santa-Luciae

2010. International Year of Biodiversity. Multicoloured.

1394	30c. Type **256**	25	25
1395	75c *Iguana cf. iguana*	55	55
1396	95c. Hercules beetle (*Dynastes hercules reidi*)	1·25	1·25
1397	$2.50 White breasted thrasher (*Ramphocinclus brachyurus sanctaeluciae*)	1·50	1·50

257 Township and Gros Islet

2010. 25th Anniv of Gros Islet's Township

1398	**257**	95c. multicoloured	55	55

2011. Queen Elizabeth II and Prince Philip 'A Lifetime of Service'. Multicoloured.

1399	$1.50 Formal portrait of Queen Elizabeth II (wearing tiara) and Prince Philip (in uniform), c. 1972	1·25	1·25
1400	$1.50 Prince Philip, 1960s	1·25	1·25
1401	$2 Formal portrait of Queen Elizabeth II (wearing tiara and sash) and Prince Philip, c. 1952	1·75	1·75
1402	$2 Queen Elizabeth II (wearing tiara and pale blue dress) and Prince Philip, 1960s	1·75	1·75
1403	$2.50 Queen Elizabeth II (wearing pearls), c. 1955	2·00	2·00
1404	$2.50 Queen Elizabeth II (wearing tiara, pendant and sash) and Prince Philip (wearing white uniform), c. 1955	2·00	2·00
MS1405	175×164 mm. Nos. 1399/404 and three stamp-size labels	10·00	10·00
MS1406	110×70 mm. $6 Princess Elizabeth and Prince Philip, c. 1949	5·00	5·00

Diamond-shaped designs as T **267** of St. Helena.

OFFICIAL STAMPS

1983. Nos. 537/48 optd OFFICIAL.

O1	5c. Type **120**	20	20
O2	10c. Douglas DC-10-30	30	20
O3	15c. Local bus	40	30
O4	20c. "Geestcrest" (freighter)	50	30
O5	25c. Britten Norman Islander aircraft	60	30
O6	30c. "Charles" (pilot boat)	70	30
O7	50c. Boeing 727-200	90	40
O8	75c. "Cunard Countess" (liner)	1·10	60
O9	$1 Lockheed TriStar 500	1·50	85
O10	$2 "Booklet Vulcan" (cargo liner)	2·00	2·00
O11	$5 Boeing 707-420 airliner	3·50	3·75
O12	$10 "Queen Elizabeth 2" (liner)	6·50	7·50

1985. Nos. 797/811 optd OFFICIAL.

O13	5c. Type **156**	60	1·25
O14	10c. Officer, Grenadier Company, 14th Regiment, 1780	60	1·25
O15	20c. Officer, Battalion Company, 46th Regiment, 1781	70	90
O16	25c. Officer, Royal Artillery, c. 1782	70	90
O17	30c. Officer, Royal Engineers, 1782	80	1·00
O18	35c. Officer, Battalion Company, 54th Regiment, 1782	90	1·00
O19	45c. Private, Grenadier Company, 14th Regiment, 1782	1·00	1·00
O20	50c. Gunner, Royal Artillery, 1796	1·00	1·00
O21	65c. Private, Battalion Company, 85th Regiment, c. 1796	1·25	1·50
O22	75c. Private, Battalion Company, 76th Regiment, 1796	1·25	2·25
O23	90c. Private, Battalion Company, 81st Regiment, c. 1796	1·50	2·25
O24	$1 Sergeant 74th (Highland) Regiment, 1796	1·75	2·25
O25	$2.50 Private, Light Company, 93rd Regiment, 1803	2·75	4·00
O26	$5 Private, Battalion Company, 1st West India Regiment, 1803	4·00	4·00
O27	$15 Officer, Royal Artillery, 1850	9·00	9·00

1990. Nos. 1081/2, 1039/40, 1085 and 1042/48 optd OFFICIAL.

O28	10c. Chinna	30	90
O29	15c. Latanier	30	90
O30	20c. Type **186**	40	60
O31	25c. L'encens	40	60
O32	50c. Bois lele	50	75
O33	80c. Bois d'amande	60	80
O34	95c. Mahot piman grand bois	1·00	1·25
O35	$1 Balata	1·00	1·00
O36	$1.50 Pencil cedar	1·50	2·00
O37	$2.50 Bois cendre	2·75	3·25
O38	$5 Lowye cannelle	4·75	6·00
O39	$25 Chalantier grand bois	13·00	18·00

POSTAGE DUE STAMPS

D1

1930

D1	**D1**	1d. black on blue	9·00	19·00
D2	**D1**	2d. black on yellow	20·00	48·00

D2

1933

D3	**D2**	1d. black	5·00	7·50
D4	**D2**	2d. black	20·00	9·50
D5	**D2**	4d. black	10·00	48·00
D6	**D2**	8d. black	10·00	60·00

D3

1949

D7a	**D3**	2c. black	10	9·50
D8a	**D3**	4c. black	50	13·00
D9	**D3**	8c. black	3·25	26·00
D10a	**D3**	16c. black	4·50	65·00

D4 St. Lucia Coat of Arms

1981

D13	**D4**	5c. purple	10	65
D17	**D4**	5c. red	10	25
D18	**D4**	15c. green	10	25
D19	**D4**	25c. orange	10	25
D20	**D4**	$1 blue	45	1·00

Pt. 6

STE MARIE DE MADAGASCAR

An island off the east coast of Madagascar. From 1898 used the stamps of Madagascar and Dependencies.

100 centimes = 1 franc.

1894. "Tablet" key-type inscr "STE MARIE DE MADAGASCAR" in red (1, 5, 15, 25, 75c., 1f.) or blue (others).

1	**D**	1c. black on blue	2·30	3·25
2	**D**	2c. brown on buff	2·50	2·50
3	**D**	4c. brown on grey	5·50	9·00
4	**D**	5c. green on green	8·75	32·00
5	**D**	10c. black on lilac	19·00	28·00
6	**D**	15c. blue	50·00	65·00
7	**D**	20c. red on green	16·00	22·00
8	**D**	25c. black on pink	9·50	10·50
9	**D**	30c. brown on drab	19·00	36·00
10	**D**	40c. red on yellow	28·00	19·00
11	**D**	50c. red on pink	65·00	70·00
12	**D**	75c. brown on orange	80·00	60·00
13	**D**	1f. green	60·00	65·00

Pt. 6

ST PIERRE ET MIQUELON

A group of French islands off the S. coast of Newfoundland. The group became an Overseas Department of France on 1 July 1976. The stamps of France were used in the islands from 1 April 1978 until 3 February 1986. Separate issues for the group were reintroduced in 1986.

1885. 100 centimes = 1 franc.
2002. 100 cents = 1 euro.

1885. Stamps of French Colonies surch S P M and value in figures only.

1	J	5 on 2c. brown on buff	£6500	£2250
4	J	5 on 4c. brown on grey	£375	£250
8	J	05 on 20c. red on green	60·00	50·00
9	H	05 on 35c. black on yellow	£130	£100
5	H	05 on 40c. red on yellow	£130	30·00
10	H	05 on 75c. red	£300	£200
11	H	05 on 1f. green	32·00	14·00
6	H	10 on 40c. red on yellow	30·00	18·00
7	H	15 on 40c. red on yellow	23·00	25·00
3	H	25 on 1f. green	£2750	£1600

The surcharge on No. 1 is always inverted.

1891. French Colonies "Commerce" type surch 15c. S P M.

15	J	15c. on 30c. brown on drab	70·00	33·00
16	J	15c. on 35c. black on orange	£550	£425
17	J	15c. on 40c. red on yellow	£140	85·00

1891. Stamps of French Colonies "Commerce" type, optd ST PIERRE M-on.

23	J	1c. black on blue	14·50	22·00
24	J	2c. brown on buff	18·00	30·00
25	J	4c. brown on grey	21·00	26·00
26	J	5c. green on green	23·00	24·00
22	J	10c. black on lilac	50·00	36·00
28	J	15c. blue on blue	50·00	35·00
29	J	20c. red on green	£110	£100
30	J	25c. black on pink	50·00	14·50
31	J	30c. brown on drab	£140	£130
32	J	35c. black on orange	£450	£350
33	J	40c. red on yellow	£110	90·00
34	J	75c. red on pink	£130	£120
35	J	1f. green	£120	£100

1891. Stamps of French Colonies, "Commerce" type, surch ST-PIERRE M-on and new value in figures and words (cent.) above and below opt.

36	J	1c. on 5c. green and green	7·25	11·00
37	J	1c. on 10c. black on lilac	11·50	28·00
38	J	1c. on 25c. black on pink	4·50	9·25
39	J	2c. on 10c. black on lilac	7·25	12·00
40	J	2c. on 15c. blue on blue	12·00	14·00
41	J	2c. on 25c. black on pink	7·50	5·50
42	J	4c. on 20c. red on green	7·25	6·50
43	J	4c. on 25c. black on pink	5·50	9·25
44	J	4c. on 30c. brown on drab	30·00	23·00
45	J	4c. on 40c. red on yellow	60·00	23·00

1892. Nos. 26 and 30 surch with figure only on top of opt.

49	J	1c. on 5c. green on green	8·75	11·00
46	J	1 on 25c. black on pink	4·50	10·00
50	J	2 on 5c. green on green	8·25	21·00
47	J	2 on 25c. black on pink	2·75	11·50
51	J	4 on 5c. green on green	7·25	11·00
48	J	4 on 25c. black on pink	2·00	8·25

1892. Postage Due stamps of French Colonies optd T ST-PIERRE M-on P.

52	U	10c. black	55·00	65·00
53	U	20c. black	38·00	50·00
54	U	30c. black	32·00	50·00
55	U	40c. black	27·00	28·00
56	U	60c. black	£140	£140
57	U	1f. brown	£160	£160
58	U	2f. brown	£250	£250
59	U	5f. brown	£375	£375

1892. "Tablet" key-type inscr "ST PIERRE ET MIQUELON".

60	D	1c. black and red on blue	70	90
61	D	2c. brown and blue on buff	2·30	3·00
62	D	4c. brown and blue on grey	1·50	1·80
63	D	5c. green and red	4·50	4·00
64	D	10c. black and blue on lilac	11·50	6·75
74	D	10c. red and blue	4·75	1·80
65	D	15c. blue and red	30·00	6·50
75	D	15c. grey and red	65·00	70·00
66	D	20c. red and blue on green	26·00	32·00
67	D	25c. black and red on pink	22·00	2·30
76	D	25c. blue and red	9·25	38·00
68	D	30c. brown and blue on drab	16·00	16·00
77	D	35c. black and red on yellow	6·50	11·00
69	D	40c. red and blue on yellow	10·00	14·50
70	D	50c. red and blue on pink	50·00	32·00
78	D	50c. brown and red on blue	23·00	60·00
71	D	75c. brown and red on orange	26·00	50·00
72	D	1f. green and red	50·00	40·00

17 Fisherman

18 Glaucous Gull

19 Fishing Brigantine

1909

79	17	1c. brown and red	20	10
80	17	2c. blue and brown	20	30
81	17	4c. brown and violet	45	1·10
82	17	5c. olive and green	1·80	65
109	17	5c. black and blue	35	2·00
83	17	10c. red and pink	1·40	1·20
110	17	10c. olive and green	35	5·50
111	17	10c. mauve and bistre	1·20	1·60
84	17	15c. red and purple	1·40	2·75
85	17	20c. purple and brown	1·40	6·00
86	18	25c. blue and deep blue	4·00	4·75
112	18	25c. green and brown	2·00	1·50
87	18	30c. brown and orange	4·75	8·00
113	18	30c. red and carmine	2·30	7·25
114	18	30c. blue and red	60	6·25
115	18	30c. green and olive	2·75	5·75
88	18	35c. brown and green	2·00	7·25
89	18	40c. green and brown	4·50	6·50
90	18	45c. green and violet	1·60	7·25
91	18	50c. green and brown	5·75	8·00
116	18	50c. light blue and blue	90	4·50
117	18	50c. mauve and bistre	2·75	2·50
118	18	60c. red and blue	1·70	6·75
119	18	65c. brown and mauve	3·75	8·25
92	18	75c. green and brown	2·20	3·75
120	18	90c. red and scarlet	29·00	70·00
93	19	1f. blue and green	5·00	5·25
121	19	1f.10 red and green	5·00	12·00
122	19	1f.50 blue and ultramarine	15·00	36·00
94	19	2f. brown and violet	8·75	11·00
123	19	3f. mauve on pink	14·00	40·00
95	19	5f. green and brown	12·50	19·00

1912. "Tablet" issue surch in figures.

96A		05 on 2c. brown and blue on buff	4·00	11·00
97A		05 on 4c. brown and blue on grey	75	4·00
98A		05 on 15c. blue and red	1·00	7·25
99A		05 on 20c. red and blue on green	90	5·25
100A		05 on 25c. black and red on pink	45	4·00
101A		05 on 30c. brown and blue on drab	55	6·75
102A		05 on 35c. black and red on yellow	1·40	7·75
103A		10 on 40c. red and blue on yellow	1·10	5·75
104A		10 on 50c. red and blue	1·00	7·50
105A		10 on 75c. brown and red on orange	3·00	9·75
106A		10 on 1f. green and red	3·75	11·50

1915. Red Cross. Surch 5c and red cross.

107	17	10c.+5c. red and pink	90	3·25
108	17	15c.+5c. red and purple	2·30	6·50

1924. Surch with new value.

124	17	25c. on 15c. red and purple	1·60	6·75
125	19	25c. on 2f. brown & violet	1·70	7·25
126	19	25c. on 5f. green & brown	1·00	7·50
127	18	65 on 45c. green and violet	3·00	9·25
128	18	85 on 75c. green and brown	2·50	9·00
129	18	90c. on 75c. red and scarlet	4·25	11·50
130	19	1f.25 on 1f. ultramarine and blue	2·40	10·00
131	19	1f.50 on 1f. blue and light blue	3·75	11·00
132	19	3f. on 5f. mauve and brown	4·75	11·00
133	19	10f. on 5f. green and red	17·00	46·00
134	19	20f. on 5f. red and violet	28·00	60·00

1931. International Colonial Exhibition, Paris, key-types inscr "ST PIERRE ET MIQUELON".

135	E	40c. green and black	4·50	11·50
136	F	50c. mauve and black	5·75	5·50
137	G	90c. red and black	4·50	10·50
138	H	1f.50 blue and black	6·75	8·25

27 Map of St. Pierre et Miquelon

28 Galantry Lighthouse

29 "Jacques Coeur" (trawler)

1932

139	27	1c. blue and purple	10	6·00
140	28	2c. green and black	10	2·00
141	29	4c. brown and red	30	5·75
142	29	5c. brown and mauve	80	2·75
143	28	10c. black and purple	70	7·00
144	28	15c. mauve and blue	1·50	7·50
145	27	20c. red and black	1·80	7·75
146	27	25c. green and mauve	4·75	2·30
147	29	30c. green and olive	5·00	8·00
148	29	40c. brown and blue	3·75	6·25
149	28	45c. green and red	4·75	7·75
150	28	50c. green and brown	3·50	1·00
151	29	65c. red and brown	6·00	4·50
152	27	75c. red and green	4·25	5·00
153	27	90c. scarlet and red	5·00	8·75
154	29	1f. scarlet and red	5·00	7·75
155	27	1f.25 red and blue	6·75	8·50
156	27	1f.50 blue and deep blue	6·50	6·75
157	29	1f.75 brown and black	7·75	8·00
158	29	2f. green and black	20·00	30·00
159	28	3f. brown and green	26·00	38·00
160	28	5f. brown and red	34·00	60·00
161	29	10f. mauve and green	65·00	£110
162	27	20f. green and red	60·00	£120

1934. 400th Anniv of Cartier's Discovery of Canada. Optd JACQUES CARTIER 1534 - 1934.

163	28	50c. green and brown	7·25	11·00
164	27	75c. red and green	7·50	12·00
165	27	1f.50 blue and deep blue	8·75	14·50
166	29	1f.75 brown and black	9·75	16·00
167	28	5f. brown and red	37·00	65·00

32 Commerce

1937. International Exhibition, Paris.

168	32	20c. violet	1·50	9·25
169	-	30c. green	1·50	9·25
170	-	40c. red	1·50	8·25
171	-	50c. brown and blue	1·50	4·50
172	-	90c. red	1·50	4·50
173	-	1f.50 blue	1·50	5·50
MS173a		120×100 mm. 3f. blue. Imperf	18·00	70·00

DESIGNS—VERT: 50c. Agriculture. HORIZ: 30c. Sailing ships; 40c. Women of three races; 90c., 3f. France extends Torch of Civilization; 1f.50, Diane de Poitiers.

38 Pierre and Marie Curie

1938. International Anti-cancer Fund.

174	38	1f.75+50c. blue	10·00	25·00

39 Dog Team

1938

175	39	2c. green	10	4·00
176	39	3c. brown	10	3·75
177	39	4c. purple	60	4·00
178	39	5c. red	10	4·25
179	39	10c. brown	10	4·25
180	39	15c. purple	20	4·25
181	39	20c. violet	30	5·75
182	39	25c. blue	2·50	9·75
183	-	30c. purple	30	4·00
184	-	35c. green	1·40	7·00
185	-	40c. blue	65	7·00
186	-	45c. green	1·70	7·00
187	-	50c. red	90	4·50
188	-	55c. blue	5·75	11·00
189	-	60c. violet	1·30	6·75
190	-	65c. brown	5·75	16·00
191	-	70c. orange	2·00	6·75
192	-	80c. violet	3·00	7·75
193	-	90c. blue	2·75	6·00
194	-	1f. red	12·00	28·00
195	-	1f. olive	1·30	3·75
196	-	1f.25 red	2·50	9·25
197	-	1f.40 brown	3·00	7·50
198	-	1r.50 green	85	4·75
199	-	1r.60 purple	3·00	7·25
200	-	1r.75 blue	3·75	8·25
201	-	2r. purple	1·40	5·50
202	-	2f.25 blue	2·75	7·00
203	-	2f.50 orange	2·00	4·50
204	-	3f. brown	1·10	6·25
205	-	5f. red	90	7·75
206	-	10f. blue	1·70	4·50
207	-	20f. olive	2·75	8·00

DESIGNS: 30 to 70c. St. Pierre harbour; 80c. to 1f.75, Pointe aux Canons lighthouse (wrongly inscr "PHARE DE LA TORTUE"); 2 to 20f. Soldiers' Cove, Langlade.

41

1939. New York World's Fair.

208	41	1f.25 red	1·40	9·00
209	41	2f.25 blue	1·40	9·00

42 Storming the Bastille

1939. 150th Anniv of French Revolution.

210	42	45c.+25c. green & black	13·00	20·00
211	42	70c.+30c. brown and black	13·00	18·00
212	42	90c.+35c. orange and black	13·00	18·00
213	42	1f.25+1f. red and black	13·00	18·00
214	42	2f.25+2f. blue and black	13·00	18·00

1941. Free French Plebiscite. Stamps of 1938 optd Noel 1941 FRANCE LIBRE F.N.F.L. or surch also.

215A	39	10c. brown	80·00	95·00
216A	39	20c. violet	85·00	£100
217A	39	25c. blue	95·00	£100
218A	-	40c. blue	95·00	95·00
219A	-	45c. green	95·00	£100
220A	-	65c. brown	£100	£100
221A	-	70c. orange	£100	£100
222A	-	80c. violet	80·00	95·00
223A	-	90c. blue	85·00	95·00
224A	-	1f. green	85·00	95·00
225A	-	1f.25 red	85·00	95·00

226A	-	1f.40 brown	85·00	95·00
227A	-	1f.60 purple	£110	£120
228A	-	1f.75 blue	£120	£120
229A	-	2f. purple	£100	£120
230A	-	2f.25 blue	£110	£120
231A	-	2f.50 orange	£110	£120
232A	-	3f. brown	£110	£120
233A	39	10f. on 10c. brown	£130	£130
234A	-	20f. on 90c. blue	£130	£130

"F.N.F.L." = Forces Navales Francaises Libres (Free French Naval Forces).

1941. Various stamps overprinted FRANCE LIBRE F. N. F. L. or surch also. (a) Nos. 111 and 114.

245	17	10c. mauve and bistre	£1300	£1300
246	18	30c. blue and lake	£1300	£1300

(b) On stamps of 1932.

247	28	2c. green and black	£225	£250
248	29	4c. brown and red	75·00	95·00
249	29	5c. brown and mauve	£800	£850
250	29	40c. brown and blue	19·00	38·00
251	28	45c. green and red	£180	£190
252	28	50c. green and brown	12·00	34·00
253	29	65c. red and brown	65·00	70·00
254	29	1f. red and brown	£375	£400
255	29	1f.75 brown and black	15·00	38·00
256	29	2f. green and black	25·00	40·00
257	28	5f. brown and red	£375	£375
258	29	5f. on 1f.75 brown & blk	12·00	34·00

(c) On stamps of 1938.

259	39	2c. green	£425	£475
260	39	3c. brown	£150	£150
261	39	4c. purple	£130	£130
262	39	5c. red	£850	£850
263	39	10c. brown	8·25	10·00
264	39	15c. purple	£1600	£1600
265	39	20c. violet	£170	£180
266	39	20c. on 10c. brown	10·00	25·00
267	39	25c. blue	7·50	22·00
268	39	30c. on 10c. brown	6·75	13·00
269	-	35c. green	£800	£800
270	-	40c. blue	11·00	14·00
271	-	45c. green	14·50	28·00
272	-	55c. blue	£11000	£11000
273	-	60c. violet	£600	£600
274	-	60c. on 90c. blue	11·50	12·50
275	-	65c. brown	16·00	60·00
276	-	70c. orange	60·00	70·00
277	-	80c. violet	£450	£450
278	-	90c. blue	13·00	34·00
279	-	1f. green	14·50	27·00
280	-	1f.25 red	17·00	42·00
281	-	1f.40 brown	11·00	38·00
282	-	1f.50 green	£750	£800
283	-	1f.50 on 90c. blue	18·00	15·00
284	-	1f.60 purple	14·00	34·00
285	-	2f. purple	85·00	95·00
286	-	2f.25 blue	10·50	25·00
287	-	2f.50 orange	11·00	60·00
288	7	2f.50 on 10c. brown	14·00	13·00
289	-	3f. brown	£12000	£12000
290	-	5f. red	£2250	£2250
291	7	10f. on 10c. brown	55·00	90·00
292	-	20f. olive	£900	£1000
293	-	20f. on 90c. blue	75·00	95·00

(d) On Nos. 208/9.

294	41	1f.25 red	12·00	17·00
295	41	2f.25 blue	10·50	11·00
296	41	2f.50 on 1f.25 red	12·00	32·00
297	41	3f. on 2f.25 blue	17·00	36·00

1942. Stamps of 1932 overprinted FRANCE LIBRE F. N. F. L. or surch also.

304	27	20c. red and black	£400	£425
305	27	75c. red and green	13·00	36·00
306	27	1f.25 red and blue	11·00	28·00
307	27	1f.50 blue and deep blue	£475	£500
308	27	10f. on 1f.25 red and blue	50·00	65·00
309	27	20f. on 75c. red and green	65·00	90·00

1942. Social Welfare Fund. Nos. 279 and 287 further surch OEUVRES SOCIALES, cross and premium.

320	1f.+50c. green	60·00	80·00
321	2f.50+1f. orange	60·00	80·00

47 Fishing Schooner

48 Airliner

1942. (a) Postage.

322	47	5c. blue	10	3·25
323	47	10c. pink	10	3·50
324	47	25c. green	10	4·50
325	47	30c. black	25	2·75
326	47	40c. blue	35	3·50
327	47	60c. purple	45	2·00
328	47	1f. violet	60	2·75
329	47	1f.50 red	1·00	3·00
330	47	2f. brown	1·30	3·00
331	47	2f.50 blue	1·80	2·75
332	47	4f. orange	90	5·75
333	47	5f. purple	1·00	4·50
334	47	10f. blue	90	3·25
335	47	20f. green	1·30	4·50

(b) Air.

336	48	1f. orange	65	5·00
337	48	1f.50 red	1·00	2·75
338	48	5f. purple	75	3·00
339	48	10f. black	1·10	2·75
340	48	25f. blue	1·20	7·50
341	48	50f. green	1·20	8·00
342	48	100f. red	1·40	10·00

49

1944. Mutual Aid and Red Cross Funds.

343	49	5f.+20f. blue	75	8·75

50 Felix Eboue

1945. Eboue.

344	50	2f. black	45	6·00
345	50	25f. green	90	7·75

1945. Surch.

346	47	50c. on 5c. blue	20	3·50
347	47	70c. on 5c. blue	35	7·00
348	47	80c. on 5c. blue	45	7·25
349	47	1f.20 on 5c. blue	30	5·50
350	47	2f.40 on 25c. green	40	4·25
351	47	3f. on 25c. green	55	3·50
352	47	4f.50 on 25c. green	75	7·75
353	47	15f. on 2f.50 blue	45	4·25

52 "Victory"

1946. Air. Victory.

354	52	8f. red	45	8·25

53 Legionaries by Lake Chad

1946. Air. From Chad to the Rhine.

355	53	5f. red	90	9·00
356	53	10f. lilac	90	9·00
357	53	15f. black	90	9·50
358	53	20f. violet	1·70	9·50
359	53	25f. brown	1·70	11·50
360	53	50f. black	1·80	11·50

54 Soldiers' Cove, Langlade

55 Allegory of Fishing

56 Douglas DC-4 and Wrecked Fishing Schooner

1947

361	54	10c. brown (postage)	10	1·70
362	54	30c. violet	10	3·25
363	54	40c. purple	10	3·00
364	54	50c. blue	10	2·50
365	55	60c. red	30	3·00
366	55	80c. blue	30	3·50
367	55	1f. green	55	1·80
368	-	1f.20 green	55	7·25
369	-	1f.50 black	90	2·30
370	-	2f. red	1·00	45
371	-	3f. violet	2·00	2·00
372	-	3f.60 red	2·30	4·50
373	-	4f. purple	2·75	1·20
374	-	5f. yellow	2·30	45
375	-	6f. blue	2·75	4·00
376	-	8f. sepia	5·00	1·80
377	-	10f. green	3·50	1·00
378	-	15f. green	3·25	1·30
379	-	17f. blue	6·25	5·75
380	-	20f. red	2·75	2·30
381	-	25f. blue	3·75	3·75
382	-	50f. green and red (air)	6·75	10·00
383	56	100f. green	11·00	22·00
384	-	200f. blue and red	12·00	27·00

DESIGNS—As Type **55**: 1f.20 to 2f. Cross and fishermen; 3f. to 4f. Weighing Atlantic cod; 5, 6, 10f. Trawler "Colonel Pleven"; 8, 17f. Red fox; 15, 20, 25f. Windswept mountain landscape. As Type **56**: 50f. Airplane and fishing village; 200f. Airplane and snow-bound fishing schooner.

58 People of Five Races, Aircraft and Globe

1949. Air. 75th Anniv of U.P.U.

395	58	25f. multicoloured	10·00	24·00

59 Doctor and Patient

1950. Colonial Welfare Fund.

396	59	10f.+2f. red and brown	7·25	20·00

60

1952. Centenary of Military Medal.

397	60	8f. blue, yellow and green	2·75	8·00

61 Normandy Landings, 1944

1954. Air. 10th Anniv of Liberation.

398	61	15f. red and brown	6·00	4·50

62 Refrigeration Plant

63 Codfish

64 Dog and Coastal Scene

1955

399	62	30c. blue & dp bl (postage)	20	6·00
400	63	40c. brown and blue	35	7·00
401	62	50c. brown, grey and black	35	5·00
402	63	1f. brown and green	45	7·25
403	63	2f. indigo and blue	1·10	7·00
404	62	3f. purple	1·20	2·75
405	-	4f. purple, red and lake	3·25	7·50
406	-	10f. brown, blue & turq	3·25	2·30
407	-	20f. multicoloured	1·50	1·80
408	-	25f. brown, green and blue	2·75	8·00
409	62	40f. turquoise	2·30	6·25
410	64	50f. multicoloured (air)	30·00	60·00
411	-	100f. black and grey	12·00	34·00
412	-	500f. indigo and blue	55·00	65·00

DESIGNS—As Type **62/3**: 4, 10f. Pointe aux Canons Lighthouse and fishing dinghies; 20f. Ice hockey players; 25f. American minks. As Type **64**: 100f. Sud Aviation Caravelle airliner over St. Pierre and Miquelon; 500f. Douglas DC-3 over St. Pierre port.

65 Trawler "Galantry"

1956. Economic and Social Development Fund.

413	65	15f. sepia and brown	1·80	90

66 "Human Rights"

1958. 10th Anniv of Declaration of Human Rights.

414	66	20f. brown and blue	55	1·00

67 "Picea"

1959

415	67	5f. multicoloured	45	8·50

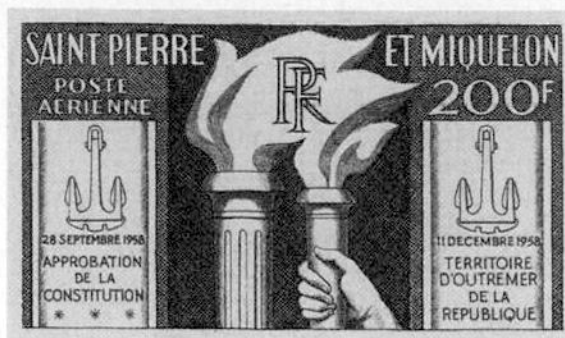

68 Flaming Torches

1959. Air. Adoption of Constitution.
416 **68** 200f. green, lake and violet 5·50 32·00

69 "Cypripedium acaule"

1962. Flowers.
417 **69** 25f. purple, orange and green (postage) 2·30 1·10
418 - 50f. red and green 3·00 14·50
419 - 100f. orange, red and green (air) 4·50 15·00
DESIGNS—VERT: 50f. "Calopogon pulchellus". HORIZ—48×27 mm: 100f. "Sarracenia purpurae".

70 Submarine "Surcouf" and Map

1962. Air. 20th Anniv of Adherence to Free French Government.
420 **70** 500f. black, blue and red 90·00 £130

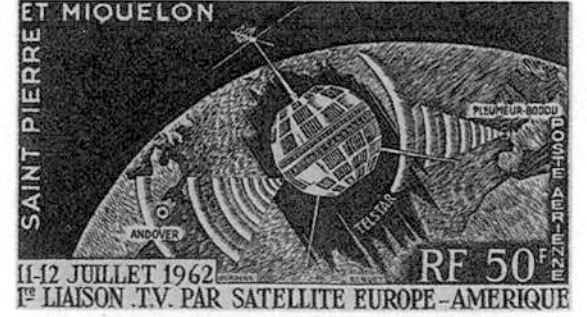

71 "Telstar" Satellite and part of Globe

1962. Air. 1st Transatlantic TV Satellite Link.
421 **71** 50f. brown, green and sepia 2·30 14·50

72 Eiders

1963. Birds.
422 **72** 50c. bistre, black and blue 45 4·50
423 - 1f. brown, mauve and blue 90 5·25
424 - 2f. brown, black and blue 90 4·75
425 - 6f. bistre, blue and turquoise 2·30 7·50
DESIGNS: 1f. Rock ptarmigan; 2f. Semi-palmated plovers; 6f. Blue-winged teal.

73 Dr. A. Calmette

1963. Birth Centenary of Dr. Albert Calmette (bacteriologist).
426 **73** 30f. brown and blue 4·50 9·00

74 Landing of Governor from "Garonne"

1963. Air. Bicentenary of Arrival of First Governor (Dangeac) in St. Pierre and Miquelon.
427 **74** 200f. blue, green and brown 7·25 36·00

75 Centenary Emblem

1963. Red Cross Centenary.
428 **75** 25f. red, grey and blue 2·75 6·50

76 Globe and Scales of Justice

1963. 15th Anniv of Declaration of Human Rights.
429 **76** 20f. orange, purple and blue 3·75 10·00

77 "Philately"

1964. "PHILATEC 1964" International Stamp Exhibition, Paris.
430 **77** 60f. blue, green and purple 5·50 26·00

78 Common Rabbits

1964. Fauna.
431 **78** 3f. chocolate, brown & grn 2·00 7·00
432 - 4f. sepia, blue and green 3·00 7·25
433 - 5f. brown, sepia and blue 3·25 8·75
434 - 34f. brown, green and blue 4·50 11·00
ANIMALS: 4f. Red fox; 5f. Roe deer; 34f. Charolais bull.

79 Potez 842 Airliner and Map

1964. Air. 1st St. Pierre–New York Airmail Flight.
435 **79** 100f. brown and blue 6·50 23·00

80 Syncom Communications Satellite, Telegraph Poles and Morse Key

1965. Centenary of I.T.U.
436 **80** 40f. blue, brown and purple 9·25 12·00

81 Rocket "Diamant"

1966. Air. Launching of First French Satellite.
437 **81** 25f. brown, blue and red 3·50 20·00
438 **81** 30f. brown, blue and red 3·75 21·00

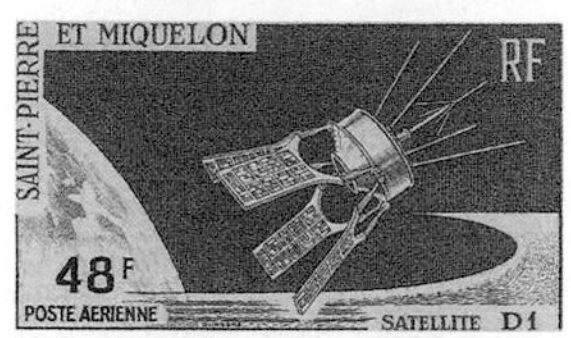

82 Satellite "D1"

1966. Air. Launching of Satellite "D1".
439 **82** 48f. blue, green and lake 3·25 8·00

83 "Revanche" and Settlers

1966. Air. 150th Anniv of Return of Islands to France.
440 **83** 100f. multicoloured 6·00 20·00

84 "Journal Officiel" and Old and New Printing Presses

1966. Air. Centenary of "Journal Officiel" Printing Works.
441 **84** 60f. plum, lake and blue 5·50 18·00

85 Map and Fishing Dinghies

1967. Air. Pres. De Gaulle's Visit.
442 **85** 25f. brown, blue and red 16·00 17·00
443 - 100f. blue, turquoise & pur 23·00 65·00
DESIGN: 100f. Maps and cruiser "Richelieu".

86 Trawler and Harbour Plan

1967. Opening of St. Pierre's New Harbour.
444 **86** 48f. brown, blue and red 8·00 10·50

87 Map and Control Tower

1967. Opening of St. Pierre Airport.
445 **87** 30f. multicoloured 4·00 8·00

88 T.V. Receiver, Aerial and Map

1967. Inauguration of Television Service.
446 **88** 40f. red, green and olive 5·50 10·50

89 Speed Skating

1968. Air. Winter Olympic Games, Grenoble. Multicoloured.
447 50f. Type **89** 6·50 14·50
448 60f. Ice-hockey goalkeeper 7·25 16·00

90 Bouquet, Sun and W.H.O. Emblem

1968. 20th Anniv of W.H.O.
449 **90** 10f. red, yellow and blue 4·50 12·50

91 J. D. Cassini (discoverer of group), Compasses and Chart

1968. Famous Visitors to St. Pierre and Miquelon (1st series).
450 **91** 4f. brown, yellow and lake 4·50 7·75
451 - 6f. multicoloured 5·75 10·50
452 - 15f. multicoloured 6·00 12·50
453 - 25f. multicoloured 7·75 13·00
CELEBRITIES: 6f. Rene de Chateaubriand and warship; 15f. Prince de Joinville, "Belle Poule" (sail frigate) and "Cassard" (survey ship); 25f. Admiral Gauchet and flagship "Provence" (Ile aux Chiens expedition).

92 Human Rights Emblem

1968. Human Rights Year.
454 **92** 20f. red, blue and yellow 7·75 18·00

93 War Memorial, St. Pierre

1968. Air. 50th Anniv of Armistice.
455 **93** 500f. multicoloured 20·00 55·00

94 Concorde in Flight

1969. Air. 1st Flight of Concorde.
456 **94** 34f. brown and olive 28·00 46·00

95 Mountain Stream, Langlade

1969. Tourism.

457	**95**	5f. brn, bl & grn (postage)	3·00	10·50
458	-	15f. brown, green and blue	3·25	13·00
459	-	50f. purple, olive & bl (air)	10·00	21·00
460	-	100f. brown, indigo & blue	16·00	23·00

DESIGNS: 15f. River bank, Debon, Langlade; 50f. Wild horses, Miquelon; 100f. Gathering wood, Miquelon. The 50f. and 100f. are larger 48×27 mm.

96 Treasury

1969. Public Buildings and Monuments.

461	**96**	10f. black, red and blue	2·75	8·00
462	-	25f. red, ultramarine & blue	3·75	8·25
463	-	30f. brown, green and blue	4·50	16·00
464	-	60f. black, red and blue	8·00	21·00

DESIGNS: 25f. Maritime Fisheries Scientific and Technical Institute; 30f. Unknown Sailor's Monument; 60f. St. Christopher's College.

97 "L'Estoile" and Granville, 1690

1969. Maritime Links with France.

465	**97**	34f. lake, green and emerald (postage)	8·50	13·50
466	-	40f. green, red and bistre	11·50	14·00
467	-	48f. multicoloured	12·50	16·00
468	-	200f. black, lake and green (air)	35·00	44·00

DESIGNS—As Type **97**: 40f. "La Jolie" and St. Jean de Luz, 1750; 48f. "La Juste" and La Rochelle, 1860; 48×27 mm. 200f. "L'Esperance" and St. Malo, 1600.

98 Pierre Loti, Sailing Ship and Book Titles

1969. Air. Pierre Loti (explorer and writer) Commemoration.

469	**98**	300f. multicoloured	50·00	60·00

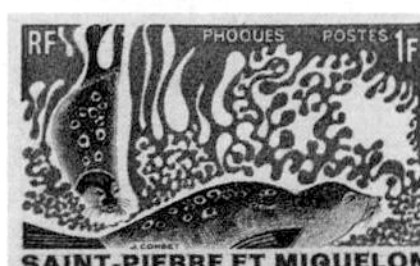

99 Ringed Seals

1969. Marine Animals.

470	**99**	1f. brown, purple and lake	5·50	10·50
471	-	3f. blue, green and red	5·50	10·50
472	-	4f. green, brown and red	5·50	10·50
473	-	6f. violet, green and red	5·50	10·50

DESIGNS: 3f. Sperm whales; 4f. Long-finned pilot whale; 6f. Common dolphins.

100 I.L.O. Building, Geneva

1969. 30th Anniv of International Labour Organization.

474	**100**	20f. brown, slate and salmon	6·50	12·00

101 New U.P.U. Building, Berne

1970. New U.P.U. Headquarters Building, Berne.

475	**101**	25f. brown, blue and red	6·50	12·50
476	**101**	34f. slate, brown & purple	11·00	18·00

102 Rocket and Japanese Women

1970. Air. World Fair "EXPO 70", Osaka, Japan.

477	**102**	34f. brown, lake and blue	12·00	24·00
478	-	85f. blue, red and orange	20·00	44·00

DESIGN—HORIZ: 85f. "Mountain Landscape" (Y. Taikan) and Expo "star".

103 Rowing Fours

1970. World Rowing Championships, St. Catherine, Canada.

479	**103**	20f. brown, blue & lt blue	6·50	16·00

104 "Rubus chamaemorus"

1970. Fruit Plants.

480	**104**	3f. green, purple & brown	2·50	6·50
481	-	4f. yellow, red and green	2·50	6·50
482	-	5f. red, green and violet	2·75	8·00
483	-	6f. violet, green and purple	3·75	4·50

PLANTS: 4f. "Fragaria vesca"; 5f. "Rubus idaeus"; 6f. "Vaccinium myrtillus".

105 Ewe and Lamb

1970. Livestock Breeding.

484	**105**	15f. brown, purple & green	8·50	9·25
485	-	30f. brown, grey and green	9·25	12·50
486	-	34f. brown, purple & green	13·00	22·00
487	-	48f. purple, brown & blue	14·50	16·00

DESIGNS: 30f. Animal quarantine station; 34f. Charolais bull; 48f. Refrigeration plant and "Narrando" (trawler).

106 Etienne Francois, Duke of Choiseul, and Warships

1970. Air. Celebrities of St. Pierre and Miquelon.

488	**106**	25f. brown, blue & purple	6·50	8·25
489	-	50f. brown, purple & green	10·50	27·00
490	-	60f. brown, green & purple	12·00	29·00

DESIGNS: 50f. Jacques Cartier and "Grande Hermine"; 60f. Sebastien Le Gonard de Sourdeval and 17th-century French galleons.

107 "St. Francis of Assisi", 1900

1971. Fisheries' Protection Vessels.

491	**107**	30f. red, blue and turquoise	20·00	27·00
492	-	35f. brown, green and blue	21·00	18·00
493	-	40f. brown, blue and green	23·00	28·00
494	-	80f. black, green and blue	23·00	48·00

DESIGNS: 35f. "St. Jehanne", 1920; 40f. "L'Aventure", 1950; 80f. "Commandant Bourdais", 1970.

108 "Aconite"

1971. 30th Anniv of Allegiance to Free French Movement. British Corvettes on loan to Free French.

495	**108**	22f. black, green and blue	18·00	28·00
496	-	25f. brown, turquoise & bl	19·00	36·00
497	-	50f. black, turquoise & blue	36·00	60·00

DESIGNS: 25f. "Alyssum"; 50f. "Mimosa".

109 Ship's Bell

1971. St. Pierre Museum. Multicoloured.

498	20f. Type **109**	6·50	16·00
499	45f. Navigational instruments and charts (horiz)	10·00	14·00

110 De Gaulle in Uniform (June 1940)

1971. 1st Death Anniv of De Gaulle.

500	**110**	35f. black and red	7·25	13·00
501	**110**	45f. black and red	10·00	32·00

111 Haddock

1972. Ocean Fish.

502	**111**	2f. indigo, red and blue	3·75	10·00
503	-	3f. brown and green	3·75	10·00
504	-	5f. red and blue	4·50	5·50
505	-	10f. green and emerald	7·25	20·00

DESIGNS: 3f. American plaice; 5f. Deepwater redfish; 10c. Atlantic cod.

112 De Gaulle and Servicemen

1972. Air. General De Gaulle Commemoration.

506	**112**	100f. brown, green & pur	20·00	36·00

113 Long-tailed Ducks

114 Montcalm and Warships

1973. Currency Revaluation.

507	**113**	6c. brown, purple and blue (postage)	1·70	5·75
508	-	10c. black, red and blue	2·50	4·50
509	-	20c. bistre, ultram & bl	3·00	6·00
510	**113**	40c. brown, green & violet	3·50	6·00
511	-	70c. black, red and green	5·50	4·00
512	-	90c. bistre, blue and purple	9·50	27·00
513	**114**	1f.60 violet, indigo and blue (air)	12·50	12·00
514	-	2f. purple, green and violet	9·25	8·00
515	-	4f. green, mauve & brown	20·00	11·00

DESIGNS—As Type **113**: 10, 70c. Atlantic puffins; 20, 90c. Snowy owls. As Type **114**: HORIZ: 4f. La Salle, map and warships. VERT: 2f. Frontenac and various scenes.

116 Swimming Pool

1973. Inauguration of St. Pierre Cultural Centre.

521	**116**	60c. brown, blue and red	4·50	7·75
522	-	1f. purple, orange and blue	6·50	10·50

DESIGN: 1f. Centre building.

117 Transall C-160 in Flight

1973. Air.

523	**117**	10f. multicoloured	75·00	65·00

118 Met Balloon and Weather Ship

1974. World Meteorological Day.

524	**118**	1f.60 blue, green and red	11·50	21·00

119 Northern Gannet with Letter

1974. Centenary of Universal Postal Union.

525	**119**	70c. ultramarine, bl & red	4·50	9·25
526	**119**	90c. blue, red and lake	5·50	11·50

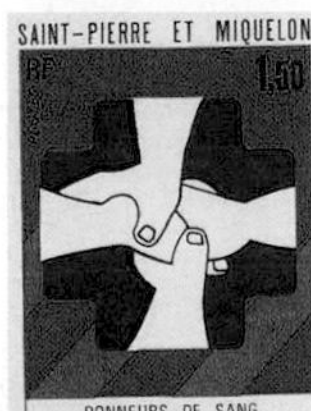

120 Clasped Hands on Red Cross

1974. Campaign for Blood Donors.

527	**120**	1f.50 multicoloured	10·00	21·00

121 Arms and Map of Islands

1974. Air.

528	**121**	2f. multicoloured	24·00	20·00

122 Banknotes in "Fish" Money-box

1974. Centenary of St. Pierre Savings Bank.

529	**122**	50c. brown, blue and black	5·00	11·50

123 Copernicus and Famous Scientists

1974. Air. 500th Birth Anniv (1973) of Nicholas Copernicus (astronomer).

530	**123**	4f. violet, red and blue	23·00	26·00

124 St. Pierre Church and Caspian Tern, Black-legged Kittiwake and Great Auk

1974. Island Churches.

531	**124**	6c. black, brown and green	5·75	7·00
532	-	10c. indigo, blue & brown	6·00	6·50
533	-	20c. multicoloured	14·00	7·25

DESIGNS: 10c. Miquelon Church and fishes; 20c. Our Lady of the Seamen Church and fishermen.

125 Red Admiral

1975. Butterflies. Multicoloured.

534		1f. Type **125**	9·25	7·00
535		1f.20 Orange tiger	12·00	9·00

126 Cod and St. Pierre et Miquelon Stamp of 1909

1975. Air. "Arphila 75" International Stamp Exhibition, Paris.

536	**126**	4f. red, indigo and blue	26·00	32·00

127 "Pottery" (Potter's wheel and products)

1975. Artisan Handicrafts.

537	**127**	50c. purple, brown & green	5·50	9·00
538	-	60c. blue and yellow	6·00	9·00

DESIGN: 60c. "Sculpture" (wood carving of Virgin and Child).

128 Pointe-Plate Lighthouse and Sea-birds

1975. Lighthouses.

539	**128**	6c. black, violet and green	3·75	7·00
540	-	10c. purple, green and slate	5·50	8·50
541	-	20c. brown, indigo & blue	13·50	9·25

DESIGNS: 10c. Galantry lighthouse, Atlantic puffin and pintail; 20c. Cap Blanc lighthouse and blue whale.

129 Judo

1975. Air. "Pre-Olympic Year". Olympic Games, Montreal (1976).

542	**129**	1f.90 blue, red and violet	11·50	15·00

130 Concorde in Flight

1976. Air. Concorde's 1st Commercial Flight.

543	**130**	10f. indigo, blue and red	25·00	29·00

131 President Pompidou

1976. President Pompidou Commemoration.

544	**131**	1f.10 grey and purple	6·50	16·00

132 Alexander Graham Bell and Early Telephone

1976. Air. Telephone Centenary.

545	**132**	5f. blue, orange and red	7·25	17·00

133 Washington and Lafayette

1976. Bicentenary of American Revolution.

546	**133**	1f. multicoloured	2·75	5·00

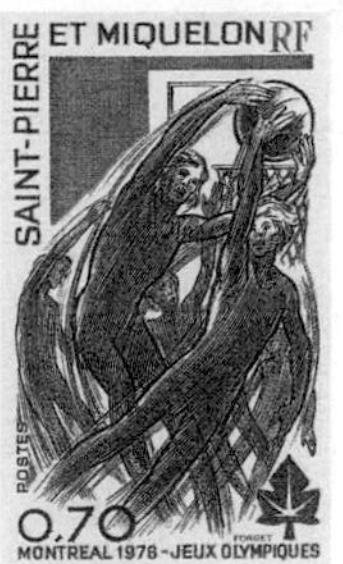

134 Basketball

1976. Olympic Games, Montreal.

547	**134**	70c. agate, blue and brown	6·00	12·50
548	-	2f.50 turquoise, green and emerald	12·00	23·00

DESIGN—HORIZ: 2f.50, Swimming.

135 Vigie Dam

1976

549	**135**	2f.20 brown, blue & turq	7·00	18·00

136 "Croix de Lorraine"

1976. Stern Trawlers. Multicoloured.

550		1f.20 Type **136**	13·00	12·00
551		1f.50 "Geolette"	29·00	24·00

1986. Nos. 2444 etc of France optd ST-PIERRE ET MIQUELON.

552	**916**	5c. green	20	4·00
553	**916**	10c. red	20	4·00
554	**916**	20c. green	20	4·00
555	**916**	30c. red	20	4·00
556	**916**	40c. brown	20	4·00
557	**916**	50c. mauve	20	4·00
558	**916**	1f. green	20	4·00
559	**916**	1f.80 green	35	4·25
560	**916**	2f. green	45	4·25
561	**916**	2f.20 red	55	1·80
562	**916**	2f. brown	55	5·00
563	**916**	3f.20 blue	55	5·00
564	**916**	4f. red	75	5·25
565	**916**	5f. blue	90	6·25
566	**916**	10f. violet	1·80	8·00

138 Open Book

1986. 450th Anniv of Discovery of Islands by Jacques Cartier and 1st Anniv of New Constitution.

567	**138**	2f.20 brown, deep brown and green	90	4·75

139 Statue and Harbour

1986. Centenary of Statue of Liberty.

568	**139**	2f.50 blue and red	1·10	2·40

141 Atlantic Cod and Detection Equipment

1986. Fishing.

578	**141**	1f. red	45	4·25
579	**141**	1f.10 orange	45	4·25
580	**141**	1f.30 red	55	4·25
581	**141**	1f.40 blue	55	4·25
582	**141**	1f.40 red	85	4·25
583	**141**	1f.50 blue	90	4·25
584	**141**	1f.60 green	1·00	4·25
585	**141**	1f.70 green	1·20	4·25

142 "Nativity" (stained glass window, L. Balmet)

1986. Christmas.

586	**142**	2f.20 multicoloured	1·00	4·75

143 Buff Cap ("Hygrophorus pratensis")

1987

587	**143**	2f.50 brown and ochre	1·80	5·00

See also Nos. 598, 609 and 645.

144 Dunan and Hospital

1987. Dr. Francois Dunan Commemoration.
588 **144** 2f.20 black, brown and blue 1·30 4·75

145 Ocean-racing Yachts

1987. Transatlantic Yacht Race (Lorient–St. Pierre et Miquelon–Lorient).
589 **145** 5f. brown, dp blue & blue 2·75 5·50

146 Maps

1987. Visit of President Francois Mitterand.
590 **146** 2f.20 multicoloured 1·30 5·00

147 Schooner on Slipway and Share Certificate

1987. Centenary of Marine Slipway.
591 **147** 2f.50 brown and light brown 2·00 5·00

148 Hawker Siddeley H.S. 748 (St. Pierre–Montreal first flight, 1987)

1987. Air. Airplanes named "Ville de St. Pierre".
592 **148** 5f. blue, green & turquoise 3·25 5·50
593 - 10f. dp blue, blue & orge 5·50 7·75
DESIGN: 10f. Flying boat "Ville de Saint-Pierre" (first flight, 1939).

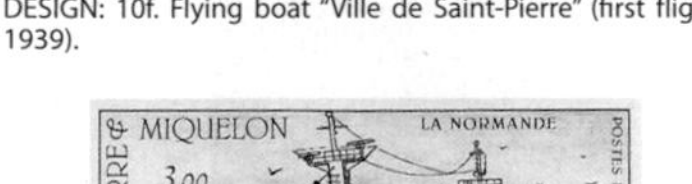

149 "La Normande" (trawler)

1987
594 **149** 3f. multicoloured 3·00 6·25

150 "St. Christopher carrying Christ Child" (stained glass window by L. Balmet) and Scout Emblem

1987. Christmas. 50th Anniv of Scouting.
595 **150** 2f.20 multicoloured 1·80 4·50

151 Horses and Ducks

1987. Natural Heritage. Le Grand Barachois. Each orange, green and brown.
596 3f. Type **151** 2·40 5·25
597 3f. Canada geese, gulls and seals 2·40 5·25
Nos. 596/7 were printed together, se-tenant, with intervening half stamp size label, each strip forming a composite design.

1988. Fungi. As T 143.
598 2f.50 black, orange and brown 1·40 4·50
DESIGN: "Russula paludosa".

152 Ice Hockey Goalkeeper

1988. Winter Olympic Games, Calgary.
599 **152** 5f. blue and red 2·00 6·00

153 Thomas and Camera

1988. Birth Centenary of Dr. Louis Thomas (photographer).
600 **153** 2f.20 brown, deep brown and blue 1·00 4·50

154 Airship "Hindenburg"

1988. Air. Aircraft. Each black, blue and purple.
601 5f. Type **154** 3·25 5·50
602 10f. Douglas DC-3 5·50 8·00

1988. "Philexfrance 89" International Stamp Exhibition, Paris. No. 2821 of France optd ST-PIERRE ET MIQUELON.
603 **1073** 2f.20 red, black and blue 1·70 4·75

156 "Nellie J. Banks" and Crates

1988. 50th Anniv of End of Prohibition and Last Liquor Smuggling Run from St. Pierre to Canada.
604 **156** 2f.50 ultramarine, brn & bl 2·30 5·00

157 "Le Marmouset" (stern trawler)

1988
605 **157** 3f. multicoloured 2·00 5·00

158 Ross Cove

1988. Natural Heritage. Each brown, deep blue and blue.
606 2f.20 Type **158** 2·00 4·50
607 13f.70 Cap Perce 4·50 13·50

159 Stained Glass Window

1988. Christmas.
608 **159** 2f.20 multicoloured 1·20 4·50

1989. Fungi. As T 143.
609 2f.50 brown and red 1·40 4·50
DESIGN: 2f.50, "Tricholoma virgatum".

160 Judo

1989. 25th Anniv of Judo in St. Pierre.
610 **160** 5f. black, green and orange 2·30 5·50

161 "Liberty" (Roger Druet)

1989. Bicentenary of French Revolution and Declaration of Rights of Man. Multicoloured.
611 2f.20 Type **161** 1·10 4·50
612 2f.20 "Equality" 1·10 4·50
613 2f.20 "Fraternity" 1·10 4·50

162 Piper Aztec

1989. Air.
614 **162** 20f. brown, light brown and blue 7·75 9·50

163 Tower of Bastille and Phrygian Cap on Tree

1989. "Philexfrance '89" International Stamp Exhibition, Paris (2nd issue) and Bicentenary of French Revolution (2nd issue). Sheet 150×140 mm containing T 163 and similar vert designs, each ultramarine, scarlet and black.
MS615 5f. Type **163**; 5f. Two towers of Bastille and brigantine; 5f. Raising tree of liberty; 5f. People cheering 11·00 28·00

164 Fisherman in Boat

1989. Natural Heritage. Ile aux Marins. Each brown, blue and green.
616 2f.20 Type **164** 1·80 4·50
617 13f.70 Boy flying kite from boat 5·50 13·00

165 "Le Malabar" (ocean-going tug)

1989
618 **165** 3f. multicoloured 2·10 4·50

166 Georges Landry and Emblem

1989. Centenary of Islands' Bank.
619 **166** 2f.20 blue and brown 1·30 4·50

167 "Christmas" (Magali Olano)

1989. Christmas.
620 **167** 2f.20 multicoloured 1·30 4·50

1990. Stamps of France optd ST-PIERRE ET MIQUELON.
621 **1118** 10c. brown 60 3·75
622 **1118** 20c. green 60 3·75
623 **1118** 50c. violet 60 3·75
624 **1118** 1f. orange 75 3·75
625 **1118** 2f. green 1·00 4·00
626 **1118** 2f. blue 1·00 4·00
627 **1118** 2f.10 green 85 4·00
628 **1118** 2f.20 green 2·00 4·00
629 **1118** 2f.30 red 1·20 3·75
630 **1118** 2f.40 green 2·10 4·25
631 **1118** 2f.50 red 1·80 4·00
632 **1118** 2f.70 green 2·00 2·75
633 **1118** 3f.20 blue 1·40 4·00
634 **1118** 3f.40 blue 2·00 4·25
635 **1118** 3f.50 green 1·60 4·50
636 **1118** 3f.80 mauve 1·40 4·00
637 **1118** 3f.80 blue 1·70 3·25
638 **1118** 4f. mauve 2·00 4·50
639 **1118** 4f.20 mauve 2·30 4·50
640 **1118** 4f.40 blue 1·80 4·50
641 **1118** 4f.50 mauve 2·00 4·00
642 **1118** 5f. blue 2·30 4·50
643 **1118** 10f. violet 3·25 5·75

The 2f.50 exists both perforated (ordinary gum) and imperforate (self-adhesive).

1990. Fungi. As T 143.
645 2f.50 brown, black and orange 1·40 4·50
DESIGN: 2f.50, Hedgehog fungus ("Hydnum repandum").

168 "Pou du Ciel" and Gull

1990. Air.
646 **168** 5f. green, blue and brown 2·00 5·00

169 De Gaulle and Soldiers

1990. 50th Anniv of De Gaulle's Call to Resist.
647 **169** 2f.30 purple, red and blue 1·20 4·25
For design as T **169** but inscr "1890–1970", see No. 653.

170 Runner and Map

1990. Miquelon 25 km Race.
648 **170** 5f. black, blue and brown 2·50 4·50

171 Moose, Micmac Canoe and Woman

1990
649 **171** 2f.50 orange, brown & bl 1·30 4·50

172 "Saint-Denis" and "Saint-Pierre" at Moorings

1990. Trawlers.
650 **172** 3f. multicoloured 1·90 4·50

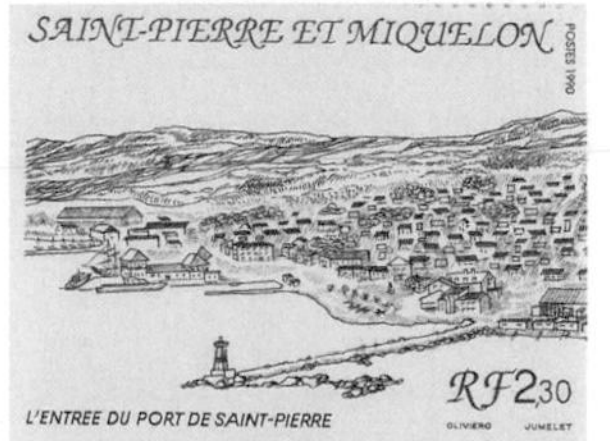

173 Entrance to Saint-Pierre Port

1990. St.-Pierre. Each brown, green and blue.
651 2f.30 Type **173** 1·60 4·50
652 14f.50 Interpeche fish factory 4·50 7·25
Nos. 651/2 were issued together, se-tenant, with intervening label, forming a composite design of part of St.-Pierre coastline.

1990. Birth Centenary of Charles de Gaulle (French statesman). As T 169 but Inscr "1890–1970". Each purple, red and blue.
653 1f.70 Type **169** 1·00 1·60
654 2f.30 De Gaulle and trawler 1·20 1·80

174 Christmas Scene (Cindy Lechevallier)

1990. Christmas.
655 **174** 2f.30 multicoloured 1·40 4·50

175 Short-tailed Swallowtail on "Heracleum maximum"

1991
656 **175** 2f.50 multicoloured 1·40 4·50

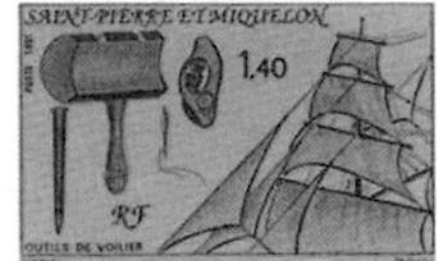

176 Sail-makers' Tools and Sails

1991
657 **176** 1f.40 green and yellow 1·20 2·75
658 **176** 1f.70 red and yellow 1·40 3·25

177 Ile aux Marins

1991. Old Views.
659 **177** 1f.70 blue 90 3·25
660 - 1f.70 blue 90 3·25
661 - 1f.70 blue 90 3·25
662 - 1f.70 blue 90 3·25
663 **177** 2f.50 red 1·20 3·50
664 - 2f.50 red 1·20 3·50
665 - 2f.50 red 1·20 3·50
666 - 2f.50 red 1·20 3·50
DESIGNS: Nos. 660, 664, Langlade; 661, 665, Miquelon; 662, 666, Saint-Pierre.

178 Piper Tomahawk

1991. Air.
667 **178** 10f. blue, turquoise & brown 4·50 6·50

179 Musicians

1991. Centenary of Lyre Music Society.
668 **179** 2f.50 red, brown & orange 1·80 4·50

180 Oars

1991. St. Pierre–Newfoundland Crossing by Rowing Boat.
669 **180** 2f.50 multicoloured 1·70 4·50

181 Pelota Players

1991. Basque Sports.
670 **181** 5f. green and red 2·00 4·75

182 Fishermen

1991. Natural Heritage. Multicoloured.
671 2f.50 Type **182** 1·40 4·00
672 14f.50 Canada geese and shore 5·50 11·50
Nos. 671/2 were issued together, se-tenant, forming a composite design of Savoyard.

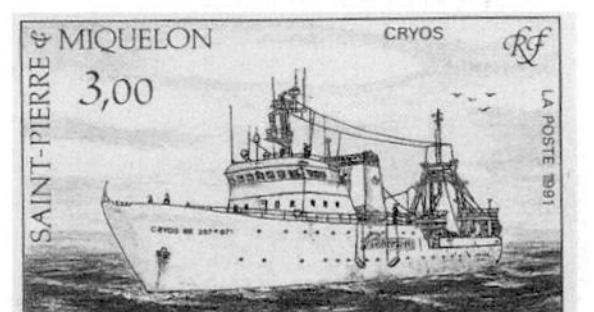

183 "Cryos" (stern trawler)

1991
673 **183** 3f. multicoloured 2·50 4·50

184 Free French Central Bank 100f. Note

1991. 50th Anniv of Central Economic Co-operation Bank.
674 **184** 2f.50 multicoloured 1·50 4·50

185 Naval Forces and Cross of Lorraine

1991. Christmas. 50th Anniv of Adherence to Free French Government.
675 **185** 2f.50 multicoloured 1·30 4·25

186 Muselier and Harbour

1992. 110th Birth Anniv of Admiral E. Muselier (commander of 1941 Free French landing force).
676 **186** 2f.50 multicoloured 1·40 4·00

187 Ice Skating

1992. Winter Olympic Games, Albertville.
677 **187** 5f. blue, ultramarine & mve 1·80 4·50

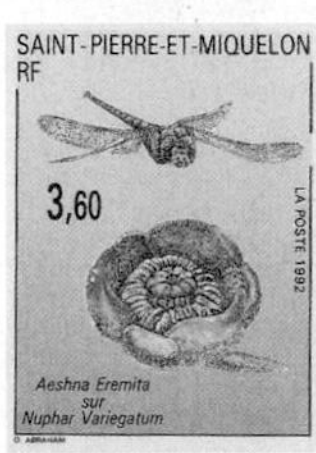

188 "Aeshna eremita" and "Nuphar variegatum"

1992
678 **188** 3f.60 multicoloured 1·70 4·25

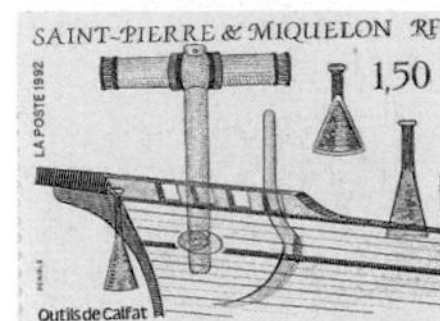

189 Boat-building Tools and Stern of Ship

1992
679 **189** 1f.50 brown and blue 80 4·00
680 **189** 1f.80 blue and azure 90 4·00

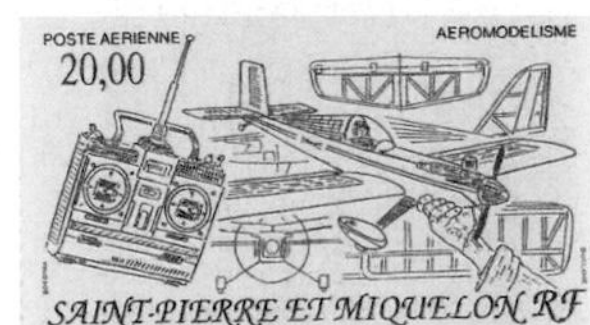

190 Model Airplane and Remote Control

1992
681 **190** 20f. red, orange and brown 6·50 8·75

191 Ile aux Marins Lighthouse

1992. Lighthouses. Multicoloured.
682 2f.50 Type **191** 1·50 3·50
683 2f.50 Galantry 1·50 3·50
684 2f.50 Old Rouge Feu lighthouse, St. Pierre 1·50 3·50
685 2f.50 Pointe-Plate 1·50 3·50

192 Cones and Common Flicker

1992. Natural Heritage. Dolisie Valley, Langlade. Multicoloured.
686 2f.50 Type **192** 1·70 4·00
687 15f.10 Valley and berries 4·50 6·75

193 Columbus and Map on Sails

1992. 500th Anniv of Discovery of America by Columbus.

688	**193**	5f.10 multicoloured	2·30	4·75

194 Baron de l'Esperance, Map and Settlers

1992. 230th Anniv (1993) of Resettlement by French of Miquelon.

689	**194**	2f.50 brown, blue and red	1·30	4·00

195 Nativity

1992. Christmas.

690	**195**	2f.50 multicoloured	1·30	4·00

196 Birot and Free French Corvette

1993. 50th Death Anniv (1992) of Commander R. Birot.

691	**196**	2f.50 multicoloured	1·60	4·00

197 Divers and Wreck of "L'Hortense"

1993. Deep Sea Diving.

692	**197**	5f. multicoloured	2·50	4·50

198 Longhorn Beetle on "Cichorium intybus"

1993

693	**198**	3f.60 multicoloured	2·50	4·25

199 Cutting up Cod

1993

694	**199**	1f.50 multicoloured	1·40	4·00
695	**199**	1f.80 multicoloured	1·40	4·00

200 Greater Shearwater

1993. Air. Migratory Birds. Multicoloured.

696	5f. Type **200**	3·00	4·25
697	10f. American golden plover	4·00	5·50

201 Fleet of Ships

1993. Bicentenary of Settlement of Madeleine Islands.

698	**201**	5f.10 blue, green & brown	2·50	4·50

1993. No. 3121 of France optd ST-PIERRE ET MIQUELON.

699	**1118**	(–) red	1·20	4·00

202 Short-spined Seascorpion

1993. Fishes. Multicoloured.

700	2f.80 Type **202**	1·80	2·75
701	2f.80 Fishermen and capelin ("Le Capelan")	1·80	2·75
702	2f.80 Ray ("Le Raie")	1·80	2·75
703	2f.80 Atlantic halibut ("Le Fletan")	1·80	2·75

203 Pine Cones, Otter and Left Bank

1993. Natural Heritage. Sylvain Hills. Multicoloured.

704	2f.80 Type **203**	1·80	3·00
705	16f. Otter on all fours, pine cones and right bank	6·50	7·25

Nos. 704/5 were issued together, se-tenant, with intervening ¾ stamp-size label, forming a composite design of an otter pool.

204 Prefect's Residence

1993

707	**204**	3f.70 blue, yellow & brn	2·00	3·25

205 Father Christmas waving to Child

1993. Christmas.

708	**205**	2f.80 multicoloured	2·00	3·00

206 Blaison and "Surcouf" (Free French submarine)

1994. 50th Death Anniv (1992) of Commander Louis Blaison.

709	**206**	2f.80 multicoloured	2·00	3·25

207 Player lining up Shot

1994. 1st French Overseas Territories Petanque Championship.

710	**207**	5f.10 multicoloured	2·50	3·75

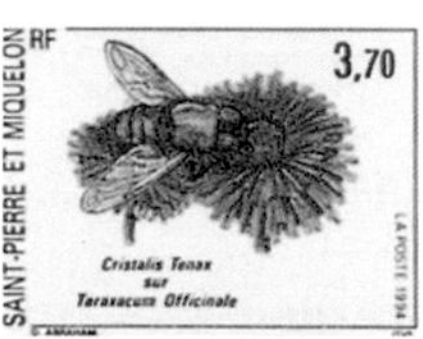

208 "Cristalis tenax" on Dandelion

1994

711	**208**	3f.70 multicoloured	1·80	3·50

209 Drying Atlantic Cod

1994

712	**209**	1f.50 black and green	85	3·00
713	**209**	1f.80 multicoloured	1·10	3·00

210 Ballot Box and Women outside Town Hall

1994. 50th Anniv of Women's Suffrage.

714	**210**	2f.80 multicoloured	1·40	3·00

211 "Saint-Pierre" (sail hospital ship)

1994. Centenary of Society of Sea Works.

715	**211**	2f.80 multicoloured	1·70	4·00

212 "Miquelon" (trawler)

1994. Ships. Multicoloured.

MS716 2f.80 Type **233**; 2f.80 "Ile de St. Pierre" (trawler); 3f.70 "St. Georges XII" (pleasure cruiser); 3f. 70"St. Eugene IV" (pleasure cruiser)	5·25	5·25

213 Poolside

1994. Natural Heritage. Miranda Pool. Mult.

720	2f.80 Type **213**	1·40	2·50
721	16f. Pool	5·50	7·25

Nos. 720/1 were issued together se-tenant with intervening ½ stamp-size label, forming a composite design.

214 Parochial School

1994

722	**214**	3f.70 black, blue and red	1·70	3·25

215 Envelope, Magnifying Glass and Tweezers holding "Stamp"

1994. 1st European Stamp Salon, Flower Gardens, Paris.

723	**215**	3f.70 blue, green and yellow	2·00	3·50

216 House and Christmas Tree

1994. Christmas.

724	**216**	2f.80 multicoloured	1·70	3·00

217 Pasteur

1995. Death Centenary of Louis Pasteur (chemist).

725	**217**	2f.80 multicoloured	1·70	3·00

218 Sports Pictograms

1995. Triathlon.

726	**218**	5f.10 multicoloured	2·20	3·50

219 "Dicranum scoparium" and "Cladonia cristatella"

1995

727 **219** 3f.70 multicoloured 1·60 3·25

220 Cooper at Work

1995

728 **220** 1f.50 multicoloured 70 3·00
729 **220** 1f.80 multicoloured 90 3·00

221 Arctic Terns

1995. Air. Migratory Birds.

730 **221** 10f. multicoloured 4·50 4·50

222 Crab

1995. Crustaceans and Molluscs. Multicoloured.

731 2f.80 Winkle 2·00 3·00
732 2f.80 Type **222** 2·00 3·00
733 2f.80 Scallop 2·00 3·00
734 2f.80 Lobster 2·00 3·00

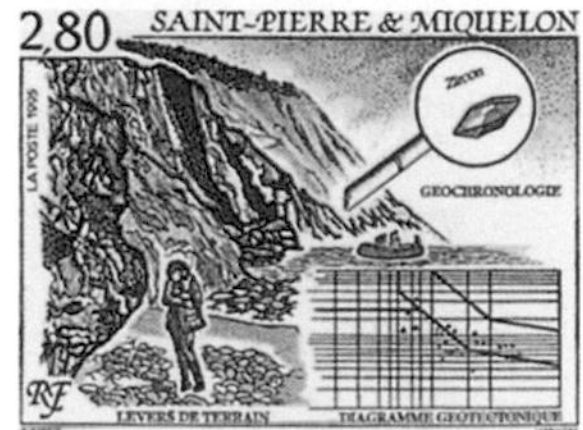

223 Geologists working at Cliff Face

1995. Geological Research. Multicoloured.

735 2f.80 Type **223** 1·80 2·75
736 16f. Geological map of Langlade 4·50 6·25

224 Sister Cesarine

1995. 150th Birth Anniv of Sister Cesarine.

737 **224** 1f.80 multicoloured 1·10 3·00

225 Building

1995. Francoforum.

738 **225** 3f.70 grey, blue and red 1·70 3·25

226 De Gaulle and French Flag

1995. 25th Death Anniv of Charles de Gaulle (French President, 1958–69).

739 **226** 14f. multicoloured 4·50 5·25

227 Shop Window

1995. Christmas.

740 **227** 2f.80 multicoloured 2·30 3·00

228 Levasseur and Free French Corvette

1996. 50th Death Anniv (1997) of Commander Jean Levasseur.

741 **228** 2f.80 multicoloured 2·50 3·25

229 Boxers

1996

742 **229** 5f.10 multicoloured 2·75 3·50

230 "Cladonia verticillata" and "Polytrichum juniperinum"

1996. Mosses and Lichens.

743 **230** 3f.70 multicoloured 2·50 3·25

231 Blacksmiths at Work

1996

744 **231** 1f.50 multicoloured 1·00 2·75
745 **231** 1f.80 multicoloured 1·10 3·00

232 Whimbrel

1996. Air. Migratory Birds.

746 **232** 15f. multicoloured 7·25 5·25

233 "Rader II" (pilot boat)

1996. Ships. Sheet 143×100 mm. containing T 233 and similar horiz designs. Multicoloured.

MS747 3f. Type **233**; 3f. "Lanelape" (ferry); 3f. "Pinta" (ferry); 3f. "Pascal-Annie" (trawler) 5·25 5·25

234 The Cape

1996. Miquelon. Multicoloured.

748 3f. Type **234** 1·30 2·50
749 15f.50 The village 4·50 5·00

Nos. 748/9 were issued together, se-tenant, with intervening ¾ stamp-size label, forming a composite design.

235 Customs House

1996. Centenary of Customs House, St. Pierre.

750 **235** 3f.80 blue and black 1·60 3·00

236 1947 Postage Due Design

1996. 50th Paris Autumn Stamp Show.

751 **236** 1f. multicoloured 55 2·75

237 Crib in St. Pierre Cathedral

1996. Christmas.

752 **237** 3f. multicoloured 1·60 3·00

238 Colmay

1997. 32nd Death Anniv of Commandant Constant Colmay.

753 **238** 3f. multicoloured 1·60 3·00

239 Common Cormorant and "Sedum rosea"

1997

754 **239** 3f.80 multicoloured 2·00 3·00

240 Salting House

1997

755 **240** 1f.70 multicoloured 85 3·00

241 "Doris" (rowing boat) and Construction Plan

1997

756 **241** 2f. multicoloured 85 3·00

242 Player, Ball and Net

1997. Volleyball.

757 **242** 5f.20 multicoloured 2·00 3·25

243 Peregrine Falcon

1997. Air. Migratory Birds.

758 **243** 5f. multicoloured 2·50 3·25

244 Statue of Liberty, "L'Oiseau Blanc" and Eiffel Tower

1997. Air. 70th Anniv of Disappearance of Charles Nungesser and Francois Coli (aviators) on attempted Non-stop Flight between Paris and New York.

759 **244** 14f. black, blue and brown 4·50 5·25

245 Atlantic Salmon

1997. Fishes. Multicoloured.

760 3f. Type **245** 1·30 3·00
761 3f. Lumpsucker ("Poule d'Eau") 1·30 3·00
762 3f. Atlantic mackerel ("Maquereau") 1·30 3·00
763 3f. Porbeagle ("Requin Marache") 1·30 3·00

1997. No. 3407 of France (no value expressed) optd ST-PIERRE ET MIQUELON. Ordinary gum or self-adhesive.

764 **1313** (3f.) red 85 2·75

1997. Nos. 3415 etc. of France optd ST-PIERRE ET MIQUELON.

765 **1313** 10c. brown 1·30 2·50
766 **1313** 20c. green 1·30 2·50
767 **1313** 50c. violet 1·50 2·50
768 **1313** 1f. orange 1·60 2·75
769 **1313** 2f. blue 1·70 2·75
770 **1313** 2f.70 green 85 2·75
773 **1313** 3f.50 green 2·00 3·00
775 **1313** 3f.80 blue 1·00 3·00

776	1313	4f.20 red	2·30	3·00
778	1313	4f.40 blue	2·30	3·00
779	1313	4f.50 mauve	2·30	3·00
780	1313	5f. blue	2·30	3·25
781	1313	6f.70 green	2·50	3·25
782	1313	10f. violet	3·25	3·00

246 Cap aux Basques

1997. Multicoloured.. Multicoloured..
785 3f. Type **246** 1·60 2·50
786 15f.50 Diamant 4·50 4·00

Nos. 785/6 were issued together, se-tenant, with intervening ¾ stamp-size label, forming a composite design.

247 Post Office

1997. Public Buildings.
787 **247** 3f.80 multicoloured 2·00 3·00

248 Nativity

1997. Christmas.
788 **248** 3f. multicoloured 2·75 3·00

249 Savary and Building

1998. 10th Death Anniv of Alain Savary (Governor).
789 **249** 3f. multicoloured 2·00 3·00

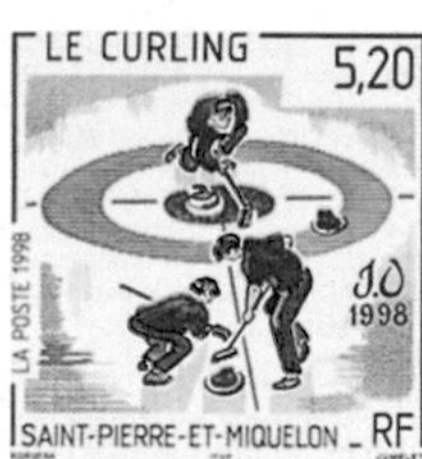
250 Curling

1998. Winter Olympic Games, Nagano, Japan.
790 **250** 5f.20 red, blue and scarlet 2·50 3·25

251 Irises and Horses

1998
791 **251** 3f.80 multicoloured 2·75 3·00

252 Lifting Blocks of Ice

1998. Work on the Ice. Multicoloured.
792 1f.70 Type **252** 1·40 2·75
793 2f. Cutting out blocks of ice 1·40 2·75

253 Head of American Bald Eagle

1998
794 **253** 10f. multicoloured 4·75 4·50

1998. "Philexfrance 99" International Stamp Exhibition, Paris. No. 3460 of France optd ST-PIERRE ET MIQUELON.
795 **1334** 3f. red and blue 2·00 2·75

254 Yellow House

1998. Local Houses. Multicoloured.
796 3f. Type **254** 2·00 2·75
797 3f. Pink house 2·00 2·75
798 3f. White house 2·00 2·75
799 3f. Grey house 2·00 2·75

255 Map of Gulf of St. Lawrence

1998. France in North America.
800 **255** 3f. multicoloured 1·80 2·75

256 Pointe Plate

1998. Natural Heritage. Multicoloured.
801 3f. Type **256** 2·00 2·75
802 15f.50 Cap Bleu 5·00 3·75

Nos. 801/2 were issued together, se-tenant, with intervening ¾ stamp-size label, forming a composite design.

257 Map of the Americas and Map of France on Football

1998. France, World Cup Football Champion.
803 **257** 3f. multicoloured 2·75 2·75

258 War Memorial

1998
804 **258** 3f.80 purple, red and blue 3·00 3·00

259 Santa Claus delivering Presents

1998. Christmas.
805 **259** 3f. multicoloured 2·75 2·75

260 Letournel

1999. 5th Death Anniv of Emile Letournel (orthopaedic surgeon).
806 **260** 3f. olive, green and brown 1·80 2·75

261 Ile-aux-marins Shore

1999
807 **261** 5f.20 multicoloured 2·30 3·25

262 *Rubus chamaemorus*

1999
808 **262** 3f.80 multicoloured 2·30 3·00

1999. Nos. 3553 of France optd ST-PIERRE ET MIQUELON. Ordinary or self-adhesive gum.
809 **1376** 3f. red and blue 1·80 2·75

No. 809 is denominated in both French francs and euros.

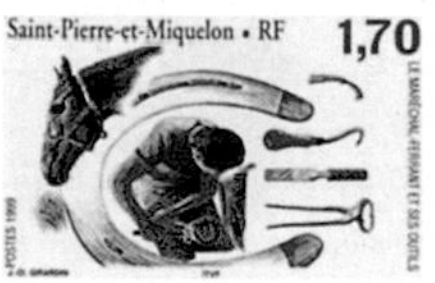
263 Horseshoe, Farrier and Tools

1999. The Farrier. Multicoloured.
811 1f.70 Type **263** 1·80 2·75
812 2f. Farrier at work 2·00 3·00

264 Northern Pintail

1999. Air. Migratory Birds.
813 **264** 20f. multicoloured 10·50 7·75

265 France 1849 20c. St. Pierre et Miquelon 1885 5c. on 2c. and 1909 1c. Stamps

1999. "Philexfrance 99" International Stamp Exhibition, Paris (2nd issue). 150th Anniv of First French Postage Stamp. Sheet 132×159 mm containing T 265 and similar vert designs. Multicoloured.
MS814 3f. Type **265**; 3f. St. Pierre et Miquelon 1932 40c. and 1941 1f.25 stamps; 3f. St.Pierre et Miquelon 1957 50f. and 1967 100f. stamps; 3f. St. Pierre et Miquelon 1986 2f.20 and 1999 3f. stamps 5·00 5·00

266 "Bearn" (steam tug)

1999. Ships. Sheet 143×100m containing T 266 and similar horiz designs. Multicoloured.
MS815 3f. Type **266** ; 3f. "Pro-Patria" (mail ship); 3f. "Eminie" (deep sea fishing boat); 3f. "Colombier" (coastal patrol vessel) 4·50 4·50

267 Cars and Quayside

1999. Place du General de Gaulle. Multicoloured.
816 3f. Type **267** 2·50 3·25
817 15f.50 Boats 5·75 6·25

268 Maps of St. Pierre et Miquelon and France

1999. Visit of President Jacques Chirac of France.
818 **268** 3f. multicoloured 2·75 2·75

269 Interior

1999. Museum and Archives.
819 **269** 5f.40 mauve 3·50 3·25

270 House and Snowman (Best Wishes)

1999. Greetings Stamp.
820 **270** 3f. multicoloured 2·50 2·75

271 "Bonjour l'An 2000"

2000. New Millennium.
821 **271** 3f. multicoloured 3·00 2·75

272 Humpback Whale

2000. Whales.

822	**272**	3f. black and blue	2·50	2·75
823	-	5f.70 black and green	3·75	3·50

DESIGN: 5f.70, Fin whale.

273 "Les Graves"

2000. Art.

824	**273**	5f.20 multicoloured	4·00	3·25

274 *Vaccinium vitis-idaea*

2000

825	**274**	3f.80 multicoloured	3·25	3·00

275 Wood on Dog-sled

2000. The Collection of Wood.

826	**275**	1f.70 blue and black	2·75	2·75
827	**275**	2f. brown and black	2·75	2·75

276 Fishermen, 1904

2000. The Twentieth Century, 1900–1950 (1st issue). Multicoloured.

828		3f. Type **276** (abandonment of fishing and drying rights on French shore)	3·00	2·75
829		3f. Women carrying dried cod, 1905	3·00	2·75
830		3f. Conscripts leaving New York for Le Havre, 1915	3·00	2·75
831		3f. Assault on Souain Hill, 1915	3·00	2·75
832		3f. People on pack ice and icebound ships (isolation of St. Pierre during exceptional weather), 1923	3·00	2·75
833		3f. Unloading contraband during American prohibition era, 1925	3·00	2·75
834		3f. St. Pierre et Miquelon Pavilion at International Colonial Exhibition, Paris, 1931	3·00	2·75
835		3f. Procession flying French and American flags (end of prohibition in America), 1933	3·00	2·75
836		3f. Admiral Muselier of Free French Naval Forces inspecting seamen (loss of *Mimosa* off Terre-Neuve), 1942	3·00	2·75
837		3f. Army vehicles crossing the Rhine, 1945	3·00	2·75

See also Nos. 842/51.

Nos. 818, 820/4, 826/7 and 838 and subsequent St. Pierre et Miquelon issues are denominated both in francs and in euros. As no cash for the latter is in circulation, the catalogue continues to use the franc value.

277 *L'Inger* (wrecked galleon)

2000

838	**277**	5f.40 green	4·00	3·25

278 Houses behind Boat Sheds

2000. Salt Works. Multicoloured.

839		3f. Type **278**	3·00	2·75
840		15f.50 Church behind boat sheds	5·00	3·75

279 Angels, Village and "2000"

2000. Christmas.

841	**279**	3f. multicoloured	3·00	2·75

280 Frozen Fish Factory, 1951

2000. The Twentieth Century, 1950–2000 (2nd issue). Multicoloured.

842		2f. Type **280**	3·00	2·75
843		2f. *Ravenel* (loss of trawler and crew, 1960)	3·00	2·75
844		2f. General de Gaulle meeting ex-servicemen during visit to St. Pierre, 1967	3·00	2·75
845		2f. First television images (inauguration of local station), 1967	3·00	2·75
846		2f. Construction of new port, 1970	3·00	2·75
847		2f. Construction of new college, 1977	3·00	2·75
848		2f. View over islands (change of status to Collective Territoriale and resumption of stamp issues, 1986)	3·00	2·75
849		2f. Eric Tarbarly's racing yacht (Tarbarly's stop-off in St. Pierre during Round the World Yacht Race, 1987)	3·00	2·75
850		2f. Oil rig and map (exploitation of off-shore oil services, 1992)	3·00	2·75
851		2f. Runway extension, White Point Airport, 1999	3·00	2·75

281 Rough-legged Buzzard

2000. Air.

852	**281**	5f. multicoloured	3·75	3·25

282 "2001"

2000. New Millennium.

853	**282**	3f. multicoloured	3·00	2·75

283 Killer Whale

2001. Whales.

854	**283**	3f. black and blue	3·00	2·75
855	-	5f.70 black and green	4·00	3·50

DESIGN: 5f.70, Long-finned pilot whale.

284 "Reflections"

2001

856	**284**	5f.20 multicoloured	3·75	3·25

285 Apple

2001

857	**285**	3f.80 multicoloured	3·25	3·00

286 "Hay gathering"

2001

858	**286**	1f.70 multicoloured	2·75	2·75
859	**286**	2f. multicoloured	2·75	2·75

287 Great Blue Heron

2001. Air.

860	**287**	15f. multicoloured	6·50	3·75

288 Lake in Autumn

2001. Seasons (1st series). Multicoloured.

861		3f. Type **288**	1·80	1·60
862		3f. Lake in winter	1·80	1·60

See also Nos. 871/2.

289 Porch (Maison Jugan)

2001. Porches. Multicoloured.

863		3f. Type **289**	1·80	1·60
864		3f. Marie de L'ile-aux-Marins	1·80	1·60
865		3f. Maison Voge	1·80	1·60
866		3f. Maison Guillou	1·80	1·60

290 Trees, Houses and River

2001. Landscapes. Multicoloured.

867		10f. Type **290**	3·50	2·30
868		10f. Cliff-top houses and church	3·50	2·30

291 Airport

2001. Saint-Pierre Pointe Blanche Airport.

869	**291**	5f. multicoloured	2·30	2·00

292 *Marie-Therese*

2001. Wreck of Marie-Therese off Pointe-du Diamant.

870	**292**	5f.40 green	2·50	2·10

2001. Seasons (2nd series). As T 288. Multicoloured.

871		3f. Lake in spring	1·80	1·60
872		3f. Lake in summer	1·80	1·60

293 Commander Jacques Pepin Lehalleur and *Alysse* (corvette)

2001

873	**293**	3f. multicoloured	1·80	1·60

294 Father Christmas

2001. Christmas.

874	**294**	3f. multicoloured	1·80	1·60

2002. Nos. 3770/82 and 3784/90 of France optd ST-PIERRE ET MIQUELON. (a) With face value. Ordinary gum.

875	**1318**	1c. yellow	1·30	1·40
876	**1318**	2c. brown	1·30	1·40
877	**1318**	5c. green	1·30	1·40
878	**1318**	10c. violet	1·30	1·40
879	**1318**	20c. orange	1·40	1·40
880	**1318**	41c. green	1·80	1·60
881	**1318**	50c. blue	1·80	1·60
882	**1318**	53c. green	1·90	1·60
883	**1318**	58c. blue	2·00	1·70
883a	**1318**	58c. green	1·90	1·60
884	**1318**	64c. orange	2·00	1·70
885	**1318**	67c. blue	2·30	1·70
886	**1318**	69c. mauve	2·30	1·70
887	**1318**	70c. green	2·30	1·80
888	**1318**	90c. blue	2·75	1·80
889	**1318**	€1 turquoise	2·75	1·80
890	**1318**	€1.02 green	2·75	1·80
891	**1318**	€1.11 purple	3·00	2·00
892	**1318**	€1.90 purple	4·25	2·30
893	**1318**	€2 violet	4·50	2·30

(b) (i) No value expressed.

897	**1318**	(41c.) green	1·80	1·50

(ii) Self-adhesive gum.

900	**1318**	(46c.) red	1·60	1·50

295 Magnifying Glass, Birds and Map

2002. "The Archipelago and the Euro".

908	**295**	€1 multicoloured	2·50	1·80

296 Common Seal (*Phoca vitulina*)

2002. Seals (1st series).
909 **296** 46c. black and brown 1·80 1·60
910 - 87c. black and brown 2·50 2·00
DESIGN: 87c. Grey seal (*Halichoerus grypus*).
See also Nos. 926/7.

297 "La Pomme de Pre"

2002
911 **297** 58c. multicoloured 2·00 1·60

298 Laranaga Farm

2002
912 **298** 79c. green 2·50 1·90

299 Mending Nets

2002
913 **299** 26c. orange 1·50 1·60
914 **299** 30c. blue 1·60 1·60

300 Atlantic Puffin

2002
915 **300** €2.50 multicoloured 5·50 3·00

301 West Point

2002
916 **301** 75c. multicoloured 2·30 2·00

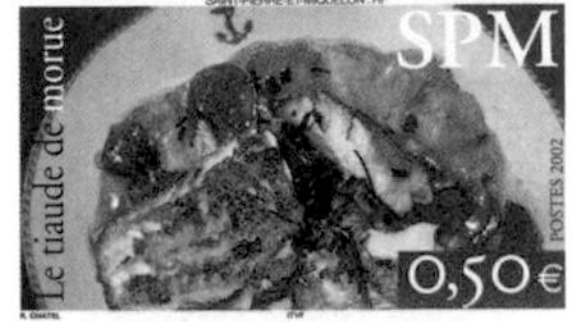

302 "Le Tiaude de Morue" (cod dish)

2002. Traditional Dishes.
917 **302** 50c. multicoloured 1·80 1·70

2002. No. 3752 of France (no value expressed) optd ST-PIERRE ET MIQUELON.
918 **1318** (41c.) red 1·80 1·40

303 Arctic Hare (*Lepus timidus*)

2002
921 **303** 46c. multicoloured 1·80 1·70

304 *Le Troutpool*

2002. Wreck of Le Troutpool off Pointe-du Diamant.
922 **304** 84c. green 2·50 2·00

305 Grand Colombier Island and Sea Bird

2002. L'Anse a Henry Cove.
923 **305** €2 blue, black and yellow 4·00 3·25
924 - €2 blue and black 4·00 3·25
DESIGN: No. 924, Saint Pierre Island Nos. 923/4 were issued together, se-tenant, forming a composite design.

306 Yacht with Christmas Tree on Sail

2002. Christmas.
925 **306** 46c. multicoloured 1·80 1·60

307 Harp Seal (*Phoca groenlandica*)

2003. Seals (2nd series).
926 **307** 46c. black and blue 1·80 1·60
927 - 87c. black and blue 2·50 1·90
DESIGNS: Type **307**; 87c. Hooded seal (*Cystophora cristata*).

308 Francois Maurer

2003. 3rd Death Anniv of Monseigner Francois Maurer (bishop of St. Pierre et Miquelon).
928 **308** 46c. multicoloured 1·80 1·70

309 Capandeguy Farm

2003
929 **309** 79c. brown 2·40 1·90

310 "Les Bleuets" (Marie-Laure Drillet)

2003
930 **310** 75c. multicoloured 2·30 1·90

311 "Le Poulieur" (the pulley man)

2003
931 **311** 30c. blue 1·60 1·60

312 Maison Patrice, Maison Jezequel and Maison Jugan (houses)

2003. International Traditional Architecture Congress. Traditional architecture. Multicoloured.
932 €2 Type **312** 5·00 3·75
933 €2 Notre-Dame des Marins and Maison Borotra 5·00 3·75
Nos. 932/3 were issued together, se-tenant, forming a composite design.

313 Northern Gannet

2003. Air.
934 **313** €2.50 multicoloured 5·50 4·50

314 Player

2003. Centenary of Associations Sportives de Saint-Pierre et Miquelon (ASSP).
935 **314** 50c. multicoloured 1·80 1·70

315 White-tailed Deer (*Odocoileus virginianus*)

2003
936 **315** 50c. multicoloured 1·80 1·70

317 Lions Club Emblem

2003. 50th Anniv of Lions Club (charitable organization).
938 **317** 50c. multicoloured 1·80 1·70

318 *L' Afrique*

2003. Shipwrecks (1st series). L'Afrique (1920).
939 **318** 90c. black 2·75 2·00
See also No. 953.

319 Snow-covered Trees and Icicles

2003. Christmas.
940 **319** 50c. multicoloured 1·80 1·70

320 Joseph Lehuenen

2004. Joseph Lehuenen (politician and historian) Commemoration.
941 **320** 50c. brown 1·80 1·70

321 Anse a Rodrigue

2004
942 **321** 75c. multicoloured 2·75 2·50

322 Atlantic White-sided Dolphin (*Lagenorhynchus acutus*)

2004. Dolphins.
943 **322** 50c. purple and black 1·80 1·70
944 - €1.08 brown and black 3·25 3·25
DESIGN: €1.08 Harbour porpoise (*Phocoena phocoena*).

323 Ollivier Farm

2004
945 **323** 90c. orange 3·00 2·75

316 Strawberries

2003. Langdale Strawberry Jam.
937 **316** 50c. multicoloured 1·80 1·70

324 "Back from Fishing"

2004

946	**324**	30c. multicoloured	1·40	1·40

325 Pro Patria Postal Ship and Sail Ships

2003. St. Pierre et Miquelon Port (circa 1928).

947	€2 black, violet and magenta	6·00	6·00
948	€2 black, violet and blue	6·00	6·00

DESIGNS: €2×2 Type **325**; Sail ships and prow of schooner.

Nos. 947/8 were issued together, se-tenant, forming a composite design.

326 Canada Geese

2004. Air. Migrant Birds.

949	**326**	€2.50 multicoloured	8·00	7·50

327 Map

2004. 500th Anniv of Mi'kmaq (aboriginal Indians) Village.

950	**327**	50c. multicoloured	1·90	2·00

2004. No. 950 optd 1re liason postale à la lame Miquelon - Terre Neuve Associations des Gangos.

951	50c. multicoloured	2·00	2·10

329 Fox

2004

952	**329**	50c. multicoloured	2·10	2·30

330 "Bread, Butter and Poor Cod"

2004

953	**330**	90c. multicoloured	3·00	3·25

331 Ribs of Ship

2004. Shipwrecks (2nd series). Fulwood (1828).

954	**331**	75c. lilac	2·75	3·00

332 *Le Cap Blanc*

2004. Transport Ships. Multicoloured.

MS955 170×115 mm. 50c. ×4, Type **332**; *Le Lisbet-C; Le Shamrock; L'Aldona* 8·00 8·00

333 Footballers

2004. 50th Anniv of SIAA.

956	**333**	44c. multicoloured	1·80	1·90

334 Snow Globe

2004. Christmas.

957	**334**	50c. multicoloured	2·00	2·10

2005. Nos. 4016/4028 of France optd ST-PIERRE ET MIQUELON. (i) With face value.

958	**1586**	1c. yellow	1·00	1·30
959	**1586**	5c. agate	1·10	1·30
960	**1586**	10c. violet	1·20	1·30
961	**1586**	60c. black	1·20	1·30
965	**1586**	55c. ultramarine	1·90	2·00
966	**1586**	58c. yellow	2·00	2·10
966a	**1586**	60c. ultramarine	2·10	2·30
967	**1586**	64c. green	2·20	2·40
968	**1586**	70c. green	2·30	2·40
968a	**1586**	70c. violet	2·30	2·40
969	**1586**	75c. blue	2·40	2·50
970	**1586**	82c. rose	2·50	2·50
970a	**1586**	85c. violet	2·75	2·75
970b	**1586**	86c. rose	2·75	2·75
972	**1586**	90c. indigo	2·75	2·75
973	**1586**	€1 orange	2·75	3·00
974	**1586**	€1.11 purple	3·00	3·25
974a	**1586**	€1.15 blue	3·75	4·00
975	**1586**	€1.22 purple	4·25	4·25
975a	**1586**	€1.30 purple	4·25	4·50
977	**1586**	€1.90 brown	5·00	5·25
981	**1586**	€1.98 purple	5·00	5·25
982a	**1586**	€2.11	7·00	7·25

(ii) Without face value.

983	(45c.) emerald	2·00	2·10
984	(50c.) scarlet	2·10	2·30

(b) Self-adhesive.

985	(50c.) As. No. 984	2·10	2·30

336 Henri Claireaux

2005. Henri Claireaux (politician).

1000	**336**	50c. purple	2·00	2·10

337 Anse a l'Allumette (Match Bay)

2005

1001	**337**	75c. multicoloured	2·75	3·00

338 Common Dolphin (*Delphinus delphis*)

2005. Dolphins.

1002	**338**	53c. black and vermilion	1·90	2·00
1003	-	€1.15 black and green	4·25	4·50

DESIGNS: Type **338**; €1.15 White beaked dolphin (*Lagenorhynchus albirostris*).

339 La Point au Cheval Farm

2005

1004	**339**	90c. olive	3·25	3·50

340 Fog

2005

1005	**340**	30c. multicoloured	1·30	1·40

341 Ferns, Rocks, Bird and Water

2005. Valley of the Seven Ponds. Multicoloured.

1006	€2 Type **341**	6·25	6·50
1007	€2 Water, rock, shrub and rabbit	6·25	6·50

342 Le pluvier siffleur (whistling plover)

2005. Air. Migrant Birds.

1008	**342**	€2.50 multicoloured	8·75	9·25

343 Le lieve variable (arctic hare)

2005

1009	**343**	53c. multicoloured	1·90	2·00

344 "Ben vous savez Madame..." (R. Goineau)

2005

1010	**344**	90c. multicoloured	3·25	3·50

345 *Transpacific*

2005. Shipwrecks.

1011	**345**	75c. blue	2·75	2·75

346 Delegates

2005. 20th Anniv of Collectivite Territoriale.

1012	**346**	53c. multicoloured	2·00	2·10

347 Snowman and Children

2005. Christmas.

1013	**347**	53c. multicoloured	2·00	2·10

348 Le poudrin de choquette (snow-covered trees)

2006

1014	**348**	53c. multicoloured	2·00	2·10

349 La fete des marins (sailors' festival)

2006. Festivals.

1015	**349**	53c. multicoloured	2·00	2·10

350 Albert Pen

2006. Albert Pen (senator) Commemoration.

1016	**350**	53c. chestnut	2·00	2·10

351 Le petit rorqual (*Balaenoptera acutorostrata*)

2006. Marine Mammals.

1017 **351** 53c. purple and black 2·00 2·10

1018 - €1.15 green and black 4·00 4·25

DESIGNS: 53c. Type **351**; €1.15 Le cachalot (*Physeter catodon*).

352 Coastal Houses

2006. Atmosphere.

1019 **352** 30c. multicoloured 1·30 1·30

353 Le goeland arctique (arctic seagull)

2006. Air. Migrant Birds.

1020 **353** €2.53 black and azure 9·00 9·50

354 L'Archipel au Senat (French Senate on beach)

2006

1021 **354** 53c. multicoloured 2·00 2·10

355 Hill, Houses and Beach

2006. Le Petit-Barachois. Multicoloured.

1022 €2 Type **355** 6·25 6·50

1023 €2 Cliffs, houses, boats and beach 6·25 6·50

356 "La Prohibition" (painting) (Jean-Claude Girardin)

2006. Smuggling during USA Alcohol Prohibition.

1024 **356** 75c. multicoloured 2·75 2·75

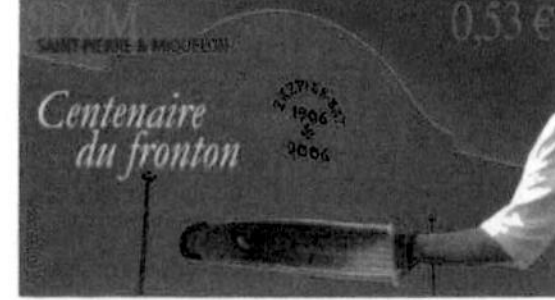

357 Pelota Bat, Ball and Wall

2006. Festivals. Centenary of Pelota Wall.

1025 **357** 53c. multicoloured 2·00 2·10

358 "Spiranthe de Romanzoff"

2006. Orchids.

1026 **358** 53c. black, green and yellow 2·00 2·10

1027 - 53c. multicoloured 2·00 2·10

1028 - 53c. black, green and red 2·00 2·10

1029 - 53c. black, green and yellow 2·00 2·10

DESIGNS: Type **358** (hooded lady's tresses); "Arethusa"; "Habenaire papillon" (small purple fringed orchid); "Habenaire laceree" (ragged fringed orchid).

359 Dugue Farm

2006

1030 **359** 95c. black 3·25 3·50

360 *Penny Fair*

2006. Shipwrecks.

1031 **360** 95c. black 3·25 3·50

361 *Anahitra*

2006. Ships. Multicoloured.

1032 54c. Type **361** 2·00 2·10

1033 54c. *Maria Galanta* 2·00 2·10

1034 54c. *Saint-Eugène V* 2·00 2·10

1035 54c. *Atlantic Jet* 2·00 2·10

362 Baubles<italic />

2006. Christmas.

1036 **362** 54c. multicoloured 2·00 2·10

363 Sister Hilarion

2007. Sister Hilarion Commemoration.

1037 **363** 54c. red and black 2·00 2·10

364 Horses and Sunset

2007

1038 **364** €1.01 multicoloured 3·50 3·75

365 *Plactopecten magellanicus* (La Royale de Miquelon)

2007

1039 **365** €1 multicoloured 3·50 3·75

366 Building Facade

2007. Bicentenary of Court of Auditors.

1040 **366** 54c. blue and vermilion 2·00 2·10

367 Yellow-rumped Warbler (Paruline acroupion jaune)

2007

1041 **367** 44c. multicoloured 1·80 1·90

368 Eider Ducks (L'eider)

2007. Air. Migrant Birds.

1042 **368** €1.50 multicoloured 5·25 5·75

369 *Les Mi'Kmaqs a Miquelon* (Jean-Claude Roy)

2007

1043 **369** 80c. multicoloured 3·00 3·25

370 'La brume de capelan' (fog of small fish)

2007

1044 **370** 30c. multicoloured 1·30 .1·30

371 Seagull

2007. Port Saint-Pierre Harbour. Multicoloured.

1045 **371** €2.40 Type **371** 7·25 7·50

1046 €2.40 Cruiser, buoy and lighthouses 7·25 7·50

Nos. 1095-6 were issued se-tenant, with No. 1096 inverted, in strips of two stamps surrounding a central label, the wholw forming a composite design of the square.

372 Delamaire Farm

2007

1047 **372** €1.06 black 4·00 4·25

373 *Drosera intermedia* (spoon leaved sundew)

2007. Carnivorous Plants. Multicoloured.

1048 54c. Type **373** 2·00 2·10

1049 54c. *Utricularia cornuta* (horned bladderwort) 2·00 2·10

1050 54c. *Pinguicula vulgaris* (common butterwort) 2·00 2·10

1051 54c. *Sarracenia purpurea* (pitcher plant) 2·00 2·10

374 *Le Petit Miquelon*

2007. Passenger Boats. Sheet 170×115 mm containing T 374 and similar horiz designs. Multicoloured.

MS1052 54c.×4, Type **374**; *La Marguerite; L'Ile-aux-Marins; Le Mousse* 7·75 8·00

375 Hunter and White-tailed Deer (Actual size 79×25 mm) (image scaled to 63% of original size)

2007

1053 **375** €1.65 multicoloured 6·25 6·50

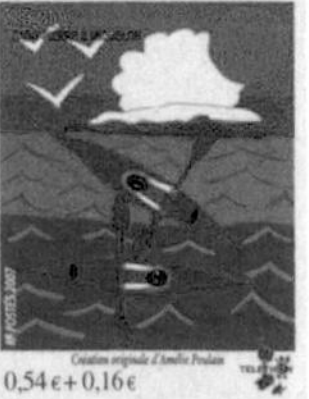

376 Canoeists (Amelie Poulain)

2007. Telethon.

1054 **376** 54c.+16c. multicoloured 2·75 2·75

377 Santa and Elves

2007. Christmas.

1055	**377**	54c. multicoloured	2·10	2·20

378 Rene Autin

2008. Rene Autin (member of Kieffer Commandos, 177 Free French, attached to the British commandos, who landed on Sword Beach in Normandy on D-Day, 1944) Commemoration.

1056	**378**	54c. red and black	2·30	2·40

379 'Regard envieux' (looking enviously)

2008

1057	**379**	€1.01 multicoloured	4·00	4·25

380 Cod Cages

2008. Aquaculture.

1058	**380**	€1 multicoloured	4·25	4·25

381 Tern, Shoreline and Butterfly

2008. Natural Heritage. Conservation of Littoral Zone–Langdale Dunes. Multicoloured.

1059	€2.40 Type **381**	8·50	9·00
1060	€2.40 Shore lark	8·50	9·00

Nos. 1059/60 were issued together, se-tenant, forming a composite design of the fore shore.

382 'Paruline a gorge noir'

2008. Black-throated Green Warbler.

1061	**382**	47c. multicoloured	2·30	2·40

383 Jam Jars, Bear, Ducks and Barrel

2008. Local Crafts.

1062	**383**	33c. black and olive	1·50	1·60

2008. Nos. 4407/9 and 4417/18 of France optd with T 137. (i) With face value. Ordinary gum.

1063	**1743**	1c. yellow	1·00	1·00
1065	**1743**	5c. agate	1·00	1·00
1067	**1743**	10c. black	1·00	1·00

(ii) Without face value.

1073	(50c.) emerald	2·40	2·40
1074	(55c.) scarlet	2·75	2·75

385 Return from Fishing (Michelle Foliot)

2008

1081	**385**	80c. multicoloured	3·75	4·00

386 Arlequin plongeur (harlequin duck)

2008. Air. Migrant Birds.

1082	**386**	€1.50 multicoloured	6·50	7·00

387 'Les deferlantes' (the waves)

2008

1083	**387**	55c. multicoloured	2·50	2·75

388 'Partir en degrat'

2008

1084	**388**	55c. multicoloured	2·50	2·75

389 Taekwondo

2008

1085	**389**	55c. multicoloured	2·50	2·75

390 Loading Sledge

2008. Ice Harvesting. Sheet 170×115 mm containing T 390 and similar horiz designs. Multicoloured.

MS1086	€1×4, Type **390**: Moving ice; Transporting ice; Sawing ice	16·00	17·00

391 Hunter and Hare (image scaled to 61% of original size)

2008

1087	**391**	€1.65 multicoloured	7·25	7·50

392 Christmas Window

2008. Christmas.

1088	**392**	55c. multicoloured	2·75	3·00

393 'Bruant fauve'

2009. Fox Sparrow.

1089	**393**	47c. multicoloured	2·40	2·50

394 'Couleurs d'hiver'

2009. Colours of Winter.

1090	**394**	€1 multicoloured	4·75	5·00

395 Henri Moraze

2009. Henri Moraze (entrepreneur) Commemoration.

1091	**395**	56c. orange-brown and black	3·00	3·25

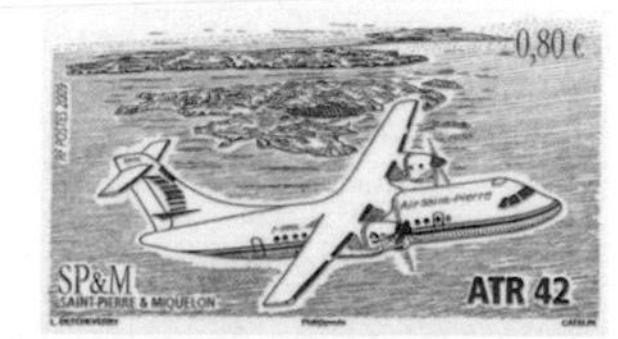

396 ATR 42

2009. Aviation.

1092	**396**	80c. new blue and black	4·00	4·25

2009. Local Crafts. As Type 383.

1093	33c. indigo and emerald	1·50	1·60

397 *Le banc bleu* (Raphaele Goineau)

2009

1094	**397**	56c. multicoloured	2·75	3·00

398 Place Mgr Francois Maurer

2009. Place Mgr Francois Maurer. Each reddish brown and cobalt.

1095	€2.50 Type **398**	11·00	11·50
1096	€2.50 Place Mgr Francois Maurer, right	11·00	11·50

Nos. 1095-1096 were issued se-tenant, with No. 1096 inverted, in strips of two stamps surrounding a central label, the whole forming a composite design of the square.

399 Tennis Racquet and Lighthouse

2009. Tennis in Saint Pierre et Miquelon.

1097	**399**	€1.05 multicoloured	4·75	5·00

400 Seaman and Ships

2009. Centenary of First Stamp.

1098	**400**	€1 multicoloured	4·50	4·75

401 Duck Shoot (image scaled to 61% of original size)

2009

1099	**401**	€1.50 multicoloured	7·25	7·50

402 Moving Building

2009. The Radio Before–After.

1100	**402**	56c. multicoloured	2·75	3·00

403 Tide Hut (Maree de cabane)

2009

1101	**403**	80c. multicoloured	4·00	4·25

404 Yachts, Men and Ice Floes (les glaces dans le port de Saint-Pierre)

2009. St. Pierre Port blocked by Ice. Sheet 170×115 mm containing T 404 and similar horiz designs.

MS1102		56c.×4, Type **404**; Ship and man driving ox (La marche sue la glace); Lighthouse and ice floes (Le phare de la Point-aux-Canons); Ships caught in ice (Les bateaux de peche dans le glaces)	10·50	11·00

405 The Nativity

2008. Christmas.

1103	**405**	56c. multicoloured	2·75	3·00

406 Richard Bartlett

2010. Richard Bartlett (with Free French Forces during WW II and president of Aero Club of St Pierre et Miquelon) Commemoration.

1104	**406**	56c. salmon and black	2·75	3·00

407 'Paruline noir et blanc'

2010. Black and White Warbler.

1105	**407**	47c. multicoloured	2·40	2·50

408 'La pêche au crabe'

2010. Crab Fishing.

1106	**408**	€1 multicoloured	4·50	4·75

409 'Le cap de Miquelon' and Eider Ducks

2010. Natural Heritage. Cape of Miquelon. Multicoloured.

1107	€2.50 Type **409**	11·00	11·50
1108	€2.50 Cape and buoy	11·00	11·50

Nos. 11107/8 were issued se-tenant, strips of two stamps surrounding a illustrated label, the strip forming a composite design of the Cape.

PARCEL POST STAMPS

1901. Optd COLIS POSTAUX.

P79	**D**	10c. black on lilac	£130	£140

1901. Optd Colis Postaux.

P80	**D**	10c. red	20·00	28·00

1917. Nos. 83 and 85 optd Colis Postaux.

P109	**17**	10c. red and pink	2·30	11·00
P110	**17**	20c. purple and brown	75	5·50

1941. Free French Plebiscite. No. P110 optd FRANCE LIBRE F. N. F. L.

P303	**17**	20c. purple and brown	£700	£750

POSTAGE DUE STAMPS

1892. Postage Due stamps of French Colonies optd ST-PIERRE M-on.

D60	**U**	5c. black	75·00	90·00
D61	**U**	10c. black	29·00	20·00
D62	**U**	15c. black	20·00	16·00
D63	**U**	20c. black	18·00	17·00
D64	**U**	30c. black	23·00	21·00
D65	**U**	40c. black	12·00	26·00
D66	**U**	60c. black	90·00	90·00
D67	**U**	1f. brown	£150	£150
D68	**U**	2f. brown	£150	£150

1925. Postage Due type of France optd SAINT-PIERRE-ET-MIQUELON or surch also centimes a percevoir and value in figures.

D135	**D11**	5c. blue	50	3·25
D136	**D11**	10c. brown	55	5·75
D137	**D11**	20c. olive	45	4·75
D138	**D11**	25c. red	75	4·75
D139	**D11**	30c. red	85	6·50
D140	**D11**	45c. green	1·20	6·50
D141	**D11**	50c. red	1·60	5·00
D142	**D11**	60c. on 50c. brown	1·70	9·25
D143	**D11**	1f. red	2·00	8·00
D144	**D11**	2f. on 1f. red	2·30	12·50
D145	**D11**	3f. mauve	9·25	32·00

D30 Newfoundland Dog

1932

D163	**D30**	5c. black and blue	1·00	8·00
D164	**D30**	10c. black and green	2·00	8·25
D165	**D30**	20c. black and red	3·50	9·00
D166	**D30**	25c. black and purple	4·75	9·00
D167	**D30**	30c. black and orange	6·00	11·00
D168	**D30**	45c. black and blue	8·25	13·00
D169	**D30**	50c. black and green	13·00	24·00
D170	**D30**	60c. black and red	12·00	32·00
D171	**D30**	1f. black and brown	30·00	65·00
D172	**D30**	2f. black and purple	44·00	50·00
D173	**D30**	3f. black and brown	50·00	65·00

D40 Atlantic Cod

1938

D208	**D40**	5c. black	10	5·75
D209	**D40**	10c. purple	10	7·00
D210	**D40**	15c. green	10	7·50
D211	**D40**	20c. blue	10	7·50
D212	**D40**	30c. red	30	7·25
D213	**D40**	50c. green	65	7·00
D214	**D40**	60c. blue	1·20	7·75
D215	**D40**	1f. red	1·20	7·50
D216	**D40**	2f. brown	1·50	11·50
D217	**D40**	3f. violet	2·40	11·50

1941. Free French Plebiscite. Nos. D208/17 optd NOEL 1941 F N F L.

D235	**D40**	5c. black	50·00	55·00
D236	**D40**	10c. purple	55·00	55·00
D237	**D40**	15c. green	55·00	55·00
D238	**D40**	20c. blue	50·00	55·00
D239	**D40**	30c. red	46·00	55·00
D240	**D40**	50c. green	65·00	70·00
D241	**D40**	60c. blue	£120	£120
D242	**D40**	1f. red	£120	£120
D243	**D40**	2f. brown	£130	£130
D244	**D40**	3f. violet	£140	£140

1941. Postage Due stamps of 1932 optd FRANCE LIBRE F. N. F. L. or surch also.

D298	**D30**	25c. black and purple	£325	£325
D299	**D30**	30c. black and orange	£325	£325
D300	**D30**	50c. black and green	£1100	£1100
D301	**D30**	2f. black and purple	75·00	70·00
D302	**D30**	3f. on 2f. black & pur	55·00	37·00

1941. Free French Plebiscite. Nos. D208/17 optd FRANCE LIBRE F. N. F. L.

D310	**D40**	5c. black	55·00	60·00
D311	**D40**	10c. purple	10·50	24·00
D312	**D40**	15c. green	10·00	24·00
D313	**D40**	20c. blue	9·75	16·00
D314	**D40**	30c. red	14·00	19·00
D315	**D40**	50c. green	9·25	29·00
D316	**D40**	60c. blue	10·00	30·00
D317	**D40**	1f. red	32·00	50·00
D318	**D40**	2f. brown	11·00	50·00
D319	**D40**	3f. violet	£450	£475

D57 Arms and Galleon

1947

D385	**D57**	10c. orange	20	2·00
D386	**D57**	30c. blue	20	1·00
D387	**D57**	50c. green	30	65
D388	**D57**	1f. red	45	6·25
D389	**D57**	2f. green	1·60	6·75
D390	**D57**	3f. violet	2·30	7·50
D391	**D57**	4f. brown	2·30	7·75
D392	**D57**	5f. green	3·00	5·50
D393	**D57**	10f. black	3·75	4·50
D394	**D57**	20f. red	3·00	4·75

D115 Newfoundland Dog and Shipwreck Scene

1973

D516	**D115**	2c. black and brown	2·75	6·00
D517	**D115**	10c. black and violet	3·25	6·50
D518	**D115**	20c. black and blue	3·75	7·75
D519	**D115**	30c. black and red	5·50	10·50
D520	**D115**	1f. black and blue	11·00	25·00

1986. Nos. D2493/2502 of France optd ST-PIERRE ET MIQUELON.

D569	10c. brown and black	2·00	4·00
D570	20c. black	2·00	4·00
D571	30c. red, brown and black	2·00	4·00
D572	40c. blue, brown and black	2·00	4·00
D573	50c. red and black	2·00	4·00
D574	1f. black	2·00	4·25
D575	2f. yellow and black	2·20	4·75
D576	3f. black and red	2·30	5·25
D577	4f. brown and black	2·75	6·00
D578	5f. brown, red and black	3·25	6·75

Pt. 9, Pt. 14

ST THOMAS & PRINCE ISLANDS

Two islands in the Gulf of Guinea off the west coast of Africa. A colony and then an Overseas Province of Portugal until 1975, when it became an independent republic.

1870. 1000 reis = 1 milreis.
1913. 100 centavos = 1 escudo.
1977. 100 cents = 1 dobra.

1870. "Crown" key-type inscr "S. THOME E PRINCIPE".

17	**P**	5r. black	4·50	3·00
18	**P**	10r. orange	31·00	16·00
29	**P**	10r. green	14·00	8·50
20	**P**	20r. bistre	6·75	4·25
30	**P**	20r. red	7·00	5·00
21	**P**	25r. red	3·50	2·10
31	**P**	25r. lilac	5·75	3·50
22	**P**	40r. blue	10·00	7·50
32	**P**	40r. yellow	10·00	8·50
25	**P**	50r. green	31·00	23·00
33a	**P**	50r. blue	4·50	3·50
26	**P**	100r. lilac	16·00	8·75
15	**P**	200r. orange	20·00	16·00
16	**P**	300r. brown	20·00	16·00

1887. "Embossed" key-type inscr "S. THOME E PRINCIPE".

38	**Q**	5r. black	8·25	6·50
42	**Q**	10r. green	14·00	4·75
43	**Q**	20r. red	16·00	5·00
44	**Q**	25r. mauve	9·00	5·00
45	**Q**	40r. brown	5·25	3·00
46	**Q**	50r. blue	11·50	2·75
47	**Q**	100r. brown	9·00	4·75
48	**Q**	200r. lilac	31·00	17·00
49	**Q**	300r. orange	23·00	17·00

1889. Stamps of 1887 surch. No gum.

50	5r. on 10r. green	65·00	55·00
51	5r. on 20r. red	65·00	55·00
52	50r. on 40r. brown	£250	£200

1895. "Figures" key-type inscr "S. THOME E PRINCIPE".

60	**R**	5r. yellow	3·50	1·40
61	**R**	10r. mauve	1·30	80
53	**R**	15r. brown	3·50	2·10
54	**R**	20r. lilac	3·50	2·30
62	**R**	25r. green	1·90	80
63	**R**	50r. blue	3·50	1·40
55	**R**	75r. pink	9·00	5·50
64	**R**	80r. green	20·00	16·00
56	**R**	100r. brown on buff	8·75	6·50
57	**R**	150r. red on pink	11·50	8·50
58	**R**	200r. blue on blue	16·00	13·00
59	**R**	300r. blue on brown	18·00	14·50

1898. "King Carlos" key-type inscr "S. THOME E PRINCIPE". Name and value in red (500r.) or black (others).

66	**S**	2½r. grey	50	35
67	**S**	5r. red	70	35
68	**S**	10r. green	70	50
69	**S**	15r. brown	2·10	1·70
113	**S**	15r. green	2·20	1·30
70	**S**	20r. lilac	1·30	75
71	**S**	25r. green	80	50
114	**S**	25r. red	2·20	1·10
72	**S**	50r. blue	1·20	75
115	**S**	50r. brown	9·00	5·75
116	**S**	65r. blue	17·00	10·50
73	**S**	75r. pink	21·00	11·50
117	**S**	75r. purple	4·75	2·10
74	**S**	80r. mauve	10·50	5·00
75	**S**	100r. blue on blue	3·50	3·25
118	**S**	115r. brown on pink	16·00	11·50
119	**S**	130r. brown on yellow	16·00	11·50
76	**S**	150r. brown on yellow	4·25	3·00
77	**S**	200r. purple on pink	8·00	5·75
78	**S**	300r. blue on pink	11·50	6·25
120	**S**	400r. blue on cream	23·00	13·00
79	**S**	500r. black on blue	12·50	9·00
80	**S**	700r. mauve on yellow	25·00	19·00

1902. Surch with new value.

121	**S**	50r. on 65r. blue	7·00	4·25
85	**R**	65r. on 5r. yellow	8·00	5·50
86	**R**	65r. on 10r. mauve	8·00	5·00
87	**R**	65r. on 15r. brown	8·00	5·00
81	**Q**	65r. on 20r. red	10·00	6·50
88	**R**	65r. on 20r. lilac	4·50	3·00
83	**Q**	65r. on 25r. mauve	5·75	3·75
84	**Q**	65r. on 100r. brown	10·50	6·50
90	**Q**	115r. on 10r. green	10·00	6·50
92	**R**	115r. on 25r. green	8·00	5·00
89	**P**	115r. on 50r. green	20·00	6·50
93	**R**	115r. on 150r. red on pink	8·00	5·00
94	**R**	115r. on 200r. blue on blue	8·00	5·00
91	**Q**	115r. on 300r. orange	10·00	6·50
95	**Q**	130r. on 5r. black	10·00	6·50
98	**R**	130r. on 75r. pink	8·00	5·00
99	**R**	130r. on 100r. brn on buff	8·00	5·00
97	**Q**	130r. on 200r. lilac	12·50	6·50
100	**R**	130r. on 300r. blue on brown	8·00	5·00
108	**V**	400r. on 2½r. brown	2·10	2·10
101	**P**	400r. on 10r. yellow	95·00	70·00
102	**Q**	400r. on 40r. brown	18·00	13·00
103	**Q**	400r. on 50r. blue	8·00	5·00
105	**R**	400r. on 50r. blue	2·20	2·10
107	**R**	400r. on 80r. green	4·50	3·50

1903. Stamps of 1898 optd PROVISORIO.

109	15r. brown	4·00	1·80
110	25r. green	4·50	1·80
111	50r. blue	2·50	1·00
112	75r. pink	10·00	7·50

1911. Stamps of 1898 optd REPUBLICA.

122	2½r. grey	50	45
123	5r. orange	50	25
124	10r. green	50	45
125	15r. green	50	45
126	20r. lilac	50	45
127	25r. red	50	45
128	50r. brown	50	45
129	75r. purple	50	45
130	100r. blue on blue	1·20	90
131	115r. brown on pink	2·30	1·50
132	130r. brown on yellow	2·30	1·50
267	200r. purple on pink	3·50	2·10
134	400r. blue on cream	3·25	1·30
268	500r. black on blue	2·50	2·10
136	700r. mauve on yellow	3·25	1·30

1912. "King Manoel" key type inscr "S. THOME E PRINCIPE" and optd REPUBLICA.

137	**T**	2½r. lilac	50	45
138	**T**	5r. black	50	45
139	**T**	10r. green	50	45
140	**T**	20r. red	2·10	1·20
141	**T**	25r. brown	1·20	75
142	**T**	50r. blue	1·20	75

143	T	75r. brown	1·20	80
144	T	100r. brown on green	2·10	1·10
145	T	200r. green on orange	3·25	3·00
146	T	300r. black on blue	5·00	2·00

1913. Nos. 109 and 111/2 optd REPUBLICA.

159	S	15r. brown	3·75	3·25
243	S	50r. blue	1·50	1·10
272	S	75r. pink	15·00	10·00

1913. Stamps of 1902 optd REPUBLICA.

244	S	50r. on 65r. blue	1·50	1·10
245	Q	115r. on 10r. green	4·50	3·25
246	R	115r. on 25r. green	1·40	70
164	P	115r. on 50r. green	£225	£180
247	R	115r. on 150r. red on pink	1·40	1·70
248	R	115r. on 200r. blue on blue	1·40	70
249	Q	115r. on 300r. orange	4·50	3·25
250	Q	130r. on 5r. black	9·50	5·00
251	R	130r. on 75r. pink	1·40	70
252	R	130r. on 100r. brn on buff	2·50	2·30
253	Q	130r. on 200r. lilac	3·00	2·10
254	R	130r. on 300r. blue on brown	2·20	1·30
197	V	400r. on 2½r. brown	4·75	2·25
198	Q	400r. on 50r. blue	£130	£110
200	R	400r. on 50r. blue	4·75	4·25
202	R	400r. on 80r. green	5·00	3·50

1913. Surch REPUBLICA S. TOME E PRINCIPE and new value on "Vasco da Gama" stamps of (a) Portuguese Colonies.

203	¼c. on 2½r. green	2·10	1·40
204	½c. on 5r. red	2·10	1·40
205	1c. on 10r. purple	2·10	1·40
206	2½c. on 25r. green	2·10	1·40
207	5c. on 50r. blue	2·10	1·40
208	7½c. on 75r. brown	4·00	3·50
209	10c. on 100r. brown	2·10	1·40
210	15c. on 150r. brown	2·30	1·70

(b) Macao.

211	¼c. on ½c. green	3·00	2·00
212	½c. on 1a. red	3·00	2·00
213	1c. on 2a. purple	3·00	2·00
214	2½c. on 4a. green	3·00	2·00
215	5c. on 8a. blue	3·25	2·75
216	7½c. on 12a. brown	5·50	4·25
217	10c. on 16a. brown	3·25	2·20
218	15c. on 24a. brown	3·25	2·20

(c) Portuguese Timor.

219	¼c. on ½a. green	3·00	2·00
220	½c. on 1a. red	3·00	2·00
221	1c. on 2a. purple	3·00	2·00
222	2½c. on 4a. green	3·00	2·00
223	5c. on 8a. blue	3·25	2·75
224	7½c. on 12a. brown	5·50	4·25
225	10c. on 16a. brown	3·25	2·20
226	15c. on 24a. brown	3·25	2·20

1914. "Ceres" key-type inscr "S. TOME E PRINCIPE" Name and value in black.

276	U	¼c. green	45	35
281	U	½c. black	45	35
282	U	1c. green	45	35
283	U	1½c. brown	2·75	2·50
284	U	2c. red	45	35
285	U	2c. grey	45	35
286	U	2½c. violet	45	35
287	U	3c. orange	45	35
288	U	4c. purple	45	35
289	U	4½c. grey	45	35
290	U	5c. blue	70	65
291	U	6c. mauve	45	35
292	U	7c. blue	45	35
293	U	7½c. brown	70	9·50
294	U	8c. grey	70	50
295	U	10c. brown	70	50
296	U	12c. green	85	65
297	U	15c. pink	85	65
298	U	20c. green	85	65
299	U	24c. blue	1·70	1·30
300	U	25c. brown	1·70	1·30
239	U	30c. brown on green	3·75	1·90
301	U	30c. green	1·30	85
240	U	40c. brown on pink	3·75	1·90
302	U	40c. turquoise	1·30	85
241	U	50c. orange on orange	9·25	6·00
303	U	50c. mauve	1·30	85
304	U	60c. blue	1·30	85
305	U	60c. pink	2·75	1·30
306	U	80c. red	3·00	1·00
242	U	1e. green on blue	9·25	4·75
307	U	1e. pink	4·25	2·10
308	U	1e. blue	2·30	1·50
309	U	2e. purple	2·75	2·30
310	U	5e. brown	26·00	7·00
311	U	10e. pink	41·00	15·00
312	U	20e. green	£130	55·00

1919. No. 109 surch REPUBLICA and new value.

255	S	2½r. on 15r. brown	1·50	1·10

1919. No. 122 surch with new value.

256	½c. on 2½r. grey	7·25	5·75
257	1c. on 2½r. grey	5·00	3·25
258	2½c. on 2½r. grey	2·00	1·40

1919. "Ceres" key-types of St. Thomas and Prince Islands surch.

259	U	½c. on ¼c. green	4·50	3·50
260	U	2c. on ¼c. green	4·50	3·50
261	U	2½c. on ¼c. green	15·00	11·00

1919. "Ceres" key-type of St. Thomas and Prince Islands surch $04 Centavos and with old value blocked out.

262	4c. on 2½c. violet	2·00	1·40

1923. Stamps of 1913 (optd REPUBLICA) surch DEZ CENTAVOS and bars.

313	R	10c. on 115r. on 25r. green	95	70
314	R	10c. on 115r. on 150r. red on pink	95	70
316	R	10c. on 115r. on 200r. blue on blue	95	70
317	R	10c. on 130r. on 75r. pink	95	70
318	R	10c. on 130r. on 100r. brown on buff	95	70
319	R	10c. on 130r. on 300r. blue on brown	95	70

1925. Stamps of 1902 surch Republica 40 C. and bars over original surcharge.

321	V	40c. on 400r. on 2½r. brown	1·90	90
322	R	40c. on 400r. on 80r. green	1·90	90

1931. Nos. 307 and 309 surch.

323	U	70c. on 1e. pink	4·00	2·00
324	U	1e.40 on 2e. purple	4·75	2·40

32 Ceres

1934

325	32	1c. brown	45	30
326	32	5c. brown	45	30
327	32	10c. mauve	45	30
328	32	15c. black	45	30
329	32	20c. grey	45	30
330	32	30c. green	45	30
331	32	40c. red	45	30
332	32	45c. turquoise	80	75
333	32	50c. brown	65	60
334	32	60c. green	1·00	60
335	32	70c. brown	1·00	60
336	32	80c. green	60	35
337	32	85c. red	5·00	2·00
338	32	1e. purple	1·50	70
339	32	1e.40 blue	4·00	2·00
340	32	2e. mauve	4·00	2·00
341	32	5e. green	9·00	6·00
342	32	10e. brown	25·00	13·50
343	32	20e. orange	£100	55·00

1938. As T 54 and 56 of Macao, but inscr "S. TOME".

344	54	1c. green (postage)	35	30
345	54	5c. brown	35	30
346	54	10c. red	35	30
347	54	15c. purple	35	30
348	54	20c. grey	35	30
349	-	30c. purple	35	30
350	-	35c. green	65	45
351	-	40c. brown	65	45
352	-	50c. mauve	65	45
353	-	60c. black	65	45
354	-	70c. violet	65	45
355	-	80c. orange	65	45
356	-	1e. red	1·30	80
357	-	1e.75 blue	2·20	1·20
358	-	2e. red	29·00	8·25
359	-	5e. green	29·00	9·25
360	-	10e. blue	34·00	10·00
361	-	20e. brown	55·00	4·00
362	56	10c. red (air)	£130	95
363	56	20c. violet	65·00	46·00
364	56	50c. orange	3·75	3·50
365	56	1e. blue	12·00	3·50
366	56	2e. red	9·50	6·50
367	56	3e. green	12·00	5·25
368	56	5e. brown	20·00	16·00
369	56	9e. red	22·00	16·00
370	56	10e. mauve	22·00	16·00

DESIGNS: 30 to 50c. Mousinho de Albuquerque; 60c. to 1e. Dam; 1e.75 to 5e. Prince Henry the Navigator; 10, 20e. Afonso de Albuquerque.

See also Nos. 374/400.

37 Portuguese Colonial Column

1938. President's Colonial Tour.

371	37	80c. green	3·75	2·10
372	37	1e.75 blue	13·00	7·00
373	37	20e. brown	80·00	41·00

1939. As Nos. 344/70 but inscr "S. TOME e PRINCIPE".

374	54	1c. green (postage)	35	30
375	54	5c. brown	35	30
376	54	10c. red	35	30
377	54	15c. purple	35	30
378	54	20c. grey	35	30
379	-	30c. purple	35	30
380	-	35c. green	35	30
381	-	40c. brown	45	30
382	-	50c. mauve	45	45
383	-	60c. black	95	60
384	-	70c. violet	1·10	60
385	-	80c. orange	1·10	60
386	-	1e. red	1·30	85
387	-	1e.75 blue	2·20	1·20
388	-	2e. red	3·75	2·00
389	-	5e. green	8·25	5·00
390	-	10e. blue	23·00	8·25
391	-	20e. brown	30·00	10·00
392	56	10c. red (air)	70	60
393	56	20c. violet	70	60
394	56	50c. orange	70	60
395	56	1e. blue	70	60
396	56	2e. red	1·70	95
397	56	3e. green	2·20	1·40
398	56	5e. brown	6·50	3·50
399	56	9e. red	12·50	7·00
400	56	10e. mauve	13·00	7·25

41 Cola Nuts

1948. Fruits.

401	41	5c. black and yellow	85	30
402	-	10c. black and orange	1·10	75
403	-	30c. slate and grey	5·75	3·00
404	-	50c. brown and yellow	6·50	4·75
405	-	1e. red and pink	7·25	4·75
406	-	1e.75 blue and grey	13·00	8·25
407	-	2e. black and green	11·50	4·75
408	-	5e. brown and mauve	38·00	18·00
409	-	10e. black and mauve	40	19·00
410	-	20e. black and grey	£880	60·00

MS410a 149×136 mm. Nos. 401/10 (sold at 42e.50) £225 £250

DESIGNS: 10c. Bread-fruit; 30c. Custard-apple; 50c. Cocoa beans; 1e. Coffee; 1e.75, Dendem; 2e. Abacate; 5e. Pineapple; 10e. Mango; 20e. Coconuts.

42 Our Lady of Fatima

1948. Honouring the Statue of Our Lady of Fatima.

411	42	50c. violet	10·50	7·75

43 Letter and Globe

1949. 75th Anniv of U.P.U.

412	43	3e.50 black	11·00	7·75

44 Bells and Dove

1950. Holy Year.

413	44	2e.50 blue	4·00	2·50
414	44	4e. orange	8·25	6·00

45 Our Lady of Fatima

1951. Termination of Holy Year.

415	45	4e. indigo and blue	3·75	3·25

46 Doctor examining Patients

1952. 1st Tropical Medicine Congress, Lisbon.

416	46	10c. blue and brown	50	35

48 J. de Santarem

1952. Portuguese Navigators. Multicoloured.

417	10c. Type **48**	20	15
418	30c. P. Escobar	20	15
419	50c. F. de Po	35	20
420	1e. A. Esteves	45	30
421	2e. L. Goncalves	1·10	50
422	3e.50 M. Fernandes	1·10	50

49 Cloisters of Monastery

1953. Missionary Art Exhibition.

423	49	10c. brown and green	15	10
424	49	50c. brown and orange	95	75
425	49	3e. indigo and blue	3·25	1·80

50 Portuguese Stamp of 1853 and Arms of Portuguese Overseas Province

1953. Centenary of First Portuguese Postage Stamps.

426	50	50c. multicoloured	1·60	90

51 Route of President's Tour

1954. Presidential Visit.

427	51	15c. multicoloured	20	15

428	51	5e. multicoloured	1·70	1·10

52 Father M. de Nobrega and View of Sao Paulo

1954. 4th Centenary of Sao Paulo.

429	52	2e.50 multicoloured	85	55

53 Exhibition Emblem, Globe and Arms

1958. Brussels International Exhibition.

430	53	2e.50 multicoloured	1·10	65

54 "Cassia occidentalis"

1958. 6th International Congress of Tropical Medicine.

431	54	5e. multicoloured	3·75	2·30

55 Points of Compass

1960. 500th Death Anniv of Prince Henry the Navigator.

432	55	10e. multicoloured	1·60	85

56 "Religion"

1960. 10th Anniv of African Technical Co-operation Commission.

433	56	1e.50 multicoloured	70	45

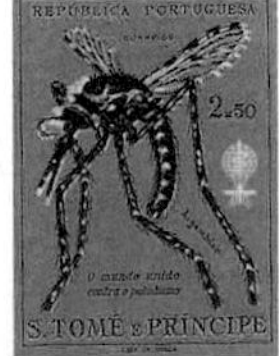

57 Fishing

1962. Sports. Multicoloured.

434	50c. Type **57**	20	15
435	1e. Gymnastics	85	20
436	1e.50 Handball	90	35
437	2e. Sailing	1·10	55
438	2e.50 Running	1·40	1·10
439	20e. Skin-diving	4·00	2·10

58 "Anopheles gambiae"

1962. Malaria Eradication.

440	58	2e.50 multicoloured	2·10	1·10

59 Map of Africa and Boeing 707 and Lockheed L.1049G Super Constellation Airliners

1963. 10th Anniv of Transportes Aereos Portugueses (airline).

441	59	1e.50 multicoloured	95	65

60 F. de Oliveira Chamico

1964. Centenary of National Overseas Bank.

442	60	2e.50 multicoloured	1·00	80

61 I.T.U. Emblem and St. Gabriel

1965. Centenary of I.T.U.

443	61	2e.50 multicoloured	2·10	1·40

62 Infantry Officer, 1788

1965. Portuguese Military Uniforms. Multicoloured.

444	20c. Type **62**	25	20
445	35c. Infantry sergeant, 1788	25	20
446	40c. Infantry corporal, 1788	25	25
447	1e. Infantryman, 1788	2·00	80
448	2e.50 Artillery officer, 1806	2·00	85
449	5e. Light infantryman, 1811	3·00	1·90
450	7e.50 Infantry sapper, 1833	2·75	2·50
451	10e. Lancers officer, 1834	5·75	3·75

65 Arts and Crafts School and Anti-Tuberculosis Clinic

1966. 40th Anniv of National Revolution.

452	65	4c. multicoloured	1·10	65

66 C. Rodrigues and Steam Corvette "Vasco da Gama"

1967. Cent of Military Naval Association. Mult.

453	1e.50 Type **66**	1·70	65
454	2e.50 A. Kopke, microscope and "Glossina palpalis" (insect)	2·50	1·10

67 Apparition appearing to Children and Valinhos Monument

1967. 50th Anniv of Fatima Apparitions.

455	67	2e.50 multicoloured	45	30

68 Medal of the Jeronimos Monastery

1968. 500th Birth Anniv of Pedro Cabral (explorer).

456	68	1e.50 multicoloured	90	60

69 Island Route-map and Monument

1969. Birth Centenary of Admiral Gago Coutinho.

457	69	2e. multicoloured	65	30

70 Da Gama's Fleet and Fireship

1969. 500th Birth Anniv of Vasco da Gama (explorer).

458	70	2e.50 multicoloured	85	55

71 L. A. Rebello da Silva

1969. Cent of Overseas Administrative Reforms.

459	71	2e.50 multicoloured	55	45

72 Manoel Gate, Guarda See

1969. 500th Birth Anniv of King Manoel I.

460	72	4e. multicoloured	65	55

73 Pero Escobar and Joao de Santarem

1969. 500th Anniv of Discovery of St. Thomas and Prince Islands.

461	73	2e.50 multicoloured	55	45

74 President A. Tomas

1970. Presidential Visit.

462	74	2e.50 multicoloured	60	25

75 Marshal Carmona

1970. Birth Centenary of Marshal Carmona.

463	75	5e. multicoloured	85	55

76 Stamps on Coffee Plant

1970. Stamp Centenary. Multicoloured.

464	1e. Type **76**	30	15
465	1e.50 Head Post Office, St. Thomas (horiz)	65	20
466	2e.50 Se Cathedral, St. Thomas	85	35

77 "Descent from the Cross" and Caravel at St. Thomas

1972. 400th Anniv of Camoens' "The Lusiads" (epic poem).

467	77	20e. multicoloured	2·75	1·10

78 Running and Throwing the Javelin

1972. Olympic Games, Munich.

468	78	1e.50 multicoloured	45	25

79 Fairey IIID Seaplane "Lusitania" and Cruiser "Gladiolus" off Rock of San Pedro

1972. 50th Anniv of 1st Flight, Lisbon–Rio de Janeiro.

469	79	2e.50 multicoloured	55	30

80 W.M.O. Emblem

1973. Cent of World Meteorological Organization.

470	80	5e. multicoloured	85	65

81 Flags of Portugal and St. Thomas and Prince Islands

1975. Independence.

471	**81**	3e. multicoloured	30	10
472	**81**	10e. multicoloured	90	40
473	**81**	20e. multicoloured	1·80	80
474	**81**	50e. multicoloured	4·40	2·20

82 National Flag

1975. Independence Proclamation.

475	**82**	1e.50 multicoloured	20	10
476	**82**	4e. multicoloured	35	15
477	**82**	7e.50 multicoloured	65	30
478	**82**	20e. multicoloured	1·80	80
479	**82**	50e. multicoloured	4·50	2·50

83 Diagram and Hand

1976. National Reconstruction Fund.

480	**83**	1e. multicoloured	10	10
481	**83**	1e.50 multicoloured	15	10
482	**83**	2e. multicoloured	20	10

1976. Optd Rep. Democr. 12-7-75.

483	**48**	10c. Joao de Santarem		
484	**62**	20c. Infantry officer, 1788		
485	-	30c. Pedro Escobar (No. 418)		
486	-	35c. Infantry sergeant, 1788		
487	-	40c. Infantry corporal, 1788		
488	-	50c. Fernao de Po (No. 419)		
489	-	1e. Alvaro Esteves (No. 420)		
490	-	2e.50 Rebello da Silva (No. 459)		
491	**73**	2e.50 Escobar and Santarem		
492	-	3e.50 Martim Fernandes (No. 422)		
493	-	4e. Manoel Gate (No. 460)		
494	-	5e. W.M.O. emblem (No. 470)		
495	-	7e.50 Infantry sapper, 1833 (No. 450)		
496	-	10e. Compass rose (No. 432)		

85 President Pinto da Costa and National Flag

1976. 1st Anniv of Independence.

497	2e. Type **85**	25	10
498	3e.50 Proclamation of Independence, 12 July 1975	30	15
499	4e.50 As 3e.50	45	30
500	12e.50 Type **85**	90	50

1977. 2nd Anniv of Independence. No. 439 optd Rep. Democr. 12-7-77.

501	20e. multicoloured	2·30	1·10
MS501	135×115 mm. No. 501	10·00	8·00

CHARITY TAX STAMPS

The notes under this heading in Portugal also apply here.

1925. Marquis de Pombal Commemoration. As stamps of Portugal, but additionally inscr "S. TOME E PRINCIPE".

C323	**C73**	15c. black and orange	85	45
C324	-	15c. black and orange	85	45
C325	**C75**	15c. black and orange	85	45

1946. Fiscal stamps as in Type C 1 of Portuguese Colonies surch Assistencia and new value.

C401	50c. on 1e. green	25·00	23·00
C402	50c. on 4e. red	30·00	30·00
C403	1e. on 4e. red	30·00	30·00
C404	1e. on 5e. red	30·00	30·00
C407	1e. on 6e. green	25·00	23·00
C408	1e. on 7e. green	32·00	23·00
C409	1e. on 10e. red	25·00	30·00
C410	1e.50 on 7e. green	29·00	23·00
C411	1e.50 on 8e. green	29·00	27·00
C412	2e.50 on 7e. green	29·00	27·00
C413	2e.50 on 9e. green	29·00	27·00
C414	2e.50 on 10e. green	25·00	23·00

40 Arms

1948. Value in black.

C415	**40**	50c. green	1·30	1·10
C416	**40**	1e. pink	3·25	2·40
C417	**40**	1e. green	1·40	1·00
C418	**40**	1e.50 brown	4·00	3·00

1965. (a) Surch um escudo 1$00 and two heavy bars.

C452	1e. on 5e. yellow	1·80	1·30

(b) Surch Um escudo.

C453	1e. on 1e. green	2·30	2·20

(c) As No. C 417 but inscr "UM ESCUDO" at foot, surch 1$00.

C454	1e. on 1e. green	1·80	1·50

(d) Previous surch "Cinco escudos" obliterated and further surch Um escudo 1$00.

C455	1e. on 5e. yellow	4·00	3·25

NEWSPAPER STAMPS

1892. Surch 2½ RS. No gum.

N53	**Q**	2½r. on 5r. black	£880	65·00
N54	**Q**	2½r. on 10r. green	£100	95
N55	**Q**	2½r. on 20r. red	£160	£130

1893. "Newspaper" key-type inscr "S. THOME E PRINCIPE".

N59	**V**	2½r. brown	1·40	3·00

1899. No. N59 optd PROVISORIO.

N81	2½r. brown	75·00	35·00

POSTAGE DUE STAMPS

1904. "Due" key-type inscr "S. THOME E PRINCIPE". Name and value in black.

D121	**W**	5r. green	1·20	1·10
D122	**W**	10r. grey	1·70	1·40
D123	**W**	20r. brown	1·70	1·40
D124	**W**	30r. orange	1·70	1·40
D125	**W**	50r. brown	3·00	2·10
D126	**W**	60r. brown	4·25	4·75
D127	**W**	100r. mauve	7·00	4·25
D128	**W**	130r. blue	7·00	4·25
D129	**W**	200r. red	7·25	5·50
D130	**W**	500r. lilac	13·50	10·50

1911. As last optd REPUBLICA.

D137	5r. green	50	45
D138	10r. grey	50	45
D139	20r. brown	50	45
D140	30r. orange	50	45
D141	50r. brown	60	55
D142	60r. brown	1·70	1·20
D143	100r. mauve	1·70	1·20
D144	130r. blue	1·70	1·20
D145	200r. red	1·30	1·20
D146	500r. lilac	3·50	2·50

1921. "Due" key-type inscr "S. TOME E PRINCIPE". Currency changed.

D313	½c. green	65	55
D314	1c. grey	65	55
D315	2c. brown	65	55
D316	3c. orange	65	55
D317	5c. brown	65	55
D318	6c. brown	30	30
D319	10c. mauve	70	60
D320	13c. blue	70	60
D321	20c. red	70	60
D322	50c. lilac	1·80	1·40

1925. Nos. C323/5 optd MULTA.

D323	**C73**	30c. black and orange	85	45
D324	-	30c. black and orange	85	45
D325	**C75**	30c. black and orange	85·00	45

D14

1925. Numerals in red, name in black.

D417	**D 14**	10c. brown and yellow	25	20
D418	**D 14**	30c. brown and blue	25	20
D419	**D 14**	50c. blue and pink	25	20
D420	**D 14**	1e. blue and olive	30	25
D421	**D 14**	2e. green and orange	35	35
D422	**D 14**	5e. brown and lilac	65	45

APPENDIX

The following stamps have either been issued in excess of postal needs or have not been available to the public in reasonable quantities at face value. Such stamps may later be given full listing if there is evidence of regular postal use.

1977

400th Birth Anniv of Rubens. 1, 5, 10, 15, 20, 50e.
150th Death Anniv of Beethoven. 20, 30, 50e.
Centenary of U.P.U. Surch on Navigators and Military Uniforms issues of Portuguese administration. 1e. on 10c., 3e. on 30c., 3e.50 on 3e.50, 5e. on 50c., 10e. on 10c., 15e. on 3e.50, 20e. on 30e. on 30c., 35e. on 35c., 40e. on 40c.
Christmas. 5, 10, 25, 50, 70d.
60th Anniv of Russian Revolution. 15, 30, 40, 50d.
1st Death Anniv of Mao Tse-tung. 50d.

1978

Nobel Peace Prizes to International Organizations. Surch on Navigators and Military Uniforms issues of Portuguese administration. 3d. on 30c., 5d. on 50c., 10d. on 10c., 15d. on 3e.50, 20d. on 20c., 35d. on 35c.
3rd Anniv of Independence. 5d.×3.
3rd Anniv of Admission to United Nations. Surch on Military Uniform issue. 40d. on 40c.
International Stamp Exhibition, Essen. 10d.×5.
Centenary of U.P.U. 5d.×4, 15d.×4.
1st Anniv of New Currency. 5d.×5, 8d.×5.
World Cup Football Championship, Argentina. 3d.×4, 25d.×3.

1979

World Cup Winners. Optd on 1978 World Cup issues. 3d.×4, 25d.×3.
Butterflies. 50c., 10d., 11d.×4.
Flowers. 1d., 8d.×4, 25d.
Telecommunications Day and 50th Anniv of C.C.I.R. 1, 11, 14, 17d.
International Year of the Child. 1, 7, 14, 17d.
450th Death Anniv of Durer. 50c.×2, 1, 7, 8, 25d.
History of Aviation. 50c., 1, 5, 7, 8, 17d.
History of Navigation. 50c., 1, 3, 5, 8, 25d.
Birds. Postage 50c.×2, 1, 7, 8d.; Air 100d.

1980

Fishes. Postage 50c., 1, 5, 7, 8d.; Air 50d.
Balloons. 50c., 1, 3, 7, 8, 25d.
Airships. 50c., 1, 3, 7, 8, 17d.
Olympic Games. 50c., 11d.×4.
Death Centenary of Sir Rowland Hill. 50c., 1, 8, 20d.
10th Anniv of First Manned Moon Landing. 50c., 1, 14, 17d.

1981

Olympic Games, Moscow. Optd on 1977 Mao Tse-tung issue. 50d.
Olympic Games, Moscow. Overprint on 60th Anniv of Revolution. Either silver or black. 15; 30; 40; 50d.×2
Mammals. 50c.×2; 1; 7; 8d.
Shells. 50c.×2; 1d.; 1d.50; 11; 17d.
Philatelia 81, Frankfurt. Johann Wolfgang von Goethe Commemoration. 25d.
Josip Broz Tito Commemoration. 17d.×2
Wedding of Prince Charles and Lady Diana Spencer. Overprint in white on Ludwig von Beethoven Commemoration issues of Portuguese Administration. 20; 30; 50d.
Chess. 1d.50×4; 30d.×4
Chess. Overprint in red on Chess. 30d.×2
Birth Centenary of Pablo Picasso. 14; 17d.×4; 20d.×2
Paintings of Dogs. 1d.50×5; 50d.×2
Paintings of Cats. 1d.50×5; 50d.×2
Central African Games. 17d.×4; 50d.
Fruit. 11d.×3; 30d.×3

1982

Birth Centenary of Josip Broz Tito (1992). Overprint on Josip Broz Tito Commemoration. 17d.×2
World Cup Football Championship, Spain. 15d.×4; 25d.×2
PhilexFrance 82 International Stamp Exhibition. 15d.×2
Centenary of Robert Koch's discovery of TB Bacillus. 25d.
150th Death Anniv of Johann Wolfgang von Goethe. 50d.
21st Birth Anniv of Diana, Princess of Wales. 75d.
75th Anniv of Scouting Movement. 15d.; 30d.
Birth Centenary of Igor Strvinsky. 30d.×2
250th Birth Anniv of George Washington. 30d.×2
Dinosaurs. 6; 16d.×4; 50d.
Navigators. 50c.; 18d.×4; 50d.
Second Anniv of Trabalho Assembly. Overprint in silver on Argel Accord issues of Portuguese Administration. 3; 10; 20; 50e.
Third Trabalho Assembly. 8; 12; 16; 30d.
Pablo Picasso Commemoration. 18d.×3; 25d.×2
Railways. 9; 16d.×4; 50d.

1983

Paintings by Peter Paul Rubens. 16d.×2; 18d.
Pascoa 83. Painting by Peter Paul Rubens. 18d.
Painting by Rembrandt. 16d.×2; 18d.
Paintings by Raphael. 16d.×2
Pascoa 83. Paintings by Raphael. 18d.×2
Brasiliana '83. Airships. 25d.×2
Centenary of Montgolfier Brothers' First Flight. 18d.×4; 20d.×3
UPU Congress, Hamburg. Overprint in gold on Centenary of UPU. 15d.×4
Christmas. 30d.×2
Cars. 12d×4; 20d.×4
Medicinal Plants. 50c.; 1; 5d.50; 15d.50; 16; 20; 46; 50d.
Olympic Games, Los Angeles. 16d.×4; 18d.×4
Birds. 50c.; 1d.50; 2; 3; 4; 5d.50; 7; 10; 11; 12; 14; 15d.50; 16; 17 18d.50; 20; 25; 30; 42; 46; 100d.

1984

Lubrapex 84, Lisbon. 16; 30d.
25th Anniv of UN International Maritime Organization. 50c.×3; 7d.×3; 8d.×3; 15d.×3
UPU Congress, Hamburg. Overprint in black on 25th Anniv of UN International Maritime Organization. 50c.×3;
Eradication of Malaria. 8; 16; 30d.
International Food Day. 8; 16; 46d.
Fungi. 10; 20; 30d.
Christmas. 30d.

1985

Conference of Portuguese Countries in Africa. 25d.
First Anniv of Reinstatement of Flights between Lisbon and St. Thomas. 25; 30d.
Flowers. 16; 20; 30d.

1986

Halley's Comet. 5; 6; 10; 16d.
Fungi. 6; 25; 30d.
World Cup Football Championship, Mexico. 25d.×4
Olympic Games, Seoul (1988). 25d.×4
Cars. 50c.; 6; 16; 30d.
Railways. 50c.; 6; 20d.
International Year of Peace. 8; 10; 16; 20d.
Lubrapex 86, Lisbon. 1d.×2; 2d.; 46d.
Christmas. 50c.; 1; 16; 20d.

1987

Flora and Fauna. 1d.×4; 2d.×4; 10d.×4; 20d.×4
Sport. 50c.; 20; 30d.
500th Anniv of Christopher Columbus' voyage to the Americas (1992). 15; 20d.×2
Fungi. 6; 25; 30d.
Railways. 5; 10; 20d.
Christmas. 1; 5; 15; 20d.
Scout Jamboree, Australia. 50c.

1988

70th Anniv of October Revolution. 25d.
World Cup Football Championship Winners. Overprint in gold on World Cup Football Championship, Mexico. 25d.×4
Fungi. 10d.×4; 20d.
Medicinal Plants. 5d.×3; 10d.; 20d.
Electric Locomotives. 10d.×6
150th Birth Anniv of Ferdinand Graf von Zeppelin. 10d.×5
Butterflies. 10d.×3
Automatic Telephone Exchange. 10; 25d.
Scout Jamboree, Australia. 10d.×3
125th Anniv of International Red Cross. 50c.; 5; 20d.
Sport. 50d.×4
Winter Olympic Games, Albertville. 5d.
Italia 90. 50d.×3
Christmas. 10d.×3; 30d.

1989

Fruit. 50c.; 1; 5; 10; 25; 50d.×2; 60d.; 100; 250; 500d.
Bicentenary of French Revolution. 10d.×3
Orchids. 20d.×2
Humming Birds. 20d.×3
Italia 90. 10d.×3; 20d.
Olympic Games, Barcelona (1992). 5d.×3; 35d.
Ships. 20d.×5
Railways. 20d.×5
Butterflies. 20d.×5
25th Anniv of Bank. 25d.
International Telecommunications Day. 60d.
Christmas. 25d.×4

1990

70th Anniv of Arthur Eddington Expedition to St. Thomas. 60d.×3
Orchids. 20d.×5
Railways. 5; 20d.; 25d.×3
Italia 90. 25d.×4
Butterflies. 15d.×5; 25d.
Fungi. 20d.×5
Christmas. 25d.×4
700th Anniv of Swiss Confederation. 20d.
Death Centenary of Vincent Van Gogh. 20d.
Art. 10d.×6; 25d.×2

1991

Flora and Fauna. 1; 5; 10; 50d.×2; 70d.; 75d.×; 80d.; 100; 250; 500d.
Railways. 75d.×6
Birds. 75d.×4; 200d.
Art. 50d.; 75d.×2; 100; 200d.
Fungi. 50d.×2; 75d.; 125; 200d.
Flowers. 50d.×2; 100d.×2; 200d.
500th Anniv of Christopher Columbus' voyage to the Americas (1992). 50d.×2; 75d.; 125d.; 200d.
Philanippon 91 International Stamp Exhibition. Butterflies. 125d.×2
Fauna. 25d.×6
Castles. 25d.×6
Butterflies. 125d.×4
Postal Express. 3000d.

1992

Marine Mammals. 450d.×4
Visit of Pope John Paul II. 120d.×8; 150d.×8; 180d.×4; 200d.×8; 250d.×4

Flora and Fauna. 1000d.; 1500; 2000; 2500d.
Environmental Protection Conference, Brazil. 65; 110; 150; 200; 275d.
Olympic Games, Barcelona. 50d.×6
Fungi. 75; 100; 125; 200; 500d.
Birds. 75; 100; 125; 200; 500d.
Olympic Games, Barcelona. 50; 300d.×6
Olympic Games, Barcelona 300d.×2
Railway. 75; 100; 125; 200; 500d.
Birth Centenary of Marcelo da Veiga. 10; 40; 50; 100d.
Butterflies. 75; 100; 125; 200; 500d.

1993

Fungi. 800d.×5
Butterflies and Flowers. 500d.×5
Birds. 500d.×5
Railways. 800d.×5
Flora. 500d.×5
World Cup Football Championship, Atlanta. 800d.×8
Dinosaurs. 500d.×6
UCCLA. 100d.; 150d.; 200d.; 250d.×2; 300d.; 350d.; 400d.; 500d.
Olympic Games, Atlanta. 800d.×8

1994

World Cup Football Championship, Brazil. 500d.
60th Birth Anniv of Elvis Presley. 10d.×18
Marilyn Monroe Commemoration. 10d.×9
UPU Congress. 1000d.
Butterflies. 1200d.×5
Cinema. 100d.×9
Independence. 350d.
Horses. 1000d.×9
Flowers and Fruit. 350; 370; 380; 800; 1000d.
Crafts. 350d.×2; 400d.; 500d.×2; 1000d.
United Nations. Overprint in black on Crafts. 350d.×2; 400d.; 500d.×2; 1000d.
Railways. 1000d.×6
Cats. 1000d.×9
Cats and Dogs. 1000d.×9
Dogs. 1000d.×18
Orchids. 1000d.×9
Art. 100d.×9
New Year. Year of the Rat. 1000d.×9
Fungi. 1000d.×15
Christmas. 750d.×9

Pt. 1

ST VINCENT

One of the Windward Islands, British West Indies.

1861. 12 pence = 1 shilling; 20 shillings = 1 pound.
1949. 100 cents = 1 West Indian dollar.

1

3

7

1861

36	7	½d. orange	7·00	7·00
47	7	½d. green	1·00	60
18	1	1d. black	60·00	12·00
29	1	1d. green	£170	5·00
39	1	1d. drab	65·00	3·00
48b	1	1d. red	1·60	85
61	1	2½d. blue	7·00	1·75
6	1	4d. blue	£275	£110
51	1	4d. brown	90·00	75
56	1	4d. yellow	1·60	11·00
62	1	5d. sepia	6·00	26·00
4	1	6d. green	60·00	19·00
57	1	6d. purple	2·25	20·00
11	1	1s. grey	£275	£120
13	1	1s. blue	£375	90·00
14	1	1s. brown	£500	£160
45	1	1s. red	£150	60·00
58	1	1s. orange	5·50	14·00
53	3	5s. lake	28·00	55·00

1880. Surch in figures.

33	½d. on half 6d. green	£160	£170
28	1d. on half 6d. green	£550	£375

1881. Surch in words.

34	1d. on 6d. green	£450	£350
63	3d. on 1d. mauve	5·00	22·00
60a	5d. on 6d. lake	1·25	1·75

1881. Surch in figures.

54	2½d. on 4d. brown	80·00	£120
35	4d. on 1s. orange	£1600	£800

1882. Surch in figures and words.

40	2½d. on 1d. red	24·00	1·50
55a	2½d. on 1d. blue	1·50	35
59	5d. on 4d. brown	28·00	45·00

1885. No. 40 further surch 1d and bars.

46	1d. on 2½d. on 1d. lake	28·00	22·00

13

1899

67	13	½d. mauve and green	2·75	2·50
68	13	1d. mauve and red	4·50	1·50
69	13	2½d. mauve and blue	5·00	2·00
70	13	3d. mauve and green	4·00	17·00
71	13	4d. mauve and orange	5·50	21·00
72	13	5d. mauve and black	7·00	17·00
73	13	6d. mauve and brown	13·00	50·00
74	13	1s. green and red	15·00	50·00
75	13	5s. green and blue	85·00	£150

1902. As T 13, but portait of King Edward VII.

85a	½d. purple and green	1·25	1·25
77	1d. purple and red	4·25	30
78	2d. purple and black	5·00	4·50
79	2½d. purple and blue	5·00	3·50
80	3d. purple and green	5·00	4·75
81	6d. purple and brown	11·00	38·00
90a	1s. green and red	12·00	65·00
83	2s. green and violet	25·00	60·00
91	2s. purple and blue on blue	23·00	42·00
84	5s. green and blue	75·00	£130
92	5s. green and red on yellow	17·00	50·00
93	£1 purple and black on red	£275	£350

17 Seal of the Colony

1907

94	17	½d. green	3·25	2·25
95	17	1d. red	3·50	15
96	17	2d. orange	1·50	6·50
97	17	2½d. blue	38·00	8·50
98	17	3d. violet	8·00	15·00

18 Seal of the Colony

1909

102	18	½d. green	1·75	60
99	18	1d. red	1·25	30
104	18	2d. grey	5·00	9·50
105	18	2½d. blue	8·00	3·75
106	18	3d. purple on yellow	2·50	11·00
107	18	6d. purple	16·00	8·50
101	18	1s. black on green	4·25	9·00
139	18	2s. blue and purple	7·50	13·00
140	18	5s. red and green	18·00	32·00
141	18	£1 mauve and black	95·00	£140

19

1913

108	19	½d. green	75	20
109	19	1d. red	80	75
132b	19	1½d. brown	3·75	15
133	19	2d. grey	2·50	1·00
111	19	2½d. blue	50	75
134	19	3d. blue	1·00	6·00
135	19	3d. purple on yellow	1·00	1·50
113	19	4d. red on yellow	80	2·00
136	19	5d. green	1·00	7·50
137	19	6d. purple	1·50	3·50
116	19	1s. black on green	1·50	3·75
138a	19	1s. brown	3·25	17·00

1915. Surch ONE PENNY.

121	1d. on 1s. black on green	9·00	38·00

1916. Optd WAR STAMP. in two lines.

122	1d. red	10·00	15·00

1916. Optd WAR STAMP. in one line.

126	1d. red	60	1·50

1935. Silver Jubilee. As T 32a of St. Helena.

142	1d. blue and red	40	4·75
143	1½d. blue and grey	1·00	4·50
144	2½d. brown and blue	2·00	5·00
145	1s. grey and purple	5·00	7·50

1937. Coronation. As T 32b of St. Helena.

146	1d. violet	35	1·25
147	1½d. red	40	1·25
148	2½d. blue	45	2·25

25

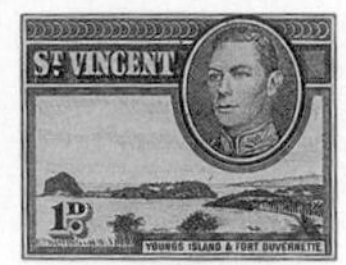

26 Young's Island and Fort Duvernette

1938

149	25	½d. blue and green	20	10
150	26	1d. blue and brown	20	10
151	-	1½d. green and red	20	10
152	25	2d. green and black	40	35
153	-	2½d. black and green	20	40
153a	-	2½d. green and brown	40	20
154	25	3d. orange and purple	20	10
154a	-	3½d. blue and green	75	2·50
155	25	6d. black and lake	1·50	40
156	-	1s. purple and green	1·50	80
157	25	2s. blue and purple	6·00	75
157a	25	2s.6d. brown and blue	1·25	3·50
158	25	5s. red and green	13·00	2·50
158a	25	10s. violet and brown	4·50	9·00
159	25	£1 purple and black	26·00	15·00

DESIGNS—HORIZ: 1½d. Kingstown and Fort Charlotte; 2½d. (No. 153), 3½d. Bathing beach at Villa; 2½d. (No. 153a), 1s. Victoria Park, Kingstown.

1946. Victory. As T 33a of St. Helena.

160	1½d. red	10	10
161	3½d. blue	10	10

1948. Silver Wedding. As T 33b/c of St Helena.

162	1½d. red	10	10
163	£1 mauve	26·00	30·00

1949. As 1938 issue, but values in cents and dollars.

164		1c. blue and green	20	1·75
164a		1c. green and black	30	2·50
165	26	2c. blue and brown	15	50
166	-	3c. green and red	50	1·00
166a	25	3c. orange and purple	5·00	2·50
167	25	4c. green and black	35	20
167a	25	4c. blue and green	30	20
168	-	5c. green and brown	15	10
169	25	6c. orange and purple	50	1·25
169a	-	6c. green and red	30	2·25
170	-	7c. black and blue	5·50	1·50
170a	-	10c. black and turquoise	50	20
171	25	12c. black and lake	35	15
172	-	24c. purple and green	35	55
173	25	48c. blue and purple	4·50	6·00
174	25	60c. brown and blue	2·00	5·50
175	25	$1.20 red and green	4·25	4·25
176	25	$2.40 violet and brown	6·00	10·00
177	25	$4.80 purple and black	13·00	20·00

DESIGNS—HORIZ: 3c. (No. 166), 6c. (No. 169a) Kingstown and Fort Charlotte; 5, 24c. Victoria Park, Kingstown; 7, 10c. Bathing beach at Villa.

1949. U.P.U. As T 33d/g of St. Helena.

178	5c. blue	20	20
179	6c. purple	1·50	2·25
180	12c. mauve	20	2·25
181	24c. green	20	1·00

1951. Inauguration of B.W.I. University College. As T 10a/b of St. Kitts-Nevis.

182	18	3c. green and red	30	65
183	19	12c. black and purple	30	1·75

1951. New Constitution. Optd NEW CONSTITUTION 1951.

184	-	3c. green and red (No. 166)	20	1·75
185	25	4c. green and black	20	60
186	-	5c. green & brn (No. 168)	20	60
187	25	12c. black and lake	1·25	1·25

1953. Coronation. As T 33h of St. Helena.

188	4c. black and green	30	20

30

31

1955

189	30	1c. orange	10	10
190	30	2c. blue	10	10
191	30	3c. grey	30	10
192	30	4c. brown	20	10
215	30	5c. red	15	10
216	30	10c. lilac	15	10
195	30	15c. blue	2·25	1·00
218	30	20c. green	45	10
197	30	25c. sepia	50	10
198a	31	50c. brown	5·50	2·75
199	31	$1 green	8·00	1·00
200	31	$2.50 blue	9·00	10·00

1958. British Caribbean Federation. As T 27a of St. Kitts-Nevis.

201	31	3c. green	40	20
202	31	6c. blue	45	1·25
203	31	12c. red	50	50

1963. Freedom from Hunger. As T 63a of St. Helena.

204	8c. violet	45	50

1963. Cent of Red Cross. As T 63b of St. Helena.

205	4c. red and black	15	20
206	8c. red and blue	35	50

32 Scout Badge and Proficiency Badges

1964. 50th Anniv of St. Vincent Boy Scouts Association.

221	32	1c. green and brown	10	10
222	32	4c. blue and purple	10	10
223	32	20c. yellow and violet	30	10
224	32	50c. red and green	45	70

33 Tropical Fruits

1965. Bicentenary of Botanic Gardens. Mult.

225	1c. Type **33**	10	10
226	4c. Breadfruit and H.M.S. "Providence" (sloop), 1793	10	10
227	25c. Doric Temple and pond (vert)	15	10
228	40c. Talipot palm and Doric Temple (vert)	30	1·25

1965. Cent of I.T.U. As T 64a of St. Helena.

229	4c. blue and green	15	10
230	48c. ochre and orange	35	45

37 Boat-building, Bequia

1965. Multicoloured.. Multicoloured..

231	1c. Type **37** (inscr "BEOUIA")	10	1·00
231a	1c. Type **37** (inscr "BEQUIA")	65	40
232	2c. Friendship Beach, Bequia	10	10
233	3c. Terminal Building, Arnos Vale Airport	1·00	10
261	4c. Woman with bananas	30	30
235	5c. Crater Lake	15	10
236	6c. Carib stone	15	40
237	8c. Arrowroot	30	10
238	10c. Owia Salt Pond	30	10
239	12c. Deep water wharf	70	10
240	20c. Sea island cotton	30	10
241	25c. Map of St. Vincent and islands	35	10
242	50c. Breadfruit	50	30
243	$1 Baleine Falls	3·00	30
244	$2.50 St. Vincent amazon	18·00	11·00
245	$5 Arms of St. Vincent	3·00	14·00

Nos. 261, 236/7 and 240/5 are vert.

1966. Churchill Commem. As T 64b of St. Helena.

246	1c. blue	10	10
247	4c. green	20	10
248	20c. brown	35	30
249	40c. violet	55	1·00

1966. Royal Visit. As T 48a of St. Kitts-Nevis.

250	4c. black, green and blue	50	20
251	25c. black and mauve	1·50	80

1966. Inauguration of W.H.O. Headquarters, Geneva. As T 64e of St. Helena.

252	4c. black, green and blue	25	10
253	25c. black, purple and ochre	50	80

1966. 20th Anniv of UNESCO. As T 64f/h of St. Helena.

254	4c. multicoloured	20	10
255	8c. yellow, violet and olive	40	10
256	25c. black, purple and orange	1·00	60

38 Coastal View of Mount Coke Area

1967. Autonomous Methodist Church. Mult.

257	2c. Type **38**	25	10
258	8c. Kingstown Methodist Church	10	10
259	25c. First licence to perform marriages	25	10
260	35c. Conference Arms	25	10

39 Meteorological Institute

1968. World Meteorological Day.

262	**39**	4c. multicoloured	10	10
263	**39**	25c. multicoloured	10	10
264	**39**	35c. multicoloured	15	15

40 Dr. Martin Luther King and Cotton Pickers

1968. Dr. Martin Luther King Commem.

265	**40**	5c. multicoloured	10	10
266	**40**	25c. multicoloured	10	10
267	**40**	35c. multicoloured	15	15

41 Speaker addressing Demonstrators

1968. Human Rights Year.

268	**41**	3c. multicoloured	10	10
269	-	35c. blue	20	10

DESIGN—VERT: 35c. Scales of Justice and Human Rights emblem.

43 Male Masquerader

1969. St. Vincent Carnival.

270	**43**	1c. multicoloured	10	20
271	-	5c. red and brown	10	10
272	-	8c. multicoloured	10	10
273	-	25c. multicoloured	15	10

DESIGNS—VERT: 5c. Steel bandsman; 25c. Queen of Bands. HORIZ: 8c. Carnival revellers.

1969. Methodist Conference. Nos. 241, 257/8 and 260 optd METHODIST CONFERENCE MAY 1969.

274	**38**	2c. multicoloured	10	15
275	-	8c. multicoloured	15	25
276	-	25c. multicoloured	15	25
277	-	35c. multicoloured	75	2·00

48 "Strength in Unity"

1969. 1st Anniv of C.A.R.I.F.T.A.

278	**48**	2c. black, buff and red	10	10
279	-	5c. multicoloured	15	10
280	**48**	8c. black, buff and green	10	10
281	-	25c. multicoloured	35	15

DESIGN—VERT: 5, 25c. Map.

50 Flag of St. Vincent

1969. Statehood.

282	**50**	4c. multicoloured	10	10
283	-	10c. multicoloured	10	10
284	-	50c. grey, black and orange	35	20

DESIGNS: 10c. Battle scene with insets of Petroglyph and Carib Chief Chatoyer; 50c. Carib House with maces and scales.

51 Green-backed Heron ("Green Heron")

1970. Multicoloured.. Multicoloured..

285	½c. House wren	10	1·25
286a	1c. Type **51**	30	1·50
287	2c. Lesser Antillean bullfinches ("Bullfinches")	15	40
288	3c. St. Vincent amazon ("St. Vincent Parrot")	15	30
289	4c. Rufous-throated solitaire ("Soufriere Bird")	20	30
364	5c. Red-necked pigeon ("Ramier")	30	20
291	6c. Bananaquits	30	40
292	8c. Purple-throated Carib ("Hummingbird")	40	30
293	10c. Mangrove cuckoo	30	10
294	12c. Common black hawk ("Black Hawk")	40	10
295	20c. Bare-eyed thrush	40	15
296	25c. Lesser Antillean tanager ("Prince")	50	20
297	50c. Blue hooded euphonia	2·00	75
298	$1 Barn owl	5·50	2·00
299	$2.50 Yellow-bellied elaenia ("Crested Elaenia")	3·25	5·50
300	$5 Ruddy quail dove	3·50	6·50

Nos. 285, 289, 364, 293/4 and 298/9 are vert.

52 de Havilland DHC-6 Twin Otter 100

1970. 20th Anniv of Regular Air Services. Multicoloured.

301	5c. Type **52**	10	10
302	8c. Grumman Goose	15	10
303	10c. Hawker Siddeley H.S.748	20	10
304	25c. Douglas DC-3	65	30

53 "Children's Nursery"

1970. Centenary of British Red Cross. Mult.

305	3c. Type **53**	10	10
306	5c. "First Aid"	15	10
307	12c. "Voluntary Aid Detachment"	35	1·00
308	25c. "Blood Transfusion"	55	50

54 "Angel and the Two Marys at the Tomb" (stained-glass window)

1970. 150th Anniv of St. George's Cathedral, Kingstown. Multicoloured.

309	½c. Type **54**	10	10
310	5c. St. George's Cathedral (horiz)	10	10
311	25c. Tower, St. George's Cathedral	15	10
312	35c. Interior, St. George's Cathedral (horiz)	15	10
313	50c. Type **54**	20	30

55 "The Adoration of the Shepherds" (Le Nain)

1970. Christmas. Multicoloured.

314	8c. "The Virgin and Child" (Bellini) (vert)	10	10
315	25c. Type **55**	10	10
316	35c. As 8c.	10	10
317	50c. Type **55**	15	20

56 New Post Office and 6d. Stamp of 1861

1971. 110th Anniv of First St. Vincent Stamps. Multicoloured.

318	2c. Type **56**	10	10
319	4c. 1d. stamp of 1861 and new Post Office	10	10
320	25c. Type **56**	10	10
321	$1 As 4c.	35	45

57 Trust Seal and Wildlife

1971. St. Vincent's National Trust. Mult.

322	12c. Type **57**	40	1·10
323	30c. Old cannon, Fort Charlotte	20	25
324	40c. Type **57**	50	40
325	45c. As 30c.	30	1·25

58 "Madonna appearing to St. Anthony" (Tiepolo)

1971. Christmas. Multicoloured.

326	5c. Type **58**	10	10
327	10c. "The Holy Family on the Flight into Egypt" (detail, Pietro da Cortona)	10	10
328	25c. Type **58**	10	10
329	$1 As 10c.	40	35

59 Careening

1971. The Grenadines of St. Vincent. Multicoloured.

330	1c. Type **59**	10	10
331	5c. Seine fishermen	10	10
332	6c. Map of the Grenadines	10	10
333	15c. Type **59**	20	10
334	20c. As 5c.	20	10
335	50c. As 6c.	65	1·00
MS336	177×140 mm. Nos. 330/5	6·00	9·50

60 Private, Grenadier Company, 32nd Foot (1764)

1972. Military Uniforms.

337	**60**	12c. multicoloured	50	30
338	-	30c. multicoloured	55	50
339	-	50c. multicoloured	60	1·25

DESIGNS: 30c. Officer, Battalion Company, 31st Foot (1772); 50c. Private, Grenadier Company, 6th Foot (1772).

61 Breadnut Fruit

1972. Fruit. Multicoloured.

340	3c. Type **61**	10	40
341	5c. Pawpaw	10	20
342	12c. Plumrose or roseapple	15	50
343	25c. Mango	35	70

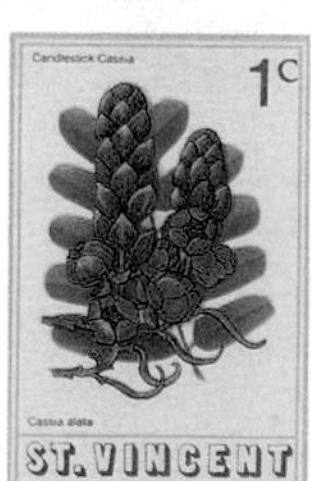

62 Candlestick Cassia

1972. Flowers. Multicoloured.

344	1c. Type **62**	10	10
345	30c. Lobster claw	10	10
346	40c. White trumpet	15	15
347	$1 Soufriere tree	35	1·25

63 Sir Charles Brisbane and Coat of Arms

1972. Birth Bicentenary of Sir Charles Brisbane.

348	**63**	20c. brown, gold and red	15	10
349	-	30c. yellow, mauve & black	35	10
350	-	$1 multicoloured	60	70

MS351	171×111 mm. Nos. 348/50 (sold at $2)	4·00	6·50

DESIGNS: 30c. H.M.S. "Arethusa", 1807; $1 H.M.S. "Blake", 1808.

1972. Royal Silver Wedding. As T 103 of St. Helena, but with Arrowroot and Breadfruit in background.

352	30c. brown	10	10
353	$1 green	20	20

65 Sighting of St. Vincent

1973. 475th Anniv of Columbus's Third Voyage to the West Indies. Multicoloured.

354	5c. Type **65**	20	30
355	12c. Caribs watching Columbus's fleet	25	50
356	30c. Christopher Columbus	40	70
357	50c. "Santa Maria"	70	2·25

66 "The Last Supper" (French stained-glass window)

1973. Easter.

358	**66**	15c. multicoloured	10	10
359	-	60c. multicoloured	20	20
360	-	$1 multicoloured	20	20

Nos. 358/60 are in the form of a triptych and make a composite design depicting "The Last Supper".

67 William Wilberforce and Poster

1973. 140th Death Anniv of William Wilberforce. Multicoloured.

369	30c. Type **67**	15	10
370	40c. Slaves cutting cane	20	15
371	50c. Wilberforce and medallion	20	15

68 P.P.F. Symbol

1973. 21st Anniv of International Planned Parenthood Federation. Multicoloured.

372	12c. Type **68**	10	10
373	40c. "IPPF" and symbol	20	20

1973. Royal Wedding. As T 103a of St. Helena. Multicoloured, background colours given.

374	50c. blue	15	10
375	70c. green	15	10

69 Administration Block, Mona

1973. 25th Anniv of West Indies University. Multicoloured.

376	5c. Type **69**	10	10
377	10c. University Centre, Kingstown	10	10
378	30c. Aerial view, Mona University	15	10
379	$1 University coat of arms (vert)	35	60

1973. Nos. 297, 292 and 298 surch.

380	30c. on 50c. multicoloured	1·25	1·00
381	40c. on 8c. multicoloured	1·25	1·00
382	$10 on $1 multicoloured	3·00	8·50

71 "The Descent from the Cross" (Sansovino)

1974. Easter. Multicoloured.

383	5c. Type **71**	10	10
384	30c. "The Deposition" (English, 14th-century)	10	10
385	40c. "Pieta" (Fernandez)	10	10
386	$1 "The Resurrection" (French, 16th-century)	20	25

72 "Istra"

1974. Cruise Ships. Multicoloured.

387	15c. Type **72**	15	10
388	20c. "Oceanic"	20	10
389	30c. "Aleksandr Pushkin"	20	10
390	$1 "Europa"	35	1·25
MS391	134×83 mm. Nos. 387/90	1·00	3·00

73 U.P.U. Emblem

1974. Centenary of U.P.U. Multicoloured.

392	5c. Type **73**	10	10
393	12c. Globe within posthorn	10	10
394	60c. Map of St. Vincent and hand-cancelling	20	10
395	90c. Map of the World	25	30

74 Royal Tern

1974. Multicoloured.. Multicoloured..

396	30c. Type **74**	1·50	90
397	40c. Brown pelican	1·50	90
398	$10 Magnificent frigate bird ("Frigatebird")	5·00	7·00

75 Scout Badge and Emblems

1974. Diamond Jubilee of Scout Movement in St. Vincent.

399	**75**	10c. multicoloured	10	10
400	**75**	25c. multicoloured	20	10
401	**75**	45c. multicoloured	20	15
402	**75**	$1 multicoloured	35	1·40

76 Sir Winston Churchill

1974. Birth Centenary of Sir Winston Churchill. Multicoloured.

403	25c. Type **76**	10	10
404	35c. Churchill in military uniform	15	10
405	45c. Churchill in naval uniform	15	10
406	$1 Churchill in air force uniform	20	50

77 The Shepherds

1974. Christmas.

407	**77**	3c. blue and black	10	10
408	-	3c. blue and black	10	10
409	-	3c. blue and black	10	10
410	-	3c. blue and black	10	10
411	**77**	8c. green and black	10	10
412	-	35c. pink and black	10	10
413	-	45c. brown and black	10	10
414	-	$1 mauve and black	20	50

DESIGNS: Nos. 408, 411, Mary and crib; Nos. 409, 413, Joseph, ox and ass; Nos. 410, 414, The Magi.

78 Faces

1975. Kingstown Carnival. Mult.

415	1c. Type **78**	10	10
416	15c. Pineapple women	15	15
417	25c. King of the Bands	15	15
418	35c. Carnival dancers	15	15
419	45c. Queen of the Bands	15	20
420	$1.25 "African Splendour"	25	55
MS421	146×128 mm. Nos. 415/20	1·00	3·00

79 French Angelfish

1975. Marine Life. Multicoloured.

422	1c. Type **79**	15	80
423	2c. Spot-finned butterflyfish	15	1·00
424	3c. Yellow jack	15	55
425	4c. Spanish mackerel	20	10
426	5c. French grunt	20	45
427	6c. Spotted goatfish	20	1·00
428	8c. Ballyhoo	20	2·75
429	10c. Sperm whale	50	10
430	12c. Humpback whale	50	2·50
431	15c. Scribbled cowfish	1·25	2·50
432	15c. Skipjack tuna	3·50	2·50
433	20c. Queen angelfish	30	10
434	25c. Princess parrotfish	30	20
435	35c. Red hind	65	2·75
436	45c. Atlantic flyingfish	80	1·25
437	50c. Porkfish	50	3·00
438	70c. Yellow-finned tuna	6·50	3·25
439	90c. Pompano	6·50	70
440	$1 Queen triggerfish	50	20
441a	$2.50 Sailfish	75	1·25
442	$5 Dolphin (fish)	3·25	2·50
443	$10 Blue marlin	2·00	7·50

80 Cutting Bananas

1975. Banana Industry. Multicoloured.

447	25c. Type **80**	10	10
448	35c. Packaging Station, La Croix	10	10
449	45c. Cleaning and boxing	15	10
450	70c. Shipping bananas aboard "Geestide" (freighter)	35	30

81 Snorkel Diving

1975. Tourism. Multicoloured.

451	15c. Type **81**	40	15
452	20c. Aquaduct Golf Course	1·50	1·50
453	35c. Steel band at Mariner's Inn	45	15
454	45c. Sunbathing at Young Island	45	15
455	$1.25 Yachting marina	1·40	3·00

82 George Washington, John Adams, Thomas Jefferson and James Madison

1975. Bicentenary of American Revolution.

456	**82**	½c. black and mauve	10	20
457	-	1c. black and green	10	20
458	-	1½c. black and mauve	10	20
459	-	5c. black and green	10	10
460	-	10c. black and blue	10	10
461	-	25c. black and yellow	10	10
462	-	35c. black and blue	10	10
463	-	45c. black and red	10	10
464	-	$1 black and orange	20	40
465	-	$2 black and green	30	85
MS466		179×156 mm. Nos. 456/65	1·00	1·50

PRESIDENTS: 1c. Monroe, Quincy Adams, Jackson, van Buren; 1½c. W. Harrison, Tyler, Polk, Taylor; 5c. Fillmore, Pierce, Buchanan, Lincoln; 10c. Andrew Johnson, Grant, Hayes, Garfield; 25c. Arthur, Cleveland, B. Harrison, McKinley; 35c. Theodore Roosevelt, Taft, Wilson, Harding; 45c. Coolidge, Hoover, Franklin Roosevelt, Truman; $1 Eisenhower, Kennedy, Lyndon Johnson, Nixon; $2 Pres. Ford and White House.

83/4 "Shepherds"

1975. Christmas.

467A	3c. black and mauve	10	25

No.	Type	Description	Unused	Used
468A		3c. black and mauve	10	25
469A		3c. black and mauve	10	25
470A		3c. black and mauve	10	25
471A		8c. black and blue	10	25
472A		8c. black and blue	10	25
473A		35c. black and yellow	15	20
474A		35c. black and yellow	15	20
475A	**83**	45c. black and green	15	30
476A	**84**	45c. black and green	15	30
477A	-	$1 black and purple	30	80
478A	-	$1 black and purple	30	80

DESIGNS: No. 467, "Star of Bethlehem"; No. 468, "Holy Trinity"; No. 469, As Type **83**; No. 470, "Three Kings"; Nos. 471/2, As No. 467; Nos. 473/4, As No. 468; Nos. 475/6, Types **83/4**; Nos. 477/8, As No. 470. The two designs of each value (Nos. 471/8) differ in that the longest side is at the foot or at the top as shown in Types **83/4**.

85 Carnival Dancers

1976. Kingstown Carnival. Mult.

No.	Description	Unused	Used
479	1c. Type **85**	10	10
480	2c. Humpty-Dumpty people	10	10
481	5c. Smiling faces	10	10
482	35c. Dragon worshippers	15	10
483	45c. Carnival tableaux	20	10
484	$1.25 Bumble-bee dancers	30	50

1976. Nos. 424 and 437 surch.

No.	Description	Unused	Used
485	70c. on 3c. Horse-eyed jack	35	1·00
486	90c. on 50c. Porkfish	35	1·25

87 Blue-headed Hummingbird and Yellow Hibiscus

1976. Hummingbirds and Hibiscuses. Mult.

No.	Description	Unused	Used
487	5c. Type **87**	30	15
488	10c. Antillean crested hummingbird ("Crested Hummingbird") and pink hibiscus	55	15
489	35c. Purple-throated carib and white hibiscus	45	10
490	45c. Blue-headed hummingbird and red hibiscus	45	10
491	$1.25 Green-throated carib and peach hibiscus	1·40	4·00

1976. West Indian Victory in World Cricket Cup. As Nos. 431/2 of St. Lucia.

No.	Description	Unused	Used
492	15c. Map of the Caribbean	60	25
493	45c. Prudential Cup	80	1·00

88 St. Mary Church, Kingstown

1976. Christmas. Multicoloured.

No.	Description	Unused	Used
494	35c. Type **88**	15	10
495	45c. Anglican Church, Georgetown	15	10
496	50c. Methodist Church, Georgetown	20	10
497	$1.25 St. George's Cathedral, Kingstown	40	60

89 Barrancoid Pot-stand

1977. National Trust. Multicoloured.

No.	Description	Unused	Used
498	5c. Type **89**	10	10
499	45c. National Museum	15	10
500	70c. Carib sculpture	20	20
501	$1 Ciboney petroglyph	30	50

90 William I, William II, Henry I and Stephen

1977. Silver Jubilee. Multicoloured.

No.	Description	Unused	Used
502	½c. Type **90**	10	30
503	1c. Henry II, Richard I, John, Henry III	10	30
504	1½c. Edward I, Edward II, Edward III, Richard II	10	30
505	2c. Henry IV, Henry V, Henry VI, Edward IV	10	30
506	5c. Edward V, Richard III, Henry VII, Henry VIII	10	10
507	10c. Edward VI, Lady Jane Grey, Mary I, Elizabeth I	10	10
508	25c. James I, Charles I, Charles II, James II	10	10
509	35c. William III, Mary II, Anne, George I	10	10
510	45c. George II, George III, George IV	10	10
511	75c. William IV, Victoria, Edward VII	15	25
512	$1 George V, Edward VIII, George VI	20	40
513	$2 Elizabeth II leaving Westminster Abbey	30	60
MS514	170×146 mm. Nos. 502/13	1·00	2·00

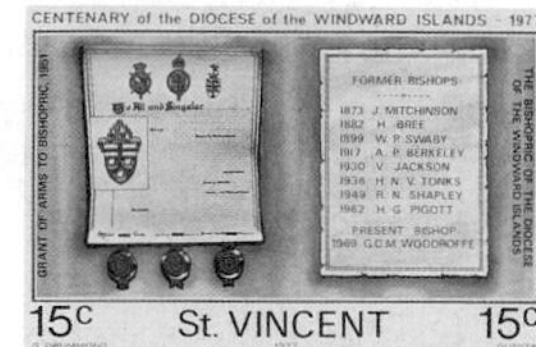

91 Grant of Arms

1977. Centenary of Windward Islands Diocese. Multicoloured.

No.	Description	Unused	Used
527	15c. Type **91**	10	10
528	35c. Bishop Berkeley and mitres	10	10
529	45c. Map and arms of diocese	10	10
530	$1.25 St. George's Cathedral and Bishop Woodroffe	30	55

1977. Kingstown Carnival. Nos. 426, 429, 432/3 and 440 optd CARNIVAL 1977 JUNE 25TH - JULY 5TH.

No.	Description	Unused	Used
531	5c. French grunt	10	10
532	10c. Sperm whale	10	10
533	15c. Skipjack tuna	10	10
534	20c. Queen angelfish	10	10
535	$1 Queen triggerfish	40	50

93 Guide and Emblem

1977. 50th Anniv of St. Vincent Girl Guides. Multicoloured.

No.	Description	Unused	Used
536	5c. Type **93**	10	10
537	15c. Early uniform, ranger, guide and brownie	10	10
538	20c. Early uniform and guide	10	10
539	$2 Lady Baden-Powell	40	75

1977. Royal Visit. No. 513 optd CARIBBEAN VISIT 1977.

No.	Description	Unused	Used
540	$2 Queen Elizabeth leaving Westminster Abbey	30	30

95 Map of St. Vincent

1977. Surch as in T 95.

No.	Type	Description	Unused	Used
541	**95**	20c. light blue and blue	15	15
542	**95**	40c. light orange and orange	25	20
543	**95**	40c. pink and mauve	20	15

Nos. 541/3 were originally printed without face values.

96 Opening Verse and Scene

1977. Christmas. Scenes and Verses from the carol "While Shepherds Watched their Flocks by Night". Multicoloured.

No.	Description	Unused	Used
544	5c. Type **96**	10	10
545	10c. Angel consoling shepherds	10	10
546	15c. View of Bethlehem	10	10
547	25c. Nativity scene	10	10
548	50c. Throng of angels	10	10
549	$1.25 Praising God	30	65
MS550	150×170 mm. Nos. 544/9	1·00	1·75

97 "Cynthia cardui" and "Bougainvillea glabra var alba"

1978. Butterflies and Bougainvilleas. Multicoloured.

No.	Description	Unused	Used
551	5c. Type **97**	15	10
552	25c. "Dione juno" and "Golden Glow"	15	10
553	40c. "Anartia amathea" and "Mrs McLean"	20	10
554	50c. "Hypolimnas misippus" and "Cyphen"	25	10
555	$1.25 "Pseudolycaena marsyas" and "Thomasii"	50	80

97a Westminster Abbey

1978. 25th Anniv of Coronation. Multicoloured.

No.	Description	Unused	Used
556	40c. Type **97a**	10	10
557	50c. Gloucester Cathedral	10	10
558	$1.25 Durham Cathedral	15	15
559	$2.50 Exeter Cathedral	15	25
MS560	130×102 mm. Nos. 556/9	40	1·00

98 Rotary International Emblem and Motto

1978. International Service Clubs. Emblems and Mottoes. Multicoloured.

No.	Description	Unused	Used
561	40c. Type **98**	15	10
562	50c. Lions International	15	10
563	$1 Jaycees	35	50

99 "Co-operation in Education Leads to Mutual Understanding and Respect"

1978. 10th Anniv of Project School to School (St. Vincent–Canada school twinning project). Multicoloured.

No.	Description	Unused	Used
564	40c. Type **99**	10	10
565	$2 "Co-operation in Education Leads to the Elimination of Racial Intolerance" (horiz)	40	50

100 Arnos Vale Airport

1978. 75th Anniv of Powered Flight. Mult.

No.	Description	Unused	Used
566	10c. Type **100**	10	10
567	40c. Wilbur Wright landing Wright Flyer I	15	10
568	50c. Orville Wright in Wright Flyer III	15	10
569	$1.25 Orville Wright and Wright Flyer I airborne	45	80

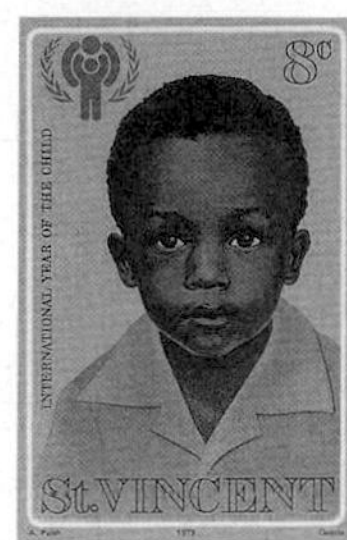

101 Young Child

1979. International Year of the Child.

No.	Type	Description	Unused	Used
570	**101**	8c. black, gold and green	10	10
571	-	20c. black, gold and lilac	10	10
572	-	50c. black, gold and blue	15	10
573	-	$2 black, gold and flesh	50	50

DESIGNS: 20, 50c., $2 Different portraits of young children.

1979. Soufriere Eruption Relief Fund. As T 95 but surch SOUFRIERE RELIEF FUND 1979 and premium.

No.	Type	Description	Unused	Used
574	**95**	10c.+5c. blue and lilac	10	15
575	**95**	50c.+25c. brown and buff	20	20
576	**95**	$1+50c. brown and grey	25	30
577	**95**	$2+$1 green and light green	40	50

103 Sir Rowland Hill

1979. Death Cent of Sir Rowland Hill. Mult.

No.	Description	Unused	Used
578	40c. Type **103**	15	10
579	50c. Penny Black and Two Penny Blue stamps	15	15
580	$3 1861 1d. and 6d. stamps	40	1·10
MS581	170×123 mm. Nos. 578/80, 594/5 and 599	1·40	2·50

104 First and Latest Buccament Postmarks and Map of St. Vincent

1979. Post Office of St. Vincent. Early and modern postmarks. Multicoloured.

No.	Description	Unused	Used
582	1c. Type **104**	10	10
583	2c. Sion Hill	10	10
584	3c. Cumberland	10	50
585	4c. Questelles	10	30
586	5c. Layou	10	10
587	6c. New Ground	10	10
588	8c. Mesopotamia	10	10
589	10c. Troumaca	10	10
590	12c. Arnos Vale	10	30
591	15c. Stubbs	10	30
592	20c. Orange Hill	10	30
593	25c. Calliaqua	10	10
594	40c. Edinboro	20	20
595	50c. Colonarie	20	25
596	80c. Biabou	30	35
597	$1 Chateaubelair	30	50
598	$2 Head P.O. Kingstown	35	80

599	$3 Barrouallie	40	1·25
600	$5 Georgetown	60	2·00
601	$10 Kingstown	1·25	4·00

1979. Opening of St. Vincent and the Grenadines Air Service. Optd ST VINCENT AND THE GRENADINES AIR SERVICE 1979.

602	10c. Type **100**	10	10

106 National Flag and "Ixora occinea" (flower)

1979. Independence. Multicoloured.

603	20c. Type **106**	15	10
604	50c. House of Assembly and "Ixora stricta" (flower)	20	10
605	80c. Prime Minister R. Milton Cato and "Ixora williamsii" (flower)	25	20

1979. Independence. Nos. 422, 425/30, 432, 437/41 and 443 optd INDEPENDENCE 1979.

606	1c. Type **79**	10	10
607	4c. Spanish mackerel	10	10
608	5c. French grunt	10	10
609	6c. Spotted goatfish	10	10
610	8c. Ballyhoo	10	10
611	10c. Sperm whale	15	15
612	12c. Humpback whale	15	15
613	15c. Skipjack tuna	10	15
614	25c. Princess parrotfish	10	20
615	50c. Porkfish	15	35
616	70c. Yellow-finned tuna	20	45
617	90c. Pompano	20	50
618	$1 Queen triggerfish	20	50
619	$2.50 Sailfish	35	1·00
620	$10 Blue marlin	1·10	4·25

108 Virgin and Child

1979. Christmas. Scenes and quotations from "Silent Night" (carol). Multicoloured.

621	10c. Type **108**	10	10
622	20c. Jesus sleeping	10	10
623	25c. Shepherds	10	10
624	40c. Angel	10	10
625	50c. Angels holding Jesus	10	10
626	$2 Nativity	40	45
MS627	151×170 mm. Nos. 621/6	70	1·25

109 "Polistes cinctus" (wasp) and Oleander

1979. Flowers and Insects. Different varieties of oleander. Multicoloured.

628	5c. Type **109**	10	10
629	10c. "Pyrophorus noctiluca" (click beetle)	10	10
630	25c. "Stagmomantis limbata" (mantid)	10	10
631	50c. "Psiloptera lampetis" (beetle)	10	10
632	$2 "Diaprepies abbreviatus" (weevil)	30	30

1980. Centenary of St. Vincent "Arms" Stamps. Sheet 116×72 mm containing designs as T 31.

MS633	116×72 mm. 50c. brown; $1 green; $2.50 blue	50	75

110 Queen Elizabeth II

1980. "London 1980" International Stamp Exhibition. Multicoloured.

634	80c. Type **110**	15	20
635	$1 Great Britain 1954 3d. and St. Vincent 1954 5c. definitives	20	30
636	$2 Unadopted postage stamp design of 1971	35	60
MS637	165×115 mm. Nos. 596/8 and 634/8	75	1·50

111 Steel Band

1980. Kingstown Carnival. Multicoloured.

638	20c. Type **111**	15	65
639	20c. Steel band (different)	15	65

112 Football

1980. "Sport for All". Multicoloured.

640	10c. Type **112**	10	10
641	60c. Cycling	30	15
642	80c. Basketball	40	40
643	$2.50 Boxing	40	1·25

1980. Hurricane Relief. Nos. 640/3 surch HURRICANE RELIEF 50c.

644	**112**	10c.+50c. multicoloured	15	20
645	-	60c.+50c. multicoloured	40	45
646	-	80c.+50c. multicoloured	45	50
647	-	$2.50+50c. mult	40	85

114 Brazilian Agouti

1980. Wildlife. Multicoloured.

648	25c. Type **114**	10	10
649	50c. Giant toad	15	10
650	$2 Small Indian mongoose	40	55

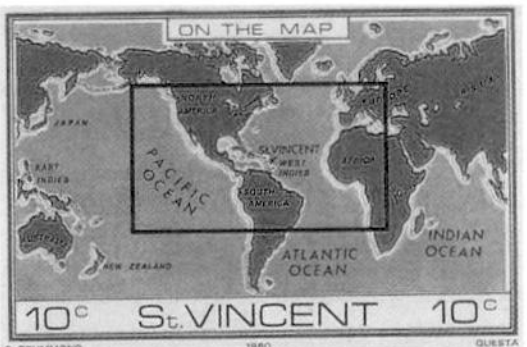

115 Map of World showing St. Vincent

1980. St. Vincent "On the Map". Maps showing St. Vincent. Multicoloured.

651	10c. Type **115**	10	10
652	50c. Western hemisphere	25	10
653	$1 Central America	40	15
654	$2 St. Vincent	60	30
MS655	143×95 mm. No. 654	70	75

116 "Ville de Paris" (French ship of the line), 1782

1981. Sailing Ships. Multicoloured.

656	50c. Type **116**	25	15
657	60c. H.M.S. "Ramillies" (ship of the line), 1782	25	25
658	$1.50 H.M.S. "Providence" (sloop), 1793	40	70
659	$2 "Dee" (paddle-steamer packet)	50	80

117 Arrowroot Cultivation

1981. Agriculture. Multicoloured.

660	25c. Type **117**	10	20
661	25c. Arrowroot processing	10	20
662	50c. Banana cultivation	10	30
663	50c. Banana export packaging station	10	30
664	60c. Coconut plantation	15	30
665	60c. Copra drying frames	15	35
666	$1 Cocoa cultivation	15	50
667	$1 Cocoa beans and sun drying frames	15	50

1981. Royal Wedding. Royal Yachts. As T 14a/b of St. Kitts. Multicoloured.

668	60c. "Isabella"	15	15
669	60c. Prince Charles and Lady Diana Spencer	30	30
670	$2.50 "Alberta" (tender)	30	30
671	$2.50 As No. 669	70	70
672	$4 "Britannia"	35	40
673	$4 As No. 669	1·00	1·25
MS674	120×109 mm. $5 As No. 669	75	75

118/19 Kingstown General Post Office

1981. U.P.U. Membership.

677	**118**	$2 multicoloured	40	90
678	**119**	$2 multicoloured	40	90

Nos. 677/8 were printed together, se-tenant, forming the composite design illustrated.

120 St. Vincent Flag with Flags of other U.N. Member Nations

1981. 1st Anniv of U.N. Membership. Mult.

679	$1.50 Type **120**	25	25
680	$2.50 Prime Minister Robert Milton Cato	35	50

Nos. 679/80 are inscribed "ST. VINCENT and the GRENADINES".

121 Silhouettes of Figures at Old Testament Reading and Bible Extract

1981. Christmas. Designs showing silhouettes of figures. Multicoloured.

681	50c. Type **121**	25	10
682	60c. Madonna and angel	30	10
683	$1 Madonna and Bible extract	45	25
684	$2 Joseph and Mary travelling to Bethlehem	65	50
MS685	129×127 mm. Nos. 681/4	1·00	1·40

122 Sugar Boilers

1982. 1st Anniv of Re-introduction of Sugar Industry. Multicoloured.

686	50c. Type **122**	20	15
687	60c. Sugar drying plant	20	20
688	$1.50 Sugar mill machinery	40	75
689	$2 Crane loading sugar cane	50	1·00

123 Butterfly Float

1982. Carnival 1982 Multicoloured.

690	50c. Type **123**	20	15
691	60c. Angel dancer (vert)	20	15
692	$1.50 Winged dancer (vert)	50	80
693	$2 Eagle float	70	1·50

124 Augusta of Saxe-Gotha, Princess of Wales, 1736

1982. 21st Birthday of Princess of Wales. Multicoloured.

694	50c. Type **124**	15	20
695	60c. Coat of arms of Augusta of Saxe-Gotha	15	25
696	$6 Diana, Princess of Wales	1·10	1·25

125 Scout Emblem

1982. 75th Anniv of Boy Scout Movement. Multicoloured.

697	$1.50 Type **125**	70	1·00
698	$2.50 75th anniversary emblem	90	1·50

1982. Birth of Prince William of Wales. Nos. 694/6 optd ROYAL BABY.

699	50c. Type **124**	10	20
700	60c. Coat of arms of Augusta of Saxe-Gotha	10	25
701	$6 Diana, Princess of Wales	60	1·50

126 De Havilland Gipsy Moth, 1932

1982. 50th Anniv of Airmail Service. Mult.

702	50c. Type **126**	55	30
703	60c. Grumman Goose, 1952	65	40
704	$1.50 Hawker Siddeley H.S.748, 1968	1·25	1·50
705	$2 Britten Norman "long nose" Trislander, 1982	1·40	2·00

127 "Geestport" (freighter)

1982. Ships. Multicoloured.

706	45c. Type **127**	40	25
707	60c. "Stella Oceanis" (liner)	50	40
708	$1.50 "Victoria" (liner)	80	1·50
709	$2 "Queen Elizabeth 2" (liner)	1·00	2·00

128 "Pseudocorynactis caribbeorum"

1983. Marine Life. Multicoloured.

710	50c. Type **128**	65	25
711	60c. "Actinoporus elegans" (vert)	75	40
712	$1.50 "Arachnanthus nocturnus" (vert)	1·40	2·25
713	$2 Reid's seahorse (vert)	1·60	2·50

129 Satellite View of St. Vincent

1983. Commonwealth Day. Multicoloured.

714	45c. Type **129**	15	20
715	60c. Flag of St. Vincent	20	25
716	$1.50 Prime Minister R. Milton Cato	30	65
717	$2 Harvesting bananas	45	90

Nos. 714/17 are inscribed "St. Vincent and The Grenadines".

1983. No. 681 surch 45c.

718	**121**	45c. on 50c. Mult	40	30

131 Symbolic Handshake

1983. 10th Anniv of Treaty of Chaguaramas. Multicoloured.

719	45c. Type **131**	15	20
720	60c. Commerce emblem	20	30
721	$1.50 Caribbean map	50	1·40
722	$2 Flags of member countries and map of St. Vincent	75	1·60

132 William A. Smith (founder)

1983. Centenary of Boys' Brigade. Mult.

723	45c. Type **132**	20	25
724	60c. On parade	25	35
725	$1.50 Craftwork	55	1·50
726	$2 Community service	70	1·60

133 Ford "Model T" (1908)

1983. Leaders of the World. Automobiles (1st series).

727	**133**	10c. multicoloured	10	10
728	-	10c. multicoloured	10	10
729	-	60c. multicoloured	10	15
730	-	60c. multicoloured	10	15
731	-	$1.50 multicoloured	15	20
732	-	$1.50 multicoloured	15	20
733	-	$1.50 multicoloured	15	20
734	-	$1.50 multicoloured	15	20
735	-	$2 multicoloured	15	20
736	-	$2 multicoloured	15	20
737	-	$2 multicoloured	15	20
738	-	$2 multicoloured	15	20

DESIGNS: (the first in each pair shows technical drawings and the second paintings of the cars). Nos. 727/8, Ford "Model T" (1908); 729/30, Supercharged Cord "812" (1937); 731/2, Citroen "Open Tourer" (1937); 733/4, Mercedes Benz "300SL Gull-Wing" (1954); 735/6, Rolls-Royce "Phantom I" (1925); 737/8, Ferrari "Boxer 512BB" (1967).

See also Nos. 820/9, 862/7, 884/91 and 952/63.

134 Appearance of the Nativity Star

1983. Christmas. Multicoloured.

739	10c. Type **134**	10	10
740	50c. Message of the Angel	20	10
741	$1.50 The Heavenly Host	40	75
742	$2.40 Worshipping Jesus	55	1·25
MS743	130×130 mm. Nos. 739/42	1·25	1·75

135 "King Henry VIII"

1983. Leaders of the World. Railway Locomotives (1st series). First in each pair shows technical drawings and the second the locomotive at work.

744	**135**	10c. multicoloured	10	10
745	-	10c. multicoloured	10	10
746	-	10c. multicoloured	10	10
747	-	10c. multicoloured	10	10
748	-	25c. multicoloured	10	10
749	-	25c. multicoloured	10	10
750	-	50c. multicoloured	15	20
751	-	50c. multicoloured	15	20
752	-	60c. multicoloured	15	20
753	-	60c. multicoloured	15	20
754	-	75c. multicoloured	15	25
755	-	75c. multicoloured	15	25
756	-	$2.50 multicoloured	20	35
757	-	$2.50 multicoloured	20	35
758	-	$3 multicoloured	25	50
759	-	$3 multicoloured	25	50

See also Nos. 792/807, 834/41, 872/83, 893/904 and 1001/8.

136 Fort Duvernette

1984. Fort Duvernette. Multicoloured.

760	35c. Type **136**	20	30
761	45c. Soldiers on fortifications	25	30
762	$1 Cannon facing bay	40	60
763	$3 Map of St. Vincent and mortar	1·25	1·75

137 White Frangipani

1984. Flowering Trees and Shrubs. Mult.

764	5c. Type **137**	20	10
765	10c. Genip	25	10
766	15c. Immortelle	30	10
767	20c. Pink poui	30	10
768	25c. Buttercup	30	10
769	35c. Sandbox	45	10
770	45c. Locust	45	10
771	60c. Colville's glory	50	30
772	75c. Lignum vitae	50	45
773	$1 Golden shower	50	1·00
774	$5 Angelin	1·25	6·50
775	$10 Roucou	1·75	11·00

138 Trench Warfare, First World War

1984. Leaders of the World. British Monarchs. Multicoloured.

776	1c. Type **138**	10	10
777	1c. George V and trenches	10	10
778	5c. Battle of Bannockburn	10	10
779	5c. Edward II and battle	10	10
780	60c. George V	15	20
781	60c. York Cottage, Sandringham	15	20
782	75c. Edward II	15	20
783	75c. Berkeley Castle	15	20
784	$1 Coat of arms of Edward II	15	25
785	$1 Edward II (different)	15	25
786	$4 Coat of arms of George V	35	60
787	$4 George V and Battle of Jutland	35	60

Nos. 776/7, 778/9, 780/1, 782/3, 784/5 and 786/7 were printed together, se-tenant, each pair forming a composite design.

139 Musical Fantasy Costume

1984. Carnival 1984. Costumes. Multicoloured.

788	35c. Type **139**	15	15
789	45c. African princess	15	20
790	$1 Market woman	35	40
791	$3 Carib hieroglyph	80	1·75

1984. Leaders of the World. Railway Locomotives (2nd series). As T 135, the first in each pair shows technical drawings and the second the locomotive at work.

792	1c. multicoloured	10	10
793	1c. multicoloured	10	10
794	2c. multicoloured	10	10
795	2c. multicoloured	10	10
796	3c. multicoloured	10	10
797	3c. multicoloured	10	10
798	50c. multicoloured	20	30
799	50c. multicoloured	20	30
800	75c. multicoloured	20	35
801	75c. multicoloured	20	35
802	$1 multicoloured	20	35
803	$1 multicoloured	20	35
804	$2 multicoloured	25	40
805	$2 multicoloured	25	40
806	$3 multicoloured	25	50
807	$3 multicoloured	25	50

DESIGNS: Nos. 792/3, Class 141-R Liberation, France (1945); 794/5, Diesel locomotive "Dread-nought", Great Britain (1967); 796/7, No. 242A1, France (1946); 798/9, Class "Dean Goods", Great Britain (1883); 800/1, Hetton Colliery No. 1, Great Britain (1822); 802/3, "Pen-y-Darren", Great Britain (1804); 804/5, "Novelty", Great Britain (1829); 806/7, Class 44, Germany (1925).

140 Slaves tilling Field

1984. 150th Anniv of Emancipation of Slaves on St. Vincent. Multicoloured.

808	35c. Type **140**	15	20
809	45c. Sugar-cane harvesting	15	25
810	$1 Cutting sugar-cane	30	70
811	$3 William Wilberforce and African slave caravan	1·00	2·75

141 Weightlifting

1984. Leaders of the World. Olympic Games, Los Angeles. Multicoloured.

812	1c. Judo	10	10
813	1c. Type **141**	10	10
814	3c. Pursuit cycling	10	10
815	3c. Cycle road-racing	10	10
816	60c. Women's backstroke swimming	15	15
817	60c. Men's butterfly swimming	15	15
818	$3 Sprint start	40	55
819	$3 Finish of long distance race	40	55

1984. Leaders of the World. Automobiles (2nd series). As T 133, the first in each pair shows technical drawings and the second paintings.

820	5c. black, drab and green	10	10
821	5c. multicoloured	10	10
822	20c. black, pink and blue	10	10
823	20c. multicoloured	10	10
824	55c. black, green and brown	20	20
825	55c. multicoloured	20	20
826	$1.50 black, light turquoise and turquoise	25	30
827	$1.50 multicoloured	25	30
828	$2.50 black, turquoise and lilac	30	35
829	$2.50 multicoloured	30	35

DESIGNS: Nos. 820/1, Austin-Healey "Sprite" (1958); 822/3, Maserati "Ghibli Coupe" (1971); 824/5, Pontiac "GTO" (1964); 826/7, Jaguar "D-Type" (1957); 828/9, Ferrari "365 GTB4 Daytona" (1970).

142 Grenadier, 70th Regt of Foot, 1773

1984. Military Uniforms. Multicoloured.

830	45c. Type **142**	50	30
831	60c. Grenadier, 6th Regt of Foot, 1775	60	35
832	$1.50 Grenadier, 3rd Regt of Foot, 1768	80	1·10
833	$2 Battalion Company Officer, 14th Regt of Foot, 1780	90	1·60

1984. Leaders of the World. Railway Locomotives (3rd series). As T 135, the first in each pair shows technical drawings and the second the locomotive at work.

834	5c. multicoloured	10	10
835	5c. multicoloured	10	10
836	40c. multicoloured	15	15
837	40c. multicoloured	15	15
838	75c. multicoloured	15	20
839	75c. multicoloured	15	20
840	$2.50 multicoloured	50	65
841	$2.50 multicoloured	50	65

DESIGNS: Nos. 834/5, 20th Class, Rhodesia (1954); 836/7, "Southern Maid", Great Britain (1928); 838/9, "Prince of Wales", Great Britain (1911); 840/1, Class 05, Germany (1935).

143 N. S. Taylor

1985. Leaders of the World. Cricketers. The first in each pair shows a head portrait and the second the cricketer in action.

842	**143**	5c. multicoloured	10	10
843	-	5c. multicoloured	10	10
844	-	35c. multicoloured	30	20
845	-	35c. multicoloured	30	20
846	-	50c. multicoloured	30	30
847	-	50c. multicoloured	30	30
848	-	$3 multicoloured	50	1·25
849	-	$3 multicoloured	50	1·25

DESIGNS: Nos. 842/3, N. S. Taylor; 844/5, T. W. Graveney; 846/7, R. G. D. Willis; 848/9, S. D. Fletcher.

144 Eye Lash Orchid

1985. Orchids. Multicoloured.

850	35c. Type **144**	20	30
851	45c. "Ionopsis utricularioides"	20	30
852	$1 "Epidendrum secundum"	30	65
853	$3 "Oncidium altissimum"	40	2·00

145 Brown Pelican

1985. Leaders of the World. Birth Bicentenary of John J. Audubon (ornithologist). Multicoloured.

854	15c. Type **145**	10	10
855	15c. Green-backed heron ("Green Heron")	10	10
856	40c. Pileated woodpecker	15	20
857	40c. Common flicker	15	20
858	60c. Painted bunting	15	30
859	60c. White-winged crossbill	15	30
860	$2.25 Red-shouldered hawk	30	90
861	$2.25 Common caracara ("Crested Caracara")	30	90

1985. Leaders of the World. Automobiles (3rd series). As T 133, the first in each pair shows technical drawings and the second paintings.

862	1c. black, yellow and green	10	10
863	1c. multicoloured	10	10
864	55c. black, blue and grey	15	25
865	55c. multicoloured	15	25
866	$2 black, yellow and purple	30	70
867	$2 multicoloured	30	70

DESIGNS: Nos. 862/3, Lancia "Aprilia", (1937); 864/5, Pontiac "Firebird Trans Am", (1973); 866/7, Cunningham "C-5R", (1953).

146 Pepper

1985. Herbs and Spices. Multicoloured.

868	25c. Type **146**	10	10
869	35c. Sweet marjoram	10	15
870	$1 Nutmeg	20	65
871	$3 Ginger	60	2·50

1985. Leaders of the World. Railway Locomotives (4th series). As T 135, the first in each pair shows technical drawings and the second the locomotive at work.

872	1c. multicoloured	10	10
873	1c. multicoloured	10	10
874	10c. multicoloured	10	10
875	10c. multicoloured	10	10
876	40c. multicoloured	15	30
877	40c. multicoloured	15	30
878	60c. multicoloured	15	30
879	60c. multicoloured	15	30
880	$1 multicoloured	25	40
881	$1 multicoloured	25	40
882	$2.50 multicoloured	40	60
883	$2.50 multicoloured	40	60

DESIGNS: Nos. 872/3, "Glen Douglas", Great Britain (1913); 874/5, "Fenchurch", Great Britain (1872); 876/7, No. 1 Stirling "single", Great Britain (1870); 878/9, No. 158A, Great Britain (1866); 880/1, Jones Goods locomotive No. 103, Great Britain (1893); 882/3, "The Great Bear", Great Britain (1908).

1985. Leaders of the World. Automobiles (4th series). As T 133, the first in each pair shows technical drawings and the second paintings.

884	25c. black, grey and red	10	10
885	25c. multicoloured	10	10
886	60c. black, pink and orange	15	20
887	60c. multicoloured	15	20
888	$1 black, blue and violet	15	25
889	$1 multicoloured	15	25
890	$1.50 black, blue and red	20	30
891	$1.50 multicoloured	20	30
MS892	180×121 mm. $4 ×2 As Nos. 890/1; $5 ×2 As Nos. 888/9	1·75	4·50

DESIGNS: Nos. 884/5, Essex "Coach" (1922); 886/7, Nash "Rambler" (1950); 888/9, Ferrari "Tipo 156" (1961); 890/1, Eagle-Weslake "Type 58" (1967).

1985. Leaders of the World. Railway Locomotives (5th series). As T 135, the first in each pair shows technical drawings and the second the locomotive at work.

893	**151**	5c. multicoloured	10	10
894	-	5c. multicoloured	10	10
895	-	30c. multicoloured	15	20
896	-	30c. multicoloured	15	20
897	-	60c. multicoloured	20	30
898	-	60c. multicoloured	20	30
899	-	75c. multicoloured	20	30
900	-	75c. multicoloured	20	30
901	-	$1 multicoloured	25	40
902	-	$1 multicoloured	25	40
903	-	$2.50 multicoloured	30	60
904	-	$2.50 multicoloured	30	60

DESIGNS: Nos. 893/4, "Loch", Isle of Man (1874); 895/6, Class 47XX, Great Britain (1919); 897/8, Class 121, France (1876); 899/900, Class 24, Germany (1927); 901/2, Tank locomotive No. 1008, Great Britain (1889); 903/4, Class PS-4, U.S.A. (1926).

147 Bamboo Flute

1985. Traditional Musical Instruments. Mult.

905	25c. Type **147**	10	15
906	35c. Quatro (four-stringed guitar)	10	25
907	$1 Ba-ha (bamboo pipe) (vert)	25	55
908	$2 Goat-skin drum (vert)	35	1·10
MS909	141×100 mm. Nos. 905/8	1·60	4·50

148 Queen Elizabeth the Queen Mother

1985. Leaders of the World. Life and Times of Queen Elizabeth the Queen Mother. Various portraits.

910	**148**	35c. multicoloured	10	25
911	-	35c. multicoloured	10	25
912	-	85c. multicoloured	10	30
913	-	85c. multicoloured	10	30
914	-	$1.20 multicoloured	15	35
915	-	$1.20 multicoloured	15	35
916	-	$1.60 multicoloured	15	35
917	-	$1.60 multicoloured	15	35
MS918		85×114 mm. $2.10 multicoloured; $2.10 multicoloured	50	1·50

Each value issued in pairs showing a floral pattern across the bottom of the portraits which stops short of the left-hand edge on the first stamp and of the right-hand edge on the second.

149 Elvis Presley

1985. Leaders of the World. Elvis Presley (entertainer). Various portraits. Multicoloured, background colours given.

919	**149**	10c. multicoloured	15	15
920	-	10c. multicoloured (blue)	15	15
921	-	60c. multicoloured (brown)	20	35
922	-	60c. multicoloured (grey)	20	35
923	-	$1 multicoloured (brown)	20	55
924	-	$1 multicoloured (blue)	20	55
925	-	$5 mult (light blue)	40	1·75
926	-	$5 multicoloured (blue)	40	1·75
MS927		Four sheets each 145×107 mm. (a) 30c. As Nos. 919/20 each ×2. (b) 50c. As Nos. 921/2 each ×2. (c) $1.50 As Nos. 923/4 each ×2. (d) $4.50 As Nos. 925/6 each ×2. Set of 4 sheets	21·00	20·00

150 Silos and Conveyor Belt

1985. St. Vincent Flour Milling Industry. Multicoloured.

928	20c. Type **150**	10	15
929	30c. Roller mills	10	20
930	75c. Administration building	20	35
931	$3 Bran finishers	50	1·40

1985. Royal Visit. Nos. 672/3, 697/8, 711, 724 and 912/13 optd CARIBBEAN ROYAL VISIT 1985 or surch also.

932	-	60c. multicoloured (711)	1·50	2·00
933	-	60c. multicoloured (724)	1·75	2·25
934	-	85c. multicoloured (912)	4·50	6·50
935	-	85c. multicoloured (913)	4·50	6·50
936	**125**	$1.50 multicoloured	1·60	3·25
937	-	$1.60 on $4 mult (672)	70	2·25
938	-	$1.60 on $4 mult (673)	11·00	17·00
939	-	$2.50 multicoloured (698)	1·75	4·00

No. 938 shows a new face value only.

151 Michael Jackson

1985. Leaders of the World. Michael Jackson (entertainer). Various portraits. Multicoloured.

940	**151**	60c. multicoloured	15	30
941	-	60c. multicoloured	15	30
942	-	$1 multicoloured	15	45
943	-	$1 multicoloured	15	45
944	-	$2 multicoloured	20	60
945	-	$2 multicoloured	20	60
946	-	$5 multicoloured	30	1·00
947	-	$5 multicoloured	30	1·00
MS948		Four sheets, each 144×109 mm. (a) 45c. As Nos. 940/1 each ×2. (b) 90c. As Nos. 942/3 each ×2. (c) $1.50 As Nos. 944/5 each ×2. (d) $4 As Nos. 946/7 each ×2. Set of 4 sheets	3·25	7·50

Each value issued in pairs, the left-hand design showing the face value at top left (as on Type **151**) and the right-hand design at top right.

152 "The Serenaders" (Kim de Freitas)

1985. Christmas. Children's Paintings. Mult.

949	25c. Type **152**	10	15
950	75c. "Poinsettia" (Jackie Douglas)	20	40
951	$2.50 "Jesus our Master" (Bernadette Payne)	55	2·00

153 "Santa Maria"

1986. 500th Anniv (1992) of Discovery of America by Columbus (1st issue). Multicoloured.

952	60c. Type **153**	50	65
953	60c. Christopher Columbus	50	65
954	$1.50 Columbus at Spanish Court	70	1·40
955	$1.50 King Ferdinand and Queen Isabella of Spain	70	1·40
956	$2.75 "Santa Maria" and fruits	1·00	2·25
957	$2.75 Maize and fruits	1·00	2·25
MS958	95×85 mm. $6 Christopher Columbus (different)	2·50	6·00

See also Nos. 1125/31, 1305/24, 1639/57, 1677/85, 1895/1901 and 1981/2.

1986. Leaders of the World. Automobiles (5th series). As T 133, the first in each pair shows technical drawings and the second paintings.

959	30c. black, blue and orange	10	15
960	30c. multicoloured	10	15
961	45c. black, grey and blue	10	15
962	45c. multicoloured	10	15
963	60c. black, blue and red	15	20
964	60c. multicoloured	15	20
965	90c. black, yellow and blue	15	25
966	90c. multicoloured	15	25
967	$1.50 black, lilac and mauve	20	40
968	$1.50 multicoloured	20	40
969	$2.50 black, blue and light blue	20	50
970	$2.50 multicoloured	20	50

DESIGNS: Nos. 959/60, Cadillac "Type 53" (1916); 961/2, Triumph "Dolomite" (1939); 963/4, Panther "J-72" (1972); 965/6, Ferrari "275 GTB/4" (1967); 967/8, Packard "Caribbean" (1953); 969/70, Bugatti "Type 41 Royale" (1931).

154 Guide Salute and Handclasp

1986. 75th Annivs of Girl Guide Movement and Boy Scouts of America. Two sheets, each 85×113 mm, containing vert designs as T 154. Multicoloured.

MS971	$5 Type **154**; $5 Palette and paintbrushes	2·00	5·00
MS972	$6 Cross-tied logs; $6 Lord Baden-Powell	2·00	6·00

The two stamps in each sheet were printed together, se-tenant, in horizontal pairs, each forming a composite design.

Nos. **MS**971/2 exist with plain or decorative margins.

Overprints on these miniature sheets commemorating "Capex '87" International Stamp Exhibition, Toronto, were not authorised by the St. Vincent administration.

155 Halley's Comet

1986. Appearance of Halley's Comet. Multicoloured.

973	45c. Type **155**	40	30
974	60c. Edmond Halley	40	30
975	75c. Newton's telescope and astronomers	50	55
976	$3 Amateur astronomer on St. Vincent	70	2·75
MS977	155×104 mm. Nos. 973/6	2·00	4·50

1986. 60th Birthday of Queen Elizabeth II (1st issue). As T 162a of St. Lucia. Multicoloured.

978	10c. Queen Elizabeth II	10	10
979	90c. Princess Elizabeth	20	30
980	$2.50 Queen gathering bouquets from crowd	35	80
981	$8 In Canberra, 1982 (vert)	1·00	2·25
MS982	85×115 mm. $10 Queen Elizabeth II (different)	3·00	6·00

See also Nos. 996/1000.

156 Mexican Player

1986. World Cup Football Championship, Mexico. Multicoloured.

983	1c. Football and world map (horiz)	10	10
984	2c. Type **156**	10	10
985	5c. Mexican player (different)	10	10

986	5c. Hungary v Scotland	10	10
987	10c. Spain v Scotland	10	10
988	30c. England v U.S.S.R. (horiz)	20	20
989	45c. Spain v France	30	30
990	75c. Mexican team (56×36 mm)	45	45
991	$1 England v Italy	45	65
992	$2 Scottish team (56×36 mm)	60	1·50
993	$4 Spanish team (56×36 mm)	1·00	2·75
994	$5 English team (56×36 mm)	1·00	3·75
MS995	Six sheets, each 84×114 mm. (a) $1.50 As Type **156**. (b) $1.50 As No. 993.(c) $2.25 As No. 992. (d) $2.50 As No. 990. (e) $3 As No. 989. (f) $5.50 As No. 994. Set of 6 sheets	7·50	11·00

157 Queen Elizabeth at Victoria Park, Kingstown

1986. 60th Birthday of Queen Elizabeth II (2nd issue). Scenes from 1985 Royal Visit. Multicoloured.

996	45c. Type **157**	50	30
997	60c. Queen and Prime Minister James Mitchell, Bequia	65	55
998	75c. Queen, Prince Philip and Mr. Mitchell, Port Elizabeth, Bequia	75	65
999	$2.50 Queen, Prince Philip and Mr. Mitchell watching Independence Day parade, Victoria Park	1·50	2·50
MS1000	121×85 mm. $3 Queen at Victoria Park	3·50	4·50

1986. Leaders of the World. Railway Locomotives (6th series). As T 135. Multicoloured.

1001	30c. multicoloured	10	10
1002	30c. multicoloured	10	10
1003	50c. multicoloured	15	20
1004	50c. multicoloured	15	20
1005	$1 multicoloured	20	30
1006	$1 multicoloured	20	30
1007	$3 multicoloured	35	70
1008	$3 multicoloured	35	70

DESIGNS: Nos. 1001/2, Class ED41 BZZB electric rack and adhesion locomotive, Japan (1926); 1003/4, "The Judge", Chicago Railroad Exposition, U.S.A. (1883); 1005/6, Class E60C electric locomotive, U.S.A. (1973); 1007/8, Class SD40-2 diesel locomotive, U.S.A. (1972).

1986. Royal Wedding (1st issue). As T 164a of St. Lucia. Multicoloured.

1009	60c. Profile of Prince Andrew	20	25
1010	60c. Miss Sarah Ferguson	20	25
1011	$2 Prince Andrew with Mrs. Nancy Reagan (horiz)	45	75
1012	$2 Prince Andrew in naval uniform (horiz)	45	75
MS1013	115×85 mm. $10 Duke and Duchess of York in carriage after wedding (horiz)	2·50	4·50

See also Nos. 1022/5.

158 "Acrocomia aculeata"

1986. Timber Resources of St. Vincent. Mult.

1014	10c. Type **158**	40	20
1015	60c. "Pithecellobium saman"	1·25	80
1016	75c. White cedar	1·60	95
1017	$3 "Andira inermis"	3·50	4·50

159 Cadet Force Emblem and Cadets of 1936 and 1986

1986. 50th Anniv of St. Vincent Cadet Force (45c., $2) and 75th Anniv of St. Vincent Girls' High School (others). Multicoloured.

1018	45c. Type **159**	40	30
1019	60c. Grimble Building, Girls' High School (horiz)	45	40
1020	$1.50 High School pupils (horiz)	1·00	1·75
1021	$2 Cadets on parade (horiz)	1·50	2·25

1986. Royal Wedding (2nd issue). Nos. 1009/12 optd Congratulations to T.R.H. The Duke & Duchess of York.

1022	60c. Profile of Prince Andrew	1·10	1·40
1023	60c. Miss Sarah Ferguson	1·10	1·40
1024	$2 Prince Andrew with Mrs. Nancy Reagan (horiz)	1·50	2·75
1025	$2 Prince Andrew in naval uniform (horiz)	1·50	2·75

160 King Arthur

1986. The Legend of King Arthur. Multicoloured.

1026	30c. Type **160**	40	40
1027	45c. Merlin taking baby Arthur	50	50
1028	60c. Arthur pulling sword from stone	60	60
1029	75c. Camelot	70	70
1030	$1 Arthur receiving Excalibur from the Lady of the Lake	80	80
1031	$1.50 Knights at the Round Table	1·00	1·50
1032	$2 The Holy Grail	1·25	1·75
1033	$5 Sir Lancelot jousting	2·00	3·00

161 Statue of Liberty Floodlit

1986. Centenary of Statue of Liberty. Designs showing aspects of the Statue.

1034	161	15c. multicoloured	10	10
1035	-	25c. multicoloured	10	15
1036	-	40c. multicoloured	15	25
1037	-	55c. multicoloured	20	30
1038	-	75c. multicoloured	25	45
1039	-	90c. multicoloured	25	60
1040	-	$1.75 multicoloured	35	1·10
1041	-	$2 multicoloured	35	1·25
1042	-	$2.50 multicoloured	40	1·60
1043	-	$3 multicoloured	40	1·75
MS1044		Three sheets, each 85×115 mm. $3.50; $4; $5. Set of 3 sheets	2·75	7·50

162 Fishing for Tri Tri

1986. Freshwater Fishing. Multicoloured.

1045	75c. Type **162**	25	40
1046	75c. Plumier's goby ("Tri Tri")	25	40
1047	$1.50 Crayfishing	35	80
1048	$1.50 Crayfish	35	80

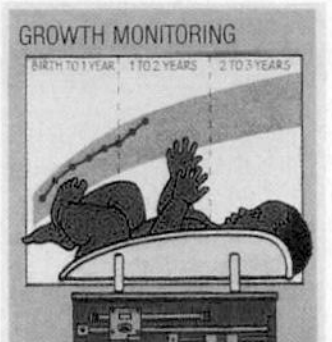

163 Baby on Scales

1987. Child Health Campaign. Multicoloured.

1049	10c. Type **163**	10	10
1050	50c. Oral rehydration therapy	45	55
1051	75c. Breast feeding	55	90
1052	$1 Nurse giving injection	60	1·25

1987. World Population Control. Nos. 1049/52 optd WORLD POPULATION 5 BILLION 11TH JULY 1987.

1053	10c. Type **163**	10	10
1054	50c. Oral rehydration therapy	40	55
1055	75c. Breast feeding	50	90
1056	$1 Nurse giving injection	55	1·25

165 Hanna Mandlikova

1987. International Lawn Tennis Players. Mult.

1057	40c. Type **165**	20	25
1058	60c. Yannick Noah	20	35
1059	80c. Ivan Lendl	20	50
1060	$1 Chris Evert	20	50
1061	$1.25 Steffi Graf	20	60
1062	$1.50 John McEnroe	20	65
1063	$1.75 Martina Navratilova with Wimbledon trophy	20	75
1064	$2 Boris Becker with Wimbledon trophy	30	85
MS1065	115×85 mm. $2.25 As No. 1063; $2.25 As No. 1064	1·40	4·00

166 Miss Prima Donna, Queen of the Bands, 1986

1987. 10th Anniv of Carnival. Multicoloured.

1066	20c. Type **166**	10	15
1067	45c. Donna Young, Miss Carnival, 1985	15	15
1068	55c. Miss St. Vincent and the Grenadines, 1986	15	15
1069	$3.70 "Spirit of Hope" costume, 1986	50	1·60

The 45c. value is inscribed "Miss Carival" in error.

1987. 10th Death Anniv of Elvis Presley (entertainer). Nos. 919/26 optd THE KING OF ROCK AND ROLL LIVES FOREVER AUGUST 16TH 1977–1987.

1070	149	10c. multicoloured	10	20
1071	-	10c. multicoloured (blue)	10	20
1072	-	60c. mult (brown)	20	35
1073	-	60c. multicoloured (grey)	20	35
1074	-	$1 multicoloured (brown)	20	60
1075	-	$1 multicoloured (blue)	20	60
1076	-	$5 mult (light blue)	60	2·25
1077	-	$5 multicoloured (blue)	60	2·25
MS1078		Four sheets, each 145×107 mm. (a) 30c. As Nos. 1070/1 each ×2. (b) 50c. As Nos. 1072/3 each ×2. (c) $1.50, As Nos. 1074/5 each ×2. (d) $4.50, As Nos. 1076/7 each ×2	7·50	10·00

168 Queen Victoria, 1841

1987. Royal Ruby Wedding and 150th Anniv of Queen Victoria's Accession. Multicoloured.

1079	15c. Type **168**	10	10
1080	75c. Queen Elizabeth and Prince Andrew, 1960	20	35
1081	$1 Coronation, 1953	20	40
1082	$2.50 Duke of Edinburgh, 1948	50	1·50
1083	$5 Queen Elizabeth II, c. 1980	1·50	2·25
MS1084	85×115 mm. $6 Princess Elizabeth with Prince Charles at his Christening, 1948	1·75	4·50

169 Karl Benz and Benz Three-wheeler (1886)

1987. Century of Motoring. Multicoloured.

1085	$1 Type **169**	40	60
1086	$2 Enzo Ferrari and Ferrari "Dino 206SP" (1966)	50	1·10
1087	$4 Charles Rolls and Sir Henry Royce and Rolls-Royce "Silver Ghost" (1907)	65	1·50
1088	$5 Henry Ford and Ford "Model T" (1908)	65	1·75
MS1089	Four sheets, each 144×75 mm. (a) $3 As Type **169**. (b) $5 As No. 1086. (c) $6 As No. 1087. (d) $8 As No. 1088. Set of 4 sheets	7·50	15·00

170 Everton Football Team

1987. English Football Teams. Mult.

1090	$2 Type **170**	1·25	1·25
1091	$2 Manchester United	1·25	1·25
1092	$2 Tottenham Hotspur	1·25	1·25
1093	$2 Arsenal	1·25	1·25
1094	$2 Liverpool	1·25	1·25
1095	$2 Derby County	1·25	1·25
1096	$2 Portsmouth	1·25	1·25
1097	$2 Leeds United	1·25	1·25

171 Five Cent Coins

1987. East Caribbean Currency. Mult.

1098	5c. Type **171**	20	10
1099	6c. Two cent coins	20	10
1100	10c. Ten cent coins	20	10
1101	12c. Two and ten cent coins	30	10
1102	15c. Five cent coins	30	10
1103	20c. Ten cent coins	35	10
1104	25c. Twenty-five cent coins	40	15
1105	30c. Five and twenty-five cent coins	40	15
1106	35c. Twenty-five and ten cent coins	40	20

1107	45c. Twenty-five and two ten cent coins	50	30
1108	50c. Fifty cent coins	50	30
1109	65c. Fifty, ten and five cent coins	60	45
1110	75c. Fifty and twenty-five cent coins	60	50
1111	$1 One dollar note (horiz)	75	65
1112	$2 Two one dollar notes (horiz)	1·25	1·75
1113	$3 Three one dollar notes (horiz)	1·25	2·50
1114	$5 Five dollar note (horiz)	2·25	5·00
1115	$10 Ten dollar note (horiz)	2·75	8·00
1115s	$20 Twenty dollar note (horiz)	11·00	17·00

172 Charles Dickens

1987. Christmas. 175th Birth Anniv of Charles Dickens. Multicoloured.

1116	6c. Type **172**	40	70
1117	6c. "Mr. Fezziwig's Ball"	40	70
1118	25c. Type **172**	45	70
1119	25c. "Scrooge's Third Visitor"	45	70
1120	50c. Type **172**	50	90
1121	50c. "The Cratchits' Christmas"	50	90
1122	75c. Type **172**	50	1·25
1123	75c. "A Christmas Carol"	50	1·25
MS1124	141×101 mm. $5 Teacher reading to class	1·75	4·50

Nos. 1116/17, 1118/19, 1120/1 and 1122/3 were printed together, se-tenant, each pair forming a composite design showing an open book. The first design in each pair shows Type **172** and the second a scene from "A Christmas Carol".

173 "Santa Maria"

1988. 500th Anniv (1992) of Discovery of America by Columbus (2nd issue). Multicoloured.

1125	15c. Type **173**	30	20
1126	75c. "Nina" and "Pinta"	40	60
1127	$1 Compass and hourglass	40	60
1128	$1.50 Claiming the New World for Spain	45	1·40
1129	$3 Arawak village	60	2·00
1130	$4 Blue and yellow macaw, Cuban tody, pineapple and maize	80	2·25
MS1131	114×86 mm. $5 Columbus, Arms and "Santa Maria"	2·50	3·00

174 Brown Pelican

1988

1132	**174**	45c. multicoloured	30	30

175 Windsurfing

1988. Tourism. Multicoloured.

1133	10c. Type **175**	10	10
1134	45c. Scuba diving	20	25
1135	65c. Aerial view of Young Island (horiz)	30	60
1136	$5 Cruising yacht (horiz)	2·10	3·50
MS1136a	115×85 mm. $10 Two windsurfers off St. Vincent (60×40 mm)	2·75	6·00

176 "Nuestra Senora del Rosario" (Spanish galleon) and Spanish Knight's Cross

1988. 400th Anniv of Spanish Armada. Mult.

1137	15c. Type **176**	25	10
1138	75c. "Ark Royal" (galleon) and English Armada medal	45	40
1139	$1.50 English fleet and Drake's dial	60	85
1140	$2 Dismasted Spanish galleon and 16th-century shot	65	1·00
1141	$3.50 Attack of English fireships at Calais and 16th-century grenade	80	2·00
1142	$5 "Revenge" (English galleon) and Drake's Drum	90	2·25
MS1143	123×92 mm. $8 Sighting the Armada	2·00	4·50

177 D. K. Lillee

1988. Cricketers of 1988 International Season. Multicoloured.

1144	15c. Type **177**	50	30
1145	50c. G. A. Gooch	70	50
1146	75c. R. N. Kapil Dev	90	70
1147	$1 S. M. Gavaskar	1·00	85
1148	$1.50 M. W. Gatting	1·25	1·50
1149	$2.50 Imran Khan	1·25	2·00
1150	$3 I. T. Botham	1·25	2·25
1151	$4 I. V. A. Richards	1·25	2·50
MS1152	130×80 mm. $2 As $4. $3.50, As $3	2·25	5·50

178 Athletics

1988. Olympic Games, Seoul. Multicoloured.

1153	10c. Type **178**	10	10
1154	50c. Long jumping (vert)	20	25
1155	$1 Triple jumping	40	50
1156	$5 Boxing (vert)	2·10	2·75
MS1157	85×63 mm. $10 Olympic flame	4·75	6·50

179 Babe Ruth

1988. Famous Baseball Players (1st series).

1158	**179**	$2 multicoloured	1·40	1·40

See also Nos. 1264/75, 1407, 1408/88, 2152/4, 2155/6, 2426 and 3004/12.

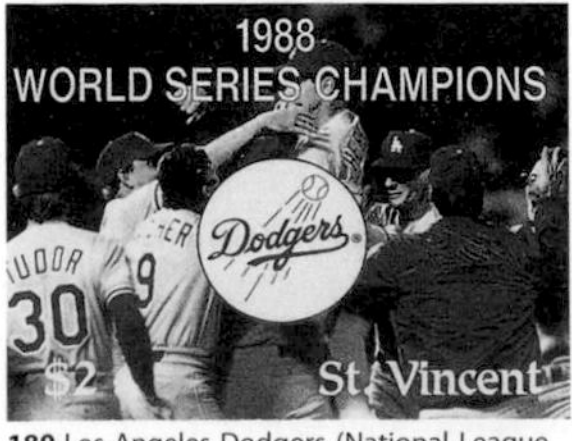

180 Los Angeles Dodgers (National League Champions)

1988. 1988 Baseball World Series. Sheet 115×85 mm containing T 180 and similar horiz design. Multicoloured.

MS1159	$2 Type **180**; $2 Team logos of Dodgers and Oakland Athletics	2·00	2·25

180a Minnie Mouse in Railway Van Loaded with Candy

1988. Christmas. "Mickey's Christmas Train". Multicoloured.

1160	1c. Type **180a**	10	10
1161	2c. Mordie and Ferdie in wagon with toys	10	10
1162	3c. Chip n' Dale in wagon with Christmas trees	10	10
1163	4c. Donald Duck's nephews riding with reindeer	10	10
1164	5c. Donald and Daisy Duck in restaurant car	10	10
1165	10c. Grandma Duck, Uncle Scrooge McDuck, Goofy and Clarabelle carol singing in carriage	10	10
1166	$5 Mickey Mouse driving locomotive	3·25	3·50
1167	$6 Father Christmas in guard's van	4·00	4·50
MS1168	Two sheets, each 127×102 mm. (a) $5 Mickey Mouse and nephews at railway station. (b) $5 Mickey and Minnie Mouse on carousel. Set of 2 sheets	7·00	8·00

181 Mickey Mouse as Snake Charmer

1989. "India-89" International Stamp Exhibition, New Delhi. Multicoloured.

1169	1c. Type **181**	10	10
1170	2c. Goofy with chowsingha antelope	10	10
1171	3c. Mickey and Minnie Mouse with common peafowl	10	10
1172	5c. Goofy with Briolette Diamond and Mickey Mouse pushing mine truck	10	10
1173	10c. Clarabelle with Orloff Diamond	10	10
1174	25c. Mickey Mouse as tourist and Regent Diamond, Louvre, Paris	20	15
1175	$4 Minnie and Mickey Mouse with Kohinoor Diamond	3·50	4·00
1176	$5 Mickey Mouse and Goofy with Indian rhinoceros	3·50	4·00
MS1177	Two sheets, each 127×102 mm. (a) $6 Mickey Mouse riding Indian elephant. (b) $6 Mickey Mouse as postman delivering Hope Diamond to Smithsonian Museum, U.S.A. (vert). Set of 2 sheets	8·50	10·00

182 Harry James

1989. Jazz Musicians. Multicoloured.

1178	10c. Type **182**	40	20
1179	15c. Sidney Bechet	50	20
1180	25c. Benny Goodman	60	20
1181	35c. Django Reinhardt	65	20
1182	50c. Lester Young	80	35
1183	90c. Gene Krupa	95	85
1184	$3 Louis Armstrong	3·00	3·00
1185	$4 Duke Ellington	3·00	3·25
MS1186	Two sheets, each 107×92 mm. (a) $5 Charlie Parker. (b) $5 Billie Holiday. Set of 2 sheets	9·00	8·00

183 Birds in Flight

1989. Wildlife Conservation. Noah's Ark. Multicoloured.

1187	40c. Type **183**	30	30
1188	40c. Rainbow (left side)	30	30
1189	40c. Noah's Ark on mountain	30	30
1190	40c. Rainbow (right side)	30	30
1191	40c. Birds in flight (different)	30	30
1192	40c. Cow elephant	30	30
1193	40c. Bull elephant	30	30
1194	40c. Top of eucalyptus tree	30	30
1195	40c. Kangaroos	30	30
1196	40c. Hummingbird	30	30
1197	40c. Lions	30	30
1198	40c. White-tailed deer	30	30
1199	40c. Koala in fork of tree	30	30
1200	40c. Koala on branch	30	30
1201	40c. Hummingbird approaching flower	30	30
1202	40c. Keel-billed toucan and flower	30	30
1203	40c. Keel-billed toucan facing right	30	30
1204	40c. Camels	30	30
1205	40c. Giraffes	30	30
1206	40c. Mountain sheep	30	30
1207	40c. Ladybirds on leaf	30	30
1208	40c. Swallowtail butterfly	30	30
1209	40c. Swallowtail butterfly behind leaves	30	30
1210	40c. Pythons	30	30
1211	40c. Dragonflies	30	30

Nos. 1187/1211 were printed together, se-tenant, forming a composite design showing Noah's Ark and animals released after the Flood.

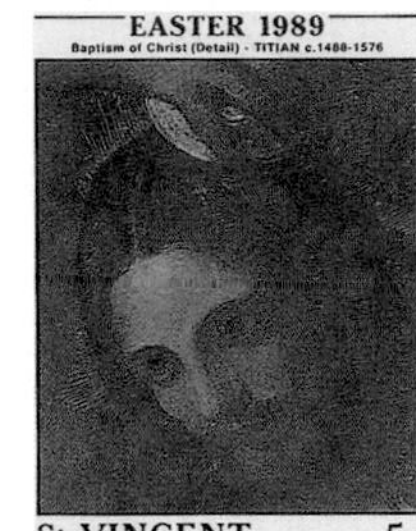

183a "Baptism of Christ" (detail)

1989. Easter. 500th Birth Anniv of Titian (artist). Multicoloured.

1212	5c. Type **183a**	10	20
1213	30c. "Temptation of Christ"	25	15
1214	45c. "Ecce Homo"	40	25
1215	65c. "Noli Me Tangere" (fragment)	55	55
1216	75c. "Christ carrying the Cross" (detail)	60	65
1217	$1 "Christ crowned with Thorns" (detail)	70	75
1218	$4 "Lamentation over Christ" (detail)	2·75	3·50
1219	$5 "The Entombment" (detail)	3·25	4·00
MS1220	(a) 98×111 mm. $6 "Pietà" (detail). (b) 114×95 mm. $6 "The Deposition" (detail). Set of 2 sheets	7·00	8·00

184 "Ile de France"

1989. Ocean Liners. Multicoloured.

1221	10c. Type **184**	1·00	40
1222	40c. "Liberte"	1·75	30
1223	50c. "Mauretania I" (launched 1906)	1·75	50
1224	75c. "France"	2·25	1·25
1225	$1 "Aquitania"	2·25	1·25
1226	$2 "United States"	3·00	3·00
1227	$3 "Olympic"	3·50	3·75
1228	$4 "Queen Elizabeth"	3·50	4·00
MS1229	Two sheets, each 141×108 mm. (a) $6 "Queen Mary" (85×28 mm). (b) $6 "Queen Elizabeth 2" (85×28 mm). Set of 2 sheets	17·00	13·00

185 Space Shuttle deploying West German Satellite, 1983

1989. International Co-operation in Space. Mult.

1230	40c. Type **185**	80	20
1231	60c. Vladimir Remek (Czech cosmonaut) and "Soyuz 28", 1978	1·10	50
1232	$1 Projected "Hermes" space plane and "Columbus" Space Station	1·50	1·00
1233	$4 Ulf Merbold (West German astronaut), 1983 and proposed European Spacelab	3·50	4·75
MS1234	93×67 mm. $5 Meeting in space of "Apollo/Soyuz" mission crews, 1975	3·00	4·00

186 "Mercury 9" Capsule and Astronaut L. Gordon Cooper

1989. 25th Anniv of Launching of "Telstar II" Communications Satellite (1988). Each showing satellite and T.V. screen. Multicoloured.

1235	15c. Type **186**	20	15
1236	35c. Martin Luther King addressing crowd, 1963	30	20
1237	50c. Speed skater, Winter Olympic Games, Innsbruck, 1964	45	50
1238	$3 Pope John XXIII blessing crowd	1·75	2·75
MS1239	107×77 mm. $5 Launch of "Telstar II", 1963	2·75	3·50

187 Head of St. Vincent Amazon

1989. Wildlife Conservation. St. Vincent Amazon ("St. Vincent Parrot"). Multicoloured.

1240	10c. Type **187**	70	30
1241	20c. St. Vincent amazon in flight	1·25	45
1242	40c. Feeding (vert)	2·00	65
1243	70c. At entrance to nest (vert)	2·75	3·25

188 Blue-hooded Euphonia ("Misletoe Bird")

1989. Birds of St. Vincent. Multicoloured.

1244	25c. Type **188**	45	25
1245	75c. Common black hawk ("Crab Hawk")	1·00	65
1246	$2 Mangrove cuckoo ("Coucou")	1·75	2·00
1247	$3 Hooded tanager ("Prince Bird")	2·00	3·00
MS1248	Two sheets. (a) 75×105 mm. $5 Rufous-throated solitaire ("Soufriere Bird") (vert). (b) 105×75 mm. $5 Purple-throated carib ("Doctor Bird"). Set of 2 sheets	5·50	7·00

188a "Autumn Flowers in Front of the Full Moon" (Hiroshige)

1989. Japanese Arts. Multicoloured.

1249	10c. Type **188a**	30	20
1250	40c. "Hibiscus" (Hiroshige)	45	25
1251	50c. "Iris" (Hiroshige)	50	30
1252	75c. "Morning Glories" (Hiroshige)	70	50
1253	$1 "Dancing Swallows" (Hiroshige)	2·00	85
1254	$2 "Sparrow and Bamboo" (Hiroshige)	2·75	2·25
1255	$3 "Yellow Bird and Cotton Rose" (Hiroshige)	2·75	2·75
1256	$4 "Judos Chrysanthemums in a Deep Ravine in China" (Hiroshige)	2·75	3·00
MS1257	Two sheets, each 102×76 mm. (a) $6 "Rural Cottages in Spring" (Sotatsu). (b) $6 "The Six Immortal Poets portrayed as Cats" (Kuniyoshi) (vert). Set of 2 sheets	7·00	8·50

189 Schooner

1989. "Philexfrance 89" International Stamp Exhibition, Paris and Bicentenary of French Revolution. 18th-century French Naval Vessels. Multicoloured.

1258	30c. Type **189**	80	30
1259	55c. Corvette	1·00	50
1260	75c. Frigate	1·40	1·10
1261	$1 Ship of the line	1·60	1·40
1262	$3 "Ville de Paris" (ship of the line)	4·25	6·00
MS1263	76×108 mm. $6 Map of St. Vincent in 18th century (vert)	3·50	4·50

190 Johnny Bench

1989. Famous Baseball Players (2nd series). Multicoloured.

1264	$2 Type **190**	85	1·00
1265	$2 Red Schoendienst	85	1·00
1266	$2 Carl Yastrzemski	85	1·00
1267	$2 Ty Cobb	85	1·00
1268	$2 Willie Mays	85	1·00
1269	$2 Stan Musial	85	1·00
1270	$2 Ernie Banks	85	1·00
1271	$2 Lou Gehrig	85	1·00
1272	$2 Jackie Robinson	85	1·00
1273	$2 Bob Feller	85	1·00
1274	$2 Ted Williams	85	1·00
1275	$2 Al Kaline	85	1·00

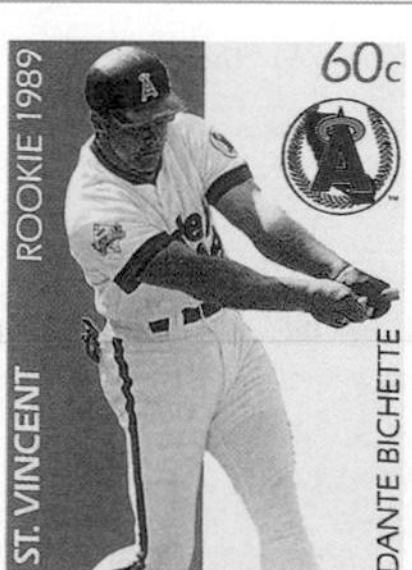

191 Dante Bichette, 1989

1989. Major League Baseball Rookies. Mult.

1276	60c. Type **191**	40	50
1277	60c. Carl Yastrzemski, 1961	40	50
1278	60c. Randy Johnson, 1989	40	50
1279	60c. Jerome Walton, 1989	40	50
1280	60c. Ramon Martinez, 1989	40	50
1281	60c. Ken Hill, 1989	40	50
1282	60c. Tom McCarthy, 1989	40	50
1283	60c. Gaylord Perry, 1963	40	50
1284	60c. John Smoltz, 1989	40	50
1285	60c. Bob Milacki, 1989	40	50
1286	60c. Babe Ruth, 1915	40	50
1287	60c. Jim Abbott, 1989	40	50
1288	60c. Gary Sheffield, 1989	40	50
1289	60c. Gregg Jeffries, 1989	40	50
1290	60c. Kevin Brown, 1989	40	50
1291	60c. Cris Carpenter, 1989	40	50
1292	60c. Johnny Bench, 1968	40	50
1293	60c. Ken Griffey Jr. 1989	40	50

192 Chris Sabo

1989. Major League Baseball Award Winners. Multicoloured.

1294	60c. Type **192**	40	50
1295	60c. Walt Weiss	40	50
1296	60c. Willie Mays	40	50
1297	60c. Kirk Gibson	40	50
1298	60c. Ted Williams	40	50
1299	60c. Jose Canseco	40	50
1300	60c. Gaylord Perry	40	50
1301	60c. Orel Hershiser	40	50
1302	60c. Frank Viola	40	50

193 All-Star Game Line-up (image scaled to 37% of original size)

1989. American League v National League All-Star Game, 1989. Sheet 115×81 mm. Imperf.

MS1303	**193**	$5 multicoloured	2·40	2·75

194 St. Vincent Amazon

1989

1304	**194**	55c. multicoloured	1·00	35

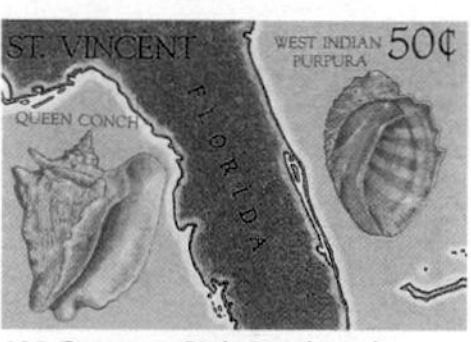

195 Queen or Pink Conch and Wide-mouthed Purpura Shells

1989. 500th Anniv (1992) of Discovery of America by Columbus (3rd issue).

1305	**195**	50c. multicoloured	45	50
1306	-	50c. multicoloured	45	50
1307	-	50c. ultramarine, blk & bl	45	50
1308	-	50c. ultramarine, blk & bl	45	50
1309	-	50c. multicoloured	45	50
1310	-	50c. multicoloured	45	50
1311	-	50c. multicoloured	45	50
1312	-	50c. black and blue	45	50
1313	-	50c. multicoloured	45	50
1314	-	50c. multicoloured	45	50
1315	-	50c. multicoloured	45	50
1316	-	50c. multicoloured	45	50
1317	-	50c. multicoloured	45	50
1318	-	50c. multicoloured	45	50
1319	-	50c. multicoloured	45	50
1320	-	50c. multicoloured	45	50
1321	-	50c. multicoloured	45	50
1322	-	50c. multicoloured	45	50
1323	-	50c. multicoloured	45	50
1324	-	50c. multicoloured	45	50

DESIGNS: No. 1306, Caribbean reef fishes; 1307, Sperm whale; 1308, Fleet of Columbus; 1309, Sharksucker (fish); 1310, Columbus planting flag; 1311, Navigational instruments; 1312, Sea monster; 1313, Kemp's ridley turtle; 1314, Magnificent frigate bird; 1315, Caribbean manatee; 1316, Caribbean monk seal; 1317, Mayan chief, dugout canoe and caravel; 1318, Blue-footed boobies ("Masked Boobies"); 1319, Venezuelan pile village; 1320, Atlantic wing oyster and lion's-paw scallop; 1321, Great hammerhead and short-finned mako; 1322, Brown pelican and hyacinth macaw ("Hyacinthine Macaw"); 1323, Venezuelan bowmen; 1324, Capuchin and squirrel monkeys.

Nos. 1305/24 were printed together, se-tenant, forming a composite design of a map of the Caribbean showing the voyages of Columbus.

196 Command Module "Columbia" returning to Earth

1989. 20th Anniv of First Manned Landing on Moon. Multicoloured.

1325	35c. Type **196**	90	30
1326	75c. Lunar module "Eagle" landing	1·75	80
1327	$1 "Apollo 11" launch	1·75	80
1328	$2 Buzz Aldrin on Moon	2·50	2·50
1329	$2 Lunar module "Eagle"	2·50	2·50
1330	$2 Earth rise from the Moon	2·50	2·50
1331	$2 Neil Armstrong	2·50	2·50
1332	$3 "Eagle" and "Columbia" in Moon orbit	2·75	2·75
MS1333	Two sheets, each 108×79 mm. (a) $3 Command Module "Columbia". $3 Lunar Module "Eagle". (b) $6 Neil Armstrong stepping on to Moon (vert). Set of 2 sheets	9·50	12·00

197 Jay Howell and Alejandro Pena

1989. Centenary of the Los Angeles Dodgers (1st issue). Baseball Players. Multicoloured.

1334	60c. Type **197**	35	45
1335	60c. Mike Davis and Kirk Gibson	35	45
1336	60c. Fernando Valenzuela and John Shelby	35	45
1337	60c. Jeff Hamilton and Franklin Stubbs	35	45
1338	60c. Aerial view of Dodger Stadium (no inscription)	35	45
1339	60c. Ray Searage and John Tudor	35	45
1340	60c. Mike Sharperson and Mickey Hatcher	35	45
1341	60c. Coaching staff	35	45
1342	60c. John Wetteland and Ramon Martinez	35	45
1343	60c. Tim Belcher and Tim Crews	35	45
1344	60c. Orel Hershiser and Mike Morgan	35	45
1345	60c. Mike Scioscia and Rick Dempsey	35	45
1346	60c. Dave Anderson and Alfredo Griffin	35	45
1347	60c. Dodgers' emblem	35	45
1348	60c. Kal Daniels and Mike Marshall	35	45
1349	60c. Eddie Murray and Willie Randolph	35	45
1350	60c. Tom Lasorda and Jose Gonzalez	35	45
1351	60c. Lenny Harris, Chris Gwynn and Billy Bean	35	45

See also Nos. 1541/58.

198 "Eurema venusta"

1989. Butterflies. Multicoloured.

1352	6c. Type **198**	25	15
1353	10c. "Historis odius"	30	15
1354	15c. "Cynthia virginiensis"	40	15
1355	75c. "Leptotes cassius"	80	65
1356	$1 "Battus polydamas"	90	75

1357 $2 "Astraptes talus" 2·00 2·25
1358 $3 "Danaus gilippus" 2·50 2·75
1359 $5 "Myscelia antholia" 3·50 4·00
MS1360 Two sheets, each 76×103 mm. (a) $6 "Danaus plexippus" (vert). (b) $6 "Eurema daira" (vert). Set of 2 sheets 8·00 9·00

199 Young Footballers

1989. World Cup Football Championship, Italy (1990) (1st issue). Multicoloured.
1361 10c. Type **199** 35 20
1362 55c. Youth football teams 70 30
1363 $1 St. Vincent team in training 1·25 90
1364 $5 National team with trophies 3·00 4·50
MS1365 Two sheets, each 103×73 mm. (a) $6 Youth team. (b) $6 National team. Set of 2 sheets 12·00 11·00
See also Nos. 1559/63.

200 St. Vincent Amazon ("St. Vincent Parrott")

1989. Wildlife. Multicoloured.
1366 65c. Type **200** 75 65
1367 75c. Whistling warbler 90 75
1368 $5 Black snake 4·00 6·00
MS1369 97×70 mm. $6 Volcano plant (vert) 4·50 6·50

1989. California Earthquake Relief Fund. Nos. 1276/302 surch +10c CALIF. EARTHQUAKE RELIEF.
1370 60c.+10c. Type **191** 60 70
1371 60c.+10c. Carl Yastrzemski 60 70
1372 60c.+10c. Randy Johnson 60 70
1373 60c.+10c. Jerome Walton 60 70
1374 60c.+10c. Ramon Martinez 60 70
1375 60c.+10c. Ken Hill 60 70
1376 60c.+10c. Tom McCarthy 60 70
1377 60c.+10c. Gaylord Perry 60 70
1378 60c.+10c. John Smoltz 60 70
1379 60c.+10c. Bob Milacki 60 70
1380 60c.+10c. Babe Ruth 60 70
1381 60c.+10c. Jim Abbott 60 70
1382 60c.+10c. Gary Sheffield 60 70
1383 60c.+10c. Gregg Jeffries 60 70
1384 60c.+10c. Kevin Brown 60 70
1385 60c.+10c. Cris Carpenter 60 70
1386 60c.+10c. Johnny Bench 60 70
1387 60c.+10c. Ken Griffey Jr 60 70
1388 60c.+10c. Type **192** 60 70
1389 60c.+10c. Walt Weiss 60 70
1390 60c.+10c. Willie Mays 60 70
1391 60c.+10c. Kirk Gibson 60 70
1392 60c.+10c. Ted Williams 60 70
1393 60c.+10c. Jose Canseco 60 70
1394 60c.+10c. Gaylord Perry 60 70
1395 60c.+10c. Orel Hershiser 60 70
1396 60c.+10c. Frank Viola 60 70

201a Mickey Mouse and Minnie Mouse by Seagull Monument, Utah

1989. "World Stamp Expo '89" International Stamp Exhibition, Washington (1st issue). Walt Disney cartoon characters and U.S. monuments. Multicoloured.
1397 1c. Type **201a** 10 10
1398 2c. Mickey Mouse and Goofy at Lincoln Memorial 10 10
1399 3c. Mickey and Minnie Mouse at Crazy Horse Memorial, South Dakota 10 10
1400 4c. Mickey Mouse saluting "Uncle Sam" Wilson statue, New York 10 10
1401 5c. Goofy and Mickey Mouse at Benjamin Franklin Memorial, Philadelphia 10 10
1402 10c. Goofy and Mickey Mouse at George Washington statue, New York 10 10
1403 $3 Mickey Mouse at John F. Kennedy's birthplace, Massachusetts 3·50 4·00
1404 $6 Mickey and Minnie Mouse at Mount Vernon, Virginia 5·50 6·00
MS1405 Two sheets, each 127×100 mm. (a) $5 Mickey and Minnie Mouse over Mount Rushmore, South Dakota. (b) $5 Mickey Mouse and Donald Duck at Stone Mountain, Georgia. Set of 2 sheets 9·00 10·00

201b Washington Monument

1989. "World Stamp Expo '89" International Stamp Exhibition, Washington (2nd issue). Sheet 61×78 mm.
MS1406 **201b** $5 multicoloured 2·10 2·50

202 Nolan Ryan

1989. Famous Baseball Players (3rd series).
1407 **202** $2 multicoloured 85 1·00

203 Early Wynn

1989. Famous Baseball Players (4th series). As T 203.
1408-1488 30c.×81 30c x 81 multicoloured. Set of 81 16·00 18·00

204 Arms and 1979 Independence 50c. Stamp

1989. 10th Anniv of Independence.
1489 **204** 65c. multicoloured 1·00 70
MS1490 57×77 mm. $10 multicoloured 5·00 6·50

204a Holy Family (detail, "The Adoration of the Magi") (Botticelli)

1989. Christmas. Paintings by Botticelli and Da Vinci. Multicoloured.
1491 10c. Type **204a** 15 10
1492 25c. Crowd (detail, "The Adoration of the Magi") (Botticelli) 25 15
1493 30c. "The Madonna of the Magnificat" (detail) (Botticelli) 25 15
1494 40c. "The Virgin and Child with St. Anne and St. John the Baptist" (detail) (Da Vinci) 30 20
1495 55c. Angel (detail, "The Annunciation") (Da Vinci) 40 30
1496 75c. Virgin Mary (detail, "The Annunciation") (Da Vinci) 50 50
1497 $5 "Madonna of the Carnation" (detail) (Da Vinci) 3·00 4·25
1498 $6 "The Annunciation" (detail) (Botticelli) 3·50 4·75
MS1499 Two sheets, each 70×94 mm. (a) $5 "The Virgin of the Rocks" (detail) (Da Vinci). (b) $5 Holy Family (detail, "The Adoration of the Magi") (Botticelli). Set of 2 sheets 5·50 6·50

205 Boy Scout, 1989

1989. 75th Anniv of Boy Scout and 60th Anniv of Girl Guide Movements in St. Vincent. Mult.
1500 35c. Type **205** 55 50
1501 35c. Guide, ranger and brownie 55 50
1502 55c. Boy scout in original uniform 75 50
1503 55c. Mrs. Jackson (founder of St. Vincent Girl Guides) 75 50
1504 $2 Scouts' 75th Anniv logo 2·00 3·25
1505 $2 Mrs. Russell (Girl Guide leader, 1989) 2·00 3·25
MS1506 Two sheets, each 105×75 mm. (a) $5 Scout in canoe. (b) Scout and Guide with flagpoles (horiz). Set of 2 sheets 9·00 10·00

206 Man and Blind Girl

1990. 25th Anniv (1989) of Lions Club of St. Vincent. Multicoloured.
1507 10c. Type **206** 40 20
1508 65c. Handing out school books (horiz) 70 50
1509 75c. Teacher explaining diabetes (horiz) 80 60
1510 $2 Blood sugar testing machine (horiz) 1·75 2·00
1511 $4 Distributing book on drugs (horiz) 2·75 4·00

206a Scuttling of "Admiral Graf Spee" (German pocket battleship), 1939

1990. 50th Anniv of Second World War. Mult.
1512 5c. Type **206a** 50 35
1513 10c. General de Gaulle and French resistance, 1940 60 30
1514 15c. British tank, North Africa, 1940 65 30
1515 25c. U.S.S. "Reuben James" (destroyer) in periscope sight, 1941 80 30
1516 30c. General MacArthur and map of S.W. Pacific, 1942 80 35
1517 40c. American parachute drop on Corregidor, 1945 80 40
1518 55c. H.M.S. "King George V" (battleship) engaging "Bismarck" (German battleship), 1941 90 55
1519 75c. American battleships entering Tokyo Bay, 1945 1·00 70
1520 $5 Hoisting the Soviet flag on the Reichstag, Berlin, 1945 3·50 4·00
1521 $6 American aircraft carriers, Battle of Philippines Sea, 1944 4·00 4·25
MS1522 100×70 mm. $6 Japanese Mitsubishi A6M Zero-Sen fighter, Battle of Java Sea, 1942 3·75 4·25

207 Two Pence Blue

1990. 150th Anniv of the Penny Black.
1523 **207** $2 black, green and mauve 1·25 1·50
1524 - $4 black and mauve 2·50 3·25
MS1525 130×99 mm. – $6 black, red and yellow 4·00 4·75
DESIGN: $4, $6 Penny Black.

207a Scrooge McDuck as 18th-century Admiral

1990. "Stamp World London '90" International Stamp Exhibition. British Uniforms. Walt Disney cartoon characters. Multicoloured.
1526 5c. Type **207a** 20 15
1527 10c. Huey as Light Infantry bugler, 1854 25 15
1528 15c. Minnie Mouse as Irish Guards drummer, 1900 35 20
1529 25c. Goofy as Seaforth Highlanders lance-corporal, 1944 45 30
1530 $1 Mickey Mouse as 58th Regiment ensign, 1879 1·25 1·00
1531 $2 Donald Duck as Royal Engineers officer, 1813 1·90 2·00
1532 $4 Mickey Mouse as Duke of Edinburgh's Royal Regiment drum major 3·00 3·50
1533 $5 Goofy as Cameronians sergeant piper, 1918 3·00 3·50
MS1534 Two sheets, each 120×100 mm. (a) $6 Goofy as officer in King's Lifeguard of Foot, 1643. (b) $6 Mickey Mouse as Grenadier Guards drummer (vert). Set of 2 sheets 7·00 8·00

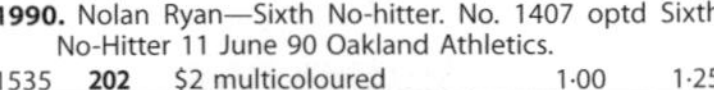
1990. Nolan Ryan—Sixth No-hitter. No. 1407 optd Sixth No-Hitter 11 June 90 Oakland Athletics.
1535 **202** $2 multicoloured 1·00 1·25

208a Queen Elizabeth signing Visitor's Book

1990. 90th Birthday of Queen Elizabeth the Queen Mother.
1536 **208a** $2 black, green and mauve 1·50 1·75
1537 - $2 black, green and mauve 1·50 1·75

1538 -	$2 black, green and mauve	1·50	1·75
MS1539	90×75 mm. $6 multicoloured	3·50	4·50

DESIGNS: No. 1537, **MS**1539, Queen Elizabeth in evening dress; 1538, Queen Elizabeth the Queen Mother in Coronation robes, 1953.

1990. Nolan Ryan—300th Win. No. 1407 optd 300th Win Milwaukee Brewers July 31, 1990.

1540	**202**	$2 multicoloured	1·00	1·25

1990. Cent of Los Angeles Dodgers (2nd issue). Baseball Players. As T 197. Multicoloured.

1541	60c. Mickey Hatcher and Jay Howell	35	50
1542	60c. Juan Samuel and Mike Scioscia	35	50
1543	60c. Lenny Harris and Mike Hartley	35	50
1544	60c. Ramon Martinez and Mike Morgan	35	50
1545	60c. Aerial view of Dodger Stadium (inscr "DODGER STADIUM")	35	50
1546	60c. Stan Javier and Don Aase	35	50
1547	60c. Ray Searage and Mike Sharperson	35	50
1548	60c. Tim Belcher and Pat Perry	35	50
1549	60c. Dave Walsh, Jose Vizcaino, Jim Neidlinger, Jose Offerman and Carlos Hernandez	35	50
1550	60c. Hubie Brooks and Orel Hershiser	35	50
1551	60c. Tom Lasorda and Tim Crews	35	50
1552	60c. Fernando Valenzuela and Eddie Murray	35	50
1553	60c. Kal Daniels and Jose Gonzalez	35	50
1554	60c. Dodgers emblem	35	50
1555	60c. Chris Gwynn and Jeff Hamilton	35	50
1556	60c. Kirk Gibson and Rick Dempsey	35	50
1557	60c. Jim Gott and Alfredo Griffin	35	50
1558	60c. Ron Perranoski, Bill Russell, Joe Ferguson, Joe Amalfitano, Mark Cresse, Ben Hines and Manny Mota	35	50

210 Maradona, Argentina

1990. World Cup Football Championship, Italy (2nd issue). Multicoloured.

1559	10c. Type **210**	40	15
1560	75c. Valderrama, Colombia	85	75
1561	$1 Francescoli, Uruguay	1·10	95
1562	$5 Ceulemans, Belgium	4·25	5·50
MS1563	Two sheets, each 101×85 mm. (a) $6 Klinsmann, West Germany. (b) $6 Careca, Brazil. Set of 2 sheets	7·50	8·50

1990. 95th Anniv of Rotary International. Nos. 1230/8 optd with Rotary emblem.

1564	10c. Type **186**	50	20
1565	40c. "Liberte"	1·00	40
1566	50c. "Mauretania I" (launched 1906)	75	45
1567	75c. "France"	1·00	70
1568	$1 "Aquitania"	1·00	90
1569	$2 "United States"	2·00	1·90
1570	$3 "Olympic"	2·25	2·75
1571	$4 "Queen Elizabeth"	2·25	3·00
MS1572	Two sheets, each 141×108 mm. (a) $6 "Queen Mary" (85×28 mm). (b) $6 "Queen Elizabeth 2" (85×28 mm). Set of 2 sheets	8·00	10·00

1990. Olympic Medal Winners, Seoul. Nos. 1153/6 optd.

1573	10c. Type **178** (optd **JOE DELOACH U.S.A. STEVE LEWIS U.S.A. PAUL ERANG KENYA**)	20	20
1574	50c. Long jumping (optd **CARL LEWIS U.S.A.**)	60	60
1575	$1 Triple jumping (optd **HRISTO MARKOV BULGARIA**)	90	90
1576	$5 Boxing (optd **HENRY MASKE E. GERMANY**)	3·25	4·00
MS1577	85×63 mm. $10 Olympic flame (optd **FINAL MEDAL STANDINGS**)	6·50	7·50

213 "Dendrophylax funalis" and "Dimerandra emarginata"

1990. "EXPO 90" International Garden and Greenery Exposition, Osaka. Orchids. Mult.

1578	10c. Type **213**	35	20
1579	15c. "Epidendrum elongatum"	40	25
1580	45c. "Comparettia falcata"	60	30
1581	60c. "Brassia maculata"	75	60
1582	$1 "Encyclia cochleata" and "Encyclia cordigera"	90	80
1583	$2 "Cyrtopodium punctatum"	1·50	1·90
1584	$4 "Cattleya labiata"	2·50	3·50
1585	$5 "Bletia purpurea"	2·75	3·50
MS1586	Two sheets, each 108×78 mm. (a) $6 "Vanilla planifolia Jackson". (b) $6 "Ionopsis utricularioides". Set of 2 sheets	7·50	8·50

214 "Miraculous Draught of Fishes" (detail, Rubens)

1990. Christmas. 350th Death Anniv of Rubens. Multicoloured.

1587	10c. Type **214**	30	20
1588	45c. "Crowning of Holy Katherine" (detail)	55	25
1589	50c. "St. Ives of Treguier" (detail)	60	30
1590	65c. "Allegory of Eternity" (detail)	75	45
1591	$1 "St. Bavo receives Monastic Habit of Ghent" (detail)	1·10	80
1592	$2 "Crowning of Holy Katherine" (different detail)	1·75	1·75
1593	$4 "St. Bavo receives Monastic Habit of Ghent" (different detail)	3·25	3·50
1594	$5 "Communion of St. Francis" (detail)	3·25	3·50
MS1595	Four sheets. (a) 70×100 mm. $6 "Allegory of Eternity" (different detail). (b) 70×100 mm. $6 As 50c. (c) 100×70 mm. $6 As Type **214** (horiz). (d) 100×70 mm. $6 "St. Bavo receives Monastic Habit of Ghent" (different detail) (horiz). Set of 4 sheets	12·50	13·00

215 Geoffrey Chaucer

1990. International Literacy Year (1st issue). Chaucer's "Canterbury Tales". Mult.

1596	40c. Type **215**	55	55
1597	40c. "When April with his showers"	55	55
1598	40c. "When Zephyr also has ..."	55	55
1599	40c. "And many little birds ..."	55	55
1600	40c. "And palmers to go seeking out ..."	55	55
1601	40c. Quill in ink well and open book	55	55
1602	40c. Green bird in tree	55	55
1603	40c. Brown bird in tree and franklin's head	55	55
1604	40c. Purple bird in tree and banner	55	55
1605	40c. Canterbury	55	55
1606	40c. Knight's head	55	55
1607	40c. Black bird in tree and squire's head	55	55
1608	40c. Friar	55	55
1609	40c. Franklin	55	55
1610	40c. Prioress and monk holding banner	55	55
1611	40c. Summoner, Oxford clerk and parson	55	55
1612	40c. Sergeant-at-Law and knight on horseback	55	55
1613	40c. Squire	55	55
1614	40c. "In fellowship ..."	55	55
1615	40c. Cockerel and horse's legs	55	55
1616	40c. Hens	55	55
1617	40c. Hen and rabbit	55	55
1618	40c. Horses' legs and butterfly	55	55
1619	40c. "And briefly, when the sun ..."	55	55

Nos. 1596/1619 were printed together, se-tenant, forming a composite design.

See also Nos. 1777/88 and 1790/1801.

215a Self-portrait, 1889

1990. Death Centenary of Vincent van Gogh (artist). Multicoloured.

1620	1c. Type **215a**	45	45
1621	5c. Self-portrait, 1886	45	45
1622	10c. Self-portrait with hat and pipe, 1888	45	45
1623	15c. Self-portrait at easel, 1888	45	45
1624	20c. Self-portrait, 1887	1·00	1·25
1625	45c. Self-portrait, 1889 (different)	1·25	1·25
1626	$5 Self-portrait with pipe, 1889	3·00	4·00
1627	$6 Self-portrait wearing straw hat, 1887	3·00	4·00

215b "The Photographer"

1990. Hummel Figurines. Multicoloured.

1628	10c. Type **215b**	30	15
1629	15c. "Ladder and Rope"	40	15
1630	40c. "Druggist"	60	30
1631	60c. "Hello"	75	45
1632	$1 "Boots"	1·00	80
1633	$2 "The Artist"	1·40	1·75
1634	$4 "Waiter"	2·50	3·25
1635	$5 "The Postman"	2·75	3·25
MS1636	Two sheets, each 94×121 mm. (a) Nos. 1628, 1631/2 and 1635. (b) Nos. 1629/30 and 1633/4. Set of 2 sheets	10·00	11·00

216 American Football Game

1991. 25th Anniv of Super Bowl American Football Championship (1st issue). T 216 and similar vert designs. Multicoloured.

MS1637	Twenty-five sheets, each 127×101 mm, containing 50c. ×2 as horiz pairs forming composite designs of game scenes or 50c. ×3 (final sheet) showing Vince Lombardi Trophy and helmets of participating teams. Set of 25 sheets	15·00	

217 Programme Cover of XXV Super Bowl

1991. 25th Anniv of Super Bowl American Football Championships (2nd issue). T 217 and similar multicoloured designs, each showing a different programme cover illustration. Imperf.

MS1638	Twenty-five sheets, 125×99 mm or 99×125 mm, each with a face value of $2. Set of 25 sheets	29·00	

218 U.S.A. 1893 1c. Columbus Stamp

1991. 500th Anniv (1992) of Discovery of America by Columbus (4th issue). Designs showing U.S.A. 1893 Columbian Exposition, Chicago, stamps (Nos. 1639/54) or ships (others). Multicoloured.

1639	1c. Type **218**	70	80
1640	2c. Columbus 2c.	70	80
1641	3c. Columbus 3c.	70	80
1642	4c. Columbus 4c.	70	80
1643	5c. Columbus 5c.	70	80
1644	6c. Columbus 6c.	70	80
1645	8c. Columbus 8c.	70	80
1646	10c. Columbus 10c.	70	80
1647	15c. Columbus 15c.	70	80
1648	30c. Columbus 30c.	70	80
1649	50c. Columbus 50c.	70	80
1650	$1 Columbus $1	70	80
1651	$2 Columbus $2	1·00	1·10
1652	$3 Columbus $3	1·40	1·50
1653	$4 Columbus $4	2·00	2·10
1654	$5 Columbus $5	2·40	2·50
1655	$10 "Santa Maria", scarlet macaw and tropical flower	5·00	5·50
1656	$10 Logo, "Santa Maria" and Amerindian hut	5·00	5·50
MS1657	Two sheets, each 98×72 mm. (a) $6 Sailors on ship's fo'c'sle. (b) $6 Ship's figurehead. Set of 2 sheets	8·00	9·00

219 Pebbles and Hoppy boxing

1991. Sports. Characters from the "Flintstones" cartoons. Multicoloured.

1658	10c. Type **219**	40	10
1659	15c. Fred Flintstone and Dino playing football	55	15
1660	45c. Fred losing rowing race to Barney Rubble	75	30
1661	55c. Betty Rubble, Wilma Flintstone and Pebbles in dressage competition	90	50
1662	$1 Fred playing basketball	1·50	1·00
1663	$2 Bamm Bamm wrestling Barney with Fred as referee	2·00	1·75
1664	$4 Fred and Barney playing tennis	3·00	3·50
1665	$5 Fred, Barney and Dino cycling	3·25	3·50
MS1666	Two sheets, each 117×95 mm. (a) $6 Fred at the plate in baseball game. (b) $6 Fred running to home-plate. Set of 2 sheets	7·50	8·00

220 Board Meeting

1991. "The Jetsons" (cartoon film). Mult.

1667	5c. Type **220**	15	10
1668	20c. Jetsons with Dog	30	15
1669	45c. Judy and Apollo Blue	50	25
1670	50c. Cosmo Spacely and George Jetson	50	35
1671	60c. George and Elroy catching cogs (horiz)	70	50
1672	$1 Judy, Apollo, Elroy and Teddy in cavern (horiz)	1·00	1·00
1673	$2 Drill destroying the cavern (horiz)	1·50	1·50
1674	$4 Jetsons celebrating with the Grungees	2·75	3·00
1675	$5 The Jetsons returning home	2·75	3·00
MS1676	Two sheets, each 114×76 mm. (a) $6 The Jetsons in spacecraft (horiz). (b) $6 The Jetsons in control room (horiz). Set of 2 sheets	7·00	8·00

220a "Sanger 2" (projected space shuttle)

1991. 500th Anniv (1992) of Discovery of America by Columbus, (5th issue). History of Exploration. Multicoloured.

1677	5c. Type **220a**	15	15
1678	10c. "Magellan" satellite, 1990	15	15
1679	25c. "Buran" space shuttle	25	25
1680	75c. Projected "Freedom" space station	65	65
1681	$1 Projected Mars mission space craft	80	80
1682	$2 "Hubble" telescope, 1990	1·60	1·75
1683	$4 Projected Mars mission "sailship"	2·50	2·75
1684	$5 Projected "Craf" satellite	2·50	2·75
MS1685	Two sheets, each 105×71 mm. (a) $6 Bow of caravel (vert). (b) $6 Caravel under full sail. Set of 2 sheets	7·00	8·25

220b Queen and Prince Philip in Spain, 1988

1991. 65th Birthday of Queen Elizabeth II. Multicoloured.

1686	5c. Type **220b**	15	15
1687	60c. Queen and Prince Philip in landau	60	45
1688	$2 Queen at Caen Hill Waterway, 1990	1·75	1·75
1689	$4 Queen at Badminton, 1983	3·00	3·25
MS1690	68×91 mm. $5 Queen Elizabeth II in 1988 and Prince Philip in 1989	4·00	4·25

1991. 10th Wedding Anniv of the Prince and Princess of Wales. As T 220b. Multicoloured.

1691	20c. Prince and Princess in hard hats, 1987	75	20
1692	25c. Portraits of Prince and Princess and sons	75	20
1693	$1 Prince Henry and Prince William, both in 1988	1·25	90
1694	$5 Princess Diana in France and Prince Charles in 1987	6·00	4·75
MS1695	68×90 mm. $5 Princes Harry and William in Majorca, and Princess Diana presenting polo trophy to Prince Charles	5·00	4·25

221 Class D51 Steam Locomotive

1991. "Phila Nippon '91" International Stamp Exhibition, Tokyo. Japanese Trains. Mult.

1696	75c. Type **221**	65	65
1697	75c. Class 9600 steam locomotive	65	65
1698	75c. Goods wagons and chrysanthemum emblem	65	65
1699	75c. Passenger coach	65	65
1700	75c. Decorated Class C57 steam locomotive	65	65
1701	75c. Oil tanker wagon	65	65
1702	75c. Class C53 steam locomotive	65	65
1703	75c. First Japanese steam locomotive	65	65
1704	75c. Class C11 steam locomotive	65	65
1705	$1 Class 181 electric unit	65	65
1706	$1 Class EH10 electric locomotive	65	65
1707	$1 Passenger coaches and Special Express symbol	65	65
1708	$1 Class 1 electric tramcar, Sendai City	65	65
1709	$1 Class 485 electric unit	65	65
1710	$1 Street-cleaning tram, Sendai City	65	65
1711	$1 "Hikari" express train	65	65
1712	$1 Class ED11 electric locomotive	65	65
1713	$1 Class EF66 electric locomotive	65	65
MS1714	Four sheets, each 108×77 mm. (a) $6 Class C55 steam locomotive (vert). P13×13½. (b) $6 Series 400 electric train. (c) $6 Class C62 steam locomotive (vert). (d) $6 "Super Hitachi" electric train. Set of 4 sheets	15·00	16·00

222 Marcello Mastroianni (actor)

1991. Italian Entertainers. Multicoloured.

1715	$1 Type **222**	70	70
1716	$1 Sophia Loren (actress)	70	70
1717	$1 Mario Lanza (singer)	70	70
1718	$1 Federico Fellini (director)	70	70
1719	$1 Arturo Toscanini (conductor)	70	70
1720	$1 Anna Magnani (actress)	70	70
1721	$1 Giancarlo Giannini (actor)	70	70
1722	$1 Gina Lollobrigida (actress)	70	70
1723	$1 Enrico Caruso (operatic tenor)	70	70
MS1724	117×80 mm. $6 Luciano Pavarotti (operatic tenor) (horiz)	5·50	6·00

223 Madonna

1991. Madonna (American singer). Mult.

1725	$1 Type **223**	95	95
1726	$1 In strapless dress	95	95
1727	$1 Wearing necklaces, looking right	95	95
1728	$1 In green dress	95	95
1729	$1 Wearing necklaces, looking to front	95	95
1730	$1 With wrist bangles	95	95
1731	$1 With hand to face	95	95
1732	$1 In purple dress	95	95
1733	$1 With microphone	95	95
MS1734	79×118 mm. $6 Madonna (25×40 mm)	6·50	7·00

224 John Lennon

1991. John Lennon (British musician). Mult.

1735	$1+2c. Type **224**	1·00	90
1736	$1+2c. With Beatle hair cut	1·00	90
1737	$1+2c. In cap	1·00	90
1738	$1+2c. In red polka-dot shirt	1·00	90
1739	$1+2c. In green polo-neck jumper and jacket	1·00	90
1740	$1+2c. In glasses and magenta jacket	1·00	90
1741	$1+2c. With long hair and glasses	1·00	90
1742	$1+2c. In black jumper	1·00	90
1743	$1+2c. In polo-neck jumper	1·00	90

225 Free French Resistance Fighters, 1944

1991. Anniversaries and Events. Multicoloured.

1744	10c. Type **225**	30	25
1745	45c. De Gaulle with Churchill, 1944	1·00	55
1746	50c. Protestor with banner	45	45
1747	65c. Tales around the camp fire (vert)	70	50
1748	75c. Liberation of Paris, 1944	70	60
1749	75c. Building Berlin Wall	70	60
1750	90c. German flag and protestors' shadows	1·00	80
1751	$1 Presidents Bush and Gorbachev shaking hands	80	80
1752	$1 "Marriage of Figaro"	2·50	1·50
1753	$1.50 British trenches and Mafeking Siege 3d. stamp	1·75	2·00
1754	$1.50 Class P-36 steam locomotive, Trans-Siberian Railway	1·75	2·00
1755	$1.50 Map of Switzerland and woman in traditional costume	1·75	2·00
1756	$1.65 Lilienthal's signature and "Flugzeug Nr. 13 Doppeldecker"	2·00	2·25
1757	$2 Street fighting, Kiev	2·50	2·75
1758	$2 Gottfried Leibniz (mathematician)	2·50	2·75
1759	$3 "The Clemency of Titus"	3·75	3·75
1760	$3.50 Angelfish and scout diver	2·75	2·75
MS1761	Four sheets. (a) 101×72 mm. $4 Arms of Berlin. (b) 77×116 mm. $4 Mozart and signature (vert). (c) 77×116 mm. $5 President De Gaulle (vert). (d) 117×89 mm. $5 Scout badge and Jamboree emblem. Set of 4 sheets	13·00	15·00

ANNIVERSARIES AND EVENTS: Nos. 1744/5, 1748, **MS**1761c, Birth centenary of Charles de Gaulle (French statesman); Nos. 1746, 1749/51, **MS**1761a, Bicentenary of Brandenburg Gate, Berlin; Nos. 1747, 1753, 1760, **MS**1761d, 50th death anniv of Lord Baden-Powell and World Scout Jamboree, Korea; Nos. 1752, 1759, **MS**1761b, Death bicentenary of Mozart; No. 1754, Centenary of Trans-Siberian Railway; No. 1755, 700th anniv of Swiss Confederation; No. 1756, Centenary of Otto Lilienthal's gliding experiments; No. 1757, 50th anniv of capture of Kiev; No. 1758, 750th anniv of Hanover.

226 Myrvyn Bennion

1991. 50th Anniv of Japanese Attack on Pearl Harbor. Recipients of Congressional Medal of Honor. Multicoloured.

1762	$1 Type **226**	60	70
1763	$1 George Cannon	60	70
1764	$1 John Finn	60	70
1765	$1 Francis Flaherty	60	70
1766	$1 Samuel Fuqua	60	70
1767	$1 Edwin Hill	60	70
1768	$1 Herbert Jones	60	70
1769	$1 Isaac Kidd	60	70
1770	$1 Jackson Pharris	60	70
1771	$1 Thomas Reeves	60	70
1772	$1 Donald Ross	60	70
1773	$1 Robert Scott	60	70
1774	$1 Franklin van Valkenburgh	60	70
1775	$1 James Ward	70	70
1776	$1 Cassin Young	60	70

226a Mickey Mouse, Goofy and Pluto as Pauper Pals

1991. International Literacy Year (1990) (2nd issue). Scenes from Disney cartoon films. Multicoloured. (a) "The Prince and The Pauper".

1777	5c. Type **226a**	30	25
1778	10c. Mickey as the bored prince	30	25
1779	15c. Donald Duck as the valet	35	30
1780	25c. Mickey as the prince and the pauper	40	30
1781	60c. Exchanging clothes	80	55
1782	75c. Prince and pauper with suit of armour	90	65
1783	80c. Throwing food from the battlements	1·00	70
1784	$1 Pete as Captain of the Guard	1·25	85
1785	$2 Mickey and Donald in the dungeon	2·00	1·75
1786	$3 Mickey and Donald at dungeon window	2·50	2·25
1787	$4 Goofy rescuing Mickey and Donald	3·00	3·00
1788	$5 Crowning the real prince	3·00	3·00
MS1789	Four sheets, each 127×101 mm. (a) $6 Crowning the wrong prince. (b) $6 Pete holding Mickey. (c) $6 The pauper on the throne. (d) $6 Mickey telling troops to seize the guard. Set of 4 sheets	14·00	15·00

(b) "The Rescuers Down Under".

1790	5c. Miss Bianca	30	25
1791	10c. Bernard	30	25
1792	15c. Matre d'Francoise	35	30
1793	25c. Wilbur the Albatross	45	25
1794	60c. Jake the Kangaroo Mouse	80	55
1795	75c. Bernard, Bianca and Jake in the outback	90	65
1796	80c. Bianca and Bernard to the rescue	1·00	70
1797	$1 Marahute the Eagle	1·25	85
1798	$2 Cody and Marahute with eggs	2·00	1·75
1799	$3 McLeach and his pet, Joanna the Goanna	2·50	2·50
1800	$4 Frank the Frill-necked Lizard	3·00	3·00
1801	$5 Red Kangaroo, Krebbs Koala and Polly Platypus	3·00	3·25
MS1802	Four sheets, each 127×102 mm. (a) $6 The Rescuers. (b) $6 Ethiopian and Japanese mice delegates. (c) $6 Wilbur carrying Bianca and Bernard. (d) $6 Wilbur in pain. Set of 4 sheets	14·00	15·00

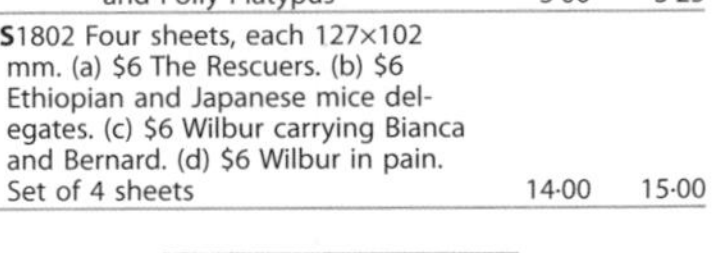

227 Hans-Dietrich Genscher and "Winged Victory" Statue

1991. European History. Multicoloured.

1803	$1 Type **227**	1·75	1·25
1804	$1 Destruction of Berlin Wall	1·75	1·50
1805	$1 Churchill, De Gaulle and Appeal to the French, 1940	1·75	1·50
1806	$1 Eisenhower, De Gaulle and D-Day, 1944	1·75	1·50
1807	$1 Brandenburg Gate, Berlin (bicentenary)	1·75	1·50
1808	$1 Chancellor Helmut Kohl and meeting of Berlin mayors, 1989	1·75	1·50
1809	$1 De Gaulle with Chancellor Adenauer	1·75	1·50
1810	$1 Pres. Kennedy's visit to Europe, 1961, Washington and Lafayette	1·75	1·50

MS1811 106×88 mm. $6 Casablanca Conference, 1942, and demolition of Berlin Wall (24½×39 mm) 4·75 6·00

1991. Famous Golfers. As T 227. Mult.

1812	$1 Gary Player	1·75	1·25
1813	$1 Nick Faldo	1·75	1·25
1814	$1 Severiano Ballesteros	1·75	1·25
1815	$1 Ben Hogan	1·75	1·25
1816	$1 Jack Nicklaus	1·75	1·25
1817	$1 Greg Norman	1·75	1·25
1818	$1 Jose-Maria Olazabal	1·75	1·25
1819	$1 Bobby Jones	1·75	1·25

1991. Famous Entertainers. As T 277. Mult.

1820	$2 Michael Jackson	1·75	1·75
1821	$2 Madonna	1·75	1·75
1822	$2 Elvis Presley	1·75	1·75
1823	$2 David Bowie	1·75	1·75
1824	$2 Prince	1·75	1·75
1825	$2 Frank Sinatra	1·75	1·75
1826	$2 George Michael	1·75	1·75
1827	$2 Mick Jagger	1·75	1·75

MS1828 Two sheets, each 110×82 mm. (a) $6 Madonna (29×43 mm). (b) $6 Elvis Presley (29×43 mm). Set of 2 sheets 10·00 10·00

1991. Famous Chess Masters. As T 227. Mult.

1829	$1 Francoise Philidor	1·25	1·00
1830	$1 Karl Anderssen	1·25	1·00
1831	$1 Wilhelm Steinitz	1·25	1·00
1832	$1 Alexandrovich Alekhine	1·25	1·00
1833	$1 Boris Spassky	1·25	1·00
1834	$1 Robert Fischer	1·25	1·00
1835	$1 Anatoly Karpov	1·25	1·00
1836	$1 Garry Kasparov	1·25	1·00

1991. Nobel Prize Winners. As T 227. Mult.

1837	$1 Albert Einstein (mathematical physicist)	1·40	1·00
1838	$1 Wilhelm Rontgen (physicist)	1·40	1·00
1839	$1 William Shockley (chemist)	1·40	1·00
1840	$1 Charles Townes (physicist)	1·40	1·00
1841	$1 Lev Landau (physicist)	1·40	1·00
1842	$1 Guglielmo Marconi (applied physicist)	1·40	1·00
1843	$1 Willard Libby (chemist)	1·40	1·00
1844	$1 Ernest Lawrence (nuclear physicist)	1·40	1·00

228 Walt Disney Characters decorating Christmas Tree, 1982

1991. Christmas. Walt Disney Christmas Cards. Multicoloured.

1845	10c. Type **228**	15	15
1846	45c. Mickey and Moose, 1980	40	30
1847	55c. Mickey, Pluto and Donald carrying bauble, 1970	50	40
1848	75c. Duckling and egg shell, 1943	70	70
1849	$1.50 Walt Disney characters decorating globe, 1941	1·25	1·50
1850	$2 The Lady and the Tramp by Christmas tree, 1986	1·50	1·75
1851	$4 Walt Disney characters carol singing, 1977	2·75	3·25
1852	$5 Mickey in fairy-tale castle, 1965	2·75	3·50

MS1853 Two sheets. (a) 102×128 mm. $6 Characters in balloon basket, 1966. (b) 128×102 mm. $6 Characters in national costumes, 1966. Set of 2 sheets 9·00 9·50

229 Kings Hill

1992. Preserving the Environment. Mult.

1854	10c. Type **229**	20	20
1855	55c. Planting sapling	50	45
1856	75c. Doric Temple, Botanic Gardens	60	65
1857	$2 18th-century map of Kings Hill	1·40	2·00

229a Kingstown from the Cliffs

1992. 40th Anniv of Queen Elizabeth II's Accession. Multicoloured.

1858	10c. Type **229a**	20	15
1859	20c. Deep water wharf, Kingstown	35	15
1860	$1 Residential suburb, Kingstown	60	60
1861	$5 Kingstown from the interior	2·75	3·25

MS1862 Two sheets, each 75×92 mm. (a) $6 Deep water wharf (different). (b) $6 Beach. Set of 2 sheets 9·00 9·50

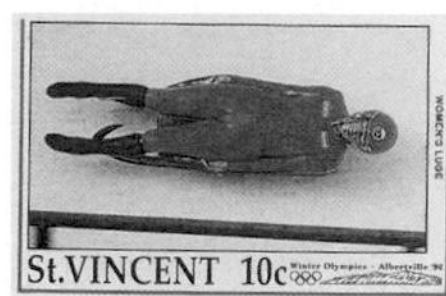

230 Women's Luge

1992. Winter Olympic Games, Albertville (1st issue). Multicoloured.

1863	10c. Type **230**	15	15
1864	15c. Women's figure skating (vert)	20	20
1865	25c. Two-man bobsleigh	25	25
1866	30c. Mogul skiing (vert)	30	30
1867	45c. Nordic combination	40	40
1868	55c. Ski jumping	55	55
1869	75c. Men's giant slalom	65	65
1870	$1.50 Women's slalom (vert)	1·10	1·10
1871	$5 Ice hockey	3·25	3·75
1872	$8 Biathlon (vert)	4·25	5·00

MS1873 Two sheets, each 100×70 mm. (a) $6 Women's speed skating (vert). (b) $6 Men's downhill skiing (vert). Set of 2 sheets 9·50 11·00

See also Nos. 1966/80.

231 Women's Synchronized Swimming

1992. Olympic Games, Barcelona. Multicoloured.

1874	10c. Type **231**	20	20
1875	15c. Men's high jump (vert)	20	20
1876	25c. Men's small-bore rifle shooting	30	20
1877	30c. Men's 200 m (vert)	30	20
1878	45c. Men's judo (vert)	35	25
1879	55c. Men's 200 m freestyle swimming	40	30
1880	75c. Men's javelin (vert)	50	50
1881	$1.50 Men's 4000 m pursuit cycling (vert)	4·00	2·00
1882	$5 Boxing	2·75	3·75
1883	$8 Women's basketball (vert)	11·00	11·00

MS1884 Two sheets, each 100×70 mm. (a) $15 Sailboarding (vert). (b) $15 Men's singles tennis (vert). Set of 2 sheets 19·00 19·00

231a The Wolf as General of Spanish Moors

1992. International Stamp Exhibitions. Walt Disney cartoon characters. Multicoloured. (a) "Granada '92", Spain. The Three Pigs in Spanish Uniforms.

1885	15c. Type **231a**	20	10
1886	40c. Pig as captain of infantry	40	25
1887	$2 Pig as halberdier	1·25	1·50
1888	$4 Pig as nobleman	2·25	3·00

MS1889 128×102 mm. $6 Nobleman at castle window 3·00 3·75

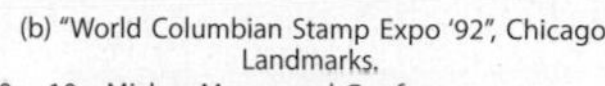

(b) "World Columbian Stamp Expo '92", Chicago Landmarks.

1890	10c. Mickey Mouse and Goofy looking at Picasso sculpture (horiz)	20	15
1891	50c. Mickey and Donald Duck admiring Robie House (horiz)	45	35
1892	$1 Calder sculpture in Sears Tower (horiz)	80	65
1893	$5 Goofy In Buckingham Memorial Fountain (horiz)	2·50	3·00

MS1894 128×102 mm. $6 Mickey painting Minnie 3·00 3·75

232 "Nina"

1992. 500th Anniv of Discovery of America by Columbus (6th issue). "World Columbian Stamp Expo '92", Chicago. Multicoloured.

1895	5c. Type **232**	40	40
1896	10c. "Pinta"	40	30
1897	45c. "Santa Maria"	75	50
1898	55c. Fleet leaving Palos, 1492	75	55
1899	$4 Christopher Columbus (vert)	3·00	3·50
1900	$5 Arms of Columbus (vert)	3·00	3·50

MS1901 Two sheets, each 115×86 mm. (a) $6 "Santa Maria" sighting land (42½×57 mm). (b) $6 Route of voyage (42½×57 mm). Set of 2 sheets 8·50 10·00

233 Elvis looking Pensive

1992. 15th Death Anniv of Elvis Presley (1st issue). Multicoloured.

1902	$1 Type **233**	1·25	1·00
1903	$1 Wearing black and yellow striped shirt	1·25	1·00
1904	$1 Singing into microphone	1·25	1·00
1905	$1 Wearing wide-brimmed hat	1·25	1·00
1906	$1 With microphone in right hand	1·25	1·00
1907	$1 In Army uniform	1·10	1·00
1908	$1 Wearing pink shirt	1·25	1·00
1909	$1 In yellow shirt	1·25	1·00
1910	$1 In jacket and bow tie	1·25	1·00

MS1911 76×107 mm. $6 In blue shirt (28½×42½ mm) 6·50 7·00

See also Nos. 2029/37, 2038/46 and 2047/9.

234 Bonnie Blair

1992. Bonnie Blair's Victories in 500 m Speed Skating at Calgary and Albertville Olympic Games. Multicoloured.

1912	$3 Type **234**	2·25	2·50

MS1913 185×127 mm. $2 Turning corner (horiz); $2 With skates in arms (43×51 mm); $2 On straight (horiz) 4·50 4·75

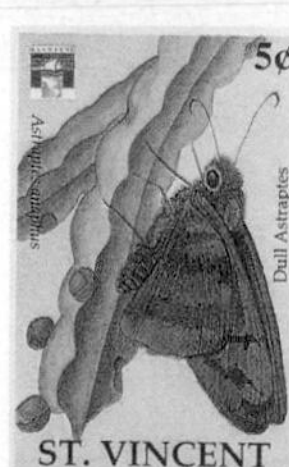

235 "Astraptes anaphus"

1992. "Genova '92" International Thematic Stamp Exhibition (1st issue). Butterflies. Multicoloured.

1914	5c. Type **235**	30	40
1915	10c. "Anartia jatrophae" (horiz)	30	20
1916	35c. "Danaus eresimus"	55	40
1917	45c. "Battus polydamus"	60	45
1918	55c. "Junonia evarete" (horiz)	70	50
1919	65c. "Urbanus proteus"	80	60
1920	75c. "Pyrgus oileus" (horiz)	90	65
1921	$1 "Biblis hyperia"	1·00	75
1922	$2 "Eurema daira"	1·50	1·50
1923	$3 "Leptotes cassius" (horiz)	1·75	2·00
1924	$4 "Ephyriades brunnea" (horiz)	2·25	2·50
1925	$5 "Victorina stelenes"	2·50	2·75

MS1926 Three sheets, each 98×72 mm. (a) $6 Phoebis sennae. (b) $6 Heliconius charitonius (horiz). (c) $6 Dryas julia (horiz). Set of 3 sheets 12·00 13·00

See also Nos. 1940/52.

236 "Collybia subpruinosa"

1992. Fungi. Multicoloured.

1927	10c. Type **236**	30	20
1928	15c. "Gerronema citrinum"	40	20
1929	20c. "Amanita antillana"	45	30
1930	45c. "Dermoloma atrobrunneum"	60	35
1931	50c. "Inopilus maculosus"	70	40
1932	65c. "Pulveroboletus brachyspermus"	80	55
1933	75c. "Mycena violacella"	90	60
1934	$1 "Xerocomus brasiliensis"	1·00	70
1935	$2 "Amanita ingrata"	1·50	1·75
1936	$3 "Leptonia caeruleocapitata"	1·75	2·25
1937	$4 "Limacella myochroa"	2·25	2·75
1938	$5 "Inopilus magnificus"	2·50	2·75

MS1939 Three sheets, each 101×68 mm. (a) $6 "Limacella guttata". (b) $6 "Amanita agglutinata". (c) $6 "Trogia buccinalis". Set of 3 sheets 11·00 12·00

No. 1936 is inscribed "Leptonia caeruleocaptata" in error.

237 Rufous-breasted Hermit

1992. "Genova '92" International Thematic Stamp Exhibition (2nd issue). Hummingbirds. Multicoloured.

1940	5c. Type **237**	30	40
1941	15c. Hispaniolan emerald	35	20
1942	45c. Green-throated carib	60	35
1943	55c. Jamaican mango	70	45
1944	65c. Vervain hummingbird	80	60
1945	75c. Purple-throated carib	90	70
1946	90c. Green mango	90	75
1947	$1 Bee hummingbird	1·00	80
1948	$2 Cuban emerald	1·75	1·75
1949	$3 Puerto Rican emerald	1·90	2·00
1950	$4 Antillean mango	2·40	2·75
1951	$5 Streamertail	2·75	2·75

MS1952 Three sheets, each 98×67 mm. (a) $6 Bahama woodstar. (b) $6 Antillean crested hummingbird. (c) $6 Blue-headed hummingbird. Set of 3 sheets 14·00 14·00

I 3 mm serif characters, no line through "c"
II 3 mm serif characters, line through "c"
III 3.5 mm sanserif characters, line through "c"
IV 3.5 mm broad serif characters
V 2.5 mm sanserif characters, line through "c"
VI 4.25 mm serif characters, no line through "c"
VII 3 mm thin serif numerals, sanserif "c", no line
VIII 2.5 mm sanserif characters, no line through "c"

20c	20¢	10¢	10¢
I	II	III	IV

20¢	20c	20c	20c
V	VI	VII	VIII

1993. Various issues surcharged. Original values obliterated by circle or rectangle. (a) On stamps of St. Vincent.

No.	Description	Unused	Used
V1953	10c. on 2c. (No. 287) (II)	60·00	
V1954	10c. on 6c. (No. 1099)		
V1955	10c. on 12c. (No. 1101) (IV)		
V1956	10c. on 15c. (No. 1115e) (III)		
V1957	10c. on 25c. (No. 296) (II)	45·00	
V1958	10c. on 25c. (No. 1115g) (III)		15·00
V1959	10c. on 35c. (No. 1106) (II)		
V1960	10c. on 35c. (No. 788) (II)	25·00	15·00
V1961	10c. on 45c. (No. 1115j) (III)		15·00
V1962	10c. on 45c. (No. 770) (II)		
V1963	10c. on 45c. (No. 1134) (II)	13·00	
V1964	10c. on 60c. (No. 687)		40·00
V1965	10c. on 60c. (No. 715) (II)	25·00	
V1966	10c. on 60c. (No. 720) (II)	13·00	5·00
V1967	10c. on 65c. (No. 1115l) (II)	25·00	
V1968	10c. on 70c. (No. 500) (II)	25·00	
V1969	10c. on 75c. (No. 1115m) (II)	20·00	
V1970	10c. on $1 (No. 773) (II)		
V1971	10c. on $1.25 (No. 555) (II)	25·00	
V1972	10c. on $1.50 (No. 688) (II)		
V1973	10c. on $1.50 (No. 725) (II)	25·00	
V1974	10c. on $2 (No. 573) (II)	25·00	
V1975	10c. on $2 (No. 689)		
V1977	10c. on $2.50 (No. 643) (II)	13·00	
V1978	20c. on ½c. (No. 285) (II)	7·50	5·00
V1979	20c. on 1c. (No. 344) (V)	40·00	25·00
V1980	20c. on 6c. (No. 1116) (II)	45·00	
V1981	20c. on 6c. (No. 1117) (II)	45·00	
V1982	20c. on 25c. (No. 949) (VIII)		45·00
V1988	20c. on 35c. (No. 808) (I)		
V1989	20c. on 35c. (No. 1181) (I)*		
V1990	20c. on 45c. (No. 723) (VIII)		
V1991	20c. on 45c. (No. 1134) (VIII)		
V1992	20c. on 60c. (No. 641) (I)	75·00	25·00
V1993	20c. on 60c. (No. 657) (VI)		
V1994	20c. on 60c. (No. 682) (I)	90·00	
V1995	20c. on 60c. (No. 687) (I)	7·50	10·00
V1996	20c. on 60c. (No. 711) (I)	7·50	10·00
V1997	20c. on 60c. (No. 720) (VIII)		
V1998	20c. on 60c. (No. 724) (I)	10·00	5·00
V1999	20c. on 60c. (No. 771) (I, surch lower left))	12·00	5·00
V2000	20c. on 60c. (No. 831) (I)		5·00
V2001	20c. on 70c. (No. 500) (I)		
V2002	20c. on 75c. (No. 1045) (I)		
V2003	20c. on 75c. (No. 1046) (I)		
V2004	20c. on 75c. (No. 1051) (V)	38·00	25·00
V2005	20c. on 75c. (No. 1115m) (I)	15·00	5·00
V2006	20c. on $1 (No. 563) (I)	25·00	7·50
V2007	20c. on $1 (No. 666) (I)	35·00	25·00
V2008	20c. on $1 (No. 667) (I)	35·00	25·00
V2009	20c. on $1 (No. 683) (I)	25·00	
V2010	20c. on $1 (No. 907) (I)		25·00
V2014	20c. on $1.25 (No. 455) (I)	15·00	
V2015	20c. on $1.25 (No. 497) (I)	15·00	
V2016	20c. on $1.25 (No. 530) (II)		
V2017	20c. on $1.25 (No. 555) (VII)		40·00
V2020	20c. on $1.50 (No. 708) (I)		
V2021	20c. on $1.50 (No. 712) (II)	7·50	10·00
V2022	20c. on $1.50 (No. 721) (V	22·00	25·00
V2023	20c. on $1.50 (No. 725) (II)		
V2024	20c. on $1.50 (No. 832) (I)	18·00	7·50
V2025	20c. on $1.50 (No. 1020) (II)	32·00	19·00
V2026	20c. on $1.50 (No. 1047) (I)	25·00	9·00
V2027	20c. on $1.50 (No. 1048) (I)	25·00	9·00
V2030	20c. on $2 (No. 659) (I)	20·00	
V2031	20c. on $2 (No. 684) (I)	20·00	
V2032	20c. on $2 (No. 689) (I)		
V2033	20c. on $2 (No. 709) (VIII)		
V2034	20c. on $2 (No. 713) (II)	20·00	25·00
V2035	20c. on $2 (No. 722) (V)	7·50	12·00
V2036	20c. on $2 (No. 726) (V)	7·50	7·50
V2037	20c. on $2 (No. 833) (I)	22·00	7·50
V2038	20c. on $2 (No. 1021) (II)		
V2039	20c. on $2.50 (No. 951) (I)	10·00	16·00
V2043	20c. on $3 (No. 763) (II)		20·00
V2045	20c. on $3 (No. 811) (I)		7·50
V2046	20c. on $3 (No. 853) (I)	20·00	12·00
V2047	20c. on $3 (No. 871) (I)	10·00	12·00
V2051	20c. on $3.70 (No. 1069) (I)	40·00	20·00
V2052	20c. on $4 (No. 1511) (V)	38·00	25·00

(b) On stamps of St. Vincent Grenadines.

No.	Description	Unused	Used
V2053	10c. on 1c. (No. 35A) (II)		38·00
V2054	10c. on 1c. (No. 110) (II)		
V2055	10c. on 6c. (No. 115) (II)	22·00	
V2056	10c. on 35c. (No. 307) (II)		
V2057	10c. on 45c. (No. 246) (II)	28·00	
V2058	10c. on 45c. (No. 268) (III)		
V2059	10c. on 90c. (No. 165) (II)	28·00	
V2060	10c. on $1 (No. 309) (II)		
V2061	10c. on $2 (No. 253) (II)		
V2065	20c. on 20c. (No. 347) (I)		15·00
V2066	20c. on 35c. (No. 386) (I)	28·00	7·50
V2067	20c. on 45c. (No. 246) (VI)		12·00
V2068	20c. on 45c. (No. 348) (II)		12·00
V2069	20c. on 45c. (No. 496) (II)		
V2070	20c. on 50c. (No. 72) (I)	15·00	10·00
V2071	20c. on 60c. (No. 247) (VI)	75·00	25·00
V2073	20c. on 75c. (No. 428) (II)		15·00
V2074	20c. on 75c. (No. 556) (II)		30·00
V2075	20c. on 75c. (No. 561) (V)	38·00	
V2076	20c. on 90c. (No. 165) (I)	25·00	12·00
V2077	20c. on $1 (No. 73) (I)	20·00	10·00
V2078	20c. on $1.25 (No. 138) (II)		
V2079	20c. on $1.25 (No. 501) (II)		25·00
V2081	20c. on $1.50 (No. 238) (VII)		
V2082	20c. on $1.50 (No. 248) (VI)		
V2083	20c. on $1.50 (No. 252) (I)	25·00	10·00
V2084	20c. on $2 (No. 105) (II)		22·00
V2085	20c. on $2 (No. 166) (I)		19·00
V2086	20c. on $2 (No. 183) (II)	15·00	15·00
V2087	20c. on $2 (No. 228) (I)	65·00	15·00
V2088	20c. on $2 (No. 253) (I)		
V2092	20c. on $2.50 (No. 239) (VII)	75·00	
V2093	20c. on $3 (No. 159) (II)		12·00
V2094	20c. on $3 (No. 310) (I)		25·00
V2095	20c. on $3 (No. 363) (I)	28·00	10·00
V2096	20c. on $3 (No. 389) (I)	17·00	
V2097	20c. on $3 (No. 480) (II)	20·00	
V2098	20c. on $3 (No. 664) (II)		
V2103	20c. on $3.50 (No. 557) (V)	20·00	
V2104	20c. on $4 (No. 498) (V)	20·00	

These stamps were not available from the Philatelic Bureau but could be bought at post offices or retail outlets. The 10c. surcharges were primarily designed for fiscal use but were also valid for postage.

In most cases the obliteration of the original value and the application of the surcharge were two separate operations, resulting in inconsistent spacing between the two. Manuscript obliterations and surcharging are known.

Numbers have been left for stamps known to have been surcharged but which have not been reported used postally.

*No. V1989 is known only with double surcharge.

238 Coral Vine

1992. Medicinal Plants. Multicoloured.

No.	Description	Unused	Used
1953	75c. Type **238**	70	85
1954	75c. Cocoplum	70	85
1955	75c. Angel's trumpet	70	85
1956	75c. Lime	70	85
1957	75c. White ginger	70	85
1958	75c. Pussley	70	85
1959	75c. Sea grape	70	85
1960	75c. Indian mulberry	70	85
1961	75c. Plantain	70	85
1962	75c. Lignum vitae	70	85
1963	75c. Periwinkle	70	85
1964	75c. Guava	70	85
MS1965	Three sheets, each 98×69 mm. (a) $6 Wild sage. (b) $6 Clover tree. (c) $6 Aloe. Set of 3 sheets	10·50	11·00

239 Kristi Yamaguchi (U.S.A.) (figure skating)

1992. Winter Olympic Games, Albertville (2nd issue). Gold Medal Winners. Multicoloured.

No.	Description	Unused	Used
1966	$1 Type **239**	80	1·00
1967	$1 Pernilla Wiberg (Sweden) (giant slalom skiing)	80	1·00
1968	$1 Lyubov Yegorova (C.I.S.) (10 km cross-country skiing)	80	1·00
1969	$1 Josef Polig (Italy) (combined alpine skiing)	80	1·00
1970	$1 Fin Christian-Jagge (Norway) (slalom skiing)	80	1·00
1971	$1 Kerrin Lee-Gartner (Canada) (downhill skiing)	80	1·00
1972	$1 Steffania Belmondo (Italy) (30 km cross-country skiing)	80	1·00
1973	$1 Alberto Tomba (Italy) (giant slalom skiing)	80	1·00
1974	$1 Fabrice Guy (France) (nordic combined skiing)	80	1·00
1975	$1 Patrick Ortlieb (Austria) (downhill skiing)	80	1·00
1976	$1 Vegard Ulvang (Norway) (nordic cross-country skiing)	80	1·00
1977	$1 Edgar Grospiron (France) (freestyle mogul skiing)	80	1·00
1978	$1 Andre Aamodt (Norway) (super giant slalom skiing)	80	1·00
1979	$1 Viktor Petrenko (C.I.S.) (figure skating)	80	1·00
MS1980	Two sheets. (a) 108×78 mm. $6 Kristi Yamaguchi (U.S.A.) (figure skating) (different). (b) 111×81 mm. $6 Alberto Tomba (Italy) (giant slalom skiing) (different). Set of 2 sheets	8·50	9·50

No. 1968 is inscribed "LYUBOV EGOROVA" in error.

239a Columbus meeting Amerindians

1992. 500th Anniv of Discovery of America by Columbus (7th issue). Organization of East Caribbean States. Multicoloured.

No.	Description	Unused	Used
1981	$1 Type **239a**	1·00	75
1982	$2 Ships approaching island	2·00	2·50

240 "Pinocchio"

1992. Opening of Euro-Disney Resort, Paris. Multicoloured.

No.	Description	Unused	Used
1983	$1 Type **240**	1·40	1·40
1984	$1 "Alice in Wonderland"	1·40	1·40
1985	$1 "Bambi"	1·40	1·40
1986	$1 "Cinderella"	1·40	1·40
1987	$1 "Snow White and the Seven Dwarfs"	1·40	1·40
1988	$1 "Peter Pan"	1·40	1·40
MS1989	187×101 mm. $5 Mickey Mouse (56×76 mm)	4·50	5·00

240a Jacob K. Javits Convention Centre

1992. Postage Stamp Mega Event, New York. Sheet 100×70 mm.

No.	Description	Unused	Used
MS1990	**240a** $6 multicoloured	4·50	5·50

No. **MS**1990 is inscribed "Jaritts" in error.

241 Spanish Galleon and Paddle-steamer

1992. First use of Adhesive Stamps on Trans-Atlantic Mail, 1840, Commemoration. Sheet 100×70 mm.

No.	Description	Unused	Used
MS1991	**241** $6 multicoloured	7·00	7·50

241a "Hospitality refused to the Virgin Mary and Joseph (detail) (Metsys)

1992. Christmas. Religious Paintings. Multicoloured.

No.	Description	Unused	Used
1992	10c. Type **241a**	20	20
1993	40c. "The Nativity" (detail) (Durer)	40	30
1994	45c. "The Nativity" (Geertgen Tot Sint Jans)	40	30
1995	50c. "The Nativity" (Jacopo Tintoretto)	50	35
1996	55c. "The Nativity" (detail) (Follower of Calcar)	50	35
1997	65c. "The Nativity" (Workshop of Fra Angelico)	60	50
1998	75c. "The Nativity" (Master of the Louvre Nativity)	65	50
1999	$1 "The Nativity" (detail) (Lippi)	80	75
2000	$2 "The Nativity" (Petrus Christus)	1·50	1·50
2001	$3 "The Nativity" (detail) (Edward Burne-Jones)	2·00	2·50
2002	$4 "The Nativity" (detail) (Giotto)	2·50	3·00
2003	$5 "Birth of Christ" (detail) (Domenico Ghirlandaio)	2·75	3·25
MS2004	Three sheets, each 72×99 mm. (a) $6 "Birth of Christ" (detail) (Gerard Horenbout). (b) $6 "The Nativity" (detail) (Botticelli). (c) $6 "The Nativity" (detail) (Jean Fouquet). Set of 3 sheets	12·00	13·00

242 Gaston

1992. Walt Disney's "Beauty and the Beast" (cartoon film). Multicoloured.

No.	Description	Unused	Used
2005	2c. Type **242**	30	30
2006	3c. Belle and her father, Maurice	30	60
2007	5c. Lumiere, Mrs. Potts and Cogsworth	35	60
2008	10c. Philippe	35	60
2009	15c. Beast and Lumiere	45	60
2010	20c. Lumiere and Feather Duster	45	60
2011	60c. Belle and Gaston	70	75
2012	60c. Maurice	70	75
2013	60c. The Beast	70	75
2014	60c. Mrs. Potts	70	75
2015	60c. Belle and enchanted vase	70	75
2016	60c. Belle discovers enchanted rose	50	50
2017	60c. Belle with wounded Beast	70	75
2018	60c. Belle	70	75
2019	60c. Household objects alarmed	70	75
2020	60c. Belle and Chip (vert)	70	75
2021	60c. Lumiere (vert)	70	75
2022	60c. Cogsworth (vert)	70	75
2023	60c. Armoire (vert)	50	50
2024	60c. Belle and Beast (vert)	70	75
2025	60c. Feather Duster (vert)	70	75
2026	60c. Footstool (vert)	70	75
2027	60c. Belle sitting on stone (vert)	70	75
MS2028	Five sheets. (a) 127×103 mm. $6 Lumiere (vert). (b) 127×103 mm. $6 Belle reading book (vert). (c) 127×103 mm. $6 The Beast (vert). (d) 127×103 mm. $6 Belle dancing (vert). (e) 103×127 mm. $6 Lumiere, Chip and Mrs. Potts. Set of 5 sheets	20·00	22·00

1992. 15th Death Anniv of Elvis Presley (2nd issue). Nos. 1902/10 optd 15th Anniversary.

No.	Description	Unused	Used
2029	$1 Elvis looking pensive	1·50	1·00
2030	$1 Wearing black and yellow striped shirt	1·50	1·00
2031	$1 Singing into microphone	1·50	1·00
2032	$1 Wearing wide-brimmed hat	1·50	1·00
2033	$1 With microphone in right hand	1·50	1·00
2034	$1 In Army uniform	1·50	1·00
2035	$1 Wearing pink shirt	1·50	1·00
2036	$1 In yellow shirt	1·50	1·00

2037	$1 In jacket and bow tie	1·50	1·00

1992. 15th Death Anniv of Elvis Presley (3rd issue). Nos. 1820/7 optd 15th Anniversary Elvis Presley's Death August 16, 1977.

2038	$2 Michael Jackson	2·50	1·90
2039	$2 Madonna	2·50	1·90
2040	$2 Elvis Presley	2·50	1·90
2041	$2 David Bowie	2·50	1·90
2042	$2 Prince	2·50	1·90
2043	$2 Frank Sinatra	2·50	1·90
2044	$2 George Michael	2·50	1·90
2045	$2 Mick Jagger	2·50	1·90
MS2046	110×82 mm. $6 Elvis Presley (29×43 mm)	11·00	8·00

244a Elvis Presley

1992. 15th Death Anniv of Elvis Presley (4th issue). Multicoloured.

2047	$1 Type **244a**	1·75	1·75
2048	$1 Elvis with guitar	1·75	1·75
2049	$1 Elvis with microphone	1·75	1·75

245 Fifer Pig building House of Straw

1992. Walt Disney Cartoon Films. As T 245.

2050-2138	60c. ×89 multicoloured. Set of 89	35·00	40·00
MS2139	Twenty sheets, each 128×103 mm or 103×128 mm. $6 ×20 multicoloured. Set of 20 sheets	70·00	75·00

Nos. 2050/2138 were printed as ten se-tenant sheetlets, each of nine different designs except for that for "Darkwing Duck" which contains eight vertical designs (Nos. 2131/8). The other nine sheetlets depict scenes from "The Three Little Pigs", "Thru the Mirror", "Clock Cleaners", "Orphans Benefit", "The Art of Skiing", "Symphony Hour", "How to Play Football", "The Small One" and "Chip N' Dale Rescue Rangers".

No. **MS**2139 contains two sheets for each film, one sheet for "The Three Little Pigs" being in a vert format. The Stamp designs for "The Three Little Pigs" (horiz sheet), "How to Play Football" (one), "Chip N'Dale Rescue Rangers" (both) and "Darkwing Duck" (both) are vert.

For Nos. 2050/8 and **MS**2139a/b ("The Three Little Pigs") with different face values see Nos. 2852/61.

246 Scottie Pippen

1992. Olympic Gold Medal Winners, Barcelona. Members of U.S.A. basketball team. Multicoloured.

2140	$2 Type **246**	1·50	1·25
2141	$2 Earvin "Magic" Johnson	1·50	1·25
2142	$2 Larry Bird	1·50	1·25
2143	$2 Christian Laettner	1·50	1·25
2144	$2 Karl Malone	1·50	1·25
2145	$2 David Robinson	1·50	1·25
2146	$2 Michael Jordan	1·50	1·25
2147	$2 Charles Barkley	1·50	1·25
2148	$2 John Stockton	1·50	1·25
2149	$2 Chris Mullin	1·50	1·25
2150	$2 Clyde Drexler	1·50	1·25
2151	$2 Patrick Ewing	1·50	1·25

247 Tom Seaver

1992. Famous Baseball Players (5th issue). Multicoloured.

2152	$2 Type **247**	1·40	1·60
2153	$2 Roberto Clemente	1·40	1·60
2154	$2 Hank Aaron	1·40	1·60

248 Don Mattingly

1992. Famous Baseball Players (6th issue). Multicoloured.

2155	$5 Type **248**	3·00	3·75
2156	$5 Howard Johnson	3·00	3·75

249 Earth and U.N. Emblem

1992. Anniversaries and Events. Mult.

2157	10c. Type **249**	40	20
2158	45c. Airship LZ-11 "Viktoria Luise" over Kiel Regatta, 1912 (vert)	1·25	35
2159	75c. Adenauer and German flag	1·25	50
2160	75c. Trophy and Bill Koch (skipper) of "America III", 1992	75	50
2161	$1 Konrad Adenauer	75	60
2162	$1 Snow leopard and emblem	1·75	60
2163	$1.50 Caribbean manatee	2·00	2·00
2164	$2 Humpback whale	4·50	2·50
2165	$3 Adenauer and Pres. Kennedy, 1962	1·60	2·25
2166	$3 Doctor checking patient's eye	3·00	3·00
2167	$4 "Discovery" space shuttle (vert)	4·25	5·00
2168	$4 Adenauer and Pope John XXIII, 1960	5·50	5·00
2169	$5 Schumacher and racing car	4·50	5·00
2170	$6 Zeppelin LZ-1 over Lake Constance, 1900	5·00	5·50
MS2171	Five sheets. (a) 70×100 mm. $6 Cabin of airship LZ-127 "Graf Zeppelin". (b) 70×100 mm. $6 Douglas DC-6 airplane from Berlin Airlift. (c) 100×70 mm. $6 Konrad Adenauer making speech. (d) 70×100 mm. $6 Woolly spider monkey. (e) 119×89 mm. $6 Schumacher winning race. Set of 5 sheets	20·00	23·00

ANNIVERSARIES AND EVENTS: Nos. 2157, 2167, International Space Year; Nos. 2158, 2170, **MS**2171a, 75th death anniv of Count Ferdinand von Zeppelin; Nos. 2159, 2161, 2165, 2168, **MS**2171b/c, 25th death anniv of Konrad Adenauer (German statesman); No. 2160, Americas Cup Yachting Championship; Nos. 2162/4, **MS**2171d, Earth Summit '92, Rio; No. 2166, 75th anniv of International Association of Lions Clubs; No. 2169, **MS**2171e, Michael Schumacher's Victory in 1992 Belgium Grand Prix.

249a Care Bear and American White Pelican

1992. Ecology. Multicoloured.

2172	75c. Type **249a**	1·25	80
MS2173	101×72 mm. $2 Care Bear in hot air balloon (horiz)	1·40	2·00

250 Farmer, Fisherman and Emblem

1993. International Conference on Nutrition, Rome.

2174	**250** 65c. multicoloured	1·25	85

251 Coastal Village

1993. "Uniting the Windward Islands". Mult.

2175	10c. Type **251**	55	20
2176	40c. Children from different islands	1·10	60
2177	45c. Children and palm tree	1·10	60

252 Fisherman holding Catch

1993. Fishing. Multicoloured.

2178	5c. Type **252**	15	15
2179	10c. Fish market	15	15
2180	50c. Fishermen landing catch	60	60
2181	$5 Fishing with nets	3·00	4·25

253 Brown Pelican

1993. Migratory Birds. Multicoloured.

2182	10c. Type **253**	85	50
2183	25c. Red-necked grebe (horiz)	1·25	40
2184	45c. Belted kingfisher (horiz)	1·50	40
2185	55c. Yellow-bellied sapsucker	1·60	40
2186	$1 Great blue heron	2·00	85
2187	$2 Common black hawk ("Crab Hawk") (horiz)	2·75	2·00
2188	$4 Yellow warbler	3·25	3·75
2189	$5 Northern oriole (horiz)	3·25	3·75
MS2190	Two sheets, each 100×70 mm. (a) $6 Blue-winged teal (horiz). (b) $6 White ibis (horiz). Set of 2 sheets	10·00	11·00

254 Sergeant Major

1993. Fishes. Multicoloured.

2191	5c. Type **254**	50	50
2192	10c. Rainbow parrotfish	55	30
2193	55c. Hogfish	80	30
2194	75c. Porkfish	1·00	40
2195	$1 Spot-finned butterflyfish	1·10	75
2196	$2 Buffalo trunkfish	1·75	1·75
2197	$4 Queen triggerfish	2·50	3·25
2198	$5 Queen angelfish	2·50	3·25
MS2199	Two sheets, each 100×70 mm. (a) $6 Bigeye (vert). (b) $6 Small-mouthed grunt (vert). Set of 2 sheets	8·00	9·50

254a "The Woman with Gambling Mania"

1993. Bicentenary of the Louvre, Paris. As T 254a.

2200-39	$1×40 multicoloured	21·00	23·00
MS2240	Three sheets, either 70×100 mm or 100×70 mm. $6 ×3 multicoloured. P 14½. Set of 3 sheets	13·00	15·00

Nos. 2200/39 were printed as five se-tenant sheetlets showing paintings by Gericault, Ingres, Le Sueur and Poussin, Poussin, and Boucher, Brueghel, Dumont, Gainsborough, Goya and Van Eyck.

The three sheets of No. **MS**2240 depict paintings by Chassériau (52×85 mm), Delacroix and Ingres (both 85×52 mm).

255 Hexagonal Muricop

1993. Shells. Multicoloured.

2241	10c. Type **255**	30	30
2242	15c. Caribbean vase	30	30
2243	30c. Measled cowrie	40	30
2244	45c. Dyson's keyhole limpet	50	25
2245	50c. Atlantic hairy triton	50	40
2246	65c. Orange-banded marginella	60	45
2247	75c. Bleeding tooth	70	50
2248	$1 Queen or pink conch	80	65
2249	$2 Hawk-wing conch	1·25	1·40
2250	$3 Musice volute	1·75	2·25
2251	$4 Alphabet cone	2·25	2·75
2252	$5 Antillean or incomparable cone	2·25	2·75
MS2253	Three sheets, each 103×76 mm. (a) $6 Wide-mouthed purpura ("Purpura patula") (horiz). (b) $6 Netted olive ("Oliva reticularis") (horiz). (c) $6 Flame auger ("Terebra taurina") (horiz). Set of 3 sheets	14·00	15·00

256 Ishihara holding Tennis Racket

1993. 7th Death Anniv of Yujiro Ishihara (Japanese actor).

2254	**256** 55c. black, grey and blue	1·10	90
2255	- 55c. black, grey and blue	1·10	1·00
2256	- 55c. black, grey and blue	1·10	1·00
2257	- 55c. multicoloured	1·10	1·00
2258	- 55c. multicoloured	1·10	1·00
2259	- $1 multicoloured	1·10	1·00
2260	- $1 multicoloured	1·10	1·00
2261	- $1 multicoloured	1·10	1·00
2262	- $1 multicoloured	1·10	1·00
MS2263	Four sheets, each 180×140 mm. (a) 55c., $1, $2 ×2 multicoloured. (b) 55c. black, grey and gold; $1 multicoloured; $2 black, grey and gold; $2 multicoloured. (c) 55c., $2, $4, multicoloured. (d) 55c., $4 ×2 multicoloured. Set of 4 sheets	20·00	21·00

DESIGNS—VERT (as T **256**)—No. 2255, Ishihara holding camera; No. 2256, In striped shirt; No. 2257, Holding drink and cigarette; No. 2258, On board yacht; No. 2259, In naval uniform; No. 2260, In jacket and tie; No. 2261, Wearing sunglasses; No. 2262, Wearing pink shirt; No. **MS**2263b, 55c. As No. 2255, $1 In formal suit, $2 In white jacket, $2 With guitar. (28×37 mm)—No. **MS**2263a, 55c. As No. 2259, $1 Laughing, $2 In striped shirt, $2 As No. 2258. HORIZ: (56×37 mm)—No. **MS**2263c, 55c. In yellow shirt with actress; No. **MS**2263d, 55c. With cigarette, $4 As No. 2262, $4 As 2261.

256a Queen Elizabeth II at Coronation (photograph by Cecil Beaton)

1993. 40th Anniv of Coronation.

2264	**256a** 45c. multicoloured	65	75
2265	- 65c. multicoloured	75	85
2266	- $2 green and black	1·40	1·60

2267 - $4 multicoloured 1·90 2·00

MS2268 – 70×100 mm. $6 multicoloured 5·00 5·50

DESIGNS: 65c. Queen Elizabeth opening Parliament; $2 Queen Elizabeth during Coronation; $4 Queen Elizabeth with corgi. (28½×42½)—$6 "Queen Elizabeth as a Young Girl" (detail).

257 "Erynnyis ello"

1993. Moths. Multicoloured.

2269 10c. Type **257** 20 20
2270 50c. "Aellopos tantalus" 55 30
2271 65c. "Erynnyis alope" 60 40
2272 75c. "Manduca rustica" 70 50
2273 $1 "Xylophanes pluto" 80 65
2274 $2 "Hyles lineata" 1·50 1·75
2275 $4 "Pseudosphinx tetrio" 2·50 3·00
2276 $5 "Protambulyx strigilis" 2·50 3·00

MS2277 Two sheets, each 100×70 mm. (a) $6 "Utetheisa ornatrix". (b) $6 "Xylophanes tersa". Set of 2 sheets 7·50 8·50

258 Early Astronomical Quadrant

1993. Anniversaries and Events. Red and black (Nos. 2281, 2293) or multicoloured (others).

2278 45c. Type **258** 40 25
2279 45c. "Massacre in Korea" (Picasso) (horiz) 40 25
2280 45c. Marc Girardelli (Luxembourg) (giant slalom) (horiz) 40 25
2281 45c. Willy Brandt and Pres. Nixon, 1971 (horiz) 40 25
2282 45c. Count Johannes and Countess Gloria of Thurn and Taxis 40 25
2283 65c. Count and Countess of Thurn and Taxis with children (horiz) 60 40
2284 65c. Masako Owada and engagement photographs (horiz) 60 40
2285 $1 "Family of Saltimbanques" (Picasso) (horiz) 60 50
2286 $1 Princess Stephanie of Monaco 60 60
2287 $1 "Deux Tetes" (left detail) (S. Witkiewicz) 80 80
2288 $2 Countess Gloria of Thurn and Taxis 1·25 1·25
2289 $3 "Deux Tetes" (right detail) (S. Witkiewicz) 1·50 1·50
2290 $4 Launch of American space shuttle 2·25 2·75
2291 $4 "La Joie de Vivre" (Picasso) (horiz) 2·25 2·75
2292 $5 Paul Accola (Switzerland) (downhill skiing) (horiz) 2·75 3·25
2293 $5 Willy Brandt and Robert F. Kennedy, 1967 (horiz) 2·75 3·25
2294 $5 Prince Naruhito in traditional dress and engagement photographs (horiz) 2·75 3·25
2295 $5 Pres. Clinton with school children (horiz) 2·75 3·25
2296 $6 Bogusz Church, Gozlin (horiz) 3·00 3·50

MS2297 Seven sheets. (a) 110×76 mm. $5 Copernicus. (b) 110×76 mm. $6 "Woman eating a Melon and Boy writing" (detail) (Picasso). (c) 110×76 mm. $6 Thommy Moe (U.S.A.) (downhill skiing). (d) 110×76 mm. $6 Willy Brandt at signing of Common Declaration, 1973 (horiz). (e) 110×76 mm). $6 Masako Owada. (f) 76×110 mm. $6 "Dancing" (detail) (Wladyslaw Roguski). (g) 76×110 mm. $6 Pres. Clinton wearing stetson. Set of 7 sheets 24·00 25·00

ANNIVERSARIES AND EVENTS: Nos. 2278, 2290, **MS**2297a, 450th death anniv of Copernicus (astronomer); Nos. 2279, 2285, 2291, **MS**2297b, 20th death anniv of Picasso (artist); Nos. 2280, 2292, **MS**2297c, Winter Olympic Games '94, Lillehammer; Nos. 2281, 2293, **MS**2297d, 80th birth anniv of Willy Brandt (German politician); Nos. 2282/3, 2288, 500th anniv (1990) of Thurn and Taxis postal service; Nos. 2284, 2294, **MS**2297e, Marriage of Crown Prince Naruhito of Japan; No. 2286, Marriage of Princess Stephanie of Monaco; Nos. 2287, 2289, 2296, **MS**2297f, "Polska '93" International Stamp Exhibition, Poznan; No. 2295, **MS**2297g, Inauguration of U.S. President William Clinton.

259 Supermarine Spitfire

1993. Aviation Anniversaries. Multicoloured.

2298 50c. Type **259** 75 30
2299 $1 Eckener and airship "Graf Zeppelin" over Egypt, 1931 1·25 90
2300 $1 Blanchard and Pres. Washington with balloon, 1793 1·25 90
2301 $2 De Havilland Mosquito Mk VI 1·90 2·00
2302 $2 Eckener and "Graf Zeppelin" over New York, 1928 1·90 2·00
2303 $3 Eckener and "Graf Zeppelin" over Tokyo, 1929 2·75 3·00
2304 $4 Blanchard's balloon ascending from Walnut St. Prison, Philadelphia 3·00 3·25

MS2305 Three sheets, each 100×70 mm. (a) $6 Hawker Hurricane Mk I. (b) $6 Dr. Hugo Eckener (vert). (c) $6 Blanchard's balloon (vert). Set of 3 sheets 12·00 14·00

ANNIVERSARIES: Nos. 2298, 2301, **MS**2305a, 75th anniv of Royal Air Force; Nos. 2299, 2302/3, **MS**2305b, 125th birth anniv of Hugo Eckener (airship commander); Nos. 2300, 2304, **MS**2305c, Bicentenary of first airmail flight.

No. 2303 is inscr "Toyko" in error.

260 First Ford Car, Model "T" and "V8"

1993. Centenaries of Henry Ford's First Petrol Engine (Nos. 2306, 2309) and Karl Benz's First Four-wheeled car (others). Multicoloured.

2306 $1 Type **260** 90 60
2307 $2 Benz racing car, 1908, "Stuttgart" and "540K" 1·75 1·75
2308 $3 Benz car, 1894, "Tourenwagen" and "Blitzen Benz" 2·25 2·75
2309 $4 Ford "Runabout", 1903, Model "T" Tourer and saloon, 1935 2·50 3·00

MS2310 Two sheets, each 100×70 mm. (a) $6 Henry Ford. (b) $6 Karl Benz. Set of 2 sheets 9·00 10·00

261 Pope John Paul II and Denver Skyline

1993. Papal Visit to Denver, Colorado, U.S.A.

2311 $1 Type **261** 1·00 80

MS2312 100×70 mm. $6 Pope and clock tower 4·75 5·50

262 Corvette of 1953

1993. 40th Anniv of Corvette Range of Cars. Multicoloured.

2313 $1 Type **262** 80 1·00
2314 $1 1993 model 80 1·00
2315 $1 1958 model 80 1·00
2316 $1 1960 model 80 1·00
2317 $1 "40" and symbolic chequered flag emblem 80 1·00
2318 $1 1961 model 80 1·00
2319 $1 1963 model 80 1·00
2320 $1 1968 model 80 1·00
2321 $1 1973 model 80 1·00
2322 $1 1975 model 80 1·00
2323 $1 1982 model 80 1·00
2324 $1 1984 model 80 1·00

263 Gedung Shrine, 1920

1993. Asian International Stamp Exhibitions. Multicoloured. As T 263. (a) "Indopex '93", Surabaya, Indonesia. Horiz designs.

2325-54 5, 10, 20, 45, 55, 75c., $1 ×2, $1.50 ×18, $2, $4, $5 ×2. Set of 30 23·00 25·00

MS2355 Three sheets. (a) 105×135 mm. $6 Relief of Sudamala epic, Mt. Lawu. (b) 105×135 mm. $6 Plaque from Banyumas, Java. (c) 135×105 mm. $6 Panel from Ramayana reliefs (vert). Set of 3 sheets 11·00 13·00

Nos. 2325/32 and 2351/4 show Indonesian scenes, Nos. 2333/50 masks (Nos. 2333/8) or paintings (Nos. 2339/50).

(b) "Taipei '93", Taiwan. Horiz designs.

2356-85 5, 10, 20, 45, 55, 75c., $1×2, $1.50×18, $2, $4, $5×2 Set of 30 23·00 25·00

MS2386 Three sheets, each 135×105 mm. (a) $6 Two Stone Guardians, Longmen Caves, Henan. (b) $6 Stone guardian, Longmen Caves, Henan (vert). (c) $6 Giant Buddha, Yungung Caves (vert). Set of 3 sheets 11·00 13·00

Nos. 2356/63 and 2382/5 show Chinese scenes, Nos. 2364/81 kites. (Nos. 2364/9) or paintings (Nos. 2370/81).

(c) "Bangkok '93", Thailand. Vert (5, 55c., $2, $4) or horiz (others).

2387-2416 5, 10, 20, 45, 55, 75c., $1×2, $1.50×18, $2, $4, $5×2 Set of 30 23·00 25·00

MS2417 Three sheets, each 105×135 mm. (a) $6 Masked dancer. (b) $6 Standing Buddha, Hua Hin (vert). (c) $6 Carved roof boss, Dusit Mahaprasad (vert). Set of 3 sheets 11·00 13·00

Nos. 2387/4 and 2413/16 show Thai scenes, Nos. 2395/2412 murals from Buddhaisawan Chapel (Nos. 2395/2400), paintings (Nos. 2401/6) or sculptures (Nos. 2407/12).

264 Players from St. Vincent and Mexico

1993. Qualifying Rounds for World Cup Football Championship, U.S.A. Multicoloured.

2418 5c. Type **264** 15 20
2419 10c. Honduras match 15 15
2420 65c. Costa Rica match 55 35
2421 $5 St. Vincent goalkeeper 3·25 4·75

265 Fish Delivery Van

1993. Japanese Aid for Fishing Industry. Multicoloured.

2422 10c. Type **265** 20 10
2423 50c. Fish aggregation device (vert) 45 30
2424 75c. Game fishing launch 60 50
2425 $5 Fish market 3·25 4·75

1993. Famous Baseball Players (7th issue). As T 247. Multicoloured.

2426 $2 Reggie Jackson 1·10 1·25

265a "Adoration of the Magi" (detail) (Durer)

1993. Christmas. Religious Paintings. Black, yellow and red (Nos. 2427/9, 2434) or multicoloured (others).

2427 10c. Type **265a** 20 10
2428 35c. "Adoration of the Magi" (different detail) (Durer) 40 20
2429 40c. "Adoration of the Magi" (different detail) (Durer) 45 25
2430 50c. "Holy Family with Saint Francis" (detail) (Rubens) 55 30
2431 55c. "Adoration of the Shepherds" (detail) (Rubens) 55 30
2432 65c. "Adoration of the Shepherds" (different detail) (Rubens) 65 40
2433 $1 "Holy Family" (Rubens) 90 90
2434 $5 "Adoration of the Magi" (different detail) (Durer) 2·50 4·50

MS2435 Two sheets, each 103×127 mm. (a) $6 "Adoration of the Magi" (different detail) (Dürer) (horiz). (b) $6 "Holy Family with Sts. Elizabeth and John" (detail) (Rubens). Set of 2 sheets 8·00 9·00

267 Barbra Streisand

1993. Barbra Streisand's Grand Garden Concert.

2436 **267** $2 multicoloured 1·40 1·40

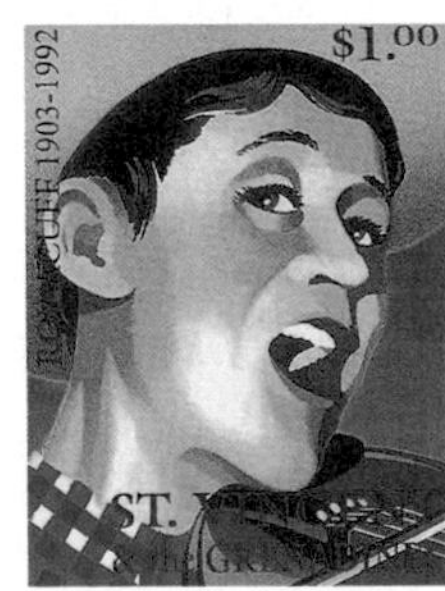

268 Roy Acuff

1994. Legends of Country Music. Multicoloured.

2437 $1 Type **268** 65 75
2438 $1 Patsy Cline in pink shirt 65 75
2439 $1 Jim Reeves in dinner jacket 65 75
2440 $1 Hank Williams in brown jacket 65 75
2441 $1 Hank Williams in purple jacket 65 75
2442 $1 Roy Acuff with microphone 65 75
2443 $1 Patsy Cline wearing white scarf 65 75
2444 $1 Jim Reeves with microphone 65 75
2445 $1 Jim Reeves in orange jacket 65 75
2446 $1 Patsy Cline with microphone 65 65
2447 $1 Hank Williams in grey jacket 65 75
2448 $1 Roy Acuff in grey jacket 65 75

269 Mobile Library

1994. Centenary of Library Service. Multicoloured.

2449 5c. Type **269** 10 20
2450 10c. Old Public Library building 10 10
2451 $1 Family reading 65 85
2452 $1 Line of books joining youth and old man 65 85

270 Woman planting Breadfruit

1994. Bicent of Introduction of Breadfruit. Mult.

2453	10c. Type **270**	15	10
2454	45c. Captain Bligh with bread-fruit plant	75	30
2455	65c. Slice of breadfruit	50	40
2456	$5 Breadfruit growing on branch	3·25	4·75

271 Family Picnic

1994. Int Year of the Family (1st issue). Mult.

2457	10c. Type **271**	15	10
2458	50c. Family in church	40	30
2459	65c. Working in the garden	50	35
2460	75c. Jogging	55	55
2461	$1 Family group (vert)	70	70
2462	$2 On the beach	1·40	1·75

See also No. 2836.

271a Hong Kong 1992 $2.30 Olympic Games stamp and "Hong Kong Harbour in 19th Century"

1994. "Hong Kong '94" International Stamp Exhibition (1st issue). Multicoloured.

2463	40c. Type **271a**	35	50
2464	40c. St. Vincent 1991 $3.50 Scouts Jamboree stamp and "Hong Kong Harbour in 19th Century"	35	50

Nos. 2463/4 were printed together, se-tenant, forming the complete painting.

See also Nos. 2465/94 and 2495/500.

271b Bowl with Bamboo and Sparrows

1994. "Hong Kong '94" International Stamp Exhibition (2nd issue). As T 271b. Multicoloured.

2465-2494	40c.×12, 45c.×12, 50c.×6 Set of 30	7·50	8·50

Nos. 2465/94 were printed as five se-tenant sheetlets, each of six different designs, depicting Ching porcelain (40c.), dragon boat races (40c.), seed-stitch purses (45c.), junks (45c.) and Qing ceramic figures (vert designs) (50c.).

272 Bird on a Flowering Spray Plate, Qianlong

1994. "Hong Kong '94" International Stamp Exhibition (3rd issue). Multicoloured.

2495	50c. Type **272**	75	75
2496	50c. Large decorated dish, Kangxi	75	75
2497	50c. Cocks on rocky ground plate, Yongzheng	75	75
2498	50c. Green decorated dish, Yuan	75	75
2499	50c. Porcelain pug dog	75	75
2500	50c. Dish decorated with Dutch ship, Qianlong	75	75

MS2501 Two sheets, each 126×95 mm. (a) $2 Dr. Sun Yat-sen. (b) $2 Chiang Kai-shek. Set of 2 sheets — 3·00 — 3·50

No. 2497 is incorrectly inscribed "Cocks on a Rocky Groung".

273 Blue Flasher

1994. Butterflies. Multicoloured.

2502	50c. Type **273**	60	55
2503	50c. Tiger swallowtail	60	55
2504	50c. Lustrous copper	60	55
2505	50c. Tailed copper	60	55
2506	50c. Blue copper	60	55
2507	50c. Ruddy copper	60	55
2508	50c. Viceroy	60	55
2509	50c. California sister	60	55
2510	50c. Mourning cloak	60	55
2511	50c. Red passion-flower	60	55
2512	50c. Small flambeau	60	55
2513	50c. Blue wave	60	55
2514	50c. Chiricahua metalmark	60	55
2515	50c. Monarch	60	55
2516	50c. Anise swallowtail	60	55
2517	50c. Buckeye	60	55

274 Antonio Cabrini

1994. Juventus Football Club (Italy) Commemoration. Past and present players. Multicoloured.

2518	$1 Type **274**	1·00	90
2519	$1 Michel Platini and Roberto Baggio	1·00	90
2520	$1 Roberto Bettega	1·00	90
2521	$1 Gaetano Scirea	1·00	90
2522	$1 Jurgen Kohler	1·00	90
2523	$1 Marco Tardelli	1·00	90
2524	$1 Paolo Rossi	1·00	90
2525	$1 Giuseppe Furino	1·00	90
2526	$1 Dino Zoff	1·00	90
2527	$1 Franco Causio	1·00	90
2528	$1 Claudio Gentile	1·00	90

MS2529 100×70 mm. $6 U.E.F.A. Cup, Cup Winners Cup and European Cup trophies (all won by Juventus) (horiz) — 4·25 — 5·00

275 "Epidendrum ibaguense"

1994. Orchids. Multicoloured.

2530	10c. Type **275**	50	30
2531	25c. "Ionopsis utricularioides"	60	30
2532	50c. "Brassavola cucullata"	75	50
2533	65c. "Enclyclia cochleata"	90	60
2534	$1 "Liparis nervosa"	1·00	75
2535	$2 "Vanilla phaeantha"	1·60	1·75
2536	$4 "Elleanthus cephalotus"	2·50	3·25
2537	$5 "Isochilus linearis"	2·50	3·25

MS2538 Two sheets, each 100×70 mm. (a) $6 "Rodriguezia lanceolata". (b) $6 "Eulophia alta". Set of 2 sheets — 8·00 — 9·00

276 Dimorphodon

1994. Prehistoric Animals (1st series). Multicoloured.

2539	75c. Type **276**	60	65
2540	75c. Camarasaurus	60	65
2541	75c. Spinosaurus	60	65
2542	75c. Allosaurus	60	65
2543	75c. Rhamphorhynchus	60	65
2544	75c. Pteranodon and body of Allosaurus	60	65
2545	75c. Eudimorphodon	60	65
2546	75c. Ornithomimus	60	60
2547	75c. Protoavis	60	60
2548	75c. Pteranodon	60	65
2549	75c. Quetzalcoatlus	60	65
2550	75c. Lesothosaurus	60	65
2551	75c. Heterodontosaurus	60	65
2552	75c. Archaeopteryx	60	65
2553	75c. Cearadactylus	60	65
2554	75c. Anchisaurus	60	65

Nos. 2539/46 and 2547/54 respectively were printed together, se-tenant, forming composite designs.

See also Nos. 2556/604.

277 Triceratops

1994. "Hong Kong '94" International Stamp Exhibition (4th issue). Prehistoric Animals. Sheet 206×121 mm, containing T 277 and similar multicoloured designs.

MS2555 $1.50, Type **277**; $1.50, Tyrannosaurus rex (vert); $1.50, Diplodocus; $1.50, Stegosaurus (vert) — 4·75 — 5·00

278 Albertosaurus

1994. Prehistoric Animals (2nd series). As T 278. Multicoloured.

2556-2603	75c. ×48. Set of 48	20·00	23·00

MS2604 Four sheets, each 115×86 mm. (a) $6 Tyrannosaurus rex. (b) $6 Triceratops. (c) $6 Pteranodon and Diplodocus carnegii. (d) $6 Styracosaurus (vert). Set of 4 sheets — 14·00 — 15·00

Nos. 2556/2603 were printed together, se-tenant, as four sheetlets of 12 with Nos. 2556/79 being horizontal and Nos. 2580/2603 vertical. The species depicted are Albertosaurus, Chasmosaurus, Brachiosaurus, Coelophysis, Deinonychus, Anatosaurus, Iguanodon, Baryonyx, Steneosaurus, Nanotyrannus, Camptosaurus, Camarasaurus, Hesperonis, Mesosaurus, Plesiosaurus Doli-chorhynchops, Squalicorax, Tylosaurus, Plesiosoar, Stenopterygius Ichthyosaurus, Steneosaurus, Eurhinosaurus Longirostris, Cryptocleidus Oxoniensis, Caturus, Protostega, Dimorphodon, Pterodactylus, Rhamphorhynchus, Pteranodon, Gallimimus, Stegosaurus, Acanthopholis, Trach-odon, Thecodonts, Ankylosaurus, Compsognathus, Protoceratops, Quetzalcoatlus, Diplodocus, Spinosaurus, Apatosaurus, Ornitholestes, Lesothosaurus, Trachodon, Protoavis, Oviraptor, Coelophysis, Ornitholestes and Archaeopteryx.

279 Mickey Mouse as Pilot

1994. 65th Anniv (1993) of Mickey Mouse. Walt Disney cartoon characters. Multicoloured.

2605	5c. Type **279**	30	30
2606	10c. Mickey in Foreign Legion	30	30
2607	15c. Mickey as frontiersman	40	40
2608	20c. Mickey, Goofy and Donald Duck	40	40
2609	35c. Horace Horsecollar and Clarabelle Cow	50	50
2610	50c. Minnie Mouse, Frankie and Figuro	60	60
2611	75c. Donald and Pluto	70	70
2612	80c. Mickey holding balloons	75	75
2613	85c. Daisy Duck and Minnie	75	75
2614	95c. Minnie	80	80
2615	$1 Mickey in red trousers	80	80
2616	$1.50 Mickey raising hat	1·40	1·40
2617	$2 Mickey with hands in pockets	1·60	1·60
2618	$3 Mickey and Minnie	2·50	2·50
2619	$4 Mickey with birthday cake	2·75	2·75
2620	$5 Mickey as Uncle Sam	2·75	2·75

MS2621 Four sheets. (a) 102×127 mm. $6 Pluto looking at portrait of Mickey. (b) 127×102 mm. $6 Mickey and camera (horiz). (c) 127×102 mm. $6 Minnie disco dancing (horiz). P 14×13½. (d) 127×102 mm. $6 Donald with Mickey's baby photo (horiz). Set of 4 sheets — 18·00 — 18·00

280 Argentine Team

1994. World Cup Football Championship, U.S.A. Competing teams. Multicoloured.

2622	50c. Type **280**	45	45
2623	50c. Belgium	45	45
2624	50c. Bolivia	45	45
2625	50c. Brazil	45	45
2626	50c. Bulgaria	45	45
2627	50c. Cameroun	45	45
2628	50c. Colombia	45	45
2629	50c. Germany	45	45
2630	50c. Greece	45	45
2631	50c. Netherlands	45	45
2632	50c. Republic of Ireland	45	45
2633	50c. Italy	45	45
2634	50c. Mexico	45	45
2635	50c. Morocco	45	45
2636	50c. Nigeria	40	40
2637	50c. Norway	45	45
2638	50c. Rumania	45	45
2639	50c. Russia	45	45
2640	50c. Saudi Arabia	45	45
2641	50c. South Korea	45	45
2642	50c. Spain	45	45
2643	50c. Sweden	45	45
2644	50c. Switzerland	45	45
2645	50c. U.S.A.	45	45

281 Marilyn Monroe

1994. Marilyn Monroe (American film star) Commemoration. Different portraits. Multicoloured.

2646	$1 Type **281**	75	75
2647	$1 Asleep	75	75
2648	$1 With long hair style and pendulum earrings	75	75
2649	$1 Wearing striped sweater	75	75
2650	$1 With gloved hand to face	75	75
2651	$1 With bare hand to face	75	75
2652	$1 In black and white dress	75	75
2653	$1 In sequined evening dress	75	75
2654	$1 With short hair and no earrings	75	75

282 Capt. Jean-Luc Picard

1994. "Star Trek – The Next Generation" (T.V. series). Multicoloured.

2655	$2 Type **282**	1·25	1·25
2656	$2 Commander William Riker	1·25	1·25

2657	$2 Lt.-Commander Data	1·25	1·25
2658	$2 Lt. Worf	1·25	1·25
2659	$2 Crew members	1·25	1·25
2660	$2 Dr. Beverley Crusher	1·25	1·25
2661	$2 Lt. Worf and Lt. Tasha Yar	1·25	1·25
2662	$2 Q wearing hat	1·25	1·25
2663	$2 Counsellor Deanna Troi	1·25	1·25
MS2664	83×101 mm. $10 As No. 2659 (59×40 mm)	6·50	7·00

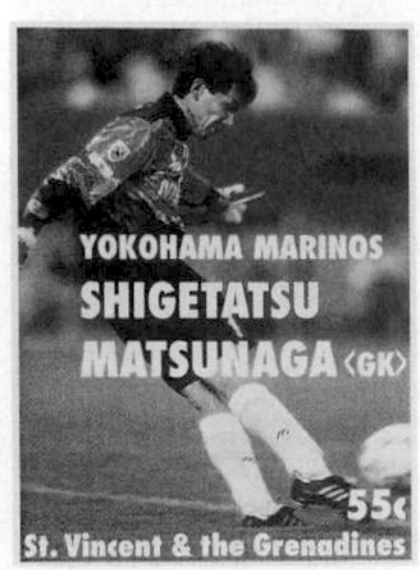

283 Shigetatsu Matsunaga (Yokohama Marinos)

284 Jef United Team

1994. Japanese Professional Football League. (a) As T 283 showing individual players and league emblem. Multicoloured.

2665-2676	55c. ×8, $1.50 ×4. Set of 12	8·50	9·00

DESIGNS: 55c. Masami Ihara (Yokohama Marinos); Shunzoh Ohno (Kashima Antlers); Luiz Carlos Pereira (Verdy Kawasaki); Tetsuji Hashiratani (Verdy Kawasaki); Carlos Alberto Souza dos Santos (Kashima Antlers); Yasuto Honda (Kashima Antlers); Kazuyoshi Miura (Verdy Kawasaki); $1.50, League emblem; Takumi Horiike (Shimizu S-Pulse); Rui Ramos (Verdy Kawasaki); Ramon Angel Diaz (Yokohama Marinos).

(b) As T 284 showing teams.

2677-2688	55c. ×8, $1.50 ×4. Set of 12	10·00	10·00

DESIGNS: 55c. Verdy Yomiuri; Yokohama Marinos; A. S. Flugels; Bellmare; Shimizu S-Pulse; Jubilo Iwata; Panasonic Gamba Osaka; $1.50, Kashima Antlers; Red Diamonds; Nagoya Grampus Eight; Sanfrecce Hiroshima.

(c) As T 284 showing players and teams.

2689-2694	55c.×3, $1.50×2, $3 A. S. Flugels	5·00	5·00
2695-2700	55c.×3, $1.50×2, $3 Bellmare	5·00	5·00
2701-2706	55c.×3, $1.50×2, $3 Panasonic Gamba Osaka	5·00	5·00
2707-2712	55c.×3, $1.50×2, $3 Jef United	5·00	5·00
2713-2718	55c.×3, $1.50×2, $3 Jubilo Iwata	5·00	5·00
2719-2724	55c.×3, $1.50×2, $3 Kashima Antlers	5·00	5·00
2725-2730	55c.×3, $1.50×2, $3 Nagoya Grampus Eight	5·00	5·00
2731-2736	55c.×3, $1.50×2, $3 Sanfrecce Hiroshima	5·00	5·00
2737-2742	55c.×3, $1.50×2, $3 Shimizu S-Pulse	5·00	5·00
2743-2748	55c.×3, $1.50×2, $3 Red Diamonds	5·00	5·00
2749-2754	55c.×3, $1.50×2, $3 Verdy Kawasaki	5·00	5·00
2755-2760	55c.×3, $1.50×2, $3 Yokohama Marinos	5·00	5·00

Prices quoted are for se-tenant sheetlets of six stamps.

284a Fred Whipple and Halley's Comet

1994. 25th Anniv of First Manned Moon Landing. Multicoloured.

2761	$1 Type **284a**	95	95
2762	$1 Robert Gilruth and "Gemini 12"	95	95
2763	$1 George Mueller and space walk from "Gemini 4"	95	95
2764	$1 Charles Berry and Johnsville Centrifuge	95	95
2765	$1 Christopher Kraft and "Apollo 4"	95	95
2766	$1 James van Allen and "Explorer 1"	95	95
2767	$1 Robert Goddard and Goddard liquid-fuel rocket	95	95
2768	$1 James Webb and "Spirit of 76" flight	95	95
2769	$1 Rocco Patrone and "Apollo 8"	95	95
2770	$1 Walter Dornberger and German rocket	95	95
2771	$1 Alexander Lippisch and Messerschmitt ME 163B Komet (airplane)	95	95
2772	$1 Kurt Debus and "A4b" rocket	95	95
2773	$1 Hermann Oberth and projected spaceship	95	95
2774	$1 Hanna Reitsch and "Reichenberg" flying bomb	95	95
2775	$1 Ernst Stuhlinger and "Explorer 1"	95	95
2776	$1 Werner von Braun and rocket-powered Heinkel He 112	95	95
2777	$1 Arthur Rudolph and rocket motor	95	95
2778	$1 Willy Ley and rocket airplane	95	95
MS2779	Two sheets, each 131×109 mm. (a) $6 Eberhardt Rees and German rocket (50×37 mm). (b) $6 Hogler Toftoy (50×37 mm)	8·00	9·00

284b Supply Convoy

1994. 50th Anniv of D-Day. Multicoloured.

2780	40c. Type **284b**	75	25
2781	$5 Unloading beached supply ship	3·00	3·75
MS2782	106×76 mm. $6 Liberty ship	3·50	4·25

285 Yorkshire Terrier Bitch

1994. Chinese New Year ("Year of the Dog"). Multicoloured.

2783	10c. Type **285**	60	35
2784	25c. Yorkshire terrier dog	65	30
2785	50c. Golden retriever	75	70
2786	50c. Pomeranian	75	70
2787	50c. English springer spaniel	75	70
2788	50c. Bearded collie	75	70
2789	50c. Irish wolfhound	75	70
2790	50c. Pekingese	75	70
2791	50c. Irish setter	75	70
2792	50c. Old English sheepdog	75	70
2793	50c. Basset hound	75	70
2794	50c. Cavalier King Charles spaniel	75	70
2795	50c. Kleiner Munsterlander	75	70
2796	50c. Shetland sheepdog	75	70
2797	50c. Dachshund	75	70
2798	65c. Bernese mountain dog	1·00	65
2799	$1 Vorstehhund	1·50	80
2800	$2 Tibetan terrier	2·25	1·75
2801	$4 West Highland terrier	3·25	3·25
2802	$5 Shih tzu	3·50	3·50
MS2803	Two sheets, each 100×100 mm. (a) $6 Afghan hound with puppy. (b) $6 German shepherd. Set of 2 sheets	6·50	7·00

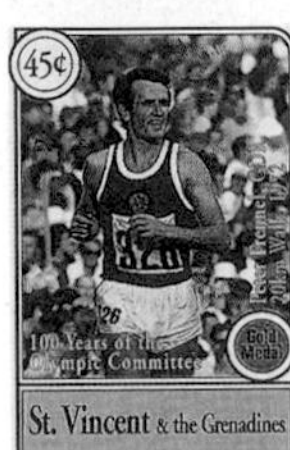

285a Peter Fennel (Germany) (20 km walk, 1972)

1994. Centenary of International Olympic Committee. Gold Medal Winners.

2804	45c. Type **285a**	60	25
2805	50c. Kijung Son (Japan) (marathon), 1936 (vert)	65	30
2806	75c. Jesse Owens (U.S.A.) (100 and 200 m), 1936 (vert)	90	80
2807	$1 Greg Louganis (U.S.A.) (diving), 1984 and 1988 (vert)	1·00	1·10
MS2808	106×76 mm. 86 Katja Seizinger (Germany) (women's downhill skiing), 1944 (horiz)	3·50	4·00

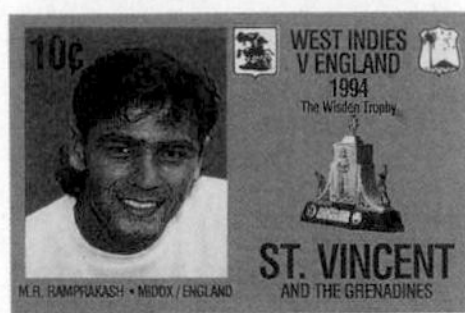

286 Mark Ramprakash (England) and Wisden Trophy

1994. Centenary of First English Cricket Tour to the West Indies (1995). Multicoloured.

2809	10c. Type **286**	45	20
2810	30c. Phil Simmonds (West Indies) and Wisden Trophy	65	25
2811	$2 Garfield Sobers (West Indies) (vert)	1·75	2·00
MS2812	76×96 mm. $3 First English touring team, 1895 (black and brown)	2·25	2·75

286a Oryon Waterfall

1994. "Philakorea '94" International Stamp Exhibition, Seoul. Multicoloured.

2813	10c. Type **286a**	30	20
2814	45c. Indoor sports stadium, Pyongyang (horiz)	40	25
2815	50c. Illuminated character with house at bottom right	40	50
2816	50c. Illuminated character with red dots in centre	40	50
2817	50c. Illuminated character with animal at right	40	50
2818	50c. Illuminated character with flowers at bottom right	40	50
2819	50c. Illuminated character with dragon at left	40	50
2820	50c. Illuminated character with house at top	40	50
2821	50c. Illuminated character with dragon at top	40	50
2822	50c. Illuminated character with sun at top	40	50
2823	50c. Fish and character	40	50
2824	50c. Two pheasants and character	40	50
2825	50c. Plant and cabinet	40	50
2826	50c. Vases and cabinet	40	50
2827	50c. Books on decorated cabinet	40	50
2828	50c. Pheasant, decorated cabinet and vase	40	50
2829	50c. Pheasant and lamp on table	40	50
2830	50c. Cabinet, vase and table	40	50
2831	65c. Pombong, Chonhwadae	50	50
2832	75c. Uisangdae, Naksansa	55	60
2833	$1 Buddha of the Sokkuram Grotto, Kyangju (horiz)	60	70
2834	$2 Moksogwon (horiz)	1·10	1·40
MS2835	Two sheets. (a) 70×100 mm. $4 Chongdong Mirukbul (vert). (b) 100×70 mm. Tiger hunting scene (embroidery). Set of 2 sheets	4·25	4·75

Nos. 2825/6 and 2830 are inscr "Bookshlef" in error.

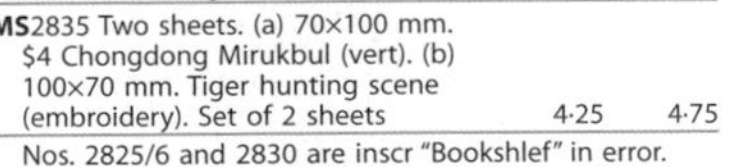

287 St. Vincent Family

1994. International Year of the Family (2nd issue).

2836	**287**	75c. multicoloured	65	65

288 Sir Shridath Ramphal and Map of Guyana

1994. First Recipients of Order of the Caribbean Community. Multicoloured.

2837	$1 Type **288**	70	50
2838	$2 Derek Walcott and map of St. Lucia	2·75	2·25
2839	$5 William Demas and map of Trinidad (horiz)	3·75	5·00

No. 2838 is inscribed "Wilcott" in error.

289 Twin-engined Airliner, Bequia Airport

1994. 50th Anniv of I.C.A.O. Multicoloured.

2840	10c. Type **289**	40	40
2841	65c. Union Island Airport	80	60
2842	75c. L.I.A.T. 8-100 at E. T. Joshua Airport	85	70
2843	$1 Aircraft and logo	1·00	1·25
2844	$1 Britten Norman Islander at J. F. Mitchell Airport, Bequia	1·00	1·25

290 "The Annunciation"

1994. Christmas. Religious Paintings from Jean de Berry's "Book of Hours". Multicoloured.

2845	10c. Type **290**	25	10
2846	45c. "The Visitation"	60	25
2847	50c. "The Nativity"	65	30
2848	65c. "The Purification of the Virgin" (detail)	80	40
2849	75c. "Presentation of Jesus in the Temple"	90	45
2850	$5 "Flight into Egypt"	4·00	6·00
MS2851	110×126 mm. $6 "Adoration of the Magi" (detail)	4·50	5·50

No. 2847 is inscribed "The Annunciation" in error.

1995. Chinese New Year ("Year of the Pig") (1st issue). Designs as Nos. 2050/8, but with different face values and with Year of the Pig logo.

2852	30c. Type **245**	60	50
2853	30c. Fiddler Pig building house of sticks	60	50
2854	30c. Practical Pig building house of bricks	60	50
2855	30c. The Big Bad Wolf	60	50
2856	30c. Wolf scaring Fiddler and Fifer Pig	60	50
2857	30c. Wolf blowing down straw house	60	50
2858	30c. Wolf in sheep costume	60	50
2859	30c. Wolf blowing down stick house	60	50
2860	30c. Wolf attempting to blow down brick house	60	50
MS2861	Two sheets. (a) 103×128 mm. $3 Original sketch of Practical Pig building house of brick. (b) 128×103 mm. $3 Practical Pig playing piano (vert). Set of 2 sheets	5·50	5·50

See also Nos. 2900/3.

291 Mealy Amazon Parrot

1995. Parrots. Multicoloured.

2862	$1 Type **291**	1·10	90
2863	$1 Nanday conure	1·10	90
2864	$1 Black-headed caique	1·10	90
2865	$1 Scarlet macaw	1·10	90
2866	$1 Red-masked conure	1·10	90
2867	$1 Blue-headed parrot	1·10	90
2868	$1 Hyacinth macaw	1·10	90
2869	$1 Sun conure	1·10	90
2870	$1 Blue and yellow macaw	1·10	90
MS2871	104×76 mm. $5 White-eared conure (vert)	4·00	4·50

Nos. 2862/70 were printed together, se-tenant, forming a composite design.

292 Snowshoe

1995. Cats. Multicoloured.

2872	$1 Type **292**	1·10	90
2873	$1 Abyssinian	1·10	90
2874	$1 Ocicat	1·10	90
2875	$1 Tiffany	1·10	90
2876	$1 Russian blue	1·10	90
2877	$1 Siamese	1·10	90
2878	$1 Bi-colour	1·10	90
2879	$1 Malayan	1·10	90
2880	$1 Manx	1·10	90
MS2881	104×76 mm. $6 Birman (vert)	4·75	5·50

Nos. 2872/80 were printed together, se-tenant, forming a composite design.

293 Blue-faced Booby ("Masked Booby")

1995. Birds. Multicoloured.

2882	75c. Type **293**	70	60
2883	75c. Pair of blue-faced boobies	70	60
2884	75c. Blue-faced booby preening	70	60
2885	75c. Blue-faced booby stretching	70	60
2886	75c. Great egrets	70	60
2887	75c. Roseate spoonbills	70	60
2888	75c. Ring-billed gull	70	60
2889	75c. Ruddy quail dove	70	60
2890	75c. Royal terns	70	60
2891	75c. Killdeer plover ("Killdeer")	70	60
2892	75c. Osprey	70	60
2893	75c. Magnificent frigate bird	70	60
2894	75c. Blue-faced boobies ("Masked Booby")	70	60
2895	75c. Green-backed heron	70	60
2896	75c. Double-crested cormorants ("Cormorant")	70	60
2897	75c. Brown pelican	70	60
MS2898	Two sheets, each 100×69 mm. (a) $5 Greater flamingo ("Flamingo") (vert). (b) $6 American Purple gallinule ("Purple Gallinule") (vert). Set of 2 sheets	9·00	10·00

Nos. 2886/97 were printed together, se-tenant, forming a composite design.

294 Churchill, Roosevelt and Stalin at Yalta Conference

1995. 50th Anniv of V.E. Day.

2899	**294**	$1 multicoloured	1·25	1·00

295 Pig

1995. Chinese New Year ("Year of the Pig") (2nd issue). Multicoloured, central panel in colours indicated.

2900	75c. Type **295** (green)	55	65
2901	75c. Pig (brown)	55	65
2902	75c. Pig (red)	55	65
MS2903	71×101 mm. $2 Two pigs (horiz)	1·25	1·50

296 National Flag and Globe

1995. 18th World Scout Jamboree, Netherlands. Multicoloured.

2904	$1 Type **296**	70	50
2905	$4 Lord Baden-Powell	2·25	2·75
2906	$5 Handshake	2·50	3·00
MS2907	Two sheets, each 81×112 mm. (a) $6 Scout greeting. (b) $6 Scout salute. Set of 2 sheets	7·00	8·50

296a Tank of U.S. First Army

1995. 50th Anniv of End of Second World War in Europe. Multicoloured.

2908	$2 Type **296a**	1·25	1·25
2909	$2 V2 rocket	1·25	1·25
2910	$2 Consolidated B-24 Liberator bombers	1·25	1·25
2911	$2 French troops advancing to Strasbourg	1·25	1·25
2912	$2 Gloster G.41 Meteor fighter	1·25	1·25
2913	$2 Berlin on fire	1·25	1·25
2914	$2 Soviet tanks in Berlin	1·25	1·25
2915	$2 "Chicago Daily Tribune" headline	1·25	1·25
MS2916	107×77 mm. $6 Sortie markings on aircraft (57×42½)	3·50	4·00

No. 2909 is inscribed "Y2" in error.

297 Globe and Peace Dove

1995. 50th Anniv of United Nations. Multicoloured.

2917	$2 Type **297**	1·10	1·40
2918	$2 Liberty	1·10	1·40
2919	$2 U.N. Building, New York, and peace dove	1·10	1·40
MS2920	71×107 mm. $6 Asian child	2·75	3·50

Nos. 2917/19 were printed together, se-tenant, forming a composite design.

No. **MS**2920 is inscribed "1945–1955" in error.

298 Women preparing Food

1995. 50th Anniv of F.A.O. Multicoloured.

2921	$2 Type **298**	1·10	1·40
2922	$2 Woman mixing food	1·10	1·40
2923	$2 Harvesting grain	1·10	1·40
MS2924	76×106 mm. 76×106 mm. $6 Baby and logo	2·75	3·50

Nos. 2921/3 were printed together, se-tenant, forming a composite design.

No. **MS**2924 is inscribed "1945–1955" in error.

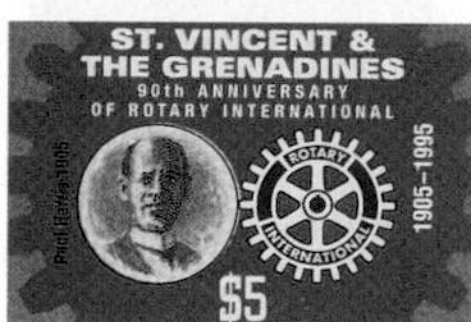

299 Paul Harris (founder) and Logo

1995. 90th Anniv of Rotary International.

2925	**299**	$5 multicoloured	2·50	3·25
MS2926		113×79 mm. $6 National flag and logo	2·75	3·50

299a Queen Elizabeth the Queen Mother (pastel drawing)

1995. 95th Birthday of Queen Elizabeth the Queen Mother.

2927	**299a**	$1.50 brown, light brown and black	2·00	1·50
2928	-	$1.50 multicoloured	2·00	1·50
2929	-	$1.50 multicoloured	2·00	1·50
2930	-	$1.50 multicoloured	2·00	1·50
MS2931		102×127 mm. $6 multicoloured	4·75	4·75

DESIGNS: No. 2928, Wearing blue hat; 2929, At desk (oil painting); 2930, Wearing mauve dress; No. **MS**2931, wearing yellow dress.

1995. 50th Anniv of End of Second World War in the Pacific. As T 296a. Multicoloured.

2932	$2 Douglas Devastator torpedo bomber	1·25	1·25
2933	$2 Doolittle's North American B-25 Mitchell "Ruptured Duck"	1·25	1·25
2934	$2 Curtiss SB2C Helldiver bomber	1·25	1·25
2935	$2 U.S.S. "Yorktown" (aircraft carrier)	1·25	1·25
2936	$2 U.S.S. "Wasp" (aircraft carrier)	1·25	1·25
2937	$2 U.S.S. "Lexington" (aircraft carrier) sinking	1·25	1·25
MS2938	107×77 mm. $6 American aircraft carriers	3·75	4·50

300 Head of Humpback Whale

1995. Marine Life. Multicoloured.

2939	90c. Type **300**	70	70
2940	90c. Green turtles	70	70
2941	90c. Bottlenose dolphin	70	70
2942	90c. Monk seals	70	70
2943	90c. Krill	70	70
2944	90c. Blue sharks	70	70
2945	90c. Porkfish	70	70
2946	90c. Reef butterflyfish	70	70
2947	90c. Shipwreck	70	70
2948	$1 Beaugregory (fish) (horiz)	70	70

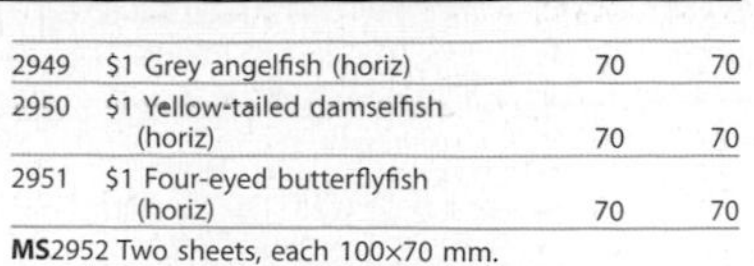

2949	$1 Grey angelfish (horiz)	70	70
2950	$1 Yellow-tailed damselfish (horiz)	70	70
2951	$1 Four-eyed butterflyfish (horiz)	70	70
MS2952	Two sheets, each 100×70 mm. (a) $6 Sea anemones. (b) $6 "Physalia physalis" (jellyfish). Set of 2 sheets	7·00	7·50

Nos. 2939/47 were printed together, se-tenant, forming a composite design.

301 Symbolic Disabled Athlete

1995. Paralympic Games '95, Connecticut.

2953	**301**	$1 yellow, blue and black	1·00	1·00

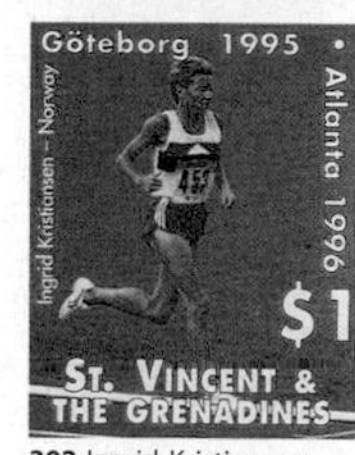

302 Ingrid Kristiansen

1995. World Athletic Championships, Gothenburg. Norwegian Athletes. Multicoloured.

2954	$1 Type **302**	70	70
2955	$1 Trine Hattestad	70	70
2956	$1 Grete Waitz	70	70
2957	$1 Vebjorn Rodal	70	70
2958	$1 Geir Moen	70	70
2959	$1 Steinar Hoen (horiz)	70	70

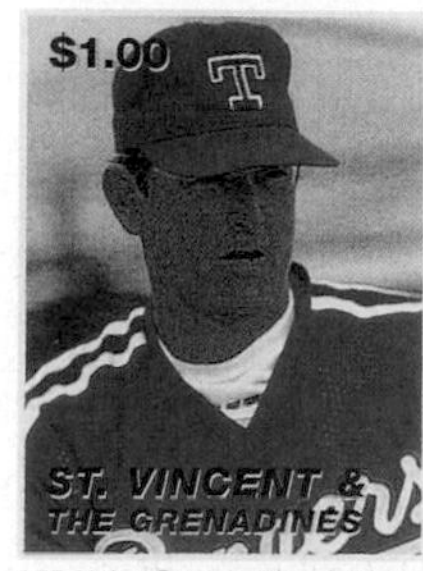

303 Nolan Ryan in Blue Jersey

1995. Retirement of Nolan Ryan (baseball player) (1993). Multicoloured.

2960	$1 Type **303**	80	80
2961	$1 With glove	80	80
2962	$1 In white jersey	80	80
2963	$1 Making pitch from left	80	80
2964	$1 Texas Rangers "All Star Game" emblem	80	80
2965	$1 Making pitch from right	80	80
2966	$1 Bleeding from blow to mouth	80	80
2967	$1 Preparing to pitch	80	80
2968	$1 Waving cap	80	80
2969	$1 Wearing "NY" cap	80	80
2970	$1 Wearing stetson with dog	80	80
2971	$1 Wearing "T" cap	80	80
2972	$1 Throwing American football	80	80
2973	$1 Nolan Ryan Foundation emblem	80	80
2974	$1 With son	80	80
2975	$1 Laughing	80	80
2976	$1 With family	80	80
2977	$1 Wearing "H" cap	80	80
MS2978	146×101 mm. $6 After final game for Texas Rangers	3·00	3·50

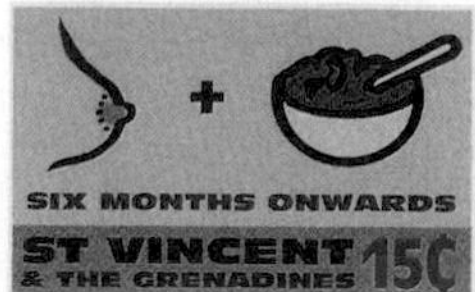

304 Breast and Bowl of Baby Food

1995. "Baby Friendly" Campaign. Multicoloured.

2979	15c. Type **304**	40	15

2980 20c. Hands squeezing milk into bowl (vert) 40 15
2981 90c. Breast-feeding (vert) 1·00 45
2982 $5 Breast-feeding emblem (vert) 3·50 4·50

305 Aerial View of Leeward Coastal Road

1995. 25th Anniv of Caribbean Development Bank. Multicoloured.

2983 10c. Type **305** 25 25
2984 15c. Feeder roads project 30 25
2985 25c. "Anthurium andraeanum" (flower) 30 25
2986 50c. Coconut palm tree (vert) 35 35
2987 65c. Fairhall Housing Scheme 45 45

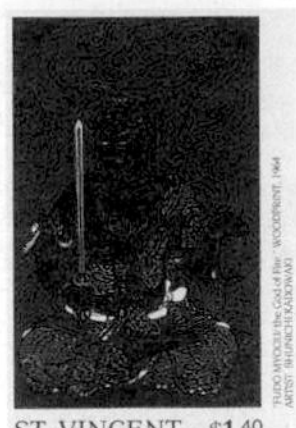

306 "The God of Fire" (woodcut) (Shunichi Kadowaki)

1995. Japanese Art.

2988 **306** $1.40 multicoloured 1·00 1·25

307 Jean Shiley (U.S.A.) (high jump)

1995. Olympic Games, Atlanta (1996) (1st issue). Multicoloured.

2989 $1 Type **307** 75 75
2990 $1 Ruth Fuchs (Germany) (javelin) 75 75
2991 $1 Alessandro Andrei (Italy) (shot put) 75 75
2992 $1 Dorando Pietri (Italy) (marathon) 75 75
2993 $1 Heide Rosendahl (Germany) (long jump) 75 75
2994 $1 Mitsuoki Watanabe (Japan) (gymnastics) 75 75
2995 $1 Yasuhiro Yamashita (Japan) (judo) 75 75
2996 $1 Dick Fosbury (U.S.A.) (high jump) 75 75
2997 $2 Long jumper and dove 1·10 1·10
2998 $2 Hurdler and deer 1·10 1·10
2999 $2 Sprinter and cheetah 1·10 1·10
3000 $2 Marathon runner and tiger 1·10 1·10
3001 $2 Gymnast and dove 1·10 1·10
3002 $2 Rower and blue-winged teal 1·10 1·10
MS3003 Two sheets. (a) 70×100 mm. $5 Magic Johnson (U.S.A.) (basket-ball). (b) 106×76 mm. $5 Swimmers hand (horiz). Set of 2 sheets 7·50 7·50

See also Nos. 3357/3400.

308 Frank Thomas

1995. Famous Baseball Players (8th series). Multicoloured.

3004 $1 Type **308** 60 60
3005 $1 Cal Ripken Jnr wearing "8" jersey and helmet 60 60
3006 $1 Ken Griffey Jnr wearing "S" cap 60 60
3007 $1 Ken Griffey Jnr wearing turquoise-blue jersey 60 60
3008 $1 Frank Thomas in "Sox" cap with bat on shoulder 60 60
3009 $1 Cal Ripken Jnr with ball and glove 60 60
3010 $1 Cal Ripkin Jnr wearing Orioles cap 60 60
3011 $1 Ken Griffey Jnr wearing "Seattle" jersey and helmet 60 60
3012 $1 Frank Thomas wearing "Chicago 35" jersey 60 60

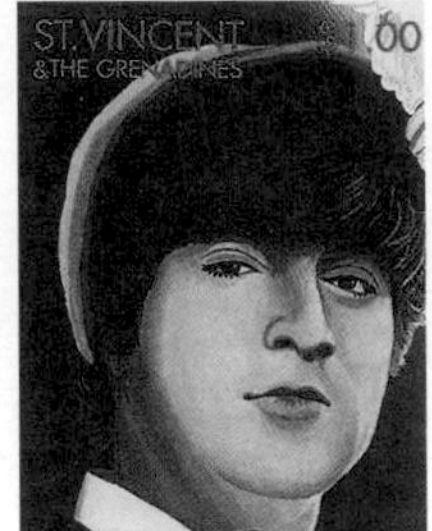

309 John Lennon

1995. Centenary of Cinema. Entertainers. Mult.

Set of 51 28·00 30·00
3013-3021 $1×9 John Lennon (as T **309**) 6·00
3022-3030 $1×9 Elvis Presley 6·00
3031-3036 $1×6 Elvis Presley 4·50
3037-3045 $1×9 Marilyn Monroe (with stairway in centre of sheetlet) 5·00
3046-3054 $1×9 Marilyn Monroe (with superimposed full length portrait) 5·00
3055-3063 $1×9 Marilyn Monroe (design with hand raised in centre of top row) 5·00
MS3064 Four sheets. (a) 110×80 mm. $6 John Lennon. (b) 80×110 mm. $6 Elvis Presley. (c) 80×110 mm. $6 Marilyn Monroe wearing red jacket. (d) 70×100 mm. $6 Marilyn Monroe in black slip. Set of 4 sheets 14·00 14·00

310 Heinrich Boll (1972 Literature)

1995. Centenary of Nobel Prize Trust Fund. Multicoloured.

3065-3112 $1 ×48. Set of 48 32·00 35·00
MS3113 Four sheets, each 74×104 mm. (a) $6 Adolf Windaus (1928 Chemistry). (b) $6 Hideki Yukawa (1949 Physics). (c) $6 Bertha von Suttner (1905 Peace). (d) $6 Karl Landsteiner (1930 Medicine). Set of 4 sheets 16·00 16·00

DESIGNS: No. 3065, Type **310**; 3066, Walther Bothe (1954 Physics); 3067, Richard Kuhn (1938 Chemistry); 3068, Hermann Hesse (1946 Literature); 3069, Knut Hamsun (1920 Literature); 3070, Konrad Lorenz (1973 Medicine); 3071, Thomas Mann (1929 Literature); 3072, Fridtjof Nansen (1922 Peace); 3073, Fritz Pregl (1923 Chemistry); 3074, Christian Lange (1921 Peace); 3075, Otto Loewi (1936 Medicine); 3076, Erwin Schrodinger (1933 Physics); 3077, Giosue Carducci (1906 Literature); 3078, Wladyslaw Reymont (1924 Literature); 3079, Ivan Bunin (1933 Literature); 3080, Pavel Cherenkov (1958 Physics); 3081, Ivan Pavlov (1904 Medicine); 3082, Pyotr Kapitza (1978 Physics); 3083, Lev Landau (1962 Physics); 3084, Daniel Bovet (1957 Medicine); 3085, Henryk Sienkiewicz (1905 Literature); 3086, Aleksandr Prokhorov (1964 Physics); 3087, Julius von Jauregg (1927 Medicine); 3088, Grazia Deledda (1926 Literature); 3089, Bjornstjerne Bjornson (1903 Literature); 3090, Frank Kellogg (1929 Peace); 3091, Gustav Hertz (1925 Physics); 3092, Har Khorana (1968 Medicine); 3093, Kenichi Fukui (1981 Chemistry); 3094, Henry Kissinger (1973 Peace); 3095, Martin Luther King Jr. (1964 Peace); 3096, Odd Hassel (1969 Chemistry); 3097, Polykarp Kusch (1955 Physics); 3098, Ragnar Frisch (1969 Economics); 3099, Willis Lamb Jr. (1955 Physics); 3100, Sigrid Undset (1928 Literature); 3101, Robert Barany (1914 Medicine); 3102, Ernest Walton (1951 Physics); 3103, Alfred Fried (1911 Peace); 3104, James Franck (1925 Physics); 3105, Werner Forssmann (1956 Medicine); 3106, Yasunari Kawabata (1968 Literature); 3107, Wolfgang Pauli (1945 Physics); 3108, Jean-Paul Sartre (1964 Literature); 3109, Aleksandr Solzhenitsyn (1970 Literature); 3110, Hermann Staudinger (1953 Chemistry); 3111, Igor Tamm (1958 Physics); 3112, Samuel Beckett (1969 Literature).

311 ET4-03 Electric Train, Germany

1995. History of Transport. Modern passenger trains (Nos. 3114/19) or classic cars (Nos. 3120/5). Multicoloured.

3114 $1.50 Type **311** 1·25 1·00
3115 $1.50 TGV express train, France 1·25 1·10
3116 $1.50 Class 87 electric locomotive, Great Britain 1·25 1·10
3117 $1.50 Class "Beijing" diesel locomotive, China 1·25 1·10
3118 $1.50 Amtrak turbotrain, U.S.A. 1·25 1·10
3119 $1.50 Class RC4 electric train, Sweden 1·25 1·10
3120 $1.50 Duesenberg Model "J", 1931 1·25 1·10
3121 $1.50 Sleeve-valve Minerva, 1913 1·25 1·10
3122 $1.50 Delage "D.8. SS", 1933 1·25 1·00
3123 $1.50 Bugatti "Royale Coupe De Ville", 1931–32 1·25 1·00
3124 $1.50 Rolls Royce "Phantom I Landauette", 1926 1·25 1·00
3125 $1.50 Mercedes Benz "S236/120/180PS", 1927 1·25 1·10
MS3126 Two sheets, each 105×75 mm. (a) $5 Hispano-Suiza Type "H6B" sports car, 1924 (85×28½ mm). (b) $6 Eurostar train, Great Britain and France (85×28½ mm). Set of 2 sheets 8·00 9·00

Nos. 3120/5 also include the "Singapore '95" International Stamp Exhibition logo.

312 Grey Wolf

1995. Centenary (1992) of Sierra Club (environmental protection society). Multicoloured.

3127 $1 Type **312** 85 75
3128 $1 Grey wolf cub 85 75
3129 $1 Head of grey wolf 85 75
3130 $1 Hawaiian goose 85 75
3131 $1 Pair of Hawaiian geese 85 75
3132 $1 Head of jaguar 85 75
3133 $1 Liontail macaque 85 75
3134 $1 Sand cat kitten 85 75
3135 $1 Three sand cat kittens 85 75
3136 $1 Orang-utan in tree (horiz) 85 75
3137 $1 Orang-utan on ground (horiz) 85 75
3138 $1 Young orang-utan (horiz) 85 75
3139 $1 Jaguar lying down (horiz) 85 75
3140 $1 Head of jaguar (horiz) 85 75
3141 $1 Pair of sand cats (horiz) 85 75
3142 $1 Hawaiian goose (horiz) 85 75
3143 $1 Three liontail macaques (horiz) 85 75
3144 $1 Head of liontail macaque (horiz) 85 75

Nos. 3136/8 are inscribed "Orangutang" in error.

313 River Nile, Egypt

1995. Natural Landmarks. Multicoloured.

3145 $1.10 Type **313** 1·00 85
3146 $1.10 River Yangtze, China 1·00 85
3147 $1.10 Niagara Falls, U.S.A.–Canada border 1·00 85
3148 $1.10 Victoria Falls, Zambia–Zimbabwe border 1·00 85
3149 $1.10 Grand Canyon, U.S.A. 1·00 85
3150 $1.10 Sahara Desert, Algeria 1·00 85
3151 $1.10 Mt. Kilimanjaro, Tanzania 1·00 85
3152 $1.10 River Amazon, Brazil 1·00 85
MS3153 106×76 mm. $6 Haleakala Crater, Hawaii 4·50 4·75

314 Lionel Santa Handcar

1995. Christmas. Antique Disney Toys. Mult.

3154 1c. Type **314** 10 10
3155 2c. Mickey Mouse "choo-choo" 10 10
3156 3c. Minnie Mouse pram 10 10
3157 5c. Mickey Mouse acrobats pull-toy 10 10
3158 10c. Mickey and Pluto clock-work cart 20 10
3159 25c. Mickey Mouse motorcycle 55 10
3160 $3 Lionel Mickey Mouse handcar 3·50 3·75
3161 $5 Casey Jr. Disneyland train 5·50 6·00
MS3162 Two sheets. (a) 127×100 mm. $6 Lionel streamlined locomotive and Mickey Mouse wagon. (b) 100×127 mm. $6 "Silver Link" locomotive and Mickey the Stoker tender. Set of 2 sheets 9·00 10·00

314a Croton

1996. Crotons. Multicoloured.

3162a 10c. Type **314a** 50 20
3162b 15c. *Codiaeum* "prince of monaco" 50 20
3162c 20c. *Codiaeum variagatum* "craigii" 5·00
3162d 40c. *Codiaeum variagatum* "gloriosum" 50 50
3162e 50c. *Croton* "ebureum" (vert) 50 50
3162f 60c. *Croton* "volutum ramshorn" (vert) 50 50
3162g 70c. *Codiaeum variagatum* "narrenii" (vert) 50 50
3162h 90c. *Croton* "undutatum" (vert) 1·00 1·00
3162i $1 *Codiaeum variagatum* "caribbean star" 1·00 1·00
3162j $1.10 *Codiaeum variagatum* "gloriosa" 1·00 1·00
3162k $1.40 *Codiaeum variagatum croton* "katonii" 1·50 1·50
3162l $2 *Codiaeum variagatum* "appleleaf" ("croton") 2·00 2·00
3162m $5 *Codiaeum variagatum tapestry* "croton" 3·00 3·00
3162n €10 *Codiaeum variagatum* "cornutum" 5·00 5·00
3162o $20 *Codiaeum variagatum* "punctatum aureum" 10·00 10·00

315 Symbolic Rat

1996. Chinese New Year ("Year of the Rat").

3163 **315** 75c. black, mauve and green 50 60
3164 - 75c. black, red and green 50 60
3165 - 75c. black, purple and green 50 60
MS3166 100×50 mm. $1 Type **315**; $1 As No. 3164; $1 As No. 3165 1·50 1·60
MS3167 71×102 mm. $2 black, red and green 1·25 1·50

DESIGNS: Nos. 3164/5, Different rats.

316 Spock giving Vulcan Salute

1996. 30th Anniv of "Star Trek" Television Series. Multicoloured.

3168	$1 Type **316**	60	55
3169	$1 Capt. Kirk and Spock dressed as gangsters	60	55
3170	$1 Kirk in front of computer	60	55
3171	$1 Kirk with Tribbles	60	55
3172	$1 Kirk, Spock and Lt. Uhura in front of Time Portal	60	55
3173	$1 Uhura and Lt. Sulu	60	55
3174	$1 Romulan commander and crew	60	55
3175	$1 City and planet	60	55
3176	$1 Khan	60	55
3177	$1 Spock with phaser	60	55
3178	$1 Capt. Kirk	60	55
3179	$1 Lt. Uhura	60	55
3180	$1 Lt. Sulu	60	55
3181	$1 Starship U.S.S. "Enterprise"	50	55
3182	$1 Dr. McCoy	60	55
3183	$1 Chief Engineer Scott	60	55
3184	$1 Kirk, Spock and McCoy	60	55
3185	$1 Chekov	60	55
MS3186	152×107 mm. $6 Spock and Uhura	3·25	3·50

317 Goofy the Stamp Dealer

1996. Occupations (1st series). Walt Disney Cartoon Characters at Work. Multicoloured.

3187-3132	Set of 62	42·00	42·00
3187-3195	10c. ×9 (Type **317**; Supermarket assistant; Car salesman; Florist; Fast food assistant; Street vendor; Gift shop assistant; Hobby shop assistant; Baker)	1·60	
3196-3204	50c. ×9 (Delivery man; Truck driver; Aircraft flight crew; Train crew; Bus driver; Tour guide; Cycle messenger; Tram conductor; Air traffic controller)	5·00	
3205-3213	75c. ×9 (Postal inspector; Traffic policeman; Private detectives; Highway Patrolman; Justice of the Peace; Security guard; Judge and lawyer; Sheriff; Court stenographer)	6·00	
3214-3222	90c. ×9 (Basketball player; Referee; Athletic coach; Ice skater; Golfer and caddy; Sports commentator; Tennis players; Football coach; Racing car driver)	9·00	
3223-3231	95c. ×9 (Paleontologist; Archaeologist; Inventor; Astronaut; Chemist; Engineer; Computer expert; Astronomer; Zoologist)	8·00	
3232-3239	$1.10 ×8 (Classroom teacher; Nursery school teacher; Music teacher; Electronic teacher; School psychologist; School principal; Professor; Graduate (all vert))	8·00	
3240-3248	$1.20 ×9 (Ship builders; Fisherman; Pearl diver; Underwater photographer; Bait and tackle shop owner; Swim suit models; Marine life painter; Life guard; Lighthouse keeper)	9·00	
MS3249	Seven sheets, each 127×102 mm. (a) $6 Ice cream seller. (b) $6 Tug boat captain (vert). (c) $6 Members of Jury (vert). (d) $6 Cheerleaders (vert). (e) $6 Oceanographer. (f) $6 Librarian (vert). (g) $6 Deep sea diver (vert). Set of 7 sheets	35·00	40·00

See also Nos. 3510/56.

317a "Moses striking Rock" (Abraham Bloemaert)

1996. 125th Anniv of Metropolitan Museum of Art, New York. Multicoloured.

3250-3257	75c. ×8 (Type **317a**; "The Last Communion" (Botticelli); "The Musicians" (Caravaggio); "Francesco Sassetti and Son" (Ghirlandaio); "Pepito Costa y Bunells" (Goya); "Saint Andrew" (Martini); "The Nativity" (The Dutch School); "Christ Blessing" (Solario))	4·00	
3258-3266	90c. ×9 ("Madame Cezanne"; "Still Life with Apples and Pears"; "Man in a Straw Hat"; "Still Life with a Ginger Jar"; "Madame Cezanne in a Red Dress"; "Still Life with Crockery"; "Dominique Aubert"; "Still Life with Flowers"; "The Card Players" (all by Cezanne))	4·50	
3267-3275	$1 ×9 ("Bullfight" (Goya); "Portrait of a Man" (Hals); "Mother and Son" (Sully); "Portrait of a Young Man" (Memling); "Matilde Stoughton de Jaudenes" (Stuart); "Josef de Jaudenes y Nebot" (Stuart); "Mont Sainte-Victoire" (Cezanne); "Gardanne" (Cezanne); "Empress Eugenie" (Winterhalter))	4·75	
3276-3284	$1.10 ×9 ("The Dissolute Household" (Steen); "Gerard de Lairesse" (Rembrandt); "Juan de Pareja" (Velazquez); "Curiosity" (Ter Borch); "The Companions of Rinaldo" (Poussin); "Don Gaspar de Guzman" (Velazquez); "Merry Company on a Terrace" (Steen); "Pilate washing Hands" (Rembrandt); "Portrait of a Man" (Van Dyck))	5·00	
MS3285	Four sheets, each 95×70 mm. (a) $6 "Hagar in the Wilderness" (Corot) (81×53 mm). (b) $6 "Two Young Peasant Women" (Pissarro) (81×53 mm). (c) $6 "Young Ladies from the Village" (Courbet) (81×53 mm). (d) $6 "Allegory of the Planets and Continents" (Tiepolo) (81×53 mm). Set of 4 sheets	13·00	15·00

318 Alien Band

319 Yoda

1996. "Star Wars" (film trilogy). Multicoloured. (a) As T 318.

3286	35c. Type **318**	1·00	90
3287	35c. Darth Vader in battle	1·00	90
3288	35c. Fighter ship	1·00	90
3289	35c. Space craft orbiting planet	1·00	90
3290	35c. Space craft and shuttle	1·00	90
3291	35c. Luke Skywalker on space bike	1·00	90

(b) As T 319. Self-adhesive.

3292	$1 Darth Vader	1·90	1·75
3293	$1 Type **319**	1·90	1·75
3294	$1 Storm trooper	1·90	1·75
MS3295	148×71 mm. $2 ×3 Designs as Nos. 3292/4 but triangular, 65×36½ mm.	6·00	6·50

320 "Anteos menippe"

1996. Butterflies. Multicoloured.

3296	70c. Type **320**	50	40
3297	90c. "Papilio lycophron"	60	60
3298	90c. "Prepona buckleyana"	60	60
3299	90c. "Parides agavus"	60	60
3300	90c. "Papilio cacicus"	60	60
3301	90c. "Euryades duponchelli"	60	60
3302	90c. "Diaethria dymena"	60	60
3303	90c. "Orimba jansoni"	60	60
3304	90c. "Polystichtis siaka"	60	60
3305	90c. "Papilio machaonides"	60	60
3306	$1 "Eunica alcmena"	70	70
3307	$1.10 "Doxocopa lavinia"	80	80
3308	$2 "Tithorea tarricina"	1·40	1·60
MS3309	Two sheets, each 75×104 mm. (a) $5 "Adelpha albia". (b) $6 "Themone pais". Set of 2 sheets	6·50	7·50

Nos. 3297/3305 were printed together, se-tenant, the backgrounds forming a composite design.

321 Michael Jordan (basketball player)

1996. Sports Legends. (a) As T 321. Multicoloured. Perf.

3310	$2 Type **321**	1·25	1·40
3311	$2 Joe Montana (American footballer)	1·25	1·40

(b) Size 69×103 mm. Imperf.

3312	$6 Michael Jordan	6·00	8·50
3313	$10 Joe Montana	8·00	11·00

322 The Monkey King

1996. "CHINA '96" 9th Asian International Stamp Exhibition (1st issue). Chinese Animated Films – "Uproar in Heaven" (Nos. 3314/18) and "Nezha conquers the Dragon King" (Nos. 3319/23). Multicoloured.

3314	15c. Type **322**	20	25
3315	15c. Monkey King flying towards illuminated pole	20	25
3316	15c. Monkey King and flying horses	20	25
3317	15c. Monkey King picking fruit	20	25
3318	15c. Monkey King drinking from flask	20	25
3319	15c. Nezha waking up	20	25
3320	15c. Nezha swimming with fish	20	25
3321	15c. Nezha on back of sea serpent	20	25
3322	15c. Nezha with sword	20	25
3323	15c. Nezha in battle	20	25
MS3324	Two sheets, each 85×105 mm. (a) 75c. Monkey King (vert). (b) 75 c. Nezha (vert). Set of 2 sheets	1·40	1·60

323 Chongqing Dazu Buddha

1996. "CHINA '96" 9th Asian International Stamp Exhibition (2nd issue). Sheet 115×80 mm.

MS3325	**323** $2 multicoloured	1·40	1·60

323a Queen Elizabeth II

1996. 70th Birthday of Queen Elizabeth II. Showing different photographs. Multicoloured.

3326	$2 Type **323a**	1·50	1·50
3327	$2 Wearing Garter robes	1·50	1·50
3328	$2 Wearing pink hat and coat	1·50	1·50
MS3329	125×103 mm. $6 On Buckingham Palace balcony (horiz)	4·25	4·50

324 West Indian Boy

1996. 50th Anniv of UNICEF. Multicoloured.

3330	$1 Type **324**	60	55
3331	$1.10 European girl	70	65
3332	$2 South-east Asian girl	1·25	1·40
MS3333	104×74 mm. $5 Arab boy	2·50	3·00

325 Menorah and The Knesset

1996. 3000th Anniv of Jerusalem. Multicoloured.

3334	$1 Type **325**	80	55
3335	$1.10 The Montefiore Windmill	80	70
3336	$2 Shrine of the Book	1·40	1·60
MS3337	104×74 mm. $5 Old City, Jerusalem	2·75	3·00

The captions on Nos. 3334 and 3336 were transposed in error.

326 Walter Winchell

1996. Centenary of Radio. Entertainers. Mult.

3338	90c. Type **326**	55	50
3339	$1 Fred Allen	60	55
3340	$1.10 Hedda Hopper	70	65
3341	$2 Eve Arden	1·25	1·40
MS3342	72×102 mm. $6 Major Bowes	3·00	3·50

327 Bananaquit

1996. Birds. Multicoloured.

3343 60c. Type **327** 60 45
3344 $1 Rufous-throated solitare 75 60
3345 $1 Caribbean martin (horiz) 75 80
3346 $1 Broad-winged hawk (horiz) 75 80
3347 $1 White-tailed tropic bird (horiz) 75 80
3348 $1 Black-winged stilt (horiz) 75 80
3349 $1 Bridled tern (horiz) 75 80
3350 $1 Antillean euphonia (horiz) 75 80
3351 $1 Ruddy turnstone (horiz) 75 80
3352 $1 Green-throated carib (horiz) 75 80
3353 $1 Yellow-crowned night heron (horiz) 75 80
3354 $1.10 Lesser Antillean tanager 80 85
3355 $2 Purple-throated carib 1·40 1·60
MS3356 Two sheets, each 89×92 mm. (a) $5 Red-billed whistling duck. (b) $6 St. Vincent amazon. Set of 2 sheets 7·00 8·00

Nos. 3345/53 were printed together, se-tenant, with the backgrounds forming a composite design.

328 Maurice King (St. Vincent) (weightlifting), Pan American Games, 1959

1996. Olympic Games, Atlanta (2nd issue). Multicoloured.

3357 20c. Type **328** 30 30
3358 70c. Eswort Coombs (St. Vincent) (400 m sprint, World University Student Games) 50 40
3359 90c. Pamenos Ballantyne (St. Vincent) (O.E.C.S. road-running) and Benedict Ballantyne (St. Vincent) (Guinness Half-marathon, 1994) 60 60
3360 90c. Ancient Greek runners, Olympia (horiz) 60 60
3361 $1 London landmarks (horiz) 60 60
3362 $1 Women's archery (Korea), 1988, 1992 60 60
3363 $1 Gymnastics (Japan),1960–76 60 60
3364 $1 Basketball (U.S.A.), 1936, 1948–68, 1976, 1984 and 1992 60 60
3365 $1 Soccer (Spain), 1992 60 60
3366 $1 Water polo (Hungary), 1956 60 60
3367 $1 Baseball (Cuba), 1992 60 60
3368 $1 Kayak (Germany), 1980 60 60
3369 $1 Fencing (France), 1980 60 60
3370 $1 Cycling (Germany), 1908, 1964, 1972–76 and 1992 60 60
3371 $1 Vitaly Shcherbo (Russia) (gymastics), 1992 60 60
3372 $1 Fu Mingxia (China) (diving), 1992 60 60
3373 $1 Wilma Rudolph (U.S.A.) (track and field), 1960 60 60
3374 $1 Rafer Johnson (U.S.A.) (decathlon), 1960 60 60
3375 $1 Teofilo Stevenson (Cuba) (boxing), 1972–80 60 60
3376 $1 Babe Didrikson (U.S.A.) (track and field), 1932 60 60
3377 $1 Kyoko Iwasaki (Japan) (swimming), 1992 60 60
3378 $1 Yoo Namkyu (Korea) (table tennis), 1988 60 60
3379 $1 Michael Gross (Germany) (swimming), 1984–88 60 60
3380 $1 Yasuhiro Yamashita (Japan) (judo), 1984 (horiz) 60 60
3381 $1 Peter Rono (Kenya) (1500m race), 1988 (horiz) 60 60
3382 $1 Aleksandr Kourlovitch (Russia) (weightlifting), 1988 (horiz) 60 60
3383 $1 Juha Tiainen (Finland) (hammer throw), 1984 (horiz) 60 60
3384 $1 Sergei Bubka (Russia) (pole vault), 1988 (horiz) 60 60
3385 $1 Q. F. Newall (Great Britain) (archery), 1908 (horiz) 60 60
3386 $1 Nadia Comaneci (Rumania) (gymnastics), 1976 (horiz) 60 60
3387 $1 Carl Lewis (U.S.A.) (long jump), 1988 (horiz) 60 60
3388 $1 Bob Mathias (U.S.A.) (decathlon), 1948 (horiz) 60 60
3389 $1 Chuhei Nambu (Japan) (triple jump), 1932 (horiz) 60 60
3390 $1 Duncan McNaughton (Canada) (high jump), 1932 (horiz) 60 60
3391 $1 Jack Kelly (U.S.A.) (single sculls), 1920 (horiz) 60 60
3392 $1 Jackie Joyner-Kersee (U.S.A.) (heptathlon), 1988 (horiz) 60 60
3393 $1 Tyrell Biggs (U.S.A.) (super heavyweight boxing), 1984 (horiz) 60 60
3394 $1 Larisa Latynina (Russia) (gymnastics), 1964 (horiz) 60 60
3395 $1 Bob Garrett (U.S.A.) (discus), 1896 (horiz) 60 60
3396 $1 Paavo Nurmi (Finland) (5000m), 1924 (horiz) 60 60
3397 $1 Eric Lemming (Sweden) (javelin), 1908 (horiz) 60 60
3398 $1.10 Rodney Jack (St. Vincent) (1995 Caribbean Nations Football Cup) 70 70
3399 $1.10 Dorando Pietri (Italy) (marathon), 1908 70 70
3400 $2 Yachting (horiz) 1·25 1·50
MS3401 Four sheets. (a) 74×104 mm. $5 Olympic flag (horiz). (b) 74×104 mm. $5 Carl Lewis (U.S.A.) (relay). (c) 104×74 mm. $5 Hannes Kolehmainen (Finland) (marathon), 1920 (horiz). (d) 104×74 mm. $5 Alexander Ditiatin (Russia) (gymnastics), 1980 (horiz). Set of 4 sheets 11·00 12·00

No. 3371 is inscribed "GYMNASTIECS" in error.

329 Notre Dame Cathedral, Paris

1996. "The Hunchback of Notre Dame". Scenes from the Disney cartoon film. Multicoloured.

3402–3207 10c. ×6 (Type **329**; People watching puppet show; Judge Frollo on black horse; Quasimodo and his parents captured; Gargoyles; Quasimodo) 1·75
3408–3416 30c. ×9 (Captain Phoebus meets Esmeralda; Captain Phoebus and Judge Frollo; Esmeralda dancing; Esmeralda and candidates for King of Fools; Quasimodo wearing crown; Quasimodo pelted; Quasimodo carrying Esmeralda; Phoebus on black horse; Quasimodo, Esmeralda and a wounded Phoebus (all horiz)) 3·25
3417–3425 $1 ×9 (Quasimodo chained to bell tower; Three gargoyles and Quasimodo; Quasimodo pulling down pillars; Quasimodo rescuing Esmeralda; Phoebus leading citizens; Quasimodo throwing wood; Quasimodo weeping over Esmeralda; Quasimodo and Frollo fighting; Quasimodo and Esmeralda on ledge (all horiz)) 7·00
3426–3433 $1 ×8 (Quasimodo; Phoebus; Laverne and Hugo; Clopin; Frollo; Esmeralda; Victor; Djali) 6·50
MS3434 Five sheets. (a) 124×102 mm. $6 Quasimodo, Phoebus and Esmerelda (horiz). (b) 124×102 mm. $6 Esmerelda. (c) 124×102 mm. $6 Quasimodo cheering. (d) 104×126 mm. $6 Esmerelda and Quasimodo (horiz). (e) 104×126 mm. $6 Esmerelda and Phoebus (horiz). Set of 5 sheets 24·00 26·00

No. 3416 is inscribed "wonded phoebus" in error.

330 French Angelfish

1996. Fishes. Multicoloured.

3435 70c. Type **330** 50 40
3436 90c. Red-spotted hawkfish 60 50
3437 $1 Barred hamlet 60 60
3438 $1 Flamefish 60 60
3439 $1 Caribbean long-nosed butterflyfish 60 60
3440 $1 Royal gramma ("Fairy Basslet") 60 60
3441 $1 Red-tailed parrotfish 60 60
3442 $1 Black-barred soldierfish 60 60
3443 $1 Three-spotted damselfish 60 60
3444 $1 Candy basslet 60 60
3445 $1 Spot-finned hogfish 60 60
3446 $1 Jackknife fish 60 60
3447 $1 Surgeon fish 60 60
3448 $1 Muttonfish 60 60
3449 $1 Seahorse 60 60
3450 $1 Comber fish 60 60
3451 $1 Angel shark 60 60
3452 $1 Moray eel 60 60
3453 $1 Bicolour parrotfish 60 60
3454 $1 "Tritonium nodiferum" (sea snail) 60 60
3455 $1.10 Balloonfish ("Spiny Puffer") 70 70
3456 $2 Grey triggerfish 1·25 1·50
MS3457 Two sheets, each 106×76 mm. (a) $5 Queen Triggerfish. (b) $6 Blue Marlin. Set of 2 sheets 6·00 7·00

Nos. 3446/54 were printed together, se-tenant, with the backgrounds forming a composite design.
No. 3445 is inscribed "HOFGFISH" in error.

331 "Beloperone guttata"

1996. Flowers. Multicoloured.

3458 70c. Type **331** 50 40
3459 90c. "Datura candida" 60 60
3460 90c. "Amherstia nobilis" 60 60
3461 90c. "Ipomoea acuminata" 60 60
3462 90c. "Bougainvillea glabra" 60 60
3463 90c. "Cassia alata" 60 60
3464 90c. "Cordia sebestena" 60 60
3465 90c. "Opuntia dilenii" 60 60
3466 90c. "Cryptostegia grandiflora" 60 60
3467 90c. "Rodriguezia lanceolata" 60 60
3468 $1 "Epidendrum elongatum" 70 60
3469 $1.10 "Petrea volubilis" 70 70
3470 $2 "Oncidium altissimum" 1·50 1·60
MS3471 Two sheets, each 78×64 mm. (a) $5 "Hibiscus rosa-sinensis". (b) $5 "Acalypha hispida". Set of 2 sheets 5·50 6·50

Nos. 3459/67 were printed together, se-tenant, with the backgrounds forming a composite design.

332 "Doric", 1923

1996. Passenger Ships. Multicoloured.

3472 $1.10 Type **332** 80 80
3473 $1.10 "Nerissa", 1926 80 80
3474 $1.10 "Howick Hall", 1910 80 80
3475 $1.10 "Jervis Bay", 1922 80 80
3476 $1.10 "Vauban", 1912 80 80
3477 $1.10 "Orinoco", 1928 80 80
3478 $1.10 "Lady Rodney", 1929 80 80
3479 $1.10 "Empress of Russia", 1913 80 80
3480 $1.10 "Providence", 1914 80 80
3481 $1.10 "Reina Victori-Eugenia", 1913 80 80
3482 $1.10 "Balmoral Castle", 1910 80 80
3483 $1.10 "Tivives", 1911 80 80
MS3484 Two sheets, each 106×76 mm. (a) $6 "Aquitania", 1914. (b) $6 "Imperator", 1913. Set of 2 sheets 6·50 7·50

333 Elvis Presley

1996. Elvis Presley (singer) Commemoration. Different portraits. Multicoloured.

3485 $2 Type **333** 1·10 1·10
3486 $2 Wearing checked shirt with guitar 1·10 1·10
3487 $2 Playing piano 1·10 1·10
3488 $2 Wearing black jacket and playing guitar 1·10 1·10
3489 $2 Wearing white shirt and black tie 1·10 1·10
3490 $2 Singing into studio microphone 1·10 1·10

334 Sandy Koufax (baseball player)

1996. Sports Legends. Sandy Koufax. Multicoloured.

3491 $2 Type **334** 1·00 1·25
3492 $2 Pitching ball 1·00 1·25
3493 $2 Preparing to pitch with arm raised 1·00 1·25
3494 $6 Sandy Koufax (69×103 mm) 3·00 4·50

335 Richard Petty's 1990 Pontiac

1996. Richard Petty (stock car driver) Commemoration. Multicoloured.

3495 $2 Type **335** 1·10 1·25
3496 $2 Richard Petty 1·10 1·25
3497 $2 1972 Plymouth 1·10 1·25
3498 $2 1974 Dodge 1·10 1·25
MS3499 Two sheets. (a) 104×74 mm. $5 1970 Plymouth "Superbird" (84×28 mm). (b) 64×48 mm. $6 1996 25th Anniversary STP Pontiac. Set of 2 sheets 6·00 7·00

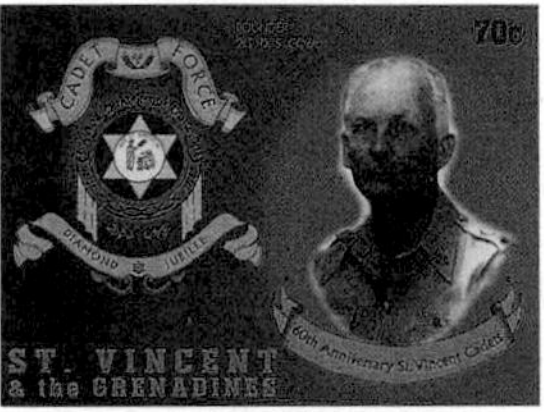

336 D.S. Cozier (founder) and Cadet Force Emblem

1996. 60th Anniv of St. Vincent Army Cadet Force. Multicoloured.

3500 70c. Type **336** 45 45
3501 90c. Emblem and first cadets with Cozier 55 55

337 "Virgin and Child" (detail, Memling)

1996. Christmas. Religious Paintings. Multicoloured.

3502 70c. Type **337** 60 40
3503 90c. "St. Anthony" (detail, Memling) 65 50
3504 $1 "Madonna and Child" (detail, D. Bouts) 75 55
3505 $1.10 "Virgin and Child" (detail, Lorenzo Lotto) 80 65
3506 $2 "St. Roch" (detail, Lotto) 1·60 1·75
3507 $5 "St. Sebastian" (detail, Lotto) 3·25 4·25
MS3508 Two sheets, each 106×76 mm. (a) $5 "Virgin and Child with St. Roch and St. Sebastian" (Lotto). (b) $5 "Virgin and Child with St. Anthony and Donor" (Memling). Set of 2 sheets 6·50 7·50

338 Sylvester Stallone in "Rocky IV"

1996. 20th Anniv of "Rocky" (film). Sheet 143×182 mm.

MS3509	**338** $2 ×3 multicoloured	3·00	3·50

No. **MS**3509 was printed with an enlarged illustrated left-hand margin.

1996. Occupations (2nd series). Multicoloured. As Nos. 3196/3248, but all with face value of 10c.

3510-3517	10c. ×8 As Nos. 3196/9 and 3201/4	1·75	
3518-3525	10c. ×8 As Nos. 3205/8 and 3210/13	1·75	
3526-3533	10c. ×8 As Nos. 3214/17 and 3519/22	1·75	
3534-3541	10c. ×8 As Nos. 3523/6 and 3528/31	1·75	
3542-3548	10c. ×7 As Nos. 3232/4 and 3236/9 (all vert)	1·75	
3549-3556	10c. ×8 As Nos. 3240/3 and 3245/8	1·75	

339 Symbolic Ox

1997. Chinese New Year ("Year of the Ox").

3557	**339**	75c. black, orange andpink	50	55
3558	-	75c. black, green and lilac	50	55
3559	-	75c. black, pink and red	50	55
MS3560		97×48 mm. Nos. 3557/9	1·10	1·25
MS3561		71×101 mm. $2 black, orange and yellow	1·25	1·50

DESIGNS: Nos. 3558/9, **MS**3561, Different oxen.

340 Lieut. Tuvok

1997. "Star Trek Voyager" (television series). Multicoloured.

3562	$2 Type **340**	1·10	1·10
3563	$2 Kes	1·10	1·10
3564	$2 Tom Paris	1·10	1·10
3565	$2 The Doctor	1·10	1·10
3566	$2 Captain Katherine Janeway	1·10	1·10
3567	$2 B'Elanna Torres	1·10	1·10
3568	$2 Neelix	1·10	1·10
3569	$2 Harry Kim	1·10	1·10
3570	$2 First Officer Chakotay	1·10	1·10
MS3571	88×120 mm. $6 Crew of the "Star Trek Voyager" (28×45 mm)	3·50	3·75

341 Mickey Mantle

1997. Sports Legends. Mickey Mantle (baseball player). Multicoloured. Perf ($2) or imperf. ($6).

3572	$2 Type **341**	1·00	1·10
3573	$6 Mickey Mantle (67×100 mm)	3·50	5·00

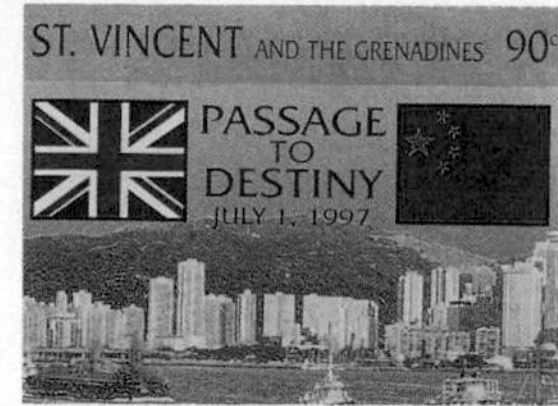

342 Hong Kong Waterfront

1997. "Hong Kong '97" International Stamp Exhibition. Designs showing the Hong Kong waterfront by day (Nos. 3574/8) or night (Nos. 3579/83). Multicoloured.

3574	90c. Type **342**	60	60
3575	90c. Two ferries in foreground	60	60
3576	90c. Construction site on waterfront	60	60
3577	90c. One launch	60	60
3578	90c. Hong Kong Bank and yellow building in centre	60	60
3579	90c. Large building with spire on right	60	60
3580	90c. Electronic billboards including HITACHI	60	60
3581	90c. Mansions on hillside at right	60	60
3582	90c. Toshiba and NEC billboards in centre	60	60
3583	90c. Hong Kong bank building under Union Jack	60	60
MS3584	Three sheets, each 127×85 mm. (a) $2 Boy and girl at Full Moon Festival; $2 Couple on bridge; $2 Two girls with lanterns. (b) $2 Incense candles; $2 Buddhist monk at Polin Monastery; $2 Orchids. (c) $2 Wanchai Market; $2 Chinese couple in street; $2 Man choosing fruit. (all designs 34×25 mm). Set of 3 sheets	9·50	11·00

Nos. 3574/83 were printed together, se-tenant, forming two composite designs.

342a Lord Howe Island, Australia

1997. 50th Anniv of UNESCO. Multicoloured.

3585	70c. Type **342a**	50	40
3586	90c. Uluru-kata Tjuta National Park, Australia	60	50
3587	$1 Cave paintings, Kakadu National Park, Australia	65	55
3588	$1.10 Te Wahipounamu National Park, New Zealand	70	75
3589	$1.10 Castle, Himeji-jo, Japan	70	75
3590	$1.10 Temple, lake and gardens, Kyoto, Japan	70	75
3591	$1.10 Walkway, Kyoto, Japan	70	75
3592	$1.10 Buddha, Temple of Ninna, Japan	70	75
3593	$1.10 View from castle, Himeji-jo, Japan	70	75
3594	$1.10 Forest, Shirakami-sanchi, Japan	70	75
3595	$1.10 Forest and mountains, Yakushima, Japan	70	75
3596	$1.10 Forest, Yakushima,Japan	70	75
3597	$1.10 City of San Gimignano, Italy	70	75
3598	$1.10 Cathedral of Santa Maria Asunta, Pisa, Italy	70	75
3599	$1.10 Cathedral of Santa Maria Fiore, Florence, Italy	70	75
3600	$1.10 Archaeological site, Valley of the Boyne, Ireland	70	75
3601	$1.10 Church of St. Savin-sur-Gartempe, France	70	75
3602	$1.10 Regency mansion, Bath, England	70	75
3603	$1.10 Rooftop view of Bath, England	70	75
3604	$1.10 Street in Bath, England	70	75
3605	$1.10 Monastery of Rossanou, Meteora, Greece	70	75
3606	$1.10 Ceiling painting, Mount Athos, Greece	60	65
3607	$1.10 Monastery Osios Varlaam, Meteora, Greece	70	75
3608	$1.10 Ruins, Athens, Greece	70	75
3609	$1.10 Carvings, Acropolis Museum, Athens, Greece	70	75
3610	$1.10 Painted cloisters, Mount Athos, Greece	70	75
3611	$1.10 The port of Zovgraphov Monastery, Greece	70	75
3612	$1.10 Painting above door, Mount Athos, Greece	70	75
3613	$1.50 Palace, Wudang Mountains, China (horiz)	85	90
3614	$1.50 Caves, Mogao, China (horiz)	85	90
3615	$1.50 House, Taklamakan Desert, China (horiz)	85	90
3616	$1.50 Section going through forest, Great Wall, China (horiz)	85	90
3617	$1.50 Section going through desert, Great Wall, China (horiz)	85	90
3618	$1.50 House and church, Quedlinburg, Germany (horiz)	80	90
3619	$1.50 Decorated house fronts, Quedlinburg (horiz)	85	90
3620	$1.50 Decorative house windows, Quedlinburg, Germany (horiz)	85	90
3621	$1.50 House front, Quedlinburg, Germany (horiz)	85	90
3622	$1.50 Church spires, Quedlinburg (horiz)	85	90
3623	$1.50 Valley of the Ingenios, Cuba (horiz)	85	90
3624	$1.50 City of Zacatecas, Mexico (horiz)	85	90
3625	$1.50 Lima, Peru (horiz)	85	90
3626	$1.50 Monastic ruins, Paraguay (horiz)	85	90
3627	$1.50 Mayan ruins, Copan, Honduras (horiz)	85	90
3628	$2 Tongariro National Park, New Zealand (horiz)	1·25	1·40
3629	$5 Tongariro National Park, New Zealand	2·75	3·25
MS3630	Seven sheets, each 127×102 mm. (a) $5 Great Wall, China (horiz). (b) $5 Venice, Italy (horiz). (c) $5 Dunbuang Oasis, China (horiz). (d) $5 Wall, Quedlinburg, Germany (horiz). (e) $5 Meteora Monastery, Greece (horiz). (f) $5 Himeji-jo, Japan (horiz). (g) $5 Dome of the Rock, Jerusalem (horiz). Set of 7 sheets	17·00	18·00

343 Microwave Radio Relay Tower, Dorsetshire Hill

1997. 125th Anniv of Telecommunications in St. Vincent. Multicoloured (except 70c.).

3631	5c. Type **343**	10	20
3632	10c. Cable and Wireless headquarters, Kingstown	15	20
3633	20c. Microwave relay tower (vert)	20	25
3634	35c. Cable and Wireless complex, Arnos Vale	30	35
3635	50c. Cable and Wireless tower, Mount St. Andrew	40	40
3636	70c. "Docia" (cable ship), 1872 (black and violet)	80	50
3637	90c. Eastern telecommunications network map, 1872	90	65
3638	$1.10 World telegraph map, 1876	1·00	85

344 Smooth-billed Ani

1997. Birds of the World. Multicoloured.

3639	60c. Type **344**	50	40
3640	70c. Belted kingfisher	50	40
3641	90c. Blackburnian warbler	60	50
3642	$1 Blue grosbeak	65	65
3643	$1 Bananaquit	65	65
3644	$1 Cedar waxwing	65	65
3645	$1 Ovenbird	65	65
3646	$1 Hooded warbler	65	65
3647	$1 Common flicker ("Flicker")	65	65
3648	$1.10 Blue tit	70	70
3649	$2 Chaffinch	1·25	1·40
3650	$2 Song thrush	1·25	1·40
3651	$2 European robin	1·25	1·40
3652	$2 Blackbird	1·25	1·40
3653	$2 Great spotted woodpecker	1·25	1·40
3654	$2 Winter wren ("Wren")	1·25	1·40
3655	$2 River kingfisher ("Kingfisher")	1·25	1·40
3656	$5 Ruddy turnstone	2·75	3·25
MS3657	Two sheets, each 101×75 mm. (a) $5 St. Vincent amazon. (b) $5 Tawny owl. Set of 2 sheets	6·00	6·50

Nos. 3642/7 and 3650/5 respectively were printed together, se-tenant, with the backgrounds forming composite designs.

345 Mandarin Duck

1997. Sea Birds. Multicoloured.

3658	70c. Type **345**	50	40
3659	90c. Green-backed heron ("Green Heron")	60	50
3660	$1 Ringed teal	65	55
3661	$1.10 Blue-footed booby and chick	70	70
3662	$1.10 Crested auklet (vert)	70	70
3663	$1.10 Whiskered auklet (vert)	70	70
3664	$1.10 Pigeon guillemot (vert)	70	70
3665	$1.10 Adelie penguins (vert)	70	70
3666	$1.10 Rockhopper penguin (vert)	70	70
3667	$1.10 Emperor penguin and chick (vert)	70	70
3668	$2 Comb-crested jacana ("Australian Jacana") (vert)	1·25	1·40
3669	$5 Reddish egret (vert)	2·75	3·25
MS3670	Two sheets, each 101×75 mm. (a) $5 Greater flamingo ("Flamingo"). (b) $5 Snowy egret. Set of 2 sheets	6·00	6·50

Nos. 3662/7 were printed together, se-tenant, with the backgrounds forming a composite design.

346 Frank Robinson

1997. Baseball Legends. Multicoloured. Imperf ($6) or perf (others). Self-adhesive (No. MS3688).

3671	$1 Type **346**	50	55
3672	$1 Satchel Paige	50	55
3673	$1 Billy Williams	50	55
3674	$1 Reggie Jackson	50	55
3675	$1 Roberto Clemente	50	55
3676	$1 Ernie Banks	50	55
3677	$1 Hank Aaron	50	55
3678	$1 Roy Campanella	50	55
3679	$1 Willie McCovey	50	55
3680	$1 Monte Irvin	50	55
3681	$1 Willie Stargell	50	55
3682	$1 Rod Carew	50	55
3683	$1 Ferguson Jenkins	50	55
3684	$1 Bob Gibson	50	55
3685	$1 Lou Brock	50	55
3686	$1 Joe Morgan	50	55
3687	$6 Jackie Robinson (67×101 mm)	3·00	3·50
MS3688	133×67 mm. $1 ×8 Jackie Robinson (32×46 mm)	1·50	1·60

346a Girl sewing ("Curly-Locks")

1997. 300th Anniv of Mother Goose Nursey Rhymes. Sheet, 102×72 mm.

MS3689	**346a** $5 multicoloured	3·00	3·25

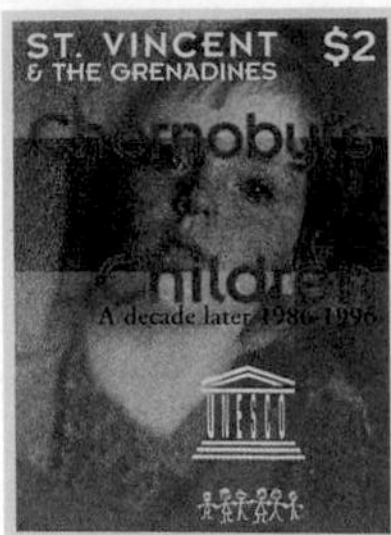

347 Child's Face and UNESCO Emblem

1997. 10th Anniv of Chernobyl Nuclear Disaster. Multicoloured.

3690	$2 Type **347**	1·00	1·25
3691	$2 As Type **347** but inscribed "CHABAD'S CHILDREN OF CHERNOBYL" at foot	1·00	1·25

347a Paul Harris and Thai Children Receiving Blankets

1997. 50th Death Anniv of Paul Harris (founder of Rotary International).

3692	**347a** $2 multicoloured	1·00	1·25
MS3693	78×108 mm. $5 Luis Vincente Giay (International President) with President Carter of the United States	2·50	3·00

347b Queen Elizabeth II

1997. Golden Wedding of Queen Elizabeth and Prince Philip. Multicoloured.

3694	$1.10 Type **347b**	90	1·00
3695	$1.10 Royal coat of arms	90	1·00
3696	$1.10 Queen Elizabeth and Prince Philip	90	1·00
3697	$1.10 Queen Elizabeth and Prince Philip on royal visit	90	1·00
3698	$1.10 Buckingham Palace	90	1·00
3699	$1.10 Prince Philip in naval uniform	90	1·00
MS3700	100×70 mm. $5 Queen Elizabeth on Coronation day	3·25	3·50

347c Bicycle Postman, India, 1800s

1997. "Pacific '97" International Stamp Exhibition, San Francisco. Death Centenary of Heinrich von Stephan (founder of the U.P.U.).

3701	**347c** $2 violet and black	1·00	1·25
3702	- $2 brown and black	1·00	1·25
3703	- $2 blue and black	1·00	1·25
MS3704	82×118 mm. $5 brown	2·75	3·25

DESIGNS: No. 3702, Von Stephan and Mercury; 3703, Ox-drawn postal cart, Indochina; **MS**3704, Von Stephan and post rider, Indochina.

347d "Furukawa River, Hiroo"

1997. Birth Bicentenary of Hiroshige (Japanese painter). "One Hundred Famous Views of Edo". Multicoloured.

3705	$1.50 Type **347d**	1·00	1·10
3706	$1.50 "Chiyogaike Pond, Meguro"	1·00	1·10
3707	$1.50 "New Fuji, Meguro"	1·00	1·10
3708	$1.50 "Moon-viewing Point"	1·00	1·10
3709	$1.50 "Ushimachi, Takanawa"	1·00	1·10
3710	$1.50 "Original Fuji, Meguro"	1·00	1·10
MS3711	Two sheets, each 102×127 mm. (a) $5 "Gotenyama, Shinagawa". (b) $5 "Shinagawa Susaki". Set of 2 sheets	6·00	6·50

348 Couple with Dog

1997. 175th Anniv of Brothers Grimm's Third Collection of Fairy Tales. "Old Sultan" (Nos. 3712/14) and "The Cobbler and the Elves" (Nos. 3715/17). Multicoloured.

3712	$2 Type **348**	1·10	1·10
3713	$2 Sheepdog on hillside	1·10	1·10
3714	$2 Wolf and sheepdog	1·10	1·10
3715	$2 The cobbler	1·10	1·10
3716	$2 The elves	1·10	1·10
3717	$2 Cobbler with elf	1·10	1·10
MS3718	Two sheets. (a) 124×96 mm. $5 Couple and baby with Old Sultan. (b) 96×124 mm. $5 Elf. Set of 2 sheets	5·50	6·50

349 Deng Xiaoping

1997. Deng Xiaoping (Chinese statesman) Commemoration.

3719	**349** $2 brown	1·00	1·10
3720	- $2 brown	1·00	1·10
3721	- $2 brown	1·00	1·10
3722	- $2 brown	1·00	1·10
3723	- $2 blue and light blue	1·00	1·10
3724	- $2 blue and light blue	1·00	1·10
3725	- $2 blue and light blue	1·00	1·10
3726	- $2 blue and light blue	1·00	1·10
3727	- $2 black	1·00	1·10
3728	- $2 black	1·00	1·10
3729	- $2 black	1·00	1·10
3730	- $2 black	1·00	1·10
MS3731	76×106 mm. $5 multicoloured	2·50	3·00

DESIGNS: No. 3720, Looking left; 3721, In military uniform; 3722, Full face; 3723, Looking right; 3724, Smiling; 3725, With head tilted to right; 3726, Looking down; 3727, Looking right; 3728, Looking left; 3729, Full face; 3730, Facing left and smiling; **MS**3731 Deng Xiaoping and Xhue Lin.

350 Alphonso Theodore Roberts

1997. Inaugural Cricket Test Match at Arnos Vale. Multicoloured.

3732	90c. Type **350**	1·00	50
3733	$5 Arnos Vale cricket ground (horiz)	3·25	3·50

351 "Cinemax" Mardi Gras Band

1997. 20th Anniv of Vincy Mas Carnival. Multicoloured.

3734	10c. Type **351**	15	20
3735	20c. Queen of the Bands "Jacintha Ballantyne"	20	20
3736	50c. Queen of the Bands "Out of the Frying Pan and into the Fire" (vert)	40	40
3737	70c. King of the Bands "Conquistodore"	50	40
3738	90c. Starlift Steel Orchestra	60	50
3739	$2 Frankie McIntosh (musical arranger) (vert)	1·25	1·50

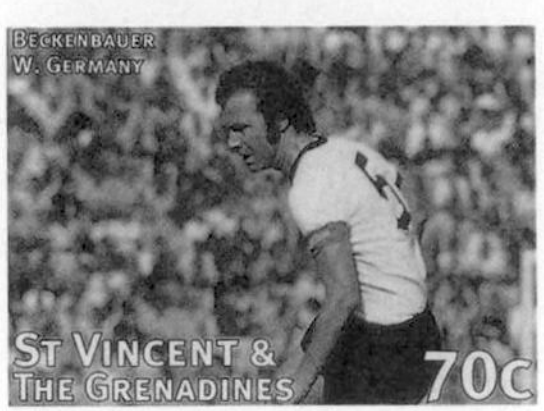

351a Beckenbauer, West Germany

1997. World Cup Football Championship, France (1998). As T 351a.

3740	70c. multicoloured	50	40
3741	90c. brown	60	50
3742	$1 multicoloured	70	60
3743-3750	$1 ×8 (black; multicoloured; black; black; black; black; multicoloured; black)	4·00	
3751-3758	$1 ×8 (each multicoloured)	4·00	
3759-3766	$1 ×8 (multicoloured; black; multicoloured; black; black; multicoloured; black; multicoloured)	4·00	
3767-3774	$1 ×8 (blue; multicoloured; blue; multicoloured; multicoloured; blue; multicoloured; blue)	4·00	
3775	$1.10 brown	75	70
3776	$2 multicoloured	1·25	1·40
3777	$10 black	6·00	7·00
MS3778	Four sheets, each 102×127 mm. (a) $5 multicoloured. (b) $5 multicoloured. (c) $5 black. (d) $5 black. Set of 4 sheets	12·00	13·00

DESIGNS—HORIZ: No. 3741, Moore, England; 3742, Lato, Poland; 3759, Argentine and West German players, 1986; 3760 and 3769, English and West German players, 1966; 3761, Goalmouth melee, 1986; 3762, Italian and West German players, 1982; 3763 and 3770, English player heading ball, 1966; 3764, Argentine player with ball, 1978; 3765, Argentine player chasing ball, 1978; 3766, Dutch player with ball, 1974; 3767, Wembley Stadium, England, 1966; 3768, West German player with ball; 3771, English player in air heading ball; 3772, German player tackling English player; 3773, Celebrating English team; 3774, Celebrating German player; 3775, Pele, Brazil; 3776, Maier, West Germany; 3777, Eusebio, Portugal; **MS**3778d, Paulao, Angola. VERT: No. 3743, Argentine player kicking ball; 3744, Argentine player holding trophy; 3745, Goalmouth melee; 3746, Dutch player; 3747, Celebrating Argentine player; 3748, Argentine tackling Dutch player; 3749, Argentine and two Dutch players; 3750, Players attempting to head ball; 3751, Bergkamp, Netherlands; 3752, Seaman, England; 3753, Schmeichel, Denmark; 3754, Ince, England; 3755, Futre, Portugal; 3756, Ravanelli, Italy; 3757, Keane, Republic of Ireland; 3758, Gascoigne, England; **MS**3778a, Salvatori Schillaci, Italy; **MS**3778b, Ally McCoist, Scotland; **MS**3778c, Mario Kempes, Argentina.

352 Hand above Globe of Flowers

1997. 10th Anniv of the Signing of the Montreal Protocol on Substances that Deplete the Ozone Layer.

3779	**352** 90c. multicoloured	75	65

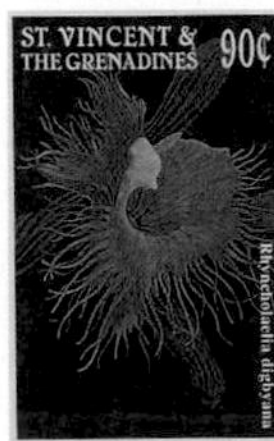

353 "Rhyncholaelia digbyana"

1997. Orchids of the World. Multicoloured.

3780	90c. Type **353**	65	50
3781	$1 "Laeliocattleya" "Chitchat Tangerine"	70	70
3782	$1 "Eulophia speciosa"	70	70
3783	$1 "Aerangis rhodosticta"	70	70
3784	$1 "Angraecum infundibularea"	70	70
3785	$1 "Calanthe sylvatica"	70	70
3786	$1 "Phalaenopsis mariae"	70	70
3787	$1 "Paphiopedilum insigne"	70	70
3788	$1 "Dendrobium nobile"	70	70
3789	$1 "Aerangis kotschyana"	70	70
3790	$1 "Cyrtorchis chailluana"	70	70
3791	$1.10 "Doritis pulcherrima"	75	75
3792	$2 "Phalaenopsis" "Barbara Moler"	1·40	1·60
MS3793	Two sheets, each 106×81 mm. (a) $5 "Sanguine broughtonia" (50×37 mm). (b) $5 "Brassavola nodosa" "Lady of the Night" (50×37 mm). Set of 2 sheets	6·00	5·50

354 Snow Leopard

1997. Sierra Club Conservation. Multicoloured.

3794-3802	20c. ×9 (Type **354**; Polar bear; Plants, Isle Royale National Park; Waterway, Isle Royale National Park; Denali National Park at night; Denali National Park; Plants, Joshua Tree National Park; Mountains, Joshua Tree National Park; Rock, Joshua Tree National Park)	90	
3803-3811	40c. ×9 (Mountain gorilla showing teeth; Mountain gorilla; Young mountain gorilla; Snow leopard; Young snow leopard; Polar bear; Polar bear cub; Denali National Park; Isle Royale National Park (all vert))	1·75	
3812-3820	50c. ×9 (Sifaka with young; Sifaka on branch; Head of sifaka; Peregrine falcon; Peregrine falcon with stretched wings; Galapagos tortoise; Waterfall, African rainforest; Tree, African rainforest; China's Yellow Mountains (all vert))	2·25	
3821-3829	60c. ×9 (Head of red panda; Red panda on branch; Red panda on ground; Peregrine falcon with chicks; Head of Galapagos tortoise; Galapagos tortoise on grass; African rainforest; Tops of trees, China's Yellow Mountains; Gorge, China's Yellow Mountains)	2·50	
3830-3838	70c. ×9 (Mountain lion; Siberian tiger; Head of Siberian tiger; Red wolf; Black bear; Lake, Wolong National Reserve; Belize rainforest; Base of tree, Belize rainforest; Mountains, Wolong National Reserve)	3·00	
3839-3847	90c. ×9 (Siberian tiger; Head of mountain lion; Mountain lion cubs; Black bear on branch; Head of black bear; Red wolf; Head of red wolf; Belize rainforest; Wolong National Reserve (all vert))	4·00	
3848-3856	$1 ×9 (Indri hanging from tree; Indri face on; Indri holding onto tree; Gopher tortoise inside shell; Gopher tortoise on ground; Black-footed ferret facing forward; Head of black-footed ferret; Haleakala National Park; Grand Teton National Park (all vert))	4·50	
3857-3865	$1.10 ×9 (Black-footed ferret; Gopher tortoise; River, Grand Teton National Park; Hillside, Grand Teton National Park; River, Haleakala National Park; Plants, Haleakala National Park; Misty view of Madagascar rainforest; Trees, Madagascar rainforest; Cleared forest, Madagascar rainforest)	5·25	
MS3866	Three sheets, each 110×80 mm. $5 Lake, Olympic National Park. (b) $5 Hillside, Olympic National Park (vert). (c) $5 Snow-covered Mountains, Olympic National Park (vert) Set of 3 sheets	7·50	8·00

355 Raised Stern of "Titanic"

1997. 85th Anniv of the Sinking of the "Titanic" (liner). Multicoloured.

3867	$1 Type **355**	1·25	1·25
3868	$1 Lifeboat rowing away	1·25	1·25
3869	$1 One funnel and lifeboat being lowered into water	1·25	1·25

3870	$1 Two funnels	1·25	1·25
3871	$1 One funnel in water and lifeboat rowing away	1·25	1·25

Nos. 3867/71 were printed together, se-tenant, forming a composite design.

1997. 30th Anniv of The Doors (rock group) and Rock and Roll Hall of Fame, Cleveland. Multicoloured.

3872	90c. Type **356**	75	50
3873	95c. "Waiting for the Sun" album cover, April 1968	75	65
3874	$1 Rock and Roll Hall of Fame and Museum, Cleveland, Ohio	80	65
3875	$1 "L.A. Women" album cover, April 1971	80	65
3876	$1.10 "The Soft Parade" album cover, July 1969	80	65
3877	$1.20 "Strange Days" album cover, October 1967	85	70
3878	$1.50 Rock and Roll Hall of Fame guitar logo	1·10	1·25
3879	$1.50 "The Doors" album cover, January 1967	1·10	1·25

357 Joe "King" Oliver

1997. New Orleans School of Jazz Commemoration. Multicoloured.

3880	$1 Type **357**	75	75
3881	$1 Louis Armstrong	75	75
3882	$1 Sidney Bechet	75	75
3883	$1 Nick Larocca	75	75
3884	$1 Louis Prima	75	75
3885	$1 "Buddy" Charles Bolden	75	75

357a Constantin Brancusi

1997. Millennium Series. Famous People of the Twentieth Century. (a) Sculptors.

3886	$1.10 Type **357a**	75	75
3887	$1.10 "The New Born" (Brancusi) (56×42 mm)	75	75
3888	$1.10 "Four Elements" (Calder) (56×42 mm)	75	75
3889	$1.10 Alexander Calder	75	75
3890	$1.10 Isamu Noguchi	75	75
3891	$1.10 "Dodge Fountain" (Noguchi) (56×42 mm)	75	75
3892	$1.10 "The Shuttlecock" (Oldenburg) (56×42 mm)	75	75
3893	$1.10 Claes Oldenburg	75	75

(b) Opera Singers.

3894	$1.10 Lily Pons	90	90
3895	$1.10 Lily Pons in Donizetti's "Lucia di Lammermoor" (56×42 mm)	90	90
3896	$1.10 Maria Callas in Bellini's "I Puritani" (56×42 mm)	90	90
3897	$1.10 Maria Callas	90	90
3898	$1.10 Beverly Sills	90	90
3899	$1.10 Beverly Sills in Donizetti's "La Fille du Regiment" (56×42 mm)	90	90
3900	$1.10 Jessye Norman in Schoenberg's "Erwartung" (56×42 mm)	90	90
3901	$1.10 Jessye Norman	90	90
3902	$1.10 Enrico Caruso	90	90
3903	$1.10 Enrico Caruso in Verdi's "Rigoletto" (56×42 mm)	90	90
3904	$1.10 Mario Lanza in "The Seven Hills of Rome" (56×42 mm)	90	90
3905	$1.10 Mario Lanza	90	90
3906	$1.10 Luciano Pavarotti	90	90
3907	$1.10 Luciano Pavarotti in Donizetti's "L'Elisir d'Amore" (56×42 mm)	90	90
3908	$1.10 Placido Domingo in Puccini's "Tosca" (56×42 mm)	90	90
3909	$1.10 Placido Domingo	90	90

358 Diana, Princess of Wales

1997. Diana, Princess of Wales Commemoration. Multicoloured.

3910	$2 Type **358**	1·10	1·10
3911	$2 Wearing pearl-drop earrings	1·10	1·10
3912	$2 Wearing black jacket	1·10	1·10
3913	$2 Wearing blue jacket and pearl earrings	1·10	1·10
3914	$2 Wearing tiara	1·10	1·10
3915	$2 In black evening dress	1·10	1·10
3916	$2 Wearing blue jacket	1·10	1·10
3917	$2 Wearing beige blouse	1·10	1·10
MS3918	Two sheets, each 100×70 mm. (a) $6 Wearing light blue jacket. (b) $6 Wearing white blouse. Set of 2 sheets	6·50	7·00

359 "The Sistine Madonna" (detail, Raphael)

1997. Christmas. Paintings and Sculptures. Multicoloured.

3919	60c. Type **359**	45	35
3920	70c. "Angel" (Edward Burne-Jones)	50	40
3921	90c. "Cupid" (sculpture, Etienne-Maurice Flaconet)	60	50
3922	$1 "Saint Michael" (sculpture, Hubert Gerhard)	70	55
3923	$1.10 "Apollo and the Hoare" (Giambattista Tiepolo)	75	65
3924	$2 "Madonna in a Garland of Flowers" (detail, Rubens and Brueghel the Elder)	1·25	1·75
MS3925	Two sheets, each 106×95 mm. (a) $5 "Madonna in a Garland of Flowers" (different detail, Rubens and Brueghel the Elder). (b) $5 "The Sacrifice of Isaac" (Giambattista Tiepolo) (detail) (horiz). Set of 2 sheets	6·00	6·50

360 Symbolic Tiger

1998. Chinese New Year ("Year of the Tiger").

3926	**360**	$1 black, grey and brown	60	65
3927	-	$1 black, silver and brown	60	65
3928	-	$1 black, lilac and pink	60	65
MS3929		71×101 mm. $2 black, lilac and orange	1·25	1·40

DESIGNS: Nos. 3927/9, Different tigers.

361 Children and School Savings Bank

1998. Economic Development. Multicoloured.

3930	20c. Type **361**	20	15
3931	90c. Agricultural workers and Credit Union Office (vert)	55	40
3932	$1.10 Freighter at quay	65	70

362 Ice Hockey

1998. Winter Olympic Games, Nagano. Mult.

3933	70c. Type **362**	50	40
3934	$1.10 Bobsleigh	70	70
3935	$1.10 Bjorn Daehlie (Norway) (Gold medal, Nordic skiing, 1994)	70	70
3936	$1.10 Gillis Grafstrom (Sweden) (Gold medal, figure skating, 1924, 1928)	70	70
3937	$1.10 Sonja Henie (Norway) (Gold medal, figure skating, 1928, 1932)	70	70
3938	$1.10 Ingemar Stenmark (Sweden) (Gold medal, slalom and giant slalom, 1980)	70	70
3939	$1.10 Christan Jagge (Norway) (Gold medal, slalom, 1992)	70	70
3940	$1.10 Tomas Gustafson (Sweden) (Gold medal, 5000m speed skating, 1992)	70	70
3941	$1.10 Johann Olav Koss (Norway) (Gold medal, 1500m speed skating, 1992, 1994)	70	70
3942	$1.10 Thomas Wassberg (Sweden) (Gold medal, 50km cross country skiing, 1984)	70	70
3943	$1.50 Downhill (red suit) (vert)	90	90
3944	$1.50 Two-man bobsleigh (vert)	90	90
3945	$1.50 Ski jump (red suit) (vert)	90	90
3946	$1.50 Downhill (red and white suit) (vert)	90	90
3947	$1.50 Luge (vert)	90	90
3948	$1.50 Biathlon (vert)	90	90
3949	$1.50 Downhill (yellow and red suit) (vert)	90	90
3950	$1.50 Figure skating (vert)	90	90
3951	$1.50 Ski jump (green suit)(vert)	90	90
3952	$1.50 Speed skating (vert)	90	90
3953	$1.50 Four-man bobsleigh (vert)	90	90
3954	$1.50 Cross-country skiing (vert)	90	90
3955	$2 Pairs figure skating	1·25	1·40
3956	$2 Aerials (vert)	1·25	1·40
MS3957	Two sheets. (a) 110×80 mm. $5 Ice Hockey. (b) 80×100 mm. $5 Slalom skiing (vert). Set of 2 sheets	6·00	7·00

Nos. 3943/8 and 3949/54 respectively were printed together, se-tenant, with the backgrounds forming composite designs.

363 Rock-iguana (Anegada)

1998. Endangered Species of the Caribbean. Multicoloured.

3958	50c. Type **363**	40	25
3959	70c. "Papilio homerus" (butterfly) (Jamaica)	50	35
3960	90c. Blossom-bat (Cuba)	55	40
3961	$1 Haitian solenodon (Dominican Republic)	60	50
3962	$1.10 Hawksbill turtle (Grenada)	60	65
3963	$1.10 Roseate spoonbill	60	65
3964	$1.10 Golden swallow	60	65
3965	$1.10 Short-snouted spinner dolphin	60	65
3966	$1.10 Queen or pink conch ("Strombus gigas")	60	65
3967	$1.10 American manatee	60	65
3968	$1.10 Loggerhead turtle	60	65
3969	$1.10 Magnificent frigate bird	60	65
3970	$1.10 Humpback whale	60	65
3971	$1.10 "Marpesia petreus" (butterfly)	60	65
3972	$1.10 St. Lucia whiptail	60	65
3973	$1.10 St. Lucia oriole	60	65
3974	$1.10 Green turtle	60	65
3975	$2 Black-billed whistling duck (Barbuda)	1·25	1·40
MS3976	Two sheets, each 102×90 mm. (a) $5 St. Vincent amazon ("St. Vincent Parrot"). (b) $5 Antiguan Racer (snake). Set of 2 sheets	5·50	6·00

Nos. 3963/8 and 3969/74 respectively were printed together, se-tenant, forming composite background designs.

364 "Gymnopilus spectabilis" and "Atildes halesus" (butterfly)

1998. Fungi. Multicoloured.

3977	10c. Type **364**	20	20
3978	20c. "Entoloma lividium"	40	25
3979	70c. "Pholiota flammans"	55	35
3980	90c. "Panaeolus semiovatus"	60	40
3981	$1 "Stropharia rugosoannulata"	60	65
3982	$1 "Amanita caesarea"	60	65
3983	$1 "Amanita muscaria"	60	65
3984	$1 "Amanita ovoidea"	60	65
3985	$1 "Amanita phalloides"	60	65
3986	$1 "Amanitopsis inaurata"	60	65
3987	$1 "Amanitopsis vaginata"	60	65
3988	$1 "Psalliota campestris"	60	65
3989	$1 "Psalliota arvensis"	60	65
3990	$1 "Coprinus comatus"	60	65
3991	$1.10 "Tricholoma sulphureum"	60	65
3992	$1.10 "Coprinus picaceus"	60	65
3993	$1.10 "Stropharia umbonatescens"	60	65
3994	$1.10 "Hebeloma crustuliniforme"	60	65
3995	$1.10 "Cortinarius collinitus"	60	65
3996	$1.10 "Cortinarius violaceus"	60	65
3997	$1.10 "Cortinarius armillatus"	60	65
3998	$1.10 "Tricholoma aurantium"	60	65
3999	$1.10 "Russula virescens"	60	65
4000	$1.10 "Clitocybe infundibuliformis"	60	65
MS4001	Two sheets. (a) 70×100 mm. $6 "Hygrocybe conica". (b) 100×70 mm. $6 "Amanita caesarea". Set of 2 sheets	6·50	7·00

365 "Amarynthis meneria meneria"

1998. Butterflies. Multicoloured.

4002	20c. Type **365**	40	25
4003	50c. "Papilio polyxenes"	50	30
4004	70c. "Emesis fatima fatima" (vert)	55	35
4005	$1 "Anartia amathea"	60	55
4006	$1 "Heliconius erato" (vert)	60	65
4007	$1 "Danaus plexippus" (vert)	60	65
4008	$1 "Papilio phorcas" (vert)	60	65
4009	$1 "Morpho peleides" (vert)	60	65
4010	$1 "Pandoriana pandora" (vert)	60	65
4011	$1 "Basilarchia astyanax" (vert)	60	65
4012	$1 "Vanessa cardui" (vert)	60	65
4013	$1 "Colobura dirce" (vert)	60	65
4014	$1 "Heraclides cresphontes" (vert)	60	65
MS4015	Two sheets, each 100×70 mm. (a) $6 "Colias eurytheme". (b) $6 "Everes comyntas". Set of 2 sheets	6·50	7·00

Nos. 4006/14 were printed together, se-tenant, with the backgrounds forming a composite design.

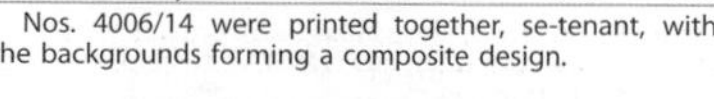

366 Pluto waking Mickey

1998. 70th Birthday of Disney's Mickey Mouse (1st issue). Multicoloured.

4016	2c. Type **366**	10	10
4017	3c. Mickey and Pluto on morning run	10	10
4018	4c. Singing in the bath	10	10
4019	5c. Breakfast time	15	10
4020	10c. Mickey going to school	20	10
4021	65c. Mickey playing basketball	90	50
4022	$1.10 Mickey as drum major (vert)	1·10	1·10
4023	$1.10 Mickey with hat and cane (vert)	1·10	1·10

4024 $1.10 Mickey in bow tie and tails (vert) 1·10 1·10
4025 $1.10 Mickey the magician (vert) 1·10 1·10
4026 $1.10 Mickey as circus musician (vert) 1·10 1·10
4027 $1.10 Mickey as cowboy (vert) 1·10 1·10
4028 $3 Mickey in soup kitchen 2·50 2·50
4029 $4 Mickey and Minnie in restaurant 2·75 2·75
4030 $5 Mickey and Pluto praying 2·75 2·75
MS4031 Four sheets, each 127×104 mm. (a) $5 Mickey reading paper (vert). (b) $6 Using computer (vert). (c) $6 Dancing at piano (vert). (d) $6 Blowing trumpet. Set of 4 sheets 12·00 13·00

See also Nos. 4179/96.

367 Winnie the Pooh in Window

1998. Stories of Winnie the Pooh. Multicoloured.
4032 $1 Type **367** 95 95
4033 $1 Eeyore, Kanga and Roo 95 95
4034 $1 Winnie the Pooh with balloon 95 95
4035 $1 Pooh stuck in Rabbit's burrow 95 95
4036 $1 Christopher Robin pulling Pooh 95 95
4037 $1 Piglet sweeping leaves 95 95
4038 $1 Pooh asleep 95 95
4039 $1 Eeyore 95 95
4040 $1 Pooh and Tigger 95 95
MS4041 127×102 mm. $6 Tigger, Pooh and Piglet 4·75 5·50

368 Australian Terrier

1998. Dogs of the World. Multicoloured.
4042 70c. Type **368** 50 35
4043 90c. Bullmastiff 60 45
4044 $1.10 Pomeranian 60 65
4045 $1.10 Beagle (horiz) 60 65
4046 $1.10 German shepherd and cockerel (horiz) 60 65
4047 $1.10 Pointer (horiz) 60 65
4048 $1.10 Vizsla (horiz) 60 65
4049 $1.10 Bulldog (horiz) 60 65
4050 $1.10 Shetland sheepdogs (horiz) 60 65
4051 $1.10 Tyrolean hunting dog (horiz) 60 65
4052 $1.10 King Charles spaniel (horiz) 60 65
4053 $1.10 Fox terriers (horiz) 60 65
4054 $1.10 Bernese mountain dog (horiz) 60 65
4055 $1.10 Papillon (horiz) 60 65
4056 $1.10 German shepherd (horiz) 60 65
4057 $2 Dandie dinmont terrier 1·25 1·40
MS4058 Two sheets, each 106×76 mm. (a) $6 Scottish Terrier and bush. (b) $6 Scottish Terrier lying down. Set of 2 sheets 6·50 7·00

Nos. 4045/50 and 4051/6 respectively were printed together, se-tenant, with the backgrounds forming composite designs.

The captions on Nos. 4052 and 4055 are transposed in error.

1998. "Israel 98" International Stamp Exhibition, Tel-Aviv. Nos. 3334/6 optd 98 in emblem.
4059 $1 Type **325** 60 45
4060 $1.10 The Montefiore Windmill 60 65
4061 $2 Shrine of the Book 1·25 1·40
MS4062 104×74 mm. $5 Old City, Jerusalem 3·25 3·50

370 L.M.S. No. 5596 "Bahamas"

1998. Railway Steam Locomotives of the World. Multicoloured.
4063 10c. Type **370** 20 20
4064 20c. Ex.Mza 1400 40 20
4065 50c. "Mallard" 60 35
4066 70c. Tank locomotive "Monarch" 60 40
4067 90c. "Big Chief" 60 40
4068 $1.10 L.M.S. No. 6228 "Duchess of Rutland" 65 70
4069 $1.10 Holmes J36 65 70
4070 $1.10 "Patentee" 65 70
4071 $1.10 "Kingfisher" 65 70
4072 $1.10 No. 23 "St Pierre" 65 70
4073 $1.10 South African Railways Class 19c 65 70
4074 $1.10 South African Railways Class 6J 65 70
4075 $1.10 No. 92220 "Evening Star" 65 70
4076 $1.10 No. 1 65 70
4077 $1.10 "The Hadrian Flyer" 65 70
4078 $1.10 Class "Highland Jones Goods" No. 103 65 70
4079 $1.10 No. 34023 "Blackmore Vale" 65 70
4080 $1.10 S.E.C.R. No. 27 65 70
4081 $1.10 Class "Brighton Terrier" "Stepney" 65 70
4082 $1.10 R.E.N.F.E. No. 2184 65 70
4083 $1.10 Southern Railway No. 24 "Calbourne" 65 70
4084 $1.10 "Clun Castle" 65 70
MS4085 Two sheets, each 101×70 mm. (a) $5 "Caledonia". (b) $5 No. 6000 "King George V". Set of 2 sheets 5·50 6·00

The identification of the locomotive on No. 4084 has been reported as incorrect.

371 Guianan Cock of the Rock ("Cock-of-the-rock")

1998. Birds of the World. Multicoloured.
4086 50c. Type **371** 45 30
4087 60c. Resplendant quetzal ("Quetzal") 55 40
4088 70c. American wood stork ("Wood Stork") 55 40
4089 90c. St. Vincent amazon (species inscr at right) 60 65
4090 90c. Keel-billed toucan ("Toucan") (horiz) 60 65
4091 90c. Racquet-tailed motmot 60 65
4092 90c. Red-billed quelea 60 65
4093 90c. Major Mitchell's cockatoo ("Leadbeater's Cockatoo") 60 65
4094 90c. Green-winged macaw ("Scarlet Macaw") 60 65
4095 90c. Bare-throated bellbird 60 65
4096 90c. Tucaman amazon 60 65
4097 90c. White-winged tanager ("Black-lored Red Tanager") 60 65
4098 90c. Tucuman amazon ("Fig parrot") 60 65
4099 90c. St. Vincent amazon (species inscr at top) 60 65
4100 90c. Peach-faced love birds 60 65
4101 90c. Blue-fronted amazon 60 65
4102 90c. Yellow-billed amazon 60 65
4103 $1 Greater bird of paradise (horiz) 60 65
4104 $1.10 Sun-bittern (horiz) 70 75
4105 $2 Green honeycreeper (horiz) 1·10 1·25
MS4106 Two sheets, each 98×62 mm. (a) $5 Hyacinth macaw. (b) $5 Blue-headed hummingbird. Set of 2 sheets 5·50 6·00

Nos. 4091/4102 were printed together, se-tenant, with the backgrounds forming a composite design.

372 White Whale

1998. International Year of the Ocean. Multicoloured.
4107 70c. Type **372** 45 35
4108 90c. Atlantic manta 50 40
4109 $1 Harlequin wrasse and brown pelican (vert) 60 65
4110 $1 Blue surgeonfish (vert) 60 65
4111 $1 Spotted trunkfish and sailing ship (vert) 60 65
4112 $1 Regal angelfish (vert) 60 65
4113 $1 Porcupine fish (vert) 60 65
4114 $1 Clownfish (vert) 60 65
4115 $1 Lion fish (vert) 60 65
4116 $1 Moray eel (vert) 60 65
4117 $1 French angelfish (vert) 60 65
4118 $1 Lemonpeel angelfish, flying fish and herring gulls (vert) 60 65
4119 $1 Narwhal (vert) 60 65
4120 $1 Panther grouper, atlantic puffin and house (vert) 60 65
4121 $1 Fur seal and jellyfish (vert) 60 65
4122 $1 Spiny boxfish (vert) 60 65
4123 $1 Loggerhead turtle (vert) 60 65
4124 $1 Opah (vert) 60 65
4125 $1 Clown triggerfish (vert) 60 65
4126 $1 Bighead searobin (vert) 60 65
4127 $1.10 Forceps butterflyfish, moorish idol and copper-band butterflyfish 70 70
4128 $2 Octopus 1·10 1·25
MS4129 Two sheets, each 98×73 mm. (a) $5 Seahorse (vert). (b) $5 Australian Seadragon (vert). Set of 2 sheets 5·50 6·00

Nos. 4109/17 and 4118/26 respectively were printed together, se-tenant, with the backgrounds forming composite designs.

No. 4109 is inscribed "Harlequin Warasse" in error.

372a Flags of St. Vincent and CARICOM

1998. 25th Anniv of Caribbean Community.
4130 **372a** $1 multicoloured 60 60

372b Stylized "50"

1998. 50th Anniv of Organization of American States.
4131 **372b** $1 violet, green and black 60 60

373 "Landscape"

1998. 25th Death Anniv of Pablo Picasso (painter). Multicoloured.
4132 $1.10 Type **373** 60 50
4133 $2 "The Death of the Female Torero" 1·10 1·25
4134 $2 "The Kiss" 1·10 1·25
MS4135 102×127 mm. $5 "Flute Player" (vert) 3·25 3·50

373a 365 GTS

1998. Birth Centenary of Enzo Ferrari (car manufacturer). Multicoloured.
4136 $2 Type **373a** 1·40 1·50
4137 $2 Testarossa 1·40 1·50
4138 $2 365 GT4 B B 1·40 1·50
MS4139 104×70 mm. $6 Dino 206 GT (91×34 mm) 3·50 4·00

373b Presentation of Silver Buffalo award to John Glenn (U.S. astronaut)

1998. 19th World Scout Jamboree, Chile.
4140 **373b** $2 lilac, violet and black 1·10 1·25
4141 - $2 brown, violet and black 1·10 1·25
4142 - $2 brown, violet and black 1·10 1·25
MS4143 70×100 mm. $5 blue, brown and black 3·25 3·50

DESIGNS—HORIZ: No. 4141, Herb Shriner learning knot-tying, 1960; 4142, Breaking camp, 1940s. VERT: No. **MS**4143, Lord Baden-Powell in court dress.

373c Mahatma Gandhi

1998. 50th Death Anniv of Mahatma Gandhi.
4144 **373c** $1 multicoloured 1·00 1·00
MS4145 107×76 mm. $5 brown, purple and black 5·00 4·25

DESIGN—HORIZ: $5 Gandhi at conference table.

373d AEW 1 (Airborne Early Warning)

1998. 80th Anniv of Royal Air Force. Multicoloured.
4146 $2 Type **373d** 1·25 1·25
4147 $2 Eurofighter EF-2000 1·25 1·25
4148 $2 Sepecat Jaguar GR1A 1·25 1·25
4149 $2 BAe Hawk T1A trainer 1·25 1·25
4150 $2 Two Sepecat Jaguar GR1s 1·25 1·25
4151 $2 Panavia Tornado F3 1·25 1·25
4152 $2 Three BAe Harrier GR7s 1·25 1·25
4153 $2 Panavia Tornado F3 IDV 1·25 1·25
MS4154 Four sheets, each 90×70 mm. (a) $6 Bristol F2B fighter and Falcon (bird). (b) $6 Bristol F2B fighter and Golden Eagle (bird). (c) $6 Mosquito and Eurofighter EF-2000. (d) $6 Vulcan B2 and Eurofighter EF-2000 Set of 4 sheets 13·00 14·00

1998. 1st Death Anniv of Diana, Princess of Wales. As T 317a of Sierra Leone. Multicoloured.
4155 $1.10 Diana, Princess of Wales 65 65

374 H. Daisley (64 years of service)

1998. 150th Anniv of Local Court of Ancient Order of Foresters. Multicoloured (except 70c.).
4156 10c. Type **374** 15 15
4157 20c. R. Jack (71 years of service) 20 15
4158 50c. Ancient Order of Foresters' arms 35 30
4159 70c. Bow and arrow symbol (green and black) 45 45
4160 90c. Court's headquarters 55 55

375 Bi-colour Longhair

1998. Christmas. Cats. Multicoloured.
4161 20c. Type **375** 20 15
4162 50c. Korat 35 25
4163 60c. Seal-point Siamese 45 40
4164 70c. Red self longhair 50 50
4165 90c. Black longhair 55 55
4166 $1.10 Red tabby exotic shorthair 65 70
MS4167 Two sheets, each 75×66 mm. (a) $5 Seal-point Colourpoint. (b) $5 Tortoiseshell Shorthair. Set of 2 sheets 5·50 6·00

376 Flautist

1998. 900th Birth Anniv of St. Hildegard von Bingen (German mystic). Multicoloured.

4168	$1.10 Type **376**	65	70
4169	$1.10 St. Hildegard and abbey	65	70
4170	$1.10 Viola player	65	70
4171	$1.10 Pope Eugenius	65	70
4172	$1.10 Town of Bingen	65	70
4173	$1.10 St. Hildegard	65	70
MS4174	85×110 mm. $5 St. Hildegard	3·25	3·50

377 Rabbit facing Right

1999. Chinese New Year ("Year of the Rabbit"). Designs showing stylized rabbits. Multicoloured (except No. MS4178).

4175	$1 Type **377**	60	65
4176	$1 Rabbit facing front	60	65
4177	$1 Rabbit facing left	60	55
MS4178	70×100 mm. $2 As No. 4176 (black, lilac and pink)	1·25	1·40

378 Mickey Mouse

1999. 70th Birthday of Mickey Mouse (2nd issue). Walt Disney characters playing Winter sports. Multicoloured.

4179	$1.10 Type **378**	85	85
4180	$1.10 Goofy on skis wearing goggles	85	85
4181	$1.10 Donald Duck skiing in yellow sweatshirt	85	85
4182	$1.10 Goofy and Mickey in red bobsleigh	85	85
4183	$1.10 Goofy on skis in yellow	85	85
4184	$1.10 Minnie on skis with yellow bow	85	85
4185	$1.10 Daisy Duck on skis wearing purple bow	85	85
4186	$1.10 Mickey on skis wearing goggles	85	85
4187	$1.10 Goofy and Mickey in green bobsleigh	85	85
4188	$1.10 Goofy on skis in blue	85	85
4189	$1.10 Minnie snowboarding	85	85
4190	$1.10 Donald on skis in blue sweatshirt	85	85
4191	$1.10 Minnie skiing with blue and purple bow	85	85
4192	$1.10 Mickey snowboarding	85	85
4193	$1.10 Goofy on skis in blue and purple vest	85	85
4194	$1.10 Donald skiing in blue and purple sweatshirt	85	85
4195	$1.10 Mickey snowboarding in yellow hat and goggles	85	85
4196	$1.10 Daisy skiing in blue and purple	85	85
MS4197	Three sheets. (a) 102×127 mm. $5 Mickey Mouse. (b) 127×102 mm. $5 Minnie Mouse. (c) 127×102 mm. $5 Goofy (horiz). Set of 3 sheets	11·00	11·00

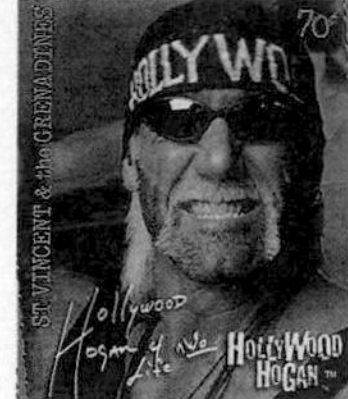

379 Hollywood Hogan

1999. World Championship Wrestling. Mult.

4198	70c. Type **379**	40	40
4199	70c. Sting	40	40
4200	70c. Bret Hart	40	40
4201	70c. Giant	40	40
4202	70c. Kevin Nash	40	40
4203	70c. Randy Savage	40	40
4204	70c. Diamond Dallas	40	40
4205	70c. Goldberg	40	40

380 Plateosaurus

1999. "Australia '99" World Stamp Exhibition, Melbourne. Prehistoric Animals. Mult.

4206	70c. Type **380**	45	50
4207	70c. Struthiomimus	45	50
4208	70c. Indricotherium	45	50
4209	70c. Giant moa	45	50
4210	70c. Deinonychus	45	50
4211	70c. Sabre tooth tiger	45	50
4212	70c. Dawn horse	45	50
4213	70c. Peittacosaurus	45	50
4214	70c. Giant ground sloth	45	50
4215	70c. Woolly rhinoceros	45	50
4216	70c. Mosasaur	45	50
4217	70c. Mastodon	45	50
4218	70c. Syndyoceras	45	50
4219	90c. Euoplacephalus	50	55
4220	90c. Rhamphorhynchus	45	50
4221	90c. Pteranodon	50	55
4222	90c. Archaeopteryx	50	55
4223	90c. Dimetrodon	35	40
4224	90c. Stegasaurus	50	55
4225	90c. Parasaurolophus	50	55
4226	90c. Iguanadon	50	55
4227	90c. Triceratops	50	55
4228	90c. Tyrannosaurus	50	55
4229	90c. Ichthyosaurus	50	55
4230	90c. Plesiosaurus	50	55
4231	90c. Hesperornis	50	55
4232	$1.10 Pachycephalosaurus	65	65
4233	$1.40 Dilophosaurus	75	80
MS4234	Two sheets, each 107×77 mm. (a) $5 Diplodocus. (b) $5 Woolly Mammoth (vert). Set of 2 sheets	6·00	6·50

381 African Elephant and Acacia Tree

1999. Fauna and Flora. Multicoloured.

4235	10c. Type **381**	30	25
4236	20c. Green turtle and coconut palm seedling	40	25
4237	25c. White ibis and mangrove tree	50	25
4238	50c. Tiger swallowtail and ironweed	50	30
4239	70c. Eastern box turtle and Jack-in-the-Pulpit (plant) (vert)	50	40
4240	70c. Basilisk lizard and strangler fig (vert)	50	55
4241	70c. Scarlet macaw ("Macaw") and kapok trees (vert)	50	55
4242	70c. Howler monkey and cecropia tree (vert)	50	55
4243	70c. Keel-billed toucan ("Toucan") and cecropia tree (vert)	50	55
4244	70c. Poison-arrow frog and bromiliad (vert)	50	55
4245	70c. "Heliconius phyllis" (butterfly) and rattlesnake orchid (vert)	50	55
4246	70c. Black-mantled goshawk ("Bat-eating Hawk") and tree fern (vert)	50	55
4247	70c. Jaguar and tillandsia (vert)	50	55
4248	70c. Margay and sierra palm (vert)	50	55
4249	70c. Lesser bird of paradise and aristolchia (vert)	50	55
4250	70c. Parides (butterfly) and erythrina (vert)	50	55
4251	70c. Fer-de-Lance (snake) and zebra plant (vert)	50	55
4252	70c. Red-tailed hawk and ocitillo (vert)	50	55
4253	70c. Mourning dove and organ pipe cactus (vert)	50	55
4254	70c. Burrowing owl and paloverde tree (vert)	50	55
4255	70c. Cactus wren and saguaro cactus (vert)	50	55
4256	70c. Puma and ocitillo (vert)	50	55
4257	70c. Grey fox and organ pipe cactus (vert)	50	55
4258	70c. Coyote and prickly pear cactus (vert)	50	55
4259	70c. Gila woodpecker and saguaro cactus (vert)	50	55
4260	70c. Collared lizard and barrel cactus (vert)	50	55
4261	70c. Gila monster (lizard) and cowblinder cactus (vert)	50	55
4262	70c. Roadrunner and hedgehog cactus (vert)	50	55
4263	70c. Jack rabbit and saguaro cactus (vert)	50	55
4264	90c. Praying mantis and milkweed (vert)	55	55
4265	$1.10 Spotted-sided finch and bottle brush (vert)	65	65
4266	$1.40 Koala and gum tree (vert)	70	80
MS4267	Two sheets, each 110×85 mm. (a) $5 Alligator and Water Lilies. (b) $5 Rivoli's Hummingbird ("Rivolis hummingbird"). Set of 2 sheets	6·00	6·50

Nos. 4240/51 and 4252/63 were each printed together, se-tenant, the backgrounds forming composite designs.

No. 4253 is inscribed "MORNING DOVE", No. 4265 "ZEBRA FINCH", both in error.

382 Lilenthal's Glider, 1894

1999. Aircraft. Multicoloured.

4268	60c. Montgolfier Balloon, 1783 (vert)	45	30
4269	70c. Type **382**	45	35
4270	90c. "Zeppelin" (airship)	50	40
4271	$1 Wilbur Wright and "Flyer", 1903	60	45
4272	$1.10 M-130 Clipper	70	75
4273	$1.10 DC-3, 1937	70	75
4274	$1.10 Staggerwing Beech CVR FT C-17L	70	75
4275	$1.10 Hughes H-1 Racer	70	75
4276	$1.10 Gee Bee Model R-1, 1932	70	75
4277	$1.10 Lockheed 8 Sirius Tingmissartoq seaplane	70	75
4278	$1.10 Fokker T-2, 1923	70	75
4279	$1.10 Curtiss CW-16E seaplane	70	75
4280	$1.10 Dayton Wright DH-4 Bomber	70	75
4281	$1.10 Sopwith Camel	70	75
4282	$1.10 Sopwith Dove	70	75
4283	$1.10 Jeannin Stahl Taube	70	75
4284	$1.10 Fokker DR-1 triplane	70	75
4285	$1.10 Albatross Diva	70	75
4286	$1.10 Sopwith Pup	70	75
4287	$1.10 SPAD XIII Smith IV	70	75
MS4288	Two sheets, each 110×85 mm. (a) $5 Lebauldy-Juillot airship No. 1 "La Jaune", 1903. (b) $5 Bleriot XI crossing Channel, 1914. Set of 2 sheets	5·50	6·00

Nos. 4272/9 and 4280/7 were each issued, se-tenant, with the backgrounds forming composite designs.

No. **MS**4288a is inscribed "LE BANDY AIRSHIP" in error.

383 NSYNC

1999. NSYNC (pop group) Commemoration.

4289	**383** $1 multicoloured	60	60

384 Galileo Galilei (astronomer, 1609)

1999. Space Exploration. Multicoloured.

4290	20c. Type **384**	20	15
4291	50c. Konstantin Tsiolkovsky (aeronautical engineer, 1903)	40	45
4292	70c. Robert Goddard (rocket scientist, 1926)	45	35
4293	90c. Sir Isaac Newton (physicist, 1668) (vert)	50	40
4294-4302	$1 ×9 ("Explorer" rocket, 1958; "Lunokhod Explorer", 1970; "Viking Lander", 1975; A - I (SL-3) rocket, 1959; Edward White (astronaut), 1965; "Salyut 1" space station, 1971; Ancient observatory; "Freedom 7" rocket, 1961; "Ariane" rocket, 1980s (all vert))	5·00	
4303-4311	$1 ×9 ("Luna 3", 1959; "Soyuz 11", 1971; "MIR" space station, 1986; "Sputnik 1", 1957; "Apollo 4", 1967; Bruce McCandles (astronaut), 1984; Sir William Herschel's telescope, 1781; John Glenn (astronaut), 1962; Space shuttle "Columbia", 1981	5·00	
4312-4320	$1 ×9 (Yuri Gagarin (cosmonaut), 1961; "Lunar Rover", 1971; "Mariner 10", 1974–5; Laika (first dog in space), 1957; Edwin Aldrin on Moon, 1969; "Skylab" space station, 1973; German "V-2" rocket, 1942; "Gemini 4" rocket, 1965; Hubble telescope, 1990; (all vert))	5·00	
MS4321	Two sheets, each 85×110 mm. (a) $5 Space Shuttle "Atlantis" docking with "MIR". (b) $5 Saturn 5 rocket, 1969 (vert). Set of 2 sheets	6·00	7·00

Nos. 4294/302, 4303/11 and 4312/20 were each printed together, se-tenant, with the backgrounds forming composite designs.

No. 4297 is inscribed "1957-R7 Rocket", No. 4303 "LUNA 9", No. 4312 "1962" and No. 4316 "NEIL ARMSTRONG" all in error.

385 Prince Edward

1999. Royal Wedding. Multicoloured.

4322	$3 Type **385**	1·75	1·75
4323	$3 Miss Sophie Rhys-Jones and Prince Edward	1·75	1·75
4324	$3 Miss Sophie Rhys-Jones	1·75	1·75
MS4325	78×108 mm. $6 Prince Edward and Miss Sophie Rhys-Jones (horiz)	3·25	3·50

385a Steam Locomotive and Power Station

1999. "iBRA '99" International Stamp Exhibition, Nuremberg.

4326	**385a** $1 multicoloured	60	60

No. 4326 is inscribed "THE KRAUSS-MAFFEI V-200 DIESEL LOCOMOTIVE: GERMANY 1852" in error.

385b "Admiring the Irises at Yatsuhashi"

1999. 150th Death Anniv of Katsushika Hokusai (Japanese artist). Multicoloured.

4327	$1.10 Type **385b**	65	70
4328	$1.10 "Sea Life" (turtle facing top left)	65	70
4329	$1.10 "Admiring the Irises at Yatsuhashi" (different)	65	70
4330	$1.10 "Pilgrims bathing in Roben Waterfall"	65	70
4331	$1.10 "Sea Life" (turtle facing top right)	65	70
4332	$1.10 "Farmers crossing a Suspension Bridge"	65	70
4333	$1.10 "Landscape with a Hundred Bridges" (mountains)	65	70
4334	$1.10 "Sea Life" (turtle facing bottom left)	65	70
4335	$1.10 "Landscape with a Hundred Bridges" (Japanese inscr at top)	65	70
4336	$1.10 "A View of Aoigaoka Waterfall in Edo"	65	70
4337	$1.10 "Sea Life" (crab)	65	70
4338	$1.10 "Women on the Beach at Enoshima"	65	70
MS4339	Two sheets, each 71×102 mm. (a) $5 "In the Horse-washing Waterfall". (b) $5 "Fisherman at Kajikazawa". Set of 2 sheets	5·50	6·00

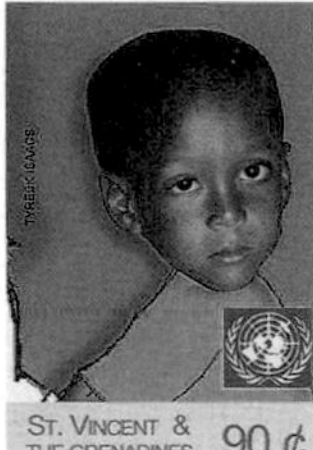

385c Tyreek Isaacs

1999. 10th Anniv of United Nations Rights of the Child Convention. Multicoloured.

4340	90c. Type **385c**	50	50
4341	90c. Fredique Isaacs	50	50
4342	90c. Jerome Burke III	50	50
4343	90c. Kellisha Roberts	50	50
4344	$3 Girl with ribbons in hair	1·75	1·75
4345	$3 Girl in straw hat	1·75	1·75
4346	$3 Girl with kitten	1·75	1·75
MS4347	110×80 mm. $5 Japanese child	3·00	3·25

385d Pacific Steam Locomotive for "Fleche d'Or"

1999. "PhilexFrance '99" International Stamp Exhibition, Paris. Railway Locomotives. Two sheets, each 106×81 mm containing horiz designs as T 385d. Multicoloured.

MS4348	(a) $6 Type **385d**. (b) $6 Quadrt electric high-speed locomotive, 1940. Set of 2 sheets	7·00	7·50

385e Faust, Helena and Euphonon

1999. 250th Birth Anniv of Johann von Goethe (German writer).

4349	**385e**	$3 grey and black	1·60	1·75
4350	-	$3 blue, purple and black	1·60	1·75
4351	-	$3 blue and black	1·60	1·75
4352	-	$3 mauve and black	1·60	1·75
4353	-	$3 cinnamon and black	1·60	1·75
MS4354		Two sheets, each 78×108 mm. (a) $5 brown and black. (b) $5 brown, deep brown and black. Set of 2 sheets	5·50	6·00

DESIGNS—HORIZ: No. 4350, Von Goethe and Von Schiller; 4351, Mephistopheles leading the Lemures to Faust; 4352, Faust dying; 4353, Faust's spirit being carried by angels. VERT: No. **MS**4354a, Von Goethe; **MS**4354b, Immortal soul of Faust.

386 I. M. Pei

1999. Year of the Elder Person. Multicoloured.

4355	70c. Type **386**	45	50
4356	70c. Billy Graham	45	50
4357	70c. Barbara Cartland	45	50
4358	70c. Mike Wallace	45	50
4359	70c. Jeanne Moreau	45	50
4360	70c. B. B. King	45	50
4361	70c. Elie Wiesel	45	50
4362	70c. Arthur Miller	45	50
4363	70c. Colin Powell	45	50
4364	70c. Jack Palance	45	50
4365	70c. Neil Simon	45	50
4366	70c. Eartha Kitt	45	50
MS4367	115×134 mm. $1.10 Thomas Saunders; $1.10 Mother Sarah Baptiste; $1.10 Sir Sydney Gun-Munro; $1.10 Dr. Earle Kirby	4·75	5·50

387 Henry Alphaeus Robertson

1999. World Teachers' Day. Multicoloured.

4368	$2 Type **387**	1·10	1·25
4369	$2 Yvonne Francis-Gibson	1·10	1·25
4370	$2 Edna Peters	1·10	1·25
4371	$2 Christopher Wilberforce Prescod	1·10	1·25

387a Lady Elizabeth Bowes-Lyon, 1909

1999. "Queen Elizabeth the Queen Mother's Century".

4372	**387a**	$2 black and gold	1·25	1·25
4373	-	$2 black and gold	1·25	1·25
4374	-	$2 multicoloured	1·25	1·25
4375	-	$2 multicoloured	1·25	1·25
MS4376		153×156 mm. $6 multicoloured	4·50	4·50

DESIGNS: No. 4373, King George VI and Queen Elizabeth with Princess Elizabeth, 1930; 4374, Queen Mother at Badminton, 1977; 4375, Queen Mother waving, 1983. 37×50 mm: No. **MS**4376, Queen Mother wearing yellow dress, 1987.

No. **MS**4376 shows the Royal Arms embossed in gold.

388 "The Resurrection" (Durer)

1999. Christmas. Religious Paintings. Multicoloured.

4377	20c. Type **388**	20	15
4378	50c. "Christ in Limbo" (Durer)	35	30
4379	70c. "Christ falling on the Way to Calvary" (Raphael)	45	35
4380	90c. "St. Ildefonso with the Madonna and Child" (Rubens)	50	40
4381	$5 "The Crucifixion" (Raphael)	3·00	3·75
MS4382	76×106 mm. $6 "The Sistine Madonna" (Raphael)	3·50	3·75

No. 4378 is inscribed "Christ in Llmbo" in error.

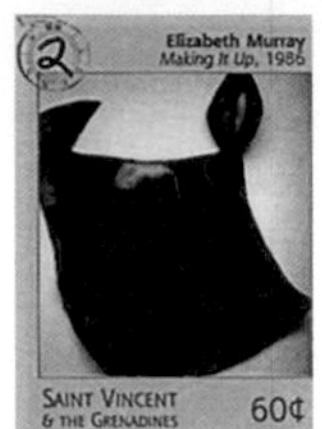

389 Mail Coach, 1800

1999. 125th Anniv of Universal Postal Union. Multicoloured.

4383	$3 Type **389**	1·75	1·75
4384	$3 Sea plane leaving liner	1·75	1·75
4385	$3 Concorde	1·75	1·75

390 "Making It Up" (Elizabeth Murray)

1999. New Millennium. Sculpture of the Twentieth Century. Multicoloured.

4386	60c. Type **390**	35	40
4387	60c. "The Brass Family" (Alexander Calder)	35	40
4388	60c. "Tent" (Charles William Moss)	35	40
4389	60c. "Dolphin Fountain" (Gaston Lachaise)	35	40
4390	60c. "Soft Toilet" (Claes Oldenbury)	35	40
4391	60c. "Nature Study, Velvet Eyes" (Louise Bourgeois)	35	40
4392	60c. "Woman with Dog" (Duane Hanson)	35	40
4393	60c. "Bird in Space" (Brancusi)	35	40
4394	60c. "Lectern Sentinel" (David Smith)	35	40
4395	60c. "Untitled" (Dan Flavin)	35	40
4396	60c. "Unique forms of continue in space" (Boccioni)	35	40
4397	60c. "Walk, Don't Walk" (George Segal)	35	40
4398	60c. "Untitled Box No. 3" (Lucas Samaras)	35	40
4399	60c. "Bicycle Wheel" (Marcel Duchamp)	35	40
4400	60c. "Humpty Dumpty" (Isamu Noguchi)	35	40
4401	60c. "Untitled" (Donald Judd) (59×39 mm)	35	40
4402	60c. "Dawn's Wedding Chapel II" (Louise Nevelson)	35	40

390a Portraits forming Forehead

1999. Faces of the Millennium: "Mona Lisa" (Leonardo da Vinci). Showing collage of miniature details of paintings. Multicoloured.

4403	$1.10 Type **390a**	65	70
4404	$1.10 Forehead (face value at right)	65	70
4405	$1.10 Side of face (face value at left)	65	70
4406	$1.10 Side of face (face value at right)	65	70
4407	$1.10 Cheek (face value at left)	65	70
4408	$1.10 Cheek (face value at right)	65	70
4409	$1.10 Hair (face value at left)	65	70
4410	$1.10 Hair and shoulder (face value at right)	65	70

Nos. 4403/10 were printed together, se-tenant, in sheetlets of 8 with the stamps arranged in two vertical columns separated by a gutter also containing miniature portraits. When viewed as a whole, the sheetlet forms the "Mona Lisa".

391 Clyde Tombaugh and Pluto

1999. New Millennium. 80th Anniv of Discovery of the Planet Pluto by Clyde Tombaugh.

4411	**391**	60c. multicoloured	1·00	75

No. 4411 shows a white frame. The design also occurs as No. 4469 with a multicoloured frame and different perforation.

1999. Faces of the Millennium: Diana, Princess of Wales. As T 329a of Sierra Leone, showing collage of miniature flower photographs. Mult.

4412	$1 Flowers forming top of head (face value at left)	60	65
4413	$1 Top of head (face value at right)	60	65
4414	$1 Ear (face value at left)	60	65
4415	$1 Eye and temple (face value at right)	60	65
4416	$1 Cheek (face value at left)	60	65
4417	$1 Cheek (face value at right)	60	65
4418	$1 Blue background (face value at left)	60	65
4419	$1 Chin (face value at right)	60	65

Nos. 4412/19 were printed together, se-tenant, in sheetlets of 8 with the stamps arranged in two vertical columns separated by a gutter also containing miniature photographs. When viewed as a whole, the sheetlet forms a portrait of Diana, Princess of Wales.

392 Dragon

2000. Chinese New Year ("Year of the Dragon"). Multicoloured.

4420	$2 Type **392** (blue and lilac background)	1·10	1·25
4421	$2 Dragon (cinnamon and brown background)	1·10	1·25
4422	$2 Dragon (orange and cerise background)	1·10	1·25
MS4423	70×101 mm. $4 Dragon	2·00	2·50

393 Stoplight Parrotfish

2000. Tropical Fish. Multicoloured.

4424	10c. Type **393**	15	15
4425	20c. Spot-finned hogfish	20	15
4426	70c. Beaugregory	45	35
4427	90c. Porkfish	50	40
4428	$1 Barred hamlet	60	45
4429	$1.10 Porcupinefish	65	70
4430	$1.10 Blue tang	65	70
4431	$1.10 Blue-headed wrasse	65	70
4432	$1.10 Queen angelfish (juvenile)	65	70
4433	$1.10 Lined seahorse	65	70
4434	$1.10 Small-mouthed grunt	65	70
4435	$1.10 French angelfish	65	70
4436	$1.10 Smooth trunkfish	65	70
4437	$1.10 Sargassum triggerfish	65	70
4438	$1.10 Indigo hamlet	65	70
4439	$1.10 Yellow-headed jawfish	65	70
4440	$1.10 Peppermint basslet	65	70
4441	$1.40 Queen triggerfish	75	80
MS4442	Two sheets, each 183×80 mm. (a) $5 Four-eyed Butterflyfish. (b) $5 Cherub ("Pygmy") Angelfish. Set of 2 sheets	5·50	6·00

Nos. 4429/34 and 4435/40 were each printed together, se-tenant, with the backgrounds forming composite designs.

No. 4438 is inscribed "Indigo Halmet" in error.

394 High Hat

2000. Marine Life. Multicoloured.

4443 50c. Type **394** 35 40
4444 50c. Sergeant major 35 40
4445 50c. Hawksbill turtle 35 40
4446 50c. Horse-eyed jacks 35 40
4447 50c. Horse-eyed jacks and middle of humpback whale 35 40
4448 50c. Head of humpback whale and horse-eyed jacks 35 40
4449 50c. Black-capped basslet ("Gramma") 35 40
4450 50c. Common dolphins 35 40
4451 50c. French grunts and flipper of humpback whale 35 40
4452 50c. Great barracuda 35 40
4453 50c. Bottle-nosed dolphins 35 40
4454 50c. Reid's seahorse 35 40
4455 50c. French grunt and southern stingray 35 40
4456 50c. French grunts 35 40
4457 50c. Indigo hamlet 35 40
4458 50c. Basking shark 35 40
4459 50c. Nassau grouper 35 40
4460 50c. Nurse shark and jackknife-fish ("Ribbonfish") 35 40
4461 50c. Southern stingray 35 40
4462 50c. Blue shark and southern stingray 35 40
4463 50c. Spanish hogfish 35 40
4464 90c. Spotfin hogfish 50 45
4465 $1 Royal gramma 60 55
4466 $2 Queen angelfish 1·10 1·25

MS4467 Two sheets, each 106×76 mm. (a) $5 Rock Beauty. (b) $5 Banded Butterflyfish. Set of 2 sheets 5·50 6·00

Nos. 4444/63 were printed together, se-tenant, with the backgrounds forming a composite design.

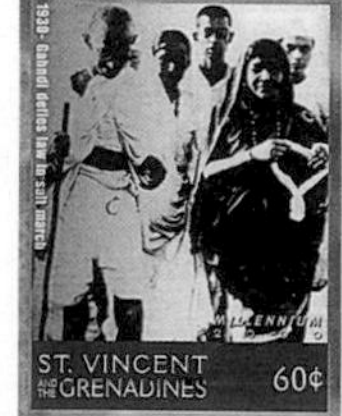

394a Mahatma Gandhi and Supporters, 1930

2000. New Millennium. People and Events of Twentieth Century (1930–39). Multicoloured.

4468 60c. Type **394a** 45 50
4469 60c. As Type **391**, but with multicoloured frame 45 50
4470 60c. Empire State Building, New York (opened 1931) 45 50
4471 60c. Declaration of Republic, Spain, 1931 45 50
4472 60c. Pres. Franklin D. Roosevelt ("New Deal" inaugurated, 1933) 45 50
4473 60c. Reichstag on fire, 1933 45 50
4474 60c. Mao Tse-tung (Communist Revolution in China, 1934) 45 50
4475 60c. General Franco (Spanish Civil War, 1936) 45 50
4476 60c. King Edward VIII and Abdication document, 1936 45 50
4477 60c. Diego Rivera (Mexican muralist) (50th birthday, 1936) 45 50
4478 60c. Golden Gate Bridge, San Francisco (opened 1937) 45 50
4479 60c. Atomic cloud (first atomic reaction, 1939) 45 50
4480 60c. Troops and newspaper vendor (start of Second World War, 1939) 45 50
4481 60c. New York World's Fair emblem, 1939 45 50
4482 60c. New Dalai Lama chosen in Tibet, 1939 45 50
4483 60c. Explosion of *Hindenburg* (airship), 1937 (59×39 mm) 45 50
4484 60c. Igor Sikorsky and VS-300, first successful helicopter, 1939 45 50

No. 4468 is inscribed "Gahndi" in error.

394b Sigmund Freud (*Interpretation of Dreams* published, 1900)

2000. New Millennium. People and Events of Twentieth Century (1900–50). Multicoloured.

4485 20c. Type **394b** 25 30
4486 20c. Guglielmo Marconi (first long distance wireless transmission, 1901) 25 30
4487 20c. Orville and Wilbur Wright (construction of Wright *Flyer III* powered aircraft, 1903) 25 30
4488 20c. Albert Einstein (Theory of Relativity, 1905) 25 30
4489 20c. Henry Ford and Model T, 1908 25 30
4490 20c. Alfred Wegener (German meteorologist) (Theory of Continental Drift, 1912) 25 30
4491 20c. Lord Kitchener on recruiting poster (beginning of First World War, 1914) 25 30
4492 20c. Lenin (Russian Revolution, 1917) 25 30
4493 20c. James Joyce (*Ulysses*, published 1922) 25 30
4494 20c. Alexander Fleming (Scottish bacteriologist) (discovery of Penicillin, 1928) 25 30
4495 20c. Edwin Hubble (Hubble's Law on expansion of Universe, 1929) 25 30
4496 20c. Mao Tse-tung and map of Long March, 1934 25 30
4497 20c. Alan Turing (English mathematician) (Theory of digital computing, 1937) 25 30
4498 20c. Berlin researchers (discovery of frission, 1938) 25 30
4499 20c. German Troops and headline (start of Second World War, 1939) 25 30
4500 20c. Churchill, Roosevelt and Stalin (Yalta Conference, 1945) 25 30
4501 20c. Gandhi and Nehru (Independence of India, 1947) 25 30
4502 20c. William Shockley (U.S. physicist) (development of miniature transistor, 1947) 25 30

394c "Robert Rich, Earl of Warwick"

2000. 400th Birth Anniv of Sir Anthony van Dyck. Multicoloured.

4503 $1 Type **394c** 60 65
4504 $1 "James Stuart, Duke of Lennox and Richmond" 60 65
4505 $1 "Sir John Suckling" 60 65
4506 $1 "Sir Robert Shirley" 60 65
4507 $1 "Teresia, Lady Shirley" 60 65
4508 $1 "Thomas Wentworth, Earl of Strafford" (with dog) 60 65
4509 $1 "Thomas Wentworth, Earl of Strafford" 60 65
4510 $1 "Lady Anne Carr, Countess of Bedford" 60 65
4511 $1 "Portrait of a Member of the Charles Family" 60 65
4512 $1 "Thomas Howard, Earl of Arundel" 60 65
4513 $1 "Diana Cecil, Countess of Oxford" 60 65
4514 $1 "The Violincellist" 60 65
4515 $1 "The Apostle Peter" 60 65
4516 $1 "St. Matthew" 60 65
4517 $1 "St. James the Greater" 60 65
4518 $1 "St. Bartholomew" 60 65
4519 $1 "The Apostle Thomas" 60 65
4520 $1 "The Apostle Jude (Thaddeus)" 60 65
4521 $1 "The Vision of St. Anthony" 60 65
4522 $1 "The Mystic Marriage of St. Catherine" 60 65
4523 $1 "The Vision of the Blessed Herman Joseph" 60 65
4524 $1 "Madonna and Child enthroned with Sts. Rosalie, Peter and Paul" 60 65
4525 $1 "St. Rosalie interceding for the Plague stricken of Palermo" 60 65
4526 $1 "Francesco Orero in Adoration of the Crucifixion" 60 65

MS4527 Three sheets. (a) 102×127 mm. $5 "William Fielding, Earl of Denbigh". (b) 127×102 mm. $5 "The Mystic Marriage of St. Catherine". (c) 102×127 mm. $5 "St. Augustine in Ecstasy" (horiz). Set of 3 sheets 7·50 8·00

395 *Brassavola nodosa*

2000. "The Stamp Show 2000" International Stamp Exhibition, London. Orchids of the Caribbean. Mult.

4528 70c. Type **395** 45 35
4529 90c. *Bletia purpurea* 50 40
4530 $1.40 *Brassavola cucullata* 80 75
4531 $1.50 *Brassavola cordata* (vert) 85 90
4532 $1.50 *Brassia caudata* (vert) 85 90
4533 $1.50 *Broughotnia sanguinea* (vert) 85 90
4534 $1.50 *Comparettia falcata* (vert) 85 90
4535 $1.50 *Clowesia rosea* (vert) 85 90
4536 $1.50 *Caularthron bicornutum* (vert) 85 90
4537 $1.50 *Cyrtopodium punctatum* (vert) 85 90
4538 $1.50 *Dendrophylax funalis* (vert) 85 90
4539 $1.50 *Dichaea hystricina* (vert) 85 90
4540 $1.50 *Cyrtopodium andersonii* (vert) 85 90
4541 $1.50 *Epidendrum secundum* (vert) 85 90
4542 $1.50 *Dimerandra emarginata* (vert) 85 90
4543 $1.50 *Oncidium urophyllum* (vert) 85 90
4544 $1.50 *Oeceoclades maculata* (vert) 85 90
4545 $1.50 *Vanilla planifolia* (vert) 85 90
4546 $1.50 *Isolhilus linearis* (vert) 85 90
4547 $1.50 *Ionopsis utricularioides* (vert) 85 90
4548 $1.50 *Nidema boothii* (vert) 85 90

MS4549 Two sheets, each 123×100 mm. (a) $5 *Edidendrum altissimum* (vert). (b) $5 *Neocogniauxia hexaptera* (vert). Set of 2 sheets 5·50 6·00

Nos. 4531/6, 4537/42 and 4543/8 were each printed together, se-tenant, with the backgrounds forming maps of the Caribbean.

395a In Grey Check Suit

2000. 18th Birthday of Prince William. Multicoloured.

4550 $1.40 Type **395a** 85 90
4551 $1.40 Wearing scarf 85 90
4552 $1.40 In blue suit 85 90
4553 $1.40 Wearing blue jumper 85 90

MS4554 100×80 mm. $5 Wearing Eton uniform (37×50 mm) 3·25 3·50

395b Hale Bopp Comet passing Calisto

2000. "EXPO 2000" International Stamp Exhibition, Anaheim, U.S.A. Spacecraft. Multicoloured.

4555 $1.50 Type **395b** 85 90
4556 $1.50 "Galileo" spacecraft 85 90
4557 $1.50 "Ulysse" spacecraft 85 90
4558 $1.50 "Pioneer 11" 85 90
4559 $1.50 "Voyager 1" 85 90
4560 $1.50 "Pioneer 10" 85 90
4561 $1.50 "Cassini" spacecraft 85 90
4562 $1.50 "Pioneer 11" approaching Saturn 85 90
4563 $1.50 "Voyager 1" and Ariel 85 90
4564 $1.50 "Huygens" spacecraft 85 90
4565 $1.50 "Deep Space 4 Champollion" 85 90
4566 $1.50 "Voyager 2" 85 90
4567 $1.50 "Voyager 2" passing Umbriel 85 90
4568 $1.50 "Pluto Project" 4·75 90
4569 $1.50 "Voyager 1" approaching Pluto 85 90
4570 $1.50 Oort Cloud (part of asteroid belt) 85 90
4571 $1.50 "Pluto Kuiper Express" spacecraft 85 90
4572 $1.50 "Voyager 2" above Neptune 85 90

MS4573 Two sheets, each 105×75 mm. (a) $5 "Pluto Project" spacecraft. (b) $5 "Stardust" spacecraft approaching Wild 2 Comet. Set of 2 sheets 5·50 6·00

Nos. 4555/60, 4561/6 and 4567/72 were each printed together, se-tenant, with the backgrounds forming composite designs.

395c *Pane, Amore e Fantasia*, 1954

2000. 50th Anniv of Berlin Film Festival. Mult.

4574 $1.40 Type **395c** 80 85
4575 $1.40 Lord Olivier in *Richard III*, 1956 80 85
4576 $1.40 *Smultronstallet*, 1958 80 85
4577 $1.40 Sidney Poitier in *The Defiant Ones*, 1958 80 85
4578 $1.40 *The Living Desert*, 1954 80 85
4579 $1.40 *A Bout de Souffle*, 1960 80 85

MS4580 95×103 mm. $5 Jean-Luc Godard (director), 1960 3·25 3·50

395d George Stephenson and *Locomotion No. 1*, 1825

2000. 175th Anniv of Stockton and Darlington Line (first public railway). Multicoloured.

4581 $3 As Type **395d** 1·90 1·90
4582 $3 Camden and Amboy Railroad locomotive *John Bull*, 1831 1·90 1·90

No. 4582 is inscribed "Camoen" in error.

396 Albert Einstein

2000. Election of Albert Einstein (mathematical physicist) as Time Magazine "Man of the Century". Multicoloured.

4583 $2 Type **396** 1·10 1·25
4584 $2 Two portraits, one with hands clasped 1·10 1·25
4585 $2 Two portraits, one standing by painting 1·10 1·25

396a LZ-6 *Delag*, 1909

2000. Centenary of First Zeppelin Flight.

4586 **396a** $3 blue, black and mauve 1·75 1·75
4587 - $3 blue, black and mauve 1·75 1·75
4588 - $3 green, black and mauve 1·75 1·75

MS4589 116×76 mm. $5 green, black and mauve 3·25 3·50

DESIGNS: No. 4587, LZ-127 *Graf Zeppelin*, 1928; 4588, LZ-129 *Hindenburg*, 1936. 50×38 mm: No. **MS**4589, LZ-9 ZII (*Ersatz*), 1911.

No. 4588 is inscribed "(129) Hindenberg" in error.

396b Mildred Didrikson (javelin), 1932

2000. Olympic Games, Sydney. Multicoloured.

4590	$2 Type **396b**	1·25	1·25
4591	$2 Man on vaulting horse	1·25	1·25
4592	$2 Olympic Stadium, Barcelona (1992) and Spanish flag	1·25	1·25
4593	$2 Ancient Greek horse racing	1·25	1·25

396c Ian Allen

2000. West Indies Cricket Tour and 100th Test Match at Lord's.

4594	**396c**	10c. multicoloured	20	20
4595	-	20c. black and yellow	35	20
4596	-	$1.10 multicoloured	70	70
4597	-	$1.40 multicoloured	90	1·00
MS4598		121×114 mm. $5 multicoloured	3·25	3·50

DESIGNS—VERT: 20c. T. Michael Findlay; $1.10, Winston Davis; $1.40, Nixon McLean. HORIZ: $5 Lord's Cricket Ground.

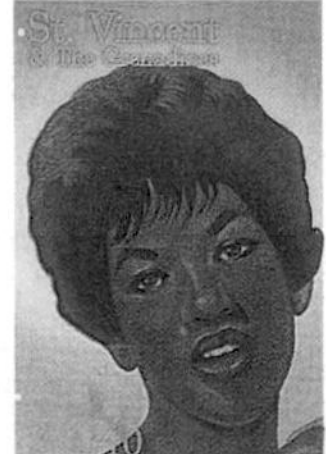

396d Member of The Chantels (value at left and hair clear of perforations)

2000. Girl Pop Groups. Multicoloured.

4599	$1.40 Type **396d**	75	80
4600	$1.40 Member of The Chantels (value at right on background)	75	80
4601	$1.40 Member of The Chantels (value at right on neck)	75	80
4602	$1.40 Member of The Chantels (value at left and hair over perforations)	75	80
4603	$1.40 Member of The Chantels (value at left on background)	75	80
4604	$1.40 Member of The Marvelettes (value on background)	75	80
4605	$1.40 Member of The Marvelettes (with curl on forehead)	75	80
4606	$1.40 Member of The Marvelettes (with gap in teeth)	75	80
4607	$1.40 Member of The Marvelettes (with long hair)	75	80
4608	$1.40 Member of The Marvelettes (looking to left)	75	80

397 Mario Andretti in Racing Car

2000. Election of Mario Andretti as "Driver of the Century".

4609	**397**	$1.10 brown and red	65	70
4610	-	$1.10 multicoloured	65	70
4611	-	$1.10 multicoloured	65	70
4612	-	$1.10 brown and red	65	70
4613	-	$1.10 brown and red	65	70
4614	-	$1.10 multicoloured	65	70
4615	-	$1.10 multicoloured	65	70
4616	-	$1.10 brown and red	65	70
MS4617		155×114 mm. $5 black and red	3·00	3·25

DESIGNS: No. 4610, In white overalls; 4611, With hands together; 4612, During race; 4613, Standing by saloon car; 4614, With "abc" trophy; 4615, In red overalls; 4616, Watching race; **MS**4617, Holding trophy.

398 Clarinet-player

2000. The Art of Jazz. Multicoloured.

4618	$1.40 Type **398**	75	80
4619	$1.40 Pianist	65	70
4620	$1.40 Trumpeter	65	70
4621	$1.40 Guitarist	65	70
4622	$1.40 Bass-player	65	70
4623	$1.40 Saxophonist	65	70

399 Michael Palin

2000. 30th Anniv of Monty Python. Multicoloured.

4624	$1.40 Type **399**	75	80
4625	$1.40 Eric Idle	75	80
4626	$1.40 John Cleese	75	80
4627	$1.40 Graham Chapman	75	80
4628	$1.40 Terry Gilliam	75	80
4629	$1.40 Terry Jones	75	80

400 Barbara Taylor Bradford

2000. Great Writers of the 20th Century: Barbara Taylor Bradford. Sheet 128×88 mm.

MS4630	**400**	$5 multicoloured	3·00	3·25

401 Betty Boop in "Jack and Jill"

2000. Betty Boop (cartoon character). Illustrating nursery rhymes. Multicoloured.

4631	$1 Type **401**	60	65
4632	$1 "Three Blind Mice"	60	65
4633	$1 "Wee Willie Winky"	60	65
4634	$1 "Hey Diddle Diddle"	60	65
4635	$1 "Mother Goose"	60	65
4636	$1 "Little Miss Muffet"	60	65
4637	$1 "Three Little Kittens"	60	65
4638	$1 "Rub-a-Dub-Dub"	60	65
4639	$1 "Little Jack Horner"	60	65
MS4640	Two sheets, each 133×91 mm. (a) $5 "Little Bo Peep". (b) $5 "Old Woman that lived in a Shoe". Set of 2 sheets	5·50	6·00

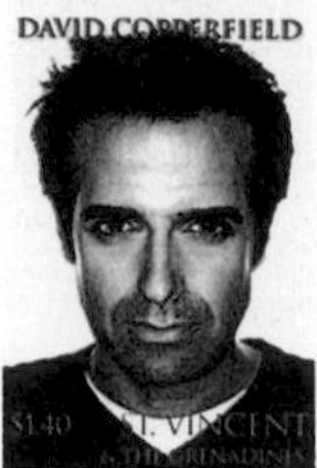

402 David Copperfield

2000. David Copperfield (conjurer). Each incorporating a similar portrait. Multicoloured.

4641	$1.40 Type **402**	75	80
4642	$1.40 David Copperfield levitating (dressed in black)	75	80
4643	$1.40 As No. 4642, but faint figure in brown	75	80
4644	$1.40 As No. 4642, but figure replaced by two large bubbles	75	80

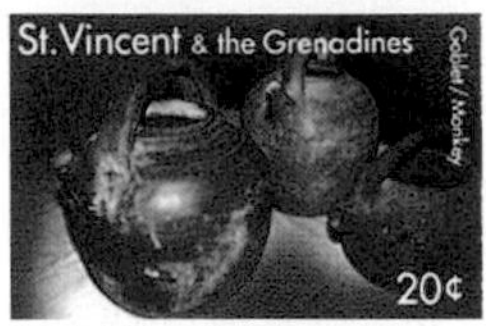

403 Goblet or Monkey

2000. Local Utensils. Multicoloured.

4645	20c. Type **403**	20	15
4646	50c. Goose (iron)	35	25
4647	70c. Boley and calabash (vert)	45	40
4648	$1 Three flat irons	60	75

404 Pink Ginger Lily

2000. Flowers. Multicoloured.

4649	90c. Type **404**	55	60
4650	90c. *Thumbergia grandiflora*	55	60
4651	90c. Red ginger lily	55	60
4652	90c. Madagascar jasmine	55	60
4653	90c. Cluster palm	55	60
4654	90c. Red torch lily	55	60
4655	90c. *Salvia splendens*	55	60
4656	90c. Balsamapple	55	60
4657	90c. Rostrata	55	60
MS4658	Two sheets. (a) 65×82 mm. $5 Red Flamingo (b) 82×65 mm. $5 Balsamapple (horiz). Set of 2 sheets	5·50	6·00

Nos. 4649, 4651 and 4654 are all inscribed "Lilly" in error.

405 Queen Elizabeth the Queen Mother

2000. Queen Elizabeth the Queen Mother's 100th Birthday.

4659	**405**	$1.40 multicoloured	1·00	1·00

2000. Faces of the Millennium: Queen Elizabeth the Queen Mother. As T 329a of Sierra Leone, showing collage of flower photographs. Multicoloured.

4660	$1 Top of head (face value at left)	75	65
4661	$1 Top of head (face value at right)	75	65
4662	$1 Eye and temple (face value at left)	75	65
4663	$1 Temple (face value at right)	75	65
4664	$1 Cheek (face value at left)	75	65
4665	$1 Cheek (face value at right)	75	65
4666	$1 Chin (face value at left)	75	65
4667	$1 Neck (face value at right)	75	65

Nos. 4660/7 were printed together, se-tenant, in sheetlets of 8 with the stamps arranged in two vertical columns separated by a gutter also containing miniature photographs. When viewed as a whole, the sheetlet forms a portrait of the Queen Mother.

406 Ida Cox

2000. New Millennium. "The Birth of The Blues". Showing singers and musicians. Multicoloured.

4668	$1.40 Type **406**	75	80
4669	$1.40 Lonnie Johnson	75	80
4670	$1.40 Muddy Waters	75	80
4671	$1.40 T-Bone Walker	75	80
4672	$1.40 Howlin' Wolf	75	80
4673	$1.40 Sister Rosetta Thorpe	75	80
4674	$1.40 Bessie Smith	75	80
4675	$1.40 Willie Dixon	75	80
4676	$1.40 Gertrude "Ma" Rainey	75	80
4677	$1.40 W. C. Handy	75	80
4678	$1.40 Leadbelly	75	80
4679	$1.40 Big Bill Broonzy	75	80
MS4680	Two sheets, each 80×120 mm. (a) $5 Billie Holiday. (b) $5 Robert Johnson. Set of 2 sheets	5·50	6·00

407 U.S.S. *Shaw* exploding, Pearl Harbor, 1941

2000. Wars of the Twentieth Century. Multicoloured.

4681	$1 Type **407**	75	75
4682	$1 American B-24 LIberators bombing Ploesti oil fields, 1943	75	75
4683	$1 Soviet T-34 tank, Germany, 1945	75	75
4684	$1 U.S.S. *New Jersey* (battleship) off North Korea, 1951	75	75
4685	$1 American F-86 Sabre fighter over North Korea, 1951	75	75
4686	$1 U.S.S. *Enterprise* (aircraft carrier) off Indo-China	75	75
4687	$1 American B-52 bomber over Vietnam, 1972	75	75
4688	$1 American armoured personnel carrier, Tay Ninh, 1967	75	75
4689	$1 Two Israeli F-4 Phantoms, 1967	75	75
4690	$1 Abandoned Egyptian T-72 tanks, 1967	75	75
4691	$1 SAM 6 rocket launchers, Cairo, 1973	75	75
4692	$1 Israeli M-48 tanks in desert, 1973	75	75
4693	$1 H.M.S. *Invincible* (aircraft carrier) on way to Falkland Islands, 1982	75	75
4694	$1 British Harriers and H.M.S. *Hermes* (aircraft carrier), Falkland Islands, 1982	75	75
4695	$1 Iraqi SS-1 Scud-B mobile missile launcher, 1990	75	75
4696	$1 American M1-A1 Abrams tanks, advancing, Gulf War, 1990	75	75
MS4697	Two sheets. (a) 85×110 mm. $5 Nucleur bomb test, Pershing II missile and B-52 bomber (55×40 mm). (b) 106×81 mm. $5 Israeli F-4 fighter-bomber, 1973. Set of 2 sheets	7·50	7·50

No. 4683 is inscribed "SOVIETIC", 4693 "H.M.S. HERMES" and 4696 "NOTHWARD", all in error.

408 Leopold Anthony

2000. Local Musicians.

No.	Type	Description	Unused	Used
4698	408	$1.40 multicoloured	75	80
4699	-	$1.40 black and buff	75	80
4700	-	$1.40 multicoloured	75	80
4701	-	$1.40 multicoloured	75	80

DESIGNS: No. 4699, "Shake" Kean (trumpeter); 4700, Olsen V. Peters (cornet-player); 4701, Patrick E. Prescod (pianist).

409 Government House

2000. 21st Anniv of Independence. Multicoloured.

No.	Description	Unused	Used
4702	10c. Type **409**	20	10
4703	15c. House of Assembly in session	20	10
4704	50c. House of Assembly building	45	25
4705	$2 Government Financial Complex	1·50	1·75

410 Blue and Yellow Macaw ("Blue and Gold Macaw")

2000. Birds. Multicoloured.

No.	Description	Unused	Used
4706	50c. Type **410**	60	30
4707	90c. English fallow budgerigar	75	50
4708	$1 Superb parrot ("Barraband Parakeet")	90	70
4709	$2 Dominant pied blue	1·40	1·40
4710	$2 Canary ("Stafford Canary")	1·40	1·40
4711	$2 Masked lovebird	1·40	1·40
4712	$2 Canary ("Parisian Full Canary")	1·40	1·40
4713	$2 Scarlet macaw	1·40	1·40
4714	$2 Blue-fronted amazon	1·40	1·40
4715	$2 Buffon's macaw	1·40	1·40
4716	$2 Canada goose (horiz)	1·40	1·40
4717	$2 Mandarin duck (horiz)	1·40	1·40
4718	$2 Gouldian finch (horiz)	1·40	1·40
4719	$2 English short-faced tumbler	1·40	1·40
4720	$2 Diamond dove	1·40	1·40
4721	$2 Norwich cropper	1·40	1·40
MS4722	Two sheets, each 96×67 mm. (a) $5 Budgerigar (horiz). (b) $5 Common Peafowl (horiz). Set of 2 sheets	7·50	8·00

No. 4707 is inscribed "Budgerigan", 4708 "Pazakeet", 4711 "Macked", 4713 "Searlet" and 4721 "Nozwich", all in error. There are also many mistakes in the Latin species names shown on the stamps.

411 Rebecca wearing Checked Coat in Shop

2000. Shirley Temple in Rebecca of Sunnybrook Farm. Showing scenes from the film. Multicoloured.

No.	Description	Unused	Used
4723	90c. Type **411**	50	55
4724	90c. Rebecca with parents	50	55
4725	90c. Rebecca being reprimanded	50	55
4726	90c. Rebecca singing with mother at piano	50	55
4727	90c. Rebecca with man by fence	50	55
4728	90c. Tea time	50	55
4729	$1.10 Rebecca in check coat with microphone (vert)	50	55
4730	$1.10 Rebecca in straw hat with chick (vert)	50	55
4731	$1.10 Rebecca in black and white dress with microphone (vert)	50	55
4732	$1.10 Rebecca in red dress with woman (vert)	50	55
MS4733	106×76 mm. $1.10 Rebecca dancing with Bill "Bojangles" Robinson (vert)	65	75

412 Angel praying

2000. Christmas. Multicoloured.

No.	Description	Unused	Used
4734	20c. Type **412**	30	15
4735	70c. Heads of two angels looking down	55	35
4736	90c. Heads of two angels, one looking down	70	40
4737	$5 Angel in red with arms folded	3·75	4·25
MS4738	110×121 mm. $5 Angel's head	3·75	4·25

413 Two Supermarine Spitfires

2000. 60th Anniv of the Battle of Britain. Multicoloured (except No. 4742).

No.	Description	Unused	Used
4739	90c. Type **413**	75	75
4740	90c. Supermarine Spitfire over countryside	75	75
4741	90c. Dornier DO217 on fire	75	75
4742	90c. Two Gloster Gladiators (black, violet and grey)	75	75
4743	90c. Two Hawker Hurricanes attacking German fighters	75	75
4744	90c. Junkers JU87-Stuka (face value at bottom left)	75	75
4745	90c. Two Supermarine Spitfires (different)	75	75
4746	90c. Junkers JU88 on fire	75	75
4747	90c. Junkers JU87-Stuka (face value at bottom right)	75	75
4748	90c. Westland Lysander and Gloster Gladiator	75	75
4749	90c. Messerschmitt BF109	75	75
4750	90c. Heinkel HE111 under attack	75	75
4751	90c. Hawker Hurricanes from below	75	75
4752	90c. Bristol Blenheim	75	75
4753	90c. Two Supermarine Spitfires over fields	75	75
4754	90c. Messerschmitt BF110	75	75
MS4755	Two sheets, each 79×59 mm. (a) $5 Supermarine Spitfire (42×27½ mm). (b) $5 Hawker Hurricane (42×27½ mm). Set of 2 sheets	7·50	8·00

414 Symbolic Snake on Background of Chinese Characters

2001. Chinese New Year ("Year of the Snake").

No.	Type	Description	Unused	Used
4756	414	$1 purple, blue and black	60	65
4757	-	$1 purple, mauve and black	60	65
4758	-	$1 purple, green and black	60	65
MS4759		64×93 mm. $2 purple, red and black	1·10	1·25

DESIGNS: Nos. 4757/8 showing different snakes.

415 "Diana the Huntress" (women hunters and dog) (Rubens)

2001. "EspaNa 2000" International Stamp Exhibition, Madrid. Rubens Paintings from the Prado Museum. Multicoloured.

No.	Description	Unused	Used
4760	10c. Type **415**	15	15
4761	90c. "Adoration of the Magi"	50	40
4762	$1 "Diana the Huntress" (Diana with dogs)	60	45
4763	$2 "Prometheus carrying Fire"	1·10	1·25
4764	$2 "Vulcan forging Jupiter's Thunderbolt"	1·10	1·25
4765	$2 "Saturn devouring one of his Sons"	1·10	1·25
4766	$2 "Polyphemus"	1·10	1·25
4767	$2 "St. Matthias"	1·10	1·25
4768	$2 "Death of Seneca"	1·10	1·25
4769	$2 "Maria de Medici, Queen of France"	1·10	1·25
4770	$2 "Achilles discovered by Ulysses"	1·10	1·25
4771	$2 "Heraclitus, the Mournful Philosopher" (full length)	1·10	1·25
4772	$2 "Heraclitus, the Mournful Philosopher" (head and shoulders)	1·10	1·25
4773	$2 "Anne of Austria, Queen of France" (head and shoulders)	1·10	1·25
4774	$2 "Anne of Austria, Queen of France" (full length)	1·10	1·25
MS4775	Two sheets. (a) 95×150 mm. $5 "Holy Family with St. Anne". (b) 130×119 mm. $5 "Judgement of Solomon". Set of 2 sheets	5·50	6·00

416 "The Concert" (Hendrick ter Brugghen)

2001. Bicentenary of the Rijksmuseum, Amsterdam. Paintings. Multicoloured.

No.	Description	Unused	Used
4776	$1.40 Type **416**	75	80
4777	$1.40 "Vertumnus and Pomona" (Paulus Moreleese)	75	80
4778	$1.40 "Elegant Couples courting" (couple standing) (Willem Buytewech)	75	80
4779	$1.40 "Sick Woman" (Jan Steen)	75	80
4780	$1.40 "Elegant Couples courting" (couple seated) (Buytewech)	75	80
4781	$1.40 "Don Ramon Satue" (Goya)	75	80
4782	$1.40 "Spendthrift" (Thomas Asselijn)	75	80
4783	$1.40 "Art Gallery of Jan Gildemeester Jansz" (Adriaan de Lelie)	75	80
4784	$1.40 "Raampoortje, Amsterdam" (Wouter van Troostwijk)	75	80
4785	$1.40 "Winter Landscape" (Barend Koekkoek)	75	80
4786	$1.40 "The Procuress" (elderly woman) (Dirck van Baburen)	75	80
4787	$1.40 "The Procuress" (couple) (Van Baburen)	75	80
4788	$1.40 "Music Party" (Rembrandt)	75	80
4789	$1.40 "Rutger Schimmelpenninck and Family" (Pierre Paul Prud'hon)	75	80
4790	$1.40 "Anna accused by Tobit of stealing a Kid" (Rembrandt)	75	80
4791	$1.40 "Syndics of the Amsterdam Goldsmiths' Guild" (Thomas de Keyser)	75	80
4792	$1.40 "Portrait of a Lady" (De Keyser)	75	80
4793	$1.40 "Marriage Portrait of Issac Massa and Beatrix van der Laen" (Hals)	75	80
MS4794	Three sheets. (a) 119×82 mm. $5 "Donkey riding on the Beach" (Isaac Israels). (b) 119×82 mm. $5 "Landscape with Stone Bridge" (Rembrandt) (horiz). (c) 102×108 mm. $5 "Still Life of Peacocks" (Rembrandt) (horiz). Set of 3 sheets	7·50	8·00

417 "Kadabra No. 64"

2001. "Pokemon" (children's cartoon series). Multicoloured.

No.	Description	Unused	Used
4795	90c. Type **417**	50	55
4796	90c. "Spearow No. 21"	50	55
4797	90c. "Kakuna No. 14"	50	55
4798	90c. "Koffing No. 109"	50	55
4799	90c. "Tentacruel No. 73"	50	55
4800	90c. "Cloyster No. 91"	50	55
MS4801	74×115 mm. $3 "Meowth No. 52"	1·75	1·90

418 Barred Owl

2001. "Hong Kong 2001" Stamp Exhibition. Birds of Prey. Multicoloured.

No.	Description	Unused	Used
4802	10c. Type **418**	60	40
4803	90c. Lammergeier	80	80
4804	90c. Common caracara ("Crested Caracara")	80	80
4805	90c. Tengmalm's owl ("Boreal Owl")	80	80
4806	90c. Harpy eagle	80	80
4807	90c. Bay owl ("Oriental Bay Owl")	80	80
4808	90c. Hawk owl	80	80
4809	90c. Laughing falcon	80	80
4810	$1 Californian condor	1·00	85
4811	$1.10 Bateleur	1·10	1·10
4812	$1.10 Northern hobby ("Hobby")	1·10	1·10
4813	$1.10 Osprey	1·10	1·10
4814	$1.10 Northern goshawk ("Goshawk")	1·10	1·10
4815	$1.10 African fish eagle	1·10	1·10
4816	$1.10 Egyptian vulture	1·10	1·10
4817	$2 Mississippi kite	1·75	2·00
MS4818	Two sheets, each 72×100 mm. (a) $5 Great grey owl. (b) $5 American kestrel. Set of 2 sheets	8·50	9·00

Nos. 4804/9 and 4811/16 were each printed together, se-tenant, the backgrounds forming a composite design.

419 Northern Eagle Owl ("Eagle Owl")

2001. Owls. Multicoloured.

No.	Description	Unused	Used
4819	10c. Type **419**	30	30
4820	20c. Barn owl	50	30
4821	50c. Great grey owl	75	50
4822	70c. Long-eared owl	80	65
4823	90c. Tawny owl	1·00	80
4824	$1 Hawk owl	1·10	85
4825	$1.40 Ural owl (horiz)	1·40	1·50
4826	$1.40 Tengmalm's owl (horiz)	1·40	1·50
4827	$1.40 African marsh owl ("Marsh Owl") (horiz)	1·40	1·50
4828	$1.40 Brown fish owl (horiz)	1·40	1·50
4829	$1.40 Little owl (horiz)	1·40	1·50
4830	$1.40 Short-eared owl (horiz)	1·40	1·50
MS4831	Two sheets. (a) 85×109 mm. $5 Hume's Owl. (b) 109×85 mm. $5 Snowy Owl. Set of 2 sheets	8·50	9·00

Nos. 4825/30 were printed together, se-tenant, the backgrounds forming a composite design.

Nos. 4819 and 4823 are inscribed "EAGEL" or "TWANY", both in error.

420 Woman on Beach

2001. United Nations Women's Human Rights Campaign. Multicoloured.

4832	90c. Type **420**	50	40
4833	$1 "Caribbean Woman II"	60	60

421 *Amanita fulva*

2001. Fungi. Multicoloured.

4834	20c. Type **421**	30	20
4835	90c. *Hygrophorus speciosus*	65	45
4836	$1.10 *Amanita phalloides*	85	80
4837	$1.40 *Amanita muscari*	95	1·00
4838	$1.40 *Boletus zelleri*	95	1·00
4839	$1.40 *Coprinus picaceus*	95	1·00
4840	$1.40 *Stropharia aeruginosa*	95	1·00
4841	$1.40 *Lepistra nuda*	95	1·00
4842	$1.40 *Hygrophorus conicus*	95	1·00
4843	$1.40 *Lactarius deliciosus*	95	1·00
4844	$1.40 *Hygrophorus psittacinus*	95	1·00
4845	$1.40 *Tricholomopsis rutilans*	95	1·00
4846	$1.40 *Hygrophorus coccineus*	95	1·00
4847	$1.40 *Collybia iocephala*	95	1·00
4848	$1.40 *Gyromitra esculenta*	95	1·00
4849	$1.40 *Lactarius peckii*	95	1·00
4850	$1.40 *Lactarius rufus*	95	1·00
4851	$1.40 *Cortinarius elatior*	95	1·00
4852	$1.40 *Boletus luridus*	95	1·00
4853	$1.40 *Russula cyanoxantha*	95	1·00
4854	$1.40 *Craterellus cornucopioides*	95	1·00
4855	$2 *Cantharellus cibarius*	1·60	1·75
MS4856	Three sheets. (a) 96×70 mm. $5 *Cyathus olla*. (b) 70×96 mm. $5 *Lycoperdon pyriforme* (horiz). (c) 70×96 mm. $5 *Pleurotus ostreatus* (horiz). Set of 3 sheets	9·00	10·00

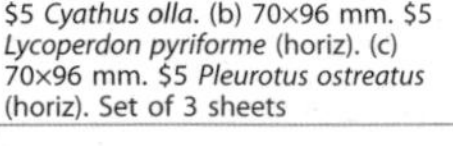

422 *Ancyluris formosissima*

2001. Butterflies and Moths of the World. Multicoloured.

4857	20c. Type **422**	30	15
4858	50c. *Callicore cynosura*	50	30
4859	70c. *Nessaea obrinus*	65	40
4860	$1 *Euphaedra neophron*	80	85
4861	$1 *Milionia grandis*	80	85
4862	$1 *Marpesia petreus*	80	85
4863	$1 *Bocotus bacotus*	80	85
4864	$1 *Arctia vilica*	80	85
4865	$1 *Arctia flavia*	80	85
4866	$1 *Baorisa hiroglyphica*	80	85
4867	$1 *Euplagia quadripuntaria*	80	85
4868	$1 *Calisthenia salvinii*	80	85
4869	$1 *Persiama vaninka*	80	85
4870	$1 *Metamorpha stelenes*	80	85
4871	$1 *Diaethria aurelia*	80	85
4872	$1 *Perisama conplandi*	80	85
4873	$1 *Mesene phareus*	80	85
4874	$1 *Callisthenia salvinii*	80	85
4875	$1 *arpella districta*	80	85
4876	$2 *Eunica alcmena*	1·60	1·75
MS4877	Two sheets, each 85×110 mm. (a) $5 *Thecla coronata*. (b) $5 *Anaxita drucei*. Set of 2 sheets	8·00	8·50

Nos. 4857, 4860 and 4867 are inscribed "ANCYCLURIS", "HEOPHRON", "QUADRIPUNTAMA" or "THECKA", all in error.

423 *Tithorea harmonia*

2001. Butterflies of the Caribbean. Multicoloured.

4878	10c. Type **423**	30	30
4879	20c. *Callicore maimuna*	30	20
4880	50c. *Colobura dirce*	50	30
4881	90c. *Danaus plexippus*	75	70
4882	90c. *Theope eudocia*	75	80
4883	90c. *Cepheuptychia cephus*	75	80
4884	90c. *Actinote pellenea*	75	80
4885	90c. *Catonephele numilia*	75	80
4886	90c. *Anteos clorinde*	75	80
4887	90c. *Phoebis philea*	75	80
4888	90c. *Eumaeus atala*	75	80
4889	90c. *Papilio cresphontes*	75	80
4890	90c. *Prepona meander*	75	80
4891	90c. *Anartia iatrophae*	75	80
4892	90c. *Mesene phareus*	75	80
4893	90c. *Battus polydamas*	75	80
4894	$1 *Doxocopa cherubima*	80	85
4895	$2 *Menander menander*	1·60	1·75
MS4896	Two sheets, each 68×98 mm. (a) $5 *Eueides heliconius*. (b) $5 *Morpho peleides* (vert). Set of 2 sheets	8·00	8·50

Nos. 4885 and 4894 are inscribed "numili" or "cherubina", both in error.

424 *Eunica alcmena*

2001. Butterflies and Moths of the Rainforest. Multicoloured.

4897	10c. Type **424**	30	30
4898	70c. *Euphaedra medon*	65	45
4899	90c. *Prepona praeneste*	75	70
4900	90c. *Cepora aspasia*	75	80
4901	90c. *Morpho aega*	75	80
4902	90c. *Mazuca amoeva*	75	80
4903	90c. *Amphicallia bellatrix*	75	80
4904	90c. *Helicopsis cupido*	75	80
4905	90c. *Cithaerias esmeralda*	75	80
4906	$1 *Euphaedra neophron*	80	85
4907	$1.10 *Asterope rosa*	85	90
4908	$1.10 *Marpesia petreus*	85	90
4909	$1.10 *Dismorphia amphione*	85	90
4910	$1.10 *Euphaedra eleus*	85	90
4911	$1.10 *Prepona deiphile*	85	90
4912	$1.10 *Phoebis avellaneda*	85	90
MS4913	Two sheets. (a) 100×70 mm. $5 *Heliconius sapho*. (b) 70×100 mm. $5 *Utethesia ornatrix*. Set of 2 sheets	8·00	8·50

Nos. 4897 and 4911 are inscribed "alamena" or "Phoebus", both in error.

425 Princess Victoria in Blue Dress

2001. Death Centenary of Queen Victoria. Multicoloured.

4914	$1.10 Type **425**	65	70
4915	$1.10 Queen Victoria wearing jewelled hair band	65	70
4916	$1.10 Queen Victoria wearing floral hair wreath	65	70
4917	$1.10 Queen Victoria wearing crown	65	70
4918	$1.10 Queen Victoria wearing pearls and black hair band	65	70
4919	$1.10 Queen Victoria in white veil and blue sash	65	70
MS4920	96×120 mm. $5 Queen Victoria in white cap (39×51 mm)	3·00	3·25

426 Mao Tse-tung in 1924

2001. 25th Death Anniv of Mao Tse-tung (Chinese leader). Multicoloured.

4921	$2 Type **426**	1·10	1·25
4922	$2 Mao in 1938	1·10	1·25
4923	$2 Mao in 1945	1·10	1·25
MS4924	146×139 mm. $5 Mao in grey suit	2·75	3·25

427 "Impression, Sunrise", 1873

2001. 75th Death Anniv of Claude-Oscar Monet (French painter). Multicoloured.

4925	$2 Type **427**	1·10	1·25
4926	$2 "Hay Stacks, End of Summer", 1891	1·10	1·25
4927	$2 "Regatta at Argenteuil", 1872	1·10	1·25
4928	$2 "Venice at Dusk", 1908	1·10	1·25
MS4929	137×110 mm. $5 "Parisians enjoying the Parc Monceau", 1878 (vert)	3·00	3·25

428 Princess Elizabeth

2001. 75th Birthday of Queen Elizabeth II. Multicoloured.

4930	$1.10 Type **428**	80	80
4931	$1.10 Queen Elizabeth in grey suit	80	80
4932	$1.10 Queen Elizabeth in blue dress	80	80
4933	$1.10 Queen Elizabeth in tiara	80	80
4934	$1.10 Queen Elizabeth in blue hat and coat	80	80
4935	$1.10 Queen Elizabeth in green hat and coat	80	80
MS4936	86×121 mm. $5 Queen Elizabeth in Guards Uniform (38×50 mm)	3·75	4·00

429 Queen Elizabeth II

2001. Golden Jubilee (1st issue).

4937	**429** $1 multicoloured	1·00	1·00

See also Nos. 5111/15.

No. 4937 was printed in sheetlets of 8, containing two vertical rows of four, separated by a large illustrated central gutter. Both the stamp and the illustration on the central gutter are made up of a collage of miniature flower photographs.

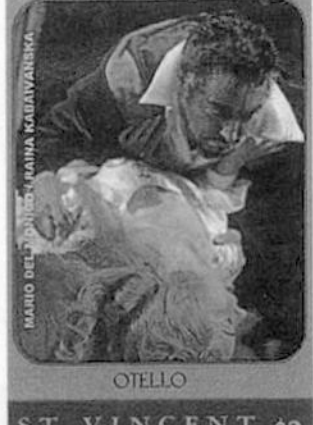

430 Mario del Monaco and Raina Kabaivanska as Othello and Desdemona

2001. Death Centenary of Giuseppe Verde (Italian composer). Multicoloured.

4938	$2 Type **430**	1·75	1·75
4939	$2 Iago's costume from *Othello*, 1898	1·75	1·75
4940	$2 Othello's costume, 1898	1·75	1·75
4941	$2 Anna Tomowa-Sintow, as Desdemona	1·75	1·75
MS4942	78×110 mm. $5 Nicolai Ghiaurov as King Philip in *Don Carlos* (opera)	3·75	4·00

Nos. 4938 and 4939 are inscribed "MONICO" or "LAGO", both in error.

431 "Countess de Toulouse-Lautrec"

2001. Death Centenary of Henri de Toulouse-Lautrec (French painter). Multicoloured.

4943	$3 Type **431**	1·75	1·90
4944	$3 "Carmen"	1·75	1·90
4945	$3 "Madame Lily Grenier"	1·75	1·90
MS4946	66×85 mm. $5 "Jane Avril"	3·00	3·25

432 "Courtesan Sumimoto" (Isoda Koryusai)

2001. "Philanippon '01" International Stamp Exhibition, Tokyo. Japanese Paintings. Multicoloured.

4947	10c. Type **432**	15	15
4948	15c. "Oiran at Shinto Shrine" (Kiyonaga)	15	15
4949	20c. "Cockerel" (horiz)	20	20
4950	20c. "Two Girls on a Veranda" (Kiyonaga)	20	20
4951	50c. "On Banks of the Sumida" (Kiyonaga)	35	25
4952	70c. "Three Ducks" (horiz)	45	35
4953	90c. "Flock of Ducks in Flight" (horiz)	50	40
4954	$1 "Three Pigeons" (horiz)	60	45
4955	$1.10 "Guineafowl" (horiz)	65	50
4956	$1.40 "Girl on River Bank" (Harunobu)	70	75
4957	$1.40 "Horseman guided by Peasant Girl" (Harunobu)	70	75
4958	$1.40 "Komachi praying for Rain" (Harunobu)	70	75
4959	$1.40 "Washing Clothes in the Stream" (Harunobu)	70	75
4960	$1.40 "Girls by Lespedeza Bush in Moonlight" (Harunobu)	70	75
4961	$1.40 "Warming Sake with Maple Leaves" (Harunobu)	70	75
4962	$1.40 "Young Samurai on Horseback" (Harunobu)	70	75
4963	$1.40 "Ide no Tamagawa" (Harunobu)	70	75
4964	$1.40 "Otani Oniji II as Edohei" (Sharaku)	70	75
4965	$1.40 "Iwai Hanshiro IV" (Sharaku)	70	75
4966	$1.40 "Segawa Kikunojo III" (Sharaku)	70	75

4967	$1.40 "Ichikawa Komazo II as Shiga Daishichi" (Sharaku)	70	75
4968	$1.40 "Toriwagi, Geisha of Kanaya, writing" (Eishi)	70	75
4969	$1.40 "Courtesan preparing for Doll Festival" (Eishi)	70	75
4970	$1.40 "Two Court Ladies in a Garden" (Eishi)	70	75
4971	$1.40 "Lady with a Lute" (Eishi)	70	75
4972	$2 "Wading birds" (horiz)	1·10	1·25
MS4973	Five sheets, each 110×77 mm. (a) $5 "Gathering Lotus Flowers" (Harunobu). (b) $5 "Boy spying on Lovers" (Harunobu). (c) $5 "Peasants ferried across the Sumida" (Hokkei). (d) $5 "Shadows on the Shoji" (Kikugawa Eizan). (e) $5 "Tayu Komurasaki and Hanamurasaki of the Kado Tamaya" (Kitao Masanobu). Set of 5 sheets	13·00	14·00

Nos. 4949, 4952/5 and 4972 are all details from "A Variety of Birds" by Nishiyama Hoen.

433 Dale Earnhardt Jr (son)

2001. Dale Earnhardt (stock car racing driver) Commemoration. Multicoloured.

4974	$2 Type **433**	1·25	1·40
4975	$2 Father and son with Winston Trophy	1·25	1·40
4976	$2 Dale Earnhardt in black and white overalls	1·25	1·40
4977	$2 Earnhardt with racing trophy	1·25	1·40
4978	$2 Congratulating son	1·25	1·40
4979	$2 Dale Earnhardt Jr holding trophy aloft	1·25	1·40

434 Crown Prince Haakon and Mette-Marit Tjessem Høiby

2001. Wedding of Crown Prince Haakon of Norway and Mette-Marit Tjessem Høiby.

4980	**434**	$5 multicoloured	3·00	3·25

435 Mammoth

2001. Prehistoric Animals. Multicoloured.

4981	10c. Type **435**	15	15
4982	20c. Pinacosaurus	20	20
4983	90c. Oviraptor	55	60
4984	90c. Head of Saltasaurus	55	60
4985	90c. Head of Apatosaurus	55	60
4986	90c. Head of Brachiosaurus	55	60
4987	90c. Troodon with body of Saltasaurus	55	60
4988	90c. Deinonychus with bodies of Apatosaurus and Brachiosaurus	55	60
4989	90c. Segnosaurus	55	60
4990	90c. Iguanodon	55	60
4991	90c. Hypacrosaurus	55	60
4992	90c. Ceratosaurus	55	60
4993	90c. Hypsilophodon	55	60
4994	90c. Herrerasaurus	55	60
4995	90c. Velociraptor	55	60
4996	$1 Centrosaurus	60	60
4997	$1.40 Protoceratops	75	80
4998	$1.40 Pteranodon	75	80
4999	$1.40 Archaeopteryx	75	80
5000	$1.40 Eudimorphodon	75	80
5001	$1.40 Shonisaurus	75	80
5002	$1.40 Elasmosaurus	75	80
5003	$1.40 Kronosaurus	75	80
5004	$1.40 Allosaurus	75	80
5005	$1.40 Dilophosaurus	75	80
5006	$1.40 Lambeosaurus	75	80
5007	$1.40 Coelophysis	75	80
5008	$1.40 Ornitholestes	75	80
5009	$1.40 Eustreptospondylus	75	80
5010	$2 Bactrosaurus	1·25	1·40
MS5011	Four sheets. (a) 105×78 mm. $5 Stegosaurus (50×38 mm). (b) 78×105 mm. $5 Parasaurolophus (38×50 mm). (c) 78×105 mm. $5 Tyrannosaurus (38×50 mm). (d) 78×105 mm. $5 Triceratops (50×38 mm). Set of 4 sheets	12·00	13·00

Nos. 4984/9, 4990/5, 4998/5003 and 5004/9 were each printed together, se-tenant, with the backgrounds forming composite designs.

436 Hong Myung-Bo and South Korean Flag

2001. World Cup Football Championship, Japan and Korea (2002). Multicoloured.

5012	$1.40 Type **436**	90	90
5013	$1.40 Hidetoshi Nakata and Japanese flag	90	90
5014	$1.40 Ronaldo and Brazilian flag	90	90
5015	$1.40 Paolo Maldini and Italian flag	90	90
5016	$1.40 Peter Schmeichel and Danish flag	90	90
5017	$1.40 Raul Blanco and Spanish flag	90	90
5018	$1.40 Kim Bong Soo and South Korean Flag	90	90
5019	$1.40 Masami Ihara and Japanese flag	90	90
5020	$1.40 Marcel Desailly and French flag	90	90
5021	$1.40 David Beckham and English flag	90	90
5022	$1.40 Carlos Valderrama and Colombian flag	90	90
5023	$1.40 George Popescu and Rumanian flag	90	90
MS5024	Two sheets, each 98×70 mm. (a) $5 International Stadium, Yokohama, Japan (64×32 mm). (b) $5 World Cup Stadium, Seoul, South Korea (64×32 mm). Set of 2 sheets	5·50	6·00

No. 5015 is inscribed "Paola" in error.

437 John F. Kennedy at Democratic Convention, 1956

2001. John F. Kennedy (American President) Commemoration. Multicoloured (except Nos. 5029, MS5037a).

5025	$1.40 Type **437**	70	80
5026	$1.40 Campaigning in New York, 1959	70	80
5027	$1.40 In rocking chair in the White House, 1960	70	80
5028	$1.40 With Robert Kennedy (brother)	70	80
5029	$1.40 Announcing Cuban Blockade, 1962 (black & red)	70	80
5030	$1.40 John Kennedy Jr (son) at father's funeral, 1963	70	80
5031	$1.40 With son, John Jr	70	80
5032	$1.40 With Jacqueline	70	80
5033	$1.40 With daughter, Caroline	70	80
5034	$1.40 With family, 1963	70	80
5035	$1.40 Sailing with wife	70	80
5036	$1.40 President and Mrs. Kennedy in evening dress	70	80
MS5037	Two sheets, each 121×88 mm. (a) $5 President John F. Kennedy (violet and black). (b) $5 With children at Hyannis Port. Set of 2 sheets	5·50	6·00

438 Princess Diana on Remembrance Day

2001. 40th Birth Anniv of Diana, Princess of Wales. Multicoloured.

5038	$1.40 Type **438**	75	80
5039	$1.40 Princess Diana in pink dress	75	80
5040	$1.40 On wedding day	75	80
MS5041	72×95 mm. $5 Princess Diana in evening dress	3·25	3·50

439 Japanese Aircraft bombing Pearl Harbor

2001. 60th Anniv of Japanese Attack on Pearl Harbor. Multicoloured.

5042	$1.40 Type **439**	1·00	1·00
5043	$1.40 Japanese pilot wearing hachimaki (headband)	1·00	1·00
5044	$1.40 Emperor Hirohito of Japan	1·00	1·00
5045	$1.40 Admiral Yamamoto	1·00	1·00
5046	$1.40 Japanese planes over *Akagi* (aircraft carrier)	1·00	1·00
5047	$1.40 Japanese "Kate" torpedo bomber	1·00	1·00
5048	$1.40 Japanese fighters over Ewa Marine base, Hawaii	1·00	1·00
5049	$1.40 Dorie Miller engaging Japanese planes	1·00	1·00
5050	$1.40 Japanese aircraft attacking U.S.S. *Nevada* (battleship)	1·00	1·00
5051	$1.40 Sinking of U.S.S. *Oklahoma* (battleship)	1·00	1·00
5052	$1.40 Japanese plane taking off from Akagi	1·00	1·00
5053	$1.40 American casualty on stretcher	1·00	1·00
MS5054	Two sheets. (a) $5 Wheeler Field under attack. (b) $5 Dorie Miller receiving Navy Cross from Admiral Nimitz, 1942 (vert). Set of 2 sheets	7·50	8·00

440 *Rhodogastria crokeri*

2001. Butterflies and Moths. Multicoloured.

5055	70c. Type **440**	55	40
5056	90c. *Gnammia virgo*	65	45
5057	$1 *Zeuzera pyrina*	70	50
5058	$1.40 *Anthela ocellata*	90	95
5059	$1.40 *Euproctis hemicyclia*	90	95
5060	$1.40 *Epicoma melanostica*	90	95
5061	$1.40 *Erateina staudingeri*	90	95
5062	$1.40 *Pseudoips fagana*	90	95
5063	$1.40 *Estigmene acrea*	90	95
5064	$1.40 *Phalera bucephala*	90	95
5065	$1.40 *Deilephila elpenor*	90	95
5066	$1.40 *Protambulyx strigilis*	90	95
5067	$1.40 *Cizara ardeniae*	90	95
5068	$1.40 *Oenochroma vinaria*	90	95
5069	$1.40 *Oenosandra boisduvalii*	90	95
5070	$2 *Campylotes desgodinsi*	1·60	1·75
MS5071	Two sheets, each 96×70 mm. (a) $5 *Lymantria dispar*. (b) $5 *Rothschildia orizaba* (Silkworm). Set of 2 sheets	7·50	8·00

Nos. 5058/63 and 5064/9 were each printed together, se-tenant, with the backgrounds forming composite designs.

Nos. 5066 and 5068 are inscribed "strigus" or "vinerea", both in error.

441 Bumble Bee

2001. Island Fauna. Multicoloured.

5072	$1.40 Type **441**	1·00	1·00
5073	$1.40 Green darner dragonfly	1·00	1·00
5074	$1.40 Small lacewing butterfly	1·00	1·00
5075	$1.40 Black widow spider	1·00	1·00
5076	$1.40 Praying mantis	1·00	1·00
5077	$1.40 Firefly	1·00	1·00
5078	$1.40 Caspian tern (horiz)	1·00	1·00
5079	$1.40 White-tailed tropicbird (horiz)	1·00	1·00
5080	$1.40 Black-necked stilt (horiz)	1·00	1·00
5081	$1.40 Black-bellied plover (horiz)	1·00	1·00
5082	$1.40 Black-winged stilt (horiz)	1·00	1·00
5083	$1.40 Ruddy turnstone (horiz)	1·00	1·00
MS5084	Two sheets. (a) 65×96 mm. $5 Blue Night Butterfly (horiz). (b) 107×77 mm. $5 Brown Pelican. Set of 2 sheets	7·50	8·00

Nos. 5072/7 (insects) and 5078/83 (shore birds) were each printed together, se-tenant, with the backgrounds forming composite designs.

442 "Madonna and Child" (Francesco Guardi)

2001. Christmas. Religious Paintings. Multicoloured.

5085	10c. Type **442**	20	20
5086	20c. "Immaculate Conception" (Giambattista Tiepolo)	30	20
5087	70c. "Adoration of the Magi" (Tiepolo)	65	40
5088	90c. "The Virgin" (Tintoretto)	75	50
5089	$1.10 "Annunciation" (Veronese)	90	90
5090	$1.40 "Madonna della Quaglia" (Pisanello)	1·10	1·40
MS5091	76×136 mm. $5 "Madonna and Child" (Tiepolo)	3·50	4·00

443 Bo Le in the Mountains

2001. Chinese New Year ("Year of the Horse"). Legend of Bo Le. Multicoloured.

5092	$1.10 Type **443**	65	70
5093	$1.10 Horse and cart	65	70
5094	$1.10 Bo Le accosting cart driver	65	70
5095	$1.10 Horse drinking	65	70
5096	$1.10 Bo Le covering horse with cloak	65	70
5097	$1.10 Horse rearing	65	70

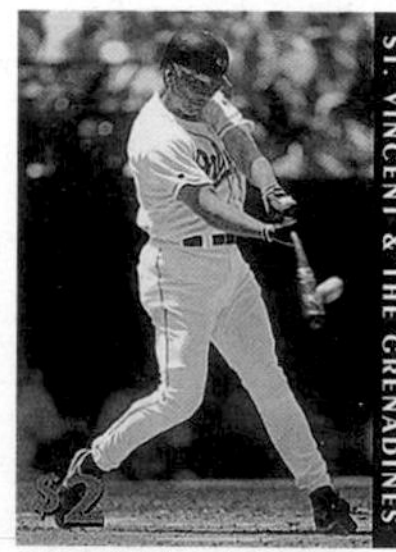

444 Cal Ripken Jr. batting

2001. Retirement of Cal Ripken Jr. (American baseball player). Multicoloured.

5098	$2 Cal Ripken Jr. greeting spectators (73×61 mm)	1·00	1·25
5099	$2 Type **444**	1·00	1·25
5100	$2 Cal Ripken Jr. running	1·00	1·25
5101	$2 Wearing white Orioles shirt, bareheaded	1·00	1·25
5102	$2 Wearing orange shirt and black helmet	1·00	1·25
5103	$2 Holding trophy	1·00	1·25
5104	$2 Cal Ripken Jr. acknowledging applause	1·00	1·25
MS5105	196×240 mm. $6 Cal Ripken Jr. (40×60 mm)	3·00	3·50

445 U. S. Flag as Statue of Liberty and St. Vincent Flag

2001. "United We Stand". Support for Victims of 11 September 2001 Terrorist Attacks.

5106 **445** $2 multicoloured 1·25 1·40

446 Vermont Nature Trails

2001. Tourism. Multicoloured.

5107	20c. Type **446**	30	15
5108	70c. Tamarind Beach Hotel, Kanouan (horiz)	60	35
5109	90c. The Tobago Cays (horiz)	70	55
5110	$1.10 Trinity Falls	85	85

2002. Golden Jubilee (2nd issue). As T 110 of St. Kitts. Multicoloured.

5111	$2 Queen Elizabeth with Duke of Edinburgh, on aircraft steps	1·60	1·60
5112	$2 Queen Elizabeth with Princess Margaret	1·60	1·60
5113	$2 Queen Elizabeth wearing pearls and blue dress	1·60	1·60
5114	$2 Princess Elizabeth on her wedding day	1·60	1·60
MS5115	76×108 mm. $5 Queen Elizabeth wearing orange coat	4·50	5·00

447 Pan American Health Organization Centenary Logo

2002. Centenary of Pan American Health Organization. Multicoloured.

5116	20c. Type **447**	25	15
5117	70c. Dr. Gideon Cordice	55	40
5118	90c. Dr. Arthur Cecil Cyrus	70	55
5119	$1.10 PAHO Headquarters, Barbados (horiz)	85	85

448 Girls from "Section of the Bands"

2002. 25th Anniv of Vincy Mas Carnival. Multicoloured.

5120	10c. Type **448**	20	15
5121	20c. Michael Ollivierre from "Cocktail" (horiz)	25	15
5122	70c. Tyson Constantine, from "Snake in the Grass"	55	40
5123	90c. Bridgette Creese from "Joy-C"	70	55
5124	$1.10 Shanelle McKenzie, from "Heatwave" (horiz)	85	80
5125	$1.40 Sion Hill Steel Orchestra (horiz)	1·00	1·25

2002. International Year of Mountains. As T 115 of St. Kitts, but vert. Multicoloured.

5126	$1.40 Mount Ararat, Turkey	75	80
5127	$1.40 Mount Ama Dablam, Nepal	75	80
5128	$1.40 Mount Cook, New Zealand	75	80
5129	$1.40 Mount Kilimanjaro, Tanzania	75	80
5130	$1.40 Mount Kenya, Kenya	75	80
5131	$1.40 Giant's Castle, South Africa	75	80
MS5132	100×120 mm. $5 Mount Aconcagua, Argentina	3·00	3·25

Nos. 5131 and **MS**5132 are inscribed "AMERICA" or "ACONCAG", both in error.

2002. Winter Olympic Games, Salt Lake City. As T 111 of St. Kitts. Multicoloured.

5133	$3 Rifle shooting (biathlon)	1·75	1·90
5134	$3 Slalom skiing	1·75	1·90
MS5135	84×115 mm. Nos. 5133/4	3·50	3·75

449 Malachite Butterfly

2002. U.N. Year of Eco Tourism. Multicoloured.

5136	$2 Type **449**	1·50	1·50
5137	$2 Manatee	1·50	1·50
5138	$2 Fallow deer	1·50	1·50
5139	$2 Castor bean plant	1·50	1·50
MS5140	75×90 mm. $6 Diver and windsurfer	3·50	4·00

2002. 20th World Scout Jamboree, Thailand. As T 116 of St. Kitts. Multicoloured.

5141	$5 Scout blowing Kudu horn	2·75	3·00
5142	$5 Scouts rolling up bedding	2·75	3·00
5143	$5 Lord Baden-Powell and Dan Beard (early Scout leaders)	2·75	3·00
MS5144	85×118 mm. $5 Scout's head (vert)	2·75	3·00

450 Former Slaves celebrating Freedom

2002. Emancipation Day (1834) Commemoration. Each black and yellow.

5145	$2 Type **450**	1·10	1·25
5146	$2 Lt. Governor, 1834	1·10	1·25
5147	$2 Freedom Celebrations	1·10	1·25
5148	$2 Britannia with former slaves	1·10	1·25

451 Elvis Presley

2002. 25th Death Anniv of Elvis Presley. Multicoloured.

5149	$1 Type **451**	90	50
5150	$1.25 Elvis Presley playing guitar	1·00	1·00
5151	$1.25 In Army uniform	1·00	1·00
5152	$1.25 Wearing checked jacket	1·00	1·00
5153	$1.25 In striped shirt	1·00	1·00
5154	$1.25 Wearing striped T shirt	1·00	1·00
5155	$1.25 Elvis Presley laughing	1·00	1·00

452 World Trade Centre Buildings, New York

2002. 1st Anniv of Terrorist Attacks on U.S.A. Sheet, 141×98 mm.

MS5156 **452** $6 multicoloured 3·00 3·25

453 Teddy Bear in Red Kimono

2002. Centenary of the Teddy Bear. Multicoloured.

5157	$2 Type **453**	1·10	1·25
5158	$2 White teddy bear in bridal dress	1·10	1·25
5159	$2 Teddy bear in traditional Japanese costume with black cap	1·10	1·25
5160	$2 Teddy bear in black and orange outfit	1·10	1·25
5161	$2 Mother bear with baby bear	1·10	1·25
5162	$2 Teddy bear in red kimono with flowers on head	1·10	1·25
5163	$2 Two teddy bears	1·10	1·25
5164	$2 Two teddy bears with bees	1·10	1·25
5165	$2 Teddy bear seated on rock	1·10	1·25
5166	$2 Cowboy teddy (35×48 mm)	1·10	1·25
5167	$2 Fisherman teddy (35×48 mm)	1·10	1·25
5168	$2 Camper teddy (35×48 mm)	1·10	1·25
5169	$2 Hiker teddy (35×48 mm)	1·10	1·25
MS5170	Two sheets, each 75×57 mm. (a) $5 Teddy bears designed by Tomoko Suenaga (horiz). (b) $5 Teddy bears designed by Terumi Yoshikawa (horiz). Set of 2 sheets	5·50	6·00

Nos. 5157/61 (Japanese bears), 5162/5 (Japanese bears) and 5166/9 (outdoor bears). The backgrounds of Nos. 5166/9 form a composite design.

454 Waterloo Medal and Charge of the Scots Greys

2002. British War Medals. Nine sheets containing vert designs as T 454. Multicoloured.

MS5171 Nine sheets. (a) 165×100 mm. $5 Type **454**. (b) 165×100 mm. $5 Zulu War medal with 1879 clasp and Rorke's Drift. (c) 165×100m. $5 South Africa War medal with clasps for defence of Ladysmith and Orange Free State, and British infantry under fire. (d) $5 1914–15 Star and British troops in trench. (e) $5 1916 medal and British troops advancing during Battle of the Somme. (f) $5 Victory medal, 1919. (g) $5 Atlantic Star with aircrew clasp, and convoy. (h) $5 1939–45 Star with Battle of Britain clasp, and squadron scramble. (i) $5 Africa Star with 8th Army clasp, and desert. Set of 9 sheets 27·00 29·00

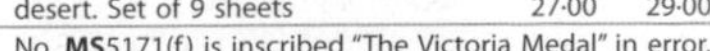

No. **MS**5171(f) is inscribed "The Victoria Medal" in error.

455 Dimples and Grandfather

2002. Shirley Temple in Dimples. Scenes from the film. Multicoloured.

5172	$1.40 Type **455**	75	80
5173	$1.40 Dimples singing for dinner guests	75	80
5174	$1.40 Dimples in black and white dress with grandfather	75	80
5175	$1.40 Singing in minstrel show	75	80
5176	$1.40 Grandfather covering Dimples with blanket	75	80
5177	$1.40 Dimples taking tea with rich widow	75	80
5178	$2 Conducting street band (vert)	1·10	1·25
5179	$2 Dimples in bonnet and Grandfather in top hat (vert)	1·10	1·25
5180	$2 Dimples adjusting cravat (vert)	1·10	1·25
5181	$2 Dimples with rich widow (vert)	1·10	1·25
MS5182	105×75 mm. $5 Tap-dancing in minstrel show (vert)	2·75	3·00

456 Ji Sung Park (South Korea) and Dietmar Hamann (Germany)

2002. World Cup Football Championship, Japan and Korea. Multicoloured.

5183	$1.40 Type **456**	75	80
5184	$1.40 Miroslav Klose (Germany) and Tae Young Kim (South Korea)	75	80
5185	$1.40 Chong Gug Song (South Korea) and Christoph Metzelder (Germany)	75	80
5186	$1.40 Tae Young Kim (South Korea) and Gerald Asamoah (Germany)	75	80
5187	$1.40 Torsten Frings (Germany) and Ji Sung Park (South Korea)	75	80
5188	$1.40 Oliver Neuville (Germany) and Tae Young Kim (South Korea)	75	80
5189	$1.40 Kleberson (Brazil) and Emre Belozoglu (Turkey)	75	80
5190	$1.40 Cafu (Brazil)	75	80
5191	$1.40 Roberto Carlos (Brazil)	75	80
5192	$1.40 Yildiray Basturk (Turkey)	75	80
5193	$1.40 Tugay Kerimoglu (Turkey) and Rivaldo (Brazil)	75	80
5194	$1.40 Bulent (Turkey)	75	80
MS5195	Four sheets, each 82×82 mm. (a) $3 Michael Ballack (Germany); $3 Oliver Kahn (Germany). (b) $3 Tae Young Kim (South Korea); $3 Du Ri Cha (South Korea). (c) $3 Ronaldo (Brazil); $3 Cafu (Brazil). (d) $3 Bulent (Turkey); $3 Yildiray Basturk (Turkey). Set of 4 sheets	12·00	13·00

457 Queen Elizabeth the Queen Mother in Floral Hat

2002. Queen Elizabeth the Queen Mother Commemoration. Multicoloured.

5196 $2 Type **457** 1·60 1·60

5197 $2 Queen Mother in blue hat and dress 1·60 1·60

5198 $2 Queen Mother in lavender hat and coat 1·60 1·60

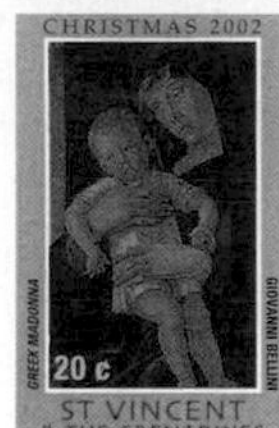

458 "Greek Madonna" (Giovanni Bellini)

2002. Christmas. Religious Paintings. Multicoloured.

5199 20c. Type **458** 30 15

5200 90c. "Kneeling Agostino Barbarigo" (Bellini) 70 40

5201 $1.10 "Presentation of Jesus in the Temple" (Perugino) 85 60

5202 $1.40 "Madonna and Child with Infant St. John" (Perugino) 1·00 1·00

5203 $1.50 "San Giobbe Altarpiece" (Bellini) 1·10 1·40

MS5204 105×78 mm. $5 "Madonna and Child with Sts John the Baptist and Sebastian" (horiz) 3·50 3·75

No. 5202 is inscribed "MADDONA" in error.

459 Space Rocket in From the Earth to the Moon (Jules Verne)

2002. Famous Science Fiction Authors. Three sheets, each 150×108 mm, containing vert designs as T 459. Multicoloured.

MS5205 Three sheets. (a) $5 Type **459**. (b) $5 Book cover for *The Time Machine* (H. G. Wells). (c) $5 Book cover for *The War of the Worlds* (H. G. Wells). Set of 3 sheets 9·00 9·50

460 Magnifying Glass and Globe

2002. 50th Anniv of International Federation of Stamp Dealers' Associations.

5206 **460** $2 multicoloured 1·25 1·40

461 Kid

2003. Chinese New Year ("Year of the Goat (Ram)"). Multicoloured.

5207 $1 Type **461** 60 65

5208 $1 Goat with chicken 60 65

5209 $1 Nanny-goat feeding kid 60 65

5210 $1 Porcelain figure of rider on goat 60 65

5211 $1 Brown and white goat on heathland 60 65

5212 $1 Black and white goat in wood 60 65

462 Westminster Abbey

2003. 50th Anniv of Coronation. Multicoloured.

5213 $2 Type **462** 1·40 1·40

5214 $2 Queen Elizabeth II in Coronation Coach leaving Buckingham Palace 1·40 1·40

5215 $2 Coronation Coach in procession 1·40 1·40

5216 $2 Queen and Duke of Edinburgh in Coronation Coach 1·40 1·40

5217 $2 Queen arriving at Westminster Abbey 1·40 1·40

5218 $2 In procession along nave of Westminster Abbey 1·40 1·40

5219 $2 Queen in Chair of State 1·40 1·40

MS5220 96×66 mm. $5 Queen wearing Imperial State Crown and Coronation robes (37×50 mm) 3·75 4·00

463 *Columbia* Crew

2003. Columbia Space Shuttle Commemoration. Three sheets, each 177×113 mm, containing T 463 and similar horiz designs. Multicoloured.

MS5221 $2 Type **463**; $2 *Columbia* Space Shuttle on launchpad; $2 *Columbia* in flight; $2 Astronaut David Brown inside *Columbia* 4·50 5·00

MS5222 $2 Type **463**; $2 Mission Commander Rick Husband inside *Columbia*; $2 *Columbia* on runway; $2 *Columbia* in orbit and satellite 4·50 5·00

MS5223 $2 Type **463**; $2 Pilot William McCool in cockpit; $2 William McCool; $2 *Columbia* in orbit over Earth 4·50 5·00

464 Embroidery Teddy Bear

2003. Centenary of the Teddy Bear. Embroidered Fabric Teddy Bears. Self-adhesive. Imperf.

5224 **464** $15 ochre, brown and black 7·50 8·00

MS5225 125×158 mm. No. 5224×4 26·00 29·00

465 "Composition avec Femme aux cheveux mi-longs"

2003. 30th Death Anniv of Pablo Picasso (artist). Multicoloured (except $1).

5226 60c. Type **465** 45 40

5227 70c. "La Soeur de l'Artiste" (vert) 55 40

5228 90c. "Maternite" (vert) 70 55

5229 $1 "Tete d'Homme" (vert) 80 60

5230 $1.10 "Deux Enfants assis (Claude et Paloma)" (vert) 85 85

5231 $1.40 "Femme a la Collerette bleue" (vert) 1·00 1·10

MS5232 203×165 mm. $2 "Corrida"; $2 "Composition a la Mandoline"; $2 "Le Peintre et son Modele"; $2 "Femme couchee sous la Lampe" 4·50 5·00

MS5233 (a) 82×105 mm. $5 "Femme espagnole sur fond orange". Imperf. (b) 102×81 mm. $5 "Femme etendue". Imperf 6·50 7·00

466 "Portrait of Jacques de Gheyn III"

2003. Paintings by Rembrandt. Multicoloured.

5234 $1 Type **466** 70 45

5235 $1.10 "Young Man in a Black Beret" 75 55

5236 $1.40 "Hendrickje Stoffels" 90 75

5237 $2 "The Polish Rider" (horiz) 1·50 1·75

MS5238 185×175 mm. $2 "Belthazzar sees the Writing on the Wall" (detail); $2 "Portrait of a Young Man (Titus?)"; $2 "Jacob blessing the Sons of Joseph" (detail); $2 "King Uzziah stricken with Leprosy" 4·50 5·00

MS5239 158×115 mm. $5 "The Stoning of St. Stephen" 3·00 3·50

467 "A Gathering of Sorcerers on the Tokaido Road" (detail) (Utagawa Kunisada)

2003. Japanese Art. Ghosts and Demons. Multicoloured.

5240 70c. Type **467** 45 30

5241 $1.10 "Kiyohime and the Moon" (Yoshu Chikanobu) 65 50

5242 $1.40 "A Gathering of Sorcerers on the Tokaido Road" (different detail) (Utagawa Kunisada) 75 70

5243 $3 "A Gathering of Sorcerers on the Tokaido Road" (different detail) (Utagawa Kunisada) 1·75 1·90

MS5244 148×148 mm. $2 "Snake Mountain" (Utagawa Kuniyoshi); $2 "Sadanobu and Oni" (Tsukioka Yoshitoshi); $2 "Shoki" (Tsukioka Yoshitoshi); $2 "The Nightly Weeping Rock" (Utagawa Kuniyoshi) 4·00 4·50

MS5245 117×85 mm. $5 "The Ghosts of Matahachi and Kikuno" (detail) (Utagawa Kumsada) 2·75 3·25

468 Prince William as Teenager

2003. 21st Birthday of Prince William of Wales. Multicoloured.

MS5246 148×78 mm. $3 Type **468**; $3 Prince William in black and yellow polo shirt; $3 Wearing blue t-shirt 6·00 6·50

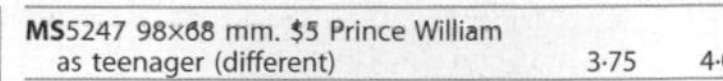

MS5247 98×68 mm. $5 Prince William as teenager (different) 3·75 4·00

469 Lady Diana Spencer as Young Girl

2003. 5th Death Anniv of Diana, Princess of Wales. Two sheets, each 132×146 mm, containing vert designs as T 469. Multicoloured.

MS5248 $2 Type **469**; $2 Princess Diana with Prince Charles on their wedding day; $2 With Prince William and baby Prince Harry; $2 Wearing mauve jacket 5·00 5·50

MS5249 $2 Princess Diana wearing tiara and yellow dress; $2 Wearing white dress; $2 Wearing mauve cardigan; $2 Wearing mauve dress 5·00 5·50

470 Antonin Magne (1931)

2003. Centenary of Tour de France Cycle Race. Multicoloured.

MS5250 157×97 mm. $2 Type **470**; $2 Andre Leducq (1932); $2 Georges Speicher (1933); $2 Antonin Magne (1934) 5·00 5·50

MS5251 157×97 mm. $2 Romain Maes (1935); $2 Silvere Maes (1936); $2 Roger Lapebie (1937); $2 Gino Bartali (1938) 5·00 5·50

MS5252 157×97 mm. $2 Silvere Maes (1939); $2 Jean Lazarides (1946) (additionally inscr "FIVE DAY RACE"); $2 Jean Robic (1947); $2 Gino Bartali (1948) 5·00 5·50

MS5253 Three sheets, each 106×78 mm. (a) $5 Antonin Magne (1931, 1934). (b) $5 Fausto Coppi (1949). (c) $5 Ferdinand Kubler (1950) Set of 3 sheets 9·00 10·00

471 Linny

2003. Centenary of Circus Clowns. Multicoloured.

MS5254 116×199 mm. $2 Type **471**; $2 Bruce Feiler; $2 Segey Provirin; $2 Weezle 4·25 4·75

MS5255 145×218 mm. $2 Mermaids (acrobats); $2 Robert Wolf (sword swallower); $2 Elbrus Pilev's Group (horsewoman); $2 Stinky (gymnast) 4·25 4·75

No. **MS**5254 is cut in the shape of a clown on a bicycle and No. **MS**5255 in the shape of a circus elephant.

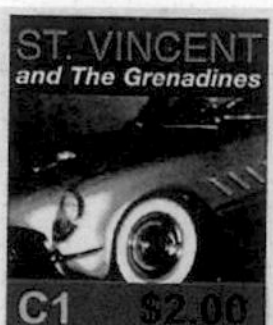

472 C1 Corvette

2003. 50th Anniv of General Motors Chevrolet Corvette. Multicoloured.

MS5256 163×202 mm. $2 Type **472**; $2 C2 Corvette; $2 C3 Corvette; $2 C4 Corvette; $2 C5 Corvette 6·00 7·00

MS5257 163×202 mm. $3 Corvette (1953); $3 Corvette (2003) (both 50×38 mm) 3·75 4·25

473 Cadillac Eldorado (1953)

2003. Centenary of General Motors Cadillac. Multicoloured.

MS5258 110×150 mm. $2 Type **473**; $2 Cadillac Eldorado (2002); $2 Cadillac Eldorado (1967); $2 Cadillac Series 62 (1962) — 5·00 6·00

MS5259 102×75 mm. $5 Cadillac LaSalle (1927) — 3·50 3·75

2003. Centenary of Powered Flight. As T 126 of St. Kitts. Multicoloured.

MS5260 176×96 mm. $2 Handley Page Heyford; $2 Heinkel He 111B; $2 Gloster Gauntlet; $2 Curtiss BF2C-1 — 5·00 5·50

MS5261 176×96 mm. $2 Mitsubishi A6M Reisen; $2 Dewoitine D520; $2 Messerschmitt Bf 109E; $2 Republic P-47 Thunderbolt — 5·00 5·50

MS5262 Two sheets, each 106×75 mm. (a) $5 Fairy Flycatcher. (b) $5 Bristol Type 142 Blenheim IV Set of 2 sheets — 6·50 7·00

474 Owia Salt Pond

2003. International Year of Freshwater. Multicoloured.

MS5263 150×88 mm. $3 Type **474**; $3 The Soufriere; $3 Falls of Baleine — 5·50 6·50

MS5264 100×70 mm. $5 Trinity Falls — 3·50 3·75

475 Musicians

2003. Centenary of Salvation Army in St. Vincent. Multicoloured.

5265	70c. Type **475**	70	45
5266	90c. District Temple	1·00	60
5267	$1 Christmas Kettle Appeal Fund	1·10	75
5268	$1.10 Salvation Army Headquarters (horiz)	1·25	90

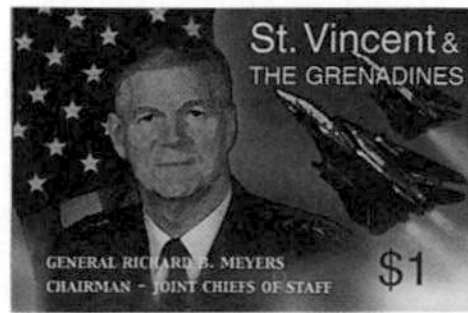

476 General Richard Meyers and Fighter Planes

2003. Operation Iraqi Freedom. Multicoloured.

MS5269 184×129 mm. $1 Type **476**; $1 Lt. General David McKiernan, troops and helicopter; $1 Lt. General Michael Moseley and bomber; $1 Vice Admiral Timothy Keating and warships; $1 Lt. General Jay Garner (retired) and troops; $1 General Tommy Franks and troops; $1 Lt. General Earl Hailston and marines in desert; $1 General John Jumper and fighter plane — 4·75 5·50

MS5270 135×135 mm. $1.50 Private Jessica Lynch and rescuers; $1.50 General Tommy Franks and troops; $1.50 Troops and Spectre Gunship; $1.50 Stryker Vehicle; $1.50 USS *Constellation* (aircraft carrier); $1.50 USS *Kitty Hawk* (aircraft carrier) — 5·50 6·50

477 Jean Grey

2003. X2: X-Men United (film based on Marvel comic characters). Multicoloured.

MS5271 124×165 mm. $2 Type **477**; $2 Storm; $2 Wolverine; $2 Cyclops — 4·25 4·75

MS5272 124×165 mm. $2 Magneto; $2 Mystique; $2 Stryker; $2 Lady Deathstroke — 4·25 4·75

MS5273 124×165 mm. $2 Nightcrawler; $2 Professor X; $2 Iceman; $2 Rogue — 4·25 4·75

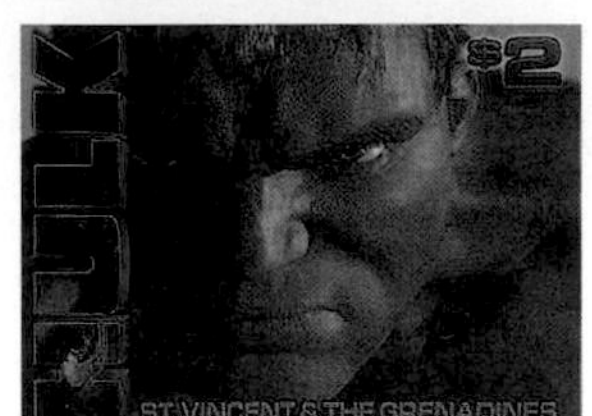

478 The Hulk

2003. The Hulk (film based on Marvel comic characters). Multicoloured.

MS5274 124×165 mm. $2 Type **478**; $2 The Hulk (head and shoulders, inscr "HULK" at right); $2 The Hulk (head and shoulders, inscr "HULK" at left); $2 As Type **477** (inscr "HULK" at right) — 4·25 4·50

MS5275 124×165 mm. $2 The Hulk in wreckage; $2 Crouching in rubble; $2 With fists raised; $2 Punching rubble — 4·25 4·50

No. **MS**5274 depicts scenes from *The Hulk* film and **MS**5275 depicts the Marvel comic character.

479 Spider-man

2003. Spider-Man 2 (film based on Marvel comic characters). Multicoloured.

MS5276 124×165 mm. $2 Type **479**; $2 With arm raised, brandishing weapon; $2 Suspended from building; $2 Clinging to building — 4·25 4·75

480 Father Christmas and Beach (Andrew Gonsalves)

2003. Christmas. Childrens Paintings. Multicoloured.

5277	70c. Type **480**	55	35
5278	90c. Father Christmas on raft pulled by dolphin (Georgia Gravel)	70	45
5279	$1.10 Father Christmas on beach (Adam Gravel) (vert)	85	85

481 *Lutjanus kasmira*

2003. Marine Life of the Caribbean. Multicoloured.

5280	70c. Type **481**	55	35
5281	90c. *Chaetadon collare*	70	50
5282	$1.10 *Istiophorus platypterus*	85	80
5283	$2 *Pomacanthus paru* (inscr "Pomacanthidae")	1·75	2·00

MS5284 118×106 mm. $2 *Equetus lanceolatus*; $2 *Hypoplectrus gutavariusi*; $2 *Pomacentridae*; $2 *Cichlidae* — 5·00 5·50

MS5285 67×96 mm. $5 Dolphins — 3·25 3·50

482 Chihuahua

2003. Dogs and Cats. Multicoloured.

5286	10c. Type **482**	25	15
5287	20c. Bulldog	35	15
5288	50c. British shorthair cat	50	25
5289	60c. Weimaraner (dog)	60	35
5290	$1 Burmese cat	75	55
5291	$1.40 American shorthair cat	1·00	75
5292	$3 Havana brown cat	2·00	2·25
5293	$5 Dalmatian	3·25	3·75

MS5294 119×109 mm. $2 Dachshund; $2 Collie; $2 Springer spaniel; $2 Hamilton hound — 5·00 5·50

MS5295 119×109 mm. $2 Osicat; $2 Manx; $2 Somali; $2 Angora — 5·00 5·50

MS5296 Two sheets, each 66×96 mm. (a) $5 Golden retriever. (b) $5 Abyssinian cat. Set of 2 sheets — 6·50 7·50

483 *Laelia lobata*

2003. Orchids of the Caribbean. Multicoloured.

5297	40c. Type **483**	50	25
5298	90c. *Miltoniopsis phalaenopsis*	75	45
5299	$1 *Phalaenopsis violacea*	85	55
5300	$3 *Trichopilia fragrans*	2·50	2·75

MS5301 116×109 mm. $2 *Masdevallia uniflora*; $2 *Laelia flava*; $2 *Barkeria lindleyana*; $2 *Laelia tenebrosa* — 5·50 6·00

MS5302 66×96 mm. $5 *Cattleya lawrenceana* — 3·50 3·75

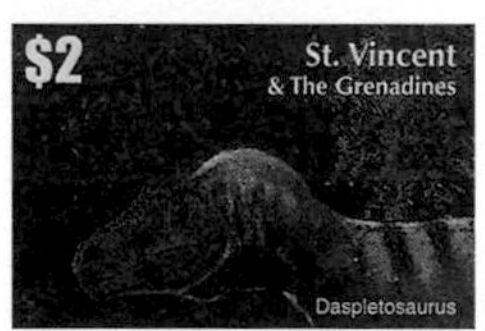

484 Daspletosaurus

2003. Prehistoric Animals. Multicoloured.

MS5303 178×118 mm. $2 Type **484**; $2 Utahraptor; $2 Scutellosaurus; $2 Scelidosaurus — 5·00 5·50

MS5304 178×118 mm. $2 Syntarsus; $2 Velociraptor; $2 Mononikus; $2 Massospondylus — 5·00 5·50

MS5305 Two sheets, each 98×68 mm. (a) $5 Giganotosaurus (vert). (b) $5 Pterodactylus (vert) Set of 2 sheets — 6·50 7·00

485 Marilyn Monroe (1st issue)

2003. 50th Anniv of Playboy Magazine. T 485 and similar vert designs showing Playboy magazine covers.

MS5306 240×152 mm. $1.50 Type **485** (black, grey and brown); $1.50 Playboy bunny logo; $1.50 Man with bunny's head; $1.50 Playboy model; $1.50 Woman licking stamp; $1.50 Fiftieth anniversary issue (January 2004) (black, ochre and rose) — 5·50 6·50

486 Monkey

2004. Chinese New Year ("Year of the Monkey").

MS5307 75×93 mm. **486** $1.40×4 black, brown and cream — 3·25 3·50

MS5308 70×100 mm. **486** $3 black, brown and pink — 1·75 2·00

487 "Apricot Blossoms"

2004. Hong Kong 2004 International Stamp Exhibition. Paintings by Ma Yuan. Multicoloured.

MS5309 123×118 mm. $2 Type **487**; $2 "Peach Blossoms"; $2 "Watching the Deer by a Pine Shaded Stream"; $2 "Drinking in the Moonlight" — 4·00 4·50

MS5310 120×80 mm. $5 "On a Mountain Path in Spring". Imperf — 2·50 3·00

488 Concorde SST and Map showing Anchorage, Alaska

2004. Last Flight of Concorde (2003). Multicoloured.

MS5311 131×90 mm. $3 Type **488**; $3 Concorde SST and map showing Los Angeles; $3 Concorde SST — 6·00 6·00

489 Marilyn Monroe

2004. Marilyn Monroe (actress) Commemoration. Multicoloured.

MS5312 Two sheets. (a) 127×111 mm. $2×4, Type **489**; Wearing blue dress; Wearing strapless white dress; Wearing strapless black dress. (b) 125×125 mm. $2×4, Wearing pearl earrings; Leaning head on back of hand; Looking slightly right; Wearing cluster earrings — 8·00 9·00

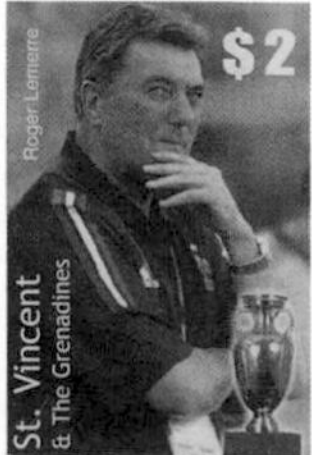

490 Roger Lemerre

2004. European Football Championship 2004, Portugal. Commemoration of Match between France and Italy (2000). Multicoloured.

MS5313 147×85 mm. $2×4, Type **490**, Marco Delvecchio; David Trezeguet; De Kuip Stadium, Rotterdam — 4·50 5·00

MS5314 98×85 mm. $5 French team, 2000 (51×38 mm) — 3·50 3·75

491 Baron Pierre de Coubertin (founder of the International Olympic Committee)

2004. Olympic Games, Athens. Multicoloured.

5315 70c. Type **491** 50 35
5316 $1 Olympic pin, St Louisa (1904) 60 50
5317 $1.40 Water polo, Berlin (1936) (horiz) 75 75
5318 $3 Greek ceramic vase 1·75 1·90

492 George Herman Ruth Jr

2004. Centenary of Baseball World Series. T 492 and similar vert designs showing George Herman Ruth Jr. ("Babe Ruth"). Multicoloured.

5319- $2×4 Type **492**; From front;
5322 Leaning on bat; Swinging bat 4·00 4·50

493 Air Chief Marshal Sir Trafford Leigh-Mallory

2004. 60th Anniv of D-Day Landings.

5323 **493** 70c. multicoloured 65 40
5324 - 90c. multicoloured 75 55
5325 - $1 multicoloured 80 60
5326 - $1.10 multicoloured 90 85
5327 - $1.40 multicoloured 1·10 1·10
5328 - $1.50 multicoloured 1·25 1·50

MS5329 Two sheets each 177×107 mm. (a) $2×4, maroon and black; maroon and black; multicoloured; purple and black. (b) $2×4, multicoloured; multicoloured; indigo, ochre and black; indigo; blue and black 10·00 11·00

MS5330 Two sheets each 100×69 mm. (a) $5 maroon, blue and black. (b) $5 maroon and ultramarine 7·00 8·00

DESIGNS: No. 5323, Type **493**; 5324, Lt. Col. Maureen Gara; 5325, Gen. Omar Bradley; 5326, Jean Valentine; 5327, Jack Culshaw; 5328, Gen. Dwight Eisenhower; **MS**5329a $2×4, Rangers take Pointe du Hoc; In trenches at Pointe du Hoc; Press headlines; British liberate Hermanville. **MS**5329b $2×4, British land on Gold Beach; Landing craft on Gold Beach; Canadians at Juno Beach; Troops and tanks on Juno Beach; **MS**5330a $5 Codebreakers; **MS**5330b $5 Soldiers preparing to board landing craft.

494 Queen Juliana

2004. Queen Juliana of the Netherlands.

5331 **494** $2 multicoloured 1·25 1·40

495 Children

2004. General Employees' Co-Operative Credit Union. Multicoloured.

5332 70c. Type **495** 50 35
5333 90c. General Employees' Co-Operative Credit Union headquarters 60 50
5334 $1.10 Calvin Nicholls (former director) (vert) 75 75
5335 $1.40 Bertrand Neehall (vert) 90 1·00

496 Ronald Reagan

2004. Ronald Reagan (President of USA 1981–89).

5336 **496** $1.40 multicoloured 90 1·00
5337 - $1.40 purple and black 90 1·00
5338 - $1.40 multicoloured 90 1·00

DESIGNS: No. 5336, Type **496**; 5337, In front of flag; 5338, Giving speech.

497 2 Ct Narrow Gauge Locomotive VV12

2004. Bicentenary of Steam Locomotives. Multicoloured.

MS5339 Three sheets, each 181×123 mm. (a) $2×4, Type **497**; Gambler LNV9701; No. 4 Snowdon; *Hiawatha* 3-1. (b) $2×4, CO1604–1; CP steam locomotive N135; 6042-6; E1 Narrow gauge 0-4-0T. (c) $2×4, Standard Boston and Maine No. 410; AG locomotive; BA101 Antigua locomotive; Aster 1449 13·00 14·00

MS5340 Three sheets, each 96×67 mm. (a) $5 Union Pacific 844. (b) $5 NA12A 01-06-00. (c) *Holy War 1* (vert) 9·00 10·00

498 Halimah DeShong (former netball player)

2004. 25th Anniv of Independence. Multicoloured.

5341 10c. Type **498** 20 15
5342 20c. Winston Davis (cricket player) 60 35
5343 70c. Pamenoa Ballantyne (athlete) (horiz) 50 50
5344 70c. Miss Carnival (2003) 50 50
5345 70c. Flag of St Vincent (horiz) 75 50
5346 90c. Rodney "Chang" Jack (football player) (horiz) 60 60
5347 90c. Breadfruit 60 60
5348 90c. Cecil "Blazer" Williams (playwright) 60 60
5349 $1.10 St Vincent parrot 1·50 80
5350 $5 George McIntosh (pharmacist) 3·00 3·25
5351 $5 Ebenezer Theodore Joshua (former Chief Minister and member of Parliament) (horiz) 3·00 3·25
5352 $5 Captain Hugh Mulzac (merchant marine naval officer) 3·00 3·25
5353 $10 Robert Milton Cato (socialist political leader) 5·50 6·50
5354 $10 His Excellency Joseph Chatoyer (Carib chief) 5·50 6·50

499 Players

2004. National Football Team.

5355 **499** 90c. multicoloured 85 75

500 David Ginola (France)

2004. Centenary of FIFA (Federation Internationale de Football Association). Multicoloured.

MS5356 192×97 mm. $2 Type **500**; $2 Paul Scholes (England); $2 Jurgen Kohler (Germany); $2 Ian Rush (Wales inscr. "England") 4·50 5·00

MS5357 107×87 mm. $6 Alan Shearer (England) 3·75 4·00

501 "Lion and His Keeper" (1954)

2004. 25th Death Anniv of Norman Rockwell (artist). Multicoloured.

5358 90c. Type **501** 60 45
5359 $1 "Weighing In" (1958) 70 55
5360 $1.40 "The Young Lawyer" (1927) 90 90
5361 $2 "The Bodybuilder" (1922) 1·25 1·40

MS5362 66×88 mm. $5 "Triple Self Portrait" (1960). Imperf 3·00 3·25

502 "Head of a Young Girl" (Jean-Baptiste Greuze)

2004. 300th Anniv of St. Petersburg. "Treasures of the Hermitage". Multicoloured.

5363 10c. Type **502** 15 15
5364 20c. "Two Actresses" (Jean-Baptiste Santerre) 35 25
5365 40c. "An Allegory of History" (Jose de Ribera) 45 35
5366 60c. "A Young Woman Trying on Earrings" (Rembrandt van Rijn) 50 50
5367 $1.40 "Count N. D. Guriev" (Jean Auguste-Dominique Ingres) 90 90
5368 $1.40 "Portrait of an Actor" (Domenico Fetti) 90 90
5369 $1.40 "Napoleon Bonaparte on the Bridge and Arcole" (Baron Antoine-Jean Gros) 90 90
5370 $1.40 "A Young Man with a Glove" (Frans Hals) 90 90
5371 $1.40 "Portrait of General Alexei Yermolov" (George Dawe) 90 90
5372 $1.40 "A Scholar" (Rembrandt van Rijn) 90 90
5373 $1.40 "Landscape with Obelisk" (Hubert Robert) 90 90
5374 $1.40 "At the Hermit's" (Hubert Robert) 90 90
5375 $1.40 "Landscape with Ruins" (Hubert Robert) 90 90
5376 $1.40 "Landscape with Terrace and Cascade" (Hubert Robert) 90 90
5377 $1.40 "A Shepherdess" (Jan Siberecht) 90 90
5378 $1.40 "Landscape with a Waterfall" (Hubert Robert) 90 90
5379 $2 "The Girlhood of the Virgin" (Francisco de Zurbaran) 1·25 1·40
5380 $5 "Portrait of a Woman" (Fran Pourbus the Elder) 3·00 3·25

MS5381 Three sheets. (a) 78×83 mm. $5 "Three Men at a Table" (Diego Rodriguez De Silva). (b) 97×72 mm. $5 "The Bean King" (Jacob Jordeans). (c) 88×76 mm. $5 "Family Portrait" (Cornelis de Vos). Imperf 8·50 9·50

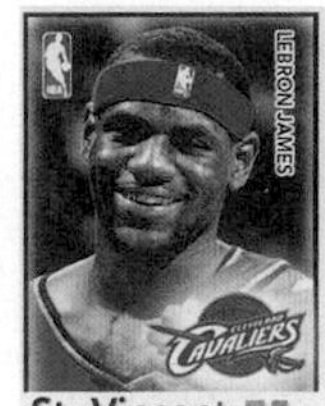

503 Lebron James (Cleveland Cavaliers)

2004. National Basketball Association (1st series). Multicoloured.

5382 75c. Type **503** 85 70
5383 75c. Gary Payton (Los Angeles Lakers) 85 70
5384 75c. Adonal Foyle (Golden State Warriors) 85 70
5385 75c. Peja Stojakovic (Sacramento Kings) 85 70

See also Nos. 5434/5.

504 Elvis Presley

2004. 50th Anniv of "That's Alright Mama" (record by Elvis Presley).

5386 **504** $2 multicoloured 1·40 1·40
5387 - $2 multicoloured 1·40 1·40
5388 - $2 multicoloured 1·40 1·40
5389 - $2 multicoloured 1·40 1·40
5390 - $2 blue, green and black 1·40 1·40
5391 - $2 magenta, blue and black 1·40 1·40
5392 - $2 blue, magenta and black 1·40 1·40
5393 - $2 green, blue and black 1·40 1·40

DESIGNS: No. 5386, Type **504**; Nos. 5387, Singing (from front); 5388, Singing (from side); 5389, Kissing guitar; 5390, Microphone touching mouth; 5391, Dancing; 5392, Dancing with guitar; 5393, Playing guitar.

505 Captain Thomas Masterman Hardy

2004. Bicentenary of the Battle of Trafalgar. Multicoloured.

5394 50c. Type **505** 65 40
5395 $1 Napoleon Bonaparte 1·00 75
5396 $1.50 Admiral Lord Horatio Nelson 1·50 1·50
5397 $3 Admiral Cuthbert Collingwood 2·50 2·75

MS5398 Two sheets. (a) 93×67 mm. $5 HMS *Victory*. (b) 93×74 mm. $5 Lord Nelson briefing his officers 8·00 8·50

506 Deng Xiaoping

2004. Birth Centenary of Deng Xiaoping (leader of China, 1978—89). Sheet 96×66 mm.
MS5399 **506** $5 multicoloured 3·00 3·25

507 "Santa's Helpers"

2004. Christmas. Paintings by Norman Rockwell. Multicoloured.
5400 70c. Type **507** 50 30
5401 90c. "Tiny Tim" 60 45
5402 $1.10 "Department Store Santa" 80 80
5403 $3 "The Muggleton Stage Coach" 1·75 2·00
MS5404 64×84 mm. $5 "Extra Good Boys and Girls". Imperf 3·00 3·25

508 Subway Token, New York (1953)

2004. Subways. Multicoloured (except 5419/21).
5405 $1 Type **508** 70 70
5406 $1 Kiosk on 23rd Street, New York (early 1900s) 70 70
5407 $1 Hi-V 3398 subway car, New York (1935) 70 70
5408 $1 R6 1208 subway car interior, New York (1936) 70 70
5409 $1 Construction of Harlem River tunnel, New York (1904) 70 70
5410 $1 Underground construction, New York (early 1900's) 70 70
5411 $1 Above ground construction (men on ground), New York (early 1900s) 70 70
5412 $1 Above ground construction (men on crane), New York (early 1900s) 70 70
5413 $1.40 Moscow metro 1·00 1·00
5414 $1.40 Tokyo metro 1·00 1·00
5415 $1.40 Mexico City metro 1·00 1·00
5416 $1.40 Paris metro 1·00 1·00
5417 $1.40 Hong Kong metro 1·00 1·00
5418 $1.40 Prague metro 1·00 1·00
5419 $1.40 Thames tunnel (1859) (maroon and violet) 1·00 1·00
5420 $1.40 City and South London Railway locomotives (1890) (maroon and violet) 1·00 1·00
5421 $1.40 East London line (1940) (chocolate, violet and black) 1·00 1·00
5422 $1.40 Piccadilly line (1930) 1·00 1·00
5423 $1.40 Victoria line (1960) 1·00 1·00
5424 $1.40 Jubilee line (1990) 1·00 1·00
MS5425 Three sheets, each 91×71 mm. (a) $5 "A" train, New York. (b) $5 London Underground. (c) $5 1992 Tube, Central Line, London 9·00 9·50

509 Origami Rooster

2005. Chinese New Year ("New Year of the Rooster").
5426 **509** 75c. multicoloured 75 75

510 Mahatma Gandhi

2005. International Year of Peace. Multicoloured.
5427 $3 Type **510** 2·25 2·25
5428 $3 Elie Wiesel (Nobel Peace Prize winner, 1986) 2·25 2·25
5429 $3 Rigoberta Menchu Tum (Nobel Peace Prize winner, 1992) 2·25 2·25

511 Ploughing Fields

2005. International Year of Rice (2004). Multicoloured.
5430 $3 Type **511** 1·75 2·00
5431 $3 Man and boy in rice field 1·75 2·00
5432 $3 Man in rice field 1·75 2·00
MS5433 99×67 mm. $5 Boy eating rice (vert) 3·00 3·25

512 Kirk Hinrich (Chicago Bulls)

2005. National Basketball Association (2nd series). Multicoloured.
5434 75c. Type **512** 1·00 75
5435 $3 Steve Francis 2·50 2·50

513 Jehanzeb Khan (disabled by polio)

2005. Centenary of Rotary International. Multicoloured.
5436 $3 Type **513** 1·75 2·00
5437 $3 Jonas Salk and polio vaccine 1·75 2·00
5438 $3 Baby receiving oral polio vaccine 1·75 2·00

514 Prince Charles and Mrs. Camilla Parker-Bowles

2005. Royal Wedding. Multicoloured.
5439 $2 Type **514** 1·60 1·60
5440 $2 Wearing dark outer coats and looking left (horiz) 1·60 1·60

515 Pope John Paul II

2005. Commemoration of Pope John Paul II.
5441 $2 Wearing evening dress 1·60 1·60
5442 **515** $3 multicoloured 2·25 2·25

516 1939 20c. Vatican City Stamp

2005. Vacant See.
5443 **516** 70c. multicoloured 1·00 75

517 Red Irish Lord

2005. Predatory Fish. Multicoloured.
5444 $1 Type **517** 75 55
5445 $1.10 Deep Sea anglerfish 85 70
5446 $1.40 Viperfish 1·10 1·10
5447 $2 Lionfish 1·60 1·75
MS5448 110×70 mm. $5 Gulper eel 3·50 3·75

518 Mexican Long-tongued Bat

2005. Bats. Multicoloured.
MS5449 167×150 mm. $1.60×6, Type **518**; Wahlberg's fruit bat; Common vampire bat; false vampire bat; Horseshoe bat; Spear-nosed long-tongued bat 6·50 7·50
MS5450 112×83 mm. $5 Greater long-nosed bat 3·25 3·50

519 USSR T-34-85 Medium Tank

2005. 60th Anniv of Victory in Europe. Multicoloured.
5451 $2 Type **519** 1·60 1·60
5452 $2 German Tiger tank 1·60 1·60
5453 $2 USA LVT(A)-1 1·60 1·60
5454 $2 Great Britain Cruiser tank Mark VI 1·60 1·60
MS5455 100×70 mm. $5 Winston Churchill (vert) 4·00 4·00

520 Maimonides (statue)

2005. 800th Death Anniv of Moses Maimonides (Rabbi Moses Ben Maimon (Jewish scholar)) (2004).
5456 **520** $2 multicoloured 1·75 1·75

521 Field-Digger Wasp (*Mellinus arvensis*)

2005. Insects. Multicoloured.
5457 $2 Type **521** 1·50 1·50
5458 $2 Water spider (*Argyronetidae*) 1·50 1·50
5459 $2 Yellow crab spider (*Thomisus onustus*) 1·50 1·50
5460 $2 Mantid (*Empusa pennata*) 1·50 1·50
MS5461 70×100 mm. $5 Praying mantis (*Mantis religiosa*) 3·50 3·75

522 Butterwort (*Pinguicula rotundifolia*)

2005. Carnivorous Plants. Multicoloured.
5462 $2 Type **522** 1·50 1·50
5463 $2 Common sundew (*Drosera rotundifolia*) 1·50 1·50
5464 $2 Venus's flytrap (*Dionaea muscipula*) 1·50 1·50
5465 $2 Butterwort (*Pinguicula gypsicola*) 1·50 1·50
MS5466 69×99 mm. $5 Pitcher plant (*Nepenthes mixta*) 3·50 3·75

523 *The Brave Tin Soldier*

2005. Birth Bicentenary of Hans Christian Andersen (writer). Multicoloured.
5467 $3 Type **523** 1·75 2·00
5468 $3 *The Top and Ball* 1·75 2·00
5469 $3 *Ole-Luk-Oie, the Dream-God* 1·75 2·00
MS5470 100×70 mm. $5 *The Snow Queen* (50×38 mm) 3·00 3·25

524 Princess Aouda held Captive

2005. Death Centenary of Jules Verne (writer). Multicoloured.
5471-5474 $2×4 *Around the World in Eighty Days*: Type **524**; Phineas Fogg (David Niven) at train window (scene from 1956 film); Phineas Fogg; Passepartout 5·00 5·50
5475-5478 $2×4 *Twenty Thousand Leagues under the Sea*: Captain Nemo and *Nautilus* at surface; Captain Nemo looking through porthole; *Nautilus* crew watching giant octopus; Crew wearing helmets 5·00 5·50
5479-5482 $2×4 *Master of the World*: Terror (machine) on land; Terror at sea; Street scene; Terror in flight 5·00 5·50
5483-5486 $2×4 *From the Earth to the Moon*: Crew experiencing weightlessness; Space capsule on way to Moon; Take-off; Crew and space capsule 5·00 5·50
5487-5490 $2×4 *The Castle of the Carpathians*: Flying nyctalops; Crowd and ghost of La Stilla; Count Franz de Telek and Baron Rodolphe de Gortz; Orfanik (head conjuror) 5·00 5·50

MS5491 Five sheets, each 100×70 mm. (a) $5 Hot air balloon. (b) $5 Helicopter. (c) $5 Tank. (d) $5 Atomic bomb. (e) $5 Blitzkrieg of Second World War 17·00 18·00

525 Friedrich von Schiller

2005. Death Bicentenary of Friedrich von Schiller (poet and dramatist). Multicoloured.

5492 $3 Type **525** 1·75 2·00
5493 $3 In close-up (facing right) 1·75 2·00
5494 $3 In close-up (facing left) 1·75 2·00
MS5495 70×100 mm. $5 Friedrich von Schiller 3·00 3·25

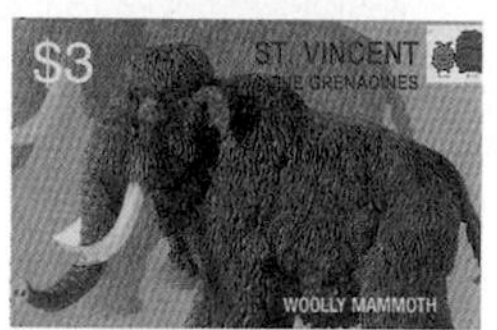

526 Woolly Mammoth

2005. Expo 2005 Exhibition, Aichi, Japan. Sheet, 178×62 mm, containing T 526 and similar horiz designs. Multicoloured.

MS5496 $2 Type **526**; $2 Woolly mammoth with long winter coat; $2 Woolly mammoth with huge upward curving tusks 3·75 4·25

527 SBD-3 *Dauntless*

2005. 60th Anniv of Victory in Japan Day. Multicoloured.

5497 $2 Type **527** 1·60 1·60
5498 $2 Mitsubishi Zero A6M5 1·60 1·60
5499 $2 USS *Yorktown* (aircraft carrier) 1·60 1·60
5500 $2 USS *Hornet* (aircraft carrier) 1·60 1·60
MS5501 100×70 mm. $5 Gen. Douglas MacArthur signing Japanese surrender 3·50 3·75

528 Panda

2005. Taipei 2005 International Stamp Exhibition. Multicoloured.

5502 $2 Type **528** 1·40 1·40
5503 $2 Formosan rock monkey 1·40 1·40
5504 $2 Formosan black bear 1·40 1·40
5505 $2 Formosan sika deer 1·40 1·40

2005. Christmas. As T 155 of St. Kitts. Multicoloured.

5506 70c. "The Small Cowper Madonna" (detail) (Raphael) 50 30
5507 90c. "Madonna of the Grand Duke" (detail) (Raphael) 60 45
5508 $1.10 "The Sistine Madonna" (detail) (Raphael) 80 70
5509 $3 "The Alba Madonna" (detail) (Raphael) 1·75 2·25
MS5510 96×67 mm. $6 "Adoration of the Magi" (Rogier van der Weyden) 3·50 3·75

529 Dog

2005. Chinese New Year ("Year of the Dog").

5511 **529** $1 multicoloured 80 70

530 Pope Benedict XVI

2005. Election of Pope Benedict XVI.

5512 **530** $2 multicoloured 1·90 1·90

531 "Panda" (Lauren Van Woy)

2006. "Kids-Did-It!" Designs. Showing children's paintings. Multicoloured.

5513 $2 Type **531** 1·40 1·40
5514 $2 "Giraffe" (Megan Albe) 1·40 1·40
5515 $2 "Orange Koala" (Holly Cramer) 1·40 1·40
5516 $2 "Red Monkey" (Roxanne Hanson) 1·40 1·40
5517 $2 "Flower Spot" (Tom Brier) 1·40 1·40
5518 $2 "Flower Vase" (Jessie Abrams) 1·40 1·40
5519 $2 "Green Flower Vase" (Nick Abrams) 1·40 1·40
5520 $2 "Red Sunflowers" (Bianca Saad) 1·40 1·40
5521 $2 "Snail" (Cortland Bobczynski) 1·40 1·40
5522 $2 "Blue Ladybug" (Jackie Wicks) 1·40 1·40
5523 $2 "Red Ladybug" (Emily Hawk) 1·40 1·40
5524 $2 "Snail Boy" (Micah Bobczynski) 1·40 1·40

532 St. Vincent Amazon Parrots

2006. 30th Anniv of the OPEC Fund for International Development. Multicoloured.

5525 $3 Type **532** 2·00 2·00
5526 $3 Waterfall in forest 2·00 2·00
5527 $3 Garden 2·00 2·00
5528 $3 Pair of St. Vincent Amazons 2·00 2·00

533 Duke and Duchess of York and Princess Elizabeth at her Christening

2006. 80th Birthday of Queen Elizabeth II. Multicoloured.

5529 $2 Type **533** 1·40 1·40
5530 $2 Princess Elizabeth making her first radio broadcast, 1940 1·40 1·40
5531 $2 Queen Elizabeth II at her Coronation, 1953 1·40 1·40
5532 $2 With Duke of Edinburgh, Princes Charles, Andrew and Edward and Princess Anne, c. 1965 1·40 1·40
5533 $2 Painting of Princesses Elizabeth and Margaret, c. 1937 1·40 1·40
5534 $2 Princess Elizabeth in ATS uniform, 1945 1·40 1·40
5535 $2 Wedding of Princess Elizabeth and Duke of Edinburgh, 1947 1·40 1·40
5536 $2 Awarding World Cup to England football captain Bobby Moore, 1966 1·40 1·40

534 Queen Angelfish

2006

5537 **534** 20c. multicoloured 15 20

535 Marilyn Monroe

2006. 80th Birth Anniv of Marilyn Monroe (actress).

5547 **535** $3 multicoloured 1·75 2·00

536 Poster for Winter Olympic Games, Lake Placid, 1932

2006. Winter Olympic Games, Turin. Multicoloured.

5548 75c. Type **536** 55 35
5549 90c. US 1932 Winter Olympics 2c. skiing stamp (horiz) 60 45
5550 $2 Poster for Winter Olympic Games, Chamonix, 1924 1·40 1·40
5551 $3 Letter postmarked for Winter Olympic Games, Chamonix, 1924 1·75 2·00

537 Nelson Mandela

2006. Washington 2006 International Stamp Exhibition.

5552 **537** $3 multicoloured 1·75 2·00

538 USS *Akron* (ZRS-4)

2006. 50th Death Anniv of Ludwig Durr (Zeppelin engineer). Multicoloured.

5553 $4 Type **538** 2·25 2·50
5554 $4 A-170 airship 2·25 2·50
5555 $4 Altair-Z experimental airship 2·25 2·50

539 "King Creole"

2006. 50th Anniv of Elvis Presley's Film Debut. Sheet 190×127 mm containing T 539 and similar vert designs showing film posters. Multicoloured.

5556 $3 Type **539** 1·75 1·75
5557 $3 "Love Me Tender" 1·75 1·75
5558 $3 "Loving You" 1·75 1·75
5559 $3 "Roustabout" 1·75 1·75

540 "Celebrating 50 Years of Service"

2006. 50th Anniv of LIAT (Leeward Islands Air Transport) Airline. Multicoloured.

5560 20c. Type **540** 30 15
5561 50c. DeHavilland DH8-300 in flight 50 35
5562 70c. HS-748 Hawker Siddely aircraft on ground 60 50
5563 90c. DeHavilland DH8-100 in flight 80 65
MS5564 99×70 mm. $5 Frank Delisle (founder) and first Beechcraft Twin Bonanza (vert) 3·25 3·50

541 Christopher Columbus

2006. 500th Death Anniv of Christopher Columbus. Multicoloured.

5565 50c. Type **541** 35 20
5566 70c. Christopher Columbus and Queen Isabella of Castile (horiz) 50 35
5567 $2 *Santa Maria* 1·40 1·50
5568 $3 *Santa Maria, Nina* and *Pinta* (horiz) 1·75 1·90
MS5569 70×100 mm. $5 *Pinta* 3·25 3·50

542 Titan Centaur Rocket taking-off, Cape Canaveral ("Viking I")

2006. Space Anniversaries. Multicoloured.

MS5570 Two sheets, each 150×100 mm. (a) $1.50×6 Type **542**; "Viking I", 1976; "Viking I" Lander on Mars, 1976; "Apollo XI" Landing Module on Moon, 1969; "Apollo XI" Command Module, 1969; "Apollo XI" launching by Saturn V rocket, 1969. (b) $2.50×4 SS Mir; "Sputnik 1"; "Soyuz"; "Luna 9" 11·00 12·00
MS5571 Two sheets, each 100×70 mm. (a) $6 Artist's concept of crew exploration vehicle ("Return to the Moon"). (b) $6 Space Station MIR, 1986–81 7·00 8·00

The stamps and margins of **MS**5570(b) form a composite background design.

543 Great White Shark

2006. Endangered Species. Great White Shark (Carcharodon carcharias). Multicoloured.

5572	$1 Type **543**	75	75
5573	$1 With dolphins	75	75
5574	$1 Swimming to left	75	75
5575	$1 In close-up, showing teeth	75	75
MS5576	98×148 mm. Nos. 5572/5, each ×2	5·50	6·00

544 Princess Amalia

2006. Princess Amalia Alexia of the Netherlands. Multicoloured.

5577	$1.50 Type **544**	1·10	1·10
5578	$1.50 Princess Amalia (head and shoulders)	1·10	1·10
5579	$1.50 As baby	1·10	1·10

545 Cherub

2006. Christmas. Showing details from painting "Enthroned Madonna with Child, Encircled by Saints" by Rubens. Multicoloured.

5580	20c. Type **545**	20	10
5581	70c. Baby Jesus	45	30
5582	90c. Four saints	65	45
5583	$1.10 Virgin Mary	80	60
5584	$2 As Type **545**	1·40	1·60
5585	$2 As No. 5581	1·40	1·60
5586	$2 As No. 5582	1·40	1·60
5587	$2 As No. 5583	1·40	1·60

546 Captains waving Union Jack Flags

2006. Last Flights of Concorde, (2003). Multicoloured.

5588	$1.40 Type **546**	1·50	1·50
5589	$1.40 Concorde landing at Heathrow Airport	1·50	1·50
5590	$1.40 Concorde G-BOAF ("The Filton flypast")	1·50	1·50
5591	$1.40 "Concorde Comes Home to Filton"	1·50	1·50

Nos. 5588/9 show the last commercial flight on 24 October 2003 and Nos. 5590/1 show the last ever Concorde flight on 26 November 2003.

547 Pres. Chen Shui-bian of Taiwan and Ralph Gonsalves (St. Vincent Prime Minister)

2006. 25th Anniv of Diplomatic Relations with Taiwan. Multicoloured.

5592	10c. Type **547**	15	15
5593	20c. Pres. Chen, Ralph Gonsalves and woman in St. Vincent parrot costume	20	15
5594	50c. Pres. Chen and Ralph Gonsalves shaking hands	30	25
5595	70c. Pres. Chen on visit to St. Vincent, 2005	45	35
5596	90c. Ralph Gonsalves and Pres. Chen	60	45
5597	$1.10 Taiwan Premier Yu Shyi-kun and Ralph Gonsalves	75	70
5598	$1.40 St. Vincent schoolchildren waving Taiwan flags	1·00	1·10
MS5599	Three sheets, each 98×68 mm. (a) $5 Pres. Chen and Ralph Gonsalves looking at documents. (b) $5 Milton Cato (first St. Vincent Prime Minister) establishing relations with Taiwan, 1979. (c) $5 Ralph Gonsalves, his wife and Premier Yu Shyi-kun	8·00	9·00

2006. 400th Birth Anniv of Rembrandt Harmenszoon van Rijn (artist). As T 157 of St. Kitts showing paintings. Multicoloured.

5600	50c. "The Jewish Physician Ephraim Bueno"	40	25
5601	75c. "Portrait of Ariantje Hollaer, Wife of Hendrick Martensz-Sorgh"	60	45
5602	$1 "An Old Man in a Fur Cap"	75	60
5603	$2 "Saskia van Uylenburgh"	1·40	1·50
5604	$2 "The Denial of St. Peter" (detail, woman)	1·40	1·50
5605	$2 "The Raising of Lazarus" (detail, Jesus Christ)	1·40	1·50
5606	$2 "The Denial of St. Peter" (detail, St. Peter)	1·40	1·50
5607	$2 "The Raising of Lazarus" (detail, Lazarus)	1·40	1·50
5608	$2 "Portrait of Titia van Uylenburgh"	1·40	1·50
5609	$2 "The Standing Syndic"	1·40	1·50
5610	$2 "Polish Officer" (detail)	1·40	1·50
5611	$2 "Seated Girl, in Profile to Left, Half Nude"	1·40	1·50
MS5612	Two sheets, each 70×100 mm. (a) $5 "Man Standing in Front of a Doorway". Imperf. (b) 70×100 mm. $5 "Two Young Negroes". Imperf	6·00	7·00

548 Wolfgang Amadeus Mozart

2007. 250th Birth Anniv of Wolfgang Amadeus Mozart. Sheet 100×70 mm.

MS5613	**548** $5 multicoloured	3·75	3·75

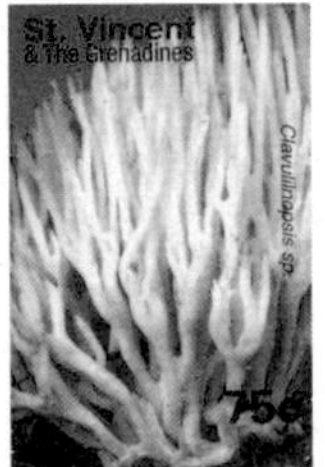

549 *Clavulilnopsis* sp.

2007. Mushrooms of the Caribbean. Multicoloured.

5614	75c. Type **549**	60	40
5615	90c. *Cortinarius* sp.	75	50
5616	$2 *Cortinarius* cf.	1·60	1·75
5617	$3 *Conocybe* spp	1·90	2·25
MS5618	100×70 mm. $6 *Galerina paludosa*	3·50	3·75

550 Lord Baden-Powell (founder) standing on Globe

2007. Centenary of Scouting. Multicoloured.

5619	$4 Type **550**	2·25	2·50
MS5620	80×110 mm. $6 Lord Baden-Powell and peace dove (horiz)	3·50	3·75

551 Congressman Kennedy

2007. 90th Birth Anniv of John F. Kennedy (US President 1960–3). Multicoloured.

5621	$3 Type **551**	1·75	1·90
5622	$3 Campaigning on crutches	1·75	1·90
5623	$3 Outdoors, wearing white t-shirt	1·75	1·90
5624	$3 Full-face portrait	1·75	1·90
5625	$3 *PT-109*	1·75	1·90
5626	$3 *PT-109* crew	1·75	1·90
5627	$3 Lieutenant Kennedy	1·75	1·90
5628	$3 Japanese destroyer	1·75	1·90

Nos. 5621/4 ("Elected to the House of Representatives 1947–53) and 5625/8 ("John Fitzgerald Kennedy Joins the Navy 1941–5).

552 Pigs (painting on fan by Liu Kuiling)

2007. Chinese New Year ("Year of the Pig").

5629	**552** $1.50 multicoloured	1·00	1·00

553 Bahama Yellowthroat

2007. Birds of the Caribbean. Multicoloured.

5630	$2 Type **553**	1·60	1·60
5631	$2 Arrow-headed warbler	1·60	1·60
5632	$2 Northern jacana	1·60	1·60
5633	$2 Loggerhead kingbird	1·60	1·60
MS5634	100×70 mm. $6 Louisiana waterthrush (horiz)	4·75	4·75

554 *Ancyluris jurgensenii*

2007. Butterflies of the Caribbean. Multicoloured.

5635	$2 Type **554**	1·60	1·60
5636	$2 *Arcas cypria*	1·60	1·60
5637	$2 *Stalachtis phlegia*	1·60	1·60
5638	$2 *Xamia xami*	1·60	1·60
MS5639	100×70 mm. $5 *Theritas coronata*	4·00	4·00

555 *Stanhopea grandiflora*

2007. Orchids. Multicoloured.

5640	$2 Type **555**	1·60	1·60
5641	$2 *Psychopsis papilio*	1·60	1·60
5642	$2 *Vanilla planifolia*	1·60	1·60
5643	$2 *Tetramicra canaliculata*	1·60	1·60
MS5644	100×70 mm. $5 *Trichopilia fragrans* (*horiz*)	4·00	4·00

556 Cameron Cuffy

2007. World Cup Cricket, West Indies. Mult.

5645	30c. Type **556**	20	20
5646	30c. Ian Allen	20	20
5647	$1.05 Neil Williams	60	60
5648	$1.35 Wilfred Slack	75	75
5649	$1.35 Michael Findlay	75	75
5650	$1.65 Winston Davis	90	90
5651	$1.65 Nixon McLean	90	90
5652	$2.10 Alphonso (Alfie) Roberts	2·10	2·10
MS5653	117×90 mm. $6 Arnos Vale Stadium, St. Vincent (horiz)	4·75	4·75

557 Dino 166 F2, 1968

2007. 60th Anniv of Ferrari Cars. Multicoloured.

5654	$1.40 Type **557**	80	80
5655	$1.40 246 F1, 1958	80	80
5656	$1.40 308 GTS, 1977	80	80
5657	$1.40 365 P Speciale, 1966	80	80
5658	$1.40 Enzo Ferrari, 2002	80	80
5659	$1.40 F40, 1987	80	80
5660	$1.40 348 Spider, 1993	80	80
5661	$1.40 212 Inter, 1951	80	80

558 Queen Elizabeth II and Duke of Edinburgh

2007. Diamond Wedding of Queen Elizabeth II and Duke of Edinburgh. Multicoloured.

5662	$1.40 Type **558**	80	80
5663	$1.40 In evening dress, in recent years	80	80
MS5664	72×102 mm. $6 In evening dress (Duke wearing military uniform), c. 1965 (vert)	4·75	4·75

559 Diana, Princess of Wales

2007. 10th Death Anniv of Diana, Princess of Wales. Multicoloured.

5665	$2 Type **559**	1·60	1·60
5666	$2 Wearing dark blue pin-striped jacket and dress	1·60	1·60
5667	$2 Wearing black and white jacket	1·60	1·60
5668	$2 Wearing white V-necked dress	1·60	1·60
MS5669	Two sheets, each 72×102 mm. (a) $6 Wearing hat and spotted blouse. (b) $6 Wearing Red Cross uniform	9·50	9·50

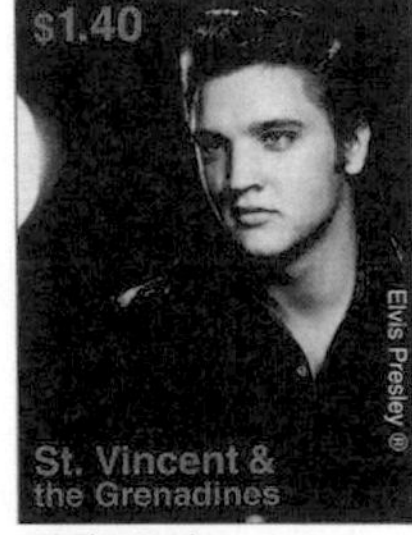

560 Elvis Presley

2007. 30th Death Anniv of Elvis Presley. Multicoloured.

5670	$1.40 Type **560**	80	80
5671	$1.40 Wearing V-necked sweater	80	80
5672	$1.40 Wearing cable-knit sweater	80	80
5673	$1.40 Wearing striped shirt	80	80
5674	$1.40 Wearing jacket and tie	80	80
5675	$1.40 Wearing western shirt	80	80

561 Pope Benedict XVI

2007. 80th Birthday of Pope Benedict XVI.

5676	**561**	$1.50 multicoloured	85	85

562 Capt. Havildar Lachhiman Gurung

2007. 150th Anniv of the First Presentation of the Victoria Cross. Multicoloured.

5677	$1.40 Type **562**	80	80
5678	$1.40 Ernest Alvia ('Smokey') Smith	80	80
5679	$1.40 Nk. Yeshwant Ghadge	80	80
5680	$1.40 Lieut. Colonel Eric Charles Twelves Wilson	80	80
5681	$1.40 Warrant Officer Class 2 Keith Payne	80	80
5682	$1.40 Lance Corporal Rambahadur Limbu	80	80
MS5683	100×70 mm. $6 Piper James Richardson	4·75	4·75

563 Delano Bart, St. Kitts & Nevis

2007. Holocaust Remembrance. Multicoloured.

5684	$1.40 Type **563**	80	80
5685	$1.40 Margaret H. Ferrari, St. Vincent & the Grenadines	80	80
5686	$1.40 Ali'ioaiga F. Elisaia, Samoa	80	80
5687	$1.40 Daniele D. Bodini, San Marino	80	80
5688	$1.40 Pavle Jevremovic, Serbia	80	80
5689	$1.40 Joe R. Pemagbi, Sierra Leone	80	80
5690	$1.40 Peter Burian, Slovakia	80	80
5691	$1.40 Sanja Stiglic, Slovenia	80	80

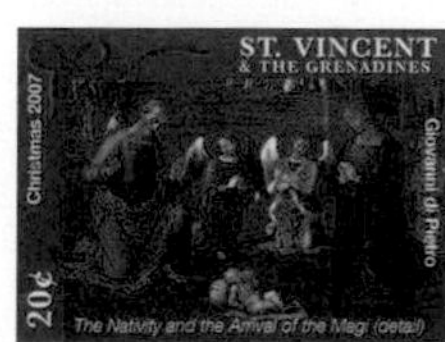

564 *The Nativity and the Arrival of the Magi* (Giovanni di Pietro)

2007. Christmas. Multicoloured.

5692	20c. Type **564**	10	10
5693	70c. *The Annunciation* (Benozzo Gozzoli)	40	40
5694	90c. *The Nativity* (Benozzo Gozzoli)	55	55
5695	$1.10 *The Journey of the Magi* (Sassetta)	65	65

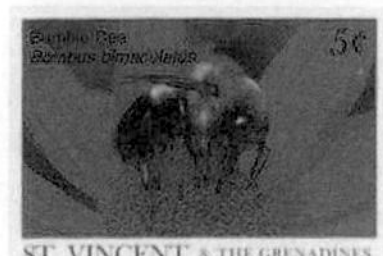

565 *Bombus bimaculatus* (bumble bee)

2007. Insects. Multicoloured.

5696	5c. Type **565**	10	10
5697	10c. *Stagmomantis carolina* (praying mantis)	15	15
5698	30c. *Photinus pyralis* (firefly) (vert)	20	20
5699	$1.35 *Anax junius* (green darner dragonfly) (vert)	75	75

566 Rat

2008. Chinese New Year ('Year of the Rat').

5700	**566**	$1.50 multicoloured	85	85

567 Bob Mathias (USA) (decathlon gold medallist)

2008. Olympic Games, Beijing. T 567 and similar vert designs showing scenes from Olympic Games, Helsinki, 1952. Multicoloured.

5701	$1.40 Type **567**	85	85
5702	$1.40 Poster for Olympic Games, Helsinki, 1952	85	85
5703	$1.40 Josy Barthel (Luxembourg) winning 1500 metres	85	85
5704	$1.40 Lis Hartel (Denmark) (dressage silver medallist)	85	85

568 Hummer H3

2008. Hummer H3. Multicoloured.

5705	$1.50 Type **568**	85	85
5706	$1.50 BNE 904 off-road on rocky track	85	85
5707	$1.50 Crossing muddy water in forest	85	85
5708	$1.50 Ascending sand hill in forest	85	85
MS5709	100×70 mm. $6 In silhouette	4·75	4·75

569 Yachts

2008. 32nd Americas Cup Yachting Championship, Valencia, Spain. Multicoloured.

5710	$1.20 Type **569**	75	75
5711	$1.80 Yachts from Germany and France	1·00	1·00
5712	$3 Two yachts, 'Fly Emirates' (on sail) in foreground	2·25	2·25
5713	$5 Two yachts, magenta sail at left	3·75	3·75

570 Taipei 101 Tower

2008. Taipei 2008 International Stamp Exhibition. Multicoloured.

5714	$1.50 Type **570**	85	85
5715	$1.50 Chinese pagoda	85	85
5716	$1.50 High speed railway	85	85
5717	$1.50 Lion dance	85	85
MS5718	100×70 mm. $5 National Taiwan Democracy Memorial Hall (51×37 mm)	3·75	3·75

571 Elvis Presley holding Rifle

2008. 50th Anniv of Elvis Presley's Induction into the US Army. Sheet 160×130 mm containing T 571 and similar vert designs showing him in Army uniform. Multicoloured.

MS5719	Type **571**; In Army uniform (against wall); Seated in red car; In Army uniform (against car)	3·50	3·50

The stamps within **MS**5719 share a composite background design.

572 Machu Picchu, Peru

2008. Seven New Wonders of the World. Sheet 155×120 mm containing T 572 and similar horiz designs. Multicoloured.

MS5720	Type **572**; Petra, Jordan; Chichén Itza, Mexico; Colosseum, Rome; Taj Mahal, India; Statue of Christ the Redeemer, Brazil; The Great Wall of China	6·25	6·25

The stamps within **MS**5720 form a composite background design.

573 *Queen Victoria*

2008. Historic meeting of 3 queens

5721	$3 Type **573**	2·25	2·25
5722	$3 *Queen Elizabeth II*	2·25	2·25
5723	$3 *Queen Mary II*	2·25	2·25

574 Pope Benedict XVI

2008. 1st Visit of Pope Benedict XVI to the United States.

5724	**574**	$2 multicoloured	2·10	2·10

575 Arms

2008. 60th Anniv of the University of the West Indies. Multicoloured.

5725	10c. Type **575**	15	15
5726	30c. Scroll	20	20
5727	90c. UWDEC Media Centre (horiz)	55	55
5728	$1.05 Anniversary emblem	65	65
MS5729	70×100 mm. $6 Scroll and anniversary emblem (horiz)	4·75	4·75

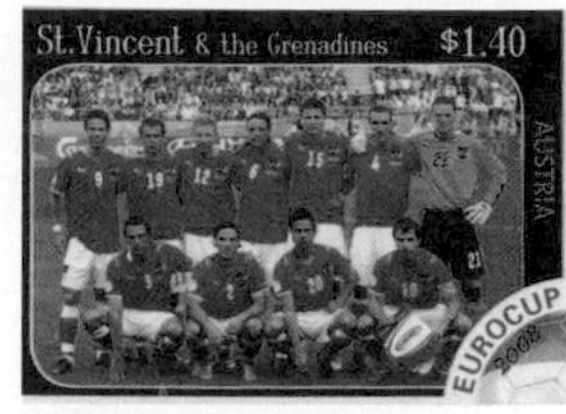

576 Austrian Team

2008. Eurocup 2008 European Football Championship, Austria and Switzerland. T 576 and similar horiz designs showing teams and stadiums. Multicoloured.

MS5730	Sixteen sheets, each 187×115 mm. (a) $1.40×6 As Type **576**×4 Tivoli Stadium, Innsbruck, Austria; St. Jakob Park Stadium, Basel, Switzerland. (b) $1.40×6 Croatian team×4; Tivoli Stadium; Stade de Geneve, Geneva, Switzerland. (c) $1.40×6 Czech Republic team×4; Tivoli Stadium; Stade de Suisse, Wankdorf, Bern, Switzerland. (d) $1.40×6 French team×4; Tivoli Stadium; Letzigrund Stadium, Zurich, Switzerland. (e) $1.40×6 German team×4; Worthersee Stadium, Hypo Arena, Klagenfurt, Austria; St. Jakob Park Stadium. (f) $1.40×6 Greek team×4; Worthersee Stadium, Hypo Arena; Stade de Suisse. (g) $1.40×6 Italian team×4; Worthersee Stadium, Hypo Arena; Stade de Geneve. (h) $1.40×6 Netherlands team×4; Worthersee Stadium, Hypo Arena; Letzigrund Stadium. (i) $1.40×6 Polish team×4; Wals-Siezenheim Stadium, Salzburg, Austria; St. Jakob Park Stadium. (j) $1.40×6 Portuguese team×4; Wals-Seizenheim Stadium; Stade de Suisse. (k) Romanian team×4; Wals-Seizenheim Stadium; Stade de Geneve. (l) $1.40×6 Russian team×4; Wals-Seizenheim Stadium; Letzigrund Stadium. (m) $1.40×6 Spanish team×4; Ernst Happel Stadium, Vienna, Austria; St. Jakob Park Stadium. (n) $1.40×6 Swedish team×4; Ernst Happel Stadium; Stade de Suisse. (o) $1.40×6 Swiss team×4; Ernst Happel Stadium; Stade de Geneve. (p) $1.40×6 Turkish team×4; Ernst Happel Stadium; Letzigrund Stadium	60·00	60·00
MS5731	280×215 mm. 65c.×16 National teams: Czech Republic; Turkey; Switzerland; Portugal; Austria; Croatia; Poland; Germany; France; Netherlands; Romania; Italy; Greece; Sweden; Russia; Spain	8·00	8·00

577 Three Teenagers

2008. 50th Anniv of the Credit Union. Multicoloured.

5732	10c. Type **577**	15	15
5733	30c. Man (vert)	25	25
5734	90c. Woman (vert)	55	55
5735	$1.05 Elderly man (vert)	65	65
MS5736	100×71 mm. $6 Kingstown Co-operative Credit Union Financial Centre	4·75	4·75

578 Valentina Tereshkova (first woman in Space)

2008. 50 Years of Space Exploration and Satellites. Multicoloured.

5737	$1.40 Type **578**	85	85
5738	$1.40 Valentina Tereshkova wearing black jacket and white tie-neck blouse	85	85
5739	$1.40 *Vostok 6*	85	85
5740	$1.40 Valentina Tereshkova wearing orange space suit	85	85

5741 $1.40 Statue of Valentina Tereshkova 85 85
5742 $1.40 Valentina Tereshkova wearing space suit (without helmet) 85 85
5743 $1.40 Titan IIIE/Centaur rocket with *Viking I* 85 85
5744 $1.40 Technical drawing of *Viking I* Orbiter/Lander 85 85
5745 $1.40 *Viking I* Lander landing on Mars 85 85
5746 $1.40 *Viking I* orbiting Mars 85 85
5747 $1.40 Technical drawing of *Viking I* Lander 85 85
5748 $1.40 Picture of Mars surface from *Viking I* 85 85
5749 $1.40 *Pioneer 11* and Saturn 85 85
5750 $1.40 Atlas Centaur 27 rocket with *Pioneer 10* 85 85
5751 $1.40 Pioneer plaque 85 85
5752 $1.40 *Pioneer 10* and Jupiter 85 85
5753 $1.40 *Pioneer 10* and *11* technical drawing 85 85
5754 $1.40 Pioneer programme spacecraft 85 85
5755 $2 *Mariner 4* Mars Encounter Imaging Geometry 1·60 1·60
5756 $2 *Mariner 4* 1·60 1·60
5757 $2 Atlas Agena D rocket launching *Mariner 4* 1·60 1·60
5758 $2 *Mariner 4* passing Mars 1·60 1·60
5759 $2 *Freedom 7* 1·60 1·60
5760 $2 Astronaut Alan Shepard 1·60 1·60
5761 $2 *Vostok* 1·60 1·60
5762 $2 Cosmonaut Yuri Gagarin (first man in space) 1·60 1·60
5763 $2 *Luna 2* 1·60 1·60
5764 $2 Soviet pennants for *Luna 2* 1·60 1·60
5765 $2 *Luna 2* rocket launch aboard Luna 8K72 1·60 1·60
5766 $2 *Luna 2* above Moon 1·60 1·60

579 The Nativity

2008. Christmas. Designs showing nativity paintings.
5767 **579** 75c. multicoloured 45 45
5768 **579** 90c. multicoloured 55 55
5769 **579** $2 multicoloured 1·60 1·60
5770 **579** $3 multicoloured 2·25 2·25

580 Pres. Barack Obama

2009. Inauguration of Pres. Barack Obama. Multicoloured.
5771 $1.75 Type **580** 1·60 1·60
MS5772 132×94 mm. $2.75 Pres. Obama, state of Pres. Abraham Lincoln in background (26×33 mm) ×4 2·10 2·10
MS5773 132×94 mm. $6.50 No. 5771; $6.50 Vice President Joseph Biden 10·50 10·50

581 Ox

2009. Chinese New Year. Year of the Ox. Sheet 190×90 mm.
MS5774 $2.50 Type **581**×4 1·90 1·90

582 Arms of St. Vincent

2009
5775 **582** $1.30 deep lilac and grey 80 80

583 First Inaugural Address, 1861

2009. Birth Bicentenary of Abraham Lincoln (US President 1861–5). T 583 and similar vert designs. Multicoloured.
MS5776 126×180 mm. $2×6 Type **583**; Abraham Lincoln (older); With Union troops; Reward poster for his killer; Abraham Lincoln (younger, US flag in background); Detail from *First Reading of the Emancipation Proclamation of PresidentLincoln* by Francis Bicknell Carpenter 9·50 9·50
MS5777 100×70 mm. $6 Head of Abraham Lincoln statue (37×50 mm) 4·75 4·75

584 Goalkeeper Gianluigi Buffon

2009. Juventus Football Club, Turin, Italy. Sheet 173×134 mm containing T 584 and similar horiz designs. Multicoloured.
MS5778 Type **584**; Mauro Camoranesi celebrating with David Trezeguet; Juventus captain Alessandro Del Piero celebrating a goal; Pavel Nedved (Czech Republic) celebrating with Mohammad Sissoko; Juventus fans inside their Stadio Olimpico di Torino; French striker David Trezeguet celebrating a goal; Zinedine Zidane (as Juventus player) celebrating; Italian striker Christian Vieri playing against Argentinian club River Plate 9·00 9·00

585 Biplane and Astronaut on USA Ohio State Quarter

2009. International Year of Astronomy. 40th Anniv of First Moon Landing. Sheet 150×100 mm containing T 585 and similar vert designs. Multicoloured.
MS5779 Type **585**; Apollo 11 Command Module; Apollo 11 badge; Apollo 11 Lunar Module; Diagram of Apollo 11 and Moon's surface; Astronaut Neil Armstrong 9·50 9·50

586 Pope Benedict XVI

2009. Visit of Pope Benedict XVI to Jordan. Sheet 100×150 mm. Multicoloured.
MS5780 $1.50, $2, $2.50, $3 all As Type **586** 7·00 7·00

587 Yorkshire Terrier

2009. 125th Anniv of the American Kennel Club. Multicoloured.
MS5781 140×160 mm. $1.60×9 Type **587**; German shepherd dog; Golden retriever; Beagle; Dachshund; Boxer; Poodle; Shih tzu; Miniature schnauzer 10·00 10·00
MS5782 100×120 mm. $3.25×4 Yorkshire terrier in pink basket with flowers at right; Yorkshire terrier (in front of basket); Yorkshire terrier (in close-up, white flowers at left); Yorkshire terrier (on red bench) 6·75 6·75

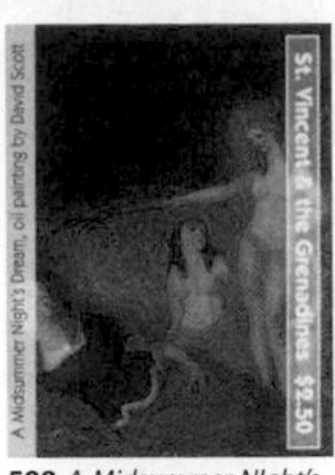

588 *A Midsummer Night's Dream* (David Scott)

2009. Birth Bicentenary of Felix Mendelssohn (composer). Sheet 164×94 mm containing T 588 and similar vert designs. Multicoloured.
MS5783 Type **588**; *Felix Mendelssohn* (Eduard Magnus); *Cécile Jeanrenaud* (Eduard Magnus); Score for *On Wings of Song* in Mendelssohn's hand; Gewandhausorchester; Drawing of interior of Church of the Holy Ghost by Mendelssohn 11·75 11·75

589 Michael Jackson

2009. Michael Jackson Commemoration. Multicoloured.
MS5784 120×157 mm. $2.25 Type **589**; $2.25 Wearing white; $2.75 As Type **589**; $2.75 Wearing white 7·75 7·75
MS5785 158×112 mm. $2.50×4 Wearing pink and brown jacket; Wearing white jacket; Wearing silver jacket; Wearing white jacket with zip and black collar 6·00 6·00

(589a)

2009. Michael Jackson Commemoration (2nd issue). As Nos. 940/8 but with new face values and optd with T 589a.
5785a 45c. Type **151** 75 75
5785b 45c. Wearing red and blue T shirt and dark jacket and hat 75 75
5785c 90c. Wearing red and white jacket, holding microphone 1·40 1·40
5785d 90c. Wearing black T shirt over white shirt 1·40 1·40
5785e $1.50 Wearing black, red and gold jacket and white shirt 1·40 1·40
5785f $1.75 Wearing red and gold jacket 1·60 1·60
5785g $4 Wearing white cap 3·25 3·25
5785h $4 Wearing red and gold jacket and white gloves 3·25 3·25
MS5785i 144×109 mm. Nos. 5785*a*/*b*, each ×2 3·00 3·00
MS5785j 144×109 mm. Nos. 5785*c*/*d*, each ×2 5·50 5·50
MS5785k 144×109 mm. Nos. 5785*e*/*f*, each ×2 6·50 6·50
MS5785l 144×109 mm. Nos. 5785*g*/*h*, each ×2 13·00 13·00

590 Michelangelo

2009. 25th Anniv of Teenage Mutant Ninja Turtles. Sheet 107×174 mm containing T 590 and similar horiz designs. Multicoloured.
MS5786 Type **590**; Donatello; Leonardo; Raphael 8·00 8·00

591 Elvis Presley

2009. Elvis Presley Commemoration. T 591 and similar vert designs. Multicoloured.
MS5787 160×130 mm. $2.50×4 Type **591**; With both arms raised; With arm raised; Standing sideways 8·00 8·00
MS5788 90×125 mm. $6 Elvis Presley as Lucky Johnson in *Viva Las Vegas*, 1964 4·75 4·75
MS5789 125×90 mm. $6 Poster for *Viva Las Vegas* 8·00 8·00
MS5790 125×90 mm. $6 Elvis Presley wearing red shirt 8·00 8·00
MS5791 90×125 mm. $6 Wearing red shirt and brown jacket 8·00 8·00

592 Penguins swimming

2009. Philakorea 2009 International Stamp Exhibition. Preserve the Polar Regions and Glaciers. Designs showing collage of Arctic penguins made from scraps of material. Multicoloured.
MS5792 120×100 mm. $3×4 Type **592**; Penguin walking with beak open and wings raised; Penguins with wings raised; Adult and chick 3·50 3·50
MS5793 100×70 mm. $6 Penguins with chick (37×70 mm) 8·00 8·00

593 White-rumped Sandpiper (*Calidris fuscicollis*)

2009. Water Birds of St. Vincent. Multicoloured.
5794 $1.20 Type **593** 80 80
5795 $1.80 Tricolored heron (*Egretta tricolor*) 90 90
5796 $3 Masked booby (*Sula dactylatra*) 2·50 2·50
5797 $5 Red-footed booby (*Sula sula*) (vert) 3·75 3·75
MS5798 90×119 mm. $2.50×4 Brown pelican (*Pelecanus occidentalis*); Great blue heron (*Ardea herodias*); Snowy egret (*Egretta thula*); Pied-billed grebe (*Podilymbus podiceps*) (all vert) 9·50 9·50
MS5799 70×100 mm. $3×2 Ring-billed gull (*Larus delawarensis*); Short-billed dowitcher (*Limnodromus griseus*) (both vert) 4·25 4·25

594 Samuel de Champlain

2009. New York State's Quadricentennial Celebrations. Sheet 130×78 mm containing T 594 and similar vert designs. Multicoloured.

MS5800	Type **594** (400th anniv of his discovery of Lake Champlain); Robert Fulton (bicentenary of first New York–Albany steamboat voyage); Henry Hudson (400th anniv of his discovery of Manhattan); USA 1909 2c. Hudson-Fulton Celebration stamp	9·50	9·50

595 Journey of the Magi

2009. Christmas. Multicoloured.

5801	90c. Type **595**	55	55
5802	$1.80 Shepherds and infant Jesus	1·00	1·00
5803	$2.50 Magi and infant Jesus	1·75	1·75
5804	$3 Virgin Mary and infant Jesus	2·25	2·25

Haiti Earthquake Relief Fund

595a

2010. Haiti Earthquake Relief Fund

MS5804a	$2.50×4 Brown pelican (*Pelecanus occidentalis*); Great blue heron (*Ardea herodias*); Snowy egret (*Egretta thula*); Pied-billed grebe (*Podilymbus podiceps*)	9·00	9·00

596 Australia

2010. World Cup Football, South Africa. Designs showing teams. Multicoloured.

MS5805	170×132 mm. $1.75×8 Type **596**; Japan; North Korea; South Korea; Honduras; Mexico; United States; New Zealand	12·75	12·75
MS5806	170×132 mm. $1.75×8 Denmark; France; Greece; Portugal; Serbia; Slovakia; Slovenia; Switzerland	12·75	12·75
MS5807	170×132 mm. $1.75×8 Algeria; Cameroon; Côte D'Ivoire; Ghana; Nigeria; Chile; Paraguay; Uruguay	12·75	12·75
MS5808	170×132 mm. $1.75×8 South Africa; Brazil; Spain; Netherlands; Italy; Germany; Argentina; England	12·75	12·75

597 Engine of Ferrari 312 B, 1970

2010. Ferrari Cars. Multicoloured.

5809	$1.25 Type **597**	80	80
5810	$1.25 312 B, 1970 (car no. 25)	80	80
5811	$1.25 Engine of 126 CX, 1981	80	80
5812	$1.25 126 CX, 1981	80	80
5813	$1.25 Engine of DINO 308 GT4, 1973	80	80
5814	$1.25 DINO 308 GT4, 1973	80	80
5815	$1.25 Gears of 400 Automatic, 1976	80	80
5816	$1.25 400 Automatic, 1976	80	80

598 Oval Office

2010. 50th Anniv of Election of President John F. Kennedy. Multicoloured.

MS5817	150×100 mm. $2×6 Type **598**; John F. Kennedy; Jackie Kennedy; Lady Bird Johnson; Lyndon B. Johnson; White House	4·25	4·25
MS5818	130×100 mm. $2.75×4 John F. Kennedy (photographed indoors); John F. Kennedy Presidential Library and Museum; Statue of John F. Kennedy, Regents Park, London; Presidential Seal	7·50	7·50

599 Elvis Presley

2010. 75th Birth Anniv of Elvis Presley. Multicoloured.

MS5819	180×159 mm. $2.75×4 Wearing black leather: Type **599**; Playing guitar; Singing, holding guitar; Facing left	7·50	7·50
MS5820	168×129 mm. $2.75×4 Wearing jacket, with guitar; Wearing jacket, hands raised to face; Wearing jacket, right hand on head; Wearing T shirt	7·50	7·50

600 Leatherback Turtle (Dermochelys coriacea)

2010. Caribbean Marine Life. Multicoloured.

5821	25c. Type **600**	15	15
5822	80c. Caesar grunt (*Haemulon carbonarium*)	70	70
5823	$1 Atlantic tarpon (*Megalops atlanticus*)	80	80
5824	$5 Moray eel (*Strophidon sathete*)	2·50	2·50
MS5825	170×101 mm. $2×6 Caribbean reef shark (*Carcharhinus perezi*); Loggerhead sea turtle (*Caretta caretta*); Great barracuda (*Sphyraena barracuda*); Caribbean lobster (*Metanephrops binghami*); Royal gramma (*Gramma loreto*); Southern stingray (*Dasyatis americana*)	5·50	5·50

The stamps and margins of **MS**5825 form a composite background design of a coral reef

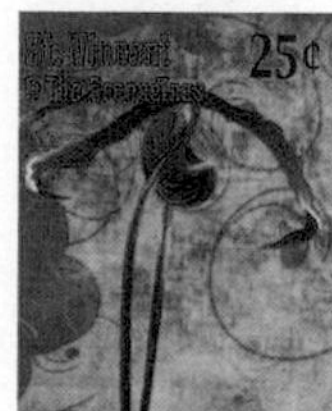

601 Phragmipedium popowii

2010. Orchids of the Caribbean

5826	25c. Type **601**	15	15
5827	80c. *Cattleya dowiana*	70	70
5828	$1 *Brassavola subulifolia*	80	80
5829	$5 *Brassavola acaulis*	2·50	2·50
MS5830	150×101 mm. $2×6 *Cattleya gaskelliana; Cattleya aurea; Cattleya mendelii; Cattleya schrodera; Cypripedium dickinsonianum; Phragmipedium longifolium* (all horiz)	5·50	5·50

The stamps and margins of **MS**5830 form a composite background design

602 Huito (Genipa americana)

2010. Flowers of St. Vincent and the Grenadines

5831	25c. Type **602**	15	15
5832	80c. Tiny bladderwort (*Utricularia pusilla*)	70	70
5833	$1 Purple coral tree (*Erythrina fusca*)	80	80
5834	$5 Apple guava (*Psidium guajava*)	2·50	2·50
MS5835	170×100 mm. $2×6 Soufriere tree (*Spachea elegans*); Guajacum (*Guaiacum officinale*); Nipplefruit (*Solanum mammosum*); Alpine bladderworts (*Utricularia alpina*); Foetid passion flower (*Passiflora foetida*); Shoreline purslane (*Sesuvium portulacastrum*) (all horiz)	5·50	5·50

The stamps and margins of **MS**5835 form a composite background design of a forested coastline.

603 Two Guides

2010. Centenary of Girlguiding. Multicoloured.

MS5836	150×100 mm. $2.75×4 Type **603**; Four guides; Four guides lying in circle; Three guides	7·50	7·50
MS5837	70×100 mm. $6 Guide holding '100' placard	4·50	4·50

OFFICIAL STAMPS

1982. Nos. 668/73 optd OFFICIAL.

O1	60c. "Isabella"	15	15
O2	60c. Prince Charles and Lady Diana Spencer	40	50
O3	$2.50 "Alberta" (tender)	15	25
O4	$2.50 Prince Charles and Lady Diana Spencer	55	70
O5	$4 "Britannia"	25	30
O6	$4 Prince Charles and Lady Diana Spencer	80	90

APPENDIX

The following issues for individual islands in the Grenadines have either been issued in excess of postal needs, or have not been made available to the public in reasonable quantities at face value. Miniature sheets, imperforate sheets etc. are excluded from this listings.

Bequia

2009

Dogs of the World. 75c., 90c., $2, $2.50×4, $3
The Three Stooges. $2×6
Visit of Pope Benedict XVI to Israel. $2.50×4
Elvis Presley Commemoration. Madison Square Gardens, 1972. $2.50×4
40th Anniv of First Manned Moon Manding. $2.50×4

Mayreau

2009

5 Years of the Pontificate of Pope Benedict XVI. $2.75×4
Endangered Species. Spotted Eagle Ray (*Aetobatus narinari*). $3×4

Mustique

2009

Dogs of the World. $2×6
Elvis Presley Commemoration. $2.50×4

Union Island

2009

50 Years of Space Exploration and Satellites. $2×8, $2.50×8
40th Anniv of First Manned Moon Landing $2×6; $2.50×4

Pt. 1, Pt. 7

SAMOA

Islands in the W. Pacific administered jointly from 1889–99 by Gt. Britain, Germany and the U.S.A. In 1899 the eastern islands were assigned to the U.S.A. and the western to Germany. The latter were occupied by British forces in 1914 and were taken over by New Zealand, under mandate, in 1920. W. Samoa was under United Nations trusteeship until it became independent on 1 January 1962.

Samoa.
1877. 12 pence = 1 shilling; 20 shillings = 1 pound.
1967. 100 sene or cents = 1 tale or dollar.

German Colony.
100 pfennig = 1 mark.

INDEPENDENT KINGDOM

1

1877

15	1	1d. blue	35·00	£650
16	1	3d. red	60·00	£700
17	1	6d. violet	50·00	£450
20	1	9d. brown	70·00	£400
7b	1	1s. yellow	£100	£250
18	1	2s. brown	£225	
19	1	5s. green	£500	

The majority of the stamps of T 1 found in old collections are worthless reprints. A 2d. stamp exists but was never issued.

2 Palm Trees **3** King Malietoa Laupepa **8**

1886

57a	2	½d. brown	3·75	1·75
88	2	½d. green	2·50	3·75
58a	2	1d. green	9·00	1·75
89	2	1d. brown	3·50	3·75
59c	2	2d. orange	5·00	9·50
60	3	2½d. red	4·00	10·00
81	3	2½d. black	1·75	3·50
61	2	4d. blue	17·00	9·00
72a	8	5d. red	4·50	19·00
62	2	6d. lake	14·00	3·00
63	2	1s. red	13·00	3·75
64b	2	2s.6d. violet	4·75	9·50

1893. Surch FIVE PENCE and bar.

65	2	5d. on 4d. blue	75·00	50·00

1893. Surch 5d and bar.

69	2	5d. on 4d. blue	35·00	38·00

1893. Surch Surcharged and value in figures.

75	2	1½d. on 2d. orange	5·50	7·50
84	2	2½d. on 1d. green	75	3·00
85	2	2½d. on 1s. red	8·50	15·00
87	2	2½d. on 2s.6d. violet	10·00	23·00

1895. Surch R 3d.

76	2	3d. on 2d. orange	9·50	12·00

1899. Optd PROVISIONAL GOVT.

90	2	½d. green	3·25	4·25
91	2	1d. brown	3·75	14·00
92	2	2d. orange	2·50	9·00
93	2	4d. blue	70	15·00
94	8	5d. red	3·75	11·00
95	2	6d. lake	1·50	11·00
96	2	1s. red	1·50	38·00
97	2	2s.6d. violet	4·75	25·00

GERMAN COLONY

1900. Stamps of Germany optd Samoa.

G1	8	3pf. brown	11·50	16·00
G2	8	5pf. green	15·00	21·00
G3	9	10pf. red	11·50	21·00
G4	9	20pf. blue	23·00	36·00
G5	9	25pf. orange	48·00	95·00
G6	9	50pf. brown	48·00	90·00

1901. "Yacht" key-type inscr "SAMOA".

G7	N	3pf. brown	1·30	1·40
G8	N	5pf. green	1·30	1·40
G9	N	10pf. red	1·30	1·40
G10	N	20pf. blue	1·30	2·75
G11	N	25pf. black & red on yell	1·40	15·00
G12	N	30pf. black & orge on buff	1·70	12·50
G13	N	40pf. black and red	1·70	15·00
G14	N	50pf. black & pur on buff	1·70	16·00
G15	N	80pf. black & red on pink	3·50	37·00
G16	O	1m. red	4·25	75·00
G17	O	2m. blue	5·75	£130
G18	O	3m. black	9·50	£180
G19	O	5m. red and black	£180	£650

NEW ZEALAND DEPENDENCY

(under Mandate from League of Nations and United Nations).

1914. "Yacht" key-types as German Cameroons, but inscr "SAMOA", surch G.R.I. and value in British currency.

101	N	½d. on 3pf. brown	55·00	15·00
102	N	½d. on 5pf. green	60·00	18·00
103	N	1d. on 10pf. red	£100	40·00
104	N	2½d. on 20pf. blue	60·00	13·00
105	N	3d. on 25pf. black and red on yellow	70·00	40·00
106	N	4d. on 30pf. black and orange on buff	£130	60·00
107	N	5d. on 40pf. black and red	£130	70·00
108	N	6d. on 50pf. black and purple on buff	65·00	35·00
109	N	9d. on 80pf. black and red on rose	£200	£100
110	O	1s. on 1m. red	£3250	£3500
112	O	2s. on 2m. blue	£3500	£3000
113	O	3s. on 3m. black	£1400	£1200
114	O	5s. on 5m. red and black	£1100	£1000

1914. Stamps of New Zealand (King Edward VII) optd SAMOA.

115	51	½d. green	1·25	30
116	50	1d. red	1·25	10
117	51	2d. mauve	1·25	1·00
118	26	2½d. blue (B)	1·75	1·75
119	51	6d. red	1·75	1·75
121	51	1s. orange	8·00	19·00

1914. Large stamps of New Zealand (Queen Victoria) optd SAMOA.

127	F4	2s. blue	6·00	5·50
123	F4	2s.6d. brown	5·50	12·00
129	F4	3s. violet	16·00	65·00
124	F4	5s. green	19·00	11·00
125	F4	10s. brown	35·00	28·00
126	F4	£1 red	80·00	45·00

1916. Stamps of New Zealand (King George V) optd SAMOA.

134	62	½d. green	70	1·25
135	62	1½d. grey	50	25
136	62	1½d. brown	30	50
137	62	2d. yellow	1·50	20
139	62	2½d. blue	1·25	50
140	62	3d. brown	50	1·00
141a	62	6d. red	1·50	1·25
142	62	1s. orange	3·50	1·50

1920. Stamps of New Zealand (Victory issue. Nos. 453/8) optd SAMOA.

143	64	½d. green	6·50	13·00
144	65	1d. red	3·00	17·00
145	-	1½d. orange	2·00	9·00
146	-	3d. brown	8·00	9·00
147	-	6d. violet	4·50	7·00
148	-	1s. orange	13·00	11·00

16 Native Hut

1921

153	16	½d. green	4·50	1·75
150	16	1d. lake	7·00	1·25
151	16	1½d. brown	1·25	18·00
152	16	2d. yellow	2·25	2·50
157	16	2½d. blue	1·75	8·00
158	16	3d. sepia	1·75	4·50
159	16	4d. violet	1·75	3·50
160	16	5d. blue	1·75	7·50
161	16	6d. red	1·75	6·50
162	16	8d. brown	1·75	13·00
163	16	9d. olive	2·00	35·00
164	16	1s. orange	1·75	28·00

1926. Stamps of New Zealand (King George V) optd SAMOA.

167	71	2s. blue	5·00	18·00
168	71	3s. mauve	23·00	45·00

1932. Stamps of New Zealand (Arms type) optd SAMOA.

171	F6	2s.6d. brown	16·00	50·00
172	F6	5s. green	26·00	55·00
173	F6	10s. red	50·00	£100
174	F6	£1 pink	75·00	£140
175	F6	£2 violet	£800	
176	F6	£5 blue	£2250	

1935. Silver Jubilee. Stamps of 1921 optd SILVER JUBILEE OF KING GEORGE V 1910-1935.

177	16	1d. lake	30	30
178	16	2½d. blue	60	65
179	16	6d. red	2·75	4·50

18 Samoan Girl **19** Apia

1935

180	18	½d. green	10	35
181	19	1d. black and red	10	10
182	-	2d. black and orange	3·50	3·50
183	-	2½d. black and blue	10	10
184	-	4d. grey and brown	70	15
205	-	5d. brown and blue	2·25	50
185	-	6d. mauve	50	10
186	-	1s. violet and brown	30	10
187	-	2s. green and purple	80	50
188	-	3s. blue and orange	1·50	3·50

DESIGNS—HORIZ: 2d. River scene; 4d. Samoan canoe and house; 5d. Apia post office; 6d. R. L. Stevenson's home, "Vailima"; 1s. Stevenson's tomb. VERT: 2½d. Samoan chief and wife; 2s. Lake Lanuto'o; 3s. Falefa Falls.

1935. Stamps of New Zealand (Arms types) optd WESTERN SAMOA.

207	F6	2s.6d. brown	11·00	24·00
208	F6	5s. green	21·00	16·00
209	F6	10s. red	20·00	17·00
234	F6	£1 pink	15·00	55·00
211	F6	30s. brown	£200	£300
235	F6	£2 violet	70·00	£160
213	F6	£3 green	£275	£375
194	F6	£5 blue	£225	£450

28 Coastal Scene **31** Robert Louis Stevenson

1939. 25th Anniv of New Zealand Control.

195	28	1d. olive and red	1·00	25
196	-	1½d. blue and brown	1·75	75
197	-	2½d. brown and blue	1·75	1·00
198	31	7d. violet and green	8·00	4·00

DESIGNS—HORIZ: 1½d. Map of Western Samoa; 2½d. Samoan dancing party.

32 Samoan Chief

1940. Surch.

199	32	3d. on 1½d. brown	75	20

1946. Peace stamps of New Zealand optd WESTERN SAMOA.

215	132	1d. green	40	15
216	-	2d. purple (No. 670)	40	15
217	-	6d. brown and orange (No. 674)	80	15
218	139	8d. black and red	40	15

35 Making Siapo Cloth **36** Native Houses and Flags

1952

219	35	½d. red and brown	10	1·75
220	36	1d. olive and green	10	30
221	-	2d. red	10	10
222	-	3d. blue and indigo	40	20
223	-	5d. brown and green	8·00	70
224	-	6d. blue and mauve	1·00	10
225	-	8d. red	30	30
226	-	1s. sepia and blue	15	10
227	-	2s. brown	1·00	25
228	-	3s. brown and olive	2·00	2·00

DESIGNS—VERT (as Type **35**): 2d. Seal of Samoa; 5d. Tooth-billed pigeon. (As Type **36**): 3s. Samoan chieftainess. HORIZ (as Type **35**): 1s. Thatching native hut. (As Type **36**): 3d. Malifa Falls, wrongly inscr on stamp "Aleisa Falls"; 6d. Bonito fishing canoe; 8d. Cacao harvesting; 2s. Preparing copra.

1953. Coronation. As T 1a of Tokelau Islands.

229	1a	2d. brown	1·00	15
230	-	6d. grey	1·00	35

DESIGN: 6d. Westminster Abbey.

48 Map of Samoa, and the Mace

1958. Inaug of Samoan Parliament. Inscr "FONO FOU 1958".

236	-	4d. red (As T **36**)	25	30
237	-	6d. violet (As No. 221)	25	30
238	48	1s. blue	75	50

INDEPENDENT STATE

49 Samoan Fine Mat

1962. Independence.

239	49	1d. brown and red	10	10
240	-	2d. multicoloured	10	10
241	-	3d. brown, green and blue	10	10
242	-	4d. multicoloured	15	20
243	-	6d. yellow and blue	80	20
261	-	8d. turquoise, green and blue	30	10
245	-	1s. brown and green	20	10
246	-	1s.3d. green and blue	1·00	45
247	-	2s.6d. red and blue	2·25	1·75
248	-	5s. multicoloured	2·50	2·25

DESIGNS—HORIZ: 2d. Samoa College; 3d. Public library; 4d. Fono house; 6d. Map of Samoa; 8d. Airport; 1s.3d. "Vailima"; 2s.6d. Samoan flag; 5s. Samoan Seal. VERT: 1s. Samoan orator.

59 Seal and Joint Heads of State

1963. 1st Anniv of Independence.

249	59	1d. sepia and green	10	10
250	59	4d. sepia and blue	10	10
251	59	8d. sepia and pink	10	10
252	59	2s. sepia and orange	20	15

60 Signing the Treaty

1964. 2nd Anniv of New Zealand–Samoa Treaty of Friendship.

253	60	1d. multicoloured	10	10
254	60	8d. multicoloured	10	10
255	60	2s. multicoloured	20	10
256	60	3s. multicoloured	20	30

62 Red-tailed Tropic Bird

1965. Air.

263	62	8d. black, orange and blue	50	10
264	-	2s. black and blue	75	20

DESIGN: 2s. Flyingfish.

64 Aerial View of Deep Sea Wharf

1966. Opening of First Deep Sea Wharf, Apia. Mult.

265	1d. Type **64**	10	10
266	8d. Aerial view of wharf and bay	15	10
267	2s. As 8d.	25	25
268	3s. Type **64**	30	35

66 W.H.O. Building

1966. Inaug of W.H.O. Headquarters, Geneva.

269	**66**	3d. ochre, blue and slate	35	10
270	-	4d. multicoloured	40	15
271	**66**	6d. lilac, green and olive	45	20
272	-	1s. multicoloured	80	25

DESIGN: 4d. and 1s. W.H.O. Building on flag.

1966. Hurricane Relief Fund. No. 244 surch HURRICANE RELIEF 6d.

273	8d.+6d. turquoise, green & bl	10	10

69 Hon. Tuatagaloa L. S. (Minister of Justice)

1967. 5th Anniv of Independence.

274	**69**	3d. sepia and violet	10	10
275	-	8d. sepia and blue	10	10
276	-	2s. sepia and olive	10	10
277	-	3s. sepia and mauve	15	15

DESIGNS: 8d. Hon. F. C. F. Nelson (Minister of Works, Marine and Civil Aviation); 2s. Hon. To'omata T. L. (Minister of Lands); 3s. Hon. Fa'alava'au G. (Minister of Post Office, Radio and Broadcasting).

73 Samoan Fales (houses), 1890

1967. Centenary of Mulinu'u as Seat of Government. Multicoloured.

278	8d. Type **73**	15	10
279	1s. Fono (Parliament) House, 1967	15	10

75 Caruncleated Honeyeater ("Wattled Honey-eater")

1967. Decimal Currency. Birds. Multicoloured.

280	1s. Type **75**	10	10
281	2s. Pacific pigeon	10	10
282	3s. Samoan starling	10	10
283	5s. White-vented flycatcher ("Samoan Broadbill")	10	10
284	7s. Red-headed parrot finch	10	10
285	10s. Purple swamphen	15	10
286	20s. Barn owl	1·25	40
287	25s. Tooth-billed pigeon	50	15
288	50s. Island thrush	50	30
289	$1 Samoan fantail	75	1·75
289a	$2 Black-breasted honeyeater ("Mao")	2·00	4·00
289b	$4 Savaii-white eye ("Samoan White-eye")	25·00	13·00

Nos. 289a/b are larger, 43×28 mm.

85 Nurse and Child

1967. South Pacific Health Service. Mult.

290	3s. Type **85**	15	15
291	7s. Leprosarium	20	15
292	20s. Mobile X-ray unit	35	30
293	25s. Apia Hospital	40	35

89 Thomas Trood

1968. 6th Anniv of Independence. Multicoloured.

294	2s. Type **89**	10	10
295	7s. Dr. Wilhelm Solf	10	10
296	20s. J. C. Williams	10	10
297	25s. Fritz Marquardt	15	10

93 Cocoa

1968. Agricultural Development.

298	**93**	3s. brown, green and black	10	10
299	-	5s. green, yellow and brown	10	10
300	-	10s. red, brown and yellow	10	10
301	-	20s. bistre, yellow and olive	15	15

DESIGNS: 5s. Breadfruit; 10s. Copra; 20s. Bananas.

97 Women weaving Mats

1968. 21st Anniv of South Pacific Commission. Multicoloured.

302	7s. Type **97**	10	10
303	20s. Palm trees and bay	15	10
304	25s. Sheltered cove	15	15

1968. 40th Anniv of Kingsford-Smith's Trans-Pacific Flight. No. 285 surch 1928-1968 KINGSFORD-SMITH TRANSPACIFIC FLIGHT 20 SENE.

305	20s. on 10s. multicoloured	10	10

101 Bougainville's Route

1968. Bicent of Bougainville's Visit to Samoa.

306	**101**	3s. blue and black	10	20
307	-	7s. ochre and black	15	20
308	-	20s. multicoloured	45	30
309	-	25s. multicoloured	60	40

DESIGNS: 7s. Louis de Bougainville; 20s. Bougainvillea flower; 25s. Ships "La Boudeuse" and "L'Etoile".

105 Globe and Human Rights Emblem

1968. Human Rights Year.

310	**105**	7s. blue, brown and gold	10	10
311	**105**	20s. orange, green and gold	10	15
312	**105**	25s. violet, green and gold	15	15

106 Dr. Martin Luther King

1968. Martin Luther King.

313	**106**	7s. black and green	15	10
314	**106**	20s. black and purple	15	10

107 Polynesian Version of Madonna and Child

1968. Christmas.

315	**107**	1s. multicoloured	10	10
316	**107**	3s. multicoloured	10	10
317	**107**	20s. multicoloured	10	10
318	**107**	30s. multicoloured	15	15

108 Frangipani "Plumeria acuminata"

1969. 7th Anniv of Independence. Multicoloured.

319	2s. Type **108**	10	10
320	7s. Hibiscus (vert)	10	10
321	20s. Red-ginger (vert)	15	10
322	30s. Moso'oi	20	80

109 R. L. Stevenson and "Treasure Island"

1969. 75th Death Anniv of Robert Louis Stevenson. Multicoloured.

323	3s. Type **109**	10	10
324	7s. R. L. Stevenson and "Kidnapped"	15	10
325	20s. R. L. Stevenson and "Dr. Jekyll and Mr. Hyde"	15	50
326	22s. R. L. Stevenson and "Weir of Hermiston"	15	50

110 Weightlifting

1969. 3rd South Pacific Games, Port Moresby.

327	**110**	3s. black and green	10	10
328	-	20s. black and blue	10	10
329	-	22s. black and orange	15	15

DESIGNS: 20s. Yachting; 22s. Boxing.

113 U.S. Astronaut on the Moon and the Splashdown near Samoan Islands

1969. First Man on the Moon.

330	**113**	7s. multicoloured	15	15
331	**113**	20s. multicoloured	15	15

114 "Virgin with Child" (Murillo)

1969. Christmas. Multicoloured.

332	1s. Type **114**	10	10
333	3s. "The Holy Family" (El Greco)	10	10
334	20s. "The Nativity" (El Greco)	20	10
335	30s. "The Adoration of the Magi" (detail) (Velazquez)	25	15
MS336	116×126 mm. Nos. 332/5	75	1·25

115 Seventh Day Adventists Sanatorium, Apia

1970. 8th Anniv of Independence.

337	**115**	2s. brown, slate and black	10	10
338	-	7s. violet, buff and black	10	10
339	-	20s. rose, lilac and black	15	10
340	-	22s. green, buff and black	15	15

DESIGNS—HORIZ: 7s. Rev. Father Violette and Roman Catholic Cathedral, Apia; 22s. John Williams, 1797–1839, and London Missionary Society Church, Sapapali'i. VERT: 20s. Mormon Church of Latter Day Saints, Tuasivi-on-Safotulafai.

119 Wreck of "Adler" (German steam gunboat)

1970. Great Apia Hurricane of 1889. Mult.

341	5s. Type **119**	30	10
342	7s. U.S.S. "Nipsic" (steam sloop)	30	10
343	10s. H.M.S. "Calliope" (steam corvette)	30	25
344	20s. Apia after the hurricane	50	75

120 Sir Gordon Taylor's Short S.25 Sandringham 7 Flying Boat "Frigate Bird III"

1970. Air. Multicoloured.

345	3s. Type **120**	45	10
346	7s. Polynesian Airlines Douglas DC-3	55	10
347	20s. Pan-American Airways Sikorsky S-42A flying boat "Samoan Clipper"	75	60
348	30s. Air Samoa Britten Norman Islander	75	1·75

121 Kendal's Chronometer and Cook's Sextant

1970. Cook's Exploration of the Pacific.

349	**121**	1s. red, silver and black	15	15
350	-	2s. multicoloured	15	15
351	-	10s. black, blue and gold	35	25
352	-	30s. multicoloured	1·00	80

DESIGN—VERT: 2s. Cook's statue, Whitby; 10s. Cook's head. HORIZ (83×25 mm): 30s. Cook, H.M.S. "Endeavour" and island.

122 "Peace for the World" (F. B. Eccles)

1970. Christmas. Multicoloured.

353	2s. Type **122**	10	10
354	3s. "The Holy Family" (W. E. Jahnke)	10	10
355	20s. "Mother and Child" (F. B. Eccles)	15	10
356	30s. "Prince of Peace" (Meleane Fe'ao)	20	15
MS357	111×158 mm. Nos. 353/6	60	1·25

123 Pope Paul VI

1970. Visit of Pope Paul to Samoa.

358	**123**	8s. black and blue	15	15
359	**123**	20s. black and red	35	15

124 Native and Tree

1971. Timber Industry. Multicoloured.

360	3s. Type **124**	10	10
361	8s. Bulldozer in clearing	15	10
362	20s. Log in sawmill	30	10
363	22s. Floating logs and harbour	30	15

The 8s. and 20s. are horiz.

125 Fautasi (large canoe) in Apia Harbour and first stamps of Samoa and U.S.A. (image scaled to 57% of original size)

1971. "Interpex" Stamp Exhibition, New York. Sheet 138×80 mm.

MS364	**125** 70s. multicoloured	85	1·40

126 Siva Dance

1971. Tourism. Multicoloured.

365	5s. Type **126**	30	10
366	7s. Samoan cricket	2·25	60
367	8s. Hideaway Hotel	75	35
368	10s. Aggie Grey and her hotel	75	60

127 "Queen Salamasina"

1971. Myths and Legends of Old Samoa (1st series). Multicoloured.

369	3s. Type **127**	10	10
370	8s. "Lu and his Sacred Hens"	15	10
371	10s. "God Tagaloa fishes Samoa from the sea"	20	10
372	22s. "Mount Vaea and the Pool of Tears"	35	40

128 "The Virgin and Child" (Bellini)

1971. Christmas.

373	**128**	2s. multicoloured	10	10
374	**128**	3s. multicoloured	10	10
375	-	20s. multicoloured	30	10
376	-	30s. multicoloured	40	20

DESIGN: 20, 30s. "The Virgin and Child with St. Anne and John the Baptist" (Leonardo da Vinci).

129 Map and Scales of Justice

1972. 1st South Pacific Judicial Conference.

377	**129**	10s. multicoloured	15	15

130 Asau Wharf, Savaii

1972. 10th Anniv of Independence. Mult.

378	1s. Type **130**	10	10
379	8s. Parliament Building	10	10
380	10s. Mothers' Centre	10	10
381	22s. "Vailima" Residence and rulers	20	25

131 Flags of Member Countries

1972. 25th Anniv of South Pacific Commission. Multicoloured.

382	3s. Type **131**	10	15
383	7s. Flag and Afoafouvale Misi-moa (Secretary-General)	10	15
384	8s. H.Q. building, Noumea (horiz)	15	15
385	10s. Flags and area map (horiz)	15	15

132 Expedition Ships

1972. 250th Anniv of Sighting of Western Samoa by Jacob Roggeveen. Multicoloured.

386	2s. Type **132**	15	10
387	8s. Ships in storm (horiz)	40	10
388	10s. Ships passing island (horiz)	40	10
389	30s. Route of voyage (85×25 mm)	1·25	1·50

133 Bull Conch and Reef Heron

1972. Multicoloured.. Multicoloured..

390	1s. Type **133**	30	30
391	2s. "Oryctes rhinoceros" (beetle)	30	30
392	3s. Skipjack tuna	30	1·00
393	4s. Painted crab	30	30
394	5s. Melon butterflyfish	35	30
395	7s. "Danaus hamata" (butterfly)	2·00	1·00
396	10s. Trumpet triton	2·00	1·00
397	20s. "Chrysochroa abdominalis" (beetle)	1·25	30
398	50s. Spiny lobster	2·00	2·75
399	$1 "Gnathothlibus erotus" (moth) (29×45 mm)	6·50	4·50
399a	$2 Green turtle (29×45 mm)	4·50	2·75
399b	$4 Black marlin (29×45 mm)	2·50	7·00
399c	$5 Green tree lizard (29×45 mm)	2·50	10·00

134 "The Ascension"

1972. Christmas. Stained-glass windows. Mult.

400	1s. Type **134**	10	10
401	4s. "The Blessed Virgin, and Infant Christ"	10	10
402	10s. "St. Andrew blessing Samoan canoe"	10	10
403	30s. "The Good Shepherd"	40	30
MS404	70×159 mm. Nos. 400/3	90	1·25

135 Erecting a Tent

1973. Boy Scout Movement. Multicoloured.

405	2s. Saluting the flag	10	10
406	3s. First-aid	10	10
407	8s. Type **135**	25	10
408	20s. Samoan action-song	60	85

136 Hawker Siddeley H.S.748

1973. Air. Multicoloured.

409	8s. Type **136**	45	15
410	10s. Hawker Siddeley H.S.748 in flight	55	15
411	12s. Hawker Siddeley H.S.748 on runway	60	35
412	22s. B.A.C. One Eleven	85	60

137 Apia General Hospital

1973. 25th Anniv of W.H.O. Multicoloured.

413	2s. Type **137**	10	10
414	8s. Baby clinic	15	10
415	20s. Filariasis research	30	20
416	22s. Family welfare	30	30

138 Mother and Child, and Map

1973. Christmas. Multicoloured.

417	3s. Type **138**	10	10
418	4s. Mother and child, and village	10	10
419	10s. Mother and child, and beach	10	10
420	30s. Samoan stable	55	50
MS421	144×103 mm. Nos. 417/20	65	75

139 Boxing

1973. Commonwealth Games, Christchurch. Mult.

422	8s. Type **139**	10	10
423	10s. Weightlifting	10	10
424	20s. Bowls	20	10
425	30s. Athletics stadium	35	45

1974. Myths and Legends of Old Samoa (2nd series). As T 127. Multicoloured.

426	2s. Tigilau and sacred dove	10	10
427	8s. Pili, his sons and fishing net	10	10
428	20s. Sina and the origin of the coconut	30	10
429	30s. The warrior, Nafanua	45	55

140 Mail-van at Faleolo Airport

1974. Centenary of U.P.U. Multicoloured.

430	8s. Type **140**	35	10
431	20s. "Mariposa" (cargo liner) at Apia wharf	50	15
432	22s. Early post office, Apia and letter	50	25
433	50s. William Willis and "Age Unlimited" (sailing raft) (87×29 mm)	95	1·25
MS434	140×82 mm. No. 433	70	1·75

141 "Holy Family" (Sebastiano)

1974. Christmas. Multicoloured.

435	3s. Type **141**	10	10
436	4s. "Virgin and Child with Saints" (Lotto)	10	10
437	10s. "Madonna and Child with St. John" (Titian)	20	10
438	30s. "Adoration of the Shepherds" (Rubens)	55	45
MS439	128×87 mm. Nos. 435/8	80	1·40

142 Winged Passion Flower

1975. Tropical Flowers. Multicoloured.

440	8s. Type **142**	10	10
441	20s. Gardenia (vert)	20	15
442	22s. "Barringtonia samoensis" (vert)	20	15
443	30s. Malay apple	25	60

143 "Joyita" (inter-island coaster) loading at Apia

1975. "Interpex 1975" Stamp Exhibition, New York, and "Joyita" Mystery. Multicoloured.

444	1s. Type **143**	10	10
445	8s. "Joyita" sails for Tokelau Islands	15	10
446	20s. Taking to rafts	20	25
447	25s. "Joyita" abandoned	25	30
448	50s. Discovery of "Joyita" north of Fiji	50	1·25
MS449	150×100 mm. Nos. 444/8. Imperf	1·50	3·50

144 "Pate" Drum

1975. Musical Instruments. Multicoloured.

450	8s. Type **144**	10	10
451	20s. "Lali" drum	20	10
452	22s. "Logo" drum	20	10
453	30s. "Pu" shell horn	35	30

145 "Mother and Child" (Meleane Fe'ao)

1975. Christmas. Multicoloured.

454	3s. Type **145**	10	10
455	4s. "The Saviour" (Polataia Tuigamala)	10	10
456	10s. "A Star is Born" (Iosua To'afa)	10	10
457	30s. "Madonna and Child" (Ernesto Coter)	30	45
MS458	101×134 mm. Nos. 454/7	60	1·25

146 "The Boston Massacre, 1770" (Paul Revere)

1976. Bicent of American Revolution. Mult.

459	7s. Type **146**	25	10
460	8s. "The Declaration of Independence" (John Trumbull)	25	10
461	20s. "The Ship that Sank in Victory, 1779" (J. L. G. Ferris)	35	10
462	22s. "Pitt addressing the Commons, 1782" (R. A. Hickel)	35	10
463	50s. "Battle of Princeton" (William Mercer)	60	1·00
MS464	160×125 mm. Nos. 459/63	4·00	8·00

147 Mullet Fishing

1976. Fishing. Multicoloured.

465	10s. Type **147**	10	10
466	12s. Fish traps	15	10
467	22s. Samoan fisherman	30	10
468	50s. Net fishing	85	80

148 Paul Revere's Ride

1976. "Interphil" Stamp Exhibition. Sheet 120×80 mm.

MS469	**148** $1 gold, black and green	1·00	1·00

149 Boxing

1976. Olympic Games, Montreal. Multicoloured.

470	10s. Type **149**	10	10
471	12s. Wrestling	10	10
472	22s. Javelin	15	10
473	50s. Weightlifting	45	50

150 Mary and Joseph going to Bethlehem

1976. Christmas. Multicoloured.

474	3s. Type **150**	10	10
475	5s. The Shepherds	10	10
476	22s. The Holy Family	15	10
477	50s. The Magi	55	65
MS478	124×115 mm. Nos. 474/7	80	1·75

151 Queen Elizabeth and View of Apia

1977. Silver Jubilee and Royal Visit. Mult.

479	12s. Type **151**	10	10
480	26s. Presentation of Spurs of Chivalry	15	20
481	32s. Queen and Royal Yacht "Britannia"	65	25
482	50s. Queen leaving Abbey	20	60

152 Map of Flight Route

1977. 50th Anniv of Lindbergh's Transatlantic Flight. Multicoloured.

483	22s. Type **152**	25	10
484	24s. In flight	35	15
485	26s. Landing	35	15
486	50s. Col. Lindbergh	80	75
MS487	194×93 mm. Nos. 483/6	2·40	2·75

Designs show the "Spirit of St. Louis".

153 3d. Express Stamp and First Mail Notice

1977. Stamp Centenary.

488	**153**	12s. yellow, red and brown	20	10
489	-	13s. multicoloured	20	30
490	-	26s. multicoloured	30	30
491	-	50s. multicoloured	60	1·60

DESIGNS: 13s. Early cover and 6d. Express; 26s. Apia P.O. and 1d. Express; 50s. Schooner "Energy" (1877) and 6d. Express.

154 Apia Automatic Telephone Exchange

1977. Telecommunications Project. Mult.

492	12s. Type **154**	15	10
493	13s. Mulinuu radio terminal	15	10
494	26s. Old and new telephones	30	20
495	50s. Global communication	50	70

155 "Samoan Nativity" (P. Feata)

1977. Christmas. Multicoloured.

496	4s. Type **155**	10	10
497	6s. "The Offering" (E. Saofaiga)	10	10
498	25s. "Madonna and Child" (F. Tupou)	20	10
499	50s. "Emmanuel" (M. Sapa'u)	35	40
MS500	117×159 mm. Nos. 496/9	55	85

156 Polynesian Airlines Boeing 737

1978. Aviation Progress. Multicoloured.

501	12s. Type **156**	15	10
502	24s. Wright brothers' Flyer I	30	20
503	26s. Kingsford Smith's Fokker F.V11a/3m "Southern Cross"	30	20
504	50s. Concorde	75	85
MS505	150×120 mm. Nos. 501/4	1·75	2·75

157 Hatchery, Aleipata

1978. Hawksbill Turtle Conservation Project. Mult.

506	24s. Type **157**	1·75	30
507	$1 Hawksbill turtle	4·25	1·60

158 Pacific Pigeon

1978. 25th Anniv of Coronation.

508	-	26s. black, brown & mauve	20	30
509	-	26s. multicoloured	20	30
510	**158**	26s. black, brown & mve	20	30

DESIGNS: No. 508, King's Lion; 509, Queen Elizabeth II.

159 Flags of Western Samoa and Canada with Canadian National Tower

1978. "Capex '78" International Stamp Exhibition, Toronto. Sheet 119×79 mm.

MS511	**159** $1 blue, red and black	75	1·40

160 Captain Cook

1978. 250th Birth Anniv of Captain Cook. Mult.

512	12s. Type **160**	25	15
513	24s. Cook's Cottage, Gt. Ayton, Yorkshire	25	20
514	26s. Old drawbridge over the river Esk, Whitby	25	30
515	50s. H.M.S. "Resolution"	80	1·40

161 Thick-edged Cowrie

1978. Shells. Multicoloured.

516	1s. Type **161**	10	10
517	2s. Controversial Isabelle cowrie	10	10
518	3s. Money cowrie	15	10
519	4s. Eroded cowrie	15	10
520	6s. Honey cowrie	15	75
521	7s. Asellus or banded cowrie	15	10
522	10s. Globular or globe cowrie	15	10
523	11s. Mole cowrie	15	10
524	12s. Children's cowrie	15	10
525	13s. Flag cone	15	10
526	14s. Soldier cone	15	10
527	24s. Textile or cloth-of-gold cone	15	10
528	26s. Lettered cone	15	10
529	50s. Tesselate or tiled cone	20	15
530	$1 Black marble cone	35	60
530a	$2 Marlin-spike auger	55	70
530b	$3 Scorpion conch	75	1·25
530c	$5 Common or major harp	1·50	2·25

Nos. 530a/c are larger, 36×26 mm.

162 "Madonna on the Crescent"

1978. Christmas. Woodcuts by Durer. Mult.

531	**162**	4s. black and brown	10	10
532	-	6s. black and green	10	10
533	-	26s. black and blue	15	10
534	-	50s. black and violet	35	50
MS535		103×154 mm. Nos. 531/4	70	1·00

DESIGNS: 6s. "Nativity"; 26s. "Adoration of the Kings"; 50s. "Annunciation".

163 Boy with Coconuts

1979. International Year of the Child. Mult.

536	12s. Type **163**	15	10
537	24s. White Sunday	20	15
538	25s. Children at pump	20	15
539	50s. Girl with ukulele	60	80

164 "Charles W. Morgan"

1979. Sailing Ships (1st series). Whaling Ships. Multicoloured.

540	12s. Type **164**	20	10
541	14s. "Lagoda"	20	10
542	24s. "James T. Arnold"	25	20
543	50s. "Splendid"	45	85

See also Nos. 561/4 and 584/7.

165 Launch of "Apollo 11"

1979. 10th Anniv of Moon Landing.

544	**165**	12s. brown and red	15	10
545	-	14s. multicoloured	15	10
546	-	24s. multicoloured	15	10
547	-	26s. multicoloured	15	10
548	-	50s. multicoloured	25	35
549	-	$1 multicoloured	50	1·10
MS550		90×130 mm. No. 549	75	1·75

DESIGNS—HORIZ: 14s. Lunar module and astronaut on Moon; 26s. Astronaut on Moon; $1 Command module after splashdown. VERT: 24s. View of Earth from Moon; 50s. Lunar and Command modules in Space.

No. **MS**550 is inscribed "Spashdown" in error.

166 Sir Rowland Hill (statue) and Penny Black

1979. Death Cent of Sir Rowland Hill. Mult.

551	12s. Type **166**	15	10
552	24s. Two-penny Blue with "Maltese Cross" postmark	15	15
553	26s. Sir Rowland Hill and Penny Black	15	15
554	$1 Two-penny Blue and Sir Rowland Hill	45	75
MS555	128×95 mm. Nos. 551/4	80	1·60

167 Anglican Church, Apia

1979. Christmas. Churches.

556	**167**	4s. black and blue	10	10
557	-	6s. black and yellow	10	10
558	-	26s. black and brown	15	10
559	-	50s. black and lilac	30	30
MS560		150×124 mm. Nos. 556/9	60	1·25

DESIGNS: 6s. Congregational Christian, Leulumoega; 26s. Methodist, Piula; 50s. Protestant, Apia.

1980. Sailing Ships (2nd series). Whaling Ships. As T 164. Multicoloured.

561	12s. "William Hamilton"	25	10
562	14s. "California"	25	10
563	24s. "Liverpool II"	25	15
564	50s. "Two Brothers"	35	75

168 "Equipment for a Hospital"

1980. Anniversaries. Multicoloured.

565	12s. Type **168**	60	10
566	13s. John Williams, dove with olive twig and commemorative inscription	45	1·10
567	14s. Dr. Wilhelm Solf (instigator), flag and commemorative inscription	1·00	15
568	24s. Cairn Monument	1·00	30
569	26s. Williams Memorial, Savai'i	70	30
570	50s. Paul P. Harris (founder)	1·25	2·50

COMMEMORATIONS: 12, 50s. 75th anniv of Rotary International; 13, 26s. 150th anniv of John Williams (missionary) arrival in Samoa; 14, 24s. 80th anniv of raising of German flag.

169 Samoan Village Scene (image scaled to 58% of original size)

1980. "London 1980" International Stamp Exhibition. Sheet 140×81 mm.

MS571	**169**	$1 multicoloured	60	1·00

170 Queen Elizabeth the Queen Mother in 1970

1980. 80th Birthday of The Queen Mother.

572	**170**	50s. multicoloured	30	30

171 1964 2nd Anniversary of New Zealand–Samoa Treaty of Friendship 2s. Commemorative and "Zeapex '80" Emblem (image scaled to 75% of original size)

1980. "Zeapex '80" International Stamp Exhibition, Auckland. Sheet 130×80 mm.

MS573	**171**	$1 multicoloured	60	1·00

172 Afiamalu Satellite Earth Station

1980. Afiamalu Satellite Earth Station. Mult.

574	12s. Type **172**	15	10
575	14s. Satellite station (different)	20	10
576	24s. Satellite station and map of Savai'i and Upolu	30	15
577	50s. Satellite and globe	60	75

173 Afiamalu Satellite Earth Station 24s. Commemorative Stamp and "Sydpex 80" Emblem (image scaled to 73% of original size)

1980. "Sydpex 80" International Stamp Exhibition, Sydney. Sheet 130×80 mm. Imperf.

MS578	**173**	$2 multicoloured	1·00	1·00

174 "The Saviour" (J. Poynton)

1980. Christmas. Paintings. Multicoloured.

579	8s. Type **174**	10	10
580	14s. "Madonna and Child" (Lealofi F. Siaopo)	10	10
581	27s. "Nativity" (Pasila Feata)	15	10
582	50s. "Yuletide" (R. P. Aiono)	25	40
MS583	90×105 mm. Nos. 579/82	1·00	1·50

1981. Sailing Ships (3rd series). As T 164. Mult.

584	12s. "Ocean" (whaling ship)	30	15
585	18s. "Horatio" (whaling ship)	40	20
586	27s. H.M.S. "Calliope" (screw corvette)	55	25
587	32s. H.M.S. "Calypso" (screw corvette)	60	50

175 President Franklin D. Roosevelt and Hyde Park (family home)

1981. Int Year for Disabled Persons. President Franklin D. Roosevelt Commem. Multicoloured.

588	12s. Type **175**	15	10
589	18s. Roosevelt's inauguration, 4 March 1933	15	10
590	27s. Franklin and Eleanor Roosevelt	20	15
591	32s. Roosevelt's Lend-lease Bill (Atlantic convoy, 1941)	25	20
592	38s. Roosevelt the philatelist	25	25
593	$1 Campobello House (summer home)	50	90

176 Hotel Tusitala

1981. Tourism. Multicoloured.

594	12s. Type **176**	15	10
595	18s. Apia Harbour	25	15
596	27s. Aggie Greys' Hotel	25	20
597	32s. Preparation for Ceremonial Kava	30	30
598	54s. Piula water pool	55	55

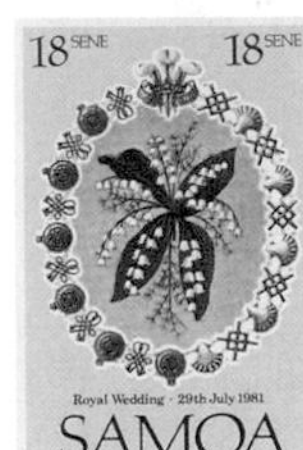

177 Wedding Bouquet from Samoa

1981. Royal Wedding. Multicoloured.

599	18s. Type **177**	15	10
600	32s. Prince Charles as Colonel-in-Chief, Gordon Highlanders	20	10
601	$1 Prince Charles and Lady Diana Spencer	30	50

178 Tattooing Instruments

1981. Tattooing. Multicoloured.

602	12s. Type **178**	30	20
603	18s. First stage of tattooing	35	25
604	27s. Progessive stage	40	30
605	$1 Completed tattoo	60	70

179 Black Marlin

1981. "Philatokyo '81" International Stamp Exhibition, Tokyo. Sheet 130×80 mm.

MS606	**179**	$2 multicoloured	1·00	1·00

180 "Thespesia populnea"

1981. Christmas. Flowers. Multicoloured.

607	11s. Type **180**	15	10
608	15s. Copper leaf	15	15
609	23s. "Allamanda cathartica"	20	25
610	$1 Mango	60	1·00
MS611	86×120 mm. Nos. 607/10	1·10	2·25

181 George Washington's Pistol

1982. 250th Birth Anniv of George Washington.

612	**181** 23s. black, brown & stone	25	30
613	- 25s. black, brown & stone	25	30
614	- 34s. black, brown & stone	30	40
MS615	104×103 mm. $1 Washington taking Oath of Office as President	70	1·00

DESIGNS: 25s. Mount Vernon (Washington's home); 34s. George Washington.

182 "Forum Samoa" (container ship)

1982. 20th Anniv of Independence. Mult.

616	18s. Type **182**	1·00	20
617	23s. "Air services"	1·25	30
618	25s. N.P.F. (National Provident Fund) Building, Apia	50	30
619	$1 "Telecommunications"	1·50	1·00

183 Scouts map-reading and "75"

1982. 75th Anniv of Boy Scout Movement. Mult.

620	5s. Type **183**	10	10
621	38s. Scout salute and "75"	30	40
622	44s. Scout crossing river by rope and "75"	40	50
623	$1 "Tower" of Scouts and "75"	90	1·00
MS624	93×81 mm. $1 As No. 623 but with portrait of Lord Baden-Powell replacing emblem (47×35 mm)	1·25	1·25

184 Boxing

1982. Commonwealth Games, Brisbane. Mult.

625	23s. Type **184**	20	20
626	23s. Hurdling	20	20
627	34s. Weightlifting	25	30
628	$1 Bowling	75	1·50

185 "Mary and Joseph" (Emma Dunlop)

1982. Christmas. Children's Pictures. Mult.

629	11s. Type **185**	15	10
630	15s. "Mary, Joseph and Baby Jesus" (Marie Tofaeono)	15	15
631	38s. "Madonna and Child" (Ralph Laban and Fetalaiga Fareni)	40	30
632	$1 "Mother and Child" (Panapa Pouesi)	90	2·25
MS633	130×119 mm. Nos. 629/32	1·60	2·25

186 Satellite View of Australasia

1983. Commonwealth Day. Multicoloured.

634	14s. Type **186**	10	10
635	29s. Flag of Samoa	25	20
636	43s. Harvesting copra	25	25
637	$1 Head of State Malietoa Tanumafili II	50	80

187 Douglas DC-1

1983. Bicentenary of Manned Flight and 50th Anniv of Douglas Commercial Aircraft. Sheet, 215×113 mm, containing horiz designs as T 187. Multicoloured.

MS638	32s.×10, each design showing a different Douglas aircraft from the DC-1 to the DC-10	3·25	3·25

188 Pole vaulting

1983. South Pacific Games. Multicoloured.

639	8s. Type **188**	35	10
640	15s. Netball	45	20
641	25s. Tennis	70	50
642	32s. Weightlifting	70	50
643	35s. Boxing	75	1·00
644	46s. Football	90	1·40
645	48s. Golf	2·25	1·50
646	56s. Rugby	1·40	2·00

189 Lime

1983. Fruit. Multicoloured.

647	1s. Type **189**	10	1·00
648	2s. Starfruit	10	1·25
649	3s. Mangosteen	10	1·25
650	4s. Lychee	10	1·25
651	7s. Passion fruit	15	1·25
652	8s. Mango	15	1·25
653	11s. Pawpaw	20	1·00
654	13s. Pineapple	20	1·00
655	14s. Breadfruit	20	1·00
656	15s. Banana	30	1·00
657	21s. Cashew nut	2·00	2·00
658	25s. Guava	2·00	1·00
659	32s. Water melon	3·50	1·75
660	48s. Sasalapa	2·25	2·50
661	56s. Avocado	2·25	2·50
662	$1 Coconut	2·25	2·00
663	$2 Vi apple (25×35½ mm)	2·50	3·00
664	$4 Grapefruit (25×35½ mm)	2·50	4·50
665	$5 Orange (25×35½ mm)	3·00	4·75

190 On Parade

1983. Centenary of Boys' Brigade. Sheet 120×83 mm.

MS668	**190** $1 multicoloured	2·50	2·00

191 Togitogiga Falls, Upolu

1984. Scenic Views. Multicoloured.

669	25s. Type **191**	30	15
670	32s. Lano Beach, Savai'i	40	60
671	48s. Mulinu'u Point, Upolu	55	1·10
672	56s. Nu'utele Island	55	1·75

192 Apia Harbour

1984. 250th Anniv of "Lloyd's List" (newspaper). Multicoloured.

673	32s. Type **192**	25	20
674	48s. Apia hurricane, 1889	50	45
675	60s. "Forum Samoa" (container ship)	50	50
676	$1 "Matua" (inter-island freighter)	75	80

1984. Universal Postal Union Congress, Hamburg. No. 662 optd 19th U.P.U. CONGRESS HAMBURG 1984.

677	$1 Coconut	1·40	80

194 Olympic Stadium

1984. Olympic Games, Los Angeles. Multicoloured.

678	25s. Type **194**	20	20
679	32s. Weightlifting	20	25
680	48s. Boxing	30	45
681	$1 Running	60	80
MS682	170×120 mm. Nos. 678/81	1·40	1·60

195 Government Aircraft Factory N24A Nomad

1984. "Ausipex" International Stamp Exhibition, Melbourne. Sheet 131×80 mm.

MS683	**195** $2.50 multicoloured	4·75	6·00

196 "Faith"

1984. Christmas. "The Three Virtues" (Raphael). Multicoloured.

684	25s. Type **196**	40	15
685	35s. "Hope"	50	40
686	$1 "Charity"	1·75	3·25
MS687	63×76 mm. Nos. 684/6	3·25	4·75

197 "Dendrobium biflorum"

1985. Orchids (1st series). Multicoloured.

688	48s. Type **197**	45	35
689	56s. "Dendrobium vaupelianum Kraenzl"	50	45
690	67s. "Glomera montana"	60	70
691	$1 "Spathoglottis plicata"	80	1·40

See also Nos. 818/21.

198 Ford "Model A", 1903

1985. Veteran and Vintage Cars. Multicoloured.

692	48s. Type **198**	1·50	60
693	56s. Chevrolet "Tourer", 1912	1·60	85
694	67s. Morris "Oxford", 1913	1·75	1·75
695	$1 Austin "Seven", 1923	2·25	3·25

199 "Dictyophora indusiata"

1985. Fungi. Multicoloured.

696	48s. Type **199**	1·10	55
697	56s. "Ganoderma tornatum"	1·25	85
698	67s. "Mycena chlorophos"	1·60	1·75
699	$1 "Mycobonia flava"	2·25	3·50

200 The Queen Mother at Liverpool Street Station

1985. Life and Times of Queen Elizabeth the Queen Mother. Multicoloured.

700	32s. At Glamis Castle, aged 9	50	25
701	48s. At Prince Henry's christening with other members of the Royal Family	60	35
702	56s. Type **200**	2·50	1·25
703	$1 With Prince Henry at his christening (from photo by Lord Snowdon)	80	2·25
MS704	91×73 mm. $2 Arriving at Tattenham Corner Station with the Queen	3·25	1·75

201 Map of Pacific and Exhibition Logo

1985. "Expo '85" World Fair, Japan. Sheet 70×45 mm.

MS705	**201** $2 multicoloured	1·50	2·00

202 I.Y.Y. Emblem and Map (Alaska–Arabian Gulf)

1985. International Youth Year. Designs showing background map and emblem (Nos. 706 and 710) or raised arms (others). Multicoloured.

706	60s. Type **202**	40	70
707	60s. Raised arms (Pakistan–Mexico)	40	70
708	60s. Raised arms (Central America–China)	40	70
709	60s. Raised arms (Japan–Greenland)	40	70
710	60s. Type **202** (Iceland–Siberia)	40	70

Nos. 706/10 were printed together in horizontal strips of 5, the background forming a composite design of three continuous world maps.

203 "System"

1985. Christmas. Designs showing illustrations by Millicent Sowerby for R. L. Stevenson's "A Child's Garden of Verses". Multicoloured.

711	32s. Type **203**	20	25
712	48s. "Time to Rise"	30	35
713	56s. "Auntie's Skirts"	35	40
714	$1 "Good Children"	65	2·00
MS715	87×109 mm. Nos. 711/14	2·25	4·25

204 "Hypolimnas bolina"

1986. Butterflies. Multicoloured.

716	25s. Type **204**	35	35
717	32s. "Belenois java"	40	35
718	48s. "Deudorix epijarbas"	60	50
719	56s. "Badamia exclamationis"	65	90
720	60s. "Danaus hamata"	65	90
721	$1 "Catochrysops taitensis"	1·00	2·00

205 Halley's Comet over Apia

1986. Appearance of Halley's Comet. Mult.

722	32s. Type **205**	30	20
723	48s. Edmond Halley	35	35
724	60s. Comet passing Earth	45	50
725	$2 Preparing "Giotto" spacecraft	1·00	2·00

1986. 60th Birthday of Queen Elizabeth II. As T 145a of St. Helena. Multicoloured.

726	32s. Engagement photograph, 1947	15	20
727	48s. Queen with Liberty Bell, U.S.A., 1976	15	35
728	56s. At Apia, 1977	20	40
729	67s. At Badminton Horse Trials, 1978	30	45
730	$2 At Crown Agents Head Office, London, 1983	60	1·25

206 U.S.S. "Vincennes" (frigate)

1986. "Ameripex '86" International Stamp Exhibition, Chicago. Multicoloured.

731	48s. Type **206**	35	40
732	56s. Sikorsky S-42A flying boat	40	50
733	60s. U.S.S. "Swan" (patrol boat)	40	50
734	$2 "Apollo 10" descending	1·00	2·50

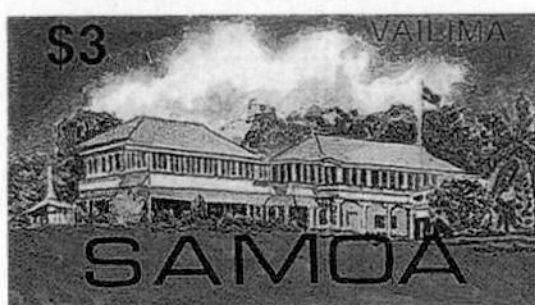

207 Vailima

1986. "Stampex '86" Stamp Exhibition, Adelaide. Sheet 158×97 mm.

MS735	**207** $3 multicoloured	4·50	5·00

208 High-finned Grouper

1986. Fishes. Multicoloured.

736	32s. Type **208**	40	40
737	48s. Scarlet-finned squirrelfish	60	45
738	60s. Yellow-edged lyretail ("Lunartail grouper")	70	90
739	67s. Yellow-striped snapper	70	1·50
740	$1 Big-scaled soldierfish	90	2·25

209 Samoan Prime Ministers, American Presidents and Parliament House

1986. Christmas. 25th Anniv of United States Peace Corps. Multicoloured.

741	45s. Type **209**	25	40
742	60s. French and American Presidents, Samoan Prime Minister and Statue of Liberty	35	60
MS743	131×72 mm. Nos. 741/2	3·00	4·50

No. **MS**743 also commemorates the Centenary of the Statue of Liberty.

210 "Hibiscus rosa-sinensis" and Map of Samoa

1987. 25th Anniv of Independence. Mult.

744	15s. Type **210**	20	10
745	45s. Parliament Building, Apia	25	30
746	60s. Longboat race at Independence celebration	30	40
747	70s. Peace dove and laurel wreath	35	70
748	$2 Head of State Malietoa Tanumafili II and national flag (horiz)	1·00	2·25

211 Gulper ("Eurypharynx")

1987. Deep Ocean Fishes. Multicoloured.

749	45s. Type **211**	45	30
750	60s. Hatchetfish	50	60
751	70s. Bearded angelfish	60	1·00
752	$2 Swallower ("Saccopharynx")	1·00	3·25

212 Workmen trimming Logs and building Fale (traditional house)

1987. "Capex 87" International Stamp Exhibition, Toronto. Sheet 122×66 mm.

MS753	**212** $3 multicoloured	1·90	1·90

213 Lefaga Beach, Upolu

1987. Coastal Scenery. Multicoloured.

754	45s. Type **213**	70	30
755	60s. Vaisala Beach, Savaii	90	40
756	70s. Solosolo Beach, Upolu	95	75
757	$2 Neiafu Beach, Savaii	1·75	3·50

214 Abel Tasman

1987. Bicentenary of Australian Settlement (1988) (1st issue). Explorers of the Pacific. Mult.

758	40s. Type **214**	50	25
759	45s. Capt. James Cook	65	40
760	80s. Comte Louis-Antoine de Bougainville	80	80
761	$2 Comte Jean de la Perouse	1·40	3·00
MS762	90×73 mm. No. 761	1·40	1·75

See also Nos. 768/72.

1987. "Hafnia" International Stamp Exhibition, Copenhagen. No. MS762 optd with Hafnia emblem.

MS763	90×73 mm. $2 Comte Jean de la Perouse	2·75	2·25

216 Christmas Tree

1987. Christmas. Multicoloured.

764	40s. Type **216**	30	25
765	45s. Family going to church	40	35
766	50s. Bamboo fire-gun	45	40
767	80s. Inter-island transport	1·10	1·25

217 Samoa Coat of Arms and Australia Post Logo

1988. Bicentenary of Australian Settlement (2nd issue). Postal Services. Multicoloured.

768	45s. Type **217**	80	90
769	45s. Samoan mail van and Boeing 727 airplane	80	90
770	45s. Loading Boeing 727 mail plane	80	90
771	45s. Australian mail van and Boeing 727	80	90
772	45s. "Congratulations Australia" message on airmail letter	80	90

Nos. 768/72 were printed together, se-tenant, Nos. 769/71 forming a composite design.

218 Airport Terminal and Douglas DC-9 Airliner taking off

1988. Opening of Faleolo Airport. Mult.

773	40s. Type **218**	60	40
774	45s. Boeing 727	65	40
775	60s. De Havilland D.H.C.6 Twin Otter	80	70
776	70s. Boeing 737	90	1·40
777	80s. Boeing 727 and control tower	1·00	1·50
778	$1 Douglas DC-9 over "fale" (house)	1·10	1·75

219 "Expo '88" Pacific Islands Village

1988. "Expo '88" World Fair, Brisbane. Mult.

779	45s. Type **219**	30	30
780	70s. Expo Complex and monorail	1·00	1·00
781	$2 Map of Australia showing Brisbane	1·50	2·75

220 Mormon Temple, Apia

1988. Centenary of Arrival of the Latter-Day Saints in Samoa. Sheet 86×77 mm.

MS782	**220** $3 multicoloured	1·50	2·00

221 Athletics

1988. Olympic Games, Seoul. Multicoloured.

783	15s. Type **221**	10	10
784	60s. Weightlifting	30	35
785	80s. Boxing	90	45
786	$2 Olympic stadium	90	1·25
MS787	85×100 mm. Nos. 783/6	1·90	2·40

222 Spotted Triller ("Polynesian Triller")

1988. Birds. Multicoloured.

788	10s. Type **222**	1·25	45
789	15s. Samoan wood rail	1·50	40
790	20s. Flat-billed kingfisher	1·75	1·25
791	25s. Samoan fantail	1·75	50
797a	25s. Many-coloured fruit dove (25×40 mm)	9·50	2·75
792	35s. Scarlet robin	1·75	1·00
793	40s. Black-breasted honeyeater ("Mao")	1·75	1·40
794	50s. Cardinal honeyeater	2·00	50
795	65s. Yellow-fronted whistler ("Samoan Whistler")	2·00	60
796	75s. Many-coloured fruit dove	2·50	2·25
798	75s. Silver gull (45×28 mm)	2·00	1·50
797	85s. White-throated pigeon	2·50	1·00
799	85s. Great frigate bird (45×28 mm)	2·00	1·50
800	90s. Reef heron ("Eastern Reef Heron") (45×28 mm)	3·50	1·25

801	$3 Short-tailed albatross (45×28 mm)	1·50	1·60
802	$10 White tern ("Common Fairy Tern") (45×28 mm)	3·50	6·00
803	$20 Shy albatross (45×28 mm)	6·50	12·00

See also No. **MS**1004.

223 Forest

1988. National Conservation Campaign. Mult.

807	15s. Type **223**	80	15
808	40s. Samoan handicrafts	55	30
809	45s. Forest wildlife	2·50	45
810	50s. Careful use of water (horiz)	1·00	65
811	60s. Fishing (horiz)	1·25	85
812	$1 Coconut plantation (horiz)	1·25	2·00

224 Congregational Church of Jesus, Apia

1988. Christmas. Samoan Churches. Mult.

813	15s. Type **224**	25	10
814	40s. Roman Catholic Church, Leauva'a	50	25
815	45s. Congregational Christian Church, Moataa	50	30
816	$2 Baha'i Temple, Vailima	1·50	2·75
MS817	143×64 mm. Nos. 813/16	2·75	3·00

225 "Phaius flavus"

1989. Orchids (2nd series). Multicoloured.

818	15s. Type **225**	15	10
819	45s. "Calanthe triplicata"	35	30
820	60s. "Luisia teretifolia"	40	35
821	$3 "Dendrobium mohlianum"	1·75	2·00

226 "Eber" (German gunboat)

1989. Cent of Great Apia Hurricane. Mult.

822	50s. Type **226**	1·75	1·75
823	65s. "Olga" (German corvette)	1·90	1·90
824	85s. H.M.S. "Calliope" (screw corvette)	2·00	2·00
825	$2 U.S.S. "Vandalia" (corvette)	2·25	2·25

227 Samoan Red Cross Youth Group on Parade

1989. 125th Anniv of Int Red Cross. Mult.

826	50s. Type **227**	30	30
827	65s. Blood donors	40	45
828	75s. Practising first aid	45	55
829	$3 Red Cross volunteers carrying patient	1·60	2·25

1989. 20th Anniv of First Manned Landing on Moon. As T 50a of St. Kitts. Multicoloured.

830	18s. Saturn rocket on mobile launcher	40	15
831	50s. Crew of "Apollo 14" (30×30 mm)	60	35
832	65s. "Apollo 14" emblem (30×30 mm)	75	45
833	$2 Tracks of lunar transporter	1·60	1·75
MS834	100×83 mm. $3 Aldrin with U.S. flag on Moon	3·50	4·00

228 Virgin Mary and Joseph

1989. Christmas. Multicoloured.

835	18s. Type **228**	30	10
836	50s. Shepherds	75	30
837	55s. Donkey and ox	80	35
838	$2 Three Wise Men	2·50	4·25

1989. "World Stamp Expo '89" International Stamp Exhibition, Washington. Sheet 91×105 mm containing designs as Nos. 824/5. Multicoloured. Imperf.

MS839	85s. H.M.S. "Calliope" $2 U.S.S. "Vandalia"	3·75	4·50

229 Pao Pao Outrigger

1990. Local Transport. Multicoloured.

840	18s. Type **229**	35	20
841	55s. Fautasi (large canoe)	85	65
842	60s. Polynesian Airlines De Havilland Twin Otter aircraft	1·75	1·40
843	$3 "Lady Samoa" (ferry)	3·75	5·50

230 Bismarck and Brandenburg Gate, Berlin

1990. Treaty of Berlin, 1889, and Opening of Berlin Wall, 1989. Multicoloured.

844	75s. Type **230**	2·00	3·00
845	$3 "Adler" (German steam gunboat)	6·00	7·00

Nos. 844/5 were printed together, se-tenant, forming a composite design showing Berliners on the Wall near the Brandenburg Gate.

231x Penny Black and Alexandra Palace, London (image scaled to 58% of original size)

1990. "Stamp World London 90" Int Stamp Exn.

846	**231** $3 multicoloured	2·50	3·00

233 1964 2nd Anniv of Treaty of Friendship 3s. Commemorative and "NZ 1990" Logo (image scaled to 71% of original size)

1990. "New Zealand 1990" International Stamp Exhibition, Auckland. Sheet 130×85 mm.

MS851	**233** $3 multicoloured	3·00	4·00

234 "Virgin and Child" (Bellini)

1990. Christmas. Paintings. Multicoloured.

852	18s. Type **234**	30	10
853	50s. "Virgin and Child with St. Peter and St. Paul" (Bouts)	70	30
854	55s. "School of Love" (Correggio)	75	35
855	$3 "Virgin and Child" (Cima)	3·25	5·50

The 55s. value should have shown "The Madonna of the Basket" by the same artist and is so inscribed.

235 William Draper III (administrator) and 40th Anniv Logo

1990. 40th Anniv of United Nations Development Programme.

856	**235** $3 multicoloured	1·90	3·50

236 Black-capped Lory

1991. Parrots. Multicoloured.

857	18s. Type **236**	75	40
858	50s. Eclectus parrot	1·25	60
859	65s. Scarlet macaw	1·25	85
860	$3 Palm cockatoo	2·75	4·50

1991. 65th Birthday of Queen Elizabeth II and 70th Birthday of Prince Philip. As T 165a of St. Helena. Multicoloured.

861	75s. Prince Philip in the countryside	90	1·25
862	$2 Queen wearing yellow lei	1·50	1·75

237 Peter Fatialofa (Samoan captain)

1991. World Cup Rugby Championships. Sheet 121×75 mm.

MS863	**237** $5 multicoloured	8·50	9·00

238 "O Come All Ye Faithful"

1991. Christmas. Carols (1st series). Mult.

864	20s. Type **238**	55	10
865	60s. "Joy to the World"	95	40
866	75s. "Hark the Herald Angels Sing"	1·25	70
867	$4 "We wish you a Merry Christmas"	4·25	6·50

See also Nos. 886/9 and 907/11.

239 "Herse convolvuli"

1991. "Phila Nippon '91" International Stamp Exhibition, Tokyo. Samoan Hawkmoths. Mult.

868	60s. Type **239**	1·00	70
869	75s. "Gnathothlibus erotus"	1·10	80
870	85s. "Deilephila celerio"	1·25	1·00
871	$3 "Cephonodes armatus"	4·00	5·25

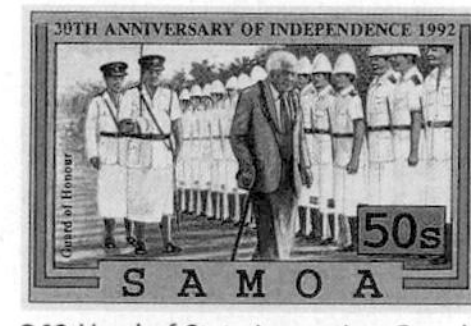

240 Head of State inspecting Guard of Honour

1992. 30th Anniv of Independence. Mult.

872	50s. Type **240**	70	30
873	65s. Siva ceremony	75	50
874	$1 Commemorative float	1·25	1·50
875	$3 Raising Samoan flag	3·75	5·00

1992. 40th Anniv of Queen Elizabeth II's Accession. As T 168a of St. Helena. Mult.

876	20s. Queen and Prince Philip with umbrellas	55	15
877	60s. Queen and Prince Philip on Royal Yacht	1·50	80
878	75s. Queen in multicoloured hat	1·00	75
879	85s. Three portraits of Queen Elizabeth	1·10	85
880	$3 Queen Elizabeth II	2·25	3·50

241 Samoa Express 1d. Stamp, 1877

1992. 500th Anniv of Discovery of America by Columbus. Sheet 91×70 mm.

MS881	**241** $4 multicoloured	3·00	4·00

242 Weightlifting

1992. Olympic Games, Barcelona. Multicoloured.

882	60s. Type **242**	80	70
883	75s. Boxing	90	80
884	85s. Running	1·00	1·00
885	$3 Montjuic Olympic Stadium, Barcelona	3·00	4·00

1992. Christmas. Carols (2nd series). As T 238. Multicoloured.

886	50s. "God rest you Merry Gentlemen"	55	30

887	60s. "While Shepherds watched their Flocks by Night"	65	55
888	75s. "Away in a Manger, no Crib for a Bed"	75	70
889	$4 "O Little Town of Bethlehem"	3·25	5·00

243 Narrow-banded Batfish

1993. Fishes. Multicoloured.

890	60s. Type **243**	70	60
891	75s. Clown surgeonfish	85	85
892	$1 Black-tailed snapper	1·25	1·75
893	$3 Long-nosed emperor	2·75	4·25

244 Samoan Players performing Traditional War Dance

1993. Rugby World Cup Seven-a-Side Championship, Edinburgh. Multicoloured.

894	60s. Type **244**	1·25	65
895	75s. Two players (vert)	1·40	75
896	85s. Player running with ball and badge (vert)	1·50	1·10
897	$3 Edinburgh Castle	4·25	6·00

245 Flying Foxes hanging from Branch

1993. Endangered Species. Flying Foxes. Mult.

898	20s. Type **245**	90	30
899	50s. Flying fox with young	1·40	70
900	60s. Flying foxes hunting for food	1·60	1·00
901	75s. Flying fox feeding from plant	1·75	1·60

246 Exhibition Emblem

1993. "Taipei '93" Asian International Stamp Exhibition, Taiwan. Sheet 137×64 mm.

MS902	**246** $5 yellow, blue and black	8·50	10·00

247 Globe, Letter and Flowers

1993. World Post Day. Multicoloured.

903	60s. Type **247**	55	45
904	75s. Post Office counter	70	80
905	85s. Hands exchanging letter	80	90
906	$4 Globe, national flags and letter	3·50	6·00

1993. Christmas Carols (3rd series). As T 238. Multicoloured.

907	20s. "Silent Night"	45	10
908	60s. "As with Gladness Men of Old"	85	45
909	75s. "Mary had a Baby yes, Lord"	1·00	55
910	$1.50 "Once in Royal David's City"	2·00	3·00
911	$3 "Angels from the Realms of Glory"	4·00	6·00

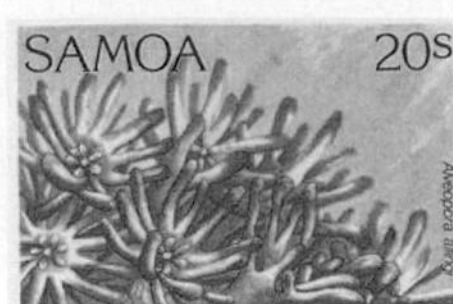

248 "Alveopora allingi"

1994. Corals. Multicoloured.

912	20s. Type **248**	30	10
913	60s. "Acropora polystoma"	65	45
914	90s. "Acropora listeri"	90	90
915	$4 "Acropora grandis"	2·75	5·00

1994. "Hong Kong '94" International Stamp Exhibition. Nos. 912/15 optd HONG KONG '94 and emblem.

916	20s. Type **248**	35	10
917	60s. "Acropora polystoma"	65	45
918	90s. "Acrophora listeri"	90	90
919	$4 "Acropora grandis"	2·75	5·00

249 Samoan Rugby Management Team

1994. Samoan National Rugby Team. Mult.

920	70s. Type **249**	70	60
921	90s. Test match against Wales	80	80
922	95s. Test match against New Zealand	80	80
923	$4 Apia Park Stadium	3·50	6·00

250 "Anaphaeis java" and "Acraea andromacha" (butterflies)

1994. "Philakorea '94" International Stamp Exhibition, Seoul. Sheet 99×82 mm.

MS924	**250** $5 multicoloured	3·00	5·00

251 Solo Singer and Choir

1994. Teuila Tourism Festival. Multicoloured.

925	70s. Type **251**	1·00	45
926	90s. Fire dancer	1·10	65
927	95s. Festival float	1·10	65
928	$4 Band outside hotel	5·50	7·00

252 "Equator" (schooner)

1994. Death Centenary of Robert Louis Stevenson (author). Multicoloured.

929	70s. Type **252**	60	50
930	90s. Robert Louis Stevenson	70	80
931	$1.20 Stevenson's tomb, Mt. Vaea	95	1·25
932	$4 Vailima House (horiz)	3·25	5·50

253 Santa Claus on House

1994. Christmas. Children's Paintings. Mult.

933	70s. Type **253**	60	50
934	95s. Star over house and palm trees	70	70
935	$1.20 Family outing	95	1·25
936	$4 "Merry Christmas"	3·25	6·00

254 Lotofaga Beach, Aleipata

1995. Scenic Views. Multicoloured.

937	5s. Type **254**	15	50
938	10s. Nuutele Island	15	50
939	30s. Satuiatua, Savaii	15	40
940	50s. Sinalele, Aleipata	30	40
941	60s. Paradise Beach, Lefaga	35	40
942	70s. Houses at Piula Cave	45	50
943	80s. Taga blowholes	45	50
944	90s. View from East Coast road	45	50
945	95s. Outrigger canoes, Leu-lumoega	45	50
946	$1 Parliament Building	50	50

255 Under-12s Rugby Players

1995. World Cup Rugby Championship, South Africa. Multicoloured.

957	70s. Type **255**	55	55
958	90s. Secondary school players	70	70
959	$1 Samoan and New Zealand test match	75	75
960	$4 Ellis Park Stadium, Johan-nesburg	2·75	4·75

1995. 50th Anniv of End of Second World War. As T 182a of St. Helena. Multicoloured.

961	70s. Vought Sikorsky OS2U Kingfisher (seaplane)	65	55
962	90s. Chance Vought F4U Corsair (fighter)	80	70
963	95s. American transport ship and landing craft	85	75
964	$3 American marines landing on Samoa	3·00	4·50
MS965	75×85 mm. $4 Reverse of 1939–45 War Medal (vert)	1·75	2·75

256 Leatherback Turtle

1995. Year of the Sea Turtle. Multicoloured.

966	70s. Type **256**	55	55
967	90s. Loggerhead turtle	70	70
968	$1 Green turtle	75	75
969	$4 Pacific ridley turtle	2·75	4·25

257 *Phaius tankervilleae*

1995. "Singapore '95" International Stamp Exhibition. Orchids. Sheet 76×100 mm.

MS970	**257** $5 multicoloured	3·25	4·25

See also No. **MS**1006.

1995. 50th Anniv of United Nations. As T 201a of St. Lucia. Multicoloured.

971	70s. Hospital lorry, Bosnia, 1995	85	55
972	90s. Bell Sioux helicopter and ambulance, Korea, 1952	1·40	85
973	$1 Bell 212 helicopter, Bosnia, 1995	1·60	1·00
974	$4 R.N.Z.A.F. Hawker Siddeley Andover, Somalia, 1995	3·50	5·00

258 Madonna and Child

1995. Christmas. Multicoloured.

975	25s. Type **258**	30	10
976	70s. Wise Man wearing green turban	65	50
977	90s. Wise Man with Child in manger	75	65
978	$5 Wise Man wearing red turban	3·50	6·50

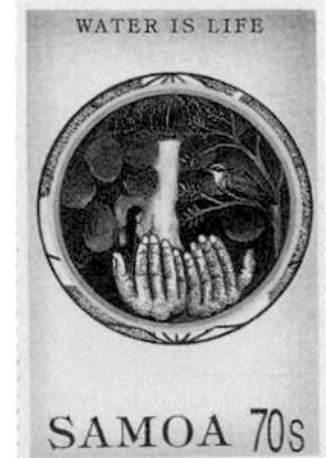

259 Hands cupped under Waterfall and Bird

1996. Environment. Water Resources. Mult.

979	70s. Type **259**	50	50
980	90s. Young girl and "WATER FOR LIFE" slogan	65	65
981	$2 Village and waterfall	1·40	2·00
982	$4 Irrigation system	2·75	3·75

1996. 70th Birthday of Queen Elizabeth II. As T 55 of Tokelau each incorporating a different photograph of the Queen. Multicoloured.

983	70s. Main Street, Apia	50	40
984	90s. Beach scene, Neiafu	65	50
985	$1 Vailima House (Head of State's residence)	75	60
986	$3 Parliament Building	2·00	3·75
MS987	64×66 mm. $5 Queen Elizabeth II	3·25	4·00

260 Moon Hare preparing Elixir of Life

1996. Moon Festival. Sheet 103×83 mm.

MS988	**260** $2.50 multicoloured	1·75	2·50

No. **MS**988 also includes the "CHINA '96" International Stamp Exhibition logo on the sheet margin.

261 Meeting Venue

1996. 63rd Session of the EU-ACP Council of Ministers. Sheet 135×71 mm.

MS989	**261** $5 multicoloured	3·25	4·50

262 Boxing

1996. Centenary of Modern Olympic Games. Mult.

990	70s. Type **262**	60	40
991	90s. Running	70	55
992	$1 Weightlifting	80	60
993	$4 Throwing the javelin	2·75	5·00

263 Festival Logo

1996. 7th Pacific Festival of Arts, Apia. Mult.

994	60s. Type **263**	40	35
995	70s. Decorated pottery	50	40
996	80s. Textile pattern	55	55
997	90s. Traditional dancing	60	60
998	$1 Carved poles	70	70
999	$4 Man wearing traditional headdress and necklace	2·00	4·25

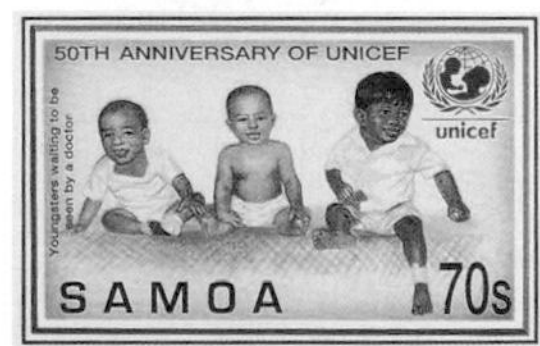

264 Young Children

1996. 50th Anniv of UNICEF. Multicoloured.

1000	70s. Type **264**	45	40
1001	90s. Children in hospital	60	60
1002	$1 Child receiving injection	70	70
1003	$4 Mothers and children	2·00	4·00

1997. "HONG KONG '97" International Stamp Exhibition. Sheet, 130×90 mm, containing No. 797a.

MS1004	$3 Many-coloured Fruit Dove	1·75	2·25

266 First U.S.A. and Samoa Postage Stamps

1997. "Pacific '97" International Stamp Exhibition, San Francisco. Sheet 96×70 mm.

MS1005	**266** $5 multicoloured	2·75	3·50

1997. Return of Hong Kong to China. Sheet 130×90 mm, containing design as T 257, but with new value.

MS1006	**257** $2.50, multicoloured	1·50	2·25

1997. Golden Wedding of Queen Elizabeth and Prince Philip. As T 192a of St. Lucia. Mult.

1007	70s. Queen Elizabeth	1·00	1·25
1008	70s. Prince Philip carriage-driving at Royal Windsor Horse Show, 1996	1·00	1·25
1009	90s. Queen Elizabeth and horse	1·10	1·40
1010	90s. Prince Philip laughing	1·10	1·40
1011	$1 Prince Philip and Prince Edward with Zara Phillips on horseback, 1993	1·25	1·50
1012	$1 Queen Elizabeth and Prince William	1·25	1·50
MS1013	111×70 mm. $5 Queen Elizabeth and Prince Philip in landau (horiz)	4·00	4·50

Nos. 1007/8, 1009/10 and 1011/12 respectively were printed together, se-tenant, with the backgrounds forming composite designs.

267 Dolphin on Surface

1997. 26th Anniv of Greenpeace (environmental organization). Multicoloured.

1014	50s. Type **267**	45	35
1015	60s. Two dolphins swimming underwater	55	45
1016	70s. Heads of two dolphins underwater	60	65
1017	$1 Dolphin "laughing"	75	1·25
MS1018	113×91 mm. $1.25 ×4. As Nos. 1014/17	2·75	3·50

268 Christmas Bells

1997. Christmas. Multicoloured.

1019	70s. Type **268**	45	35
1020	80s. Christmas bauble	50	40
1021	$2 Candle	1·40	2·00
1022	$3 Christmas star	1·60	2·75

269 Mangrove Fruit

1998. Mangroves. Multicoloured.

1023	70s. Type **269**	40	35
1024	80s. Mangrove seedlings	45	40
1025	$2 Mangrove roots	1·25	2·00
1026	$4 Mangrove tree on seashore	2·25	3·50

1998. Diana, Princess of Wales Commemoration. As T 98 of Tokelau. Multicoloured.

1027	50s. Wearing red jacket, 1990	30	40
MS1028	145×70 mm. $1.40 As 50s.; $1.40 Wearing tweed jacket, 1981; $1.40 Wearing red dress, 1988; $1.40 Carrying bouquets, 1993 (sold at $5.60+75s. charity premium)	1·90	3·00

270 Westland Wallace

1998. 80th Anniv of the Royal Air Force. Mult.

1029	70s. Type **270**	70	35
1030	80s. Hawker Fury Mk I	70	40
1031	$2 Vickers Varsity	1·50	1·75
1032	$5 BAC Jet Provost	3·00	4·50
MS1033	110×77 mm. $2 Norman Thompson N.T.2b; $2 Nieuport 27 Scout; $2 Miles Magister; $2 Bristol Bomber	5·00	5·50

271 Christmas Star

1998. Christmas. Multicoloured.

1034	70s. Type **271**	50	35
1035	$1.05 Bell	70	60
1036	$1.40 Bauble	85	80
1037	$5 Cross	3·25	5·00

272 Outrigger Canoe

1999. "Australia '99" World Stamp Exhibition, Melbourne. Maritime Heritage. Multicoloured.

1038	70s. Type **272**	40	35
1039	90s. "Heemskerk" and "Zeehan" (Tasman), 1642	90	55
1040	$1.05 H.M.S. "Resolution" and H.M.S. "Adventure" (Cook), 1773	1·25	1·00
1041	$6 New Zealand scow schooner, 1880	3·75	5·50

1999. Royal Wedding. Vert designs as T 197a of St. Helena. Multicoloured.

1042	$1.50 Photographs of Prince Edward and Miss Sophie Rhys-Jones	75	75
1043	$6 Engagement photograph	3·00	4·25

1999. 30th Anniv of First Manned Landing on Moon. As T 94a of St. Kitts. Multicoloured.

1044	70s. Lift-off	40	35
1045	90s. Lunar lander separating from service module	45	40
1046	$3 Buzz Aldrin on Moon's surface	1·50	2·25
1047	$5 Command module descending on parachutes	2·50	3·75
MS1048	90×80 mm. $5 Earth as seen from Moon (circular, 40 mm diam)	2·75	3·50

1999. "Queen Elizabeth the Queen Mother's Century". As T 199 of St. Helena. Multicoloured.

1049	70s. Talking to air-raid victims, 1940	60	35
1050	90s. King, Queen and Princess Elizabeth at garden party, South Africa, 1947	70	40
1051	$2 Reviewing scouts at Windsor, 1991	1·25	1·50
1052	$6 With Princess Eugenie, 1998	2·75	4·50
MS1053	145×70 mm. $5 Lady Elizabeth Bowes-Lyon, 1923, and Charlie Chaplin film	4·75	6·00

273 Hibiscus and Star

1999. Christmas and Millennium. Multicoloured.

1054	70s. Type **273**	50	35
1055	90s. Poinsettia and star	60	40
1056	$2 Christmas cactus and star	1·40	1·40
1057	$6 Southern Cross constellation and Samoan flag	4·50	6·00

274 Sunrise

2000. New Millennium. Multicoloured.

1058	70s. Type **274**	1·00	1·00
1059	70s. Sunset	1·00	1·00

274a The Count on Ladder

2000. "Sesame Street" (children's T.V. programme). Multicoloured.

1060	90s. Type **274a**	45	60
1061	90s. Ernie on trapeze	45	60
1062	90s. Grover swinging on rope	45	60

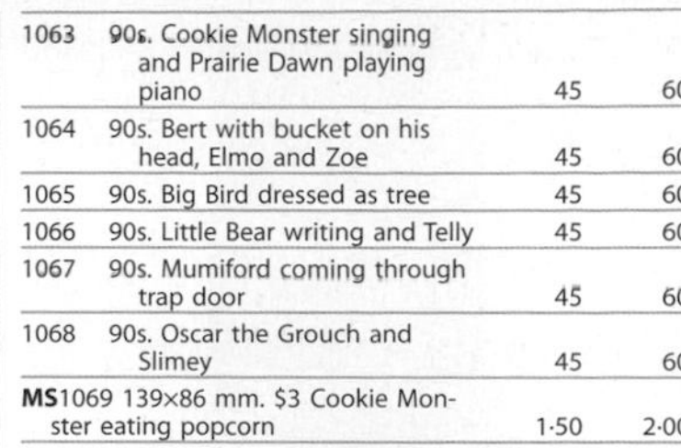

1063	90s. Cookie Monster singing and Prairie Dawn playing piano	45	60
1064	90s. Bert with bucket on his head, Elmo and Zoe	45	60
1065	90s. Big Bird dressed as tree	45	60
1066	90s. Little Bear writing and Telly	45	60
1067	90s. Mumiford coming through trap door	45	60
1068	90s. Oscar the Grouch and Slimey	45	60
MS1069	139×86 mm. $3 Cookie Monster eating popcorn	1·50	2·00

Nos. 1060/8 were printed together, se-tenant, with the backgrounds forming a composite design.

275 Fire Dancing

2001. Siva afi Fire Dancing. Multicoloured.

1070	25s. Type **275**	25	10
1071	50s. Dancer with torch	40	25
1072	90s. Dancer with arms crossed	65	55
1073	$1 Three dancers	70	60
1074	$4 Pati Levasa, World Fire Dance Champion	2·50	3·50

276 *Vagrans egista*

2001. Butterflies. Multicoloured. Self-adhesive.

1075	70s. Type **276**	80	1·10
1076	$1.20 *Jamides bochus*	1·00	1·40
1077	$1.40 *Papilio godeffroy*	1·00	1·40
1078	$2 *Acraea andromacha*	1·25	1·75
1079	$3 *Eurema hecabe*	1·50	2·00

277 Snorkellers

2002. U.N. Year of Eco Tourism. Multicoloured.

1080	60s. Type **277**	55	75
1081	95s. Canoeists	80	1·25
1082	$1.90 Wood-carver and children	1·10	1·50
1083	$3 Children by waterfall	1·40	1·75

Nos. 1080/3 were printed together, se-tenant, in horizontal strips of 4 and a central label showing the U.N. symbol, with the backgrounds forming a composite design.

278 Buses, Traditional Huts and Man with Baseball Bat

2000. 40th Anniv of Independence. Designs showing the Samoan flag in the background. Multicoloured. Self-adhesive.

1084	25s. Type **278**	50	25
1085	70s. Local dancers and conch blower	45	35
1086	95s. Ferry, aircraft and office workers	1·00	55
1087	$5 Church, police parade and rugby player	4·75	4·75
MS1088	110×85 mm. No. 1087	4·75	5·50

279 Woman holding Fish

2002. Faces of Samoa. Multicoloured.

1089	5s. Type **279**	10	20
1090	10s. Boy with grandparents selling fruit	15	20
1091	20s. Young men collecting wood	20	20
1092	25s. Two young boys laughing	20	20
1093	35s. Mother and daughter	30	30
1094	50s. Baby boy	40	40
1095	60s. Male traditional dancer	45	45
1096	70s. Female traditional dancer	45	45
1097	80s. Woman laughing	55	55
1098	90s. Women's choir	65	65
1099	95s. Two women with flowers in their hair	65	65
1100	$1 Young boy under shower	70	70
1101	$1.20 Young girl with pigtails	75	75
1102	$1.85 Man in shirt and tie	1·10	1·25
1103	$10 Children awaiting confirmation	5·50	6·50

280 Local Couple on Rock

2002. Samoan Scenes. Multicoloured.

1104	95s. Type **280**	90	65
1105	$1.20 Local couple on beach	1·10	90
1106	$1.40 Waterfall	1·25	1·40
1107	$2 Local girl in sea	1·75	2·25
MS1108	120×920 mm. Nos. 1105 and 1107	2·50	3·00

281 *Alpinia pupurata*

2002. Ginger Flowers. Multicoloured.

1109	25s. Type **281**	30	15
1110	$1.05 *Alpinia samoensis*	1·00	65
1111	$1.20 *Etlingeria cevuga*	1·10	75
1112	$4 *Hedychium flavescens*	2·75	4·00

282 "Return to Paradise" Bus

2003. Buses. Multicoloured. Self-adhesive.

1113	25s. Type **282**	85	25
1114	70s. "Misileti Fatu" bus	1·75	1·00
1115	90s. "Jungle Boys" bus	2·00	1·50
1116	95s. "Sun Rise Transport" bus	2·00	1·50
1117	$4 "Laifoni" bus	5·50	6·50

283 Turtles, Aleipata

2003. Establishment of Marine Protected Areas. Multicoloured.

1118	25s. Type **283**	75	15
1119	$5 Crab and mangrove, Safata	3·25	4·25

284 Vanya Taule'alo

2003. Art of Samoa (1st series). Showing artists and their work. Multicoloured.

1120	25s. Type **284**	30	15
1121	70s. Michel Tuffery	60	40
1122	90s. Momoe von Reiche	75	60
1123	$1 Fatu Feu'u	80	75
1124	$4 Lily Laita	2·25	3·25

285 David Tua (boxing)

2003. Sporting Legends of Samoa. Multicoloured.

1125	25s. Type **285**	30	15
1126	70s. Beatrice Faumuina (discus)	65	45
1127	90s. Michael Jones (rugby)	80	70
1128	95s. Rita Fatialofa (netball)	85	75
1129	$4 Jesse Sapolu (American football)	2·75	4·00

286 Bicoloured Angelfish

2003. Angelfish. Multicoloured.

1130	25s. Type **286**	55	20
1131	60s. Flame angelfish	90	45
1132	90s. Regal angelfish	1·50	70
1133	$5 Emperor angelfish	4·75	5·50
MS1134	123×98 mm. $5 No. 1133	4·50	5·50

287 *Heliconia caribaea*

2004. Flowers of the Tropics. Multicoloured.

1135	70s. Type **287**	60	45
1136	80s. *Heliconia psittacorum* "Andromeda"	75	60
1137	90s. *Hibiscus rosa-sinensis* var.	85	65
1138	$4 *Plumeria rubra var. acutifolia*	3·00	4·00

288 Black-naped Tern

2004. Sea Birds. Multicoloured.

1139	25s. Type **288**	60	25
1140	60s. Crested tern	90	55
1141	70s. Common noddy (vert)	90	65
1142	90s. Lesser frigate bird (vert)	1·10	75
1143	$4 Reef heron	4·00	5·50
MS1144	191×92 mm. Nos. 1139/43	6·75	7·50

289 *Chaetodon meyeri*

2004. Butterfly Fish. Multicoloured.

1145	50s. Type **289**	65	30
1146	90s. *Chaetodon punctatofasciatus* (horiz)	1·00	60
1147	$1 *Chaetodon ephippium* (horiz)	1·10	75
1148	$4 *Chaetodon flavirostris*	3·50	4·50
MS1149	100×61 mm. $4 As No. 1148	3·50	4·50

The top right corner of No. **MS**1149 is die-cut round the shape of a sea anemone.

290 Samoan Woman

2004. Samoan Women. Multicoloured.

1150	25s. Type **290**	40	15
1151	70s. Two women and beach scene (vert)	65	45
1152	90s. Woman resting head on hands	75	65
1153	$4 Woman during Kava ceremony (vert)	2·75	4·75

291 Three Children in Canoe

2005. Island of Savaii. Multicoloured.

1154	25s. Type **291**	55	15
1155	70s. Tourists on steps to building	80	45
1156	90s. Walkway through forest (vert)	1·00	65
1157	$4 Coastline (vert)	3·75	5·50

292 Spinner Dolphin

2005. Dolphins. Sheet 154×110 mm containing T 292 and similar square designs. Multicoloured.

MS1158	$1 Type **292**; $1.75 Rough-toothed dolphin; $4 Bottlenose dolphin	6·00	7·00

293 Sau Sau, Dawn of the First Humans

2005. Legends. Multicoloured.

1159	25s. Type **293**	30	20
1160	70s. Tuimanu'a and the flying fox	65	50
1161	90s. Fonuea and Salofa escape famine	85	75
1162	$4 Patea the sea demon	3·25	4·50

294 Samoan Prime Minister Tuila'epa Sailele Malielegaoi and Chinese Premier Wen Jiabao

2005. 30th Anniv of Samoa–People's Republic of China Diplomatic Relations. Multicoloured.

1163	25c. Type **294**	30	20
1164	50c. Samoa Aquatic Centre, Faleata	50	35
1165	$1 Wooden bowl	90	80
1166	$4 Chinese astronauts	3·25	4·25
MS1167	90×82 mm. Nos. 1163/6	4·50	5·50

295 Europa Stamps and Globe

2005. 50th Anniv of First Europa Stamp.

1168	**295**	60s. multicoloured	50	30
1169	-	$3 multicoloured	2·50	2·75
1170	-	$4 multicoloured	3·00	3·25
1171	-	$10 multicoloured	6·50	7·50
MS1172		122×78 mm. Nos. 1168/71	11·00	12·00

DESIGNS: Nos. 1169 to **MS**1172 showing globe and Europa stamps.

296 Sunset over Bay

2006. Samoan Sunsets. Multicoloured.

1173	60s. Type **296**	65	35
1174	90s. Canoe just offshore at sunset	1·00	70
1175	$1 Two people watching sunset over lagoon	1·10	1·00
1176	$4 Man on beach at sunset	5·50	6·50

2006. 80th Birthday of Queen Elizabeth II. As T 237 of St. Helena. Multicoloured.

1177	$1 Princess Elizabeth as young girl	90	65
1178	$1.75 Queen in uniform and baby Prince Charles	1·50	1·25
1179	$4 Queen Elizabeth (black/white photo)	3·25	3·75
1180	$5 Wearing turquoise hat with white rose decoration	3·50	4·25
MS1181	144×75 mm. $1.75 Queen in uniform for Trooping the Colour and Prince Charles as baby; $5 As No. 1179	5·00	5·50

297 Humphead Wrasse on Reef

2006. Endangered Species. Humphead Wrasse (Cheilinus undulatus). Sheet 205×135 mm containing T 297 and similar horiz designs. Multicoloured.

MS1182	$1.50×2 Type **297**; $2.30×2 Two wrasse on reef; $2.50×2 One wrasse; $3.60×2 Two wrasse	17·00	19·00

298 *Cypraea cribraria*

2007. Cowrie Shells of Samoa. Multicoloured. Self-adhesive.

1183	$1.60 Type **298**	1·25	1·25
1184	$2.10 *Cypraea aurantium*	1·75	1·75
1185	$2.40 *Cypraea mauritiana*	2·25	2·25
1186	$3.10 *Ovula ovum*	2·75	2·75

299 Piula College, Upolu

2007. Churches of Samoa. Multicoloured.

1187	50s. Type **299**	40	40
1188	50s. Anglican Church, Apia	40	40
1189	50s. SDA Church, Fusi Saolu-afata	40	40
1190	50s. Protestant Church, Apia	40	40
1191	$1 Methodist Church, Matafele	80	80
1192	$1 Mauga, Apia	80	80
1193	$1 EFKS, Apia	80	80
1194	$1 Malua Theological College	80	80
1195	$2 Mulivai Cathedral, Apia	1·75	1·75
1196	$2 LDS Temple, Pesega	1·75	1·75
1197	$2 EFKS, Sapapaii	1·75	1·75
1198	$2 Bahai Temple, Apia	1·75	1·75
MS1199	211×124 mm. Nos. 1187/98	12·00	12·00

300 Mana the Mascot

2007. 13th South Pacific Games, Samoa. Mult.

1200	$1 Type **300**	90	90
1201	$1 Ele Opeloge (women's weightlifting Commonwealth Record Holder)	90	90
1202	$1 Apia Park	90	90
1203	$1 Aquatic Centre	90	90
MS1204	97×76 mm. No. 1200	90	90

301 Pineapples

2007. Tropical Fruit. Multicoloured. Self-adhesive.

1205	$1.60 Type **301**	1·25	1·25
1206	$2.10 Coconuts	1·75	1·75
1207	$2.40 Pawpaws	2·25	2·25
1208	$3.10 Mangoes	2·75	2·75

302 Cycling

2008. Olympic Games, Beijing. Sheet 151×94 mm containing T 302 and similar vert designs. Multicoloured.

MS1209	50s. Type **302**; $1 Boxing; $1.50 Wrestling; $2 Athletics	3·50	3·50

303 Pacific Robin (Petroica multicolor)

2009. Endangered Species. Multicoloured.

MS1210	50s. Type **303**×2; $2 Polynesian triller (*Lalage maculosa*)×2; $2.70 Polynesian starling (*Aplonis tabuensis*)×2; $5 Wattled honeyeater (*Foulehaio carunculatus*)×2	13·00	13·00

304 Peonies

2010. China 2009 World Stamp Exhibition and Peony Festival, Luoyang, China

1211	$1 multicoloured	1·00	1·00

Pt. 8

SAN MARINO

An independent republic lying near the east coast of the Italian peninsula.

1877. 100 centesimi = 1 lira.
2002. 100 cents = 1 euro.

1

1877

1	1	2c. green	21·00	6·50
18	1	2c. blue	12·00	6·50
32	1	2c. purple	9·00	6·50
2	2	5c. yellow	£170	14·00
33	2	5c. green	6·75	4·25
3	2	10c. blue	£200	14·00
20	2	10c. green	6·75	3·25
34	2	10c. red	6·75	4·25
21	2	15c. red	£180	55·00
4	2	20c. red	28·00	7·50
35	2	20c. lilac	6·75	4·25
5	2	25c. purple	£170	21·00
36	2	25c. blue	6·75	5·25
6	2	30c. brown	£1000	70·00
22	2	30c. yellow	7·75	7·50
7	2	40c. mauve	£1000	70·00
23	2	40c. brown	7·75	7·50
24	2	45c. green	7·75	7·50
25	2	65c. brown	7·75	7·50
26	2	1l. red and yellow	£2000	£650
37	2	1l. blue	£1900	£550
27	2	2l. brown and buff	90·00	£225
28	2	5l. red and blue	£200	£200

2

1892. Surch Cmi. and figure of value.

10c	5c. on 10c. blue	85·00	15·00
12	5c. on 30c. brown	£300	50·00
16	10c. on 20c. red	75·00	8·50

1892. Surch 10 10.

17	10(c.) on 20c. red	£375	13·00

13 Government Palace

14 Government Palace

15 Interior of Government Palace

1894. Opening of Government Palace and Installation of Captains-Regent.

29	13	25c. purple and blue	5·50	2·10
30	14	50c. purple and red	55·00	5·25
31	15	1l. purple and green	33·00	8·50

17 Statue of Liberty

1899

38	17	2c. brown	1·70	1·40
39	17	5c. orange	4·50	3·00

See also Nos. 86/91.

18

19 Mt. Titano

1903

40	18	2c. lilac	14·50	5·25
73	18	2c. brown	45	75
74	19	5c. green	45	75
111	19	5c. purple	40	25
42	19	10c. pink	6·75	2·10
75	19	10c. orange	45	75
112	19	10c. green	40	25
76	19	15c. green	45	75
113	19	15c. purple	40	25
43	19	20c. orange	£130	32·00
77	19	20c. brown	45	75
114	19	20c. green	40	25
44	19	25c. blue	18·00	5·25
78	19	25c. grey	45	75
115	19	25c. violet	40	25
45	19	30c. red	6·75	10·50
79	19	30c. mauve	45	75
116	19	30c. orange	18·00	1·30
46	19	40c. red	12·00	13·00
80	19	40c. pink	1·30	1·10
117	19	40c. brown	65	25
47	19	45c. yellow	9·00	12·00
81	19	50c. purple	1·80	1·60
118	19	50c. grey	65	25
119	19	60c. red	65	25
48	19	65c. brown	9·00	12·00
82	19	80c. blue	2·20	2·75
83	19	90c. brown	2·20	2·75
49	19	1l. green	28·00	17·00
120	19	1l. blue	65	65
50	19	2l. violet	£850	£225
85	19	2l. red	34·00	21·00
121	19	2l. green	6·75	4·75
122	19	5l. blue	18·00	18·00

1905. Surch 1905 15.

52	15c. on 20c. orange	11·00	6·50

22

23

1907

53a	22	1c. brown	5·50	2·10
54	23	15c. grey	18·00	5·25

1917. For Combatants. Surch 1917 Pro combattenti and value.

55	18	25c. on 2c. lilac	4·50	4·25
56	19	50c. on 2l. violet	50·00	38·00

1918. Surch Cent. 20 1918.

57	23	20c. on 15c. grey	3·50	2·75

26 Statue of Liberty

1918. War Casualties Fund. Inscr as in T 26.

58	26	2c.(+5c.) black and lilac	70	1·10
59	26	5c.(+5c.) black and green	70	1·10
60	26	10c.(+5c.) black and red	70	1·10
61	26	20c.(+5c.) black and orange	70	1·10
62	26	25c.(+5c.) black and blue	70	1·10
63	26	45c.(+5c.) black and brown	70	1·10
64	-	1l.(+5c.) black and green	20·00	21·00
65	-	2l.(+5c.) black and lilac	20·00	19·00
66	-	3l.(+5c.) black and red	20·00	18·00

DESIGN—HORIZ: 1, 2, 3l. San Marino.

1918. Italian Victory over Austria and Premium for War Casualties Fund. Optd 3 Novembre 1918.

67	26	20c.(+5c.) black and orange	2·20	3·75
68	26	25c.(+5c.) black and blue	2·20	3·75
69	26	45c.(+5c.) black and brown	2·20	3·75
70	-	1l.(+5c.) black and green	9·00	6·50
71	-	2l.(+5c.) black and lilac	18·00	13·00
72	-	3l.(+5c.) black and red	22·00	15·00

DESIGN—HORIZ: 1, 2, 3l. As Nos. 64/66.

1922. Re-issue of T 17. Colours changed.

86	17	2c. purple	20	30
87	17	5c. green	20	30
88	17	10c. brown	40	30
89	17	20c. brown	40	30
90	17	25c. blue	40	30
91	17	45c. red	4·00	2·10

30 Arbe (Rab)

1923. Delivery to San Marino of Italian Flag flown on Arbe, after the island returned to Yugoslavia.

92	30	50c. green	55	55

31 St. Marinus

1923. San Marino Mutual Aid Society.

93	31	30c. brown	55	55

32 Mt. Titano

33 "Liberty"

1923. Red Cross Fund.

94	32	5c.+5c. green	40	30
95	32	10c.+5c. orange	75	30
96	32	15c.+5c. green	3·25	30
97	32	25c.+5c. red	2·20	85
98	32	40c.+5c. purple	7·75	3·25
99	32	50c.+5c. grey	14·50	45
100	33	1l.+5c. blue and black	5·00	7·50

34

1923. San Marino Volunteers in the Great War.

101	34	1l. brown	14·50	10·50

35 Garibaldi

36

1924. 75th Anniv of Garibaldi's Refuge in San Marino.

102	35	30c. purple	2·75	1·80
103	35	50c. brown	3·00	2·50
104	35	60c. red	4·50	3·75

105	**36**	1l. blue	10·00	6·00
106	**36**	2l. green	13·50	7·50

1924. Red Cross stamps of 1918 surch.

107	**26**	30c. on 45c. black & brown	2·00	1·10
108	-	60c. on 1l. black and green	7·00	5·25
109	-	1l. on 2l. black and lilac	20·00	15·00
110	-	2l. on 3l. black and red	18·00	13·00

1926. Surch.

123	**19**	75c. on 80c. blue	1·90	85
124	**19**	1l.20 on 90c. brown	1·90	85
125	**19**	1l.25 on 90c. brown	4·00	3·25
126	**19**	2l.50 on 80c. blue	7·75	8·50

40 Onofri

1926. Death Centenary of Antonio Onofri, "Father of the Country".

127	**40**	10c. black and blue	90	25
128	**40**	20c. black and green	90	65
129	**40**	45c. black and violet	90	85
130	**40**	65c. black and green	90	85
131	**40**	1l. black and orange	5·50	5·25
132	**40**	2l. black and mauve	5·50	5·25

1926. No. E92 surch Lire 1,85.

133	**19**	1l.85 on 60c. violet	55	75

1927. Surch.

134	**40**	"1,25" on 1l. black & orge	5·00	3·25
135	**40**	"2,50" on 2l. black & mauve	13·00	9·50
136	**40**	"5" on 2l. black and mauve	55·00	50·00

1927. Unissued Express stamp (No. 115 surch ESPRESSO 50) surch L. 1,75.

137	**19**	1l.75 on 50c. on 25c. violet	85	80

44 San Marino War Memorial

1927. War Cenotaph Commemoration.

138	**44**	50c. purple	1·30	2·10
139	**44**	1l.25 blue	4·00	2·10
140	**44**	10l. violet	23·00	22·00

45 Franciscan Convent and Capuchin Church

1928. 700th Death Anniv of St. Francis of Assisi.

141	**45**	50c. red	34·00	6·50
142	**45**	1l.25 blue	8·00	7·50
143	-	2l.50 brown	8·00	7·50
144	-	5l. violet	39·00	32·00

DESIGN: 2l.50, 5l. Death of St. Francis.

46 La Rocca Fortress

47 Government Palace

48 Statue of Liberty

1929

145	**46**	5c. blue and purple	1·00	65
146	**46**	10c. mauve and blue	1·00	65
147	**46**	15c. green and orange	1·00	65
148	**46**	20c. red and blue	1·00	65
149	**46**	25c. black and green	1·00	65
150	**46**	30c. red and grey	1·00	65
151	**46**	50c. green and purple	1·00	65
152	**46**	75c. grey and red	1·00	65
153	**47**	1l. green and brown	1·00	65
154	**47**	1l.25 black and blue	1·30	65
155	**47**	1l.75 orange and green	8·75	1·60
156	**47**	2l. red and blue	2·00	1·60
157	**47**	2l.50 blue and red	2·00	1·60
158	**47**	3l. blue and orange	2·00	1·60
159	**47**	3l.70 purple and green	2·00	2·75
160	**48**	5l. green and violet	10·00	2·75
161	**48**	10l. blue and brown	20·00	10·50
162	**48**	15l. purple and green	90·00	85·00
163	**48**	20l. red and blue	£350	£375

50 Mt. Titano

1931. Air.

164	**50**	50c. green	9·00	7·50
165	**50**	80c. red	9·00	7·50
166	**50**	1l. brown	6·75	4·25
167	**50**	2l. purple	6·75	4·25
168	**50**	2l.60 blue	49·00	55·00
169	**50**	3l. grey	49·00	55·00
170	**50**	5l. green	16·00	4·25
171	**50**	7l.70 brown	16·00	8·50
172	**50**	9l. orange	18·00	10·50
173	**50**	10l. blue	£425	£400

51 G.P.O., San Marino

1932. Inauguration of New G.P.O.

174	**51**	20c. green	9·00	8·50
175	**51**	50c. red	13·50	13·00
176	**51**	1l.25 blue	£250	£130
177	**51**	1l.75 brown	£250	85·00
178	**51**	2l.75 violet	44·00	32·00

52 San Marino Railway Station

1932. Opening of San Marino Electric Railway, Rimini.

179	**52**	20c. green	3·00	2·10
180	**52**	50c. red	4·25	3·25
181	**52**	1l.25 blue	14·50	10·50
182	**52**	5l. brown	80·00	70·00

53 Garibaldi

1932. 50th Death Anniv of Garibaldi.

183	**53**	10c. brown	7·50	3·25
184	**53**	20c. violet	7·50	3·25
185	**53**	25c. green	7·50	3·25
186	**53**	50c. brown	12·00	7·50
187	-	75c. red	20·00	10·50
188	-	1l.25 blue	36·00	15·00
189	-	2l.75 orange	85·00	43·00
190	-	5l. green	£350	£350

DESIGN: 75c. to 5l. Garibaldi's arrival at San Marino.

1933. Air. LZ-127 "Graf Zeppelin". Surch ZEPPELIN 1933 under airship and new value.

191	**50**	3l. on 50c. orange	8·25	£110
192	**50**	5l. on 80c. green	44·00	£110
193	**50**	10l. on 1l. blue	44·00	£160
194	**50**	12l. on 2l. brown	44·00	£160
195	**50**	15l. on 2l.60 red	48·00	£160
196	**50**	20l. on 3l. green	48·00	£275

1933. 20th Italian Philatelic Congress. Surch 28 MAGGIO 1933 CONVEGNO FILATELICO and new value.

197	**51**	25c. on 2l.75 violet	13·50	10·50
198	**51**	50c. on 1l.75 brown	26·00	21·00
199	**51**	75c. on 2l.75 violet	65·00	43·00
200	**51**	1l.25 on 1l.75 brown	£400	£400

1934. Philatelic Exn. Surch 12-27 APRILE 1934 MOSTRA FILATELICA and value with wheel.

201		25c. on 1l.25 blue	1·80	2·10
202		50c. on 1l.75 brown	3·50	3·25
203		75c. on 50c. red	7·00	6·50
204		1l.25 on 20c. green	32·00	42·00

1934. Surch with value and wheel.

205		3l.70 on 1l.25 blue	90·00	75·00
206		3l.70 on 2l.75 violet	90·00	95·00

58 Ascent to Mt. Titano

1935. 12th Anniv of San Marino Fascist Party.

207	**58**	5c. black and brown	40	25
208	**58**	10c. black and violet	40	25
209	**58**	20c. black and orange	40	25
210	**58**	25c. black and green	40	25
211	**58**	50c. black and bistre	40	25
212	**58**	75c. black and red	1·20	2·75
213	**58**	1l.25 black and blue	4·75	6·00

59 Delfico

1935. Death Centenary of Melchiorre Delfico (historian of San Marino).

214	**59**	5c. black and purple	95	1·10
215	**59**	7½c. black and brown	95	1·10
216	**59**	10c. black and green	95	1·10
217	**59**	15c. black and red	24·00	7·50
218	**59**	20c. black and orange	1·90	2·10
219	**59**	25c. black and green	1·90	2·10
220	-	30c. black and violet	1·90	2·10
221	-	50c. black and green	4·75	6·50
222	-	75c. black and red	12·00	12·00
223	-	1l.25 black and blue	3·25	4·25
224	-	1l.50 black and brown	55·00	48·00
225	-	1l.75 black and orange	85·00	85·00

DESIGN—25×35 mm: 30c. to 1l.75, Statue of Delfico.

1936. Surch. (a) Postage.

226	**40**	80c. on 45c. black & violet	4·00	3·75
227	**40**	80c. on 65c. black & green	4·00	3·75
228	**45**	2l.05 on 1l.25 blue	6·50	6·50
229	-	2l.75 on 2l.50 brown (No. 143)	24·00	26·00

(b) Air.

230	**50**	75c. on 50c. green	2·20	3·75
231	**50**	75c. on 80c. red	13·50	12·50

63 St. Marinus and St. Leo

1937. Independence Monument. Sheet 125×105 mm.

MS232	**63**	5l.	16·00	21·00

64 Abraham Lincoln

1938. Dedication of Bust of Abraham Lincoln. Sheets (each 125×105 mm).

MS232a	**64**	3l. blue	3·50	3·25
MS232b		5l. red	24·00	13·00

1941. Surch 10.

233	**19**	10c. on 15c. purple	20	25
234	**19**	10c. on 30c. orange	1·30	1·10

1942. Air. Surch Lire 10 and bars.

235	**50**	10l. on 2l.60 blue	£140	£130
236	**50**	10l. on 3l. grey	30·00	32·00

67 Gajarda Tower, Arbe, and Flags of Italy and San Marino

1942. Restoration of Italian Flag to Arbe (Rab) annexed by Italy in 1941.

237	**67**	10c. red and bistre (postage)	15	10
238	**67**	15c. red and brown	15	10
239	**67**	20c. grey and green	15	10
240	**67**	25c. blue and green	20	10
241	**67**	50c. brown and red	20	10
242	**67**	75c. grey and red	20	10
243	-	1l.25 light blue and blue	20	10
244	-	1l.75 grey and brown	45	25
245	-	2l.75 blue and bistre	65	55
246	-	5l. brown and green	4·50	4·25
247	-	25c. grey and brown (air)	30	10
248	-	50c. brown and green	30	10
249	-	75c. brown and blue	30	10
250	-	1l. brown and bistre	85	75
251	-	5l. blue and bistre	8·25	6·25

DESIGNS—HORIZ: Nos. 243/6, Galleon in Arbe Harbour. VERT: Nos. 247/51, Granda Belfry, Arbe.

1942. Italian Philatelic Congress. Surch GIORNATA FILATELICA RIMINI - SAN MARINO 3 AGOSTO 1942 (1641 d. F. R.) C. – 30.

252	**67**	30c. on 10c. red and bistre	20	25

1942. Surch.

253		30c. on 20c. grey and green	20	30
254	-	20l. on 75c. black and red (No. 222)	17·00	16·00

71 Printing Press

1943. Press Propaganda.

255	**71**	10c. green	15	15
256	**71**	15c. brown	15	15
257	**71**	20c. brown	15	15
258	**71**	30c. purple	15	15
259	**71**	50c. blue	15	15
260	**71**	75c. red	15	15
261	**72**	1l.25 blue	15	15
262	**72**	1l.75 violet	30	20
263	**72**	5l. blue	1·00	1·20
264	**72**	10l. brown	5·75	4·75

72 Newspapers

1943. Philatelic Exhibition. Optd GIORNATA FILATELICA RIMINI - SAN MARINO 5 LUGLIO 1943 (1642 d. F. R.).

265	**71**	30c. purple	10	15
266	**71**	50c. blue	10	15

74 Gateway

75 War Memorial

1943. Fall of Fascism. Unissued series for 20th Anniv of Fascism optd 28 LVGLIO 1943 1642 d. F.R. (the "d." is omitted on T 74) and bars cancelling commemorative inscription.

267	**74**	5c. brown (postage)	20	25
268	**74**	10c. orange	20	25

269	74	20c. blue	20	25
270	74	25c. green	20	25
271	74	30c. purple	20	25
272	74	50c. violet	20	25
273	74	75c. red	20	25
274	75	1l.25 blue	20	25
275	75	1l.75 orange	20	25
276	75	2l.75 brown	45	60
277	75	5l. green	1·00	1·20
278	75	10l. violet	1·70	2·10
279	75	20l. blue	6·00	4·75
280	-	25c. brown (air)	20	25
281	-	50c. purple	20	25
282	-	75c. brown	20	25
283	-	1l. purple	20	25
284	-	2l. blue	20	25
285	-	5l. orange	1·10	25
286	-	10l. green	1·80	1·40
287	-	20l. black	7·00	7·00

DESIGN—Air: Nos. 280/7, Map of San Marino.

1943. Provisional Govt. Optd GOVERNO PROVVISORIO over ornamentation.

288	74	5c. brown (postage)	20	20
289	74	10c. orange	20	20
290	74	20c. blue	20	20
291	74	25c. green	20	20
292	74	30c. purple	20	20
293	74	50c. violet	20	20
294	74	75c. red	20	20
295	75	1l.25 blue	20	20
296	75	1l.75 orange	25	20
297	75	5l. green	80	65
298	75	20l. blue	3·25	2·40
299	-	25c. brown (air)	20	25
300	-	50c. red	20	25
301	-	75c. brown	20	25
302	-	1l. purple	20	25
303	-	5l. orange	65	1·20
304	-	20l. black	4·00	3·25

78 St. Marinus

79 Mt. Titano

1944

305	78	20l.+10l. brown (postage)	2·75	2·75
306	79	20l.+10l. green (air)	2·20	2·75

80 Govt Palace

81 Govt Palace

1945. 50th Anniv of Government Palace.

307	80	25l. purple (postage)	27·00	8·50
308	81	25l. brown (air)	39·00	7·50

MS308a 180×120 mm comprising 10l. blue and15l. green (angels and crowd scene, horiz); 25l. red (Palace, vert). Perf or imperf £375 £225

82 Arms of Montegiardino

83 Arms of San Marino

1945. Arms Types.

309	-	10c. blue	30	25
310	82	20c. red	30	25
311	-	40c. orange	30	25
312	82	60c. grey	30	25
313	-	80c. green	30	25
314	-	1l. red	55	25
315	-	1l.20 violet	55	25
316	-	2l. brown	55	25
317	-	3l. blue	55	25
317a	-	4l. orange	55	25
318	-	5l. brown	55	25
319	-	10l. red and brown	4·25	3·25
318a	-	15l. blue	5·00	3·25
320	-	20l. red and blue	9·50	4·25
321	-	20l. brown and blue	22·00	4·25
322	82	25l. blue and brown	21·00	7·50
323	83	50l. blue and green	33·00	19·00

DESIGNS (Arms of San Marino and villages in the Republic): 10c., 1l., 1l.20, 15l. Faetano; 40c., 5l. San Marino; 80c., 2, 3, 4l. Fiorentino; 10l. Borgomaggiore; 20l. (2) Serravalle.

84 U.N.R.R.A. Aid for San Marino

1946. U.N.R.R.A.

324	84	100l. red, purple and orange	22·00	10·50

85 Airplane and Mt. Titano

1946. Air.

325	-	25c. grey	30	25
326	85	75c. red	30	25
327	-	1l. brown	30	25
328	85	2l. green	30	25
329	85	3l. violet	30	25
330	-	5l. blue	55	25
331	-	10l. red	55	25
334	-	20l. purple	2·50	2·75
332	-	35l. red	13·00	7·00
335	-	50l. green	20·00	10·50
333	-	100l. brown	3·25	1·50

DESIGNS—HORIZ: 25c., 1, 10l. Wings over Mt. Titano; 100l. Airplane over globe. VERT: 5, 20, 35, 50l. Four aircraft over Mt. Titano.

1946. Stamp Day. Surch L.10.

336	83	50l.+10l. blue and green	33·00	15·00

1946. National Philatelic Convention. Nos. 329/31 but colours changed and without "POSTA AEREA" surch CONVEGNO FILATELICO 30 NOVEMBRE 1946 and premium.

336a	85	3l.+25l. brown	2·20	1·10
336b	-	5l.+25l. orange	2·20	1·10
336c	-	10l.+50l. blue	18·00	9·00

87 Quotation from F.D.R. on Liberty

88 Franklin D. Roosevelt

1947. In Memory of President Franklin D. Roosevelt.

336d	87	1l. brn & ochre (postage)	30	25
336e	88	2l. brown and blue	30	25
336f	-	5l. multicoloured	30	25
336g	-	15l. multicoloured	30	25
336h	87	50l. brown and red	2·20	30
336i	88	100l. brown and violet	4·50	1·30

DESIGN—HORIZ: 5l., 15l. Roosevelt and flags of San Marino and U.S.A.

336j		1l. brown and blue (air)	30	25
336k		2l. brown and red	30	25
336l		5l. multicoloured	30	25
336m		20l. brown and purple	85	25
336n		31l. brown and orange	1·70	25
336o		50l. brown and red	4·50	1·10
336p		100l. brown and blue	6·75	2·10
336q		200l. multicoloured	44·00	22·00

DESIGNS—HORIZ: 1, 3, 50l. Roosevelt and eagle; 2, 20, 100l. Roosevelt and San Marino arms. VERT: 5, 200l. Roosevelt and flags of San Marino and U.S.A.

1947. Surch in figures.

336r	87	3 on 1l. brown and ochre (postage)	55	30
336s	88	4 on 2l. brown and blue	65	30
336t	-	6 on 5l. mult (No. 336f)	65	45
336u	-	3 on 1l. brown and blue (No. 336j) (air)	55	30
336v	-	4 on 2l. brown and red (No. 336k)	70	30
336w	-	6 on 5l. mult (No. 336l)	70	45

1947. No. 317a surch.

337		6l. on 4l. orange	35	25
338		21l. on 4l. orange	1·90	85

91 St. Marinus founding Republic

1947. Reconstruction.

339	91	1l. mauve & green (postage)	30	25
340	91	2l. green and mauve	30	25
341	91	4l. green and brown	30	25
342	91	10l. blue and orange	55	25
343	91	25l. mauve and red	3·50	2·10
344	91	50l. brown and green	48·00	20·00
345	91	25l. blue and orange (air)	2·20	2·40
346	91	50l. blue and brown	5·50	5·00

Nos. 343/6 are larger (24½×32 mm) and have two rows of ornaments forming the frame.

1947. Air. Rimini Philatelic Exhibition. No. 333 optd Giornata Filatelica Rimini - San Marino 8 Luglio 1947.

347		100l. brown	3·25	1·40

1947. Reconstruction. Surch + and value in figures.

348		1l.+1 mauve and green	20	20
349		1l.+2 mauve and green	20	20
350		1l.+3 mauve and green	20	20
351		1l.+4 mauve and green	20	20
352		1l.+5 mauve and green	20	20
353		2l.+1 green and mauve	20	20
354		2l.+2 green and mauve	20	20
355		2l.+3 green and mauve	20	20
356		2l.+4 green and mauve	20	20
357		2l.+5 green and mauve	20	20
358		4l.+1 green and brown	11·00	5·25
359		4l.+2 green and brown	11·00	5·25

94 Mt. Titano, Statue of Liberty and 1847 U.S.A. Stamp

95 Mt. Titano and 1847 U.S.A. Stamp

1947. Centenary of First U.S.A. Postage Stamp.

360	94	2l. brown & pur (postage)	30	25
361	-	3l. grey, red and blue	30	25
362	94	6l. green and blue	30	25
363	-	15l. violet, red and blue	1·10	55
364	-	35l. brown, red and blue	4·25	1·60
365	-	50l. green, red and blue	5·00	1·60
366	95	100l. brown and violet (air)	26·00	16·00

DESIGNS: 3, 35l. U.S.A. stamps, 5c. and 10c. of 1847 and 90c. of 1869 and flags of U.S.A. and San Marino; 15, 50l. Similar but differently arranged.

96 Worker and San Marino Flag

1948. Workers' Issue.

367	96	5l. brown	4·50	55
368	96	8l. green	4·50	55
369	96	30l. red	7·75	1·10
370	96	50l. brown and mauve	17·00	3·25
371	96	100l. blue and violet	55·00	48·00

See also Nos. 506/7.

1948. Surch L.100 between circular ornaments.

372	59	100l. on 15c. black and red	£110	32·00

1948. Air. Surch POSTA AEREA 200.

373	91	200l. on 25l. mauve and red (No. 343)	70·00	29·00

99 Faetano

100 Mt. Titano

1949

374	-	1l. blue and black	55	25
375	-	2l. red and purple	55	25
376	99	3l. blue and violet	55	25
377	-	4l. violet and black	55	25
378	-	5l. brown and purple	55	25
379	99	6l. black and blue	1·70	80
380	100	8l. brown and deep brown	1·70	25
381	-	10l. blue and black	1·10	25
382	-	12l. violet and red	4·00	1·30
383	-	15l. red and violet	9·00	1·90
383a	99	20l. brown and blue	39·00	2·75
384	-	35l. violet and green	17·00	5·25
385	-	50l. brown and red	10·00	2·10
385a	-	55l. green and blue	£130	50·00
386	100	100l. green and brown	£140	75·00
387	-	200l. brown and blue	£140	£110

DESIGNS—HORIZ: 1, 5, 35l. Guaita Tower and walls; 2, 12, 50l. Serravalle and Mt. Titano; 4, 15, 55l. Franciscan Convent and Capuchin Church. VERT: 10, 200l. Guaita Tower.

For similar stamps see Nos. 491/5, 522a/7a and 794/9.

1949. Stamp Day. Optd Giornata Filatelica San Marino-Riccione 28-6-1949.

388	91	1l. mauve and green	55	25
389	91	2l. green and mauve	85	25

104 Garibaldi

1949. Centenary of Garibaldi's Retreat from Rome. (a) Postage. Portraits as T 104. (i) Size 22×28 mm.

390	-	1l. red and black	30	25
391	-	2l. blue and brown	30	25

392	104	3l. green and red	30	25
393	-	4l. brown and blue	30	25

(ii) Size 27×37 mm.

394		5l. brown and mauve	45	25
395		15l. blue and red	2·20	1·20
396		20l. red and violet	4·00	1·90
397	104	50l. violet and purple	40·00	15·00

105 Garibaldi in San Marino

(b) Air. (i) Size 28×22 mm.

398	105	2l. blue and purple	55	25
399	105	3l. black and green	55	25
400	105	5l. green and blue	55	25

(ii) Size 37×27 mm.

401		25l. violet and green	6·00	2·40
402		65l. black and green	17·00	9·50

PORTRAITS—VERT: 1, 20l. Francesco Nullo; 2, 5l. Anita Garibaldi; 4, 15l. Ugo Bassi.

See also Nos. 538/44.

106 Mail Coach and Mt. Titano

1949. 75th Anniv of U.P.U.

403	106	100l. purple & blue (postage)	28·00	12·00
404	106	200l. blue (air)	4·50	2·10
405	106	300l. brown, light brown and purple	9·00	4·75

107 Mt. Titano from Serravalle

108 Second and Guaita Towers

109 Guaita Tower

1950. Air. Views.

406	107	2l. green and violet	55	55
407	-	3l. brown and blue	55	55
408	108	5l. red and brown (22×28 mm)	55	55
409	-	10l. blue and green	4·50	1·10
410	-	15l. violet and black	6·00	1·30
411	-	55l. green and blue	55·00	18·00
412	107	100l. black and red (37×27 mm)	44·00	14·00
413	108	250l. brown and violet	£225	48·00
414	109	500l. brown and green (37×27 mm)	£110	£100
415	109	500l. purple, green and blue	£325	£150

DESIGNS—As Type **107**: 3l. Distant view of Domagnano; 10l. Domagnano; 15l. San Marino from St. Mustiola. 27×37 mm: 55l. Borgo Maggiore.

1950. Air. 28th Milan Fair. As Nos. 408, 410 and 411 but in different colours, optd XXVIII FIERA INTERNAZIONALE DI MILANO APRILE 1950.

416		5l. green and blue	55	25
417		15l. black and red	1·10	55
418		55l. brown and violet	8·25	4·75

111 Government Palace

1951. Red Cross.

419	111	25l. purple, red and brown	14·50	7·50
420	-	75l. brown, red & lt brown	22·00	10·50
421	-	100l. black, red and brown	30·00	14·00

DESIGNS—HORIZ: 75l. Archway of Murata Nuova. VERT: 100l. Guaita Tower.

1951. Air. Stamp Day. No. 415 surch Giornata Filatelica San Marino - Riccione 20-8-1951 L. 300.

422	109	300l. on 500l. purple, green and blue	£100	43·00

113 Flag, Douglas DC-6 Airliner and Mt. Titano

1951. Air.

423	113	1000l. blue and brown	£850	£550

108 Second and Guaita Towers

1951. Air. Italian Flood Relief Fund. Surch Pro-alluvionati italiani 1951 L. 100 and bars.

424	108	100l. on 250l. brown and violet	13·00	6·00

115 "Columbus at the Council of Salamanca" (after Barabino)

1952. 500th Birth Anniv (1951) of Christopher Columbus.

425	115	1l. orange & grn (postage)	55	25
426	-	2l. brown and violet	55	25
427	-	3l. violet and brown	55	25
428	-	4l. blue and brown	55	25
429	-	5l. green and turquoise	55	60
430	-	10l. brown and black	1·70	85
431	-	15l. red and black	2·20	1·40
432	-	20l. blue and green	3·25	1·70
433	-	25l. purple and brown	18·00	5·25
434	115	60l. brown and violet	28·00	10·50
435	-	80l. grey and black	60·00	27·00
436	-	200l. green and blue	£120	60·00
437	-	200l. blue and black (air)	55·00	32·00

DESIGNS—HORIZ: 2, 25l. Columbus and fleet; 3, 10, 20l. Landing in America; 4, 15, 80l. Red Indians and American settlers; 5, 200l. (No. 436) Columbus and Map of America; 200l. (No. 437) Columbus, Statue of Liberty (New York) and skyscrapers.

1952. Trieste Fair. As Columbus issue of 1952, but colours changed, optd FIERA DI TRIESTE 1952.

438		1l. violet and brown (postage)	30	25
439		2l. red and black	30	25
440		3l. green and turquoise	30	25
441		4l. brown and black	55	25
442		5l. mauve and violet	85	55
443		10l. blue and brown	2·20	1·10
444		15l. brown and blue	6·75	2·75
445		200l. brown and black (air)	90·00	43·00

117 Rose

118 Cyclamen, Douglas DC-6 Airliner, Rose, San Marino and Riccione

1952. Air. Stamp Day and Philatelic Exhibition.

446	-	1l. purple and violet	55	25
447	-	2l. green and blue	55	25
448	117	3l. red and brown	55	25
449	118	5l. brown and purple	1·70	25
450	118	25l. green and violet	4·50	1·70
451	118	200l. multicoloured	£100	45·00

DESIGNS—As Type **117**: 1l. Cyclamen; 2l. San Marino and Riccione.

119 Airplane over San Marino

1952. Air. Aerial Survey of San Marino.

452	119	25l. green and yellow	4·00	1·60
453	-	75l. violet and brown	10·00	4·75

DESIGN: 75l. Airplane over Mt. Titano.

120 "The Discus Thrower"

121 Tennis

1953. Sports.

454	120	1l. black & brn (postage)	15	25
455	121	2l. brown and black	15	25
456	-	3l. blue and black	15	25
457	-	4l. blue and green	15	25
458	-	5l. green and brown	15	25
459	-	10l. red and blue	1·40	25
460	-	25l. brown and black	6·00	1·70
461	-	100l. black and brown	19·00	7·50
462	-	200l. turquoise & grn (air)	25·00	9·75

DESIGNS—As Type **120**: 3l. Running. As Type **121**: HORIZ: 4l. Cycling; 5l. Football; 100l. Roller skating; 200l. Skiing. VERT: 10l. Model glider flying; 25l. Shooting.

See also No. 584.

1953. Stamp Day and Philatelic Exn. As No. 461 but colour changed, optd GIORNATA FILATELICA S. MARINO - RICCIONE 24 AGOSTO 1953.

463		100l. green and turquoise	40·00	16·00

123 Narcissus

1953. Flowers.

464	123	1l. blue, green and yellow	15	25
465	-	2l. blue, green and yellow	15	25
466	-	3l. blue, green and yellow	15	25
467	-	4l. blue, green and yellow	15	25
468	-	5l. green and red	15	25
469	-	10l. blue, green and yellow	1·40	60
470	-	25l. blue, green and pink	5·50	2·75
471	-	80l. blue, green and red	28·00	16·00

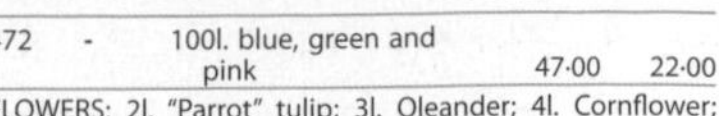

472	-	100l. blue, green and pink	47·00	22·00

FLOWERS: 2l. "Parrot" tulip; 3l. Oleander; 4l. Cornflower; 5l. Carnation; 10l. Iris; 25 l; Cyclamen; 80l. Geranium; 100l. Rose.

124 Douglas DC-6 Airliner over Mt. Titano and Arms

1954. Air.

473	124	1000l. brown and blue	75·00	38·00

125 Walking

1954. Sports.

474	125	1l. mauve and violet	10	15
475	-	2l. violet and green	10	15
476	-	3l. chestnut and brown	10	15
477	-	4l. blue and turquoise	10	15
478	-	5l. brown and green	10	15
479	-	8l. lilac and purple	10	15
480	-	12l. red and black	55	25
481	-	25l. green and blue	3·25	30
482	125	80l. green and blue	4·50	1·10
483	-	200l. brown and lilac	12·00	4·25
484	-	250l. multicoloured	90·00	43·00

DESIGNS—HORIZ: 2l. Fencing; 3l. Boxing; 5l. Motor-cycle racing; 8l. Throwing the javelin; 12l. Car racing. VERT: 4, 200, 250l. Gymnastics; 25l. Wrestling.

The 200l. measures 27×37 mm and the 250l. 28×37½ mm.

126 Statue of Liberty

1954

485	126	20 1. blue & brn (postage)	1·10	30
486	126	60l. green and red	4·00	80
487	126	120l. brown and blue (air)	2·20	1·30

127 Hurdling

1955. Air. 1st Int Exhibition of Olympic Stamps.

488	127	80l. black and red	3·25	1·20
489	-	120l. red and green	5·50	2·20

DESIGN—HORIZ: 120l. Relay racing.

128 Yacht

1955. 7th International Philatelic Exhibition.

490	128	100l. black and blue	8·25	3·25

See also No. 518.

1955. Views as T 99.

491		5l. brown and blue	10	15
492		10l. green and orange	10	15
493		15l. red and green	10	15
494		25l. violet and brown	20	20

495		35l. red and lilac	20	20

DESIGNS—HORIZ: 5, 25l. Archway of Murata Nuova. VERT: 10, 35l. Guaita Tower; 15l. Government Palace.
See also Nos. 519/21 and 797/9.

129 Ice Skating

1955. Winter Olympic Games, Cortina D'Ampezzo.

496	**129**	1l. brown & yell (postage)	15	15
497	-	2l. blue and red	15	15
498	-	3l. black and brown	15	15
499	-	4l. brown and green	15	15
500	-	5l. blue and red	15	15
501	-	10l. blue and pink	15	20
502	-	25l. black and red	1·70	75
503	-	50l. brown and blue	4·00	1·30
504	-	100l. black and green	11·50	4·50
505	-	200l. black and orange (air)	55·00	21·00

DESIGNS—HORIZ: 2, 25l. Skiing; 3, 50l. Bobsleighing; 5, 100l. Ice hockey; 200l. Ski jumping. VERT: 4l. Slalom racing; 10l. Figure skating.

1956. Winter Relief Fund. As T 96 but additionally inscr "ASSISTENZA INVERNALE".

506		50l. green	14·50	8·00

1956. 50th Anniv of "Arengo" (San Marino Parliament). As T 96 but additionally inscr "50° ANNIVERSARIO ARENGO 25 MARZO 1906".

507		50l. blue	14·50	8·00

130 Pointer

1956. Dogs. 25l. to 100l. have multicoloured centres.

508	**130**	1l. brown and blue	10	25
509	-	2l. grey and red	10	25
510	-	3l. brown and blue	10	25
511	-	4l. grey and blue	10	25
512	-	5l. brown and red	10	25
513	-	10l. brown and blue	10	25
514	-	25l. blue	4·00	1·10
515	-	60l. red	13·00	4·75
516	-	80l. blue	17·00	6·50
517	-	100l. red	26·00	12·00

DOGS: 2l. Borzoi; 3l. Sheepdog; 4l. Greyhound; 5l. Boxer; 10l. Great Dane; 25l. Irish setter; 60l. Alsatian; 80l. Rough collie; 100l. Foxhound.

1956. Philatelic Exn. As T 128 but inscr "1956".

518	**128**	100l. brown and green	3·25	1·70

1956. International Philatelic Congress. Designs as Nos. 491/5 but larger and new values inscr "CONGRESSO INTERNAZ. PERITI FILATELICI SAN MARINO SALSOMAGGIORE 6–8 OTTOBRE 1956".

519		20l. brown and blue	2·20	55
520		80l. red and violet	4·50	2·10
521		100l. green and orange	7·00	3·75

SIZES—26½×37 mm: 20l. Guaita Tower; 100l. Government Palace. (36½×27 mm): 8l. Archway of Murata Nuova.

1956. Air. No. 504 optd with an airplane and POSTA AEREA.

522		100l. black and green	5·00	2·75

1957. Views as T 99.

522a		1l. green and deep green	10	10
523		2l. red and green	10	15
524		3l. brown and blue	15	15
524a		4l. blue and brown	20	15
525		20l. green and deep green	30	15
525a		30l. violet and brown	65	30
526		60l. violet and brown	3·25	1·20
526a		115l. brown and blue	1·10	65
527		125l. blue and black	85	55
527a		500l. black and green	£170	80·00

DESIGNS—VERT: 2l. Borgo Maggiore Church; 3, 30l. Town gate, San Marino; 4, 125l. View of San Marino from southern wall; 20, 115l. Borgo Maggiore market place. HORIZ: 1, 60l. View of San Marino from Hospital Avenue. 37½×28 mm: 500l. Panorama of San Marino.
See also Nos. 794/6.

132 Marguerites

1957. Flowers. Multicoloured.

528		1l. Type **132**	10	15
529		2l. Polyanthuses	10	15
530		3l. Lilies	10	15
531		4l. Orchid	10	15
532		5l. Lilies of the valley	10	15
533		10l. Poppies	10	15
534		25l. Pansies	45	20
535		60l. Gladiolus	1·10	60
536		80l. Wild roses	2·10	90
537		100l. Anemones	3·25	1·70

104 Garibaldi

1957. 150th Birth Anniv of Garibaldi. As T 104 but inscr "COMMEMORAZIONE 150° NASCITA G. GARIBALDI 1807 1957. (a) Size 22×28 mm.

538	-	2l. blue and violet (as No. 391)	15	15
539	-	3l. green and red (as No. 390)	15	15
540	**104**	5l. drab and brown	15	15

(b) Size 26½×37 mm.

541	-	15l. violet and blue (as No. 395)	20	20
542	-	25l. black and green (as No. 396)	55	45
543	-	50l. brown and violet (as No. 394)	1·70	1·30
544	**104**	100l. violet and brown	3·25	1·60

134 St. Marinus and Fair Entrance

1958. 36th Milan Fair.

545	**134**	15l. yellow & bl (postage)	30	25
546	-	60l. green and red	55	55
547	-	125l. blue and brown (air)	4·25	3·00

DESIGNS—HORIZ: 60l. Italian pavilion and giant arch. VERT: 125l. Bristol 173 Rotocoach helicopter and airplane over fair.

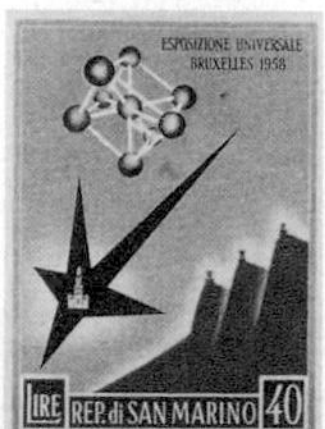

135 Exhibition Emblem, Atomium and Mt. Titano

1958. Brussels International Exhibition.

548	**135**	40l. sepia and green	30	25
549	**135**	60l. lake and blue	70	45

136 View of San Marino

1958. Air.

550	**136**	200l. blue and brown	8·00	2·75
551	-	300l. violet and red	8·00	2·75

DESIGN: 300l. Mt. Titano.

137 Wheat

1958. Fruit and Agricultural Products.

552	**137**	1l. yellow and blue	10	10
553	-	2l. red and green	10	10
554	-	3l. orange and blue	10	10
555	-	4l. red and green	10	10
556	-	5l. yellow, green and blue	10	10
557	**137**	15l. yellow, brown & blue	10	10
558	-	25l. multicoloured	55	10
559	-	40l. multicoloured	1·30	45
560	-	80l. multicoloured	2·20	1·40
561	-	125l. multicoloured	6·00	3·25

DESIGNS: 2, 125l. Maize; 3, 80l. Grapes; 4, 25l. Peaches; 5, 40l. Plums.

138 Naples 10 grana stamp of 1858 and Bay of Naples

1958. Centenary of First Naples Postage Stamps.

562	**138**	25l. brown & blue (postage)	30	25
563	**138**	125l. brown and bistre (air)	4·25	2·00

The Naples stamp on No. 563 is the 50gr.

139 Mediterranean Gull

1959. Air. Native Birds.

564	**139**	5l. black and green	30	20
565	-	10l. brown, black and blue	30	20
566	-	15l. multicoloured	55	25
567	-	120l. multicoloured	2·20	75
568	-	250l. black, yellow & green	4·50	2·20

BIRDS: 10l. Common kestrel; 15l. Mallard; 120l. Feral rock dove; 250l. Barn swallow.

140 P. de Coubertin (founder)

1959. Pre-Olympic Games Issue.

569	**140**	2l. black & brn (postage)	10	10
570	-	3l. sepia and mauve	10	10
571	-	5l. green and blue	10	10
572	-	30l. black and violet	10	10
573	-	60l. sepia and green	35	20
574	-	80l. green and lake	45	20
575	-	120l. brown (air)	7·75	2·50

PORTRAITS—As Type **140**: 3l. A. Bonacossa; 5l. A. Brundage; 30l. C. Montu; 60l. J. S. Edstrom; 80l. De Baillet-Latour. HORIZ: (36×21½ mm): 120l. De Coubertin and Olympic Flame. All, except the founder, De Coubertin are executives of the Olympic Games Committee.

141 Vickers Viscount 700 Airliner over Mt. Titano

1959. Air. Alitalia Inaugural Flight, Rimini–London.

576	**141**	120l. violet	3·00	1·70

142 Abraham Lincoln and Scroll

1959. Abraham Lincoln's 150th Birth Anniv. Inscr "ABRAMO LINCOLN 1809–1959".

577	**142**	5l. brn & sepia (postage)	10	10
578	-	10l. green and blue	10	10
579	-	15k. grey and green	10	10
580	-	70k. violet	20	50
581	-	200l. blue (air)	10·50	3·75

DESIGNS—Portraits of Lincoln with: HORIZ: 10l. Map of San Marino; 15l. Govt Palace, San Marino; 200l. Mt. Titano. VERT: 70l. Mt. Titano.

143 1859 Romagna ½b. stamp and Arch of Augustus, Rimini

1959. Romagna Stamp Centenary. Inscr "1859–1959".

582	**143**	30l. brown & sepia (postage)	30	25
583	-	120l. green and black (air)	3·00	2·00

DESIGN: 120 1. 1989 Romagna 3l. stamp and view of Bologna.

1959. World University Games, Turin. Inscr "UNIVERSITY TORINO 1959".

584	**120**	30l. red	90	65

144 Portal of Messina Cathedral and ½gr. Sicily stamp

1959. Centenary of First Sicilian Postage Stamp.

585	**144**	1l. brown & yell (postage)	10	10
586	-	2l. red and green	10	10
587	-	3l. slate and blue	10	10
588	-	4l. brown and red	10	10
589	-	5l. purple and blue	10	10
590	-	25l. multicoloured	15	20
591	-	60l. multicoloured	20	25
592	-	200l. multicoloured (air)	3·50	1·40

DESIGNS—VERT: 2l. Selinunte Temple (1gr.); 3l. Erice Church (2gr.); 4l. "Concordia" Temple, Agrigento (5gr.); 5l. "Castor and Pollux" Temple, Agrigento (10gr.); 25l. "St. John of the Hermits" Church, Palermo (20gr.). HORIZ: 60l. Taormina (50gr.); 200l. Bay of Palermo (50gr.).

145 Golden Oriole

1960. Birds.

593	**145**	1l. yellow, olive and blue	20	20
594	-	2l. brown, red and green	20	20
595	-	3l. red, brown and green	20	20
596	-	4l. black, brown and green	20	20
597	-	5l. red, brown and green	20	25
598	-	10l. multicoloured	30	25
599	-	25l. multicoloured	1·10	50
600	-	60l. multicoloured	2·20	1·40
601	-	80l. multicoloured	3·50	2·75
602	-	110l. multicoloured	6·75	4·75

DESIGNS—VERT: 2l. Nightingale; 4l. Hoopoe; 10l. Eurasian goldfinch; 25l. River kingfisher; 80l. Green woodpecker; 110l. Red-breasted flycatcher. HORIZ: 3l. Eurasian woodcock; 5l. Red-legged partridge; 60l. Common pheasant.

146 Putting the Shot

1960. Olympic Games.

603	**146**	1l. violet and red (postage)	10	10
604	-	2l. orange and black	10	10
605	-	3l. violet and brown	10	10
606	-	4l. brown and red	10	10
607	-	5l. blue and brown	10	10
608	-	10l. blue and brown	10	10
609	-	15l. violet and green	10	15
610	-	25l. orange and green	10	15
611	-	60l. brown and green	45	20
612	-	110l. red, black and green	65	30
613	-	20l. violet (air)	10	30
614	-	40l. red and brown	30	25
615	-	80l. yellow and blue	30	25
616	-	125l. brown and red	55	55
MS616a		90×125 mm. 1, 2, 3, 60l. brown, green and light green	3·25	3·25
MS616b		90×127 mm. 4, 10, 20, 40l. brown, red and light red	3·25	3·25
MS616c		145×100 mm. 5, 15, 25, 80, 110, 125l. brown, deep brown and light green	5·75	5·75

DESIGNS—VERT: 2l. Gymnastics; 3l. Long-distance walking; 4l. Boxing; 10l. Cycling; 20l. Handball; 40l. Breasting the tape; 60l. Football. HORIZ: 5l. Fencing; 15l. Hockey; 25l. Rowing; 80l. Diving; 110l. Horse-jumping; 125l. Rifle shooting.

147 Melvin Jones (founder) and Lions International H.Q.

1960. Lions International Commemoration.

617		30l. brown and violet (postage)	30	30
618	**147**	45l. brown and violet	55	30
619	-	60l. red and blue	30	30
620	-	115l. green and black	55	60
621	-	150l. brown and violet	4·00	2·50
622	-	200l. blue and green (air)	21·00	8·00

DESIGNS—VERT: 30l. Mt. Titano; 60l. San Marino Government Palace. HORIZ: 115l. Pres. Clarence Sturm; 150l. Vice-Pres. Finis E. Davis; 200l. Globe. All designs except Type **147** bear the Lions emblem.

148 Riccione

1960. 12th Riccione–San Marino Stamp Day. Centres multicoloured.

623	**148**	30l. red (postage)	20	20
624	**148**	125l. blue (air)	3·00	1·40

149 "Youth with Basket of Fruit"

1960. 350th Death Anniv of Caravaggio (painter).

625	**149**	200l. multicoloured	18·00	8·00

150 Hunting Roe Deer

1961. Hunting (1st issue). Historical Scenes.

626	**150**	1l. blue and mauve	10	10
627	-	2l. red and brown	10	10
628	-	3l. black and red	10	10
629	-	4l. red and blue	10	10
630	-	5l. brown and green	10	10
631	-	10l. violet and orange	10	10
632	-	30l. blue and yellow	15	15
633	-	60l. brown, orange & black	20	20
634	-	70l. red, purple and green	30	20
635	-	115l. blue, purple & black	85	35

DESIGNS—VERT: 2l. 16th-cent falconer; 10l. 16th-cent falconer (mounted); 60l. 17th-century hunter with rifle and dog. HORIZ: 3l. 16th-cent wild boar hunt; 4l. Duck-shooting with crossbow (16th-cent); 5l. 16th-cent stag hunt with bow and arrow; 30l. 17th-cent huntsman with horn and dogs; 70l. 18th-cent hunter and beater; 115l. Duck-shooting with bow and arrow (18th-cent).

See also Nos. 679/88.

151 Bell 47J Ranger Helicopter near Mt. Titano

1961. Air.

636	**151**	1000l. red	60·00	44·00

152 Guaita Tower, Mt. Titano and 1858 Sardinian Stamp

1961. Centenary of Italian Independence Philatelic Exhibition, Turin.

637	**152**	30l. multicoloured	35	50
638	**152**	70l. multicoloured	55	70
639	**152**	200l. multicoloured	1·80	1·20

153 Mt. Titano

1961. Europe.

640	**153**	500l. green and brown	50·00	22·00

155 King Enzo's Palace, Bologna

1961. Bologna Stamp Exn. Inscr "BOLOGNA".

641	**155**	30l. black and blue	15	15
642	-	70l. black and myrtle	20	20
643	-	100l. black and brown	20	30

DESIGNS: 70l. Gateway of Merchant's Palace; 100l. Towers of Garisenda and Asinelli, Bologna.

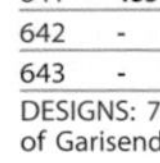

156 Duryea, 1892

1962. Veteran Motor Cars.

644	**156**	1l. blue and brown	10	15
645	-	2l. orange and blue	10	15
646	-	3l. orange and black	10	15
647	-	4l. red and black	10	15
648	-	5l. orange and violet	10	15
649	-	10l. orange and black	10	15
650	-	15l. red and black	10	15
651	-	20l. blue and black	10	30
652	-	25l. orange and black	10	30
653	-	30l. buff and black	10	30
654	-	50l. mauve and black	15	30
655	-	70l. green and black	20	30
656	-	100l. red, yellow and black	55	50
657	-	115l. green, orange & black	80	60
658	-	150l. yellow, orange & black	1·00	90

MOTOR CARS—HORIZ: 2l. Panhard and Levassor, 1895; 3l. Peugeot "Vis-a-vis", 1895; 4l. Daimler, 1899; 10l. Decauville, 1900; 15l. Wolseley, 1901; 20l. Benz, 1902; 25l. Napier, 1903; 50l. Oldsmobile, 1904; 100l. Isotta Fraschini, 1908; 115l. Bianchi, 1910; 150l. Alfa, 1910. VERT: 5l. F.I.A.T., 1899; 30l. White, 1903; 70l. Renault, 1904.

157 Wright Type A Biplane

1962. Vintage Aircraft.

659	**157**	1l. black and yellow	10	20
660	-	2l. brown and green	10	20
661	-	3l. brown and green	10	20
662	-	4l. black and bistre	10	20
663	-	5l. red and blue	10	20
664	-	10l. brown and green	10	30
665	-	30l. bistre and blue	10	35
666	-	60l. bistre and violet	35	35
667	-	70l. black and orange	35	50
668	-	115l. bistre, black & green	1·70	1·00

DESIGNS: 2l. Archdeacon-Voisin "Boxkite" float glider; 3l. Albert and Emile Bonnet-Labranche biplane; 4l. Glenn Curtiss "June Bug"; 5l. Henri Farman H.F.III biplane; 10l. Bleriot XI, 30l. Hubert Latham's Antoinette IV; 60l. Alberto Santos-Dumont's biplane "14 bis"; 70l. Alliott Verdon Roe's Triplane II; 115l. Faccioli's airplane.

158 Roping Down

1962. Mountaineering.

669	**158**	1l. bistre and black	10	15
670	-	2l. turquoise and black	10	15
671	-	3l. purple and black	10	15
672	-	4l. blue and black	10	15
673	-	5l. orange and black	10	15
674	-	15l. yellow and black	10	15
675	-	30l. red and black	10	15
676	-	40l. blue and black	10	15
677	-	85l. green and black	20	20
678	-	115l. blue and black	65	65

DESIGNS: 2l. Sassolungo; 3l. Mt. Titano; 4l. Three Lavaredo peaks; 5l. The Matterhorn; 15l. Skier; 30l. Climber negotiating overhang; 40l. Step-cutting in ice; 85l. Aiguille du Geant; 115l. Citadel on Mt. Titano.

159 Hunter and Retriever

1962. Hunting (2nd issue). Modern scenes.

679	**159**	1l. deep purple and green	10	15
680	-	2l. blue and orange	10	15
681	-	3l. black and blue	10	15
682	-	4l. sepia and brown	10	15
683	-	5l. brown and green	10	15
684	-	15l. black and green	10	15
685	-	50l. sepia and green	30	30
686	-	70l. turquoise and red	30	30
687	-	100l. black and red	30	30
688	-	150l. green and lilac	90	55

DESIGNS—HORIZ: 3l. Marsh ducks (with decoys); 4l. Roe deer; 5l. Grey partridge; 15l. Northern lapwing; 50l. Partridge; 70l. Marsh geese; 100l. Wild boar. VERT: 2l. Huntsman and hounds; 150l. Hunter shooting pheasant.

160 Arrows encircling "Europa"

1962. Europa.

689	**160**	200l. red and black	3·25	1·40

161 Egyptian Merchant Ship, 2000 B.C.

1963. Historical Ships.

690	**161**	1l. blue and orange	10	15
691	-	2l. sepia and purple	10	15
692	-	3l. sepia and mauve	10	15
693	-	4l. dull purple and grey	10	15
694	-	5l. sepia and yellow	10	15
695	-	10l. brown and green	10	15
696	-	30l. sepia and blue	55	55
697	-	60l. blue and green	55	60
698	-	70l. red and deep grey	55	70
699	-	115l. brown and blue	3·75	2·00

DESIGNS—HORIZ: 2l. Greek trier, 5th-cent, B.C.; 3l. Roman trireme, 1st-cent, B.C.; 4l. Viking longship, 10th-cent; 5l. The "Santa Maria"; 30l. Gallery, c. 1600; 115l. "Duncan Dunbar" (full-rigged merchantman), 1550. VERT: 10l. Carrack, c. 1550; 60l. "Sovereign of the Seas" (English galleon), 1637; 70l. "Fyn" (Danish ship of the line), c. 1750.

162 "The Fornarina" (or "The Veiled Woman")

1963. Paintings by Raphael. Multicoloured.

700		30l. Type **162**	10	20
701		70l. Self portrait	15	20
702		100l. Sistine Madonna (detail of woman praying)	20	30
703		200l. "Portrait of a Young Woman" (Maddalena Strozzi)	55	80

The 200l. is larger, 27×44 mm.

163 Saracen Game, Arezzo

1963. Ancient Tournaments.

704	**163**	1l. mauve	10	15
705	-	2l. black	10	15
706	-	3l. black	10	15
707	-	4l. violet	10	15
708	-	5l. violet	10	15
709	-	10l. green	10	15
710	-	30l. red	10	15
711	-	60l. blue	15	15
712	-	70l. brown	20	20
713	-	115l. black	55	30

TOURNAMENTS—HORIZ: 2l. 14th-century, French cavaliers; 4l. 15th-century, Presenting arms to an English cavalier; 30l. Quintana game, Foligno; 70l. 15th-century, Cavaliers (from castle mural, Malpaga). VERT: 3l. Crossbow Champion-ships, Gubbio; 5l. 16th-century, Cavaliers, Florence; 10l. Quintana game, Ascoli Piceno; 60l. Palio (horse-race), Siena; 115l. 13th-century, The Crusades: cavaliers' challenge.

164 Peacock

1963. Butterflies. Multicoloured.

714		25l. Type **164**	20	20
715		30l. "Nessaea obrinus"	20	20
716		60l. Large tortoiseshell	20	20
717		70l. Peacock (horiz)	35	45
718		115l. "Papilio blumei" (horiz)	65	55

165 Corner of Government Palace, San Marino

1963. San Marino–Riccione Stamp Fair.

719	**165**	100l. black and blue	20	20
720	-	100l. blue and sepia	20	20

DESIGN: No. 720, Fountain, Riccione.

166 Pole Vaulting

1963. Olympic Games, Tokyo (1964) (1st issue).

721		1l. purple and orange	10	10
722	**166**	2l. sepia and green	10	10
723	-	3l. sepia and blue	10	10
724	-	4l. sepia and blue	10	10
725	-	5l. sepia and red	10	10
726	-	10l. mauve and purple	10	10
727	-	30l. purple and grey	10	10
728	-	60l. sepia and yellow	10	10
729	-	70l. sepia and blue	35	10
730	-	115l. sepia and green	45	10

SPORTS—HORIZ: 1l. Hurdling; 3l. Relay-racing; 4l. High jumping (men); 5l. Football; 10l. High jumping (women); 60l. Throwing the javelin; 70l. Water polo; 115l. Throwing the hammer. VERT: 30l. Throwing the discus.

See also Nos. 743/52.

167 "E" and Flag of San Marino

1963. Europa.

731	**167**	200l. blue and brown	1·00	45

168 Tupolev Tu-104A Jetliner

1963. Air. Contemporary Aircraft.

732	**168**	5l. purple, brown and blue	15	15
733	-	10l. blue and red	15	15
734	-	15l. red, mauve and violet	15	15
735	-	25l. red, mauve and violet	15	15
736	-	50l. red and blue	20	15
737	-	75l. orange and green	20	15
738	-	120l. red and blue	35	30
739	-	200l. black and yellow	65	20
740	-	300l. black and orange	90	45
741	-	500l. multicoloured	7·25	5·50
742	-	1000l. multicoloured	4·00	2·75

DESIGNS—HORIZ: 15l. Douglas DC-8 jetliner; 25, 1000l. Boeing 707 jetliner (different views); 50l. Vickers Viscount 837 airliner; 120l. Vickers VC-10; 200l. Hawker Siddley Comet 4C jetliner; 300l. Boeing 727-100 jetliner. VERT: 10l. Boeing 707 jetliner; 75l. Sud Aviation SE 210 Caravelle jetliner; 500l. Rolls Royce Dart 527 turboprop engine.

169 Running

1964. Olympic Games, Tokyo (2nd issue).

743	**169**	1l. brown and green	15	10
744	-	2l. brown and sepia	15	10
745	-	3l. brown and black	15	10
746	-	4l. blue and red	15	10
747	-	5l. brown and blue	15	10
748	-	15l. purple and orange	15	10
749	-	30l. blue and light blue	15	10
750	-	70l. brown and green	15	10
751	-	120l. brown and blue	30	10
752	-	150l. purple and red	45	30

DESIGNS—VERT: 2l. Gymnastics; 3l. Basketball; 120l. Cycling; 150l. Fencing. HORIZ: 4l. Pistol-shooting; 5l. Rowing; 15l. Long jumping; 30l. Diving; 70l. Sprinting.

1964. "Towards Tokyo" Sports Stamp Exn, Rimini. As Nos. 749/50, but inscr "VERSO TOKIO" and colours changed.

753		30l. blue and violet	20	15
754		70l. brown and turquoise	20	15

170 Murray Blenkinsop Rack Locomotive (1812)

1964. "Story of the Locomotive".

755	**170**	1l. black and buff	10	10
756	-	2l. black and green	10	10
757	-	3l. black and violet	10	10
758	-	4l. black and yellow	10	10
759	-	5l. black and salmon	10	10
760	-	15l. black and green	15	10
761	-	20l. black and pink	15	15
762	-	50l. black and blue	20	15
763	-	90l. black and orange	30	15
764	-	110l. black and blue	45	30

LOCOMOTIVES: 2l. "Puffing Billy" (1813–14); 3l. "Locomotion" (1825); 4l. "Rocket" (1829); 5l. "Lion" (1838); 15l. "Bayard" (1839); 20l. Crampton type No. 125, France (1849); 50l. "Little England" (1851); 90l. "Spitfire", Canada (1855); 110l. Rogers, U.S.A. (c. 1865).

171 Baseball Players

1964. 7th European Baseball Championships, Milan.

765	**171**	30l. sepia and green	20	15
766	-	70l. black and red	35	30

DESIGN: 70l. Player pitching ball.

172 "E" and Part of Globe

1964. Europa.

767	**172**	200l. red, blue & light blue	3·00	55

173 Pres. Kennedy giving Inaugural Address

1964. 1st Death Anniv of John F. Kennedy (President of U.S.A.). Multicoloured.

768		70l. Type **173**	20	15
769		130l. Pres. Kennedy and U.S. flag (vert)	20	30

174 Cyclists at Government Palace

1965. Cycle Tour of Italy.

770	**174**	30l. sepia	15	15
771	-	70l. purple	15	15
772	-	200l. red	30	30

DESIGNS—Cyclists passing: 70l. "The Rock"; 200l. Mt. Titano.

175 Brontosaurus

1965. Prehistoric Animals.

773	**175**	1l. purple and green	10	15
774	-	2l. black and blue	10	15
775	-	3l. yellow and green	10	15
776	-	4l. brown and blue	10	15
777	-	5l. purple and green	10	15
778	-	10l. purple and green	10	15
779	-	75l. blue and turquoise	30	20
780	-	100l. purple and green	40	55
781	-	200l. purple and green	80	60

ANIMALS—VERT: 2l. Brachyosaurus. HORIZ: 3l. Pteranodon; 4l. Elasmosaurus; 5l. Tyrannosaurus; 10l. Stegosaurus; 75l. Thamatosaurus Victor; 100l. Iguanodon; 200l. Triceratops.

176 Rooks on Chessboard

1965. Europa.

782	**176**	200l. multicoloured	50	40

177 Dante

1965. 700th Anniv of Dante's Birth.

783	**177**	40l. sepia and blue	20	15
784	-	90l. sepia and red	20	15
785	-	130l. sepia and brown	35	15
786	-	140l. sepia and blue	35	30

DESIGNS: 90l. "Hell"; 130l. "Purgatory"; 140l. "Paradise".

178 Mt. Titano and Flags

1965. Visit of Pres. Saragat of Italy.

787	**178**	115l. multicoloured	30	30

179 Trotting

1966. Equestrian Sports. Multicoloured.

788		10l. Type **179**	20	15
789		20l. Cross-country racing (vert)	20	15
790		40l. Horse-jumping	20	15
791		70l. Horse-racing	20	15
792		90l. Steeple-chasing	20	15
793		170l. Polo (vert)	35	20

1966. New values in previous designs.

794		5l. brown and blue (as No. 522a)	15	10
795		10l. green and black (as No. 524)	15	10
796		15l. violet and brown (as No. 524a)	15	10
797		40l. red and lilac (as No. 491)	15	10
798		90l. blue and black (as No. 492)	15	10
799		140l. orange and violet (as No. 493)	35	10

180 "La Bella"

1966. Paintings by Titian. Multicoloured.

800		40l. Type **180**	20	15
801		90l. "The Three Graces"	20	15
802		100l. "The Three Graces"	20	20
803		170l. "Sacred and Profane Love"	45	45

The 90 and 100l. show different details from the picture.

181 Stone Bass

1966. Sea Animals. Multicoloured.

804		1l. Type **181**	15	15
805		2l. Cuckoo wrasse	15	15
806		3l. Common dolphin	15	15
807		4l. John Dory	15	15
808		5l. Octopus (vert)	15	15
809		10l. Red scorpionfish	15	15
810		40l. Eyed electric ray (vert)	15	15
811		90l. Medusa (vert)	15	15
812		115l. Long-snouted seahorse (vert)	35	20
813		130l. Dentex seabream	35	20

182 Our Lady of Europe

1966. Europa.

814	182	200l. multicoloured	45	35

183 Peony

1967. Flowers. Multicoloured.

815	5l. Type **183**	10	15
816	10l. Campanula	10	15
817	15l. Pyrenean poppy	10	15
818	20l. Purple deadnettle	10	15
819	40l. Hemerocallis	10	15
820	140l. Gentian	10	15
821	170l. Thistle	35	15

Each flower has a different background view of Mt. Titano.

184 St. Marinus

1967. Paintings by Francesco Barbieri (Guercino). Multicoloured.

822	40l. Type **184**	10	20
823	170l. "St. Francis"	45	45
824	190l. "Return of the Prodigal Son" (45×37 mm)	50	45

185 Map of Europe

1967. Europa.

825	185	200l. green and orange	65	35

186 Caesar's Mushroom

1967. Fungi. Multicoloured.

826	5l. Type **186**	15	10
827	15l. The Miller	15	10
828	20l. Parasol mushroom	15	10
829	40l. Cep	15	10
830	50l. "Russula paludosa"	15	10
831	170l. St. George's mushroom	35	30

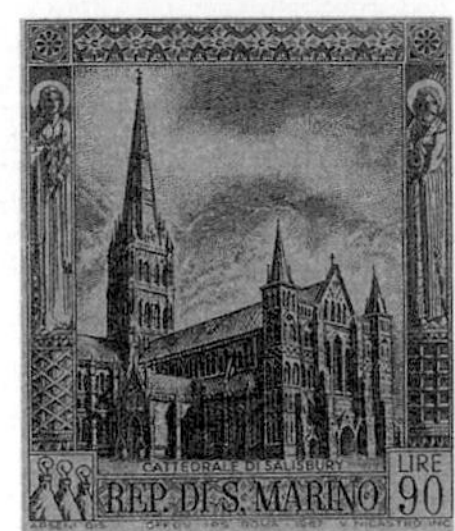

187 Salisbury Cathedral

1967. Gothic Cathedrals.

832	-	20l. violet on cream	15	15
833	-	40l. green on cream	15	15
834	-	80l. blue on cream	15	15
835	187	90l. sepia on cream	15	15
836	-	170l. red on cream	40	35

DESIGNS: 20l. Amiens; 40l. Siena; 80l. Toledo; 170l. Cologne.

188 Cimabue Crucifix, Florence

1967. Christmas.

837	188	300l. brown and violet	80	50

189 Arms of San Marino

1968. Arms of San Marino Villages. Mult.

838	2l. Type **189**	10	15
839	3l. Penna Rossa	10	15
840	5l. Fiorentino	10	15
841	10l. Montecerreto	10	15
842	25l. Serravalle	10	15
843	35l. Montegiardino	10	15
844	50l. Faetano	10	15
845	90l. Borgo Maggiore	10	15
846	180l. Montelupo	30	15
847	500l. State crest	55	35

190 Europa "Key"

1968. Europa.

848	190	250l. brown	65	45

191 "The Battle of San Romano" (detail, P. Uccello)

1968. 671st Birth Anniv of Paolo Uccello (painter).

849	191	50l. black on lilac	10	15
850	-	90l. black on lilac (vert)	10	15
851	-	130l. black on lilac	10	15
852	-	230l. black on pink	55	35

All stamps show details of "The Battle of San Romano".

192 "The Nativity" (detail, Botticelli)

1968. Christmas.

853	192	50l. blue	15	15
854	192	90l. red	20	15
855	192	180l. sepia	35	30

193 "Peace"

1969. "The Good Government" (frescoes) by Ambrogio Lorenzetti.

856	193	50l. blue	10	10
857	-	80l. sepia	15	10
858	-	90l. violet	20	10
859	-	180l. red	35	20

DESIGNS—VERT: 80l. "Justice"; 90l. "Temper- ance". HORIZ: 180l. View of Siena.

194 "Young Soldier" (Bramante)

1969. 525th Birth Anniv of Donato Bramante (architect and painter). Multicoloured.

860	50l. Type **194**	20	15
861	90l. "Old Soldier" (Bramante)	35	15

195 Colonnade

1969. Europa.

862	195	50l. green	35	20
863	195	180l. purple	1·00	20

196 Benched Carriage ("Char-a-banc")

1969. Horses and Carriages. Multicoloured.

864	5l. Type **196**	10	15
865	10l. Barouche	10	15
866	25l. Private drag	10	15
867	40l. Hansom cab	10	15
868	50l. Curricle	10	15
869	90l. Wagonette	10	20
870	180l. Spider phaeton	35	30

197 Mt. Titano

1969. Paintings by R. Viola. Multicoloured.

871	20l. Type **197**	20	15
872	180l. "Pier at Rimini"	45	30
873	200l. "Pier at Riccione" (horiz)	45	45

198 "Faith"

1969. Christmas. "The Theological Virtues" by Raphael.

874	198	20l. violet and orange	20	15
875	-	180l. violet and green	35	30
876	-	200l. violet and buff	45	45

DESIGNS: 180l. "Hope"; 200l. "Charity".

199 "Aries"

1970. Signs of the Zodiac. Multicoloured.

877	1l. Type **199**	10	10
878	2l. "Taurus"	10	10
879	3l. "Gemini"	10	10
880	4l. "Cancer"	10	10
881	5l. "Leo"	10	10
882	10l. "Virgo"	10	10
883	15l. "Libra"	10	10
884	20l. "Scorpio"	10	10
885	70l. "Sagittarius"	10	30
886	90l. "Capricorn"	10	30
887	100l. "Aquarius"	30	35
888	180l. "Pisces"	45	55

200 "Flaming Sun"

1970. Europa.

889	200	90l. red and green	35	20
890	200	180l. red and yellow	55	45

201 "The Fleet in the Bay of Naples" (Pieter Brueghel the Elder)

1970. 10th "Europa" Stamp Exhibition, Naples.

891	201	230l. multicoloured	45	40

202 St. Francis' Gate

1970. 65th Anniv of Rotary International and 10th Anniv of San Marino Rotary Club. Multicoloured.

892	180l. Type **202**	35	35
893	220l. "Rocco" Fort, Mt. Titano	55	55

203 "Girl with Mandolin"

1970. Death Bicentenary of Giambattista Tiepolo (painter).

894	50l. Type **203**	20	15
895	180l. "Girl with Parrot"	20	45
896	220l. "Rinaldo and Armida Surprised"	20	60

SIZES: 180l. As Type **203**; 220l. 57×37 mm.

204 Black Pete

1970. 4th Death Anniv of Walt Disney (film producer). Cartoon Characters. Multicoloured.

897	1l. Type **204**	15	15
898	2l. Gyro Gearloose	15	15
899	3l. Pluto	15	15
900	4l. Minnie Mouse	15	15
901	5l. Donald Duck	15	15
902	10l. Goofy	15	15
903	15l. Scrooge McDuck	15	15
904	50l. Hewey, Dewey and Louie	80	35
905	90l. Mickey Mouse	1·30	1·10
906	220l. Walt Disney and scene from "The Jungle Book" (horiz)	7·25	5·50

205 "Customs House, Venice"

1971. "Save Venice" Campaign. Paintings by Canaletto. Multicoloured.

907	20l. Type **205**	20	20
908	180l. "Grand Canal, Balbi Palace and Rialto Bridge, Venice"	80	55
909	200l. "St. Mark's and Doge's Palace"	90	60

206 Congress Building and San Marino Flag

1971. Italian Philatelic Press Union Congress, San Marino. Multicoloured.

910	20l. Type **206**	10	10
911	90l. Government Palace door and emblems (vert)	10	10
912	180l. Type **206**	35	20

207 Europa Chain

1971. Europa.

913	**207**	50l. blue and yellow	35	15
914	**207**	90l. orange and blue	55	20

208 "Duck" Jug with "Lasa" Decoration

1971. Etruscan Art (1st series).

915	**208**	50l. black and orange	10	15
916	-	80l. black and green	10	15
917	-	90l. black and green	10	20
918	-	180l. black and orange	55	30

DESIGNS—VERT: 80l. Head of Hermes (bust); 90l. Man and Wife (relief on sarcophagus). HORIZ: 180l. Chimera (bronze).

See also Nos. 1018/21.

209 Day Lily

1971. Flowers. Multicoloured.

919	1l. Type **209**	10	10
920	2l. "Phlox paniculata"	10	10
921	3l. Wild pink	10	10
922	4l. Globe flower	10	10
923	5l. "Centaurea dealbata"	10	10
924	10l. Peony	10	10
925	15l. Christmas rose	10	10
926	50l. Pasque flower	10	10
927	90l. "Gaillardia aristata"	10	10
928	220l. "Aster dumosus"	45	30

210 "Allegory of Spring" (detail, Botticelli)

1972. "Allegory of Spring" by Sandro Botticelli. Multicoloured.

929	50l. Type **210**	20	20
930	190l. The Three Graces (27×37 mm)	55	35
931	220l. Flora	65	50

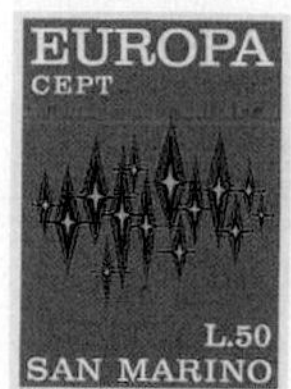

211 "Communications"

1972. Europa.

932	**211**	50l. multicoloured	65	15
933	**211**	90l. multicoloured	55	20

212 "Taming the Bear"

1972. "Life of St. Marinus". 16th-century paintings from former Government Palace.

934	**212**	25l. black and buff	10	10
935	-	55l. black and orange	15	10
936	-	100l. black and blue	20	10
937	-	130l. black and yellow	30	20

DESIGNS: 55l. "The Conversion of Donna Felicissima"; 100l. "Hostile archers turned to stone"; 130l. "Mount Titano given to St. Marinus".

213 House Sparrow

1972. Birds. Multicoloured.

938	1l. Type **213**	20	15
939	2l. Firecrest	20	15
940	3l. Blue tit	20	15
941	4l. Ortulan bunting	20	15
942	5l. Bluethroat	20	15
943	10l. Northern bullfinch	20	15
944	25l. Linnet	20	15
945	50l. Black-eared wheatear	20	15
946	90l. Sardinian warbler	35	15
947	220l. Western greenfinch	45	15

214 "Healthy Man"

1972. World Heart Month. Multicoloured.

948	50l. Type **214**	20	10
949	90l. "Sick Man" (horiz)	20	10

215 Veterans Emblem

1972. "Veterans of Philately" Award of Italian Philatelic Federation.

950	**215**	25l. gold and blue	35	30

216 Plane over Mt. Titano

1972. Air.

951	**216**	1000l. multicoloured	2·00	1·60

217 Five-Cent Coin of 1864

1972. San Marino Coinage.

952	**217**	5l. bronze, black and grey	20	10
953	-	10l. bronze, black & orge	20	10
954	-	15l. silver, black and red	20	10
955	-	20l. silver, black and purple	20	10
956	-	25l. silver, black and blue	20	10
957	-	50l. silver, black and blue	20	10
958	-	55l. silver, black and ochre	20	10
959	-	220l. gold, black and green	45	20

COINS (obverse and reverse on each stamp): 10l. 10c. of 1935; 15l. 1l. of 1906; 20l. 5l. of 1898; 25l. 5l. of 1937; 50l. 10l. of 1932; 55l. 20l. of 1938; 220l. 20l. of 1925.

218 New York, 1673

1973. "Interpex" Stamp Exhibition and Important Cities of the World (1st series). New York.

960	**218**	200l. brown, grey & black	35	35
961	-	300l. blue, lilac & deep lilac	45	55

DESIGN: 300l. New York, 1973.

See also Nos. 1032/3, 1075/6, 1144/5, 1160/1, 1197/8, 1215/16, 1230/1, 1259/60, 1271/2, 1306/7, 1331/2, 1358/9 and 1524/5.

219 Printing Press

1973. Tourist Press Congress.

962	**219**	50l. multicoloured	35	30

220 "Sportsmen"

1973. Youth Games.

963	**220**	100l. multicoloured	35	30

221 Europa "Posthorn"

1973. Europa.

964	**221**	20l. green, blue and flesh	30	20
965	**221**	180l. mauve, red and blue	85	35

222 Grapes

1973. Fruits. Multicoloured.

966	1l. Type **222**	10	10
967	2l. Mandarines	10	10
968	3l. Apples	10	10
969	4l. Plums	10	10
970	5l. Strawberries	10	10
971	10l. Pears	10	10
972	25l. Cherries	10	10
973	50l. Pomegranate	10	10
974	90l. Apricots	10	10
975	200l. Peaches	45	20

223 Couzinet 70 F-AMBV "Arc en Ciel"

1973. Aircraft.

976	**223**	25l. blue, yellow and gold	10	10
977	-	55l. blue, grey and gold	10	10
978	-	60l. blue, pink and gold	10	10
979	-	90l. blue, bistre and gold	10	10
980	-	220l. blue, orange and gold	45	35

AIRCRAFT: 55l. Macchi Castoldi MC-72-181 seaplane; 60l. Tupolev ANT-9; 90l. Ryan NYP "Spirit of St. Louis" (Charles Lindburgh's plane); 220l. Handley Page H.P.42.

224 Crossbowman, Serravalle Castle

1973. San Marino's Victory in Crossbow Tournament, Masa Marittima. Multicoloured.

No.	Type	Description	Unused	Used
981		5l. Type **224**	10	10
982		10l. Crossbowman, Pennarossa Castle	10	10
983		15l. Drummer, Montegiardino Castle	10	10
984		20l. Trumpeter, Fiorentino Castle	10	10
985		30l. Crossbowman, Montecerreto Castle	10	10
986		40l. Crossbowman, Borgo Maggiore Castle	10	10
987		50l. Trumpeter, Guaita Castle	10	10
988		80l. Crossbowman, Faetano Castle	10	10
989		200l. Crossbowman, Montelupo Castle	55	30

225 "Adoration of the Magi" (detail)

1973. Christmas. 600th Birth Anniv of Gentile da Fabriano. Details of Gentile's altarpiece "Adoration of the Magi".

No.	Type	Description	Unused	Used
990	225	5l. multicoloured	10	10
991	-	30l. multicoloured	10	10
992	-	115l. multicoloured	20	15
993	-	250l. multicoloured	45	35

226 Combat Shield (16th-century)

1974. Ancient Weapons from "Cesta" Museum, San Marino.

No.	Type	Description	Unused	Used
994	226	5l. black brown and green	10	10
995	-	10l. black, blue & brown	10	10
996	-	15l. black, blue & lt blue	10	10
997	-	20l. black, blue & brown	10	10
998	-	30l. black, brown & blue	10	10
999	-	50l. black, blue and pink	10	10
1000	-	80l. black, blue and lilac	10	10
1001	-	250l. black and yellow	45	30

DESIGNS: 10l. German armour (16th-century); 15l. Crested morion (16th-century); 20l. Horse head-armour (15th–16th century); 30l. Italian morion with crest (16th–17th century); 50l. Gauntlets and sword pommel (16th-century); 80l. Sallet helmet (16th-century); 250l. Sforza shield (16th-century).

227 "The Joy of Living" (Emilio Greco)

1974. Europa. Sculpture.

No.	Type	Description	Unused	Used
1002	227	100l. black and brown	45	30
1003	-	200l. black and green	90	40

DESIGN: 200l. "The Joy of Living" (complete sculpture).

228 "Sea and Mountains"

1974. San Marino–Riccione Stamp Fair.

No.	Type	Description	Unused	Used
1004	228	50l. multicoloured	35	30

229 Arms of Sansepolcro

1974. 9th Crossbow Tournament, San Marino. Arms. Multicoloured.

No.	Type	Description	Unused	Used
1005		15l. Type **229**	55	20
1006		20l. Massa Marittima	55	20
1007		50l. San Marino	55	30
1008		115l. Gubbio	55	60
1009		300l. Lucca	55	90

230 U.P.U. Emblem and Shadow

1974. Centenary of Universal Postal Union.

No.	Type	Description	Unused	Used
1010	230	50l. multicoloured	20	15
1011	230	90l. multicoloured	35	15

231 Glider

1974. Air. 50th Anniv of Gliding in Italy.

No.	Type	Description	Unused	Used
1012	231	40l. blue, green and brown	20	15
1013	-	120l. blue, lt blue & pur	20	20
1014	-	500l. violet, mauve & purple	65	60

DESIGNS: 120, 500l. Gliders in "air currents" (both different).

232 Mt. Titano and Verses of Hymn

1974. Death Centenary of Niccolo Tommaseo (writer).

No.	Type	Description	Unused	Used
1015	232	50l. black, green and red	20	15
1016	-	150l. black, yellow & blue	35	20

DESIGN: 150l. Portrait of Tommaseo.

233 "Madonna and Child" (4th-century painting)

1974. Christmas.

No.	Type	Description	Unused	Used
1017	233	250l. multicoloured	85	45

234 "Dancing Scene", Tomb of the Leopards, Tarquinia

1975. Etruscan Art (2nd series). Tomb Paintings. Multicoloured.

No.	Type	Description	Unused	Used
1018		20l. Type **234**	10	10
1019		30l. "Chariot Race", Tomb of the Hill, Chiusi	10	10
1020		180l. "Achilles and Troillus", Tomb of the Bulls, Tarquinia	35	30
1021		220l. "Dancers", Tomb of the Triclinium, Tarquinia	45	45

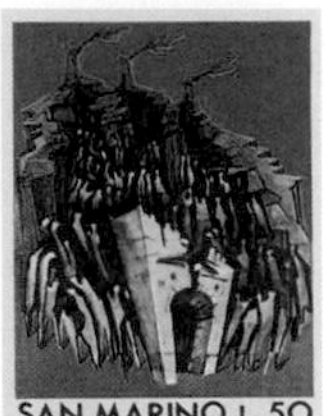

235 "Escape Tunnel"

1975. 30th Anniv of Escape of 100,000 Italian War Refugees to San Marino.

No.	Type	Description	Unused	Used
1022	235	50l. multicoloured	35	30

236 "The Blessing"

1975. Europa. Details from "St. Marinus" by Guercino. Multicoloured.

No.	Type	Description	Unused	Used
1023		100l. Type **236**	55	30
1024		200l. "St. Marinus"	1·10	40

237 "The Virgin Mary"

1975. Holy Year. Details from Frescoes by Giotto from Scrovegni Chapel, Padua. Multicoloured.

No.	Type	Description	Unused	Used
1025		10l. Type **237**	10	15
1026		40l. "Virgin and Child"	10	15
1027		50l. "Heads of Angels"	10	15
1028		100l. "Mary Magdalene" (horiz)	10	15
1029		500l. "Heads of Saints" (horiz)	55	55

238 "Aphrodite" (sculpture)

1975. 15th Europa Stamp Exhibition, Naples.

No.	Type	Description	Unused	Used
1030	238	50l. black, grey and violet	35	30

239 Congress Emblem

1975. "Eurocophar" International Pharmaceutical Congress, San Marino.

No.	Type	Description	Unused	Used
1031	239	100l. multicoloured	35	30

240 Tokyo, 1835

1975. Important Cities of the World (2nd series). Tokyo. Multicoloured.

No.	Type	Description	Unused	Used
1032		200l. Type **240**	35	50
1033		300l. Tokyo, 1975	45	70

241 "Woman on Balcony"

1975. International Women's Year. Paintings by Gentilini. Multicoloured.

No.	Type	Description	Unused	Used
1034		50l. Type **241**	20	10
1035		150l. "Heads of Two Women" (horiz)	40	20
1036		230l. "Profile of Girl"	50	50

242 "Head of the Child" (detail)

1975. Christmas. 500th Birth Anniv of Michelangelo. Painting "Doni Madonna" and details. Multicoloured.

No.	Type	Description	Unused	Used
1037		50l. Type **242**	10	15
1038		100l. "Head of Virgin" (detail)	20	20
1039		250l. "Doni Madonna"	35	50

243 "Modesty"

1976. "The Civil Virtues". Sketches by Emilio Greco.

No.	Type	Description	Unused	Used
1039a	-	5l. black and lilac	10	10
1040	243	10l. black and stone	10	10
1041	-	20l. black and lilac	10	10
1041a	-	35l. black and stone	10	10
1042	-	50l. black and green	10	10
1043	-	70l. black and pink	10	10
1044	-	90l. black and pink	10	10
1045	-	100l. black and pink	10	10
1046	-	120l. black and blue	20	10
1047	-	150l. black and lilac	20	10
1048	-	160l. black and green	30	15
1049	-	170l. black and flesh	30	20
1050	-	220l. black and grey	30	20
1051	-	250l. black and yellow	30	30
1052	-	300l. black and grey	55	35
1053	-	320l. black and mauve	55	45
1054	-	500l. black and stone	55	35
1055	-	1000l. black and blue	1·10	1·10
1055a	-	2000l. black and cream	3·25	2·50

DESIGNS: 5l. "Wisdom"; 20, 160l. "Temperance"; 35l. "Love"; 50, 70l. "Fortitude"; 90, 220l. "Prudence"; 100, 120l. "Altruism"; 150, 170l. "Hope"; 250l. "Justice"; 300, 320l. "Faith"; 500l. "Honesty"; 1000l. "Industry"; 2000l. "Faithfulness".

244 Capitol, Washington

1976. Bicentenary of American Revolution and "Interphil 1976" International Stamp Exhibition, Philadelphia. Multicoloured.

1056	70l. Type **244**	20	15
1057	150l. Statue of Liberty, New York	20	20
1058	180l. Independence Hall, Philadelphia	35	35

245 Emblem and Maple Leaf

1976. Olympic Games, Montreal.

1059	**245**	150l. black and red	35	65

246 Polychrome Plate (U. Bruno)

1976. Europa. Handicrafts. Multicoloured.

1060	150l. Type **246**	65	30
1061	180l. Silver plate (A. Ruscelli)	80	45

247 S.U.M.S. Emblem

1976. Centenary of San Marino Social Welfare Union.

1062	**247**	150l. red, yellow and lilac	35	35

248 Children of Different Races

1976. 30th Anniv of UNESCO.

1063	**248**	180l. brown, orange & blue	30	25
1064	**248**	220l. brown, buff & sepia	40	50

249 "San Marino"

1976. "Italia '76" International Stamp Exhibition, Milan.

1065	**249**	150l. multicoloured	35	35

250 "The Annunciation"

1976. Christmas. 400th Death Anniv of Titian. Multicoloured.

1066	150l. Type **250**	35	45
1067	300l. "The Nativity"	55	80

251 Mount Titano and Emblem

1977. "San Marino 77" International Stamp Exhibition (1st issue).

1068	**251**	80l. red, green and olive (postage)	10	10
1069	**251**	170l. yellow, violet & blue	20	20
1070	**251**	200l. orange, ultram & blue	35	35
1071	**251**	200l. ochre, green and blue (air)	45	35

See also No. 1082.

252 "San Marino" (Ghirlandaio)

1977. Europa. Landscapes. Multicoloured.

1072	170l. Type **252**	90	35
1073	200l. "San Marino" (Guercino)	1·10	55

253 Leonardo da Vinci's Drawing of "Helicopter"

1977. Centenary of Enrico Forlanini's First Vertical Flight Experiment.

1074	**253**	120l. multicoloured	35	30

254 University Square, 1877

1977. Centenary of Rumanian Independence. Important Cities of the World (3rd series). Bucharest.

1075	**254**	200l. green and blue	35	45
1076	-	400l. brown and stone	55	80

DESIGN: 400l. City centre, 1977.

255 Design of First San Marino Stamp

1977. Centenary of San Marino Postage Stamps.

1077	**255**	40l. green	10	10
1078	**255**	70l. blue	10	10
1079	**255**	170l. red	10	15
1080	**255**	500l. brown	40	45
1081	**255**	1000l. lilac	55	85

256 "St. Marinus Blessing" (Retrosi)

1977. "San Marino 1977" International Stamp Exhibition (2nd issue).

1082	**256**	1000l. multicoloured	2·75	2·00

257 Medicinal Plants

1977. Italian Pharmacists' Union Congress.

1083	**257**	170l. multicoloured	35	35

258 Woman gripped by Octopus

1977. World Rheumatism Year.

1084	**258**	200l. multicoloured	35	40

259 Angel

1977. Christmas.

1085	**259**	170l. black, grey & silver	20	20
1086	-	230l. black, grey & silver	35	30
1087	-	300l. black, grey & silver	45	35

DESIGNS: 230l. Palm tree and olive; 300l. The Virgin.

260 Baseball Player

1978. World Baseball Championships.

1088	**260**	90l. black, blue and ultramarine	10	15
1089	**260**	120l. black, light green and green	10	20

261 San Francesco Gate

1978. Europa. Architecture.

1090	**261**	170l. blue and light blue	1·20	35
1091	-	200l. brown and stone	1·60	55

DESIGN: 200l. Ripa Gate.

262 Feather

1978. World Hypertension Month.

1092	**262**	320l. black, blue and red	55	55

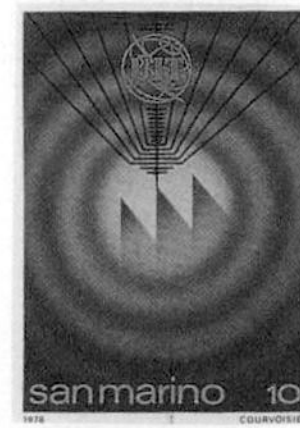

263 Mt. Titano and Antenna

1978. San Marino's Admission to the I.T.U.

1093	**263**	10l. yellow and red	10	10
1094	**263**	200l. blue and violet	20	20

264 Hawk and Slender-billed Gull

1978. 30th San Marino–Riccione Stamp Fair.

1095	**264**	120l. multicoloured	20	20
1096	**264**	170l. multicoloured	35	35

265 Wright "Flyer I"

1978. Air. 75th Anniv of First Powered Flight.

1097	**265**	10l. multicoloured	20	10
1098	**265**	50l. multicoloured	20	10
1099	**265**	200l. multicoloured	35	20

266 Allegory of Human Rights

1978. 30th Anniv of Declaration of Human Rights.

1100	**266**	200l. multicoloured	35	35

267 Holly

1978. Christmas. Multicoloured.

1101	10l. Type **267**	10	10
1102	120l. Star	20	10
1103	170l. Snowflakes	35	20

268 Albert Einstein

1979. Birth Cent of Albert Einstein (physicist).

1104	**268**	120l. brown, sepia and grey	35	30

269 Motor-coach, 1915

1979. Europa. Multicoloured.

1105		170l. Type **269**	2·40	60
1106		220l. Horse-drawn stage-coach	3·00	80

270 San Marino Crossbowmen Federation Emblem

1979. 14th Crossbow Tournament.

1107	**270**	120l. multicoloured	35	30

271 Maigret (G. Simenon)

1979. Fictional Detectives. Multicoloured.

1108		10l. Type **271**	10	15
1109		80l. Perry Mason (S. Gardner)	10	15
1110		150l. Nero Wolfe (R. Stout)	10	15
1111		170l. Ellery Queen (F. Dannay and M. B. Lee)	10	15
1112		220l. Sherlock Holmes (A. Conan Doyle)	45	35

272 Water Skiing

1979. Water Skiing Championships, Castelgandolfo.

1113	**272**	150l. green, blue & black	35	35

273 St. Apollonia

1979. 13th International Stomatology Congress.

1114	**273**	170l. multicoloured	35	35

274 "Knowledge"

1979. International Year of the Child. Mult.

1115		20l. Type **274**	15	10
1116		120l. "Friendship"	20	10
1117		170l. "Equality"	20	15
1118		220l. "Love"	35	35
1119		350l. "Existence"	65	50

275 Horse Chestnut and Red Deer

1979. Environment Protection. Trees and Animals. Multicoloured.

1120		5l. Type **275**	20	10
1121		10l. Cedar of Lebanon and golden eagle	20	10
1122		35l. Flowering dogwood and common racoon	20	10
1123		50l. Banyan and tiger	20	10
1124		70l. Stone pine and hoopoe	20	10
1125		90l. Larch and yellow-throated marten	20	10
1126		100l. Tasmanian blue gum and koala	20	10
1127		120l. Date palm and dromedary	20	10
1128		150l. Silver maple and American beaver	30	20
1129		170l. Baobab and African elephant	35	30

276 "Disturbing Muses"

1979. 1st Death Anniv of Giorgio de Chirico (painter). Multicoloured.

1130		40l. Type **276**	10	10
1131		150l. "Ancient Horses"	35	20
1132		170l. "Self-portrait"	35	30

277 St. Joseph

1979. Christmas. "The Holy Family" (fresco) by Antonio Alberti or details from it.

1133		80l. Type **277**	20	15
1134		170l. Infant Jesus	30	15
1135		220l. Magus	40	35
1136		320l. "The Holy Family"	65	60

278 St. Benedict of Nursia

1980. 1500th Birth Anniv of Saint Benedict of Nursia (founder of Benedictine Order).

1137	**278**	170l. multicoloured	35	35

279 Cigarette Ends

1980. Anti-smoking Campaign. Multicoloured.

1138		120l. Type **279**	20	20
1139		220l. Face hidden by cigarettes	35	35
1140		520l. Face wreathed in smoke	65	65

280 Naples

1980. "Europa" Stamp Exhibition, Naples.

1141	**280**	170l. multicoloured	35	35

281 Giovanbattista Belluzzi (military architect)

1980. Europa. Multicoloured.

1142		170l. Type **281**	1·80	45
1143		220l. Antonio Orafo (silver and goldsmith)	2·75	50

282 London, 1850

1980. "London 1980" International Stamp Exhibition and Important Cities of the World (4th series). London.

1144	**282**	200l. brown and green	35	45
1145	-	400l. blue and lilac	55	80

DESIGN: 400l. London, 1980.

283 Cycling

1980. Olympic Games, Moscow.

1146	**283**	70l. black, emerald & green	10	10
1147	-	90l. black, orange & brown	10	10
1148	-	170l. black, red & mauve	20	20
1149	-	350l. black, blue & dp blue	55	55
1150	-	450l. black, violet & blue	80	65

DESIGNS: 90l. Basketball; 170l. Running; 350l. Gymnastics; 450l. High jumping.

284 Stolz and Score of "Philatelic Waltz"

1980. Birth Centenary of Robert Stolz (composer).

1151	**284**	120l. blue and black	35	30

285 Weightlifting

1980. European Junior Weightlifting Championship.

1152	**285**	170l. red, black and green	35	35

286 City Fortifications

1980. World Tourism Conference, Manila.

1153	**286**	220l. multicoloured	40	40

287 "The Annunciation" (detail)

1980. Christmas. Details of Paintings by Andrea del Sarto. Multicoloured.

1154		180l. "Madonna of the Harpies" (detail)	35	30
1155		250l. "Annunciation" (Mary)	55	45
1156		500l. Type **287**	1·10	85

288 St. Joseph's Eve Bonfire

1981. Europa. Multicoloured.

1157		200l. Type **288**	2·10	35
1158		300l. National Day fireworks	3·00	55

289 Hands holding Broken Branch

1981. International Year of Disabled Persons.

1159	**289**	300l. yellow, green and light green	45	55

290 "St. Charles' Square, 1817" (Jakob Alt)

1981. "WIPA 1981" International Stamp Exn and Important Cities of the World (5th series). Vienna. Multicoloured.

1160		200l. Type **290**	35	25
1161		300l. St. Charles' Square, 1981	55	50

291 Motor Cyclist

1981. San Marino Motor Cycle Grand Prix.

1162	**291**	200l. multicoloured	35	30

292 Girl playing Pipes

1981. Birth Bimillenary of Virgil (poet).

1163	**292**	300l. grey and silver	35	35
1164	-	550l. grey and silver	65	65
1165	-	1500l. grey and silver	2·20	1·90

DESIGNS: 550l. Soldier; 1500l. Shepherd.

293 House

1981. Urban Development Scheme. Multicoloured.

1167	20l. Type **293**	10	15
1168	80l. Tree (provision of green belts)	10	15
1169	400l. Gas flame (power plants)	55	55

294 Judo

1981. European Junior Judo Championships, San Marino.

1170	**294**	300l. multicoloured	50	45

295 "Girl with Dove" (Picasso)

1981. Birth Centenary of Pablo Picasso (artist). Multicoloured.

1171	150l. Type **295**	20	20
1172	200l. "Homage to Picasso" (detail, Renato Guttuso)	55	50

296 Bread

1981. World Food Day.

1173	**296**	300l. multicoloured	50	45

297 King presenting Gift

1981. Christmas. 500th Birth Anniv of Benvenuto Tisi da Garofalo (artist). Details from "Adoration of the Magi and St. Bartholomew". Multicoloured.

1174	200l. Type **297**	30	30
1175	300l. Kneeling King	50	45
1176	600l. Virgin and Child	1·00	95

298 Cancellation and "San Marino 82" Emblem

1982. Centenary of Postal Stationery.

1177	**298**	200l. multicoloured	35	35

299 "The Cicada and the Ant" (Aesop fable)

1982. Centenary of Savings Bank.

1178	**299**	300l. multicoloured	50	45

300 Assembly of Heads of Families, 1906

1982. Europa. Multicoloured.

1179	300l. Type **300**	4·50	90
1180	450l. Napoleon at the border of San Marino, 1797	6·75	1·30

301 Archimedes

1982. Pioneers of Science.

1181	**301**	20l. red and black	10	10
1182	-	30l. blue and black	10	10
1183	-	40l. brown and black	10	10
1184	-	50l. green and black	10	10
1185	-	60l. red and black	10	10
1186	-	100l. brown and black	10	10
1187	-	150l. brown and black	10	10
1188	-	200l. brown and black	35	30
1189	-	250l. red and black	35	30
1190	-	300l. green and black	45	45
1191	-	350l. green and black	55	35
1192	-	400l. red and black	65	50
1193	-	450l. red and black	65	60
1194	-	1000l. red and black	1·80	1·00
1195	-	1400l. red and black	2·50	2·00
1196	-	5000l. black and blue	6·75	5·25

DESIGNS: 30l. Copernicus; 40l. Isaac Newton; 50l. Antoine Lavoisier; 60l. Marie Curie; 100l. Robert Koch; 150l. Alexander Fleming; 200l. Thomas Edison; 250l. Alessandro Volta; 300l. Guglielmo Marconi; 350l. Evangelista Torricelli; 400l. Carl Linnaeus; 450l. Hippocrates; 1000l. Pythagoras; 1400l. Leonardo da Vinci; 5000l. Galileo.

302 "Notre Dame", 1806 (J. Hill)

1982. "Philexfrance 82" International Stamp Exhibition and Important Cities of the World (6th series). Paris.

1197	**302**	300l. buff and black	45	55
1198	-	450l. multicoloured	65	80

DESIGN: 450l. Notre Dame and Ile de Cite, 1982.

303 Hands and Birds

1982. 800th Birth Anniv of St. Francis of Assisi.

1199	**303**	200l. multicoloured	35	35

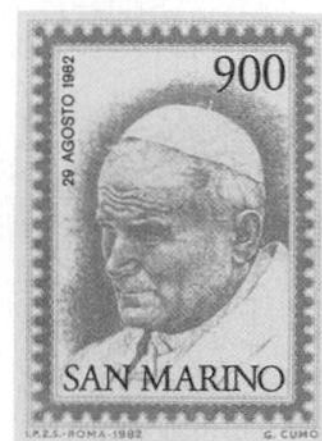

304 Pope John Paul II

1982. Visit of Pope John Paul II to San Marino.

1200	**304**	900l. purple, deep green and green	1·40	1·30

305 Globe encircled by Flag Stamps

1982. 5th Anniv of International Association of Stamp Philatelic Catalogue Editors (ASCAT).

1201	**305**	300l. multicoloured	50	45

306 Face besplattered with Blood

1982. 15th International Congress of Amnesty International, Rimini.

1202	**306**	700l. red and black	1·00	90

307 "Accipe Lampadam Ardentem" (detail)

1982. Christmas. Paintings by Gregorio Sciltian. Multicoloured.

1203	200l. Type **307**	40	35
1204	300l. "Madonna della Citta" (detail)	60	55
1205	450l. Angel (detail, "Accipe Sal Sapientiae")	1·00	80

308 Refugee

1982. "For Refugees".

1206	**308**	300l.+100l. mult	50	45

309 Begni Building and Quill

1983. Centenary of Secondary School.

1207	**309**	300l. multicoloured	50	45

310 Formula One Racing Cars

1983. San Marino Formula One Grand Prix.

1208	**310**	50l. multicoloured	10	10
1209	**310**	350l. multicoloured	45	80

311 Auguste Piccard and Stratosphere Balloon "F.N.R.S."

1983. Europa. Multicoloured.

1210	400l. Type **311**	3·25	1·50
1211	500l. Piccard and bathyscaphe	4·00	1·90

312 Amateur Radio Operator

1983. World Communications Year.

1212	**312**	400l. black, blue and red	55	55
1213	-	500l. black, brown & red	85	85

DESIGN: 500l. Postman on bicycle.

313 Montgolfier Balloon

1983. Bicentenary of Manned Flight.

1214	**313**	500l. multicoloured	80	65

314 "Rio de Janeiro, 1845" (Richard Bate)

1983. "Brasiliana 83" International Stamp Exhibition and Important Cities of the World (7th series). Rio de Janeiro. Multicoloured.

1215	400l. Type **314**	55	60

1216		1400l. Rio de Janeiro, 1983	1·90	1·70

315 Feeding Colt

1983. World Food Programme.

1217	**315**	500l. multicoloured	85	70

316 "Madonna of the Grand Duke"

1983. Christmas. 500th Birth Anniv of Raphael. Multicoloured.

1218		300l. Type **316**	45	55
1219		400l. "Madonna of the Goldfinch" (detail)	55	80
1220		500l. "Madonna of the Chair" (detail)	80	1·10

317 Demetrius Vikelas

1984. 90th Anniv of International Olympic Committee. I.O.C. Presidents.

1221	**317**	300l. black and green	80	70
1222	-	400l. purple and blue	1·00	90
1223	-	550l. lilac and green	1·40	1·10

DESIGNS: 400l. Lord Killanin; 550l. Juan Samaranch.

318 Bridge

1984. Europa. 25th Anniv of C.E.P.T.

1224	**318**	400l. yellow, violet & black	3·25	1·30
1225	**318**	550l. yellow, red & black	4·50	1·70

319 Flag Waver

1984. Flag Wavers. Multicoloured.

1226		300l. Type **319**	45	45
1227		400l. Waver with two flags	65	65

320 Male Athlete

1984. Olympic Games, Los Angeles. Sheet 151×110 mm containing T 320 and similar vert designs. Multicoloured.

MS1228		550l. Type **320**; 1000l. Female athlete	25·00	2·75

321 Motocross

1984. World Motocross Championship.

1229	**321**	450l. multicoloured	65	65

322 Collins Street, 1839

1984. "Ausipex 84" International Stamp Exhibition, and Important Cities of the World (8th series). Melbourne. Multicoloured.

1230		1500l. Type **322**	2·20	2·30
1231		2000l. Collins Street, 1984	2·75	3·00

323 Pres. Pertini and San Marino City

1984. Visit of President Sandro Pertini of Italy.

1232	**323**	1950l. multicoloured	3·00	3·00

324 "Universe"

1984. Youth Philately. Multicoloured.

1233		50l. Type **324**	10	15
1234		100l. Caveman and modern man framed by television ("The Evolution of Life")	20	20
1235		150l. Pipe smoker driving car ("The World in which we Live")	20	20
1236		200l. Man with fig leaf and snake with apple ("Mankind")	30	30
1237		450l. Scientist with H-bomb ("Science")	60	60
1238		550l. Man in barrel with books and candle ("Philosophy")	90	85

325 Angel with Book

1984. Christmas. Designs showing details of "Madonna of San Girolamo" by Correggio. Mult.

1239		400l. Type **325**	65	80
1240		450l. Virgin and Child	90	65
1241		550l. Attendant	1·00	1·10

326 Johann Sebastian Bach and Score

1985. Europa.

1242	**326**	450l. black and brown	3·25	1·60
1243	-	600l. black and green	4·50	2·30

DESIGN: 600l. Vincenzo Bellini and score.

327 State Flags, Stadium and Swimming Pictogram

1985. 1st Small States Games. Multicoloured.

1244		50l. Type **327**	20	15
1245		350l. Flags, stadium and running pictogram	45	45
1246		400l. Flags, stadium and shooting pictogram	55	55
1247		450l. Flags, stadium and cycling pictogram	65	60
1248		600l. Flags, stadium and handball pictogram	1·00	90

328 Sunset and Birds

1985. Emigration.

1249	**328**	600l. multicoloured	1·00	90

329 Face and Hand holding Dove

1985. International Youth Year.

1250	**329**	400l. yellow, blue and gold	55	55
1251	-	600l. gold, blue and yellow	1·00	90

DESIGN: 600l. Girl's face, dove and horse's head.

330 Camera and San Marino

1985. 18th Int Federation of Photographic Art Congress.

1252	**330**	450l. multicoloured	80	80

331 Sun breaking through Clouds and Sapling

1985. 10th Anniv of Helsinki European Security and Co-operation Conference.

1253	**331**	600l. multicoloured	1·00	1·00

332 Don Abbondio and Don Rodrigo's Henchmen

1985. Birth Bicentenary of Alessandro Manzoni (writer). Scenes from "I Promessi Sposi".

1254	**332**	400l. green	55	55
1255	-	450l. brown	65	65
1256	-	600l. blue	90	90

DESIGNS: 450l. Forcing curate to bless wedding; 600l. Plague in Milan.

333 Common Carp caught on Hook

1985. World Angling Championships, River Arno, Florence.

1257	**333**	600l. multicoloured	1·00	1·00

334 Cat (after Pompeian mosaic)

1985. International Feline Federation Congress.

1258	**334**	600l. multicoloured	1·00	1·00

335 Colosseum, 85 A.D.

1985. "Italia 85" International Stamp Exhibition, and Important Cities of the World (9th series). Rome. Multicoloured.

1259		1000l. Type **335**	1·40	1·30
1260		1500l. Colosseum, 1985	2·10	1·80

336 Flying Angel

1985. Christmas. Multicoloured.

1261		400l. Type **336**	80	80
1262		450l. Madonna and Child	90	90
1263		600l. Angel resting	1·10	1·30

337 Aerial View of Cailungo Hospital

1986. 30th Anniv of Social Security Institute (450l.) and World Health Day (650l.). Mult.

1264		450l. Type **337**	65	65
1265		650l. Front view of Cailungo hospital	90	90

338 "Giotto" Space Probe

1986. Appearance of Halley's Comet. Mult.

1266		550l. Type **338**	1·00	90
1267		1000l. "Adoration of the Magi" (Giotto)	1·70	1·70

339 Player and Emblem

1986. World Table Tennis Championships, Rimini.

1268	**339**	450l. blue, ultram & red	80	80

340 Deer

1986. Europa. Multicoloured.

1269		550l. Type **340**	13·00	5·50
1270		650l. Common kestrel	15·00	7·75

341 Water Tower, 1870 (lithograph, Charles Shober)

1986. "Ameripex" International Stamp Exhibition, and Important Cities of the World (10th series). Chicago. Multicoloured.

1271		2000l. Type **341**	2·75	2·30
1272		3000l. Water tower, 1986	4·00	3·50

342 Swallows

1986. International Peace Year.

1273	**342**	550l. multicoloured	1·00	95

343 Head of Soldier

1986. 15th Anniv of Establishment of Diplomatic Relations with Chinese People's Republic. Terracotta Figures from Qin Shi Huang's Tomb. Sheet 153×95 mm, containing T 343 and similar designs.

MS1274		550l. black and blue; 650l. black and brown; 2000l. black and magenta	5·50	5·50

DESIGNS—VERT: 650l. Head of horse. VERT: 2000l. Head of soldier (different).

344 "Apollo dancing with the Muses" (detail, Giulio Romano)

1986. 25th Anniv of San Marino Choral Society.

1275	**344**	450l. multicoloured	80	70

345 Boules Player

1986. European Boules Championships, San Marino.

1276	**345**	550l. multicoloured	90	85

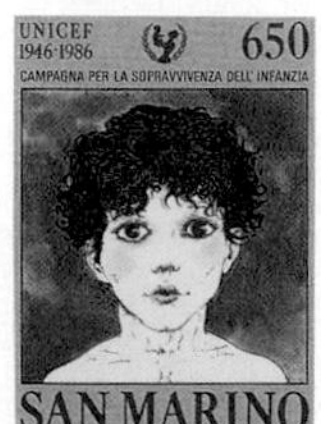

346 Boy

1986. 40th Anniv of UNICEF. Child Survival Campaign.

1277	**346**	650l. multicoloured	1·10	1·00

347 "St. John the Baptist"

1986. Christmas. Triptych by Hans Memling. Mult.

1278		450l. Type **347**	1·10	85
1279		550l. "Madonna and Child"	1·30	70
1280		650l. "St. John the Evangelist"	1·40	1·20

348 Motor Car and Route Map (Paris–Peking Rally, 1907)

1987. Motor Rallies. Multicoloured.

1281		500l. Type **348**	65	65
1282		600l. Peugeot "205" (15th San Marino Rally)	80	80
1283		700l. Motor car and crowds (60th anniv of Mille Miglia)	1·10	1·10

349 Sketch of Church

1987. Europa. Architecture. Our Lady of Consolation Church, Borgomaggiore (Giovanni Michelucci).

1284	**349**	600l. black and red	14·00	6·75
1285	-	700l. black and yellow	16·00	7·75

DESIGN: 700l. Church interior.

350 Modern Sculpture (Reffi Busignani)

1987. Modern Sculptures in San Marino. Designs showing works by artists named. Multicoloured.

1286		50l. Type **350**	10	15
1287		100l. Bini	10	15
1288		200l. Guguianu	35	30
1289		300l. Berti	45	45
1290		400l. Crocetti	55	55
1291		500l. Berti	80	80
1292		600l. Messina	1·00	95
1293		1000l. Minguzzi	1·60	1·50
1294		2200l. Greco	3·50	3·25
1295		10000l. Sassu	17·00	17·00

351 "Chromatic Invention" (Corrado Cagli)

1987. Art Biennale.

1300	-	500l. blue, black and red	80	80
1301	**351**	600l. multicoloured	95	90

DESIGN: 500l. "From My Brazilian Diary—Virgin Forest" (Emilio Vedova).

352 Baroudeur Microlight, San Marino Air Club

1987

1302	**352**	600l. multicoloured	1·00	1·00

353 Bust of Mahatma Gandhi in Gandhi Square, San Marino

1987. "A Society based on Non-violence".

1303	**353**	500l. multicoloured	85	85

354 Olympic Rings and Hurdler in "Stamp"

1987. "Olymphilex" Olympic Stamp Exhibition and World Light Athletics Championships, Rome.

1304	**354**	600l. multicoloured	1·00	1·00

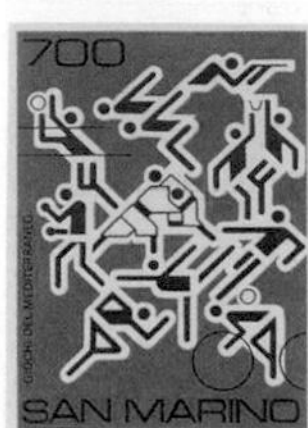

355 Sports Pictograms

1987. Mediterranean Games, Syria.

1305	**355**	700l. red, blue and black	1·10	1·10

356 "View from Round Tower, 1836" (anon)

1987. "Hafnia 87" International Stamp Exhibition, and Important Cities of the World (11th series). Copenhagen. Multicoloured.

1306		1200l. Type **356**	2·20	2·00
1307		2200l. View from Round Tower, 1987	4·00	3·75

357 "The Annunciation" (detail)

1987. Christmas. 600th Birth Anniv of Fra Giovanni of Florence (Beato Angelico). Mult.

1308		600l. Type **357**	1·30	1·20
1309		600l. Madonna and Child (detail, Triptych of Cortona)	1·30	1·20
1310		600l. Saint (detail, "The Annunciation")	1·30	1·20

358 1923 30c., 1944 20l.+10l. and 1975 200l. Stamps of St. Marinus

1988. Thematic Collecting. Multicoloured.

1311		50l. Type **358**	10	15
1312		150l. Aerogramme and 1933 3l. LZ-127 "Graf Zeppelin" stamp (transport)	20	20
1313		300l. 1954 5l. and 1981 200l. motor cycle racing stamps and 1986 meter mark showing motor cycle (sport)	50	50
1314		350l. 1978 200l. human rights stamp on cover and 1982 200l. St. Francis of Assisi stamp (art)	60	60
1315		1000l. 1949 50l. Garibaldi stamp, 1985 450l. Europa stamp and 1952 1l. Columbus stamp (famous people)	1·60	1·60

See also Nos. 1340/4 and 1393/7.

359 Maglev Monorail Train and Globe

1988. Europa. Transport and Communications. Multicoloured.

1316		600l. Type **359**	7·75	3·25
1317		700l. Optical fibres and globe	11·00	4·50

360 Carlo Malagola and Palazzo della Mercanzia

1988. 900th Anniv of Bologna University. Mult.

1318		550l. Type **360**	80	80
1319		650l. Pietro Ellero and Palazzo del Podesta	90	90

1320 1300l. Giosue Carducci and Pala dei Mercanti 1·80 1·80
1321 1700l. Giovanni Pascoli and Atheneum 2·30 2·30

361 "La Strada"

1988. Award of Celebrities of Show Business Prize to Federico Fellini (film director). Film posters. Multicoloured.

1322 300l. Type **361** 45 45
1323 900l. "La Dolce Vita" 1·30 1·30
1324 1200l. "Amarcord" 1·90 1·90

362 Mt. Titano from Beach

1988. 40th Riccione Stamp Fair.

1325 **362** 750l. blue, green and mauve 1·10 1·10

363 Healthy Tree with Diseased Roots

1988. Present Day Problems. International AIDS Congress, San Marino.

1326 **363** 250l. multicoloured 40 40
1327 - 350l. red and black 55 55
1328 - 650l. multicoloured 95 95
1329 - 1000l. multicoloured 1·70 1·70

DESIGNS: 350l. "AIDS" crumbling; 650l. Knotted cord and emblem of virus; 1000l. Printed information.

364 Man Running

1988. Olympic Games, Seoul. Sheet 118×103 mm containing T 364 and similar vert designs, each black, magenta and yellow.

MS1330 650l. Type **364**; 750l. Hurdling; 1300l. Woman running 4·25 4·25

365 "Kurhaus, Scheveningen, 1885" (anon)

1988. "Filacept" International Stamp Exhibition, and Important Cities of the World (12th series). The Hague. Multicoloured.

1331 1600l. Type **365** 2·20 1·70
1332 3000l. Kurhaus, Scheveningen, 1988 4·50 3·50

366 "Angel with Violin"

1988. Christmas. 550th Birth Anniv of Melozzo da Forli. Multicoloured.

1333 650l. Type **366** 1·10 90
1334 650l. "Angel of the Annunciation" (20×37 mm) 1·10 90
1335 650l. "Angel with Mandolin" 1·10 90

367 Bird in Tree (Federica Sparagna)

1989. "Nature is Beautiful. Nature is Useful. Nature is ...". Multicoloured.

1336 200l. Type **367** 40 30
1337 500l. Birds beneath tree (Giovanni Monteduro) 95 80
1338 650l. Landscape (Rosa Mannarino) 1·20 1·00

Nos. 1336/8 depict the first three winning entries in a children's drawing competition.

368 Sledging

1989. Europa. Children's Games. Sheet 115×80 mm containing T 368 and similar vert design. Multicoloured.

MS1339 60l. Type **368**; 750l. Hopscotch 28·00 14·50

1989. Postal History. As T 358. Multicoloured.

1340 100l. "San Marino 1977" Exhibition 1000l. stamp on cover (postal tariffs) 10 10
1341 200l. 1988 350l. stamp on cover (cancellations) 35 20
1342 400l. Parcel receipt (parcel post) 65 65
1343 500l. Essay by Martin Riester, 1865 90 80
1344 1000l. 1862 handstamp on cover (pre-stamp period) 1·70 1·60

369 Emblem

1989. Sport. Multicoloured.

1345 650l. Type **369** (30th anniv of San Marino Olympic Committee) 1·00 95
1346 750l. Emblems (admission of San Marino Football Federation to UEFA and FIFA) 1·20 1·10
1347 850l. Tennis racquet and ball (San Marino championships) 1·30 1·30
1348 1300l. Formula 1 racing car (San Marino Grand Prix, Imola) 1·80 1·80

370 Oath of the Tennis Court

1989. Bicentenary of French Revolution. Mult.

1349 700l. Type **370** 1·10 1·10
1350 1000l. Arrest of Louis XVI 1·60 1·40
1351 1800l. Napoleon's army 3·00 2·50

371 "Marguerite and Armand"

1989. Award of Celebrities of Show Business Prize to Rudolph Nureyev (ballet dancer). Mult.

1352 1200l. Type **371** 2·10 2·10
1353 1500l. "Apollo Musagete" 2·50 2·40
1354 1700l. Ken Russell's film "Valentino" 3·00 2·75

372 "Angel of the Annunciation"

1989. Christmas. Details of the polyptych in Church of Servants of Mary. Multicoloured.

1355 650l. Type **372** 1·10 90
1356 650l. "Nativity" (50×40 mm) 1·10 90
1357 650l. Mary ("Annunciation") 1·10 90

373 Capitol, 1850

1989. "World Stamp Expo '89" Int Stamp Exhibition, and Important Cities of the World (13th series). Washington D.C. Multicoloured.

1358 2000l. Type **373** 2·75 2·30
1359 2500l. Capitol, 1989 3·25 3·00

374 Old Post Office

1990. Europa. Post Office Buildings. Mult.

1360 700l. Type **374** 3·25 1·40
1361 800l. Dogana Post Office 4·00 1·60

375 "Martyrdom of St. Agatha" (Tiepolo) and Cardinal Alberoni leaving City

1990. 250th Anniv of End of Cardinal Alberoni's Occupation of San Marino.

1362 **375** 3500l. multicoloured 6·00 4·25

376 Map pinpointing San Marino

377 Statue, Government Palace

1990. European Tourism Year. Multicoloured.

1366 50l. Type **377** 10 10
1367 50l. Liberty Statue and English inscription 10 10
1368 50l. Government Palace and German inscription 10 10
1369 50l. Man with flag and French inscription 10 10
1370 600l. Type **376** 85 55
1371 600l. Aerial view showing villages 85 55
1372 600l. First Tower 85 55

See also Nos. 1424/7.

378 West Germany (winners 1954, 1974)

1990. World Cup Football Championship, Italy. Previous Winners. Sheet 120×114 mm containing T 378 and similar vert designs. Multicoloured.

MS1373 700l Type **378**; 700l. Italy (1934, 1938, 1982); 700l. England (1966); 700l. Uruguay (1930, 1950); 700l. Brazil (1958, 1962, 1970); 700l. Argentina (1978, 1986) 7·25 7·00

379 Olivier in "Hamlet"

1990. Award of Celebrities of Show Business Prize to Laurence Olivier (actor). Multicoloured.

1374 600l. Type **379** 1·20 1·20
1375 700l. "Richard III" 1·40 1·40
1376 1500l. "The Runner" 3·25 2·75

Nos. 1374/6 are wrongly inscribed "Lawrence".

380 Mt. Titano and State Flags

1990. Visit of President Francesco Cossiga of Italy.

1377 **380** 600l. multicoloured 1·00 85

381 Pinocchio

1990. Death Centenary of Carlo Collodi (writer). Characters from "Pinocchio". Multicoloured.

1378 250l. Type **381** 45 45
1379 400l. Geppetto 65 65
1380 450l. Blue fairy 85 85
1381 600l. Cat and wolf 1·10 1·10

382 Pre-Columbian Civilizations

1990. 500th Anniv (1992) of Discovery of America by Columbus (1st issue). Multicoloured.

1382 1500l. Type **382** 2·20 2·20
1383 2000l. Produce of the New World 3·00 3·00

See also Nos. 1401/2 and 1417/18.

383 Mary and Two Kings

1990. Christmas. Details of Cuciniello Crib. Mult.

1384	750l. Type **383**	1·30	1·20
1385	750l. Baby Jesus in manger and third King	1·30	1·20

Nos. 1384/5 were issued together, se-tenant, forming a composite design.

384 Swallowtail on "Ephedra major"

1990. Flora and Fauna. Multicoloured.

1386	200l. Type **384**	30	30
1387	300l. "Apoderus coryli" (weevil) and hazelnut	55	55
1388	500l. Garden dormouse and acorns of holm oak	85	85
1389	1000l. Green lizard and "Ophrys bertolonii" (orchid)	1·70	1·70
1390	2000l. Firecrest on black pine	3·25	3·25

385 Launch of "Ariane-4"

1991. Europa. Europe in Space. Multicoloured.

1391	750l. Type **385**	3·25	3·25
1392	800l. "E.R.S.-1." survey satellite	4·00	4·00

1991. World of Stamps. As T 358. Multicoloured.

1393	100l. Stamp shop	20	15
1394	150l. Stamp club	30	20
1395	200l. Exhibition	40	35
1396	450l. Stamp album and catalogues	80	70
1397	1500l. Philatelic publications (25th anniv of Italian Philatelic Press Union)	2·75	2·40

386 Torch Bearer leaving Athens

1991. Olympic Games, Barcelona (1992) (1st issue). Multicoloured.

1398	400l. Type **386**	70	70
1399	600l. Torch bearer passing through San Marino	1·10	1·10
1400	2000l. Torch bearer arriving in Barcelona	3·50	3·00

See also No. **MS**1434.

1991. 500th Anniv (1992) of Discovery of America by Columbus (2nd issue). As T 382. Mult.

1401	750l. Navigational dividers, quadrant, hour-glass, compass and route map	1·10	1·10
1402	3000l. "Santa Maria", "Nina" and "Pinta"	5·00	4·50

387 Cat

1991. Pets. Multicoloured.

1403	500l. Type **387**	80	65
1404	550l. Hamster on wheel	90	80
1405	750l. Great Dane and Pomeranian	1·20	1·10
1406	1000l. Aquarium fishes	1·60	1·50
1407	1200l. Canaries in cage	2·00	1·80

388 Players, Balls and Baskets

1991. Centenary of Basketball. Multicoloured.

1408	650l. Type **388**	1·10	1·00
1409	750l. James Naismith (inventor) and players	1·40	1·30

389 James Clerk-Maxwell (physicist)

1991. 100 Years of Radio (1st issue).

1410	**389**	750l. multicoloured	1·10	1·10

Clerk-Maxwell formulated the theory of electromagnetic radiation.

See also Nos. 1431, 1452, 1479 and 1521/2.

390 Dove and Broken Chain (unification of Germany)

1991. "Birth of a New Europe". Sheet 120×72 mm containing T 390 and similar vert designs. Multicoloured.

MS1411	1500l. Type **390**; 1500l. Pres. Gorbachev of Soviet Union, Pres. Bush of United States and rainbow (stategic arms talks); 1500l. Flower breaking through barbed wire (Eastern European democracy)	7·25	7·25

391 Keep

1991. Christmas. La Rocca Fortress. Multicoloured.

1412	600l. Type **391** (postage)	1·00	90
1413	750l. Inland view of fortress	1·30	1·10
1414	1200l. Fortress on crag (air)	2·10	1·80

392 "Bianca and Falliero" (Pesaro production)

1992. Birth Bicentenary of Gioachino Rossini (composer). Scenes from productions of his operas. Multicoloured.

1415	750l. Type **392**	1·30	1·30
1416	1200l. "The Barber of Seville" (La Scala Theatre, Milan)	2·30	2·20

1992. 500th Anniv of Discovery of America by Columbus (3rd issue). As T 382. Multicoloured.

1417	1500l. Amerindians watching fleet	2·20	2·20
1418	2000l. Route map of the four voyages	3·00	3·00

393 Roses

1992. Plants. Multicoloured.

1419	50l. Type **393**	20	20
1420	200l. Ficus as house plant	20	20
1421	300l. Orchid in conservatory	40	40
1422	450l. Cacti in pots	60	60
1423	5000l. Pelargoniums in trough	7·50	7·00

1992. Tourism. Multicoloured. (a) As T 377.

1424	50l. Man with crossbow and Italian inscription	10	15
1425	50l. Tennis player and English inscription	10	15
1426	50l. Motor cycle rider and French inscription	10	15
1427	50l. Ferrari racing car and German inscription	10	15

394 Courting Couple

(b) As T 394.

1428	600l. Type **394**	80	55
1429	600l. Man in restaurant	80	55
1430	600l. Woman reading on veranda	80	55

1992. 100 Years of Radio (2nd issue). As T 389. Multicoloured.

1431	750l. Heinrich Rudolf Hertz (physicist)	1·20	1·20

Hertz proved Clerk-Maxwell's theory.

395 Egg-shaped Globe and Caravel

1992. Europa. 500th Anniv of Discovery of America. Multicoloured.

1432	750l. Type **395**	1·20	1·20
1433	850l. Caravel and island inside broken egg	1·40	1·40

396 Football

1992. Olympic Games, Barcelona (2nd Issue). Sheet 137×105 mm containing T 396 and similar multicoloured designs.

MS1434	1250l. Type **396**; 1250l. Shooting (horiz); 1250l. Swimming; 1250l. Running	7·25	7·25

397 Inedible Mushrooms

1992. 3rd Titano Mycological Exhibition, Borgo Maggiore. Multicoloured.

1435	250l. Type **397**	55	50
1436	250l. Inedible mushrooms (different)	55	50
1437	350l. Edible mushrooms in bowl	65	70
1438	350l. Edible mushrooms on cloth	65	70

Stamps of the same value were issued together, se-tenant, each pair forming a composite design.

398 View and Arms of San Marino

1992. Admission of San Marino to United Nations Organization. Multicoloured.

1439	1000l. Type **398**	1·40	1·40
1440	1000l. View of San Marino (different) and United Nations emblem	1·40	1·40

399 "La Sacra Conversazione"

1992. Christmas. 500th Death Anniv of Piero della Francesca (artist). Multicoloured.

1441	750l. Type **399**	1·10	90
1442	750l. Close-up of Madonna	1·10	90
1443	750l. Close-up of shell decoration	1·10	90

400 Tennis Player

1993. Sporting Events. Multicoloured.

1444	300l. Type **400** (Italian and San Marino Youth Games)	35	35
1445	400l. Cross-country skiers (European Youth Olympic Days (winter), Aosta, Italy)	50	50
1446	550l. Runners (European Youth Olympic Days (summer), Eindhoven, Netherlands)	65	65
1447	600l. Fisherman (Freshwater Angling Clubs World Championship, Ostellato, Italy)	70	70
1448	700l. Runners breasting tape (Small States Games, Malta)	90	90
1449	1300l. Sprinters (Mediterranean Games, Rousillon, France)	2·75	1·70

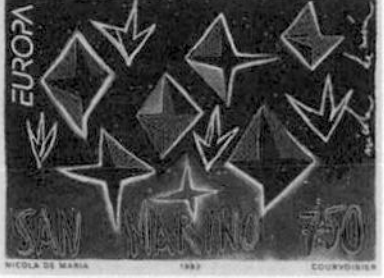

401 Stars

1993. Europa. Contemporary Art.

1450	**401**	750l. multicoloured	1·10	1·10
1451	-	850l. blue and orange	1·30	1·30

DESIGN: 850l. Silhouette.

1993. 100 Years of Radio (3rd issue). As T 389. Multicoloured.

1452	750l. Edouard Branly (physicist) and his "radioconductor"	1·10	1·10

Branly developed a method of revealing Hertzian waves.

402 Finish of World Championship 100 Metres Race, Tokyo, 1991

1993. Inauguration of State Television. Sheet 140×70 mm containing T **402** and similar horiz designs. Multicoloured.

MS1453	2000l. Type **402**; 2000l. Hologram of satellite over San Marino by night; 2000l. Neil Armstrong on the Moon, 1969	7·25	7·25

404 Scarce Swallowtail ("Iphidides podalirius") on Wild Apple

1993. Butterflies. Multicoloured.

1454	250l. Type **404**	40	35
1455	250l. Clouded yellow ("Colias crocea") on wild vetch	40	35
1456	250l. Glanville's fritillary ("Melitaea anxia")	40	35
1457	250l. Camberwell beauty ("Nymphalis antiopa") on white willow	40	35

405 Denmark

1993. "The European Village". Sheet 145×170 mm containing T **405** and similar vert designs, each representing a European Community member. Multicoloured.

MS1458	750l. Type **405**; 750l. England; 750l. Eire; 750l. Luxembourg; 750l. Germany; 750l. Netherlands; 750l. Belgium; 750l. Portugal; 750l. Italy; 750l. Spain; 750l. France; 750l. Greece	10·50	10·50

406 Carlo Goldoni

1993. Death Anniversaries. Multicoloured.

1459	550l. Type **406** (dramatist, bicentenary)	55	55
1460	650l. Horace (Quintus Horatius Flaccus) (poet) (2000th anniv)	80	80
1461	850l. Scene from opera "Orpheus" by Claudio Monteverdi (composer, 350th anniv) (horiz)	1·00	1·00
1462	1850l. Guy de Maupassant (writer, centenary) (horiz)	2·30	2·30

407 San Marino

1993. Christmas. Multicoloured.

1463	600l. Type **407**	65	65
1464	750l. "Adoration of the Child" (Gerrit van Honthorst) (horiz)	90	90
1465	850l. "Adoration of the Shepherds" (Van Honthorst)	1·20	1·20

408 Long-haired Dachshund

1994. 10th International Dog Show. Multicoloured.

1466	350l. Type **408**	45	45
1467	400l. Afghan hound	50	50
1468	450l. Belgian tervuren shepherd dog	55	55
1469	500l. Boston terrier	60	60
1470	550l. Mastiff	65	65
1471	600l. Malamute	80	80

409 Ernst Vettori (90 metre ski jumping)

1994. Winter Olympic Games, Lillehammer, Norway. 1992 Gold Medal Winners. Sheet 164×112 mm containing T **409** and similar square designs. Multicoloured.

MS1472	750l. ×2, Type **409**; 750l. ×2, Patrick Ortlieb (downhill skiing); 750l. ×2, Alberto Tomba (giant slalom); 750l. Natalia Mishkutionok and Arthur Dmitriev (pairs figure skating)	7·25	7·25

410 Gate

1994. Gardens. Multicoloured.

1473	100l. Type **410**	20	20
1474	200l. Pergola	20	20
1475	300l. Well	45	45
1476	450l. Gazebo	55	55
1477	1850l. Pond	2·10	2·10

411 Olympic Flags

1994. Centenary of International Olympic Committee.

1478	**411**	600l. multicoloured	1·20	1·10

1994. 100 Years of Radio (4th issue). As T 389. Multicoloured.

1479	750l. Aleksandr Stepanovich Popov	1·10	1·10

Popov was the first to use a suspended wire as an aerial.

412 Players

1994. World Cup Football Championship, U.S.A. Multicoloured.

1480	600l. Type **412**	70	70
1481	600l. Player kicking ball	70	70
1482	600l. Player heading ball	70	70
1483	600l. Players tackling	70	70
1484	600l. Goalkeeper saving goal	70	70

413 Route Map

1994. Europa. Discoveries. Exploration of Sun by "Ulysses" Space Probe. Multicoloured.

1485	750l. Type **413**	1·10	1·10
1486	850l. "Ulysses" approaching Sun	1·30	1·30

414 Government Palace

1994. Centenary of Government Palace. Mult.

1487	150l. Type **414**	20	20
1488	600l. Tower and San Marino from ramparts	65	65
1489	650l. Clock-tower	80	80
1490	1000l. Government chamber (horiz)	1·10	1·10

415 St. Mark's Basilica

1994. 900th Anniv of Dedication of St. Mark's Basilica, Venice.

1491	**415** 750l. multicoloured	6·00	6·00
MS1492	80×115 mm. No. 1491 together with No. 2276 of Italy	4·00	3·50

416 Angels playing Musical Instruments

1994. Christmas. 500th Death Anniv of Giovanni Santi (painter). Details of "The Enthroned Madonna and Child with Saints". Multicoloured.

1493	600l. Type **416**	70	70
1494	750l. Madonna and Child	90	90
1495	850l. Angel playing harp	1·10	1·10

417/420 "Italy on the Road in a Sea of Flowering Greenery"

1994. Centenary of Italian Touring Club.

1496	**417**	1000l. multicoloured	1·10	90
1497	**418**	1000l. multicoloured	1·10	90
1498	**419**	1000l. multicoloured	1·10	90
1499	**420**	1000l. multicoloured	1·10	90

Nos. 1496/9 were issued together, se-tenant, forming the composite design illustrated.

421 Cyclist

1995. Sporting Events. Multicoloured.

1500	100l. Type **421** (Junior World Cycling Championships, Italy and San Marino)	20	20
1501	500l. Volleyball (centenary)	55	55
1502	650l. Skater (Men's Speed-skating Championships, Baselga di Pine, Italy)	90	80
1503	850l. Sprinter (World Athletics Championships, Gothenburg, Sweden)	1·20	1·10

422 Flora and Fauna

1995. European Nature Conservation Year. Mult.

1504	600l. Type **422**	65	60
1505	600l. Frog, lizard and water lily	65	60
1506	600l. Water lily, bird and ladybirds	65	60
1507	600l. Butterfly, white-headed duckling and frog	65	60
1508	600l. Mallard and duckling	65	60

Nos. 1504/8 were issued together, se-tenant, forming a composite design of river life.

423 U.N. Emblem

1995. 50th Anniv of U.N.O. Multicoloured.

1509	550l. Type **423**	65	65
1510	600l. Rose with emblem	80	80
1511	650l. Hourglass	90	90
1512	1200l. Rainbow and emblem forming "50"	1·20	1·20

424 Mute Swans over Coastline

1995. Europa. Peace and Freedom. Multicoloured.

1513	750l. Type **424**	1·00	1·00
1514	850l. Landscape	1·20	1·20

425 Basilica and "Legend of the True Cross" (detail of fresco, Agnolo Gaddi)

1995. 700th Anniv of Santa Croce Basilica, Florence. Multicoloured.

1515	1200l. Type **425**	1·30	1·30

1516	1250l. Pazzi Chapel and "Madonna and Child with Saints" (Andrea della Robbia)	1·60	1·60

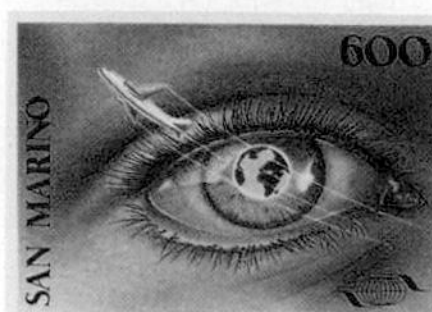

426 Eye and Airplane

1995. 20th Anniv of World Tourism Organization. Multicoloured.

1517	600l. Type **426**	55	55
1518	750l. Five ribbons (continents) around La Rocca fortress	85	85
1519	850l. Airplane and postcards circling globe	95	95
1520	1200l. Five ribbons around globe	1·30	1·30

427 Guglielmo Marconi and Transmitter

1995. 100 Years of Radio (5th issue). Centenary of First Radio Transmission. Multicoloured.

1521	850l. Type **427**	1·10	90
1522	850l. Radio frequency dial	1·10	90

428 *The General*, 1928 (1)

1995. Centenary of Motion Pictures. Sheet 187×120 mm containing T 428 and similar horiz designs. Black "The General" or multicoloured (others).

MS1523 250l. ×4, Buster Keaton in *The General*; 250l. ×4, Burt Lancaster and Claudia Cardinale in *The Leopard*; 250l. ×4, Bruno Bozzetto's *Allegro non Troppo* (animated film); 250l. ×4, Mel Gibson in *Braveheart* 5·00 5·00

Each film is represented by four different frames, numbered from 1 to 4.

429 Qianmen Complex, 1914

1995. "Beijing 1995" International Stamp and Coin Exhibition, Peking, and Important Cities of the World (14th series). Multicoloured.

1524	1500l. Type **429**	1·90	1·10
1525	1500l. Qianmen complex, 1995	1·90	1·10

430 "The Anunciation" (detail of illuminated MS)

1995. "Neri of Rimini" Art and Literature Exn.

1526	**430**	650l. multicoloured	1·20	1·00

431 Reindeer pulling Sleigh

1995. Christmas. Multicoloured.

1527	750l. Type **431**	1·40	1·10
1528	750l. Children dancing around Christmas tree	1·40	1·10
1529	750l. Wise Men approaching stable with crib	1·40	1·10

Nos. 1527/9 were issued together, se-tenant, forming a composite design.

432 Cheetah

1995. Inaug of San Marino Express Mail Service.

1530	**432**	6000l. multicoloured	8·00	8·00

433 Throwing the Discus

1996. Centenary of Modern Olympic Games. Mult.

1531	100l. Type **433**	15	15
1532	500l. Wrestling	65	60
1533	650l. Long jumping	90	85
1534	1500l. Throwing the javelin	2·10	1·80
1535	2500l. Running	3·50	3·00

434 Dolphin swimming

1996. 3rd "Nature World" Exhibition, Rimini. Mult.

1536	50l. Type **434**	10	10
1537	100l. Frog on leaf	15	15
1538	150l. Emperor penguins in snow	20	20
1539	1000l. Butterfly on flower	1·20	1·20
1540	3000l. Mallards flying over water	3·25	3·25

435 Mother Teresa of Calcutta

1996. Europa. Famous Women.

1541	**435**	750l. multicoloured	2·30	1·60

436 Marco Polo and Palace in the Forbidden City

1996. 700th Anniv (1995) of Marco Polo's Return from Asia and "China '96" International Stamp Exhibition, Peking.

1542	**436**	1250l. multicoloured	3·25	2·20

437 Great Wall of China

1996. 25th Anniv of San Marino–China Diplomatic Relations. Multicoloured.

1543	750l. Type **437**	1·40	85
1544	750l. Walled rampart, San Marino	1·40	85
MS1545	110×75 mm. Nos. 1543/4	2·75	2·75

Nos. 1543/4 were issued together, se-tenant, forming a composite design.

438 Traditional Weaving

1996. "Medieval Days" Traditional Festival. Mult.

1546	750l. Type **438**	90	65
1547	750l. Potter	90	65
1548	750l. Traditional craftswoman	90	65
1549	750l. Playing traditional game	90	65
1550	750l. Trumpeters (horiz)	90	65
1551	750l. Flag display (horiz)	90	65
1552	750l. Crossbow tournament (horiz)	90	65
1553	750l. Dancing and playing musical instruments (horiz)	90	65

439 Front Page

1996. Centenary of "La Gazzetta dello Sport" (newspaper).

1554	**439**	1850l. multicoloured	3·00	2·30

440 Applauding Crowd

1996. 33rd "Festivalbar" Song Festival.

1555	**440**	2000l. multicoloured	3·00	2·40

441 Enrico Caruso and "O Sole Mio"

1996. Italian Music. Singers and Their Songs. Multicoloured.

1556	750l. Type **441**	1·00	90
1557	750l. Armando Gill and "Come Pioveva"	1·00	90
1558	750l. Ettore Petrolini and "Gastone"	1·00	90
1559	750l. Vittorio de Sica and "Parlami d'Amore Mariu"	1·00	90
1560	750l. Odoardo Spadaro and "La porti un bacione a Firenze"	1·00	90
1561	750l. Alberto Rabagliati and "O mia bela Madonina"	1·00	90
1562	750l. Beniamino Gigli and "Mamma"	1·00	90
1563	750l. Claudio Villa and "Luna rossa"	1·00	90
1564	750l. Secondo Casadei and "Romagna Mia"	1·00	90
1565	750l. Renato Rascel and "Arrivederci Roma"	1·00	90
1566	750l. Fred Buscaglione and "Guarda che luna"	1·00	90
1567	750l. Domenico Modugno and "Nel blu, dipinto di blu"	1·00	90

442 Yellowstone National Park, United States

1996. 50th Anniv of UNESCO. World Heritage Sites. Multicoloured.

1568	450l. Type **442**	55	55
1569	500l. Prehistoric cave paintings, Vezere Valley, France	65	65
1570	650l. San Gimignano, Italy	90	80

1571	1450l. Wies Pilgrimage Church, Germany	2·20	1·90

443 Hen and Chicks

1996. 50th Anniv of UNICEF. Multicoloured.

1572	550l. Type **443**	80	65
1573	1000l. Chicks in nest	1·40	1·30

444 Playing Lotto

1996. Christmas. Multicoloured.

1574	750l. Type **444**	85	65
1575	750l. Hanging decoration	85	65
1576	750l. Father Christmas on sleigh and child reading book	85	65
1577	750l. Christmas tree	85	65
1578	750l. Bowls of fruit and nuts	85	65
1579	750l. Snowflakes and shooting star	85	65
1580	750l. Children's toys	85	65
1581	750l. Presents	85	65
1582	750l. Hanging Father Christmas decoration	85	65
1583	750l. Nativity scene	85	65
1584	750l. Mistletoe	85	65
1585	750l. Stocking hanging on mantelpiece	85	65
1586	750l. Family celebrating	85	65
1587	750l. Christmas tree outside window and party	85	65
1588	750l. Snowman outside window and party	85	65
1589	750l. Calendar pages and bottle of champagne (New Year's celebrations)	85	65

Nos. 1574/89 were issued together, se-tenant, forming a composite design.

445 Hong Kong, 1897

1997. Important Cities of the World (15th series). Sheet 84×94 mm containing T 445 and similar horiz design. Multicoloured.

MS1590 750l. Type **445**; 750l. Hong Kong, 1997 2·10 2·10

446/449 Championship Races

1997. World Skiing Championships, Sestriere.

1591	**446**	1000l. multicoloured	1·10	1·10
1592	**447**	1000l. multicoloured	1·10	1·10
1593	**448**	1000l. multicoloured	1·10	1·10
1594	**449**	1000l. multicoloured	1·10	1·10

Nos. 1591/4 were issued together, se-tenant, forming the composite design illustrated.

450 Acquaviva

1997. Communes. Multicoloured.

1595	100l. Type **450**	15	15
1596	200l. Borgomaggiore	20	20
1597	250l. Chiesanuova	35	30
1598	400l. Domagnano	55	50
1599	500l. Faetano	65	60
1600	550l. Fiorentino	80	65
1601	650l. Montegiardino	90	80
1602	750l. Serravalle	1·10	90
1603	5000l. San Marino	6·50	5·75

451 St. Marinus tames the Bear

1997. Europa. Tales and Legends. Multicoloured.

1604	650l. Type **451**	90	90
1605	750l. Felicissima begs St. Marinus to cure her son Verissimus	1·20	1·20

452 Bicycle and Stopwatch

1997. Sporting Events in San Marino. Each with Mt. Titano in the background. Multicoloured.

1606	500l. Type **452** (80th Giro d'Italia cycle race)	60	60
1607	550l. Tennis racket and ball (men's tennis championships)	65	65
1608	750l. Ferrari Formula One racing car (17th San Marino Grand Prix)	90	90
1609	850l. Juventus badge, football and trophy (Republic of San Marino Trophy football championship)	1·00	1·00
1610	1000l. Boules (World Petanque Championship)	1·20	1·20
1611	1250l. Motor cycle (World 250cc Motocross Championship)	1·50	1·40
1612	1500l. Car dashboard (Mille Miglia (classic car rally))	1·90	1·70

453 Scanning the Heavens

1997. 5th International Symposium on Unidentified Flying Objects and Associated Phenomena, San Marino.

1613	**453**	750l. multicoloured	1·00	85

454 Stone Pine

1997. Trees. Multicoloured.

1614	50l. Type **454**	15	15
1615	800l. White oak	85	95
1616	1800l. Walnut	2·50	2·20
1617	2000l. Pear	3·00	2·50

455 Count Giovanni Barbavera di Grevellona

1997. 120th Anniv of First San Marino Postage Stamp.

1618	**455**	800l. brown and green	90	90
1619	-	800l. brown and blue	90	90
1620	-	800l. brown and mauve	90	90
1621	-	800l. brown and red	90	90

DESIGNS: No. 1618, Type **455** (Director-General of Italian Post Office and co-signatory of postal convention between Italy and San Marino); 1619, Italian Government Printing Works, Turin, and Enrico Repettati (chief engraver); 1620, "San Marino-Philatelist" (monthly magazine) and Otto Bickel (collectables dealer) holding illustrated envelopes; 1621, Alfredo Reffi (stamp dealer and postcard publisher) and postcard.

456 First Tower and Dal Monte

1997. Beatification of Father Bartolomeo Maria dal Monte.

1622	**456**	800l. multicoloured	1·10	90

457 Quadratino (Antonio Rubino)

1997. Italian Comic Strips. Multicoloured.

1623	800l. Type **457**	1·10	1·10
1624	800l. Signor Bonaventura (Sergio Tofano)	1·10	1·10
1625	800l. Kit Carson (Rino Albertarelli)	1·10	1·10
1626	800l. Cocco Bill (Benito Jacovitti)	1·10	1·10
1627	800l. Tex Willer (Gian Bonelli and Aurelio Galleppini)	1·10	1·10
1628	800l. Diabolik (Angela and Luciana Giussani and Franco Paludetti)	1·10	1·10
1629	800l. Valentina (Guido Crepax)	1·10	1·10
1630	800l. Corto Maltese (Hugo Pratt)	1·10	1·10
1631	800l. Sturmtruppen (Franco Bonvicini)	1·10	1·10
1632	800l. Alan Ford (Max Bunker)	1·10	1·10
1633	800l. Lupo Alberto (Guido Silvestri)	1·10	1·10
1634	800l. Pimpa (Francesco Tullio Altan)	1·10	1·10
1635	800l. Bobo (Sergio Staino)	1·10	1·10
1636	800l. Zanardi (Andrea Pazienza)	1·10	1·10
1637	800l. Martin Mystere (Alfredo Castelli and Giancarlo Alessandrini)	1·10	1·10
1638	800l. Dylan Dog (Tiziano Sclavi and Angelo Stano)	1·10	1·10

458 St. Francis of Assisi and Dove

1997. Voluntary and Charitable Service. Mult.

1639	550l. Type **458** (voluntary aid after Assisi earthquake)	65	65
1640	650l. Mariele Ventre (organizer of Zecchino d'Oro) and children (40th anniv of Antoniano in Bologna (charitable organization))	80	80
1641	800l. Children around globe (40th anniv of Zecchino d'Oro (children's song festival))	1·10	1·00

459 "Adoration of the Magi" (detail of altarpiece by Giorgio Vasari, San Fortunato Abbey, Rimini)

1997. Christmas.

1642	**459**	800l. multicoloured	1·30	1·10

460 Beetle

1997. 60th Anniv of Volkswagen (motor manufacturer). Sheet 154×115 mm containing T 460 and similar horiz designs. Multicoloured.

MS1643	800l. Type **460**; 800l. Golf Mk I; 800l. New Beetle; 800l. Golf Mk IV	3·50	3·50

461 Rainbow over Grass and Sunflower erupting from Globe

1998. World Day of the Sick. Multicoloured.

1644	650l. Type **461**	85	80
1645	1500l. Dove and rainbow over waves and globe	1·90	1·80

462 125S Racing Car, 1947

1998. Birth Centenary of Enzo Ferrari (motor manufacturer). Racing Cars. Multicoloured.

1646	800l. Type **462**	1·20	1·20
1647	880l. Model 375, 1950 (wrongly inscr "500 F2, 1952")	1·20	1·20
1648	800l. Lancia D50, 1956 (wrongly inscr "801")	1·20	1·20
1649	800l. Racing car (wrongly inscr "246 Dino")	1·20	1·20
1650	800l. Model 156, 1961	1·20	1·20
1651	800l. John Surtees' 158, 1964	1·20	1·20
1652	800l. Niki Lauda's 312T, 1975	1·20	1·20
1653	800l. Jody Scheckter's 312T4, 1979	1·20	1·20
1654	800l. Model 126C, 1981	1·20	1·20
1655	800l. Michelo Alboreto's 156/85, 1985	1·20	1·20
1656	800l. Model 639, 1989	1·20	1·20
1657	800l. Michael Schumacher's F310, 1996	1·20	1·20

463 Verse of "Infinity", 1819

1998. Birth Bicentenary of Giacomo Leopardi (poet). Multicoloured.

1658	550l. Type **463**	80	65
1659	650l. "A Village Saturday", 1829	95	80
1660	900l. "Nocturne of a Wandering Asian Shepherd", 1822–30	1·30	1·10
1661	2000l. "To Sylvia", 1828	2·75	2·40

464 Installation of Captains Regent

1998. Europa. National Festivals. Multicoloured.

1662	650l. Type **464**	1·10	90
1663	1200l. Religious procession (Feast Day of Patron Saint)	2·20	1·90

465 Emigrants on Ship, Passport and Ticket

1998. Museum of the Emigrant. Multicoloured.

1664	800l. Type **465**	1·20	95
1665	1500l. Emigrants working, restaurant, work permit, pay slip, money and residency permit	2·40	1·70

466 Goalkeeper reaching for Ball

1998. World Cup Football Championship, France. Multicoloured.

1666	650l. Type **466**	1·40	1·70
1667	800l. Two players challenging for ball	1·90	1·90
1668	900l. Three players challenging for ball	2·20	1·90

467 Launch of Space Shuttle, Cape Canaveral

1998. San Marino Flag in Space. Sheet 140×70 mm containing T 467 and similar horiz designs. Multicoloured.

MS1669	2000l. Type **467**; 2000l, Space capsule in orbit and San Marino flag; 2000l. Space shuttle returning to Earth	7·75	7·75

468 "20,000 Leagues Under the Sea" (Jules Verne)

1998. Science Fiction Novels. Multicoloured.

1670	800l. Type **468**	1·00	80
1671	800l. "War of the Worlds" (H. G. Wells) (centenary of publication)	1·00	80
1672	800l. "Brave New World" (Aldous Huxley)	1·00	80
1673	800l. "1984" (George Orwell)	1·00	80
1674	800l. "Foundation Trilogy" (Isaac Asimov)	1·00	80
1675	800l. "City" (Clifford D. Simak)	1·00	80
1676	800l. "Fahrenheit 451" (Ray Bradbury)	1·00	80
1677	800l. "The Seventh Victim" (Robert Sheckley)	1·00	80
1678	800l. "The Space Merchants" (Frederik Pohl and Cyril Kornbluth)	1·00	80
1679	800l. "The Coming Dark Age" (Roberto Vacca)	1·00	80

1680 800l. "Stranger in a Strange Land" (Robert Heinlein) 1·00 80

1681 800l. "A Clockwork Orange" (Anthony Burgess) 1·00 80

1682 800l. "The Drowned World" (James Ballard) 1·00 80

1683 800l. "Dune" (Frank Herbert) 1·00 80

1684 800l. "2001 A Space Odyssey" (Arthur Clarke) 1·00 80

1685 800l. "Do Androids Dream of Electric Sheep?" (Philip K. Dick) 1·00 80

469 Sailing Dinghy and Factory Chimneys

1998. International Stamp Fair, Riccione. Mult.

1686 800l. Type **469** 1·00 95

1687 1500l. Dolphin jumping through stamp and factory chimneys 1·80 1·80

470 Pope John Paul II

1998. "Italia 98" International Stamp Exhibition, Milan (1st issue).

1688 **470** 800l. multicoloured 2·20 1·10

See also No. 1695.

471 Boy and Tree of Santa Clauses

1998. Christmas. Multicoloured.

1689 800l. Type **471** 1·10 90

1690 800l. Pacific Island child 1·10 90

1691 800l. Boy in clogs and rabbit 1·10 90

1692 800l. Girl and dog 1·10 90

Nos. 1689/92 were issued together, se-tenant, forming a composite design of a tree of Santa Clauses bearing gifts.

472 Woman

1998. 50th Anniv of Universal Declaration of Human Rights. Multicoloured.

1693 900l. Type **472** 1·00 1·10

1694 900l. Man 1·00 1·10

Nos. 1693/4 were issued together, se-tenant, forming a composite design.

473 "The Joy of Living" (Emilio Greco)

1998. "Italia 98" International Stamp Exhibition (2nd issue). Art Day.

1695 **473** 1800l. multicoloured 2·50 2·20

DENOMINATION. From No. 1696 to No. 1890 San Marino stamps are denominated both in lire and in euros. As no cash for the latter is in circulation, the catalogue continues to use the lira value.

474 "The Coronation of Poppea" (Claudio Monteverdi)

1999. 400 Years of Opera. Multicoloured.

1696 800l. Type **474** 1·10 90

1697 800l. "Dido and Aeneas" (Henry Purcell) 1·10 90

1698 800l. "Orpheus and Eurydice" (Christoph Willibald Gluck) 1·10 90

1699 800l. "Don Juan" (Wolfgang Amadeus Mozart) 1·10 90

1700 800l. "The Barber of Seville" (Gioacchino Rossini) 1·10 90

1701 800l. "Norma" (Vincenzo Bellini) 1·10 90

1702 800l. "Lucia di Lammermoor" (Gaetano Donizetti) 1·10 90

1703 800l. "Aida" (Giuseppe Verdi) 1·10 90

1704 800l. "Faust" (Charles Gounod) 1·10 90

1705 800l. "Carmen" (Georges Bizet) 1·10 90

1706 800l. "The Ring of the Nibelung" (Richard Wagner) 1·10 90

1707 800l. "Boris Godunov" (Modest Musorgsky) 1·10 90

1708 800l. "Tosca" (Giacomo Puccini) 1·10 90

1709 800l. "The Love for Three Oranges" (Sergei Prokofiev) 1·10 90

1710 800l. "Porgy and Bess" (George Gershwin) 1·10 90

1711 800l. "West Side Story" (Leonard Bernstein) 1·10 90

475 Hand writing with Quill Pen

1999. 12th World Hang-gliding Championship, Montecucco, Italy. Multicoloured.

1712 800l. Type **475** 1·10 95

1713 1800l. Hang-glider with balloon 2·50 2·10

476 Mountain Pine

1999. San Marino Bonsai Exhibition. Mult.

1714 50l. Type **476** 15 15

1715 300l. Olive 40 35

1716 350l. Scots pine 45 45

1717 500l. Pedunculate oak 65 60

477 Eastern Slopes of Mount Titano

1999. Europa. Parks and Gardens. Multicoloured.

1718 650l. Type **477** 95 80

1719 1250l. Cesta Tower, Mount Titano 1·80 1·40

478 Emblem and Town Hall, Treviso

1999. World Cycling Championships, Treviso and Verona, Italy. Multicoloured.

1720 900l. Type **478** 1·20 1·10

1721 3000l. Emblem and amphitheatre, Verona 4·00 3·50

479 Article 1 of First Treaty (1874) and Swiss Parliament Building

1999. 125th Anniv of Universal Postal Union. Multicoloured.

1722 800l. Type **479** 1·10 95

1723 3000l. World map highlighting original U.P.U. signatories, 1875 4·00 3·50

480 Garibaldi (after Lorusso) and Crowds in front of the Quirinale, Rome

1999. 150th Anniv of Garibaldi's Refuge in San Marino after Fall of the Roman Republic.

1724 **480** 1250l. multicoloured 1·80 1·60

481 "50" and People climbing Ladder to Council Emblem

1999. 50th Anniv of Council of Europe.

1725 **481** 1300l. multicoloured 1·90 1·70

482 European Brown Hare

1999. Animals. Multicoloured.

1726 500l. Type **482** 60 60

1727 650l. Eurasian red squirrel 85 80

1728 1100l. Eurasian badger 1·30 1·30

1729 1250l. Red fox 1·60 1·40

1730 1850l. North African crested porcupine 2·50 2·20

483 Pilgrimage Route Map and Canterbury Cathedral

1999. Holy Year 2000. Multicoloured.

1731 650l. Type **483** 90 80

1732 800l. Priest blessing pilgrim (fresco, Novalesa Abbey) and Rheims Cathedral 1·10 1·00

1733 900l. Hospice welcoming pilgrims (fresco, St. James's Chapel, Briancon) and Pavia Cathedral 1·20 1·10

1734 1250l. Pilgrims on the road (bas-relief, Fidenza Cathedral) and Fidenza Cathedral 1·70 1·40

1735 1500l. "Mount of Joy" (Sir Charles Eastlake) and St. Peter's Cathedral, Rome 2·10 1·90

484 Fregoso Castle, Sant'Agata Feltria

1999. Architecture of Montefeltro. Multicoloured.

1736 50l. Type **484** 15 15

1737 250l. Feltresca Castle, San Leo 20 30

1738 650l. Ducal Palace, Urbino 85 80

1739 1300l. Ubaldinesca Castle, Sassocorvaro 1·80 1·60

1740 6000l. Il Montale and La Rocca fortress, San Marino 8·00 7·25

485 St. Martin tearing Cloak in Half

1999. 50th Anniv of San Marino Red Cross.

1741 **485** 800l. multicoloured 1·40 1·10

486 Team Photograph (Italian championship, 1901)

1999. Centenary of A. C. Milan Football Club. Sheet 155×115 mm containing T 486 and similar horiz designs. Multicoloured.

MS1742 800l. Type **486**; 800l. Players Gren, Nordahl and Liedholm, 1950s; 800l. Team photograph, Wembley (goalkeeper in front row) (European Championship, 1963); 800l. Team photograph, Vienna (goalkeeper in back row), 1990; 800l. Team and children celebrating Italian Championship, 1994; 800l. Team with trophy (Italian Championship, 1999) 7·25 7·25

487 Nativity

1999. Christmas.

1743 **487** 800l. multicoloured 1·40 1·10

488 18/50 h.p. Horch

1999. Centenary of Audi (car manufacturer). Sheet 155×115 mm containing T 488 and similar horiz designs. Multicoloured.

MS1744 1500l. Type **488**; 1500l. Audi TT; 1500l. Audi A8; 1500l. Auto Union racing car 7·75 7·75

489 Tank, Soldiers and Civilians (First and Second World Wars)

2000. The Twentieth Century. Multicoloured.

1745 650l. Type **489** 70 70

1746 650l. Syringe being filled, scanner and DNA molecular structure (science and medicine) 70 70

1747 650l. Washing machine, underground train and lamp (electricity) 70 70

1748 650l. Switchboard operators, radio and computer (telecommunications) 70 70

1749 650l. Wright *Flyer*, Boeing 727 airship and astronaut on Moon (conquest of space) 70 70

1750 650l. Factory chimneys and rubbish (pollution) 70 70

1751 650l. Sports car, lorry and traffic jam (development of motor vehicles) 70 70

1752 650l. Submarine and mushroom cloud (atomic energy) 70 70

1753 650l. Charlie Chaplin in *Modern Times*, comic strip and chair (cinema, comics and design) 70 70

1754 650l. Crossword puzzle, art gallery and car towing caravan (leisure activities) 70 70
1755 650l. Advertising posters (publicity) 70 70
1756 650l. Cyclist, stadium and footballers (sport) 70 70

490 St. John Lateran Basilica, Rome, Pilgrim (detail of engraving by G. Perugino) and Mt. Titano

2000. Holy Year 2000. Sheet 155×115 mm containing T 490 and similar horiz designs. Multicoloured.
MS1757 1000l. Type **490**; 1000l. St. Paul without the Walls Basilica, Rome, St. Marinus (statue) and La Rocca fortress; 1000l. St. Mary Major Basilica, Rome, with Madonna and Child; 1000l. St. Peter's Basilica, Rome, and St. Marinus (detail of painting by Pompeo Batoni) 5·50 5·50

491 Emblem and La Rocca Fortress

2000. 40th Anniv of San Marino Rotary Club. Mult.
1758 650l. Type **491** 1·00 80
1759 800l. Government Palace, Arms and Statue of Liberty, San Marino 1·20 1·00

492 I.I.S.A. Emblem, Government Palace, Fiera di Bologna Towers and Statue of Liberty, San Marino

2000. International Institute of Administrative Science Conference, Bologna (1760) and European City of Culture (others). Multicoloured.
1760 650l. Type **492** 85 80
1761 800l. Guglielmo Marconi's workbench, radio aerial, San Pietro Cathedral, clock tower, Tubertini dome and St. Petronius Basilica 1·10 95
1762 1200l. Microchip, musical instruments, St. Petronius Basilica, Santa Maria della Vita Church and Asinelli and Garisenda Towers 1·60 1·40
1763 1500l. Books, detail of still life by Giorgio Morandi, campanile and apse of St. Giacomo Maggiore and St. Francis Churches and Arengo Tower 2·10 1·90

493 Vincenzo Muccioli (founder of San Patrignano Community) and Drug Addict

2000. 5th Anniv of Rainbow International Association Against Drugs. Multicoloured.
1764 650l. Type **493** 90 80
1765 1200l. Blocks spelling "rainbow" in sky 1·70 1·40
1766 2400l. Muccioli and reformed addicts 3·50 3·00

494 "Building Europe"

2000. Europa.
1767 **494** 800l. multicoloured 1·40 1·10

495 "2000"

2000. "Stampin' the Future". Winning Entries in Children's International Painting Competition.
1768 **495** 800l. multicoloured 1·10 95

496 Dog and Butterfly

2000. Olympic Games, Sydney. Multicoloured.
1769 1000l. Type **496** 1·10 1·10
1770 1000l. Hippopotamus and penguin 1·10 1·10
1771 1000l. Elephant and ladybird 1·10 1·10
1772 1000l. Rabbit and snail 1·10 1·10

497 Bicycles

2000. Centenary of International Cycling Union.
1773 **497** 1200l. multicoloured 1·70 1·30

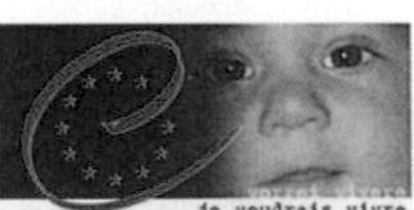

498 Child hiding beneath Soldier's Helmet

2000. 10th Anniv of International Convention on Children's Rights. Multicoloured.
1774 650l. Type **498** 90 80
1775 800l. Child cowering away from frightening shadow 1·10 95
1776 1200l. Child in flower 1·60 1·40
1777 1500l. Childhood fantasies tumbling from book 2·00 1·80

499 Council Emblem and child's face

2000. 50th Anniv of the European Convention on Human Rights.
1778 **499** 800l. multicoloured 1·10 90

500 Basilica of the Saint

2000. Churches of Montefeltro. Multicoloured.
1779 650l. Type **500** 90 80
1780 800l. Church of St. Mary of Antico, Maiolo 1·10 95
1781 1000l. St. Lawrence's Church, Talamello 1·30 1·20
1782 1500l. Parish Church, San Leo 2·00 1·70
1783 1800l. Sanctuary of Our Lady of Graces, Pennabilli 2·40 2·10

501 "Virgin and Child" (Ludovico Carracci)

2000. Christmas.
1784 **501** 800l. multicoloured 4·50 2·20

502 Melchiorre Delfico (author of *History of the Republic of San Marino*) and Title Page

2000. 1700th Anniv of San Marino (1st issue). Multicoloured.
1785 800l. Type **502** 1·00 1·00
1786 800l. Guiseppe Garibaldi (painting) 1·00 1·00
1787 800l. Abraham Lincoln and passage from his letter to the Captains Regent, 1861 1·00 1·00
1788 800l. Refugees arriving in San Marino, 1943–45 1·00 1·00
1789 800l. Roman jewels 1·00 1·00
1790 800l. 1463 map of San Marino 1·00 1·00
1791 800l. Napoleon Bonaparte 1·00 1·00
1792 800l. "L'Arengo" (detail) (postcard, 1906) 1·00 1·00
1793 800l. Child, class and swimming pool 1·00 1·00
1794 800l. Young man, construction site and computers 1·00 1·00
1795 800l. Woman, street scene and church 1·00 1·00
1796 800l. Man, dancers and building 1·00 1·00
1797 1200l. St. Marinus (detail) (Francesco Manzocchi di Forl) 1·40 1·40
1798 1200l.15 th-century painting of St. Marinus 1·40 1·40
1799 1200l. St. Marinus (painting, School of Guercino) 1·40 1·40
1800 1200l. "St. Marinus in glory" (anon) 1·40 1·40
1801 1200l. Double throne of Captains Regent 1·40 1·40
1802 1200l. Title page of 17th-century edition of Republican Statutes 1·40 1·40
1803 1200l. Parade of Palace guards 1·40 1·40
1804 1200l. Flags 1·40 1·40

See also Nos. 1846/9.

503 Michael Schumacher and Ferrari Racing Car

2001. Michael Schumacher Drivers' Champion and Ferrari. Constructors' Champion (2000). Sheet 110×75 mm containing T 503 and similar horiz designs. Multicoloured.
MS1805 1500l. Type **503**; 1500l. Schumacher, racing car and engineers 5·00 5·00

504 Verdi and Scene from *Nabucco*

2001. Death Centenary of Guiseppe Verdi (composer). Scenes from named operas. Multicoloured.
1806 800l. Type **504** 80 80
1807 800l. *Ernani* 80 80
1808 800l. *Rigoletto* 80 80
1809 800l. *Il Trovatore* 80 80
1810 800l. *La Traviata* 80 80
1811 800l. *I Vespri Siciliani* 80 80
1812 800l. *Un Ballo in Maschera* 80 80
1813 800l. *La Forza del Destino* 80 80
1814 800l. *Don Carlos* 80 80
1815 800l. *Aida* 80 80
1816 800l. *Otello* 80 80
1817 800l. *Falstaff* 80 80

505 Malatestian Temple (by Leon Battista Alberti), Rimini

2001. Commemoration of Malatesta Family (Lords of Rimini). Multicoloured.
1818 800l. Type **505** 1·10 95
1819 1200l. "Christ's Devotion" (Giovanni Bellini) 1·70 1·40

506 Yacht

2001. 10th Anniv of "San Marino 24 Hour Yacht Race". Multicoloured.
1820 1200l. Type **506** 1·40 1·40
1821 1200l. Yacht with green and purple spinnaker 1·40 1·40
1822 1200l. Yacht with brown and white sails 1·40 1·40
1823 1200l. Yacht with white spinnaker 1·40 1·40

507 Bowls and Athletics

2001. 9th European Small States Games. Multicoloured.
1824 800l. Type **507** 95 95
1825 800l. Swimming 95 95
1826 800l. Cycling 95 95
1827 800l. Target and skeet shooting 95 95
1828 800l. Judo 95 95
1829 800l. Tennis and table tennis 95 95
1830 800l. Basketball and volleyball 95 95
1831 800l. RASTA (mascot) 95 95

508 Safe containing Water and Forest

2001. Europa. Water Resources. Multicoloured.
1832 800l. Type **508** 1·40 1·10
1833 1200l. Mountain, tap and running water 2·20 1·70

509 *Santa Maria* and *Dahlia variablis*

2001. "Euroflora 2001" International Flower Show, Genoa. Multicoloured.

1834 800l. Type **509** 1·10 95
1835 1200l. *Santa Maria* and *Zantedeschia aethiopica* 2·00 1·40
1836 1500l. *Santa Maria* and rose "Helen Troubel" 1·90 1·90
1837 2400l. Faro Tower, Genoa and *Amaryllis hippeastrum* 3·00 3·00

510 Ellis Island Immigration Museum, New York

2001. "Emigration of the Sammarinese" Exhibition, New York and 25th Anniv of San Marino Social Club, Detroit. Multicoloured.

1838 1200l. Type **510** 1·70 1·40
1839 2400l. San Marino Social Club, Detroit 4·00 3·00

511 Early Stringed Instrument and Ceramics

2001. Inauguration of State Museum. Multicoloured.

1840 550l. Type **511** 55 55
1841 800l. Painting and gallery 90 90
1842 1500l. Ancient ceramics 1·70 1·70
1843 2000l. European artifacts 2·20 2·20

512 Figure reaching Downwards

2001. 50th Anniv of United Nations High Commissioner for Refugees. Multicoloured.

1844 1200l. Type **512** 1·40 1·40
1845 1200l. Figure reaching upwards 1·40 1·40

Nos. 1844/5 were issued together, se-tenant, forming a composite design.

513 Mount Titan

2001. 1700th Anniv of San Marino (2nd issue). Scenes of Mount Titan. Multicoloured.

1846 1200l. Type **513** 1·40 1·40
1847 1200l. Three Towers, Mount Titan 1·40 1·40
1848 1200l. Fields below Mount Titan 1·40 1·40
1849 1200l. Urban infrastructure below Mount Titan 1·40 1·40

514 Old Bakery Mill Silo and Woman surrounded by People

2001. 125th Anniv of San Marino Social Welfare Union (S.U.M.S.). Multicoloured.

1850 1200l. Type **514** 1·40 1·30
1851 1200l. New Bakery Mill Silo headquarters and woman giving sheaves of corn to crowd 1·40 1·30

515 Banner

2001. "Defence of Nature" Exhibition of Works by Joseph Beuys (artist), San Marino.

1852 **515** 2400l. multicoloured 4·00 2·50

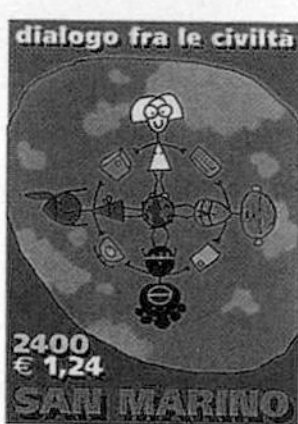

516 Children encircling Globe

2001. United Nations Year of Dialogue among Civilizations.

1853 **516** 2400l. multicoloured 4·00 2·50

517 Angel playing Lute

2001. Christmas. Multicoloured.

1854 800l. Type **517** 1·20 1·00
1855 800l. Woman with basket and king riding on camel 1·20 1·00
1856 800l. King riding camel, woman leading sheep, and woman with parcel 1·20 1·00
1857 800l. Man with parcel and Holy Family on Mount Titano 1·20 1·00
1858 800l. Sheep, birds and man with lantern 1·20 1·00
1859 800l. Ascending angel with trumpet 1·20 1·00
1860 800l. Angel with lyre 1·20 1·00
1861 800l. King with blue crown riding camel 1·20 1·00
1862 800l. Women with parcel, basket and dog 1·20 1·00
1863 800l. Shepherd and sheep 1·20 1·00
1864 800l. Descending angel with trumpet 1·20 1·00
1865 800l. Woman with parcel and angel with trumpet 1·20 1·00
1866 800l. Angel playing violin 1·20 1·00
1867 800l. Man with parcels on sledge 1·20 1·00
1868 800l. Woman with parcel in right hand 1·20 1·00
1869 800l. Angel playing drum 1·20 1·00

Nos. 1854/69 were issued together, se-tenant, forming a composite design.

518 Coins and Map of Euro Zone

2001. Introduction of Euro Coins and Banknotes (2002). Multicoloured.

1870 1200l. Type **518** 1·70 1·30
1871 2400l. Banknotes and map of Euro Zone 3·50 2·50

519 Rabbits

2002. New Currency. Multicoloured.

1872 1c. Type **519** 10 10
1873 2c. Sunset 10 10
1874 5c. Cactus flower 10 10
1875 10c. Field of grain 30 15
1876 25c. Alpine landscape 70 50
1877 50c. Olive leaves 1·40 1·10
1878 €1 Sparrows 2·75 2·20
1879 €5 Baby 13·50 10·50

520 Hippopotamus Ice Skating

2002. Winter Olympic Games, Salt Lake City. Multicoloured.

1885 41c. Type **520** 1·00 1·00
1886 41c. Dog skiing 1·00 1·00
1887 41c. Elephant playing ice hockey 1·00 1·00
1888 41c. Rabbit cross-country skiing 1·00 1·00

521 Poggiali racing

2002. Manuel Poggiali—2001 125cc. Motorcycle World Champion. Multicoloured.

1889 62c. Type **521** 1·50 1·30
1890 62c. Side view of Poggiali racing 1·50 1·30

522 Trapeze Artist

2002. Europa. Circus. Multicoloured.

1891 36c. Type **522** 8·00 4·50
1892 62c. Equestrienne performer 14·00 7·00

523 Players and Ball (finals, 1934)

2002. World Cup Football Championship, Japan and South Korea. Winning Italian Teams. Sheet 155×116 mm, containing T 523 and similar horiz designs. Multicoloured.

MS1893 41c. Type **523** (score wrongly inscr as 4-2); 41c. Player heading ball (finals, 1938) (score wrongly inscr as 1-0); 41c. Players jumping (semi-finals, 1970); 41c. Italy and Brazil players at goal mouth (finals, 1982); 41c. Player tackling (third-place playoff, 1990); 41c. Italy and Nigeria (No 10 players at goal (second round, 1994)) 7·00 7·00

524 Cyclist

2002. Priority Mail Stamps. Multicoloured.

1894 62c. Type **524** 2·10 1·30
1895 €1.24 Hurdler 4·00 2·75

525 Three Towers, Mount Titano

2002. International Year of Mountains. Mult.

1896 41c. Type **525** 1·00 85
1897 41c. Tower and wall on Mount Titano 1·00 85
1898 41c. Tower on peak 1·00 85

526 Map of Europe as Tree

2002. 10th Anniv of Maastricht Treaty.

1899 **526** €1.24 multicoloured 3·50 2·75

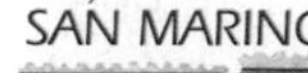

527 1877 2c. and 10c. Stamps

2002. 125th Anniv of First San Marino Stamps. Sheet 140×71 mm, containing T 527 and similar square designs depicting stamps (issued in 1877). Multicoloured.

MS1900 €1.24, Type **527**; €1.24, 10c. and 20c. stamps; €1.24, 20c. and 30c. stamps; €1.24, 30c. and 40c. stamps 13·50 13·50

528 Blacksmith working at Anvil

2002. Traditional Crafts. Multicoloured.

1901 26c. Type **528** 70 60
1902 36c. Broom-maker tying grass bundle 90 80
1903 41c. Chair-mender repairing chair seat 1·00 90
1904 77c. Scribe writing at table 2·20 1·70
1905 €1.24 Knife-grinder sharpening knife at wheel 3·75 3·00
1906 €1.55 Charcoal burner and wood clamp 5·25 3·50

529 Emblems, World Map, Aerial and Morse Code Notation

2002. International Amateur Radio Union Region 1 Conference. Multicoloured.

1907 36c. Type **529** 1·00 80
1908 62c. Emblems, national flag, world map, aerial and Morse code notation 2·10 1·50

530 Government Palace

2002. Tourism. Sheet 150×116 mm, containing T 530 and similar multicoloured designs showing places of interest.

MS1909	62c. Type **530**; 62c. Guaita (First Tower), Mount Titan (44×30 mm); 62c. Cesta (Second Tower) and Montale (Third Tower), Mount Titan (44×30 mm); 62c. Basilicia del Santo and San Pietro Church; 62c. Capuchin Church; 62c. St. Francis gate (39×39 mm)	11·00	9·25

531 Woman's Mouth

2002. Greetings Stamps. Multicoloured.

1910	41c. Type **531**	1·30	90
1911	41c. Child's face and "Hello"	1·30	90
1912	41c. Man's face and "best wishes"	1·30	90
1913	41c. Baby's face and "Ehi"	1·30	90
1914	41c. Man's perplexed face	1·30	90
1915	41c. Hand covering smiling face and "sorry"	1·30	90

532 Child's and Adults Hands

2002. Christmas. Sheet 185×144 mm, containing T 532 and similar vert designs. Multicoloured.

MS1916	41c. Type **532**; 41c. Mother wearing earrings and baby; 41c. Baby at breast; 41c. Mother and baby sleeping; 41c. Adult hands holding baby; 41c. Mother and baby wrapped in shawl; 41c. Wakeful baby against mother's left shoulder; 41c. Baby with finger in mouth laughing with mother; 41c. Baby asleep against mother's left shoulder; 41c. Baby looking away from smiling mother; 41c. Baby with arm extended towards mother's face; 41c. Two babies	15·00	12·50

533 Mushrooms and Artichokes

2003. Italian Cuisine. Multicoloured.

1917	41c. Type **533**	1·20	90
1918	41c. Cooked meats	1·20	90
1919	41c. Spaghetti	1·20	90
1920	41c. Cappelletti	1·20	90
1921	41c. Prawns	1·20	90
1922	41c. Mixed seafood	1·20	90
1923	41c. Ravioli	1·20	90
1924	41c. Tagliatelle	1·20	90
1925	41c. Chicken and potatoes	1·20	90
1926	41c. Fish	1·20	90
1927	41c. Fruit tart	1·20	90
1928	41c. Chocolate pudding	1·20	90
1929	41c. Scrambled eggs	1·20	90
1930	41c. Pancetta	1·20	90
1931	41c. Pastries	1·20	90

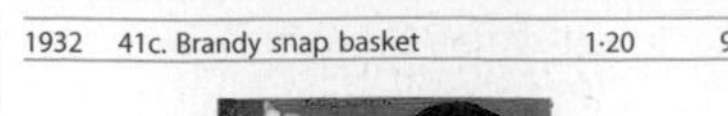

1932	41c. Brandy snap basket	1·20	90

534 "Woman with Mango" (Paul Gauguin)

2003. Artists' Anniversaries. Multicoloured.

1933	52c. Type **534** (death centenary)	1·40	1·40
1934	62c. "Wheat-field with flight of crows" (Vincent Van Gogh) (150th birth anniv)	1·60	1·50
1935	€1.55 "Portrait of a young woman" (Parmigianino) (500th birth anniv)	4·25	4·00

535 Combination Skiing

2003. World Nordic Skiing Championship, Val di Femme. Sheet 156×116 mm containing T 535 and similar vert designs. Multicoloured.

MS1936	Type **535**; 77c. Ski jumping; 77c. Cross-country skiing	6·50	6·00

536 Molvedo (horse)

2003. Horse Racing. Showing champion race horses. Multicoloured.

1937	11c. Type **536**	25	25
1938	15c. Tornese	40	40
1939	26c. Ribot	65	65
1940	€1.55 Varenne	4·25	4·25

537 Partially submerged Woman's Head (Armando Testa)

2003. Europa. Poster Art. Multicoloured.

1941	28c. Type **537**	4·00	4·00
1942	77c. "Jane Avril" (Toulouse Latrec)	10·50	10·50

538 Girolamo Fracastoro

2003. 550th Death Anniv of Girolamo Fracastoro (writer and scientist) Centenary of Veronafil Exhibition.

1943	**538**	77c. multicoloured	2·10	2·10

539 Bridge over Winter Canal

2003. 300th Anniv of St. Petersburg. Multicoloured.

1944	15c. Type **539**	40	40
1945	26c. Bartolomeo Francesco Rastrelli (architect)	65	65
1946	36c. Trinity bridge over River Neva	95	95
1947	41c. Aleksander Sergeyevich Pushkin (writer)	1·10	1·10
1948	77c. Queen Catherine II	2·10	2·10
1949	€1.55 Tsar Peter I	4·00	4·00

540 Wright *Flyer I*

2003. Centenary of Powered Flight. Multicoloured.

1950	36c. Type **540**	95	95
1951	41c. Bleriot XI	1·10	1·10
1952	62c. Aermacchi MB339	1·70	1·70
1953	77c. Aermacchi MB339s of Frecce Tricolori (Italian acrobatic flying team)	2·10	2·10

541 Stagecoach on Road

2003. 120th Anniv of First Daily Mail Coach between Rimini and San Marino. Multicoloured.

1954	41c. Type **541**	1·10	1·10
1955	77c. Stagecoach in town	2·10	2·10

542 Chain Wheel (Tour de France)

2003. Centenary of Tour de France Cycle Race. Hamilton 2003 World Championship Road Race, Hamilton, Canada. Sheet 155×115 mm containing T 542 and similar circular design. Multicoloured.

MS1956	77c. Type **542**; 77c. Front wheel (Hamilton 2003)	4·25	4·25

543 Go-Carting

2003. Children's Games. Multicoloured.

1957	36c. Type **543**	95	95
1958	41c. Blind man's buff	1·10	1·10
1959	62c. Hoops	1·70	1·70
1960	77c. Marbles	2·10	2·10
1961	€1.24 Dance	3·25	3·25
1962	€1.55 Tug-of-war	4·00	4·00

544 Masked Puppet

2003. Puppetry. Multicoloured.

1963	41c. Type **544**	1·10	1·10
1964	41c. Blowing trumpet	1·10	1·10
1965	41c. Male puppet offering flower to female	1·10	1·10
1966	41c. Two puppets with sticks	1·10	1·10

Nos. 1963/6 were issued together, se-tenant, forming a composite design of a puppet theatre.

545 Two Players and Ball

2003. Rugby World Cup Championship, Australia. Multicoloured.

1967	41c. Type **545**	1·10	1·10
1968	62c. Player about to throw ball	1·70	1·70
1969	77c. Two players fighting for possession	2·10	2·10
1970	€1.55 Player with ball	4·00	4·00

546 Angel

2003. Christmas. Sheet 186×143 mm containing T 546 and similar horiz designs. Multicoloured.

MS1971	41c. ×16, Type **546** (1/2); Shepherds and three kings (3/4); Holy family (5/6); Christmas cards (7/8); Decorated tree (9); Filled stocking (10); Wreath (11/12); Child and snowman (13/14); Father Christmas (15/16); Children and toys (17/18); Toys (19); Angels singing (20/21); Children and cake (22); Girl and games (23); Cornucopia (24); San Marino arms (25)	17·00	17·00

MS1971 was arranged in the shape of a snakes and ladders board, with seven stamps (1/2; 3/4; 5/6; 7/8; 20/21; 22; 23) reversed and two (9; 10) at right angles. The numbers on the board are given in brackets.

547 Theatre Emblem

2003. Reopening of La Fenice Theatre, Venice.

1972	**547**	$3.72 multicoloured	10·00	10·00

548 "Ballet" (Edgar Degas) and Tango Dancers

2004. 50th Anniv of Latin Union (inter-government organization). Multicoloured.

1973	41c. Type **548**	1·10	1·10
1974	77c. "Don Quixote" (Miguel De Cervantes) and "Donna Flor and her Two Husbands" (Jorge Amado)	2·10	2·10
1975	€1.55 "Susanna and the Elders" (Tintoretto) and "Sunday Afternoon" (Fernando Botero)	4·00	4·00

549 Building Facade and Coloured Spheres

2004. Venice Carnival. Multicoloured.

1976	77c. Type **549**	2·10	2·10
1977	€1.55 Masked woman	4·00	4·00

550 Manuel Poggiali

2004. Manuel Poggiali—2003 250cc. Motorcycle World Champion.
1978 **550** €1.55 multicoloured 4·00 4·00
See also 1889/90.

551 Bonsai Tree

2004. 20th European Bonsai Association Convention, San Marino.
1979 45c. Type **551** 1·20 1·20
1980 60c. Bonsai (different) 1·60 1·60

552 Government Palace, San Marino and Tian-An-Men Palace, China

2004. 55th Anniv of People's Republic of China. Sheet 180×166 mm containing T 552 and similar horiz designs. Multicoloured.
MS1981 80c. ×3, Type **552**; San Marino mountain and Great Wall, China; Temple of Heaven Pagoda, China and San Marino Tower 6·25 6·25

553 Emblem

2004. Centenary of FIFA (Federation Internationale de Football Association).
1982 **553** €2.80 multicoloured 7·25 7·25

554 "Autoshipplane"

2004. Europa. Tourism. Multicoloured.
1983 45c. Type **554** 1·30 1·30
1984 80c. "Boatcampertrainbus" (horiz) 2·75 2·75

555 Chariot Racing, Boxers and Javelin Thrower

2004. Olympic Games 2004, Athens. Multicoloured.
1985 90c. Type **555** 2·40 2·40
1986 90c. Runner, discus thrower and wrestlers 2·40 2·40
1987 90c. Relay runner, cyclist and golfer 2·40 2·40
1988 90c. Racquet player, weightlifter and gymnasts 2·40 2·40
Nos. 1985/8 were issued together, se-tenant, forming a composite design.

556 Volkswagen Golf

2004. 50th Anniv of Volkswagen (car manufacturers). Multicoloured.
1989 €1.50 Type **556** (30th anniv of Golf) 4·00 4·00
1990 €1.50 Early and modern Beetles ("50" upright) 4·00 4·00
1991 €1.50 Early and modern Beetles ("50" diagonal) 4·00 4·00
1992 €1.50 Golf (different) 4·00 4·00

557 *Hansel and Gretel* (Jakob and Wilhelm Grimm)

2004. Fairytales.
1993 45c. Type **557** 1·20 1·20
1994 60c. *Little Red Riding Hood* (Jakob and Wilhelm Grimm) 1·60 1·60
1995 80c. *Pinocchio* (Carlo Collodi) 2·10 2·10
1996 €1 *Puss in Boots* (Charles Perrault) 2·75 2·75

558 Francesco Petrarca (Petrarch)

2004. Writers' Anniversaries. Multicoloured.
1997 45c. Type **558** (700th birth anniv) 1·20 1·20
1998 €1.50 Oscar Wilde (150th birth anniv) 4·00 4·00
1999 €2.20 Anton Chekov (death centenary) 5·75 5·75

559 Manuel de Nobrega and Josa Anchieta (founders)

2004. 450th Anniv of Founding of San Paulo, Brazil. Multicoloured.
2000 60c. Type **559** 1·60 1·60
2001 80c. Mario Andrade and Antonio Machado (writers) 2·10 2·10
2002 €1.40 Modern San Paulo and Imaculada Conceicao da Luz monastery 3·75 3·75

560 Three Men

2004. 25th Meeting for Friendship Among Peoples, Rimini, Italy (Meeting Rimini). Sheet 155×115 mm containing T 560 and similar horiz designs. Multicoloured.
MS2003 €1 ×4 Type **560**; Two women and child; Family; Priests 10·50 10·50
The stamps and margin of No.**MS**2003 form a composite design.

561 "Rebecca at the Well" (Giovanni Battista Piazzetta)

2004. Artists' Anniversaries. Multicoloured.
2004 45c. Type **561**(250th death anniv) 1·20 1·20
2005 €1.40 "Piazza Navona" (Scipione Gino Bonichi) (birth centenary) 3·75 3·75
2006 €1.70 "The Persistence of Memory" (Salvador Dali) (birth centenary) 4·50 4·50

562 Cherubs and Musical Instruments

2004. Christmas. Designs showing cherubs. Multicoloured.
2007 60c. Type **562** 1·60 1·60
2008 60c. Holding bag of presents 1·60 1·60
2009 60c. Carrying Christmas tree 1·60 1·60
2010 60c. Holding cornucopia 1·60 1·60

563 Antonio Salieri and 18th-century Auditorium

2004. Re-opening of La Scala Theatre, Milan. Sheet 132×172 mm containing T 563 and similar horiz designs. Multicoloured.
MS2011 $1.50×3, Type **563**; 19th-century and modern theatre building facade; Ricardo Muti and modern auditorium 12·00 12·00
The stamps of No.**MS**2011 merge with the score of "Europa riconosciuta" (opera by Antonio Salieri) in the margin to form a composite design.

564 Manuel Fangio (1956)

2005. Ferrari—World Champion Racing Team. Showing World Champions and their cars. Multicoloured.
2012 1c. Type **564** 15 15
2013 4c. Niki Lauda (1975–77) 15 15
2014 5c. John Surtees (1964) 15 15
2015 45c. Michael Schumacher (2000–04) 1·20 1·20
2016 62c. Race car 1·70 1·70
2017 €1.50 Alberto Ascari (1952–3) 4·00 4·00

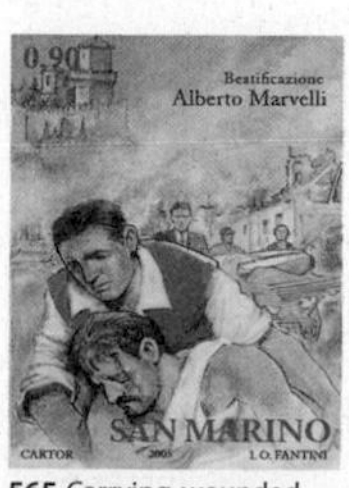

565 Carrying wounded Man

2005. Beatification of Alberto Marvelli. Multicoloured.
2018 90c. Type **565** 2·40 2·40
2019 €1.80 Pope John Paul II and Alberto Marvelli 4·75 4·75

566 "In the Hollow of a Wave off the Coast at Kanagawa" (Hokusai Katsushika) and Faces of Victims

2005. Support For Victims of the Tsunami Disaster.
2020 **566** €1.50 multicoloured 4·00 4·00

567 Weightlifter

2005. Centenary of International Weightlifting Federation.
2021 **567** €2.20 multicoloured 5·75 5·75

568 Soldier scaling Cliff

2005. Alpine Troops. Multicoloured.
2022 36c. Type **568** 1·10 1·10
2023 45c. Soldier picking flower 1·20 1·20
2024 62c. Soldier, mother and child 1·70 1·70
2025 €1 Map of faces 2·75 2·75

569 NCO and Third Tower

2005. Militia. Showing militia men. Multicoloured.
2026 36c. Type **569** 1·10 1·10
2027 45c. Dress uniform and Second Tower 1·20 1·20
2028 62c. Standard bearer and Palazzo Pubblico 1·70 1·70
2029 €1.50 Two militia men and First Tower 4·00 4·00

570 Bread

2005. Europa. Gastronomy. Multicoloured.
2030 62c. Type **570** 1·70 1·70
2031 €1.20 Wine 3·25 3·25

571 Ship, Courier, Letter and Train

2005. History of the Letter. Multicoloured.
2032 36c. Type **571** 1·10 1·10
2033 45c. Man reading letter 1·20 1·20
2034 60c. Three men 1·60 1·60
2035 62c. Man and woman 1·70 1·70

572 1864 5 cent Coin

2005. Coins. Multicoloured.

2036	36c. Type **572**	1·10	1·10
2037	45c. 1898 5 lira coin	1·20	1·20
2038	€1.10 and 20 lira gold coins	2·75	2·75
2039	€2.20 Modern euro coins	5·75	5·75

573 Erminio Macario

2005. Variety Performers. Multicoloured.

2040	45c. Type **573**	1·20	1·20
2041	45c. Wanda Osiris	1·20	1·20
2042	45c. Toto	1·20	1·20
2043	45c. Anna Magnani	1·20	1·20
2044	45c. Aldo Fabrizi	1·20	1·20
2045	45c. Renato Rascel	1·20	1·20
2046	45c. Nino Taranto	1·20	1·20
2047	45c. Delia Scala	1·20	1·20
2048	45c. Tino Scotti	1·20	1·20
2049	45c. Carlo Dapporto	1·20	1·20

574 Face and Kite

2005. 150th Birth Anniv of Giovanni Pascoli (writer). Multicoloured.

2050	36c. Type **574**	1·10	1·10
2051	45c. Mount Titan	1·20	1·20
2052	€1 Family home and horse	2·75	2·75
2053	€2 Tower and Giovanni Pascoli	5·25	5·25

575 Ferrari Wine Label

2005. Wine. Designs showing wine labels. Multicoloured.

2054	45c. Type **575**	1·20	1·20
2055	45c. Amarone della Valpolicella	1·20	1·20
2056	45c. Canevel	1·20	1·20
2057	45c. Biondi-Santi	1·20	1·20
2058	45c. Vecchioflorio	1·20	1·20
2059	45c. Verdicchio dei Castellidijesi	1·20	1·20
2060	45c. Sassicaia (vert)	1·20	1·20
2061	45c. Piano di Monte Vergine dei Feudi di San Gregorio (vert)	1·20	1·20
2062	45c. Tocai Friulano (vert)	1·20	1·20
2063	45c. Barolo (vert)	1·20	1·20

576 Devil and Angel as Gondoliers

2005. Venice Regatta. Multicoloured.

2064	€1.40 Type **576**	3·75	3·75
2065	€2 Gondolier wearing traditional costume (vert)	5·25	5·25

577 Dahlia

2005. Self-adhesive.

2066	**577** (20g.) multicoloured	1·20	1·20

578 Panel, St. John the Baptist (Lorenzo Ghiberti) (550th death anniv)

2005. Anniversaries. Multicoloured.

2067	36c. Type **578**	95	95
2068	62c. "The Annunciation" (Beato Angelico) (550th death anniv)	1·70	1·70
2069	€1 Jules Verne and illustrations (writer) (death centenary)	2·75	2·75
2070	€2 Hans Christian Andersen and illustrations (writer) (birth bicentenary)	3·50	3·50

579 The Annunciation

2005. Christmas. Multicoloured.

2071	62c. Type **579**	1·70	1·70
2072	€1.55 The Nativity	4·25	4·25
2073	€2.20 Three Wise Men	6·00	6·00

580 Pope Clement XIV

2005. 300th Birth Anniv of Pope Clement XIV. Multicoloured.

2074	80c. Type **580**	2·10	2·10
2075	€1 Pope Clement XIV facing left	2·75	2·75

581 Ski Jump, Snow Board and Flags

2006. Winter Olympic Games, Turin. Multicoloured.

2076	45c. Type **581**	1·20	1·20
2077	45c. Ski run, village and flags	1·20	1·20
2078	45c. Cross-country skiing, bob-sleigh, ice hockey and finish line	1·20	1·20
2079	45c. Ice skating, cross-country skiing and chair lift	1·20	1·20

Nos. 2076/9 were issued together, se-tenant, forming a composite design.

582 Palazzo Pubblico

2006. Centenary of Arengo of Patriarchs (first governing body). Multicoloured.

2080	45c. Type **582**	1·20	1·20
2081	62c. Statue of Liberty, Piazza della Liberta	1·70	1·70
2082	€1.50 Basilica Del Santo Marino	4·00	4·00

583 Christopher Columbus and Native American

2006. 500th Death Anniv of Christopher Columbus (explorer). Multicoloured.

2083	90c. Type **583**	2·40	2·40
2084	€1.80 Holding globe and compasses	4·75	4·75

584 Palazzo Mentcitorio, Rome and Palazzo Pubblico, San Marino

2006. Le Due Repubbliche (two republics) Philatelic Exhibition. Sheet 121×90 mm containing T 584 and similar horiz design. Multicoloured.

MS2085	62c.×2, Type **584**; Type **1365** of Italy	33·00	33·00

No. **MS**2085 is identical to **MS**3011 of Italy. Nos. **MS**2085 of San Marino and Nos. 3010/**MS**3011 of Italy were all issued on the same day.

585 "Bathers" (Paul Cezanne)

2006. Art. Multicoloured.

2086	36c. Type **585**	1·10	1·10
2087	45c. "Bathsheba with Letter from David" (Rembrandt)	1·20	1·20
2088	60c. "Coronation of the Virgin" (Gentile da Fabriano)	1·60	1·60
2089	€1.80 "The Room of Spouses" (Andrea Mantegna)	4·75	4·75

586 Emblem, Flag and Ball

2006. World Cup Football Championship, Germany.

2090	**586** €2.20 multicoloured	5·75	5·75

587 Flag Throwers

2006. 50th Anniv of Crossbow Federation. Multicoloured.

2091	36c. Type **587**	95	95
2092	45c. Standard bearers	1·20	1·20
2093	62c. Archer preparing to shoot	1·70	1·70
2094	€1 Two archers positioning arrows	2·75	2·75
2095	€1.50 Three flag throwers	4·00	4·00
2096	€2.80 Arms master holding target full of arrows	7·50	7·50

588 Butterfly (Sara Santolini)

2006. Europa. Integration. Multicoloured.

2097	45c. Type **588**	1·20	1·20
2098	62c. Vitruvian man (after Leonardo da Vinci) (Marco Moliari and Clementina Casadei)	1·70	1·70

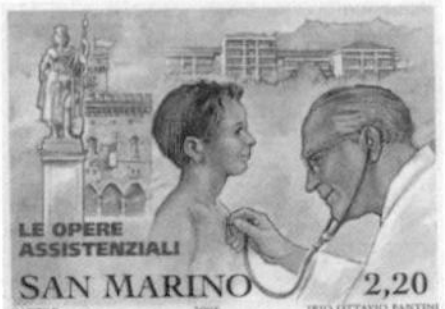

589 Doctor and Child

2006. Military Order of Malta.

2099	€2.20 multicoloured	5·75	5·75

590 Hand in Ring

2006. 125th Anniv of International Gymnastic Federation. Multicoloured.

2100	15c. Type **590**	40	40
2101	€2.80 Gymnast	7·50	7·50

591 Second Tower

2006. 40th Anniv of Italian Philatelic Press Union. Multicoloured.

2102	90c. Type **591**	2·40	2·40
2103	€2.20 Archway, Palazzo Strozzi and "Gli Amanti" (sculpture) (Giacomo Maria Cavina)	5·75	5·75

592 Grandmother's Face

2006. Italy—2006 Football World Cup Champions.

2104	**592** €1 multicoloured	2·75	2·75

593 Scene from "Rome Open City" (film)

2006. Anniversaries. Multicoloured.

2105	5c. Type **593** (Roberto Rosellini (director) (birth centenary))	25	25
2106	65c. Top hat (Luchino Visconti (director) (birth centenary))	1·70	1·70
2107	85c. Friar (Iacopone da Todi (writer) (700th death anniv)	2·30	2·30
2108	€1.40 "K 551" (Wolfgang Amadeus Mozart (composer) (250th birth anniv))	3·75	3·75

594 Joseph (detail)

2006. Christmas. Showing details from "La Natività" by Giovan Battista Tiepolo. Multicoloured.

2109	60c. Type **594**	1·60	1·60
2110	60c. Angel	1·60	1·60
2111	65c. Infant Jesus	1·70	1·70
2112	65c. Virgin Mary	1·70	1·70
2113	€2.80 "La Nativita" (29×40 mm)	7·25	7·25

595 Duke Guidubaldo de Montefeltro (founder), "Ideal City" (painting) and Carlo Bo (rector, 1947–2001)

2006. 500th Anniv of Urbino University.

2119	**595**	€2.20 multicoloured	5·75	5·75

596 San Marino Flag and EU Emblem

2007. San Merino's Presidency of Council of Europe Council of Ministers.

2120	**596**	65c. multicoloured	1·70	1·70

597 "Self Portrait" (painting)

2006. Gina Lollobrigida, Artist. Designs showing Gina Lollobrigida's work. Multicoloured.

2121	65c. Type **597**	1·70	1·70
2122	85c. "Potato Seller" (photograph)	2·30	2·30
2123	€1 "Esmeralda" (sculpture)	2·75	2·75
2124	€3.20 Gina Lollobrigida with Mother Teresa (as ambassador for FAO)	8·50	8·50

598 Alessandro Glaray and Philatelic Material

2007. Alessandro Glaray (philatelic expert) Commemoration.

2125	**598**	€1.80 multicoloured	4·75	4·75

599 Arriving in San Marino with Anita and the Thousand

2007. Birth Bicentenary of Giuseppe Garibaldi (soldier and nationalist). Multicoloured.

2126	65c. Type **599**	1·70	1·70
2127	€1.40 Arriving in Marsala (the Kingdom of Two Sicilies war) and fighting in Uruguayan War of Independence	3·75	3·75
2128	€2 Handshake at Teano ending Italian War of Independence	5·25	5·25

600 Window Dresser's Tool

2007. Birth Centenary of Bruno Munari (artist, designer, writer, and educator).

2129	**600**	36c. yellow and black	95	95
2130	-	65c. blue and black	1·70	1·70
2131	-	€1.40 magenta and black	3·75	3·75
2132	-	€2 green and black	5·25	5·25

DESIGNS: 36c. Type **600**; 65c. Milk carton; €1.40 Roll-up shutter lock; €2 Garage lamp.

601 Cherubs, Church of the Immaculate Conception, Palermo

2007. San Gabriel International Philatelic Art Award, Legnago.

2133	**601**	€1.50 multicoloured	4·00	4·00

602 Scouts, Globe, Compass and Brownsea Island

2007. Europa. Centenary of Scouting. Multicoloured.

2134	60c. Type **602**	1·60	1·60
2135	65c. Scout master, scout and Three Towers	1·70	1·70

603 High Jump

2007. World Athletics Championships, Osaka. Multicoloured.

2136	60c. Type **603**	1·60	1·60
2137	85c. Long jump (horiz)	2·30	2·30
2138	€1.50 Runner (horiz)	4·00	4·00

603a Striker

2007. European Baseball Cup, San Marino. Multicoloured.

2139	65c. Type **603a**	1·70	1·70
2140	€1 Pitcher	2·75	2·75

604 Cliffs and Postilion (detail from 'Theatrum civitatum et admirandorum Italiae' by Joan (Johannes) Blaeu)

2007. 400th Anniv of Mail Services. Sheet 110×83 mm.

MS2141	€4.50 multicoloured	12·00	12·00

The stamp and margin of **MS**2141 form a composite design.

605 Catalogues, Albums and Magazines

2007. 30th Anniv of Constitution of ASCAT (association of philatelic editors). Riccione International Stamp Fair.

2142	**605**	65c. multicoloured	1·70	1·70

606 La Guaita (Rocca) Tower, San Marino

2007. The Oldest (San Marino–301) and Newest (Slovakia–1993) Republics of Europe. Mult.

2143	65c. Type **606**	1·70	1·70
2144	65c. Orava Castle, Slovakia	1·70	1·70

Stamps of a similar design were issued by Slovakia.

607 Port (Quinta do Estanho, Portugal)

2007. European Wines. Sheet 185×143 mm. T 607 and similar multicoloured designs.

MS2145	65c.×8, Type **607**; Champagne (Tarlant, France) (horiz); Champagne (Bauget-Jouette, France) (horiz); Zlahtina white wine (Katunar, Croatia); Reisling (Petri, Germany); Tokaji (Chateau Pajzos, Hungary) (horiz); Ribera del Duero (Carmelo Rodero, Spain) (horiz); Teodor Belo (Simcic, Slovenia)	14·00	14·00

608 Palazzo del Governo

2007. Christmas. Multicoloured.

2146	60c. Type **608**	1·60	1·60
2147	65c. Santa Claus	1·70	1·70
2148	85c. Holy Family and Three Towers, San Marino	2·30	2·30

609 Arturo Toscanni (conductor)

2007. Artistes' Anniversaries. Multicoloured.

2149	60c. Type **609** (50th death anniv)	1·60	1·60
2150	65c. *Paolina Borghese* (sculpture) (Antonio Canova) (250th birth anniv)	1·70	1·70
2151	€1 Harlequin (Carlos Goldoni) (comedic playwright) (300th birth anniv)	2·75	2·75
2152	€1.80 *Via Toscanella* (painting) (Ottone Rosai) (50th death anniv)	4·75	4·75

610 Woman holding Scales

2007. Equal Opportunities for All.

2153	**610**	€1 multicoloured	3·25	3·25

611 *Crocefissione* (Crucifixion) (Giovanni Bellini)

2008. Capolavori che ritornano

2154	36c. Type **611**	1·10	1·10
2155	60c. *Madonna con bambino e San Giovannino* (Madonna with Child and Saint John) (Jacopo Bassano)	1·60	1·60
2156	65c. *Venere e Amore* (Venus and Love) (Gian Antonio Pellegrini)	1·70	1·70
2157	85c. *Testa di vecchio* (Old Man's Face) (Giandomenico Tiepolo)	2·30	2·30

612 'Aria' (air) (Andrea Lisi)

2008. International Year of Planet Earth. Drawings by Faculty of Industrial Design Students, University of San Marino. Multicoloured.

2158	60c. Type **612**	1·60	1·60
2159	85c. Uomo	2·30	2·30
2160	€1.40 Aqua	3·75	3·75
2161	€2 Terra	5·25	5·25

613 Emblem

2008. Centenary of Inter Football Club.

2162	**613**	€1 multicoloured	2·75	2·75

614 Pianello, Old Public Palace, First Post Office and 'Affrancata' (cancellation)

2008. 175th Anniv of Post Office in San Marino.

2163	**614**	€1.80 multicoloured	4·75	4·75

615 Bernadette Soubirous and First Miracle

2008. 150th Anniv of Apparition at Lourdes. Multicoloured.

2164	36c. Type **615**	1·10	1·10
2165	60c. Pilgrims and Basilica	1·60	1·60
2166	€2 Bernadette Soubirous and Madonna	5·25	5·25

616 Globe as Pangea

2008. European Year of Intercultural Dialogue.

2167	**616**	65c. multicoloured	1·70	1·70

617 Concetto Marchesi

2008. 130th Birth Anniv of Concetto Marchesi (academic and politician).

2168	**617**	€1 multicoloured	2·75	2·75

618 Table Tennis

2008. Olympic Games, Beijing. Sheet 137×105 mm containing T 618 and similar horiz design. Multicoloured.

MS2169 36c. Type **618**; 65c. Fencing; 85c. Swimming 5·00 5·00

619 Envelopes as Ships

2008. Europa. The Letter. Multicoloured.

2170	60c. Type **619**	1·60	1·60
2171	65c. Couple on globe releasing envelopes as doves	1·70	1·70

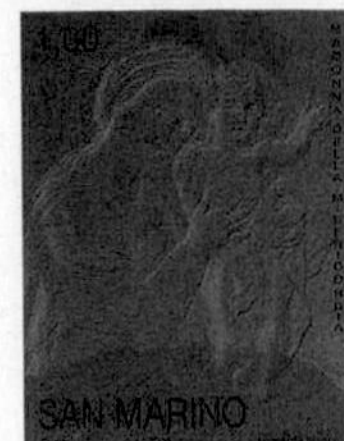

620 *Our Lady of Mercy*

2008. Art for Basilica of the Annunciation, Nazareth.

2172	**620**	€1 multicoloured	2·75	2·75

621 Statues of Liberty of San Marino and USA

2008. 30th Anniv of San Marino–USA Friendship Association.

2173	**621**	€1.50 multicoloured	4·00	4·00

622 Posters for *La Boheme* and *Madame Butterfly*

2008. Anniversaries. Multicoloured.

2174	60c. Type **622** (Giacomo Puccini) (composer) (150th birth anniv)	1·60	1·60
2175	€1 *Rotonda di Palmieri* and *Vita Militare* (Giovanni Fattori) (artist) (death centenary)	2·75	2·75
2176	€1.40 Book covers for *Don Camillo* and *Diario Clandestino* (Giovannino Guareschi) (writer) (birth centenary)	3·75	3·75
2177	€1.70 *The Print Collectors* and ceramic bust (Honoré Daumier) (artist) (birth bicentenary)	4·50	4·50

623 Chronometer and Cyclist

2008. World Road Cycling Championships, Varese. Multicoloured.

2178	85c. Type **623**	2·30	2·30
2179	€3.85 Rider and cycle	8·50	8·50

624 Andrea Palladio and Villa Pojana

2008. 500th Birth Anniv of Andrea Palladio (architect).

2180	**624**	€1 multicoloured	2·75	2·75

625 Angel

2008. Christmas. Multicoloured.

2181	36c. Type **625**	1·30	1·30
2182	60c. Holy Family	1·90	1·90
2183	€1 Angel carrying gift	3·25	3·25

626 Polar Landscape

2008. International Polar Year. Multicoloured.

2184	60c. Type **626**	1·90	1·90
2185	€1 Penguins	3·25	3·25
2186	€1.20 Research helicopter	4·00	4·00

627 Tamburino (character from *Cuore*)

2008. Writers. Multicoloured.

2187	60c. Type **627** (Edmondo de Amicis) (death centenary)	1·90	1·90
2188	€2.20 Scene from *La Lune e i falo* (Cesare Pavese) (birth centenary)	7·25	7·25

628 Second Tower (Cesta Fortress)

2008. Inclusion of Historic Centre and Mount Titano in UNESCO World Heritage Lists. Sheet 185×143 mm containing T 628 and similar vert designs. Multicoloured.

MS2189 €1×6, Type **628**; San Marino Basilica; Piazza della Liberta, Il Palazzo Pubblico; Contrada Omerelli; Contrada delle Mura; First Tower (Guaita) 19·00 19·00

629 Two-handled Amphora (Libero Cellarosi)

2009. Sammarinese Ceramists. Multicoloured.

2190	36c. Type **629**	1·30	1·30
2191	60c. Amphora (Umberto Masi)	1·90	1·90
2192	85c. Vase (Giorgio Monti)	2·75	2·75

630 *Dinamismo di un cane al guinzaglio* (Giacomo Balla)

2009. Centenary of Futurist Manifesto. Sheet 185×143 mm containing T 630 and similar multicoloured designs.

MS2193 60c.×10, Type **630**; *Treno armato* (Gino Severini) (vert); *Studio per centrale electtrica* (Antonio Sant'elia) (vert); *Zang Tumb Tumb* (Filippo Tommaso Marinetti); *Cavaliere rosso* (Carlo Carra); *Risveglio di una città* (Luigi Russolo); *Dinamismo di un ciclista* (Umberto Boccioni); *Natura morta con uvovo rosso* (Ardengo Soffici) (vert); *Forme uniche nella continuità dello spazio* (Umberto Boccioni) (vert); *Serata futurista* (Umberto Boccioni); 19·00 19·00

631 Emblem

2009. 50th Anniv of Comitato Olimpico Nazionale di San Marino (CONS) (Olympic committee).

2194	**631**	€1.80 multicoloured	5·75	5·75

632 Saturn and Astronomical Instruments

2009. Europa. Astronomy. Multicoloured.

2195	60c. Type **632**	1·90	1·90
2196	65c. Solar system	2·10	2·10

633 Hot Air Balloon and Doves

2009. World Air Games, Turin. Multicoloured.

2197	60c. Type **633**	1·90	1·90
2198	85c. Glider with a dove on each wing	2·75	2·75
2199	€1.50 Dove swinging below helicopter	4·75	4·75
2200	€1.80 Dove surfing on aircraft trail	6·00	6·00

634 Emblem

2009. ICPO–Interpol European Regional Conference, San Marino.

2201	**634**	€2 multicoloured	6·50	6·50

635 Shanghai Financial Centre and China Pavilion

2009. Expo 2010, Shanghai, China.

2202	**635**	€2.20 multicoloured	6·75	6·75

636 August Dauphin (Edgar Allan Poe)

2009. Writers' Anniversaries. Designs showing symbols of characters. Multicoloured.

2203	36c. Type **636** (birth bicentenary)	1·30	1·30
2204	85c. Sherlock Holmes (Arthur Conan Doyle) (150th birth anniv)	2·75	2·75
2205	€1.40 Philip Marlowe (Raymond Chandler) (50th death anniv)	4·50	4·50

637 Tessano

2009. Wines of San Marino. Sheet 137×105 mm containing T 637 and similar horiz designs showing wine bottles. Multicoloured.
MS2206 60c.×6, Type **637**; Brugneto; Riserva Titano; Caldese; Roncale; Moscato Spumante 9·50 9·50

638 Athletics

2009. Mediterranean Games, Pescara. Multicoloured.

2207	60c. Type **638**	1·90	1·90
2208	€1.40 Cycling	4·50	4·50
2209	€1.70 Wrestling	5·25	5·25

639 'Braille'

2009. Birth Bicentenary of Louis Braille (inventor of Braille writing for the blind).
2210 **639** €1.50 multicoloured 4·75 4·75
No. 2210 is embossed with Braille writing.

640 '30' enclosing Dove

2009. 30th (2010) Meeting for Friendship Among Peoples, Rimini.
2211 **640** €1.80 multicoloured 6·00 6·00

641 Centenary Emblem, Club Colours and Player

2009. Centenary of Bologna Football Club.
2212 **641** €1 multicoloured 3·25 3·25

642 Statue of Liberty

2009. European Year of Creativity and Innovation. Stereoscopic Stamps. Three sheets, each 150×43 mm containing T 642 and similar horiz designs. Multicoloured.

MS2213 €1×2, Type **642**×2	6·50	6·50
MS2214 €1×2, Palazzo Pubblico interior×2	6·50	6·50
MS2215 €1×2, Statue of St. Marinus×2	6·50	6·50

The stamps of Nos. **MS**2213/**MS**2215, whilst showing the same image, differ slightly.

643 Cat (Natascia Stefanelli)

2009. Pet Photograph Competition Winners. Multicoloured.

2216	36c. Type **643**	1·30	1·30
2217	60c. Cocker spaniel (Tina Woodcock)	1·90	1·90
2218	65c. Duck (Ettore Zonzini)	2·10	2·10
2219	75c. Goat, foal and dog (Anna Rosa Francioni)	2·50	2·50
2220	85c. Tiny tortoise (Maria Eleonora Vaglio)	2·75	2·75
2221	€1.20 Basset hound (Lorenzo Zamagni)	3·75	3·75

644 Dante and Virgil and Three Wild Beasts (from 15th-century Codex Urbinate Latino 365, Vatican Apostolic Library)

2009. Italia 2009 International Stamp Exhibition, Rome. Italian Language.
2222 **644** 60c. multicoloured 1·90 1·90
A stamp of a similar design was issued by Italy and Vatican City.

645 Joseph

2009. Christmas. Rest on the Flight into Egypt (Caravaggio). Sheet 137×105 mm containing T 645 and similar multicoloured design.
MS2223 €1.50 Type **645**; €2 Virgin and Child (vert) 4·75 4·75

646 Narcissi

2010. Flowers. Multicoloured.

2224	10c. Type **646**	20	20
2225	85c. Hyacinth	2·50	2·50
2226	€1 Muscari	3·50	3·50
2227	€1.50 Tulips	3·75	3·75

647 Ski Jump, Snowboarding, Ice Hockey and Speed Skating

2010. Winter Olympic Games, Vancouver. Multicoloured.
MS2228 65c. Type **647**; 85c. Downhill skiing, Nordic skiing, Curling and Bob sleigh; €1 Speed skating (different), Ice dance and Grand Slalom 7·50 7·50

648 Third Tower

2010. Expo 2010, Shanghai
MS2229 65c. Type **648**; €1 Second tower; €1.50 First Tower; €1.80 Government Building and the Statue of Liberty (36×51 mm) 15·00 15·00

649 La Republica (V. Pochini) and First Tower (Guaita)

2010. 50th Anniv of Association of Blood and Organ Donors (AVSSO)
2230 **649** €1.80 multicoloured 5·25 5·25

650 Flying Girl with Open Book as Wings

2010. Europa . Multicoloured.

2231	60c Type **650**	3·50	3·50
2232	65c. Girl sleeping on open book, amongst clouds containing characters and planets	3·75	3·74

651 Gino Bartali (10th death anniv)

2010. Cyclists' Anniversaries. Multicoloured.

2233	€1.40 Type **651**	4·25	4·25
2234	€1.50 Fausto Coppi (50th death anniv)	4·25	2·25

Nos. 2233/4 were printed, *se-tenant*, forming a composite design

652 Player and Net

2010. World Men's Volleyball Championship, Italy
2235 **652** €1 multicoloured 3·00 3·00

653 Emblem and Players

2010. World Cup Football Championships, South Africa
2236 **653** €1.50 multicoloured 8·50 8·50

654 La Republica (V. Pochini) and First Tower (Guaita)

2010. San Marino–Japan. Multicoloured.
MS2237 €1.50×4, Type **654**; Himej Castle; *Apparizione di San Marino al suo popolo* (E. Retrosi) (mural); *Tokaido-Gojyusantugi* (Nihonbashi in the Morning) 18·00 18·00
Stamps of a similar design were issued by Japan

655 San Marino from East

2010. 50th Anniv of San Marino Lions Club. Multicoloured.

2238	36c. Type **655**	90	90
2239	60c. San Marino, aerial view	1·90	1·90

656 'inter', Italian Flag and Football

2010. Inter Football Club, winners of Italian Football League, Italian Cup and European Champions League. Multicoloured.

2240	€1 Type **656**	3·00	3·00
2241	€1 '3 volte', Italian shield enclosing '18'	3·00	3·00
2242	€1 'campione' and 'Campione d'Europa'	3·00	3·00

657 The Birth of Venus (Sandro Botticelli)

2010. Art. Multicoloured.

2243	€1 Type **657**	3·00	3·00
2244	€1.40 *The Tempest* (Giorgione da Castelfranco Veneto)	3·75	3·75
2245	€1.45 *Supper at Emmaus* (Michelangelo Merisi da Caravaggio)	4·25	4·25
2246	€1.50 *Football Players* (Henri Rousseau)	5·00	5·00

658 Second Tower

2010. San Marino–Gibraltar. Multicoloured.
MS2247 €1.50×4, Type **658**; Moresco Castle, Gibraltar; Mount Titano; Rock of Gibraltar 16·00 16·00
Stamps of a similar design were issued by Gibraltar

EXPRESS LETTER STAMPS

E22 Mt. Titano and "Liberty"

1907

E53	E22	25c. pink	27·00	10·50

1923. Optd ESPRESSO.

E92	19	60c. violet	55	55

1923. Surch Cent. 60.

E93	E22	60c. on 25c. pink	55	55

E34

1923. Red Cross.

E101	E34	60c.+5c. red	2·20	2·10

1926. No. E92 surch Lire 1,25.

E134	E19	1l.25 on 60c. violet	1·10	1·10

1927. No. E93 surch L. 1,25 and bars over old surch.

E138	E22	1l.25 on 60c. on 25c. pink	80	85

E50 Statue of Liberty and View of San Marino

1929. As Type E 50 but without "UNION POSTALE UNIVERSELLE" and inscr "ESPRESSO".

E164	E50	1l.25 green	30	20

1929. Optd UNION POSTALE UNIVERSELLE as in Type E 50.

E165		2l.50 blue	70	80

E78

1943

E305	E78	1l.25 green	15	15
E306	E78	2l.50 orange	15	15

E79 Mt. Titano

1945

E307	E79	2l.50 green	20	15
E308	E79	5l. orange	20	15
E309	E79	5l. red	1·40	60
E310	E79	10l. blue	3·25	1·90
E419	E79	60l. red	15·00	5·50

E87 Pegasus and Mt. Titano

1946

E337	E87	30l. blue	7·25	4·25
E420	E87	80l. blue	24·00	9·50

1947. Surch.

E339	E79	15l. on 5l. red	60	25
E340	E79	15l. on 10l. blue	60	25
E374	E 87	35l. on 30l. blue	46·00	31·00
E341	E 87	60l. on 30l. blue	5·50	5·50
E545	E 79	75l. on 60l. red	4·25	2·50
E375	E 87	80l. on 30l. blue	49·00	22·00
E546	E 87	100l. on 80l. blue	4·25	2·50
E783	E 180	120l. on 75l. black and yellow	15	15
E784	E 180	135l. on 100l. black and orange	15	15

E180 Crossbow and Three "Castles"

1966

E800	E180	75l. black and yellow	15	15
E801	E180	80l. black and purple	15	15
E802	E180	100l. black and orange	15	15

No. E800 has crossbow in white without "shadows".

PARCEL POST STAMPS Unused and used prices are for complete pairs

P46

1928

P145	P46	5c. purple and blue	30	25
P146	P46	10c. blue and light blue	30	25
P147	P46	20c. black and blue	30	25
P148	P46	25c. red and blue	30	25
P149	P46	30c. ultramarine & blue	40	25
P150	P46	30c. orange and blue	40	25
P151	P46	60c. red and blue	40	25
P152	P46	1l. violet and red	40	25
P153	P46	2l. green and red	80	1·30
P154	P46	3l. bistre and red	1·30	2·10
P155	P46	4l. grey and red	1·60	2·75
P156	P46	10l. mauve and red	4·75	4·25
P157	P46	12l. lake and red	13·50	12·00
P158	P46	15l. green and red	21·00	21·00
P159	P46	20l. purple and red	34·00	34·00

1945

P309	5c. purple and red	20	15
P310	10c. brown and black	20	15
P311	20c. red and green	20	15
P312	25c. yellow and black	20	15
P313	30c. mauve and red	20	15
P314	50c. violet and black	20	15
P315	60c. red and black	20	15
P316	1l. brown and blue	35	15
P317	2l. brown and blue	35	15
P318	3l. grey and brown	35	15
P319	4l. green and brown	35	15
P320	10l. grey and violet	80	15
P770	10l. green and red	15	15
P321	12l. green and blue	4·25	4·75
P322	15l. green and violet	3·00	2·40
P323	20l. violet and brown	3·00	2·40
P324	25l. red and blue	80·00	37·00
P771	50l. yellow and red	15	15
P455	300l. violet and red	£275	£170
P773	300l. violet and brown	35	35
P526	500l. brown and red	3·25	5·25
P775	1000l. green and brown	1·10	1·10

1948. Nos. P324 and P771 surch in figures and wavy lines on each half of design.

P524	100l. on 50l. yellow and red	85	1·70
P375	200l. on 25l. red & blue	£350	£180

POSTAGE DUE STAMPS

D18

1897

D38	D18	5c. brown and green	1·10	55
D39	D18	10c. brown and green	1·10	55
D40	D18	30c. brown and green	2·75	1·10
D41	D18	50c. brown and green	7·25	2·10
D42	D18	60c. brown and green	29·00	7·50
D43	D18	1l. brown and pink	13·50	6·50
D44	D18	3l. brown and pink	40·00	20·00
D45	D18	5l. brown and pink	£250	65·00
D46	D18	10l. brown and pink	80·00	36·00

1924

D102	5c. brown and red	80	1·10
D103	10c. brown and red	80	1·10
D104	30c. brown and red	1·30	1·10
D105	50c. brown and red	1·90	1·30
D106	60c. brown and red	10·00	7·25
D107	1l. brown and green	16·00	12·00
D108	3l. brown and green	50·00	37·00
D109	5l. brown and green	70·00	55·00
D110	10l. brown and green	£400	£350

1925

D112	5c. brown and red	40	25
D113	10c. brown and blue	85	60
D114	15c. brown and blue	40	25
D115	20c. brown and blue	40	25
D116	25c. brown and blue	65	60
D117	30c. brown and blue	85	55
D118	40c. brown and blue	4·00	3·75
D119	50c. brown and blue	1·90	2·10
D120	60c. brown and blue	4·00	1·10
D121	1l. brown and orange	7·75	1·60
D122	2l. brown and orange	2·30	2·10
D123	3l. brown and orange	£110	46·00
D124	5l. brown and orange	28·00	7·50
D125	10l. brown and orange	44·00	16·00
D126	15l. brown and orange	3·50	2·10
D127	25l. brown and orange	55·00	34·00
D128	30l. brown and orange	10·50	14·00
D129	50l. brown and orange	14·00	14·00

1931. As Type D 18 but with centre obliterated in black and new value superimposed in silver.

D164	15c. on 5c. blue	55	55
D165	15c. on 10c. blue	55	55
D166	15c. on 30c. blue	55	55
D167	20c. on 5c. blue	55	55
D168	20c. on 10c. blue	65	55
D169	20c. on 30c. blue	65	55
D170	25c. on 5c. blue	2·40	1·60
D171	25c. on 10c. blue	2·40	1·60
D172	25c. on 30c. blue	21·00	13·00
D173	40c. on 10c. blue	2·50	1·10
D174	40c. on 10c. blue	3·00	1·60
D175	40c. on 30c. blue	3·00	1·60
D176	2l. on 5c. blue	80·00	46·00
D177	2l. on 10c. blue	£150	85·00
D178	2l. on 30c. blue	£110	70·00

1936. Surch in figures and words and bars. Nos. D233/8 and D242 are brown and blue; the rest brown and orange.

D233	10c. on 5c.	55	55
D234	25c. on 30c.	16·00	16·00
D235	50c. on 5c.	4·00	1·60
D237	1l. on 30c.	60·00	9·50
D238	1l. on 40c.	12·00	9·50
D239	1l. on 3l.	60·00	2·25
D240	1l. on 25l.	£120	28·00
D241	2l. on 15l.	55·00	33·00
D242	3l. on 20c.	42·00	28·00
D243	25l. on 50l.	3·00	3·00

D82

1945

D309	D82	5c. green	30	15
D310	D82	10c. brown	30	15
D311	D82	15c. red	30	15
D312	D82	20c. blue	30	15
D313	D82	25c. violet	30	15
D314	D82	30c. mauve	30	15
D315	D82	40c. yellow	30	15
D316	D82	50c. grey	30	15
D317	D82	60c. brown	30	15
D318	D82	1l. orange	30	15
D319	D82	2l. red	30	15
D320	D82	5l. violet	30	15
D321	D82	10l. blue	1·10	80
D322	D82	20l. green	18·00	12·00
D323	D82	25l. brown	18·00	12·00
D324	D82	50l. brown	18·00	12·00

Pt. 20

SANTANDER

One of the states of the Granadine Cofederation.

A department of Columbia from 1886, now uses Colombian stamps.

100 centavos = 1 peso.

1

1884. Imperf.

1	1	1c. blue	35	30
2	1	5c. red	65	65
3	1	10c. violet	2·40	2·30

2

1886. Imperf.

4	2	1c. blue	1·20	1·20
5	2	5c. red	45	45
6	2	10c. lilac	65	65

1887. As T 1 but inscr "REPUBLICA DE COLOMBIA". Imperf.

7	1c. blue	35	30
8	5c. red	2·20	2·10
9	10c. violet	7·25	7·00

3 4 5

1890. Perf.

10	3	1c. blue	45	45
11	4	5c. red	1·70	1·60
12	5	10c. violet	55	55

6

1895

14	6	5c. red on buff	1·30	1·20

7

1895

15	7	5c. brown	90	85
16	7	5c. green	90	85

8 9 10

1899

17	8	1c. black on green	45	45
18	9	5c. black on red	45	45
19	10	10c. blue	1·00	95

F11

1903. Fiscal stamp as Type F 11 optd Provisional. Correos de Santander. Imperf.

21	F11	50c. red	75	75

Pt. 1

SARAWAK

Formerly an independent state on the north coast of Borneo under British protection. Under Japanese occupation from 1941 until 1945. A Crown Colony from 1946 until September 1963, when it became a state of the Federation of Malaysia.

100 cents = 1 dollar (Malayan or Malaysian).

1 Sir James Brooke

1869

1	1	3c. brown on yellow	55·00	£225

2 Sir Charles Brooke

1871

3	2	2c. mauve on lilac	19·00	17·00
2	2	3c. brown on yellow	2·25	3·50
4	2	4c. brown on yellow	5·00	3·00
5	2	6c. green on green	4·50	3·75
6	2	8c. blue on blue	4·25	5·00
7	2	12c. red on red	9·00	6·50

4 Sir Charles Brooke

1888

8	4	1c. purple and black	4·50	1·25
9	4	2c. purple and red	5·50	3·00
10	4	3c. purple and blue	7·50	5·00
11	4	4c. purple and yellow	32·00	65·00
12	4	5c. purple and green	27·00	4·25
13	4	6c. purple and brown	24·00	60·00
14	4	8c. green and red	16·00	4·75
15	4	10c. green and purple	45·00	14·00
16	4	12c. green and blue	16·00	12·00
17	4	16c. green and orange	55·00	90·00
18	4	25c. green and brown	60·00	45·00
19	4	32c. green and black	48·00	70·00
20	4	50c. green	65·00	£120
21	4	$1 green and black	£100	£100

1889. Surch in words (1c.) or figures (others).

22		1c. on 3c. purple and blue (surch **One Cent.**)	65·00	40·00
23		1c. on 3c. purple and blue (surch **one cent.**)	3·25	2·75
27	2	1c. on 3c. brown on yellow (surch **ONE CENT**)	1·40	2·00
24		2c. on 8c. green and red	3·50	8·00
25		5c. on 12c. green and blue	29·00	55·00

11 Sir Charles Brooke

1895. Various frames.

28c	11	2c. red	22·00	4·50
29	11	4c. black	14·00	3·50
30	11	6c. violet	17·00	9·00
31	11	8c. green	38·00	6·00

1889. Surch in figures and words.

32	2	2c. on 3c. brown on yellow	2·75	1·75
33	2	2c. on 12c. red on red	3·25	3·75
34	2	4c. on 6c. green on green	45·00	90·00
35	2	4c. on 8c. blue on blue	7·00	11·00

1899. As T 4, but inscr "POSTAGE POSTAGE".

36		1c. blue and red	1·25	1·25
37		2c. green	2·00	90
38		3c. purple	17·00	65
39a		4c. red	2·50	15
40		8c. yellow and black	2·25	80
41		10c. blue	3·75	1·00
42		12c. mauve	5·50	4·50
43		16c. brown and green	6·50	1·75
44		20c. brown and mauve	5·50	6·00
45		25c. brown and blue	8·50	5·50
46		50c. green and red	28·00	32·00
47		$1 red and green	90·00	£120

17 Sir Charles Vyner Brooke

1918

76	17	1c. blue and red	1·50	35
51	17	2c. green	2·50	1·50
77	17	2c. purple	2·25	1·25
52	17	3c. purple	3·25	2·75
64	17	3c. green	3·50	1·25
53	17	4c. red	7·50	3·75
79	17	4c. purple	1·75	10
66	17	5c. orange	1·75	2·00
81	17	6c. purple	1·25	30
54	17	8c. yellow and black	13·00	65·00
82	17	8c. red	3·25	26·00
55	17	10c. blue	5·00	5·00
83	17	10c. black	1·75	1·25
56	17	12c. purple	18·00	42·00
84	17	12c. blue	3·25	35·00
85	17	16c. brown and green	3·25	4·00
86	17	20c. bistre and violet	3·25	7·50
87	17	25c. brown and blue	6·00	8·50
71	17	30c. brown and grey	3·75	4·25
89	17	50c. green and red	12·00	24·00
90	17	$1 pink and green	17·00	24·00

1923. Surch in words.

72		1c. on 10c. blue	10·00	60·00
73		2c. on 12c. purple	6·50	48·00

19 Sir Charles Vyner Brooke

1932

91	19	1c. blue	80	1·00
92	19	2c. green	1·00	2·25
93	19	3c. violet	4·00	1·00
94	19	4c. orange	9·00	75
95	19	5c. lake	6·50	1·25
96	19	6c. red	7·00	11·00
97	19	8c. yellow	9·00	8·50
98	19	10c. black	2·25	3·25
99	19	12c. blue	4·00	9·50
100	19	15c. brown	6·50	10·00
101	19	20c. orange and violet	6·50	8·00
102	19	25c. yellow and brown	10·00	22·00
103	19	30c. brown and red	9·50	35·00
104	19	50c. red and olive	14·00	13·00
105	19	$1 green and red	22·00	35·00

21 Sir Charles Vyner Brooke

1934

106	21	1c. purple	1·25	10
107	21	2c. green	1·50	10
107a	21	2c. black	4·75	1·60
108	21	3c. black	1·25	10
108a	21	3c. green	7·50	4·50
109	21	4c. purple	2·00	15
110	21	5c. violet	2·00	10
111	21	6c. red	2·75	60
111a	21	6c. brown	8·50	8·00
112	21	8c. brown	2·25	10
112a	21	8c. red	9·00	10
113	21	10c. red	4·25	40
114	21	12c. blue	3·00	25
114a	21	12c. orange	7·50	4·75
115	21	15c. orange	7·50	10·00
115a	21	15c. blue	9·00	15·00
116	21	20c. green and red	7·50	1·25
117	21	25c. violet and orange	7·50	1·50
118	21	30c. brown and violet	7·50	2·50
119	21	50c. violet and red	9·00	75
120	21	$1 red and brown	4·00	75
121	21	$2 purple and violet	24·00	24·00
122	21	$3 red and green	45·00	50·00
123	21	$4 blue and red	45·00	80·00
124	21	$5 red and brown	65·00	85·00
125	21	$10 black and yellow	30·00	85·00

1945. Optd B M A.

126		1c. purple	1·25	60
127		2c. black	3·50	1·25
128		3c. green	1·25	1·75
129		4c. purple	3·25	50
130		5c. violet	4·50	1·25
131		6c. brown	4·00	75
132		8c. red	15·00	20·00
133		10c. red	1·75	70
134		12c. orange	4·50	3·75
135		15c. blue	8·50	40
136		20c. green and red	4·50	4·00
137		25c. violet and orange	5·00	2·75
138		30c. brown and violet	9·00	3·00
139		50c. violet and red	1·75	35
140		$1 red and brown	2·50	3·75
141		$2 purple and violet	9·00	18·00
142		$3 red and green	32·00	90·00
143		$4 blue and red	32·00	60·00
144		$5 red and brown	£190	£250
145		$10 black and yellow	£180	£250

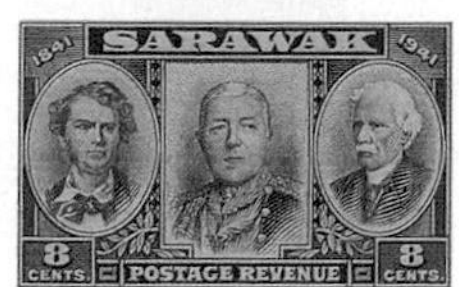

23 Sir James Brooke, Sir Charles Vyner Brooke and Sir Charles Brooke

1946. Centenary Issue.

146	23	8c. red	3·25	1·00
147	23	15c. blue	3·75	2·00
148	23	50c. black and red	3·75	2·50
149	23	$1 black and brown	3·75	35·00

1947. Optd with the Royal Cypher.

150	21	1c. purple	20	30
151	21	2c. black	25	15
152	21	3c. green	25	15
153	21	4c. purple	25	15
154	21	6c. brown	35	90
155	21	8c. red	1·00	10
156	21	10c. red	35	20
157	21	12c. orange	70	1·00
158	21	15c. blue	50	40
159	21	20c. green and red	2·25	50
160	21	25c. violet and orange	65	30
161	21	50c. violet and red	1·25	40
162	21	$1 red and brown	1·50	90
163	21	$2 purple and violet	4·00	4·25
164	21	$5 red and brown	4·00	3·25

1948. Silver Wedding. As T 33b/c of St. Helena.

165		8c. red	30	30
166		$5 brown	48·00	50·00

1949. U.P.U. As T 33d/g of St. Helena.

167		8c. red	1·25	60
168		15c. blue	3·50	2·50
169		25c. green	2·00	1·50
170		50c. violet	2·00	7·00

25 "Trogonoptera brookiana"

26 Western Tarsier

27 Kayan Tomb

1950

171	25	1c. black	75	30
172	26	2c. orange	30	40
173	27	3c. green	30	80
174	-	4c. brown	65	20
175	-	6c. blue	40	20
176	-	8c. red	1·00	30
177	-	10c. orange	2·50	6·00
186	-	10c. orange	1·75	50
178	-	12c. violet	3·50	1·50
179	-	15c. blue	3·50	15
180	-	20c. brown and orange	2·75	30
181	-	25c. green and red	3·75	30
182	-	50c. brown and violet	7·00	45
183	-	$1 green and brown	25·00	4·50
184	-	$2 blue and red	38·00	16·00
185	-	$5 multicoloured	30·00	16·00

DESIGNS—VERT: 4c. Kayan boy and girl; 6c. Beadwork; 50c. Iban woman. HORIZ: 8c. Dayak dancer; 10c. (No. 177) Malayan Pangolin; 10c. (No. 186) Map of Sarawak; 12c. Kenyah boys; 15c. Fire-making; 20c. Kelemantan rice barn; 25c. Pepper vines; $1 Kelabit smithy; $2 Map of Sarawak; $5 Arms of Sarawak.

1953. Coronation. As T 33h of St. Helena.

187		10c. black and blue	1·60	1·75

47 Barong Panau (sailing prau)

51 Queen Elizabeth II

52 Queen Elizabeth II (after Annigoni)

1955

188	-	1c. green	10	30
189	-	2c. orange	30	55
190	-	4c. brown	1·50	60
191	-	6c. blue	3·75	3·25
192	-	8c. red	40	30
193	-	10c. green	30	10
194	47	12c. plum	3·75	55
195	-	15c. blue	2·25	30
196	-	20c. olive and brown	1·00	10
197	-	25c. sepia and green	6·50	20
198	51	30c. brown and lilac	8·00	30
199	51	50c. black and red	2·50	30
200	52	$1 green and brown	14·00	2·50
201	52	$2 violet and green	22·00	3·75
202	-	$5 multicoloured	32·00	19·00

DESIGNS—VERT (as Type **47**): 1c. Logging; 2c. Young orang-utan; 4c. Kayan dancing. HORIZ: 6c. Malabar pied hornbill ("Hornbill"); 8c. Shield with spears; 10c. Kenyah ceremonial carving; 15c. Turtles; 20c. Melanau basket-making; 25c. Astana, Kuching; $5 Arms of Sarawak.

1963. Freedom from Hunger. As T 63a of St. Helena.

203		12c. sepia	1·50	2·00

53 "Vanda hookeriana"

1965. As Nos. 155/21 of Kedah, but with Arms of Sarawak inset as in T 53.

212	53	1c. multicoloured	10	1·10
213	-	2c. multicoloured	30	2·50
214	-	5c. multicoloured	1·50	10
215	-	6c. multicoloured	60	2·00
216	-	10c. multicoloued	80	10
217	-	15c. multicoloured	1·50	10
218	-	20c. multicoloured	2·00	50

The higher values used in Sarawak were Nos. 20/7 of Malaysia (National issues).

54 "Precis orithya"

1971. Butterflies. As Nos. 124/30 of Kedah, but with Sarawak Arms as in T 54.

219		1c. multicoloured	65	2·25
220		2c. multicoloured	70	2·25
221		5c. multicoloured	1·75	10
222		6c. multicoloured	1·75	2·50
223		10c. multicoloured	1·75	10

224	**54**	15c. multicoloured	2·75	10
225	-	20c. multicoloured	2·75	1·25

The higher values in use with this issue were Nos. 64/71 of Malaysia (National issues).

55 "Precis orithya" (different crest at right)

1977. As Nos. 219/21 and 223/5, but showing new State Crest.

226		1c. multicoloured	6·50	13·00
227		2c. multicoloured	13·00	9·50
228		5c. multicoloured	80	70
230		10c. multicoloured	50	30
231	**55**	15c. multicoloured	1·25	20
232	-	20c. multicoloured	3·50	2·25

56 "Rhododendron scortechinii"

1979. As Nos. 135/41 of Kedah, but with Arms of Sarawak as in T 56.

233	1c. "Rafflesia hasseltii"	10	50
234	2c. "Pterocarpus indicus"	10	50
235	5c. "Lagerstroemia speciosa"	20	70
236	10c. "Durio zibethinus"	20	10
237	15c. "Hibiscus rosa-sinensis"	20	10
238	20c. Type **56**	60	10
239	25c. "Etlingera elatior" (inscr "Phaeomeria speciosa")	65	70

57 Coffee

1986. As Nos. 152/8 of Kedah, but with Arms of Sarawak as in T 57.

247	1c. Type **57**	10	30
248	2c. Coconuts	10	30
249	5c. Cocoa	15	20
250	10c. Black pepper	15	10
251	15c. Rubber	25	10
252	20c. Oil palm	25	10
253	30c. Rice	35	15

Nos. 247/53 exist with slightly different versions to state arms at right.

58 *Nelumbium nelumbo* (sacred lotus)

2007. Garden Flowers. As Nos. 210/15 of Johore, but with Arms of Sarawak as in T 58. Multicoloured.

261	5s. Type **58**	10	10
262	10s. *Hydrangea macrophylla*	15	10
263	20s. *Hippeastrum reticulatum*	25	15
264	30s. *Bougainvillea*	40	20
265	40s. *Ipomoea indica*	50	30
266	50s. *Hibiscus rosa-sinensis*	65	35

JAPANESE OCCUPATION

(1) "Imperial Japanese Government"

1942. Stamps of Sarawak optd with T 1.

J1	**21**	1c. purple	38·00	85·00
J2	**21**	2c. green	£160	£200
J3	**21**	2c. black	£150	£160
J4	**21**	3c. black	£500	£500
J5	**21**	3c. green	80·00	£110
J6	**21**	4c. purple	£110	£120
J7	**21**	5c. violet	£130	£140
J8	**21**	6c. red	£180	£180
J9	**21**	6c. brown	£120	£130
J10	**21**	8c. brown	£450	£450
J11	**21**	8c. red	75·00	£120
J12	**21**	10c. red	£110	£130
J13	**21**	12c. blue	£190	£200
J14	**21**	12c. orange	£180	£200
J15	**21**	15c. orange	£550	£550
J16	**21**	15c. blue	£150	£160
J17	**21**	20c. green and red	90·00	£110
J18	**21**	25c. violet and orange	£130	£150
J19	**21**	30c. brown and violet	90·00	£120
J20	**21**	50c. violet and red	75·00	£110
J21	**21**	$1 red and brown	£150	£170
J22	**21**	$2 purple and violet	£325	£400
J23	**21**	$3 red and green	£2750	£2750
J24	**21**	$4 blue and red	£325	£475
J25	**21**	$5 red and brown	£325	£475
J26	**21**	$10 black and yellow	£325	£475

Pt. 8

SARDINIA

A former Italian kingdom, including the island of Sardinia, a large part of the mainland and parts of what is now south-east France. The kingdom of Italy was formed by the adhesion of other Italian states to Sardinia, whose king became the first ruler of united Italy.

100 centesimi = 1 lira.

1 Victor Emmanuel II

1851. Imperf.

1	**1**	5c. black	£12000	£2250
3	**1**	20c. blue	£11000	£275
7	**1**	40c. pink	£20000	£5000

1853. Embossed on coloured paper. Imperf.

9	5c. on green	£20000	£1400
10	20c. on blue	£18000	£225
11	40c. on pink	£13000	£1200

1854. Embossed on white paper. Imperf.

13	5c. green	£41000	£750
15	20c. blue	£20000	£190
18	40c. red	£118000	£3250

2 Victor Emmanuel II

1855. Head embossed. Imperf.

28	**2**	5c. green	8·50	21·00
35	**2**	10c. grey	32·00	£130
39	**2**	10c. brown	£120	£110
40	**2**	10c. bistre	8·50	21·00
47	**2**	20c. blue	£225	29·00
55	**2**	40c. red	32·00	65·00
59	**2**	80c. yellow	32·00	£400
61	**2**	3l. bronze	£550	£3500

For Type **2** perf, see Italy Nos. 1/4.

NEWSPAPER STAMPS

N3

1861. Numerals embossed. Imperf.

N62	**N3**	1c. black	10·50	19·00
N63	**N3**	2c. black	£225	£140

For 2c. stamps of similar types in yellow see Italy No. N5.

Pt. 3

SASENO

An island off the W. coast of Albania, temporarily occupied by Italy.

100 centesimi = 1 lira.

1923. Stamps of Italy optd SASENO.

1	**38**	10c. red	20·00	37·00
2	**38**	15c. grey	20·00	37·00
3	**41**	20c. orange	20·00	37·00
4	**39**	25c. blue	20·00	37·00
5	**39**	30c. brown	20·00	37·00
6	**39**	50c. mauve	20·00	37·00
7	**39**	60c. red	20·00	37·00
8	**34**	1l. brown and green	20·00	37·00

Pt. 19

SAUDI ARABIA

Formerly under Turkish rule, the Hejaz became an independent kingdom in 1916 but was conquered in 1925 by the Sultan of Nejd. In 1926 the two kingdoms were combined. In 1932 the name of the state was changed to the Saudi Arabian Kingdom.

1916. 40 paras = 1 piastre.
1929. 110 guerche = 10 riyal = 1 gold sovereign.
1952. 440 guerche = 40 riyal = 1 gold sovereign.
1960. 100 halalah = 20 guerche = 1 riyal.
(1 piastre = 1 guerche.)

A. HEJAZ

5 From Stucco Work over Entrance to Cairo Railway Station

1916. As T 5 (various Arabic designs). Perf or roul.

11	**5**	1pa. purple	6·25	2·20
12	-	⅛pi. yellow	6·75	3·25
13	-	¼pi. green	6·75	3·25
14	-	½pi. red	7·75	4·75
15	-	1pi. blue	8·00	4·75
16	-	2pi. purple	37·00	16·00

7 "1340 Hashemite Kingdom 1340"

1921. Optd with T 7.

21	1pa. purple	50·00	26·00
22	⅛pi. yellow	95·00	28·00
23	¼pi. green	20·00	10·00
24	½pi. red	23·00	12·50
26	1pi. blue	20·00	11·00
28	2pi. purple	28·00	16·00

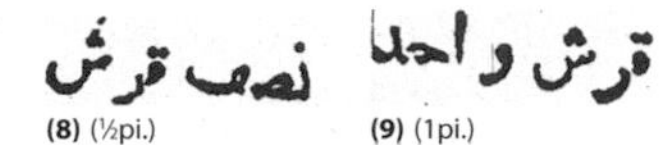

(8) (½pi.) **(9)** (1pi.)

1921. No. 21 surch with T 8 or 9.

29	**5**	½pi. on 1pa. purple	£550	£250
30	**5**	1pi. on 1pa. purple	£550	£250

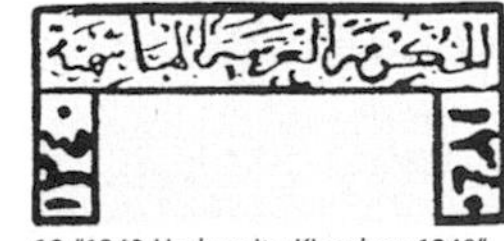

10 "1340 Hashemite Kingdom 1340"

1922. Nos. 11 to 16 optd with T 10.

31		1pa. purple	5·00	4·75
32	-	⅛pi. yellow	16·00	13·50
33	-	¼pi. green	6·25	4·75
34	-	½pi. red	4·00	3·50
35	-	1pi. blue	4·00	1·50
36	-	2pi. claret	11·00	10·50

1922. No. 31 surch with T 8 or 9.

37	**5**	½pi. on 1pa. purple	42·00	23·00
38	**5**	1pi. on 1pa. purple	4·00	1·60

11 Meccan Sherifian Arms

1922

39	**11**	⅛pi. brown	3·25	90
57	**11**	¼pi. green	10·00	10·00
41	**11**	½pi. red	3·25	65
42	**11**	1pi. blue	3·25	65
43	**11**	1½pi. lilac	3·25	90
44	**11**	2pi. orange	3·50	1·00
45	**11**	3pi. brown	3·25	90
46	**11**	5pi. green	3·25	90
58	-	10pi. purple and mauve	7·75	7·75

DESIGN: 10pi. As T **11** but with different corner ornaments in the centre motif.

(12) (¼pi.) **(13)** (10pi.)

1923. Surch with T 12 or 13.

47	**11**	¼pi. on ⅛pi. brown	60·00	55·00
49	**11**	10pi. on 5pi. olive	90·00	47·00

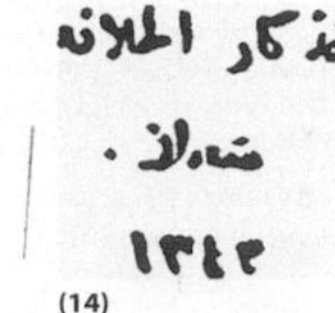

(14)

1924. Proclamation of King Hussein as Caliph. Optd with T 14.

50	⅛pi. brown	7·75	5·00
51	½pi. red	5·00	2·20
52	1pi. blue	7·75	5·00
53	1½pi. lilac	7·75	5·00
54	2pi. orange	7·75	5·00
55	3pi. brown	7·75	5·00
56	5pi. green	9·00	7·75

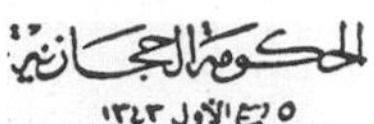

15 "Hejaz Government. 4th October, 1924"

1924. Optd with T 15.

66	1pa. purple (No. 11)	21·00	21·00
77	1pa. purple (No. 31)	£275	£275
59	⅛pi. yellow (No. 12)	28·00	28·00
78	⅛pi. yellow (No. 32)	£4000	£3250
68	¼pi. green (No. 13)	33·00	33·00
79	¼pi. green (No. 33)	£110	£110
71	½pi. red (No. 14)	50·00	50·00
76	½pi. red (No. 24)	£4500	
80	½pi. red (No. 34)	£160	£150
86	½pi. red (No. 41)	£1700	£1700
84	½pi. on 1pa. purple (No. 37)	£160	£160
73	1pi. blue (No. 15)	55·00	55·00
81	1pi. blue (No. 35)	£225	£180
85	1pi. on 1pa. purple (No. 38)	£120	£120
74	2pi. purple (No. 16)	60·00	55·00
83	2pi. purple (No. 36)	£275	£275
87	10pi. purple and mauve (No. 58)	£3250	£3250

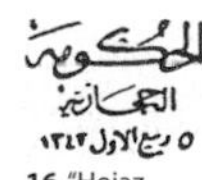

16 "Hejaz Government, 4th October, 1924"

1924. Optd with T 16 (or smaller size). (a) On No. 13.

90	¼pi. green	£110	£110

(b) On Nos. 39 etc.

105	**11**	⅛pi. brown	7·75	7·75
96	**11**	¼pi. green	28·00	28·00
116	**11**	½pi. red	7·75	7·75
98	**11**	1pi. blue	14·50	14·50
99	**11**	1½pi. lilac	7·75	7·75
119	**11**	2pi. orange	12·50	12·50
120	**11**	3pi. brown	12·50	10·00
103	**11**	5pi. green	21·00	12·50
104	-	10pi. purple and mauve	28·00	28·00

(c) On Nos. 50/6.

136	⅛pi. brown	65·00	65·00
137	½pi. red	£150	£150
138	1pi. blue	£100	90·00
139	1½pi. lilac	£120	£110
134	2pi. orange	£180	£160
146	3pi. brown	£180	£180
142	5pi. green	65·00	65·00

For similar overprint see Nos. 172/6.

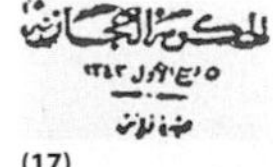

(17)

1925. Stamps of 1922 surch as Type 17.

148	¼pi. on ⅛pi. brown	£170
149	¼pi. on ½pi. red	£170
150	1pi. on 2pi. orange	£170
151	1pi. on 3pi. brown	£170
153	10pi. on 5pi. green	£170

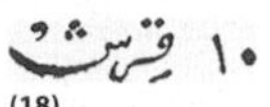

(18)

1925. Nos. 148/53 further surch with values in larger type as Type 18.

154	¼pi. on ¼pi. on ⅛pi. brown	85·00	85·00
155	¼pi. on ¼pi. on ½pi. red	50·00	50·00
157	1pi. on 1pi. on 2pi. orange	50·00	50·00
158	1pi. on 1pi. on 3pi. brown	39·00	39·00
160	10pi. on 10pi. on 5pi. green	28·00	28·00

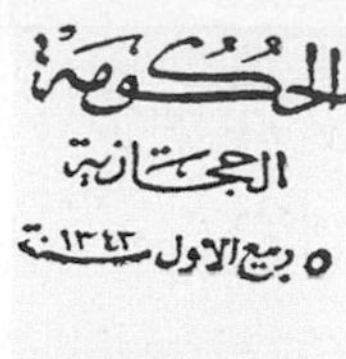
(19)

1925. Stamps of 1922 surch as T 19.

165	⅛pi. on ½pi. red	23·00	18·00
166	¼pi. on ½pi. red	23·00	18·00
167	1pi. on ½pi. red	23·00	18·00
173c	1pi. on 1½pi. lilac	14·50	14·50
174	1pi. on 2pi. orange	14·50	14·50
175	1pi. on 3pi. brown	14·50	14·50
176	10pi. on 5pi. green	23·00	23·00

20

(24)

1925. As T 20 (various Arabic designs) optd with T 24.

177C	⅛pi. brown	2·75	2·75
178C	¼pi. blue	2·75	2·75
179C	½pi. red	3·25	3·25
180C	1pi. green	3·25	3·25
181C	1½pi. orange	3·25	3·25
182C	2pi. blue	4·00	4·00
183B	3pi. green	3·25	3·25
184A	5pi. brown	6·50	6·50
185C	10pi. green and red	8·75	8·75

B. NEJDI OCCUPATION OF HEJAZ

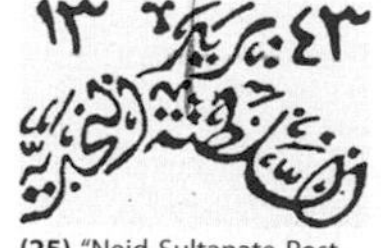
(25) "Nejd Sultanate Post 1343"

1925. Various stamps optd with T 25. (A.) Stamps of Turkey.

190	30	5pa. bistre (No. 583)	36·00	22·00
191	30	10pa. green (No. 503)	25·00	19·00

26

(B.) Hejaz Fiscal stamps. (i) Notarial stamps.

192	26	1pi. violet	31·00	31·00
193a	26	1pi. blue	39·00	39·00

27

(ii) Bill stamp.

194	27	1pi. violet	22·00	22·00

28

(iii) Railway Tax stamps.

195	28	1pi. blue	25·00	25·00
196	28	2pi. orange	33·00	33·00
197	28	3pi. lilac	39·00	39·00

(C.) Hejaz Postage stamps (1922 issue).

198	11	⅛pi. brown	33·00	33·00
198ca	11	¼pi. red	39·00	39·00
199a	11	½pi. red	25·00	25·00
200	11	1½pi. lilac	33·00	33·00
201	11	2pi. orange	55·00	55·00
202	11	3pi. red	33·00	33·00

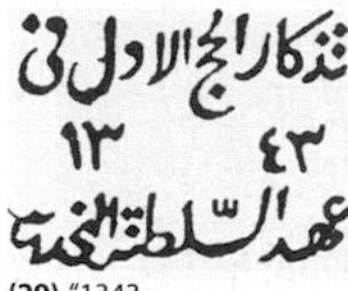
(29) "1343 Commemoration of First Pilgrimage under Sultan of Nejd"

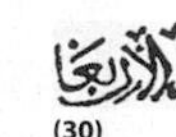
(30) "Wednesday"

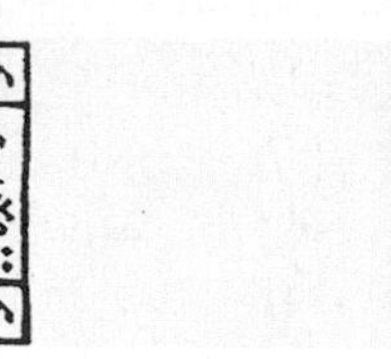
(31)

1925. Pilgrimage Commemoration. Various stamps optd with T 29 and 30 and surch as T 31. (a) 1914 pictorial stamps of Turkey.

210	1pi. on 10pa. green (No. 503)	£110	85·00
211	5pi. on 1pi. blue (No. 518)	£110	85·00

(b) 1916 stamps of Hejaz.

212	2pi. on 1pa. purple	£150	£110
213	4pi. on⅛pi. yellow	£500	£250

(c) Railway Tax stamp of Hejaz.

214	28	3pi. lilac	£375	£130

(32) "Nejd Sultanate Post"

1925. Various stamps optd with T 32. (A.) Stamps of Turkey.

215	30	5pa. bistre	17·00	16·00
216	-	10pa. green (No. 503)	22·00	19·00

(B.) Hejaz Fiscal stamps. (i) Notarial stamp.

217	26	2pi. blue	31·00	25·00

(ii) Railway Tax Stamps.

218	28	1pi. blue	36·00	16·00
219	28	2pi. orange	39·00	16·00
220	28	3pi. lilac	33·00	22·00
221	28	5pi. green	31·00	19·00

28

(C.) Hejaz Postage stamps. (i) Nos. 35/6.

222	1pi. blue	60·00	60·00
223	2pi. purple	85·00	85·00

(ii) Stamps of 1922 (some in new colours).

224	11	⅛pi. brown	£6000	
225	11	½pi. red	22·00	10·00
226	11	1pi. violet	25·00	22·00
227	11	1½pi. pink	45·00	28·00
228	11	2pi. orange	£130	85·00
229	11	2pi. purple	85·00	65·00
230	11	3pi. red	33·00	25·00
231	11	5pi. red	45·00	39·00

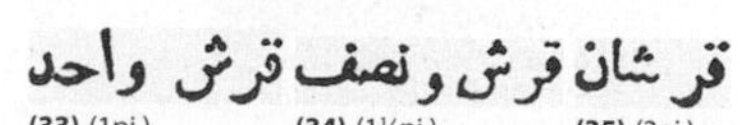
(33) (1pi.) (34) (1½pi.) (35) (2pi.)

1925. Stamps optd with T 32 further surch with T 33/5.

239	1pi. on ½pi. red	11·00	3·25
241	1½pi. on ½pi. red	13·50	3·25
243	2pi. on 3pi. red	22·00	4·50

(36) "Postage of Nejd, 1344, Commemoration of Medina"

1925. Capture of Medina. Railway Tax stamps of Hejaz optd with T 36.

244	28	1pi. on 10pi. mauve and violet	£110	80·00
245	28	2pi. on 50pi. red and blue	£110	80·00
246	28	3pi. on 100pi. brown	£110	80·00
247	28	4pi. on 500pi. red	£110	80·00
248	28	5pi. on 1000pi. violet and red	£110	80·00

(37) "Commemoration of Jeddah, 1344, Postage of Nejd"

1925. Capture of Jeddah. Optd with T 37.

249	1pi. on 10pi. mauve and violet	£110	80·00
250	2pi. on 50pi. red and blue	£110	80·00
251	3pi. on 100pi. brown	£110	80·00
252	4pi. on 500pi. red	£110	80·00
253	5pi. on 1000pi. violet and red	£110	80·00

C. HEJAZ AND NEJD

38

39

1926

254	38	⅛pi. violet	31·00	19·00
261	38	⅛pi. orange	22·00	2·50
255	38	¼pi. grey	31·00	19·00
262	38	¼pi. green	13·50	1·50
256	38	1pi. blue	33·00	22·00
263	38	1pi. red	11·00	1·50
257	39	2pi. green	31·00	19·00
264	39	2pi. purple	11·00	1·50
259	39	3pi. pink	45·00	28·00
265	39	3pi. blue	11·00	1·50
266	39	5pi. brown	22·00	2·50

(40) "Islamic Congress, 1 June, 1926"

1926. Pan-Islamic Congress, Cairo. Optd with T 40.

275	38	⅛pi. orange	16·00	6·25
276	38	¼pi. green	16·00	6·25
277	38	1pi. red	16·00	6·25
278	39	2pi. purple	16·00	6·25
279	39	3pi. blue	16·00	6·25
280	39	5pi. brown	16·00	6·25

41 Tougra of Ibn Saud

1926

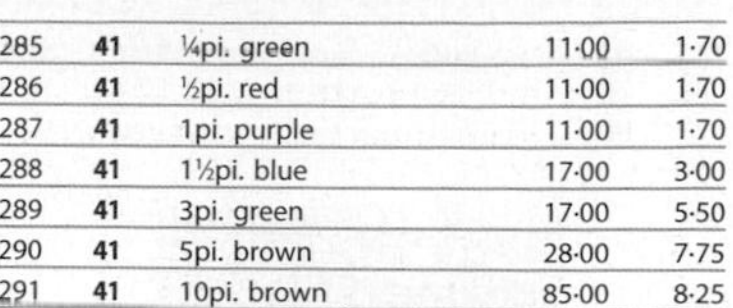

284	41	⅛pi. brown	11·00	80
285	41	¼pi. green	11·00	1·70
286	41	½pi. red	11·00	1·70
287	41	1pi. purple	11·00	1·70
288	41	1½pi. blue	17·00	3·00
289	41	3pi. green	17·00	5·50
290	41	5pi. brown	28·00	7·75
291	41	10pi. brown	85·00	8·25

42 "25th Rajab 1345"

1927. Establishment of Kingdom. Optd with T 42.

294	⅛pi. brown	16·00	7·75
295	¼pi. green	16·00	7·75
296	½pi. red	16·00	7·75
297	1pi. purple	16·00	7·75
298	1½pi. blue	16·00	7·75
299	3pi. green	16·00	7·75
300	5pi. brown	16·00	7·75
301	10pi. brown	16·00	7·75

43

1929

302	43	1¾g. blue	25·00	3·25
303	43	20g. violet	75·00	12·50
304	43	30g. green	£120	22·00

44

1930. 4th Anniv of King Ibn Saud's Accession.

305	44	½g. red	22·00	4·75
306	44	1½g. violet	22·00	3·25
307	44	1¾g. blue	22·00	4·50
308	44	3½g. green	22·00	5·00
309	44	5g. purple	33·00	8·25

45

1931

310	45	⅛g. yellow	22·00	3·25
311	45	¼g. green	22·00	2·20
312	45	1¾g. blue	60·00	3·25

46

1932

313	46	¼g. green	25·00	3·00
314a	46	½g. red	60·00	4·50
315	46	2¼g. blue	£110	3·25

D. SAUDI ARABIA

47

1932. Proclamation of Emir Saud as Heir Apparent.

316	47	¼g. green	11·00	6·75
317	47	½g. red	11·00	7·25
318	47	1½g. blue	22·00	22·00
319	47	3g. green	28·00	28·00
320	47	3½g. blue	33·00	10·50
321	47	5g. yellow	55·00	47·00
322	47	10g. orange	£110	
323	47	20g. violet	£150	
324	47	30g. violet	£200	

325	**47**	¼s. purple	£275	
326	**47**	½s. brown	£600	
327	**47**	1s. purple	£1500	

48

1934. Charity Tax. Fund for Wounded in War with Yemen.

328	**48**	½g. red	£225	14·50

49

1934

329A	**49**	⅛g. yellow	7·25	55
330A	**49**	¼g. green	9·50	55
331Aa	**49**	½g. red	5·00	20
332B	**49**	⅞g. blue	9·50	1·00
333Aa	**49**	1g. green	6·50	45
334Ba	**49**	2g. green	21·00	3·25
335B	**49**	2⅞g. violet	9·50	1·00
336Ba	**49**	3g. blue	30·00	1·10
337A	**49**	3½g. blue	32·00	2·50
338Aa	**49**	5g. orange	7·75	65
339Aa	**49**	10g. violet	22·00	1·90
340Aa	**49**	20g. purple	31·00	1·20
341A	**49**	100g. mauve	£130	5·50
342A	**49**	200g. brown	1·60	9·00

50 General Hospital, Mecca

1936. Charity. Medical Aid. Perf or roul. (a) Three palm trees.

345	**50**	⅛g. red (37×20 mm)	£850	25·00
346	**50**	⅛g. red (30½×18 mm)	£120	2·75

(b) One palm tree.

348		⅛g. red (30½×18 mm)	10·00	1·00
351		¼g. red (30½×18 mm)	12·50	20

53 Egyptian Royal Yacht "Fakhr el Bihar", Radhwa

1945. Meeting of King Ibn Saud and King Farouk of Egypt at Radhwa.

352	**53**	½g. red	13·50	2·20
353	**53**	3g. blue	16·00	5·50
354	**53**	5g. violet	50·00	11·00
355	**53**	10g. purple	£110	22·00

54 Map of Saudi Arabia, Flags and Emblem

1946. Obligatory Tax. Return of King Ibn Saud from Egypt.

356b	**54**	½g. mauve	50·00	10·00

55 Airliner

1949. Air.

357	**55**	1g. green	5·25	20
358	**55**	3g. blue	6·75	35
359	**55**	4g. orange	6·75	35
360	**55**	10g. violet	18·00	80
361	**55**	20g. brown	17·00	2·75
362	**55**	100g. purple	£160	18·00

56 Arms of Saudi Arabia and Afghanistan

1950. Visit of King Mohamed Zahir Shah of Afghanistan.

363	**56**	½g. red	11·00	1·50
364	**56**	3g. blue	18·00	1·50

57 Al-Murabba Palace, Riyadh

1950. 50th Anniv of Capture of Riyadh by King Abdulaziz Ibn Saud. Centres in purple.

365	**57**	½g. purple	11·00	2·20
366	**57**	1g. blue	17·00	3·25
367	**57**	3g. violet	28·00	5·50
368	**57**	5g. orange	55·00	10·00
369	**57**	10g. green	95·00	21·00

58 Arms of Saudi Arabia and Jordan

1951. Visit of King Talal of Jordan.

370	**58**	½g. red	8·25	1·70
371	**58**	3g. blue	28·00	2·75

59 Arabs and Diesel Goods Train

1952. Inaug of Dammam–Riyadh Railway.

372	**59**	½g. brown	12·50	4·00
373	**59**	1g. green	14·50	4·50
374	**59**	3g. mauve	25·00	4·00
375	**59**	10g. red	49·00	17·00
376	**59**	20g. blue	£100	39·00

60 Arms of Saudi Arabia and Lebanon

1953. Visit of President Chamoun of Lebanon.

377	**60**	½g. red	7·25	2·00
378	**60**	3g. blue	19·00	4·50

61

1953. Visit of Governor-General of Pakistan.

379	**61**	½g. red	11·00	2·00
380	**61**	3g. blue	23·00	4·50

62 Arms of Saudi Arabia and Jordan

1953. Visit of King Hussein of Jordan.

381	**62**	½g. red	11·00	2·00
382	**62**	3g. blue	23·00	4·50

1955. Arab Postal Union. As T 96a of Syria but smaller, 20×34 mm. Inscr "ROYAUME DE L'ARABIE SOUDITE" at top.

383		½g. green	4·50	1·10
384		3g. violet	13·50	2·20
385		4g. brown	19·00	6·25

1960. Inaug of Arab League Centre, Cairo. As T 154a of Syria, but inscr "S.A.K.".

386		2p. green and black	3·25	1·70

63 Congress Building

1960. Arab Postal Union Congress, Riyadh.

387	**63**	2p. blue	1·80	1·10
388	**63**	5p. purple	4·25	1·70
389	**63**	10p. green	9·00	2·20

64 Radio Mast and Globe

1960. Inauguration of Direct Radio Service.

390	**64**	2p. red and black	2·10	1·50
391	**64**	5p. purple and claret	5·00	2·20
392	**64**	10p. indigo and blue	10·00	4·25

65 Refugee Camp

1960. World Refugee Year.

393	**65**	2p. blue	45	20
394	**65**	8p. violet	45	20
395	**65**	10p. green	2·00	90

66 Gas Oil Plant

(I) **(II)**

1960. Cartouche of King Saud as Type I. Size 27½×22 mm. (a) Postage. (i) Type 66.

396		½p. orange and red	1·90	35
397		1p. red and blue	1·90	35
398		2p. blue and red	1·90	35
399		3p. green and violet	1·90	35
400		4p. purple and green	1·90	35
401		5p. red and purple	1·90	35
471		5p. red and brown	28·00	65
402		6p. lilac and brown	1·90	35
534		6p. chocolate and brown	85·00	7·25
403		7p. green and violet	1·90	35
404		8p. black and green	3·25	35
405		9p. brown and blue	5·50	35
406		10p. red and blue	2·75	45
539		11p. orange and green	6·25	45
540		12p. green and brown	6·25	45
541		13p. blue and mauve	6·25	55
542		14p. brown and lilac	9·00	55
543		15p. brown and mauve	10·00	80
544		16p. red and green	12·50	80
545		17p. brown and mauve	20·00	2·20
546		18p. blue and black	12·50	80
547		19p. yellow and brown	12·50	80
407		20p. black and brown	10·00	80
549		23p. red and orange	12·50	1·00
550		24p. yellow and green	12·50	1·10
551		26p. brown and purple	18·00	1·10
552		27p. black and red	18·00	1·10
553		31p. red and green	31·00	2·20
554		33p. black and brown	28·00	2·20
408		50p. green and brown	28·00	2·20
409		75p. purple and red	47·00	4·50
410		100p. brown and blue	75·00	4·25
411		200p. green and black	£130	9·50

67 Wadi Hanifa Dam, near Riyadh

(ii) Type 67.

412		½p. orange and bistre	2·00	35
413		1p. purple and olive	2·00	35
414		2p. brown and blue	2·00	35
415		3p. blue and brown	2·00	35
416		4p. chestnut and brown	2·00	35
417		5p. purple and black	2·00	35
418		6p. red and black	2·00	35
419		7p. green and red	2·00	35
563		7p. black and brown	18·00	45
420		8p. purple and blue	3·25	35
564		8p. brown and blue	£100	7·25
421		9p. red and brown	5·50	35
422		10p. lake and green	2·75	45
567		11p. green and red	8·25	2·75
568		12p. blue and orange	8·25	55
569		13p. mauve and green	8·25	55
570		14p. green and brown	8·25	55
571		15p. green and brown	8·25	2·75
572		16p. lilac and red	10·00	55
573		17p. blue and purple	10·00	3·25
574		18p. blue and green	10·00	55
575		19p. brown and black	12·50	80
423		20p. green and brown	10·00	80
480		20p. green and red	31·00	2·10
577		23p. purple and brown	10·50	2·75
578		24p. blue and red	12·50	80
579		26p. yellow and green	16·00	1·00
580		27p. purple and blue	16·00	1·00
581		31p. blue and black	16·00	1·10
582		33p. purple and green	16·00	1·10
424		50p. brown and black	28·00	2·20
425		75p. grey and brown	75·00	4·50
426		100p. turquoise and blue	65·00	4·25
427		200p. green and purple	£130	9·50

68 Vickers Viscount 800

(b) Air. Type 68.

428		1p. green and purple	90	35
429		2p. purple and green	90	35
430		3p. blue and red	90	35
431		4p. purple and blue	90	35
432		5p. red and green	90	35
433		6p. violet and brown	1·60	45
484		6p. green and orange	13·50	1·50
434		8p. green and red	1·80	45
435		9p. brown and violet	2·75	55
436		10p. purple and black	7·75	90
437		15p. brown and blue	7·75	65
438		20p. green and brown	7·75	80
439		30p. green and brown	18·00	2·20
440		50p. blue and green	39·00	1·60
441		100p. brown and grey	80·00	4·50
442		200p. black and purple	£110	6·75

Some values vary in size.

For similar design to Type **68** with King Saud cartouche but with different airplane, see Nos. 585/610c.

For designs with Type II cartouche, see Nos. 755 etc (1966 issue).

69 Globe, Pylon and Telegraph Pole

1960. 6th Anniv (1959) of Arab Telecommunications Union.

443	**69**	3p. purple	2·00	35
444	**69**	6p. black	3·25	80
445	**69**	8p. brown	5·50	1·00

71 Damman Port

1961. Opening of Damman Port Extension.

446	**71**	3p. violet	2·20	20
447	**71**	6p. blue	3·25	1·00
448	**71**	8p. green	5·50	65

1962. Arab League Week. As T 178 of Syria but larger, 25×41 mm. Inscr "S.A.K.".

449		3p. green	1·90	20
450		6p. mauve	4·00	45
451		8p. green	5·50	65

72 Campaign Emblem

1962. Malaria Eradication.

452	**72**	3p. red and blue	1·50	20
453	**72**	6p. green and blue	2·20	45
454	**72**	8p. black and purple	3·25	65
MS455		89×110 mm. Imperf	31·00	31·00

73 Koran

1963. 1st Anniv of Islamic Institute, Medina.

456	**73**	2½p. purple and orange	1·50	35
457	**73**	7½p. blue and green	2·50	55
458	**73**	9½p. green and black	4·00	65

74 Emblem within Hands

1963. Freedom From Hunger.

459	**74**	2½p. mauve and orange	1·50	35
460	**74**	7½p. purple and pink	1·70	45
461	**74**	9p. brown and blue	3·25	80

75 Boeing 707 over Airport

1963. Opening of Dhahran Airport and Inauguration of Jet Service.

462	**75**	1p. violet and brown	1·50	20
463	**75**	3½p. blue and green	4·50	45
464	**75**	6p. green and red	7·25	80
465	**75**	7½p. mauve and blue	7·25	90
466	**75**	9½p. red and violet	10·00	1·00

76 "Flame of Freedom"

1964. 15th Anniv of Declaration of Human Rights.

493	**76**	3p. blue, violet and orange	4·75	45
494	**76**	6p. blue, green & light blue	5·50	1·00
495	**76**	9p. blue, brown and pink	11·00	1·50

77 Arms and King Faisal

1964. Installation of King Faisal.

496	**77**	4p. blue and green	6·25	55

80 Boeing 720-B

1964. Air. Type **80**. Cartouche of King Saud as Type 1 (illus next to T **66**).

585	1p. green and purple	£120	4·25
586	2p. purple and green	£4250	£150
587	3p. blue and red	14·50	35
588	4p. purple and blue	9·00	35
589	5p. red and green	£2750	£600
590	6p. grey and brown	£170	2·75
591	7p. green and mauve	10·00	55
592	8p. green and red	£120	2·75
593	9p. brown and violet	9·00	45
594	10p. purple and black	£120	9·00
595	11p. buff and green	£120	29·00
596	12p. grey and orange	9·00	45
597	13p. green and myrtle	6·75	45
598	14p. orange and blue	6·75	55
599	15p. brown and blue	£120	9·00
600	16p. blue and black	10·00	80
601	17p. brown and ochre	8·25	55
602	18p. green and blue	8·25	55
603	19p. orange and mauve	9·00	80
604	20p. green and brown	£225	10·00
605	23p. brown and green	£250	18·00
606	24p. brown and blue	8·25	80
607	26p. green and red	8·25	80
608	27p. green and brown	9·00	80
609	31p. red and mauve	12·50	80
610	33p. purple and red	14·50	80
610a	50p. blue and green		
610b	100p. brown and grey		
610c	200p. brown and purple		

For Type **80** with Type II cartouche, see Nos. 806 etc (1966 issue).

81 Kaaba, Mecca

1965. Moslem League Conference, Mecca.

611	**81**	4p. black and brown	5·50	55
612	**81**	6p. black and mauve	7·75	1·00
613	**81**	10p. black and green	11·00	1·50

82 Arms of Saudi Arabia and Tunisia

1965. Visit of President Bourguiba of Tunisia.

614	**82**	4p. silver and mauve	3·50	1·10
615	**82**	8p. silver and violet	6·75	2·20
616	**82**	10p. silver and blue	9·00	3·00

83 Highway

1965. Opening of Arafat–Taif Highway.

617	**83**	2p. black and red	2·10	20
618	**83**	4p. black and blue	4·00	55
619	**83**	6p. black and violet	5·50	90
620	**83**	8p. black and green	7·25	1·10

84 I.C.Y. Emblem

1965. International Co-operation Year.

621	**84**	1p. brown and yellow	65	20
622	**84**	2p. green and orange	1·30	45
623	**84**	3p. green and blue	2·00	65
624	**84**	4p. black and green	2·75	90
625	**84**	10p. purple and orange	6·75	2·20

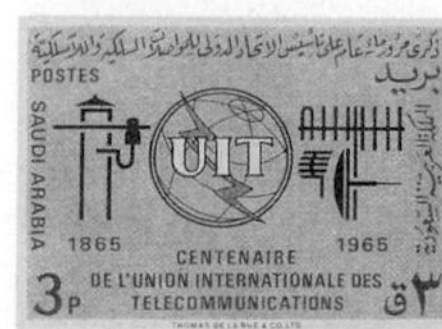

85 I.T.U. Symbol and Emblems

1965. Centenary of I.T.U.

626	**85**	3p. black and blue	1·30	35
627	**85**	4p. green and violet	1·80	45
628	**85**	8p. brown and green	3·50	90
629	**85**	10p. green and orange	4·50	1·10

86 Lamp and Burning Library

1966. Burning of Algiers Library in 1962.

630	**86**	1p. red	1·50	10
631	**86**	2p. red	3·00	20
632	**86**	3p. purple	4·00	45
633	**86**	4p. violet	5·50	55
634	**86**	5p. mauve	6·75	65
635	**86**	6p. red	8·25	80

87 A.P.U. Emblem

1966. 10th Anniv (1964) of Arab Postal Union's Permanent Office, Cairo.

636	**87**	3p. green and purple	1·80	45
637	**87**	4p. green and blue	1·80	45
638	**87**	6p. green and purple	5·50	1·00
639	**87**	7p. olive and green	5·50	1·00

88 Dagger on Deir Yassin, Palestine

1966. Deir Yassin Massacre.

640	**88**	2p. black and green	2·20	45
641	**88**	4p. black and brown	4·00	90
642	**88**	6p. black and blue	5·50	1·30
643	**88**	8p. black and orange	8·25	1·80

89 Scout Badges

1966. Arab Scout Jamboree.

644	**89**	4p. multicoloured	6·25	2·10
645	**89**	8p. multicoloured	6·25	2·10
646	**89**	10p. multicoloured	12·50	3·25

90 W.H.O. Building

1966. Inaug of W.H.O. Headquarters, Geneva.

647	**90**	4p. multicoloured	1·80	80
648	**90**	6p. multicoloured	3·75	1·10
649	**90**	10p. multicoloured	6·75	1·80

91 UNESCO Emblem

1966. 20th Anniv of UNESCO.

650	**91**	1p. multicoloured	1·90	10
651	**91**	2p. multicoloured	1·90	35
652	**91**	3p. multicoloured	2·50	45
653	**91**	4p. multicoloured	2·50	55
654	**91**	10p. multicoloured	3·50	1·30

92 Radio Mast, Telephone and Map

1966. 8th Arab Telecommunications Union Congress, Riyadh.

655	**92**	1p. multicoloured	1·10	20
656	**92**	2p. multicoloured	2·10	45
657	**92**	4p. multicoloured	4·00	80
658	**92**	6p. multicoloured	6·25	1·30
659	**92**	7p. multicoloured	6·75	1·60

1966. As 1960 and 1964 issues, but with cartouche of King Faisal as Type II (see above No. 396). (a) Postage. (i) Type 66.

755	1p. red and blue	14·50	1·50
756	2p. blue and red	9·00	80
662	3p. green and violet	22·00	80
663	4p. purple and green	12·50	45
759	5p. red and purple	31·00	2·20
760	6p. chocolate and brown	39·00	2·75
666	7p. green and lilac	50·00	2·75
667	8p. green and turquoise	9·00	45
668	9p. brown and blue	6·25	45
669	10p. red and blue	7·25	80
765	11p. orange and green	48·00	2·75
671	12p. green and brown	7·25	1·10
672	13p. blue and mauve	65·00	45
673	14p. brown and lilac	60·00	3·50
674	15p. brown and mauve	18·00	1·00
675	16p. red and green	22·00	1·10
676	17p. brown and mauve	16·00	80
677	18p. blue and black	22·00	2·50
678	19p. yellow and brown	25·00	2·50
679	20p. brown and light brown	20·00	2·50
680	23p. red and orange	31·00	2·75
681	24p. yellow and green	14·50	1·10
681a	26p. brown and purple	£225	
682	27p. black and red	55·00	5·50
683	31p. red and green	18·00	1·10
684	33p. black and brown	31·00	1·70
685	50p. green and brown	£600	£225
686	100p. brown and blue	£475	60·00
687	200p. green and black	£600	90·00

(ii) Type 67.

688	1p. purple and green	£250	36·00
689	2p. brown and blue	30·00	2·50
690	3p. blue and brown	18·00	1·20
691	4p. orange and brown	25·00	55
782	5p. purple and black	39·00	2·75
783	6p. red and black	36·00	2·20
694	7p. black and brown	29·00	2·75
695	8p. brown and blue	18·00	80
696	9p. red and brown	12·50	1·20
697	10p. brown and green	25·00	2·20
698	11p. green and red	18·00	2·20
699	12p. purple and orange	10·50	2·20
700	13p. mauve and green	36·00	2·20
701	14p. green and brown	30·00	2·20
702	15p. green and brown	30·00	2·75
703	16p. lilac and red	42·00	5·00
704	17p. blue and purple	50·00	2·75
705	18p. blue and green	36·00	4·00
706	19p. brown and black	12·50	1·20
707	20p. green and brown	£120	3·50
708	23p. purple and brown	£425	7·25
708a	24p. blue and red	90·00	9·00
709	26p. yellow and green	11·00	1·10
711	27p. purple and blue	12·50	1·20
712	33p. purple and green	65·00	3·50
713	50p. brown and black	£275	55·00
714	100p. blue and deep blue	£450	£120
715	200p. green and purple	£450	£120

(b) Air. Type 80.

806	1p. green and purple	10·00	35
807	2p. purple and green	12·50	35
718	3p. blue and red	31·00	80
719	4p. purple and blue	16·00	35
720	5p. red and green	£2750	£650
721	6p. grey and brown	£200	14·50
812	7p. green and mauve	14·50	2·50
813	8p. green and red	60·00	10·00
724	9p. brown and violet	8·25	80
725	10p. brown and black	25·00	1·50
726	11p. brown and green	20·00	80
727	12p. grey and orange	75·00	5·50
728	13p. green and myrtle	22·00	1·50

729	14p. orange and blue	21·00	2·50
730	15p. brown and blue	18·00	1·10
731	16p. blue and black	25·00	4·25
732	17p. brown and stone	22·00	2·20
733	18p. green and blue	21·00	3·50
734	19p. orange and mauve	29·00	1·50
735	20p. green and brown	£275	20·00
736	23p. brown and green	36·00	4·25
737	24p. brown and blue	42·00	4·25
741	33p. purple and red	18·00	80
742	50p. blue and green		
743	100p. brown and grey	£1200	£450
744	200p. black and purple		

93 Moot Emblem

1967. 2nd Rover Moot, Mecca.

745	**93**	1p. multicoloured	3·00	80
746	**93**	2p. multicoloured	3·00	80
747	**93**	3p. multicoloured	4·50	80
748	**93**	4p. multicoloured	5·50	80
749	**93**	10p. multicoloured	12·50	2·20

94 Meteorological Apparatus

1967. World Meteorological Day.

750	**94**	1p. mauve	1·30	20
751	**94**	2p. violet	2·75	20
752	**94**	3p. green	2·75	35
753	**94**	4p. green	9·00	35
754	**94**	10p. blue	12·50	80

96 Route Map and Dates

1968. Inauguration of Dammam–Jeddah Highway.

834	**96**	1p. multicoloured	2·20	35
835	**96**	2p. multicoloured	2·20	35
836	**96**	3p. multicoloured	4·25	35
837	**96**	4p. multicoloured	4·25	65
838	**96**	10p. multicoloured	12·50	1·10

97 The Prophet's Mosque, Medina

1968. (a) Type 97.

839	**97**	1p. green and orange	3·50	45
840	**97**	2p. green and brown	10·00	45
857	**97**	3p. green and violet	5·00	55
945	**97**	4p. green and brown	7·75	55
843	**97**	5p. green and purple	20·00	1·50
860	**97**	6p. green and black	16·00	1·50
948	**97**	10p. green and brown	20·00	1·50
949	**97**	20p. green and brown	25·00	2·75
864	**97**	50p. green and purple	28·00	9·00
865	**97**	100p. green and blue	28·00	9·00
866	**97**	200p. green and red	30·00	10·00

98 Prophet's Mosque Extension

(b) Type 98.

952	**98**	1p. green and orange	7·25	35
953	**98**	2p. green and brown	12·50	35
954	**98**	3p. green and black	10·00	55
868	**98**	4p. green and red	11·00	80
851	**98**	5p. green and red	7·25	90
852	**98**	6p. green and blue	10·00	80
870a	**98**	8p. green and red	36·00	2·75
871	**98**	10p. green and brown	13·50	80
940	**98**	20p. green and violet	29·00	3·50

99 Ancient Wall Tomb, Madayin Saleh

(c) Type 99.

876	**99**	2p. brown and blue	31·00	5·50
878	**99**	4p. cinnamon and brown	8·25	1·10
880	**99**	7p. brown and orange	60·00	14·50
881	**99**	10p. brown and green	20·00	2·75
883	**99**	20p. brown and purple	22·00	2·20

100 Colonnade, Sacred Mosque, Mecca

(d) Type 100.

887	**100**	3p. grey and red	£600	£150
888	**100**	4p. grey and green	9·00	80
891	**100**	10p. grey and purple	13·50	1·30

101 Camels and Oil Derrick

(e) Type 101.

898	**101**	4p. red and lilac	33·00	5·50
901	**101**	10p. red and blue	30·00	4·25

102 Arab Stallion

(f) Type 102.

908	**102**	4p. brown and purple	9·00	1·10
911	**102**	10p. brown and black	22·00	4·25
912	**102**	14p. brown and blue	36·00	9·00
913	**102**	20p. brown and green	12·50	2·75

103 Holy Ka'aba, Mecca

(g) Type 103.

918	**103**	4p. black and green	12·50	1·10
920	**103**	6p. black and purple	7·25	55
924	**103**	8p. black and red	42·00	4·25
921	**103**	10p. black and red	27·00	2·20

104 Saker Falcon

1968. Air.

1022	**104**	1p. brown and green	15·00	1·00
1023	**104**	4p. brown and red	£375	30·00
1024	**104**	10p. brown and blue	50·00	7·00
1025	**104**	20p. brown and green	£125	12·00

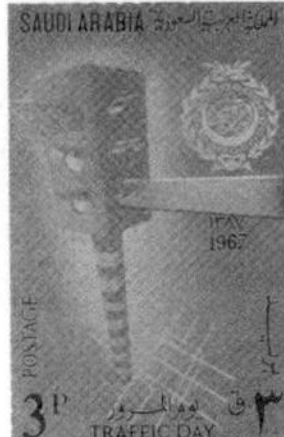

105 Traffic Signals

1969. Traffic Day.

1026	**105**	3p. blue, green and red	3·25	35
1027	**105**	4p. brown, green and red	3·25	35
1028	**105**	10p. purple, green and red	6·25	1·20

106 Scout Emblem, Camp and Flag

1969. 3rd Arab Rover Moot, Mecca.

1029	**106**	1p. multicoloured	2·00	80
1030	**106**	4p. multicoloured	6·25	1·60
1031	**106**	10p. multicoloured	18·00	6·75

107 W.H.O. Emblem

1969. 20th Anniv (1968) of W.H.O.

1032	**107**	4p. yellow, blue and deep blue	13·50	80

108 Conference Emblem

1970. Islamic Foreign Ministers' Conf, Jeddah.

1033	**108**	4p. black and blue	4·00	35
1034	**108**	10p. black and brown	5·50	55

109 Satellite, Dish Aerial and Open Book

1970. World Telecommunications Day.

1035	**109**	4p. blue, mauve and ultramarine	6·75	55
1036	**109**	10p. blue, mauve & green	13·50	2·00

110 Steel Rolling-mill

1970. Inauguration (1967) of First Saudi Arabian Steel Rolling-mill.

1037	**110**	3p. multicoloured	4·00	35
1038	**110**	4p. multicoloured	6·25	45
1039	**110**	10p. multicoloured	11·00	1·00

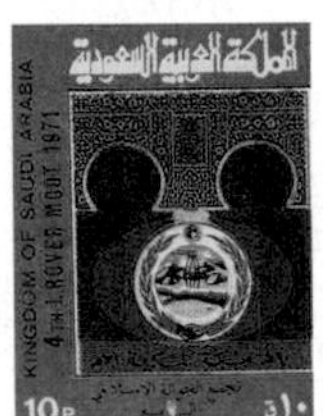

112 Emblem and Arab Archway

1971. 4th Arab Rover Moot, Mecca.

1049	**112**	10p. multicoloured	12·50	1·20

113 Global Emblem

1971. World Telecommunications Day.

1050	**113**	4p. black and blue	3·25	35
1051	**113**	10p. black and lilac	6·75	80

114 University "Tower" Emblem

1971. 4th Anniv of Inauguration of King Abdulaziz National University.

1052	**114**	3p. black and green	2·50	35
1053	**114**	4p. black and brown	5·00	80
1054	**114**	10p. black and blue	9·00	1·50

115 I.E.Y. Emblem

1971. International Education Year (1970).

1055	**115**	4p. red and green	7·75	35

116 Arab League Emblem

1971. Arab Propaganda Week.

1056	**116**	10p. multicoloured	9·00	1·20

117 O.P.E.C. Emblem

1971. 10th Anniv of O.P.E.C.

1057	**117**	4p. blue	9·00	35

O.P.E.C. = Organization of Petroleum Exporting Countries.

118 Globe

1972. World Telecommunications Day.

1058	**118**	4p. multicoloured	9·00	35

119 Telephone within Dial

1972. Inauguration of Automatic Telephone System (1969).

1059	**119**	1p. black, green and red	3·25	35
1060	**119**	4p. black, turquoise & green	3·25	35
1061	**119**	5p. black, green & mauve	5·00	45
1062	**119**	10p. black, green & brn	11·00	1·10

120 Writing in Book

1973. World Literacy Day (1972).

1063	**120**	10p. multicoloured	12·50	90

121 Mosque, Mecca, and Moot Emblem

1973. 5th Arab Rover Moot, Mecca. Mult.

1064	4p. Type **121**	5·00	1·00
1065	6p. Holy Ka'aba, Mecca	10·00	1·50
1066	10p. Rover encampment	16·00	3·75

122 Globe and Map of Palestine

1973. Universal Palestine Week.

1067	**122**	4p. red, yellow and grey	5·50	20
1068	**122**	10p. red, yellow and blue	10·00	1·20

123 Leaf and Emblem

1973. International Hydrological Decade.

1069	**123**	4p. multicoloured	9·00	35

124 A.P.U. Emblem

1973. 25th Anniv of Founding of Arab Postal Union at Sofar Conference.

1070	**124**	4p. multicoloured	6·75	35
1071	**124**	10p. multicoloured	16·00	1·90

125 Balloons

1973. Universal Children's Day (1971).

1072	**125**	4p. multicoloured	11·00	35

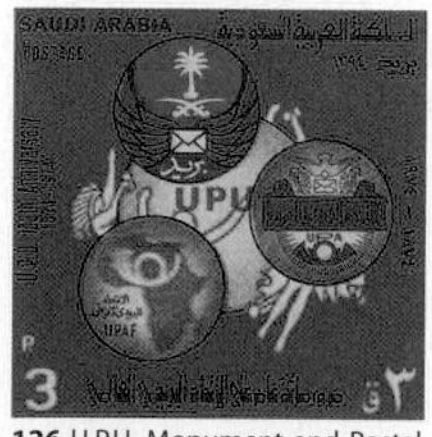

126 U.P.U. Monument and Postal Emblem

1974. Centenary of U.P.U.

1073	**126**	3p. multicoloured	55·00	6·25
1074	**126**	4p. multicoloured	75·00	11·00
1075	**126**	10p. multicoloured	90·00	12·50

127 Handclasp and UNESCO Emblem

1974. International Book Year (1972).

1076	**127**	4p. multicoloured	4·25	35
1077	**127**	10p. multicoloured	16·00	1·30

128 Desalination Works

1974. Inauguration of Sea-water Desalination Plant, Jeddah (1971).

1078	**128**	4p. blue and orange	3·25	35
1079	**128**	6p. lilac and green	6·25	45
1080	**128**	10p. black and red	10·00	1·10

129 Interpol Emblem

1974. 50th Anniv (1973) of International Criminal Police Organization (Interpol).

1081	**129**	4p. blue and red	10·00	45
1082	**129**	10p. blue and green	20·00	2·30

130 Tower, Emblem and Hand with Letter

1974. 3rd Session of Arab Postal Studies Consultative Council, Riyadh.

1083	**130**	4p. multicoloured	10·00	35

131 New Headquarters Building

1974. Inauguration (1970) of New U.P.U. Headquarters, Berne.

1084	**131**	3p. multicoloured	4·25	45
1085	**131**	4p. multicoloured	9·50	80
1086	**131**	10p. multicoloured	12·50	2·50

132 Armed Forces and Flame

1974. King Faisal Military Cantonment (1971).

1087	**132**	3p. multicoloured	3·25	35
1088	**132**	4p. multicoloured	6·25	45
1089	**132**	10p. multicoloured	16·00	2·50

133 Red Crescent "Flower"

1974. 10th Anniv (1973) of Saudi Arabian Red Crescent Society.

1090	**133**	4p. multicoloured	2·50	45

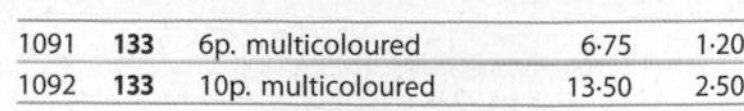

1091	**133**	6p. multicoloured	6·75	1·20
1092	**133**	10p. multicoloured	13·50	2·50

134 Scout Emblem and Minarets

1974. 6th Arab Rover Moot, Mecca.

1093	**134**	4p. multicoloured	6·75	45
1094	**134**	6p. multicoloured	13·50	90
1095	**134**	10p. multicoloured	20·00	2·50

135 Reading Braille

1975. Day of the Blind.

1096	**135**	4p. multicoloured	5·50	45
1097	**135**	10p. multicoloured	10·50	1·00

136 Anemometer and U.N. Emblem as Weather Balloon

1975. Centenary (1973) of World Meteorological Organization.

1098	**136**	4p. multicoloured	12·50	55

137 King Faisal

1975. King Faisal Memorial Issue.

1099	**137**	4p. purple and green	4·00	45
1100	**137**	16p. green and violet	5·50	1·00
1101	**137**	23p. violet and green	11·00	1·70
MS1102		71×80 mm. 40p. As T **137** but larger	£475	£475

138 Conference Emblem

1975. 6th Islamic Conference of Foreign Ministers, Jeddah.

1103	**138**	10p. black and brown	7·25	80

139 Wheat and Sun

1975. 29th Anniv of Charity Society.

1104	**139**	4p. multicoloured	4·75	35
1105	**139**	10p. multicoloured	12·50	55

140 Kaaba, Handclasp and Globe

1975. Moslem Organizations Conference, Mecca.

1106	**140**	4p. multicoloured	10·00	35
1107	**140**	10p. multicoloured	22·00	55

141 Lockheed TriStar and Douglas DC-3 Aircraft

1975. 30th Anniv of National Airline "Saudia".

1108	**141**	4p. multicoloured	12·50	45
1109	**141**	10p. multicoloured	20·00	80

142 Mecca and Riyadh

1975. Conference Locations.

1110	**142**	10p. multicoloured	16·00	80

143 Friday Mosque, Medina, and Juwatha Mosque, Al-Hasa

1975. Islamic Holy Places.

1111	**143**	4p. multicoloured	9·00	35
1112	**143**	10p. multicoloured	12·50	80

144 F.A.O. Emblem

1975. 10th Anniv (1973) of World Food Programme.

1113	**144**	4p. multicoloured	6·75	20
1114	**144**	10p. multicoloured	19·00	80

145 Conference Emblem

1976. Islamic Solidarity Conference of Science and Technology, Mecca.

1115	**145**	4p. multicoloured	22·00	55

146 Map and T.V. Screen

1976. 10th Anniv (1975) of Saudi Arabian Television Service.

1116	**146**	4p. multicoloured	29·00	55

147 Ear of Wheat, Atomic Symbol and Graph

1976. 2nd Five-year Plan.

1117	**147**	20h. multicoloured	6·25	35
1118	**147**	50h. multicoloured	10·00	80

148 Quba Mosque, Medina

1976. Size 36×26 mm. (a) Type 148.

1122	20h. grey and orange	3·25	35
1128	50h. lilac and green	4·25	35

149 Holy Kaaba, Mecca

(b) Type 149.

1137	5h. black and lilac	35	35
1138	10h. black and lilac	35	35
1139	15h. black and orange	55	35
1140	20h. black and blue	6·25	35
1141	25h. black and yellow	1·70	35
1142	30h. black and green	2·20	35
1143	35h. black and brown	1·20	35
1144	40h. black and green	5·50	35
1145	45h. black and purple	1·70	35
1146	50h. black and red	1·70	35
1149	65h. black and blue	2·00	35
1151	1r. black and green	2·75	45
1152	2r. black and green	11·00	55

150 Oil Rig, Al-Khafji

(c) Type 150.

1167	5h. blue and orange	35	35
1168	10h. green and orange	35	35
1169	15h. brown and orange	35	35
1170	20h. green and orange	35	35
1171	25h. purple and orange	35	35
1172	30h. blue and orange	35	35
1173	35h. brown and orange	45	35
1174	40h. purple and orange	45	35
1175	45h. mauve and orange	55	35
1176b	50h. pink and orange	80	35
1177	55h. green and orange	31·00	5·50
1179	65h. brown and orange	1·70	55
1180	1r. green and orange	2·20	90
1181	2r. purple and red	5·00	1·50

For smaller designs see Nos. 1283/1325 and 1435/7.

151 Globe and Telephones

1976. Telephone Centenary.

1191	**151**	50h. multicoloured	10·00	55

152 Emblem and Heads of State

1976. Arab League Summit Conference.

1192	**152**	20h. green and blue	6·25	35

153 Kaaba and Spinning Wheel

1976. 50th Anniv of Manufacture of Kaaba Covering.

1193	**153**	20h. multicoloured	11·00	55

154 Eye and W.H.O. Emblem

1976. World Health Day. Prevention of Blindness.

1194	**154**	20h. multicoloured	16·00	55

155 Emblem

1976. Islamic Jurisprudence Conference.

1195	**155**	20h. multicoloured	11·00	55

156 Emblem

1977. 25th Anniv of Sharia Law College, Mecca.

1196	**156**	4p. green, yellow and mauve	10·00	55

157 King Khaled

1977. 2nd Anniv of Installation of King Khaled. (a) With incorrect dates at foot.

1197	**157**	20h. brown and green	25·00	25·00
1198	**157**	80h. black and green	25·00	25·00

(b) With corrected dates.

1199	20h. brown and green	2·75	35
1200	80h. black and green	5·50	45

On Nos. 1197/8 the two Arabic dates end with the same characters. On the correct version of the design, the characters differ.

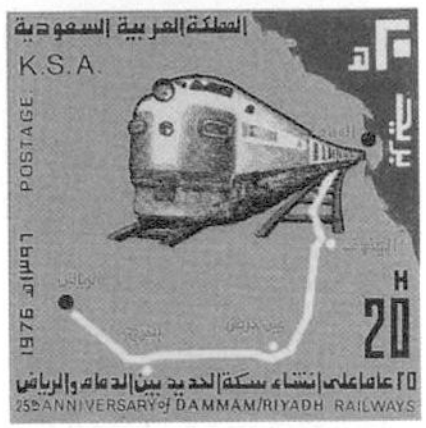

158 Diesel Train and Route Map

1977. 25th Anniv (1976) of Dammam–Riyadh Railway.

1201	**158**	20h. multicoloured	31·00	2·50

159/62 "The Four Imams" (image scaled to 61% of original size)

1977

1202	**159**	20h. blue, yellow and grey	10·00	1·10
1203	**160**	20h. blue, yellow and grey	10·00	1·10
1204	**161**	20h. blue, yellow and grey	10·00	1·10
1205	**162**	20h. blue, yellow and grey	10·00	1·10

Nos. 1202/5 were issued together, se-tenant, forming the composite design illustrated.

163 Moenjodaro Ruins, Pakistan

1977. "Save Moenjodaro" Campaign.

1206	**163**	50h. multicoloured	11·00	55

164 Map by al-Idrisi

1977. 1st International Arab History Symposium.

1207	**164**	20h. multicoloured	4·00	35
1208	**164**	50h. multicoloured	7·75	55

165 King Faisal Hospital, Riyadh

1977. Opening of King Faisal Hospital.
1209 **165** 20h. multicoloured 4·75 35
1210 **165** 50h. multicoloured 7·25 55

166 A.P.U. Emblem

1977. 25th Anniv of Arab Postal Union.
1211 **166** 20h. multicoloured 2·50 35
1212 **166** 80h. multicoloured 5·50 80

167 Kaaba, Book and Lighthouse

1977. 1st World Conference on Muslim Education.
1213 **167** 20h. blue and yellow 6·25 55

168 Taif–Abha–Jizan Road and Route Map

1978. Opening of Taif–Abha–Jizan Road.
1214 **168** 20h. multicoloured 2·50 20
1215 **168** 80h. multicoloured 5·50 55

169 Mount Arafat, Pilgrims and Kaaba

1978. Pilgrimage to Mecca.
1216 **169** 20h. multicoloured 2·50 20
1217 **169** 80h. multicoloured 5·50 55

170 Posthorn Dhow

1979. 2nd Gulf Postal Organization Conf, Dubai.
1218 **170** 20h. multicoloured 2·00 20
1219 **170** 50h. multicoloured 4·00 45

171 5g. Stamp of 1930

1979. 50th Anniv of First Commemorative Stamp Issue.
1220 **171** 20h. multicoloured 2·20 20
1221 **171** 50h. multicoloured 5·00 35
1222 **171** 115h. multicoloured 7·25 1·20

MS1223 100×75 mm. **171** 100h. multi-coloured. Imperf £120 £120

172 Crown Prince Fahd

1979. Crown Prince Fahd's Birthday.
1224 **172** 20h. multicoloured 2·75 20
1225 **172** 50h. multicoloured 5·50 45

173 Dome of the Rock, Jerusalem

1979. Solidarity with Palestinians.
1226 **173** 20h. multicoloured 2·75 55
For similar design see No. 1354.

174 Golden Door of Kaaba, Mecca

1979. Installation of New Gold Doors on Kaaba.
1227 **174** 20h. multicoloured 2·20 20
1228 **174** 80h. multicoloured 5·00 55

175 The Kaaba, Mecca

1979. Pilgrimage to Mecca.
1229 **175** 20h. multicoloured 1·50 20
1230 **175** 50h. multicoloured 4·00 55

176 "Birds in a Forest"

1980. International Year of the Child. Children's Paintings. Multicoloured.
1231 20h. Type **176** 13·50 35
1232 50h. "Paper Lanterns" 22·00 1·20

177 King Abdulaziz Ibn Saud

1980. 80th Anniv of Saudi Armed Forces.
1233 **177** 20h. multicoloured 2·00 20
1234 **177** 80h. multicoloured 5·00 80

178 Emblem

1980. 35th Anniv of Arab League.
1235 **178** 20h. green, black and blue 2·50 35

179 Globe and Books

1980. 50th Anniv of Int Bureau of Education.
1236 **179** 50h. multicoloured 3·25 35

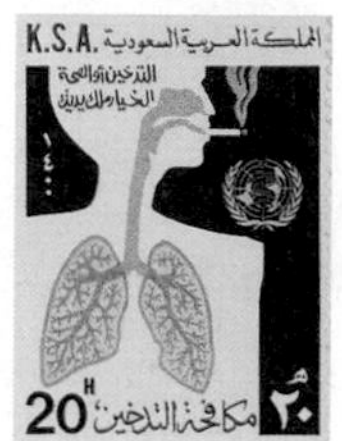

180 Polluted Air Passages and W.H.O. Emblem

1980. Anti-smoking Campaign.
1237 **180** 20h. multicoloured 2·50 20
1238 - 50h. black, red and blue 5·50 55
DESIGN: 50h. Cigarette crossed through and W.H.O. emblem.

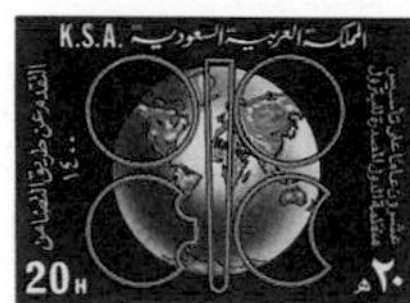

181 O.P.E.C. Emblem and Globe

1980. 20th Anniv of Organization of Petroleum Exporting Countries. Multicoloured.
1239 20h. Type **181** 2·20 20
1240 50h. Figures supporting O.P.E.C. emblem 3·75 55

182 Pilgrims leaving Airplane

1980. Pilgrimage to Mecca.
1241 **182** 20h. multicoloured 1·30 20
1242 **182** 50h. multicoloured 2·50 55

183 Kaaba, Mecca

1981. 3rd Islamic Summit Conference, Mecca. Multicoloured, frame colours given in brackets.
1243 20h. Type **183** (mauve) 1·30 35
1244 20h. Prophet's Mosque, Medina (blue) 1·30 35
1245 20h. Dome of the Rock, Jerusalem (black) 1·30 35
1246 20h. Conference emblem (35×35 mm) 1·30 35

184 Thour Cave, Mecca, and Quba Mosque, Medina, on Map

1981. 1400th Anniv of Hegira.
1247 **184** 20h. multicoloured 1·00 25
1248 **184** 50h. multicoloured 2·00 45
1249 **184** 80h. multicoloured 4·25 60

185 Royal Corporation of Jubeil and Yanbou Emblem

1981. Industry Week.
1250 **185** 20h. brown, orange & silver 1·00 35
1251 **185** 80h. brown, orge & gold 3·25 60

186 Satellite Earth Station

1981. Telecommunications Achievements.
1252 - 20h. gold, black and blue 55 35
1253 - 80h. multicoloured 3·50 60
1254 **186** 115h. multicoloured 4·00 80
DESIGNS—As T **186**: 20h. Modern telephone and graph. 36×36 mm: 80h. Microwave antenna on map of Saudi Arabia.

187 Emblem of Arab Towns Organization

1981. Arab Towns Day.
1255 **187** 20h. multicoloured 55 35
1256 **187** 65h. multicoloured 1·70 60
1257 **187** 80h. multicoloured 2·20 60
1258 **187** 115h. multicoloured 3·25 95

188 Douglas DC-9-80 Super Eighty Jetliner

1981. Inauguration of King Abdulaziz International Airport, Jeddah. Multicoloured.
1259 20h. Type **188** 90 35
1260 80h. Airplane over departure halls in form of tents 3·50 60

189 Flags of participating Countries and Saudi Team Emblem

1981. World Cup Football Championship Preliminary Round, Riyadh.
1261 **189** 20h. multicoloured 2·75 35
1262 **189** 80h. multicoloured 5·50 60

190 Blind Person reading Braille

1981. Int Year of Disabled Persons. Mult.

1263	20h. Type **190**	2·50	35
1264	50h. Disabled person in wheel-chair weaving on loom	4·00	45

191 Wheat and Cogwheel on Graph

1981. 3rd Five-year Plan.

1265	**191**	20h. multicoloured	2·00	35

192 King Abdulaziz Ibn Saud and Map of Saudi Arabia

1981. 50th Anniv of Unification of Saudi Arabia.

1266	**192**	5h. multicoloured	35	35
1267	**192**	10h. multicoloured	35	35
1268	**192**	15h. multicoloured	35	35
1269	**192**	20h. multicoloured	45	35
1270	**192**	50h. multicoloured	1·00	45
1271	**192**	65h. multicoloured	1·50	60
1272	**192**	80h. multicoloured	3·75	60
1273	**192**	115h. multicoloured	4·75	80
MS1274		100×74 mm. 10r. King Abdulaziz Ibn Saud, map and unification decree. Imperf	£120	£120

193 Pilgrims passing through Almasa'a Arcade

1981. Pilgrimage to Mecca.

1275	**193**	20h. multicoloured	2·00	25
1276	**193**	65h. multicoloured	4·00	60

194 Tractor

1981. World Food Day.

1277	**194**	20h. multicoloured	3·25	35

For similar design see No. 1343.

195 Conference Emblem

1981. 2nd Session of Gulf Co-operation Council Summit Conference, Riyadh.

1278	**195**	20h. multicoloured	1·00	35
1279	**195**	80h. multicoloured	3·25	80

196 University Emblem

1982. 25th Anniv of King Saud University.

1280	**196**	20h. multicoloured	1·20	35
1281	**196**	50h. multicoloured	2·75	60

1982. As T 149/150 but in smaller size, 25×20 mm. (a) Type 149.

1283	10h. black and lilac	35	35
1284	15h. black and orange	35	35
1285d	20h. black and blue	35	35
1291c	50h. black and red	45	35
1294c	65h. black and blue	1·00	35
1301c	1r. black and green	2·20	35

(b) Type 150.

1306a	5h. blue and orange	35	35
1307c	10h. green and orange	35	35
1308c	15h. brown and orange	35	35
1309c	20h. green and orange	35	35
1310	25h. purple and orange	35	35
1315c	50h. red and orange	45	35
1318c	65h. brown and orange	55	35
1325c	1r. green and orange	80	45

197 Riyadh Postal Building

1982. New Postal Buildings. Multicoloured.

1330	20h. Type **197**	55	35
1331	65h. Jeddah	1·50	60
1332	80h. Dammam	2·10	60
1333	115h. Postal mechanized sorting	2·75	95
MS1334	Four sheets, each 8×70 mm. (a) No. 1330; (b) No. 1331; (c) No. 1332; (d) No. 1333. Imperf (each sold at 3000h.)	£130	£130

198 Riyadh Television Centre

1982. Riyadh Television Centre.

1335	**198**	20h. multicoloured	1·70	35

199 Football and King's Cup

1982. 25th Anniv of King's Cup Football Championship.

1336	**199**	20h. multicoloured	1·20	35
1337	**199**	65h. multicoloured	2·50	60

200 A.P.U. Emblem and Map

1982. 30th Anniv of Arab Postal Union. Mult.

1338	20h. A.P.U. Emblem and Arabic "30"	1·00	35
1339	65h. Type **200**	2·75	60

201 Pilgrims at Muzdalefa looking for Stones to stone the Devil

1982. Pilgrimage to Mecca.

1340	**201**	20h. multicoloured	1·00	35
1341	**201**	50h. multicoloured	2·75	60

202 Saudi Arabian and World Standards Organizations Emblems

1982. World Standards Day.

1342	**202**	20h. multicoloured	2·00	45

203 Tractor

1982. World Food Day.

1343	**203**	20h. multicoloured	1·70	35

For similar design see No. 1277.

204 King Fahd

1983. Installation of King Fahd.

1344	**204**	20h. multicoloured	45	25
1345	**204**	50h. multicoloured	1·00	45
1346	**204**	65h. multicoloured	1·50	60
1347	**204**	80h. multicoloured	1·70	80
1348	**204**	115h. multicoloured	2·75	1·00

205 Crown Prince Abdullah

1983. Installation of Crown Prince.

1349	**205**	20h. multicoloured	45	25
1350	**205**	50h. multicoloured	1·00	45
1351	**205**	65h. multicoloured	1·50	60
1352	**205**	80h. multicoloured	1·70	80
1353	**205**	115h. multicoloured	2·75	1·00

206 Dome of the Rock, Jerusalem

1983. Solidarity with Palestinians.

1354	**206**	20h. multicoloured	1·00	45

For similar design but inscribed "K.S.A." see No. 1226.

207 Container Ship "Bar'zan"

1983. 6th Anniv of United Arab Shipping Company. Multicoloured.

1355	20h. Type **207**	80	35
1356	65h. "Al Drieya" (container ship)	2·75	95

208 Stoning the Devil

1983. Pilgrimage to Mecca.

1357	**208**	20h. multicoloured	55	35
1358	**208**	65h. multicoloured	2·00	45

209 Saudi Arabia Post and U.P.U. Emblems

1983. World Communications Year. Mult.

1359	20h. Type **209**	45	35
1360	80h. Saudi Arabia telephone and I.T.U. emblems	2·00	45

210 Terminal Building

1983. Opening of King Khaled International Airport, Riyadh. Multicoloured.

1361	20h. Type **210**	80	25
1362	65h. Embarkation wing of terminal	2·20	95

211 Wheat and F.A.O. Emblem

1983. World Food Day.

1363	**211**	20h. multicoloured	2·00	45

212 Al Aqsa Mosque, Jerusalem

1983. Solidarity with Palestinians.

1364	**212**	20h. brown, blue & green	80	35

213 Riyadh

1984. Saudi Cities. (a) Riyadh.

1365	**213**	20h. multicoloured	35	35
1366	**213**	50h. multicoloured	45	35

1370 **213** 75h. multicoloured 1·00 60
1371 **213** 150h. multicoloured 2·50 1·30

214 Shobra Palace, Taif

(b) Taif.
1367 **214** 20h. multicoloured 35 35
1368 **214** 50h. multicoloured 1·00 60
1374 **214** 75h. multicoloured 1·00 60
1375 **214** 150h. multicoloured 2·50 1·30

215 Jeddah

(c) Jeddah.
1377 **215** 50h. multicoloured 1·50 80
1378 **215** 75h. multicoloured 1·50 80
1379 **215** 150h. multicoloured 2·50 1·30

216 Dammam

(d) Dammam.
1380 **216** 50h. multicoloured 80 45
1381 **216** 75h. multicoloured 1·00 60
1382 **216** 150h. multicoloured 2·00 1·00

217 Abha

(e) Abha.
1383 **217** 1r. multicoloured 1·10 1·20
1384 **217** 2r. multicoloured 2·20 2·30

223 Family and House

1984. 10th Anniv of Estate Development Fund.
1385 **223** 20h. multicoloured 80 35

224 Solar Panels and Symbols

1984. Al-Eyenah Solar Village. Multicoloured.
1386 20h. Type **224** 55 35
1387 80h. Sun and solar panels 1·70 45
MS1388 Two sheets, each 80×80 mm. Imperf. (a) 100h. As Type **224**; (b) As No. 1387, but both larger 85·00 85·00

225 Al-Kheef Mosque, Mina

1984. Pilgrimage to Mecca. Multicoloured.
1389 20h. Type **225** 80 25
1390 65h. Al-Kheef Mosque, Mina (different) 2·20 45

226 Olympic and Saudi Football Federation Emblems

1984. Qualification of Saudi Football Team for Olympic Games.
1391 **226** 20h. multicoloured 1·90 45
1392 **226** 115h. multicoloured 7·75 1·50

Nos. 1391/2 have the incorrect spellings "Gamos" and "Olympied".

227 Wheat and F.A.O. Emblem

1984. World Food Day.
1393 **227** 20h. green, buff and black 80 35

228 Olympic Rings and "90"

1984. 90th Anniv of Int Olympic Committee.
1394 **228** 20h. multicoloured 1·50 45
1395 **228** 50h. multicoloured 3·50 80

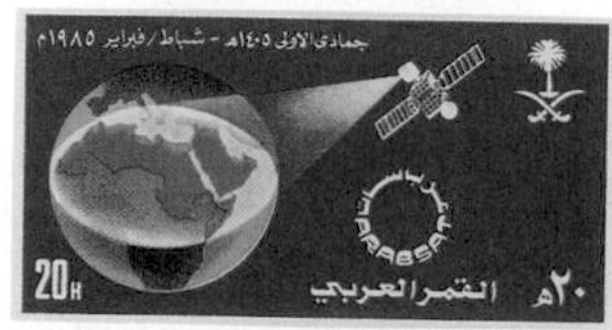

229 "Arabsat" and Globe

1985. Launch of "Arabsat" Satellite.
1396 **229** 20h. multicoloured 2·75 35

230 Emblem and Koran

1985. International Koran Reading Competition.
1397 **230** 20h. multicoloured 55 35
1398 **230** 65h. multicoloured 1·50 60

231 King Fahd and Jubail Industrial Complex

1985. Five Year Plan. Multicoloured.
1399 20h. Type **231** 55 35
1400 50h. King Fahd, T.V. tower, dish aerial and microwave tower 1·50 35
1401 65h. King Fahd and agricultural landscape 1·70 35
1402 80h. King Fahd and Yanbu industrial complex 2·50 45

232 I.Y.Y. Emblem

1985. International Youth Year.
1403 **232** 20h. multicoloured 45 35
1404 **232** 80h. multicoloured 1·70 45

233 Map and Wheat

1985. "Self Sufficiency in Wheat Production".
1405 **233** 20h. multicoloured 80 35

234 Loading Berth, Yanbu

1985. Abqaiq–Yanbu Oil Pipeline. Multicoloured.
1406 20h. Type **234** 80 35
1407 65h. Pipeline and map 2·00 60

235 "Arabsat 2" Satellite and Launch of "Discovery" (space shuttle)

1985. 1st Arab Astronaut, Prince Sultan Ibn Salman Al-Saud. Multicoloured.
1408 20h. Type **235** 1·20 60
1409 115h. Space shuttle and mission emblem (51×26 mm) 6·75 3·25

236 "40" and U.N. Emblem

1985. 40th Anniv of U.N.O.
1410 **236** 20h. light blue, blue and green 90 35

237 Highway and Map of Route

1985. Mecca–Medina Highway.
1411 **237** 20h. multicoloured 55 35
1412 **237** 65h. multicoloured 1·70 45

238 Coded Envelope and Post Emblem

1985. Post Code Publicity.
1413 **238** 20h. multicoloured 80 35

239 Trophy and Football

1985. Victory in 8th (1984) Asian Football Cup Championship.
1414 **239** 20h. multicoloured 55 25
1415 **239** 65h. multicoloured 1·90 60
1416 **239** 115h. multicoloured 3·25 1·20

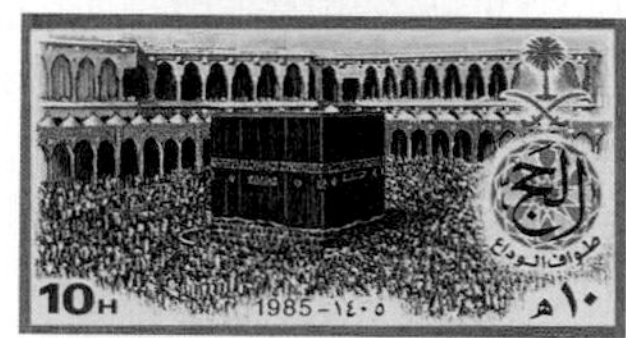

240 Pilgrims around Kaaba

1985. Pilgrimage to Mecca.
1417 **240** 10h. multicoloured 35 35
1418 **240** 15h. multicoloured 35 35
1419 **240** 20h. multicoloured 45 35
1420 **240** 65h. multicoloured 1·10 35

241 Olympic Rings and Council Emblem

1985. 1st Arabian Gulf Co-operation Council Olympic Day.
1421 **241** 20h. multicoloured 60 40
1422 **241** 115h. multicoloured 3·00 65

242 Irrigation System

1985. World Food Day.
1423 **242** 20h. multicoloured 1·30 65
1424 **242** 65h. multicoloured 4·00 1·40

243 King Abdulaziz and Horsemen

1985. International Conference on King Abdulaziz.
1425 **243** 15h. multicoloured 25 25
1426 **243** 20h. multicoloured 35 25
1427 **243** 65h. multicoloured 1·20 65
1428 **243** 80h. multicoloured 1·60 90
MS1429 120×100 mm. Nos. 1425/8. Imperf (sold at 10r.) 34·00 34·00

244 Building within Roll of Printed Paper

1985. King Fahd Holy Koran Press Compound, Medina. Multicoloured.

1430		20h. Type **244**	35	35
1431		65h. Open book sculpture within roll of printed paper	1·80	50

245 O.P.E.C. Emblem and "25"

1985. 25th Anniv of Organization of Petroleum Exporting Countries.

1432	**245**	20h. sepia, brown and black	50	35
1433	**245**	65h. multicoloured	2·40	50

246 Doves and I.P.Y. Emblem

1986. International Peace Year.

1434	**246**	20h. multicoloured	1·60	65

1986. As T 149 but size 29×19 mm.

1435		10h. black and violet	9·75	9·75
1436		20h. black and blue	16·00	16·00
1437		50h. black and red	33·00	28·00

247 Riyadh

1986. 50th Anniv of Riyadh Municipality.

1438a	**247**	20h. multicoloured	60	50
1439	**247**	65h. multicoloured	1·80	65

248 Child in Droplet

1986. World Health Day.

1440	**248**	20h. multicoloured	60	50
1441	**248**	50h. multicoloured	1·80	65

249 Electricity Pylon and Flashes

1986. 10th Anniv of General Electricity Corporation.

1442	**249**	20h. multicoloured	60	50
1443	**249**	65h. multicoloured	1·80	65

250 Route Map of Cable

1986. Inauguration of Singapore–Marseilles Communications Cable.

1444	**250**	20h. blue, black and green	95	50
1445	**250**	50h. multicoloured	1·80	65

251 Houses and Soldier

1986. National Guards Housing Project, Riyadh.

1446	**251**	20h. multicoloured	60	50
1447	**251**	65h. multicoloured	1·80	65

252 Holy Kaaba

1986

1448	**252**	30h. black and green	50	50
1449	**252**	40h. black and mauve	60	50
1450	**252**	50h. black and green	1·20	75
1451a	**252**	75h. black and blue	1·20	75
1451b	**252**	100h. black and green	1·80	1·00
1452a	**252**	150h. black and mauve	2·75	1·50
1454	**252**	2r. black and blue	3·50	1·90

253 Mount Arafat, Pilgrims and Kaaba

1986. Pilgrimage to Mecca. Multicoloured.

1460		20h. Type **253**	2·75	2·30
1461		20h. Pilgrims leaving jet airliner	2·75	2·30
1462		20h. Stoning the Devil	2·75	2·30
1463		20h. Pilgrims at Muzdalefa looking for stones to stone the Devil	2·75	2·30
1464		20h. Pilgrims passing through Almasa'a Arcade	2·75	2·30
1465		20h. Kaaba, Mecca	2·75	2·30
1466		20h. Pilgrims around Kaaba	2·75	2·30
1467		20h. Al-Kheef Mosque, Mina	2·75	2·30

254 Refinery

1986. 50th Anniv of Discovery of Oil in Saudi Arabia. Multicoloured.

1468		20h. Type **254**	70	50
1469		65h. Oil derrick on map	2·40	65

255 Palm Tree and Wheat in Globe

1986. World Food Day. Multicoloured.

1470		20h. Type **255**	50	50
1471		115h. Corn cob and wheat in leaves of flower	2·20	1·10

256 Scroll behind Dagger and Pool of Blood

1986. 4th Anniv of Massacre of Palestinian Refugees at Sabra and Shatila Camps, Lebanon.

1472	**256**	80h. multicoloured	1·40	75
1473	**256**	115h. multicoloured	2·40	1·10

257

1986. University Crests. (a) Imam Mohammed ibn Saud Islamic University, Riyadh.

1474	**257**	15h. black and green	50	50
1475	**257**	20h. black and blue	50	50
1476	**257**	50h. black and blue	70	65
1477	**257**	65h. black and blue	1·10	65
1478	**257**	75h. black and blue	1·20	75
1479	**257**	100h. black and pink	1·40	75
1480	**257**	150h. black and red	3·00	1·30

258

(b) Umm al-Qura University, Mecca.

1481	**258**	50h. black and blue	1·10	65
1482	**258**	65h. black and blue	1·20	65
1483	**258**	75h. black and blue	1·20	75
1484	**258**	100h. black and pink	2·20	1·10
1485	**258**	150h. black and red	3·25	2·00

259

(c) King Saud University, Riyadh.

1487	**259**	50h. black and blue	1·10	65
1488	**259**	75h. black and blue	1·20	75
1489	**259**	100h. black and pink	2·20	1·10
1490	**259**	150h. black and pink	3·00	1·30

260

(d) King Abulaziz University, Jeddah.

1493	**260**	50h. black and blue	70	65
1494	**260**	75h. black and blue	1·20	75
1496	**260**	150h. black and red	3·00	1·30

261

(e) King Faisal University, Al-Hasa.

1499	**261**	50h. black and blue	70	65
1500	**261**	75h. black and blue	1·20	75
1502	**261**	150h. black and red	3·00	1·00

262

(f) King Fahd University of Petroleum and Minerals, Dhahran.

1505	**262**	50h. black and blue	70	65
1506	**262**	75h. black and blue	1·20	75
1508	**262**	150h. black and pink	2·40	1·00

263

(g) Islamic University, Medina.

1511	**263**	50h. black and blue	1·10	65
1512	**263**	75h. black and blue	1·20	75
1514	**263**	150h. black and red	2·40	50

264 Road Bridge and Aerial View of Causeway (left)

1986. Saudi Arabia–Bahrain Causeway. Mult.

1515		20h. Type **264**	1·60	65
1516		20h. Road bridge and aerial view of causeway (right)	1·60	65

265 Olympic Torch and Rings

1986. 90th Anniv of Modern Olympic Games.

1517	**265**	20h. multicoloured	1·80	50
1518	**265**	100h. multicoloured	9·75	2·75

266 Oil Derrick and Refinery

1987. 25th Anniv of General Petroleum and Mineral Organization.

1519	**266**	50h. multicoloured	1·10	65
1520	**266**	100h. multicoloured	2·20	1·10

267 Mosque and Model of Extension

1987. Restoration and Extension of Quba Mosque, Medina.

1521	**267**	50h. multicoloured	1·20	65
1522	**267**	75h. multicoloured	1·80	75

268 Drill-press Operator

1987. Technical and Vocational Training. Mult.

1523		50h. Type **268**	2·40	1·30
1524		50h. Lathe operator	2·40	1·30
1525		50h. Laboratory technician	2·40	1·30
1526		50h. Welder	2·40	1·30

Nos. 1523/6 were printed together, se-tenant, each block forming an overall design of a cogwheel.

269 Pyramid, Riyadh T.V. Tower, King Khaled International Airport and Fort

1987. "Saudi Arabia—Yesterday and Today" Exhibition, Cairo.

1527	**269**	50h. multicoloured	1·10	65
1528	**269**	75h. multicoloured	2·20	1·00

270 Dish Aerials and Satellite

1987. King Fahd Space Communications City, Umm al Salam, Jeddah. Multicoloured.

1529	50h. Type **270**	1·10	65
1530	75h. Dish aerials and City buildings (51×26 mm)	2·20	1·00

271 Map and Rifleman

1987. Afghan Resistance to Occupation.

1531	**271**	50h. multicoloured	1·10	65
1532	**271**	100h. multicoloured	2·20	1·10

272 Mosque and Pilgrims

1987. Pilgrimage to Mecca.

1533	**272**	50h. multicoloured	1·20	65
1534	**272**	75h. multicoloured	1·80	75
1535	**272**	100h. multicoloured	2·20	1·10

273 Emblems

1987. 1st Anniv of Disabled Children's Care Home.

1536	**273**	50h. multicoloured	95	50
1537	**273**	75h. multicoloured	1·30	65

274 Emblems and Hands writing on Airmail Envelope

1987. World Post Day.

1538	**274**	50h. multicoloured	95	50
1539	**274**	150h. multicoloured	2·40	1·30

275 Combine Harvester within Leaf

1987. World Food Day.

1540	**275**	50h. multicoloured	1·10	50
1541	**275**	75h. multicoloured	1·60	65

276 Woman and Children in Hand

1987. 25th Anniv of First Social Welfare Society.

1542	**276**	50h. multicoloured	1·10	50
1543	**276**	100h. multicoloured	2·20	1·00

277 Dome of the Rock, Jerusalem

1987

1544	**277**	75h. multicoloured	2·75	65
1545	**277**	150h. multicoloured	5·50	1·40

278 Mosque

1987. Expansion of Prophet's Mosque, Medina.

1546	**278**	50h. multicoloured	1·10	50
1547	**278**	75h. multicoloured	1·60	65
1548	**278**	150h. multicoloured	3·00	1·30
MS1549		110×70 mm. Imperf (sold at 300h.)	65·00	65·00

279 Dome of the Rock, Horseman and Battle Scene

1987. 800th Anniv of Battle of Hattin.

1550	**279**	75h. multicoloured	2·75	65
1551	**279**	150h. multicoloured	5·50	1·40

280 Emblem

1987. 8th Supreme Council Session of Gulf Co-operation Council, Riyadh.

1552	**280**	50h. multicoloured	1·10	50
1553	**280**	75h. multicoloured	1·80	65

281 Road as "3" and Ship

1988. 3rd International Roads Federation (Middle East Region) Meeting, Riyadh.

1554	**281**	50h. multicoloured	1·60	90
1555	**281**	75h. multicoloured	2·20	1·10

282 Aerial View of Stadium and Sports Pictograms

1988. Inauguration of International King Fahd Stadium, Riyadh. Multicoloured.

1556	50h. Type **282**	1·10	50
1557	150h. Side view of stadium and sports pictograms (51×26 mm)	3·50	1·60

283 Anniversary Emblem and W.H.O. Building

1988. World Health Day. 40th Anniv of W.H.O.

1558	**283**	50h. multicoloured	1·30	50
1559	**283**	75h. multicoloured	1·60	65

284 Blood Transfusion and Blood Drop

1988. Blood Donation.

1560	**284**	50h. multicoloured	1·10	50
1561	**284**	75h. multicoloured	1·60	65

285 Mosque, Holy Kaaba and King Fahd

1988. Appointment of King Fahd as Custodian of Two Holy Mosques.

1562	**285**	50h. multicoloured	85	50
1563	**285**	75h. multicoloured	1·10	65
1564	**285**	150h. multicoloured	2·40	1·10
MS1565		120×85 mm. As No. 1563 but 63×32 mm (sold at 3r.)	80·00	80·00

286 Clean Air, Land and Sea

1988. Environmental Protection.

1566	**286**	50h. multicoloured	1·20	50
1567	**286**	75h. multicoloured	1·80	65

287 Palestinian Flag, Hand holding Stone and Crowd

1988. Palestinian "Intifada" Movement.

1568	**287**	75h. multicoloured	1·80	65
1569	**287**	150h. multicoloured	3·50	1·40

288 Pilgrims at al-Sail al-Kabir Miqat

1988. Pilgrimage to Mecca.

1570	**288**	50h. multicoloured	1·30	50
1571	**288**	75h. multicoloured	2·20	90

289 Ear of Wheat

1988. World Food Day.

1572	**289**	50h. multicoloured	1·60	90
1573	**289**	75h. multicoloured	2·40	1·30

290 Mosque

1988. Expansion of Qiblatayn Mosque, Medina.

1574	**290**	50h. multicoloured	1·20	50
1575	**290**	75h. multicoloured	1·80	65

291 Footballer and Trophy on Globe

1989. World Youth Football Cup, Saudi Arabia.

1576	**291**	75h. multicoloured	2·10	1·00
1577	**291**	150h. multicoloured	4·00	1·90

292 W.H.O. Emblem and Means of Communications

1989. World Health Day.

1578	**292**	50h. multicoloured	1·30	50
1579	**292**	75h. multicoloured	2·20	65

293 Shuaibah Desalination Plant, Red Sea

1989. 1st Anniv of Sea Water Desalination and Electricity Power Station.

1580	**293**	50h. multicoloured	95	50
1581	**293**	75h. multicoloured	1·30	90

294 Palestinian Flag and Dome of the Rock, Jerusalem

1989. "Freedom of Palestine".

1582	**294**	50h. multicoloured	1·10	40
1583	**294**	75h. multicoloured	1·80	50

295 Attan'eem Miqat, Mecca

1989. Pilgrimage to Mecca.

1584	**295**	50h. multicoloured	1·10	40
1585	**295**	75h. multicoloured	1·60	50

296 Ears of Wheat encircling Globe

1989. World Food Day.

1586	**296**	75h. multicoloured	95	65
1587	**296**	150h. multicoloured	1·80	1·40

297 Hands holding Trophy aloft

1989. 3rd World Under-16 JVC Cup Soccer Championship, Scotland.

1588	**297**	75h. multicoloured	1·30	65
1589	**297**	150h. multicoloured	2·75	1·40

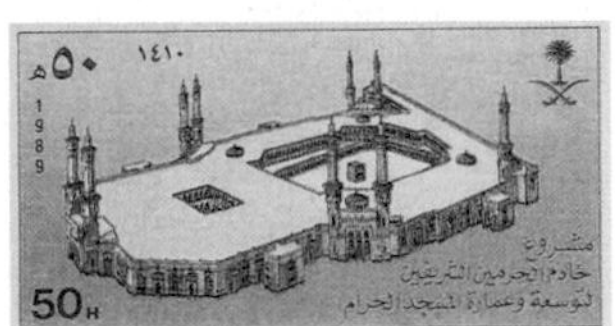

298 Mosque after Expansion

1989. Expansion of Holy Mosque, Mecca.

1590	**298**	50h. multicoloured	95	50
1591	**298**	75h. multicoloured	1·30	90
1592	**298**	150h. multicoloured	2·75	1·40
MS1593		105×80 mm. 5r. As T **298** but larger. Imperf or perf	48·00	48·00

299 Emblem and Arabic Letters

1990. International Literacy Year.

1595	**299**	50h. multicoloured	1·20	50
1596	**299**	75h. multicoloured	1·80	65

300 "Aloe sheilaa"

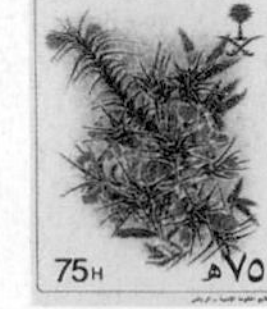

301 "Blopharis ciliaris"

302 "Pergularia tormentosa"

303 "Talinam cuneifolium"

304 "Echium horridum"

305 "Cleome arabica"

306 "Iris sisyrinchium"

308 "Cistanche phelypaea"

309 "Plumbago zeylanica"

310 "Cappario cartilaginea"

311 "Peganum harmala"

312 Acacia

313 "Cagea reticulata"

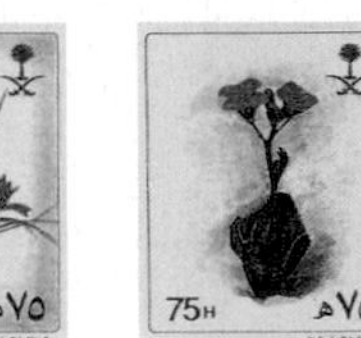

314 "Diplotakis harra"

315 "Anvillea garcini"

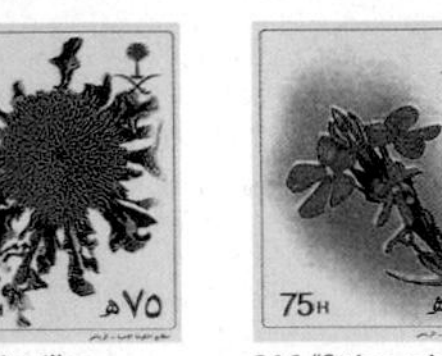

316 "Striga asiatica"

317 "Rhanterium eppaposum"

318 "Oenostachys abyssinica"

319 "Roemeria dodecandra"

320 Poppy

1990. Flowers.

1597	**300**	50h. multicoloured	60	40
1598	**301**	50h. multicoloured	60	40
1599	**302**	50h. multicoloured	60	40
1600	**303**	50h. multicoloured	60	40
1601	**304**	50h. multicoloured	60	40
1602	**305**	50h. multicoloured	60	40
1603	**306**	50h. multicoloured	60	40
1604	**307**	50h. multicoloured	60	40
1605	**308**	50h. multicoloured	60	40
1606	**309**	50h. multicoloured	60	40
1607	**310**	50h. multicoloured	60	40
1608	**311**	50h. multicoloured	60	40
1609	**312**	50h. multicoloured	60	40
1610	**313**	50h. multicoloured	60	40
1611	**314**	50h. multicoloured	60	40
1612	**315**	50h. multicoloured	60	40
1613	**316**	50h. multicoloured	60	40
1614	**317**	50h. multicoloured	60	40
1615	**318**	50h. multicoloured	60	40
1616	**319**	50h. multicoloured	60	40
1617	**320**	50h. multicoloured	60	40
1618	**300**	75h. multicoloured	95	50
1619	**301**	75h. multicoloured	95	50
1620	**302**	75h. multicoloured	95	50
1621	**303**	75h. multicoloured	95	50
1622	**304**	75h. multicoloured	95	50
1623	**305**	75h. multicoloured	95	50
1624	**306**	75h. multicoloured	95	50
1625	**307**	75h. multicoloured	95	50
1626	**308**	75h. multicoloured	95	50
1627	**309**	75h. multicoloured	95	50
1628	**310**	75h. multicoloured	95	50
1629	**311**	75h. multicoloured	95	50
1630	**312**	75h. multicoloured	95	50
1631	**313**	75h. multicoloured	95	50
1632	**314**	75h. multicoloured	95	50
1633	**315**	75h. multicoloured	95	50
1634	**316**	75h. multicoloured	95	50
1635	**317**	75h. multicoloured	95	50
1636	**318**	75h. multicoloured	95	50
1637	**319**	75h. multicoloured	95	50
1638	**320**	75h. multicoloured	95	50
1639	**300**	150h. multicoloured	1·90	1·10
1640	**301**	150h. multicoloured	1·90	1·10
1641	**302**	150h. multicoloured	1·90	1·10
1642	**303**	150h. multicoloured	1·90	1·10
1643	**304**	150h. multicoloured	1·90	1·10
1644	**305**	150h. multicoloured	1·90	1·10
1645	**306**	150h. multicoloured	1·90	1·10
1646	**307**	150h. multicoloured	1·90	1·10
1647	**308**	150h. multicoloured	1·90	1·10
1648	**309**	150h. multicoloured	1·90	1·10
1649	**310**	150h. multicoloured	1·90	1·10
1650	**311**	150h. multicoloured	1·90	1·10
1651	**312**	150h. multicoloured	1·90	1·10
1652	**313**	150h. multicoloured	1·90	1·10
1653	**314**	150h. multicoloured	1·90	1·10
1654	**315**	150h. multicoloured	1·90	1·10
1655	**316**	150h. multicoloured	1·90	1·10
1656	**317**	150h. multicoloured	1·90	1·10
1657	**318**	150h. multicoloured	1·90	1·10
1658	**319**	150h. multicoloured	1·90	1·10
1659	**320**	150h. multicoloured	1·90	1·10

321 "20" within Crescent and Circle

1990. 20th Anniv of Islamic Conference Organization.

1660	**321**	75h. multicoloured	95	50
1661	**321**	150h. multicoloured	1·80	1·00

322 Globe and W.H.O. Emblem

1990. World Health Day.

1662	**322**	75h. multicoloured	1·30	65
1663	**322**	150h. multicoloured	2·75	1·30

323 White Horse

1990. 25th Anniv of Horsemanship Club. Mult. (a) Size 38×29 mm.

1664	50h. Type **323**	1·30	50
1665	50h. Brown horse	1·30	50
1666	50h. White horse with dark muzzle	1·30	50
1667	50h. Chestnut horse	1·30	50

(b) Size 36×27 mm.

1668	50h. As No. 1667	1·30	50
1669	75h. As No. 1665	1·60	90
1670	100h. Type **323**	2·20	1·10
1671	150h. As No. 1666	3·25	1·60

324 El Johfah Miqat, Rabegh

1990. Pilgrimage to Mecca.

1672	**324**	75h. multicoloured	1·30	65
1673	**324**	150h. multicoloured	2·75	1·40

325 T.V. Tower and Centre

1990. 25th Anniv of Saudi Television.

1674	**325**	75h. multicoloured	1·30	65
1675	**325**	150h. multicoloured	2·75	1·40

326 Ornament

1990. Islamic Heritage Year. Multicoloured.

1676	75h. Type **326**	1·30	90
1677	75h. Mosque	1·30	90
1678	75h. Arabic script	1·30	90
1679	75h. Decoration with stylized minarets	1·30	90

Nos. 1676/9 were issued together, se-tenant, each block having a composite design of a stylized rosette in the centre.

327 Boeing 747-300/400 and International Flights Route Map

1990. 45th Anniv of Saudi Airlines. Multicoloured.

1680	75h. Type **327**	95	65
1681	75h. Douglas DC-10 airliner and domestic flights route map	95	65
1682	150h. Type **327**	1·90	1·30
1683	150h. As No. 1681	1·90	1·30

328 Anniversary Emblem

1990. 30th Anniv of Organization of Petroleum Exporting Countries.

1684	**328**	75h. multicoloured	1·80	65
1685	**328**	150h. multicoloured	3·50	2·10

329 World Map

1990. World Food Day.

1686	**329**	75h. multicoloured	1·30	65
1687	**329**	150h. multicoloured	3·00	1·40

330 Industrial Site, Irrigation System and Oil Refinery

1990. 5th Five Year Plan. Multicoloured.

1688	75h. Type **330**	1·60	90
1689	75h. Radio tower, road and mine	1·60	90
1690	75h. Monument, sports stadium and vocational training	1·60	90
1691	75h. Television tower, environmental protection and modern building	1·60	90

331 Arabic Script and Decoration

1991. Battle of Badr, 624 A.D.

1692	**331**	75h. green and orange	1·20	65
1693	**331**	150h. dp blue, blue & green	2·40	1·30

332 Tidal Wave, Erupting Volcano and Earthquake-damaged House

1991. World Health Day. Natural Disasters Relief.

1694	**332**	75h. multicoloured	1·20	65
1695	**332**	150h. multicoloured	2·40	1·30

333 Mountain Gazelle

334 Ibex

335 Arabian Oryx

336 Sand Fox

337 Bat

338 Striped Hyena

339 Sand Cat

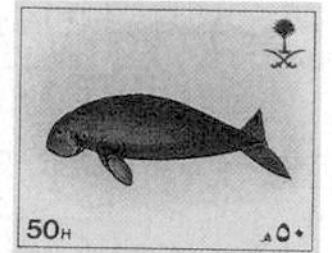

340 Dugong

341 Arabian Leopard

342 Flag and Map of Kuwait

1991. Animals.

1696	**333**	25h. multicoloured	50	25
1697	**334**	25h. multicoloured	50	25
1698	**335**	25h. multicoloured	50	25
1699	**336**	25h. multicoloured	50	25
1700	**337**	25h. multicoloured	50	25
1701	**338**	25h. multicoloured	50	25
1702	**339**	25h. multicoloured	50	25
1703	**340**	25h. multicoloured	50	25
1704	**341**	25h. multicoloured	50	25
1705	**333**	50h. multicoloured	1·10	65
1706	**334**	50h. multicoloured	1·10	65
1707	**335**	50h. multicoloured	1·10	65
1708	**336**	50h. multicoloured	1·10	65
1709	**337**	50h. multicoloured	1·10	65
1710	**338**	50h. multicoloured	1·10	65
1711	**339**	50h. multicoloured	1·10	65
1712	**340**	50h. multicoloured	1·10	65
1713	**341**	50h. multicoloured	1·10	65
1714	**333**	75h. multicoloured	1·60	1·10
1715	**334**	75h. multicoloured	1·60	1·10
1716	**335**	75h. multicoloured	1·60	1·10
1717	**336**	75h. multicoloured	1·60	1·10
1718	**337**	75h. multicoloured	1·60	1·10
1719	**338**	75h. multicoloured	1·60	1·10
1720	**339**	75h. multicoloured	1·60	1·10
1721	**340**	75h. multicoloured	1·60	1·10
1722	**341**	75h. multicoloured	1·60	1·10
1723	**333**	100h. multicoloured	2·20	1·40
1724	**334**	100h. multicoloured	2·20	1·40
1725	**335**	100h. multicoloured	2·20	1·40
1726	**336**	100h. multicoloured	2·20	1·40
1727	**337**	100h. multicoloured	2·20	1·40
1728	**338**	100h. multicoloured	2·20	1·40
1729	**339**	100h. multicoloured	2·20	1·40
1730	**340**	100h. multicoloured	2·20	1·40
1731	**341**	100h. multicoloured	2·20	1·40
1732	**333**	150h. multicoloured	3·25	2·30
1733	**334**	150h. multicoloured	3·25	2·30
1734	**335**	150h. multicoloured	3·25	2·30
1735	**336**	150h. multicoloured	3·25	2·30
1736	**337**	150h. multicoloured	3·25	2·30
1737	**338**	150h. multicoloured	3·25	2·30
1738	**339**	150h. multicoloured	3·25	2·30
1739	**340**	150h. multicoloured	3·25	2·30
1740	**341**	150h. multicoloured	3·25	2·30

342 Flag and Map of Kuwait

1991. Liberation of Kuwait.

1741	**342**	75h. multicoloured	1·30	1·00
1742	**342**	150h. multicoloured	3·00	1·90

343 Rainbow and Arrows

1991. World Telecommunications Day.

1743	**343**	75h. multicoloured	1·20	65
1744	**343**	150h. multicoloured	2·40	1·30

344 Thee el Halifa Miqat, Medina

1991. Pilgrimage to Mecca.

1745	**344**	75h. multicoloured	1·20	65
1746	**344**	150h. multicoloured	2·40	1·30

345 Blackboard and I.L.Y. Emblem

1991. International Literacy Year.

1747	**345**	75h. multicoloured	1·80	1·00
1748	**345**	150h. multicoloured	3·50	1·90

346 Olive Branch and F.A.O. Emblem

1991. World Food Day.

1749	**346**	75h. multicoloured	1·20	65
1750	**346**	150h. multicoloured	2·40	1·40

347 Child's Profile and Emblem

1991. World Children's Day.

1751	**347**	75h. multicoloured	1·80	1·10
1752	**347**	150h. multicoloured	3·50	2·30

348 Arabian Woodpecker

349 Arabian Bustard

350 Crested Lark

351 Turtle Dove

352 Western Reef Heron

353 Arabian Chukar

354 Hoopoe

355 Peregrine Falcon

356 Houbara Bustard

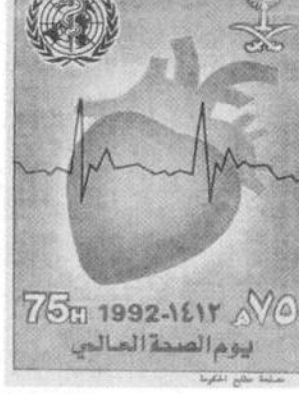

357 Heart and Cardiograph

1992. Birds.

1753	**348**	25h. multicoloured	70	40
1754	**349**	25h. multicoloured	70	40
1755	**350**	25h. multicoloured	70	40
1756	**351**	25h. multicoloured	70	40
1757	**352**	25h. multicoloured	70	40
1758	**353**	25h. multicoloured	70	40
1759	**354**	25h. multicoloured	70	40
1760	**355**	25h. multicoloured	70	40
1761	**356**	25h. multicoloured	70	40
1762	**348**	50h. multicoloured	1·30	90
1763	**349**	50h. multicoloured	1·30	90
1764	**350**	50h. multicoloured	1·30	90
1765	**351**	50h. multicoloured	1·30	90
1766	**352**	50h. multicoloured	1·30	90
1767	**353**	50h. multicoloured	1·30	90
1768	**354**	50h. multicoloured	1·30	90
1769	**355**	50h. multicoloured	1·30	90
1770	**356**	50h. multicoloured	1·30	90
1771	**348**	75h. multicoloured	1·60	1·00
1772	**349**	75h. multicoloured	1·60	1·00
1773	**350**	75h. multicoloured	1·60	1·00
1774	**351**	75h. multicoloured	1·60	1·00
1775	**352**	75h. multicoloured	1·60	1·00
1776	**353**	75h. multicoloured	1·60	1·00
1777	**354**	75h. multicoloured	1·60	1·00
1778	**355**	75h. multicoloured	1·60	1·00
1779	**356**	75h. multicoloured	1·60	1·00
1780	**348**	100h. multicoloured	3·00	2·10
1781	**349**	100h. multicoloured	3·00	2·10
1782	**350**	100h. multicoloured	3·00	2·10
1783	**351**	100h. multicoloured	3·00	2·10
1784	**352**	100h. multicoloured	3·00	2·10
1785	**353**	100h. multicoloured	3·00	2·10
1786	**354**	100h. multicoloured	3·00	2·10
1787	**355**	100h. multicoloured	3·00	2·10
1788	**356**	100h. multicoloured	3·00	2·10
1789	**348**	150h. multicoloured	4·50	3·25
1790	**349**	150h. multicoloured	4·50	3·25
1791	**350**	150h. multicoloured	4·50	3·25
1792	**351**	150h. multicoloured	4·50	3·25
1793	**352**	150h. multicoloured	4·50	3·25
1794	**353**	150h. multicoloured	4·50	3·25
1795	**354**	150h. multicoloured	4·50	3·25
1796	**355**	150h. multicoloured	4·50	3·25
1797	**356**	150h. multicoloured	4·50	3·25

357 Heart and Cardiograph

1992. World Health Day.

1798	**357**	75h. multicoloured	1·30	65
1799	**357**	150h. multicoloured	2·75	1·40

358 Arabic Script

1992. Battle of Mt. Uhod (between Mecca and Medina, 625 A.D.) Commemoration.

1800	**358**	75h. green and orange	1·30	65
1801	**358**	150h. dp blue, blue & green	2·75	1·40

359 Mosque, Yalamlam Miqat

1992. Pilgrimage to Mecca.

1802	**359**	75h. multicoloured	1·50	65
1803	**359**	150h. multicoloured	3·00	1·40

360 Human Pyramid inside House

1992. Population and Housing Census.

1804	**360**	75h. multicoloured	1·10	65
1805	**360**	150h. multicoloured	2·00	1·30

361 Vegetables

1992. World Food Day. Multicoloured.

1806	75h. Type **361**	1·50	65
1807	150h. Fruits	3·25	1·30

362 Decree of Regional System

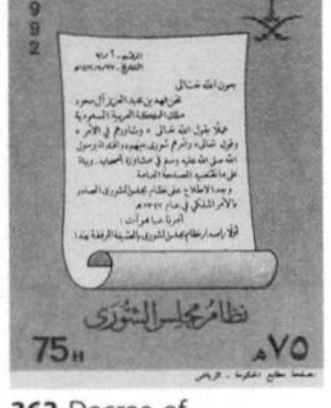

363 Decree of Consultative Council

364 Decree of Essential Governing

1992. Declaration of Basic Law of Government.

1808	**362**	75h. black, silver & green	1·10	50
1809	**363**	75h. black, silver & green	1·10	50
1810	**364**	75h. black, silver & green	1·10	50
1811	**362**	150h. multicoloured	2·30	1·10
1812	**363**	150h. multicoloured	2·30	1·10
1813	**364**	150h. multicoloured	2·30	1·10

365 Flags, Globe and King Fahd Stadium

1993. Continental Cup Football Championship, Saudi Arabia.

1815	**365**	75h. multicoloured	2·00	65
1816	**365**	150h. multicoloured	4·00	1·30

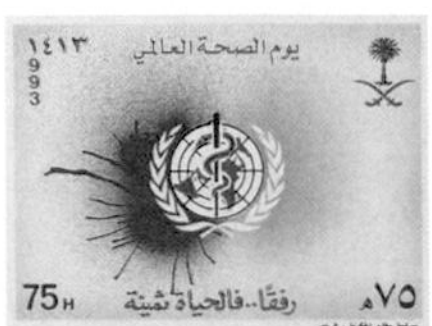

366 Blood Spot and W.H.O. Emblem

1993. World Health Day.

1817	**366**	75h. multicoloured	1·30	65
1818	**366**	150h. multicoloured	2·75	1·30

367 Arabic Script

1993. Battle of Khandaq (between Mecca and Medina, 627 A.D.) Commemoration.

1819	**367**	75h. green and orange	1·20	65
1820	**367**	150h. dp blue, blue & green	2·00	1·30

368 I.T.U. Emblem

1993. 25th Anniv of World Telecommunications Day.

1821	**368**	75h. multicoloured	1·20	65
1822	**368**	150h. multicoloured	2·00	1·30

369 That Irq Miqat

1993. Pilgrimage to Mecca.

1823	**369**	75h. multicoloured	1·20	65
1824	**369**	150h. multicoloured	2·00	1·30

370 Desert, Oasis, Mountains and Sea Environments

1993. World Food Day.

1825	**370**	75h. multicoloured	1·50	65
1826	**370**	150h. multicoloured	3·25	1·30

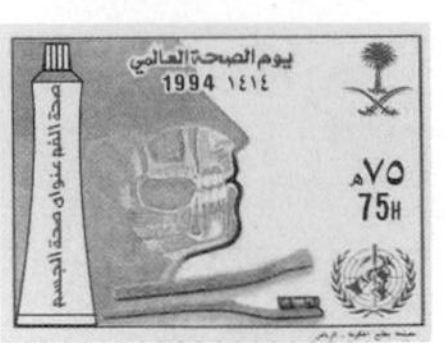

371 X-ray of Teeth and Cleaning Implements

1994. World Health Day.

1827	**371**	75h. multicoloured	1·30	65
1828	**371**	150h. multicoloured	2·75	1·30

372 "100" and Olympic Rings

1994. Centenary of International Olympic Committee.

1829	**372**	75h. multicoloured	1·50	65
1830	**372**	150h. multicoloured	3·25	1·30

373 Namirah Mosque and Tents

1994. Pilgrimage to Mecca.

1831	**373**	75h. multicoloured	1·20	65
1832	**373**	150h. multicoloured	2·00	1·30

374 Arabic Script

1994. Battle of Khaibar Commemoration.

1833	**374**	75h. green and gold	1·30	65
1834	**374**	150h. blue, silver and green	2·75	1·30

375 Flag, International and Saudi Football Federation Emblems and Player

1994. Qualification of Saudi Arabian Team to Final Rounds of World Cup Football Championship, U.S.A. Multicoloured.

1835	75h. Type **375**	1·30	65
1836	150h. Maps of United States and Saudi Arabia and player (51×27 mm)	2·75	1·30

376 Council Building

1994. Establishment of Consultative Council (advisory body). Multicoloured.

1837	75h. Type **376**	1·30	65
1838	150h. Council building (closer view)	2·75	1·30
MS1839	120×80 mm. Nos. 1837/8. Imperf (sold at 5r.)	47·00	47·00

377 King Abdul Aziz Port, Dammam

1994. Saudi Ports. (a) Dammam.

1839a	**377**	25h. multicoloured	1·10	50
1839b	**377**	50h. multicoloured	1·10	50
1840	**377**	75h. multicoloured	1·30	65
1841	**377**	100h. multicoloured	1·70	90
1842	**377**	150h. multicoloured	2·75	1·30

378 Islam Port, Jeddah

(b) Jeddah.

1845	**378**	25h. multicoloured	65	40
1846	**378**	50h. multicoloured	1·50	90
1847	**378**	75h. multicoloured	2·10	1·30
1848	**378**	100h. multicoloured	3·00	1·60
1849	**378**	150h. multicoloured	4·25	2·50

379 Jubail Port

(c) Jubail.

1853	**379**	2r. multicoloured	3·75	1·60
1854	**379**	4r. multicoloured	5·25	2·50

380 Yanbu Port

(d) Yanbu.

1856	**380**	100h. multicoloured	2·75	1·60
1858	**380**	2r. multicoloured	5·25	3·25

385 Crops inside Greenhouse

1994. World Food Day. Multicoloured.

1880	75h. Type **385**	2·00	65
1881	150h. Crops on globe (36×37 mm)	4·25	1·40

386 U.N. Emblem

1995. 50th Anniv of U.N.O. Multicoloured.

1882	75h. Type **386**	1·30	65
1883	150h. U.N. headquarters, New York (26×52 mm)	2·75	1·30

387 Emblem and Map of Member Countries

1995. 50th Anniv of Arab League.

1884	**387**	75h. yellow, mauve and green	1·20	65
1885	-	150h. gold and green	2·40	1·30

DESIGN—36×27 mm: 150h. Anniversary emblem.

388 Emblem and Family

1995. Protection of Refugees.

1886	**388**	75h. multicoloured	1·20	65
1887	**388**	150h. multicoloured	2·40	1·30

389 Mish'ar el Haram Mosque, Muzdalefah

1995. Pilgrimage to Mecca.

1888	**389**	75h. multicoloured	1·20	65
1889	**389**	150h. multicoloured	2·40	1·30

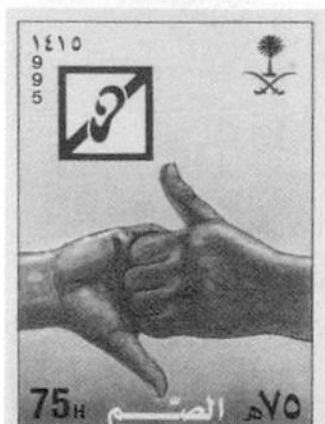

390 Hand Sign and International Symbol

1995. Deaf Week. Multicoloured.

1890	75h. Type **390**	1·30	65
1891	150h. International symbol (ear) and hand sign	2·75	1·30

391 Anniversary Emblem

1995. 50th Anniv of Saudia (national airline). Mult.

1892	75h. Type **391**	1·30	65
1893	150h. Tailfins (horiz)	2·75	1·30

392 Ears of Wheat and Anniversary Emblem

1995. 50th Anniv of F.A.O. Multicoloured.

1894	75h. Type **392**	2·00	65
1895	150h. Anniversary emblem illuminating globe	4·00	1·40

393 Al-Khaif Mosque, Mecca

1996. Pilgrimage to Mecca.

1896	**393**	150h. multicoloured	3·00	1·40
1897	**393**	2r. multicoloured	3·75	1·90
1898	**393**	3r. multicoloured	6·00	2·75

394 Emblems and Pictograms

1996. Olympic Games, Atlanta, U.S.A.

1899	**394**	150h. multicoloured	3·00	1·40
1900	**394**	2r. multicoloured	4·50	1·90

395 Sunrise over City

1996. World Health Day.

1901	**395**	2r. multicoloured	3·25	1·60
1902	**395**	3r. multicoloured	5·75	2·50

396 River and Emblem

1996. 50th Anniv (1995) of F.A.O.

1903	**396**	2r. multicoloured	4·75	1·90
1904	**396**	3r. multicoloured	7·25	2·75

397 Anniversary Emblem

1996. 50th Anniv of UNICEF.

1905	**397**	150h. multicoloured	2·75	1·30
1906	**397**	2r. multicoloured	3·75	1·60

398 Power Station

1997. Opening of Rabigh Power Station. Mult.

1907	150h. Type **398**	2·75	1·30
1908	2r. Power station and pylon (54×29 mm)	3·75	1·60

399 Emblem and Map

1997. 25th Anniv of King Abdul Aziz Research Centre.

1909	**399**	150h. multicoloured	2·75	1·30
1910	**399**	2r. multicoloured	3·75	1·60

400 Sunrise and Arabic Inscription

1997. Mecca.

1911	**400**	1r. green, yellow and black	1·70	90
1912	**400**	2r. multicoloured	3·75	1·60

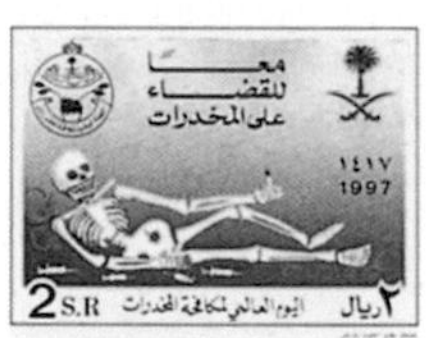

401 Skeleton

1997. Anti-drugs Campaign.

1913	**401**	150h. multicoloured	4·50	2·75
1914	**401**	2r. multicoloured	6·00	3·75

402 King Fahd

1997. 74th Birthday of King Fahd.

1915	**402**	100h. multicoloured	1·70	90
1916	**402**	150h. multicoloured	2·75	1·30
1917	**402**	2r. multicoloured	3·75	1·60

MS1918 103×117 mm. **402** 5r. multicoloured 24·00 24·00

403 Arabic Script

1997. Battle of Honain, 630.

1919	**403**	150h. multicoloured	2·75	1·30
1920	**403**	2r. multicoloured	3·75	1·60

404 Shrine

1997. Pilgrimage to Mecca. Multicoloured.

1921	1r. Type **404**	1·70	90
1922	2r. Shrine and Kaaba (39×39 mm)	3·75	1·60

405 W.H.O. Emblem

1997. World Health Day.

1923	**405**	150h. multicoloured	2·75	1·30
1924	**405**	2r. multicoloured	3·75	1·60

406 Library

1997. Inauguration of King Fahd National Library. Multicoloured.

1925	1r. Type **406**	1·70	90
1926	2r. Books and library emblem	3·75	1·60

407 Hand over Globe of Flora and Fauna

1997. International Anti-ozone Day. 10th Anniv of Montreal Protocol.

1927	**407**	1r. multicoloured	1·70	1·00
1928	**407**	2r. multicoloured	3·75	1·60

408 Emblem

1997. King Abdul Aziz Public Library. Mult.

1929	150h. Type **408**	3·25	1·40
1930	2r. Library and emblem	4·25	1·90

409 Emblem

1997. 3rd Gulf Co-operation Council Stamp Exhibition, Riyadh.

1931	**409**	1r. multicoloured	2·00	1·00

410 Emblem

1998. Prince Salman Centre.

1932	**410**	1r. multicoloured	2·00	1·00

411 Arabic Script

1998. Battle of Tabuk Commemoration.

1933	**411**	1r. multicoloured	2·00	1·00

412 Globe as Vegetable

1998. World Food Day.

1934	**412**	2r. multicoloured	4·50	2·10

413 Mother and Child, House and Sun

1998. Disabled Persons Day.

1935	**413**	1r. multicoloured	2·00	1·10

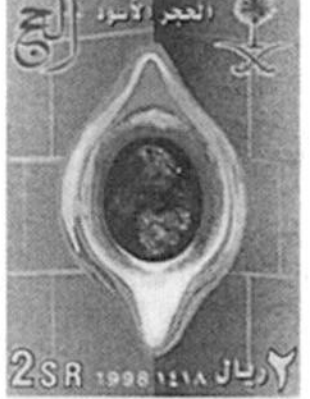

414 Detail of Corner of Kaaba

1998. Pilgrimage to Mecca.

1936	**414**	2r. multicoloured	4·50	1·90

415 Bishah-Tal Reservoir

1998. Inauguration of King Fahd Dam.

1937	**415**	1r. multicoloured	2·00	1·00

416 Mother with Child and W.H.O. Emblem

1998. World Health Day.

1938	**416**	1r. multicoloured	2·00	1·00

417 Emblem and Flag

1998. 6th General Assembly of Islamic Organization for Education, Science and Culture, Riyadh.

1939	**417**	1r. multicoloured	2·00	1·00

418 Dove with Envelope over Globe

1998. Arabic Stamp Day.

1940	**418**	2r. multicoloured	4·00	1·90

419 Horses

1999. Centenary of Saud Dynasty. Multicoloured.

1941	1r. Type **419**	3·50	2·10
1942	1r. Restored buildings in Riyadh (51×27 mm)	3·50	2·10
1943	1r. Emblem of National Cultural Festivals and traditional buildings	3·50	2·10
1944	1r. Airplane, tanks, ships and armed forces coat of arms (36×37 mm)	3·50	2·10
1945	1r. Fort	3·50	2·10
1946	2r. King Abdul Aziz, emblem and outline map of Saudi Arabia	7·00	4·25
MS1947	Five sheets. Imperf (with simulated perforations). (a) 121×81 mm. No. 1941; (b0 125×85 mm. No. 1942; (c) 124×94 mm. No. 1943; (d) 120×90 mm. No. 1944; (e) 121×92 mm. Nos. 1945/6 (set sold at 25r.)	£160	£160

420 Airplane over Airport

1999. Inauguration of King Fahd International Airport. Multicoloured.

1948	1r. Type **420**	2·00	1·00
1949	2r. Air traffic control tower and airplane (26×37 mm)	4·00	1·90

421 Hand holding Globe as Apple

1999. World Food Day.

1950	**421**	1r. multicoloured	4·00	1·60

422 Zam-Zam Fountain and Holy Kaaba

1999. Pilgrimage to Mecca.

1951	**422**	2r. multicoloured	4·00	1·90

423 Emblem on Open Book

1999. Academy for Security Sciences.

1952	**423**	150h. multicoloured	3·25	1·40

424 Emblem and Traffic Lights

1999. Gulf Co-operation Council Traffic Week.

1953	**424**	1r. multicoloured	2·00	1·00

425 Emblem

1999. International Koran Reading Competition.

1954	**425**	1r. multicoloured	2·00	1·00

426 Emblem

1999. 125th Anniv of the Universal Postal Union.

1955	**426**	1r. multicoloured	4·00	1·60

300 "Aloe sheilaa"

2000. Flowers. As T 300/20.

1956	**300**	1r. multicoloured	3·25	2·75
1957	**301**	1r. multicoloured	3·25	2·75
1958	**302**	1r. multicoloured	3·25	2·75
1959	**303**	1r. multicoloured	3·25	2·75
1960	**304**	1r. multicoloured	3·25	2·75
1961	**305**	1r. multicoloured	3·25	2·75
1962	**306**	1r. multicoloured	3·25	2·75
1963	**307**	1r. multicoloured	3·25	2·75
1964	**308**	1r. multicoloured	3·25	2·75
1965	**309**	1r. multicoloured	3·25	2·75
1966	**310**	1r. multicoloured	3·25	2·75
1967	**311**	1r. multicoloured	3·25	2·75
1968	**312**	1r. multicoloured	3·25	2·75
1969	**313**	1r. multicoloured	3·25	2·75
1970	**314**	1r. multicoloured	3·25	2·75
1971	**315**	1r. multicoloured	3·25	2·75
1972	**316**	1r. multicoloured	3·25	2·75
1973	**317**	1r. multicoloured	3·25	2·75
1974	**318**	1r. multicoloured	3·25	2·75
1975	**319**	1r. multicoloured	3·25	2·75
1976	**320**	1r. multicoloured	3·25	2·75

427 Medina

2000. Pilgrimage to Mecca.

1998	**427**	1r. multicoloured	2·00	1·00
1999	**427**	2r. multicoloured	4·00	2·20

428 Organization Emblem

2000. 50th Anniv of World Meteorological Organization.

2000	**428**	1r. multicoloured	2·30	1·40

429 Door and Dome

2000. 75th Anniv of Council of State.

2001	**429**	1r. multicoloured	2·75	2·20

430 Tap enclosed in Water Droplet

2000. Water Conservation Campaign.

2002	**430**	1r. multicoloured	2·75	2·20

431 Rainbow, Palm Tree and Wall

2000. Ryadh, Arabian Cultural Capital, 2000.

2003	**431**	1r. multicoloured	2·75	2·20

432 Emblem

2000. Altaif 2000. 24th Arab Scout Camp.

2004	**432**	1r. multicoloured	2·75	2·20

433 Aerial View of City

434 City enclosed in Oval

2000. Buraydah City.

2005	**433**	50h. multicoloured	1·30	1·10
2006	**434**	50h. multicoloured	1·30	1·10
2007	**433**	1r. multicoloured	2·75	2·20
2008	**434**	1r. multicoloured	2·75	2·20
2009	**433**	2r. multicoloured	5·25	4·50
2010	**434**	2r. multicoloured	5·25	4·50

435 Al Khafji Oil Rig

2000

2011	**435**	25h. lilac and orange	2·10	1·80

436 Port Tower

2000. Jazan Port.

2012	**436**	50h. multicoloured	1·30	1·10
2013	**436**	1r. multicoloured	2·75	2·20
2014	**436**	2r. multicoloured	5·25	4·50

437 Anniversary Emblem

2000. 50th Anniv of United Nations High Commissioner for Refugees.

2015	**437**	2r. multicoloured	5·25	3·25

438 Printing Press and Building

2000. King Fahd Koran Printing Complex.

2016	**438**	50h. multicoloured	1·30	1·10
2017	**438**	1r. multicoloured	2·75	2·20
2018	**438**	2r. multicoloured	5·25	4·50

439 Emblem

2000. King Abdul Aziz Science and Technology City.

2019	**439**	1r. multicoloured	3·00	1·10

440 University Emblem

2000. King Khaled University.

2020	**440**	1r. multicoloured	3·00	1·10

441 Mosque and Pilgrims

2001. Pilgrimage to Mecca. Designs showing Hajj sites. Multicoloured.

2021	1r. Type **441**	2·75	2·20
2022	1r. Holy Kabba	2·75	2·20
2023	1r. Attan'eem Miqat, Mecca	2·75	2·20
2024	1r. El Johfah Miqat, Rabergh	2·75	2·20
2025	1r. Thee el Haifa, Miqat	2·75	2·20
2026	1r. Al-Kheef Mosque	2·75	2·20
2027	1r. That Irq Miqat	2·75	2·20
2028	1r. Mosque, Yalamlam	2·75	2·20

442 Profiles

2001. King Aziz Institute for Persons of Talent.

2029	**442**	1r. multicoloured	2·75	2·20

443 Mohammed Al Durra and Father

2001. Al Asqa Intifada. Multicoloured.

2030	1r. Type **443**	3·25	2·75
2031	2r. Father and child enclosed in barbed wire (vert)	6·00	5·00
MS2032	110×95 mm. 5r. No. 1988 enlarged. Imperf	75·00	75·00

444 Building Facade

2001. King Abdul Aziz History Centre. Multicoloured.

2033	1r. Type **444**	2·75	2·20
2034	1r. Corner of building	2·75	2·20
2035	1r. Towers and wall	2·75	2·20
2036	1r. Aerial view of complex	2·75	2·20

445 Buildings

2001. Folk Art. Multicoloured.

2037	1r. Type **445**	2·75	2·20
2038	1r. Horse	2·75	2·20
2039	1r. Doorways	2·75	2·20
2040	1r. Desert	2·75	2·20
2041	1r. Gate	2·75	2·20

446 Handshake

2001. World Teachers' Day.

2042	**446**	1r. multicoloured	2·75	2·20

447 Symbols of Industry

2002. Seventh Five Year Plan.

2043	**447**	1r. multicoloured	2·75	2·20

448 Islamic Education, Scientific and Culture Organization (ISESCO) Emblem

2002. First Conference of Islamic Ministers of Higher Education and Scientific Research.

2044	**448**	1r. multicoloured	2·75	2·20

449 Tents and Pilgrims

2002. Pilgrimage to Mecca.

2045	**449**	1r. multicoloured	2·75	2·20

450 King Fahd

2002. 20th Anniv of King Fahd's Accession to the Throne. Multicoloured.

2046	1r. Type **450**	2·75	2·20
MS2047	98×128 mm. 3r. As Type **450** plus a montage of other stamps issued during his reign. Imperf	8·00	8·00

451 King Fahd Port, Yanbu

2002

2048	**451**	1r. multicoloured	2·75	2·20
2049	**451**	2r. multicoloured	5·25	4·50

452 Ship at Dockside, King Fahd Port, Jubail

2002. King Fahd Port, Jubail.

2050	**452**	1r. multicoloured	2·75	2·20
2051	**452**	2r. multicoloured	5·25	4·50

453 Pilgrims and Tunnel, Mecca

2003. Pilgrimage to Mecca.

2052	**453**	1r. multicoloured	2·75	2·20

454 Water Droplet

2003. Water Conservation. Multicoloured.

2053	1r. Type **454**	2·75	2·20
2054	1r. Two droplets (vert)	2·75	2·20

455 Fire Fighters

2003. Civil Defence.

2055	**455**	1r. multicoloured	2·75	2·20

456 Emblem and Red Crescent Workers

2003. Saudi Red Crescent (aid organization).

2056	**456**	1r. multicoloured	2·75	2·20

457 *Cirrhilabrus rubriventralis*

2003. Red Sea Fish. Multicoloured.

2057	1r. Type **457**	2·75	2·20
2058	1r. *Cryptocentrus caeruleopunctatus*	2·75	2·20
2059	1r. *Plesiops nigricans*	2·75	2·20
2060	1r. Arabian angelfish (*Pomacanthus asfur*)	2·75	2·20
2061	1r. *Cheilinus abudjubbe*	2·75	2·20
2062	1r. *Pomacentrus albicaudatus*	2·75	2·20
2063	1r. *Caesio suevicus*	2·75	2·20
2064	1r. *Chaetodon austriacus*	2·75	2·20
2065	1r. *Thalassoma klumzinger* (inscr "klumzingeri")	2·75	2·20
2066	1r. *Oxymonacanthus halli*	2·75	2·20
2067	1r. Two-banded anemonefish (*Amphiprion bicinctus*)	2·75	2·20
2068	1r. *Canthigaster pygmaea*	2·75	2·20
2069	2r. *Cirrhilabrus rubriventralis*	2·75	2·20
2070	2r. *Cryptocentrus caeruleopunctatus*	2·75	2·20
2071	2r. *Plesiops nigricans*	2·75	2·20
2072	2r. Arabian angelfish (*Pomeacanthus asfur*)	2·75	2·20
2073	2r. *Cheilinus abudjubbe*	2·75	2·20
2074	2r. *Pomacentrus albicaudatus*	2·75	2·20
2075	2r. *Caesio suevicus*	2·75	2·20
2076	2r. *Chaetodon austriacus*	2·75	2·20
2077	2r. *Thalassoma klumzingeri*	2·75	2·20
2078	2r. *Oxymonacanthus halli*	2·75	2·20
2079	2r. Two-banded anemonefish (*Amphiprion bicinctus*)	2·75	2·20
2080	2r. *Canthigaster pygmaea*	2·75	2·20

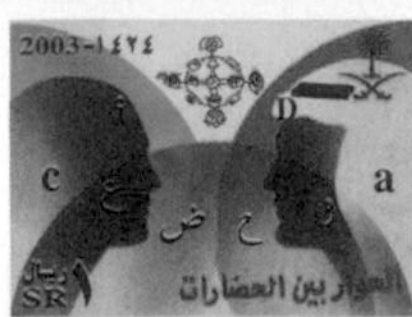
458 Faces

2003. Dialogue among Civilzations.

2081	**458**	1r. multicoloured	2·75	2·20

459 Hands enclosing Light Bulb

2003. Electricity Consumption Campaign.

2082	**459**	1r. multicoloured	2·75	2·20

460 Envelope and Postman

2003. Post Day.

2083	**460**	1r. multicoloured	2·75	2·20

461 "9" enclosing Emblem and Fireworks

2003. Ninth Gulf Co-operation Council Philatelic Exhibition, Riyadh.

2084	**461**	1r. multicoloured	2·75	2·20

462 1930 Hedjaz and Nedjde 5g. Stamp

2003. 75th Anniv of First Saudi Stamp.

2085	**462**	1r. multicoloured	3·25	2·75

463 Adult and Child

2003. Council for the Disabled.

2086	**463**	1r. multicoloured	2·75	2·20

464 Horse Race

2003. King Abdul Aziz Equestrian Centre, Riyadh.

2087	**464**	1r. multicoloured	2·75	2·20

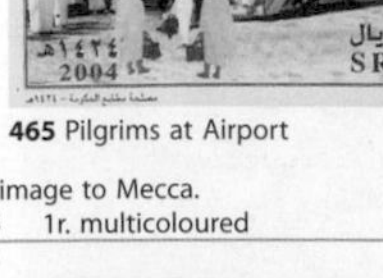
465 Pilgrims at Airport

2003. Pilgrimage to Mecca.

2088	**465**	1r. multicoloured	2·75	2·20

466 Mosque

467 Mosque

468 Mosque

469 Mosque

470 Mosque

471 Mosque

472 Mosque

473 Mosque

2003. Mosques of Saudi Arabia.

2089	**466**	1r. multicoloured	2·75	2·20
2090	**467**	1r. multicoloured	2·75	2·20
2091	**468**	1r. multicoloured	2·75	2·20
2092	**469**	1r. multicoloured	2·75	2·20
2093	**470**	1r. multicoloured	2·75	2·20
2094	**471**	1r. multicoloured	2·75	2·20
2095	**472**	1r. multicoloured	2·75	2·20
2096	**473**	1r. multicoloured	2·75	2·20
2097	**466**	2r. multicoloured	5·25	4·50
2098	**467**	2r. multicoloured	5·25	4·50
2099	**468**	2r. multicoloured	5·25	4·50
2100	**469**	2r. multicoloured	5·25	4·50
2101	**470**	2r. multicoloured	5·25	4·50
2102	**471**	2r. multicoloured	5·25	4·50
2103	**472**	2r. multicoloured	5·25	4·50
2104	**473**	2r. multicoloured	5·25	4·50

474 McDonnell-Douglas MD 11-F

2004. Aircraft. Multicoloured.

2105	1r. Type **474**	2·75	2·20
2106	1r. Boeing 747-400	2·75	2·20
2107	1r. Boeing 777-268	2·75	2·20
2108	1r. McDonnell-Douglas MD-90-30	2·75	2·20

475 Rose and Town Square

2004. Tabuk.

2109	**475**	1r. multicoloured	2·75	2·20
2110	**475**	2r. multicoloured	5·25	4·50

476 Scales and Book

2004. Legal System.

2111	**476**	1r. multicoloured	2·75	2·20

477 Tower and City Walls

2004. Hail City.

2112	**477**	1r. multicoloured	2·75	2·20
2113	**477**	2r. multicoloured	5·25	4·50

478 World Map and Binary Code

2004. World Conferences on Information Technology, Geneva and Tunis.

2114	**478**	1r. multicoloured	2·75	2·20

479 Dunes

2004. Tourism. Multicoloured.

2115	2r. Type **479**	5·25	4·50
2116	2r. Cable cars	5·25	4·50
2117	2r. Coastline	5·25	4·50
2118	2r. Mountains	5·25	4·50

480 Clasped Hands

2004. Peace.

2119	**480**	2r. multicoloured	5·25	4·50

481 Pilgrims

2005. Pilgrimage to Mecca.

2120	**481**	1r. multicoloured	3·25	2·75

482 Emblem

2005. Municipal Elections.

2121	**482**	1r. multicoloured	3·25	2·75

483 Emblem

2005. 1st Islamic Solidarity Games, Makkah, Madinah, Jeddah and Taif.

2122	**483**	1r. multicoloured	2·75	2·20

484 Emblem

2005. National Anti-Terrorism Campaign. Multicoloured.

2123	1r. Type **484**	2·75	2·20
MS2124	108×74 mm. 1r. As Type **484**. Imperf	13·50	13·50

485 Towers

2005. Arar City.

2125	**485**	1r. multicoloured	2·75	2·20

486 Pot (1500 BC)

2005. Cultural Heritage. Multicoloured.

2126	1r. Type **486**	2·75	2·20
2127	1r. Bronze lion head (500 BC)	2·75	2·20

2128	1r. Gold mask	2·75	2·20
2129	1r. Inscribed tablet	2·75	2·20
2130	2r. Castleb	5·25	4·50
2131	2r. Omar bin al Khattab Mosque	5·25	4·50
2132	2r. Palace	5·25	4·50
2133	2r. Zaa'bal Fortress	5·25	4·50

487 King Fahd

2005. King Fahd Bin Abdul Aziz Commemoration. Multicoloured.

2134	2r. Type **487**	4·25	3·50
2135	3r. As No. 2134	6·50	5·25
MS2136	80×106 mm. 5r. King Fahd facing left. Imperf	27·00	27·00

488 Mecca

2005. Pilgrimage to Mecca.

2137	**488**	2r. multicoloured	5·25	4·50

489 King Abdullah Bin Abdul Aziz

2005. Accession of King Abdullah Bin Abdul Aziz and Installation of Sultan bin Abdul Aziz al-Saud as Heir Apparent. Multicoloured.

2138	2r. Type **489**	5·25	4·50
2139	2r. Sultan bin Abdul Aziz al-Saud	5·25	4·50
2140	3r. As Type **489**	6·50	5·25
2141	3r. As No. 2139	6·50	5·25
MS2142	106×81 mm. 5r. King Abdullah Bin Abdul Aziz and Sultan bin Abdul Aziz al-Saud. Imperf	42·00	42·00

490 Emblem

2005. Mecca—Capital of Islamic Culture. Multicoloured.

2143	3r. Type **490**	7·75	6·50
MS2144	80×105 mm. 5r. Ka'ba. Imperf	40·00	40·00

491 Emblem

2005. National Society for Human Rights. Multicoloured.

2145	2r. Type **491**	5·25	4·50
MS2146	80×105 mm. 5r. Emblem (different). Imperf	40·00	40·00

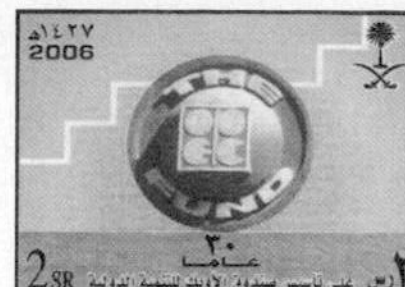

492 Emblem

2006. 30th Anniv of OPEC Development Fund.

2147	**492**	2r. multicoloured	5·25	4·50

493 Medals and King Faisal

2006. King Faisal International Prize.

2148	**493**	2r. multicoloured	5·25	4·50
2149	**493**	3r. multicoloured	7·25	6·25

494 Post Boxes

2006. Postal Address System.

2150	**494**	2r. multicoloured	5·25	4·50

495 Script

2006. 50th Anniv of King Saud University.

2151	**495**	2r. multicoloured	5·25	4·50

496 Stylized Players

2006. World Cup Football Championship, Germany. Multicoloured.

2152	2r. Type **496**	5·25	4·50
2153	3r. Championship emblem	7·25	6·25

497 Flag

2006. 25th Anniv of Gulf Co-operation Council. Multicoloured.

2154	**497** 2r. multicoloured	5·25	4·50
MS2155	165×105 mm. 5r. Flags of member states. Imperf	42·00	42·00

Stamps of similar designs were issued by Kuwait, Oman, Qatar, United Arab Emirates and Bahrain.

497a Emblem

2006. Centre for Organ Transplantation.

2155a	**497a**	2r. multicoloured	5·25	4·50

498 City Centre

2006. Al Medina Al Munawarah. Multicoloured.

2156	2r. Type **498**	5·25	4·50
MS2157	105×80 mm. 5r. As No. 2156 and doorway. Imperf	42·00	42·00

499 Open Book

2006. International Book Fair, Riyadh.

2158	**499**	2r. multicoloured	5·25	4·50

500 Child's Face enclosed in Map

2006. National Day.

2159	**500**	2r. multicoloured	5·25	4·50

501 Horse

2006. Arabian Horse. Multicoloured.

2160	2r. Type **501**	5·25	4·50
2161	2r. Bay facing left	5·25	4·50
2162	2r. Chestnut facing right	5·25	4·50
2163	2r. Roan facing left	5·25	4·50
2164	2r. Grey cantering	5·25	4·50
2165	2r. Mare and foal	5·25	4·50

502 King Abdullah Bin Abdul Aziz and Mecca

2006. Pilgrimage to Mecca.

2166	**502**	2r. multicoloured	5·25	4·50

503 Abdullah bin Abdul Aziz Al Saud and Patients

2007. Kingdom of Humanity. Multicoloured.

2167	2r. Type **503**	5·25	4·50
MS2168	105×80 mm. 5r. Abdullah bin Abdul Aziz Al Saud and patients (different)	42·00	42·00

(B)

504 Emblem

2007. KSA—Winner of Football Cup for Mentally Disabled Championship.

2169	**504**	2r. multicoloured	5·25	4·50

505 Map and Immunization Campaign Emblem

2007. Polio Free Saudi Arabia Campaign.

2170	**505**	2r. multicoloured	5·25	4·50

506 *Junonia hierta*

2007. Butterflies. Multicoloured.

2171	2r. Type **506**	5·25	4·50
2172	2r. *Melitaea deserticola*	5·25	4·50
2173	2r. *Funonia orithya cheesmani*	5·25	4·50
2174	2r. *Eyrema hecabe*1	5·25	4·50
2175	2r. *Papilio demoleus*	5·25	4·50
2176	2r. Inscr 'Colotis calas'	5·25	4·50
2177	2r. *Colotis phisadia*	5·25	4·50
2178	2r. *Vanessa cardui*	5·25	4·50
2179	3r. *Junonia hierta*	7·25	6·25
2180	3r. *Melitaea deserticola*	7·25	6·25
2181	3r. *Funonia orithya cheesmani*	7·25	6·25
2182	3r. *Eyrema hecabe*	7·25	6·25
2183	3r. *Papilio demoleus*	7·25	6·25
2184	3r. Inscr 'Colotis calas'	7·25	6·25
2185	3r. *Colotis phisadia*	7·25	6·25
2186	3r. *Vanessa cardui*	7·25	6·25

507 Emblem

2007. Postal Events. Multicoloured.

2187	2r. Type **507** (PosTech 2007 (global conference on technology), Jeddah)	5·25	4·50
2188	2r. Flags of member countries (Steering Committee of GCC countries)	5·25	4·50
2189	2r. 13	5·25	4·50
2190	2r. UPU emblem (Arab Regional Postal Roundtable, Jeddah)	5·25	4·50

508 Woman teaching

2007. Female Participation in Science and Education Campaign. Multicoloured.

2191	2r. Type **508**	5·25	4·50
2192	2r. Woman using microscope	5·25	4·50
2193	2r. Women students	5·25	4·50
2194	2r. Women using computers	5·25	4·50

509 '3' and Flags of Member States

2007. 3rd OPEC Summit, Riyadah.

2195	**509**	2r. multicoloured	5·25	4·50

510 Map Outline enclosing People and Symbols of Saudi Arabia

2007. National Day.

2196	**510**	2r. multicoloured	5·25	4·50

511 King Abdullah Bin Abdul Aziz and Mecca

2007. Pilgrimage to Mecca.

2197	**511**	2r. multicoloured	5·25	4·50

512 Emblem

2007. King Abdullah Bin Abdul Aziz Centre for National Dialogue.

2198	**512**	2r. multicoloured	5·75	4·75

513 Al majaheem

2008. Camels. Multicoloured.

2199	2r. Type **513**	5·25	4·50
2200	2r. Al wad'h	5·25	4·50
2201	2r. Al shog'h	5·25	4·50
2202	2r. Al shoe'l	5·25	4·50
MS2203	105×75 mm. Size 23×17 mm. Nos 2199/202. Imperf	42·00	42·00

No. **MS**2203 was sold for 5r.

514 Refinery

2008. 75th Anniv of Saudi Aramco. Multicoloured.

2204	2r. Type **514**	5·25	4·50
2205	2r. Diver	5·25	4·50
2206	2r. Refinery (child's drawing)	5·25	4·50
2207	2r. Men with flags (child's drawing)	5·25	4·50

515 King Abdullah bin Abdul Aziz Al Saud and City

2008. Riyadh–50 Years of Development.

2208	**515**	2r. multicoloured	5·75	4·75

515a Emblem

2008. Centenary of International Electrotechnical Commission.

2209	**515a**	2r. multicoloured	5·75	4·75

516 Pigeon (image scaled to 70% of original size)

2008. Arab Post Day. Sheet 170×60 mm containing T 516 and similar horiz design. Multicoloured.

MS2210	5r.×2, Type **516**; Camels	60·00	60·00

517 King Abdullah Bin Abdul Aziz and Mecca

2008. Pilgrimage to Mecca.

2211	**517**	2r. multicoloured	5·75	4·75

518 King Abdullah Bin Abdul Aziz and KAUST Breakwater Beacon

2009. King Abdullah University of Science and Technology (KAUST). Multicoloured.

2212	2r. Type **518**	5·75	4·75

519 Emblem

2009. Al Quds—Capital of Arab Culture.

2213	**519**	2r. multicoloured	5·75	4·75

520 King Abdullah Bin Abdul Aziz and Flags

2009. 79th National Day.

2214	**520**	2r. multicoloured	5·75	4·75

521 Pilgrims and Mecca

2009. Pilgrimage to Mecca.

2215	**521**	2r. multicoloured	5·75	4·75

522 '50'

2010. 50th Anniv of OPEC.

2216	**522**	2r. multicoloured	5·75	4·75

NEWSPAPER STAMPS
NEJDI OCCUPATION OF HAJAZ

(N29)

1925. Nos. 198 and 199a optd with Type N 29.

N208	**11**	⅛pi. brown	£2250
N209	**11**	½pi. red	£5500

OFFICIAL STAMPS
SAUDI ARABIA

O52

1939

O347	**O52**	3g. blue	5·50	3·25
O348	**O52**	5g. mauve	9·00	4·00
O349	**O52**	20g. brown	14·50	8·25
O350	**O52**	50g. turquoise	33·00	16·00
O351	**O52**	100g. olive	£120	65·00
O352	**O52**	200g. purple	95·00	49·00

O72

1961. Size 18½×22½ mm.

O449	**O72**	1p. black	1·60	45
O450	**O72**	2p. green	2·50	65
O451	**O72**	3p. bistre	3·50	1·10
O452	**O72**	4p. blue	4·75	1·30
O453	**O72**	5p. red	5·50	1·80
O454	**O72**	10p. purple	7·75	3·50
O455	**O72**	20p. violet	16·00	6·75
O456	**O72**	50p. brown	39·00	18·00
O457	**O72**	100p. green	80·00	36·00

1964. Size 21×26 mm.

O497	1p. black	2·00	65
O498	2p. green	3·50	1·20
O504	3p. ochre	6·75	2·75
O505	4p. blue	6·75	2·75
O501	5p. red	9·50	3·25
O507	6p. purple	13·50	3·25
O508	7p. green	13·50	3·25
O509	8p. red	13·50	3·25
O510	9p. red	£300	
O511	10p. brown	55·00	3·25
O512	11p. green	£100	
O513	12p. violet	£550	
O514	13p. blue	18·00	5·00
O515	14p. violet	18·00	5·00
O516	15p. orange	£325	
O517	16p. black	£325	
O518	17p. green	£325	
O519	18p. yellow	£325	
O520	19p. purple	£325	
O520a	20p. blue		
O521	23p. blue	£450	
O522	24p. green	£325	
O523	26p. bistre	£325	
O524	27p. lilac	£325	
O525	31p. brown	£450	
O526	33p. green	£325	
O527	50p. green	£650	
O528	100p. green	£1500	

O111

1970

O1040	**O111**	1p. brown	5·25	1·70
O1041	**O111**	2p. green	5·25	1·70
O1042	**O111**	3p. mauve	6·75	2·75
O1043	**O111**	4p. blue	8·25	3·25
O1044	**O111**	5p. red	8·25	3·25
O1045	**O111**	6p. orange	8·25	3·25
O1046	**O111**	7p. red	£200	
O1047	**O111**	8p. violet		
O1048	**O111**	9p. blue		
O1049	**O111**	10p. blue	11·00	5·25
O1050	**O111**	11p. green		
O1050a	**O111**	12p. brown		
O1051	**O111**	20p. blue	27·00	8·25
O1051b	**O111**	23p. brown	£450	
O1052	**O111**	31p. purple	85·00	36·00
O1053	**O111**	50p. brown		
O1054	**O111**	100p. green		

POSTAGE DUE STAMPS
A. HEJAZ

D7 From Old Door at El Ashra Barsbai, Shari El Ashrafuga, Cairo

(D11)

1917

D17	**D7**	20pa. red	4·75	3·25
D18	**D7**	1pi. blue	4·75	3·25
D19	**D7**	2pi. purple	4·75	3·25

1921. Nos. D17/19 optd with T 7.

D31	20pa. red	31·00	4·75
D33	1pi. blue	10·00	6·25
D34	2pi. purple	17·00	12·50

1922. Nos. D17/19 optd with T 10.

D39	20pa. red	39·00	45·00
D40	1pi. blue	5·50	5·50
D41	2pi. purple	5·50	5·50

1923. Optd with Type D 11.

D47A	**11**	½pi. red	6·25	2·30
D48A	**11**	1pi. blue	11·00	2·50
D49A	**11**	2pi. orange	6·25	3·25

1924. Nos. D47/9 optd with T 14.

D57	½pi. red	£3750
D58	1pi. blue	£3750
D59	2pi. orange	£3750

1925. Nos. D17/19 optd with T 15.

D88a	20pa. red	£550	£550
D91	1pi. blue	49·00	42·00
D92	2pi. purple	23·00	23·00

1925. Nos. D17/19 optd with T 16.

D93a	20pa. red	£375	
D94	1pi. blue	39·00	39·00
D96	2pi. claret	31·00	45·00

No. D93a has the overprint inverted.

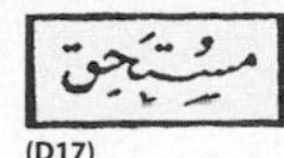
(D17)

1925. Stamps of 1924 (optd T 16) optd with Type D 17.

D149	½pi. red (No. 116)	£130
D150	1½pi. lilac (No. 99)	£130
D151	2pi. orange (No. 119)	£190
D152	3pi. brown (No. 120)	£130
D153	5pi. green (No. 103)	£130

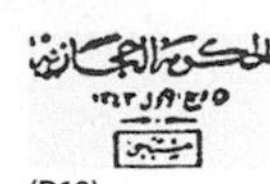
(D18)

1925. Stamps of 1922 optd with Type D 18.

D154		⅛pi. brown	60·00
D155		½pi. red	65·00
D156		1pi. blue	65·00
D157		1½pi. lilac	65·00
D158		2pi. orange	65·00
D160		3pi. brown	65·00
D161		5pi. green	95·00
D162	-	10pi. purple and mauve	95·00

1925. Nos. D154/62 optd with Type D 17.

D163	11	⅛pi. brown	33·00	31·00
D164	11	½pi. red	42·00	42·00
D165	11	1pi. blue	31·00	31·00
D166	11	1½pi. lilac	33·00	31·00
D167	11	2pi. orange	33·00	32·00
D168	11	3pi. brown	33·00	32·00
D170	11	5pi. green	33·00	32·00
D171	-	10pi. purple and mauve	49·00	42·00

D25

1925. Optd with T 24.

D186	D 25	½pi. blue	5·00
D187	D 25	1pi. orange	5·00
D188	D 25	2pi. brown	5·00
D189	D 25	3pi. pink	5·00

These stamps without overprint were not officially issued.

B. NEJDI OCCUPATION OF HEJAZ

1925. Nos. D47/9 of Hejaz optd with T 25.

D203A	11	½pi. red	39·00
D204Ac	11	1pi. blue	£110
D205Ac	11	2pi. orange	£110

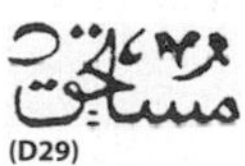
(D29)

(D33)

1925. Hejaz Postage Stamps of 1922 optd with Type D 29.

D206	½pi. red	45·00
D207	3pi. red	45·00

1925. Postage stamps optd with T 32 further optd with Type D 33.

D232	28	1pi. blue	33·00
D233	28	2pi. orange	33·00
D234	11	3pi. red	25·00
D236	28	5pi. green	55·00

1925. No. D40 of Hejaz optd with T 32.

D238	D 7	1pi. blue	£150

C. HEJAZ AND NEJD

D40

1926

D267	D 40	½pi. red	5·50	2·20
D270	D 40	2pi. orange	5·50	2·20
D272	D 40	6pi. brown	5·50	2·20

1926. Pan-Islamic Congress, Cairo. Optd with T 40.

D281	½pi. red	11·00	7·75
D282	2pi. orange	11·00	7·75
D283	6pi. brown	11·00	7·75

D42 Tougra of Ibn Saud

1927

D292	D 42	1pi. grey	16·00	2·20
D293	D 42	2pi. violet	19·00	2·20

D. SAUDI ARABIA

1935. No. 331a optd T in a circle.

D343	49	½g. red	£325

D52

1937

D347	D52	½g. brown	23·00	23·00
D348	D52	1g. blue	23·00	23·00
D349	D52	2g. purple	32·00	14·50

D72

1961

D449	D72	1p. violet	9·50	9·50
D450	D72	2p. green	17·00	7·25
D451	D72	4p. red	19·00	19·00

Pt. 7

SAXONY

A former kingdom in S. Germany. Stamps superseded in 1868 by those of the North German Federation.

10 pfennige = 1 neugroschen; 30 neugroschen = 1 thaler.

1

1850. Imperf.

1	1	3pf. red	£8500	£8500

2

1851. Imperf.

7	2	3pf. green	£170	£130

3 Friedrich August II

1851. Imperf.

10	3	½ngr. black on grey	95·00	16·00
12	3	1ngr. black on pink	£130	12·50
13	3	2ngr. black on blue	£350	85·00
14	3	3ngr. black on yellow	£200	32·00

4 King Johann I

1855. Imperf.

16	4	½ngr. black on grey	12·50	5·25
18	4	1ngr. black on pink	12·50	5·25
20	4	2ngr. black on blue	25·00	21·00
23	4	3ngr. black on yellow	27·00	16·00
24	4	5ngr. red	£120	75·00
28	4	10ngr. blue	£325	£325

5

6

1863. Perf.

31	5	3pf. green	2·75	55·00
36	5	½ngr. orange	2·75	3·75
39	6	1ngr. pink	1·60	3·25
40	6	2ngr. blue	3·75	8·50
42	6	3ngr. brown	5·25	16·00
45	6	5ngr. blue	26·00	65·00
46	6	5ngr. purple	42·00	65·00
47	6	5ngr. grey	32·00	£375

Pt. 7

SCHLESWIG-HOLSTEIN

Two former Duchies of the King of Denmark which, following a revolt, established a Provisional Government in 1848. Danish stamps were in use from 1851 in Schleswig and 1853 in Holstein.

The Duchies were invaded by Prussia and Audtria in 1864 and, by the Convention of Gastein in 1865, were placed under joint sovereignty of those countries, with Holstein administered by Austria.

The Duchies were annexed by Prussia in 1867 adn from 1868 used the stamps of the North German Confederation.

96 skilling = 1 Rigsbankdaler (Danish). 16 schilling = 1 mark.

SCHLESWIG-HOLSTEIN

1

2

1850. Imperf.

2a	1	1s. blue	£425	£7500
4	1	2s. pink	£750	£9500

1865. Inscr "SCHLESWIG-HOLSTEIN". Roul.

6	2	½s. pink	48·00	60·00
7	2	1¼s. green	23·00	26·00
8	2	1⅓s. mauve	60·00	£160
9	2	2s. blue	65·00	£325
10	2	4s. bistre	85·00	£1700

SCHLESWIG

1864. Inscr "HERZOGTH. SCHLESWIG". Roul.

24	½s. green	42·00	75·00
21	1¼s. green	60·00	26·00
25	1¼s. lilac	75·00	32·00
27	1⅓s. pink	38·00	85·00
28	2s. blue	38·00	65·00
22	4s. red	£130	£650
29	4s. bistre	42·00	£110

HOLSTEIN

6

1864. Imperf.

51	6	1¼s. blue	70·00	75·00

9

1864. Roul.

59	9	1¼s. blue	55·00	26·00

10

1865. Roul.

61	10	½s. green	85·00	£130
62	10	1¼s. mauve	65·00	32·00
63	10	1⅓s. pink	80·00	60·00
64	10	2s. blue	70·00	65·00
65	10	4s. bistre	75·00	£110

On the 1⅓s. and 4s. the word "SCHILLING" is inside the central oval.

1868. Inscr "HERZOGTH. HOLSTEIN". Roul.

66	2	1¼s. purple	95·00	32·00
67	2	2s. blue	£190	£200

Pt. 1

SELANGOR

A state of the Federation of Malaya, incorporated in Malaysia in 1963.

100 cents = 1 dollar (Straits or Malayan).

1881. Stamps of Straits Settlements optd SELANGOR.

3	5	2c. brown	£150	£160
35	5	2c. red	17·00	2·75

1882. Straits Settlements stamp optd S.

8	2c. brown	£3750

1891. Stamp of Straits Settlements surch SELANGOR Two CENTS.

44	2c. on 24c. green	42·00	70·00

40

1891

49	40	1c. green	1·50	25
50	40	2c. red	3·50	1·00
51	40	2c. orange	2·50	1·00
52	40	5c. blue	24·00	5·00

1894. Surch 3 CENTS.

53	3c. on 5c. red	5·00	50

42

43

1895

54	42	3c. purple and red	6·50	30
55	42	5c. purple and yellow	9·50	30
56	42	8c. purple and blue	48·00	7·00
57	42	10c. purple and orange	12·00	2·75
58	42	25c. green and red	80·00	55·00
59	42	50c. purple and black	85·00	28·00
60	42	50c. green and black	£425	£120
61	43	$1 green	60·00	£140
62	43	$2 green and red	£250	£300
63	43	$3 green and yellow	£600	£550
64	43	$5 green and blue	£300	£375
65	43	$10 green and purple	£750	£1100
66	43	$25 green and orange	£4000	£4000

1900. Surch in words.

66a	42	1c. on 5c. purple & yellow	65·00	£130
66b	42	1c. on 50c. green and black	4·00	30·00
67	42	3c. on 50c. green and black	4·50	27·00

46 Mosque at Palace, Klang

47 Sultan Suleiman

1935

68	46	1c. black	30	10
69	46	2c. green	90	10
70	46	2c. orange	4·25	75
71	46	3c. green	2·50	8·00
72	46	4c. orange	50	10
73	46	5c. brown	70	10
74	46	6c. red	8·00	10
75	46	8c. grey	60	10
76	46	10c. purple	60	10
77	46	12c. blue	1·50	10
78	46	15c. blue	12·00	32·00
79	46	25c. purple and red	1·00	60
80	46	30c. purple and orange	1·00	85
81	46	40c. red and purple	1·50	1·00
82	46	50c. black on green	1·00	15

83	**47**	$1 black and red on blue	11·00	90
84	**47**	$2 green and red	35·00	9·50
85	**47**	$5 green and red on green	95·00	23·00

48 Sultan Hisamud-din Alam Shah

1941

86	**48**	$1 black and red on blue	24·00	6·00
87	**48**	$2 green and red	48·00	40·00

1948. Silver Wedding. As T 33b/c of St. Helena.

88	10c. violet	20	30
89	$5 green	27·00	22·00

49 Sultan Hisamud-din Alam Shah

1949

90	**49**	1c. black	10	60
91	**49**	2c. orange	30	1·50
92	**49**	3c. green	4·50	1·50
93	**49**	4c. brown	60	10
94a	**49**	5c. purple	30	1·50
95	**49**	6c. grey	30	40
96	**49**	8c. red	2·50	1·00
97	**49**	8c. green	1·00	1·75
98	**49**	10c. purple	20	10
99	**49**	12c. red	1·25	3·50
100	**49**	15c. blue	9·00	10
101	**49**	20c. black and green	6·00	35
102	**49**	20c. blue	1·00	10
103	**49**	25c. purple and orange	2·00	20
104	**49**	30c. red and purple	2·00	2·25
105	**49**	35c. red and purple	1·25	1·50
106	**49**	40c. red and purple	12·00	7·00
107	**49**	50c. black and blue	3·50	10
108	**49**	$1 blue and purple	3·50	60
109	**49**	$2 green and red	15·00	60
110	**49**	$5 green and brown	48·00	2·25

1949. U.P.U. As T 33d-g of St. Helena.

111	10c. purple	30	10
112	15c. blue	2·50	2·50
113	25c. orange	35	4·50
114	50c. black	1·00	6·00

1953. Coronation. As T 33h of St. Helena.

115	10c. black and purple	2·00	10

1957. As Nos. 92-102 of Kedah but inset portrait of Sultan Hisamud-din Alam Shah.

116	1c. black	10	2·25
117	2c. red	30	1·00
118	4c. sepia	10	10
119	5c. lake	10	10
120	8c. green	3·50	3·00
121	10c. sepia	2·50	10
122	10c. purple	11·00	10
123	20c. blue	2·75	20
124	50c. black and blue	40	10
125	$1 blue and purple	6·50	10
126	$2 green and red	7·00	2·75
127a	$5 brown and green	14·00	2·25

51 Sultan Salahuddin Abdul Aziz Shah

1961. Coronation of the Sultan.

128	**50**	10c. multicoloured	20	10

51 Sultan Salahuddin Abdul Aziz Shah

1961. As Nos. 116 etc but with inset portrait of Sultan Salahuddin Abdul Aziz as in T 51.

129	1c. black	1·00	2·50
130	2c. red	1·75	2·75
131	4c. sepia	2·00	10
132	5c. lake	2·00	10
133	8c. green	6·00	6·00
134	10c. purple	1·50	10
135	20c. blue	11·00	1·75

52 "Vanda hookeriana"

1965. As Nos. 115-121 of Kedah but with inset portrait of Sultan Salahuddin Abdul Aziz Shah as in T 52.

136	**52**	1c. multicoloured	10	20
137	-	2c. multicoloured	10	1·75
138	-	5c. multicoloured	80	10
139	-	6c. multicoloured	15	10
140	-	10c. multicoloured	15	10
141	-	15c. multicoloured	1·25	10
142	-	20c. multicoloured	1·90	70

The higher values used in Selangor were Nos. 20-7 of Malaysia (National issues).

53 "Parthenos sylvia"

1971. Butterflies. As Nos. 124-130 of Kedah, but with portrait of Sultan Salahuddin Abdul Aziz Shah as in T 53.

146		1c. multicoloured	75	2·00
147		2c. multicoloured	1·50	2·00
148	**53**	5c. multicoloured	1·50	20
149	-	6c. multicoloured	1·50	2·00
150	-	10c. multicoloured	1·50	10
151	-	15c. multicoloured	1·50	10
152	-	20c. multicoloured	1·50	50

The higher values in use with this issue were Nos. 64-71 of Malaysia (National issues).

54 "Lagerstroemia speciosa"

1979. Flowers. As Nos. 135-141 of Kedah but with portrait of Sultan Salahuddin Abdul Aziz Shah as in T 54.

158	1c. "Rafflesia hasseltii"	10	1·00
159	2c. "Pterocarpus indicus"	10	1·00
160	5c. Type **54**	10	10
161	10c. "Durio zibethinus"	15	10
162	15c. "Hibiscus rosa sinensis"	15	10
163	20c. "Rhododendron scortechinii"	20	10
164	25c. "Etlingera elatior" (inscr "Phaeomeria speciosa")	40	10

55 Sultan Salahuddin Abdul Aziz Shah and Royal Crest

1985. Silver Jubilee of Sultan.

173	**55**	15c. multicoloured	1·50	10
174	**55**	20c. multicoloured	1·50	15
175	**55**	$1 multicoloured	7·00	9·00

56 Black Pepper

1986. As Nos. 152-158 of Kedah but with portrait of Sultan Salahuddin Abdul Aziz Shah as in T 56.

176	1c. Coffee	10	30
177	2c. Coconuts	10	30
178	5c. Cocoa	15	10
179	10c. Type **56**	15	10
180	15c. Rubber	25	10
181	20c. Oil palm	25	15
182	30c. Rice	30	15

2003. As Type 56 but redenominated 'sen'. Multicoloured.

183	30s. Rice	1·25	10

57 *Nelumbium nelumbo* (sacred lotus)

2007. Garden Flowers. As Nos. 210-215 of Johore, but with portrait of Sultan Sharafuddin Idris Shah and Arms of Selangor as in T 57. Multicoloured.

184	5s. Type **57**	10	10
185	10s. *Hydrangea macrophylla*	15	10
186	20s. *Hippeastrum reticulatum*	25	15
187	30s. *Bougainvillea*	40	20
188	40s. *Ipomoea indica*	50	30
189	50s. *Hibiscus rosa-sinensis*	65	35

Pt. 6, Pt. 14

SENEGAL

A French colony incorporated in French West Africa in 1944. In 1958 Senegal became an autonomous State within the French Community and in 1959 joined the Sudan to form the Mali Federation. In 1960 the Federation broke up with Mali and Senegal becoming independent republics.

100 centimes = 1 franc.

1887. Stamps of French Colonies, "Commerce" type, surch in figures.

1	J	5 on 20c. red on green	£170	£180
2	J	5 on 30c. brown on drab	£225	£225
3	J	10 on 4c. brown on green	£100	85·00
4c	J	10 on 20c. red on green	£425	£425
5a	J	15 on 20c. red on green	80·00	80·00

1892. Stamps of French Colonies, "Commerce" type, surch SENEGAL and new value.

6	75 on 15c. blue on blue	£425	£150
7	1f. on 5c. green on green	£425	£170

1892. "Tablet" key-type inscr "SENEGAL ET DEPENDANCES".

8	D	1c. black and red on blue	90	75
9	D	2c. brown and blue on buff	4·50	4·25
10	D	4c. red and blue on grey	1·00	1·20
21	D	5c. green and red	4·25	35
12	D	10c. black and blue on lilac	10·00	4·50
22	D	10c. red and blue	6·50	20
13	D	15c. blue and red	17·00	90
23	D	15c. grey and red	6·50	50
14	D	20c. red and blue on green	7·50	8·00
15	D	25c. black and red on pink	4·25	1·00
24	D	25c. blue and red	32·00	70·00
16	D	30c. brown & blue on drab	11·50	13·00
17	D	40c. red and blue on yellow	48·00	50·00
18	D	50c. red and blue on pink	12·50	23·00
25	D	50c. brown and red on blue	60·00	75·00
19	D	75c. brown & red on orange	14·00	30·00
20	D	1f. green and red	17·00	25·00

1903. Surch.

26	5 on 40c. red & blue on yell	12·00	36·00
27	10 on 50c. red and blue on pink	20·00	50·00
28	10 on 75c. brown and red on orange	50·00	38·00
29	10 on 1f. green and red	£120	£120

1906. "Faidherbe", "Palms" and "Balay" key types inscr "SENEGAL".

33	I	1c. grey and red	1·80	75
34	I	2c. brown and blue	1·60	75·00
34	I	2c. brown and red	1·60	75
35	I	4c. brown and red on blue	2·50	1·40
36	I	5c. green and red	3·75	35
37	I	10c. pink and blue	13·50	35
38	I	15c. violet and red	11·00	4·25
39	J	20c. black and red on blue	4·00	3·25
40	J	25c. blue and red	2·30	85
41	J	30c. brown and red on pink	5·00	6·00
42	J	35c. black and red on yellow	14·00	1·40
43	J	40c. red and blue on blue	8·25	11·00
44	J	45c. brown & red on green	13·50	17·00
45	J	50c. violet and red	9·75	7·75
46	J	75c. green & red on orange	5·75	7·75
47	K	1f. black and red on blue	16·00	55·00
48	K	2f. blue and red on pink	21·00	60·00
49	K	5f. red and blue on yellow	60·00	95·00

1912. Surch.

58A	05 on 15c. grey and red	45	90
59A	05 on 20c. red and blue on green	1·90	8·50
60A	05 on 30c. brown and blue on drab	1·40	7·00
61A	10 on 40c. red and blue on yellow	1·70	6·00
62A	10 on 50c. red and blue	4·00	12·00
63A	10 on 75c. brown and red on orange	8·25	22·00

33 Market

1914

64	33	1c. violet and brown	35	10
65	33	2c. blue and black	35	50
66	33	4c. brown and grey	50	90
67	33	5c. green and light green	1·40	75
91	33	5c. red and black	35	55
68	33	10c. pink and red	2·00	80
92	33	10c. green and light green	85	1·30
113	33	10c. blue and purple	55	55
69	33	15c. purple and brown	80	55
70	33	20c. grey and brown	1·10	1·00
114	33	20c. green	65	2·50
115	33	20c. blue and grey	1·80	10
71	33	25c. blue and ultramarine	3·75	1·00
93	33	25c. black and red	1·90	60
72	33	30c. pink and black	1·00	80
94	33	30c. carmine and red	3·00	7·50
116	33	30c. blue and grey	80	35
117	33	30c. green and olive	2·30	90·00
73	33	35c. violet and orange	1·50	2·75
74	33	40c. green and violet	2·50	60
75	33	45c. brown and blue	2·30	7·50
95	33	45c. blue and red	3·00	6·50
118	33	45c. red and carmine	80	1·20
119	33	45c. red and brown	6·00	13·00
76	33	50c. blue and purple	4·00	5·50
96	33	50c. blue and ultramarine	1·80	1·90
120	33	50c. green and red	2·00	30·00
121	33	60c. violet on pink	1·00	6·50
122	33	65c. green and red	4·50	7·25
77	33	75c. pink and grey	2·00	3·25
123	33	75c. light blue and blue	1·20	1·10
124	33	75c. blue and pink	2·30	65
125	33	90c. carmine and red	4·00	4·25
78	33	1f. black and violet	2·50	1·30
126	33	1f. blue	70	60
127	33	1f. blue and black	2·00	45
128	33	1f.10 black and green	6·25	12·50
129	33	1f.25 red and green	1·50	1·40
130	33	1f.50 light blue and blue	4·00	90
131	33	1f.75 green and brown	14·50	1·20
79	33	2f. blue and pink	3·75	9·00
97	33	2f. brown and blue	4·75	85
132	33	3f. mauve on pink	4·25	75
80	33	5f. violet and green	5·00	1·40

1915. Surch 5c and red cross.

89	10c.+5c. pink and red	1·80	2·75
90	15c.+5c. purple & brown	1·50	9·00

1922. Surch.

102	0.01 on 15c. purple & brn	45	6·25
103	0.02 on 15c. purple & brn	45	7·00
104	0.04 on 15c. purple & brn	45	5·50
105	0.05 on 15c. purple & brn	45	7·00
106	25c. on 5f. violet on green	1·20	7·50
98	60 on 15c. purple and pink	55	35
99	65 on 15c. purple & brown	2·30	6·75
100	85 on 15c. purple & brown	1·90	8·25
101	85 on 75c. pink and grey	2·00	8·25
107	90c. on 75c. pink and red	1·80	3·50
108	1f.25 on 1f. blue	55	3·50
109	1f.50 on 1f. lt blue & blue	1·30	45
110	3f. on 5f. brown and purple	1·40	55
111	10f. on 5f. red and blue	5·50	2·50
112	20f. on 5f. brown & mauve	10·00	8·25

1931. "Colonial Exhibition" key-types.

135	E	40c. green and black	3·75	4·25
136	F	50c. mauve and black	4·00	5·75
137	G	90c. red and black	3·75	4·25
138	H	1f.50 blue and black	6·50	5·50

38 Faidherbe Bridge, Dakar

39 Senegalese Girl

1935

139	38	1c. blue (postage)	35	2·50
140	38	2c. brown	20	3·00
141	38	3c. violet	55	6·75
142	38	4c. blue	45	5·75
143	38	5c. orange	40	1·10
144	38	10c. purple	65	1·50
145	38	15c. black	70	90
146	38	20c. red	80	2·10
147	38	25c. brown	1·30	40
148	38	30c. green	1·20	3·00
149	39	35c. green	1·90	3·00
150	38	40c. red	65	1·00
151	38	45c. green	1·50	2·50
152	A	50c. orange	85	20
153	39	55c. brown	3·00	3·25
154	A	60c. violet	1·00	3·25
155	A	65c. violet	1·90	35
156	A	70c. brown	2·75	6·50
157	A	75c. brown	2·75	1·80
158	39	80c. violet	3·25	2·50
159	A	90c. red	2·50	2·75
160	39	90c. violet	2·30	3·25
161	A	1f. violet	17·00	5·50
162	39	1f. red	2·50	1·40
163	39	1f. brown	70	75
164	A	1f.25 brown	1·80	4·25
165	A	1f.25 red	1·70	5·75
166	A	1f.40 green	1·90	5·50
167	A	1f.50 blue	1·30	55
168	A	1f.60 blue	2·30	4·50
169	A	1f.75 green	2·30	1·70
170	39	1f.75 blue	2·50	3·50
171	A	2f. blue	2·50	60
172	39	2f.25 blue	2·75	3·50
173	39	2f.50 black	2·30	3·00
174	A	3f. green	1·40	1·50
175	A	5f. brown	2·50	1·30
176	A	10f. red	3·75	3·00
177	A	20f. grey	2·50	1·80
178	B	25c. brown (air)	2·30	5·25
179	B	50c. red	2·00	4·50
180	B	1f. purple	1·30	80
181	B	1f.25 green	1·30	2·75
182	B	1f.90 blue	1·70	4·50
183	B	2f. blue	2·30	75
184	B	2f.90 red	1·20	5·50
185	B	3f. green	1·60	1·90
186	C	3f.50 violet	2·75	1·50
187	B	4f.50 green	1·10	3·25
188	C	4f.75 orange	1·90	3·75
189	B	4f.90 brown	2·30	4·00
190	C	6f.50 blue	1·50	3·25
191	B	6f.90 orange	1·80	4·75
192	C	8f. black	3·25	4·00
193	C	15f. red	3·25	3·50

DESIGNS—HORIZ: A, Djourbel Mosque; B, Airplane over village; C, Airplane over camel caravan.

1937. International Exhibition, Paris. As Nos. 168/73 of St.-Pierre et Miquelon.

194	20c. violet	2·00	6·25
195	30c. green	1·30	3·75
196	40c. red	1·30	3·25
197	50c. brown	90	3·50
198	90c. red	1·50	2·00
199	1f.50 blue	1·30	4·50
MS200	120×100 mm. 3f. purple. Imperf	12·00	36·00

1938. International Anti-cancer Fund. As T 38 of St.-Pierre et Miquelon.

201	1f.75+50c. blue	5·50	24·00

40 René Caillié

1939. Death Centenary of René Caillié (explorer).

202	40	90c. orange	50	35
203	40	2f. violet	55	45
204	40	2f.25 blue	65	55

1939. New York World's Fair. As T 41 of St.-Pierre et Miquelon.

205	1f.25 red	85	3·75
206	2f.25 blue	1·20	4·50

1939. 150th Anniv of French Revolution. As T 42 of St.-Pierre et Miquelon.

207	45c.+25c. green and black (postage)	9·25	19·00
208	70c.+30c. brown and black	9·25	19·00
209	90c.+35c. orange and black	9·25	19·00
210	1f.25+1f. red and black	9·50	19·00
211	2f.25+2f. blue and black	9·50	19·00
212	4f.75+4f. black & orge (air)	16·00	20·00

1941. National Defence Fund. Surch SECOURS NATIONAL and value.

213	+1f. on 50c. (No. 152)	2·75	2·30
214	+2f. on 80c. (No. 158)	8·50	14·50
215	+2f. on 1f.50 (No. 167)	11·00	20·00
216	+3f. on 2f. (No. 171)	8·50	17·00

1942. Air. Colonial Child Welfare Fund. As Nos. 98g/i of Niger.

216a	1f.50+3f.50 green	65	2·30
216b	2f.+6f. brown	80	4·25
216c	3f.+9f. red	65	2·30

40c "Vocation"

1942. Air. "Imperial Fortnight".

216d	40c	1f.20+1f.80 blue and red	65	4·50

40d Aeroplane over Camel Caravan

1942. Air. As T 40d, but inscr "SENEGAL" and similar design.

217	40d	50f. green and yellow	2·30	4·50
218	-	100f. blue and red	2·50	5·50

DESIGN—48×26 mm: 100f. Twin-engined airliner landing.

1944. Stamps of 1935 surch.

219	38	1f.50 on 15c. black	1·70	60
220	A	1f.50 on 65c. violet	75	55
221	38	4f.50 on 15c. black	1·00	1·40
222	38	5f.50 on 2c. brown	1·80	1·80
223	A	5f.50 on 65c. violet	1·40	1·00
224	38	10f. on 15c. black	1·80	75
225	A	50f. on 65c. violet	1·50	1·80

1944. No. 202 surch.

226	20f. on 90c. orange	1·80	3·75
227	50f. on 90c. orange	5·25	3·75

42 African Buffalo

1960. Niokolo-Koba National Park.

228	-	5f. purple, black and green	20	10
229	42	10f. purple, black and green	45	15
230	-	15f. purple, brown and sepia	50	30
231	-	20f. brown, green & chest	70	30
232	-	25f. brown, choc & green	1·00	40
233	-	85f. multicoloured	2·25	1·00

ANIMALS—VERT: 5f. Roan antelope; 15f. Warthog; 20f. Giant eland; 85f. Waterbuck. HORIZ: 25f. Bushbuck.

43 African Fish Eagle

1960. Air.

234		50f. multicoloured	2·50	90
235		100f. multicoloured	5·50	1·40
236		200f. multicoloured	10·50	4·50
237		250f. multicoloured	13·50	5·50
238	43	500f. multicoloured	29·00	7·50

BIRDS—VERT: 50f. Carmine bee-eater; 200f. Violet turaco; 250f. Red bishop. HORIZ: 100f. Abyssinian roller.

44 Mother and Child

1961. Independence Commemoration.

239	**44**	25f. brown, blue and green	55	20

45 Pirogue Race

1961. Sports.

240	-	50c. brown, blue and sepia	10	10
241	**45**	1f. purple, turquoise & green	10	10
242	-	2f. sepia, bistre and blue	10	10
243	-	30f. purple and red	90	55
244	-	45f. black, blue and brown	1·50	65

DESIGNS: 50c. African wrestling; 2f. Horse race; 30f. African dancers; 45f. Lion game.

46 Senegal Flag, U.N. Emblem and H.Q. Building

1962. 1st Anniv of Admission of Senegal to U.N.O.

245	**46**	10f. red, ochre and green	15	15
246	**46**	30f. green, ochre and red	30	25
247	**46**	85f. multicoloured	1·10	55

47 I.T.U. Emblems, African Map and Telephonist

1962. 1st I.T.U. African Plan Sub-Committee Meeting, Dakar.

248	**47**	25f. multicoloured	55	20

47a European, African and Airliners

1962. Air. "Air Afrique" Airline.

249	**47a**	25f. purple, brown & green	35	20

47b Campaign Emblem

1962. Malaria Eradication.

250	**47b**	25f.+5f. turquoise	40	35

47c Union Flag

1962. 1st Anniv of Union of African and Malagasy States.

251	**47c**	30f. turquoise	40	35

47d Globe and Emblem

1963. Freedom from Hunger.

252	**47d**	25f.+5f. olive, brn & vio	35	35

48 Boxing

1963. Dakar Games. Inscr as in T 48. Centres brown; inscr and frame colours given.

253	**48**	10f. red and green	15	10
254	-	15f. ochre and blue	20	15
255	-	20f. red and blue	25	15
256	-	25f. green and blue	40	20
257	-	30f. red and green	85	25
258	-	85f. blue	1·75	1·00

DESIGNS—HORIZ: 15f. Diving; 20f. High- jumping. VERT: 25f. Football; 30f. Basketball; 85f. Running.

49 Main Motif of U.P.U. Monument, Berne

1963. 2nd Anniv of Admission to U.P.U.

259	**49**	10f. red and green	20	15
260	**49**	15f. brown and blue	20	20
261	**49**	30f. blue and brown	45	25

50 "Charaxes varanes"

1963. Butterflies. Butterflies in natural colours; inscr in black; background colours given.

262	**50**	30f. blue	1·00	40
263	-	45f. orange	1·75	60
264	-	50f. yellow	1·75	1·00
265	-	85f. red	4·25	1·75
266	-	100f. blue	5·50	2·50
267	-	500f. green	17·00	7·50

BUTTERFLIES: 45f. "Papilio nireus"; 10f. "Colotis danae"; 85f. "Epiphora bauhiniae"; 100f. "Junonia hierta"; 500f. "Danaus chrysippus".

1963. Air. 2nd Anniv of African and Malagasian Posts and Telecommunications Union. As No. 36 of Rwanda.

268		85f. multicoloured	1·10	55

51 G. Berger, Owl and "Prospective" (book)

1963. 3rd Death Anniv of Prof. Gaston Berger (educationalist).

269	**51**	25f. multicoloured	55	20

51a Airline Emblem

1963. Air. 1st Anniv of "Air Afrique" and "DC-8" Service Inauguration.

270	**51a**	50f. multicoloured	1·25	55

52 Globe, Scales of Justice and Flag

1963. 15th Anniv of Declaration of Human Rights.

271	**52**	60f. multicoloured	90	40

53 Mother and Child

1963. Senegalese Red Cross.

272	**53**	25f. multicoloured	55	25

54 Temple Gods, Abu Simbel

1964. Air. Nubian Monument Preservation Fund.

273	**54**	25f.+5f. brown, green and turquoise	1·40	70

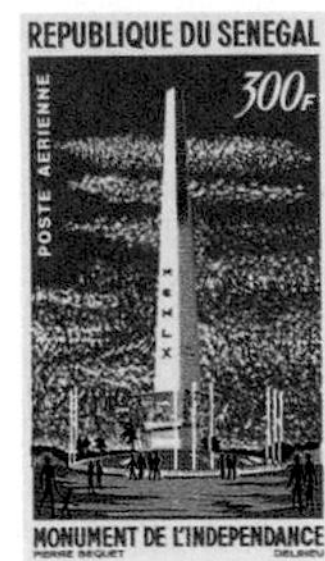

55 Independence Monument

1964. Air.

274	**55**	300f. multicoloured	4·00	2·00

56 Allegorical Figures of Twin Towns

1964. Air. World Twin Towns Federation Congress, Dakar.

275	**56**	150f. brown, black & turq	3·25	1·40

57 Titanium Sand Dredger

1964. Senegal Industries.

276	**57**	5f. brown, turquoise & lake	15	15
277	-	10f. blue, brown and green	15	10
278	-	15f. brown, green and blue	20	10
279	-	20f. purple, bistre and blue	25	10
280	-	25f. black, ochre and blue	65	10
281	-	85f. brown, blue and red	2·25	1·10

DESIGNS: 10f. Titanium sorting works; 15f. Rufisque cement works; 20f. Loading phosphate at Pallo; 25f. Working phosphate at Taiba; 85f. Mineral wharf, Dakar.

58 "Supporting the Globe"

1964. Air. "Europafrique".

282	**58**	50f. multicoloured	1·25	55

59 Basketball

1964. Air. Olympic Games, Tokyo.

283	**59**	85f. brown and blue	2·00	70
284	-	100f. purple and green	2·25	90

DESIGN: 100f. Pole-vaulting.

60 "Syncom 2" Satellite and Rocket

1964. Air. Space Telecommunications.

285	**60**	150f. blue, brown and green	2·25	1·25

60a "Co-operation"

1964. French, African and Malagasy Co-operation.

286	**60a**	100f. brown, red and green	1·75	90

61 Church of Ste. Therese, Dakar

1964. Religious Buildings.

287	**61**	5f. lake, green and blue	10	10
288	-	10f. brown, black and blue	15	10
289	-	15f. slate, brown and blue	45	15

DESIGNS—HORIZ: 10f. Touba Mosque. VERT: 15f. Dakar Mosque.

62 Pres. Kennedy

1964. Air. Pres. Kennedy Commemoration.

290	**62**	100f. brown, yellow & green	2·00	1·00
MS291		90×129 mm. No. 290 (×4)	8·00	4·00

63 Child and Microscope

1965. Anti-leprosy Campaign.

292	**63**	20f. black, green and brown	25	20
293	-	65f. multicoloured	90	45

DESIGN: 65f. Peycouk Village.

64 Haute Casamance

1965. Senegal Landscapes.

294	**64**	25f. green, brown and blue (postage)	25	15
295	-	30f. blue, green and brown	30	15
296	-	45f. turquoise, green & brown	75	55
297	-	100f. black, green and bistre (air)	1·50	1·10

DESIGNS: 30f. Sangalkam; 45f. Senegal River forest region; 100f. Banks of Gambia River, East Senegal (48×27 mm).

65 A. Seck (Director of Posts, 1873–1931)

1965. Postal Services Commemoration.

298	**65**	10f. black and brown	15	15
299	-	15f. brown and green	20	15

DESIGN—HORIZ: 15f. P.T.T. Headquarters, Dakar.

66 Berthon-Ader Telephone

1965. I.T.U. Centenary.

300	**66**	50f. brown, bistre and green	50	30
301	-	60f. red, green and blue	1·00	60
302	-	85f. purple, red and blue	1·10	50

DESIGNS: 60f. Cable-ship "Alsace"; 85f. Picard's submarine telegraph cable relay apparatus.

67 Ploughing with Oxen

1965. Rural Development.

303	**67**	25f. brown, violet and green	35	25
304	-	60f. multicoloured	90	45
305	-	85f. black, red and green	1·25	55

DESIGNS—VERT: 50f. Millet cultivation. HORIZ: 85f. Rice cultivation, Casamance.

68 Goree Pirogue under Sail

1965. Senegal Pirogues. Multicoloured.

306		10f. Type **68**	20	15
307		20f. Large pirogue at Seumbedioune	35	15
308		30f. One-man pirogue at Fadiouth Island	85	20
309		45f. One-man pirogue on Senegal River	1·50	65

69 Woman holding Child and U.N. Emblems

1965. Air. International Co-operation Year.

310	**69**	50f. brown, green and blue	90	30

70 "Fruit of Cashew Tree"

1965. Fruits. Multicoloured.

311		10f. Type **70**	15	10
312		15f. Papaw	20	15
313		20f. Mango	25	10
314		30f. Groundnuts	65	15

71 "The Gentleman of Fashion"

1966. Goree Puppets.

315	**71**	1f. blue, brown and red	10	10
316	-	2f. orange, brown and blue	10	10
317	-	3f. blue, brown and red	10	10
318	-	4f. green, brown and violet	10	10

PUPPETS: 2f. "The Lady of Fashion"; 3f. "The Pedlar"; 4f. "The Pounder".

72 Tom-tom Player

1966. World Festival of Negro Arts, Dakar ("Announcement").

319	**72**	30f. brown, red and green	75	15

See also Nos. 327/30.

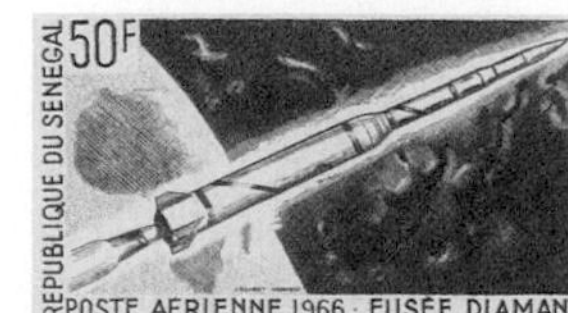

73 Rocket "Diamant"

1966. Air. French Satellites.

320	**73**	50f. red, blue and brown	70	40
321	-	50f. black, brown and green	70	40
322	-	90f. blue, brown and slate	1·75	75

DESIGNS: No. 321, Satellite "A1"; 322, Rocket "Scout" and satellite "FR1".

74 Little Tuna

1966. Senegal Fishes. Multicoloured.

323		20f. Type **74**	50	25
324		30f. White grouper	90	35
325		50f. Peacock wrasse	1·90	65
326		100f. West African parrotfish	3·50	1·25

1966. World Festival of Negro Arts, Dakar. As T 72.

327		15f. lake, orange and blue	15	15
328		30f. lake, yellow and blue	35	20
329		75f. black, lake and blue	1·25	55
330		90f. lake, black and orange	1·40	65
MS331		140×110 mm. Nos. 327/30	3·25	1·60

DESIGNS: 15f. Statuette ("Sculpture"); 30f. Musical instrument ("Music"); 75f. Carving ("Dance"); 90f. Ideogram.

75 Satellite "D1"

1966. Air. Launching of Satellite "D 1".

332	**75**	100f. blue, lake and violet	1·50	65

76 Arms of Senegal

1966

333	**76**	30f. multicoloured	55	15

76a Douglas DC-8F Jet Trader and "Air Afrique" Emblem

1966. Air. Inauguration of DC-8F Air Services.

334	**76a**	30f. yellow, black & brown	55	20

77 "Argemone mexicana"

1966. Flowers. Multicoloured.

335		45f. Type **77**	1·00	20
336		55f. "Dichrostachys glomerata"	1·00	25
337		60f. "Haemanthus multiflorus"	1·25	35
338		90f. "Adansonia digitata"	1·75	50

78 Couzinet 70 "Arc en Ciel"

1966. Air. 30th Anniv of Disappearance of Jean Mermoz (aviator).

339	**78**	20f. slate, purple and blue	70	20
340	-	35f. slate, brown and green	85	20
341	-	100f. lake, emerald & green	1·50	45
342	-	150f. lake, black and blue	3·00	1·00

DESIGNS—HORIZ: 35f. Latecoere 300 flying boat "Croix du Sud"; 100f. Map of Mermoz's last flight across Atlantic Ocean. VERT: 150f. Jean Mermoz.

79 Port of Ile de Goree

1966. Tourism.

343	**79**	20f. lake, blue and black	20	15
344	-	25f. sepia, green and red	1·75	30
345	-	30f. blue, red and green	30	10
346	-	50f. blue, green and red	50	20
347	-	90f. black, green and blue	1·10	45

DESIGNS: 25f. Liner "France" at Dakar; 30f. N'Gor Hotel and tourist cabins; 50f. N'Gor Bay and Hotel; 90f. Town Hall, Dakar.

80 Laying Water Mains

1967. International Hydrological Decade.

348	**80**	10f. blue, green and brown	15	15
349	-	20f. brown, green and blue	30	20
350	-	30f. blue, orange and black	35	20
351	-	50f. lake, flesh and blue	75	20

DESIGNS—HORIZ: 20f. Cattle at trough. VERT: 30f. Decade emblem; 50f. Obtaining water from primitive well.

81 Terminal Building, Dakar-Yoff Airport

1967. Air.

352	**81**	200f. indigo, blue & brown	2·75	1·00

82 Lions Emblem

1967. 50th Anniv of Lions International.

353	**82**	30f. multicoloured	65	45

83 Blaise Diagne

1967. 95th Birth Anniv of Blaise Diagne (statesman).

354	**83**	30f. brown, green & purple	55	20

84 Spiny Mimosa

1967. Air. Flowers. Multicoloured.

355		100f. Type **84**	2·50	75
356		150f. Barbary fig	3·50	1·40

85 "Les Demoiselles d'Avignon" (Picasso)

1967. Air.
357 **85** 100f. multicoloured 3·00 1·10

86 Carved Eagle and Kudu's Head

1967. "EXPO 67" World Fair, Montreal.
358 **86** 90f. black and red 1·50 50
359 - 150f. multicoloured 2·00 75
DESIGN: 150f. Maple leaf and flags.

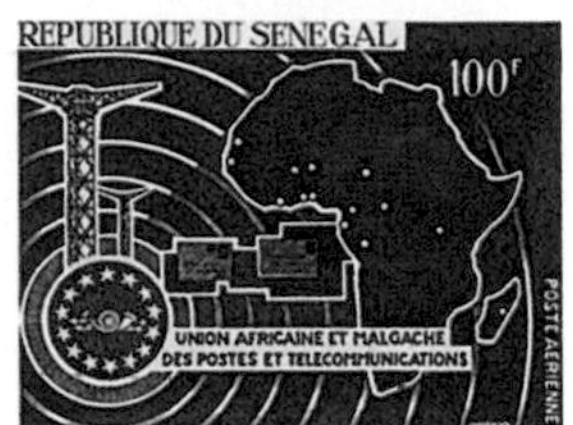

86a Map, Letters and Pylons

1967. Air. 5th Anniv of UAMPT.
360 **86a** 100f. red, green and violet 90 50

87 I.T.Y. Emblem

1967. International Tourist Year.
361 **87** 50f. black and blue 80 35
362 - 100f. black, green & orange 2·75 1·00
DESIGN: 100f. Tourist photographing hippo-potamus.

88 Currency Tokens

1967. 5th Anniv of West African Monetary Union.
363 **88** 30f. violet, purple and grey 25 15

89 "Lyre" Stone, Kaffrine

1967. 6th Pan-American Prehistory Congress, Dakar.
364 **89** 30f. red, blue and green 90 15
365 - 70f. red, brown and blue 1·60 90
DESIGN: 70f. Ancient bowl, Bandiala.

90 Nurse feeding Baby

1967. Senegalese Red Cross.
366 **90** 50f. lake, red and green 50 25

91 Human Rights Emblem

1968. Human Rights Year.
367 **91** 30f. gold and green 35 20

92 Chancellor Adenauer

1968. Air. Adenauer Commemoration.
368 **92** 100f. sepia, red and green 1·40 55
MS369 120×171 mm. No. 368×4 5·50 2·20

93 Weather Balloon, Flourishing Plants and W.M.O. Emblem

1968. Air. World Meteorological Day.
370 **93** 50f. green, blue and black 90 40

94 Parliament Building, Dakar

1968. Inter-Parliamentary Union Meeting, Dakar.
371 **94** 30f. red 55 15

95 Spiny Lobster

1968. Marine Crustacea. Multicoloured.
372 10f. Type **95** 15 10
373 20f. Sea crawfish 25 15
374 35f. Prawn 75 20
375 100f. Gooseneck barnacle 2·40 1·00

96 Lesser Pied Kingfisher

1968. Birds. Multicoloured.
376 5f. Type **96** (postage) 35 10
377 15f. African jacana 65 10
378 70f. African darter 2·25 1·10
379 250f. Village weaver (air) 6·75 1·50
380 300f. Comb duck 10·50 2·50
381 500f. Bateleur 18·00 6·75
Nos. 379/81 are 45½×26 mm.

97 Ox and Syringe

1968. Campaign for Prevention of Cattle Plague.
382 **97** 30f. red, green and blue 55 20

98 Hurdling

1968. Air. Olympic Games, Mexico.
383 **98** 20f. brown, green and blue 45 15
384 - 30f. brown, ochre & purple 65 15
385 - 50f. lake, brown and blue 1·25 35
386 - 75f. bistre, brown and green 2·00 60
DESIGNS: 30f. Throwing the javelin; 50f. Judo; 75f. Basket-ball.

98a "Young Girl reading a Letter" (J. Raoux)

1968. Air. "Philexafrique". Stamp Exhibition, Abidjan (1st issue) (1969).
387 **98a** 100f. multicoloured 3·00 2·25

99 Senegalese Boy

1968. 20th Anniv of W.H.O.
388 **99** 30f. black, red and green 25 25
389 **99** 45f. black, green and brown 60 20

101 Faculty Building

1969. Faculty of Medicine and Pharmaceutics, and Sixth "Medical Days", Dakar.
391 **101** 30f. blue and green 55 20
392 - 50f. green, red and brown 60 25
DESIGN—VERT: 50f. Emblem of "Medical Days".

101a Modern Dakar and Senegal Stamp of 1935

1969. Air. "Philexafrique". Stamp Exhibition, Abidjan, Ivory Coast (2nd issue).
393 **101a** 50f. violet, slate and green 1·25 1·25

102 Panet, Camels and Route-map

1969. 150th Birth Anniv of Leopold Panet, first Explorer of the Mauritanian Sahara.
394 **102** 75f. brown and blue 1·50 75

103 AITY Emblem

1969. Air. African International Tourist Year.
395 **103** 100f. red, green and blue 1·10 45

104 I.L.O. Emblem

1969. 50th Anniv of I.L.O.
396 **104** 30f. black and turquoise 25 15
397 **104** 45f. black and red 40 20

105 Pres. Lamine Gueye

1969. Air. President Gueye Memorial.
398 **105** 30f. black, buff and brown 25 15
399 - 45f. black, blue and brown 65 20
MS400 120×160 mm. Nos. 398/9×2 1·90 80
DESIGN: 45f. Pres. Lamine Gueye (different).

106 Arms of Casamance

1969. Senegal Arms. Multicoloured.

401		15f. Type **106**	15	10
402		20f. Arms of Ile de Goree	45	15

107 Bank Emblem

1969. 5th Anniv of African Development Bank.

403	**107**	30f. brown, green and slate	25	15
404	**107**	45f. brown and green	35	20

108 Mahatma Gandhi

1969. Birth Centenary of Mahatma Gandhi.

405	**108**	50f. multicoloured	45	25
MS406		100×129 mm. No. 405 in block of 4	1·90	1·20

109 "Transmission of Thought" (O. Faye)

1969. Air. Tapestries. Multicoloured.

407		25f. Type **109**	60	20
408		30f. "The Blue Cock" (Mamadou Niang)	35	20
409		45f. "The Fairy" (Papa Sidi Diop)	1·25	50
410		50f. "Fari" (A. N'Diaye)	1·50	75
411		75f. "Lunaris" (J. Lurcat)	2·00	70

SIZES—VERT: 30f., 45f. 37×49 mm. HORIZ: 50f. 49×37 mm.

110 Baila Bridge

1969. Air. Europafrique.

412	**110**	100f. multicoloured	1·25	45

111 Rotary Emblem and "Sailing Ship"

1969. 30th Anniv of Dakar Rotary Club.

413	**111**	30f. yellow, black and blue	35	20

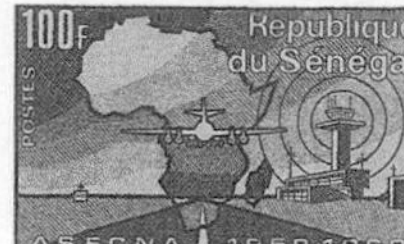

112 Airliner, Map and Airport

1969. 10th Anniv of ASECNA.

414	**112**	100f. slate	90	35

113 Cape Skiring, Casamance

1969. Tourism.

415	**113**	20f. green, lake and blue	45	15
416	-	30f. lake, brown and blue	65	15
417	-	35f. black, brown and blue	2·50	65
418	-	45f. lake and blue	1·10	55

DESIGNS: 30f. Tourist camp, Niokolo-Koba; 35f. Herd of African elephants, Niokolo-Koba Park; 45f. Millet granaries on stilts, Fadiouth Island.

114 Lecrivain, Latecoere 25 Airplane and Route

1970. Air. 40th Anniv of Disappearance of Emile Lecrivain (aviator).

419	**114**	50f. lake, slate and green	1·00	40

115 Bottle-nosed Dolphins

1970

420	**115**	50f. multicoloured	2·50	1·10

116 R. Maran (Martinique)

1970. Air. Negro Celebrities (1st series).

421	**116**	30f. brown, green and lake	25	15
422	-	45f. brown, blue and pink	65	25
423	-	50f. brown, green & yellow	75	35

PORTRAITS: 45f. M. Garvey (Jamaica); 50f. Dr. P. Mars (Haiti).

See also Nos. 457/60.

117 Sailing Pirogue and Obelisk

1970. Air. 10th Anniv of Independence.

424	**117**	500f. multicoloured	6·50	3·25
MS425		72×104 mm. No. 424 (sold at 600f.)	7·75	3·75

118 Lenin

1970. Birth Centenary of Lenin.

426	**118**	30f. brown, stone and red	1·40	55
MS427		67×97 mm. 50f. As No. 426 but larger	2·20	90

119 Bay of Naples, and Post Office, Dakar

1970. Air. 10th "Europa" Stamp Exn, Naples.

428	**119**	100f. multicoloured	1·25	55

1970. New U.P.U. Headquarters Building, Berne. As T 101 of St. Pierre et Miquelon.

429		30f. plum, blue and lake	25	15
430		45f. brown, lake and green	45	20

121 Nagakawa and Mt. Fuji

1970. Air. World Fair "EXPO 70", Osaka, Japan.

431	-	25f. red, green and lake	45	15
432	**121**	75f. red, blue and green	1·25	30
433	-	150f. red, brown and blue	1·90	70

DESIGNS—VERT: 25f. "Woman playing guitar" (Hokusai) and Sun tower; 150f. "Nanboku Beauty" (Shuncho).

122 Harbour Quayside, Dakar

1970. Air. Industrial and Urban Development.

434	**122**	30f. blue, black and red	75	15
435	-	100f. brown, green & slate	1·40	45

DESIGN: 100f. Aerial view of city centre, Dakar.

123 Beethoven, Napoleon and "Evocation of Eroica" Symphony

1970. Air. Birth Bicentenary of Beethoven.

436	**123**	50f. brown, orange and green	1·25	35
437	-	100f. red and blue	2·50	1·25

DESIGN: 100f. Beethoven with quillpen and scroll.

124 Heads of Four Races

1970. Air. 25th Anniv of U.N.O.

438	**124**	100f. multicoloured	1·60	90

125 Looms and Textile Works, Thies

1970. "Industrialization".

439	**125**	30f. red, blue and green	30	15
440	-	45f. blue, brown and red	65	20

DESIGN: 45f. Fertilizer plant, Dakar.

126 Scouts in Camp

1970. 1st African Scouting Conference, Dakar. Multicoloured.

441		30f. Type **126**	30	20
442		100f. Scout badge, Lord Baden-Powell and map	1·40	45

127 Three Heads and Sun

1970. International Education Year.

443	**127**	25f. brown, blue & orange	25	15
444	-	40f. multicoloured	45	20

DESIGN: 40f. Map of Africa on Globe, and two heads.

128 Arms of Senegal

1970

445	**128**	30f. multicoloured	35	15
446	**128**	35f. multicoloured	35	15
446a	**128**	50f. multicoloured	35	15
446b	**128**	65f. multicoloured	35	15
803	**128**	95f. multicoloured	35	30

129 De Gaulle, Map, Ears of Wheat and Cogwheel

1970. Air. "De Gaulle the De-colonizer". Mult.

447		50f. Type **129**	1·25	90
448		100f. De Gaulle, and map within "sun"	3·00	1·90

130 Refugees

1971. 20th Anniv of U.N. High Commissioner for Refugees. Multicoloured.

449	40f. Type **130** (postage)	65	20
450	100f. Building house (air)	1·10	80

No. 450 is 46×27 mm.

131 "Mbayang" Horse

1971. Horse-breeding Improvement Campaign. Multicoloured.

451	25f. "Madjiguene"	65	40
452	40f. Type **131**	90	45
453	100f. "Pass"	2·25	1·50
454	125f. "Pepe"	2·75	1·60

132 European Girl and African Boy

1971. Racial Equality Year. Multicoloured.

455	30f. Type **132**	25	15
456	50f. People of four races (horiz) (37×30 mm)	80	25

133 Phillis Wheatley

1971. Air. Negro Celebrities (2nd series). Mult.

457	25f. Type **133**	20	15
458	40f. J. E. K. Aggrey	35	20
459	60f. A. Le Roy Locke	80	25
460	100f. Booker T. Washington	1·10	45

134 "Telephones"

1971. World Telecommunications Day.

461	**134**	30f. brown, green & purple	25	15
462	-	40f. brown, red and blue	65	20

DESIGN: 40f. "Telecommunications" theme.

135 "Napoleon as First Consul" (Ingres)

1971. Air. 150th Death Anniv of Napoleon. Mult.

463	15f. Type **135**	55	25
464	25f. "Napoleon in 1809" (Lefevre)	70	30
465	35f. "Napoleon on his Death-bed" (Rouget)	1·25	45
466	50f. "The Awakening to Immortality" (bronze by Rude)	2·25	1·10

136 Pres. Nasser

1971. Air. Nasser Commemoration.

467	**136**	50f. multicoloured	45	25

137 Hayashida (drummer)

1971. 13th World Scout Jamboree, Asagiri, Japan. Multicoloured.

468	35f. Type **137**	65	15
469	50f. Japonica	90	45
470	65f. Judo	1·25	55
471	75f. Mt. Fuji	1·60	90

138 A. Nobel

1971. Air. 75th Death Anniv of Alfred Nobel (scientist and philanthropist).

472	**138**	100f. multicoloured	1·50	60

139 Persian Flag and Senegal Arms

1971. Air. 2500th Anniv of Persian Empire.

473	**139**	200f. multicoloured	2·25	1·00

140 Map and Emblem

1971. 25th Anniv of UNICEF. Multicoloured.

474	35f. Type **140**	35	20
475	100f. Nurse, children and UNICEF emblem	1·25	55

141 UAMPT Headquarters, Brazzaville, and arms of Senegal

1971. Air. 10th Anniv of UAMPT.

476	**141**	100f. multicoloured	1·10	40

142 Louis Armstrong

1971. Air. Louis Armstrong Commemoration.

477	**142**	150f. brown and gold	3·75	1·60

143 Trying for Goal

1971. 6th African Basketball Championships, Dakar. Multicoloured.

478	35f. Type **143**	55	15
479	40f. Players reaching for ball	75	25
480	75f. Championships emblem	1·25	60

144 Ice-skating

1971. Air. Winter Olympic Games, Sapporo, Japan. Multicoloured.

481	5f. Type **144**	15	10
482	10f. Bobsleighing	15	10
483	125f. Alpine skiing	1·75	60

145 "Il Fonteghetto della Farina" (detail, Canaletto)

1972. Air. UNESCO "Save Venice" Campaign. Multicoloured.

484	50f. Type **145**	90	55
485	100f. "Giudecca e S. Giorgio Maggiore" (detail, Guardi) (vert)	1·90	1·10

146 "Albouri and Queen Seb Fall" (scene from "The Exile of Albouri")

1972. International Theatre Day. Multicoloured.

486	35f. Type **146** (postage)	65	20
487	40f. Scene from "The Merchant of Venice"	65	25
488	150f. Daniel Sorano as "Shylock" ("The Merchant of Venice") (vert) (air)	3·25	1·50

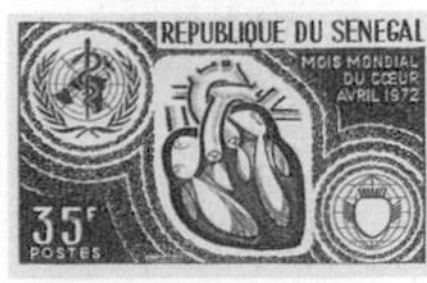

147 Human Heart

1972. World Heart Month.

489	**147**	35f. brown and blue	25	15
490	-	40f. purple, green & emerald	55	20

DESIGN: 40f. Doctor and patient.

148 Vegetation in Desert

1972. U.N. Environmental Conservation Conf, Stockholm. Multicoloured.

491	35f. Type **148** (postage)	65	20
492	100f. Oil slick on shore (air)	1·60	60

149 Tartarin of Tarascon shooting Lion

1972. 75th Death Anniv of Alphonse Daudet (writer).

493	**149**	40f. red, green and brown	1·10	30
494	-	100f. brown, lt blue & blue	1·25	50

DESIGN: 100f. Daudet and scene from "Tartarin de Tarascon".

150 Musical Instruments

1972. Belgica 72 Stamp Exhibition, Brussels. Sheet 111×95 mm.

MS495	**150** 150f. red	2·20	75

151 Wrestling

1972. Olympic Games, Munich. Multicoloured.

496	15f. Type **151**	20	15
497	20f. Running (100 m)	45	15
498	100f. Basketball	1·40	45
499	125f. Judo	1·75	55
MS500	91×71 mm. 240f. Torch runner	2·50	1·10

152 Emperor Haile Selassie and Flags

1972. Air. Emperor Haile Selassie's 80th Birthday.

501	**152**	100f. multicoloured	1·25	55

153 Children reading Book

1972. International Book Year.

502	**153**	50f. multicoloured	45	20

154 "Senegalese Elegance"

1972. (1st issue).

502a	**154**	5f. blue	10	10
502b	**154**	10f. red	15	10
502c	**154**	15f. orange	15	10
502d	**154**	20f. purple	15	10
503	**154**	25f. black	20	10
503a	**154**	30f. brown	15	10
504	**154**	40f. blue	55	10
504a	**154**	45f. orange	10	10
504b	**154**	50f. red	35	10
504c	**154**	60f. green	60	10
504d	**154**	75f. purple	55	35
504e	**154**	90f. red	65	35
504f	**154**	125f. blue	80	20
504g	**154**	145f. orange	90	25
504h	**154**	180f. blue	1·10	45

See also Nos. 1334/45 and 1544/6.

155 Alexander Pushkin

1972. Pushkin (writer) Commemoration.

505	**155**	100f. purple and pink	1·50	50

156 Africans and 500f. Coin

1972. 10th Anniv of West African Monetary Union.

506	**156**	40f. brown, grey and blue	60	15

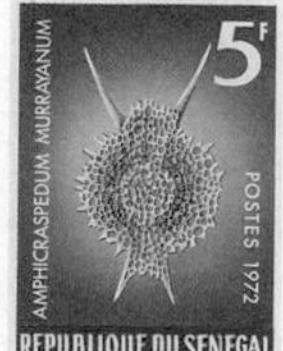

157 "Amphicraspedum murrayanum"

1972. Protozoans and Marine Life. Multicoloured.

507	5f. Type **157** (postage)	10	10
508	10f. "Pterocanium tricolpum"	15	10
509	15f. "Ceratospyris polygona"	75	10
510	20f. "Cortiniscus typicus"	20	10
511	30f. "Theopera cortina"	75	10
512	50f. Swordfish (air)	1·40	50
513	65f. Killer whale	1·75	65
514	75f. Whale shark	2·50	1·25
515	125f. Fin whale	4·25	1·50

Nos. 512/15 are size 45×27 mm.

1972. No. 353 surch 1872-1972 and value.

516	**83**	100f. on 30f. brown, green and chestnut	1·40	60

159 Melchior

1972. Christmas. Nativity Scene and Three Kings. Multicoloured.

517	10f. Type **159**	15	15
518	15f. Gaspard	20	15
519	40f. Balthazar	90	20
520	60f. Joseph	1·10	40
521	100f. Mary and Baby Jesus (African representation)	1·50	65

160 "Sharing the Load"

1973. Europafrique.

522	**160**	65f. black and green	1·00	30

161 Palace of the Republic

1973. Air.

523	**161**	100f. multicoloured	1·10	60

162 Station and Aerial

1973. Inauguration of Satellite Earth Station, Gandoul.

524	**162**	40f. multicoloured	35	20

163 Hotel Teranga

1973. Air. Opening of Hotel Teranga, Dakar.

525	**163**	100f. multicoloured	1·10	60

164 "Lions" African Emblem

1973. Air. 15th Lions International District 403 Congress, Dakar.

526	**164**	150f. multicoloured	1·75	85

165 Stages of Eclipse

1973. Eclipse of the Sun. Multicoloured.

527	35f. Type **165**	55	15
528	65f. Eclipse in diagramatic form	90	25
529	150f. Eclipse and "Skylab 1"	1·90	75

166 Symbolic Torch

1973. 10th Anniv of Organization of African Unity.

530	**166**	75f. multicoloured	80	40

1973. "Drought Relief". African Solidarity. No. 451 surch SECHERESSE SOLIDARITE AFRICAINE and value.

531	100f. on 25f. multicoloured	1·50	75

168 "Couple with Mimosa" (Chagall)

1973. Air.

532	**168**	200f. multicoloured	5·00	2·25

169 "Riccione 1973"

1973. Air. Int Stamp Exhibition, Riccione (Italy).

533	**169**	100f. violet, green and red	1·50	55

170 Crane with Letter and Telecommunications Emblem

1973. 12th Anniv of African and Malagasy Posts and Telecommunications Union.

534	**170**	100f. violet, green and red	1·10	35

171 W.H.O. Emblem and Child

1973. Centenary of W.M.O.

535	**171**	50f. multicoloured	35	15

172 Interpol H.Q., Paris

1973. 50th Anniv of International Criminal Police Organization (Interpol).

536	**172**	75f. brown, blue and green	1·00	40

173 Pres. Kennedy

1973. 10th Death Anniv of President Kennedy. Sheet 90×106 mm.

MS537	**173**	150f. blue	1·75	50

174 Flame Emblem and People

1973. 25th Anniv of Declaration of Human Rights. Multicoloured.

538	35f. Type **174**	55	15
539	65f. Emblem and drummer	70	25

175 R. Follereau (rehabilitation pioneer) and Map

1973. Air. Cent of Discovery of Leprosy Bacillus.

540	**175**	40f. brown, green & violet	75	15
541	-	100f. purple, red and green	1·50	50

DESIGN: 100f. Dr. G. Hansen (discoverer of leprosy bacillus) and laboratory equipment.

176 "Key" Emblem

1973. Air. World Twinned Towns Congress, Dakar. Multicoloured.

542	50f. Type **176**	75	20
543	125f. Arms of Dakar and meeting of citizens (horiz)	1·50	50

177 Amilcar Cabral and Weapons

1974. Amilcar Cabral (Guinea Bissau guerilla leader) Commemoration.

544	**177**	75f. multicoloured	90	40

178 Peters's Finfoot

1974. Air. Birds of Djoudj Park. Multicoloured.

545	1f. Type **178**	15	10
546	2f. White spoonbills	15	10
547	3f. Crowned cranes	15	10
548	4f. Little egret	30	10
549	250f. Greater flamingos (gold value)	6·50	2·25
550	250f. Greater flamingos (black value)	6·50	2·25

179 "Tiger attacking Wild Horse"

1974. Air. Paintings by Delacroix. Multicoloured.

551	150f. Type **179**	2·25	80
552	200f. "Tiger-hunting"	2·75	1·25

180 Athletes on Podium

1974. National Youth Week. Multicoloured.

553	35f. Type **180**	50	15
554	40f. Dancer with mask	50	20

181 World Cup, Footballers and "Munich"

1974. World Cup Football Championship. Footballers and locations.

555	25f. Type **181**	15	10
556	40f. "Hamburg"	40	15
557	65f. "Hanover"	60	20
558	70f. "Stuttgart"	1·00	25

182 U.P.U. Emblem, Letters and Transport

1974. Centenary of U.P.U.

559	**182**	100f. green, blue and lilac	1·75	75

183 Archway, and Africans at Work

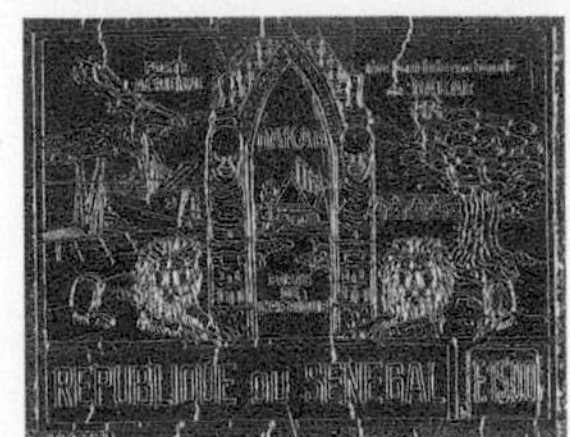

184 Dakar, "Gateway to Africa"

1974. 1st Dakar International Fair.

560	**183**	100f. brown, orange and blue (postage)	1·00	35
561	**184**	350f. silver (air)	4·50	
562	**184**	1500f. gold	20·00	

Nos. 561/2 are embossed on foil.

1975. West Germany's Victory in World Cup Football Championship, Munich. No. 566 surch 200F ALLEMAGNE RFA–HOLLANDE 2 – 1.

563	200f. on 40f. multicoloured	2·00	1·25

186 Pres. Senghor and King Baudouin

1975. Visit of King Baudouin of the Belgians.

564	**186**	65f. blue and purple	50	25
565	**186**	100f. green and orange	1·25	45

187 I.L.O. Emblem

1975. Labour Day.

566	**187**	125f. multicoloured	1·10	45

188 "Apollo" and "Soyuz" Spacecraft

1975. Air. "Apollo"–"Soyuz" Space Co-operation Project.

567	**188**	125f. green, blue and red	1·25	60

189 Spanish "Stamp", Globe and Letters

1975. "Espana 75" (Madrid) and "Arphila 75" (Paris) International Stamp Exhibitions.

568	**189**	55f. red, blue and green	85	30
569	-	95f. light brown and brown	2·00	70

DESIGN: 95f. Head of Apollo and "Arphila" Emblem.

190 Classroom and Tractor

1975. Technical Education.

570	**190**	85f. brown, blue and black	75	30

191 Dr. Schweitzer

1975. Birth Centenary of Dr. Albert Schweitzer.

571	**191**	85f. lilac and green	90	55

192 Soldier, Flag and Map of Sinai Desert 1973–74

1975. Senegalese Battalion with U.N.

572	**192**	100f. multicoloured	90	40

193 Stamps and Map of Italy

1975. Air. Riccione Stamp Exhibition.

573	**193**	125f. brown, red and lilac	1·25	75

194 Woman pounding Maize

1975. International Women's Year. Multicoloured.

574	55f. Type **194**	65	20
575	75f. Mother and child with woman doctor (horiz)	90	25

1975. Air. "Apollo"–"Soyuz" Space Link. Optd JONCTION 17 Juil. 1975.

576	**188**	125f. green, blue and red	1·40	60

196 Stylized Caduceus

1975. French Medical Congress, Dakar.

577	**196**	50f. multicoloured	55	15

197 "Massacre of Boston" (A. Chappel)

1975. Air. Bicentenary of American Revolution. (1st issue).

578	**197**	250f. brown, red and blue	2·75	1·00
579	-	500f. red and blue	5·50	2·75

DESIGN: 500f. Siege of Yorktown.

See also No. 593.

198 Emblem on Map of Africa

1976. International "Rights of Man" and Namibia Conferences, Dakar.

580	**198**	125f. multicoloured	60	30

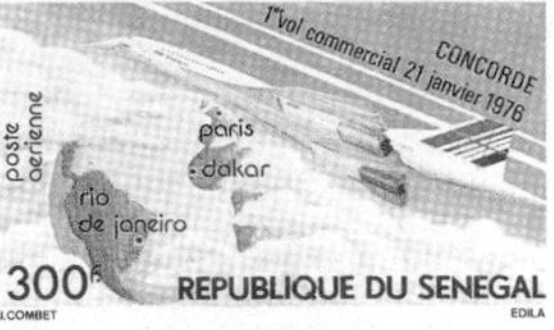

199 Concorde and Flight Locations

1976. Air. Concorde's 1st Commercial Flight.

581	**199**	300f. multicoloured	4·50	2·25

See also No. 646.

200 Deep-sea Fishing

1976. "Expo", Okinawa. Multicoloured.

582	140f. Type **200**	3·25	1·60
583	200f. Yacht-racing	2·25	1·25

201 Serval

1976. Basse Casamance National Park. Fauna. Multicoloured.

584	2f. Type **201**	10	10
585	3f. Bar-tailed godwit (marsh bird)	60	10
586	4f. Bush pig	10	10
587	5f. African fish eagle	1·60	30
588	250f. Sitatunga (males)	3·25	1·50
589	250f. Sitatunga (females)	3·25	1·50

202 Alexander Graham Bell

1976. Telephone Centenary.

590	**202**	175f. multicoloured	1·40	85

203 Map of Africa

1976. G.A.D.E.F. Scientific and Cultural Days.

591	**203**	60f. multicoloured	35	20

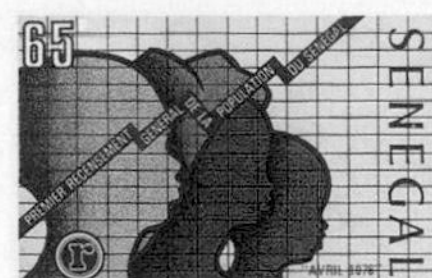

204 Heads on Graphs

1976. 1st Population Census.

592	**204**	65f. multicoloured	65	25

205 Jefferson reading Independence Declaration

1976. Bicentenary of American Revolution (2nd issue).

593	**205**	50f. black, red and blue	65	20

206 Plant Cultivation

1976. Operation "Sahel Vert".

594	**206**	60f. multicoloured	35	20

207 Scouts around Campfire

1976. 1st All African Scouts Jamboree, Jos, Nigeria. Multicoloured.

595	80f. Type **207**	45	35
596	100f. Emblem and map (vert)	90	45

208 Swimming

209 Basketball

1976. Olympic Games, Montreal. Multicoloured.

597	5f. Type **208** (postage)	10	10
598	10f. Weightlifting	10	10
599	15f. Hurdling (horiz)	15	10
600	20f. Horse-jumping (horiz)	15	10
601	25f. Steeplechasing (horiz)	15	10
602	50f. Wrestling (horiz)	55	15
603	60f. Hockey	55	20
604	65f. Running	65	20
605	70f. Gymnastics	75	25
606	100f. Cycling (horiz)	1·10	30
607	400f. Boxing (horiz) (air)	3·75	40
607a	500f. Judo	4·50	1·10
608	1000f. Basketball (41×41 mm)	7·25	3·75
608a	1500f. Running (41×41 mm)	11·00	5·50
MS609	Two sheets (a) 121×83 mm. 400f. Aerial view of stadium (58×40 mm); (b) 118×81 mm. 500f. Front view of stadium (58×40 mm)	8·50	1·70
MS609a	Two sheets. As T **209**. (a) 120×90 mm. 1000f. Boxing; (b) 90×120 mm. 1500f. Long Jump	18·00	9·50

210 Emblem and Map

1976. President Senghor's 70th Birthday. Mult.

610	40f. Type **210**	25	20
611	60f. Star over world map	35	25
612	70f. Technicians and symbol	75	30
613	200f. President Senghor and extended hands	1·90	75

211 Harvesting Tomatoes

1976. Tomato Production.

614	**211**	180f. multicoloured	2·25	1·25

212 Concorde and Route Plan

1976. Air. Dakar International Fair.

615	**212**	500f. silver	5·50	
616	**212**	1500f. gold	20·00	

213 Black Peoples' "Charter"

1977. Black Peoples' Day.

617	**213**	60f. multicoloured	65	25

214 Mohammed Ali and Joe Frazier

1977. World Boxing Championship.

618	**214**	60f. black and blue	50	15
619	-	150f. black and green	1·75	50

DESIGN—HORIZ: 150f. Mohammed Ali landing punch.

215 Dancer and Musicians

1977. 2nd World Black and African Festival of Arts and Culture, Lagos (Nigeria). Multicoloured.

620	50f. Type **215**	40	20
621	75f. Statuette and masks	85	25
622	100f. Statuette and dancers	1·00	45

216 Cog Wheels

1977. 1st Anniv of Dakar Industrial Zone.

623	**216**	70f. brown and green	40	20

217 Hauling in Net

1977. Fishing. Multicoloured.

624	25f. Type **217** (postage)		
625	5f. Fishing by trawl-line (air)		
626	10f. Harpooning		
627	15f. Pirogue breasting wave		
628	20f. Displaying prize catch		

218 Burnt Tree in "Flame"

1977. Fight Against Forest Fires. Multicoloured.

629	40f. Type **218**	55	15
630	60f. Firefighting vehicle (horiz)	1·00	55

219 Industrial and Pre-Industrial Communication

1977. World Telecommunications Day. Mult.

631	80f. Type **219**	45	35
632	100f. Printed circuit (vert)	70	45

220 Arms of Senegal

1977. 10th Anniv of International French Language Council. Multicoloured.

633	65f. Type **220**	35	20
634	250f. As No. 831 of Rwanda	2·00	1·00

221 Woman rowing on River

1977. "Amphilex 1977" International Stamp Exhibition, Amsterdam. Multicoloured.

635	50f. Type **221**	30	25
636	125f. Senegalese woman	1·00	45

222 "Viking" and Control Centre

1977. Air. "Viking" Space Mission to Mars.

637	**222**	300f. multicoloured	2·25	1·25

223 Class in Front of Blackboard

1977. Literacy Week. Multicoloured.

638	60f. Type **223**	35	25
639	65f. Man with alphabet table	35	25

224 "Mercury and Argus" (Rubens)

1977. Paintings. Multicoloured.

640	20f. Type **224**	10	10
641	25f. "Daniel and the Lions" (Rubens)	15	10
642	40f. "The Empress" (Titian)	20	15
643	60f. "Flora" (Titian)	55	20
644	65f. "Jo la belle Irlandaise" (Courbet)	75	20
645	100f. "The Painter's Studio" (Courbet)	1·40	55

1977. Air. 1st Paris–New York Commercial Flight of Concorde. Optd 22.11.77 PARIS NEW-YORK.

646	**199**	300f. multicoloured	4·25	2·25

226 "Adoration of the Kings"

1977. Christmas. Multicoloured.

647	20f. Type **226**	10	10
648	25f. Fanal (celebration)	15	10
649	40f. Family Christmas tree	55	15
650	100f. "Three Wise Men" (horiz)	1·00	40

227 Wrestler

1978. Tourism. Multicoloured.

651	10f. Type **227**	10	10
652	30f. Soumbedioun Regatta (canoes)	20	15
653	65f. Soumbedioun Regatta (race) (horiz)	45	25
654	100f. Dancers (horiz)	95	50

228 Dakar Cathedral and Parthenon, Athens

1978. UNESCO Campaign for Protection of Monuments.
655 **228** 75f. multicoloured 35 25

229 Solar Pump

1978. Sources of Energy. Multicoloured.
656 50f. Type **229** 25 15
657 95f. Electricity power station 75 30

230 Caspian and Royal Terns

1978. Saloum Delta National Park. Multicoloured.
658 5f. Type **230** 20 15
659 10f. Pink-backed pelicans 50 15
660 15f. Grey Heron and warthog 1·00 40
661 20f. Greater flamingoes 1·00 40
662 150f. Grey heron and royal terns 5·00 1·50
663 150f. Abyssinian ground horn-bill and warthog 5·00 1·50

231 Dome of the Rock

1978. Palestine Freedom-Fighters.
664 **231** 60f. multicoloured 55 20

232 Mahatma Gandhi

1978. Apostles of Non-violence. Multicoloured.
665 125f. Type **232** 85 50
666 150f. Martin Luther King 1·25 60
MS667 85×73 mm. 200f.×2 As Nos. 665/6 2·20 1·20

233 Jenner and Vaccination of Children

1978. Global Eradication of Smallpox.
668 **233** 60f. multicoloured 55 20

234 Players, and Flags of Group 1 Countries

1978. World Cup Football Championship, Argentina. Multicoloured.
669 25f. Type **234** 15 10
670 40f. Players and flags of Group 2 countries 30 15
671 65f. Players and flags of Group 3 countries 45 20
672 100f. Players and flags of Group 4 countries 85 30
MS673 Two sheets, each 99×82 mm. (a) 100f. As No. 670, 150f. Type **234**; (b) 75f. As No. 672, 125f. As No. 671 3·75 1·50

235 Symbols of Technology, Equipment and Industrialization

1978. 3rd International Fair, Dakar.
674 **235** 110f. multicoloured 75 30

236 Wright Brothers and Wright Type A

1978. Conquest of Space. Multicoloured.
675 75f. Type **236** (75th anniv of first powered flight) 65 20
676 100f. Yuri Gagarin (10th death anniv of first cosmonaut) 1·00 30
677 200f. "Apollo 8" (10th anniv of first manned moon orbit) 1·60 85
MS678 96×160 mm. 150f. Type **236**; 250f. As No. 676; 300f. As No. 677 7·25 2·30

237 Henri Dunant and Children's Ward

1978. 150th Birth Anniv of Henri Dunant (founder of the Red Cross).
679 **237** 5f. blue, black and red 10 10
680 - 20f. multicoloured 15 10
DESIGN: 20f. Henri Dunant and scenes of Red Cross aid.

237a Western Capercaillie and Schleswig-Holstein 1850 1s. stamp

1978. Air. "Philexafrique" Stamp Exhibition, Libreville, Gabon and International Stamp Fair, Essen, West Germany. Multicoloured.
681 100f. Type **237a** 2·25 1·60
682 100f. Lion and Senegal 1960 200f. Violet turaco stamp 2·25 1·60

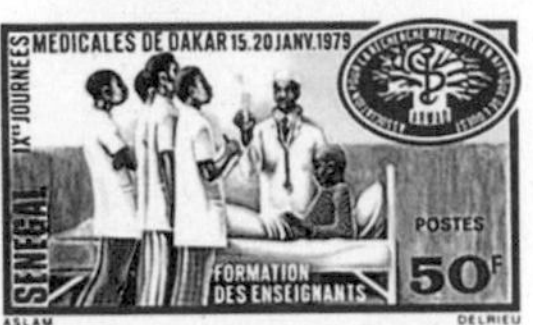

238 Telecommunications

1978. Post Office Achievements. Multicoloured.
683 50f. Type **238** 25 15
684 60f. Social welfare 30 20
685 65f. Travelling post offce 55 20

239 Doctor with Students

1979. 9th Medical Days, Dakar. Multicoloured.
686 50f. Type **239** 25 15
687 100f. Problems of pollution 70 45

240 Agriculture

1979. Professional Pride. Multicoloured.
688 30f. Type **240** 15 10
689 150f. Symbols of progress 1·00 45

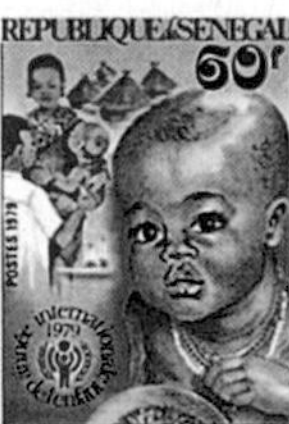

241 Open Air Class

1979. S.O.S. Children's Village. Multicoloured.
690 40f. Type **241** 20 15
691 60f. View of village 30 20

242 Young Child

1979. International Year of the Child. Mult.
692 60f. Type **242** 30 20
693 65f. Children with book 30 20

243 Baobab Flower and Tree and Independence Monument

1979. "Philexafrique" Stamp Exhibition, Libreville, Gabon. Multicoloured.
694 60f. Type **243** 1·25 90
695 150f. Drum, early telegraph apparatus and dish aerial (square, 36×36 mm) 2·50 1·60

244 Children ushered into Open Book

1979. 50th Anniv of International Bureau of Education.
696 **244** 250f. multicoloured 1·40 80

245 Hill and Senegal 100f. Stamp of 1960

1979. Death Centenary of Sir Rowland Hill.
697 **245** 500f. multicoloured 4·75 2·75

246 "Black Trees"

1979. Paintings by Friedensreich Hundertwasser. Multicoloured.
698 60f. Type **246** 1·10 65
699 100f. "Head" 2·25 1·00
700 200f. "Rainbow Windows" 3·25 1·60
MS701 Three sheets each 190×260 mm. (a) No. 698×4; (b) No. 699×4; (c) No. 700×4 27·00 14·00

247 Start of Race

1980. 1st African Athletic Championships. Mult.
702 20f. Type **247** 15 10
703 25f. Javelin 15 10
704 50f. Passing the relay baton 25 10
705 100f. Discus 75 30

248 Musicians

1980. Mudra African Arts Festival.
706 50f. Type **248** 40 15
707 100f. Dancers 85 25
708 200f. Dancers and drummer 1·50 70

249 Lions Emblem

1980. 22nd Congress of Lions' Club District 403, Dakar.
709 **249** 100f. multicoloured 75 25

250 Chimpanzees

1980. Niokolo-Koba National Park. Multicoloured.
710 40f. Type **250** 25 10
711 60f. African elephants 45 20
712 65f. Giant elands 75 20
713 100f. Spotted hyenas 1·00 30
714 200f. Wildlife on the savannah 3·00 70
715 200f. Simenti Hotel 3·00 70
MS716 133×98 mm. 125f.×4, As No. 710/13 2·50 85
Nos. 714/15 were issued together, se-tenant, forming a composite deisgn.

251 Watering Sapling

1980. Tree Planting Year.

717	**251**	60f. multicoloured	75	25
718	**251**	65f. multicoloured	95	30

252 Women with Bowls of Rice Flour and Electric Mill

1980. Rural Women. Multicoloured.

719	50f. Street market (horiz)	25	15
720	100f. Type **252**	90	30
721	200f. Drawing water (horiz)	1·50	70

253 Wrestling

1980. Olympic Games, Moscow. Multicoloured.

722	60f. Type **253**	30	20
723	65f. Running	30	20
724	70f. Games emblems	35	25
725	100f. Judo	45	30
726	200f. Basketball	1·25	70

MS727 Two sheets each 76×62 mm. (a) 75f. Type **253**; 125f. As No. 723; (b) 75f. As No. 725, 125f. As No. 726 — 2·75 — 1·50

254 Dabry, Gimie, Mermoz and Seaplane "Comte de la Vaulx"

1980. Air. 50th Anniv of First South Atlantic Airmail Flight.

728	**254**	300f. multicoloured	2·50	1·00

255 Caspian Tern, Eastern White Pelicans and Grey-headed Gulls (Pointe Kalissaye Bird Sanctuary)

1981. National Parks. Multicoloured.

729	50f. Type **255**	2·25	50
730	70f. Slender-billed gulls and gull-billed tern (Langue de Barbarie)	2·25	75
731	85f. Turtle and crab (Madeline Islands)	50	25
732	150f. White-breasted cormorant and red-billed tropic bird (Madeline Islands)	4·75	1·60

MS733 127×115 mm. 125f.×4, As Nos. 729/32 — 9·50 — 3·00

256 Healthy Activities

1981. Anti-smoking Campaign. Multicoloured.

734	75f. Type **256**	30	30
735	80f. Cancerous mouth with pipe	35	35

257 Fair Visitors beneath Tree

1981. 4th International Fair, Dakar.

736	**257**	80f. multicoloured	35	35

258 Lat Dior Damel Teigne

1982. National Heroes. Lat Dior. Multicoloured.

737	80f. Type **258**	35	25
738	500f. Lat Dior on horseback	3·25	1·25

259 "Nymphaea lotus"

1982. Flowers. Multicoloured.

739	50f. Type **259**	50	20
740	75f. "Strophanthus sarmentosus"	75	30
741	200f. "Crinum moorei"	1·75	75
742	225f. "Cochlospermum tinctorium"	2·00	1·00

260 "Euryphrene senegalensis" (male and female)

1982. Butterflies. Multicoloured.

743	45f. Type **260**	60	35
744	55f. "Hypolimnas salmacis, Precis octavia" and "Salamis cytora"	75	45
745	75f. "Cymothoe caenis" and "Cyrestis camillus"	90	55
746	80f. "Precis cebrene, Junonia terea" and "Salamis parhassus"	1·10	70

MS747 124×95 mm. 100f. As No. 743; 150f. As No. 744; 200f. As No. 745; As No. 746

261 "Rhaguva albipunctella"

1982. Harmful Insects. Multicoloured.

748	75f. Type **261**	75	45
749	80f. "Amsacta moloneyi, Tolyposporium penicillariae" and "Sclerospore graminicola" (horiz)	1·50	45
750	100f. "Amsacta moloneyi"	1·10	60

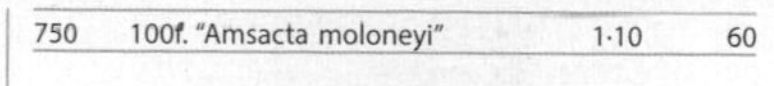

262 Flags and Three-dimensional Map of Senegambia

1982. Senegambia Confederation. Multicoloured.

751	225f. Type **262**	1·60	60
752	350f. Arms of Senegal and Gambia	2·25	90

263 Black-tailed Godwit

1982. Birds. Multicoloured.

753	45f. Type **263**	45	30
754	75f. Saddle-bill stork	95	40
755	80f. Double-spurred francolin	1·10	45
756	500f. Tawny eagle	5·75	3·25

264 Footballer and Emblem

1982. World Cup Football Championship, Spain. Multicoloured.

757	30f. Type **264**	15	15
758	50f. Footballer	20	20
759	75f. Football	55	30
760	80f. World Cup and emblem	60	35

MS761 Four sheets each 90×80 mm. (a) 75f. Type **264**; (b) 100f. As No. 758; (c) 150f. As No. 759; (d) 200f. As No. 760

265 Flag "Stamp" and Ribbon

1982. "Philexfrance 82" International Stamp Exhibition, Paris. Multicoloured.

762	100f. Type **265**	40	25
763	500f. Arms "stamp" between circling arrows	3·25	1·50

266 Exhibition Poster

1983. Stamp Exhibition, Dakar. Multicoloured.

764	60f. Type **266**	25	20
765	70f. Butterfly stamps	65	20
766	90f. Stamps and magnifying glass	75	25
767	95f. Exhibition hall and Dakar arms on stamp	75	30

267 Light Bulb

1983. Energy Conservation. Multicoloured.

768	90f. Type **267**	90	30
769	95f. Cars queueing for petrol	1·00	30
770	260f. Woman cooking	1·60	85

268 Torch on Map of Africa

1983. "For Namibian Independence". Mult.

771	90f. Type **268**	55	30
772	95f. Clenched fist and broken chain on map of Africa	60	30
773	260f. Woman with torch on map of Africa	2·25	85

269 Agency Building, Ziguinchor

1983. 20th Anniv of West African Monetary Union. Multicoloured.

774	60f. Type **269**	25	20
775	65f. Headquarters building, Dakar (vert)	25	25

270 Dakar Rotary Banner

1983. 1st Anniv of Dakar Alizes Rotary Club.

776	**270**	70f. multicoloured	50	25
777	**270**	500f. multicoloured	3·50	1·75

271 Customs Council Headquarters

1983. 30th Anniv of Customs Co-operation Council.

778	**271**	90f. multicoloured	30	30
779	**271**	300f. multicoloured	2·25	1·00

272 Anniversary Emblem

1984. 25th Anniv of Economic Commission for Africa.

780	**272**	90f. multicoloured	60	30
781	**272**	95f. multicoloured	60	30

273 Village

1984. S.O.S. Children's Village. Multicoloured.

782	90f. Type **273**	55	30
783	95f. Foster-mother and child (vert)	65	30
784	115f. Foster-family	80	40
785	260f. House (vert)	2·00	85

274 Scout Salute

1984. 75th Anniv of Boy Scout Movement. Mult.

786	60f. Type **274**	45	15
787	70f. Scout badge	55	20
788	90f. Scouts of different nations	60	30
789	95f. Lord Baden-Powell (founder)	65	35

275 Javelin-throwing

1984. Olympic Games, Los Angeles. Multicoloured.

790	90f. Type **275**	35	30
791	95f. Hurdling	65	35
792	165f. Football	1·10	70

MS793 120×90 mm. 125f. Type **275**; 175f. As No. 791; 250f. As No. 792

276 Basket of Food, Fishing and Farming

1984. World Food Day. Multicoloured. Inscr "16 OCTOBRE 1983".

794	65f. Type **276**	25	20
795	70f. Woman cooking and child (vert)	60	20
796	225f. Group and food	1·90	1·25

1984. Drought Aid. No. 785 optd Aide au Sahel 84.

797	260f. multicoloured	2·00	1·25

278 William Ponty School

1984. World Heritage. Goree Island.

798	**278**	90f. multicoloured	75	30
799	-	95f. black and blue	90	35
800	-	250f. multicoloured	2·25	85
801	-	500f. multicoloured	4·50	2·25

MS802 120×110 mm. 125f. multicoloured; 150f. black and blue; 325f. multicoloured; 675f. multicoloured 11·00 5·00

DESIGNS—VERT: 90, 120f. Type **278**; 250, 325f. Goree Historical Museum. HORIZ: 95, 150f. Map of Goree; 500, 650f. Slaves House.

279 Pump and Sprinkler

1985. Irrigation Project. Multicoloured.

810	40f. Type **279**	45	15
811	50f. Tap and dam	55	15
812	90f. Storage tanks and cattle	1·00	55
813	250f. Women at water pump	2·40	1·10

280 Globe, Envelopes and Map

1985. World Communication Year (1984).

814	**280**	90f. multicoloured	55	25
815	-	95f. blue, green and brown	60	30
816	-	350f. multicoloured	2·75	1·50

DESIGNS: 95f. Maps of Africa and Senegal and aerial; 350f. Globe, dove and map of Senegal.

281 Stringed Instrument and Flute

1985. Musical Instruments. Multicoloured.

817	50f. Type **281**	65	15
818	85f. Drums and stringed instrument	1·00	25
819	125f. Musician, stringed instruments, xylophone and drums	1·50	40
820	250f. Stringed instruments	2·50	1·10

282 Seaplane "Comte de la Vaulx" and Map

1985. Air. 55th Anniv of 1st Airmail Flight across South Atlantic.

821	**282**	250f. multicoloured	2·50	1·10

283 People and Broken Chain

1985. "Philexafrique" Int Stamp Exn, Lome, Togo. "Youth and Development". Multicoloured.

822	100f. Type **283** (political and civic education)	45	40
823	125f. Carpenter and draughtsman (professional education)	75	45
824	150f. Couple looking at planets (general education)	90	60
825	175f. Farm workers (food self-sufficiency)	1·40	80

284 Laboratory and Farm Workers

1985. International Youth Year. Multicoloured.

826	40f. Type **284**	20	15
827	50f. Young people, forms of communication and globe	20	15
828	90f. Youth building "Peace" monument	65	35
829	125f. Youth, football and globe	90	45

285 Man, Woman and Boy

1985. National Costumes. Multicoloured.

830	40f. Type **285**	20	15
831	95f. Man in straw hat and striped gown (vert)	65	35
832	100f. Seated gown (vert)	75	40
833	150f. Man and woman (vert)	1·25	60

286 Men bringing Boat Ashore

1986. Fishing at Kayar. Multicoloured.

834	40f. Type **286**	20	15
835	50f. Women waiting on shore	20	15
836	100f. Man with large fish (vert)	1·00	55
837	125f. Sorting the catch (vert)	1·50	65
838	150f. View of beach	1·75	90

287 Perruque and Ceeli

1986. Hairstyles. Multicoloured.

839	90f. Type **287**	40	30
840	125f. Ndungu, Kearly and Rasta	75	40
841	250f. Jamono, Kura and Kooraa	1·50	60
842	300f. Mbaram and Jeere	2·00	70

288 Flags and Football

1986. African Football Cup, Cairo. Multicoloured.

843	115f. Type **288**	70	35
844	125f. Footballer and map	75	45
845	135f. Lion rampant with torch ascending pyramid (horiz)	1·10	50
846	165f. Lions rampant beneath flag (horiz)	1·25	65

1986. 5th Convention of District 403 of Lions Int. No. 818 surch Ve CONVENTION MULTI-DISTRICT 8-10 MAI 1988.

847	165f. on 85f. Drums and stringed instrument	1·00	65

290 Doe and Calf

1986. Ndama Gazelle. Multicoloured.

848	15f. Type **290**	10	10
849	45f. Group of gazelle resting	75	15
850	85f. Gazelle among dead trees	1·25	30
851	125f. Gazelle running	1·75	90

291 Immunizing Child

1986. UNICEF Child Survival Campaign. Multicoloured.

852	50f. Type **291**	20	15
853	85f. Child drinking from bowl	40	35

292 Trophy, Footballers and Terracotta Offertory Vessel

1986. World Cup Football Championship, Mexico. Multicoloured. (a) As T 292.

854	125f. Type **292**	75	45
855	135f. Trophy, footballers and stucco Maya head from Palenque	80	50
856	165f. Gold breastplate, footballers and trophy	1·00	65
857	340f. Teotihuacan porcelain mask, footballers and trophy	2·00	90

(b) Nos. 854/7 optd ARGENTINA 3 R.F.A. 2.

858	125f. Type **292**	75	45
859	135f. Trophy, footballers and stucco Maya head from Palenque	80	50
860	165f. Gold breastplate, footballers and trophy	1·00	65
861	340f. Teotihuacan porcelain mask, footballers and trophy	2·00	90

294 Ostriches

1986. Guembeul Nature Reserve. Multicoloured.

862	50f. Type **294**	1·25	35
863	65f. Gazelles	55	20
864	85f. Giraffes	60	30
865	100f. Ostrich, buffalo, gazelle and giraffe	2·00	75
866	150f. Buffalo	1·40	60

295 Man with Puppet (Xuusmaanapaa)

1986. Christmas. Customs. Multicoloured.

867	70f. Type **295**	25	20
868	85f. Setting up fanal (Fente) (horiz)	65	25
869	150f. Decorating fanal (Jebele)	90	55
870	250f. Boy praying before candle and Nativity scene (horiz)	1·50	75

296 Statue of Liberty

1986. Centenary of Statue of Liberty.

871	**296**	225f. multicoloured	1·50	80

297 Jellyfish and Coral

1987. Marine Fauna. Multicoloured.

872	50f. Type **297**	30	15
873	85f. Sea urchin and starfish	75	25
874	100f. Norway lobster	1·10	35
875	150f. Common dolphin	1·50	55
876	200f. Octopus	2·25	1·10

298 Motor Cyclist and Lorry

1987. Paris–Dakar Rally. Multicoloured.

877	115f. Type **298**	1·10	40
878	125f. Thierry Sabine, helicopter, motor cyclist, lorry and car (horiz)	1·50	60
879	135f. Sabine and motor car (horiz)	1·50	45
880	340f. Eiffel Tower, car and huts	2·75	1·10

299 Hands over Antelope

1987. Endangered Fauna in Ferlo National Park. Multicoloured.

881	55f. Type **299**	20	15
882	70f. Ostriches	1·25	35
883	85f. Warthog	75	25
884	90f. Elephant	75	30

300 Spacecraft above Earth

1987. 10th Anniv of "Gemini 8"–Agena Flight.

885	**300**	320f. multicoloured	2·25	1·40

301 International Express Mail Emblem

1987. Centenary of First Senegal Stamp. Mult.

887	100f. Type **301**	65	35
888	130f. 1892 4c. Senegal and Dependencies stamp	75	45
889	140f. 1961 Senegal independence stamp	80	50
890	145f. 1935 30c. and 1f.25 Senegal stamps	85	50
891	320f. Senegal 1887 15c. on 20c. stamp and cancellation	2·25	1·10

302 Hand gripping Bloodied Claw above Map of South Africa

1987. Anti-Apartheid Campaign. Multicoloured.

892	130f. Type **302**	80	45
893	140f. Broken and bloodied chain in fist (vert)	85	50
894	145f. Skeleton with scythe, dove and globe	85	50

303 Emblem

1987. 20th Anniv of Intelsat. Multicoloured.

895	50f. Type **303**	20	15
896	125f. Satellite and emblem	75	45
897	150f. Emblem and globe	90	55
898	200f. Globe and satellite	1·25	75

304 Emblem and Crowd

1987. West African Cities Organization. Mult.

899	40f. Type **304**	15	15
900	125f. Emblem and clasped hands	75	45

305 Yacht and Sun

1987. 45th Anniv of Dakar Rotary Club.

901	**305**	500f. multicoloured	4·00	1·50

306 U.N. Building, New York

1987. 40th Anniv (1985) of U.N.O. Multicoloured.

902	85f. Type **306**	60	25
903	95f. Emblem	65	35
904	150f. Hands of different races and emblem	90	55

307 Fr. Daniel Brottier (founder) and Angel

1987. 50th Anniv of Cathedral of African Remembrance. Multicoloured.

905	130f. Type **307**	85	45
906	140f. Cathedral in 1936 and 1986	85	50

308 Hand pouring Grain into Globe

1987. World Food Day. Multicoloured.

907	130f. Type **308**	80	45
908	140f. Ear of wheat and F.A.O. emblem rising as sun (horiz)	1·10	50
909	145f. Emblem	1·25	50

SENEGAL

309 Servals

1987. Basse Casamance National Park. Mult.

910	115f. Type **309**	1·00	40
911	135f. Demidoff's galagos	1·40	45
912	150f. Bush pig	1·50	55
913	250f. Leopards	2·75	1·25
914	300f. Little egrets	11·00	3·50
915	300f. Carmine bee eaters	11·00	3·50

310 Wrestlers

1987. Senegalese Wrestling. Multicoloured.

916	115f. Type **310**	80	40
917	125f. Wrestlers and musicians	80	45
918	135f. Wrestlers (vert)	1·00	45
919	165f. Referee, wrestlers and crowd (vert)	1·25	55

311 African Open-bill Stork

1987. Djoudj National Park. Multicoloured.

920	115f. Type **311**	1·75	85
921	125f. Greater flamingos (horiz)	1·75	1·25
922	135f. Pink-backed pelican and greater flamingos (horiz)	2·60	1·25
923	300f. Pink-backed pelicans	4·75	2·00
924	350f. As No. 921	5·00	2·50
925	350f. As No. 922	5·00	2·50

312 Boy dreaming of Father Christmas's Visit

1987. Christmas. Multicoloured.

926	145f. Type **312**	85	50
927	150f. Star behind Virgin gazing at Child	90	55
928	180f. Nativity scene above people praying in church	1·25	65
929	200f. Nativity scene in candle glow	1·25	75

313 Battle of Dekhele

1988. Death Centenary of Lat-Dior. Multicoloured.

930	130f. Type **313**	1·00	45
931	160f. Lat-Dior on his horse "Maalaw"	1·00	60

314 10th Anniv Emblem and Map

1988. Dakar International Fair.

932	**314**	125f. multicoloured	75	45

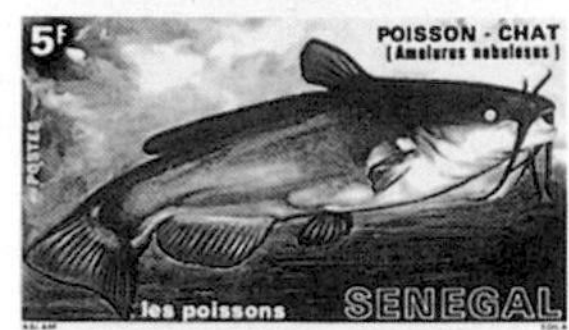

315 Brown Bullhead

1988. Fishes. Multicoloured.

933	5f. Type **315**	10	10
934	100f. Pennant coralfish	50	45
935	145f. Common barberfish	1·10	70
936	180f. Common carp	1·90	1·25

316 W.M.O. Emblem and Means of Conveying Information

1988. World Meteorology Day.

937	**316**	145f. multicoloured	90	30

317 Motor Cyclist

1988. 10th Anniv of Paris–Dakar Rally. Mult.

938	145f. Type **317**	1·25	50
939	180f. Rally car and emblem	1·50	65
940	200f. Rally cars and man	1·75	70
941	410f. Thierry Sabine and motor cyclist	3·50	1·90

318 Squid

1988. Molluscs. Multicoloured.

942	10f. Type **318**	15	10
943	20f. Truncate donax (bivalve)	15	10
944	145f. Giant East African snail	1·40	65
945	165f. Banded snail	1·75	75

319 Football, Cup and Map

1988. Africa Cup Football Championship, Rabat. Multicoloured.

946	80f. Type **319**	55	25
947	100f. Player's leg and ball (vert)	75	35
948	145f. Match scene and map of Africa (vert)	90	50
949	180f. Emblem and cup (vert)	1·25	65

320 Corps Member and Children

1988. 25th Anniv of American Peace Corps in Senegal.

950	**320**	190f. multicoloured	1·25	65

321 "Dictyota atomaria"

1988. Marine Flora. Multicoloured.

951	10f. Type **321**	10	10
952	65f. "Agarum gmelini"	75	20
953	145f. "Saccorrhiza bulbosa"	1·10	55
954	180f. "Rhodymenia palmetta"	1·75	65

1988. Riccione Stamp Fair. No. 891 optd RICCIONE 88 27-29-08-89.

955	320f. multicoloured	2·25	1·25

323 Hodori (mascot) and Stadium

1988. Olympic Games, Seoul. Multicoloured.

956	5f. Type **323**	10	10
957	75f. Athletics, swimming and football	55	25
958	300f. Hodori, flame and sports pictograms	2·10	1·00
959	410f. Emblem and athletics pictogram	2·75	1·40

324 Thierno Saidou Nourou Tall Centre

1988

960	**324**	125f. multicoloured	70	60

325 Thies Phosphate Mine

1988. Senegal Industries. Multicoloured.

961	5f. Type **325**	1·00	50
962	20f. Chemical industry	10	10
963	145f. Diourbel factory	85	50
964	410f. Mbao refinery	3·00	1·75

326 Children and Government Palace

1988. Postcards of 1900. Multicoloured.

965	20f. Type **326**	10	10
966	145f. Wrestlers and St. Louis Grand Mosque	1·10	50
967	180f. Old Dakar railway station and young woman	2·25	1·25
968	200f. Goree Governor's residence and young woman	1·60	70

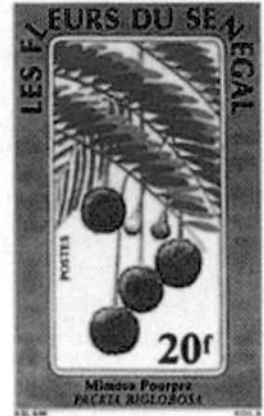

327 "Packia biglobosa"

1988. Flowers. Multicoloured.

969	20f. Type **327**	10	10
970	60f. "Euphorbia pulcherrima"	20	15
971	65f. "Cyrtosperma senegalense"	25	20
972	410f. "Bombax costatum"	3·00	1·40

328 Mask, Rally Car and Eiffel Tower

1989. 11th Paris–Dakar Rally. Multicoloured.

973	10f. Type **328**	10	10
974	145f. Crash helmet and sand dunes	1·25	55
975	180f. Turban and motor cyclist	1·50	70
976	220f. Motor cyclist and Thierry Sabine	2·00	85

329 Teranga Hotel

1989. Tourism (1st series). Multicoloured.

977	10f. Type **329**	10	10
978	80f. Thatched hut and shades on beach	55	25
979	100f. Saly hotel	65	35
980	350f. Dior hotel	2·50	1·25

330 Senegal Tourism Emblem

1989. Tourism (2nd series). Multicoloured.

981	130f. Type **330**	75	45
982	140f. Rural tourism (horiz)	85	50
983	145f. Fishing (horiz)	1·40	70
984	180f. Water sports (horiz)	1·25	70

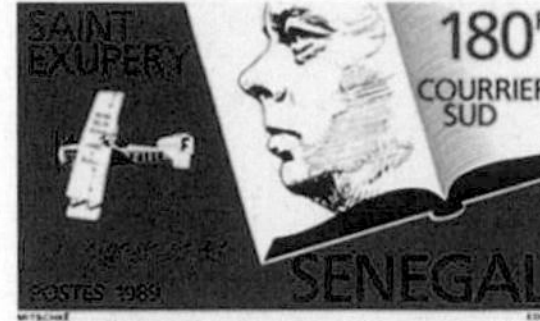

331 Saint-Exupery and Scene from "Courrier Sud"

1989. 45th Anniv of Disappearance of Antoine de Saint-Exupery (pilot and writer).

985	**331**	180f. black, orange and grey	1·40	50
986	-	220f. black, blue and grey	1·75	75
987	-	410f. multicoloured	3·50	1·25

DESIGNS: 220f. Scene from "Vol de Nuit"; 410f. Scene from "Pilote de Guerre".

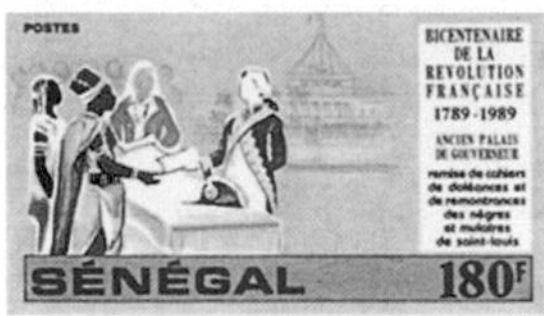

332 Presentation of Lists of Grievances by People of St. Louis

1989. Bicentenary of French Revolution. Mult.

988	180f. Type **332**	1·25	1·00
989	220f. Declaration of Rights of Man, quill pen in hand and phrygian cap (vert)	1·25	1·10
990	300f. Revolutionaries and flag	2·75	1·50

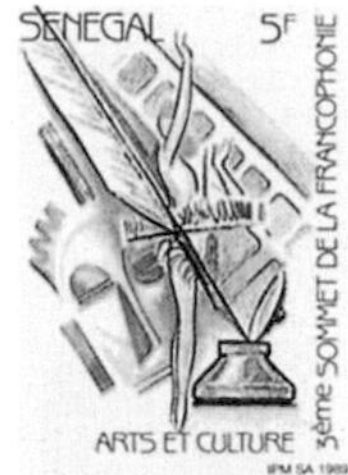

333 Arts and Culture

1989. 3rd Francophone Summit. Multicoloured.

991	5f. Type **333**	10	10
992	30f. Education (horiz)	15	10
993	100f. Communication (horiz)	65	35
994	200f. Development (horiz)	1·25	75

1989. No. 960 surch.

995	555f. on 125f. multicoloured	3·50	1·25

335 Stamps

1989. "Philexfrance 89" International Stamp Exhibition, Paris. Multicoloured.

996	10f. Type **335**	10	10
997	25f. Stamp on map of France (vert)	10	10
998	75f. Couple viewing stamp on easel (vert)	55	25
999	145f. Sticking stamp on envelope (vert)	1·10	55

336 "30" Dish Aerial and Envelope

1989. 30th Anniv Meeting of West African Post and Telecommunications Administrations Conference, Dakar. Multicoloured.

1000	25f. Type **336**	10	10
1001	30f. Telephone handset, punched tape and map on stamp	15	10
1002	180f. Map of Africa, stamp and telephone earpiece	1·40	70

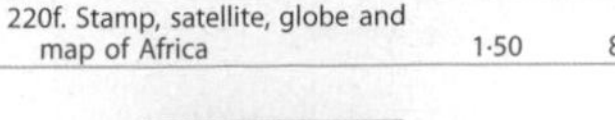

1003	220f. Stamp, satellite, globe and map of Africa	1·50	85

337 Record Stacks and 1922 Postcard

1989. 75th Anniv (1988) of Senegal Archives. Mult.

1004	15f. Type **337**	10	10
1005	40f. 1825 document	15	10
1006	145f. 1825 document and archive building	1·10	55
1007	180f. Bound volume	1·25	70

338 Jar with Lid

1989. Pottery. Multicoloured.

1008	15f. Type **338**	10	10
1009	30f. Potter at work	15	10
1010	75f. Stacked pots	65	25
1011	145f. Woman carrying pots	1·25	55

339 Nehru

1989. Birth Centenary of Jawaharlal Nehru (Indian statesman).

1012	**339**	220f. multicoloured	1·25	85
1013	-	410f. black, red & yellow	2·75	1·40

DESIGN—HORIZ: 410f. Nehru (different).

340 Swimming Crab

1989. Marine Life. Multicoloured.

1014	10f. Type **340**	10	10
1015	60f. Long-snouted seahorse (vert)	60	25
1016	145f. Barnacles	1·25	55
1017	220f. Sand-hopper	1·50	85

341 Clasped Hand and People of Different Races

1989. World AIDS Day. Multicoloured.

1018	5f. Type **341**	10	10
1019	100f. People under umbrella	40	35
1020	145f. Fist smashing AIDS virus	85	55
1021	180f. Hammer smashing AIDS virus	1·10	70

342 Pilgrims

1989. Centenary of Pilgrimage to Our Lady of Popenguine. Multicoloured.

1022	145f. Type **342**	90	55
1023	180f. Our Lady of Popenguine Church	1·40	70

343 White-breasted Cormorant and African Darter, Djoudj

1989. National Parks. Multicoloured.

1024	10f. Type **343**	25	15
1025	45f. Grey-headed gulls, Langue de Barbarie	90	35
1026	100f. Blue-checked bee eater and long-crested eagle, Basse Casamance	1·50	85
1027	180f. Western reef herons, Saloum	4·25	1·75

344 Boy looking at Christmas Tree

1989. Christmas. Multicoloured.

1028	10f. Type **344**	10	10
1029	25f. Teddy bear and bauble hanging from tree	10	10
1030	30f. Animals around Baby Jesus	15	10
1031	200f. Madonna and Child	1·25	75

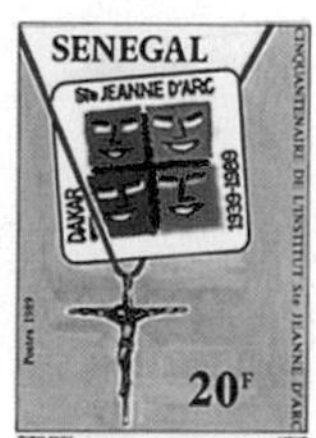

345 Crucifix and Anniversary Emblem

1989. 50th Anniv of St. Joan of Arc Institute, Dakar. Multicoloured.

1032	20f. Type **345**	10	10
1033	500f. Emblem and Institute building	3·50	1·40

346 "Hydravion"

1989. 79th Anniv of First Flight of Henri Fabre's Seaplane. Multicoloured.

1034	125f. Type **346**	75	55
1035	130f. Fabre working on engine of "Hydravion"	1·10	55
1036	475f. Technical drawings and Fabre (vert)	3·50	1·00
MS1037	141×101 mm. 700f. As No. 1036	5·50	2·75

347 Basketball

1990. Olympic Games, Barcelona (1992). Mult.

1038	10f. Type **347**	10	10
1039	130f. High jumping	50	20
1040	180f. Throwing the discus	1·00	35
1041	190f. Running	1·10	45
1042	315f. Lawn tennis	2·00	55
1043	475f. Show jumping	2·75	65
MS1044	85×85 mm. 600f. Football	3·75	1·00

348 Rally Car

1990. 12th Paris–Dakar Rally. Multicoloured.

1045	20f. Type **348**	10	10
1046	25f. Motor cycle and sidecar	10	10
1047	180f. Crowd cheering winning driver	1·40	70
1048	200f. Thierry Sabine and car	1·40	75

349 Piazza della Signoria, Florence, and Footballer

1990. World Cup Football Championship, Italy. Multicoloured.

1049	45f. Type **349**	20	15
1050	140f. Piazza Navona, Rome	1·00	25
1051	180f. "Virgin with St. Anne and Infant Jesus" (Leonardo da Vinci)	1·25	30
1052	220f. "Giuseppe Garibaldi" (oil painting)	1·40	55
1053	300f. "Sistine Madonna" (Raphael)	2·00	75
1054	415f. "Virgin and Child" (Danielle da Volterra)	2·75	1·10
MS1055	83×78 mm. 700f. Christopher Columbus statue, Milan (51×39 mm)	4·00	1·90

350 Footballer

1990. African Nations Cup Football Championship, Algeria. Multicoloured.

1056	20f. Type **350**	10	10
1057	60f. Goalkeeper	25	20
1058	100f. Clasped hands and pennants	75	35
1059	500f. Trophy	3·50	1·75

351 Facsimile Telegraphy

1990. Postal Services. Multicoloured.

1060	5f. Type **351**	10	10
1061	15f. Express mail service	10	10
1062	100f. Postal cheques	65	35
1063	180f. Savings	1·25	40

352 Hands and Umbrella protecting Children

1990. Louga S.O.S. Children's Village. Mult.

1064	5f. Type **352**	10	10
1065	500f. Children under umbrella	3·25	1·25

353 Envelopes on Map

1990. 20th Anniv of Multinational Postal Training School, Abidjan. Multicoloured.

1066	145f. Type **353**	1·00	55
1067	180f. Man carrying wreath containing envelope	1·25	70

354 Excursion by Pirogue, Basse-Casamance

1990. Tourism. Multicoloured.

1068	10f. Type **354**	10	10
1069	25f. Hotel and beach, Goree	10	10
1070	30f. Houses on stilts, Fadiouth	15	10
1071	40f. Rose Lake and salt drying	15	10

355 Camp

1990. Scouting. Multicoloured.

1072	30f. Type **355**	15	10
1073	100f. Scouts trekking alongside lake	75	35
1074	145f. Scouts trekking through hilly landscape	1·00	55
1075	200f. Scout and emblem (vert)	1·25	75

356 "Cassia tora"

1990. Medicinal Plants. Multicoloured.

1076	95f. Type **356**	65	35
1077	105f. "Tamarind"	75	40
1078	125f. "Cassia occidentalis"	90	45
1079	175f. "Leptadenia hastata"	1·25	65

357 Angels and Tree

1990. Christmas.

1080	**357**	25f. multicoloured	10	10

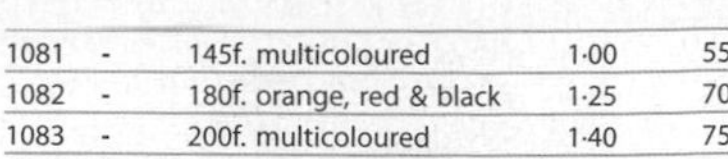

1081	-	145f. multicoloured	1·00	55
1082	-	180f. orange, red & black	1·25	70
1083	-	200f. multicoloured	1·40	75

DESIGNS: 145f. Angel trumpeting stars; 180f. Adoration of Three Kings; 200f. Donkey and cow gazing at Child.

358 Anniversary Emblem

1991. 125th Anniv (1988) of International Red Cross and 25th Anniv of Senegal Red Cross.

1084	**358**	180f. multicoloured	1·25	45

359 Rally Car

1991. 13th Paris–Dakar Rally. Multicoloured.

1085	15f. Type **359**	10	10
1086	15f. Car and motor cycle at night	75	35
1087	180f. Rally car (different)	1·25	75
1088	220f. Motor cycles	1·60	90

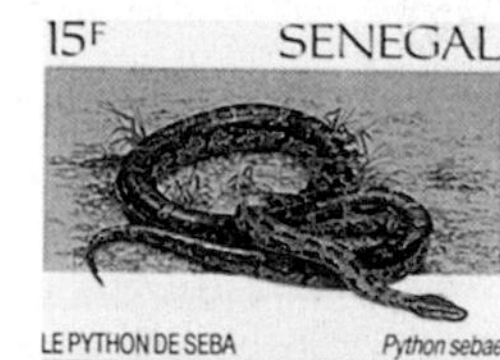

360 African Python

1991. Reptiles. Multicoloured.

1089	15f. Type **360**	10	10
1090	60f. Common green turtle	65	15
1091	100f. Nile crocodile	1·10	25
1092	180f. Senegal chameleon	1·75	90

361 Sphinx, House of Slaves, Frescoes, Kirdi Houses and Mohammed's Tomb

1991. "Fespaco". 12th Pan-African Cinema and Television Festival. Multicoloured.

1093	30f. Type **361**	10	10
1094	60f. Dogon mask, B. Dioulasso Mosque, drawing of Osiris, and camel rider	25	15
1095	100f. Rabat, "Seated Scribe" (Egyptian statue), drum and camels	75	25
1096	180f. Pyramids of Egypt, Djenne Mosque, Guinean mask, Moroccan architecture and Moorish door decorations	1·25	75

362 Nobel

1991. 95th Death Anniv of Alfred Nobel (founder of Nobel prizes). Multicoloured. Self-adhesive.

1097	145f. Type **362**	1·00	75
1098	180f. Nobel and prize presentation (horiz)	1·25	90

363 Oribi

1991. National Parks. Multicoloured.

1099	5f. Type **363**	10	10
1100	10f. Dorcas gazelle	10	10
1101	180f. Kob	1·25	45
1102	555f. Hartebeest	4·50	2·25

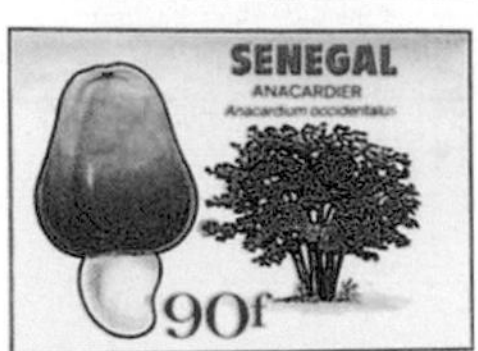

364 Cashew

1991. Trees and their Fruit. Multicoloured.

1103	90f. Type **364**	65	25
1104	100f. Mango	75	25
1105	125f. Sugar-palm (vert)	90	35
1106	145f. Oil palm (vert)	1·00	45

365 Ader, Motor Car and Telephone

1991. Air. Centenary (1990) of First Heavier than Air Powered Flight. Multicoloured.

1107	145f. Type **365**	1·10	40
1108	180f. Clement Ader and his monoplane "Eole"	1·25	55
1109	615f. "Eole" and Ader (vert)	4·25	2·00
MS1110	132×96 mm. 940f. As No. 1105	6·25	2·75

366 Columbus and Haitians

1991. 500th Anniv (1992) of Discovery of America by Columbus. Multicoloured.

1111	100f. Type **366**	65	25
1112	145f. Arms of Castile and Leon (vert)	90	40
1113	180f. "Santa Maria" and Columbus	1·10	45
1114	200f. Vicente Yanez Pinzon and "Nina"	1·25	55
1115	220f. Martin Alonzo Pinzon and "Pinta"	1·40	60
1116	500f. Details of charts	3·25	1·25
1117	625f. Compass rose and Columbus with charts	4·00	1·75

367 Armstrong

1991. 20th Death Anniv of Louis Armstrong (musician). Multicoloured.

1118	10f. Type **367**	10	10
1119	145f. Armstrong singing	90	40
1120	180f. Armstrong and trumpets	1·40	45
1121	220f. Armstrong playing trumpet	2·00	90

368 Yuri Gagarin and "Vostok 1"

1991. 30th Anniv of First Man in Space. Mult.

1125	15f. Type **368**	10	10
1126	145f. "Vostok 1" and Gagarin in spacesuit	90	40
1127	180f. Gagarin in spacesuit and "Vostok 1" (different)	1·25	45
1128	220f. Globe, "Vostok 1" and Gagarin in flying kit	1·50	90

369 Flags and Water dripping into Bowl

1991. "Water, Source of Life". Senegal–Saudi Arabia Rural Water Supply Co-operation. Mult.

1129	30f. Type **369**	10	10
1130	145f. Tap and village	90	40
1131	180f. Tap dripping and flags	1·25	45
1132	220f. Water tower and village	1·50	90

370 Star and Crescents

1991. 6th Summit Meeting of Islamic Conference Organization, Dakar. Multicoloured.

1133	15f. Type **370**	10	10
1134	145f. Hands	90	40
1135	180f. Conference centre and accommodation	1·25	45
1136	220f. Grand Mosque, Dakar	1·50	90

371 Player shooting at Basket

1991. Centenary of Basketball. Multicoloured.

1137	125f. Type **371**	75	35
1138	145f. Player approaching basket	1·00	40
1139	180f. King and Queen of the Basket	1·10	45
1140	220f. Lion, trophies and ball	1·50	60

372 Giving Blessing

1991. Christmas. Multicoloured.

1141	5f. Type **372**	10	10
1142	145f. Madonna and Child	90	40
1143	160f. Angels and star	1·25	45
1144	220f. Animals and Baby Jesus	1·50	90

373 Bust of Mozart and Score

1991. Death Bicentenary of Wolfgang Amadeus Mozart (composer). Multicoloured.

1145	5f. Type **373**	10	10
1146	150f. Mozart conducting	1·00	40
1147	180f. Mozart at keyboard	1·25	45
1148	220f. Mozart and score	1·50	90

374 Flags on Player's Sock

1992. 18th African Nations Cup Football Championship. Multicoloured.

1149	10f. Type **374**	10	10
1150	145f. Footballs forming "92"	70	45
1151	200f. Cup and mascot	1·25	65
1152	220f. Players	1·50	1·00

1992. Papal Visit. No. 1143 surch VISITE DU PAPE JEAN PAUL II AU SENEGAL 19-23/02/92 180F.

1153	180f. on 160f. multicoloured	1·60	1·10

376 Saloum Delta

1992. National Parks. Multicoloured.

1154	10f. Type **376**	35	15
1155	125f. Djoudj	1·50	60
1156	145f. Niokolo-Koba	2·10	65
1157	220f. Basse Casamance	3·00	1·75

377 Oil Wells, Flag and Bombs

1992. Participation of Senegal Contingent in Gulf War. Multicoloured.

1158	30f. Type **377**	15	10
1159	145f. Senegalese officer	70	45
1160	180f. Kaaba and Senegalese guard	1·10	55
1161	220f. Map, dove and flag	1·50	75

378 Frozen Fish

1992. Fish Products. Multicoloured.

1162	5f. Type **378**	10	10
1163	60f. Sandwich seller and platters of fish	40	20
1164	100f. Woman filleting fish	1·10	40
1165	150f. Women packing prawns	1·10	75

379 Niokolo Complex

1992. Tourist Sites. Multicoloured.

1166	5f. Type **379**	10	10
1167	10f. Basse Casamance	10	10
1168	150f. Dakar	1·10	45
1169	200f. Saint-Louis	1·60	80

380 Teacher and Pupils carrying Saplings

1992. Reforestation by Schoolchildren. Mult.

1170	145f. Type **380**	1·00	45
1171	180f. Planting sapling	1·25	55
1172	200f. Planting saplings (different)	1·40	90
1173	220f. Watering-in sapling (vert)	1·75	1·10

381 People with Cleaning Materials

1992. Manpower Services Operation, Setal. Mult.

1174	25f. Type **381**	10	10
1175	145f. Clearing road	70	45
1176	180f. Sweeping streets (vert)	1·10	55
1177	220f. Painting kerbstones (vert)	1·50	1·00

382 Education

1992. Rights of the Child. Multicoloured.

1178	20f. Type **382**	10	10
1179	45f. Vocational training	20	15
1180	165f. Instruction	1·10	55
1181	180f. Health	1·25	55

383 Customs Post (Free Trade)

1992. African Integration. Multicoloured.

1182	10f. Type **383**	10	10
1183	30f. Silhouettes (youth activities)	15	10
1184	145f. Communications equipment	1·10	45
1185	220f. Women's movements	1·50	75

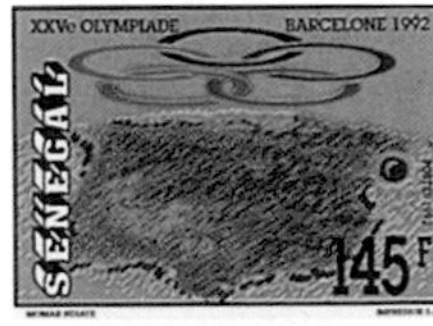

384 Rings and Map of Spain

1992. Olympic Games, Barcelona. Multicoloured.

1186	145f. Type **384**	70	45
1187	180f. Runner (vert)	1·10	55
1188	200f. Sprinter	1·40	90
1189	300f. Athlete carrying torch (vert)	2·00	1·50

385 Passenger Carriages

1992. "The Blue Train". Multicoloured.

1190	70f. Type **385**	45	30
1191	145f. Diesel locomotives and carriages	1·00	55
1192	200f. Train and track on map	1·40	90
1193	220f. Railway station	1·50	1·00

386 Sealife around Map of Antarctic

1992. International Maritime Heritage Year.

1194	386	25f. black, blue & yellow	10	10
1195	-	100f. multicoloured	70	25

1196	-	180f. multicoloured	1·25	55
1197	-	220f. multicoloured	1·50	75

DESIGNS—VERT: 100f. Marine life caught in sun ray; 180f. United Nations seminar; 220f. Fish, ship, flags and hands holding globe.

387 Coral

1992. Corals.

1198	**387**	50f. multicoloured	35	15
1199	-	100f. multicoloured	90	25
1200	-	145f. multicoloured (vert)	1·25	45
1201	-	220f. multicoloured	2·00	1·00

DESIGNS: 100f. to 220f. Different corals.

388 Adenauer

1992. 25th Death Anniv of Konrad Adenauer (German statesman). Multicoloured.

1202	5f. Type **388**	10	10
1203	145f. Schaumburg Palace and flags (horiz)	1·00	45
1204	180f. German flag and hand-shake (horiz)	1·25	55
1205	220f. Map, flag and emblem of Germany (horiz)	1·50	75

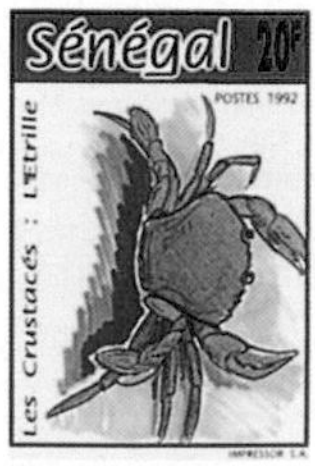

389 Crab

1992. Crustaceans. Multicoloured.

1206	20f. Type **389**	10	10
1207	30f. Sea spider	25	10
1208	180f. Crayfish	1·50	55
1209	200f. King prawn	1·75	1·00

390 "Parkia biglobosa"

1992. Flowers and their Fruits. Multicoloured.

1210	10f. Type **390**	10	10
1211	50f. Desert date	35	15
1212	200f. "Parinari macrophylla"	1·50	65
1213	220f. Cactus	1·75	1·00

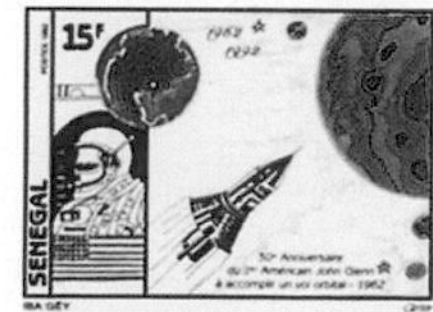

391 Rocket and Earth

1992. 30th Anniv of First American Manned Orbit of the Earth. Multicoloured.

1214	15f. Type **391**	10	10
1215	145f. American flag and John Glenn	1·00	55
1216	180f. Rocket launch and globe	1·25	90
1217	200f. Astronaut and rocket on launch-pad (vert)	1·40	1·00

392 Bakari II and Map from 14th-century Catalan Atlas

1992. Bakari II. Multicoloured.

1218	100f. Type **392**	65	25
1219	145f. Giant Mexican carved head and map from 15th-century atlas	1·00	45

393 Picture Frame and Obelisk

1992. Dakar Biennale. Multicoloured.

1220	20f. Type **393**	10	10
1221	50f. Mask hanging from window frame	35	10
1222	145f. Open book	1·00	65
1223	220f. Traditional string instrument	1·75	1·00

394 Children dancing round Decorated Globe

1992. Christmas. Multicoloured.

1224	15f. Type **394**	10	10
1225	145f. People around tree (vert)	1·00	55
1226	180f. Jesus (vert)	1·25	65
1227	200f. Father Christmas (vert)	1·40	90

1993. 15th Paris–Dakar Rally. Nos. 941 and 975 surch Dakar le 17-01-93 and new value.

1228	145f. on 180f. multicoloured	1·10	90
1229	220f. on 410f. multicoloured	1·60	1·10

396 First Aid Post

1993. Accident Prevention Campaign. Mult.

1230	20f. Type **396** (prevention, security and first aid)	10	10
1231	25f. The Sonacos incident (re-inforcement of preventative measures) (36×28 mm)	10	10
1232	145f. Chemical accident (need for vigilance and security) (36×28 mm)	1·00	55
1233	200f. Helicopter rescue (rapid and efficient intervention at air disasters)	1·25	90

397 Seck

1993. 120th Birth Anniv of Abdoulaye Seck (Director of Posts and Telecommunications).

1234	**397**	220f. multicoloured	1·50	65

398 Spotted Hyena

1993. Wild Animals. Multicoloured.

1235	30f. Type **398**	10	10
1236	50f. Lioness	10	10
1237	70f. Leopard	25	10
1238	150f. Giraffe (vert)	50	25
1239	180f. Stag	75	30

399 Decorated Tree, Children playing and Father Christmas

1993. Christmas. Multicoloured.

1240	5f. Type **399**	10	10
1241	80f. Children decorating tree and Father Christmas	20	15
1242	145f. Children visiting Father Christmas	35	25
1243	150f. Girl tugging Father Christmas's beard	35	25

400 U.S. Flag and Kennedy

1993. 30th Anniv of Assassination of President John F. Kennedy of the United States. Mult.

1244	80f. Type **400**	20	15
1245	555f. Kennedy and White House	1·90	95

402 Vehicles and Tree at Sunset

1994. 16th Anniv of Paris–Dakar Rally. Mult.

1250	145f. Type **402**	50	25
1251	180f. Boys with camel	60	30
1252	220f. Rally cars	75	35

403 Diplodocus

1994. Prehistoric Animals. Multicoloured.

1253	100f. Type **403**	25	15
1254	175f. Brontosaurus	40	25
1255	215f. Triceratops	50	35
1256	290f. Stegosaurus	1·25	45
1257	300f. Tyrannosaurus	1·75	1·10

404 Black-headed Herons

1994. Birds of Kalissaye National Park. Mult.

1258	100f. Type **404**	50	20
1259	275f. Caspian terns	1·10	45

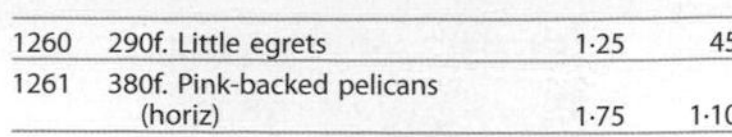

1260	290f. Little egrets	1·25	45
1261	380f. Pink-backed pelicans (horiz)	1·75	1·10

405 Dried Moray Fat

1994. Produce of the Sea. Multicoloured.

1262	5f. Type **405**	10	10
1263	90f. Sifting shellfish	20	15
1264	100f. Salted shark	40	25
1265	200f. Smoking small fry	70	40

406 "Stop Sand Extraction"

1994. Coastal Protection. Multicoloured.

1266	5f. Type **406**	10	10
1267	75f. Prevention of sand dunes	20	15
1268	100f. Horizontal and vertical barrages	25	15
1269	200f. Cleanliness of beaches	50	35

407 Water Store, Goree, and Railway Station, Rufisque

1994. Preservation of Heritage Sites. Mult.

1270	100f. Type **407**	30	20
1271	175f. Soudan House	40	25
1272	215f. Goree Island	50	35
1273	275f. Pinet Laprade Fort, Sedhiou	90	45

408 Red-flowered Kapok

1994. Flowers. Multicoloured.

1274	30f. Type **408**	10	10
1275	75f. Golden trumpet	20	15
1276	100f. Rose periwinkle	25	15
1277	1000f. Glory-bower	3·50	2·10

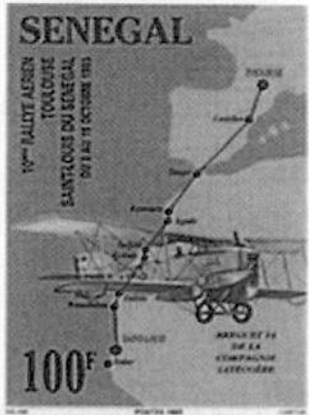

409 Breguet 14 Biplane over Route Map

1994. 10th Toulouse–Saint-Louis Aerial Rally (1993). Multicoloured.

1278	100f. Type **409**	40	15
1279	145f. Henri Guillaumet and route map	50	25
1280	180f. Jean Mermoz and route map	60	30
1281	220f. Antoine Saint-Exupery and route map	75	35

410 Head of Elephant with Ear forming Map of Africa

1994. S.O.S. Elephant Conservation Programme. Multicoloured.

1282	30f. Type **410**	20	10
1283	60f. Elephant within "SOS"	25	10
1284	90f. Pair of elephants with trunks forming "SOS"	40	15
1285	145f. Dead elephant and tusks	50	25

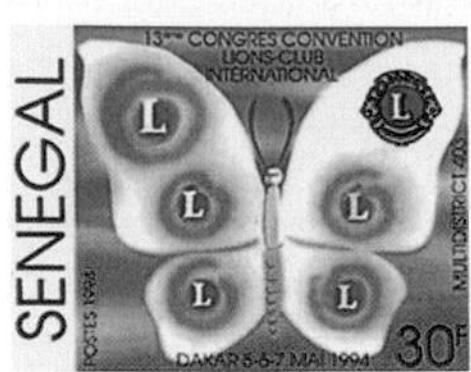

411 Emblems on Butterfly

1994. 13th Congress of District 403 of Lions Clubs International, Dakar. Multicoloured.

1286	30f. Type **411**	20	10
1287	60f. Emblem over butterfly	30	10
1288	175f. "L's and emblem	60	25
1289	215f. Emblem on rainbow	90	35

412 "Stamp" showing Children playing

1994. African Children's Day. Children's Drawings. Multicoloured.

1290	175f. Type **412**	40	25
1291	215f. Preparing meal outside house	50	35

413 Flags and Football

1994. World Cup Football Championship, U.S.A. Multicoloured.

1292	45f. Type **413**	10	10
1293	175f. World map forming part of football	65	25
1294	215f. Player dribbling ball (horiz)	75	35
1295	665f. Players with ball (horiz)	2·10	1·10

414 Slave House

1994. World Heritage Site, Goree.

1296	**414**	500f. multicoloured	1·60	1·10

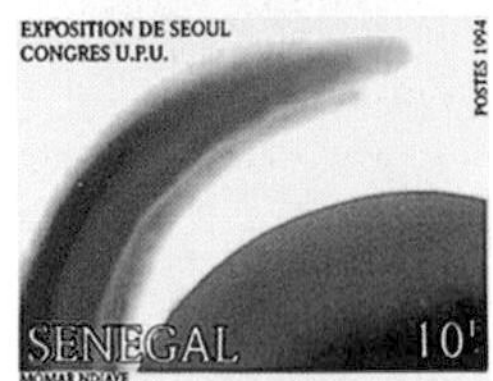

415 Rainbow over Globe

1994. 21st Universal Postal Union Congress and "Philakorea 1994" International Stamp Exhibition, Seoul. Multicoloured.

1297	10f. Type **415**	10	10
1298	175f. "Stamp" forming wing of dove	40	25
1299	260f. "Stamp" forming sail of boat	65	45

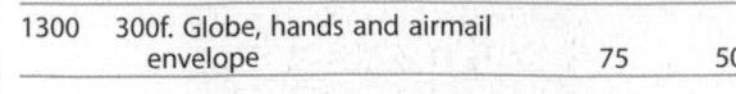

1300	300f. Globe, hands and airmail envelope	75	50

416 Peace Dove, People of Different Cultures and Flags

1994. International Year of the Family. Mult.

1301	5f. Type **416**	10	10
1302	175f. People of different cultures, flags and globe	65	25
1303	215f. Globe and mothers with children	75	35
1304	290f. Globe, dove and family	1·00	45

417 "Murex saxatilis"

1994. Shells. Multicoloured.

1305	20f. Type **417**	10	10
1306	45f. "Nerita senegalensis" (vert)	10	10
1307	75f. "Polymita picea"	20	15
1308	175f. "Scalaria pretiosa" (vert)	65	25
1309	215f. Glory of the sea cone (vert)	75	65

418 Golden Jackal

1994. Animals. Multicoloured.

1310	60f. Type **418**	25	10
1311	70f. African clawless otter	25	10
1312	100f. Egyptian mongoose	40	15
1313	175f. Giant ground pangolin	90	25
1314	215f. Nile monitor	1·00	35

419 Pierre de Coubertin (founder) and Anniversary Emblem

1994. Centenary of International Olympic Committee. Multicoloured.

1315	175f. Type **419**	40	25
1316	215f. Coubertin within wreath and anniversary emblem	50	35
1317	275f. Coubertin over anniversary emblem (vert)	90	45
1318	290f. Coubertin within anniversary emblem and Olympic rings (vert)	1·10	45

420 Africans greeting Portuguese

1994. 550th Anniv of First Portuguese Landing in Senegal.

1319	**420**	175f. multicoloured	65	25

421 Father Christmas and Children with Presents

1994. Christmas. Multicoloured.

1320	175f. Type **421**	40	25
1321	215f. Madonna and Child and Christmas trees	50	35
1322	275f. Adoration of the Wise Men (horiz)	90	45
1323	290f. Madonna and Child	1·10	45

422 Emblem and Ribbons

1995. Conference of District 9100 of Rotary International. Multicoloured.

1324	260f. Type **422**	90	45
1325	275f. Emblem and dove in flight	90	45

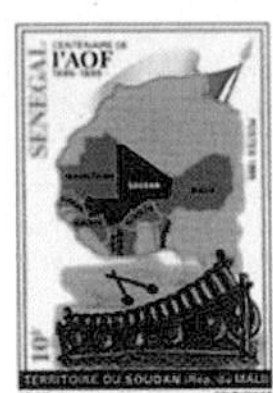

423 Sudan and Xylophone

1995. Centenary of Formation of French Governate-General of French West Africa. Map highlighting featured country. Multicoloured.

1326	10f. Type **423**	10	10
1327	15f. Dahomey and canoes	10	10
1328	30f. Ivory Coast and elephant	10	10
1329	70f. Mauritania and camel	15	10
1330	175f. Guinea, stringed instrument and plants	40	25
1331	180f. Upper Volta, cow and produce	45	30
1332	215f. Niger and Cross of Agadez	75	35
1333	225f. Senegal and lions	80	35

1995. As Nos. 502a/504h but size 21×26 mm.

1334	**154**	5f. orange	10	10
1335	**154**	10f. green	10	10
1336	**154**	20f. red	10	10
1337	**154**	25f. green	10	10
1338	**154**	30f. green	10	10
1339	**154**	40f. green	10	10
1340	**154**	50f. green	10	10
1341	**154**	60f. green	10	10
1342	**154**	70f. green	15	10
1343	**154**	80f. green	15	10
1344	**154**	100f. blue	25	15
1345	**154**	150f. blue	35	25
1346	**154**	175f. brown	40	25
1347	**154**	190f. green	40	30
1348	**154**	200f. black	50	35
1349	**154**	215f. blue	45	30
1350	**154**	225f. blue	45	30
1351	**154**	240f. brown	50	35
1352	**154**	250f. red	60	40
1353	**154**	260f. brown	50	35
1354	**154**	275f. red	65	45
1355	**154**	300f. purple	60	40
1356	**154**	320f. mauve	60	40
1357	**154**	350f. brown	70	50
1358	**154**	410f. red and brown	80	55
1363	**154**	500f. purple	1·00	70
1366	**154**	1000f. red	2·00	1·40

424 Communications, Map of West Africa and Energy Sources

1995. 1st Economic Community of West African States Trade Fair. Multicoloured.

1370	175f. Type **424**	40	25
1371	215f. Members' flags, banknotes and crops (horiz)	50	35

425 Pasteur developing Rabies Vaccine

1995. Death Centenary of Louis Pasteur (chemist). Multicoloured.

1372	275f. Type **425**	1·10	45
1373	500f. Pasteur working on pasteurization	1·60	85

426 Scene from "L'Arroseur Arrose" (dir. Lumiere Brothers)

1995. Centenary of Motion Pictures. Multicoloured.

1374	100f. Type **426**	25	15
1375	200f. First public film screening by Lumiere brothers	75	35
1376	250f. Auguste and Louis Lumiere watching screening of "Arrival by Train"	90	40
1377	275f. Presentation on cinematography by Antoine Lumiere, 1895	1·25	90

427 Animal Welfare

1995. 50th Anniv of F.A.O. Multicoloured.

1378	175f. Type **427**	40	25
1379	215f. Teaching new skills to rural communities	50	35
1380	260f. Aquaculture	1·00	45
1381	275f. Nourishment of children	1·10	90

428 People of Different Cultures

1995. 50th Anniv of U.N.O.

1382	**428**	275f. blue, violet and black	1·10	45
1383	-	1000f. multicoloured	3·25	2·10

DESIGN: 1000f. "ONU 50" and U.N. Headquarters, New York.

429 Figures dancing around Book

1995. 25th Anniv of Agency for Cultural and Technical Co-operation in French-speaking Countries. Multicoloured.

1384	150f. Type **429**	35	25
1385	500f. Panels of contestants (victory of St. Louis Military Academy in 1994 competition)	1·60	1·10

430 African buffalo

1995. Animals. Multicoloured.

1386	90f. Type **430**	20	15
1387	150f. Warthog	50	25
1388	175f. Bushbuck	1·00	25
1389	275f. African spurred tortoise	1·25	45
1390	300f. North African crested porcupine	1·25	50

431 Caspian Tern

1995. Endangered Birds. Terns. Multicoloured.

1391	90f. Type **431**	20	15
1392	145f. Gull-billed tern	35	25
1393	150f. Royal tern	65	25
1394	180f. Common tern	75	55

432 "Meganostoma eurydice"

1995. Butterflies. Multicoloured.

1395	45f. Type **432**	10	10
1396	100f. "Luehdorfia japonica"	40	15
1397	200f. Great orange-tip	1·00	35
1398	220f. Small tortoiseshell	1·25	65

433 Bassari Festivals

1995. Cultural Tourism. Multicoloured.

1399	100f. Type **433**	25	15
1400	175f. "Baawnann" (vert)	40	25
1401	220f. Pyramid-roofed houses	55	35
1402	500f. Turu Dance	1·60	1·10

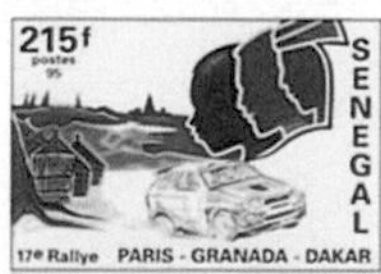

434 Rally Car and Profiles

1996. Paris–Granada–Dakar Motor Rally. Mult.

1403	215f. Type **434**	50	35
1404	275f. Motor cyclists (vert)	65	45
1405	290f. Landmarks and vehicles	65	45
1406	665f. Rally cars	1·75	1·10

435 Sea-island Cotton

1996. Flowers. Multicoloured.

1407	175f. Type **435**	40	30
1408	275f. Sorrel	75	45
1409	290f. Wood sorrel	75	45
1410	500f. Lotus water-lily	1·25	75

436 Diop in Youth and "Sphinx" (Dominique Denon)

1996. 10th Death Anniv of Cheikh Anta Diop. Mult.

1411	175f. Type **436**	40	30
1412	215f. Diop engaged in Carbon 14 dating tests	50	35

437 Saloum Delta National Park

1996. National Parks. Multicoloured.

1413	175f. Type **437**	40	30
1414	200f. Niokolo Koba	45	30
1415	220f. Madeleine Islands	50	35
1416	275f. Basse Casamance	65	45

438 Boxing

1996. Sport. Multicoloured.

1417	125f. Type **438**	30	20
1418	215f. Judo	50	35
1419	275f. Throwing the javelin	65	45
1420	320f. Throwing the discus	75	55

439 Woman

1996. Improvement of World. Multicoloured.

1421	215f. Type **439** (campaign against poverty)	50	35
1422	500f. "Drop of Hope" (balloon) over landscape (Rio de Janeiro, 1992–Dakar, 1996)	1·10	75

440 "Choose Corridor 1"

1996. "Hall of Pearls" by Serge Correa (painter). Multicoloured.

1423	260f. Type **440**	60	40
1424	320f. "Choose Symphony 1"	75	55

441 Man with Globe rejecting Drugs

1996. United Nations Decade against the Abuse and Trafficking of Drugs. Multicoloured.

1425	175f. Type **441**	40	30
1426	215f. U.N. emblem and hand holding up stop sign to drugs	50	35

442 Competitors and Statue

1996. Centenary of Modern Olympic Games.

1427	**442**	215f. multicoloured	50	35

443 Swimming

1996. Olympic Games, Atlanta, U.S.A. Mult.

1428	10f. Type **443**	10	10
1429	80f. Gymnastics	30	15
1430	175f. Running	60	30
1431	260f. Hurdling	75	40

444 "90" and Senghor

1996. 90th Birthday of Leopold Senghor (President, 1960–81). Multicoloured.

1432	175f. Type **444**	40	30
1433	275f. Senghor as young and older man (vert)	65	45

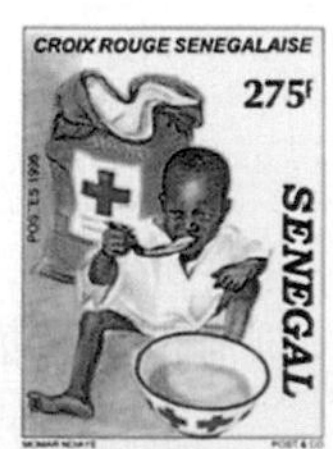

445 Sack of Food and Boy eating

1996. Senegalese Red Cross.

1434	**445**	275f. multicoloured	65	45

446 Savanna Monkey

1996. Primates. Multicoloured.

1435	10f. Type **446**	20	10
1436	30f. Patas monkey	25	10
1437	90f. Campbell's monkey	40	15
1438	215f. Chimpanzee	75	35
1439	260f. Guinea baboon	1·00	40

447 Sad and Injured Boys (child victims of armed conflicts)

1996. 50th Anniv of UNICEF. Multicoloured.

1440	75f. Type **447**	15	10
1441	275f. Nurse and child, mother feeding baby, smiling boy and boy at tap (primary health care) and breast-feeding	65	45

448 Lorry

1997. Dakar–Agades–Dakar Motor Rally. Mult.

1442	25f. Type **448**	25	10
1443	75f. Man pushing car	50	10
1444	215f. Rally car	75	30
1445	300f. Motor cyclist	1·00	45

449 Praying Mantis

1997. Insects. Multicoloured.

1446	10f. Type **449**	20	10
1447	50f. Common earwig	20	10
1448	75f. Desert locust	25	10
1449	215f. Sand tiger beetle	75	30
1450	220f. European field cricket	75	30

450 White Spoonbill

1997. Endangered Birds. Multicoloured.

1451	25f. Type **450**	10	10
1452	70f. Marabou stork	25	10
1453	175f. Western curlew	50	25
1454	215f. Saddle-bill stork	1·00	30
1455	220f. Crowned crane	1·00	30

The French and Latin inscriptions on Nos. 1453 and 1455 have been transposed.

451 Acacia

1997. Trees and their Fruits. Multicoloured.

1456	80f. Type **451**	40	10
1457	175f. Eucalyptus	50	25
1458	220f. "Khaya senegalensis"	75	30
1459	260f. Horse-tail tree	1·00	40

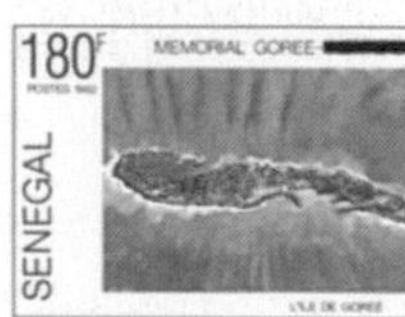

452 Goree Island

1997. Unissued stamp with part of inscription deleted by bar as in T 452.

1460	**452**	180f. multicoloured	85	30

453 African Buffaloes

1997. Mammals. Multicoloured.

1461	25f. Type **453**	20	10

1462 90f. Antelopes 35 15
1463 100f. Gnus 40 15
1464 200f. African hunting dogs 75 30
1465 240f. Cheetahs 1·00 35

454 African Fish Eagle

1997. Niokolo-Badiar National Park. Mult.
1466 30f. Type **454** 50 10
1467 90f. Hippopotamus 50 15
1468 240f. African elephant 75 35
1469 300f. Giant eland 1·00 45

455 West African Helmet

1997. Shells. Multicoloured.
1470 15f. Type **455** 20 10
1471 40f. "Pugilina meria" 30 10
1472 190f. Map cowrie 60 30
1473 200f. "Natica adansoni" 75 30
1474 300f. "Bullia miran" 1·00 45

There are errors of spelling in the Latin inscriptions.

456 Von Stephan

1997. Death Centenary of Heinrich von Stephan (founder of U.P.U.).
1475 **456** 310f. multicoloured 75 45

457 Cereal Stockpiles

1997. Security of Food Supplies. Multicoloured.
1476 190f. Type **457** 70 30
1477 200f. Woman weighing herself (post-weaning nutritional vulnerability) 90 30

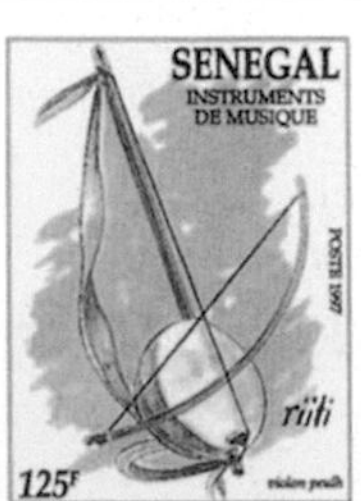
458 Riiti

1997. Musical Instruments. Multicoloured.
1478 125f. Type **458** 40 20
1479 190f. Kora (stringed instrument) 70 30
1480 200f. Tama (double-ended drum) 75 30
1481 240f. Dioung dioung (royal ceremonial drum) 1·00 35

459 Da Gama and Ship's Hold containing Spices (Spice Route)

1997. 500th Anniv of Vasco da Gama's Voyage to India via the Cape of Good Hope. Multicoloured.
1482 40f. Type **459** 20 10
1483 75f. Map of Africa, scales and Da Gama (port of call at Zanzibar) 25 10
1484 190f. "Sao Gabriel" (flagship) and Da Gama (development of caravel) 90 30
1485 200f. Compass rose over map of Africa and printing press (introduction of compass and printed maps) 90 30

460 Planche Mask, Burkina Faso

1997. Traditional Masks. Multicoloured.
1486 45f. Type **460** 25 10
1487 90f. Kpeliyehe mask, Senufo, Ivory Coast 40 15
1488 200f. Nimba mask, Baga, Guinea 80 30
1489 240f. Walu mask, Dogon, Mali 90 35
1490 300f. Dogon mask, Bandiagara, Mali 1·00 45

461 Series CC2400 Diesel-electric Locomotive

1997. Trains. Multicoloured.
1491 15f. Type **461** 25 10
1492 90f. Diesel goods locomotive 45 15
1493 100f. Mountain steam locomotive 50 15
1494 240f. Maquinista diesel locomotive 85 35
1495 310f. Series 151-A steam locomotive and goods wagons 1·00 45

462 Cat

1997. The African Golden Cat. Multicoloured.
1496 45f. Type **462** 25 10
1497 100f. Standing on branch 50 15
1498 240f. Lying on branch 75 35
1499 300f. One cat grooming another 1·00 45

463 Lorry crossing Sahara

1998. Dakar–Dakar Motor Rally. Multicoloured.
1500 20f. Type **463** 20 10
1501 45f. Motor cycle at Lac Rose 40 10
1502 190f. Off-road vehicle crossing Mauritanian desert 75 30
1503 240f. Rally car by River Senegal 1·00 35

464 Hut and Children

1998. 25th Anniv of Aldiana Club. Multicoloured.
1504 290f. Type **464** 90 55
1505 320f. Canoe, woman and fish 95 60

465 Children

1998. SOS Children's Village, Ziguinchor. Multicoloured.
1506 190f. Type **465** 60 35
1507 240f. Girl and huts 95 60

466 Diana, Princess of Wales

1998. Diana, Princess of Wales Commemoration. Multicoloured.
1508 240f. Diana wearing hat with veil 95 60

MS1509 Five sheets. (a) 141×198 mm. 200f. T **466** and different designs showing Diana, Princess of Wales; (b) 141×198 mm. 25f. As No. 1508 and 8 different designs showing Diana; (c) 131×94 mm. 1000f. With head on hand; (d) 131×94 mm. 1500f. With Princes William and Harry (e) 138×100 mm. 2000f. Wearing tiara Set of 5 sheets 26·00 14·00

467 Slave House, Goree Island

1998. 150th Anniv of Abolition of Slavery. Multicoloured.
1510 20f. Type **467** 15 10
1511 40f. Frederick Douglas (American abolitionist) 15 10
1512 190f. Mother, child and slave ship 60 35
1513 290f. Victor Schoelcher (French abolitionist and politician) 90 55

468 Museum Emblem, Museum Building and Reyane Henriette Bathily (founder)

1998. 4th Anniv of Henriette Bathily Women's Museum. Multicoloured.
1514 190f. Type **468** 60 25
1515 270f. Emblem, building and Henriette Bathily (different) 95 60

469 Brazilian Player with Football

1998. World Cup Football Championships, France. Multicoloured.
1516 25f. Type **469** 15 10
1517 50f. Mascot, legs, ball and trophy 15 10
1518 150f. Mascot, trophy and ball 45 25
1519 300f. Flags of competing countries 95 60

470 House and Car

1998. Children's Paintings. SOS Children's Village, Ziguinchor. Multicoloured.
1520 30f. Type **470** 10 10
1521 50f. Trees and rainbow 15 10
1522 180f. Sunrise and flowers 60 35
1523 300f. House, road and eyes 95 60

471 Buoy with Siren

1998. Lighthouses and Buoys. Multicoloured.
1524 50f. Type **471** 15 15
1525 100f. Mammelles lighthouse 30 20
1526 190f. Luminescent buoy 60 35
1527 240f. Port entrance lighthouse 75 45

472 Alberto Ascari

1998. Ferrari Formula I Racing Team. Two sheets containing T 472 and similar horiz designs. Multicoloured.

MS1528 (a) 158×125 mm. 100f.×6 Type **472**, Guiseppe Farina, Ricardo Patrese, Michele Alboreto, Elio de Angelis, Andrea de Cesaris; (b) 81×100 mm. 1000f. Ferrari race car Set of two sheets 7·75 4·50

473 Leaning Tower, Pisa

1998. Italia '98 International Stamp Exhibition, Milan (1st issue).
1529 **473** 290f. multicoloured 95 60

See also No. **MS**1559 and **MS**1607.

474 Seagull, Dolphin and Undersea Fauna

1998. International Year of the Ocean. Multicoloured.
1530 190f. Type **474** 60 35
1531 790f. Fish 2·60 1·50

475 Emblem and Beach

1998. Palm Beach Hotel. 50th Anniv of FRAM (travel company). Multicoloured.
1532 240f. Type **475** 75 45
1533 300f. Women and beach scene 95 60

476 Woman wearing Turban

1998. Women's Hair Styles and Headdresses.

1534 **476** 40f. brown, chocolate and black 10 10
1535 - 100f. green, deep green and black 30 20
1536 - 240f. violet, deep violet and black 75 45
1537 - 300f. blue, deep blue and black 95 60

DESIGNS: Type **476**; 100f. Long braided hair; 240f. Braided hair with beads; 300f. Turban tied in front.

477 Figure behind Bars and United Nations Emblem

1998. 50th Anniv of United Nations Declaration of Human Rights. Multicoloured.

1538 200f. Type **477** 60 35
1539 350f. Women and emblem 1·00 60

478 Seagull, Fish and Net

1998. Marine Protection. Multicoloured.

1540 50f. Type **478** 15 10
1541 100f. Fish and effluent pipe 30 20
1542 310f. Dynamite and dead fish 90 55
1543 365f. Fish and oil pollution 1·00 60

479 Smiling Woman

1998. "Senegalese Elegance" (3rd series).

1544 **479** 125f. olive 45 25
1545 **479** 290f. purple 90 55
1546 **479** 310f. purple 95 60

480 Repairing Rally Car

1999. 21st Paris—Dakar Rally. Multicoloured.

1555 150f. Type **480** 45 25
1556 175f. Digging out of sand dune 50 30
1557 240f. Motorcycle crash 75 45
1558 290f. Motorcycle and car sunk in sand 95 60

481 Romy Schneider

1999. Italia '98 International Stamp Exhibition, Milan (2nd issue). Film Actors. Three sheets containing T 481 and similar horiz designs. Multicoloured.

MS1559 (a) 140×195 mm. 200f.×9, Type **481**; Yves Montand; Catherine Deneuve; Gina Lollobrigida; Marcello Mastroianni; Sophia Loren; Frank Sinatra; Dean Martin; Marilyn Monroe; (b) 144×116 mm. 1500f. Marilyn Monroe (different); (c) 144×116 mm. 2000f. Marcello Masstroianni (different) 4·50 2·75

482 Black Coupe

1999. 40th Anniv of De Tomaso (car manufacturer). Sheet 153×103 mm containing T 482 and similar horiz designs. Multicoloured.

MS1560 250f.×4, Type **482**; White coupe; Dark blue coupe; Red coupe 3·00 1·75

483 Elvis Presley

1999. Elvis Presley (entertainer) Commemoration. Sheet 130×175 mm containing T 483 and similar vert designs. Multicoloured.

MS1561 250f. Type **483** and 8 designs showing Elvis Presley 6·00 3·50

484 Stamp and Flags

1999. PhilexFrance '99 International Stamp Exhibition, Paris. 150th Anniv of First French Stamp.

1562 **484** 240f. multicoloured 95 60

485 Ayrton Senna

1999. Formula 1 Racing Drivers. Multicoloured.

1563 200f. Type **485** 80 50

MS1564 (a) 157×120 mm. 200f.×9, Juan Manuel Fangio; Alberto Ascari; Graham Hill; Jim Clark; Jack Brabham; Jackie Stewart; Niki Lauda; Type **485** (design enlarged); Alain Prost; (b) 112×82 mm. 2000f. Ayrton Senna (different) (50×36 mm) 6·00 3·50

486 Knight on Horseback and Knight (chess piece)

1999. Chess. Multicoloured.

1565 250f. Knight and chess piece (different) 95 60

MS1566 Three sheets, each 140×200 mm. (a) 200f. Type **486** and 8 different designs showing soldiers of the Crusades and chess pieces; (b) 250f.×9 Soldiers and chess pieces; (c) 400f.×9 Soldiers and chess pieces (different) Set of 3 sheets 25·00 15·00

487 Jackie Robinson

1999. Jackie Robinson (baseball player) Commemoration. Multicoloured.

1567 250f. Type **487** 95 60

MS1568 Three sheets. (a) 132×177 mm. 1000f. Type **487** and 8 different designs showing Jackie Robinson; (b) 88×138 mm. 1500f. Looking left (36×42 mm); (c) 88×138 mm. 2000f. With raised bat Set of 3 sheets 7·50 4·50

488 Ludger Beerbaum (show jumper)

1999. Equestrian Competitors. Multicoloured.

1569 300f. Type **488** 1·10 65

MS1570 Two sheets. (a) 120×156 mm. 300f.×9, Martin Schaudi; Klaus Balkenhols; Nadine Capellmann Bifar; Willi Melliger; Type **488**; Ulrich Kirchhoff; Sally Clark; Bettina Overesch Boker; Karen O' Connor; (b) 112×82 mm. 1500f. German equestrian team (50×36 mm) Set of 2 sheets 8·50 5·00

489 Mohammed Ali

1999. 25th Anniv of Mohammed Ali—George Forman Boxing Match. Multicoloured.

1571 300f. Type **489** 95 60

MS1572 Three sheets. (a) 132×177 mm. 300f. Type **489** and 8 different designs showing Mohammed Ali; (b) 88×138 mm. 1000f. Wearing robe (36×42 mm) (c) 88×138 mm. 2000f. With raised fists (36×42 mm) 7·50 4·50

490 Pete Sampras

1999. Racquet Sports. Multicoloured.

1573 400f. Type **490** 1·30 80

MS1574 Two sheets. (a) 120×156 mm. 400f.×9, Liu Guoliang (tennis player); Martina Hingis (tennis); Deng Yaping (table tennis player); Andre Agassi (tennis); Jean-Philippe Gatien (table tennis); Anna Kournikova (tennis); Mikael Appelgren (table tennis); Type **490** (tennis); Jan-Ove Waldner (table tennis); (b) 112×82 mm. 2000f. Vladimir Samsonov, Deng Yaping and Jörg Rosskopf (table tennis players) (50×36 mm) Set of 2 sheets 12·00 7·00

491 Racing Yachts

1999. Transport. Multicoloured.

1575 250f. Type **491** 95 60
1576 325f. Bentley coupe 1·00 60
1577 350f. Prussian locomotive S10 1·10 65
1578 375f. Ducati 900 SS motorbike 1·20 70
1579 500f. Concorde super sonic aircraft 1·50 90

MS1580 Ten sheets. (a) 155×119 mm. Ships:—250f.×9, *France* (liner); United States (liner); *Finnjet* (ferry); *Chusan* (liner); *Cheers* (inscr "Sheers") (catamaran); *Vendredi 13* (racing yacht); Type **491**; *Pen Duick II* (transatlantic ketch); *Jester* (transatlantic yacht); (b) 155×119 mm. Cars:—325f.×9, Duryea (1893); Menon (1897); Renault; Fiat Zero (1912); Inscr "Spa" (1913); Packard; As No. 1525; Mercedes Benz; Morris Minor (1930); (c) 155×119 mm Steam trains:—350f.×9, *Mikado*; French locomotive 241 P (1948); French locomotive 230 K; The Milwaukee road class A locomotive (1935) Russian locomotive class 1.5; Prussian locomotive G12; As No. 1526; Inscr "Austrian locomotive KK SEB series 310"; French locomotive *Outrance* (1877) (d) 155×119 mm. 375f.×9, Zenith motorcycle and sidecar (1913) Brough Superior motor cycle (1920); Motor cycle racing, 1903; As No. 1257; Dave Thorpe (motocross rider); Suzuki 500 motorcycle; Michaux bicycle (1865); Modern solid wheel racing cycle; Woman cyclist (e) 155×119 mm. High speed trains:—450f.×9, Acela, USA; Class 332 Britain; I.C.E., Germany; Trans Europe Express locomotive, Luxembourg; California–Nevada Super Speed monorail, USA; Inter City 250, Britain; Korean high speed locomotive; Eurostar locomotive, Britain; TGV Thalys PBA, France (f) 155×119 mm. Aircraft:—500f.×9, USA; USA Maglifter launch catapult; Inscr "S.M." (USA); Concorde; Inscr "T.U. 144" (URSS); Inscr "Futur X USA"; USA X 33; Type **491**; USA X 34 space vehicle (g) 121×92 mm. 1000f. Eric Tabarly and *Pen Duick VI* (51×36 mm) (h) 121×92 mm.1500f. Walter Chrysler and Chrysler (1924) (i) 122×92 mm. 1500f. Marc Seguin and steam locomotive (36×51 mm) (j) 112×82 mm. 2000f. Bobby Julich (cycle racer) (51×36 mm) (k) 122×92 mm. TGV locomotive *Atlantique*, TGV *Mediterraneé* and *Etienne Chambron* (l) 122×92 mm. 2000f. Concorde (51×36 mm) Set of 10 sheets 65·00 38·00

492 Evacuation of Sinking Ship

1999. Sinking of Titanic (liner), 1912. Multicoloured.

1581 300f. Type **492** 95 60

MS1582	155×119 mm. 300f.×9, In shipyard; At the dockside; Pulled by tugboat; At sea; Collision with iceberg; Type **492**; Expedition to wreck; Couple lost in accident; Captain John Smith	9·00	5·00

493 Russian R.D. 107 Rocket

1999. Spacecraft. Two sheets containing T 493 and similar multicoloured designs.

MS1583	(a) 140×200 mm. 400f.×9, Type **493**; Russian Soyuz; Russian Proton; USA Atlas-Centaur; USA Atlas-Agena; USA Atlas-mercury; USA Titan 2; USA Juno 2; USA Saturn I; (b) 122×92 mm. Neil Armstrong (51×36 mm) Set of 2 sheets	12·00	7·00

494 Book, Men and National Colours

1999. International Year of the Elderly. Multicoloured.

1584	30f. Type **494**	15	10
1585	150f. Blacksmith	45	25
1586	290f. Musicians	90	55
1587	300f. Scientist (vert)	95	60

495 Death Cap (*Amanita phalloides*) (inscr "Amanite phalloide")

1999. Fungi. Senegal Scouts. Multicoloured.

1588	60f. Type **495**	20	10
1589	175f. Common ink cap (*Coprinus atramantarius*)	60	35
1590	220f. Destroying angel (*Amanita virosa*) (inscr "Amanite vireuse")	75	45
1591	250f. Field mushroom (*Agaricus campestri*) (inscr "campester")	95	60

496 Astronauts and Flag on Moon

1999. 30th Anniv of First Moon Landing. Multicoloured.

1592	25f. Type **496**	15	10
1593	145f. Neil Armstrong, flag and astronaut (vert)	45	25
1594	180f. Astronaut, flag and rocket (vert)	55	30
1595	500f. Astronaut and space shuttle (vert)	1·50	90

497 Roan Antelope (*Hippotragus equines*)

1999. Fauna. Multicoloured.

1596	60f. Type **497**	20	10
1597	90f. Oyster catcher (*Haematopus ostralegus*)	30	20
1598	300f. White-face whistling duck (*Dendrocygna viduata*) (inscr "viduada")	95	60
1599	320f. Leatherback turtle (*Dermochelys coriacea*)	95	60

498 Mother Teresa and Child

1999. 20th Anniv of Award of Nobel Peace Prize to Mother Teresa (humanitarian). Multicoloured.

1600	75f. Type **498**	20	10
1601	100f. With children	45	25
1602	290f. With priest	80	50
1603	300f. Holding laughing child	1·00	60

499 Emblem and Rainbows

1999. 125th Anniv of Universal Postal Union. Multicoloured.

1604	270f. Type **499**	90	55
1605	300f. Emblem	1·10	65

500 "Mont Sainte-Victoire seen from Bibemus Quarry"

1999. Art. Four sheets containing T 500 and similar multicoloured designs showing paintings by artists named.

MS1606	(a) Horiz. 195×141 mm. Paul Cezanne. 200f. ×9, Type **500**; "Sea at l'Estaque"; "Landscape"; "Still Life"; "Still Life with Basket"; "Still Life with Apples and Peaches"; "Bibemus Quarry"; "Woods with Millstone"; "Lake Annecy". (b) Vert. 113×163 mm. Paul Gauguin. 250f. ×4, "Te Faaturuma (Brooding Woman)"; "The Cellist (Portrait of Upaupa Scheklud)"; "Self-portrait with Halo"; "When are you getting Married?". (c) Vert. 113×163 mm. Pablo Picasso. 375f. ×4, "Cavalier with Pipe"; "Rembrandt Figure and Eros"; "Female Nude and Smoker"; "The Doves". (d) Vert. 156×120 mm. Vincent van Gogh. 2000f. "Dr. Paul Gachet" Set of 4 sheets	12·50	7·50

501 Clark Gable

1999. Italia '98 International Stamp Exhibition, Milan (3rd issue). Film Actors. Four sheets containing T 501 and similar vert designs. Multicoloured.

MS1607	(a) 136×196 mm. 250f. ×9, Type **501**; Rudolph Valentino; Errol Flynn; Cary Grant; Robert Taylor; Gary Cooper; James Dean; Humphrey Bogart; Marlon Brando. (b) 136×196 mm. 425f. ×9, Grace Kelly; Marilyn Monroe; Audrey Hepburn; Greta Garbo; Jean Harlow; Loretta Young; Jane Russell; Dorothy Lamour; Veronica Lake. (c) 140×200 mm. 450f. ×9, Ginger Rogers and Fred Astaire; Cary Grant, Katherine Hepburn and James Stewart; Melvyn Douglas and Greta Garbo; Vivien Leigh and Clark Gable; Burt Lancaster and Deborah Kerr; Humphrey Bogart and Lauren Bacall; Steve McQueen and Jacqueline Bisset; Gene Kelly and Rita Hayworth; Ingrid Bergman and Cary Grant. (d) 116×143 mm. 2000f. Grace Kelly (different) Set of 4 sheets	24·00	14·50

502 Betty Boop holding Microphone

1999. Betty Boop (cartoon character created by Max Fleischer). Multicoloured.

1608	250f. Type **502**	50	30
1609	250f. Holding guitar	50	30
1610	400f. Seated	80	50
MS1611	Five sheets. (a) 132×177 mm. 250f. ×9, Holding saxophone; Playing tambourine; 1609; Playing guitar; Wearing top hat; Holding drum sticks; Wearing headphones; 1608; Wearing patterned trousers. (b) 132×177 mm. 400f. ×9, Wearing red dress; Wearing flowered earrings, bracelets and belt; Wearing ruffled blouse and waistcoat; Wearing purple dress; 1610; Wearing black outfit; Wearing fringed waistcoat; Wearing black sleeveless dress; Wearing purple jacket and trousers. (c) 89×140 mm. 1000f. Head and shoulders. (d) 89×140 mm. 1500f. With folded arms. (e) 89×140 mm. 2000f. Wearing purple jacket Set of 5 sheets	20·00	12·00

503 Lucy (Lucille Ball)

1999. I Love Lucy (Television comedy series). Multicoloured.

1612	300f. Type **503**	60	40
1613	300f. Fred Mertz (William Fawley), Ethel Mertz (Vivian Vance) and Lucy	60	40
MS1614	Four sheets. (a) Vert. 137×182 mm. 330f. ×9, Lucy holding telephone; No. 1612; Wearing green dress with black tie; With hand raised; Wearing pearl necklace and black hat; Holding medicine bottle; Wearing hat, glasses and fur stole; Wearing purple hat; Wearing top hat. (b) Horiz. 177×132 mm. 330f. ×9, With Ethel holding boxes; Desi Arnaz, Lucy, Fred and Ethel; Fred, Ethel and Lucy wearing headscarf; Lucy and chicks; Fred, Ethel, Lucy and Desi seated at table; Ethel and Lucy; Lucy dancing wearing rolled up trousers; As No. 1613; Lucy, Ethel and Fred seated at table. (c) 89×127 mm. 1000f. Lucy holding box (36×51 mm). (d) 117×89 mm. 2000f. Lucy holding paper bag (36×51 mm) Set of 4 sheets	18·00	11·00

504 Three Stooges

1999. The Three Stooges (comedy series starring Moe Howard, Larry Fine and Curly Howard). Multicoloured.

1615	400f. Type **504**	80	50
MS1616	Three sheets. (a) Horiz. 175×140 mm. 400f. ×9, Moe and Larry lying on bed; Moe, Larry and Curly; Moe and Larry listening to telephone ("False Alarms"); Holding scissors; As No. 1615; With surgical trolley ("Dizzy Doctors"); Larry and Curly holding Moe down; Holding step ladder; Holding plank ("Tassels in the Air"). (b) Vert. 140×89 mm. 1000f. Curly and Moe with feathers. (c) Vert. 140×89 mm. 1500f. Curly as cowboy Set of 3 sheets	12·00	7·25

505 Participants and Pyramids

2001. 22nd Paris—Dakar Rally. Multicoloured.

1617	75f. Type **505**	15	10
1618	100f. Truck, four-wheel drive and rally car	20	10
1619	220f. Truck and motorcycle	45	25
1620	320f. Camel and motorcycle	65	40

506 Motorcyclist and Rally Emblem

2001. 23rd Paris—Dakar Rally. Multicoloured.

1621	190f. Type **506**	40	25
1622	220f. Emblem as face (vert)	45	25
1623	240f. Emblem containing camel (vert)	50	30
1624	790f. Emblem and four-wheel drive car	1·60	95

507 Festival of Arts and Culture Emblem

2001. Third Millennium. Multicoloured.

1625	20f. Type **507**	10	10
1626	100f. Pan African Plastic Arts festival emblem	20	10
1627	150f. National Heritage Day emblem	30	20
1628	300f. Memorial, Goree Island (anti-slavery memorial) (horiz)	60	35

508 Swimmer and Weightlifter

2001. Olympic Games, Sydney (2000). Multicoloured.

1629	40f. Type **508**	10	10
1630	80f. Taekwondo	15	10
1631	240f. Runners finishing 200m race	50	30

1632	290f. Handball match	60	35

509 Flower Seller

2001. Craft Market, Kermel. Multicoloured.

1633	50f. Type **509**	10	10
1634	90f. Wooden carvings	20	10
1635	250f. Bowls and pendants (horiz)	50	30
1636	350f. Carvings and flower seller	70	40

510 Satellite Dish, Globe and Weather Station

2001. 50th Anniv of World Meteorological Organization. Multicoloured.

1637	100f. Type **510**	20	10
1638	790f. Weather station (vert)	1·60	95

511 *Maytenus senegalensis*

2001. Medicinal Plants. Multicoloured.

1639	240f. Type **511**	50	30
1640	320f. *Boscia senegalensis*	65	40
1641	350f. *Euphorbia hirta*	70	40
1642	500f. *Guiera senegalensis*	1·00	60

512 Outline of Senegal

2001. 19th Lions International District 403 Congress, Dakar. Multicoloured.

1643	190f. Type **512**	40	25
1644	300f. Lion (vert)	60	35

513 Emblem, Tank and Runners

2001. 50th Anniv of United Nations High Commissioner for Refugees. Multicoloured.

1645	240f. Type **513**	50	30
1646	320f. Emblem, globe and runner (vert)	65	40

514 Hands holding Book

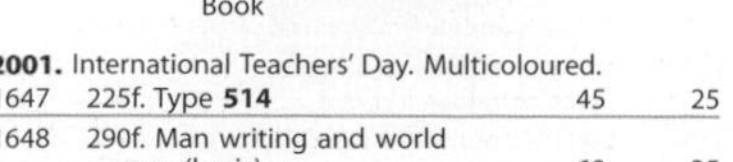

2001. International Teachers' Day. Multicoloured.

1647	225f. Type **514**	45	25
1648	290f. Man writing and world map (horiz)	60	35

515 Drummer

2001. Tourism. Multicoloured.

1649	145f. Type **515**	30	20
1650	290f. Tree, windsurfer, and beach (vert)	60	35

516 Antelope and Lioness

2001. National Parks. Multicoloured.

1651	75f. Type **516**	15	10
1652	125f. Heron and marabou stork	25	15
1653	275f. Crowned cranes and elephant	55	35
1654	300f. Zebra (vert)	60	35

517 Motorcyclists

2002. 24th Paris—Dakar Rally (inscr "2001"). Multicoloured.

1655	250f. Type **517**	50	30
1656	360f. Four-wheel drive race cars	75	45
1657	370f. Eiffel tower and motorcyclist (vert)	80	50
1658	425f. Motorcyclist (vert)	90	55

518 Trophy, Footballers and Flags

2002. African Nations Football Championship. Multicoloured.

1659	250f. Type **518**	50	30
1660	380f. Players in front of goal	80	50
1661	425f. Saving goal	90	55
1662	440f. Trophy and player (vert)	90	55

519 Peulh Woman

520 Linguere Woman

2002. Senegalese Women.

1663	**519**	5f. magenta	10	10
1664	**519**	10f. yellow	10	10
1665	**519**	20f. orange	10	10
1666	**519**	25f. red	10	10
1667	**519**	40f. magenta	10	10
1668	**519**	50f. blue	10	10
1669	**519**	60f. green	15	10
1670	**519**	70f. green	15	10
1671	**519**	100f. green	20	10
1672	**519**	150f. olive	30	20
1673	**519**	175f. brown	35	20
1674	**520**	200f. olive	40	25
1675	**520**	250f. orange	50	30
1676	**520**	290f. red	60	35
1677	**520**	300f. purple	60	35
1678	**520**	360f. violet	75	45
1679	**520**	390f. blue	80	50
1680	**520**	425f. green	90	55
1681	**520**	500f. bistre	1·00	60
1682	**520**	800f. black	1·70	1·00
1683	**520**	1000f. blue	2·10	1·30

521 Map of Africa

2002. Proclamation of African Union Act. Multicoloured.

1684	330f. Type **521**	70	40
1685	390f. Flags, hands and map (horiz)	80	50

522 Gate of the Third Millennium, Dakar

2002. New Millennium. Showing the Millennium Gate. Multicoloured.

1686	200f. Type **522**	40	25
1687	290f. Front of gate	60	35
1688	390f. Rear of gate	80	50
1689	725f. Rocks and gate	1·50	90

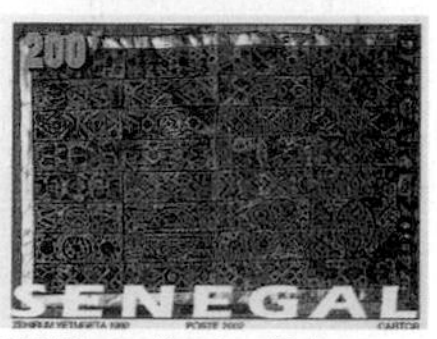

523 Woven Hanging (Zehum Yetmgeta)

2002. Dak'Art 2002 Biennial Art Exhibition. Multicoloured.

1690	200f. Type **523**	40	25
1691	330f. Sculpture (Moustapha Dime) (vert)	70	40
1692	400f. Woven Hanging (Abdoulaye Konate)	85	50
1693	425f. Two figures (painting) (Gora Mbengue)	90	55

524 Trophy and Football

2002. World Cup Football Championship, Japan and South Korea. Multicoloured.

1694	75f.+100f. Type **524**	35	20
1695	200f.+100f. Trophy and emblem (36×27 mm)	60	35
1696	290f.+50f. Stadium and football (36×27 mm)	70	40
1697	360f.+50f. Hands holding trophy and goalposts (36×27 mm)	85	50

525 Map, Star and Globe

2002. Culture and Sport. "Senegal Wins".

1698	**525**	200f. multicoloured	40	25
1699	**525**	380f. multicoloured	80	50

526 Globe, Rainbow, Skyscraper and Traditional Dwellings

2002. United Nations Year of Dialogue among Civilizations. Multicoloured.

1700	290f. Type **526**	60	35
1701	380f. Children surrounding globe	80	50

527 "Le Mbayar du Baol" (race horse)

2002. Senegalese Race Horses. Multicoloured.

1702	30f. Type **527**	10	10
1703	200f. "Le Mpar du Cayor"	40	25
1704	250f. "Le Narougor"	50	30
1705	300f. "Le Foutanke"	60	35

528 Sacred Baobab Tree

2002. International Year of Eco-Tourism. Multicoloured.

1706	90f. Type **528**	20	10
1707	250f. Pelican, Du Djoudj National Park	50	30
1708	300f. Mangroves	60	35
1709	380f. Rope bridge	80	50

529 Gorillas

2002. Fauna. Multicoloured.

1710	75f. Type **529**	15	10
1711	290f. Black rhinoceros	60	35
1712	360f. Ostrich and tortoise	75	45
1713	380f. Giraffes (vert)	80	50

530 Four-wheel Drive Race Cars

2003. 25th Paris–Dakar Rally. Multicoloured.

1714	360f. Type **530**	75	45
1715	425f. Motorcyclists	90	55

531 Hands holding Document and Rose

2003. New Partnership for Africa's Development (NEPAD). Multicoloured.

1716	200f. Type **531**	40	25
1717	250f. Map of Africa and symbols of renewal	50	30
1718	290f. Gannet and map	60	35

532 Animal Sacrifice

2003. Art. Multicoloured.

1719	250f. Type **532**	50	30
1720	360f. Faces	75	45

533 "Le Cailcedrat Mort"

2003. Sculpture. Multicoloured.

1721	200f. Type **533**	40	25
1722	300f. "Tete d'un Sorcier"	60	35
1723	380f. "Le Laard"	80	50
1724	440f. "Le Thioury"	90	55

534 Le Goumbe Lebon

2003. Traditional Costumes. Multicoloured.

1725	250f. Type **534**	50	30
1726	360f. La Badiaranke	75	45
1727	390f. Le Grand Boubou	80	50
1728	500f. Le Bowede	1·00	60

535 *Cymbium cymbium*

2003. Marine Fauna. Multicoloured.

1729	290f. Type **535**	60	35
1730	370f. Herrings	80	50
1731	380f. Catfish	80	50
1732	400f. *Chelonia mydas*	85	50

536 Motorcyclists

2004. 26th Paris–Dakar Rally (inscr "2003"). Multicoloured.

1733	390f. Type **536**	80	50
1734	500f. Four-wheel drive race car and motorcyclist	1·00	60

537 Emblem

2004. African Nations Cup Football Championship. Multicoloured.

1735	200f. Type **537**	20	10
1736	300f. Trophy, stadium, football and television (horiz)	60	35
1737	400f. Shaking hands (horiz)	85	50
1738	425f. Match play (horiz)	90	55

2004. Senegalese Women.

1739	**519**	125f. silver	25	15
1740	**520**	350f. violet	75	45
1741	**520**	600f. black	1·20	70
1742	**520**	700f. violet	1·40	85

See also Nos. 1739-1742.

538 Dakar Railway Station

2004. Cultural Heritage. Architecture. Multicoloured.

1743	240f. Type **538**	50	30
1744	370f. Podor fort	80	50
1745	390f. Town Hall	80	50
1746	500f. Notre Dame de Victoires Cathedral	1·00	60

539 Mosque, Omarienne de Guede

2004. Places of Worship. Multicoloured.

1747	200f. Type **539**	40	25
1748	225f. Popenguine Basilica (vert)	50	30
1749	250f. Grand Mosque, Touba	50	30
1750	300f. Grand Mosque, Tivaouane	60	35

540 Millet

2004. Local Cereals. Multicoloured.

1751	100f. Type **540**	20	10
1752	150f. Millet and maize (horiz)	30	20
1753	200f. Maize	40	25
1754	300f. Rice (horiz)	60	35

541 Race Truck and Motorcyclist

2005. 27th Paris–Dakar Rally. Multicoloured.

1755	450f. Type **541**	95	60
1756	550f. Emblem and dunes (vert)	1·10	65

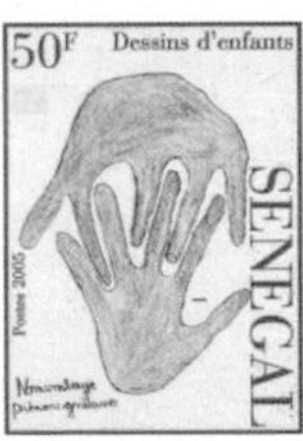

542 Hands (Mbaye Gnilane)

2005. Children's Drawings. Multicoloured.

1757	50f. Type **542**	20	20
1758	75f. Village (Pape Cheick Diack) (*horiz*)	30	30
1759	100f. Dove carrying leaf (Aly Gueye) (*horiz*)	35	35
1760	425f. School (Abdourahim Diallo) (*horiz*)	1·50	1·50

543 Tents and Race Car

2006. 28th Paris—Dakar Rally. Multicoloured.

1761	500f. Type **543**	1·80	1·80
1762	1000f. Repair to race car and men carrying vehicle doors	3·50	3·50

544 Family Discussion

2006. AIDS Awareness Campaign. Multicoloured.

1763	200f. Type **544**	75	75
1764	250f. Virus (*vert*)	90	90
1765	290f. Couples (fidelity)	1·10	1·10
1766	425f. Adults in circle	1·50	1·50

545 'Toorodo Penlh' (inscr '2005')

2006. African Dolls. Multicoloured.

1767	200f. Type **545**	75	75
1768	250f. La Reine Signare	90	90
1768a	375f. Zulu Afrique du Sud	1·30	1·30
1768b	425f. Femme Woloff-Senegal	1·50	1·50

546 Symbols of Communication

2006. World Numerical Solidarity Day. Multicoloured.

1769	200f. Type **546**	75	75
1770	250f. Globe, speaking over telephone and four clasped hands	90	90
1771	370f. Satellite, computer circuits and map of Senegal (*horiz*)	1·30	1·30
1772	380f. Hand, cable, satellite and computer (*horiz*)	1·40	1·40

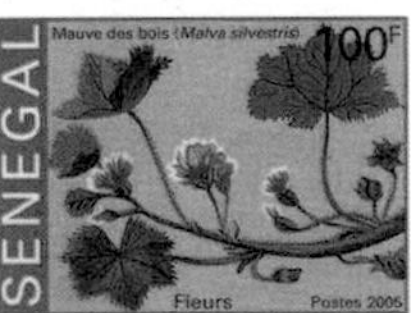

547 *Malva silvestris* (mallow)

2006. Flowering Plants. Multicoloured.

1773	100f. Type **547**	35	35
1774	150f. *Moringa oleifera* (*vert*)	55	55
1775	300f. *Cichorum intybus* (chicory) (*vert*)	1·10	1·10
1776	450f. Dandelion (*Taraxacum*)	1·60	1·60

548 Combatants sparring

2006. Traditional Wrestling. Multicoloured.

1777	100f. Type **548**	35	35
1778	200f. Wrestling	75	75
1779	250f. Mud covered wrestler (*vert*)	90	90
1780	500f. Drummers and wrestler (preparation mystique) (*vert*)	1·80	1·80

549 'Demba & Dupont' (statue of Senegalese and French soldier)

2006. Tirailleur Senegalais Day. Multicoloured.

1781	200f. Type **549**	75	75
1782	450f. Demba & Dupont	1·60	1·60

550 Leopold Senghor

2006. Birth Centenary of Leopold Sedar Senghor (poet and politician) (first president 1960—80).

1783	**550**	200f. multicoloured	75	75
1784	**550**	450f. multicoloured	1·60	1·60

551 Women struggling

2006. Campaign against Female Excision. Multicoloured.

1785	50f. Type **551**	20	20
1786	200f. Women and children	75	75
1787	350f. Health workers and woman	1·20	1·20
1788	370f. Women and girl	1·30	1·30

551a *Luscinia phoenicurus*

2006. Birds. Multicoloured.

1788a	30f. Type **551a**	10	10
1788b	75f. Inscr 'Rouge gorge bleu' (vert)	25	25
1788c	200f. *Pica pica* (magpie) (vert)	75	75
1788d	400f. Crow (vert)	1·40	1·40

552 Competitors

2007. 29th Paris—Dakar Rally. Multicoloured.

1789	450f. Type **552**	1·60	1·60
1790	550f. Motorcyclist	1·40	1·40

553 Hands Exchanging Book and Sharing Food

2007. National Solidarity Day. Multicoloured.

1791	50f. Type **553**	20	20
1792	100f. Hands holding star and map outline	35	35
1793	200f. Map outline and hands placing goods in bowl	75	75
1794	500f. Map outline and symbols of prosperity	1·80	1·80

554 Emblem

2007. Gorée Diaspora Cutural Festival. Multicoloured.

1795	50f. Type **554**	20	20
1796	200f. Art installation (horiz)	75	75
1797	450f. Building and hands writing with quill	1·60	1·60
1798	525f. Sail ship	1·90	1·90

554a *Strichnos nux vomica*

2007. Flora. Multicoloured.

1798a	200f. Type **554a**	75	75
1798b	290f. *Conium macultum*	1·10	1·10
1798c	300f. Succulent	1·20	1·20
1798d	450f. Pitcher Plant	1·60	1·60

555 Flamingoes and Monkey (Sine Saloum Delta)

2008. Tourism. Multicoloured.

1799	75f. Type **555**	25	25
1800	125f. Cockatoo, Roan antelope and cheetah (Niokolo-Koba Park)	45	45
1801	200f. Lion, giraffe and elephant (Niokolo-Koba Park)	75	75
1802	450f. Pelicans and Faidherbe Bridge (Saint Louis)	1·60	1·60

556 Preventing Tree Felling

2008. Protection of the Environment. Multicoloured.

1803	100f. Type **556**	35	35
1804	200f. No bonfires (vert)	75	75
1805	300f. Boy collecting litter	1·10	1·10
1806	450f. Trees with guards	1·60	1·60

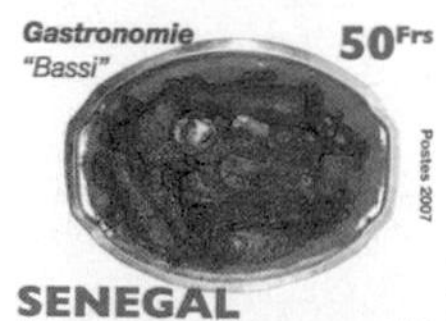

557 Bassi

2008. Gastronomy. Sheet 120×90 mm containing T 557 and similar horiz designs. Multicoloured.

MS1807	50f. Type **557**; 200f. Yassa poulet; 250f. Thieboudiene; 500f. Yassa poisson	3·50	3·50

558 Motor Cyclist and Camel

2009. 30th Paris–Dakar Rally. Multicoloured.

1808	450f. Type **558**	1·60	1·60
1809	550f. Motor cyclist and rally car (horiz)	1·90	1·90

559 Child reading Braille Book

2009. Birth Centenary of Louis Braille (inventor of Braille writing for the blind). Multicoloured.

1810	200f. Type **559**	75	75
1811	450f. Braille letters	1·60	1·60

560 Mother receiving Bouquet

2009. Mothers' Day. Multicoloured.

1812	200f. Type **560**	75	75
1813	450f. Mother and daughter hugging (vert)	1·60	1·60

561 Demonstrators (freedom of expression)

2010. Democracy and Liberty. Multicoured.

1814	150f. Type **561**	60	60
1815	250f. Woman with voting registration card (right to voter registration card)	80	80
1816	400f. Woman voting (right to vote freely and democratically)	1·20	1·20
1817	450f. Symbols of communication (freedom of press, radio and television)	1·60	1·60

Nos. 1814/17 are inscribed '2006'.

562 Coin and BCEAO Emblem

2010. Economic and Monetary Union of West Africa

1818	500f. Type **562**	10	10
1819	790f. Central Bank of States of West Africa (BCEAO) building, Dakar, UEMOA emblem and BCEAO emblem (horiz)	2·75	2·75

Nos. 1818/19 are inscribed for 11th anniversary of UEMOA.
Nos. 1818/19 are inscribed '2006'.
T **562** and similar multicoloured design.

563 Ndaw rabine

2010. Tradtional Dances. Multicoloured.

1820	100f. Type **563**	75	75
1821	200f. Niary gorom (horiz)	85	85
1822	250f. Dagathe	90	90
1823	450f. Ndaa daly	1·60	1·60

Nos. 1820/3 are inscribed '2009'.

564 Praying Mantis

2010. Insects. Multicoloured.

1824	150f. Type **564**	60	60
1825	200f. Wasp	80	80
1826	250f. Grasshopper	90	90
1827	500f. Ant	1·70	1·70

OFFICIAL STAMPS

O45 Arms of Dakar

1961. Figures of value in black.

O240	**O45**	1f. black and blue	10	10
O241	**O45**	2f. blue and yellow	10	10
O242	**O45**	5f. lake and green	10	10
O243	**O45**	10f. red and blue	10	10
O244	**O45**	25f. blue and red	45	15
O245	**O45**	50f. red and grey	75	30
O246	**O45**	85f. purple and orange	1·40	45
O247	**O45**	100f. red and green	2·25	1·10

O78 Baobab Tree

1966

O339	**O78**	1f. black and yellow	10	10
O340	**O78**	5f. black and orange	10	10
O341	**O78**	10f. black and red	10	10
O342	**O78**	20f. black and purple	15	10
O342a	**O78**	25f. black and mauve	15	10
O343	**O78**	30f. black and blue	15	10
O344	**O78**	35f. black and blue	45	10
O344a	**O78**	40f. black and blue	20	10
O1122	**O78**	50f. black and red	20	15
O345	**O78**	55f. black and green	65	20
O345a	**O78**	60f. black and green	45	20
O346	**O78**	90f. black and green	1·00	35
O347	**O78**	100f. black & brown	1·10	40
O1123	**O78**	145f. black and green	1·00	35
O1124	**O78**	180f. black & orange	1·10	45

1969. No. O345 surch.

O390	60f. on 55f. black & grn	1·10	10

POSTAGE DUE STAMPS

1903. Postage Due stamps of French Colonies surch.

D30	**U**	10 on 50c. purple	£120	£110
D31	**U**	10 on 60c. brown on buff	£110	£120
D32	**U**	10 on 1f. pink on buff	£325	£325

1906. "Natives" key-type.

D50	**L**	5c. green and red	2·00	3·25
D51	**L**	10c. purple and blue	4·50	3·75
D52	**L**	15c. blue and red on blue	3·75	10·00
D53	**L**	20c. black & red on yellow	5·50	2·75
D54	**L**	30c. red and blue on cream	8·25	12·00
D55	**L**	50c. violet and red	7·25	22·00
D56	**L**	60c. black and red on buff	10·00	17·00
D57	**L**	1f. black and red on pink	12·00	60·00

1915. "Figure" key-type.

D81	**M**	5c. green	1·00	5·00
D82	**M**	10c. red	55	2·75
D83	**M**	15c. grey	85	5·25
D84	**M**	20c. brown	90	3·50
D85	**M**	30c. blue	1·80	3·00
D86	**M**	50c. black	2·50	3·75
D87	**M**	60c. orange	3·25	9·75
D88	**M**	1r. violet	3·00	1·80

1927. Surch in figures.

D133	2f. on 1f. purple	3·25	17·00
D134	3f. on 1f. brown	3·75	14·50

D40

1935

D194	**D40**	5c. green	35	5·75
D195	**D40**	10c. orange	30	6·75
D196	**D40**	15c. violet	30	7·00
D197	**D40**	20c. olive	30	5·75
D198	**D40**	30c. brown	40	7·00
D199	**D40**	50c. purple	55	6·75
D200	**D40**	60c. yellow	1·70	7·25
D201	**D40**	1f. black	1·00	7·00
D202	**D40**	2f. blue	2·50	9·50
D203	**D40**	3f. red	1·60	8·25

D43

1961

D239	**D43**	1f. orange and red	10	10
D240	**D43**	2f. blue and red	10	10
D241	**D43**	5f. brown and red	10	10
D242	**D43**	20f. green and red	25	25
D243	**D43**	25f. purple and red	65	65

D77 Lion's Head

1966. Head in gold and black; value in black.

D339	**D77**	1f. red	15	15
D340	**D77**	2f. brown	15	15
D341	**D77**	5f. violet	20	20
D342	**D77**	10f. blue	40	40
D343	**D77**	20f. green	50	50
D344	**D77**	30f. grey	65	65
D345	**D77**	60f. blue	65	65
D346	**D77**	90f. purple	75	75

Pt. 6

SENEGAMBIA AND NIGER

A French colony later re-named Upper Senegal and Niger, and later French Sudan.

100 centimes = 1 franc.

1903. "Tablet" key-type inscr "SENEGAMBIE ET NIGER" in red (1, 5, 15, 25, 75c., 1f.) or blue (others).

22	**D**	1c. black on blue	2·00	5·75
23	**D**	2c. brown on buff	65	3·00
24	**D**	4c. brown on grey	3·00	6·50
25	**D**	5c. green	6·00	3·75
26	**D**	10c. red	8·50	4·00
27	**D**	15c. grey	30·00	18·00
28	**D**	20c. red on green	21·00	44·00
29	**D**	25c. blue	28·00	55·00
30	**D**	30c. brown on drab	14·00	55·00
31	**D**	40c. red on yellow	22·00	65·00
32	**D**	50c. brown on blue	60·00	85·00
33	**D**	75c. brown on orange	55·00	95·00
34	**D**	1f. green	70·00	£120

Pt. 3

SERBIA

A kingdom in the Balkans, S.E. Europe. Part of Yugoslavia since 1918, except during the Second World War when stamps were issued by a German sponsored Government.

1866. 40 para = 1 grosch.
1880. 100 para = 1 dinar.

2 Prince Michael (Obrenovic III)

1866. Perf.

12	2	10p. orange	£130	£170
15	2	20p. red	22·00	34·00
14	2	40p. blue	85·00	55·00

3 Prince Milan (Obrenovic IV)

1869. Perf.

42	3	10p. brown	13·50	7·25
45	3	10p. orange	3·25	9·00
31c	3	15p. orange	£100	45·00
46	3	20p. blue	2·20	4·00
39b	3	25p. red	3·25	9·00
34c	3	35p. green	6·75	8·00
47	3	40p. mauve	3·25	11·00
36	3	50p. green	13·50	22·00

5 King Milan I

1880. Perf.

54a	5	5p. green	2·20	55
55	5	10p. red	3·25	55
56	5	20p. orange	1·70	1·10
57a	5	25p. blue	2·20	1·70
58	5	50p. brown	2·20	7·25
59	5	1d. violet	16·00	17·00

6 King Alexander (Obrenovic V)

1890

60	6	5p. green	55	20
61	6	10p. red	1·90	20
62	6	15p. lilac	1·70	20
63	6	20p. orange	1·10	20
64	6	25p. blue	2·20	55
65	6	50p. brown	4·50	4·50
66	6	1d. lilac	17·00	13·50

7 King Alexander (Obrenovic V)

1894

75	7	1p. red	45	20
76	7	5p. green	5·50	20
68	7	10p. red	8·50	20
69	7	15p. lilac	13·50	35
79	7	20p. orange	8·50	35
80	7	25p. blue	4·25	35
81a	7	50p. brown	14·00	1·00
73	7	1d. green	2·20	4·50
74	7	1d. brown on blue	28·00	4·50

1900. Surch.

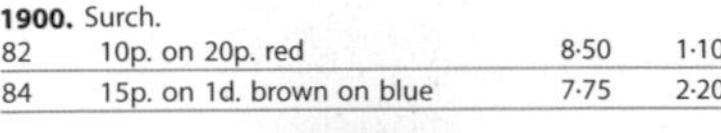

82	10p. on 20p. red	8·50	1·10
84	15p. on 1d. brown on blue	7·75	2·20

10 King Alexander (Obrenovic V)

1901

85a	10	5p. green	55	35
86	10	10p. red	55	35
87	10	15p. purple	55	35
88	10	20p. yellow	55	35
89	10	25p. blue	55	35
90	10	50p. yellow	1·10	85
91	-	1d. brown	1·70	2·75
92a	-	3d. pink	17·00	22·00
93a	-	5d. violet	17·00	22·00

The 1d. to 5d. are larger.

12 King Alexander 1 (Obrenovic V)

1903. Optd with shield.

94	12	1p. black and red	1·30	1·70
95	12	5p. black and green	1·10	55
96	12	10p. black and red	80	55
97	12	15p. black and grey	80	55
98	12	20p. black and yellow	1·10	55
99	12	25p. black and blue	1·10	55
100	12	50p. black and grey	6·75	1·70
101	12	1d. black and green	17·00	6·75
102	12	3d. black and lilac	4·75	5·00
103	12	5d. black and brown	4·75	5·50

1903. Surch with arms and new value.

104	1p. on 5d. black and brown	3·25	17·00

14 Karageorge and Petar 1

1904. Coronation. Centenary of Karageorgevic Dynasty. Dated "1804 1904".

108	14	5p. green	1·10	55
109	14	10p. red	1·10	55
110	14	15p. purple	1·10	55
111	14	25p. blue	2·00	1·10
112	14	50p. brown	2·20	2·20
113	-	1d. bistre	3·25	7·75
114	-	3d. green	4·50	11·00
115	-	5d. violet	5·50	13·50

DESIGN: 1, 3, 5d. Karageorge and insurgents, 1804.

16 Petar I

1905

116	16	1p. black and grey	35	10
117	16	5p. black and green	1·70	20
118	16	10p. black and red	4·00	20
119	16	15p. black and mauve	4·50	20
120	16	20p. black and yellow	7·75	35
121	16	25p. black and blue	11·00	35
122	16	30p. black and green	6·75	35
123	16	50p. black and brown	8·50	80
135	16	1d. black and bistre	1·30	55
136	16	3d. black and green	1·30	1·30
137	16	5d. black and violet	5·50	4·00

17 Petar I

1911

146	17	1p. black	20	10
147	17	2p. violet	20	10
169	17	5p. green	20	10
170	17	10p. red	20	10
150	17	15p. purple	45	10
171	17	15p. black	20	10
151	17	20p. yellow	45	10
172	17	20p. brown	80	45
173	17	25p. blue	20	10
153	17	30p. green	45	35
173a	17	30p. bronze	20	45
154	17	50p. brown	80	55
174	17	50p. red	65	55
155	17	1d. orange	34·00	65·00
175	17	1d. green	5·50	11·00
156	17	3d. lake	45·00	£130
176	17	3d. yellow	£225	£1700
177	17	5d. violet	9·00	29·00

19 King Petar I on the Battlefield

1915

178	19	5p. green	55	
179	19	10p. red	55	
179a	19	15p. grey	8·50	
179b	19	20p. brown	2·20	
179c	19	25p. blue	17·00	
179d	19	30p. green	11·00	
179e	19	50p. brown	45·00	

20 King Petar I and Prince Alexander

1918

194	20	1p. black	10	10
195	20	2p. olive	10	10
196	20	5p. green	10	10
197	20	10p. red	10	10
198	20	15p. sepia	10	10
199	20	20p. brown	10	10
208	20	20p. mauve	5·25	1·30
200	20	25p. blue	10	10
201	20	30p. olive	10	10
202	20	50p. mauve	10	10
220	20	1d. brown	35	15
204	20	3d. slate	1·70	1·30
205	20	5d. brown	2·75	1·70

These issues were only for sale within Serbia.

2003. No. 2864, Nos. 2927, 2928 and 2930 surch.

S235	1d. on R ultramarine	95	95
S236	12d. on 1p. violet and bistre	1·00	1·00
S236a	12d. on 20p. purple and brown-lilac	1·80	1·80
S236b	32d. on 5p. deep dull blue and orange	2·50	2·50

S24 Father Christmas and Reindeer

2003. Christmas. Multicoloured.

S237	10d. Type S **24**	90	90
S238	13d.50 Baubles	1·10	1·10
S239	26d.20 Snowflakes	1·70	1·70

S25 Bat and Virus as Ball

2005. AIDS Awareness Campaign.

S240	S25	8d. multicoloured	55	55

S26 Children

2006. Red Cross. Each vermilion and blue.

S241	8d. Type S **26**	55	55
S242	8d. Elderly couple	55	55

S27

S28

2006. Monasteries.

S243	S27	8d. multicoloured	55	55
S244	S28	8d. multicoloured	55	55

S29 Glass containing Virus

2006. AIDS Awareness Campaign.

S245	S29	8d. multicoloured	55	55

On 3rd of June 2006 Montenegro resigned from the Alliance (Serbia & Montenegro) and Serbia reverted to a single unit.

30 National Flag

2006. National Symbols. Multicoloured.

246	16d.50 Type **30**	55	55
247	20d. Arms (vert)	65	65

31 Battle Scene (detail) (Paja Jovanovic)

2006. Bicentenary of Battle of Misar.

248	31	46d. multicoloured	1·50	1·50

32 Net, Ball and Players

2006. Water Polo Championships, Belgrade. Multicoloured.

249	32	46d. multicoloured	1·50	1·50

2006. Serbia—2006 Water Polo Champions. As T 32. Multicoloured.

250	46d. Medal, players and ball	1·50	1·50

33 Train

2006. 38th "Joy in Europe" Meeting. Children's Day. Multicoloured.

251	46d. Type **33**	1·50	1·50
252	73d. Girl and bird	2·40	2·40

34 Zica Monastery

2006

253	34	8d. multicoloured	25	25

35 1866 1p. Stamp (As Type **1**)

2006. Stamp Day. 140th Anniv of First Serbian Stamp.

254	**35**	46d. multicoloured	1·50	1·50

36 Crown

2006. Museum Exhibits. Bridal Jewellery. Multicoloured.

255	16d.50 Type **36**	55	55
256	16d.50 Ring	55	55
257	46d. Earrings	1·50	1·50
258	46d. Necklace	1·50	1·50

37 Actors and Theatre Facade

2006. 50th Anniv of Theatre ATELJE 212.

259	**37**	46d. multicoloured	1·50	1·50

38 Wolfgang Amadeus Mozart

2006. Birth Anniversaries. Multicoloured.

260	46d. Type **38** (composer) (250th)	1·50	1·50
261	46d. Rembrandt Harmenszoon van Rijn (artist) (400th)	1·50	1·50

39 Wine, Apples, Bread and Candle

2006. Christmas. Multicoloured.

262	16d.50 Type **39**	55	55
263	46d. Candle and decoration	1·50	1·50

39a Athletes

2006. European Olympic Youth Festival Games, Belgrade.

263a	**39a**	8d. multicoloured	25	25

40 Santa Claus and Presents

2006. New Year.

264	**40**	46d. multicoloured	1·50	1·50

41 Children

2006. 60th Anniv of UNICEF.

265	**41**	16d.50 multicoloured	65	65

42 Battle Scene

2006. Bicentenary of the Liberation of Belgrade.

266	**42**	16d.50 multicoloured	65	65

43 Dahlia

2007. Flora. Multicoloured.

267	50p. Type **43**	15	15
268	1d. Sunflowers (horiz)	15	15
269	5d. Apple tree (horiz)	25	25

44 Western Moravia

2007. Tourism. Multicoloured.

270	10d. Type **44**	40	40
271	13d. Field and woods, Coc (37×29 mm)	55	55
272	33d. Lake and trees, Zlatibov (37×29 mm)	1·20	1·20
273	50d. Winter sports centre, Kopaomk (37×29 mm)	1·70	1·70
274	100d. National Theatre, Belgrade (29×37 mm)	3·50	3·50

45 Combatants

2007. European Judo Championships, Belgrade.

275	**45**	8d. multicoloured	25	25

46 Map and Milutin Milankovic (engineer and geophysicist)

2007. International Polar Year.

276	**46**	46d. multicoloured	1·60	1·60

47 Petar Dubrinovic

2007. Actors and Actresses. Multicoloured.

277	16d.50 Type **47**	65	65
278	16d.50 Milka Grgurova Aleksic	65	65
279	16d.50 Ljublsa Jovanovic	65	65
280	16d.50 Rahela Farari	65	65
281	16d.50 Miodrag Petrovic Skalja	65	65
282	16d.50 Branko Plesa	65	65
283	16d.50 Ljuba Tadic	65	65
284	16d.50 Danilo Bata Stojkovic	65	65

48 Crucifixion (icon)

2007. Easter. Multicoloured.

285	20d. Type **48**	65	65
286	46d. Crucifixion	1·60	1·60

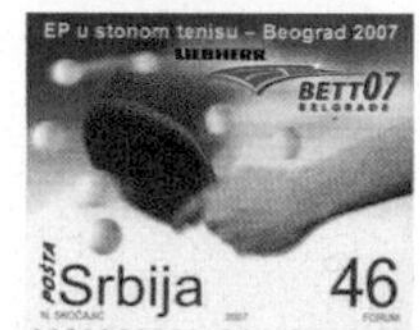

49 Hand, Paddle and Balls

2007. European Table Tennis Championship, Belgrade. Multicoloured.

287	46d. Type **49**	1·60	1·60
MS288	99×71 mm. 112d. Emblem, net and player	4·00	4·00

The stamp and margin of **MS**288 form a composite design.

49a Fresco

2007. St Sava's Temple.

288a	**49a**	10d. multicoloured	50	50

50 Rose

2007

289	**50**	40d. multicoloured	1·50	1·50

51 Black Woodpecker

2007. Endangered Species. Black Woodpecker (Dryocopus martius). Multicoloured.

290	20d. Type **51**	80	80
291	20d. Feeding young facing right	80	80
292	40d. Feeding young facing left	1·50	1·50
293	40d. Black wood pecker facing right	1·50	1·50

52 City Park, Vrnjacka Banja

2007. Nature Protection. Multicoloured.

294	40d. Type **52**	1·30	1·30
295	46d. Fountain, Pionirski Park, Belgrade	1·60	1·60

52a Hand enclosing Elderly Couple

2007. Senior Care Programme.

295a	**52a**	10d. vermilion and black	60	60

53 Scouts

2007. Europa. Centenary of Scouting. Multicoloured.

296	20d. Type **53**	65	65
297	20d. Milos Popovic (founder of Serbian Scouting)	65	65
298	20d. Robert Baden Powell (original founder)	65	65
299	46d. Scouts canoeing	1·60	1·60

54 Emblem and Map

2007. Serbia's Chairmanship of Council of Europe's Ministers' Committee, May–November 2007.

300	**54**	20d. multicoloured	65	65

55 Amelia Earhart and Lockheed *Vega 5b*

2007. 75th Anniv of Amelia Earhart's Transatlantic Flight.

301	**55**	50d. multicoloured	1·60	1·60

56 *Dositej Obradovic* (Uros Predic)

2007. Dositej Obradovic (writer, philosopher and linguist) Commemoration. Bicentenary of Return to Serbia.

302	**56**	20d. multicoloured	65	65

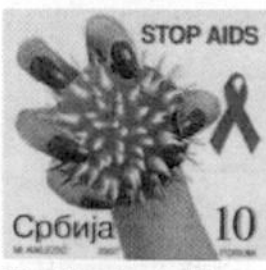

56a Hand crushing Virus

2007. AIDS Awareness Campaign.

302a	**56a**	10d. multicoloured	1·00	1·00

57 Jovan Zmaj

2007. 50th Anniv of Zmaj's Children's Games (youth cultural event).

303	**57**	20d. multicoloured	65	65

58 Prince Stefan Lazarevic (Despot 1402–1427) (fresco) and Arms

2007. Srbijafila 2007 Philatelic Exhibition. Sheet 95×53 mm containing T 58 and similar horiz design. Multicoloured.

MS304 20d. Type **58**; 46d. Court at Kalemegdan and seal	2·20	2·20

The stamps of **MS**304 form a composite background design.

59 Swimmer

2007. European Olympic Youth Festival, Belgrade. Sheet 95×53 mm containing T 59 and similar horiz design. Multicoloured.

MS305 46d.×2 Type **59**; Runner	3·25	3·25

The stamps and margins of **MS**305 form a composite background design.

60 Eventing

2007. Equestrian Sports. Multicoloured.

306	20d. Type **60**	65	65
307	20d. Carriage driving	65	65
308	40d. Dressage	1·30	1·30
309	40d. Show jumping	1·30	1·30

61 William Thomas Kelvin

2007. Scientists' Centenaries. Multicoloured.

310	40d. Type **61** (developed second law of thermodynamics and formulated the Kelvin temperature scale) (death centenary)	1·30	1·30
311	46d. Giuseppe Occhialini (expert on cosmic radiation) (birth centenary)	1·60	1·60
312	46d. Dmitrij Ivanovitch Mendeleev (developed Periodic Table) (death centenary)	1·60	1·60

62 Peter Lubarda and *Horses' Game* (1960)

2007. Birth Centenary of Peter Lubarda (artist).

313	**62**	20d. multicoloured	65	65

63 Monastery Building

2007. 600th Anniv of Kalenic Monastery.

314	**63**	20d. multicoloured	65	65

64 *Haliaeetus albicilla* (white-tailed eagle)

2007

315	**64**	46d. multicoloured	1·60	1·60

A stamp of the same design was issued by Austria.

65 Hands

2007. International Ozone Layer Protection Day.

316	**65**	20d. multicoloured	65	65

66 Ruins

2007. UNESCO World Heritage Site. Felix Romuliana, Gamzigrad. Multicoloured.

317	46d. Type **66**	1·60	1·60
318	46d. Columns surrounding tiled area with bowl	1·60	1·60

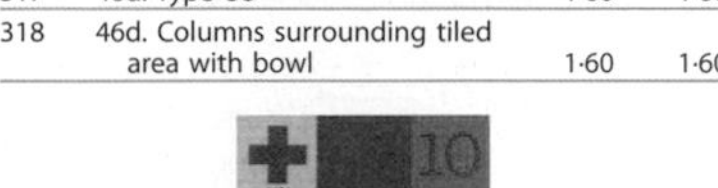

67 Emblem

2007. Red Cross. Roma Week.

319	**67**	10d. multicoloured	35	35

68 Children

2007. 39th 'Joy in Europe' Meeting. Children's Day.

320	**68**	46d. multicoloured	1·60	1·60

69 *Sputnik I*

2007. 50th Anniv of Space Exploration.

321	**69**	46d. multicoloured	1·60	1·60

70 Observatory and Medal showing Milan Nedeljkovic

2007. 120th Anniv of Astronomical Observatory, Belgrade. 150th Birth Anniv of Milan Nedeljkovic (founder).

322	**70**	20d. multicoloured	65	65

71 Erzen Derocco

2007. Stamp Day. Erzen Derocco (philatelist) Commemoration.

323	**71**	46d. multicoloured	1·60	1·60

72 *Rest after Battle* (Djura Jaksic)

2007. Artists' Anniversaries. Multicoloured.

324	20d. Type **72** (175th birth anniv)	65	65
325	46d. *Self Portrait* (Frida Kahlo) (birth centenary)	1·60	1·60
326	46d. *Boy at Window* (Uros Predic) (150th birth anniv)	1·60	1·60

73 *The Nativity* (Eremija Profeta)

2007. Christmas. Multicoloured.

327	20d. Type **73**	65	65
328	46d. *The Nativity* ('XVIII century')	1·60	1·60

74 Novi Sad Port

2007. Danube Ports and Ships. Multicoloured.

329	20d. Type **74**	65	65
330	46d. Orsova port	1·60	1·60
MS331	95×53 mm. 40d. *Sirona* (Serbia); 50d. *Orsova* (Romania)	3·00	3·00

Stamps of a similar design were issued by Romania.

75 King Milan I Obrenovic and Emperor Meiji of Japan

2007. 125th Anniv of Serbia–Japan Bi-lateral Relations.

332	**75**	46d. multicoloured	1·60	1·60

76 Ladu of Vinca (statue) and Ruins of Neolithic House

2008. Centenary of First Archaeological Dig, Vinca.

333	**76**	20d. multicoloured	65	65

77 *Cluny Museum, Paris*

2008. Art. Birth Centenary of Peda Milosavljevic. Multicoloured.

334	20d. Type **77**	65	65
335	46d. *Notre Dame, Paris*	1·60	1·60

78 Swimmer and Emblem

2008. Centenary of Swimming Federation (Fina).

336	**78**	50d. multicoloured	1·70	1·70

79 Tennis Player

2008. Olympic Games, Beijing. Multicoloured.

337	46d. Type **79**	1·60	1·60
338	50d. Hurdlers	2·00	2·00

80 Christ enclosed (detail) (King Milutin's plastanica (13th–14th century textile))

2008. Easter. Multicoloured.

339	20d. Type **80**	65	65
340	46d. Christ enclosed (detail) (15th century icon)	1·60	1·60

81 Janko Tipsarevic

2008. Olympic Tennis Team. Designs showing players. Multicoloured.

341	20d. Type **81**	65	65
342	30d. Nenad Zimonjic	90	90
343	30d. Jelena Jankovic	90	90
344	40d. Ana Ivanovic	1·30	1·30
345	46d. Novak Dokovic	1·50	1·50

82 *Cervus elaphus* (red deer)

2008. Fauna. Multicoloured.

346	20d. Type **82**	65	65
347	20d. *Meles meles* (European badger)	65	65
348	46d. *Felis silvestris* (wildcat)	1·60	1·60
349	46d. *Sus scrofa* (wild boar)	1·60	1·60

83 Singer

2008. Eurovision Song Contest, Belgrade. Sheet 95×53 mm.

MS350 multicoloured	5·75	5·75

83a Clasped Hands

2008. Senior Care Programme.
350a **83a** 10d. multicoloured 35 35

84 Quill and Envelope

2008. Europa. The Letter. Multicoloured.
351 46d. Type **84** 1·60 1·60
352 50d. Letter opener 2·00 2·00

85 Vlasina Plateau

2008. European Protection. Multicoloured.
353 20d. Type **85** 65 65
354 46d. Djavolija varos (devil's town) 1·60 1·60

86 Train and Eiffel Tower

2008. 125th Anniv of Orient Express. Multicoloured.
355 20d. Type **86** 65 65
356 50d. Train and mosque 1·60 1·60

87 Camera and Film

2008. 50th Anniv of Television Belgrade.
357 **87** 46d. multicoloured 1·60 1·60

88 Dositej Obradovic and Building

2008. Bicentenary of Grand School, Belgrade.
358 **88** 20d. multicoloured 65 65

89 Green Grapes

2008. Wine Growing. Multicoloured.
359 20d. Type **89** 65 65
360 20d. White grapes 65 65
361 46d. Black grapes 1·60 1·60
362 46d. Crimson grapes 1·60 1·60

90 Children

2008. 40th 'Joy in Europe' Meeting. Children's Day.
363 **90** 46d. multicoloured 1·60 1·60

91 Panta Mihajlovic, Early Handset and Telephone Wires

2008. Stamp Day. 125th Anniv of First Telephone in Serbia.
364 **91** 46d. multicoloured 1·60 1·60

92 Sumadija

2008. Museum Exhibits. Traditional Children's Costumes. Multicoloured.
365 46d. Type **92** 1·60 1·60
366 50d. Kumodraz 1·60 1·60

93 Danube

2008. 60th Anniv of Danube Commission.
367 **93** 46d. multicoloured 1·60 1·60

94 The Nativity (18th–century)

2008. Christmas. Multicoloured.
368 20d. Type **94** 65 65
369 46d. *The Nativity* (Dimitrije Bacevic) 1·60 1·60

95 Anniversary Emblem

2008. 50th Anniv of Dadov Theatre, Belgrade.
370 **95** 20d. multicoloured 65 65

96 TV Tower, Avala

2008
371 **96** 10d. multicoloured 35 35

97 St. Sava

2008. St. Sava's Temple.
372 **97** 10d. multicoloured 35 35

98 Don Quixote

2009. 75th Anniv of Osisani Jez (magazine).
373 **98** 20d. multicoloured 65 65

99 Louis Braille and Writing

2009. Birth Bicentenary of Louis Braille (inventor of Braille writing for the Blind).
374 **99** 46d. multicoloured 1·60 1·60

100 Buckle

2009. Cultural Heritage. Multicoloured.
375 11d. Type **100** 40 40
376 22d. Ring 75 75

No. 377 has been left for stamp not yet received.

(101)

2009. No. 247 surch as T (101).
378 22d. on 20c. multicoloured 80 80

102 Kalemegdan Fortress

2009. Tourism.
379 **102** 55d. multicoloured 1·70 1·70

103 *Mustela erminea* (stoat)

2009. Fauna. Multicoloured.
380 22d. Type **103** 65 65
381 22d. *Micromys minutus* (harvest mouse) 65 65
382 46d. *Sicista subtilis* (southern birch mouse) 1·60 1·60
383 46d. *Spermophilus citellus* (inscr 'citelluss') (European ground squirrel) 1·60 1·60

104 Dikan an Uncle Vu Koje (from *Dikan* (cartoon by Lazo Sredanovic))

2009. 70th Anniv of Politikin Zabavnik (magazine).
384 **104** 22d. multicoloured 65 65

105 *Scolopax rusticola* (Eurasian woodcock)

2009. Ecology—Balkan Mountains. Multicoloured.
385 22d. Type **105** 65 65
386 46d. *Monticola saxatilis* (rufous-tailed rock thrush) 1·60 1·60
MS387 127×67 mm. Nos. 385/6 2·30 2·30

Stamps of a similar design were issued by Bulgaria.

106 The Last Supper

2009. Easter. Design showing wood carving. Multicoloured.
388 22d. Type **106** 65 65
389 46d. Entombment of Christ 1·60 1·60

107 Vela Nigrinova

2009. Actors and Actresses. Multicoloured.
390 22d. Type **107** 65 65
391 22d. Milan Ajvaz 65 65
392 22d. Nevenka Urbanova 65 65
393 22d. Stevo Zigon 65 65
394 22d. Slobodan Perovic 65 65
395 22d. Stevan Salajic 65 65
396 22d. Neda Spasojevic 65 65
397 22d. Milos Zutic 65 65

108 Birds as Footballers

2009. 25th Summer Universiade (games), Belgrade. Multicoloured.
398 22d. Type **108** 65 65
399 46d. Birds as athletes 1·60 1·60

108a St. Sava's Temple

2009. Obligatory Tax.
399a **108a** 10d. multicoloured 1·00 1·00

109 *Self Portrait with Veil* (Milena Barelli) (birth centenary)

2009. Artists' Anniversaries. Multicoloured.
400 22d. Type **109** 65 65
401 46d. *Dead Nature with Parrot* (Jovan Bijelic) (125th birth anniv) 1·60 1·60
402 46d. *Young Woman in Pink Dress* (Paja Jovanovic) (150th birth anniv) 1·60 1·60

110 Urania (muse of astrology) (statue), Galileo's Telescope and Milky Way

2009. Europa. Astronomy. Multicoloured.
403 46d Type **110** 1·60 1·60
404 50d. Radio telescope and Horsehead nebula 1·70 1·70

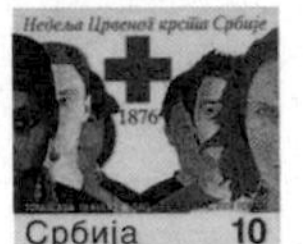

110a People of Many Nations

2009. Obligatory Tax. Red Cross Week.
404a **110a** 10d. multicoloured 1·00 1·00

111 Saint Sava's Panagia and Temple of Saint Sava

2009. 70th Anniv of Laying of Saint Sava's Temple Foundation Stone on Vracar.
405 **111** 22d. multicoloured 65 65

112 Griffon Vulture (*Gyps fulvus*) over Uvac River Gorge

2009. European Nature Protection. Multicoloured. P 13½.
406 22d. Type **112** 65 65
407 46d. Pcinja Valley 1·60 1·60

113 Kornelije Stankovic

2009. Musical Personalities. Sheet 116×126 containing T **113** and similar vert designs. Multicoloured.
MS408 22d.×8, Type **113**; Josef Marinkovic; Petar Konjovic; Stefan Hristic; Miloje Milojevic; Mihovil Logar; Ljubica; Vasilije Mokranjac 5·25 5·25

The stamps and margins of **MS**407 share a common background design.

114 *Battle at Cegar* (Boza Ilic)

2009. Bicentenary of Battle at Cegar during First Serbian Uprising. Multicoloured.
409 22d. Type **114** 65 65
410 46d. *Stevan Sindelic and Skull Tower* (lithograph by Konstantin Nenadovic) 1·60 1·60

115 *The Virgin of Studenica*

2009. 800th Anniv of Frescoes, Church of the Virgin, Studenica Monastery.
411 **115** 22d. multicoloured 65 65

116 Dimitrije Putnikovi

2009. Scientific Personalities' Anniversaries. Multicoloured.
412 22c. Type **116** (educator) (150th birth anniv) 65 65
413 22c. Pavle Savic (physicist and chemist) (birth centenary) 65 65
414 46d. Pierre Curie (chemist) (birth centenary) 1·60 1·60
415 46d. Charles Robert Darwin (naturalist and evolutionary theorist) (birth bicentenary) 1·60 1·60

117 CS No.1 (first steam locomotive) and Belgrade Railway Station

2009. 125th Anniv of Serbian Railways. Multicoloured.
416 22d. Type **117** 65 65
417 46d. Electric locomotive JZ 441and Nis Station 1·60 1·60

118 Hands and '50'

2009. 50th Golden Pen of Belgrade and Tenth International Biennial of Illustration–2009 Exhibition, Art Pavillion Cvijeta Zuzoric, Kalemegdan, Belgrade.
418 **118** 22d. bronze and black 65 65

119 Children

2009. 41st 'Joy in Europe' Meeting. Children's Day.
419 **119** 46d. multicoloured 1·60 1·60

120 Mother and Child

2009. Obligatory Tax. Red Cross Week.
420 **120** 10d. multicoloured 1·00 1·00

121 Nada Higl

2009. FINA International Swimming Championship, Rome. Gold Medallists. Multicoloured.
421 46d. Type **121** 1·60 1·60
422 46d. Milorad Cavic 1·60 1·60
423 50d. Serbian water polo team 1·70 1·70

122 Front Cover and George Hugo Paul Michel (founder)

2009. Stamp Day. Centenary (2010) of Michel Stamp Catalogues.
424 **122** 46d. multicoloured 1·60 1·60

123 *Herrerasaurus ischigualastensis*

2009. Museum Exhibition. Dinosaurs of Argentina–Giants of Patagonia. Multicoloured.
425 22d. Type **123** 65 65
426 46d. *Giganotosaurus carolinii* 1·60 1·60

124 Front Pages

2010. 75th Anniv of NIN (weekly magazine).
427 **124** 22d. multicoloured 65 65

125 Tiger

2010. Chinese New Year. Year of the Tiger. Multicoloured.
428 22d. Type **125** 65 65
429 50d. Tiger to left of horoscope circle 1·60 1·60

126 Peony

2010. European Nature Protection. Paeonia officinalis. Multicoloured.
430 22d. Type **126** 65 65
431 46d. Pink double-flowered peony 1·60 1·60

MS432 96×78 mm. Nos. 430/1 form a composite design of peonies in landscape. 2·30 2·30

127 Nordic Skiers

2010. Winter Olympic Games, Vancouver. Multicoloured.
433 22d. Type **127** 65 65
434 50d. Skier 1·60 1·60

128 Athletes as '100'

2010. Centenary of Serbian Olympic Committee.
435 **128** 22d. multicoloured 65 65

128a Pavilion, interior

2010. Expo 2010, Shanghai. Multicoloured.
435a 22d. Type **128a** 65 65
435b 50d. Pavilion, exterior 1·60 1·60

129 Frederic Chopin

2010. Birth Bicentenary of Fryderyk Franciszek Chopin (Frederic Francois Chopin) (composer).
436 **129** 50d. multicoloured 1·60 1·60

130 The Crucifixion

2010. Easter. Multicoloured.
437 22d. Type **130** 65 65
438 46d. Resurrected Christ on Easter egg 1·60 1·60

131 Military Artefacts

2010. 160th Anniv of Military Academy, Belgrade
439 **131** 22d. multicoloured 85 85

132 Zastava 750

2010. 55th Anniv of Zastava 750 (car made by Zavod Crvena Zastava)
440 **132** 22d. multicoloured 85 85

133 *Passer domesticus* (house sparrow)

2010. Birds. Multicoloured.

441		22d. Type **133**	65	65
442		33d. *Phoenicurus ochruros* (black redstart)	95	95
443		46d. *Columba livia* (rock pigeon)	2·30	2·30
444		50d. *Parus major* (great tit)	2·40	2·40

134 'K', Factory and Townscape

2010. 140th Anniv of Industrialization

445	**134**	22d. multicoloured	85	85

135 Beanstalk, White Rabbit, Girl reading and Giraffe

2010. Europa. Multicoloured.

446		66d. Type **135**	2·50	2·50
447		77d. Pumpkin, boy in hammock hanging from moon, fairy, elves and girl reaching for star	3·00	3·00

136 Players and Map of Africa

2010. World Cup Football Championships, South Africa. Multicoloured.

448		22d. Type **136**	1·10	1·10
449		50d. Players and South African and Serbian flags	2·20	2·20
MS450		85×78 mm. 177d. Players legs and football (42×35 mm)	8·00	8·00

137 Cyclists

2010. 50th Anniv of Tour de Serbie Cycle Race

451	**137**	50d. multicoloured	2·00	2·00

138 The Virgin Odigitrija (19th-century, Belgrade)

2010. Icons. Multicoloured.

452		50d. Type **138**	2·20	2·20
453		50d. The Archangel Mikhail (Andrey Rublev, 15th-century)	2·20	2·20

139 Trumpeteers and Trumpets

2010. 50th Anniv of Trumpet Festival, Guca

454	**139**	44d. multicoloured	2·00	2·00

140 Athletes

2010. Youth Olympic Games, Singapore

455	**140**	51d. multicoloured	2·30	2·30

141 Mother Teresa

2010. Birth Centenary of Agnes Gonxha Bojaxhiu (Mother Teresa) (founder of Missionaries of Charity)

456	**141**	50d. multicoloured	2·00	2·00

142 Laza Kostic (1841-1910)

2010. Literary Personalities. Multicoloured.

457		22d. Type **142**	1·40	1·40
458		22d. Branislav Nusic (1864-1938)	1·40	1·40
459		22d. Borisav Stankovi (1876-1927)	1·40	1·40
460		22d. Ivo Andric (1892-1975)	1·40	1·40
461		22d. Milos Crnjanski (1893-1977)	1·40	1·40
462		22d. Mesa Selimovic (1910-1982)	1·40	1·40
463		22d. Borislav Peki (1930-1992)	1·40	1·40
464		22d. Danilo Kis (1935-1989)	1·40	1·40

143 Decorated Plate (16th-century)

2010. 60th Anniv of Art Museum, Belgrade. Multicoloured.

465		22d. Type **143**	1·00	1·00
466		44d. Musical figurine (19th-century)	3·25	3·25

144 Postman, Letter, Pen and Main Post Office, Belgrade

2010. 170th Anniv of Serbian Post

467	**144**	46d. multicoloured	2·00	2·00

145 Pig

2010. Joy of Europe

468	**145**	46d. multicoloured	3·00	3·00

146 Birth of Christ (Arsenije Teodorovic)

2010. Christmas. Icons from Mother of God Church, Zemin. Multicoloured.

469		22d. Type **146**	1·30	1·30
470		46d. Birth of Christ (unknown)	3·25	3·25

NEWSPAPER STAMPS

1 State Arms

1866. Imperf.

N7	**1**	1p. green and pink	85·00	
N2	**1**	2p. green and blue	£3250	
N6	**1**	2p. brown and blue	£325	

1867. Perf.

N17	**2**	1p. green	28·00	£850
N18	**2**	2p. brown	45·00	£850

1868. Imperf.

N19		1p. green	80·00	
N20		2p. brown	£110	

1869. Perf.

N49a	**3**	1p. yellow	4·00	£275

4 King Milan

1872. Imperf.

N51		1p. yellow	10·00	28·00
N53	**4**	2p. black	2·20	1·10

POSTAGE DUE STAMPS

D8

1895

D87	**D8**	5p. mauve	80	55
D83	**D8**	10p. blue	8·50	55
D91	**D8**	20p. brown	55	1·10
D85	**D8**	30p. green	85	1·10
D86	**D8**	50p. red	85	1·50

D21

1918

D227	**D21**	5p. red	55	1·10
D228	**D21**	10p. green	55	1·10
D229	**D21**	20p. brown	55	1·10
D230	**D21**	30p. blue	55	1·10
D231	**D21**	50p. brown	1·30	2·20
D232	**D21**	5p. brown	55	1·10
D233	**D21**	30p. grey	1·30	1·90

GERMAN OCCUPATION

1941. Stamps of Yugoslavia on paper with coloured network optd SERBIEN reading downwards.

G1	**99**	25p. black	45	9·25
G2	**99**	50p. orange	45	4·75
G3	**99**	1d. green	45	4·75
G4	**99**	1d.50 red	45	4·75
G5	**99**	2d. red	45	4·75
G6	**99**	3d. brown	3·25	37·00
G7	**99**	4d. blue	1·90	7·50
G8	**99**	5d. blue	2·75	19·00
G9	**99**	5d.50 violet	2·75	19·00
G10	**99**	6d. blue	2·75	19·00
G11	**99**	8d. brown	3·75	28·00
G12	**99**	12d. violet	3·75	28·00
G13	**99**	16d. purple	5·50	95·00
G14	**99**	20d. blue	9·25	£325
G15	**99**	30d. pink	37·00	£1300

1941. Air. Stamps of Yugoslavia on paper with coloured network, optd SERBIEN.

G16	**80**	50p. brown	9·25	£200
G17	-	1d. green (No. 361)	9·25	£200
G18	-	2d. blue (No. 362)	9·25	£200
G19	-	2d.50 red (No. 363)	9·25	£200
G20	**80**	5d. violet	9·25	£200
G21	-	10d. red (No. 365)	9·25	£200
G22	-	20d. green (No. 366)	9·25	£200
G23	-	30d. blue (No. 367)	9·25	£200
G24	-	40d. green (No. 443)	23·00	£750
G25	-	50d. blue (No. 444)	33·00	£1300

1941. Air. As last, but without network opt, surch SERBIEN and value.

G26		1d. on 10d. red (No. 365)	6·50	£225
G27		3d. on 20d. grn (No. 366)	6·50	£225
G28		6d. on 30d. blue (No. 367)	6·50	£225
G29		8d. on 40d. grn (No. 443)	14·00	£475
G30		12d. on 50d. blue (No. 444)	23·00	£1000

1941. As Nos. G1/15, but with SERBIEN reading upwards.

G31	**99**	25p. black	45	28·00
G32	**99**	50p. orange	45	6·50
G33	**99**	1d. green	45	6·50
G34	**99**	1d.50 red	45	6·50
G35	**99**	2d. red	45	6·50
G36	**99**	3d. brown	1·40	24·00
G37	**99**	4d. blue	1·90	6·50
G38	**99**	5d. blue	1·90	12·00
G39	**99**	5d.50 violet	2·75	24·00
G40	**99**	6d. blue	2·75	24·00
G41	**99**	8d. brown	3·75	37·00
G42	**99**	12d. violet	5·00	37·00
G43	**99**	16d. purple	5·00	£120
G44	**99**	20d. blue	5·00	£375
G45	**99**	30d. pink	26·00	£1200

G4 Smederovo Fortress

1941. Smederovo Explosion Relief Fund. (a).

G46	**G4**	0.50d.+1d. brown	75	1·90
G47	-	1d.+2d. green (Refugees)	75	2·30
G48	-	1.50d.+3d. purple (Refugees)	1·30	4·25
G49	**G4**	2d.+4d. blue	1·90	5·50

(b) Sheets 149×109 mm comprising Nos. G47 and G49, colours changed and with high premiums.

MSG49a	1d.+49d. red; 2d.+48d. green. P 11½	40·00	£300
MSG49b	1d.+49d. green; 2d.+48d. red. Imperf	40·00	£300

G6 Christ and the Virgin Mary

1941. Prisoners of War Fund.

G50	**G6**	0.50d.+1.50d. red	30	5·00
G51	**G6**	1d.+3d. green	30	5·00
G52	**G6**	2d.+6d. red	30	5·00
G53	**G6**	4d.+12d. blue	30	5·00

This set also exists with an optd network, both plain and incorporating a large "E", this letter being either normal or reversed.

G7 **G8**

1942. Anti-Masonic Exn. Dated "22.X.1941".

G54	**G7**	0.50d.+1.50d. brown	55	4·25
G55	-	1d.+1d. green	55	4·25
G56	**G8**	2d.+2d. red	95	7·50
G57	-	4d.+4d. blue	95	7·50

DESIGNS—HORIZ: 1d. Hand grasping snake. VERT: 4d. Peasant demolishing masonic symbols.

G9 Kalenic

1942. Monasteries.

G58		0d.50 violet	20	45
G59	**G9**	1d. red	20	45
G60	-	1d.50 brown	1·70	6·50
G61	-	1d.50 green	20	45
G62	-	2d. purple	20	45
G63	-	3d. blue	1·70	6·50
G64	-	3d. pink	20	45
G65	-	4d. blue	20	45
G66	-	7d. green	20	45
G67	-	12d. red	30	3·25
G68	-	16d. black	1·90	3·75

DESIGNS—VERT: 0d.50, Lazarica; 1d.50, Ravanica; 12d. Gornjak; 16d. Studenica. HORIZ: 2d. Manasija; 3d. Ljubostinja; 4d. Sopocani; 7d. Zica.

1942. As Nos. G50/53, colours changed.

G68a	**G6**	0.50d.+1.50d. brown	2·30	4·75
G68b	**G6**	1d.+3d. green	2·30	4·75
G68c	**G6**	2d.+6d. red	2·30	4·75
G68d	**G6**	4d.+12d. blue	2·30	4·75

1942. Air. 1939 issue of Yugoslavia surch with airplane, "SERBIA" in cyrillic characters and new value.

G69	**99**	2 on 2d. mauve	45	2·30
G70	**99**	4 on 4d. blue	45	2·30
G71	**99**	10 on 12d. violet	45	4·75
G72	**99**	14 on 20d. blue	45	4·75
G73	**99**	20 on 30d. pink	1·10	19·00

G11 Mother and Children

1942. War Orphans Fund.

G74	**G11**	2d.+6d. violet	11·00	12·00
G75	**G11**	4d.+8d. blue	11·00	12·00
G76	**G11**	7d.+13d. green	11·00	12·00
G77	**G11**	20d.+40d. red	11·00	12·00

G12 Broken Sword

1943. War Invalids' Relief Fund.

G78	**G12**	1.50d.+1.50d. brown	2·30	3·75
G79	-	2d.+3d. green	2·30	3·75
G80	-	3d.+5d. mauve	4·75	5·50
G81	-	4d.+10d. blue	5·00	6·50

MSG81a Two sheets, each 149×110 mm. Thick paper. P 11½. (a) 1d.50+48d.50, 4d.+46d. (b) 2d.+48d., 3d.+47d. 60·00 £4000

DESIGNS—HORIZ: 2d. Fallen standard bearer; 3d. Wounded soldier (seated). VERT: 4d. Nurse tending soldier.

G13 Post Rider

1943. Postal Centenary. Inscr "15.X.1843–15.X.1943".

G82	**G13**	3d. red and lilac	1·90	5·50
G83	-	8d. red and green	1·90	5·50
G84	-	9d. green and brown	1·90	5·50
G85	-	30d. brown and green	1·90	5·50
G86	-	50d. blue and red	1·90	5·50

DESIGNS: 8d. Horse wagon; 9d. Railway mail van; 30d. Postal motor van; 50d. Junkers Ju 52/3m mail plane.

1943. Bombing of Nish Relief Fund. Monasteries issue of 1942 on paper with network, surch with Serbian inscr 20-X-1943 and value.

G87	0d.50+2d. violet	45	55·00
G88	1d.+3d. red	45	55·00
G89	1d.50+4d. green	45	55·00
G90	2d.+5d. purple	45	55·00
G91	3d.+7d. pink	45	55·00
G92	4d.+9d. blue	45	55·00
G93	7d.+15d. green	1·20	55·00
G94	12d.+25d. red	1·20	£250
G95	16d.+33d. black	2·50	£425

OFFICIAL STAMP

GO12

1943

GO78	**GO12**	3d. red	60	2·00

POSTAGE DUE STAMPS

GD2 **GD3**

1941. Unissued Postage Due stamps optd SERBIEN.

GD16	**GD2**	0d.50 violet	1·90	47·00
GD17	**GD2**	1d. red	1·90	47·00
GD18	**GD2**	2d. blue	1·90	47·00
GD19	**GD2**	3d. red	2·75	70·00
GD20	**GD3**	4d. blue	3·75	£170
GD21	**GD3**	5d. orange	3·75	£170
GD22	**GD3**	10d. violet	6·50	£425
GD23	**GD3**	20d. green	16·00	£1100

1942. Types GD 2 and GD 3 without opt. Bottom inscription on white background.

GD69	**GD2**	1d. red and green	2·75	9·25
GD70	**GD2**	2d. blue and red	2·75	9·25
GD71	**GD2**	3d. red and blue	2·75	14·00
GD72	**GD3**	4d. blue and red	2·75	14·00
GD73	**GD3**	5d. orange and blue	3·75	19·00
GD74	**GD3**	10d. violet and red	3·75	28·00
GD75	**GD3**	20d. green and red	19·00	£110

GD13

1943

GD82	**GD13**	0d.50 black	1·90	7·50
GD83	**GD13**	3d. violet	1·90	7·50
GD84	**GD13**	4d. blue	1·90	7·50
GD85	**GD13**	5d. green	1·90	7·50
GD86	**GD13**	6d. orange	2·75	19·00
GD87	**GD13**	10d. red	3·75	23·00
GD88	**GD13**	20d. blue	9·25	70·00

Pt. 3

SERBIA AND MONTENEGRO

On 4 February 2003 Yugoslavia became Serbia & Montenegro. See Yugoslavia for previous issues.

2003. 100 para = 1 dinar.

1 "e", Stars and Map of Europe

2003. Accession to the Council of Europe. Multicoloured.

1	16d. Type **1**	1·30	1·30
2	28d.70 Smaller "e", stars and map of Europe	2·20	2·20

2 The Descent from the Cross (16th-century icon)

2003. Easter. Multicoloured.

3	12d. Type **2**	90	90
4	16d. Resurrection (Dimitrije Bacevic)	1·10	1·10
5	26d.20 Mourning Christ (icon, St. Paul's Monastery, Athos) (1616)	2·00	2·00
6	28d.70 Transfiguration of Christ (Giovanni Bellini)	2·20	2·20

3 Document and Emblem

2003. 150th Anniv of First Belgrade Singers' Society.

7	**3**	16d. multicoloured	3·25	3·25

4 Pasting up Poster

2003. Europa. Poster Art. Multicoloured.

8	28d.70 Type **4**	2·20	2·20
9	50d. Pasting up poster for Balkan Express	5·50	5·50

5 *Galanthus nivalis*

2003. Flowers. Multicoloured.

10	16d. Type **5**	1·30	1·30
11	24d. *Erythronium dens canis*	1·80	1·80
12	26d.20 *Hepatica nobilis*	2·00	2·00
13	28d.70 *Anemone runculoides*	2·20	2·20

6 Ilija Stanojevic

2003. Actors and Actresses. Multicoloured.

14	16d. Type **6**	1·30	1·30
15	16d. Zivana Stokic	1·30	1·30
16	16d. Radomir Plaovic	1·30	1·30
17	16d. Milosav Aleksic	1·30	1·30
18	16d. Dobrivoje Milotinovic	1·30	1·30
19	16d. Lubinka Bobic	1·30	1·30
20	16d. Milivoje Zivanovic	1·30	1·30
21	16d. Zoran Radmilovic	1·30	1·30

7 Early Car

2003. Centenary of First Motor Vehicle in Belgrade.

22	**7**	16d. multicoloured	13·50	13·50

8 Tree overhanging River

2003. Nature Protection. Zasavica Park. Multicoloured.

23	28d.70 Type **8**	2·00	2·00
24	50d. Boat and river	3·50	3·50

9 Magnifying Glass and Stamp

2003. Communications. Multicoloured.

25	1d. Type **9**	45	45
26	8d. Parcels in post van	65	65
27	12d. Telephonist (vert)	1·00	1·00
28	16d. Post van	1·50	1·50
29	32d. Television screen	3·25	3·25

10 Prince Milan Obrenovic (military reformer)

2003. 125th Anniv of Belgrade Military Museum.

30	**10**	16d. multicoloured	1·10	1·10

11 Delfa Ivanic (founder)

2003. Centenary of Serbian Sisters (humanitarian organization).

31 **11** 16d. multicoloured 1·10 1·10

12 Serbia State Arms

2003. 125th Anniversary of Serbia and Montenegro State. Multicoloured.

32 16d. Type **12** 1·10 1·10

33 16d. Montenegro state arms 1·10 1·10

13 Model Rockets

2003. European Model Rocket Building Championship.

34 **13** 16d. multicoloured 1·10 1·10

14 Neolithic Carved Figure

2003. Philatelica Danubiana Stamp Exhibition, Belgrade. Multicoloured.

35 16d. Type **14** 1·10 1·10

36 16d. Circular head 1·10 1·10

15 17th-century Belgrade

2003. 13th Srbijafila Stamp Exhibition, Belgrade. Sheet 84×57 mm containing T 15 and similar vert design. Multicoloured.

MS37 32d.×2, Type **15**; "Serbia" as woman (sculpture) (Djordje Jovanovic) 9·00 9·00

16 Children

2003. 35th "Joy in Europe" Meeting. Children's Day. Multicoloured.

38 28d.70 Type **16** 2·20 2·20

39 50d. Stylized rabbit (horiz) 3·50 3·50

17 Newspaper Vendor

2003. 50th Anniv of the Vecernje Novost Newspaper.

40 **17** 32d. multicoloured 2·20 2·20

18 Stamp Catalogues

2003. Stamp Day.

41 **18** 16d. multicoloured 4·50 4·50

19 Emblem

2003. 50th Anniv of ULUPUDS (Fine and Applied Artists and Designers of Serbia Association).

42 **19** 16d. multicoloured 1·10 1·10

20 Actors and Theatre Building

2003. 50th Anniv of Montenegro National Theatre, Podgorica.

43 **20** 50d. multicoloured 2·20 2·20

21 Early City

2003. 850th Anniv of Pancevo City.

44 **21** 32d. multicoloured 2·20 2·20

22 Saint John the Baptist (1645)

2003. Russian Orthodox Museum Exhibits. Multicoloured.

45 16d. Type **22** 1·10 1·10

46 24d. Cross (1602) 1·60 1·60

47 26d.20 Embroidered mitre (15th-century) 1·80 1·80

48 28d.70 Iron work tabernacle (1550) 2·20 2·20

23 Nativity (Oropos) (1983)

2003. Christmas. Icons. Multicoloured.

49 12d. Type **23** 90 90

50 16d. Nativity (Belgrade) (18th-century) 1·10 1·10

51 26d.20 (Panagiota Fourka) (2000) 1·80 1·80

52 28d.70 Wise men bearing gifts (Albrecht Durer) 2·20 2·20

24 Submarine

2003. 75th Anniv of Submarine Shipping.

53 **24** 32d. multicoloured 2·10 2·10

25 Wilbur and Orville Wright and *Wright Flyer I*

2003. Centenary of Powered Flight. Multicoloured.

54 16d. Type **25** 90 90

55 28d.70 *Wright Flyer I* and horse-drawn carriages 2·10 2·10

26 Building Facade

2004. Centenary of Politika Newspaper. Multicoloured.

56 16d. Type **26** 1·10 1·10

57 16d. Typewriter (horiz) 1·10 1·10

27 *Parnassius Apollo*

2004. Endangered Species. Butterflies and Insects. Multicoloured.

58 12d. Type **27** 65 65

59 16d. *Rosalia alpine* 80 80

60 26d.20 *Aeshna virirdis* 1·80 1·80

61 28d.70 *Saga pedo* 2·10 2·10

28 Karadorde (Dorde Petrovic) (leader)

2004. Bicentenary of Serbian Rebellion against Turkey (1st issue). Multicoloured.

62 16d. Type **28** 1·10 1·10

63 16d. Children and globe 1·10 1·10

See also Nos. 70/3.

29 *Ramonda serbica*

2004. Fauna and Flora. Multicoloured.

64 16d. Type **29** 1·00 1·00

65 24d. *Ramonda nathaliae* 1·40 1·40

66 26d.20 *Heodes virgaureae* 1·60 1·60

67 28d.70 *Lysandra bellargus* 2·00 2·00

30 Early Greek and Modern Runners

2004. Olympic Games, Athens (1st issue). Multicoloured.

68 32d. Type **30** 2·30 2·30

69 56d. Early Greek and modern wrestlers 3·25 3·25

See also Nos. 90/3.

2004. Bicentenary of Serbian Rebellion against Turkey (2nd issue). As T 28. Multicoloured.

70 12d. Freedom fighters 85 85

71 16d. Pistol and flag (vert) 1·00 1·00

72 28d.70 Karadorde (vert) 1·90 1·90

73 32d. Children and globe (vert) 2·10 2·10

31 Lifting Mask from Globe

2004. Anti-Terrorism Campaign.

74 **31** 16d. multicoloured 1·00 1·00

32 Crucified Christ and Angels

2004. Easter. Multicoloured.

75 16d. Type **32** 1·10 1·10

76 28d.70 Risen Christ 2·20 2·20

33 Globes and Milutin Milankovic (geophysicist)

2004. 125th Birth Anniversaries. Multicoloured.

77 16d. Type **33** 1·00 1·00

78 16d. Albert Einstein (physicist) (vert) 1·00 1·00

34 South (Gurdich) Gate and Beskutcha Family Portal (detail)

2004. 25th Anniv of Kotor as UNESCO World Heritage Site.

79	34	16d. multicoloured	1·00	1·00

35 Vasiliji Petrovic (author)

2004. 250th Anniv of Publication of First History of Montenegro.

80	35	16d. multicoloured	1·00	1·00

36 Paragliding

2004. Europa. Holidays. Multicoloured.

81	16d. Type **36**	1·30	1·30
82	56d. Sail boat and water-skier in water (horiz)	3·50	3·50
MS83	97×55 mm. 32d. Yacht (35×29 mm); 56d. Rowing boats (35×29 mm)	6·00	6·00

37 Mosaic and Church Facade

2004. Saint Sava's Church, Belgrade. Multicoloured.

84	16d. Type **37**	1·10	1·10
85	28d.70 Church facade and statue (horiz)	2·20	2·20

38 Michael Pupin

2004. 150th Birth Anniv of Michael Idvorsky Pupin (Serbian-American physicist).

86	38	16d. lilac	1·00	1·00

39 Emblem

2004. Centenary of FIFA (Federation Internationale de Football).

87	39	28d.70 multicoloured	2·30	2·30

40 River, Ravnjak

2004. Nature Protection. Multicoloured.

88	32d. Type **40**	2·30	2·30
89	56d. Mountains, Sara	3·50	3·50

41 Early and Modern Runners and Gate of Athene Archgetis

2004. Olympic Games, Athens (2nd issue). Multicoloured.

90	16d. Type **41**	1·20	1·20
91	28d.70 Runners and Parthenon	2·40	2·40
92	32d. Long jumpers and Olympieion	2·50	2·50
93	57d.40 Hurdlers and Temple of Hephaistos	4·00	4·00

42 Guilielmo Marconi (inventor) and Antenna

2004. Establishment of First Radio Telegraph Stations in Volujica and Bar.

94	42	16d. multicoloured	1·00	1·00

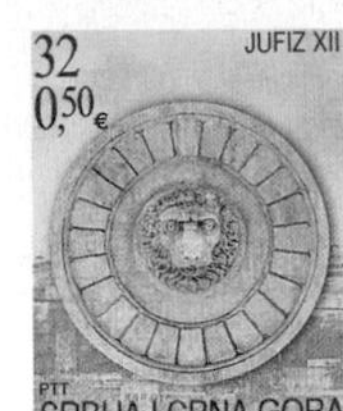

43 Lions Head Medallion

2004. Jufiz XII, National Philatelic Exhibition, Belgrade. Sheet 88×65 mm containing T 43 and similar vert design. Multicoloured.

MS95	32d.×2, Type **43**; Monument	4·25	4·25

44 Bridge (Angelka Misurovic)

2004. 35th "Joy in Europe" Meeting. Children's Day. Multicoloured.

96	32d. Type **44**	2·50	2·50
97	56d. Houses and church (Karol Sackievicz) (vert)	3·75	3·75

45 Boats

2004. 125th Anniv of Bar (Montenegrin port).

98	45	32d. multicoloured	2·30	2·30

46 Stamp and Magnifier

2004. Stamp Day.

99	46	16d. multicoloured	1·00	1·00

47 Bank Building Facade

2004. 120th Anniv of Serbian National Bank.

100	47	16d. indigo, black and cobalt	1·10	1·10
101	-	32d. multicoloured	2·20	2·20

DESIGNS: 16d. Type **47**; 32d. Mr Djordje Vajfert (Governor of the National Bank of the Kingdom of Serbia, the first Governor of the Kingdom of Serbs, Croats and Slovenes).

48 Fruit Stand

2004. Museum Exhibits. Silverware. Multicoloured.

102	16d. Type **48**	1·00	1·00
103	24d. Box	1·50	1·50
104	26d.20 Pierced bowl	1·70	1·70
105	28d.70 Cup with handles and lid	2·10	2·10

49 Lombardic Palace

2004. Architecture. Kotor Palaces. Multicoloured.

106	16d. Type **49**	1·00	1·00
107	24d. Pima Palace	1·50	1·50
108	26d.20 Grgurina Palace	1·70	1·70
109	28d.70 Bizanti Palace	2·10	2·10

50 Mary and Jesus (painting)

2004. Christmas. Multicoloured.

110	16d. Type **50**	1·00	1·00
111	28d.70 Mary and Jesus (painting) (different)	2·30	2·30

51 *Capparis spinosa*

2005. Endangered Species. Mammals and Flowers. Multicoloured.

112	16d.50 Type **51**	1·00	1·00
113	33d. *Mustela erminea*	1·70	1·70
114	41d.50 *Trollius europaeus*	2·10	2·10
115	49d.50 *Rupicapra rupicapra*	2·75	2·75

52 Great Egret (*Egretta alba*)

2005. Birds. Multicoloured.

116	16d.50 Type **52**	1·00	1·00
117	33d. Black-necked grebe (*Podiceps nigricollis*)	1·70	1·70
118	41d.50 Ferruginous duck (*Aythya nyroca*)	2·10	2·10
119	49d.50 Black stork (*Ciconia nigra*)	2·75	2·75

53 Bat, Balls and Net

2005. 50th Anniv of Montenegrin Table Tennis Association.

120	53	16d.50 multicoloured	1·00	1·00

54 18th-century Fresco

2005. Easter. Multicoloured.

121	16d.50 Type **54**	1·00	1·00
122	28d.70 Crucifixion (carving) (1602)	2·30	2·30

55 University Facade, Belgrade

2005. Centenary of First Serbian University.

123	55	16d.50 multicoloured	1·00	1·00

56 Jovan Djordjevic

2005. Actors and Actresses. Multicoloured.

124	16d. Type **56**	1·10	1·10
125	16d. Milan Predic	1·10	1·10
126	16d. Milan Grol	1·10	1·10
127	16d. Mira Trailovic	1·10	1·10
128	16d. Soja Jovanovic	1·10	1·10
129	16d. Hugo Klajn	1·10	1·10
130	16d. Mata Milosevic	1·10	1·10
131	16d. Bojan Stupica	1·10	1·10

57 Colonnade (As No. 1407)

2005. 50th Anniv of Europa Stamps. Multicoloured.

132	16d.50 Type **57**	1·20	1·20
133	16d.50 Flaming sun (As No. 1425)	1·20	1·20
134	16d.50 Europa chain (As No. 1455)	1·20	1·20
135	16d.50 Communications (As No. 1514)	1·20	1·20
136	41d.50 Europa posthorn (As No. 1553)	2·40	2·40
137	41d.50 "Widow and Child" (sculpture, Ivan Mestrovic) (As No. 1604)	2·40	2·40
138	41d.50 Bridge (As No. 2138)	2·40	2·40
139	41d.50 Combined design (As No. 132, 134 and 137)	2·40	2·40
MS140	Two sheets, each 90×69 mm. (a) Nos. 132/5 (b) Nos. 136/139	13·00	13·00

58 *The Little Mermaid*

2005. Birth Bicentenary of Hans Christian Andersen (writer). Multicoloured.

141	41d.50 Type **58**	2·10	2·10
142	58d. *Snow Queen*	3·25	3·25

59 Bread and Bowl

2005. Europa. Gastronomy. Multicoloured.

143 41d.50 Type **59** 2·10 2·10
144 73d. Fish 4·00 4·00
MS145 93×50 mm. 41d.50 Cake; 73d. Tart 6·00 6·00

60 Marko Ivanovic

2005. Boka Kotorska Sea Captains. Multicoloured.

146 16d.50 Type **60** 1·00 1·00
147 33d. Petar Zelalic 1·70 1·70
148 41d.50 Matija Balovic 2·10 2·10
149 49d.50 Ivan Bronza 2·75 2·75

61 Crvena Zvezda (Red Star Football Club, Belgrade)

2005. Sports Associations' 60th Anniversaries. Multicoloured.

150 16d.50 Type **61** 1·10 1·10
151 16d.50 Partizan Football Club, Belgrade 1·10 1·10
MS152 94×53 mm. 16d.50×2, Crvena Zvezda; Partizan 2·10 2·10

The stamps and margins of No. **MS**152 form a composite design of knights jousting.

62 Boats and River Bank

2005. 50th Anniv of Danube Regatta. Sheet 97×49 mm containing T 62 and similar horiz design. Multicoloured.

MS153 41d.50 Type **62**; 49d.50 Boats, bridge and trees 4·75 4·75

The stamps and margins of No. **MS**153 form a composite design of the start of a boat race.

63 Rings surrounding Globe

2005. International Year of Physics (154) and Centenary of Publication of Theory of Special Relativity by Albert Einstein (155). Multicoloured.

154 41d.50 Type **63** 2·10 2·10
155 58d. Albert Einstein 3·25 3·25

64 Flowering Tree and Water

2005. Nature Protection. Koviljsko Petrovaradinski Rit Special Nature Reserve. Multicoloured.

156 41d.50 Type **64** 2·10 2·10
157 58d. Reeds, shrubs and water 3·25 3·25

65 Hands, Net and Ball

2005. European Volleyball Championships, Belgrade and Rome.

158 **65** 16d.50 multicoloured 1·30 1·30

66 Ball and Emblem

2005. European Basketball Championship (Eurobasket 2005), Belgrade.

159 **66** 16d.50 multicoloured 1·00 1·00

67 Parrot

2005. 36th "Joy in Europe" Meeting. Children's Day. Multicoloured.

160 41d.50 Type **67** 2·10 2·10
161 58d. Figure with raised arms (horiz) 3·25 3·25

68 Heart-shaped Graffiti

2005. World Youth Day.

162 **68** 41d.50 multicoloured 2·10 2·10

69 Roadway and Stars

2005. Initiation of Stabilization and Association Agreement with European Union.

163 **69** 16d.50 multicoloured 1·00 1·00

70 Early Airplane and Air Balloon

2005. Centenary of International Airline Federation. Multicoloured.

164 49d.50 Type **70** 2·50 2·50
165 58d. Glider, parachute and hang glider 3·25 3·25

71 Anniversary Emblem

2005. 60th Anniv of United Nations.

166 **71** 16d.50 multicoloured 1·10 1·10

72 Envelope and Aircraft

2005. Stamp Day.

167 **72** 16d.50 multicoloured 1·10 1·10

73 Petar I

2005. 175th Death Anniv of Valdika Petar I Petrovic (St Peter Cetinjski (bishop and leader)).

168 **73** 16d.50 multicoloured 1·10 1·10

74 Nicholas I

2005. Centenary of Montenegro's First Constitution.

169 **74** 16d.50 multicoloured 1·10 1·10

75 Stevan Sremac

2005. 150th Birth Anniv of Stevan Sremac (writer).

170 **75** 16d.50 multicoloured 1·10 1·10

76 Sudenica (Djorde Krstic)

2005. Paintings of Monasteries. Multicoloured.

171 16d.50 Type **76** 1·00 1·00
172 33d. Sopocani (Paja Jovanovic) 1·70 1·70
173 41d.50 Zica (Djorde Krstic) 2·30 2·30
174 49d.50 Gracanica (Milan Milanovic) 2·75 2·75

77 "Girl with Blue Ribbon" (F. X. Winterhalter)

2005. Paintings. Multicoloured.

175 16d.50 Type **77** 1·00 1·00
176 33d. "Adoration of the Child" (Andrea Alovidi) 1·70 1·70
177 41d.50 "Madonna with the Saints" (Biagio d'Antonio) 2·30 2·30
178 49d.50 "Remorse" (Vlaho Bukovaa) 2·75 2·75

78 The Nativity

2005. Christmas. Multicoloured.

179 16d.50 Type **78** 1·00 1·00
180 46d. The Nativity (different) 2·10 2·10

79 Footprints in Snow

2005. Tourism. Multicoloured.

181 5d. Type **79** 30 30
182 13d. Frozen lake 85 85
183 16d.50 Snow covered house and trees 1·00 1·00
184 33d. Snow covered hills 1·70 1·70

80 Jovan Sterija Popovic (birth bicentenary)

2006. Writers' Anniversaries. Multicoloured.

185 33d. Type **80** 1·70 1·70
186 46d. Stevan Stojanovic Mokranjac (150th birth anniv) 2·10 2·10

81 Ski Jump

2006. Winter Olympic Games, Turin. Multicoloured.

187 53d. Type **81** 2·50 2·50
188 73d. Skier 3·25 3·25

82 Easter Egg

2006. Easter. Multicoloured.

189 16d.50 Type **82** 85 85
190 46d. Basket of eggs 2·20 2·20

83 Bridge, Novi Sad

2006. 150th Anniv of Danube Commission. Multicoloured.

191 16d.50 Type **83** 85 85
192 16d.50 Castle, Smederevo 85 85
193 46d. Belgrade from river 2·20 2·20
194 46d. Tabula Traiana 2·20 2·20

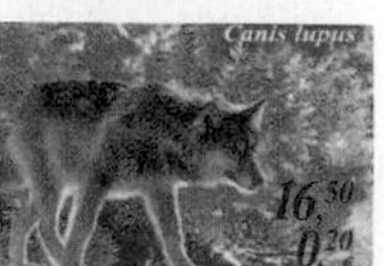

84 *Canis lupus*

2006. Fauna. Multicoloured.

195		16d.50 Type **84**	85	85
196		16d.50 *Otis tarda*	85	85
197		46d. *Vormela peregusna*	2·20	2·20
198		46d. *Ursus arctos*	2·20	2·20

85 Two Players

2006. World Cup Football Championship, Germany. Multicoloured.

199		33d. Type **85**	1·70	1·70
200		33d. Goalkeeper	2·20	2·20
MS201		95×55 mm. 46d.×2, Left of stadium (horiz); Right of stadium (horiz)	8·75	8·75

The stamps and margins of **MS**201 form a composite design.

86 Eskimo and Penguin on Beach

2006. Europa. Integration. Multicoloured.

202		46d. Type **86**	2·20	2·20
203		73d. Lion and lamb	3·50	3·50
MS204		95×55 mm. 46d. Women in park; 73d. Couple entering house	5·75	5·75

The stamps and margins of **MS**204 form a composite design.

87 Nikola Tesla

2006. 150th Birth Anniv of Nikola Tesla (inventor). Multicoloured.

205		16d.50 Type **87**	85	85
206		46d. Nikola Tesla and coil	2·20	2·20
MS207		124×70 mm. 46d. Nikola Tesla (horiz); 112d. Engine (horiz)	7·75	7·75

The stamps and margins of **MS**207 form a composite design.

88 Aqua

2006. Roses. Multicoloured.

208		16d.50 Type **88**	85	85
209		16d.50 Vendela	85	85
210		46d. Sphinx	2·20	2·20
211		46d. Red Berlin	2·20	2·20

89 Belgrade

2006

212	**89**	46d. multicoloured	2·20	2·20

90 Parkland

2006. Nature Protection. Multicoloured.

213		46d. Type **90**	2·20	2·20
214		58d. Graddski park	2·50	2·50

Pt. 2

SERBIAN OCCUPATION OF HUNGARY

100 filler = 1 korona.

BARANYA

1919. Stamps of Hungary optd 1919 Baranya or surch also. (a) "Turul" Type.

1	**7**	6f. drab	30	30
2	**7**	50f. red on blue	20	20
3	**7**	60f. green on red	55	55
4	**7**	70f. brown on green	20	20
5	**7**	80f. violet	2·75	2·75

(b) War Charity stamp of 1915.

6		50+2f. red on blue	8·50	8·50

(c) War Charity stamps of 1916.

8	**20**	10f. (+ 2f.) red	20	20
9	-	15f. (+ 2f.) violet	20	20

(d) Harvesters and Parliament Types.

10	**18**	2f. brown	20	20
11	**18**	3f. purple	30	30
12	**18**	5f. green	55	55
13	**18**	6f. blue	30	30
14	**18**	15f. purple	20	20
15	**18**	20f. brown	16·00	16·00
16	**18**	25f. blue	2·75	2·75
17	**18**	35f. brown	5·50	5·50
18	**18**	40f. green	22·00	22·00
19	**18**	50f. purple	55	55
20	**18**	75f. blue	20	20
21	**18**	80f. green	30	30
22	**19**	1k. lake	30	30
23	**19**	2k. brown	30	30
24	**19**	3k. grey and violet	30	30
25	**19**	5k. pale brown and brown	1·10	1·10
26	**19**	10k. magenta and brown	6·50	6·50

(e) Charles and Zita stamps.

27		10f. rose	20	20
28		20f. brown	20	20
29		25f. blue	1·10	1·10
30	**27**	40f. green	13·00	13·00
31	**27**	2f. brown	8·00	6·00
32	**27**	40f. green	18·00	18·00
33	**18**	45f. on 2f. brown	55	55
34		45f. on 5f. green	20·00	20·00
35		45k. on 15f. plum	20	20
36	**28**	45f. on 2f. brown	1·10	1·10

1919. Stamps of Hungary surch BARANYA and value. (a) Harvesters and Parliament Types.

42	**18**	20 on 2f. brown	8·00	8·00
43	**18**	50 on 5f. green	4·25	4·25
44	**18**	150 on 15f. purple	75	75
45	**19**	200 on 75f. blue	75	75

(b) Harvesters Type inscr "MAGYAR POSTA".

46	**18**	20 on 2f. brown	20	20
47	**18**	30 on 6f. blue	45	45
48	**18**	50 on 5f. green	10	10
49	**18**	100 on 25f. blue	10	10
50	**18**	100 on 40f. green	10	10
51	**18**	100 on 45f. orange	55	55
52	**18**	150 on 20f. brown	30	30

(c) Charles stamp optd KOZTARSASAG.

53	**27**	150 on 15f. purple	1·60	1·60

EXPRESS LETTER STAMPS

1919. No. E245 of Hungary surch 1919 Baranya 105.

E37	**E 18**	105 on 2f. green and red	1·10	1·10

1919. No. E245 of Hungary surch BARANYA 10.

E55		10 on 2f. olive and red	45	45

NEWSPAPER STAMP

1919. No. N136 of Hungary surch BARANYA 10.

N54	**N 9**	10 on 2(f). orange	10	10

POSTAGE DUE STAMPS

1919. Nos. D191 etc of Hungary optd 1919 BARANYA or surch also.

D38	**D9**	2f. red and green	4·25	4·25
D39	**D9**	10f. red and green	75	75
D40	**D9**	20f. red and geen	75	75
D41	**D9**	40 on 2f. red and green	75	75

SAVINGS BANK STAMP

1919. No. B199 of Hungary surch BARANYA 10.

B56	**B 17**	10 on 10f. purple	55	55

TEMESVAR

Temesvar was later occupied by Romania which issued stamps for this area. It was then incorporated in Romania and renamed Timosoara.

1919. Stamps of Hungary surch. (a) War Charity stamps of 1916.

1	**20**	45f. on 10f.(+2f.) red	20	20

(b) Harvesters Type.

2	**18**	10f. on 2f. brown	20	20
3	**18**	30f. on 2f. brown	30	30
4	**18**	1k.50 on 15f. purple	45	45

(c) Charles Stamp.

5	**27**	50f. on 20f. brown	30	30

POSTAGE DUE STAMPS

1919. No. D191 of Hungary surch.

D6	**D 9**	40f. on 2f. red and green	55	55
D7	**D 9**	60f. on 2f. red and green	55	55
D8	**D 9**	100f. on 2f. red and green	55	55

Pt. 1

SEYCHELLES

A group of islands in the Indian Ocean, east of Africa.

100 cents = 1 rupee.

1

1890

9	**1**	2c. green and red	2·50	1·00
28	**1**	2c. brown and green	2·00	1·75
22	**1**	3c. purple and orange	1·50	50
10	**1**	4c. red and green	2·50	1·75
29	**1**	6c. red	3·50	50
11	**1**	8c. purple and blue	14·00	1·75
12	**1**	10c. blue and brown	14·00	3·25
23	**1**	12c. brown and green	2·50	60
13	**1**	13c. grey and black	4·00	1·75
24	**1**	15c. olive and lilac	6·00	2·00
30	**1**	15c. blue	10·00	5·00
6	**1**	16c. brown and blue	11·00	4·25
31	**1**	18c. blue	9·00	1·50
32	**1**	36c. brown and red	38·00	5·00
25	**1**	45c. brown and red	23·00	35·00
7	**1**	48c. bistre and green	23·00	10·00
33	**1**	75c. yellow and violet	55·00	70·00
8	**1**	96c. mauve and red	65·00	48·00
34	**1**	1r. mauve and red	13·00	6·00
35	**1**	1r.50 grey and red	85·00	90·00
36	**1**	2r.25 mauve and green	£110	85·00

1893. Surch in figures and words in two lines.

15		3c. on 4c. red and green	1·10	1·50
16		12c. on 16c. brown and blue	4·25	4·50
19		15c. on 16c. brown and blue	22·00	3·00
20		45c. on 48c. brown and green	32·00	5·50
21		90c. on 96c. mauve and red	65·00	42·00

1896. Surch in figures and words in one line.

26		18c. on 45c. brown and red	7·50	3·00
27		36c. on 45c. brown and red	9·00	60·00

1901. Surch in figures and words.

41		2c. on 4c. red and green	3·50	2·75
37		3c. on 10c. blue and brown	2·00	75
38		3c. on 16c. brown and blue	4·50	7·00
39		3c. on 36c. brown and red	1·00	80
40		6c. on 8c. purple and blue	4·00	3·00
42		30c. on 75c. yellow and violet	2·25	5·00
43		30c. on 1r. mauve and red	12·00	42·00
44		45c. on 1r. mauve and red	6·00	45·00
45		45c. on 2r.25 mauve and green	50·00	£110

6

1903

46	**6**	2c. brown and green	1·75	2·00
47	**6**	3c. green	1·00	1·25
62	**6**	6c. red	2·00	80
49	**6**	12c. brown and green	3·50	2·50
64	**6**	15c. blue	3·00	2·00
65	**6**	18c. olive and red	3·00	6·50
66	**6**	30c. violet and green	6·00	8·00
67	**6**	45c. brown and red	3·00	9·00
54	**6**	75c. yellow and violet	10·00	32·00
69	**6**	1r.50 black and red	55·00	60·00
70	**6**	2r.25 purple and green	50·00	65·00

1903. Surch 3 cents.

57		3c. on 15c. blue	1·00	3·25
58		3c. on 18c. olive and red	2·75	45·00
59		3c. on 45c. brown and red	3·00	3·25

9

1912. Inscr "POSTAGE POSTAGE".

71	**9**	2c. brown and green	1·00	7·00
72	**9**	3c. green	4·00	60
73	**9**	6c. red	4·25	1·75
74	**9**	12c. brown and green	1·25	4·50
75	**9**	15c. blue	3·75	1·75
76	**9**	18c. olive and red	3·25	8·50
77	**9**	30c. violet and green	9·00	1·50
78	**9**	45c. brown and red	2·75	50·00
79	**9**	75c. yellow and violet	2·75	5·50
80	**9**	1r.50 black and red	8·50	1·00
81	**9**	2r.25 purple and green	70·00	2·50

11

1917. Inscr "POSTAGE & REVENUE".

98	**11**	2c. brown and green	25	15
99	**11**	3c. green	1·75	15
100	**11**	3c. black	1·00	30
101	**11**	4c. green	1·00	2·50
102	**11**	4c. olive and red	6·50	17·00
103	**11**	5c. brown	75	5·50
85	**11**	6c. red	3·50	1·00
105	**11**	6c. mauve	1·25	10
106	**11**	9c. red	3·25	4·25
107	**11**	12c. grey	2·75	20
108	**11**	12c. red	1·50	30
87	**11**	15c. blue	1·75	1·50
111	**11**	15c. yellow	1·00	2·75
112	**11**	18c. purple on yellow	2·50	16·00
113	**11**	20c. blue	1·50	35
89b	**11**	25c. black & red on yellow	3·00	14·00
90	**11**	30c. purple and olive	1·50	11·00
116	**11**	45c. purple and orange	1·25	5·00
117	**11**	50c. purple and black	2·50	2·25
93a	**11**	75c. black on green	1·40	21·00
119	**11**	1r. purple and red	22·00	18·00
121	**11**	1r.50 purple & blue on bl	14·00	22·00
122	**11**	2r.25 green and violet	16·00	14·00
123	**11**	5r. green and blue	£110	£170

1935. Silver Jubilee. As T 32a of St. Helena.

128		6c. blue and black	1·25	2·00
129		12c. green and blue	4·75	1·50
130		20c. brown and blue	3·50	4·50
131		1r. grey and purple	7·50	23·00

1937. Coronation. As T 32b of St. Helena.

132		6c. green	55	15
133		12c. orange	75	50
134		20c. blue	75	1·00

14 Coco-de-mer Palm

1938

135	**14**	2c. brown	1·50	40
136	-	3c. green	9·50	2·50
136ab	-	3c. orange	55	1·50
137	-	6c. orange	15·00	3·50
137b	-	6c. green	55	2·25
138	**14**	9c. red	17·00	3·50
138ac	-	9c. blue	7·50	3·25
139	-	12c. mauve	50·00	1·25
139ab	-	15c. red	7·50	4·50

139c	14	18c. red	10·00	60
140	-	20c. blue	45·00	6·00
140b	-	20c. yellow	2·50	3·00
141	14	25c. brown	50·00	14·00
142	-	30c. red	50·00	11·00
142ab	-	30c. blue	2·25	6·00
143a	-	45c. brown	3·00	2·50
144a	14	50c. violet	1·75	3·25
145	-	75c. blue	85·00	48·00
145ab	-	75c. mauve	2·75	6·00
146	-	1r. green	£130	75·00
146ab	-	1r. black	3·75	5·50
147a	14	1r.50 blue	5·50	14·00
148a	-	2r.25 olive	29·00	32·00
149	-	5r. red	24·00	12·00

DESIGNS—VERT: 3, 12, 15, 30, 75c., 2r.25, Giant tortoise. HORIZ: 6, 20, 45c., 1, 5r. Fishing pirogue.

1946. Victory. As T 33a of St. Helena.

150	9c. blue	10	10
151	30c. blue	30	20

1948. Silver Wedding. As T 33b-c of St. Helena.

152	9c. blue	15	60
153	5r. red	14·00	42·00

1949. U.P.U. As T 33d-g of St. Helena.

154	18c. mauve	20	25
155	50c. purple	1·75	2·40
156	1r. grey	50	35
157	2r.25 olive	35	1·25

17 Sailfish

1952. Full face portrait.

158	17	2c. lilac	75	70
159	-	3c. orange	75	30
160	-	9c. blue	60	1·75
161	-	15c. green	50	1·00
162	-	18c. lake	1·75	20
163	-	20c. yellow	2·25	1·50
164	-	25c. red	70	2·50
165	17	40c. blue	1·25	2·00
166	-	45c. brown	1·75	30
167	-	50c. violet	1·25	1·75
168	-	1r. black	5·50	4·25
169	-	1r.50 blue	12·00	17·00
170	-	2r.25 olive	18·00	19·00
171	-	5r. red	19·00	20·00
172	17	10r. green	27·00	50·00

DESIGNS—VERT: 2, 25c., 2r.25, Giant tortoise; 9, 50c., 1r.50, Coco-de-mer palm. HORIZ: 15, 20, 45c. Fishing pirogue; 18c., 1, 5r. Map of Indian Ocean.

1953. Coronation. As T 33h of St. Helena.

173	9c. black and blue	60	70

1954. Designs as 1952 but with portrait of Queen Elizabeth II.

174	2c. lilac	10	10
175	3c. orange	10	10
175a	5c. violet	2·75	30
176	9c. blue	10	10
176a	10c. blue (as 9c.)	70	2·25
177	15c. green	2·50	30
178	18c. lake	20	10
179	20c. yellow	1·50	20
180	25c. red	2·25	1·00
180a	35c. lake (as 18c.)	6·50	1·75
181	40c. blue	1·00	25
182	45c. brown	20	15
183	50c. violet	30	80
183a	70c. brown (as 45c.)	6·50	2·25
184	1r. black	1·75	40
185	1r.50 blue	7·00	11·00
186	2r.25 olive	6·50	9·00
187	5r. red	18·00	9·00
188	10r. green	28·00	18·00

NEW DESIGN: 5c. Seychelles flying fox.

21 "La Pierre de Possession"

1956. Bicent of "La Pierre de Possession".

189	21	40c. blue	15	15
190	21	1r. black	15	15

1957. No. 182 surch 5 cents and bars.

191	5c. on 45c. brown	15	10

23 Mauritius 6d. Stamp with Seychelles "B 64" Cancellation

1961. Cent of First Seychelles Post Office.

193	23	10c. blue, black and purple	25	10
194	23	35c. blue, black and green	40	10
195	23	2r.25 blue, black & brown	70	45

24 Black Parrot

40 Colony's Badge

1962. Multicoloured.. Multicoloured..

233	5c. Type **24**	35	2·25
234	10c. Vanilla vine	30	15
198	15c. Fisherman	30	10
199	20c. Denis Is. Lighthouse	40	10
200	25c. Clock Tower, Victoria	50	10
200a	30c. Anse Royale Bay	8·50	5·00
201	35c. Anse Royale Bay	1·75	1·50
202	40c. Government House	20	1·50
203	45c. Fishing pirogue	3·50	5·00
204	50c. Cascade Church	40	25
236	60c. red, blue and brown (Flying fox)	1·75	45
205	70c. ultramarine and blue (Sailfish)	7·00	3·00
206	75c. Coco-de-mer palm	2·75	4·25
237	85c. ultramarine and blue (Sailfish)	1·00	40
207	1r. Cinnamon	1·00	10
208	1r.50 Copra	5·50	6·50
209	2r.25 Map	5·50	9·00
210	3r.50 Land settlement	2·25	6·50
211	5r. Regina Mundi Convent	5·00	2·50
212	10r. Type **40**	14·00	4·00

The 30, 35, 40, 85c., 1, 1r.50, 2r.25, 3r.50 and 5r. are horiz.

No. 236 is 23×25 mm.

1963. Freedom from Hunger. As T 63a of St. Helena.

213	70c. violet	60	25

1963. Cent of Red Cross. As T 63b of St. Helena.

214	10c. red and black	25	10
215	75c. red and blue	75	60

1965. Surch.

216	45c. on 35c. (No. 201)	10	15
217	75c. on 70c. (No. 205)	20	15

1965. Cent of I.T.U. As T 64a of St. Helena.

218	5c. orange and blue	10	10
219	1r.50 mauve and green	50	25

1965. I.C.Y. As T 64b of St. Helena.

220	5c. purple and turquoise	15	10
221	40c. green and lavender	35	30

1966. Churchill Commemoration. As T 64c of St. Helena.

222	5c. blue	15	50
223	15c. green	45	10
224	75c. brown	1·25	45
225	1r.50 violet	1·40	3·25

1966. World Cup Football Championship. As T 64d of St. Helena.

226	15c. multicoloured	20	25
227	1r. multicoloured	35	40

1966. Inauguration of W.H.O. Headquarters, Geneva. As T 64e of St. Helena.

228	20c. black, green and blue	20	10
229	30c. black, purple and ochre	40	20

1966. 20th Anniv of UNESCO. As T 64f of St. Helena.

230	15c. multicoloured	20	10
231	1r. yellow, violet and olive	35	10
232	5r. black, purple and orange	80	1·00

1967. Universal Adult Suffrage. Nos. 198, 203, 206 and 210 optd UNIVERSAL ADULT SUFFRAGE 1967.

238	15c. multicoloured	10	10
239	45c. multicoloured	10	10
240	75c. multicoloured	10	10
241	3r.50 multicoloured	20	50

44 Money Cowrie, Mole Cowrie and Tiger Cowrie

1967. International Tourist Year. Mult.

242	15c. Type **44**	20	10
243	40c. Beech cone, textile or cloth of gold cone and Virgin cone	25	10
244	1r. Arthritic spider conch	35	10
245	2r.25 Subulate auger and trumpet triton shells	60	1·25

1968. Nos. 202-203 and 206 surch.

246	30c. on 40c. multicoloured	10	30
247	60c. on 45c. multicoloured	15	30
248	85c. on 75c. multicoloured	20	30

49 Farmer with Wife and Children at Sunset

1968. Human Rights Year.

249	49	20c. multicoloured	10	10
250	49	50c. multicoloured	10	10
251	49	85c. multicoloured	10	10
252	49	2r.25 multicoloured	25	1·60

50 Expedition landing at Anse Possession

1968. Bicent of First Landing on Praslin. Mult.

253	20c. Type **50**	35	10
254	50c. French warships at anchor (vert)	40	15
255	85c. Coco-de-mer and Black parrot (vert)	90	25
256	2r.25 French warships under sail	90	2·75

54 Apollo Launch

1969. First Man on the Moon. Multicoloured.

257	5c. Type **54**	10	50
258	20c. Module leaving mother ship for the Moon	15	10
259	50c. Astronauts and Space Module on the Moon	20	15
260	85c. Tracking station	25	15
261	2r.25 Moon craters with Earth on the "Horizon"	45	1·60

59 Picault's Landing, 1742

1969. Multicoloured.. Multicoloured..

262	5c. Type **59**	10	10
263	10c. U.S. satellite-tracking station	10	10
264	15c. "Konigsberg I" (German cruiser) at Aldabra, 1914	3·00	2·00
265	20c. Fleet re-fuelling off St. Anne, 1939–45	1·75	10
266	25c. Exiled Ashanti King, Prempeh	20	10
267	30c. Laying Stone of Possession, 1756	1·00	4·00
268a	40c. As 30c.	1·60	1·60
269	50c. Pirates and treasures	30	15
270	60c. Corsairs attacking merchantman	1·00	1·50
271	65c. As 60c.	6·00	8·00
272	85c. Impression of proposed airport	3·50	1·75
273a	95c. As 85c.	5·50	3·25
274	1r. French Governor capitulating to British naval officer, 1794	35	15
275	1r.50 H.M.S. "Sybille" (frigate) and "Chiffone" (French frigate) in battle, 1801	1·75	2·00
276	3r.50 Visit of the Duke of Edinburgh, 1956	1·00	2·25
277	5r. Chevalier Queau de Quincy	1·00	2·75
278	10r. Indian Ocean chart, 1574	2·75	8·00
279	15r. Badge of Seychelles	4·00	14·00

NOTE: The design of No. 264 incorrectly shows the vessel "Konigsberg II" and date "1915".

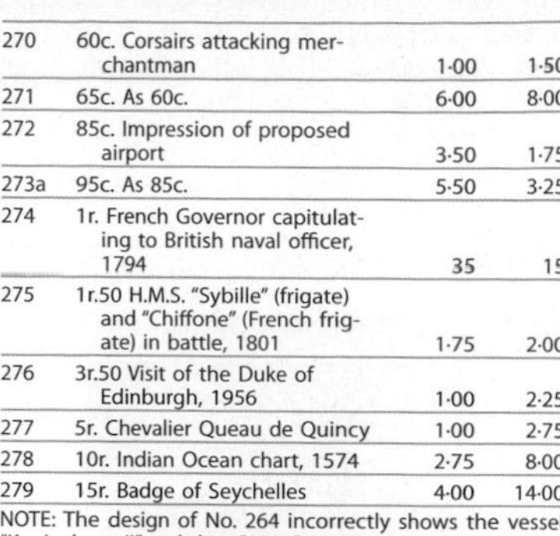

74 White Terns, French Warship and Island

1970. Bicentenary of First Settlement, St. Anne Island. Multicoloured.

280	20c. Type **74**	1·00	10
281	50c. Spot-finned flyingfish, ship and island	45	10
282	85c. Compass and chart	45	10
283	3r.50 Anchor on sea-bed	70	1·25

78 Girl and Optician's Chart

1970. Centenary of British Red Cross. Mult.

284	20c. Type **78**	30	10
285	50c. Baby, scales and milk bottles	30	10
286	85c. Woman with child and umbrella (vert)	30	10
287	3r.50 Red Cross local headquarters building	1·25	2·75

79 Pitcher Plant

1970. Flowers. Multicoloured.

288	20c. Type **79**	25	15
289	50c. Wild vanilla	30	15
290	85c. Tropic-bird orchid	80	30
291	3r.50 Vare hibiscus	1·00	2·25
MS292	81×133 mm. Nos. 288-291	2·75	13·00

80 Seychelles "On the Map"

1971. "Putting Seychelles on the Map". Sheet 152×101 mm.

MS293	**80**	5r. multicoloured	1·75	9·00

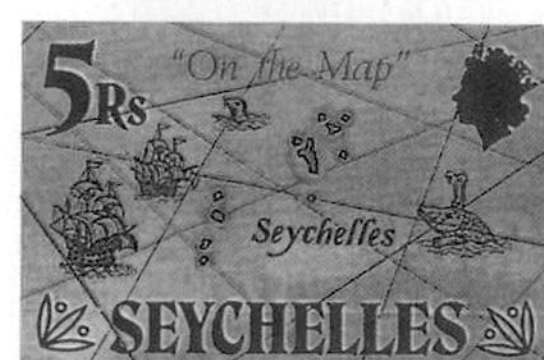

81 Piper Navajo

1971. Airport Completion. Multicoloured.

294	5c. Type **81**	30	50
295	20c. Westland Wessex HAS-1 helicopter	65	10
296	50c. Consolidated Catalina amphibian (horiz)	70	10
297	60c. Grumman Albatross	75	10
298	85c. Short "G" Class flying boat "Golden Hind" (horiz)	80	10
299	3r.50 Vickers Supermarine Walrus Mk I amphibian (horiz)	2·25	3·50

82 Santa Claus delivering Gifts (Jean-Claude Waye Hive)

1971. Christmas. Multicoloured.

300	10c. Type **82**	10	10
301	15c. Santa Claus seated on turtle (Edison Theresine)	10	10
302	3r.50 Santa Claus landing on island (Isabelle Tirant)	40	2·25

1971. Nos. 267, 270 and 272 surch.

303	40c. on 30c. multicoloured	30	55
304	65c. on 60c. multicoloured	40	75
305	95c. on 85c. multicoloured	45	1·00

1972. Royal Visit. Nos. 265 and 277 optd ROYAL VISIT 1972.

306	20c. multicoloured	15	20
307	5r. multicoloured	1·00	3·00

85 Seychelles Brush Warbler

1972. Rare Seychelles Birds. Multicoloured.

308	5c. Type **85**	60	70
309	20c. Bare-legged scops owl ("Seychelles Scoops Owl")	2·25	70
310	50c. Seychelles blue pigeon	2·25	70
311	65c. Seychelles magpie robin	2·75	75
312	95c. Seychelles paradise flycatcher ("Black Paradise Flycatcher")	3·00	2·50
313	3r.50 Seychelles kestrel	8·00	12·00
MS314	144×162 mm. Nos. 308/13	20·00	28·00

86 Fireworks Display

1972. "Festival '72". Multicoloured.

315	10c. Type **86**	10	10
316	15c. Pirogue race (horiz)	10	10
317	25c. Floats and costumes	10	10
318	5r. Water skiing (horiz)	60	1·25

1972. Royal Silver Wedding. As T 103 of St. Helena, but with Giant Tortoise and Sailfish in background.

319	95c. blue	15	10
320	1r.50 brown	15	10

1973. Royal Wedding. As T 103a of St. Helena. Multicoloured, background colours given.

321	95c. brown	10	10
322	1r.50 blue	10	10

88 Seychelles Squirrelfish

1974. Fishes. Multicoloured.

323	20c. Type **88**	25	15
324	50c. Harlequin filefish	35	15
325	95c. Pennant coralfish ("Papillon")	40	40
326	1r.50 Oriental sweetlips ("Peau d'ane canal")	85	2·50

89 Globe and Letter

1974. Centenary of U.P.U. Multicoloured.

327	20c. Type **89**	10	10
328	50c. Globe and radio beacon	20	10
329	95c. Globe and postmark	35	40
330	1r.50 Emblems within "UPU"	50	1·25

90 Sir Winston Churchill

1974. Birth Centenary of Sir Winston Churchill. Multicoloured.

331	95c. Type **90**	20	20
332	1r.50 Profile portrait	35	80
MS333	81×109 mm. Nos. 331/2	60	1·75

1975. Visit of Liner "Queen Elizabeth II". Nos. 265, 269, 273a and 275 optd VISIT OF Q.E. II and silhouette of liner.

334	20c. multicoloured	15	15
335	50c. multicoloured	20	20
336	95c. multicoloured	25	40
337	1r.50 multicoloured	35	1·75

1975. Internal Self-Government. Nos. 265, 271, 274 and 276 optd INTERNAL SELF-GOVERNMENT OCTOBER 1975.

338	20c. multicoloured	15	15
339	65c. multicoloured	25	30
340	1r. multicoloured	30	35
341	3r.50 multicoloured	75	2·50

93 Queen Elizabeth I

1975. International Women's Year. Mult.

342	10c. Type **93**	10	25
343	15c. Gladys Aylward	10	25
344	20c. Elizabeth Fry	10	10
345	25c. Emmeline Pankhurst	10	10
346	65c. Florence Nightingale	25	20
347	1r. Amy Johnson	40	35
348	1r.50 Joan of Arc	50	1·50
349	3r.50 Eleanor Roosevelt	1·00	3·50

94 Map of Praslin and Postmark

1976. Rural Posts. Multicoloured.

350	20c. Type **94**	30	10
351	65c. La Digue	40	20
352	1r. Mahe with Victoria postmark	50	25
353	1r.50 Mahe with Anse Royale postmark	60	2·00
MS354	166×127 mm. Nos. 350/3	1·50	3·00

Nos. 350-353 show maps and postmarks.

95 First Landing, 1609 (inset portrait of Premier James Mancham)

1976. Independence. Multicoloured.

355	20c. Type **95**	15	10
356	25c. The Possession Stone	15	10
357	40c. First settlers, 1770	15	15
358	75c. Chevalier Queau de Quincy	15	40
359	1r. Sir Bickham Sweet-Escott	15	20
360	1r.25 Legislative Building	20	1·00
361	1r.50 Seychelles badge	20	1·00
362	3r.50 Seychelles flag	60	2·00

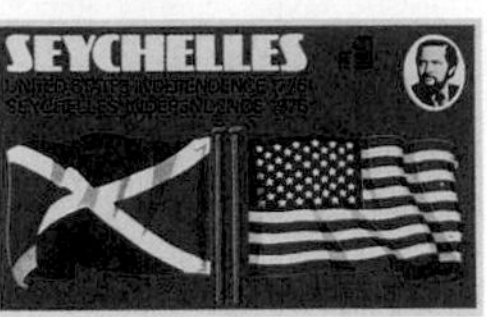

96 Flags of Seychelles and U.S.A.

1976. Seychelles Independence and American Bicent of Independence. Multicoloured.

363	1r. Type **96**	30	15
364	10r. Statehouses of Seychelles and Philadelphia	70	3·00

97 Swimming

1976. Olympic Games, Montreal.

365	**97**	20c. blue, lt blue & brown	10	10
366	-	65c. lt green, green & grey	35	10
367	-	1r. brown, blue and grey	35	10
368	-	3r.50 light red, red & grey	50	2·75

DESIGNS: 65c. Hockey; 1r. Basketball; 3r.50, Football.

98 Seychelles Paradise Flycatcher

1976. 4th Pan-African Ornithological Congress, Seychelles. Multicoloured.

369	20c. Type **98**	40	20
370	1r.25 Seychelles sunbird (horiz)	1·10	1·00
371	1r.50 Seychelles brown white eye ("The Seychelles White-eye") (horiz)	1·50	1·50
372	5r. Black parrot ("The Seychelles Black Parrot")	2·50	5·50
MS373	161×109 mm. Nos. 369-372	6·50	9·00

1976. Independence. Nos. 265, 269, 271, 273a, 274 and 276-279 optd Independence 1976 or surch also.

374	20c. Fleet re-fuelling off St. Anne, 1939–45	70	2·50
375	50c. Pirates and treasure	60	2·50
376	95c. Impression of proposed airport	2·25	2·25
377	1r. French Governor capitulating to British naval officer, 1794	55	2·25
378	3r.50 Visit of Duke of Edinburgh, 1956	2·75	4·50
379	5r. Chevalier Queau de Quincy	1·75	7·50
380	10r. Indian Ocean chart, 1574	2·50	12·00
381	15r. Badge of Seychelles	2·75	12·00
382	25r. on 65c. Corsairs attacking merchantman	3·00	16·00

100 Inauguration of George Washington

1976. Bicentenary of American Revolution.

383	**100**	1c. deep red and red	10	10
384	-	2c. violet and lilac	10	10
385	-	3c. light blue and blue	10	10
386	-	4c. brown and yellow	10	10
387	-	5c. green and yellow	10	10
388	-	1r.50 brown & light brown	30	35
389	-	3r.50 blue and green	35	70
390	-	5r. brown and yellow	40	80
391	-	10r. blue and light blue	65	1·50
MS392		141×141 mm. 25r. purple and mauve	3·00	6·50

DESIGNS: 2c. Jefferson and Louisiana Purchase; 3c. William Seward and Alaska Purchase; 4c. Pony Express, 1860; 5c. Lincoln's Emancipation Proclamation; 1r.50, Trans-continental Railroad, 1869; 3r.50, Wright Brothers flight, 1903; 5r. Henry Ford's assembly-line, 1913; 10r. J. F. Kennedy and 1969 Moon-landing; 25r. Signing Independence Declaration, 1776.

101 Silhouette of the Islands

1977. Silver Jubilee. Multicoloured.

393	20c. Type **101**	10	10
394	40c. Silhouette (different)	10	10
395	50c. The Orb (vert)	10	10
396	1r. St. Edward's Crown (vert)	10	10
397	1r.25 Ampulla and Spoon (vert)	10	15
398	1r.50 Sceptre with Cross (vert)	10	15
399	5r. Silhouette (different)	25	30
400	10r. Silhouette (different)	45	60
MS401	133×135 mm. 20c., 50c., 1r., 10r.	55	1·40

102 Cruiser "Aurora" and Flag

1977. 60th Anniv of Russian Revolution.

402	**102**	1r.50 multicoloured	55	30
MS403		101×129 mm. No. 402	80	1·10

103 Coral Scene

1977. Marine Life. Rupee face values shown as "Re" or "Rs". Multicoloured.

404A	5c. Reef fish	30	2·00
405B	10c. Hawksbill turtle	20	10
406B	15c. Coco-de-mer	20	15
407A	20c. Wild vanilla orchid	1·50	20
408A	25c. "Hypolimnas misippus" (butterfly)	1·50	1·75
409B	40c. Type **103**	20	10
410A	50c. Giant tortoise	30	10
411A	75c. Crayfish	40	10
412A	1r. Madagascar red fody ("Madagascar Fody")	1·25	10
413A	1r.25 White tern ("Fairy Tern")	1·25	20
414A	1r.50 Seychelles flying fox	1·00	20
736	3r. Seychelles gecko	6·00	6·00
415A	3r.50 As 3r.	75	3·25
416A	5r. Octopus	1·50	40
417A	10r. Tiger cowrie	1·50	2·50
418A	15r. Pitcher plant	1·50	2·50
419A	20r. Coat of arms	1·50	2·50

The 40c., 1r., 1r.25 and 1r.50 values are horizontal, 31×27 mm. The 5, 10, 15 and 20r. are vertical, 28×36 mm. The others are horizontal, 29×25 mm.

Nos. 405-412 and 414 exist with or without imprint date at foot.

For similar designs with rupee face values shown as "R" see Nos. 487a-494.

104 St. Roch Roman Catholic Church, Bel Ombre

1977. Christmas. Multicoloured.

420	20c. Type **104**	10	10
421	1r. Anglican cathedral, Victoria	10	10
422	1r.50 Roman Catholic cathedral, Victoria	15	10
423	5r. St. Mark's Anglican church, Praslin	30	45

105 Liberation Day ringed on Calendar

1978. Liberation Day. Multicoloured.

424	40c. Type **105**	10	10
425	1r.25 Hands holding bayonet, torch and flag	15	10
426	1r.50 Fisherman and farmer	15	15
427	5r. Soldiers and rejoicing people	35	40

106 Stamp Portraits of Edward VII, George V and George VI

1978. 25th Anniv of Coronation. Multicoloured.

428	40c. Type **106**	10	10
429	1r.50 Queen Victoria and Elizabeth II	15	10
430	3r. Queen Victoria Monument	25	25
431	5r. Queen's Building, Victoria	35	35
MS432	87×129 mm. Nos. 428-431	75	85

107 Gardenia

1978. Wildlife. Multicoloured.

433	40c. Type **107**	15	10
434	1r.25 Seychelles magpie robin ("Magpie Robin of Fregate Island")	1·50	70
435	1r.50 Seychelles paradise flycatcher	1·50	70
436	5r. Green turtle	1·25	1·50

108 Possession Stone

1978. Bicentenary of Victoria. Multicoloured.

437	20c. Type **108**	10	10
438	1r.25 Plan of 1782 "L' Etablissement"	15	15
439	1r.50 Clock Tower	15	15
440	5r. Bust of Pierre Poivre	40	1·75

109 Seychelles Fody

1979. Birds (1st series). Multicoloured.

441	2r. Type **109**	55	55
442	2r. Green-backed heron	55	55
443	2r. Thick-billed bulbul ("Seychelles Bulbul")	55	55
444	2r. Seychelles cave swiftlet	55	55
445	2r. Grey-headed lovebird	55	55

See also Nos. 463-467, 500-504 and 523-527.

110 Patrice Lumumba

1979. Africa Liberation Heroes.

446	**110**	40c. black, violet and lilac	10	10
447	-	2r. black, blue & light blue	20	25
448	-	2r.25 black, brown & orange	20	30
449	-	5r. black, olive and green	45	1·25

DESIGNS: 2r. Kwame Nkrumah; 2r.25, Dr. Eduardo Mondlane; 5r. Hamilcar Cabral.

111 1978 5r. Liberation Day Commemorative and Sir Rowland Hill

1979. Death Cent of Sir Rowland Hill. Mult.

450	40c. Type **111**	10	10
451	2r.25 1972 50c. Seychelles blue pigeon commemorative	25	70
452	3r. 1962 50c. definitive	35	95
MS453	112×88 mm. 5r. 1892 4c. definitive	50	55

112 Child with Book

1979. International Year of the Child. Mult.

454	40c. Type **112**	10	10
455	2r.25 Children of different races	15	30
456	3r. Young child with ball (vert)	20	50
457	5r. Girl with glove puppet (vert)	35	70

113 The Herald Angel

1979. Christmas. Multicoloured.

458	20c. Type **113**	10	10
459	2r.25 The Virgin and Child	30	40
460	3r. The Three Kings (horiz)	40	60
MS461	87×75 mm. 5r. The Flight into Egypt (horiz)	50	70

1980. No. 415 surch R.1.10.

462	1r.10 on 3r.50 Green gecko	30	50

115 Seychelles Kestrel

1980. Birds (2nd series). Seychelles Kestrel. Mult.

463	2r. Type **115**	80	65
464	2r. Pair of Seychelles kestrels	80	65
465	2r. Seychelles kestrel with eggs	80	65
466	2r. Seychelles kestrel on nest with chick	80	65
467	2r. Seychelles kestrel chicks in nest	80	65

116 10 Rupees Banknote

1980. "London 1980" International Stamp Exhibition. Currency Notes. Multicoloured.

468	40c. Type **116**	15	10
469	1r.50 25 rupees	30	15
470	2r.25 50 rupees (vert)	40	25
471	5r. 100 rupees (vert)	80	75
MS472	119×102 mm. Nos. 468-471	2·00	1·60

117 Sprinting

1980. Olympic Games, Moscow. Multicoloured.

473	40c. Type **117**	10	10
474	2r.25 Weightlifting	20	20
475	3r. Boxing	30	30
476	5r. Sailing	60	50
MS477	90×121 mm. Nos. 473-476	1·40	2·25

118 Boeing 747-200 Airliner

1980. Int Tourism Conference, Manila. Mult.

478	40c. Type **118**	10	10
479	2r.25 Bus	25	30
480	3r. Cruise liner	35	40
481	5r. "La Belle Coralline" (tourist launch)	55	65

119 Female Palm

1980. Coco-de-mer (palms). Multicoloured.

482	40c. Type **119**	10	10
483	2r.25 Male palm	25	20
484	3r. Artefacts	40	35
485	5r. Fisherman's gourd	55	55
MS486	82×140 mm. Nos. 482/5	1·60	1·60

1981. As Nos. 412-414, 415 (with new value), and 416-419 but face values redrawn as "R" instead of "Re" or "Rs".

487	1r. Madagascar red fody ("Madagascar Fody")	1·00	60
488	1r.10 Green gecko	70	1·00
489	1r.25 White tern ("Fairy Tern")	2·75	1·75
490	1r.50 Seychelles flying fox	50	75
491	5r. Octopus	1·25	1·40
492	10r. Tiger cowrie	3·25	3·50
493	15r. Pitcher plant	4·00	4·50
494	20r. Seychelles coat of arms	5·00	6·00

120 Vasco da Gama's "Sao Gabriel", 1497

1981. Ships. Multicoloured.

495	40c. Type **120**	15	10
496	2r.25 Mascarenhas' caravel, 1505	50	55
497	3r.50 Darwin's H.M.S. "Beagle", 1831	55	1·00
498	5r. "Queen Elizabeth 2" (liner), 1968	60	1·40
MS499	141×91 mm. Nos. 495/8	1·50	3·50

121 Male White Tern

1981. Birds (3rd series). White Tern. Mult.

500	2r. Type **121**	1·00	65
501	2r. Pair of white terns	1·00	65
502	2r. Female white tern	1·00	65
503	2r. Female white tern on nest and egg	1·00	65
504	2r. White tern and chick	1·00	65

1981. Royal Wedding. Royal Yachts. As T 14a/b of St. Kitts. Multicoloured.

505	1r.50 "Victoria and Albert I"	15	25
506	1r.50 Prince Charles and Lady Diana Spencer	65	75
507	5r. "Cleveland"	35	60
509	10r. "Britannia"	60	1·50
510	10r. As No. 506	1·75	3·00
MS511	120×109 mm. 7r.50 As No. 506	1·00	1·00
513	5r. As No. 506	1·25	2·00

122 Britten Norman Islander

1981. 10th Anniv of Opening of Seychelles International Airport. Aircraft. Multicoloured.

514	40c. Type **122**	15	10
515	2r.25 Britten Norman "long nose" Trislander	40	45
516	3r.50 Vickers Super VC-10 airliner	60	70
517	5r. Boeing 747-100 airliner	75	1·00

123 Seychelles Flying Foxes in Flight

1981. Seychelles Flying Fox (Roussette). Mult.

No.	Description	Unused	Used
518	40c. Type **123**	10	10
519	2r.25 Flying fox eating	30	45
520	3r. Flying fox climbing across tree branch	45	70
521	5r. Flying fox hanging from tree branch	55	1·00
MS522	95×130 mm. Nos. 518-521	1·50	3·75

124 Chinese Little Bittern (male)

1982. Birds (4th series). Chinese Little Bittern. Multicoloured.

No.	Description	Unused	Used
523	3r. Type **124**	2·00	1·00
524	3r. Chinese little bittern (female)	2·00	1·00
525	3r. Hen on nest	2·00	1·00
526	3r. Nest and eggs	2·00	1·00
527	3r. Hen with chicks	2·00	1·00

125 Silhouette Island and La Digue

1982. Modern Maps. Multicoloured.

No.	Description	Unused	Used
528	40c. Type **125**	15	10
529	1r.50 Denis and Bird Islands	25	25
530	2r.75 Praslin	30	65
531	7r. Mahe	50	2·25
MS532	92×128 mm. Nos. 528-531	1·10	5·00

126 "Education"

1982. 5th Anniv of Liberation. Multicoloured.

No.	Description	Unused	Used
533	40c. Type **126**	10	10
534	1r.75 "Health"	25	25
535	2r.75 "Agriculture"	30	45
536	7r. "Construction"	80	1·40
MS537	128×120 mm. Nos. 533-536	2·25	6·50

127 Tourist Board Emblem

1982. Tourism. Multicoloured.

No.	Description	Unused	Used
538	1r.75 Type **127**	20	35
539	1r.75 Northolme Hotel	20	35
540	1r.75 Reef Hotel	20	35
541	1r.75 Barbarous Beach Hotel	20	35
542	1r.75 Coral Strand Hotel	20	35
543	1r.75 Beau Vallon Bay Hotel	20	35
544	1r.75 Fisherman's Cove Hotel	20	35
545	1r.75 Mahe Beach Hotel	20	35

128 Tata Bus

1982. Land Transport. Multicoloured.

No.	Description	Unused	Used
546	20c. Type **128**	10	10
547	1r.75 Mini-Moke	20	30
548	2r.75 Ox-cart	25	65
549	7r. Truck	80	2·75

129 Radio Seychelles Control Room

1983. World Communications Year. Mult.

No.	Description	Unused	Used
550	40c. Type **129**	10	10
551	2r.75 Satellite Earth station	30	50
552	3r.50 Radio Seychelles television control room	45	75
553	5r. Postal services sorting office	60	1·25

130 Agricultural Experimental Station

1983. Commonwealth Day. Multicoloured.

No.	Description	Unused	Used
554	40c. Type **130**	10	10
555	2r.75 Food processing plant	25	40
556	3r.50 Unloading fish catch	40	60
557	7r. Seychelles flag	65	1·40

131 Denis Island Lighthouse

1983. Famous Landmarks. Multicoloured.

No.	Description	Unused	Used
558	40c. Type **131**	10	10
559	2r.75 Victoria Hospital	30	45
560	3r.50 Supreme Court	35	65
561	7r. State House	55	1·40
MS562	110×98 mm. Nos. 558-561	2·75	7·00

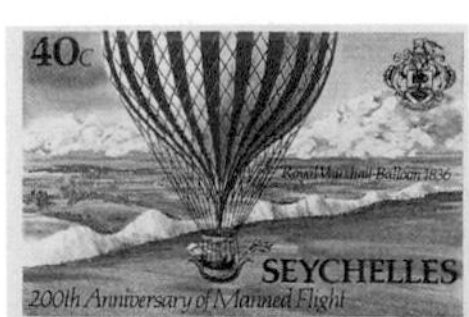

132 "Royal Vauxhall" Balloon, 1836

1983. Bicentenary of Manned Flight. Mult.

No.	Description	Unused	Used
563	40c. Type **132**	15	10
564	1r.75 De Havilland D.H.50J	30	30
565	2r.75 Grumman Albatros flying boat	35	55
566	7r. Swearingen Merlin IIIA	55	1·75

133 Douglas DC-10-30

1983. 1st International Flight of Air Seychelles.

No.	Description	Unused	Used
567	**133** 2r. multicoloured	2·00	2·00

134 Swamp Plant and Moorhen

1983. Centenary Visit to Seychelles by Marianne North (botanic artist). Multicoloured.

No.	Description	Unused	Used
568	40c. Type **134**	25	10
569	1r.75 "Wormia flagellaria"	45	30
570	2r.75 Asiatic pancratium	55	75
571	7r. Pitcher plant	95	2·50
MS572	90×121 mm. Nos. 568-571	2·75	6·50

1983. Nos. 505-507, 509-510 and 513 surch.

No.	Description	Unused	Used
573	50c. on 1r.50 "Victoria and Albert I"	15	30
574	50c. on 1r.50 Prince Charles and Lady Diana Spencer	40	1·50
575	2r.25 on 5r. "Clevland"	45	70
576	2r.25 on 5r. As No. 574	1·25	3·00
577	3r.75 on 10r. "Britannia"	75	1·10
578	3r.75 on 10r. As No. 574	1·60	3·50

136 Coconut Vessel

1984. Traditional Handicrafts. Multicoloured.

No.	Description	Unused	Used
579	50c. Type **136**	15	10
580	2r. Scarf and doll	30	70
581	3r. Coconut-fibre roses	35	1·00
582	10r. Carved fishing boat and doll	90	4·50

137 Victoria Port

1984. 250th Anniv of "Lloyd's List" (newspaper). Multicoloured.

No.	Description	Unused	Used
583	50c. Type **137**	25	10
584	2r. "Boissevain" (cargo liner)	65	55
585	3r. "Sun Viking" (liner)	90	90
586	10r. Loss of R.F.A. "Ennerdale II" (tanker)	2·40	3·50

138 Old S.P.U.P. Office

1984. 20th Anniv of Seychelles People's United Party. Multicoloured.

No.	Description	Unused	Used
587	50c. Type **138**	10	10
588	2r. Liberation statue (vert)	25	50
589	3r. New S.P.U.D. office	35	85
590	10r. President Rene (vert)	1·00	4·00

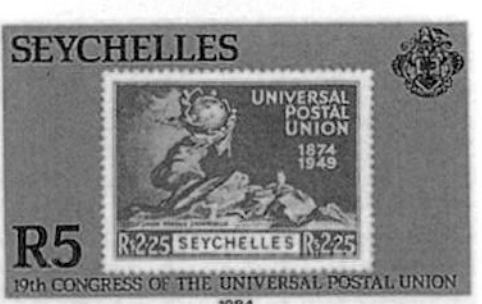

139 1949 U.P.U. 2r 25 Stamp

1984. Universal Postal Union Congress, Hamburg. Sheet 70×85 mm.

No.	Description	Unused	Used
MS591	**139** 5r. green, pink and black	1·40	2·50

140 Long Jumping

1984. Olympic Games, Los Angeles. Mult.

No.	Description	Unused	Used
592	50c. Type **140**	10	10
593	2r. Boxing	40	45
594	3r. Swimming	60	75
595	10r. Weightlifting	1·75	2·50
MS596	100×100 mm. Nos. 592-595	3·00	5·50

141 Sub-aqua Diving

1984. Water Sports. Multicoloured.

No.	Description	Unused	Used
597	50c. Type **141**	30	10
598	2r. Paraskiing	90	45
599	3r. Sailing	1·00	75
600	10r. Water-skiing	2·40	2·50

142 Humpback Whale

1984. Whale Conservation. Multicoloured.

No.	Description	Unused	Used
601	50c. Type **142**	1·50	20
602	2r. Sperm whale	2·75	1·75
603	3r. Black right whale	3·00	2·50
604	10r. Blue whale	6·00	9·00

143 Two Bare-legged Scops Owls in Tree

1985. Birth Bicentenary of John J. Audubon (ornithologist). Bare-legged Scops Owl. Mult.

No.	Description	Unused	Used
605	50c. Type **143**	1·75	50
606	2r. Owl on branch	2·50	2·25
607	3r. Owl in flight	2·75	2·75
608	10r. Owl on ground	5·50	8·50

144 Giant Tortoises

1985. "Expo '85" World Fair, Japan. Mult.

No.	Description	Unused	Used
609	50c. Type **144**	70	30
610	2r. White terns ("Fairy Tern")	2·00	1·75
611	3r. Windsurfing	2·00	2·50
612	5r. Coco-de-mer	2·00	5·00
MS613	130×80 mm. Nos. 609-612	8·50	10·00

See also No. **MS**650.

145 The Queen Mother with Princess Anne and Prince Andrew, 1970

1985. Life and Times of Queen Elizabeth the Queen Mother. Multicoloured.

614	50c. The Queen Mother in 1930	25	10
615	2r. Type **145**	60	50
616	3r. On her 75th Birthday	80	75
617	5r. With Prince Henry at his christening (from photo by Lord Snowdon)	1·10	1·50
MS618	91×73 mm. 10 r. Arriving at Blenheim Palace by Westland Wessex helicopter	3·25	2·25

146 Boxing

1985. 2nd Indian Ocean Islands Games. Mult.

619	50c. Type **146**	15	10
620	2r. Football	55	50
621	3r. Swimming	75	75
622	10r. Windsurfing	2·40	2·75

1985. Acquisition of First Air Seychelles "Airbus". As No. 413A, but additionally inscribed "AIR SEYCHELLES FIRST AIRBUS".

623	1r.25 White tern ("Fairy Tern")	2·50	2·25

147 Agriculture Students

1985. International Youth Year. Multicoloured.

624	50c. Type **147**	10	10
625	2r. Construction students building wall	55	50
626	3r. Carpentry students	70	1·00
627	10r. Science students	2·25	5·50

148 Ford "Model T" (1919)

1985. Vintage Cars. Multicoloured.

628	50c. Type **148**	50	20
629	2r. Austin "Seven" (1922)	1·50	1·00
630	3r. Morris "Oxford" (1924)	1·60	1·75
631	10r. Humber "Coupe" (1929)	3·00	6·50

149 Five Foot Transit Instrument

1986. Appearance of Halley's Comet. Mult.

632	50c. Type **149**	30	10
633	2r. Eight foot quadrant	75	70
634	3r. Comet's orbit	75	95
635	10r. Edmond Halley	1·25	3·00

150 Ballerina

1986. Visit of Ballet du Louvre Company, "Giselle". Multicoloured.

636	2r. Type **150**	50	75
637	3r. Male dancer	60	1·50
MS638	80×90 mm. 10r. Pas de deux	1·40	2·40

1986. 60th Birthday of Queen Elizabeth II. As T 145a of St. Helena. Multicoloured.

639	50c. Wedding photograph, 1947	10	10
640	1r.25 At State Opening of Parliament, 1982	25	35
641	2r. Queen accepting bouquet, Seychelles, 1972	30	50
642	3r. On board Royal Yacht "Britannia", Qatar, 1979	40	75
643	5r. At Crown Agents Head Office, London, 1983	60	1·25

151 Ferry to La Digue

1986. "Ameripex '86" Int Stamp Exhibition, Chicago. Inter-island Communications. Mult.

644	50c. Type **151**	60	10
645	2r. Telephone kiosk (vert)	1·25	70
646	3r. Post Office counter, Victoria (vert)	1·40	1·10
647	7r. Air Seychelles Britten Norman "short nose" Trislander aircraft	4·00	3·50

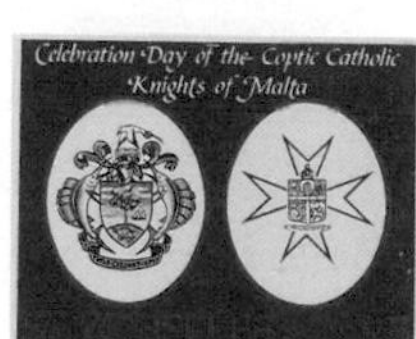

152 Crests of Seychelles and Knights of Malta

1986. Seychelles Knights of Malta Day.

648	**152** 5r. multicoloured	1·10	1·60
MS649	101×81 mm. No. 648	2·25	4·00

1986. Seychelles Philatelic Exhibition, Tokyo. Miniature sheet, 130×80 mm, containing stamps as Nos. 609-612, but without "Expo '85" inscription and emblem.

MS650	As Nos. 609-612	1·75	3·00

1986. Royal Wedding. As T 146a of St. Helena. Multicoloured.

651	2r. Prince Andrew and Miss Sarah Ferguson	35	50
652	10r. Prince Andrew boarding Wessex helicopter, 1983	1·40	3·00

1986. International Creole Day. No. 487 optd LAZOURNEN ENTERNASYONAL KREOL.

653	1r. Madagascar red fody	2·75	2·75

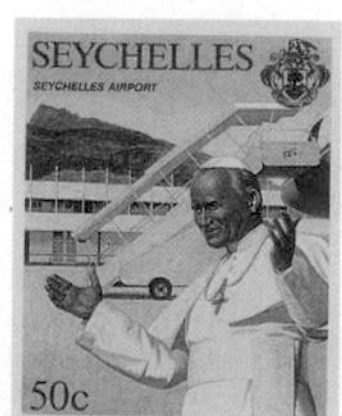

154 Pope John Paul at Seychelles Airport

1986. Visit of Pope John Paul II. Designs showing Pope and Seychelles scenes. Multicoloured.

654	50c. Type **154**	75	30
655	2r. Catholic Cathedral, Victoria	2·00	1·25
656	3r. Baie Lazare Parish Church	2·50	2·25
657	10r. Aerial view of People's Stadium	4·25	8·00
MS658	95×106 mm. Nos. 654-657	11·00	13·00

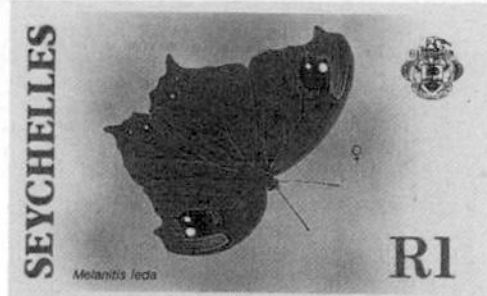

155 "Melanitis leda"

1987. Butterflies. Multicoloured.

659	1r. Type **155**	1·00	30
660	2r. "Phalanta philiberti"	1·60	1·25
661	3r. "Danaus chrysippus"	1·90	1·90
662	10r. "Euploea mitra"	5·00	8·00

156 Royal Oak Scallop

1987. Sea Shells. Multicoloured.

663	1r. Type **156**	1·25	30
664	2r. Golden thorny oyster	2·00	1·00
665	3r. Ventral or single harp and ornate pitar venus	2·25	1·60
666	10r. Silver conch	5·50	8·00

157 Statue of Liberation

1987. 10th Anniv of Liberation. Multicoloured.

667	1r. Type **157**	20	25
668	2r. Seychelles hospital (horiz)	35	50
669	3r. Orphanage village (horiz)	45	75
670	10r. Proposed Sail-fish Monument	1·00	2·50

158 Seychelles Savings Bank, Praslin

1987. Centenary of Banking in Seychelles.

671	**158** 1r. deep green and green	20	25
672	- 2r. brown and orange	35	50
673	- 10r. deep blue and blue	1·00	2·50

DESIGNS: 2r. Development Bank; 10r. Central Bank.

1987. Royal Ruby Wedding. Nos. 639-643 optd 40TH WEDDING ANNIVERSARY.

674	50c. Wedding photograph, 1947	15	15
675	1r.25 At State Opening of Parliament, 1982	25	65
676	2r. Queen accepting bouquet, Seychelles, 1972	30	65
677	3r. On board Royal Yacht "Britannia", Qatar, 1979	40	1·10
678	5r. At Crown Agents Head Office, London, 1983	60	2·00

159 Tuna-canning Factory

1987. Seychelles Fishing Industry. Mult.

679	50c. Type **159**	15	15
680	2r. Trawler	45	55
681	3r. Weighing catch	70	1·00
682	10r. Unloading net	2·25	3·50

160 Water Sports

1988. Tourism. Multicoloured.

683	1r. Type **160**	65	25
684	2r. Speedboat and yachts	1·00	65
685	3r. Yacht at anchor	1·60	1·40
686	10r. Hotel at night	3·50	6·50

161 Young Turtles making for Sea

1988. The Green Turtle. Multicoloured.

687	2r. Type **161**	1·50	2·00
688	2r. Young turtles hatching	1·50	2·00
689	3r. Female turtle leaving sea	1·75	2·25
690	3r. Female laying eggs	1·75	2·25

Nos. 687-688 and 689-690 were printed together, se-tenant, each pair forming a composite design.

162 Shot Put

1988. Olympic Games, Seoul. Multicoloured.

691	1r. Type **162**	30	25
692	2r. Type **162**	55	90
693	2r. High jump	55	90
694	2r. Gold medal winner on podium	55	90
695	2r. Athletics	55	90
696	2r. Javelin	55	90
697	3r. As No. 694	60	90
698	4r. As No. 695	80	1·10
699	5r. As No. 696	1·00	1·25
MS700	121×52 mm. 10r. Tennis	4·00	6·50

1988. 300th Anniv of Lloyd's of London. As T 152a of St. Helena. Multicoloured.

701	1r. Leadenhall Street, 1928	60	25
702	2r. "Cinq Juin" (travelling post office) (horiz)	1·60	75
703	3r. "Queen Elizabeth 2" (liner) (horiz)	3·00	1·50
704	10r. Loss of "Hindenburg" (airship), 1937	6·00	5·00

163 Police Motorcyclists

1988. 1st Anniv of Defence Forces Day. Mult.

705	1r. Type **163**	2·75	50
706	2r. Hindustan Aircraft Chetak helicopter	4·00	2·25
707	3r. "Andromanche" (patrol boat)	4·00	2·75
708	10r. BRDM armoured car	7·50	10·00

164 Father Christmas with Basket of Presents

1988. Christmas. Multicoloured.

709	50c. Type **164**	15	10
710	2r. Bird and gourd filled with presents	70	70
711	3r. Father Christmas basket weaving	90	90
712	10r. Christmas bauble and palm tree	2·50	4·50

165 "Dendrobium sp."

1988. Orchids (1st series). Multicoloured.

713	1r. Type **165**	1·25	25
714	2r. Arachnis" hybrid (horiz)	1·75	70
715	3r. "Vanda caerulea"	2·00	1·25
716	10r. "Dendrobium phalaenopsis" (horiz)	4·00	6·50

See also Nos. 767-770 and 795-798.

166 India 1976 25p. Nehru Stamp

1989. Birth Centenary of Jawaharlal Nehru (Indian statesman). Each showing flags of Seychelles and India. Multicoloured.

724	2r. Type **166**	1·25	50
725	10r. Jawaharlal Nehru	3·25	5·50

167 Pres. Rene addressing Rally at Old Party Office

1989. 25th Anniv of Seychelles People's United Party. Multicoloured.

742	1r. Type **167**	25	25
743	2r. Women with Party flags and Maison du Peuple	60	50
744	3r. President Rene making speech and Torch of Freedom	70	80
745	10r. President Rene, Party flag and Torch of Freedom	2·25	5·00

1989. 20th Anniv of First Manned Landing on Moon. As T 50a of St. Kitts. Multicoloured.

746	1r. Lift off of "Saturn 5" rocket	45	25
747	2r. Crew of "Apollo 15" (30×30 mm)	75	75
748	3r. "Apollo 15" emblem (30×30 mm)	90	1·10
749	5r. James Irwin saluting U.S. flag on Moon	1·50	2·25
MS750	100×83 mm. 10r. Aldrin alighting from "Apollo 11" on Moon	5·00	6·50

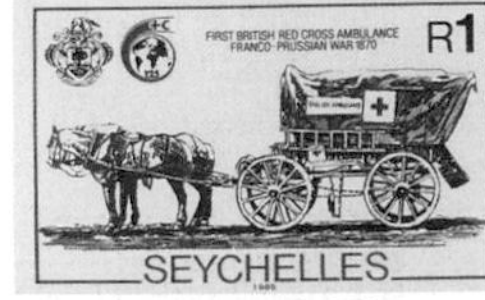

168 British Red Cross Ambulance, Franco-Prussian War, 1870

1989. 125th Anniv of International Red Cross.

751	**168**	1r. black and red	3·00	35
752	-	2r. black, green and red	3·50	1·50
753	-	3r. black and red	4·00	2·50
754	-	10r. black and red	10·00	12·00

DESIGNS: 2r. "Liberty" (hospital ship), 1914–18; 3r. Sunbeam "Standard" army ambulance, 1914–18; 10r. "White Train" (hospital train), South Africa, 1899–1902.

169 Black Parrot and Map of Praslin

1989. Island Birds. Multicoloured.

755	50c. Type **169**	2·25	55
756	2r. Sooty tern and Ile aux vaches	3·25	1·75
757	3r. Seychelles magpie robin ("Magpie Robin") and Fregate	4·00	3·00
758	5r. Roseate tern and Aride	4·25	7·50
MS759	83×109 mm. Nos. 755-758	15·00	16·00

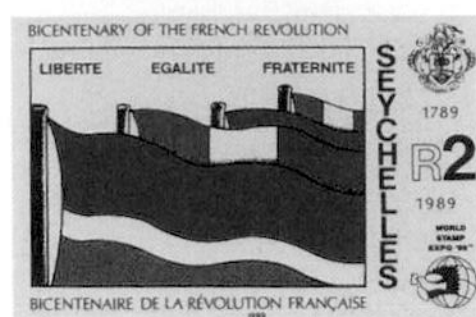

170 Flags of Seychelles and France

1989. Bicentenary of French Revolution and "World Stamp Expo '89". International Stamp Exhibition, Washington.

760	**170**	2r. multicoloured	3·50	1·50
761	-	5r. black, blue and red	4·00	6·00
MS762		78×100 mm. 10r. mult	5·50	7·50

DESIGN: 5r. Storming the Bastille, Paris, 1789; 10r. Reading Revolutionary proclamation, Seychelles, 1791.

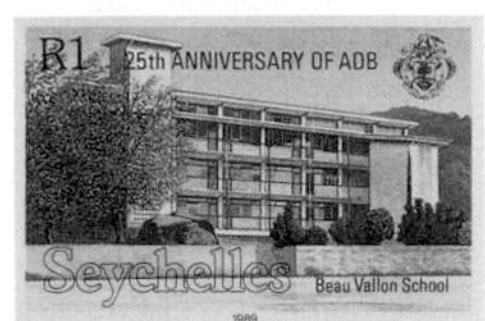

171 Beau Vallon School

1989. 25th Anniv of African Development Bank. Multicoloured.

763	1r. Type **171**	45	25
764	2r. Seychelles Fishing Authority Headquarters	80	1·00
765	3r. "Variola" (fishing boat) (vert)	2·75	2·50
766	10r. "Deneb" (fishing boat) (vert)	6·50	10·00

172 "Disperis tripetaloides"

1990. Orchids (2nd series). Multicoloured.

767	1r. Type **172**	2·75	50
768	2r. "Vanilla phalaenopsis"	3·25	1·50
769	3r. "Angraecum eburneum" subsp. "superbum"	3·75	2·50
770	10r. "Polystachya concreta"	7·50	11·00

173 Seychelles 1903 2c. and Great Britain 1880 1½d. Stamps

1990. "Stamp World London '90" International Stamp Exhibition. Each showing stamps. Mult.

771	1r. Type **173**	85	25
772	2r. Seychelles 1917 25c. and G.B. 1873 1s.	1·40	1·25
773	3r. Seychelles 1917 2c. and G.B. 1874 6d.	2·00	2·25
774	5r. Seychelles 1890 2c. and G.B. 1841 1d. red	2·75	5·00
MS775	88×60 mm. 10r. Seychelles 1961 Post Office Centenary 2r.25 and G.B. 1840 Penny Black	11·00	12·00

174 Fumiyo Sako

1990. "EXPO 90" International Garden and Greenery Exhibition, Osaka. Multicoloured.

776	2r. Type **174**	1·75	1·00
777	3r. Male and female coco-de-mer palms	2·00	1·50
778	5r. Pitcher plant and Aldabra lily	3·00	3·50
779	7r. Arms of Seychelles and gardenia	3·75	6·00
MS780	130×85 mm. Nos. 776-779	8·50	11·00

175 Air Seychelles Boeing 767-200ER over Island

1990. Air Seychelles "Boeing 767-200ER" World Record-breaking Flight (1989).

781	**175**	3r. multicoloured	4·25	3·75

1990. 90th Birthday of Queen Elizabeth the Queen Mother. As T 161a of St. Helena.

782	2r. multicoloured	1·25	75
783	10r. black and violet	3·25	4·50

DESIGNS—(21×36 mm): 2r. Queen Elizabeth in Coronation robes, 1937. (29×37 mm): 10r. Queen Elizabeth visiting Lord Roberts Workshops, 1947.

176 Adult Class

1990. International Literacy Year. Mult.

784	1r. Type **176**	75	25
785	2r. Reading a letter	1·50	1·25
786	3r. Following written instructions	2·00	2·00
787	10r. Typewriter, calculator and crossword	5·00	8·50

177 Sega Dancers

1990. Kreol Festival. Sega Dancing. Mult.

788	2r. Type **177**	2·50	2·75
789	2r. Dancing couple (girl in yellow dress)	2·50	2·75
790	2r. Female Sega dancer	2·50	2·75
791	2r. Dancing couple (girl in floral pattern skirt)	2·50	2·75
792	2r. Dancing couple (girl in red patterned skirt)	2·50	2·75

178 Beach

1990. 1st Indian Ocean Regional Seminar on Petroleum Exploration. Multicoloured.

793	3r. Type **178**	1·75	1·50
794	10r. Geological map	5·75	7·50

1991. Orchids (3rd series). As T 172. Mult.

795	1r. "Bullbophyllum intertextum"	1·75	45
796	2r. "Agrostophyllum occidentale"	2·25	1·75
797	3r. "Vanilla planifolia"	2·50	2·50
798	10r. "Malaxis seychellarum"	6·00	7·50

1991. 65th Birthday of Queen Elizabeth II and 70th Birthday of Prince Philip. As T 165a of St. Helena. Multicoloured.

799	4r. Queen in evening dress	1·60	2·25
800	4r. Prince Philip in academic robes	1·60	2·25

179 "Precis rhadama"

1991. "Phila Nippon '91" International Stamp Exhibition, Tokyo. Butterflies. Multicoloured.

801	1r.50 Type **179**	2·00	85
802	3r. "Lampides boeticus"	2·50	2·25
803	3r.50 "Zizeeria knysna"	2·75	2·50
804	10r. "Phalanta phalantha"	7·25	7·50
MS805	78×81 mm. 10r. "Eagris sabadius"	7·00	7·50

180 "The Holy Virgin, Joseph, The Holy Child and St. John" (S. Vouillemont after Raphael)

1991. Christmas. Woodcuts.

806	**180**	50c. black, brown and red	50	15
807	-	1r. black, brown and green	90	25
808	-	2r. black, brown and blue	1·75	1·10
809	-	7r. black, brown and blue	4·50	7·00

DESIGNS: 1r. "Holy Virgin, the Child and Angel" (A. Blooting after Van Dyck); 2r. "The Holy Family, St. John and St. Anna" (L. Vorsterman after Rubens); 7r. "The Holy Family, Angel and St. Cathrin" (C. Bloemaert).

1992. 40th Anniv of Queen Elizabeth II's Accession. As T 168a of St. Helena. Mult.

810	1r. Seychelles coastline	65	25
811	1r.50 Clock Tower, Victoria	80	40
812	3r. Victoria harbour	1·50	1·50
813	3r.50 Three portraits of Queen Elizabeth	1·60	1·75
814	5r. Queen Elizabeth II	1·75	2·75

181 Seychelles Brush Warbler ("Bush Warbler")

1993. Flora and Fauna. Multicoloured.

815	10c. Type **181**	1·50	1·25
816	25c. Bronze gecko (vert)	75	15
817	50c. Seychelles tree frog	1·50	20
818	1r. Seychelles splendid palm (vert)	80	25
819	1r.50 Seychelles skink (vert)	1·50	80
820	2r. Giant tenebrionid beetle	1·25	45
821	3r. Seychelles sunbird	2·00	1·25
822	3r.50 Seychelles killifish	1·75	1·25
823	4r. Seychelles magpie robin ("Magpie Robin")	2·25	1·75
824	5r. Seychelles vanilla (plant) (vert)	1·75	1·75
825	10r. Tiger chameleon	2·75	2·75
826	15r. Coco-de-mer (vert)	4·00	4·75
827	25r. Seychelles paradise flycatcher ("Paradise Flycatcher") (vert)	9·00	9·50
828	50r. Giant tortoise	16·00	21·00

182 Archbishop George Carey and Anglican Cathedral, Victoria

1993. First Visit of an Archbishop of Canterbury to Seychelles. Multicoloured.

834	3r. Type **182**	2·50	1·50
835	10r. Archbishop Carey with Air France Boeing 747-400 and Air Seychelles Boeing 737-200 airliners	6·00	8·50

183 Athletics

1993. 4th Indian Ocean Island Games. Mult.

836	1r.50 Type **183**	65	55
837	3r. Football	1·25	1·00
838	3r.50 Cycling	2·00	1·75
839	10r. Sailing	3·25	6·00

184 "Scotia" (cable ship) off Victoria, 1893

1993. Century of Telecommunications. Mult.

840	1r. Type **184**	1·75	60
841	3r. Eastern Telegraph Co office, Victoria, 1904	2·50	1·75
842	4r. HF Transmitting Station, 1971	2·75	3·00
843	10r. New Telecoms House, Victoria, 1993	5·00	7·50

1994. "Hong Kong '94" Int Stamp Exhibition. Nos. 62, 64 and 66-67 of Zil Elwannyen Sesel surch HONG KONG '94, emblem and value.

844	1r. on 2r.10 Souimanga sunbird	50	30
845	1r.50 on 2r.75 Sacred ibis	75	60
846	3r.50 on 7r. Seychelles kestrel (vert)	1·60	2·25
847	10r. on 15r. Comoro blue pigeon (vert)	3·00	5·00

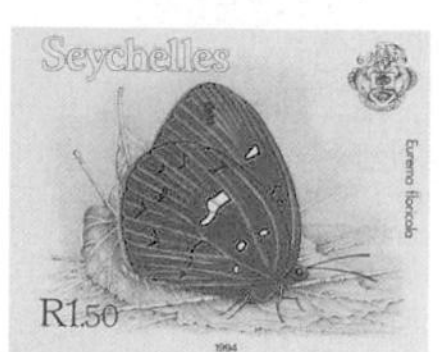

186 "Eurema floricola"

1994. Butterflies. Multicoloured.

848	1r.50 Type **186**	1·75	75
849	3r. "Coeliades forestan"	2·50	2·00
850	3r.50 "Borbo borbonica"	2·75	2·75
851	10r. "Zizula hylax"	5·50	7·50

187 Lady Elizabeth Bowes-Lyon

1995. 95th Birthday of Queen Elizabeth the Queen Mother. Multicoloured.

852	1r.50 Type **187**	85	40
853	3r. Duchess of York on wedding day, 1923	1·60	1·00
854	3r.50 Queen Elizabeth	1·75	1·40
855	10r. Queen Elizabeth the Queen Mother	3·75	6·00

188 Female Seychelles Paradise Flycatcher feeding Chick

1996. Endangered Species. Seychelles Paradise Flycatcher. Multicoloured.

856	1r. Type **188**	70	95
857	1r. Male bird in flight	70	95
858	1r. Female bird on branch	70	95
859	1r. Male bird on branch	70	95
MS860	60×53 mm. 10r. Pair on branch	6·50	7·50

189 Swimming

1996. Centenary of Modern Olympic Games. Mult.

861	50c. Type **189**	40	20
862	1r.50 Running	60	45
863	3r. Sailing	1·25	1·50
864	5r. Boxing	1·90	3·00

190 Archbishop Makarios at Table

1996. 40th Anniv of Exile of Archbishop Makarios of Cyprus to Seychelles. Multicoloured.

865	3r. Type **190**	1·50	1·00
866	10r. Archbishop Makarios in priest's robes	3·25	6·00

191 Comoro Blue Pigeon

1996. Birds. Multicoloured.

867	3r. Type **191**	1·40	1·60
868	3r. Seychelles blue pigeon	1·40	1·60
869	3r. Souimanga sunbird	1·40	1·60
870	3r. Seychelles sunbird	1·40	1·60
871	3r. Mascarene fody ("Aldabra Red-headed Fody")	1·40	1·60
872	3r. Seychelles fody	1·40	1·60
873	3r. Madagascar white eye	1·40	1·60
874	3r. Seychelles brown white-eye ("Seychelles White eye")	1·40	1·60

Nos. 867/8, 869/70, 871/2 and 873/4 respectively were printed together, se-tenant, with the background of each pair forming a composite design showing a regional map.

1997. "HONG KONG '97" International Stamp Exhibition. No. 226 of Zil Elwannyen Sesel surch R1.50 and emblem.

875	1r.50 on 2r. Little egret ("Dimorphic Little Egret")	2·50	2·50

1997. Golden Wedding of Queen Elizabeth and Prince Philip. As T 192a of St. Helena. Mult.

876	1r. Queen Elizabeth wearing red and white suit	75	1·00
877	1r. Prince Philip driving carriage	75	1·00
878	1r.50 Prince Philip	85	1·25
879	1r.50 Queen Elizabeth with horse	85	1·25
880	3r. Prince Charles and Princess Anne on horseback	1·60	1·90
881	3r. Prince Philip and Queen Elizabeth	1·60	1·90
MS882	110×70 mm. 10r. Queen Elizabeth and Prince Philip in landau (horiz)	4·25	4·75

Nos. 876/7, 878/9 and 880/1 respectively were printed together, se-tenant, with the backgrounds forming composite designs.

1998. Diana, Princess of Wales Commemoration. Sheet, 145×70 mm, containing vert designs as T 62a of Tokelau. Multicoloured.

MS883	3r. Wearing red jacket, 1992; 3r. Wearing floral dress, 1981; 3r. Wearing blue and black jacket, 1993; 3r. Wearing white dress, Nepal 1993 (sold at 12r.+2r. charity premium)	3·50	4·00

193 Powderblue Surgeonfish

1998. International Year of the Ocean. Mult.

884	3r. Type **193**	90	1·25
885	3r. Shoal of soldierfish	90	1·25
886	3r. Lionfish	90	1·25
887	3r. School of fish	90	1·25
888	3r. Coral	90	1·25
889	3r. Turtle	90	1·25

194 "Vierge du Cap" (galleon), 1721

1999. 18th-century Ships. Multicoloured.

890	1r.50 Type **194**	55	35
891	3r. "L'Elizabeth" (corvette), 1741	1·25	1·00
892	3r.50 "Curieuse" (sloop), 1768	1·25	1·75
893	10r. "La Fleche" (frigate), 1801	2·75	4·25
MS894	105×70 mm. 20r. "Le Cheval Marin" (French merchantman), 1774 (vert)	6·00	7·50

No. **MS**894 also includes the "Australia '99" World Stamp Exhibition, Melbourne, emblem on the sheet margin.

195 Royal Couple on Steps of Chapel Royal, Windsor

1999. Royal Wedding. Multicoloured.

895	3r. Type **195**	1·00	75
896	15r. In landau	4·50	6·50

196 Cathedral of the Immaculate Conception

1999. New Millennium. Multicoloured.

897	1r. Type **196**	50	30
898	1r.50 White tern at sunrise	1·75	1·00
899	2r.50 Dolphin and island	2·00	1·50
900	10r. Comet over beach	4·25	6·00

197 Lady Elizabeth Bowes-Lyon

2000. Queen Elizabeth the Queen Mother's 100th Birthday.

901	**197**	3r. multicoloured	1·50	70
902	-	5r. black and brown	2·00	1·75
903	-	7r. black and lilac	2·75	3·25
904	-	10r. multicoloured	3·25	4·25

DESIGNS: 5r. Queen Elizabeth in East End of London during Second World War; 7r. Visiting Seychelles with King George VI and Princess Elizabeth; 10r. Wearing blue hat and outfit.

198 Arrival of Jacobin Deportees (Bicentenary)

2001. Milestones in Seychelles History. Mult.

905	1r. Type **198**	75	30
906	1r.50 Victoria (160th anniv as capital)	85	40
907	3r. Father Leon des Avanchers (150th anniv of arrival)	1·60	1·00
908	3r.50 Victoria Fountain (centenary) (vert)	1·60	1·25
909	5r. Botanical Gardens (centenary)	2·25	2·50
910	10r. Independence monument (25th anniv) (vert)	3·00	4·50

199 Ruddy Shelduck

2001. Bird Life World Bird Festival. Migrant Ducks and Bare-legged Scops Owl (No. MS915). Multicoloured.

911	3r. Type **199**	2·00	2·00
912	3r. White-faced whistling duck	2·00	2·00
913	3r. Northern Shoveler	2·00	2·00
914	3r. Garganey	2·00	2·00
MS915	171×78 mm. 3r. Bare-legged scops owl ("Seychelles Scops Owl") in flight (35×30 mm); 3r. Chick in tree hole (35×30 mm); 3r. Adult tufts down (30×35 mm); 3r. Adult tufts erect (30×35 mm); 3r. Immature (35×30 mm)	7·50	8·50

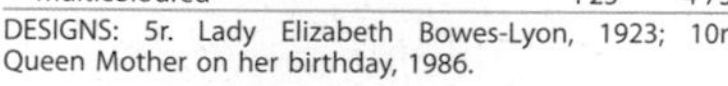

2002. Queen Elizabeth the Queen Mother Commemoration. Sheet, 145×70 mm, containing vert designs as T 215 of St. Helena.

MS916	5r. brown, gold and black; 10r. multicoloured	4·25	4·75

DESIGNS: 5r. Lady Elizabeth Bowes-Lyon, 1923; 10r. Queen Mother on her birthday, 1986.

200 Seychelles Frog

2003. Endangered Species. Frogs. Multicoloured.

917	1r. Type **200**	85	85
918	1r. Palm frog	85	85
919	1r. Thomasset's frog	85	85
920	1r. Gardiner's frog	85	85
MS921	65×65 mm. 20r. Seychelles tree frog	8·50	9·50

201 Seychelles Blenny

2003. Marine Life. Multicoloured.

922	10c. Type **201**	15	15
923	25c. African pygmy angelfish	25	10

924	50c. Seychelles anemonefish	30	15
925	1r. Indian butterflyfish	45	25
926	1r.50 Goldbar wrasse	60	35
927	2r. Picasso triggerfish	75	45
928	3r. Seychelles squirrelfish	1·10	80
929	3r.50 Palette surgeonfish	1·25	80
930	4r. Longfin batfish	1·40	1·25
931	5r. Green-beaked parrotfish ("Greenthroat Parrotfish")	1·60	1·60
932	10r. Masked moray	3·00	3·00
933	15r. Lyretail grouper	4·25	4·50
934	25r. Emperor snapper	7·50	8·50
935	50r. Whale shark	14·00	15·00

202 Emblem

2004. 20th Anniv of the Indian Ocean Commission.

936	**202**	15r. multicoloured	4·50	4·75

2004. Flora and Fauna. Nos. 819, 821 and 824-828 surch.

937	1r. on 1r.50 Seychelles skink (vert)	65	30
938	2r. on 3r. Seychelles sunbird	1·25	65
939	3r.50 on 5r. Seychelles vanilla (vert)	1·90	1·90
940	3r.50 on 10r. Tiger chameleon	1·90	1·90
941	3r.50 on 15r. Coco-de-mer (vert)	1·90	1·90
942	4r. on 25r. Paradise flycatcher (vert)	2·00	2·00
943	4r. on 50r. Giant tortoise	2·00	2·00

2005. Pope John Paul II Commemoration. As T 231 of St. Helena.

944	5r. multicoloured	2·00	2·00

204 Archbishop Makarios in Exile, 1956

2006. 50th Anniv of Exile of Archbishop Makarios of Cyprus to the Seychelles. Multicoloured.

945	3r.50 Type **204**	1·50	1·25
946	15r. Archbishop Makarios	4·50	5·00

205 Possession Stone (250th anniv of naming of Seychelles)

2006. 30th Anniv of Independence. Multicoloured.

947	50c. Type **205**	30	15
948	1r. National flag and national flags of 1977–96 and 1976	75	30
949	1r.50 Vallee de Mai, Praslin (World Heritage Site)	80	60
950	2r. School children	1·00	1·75
951	3r.50 Jacob Marie (musician) with bonm (musical arc)	1·60	1·40
952	4r. *Seychelles Progress* (tanker)	1·75	1·75
953	15r. "Selebre Sesel" emblem	4·50	5·00

206 *Solanum aldabrensis*

2007. 25th Anniv of Aldabra as a World Heritage Site. Multicoloured.

954	2r. Type **206**	1·00	1·10
955	3r.50 Dugong	1·60	1·70
956	10r. Giant tortoise	3·00	3·35

207 Kayaking

2008. Olympic Games, Beijing. Multicoloured.

957	1r. Type **207**	15	15
958	1r.50 Swimming	25	25
959	2r. Sailing	50	50
960	3r.50 Javelin throwing	70	70

208 Pair of Aldabra Drongos

2008. Endangered Species. Aldabra Drongo (Dicrurus aldabranus) and Aldabra Red-headed Fody (Foudiaeminentissima aldabrana). Multicoloured.

961	1r. Type **208**	25	25
962	1r. Pair of Aldabra red-headed fodies (in tree with foliage, looking to left)	25	25
963	1r. Pair of Aldabra red-headed fodies (on bare branch, looking to right)	25	25
964	1r. Pair of Aldabra drongos (left hand bird facing forwards)	25	25
MS965	84×60 mm. 20r. Aldabra red-headed fody and Aldabra drongo	4·75	4·75

209 Ferdinand Magellan

2009. Seafaring and Exploration. Multicoloured.

966	1r.50 Type **209**	30	30
967	3r.50 Sir Martin Frobisher	1·75	1·60
968	6r.50 Sir Francis Drake	2·75	2·50
969	8r. Henry Hudson	3·00	2·75
970	15r. Abel Tasman	5·75	5·50
971	27r. Sir John Franklin	9·25	9·00
MS972	110×70 mm. 7r. *Ascension* (East Indiaman), 1609 (400th anniv of first European landing on the Seychelles)	3·25	3·25

Nos. 966-971 were each printed in sheetlets of six stamps with enlarged illustrated margins.

2009. International Year of Astronomy. 40th Anniv of First Moon Landing. As T 257 of St. Helena. Multicoloured.

973	3r.50 X1 being loaded under Superfortress, 1951	1·75	1·60
974	7r. Lunar Landing Research Vehicle, 1964	3·25	3·00
975	8r. Apollo 11 Launch Site, 1969	3·75	3·50
976	13r. Space Transportation System 86, 1997	6·75	6·50
977	20r. Soyuz TMA-13 rolls out to Launch Pad, 2008	5·25	5·25
MS978	100×80 mm. 24r. *An American Success Story* (astronaut John Young) (Alan Bean) (39×59 mm). Wmk upright	11·00	11·00

2010. As Nos. 929/35 and new values (6r.50, 7r., 8r., 100r.)

986	3r.50 Palette surgeonfish	1·25	80
987	4r Longfin batfish	1·40	1·25
988	5r. Green-beaked parrotfish ('Greenthroat Parrotfish')	1·60	1·60
989	6r.50 Queen Coris	1·75	1·75
990	7r. White-lined goatfish	2·10	2·10
991	8r. Three-spot angelfish	2·20	2·50
992	10r. Masked moray	3·00	3·00
993	15r. Lyretail grouper	4·25	4·50
994	25r. Emperor snapper	7·50	8·50
995	50r. Whale shark	14·00	15·00
996	100r. Coral grouper	25·00	25·00

Nos. 979/85 are left for possible additions to this definitive series.

POSTAGE DUE STAMPS

D1

1951. Value in red.

D1	**D1**	2c. red and carmine	80	1·50
D2	**D1**	3c. red and green	2·25	1·50
D3	**D1**	6c. red and bistre	2·25	1·25
D4	**D1**	9c. red and orange	2·25	1·25
D5	**D1**	15c. red and violet	2·00	12·00
D6	**D1**	18c. red and blue	2·00	12·00
D7	**D1**	20c. red and brown	2·00	12·00
D8	**D1**	30c. red and claret	2·00	7·50

1980. As Type D 1 but 18×22 mm.

D11	5c. red and mauve	15	1·00
D12	10c. red and green	15	1·00
D13	15c. red and bistre	20	1·00
D14	20c. red and brown	20	1·00
D15	25c. red and violet	20	1·00
D16	75c. red and maroon	30	1·00
D17	80c. red and blue	30	1·00
D18	1r. red and purple	30	1·00

Pt. 1

SHAHPURA

One of the Indian Feudatory States. Now uses Indian stamps.

12 pies = 1 anna; 16 annas = 1 rupee.

RAJ
SHAHPURA
Postage 1 pice
1

1914. Perf (No. 1) or imperf (No. 2).

1	**1**	1p. red on grey	£750
2	**1**	1p. red on brown	£1100

1920. As T 1 but "Postage" omitted. Imperf.

3	1p. red on brown	£1300
4	1a. black on pink	£1500

Pt. 17

SHANGHAI

A seaport on the E. coast of China, which for a time had a separate postal system.

1865. 10 cash = 1 candareen. 100 candareens = 1 tael.
1890. 100 cents = 1 dollar (Chinese).

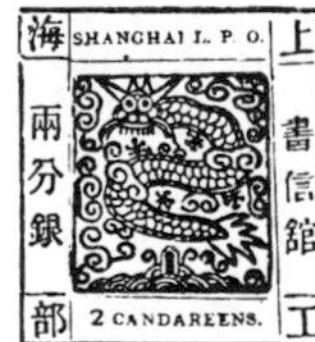

1 Dragon

1865. Value in candareens. Imperf. (a) "CANDAREEN" in singular.

28	1ca. blue	£225	£5000
12	2ca. black	£600	£8500
29	3ca. brown	£225	£5500
13	4ca. yellow	£700	£9000
14	8ca. green	£600	
15	16ca. red	£650	

(b) "CANDAREENS" in plural.

30	2ca. black	£200	
31	3ca. brown	£200	£3750
3	4ca. yellow	£1000	£6000
18	6ca. brown	£325	
20	6ca. red	£450	
4	8ca. green	£600	£6500
21	12ca. brown	£300	
22	16ca. red	£300	

2

1866. Value in cents. Frames differ. Perf.

32	**2**	2c. red	25·00	32·00
33	**2**	4c. lilac	42·00	55·00
34	**2**	8c. blue	48·00	60·00
35	**2**	16c. green	75·00	£100

6

1867. Value in candareens. Frames differ.

37	**6**	1ca. brown	10·00	14·00
59	**6**	1ca. yellow on yellow	38·00	38·00
62	**6**	1ca. yellow	22·00	30·00
73	**6**	1ca. red	£2250	£3250
38	**6**	3ca. yellow	40·00	55·00
60	**6**	3ca. pink on pink	38·00	38·00
63	**6**	3ca. red	85·00	95·00
39	**6**	6ca. grey	42·00	50·00
64	**6**	6ca. green	£125	£160
65	**6**	9ca. grey	£225	£300
40	**6**	12ca. brown	75·00	95·00

1873. Surch with value in English and Chinese.

41	**2**	1ca. on 2c. red	55·00	65·00
44	**2**	1ca. on 4c. lilac	22·00	32·00
46	**2**	1ca. on 8c. blue	48·00	55·00
48	**2**	1ca. on 16c. green	£4250	£3500
50	**2**	3ca. on 2c. red	£275	£250
52	**2**	3ca. on 16c. green	£4250	£3000

1873. Surch with value in English and Chinese.

53	**6**	1ca. on 3ca. yellow	£38000	£20000
67	**6**	1ca. on 3ca. red	£150	£140
68	**6**	1ca. on 3ca. pink on pink	£500	£425
54	**6**	1ca. on 6ca. grey	£750	£650
69	**6**	1ca. on 6ca. green	£275	£225
70	**6**	1ca. on 9ca. grey	£500	£500
56	**6**	1ca. on 12ca. brown	£1000	£900
58	**6**	3ca. on 12ca. brown	£6000	£5500

1877. Value in cash.

74	20 cash blue	15·00	15·00
75	20 cash lilac	12·00	10·00
93	20 cash green	7·50	5·00
114	20 cash grey	5·00	3·00
81	40 cash pink	16·00	15·00
94	40 cash brown	9·00	9·00
107	40 cash black	8·00	5·00
82	60 cash green	18·00	20·00
95	60 cash violet	16·00	17·00
108	60 cash red	12·00	9·00
83	80 cash blue	19·00	20·00
96	80 cash brown	15·00	15·00
109	80 cash green	8·50	7·50
84	100 cash brown	22·00	22·00
97	100 cash yellow	18·00	20·00
110	100 cash blue	12·00	12·00

1879. Surch in English and Chinese.

89	20 cash on 40 cash pink	22·00	22·00
103	20 cash on 40 cash brown	25·00	25·00
105	20 cash on 80 cash brown	13·00	12·00
111	20 cash on 80 cash green	15·00	15·00
112	20 cash on 100 cash blue	15·00	15·00
100	40 cash on 80 cash brown	12·00	12·00
101	40 cash on 100 cash yellow	15·00	16·00
90	60 cash on 80 cash blue	32·00	36·00
88	60 cash on 100 cash brown	60·00	65·00
102	60 cash on 100 cash yellow	18·00	18·00

1886. Surch 20 CASH in English and Chinese in double-lined frame.

104	20 cash on 40 cash brown	25·00	26·00

1889. Surch 100 CASH over 20 CASH in English and Chinese in double-lined frame.

113	100 cash on 20 cash on 100 cash yellow	£180	£225

16

1890. Value in cents.

119	**16**	2c. brown	3·75	4·25
142	**16**	2c. green	2·75	2·50
120	**16**	5c. pink	11·00	8·00
143	**16**	5c. red	7·50	7·25
122	**16**	10c. black	16·00	12·00
144	**16**	10c. orange	20·00	22·00
123	**16**	15c. blue	22·00	18·00
145	**16**	15c. mauve	12·00	10·00
124	**16**	20c. mauve	16·00	14·00
146	**16**	20c. brown	13·00	13·00

1892. Surch 2 Cts and in Chinese.

141		2c. on 5c. pink	£120	55·00

1893. Surch in words in English and Chinese.

147		½c. on 15c. mauve	18·00	13·00
148		1c. on 20c. brown	18·00	13·00

1893. Surch ½Ct. or 1 Ct.

149		½c. on half of 5c. pink	12·00	10·00
152		½c. on half of 5c. red	12·00	10·00
155		1c. on half of 2c. brown	3·25	3·00
156		1c. on half of 2c. green	15·00	12·00

25

1893. Inscriptions in outer frame in black.

165	**25**	½c. orange	50	50
166	**25**	1c. brown	50	50
187	**25**	2c. red	25	1·60
188	**25**	4c. orange on yellow	6·50	5·50
161	**25**	5c. blue	1·00	55
189	**25**	6c. red on pink	7·50	8·50
167	**25**	10c. green	2·50	3·00
163	**25**	15c. yellow	1·00	75
168	**25**	20c. mauve	2·50	4·25

26

1893. Jubilee of First Settlement.

176	**26**	2c. red and black	1·00	1·00

1893. Optd 1843 Jubilee 1893. Inscriptions in outer frame in black.

177	**25**	½c. orange	40	40
178	**25**	1c. brown	55	55
179	**25**	2c. red	75	75
180	**25**	5c. blue	3·25	4·25
181	**25**	10c. green	10·00	12·00
182	**25**	15c. yellow	6·50	6·50
183	**25**	20c. mauve	8·50	10·00

1896. Surch in English and Chinese.

184		4c. on 15c. yellow	10·00	8·00
185		6c. on 20c. mauve	10·00	8·00

POSTAGE DUE STAMPS

1892. T 16 optd Postage Due.

D134	2c. brown	3·00	2·75
D135	5c. pink	14·00	8·00
D130	10c. black	32·00	32·00
D138	10c. orange	18·00	15·00
D131	15c. blue	27·00	27·00
D139	15c. mauve	30·00	30·00
D132	20c. mauve	20·00	20·00
D140	20c. brown	30·00	29·00

D26

1893. Inscriptions in outer frame in black.

D169	**D26**	½c. orange	50	50
D170	**D26**	1c. brown	60	50
D171	**D26**	2c. red	60	50
D172	**D26**	5c. blue	90	90
D173	**D26**	10c. green	5·50	1·80
D174	**D26**	15c. yellow	4·25	3·75
D175	**D26**	20c. mauve	1·60	1·60

Pt. 19

SHARJAH

One of the Trucial States on the Persian Gulf. Embodies the principalities of Dibbah, Khor Fakkan and Khor al-Kalba.

On 2 December 1971, Sharjah, together with six other Gulf Shaikdoms, formed the United Arab Emirates.

1963. 100 naye paise = 1 rupee.
1966. 100 dirhams = 1 riyal.

IMPERFORATE STAMPS. Some sets also exist imperf in limited quantities.

1 Shaikh Saqr bin Sultan al Qasimi, Flag and Map

1963. Multicoloured.. Multicoloured..

1	**1**	1n.p. (postage) multicoloured	10	10
2	**1**	2n.p. multicoloured	10	10
3	**1**	3n.p. multicoloured	10	10
4	**1**	4n.p. multicoloured	10	10
5	**1**	5n.p. multicoloured	10	10
6	**1**	6n.p. multicoloured	10	10
7	**1**	8n.p. multicoloured	10	10
8	**1**	10n.p. multicoloured	25	25
9	**1**	16n.p. multicoloured	50	25
10	**1**	20n.p. multicoloured	60	25
11	**1**	30n.p. multicoloured	85	35
12	**1**	40n.p. multicoloured	95	60
13	**1**	50n.p. multicoloured	1·30	70
14	**1**	75n.p. multicoloured	2·40	1·60
15	**1**	100n.p. multicoloured	3·25	2·40
16	**1**	1r. (air) multicoloured	1·40	70
17	**1**	2r. multicoloured	2·75	1·20
18	**1**	3r. multicoloured	3·00	1·90
19	**1**	4r. multicoloured	5·00	2·75
20	**1**	5r. multicoloured	6·75	3·50
21	**1**	10r. multicoloured	12·00	7·25

The air stamps are as T **1** but additionally inscr "AIR-MAIL" in English and Arabic, and with a hawk in flight.

2 Mosquito and W.H.O. Emblem

1963. Malaria Eradication.

22	**2**	1n.p. turquoise	10	10
23	**2**	2n.p. blue	10	10
24	**2**	3n.p. blue	25	10
25	**2**	4n.p. green	35	25
26	**2**	90n.p. brown	3·75	1·80
MS26a 64×90 mm. **2** 100n.p. greenish blue (40×67 mm). Imperf			7·50	2·40

3 "Red Crescent"

1963. Red Cross Centenary.

27	**3**	1n.p. red and purple	10	10
28	**3**	2n.p. red and turquoise	10	10
29	**3**	3n.p. red and blue	10	10
30	**3**	4n.p. red and green	10	10
31	**3**	5n.p. red and brown	10	10
32	**3**	85n.p. red and green	2·40	1·20
MS32a 90×64 mm. **3** 100n.p. red and purple (67×40 mm). Imperf			5·50	3·00

4 Campaign Emblem between Hands

1963. Freedom from Hunger.

33	**4**	1n.p. green	10	10
34	**4**	2n.p. brown	10	10
35	**4**	3n.p. green	10	10
36	**4**	4n.p. blue	10	25
37	**4**	90n.p. red	2·75	1·20
MS37a 64×90 mm. **4** 100n.p. plum (40×67 mm). Imperf			3·50	2·40

1963. Surch.

38	**4**	10n.p. on 1n.p. green	35	35
39		20n.p. on 2n.p. brown	70	60
40		30n.p. on 3n.p. green	1·20	95
41		40n.p. on 4n.p. blue	1·60	1·40
42		75n.p. on 90n.p. red	3·00	2·40
43		80n.p. on 90n.p. red	3·50	2·75
44	**2**	1r. on 90n.p. brown	4·75	4·00

1964. Air. Pres. Kennedy Memorial Issue (1st issue). Nos. 16-21 optd In Memoriam John F Kennedy 1917-1963 in English and Arabic, and emblems.

45	**1**	1r. multicoloured	3·50	3·50
46	**1**	2r. multicoloured	7·25	7·25
47	**1**	3r. multicoloured	12·00	12·00
48	**1**	4r. multicoloured	14·50	14·50
49	**1**	5r. multicoloured	22·00	22·00
50	**1**	10r. multicoloured	31·00	31·00

See also Nos. 98-100.

7 Orbiting Astronomical Observatory (image scaled to 74% of original size)

1964. Scientific Space Research.

51	**7**	1n.p. blue	10	10
52	**7**	2n.p. green and brown	10	10
53	**7**	3n.p. blue and black	10	10
54	**7**	4n.p. black and bistre	10	10
55	**7**	5n.p. bistre and violet	10	10
56	**7**	35n.p. violet and blue	1·20	95
57	**7**	50n.p. brown and green	2·40	1·40
MS57a 112×80 mm. 100n.p. multicoloured (Various satellites). Imperf			8·50	2·40

DESIGNS: 2n.p. "Nimbus" weather satellite; 3n.p. "Pioneer V" space probe; 4n.p. "Explorer XIII" satellite; 5n.p. "Explorer XII" satellite; 35n.p. Project "Relay" satellite; 50n.p. Orbiting solar observatory.

8 Running (image scaled to 75% of original size)

1964. Olympic Games, Tokyo (1st issue).

58	**8**	1n.p. blue, green and yellow	10	10
59	-	2n.p. red and turquoise	10	10
60	-	3n.p. brown and green	10	10
61	-	4n.p. green and brown	10	10
62	-	20n.p. blue and brown	60	25
63	-	30n.p. bistre and pink	95	50
64	-	40n.p. violet and yellow	1·20	60
65	-	1r. brown and blue	3·00	1·80
MS65a 102×102 mm. 1r. sepia and cobalt (67×67 mm) (As No. 65). Imperf			12·00	9·75

DESIGNS: 2n.p. Throwing the discus; 3n.p. Hurdling; 4n.p. Putting the shot; 20n.p. High jumping; 30n.p. Weightlifting; 40n.p. Throwing the javelin; 1r. High diving.

See also Nos. 90-7.

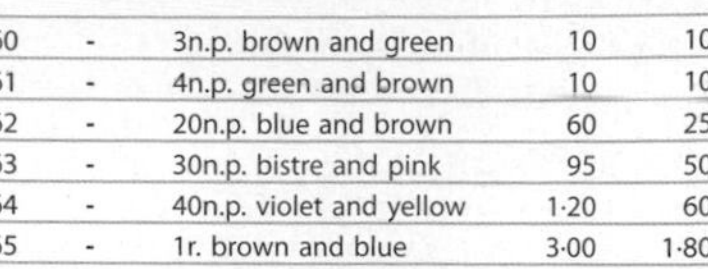

9 Flame and World Map

1964. Air. Human Rights Day.

66	**9**	50n.p. brown	70	35
67	**9**	1r. violet	1·40	85
68	**9**	150n.p. green	2·75	1·40
MS68a 90×64 mm. **9** 3r. rosine (67×40 mm). Imperf			4·75	3·00

10 Girl Scouts Marching

1964. Sharjah Girl Scouts.

69	**10**	1n.p. green	10	10
70	**10**	2n.p. green	10	10
71	**10**	3n.p. blue	25	25
72	**10**	4n.p. violet	25	25
73	**10**	5n.p. mauve	35	25
74	**10**	2r. brown	4·00	2·75
MS74a 103×76 mm. **10** 2r. vermilion (67×40 mm). Imperf			6·00	4·25

11 Khor Fakkan

1964. Air. Multicoloured.

75	10n.p. Type **11**	25	25
76	20n.p. Bedouin camp, Beni Qatab	35	25
77	30n.p. Dhaid oasis	50	25
78	40n.p. Kalba Castle	60	35
79	75n.p. Street and Wind tower, Sharjah	1·30	50
80	100n.p. Fortress	2·40	60

12 "Mr. Gus" (oil rig)

1964. Air. New York World's Fair. Multicoloured.

81	20n.p. Type **12**	70	25
82	40n.p. Unisphere	1·20	35
83	1r. New York skyline (85½×44½ mm)	3·00	85
MS83a 76×108 mm. 40n.p. multicoloured (40×67 mm) (As No. 82). Imperf		4·75	2·10

13 Scout at Attention

1964. Sharjah Boy Scouts.

84	**13**	1n.p. green	10	10
85	-	2n.p. green	10	10
86	-	3n.p. blue	10	10
87	**13**	4n.p. violet	60	50
88	-	5n.p. mauve	70	60
89	-	2r. brown	2·75	1·80

MS89a 77×103 mm. 2r. vermilion (40×67 mm) (As No. 86). Imperf 6·00 4·25

DESIGNS—HORIZ: 2, 5n.p. Scouts marching. VERT: 3n.p., 2r. Boy scout.

14 Olympic Torch

1964. Olympic Games, Tokyo (2nd issue).

90	**14**	1n.p. green	10	10
91	**14**	2n.p. blue	10	10
92	**14**	3n.p. brown	10	10
93	**14**	4n.p. turquoise	10	10
94	**14**	5n.p. violet	10	10
95	**14**	40n.p. blue	50	10
96	**14**	50n.p. brown	85	35
97	**14**	2r. brown	4·25	2·20

MS97a 108×76 mm. **14** 2r. green (57×82 mm). Imperf 12·00 9·75

15 Pres. Kennedy and Statue of Liberty

1964. Air. Pres. Kennedy Commemoration (2nd issue). Inscr in gold.

98	**15**	40n.p. blue, brown & green	2·40	1·20
99	**15**	60n.p. brown, green & blue	2·40	1·20
100	**15**	100n.p. green, blue & brown	2·40	1·20

MS100a 108×76 mm. Nos. 98-100. Imperf 12·00 9·75

16 Feral Rock Pigeon ("Rock Dove")

1965. Air. Birds. Multicoloured.

101	30n.p. Type **16**	95	25
102	40n.p. Red junglefowl	1·20	35
103	75n.p. Hoopoe	1·80	60
104	150n.p. Type **16**	3·50	1·20
105	2r. Red junglefowl	4·75	1·40
106	3r. Hoopoe	6·00	2·40

17 Early Telephone

1965. "Science, Transport and Communications".

107	**17**	1n.p. black and red	10	10
108	**A**	1n.p. black and red	10	10
109	**B**	2n.p. blue and orange	10	10
110	**C**	2n.p. blue and orange	10	10
111	**D**	3n.p. brown and green	10	10
112	**E**	3n.p. brown and green	10	10
113	**F**	4n.p. violet and green	10	10
114	**G**	4n.p. violet and green	10	10
115	**H**	5n.p. brown and green	10	10
116	**I**	5n.p. brown and green	10	10
117	**J**	30n.p. indigo and blue	25	25
118	**K**	30n.p. indigo and blue	25	25
119	**L**	40n.p. blue and yellow	50	25
120	**M**	40n.p. blue and yellow	50	25
121	**N**	50n.p. brown and blue	60	35
122	**O**	50n.p. brown and blue	60	35
123	**P**	75n.p. brown and green	60	35
124	**Q**	75n.p. brown and green	60	35
125	**R**	1r. blue and yellow	3·00	1·20
126	**S**	1r. blue and yellow	3·00	1·20

MS126a Two sheets each 153×77 mm. Nos. 119-20 and 125-6. Imperf 9·00 5·00

DESIGNS: A, Modern teleprinter; B, 1895 Car; C, 1964 American car; D, Early X-ray apparatus; E, T.V. X-ray machine; F, Early mail coach; G, "Telstar" satellite; H, Medieval ship; I, Nuclear- powered freighter "Savannah"; J, Early astronomers; K, Jodrell Bank radio-telescope; L, Greek messengers; M, "Relay" satellite; N, "Man's early flight" (Lilienthal biplane glider); O, Sud Aviation Caravelle jetliner; P, Persian waterwheel; Q, Hydro-electric dam; R, Locomotive "Fitzwilliam", 1849, Great Britain; S, Modern diesel train.

1965. Air. Churchill Commemoration (1st issue). Optd In Memoriam Sir Winston Churchill 1874-1965 in English and Arabic.

127	**15**	40n.p. multicoloured	1·20	50
128	**15**	60n.p. multicoloured	1·80	60
129	**15**	100n.p. multicoloured	2·40	70

MS129a 108×76 mm. Nos. 127-9. Imperf 14·50 12·00

See also Nos. 201-4.

18a A.P.U. Emblem

1965. 10th Anniv (1964) of Arab Postal Union's Permanent Office.

130	**18a**	5n.p. blue and yellow	10	10
131	**18a**	30n.p. blue and red	70	35
132	**18a**	65n.p. green and orange	1·80	1·10

1965. Various issues of Shaikh Saqr with portrait obliterated with bars. (a) Postage. Nos. 5, 8/13.

150	**1**	5n.p. multicoloured	10	10
151	**1**	10n.p. multicoloured	10	10
152	**1**	16n.p. multicoloured	25	25
153	**1**	20n.p. multicoloured	35	25
154	**1**	30n.p. multicoloured	50	25
155	**1**	40n.p. multicoloured	50	35
156	**1**	50n.p. multicoloured	60	50

(b) Air. (i) Nos. 16, 18-21.

157	1r. multicoloured	95	70
158	3r. multicoloured	3·00	2·40
159	4r. multicoloured	3·75	3·00
160	5r. multicoloured	5·00	3·50
161	10r. multicoloured	10·00	6·00

(ii) Nos. 75-80.

144	**11**	10n.p. multicoloured	35	25
145	-	20n.p. multicoloured	50	25
146	-	30n.p. multicoloured	60	25
147	-	40n.p. multicoloured	70	35
148	-	75n.p. multicoloured	95	35
149	-	100n.p. multicoloured	1·20	50

22 Rameses II in War Chariot

1965. Nubian Monuments Preservation.

162	**22**	5n.p. blue and yellow	10	10
163	**22**	10n.p. green and brown	10	10
164	**22**	30n.p. blue and orange	70	60
165	**22**	55n.p. violet and blue	1·20	85

23 Cable Ship "Monarch IV" and COMPAC Cable Route Map

1965. I.T.U. Centenary. Country name in gold.

166	**23**	1n.p. brown and blue	10	10
167	-	2n.p. brown and blue	10	10
168	-	3n.p. violet and green	10	10
169	-	4n.p. brown and blue	10	10
170	**23**	5n.p. brown and violet	25	10
171	-	50n.p. purple and black	60	25
172	-	1r. green and brown	1·20	50
173	-	120n.p. red and green	1·80	70

DESIGNS: 2, 120n.p. "Relay 1" satellite and tracking station, Goonhilly Down; 3, 50n.p. "Telstar" satellite and Atlas-Agena rocket on launching pad; 4n.p., 1r. "Syncom" satellite, Post Office Tower (London) and horn paraboloid reflector aerial.

24 Running

1965. Pan-American Games, Cairo.

174	**24**	50n.p. turquoise and lilac	85	35
175	-	50n.p. green and brown	85	35
176	-	50n.p. lilac and brown	85	35
177	-	50n.p. brown and green	85	35
178	-	50n.p. brown and turquoise	85	35

SPORTS: No. 175, Pole vaulting; 176, Boxing; 177, High jumping; 178, Long jumping.

25 Flags (reverse of 5r. coin)

1966. Arabian Gulf Area Monetary Conf. Circular designs on silver foil, backed with paper inscr "Walsall Security Paper" in English and Arabic. Imperf. (a) Diameter 41 mm.

179	**25**	50n.p. black	1·20	1·20
180	-	75n.p. violet	1·30	1·30

(b) Diameter 52 mm.

181	**25**	1r. purple	1·40	1·40
182	-	3r. blue	4·00	4·00

(c) Diameter 64 mm.

183	**25**	4r. green	6·00	6·00
184	-	5r. orange	6·75	6·75

COINS: 75n.p., 3r. and 5r. show the obverse (Pres. Kennedy).

1966. Rendezvous in Space. Nos. 33-6 optd 15-12-1965 Rendezvous in SPACE, two space capsules and four bars obliterating portrait or surch also in English and Arabic.

185	**4**	1n.p. green	10	10
186	**4**	2n.p. brown	10	10
187	**4**	3n.p. green	10	10
188	**4**	4n.p. blue	10	10
189	**4**	15n.p. on 1n.p. green	35	25
190	**4**	30n.p. on 2n.p. brown	50	35
191	**4**	50n.p. on 3n.p. green	1·30	85
192	**4**	1r. on 4n.p. blue	1·70	95

27 I.C.Y. Emblem and Prime Minister Harold Wilson

1986. International Co-operation Year.

193	**27**	80n.p. brown and violet	70	25
194	-	80n.p. brown and green	70	25
195	-	80n.p. green and red	70	25
196	-	80n.p. purple and blue	70	25
197	-	80n.p. blue and orange	70	25
198	-	80n.p. purple and green	70	25
199	-	80n.p. blue and grey	70	25
200	-	80n.p. purple and brown	70	25

DESIGNS—I.C.Y. emblem and "World Leaders": No. 194, Chancellor Erhard (West Germany); 195, Pres. Nasser (Egypt); 196, Pres. Johnson (U.S.A.); 197, Pope Paul VI; 198, Pres. De Gaulle (France); 199, Shaikh Isa bin Sulman al-Khalifa (Bahrain); 200, King Faisal (Saudi Arabia).

28 Sir Winston Churchill, Pen and Ink, and Books

1966. Churchill Commemoration (2nd issue). Multicoloured, printed on gold foil, backed with paper.

201	2r. Type **28**	1·20	60
202	3r. Churchill and Houses of Parliament, pen and ink	1·40	70
203	4r. Churchill and St. Paul's Cathedral	2·20	95
204	5r. Churchill and "Big Ben" (clock tower, Houses of Parliament) and Tower Bridge	2·40	1·20

MS205 102×71 mm. 1, 2, 3, and 4r. stamps in colours and designs of Nos. 201-2, 204 and 203 but smaller 16·00 11·00

29 Pennant Coralfish

1966. Fishes. Multicoloured.

206	1n.p. Type **29**	35	25
207	2n.p. Sail-finned tang	35	25
208	3n.p. Young emperor angelfish	35	25
209	4n.p. African mouthbrooder	35	25
210	5n.p. Undulate triggerfish	35	25
211	15n.p. Diamond fingerfish	1·10	25
212	20n.p. Ornate butterflyfish	1·40	25
213	30n.p. Moorish idol	1·40	25
214	40n.p. Regal angelfish	1·80	25
215	50n.p. African mouthbrooder	1·80	25
216	75n.p. Undulate triggerfish	2·20	35
217	1r. Regal angelfish	3·00	35
218	2r. Moorish idol	4·25	65
219	3r. Ornate butterflyfish	5·50	70
220	4r. Diamond fingerfish	7·25	1·30
221	5r. Young emperor angelfish	11·00	1·70
222	10r. Type **29**	22·00	3·25

30 Arms of Munich and "Souvenir Sheet"

1966. International Philatelic Federation and International Philatelic Journalists Association Congresses, Munich. Multicoloured.

223	80n.p. Type **30**	60	25
224	120n.p. Frauenkirche, Munich	85	35
225	2r. Statue and Hall of Fame, Munich (81×41 mm)	1·60	70

NEW CURRENCY SURCHARGES. During the latter half of 1966 various issues appeared surcharged in dirhams and riyals. The 1966 definitives with this surcharge are listed below as there is evidence of their postal use. Nos. 102, 107-126, 135, 145, 150-161, 174-184 and 190 also exist with these surcharges.

Earlier in 1966 Nos. 98-100, 171-173, 193-194, 196, 198 and 200-205 appeared surcharged in piastres and rials. As Sharjah did not adopt this currency their status is uncertain.

1966. Nos. 206-22 with currency names changed by overprinting in English and Arabic. (a) Optd. Dirham or Riyal.

226	**29**	1d. on 1n.p. multicoloured	25	25
227	-	2d. on 2n.p. multicoloured	25	25
228	-	3d. on 3n.p. multicoloured	25	25
229	-	4d. on 4n.p. multicoloured	25	25
230	-	5d. on 5n.p. multicoloured	25	25
231	-	15d. on 15n.p. mult	25	25
232	-	20d. on 20n.p. mult	25	25
233	-	30d. on 30n.p. mult	50	50
234	-	40d. on 40n.p. mult	70	50
235	-	50d. on 50n.p. mult	95	70
236	-	75d. on 75n.p. mult	1·40	95
237	-	1r. on 1r. multicoloured	1·90	1·40
238	-	2r. on 2r. multicoloured	4·00	3·00
239	-	3r. on 3r. multicoloured	5·75	4·00
240	-	4r. on 4r. multicoloured	7·75	5·25
241	-	5r. on 5r. multicoloured	8·50	6·00
242	**29**	10r. on 10r. multicoloured	16·00	13·50

(b) Optd Dh.

242b	2d. on 2n.p. multicoloured	25	25
242c	3d. on 3n.p. multicoloured	25	25
242f	15d. on 15n.p. mult	40	25
242g	20d. on 20n.p. mult	50	30
242h	30d. on 30n.p. mult	60	25
242i	40d. on 40n.p. mult	70	25
242j	50d. on 50n.p. mult	70	50
242k	75d. on 75n.p. mult	1·10	70

33 Greek 6th-cent Ball-player

1966. World Cup Football Championship, England. Printed on coloured metal foil-surfaced paper. Multicoloured.

243	½r. Type **33**	1·60	25
244	½r. Tsu-chu "Kick-ball" game, China, c. 175 B.C.	1·60	25
245	½r. 14th-cent ball game	1·60	25
246	½r. Blowing up ball-bladder (17th-cent)	1·60	25
247	½r. Football game, Barnet, England, c. 1750	1·60	25
248	½r. England v. Scotland game, Kennington Oval (London), 1879	1·60	25
249	½r. Victorious England team, Wembley, 1966 (56×55½ mm)	1·60	25
MS250	Six sheets comprising Nos. 243-248, but smaller, 31×36 mm, each block of four	14·50	14·50

34 Pres. Kennedy

1966. 3rd Death Anniv of Pres. Kennedy and Inauguration of Arlington Memorial.

251	50d. Type **34**	50	25
252	2r. Sharjah 50n.p. Kennedy stamp of 1964	1·90	60
253	2r.50 Pres. Kennedy's grave (77×40 mm)	2·40	95
MS254	102×126 mm. 3r. President Kennedy's grave (55×42 mm)	8·50	8·50

35 Shaikh Khalid bin Mohammed al Qasimi and Arms

1968. Multicoloured.. Multicoloured..

255	5d. Type **35** (postage)	25	25
256	10d. Flag	25	25
257	15d. Flag and arms (vert)	35	25
258	20d. Decorative pattern (vert)	35	25
259	35d. Type **35** (air)	60	35
260	40d. As 10d.	60	35
261	60d. As 15d.	85	35
262	75d. As 20d.	1·10	50
263	1r. Type **35**	1·40	50
264	2r. As 10d.	3·00	1·20
265	3r. As 15d.	4·25	2·20
266	4r. As 20d.	5·50	3·00
267	5r. Type **35**	6·75	3·00
268	10r. As 10d.	12·00	7·25

36 Freighter at Wharf

1970. 5th Anniv of Ruler's Accession. "Progress in Sharjah".

285	**36**	5d. deep violet and violet	25	25
286	**A**	5d. deep blue and blue	25	25
287	**B**	5d. brown and red	25	25
288	**C**	5d. brown and green	25	25
289	**D**	5d. brown and light brown	25	25
290	**D**	20d. brown and light brown	25	25
291	**36**	35d. deep violet and violet	35	35
292	**A**	35d. deep blue and blue	35	35
293	**B**	35d. brown and red	35	35
294	**C**	35d. brown and green	35	35
295	**D**	35d. brown and light brown	35	35
296	**36**	40d. deep violet and violet	50	35
297	**A**	40d. deep blue and blue	50	35
298	**B**	40d. brown and red	50	35
299	**C**	40d. brown and green	50	35
300	**D**	40d. brown and light brown	50	35
301	**36**	60d. deep violet and violet	70	50
302	**A**	60d. deep blue and blue	70	50
303	**B**	60d. brown and red	70	50
304	**C**	60d. brown and green	70	50
305	**D**	60d. brown and light brown	70	50

DESIGNS: A, Airport; B, Oil derrick; C, Modern building; D, Shaikh Khalid.

37 Turbines

1971. 6th Anniv of Ruler's Accession. "Progress in Sharjah".

306	**37**	5d. bl, vio & grn (postage)	
307	**A**	5d. mauve, brown & vio	
308	**B**	5d. multicoloured	
309	**C**	5d. multicoloured	
310	**B**	35d. multicoloured (air)	
311	**37**	75d. blue, violet and green	
312	**A**	75d. mauve, brown and violet	
313	**B**	75d. multicoloured	
314	**C**	75d. multicoloured	
315	**37**	1r. blue, violet and green	
316	**A**	1r. mauve, brown and violet	
317	**B**	1r. multicoloured	
318	**C**	1r. multicoloured	
319	**A**	2r. mauve, brown and violet	
320	**37**	3r. blue, violet and green	
321	**A**	3r. mauve, brown and violet	
322	**B**	3r. multicoloured	
323	**C**	3r. multicoloured	
324	**C**	5r. multicoloured	

DESIGNS—HORIZ: A, Mosque. VERT: B, Clock fountain; C, Shaikh Khalid.

38 Shaikh Rashid of Dubai and Shaikh Khalid

1971. Air. Proclamation of United Arab Emirates. Multicoloured.

325	25d. Type **38**
326	35d. Shaikh Ahmed of Umm al Qiwain and Shaikh Khalid
327	65d. United Nations and Arab League emblems
328	75d. Shaikh Rashid of Ajman and Shaikh Khalid
329	1r. Shaikh Mohamed of Fujeira and Shaikh Khalid
330	2r. Shaikh Zaid of Abu Dhabi and Shaikh Khalid

1971. Various stamps surcharged. (a) 1968 Winter Olympics issue (Appendix).

331	35d. on 5d. multicoloured

(b) Nos. 255 and 262.

332	**35**	35 on 5d. mult (postage)
334	-	60 on 75d. multicoloured

(c) 5th Anniv of Ruler's Accession (Nos. 296-300).

335	**36**	5 on 40d. dp vio & vio
336	**A**	5 on 40d. dp blue & blue
337	**B**	5 on 40d. brown and red
338	**C**	5 on 40d. brown and green
339	**D**	5 on 40d. brn & lt brn

(d) Air. Proclamation of United Arab Emirates (Nos. 325 and 328-330).

340	**38**	65d. on 25d. multicoloured
341	-	65d. on 75d. multicoloured
342	-	65d. on 1r. multicoloured
343	-	65d. on 2r. multicoloured

OFFICIAL STAMPS

1966. Optd ON STATE SERVICE in English and Arabic. Multicoloured.

O101	**1**	8n.p.	10	10
O102	**1**	10n.p.	10	10
O103	**1**	16n.p.	25	25
O104	**1**	20n.p.	35	35
O105	**1**	30n.p.	35	35
O106	**1**	40n.p.	60	60
O107	**1**	50n.p.	1·60	1·60
O108	**1**	75n.p.	4·00	4·00
O109	**1**	100n.p.	7·25	7·25

1968. As Nos. 258 and 261 but colours changed and inscr "OFFICIAL".

O269	20d. multicoloured
O270	60d. multicoloured

For later issues see **UNITED ARAB EMIRATES**.

APPENDIX

The following stamps have either been issued in excess of postal needs or have not been made available to the public in reasonable quantities at face value. Such stamps may later be given full listing if there is evidence of regular postal use.

1967

Post Day. Japanese Paintings. 1r.×3.
22nd Anniv of United Nations. 10, 30, 60d.
Olympics Preparation, Mexico, 1968. Postage 1, 2, 3, 10 d; Air 30, 60d., 2r.
Flowers and Butterflies. Postage 1, 2, 3, 4, 5, 10, 20d.; Air 30, 60d., 1, 2r.
Famous Paintings. Postage 1, 2, 3, 4, 5, 30, 40, 60, 75d.; Air 1, 2, 3, 4, 5r.

1968

Winter Olympic Games, Grenoble. Postage 1, 2, 3, 4, 5d.; Air 1, 2, 3r.
12th World Jamboree. Postage 1, 2, 3, 4, 5, 10d.; Air 30, 50, 60d., 1r.50.
Grenoble Olympic Medal Winners. Optd on Winter Olympics, Grenoble issue. Postage 1, 2, 3, 4, 5d.; Air 1, 2, 3r.
Mothers' Day. Paintings. Postage 10, 20, 30, 40d.; Air 1, 2, 3, 4r.
American Paintings. Postage 20, 30, 40, 50, 60d.; Air 1, 4, 5r.
Egyptian Art. 15, 25, 35, 45, 55, 65, 75, 95d.
Martyrs of Liberty. Air 35d.×4, 60d.×4, 1r.×4.
Olympic Games, Mexico. 10, 20, 30d., 2r., 2r. 40, 5r.
Previous Olympic Games. Air 25, 50, 75d., 1r. 50, 3, 4r.
Sportsmen and Women. Postage 20, 30, 40, 60d., 1r. 50, 2r. 50; Air 25, 50d., 1, 2r., 3r. 25, 4, 4r.
Robert Kennedy Memorial. Optd on American Paintings issue. Air 4r.
Olympic Medal Winners, Mexico. 35, 50, 60d., 1, 2, 4r.

1969

Famous Men and Women. Postage 10, 20, 25, 35, 50, 60d.; Air 1, 2, 3, 4, 5, 6r.
"Apollo 8" Moon Mission. Postage 5d.×6; Air 10, 15, 20d., 2, 3, 4r.
"Apollo 11" Moon Mission (1st series). Postage 5d.×8; Air 75d.×8, 1r.×8.
Post Day. Famous Ships. Postage 5d.×8; Air 90d.×8.
"Apollo 12" Moon Mission. Optd on Famous Ships issue. 5d.×8.

1970

UNICEF. Paintings of Children. Postage 5d.×9; Air 20, 25, 35, 40, 50, 60, 75d., 1, 3r.
Animals. Postage 3d.×14, 10, 10, 15, 15d.; Air 20, 20, 35, 35d., 1, 1, 2, 2r.
"Expo 70" World Fair, Osaka, Japan (1st series). Japanese Paintings. Postage 3d.×4; Air 1r.×4.
"Expo 70" World Fair, Osaka, Japan (2nd series). Pavilions. Postage 2, 2, 3, 3d.; Air 40d.×4.
Paintings of Napoleon. Postage 3d.×5; Air 20, 30, 40, 60d., 2r.
De Gaulle Commemoration. Postage 3d.×5; Air 20, 30, 40, 60d., 2r.
"Mercury" and "Vostok" Moon Missions. Postage 1, 2, 3, 4, 5d.; Air 25, 40, 85d., 1, 2r.
"Gemini" Space Programme. Postage 1, 2, 3, 4, 5d.; Air 25, 40, 85d., 1, 2r.
"Apollo", "Voskhod" and "Soyuz" Projects. Postage 1, 2, 3, 4, 5d.; Air 25, 40, 85d., 1, 2r.
Events of 1970. Postage 1d.×5, 5d.; Air 75d., 1, 2, 3r.
200th Birth Anniv of Beethoven. Postage 3d.×5; Air 35, 40, 60d., 1, 2r.
Mozart. Postage 3d.×5; Air 35, 40, 60d., 1, 2r.
The Life of Christ (1st series). Postage 1, 2, 3, 4, 5d.; Air 25, 40, 60d., 1, 2r.

1971

"Apollo 14" Moon Mission. Optd on 1969 "Apollo 11" issue. Postage 5d.×4; Air 75d.×4.
Post Day 1970. Cars. Postage 1, 2, 3, 4, 5d.; Air 25, 50, 60d., 2, 3r.
Post Day (1st series). American Cars. Postage 1, 2, 3, 4, 5d.; Air 35, 50d., 1, 2, 3r.
Post Day (2nd series). Trains. Postage 1, 2, 3, 4, 5d.; Air 25, 50, 60d., 1, 2r.
Pres. Nasser Commemoration. Postage 5d.×5; Air 20, 35, 40, 60d., 2r.
Safe return of "Apollo 13". Optd on 1969 "Apollo 8" issue. Air 10, 15, 20d., 2, 3, 4r.
De Gaulle Memorial. Postage 3, 4, 5, 6, 7d.; Air 40, 60, 75d., 1, 2r.
Olympics Preparation, Munich, 1972. Postage 2, 3, 4, 5, 6d.; Air 35, 40, 60d., 1, 2r.
Miracles of Christ. Postage 1, 2, 3, 4, 5d.; Air 25, 40, 60d., 1, 2r.

1972

Sport. Postage 2, 3, 4, 5, 6d.; Air 35, 40, 60d., 1, 2r.
The Life of Christ (2nd series). Postage 1, 2, 3, 4, 5d.; Air 25, 40, 60d., 1, 2r.
Winter Olympics Preparation, Sapporo. Postage 2, 3, 4, 5, 6d.; Air 35, 40, 60d., 1, 2r.
Safe Return of "Apollo 14". Optd on 1969 "Apollo 11" issue. Postage 5d.×4; Air 1r.×4.
Previous World Cup Winners. Postage 5, 10, 15, 20, 25d.; Air 35, 75d., 1, 2, 3r.
Sapporo Olympic Medal Winners. Paintings. Postage 5, 10, 15, 20, 25d.; Air 35, 75d., 1, 2, 3r.
Famous People, Churchill, De Gaulle and John Kennedy. Postage 5d.×4, 10d.×4, 35d.×4; Air 75d.×4, 1r.×4, 3r.×4.
Olympic Games, Munich. Postage 5, 10, 15, 20, 25d.; Air 35, 75d., 1, 2, 3r.
Cats. Postage 20, 25d.; Air 75d., 1, 2r.
Birds (1st series). Postage 20, 25, 75d., Air 1, 2r.
"Apollo 11" Moon Mission (2nd series). Postage 1, 1r. Air 1r.×3.
"Apollo 16" Moon Mission. Postage 1, 1r.; Air 1r.×3.

Dogs. Postage 20, 25d.; Air 75d., 1, 2r.
"Apollo 17" Moon Mission. Postage 1, 1r.; Air 1r.×3.
Munich Olympic Medal Winners. Air 5r.×20.
Horses. Postage 20, 25d.; Air 75d., 1, 2r.
"Apollo 17" Astronauts. Postage 1, 1r.; Air 1r.×3.
Butterflies. Postage 20, 25d.; Air 75d., 1, 2r.
"Luna 9" Soviet Space Programme. Postage 1, 1r.; Air 1r.×3.
Monkeys. Postage 20, 25d.; Air 75d., 1, 2r.
Birds (2nd series). Air 25, 25, 35, 35, 50, 50, 65, 65d., 1r.×6, 3, 3r.
Fish. Air 25, 35, 50, 65d., 1r.×5, 3r.
Insects. Air 25, 35, 50, 65d., 1, 3r.
Flowers. Postage 25, 35, 50, 65d., 1, 3r.; Air 1r.×4.
Fruit. Air 1r.×4.
Children. Air 1r.×4.
Eastern Antiquities. Air 25, 35, 40, 65, 75d., 1r.×4, 3r.
Planetary Exploration. Postage 1r.×3; Air 1, 1r.
13th World Jamboree. Postage 2d.×3, 3d.×3, 4d.×3, 5d.×3, 6d.×3; Air 35d.×3, 75d.×3, 1r.×3, 2r.×3, 3r.×3.

A number of issues on gold or silver foil also exist, but it is understood that these were mainly for presentation purposes, although valid for postage.

In common with the other states of the United Arab Emirates the Sharjah stamp contract was terminated on 1 August 1972, and further new issues released after that date were unauthorized.

Pt. 10

SIBERIA

Various Anti-Bolshevist governments existed in this area, culminating in Kolchak's assumption of power as "Supreme Ruler". The Kolchak Government fell in January 1920, provincial issues followed until the area was incorporated into the Soviet Union in 1922.

100 kopeks = 1 rouble.

1919. Admiral Kolchak Govt. Arms types of Russia surch in figures, or in figures and words (rouble values). Imperf or perf.

5	**22**	35 on 2k. green	40	2·10
6	**22**	50 on 3k. red	40	2·00
3	**22**	70 on 1k. orange	50	4·00
8	**23**	1r. on 4k. red	85	2·50
9	**22**	3r. on 7k. blue	3·75	6·50
10	**10**	5r. on 14k. red and blue	5·50	16·00

1920. Transbaikal Province. Ataman Semyonov regime. Arms types of Russia surch p. 1 p. Perf.

11	**23**	1r. on 4k. red	27·00	65·00
12	**14**	2r.50 on 20k. red and blue	19·00	40·00
13	**22**	5r. on 5k. red	13·50	31·00
14	**10**	10r. on 70k. orange & brn	19·00	40·00

6

1920. Amur Province. Imperf.

15	**6**	2r. red	3·50	9·75
16	**6**	3r. green	3·50	9·75
17	**6**	5r. blue	3·50	9·75
18	**6**	15r. brown	3·50	9·75
19	**6**	30r. mauve	3·50	9·75

FAR EAST REPUBLIC

1920. Vladivostok issue. Optd DBP in fancy letters or surch also. Imperf or perf. (a) On Arms types of Russia.

32	**22**	1k. orange	7·00	7·25
33	**22**	2k. green	3·25	3·00
21	**22**	3k. red	5·00	5·50
39	**10**	3k. on 35k. green and purple	10·00	10·00
22	**23**	4k. red	7·75	8·50
40	**10**	4k. on 70k. orange & brown	4·25	5·00
41	**10**	7k. on 15k. blue and purple	3·00	3·00
23	**23**	10k. blue	65·00	65·00
44	**11**	10k. on 3r.50 green & brn	7·75	9·50
24	**10**	14k. red and blue	21·00	21·00
25	**10**	15k. blue and purple	8·50	8·50
26	**14**	20k. red and blue	75·00	75·00
27	**10**	20k. on 14k. red and blue	3·50	4·75
28	**10**	25k. mauve and green	8·00	8·00
29	**10**	35k. green and purple	31·00	31·00
30	**14**	50k. green and purple	13·50	13·50
35	**15**	1r. orange and brown	16·00	22·00

(b) On Nos. 5 and 3 of Siberia.

37	**22**	35k. on 2k. green	4·00	5·00
38	**22**	70k. on 1k. orange	5·00	6·00

(c) On Postal Savings Bank stamps of Russia.

45	1k. on 5k. green on buff	10·50	10·50
46	2k. on 10k. brown on buff	19·00	19·00

10

11

1921. Chita issue. Imperf.

47	**10**	1k. orange	90	1·30
48	**10**	3k. red	45	60
49	**11**	4k. brown and red	45	60
50	**10**	5k. brown	45	60
51b	**10**	7k. blue	65	1·30
52	**11**	10k. red and blue	60	95
53	**10**	15k. red	90	1·30
54	**11**	20k. red and blue	90	1·30
55	**11**	30k. red and green	1·20	1·60
56	**11**	50k. red and black	1·80	2·75

13

1922. Vladivostok issue. 5th Anniv of Russian October Revolution. Optd 1917 7-XI 1922. Imperf.

57	**13**	2k. green	10·50	11·00
58	**13**	4k. red	12·00	13·50
59	**13**	5k. brown	12·50	19·00
60	**13**	10k. blue	14·50	19·00

PRIAMUR AND MARITIME PROVINCES

Anti-Bolshevist Government

1921. Vladivostok issue. Imperf.

61	2k. green	95	95
62	4k. red	1·50	1·50
63	5k. purple	1·70	1·70
64	10k. blue	1·90	1·90

(15)

1922. Anniv of Priamur Provisional Govt. Optd with T 15.

89	2k. green	19·00	19·00
90	4k. red	19·00	19·00
91	5k. purple	19·00	19·00
92	10k. blue	19·00	19·00

16 Trans. "Priamur Territory"

1922. Optd or surch as T 16.

93	1k. on 2k. green	4·00	4·50
94	2k. green	5·25	6·25
95	3k. on 4k. red	4·75	5·50
96	4k. red	5·75	6·25
97	5k. purple	5·25	6·25
98	10k. blue	4·75	6·50

1922. Optd as T 16. Imperf or perf. (a) On Arms types of Russia.

114	**22**	1k. orange	6·75	8·75
115	**22**	2k. green	7·50	8·25
116	**22**	3k. red	10·50	18·00
102	**23**	4k. red	7·50	9·50
118	**22**	5k. red	17·00	28·00
104	**22**	7k. blue	31·00	42·00
105	**23**	10k. blue	34·00	47·00
106	**10**	14k. red and blue	£110	£130
107	**10**	15k. blue and purple	7·50	9·50
108	**14**	20k. red and blue	9·50	12·00
109	**10**	20k. on 14k. red and blue	£150	£180
110	**10**	25k. mauve and green	27·00	35·00
111	**10**	35k. green and purple	5·75	7·75
112	**14**	50k. green and purple	8·75	10·50
113	**10**	70k. orange and brown	18·00	23·00
121	**15**	1r. orange and brown	13·50	23·00

(b) On Nos. 5 and 3 of Siberia.

122	**22**	35k. on 2k. green	65·00	75·00
123	**22**	70k. on 1k. orange	75·00	80·00

1922. Nos. 37 and 38 optd II.3.K. and three bars. Imperf and perf.

125	35k. on 2k. green	5·00	6·50
126	70k. on 1k. orange	7·25	9·25

SOVIET UNION ISSUE FOR THE FAR EAST

Д. В.
коп. 1 коп.
ЗОЛОТОМ

(18)

1923. Stamps of Russia surch as T 18. Imperf or perf.

131	**79**	1k. on 100r. red	75	85
128	**79**	2k. on 70r. purple	35	45
129	**78**	5k. on 10r. blue	35	45
130	**79**	10k. on 50r. brown	60	75

Pt. 8

SICILY

An island to the south of Italy, which, with Naples, formed the Kingdom of the Two Sicilies, until incorporated in the Kingdom of Italy.

100 grano = 1 ducato.

1 King "Bomba"

1859. Imperf.

1c	**1**	½g. yellow	£650	£1300
2b	**1**	1g. olive	£850	£180
3	**1**	2g. blue	£225	£160
4	**1**	5g. red	£800	£600
5	**1**	10g. blue	£800	£300
6	**1**	20g. grey	£950	£750
7	**1**	50g. brown	£950	£5500

Pt. 1

SIERRA LEONE

A British colony on the west coast of Africa. Achieved independence within the British Commonwealth in 1961. By vote of the Assembly on 19 April 1971, Sierra Leone was proclaimed a republic.

1859. 12 pence = 1 shilling; 20 shillings = 1 pound.
1964. 100 cents = 1 leone.

1

2

1859

16	2	½d. brown	4·75	11·00
27	2	½d. green	3·00	2·00
28	2	1d. red	10·00	1·00
29	2	1½d. lilac	3·50	6·50
25	2	2d. mauve	65·00	8·50
30	2	2d. grey	50·00	3·25
31	2	2½d. blue	14·00	1·75
32	2	3d. yellow	3·50	10·00
21	2	4d. blue	£200	6·50
33	2	4d. brown	2·50	2·75
37	1	6d. purple	2·75	7·00
22	2	1s. green	80·00	6·50
34	2	1s. brown	26·00	16·00

1893. Surch HALF PENNY.

39	2	½d. on 1½d. lilac	7·00	3·25

4

1896

41	4	½d. mauve and green	2·50	3·00
42	4	1d. mauve and red	5·00	1·75
43	4	1½d. mauve and black	4·00	22·00
44	4	2d. mauve and orange	2·50	5·00
45	4	2½d. mauve and blue	2·50	1·25
46	4	3d. mauve and grey	8·50	7·00
47	4	4d. mauve and red	9·50	13·00
48	4	5d. mauve and black	13·00	15·00
49	4	6d. mauve	8·00	26·00
50	4	1s. green and black	6·00	22·00
51	4	2s. green and blue	29·00	75·00
52	4	5s. green and red	90·00	£225
53	4	£1 purple on red	£250	£500

6

1897. T 6 optd POSTAGE AND REVENUE.

54	6	1d. purple and green	6·00	3·50

1897. T 6 optd POSTAGE AND REVENUE and surch 2½d. and bars.

55	2½d. on 3d. purple and green	11·00	18·00
59	2½d. on 6d. purple and green	8·50	18·00
63	2½d. on 1s. lilac	£110	70·00
67	2½d. on 2s. lilac	£1800	£2500

15

1903

73	15	½d. purple and green	3·00	6·00
87	15	1d. purple and red	1·50	1·00
88	15	1½d. purple and black	3·00	13·00
89	15	2d. purple and orange	4·25	4·00
90	15	2½d. purple and blue	6·00	2·00
78	15	3d. purple and grey	12·00	14·00
92	15	4d. purple and red	9·50	7·00
93	15	5d. purple and black	12·00	30·00
94	15	6d. purple	5·00	3·25
95	15	1s. green and black	7·50	9·00
96	15	2s. green and blue	27·00	28·00
97	15	5s. green and red	42·00	60·00
98	15	£1 purple on red	£225	£250

1907

99	½d. green	1·00	50
100a	1d. red	13·00	60
101	1½d. orange	2·25	2·00
102	2d. grey	1·75	1·50
103	2½d. blue	3·75	3·00
104	3d. purple on yellow	9·50	2·75
105	4d. black and red on yellow	2·25	1·60
106	5d. purple and green	17·00	5·00
107	6d. purple and light purple	16·00	8·00
108	1s. black on green	5·50	5·00
109	2s. purple and blue on blue	21·00	19·00
110	5s. green and red on yellow	42·00	60·00
111	£1 purple and black on red	£275	£200

17

20

1912

131	17	½d. green	1·25	1·00
113	17	1d. red	2·25	30
132a	17	1d. violet	4·50	20
114	17	1½d. orange	2·00	2·50
133	17	1½d. red	2·00	1·25
134	17	2d. grey	1·25	20
116a	17	2½d. blue	1·00	1·00
116b	20	3d. purple on yellow	3·75	3·25
136	17	3d. blue	1·50	1·25
137	17	4d. black and red on yellow	3·50	3·25
138	17	5d. purple and green	1·25	1·25
139	17	6d. purple and light purple	1·25	2·75
120	17	7d. purple and orange	3·00	9·00
121	17	9d. purple and black	5·00	12·00
122	17	10d. purple and red	3·00	18·00
124a	20	1s. black on green	5·50	3·25
125	20	2s. blue and purple on blue	18·00	5·50
126	20	5s. red and green on yellow	18·00	28·00
127	20	10s. red and green on green	85·00	£140
128	20	£1 black and purple on red	£200	£250
147	20	£2 blue and purple	£700	£950
148	20	£5 orange and green	£2000	£3250

21 Rice Field

22 Palms and Cola Tree

1932

155	21	½d. green	20	50
156	21	1d. violet	30	30
157	21	1½d. red	30	1·75
158	21	2d. brown	30	30
159	21	3d. blue	1·25	2·00
160	21	4d. orange	1·00	10·00
161	21	5d. green	1·75	6·00
162	21	6d. blue	1·00	4·00
163	21	1s. lake	5·00	10·00
164	22	2s. brown	5·00	6·50
165	22	5s. blue	16·00	23·00
166	22	10s. green	85·00	£140
167	22	£1 purple	£160	£250

23 Arms of Sierra Leone

1933. Cent of Abolition of Slavery and of Death of William Wilberforce. Dated "1833 1933".

168	23	½d. green	1·00	1·25
169	-	1d. black and brown	65	10
170	-	1½d. brown	6·00	4·50
171	-	2d. purple	3·25	20
172	-	3d. blue	5·00	1·75
173	-	4d. brown	6·50	10·00
174	-	5d. green and brown	7·00	11·00
175	-	6d. black and orange	9·50	7·00
176	-	1s. violet	4·75	18·00
177	-	2s. brown and blue	35·00	48·00
178	-	5s. black and purple	£150	£190
179	-	10s. black and olive	£250	£400
180	-	£1 violet and orange	£500	£600

DESIGNS—VERT: 1d. "Freedom"; 1½d. Map of Sierra Leone; 4d. Government sanatorium; 5s. African elephant. HORIZ: 2d. Old Slave Market, Freetown; 3d. Native fruit seller; 5d. Bullom canoe; 6d. Punting near Banana Is; 1s. Government buildings, Freetown; 2s. Bunce Is; 10s. King George V; £1 Freetown Harbour.

1935. Silver Jubilee. As T 32a of St. Helena.

181	1d. blue and black	1·75	2·50
182	3d. brown and blue	2·75	8·50
183	5d. green and blue	3·75	25·00
184	1s. grey and purple	22·00	17·00

1937. Coronation. As T 32b of St. Helena.

185	1d. orange	70	1·00
186	2d. purple	1·00	1·25
187	3d. blue	2·00	4·25

30 Freetown from the Harbour

1938. King George VI.

188	30	½d. black and green	15	40
189	30	1d. black and lake	40	60
190	-	1½d. red	20·00	1·00
190a	-	1½d. mauve	30	60
191	-	2d. mauve	50·00	3·00
191a	-	2d. red	30	2·00
192	30	3d. black and blue	65	50
193	30	4d. black and brown	2·50	4·50
194	-	5d. green	3·25	4·00
195	-	6d. grey	1·50	50
196	30	1s. black and green	3·50	70
196a	-	1s.3d. orange	75	60
197	30	2s. black and brown	4·50	2·75
198	-	5s. brown	10·00	15·00
199	-	10s. green	28·00	17·00
200	30	£1 blue	20·00	30·00

DESIGNS: 1½, 2, 5, 6d., 1s.3d., 5s., 10s. Rice harvesting.

1946. Victory. As T 33a of St. Helena.

201	1½d. lilac	20	10
202	3d. blue	20	30

1948. Silver Wedding. As T 33b/c of St. Helena.

203	1½d. mauve	15	15
204	£1 blue	19·00	24·00

1949. 75th Anniv of U.P.U. As T 33d/g of St. Helena.

205	1½d. purple	20	50
206	3d. blue	2·00	5·50
207	6d. grey	50	7·50
208	1s. green	35	1·00

1953. Coronation. As T 33h of St. Helena.

209	1½d. black and lilac	50	30

32 Cape Lighthouse

1956. Centres in black.

210	32	½d. lilac	1·00	2·75
211	-	1d. olive	90	40
212	-	1½d. blue	1·60	6·50
213	-	2d. brown	70	40
214	-	3d. blue	1·25	10
215	-	4d. slate	2·50	2·25
216	-	6d. violet	1·00	30
217	-	1s. red	1·25	50
218	-	1s.3d. sepia	11·00	30
219	-	2s.6d. brown	15·00	13·00
220	-	5s. green	3·75	3·75
221	-	10s. mauve	3·50	2·75
222	-	£1 orange	21·00	32·00

DESIGNS—HORIZ: 1d. Queen Elizabeth II Quay; 1½d. Piassava workers; 4d. Iron ore production, Marampa; 6d. Whale Bay, York Village; 1s.3d. Bristol 170 Freighter Mk 31 airplane and map; 10s. Law Courts, Freetown; £1 Government House. VERT: 2d. Cotton tree, Freetown; 3d. Rice harvesting; 1s. Bullom canoe; 2s.6d. Orugu railway bridge; 5s. Kuranko chief.

46 Licensed Diamond Miner

1961. Independence.

223	-	½d. brown and turquoise	20	20
224	46	1d. brown and green	1·50	10
225	-	1½d. black and green	20	20
226	-	2d. black and blue	20	10
227	-	3d. brown and blue	20	10
228	-	4d. blue and red	20	10
229	-	6d. black and purple	20	10
230	-	1s. brown and orange	20	10
231	-	1s.3d. blue and violet	20	10
232	46	2s.6d. green and black	2·75	30
233	-	5s. black and red	1·00	1·25
234	-	10s. black and green	1·00	1·25
235	-	£1 red and yellow	9·00	18·00

DESIGNS—VERT: ½d., 1s. Palm fruit gathering; 1½d., 5s. Bundu mask; 2d., 10s. Bishop Crowther and Old Fourah Bay College; £1 Forces bugler. HORIZ: 3d., 6d. Sir Milton Margai; 4d., 1s.3d. Lumley Beach, Freetown.

53 Royal Charter, 1799

55 Old House of Representatives, Freetown, 1924

1961. Royal Visit.

236	53	3d. black and red	15	10
237	-	4d. black and violet	15	1·75
238	55	6d. black and orange	20	10
239	-	1s.3d. black and blue	3·25	1·75

DESIGNS—VERT: 4d. King's Yard Gate, Freetown, 1817. HORIZ: 1s.3d. Royal Yacht "Britannia" at Freetown.

57 Campaign Emblem

1962. Malaria Eradication.

240	57	3d. red	10	10
241	57	1s.3d. green	20	10

58 Fireball Lily

1963. Flowers in natural colours; background colours given below.

242	58	½d. bistre	10	20
243	-	1d. red	10	10
244	-	1½d. green	20	20
245	-	2d. olive	20	10
246	-	3d. green	20	10
247	-	4d. blue	20	20
248	-	6d. blue	30	10
249	-	1s. green	40	10
250	-	1s.3d. green	1·50	20
251	-	2s.6d. purple	1·25	30
252	-	5s. violet	1·25	80
253	-	10s. purple	3·50	1·50
254	-	£1 blue	6·00	10·00

FLOWERS—VERT: 1½d. Stereospermum; 3d. Beniseed; 4d. Blushing hibiscus; 1s. Beautiful crinum; 2s.6d. Broken hearts; 5s. Ra-ponthi; 10s. Blue plumbago. HORIZ: 1d. Jina-gbo; 2d. Black-eyed Susan; 6d. Climbing lily; 1s.3d. Blue bells; £1 African tulip tree.

71 Threshing Machine and Corn Bins

1963. Freedom from Hunger.

255	**71**	3d. black and ochre	30	10
256	-	1s.3d. sepia and green	35	10

DESIGN: 1s.3d. Girl with onion crop.

1963. 2nd Anniv of Independence. Stamps of 1956 surch 2ND YEAR OF INDEPENDENCE PROGRESS DEVELOPMENT 1963 and value (except 2s.6d.). Centres in black. (a) Postage.

257		3d. on ½d. lilac	40	10
258		4d. on 1½d. blue	15	10
259		6d. on ½d. lilac	30	10
260		10d. on 3d. blue	50	10
261		1s.6d. on 3d. blue	30	20
262		3s.6d. on 3d. blue	40	20

(b) Air. Optd AIR MAIL in addition.

263		7d. on 1½d. blue	20	10
264		1s.3d. on 1½d. blue	20	10
265		2s.6d. brown	2·50	40
266		3s. on 3d. blue	40	20
267		6s. on 3d. blue	1·00	20
268		11s. on 10s. mauve	2·00	1·50
269		11s. on £1 orange	£650	£200

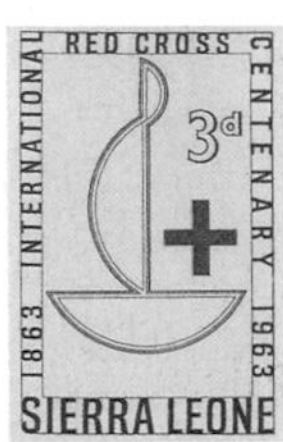

75 Centenary Emblem

1963. Centenary of Red Cross.

270	**75**	3d. red and violet	50	10
271	-	6d. red and black	50	15
272	-	1s.3d. red and green	65	20

DESIGNS: 6d. Red Cross emblem; 1s.3d. As T **75** but with lined background and value on left.

1963. Postal Commemorations. (a) Postage. Optd or surch 1853–1859–1963 Oldest Postal Service Newest G.P.O. in West Africa and value.

273		3d. (No. 214)	10	10
274		4d. on 1½d. (No. 212)	10	10
275		9d. on 1½d. (No. 212)	10	10
276		1s. on 1s.3d. (No. 231)	10	10
277	**32**	1s.6d. on ½d	15	10
278	-	2s. on 3d. (No. 214)	15	10

(b) Air. Optd or surch as above but Postage Stamp instead of Postal Service and AIRMAIL in addition.

279	**53**	7d. on 3d.	20	65
280	-	1s.3d. (No. 239)	2·00	1·50
281	-	2s.6d. on 4d. (No. 228)	1·25	60
282	**52**	3s. on 3d.	2·50	2·50
283	**55**	6s. on 6d.	1·00	1·50
284	-	£1 (No. 222)	30·00	32·00

Commemoration dates:—
1853—"First Post Office".
1859—"First Postage Stamps".
1963—"Newest G.P.O. in West Africa".

80 Lion Emblem and Map

81 Globe and Map

1964. World's Fair, New York. Imperf. Self-adhesive.

285	**80**	1d. multicoloured (postage)	10	10
286	**80**	3d. multicoloured	10	10
287	**80**	4d. multicoloured	10	10
288	**80**	6d. multicoloured	10	10
289	**80**	1s. multicoloured	15	10
290	**80**	2s. multicoloured	40	25
291	**80**	5s. multicoloured	60	75
292	**81**	7d. multicoloured (air)	10	10
293	**81**	9d. multicoloured	10	10
294	**81**	1s.3d. multicoloured	30	10
295	**81**	2s.6d. multicoloured	40	15
296	**81**	3s.6d. multicoloured	40	25
297	**81**	6s. multicoloured	65	75
298	**81**	11s. multicoloured	80	1·50

WARNING:—These self-adhesive stamps should be kept mint on their backing paper and used on cover or piece.

82 Inscription and Map

83 Pres. Kennedy and Map

1964. President Kennedy Memorial Issue. Imperf. Self-adhesive.

299	**82**	1d. multicoloured (postage)	10	10
300	**82**	3d. multicoloured	10	10
301	**82**	4d. multicoloured	10	10
302	**82**	6d. multicoloured	10	10
303	**82**	1s. multicoloured	10	10
304	**82**	2s. multicoloured	40	60
305	**82**	5s. multicoloured	60	1·75
306	**83**	7d. multicoloured (air)	10	10
307	**83**	9d. multicoloured	10	10
308	**83**	1s.3d. multicoloured	15	10
309	**83**	2s.6d. multicoloured	40	25
310	**83**	3s.6d. multicoloured	40	35
311	**83**	6s. multicoloured	65	1·75
312	**83**	11s. multicoloured	80	2·50

The note below No. 298 applies also to the above issue.

1964. Decimal Currency. Various stamps surch. (i) First issue. Surch in figures. (a) Postage.

313	-	1c. on 6d. (No. 248)	10	10
314	**53**	2c. on 3d. (No. 236)	10	10
315	-	3c. on 3d. (No. 246)	10	10
316	-	5c. on ½d. (No. 223)	10	10
317	**71**	8c. on 3d. (No. 255)	10	10
318	-	10c. on 1s.3d. (No. 250)	10	10
319	-	15c. on 1s. (No. 249)	15	10
320	**55**	25c. on 6d. (No. 238)	30	25
321	**46**	50c. on 2s.6d. (No. 232)	2·00	1·50

(b) Air. Nos. 322/5 additonally optd AIRMAIL.

322	-	7c. on 1s.3d. (No. 256)	10	10
323	-	20c. on 4d. (No. 228)	25	20
324	-	30c. on 10s. (No. 234)	40	45
325	-	40c. on 5s. (No. 233)	50	60
326	**83**	1l. on 1s.3d. (No. 308)	75	2·00
327	**83**	2l. on 11s. (No. 312)	1·25	3·50

(ii) Second issue. Surch in figures or figures and words (Nos. 332/3).

328	-	1c. on 3d. (No. 227) (postage)	10	10
329	**82**	2c. on 1d. (No. 299)	10	10
330	**82**	4c. on 3d. (No. 300)	10	10
331	-	5c. on 2d. (No. 245)	10	10
332	-	1l. on 5s. (No. 252)	1·50	3·00
333	-	2l. on £1 (No. 235)	3·00	4·75
334	**83**	7c. on 7d. (No. 306) (air)	10	10
335	**83**	60c. on 9d. (Nos. 307)	75	1·25

(iii) Third issue. Surch in figures.

336	-	1c. on 1½d. (No. 225) (postage)	10	10
337	**82**	2c. on 3d. (No. 300)	10	10
338	**80**	2c. on 4d. (No. 287)	10	10
339	-	3c. on 1d. (No. 243)	10	10
340	-	3c. on 2d. (No. 226)	10	10
341	-	5c. on 1s.3d. (No. 231)	10	10
342	**82**	15c. on 6d. (No. 302)	80	50
343	**82**	15c. on 1s. (No. 303)	1·25	90
344	-	20c. on 6d. (No. 229)	30	15
345	-	25c. on 6d. (No. 248)	35	20
346	-	50c. on 3d. (No. 227)	1·00	70
347	**80**	60c. on 5s. (No. 291)	4·00	2·25
348	**82**	1l. on 4d. (No. 301)	4·25	4·75
349	-	2l. on £1 (No. 235)	12·00	12·00
350	**81**	7c. on 9d. (air)	25	10

(iv) Fourth issue. Surch in figures.

351	**80**	1c. on 6d. (postage)	2·75	7·50
352	**80**	1c. on 2s.	2·75	7·50
353	**82**	1c. on 2s.	2·75	7·50
354	**82**	1c. on 5s.	2·75	7·50
355	**81**	2c. on 1s.3d. (air)	2·75	7·50
356	**83**	2c. on 1s.3d.	2·75	7·50
357	**83**	2c. on 3s.6d.	2·75	7·50
358	**81**	3c. on 7d.	2·75	7·50
359	**83**	3c. on 9d.	2·75	7·50
360	**81**	5c. on 2s.6d.	2·75	7·50
361	**83**	5c. on 2s.6d.	2·75	7·50
362	**81**	5c. on 3s.6d.	2·75	7·50
363	**81**	5c. on 6s.	2·75	7·50
364	**83**	5c. on 6s.	2·75	7·50

(v) Fifth issue. No. 374 further surch TWO Leones.

365		2l. on 30c. on 6d. (air)	2·50	2·00

91 Margai and Churchill

1965. Sir Milton Margai and Sir Winston Churchill Commem. Flower stamps of 1963 surch as T 91 on horiz designs or with individual portraits on vert designs as indicated. Multicoloured. (a) Postage.

366		2c. on 1d.	45	30
367		3c. on 3d. Margai	10	20
368		10c. on 1s. Churchill	1·00	20
369		20c. on 1s.3d.	1·10	20
370		50c. on 4d. Margai	90	45
371		75c. on 5s. Churchill	4·00	1·25

(b) Air. Additionally optd AIRMAIL.

372	-	7c. on 2d.	65	20
373	**58**	15c. on ½d. Margai	45	20
374	-	30c. on 6d.	2·00	35
375	-	1l. on £1	6·00	1·50
376	-	2l. on 10s. Churchill	13·00	5·50

92 Cola Plant and Nut

1965. Various shapes, backed with paper bearing advertisements. Imperf. Self-adhesive. A. Printed in green, yellow and red on silver foil. Values in colours given.

377	**92**	1c. green (postage)	25	10
378	**92**	2c. red	25	10
379	**92**	3c. yellow	25	10
380	**92**	4c. silver on green	30	10
381	**92**	5c. silver on red	30	10

B. Designs 45×49 mm showing Arms of Sierra Leone.

382		20c. mult on cream (postage)	2·25	60
383		50c. multicoloured on cream	4·00	4·00
384		40c. mult on cream (air)	4·00	4·00

C. Designs 48×44½ mm showing inscription and necklace.

385		7c. multicoloured (air)	80	15
386		15c. multicoloured	1·50	90

1966. 5th Anniv of Independence. Surch FIVE YEARS INDEPENDENCE 1961-1966 and value. (a) Postage.

387		1c. on 6d. (No. 248)	10	10
388		2c. on 4d. (No. 247)	10	10
389		3c. on 1½d. (No. 212)	10	10
390		8c. on 1s. (No. 249)	20	10
391		10c. on 2s.6d. (No. 251)	20	10
392		20c. on 2d. (No. 213)	30	10

(b) Air. Surch AIRMAIL also.

393	**75**	7c. on 3d.	15	10
394	-	15c. on 1s. (No. 249)	30	10
395	-	25c. on 2s.6d. (No. 251)	75	60
396	-	50c. on 1½d. (No. 244)	1·25	1·00
397	-	1l. on 4d. (No. 247)	2·00	2·00

97 Lion's Head

1966. First Sierra Leone Gold Coinage Commem. Circular designs, embossed on gold foil, backed with paper bearing advertisements. Imperf. (a) Postage. (i) ¼ golde coin. Diameter 1½ in.

398	**97**	2c. mauve and orange	10	10
399	-	3c. green and purple	10	10

(ii) ½ golde coin. Diameter 218in.

400	**97**	5c. red and blue	10	10
401	-	8c. turquoise and black	20	20

(iii) 1 golde coin. Diameter 3¼ in.

402	**97**	25c. violet and green	40	35
403	-	1l. orange and red	2·75	3·25

(b) Air. (i) ¼ golde coin. Diameter 1½ in.

404	**97**	7c. orange and red	15	10
405	-	30c. purple and black	20	25

(ii) ½ golde coin. Diameter 218in.

406	**97**	15c. orange and red	35	35
407	-	30c. purple and black	50	60

(iii) 1 golde coin. Diameter 3¼ in.

408	**97**	50c. green and purple	1·00	1·00
409	-	2l. black and green	4·00	4·50

DESIGN: Nos. 399, 401, 403, 405, 407 and 409, Map of Sierra Leone.

1967. Decimal Currency Provisionals. Nos. 347/8, 369/71 and 383/4 surch.

410		6½c. on 75c. on 5s. (postage)	20	15
411		7½c. on 75c. on 5s.	20	15
412		9½c. on 50c. on 4d.	25	20
413		12½c. on 20c. on 1s.3d.	35	25
414		17½c. on 50c. on 1l. on 4d.	2·00	2·50
415		17½c. on 1l. on 4d.	2·00	2·50
416		18½c. on 1l. on 4d.	2·00	2·50
417		18½c. on 60c. on 5s.	5·50	7·50
418		25c. on 50c.	80	1·00
419		11½c. on 40c. (air)	35	30
420		25c. on 40c.	80	1·00

1967. Decimal Currency. Imperf. Self-adhesive. As T 92, but embossed on white paper, backed with paper bearing advertisements. Background colours given first, and value tablet colours in brackets.

421	**92**	½c. red (red on white)	10	30
422	**92**	1c. red (red on white)	15	10
423	**92**	1½c. yellow (green on white)	20	15
424	**92**	2c. red (green on white)	35	10
425	**92**	2½c. green (yellow on white)	60	50
426	**92**	3c. red (white on red)	35	10
427	**92**	3½c. purple (white on green)	60	50
428	**92**	4c. red (white on green)	60	15
429	**92**	4½c. green (green on white)	60	50
430	**92**	5c. red (yellow on white)	60	15
431	**92**	5½c. red (green on white)	60	70

102 Eagle

1967. T 102 embossed on black paper, backed with paper bearing advertisements, or as No. 382 also with advertisements (No. 433/b).

432	**102**	9½c. red and gold on black	70	70
432a	**102**	9½c. blue & gold on black	8·50	8·50
433	-	10c. mult (red frame)	70	70
433b	-	10c. mult (black frame)	9·50	9·50
434	**102**	15c. green & gold on black	1·00	1·00
434a	**102**	15c. red and gold on black	10·00	10·00

See also Nos. 538/44.

1968. No advertisements on back and colours in value tablet reversed. Background colours given first, and value tablet colours in brackets.

435	**92**	½c. red (white on green)	10	10
436	**92**	1c. red (white on red)	15	10
437	**92**	2c. red (white on green)	5·50	6·00

438	92	2½c. green (white on yellow)	6·00	6·50
439	92	3c. red (red on white)	2·50	75

On Nos. 435 and 438 the figure "½" is larger than on Nos. 421 and 425.

1968. No advertisements on back, colours changed and new value (7c.). Background colours given.

440	2c. pink (postage)	2·50	2·25
441	2½c. green	2·50	2·25
442	3½c. yellow	2·75	2·50
442a	7c. yellow (air)	8·00	3·75

On Nos. 441/2 the fraction "½" is larger than on Nos. 425 and 427.

103 Outline Map of Africa

1968. Human Rights Year. Each value comes in six types showing the following territories: Portuguese Guinea; South Africa; Mozambique; Rhodesia; South West Africa and Angola. Imperf. Self-adhesive.

443	103	½c. multicoloured (postage)	10	10
444	103	2c. multicoloured	10	10
445	103	2½c. multicoloured	10	10
446	103	3½c. multicoloured	10	10
447	103	10c. multicoloured	15	15
448	103	11½c. multicoloured	20	20
449	103	15c. multicoloured	25	25
450	103	7½c. multicoloured (air)	15	15
451	103	9½c. multicoloured	20	20
452	103	14½c. multicoloured	25	25
453	103	18½c. multicoloured	30	30
454	103	25c. multicoloured	40	40
455	103	1l. multicoloured	3·00	5·50
456	103	2l. multicoloured	9·00	12·00

Nos. 443/56 were issued in sheets of 30 (6×5) on backing paper depicting diamonds or the coat-of-arms on the reverse. The six types occur once in each horiz row.

1968. Mexico Olympics Participation. Nos. 383/4 optd OLYMPIC PARTICIPATION MEXICO 1968 or surch also.

457	6½c. on 50c. mult (postage)	40	30
458	17½c. on 50c. multicoloured	45	35
459	22½c. on 50c. multicoloured	65	50
460	28½c. on 50c. multicoloured	85	1·50
461	50c. multicoloured	1·25	2·50
462	6½c. on 40c. mult (air)	45	30
463	17½c. on 40c. multicoloured	55	35
464	22½c. on 40c. multicoloured	70	50
465	28½c. on 40c. multicoloured	85	1·50
466	40c. multicoloured	1·25	2·50

105 1859 6d. Stamp

111 1965 15c. Self-adhesive

1969. 5th Anniv of World's First Self-adhesive Postage Stamps. Multicoloured. Self-adhesive. Imperf.

467	1c. Type **105** (postage)	10	10
468	2c. 1965 2c. self-adhesive	10	10
469	3½c. 1961 Independence £1	10	10
470	5c. 1965 20c. self-adhesive	10	10
471	12½c. 1948 Royal Silver Wedding £1	30	15
472	1l. 1923 £2	2·50	1·50
473	7½c. Type **111** (air)	20	10
474	9½c. 1967 9½c. self-adhesive	20	10
475	20c. 1964 1s.3d. self-adhesive	40	25
476	30c. 1964 President Kennedy Memorial 6s. self-adhesive	55	35
477	50c. 1933 Centenary of Abolition of Slavery £1	1·50	75
478	2l. 1963 2nd Anniv of Independence 11s.	9·00	8·00

DESIGNS—As Type **105**, Nos. 468/72; As Type **111**, Nos. 474/8.

All values are on white backing paper with advertisement printed on the reverse.

117 Ore Carrier, Globe and Flags of Sierra Leone and Japan

118 Ore Carrier, Map of Europe and Africa and Flags of Sierra Leone and Netherlands

1969. Pepel Port Improvements. Imperf. Self-adhesive, backed with paper bearing advertisements.

479	117	1c. multicoloured (postage)	10	10
480	118	2c. multicoloured	15	10
481	-	3½c. multicoloured	15	10
482	-	10c. multicoloured	20	10
483	118	18½c. multicoloured	35	25
484	-	50c. multicoloured	1·00	1·00
485	117	7½c. multicoloured (air)	20	10
486	-	9½c. multicoloured	20	10
487	117	15c. multicoloured	35	25
488	118	25c. multicoloured	45	35
489	-	1l. multicoloured	1·75	2·00
490	-	2l. multicoloured	2·25	4·50

The 3½, 9½c., 2l., 10, 50c., 1l. show respectively the flags of Great Britain and West Germany instead of the Netherlands.

119 African Development Bank Emblem

1969. 5th Anniv of African Development Bank. Imperf. Self-adhesive, backed with paper bearing advertisements.

491	119	3½c. green, gold and black (postage)	25	40
492	119	9½c. violet, gold & grn (air)	35	70

120 Boy Scouts Emblem in "Diamond"

1969. Boy Scouts Diamond Jubilee. Imperf. Self-adhesive.

493	120	1c. multicoloured (postage)	10	10
494	120	2c. multicoloured	10	10
495	120	3½c. multicoloured	15	10
496	120	4½c. multicoloured	15	15
497	120	5c. multicoloured	15	15
498	120	75c. multicoloured	5·50	2·75
499	-	7½c. multicoloured (air)	35	20
500	-	9½c. multicoloured	45	25
501	-	15c. multicoloured	70	50
502	-	22c. multicoloured	90	70
503	-	55c. multicoloured	4·00	2·00
504	-	3l. multicoloured	50·00	38·00

DESIGN—OCTAGONAL (65×51 mm): Nos. 499/504, Scout saluting, Baden-Powell and badge.

1970. Air. No. 443 surch AIRMAIL twice and new value.

505	103	7½c. on ½c. multicoloured	40	15
506	103	9½c. on ½c. multicoloured	40	15
507	103	15c. on ½c. multicoloured	65	30
508	103	28c. on ½c. multicoloured	1·25	65
509	103	40c. on ½c. multicoloured	1·75	1·75
510	103	2l. on ½c. multicoloured	7·00	16·00

122 Expo Symbol and Maps of Sierra Leone and Japan

1970. World Fair, Osaka. Imperf. Self-adhesive.

511	122	2c. multicoloured (postage)	10	10
512	122	3½c. multicoloured	10	10
513	122	10c. multicoloured	15	10
514	122	12½c. multicoloured	15	10
515	122	20c. multicoloured	20	10
516	122	45c. multicoloured	45	45
517	-	7½c. multicoloured (air)	10	10
518	-	9½c. multicoloured	15	10
519	-	15c. multicoloured	20	10
520	-	25c. multicoloured	40	20
521	-	50c. multicoloured	55	50
522	-	3l. multicoloured	1·75	5·50

DESIGN—CHRYSANTHEMUM (43×42 mm): Nos. 517/22, Maps of Sierra Leone and Japan.

123 Diamond

124 Palm Nut

1970. Imperf. Self-adhesive.

523	123	1c. multicoloured	35	30
524	123	1½c. multicoloured	35	30
525	123	2c. multicoloured	35	10
526	123	2½c. multicoloured	35	10
527	123	3c. multicoloured	45	10
528	123	3½c. multicoloured	45	10
529	123	4c. multicoloured	50	10
530	123	5c. multicoloured	60	10
531	124	6c. multicoloured	30	10
532	124	7c. multicoloured	35	15
533	124	8½c. multicoloured	50	15
534	124	9c. multicoloured	50	15
535	124	10c. multicoloured	55	15
536	124	11½c. multicoloured	80	20
537	124	18½c. multicoloured	1·75	55

1970. Air. As T 102, but on white paper.

538	102	7½c. gold and red	45	10
539	102	9½c. silver and green	50	10
540	102	15c. silver and blue	1·50	20
541	102	25c. gold and purple	2·50	50
542	102	50c. green and orange	5·50	3·25
543	102	1l. blue and silver	12·00	14·00
544	102	2l. blue and gold	20·00	29·00

126 Jewellery Box and Sewa Diadem

1970. Diamond Industry. Imperf. Self-adhesive.

545	126	2c. multicoloured (postage)	45	20
546	126	3½c. multicoloured	45	20
547	126	10c. multicoloured	70	20
548	126	12½c. multicoloured	1·00	30
549	126	40c. multicoloured	2·50	1·25
550	126	1l. multicoloured	12·00	11·00
551	-	7½c. multicoloured (air)	75	20
552	-	9½c. multicoloured	85	20
553	126	15c. multicoloured	1·50	35
554	-	25c. multicoloured	2·00	60
555	-	75c. multicoloured	7·00	6·00
556	-	2l. multicoloured	27·00	25·00

DESIGN—HORIZ (63×61 mm): Nos. 551/6, Diamond and curtain.

127 "Traffic Changeover"

1971. Changeover to Driving on the Right of the Road. Imperf. Self-adhesive.

557	127	3½c. orange, blue and black (postage)	1·50	1·00
558	127	9½c. blue, orge & blk (air)	2·00	2·50

1971. Air. Various stamps surch AIRMAIL and value (Nos. 559/61) or value only (Nos. 562/3).

559	10c. on 2d. (No. 226)	40	20
560	20c. on 1s. (No. 230)	70	45
561	50c. on 1d. (No. 243)	1·25	1·50
562	70c. on 30c. (No. 476)	2·00	4·00
563	1l. on 30c. (No. 476)	3·00	5·00

129 Flag and Lion's Head

1971. 10th Anniv of Independence. Imperf. Self-adhesive.

564	129	2c. multicoloured (postage)	15	10
565	129	3½c. multicoloured	15	10
566	129	10c. multicoloured	25	10
567	129	12½c. multicoloured	35	10
568	129	40c. multicoloured	1·10	40
569	129	1l. multicoloured	1·90	2·50
570	-	7½c. multicoloured (air)	15	10
571	-	9½c. multicoloured	15	10
572	-	15c. multicoloured	25	10
573	-	25c. multicoloured	35	35
574	-	75c. multicoloured	1·10	1·50
575	-	2l. multicoloured	3·00	6·50

DESIGN—"Map" shaped as Type **129**: Nos. 570/5, Bugles and lion's head.

130 Pres. Siaka Stevens

1972. Multicoloured. Background colour given.

576	**130**	1c. lilac	10	10
577	**130**	2c. lavender	10	10
578	**130**	4c. blue	10	10
579	**130**	5c. brown	10	10
580	**130**	7c. pink	15	10
581	**130**	10c. brown	15	10
582	**130**	15c. green	25	15
583	**130**	18c. yellow	25	15
584	**130**	20c. blue	30	15
585	**130**	25c. orange	35	15
586	**130**	50c. green	1·00	55
587	**130**	1l. mauve	1·50	1·00
588	**130**	2l. pink	2·25	3·50
589	**130**	5l. cream	3·75	8·50

131 Guma Valley Dam and Bank Emblem

1975. 10th Anniv of African Development Bank.

590	**131**	4c. multicoloured (postage)	60·00	28·00
591	**131**	15c. multicoloured (air)	1·00	80

132 Opening Ceremony

1975. New Congo Bridge Opening and 70th Birthday of President Stevens.

592	**132**	5c. multicoloured (postage)	1·60	85
593	**132**	20c. multicoloured (air)	40	25

133 Presidents Tolbert and Stevens, and Handclasp

1975. 1st Anniv of Mano River Union.

594	**133**	4c. multicoloured (postage)	30	40
595	**133**	15c. multicoloured (air)	20	20

134 "Quaid-i-Azam" (Mohammed Ali Jinnah)

1977. Birth Centenary of Mohammed Ali Jinnah (Quaid-i-Azam).

596	**134**	30c. multicoloured	1·25	30

135 Queen Elizabeth II

1977. Silver Jubilee.

597	**135**	5c. multicoloured	10	10
598	**135**	1l. multicoloured	65	80

136 College Buildings

1977. 150th Anniv of Fourah Bay College. Multicoloured.

599	5c. Type **136**	10	10
600	20c. The old college (vert)	35	60

137 St. Edward's Crown and Sceptres

1978. 25th Anniv of Coronation. Multicoloured.

601	5c. Type **137**	10	10
602	50c. Queen Elizabeth II in Coronation Coach	20	40
603	1l. Queen Elizabeth II and Prince Philip	35	60

138 "Myrina silenus"

1979. Butterflies (1st series). Multicoloured.

604	5c. Type **138**	10	10
605	15c. "Papilio nireus"	25	15
606	25c. "Catacroptera cloanthe"	40	15
607	1l. "Druryia antimachus"	1·00	1·50

See also Nos. 646/9.

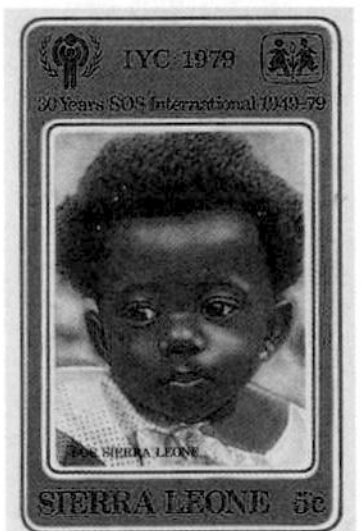

139 Young Child's Face

1979. International Year of the Child. 30th Anniv of S.O.S. International. Multicoloured.

608	5c. Type **139**	10	10
609	27c. Young child with baby	20	25
610	1l. Mother with young child	50	1·10
MS611	114×84 mm. No. 610	75	1·75

140 Presidents Stevens (Sierra Leone) and Tolbert (Liberia), Dove with Letter and Bridge

1979. 5th Anniv of Mano River Union and 1st Anniv of Postal Union.

612	**140**	5c. brown, orange & yellow	10	10
613	**140**	22c. brown, yellow & violet	10	15
614	**140**	27c. brown, blue & orange	10	15
615	**140**	35c. brown, green and red	15	20
616	**140**	1l. brown, violet and blue	50	1·00
MS617		144×73 mm. No. 616	55	1·00

141 Great Britain 1848 10d. Stamp

1979. Death Centenary of Sir Rowland Hill.

618	**141**	10c. black, brown and blue	15	10
619	-	15c. black, brown and blue	25	15
620	-	50c. black, red and yellow	60	70
MS621		90×99 mm. 1l. black, red and pink	60	80

DESIGNS: 15c. 1872 4d. stamp; 50c. 1961 £1 Independence commemorative; 1l. 1912 £1.

142 Green Turaco ("Sierra Leone Turaco")

1980. Birds. Multicoloured.

622B	1c. Type **142**	30	1·75
623B	2c. Olive-bellied sunbird ("Sierra Leone Olive-billed Sunbird")	40	1·75
624B	3c. Western black-headed oriole ("Sierra Leone Black-headed Oriole")	40	1·75
625B	5c. Spur-winged goose	40	75
626A	7c. Didric cuckoo ("White-bellied Didric Cuckoo")	1·25	60
627B	10c. Grey parrot ("Sierra Leone Grey Parrot") (vert)	40	80
628B	15c. Indian Blue quail ("African Blue Quail") (vert)	50	2·00
629B	20c. African wood owl ("West African Wood Owl") (vert)	50	2·25
630B	30c. Greater blue turaco ("Blue Plantain eater") (vert)	50	2·25
631B	40c. Blue-breasted kingfisher ("Nigerian Blue-breasted kingfisher") (vert)	60	2·50
632B	50c. African black crake ("Black Crake") (vert)	60	2·50
633A	1l. Hartlaub's duck	1·40	2·50
634A	2l. Black bee eater	2·00	4·00
635B	5l. Denham's Bustard	1·00	11·00

143 Paul P. Harris (founder), President Stevens of Sierra Leone and Rotary Emblem

1980. 75th Anniv of Rotary International.

636	**143**	5c. multicoloured	10	10
637	**143**	27c. multicoloured	10	10
638	**143**	50c. multicoloured	20	25
639	**143**	1l. multicoloured	40	55

144 "Maria", 1844

1980. "London 1980" Int Stamp Exhibition. Mult.

640	6c. Type **144**	30	10
641	31c. "Tarquah", 1902	40	35
642	50c. "Aureol", 1951	50	70
643	1l. "Africa Palm", 1974	60	1·60

145 Organization for African Unity Emblem

1980. African Summit Conference, Freetown.

644	**145**	20c. black, blue and purple	10	10
645	**145**	1l. black, purple and blue	45	45

146 "Graphium policenes"

1980. Butterflies (2nd series). Multicoloured.

646	5c. Type **146**	10	10
647	27c. "Charaxes varanes"	25	15
648	35c. "Charaxes brutus"	25	25
649	1l. "Euphaedra zaddachi"	75	1·40

147 Arrival at Freetown Airport

1980. Tourism. Multicoloured.

650	6c. Type **147**	10	10
651	26c. Welcome to tourists	10	20
652	31c. Freetown cotton tree	10	25
653	40c. Beinkongo Falls	20	30
654	50c. Sports facilities	20	40
655	1l. African elephant	1·10	95

148 Servals

1981. Wild Cats. Multicoloured.

656	6c. Type **148**	35	10
657	6c. Serval cubs	35	10
658	31c. African golden cats	60	30
659	31c. African golden cat cubs	60	30
660	50c. Leopards	75	45
661	50c. Leopard cubs	75	45
662	1l. Lions	1·00	80
663	1l. Lion cubs	1·00	80

The two designs of each value were printed together, se-tenant, in horizontal pairs, forming composite designs.

149 Soldiers (Defence)

1981. 20th Anniv of Independence and 10th Anniv of Republic. National Services. Multicoloured.

664	6c. Type **149**	65	10
665	31c. Nurses administering first aid, and ambulance (Health) (horiz)	1·75	30
666	40c. Traffic (Police Force)	3·00	1·00
667	1l. Patrol boat (Coastguard) (horiz)	3·25	3·00

150 Wedding Bouquet from Sierra Leone

1981. Royal Wedding (1st issue). Mult.

668	31c. Type **150**	10	10
669	45c. Prince Charles as helicopter pilot	15	20
670	1l. Prince Charles and Lady Diana Spencer	20	90

151 Sandringham

1981. Royal Wedding (2nd issue). Mult.

671	35c. Type **151**	10	15
672	60c. Prince Charles in outdoor clothes	15	25
673	1l.50 Prince Charles and Lady Diana Spencer	25	90
MS674	96×83 mm. 3l. Royal landau	65	65
675	70c. Type **151**	75	90
676	1l.30 As 60c.	75	90
677	2l. As 1l.50	1·50	2·00

152 "Physical Recreation"

1981. 25th Anniv of Duke of Edinburgh Award Scheme and President's Award Scheme Publicity. Multicoloured.

678	6c. Type **152**	10	10
679	31c. "Community service"	15	10
680	1l. Duke of Edinburgh	30	40
681	1l. President Siaka Stevens	30	40

153 Pineapples

1981. World Food Day. Multicoloured.

682	6c. Type **153**	10	10
683	31c. Ground nuts	15	10
684	50c. Cassava fruits	20	15
685	1l. Rice plants	50	50

154 Groundnut

1981. World Food Day (2nd issue). Agricultural Industry. Multicoloured.

686	6c. Type **154**	10	10
687	31c. Cassava	25	10
688	50c. Rice	40	25
689	1l. Pineapples	65	70

155 Scouts with Cattle

1982. 75th Anniv of Boy Scout Movement. Mult.

690	20c. Type **155**	25	10
691	50c. Scouts picking flowers	50	40
692	1l. Lord Baden-Powell	90	1·00
693	2l. Scouts fishing	1·90	2·00
MS694	101×70 mm. 3l. Scouts raising flag	1·75	3·25

1982. Nos. 668/74 surch.

695	50c. on 31c. Type **150**	1·00	70
696	50c. on 35c. Type **151**	1·00	70
697	50c. on 45c. Prince Charles as helicopter pilot	1·00	70
698	50c. on 60c. Prince Charles in outdoor clothes	1·00	70
699	90c. on 1l. Prince Charles and Lady Diana Spencer	2·00	85
699a	1l.30 on 60c. Prince Charles in outdoor clothes	2·25	2·75
699b	2l. on 35c. Type **151**	3·25	3·75
700	2l. on 1l.50 Prince Charles and Lady Diana Spencer	1·75	2·00
700a	8l. on 1l.50 Prince Charles and Lady Diana Spencer	11·00	13·00
MS701	95×83 mm. 3l.50 on 3l. Royal landau	1·00	1·00

157 Heading

1982. World Cup Football Championship, Spain. Multicoloured.

702	20c. Type **157**	45	15
703	30c. Dribbling	70	20
704	1l. Tackling	2·25	2·50
705	2l. Goalkeeping	3·50	4·25
MS706	92×75 mm. 3l. Shooting	4·75	3·00

158 Prince and Princess of Wales

1982. 21st Birthday of Princess of Wales. Mult.

707	31c. Caernarvon Castle	20	15
708	50c. Type **158**	40	15
709	2l. Princess of Wales	2·50	80
MS710	103×75 mm. 3l. Princess of Wales (different)	1·40	1·00

1982. Birth of Prince William of Wales. Nos. 707/9 optd ROYAL BABY 21.6.82.

711	31c. Caernarvon Castle	15	15
712	50c. Type **158**	30	15
713	2l. Princess of Wales	1·00	80
MS714	103×75 mm. 3l. Princess of Wales (different)	1·25	1·00

159 Washington with Troops

1982. 250th Birth Anniv of George Washington. Multicoloured.

715	6c. Type **159**	10	10
716	31c. Portrait of Washington (vert)	20	20
717	50c. Washington with horse	35	35
718	1l. Washington standing on battlefield (vert)	65	80
MS719	103×71 mm. 2l. Washington at home	75	1·25

160 Temptation of Christ

1982. Christmas. Stained-glass Windows. Mult.

720	6c. Type **160**	10	10
721	31c. Baptism of Christ	15	20
722	50c. Annunciation	20	40
723	1l. Nativity	55	90
MS724	74×104 mm. 2l. Mary and Joseph	70	1·10

1982. World Cup Football Championship Winners. Nos. 702/5 optd WORLD CUP WINNERS ITALY (3) vs. W. GERMANY (1).

725	20c. Type **157**	30	20
726	30c. Dribbling	30	30
727	1l. Tackling	80	75
728	2l. Goalkeeping	1·25	1·75
MS729	91×75 mm. 3l. Shooting	1·00	2·00

162 Long Snouted Crocodile

1982. Death Cent of Charles Darwin. Mult.

730	6c. Type **162**	1·50	20
731	31c. Rainbow lizard	2·25	75
732	50c. River turtle	2·75	2·50
733	1l. Chameleon	3·75	6·00
MS734	90×70 mm. 2l. Royal python (vert)	1·75	3·00

163 Diogenes

1983. 500th Birth Anniv of Raphael. Details from painting "The School of Athens". Multicoloured.

735	6c. Type **163**	20	10
736	31c. Euclid, Ptolemy, Zoroaster, Raphael and Sodoma	40	30
737	50c. Euclid and his pupils	55	45
738	2l. Pythagoras, Francesco Maria della Rovere and Heraclitus	1·25	1·40
MS739	101×126 mm. 3l. Plato and Aristolle (vert)	1·50	2·00

164 Agricultural Training

1983. Commonwealth Day. Multicoloured.

740	6c. Type **164**	10	10
741	10c. Tourism development	10	10
742	50c. Broadcasting training	45	45
743	1l. Airport services	1·50	1·25

165 Map of Africa and Flag of Sierra Leone

1983. 25th Anniv of Economic Commission for Africa.

744	165	1l. multicoloured	80	1·10

166 Chimpanzees in Tree

1983. Endangered Species. Multicoloured.

745	6c. Type **166**	1·50	20
746	10c. Three chimpanzees (vert)	1·75	30
747	31c. Chimpanzees swinging in tree (vert)	3·25	90
748	60c. Group of chimpanzees	5·50	7·50
MS749	115×80 mm. 3l. African elephant	3·00	2·25

167 Traditional Communications

1983. World Communications Year. Mult.

750	6c. Type **167**	10	10
751	10c. Mail via Mano River	15	10
752	20c. Satellite ground station	15	10
753	1l. British packet, c. 1805	90	65
MS754	115×85 mm. 2l. Telecommunications	80	1·25

168 Montgolfier Balloon, Paris, 1783

1983. Bicentenary of Manned Flight. Mult.

755	6c. Type **168**	35	10
756	20c. Wolfert's airship "Deutschland", Berlin, 1879 (horiz)	1·00	30
757	50c. Amundsen's airship N.1 "Norge", North Pole, 1926 (horiz)	2·75	2·25
758	1l. "Cap Sierra" sport balloon, Freetown, 1983	2·25	3·00
MS759	115×85 mm. 2l. Airship of 21st century	1·00	1·75

169 Mickey Mouse

1983. Space Ark Fantasy. Walt Disney Cartoon Characters. Multicoloured.

774 1c. Type **169** 10 10
775 1c. Huey, Dewey and Louie 10 10
776 3c. Goofy in spaceship 10 10
777 3c. Donald Duck 10 10
778 10c. Ludwig von Drake 10 10
779 10c. Goofy 10 10
780 2l. Mickey Mouse and Giraffe in spaceship 1·00 1·25
781 3l. Donald Duck floating in space 1·25 1·75
MS782 140×116 mm. 5l. Mickey Mouse leaving spaceship 3·00 3·50

170 Graduates from Union Training Programme

1984. 10th Anniv of Mano River Union. Mult.

783 6c. Type **170** 10 10
784 25c. Intra-Union trade 10 10
785 31c. Member Presidents on map 10 10
786 41c. Signing ceremony marking Guinea's accession 20 20
MS787 75×113 mm. No. 786 35 90

171 Gymnastics

1984. Olympic Games, Los Angeles. Mult.

788 90c. Type **171** 30 40
789 1l. Hurdling 30 40
790 3l. Javelin-throwing 75 1·25
MS791 104×71 mm. 7l. Boxing 1·10 2·00

172 "Apollo 11" Liftoff

1984. 15th Anniv of First Moonwalk. Mult.

792 50c. Type **172** 20 20
793 75c. Lunar module 30 30
794 1l.25 First Moonwalk 45 45
795 2l.50 Lunar exploration 85 85
MS796 99×69 mm. 5l. Family watching Moonwalk on television (horiz) 1·60 2·25

173 Concorde

1984. Universal Postal Union Congress, Hamburg. Multicoloured.

797 4l. Type **173** 3·00 1·75
MS798 100×70 mm. 4l. Heinrich von Stephan (founder of U.P.U.) 1·25 1·75

174 Citroen "Traction Avante"

1984. United Nations Decade of African Transport. Multicoloured.

799 12c. Type **174** 50 20
800 60c. Locomotive 80 45
801 90c. A.C. "Ace" 95 65
802 1l. Vauxhall "Prince Henry" 95 65
803 1l.50 Delahaye "135" 1·00 1·50
804 2l. Mazda "1105" 1·00 1·50
MS805 107×75 mm. 6l. Volkswagen "Beetle" 3·75 4·50

1984. Nos. 625, 627 and 634 surch.

811 25c. on 10c. Grey parrot (vert) 75 85
812 40c. on 10c. Grey parrot (vert) 50 70
813 50c. on 2l. Black bee eater 50 70
814 70c. on 5c. Spur-winged goose 50 70
815 10l. on 5c. Spur-winged goose 2·25 3·50

1984. "Ausipex" International Stamp Exhibition, Melbourne. Nos. 632 and 635 optd AUSIPEX 84.

818 50c. African black crake (vert) 1·50 75
819 5l. Denham's bustard 3·50 2·00

177 Portuguese Caravel

1984. History of Shipping. Multicoloured.

820B 2c. Type **177** 55 1·50
821B 5c. "Merlin" of Bristol 55 80
822B 10c. "Golden Hind" 75 70
823A 15c. "Mordaunt" 1·75 90
824B 20c. "Atlantic" (sail transport) 80 60
825B 25c. H.M.S. "Lapwing" (frigate), 1785 80 60
826B 30c. "Traveller" (brig) 80 60
827B 40c. "Amistad" (schooner) 90 60
828B 50c. H.M.S. "Teazer" (gun vessel), 1868 1·00 60
829B 70c. "Scotia" (cable ship) 1·75 2·00
830B 1l. H.M.S. "Alecto" (paddle-steamer), 1882 1·75 2·00
831B 2l. H.M.S. "Blonde" (cruiser), 1889 2·00 3·00
832B 5l. H.M.S. "Fox" (cruiser), 1895 2·75 4·50
833B 10l. "Accra" (liner) 3·25 5·50
833cA 15l. H.M.S. "Favourite" (sloop), 1829 3·00 4·00
833dA 25l. H.M.S. "Euryalus" (screw frigate), 1883 3·00 4·50

Nos. 820/2 and 824/33 come both with and without imprint dates.

178 Mail Runner approaching Mano River Depot, c. 1843

1984. 125th Anniv of First Postage Stamps. Mult.

834 50c. Type **178** 35 15
835 2l. Isaac Fitzjohn, first Postmaster, receiving letters, 1855 1·25 85
836 3l. 1859 packet franked with four 6d. stamps 1·75 1·50
MS837 100×70 mm. 5l. Sierra Leone 1859 6d. purple and Great Britain 1840 Penny Black stamps 1·50 1·60

179 "Madonna and Child" (Pisanello)

1984. Christmas. Madonna and Child Paintings by artists named. Multicoloured.

838 20c. Type **179** 10 10
839 1l. Memling 40 40
840 2l. Raphael 75 90
841 3l. Van der Werff 1·10 1·40
MS842 100×69 mm. 6l. Picasso 2·75 2·75

180 Donald Duck in "The Wise Little Hen"

1984. 50th Birthday of Donald Duck. Walt Disney Cartoon Characters. Multicoloured.

843 1c. Type **180** 10 10
844 2c. Mickey Mouse and Donald Duck in "Boat Builders" 10 10
845 3c. Panchito, Donald Duck and Jose Carioca in "The Three Caballeros" 10 10
846 4c. Donald Duck meeting Pythagoras in "Mathmagic Land" 10 10
847 5c. Donald Duck and nephew in "The Mickey Mouse Club" 10 10
848 10c. Mickey Mouse, Goofy and Donald Duck in "Donald on Parade" 10 10
849 1l. Donald Duck riding donkey in "Don Donald" 1·00 1·00
850 2l. Donald Duck in "Donald Gets Drafted" 2·00 2·00
851 4l. Donald Duck meeting children in Tokyo Disneyland 3·25 3·25
MS852 126×102 mm. 5l. Style sheet for Donald Duck 4·50 2·50

181 Fischer's Whydah

1985. Birth Bicentenary of John J. Audubon (ornithologist). Songbirds of Sierra Leone. Mult.

853 40c. Type **181** 1·75 55
854 90c. Spotted flycatcher 3·00 1·75
855 1l.30 Garden warbler 3·25 3·50
856 3l. Speke's weaver 5·50 7·50
MS857 100×70 mm. 5l. Great grey shrike 3·50 3·00

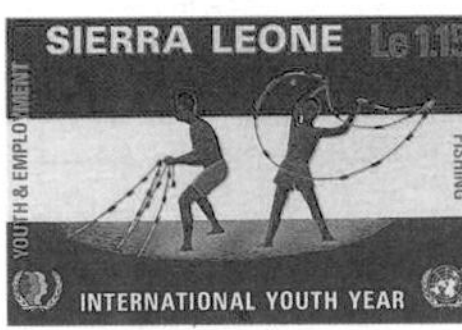

182 Fishing

1985. International Youth Year. Multicoloured.

858 1l.15 Type **182** 45 55
859 1l.50 Sawing timber 60 75
860 2l.15 Rice farming 75 95
MS861 100×70 mm. 5l. Polishing diamonds 1·75 1·50

183 Eddie Rickenbacker and Spad "XIII", 1918

1985. 40th Anniv of I.C.A.O. Multicoloured.

862 70c. Type **183** 1·50 75
863 1l.25 Samuel P. Langley and "Aerodrome A", 1903 2·00 1·75
864 1l.30 Orville and Wilbur Wright with Wright Flyer I, 1903 2·00 1·75
865 2l. Charles Lindbergh and "Spirit of St. Louis", 1927 2·25 2·75
MS866 100×69 mm. 5l. Sierra Leone Airlines Boeing 707-384C 2·00 1·75

184 "Temptation of Christ" (Botticelli)

1985. Easter. Religious Paintings. Mult.

867 45c. Type **184** 30 15
868 70c. "Christ at the Column" (Velasquez) 55 35
869 1l.55 "Pieta" (Botticelli) (vert) 90 75
870 10l. "Christ on the Cross" (Velasquez) (vert) 4·75 5·00
MS871 106×76 mm. 12l. "Man of Sorrows" (Botticelli) 4·00 4·00

185 The Queen Mother at St. Paul's Cathedral

1985. Life and Times of Queen Elizabeth the Queen Mother. Multicoloured.

872 1l. Type **185** 20 25
873 1l.70 With her racehorse, "Double Star", at Sandown (horiz) 30 40
874 10l. At Covent Garden, 1971 1·75 2·50
MS875 56×85 mm. 12l. With Princess Anne at Ascot 1·75 2·25

1985. 75th Anniv of Girl Guide Movement. Nos. 690/3 surch 75th ANNIVERSARY OF GIRL GUIDES.

876 70c. on 20c. Type **155** 30 30
877 1l.30 on 50c. Scouts picking flowers 55 55
878 5l. on 1l. Lord Baden-Powell 1·60 1·60
879 7l. on 2l. Scouts fishing 2·25 2·25
MS880 101×70 mm. 15l. on 3l. Scouts raising flag 3·75 4·00

1985. Olympic Gold Medal Winners, Los Angeles. Nos. 788/90 surch.

881 2l. on 90c. Type **171** (surch **Le2 MA YANHONJG CHINA GOLD MEDAL**) 50 55
882 4l. on 1l. Hurdling (surch **Le4 E. MOSES U.S.A. GOLD MEDAL**) 1·00 1·25
883 8l. on 3l. Javelin-throwing (surch **Le8 A. HAERKOENEN FINLAND GOLD MEDAL**) 2·00 2·10
MS884 104×71 mm. 15l. on 7l. Boxing (surch **M. TAYLOR U.S.A. GOLD MEDAL**) 3·25 3·75

188 Chater-Lea (1905) at Hill Station House

1985. Centenary of Motor Cycle and Decade for African Transport. Multicoloured.

885 1l.40 Type **188** 1·00 1·00
886 2l. Honda "XR 350 R" at Queen Elizabeth II Quay, Freetown 1·40 1·40
887 4l. Kawasaki "Vulcan" at Bo Clock Tower 2·50 2·50
888 5l. Harley-Davidson "Electra-Glide" in Makeni village 2·75 2·75
MS889 104×71 mm. 12l. Millet (1893) 4·75 4·25

189a Viola Pompose

1985. 300th Birth Anniv of Johann Sebastian Bach (composer). Multicoloured (except No. MS894).

890 70c. Type **189a** 1·00 25
891 3l. Spinet 2·50 80
892 4l. Lute 2·50 1·10
893 5l. Oboe 2·50 1·40
MS894 103×77 mm. 12l. "Johann Sebastian Bach" (Toby E. Rosenthal) (black) 5·00 3·50

1985. Nos. 707/10 and 711/14 surch.

895 70c. on 3l. Caernarvon Castle (No. 707) 30 30
896 4l. on 50c. Type **158** (No. 708) 2·00 2·50
897 5l. on 2l. Princess of Wales (No. 709) 2·75 3·00

MS898	103×75 mm. 15l. on 3l. Princess of Wales (different) (No. MS710)	8·00	6·00
899	1l.30 on 3lc. Caernarvon Castle (No. 711)	2·00	1·25
900	5l. on 50c. Type **158** (No. 712)	4·00	3·50
901	7l. on 2l. Princess of Wales (No. 713)	6·50	4·50
MS902	103×75 mm. 15l. on 3l. Princess of Wales (different) (No. MS714)	8·00	6·00

190 "Madonna and Child" (Crivelli)

1985. Christmas. "Madonna and Child" Paintings by artists named. Multicoloured.

903	70c. Type **190**	25	10
904	3l. Bouts	80	40
905	4l. Da Messina	95	55
906	5l. Lochner	1·10	65
MS907	113×85 mm. 12l. Miniature from Book of Kells	1·50	1·60

190a Snow White and Bashful

1985. 150th Birth Anniv of Mark Twain (author). Walt Disney cartoon characters illustrating Mark Twain quotations. Multicoloured.

908	1l.50 Type **190a**	1·25	1·00
909	3l. Three Little Pigs	1·50	1·60
910	4l. Donald Duck and nephew	1·60	1·75
911	5l. Pinocchio and Figaro the cat	1·75	2·00
MS912	126×101 mm. 15l. Winnie the Pooh	4·25	2·50

190b The Miller (Donald Duck) and his daughter (Daisy Duck) meet the King (Uncle Scrooge)

1985. Birth Bicentenaries of Grimm Brothers (folklorists). Walt Disney cartoon characters in scenes from "Rumpelstiltskin". Multicoloured.

913	70c. Type **190b**	20	25
914	1l. The King puts the Miller's daughter to work	35	40
915	2l. Rumpelstiltskin demands payment	50	55
916	10l. The King with gold spun from straw	2·75	3·50
MS917	126×100 mm. 15l. The King and Queen with baby	5·50	4·50

190c John Kennedy and 1954 Human Rights 8c. Stamp

1985. 40th Anniv of U.N.O. Showing United Nations (New York) stamps. Multicoloured.

918	2l. Type **190c**	50	70
919	4l. Albert Einstein (scientist) and 1958 Atomic Energy 3c.	1·00	1·60
920	7l. Maimonides (physician) and 1956 W.H.O. 8c.	3·50	4·25
MS921	110×85 mm. 12l. Martin Luther King (civil rights leader) (vert)	1·25	1·75

191 Player kicking Ball

1986. World Cup Football Championship, Mexico. Multicoloured.

922	70c. Type **191**	55	10
923	3l. Player controlling ball	1·00	50
924	4l. Player chasing ball	1·25	70
925	5l. Player kicking ball (different)	1·50	80
MS926	105×74 mm. 12l. Player kicking ball (different)	1·50	1·75

191a Times, Square, 1905

1986. Centenary of Statue of Liberty. Mult.

927	40c. Type **191a**	10	10
928	70c. Times Square, 1986	15	10
929	1l. "Tally Ho" coach, c. 1880 (horiz)	35	15
930	10l. Express bus, 1986 (horiz)	2·00	1·90
MS931	105×75 mm. 12l. Statue of Liberty	2·50	2·25

191b Johannes Kepler (astronomer) and Paris Observatory

1986. Appearance of Halley's Comet (1st issue). Multicoloured.

932	15c. Type **191b**	30	10
933	50c. N.A.S.A. Space Shuttle landing, 1985	40	10
934	70c. Halley's Comet (from Bayeux Tapestry)	40	15
935	10l. Comet of 530 A.D. and Merlin predicting coming of King Arthur	2·75	1·60
MS936	101×70 mm. 12l. Halley's Comet	1·50	1·60

See also Nos. 988/91.

191c Princess Elizabeth Inspecting Guard of Honour, Cranwell, 1951

1986. 60th Birthday of Queen Elizabeth II.

937	**191c**	10c. black and yellow	20	10
938	-	1l.70 multicoloured	55	35
939	-	10l. multicoloured	2·50	2·75
MS940		120×85 mm. 12l. black and brown	2·25	2·00

DESIGNS: 1l.70, In Garter robes; 10l. At Braemar Games, 1970; 12l. Princess Elizabeth, Windsor Castle, 1943.

192 Chicago–Milwaukee "Hiawatha Express"

1986. "Ameripex" International Stamp Exhibition, Chicago. American Trains. Multicoloured.

941	50c. Type **192**	90	40
942	2l. Rock Island Line "The Rocket"	1·75	1·75
943	4l. Rio Grande "Prospector"	2·75	3·25
944	7l. Southern Pacific "Daylight Express"	3·50	5·00
MS945	105×85 mm. 12l. Pennsylvania "Broadway Limited"	3·25	2·25

192c Prince Andrew and Miss Sarah Ferguson

1986. Royal Wedding. Multicoloured.

946	10c. Type **192c**	10	10
947	1l.70 Prince Andrew at clay pigeon shoot	30	35
948	10l. Prince Andrew in naval uniform	1·40	1·75
MS949	88×88 mm. 12l. Prince Andrew and Miss Sarah Ferguson (different)	2·25	1·60

193 "Monodora myristica"

1986. Flowers of Sierra Leone. Multicoloured.

950	70c. Type **193**	15	10
951	1l.50 "Gloriosa simplex"	20	15
952	4l. "Mussaenda erythrophylla"	35	25
953	6l. "Crinum ornatum"	50	40
954	8l. "Bauhinia purpurea"	60	60
955	10l. "Bombax costatum"	70	70
956	20l. "Hibiscus rosasinensis"	1·25	1·50
957	30l. "Cassia fistula"	1·75	2·00
MS958	Two sheets, each 101×92 mm. (a) 40l. "Clitoria ternatea" (b) 40l. "Plumbago auriculata" Set of 2 sheets	6·00	6·00

194 Handshake and Flags of Sierra Leone and U.S.A.

1986. 25th Anniv of United States Peace Corps.

959	**194**	4l. multicoloured	70	70

195 Transporting Goods by Canoe

1986. International Peace Year. Multicoloured.

960	1l. Type **195**	30	15
961	2l. Teacher and class	40	25
962	5l. Rural post office	80	50
963	10l. Fishermen in longboat	1·60	1·25

1986. Various stamps surch.

964	30l. on 2c. Type **177** (No. 820)	3·75	3·75
965	40l. on 30c. "Traveller" (brig) (No. 826)	4·25	4·25
966	45l. on 40c. "Amistad" (schooner) (No. 827)	4·50	4·50
967	50l. on 70c. "Scotia" (cable ship) (No. 829)	4·50	4·50
968	70c. on 10c. Type **191c** (No. 937)	1·25	30
969	45l. on 10l. Queen at Braemar Games, 1970 (No. 934)	6·00	2·50
MS970	120×85 mm. 50l. on 12l. black and brown (No. MS940)	2·50	3·00
971	70c. on 10c. Prince Andrew and Miss Sarah Ferguson (No. 946)	20	20
972	45l. on 10l. Prince Andrew in naval uniform (No. 948)	3·00	2·50
MS973	88×88 mm. 50l. on 12l. Prince Andrew and Miss Sarah Ferguson (different) (No. MS949)	2·50	3·00

1986. World Cup Football Championship Winners, Mexico. Nos. 922/5 optd WINNERS Argentina 3 W.Germany 2 or surch also.

974	70c. Type **191**	35	10
975	3l. Player controlling ball	75	30
976	4l. Player chasing ball	80	40
977	40l. on 5l. Player kicking ball (different)	6·50	4·50
MS978	105×74 mm. 40l. on 12l. Player kicking ball (different)	2·75	2·50

198 Mickey and Minnie Mouse as Jack and Jill

1986. "Stockholmia '86" International Stamp Exn, Sweden. Walt Disney cartoon characters in scenes from nursery rhymes. Multicoloured.

979	70c. Type **198**	10	10
980	1l. Donald Duck as Wee Willie Winkie	15	15
981	2l. Minnie Mouse as Little Miss Muffet	20	20
982	4l. Goofy as Old King Cole	40	40
983	5l. Clarabelle as Mary Quite Contrary	50	50
984	10l. Daisy Duck as Little Bo Peep	90	1·00
985	25l. Daisy Duck and Minnie Mouse in "Polly put the Kettle on"	2·00	2·75
986	35l. Goofy, Mickey Mouse and Donald Duck as the Three Men in a Tub	2·50	3·25
MS987	Two sheets, each 127×102 mm. (a) 40l. Aunt Matilda as the Old Woman in the Shoe. (b) 40l. Goofy as Simple Simon Set of 2 sheets	6·50	6·50

(198a)

1986. Appearance of Halley's Comet (2nd issue). Nos. 932/5 optd as T 198a.

988	50c. N.A.S.A. Space Shuttle landing, 1985	30	10
989	70c. Halley's Comet (from Bayeux Tapestry)	30	10
990	1l.50 on 15c. Johannes Kepler (astronomer) and Paris Observatory	30	10
991	45l. on 10l. Comet of 530 A.D. and Merlin predicting coming of King Arthur	6·00	3·75
MS992	101×70 mm. 50l. on 12l. Halley's Comet	3·25	3·75

199 "Virgin and Child with St. Dorothy"

1986. Christmas. Paintings by Titian. Mult.

993	70c. Type **199**	10	10
994	1l.50 "The Gypsy Madonna" (vert)	15	10
995	20l. "The Holy Family"	2·25	2·50
996	30l. "Virgin and Child in an Evening Landscape" (vert)	2·75	3·25
MS997	76×102 mm. 40l. "Madonna with the Pesaro Family" (vert)	7·50	7·00

200 Nomoli (soapstone figure)

1987. Bicentenary of Sierra Leone. Mult.

998	2l. Type **200**	20	20
999	5l. King's Yard Gate, Royal Hospital, 1817	80	60
MS1000	100×70 mm. 60l. Early 19th-century British warship at Freetown	3·25	3·75

201 Removing Top of Statue's Torch

1987. Centenary of Statue of Liberty (1986) (2nd issue). Multicoloured.

1001	70c. Type **201**	10	10
1002	1l.50 View of Statue's torch and New York harbour (horiz)	10	10
1003	2l. Crane lifting torch	10	10
1004	3l. Workman steadying torch	10	15
1005	4l. Statue's crown (horiz)	15	20
1006	5l. Statue of Liberty (side view) and fireworks	20	25
1007	10l. Statue of Liberty and fireworks	40	45
1008	25l. Bedloe Island, statue and fireworks (horiz)	1·00	1·40
1009	30l. Statue's face	1·25	1·75

202 Emblem, Mother and Child and Syringe

1987. 40th Anniv of UNICEF.

1010	**202**	10l. multicoloured	50	55

203 "U.S.A.", 1987

1987. America's Cup Yachting Championship. Multicoloured.

1011	1l. Type **203**	15	10
1012	1l.50 "New Zealand II", 1987 (horiz)	15	10
1013	2l.50 "French Kiss", 1987	15	10
1014	10l. "Stars and Stripes", 1987 (horiz)	75	45
1015	15l. "Australia II", 1983	1·00	75
1016	25l. "Freedom", 1980	1·75	1·40
1017	30l. "Kookaburra", 1987 (horiz)	1·75	1·60
MS1018	100×70 mm. 50l. "Constellation", 1964	2·25	2·50

204 Mickey Mouse as Mountie and Parliament Building, Ottawa

1987. "Capex '87" International Stamp Exhibition, Toronto. Walt Disney cartoon characters in Canada. Multicoloured.

1019	2l. Type **204**	20	20
1020	5l. Goofy dressed as Mountie and totem poles	35	35
1021	10l. Goofy windsurfing and Donald Duck fishing off Perce Rock	60	45
1022	20l. Goofy with mountain goat in Rocky Mountains	1·00	1·25
1023	25l. Donald Duck and Mickey Mouse in Old Quebec	1·25	1·40
1024	45l. Goofy emerging from igloo and "Aurora Borealis"	1·75	2·50
1025	50l. Goofy as gold prospector and post office, Yukon	2·00	3·00
1026	75l. Dumbo flying over Niagara Falls	3·25	4·50
MS1027	Two sheets, each 127×101 mm. (a) 100l. Mickey Mouse driving chuckwagon in Calgary Stampede. (b) 100l. Mickey Mouse and Goofy as Vikings in Newfoundland Set of 2 sheets	8·00	12·00

205 "Salamis temora"

1987. Butterflies. Multicoloured. "Sierra Leone" in black.

1028A	10c. Type **205**	1·25	40
1029B	20c. "Stugeta marmorea"	1·00	1·00
1030B	40c. "Graphium ridleyanus"	1·00	65
1031A	1l. "Papilio bromius"	1·25	40
1032Ac	2l. "Iterus zalmoxis"	1·25	60
1033A	3l. "Cymothoe sangaris"	1·50	60
1033Bd	3l. As 40c.	5·00	2·75
1034A	5l. "Graphium tynderaeus"	1·50	40
1034Bc	9l. As 3l. (No. 1033)	6·00	3·75
1035Ac	10l. "Graphium policenes"	1·25	30
1035Bc	12l. Type **205**	7·00	4·00
1035Bd	16l. As 20c.	7·00	4·00
1036Ac	20l. "Tanuetheira timon"	1·50	60
1037Ac	25l. "Danaus limniace"	1·50	30
1038Ac	30l. "Papilio hesperus"	1·75	65
1039Ac	45l. "Charaxes smaragdalis"	2·25	30
1040Ac	60l. "Charaxes lucretius"	2·00	2·25
1041Ac	75l. "Antanartia delius"	2·25	2·75
1042A	100l. "Abisara talantus"	3·25	6·00

For similar stamps but with "Sierra Leone" in blue, see Nos. 1658/72.

206 Cycling

1987. Olympic Games, Seoul (1988) (1st series). Multicoloured.

1043	5l. Type **206**	20	25
1044	10l. Three-day eventing	40	50
1045	45l. Athletics	1·75	2·00
1046	50l. Tennis	2·00	2·40
MS1047	73×84 mm. 100l. Olympic gold medal	4·00	4·50

See also Nos. 1137/41.

206a "The Quarrel"

1987. Birth Centenary of Marc Chagall (artist). Multicoloured.

1048	3l. Type **206a**	15	15
1049	5l. "Rebecca giving Abraham's Servant a Drink"	20	25
1050	10l. "The Village"	40	45
1051	20l. "Ida at the Window"	60	65
1052	25l. "Promenade"	1·00	1·10
1053	45l. "Peasants"	2·00	2·25
1054	50l. "Turquoise Plate" (ceramic)	2·25	2·25
1055	75l. "Cemetery Gate"	3·25	3·75
MS1056	Two sheets, each 110×95 mm. (a) 100l. "Wedding Feast" (stage design) (104×78 mm). (b) 100l. "The Falling Angel" (104×78 mm). Imperf Set of 2 sheets	9·00	10·00

206b "Apollo 8" Spacecraft (first manned Moon orbit), 1968

1987. Milestones of Transportation. Multicoloured.

1057	3l. Type **206b**	40	30
1058	5l. Blanchard's balloon (first U.S. balloon flight), 1793	40	30
1059	10l. Amelia Earhart's Lockheed Vega 5B (first solo transatlantic flight by woman), 1932	1·25	60
1060	15l. Vicker's Vimy (first non-stop transatlantic flight), 1919	1·50	80
1061	20l. British "Mk 1" tank (first combat tank), 1916	1·75	1·25
1062	25l. Vought-Sikorsky VS-300 (first U.S. helicopter flight), 1939	2·00	1·60
1063	30l. Wright brothers Flyer I (first powered flight), 1903	2·00	1·60
1064	35l. Bleriot XI (first cross Channel flight), 1909	2·00	2·00
1065	40l. Paraplane (first flexible-wing ultralight), 1983	2·00	2·25
1066	50l. Daimler's first motorcycle, 1885	2·00	2·50
MS1067	114×83 mm. 100l. "Rhinegold Express" (first electric express service) (horiz)	3·75	6·50

Nos. 1058/64 are horiz.

207 Evonne Goolagong

1987. Wimbledon Tennis Champions. Mult.

1068	2l. Type **207**	35	35
1069	5l. Martina Navratilova	55	55
1070	10l. Jimmy Connors	85	85
1071	15l. Bjorn Borg	1·25	1·25
1072	30l. Boris Becker	2·25	2·25
1073	40l. John McEnroe	2·50	2·50
1074	50l. Chris Evert Lloyd	2·75	2·75
1075	75l. Virginia Wade	3·50	3·50
MS1076	Two sheets, each 105×75 mm. (a) 100l. Boris Becker (different). (b) 100l. Steffi Graf Set of 2 sheets	13·00	13·00

208 Ducats, "Santa Maria" and Isaac Abravanel (financier)

1987. 500th Anniv (1992) of Discovery of America by Columbus. Multicoloured.

1077	5l. Type **208**	80	20
1078	10l. Astrolabe, "Pinta" and Abraham Zacuto (astronomer)	90	35
1079	45l. Maravedis (coins), "Nina" and Luis de Santangel (financier)	2·75	3·00
1080	50l. Carib and Spaniard with tobacco plant and Luis de Torres (translator)	3·00	3·25
MS1081	101×70 mm. 100l. Christopher Columbus and map	3·00	3·50

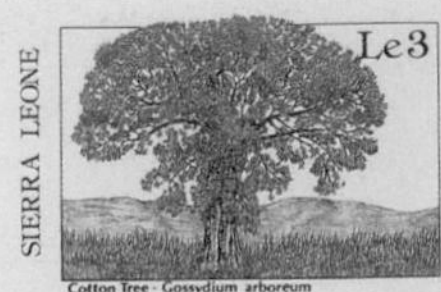

209 Cotton Tree

1987. Flora and Fauna. Multicoloured.

1082	3l. Type **209**	15	15
1083	5l. Dwarf crocodile	35	25
1084	10l. Kudu	40	35
1085	20l. Yellowbells	65	65
1086	25l. Hippopotamus and calf	1·75	1·25
1087	45l. Comet orchid	3·25	2·50
1088	50l. Baobab tree	2·25	2·50
1089	75l. Elephant and calf	4·25	5·00
MS1090	Two sheets, each 100×70 mm. (a) 100l. Bananas, Coconut Palm, Papayas and Pineapple. (b) 100l. Leopard Set of 2 sheets	5·75	7·00

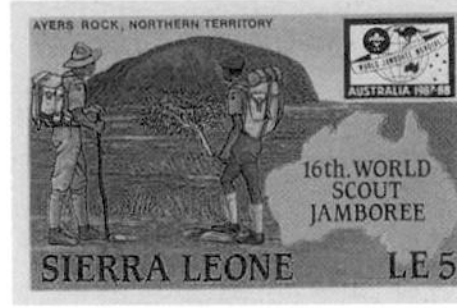

210 Scouts at Ayers Rock

1987. World Scout Jamboree, Australia. Mult.

1091	5l. Type **210**	30	20
1092	15l. Scouts sailing yacht	65	65
1093	40l. Scouts and Sydney skyline	1·75	2·50
1094	50l. Scout, Sydney Harbour Bridge and Opera House	3·25	2·75
MS1095	114×78 mm. 100l. Flags of Sierra Leone, Australia and Boy Scouts	3·00	3·50

210a White House

1987. Bicentenary of U.S. Constitution. Mult.

1096	5l. Type **210a**	15	20
1097	10l. George Washington (Virginia delegate) (vert)	30	35
1098	30l. Patrick Henry (statesman) (vert)	80	95
1099	65l. State Seal, New Hampshire	1·60	2·40
MS1100	105×75 mm. 100l. John Jay (jurist) (vert)	1·50	3·00

210b Mickey and Minnie Mouse on Space Mountain

1987. 60th Anniv of Mickey Mouse (Walt Disney cartoon character). Cartoon characters at Tokyo Disneyland. Multicoloured.

1101	20c. Type **210b**	10	10
1102	40c. Mickey Mouse at Country Bear Jamboree	10	10
1103	80c. Mickey Mouse as bandleader and Minnie Mouse, Goofy and Pluto as musicians	10	10
1104	1l. Goofy, Mickey Mouse and children in canoe and Mark Twain's river boat	10	10
1105	2l. Mickey Mouse, Goofy and Chip n'Dale on Western River Railroad	10	10
1106	3l. Goofy and Mickey Mouse as Pirates of the Caribbean	15	15
1107	10l. Mickey Mouse, Goofy and children aboard Big Thunder Mountain train	55	55
1108	20l. Mickey Mouse, Morty and Ferdie in boat and Goofy on flying carpet	1·25	1·50
1109	30l. Mickey and Minnie Mouse in kimonos at Disneyland entrance	1·75	2·00
MS1110	127×102 mm. 65l. Mickey and Minnie Mouse in kimonos at Cinderella's Castle	5·50	4·50

211 "The Annunciation" (detail) (Titian)

1987. Christmas. Religious Paintings by Titian. Multicoloured.

1111	2l. Type **211**	20	10
1112	10l. "Madonna and Child with Saints"	60	35
1113	20l. "Madonna and Child with Saints Ulfus and Brigid"	1·10	1·25
1114	35l. "The Madonna of the Cherries"	1·90	2·75
MS1115	70×100 mm. 65l. "The Pesaro Altarpiece" (vert)	3·50	4·00

211a Wedding of Princess Elizabeth and Duke of Edinburgh, 1947

1988. Royal Ruby Wedding.

1116	**211a**	2l. brown, black and grey	40	10
1117	-	3l. multicoloured	40	10
1118	-	10l. brown, black and orange	60	35
1119	-	50l. multicoloured	2·75	2·50
MS1120		76×100 mm. 65l. mult	3·00	2·50

DESIGNS: 3l. Prince Charles's christening photograph, 1949; 10l. Queen Elizabeth II with Prince Charles and Princess Anne, c. 1951; 50l. Queen Elizabeth, c. 1960; 65l. Wedding photograph, 1947.

212 "Russula cyanoxantha"

1988. Fungi. Multicoloured.

1121	3l. Type **212**	45	30
1122	10l. "Lycoperdon perlatum"	1·10	70
1123	20l. "Lactarius deliciosus"	1·90	2·00
1124	30l. "Boletus edulis"	2·25	2·75
MS1125	100×70 mm. 65l. "Amanita muscaria"	5·50	4·75

213 Golden Pheasant Panchax

1988. Fishes of Sierra Leone. Multicoloured.

1126	3l. Type **213**	15	15
1127	10l. Banded panchax	30	30
1128	20l. Jewel cichlid	50	75
1129	35l. Freshwater butterflyfish	75	1·40
MS1130	99×69 mm. 65l. Long-finned tetra	2·50	4·00

1988. Stamp Exhibitions. Nos. 1016, 1072 and 1079 optd.

1131	25l. "Freedom", 1980 (optd **INDEPENDENCE 40**, Israel)	1·10	1·40
1132	30l. Boris Becker (optd **OLYMPHILEX '88**, Seoul)	1·25	1·75
1133	45l. Maravedis (coins), "Nina" and Luis de Santangel (financier) (optd **PRAGA 88**, Prague)	1·75	2·25

214 Hands holding Coffee Beans and Woman with Cocoa

1988. International Fund for Agricultural Development. Multicoloured.

1134	3l. Type **214**	20	20
1135	15l. Tropical fruits and man climbing palm tree	70	80
1136	25l. Sheaf of rice and harvesters	1·25	1·50

215 Basketball

1988. Olympic Games, Seoul (2nd issue). Mult.

1137	3l. Type **215**	10	10
1138	10l. Judo	30	35
1139	15l. Gymnastics	45	55
1140	40l. Synchronized swimming	1·25	1·75
MS1141	73×101 mm. 65l. Sierra Leone athlete	1·90	2·50

216 Swallow-tailed Bee Eater

1988. Birds. Multicoloured.

1142	3l. Type **216**	85	75
1143	5l. Double-toothed barbet ("Tooth-billed Barbet")	1·10	1·00
1144	8l. African golden oriole	1·40	1·25
1145	10l. Red bishop	1·40	1·25
1146	12l. Red-billed shrike	1·40	1·25
1147	20l. European bee eater	1·60	1·40
1148	35l. Common gonolek ("Barbary Shrike")	2·25	2·00
1149	40l. Western black-headed oriole ("Black-headed Oriole")	2·25	2·25
MS1150	Two sheets, each 111×82 mm. (a) 65l. Purple heron. (b) 65l. Saddle-bill stork Set of 2 sheets	3·75	4·50

217 "Aureol" (liner)

1988. Ships. Multicoloured.

1151	3l. Type **217**	75	30
1152	10l. "Dunkwa" (freighter)	1·75	80
1153	15l. "Melampus" (container ship)	2·50	1·60
1154	30l. "Dumbaia" (freighter)	3·25	3·00
MS1155	95×95 mm. 65l. Loading container ship, Freetown	2·25	2·50

1988. 500th Birth Anniv of Titian (artist). As T 183a of St. Vincent. Multicoloured.

1156	1l. "The Concert" (detail)	15	10
1157	2l. "Philip II of Spain"	20	15
1158	3l. "Saint Sebastian" (detail)	20	20
1159	5l. "Martyrdom of St. Peter Martyr"	30	30
1160	15l. "St. Jerome"	90	85
1161	20l. "St. Mark enthroned with Saints"	1·10	1·10
1162	25l. "Portrait of a Young Man"	1·25	1·40
1163	30l. "St. Jerome in Penitence"	1·40	1·50
MS1164	Two sheets, each 110×95 mm. (a) 50l. "Self Portrait". (b) 50l. "Orpheus and Eurydice" Set of 2 sheets	4·00	4·50

218 Sikorsky S-58 Helicopter lowering "Mercury" Capsule to Flight Deck

1988. 25th Death Anniv of John F. Kennedy (American statesman). U.S. Space Achievements. Multicoloured.

1165	3l. Type **218**	1·25	30
1166	5l. "Liberty Bell 7" capsule descending (vert)	1·00	20
1167	15l. Launch of first manned American capsule (vert)	1·25	70
1168	40l. "Freedom 7" orbiting Earth	3·00	2·00
MS1169	98×69 mm. 65l. President Kennedy and quotation	1·90	2·25

219 Famine Relief Convoy crossing Desert

1988. 125th Anniv of Int Red Cross. Mult.

1170	3l. Type **219**	1·00	40
1171	10l. Rifle and map of Battle of Solferino, 1859	2·50	90
1172	20l. World War II hospital ship in Pacific	3·00	2·00
1173	40l. Red Cross tent and World War I German biplanes	3·75	3·25
MS1174	100×70 mm. 65l. Henri Dunant (founder), Alfred Nobel and Peace Prize scroll (horiz)	2·40	3·00

219a Donald Duck's Nephews playing as Band

1988. Christmas. "Mickey's Christmas Dance". Walt Disney cartoon characters. Multicoloured.

1175	10l. Type **219a**	80	80
1176	10l. Clarabelle	80	80
1177	10l. Goofy	80	80
1178	10l. Scrooge McDuck and Grandma Duck	80	80
1179	10l. Donald Duck	80	80
1180	10l. Daisy Duck	80	80
1181	10l. Minnie Mouse	80	80
1182	10l. Mickey Mouse	80	80
MS1183	Two sheets, each 127×102 mm. (a) 70l. Mickey Mouse dancing the Charleston. (b) 70l. Mickey Mouse jiving Set of 2 sheets	6·50	6·50

Nos. 1175/82 were printed together, se-tenant, forming a composite design.

220 "Adoration of the Magi" (detail)

1988. Christmas. Religious Paintings by Rubens. Multicoloured.

1184	3l. Type **220**	25	15
1185	3l.60 "Adoration of the Shepherds" (detail)	25	15
1186	5l. "Adoration of the Magi" (detail)	40	25
1187	10l. "Adoration of the Shepherds" (different detail)	60	40
1188	20l. "Virgin and Child surrounded by Flowers"	1·00	75
1189	40l. "St. Gregory the Great and Other Saints" (detail)	1·75	1·75
1190	60l. "Adoration of the Magi" (detail)	2·25	2·75
1191	80l. "Madonna and Child with Saints" (detail)	2·75	3·25
MS1192	Two sheets, each 76×113 mm. (a) 100l. "Virgin and Child enthroned with Saints". (b) 100l. "St. Gregory the Great and Other Saints" Set of 2 sheets	6·00	9·00

1989. Steffi Graf's "Grand Slam" Tennis Victories. No. MS1076b optd GOLD MEDALIST (No. MS1193e) or (others), each with different inscription on sheet margin, all in gold.

MS1193	105×75 mm. 100l. Steffi Graf. (a) Optd **AUSTRALIAN OPEN JANUARY 11–24, 1988 GRAFv EVERET**. (b) Optd **FRENCH OPEN MAY 23–JUNE 5, 1988 GRAFv ZVERENA**. (c) Optd **WIMBLEDON JUNE 20–JULY 4, 1988 GRAFv NAVRATILOVA**. (d) Optd **U.S. OPEN AUGUST 29–SEPTEMBER 11, 1988 GRAFv SABATINI**. (e) Optd **SEOUL OLYMPICS 1988 GRAFv SABBATINI** Set of 5 sheets	17·00	15·00

Each marginal overprint includes score of match involved.

No. **MS**1193a overprinted "EVERET" in error for "EVERT".

222 Brazil v. Sweden, 1958

1989. World Cup Football Championship, Italy (1st issue). Designs showing action from previous World Cup finals. Multicoloured.

1194	3l. Type **222**	40	30
1195	6l. West Germany v. Hungary, 1954	50	40
1196	8l. England v. West Germany, 1966	60	45
1197	10l. Argentina v. Netherlands, 1978	70	50
1198	12l. Brazil v. Czechoslovakia, 1962	75	75
1199	20l. West Germany v. Netherlands, 1974	1·00	1·00
1200	30l. Italy v. West Germany, 1982	1·40	1·60
1201	40l. Brazil v. Italy, 1970	1·75	1·90
MS1202	Two sheets, each 73×104 mm. (a) 100l. Argentina v. West Germany, 1986. (b) 100l. Uruguay v. Brazil, 1950 Set of 2 sheets	6·75	6·75

See also Nos. 1455/74.

223 Decathlon (Gold, C. Schenk, East Germany)

1989. Olympic Medal Winners, Seoul (1988). Mult.

1203	3l. Type **223**	70	30
1204	6l. Men's heavyweight judo (Gold, H. Saito, Japan)	1·00	40
1205	10l. Women's cycle road race (Silver, J. Niehaus, West Germany)	3·00	75
1206	15l. Men's single sculls (Gold, T. Lange, East Germany)	1·50	80
1207	20l. Men's 50 metres freestyle swimming (Gold, M. Biondi, U.S.A.)	1·50	1·00
1208	30l. Men's 100 m (Gold, C. Lewis, U.S.A.)	1·50	1·50
1209	40l. Dressage (Gold, West Germany)	2·75	2·00
1210	50l. Greco-Roman wrestling (57 kg) (Gold, A. Sike, Hungary)	2·50	2·75
MS1211	Two sheets, each 70×100 mm. (a) 100l. Olympic gold medal. (b) 100l. Olympic torch and rings Set of 2 sheets	6·75	6·75

224 Map of Union States, Mail Lorry and Post Office

1989. 15th Anniv of Mano River Union. Mult.

1212	1l. Type **224**	1·00	65
1213	3l. Map of West Africa and Presidents Momoh, Conte and Doe	1·25	40
1214	10l. Construction of Freetown–Monrovia Highway	1·75	1·00
MS1215	96×68 mm. 15l. Presidents signing anniversary metting communique	1·00	1·00

225 "Richard III"

1989. 425th Birth Anniv of Shakespeare. Mult.

1216	15l. Type **225**	60	60
1217	15l. "Othello" (Iago)	60	60
1218	15l. "Two Gentlemen of Verona"	60	60
1219	15l. "Macbeth" (Lady Macbeth)	60	60
1220	15l. "Hamlet"	60	60
1221	15l. "The Taming of the Shrew"	60	60
1222	15l. "The Merry Wives of Windsor"	60	60
1223	15l. "Henry IV" (Sir John Falstaff)	60	60
1224	15l. "Macbeth" (The Witches)	60	60
1225	15l. "Romeo and Juliet"	60	60
1226	15l. "Merchant of Venice"	60	60
1227	15l. "As You Like It"	60	60
1228	15l. "The Taming of the Shrew" (banquet scene)	60	60
1229	15l. "King Lear"	60	60
1230	15l. "Othello" (Othello and Desdemona)	60	60
1231	15l. "Henry IV" (Justice Shallow)	60	60
MS1232	Two sheets, each 117×82 mm. (a) 100l. Shakespeare and arms (49×36 mm). (b) 100l. Shakespeare (49×36 mm) Set of 2 sheets	8·00	8·50

226 Centenary Logo

1989. Cent of Ahmadiyya Muslim Society.

1233	**226** 3l. black and blue	30	30

1989. Japanese Art (1st series). Paintings by Seiho. As T 188a of St. Vincent. Multicoloured.

1234	3l. "Lapping Waves"	60	35
1235	6l. "Hazy Moon" (vert)	70	45
1236	8l. "Passing Spring" (vert)	70	45
1237	10l. "Mackerels"	70	45
1238	12l. "Calico Cat"	70	45
1239	30l. "The First Time to be a Model" (vert)	2·00	80
1240	40l. "Kingly Lion"	2·25	1·10
1241	75l. "After a Shower" (vert)	2·75	2·00
MS1242	Two sheets, each 102×77 mm. (a) 150l. "Dozing in the midst of all the Chirping" (Detail) (vert). (b) 150l. "Domesticated Monkeys and Rabbits" (detail) Set of 2 sheets	8·50	8·50

See also Nos. 1321/50.

227 Robespierre and Bastille

1989. "Philexfrance '89" International Stamp Exhibition, Paris and Bicentenary of French Revolution. Multicoloured.

1243	6l. Type **227**	45	35
1244	20l. Danton and Louvre	90	80
1245	45l. Queen Marie Antoinette and Notre Dame	1·40	1·25
1246	80l. Louis XVI and Palace of Versailles	2·00	2·75
MS1247	77×107 mm. 150l. Celebrating crowd, Paris (vert)	3·25	4·00

228 Sputnik Satellite in Orbit, 1957

1989. History of Space Exploration. As T 228. Multicoloured.

1248–1301	10l.×27, 15l.×27 Set of 54	22·00	23·00
MS1302	Three sheets, each 112×90 mm. 100l.×3 Set of 3 sheets	12·00	13·00

229 "Bulbophyllum barbigerum"

1989. Orchids of Sierra Leone. Multicoloured.

1303	3l. Type **229**	55	40
1304	6l. "Bulbophyllum falcatum"	85	60
1305	12l. "Habenaria macrara"	1·25	90
1306	20l. "Eurychone rothchildiana"	1·60	1·40
1307	50l. "Calyptrochilum christyanum"	2·25	2·25
1308	60l. "Bulbophyllum distans"	2·50	2·75
1309	70l. "Eulophia guineensis"	2·50	2·75
1310	80l. "Diaphananthe pellucida"	2·75	3·25
MS1311	Two sheets, each 112×80 mm. (a) 100l. "Cyrtorchis arcuata" and Pagoda, Kew Gardens. (b) 100l. "Eulophia cucullata" Set of 2 sheets	17·00	17·00

230 "Salamis temora"

1989. Butterflies. Multicoloured.

1312	6l. Type **230**	85	75
1313	12l. "Pseudacraea lucretia"	1·25	1·10
1314	18l. "Charaxes boueti" (vert)	1·60	1·40
1315	30l. "Graphium antheus" (vert)	2·25	2·00
1316	40l. "Colotis protomedia"	2·50	2·25
1317	60l. "Asterope pechueli" (vert)	3·00	2·75
1318	72l. "Coenyra aurantiaca"	3·25	3·00
1319	80l. "Precis octavia" (vert)	3·25	3·00
MS1320	Two sheets, each 100×70 mm. (a) 100l. "Charaxes cithaeron" (vert). (b) 100l. "Euphaedra themis" Set of 2 sheets	14·00	14·00

1989. Japanese Art (2nd series). Paintings by Hiroshige of "The Fifty-three Stations on the Tokaido Road". As T 188a of St. Vincent. Mult.

1321	25l. "Ferry-boat to Kawasaki"	1·00	1·00
1322	25l. "The Hilly Town of Hodogaya"	1·00	1·00
1323	25l. "Lute Players at Fujisawa"	1·00	1·00
1324	25l. "Mild Rainstorm at Oiso"	1·00	1·00
1325	25l. "Lake Ashi and Mountains of Hakone"	1·00	1·00
1326	25l. "Twilight at Numazu"	1·00	1·00
1327	25l. "Mount Fuji from Hara"	1·00	1·00
1328	25l. "Samurai Children riding through Yoshiwara"	1·00	1·00
1329	25l. "Mountain Pass at Yui"	1·00	1·00
1330	25l. "Harbour at Ejiri"	1·00	1·00
1331	25l. "Halt at Fujieda"	1·00	1·00
1332	25l. "Misty Kanaya on the Oi River"	1·00	1·00
1333	25l. "The Bridge to Kakegawa"	1·00	1·00
1334	25l. "Teahouse at Fukuroi"	1·00	1·00
1335	25l. "The Ford at Mistuke"	1·00	1·00
1336	25l. "Coolies warming themselves at Hamamatsu"	1·00	1·00
1337	25l. "Imakiri Ford at Maisaka"	1·00	1·00
1338	25l. "Pacific Ocean from Shirasuka"	1·00	1·00
1339	25l. "Futakawa Street-singers"	1·00	1·00
1340	25l. "Repairing Yoshida Castle"	1·00	1·00
1341	25l. "The Inn at Akasaka"	1·00	1·00
1342	25l. "The Bridge to Okazaki"	1·00	1·00
1343	25l. "Samurai's Wife entering Narumi"	1·00	1·00
1344	25l. "Harbour at Kuwana"	1·00	1·00
1345	25l. "Autumn in Ishiyakushi"	1·00	1·00
1346	25l. "Snowfall at Kameyama"	1·00	1·00
1347	25l. "The Frontier-station of Seki"	1·00	1·00
1348	25l. "Teahouse at Sakanoshita"	1·00	1·00
1349	25l. "Kansai Houses at Minakushi"	1·00	1·00
1350	25l. "Kusatsu Station"	1·00	1·00
MS1351	Two sheets, each 102×75 mm. (a) 120l. "Nihom Bridge, Edo". (b) 120l. "Sanjo Bridge, Kyoto" Set of 2 sheets	8·00	8·50

The English captions of the two miniature sheets of No. **MS**1351 are transposed. The sheet showing the Nihom Bridge, Edo, has a group of fishmongers in the left foreground.

231 Formosan Sika Deer

1989. "World Stamp Expo '89" International Stamp Exhibition, Washington (2nd issue). Endangered Fauna. Multicoloured.

1353	6l. Humpback whale	50	40
1354	9l. Type **231**	40	40
1355	16l. Spanish lynx	65	60
1356	20l. Goitred gazelle	60	60
1357	30l. Japanese sea lion	65	65
1358	50l. Long-eared owl	1·50	1·25
1359	70l. Lady Amherst's ("Chinese Copper") pheasant	1·50	1·50
1360	100l. Siberian tiger	2·25	2·50
MS1361	Two sheets, each 103×75 mm. (a) 150l. Mauritius kestrel (vert). (b) 150l. Japanese crested ibis (vert) Set of 2 sheets	12·00	13·00

231a Mickey Mouse and Goofy in Rolls-Royce "Phantom II Roadstar", 1934

1989. Christmas. Walt Disney cartoon characters with cars. Multicoloured.

1362	3l. Type **231a**	55	30
1363	6l. Mickey and Minnie Mouse in Mercedes-Benz "500K", 1935	70	40
1364	10l. Mickey and Minnie Mouse with Jaguar "SS-100", 1938	80	45
1365	12l. Mickey Mouse and Goofy with U.S. army jeep, 1941	90	55
1366	20l. Mickey and Minnie Mouse with Buick Roadmaster Sedan "Model 91", 1937	1·25	90
1367	30l. Mickey Mouse driving 1948 Tucker	1·50	1·25
1368	40l. Mickey and Minnie Mouse in Alfa Romeo, 1933	1·60	1·40
1369	50l. Mickey and Minnie Mouse with 1937 Cord	1·75	1·60
MS1370	Two sheets, each 127×101 mm. (a) 100l. Mickey in Fiat Topolino, 1938. (b) 100l. Mickey Mouse with gifts and Pontiac "Model 401", 1931 Set of 2 sheets	6·50	7·00

1989. Christmas. Paintings by Rembrandt. As T 204a of St. Vincent. Multicoloured.

1371	3l. "The Adoration of the Magi"	50	30
1372	6l. "The Holy Family with a Cat"	60	40
1373	10l. "The Holy Family with Angels"	70	45
1374	15l. "Simeon in the Temple"	85	55
1375	30l. "The Circumcision"	1·50	1·10
1376	90l. "The Holy Family"	3·00	3·25
1377	100l. "The Visitation"	3·00	3·25
1378	120l. "The Flight into Egypt"	3·25	3·50
MS1379	Two sheets, each 70×95 mm. (a) 150l. "The Adoration of the Shepherds" (detail). (b) 150l. "The Presentation of Jesus in the Temple" (detail) Set of 2 sheets	8·50	8·50

232 Johann Kepler (astronomer)

1990. Exploration of Mars. Designs as T 232 showing astronomers, spacecraft and Martian landscapes.

1380–1415	175l.×36 multicoloured Set of 36	65·00	75·00
MS1416	Two sheets, each 105×85 mm. (a) 150l. The "Face" on Mars. (b) 150l. Section of space station Set of 2 sheets	11·00	12·00

1990. 50th Anniv of Second World War. American Aircraft. As T 206a of St. Vincent. Multicoloured.

1417	1l. Dolittle's North American B-25 Mitchell "Ruptured Duck", 1942	30	30
1418	2l. Consolidated B-24 Liberator	40	30
1419	3l. Douglas A20J Boston attacking Japanese convoy, Bismark Sea, 1943	40	30
1420	9l. Lockheed P-38 Lightning	60	35
1421	12l. Martin B-26 Marauder	75	40
1422	16l. Boeing B-17F Flying Fortress bombers	85	55
1423	50l. North American B-25D Mitchell bomber	2·50	1·75
1424	80l. Boeing B-29 Superfortress	2·75	2·75
1425	90l. Boeing B-17G Flying Fortress bomber	2·75	3·00
1426	100l. Boeing B-29 Superfortress "Enola Gay"	3·00	3·00
MS1427	Two sheets, each 106×77 mm. (a) 150l. North American B-25 Mitchell "Ruptured Duck" taking off from U.S.S. "Hornet" 1942. (b) 150l. Boeing B-17G Flying Fortress of 447th Bomber Group Set of 2 sheets	7·50	8·00

233 Mickey Mouse at Bauxite Mine

1990. Sierra Leone Sites and Scenes. Walt Disney cartoon characters. Multicoloured.

1428	3l. Type **233**	30	15
1429	6l. Scrooge McDuck panning for gold	30	15
1430	10l. Minnie Mouse at Lungi Airport	40	20
1431	12l. Mickey Mouse at Old Fourah Bay College	40	20
1432	16l. Mickey Mouse mining bauxite	60	25
1433	20l. Huey, Dewey and Louie harvesting rice	60	30
1434	30l. Mickey and Minnie Mouse admire the Freetown Cotton Tree	70	40
1435	100l. Mickey Mouse flying over Rutile Mine	3·00	3·25
1436	200l. Mickey Mouse fishing at Goderich	3·75	4·25
1437	225l. Mickey and Minnie Mouse at Bintumani Hotel	3·75	4·25
MS1438	Two sheets, each 130×100 mm. (a) 250l. Dwarfs with diamonds. (b) 250l. Mickey and Minnie Mouse at King Jimmy Market (vert) Set of 2 sheets	9·00	9·50

234 Olivier as Antony in "Antony and Cleopatra", 1951

1990. Sir Laurence Olivier (actor) Commem. Multicoloured.

1439	3l. Type **234**	55	20
1440	9l. As King Henry V in "Henry V", 1943	65	30
1441	16l. As Oedipus in "Oedipus", 1945	80	35
1442	20l. As Heathcliffe in "Wuthering Heights", 1939	85	40

1443	30l. As Szell in "Marathon Man", 1976	1·00	55
1444	70l. As Othello in "Othello", 1964	2·25	1·40
1445	175l. As Michael in "Beau Geste", 1929	3·00	3·00
1446	200l. As King Richard III in "Richard III", 1956	3·25	3·25
MS1447	Two sheets, each 98×68 mm. (a) 250l. As Hamlet in "Hamlet", 1947. (b) 250l. As Sir Hugh Dowding in "The Battle of Britain", 1969 Set of 2 sheets	9·50	9·50

235 Penny Black

1990. 150th Anniv of the Penny Black.

1448	**235**	50l. blue	2·25	1·50
1449	**235**	100l. brown	3·00	2·75
MS1450		145×106 mm. **235** 250l. black	4·00	4·50

236 Cameroons World Cup Team

1990. World Cup Football Championship, Italy (2nd issue). Finalists. Multicoloured.

1451-1474	15l.×8 (Type **236**, Colombia, Costa Rica, Egypt, Rumania, South Korea, U.A.E., Yugoslavia) 30l.×8 (Austria, Belgium, Czechoslovakia, Netherlands, Scotland, Sweden, Uruguay, U.S.S.R.) 45l.×8 (Argentina, Brazil, England, Ireland, Italy, Spain, U.S.A., West Germany) Set of 24	14·00	15·00

No. 1452 is inscr "COLUMBIA" and No. 1465 "URAGUAY", both in error.

237 Great Crested Grebe

1990. Birds. Multicoloured.

1475	3l. Type **237**	20	20
1476	6l. Green wood hoopoe	25	25
1477	10l. African jacana	30	30
1478	12l. Pied avocet ("Avocet")	35	35
1479	20l. Peter's finfoot	40	40
1480	80l. Glossy ibis	1·25	1·50
1481	150l. Hammerkop	1·75	2·00
1482	200l. Black-throated honey-guide	2·00	2·50
MS1483	Two sheets, each 100×70 mm. (a) 250l. African palm swift. (b) 250l. Painted snipe Set of 2 sheets	7·00	8·00

1990. "Stamp World London '90" International Stamp Exhibition. British Costumes. As T 207a of St. Vincent showing Walt Disney cartoon characters. Multicoloured.

1484	3l. Mickey Mouse as a Yeoman Warder	20	15
1485	6l. Scrooge McDuck as a lamplighter	20	15
1486	12l. Goofy as a medieval knight	30	20
1487	15l. Clarabelle as Ann Boleyn	30	20
1488	75l. Minnie Mouse as Queen Elizabeth I	2·50	2·00
1489	100l. Donald Duck as a chimney sweep	2·75	2·25
1490	125l. Pete as King Henry VIII	3·00	2·50
1491	150l. Clarabell, Minnie Mouse and Daisy Duck as May dancers	3·00	2·50
MS1492	Two sheets, each 127×102 mm. (a) 250l. Donald Duck as a lawyer (vert). (b) 250l. Minnie Mouse as Queen Boadicea Set of 2 sheets	7·50	8·50

1990. 90th Birthday of Queen Elizabeth the Queen Mother. As T 208a of St. Vincent. Mult.

1493	75l. Queen Mother on Remembrance Sunday	1·75	1·25
1494	75l. Queen Mother in yellow hat	1·75	1·25
1495	75l. Waving to crowds on 85th birthday	1·75	1·25
MS1496	90×75 mm. 250l. As No. 1495	3·50	3·50

238 Golden Cat

1990. Wildlife. Multicoloured.

1497	25l. Type **238**	75	75
1498	25l. White-backed night heron	75	75
1499	25l. Bateleur ("Bateleur Eagle")	75	75
1500	25l. Marabou stork	75	75
1501	25l. White-faced whistling duck	75	75
1502	25l. Aardvark	75	75
1503	25l. Royal antelope	75	75
1504	25l. Pygmy hippopotamus	75	75
1505	25l. Leopard	75	75
1506	25l. Sacred ibis	75	75
1507	25l. Mona monkey	75	75
1508	25l. African darter	75	75
1509	25l. Chimpanzee	75	75
1510	25l. African elephant	75	75
1511	25l. Potto	75	75
1512	25l. African manatee	75	75
1513	25l. African fish eagle	75	75
1514	25l. African spoonbill	75	75
MS1515	106×76 mm. 150l. Crowned eagle (vert)	7·00	7·50

239 Rabbit

1990. Fairground Carousel Animals. Mult.

1516	5l. Type **239**	15	15
1517	10l. Horse with panther saddle	20	20
1518	20l. Ostrich	30	30
1519	30l. Zebra	40	40
1520	50l. Horse	55	55
1521	80l. Sea monster	80	80
1522	100l. Giraffe	1·00	1·00
1523	150l. Armoured horse	1·40	1·40
1524	200l. Camel	1·75	1·75
MS1525	Two sheets (a) 98×68 mm. 300l. Masked horse. (b) 68×98 mm. 300l. Baden-Powell as Centaur Set fo 2 sheets	8·50	9·50

239a Start of Men's 100 m

1990. Olympic Games, Barcelona (1992). Mult.

1526	5l. Type **239a**	20	15
1527	10l. Men's 4×400 m relay	25	20
1528	20l. Men's 100 m in progress	40	30
1529	30l. Weightlifting	50	40
1530	40l. Freestyle wrestling	55	45
1531	80l. Water polo	80	90
1532	150l. Women's gymnastics	1·40	1·75
1533	200l. Cycling	3·75	3·00
MS1534	Two sheets, each 103×75 mm. (a) 400l. Boxing (horiz). (b) 400l. Olympic flag (horiz) Set of 2 sheets	8·00	9·00

240 Morty assembling Bicycle by Christmas Tree

1990. Christmas. "The Night before Christmas". As T 240 showing Walt Disney cartoon characters in scenes from Clement Moore's poem. Multicoloured.

1535-1558	50l.×8, 75l.×8, 100l.×8 Set of 24	20·00	22·00
MS1559	Six sheets, each 129×107 mm. 400l.×6 multicoloured Set of 6 sheets	20·00	22·00

Of the stamps in No. **MS**1559 four are horizontal and two vertical.

241 "Holy Family with St. Elizabeth" (Mantegna)

1990. Christmas. Paintings. Multicoloured.

1560	10l. "Holy Family resting" (Rembrandt)	40	15
1561	20l. Type **241**	55	20
1562	30l. "Virgin and Child with an Angel" (Correggio)	70	30
1563	50l. "Annunciation" (Bernardo Strozzi)	85	45
1564	100l. "Madonna and Child appearing to St. Anthony" (Lippi)	2·00	80
1565	175l. "Virgin and Child" (Giovanni Boltraffio)	3·00	3·25
1566	200l. "Esterhazy Madonna" (Raphael)	3·25	3·25
1567	300l. "Coronation of Mary" (Andrea Orcagna)	3·75	4·25
MS1568	Two sheets, each 75×114 mm. (a) 400l. "Adoration of the Shepherds" (Bronzino). (b) 400l. "Adoration of the Shepherds" (Gerard David) Set of 2 sheets	9·00	9·50

241a Helena Fourment as "Hagar in the Wilderness" (detail)

1990. 350th Death Anniv of Rubens (1st issue). Multicoloured.

1569	5l. Type **241a**	15	10
1570	10l. "Isabella Brant"	20	15
1571	20l. "Countess of Arundel and her Party" (detail)	30	20
1572	60l. "Countess of Arundel and her Party" (different detail)	70	70
1573	80l. "Nicolaas Rockox"	90	90
1574	100l. "Adriana Perez"	1·00	1·00
1575	150l. "George Villiers, Duke of Buckingham" (detail)	1·75	2·00
1576	300l. "Countess of Buckingham"	2·50	2·75
MS1577	Two sheets, each 71×100 mm. (a) 350l. "Giovanni Carlo Dorio" (detail). (b) 350l. "Veronica Spinola Dorio" (detail) Set of 2 sheets	8·00	8·50

See also Nos. 1595/602.

242 "Chlorophyllum molybdites"

1990. Fungi. Multicoloured.

1578	3l. Type **242**	30	15
1579	5l. "Lepista nuda"	30	15
1580	10l. "Clitocybe nebularis"	40	20
1581	15l. "Cyathus striatus"	50	30
1582	20l. "Bolbitius vitellinus"	55	35
1583	25l. "Leucoagaricus naucinus"	55	40
1584	30l. "Suillus luteus"	60	45
1585	40l. "Podaxis pistillaris"	70	55
1586	50l. "Oudemansiella radicata"	80	60
1587	60l. "Phallus indusiatus"	90	70
1588	80l. "Macrolepiota rhacodes"	1·00	1·10
1589	100l. "Mycena pura"	1·25	1·25
1590	150l. "Volvariella volvacea"	1·60	1·75
1591	175l. "Omphalotus olearius"	1·90	2·25
1592	200l. "Sphaerobolus stellatus"	2·00	2·50
1593	250l. "Schizophyllum commune"	2·25	2·75
MS1594	Four sheets, each 101×70 mm. (a) 350l. "Hypholoma fasciculare" (b) 350l. "Psilocybe coprophila" (c) 350l. "Agaricus campestris" (d) 350l. "Suillus granulatus" Set of 4 sheets	15·00	15·00

243 "The Flight of St. Barbara" (detail) (Rubens)

1991. Easter. 350th Death Anniv (1990) of Rubens (2nd issue). Multicoloured.

1595	10l. Type **243**	55	15
1596	20l. "The Last Judgement" (detail)	75	20
1597	30l. "St. Gregory of Nazianzus"	85	30
1598	50l. "Doubting Thomas"	1·25	45
1599	80l. "The Way to Calvary" (detail)	2·00	1·10
1600	100l. "St. Gregory with Sts. Domitilla, Maurus and Papianus"	2·25	1·25
1601	175l. "Sts. Gregory, Maurus and Papianus"	3·50	3·75
1602	300l. "Christ and the Penitent Sinners"	5·00	6·50
MS1603	Two sheets, each 70×101 mm. (a) 400l. "The Last Judgement" (different detail). (b) 400l. "The Way to Calvary" (different detail) Set of 2 sheets	8·50	9·00

244 Krauss Class 1400 Steam Locomotive, 1895

1991. "Phila Nippon '91" International Stamp Exhibition, Tokyo. Japanese Trains. Mult.

1604	10l. Type **244**	35	20
1605	20l. Class C55 streamline steam locomotive, 1935	50	25
1606	30l. Class ED17 electric locomotive, 1931	70	40
1607	60l. Class EF13 electric locomotive, 1944	1·00	85
1608	100l. Baldwin Mikado steam locomotive, 1897	1·25	1·25
1609	150l. Class C62 steam locomotive, 1948	1·75	2·00
1610	200l. Class Kiha 81 diesel multiple unit, 1960	2·00	2·25
1611	300l. Schenectady Class 8550 steam locomotive, 1899	2·25	2·75

MS1612 Four sheets, each 106×76 mm. (a) 400l. Class 9600 steam locomotive, 1913. (b) 400l. Class D51 steam locomotive, 1936. (c) 400l. Class 7000 electric multiple unit. (d) 400l. "Hikari" express train Set of 4 sheets 15·00 15·00

245 Turquoise Killifish

1991. Fishes. Multicoloured.

1613	10l. Type **245**	45	20
1614	20l. Red-chinned panchax	65	25
1615	30l. Peters' killifish	80	40
1616	60l. Micro-walkeri killifish	1·40	90
1617	100l. Freshwater butterflyfish	1·60	1·25
1618	150l. Green panchax	2·00	2·25
1619	200l. Six-banded lyretail	2·25	2·50
1620	300l. Nile pufferfish	2·25	2·50
MS1621	Two sheets, each 96×70 mm. (a) 400l. Spot-finned squeaker. (b) 400l. Two-striped panchax Set of 2 sheets	8·50	8·50

1991. Death Centenary of Vincent van Gogh (artist). As T 215a of St. Vincent. Multicoloured.

1622	10c. "The Langlois Bridge at Arles" (horiz)	10	30
1623	50c. "Tree in Garden at Saint-Paul Hospital"	10	30
1624	1l. "Wild Flowers and Thistles in a Vase"	10	30
1625	2l. "Still Life: Vase with Oleanders and Books" (horiz)	15	30
1626	5l. "Farmhouses in a Wheatfield near Arles" (horiz)	20	20
1627	10l. "Self-portrait, September 1889"	30	15
1628	20l. "Patience Escalier"	55	20
1629	30l. "Doctor Felix Rey"	70	30
1630	50l. "The Iris"	1·00	45
1631	60l. "The Shepherdess"	1·25	65
1632	80l. "Vincent's House in Arles" (horiz)	1·60	1·00
1633	100l. "The Road Menders" (horiz)	1·75	1·10
1634	150l. "The Garden of Saint-Paul Hospital"	3·00	3·25
1635	200l. "View of the Church, Saint-Paul-de-Mausole" (horiz)	3·25	3·50
1636	250l. "Seascape at Saintes-Maries" (horiz)	3·50	3·75
1637	300l. "Pieta"	3·50	3·75
MS1638	Six sheets. (a) 102×76 mm. 400l. "Haystacks in Provence" (96×70 mm). (b) 102×76 mm. 400l. "The Trinquetaille Bridge" (96×70 mm). (c) 102×76 mm. 400l. "Vineyards with a View of Auvers" (96×70 mm). (d) 102×76 mm. 400l. "The Garden of Saint-Paul Hospital" (96×107 mm). (e) 76×102 mm. 400l. "Church at Auvers-sur-Dise" (70×96 mm). (f) 76×102 mm. 400l. "Two Poplars on a Road through the Hills" (70×96 mm). Imperf Set of 6 sheets	17·00	17·00

1991. 65th Birthday of Queen Elizabeth II. As T 220b of St. Vincent. Multicoloured.

1639	10l. The Queen and Prince Charles at polo match	25	10
1640	30l. The Queen at Windsor, 1989	35	20
1641	200l. The Queen and Princess Diana in Nigeria, 1989	2·00	2·00
1642	250l. The Queen and Prince Philip	2·25	2·25
MS1643	68×90 mm. 400l. Separate photographs of the Queen and Prince Philip in 1987 and 1988	4·25	3·75

1991. 10th Wedding Anniv of Prince and Princess of Wales. As T 220b of St. Vincent. Mult.

1644	20l. Prince and Princess of Wales in August, 1987	90	15
1645	80l. Separate photographs of Prince, Princess and sons	2·25	85
1646	100l. Prince Henry in Majorca and Prince William on his first day at school	2·00	95
1647	300l. Prince Charles at Caister, April, 1988 and Princess Diana in Hyde Park, May, 1989	4·50	4·00
MS1648	68×90 mm. 400l. Prince, Princess and Prince Henry in Majorca and Prince William going to school	5·00	4·50

246 "Graphium latreillianus" and "Ancistrochilus rothschildianus"

1991. Butterflies and Flowers. Multicoloured.

1649	10l. Type **246**	75	30
1650	30l. "Euphraedra eleus" and "Clitoria ternatea"	1·25	45
1651	50l. "Graphium antheus" and "Gloriosa simplex"	1·50	60
1652	60l. "Salamis cacta" and "Stenandriopsis guineensis"	1·75	85
1653	80l. "Kallima rumia" and "Cassia fistula"	2·25	1·25
1654	100l. "Hypolimnas salmacis" and "Amorphophallus abyssinicus"	2·25	1·50
1655	200l. "Danaus formosa" and "Nephthytis afzelii"	3·75	3·75
1656	300l. "Graphium leonidas" and "Clappertonia ficifolia"	4·50	5·50
MS1657	Four sheets, each 102×74 mm. (a) 400l. "Charaxes cynthia" and "Plumbago auriculata" (b) 400l. "Colias electo" and "Combretum grandiflorum" (c) 400l. "Cynandra opis" and "Bombax costatum" (d) 400l. "Eurema brigitta" and "Monodora myristica" Set of 4 sheets	14·00	14·00

1991. Butterflies. As Nos. 1028/42 but "Sierra Leone" in blue. Multicoloured.

1658	10c. "Danaus limniace"	7·50	75
1660	50c. "Graphium ridleyanus"	7·50	60
1661	1l. "Papilio bromius"	7·50	60
1662	2l. "Iterus ("Papilio") zalmoxis"	7·50	60
1663	5l. "Graphium tynderaeus"	24·00	80
1665	10l. "Graphium policenes"	7·50	50
1666	20l. "Tanuetheira ("Iolaus") timon"	24·00	70
1667	30l. "Cymothoe sangaris"	24·00	70
1668	50l. Type **205**	7·50	55
1669	60l. "Charaxes lucretius"	7·50	70
1670	80l. "Stugeta ("Iolaus") marmorea"	14·00	1·00
1671	100l. "Abisara talantus"	24·00	1·00
1672	300l. "Papilio hesperus"	14·00	2·75

247 Audie Murphy in "To Hell and Back"

1991. Films of Second World War. Mult.

1675	2l. Type **247**	15	10
1676	5l. Jack Palance in "Attack"	20	15
1677	10l. Greer Garson and Walter Pidgeon in "Mrs. Miniver"	20	20
1678	20l. Heavy artillery from "The Guns of Navarone"	40	30
1679	30l. Charlie Chaplin and Paulette Goddard in "The Great Dictator"	75	40
1680	50l. Steam locomotive from "The Train"	80	60
1681	60l. Diary and fountain pen from "The Diary of Anne Frank"	90	70
1682	80l. William Holden in "The Bridge on the River Kwai"	1·25	90
1683	100l. Tallulah Bankhead in "Lifeboat" and Alfred Hitchcock (director)	1·25	1·00
1684	200l. John Wayne in "Sands of Iwo Jima"	2·25	2·25
1685	300l. Van Johnson and Spencer Tracy in "Thirty Seconds over Tokyo"	3·00	3·25
1686	350l. Humphrey Bogart and Ingrid Bergman in "Casablanca"	3·25	3·50
MS1687	Three sheets, each 116×76 mm. (a) 450l. George C. Scott in "Patton". (b) 450l. Gregory Peck in "Twelve O'clock High". (c) 450l. Burning American cruiser from "Tora! Tora! Tora!" Set of 3 sheets	11·00	11·00

248 Meissen China Parrot Ornament, Munich Botanic Garden

1991. Botanical Gardens of the World. Multicoloured.

1688-1735	60l.×48 Type **248** Set of 48	24·00	25·00
MS1736	Three sheets, each 97×69 mm. (a) 600l. Munich Botanic Garden. (b) 600l. Kyoto Botanic Garden. (c) 600l. Brooklyn Botanic Garden Set of 3 sheets	13·00	15·00

Issued in 3 sheetlets of 16 stamps, depicting features and plants from Munich (Nos. 1688/1703), Kyoto (Nos. 1704/19) and Brooklyn (Nos. 1720/35).

The single designs in the three miniature sheets of No. **MS**1736 are horiz.

248a "Mary being Crowned by Two Angels"

1991. Christmas. Drawings and Paintings by Albrecht Durer.

1737	**248a**	6l. black and mauve	15	10
1738	-	60l. black and blue	35	30
1739	-	80l. multicoloured	45	40
1740	-	100l. multicoloured	65	65
1741	-	200l. multicoloured	1·60	1·60
1742	-	300l. multicoloured	2·00	2·00
1743	-	700l. multicoloured	4·75	5·00
MS1744		Two sheets, each 102×127 mm. (a) 600l. multicoloured. (b) 600l. multicoloured Set of 2 sheets	7·50	7·50

DESIGNS: 60l. "St. Christopher"; 80l. "Virgin and Child with St. Anne" (detail); 100l. "Virgin with the Pear" (detail); 200l. "Madonna and Child" (detail); 300l. "The Virgin in Half-Length" (detail); 700l. "The Madonna with the Siskin" (detail); 600l. (No. **MS**1744a) "Virgin and Child with St. Anne"; 600l. (No. **MS**1744b) "The Feast of the Rose Garlands" (detail).

249 National Theatre, Prague

1991. Anniversaries and Events. Multicoloured.

1745	50l. Type **249**	50	20
1746	100l. St. Peter's Abbey, Salzburg	70	35
1747	250l. Sea Scouts learning sailing	1·00	1·00
1748	300l. Sierra Leone scouts emblem and Lord Baden-Powell	1·00	1·00
1749	400l. Scouts playing baseball at Mt. Sorak Jamboree	1·40	1·60
1750	500l. Scene from "Idomeneo"	2·75	3·25
MS1751	Two sheets. (a) 75×105 mm. 600l. Bust of Mozart (vert). (b) 89×117 mm. 750l. 17th World Scout Jamboree emblem (vert) Set of 2 sheets	10·00	10·00

ANNIVERSARIES AND EVENTS: Nos. 1745/6, 1750, Death bicentenary of Mozart; 1747/9, 50th death anniv of Lord Baden-Powell and World Scout Jamboree, Korea.

250 Aichi D3A "Val" Dive Bomber

1991. 50th Anniv of Japanese Attack on Pearl Harbor. Multicoloured.

1752	75l. Type **250**	75	75
1753	75l. Japanese Aichi D3A "Val" dive bomber and smoke	75	75
1754	75l. Battleship Row burning	75	75
1755	75l. Planes and burning dockyard	75	75
1756	75l. Burning installations	75	75
1757	75l. Two Japanese Aichi D3A "Val" dive bombers	75	75
1758	75l. Burning ships and hangars	75	75
1759	75l. Airfield under attack	75	75
1760	75l. American Curtiss P-40C fighter	75	75
1761	75l. Japanese Mitsubishi A6M Zero-Sen fighter-bombers	75	75
1762	75l. Japanese Mitsubishi A6M Zero-Sen fighter-bombers over suburb	75	75
1763	75l. Japanese Nakajima B5N "Kate" bombers attacking ships	75	75
1764	75l. Japanese Nakajima B5N "Kate" aircraft on fire	75	75
1765	75l. Japanese Nakajima B5N "Kate" bombers over jungle	75	75
1766	75l. Mitsubishi A6M Zero-Sen fighters	75	75

1991. Christmas. Walt Disney Christmas Cards. As T 228 of St. Vincent. Multicoloured.

1767	12l. Mickey Mouse, Donald Duck and characters from "Peter Pan", 1952 (horiz)	35	10
1768	30l. Disney characters reading "Alice in Wonderland", 1950 (horiz)	45	10
1769	60l. Sleepy and animals, 1938 (horiz)	65	25
1770	75l. Mickey, Minnie, Donald and Pluto posting card, 1936 (horiz)	75	30
1771	100l. Disney cartoon characters, 1984 (horiz)	1·00	45
1772	125l. Mickey and Donald singing carols with Donald's nephews and Pluto reading, 1954 (horiz)	1·40	90
1773	150l. "101 Dalmatians", 1960 (horiz)	1·60	1·10
1774	200l. Mickey and Donald opening presents, 1948 (horiz)	2·00	1·40
1775	300l. Mickey, Minnie, Morte and Ferdie decorating tree, 1983 (horiz)	2·50	2·50
1776	400l. Donald decorating tree and nephews watching television, 1956 (horiz)	2·75	3·00
1777	500l. Characters from Disney films, 1972 (horiz)	2·75	3·00
1778	600l. Mickey, Donald, Pluto and friends singing, 1964 (horiz)	2·75	3·25
MS1779	Three sheets, each 128×102 mm. (a) 900l. Mad Hatter's tea party, 1950; (b) 900l. Disneyland, 1955. (c) 900l. Seven Dwarfs in toboggan, 1959 Set of 3 sheets	12·00	13·00

250a Minnie Mouse as Chiquita with Pluto, Cuba

1992. Mickey's World Tour. Walt Disney cartoon characters in different countries. Multicoloured.

1780	6l. Type **250a**	20	10
1781	10l. Goofy as Olympic discus champion, Greece	20	10
1782	20l. Donald and Daisy Duck as flamenco dancers, Spain	30	15
1783	30l. Goofy and Donald as guardsman, England	40	15
1784	50l. Mickey and Minnie at Paris fashion show, France	50	25
1785	100l. Goofy in the Alps, Switzerland	80	50
1786	200l. Daisy and Minnie in grass skirts, Hawaii	1·50	1·75
1787	350l. Mickey, Donald and Goofy as ancient Egyptians (horiz)	2·00	2·25
1788	500l. Daisy and Minnie as can-can dancers, France (horiz)	2·25	2·50
MS1789	Three sheets, each 83×105 mm. (a) 700l. Mickey playing bagpipes, Scotland. (b) 700l. Donald the gondolier, Italy. (c) 700l. Mickey and Goofy smashing plates, Greece Set of 3 sheets	12·00	13·00

1992. 40th Anniv of Queen Elizabeth II's Accession. As T 229a of St. Vincent. Mult.

1790	60l. State House	80	20
1791	100l. Beach	1·40	40
1792	300l. Parliament Building	3·00	2·50
1793	400l. Canoe on beach	3·00	3·00
MS1794	Two sheets, each 75×97 mm. (a) 700l. Jungle hillside. (b) 700l. Freetown Set of 2 sheets	12·00	13·00

250b "Visit of St. Thomas Aquinas to St. Bonaventure"

1992. "Granada '92" International Stamp Exhibition, Spain. Paintings by Francisco Zurbaran. Multicoloured.

1795	1l. Type **250b**	10	10
1796	10l. "St. Gregory"	15	10
1797	30l. "St. Andrew"	30	20
1798	50l. "St. Gabriel the Archangel"	40	30
1799	60l. "The Blessed Henry Suso"	40	30
1800	100l. "St. Lucy"	65	40
1801	300l. "St. Casilda"	1·75	1·25
1802	400l. "St. Margaret of Antioch"	2·00	1·75
1803	500l. "St. Apollonia"	3·25	2·25
1804	600l. "St. Bonaventure at Council of Lyons"	2·50	2·75
1805	700l. "St. Bonaventure on his Bier"	2·75	3·00
1806	800l. "The Martyrdom of St. James" (detail)	3·00	3·25

MS1807 Three sheets. (a) 95×112 mm. 900l. "The Martyrdom of St. James". (b) 95×112 mm. 900l. "The Young Virgin". (c) 112×95 mm. 900l. "St. Hugh in the Refectory". Imperf Set of 3 sheets 10·00 11·00

250c Rhamphorhynchus

1992. Prehistoric Animals. Multicoloured.

1808	50l. Type **250c**	60	60
1809	50l. Pteranodon	60	60
1810	50l. Dimorphodon	60	60
1811	50l. Pterodactyl	60	60
1812	50l. Archaeopteryx	60	60
1813	50l. Iguanodon	60	60
1814	50l. Hypsilophodon	60	60
1815	50l. Nothosaurus	60	60
1816	50l. Brachiosaurus	60	60
1817	50l. Kentrosaurus	60	60
1818	50l. Plesiosaurus	60	60
1819	50l. Trachodon	60	60
1820	50l. Hesperornis	60	60
1821	50l. Henodus	60	60
1822	50l. Steneosaurus	60	60
1823	50l. Stenopterygius	60	60
1824	50l. Eurhinosaurus	60	60
1825	50l. Placodus	60	60
1826	50l. Mosasaurus	60	60
1827	50l. Mixosaurus	60	60

MS1828 106×76 mm. No. 1820 1·75 2·00

Nos. 1808/27 were printed together, se-tenant, forming a composite design.

No. 1811 is inscribed "Pteradactyl" and No. 1826 "Mosasaurs", both in error.

251 Greater Flamingo

1992. Birds. Multicoloured.

1829	30l. Type **251**	60	50
1830	50l. African white-crested hornbill ("White-crested Hornbill")	75	50
1831	100l. Crested touraco ("Verreaux's Touraco")	1·40	65
1832	170l. Yellow-spotted barbet	2·00	1·25
1833	200l. African spoonbill	2·25	1·25
1834	250l. Saddle-bill stork	2·25	1·50
1835	300l. Red-faced lovebird ("Red Headed Lovebird")	2·50	2·50
1836	600l. Yellow-billed barbet	7·75	7·00

MS1837 Two sheets, each 72×101 mm. (a) 1000l. Fire-bellied woodpecker. (b) 1000l. Swallow-tailed bee eater Set of 2 sheets 11·00 11·00

251a Marathon

1992. Olympic Games, Albertville and Barcelona. Multicoloured.

1838	10l. Type **251a**	25	20
1839	20l. Men's parallel bars	30	25
1840	30l. Men's discus	30	25
1841	50l. Men's 110 m hurdles (horiz)	40	30
1842	60l. Women's long jump	40	30
1843	100l. Men's floor exercise (horiz)	55	45
1844	200l. Windsurfing	1·00	80
1845	250l. Women's biathlon	1·25	1·00
1846	300l. Cycle road race	4·50	2·75
1847	400l. Weightlifting	3·00	3·25
1848	500l. Men's speed skating	3·50	3·50
1849	600l. Men's downhill skiing (horiz)	4·50	5·00

MS1850 Three sheets, each 102×71 mm. (a) 900l. Football (horiz). (b) 900l. Men's single luge (horiz). (c) 900l. Pairs ice dancing Set of 3 sheets 14·00 15·00

252 Minnie Mouse and Chip decorating Christmas Tree

1992. Christmas. Walt Disney cartoon characters. Multicoloured.

1851	10l. Type **252**	25	10
1852	20l. Goofy as Father Christmas	35	10
1853	30l. Daisy Duck and Minnie decorating Christmas tree	35	10
1854	50l. Mickey Mouse, and Goofy lighting candle	50	20
1855	80l. Big Pete as Father Christmas	80	40
1856	100l. Donald Duck as Father Christmas	90	40
1857	150l. Morty and Ferdie decorating cake	1·75	1·25
1858	200l. Mickey and bauble	1·90	1·40
1859	300l. Goofy and toy Father Christmas	2·25	1·75
1860	500l. Chip and Dale with sledge	2·75	2·75
1861	600l. Donald and Dale with musical instruments	2·75	3·25
1862	800l. Huey, Dewey and Louie making patterns in snow	3·25	4·25

MS1863 Three sheets, each 128×102 mm. (a) 900l. Mickey as Father Christmas. (b) 900l. Chip and Christmas tree fairy (horiz). (c) 900l. Mickey and Minnie (horiz) Set of 3 sheets 14·00 15·00

253 Toy Pennsylvania Railroad GG-1 Electric Locomotive No. 6-18306, 1992

1992. "Genova '92" International Thematic Stamp Exhibition. Toy Trains. Designs showing electric locomotives and rolling stock manufactured by Lionel. Multicoloured.

1864	150l. Type **253**	1·25	1·25
1865	150l. Wabash Railroad Hudson locomotive No. 8610, 1985	1·25	1·25
1866	150l. Locomotive No. 1911, 1911	1·25	1·25
1867	150l. Chesapeake & Ohio locomotive No. 6-18627, 1992	1·25	1·25
1868	150l. Gang car No. 50, 1954	1·25	1·25
1869	150l. Rock Island & Peoria locomotive No. 8004, 1980	1·25	1·25
1870	150l. Western Maryland Railroad Shay locomotive No. 6-18023, 1992	1·25	1·25
1871	150l. Boston & Albany Railroad Hudson locomotive No. 784, 1986	1·25	1·25
1872	150l. Locomotive No. 6, 1906	1·25	1·25
1873	170l. Special F-3 diesel locomotive, 1947	1·25	1·25
1874	170l. Pennsylvania Railroad diesel switcher locomotive No, 6-18905, 1992	1·25	1·25
1875	170l. No. 1 Trolley, 1913	1·25	1·25
1876	170l. Seaboard Railroad diesel freight locomotive No. 602, 11008	1·25	1·25
1877	170l. Pennsylvania Railroad S-2 turbine locomotive, 1991	1·25	1·25
1878	170l. Western Pacific GP-9 diesel locomotive No. 6-18822, 1992	1·25	1·25
1879	170l. Locomotive No. 10, 1929	1·25	1·25
1880	170l. Locomotive No. 400E, 1931	1·25	1·25
1881	170l. Locomotive No. 384E, 1928	1·25	1·25
1882	170l. Pennsylvania Railroad "Torpedo" locomotive No. 238EW, 1936	1·25	1·25
1883	170l. Denver & Rio Grande Western Type PA diesel locomotive, 1992	1·25	1·25
1884	170l. Locomotive No. 408E, 1930	1·25	1·25
1885	170l. Mickey Mouse 60th Birthday boxcar No. 19241, 1991	1·25	1·25
1886	170l. Polished brass locomotive No. 54, 1913	1·25	1·25
1887	170l. Pennsylvania Railroad "Broadway Limited" locomotive No. 392E, 1936	1·25	1·25
1888	170l. Great Northern Railroad EP-5 electric locomotive No. 18302, 1988	1·25	1·25
1889	170l. Locomotive No. 6, 1918	1·25	1·25
1890	170l. Locomotive No. 400E, 1933	1·25	1·25

MS1891 Three sheets, each 119×90 mm. (a) 1000l. Joshua Lionel Cowen commemorative locomotive (50×37 mm). (b) 1000l. Trolley No. 300 (50×37 mm). (c) 1000l. Locomotive No. 381E, 1928 (50×37 mm) Set of 3 sheets 17·00 17·00

Nos. 1874 and 1877 are inscribed "Pennsylvannia" in error.

254 African Pygmy Goose ("Pigmy Goose")

1992. Birds. Multicoloured.

1892B	50c. Type **254**	25	10
1893A	1l. Spotted eagle owl	70	60
1894A	2l. Crested touraco ("Verraux's Toucan")	70	60
1895A	5l. Saddle-bill stork	70	60
1896A	10l. African golden oriole	70	50
1897A	20l. Malachite kingfisher	1·00	50
1898A	30l. Red-crowned bishop ("Fire-crowned Bishop")	1·00	50
1899A	40l. Fire-bellied woodpecker	1·00	50
1900B	50l. Red-billed fire finch	10	10
1901A	80l. Blue flycatcher ("Blue Fairy Flycatcher")	1·00	50
1902B	100l. Crested malimbe	25	10
1903B	150l. Vitelline masked weaver	10	10
1904A	170l. Great blue turaco ("Blue Plantain-eater")	1·50	40
1905B	200l. Superb sunbird	10	10
1906B	250l. Swallow-tailed bee eater	10	15
1907B	300l. Cabanis's yellow bunting ("Cabanis's Yellow Bunting")	10	10
1908B	500l. Egyptian plover ("Crocodile Bird")	20	25
1909A	750l. White-faced scops owl ("White-faced Owl")	1·25	75
1910B	1000l. African blue cuckoo shrike ("Blue Cuckoo-shrike")	40	45
1911B	2000l. White-necked bald crow ("Bare-headed Rock fowl")	80	85
1912B	3000l. African red-tailed buzzard ("Red-tailed Buzzard")	1·25	1·40
1913A	4000l. Grey-headed bush shrike	1·60	1·75
1914A	5000l. Black-backed puffback	1·90	2·00
1915A	6000l. Burchell's gonolek ("Crimson-breasted Shrike")	2·25	2·40
1915Ac	10000l. Northern shrike	4·00	4·25

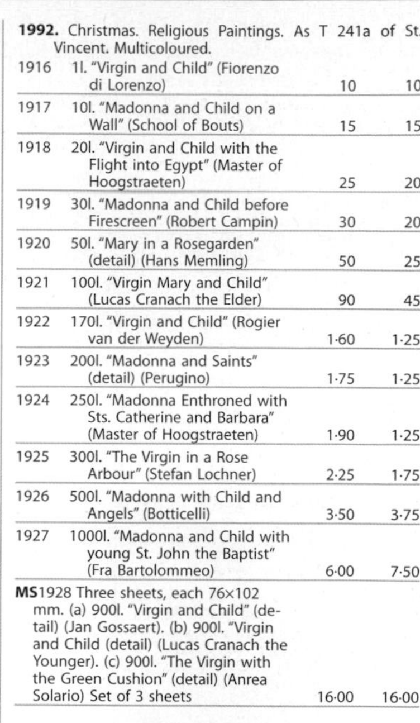

1992. Christmas. Religious Paintings. As T 241a of St. Vincent. Multicoloured.

1916	1l. "Virgin and Child" (Fiorenzo di Lorenzo)	10	10
1917	10l. "Madonna and Child on a Wall" (School of Bouts)	15	15
1918	20l. "Virgin and Child with the Flight into Egypt" (Master of Hoogstraeten)	25	20
1919	30l. "Madonna and Child before Firescreen" (Robert Campin)	30	20
1920	50l. "Mary in a Rosegarden" (detail) (Hans Memling)	50	25
1921	100l. "Virgin Mary and Child" (Lucas Cranach the Elder)	90	45
1922	170l. "Virgin and Child" (Rogier van der Weyden)	1·60	1·25
1923	200l. "Madonna and Saints" (detail) (Perugino)	1·75	1·25
1924	250l. "Madonna Enthroned with Sts. Catherine and Barbara" (Master of Hoogstraeten)	1·90	1·25
1925	300l. "The Virgin in a Rose Arbour" (Stefan Lochner)	2·25	1·75
1926	500l. "Madonna with Child and Angels" (Botticelli)	3·50	3·75
1927	1000l. "Madonna and Child with young St. John the Baptist" (Fra Bartolommeo)	6·00	7·50

MS1928 Three sheets, each 76×102 mm. (a) 900l. "Virgin and Child" (detail) (Jan Gossaert). (b) 900l. "Virgin and Child (detail) (Lucas Cranach the Younger). (c) 900l. "The Virgin with the Green Cushion" (detail) (Anrea Solario) Set of 3 sheets 16·00 16·00

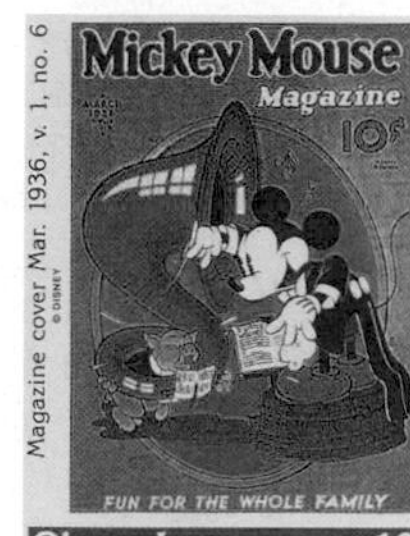

255 Mickey Mouse and Sousaphone (magazine cover, 1936)

1992. Mickey Mouse in Literature. Designs showing Walt Disney cartoon characters on magazine or book covers. Multicoloured.

1929	10l. Type **255**	25	10
1930	20l. Mickey and Minnie Mouse, 1936	30	10
1931	30l. Mickey and Donald Duck, 1936	30	10
1932	40l. Mickey, Minnie and Goofy in car, 1936	30	15
1933	50l. Mickey as Ringmaster, 1937	35	15
1934	60l. Mickey as Father Christmas, 1937	40	25
1935	70l. Donald and Goofy representing 1937 and 1938	45	25
1936	150l. Mickey and Minnie steering ship, 1935	1·25	1·10
1937	170l. Mickey and Tanglefoot the horse, 1936	1·40	1·10
1938	200l. Mickey tied up	1·60	1·25
1939	300l. Mickey and Goofy in Jungle	2·00	1·75
1940	400l. Mickey and Goofy on submarine	2·25	2·25
1941	500l. Mickey and Minnie singing and dancing, 1931	2·50	2·75

MS1942 Three sheets. (a) 127×102 mm. 900l. Mickey reading to Morty and Ferdie, 1933 (horiz). (b) 102×127 mm. 900l. Mickey with book, 1935 (horiz). (c) 102×127 mm. 900l. Mickey the hunter, 1948 Set of 3 sheets 12·00 13·00

256 Emblems

1993. Anniversaries and Events. Multicoloured.

1943	150l. Type **256**	70	70
1944	170l. Cow and cereal with emblems	80	90
1945	170l. Airship LZ-127 "Graf Zeppelin"	1·50	90
1946	200l. Starving child with W.H.O. emblem	1·00	1·00
1947	250l. Summit emblem and cottonwood tree	1·25	1·25
1948	250l. Lions Club emblem and World map	1·25	1·25

1949 300l. Emblem and African elephant 3·00 2·00
1950 300l. Columbus, King Ferdinand and Queen Isabella 2·50 2·00
1951 500l. Landing in the New World 3·25 3·00
1952 600l. American space shuttle 3·50 3·75
1953 700l. Construction drawings of "Graf Zeppelin" 3·75 4·00
MS1954 Three sheets. (a) 100×70 mm. 900l. Count Ferdinand von Zeppelin (vert). (b) 97×67 mm. 900l. Christopher Columbus (vert). (c) 100×70 mm. 900l. American astronaut on space walk Set of 3 sheets 10·50 11·50

ANNIVERSARIES AND EVENTS: Nos. 1943/4, International Conference on Nutrition, Rome; 1945, 1953, **MS**1954a, 75th death anniv of Count Ferdinand von Zeppelin (airship pioneer); 1946, United Nations World Health Organization Projects; 1947, 1949, Earth Summit '92, Rio; 1948, 75th anniv of International Association of Lions Clubs; 1950/1, **MS**1954b, 500th anniv of discovery of America by Columbus; 1952, **MS**1954c, International Space Year.

257 Joe Louis

1993. Centenary of Modern Boxing (1st issue). World Champions. Multicoloured.
1955 200l. Type **257** 1·40 1·40
1956 200l. Archie Moore 1·40 1·40
1957 200l. Muhammad Ali 1·40 1·40
1958 200l. George Foreman 1·40 1·40
1959 200l. Joe Frazier 1·40 1·40
1960 200l. Marvin Hagler 1·40 1·40
1961 200l. Sugar Ray Leonard 1·40 1·40
1962 200l. Evander Holyfield 1·40 1·40
MS1963 128×102 mm. 1000l. Muhammad Ali (different) 4·25 4·75

1993. Centenary of Modern Boxing (2nd issue). Boxing Films. As T 257. Multicoloured.
1964 200l. Wallace Beery ("The Champ") 1·40 1·40
1965 200l. William Holden ("Golden Boy") 1·40 1·40
1966 200l. John Garfield ("Body and Soul") 1·40 1·40
1967 200l. Kirk Douglas ("Champion") 1·40 1·40
1968 200l. Robert Ryan ("The Set-Up") 1·40 1·40
1969 200l. Anthony Quinn ("Requiem for a Heavyweight") 1·40 1·40
1970 200l. Elvis Presley ("Kid Galahad") 1·40 1·40
1971 200l. Jeff Bridges ("Fat City") 1·40 1·40
MS1972 Two sheets, each 128×102 mm. (a) 1000l. Errol Flynn "Gentleman Jim" (b) 1000l. Sylvester Stallone "Rocky III" Set of 2 sheets 7·00 7·50

1993. Bicentenary of the Louvre, Paris. Paintings by Delacroix. As T 255a of St. Vincent. Mult.
1973 70l. "Young Orphan at a Cemetery" 45 50
1974 70l. "Algerian Women in their Apartment" (left detail) 45 50
1975 70l. "Algerian Women in their Apartment" (right detail) 45 50
1976 70l. "Dante and Virgil" 45 50
1977 70l. "Self-portrait" 45 50
1978 70l. "Massacre of Chios" (left detail) 45 50
1979 70l. "Massacre of Chios" (right detail) 45 50
1980 70l. "Frederic Chopin" 45 50
1981 70l. "Entry of the Crusaders into Constantinople" (left detail) 45 50
1982 70l. "Entry of the Crusaders into Constantinople" (right detail) 45 50
1983 70l. "Jewish Wedding, Morocco" (left detail) 45 50
1984 70l. "Jewish Wedding, Morocco" (right detail) 45 50
1985 70l. "Death of Sardanopoulous" (left detail) 45 50
1986 70l. "Death of Sardanopoulous" (right detail) 45 50
1987 70l. "Liberty leading the People" (left detail) 45 50
1988 70l. "Liberty leading the People" (right detail) 45 50
MS1989 100×70 mm. 900l. "The Sabine Women" (Louis David) (85×53 mm) 6·00 6·50

258 "Amanita flammeola"

1993. Mushrooms. Multicoloured.
1990 30l. Type **258** 40 20
1991 50l. "Cantharellus pseudocibarius" 50 20
1992 100l. "Volvariella volvacea" 70 40
1993 200l. "Termitomyces microcarpus" 1·10 90
1994 300l. "Auricularia auricula-judae" 1·60 1·50
1995 400l. "Lentinus tuber-regium" ("Pleurotus tuberregium") 1·75 2·00
1996 500l. "Schizophyllum commune" 1·90 2·25
1997 600l. "Termitomyces robustus" 2·00 2·50
MS1998 Two sheets, each 106×76 mm. (a) 1000l. "Daldinia concentrica" (b) 1000l. "Phallus rubicundus" Set of 2 sheets 11·00 12·00

259 "Pseudacraea boisduvali"

1993. Butterflies. Multicoloured.
1999 20l. Type **259** 60 20
2000 30l. "Salamis temora" 65 25
2001 50l. "Charaxes jasius" 70 30
2002 100l. "Amblypodia anita" 1·00 40
2003 150l. "Papilio nireus" 1·25 70
2004 170l. "Danaus chrysippus" 1·25 85
2005 200l. "Meneris tulbaghia" 1·40 90
2006 250l. "Precis octavia" 1·50 1·00
2007 300l. "Palla ussheri" 1·60 1·40
2008 500l. "Catacroptera cloanthe" 1·90 1·90
2009 600l. "Cynthia cardui" 2·00 2·50
2010 700l. "Euphaedra neophron" 2·25 2·75
MS2011 Three sheets, each 100×70 mm. (a) 1000l. "Papilio zalmoxis" (b) 1000l. "Hypolimnas salmacts" (c) 1000l. "Kallimoides rumia" Set of 3 sheets 11·00 11·00

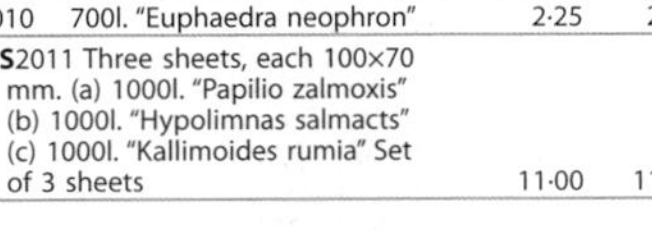

260 Black Persian

1993. Cats. Multicoloured.
2012 150l. Type **260** 90 80
2013 150l. Blue-point Siamese 90 80
2014 150l. American wirehair 90 80
2015 150l. Birman 90 80
2016 150l. Scottish fold 90 80
2017 150l. American shorthair red tabby 90 80
2018 150l. Blue and white Persian bicolour 90 80
2019 150l. Havana brown 90 80
2020 150l. Norwegian forest cat 90 80
2021 150l. Brown tortie Burmese 90 80
2022 150l. Angora 90 80
2023 150l. Exotic shorthair 90 80
2024 150l. Somali 90 80
2025 150l. Egyptian mau smoke 90 80
2026 150l. Chocolate-point Siamese 90 80
2027 150l. Mi-Ke Japanese bobtail 90 80
2028 150l. Chinchilla 90 80
2029 150l. Red Burmese 90 80
2030 150l. British shorthair brown tabby 90 80
2031 150l. Blue Persian 90 80
2032 150l. British silver classic tabby 90 80
2033 150l. Oriental ebony 90 80
2034 150l. Red Persian 90 80
2035 150l. British calico shorthair 90 80
MS2036 Two sheets, each 108×65 mm. (a) 1000l. American shorthair blue tabby. (B) 1000l. Seal-point colourpoint Set of 2 sheets 11·00 11·00

261 Gorilla

1993. Wildlife. Multicoloured.
2037 30l. Type **261** 50 30
2038 100l. Bongo 60 35
2039 150l. Potto 70 60
2040 170l. Chimpanzee 90 90
2041 200l. Dwarf galago 1·00 1·00
2042 300l. African linsang 1·25 1·25
2043 500l. Banded duiker 1·75 2·00
2044 750l. Diana monkey 2·25 3·75
MS2045 Two sheets, each 106×77 mm. (a) 1200l. African elephant. (b) 1200l. Leopard Set of 2 sheets 12·00 12·00

262 "Clerodendrum thomsonae"

1993. Flowers. Multicoloured.
2046 30l. Type **262** 40 20
2047 40l. "Passiflora quadrangularis" 45 25
2048 50l. "Hydrangea macrophylla" 45 25
2049 60l. "Begonia semperflorens" 55 30
2050 100l. "Hibiscus rosa-sinensis" 75 40
2051 150l. "Lagerstroemia indica" 1·00 75
2052 170l. "Bougainvillea glabra" 1·10 85
2053 200l. "Plumbago capensis" 1·25 1·00
2054 250l. "Gerbera jamesonae" 1·50 1·25
2055 300l. "Thunbergia alata" 1·75 1·75
2056 500l. "Gloriosa superba" 2·00 2·50
2057 900l. "Viola odorata" 3·00 4·75
MS2058 Three sheets, each 72×102 mm. (a) 1200l. "Hibiscus rosa-sinensis" (different). (b) 1200l. "Passiflora quadrangularis" (different). (c) 1200l. "Gloriosa superba" (different) Set of 3 sheets 12·00 13·00

263 Royal Family

1993. Anniversaries and Events. Black (No. 2061) or multicoloured (others).
2059 100l. Type **263** 1·25 40
2060 170l. "Woman with Hat" (Picasso) 1·50 1·00
2061 200l. Coronation procession 1·50 1·25
2062 200l. "Buste de Femme" (Picasso) 1·50 1·25
2063 250l. Early telescope 3·75 2·00
2064 600l. Queen Elizabeth II in Coronation robes (from photograph by Cecil Beaton) 3·25 3·50
2065 800l. "Maya with a Doll" (Picasso) 4·00 6·00
2066 800l. Craters on Moon 6·00 6·00
MS2067 Two sheets. (a) 100×70 mm. 1000l. "Woman of Algiers" (detail) (Picasso). (b) 73×103 mm. 1500l. "Queen Elizabeth II" (detail) (Pietro Annigoni) Set of 2 sheets 13·00 14·00

ANNIVERSARIES AND EVENTS: Nos. 2059, 2061, 2064, **MS**2067b, 40th anniv of Coronation; 2060, 2062, 2065, **MS**2067a, 20th death anniv of Picasso (artist); 2063, 2066, 450th death anniv of Copernicus (astronomer).

1993. Christmas. Religious Paintings. As T 265a of St. Vincent. Black, yellow and red (Nos. 2071/4) or multicoloured (others).
2068 50l. "Madonna of the Fish" (detail) (Raphael) 30 10
2069 100l. "Madonna of the Fish" (different detail) (Raphael) 50 20
2070 150l. "Madonna and Child enthroned with Five Saints" (detail) (Raphael) 75 30
2071 200l. "The Circumcision" (detail) (Durer) 85 55
2072 250l. "The Circumcision" (different detail) (Durer) 95 75
2073 300l. "The Circumcision" (different detail) (Durer) 1·00 1·00
2074 500l. "Holy Family with Saints and Two Angels playing Music" (detail) (Durer) 1·90 2·25
2075 800l. "The Holy Family with the Lamb" (detail) (Raphael) 2·50 4·00
MS2076 Two sheets. (a) 102×127 mm. 1200l. "Madonna of the Fish" (different detail) (Raphael). (b) 127×102 mm. 1200l. "Holy Family with Saints and Two Angels playing Music" (different detail) (Durer) Set of 2 sheets 8·50 9·00

265 Donald Duck and Toy Train

1993. Christmas. Walt Disney cartoon characters in Christmas scenes. Multicoloured.
2077 50l. Type **265** 50 10
2078 100l. Disney carol singers 75 20
2079 170l. Mickey drinking punch 1·40 70
2080 200l. Pluto with cream-covered bones 1·60 85
2081 250l. Goofy eating angel cakes 1·75 1·25
2082 500l. Donald's nephews decorating Christmas tree 3·00 3·00
2083 600l. Donald dropping Christmas cake on foot 3·25 3·75
2084 800l. Uncle Scrooge and Daisy under mistletoe 3·75 4·75
MS2085 Four sheets. (a) 127×102 mm. 1200l. Father Christmas in sleigh. (b) 102×127 mm. 1200l. Disney carol singers in wood (horiz). (c) 127×102 mm. 1200l. Father Christmas (horiz). (d) 127×102 mm. 1200l. Mickey and Minnie with turkey (horiz) Set of 4 sheets 15·00 16·00

265a Jose Brown with Goalkeeper (Agentina)

1993. World Cup Football Championship, U.S.A. (1994) (1st issue). Multicoloured.
2086 30l. Type **265a** 50 20
2087 50l. Gary Lineker (England) 75 30
2088 100l. Carlos Valderrama (Colombia) 85 35
2089 250l. Tomas Skuhravy (Czechoslovakia) and Hector Marchena (Costa Rica) 1·60 1·40
2090 300l. Butragueno (Spain) 1·75 1·75
2091 400l. Roger Milla (Cameroun) 2·25 2·50
2092 500l. Roberto Donadoni (Italy) 2·50 2·75
2093 700l. Enzo Scifo (Belgium) 2·75 3·25
MS2094 Two sheets. (a) 70×100 mm. 1200l. Mark Wright (England) and Stephane Demol (Belgium). (b) 100×70 mm. 1200l. Socrates (Brazil) Set of 2 sheets 13·00 13·00

See also Nos. 2130/5.

1994. "Hong Kong '94" International Stamp Exhibition (1st issue). As T 271a of St. Vincent. Multicoloured.
2095 200l. Hong Kong 1985 $1.70 Bauhinia stamp and Pagoda, Tiger Baum Garden 65 75
2096 200l. Sierra Leone 1989 70l. Orchid stamp and Aw Par Gardens 65 75

See also Nos. 2097/2102 and 2103/4.

1994. "Hong Kong '94" International Stamp Exhibition (2nd issue). Ching Dynasty Carved Lacquerware. As T 271b of St. Vincent. Mult.
2097 100l. Bowl 55 70
2098 100l. Four-wheeled box 55 70
2099 100l. Flower container 55 70
2100 100l. Box with human figure design 55 70
2101 100l. Shishi dog 55 70

2102	100l. Box with persimmon design	55	70

1994. "Hong Kong '94" International Stamp Exhibition (3rd issue). Nos. 2013 and 2025 optd HONG KONG '94 and emblem.

2103	150l. Blue-point Siamese	75	75
2104	150l. Egyptian mau smoke	75	75
MS2105	Two sheets, each 108×65 mm. (a) 1000l. American shorthair blue tabby. (b) 1000l. Seal-point colourpoint Set of 2 sheets	7·00	7·50

On No. **MS**2105 the overprint only appears on the margins of the miniature sheet.

267 Pekingese

1994. Chinese New Year ("Year of the Dog"). Multicoloured.

2106	100l. Type **267**	85	1·10
2107	150l. Dobermann pinscher	1·10	1·25
2108	200l. Tibetan terrier	1·25	1·40
2109	250l. Weimaraner	1·25	1·40
2110	400l. Rottweiler	1·40	1·60
2111	500l. Akita	1·40	1·60
2112	600l. Schnauzer	1·50	1·75
2113	1000l. Tibetan spaniel	1·75	1·90
MS2114	Two sheets, each 116×88 mm. (a) 1200l. Wire-haired pointing griffon. (b) 1200l. Shih Tzu Set of 2 sheets	6·00	7·00

1994. 50th Anniv of D-Day. As T 284b of St. Vincent. Multicoloured.

2115	500l. British paratroop drop	1·50	1·50
2116	750l. U.S. paratrooper jumping from aircraft	2·00	2·00
MS2117	106×76 mm. 1000l. U.S. paratrooper preparing to jump from Douglas C-47 Dakota	3·00	3·50

1994. "Philakorea '94" International Stamp Exn, Seoul. As T 286a of St. Vincent. Multicoloured.

2118	100l. Traditional wedding	40	25
2119	200l. Tiger and cubs	70	70
2120	200l. Munsa-pasal	70	70
2121	200l. Extinct Korean tiger	70	70
2122	200l. Tiger and bamboo	70	70
2123	200l. Tiger, three cubs and magpies	70	70
2124	200l. Tiger, two cubs and black-billed magpies	70	70
2125	200l. Mountain spirit	70	70
2126	200l. Tiger and black-billed magpie	70	70
2127	400l. Royal tombs, Kaesong	1·00	1·00
2128	600l. Terraced fields, Chungmu	1·50	1·75
MS2129	100×70 mm. 1200l. Tiger hunt	5·00	5·00

No. **MS**2129 is inscribed "Sierre Leone" in error.

268 Kim Ho (South Korea)

1994. World Cup Football Championship, U.S.A. (2nd issue). Multicoloured.

2130	250l. Type **268**	95	85
2131	250l. Cobi Jones (U.S.A.) ("No. 13")	95	85
2132	250l. Claudio Suarez (Mexico) ("No. 2")	95	85
2133	250l. Tomas Brolin (Sweden) ("No. 11")	95	85
2134	250l. Ruud Gullit (Holland) (red shirt without number)	95	85
2135	250l. Andreas Herzog (Austria) (white shirt without number)	95	85
MS2136	Two sheets. (a) 70×100 mm. 1500l. Player and Giant Stadium, New Jersey. (b) 100×70 mm. 1500l. Sierra Leone national team Set of 2 sheets	8·00	9·00

1994. 25th Anniv of First Manned Moon Landing. As T 284a of St. Vincent. Multicoloured.

2137	200l. Buzz Aldrin gathering Moon samples	65	65
2138	200l. Lunar Module "Eagle" on Moon's surface	65	65
2139	200l. Tranquility Base	65	65
2140	200l. Aldrin with U.S. flag	65	65
2141	200l. Plaque	65	65
2142	200l. "Apollo 11" crew with stamps	65	65
2143	200l. Edwin Aldrin	65	65
2144	200l. Michael Collins	65	65
2145	200l. Neil Armstrong	65	65
2146	200l. "Apollo 11" lift off	65	65
2147	200l. Aldrin descending to Moon's surface	65	65
2148	200l. Reflection in Aldrin's face shield	65	65
MS2149	103×73 mm. 1000l. First lunar footprint (vert)	3·00	3·50

269 White-necked Bald Crow ("Picathartes") feeding Chicks

1994. Birds. Multicoloured.

2150	50l. Type **269**	65	65
2151	100l. Adult white-necked bald crow	75	75
2152	150l. Pair of white-necked bald crows	85	85
2153	200l. Young white-necked bald crow	90	90
2154	250l. Black kite	1·00	1·00
2155	300l. Superb sunbird	1·10	1·10
2156	500l. Martial eagle	1·60	2·00
2157	800l. Red bishop	2·00	2·75
MS2158	Two sheets, each 90×65 mm. (a) 1200l. Greater flamingo (vert). (b) 1200l. White-necked bald crow (vert) Set of 2 sheets	10·00	10·00

270 "Aerangis kotschyana"

1994. Orchids. Multicoloured.

2159	50l. Type **270**	40	20
2160	100l. "Brachycorythis kalbreyeri"	50	30
2161	150l. "Diaphananthe pellucida"	65	55
2162	200l. "Eulophia guineensis"	75	65
2163	300l. "Eurychone rothschildiana"	1·00	85
2164	500l. "Tridactyle tridactylites"	1·60	1·60
2165	750l. "Cyrtorchis arcuata"	2·25	3·00
2166	900l. "Ancistrochilus rothschildianus"	2·50	3·50
MS2167	Two sheets, each 117×78 mm. (a) 1500l. "Plectrelminthus caudatus". (b) 1500l. "Polystachaya affinis" Set of 2 sheets	8·50	9·50

1994. Christmas. Religious Paintings. As T 290 of St. Vincent. Multicoloured.

2168	50l. "The Birth of the Virgin" (Murillo)	35	10
2169	100l. "Education of the Virgin" (Murillo)	45	20
2170	150l. "Annunciation" (detail) (Filippino Lippi)	75	55
2171	200l. "Marriage of the Virgin" (Bernard van Orley)	85	70
2172	250l. "The Visitation" (Nicolas Vleughels)	1·00	90
2173	300l. "Castelfranco Altarpiece" (detail) (Giorgione)	1·25	1·25
2174	400l. "Adoration of the Magi" (workshop of Bartholome Zeitblom)	1·60	1·75
2175	600l. "Presentation of Infant Jesus in the Temple" (Master of the Prado)	2·00	3·25
MS2176	Two sheets, each 115×95 mm. (a) 1500l. "Nativity Altarpiece" (detail) (Lorenzo Monaco). (b) 1500l. "Allendale Nativity" (detail) (Giorgione) Set of 2 sheets	8·00	9·00

271 Family working in Field

1994. International Year of the Family. Mult.

2177	300l. Type **271**	75	80
2178	350l. Family on beach	75	80

272 Mickey Mouse stroking Cat

1995. Christmas. Walt Disney cartoon characters. Multicoloured.

2179	50l. Type **272**	40	10
2180	100l. Goofy with Christmas tree and axe (vert)	50	20
2181	150l. Donald Duck giving Daisy Duck a plant	80	45
2182	200l. Donald finding Chipmunk in stocking (vert)	90	60
2183	250l. Minnie Mouse in airplane	1·10	85
2184	300l. Goofy in snowball (vert)	1·40	1·00
2185	400l. Goofy with Chip N' Dale at mail box	1·60	1·50
2186	500l. Mickey and Donald on sledge (vert)	1·75	1·75
2187	600l. Mickey and Minnie making snowmouse	2·00	2·50
2188	800l. Mickey and Pluto with cake (vert)	2·50	3·50
MS2189	Two sheets. (a) 108×133 mm. 1500l. Goofy caught up in Christmas lights. (b) 130×108 mm. 1500l. Mickey asleep in armchair (vert) Set of 2 sheets	9·50	10·00

273 "Madonna Duck" (after Da Vinci)

1995. Donald's Gallery of Old Masters. Donald and Daisy Duck in portraits inspired by famous paintings. Multicoloured.

2190	50l. Type **273**	25	15
2191	100l. "Portrait of a Venetian Duck" (after Tintoretto)	35	25
2192	150l. "Duck with a Glove" (after Frans Hals)	50	50
2193	200l. "Donald with a Pink" (after Massys)	60	60
2194	250l. "Pinkie Daisy" (after Lawrence)	70	70
2195	300l. "Donald's Whistling Mother" (after Whistler)	80	80
2196	400l. "El Quacko" (after El Greco)	90	90
2197	500l. "The Noble Snob" (after Rembrandt)	1·00	1·00
2198	600l. "The Blue Duck" (after Gainsborough)	1·25	1·50
2199	800l. "Modern Quack" (after Picasso)	1·40	1·60
MS2200	Two sheets, each 133×108 mm. (a) 1500l. "Soup's On" (detail) (after Brueghel). (b) 1500l. "Two Duck Dancers" (detail) (after Degas) (horiz) Set of 2 sheets	8·50	9·00

274 Ragnar Lundberg (Sweden) (1952 pole vault bronze medal)

1995. Centenary of International Olympic Committee. Medal Winners. Multicoloured.

2201	75l. Type **274**	45	45
2202	75l. Karin Janz (Germany) (1972 gymnastics silver)	45	45
2203	75l. Matthias Volz (Germany) (1936 gymnastics bronze)	45	45
2204	75l. Carl Lewis (U.S.A.) (1988 long jump gold)	45	45
2205	75l. Sara Simeoni (Italy) (1976 high jump silver)	45	45

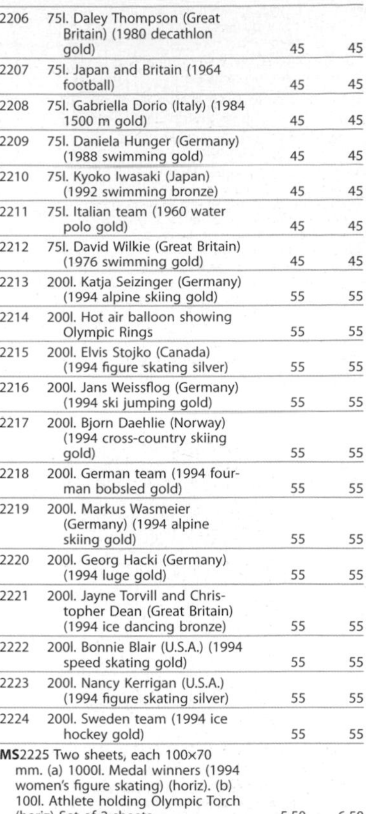

2206	75l. Daley Thompson (Great Britain) (1980 decathlon gold)	45	45
2207	75l. Japan and Britain (1964 football)	45	45
2208	75l. Gabriella Dorio (Italy) (1984 1500 m gold)	45	45
2209	75l. Daniela Hunger (Germany) (1988 swimming gold)	45	45
2210	75l. Kyoko Iwasaki (Japan) (1992 swimming bronze)	45	45
2211	75l. Italian team (1960 water polo gold)	45	45
2212	75l. David Wilkie (Great Britain) (1976 swimming gold)	45	45
2213	200l. Katja Seizinger (Germany) (1994 alpine skiing gold)	55	55
2214	200l. Hot air balloon showing Olympic Rings	55	55
2215	200l. Elvis Stojko (Canada) (1994 figure skating silver)	55	55
2216	200l. Jans Weissflog (Germany) (1994 ski jumping gold)	55	55
2217	200l. Bjorn Daehlie (Norway) (1994 cross-country skiing gold)	55	55
2218	200l. German team (1994 four-man bobsled gold)	55	55
2219	200l. Markus Wasmeier (Germany) (1994 alpine skiing gold)	55	55
2220	200l. Georg Hackl (Germany) (1994 luge gold)	55	55
2221	200l. Jayne Torvill and Christopher Dean (Great Britain) (1994 ice dancing bronze)	55	55
2222	200l. Bonnie Blair (U.S.A.) (1994 speed skating gold)	55	55
2223	200l. Nancy Kerrigan (U.S.A.) (1994 figure skating silver)	55	55
2224	200l. Sweden team (1994 ice hockey gold)	55	55
MS2225	Two sheets, each 100×70 mm. (a) 1000l. Medal winners (1994 women's figure skating) (horiz). (b) 100l. Athlete holding Olympic Torch (horiz) Set of 2 sheets	5·50	6·50

275 Ceratosaurus

1995. Prehistoric Animals. Multicoloured.

2226	200l. Type **275**	75	75
2227	200l. Brachiosaurus	75	75
2228	200l. Pteranodon	75	75
2229	200l. Stegoceras	75	75
2230	200l. Saurolophus	75	75
2231	200l. Ornithomumus	75	75
2232	200l. Compsognathus	75	75
2233	200l. Deinonychus	75	75
2234	200l. Ornitholestes	75	75
2235	200l. Archaeopteryx	75	75
2236	200l. Heterodontosaurus	75	75
2237	200l. Lesothosaurus	75	75
MS2238	130×58 mm. 100l. Triceratops (vert); 250l. Protoceratops (vert); 400l. Monoclonius (vert); 800l. Styracosaurus (vert)	3·50	3·50
MS2239	Two sheets, each 99×79 mm. (a) 2500l. Rhamphorynchus (vert). (b) 2500l. Deinonychus (vert) Set of 2 sheets	5·50	6·00

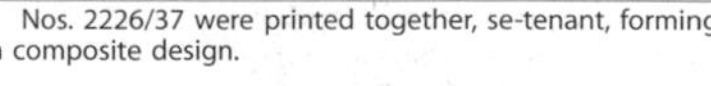
Nos. 2226/37 were printed together, se-tenant, forming a composite design.

276 Pig (on red panel)

1995. Chinese New Year ("Year of the Pig"). Multicoloured.

2240	100l. Type **276**	50	50
2241	100l. Pig facing right (on green panel)	50	50
2242	100l. Pig facing left (on green panel)	50	50
2243	100l. Pig facing right (on red panel)	50	50
MS2244	77×105 mm. 500l. Two pigs (vert)	2·00	2·75

276a Black-faced Impalas

1995. Centenary (1992) of Sierra Club (environmental protection society). Endangered Species. Multicoloured.

No.	Description	Mint	Used
2245	150l. Type **276a**	50	50
2246	150l. Herd of black-faced impalas	50	50
2247	150l. Black-faced impalas drinking	50	50
2248	150l. Bonobo with young	50	50
2249	150l. Black-footed cat in foliage	50	50
2250	150l. Close-up of black-footed cat	50	50
2251	150l. L'Hoest's monkey on all fours	50	50
2252	150l. L'Hoest's monkey squatting	50	50
2253	150l. Pair of mandrills	50	50
2254	150l. L'Hoest's monkey (vert)	50	50
2255	150l. Black-footed cat (vert)	50	50
2256	150l. Head of colobus monkey (vert)	50	50
2257	150l. Colobus monkey in tree fork (vert)	50	50
2258	150l. Head of mandrill (vert)	50	50
2259	150l. Bonobo with young (vert)	50	50
2260	150l. Bonobo asleep on log (vert)	50	50
2261	150l. Mandrill facing right (vert)	50	50
2262	150l. Colobus monkey on log (vert)	50	50

277 Denver and Rio Grande Western Railroad

1995. Railways of the World. Multicoloured.

No.	Description	Mint	Used
2263-2274	200l.×12 (Type **277**; Central of Georgia; Seaboard Air Line; Missouri Pacific Lines; Atchison, Topeka and Santa Fe; Chicago, Milwaukee, St. Paul and Pacific; Texas and Pacific; Minneapolis, St. Paul and Sault Ste. Marie; Western Pacific; Great Northern; Baltimore and Ohio; Chicago, Rock Island and Pacific)	7·00	7·50
2275-2286	200l.×12 (Southern Pacific; Belgian National; Indian; Southern Australian; Union Pacific; British Railways; German Federal; Japanese National; Pennsylvania; East African; Milwaukee; Paris-Orleans)	7·00	7·50
2287-2298	250l.×12 (Eurostar; E.T.R. 401 Pendolino express; British Rail Intercity 125; Talgo "Virgen" express, Spain; French National TGV; Amtrak "Southwest Chief" express; French National TGV "Atlantique" express; Greek "Peloponnese Express"; Japanese "Hikari" express train; Canadian National Turbotrain; Australian XPT high-speed train; Chinese SS1 electric locomotive)	7·50	8·00
2299-2310	300l.×12 (Canadian National U1-f locomotive; Union Pacific steam locomotive No. 119; LNER Class A4 No. 4468 "Mallard"; New York Central Class J3a steam locomotive; Canadian National Class U4 locomotive; Australian Class 38 locomotive; Canadian Pacific Class G3c locomotive; Southern Railway Class "West Country" locomotive; Norfolk & Western Class J locomotive; China Class RM locomotive; Russia Class P-36 locomotive; GWR Class "King" locomotive)	7·50	8·00
MS2311	Five sheets, each 107×79 mm. containing larger designs, 56½×42½ mm. (a) 1500l. British Railways No. 45627 "Sierra Leone" locomotive. (b) 1500l. China Railways Class QJ locomotive. (c) 1500l. Denver and Rio Grande Western Railroad "California Zephyr" express. (d) 1500l. China Railways Beijing-Shanghai express. (e) 1500l. China Railways first train across Yangtze Bridge, 1968 Set of 5 sheets	16·00	18·00

No. 2290 is inscribed "VIRGIN", No. 2300 "CENTRAL PACIFIC RAILWAY" and No. 2302 "J-32", all in error.

278 National Flag and Scout Emblems

1995. 18th World Scout Jamboree, Netherlands. Multicoloured.

No.	Description	Mint	Used
2312	400l. Type **278**	90	1·00
2313	500l. Lord Baden-Powell	1·00	1·25
2314	600l. Scout sign	1·10	1·40
MS2315	80×111 mm. 1500l. Scout saluting	2·75	3·25

1995. 50th Anniv of End of Second World War in Europe. As T 296a of St. Vincent, showing warships. Multicoloured.

No.	Description	Mint	Used
2316	250l. U.S.S. "Idaho" (battleship)	75	75
2317	250l. H.M.S. "Ark Royal" (aircraft carrier)	75	75
2318	250l. Admiral "Graf Spee" (German pocket battleship)	75	75
2319	250l. American destroyer	75	75
2320	250l. H.M.S. "Nelson" (battleship)	75	75
2321	250l. U.S.S. "PT 109" (motor torpedo boat)	75	75
2322	250l. U.S.S. "Iowa" (battleship)	75	75
2323	250l. "Bismarck" (German battleship)	75	75
MS2324	105×74 mm. 1500l. H.M.S. "Indomitable" (aircraft carrier) (57×42½ mm)	4·00	4·50

No. 2323 is wrongly inscr "BISMARK".

278a U.N. Emblem above Podium

1995. 50th Anniv of the United Nations. Mult.

No.	Description	Mint	Used
2325	300l. Type **278a**	60	70
2326	400l. U Thant (Secretary-General, 1961–71)	70	1·00
2327	500l. Peace dove and U.N. Building, New York	80	1·10
MS2328	105×74 mm. 1500l. Dag Hammarskjold (Secretary-General, 1953-61)	2·00	2·50

Nos. 2325/7 were printed together, se-tenant, forming a composite design.

1995. 50th Anniv of F.A.O. As T 298 of St. Vincent. Multicoloured.

No.	Description	Mint	Used
2329	300l. Fisherman in boat (horiz)	60	70
2330	400l. Boy carrying wood (horiz)	70	1·00
2331	500l. Woman with fruit (horiz)	80	1·10
MS2332	76×106 mm. 1500l. Mother and child	2·00	2·50

1995. 90th Anniv of Rotary International. As T 299 of St. Vincent. Multicoloured.

No.	Description	Mint	Used
2333	500l. National flag and Rotary logo	1·10	1·50
MS2334	105×75 mm. 1000l. Paul Harris (founder) and logo	1·60	1·75

1995. 95th Birthday of Queen Elizabeth the Queen Mother. As T 323a of St. Vincent.

No.	Description	Mint	Used
2335	400l. brown, lt brown & blk	90	1·00
2336	400l. multicoloured	90	1·00
2337	400l. multicoloured	90	1·00
2338	400l. multicoloured	90	1·00
MS2339	102×127 mm. 1500l. multicoloured	3·50	3·50

DESIGNS: No. 2335, Queen Elizabeth the Queen Mother (pastel drawing); 2336, Holding bouquet of flowers; 2337, At desk (oil painting); . 2338, Wearing pink evening dress; **MS**2339, wearing blue hat.

1995. 50th Anniv of End of Second World War in the Pacific. As T 296a of St. Vincent. Mult.

No.	Description	Mint	Used
2340	300l. American B-179 bomber	80	80
2341	300l. American B-25 bomber	80	80
2342	300l. American Consolidated B-24 Liberator bomber	80	80
2343	300l. U.S.S. "Missouri" (battleship)	80	80
2344	300l. American Douglas A-20 Boston bomber	80	80
2345	300l. American battle fleet in Lingayen Gulf	80	80
MS2346	108×76 mm. 1500l. Nose of B-29 Superfortress	3·00	3·50

279 Black-spotted Pufferfish

1995. "Singapore '95" International Stamp Exhibition (1st issue). Marine Life. Multicoloured.

No.	Description	Mint	Used
2347	300l. Type **279**	65	65
2348	300l. Coral hind	65	65
2349	300l. Hawksbill turtle	65	65
2350	300l. Hogfish	65	65
2351	300l. Emperor angelfish	65	65
2352	300l. Red-tailed butterflyfish	65	65
2353	300l. Lemon butterflyfish	65	65
2354	300l. Green-beaked parrotfish	65	65
2355	300l. Spotted reef moray	65	65
2356	300l. Pintado petrel ("Cape Pigeons")	65	65
2357	300l. Eastern white pelican ("Pelican")	65	65
2358	300l. Atlantic puffin ("Puffin")	65	65
2359	300l. Humpback whale	65	65
2360	300l. Greater shearwater	65	65
2361	300l. Bottlenose dolphin	65	65
2362	300l. Gurnards	65	65
2363	300l. Atlantic salmon	65	65
2364	300l. John Dory	65	65
MS2365	Two sheets. (a) 71×101 mm. 1500l. Ocean surgeonfish. (b) 101×71 mm. 1500l. Pennant coralfish ("Angelfish") (vert) Set of 2 sheets	6·00	6·50

Nos. 2347/55 and 2356/64 were printed together, se-tenant, forming composite designs.

280 Flame Lily

1995. "Singapore '95" International Stamp Exhibition (2nd issue). African Flora and Fauna. Multicoloured.

No.	Description	Mint	Used
2366	300l. Type **280**	1·00	1·00
2367	300l. Grant's gazelle	1·00	1·00
2368	300l. Dogbane	1·00	1·00
2369	300l. Gold-banded forester	1·00	1·00
2370	300l. Horned chameleon	1·00	1·00
2371	300l. Malachite kingfisher	1·00	1·00
2372	300l. Leaf beetle	1·00	1·00
2373	300l. Acanthus	1·00	1·00
2374	300l. African tulip tree	1·00	1·00
2375	300l. Senegal bush locust	1·00	1·00
2376	300l. Killfish	1·00	1·00
2377	300l. Bird of paradise (flower)	1·00	1·00
2378	300l. Mandrill	1·00	1·00
2379	300l. Painted reed frog	1·00	1·00
2380	300l. Large spotted acraea	1·00	1·00
2381	300l. Carmine bee eater	1·00	1·00
MS2382	Two sheets, each 103×73 mm. (a) 1500l. Elephant. (b) 1500l. Lion Set of 2 sheets	6·50	7·00

281 School Building and Emblem

1995. 150th Anniv of Sierra Leone Grammar School.

No.	Type	Description	Mint	Used
2383	**281**	300l. brown, mauve and black	70	70

281a "Holy Family" (detail) (Beccafumi)

1995. Christmas. Religious Paintings. Mult.

No.	Description	Mint	Used
2384	50l. Type **281a**	25	10
2385	100l. "The Rest on the Flight into Egypt" (detail) (Federico Barocci)	30	10
2386	150l. "The Virgin" (Jacopo Bellini)	40	15
2387	200l. "The Flight" (Cavaliere d'Arpino)	50	25
2388	600l. "Adoration of the Magi" (detail) (Francken)	1·60	2·25
2389	800l. "The Annunciation" (Cima de Conegliano)	1·75	2·50
MS2390	Two sheets, each 102×127 mm. (a) 1500l. "Virgin and Child" (detail) (Cranach). (b) 1500l. "Madonna and Child" (detail) (Berlinghiero) Set of 2 sheets	6·00	6·50

282 Mickey Mouse Doll

1995. Christmas. Disney Toys. Multicoloured.

No.	Description	Mint	Used
2391	5l. Type **282**	10	10
2392	10l. Donald Duck drum-major doll	10	10
2393	15l. Donald Duck wind-up toy	15	10
2394	20l. Donald Duck toothbrush holder	15	10
2395	25l. Mickey Mouse telephone	15	10
2396	30l. Mickey Mouse walking toy	15	10
2397	800l. Toy film projector	2·50	3·25
2398	1000l. Goofy tricycle toy	2·75	3·50
MS2399	Two sheets, each 133×107 mm. (a) 1500l. Black Mickey Mouse doll. (b) 1500l. First Mickey Mouse book Set of 2 sheets	6·00	6·50

283 Andrew Huxley (1963 Medicine)

1995. Cent of Nobel Prize Trust Fund. Mult.

No.	Description	Mint	Used
2400-2408	250l.× 9 (Type **283**; Nelson Mandela (1993 Peace); Gabriela Mistral (1945 Literature); Otto Diels (1950 Chemistry); Hannes Alfven (1970 Physics); Wole Soyinka (1986 Literature); Hans Dehmelt (1989 Physics); Desmond Tutu (1984 Peace); Leo Esaki (1973 Physics))	7·50	7·50
2409-2417	250l.× 9 (Tobias Asser (1911 Peace); Andrei Sakharov (1975 Peace); Frederic Passy (1901 Peace); Dag Hammarskjold (1961 Peace); Aung San Suu Kyi (1991 Peace); Ludwig Quidde (1927 Peace); Elie Wiesel (1986 Peace); Bertha von Suttner (1905 Peace); The Dalai Lama (1989 Peace))	7·50	7·50
2418-2426	50l.× 9 (Richard Zsigmondy (1925 Chemistry); Robert Huber (1988 Chemistry); Wilhelm Ostwald (1909 Chemistry); Johann Deisenhofer (1988 Chemistry); Heinrich Wieland (1922 Chemistry); Gerhard Herzberg (1971 Chemistry); Hans von Euler-Chelpin (1929 Chemistry); Richard Willsatter (1915 Chemistry); Fritz Haber (1918 Chemistry))	7·50	5·50
2427-2435	250l.× 9 (Maria Goeppert Mayer (1963 Physics); Irene Joliot-Curie (1935 Chemistry); Mother Teresa (1979 Peace); Selma Lagerlof (1909 Literature); Rosalyn Yalow (1977 Medicine); Dorothy Hodgkin (1964 Chemistry); Rita Levi-Montalcini (1986 Medicine); Mairead Corrigan (1976 Peace); Betty Williams (1976 Peace))	7·50	5·50

MS2436 Three sheets, each 80×110 mm. (a) 1500l. Albert Einstein (1921 Physics). (b) 1500l. Wilhelm Rontgen (1901 Physics). (c) 1500l. Sin-Itiro Tomonaga (1965 Physics) Set of 3 sheets 9·00 11·00

284 Rat

1996. Chinese New Year ("Year of the Rat"). Background colour given.

2437	**284**	200l. multicoloured (brown background)	50	55
2438	-	200l. multicoloured (pink background)	50	55
2439	-	200l. multicoloured (red background)	50	55
2440	-	200l. multicoloured (blue background)	50	55

MS2441 110×84 mm. Nos. 2437/40 2·00 2·50

MS2442 76×106 mm. 500l. multicoloured (orange background) (vert) 2·00 2·50

285 Mickey Mouse as Magician

1996. Disney Circus Performers. Cartoon Characters. Multicoloured.

2443	100l. Type **285**	50	20
2444	200l. Clarabelle Cow walking tightrope	70	50
2445	250l. Donald Duck and nephews as clowns	80	60
2446	300l. Donald as lion tamer	1·00	75
2447	800l. Minnie Mouse riding bareback	2·50	3·25
2448	1000l. Goofy on trapeze	2·75	3·50

MS2449 Two sheets, each 104×125 mm. (a) 1500l. Mickey with dinosaur (horiz). (b) 1500l. Pluto balancing ball on nose (horiz) Set of 2 sheets 7·00 8·00

286 Lumiere Brothers (cine camera inventors) and Train

1996. Centenary of Cinema. Multicoloured.

2450	250l. Type **286**	70	75
2451	250l. Georges Melies (director)	70	75
2452	250l. Toshiro Mefune (director)	70	75
2453	250l. David O. Selznick (director)	70	75
2454	250l. Character from "Metropolis"	70	75
2455	250l. Akira Kurosawa (director)	70	75
2456	250l. Charlie Chaplin (actor)	70	75
2457	250l. Marlene Dietrich (actress)	70	75
2458	250l. Steven Spielberg (director)	70	75
2459	250l. Film camera	70	75
2460	250l. Pete (dog)	70	75
2461	250l. Silver (horse)	70	75
2462	250l. Rin-Tin-Tin (dog)	70	75
2463	250l. King Kong (gorilla)	70	75
2464	250l. Flipper (dolphin)	70	75
2465	250l. Great White Shark from "Jaws"	70	75
2466	250l. Elsa (lioness)	70	75
2467	250l. Whale from "Moby Dick"	70	75

MS2468 Two sheets, each 109×80 mm. (a) 1500l. Cecil B. De Mille (producer). (b) 1500l. Lassie (dog) Set of 2 sheets 6·50 7·00

Nos. 2450/8 and 2459/67 respectively were printed together, se-tenant, forming composite designs.

1996. 125th Anniv of Metropolitan Museum of Art, New York. As T 317a of St. Vincent. Mult.

2469-76	200l.× 8 ("Honfleur" (detail) (Jongkind); "A Boat on the Shore" (detail) (Courbet); "Barges at Pontoise" (detail) (Pissarro); "The Dead Christ with Angels" (Manet); "Salisbury Cathedral" (detail) (Constable); "Lady with a Setter Dog" (detail) (Eakins); "Tahitian Women Bathing" (detail) (Gauguin); "Majas on a Balcony" (detail) (Goya))	4·00	4·25
2477-84	200l.× 8 ("In the Meadow"; "By the Seashore" (detail); "Still Life with Peaches and Grapes" (detail); "Marguerite Berard"; "Young Girl in Pink and Black Hat"; "Waitress at Duval's Restaurant" (detail); "A Road in Louveciennes" (detail); "Two Young Girls at the Piano" (detail) (all by Renoir))	4·00	4·25
2485-92	200l.× 8 ("Morning, An Overcast Day, Rouen" (detail) (Pissarro); "The Horse Fair" (detail) (Bonheur); "High Tide: The Bathers" (detail) (Homer); "The Dance Class" (Degas); "The Brioche" (detail) (Manet); "The Grand Canal, Venice" (detail) (Turner); "St. Tecia interceding for plague-stricken Este" (detail) (G. B. Tiepolo); "Bridge at Villeneuve" (detail) (Sisley))	4·00	4·25
2493-2500	200l.× 8 ("Madame Charpentier" (detail) (Renoir); "Head of Christ" (detail) (Rembrandt); "The Standard-bearer" (detail) (Rembrandt); "Girl Asleep" (Vermeer); "Lady with a Lute" (Vermeer); "Portrait of a Woman" (detail) (Rembrandt); "La Grenouillere" (detail) (Monet); "Woman with Chrysanthemums" (detail) (Degas))	4·00	4·25

MS2501 Four sheets, each 95×70 mm. (a) 1500l. "The Death of Socrates" (J. L. David) 85×56 mm). (b) 1500l. "Battle of Constantine and Licinius" (detail) (rubens) (85×56 mm). (c) 1500l. "Samson and Delilah" (detail) (rubens) (85×56 mm). (d) 1500l. "The Emblem of Christ appearing to Constantine" (detail) (Rubens) (85×56 mm) Set of 4 sheets 6·50 7·50

287 Olympic Stadium, Los Angeles, 1932

1996. Olympic Games, Atlanta. Multicoloured.

2502	100l. Type **287**	30	20
2503	150l. Archery	50	50
2504	300l. Hockey	80	90
2505	300l. Swimming	80	90
2506	300l. Equestrian	80	90
2507	300l. Boxing	80	90
2508	300l. Pommel horse exercises	80	90
2509	300l. 100 m running	80	90
2510	500l. Rings exercises	1·25	1·40
2511	600l. Pole vault	1·40	1·60

MS2512 104×75 mm. 1500l. Running (vert) 3·50 4·00

288 "Cantharellus cinnabarinus"

1996. Fungi. Multicoloured.

2513	50l. Type **288**	35	20
2514	250l. "Poronidulus conchifer" and "Aphyllophorales polyporaceae"	80	85
2515	250l. "Ceratiomyxa fruticulosa"	80	85
2516	250l. "Cortinarius semisanguineus" and "Cortinariaceae agaricales"	80	85
2517	250l. "Volvamella surrecta" and "Pluteaceae agricales"	80	85
2518	250l. "Lepiota cepaestipes"	80	85
2519	250l. "Amanita rubescans"	80	85
2520	250l. "Phyllotopsis nidulans" and "Tricholomataceas agaricales"	80	85
2521	250l. "Lysyrus gardneri" and "Clathraceae phallales"	80	85
2522	250l. "Lactarius indigo"	80	85
2523	250l. "Coprinus quadrifidus"	80	85
2524	250l. "Geopyxis carbonaria"	80	85
2525	250l. "Astraeus hygrometricus"	80	85
2526	250l. "Agaicaceae agaricales"	80	85
2527	250l. "Mycena maculata"	80	85
2528	250l. "Lactarius delciosus"	80	85
2529	250l. "Amanita fulva"	80	85
2530	300l. "Suillus grevillci"	90	95
2531	400l. "Morchella esculenta"	1·10	1·25
2532	500l. "Cortinamaceae agaricales"	1·25	1·40

MS2533 Two sheets, each 110×80 mm. (a) 1500l. "Psathyrella epimyces" (horiz). (b) 1500l. "Rhodotus parmatus" (horiz) Set of 2 sheets 6·00 6·50

289 Abyssinian Cat

1996. Cats. Multicoloured.

2534	200l. Type **289**	65	60
2535	200l. British tabby	65	60
2536	200l. Norwegian forest cat	65	60
2537	200l. Maine coon	65	60
2538	200l. Bengal	65	60
2539	200l. Asian	65	60
2540	200l. American curl	65	60
2541	200l. Devon rex	65	60
2542	200l. Tonkinese	65	60
2543	200l. Egyptian mau	65	60
2544	200l. Burmese	65	60
2545	200l. Siamese	65	60
2546	200l. British shorthair	65	60
2547	200l. Tiffany	65	60
2548	200l. Birman	65	60
2549	200l. Somali	65	60
2550	200l. Malayan	65	60
2551	200l. Japanese bobtail	65	60
2552	200l. Himalayan	65	60
2553	200l. Tortoiseshell	65	60
2554	200l. Oriental	65	60
2555	200l. Ocicat	65	60
2556	200l. Chartreux	65	60
2557	200l. Ragdoll	65	60

MS2558 Two sheets, each 110×80 mm. (a) 2000l. Persian. (b) 2000l. Burmilla Set of 2 sheets 6·50 7·00

1996. 70th Birthday of Queen Elizabeth II. As T 323a of St. Vincent. Different photographs. Multicoloured.

2559	600l. Queen Elizabeth II	1·40	1·50
2560	600l. Receiving posy	1·40	1·50
2561	600l. Carrying bouquets	1·40	1·50

MS2562 125×103 mm. 1500l. Waving from balcony 3·75 4·00

290 Three Asian Girls reading

1996. 50th Anniv of UNICEF. Multicoloured.

2563	300l. Type **290**	80	80
2564	400l. African children reading	90	1·00
2565	500l. Children in class	95	1·10

MS2566 104×74 mm. 1500l. Children's faces 3·00 3·50

291 "Pioneer" Spacecraft in Venus Orbit, 1986–1992

1996. Space Exploration. Multicoloured.

2567	300l. Type **291**	80	75
2568	300l. Hubble space telescope	80	75
2569	300l. "Voyager" space probe	80	75
2570	300l. Space Shuttle "Challenger"	80	75
2571	300l. "Pioneer II" space probe	80	75
2572	300l. "Viking I" Mars lander	80	75

MS2573 104×74 mm. 1500l. Space shuttle "Challenger" landing 3·75 4·00

Nos. 2567/72 were printed together, se-tenant, the background forming a composite design.

292 Rat

1996. Chinese Lunar Calendar. Multicoloured.

2574	150l. Type **292**	70	70
2575	150l. Ox	70	70
2576	150l. Tiger	70	70
2577	150l. Hare	70	70
2578	150l. Dragon	70	70
2579	150l. Snake	70	70
2580	150l. Horse	70	70
2581	150l. Sheep	70	70
2582	150l. Monkey	70	70
2583	150l. Cockerel	70	70
2584	150l. Dog	70	70
2585	150l. Pig	70	70

293 "Charaxes pleione"

1996. Butterflies. Multicoloured.

2586	150l. Type **293**	50	35
2587	200l. "Eurema brigitta"	70	50
2588	250l. "Precis orithya"	75	80
2589	250l. "Palla ussheri"	75	80
2590	250l. "Junonia orithya"	75	80
2591	250l. "Cymothoe sangaris"	75	80
2592	250l. "Cyrestis camillus"	75	80
2593	250l. "Precis rhadama"	75	80
2594	250l. "Precis cebrene"	75	80
2595	250l. "Hypolimnas misippus"	75	80
2596	250l. "Colotis danae"	75	80
2597	300l. "Charaxes ameliae"	80	85
2598	500l. "Kallimoides rumia"	1·25	1·40

MS2599 Two sheets, each 100×70 mm. (a) 1500l. "Papilio antimachus" (b) 1500l. "Charaxes bohemani" Set of 2 sheets 6·50 7·00

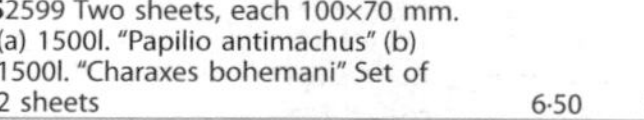

294 "Begonia multiflora" "Rambouillet"

1996. Flowers. Multicoloured.

2600	150l. "Tulipa" "Georgette"	40	30
2601	200l. "Helichrysum bracteatum" "Monstrosum"	55	60
2602	200l. Fountain	55	60
2603	200l. Type **294**	55	60
2604	200l. Narcissus "Trumpet Daffodil"	55	60
2605	200l. "Crocus speciosus"	55	60
2606	200l. "Chrysanthemum frutescens" "Marguerite"	55	60
2607	200l. Petunia "Polaris" and "Danaus gilippus" (butterfly)	55	60
2608	200l. "Cosmos pipinnatus" "Sensation" and "Papilio calguanabus" (butterfly)	55	60
2609	200l. "Anemone coronaris"	55	60
2610	200l. "Convolvulus minor"	55	60
2611	300l. "Paphiopedilum" "Claire de Lune"	80	85
2612	300l. "Cymbidium" "Peach Bloom"	80	85
2613	300l. Yacht	80	85
2614	300l. "Mitonia" "Peach Blossom"	80	85
2615	300l. "Parides gundalachianus" (butterfly)	80	85
2616	300l. "Laeliocattleya" "Grand Gate"	80	85

2617 300l. "Lycaste aromatica" 80 85
2618 300l. "Brassolaeliocattleya" "Golden Land" 80 85
2619 300l. "Cymbidium" "Southern Lace" and "Catastica teutila" (butterfly) 80 85
2620 400l. Vida "Pansy" 90 1·00
2621 500l. "Phalaenopsis" "Pink Beauty" 1·10 1·25
MS2622 Two sheets, each 80×110 mm. (a) 1500l. "Helianthus annuus" (b) 1500l. "Cymbidium" "Lucifer" Set of 2 sheets 6·00 7·00

Nos. 2602/10 and 2611/19 respectively were printed together, se-tenant, with the backgrounds forming composite designs.

295 Greek War Galley (4th-century B.C.)

1996. History of Ships. Multicoloured.
2623 300l. Type **295** 90 90
2624 300l. Roman war galley (A.D. 50) 90 90
2625 300l. Viking longship (9th-century) 90 90
2626 300l. Flemish carrack (15th-century) 90 90
2627 300l. Merchantman (16th-century) 90 90
2628 300l. Tudor galleon (16th-century) 90 90
2629 300l. Elizabethan galleon (17th-century) 90 90
2630 300l. Dutch warship (17th-century) 90 90
2631 300l. "Maestrale" (18th-century Maltese galley) 90 90
2632 300l. "Cutty Sark" (19th-century clipper) 90 90
2633 300l. "Great Britain", 1846 (steam/sail liner) 90 90
2634 300l. H.M.S. "Dreadnought", 1906 (battleship) 90 90
2635 300l. "Queen Elizabeth", 1940 (liner) 90 90
2636 300l. Ocean-going yacht, 1962 90 90
2637 300l. "United States", 1952 (liner) 90 90
2638 300l. Nuclear-powered submarine, 1950s 90 90
2639 300l. Super tanker, 1960s 90 90
2640 300l. U.S.S. "Enterprise", 1961 (aircraft carrier) 90 90
MS2641 Two sheets, each 96×66 mm. (a) 1500l. Egyptian ship (1480 B.C.) (56×42 mm). (b) 1500l. "Legend of the Seas" 1996 (cruise ship) (56×42 mm) Set of 2 sheets 8·50 9·00

No. 2634 is inscribed "Dreadnaught" in error.

1996. Christmas. Religious Paintings. As T 337 of St.Vincent. Multicoloured.
2642 200l. "Madonna of Humility" (Filippo Lippi) 60 15
2643 250l. "Coronation of the Virgin" (Lippi) 70 25
2644 400l. "The Annunciation" (Lippi) 1·25 1·10
2645 500l. "Annunciation" (different) (Lippi) 1·40 1·40
2646 600l. "Barbadori Altarpiece" (Lippi) 1·60 2·25
2647 800l. "Coronation of the Virgin" (different) (Lippi) 2·00 3·00
MS2648 Two sheets, each 76×106 mm. (a) 2000l. "Adoration of the Magi" (Rubens). (b) 2000l. "Holy Family with St. Anne" (Rubens) Set of 2 sheets 6·50 7·00

No. 2646 is inscribed "Alterpiece" in error.

296 "The Sea Dragon's Daughter"

1996. Legends of the Seas. Forty sheets, each 105×75 mm, containing T 296 and similar multicoloured designs.
MS2649 (a) 1500l. Type **296**; (b) 1500l. "Homo aquaticus"; (c) 1500l. Chinese sea fairy; (d) 1500l. Sea totem pole; (e) 1500l. "Turtle" (fantasy submarine) (horiz); (f) 1500l. Mermaid (horiz); (g) 1500l. "How the Whale got its throat" (horiz); (h) 1500l. Killer Whale crest; (i) 1500l. Odysseus and siren (horiz); (j) 1500l. "The Little Mermaid" (Hans Christian Andersen) (horiz); (k) 1500l. Squamish Indians (horiz); (l) 1500l. Boy on Dolphin; (m) 1500l. Atlantis airship (horiz); (n) 1500l. Sea Bishop (horiz); (o) 1500l. "Twenty Thousand Leagues Under the Sea" (Jules Verne); (p) 1500l. "Whale Song" (horiz); (q) 1500l. Arion (horiz); (r) 1500l. Dragonrider of Pern (horiz); (s) 1500l. Kelpie (horiz); (t) 1500l. Natsihlane on Sea Lion (horiz); (u) 1500l. Triton; (v) 1500l. Lang (dragon) (horiz); (w) 1500l. "The Flying Dutchman" (horiz); (x) 1500l. Lilith; (y) 1500l. "Queen of the Orkney Islands"; (z) 1500l. Merman; (za) 1500l. Sea Centaur; (zb) 1500l. Albatross (horiz); (zc) 1500l. "The Rime of the Ancient Mariner" (Samuel Coleridge); (zd) 1500l. Haida Eagle (horiz); (ze) 1500l. Poseidon; (zf) 1500l. Captain Ahab "Moby Dick"; (zg) 1500l. Underwater City; (zh) 1500l. Jonah and the Whale; (zi) 1500l. Waskos (horiz); (zj) 1500l. Tom Swift (horiz); (zk) 1500l. Arthropod sea monsters; (zl) 1500l. Sea Serpant; (zm) 1500l. Aphrodite (horiz); (zn) 1500l. Ship's figurehead Set of 40 sheets 48·00 55·00

297 Ox

1997. Chinese New Year ("Year of the Ox"). Multicoloured.
2650 250l. Type **297** (on purple panel) 40 50
2651 250l. Ox (on green panel) 40 50
2652 250l. Ox (on blue panel) 40 50
2653 250l. Ox (on brown panel) 40 50
MS2654 106×76 mm. Nos. 2650/3 1·60 1·75
MS2655 106×76 mm. 800l. Ox (vert) 1·40 1·75

298 Aladdin and Jasmine

1997. Christmas. Aladdin. Disney Cartoon Characters. Multicoloured.
2656 10l. Type **298** 25 10
2657 15l. Genie and Santa Claus 25 10
2658 20l. Aladdin and Jasmine on magic carpet 30 10
2659 25l. Genie as a Christmas tree 30 10
2660 30l. Genie as Santa Claus and Aladdin 30 10
2661 100l. Aladdin, Jasmine and Genie on magic carpet 1·25 30
2662 800l. Genie writing letter to Santa Claus 3·50 3·75
2663 1000l. Genie with four heads 3·75 4·25
MS2664 Two sheets, each 127×101 mm. (a) 2000l. Aladdin under a pile of gold; (b) 2000l. Aladdin and Jasmine on magic carpet (horiz) Set of 2 sheets 7·50 8·00

299 Hong Kong Skyline by Day

1997. "Hong Kong '97" International Stamp Exhibition. Two sheets, each 125×68 mm, containing T 299 and similar vert designs. Multicoloured.
MS2665 (a) 500l.×4 forming panorama of central Hong Kong by day. (b) 500l.×4 forming panorama of central Hong Kong by night Set of 2 sheets 7·50 8·00

1997. 50th Anniv of UNESCO. As T 342a of St. Vincent. Multicoloured.
2666 60l. Church, Kizhi Pogost, Russia 15 10
2667 200l. Durmitor National Park, Yugoslavia 40 15
2668 250l. Nessebar, Bulgaria 60 35
2669 300l. Roros, Norway 75 80
2670 300l. Varsovia city gate, Poland 75 80
2671 300l. Nuestra Senora Cathedral, Luxembourg 75 80
2672 300l. Tower, Vilnius, Lithuania 75 80
2673 300l. Jelling, Denmark 75 80
2674 300l. Petajavesi Church, Finland 75 80
2675 300l. Round house, Sweden 75 80
2676 300l. Berne Cathedral, Switzerland 75 80
2677 300l. Slopes of Mount Kilimanjaro, Tanzania 75 80
2678 300l. Tombs, Fasil Ghebbi, Ethiopia 75 80
2679 300l. Mount Ruwenzori National Park, Uganda 75 80
2680 300l. Nubia Monument, Abu Simbel, Egypt 75 80
2681 300l. Tsingy of Bemaraha Nature Reserve, Madagascar 75 80
2682 300l. House, Djenne, Mali 75 80
2683 300l. Traditional house, Ghana 75 80
2684 300l. House, Abomey, Benin 75 80
2685 400l. Gateway, Bukhara, Uzbekistan 85 90
2686 500l. Monastery, Petchersk, Ukraine 95 1·10
2687 500l. Tower, Himeji-jo, Japan (horiz) 95 1·10
2688 500l. Gateway, Himeji-jo, Japan (horiz) 95 1·10
2689 500l. Outer wall and turrets, Himeji-jo, Japan (horiz) 95 1·10
2690 500l. Village, Himeji-jo, Japan (horiz) 95 1·10
2691 500l. Ornate gables, Himeji-jo, Japan (horiz) 95 1·10
2692 800l. Mountains, Slovakia 1·40 1·60
MS2693 Two sheets, each 127×102 mm. (a) 2000l. Djudj National Bird Sanctuary, Senegal (horiz). (b) 2000l. The Acropolis, Athens, Greece (horiz) Set of 2 sheets 7·50 8·00

No. 2676 is inscribed "BERNA", No. 2677 "KILIMANDJARO" and No. 2686 "MONESTRY", all in error.

1997. 300th Anniv of Mother Goose Nursery Rhymes. Two sheets, each 72×102 mm, containing horiz designs as T 346a of St. Vincent.
MS2694 (a) 1500l. "Three Blind Mice". (b) 1500l. Woman in pink dress ("Myself") Set of 2 sheets 5·50 6·00

1997. 10th Anniv of Chernobyl Nuclear Disaster. As T 347 of St. Vincent. Multicoloured.
2695 1000l. Child's face and UNESCO emblem 2·00 2·50
2696 1500l. As 1000l., but inscribed "CHABAD'S CHILDREN OF CHERNOBYL" at foot 2·50 3·00

1997. Golden Wedding of Queen Elizabeth and Prince Philip. As T 347a of St. Vincent. Multicoloured (except Nos. 2699/2700).
2697 400l. Queen Elizabeth II 1·50 1·50
2698 400l. Royal coat of arms 1·50 1·50
2699 400l. Queen Elizabeth with Prince Philip in military uniform (black) 1·50 1·50
2700 400l. Queen Elizabeth with Prince Philip in naval mess dress (black) 1·50 1·50
2701 400l. St. James's Palace 1·50 1·50
2702 400l. Prince Philip 1·50 1·50
MS2703 100×70 mm. 1500l. Queen Elizabeth with Prince Philip in naval uniform 2·75 3·00

1997. Birth Bicentenary of Hiroshige (Japanese painter). "One Hundred Famous Views of Edo". As T 347d of St. Vincent. Multicoloured.
2704 400l. "Hatsune Riding Grounds, Bakuro-cho" 85 85
2706 400l. "Ryogoku Bridge and the Great Riverbank" 85 85
2707 400l. "Asakusa River, Great Riverbank, Miyato River" 85 85
2708 400l. "Silk-goods Lane, Odenma-cho" 85 85
2709 400l. "Mokuboji Temple, Uchigawa Inlet, Gozensaihata" 85 85
2710 400l. "Mannen Bridge, Fukagawa" 85 85
MS2710 Two sheets, each 102×127 mm. (a) 1500l. "Nihonbashi Bridge and Edobashi Bridge". (b) 1500l. "Tsukudajima from Eitai Bridge" Set of 2 sheets 5·00 5·50

300 Hong Kong Skyline

1997. Return of Hong Kong to China.
2711 **300** 400l. multicoloured 85 90
2712 - 500l. multicoloured 95 1·00
2713 - 550l. multicoloured 1·00 1·10
2714 - 600l. multicoloured 1·10 1·25
2715 - 650l. multicoloured 1·25 1·40
2716 - 800l. multicoloured 1·50 1·60

DESIGNS: 500l. to 650l. Different views of modern Hong Kong; 800l. Deng Xiaoping.

301 Calgary Stadium, 1988

1997. Winter Olympic Games, Nagano, Japan (1998). Multicoloured.
2717 250l. Type **301** 60 40
2718 300l. Freestyle Skiing Aerials, 1994 (vert) 75 80
2719 300l. Peggy Fleming (U.S.A.) (figure skating, 1968) (vert) 75 80
2720 300l. Japanese competitor (Nordic combined-ski jump, 1992/4) (vert) 75 80
2721 300l. German team (two-man luge, 1968 to 1992) (vert) 75 80
2722 300l. Frank-Peter Roetsch (East Germany) (biathlon, 1988) (vert) 75 80
2723 500l. Ice Hockey (vert) 1·25 1·40
2724 800l. Dan Jansen (U.S.A.) (speed skating, 1994) (vert) 1·50 1·60
MS2725 Two sheets. (a) 106×76 mm. 1500l. Jamaican bobsleigh team (vert). (b) 76×106 mm. 1500l. Johann Olav Koss (Norway) (speed skating, 1992/4) (vert) Set of 2 sheets 5·00 5·50

301a Stabile, Uruguay

1997. World Cup Football Championship, France (1998).
2726 **301a** 100l. black 30 20
2727 - 150l. black 40 30
2728 - 200l. black 50 30
2729 - 250l. black 60 40
2730 - 300l. multicoloured 80 85
2731 - 300l. multicoloured 80 85
2732 - 300l. multicoloured 80 85
2733 - 300l. multicoloured 80 85
2734 - 300l. multicoloured 80 85
2735 - 300l. multicoloured 80 85
2736 - 300l. multicoloured 80 85
2737 - 300l. multicoloured 80 85
2738 - 500l. black 95 1·10
2739 - 600l. black 1·10 1·25
MS2740 Two sheets, each 127×102 mm. (a) 1500l. brown (b) 1500l. multicoloured Set of 2 sheets 8·00 8·00

DESIGNS—VERT: No. 2727, Schavio, Italy; 2728, Kocsis, Hungary; 2729, Nejedly, Czechoslovakia; 2730, Dwight Yorke, Trinidad and Tobago; 2731, Dennis Bergkamp, Netherlands; 2732, Steve McManaman, England; 2733, Ryan Giggs, Wales; 2734, Romario, Brazil; 2735, Faustino Asprilla, Colombia; 2736, Roy Keane, Republic of Ireland; 2737, Peter Schmeichel, Denmark; 2738, Leonidas, Brazil; 2739, Ademir, Brazil. HORIZ: No. **MS**2740a, Pele, Brazil; **MS**2740b, Lato, Poland.

302 "Vindula erota"

1997. Butterflies of the World. Multicoloured.

No.	Description	Unused	Used
2741	150l. Type **302**	50	20
2742	200l. "Pereute leucodrosime"	65	20
2743	250l. "Dynastor napolean"	70	25
2744	300l. "Thauria aliris"	80	50
2745	500l. "Lycaena dispar"	1·10	1·25
2746	500l. "Graphium sarpedon"	1·10	1·25
2747	500l. "Euploe core"	1·10	1·25
2748	500l. "Papilio cresphontes"	1·10	1·25
2749	500l. "Colotis danae"	1·10	1·25
2750	500l. "Battus philenor"	1·10	1·25
2751	600l. "Papilio aegeus"	1·25	1·40
2752	600l. "Mylothris chloris"	1·25	1·40
2753	600l. "Argynnis lathonia"	1·25	1·40
2754	600l. "Elymnias agondas"	1·25	1·40
2755	600l. "Palla ussheri"	1·25	1·40
2756	600l. "Papilio glaucus"	1·25	1·40
2757	600l. "Cercyonis pegala"	1·25	1·40
2758	800l. "Amblypodia anita"	1·75	1·90
2759	1500l. "Kallimoides rumia"	3·00	3·50
2760	2000l. "Papilio dardanas"	3·50	4·00
MS2761	Two sheets, each 74×103 mm. (a) 3000l. "Hebomoia glaucippe" (horiz). (b) 3000l. "Colias eurytheme" (horiz) Set of 2 sheets	10·00	11·00

Nos. 2745/50 and 2752/7 respectively were printed together, se-tenant, with the backgrounds forming composite designs.

303 Lon Chaney in "Phantom of the Opera", 1925

1997. Famous Films. Horror classics (Nos. 2762/70) or the films of Alfred Hitchcock (Nos. 2771/9). Multicoloured.

No.	Description	Unused	Used
2762	300l. Type **303**	80	80
2763	300l. Boris Karloff in "The Mummy", 1932	80	80
2764	300l. Fredric March in "Dr. Jekyll and Mr Hyde", 1932	80	80
2765	300l. Lon Chaney Jr. in "The Wolf Man", 1941	80	80
2766	300l. Charles Laughton in "Island of Lost Souls", 1933	80	80
2767	300l. Lionel Atwill in "Mystery of the Wax Museum", 1933	80	80
2768	300l. Bela Lugosi in "Dracula", 1931	80	80
2769	300l. Vincent Price in "The Haunted Palace", 1963	80	80
2770	300l. Elsa Lanchester in "Bride of Frankenstein", 1935	80	80
2771	350l. Ray Milland in "Dial M for Murder", 1954	80	80
2772	350l. James Stewart and Kim Novak in "Vertigo", 1958	80	80
2773	350l. Cary Grant, Ingrid Bergman and Claude Rains in "Notorious", 1946	80	80
2774	350l. Farley Granger and John Dall in "Rope", 1948	80	80
2775	350l. Cary Grant in "North by Northwest", 1959	80	80
2776	350l. James Stewart and Grace Kelly in "Rear Window", 1954	80	80
2777	350l. Joan Fontaine and Laurence Olivier in "Rebecca", 1940	80	80
2778	350l. Tippi Hedren in "The Birds", 1963	80	80
2779	350l. Janet Leigh in "Psycho", 1960	80	80
MS2780	Two sheets. (a) 72×102 mm. 1500l. Alfred Hitchcock. (b) 82×82 mm. 3000l. Boris Karloff in "Son of Frankenstein" 1939 Set of 2 sheets	8·50	9·00

Nos. 2762/70 and 2771/9 respectively were printed together, se-tenant, with the backgrounds forming composite designs.

304 Shetland Sheepdog

1997. Dogs and Cats. Multicoloured.

No.	Description	Unused	Used
2781	100l. Type **304**	40	15
2782	150l. American shorthair tabby cat	50	25
2783	250l. British shorthair cat	70	55
2784	250l. Alaskan husky	70	55
2785	400l. Basset hound	90	90
2786	400l. Irish setter	90	90
2787	400l. St. Bernard	90	90
2788	400l. German shepherd	90	90
2789	400l. Dalmatian	90	90
2790	400l. Cocker spaniel	90	90
2791	400l. Chartreux cat	90	90
2792	400l. Abyssinian cat	90	90
2793	400l. Burmese cat	90	90
2794	400l. White angora cat	90	90
2795	400l. Japanese bobtail cat	90	90
2796	400l. Cymric cat	90	90
2797	500l. Turkish angora cat	95	95
2798	600l. Jack Russell terrier	1·10	1·25
MS2799	Two sheets, each 106×75 mm. (a) 1500l. Boxer (31×63 mm). (b) 1500l. Egyptian mau cat (63×31 mm) Set of 2 sheets	6·50	7·00

305 "Ansellia africana"

1997. Orchids of the World. Multicoloured.

No.	Description	Unused	Used
2800	150l. Type **305**	60	25
2801	200l. "Maxillaria praestans"	70	30
2802	250l. "Cymbidium mimi"	70	35
2803	300l. "Dendrobium bigibbum"	80	40
2804	400l. "Laelia anceps"	90	95
2805	400l. "Paphiopedilum fairrieanum"	90	95
2806	400l. "Restrepia lansbergii"	90	95
2807	400l. "Yamadara cattleya"	90	95
2808	400l. "Cleistes divaricata"	90	95
2809	400l. "Calypso bulbosa"	90	95
2810	500l. "Encyclia vitellina"	1·00	1·00
2811	800l. "Epidendrum prismatocarpum"	1·75	2·00
MS2812	Two sheets, each 76×106 mm. (a) 1500l. "Paphiopedilum tonsum" (b) 1500l. "Odontoglossum schieperianum" Set of 2 sheets	5·50	5·50

306 Daisy Duck

1997. Christmas. Disney Holidays. Multicoloured.

No.	Description	Unused	Used
2813	50l. Type **306**	20	20
2814	50l. Huey, Dewey and Louie	20	20
2815	50l. Donald Duck	20	20
2816	50l. Minnie Mouse	20	20
2817	50l. Morty and Ferdie	20	20
2818	50l. Mickey Mouse	20	20
2819	150l. As No. 2814	60	60
2820	200l. As No. 2817	75	75
2821	250l. Type **306**	90	90
2822	300l. As No. 2816	1·10	1·10
2823	400l. As No. 2818	1·25	1·40
2824	500l. As No. 2815	1·50	1·60
2825	600l. Pluto	1·75	2·00
2826	800l. Goofy	2·25	2·50
MS2827	Two sheets. (a) 114×140 mm. 2000l. Mickey Mouse in sleigh. (b) 140×114 mm. 2000l. Mickey, Donald and Daisy (horiz) Set of 2 sheets	11·00	12·00

307 Benoist Type XIV

1997. Development of the Civil Airliner. Mult.

No.	Description	Unused	Used
2828	600l. Type **307**	1·50	1·50
2829	600l. Douglas DC-3	1·50	1·50
2830	600l. Junkers JU52/3m seaplane	1·50	1·50
2831	600l. Sikorsky S-42 flying boat	1·50	1·50
2832	600l. Sud Caravelle 6	1·50	1·50
2833	600l. Boeing 707	1·50	1·50
2834	600l. De Havilland Comet	1·50	1·50
2835	600l. Airbus Industrie A300	1·50	1·50
MS2836	Two sheets, each 121×96 mm. (a) 2000l. Lockheed L.1649A Starliner (91×34 mm). (b) 2000l. Concorde (91×34 mm) Set of 2 sheets	8·00	8·50

308 "The Annunciation" (Titian)

1997. Christmas. Religious Paintings. Mult.

No.	Description	Unused	Used
2837	100l. Type **308**	35	10
2838	150l. "The Annunciation" (Titian) (different)	40	20
2839	200l. "Madonna of Foligno" (Raphael)	50	20
2840	250l. "The Annunciation" (Michelino)	60	25
2841	500l. "The Prophet Isaiah" (Michelangelo)	1·10	1·50
2842	600l. "Three Angels" (Master of the Rhenish Housebook)	1·40	1·75
MS2843	Two sheets, each 105×95 mm. (a) 2000l. "The Fall of the Rebel Angels" (Bruegel the Elder) (horiz). (b) 2000l. Angel and Monk (Anon) (horiz) Set of 2 sheets	6·00	7·00

308a With Daffodils

1998. Diana, Princess of Wales Commemoration. Multicoloured (except Nos. 2844, 2849, 2854 and 2856).

No.	Description	Unused	Used
2844	400l. Type **308a** (violet and black)	80	80
2845	400l. Carrying bouquet	80	80
2846	400l. With Mother Teresa	80	80
2847	400l. Wearing green and black jacket	80	80
2848	400l. With shawl over head	80	80
2849	400l. In evening dress (red and black)	80	80
2850	400l. Wearing choker and earrings	80	80
2851	400l. With Prince William	80	80
2852	400l. Wearing blue jacket and hat	80	80
2853	400l. Wearing white jacket	80	80
2854	400l. Wearing hat (brown and black)	80	80
2855	400l. Wearing black evening dress	80	80
2856	400l. Laughing (blue and black)	80	80
2857	400l. Wearing blue and white jacket and hat	80	80
2858	400l. Wearing green jacket with arms folded	80	80
2859	400l. Wearing black and white hat	80	80
2860	400l. Wearing open white shirt	80	80
2861	400l. Getting out of car	80	80
MS2862	Three sheets. (a) 100×70 mm. 1500l. Spooning food into bowl. (b) 100×70 mm. 1500l. Wearing grey-blue hat and jacket. (c) 70×100 mm. 1500l. Inspecting guard of honour Set of 3 sheets	8·50	9·00

309 Tiger

1998. Chinese New Year ("Year of the Tiger"). Designs with the tiger in the colour given.

No.	Type	Description	Unused	Used
2863	**309**	250l. mult (mauve)	40	50
2864	-	250l. mult (lake)	40	50
2865	-	250l. mult (purple)	40	50
2866	-	250l. mult (red)	40	50
MS2867		76×106 mm. 800l. multicoloured (vert)	1·25	1·50

310 "Metagyrphus nitens"

1998. Fauna and Flora. Multicoloured.

No.	Description	Unused	Used
2868	200l. Type **310**	35	15
2869	250l. Lord Derby's parakeet	50	25
2870	300l. Narcissus	55	20
2871	400l. "Barbus tetrazona" (fish) (horiz)	75	60
2872	450l. Japanese white-eyes (bird)	80	85
2873	450l. Rhododendron (horiz)	80	85
2874	450l. Slow loris (horiz)	80	85
2875	450l. Gentiana (flower) (horiz)	80	85
2876	450l. "Orthetrum albistylum" (dragonfly) (horiz)	80	85
2877	450l. "Coluber jugularis" (snake) (horiz)	80	85
2878	450l. Cheetah (horiz)	80	85
2879	450l. "Ornithogalum thyrsoides" (plant) (horiz)	80	85
2880	450l. Ostrich (horiz)	80	85
2881	450l. Common chameleon (horiz)	80	85
2882	450l. Fennec fox (horiz)	80	85
2883	450l. "Junonia hierta cebrene" (butterfly) (horiz)	80	85
2884	500l. "Agalychnis callidryas" (frog) (horiz)	80	85
2885	600l. Wolverine (horiz)	95	95
MS2886	Two sheets (a) 70×100 mm. 2000l. Louisiana heron ("Tricoloured Heron") (b) 100×70 mm. 2000l. "Atheris squamiger" (snake) (horiz) Set of 2 sheets	6·50	7·00

Nos. 2872/7 and 2878/83 respectively were printed together, se-tenant, with the backgrounds forming composite designs.

311 Hypsilophodon

1998. Prehistoric Animals. Multicoloured.

No.	Description	Unused	Used
2887	200l. Type **311**	40	15
2888	400l. Lambeosaurus	75	50
2889	500l. Corythosaurus	80	85
2890	500l. Tyrannosaurus (horiz)	80	85
2891	500l. Tenontosaurus (horiz)	80	85
2892	500l. Deinonychus (horiz)	80	85
2893	500l. Triceratops (horiz)	80	85
2894	500l. Maiasaura with eggs (horiz)	80	85
2895	500l. Struthiomimus (horiz)	80	85
2896	500l. Plateosaurus	80	85
2897	500l. Tyrannosaurus	80	85
2898	500l. Brachiosaurus	80	85
2899	500l. Iguanodon	80	85
2900	500l. Styracosaurus	80	85
2901	500l. Hadrosaurus	80	85
2902	600l. Stegosaurus	85	90
2903	800l. Antrodemus (horiz)	1·25	1·40
MS2904	Two sheets. (a) 73×103 mm. 2000l. Triceratops (horiz). (b) 83×108 mm. 2000l. Tyrannosaurus (horiz) Set of 2 sheets	6·50	7·00

Nos. 2890/5 and 2896/2901 respectively were printed together, se-tenant, with the backgrounds forming composite designs.

312 Phoenician Galley

1998. Ships of the World. Multicoloured.

2905	300l. Type **312**	90	90
2906	300l. Viking longship	90	90
2907	300l. Carrack	90	90
2908	300l. Venetian galley	90	90
2909	300l. Galeasse	90	90
2910	300l. Chebeck	90	90
2911	300l. Junk	90	90
2912	300l. H.M.S. "Victory" (ship of the line, 1765)	90	90
2913	300l. "Savannah" (paddle-steamer)	90	90
2914	300l. Gaissa (sailing canoe)	90	90
2915	300l. H.M.S. "Warrior" (ironclad)	90	90
2916	300l. "Preussen" (full-rigged ship)	90	90
MS2917	Two sheets, each 108×83 mm. (a) 2000l. "Santa Maria" (Columbus) (56×41 mm). (b) 2000l. "Titanic" (liner) (56×41 mm) Set of 2 sheets	7·00	7·50

1998. 70th Birthday of Mickey Mouse. Nos. 2813/18 and MS2827. Optd with Mickey Mouse and HAPPY BIRTHDAY 1998.

2918	50l. Type **306**	90	80
2919	50l. Huey, Dewey and Louie	90	80
2920	50l. Donald Duck	90	80
2921	50l. Minnie Mouse	90	80
2922	50l. Morty and Ferdie	90	80
2923	50l. Mickey Mouse	90	80
MS2924	Two sheets. (a) 114×140 mm. 2000l. Mickey Mouse in sleigh. (b) 140×114 mm. 2000l. Mickey, Donald and Daisy (horiz) Set of 2 sheets	11·00	12·00

No. **MS**2924 are overprinted on the sheet margins which are additionally overprinted "MICKEY & MINNIE — 70th ANNIVERSARY".

314 Kiara and Butterfly

1998. Disney's "Lion King" (cartoon film). Multicoloured.

2925	500l. Type **314**	1·25	1·25
2926	500l. Timon and Pumbaa	1·25	1·25
2927	500l. Kiara	1·25	1·25
2928	500l. Kiara and Kovu lying down	1·25	1·25
2929	500l. Kovu with bird	1·25	1·25
2930	500l. Kiara sitting with Kovu	1·25	1·25
2931	500l. Kiara and bird	1·25	1·25
2932	500l. Pumbaa	1·25	1·25
2933	500l. Kiara and Kovu side by side	1·25	1·25
2934	500l. Kovu	1·25	1·25
2935	500l. Kiara and Kovu back to back	1·25	1·25
2936	500l. Timon	1·25	1·25
MS2937	Two sheets, each 130×104 mm. (a) 2500l. Pumbaa and Timon. (b) 2500l. Kiara, Kovu and butterflies (horiz).	12·00	13·00

315 "Mary Magdalen Penitent" (Titian)

1998. Christmas. Religious Paintings. Mult.

2938	200l. Type **315**	35	15
2939	500l. "Lamentation of Christ" (Veronese)	75	30
2940	1500l. "Building of Noah's Ark" (Guido Reni)	2·00	2·50
2941	2000l. "Abraham and Isaac" (Rembrandt)	2·50	3·00
MS2942	Two sheets, each 70×100 mm. (a) 3000l. "The Assumption of the Virgin" (Murillo). (b) 3000l. "Adoration of the Shepherds" (Murillo) Set of 2 sheets	7·50	8·50

1998. 25th Death Anniv of Pablo Picasso (painter). As T 373 of St. Vincent. Multicoloured.

2943	400l. "Man with Straw Hat and Ice Cream Cone" (vert)	70	50
2944	600l. "Woman in a Red Arm-chair" (vert)	1·00	1·10
2945	800l. "Nude in a Garden"	1·25	1·50
MS2946	101×127 mm. 2000l. "Girl holding a Dove" (vert)	2·50	3·00

315a Dan Beard and Lord Baden-Powell, 1937

1998. 19th World Scout Jamboree, Chile. Multicoloured (except No. 2950).

2947	1500l. Type **315a**	1·75	1·90
2948	1500l. Kuwaiti Scouts	1·75	1·90
2949	1500l. Scout leader feeding bear cub	1·75	1·90
2950	1500l. William D. Boyce (founder of Lone Scouts) (purple, brown and black) (vert)	1·75	1·90
2951	1500l. Guion S. Bluford (astronaut and former Eagle scout) (vert)	1·75	1·90
2952	1500l. Ellison S. Onizuka (astronaut and former Eagle scout) (vert)	1·75	1·90
MS2953	Two sheets, each 70×100 mm. (a) 3000l. Lord and Lady Baden-Powell, 1932. (b) 3000l. Feeding bear cub from bottle Set of 2 sheets	8·00	9·00

315b Mahatma Gandhi

1998. 50th Death Anniv of Mahatma Gandhi.

2954	**315b** 600l. multicoloured	2·75	2·25
MS2955	98×59 mm. 2000l. brown and black (horiz)	3·25	3·50

1998. 80th Anniv of Royal Air Force. As T 373d of St. Vincent. Multicoloured.

2956	800l. McDonnell Douglas FRG2 Phantom	2·00	2·00
2957	800l. Pair of Panavia Tornado GR1s	2·00	2·00
2958	800l. Sepecat Jaguar GR1A	2·00	2·00
2959	800l. Lockheed C-130 Hercules	2·00	2·00
MS2960	Two sheets, each 92×70 mm.(a) 2000l. Lysander (reconnaissance) and Eurofighter EF-2000. (b) 2000l. Common buzzard and Bristol F2B fighter Set of 2 sheets	7·00	7·00

316 "Rocks and a Small Valley"

1998. Birth Bicentenary of Eugene Delacroix (painter). Multicoloured.

2961	400l. Type **316**	1·25	1·25
2962	400l. "Jewish Musicians from Magador"	1·25	1·25
2963	400l. "Moroccans travelling"	1·25	1·25
2964	400l. "Women of Algiers in their Apartment"	1·25	1·25
2965	400l. "Moroccan Military Training"	1·25	1·25
2966	400l. "Arabs skirmishing in the Mountains"	1·25	1·25
2967	400l. "Arab Chieftain reclining on a Carpet"	1·25	1·25
2968	400l. "Procession in Tangier"	1·25	1·25
MS2969	85×100 mm. 400l. "Self-portrait" (vert)	2·00	2·25

316a Diana, Princess of Wales

1998. 1st Death Anniv of Diana, Princess of Wales. Multicoloured.

2970	**316a** 600l. multicoloured	1·25	1·40

317 Rabbit

1998. Chinese New Year ("Year of the Rabbit"). Designs with the rabbit in the colour given.

2971	**317** 700l. mult (red)	1·10	1·25
2972	- 700l. mult (purple)	1·10	1·25
2973	- 700l. mult (blue)	1·10	1·25
2974	- 700l. mult (violet)	1·10	1·25
MS2975	76×106 mm. 1500l. multicoloured (vert)	2·25	2·75

318 Powder-blue Surgeonfish

1999. International Year of the Ocean. Mult.

2976	150l. Type **318**	35	15
2977	250l. Frilled anemone	50	20
2978	400l. Reef heron ("Eastern Reef Heron")	80	85
2979	400l. Dolphins	80	85
2980	400l. Humpback whale and sailing ship	80	85
2981	400l. Green-winged macaw ("Red and Green Macaw")	80	85
2982	400l. Blue tangs	80	85
2983	400l. Guitarfish and blue-striped pipefish	80	85
2984	400l. Manatees	80	85
2985	400l. Hammerhead shark	80	85
2986	400l. Blue shark	80	85
2987	400l. Lemon goby and moorish idol	80	85
2988	400l. Ribbon moray ("Ribbon Eels")	80	85
2989	400l. Loggerhead turtle	80	85
2990	500l. Blue shark	85	90
2991	500l. Tiger shark	85	90
2992	500l. Bull shark	85	90
2993	500l. Great white shark	85	90
2994	500l. Scalloped hammerhead shark	85	90
2995	500l. Oceanic white-tipped shark	85	90
2996	500l. Zebra shark	85	90
2997	500l. Leopard shark	85	90
2998	500l. Horn shark	85	90
2999	500l. Hector's dolphin	85	90
3000	500l. Tucuxi	85	90
3001	500l. Hourglass dolphin	85	90
3002	500l. Bottlenose dolphin	85	90
3003	500l. Gray's beaked whale	85	90
3004	500l. Bowhead whale	85	90
3005	500l. Fin whale	85	90
3006	500l. Gray whale	85	90
3007	500l. Blue whale	85	90
3008	600l. Red beard sponge	95	1·00
3009	800l. Dusky batfish ("Red-finned Batfish")	1·25	1·40
MS3010	Three sheets, each 110×85 mm. (a) 3000l. Purple fire goby ("Purple Fire-fish"). (b) 3000l. Spotted eagle ray. (c) 3000l. Leather-back turtle Set of 3 sheets	15·00	16·00

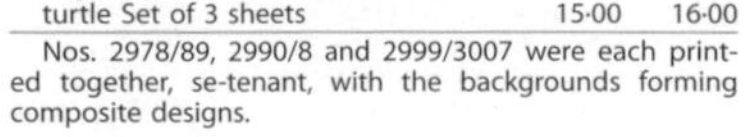

Nos. 2978/89, 2990/8 and 2999/3007 were each printed together, se-tenant, with the backgrounds forming composite designs.

319 Grumman X-29

1999. Aircraft. Multicoloured.

3011	200l. Type **319**	40	20
3012	300l. Bell XS-1 rocket aircraft	50	20
3013	400l. Mikoyan Gurevich MiG-21	60	30
3014	600l. Bleriot XI	80	85
3015	600l. Nieuport 11 "Bebe"	80	85
3016	600l. D.H.100 Vampire	80	85
3017	600l. Aerospatiale/Aeritalia ATR 72	80	85
3018	600l. Fiat CR-32	80	85
3019	600l. Curtiss P-6E Hawk	80	85
3020	600l. SAAB JA 37 Viggen	80	85
3021	600l. Piper PA-46 Malibu	80	85
3022	600l. Grumman F-14 Tomcat	80	85
3023	600l. Grumman F3F-1	80	85
3024	600l. North American F-86A Sabre	80	85
3025	600l. Cessna 377 Super Skymaster	80	85
3026	600l. General Dynamics F-16 Fighting Falcon	80	85
3027	600l. "Voyager" experimental aircraft	80	85
3028	600l. Fairchild A10A Thunderbolt II	80	85
3029	600l. Wiley Post's Lockheed Vega, 1933	80	85
3030	600l. Amelia Earhart's Lockheed Vega, 1930	80	85
3031	600l. Sopwith Tabloid	80	85
3032	600l. Vickers F.B.5 "Gun Bus"	80	85
3033	600l. Savoia-Marchetti S.M. 79-II Sparviero	80	85
3034	600l. Mitsubishi A6M3 "Zero Sen"	80	85
3035	600l. Morane-Saulnier L	80	85
3036	600l. Shorts 360	80	85
3037	600l. Tupolev TU-160	80	85
3038	600l. Mikoyan-Gurevich MiG-15	80	85
3039	800l. Fokker F.VIIa/3m "Southern Cross"	1·25	1·40
3040	1500l. Supermarine S6B (seaplane)	2·00	2·50
MS3041	Two sheets, each 98×68 mm. (a) 3000l. Ryan NYP Special "Spirit of St. Louis" (56×42 mm). (b) 3000l. Canadair CL-215 (fire-fighting amphibian) (56×42 mm) Set of 2 sheets	8·50	9·00

No. 3023 is inscribed "GUMMAN F3F-1", No. 3027 "NICK" and No. 3030 "Amella Earhart", all in error.

320 "Geranium wallichianum"

1999. "Australia '99" World Stamp Exhibition, Melbourne. Flowers. Multicoloured.

3042	150l. Type **320**	30	15
3043	200l. "Osmanthus x burkwoodii"	40	20
3044	250l. "Iris pallida dalmatica" (vert)	40	20
3045	500l. Rhododendron (vert)	70	30
3046	600l. Rose (vert)	80	80
3047	600l. "Clematis hybrida" (vert)	80	80
3048	600l. "Cardiospermum halicacabum" (vert)	80	80
3049	600l. "Fritillaria imperialis" (vert)	80	80
3050	600l. "Iris foetidiissima" (vert)	80	80
3051	600l. Pyracantha (vert)	80	80
3052	600l. "Hepatica transsilvanica" (vert)	80	80
3053	600l. "Aquilegia olympica"	80	80
3054	600l. Lilium (orange)	80	80
3055	600l. "Magnolia grandiflora"	80	80
3056	600l. "Polygonatum x hybridum"	80	80
3057	600l. "Clematis montana"	80	80
3058	600l. "Vinca minor"	80	80
3059	600l. "Jack Snipe"	80	80
3060	600l. "Alstroemeria ligtu"	80	80
3061	600l. Lilium (yellow)	80	80
3062	600l. "Marjorie fair"	80	80
3063	600l. "Anemone coronaria"	80	80
3064	600l. "Clematis ranncu lanaceae"	80	80
3065	600l. "Colchicum speciosum"	80	80
3066	600l. "Scandere"	80	80
3067	600l. "Helianthus annuus"	80	80
3068	600l. "Lady Kerkrade"	80	80
3069	600l. "Clematis x durandii"	80	80
3070	600l. "Lilium regale"	80	80
3071	800l. Papoose (vert)	1·25	1·40
3072	1500l. "Viola labradorica" (vert)	1·75	2·00

3073 2000l. "Rosa banksiae lutea" (vert) 2·25 2·50

MS3074 Four sheets. (a) 100×74 mm. 4000l. "Clerodendrum trichotomum fargesii" (b) 75×100 mm. 4000l. "Rubus fruitcosus" (vert). (c) 75×100 mm. 4000l. "Crocus angustifolius" (vert). (d) 75×100 mm. 4000l. "Holboellia" Set of 4 sheets 18·00 20·00

Nos. 3047/52, 3053/8 and 3071/3 were printed together, se-tenant, with the backgrounds forming a composite design.

Only Nos. 3042/6 and 3071/3 show the "Australia '99" emblem actually printed on the stamp.

No. 3043 is inscribed "Osmanthus burkwoodu" and No. 3069 "Clematix x durandii", both in error.

321 Red-headed Malimbe

1999. Birds of Africa. Multicoloured.

3075 400l. Type **321** 50 25
3076 500l. Common kestrel 60 30
3077 600l. Little owl 70 75
3078 600l. Eastern white pelican ("Great White Pelican") 70 75
3079 600l. Superb starling 70 75
3080 600l. Red-throated bee eater 70 75
3081 600l. Woodland kingfisher 70 75
3082 600l. Purple swamphen 70 75
3083 600l. Lesser pied kingfisher ("Pied Kingfisher") 70 75
3084 600l. African spoonbill 70 75
3085 600l. Egyptian plover ("Crocodilebird") 70 75
3086 600l. Cattle egret 70 75
3087 600l. White-fronted bee eater 70 75
3088 600l. Gray parrot ("African Grey Parrot") 70 75
3089 600l. Cinnamon-chested bee eater 70 75
3090 600l. Malachite kingfisher 70 75
3091 600l. White-throated bee eater 70 75
3092 600l. Yellow-billed stork 70 75
3093 600l. Hildebrandt's starling 70 75
3094 600l. White-faced whistling duck (horiz) 70 75
3095 600l. Black-headed heron (horiz) 70 75
3096 600l. Black-headed gonolek (horiz) 70 75
3097 600l. Malachite kingfisher (horiz) 70 75
3098 600l. African fish eagle ("Fish-eagle") (horiz) 70 75
3099 600l. African spoonbill (horiz) 70 75
3100 600l. African skimmer (horiz) 70 75
3101 600l. Black heron (horiz) 70 75
3102 600l. Allen's gallinule (horiz) 70 75
3103 600l. Montagu's harrier (horiz) 70 75
3104 600l. Booted eagle (horiz) 70 75
3105 600l. Yellow-crested helmet shrike (horiz) 70 75
3106 600l. Red-tufted malachite sunbird ("Scarlet-tufted Malachite Sunbird") (horiz) 70 75
3107 600l. Pin-tailed whydah (horiz) 70 75
3108 600l. Red-headed weaver ("Red-headed Malimbe") (horiz) 70 75
3109 600l. Violet-backed sunbird (horiz) 70 75
3110 600l. Yellow white eye (horiz) 70 75
3111 600l. Brubru shrike (horiz) 70 75
3112 600l. African paradise flycatcher ("African Paradise Monarch") (horiz) 70 75
3113 600l. Lilac-breasted roller (horiz) 70 75
3114 600l. Scops owl ("European Scops Owl") (horiz) 70 75
3115 600l. African emerald cuckoo (horiz) 70 75
3116 600l. Blue flycatcher ("Blue Monarch") (horiz) 70 75
3117 600l. African golden oriole (horiz) 70 75
3118 600l. White-throated bee eater (horiz) 70 75
3119 600l. Black-bellied seedcracker (horiz) 70 75
3120 600l. Hoopoe (horiz) 70 75
3121 600l. Scimitar-bill (horiz) 70 75
3122 600l. Bateleur (horiz) 70 75
3123 600l. Village weaver ("Black-headed Weaver") (horiz) 70 75
3124 600l. Variable sunbird (horiz) 70 75
3125 600l. Blue swallow (horiz) 70 75
3126 600l. Red-crowned bishop ("Black-winged Red Bishop") (horiz) 70 75
3127 600l. Namaqua dove (horiz) 70 75
3128 600l. Golden-breasted bunting (horiz) 70 75
3129 600l. Hartlaub's bustard (horiz) 70 75

MS3130 Six sheets, each 85×110 mm (3000l.) or 73×98 mm (4000l.). (a) 3000l. African fish eagle. (b) 3000l. Baglafecht weaver ("Richenow's Weaver"). (c) 4000l. African Pygmy kingfisher. (d) 4000l. Ruwenzori turaco. (e) 4000l. Crowned crane ("Grey Crowned Crane") (f) 4000l. Whale-headed stork ("Shoebill") Set of 6 sheets 23·00 25·00

Nos. 3078/85, 3086/93, 3094/102, 3103/11, 3112/20 and 3121/9 were each printed together, se-tenant, with the backgrounds forming composite designs.

No. 3077 is inscribed "LITLE OWL", No. 3087 "BMerops bullockoides", No. 3112 "Terpsiphonevirdis", No. 3121 "Scimitarbill", No. 3124 "Nectarina", No. 3126 "hordeaceus" and No. **MS**3130d ("Rwenzori"), all in error.

322 Diana Monkey

1999. Wildlife. Multicoloured.

3131 300l. Type **322** 60 20
3132 800l. Bush pig 1·25 1·25
3133 900l. Flap-necked chameleon 1·50 1·60
3134 900l. Golden oriole 1·50 1·60
3135 900l. European bee eater 1·50 1·60
3136 900l. Leopard 1·50 1·60
3137 900l. Lion 1·50 1·60
3138 900l. Chimpanzee 1·50 1·60
3139 900l. Senegal galago 1·50 1·60
3140 900l. Hoopoe 1·50 1·60
3141 900l. Long-tailed pangolin 1·50 1·60
3142 900l. Hippopotamus 1·50 1·60
3143 900l. African elelphant 1·50 1·60
3144 900l. Red-billed hornbill 1·50 1·60
3145 1500l. Lioness 2·25 2·50

MS3146 Two sheets, each 85×110 mm. (a) 3000l. Grey parrot. (b) 3000l. West African linsang Set of 2 sheets 9·00 10·00

Nos. 3133/8 and 3139/44 were each printed together, se-tenant, forming composite designs.

323 Steam Locomotive, Benguela Railway, Angola

1999. Famous Trains. Multicoloured.

3147 100l. The "Rocket" (vert) 30 15
3148 150l. Type **323** 35 20
3149 200l. Class 310 steam locomotive, Sudan 40 25
3150 250l. Steam locomotive, Chicago, Burlington and Quincy Railway, U.S.A. 40 25
3151 300l. Class "Terrier" tank locomotive, Great Britain 50 30
3152 400l. Dublin to Cork express train, Ireland 60 40
3153 500l. Steam locomotive "George Stephenson", Scotland 70 55
3154 600l. Shay steam locomotive 75 65
3155 800l. Class 19D, Africa 90 90
3156 800l. Double-headed train on viaduct over Kaaiman River, Africa 90 90
3157 800l. Bo-Bo electric locomotive, Egypt 90 90
3158 800l. Gmam Garratt steam locomotive, South Africa 90 90
3159 800l. Passenger train at Rabat, Morocco 90 90
3160 800l. Class 14A Garratt, Rhodesia 90 90
3161 800l. Western type steam locomotive, U.S.A. 90 90
3162 800l. "The Flying Scotsman" express, Scotland 90 90
3163 800l. Steam locomotive "Lord Nelson" 90 90
3164 800l. Steam locomotive "Mallard" 90 90
3165 800l. Steam locomotive "Evening Star" 90 90
3166 800l. Indian Railways Class WP steam locomotive No. 7418 90 90
3167 1500l. "South Wind" express, U.S.A. (horiz) 1·60 1·75

MS3168 Two sheets. (a) 76×106 mm. 3000l. Railcar on an Alpine rack railway (vert). (b) 106×76 mm. 3000l. Royal train, Rhodesia Set of 2 sheets 8·50 8·50

No. 3166 is inscribed "THE BRITIANIA" and No. **MS**3168a "MOUNTAIN CLASS GARRATT/AFRICA", both in error.

1999. "iBRA '99" International Stamp Exhibition, Nuremburg. As T 384a of St. Vincent. Mult.

3169 1500l. "Claud Hamilton" steam locomotive, Germany 2·25 2·50
3170 2000l. "Borsig" steam locomotive, 1835, Germany 2·75 3·00

1999. 150th Death Anniv of Katsushika Hokusai (Japanese artist). As T 384b of St. Vincent. Multicoloured.

3171 1000l. "People admiring Mount Fuji from a Tea House" 1·25 1·25
3172 1000l. "People on a Temple Balcony" 1·25 1·25
3173 1000l. "Sea Life" (shrimp) 1·25 1·25
3174 1000l. "Sea Life" (shells) 1·25 1·25
3175 1000l. "The Pontoon Bridge at Sano in Winter" 1·25 1·25
3176 1000l. "A Shower below the Summit" 1·25 1·25
3177 1000l. "The Hanging Cloud Bridge" 1·25 1·25
3178 1000l. "The Timber Yard by the Tate River" 1·25 1·25
3179 1000l. "Bird Drawings" (owl) 1·25 1·25
3180 1000l. "Bird Drawings" (ducks) 1·25 1·25
3181 1000l. "Travellers crossing the Oi River" 1·25 1·25
3182 1000l. "Travellers on the Tokaido Road at Hodogaya" 1·25 1·25

MS3183 Two sheets, each 100×70 mm. (a) 3000l. "A view of Mount Fuji and Travellers by a Bridge" (vert). (b) 3000l. "A Sudden Gust of Wind at Ejiri" (vert) Set of 2 sheets 8·00 8·50

1999. 10th Anniv of United Nations Rights of the Child Convention. As T 348d of St. Vincent. Multicoloured.

3184 1600l. Japanese girl holding candle 1·75 2·00
3185 1600l. Two Japanese children 1·75 2·00
3186 1600l. Japanese girl in kimono 1·75 2·00

MS3187 110×85 mm. 3000l. Baby boy (horiz) 3·75 4·25

1999. "PhilexFrance '99" International Stamp Exhibition, PAris. railway Locomotives. Two sheets, each 106×76 mm containing horiz designs as T 385d of St. Vincent. Multicoloured.

MS3188 (a) 3000l. Crampton locomotive, French Eastern Railway. (b) 3000l. De Glehn Compund locomotive, French Northern Railway Set of 2 sheets 9·00 10·00

1999. 250th Birth Anniv of Johann von Goethe (German writer). As T 384c of St. Vincent.

3189 1600l. multicoloured 2·00 2·25
3190 1600l. blue, lilac and black 2·00 2·25
3191 1600l. multicoloured 2·00 2·25
3192 1600l. blue, black and green 2·00 2·25
3193 1600l. light blue, blue and black 2·00 2·25

MS3194 Two sheets. (a) 106×76 mm. 3000l. brown and black. (b) 76×106 mm. 3000l. brown and black Set of 2 sheets 8·00 8·50

DESIGNS—HORIZ: No. 3189, Helena with her Chorus; 3190, Goethe and Schiller; 3191, Faust seated beside Helena; 3192, The Witch beseeching Faust to drink her fiery brew; 3193, Margaret placing flowers before the niche of Mater Dolorosa; No. **MS**3191a, Angelic spirit. VERT: No. **MS**3194b, Ariel.

No. 3192 is inscribed "BESEIGES" in error.

1999. "Queen Elizabeth the Queen Mother's Century". As T 386b of St. Vincent.

3195 1300l. black and gold 1·75 1·75
3196 1300l. multicoloured 1·75 1·75
3197 1300l. black and gold 1·75 1·75
3198 1300l. multicoloured 1·75 1·75

MS3199 153×157 mm. 4000l. multicoloured 6·50 7·00

DESIGNS: No. 3195, Duke and Duchess of York and Princess Elizabeth, 1926; 3196, Queen Mother, 1979; 3197, Queen Mother visiting Nairobi, 1959; 3198, Queen Mother holding bouquet, 1991. 37×50 mm: No. **MS**3199, Queen Elizabeth in Coronation robes, 1937.

No. **MS**3199 also shows the Royal Arms embossed in gold.

324 "Interpretation of a Poem of Shi-Tao" (Fu Baoshi)

1999. "China '99" International Stamp Exhibition, Beijing. Paintings of Fu Baoshi (Chinese artist). Multicoloured.

3200 400l. Type **324** 65 75
3201 400l. "Autumn of Ho-Pao" 65 75
3202 400l. "Landscape in Rain" (bridge at bottom right) 65 75
3203 400l. "Landscape in Rain" (mountain peaks) 65 75
3204 400l. "Landscape in Rain" (mountain rest house) 65 75
3205 400l. "Portrait of To-Fu" 65 75
3206 400l. "Classic Lady" (amongst green trees) 65 75
3207 400l. "Portrait of Li-Pai" 65 75
3208 400l. "Sprite of the Mountain" 65 75
3209 400l. "Classic Lady" (amongst bare trees) 65 75

MS3210 138×105 mm. 800l. "Four Seasons–Winter" (51×39 mm) (vert); 1500l. "Four Seasons–Summer" (51×39 mm) (vert) 3·25 3·75

325 Macao Skyline inside "MACAU"

1999. Return of Macao to China.

3211 **325** 1200l. multicoloured 1·25 1·40

326 Sophie Rhys-Jones

1999. Royal Wedding. Multicoloured.

3212 2000l. Type **326** 2·00 2·25
3213 2000l. Prince Edward (wearing striped shirt and black jacket) 2·00 2·25
3214 2000l. Sophie Rhys-Jones (different) 2·00 2·25
3215 2000l. Prince Edward 2·00 2·25

MS3216 117×115 mm. 4000l. Sophie Rhys-Jones and Prince Edward (horiz) 7·00 7·50

327 Dragon

2000. Chinese New Year ("Year of the Dragon"). Multicoloured.

3217 1500l. Type **327** 1·75 1·90
3218 1500l. Dragon ("LUNAR NEW YEAR" bottom right) 1·75 1·90
3219 1500l. Dragon ("LUNAR NEW YEAR" bottom left) 1·75 1·90
3220 1500l. Dragon ("LUNAR NEW YEAR" top right) 1·75 1·90

MS3221 76×106 mm. 4000l. Dragon (vert) 5·00 6·00

328 Sammy Davis Jr.

2000. 75th Birth Anniv of Sammy Davis Jr. (American entertainer).

3222 - 1000l. brown and black 1·00 1·10
3223 - 1000l. brown and black 1·00 1·10
3224 **328** 1000l. multicoloured 1·00 1·10
3225 - 1000l. multicoloured 1·00 1·10
3226 - 1000l. red and black 1·00 1·10
3227 - 1000l. red and black 1·00 1·10
MS3228 130×130 mm. 5000l. brown and black 5·00 5·50

DESIGNS: No. 3222, As young boy; 3223, Arms outstretched in front of motorcycle; 3225, Holding microphone and singing; 3226, With foot on chair: 3227, Singing with cigarette. **MS**3228, Wearing sunglasses, white shirt and waistcoat.

329 Betty Boop

2000. Betty Boop (cartoon character). Mult.

3229 800l. Wearing short flowered dress 85 90
3230 800l. Out shopping 85 90
3231 800l. Wearing baseball cap 85 90
3232 800l. Type **329** 85 90
3233 800l. Sitting on chair 85 90
3234 800l. In duffle coat and carrying book 85 90
3235 800l. Playing guitar 85 90
3236 800l. As cowgirl with lasso 85 90
3237 800l. Holding flower 85 90
MS3238 Two sheets (a) 140×101 mm. 5000l. Riding bicycle. (b) 101×140 mm. 5000l. Wearing purple coat Set of 2 sheets 9·00 10·00

Nos. 3229/37 were printed, se-tenant, with the backgrounds forming a composite design.

330 Lucille Ball in Hotel Uniform

2000. "I Love Lucy" (American T.V. comedy series). Multicoloured.

3239 800l. Type **330** 85 90
3240 800l. Behind medicine counter with hands crossed 85 90
3241 800l. In bed 85 90
3242 800l. Poking tongue out 85 90
3243 800l. Inside television set 85 90
3244 800l. Behind counter with bottle in left hand 85 90
3245 800l. Behind medicine counter with hands by sides 85 90
3246 800l. Leaning on counter holding bottle in right hand 85 90
3247 800l. Tipping medicine away 85 90
MS3248 Two sheets, each 101×140 mm. (a) 5000l. Lucy inside television set. (b) 5000l. Lucy pinching man's face Set of 2 sheets 6·00 6·25

330a Tsar Michael Romanov of Russia (elected 1613)

2000. New Millennium. People and Events of Seventeenth Century (1600–1650). Multicoloured.

3249 400l. Type **330a** 70 70
3250 400l. William Shakespeare ("Hamlet", published 1603) 70 70
3251 400l. "Thousand Peaks and Myriad Ravines" (Kung Hsien, 1620–89) 70 70
3252 400l. Francis Bacon and title page (works published 1605) 70 70
3253 400l. Captain John Smith and colonists (Jamestown, founded 1607) 70 70
3254 400l. Versailles and courtiers (succession of Louis XIV, 1643) 70 70
3255 400l. Flag, map and waterfall (French foundation of Quebec, 1608) 70 70
3256 400l. Isaac Newton (born 1642) 70 70
3257 400l. "The Rape of the Sabine Women" (Nicolas Poussin), 1636 70 70
3258 400l. Johannes Kepler ("The New Astronomy" published 1609) 70 70
3259 400l. Colonists at Cape Cod (arrival of "Mayflower" in America, 1620) 70 70
3260 400l. King James I of England and title page of Bible (King James Bible, published 1611) 70 70
3261 400l. Activities of Dutch East India Company (introduction of tea to Europe, 1610) 70 70
3262 400l. Rene Descartes and sketch of boy (doctrine "I think, therefore I am", 1641) 70 70
3263 400l. Galileo (proves Earth orbits Sun, 1632) 70 70
3264 400l. Queen Elizabeth I (died 1603) (59×39 mm) 70 70
3265 400l. Miguel de Cervantes and title page (publication of "Don Quixote", 1605) 70 70

330b Flowers forming Top of Head

2000. Faces of the Millennium: Diana, Princess of Wales. Showing collage of miniature flower photographs. Multicoloured.

3266 800l. Type **330b** (face value at left) 85 90
3267 800l. Top of head (face value at right) 85 90
3268 800l. Ear (face value at left) 85 90
3269 800l. Eye and temple (face value at right) 85 90
3270 800l. Cheek (face value at left) 85 90
3271 800l. Cheek (face value at right) 85 90
3272 800l. Blue background (face value at left) 85 90
3273 800l. Chin (face value at right) 85 90

Nos. 3266/73 were printed together, se-tenant, in sheetlets of 8 with the stamps arranged in two vertical columns separated by a gutter also containing miniature photographs. When viewed as a whole, the sheetlet forms a portrait of Diana, Princess of Wales.

331 Colonel Lloyd (Lionel Barrymore) and his Granddaughter (Shirley Temple)

2000. Shirley Temple in "The Little Colonel". Showing scenes from the film. Multicoloured.

3274 1200l. Type **331** 1·00 1·10
3275 1200l. Lloyd (Shirley Temple) and Walker (Bill Robinson) 1·00 1·10
3276 1200l. Lloyd with Henry Clay and May Lily 1·00 1·10
3277 1200l. Lloyd with soldiers 1·00 1·10
3278 1200l. Lloyd with her mother and Mom Beck 1·00 1·10
3279 1200l. Lloyd hugging her grandfather 1·00 1·10
3280 1500l. Lloyd with her grandfather's servants 1·25 1·40
3281 1500l. Walker and Lloyd tap dancing 1·25 1·40
3282 1500l. Lloyd standing in bushes 1·25 1·40
3283 1500l. Lloyd and the Colonel 1·25 1·40
MS3284 107×76 mm. 5000l. Lloyd saluting 3·00 3·25

332 Mario Andretti in Saloon Car

2000. 60th Birthday of Mario Andretti (U.S. racing driver). Multicoloured (except Nos. 3285 and 3288).

3285 600l. Type **332** (black, yellow and red) 70 75
3286 600l. Wearing racing helmet 70 75
3287 600l. Being congratulated 70 75
3288 600l. In car number 26 (black and red) 70 75
3289 600l. Changing wheel 70 75
3290 600l. Wearing white T-shirt 70 75
3291 600l. Shirtless 70 75
3292 600l. Driving GT Ferrari 70 75
MS3293 128×151 mm. 5000l. As young man with friends and first car 6·00 6·50

2000. 400th Birth Anniv of Sir Anthony Van Dyck (Flemish painter). As T 394c of St. Vincent. Mult.

3294 1000l. "Taking of Christ" (detail) 90 1·00
3295 1000l. "Ecce Homo" (1625–26) 90 1·00
3296 1000l. "Christ carrying the Cross" (soldier in black helmet) 90 1·00
3297 1000l. "Raising of Christ on the Cross" 90 1·00
3298 1000l. "The Crucifixion" (c. 1627) 90 1·00
3299 1000l. "The Lamentation" (c. 1616) 90 1·00
3300 1000l. "Taking of Christ" (complete painting) 90 1·00
3301 1000l. "The Mocking of Christ" 90 1·00
3302 1000l. "Ecce Homo" (1628–32) 90 1·00
3303 1000l. "Christ carrying the Cross" (soldier in red helmet) 90 1·00
3304 1000l. "The Crucifixion" (1629–30) 90 1·00
3305 1000l. "The Lamentation" (1618–20) 90 1·00
3306 1000l. "Portrait of a Man" 90 1·00
3307 1000l. "Anna Wake, Wife of Peeter Stevens" 90 1·00
3308 1000l. "Peeter Stevens" 90 1·00
3309 1000l. "Adriaen Stevens" 90 1·00
3310 1000l. "Maria Bosschaerts, Wife of Adriaen Stevens" 90 1·00
3311 1000l. "Portrait of a Woman" 90 1·00
3312 1000l. "Self-portrait" (1617–18) 90 1·00
3313 1000l. "Self-portrait" (1620–21) 90 1·00
3314 1000l. "Self-portrait" (1622–23) 90 1·00
3315 1000l. "Andromeda chained to the Rock" 90 1·00
3316 1000l. "Self-portrait" (late 1620s–early 1630s) 90 1·00
3317 1000l. "Mary Ruthven" 90 1·00
3318 1000l. "The Duchess of Croy with her Son" 90 1·00
3319 1000l. "Susanna Fourment and her Daughter" 90 1·00
3320 1000l. "Geronima Brignole-Sale with her Daughter Maria Aurelia" 90 1·00
3321 1000l. "Woman with her Daughter" 90 1·00
3322 1000l. "Genoese Noblewoman with her Child" 90 1·00
3323 1000l. "Paola Adorno and her Son" 90 1·00
MS3324 Six sheets. (a) 102×127 mm. 5000l. "Young Woman with a Child". (b) 102×127 mm. 5000l. "Pozia Imperiale and her Daughter Maria Frencesca". (c) 102×127 mm. 5000l. "Portrait of Mother and Daughter". (d) 127×102 mm. 5000l. "Self-portrait with Endymion Porter". (e) 127×102 mm. 5000l. "Self-portrait with Sunflower". (f) 102×127 mm. 5000l. "Woman and Child" (horiz) Set of 6 sheets 26·00 29·00

No. 3311 is inscribed "Protrait of a Women" in error.

333 Grey Parrot ("African Grey Parrot")

2000. "The Stamp Show 2000" International Stamp Exhibition, London. Parrots and Parakeets. Mult.

3325 200l. Type **333** 35 15
3326 800l. Monk parakeet 1·10 1·10
3327 800l. Lesser sulphur-crested cockatoo ("Citron-crested Cockatoo") 1·10 1·10
3328 800l. Golden conure ("Queen of Bavaria Conure") 1·10 1·10
3329 800l. Budgerigar 1·10 1·10
3330 800l. Canary-winged parakeet ("Yellow-chevroned Parakeet") 1·10 1·10
3331 800l. Cockatiel 1·10 1·10
3332 800l. Green-checked amazon ("Amazon Parrot") 1·10 1·10
3333 800l. Sun conure 1·10 1·10
3334 800l. Malabar parakeet 1·10 1·10
3335 800l. Eclectus parrot ("Grand Eclectus Parrot") 1·10 1·10
3336 800l. Jandaya conure ("Sun Parakeet") 1·10 1·10
3337 800l. Hawk-headed parrot ("Red fan Parakeet") 1·10 1·10
3338 800l. Fischer's lovebird 1·10 1·10
3339 800l. Masked lovebird ("Blue-masked Lovebird") 1·10 1·10
3340 800l. White-bellied caique ("White-bellied Rosella") 1·10 1·10
3341 800l. Plum-headed parakeet 1·10 1·10
3342 800l. Striated lorikeet 1·10 1·10
3343 800l. Eastern rosella ("Gold-mantled Rosella") 1·10 1·10
3344 1500l. Sulphur-crested cockatoo 1·90 2·25
MS3345 120×81 mm. 4000l. Blue and yellow macaw ("Blue and Gold Macaw") (37×50 mm) 7·00 7·50

Nos. 3326/34 and 3335/43 were each printed together, se-tenant, with the backgrounds forming composite designs.

No. 3327 is inscribed "Cockatto" and No. 3344 "Sulfur Crested Cockatto", both in error.

334 Herring Gull

2000. Seabirds of the World. Multicoloured.

3346 400l. Type **334** 65 35
3347 600l. Caspian tern (standing by rock) 90 60
3348 800l. Grey phalarope ("Red Phalarope") 1·10 90
3349 1000l. Wandering albatross 1·25 1·40
3350 1000l. Fork-tailed storm petrel 1·25 1·40
3351 1000l. Greater shearwater 1·25 1·40
3352 1000l. Blue-footed booby 1·25 1·40
3353 1000l. Great cormorant 1·25 1·40
3354 1000l. Atlantic puffin 1·25 1·40
3355 1000l. Caspian tern (fishing) 1·25 1·40

3356	1000l. Glaucous gull	1·25	1·40
3357	1000l. Northern gannet	1·25	1·40
3358	1000l. Long-tailed skua ("Long-tailed Jaeger")	1·25	1·40
3359	1000l. Brown pelican	1·25	1·40
3360	1000l. Great skua	1·25	1·40
3361	2000l. Magnificent frigate bird	2·25	2·50
MS3362	Two sheets, each 56×66 mm. (a) 5000l. red-billed tropic bird ("Red-tailed Tropic Bird") (vert). (b) 5000l. Brown booby (vert) Set of 2 sheets	11·00	12·00

No. **MS**3362b is inscribed "Brown Boobie" in error.
Nos. 3349/54 and 3355/60 were each printed together, se-tenant, with the backgrounds forming composite designs.

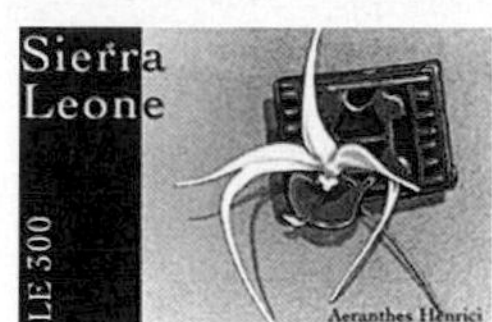

335 *Aeranthes henrici*

2000. Orchids. Multicoloured.

3363	300l. Type **335**	50	20
3364	500l. *Ophrys apifera*	70	35
3365	600l. *Disa crassicornis*	80	55
3366	1100l. *Oeleoclades maculata* (vert)	1·25	1·40
3367	1100l. *Polystachya campyloglossa* (vert)	1·25	1·40
3368	1100l. *Polystachya pubescens* (vert)	1·25	1·40
3369	1100l. *Tridactyle bicaudata* (vert)	1·25	1·40
3370	1100l. *Angraecum veitcii* (vert)	1·25	1·40
3371	1100l. *Sobennikoffia robusta* (vert)	1·25	1·40
3372	1100l. *Aerangis curnowiana* (vert)	1·25	1·40
3373	1100l. *Aerangis fastudsa* (vert)	1·25	1·40
3374	1100l. *Angraecum magdalenae* (vert)	1·25	1·40
3375	1100l. *Angraecum sororium* (vert)	1·25	1·40
3376	1100l. *Eulophia speciosa* (vert)	1·25	1·40
3377	1100l. *Ansellia africana* (vert)	1·25	1·40
3378	2000l. *Aeranthes grandiflora*	2·25	2·50
MS3379	Two sheets, each 74×64 mm. (a) 4000l. *Angraecum eburneum* (vert). (b) 4000l. *Angraecum compactum* (vert) Set of 2 sheets	11·00	12·00

Nos. 3366/71 and 3372/7 were each printed together, se-tenant, with the backgrounds forming composite designs.
No. 3367 is inscribed "Ploystachya" in error.

2000. 18th Birthday of Prince William. As T 395a of St. Vincent. Multicoloured.

3380	1100l. Prince William laughing	1·40	1·40
3381	1100l. Wearing blue shirt and grey suit	1·40	1·40
3382	1100l. In dark jacket and red-patterned tie	1·40	1·40
3383	1100l. Wearing white shirt and blue suit	1·40	1·40
MS3384	100×80 mm. 5000l. Holding bouquet of flowers (37×50 mm)	7·00	7·50

335a "Apollo 18"

2000. 25th Anniv of "Apollo–Soyuz" Joint Project. Multicoloured.

3385	1200l. Type **335a**	1·25	1·40
3386	1200l. "Soyuz 19"	1·25	1·40
3387	1200l. "Apollo 18" and "Soyuz 19" docked in orbit	1·25	1·40
MS3388	94×84 mm. 5000l. "Apollo 18" and "Soyuz 19" docking	6·50	7·00

2000. 50th Anniv of Berlin Film Festival. As T 395c of St. Vincent. Showing film scenes. Multicoloured.

3389	1100l. *Las Palabras de Max*, 1978	1·25	1·40
3390	1100l. *Ascendancy*, 1983	1·25	1·40
3391	1100l. *Deprisa, Deprisa*, 1981	1·25	1·40
3392	1100l. *Die Sehnsucht der Veronika Voss*, 1982	1·25	1·40
3393	1100l. *Heartland*, 1980	1·25	1·40
3394	1100l. *La Colmena*, 1983	1·25	1·40
MS3395	97×103 mm. 5000l. *Las Truches*, 1978	6·50	7·00

2000. 175th Anniv of Stockton and Darlington Line (first public railway). As T 395d of St. Vincent. Multicoloured.

3396	3000l. George Stephenson and *Locomotion No. 1*	3·50	3·75
3397	3000l. James Watt's original design for separate condenser engine, 1789	3·50	3·75

No. 3397 is inscribed "comdensor" in error.

335b Johann Sebastian Bach

2000. 250th Death Anniv of Johann Sebastian Bach (German composer). Sheet, 104×101 mm.

MS3398	**335b** 5000l. multicoloured	7·00	7·50

335c Albert Einstein holding Pipe

2000. Election of Albert Einstein (mathematical physicist) as Time Magazine "Man of the Century". Sheet 117×91 mm.

MS3399	**335c** 5000l. multicoloured	6·00	6·50

2000. Centenary of First Zeppelin Flight. As T 396a of St. Vincent. Multicoloured.

3400	2000l. LZ-129 *Hindenburg*, 1936	2·00	2·25
3401	2000l. LZ-4, 1908	2·00	2·25
3402	2000l. LZ-6 *Delag*, 1909	2·00	2·25
MS3403	116×76 mm. 4000l. LZ-127 *Graf Zeppelin*, 1928 (50×37 mm)	6·00	6·50

No. 3400 is inscribed "Hindenberg" in error.

2000. Olympic Games, Sydney. As T 396b of St. Vincent. Multicoloured.

3404	1500l. Forrest Smithson (hurdling), London (1908)	1·75	2·00
3405	1500l. Football	1·75	2·00
3406	1500l. Olympic Stadium, Helsinki (1952) with Finnish flag	1·75	2·00
3407	1500l. Ancient Greek wrestlers	1·75	2·00

336 Richard Petty sitting on Car with Trophy

2000. Richard Petty (stock car driver) Commem. Multicoloured.

3408	800l. Type **336**	75	85
3409	800l. In cream overalls and cap	75	85
3410	800l. In stetson and sunglasses (blue collar)	75	85
3411	800l. In plain white shirt (blue background)	75	85
3412	800l. In stetson and sunglasses (red collar)	75	85
3413	800l. Squatting with cap alongside No. 43	75	85
3414	800l. Leaning on car	75	85
3415	800l. Crouching with arm in car	75	85
3416	800l. Looking out of car No. 43	75	85
3417	800l. Car in pits	75	85
3418	800l. Standing with family	75	85
3419	800l. Standing by car with helmet on door	75	85
3420	800l. In Pontiac cap	75	85
3421	800l. In white stetson and sunglasses (green background)	75	85
3422	800l. In STP cap	75	85
3423	800l. Standing up in blue car	75	85
3424	800l. In white stetson (with STP epaulettes)	75	85
3425	800l. Sitting watching race	75	85
3426	800l. Being interviewed	75	85
3427	800l. In plain white shirt (brown background)	75	85
3428	800l. Wearing orange cap and sunglasses	75	85
3429	800l. Sitting in car (interior view)	75	85
3430	800l. Timing a race	75	85
3431	800l. In blue and red helmet	75	85
3432	800l. In white stetson and sunglasses (blue overalls)	75	85
3433	800l. Holding trophy in blue, red and white overalls	75	85
3434	800l. Sitting in white stetson and sunglasses	75	85
MS3435	Two sheets, each 110×76 mm. (a) 5000l. As No. 3423. (b) 5000l. Car No. 43 during race (horiz) Set of 2 sheets	9·00	10·00

337 Worns (German player)

2000. "Euro 2000" Football Championship. Mult.

3436	1300l. Type **337**	1·10	1·25
3437	1300l. German team	1·10	1·25
3438	1300l. Babbel (German player)	1·10	1·25
3439	1300l. Franz Beckenbauer, 1972	1·10	1·25
3440	1300l. Selessin Stadium, Liege	1·10	1·25
3441	1300l. Stefan Kuntz, (German player), 1996	1·10	1·25
3442	1300l. Walter Zenga (Italian player)	1·10	1·25
3443	1300l. Italian team	1·10	1·25
3444	1300l. Roberto Bettega (Italian player), 1980	1·10	1·25
3445	1300l. Totti (Italian player)	1·10	1·25
3446	1300l. Philips Stadium, Eindhoven	1·10	1·25
3447	1300l. Vieri (Italian player)	1·10	1·25
3448	1300l. Dimas (Portuguese player)	1·10	1·25
3449	1300l. Portuguese team	1·10	1·25
3450	1300l. Pinto (Portuguese player)	1·10	1·25
3451	1300l. Santos (Portuguese player)	1·10	1·25
3452	1300l. Gelredome Stadium, Arnhem	1·10	1·25
3453	1300l. Sousa (Portuguese player)	1·10	1·25
3454	1300l. Munteanu (Romanian player)	1·10	1·25
3455	1300l. Romanian team	1·10	1·25
3456	1300l. Petre (Romanian player)	1·10	1·25
3457	1300l. Petrescu (Romanian player)	1·10	1·25
3458	1300l. Popescu (Romanian player)	1·10	1·25
MS3459	Four sheets, each 145×95 mm. (a) 5000l. Erich Ribbeck (German trainer) (vert). (b) 5000l. Dino Zoff (Italian trainer) (vert). (c) 5000l. Humberto Coelho (Portuguese trainer) (vert). (d) 5000l. Emerich Jenei (Romanian trainer) (vert) Set of 4 sheets	15·00	17·00

337a Emperor Hung-Wu of China

2000. Monarchs of the Millennium.

3460	**337a**	1100l. multicoloured	1·10	1·25
3461	-	1100l. multicoloured	1·10	1·25
3462	-	1100l. multicoloured	1·10	1·25
3463	-	1100l. black, stone & brn	1·10	1·25
3464	-	1100l. multicoloured	1·10	1·25
3465	-	1100l. black, stone & brn	1·10	1·25
MS3466		116×131 mm.–5000l. multicoloured	6·00	6·50

DESIGNS: No. 3461, Emperor Hsuan-Te of China; 3462, King Sejong of Korea; 3463, Emperor T'ung Chin of China; 3464, Emperor T'ai-Tsu of China; 3465, Empress Yung Ching of China; **MS**3466, Kublai Khan, Great Khan of the Mongols.

2000. Popes of the Millennium. As T 337a. Each black, yellow and green (Nos. 3467/78 or black, yellow and brown (No. MS3479).

3467	1100l. Gregory VI	1·40	1·40
3468	1100l. Celestine V	1·40	1·40
3469	1100l. Honorius IV	1·40	1·40
3470	1100l. Innocent IV	1·40	1·40
3471	1100l. Innocent VII	1·40	1·40
3472	1100l. John XXII	1·40	1·40
3473	1100l. Martin IV	1·40	1·40
3474	1100l. Nicholas II	1·40	1·40
3475	1100l. Nicholas IV	1·40	1·40
3476	1100l. Urban IV	1·40	1·40
3477	1100l. Urban V	1·40	1·40
3478	1100l. Urban VI	1·40	1·40
MS3479	Two sheets, each 116×136 mm. (a) 5000l. Nicholas IV. (b) 5000l. Clement XI Set of 2 sheets	12·00	13·00

338 Bulldog

2000. Dogs and Cats. Multicoloured.

3480	500l. Type **338**	70	30
3481	800l. Brown tabby	85	60
3482	1000l. Red tabby stumpy manx	1·00	1·00
3483	1000l. Red self	1·00	1·00
3484	1000l. Maine coon	1·00	1·00
3485	1000l. Black smoke	1·00	1·00
3486	1000l. Chinchilla	1·00	1·00
3487	1000l. Russian blue cat	1·00	1·00
3488	1000l. Beagle	1·00	1·00
3489	1000l. Scottish terrier	1·00	1·00
3490	1000l. Bloodhound	1·00	1·00
3491	1000l. Greyhound	1·00	1·00
3492	1000l. German shepherd	1·00	1·00
3493	1000l. Cocker spaniel	1·00	1·00
3494	1100l. Singapura	1·00	1·00
3495	1100l. Himalayan	1·00	1·00
3496	1100l. Abyssinian	1·00	1·00
3497	1100l. Black cat	1·00	1·00
3498	1100l. Siamese	1·00	1·00
3499	1100l. North African wild cat	1·00	1·00
3500	1100l. Pointer	1·00	1·00
3501	1100l. Doberman pinscher	1·00	1·00
3502	1100l. Collie	1·00	1·00
3503	1100l. Chihuahua	1·00	1·00
3504	1100l. Afghan hound	1·00	1·00
3505	1100l. Boxer	1·00	1·00
3506	1500l. Burmese	1·40	1·50
3507	2000l. Dachshund	1·90	2·25
MS3508	Two sheets, each 48×62 mm. (a) 5000l. Calico cat (vert). (b) 5000l. Fox terrier (vert) Set of 2 sheets	12·00	13·00

Nos. 3482/7 (cats), 3489/93 (dogs), 3494/9 (cats) and 3500/505 (dogs) were printed together, se-tenant, with the backgrounds forming composite designs.

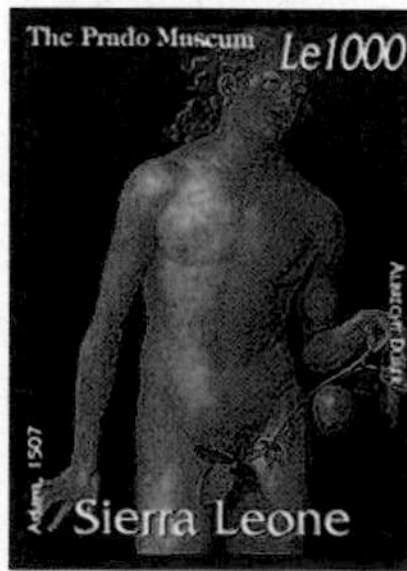

339 "Adam" (Durer)

2000. "Espana 2000" International Stamp Exhibition, Madrid. Paintings from the Prado. Multicoloured.

3509	1000l. Type **339**	80	90
3510	1000l. "Moor" (M. Vives)	80	90
3511	1000l. "Eve" (Durer)	80	90
3512	1000l. "Gypsy" (R. de Madrazo y Garreta)	80	90
3513	1000l. "Maria Guerrero" (J. Sorolla y Bastida)	80	90
3514	1000l. "Aline Masson with a White Mantilla" (R. de Madrazo y Garreta)	80	90
3515	1000l. "Madonna and Child between Sts. Catherine and Ursula" (G. Bellini) (left detail)	80	90
3516	1000l. "Madonna and Child between Sts. Catherine and Ursula" (centre detail)	80	90

3517 1000l. "Madonna and Child between Sts. Catherine and Ursula" (right detail) 80 90
3518 1000l. "Giovanni Mateo Ghiberti" (B. India) 80 90
3519 1000l. "The Marchioness of Santa Cruz" (A. Esteve) 80 90
3520 1000l. "Self Portrait" (O. Borgianni) 80 90
3521 1000l. "The Transport of Mary Magdalen" (J. Antolinez) 80 90
3522 1000l. "The Holy Family" (Goya) 80 90
3523 1000l. "Our Lady of the Immaculate Conception" (J. Antolinez) 80 90
3524 1000l. "Charles IV as Prince" (A. Mengs) 80 90
3525 1000l. "Louis XIII of France" (P. de Champaigne) 80 90
3526 1000l. "Prince Ferdinand VI" (J. Ranc) 80 90
3527 1000l. "Feliciana Bayeu" (F. Bayeu) 80 90
3528 1000l. "Tomas de Iriarte" (J. Inza) 80 90
3529 1000l. "St. Elizabeth of Portugal" (F. de Zurbaran) 80 90
3530 1000l. "The Vision of St. Francis at Porziuncola" (Murillo) (Christ with cross) 80 90
3531 1000l. "The Vision of St. Francis at Porziuncola" (St. Francis) 80 90
3532 1000l. "The Vision of St. Francis at Porziuncola" (Two women) 80 90
3533 1000l. "The Holy Family with a Little Bird" (Murillo) (Virgin Mary) 80 90
3534 1000l. "The Holy Family with a Little Bird" (Holy Child) 80 90
3535 1000l. "The Holy Family with a Little Bird" (St. Joseph) 80 90
3536 1000l. "Cardinal Carlos de Borja" (A. Procaccini) 80 90
3537 1000l. "St. Dominic de Guzman" (C. Coello) 80 90
3538 1000l. "The Dead Christ Supported by an Angel" (A. Cano) 80 90
3539 1000l. "The Seller of Fans" (woman) (J. del Castillo) 80 90
3540 1000l. "Allegory of Summer" (M. Maella) 80 90
3541 1000l. "The Seller of Fans" (man) 80 90
3542 1000l. "Portrait of a Girl" (C. de Ribera y Fieve) 80 90
3543 1000l. "The Poultry Keeper" (Il Pensionante del Saraceni) 80 90
3544 1000l. "The Death of Cleopatra" (G. Reni) 80 90
MS3545 Six sheets, each 110×91 mm. (a) 5000l. "The Two Friends" (J. Agrasot y Juan) (horiz). (b) 5000l. "The Finding of Joseph's Cup in Benjamin's Sack" (J. Amiconi). (c) 5000l. "The Execution of Tprrijos and His Companions" (A. Gisbert Pirez). (d) 5000l. "The Concert" (V. Palmaroli Gonzalez). (e) 5000l. "Lot and His Daughters" (F. Furini). (f) 5000l. "Vulcan's Forge" (Velazquez) Set of 6 sheets 25·00 28·00

2000. Faces of the Millennium: Pope John Paul II. As T 330b, showing collage of miniature religious photographs. Multicoloured.
3546 900l. Top of head (face value at left) 1·25 1·40
3547 900l. Top of head (face value at right) 1·25 1·40
3548 900l. Ear (face value at left) 1·25 1·40
3549 900l. Eye and temple (face value at right) 1·25 1·40
3550 900l. Back of neck (face value at left) 1·25 1·40
3551 900l. Cheek (face value at right) 1·25 1·40
3552 900l. Collar and top of cassock (face value at left) 1·25 1·40
3553 900l. Hand (face value at right) 1·25 1·40
Nos. 3546/53 were printed together, se-tenant, in sheetlets of 8 with the stamps arranged in two vertical columns separated by a gutter also containing miniature photographs. When viewed as a whole, the sheetlet forms a portrait of Pope John Paul II.

2000. Faces of the Millennium: Queen Elizabeth, The Queen Mother. As T 330b, showing collage of miniature flower photographs. Multicoloured.
3554 800l. Top of forehead and hat (face value at left) 1·10 1·25
3555 800l. Hat (face value at right) 1·10 1·25
3556 800l. Eye (face value at left) 1·10 1·25
3557 800l. Side of face and hat (face value at right) 1·10 1·25
3558 800l. Cheek (face value at left) 1·10 1·25
3559 800l. Cheek (face value at right) 1·10 1·25
3560 800l. Chin (face value at left) 1·10 1·25
3561 800l. Chin and neck (face value at right) 1·10 1·25
Nos. 3554/61 were printed together, se-tenant, in sheetlets of 8 with the stamps arranged in two vertical columns separated by a gutter also containing miniature photographs. When viewed as a whole, the sheetlet forms a portrait of The Queen Mother.

340 *Tuberus polypore*

2001. Fungi. Multicoloured.
3562 600l. Type **340** 75 40
3563 900l. *Cultivated agaricus* 95 85
3564 1000l. Armed stinkhorn (vert) 1·00 1·00
3565 1000l. *Red-staining inocybe* (vert) 1·00 1·00
3566 1000l. Grisette (*Amanitopsis vaginata*) (vert) 1·00 1·00
3567 1000l. *Inocybe jurana* (vert) 1·00 1·00
3568 1000l. *Xerula longipes* (vert) 1·00 1·00
3569 1000l. Matsu-take mushroom (*Tricholoma matsutake*) (vert) 1·00 1·00
3570 1000l. Orange-staining mycena (vert) 1·00 1·00
3571 1000l. *Russula amoema* (vert) 1·00 1·00
3572 1000l. *Cinnabar chanterelle*(vert) 1·00 1·00
3573 1000l. *Calodon aurantiacum* (vert) 1·00 1·00
3574 1000l. Scaly lentinus (*Lentinus lepideus*) (vert) 1·00 1·00
3575 1000l. *Gomphidius roseus* (vert) 1·00 1·00
3576 1200l. Scarlet wax cap 1·25 1·40
3577 2500l. Blue-green psilocybe 2·25 2·50
MS3578 Two sheets. (a) 98×74 mm. 5000l. Orange latex lactarius. (b) 74×98 mm. 5000l. Common morel (vert) Set of 2 sheets 11·00 12·00
Nos. 3564/9 and 3570/575 were each printed together, se-tenant, with the backgrounds forming a composite design.
No. 3567 is inscribed "Inoeybe" in error.

341 Kahat Shor (shooting coach)

2000. Israel Olympic Team Members killed at Munich (1972) Commemoration. Multicoloured.
3579 500l. Type **341** 80 80
3580 500l. Andrei Schpitzer (fencing referee) 80 80
3581 500l. Joseph Romano (weightlifter) 80 80
3582 500l. Yaakov Springer (weightlifting referee) 80 80
3583 500l. Eliazer Halffin (wrestler) 80 80
3584 500l. Amitsur Shapira (athletics coach) 80 80
3585 500l. Moshe Weinberg (wrestling referee) 80 80
3586 500l. Mark Slavin (wrestler) 80 80
3587 500l. Flag and runner with Olympic Torch 80 80
3588 500l. Joseph Gottfreund (wrestling referee) 80 80
3589 500l. Ze'ev Friedman (weightlifter) 80 80
3590 500l. David Berger (weightlifter) 80 80
MS3591 116×80 mm. 5000l. Runner with Olympic Torch (vert) 7·50 8·00

342 Tightrope Cyclist

2000. Circus. Multicoloured.
3592 800l. Type **342** 1·25 70
3593 1000l. Bear with ball 1·25 1·00
3594 1100l. Polar bear 1·25 1·25
3595 1100l. Gorilla 1·25 1·25
3596 1100l. Clown (green background) 1·25 1·25
3597 1100l. Tightrope walker 1·25 1·25
3598 1100l. Sealions 1·25 1·25
3599 1100l. Camel 1·25 1·25
3600 1100l. Clown (brown background) 1·25 1·25
3601 1100l. Tiger on tightropes 1·25 1·25
3602 1100l. Chimpanzee 1·25 1·25
3603 1100l. Dancing dogs 1·25 1·25
3604 1100l. Bear on skates with hockey stick 1·25 1·25
3605 1100l. Trapeze artists 1·25 1·25
3606 1100l. Acrobat (vert) 1·25 1·25
3607 1100l. Giraffe (vert) 1·25 1·25
3608 1100l. Bear on stilts (vert) 1·25 1·25
3609 1100l. Elephant (vert) 1·25 1·25
3610 1100l. Rearing horse (vert) 1·25 1·25
3611 1100l. Fire-eater (vert) 1·25 1·25
3612 1500l. Tiger on ball 1·60 1·75
3613 2000l. Camels 2·25 2·50
MS3614 Three sheets, each 70×90 mm. (a) 5000l. Tiger leaping through flames (vert). (b) 5000l. Human cannonball (vert). (c) 5000l. Ringmaster standing on elephant (vert) Set of 3 sheets 20·00 20·00

2000. Queen Elizabeth the Queen Mother's 100th Birthday. As T 405 of St. Vincent. Multicoloured.
3615 1100l. Queen Mother in blue hat 2·25 2·25

343 Decorative Snake

2001. Chinese New Year. "Year of the Snake". Decorative snakes. Multicoloured.
3616 800l. Type **343** (blue frame) 90 1·00
3617 800l. Snake (pink frame) 90 1·00
3618 800l. Snake (lilac frame) 90 1·00
3619 800l. Snake (green frame) 90 1·00
MS3620 65×95 mm. 2500l. Snake (vert) 2·50 3·00

344 Natal Mixands Dwarf Chameleon

2001. African Reptiles. Multicoloured.
3621 250l. Type **344** 40 15
3622 400l. Cape cobra 50 30
3623 500l. Western sand lizard 55 30
3624 600l. Pan-hinged terrapin 65 40
3625 800l. Many-horned adder 85 65
3626 1200l. Reticulated desert lizard 1·10 1·25
3627 1200l. Ball python 1·10 1·25
3628 1200l. Gabon viper 1·10 1·25
3629 1200l. Dumeril's boa 1·10 1·25
3630 1200l. Common egg-eater 1·10 1·25
3631 1200l. Helmet turtle 1·10 1·25
3632 1200l. Saw-scaled viper 1·10 1·25
3633 1200l. Namibian sand snake 1·10 1·25
3634 1200l. Angolan gartersnake 1·10 1·25
3635 1200l. Striped skaapsteker 1·10 1·25
3636 1200l. Brown housesnake 1·10 1·25
3637 1200l. Shield-nosed cobra 1·10 1·25
3638 1500l. Hawequa flat gecko 1·40 1·50
MS3639 Two sheets, each 86×56 mm. (a) 5000l. Flat-necked chameleon. (b) 5000l. Green water snake Set of 2 sheets 10·00 11·00
Nos. 3626/31 and 3632/7 were each printed together, se-tenant, with the backgrounds forming a composite map of Africa.
No. 3621 is inscribed "Chamaeleon" in error.

345 Sleeping Car No. 507, 1897

2001. "The Orient Express". Multicoloured.
3640 1000l. First sleeping car, 1872 1·00 1·00
3641 1000l. Dining car No. 193, 1886 1·00 1·00
3642 1000l. Dining car No. 2422, 1913 1·00 1·00
3643 1000l. Sleeping car Type S1 1·00 1·00
3644 1000l. Metal sleeping car No. 2645, 1922 1·00 1·00
3645 1000l. Metal sleeping car No. 2644, 1922 1·00 1·00
3646 1000l. Dining car series No. 8341 1·00 1·00
3647 1000l. Dining car series No. 3342 1·00 1·00
3648 1000l. Sleeping car series Type Z, No. 3312 1·00 1·00
3649 1000l. Sleeping car series No. 3879, 1950 1·00 1·00
3650 1000l. Sleeping car series, Type Z, No. 3311 1·00 1·00
3651 1000l. Dining car series No. 3785, 1932 1·00 1·00
3652 1100l. Type **345** 1·00 1·00
3653 1100l. Sleeping car No. 438, 1894 1·00 1·00
3654 1100l. Sleeping car No. 313, 1880 1·00 1·00
3655 1100l. Sleeping car No. 190, 1886 1·00 1·00
3656 1100l. Sleeping car No. 102, 1882 1·00 1·00
3657 1100l. Sleeping car No. 77, 1881 1·00 1·00
3658 1100l. Steam locomotive, Ostend–Vienna Express, 1910 5·50 5·50
3659 1100l. Steam locomotive East 230 No. 3175 1·00 1·00
3660 1100l. Dual-cylinder steam locomotive 1·00 1·00
3661 1100l. Steam locomotive, Simplon Orient Express, 1919 1·00 1·00
3662 1100l. Steam locomotive East 220 No. 2405 1·00 1·00
3663 1100l. Brake van of Simplon Express, c. 1906 1·00 1·00
MS3664 Four sheets, each 106×81 mm. (a) 5000l. Agatha Christie (author) (vert). (b) 5000l. Georges Nagelmackers (company founder) (vert). (c) 5000l. Mata Hari (spy) (vert). (d) 5000l. "Orient Express" leaving Constantinople Set of 4 sheets 16·00 17·00

346 Candle-bearers from "David playing the Harp" (Jan de Bray)

2001. Bicentenary of Rijksmuseum, Amsterdam. Dutch Paintings. Multicoloured.
3665 1100l. Type **346** 90 1·00
3666 1100l. Women and children from "St. Paul healing the Cripple at Lystra" (Karel Dujardin) 90 1·00
3667 1100l. Two pikemen (one wearing hat) from "The Meagre Company" (Frans Hals and Pieter Codde) 90 1·00
3668 1100l. "The Grey" (Philips Wouwermans) 90 1·00
3669 1100l. "Elegant Couple in an Interior" (Eglon van der Neer) 90 1·00
3670 1100l. "The Hut" (Adriaen van der Velde) 90 1·00
3671 1100l. "Lady reading a Letter" (Gabriel Metsu) 90 1·00
3672 1100l. "Portrait of Titus" (Rembrandt) 90 1·00
3673 1100l. "Gerard de Lairesse" (Rembrandt) 90 1·00
3674 1100l. "Family in an Interior" (Emanuel de Witte) 90 1·00
3675 1100l. "The Letter" (Gerard ter Borch) 90 1·00
3676 1100l. "Three Women and a Man in a Courtyard" (Pieter de Hooch) 90 1·00
3677 1100l. "Gentleman writing a Letter" (Gabriel Metsu) 90 1·00
3678 1100l. "Self-portrait" (Carel Fabritius) 90 1·00
3679 1100l. "Windmill at Wijk bij Duurstede" (Jacob van Ruisdael) 90 1·00
3680 1100l. "Bentheim Castle" (Jacob van Ruisdael) 90 1·00
3681 1100l. "Ships on a Stormy Sea" (Willem van der Velde the Younger) 90 1·00
3682 1100l. David from "David playing the Harp" (Jan de Bray) 90 1·00
3683 1100l. St. Paul from "St. Paul healing the Cripple at Lystra" (Karel Dujardin) 90 1·00
3684 1100l. Two pikemen (both bareheaded) from "The Meagre Company" (Frans Hals and Pieter Codde) 90 1·00
3685 1100l. Man from "Elegant Couple in an Interior" (Eglon van der Neer) 90 1·00
3686 1100l. "Laid Table with Cheese and Fruit" (Floris van Dijck) 90 1·00
3687 1100l. "Bacchanal" (Moses van Uyttenbroeck) 90 1·00
3688 1100l. The cripple from "St. Paul healing the Cripple at Lystra" (Karel Dujardin) 90 1·00

MS3689 Four sheets. (a) 118×73 mm. 5000l. "Road in the Dunes with a Coach" (Salomon van Ruysdael) (horiz) (b) 118×73 mm. 5000l. "Cows in the Meadow" (Albert Gerard Bilders) (horiz). (c) 118×78 mm. 5000l. "Lot and his Daughters" (Hendrick Goltzius) (horiz). (d) 118×83 mm. 5000l. "Arrival of Queen Wilhelmina at the Frederiksplein, Amsterdam (Otto Eerelman) (horiz) Set of 4 sheets 16·00 17·00

347 "Song of Simeon"

2001. Biblical Drawings and Paintings by Rembrandt.

3690 **347** 1000l. deep brown, brown and grey 1·00 1·00
3691 - 1000l. deep brown, brown and grey 1·00 1·00
3692 - 1000l. deep brown, brown and grey 1·00 1·00
3693 - 1000l. blue, brown and grey 1·00 1·00
3694 - 1000l. deep brown, brown and grey 1·00 1·00
3695 - 1000l. blue and brown 1·00 1·00
3696 - 1000l. red, brown and grey 1·00 1·00
3697 - 1000l. deep brown, brown and red 1·00 1·00
3698 - 1000l. deep brown, brown and red 1·00 1·00
3699 - 1000l. deep brown, brown and grey 1·00 1·00
3700 - 1000l. deep brown, brown and grey 1·00 1·00
3701 - 1000l. deep brown, brown and grey 1·00 1·00
MS3702 Four sheets 86×110 mm. (a) 5000l. multicoloured. (b) 5000l. multicoloured. (c) 5000l. multicoloured. (d) 5000l. multicoloured Set of 4 sheets 16·00 17·00

DESIGNS—HORIZ: No. 3690, Type **347**; 3691, Study for "Adoration of the Magi"; 3692, "Mary with the Child by a Window"; 3693, "The Rest on the Flight into Egypt"; 3694, "The Circumcision"; 3695, "The Shepherds worship the Child"; 3696, "The Angel rises up in the Flame of Manoah's Sacrifice"; 3697, "Tobias frightened by the Fish"; 3698, "The Angel of the Lord stands in Balaam's Path"; 3699, "The Angel appears to Hagar in the Desert"; 3700, "Jacob's Dream"; 3701, "The Healing of Tobit"; **MS**3702a, "The Angel prevents the Sacrifice of Isaac"; **MS**3702b, "Simeon's Prophecy to Mary". VERT: No. **MS**3702c, "The Adoration of the Magi"; **MS**3702d, "The Angel leaves Tobit and His Family".

2001. 60th Anniv of the Battle of Britain. As T 413 of St. Vincent. Multicoloured.

3703 1000l. St. Paul's Cathedral, London 1·25 1·25
3704 1000l. Evacuating bombed building 1·25 1·25
3705 1000l. Winston Churchill being cheered by British troops 1·25 1·25
3706 1000l. Rescuing British pilot by boat 1·25 1·25
3707 1000l. Boy Scout and children 1·25 1·25
3708 1000l. British anti-aircraft gun 1·25 1·25
3709 1000l. Searchlight and crew 1·25 1·25
3710 1000l. Royal Observer Corps post 1·25 1·25
3711 1000l. Bombed houses 1·25 1·25
3712 1000l. Sheltering in underground station 1·25 1·25
3713 1000l. Firemen 1·25 1·25
3714 1000l. Home Guard at drill 1·25 1·25
3715 1000l. ARP warden and black-out sign 1·25 1·25
3716 1000l. Pilots on stand-by 1·25 1·25
3717 1000l. Brendan "Paddy" Finucane (fighter pilot) 1·25 1·25
3718 1000l. Hawk 75 (fighter) 1·25 1·25
3719 1000l. Tower Bridge, London 1·25 1·25
3720 1000l. Surrey Home Guard 1·25 1·25
3721 1000l. Cruiser tank MK III 1·25 1·25
3722 1000l. Newfoundland gun crew 1·25 1·25
3723 1000l. Bomb damage in Plymouth 1·25 1·25
3724 1000l. Winston Churchill 1·25 1·25
3725 1000l. Bomb damage at West-minster Hall 1·25 1·25
3726 1000l. Radar screen 1·25 1·25
3727 1000l. Female telephone engineer and W.A.A.F. 1·25 1·25
3728 1000l. Women munitions workers 1·25 1·25
3729 1000l. Winston Churchill at desk 1·25 1·25
3730 1000l. Dornier DO17 (German bomber) 1·25 1·25
3731 1000l. Church fire 1·25 1·25
3732 1000l. Searchlights over London 1·25 1·25
3733 1000l. Lunch in the underground 1·25 1·25
3734 1000l. Sing song in the underground 1·25 1·25
MS3735 Four sheets. (a) 76×106 mm. 6000l. London skyline. (b) 76×106 mm. 6000l. Winston Churchill and his wife, Clementine. (c) 106×76 mm. 6000l. Supermarine Spitfire. (d) 106×76 mm. 6000l. British bomber crew preparing for mission (vert) Set of 4 sheets 32·00 35·00

No. 3719 is inscribed "LONDON BRIDGE", 3720 "SURRY", 3727 "WAFF", 3729 "DEFINSE" and **MS**3735c "SUBMARINE SPITFIRE", all in error.

348 "Piebald" from National Velvet (Enid Bagnold)

2001. Horses from Literature and Mythology. Multicoloured.

3736 1100l. Type **348** 1·40 1·40
3737 1100l. "Strider" (Tolstoy) 1·40 1·40
3738 1100l. "Black Beauty" (Anna Sewell) 1·40 1·40
3739 1100l. "Red Pony" (John Steinbeck) 1·40 1·40
3740 1100l. "Black Stallion" (Walter Farley) 1·40 1·40
3741 1100l. "Misty" from *Misty of Chincoteague* (Marguerite Henry) 1·40 1·40
3742 1100l. "Arvak" and "Alsvid" pulling Sun (Norse myth) 1·40 1·40
3743 1100l. "Pegasus" (Greek myth) 1·40 1·40
3744 1100l. Odin on "Sleipnir" (Norse myth) 1·40 1·40
3745 1100l. Roland on "Veillantif" from the "Song of Roland" 1·40 1·40
3746 1100l. Sigurd with "Grani" (Norse myth) 1·40 1·40
3747 1100l. Hector on "Galathe" from *Troilus and Cressida* (Shakespeare) 1·40 1·40
MS3748 Two sheets, each 97×67 mm. (a) 5000l. Don Quixote on "Rocinante" (Cervantes). (b) 5000l. "Xanthus" and "Balius" pulling Achilles chariot (greek myth) Set of 2 sheets 13·00 14·00

Nos. 3736/41 and 3742/7 were each printed together, se-tenant, the backgrounds forming composite designs.
No. 3745 is inscribed "Veillanfif" and No. 3747 "Truilus", both in error.

349 "Native Dancer", 1950 (racehorse)

2001. Racehorses. Multicoloured.

3749 200l. Type **349** 55 20
3750 500l. "Citation", 1945 85 40
3751 1200l. "Arkle", 1957 1·40 1·40
3752 1200l. "Golden Miller", 1927 1·40 1·40
3753 1200l. "Phar Lap", 1927 1·40 1·40
3754 1200l. "Battleship", 1927 1·40 1·40
3755 1200l. "Kelso", 1957 1·40 1·40
3756 1200l. "Nijinski", 1967 1·40 1·40
3757 1200l. "Red Rum", 1965 1·40 1·40
3758 1200l. "Sir Ken", 1947 1·40 1·40
3759 1200l. "War Admiral", 1934 1·40 1·40
3760 1200l. "Troytown", 1913 1·40 1·40
3761 1200l. "Shergar", 1981 1·40 1·40
3762 1200l. "Allez France", 1970 1·40 1·40
3763 1500l. "Spectre", 1899 1·40 1·40
3764 2000l. "Carbine", 1885 1·40 1·40
MS3765 Four sheets. (a) 100×74 mm. 5000l. "Cigar". (b) 100×74 mm. 5000l. Racing trophy. (c) 100×74 mm. 5000l. French racecourse. (horiz) (d) 74×100 mm. 5000l. "Desert Orchid" Set of 4 sheets 21·00 21·00

350 Acrocanthosaurus

2001. "Hong Kong 2001" International Stamp Exhibition. Dinosaurs. Multicoloured.

3766 1000l. Type **350** 1·25 1·25
3767 1000l. Edmontosaurus 1·25 1·25
3768 1000l. Archaeopteryx 1·25 1·25
3769 1000l. Hadrosaurus 1·25 1·25
3770 1000l. Mongolian avimimus 1·25 1·25
3771 1000l. Pachyrhinosaurus 1·25 1·25
3772 1000l. Iguanadons and log 1·25 1·25
3773 1000l. Iguanadons 1·25 1·25
3774 1000l. Albertosaurus (horiz) 1·25 1·25
3775 1000l. Pteranadon ingens (horiz) 1·25 1·25
3776 1000l. Asiatic Iguanadon (horiz) 1·25 1·25
3777 1000l. Sordes (horiz) 1·25 1·25
3778 1000l. Coelophysis (horiz) 1·25 1·25
3779 1000l. Saichania (horiz) 1·25 1·25
3780 1000l. Bactrosaurus (horiz) 1·25 1·25
3781 1000l. Triceratops (horiz) 1·25 1·25
MS3782 Five sheets. (a) 85×110 mm. 5000l. Dryosaurus. (b) 110×85 mm. 5000l. Diplodocus. (c) 110×85 mm. 5000l. Allosaurus (horiz). (d) 71×90 mm. 5000l. Stenonychosaurus. (e) 71×90 mm. 5000l. Corythosaurus Set of 5 sheets 28·00 30·00

Nos. 3771, 3774 and **MS**3782b are inscribed "PACHYRMINOSAURUS", "ALBERTO-SAUR" or "DIPLODOCIDS", all in error.

351 Benz Velo, 1898

2001. Cars. Multicoloured.

3783 1000l. Type **351** 1·25 1·25
3784 1000l. Rolls-Royce Silver Ghost, 1909 1·25 1·25
3785 1000l. Ford Model T, 1912 1·25 1·25
3786 1000l. Duesenberg SJ, 1937 1·25 1·25
3787 1000l. Grosse Mercedes, 1938–40 1·25 1·25
3788 1000l. Citroën Light 15, 1938 1·25 1·25
3789 1000l. Lincoln Zephyr, 1939 1·25 1·25
3790 1000l. Volkswagen Beetle, 1947 1·25 1·25
3791 1000l. Jaguar Mark II, 1959 1·25 1·25
3792 1000l. Ford Mustang GT500, 1968 1·25 1·25
3793 1000l. Opel/Vauxhall Senator, 1987-94 1·25 1·25
3794 1000l. Mercedes Maybach, 2002 1·25 1·25
MS3795 Two sheets, each 110×75 mm. (a) 5000l. 3-Litre Bentley Short Chassis Tourer, 1928. (b) 5000l. Ferrari 360 Modena, 1999 Set of 2 sheets 13·00 14·00

No. 3783 is inscribed "Bena" in error.

352 *Teinopalpus imperialis*

2001. Butterflies of the World. Multicoloured.

3796 1100l. Type **352** 1·50 1·50
3797 1100l. *Papilio mochaon* 1·50 1·50
3798 1100l. *Heliconius doris* 1·50 1·50
3799 1100l. *Delias argenthona* 1·50 1·50
3800 1100l. *Danaus formosa* 1·50 1·50
3801 1100l. *Precis octavia* 1·50 1·50
3802 1100l. *Danaus chrysippus* 1·50 1·50
3803 1100l. *Tithorea harmonia* 1·50 1·50
3804 1100l. *Morpho cypris* 1·50 1·50
3805 1100l. *Castnia licusi* 1·50 1·50
3806 1100l. *Dismorphia nemesis* 1·50 1·50
3807 1100l. *Saintpaulia ionanthe* 1·50 1·50
MS3808 Two sheets, each 75×55 mm. (a) 5000l. *Iphiclides podalirius*. (b) 5000l. *Colias crocea* (vert) Set of 2 sheets 13·00 14·00

Nos. 3796/8001 and 3802/7 were each printed together, se-tenant, with the backgrounds forming composite designs.
No. **MS**3808a is inscribed "podoliruis" in error.

353 *Eurema floricola*

2001. Butterflies of Africa. Multicoloured.

3809 250l. Type **353** 65 25
3810 400l. *Papilio dardanus* 85 40
3811 800l. *Amauris nossima* 1·25 80
3812 1100l. *Charaxes lucretia* 1·50 1·50
3813 1100l. *Euxanthe crossleyi* 1·50 1·50
3814 1100l. *Charaxes phoenix* 1·50 1·50
3815 1100l. *Charaxes acraeades* 1·50 1·50
3816 1100l. *Charaxes protoclea* 1·50 1·50
3817 1100l. *Charaxes lydiae* 1·50 1·50
3818 1100l. *Papilio dardanus* 1·50 1·50
3819 1100l. *Cymothoe sangaris* 1·50 1·50
3820 1100l. *Epiphora albida* 1·50 1·50
3821 1100l. African giant swallowtail 1·50 1·50
3822 1100l. *Papilio nobilis* 1·50 1·50
3823 1100l. *Charaxes hadrianus* 1·50 1·50
3824 1500l. *Gideona lucasi* 1·50 1·50
MS3825 Two sheets, each 110×85 mm. (a) 5000l. *Colotis zoe*. (b) 5000l. *Acraea ranaualona* (vert) Set of 2 sheets 13·00 14·00

Nos. 3812/17 and 3818/23 were each printed together, se-tenant, with the backgrounds forming composite designs based on the map of Africa.
Nos. 3813, 3814, 3819, 3823 and **MS**3825a are inscribed "CLOSSEX", "PHENIX", "CYMOTOE", "HADNANUS" and "CLOTIS", all in error.

2001. 25th Death Anniv of Mao Tse-tung (Chinese leader). As T 426 of St. Vincent. Multicoloured.

3826 1100l. Young Mao wearing blue 1·00 1·10
3827 1100l. Mao in green People's Army uniform 1·00 1·10
3828 1100l. Mao in blue cap 1·00 1·10
3829 1100l. Mao in khaki uniform 1·00 1·10
3830 1100l. Mao in open-necked shirt 1·00 1·10
3831 1100l. Mao in grey cap 1·00 1·10
MS3832 Two sheets, each 90×119 mm. (a) 5000l. Mao in traditional robe. (b) 5000l. Mao in blue tunic Set of 2 sheets 10·00 11·00

2001. 75th Death Anniv of Claude-Oscar Monet (French painter). As T 427 of St. Vincent. Mult.

3833 1500l. "Road to Vetheuil, Winter, 1879" 1·75 1·90
3834 1500l. "Church at Vetheuil, 1879" 1·75 1·90
3835 1500l. "Breakup of Ice near Vetheuil, 1880" 1·75 1·90
3836 1500l. "Boulevard de Pontoise, Argenteuil, 1875" 1·75 1·90
MS3837 137×110 mm. 5000l. "Irises by Pool, 1914–17" (vert) 6·50 7·00

2001. 75th Birthday of Queen Elizabeth II. As T 428 of St. Vincent. Multicoloured.

3838 2000l. Princess Elizabeth in A.T.S. uniform 2·50 2·75
3839 2000l. Princess Elizabeth and Prince Charles 2·50 2·75
3840 2000l. Coronation portrait 2·50 2·75
3841 2000l. Princess Elizabeth in Girl Guide uniform 2·50 2·75
MS3842 80×110 mm. 5000l. Queen Elizabeth in evening dress (37×50 mm) 7·50 8·00

2001. Golden Jubilee (1st issue). As T 429 of St. Vincent. Multicoloured.

3843 1000l. Queen Elizabeth II 1·50 1·75

See also Nos. 3960/4.
No. 3843 was printed in sheetlets of 8, containing two vertical rows of four, separated by a large illustrated central gutter. Both the stamp and the illustration on the central gutter are made up of a collage of miniature flower photographs.

2001. Death Centenary of Giuseppe Verdi (Italian composer). As T 430 of St. Vincent showing scenes from Aida (opera). Multicoloured.

3844 1700l. Vladimir Popov 2·50 2·50
3845 1700l. Enrico Caruso 2·50 2·50
3846 1700l. Rudolf Bockelmann 2·50 2·50
3847 1700l. Scene from *Aida* 2·50 2·50
MS3848 79×110 mm. 5000l. Aprile Millo as Aida and Barseq Tumayan as Amonasro 8·50 8·50

2001. Death Centenary of Henri de Toulouse-Lautrec (French painter). As T 431 of St. Vincent. Multicoloured.

3849 2200l. "A la Mie" 2·25 2·50
3850 2200l. "Corner of the Moulin de la Galette" 2·25 2·50
3851 2200l. "Start of the Quadrille" 2·25 2·50
MS3852 68×109 mm. 5000l. "La Gouloue" (vert) 7·00 8·00

2001. Centenary of Royal Navy Submarine Service. As T 107 of St. Kitts. Multicoloured.

3853 1100l. C29 (submarine) 1·75 1·75

3854	1100l. H.M.S. *Spartan* (submarine)	1·75	1·75
3855	1100l. H.M.S. *Exeter*(cruiser)	1·75	1·75
3856	1100l. H.M.S. *Chatham* (frigate)	1·75	1·75
3857	1100l. H.M.S. *Verdun* (destroyer)	1·75	1·75
3858	1100l. H.M.S. *Marlborough* (frigate)	1·75	1·75
MS3859	70×55 mm. 5000l. H.M.S. *Vanguard* (missle submarine)	8·00	8·50

Nos. 3854 and 3857 are inscribed "SPARTON" or "VERDUM",both in error.

354 Marlene Dietrich in Black Dress

2001. Birth Centenary of Marlene Dietrich (actress and singer).

3860	**354**	2000l. black, purple and red	1·75	2·00
3861	-	2000l. multicoloured	1·75	2·00
3862	-	2000l. black, purple and red	1·75	2·00
3863	-	2000l. black, purple and red	1·75	2·00

DESIGNS: No. 3861, Marlene Dietrich in evening dress; 3862, Wearing white fur coat; 3863, Smoking.

2001. "Philanippon '01" International Stamp Exhibition, Tokyo. Japanese Art. As T 432 of St. Vincent. Multicoloured.

3864	50l. "Iziu Chinuki No Hi" (Hokkei) (horiz)	20	20
3865	100l. "Visit to Enoshima" (Torii Kiyonaga) (horiz)	20	20
3866	150l. "Inn on a Harbour" (Sadahide) (horiz)	30	20
3867	200l. "Entrance to Foreigners' Establishment" (Sadahide) (horiz)	35	25
3868	250l. "Courtesans at Cherry Blossom Time" (Kiyonaga) (horiz)	35	25
3869	300l. "Cherry Blossom Viewing at Ueno" (Toyohara Chikanobu) (horiz)	40	25
3870	400l. "Summer Evening at Restaurant by the Sumida River" (Kiyonaga) (horiz)	45	30
3871	500l. "Ichikana Yaozo I as Samurai" (Buncho)	50	30
3872	600l. "Nakamura Noshoi II as Street Walker" (Katsukawa Shunzan)	50	30
3873	800l. "Arashi Sangoro II Hosoban" (Shokosai)	60	40
3874	1500l. "Bando Mitsuguro I" (Shunko)	85	60
3875	2000l. "Matsumoto Koshiro II" (Masanobu)	1·40	1·50
3876	2000l. "Young Woman attended by Maid" (Suzuki Harunobu)	1·75	1·90
3877	2000l. "Lovers by Lespedeza Bush" (Harunobu)	1·75	1·90
3878	2000l. "Girl contemplating a Landscape" (Harunobu)	1·75	1·90
3879	2000l. "Young Man unrolling a Hanging Scroll" (Harunobu)	1·75	1·90
3880	2000l. "Promenade" (Harunobu)	1·75	1·90
3881	2000l. "Wine Tasters" (Harunobu)	1·75	1·90
3882	2000l. "Rain in May" (Harunobu)	1·75	1·90
3883	2000l. "Lovers by the Wall" (Harunobu)	1·75	1·90
3884	2000l. "Six Girls" (standing figure with orange sash) (Eisho)	1·75	1·90
3885	2000l. "Courtesan on a Bench" (Eiri)	1·75	1·90
3886	2000l. "Courtesan and her Two Kamuro" (Harunobu)	1·75	1·90
3887	2000l. "Clearing Weather at Awazu" (Shigemasa)	1·75	1·90
3888	2000l. "Nakamura Shikan II and Nakamura Baiko" (Shigeharu)	1·75	1·90
3889	2000l. "Women making Rice Cakes" (Shunsho)	1·75	1·90
3890	2000l. "Youth sending Letter by Arrow" (Harushige)	1·75	1·90
3891	2000l. "Six Girls" (standing figure with green sash) (Eisho)	1·75	1·90
MS3892	Five sheets, each 85×120 mm. (a) 5000l. "Courtesan and Two Kamuro". (b) 5000l. "Searching for the Hermit". (c) 5000l. "Girl contemplating a Landscape" (different). (d) 5000l. "Drying Clothes". (e) 5000l. "Komachi praying for Rain". All by Harunobu Set of 5 sheets	24·00	26·00

355 General Ulysses S. Grant

2001. American Civil War. Multicoloured.

3893	2000l. Type **355**	2·00	2·25
3894	2000l. General John Hood	2·00	2·25
3895	2000l. General Jeb Stuart	2·00	2·25
3896	2000l. General Robert E. Lee	2·00	2·25
3897	2000l. General Joshua Chamberlain	2·00	2·25
3898	2000l. General "Stonewall" Jackson	2·00	2·25
3899	2000l. General George McClellan	2·00	2·25
3900	2000l. Admiral David Farragut	2·00	2·25
3901	2000l. Battle of Fredericksburg, 1862	2·00	2·25
3902	2000l. Battle of Gettysburg, 1863	2·00	2·25
3903	2000l. Naval Battle of Mobile Bay, 1864	2·00	2·25
3904	2000l. Bombardment of Fort Sumter, 1861	2·00	2·25
3905	2000l. Battle of Shiloh, 1862	2·00	2·25
3906	2000l. Battle of Bull Run, 1861 and 1862	2·00	2·25
3907	2000l. Battle of Fair Oaks, 1863	2·00	2·25
3908	2000l. Battle of Chattanooga, 1863	2·00	2·25
MS3909	Four sheets. (a) 109×157 mm. 5000l. General George Custer. (b) 109×157 mm. 5000l. General William T. Sherman. (c) 109×157 mm. 5000l. Battle of Vicksburg, 1863. (d) 157×109 mm. 5000l. Battle of Antietam, 1862 Set of 4 sheets	21·00	23·00

No. 3900 is inscribed "ADMRIAL" in error.

356 Ferrari 360 Challenge, 2001

2001. Ferrari Racing Cars. Multicoloured.

3910	100l. Type **356**	35	20
3911	500l. 712 Can Am, 1971	75	35
3912	600l. 512M, 1970	85	65
3913	1000l. F40, 1988	1·40	1·50
3914	1500l. 365 GT4/BB, 1982	1·90	2·25
3915	2000l. 365 GTB/4, 1972	2·25	2·50

357 Chinese Character with Symbolic Horse ("2002" in green)

2001. Chinese New Year ("Year of the Horse"). Each incorporating the same character and a symbolic horse. Multicoloured.

3916	1200l. Type **357**	1·60	1·75
3917	1200l. "2002" in red	1·60	1·75
3918	1200l. "2002" in orange	1·60	1·75
3919	1200l. "2002" in blue	1·60	1·75
MS3920	97×69 mm. 1200l. European toy horse on wheels (37×24 mm); 1200l. Chinese toy horse and rider (37×24 mm)	3·00	3·50

358 British Newspaper Article, Brazil, 1950

2001. World Cup Football Championship, Japan and Korea (2002). Multicoloured.

3921	1400l. Type **358**	1·60	1·60
3922	1400l. Jules Rimet (F.I.F.A. President), Switzerland, 1954	1·60	1·60
3923	1400l. Pele and other members of Brazilian team, Sweden, 1958	1·60	1·60
3924	1400l. Vava (Brazil) and Schroiff (Czechoslovakia), Chile, 1962	1·60	1·60
3925	1400l. Bobby Charlton (England), England, 1966	1·60	1·60
3926	1400l. Pele (Brazil), Mexico, 1970	1·60	1·60
3927	1400l. Daniel Passarella (Argentina) with World Cup, Argentina, 1978	1·60	1·60
3928	1400l. Karl-Heinz Rummenigge (West Germany), Spain, 1982	1·60	1·60
3929	1400l. Diego Maradona (Argentina), Mexico, 1986	1·60	1·60
3930	1400l. Roger Milla (Cameroon), Italy, 1990	1·60	1·60
3931	1400l. Romario (Brazil), U.S.A., 1994	1·60	1·60
3932	1400l. Zinedine Zidane (France), France, 1998	1·60	1·60
MS3933	Two sheets, each 88×75 mm. (a) 5000l. Detail of Jules Rimet Trophy, Uruguay, 1930. (b) 5000l. Detail of World Cup Trophy, Japan/Korea 2002 Set of 2 sheets	13·00	14·00

No. 3922 is inscribed "Rimmet" in error.

359 "Madonna of Humility" (Filippo Lippi)

2001. Christmas. Religious Paintings by Filippo Lippi. Multicoloured.

3934	300l. Type **359**	60	20
3935	600l. "Annunciation"	90	35
3936	1500l. "Annunciation" (different) (vert)	2·00	2·50
3937	2000l. "Adoration of the Child and Saints" (vert)	2·50	3·00
MS3938	136×106 mm. 5000l. "Barbadori Altarpiece" (vert)	5·50	6·50

No. **MS**3938 is inscribed "Alterpiece" in error.

360 Early Steam Fire Engine

2002. Technological Development from Steam to Electricity. Multicoloured.

3939	1100l. Type **360**	1·50	1·50
3940	1100l. Dial telephone	1·50	1·50
3941	1100l. Luxury liner	1·50	1·50
3942	1100l. Electrical battery	1·50	1·50
3943	1100l. Steam carriage, 1770	1·50	1·50
3944	1100l. Modern electric locomotive	1·50	1·50
3945	1100l. Robert Fulton and early steam ship	1·50	1·50
3946	1100l. Thomas Edison and early electric light bulb	1·50	1·50
3947	1100l. Class T9 steam locomotive, 1899	1·50	1·50
3948	1100l. Early radio and transmitting masts	1·50	1·50
3949	1100l. James Watt and diagram of steam engine	1·50	1·50
3950	1100l. Alexander Graham Bell and early telephone	1·50	1·50
3951	1100l. *The Rocket* (steam locomotive), 1829	1·50	1·50
3952	1100l. Modern TGV train	1·50	1·50
3953	1100l. Firefighting steam pump, 1863	1·50	1·50
3954	1100l. Early electric tram	1·50	1·50
3955	1100l. Steam car, 1893	1·50	1·50
3956	1100l. Modern electric monorail	1·50	1·50
MS3957	Three sheets, each 70×100 mm (a) 5000l. Class T9 steam locomotive, 1899. (b)5000l. Telephone, radio and light bulb. (c) 5000l. Benjamin Franklin (vert) Set of 3 sheets	20·00	22·00

361 S.O.S. Children's Village Logo

2002. S.O.S. Children's Villages (Kinderdorf International).

3958	**361**	2000l. multicoloured	1·75	2·00

2002. "United We Stand". Support for Victims of 11 September 2001 Terrorist Attacks. As T 445 of St. Vincent. Multicoloured.

3959	2000l. U. S. flag as Statue of Liberty and Sierra Leone flag	2·00	2·50

2002. Golden Jubilee (2nd issue). As T 110 of St. Kitts Multicoloured.

3960	2000l. Queen Elizabeth with Prince Charles and Princess Anne	2·75	3·00
3961	2000l. Queen Elizabeth in red dress and fur stole	2·75	3·00
3962	2000l. Queen Elizabeth wearing tiara and fur	2·75	3·00
3963	2000l. Queen Elizabeth wearing beige hat and coat	2·75	3·00
MS3964	76×108 mm. 5000l. Queen Elizabeth wearing grey hat and coat	7·00	7·50

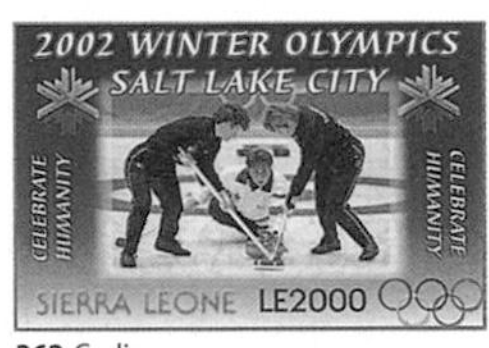

362 Curling

2002. Winter Olympic Games, Salt Lake City. Multicoloured.

3965	2000l. Type **362**	2·75	3·00
3966	2000l. Ice hockey	2·75	3·00
MS3967	88×118 mm. Nos. 3965/6	5·50	6·00

363 Jerusalem Artichoke Flower and Butterfly

2002. Flowers of Sierra Leone. Multicoloured.

3968	400l. Type **363**	55	30
3969	500l. Painted trillium and bee	70	35
3970	600l. Bell flower ("Bluebells") and moth	90	45
3971	1000l. Rough-fruited cinquefoil and moth	1·25	90
3972	1300l. Laevigata iris (43×29 mm)	1·40	1·50
3973	1300l. Wild iris ("Dietes") (43×29 mm)	1·40	1·50
3974	1300l. Day lily (43×29 mm)	1·40	1·50
3975	1300l. Cardinal flower (43×29 mm)	1·40	1·50
3976	1300l. Mountain pink (43×29 mm)	1·40	1·50
3977	1300l. Seaside gentian (43×29 mm)	1·40	1·50
3978	1300l. Hepatica americana (43×29 mm)	1·40	1·50
3979	1300l. Star of Bethlehem (43×29 mm)	1·40	1·50
3980	1300l. Wood lily (43×29 mm)	1·40	1·50
3981	1300l. Wild geranium (43×29 mm)	1·40	1·50
3982	1300l. Hedge bindweed (43×29 mm)	1·40	1·50
3983	1300l. Gloxinia (43×29 mm)	1·40	1·50
3984	1500l. Wake-robin and wasp	1·40	1·50
3985	2000l. Seashore mallow and butterfly	1·40	1·50
MS3986	Two sheets, each 117×107 mm. (a) 5000l. Dame's rocket (29×43 mm). (b) 5000l. Pinxter flower (29×43 mm) Set of 2 sheets	13·00	14·00

Nos. 3972/7 and 3978/83 were each printed together, se-tenant, with the backgrounds forming composite designs.

364 African Buffalo

2002. Sierra Leone Wildlife. Multicoloured.

3987	200l. Giraffe (vert)	75	30
3988	400l. L'Host's guenon (vert)	70	35
3989	1100l. Type **364**	1·40	1·50
3990	1100l. Wild dog	1·40	1·50
3991	1100l. Black-backed jackal	1·40	1·50
3992	1100l. Aardvark	1·40	1·50
3993	1100l. Impala	1·40	1·50
3994	1100l. Waterbuck	1·40	1·50
3995	1100l. Kudu	1·40	1·50
3996	1100l. Caracal	1·40	1·50
3997	1100l. Oribis	1·40	1·50
3998	1100l. Aardwolf	1·40	1·50
3999	1100l. Bushpig	1·40	1·50
4000	1100l. Meerkat ("Suricates")	1·40	1·50
4001	1500l. Jentink's duiker	1·40	1·50
MS4002	Two sheets, each 117×107 mm. (a) 8000l. Springbok (vert). (b) (b) 8000l. Vervet monkey (vert) Set of 2 sheets	18·00	20·00

Nos. 3989/94 and 3995/4000 were each printed together, se-tenant, with the backgrounds forming composite designs. Nos. 3991, 3997 and 4001 are inscribed "Jackel", "Orbis" and "Jentik's", all in error.

2002. Queen Elizabeth the Queen Mother Commemoration. Nos. 2335/9 surch.

4003	800l. on 400l. Queen Mother (brown, light brown and black)	1·60	1·75
4004	800l. on 400l. Holding bouquet	1·60	1·75
4005	800l. on 400l. Sitting at desk	1·60	1·75
4006	800l. on 400l. Wearing pink evening dress	1·60	1·75
MS4007	103×127 mm. 5000l. on 1500l. Wearing blue hat	7·50	8·00

2002. Shirley Temple in Wee Willie Winkie. As T 411 of St. Vincent showing scenes from the film. Multicoloured.

4008	1100l. Meeting Khoda Khan	90	1·00
4009	1100l. Priscilla looking in mirror	90	1·00
4010	1100l. With drummer boy	90	1·00
4011	1100l. Priscilla being admonished by Indian servant	90	1·00
4012	1100l. Priscilla with grandfather	90	1·00
4013	1100l. Exchanging letter with Khoda Khan in prison	90	1·00
4014	1300l. Priscilla and mother (vert)	1·00	1·10
4015	1300l. Examining Khoda Khan's locket (vert)	1·00	1·10
4016	1300l. Priscilla with mother and grandfather (vert)	1·00	1·10
4017	1300l. Priscilla with colour sergeant, holding rifle (vert)	1·00	1·10
MS4018	106×76 mm. 5000l. Priscilla on parade (vert)	5·50	6·00

2002. International Year of Mountains. As T 115 of St. Kitts. Multicoloured.

4019	2000l. Mount Etna, Italy	2·50	2·50
4020	2000l. Mount Cotopaxi, Ecuador	2·50	2·50
4021	2000l. Mount Everest, Nepal	2·50	2·50
4022	2000l. Mount Popocatepetl, Mexico	2·50	2·50
MS4023	118×68 mm. 5000l. Mount Machhapuchare, Nepal	7·00	7·50

2002. U.N. Year of Eco Tourism. As T 449 of St.Vincent, but horiz. Multicoloured.

4024	1300l. Bullom boats	1·60	1·60
4025	1300l. Dinkongor Falls	1·60	1·60
4026	1300l. Sailing canoe on River Rokel	1·60	1·60
4027	1300l. Pigmy hippopotamus	1·60	1·60
4028	1300l. Soa Chiefdom hills	1·60	1·60
4029	1300l. Long Beach	1·60	1·60
MS4030	88×103 mm. 5000l. Photo safari	6·50	7·50

366 *Spirit of St. Louis* (aircraft)

2002. 75th Anniv of First Solo Transatlantic Flight, by Charles Lindbergh.

4031	**366** 2500l. lake and red	3·00	3·25
4032	- 2500l. green and red	3·00	3·25
4033	- 2500l. lilac and red	3·00	3·25
MS4034	116×85 mm. 2500l. multicoloured (vert)	3·00	3·25

DESIGNS—HORIZ: No. 4032, *Spirit of St. Louis*, Curtisfield, 1927; 4033, Taking off from Roosevelt Field, 1927. VERT: No. **MS**4034, Charles Lindbergh.

367 Chiune Sugihara

2002. Chiune Sugihara, Japanese Consul-general to Lithuania, 1939–40, Commemoration.

4035	**367** 2000l. multicoloured	2·75	3·00

2002. 20th World Scout Jamboree, Thailand. As T 116 St. Kitts, but vert. Multicoloured.

4036	2000l. Scouts on rocks	2·50	2·50
4037	2000l. Scouts of all nations	2·50	2·50
4038	2000l. Two scouts in river, holding fish	2·50	2·50
4039	2000l. Watching demonstration	2·50	2·50
MS4040	107×122 mm. 5000l. Sailing on lake	7·00	7·50

2002. "Pokemon" (children's cartoon series). As T 417 of St. Vincent. Multicoloured.

4041	1500l. "Sudowoodo No. 185"	1·10	1·40
4042	1500l. "Aipom No. 190"	1·10	1·40
4043	1500l. "Shuckle No. 213"	1·10	1·40
4044	1500l. "Miltank No. 241"	1·10	1·40
4045	1500l. "Hitmontop No. 237"	1·10	1·40
4046	1500l. "Ledian No. 166"	1·10	1·40
MS4047	67×91 mm. 5000l. "Lugia No. 249"	5·50	6·00

368 Popeye and Olive Oyl at Helm

2002. "Popeye" (cartoon character) in New York. Multicoloured.

4048	1300l. Type **368**	1·10	1·25
4049	1300l. Popeye giving Olive Oyl spinach	1·10	1·25
4050	1300l. By Brooklyn Bridge	1·10	1·25
4051	1300l. Popeye near Statue of Liberty	1·10	1·25
4052	1300l. At the Flatiron building	1·10	1·25
4053	1300l. In front of Empire State Building	1·10	1·25
MS4054	128×89 mm. 5000l. Popeye and Olive Oyl ice skating (78×51 mm)	6·00	6·50

369 Elvis Presley

2002. 25th Death Anniv of Elvis Presley (American entertainer). Each black and brown.

4055	1000l. Type **369**	1·40	1·40
4056	1000l. Playing bi-coloured guitar	1·40	1·40
4057	1000l. Sitting in director's chair	1·40	1·40
4058	1000l. Wearing polo neck jumper	1·40	1·40
4059	1000l. In Hispanic suit	1·40	1·40
4060	1000l. Playing dark guitar	1·40	1·40

370 Michael Ballack (Germany)

2002. World Cup Football Championship, Japan and Korea. Multicoloured.

4061	1400l. Type **370**	1·10	1·10
4062	1400l. Oliver Kahn (Germany)	1·10	1·10
4063	1400l. Miroslav Klose (Germany)	1·10	1·10
4064	1400l. Diego Gavilan (Paraguay)	1·10	1·10
4065	1400l. Jose Luis Chilavert (Paraguay)	1·10	1·10
4066	1400l. Guido Alvarenga (Paraguay)	1·10	1·10
4067	1400l. Rafael Marquez (Mexico)	1·10	1·10
4068	1400l. Oscar Perez (Mexico)	1·10	1·10
4069	1400l. Jared Borgetti (Mexico)	1·10	1·10
4070	1400l. Landon Donovan (U.S.A.)	1·10	1·10
4071	1400l. Brad Friedel (U.S.A.)	1·10	1·10
4072	1400l. DaMarcus Beasley (U.S.A.)	1·10	1·10
4073	1400l. Jesper Gronkjaer (Denmark)	1·10	1·10
4074	1400l. Thomas Helveg (Denmark)	1·10	1·10
4075	1400l. Dennis Rommedahl (Denmark)	1·10	1·10
4076	1400l. Michael Owen (England)	1·10	1·10
4077	1400l. David Seaman (England)	1·10	1·10
4078	1400l. Rio Ferdinand (England)	1·10	1·10
4079	1400l. Ryuzo Morioka (Japan)	1·10	1·10
4080	1400l. Kazuyuki Toda (Japan)	1·10	1·10
4081	1400l. Atsushi Yanagisawa (Japan)	1·10	1·10
4082	1400l. Fatih Akyel (Turkey)	1·10	1·10
4083	1400l. Yildiray Basturk (Turkey)	1·10	1·10
4084	1400l. Umit Davala (Turkey)	1·10	1·10
MS4085	Eight sheets, each 82×82 mm. (a) 2500l. Rudi Voeller (coach) (Germany); 2500l. Dietmar Hamann (Germany). (b) 2500l. Julio Cesar Caceres (Paraguay); 2500l. Cesare Maldini (coach) (Paraguay). (c) 2500l. Javier Aguirre (coach) (Mexico); 2500l. Jesus Arellano (Mexico). (d) 2500l. Brian McBride (U.S.A.); 2500l. Bruce Arena (coach) (U.S.A.). (e) 2500l. Morten Olsen (coach) (Denmark); 2500l. Jon Dahl Tomasson (Denmark). (f) 2500l. David Beckham (England); 2500l. Sven Goran Eriksson (coach) (England). (g) 2500l. Philippe Troussier (coach) (Japan); 2500l. Junichi Inamoto (Japan). (h) 2500l. Vildiray Basturk (Turkey); 2500l. Senol Gunes (coach) (Turkey) Set of 8 sheets	17·00	20·00

371 "Madonna and Child between Sts. John the Baptist and Catherine of Alexandria" (Perugino)

2002. Christmas. Religious Paintings. Mult.

4086	50l. Type **371**	20	15
4087	100l. "Madonna and Child enthroned between Angels and Saints" (Ghirlandaio)	25	15
4088	150l. "The Virgin" (Giovanni Bellini)	30	15
4089	500l. "The Birth of Mary" (Ghirlandaio)	80	25
4090	5000l. "Adoration of the Magi" (Ghirlandaio)	6·50	7·50
MS4091	100×76 mm. 6000l. "Madonna enthroned with Saints" (Ghirlandaio)	7·50	8·50

372 Teddy Bear with Green and Gold Bow

2002. Centenary of the Teddy Bear (1st issue). Two sheets containing T 372 and similar vert designs. Multicoloured.

MS4092	107×115 mm. 1700l. Type **372**; 1700l. Jester teddy bear; 1700l. Bear with red and gold headband; 1700l. Bear with sash	6·00	7·00
MS4093	148×158 mm. 2000l. Baby girl bear; 2000l. School girl bear; 2000l. Bear in denim overalls; 2000l. Bear in pyjamas	6·50	7·50

See also Nos. **MS**4128/9.

373 Princess Diana

2002. 5th Death Anniv of Diana, Princess of Wales. Two sheets, each 120×130 mm, containing T 373 and similar vert design. Multicoloured.

MS4094	1700l. ×4 Type **373**	7·50	8·00
MS4095	1700l. ×4 Princess Diana (wearing tiara)	7·50	8·00

374 President John F. Kennedy

2002. Presidents John F. Kennedy (Commemoration) and Ronald Reagan. Miniature sheets containing vert designs as T 374. Multicoloured.

MS4096	122×135 mm. 1700l. Type **374**; 1700l. John Kennedy reading newspaper; 1700l. John Kennedy (looking ahead); 1700l. John Kennedy (looking left)	6·00	7·00
MS4097	114×129 mm. 1700l. John and Jacqueline Kennedy in evening dress; 1700l. John and Jacqueline Kennedy; 1700l. With John Jnr; 1700l. Jacqueline Kennedy in pink hat and coat	6·00	7·00
MS4098	143×110 mm. 1700l. ×4 containing two different portraits of Ronald Reagan	6·00	7·00
MS4099	137×165 mm. 1700l. ×4 containing two different portraits of Ronald Reagan	6·00	7·00

375 Great Blue Turaco

2003. Fauna and Flora of Africa. Miniature sheets containing T 375 and similar multicoloured designs.

MS4100	139×100 mm. 1300l. Type **375**; 1300l. Helmet bird ("Helmet Vanga"); 1300l. Red-tufted malachite sunbird ("Scarlet-tufted Malachite Sunbird"); 1300l. African pitta; 1300l. African jacana; 1300l. Carmine bee eater	10·00	11·00
MS4101	139×100 mm. 1300l. *Ancistrochilus rothschildianus*; 1300l. *Oeceoclades maculate*; 1300l. *Eulophia guineensis*; 1300l. *Angraecum distichum*; 1300l. *Disa uniflora*; 1300l. *Vanilla imperialis*	10·00	11·00

MS4102 139×100 mm. 1300l. Panther-spotted grasshopper; 1300l. Basker moth; 1300l. *Charaxes samagdalis* (butterfly); 1300l. Carpenter ant; 1300l. Worker bee; 1300l. *Libellula pulchella* (ten-spot dragonfly) 10·00 11·00

MS4103 Three sheets. (a) 63×87 mm. 5000l. European robin. (b) 87×63 mm. 5000l. *Bulbophyllum lepidum*. (c) 87×63 mm. 5000l. Common dotted border (butterfly) (horiz) Set of 3 sheets 20·00 21·00

No. **MS**4100 shows birds, **MS**4101 shows flowers and **MS**4102 insects.

376 Green Symbolic Ram

2003. Chinese New Year ("Year of the Ram"). Sheet 109×128 mm, containing T 376 and similar vert designs. Multicoloured.

MS4104 900l. Type **376**; 900l.×3 Carved ram; 900l. Red symbolic ram. 900l. Magenta symbolic ram 4·25 4·75

377 David Brown

2003. Columbia Space Shuttle Commemoration. Sheet 184×145 mm, containing T 377 and similar vert designs showing crew members. Multicoloured.

MS4105 1000l. Type **377**; 1000l. Commander Rick Husband; 1000l. Laurel Clark; 1000l. Kalpana Chawla; 1000l. Payload Commander Michael Anderson; 1000l. Pilot William McCool; 1000l. Ilan Ramon 8·00 9·00

2003. Centenary of the Teddy Bear (2nd issue). Embroidered Fabric Teddy Bears. As T 464 of St. Vincent. Self-adhesive. Imperf.

4106	12000l. ochre, silver and black	3·50	3·75
MS4107	126×157 mm. No. 4106 ×4	14·00	14·50

378 "Priest Raigo tranformed into a Rat" (Tsukioka Yoshitoshi)

2003. Japanese Art. Ghosts and Demons. Multicoloured.

4108	800l. Type **378**	1·00	60
4109	1000l. "The Spirit of Tamichi as a Great Snake" (Tsukioka Yoshitoshi)	1·25	85
4110	1500l. "The Gathering and Gossiping of Various Tools" (Utagawa Kuniyoshi)	1·75	2·00
4111	2500l. "Caricatures of Actors as Three Animals playing Ken" (Utagawa Kuniyoshi)	2·75	3·25

MS4112 148×148 mm. 2000l. "The Fox Woman leaving her Child"; 2000l. "Fox Cry"; 2000l. "The Lucky Teakettle of Morin Temple"; 2000l. "The Ghost of Okiku" (all Tsukioka Yoshitoshi) 8·50 9·50

MS4113 88×118 mm. 5000l. "Fox in a Thunderstorm" (Utagawa Kunisada) 6·00 6·50

2003. 30th Death Anniv of Pablo Picasso (artist). As T 465 of St. Vincent, but vert. Multicoloured.

4114	400l. "Verres Pipe, Carte a Jouer"	70	45
4115	500l. "Gueridon devant un Balcon"	80	50
4116	600l. "Femme au Chapeau a Plumes"	90	65
4117	700l. "Gueridon et Guitare"	1·00	1·00
4118	1000l. "Femme en Pied"	1·25	1·25
4119	3000l. "Femme Acrobate"	3·50	4·00

MS4120 205×140 mm. 2000l. "Portrait de Face"; 2000l. "Femme au Fauteuil Rouge"; 2000l. "Femme au Petit Chapeau Rond, Assise (Dora Maar)"; 2000l. "Femme aux Mains Croisees" 8·00 8·50

MS4121 (a) 82×105 mm. 5000l. "Garcon au Calecon noir". Imperf. (b) 102×81 mm. 5000l. "Les Baigneuses". Imperf 12·00 13·00

2003. Paintings by Rembrandt. As T 466 of St. Vincent. Multicoloured.

4122	800l. "Young Man with Pointed Beard"	1·00	75
4123	1000l. "Old Man with Book"	1·25	95
4124	1200l. "The Shipbuilder Jan Rijcksen and his Wife, Griet Jans" (horiz)	1·40	1·40
4125	2000l. "Portrait of a Young Jew"	2·40	3·00

MS4126 185×183 mm. 1700l. "Juno"; 1700l. "Bellona, Goddess of War"; 1700l. "Artemisia" (detail); 1700l. "Esther preparing to Intercede with Ahasuerus" (detail) (all 35×47 mm) 8·00 8·50

MS4127 110×130 mm. 5000l. "Two Scholars Disputing" 6·50 7·00

379 Teddy Bear wearing Apron and Hat

2003. Centenary of the Teddy Bear (3rd issue). German Teddy Bears. Multicoloured.

MS4128 183×129 mm. 1500l. Type **379**; 1500l. Bear wearing waistcoat, hat and water bottle; 1500l. Bear wearing pink dress 1500l. Bear with trumpet and score 6·00 7·00

MS4129 98×72 mm. 5000l. Bear in Volkswagen Beetle car (horiz) 5·00 6·00

2003. 50th Anniv of Coronation. As T 462 of St. Vincent. Multicoloured.

4130	1500l. Queen Elizabeth II holding Sovereign's Sword	1·90	1·90
4131	1500l. Ampulla and spoon	1·90	1·90
4132	1500l. Queen presented with Holy Bible	1·90	1·90
4133	1500l. Crowning of Queen	1·90	1·90
4134	1500l. Queen signing Oath	1·90	1·90
4135	1500l. Anointing of Queen	1·90	1·90
4136	1500l. Orb and Sceptre	1·90	1·90
4137	1500l. Crowd at Palace gates and Royal Family on balcony	1·90	1·90

MS4138 9×67 mm. 5000l. Queen Elizabeth II (38×50 mm) 7·50 8·00

380 Prince William

2003. 21st Birthday of Prince William of Wales. Multicoloured.

MS4139 146×85 mm. 2500l. Type **380**; 2500l. Prince William (wearing black jacket and tie); 2500l. Wearing grey sweatshirt 10·00 11·00

MS4140 96×67 mm. 5000l. Prince William 7·50 8·00

381 Peggy Williams

2003. Centenary of Circus Clowns. Multicoloured.

MS4141 116×196 mm. 2000l. Type **381**; 2000l. Nico; 2000l. Steve TJ Tatter Smith; 2000l. Uncle Dippy 7·00 7·50

MS4142 145×217 mm. 2000l. Caracal (cat) ; 2000l. Chairs (gymnast); 2000l. Elena Panova on trapeze; 2000l. Chinese Circus performer 7·00 7·50

382 "Mona Lisa"

2003. 500th Anniv of "Mona Lisa" (painting, Da Vinci).

MS4143 100×77 mm. 2000l. Type **382** (black and grey); 2000l. "Mona Lisa (black, deep brown and brown); 2000l. "Mona Lisa" (multicoloured) 7·00 8·00

MS4144 67×97 mm. 5000l. "Mona Lisa" (detail) (multicoloured) 6·50 7·00

383 Waterfalls of Mount Tonkour

2003. International Year of Freshwater. Multicoloured.

MS4145 96×138 mm. 2000l. Type **383**; 2000l. Tagbaladougou Falls; 2000l. Cascades d,Ouzoud 7·00 8·00

MS4146 67×97 mm. 5000l. Little Scarcies 6·50 7·00

384 Rotarian and People in Canoe

2003. 40th Anniv of Rotary Club in Sierra Leone. Multicoloured.

MS4147 105×77 mm. 2500l. Type **384**; 2500l. People of Sierra Leone and cacheted first day cover; 2500l. Paul Harris (founder) and girl with flowers 8·00 9·00

MS4148 97×67 mm. 6000l. Bhichai Rattakul (Rotary President) 7·00 8·00

385 Wright Brothers First Plane (USA), 1903

2003. Centenary of Powered Flight. Multicoloured.

MS4149 176×96 mm. 1500l. Wright Brothers' First Plane (U.S.A.), 1903; 1500l. Voisin-Farmin (France), 1907 (grey background); 1500l. Levavasseur Antoinette (France), 1909 (No. 29 on fuselage); 1500l. Nieuport (France) 1910 7·50 8·50

MS4150 176×96 mm. 1500l. Curtiss Triad, 1911 (inscr "Wright Brothers First Plane (U.S.A.) 1903"; 1500l. Avro Biplane, 1911 (inscr "Voisin-Farmin (France) 1907") (blue-grey background); 1500l. Curtiss America, 1913 (inscr "Levavasseur Antoinette (France) 1909"); 1500l. Farnborough Be-2, 1913 (inscr "Nieuport (France) 1910") (No. 345 on tail) 7·50 8·50

MS4150a 176×96 mm. 1500l. Curtiss Triad (U.S.A.), 1911; 1500l. Avro Biplane (British), 1911; 1500l. Curtiss America (U.S.A.), 1913; 1500l. Farnborough Be-2 (British), 1913 7·50 8·50

MS4151 Two sheets, each 106×76 mm. (a) 5000l. Voisin-Farman plane crossing finish line, Aero Club, 1908. (b) 5000l. Roland Garros and Morane-Saulnier monoplane after first non-stop Mediterranean crossing, 1913 Set of 2 sheets 7·50 8·50

No. **MS**4150 was issued with the incorrect aircraft inscriptions and **MS**4150a was issued subsequently with the correct inscriptions.

2003. Centenary of Tour de France Cycle Race. As T 470 of St.Vincent. Multicoloured.

MS4152 157×97 mm. 1500l. Ferdinand Kubler (1950); 1500l. Hugo Koblet (1951); 1500l. Fausto Coppi (1952); 1500l. Louison Bobet (1953) 7·50 8·00

MS4153 157×97 mm. 1500l. Louison Bobet 1954); 1500l. Louison Bobet (1955); 1500l. Roger Walkowiak (1956); 1500l. Jacques Anquetil (1957) 7·50 8·00

MS4154 157×97 mm. 1500l. Eddy Merckx (1970); 1500l. Eddy Merckx (1971); 1500l. Eddy Merckx (1972); 1500l. Luis Ocana (1973) 7·50 8·00

MS4155 Two sheets, each 106×77 mm. (a) 5000l. Louison Bobet (1953, 1954, 1955). (b) 5000l. Jacques Anquetil (1957). (c) 5000l. Bernard Hinault (1978) Set of 2 Sheets 12·00 13·00

386 Forrest Smithson (110 metre hurdles), USA, 1908

2003. Olympic History. Gold Medal Winners. Multicoloured.

4156	300l. Type **386**	50	25
4157	400l. Hannes Kolehmainen (10000 metres, 5000 metres and cross-country), Finland, 1912	60	30
4158	500l. Larisa Latynina (gymnastics–floor exercises), URS, 1964	65	35
4159	800l. Klaus Dibiasi (10 metre platform diving), Italy, 1976	1·00	70
4160	1000l. Archie Hahn (100 metres and 200 metres), USA, 1904	1·25	95
4161	1500l. Marcus Hurley (cycling), USA, 1904	2·00	2·00
4162	2000l. Ray Ewry (standing high jump, standing long jump and standing triple jump), USA, 1900	2·25	2·50
4163	3000l. Henry Taylor (swimming–1500 metres and 400 metres freestyle), Great Britain, 1908	3·25	3·75

387 "Madonna and Child with St. Anne and Four Saints" (detail)

2003. Christmas. Paintings by Fiorentino. Multicoloured.

4164	100l. Type **387**	25	15
4165	150l. "Madonna and Child with Two Saints" (detail)	30	15
4166	500l. "Madonna and Child enthroned with Four Saints" (detail) (Ognissanti Altarpiece)	75	30
4167	4000l. "Madonna enthroned between Two Saints" (detail)	5·00	6·00

MS4168 99×110 mm. 5000l. "Madonna with Saints" 6·50 7·50

388 Camarasaurus

2004. Prehistoric Animals. Multicoloured.

MS4169 138×99 mm. 2000l. Type **388**; 2000l. Iystrosaurus; 2000l. Ankylosaurus; 2000l. Herrerasaurus 8·50 9·50

MS4170 125×106 mm. 2000l. Apatosaurus (vert); 2000l. Styracosaurus (vert); 2000l. Plateosaurus (vert); 2000l. Pachyrhinosaurus (vert) 8·50 9·50

MS4171	Two sheets (a) 97×67 mm. 5000l. Archaeopteryx. (b) 67×96 mm. 5000l. Dunklosteus (vert)	11·00	12·00

No. **MS**4171a is incorrectly inscr "Archaeopterxy".

389 Monkey eating Fruit

2004. Chinese New Year ("Year of the Monkey"). Multicoloured.

MS4173	85×70 mm. 1200l. Type **389** (ochre background); 1200l. Type **389** (blue background); 1200l. Monkey eating fruit (facing right, mauve background); 1200l. Monkey eating fruit (facing right, orange background)	4·50	4·75
MS4174	66×96 mm. 2500l. Monkey holding fruit (42×28 mm)	4·25	4·50

390 "Taoist Ritual at the Imperial Court"

2004. Hong Kong 2004 International Stamp Exhibition. Paintings by Chiao Ping-chen. Multicoloured.

MS4175	136×139 mm. 2000l. Type **390**; 2000l. Landscape of mountains, river and lake; 2000l. "Court Ladies" (by pavilion); 2000l. "Court Ladies" (poling raft)	7·00	8·00
MS4176	90×90 mm. 5000l. "The Beauty of Traditional Chinese Architecture in Painting". Imperf	5·00	5·50

391 Cabani's Yellow Bunting

2004. 60th Anniv of British Council in Sierra Leone.

4177	**391**	500l. multicoloured	85	30
4178	**391**	1000l. multicoloured	1·25	90
4179	**391**	2000l. multicoloured	2·25	2·50
4180	**391**	3000l. multicoloured	3·00	3·75

392 Lion Emblem and Map

2004. 40th Anniv of First Self-adhesive Stamps. As T 80 (World's Fair, New York of 1964) but redrawn with face value in leones as T 392. Self-adhesive. Imperf.

4181	**392**	1000l. multicoloured	1·25	1·40

393 "Ice Cream Carrier"

2004. 25th Death Anniv of Norman Rockwell (artist) (2003). Multicoloured.

MS4182	150×180 mm. 2000l. Type **393**; 2000l. "The Voyeur"; 2000l. "Teacher's Birthday"; 2000l. Fisk Tires advertisement, 1919	7·50	8·50
MS4183	90×97 mm. 5000l. "Cousin Reginald plays Pirate"	6·00	7·00

394 Concorde over River, Rio de Janeiro

2004. Last Flight of Concorde (2003). Multicoloured.

MS4184	90×131 mm. 3000l. Type **394**; 3000l. Concorde over Brazil flag (top left of blue circle); 3000l. Concorde over Brazil flag (bottom left of blue circle)	12·00	12·00
MS4185	90×129 mm. 3000l. Concorde (pink background); 3000l. Concorde and pyramid (red background); 3000l. Concorde and pyramid (dark brown background)	12·00	12·00
MS4186	131×90 mm. 3000l. Concorde and Nairobi skyline; 3000l. Concorde over Kenyan bush (black and red background) 3000l. Concorde over Kenyan bush (red and green background)	12·00	12·00

No. **MS**4184 shows Concorde 206 G-BOAA over Rio de Janeiro, **MS**4185 Concorde G-AXDN and Egyptian pyramid and **MS**4186 Concorde G-AXDN Aircraft No. 101 over Kenya.

395 "The Birth of John the Baptist" (detail) (Tintoretto)

2004. 300th Anniv of St. Petersburg. "Treasures of the Hermitage". Multicoloured.

MS4187	144×144 mm. 1400l. Type **395**; 1400l. "Penitent Mary Magdalen" (Titian); 1400l. "The Death of St. Petronilla" (Simone Pignoni); 1400l. "The Assumption of the Virgin" (Murillo); 1400l. "St. Jerome Hears the Trumpet" (Jusepe de Ribera); 1400l. "St. George and the Dragon" (Tintoretto)	7·50	8·50
MS4187a	160×140 mm. 2000l. "Countess A. S. Stroganova and Her Son" (Louise-Elisabeth Vigee-Lebrun); 2000l. "Count G. I. Chernyshev Holding a Mask (Louise-Elisabeth Vigee-Lebrun)"; 2000l. "Self Portrait" (Louise-Elisabeth Vigee-Lebrun); 2000l. "Baron G. A. Stroganov" (Louise-Elisabeth Vigee-Lebrun)	7·50	8·50
MS4188	Two sheets. (a) 62×81 mm. 5000l. "The Apostles Peter and Paul" (El Greco). (b) 100×69 mm. 5000l. "A Visit to the Priest" (Jean-Baptiste Greuze). Both imperf	11·00	12·00

396 Marilyn Monroe

2004. Marilyn Monroe (actress) Commemoration. Multicoloured.

4189	1000l. Type **396**	1·00	1·10
4190	1000l. With short hair and sparkly earrings (cobalt background)	1·00	1·10
4191	1000l. As No. 4190 but with lavender background	1·00	1·10
4192	1000l. Wearing pink patterned shirt	1·00	1·10
MS4193	113×112 mm. 2000l. Wearing strapless top; 2000l. With arms above head; 2000l. Leaning back with shoulders hunched; 2000l. Wearing scoop-necked top	7·00	8·00

397 Yang Liwei (Chinese Astronaut)

2004. Astronauts. Multicoloured.

4194	900l. Type **397**	1·25	1·25
4195	900l. Yang Liwei wearing uniform	1·25	1·25
4196	900l. Yang Liwei wearing space suit	1·25	1·25
4197	900l. Yang Liwei showing "victory" sign	1·25	1·25
4198	1200l. "Vostok 1" (vert)	1·40	1·40
4199	1200l. John Glenn (American astronaut) (vert)	1·40	1·40
4200	1200l. Launch of "Friendship 7" (vert)	1·40	1·40
4201	1200l. Yuri Gagarin (Russian astronaut) (vert)	1·40	1·40
4202	1200l. Launch of "Shenzhou 5" (vert)	1·40	1·40
4203	1200l. Yang Liwei (vert)	1·40	1·40
MS4204	Two sheets, each 100×70 mm. (a) 5000l. John Glenn. (b) 5000l. Yang Liwei Set of 2 sheets	12·00	13·00

398 Lo Moth

2004. Butterflies and Moths. Multicoloured.

4205	200l. Type **398**	50	20
4206	300l. Hackberry butterfly	70	30
4207	400l. Red admiral	80	45
4208	4000l. Spangled fritillary	5·50	6·50
MS4209	Two sheets. (a) 144×118 mm. 1700l. Pearl crescent; 1700l. Pipevine swallowtail; 1700l. Alfalfa looper; 1700l. Tiger swallowtail. (b) 66×65 mm. 5000l. Cecropia moth Set of 2 sheets	15·00	16·00

399 *Catasetum pileatum*

2004. Orchids. Multicoloured.

4210	150l. Type **399**	60	20
4211	400l. *Cattleya araguainsis*	80	70
4212	400l. *Barkeria spectabilis*	80	70
4213	1700l. *Odontonia vesta*	2·00	2·25
4214	1700l. *Ancistro rothschildianus*	2·00	2·25
4215	1700l. *Ansellia Africana*	2·00	2·25
4216	1700l. *Aspasia epidendroides*	2·00	2·25
4217	3500l. *Catasetum fimbriatum*	2·00	2·25
MS4218	68×73 mm. 5000l. *Bulbophyllum lobbii*	7·00	8·00

400 Banded Sculpin

2004. Marine Life. Multicoloured.

4219	800l. Type **400**	1·00	60
4220	1100l. Black durgon	1·40	1·25
4221	1400l. Atlantic spadefish	1·50	1·75
4222	1400l. Queen triggerfish	1·50	1·75
4223	1700l. Peacock flounder	1·75	1·90
4224	1700l. Northern puffer	1·75	1·90
4225	1700l. Sea raven	1·75	1·90
4226	1700l. Tiger shark	1·75	1·90
MS4227	68×74 mm. 5000l. Sea lamprey (vert)	7·00	8·00

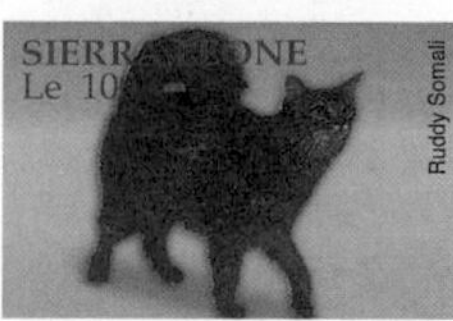

401 Ruddy Somali

2004. Cats. Multicoloured.

4228	100l. Type **401**	30	20
4229	800l. Bombay (walking right)	1·00	60
4230	1200l. Burmese (walking left)	1·40	1·25
4231	1700l. Persian (vert)	1·75	1·90
4232	1700l. Colorpoint shorthair (vert)	1·75	1·90
4233	1700l. Cornish Rex (vert)	1·75	1·90
4234	1700l. Blue Point Balinese (vert)	1·75	1·90
4235	3000l. Blue British shorthair	1·75	1·90
MS4236	83×63 mm. 5000l. Devon Rex	7·00	8·00

402 Great Pyrenees

2004. Dogs. Multicoloured.

4237	250l. Type **402**	60	25
4238	600l. Kerry blue terrier	85	50
4239	1300l. Mastiff	1·50	1·25
4240	1700l. Sealyham terrier	1·75	1·90
4241	1700l. Norwich terrier	1·75	1·90
4242	1700l. Wheaton terrier	1·75	1·90
4243	1700l. Bull terrier	1·75	1·90
4244	1800l. English sheepdog	1·75	1·90
MS4245	70×79 mm. 5000l. Greyhound	7·00	8·00

403 Belted Kingfisher

2004. Birds. Multicoloured.

4246	500l. Type **403**	85	45
4247	1000l. Burrowing owl	1·60	1·25
4248	1500l. Crested caracara	1·75	1·75
4249	1700l. Snail kite (horiz)	1·75	1·90
4250	1700l. Avocet (horiz)	1·75	1·90
4251	1700l. Greater flamingo (horiz)	1·75	1·90
4252	1700l. Bald eagle (horiz)	1·75	1·90
4253	2000l. Red headed finch	2·25	2·50
MS4254	84×64 mm. 5000l. Ring neck pheasant	7·50	8·00

404 Pope John Paul II

2004. 25th Anniv of the Pontificate of Pope John Paul II. Sheet 95×118 mm containing T 404 and similar horiz designs. Multicoloured.

MS4255	2000l. Type **404**; 2000l. Pope and John Bonica (President of International Association for the Study of Pain); 2000l. Pope in Croatia; 2000l. Pope presiding over Mass	9·50	10·00

405 Deng Xiaoping

2004. Birth Centenary of Deng Xiaoping (leader of China, 1978–89). Sheet 96×67 mm.

MS4256	5000l. multicoloured	5·00	6·00

406 Marathon, 1908

2004. Olympic Games, Athens. Multicoloured.

4257	250l. Type **406**	45	25
4258	300l. Demetrius Vikelas (President of International Olympic Committee 1894–1896)	50	25
4259	1500l. Detail of gold medal, Athens (1896)	1·75	2·00
4260	2000l. Discobolus (Greek sculpture)	2·00	2·25

407 General Dwight D. Eisenhower

2004. 60th Anniv of D-Day Landings. Multicoloured.

4261	1400l. Type **407**	1·60	1·60
4262	1400l. Rear Admiral Don. P. Moon	1·60	1·60
4263	1400l. Lieutenant General Omar N. Bradley	1·60	1·60
4264	1400l. Rear Admiral Alan G. Kirk	1·60	1·60
4265	1400l. Major General Clarence R. Huebner	1·60	1·60
4266	1400l. Major General Maxwell D. Taylor	1·60	1·60
MS4267	Six sheets each 200×117 mm. (a) 950l. ×8, LST landing craft; M4 Sherman tank; US soldier on tank; Gun of tank; 70th Tank Battalion patch; Soldier aiming rifle; 743rd Tank Battalion patch; 741st Tank Battalion patch. (b) 1000l. ×8, P-51 Mustang; Parachutists; Map of troop movements; P-38 Lightning; M4 Sherman tank and explosion; Soldiers; LCM landing craft; U.S. light cruiser. (c) 1000l. ×8, Spitfire; Typhoon; Tail of Typhoon; P-51 Mustang; C-47 Skytrain; War plane and wing of Typhoon; P-38 Lightning; U.S. Airforce patch. (d) 1000l. ×8, P-47 Thunderbolt; Parachutists, map and planes; Tank and map of troop movements; Map showing Dieppe and soldier aiming rifle; U.S. heavy cruiser; U.S. light cruiser and bow of heavy cruiser; Destroyer and bow and stern of ships; U.S. Destroyer escort. (e) 1100l. ×8 U.S. light cruiser and airships; LST landing craft and airships; Bow of LST landing craft; Hull of LST landing craft; U.S. armoured car; Soldiers; U.S. medical transport; U.S. armoured car and landing craft. (f) 1100l. ×8 Soldier aiming rifle and map of parachutists' descent; Badge of 101st Airborne "Screaming Eagles"; Parachutist and tail of plane; Cockpit of plane; General Dwight D. Eisenhower; Bernard Montgomery; 82nd Airborne Division; C-47 Skytrain and parachutists Set of 6 sheets	45·00	50·00

408 "Mona Lisa"

2004. 500th Anniv of the "Mona Lisa".

4268	**408**	2000l. multicoloured	2·00	2·25

409 Peace Dove carrying Olive Branch

2004. United Nations International Year of Peace. Sheet 143×83 mm, containing T 409 and similar designs. Multicoloured.

MS4269	3000l. ×3 Type **409**; Dove facing left; Dove with legs tucked up	8·25	8·50

410 The Smalls Lighthouse

2004. Lighthouses of Great Britain. Multicoloured.

4270	1800l. Type **410**	2·00	2·00
4271	2000l. Needles Rock lighthouse	2·00	2·00
4272	2500l. St. John's Point lighthouse	2·25	2·50
4273	3500l. Bell Rock lighthouse	3·00	3·50
4274	4000l. Eddystone lighthouse	3·50	4·00

411 Arapaho Pipe Bag

2004. American Indians. Multicoloured.

4275-83	Decorative Artifacts. 1000l. ×9, Type **411**; Apache basket; Blackfoot parfleche; Crow Elkhide robe; Iroquois moccasins; Hopi canteen; Sioux parfleche; Navajo rug; Nez Perce cradle	8·00	9·00
4284-9	Chiefs and Warriors. 1500l. ×6, Ne-O-Mon-Ne; Ma-Has-Kah; Moa-Na-Hon-Ga; Tah-Ro-Hon; Not-Chi-Mi-Ne; Shau-Hau-Napo-Tinia	8·00	9·00

412 Patas Monkeys

2004. Endangered Species. Patas Monkey. Multicoloured.

4290	1000l. Type **412**	1·25	1·25
4291	1000l. Feeding	1·25	1·25
4292	1000l. With baby	1·25	1·25
4293	1000l. Monkey	1·25	1·25

413 Carmelo Anthony (Denver Nuggets)

2004. National Basketball Association (1st series). Multicoloured.

4294	700l. Type **413**	1·00	1·00
4295	700l. Yao Ming (Houston Rockets)	1·00	1·00
4296	700l. Jermaine O'Neal (Indiana Pacers)	1·00	1·00
4297	700l. Kobe Bryant (Los Angeles Lakers)	1·00	1·00

See also Nos. 4320/1.

414 George Herman Ruth Jr

2004. Centenary of Baseball World Series.

4298	**414**	500l. multicoloured	45	50

415 LMS 8F 2-8-0, Great Central Railway

2004. Bicentenary of Steam Locomotives. Multicoloured.

MS4299	Four sheets, each 148×176 mm. (a) 1000l.×9, Type **413**; Rhodesia Railways 12 Class 4-8-2; DR German Railways 01 Class Pacific; Indian Railways Metre Gauge McArthur 2-8-2; USATC 0-6-0 T, Greece; China Railways KD6 2-8-0; Polish Feldbahn 0-8-0 T; Indian Railways MAWD 2-8-2; North British 2-10-0. (b) 1000l.×9 (horiz), Stephenson's Rocket; Indonesian State Railway B50 Class 2-4-0; Eurostar; China Railways SY Class 2-8-2; Baldwin 0-6-0, Philippines; Hunsle 0-4-2 T, Java; Bagnall 0-6-0 ST Progress; North British built 4-8-2 T; Baldwin 0-6-2 ST, Brazil. (c) 1000l.×9, B12 Class 4-6-0; Uruguay Railways Beyer Peacock Mogul 2-6-0; Ghana Railways Diesel Electric, 1950s; Bagnall 0-4-0, St. Assam; Ledo Brickworks, Upper Assam; Metregauge 2 gauge operation; Carbon converter, China; Timbre loading, China; Loading clay at Bagnall, Saddletank. (d) 1000l.×9, GWR Mogul, Severn Valley Railway; Litson Meyer 0-6-6-0, Chile; China Railways SL7 Class Pacific; Firing a Yugoslav 20-2-6-0; Lookout man warning of approaching train; Filling sandboxes, Midland Railway; Taking water; Indian Railways; Indian Railways 2'6" Gauge ZP Pacific Pulgeon; Smokebox cleaning, Wankaner	35·00	40·00
MS4300	Four sheets, each 98×68 mm. (a) 5000l. The Bullet Train. (b) 5000l. The Blue Train. (c) 5000l. The Ghan. (d) 5000l. The Hudson Line	22·00	24·00

416 Players

2004. National Football Team.

4301	**416**	2000l. multicoloured	2·00	2·25

417 Diego Simeone (Argentina)

2004. Centenary of FIFA (Federation Internationale de Football Association). Multicoloured.

MS4302	193×97 mm. 2000l.×4, Type **417**; Carcea (Brazil); Oliver Bierhoff (Germany); Kevin Keegan (England)	7·00	8·00
MS4303	108×87 mm. 5000l. David Ginola (France)	4·25	4·50

418 Elvis

2004. 50th Anniv of First Record by Elvis Presley. Multicoloured.

4304	2000l. Type **418**	2·25	2·25
4305	2000l. Holding guitar upright	2·25	2·25
4306	2000l. Leaning on guitar	2·25	2·25
4307	2000l. Playing guitar	2·25	2·25
4308	2000l. Singing into microphone (from front)	2·25	2·25
4309	2000l. Holding microphone on stand	2·25	2·25
4310	2000l. Holding microphone without stand	2·25	2·25
4311	2000l. Singing into microphone (from side)	2·25	2·25

419 *Paris*

2004. Ocean Liners. Multicoloured.

4312	600l. Type **419**	85	55
4313	800l. *Statendam*	1·10	80
4314	1000l. *Stavengerfjords*	1·25	1·10
4315	1500l. *Campania*	1·75	1·75
4316	2000l. *Drottningholm*	2·25	2·50
4317	3000l. *Lusitania*	3·25	3·75
MS4318	82×76 mm. 5000l. *United States* (horiz)	6·50	7·00

420 *Tokyo Story*

2004. Birth Centenary of Ozu Yasujiro (Japanese film director). Sheet, 190×203 mm, containing T 420 and similar vert designs. Multicoloured.

MS4319	1400l.×6, Type **420**; *Late Spring; Early Summer; Equinox Flower; Good Morning; An Autumn Afternoon*	7·00	8·00

2004. National Basketball Association (2nd series). As T 413. Multicoloured.

4320	700l. Vlade Divac (Sacramento Kings)	1·00	1·00
4321	700l. Leandro Barbosa (Phoenix Suns)	1·00	1·00

421 "Nativity with the Annunciation to the Shepherds" (Jan Joest)

2004. Christmas. Paintings. Multicoloured.

4322	1000l. Type **421**	1·25	70
4323	1500l. "Christmas Snow" (Norman Rockwell)	1·75	1·60

4324	2000l. "The Christmas Tree" (E. Osborn)	2·25	2·25
4325	5000l. "The Spirit of Christmas" (Norman Rockwell)	5·50	6·50
MS4326	55×110 mm. 8000l. "Madonna and Child Enthroned with Two Angels" (Fra Filippo Lippi)	8·50	9·50

422 Ronald and Nancy Reagan with Queen Elizabeth and Prince Philip

2004. Ronald Reagan (President of USA, 1981–1989) Commemoration. Sheet, 153×144 mm, containing T 422 and similar horiz designs. Multicoloured.

MS4327	2000l.×3, Type **422**; 2000l.×3, President Reagan and Queen Elizabeth II	9·50	11·00

423 Rooster

2005. Chinese New Year ("Year of the Rooster"). Multicoloured.

4328	600l. Type **423**	80	80
4329	600l. As Type **423** but with country name and value in different colours	80	80

424 Pres. Roosevelt addressing Congress

2005. 60th Anniv of Victory in Japan. Multicoloured.

MS4330	174×83 mm. 2000l.×4, Type **424**; Little Boy (Hiroshima bomb); Fat Man (Nagasaki bomb); Foreign Minister Shigemitsu signing surrender instrument aboard *Missouri* (battleship)	8·00	9·00
MS4331	70×80 mm. 5000l. Newspaper headlines	6·00	6·50

425 Handshake

2005. Centenary of Rotary International. Sheet, 114×103 mm, containing T 425 and similar vert designs. Multicoloured.

MS4332	1800l.×4, Type **425**; Two people shaking hands over map; Rotary emblem; Paul Harris (founder of Rotary)	7·00	8·00

426 Ships Lined Up

2005. Bicentenary of the Battle of Trafalgar. Multicoloured.

4333	500l. Type **426**	1·00	60
4334	1000l. Surrounded ship on fire	1·60	1·10
4335	2000l. Fleets of ships	2·50	2·25
4336	5000l. Line of ships shrouded in smoke	6·00	7·00
MS4337	84×119 mm. 8000l. Ships engaged in battle	9·50	10·00

427 *Little Claus and Big Claus*

2005. Birth Bicentenary of Hans Christian Andersen (artist and children's writer).

4338	**427**	3000l. multicoloured	2·75	3·25
4339	-	3000l. multicoloured	2·75	3·25
4340	-	3000l. green and black	2·75	3·25
MS4341		100×70 mm. 5000l. multicoloured	5·50	6·50

DESIGNS: No. 4338, Type **427**; 4339, *Little Ida's Flowers*; 4340, *The Tinder-Box*. **MS**4341, *The Princess and The Pea* (50×38 mm).

428 Luftwaffe Air Strikes

2005. Battle of Britain. Multicoloured.

4342	2000l. Type **428**	2·50	2·50
4343	2000l. Civilians sheltering in Underground station	2·50	2·50
4344	2000l. Pilots running to planes	2·50	2·50
4345	2000l. Fighting planes	2·50	2·50
MS4346	107×97 mm. 5000l. Winston Churchill, pilot and plane (vert)	7·00	7·50

429 Russian Soldiers

2005. Battle for Stalingrad.

4347	**429**	2000l. grey and black	2·50	2·50
4348	-	2000l. grey	2·50	2·50
4349	-	2000l. grey, stone and black	2·50	2·50
4350	-	2000l. grey, stone and blue	2·50	2·50
MS4351		107×97 mm. 5000l. grey, blue and black	6·50	7·00

DESIGNS: No. 4347, Type **429**; 4348, Destroyed German tank; 4349, Remains of German 6th Army; 4350, German Prisoners of War; **MS**4351, Russian victory at Stalingrad.

430 Pope John Paul II and French Pres. Jacques Chirac

2005. Pope John Paul II Commemoration.

4352	**430**	1800l. multicoloured	2·50	2·50

431 Glacial Polish, Toiyabe National Forest, USA

2005. Expo. World Exposition, Aichi, Japan. Multicoloured.

4353/8	1500l×6, Type **431**; African gorilla; Rock climbing, Yosemite Valley, USA; Nassau groupers; Ladybirds; Evolution Valley, USA	7·50	8·50

432 Pres. Franklin D. Roosevelt and Prime Minister Winston Churchill

2005. 60th Anniv of Victory in Europe. Multicoloured.

4359	2000l. Type **432**	2·50	2·50
4360	2000l. Louis Johnson (Secretary of Defence), Gen. Douglas Macarthur and Gen. Omar Bradley	2·50	2·50
4361	2000l. Top commanders of Allied Expeditionary Forces, 1944	2·50	2·50
4362	2000l. Prime Minister Winston Churchill	2·50	2·50
MS4363	70×80 mm. 5000l. Winston Churchill at VE Day celebrations	7·00	7·50

433 Boss Hoss Limited Edition, Germany

2005. Fire Engines. Multicoloured.

4364	900l. Type **433**	1·40	1·25
4365	1200l. Pumper 8 by 10, Austria	1·75	1·50
4366	1500l. Hydraulic platform	2·00	1·75
4367	1800l. Scania fire appliance, Australia	2·25	2·00
4368	2000l. Fire engine, Japan	2·25	2·25
4369	2000l. Fire engine, Germany	2·25	2·25
4370	2000l. Fire engine, Canada	2·25	2·25
4371	2000l. Fire engine, Ireland	2·25	2·25
4372	2000l. Mercedes Benz 2635 Thoma, Germany	2·25	2·25
4373	2000l. Dennis Sabre water tender, Ireland	2·25	2·25
4374	2000l. Microscopic fire truck, Japan	2·25	2·25
4375	2000l. Scania fire appliance, Australia	2·25	2·25
4376	2000l. Chevy fire truck	2·25	2·25
4377	2000l. 1914 International fire truck	2·25	2·25
4378	2000l. 1884 chemical fire engine	2·25	2·25
4379	2000l. 1963 Mason FD1 fire engine	2·25	2·25
MS4380	Two sheets, each 100×70 mm. (a) 5000l. 1890 Horse driven fire truck, UK. (b) 5000l. Fire engine, USA	13·00	14·00

434 Jules Verne's Tomb, Amiens

2005. Death Centenary of Jules Verne (writer). Multicoloured (except No. 4382).

4381	3000l. Type **434**	3·25	3·75
4382	3000l. Michael Arden (sepia, green and black)	3·25	3·75
4383	3000l. Jules Verne and lunar surface	3·25	3·75
MS4384	100×75 mm. 5000l. Pencil sketch of Jules Verne and hot air balloon	5·50	6·00

435 Moses Maimonides

2005. 800th Death Anniv of Moses Maimonides (Jewish rabbi, physician and philosopher) (2004).

4385	**435**	2000l. multicoloured	2·25	2·25

436 Playhouse Square Memorial, Berlin

2005. 200th Death Anniv of Friedrich Von Schiller (poet and dramatist). Multicoloured.

4386	3000l. Type **436**	3·00	3·50
4387	3000l. Statue, Munich	3·00	3·50
4388	3000l. Statue of Friedrich Von Schiller and Johann Wolfgang von Goethe	3·00	3·50
MS4389	100×70 mm. 5000l. Friedrich Von Schiller	5·50	6·00

437 Quesnard Lighthouse, Alderney

2005. Lighthouses (2nd series).

4390	**437**	4500l. multicoloured	6·00	7·00

2005. Royal Wedding. Multicoloured designs as T 514 of St. Vincent. Multicoloured.

4391	2000l. Prince Charles and Mrs. Camilla Parker-Bowles during wedding ceremony	2·50	2·50
4392	2000l. Prince Charles and Duchess of Cornwall holding posy	2·50	2·50
4393	2000l. Prince Charles and Duchess of Cornwall with their families (horiz)	2·50	2·50

438 Man and Woman in Workshop

2005. International Year of Microcredit. Each showing portrait of woman at left. Multicoloured.

MS4394	105×105 mm. 2500l. Type **438**; 2500l. Man in workshop; 2500l. Man with scales; 2500l. Woman feeding fodder to cattle	11·00	12·00

The stamps within No. **MS**4394 have a composite background design showing part of the UN emblem.

2005. Christmas. As T 155 of St. Kitts. Multicoloured.

4395	500l. "The Virgin with Grapes" (detail) (Pierre Mignard)	75	35
4396	1500l. "Adoration of the Shepherds" (detail) (Murillo)	1·60	1·60
4397	2000l. "Madonna with the Child" (detail) (Murillo)	2·25	2·50
4398	3000l. "Fountain of Life" (detail) (Holbein the Elder)	3·25	3·50
MS4399	100×70 mm. 6000l. "Adoration of the Shepherds" (different) (Murillo)	7·00	8·00

439 Elvis Presley playing Guitar

2005. 70th Birth Anniv of Elvis Presley. Multicoloured.
4400 2000l. Type **439** (blue background) 2·50 2·50
4401 2000l. Holding guitar (black background) 2·50 2·50
4402 2000l. As No. 4401 (black background) 2·50 2·50
4403 2000l. Type **439** (lilac background) 2·50 2·50
4404 2000l. Elvis singing (blue silhouette) 2·50 2·50
4405 2000l. As No. 4404 (emerald silhouette) 2·50 2·50
4406 2000l. As No. 4404 (yellow silhouette) 2·50 2·50
4407 2000l. As No. 4404 (purple and magenta silhouette) 2·50 2·50

440 "In It's Position" (Xu Beihong)

2006. Chinese New Year ("Year of the Dog"). Multicoloured.
4408 600l. Type **440** 45 45
MS4409 70×100 mm. 2000l. As Type **440** but 29×64 mm 2·50 2·50
The stamp within **MS**4409 is as Type **440** but shows more of the foreground of the painting.

441 Pope Benedict XVI

2006. Election of Pope Benedict XVI.
4410 **441** 10000l. multicoloured 12·00 13·00

2006. "Kids-Did-It!" Designs. Vert designs as T 531 of St. Vincent showing children's paintings.
4411 2000le. "Monkey" (Andrew Heye) 2·25 2·25
4412 2000le. "Red Toed Elephant" (Conrad Mazur) 2·25 2·25
4413 2000le. "Colored Giraffe" (Adeline Longstreth) 2·25 2·25
4414 2000le. "Colored Bird" (Sarah Bowen) 2·25 2·25
4415 2000le. "Green Gecko" (Nick Abrams) 2·25 2·25
4416 2000le. "Froggy" (Brett Walker) 2·25 2·25
4417 2000le. "Spots" (Maya Barba) 2·25 2·25
4418 2000le. "Orange Lizard" (Nick Abrams) 2·25 2·25
4419 2000le. "Yellow Flowers" (Christina Miller) 2·25 2·25
4420 2000le. "Poppies" (Trevor Nielsen) 2·25 2·25
4421 2000le. "Orange Flowers" (Christina Miller) 2·25 2·25
4422 2000le. "Lilies" (Lauren Van Woy) 2·25 2·25

442 Chief Medicine Crow (Crow)

2006. Great Indian Chiefs. Multicoloured.
4423 1250le. Type **442** 1·25 1·25
4424 1250le. Chief Quanah Parker (Comanche) 1·25 1·25
4425 1250le. Chief Garfield (Jicarilla) 1·25 1·25
4426 1250le. Chief Pretty Eagle (Crow) 1·25 1·25
4427 1250le. Chief Plenty Coups (Crow) 1·25 1·25
4428 1250le. Chief He Dog (Oglala) 1·25 1·25
4429 1250le. Chief Crow King (Hunkpapa) 1·25 1·25
4430 1250le. Chief Pontiac (Ottawa) 1·25 1·25
4431 1250le. Chief Naiche (Chiricahua Apache) 1·25 1·25
4432 1250le. Chief Gall (Hunkpapa) 1·25 1·25

443 Pope John Paul II, Madrid, 2003

2006. Visits of Pope John Paul II, 2003–2004. Multicoloured.
4433 2500le. Type **443** 3·00 3·00
4434 2500le. Croatia, 2003 3·00 3·00
4435 2500le. Banja Luka, Bosnia Herzegovina 3·00 3·00
4436 2500le. Slovakia, 2003 3·00 3·00
4437 2500le. Pompeii, Italy, 2003 3·00 3·00
4438 2500le. Shaking hands with Swiss President Joseph Deiss, Bern, 2004 3·00 3·00
4439 2500le. Praying at Lourdes, France, 2004 3·00 3·00
4440 2500le. Loreto, Italy, 2004 3·00 3·00

2006. Winter Olympic Games, Turin. As T 536 of St. Vincent. Multicoloured.
4441 1000le. US 1960 Winter Olympics 4c. stamp 1·25 1·00
4442 1300le. Canada 1987 Winter Olympics 36c. cross-country skiing stamp 1·60 1·60
4443 2000le. Poster for Winter Olympic Games, Calgary, 1988 2·25 2·25
4444 3000le. Poster for Winter Olympic Games, Squaw Valley, California, 1960 3·00 3·50

444 Michael Douglas (actor)

2006. Michael Douglas, "UN Messenger of Peace". Multicoloured.
4445 2000le. Type **444** 2·00 2·00
4446 2000le. UN Building, New York 2·00 2·00

445 US 1903 Stamp and Benjamin Franklin

2006. Washington 2006 International Stamp Exhibition. Sheet 91×116 mm.
MS4447 **445** 6000le. Multicoloured 5·00 6·00

446 Queen Elizabeth II

2006. 80th Birthday of Queen Elizabeth II. Multicoloured.
4448 3000le. Type **446** 3·50 3·50
4449 3000le. Wearing dark blue hat and coat 3·50 3·50
4450 3000le. Wearing blue blouse 3·50 3·50
4451 3000le. With parasol and bouquet 3·50 3·50
MS4452 125×126 mm. 6000le. Wearing diadem, 1950s 7·00 7·50

447 Zeppelin L30

2006. 50th Death Anniv of Ludwig Durr (Zeppelin engineer). Multicoloured.
4453 4000le. Type **447** 4·00 4·50
4454 4000le. Airship *Hindenburg* 4·00 4·50
4455 4000le. *Graf Zeppelin* 4·00 4·50

2006. 400th Birth Anniv of Rembrandt Harmenszoon van Rijn (artist). As T 157 of St. Kitts showing paintings. Multicoloured.
4456 800le. "Abraham Frans" (detail) 1·10 65
4457 1000le. "The Rat Catcher" (detail) 1·25 80
4458 2000le. "Young Man with Velvet Cap" (detail) 2·25 2·00
4459 3000le. "The Night Watch" (detail of man with black hat) 2·75 3·00
4460 3000le. "The Night Watch" (detail of man with brown hat) 2·75 3·00
4461 3000le. "The Night Watch" (detail of man with pale hat 2·75 3·00
4462 3000le. "The Night Watch" (detail of man with brown hat and ruffed collar) 2·75 3·00
4463 3000le. "Abraham and Isaac" (detail) 2·75 3·00
4464 3000le. "Abraham entertaining the Angels" (detail) 2·75 3·00
4465 3000le. "Return of the Prodigal Son" (detail) 2·75 3·00
4466 3000le. "Adam and Eve" (detail) 2·75 3·00
4467 8000le. "The Flute Player" (detail) 2·75 3·00
MS4468 Three sheets, each 70×100 mm. (a) 6000le. "Homer dictating to a Scribe" (detail). (b) 6000le. "Portrait of an Amsterdam Citizen as a Militiaman" (detail). (c) 6000le. "Maria Trip, Daughter of Alottte Adriaensdr" (detail). All imperf 14·00 16·00

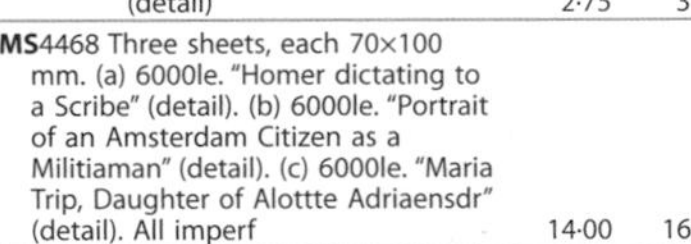

448 Marilyn Monroe

2006. 80th Birth Anniv of Marilyn Monroe (actress). Multicoloured.
4469 2000l. Type **448** 1·90 2·00
4470 2000l. Wearing brown patterned dress with narrow straps 1·90 2·00
4471 2000l. Wearing white, with hand behind head 1·90 2·00
4472 2000l. In half profile, wearing pendant earrings 1·90 2·00

449 Space Station MIR

2006. Space Anniversaries. Multicoloured. (a) "Conquering our Universe".
4473 2000le. Type **449** 2·25 2·25
4474 2000le. Space Shuttle *Challenger* 2·25 2·25
4475 2000le. *Giotto* Comet Probe 2·25 2·25
4476 2000le. Luna 9, first soft lander 2·25 2·25
4477 2000le. Viking 1 Mars Lander 2·25 2·25
4478 2000le. International Space Station 2·25 2·25

(b) International Space Station.
4479 3000le. ISS 3 June 1999 (vert) 3·00 3·00
4480 3000le. ISS 2 December 2000 (vert) 3·00 3·00
4481 3000le. ISS 15 June 2002 (vert) 3·00 3·00
4482 3000le. ISS 6 August 2005 (vert) 3·00 3·00

(c) Artist's Concept of "Journey's to the Moon".
4483 3000le. NASA's "Crew Launch" (vert) 3·00 3·00
4484 3000le. New spacecraft to rendezvous with International Space Station (vert) 3·00 3·00
4485 3000le. New lunar lander on lunar surface (vert) 3·00 3·00
4486 3000le. Parachutes deployed after re-entry (vert) 3·00 3·00

(d) CloudSat/Calipso Satellites.
4487 3000le. Launch vehicle: Boeing Delta II Rocket 3·00 3·00
4488 3000le. *Calipso* Spacecraft 3·00 3·00
4489 3000le. *CloudSat* Spacecraft 3·00 3·00
4490 3000le. Six satellites of the "A-Train": *Aura, Parasol, Calipso, CloudSat, Aqua* and *OCO 2* 3·00 3·00
MS4491 Four sheets, each 100×70 mm. (a) 6000le. Impactor with Deep Impact Probe, 2005. (b) 6000le. Apollo 11 Lunar Module *Eagle* In a landing configuration, 1969. (c) 6000le. Mars Reconnaissance Orbiter, 2005. (d) 6000le. Space Shuttle *Columbia*, 1981 (vert) 23·00 25·00

450 Mozart as Young Boy playing Piano

2006. 250th Birth Anniv of Wolfgang Amadeus Mozart (composer). Sheet 100×70 mm.
MS4492 7000le. Multicoloured 8·50 8·50

451 Angel

2006. Christmas. Multicoloured.
4493 1000l. Type **451** 1·10 75
4494 1500l. Madonna and Child 1·75 1·50
4495 2000l. Angel (facing to right) 2·25 2·00
4496 3000l. Angel (looking to left) 3·00 3·25
MS4497 150×100 mm. 2000l.×4 As Nos. 4493/6 6·50 7·50
The stamps and margins of **MS**4497 form a composite design showing the Crown of the Main Altar of the Jesuit Church in Antwerp, Belgium, by Peter Paul Rubens.
Nos. 4493/6 show portions of the design.

452 John F. Kennedy making Speech, 20 January 1961

2006. 90th Birth Anniv of John F. Kennedy (US President 1960–3). Multicoloured.

4498 2000l. Type **452** 1·90 2·00
4499 2000l. John Kennedy and Official Inaugural Program 1·90 2·00
4500 2000l. Coin with profile of John Kennedy 1·90 2·00
4501 2000l. Robert Frost and words of "The Gift Outright" recited at Inauguration, 1961 1·90 2·00
4502 2000l. Pres. Kennedy and map of Cuba (Missile Crisis 22 October 1962) 1·90 2·00
4503 2000l. Soviet Premier Khrushchev and map showing range of Soviet R-12 medium range missile 1·90 2·00
4504 2000l. Pres. Kennedy and Soviet Foreign Minister Andrei Gromyko, 22 October 1962 1·90 2·00
4505 2000l. Cuban Pres. Fidel Castro and Pres. Kennedy at the White House 1·90 2·00

453 Elvis Presley

2006. 30th Death Anniv of Elvis Presley. Multicoloured.

4506 2000l. Type **453** 2·00 2·00
4507 2000l. Wearing black and silver patterned cape 2·00 2·00
4508 2000l. In uniform in front of US flag 2·00 2·00
4509 2000l. Wearing blue jacket 2·00 2·00

454 Stylized Pig

2007. Chinese New Year ("Year of the Pig").

4510 **454** 2000l. multicoloured 2·00 2·00

455 Peace Dove and "One World One Promise" Text

2007. Centenary of Scouting and 21st World Scout Jamboree, England. Multicoloured.

MS4511 175×160 mm. 3000l. Type **455**×4 8·00 9·00
MS4512 110×80 mm. 6000l. Peace dove, text and symbols of scouting 6·00 7·00

456 Speedometer (Mach 2.23 Speed Record, 26 March 1974)

2007. Concorde. Multicoloured.

4513 2000l. Type **456** 2·25 2·25
4514 2000l. Concorde silhouette and "MACH 2.23" 2·25 2·25
4515 2000l. Concorde with RAF Red Arrows in Golden Jubilee Flypast 2·25 2·25
4516 2000l. Golden Jubilee Flypast over London, 4 June 2002 2·25 2·25

457 Diana, Princess of Wales

2007. 10th Death Anniv of Diana, Princess of Wales. Multicoloured.

4517 1500le. Type **457** 1·75 1·75
4518 1500le. Wearing pendant and blue off-the-shoulder evening dress 1·75 1·75
4519 1500le. Wearing white blouse with pie-frill neck (olive background) 1·75 1·75
4520 1500le. Wearing yellow dress (green background) 1·75 1·75
4521 1500le. Seen in half-profile (pink background) 1·75 1·75
4522 1500le. Wearing white blouse with ruffed layers (turquoise background) 1·75 1·75
MS4523 100×70 mm. 7000le. Wearing bright blue jacket and hat (horiz) 6·50 6·50

458 166 Inter, 1948

2007. 60th Anniv of Ferrari. Multicoloured.

4524 1400le. Type **458** 1·60 1·60
4525 1400le. 612 Scaglietti 1·60 1·60
4526 1400le. F50, 1995 1·60 1·60
4527 1400le. 550 Barchetta Pininfarina, 2000 1·60 1·60
4528 1400le. 250 GT Cabriolet, 1957 1·60 1·60
4529 1400le. 250 P, 1963 1·60 1·60
4530 1400le. 246 SP, 1961 1·60 1·60
4531 1400le. 126 CK, 1981 1·60 1·60

459 Pope Benedict XVI

2007. 80th Birthday of Pope Benedict XVI.

4532 **459** 1500le. Multicoloured 2·00 2·00

460 *The Annunciation* (detail) (Raphael)

2007. Christmas. Multicoloured.

4533 1000le. Type **460** 1·00 75
4534 1500le. *The Adoration of the Magi* (detail) (Raphael) 1·50 1·40
4535 2000le. *The Presentation of the Christ Child in the Temple* (detail) (Raphael) 1·90 2·00
4536 3000le. *The Nativity and the Arrival of the Magi* (detail) (Giovanni di Pietro) 2·50 3·00

461 Murray Rose (Australia) (swimming 400m & 1500m freestyle gold medallist)

2008. Olympic Games, Beijing. Designs showing scenes from 1956 Olympic Games, Melbourne. Multicoloured.

4537 1500l. Type **461** 1·50 1·60
4538 1500l. Poster for Olympic Games, Melbourne, 1956 1·50 1·60
4539 1500l. Vladimir Kuts (USSR) (10000m & 5000m gold medallist) winning race 1·50 1·60
4540 1500l. Laszlo Papp (Hungary) winning light middleweight boxing gold medal 1·50 1·60

2008. Nos. 1142/4, 1147/8, 2745/50 and 2752/7, 2905/10, 2950/2, 3086/93, 2150/4, 2954, 3112/20, 745/8, 2911/16 and 4290/3 surch

(a) Nos. 1142/4 and 1147/8

4541 800l. on 3l. Type **216** 75 75
4542 800l. on 5l. Double-toothed barbet 75 75
4543 800l. on 8l. African golden oriole 75 75
4544 800l. on 20l. European bee eater 75 75
4545 800l. on 35l. Common gonolek ('Barbary shrike') 75 75

(b) Nos. 2745/50 and 2752/7

4546 2500l. on 500l. *Lycaena dispar* 2·25 2·25
4547 2500l. on 500l. *Graphium sarpedon* 2·25 2·25
4548 2500l. on 500l. *Euploe core* 2·25 2·25
4549 2500l. on 500l. *Papilio cresphontes* 2·25 2·25
4550 2500l. on 500l. *Colotis danae* 2·25 2·25
4551 2500l. on 500l. *Battus philenor* 2·25 2·25
4552 2500l. on 600l. *Mylothis chloris* 2·25 2·25
4553 2500l. on 600l. *Argynnis lathonia* 2·25 2·25
4554 2500l. on 600l. *Elymnias agendas* 2·25 2·25
4555 2500l. on 600l. *Palla ussheri* 2·25 2·25
4556 2500l. on 600l. *Papilio glaucus* 2·25 2·25
4557 2500l. on 600l. *Cercyonis pegala* 2·25 2·25

(c) Nos. 2905/10

4558 2800l. on 300l. Type **312** 2·50 2·50
4559 2800l. on 300l. Viking longship 2·50 2·50
4560 2800l. on 300l. Carrack (surch reading downwards) 2·50 2·50
4561 2800l. on 300l. Venetian galley (surch reading downwards) 2·50 2·50
4562 2800l. on 300l. Galeasse (surch reading downwards) 2·50 2·50
4563 2800l. on 300l. Chebeck (surch reading downwards) 2·50 2·50

(d) Nos. 2950/2

4564 2800l. on 1500l. William D. Boyce (founder of Lone Scouts) (brown-purple, yellow-brown and black) (vert) 2·50 2·50
4565 2800l. on 1500l. Guion S. Bluford (astronaut and former Eagle scout) (vert) 2·50 2·50
4566 2800l. on 1500l. Ellison S. Onizuka (astronaut and former Eagle scout) (vert) (surch at top left, reading upwards) 2·50 2·50

(e) Nos. 3086/93

4567 2800l. on 600l. Cattle egret 2·50 2·50
4568 2800l. on 600l. White-fronted bee eater 2·50 2·50
4569 2800l. on 600l. Gray parrot 2·50 2·50
4570 2800l. on 600l. Cinnamon-chested bee eater 2·50 2·50
4571 2800l. on 600l. Malachite kingfisher 2·50 2·50
4572 2800l. on 600l. White-throated bee eater 2·50 2·50
4573 2800l. on 600l. Yellow-billed stork 2·50 2·50
4574 2800l. on 600l. Hildebrandt's starling 2·50 2·50

(f) Nos. 2150/4

4575 3500l. on 50l. Type **269** (surch at right of obliterator) 3·00 3·00
4576 3500l. on 100l. Adult white-necked bald crow 3·00 3·00
4577 3500l. on 150l. Pair of white-necked bald crows 3·00 3·00
4578 3500l. on 200l. Young white-necked bald crow 3·00 3·00

(g) No. 2954

4579 3500l. on 600l. Gandhi as a young man 3·00 3·00

(h) Nos. 3112/20

4580 3500l. on 600l. African paradise flycatcher ('Monarch') (horiz) 3·00 3·00
4581 3500l. on 600l. Lilac-breasted roller (horiz) 3·00 3·00
4582 3500l. on 600l. Scops owl (horiz) 3·00 3·00
4583 3500l. on 600l. African emerald cuckoo (horiz) 3·00 3·00
4584 3500l. on 600l. Blue flycatcher ('Monarch') (horiz) 3·00 3·00
4585 3500l. on 600l. African golden oriole (horiz) 3·00 3·00
4586 3500l. on 600l. White-throated bee eater (horiz) (surch at right, reading downwards) 3·00 3·00
4587 3500l. on 600l. Black-bellied seedcracker (horiz) (surch at right, reading downwards) 3·00 3·00
4588 3500l. on 600l. Hoopoe (horiz) 3·00 3·00

(i) Nos. 745/8

4589 4000l. on 6c. Type **166** (surch at right of country name) 3·75 3·75
4590 4000l. on 10c. Three chimpanzees (vert) 3·75 3·75
4591 4000l. on 31c. Chimpanzees swinging in tree (vert) 3·75 3·75
4592 4000l. on 60c. Group of chimpanzees (surch at top right) 3·75 3·75

(j) Nos. 2911/16

4593 4000l. on 300l. Junk 3·75 3·75
4594 4000l. on 300l. HMS *Victory* (ship of the line, 1765) 3·75 3·75
4595 4000l. on 300l. *Savannah* (paddle-steamer) 3·75 3·75
4596 4000l. on 300l. Gaissa (sailing canoe) 3·75 3·75
4597 4000l. on 300l. HMS *Warrior* (ironclad) 3·75 3·75
4598 4000l. on 300l. *Preussen* (full-rigged ship) 3·75 3·75

(k) Nos. 4290/3

4599 4000l. on 1000l. Type **412** 3·75 3·75
4600 4000l. on 1000l. Feeding (surch at bottom right) 3·75 3·75
4601 4000l. on 1000l. With baby (surch at centre right) 3·75 3·75
4602 4000l. on 1000l. Patas monkey 3·75 3·75

472 King David's Harp at Entrance to City of David, Jerusalem (image scaled to 48% of original size)

2008. Israel 2008 World Stamp Championship. Sheet 100×110 mm.

MS4603 **472** 7500l. multicoloured 7·50 7·50

473 Joel Palmer locates Pass through the Cascades

2008. Oregon Discovery and Exploration. Multicoloured.

4604	1500l. Type **473**	1·50	1·60
4605	1500l. Ship, coastline and Sir Francis Drake (first European to view Oregon coast) (40×25 mm)	1·50	1·60
4606	1500l. Multnomah Falls and Lewis and Clark (explorers)	1·50	1·60
4607	1500l. Ship in river estuary and Capt. Robert Gray (discovery of the Columbia River) (40×25 mm)	1·50	1·60

474 Yacht

2008. 32nd Americas Cup Yachting Championship, Valencia, Spain. Multicoloured.

4608	200l. Type **474**	30	25
4609	500l. *Shosholoza* (South Africa) and another yacht	50	40
4610	1000l. Yacht *Prada* (crew in white)	1·00	75
4611	10000l. Yachts ('Espresso' and 'Toyota' on sails)	10·00	11·00

475 Queen Elizabeth II and Prince Philip

2008. Diamond Wedding of Queen Elizabeth II and Prince Philip (2007). Multicoloured.

4612	1500l. Type **475**	1·50	1·60
4613	1500l. Queen Elizabeth II	1·50	1·60

476 Statue of Christ the Redeemer, Rio de Janeiro, Brazil

2008. Seven New Wonders of the World. Multicoloured.

4614	1500l. Type **476**	1·50	1·60
4615	1500l. Colosseum, Rome, Italy	1·50	1·60
4616	1500l. Great Wall of China	1·50	1·60
4617	1500l. Machu Picchu, Peru	1·50	1·60
4618	1500l. Petra, Jordan	1·50	1·60
4619	1500l. Chichén Itza, Mexico	1·50	1·60
MS4620	70×100 mm. 7000l. Taj Mahal, India (horiz)	6·50	6·50

477 World Map and Minaret

2008. Centenary of Khilafat Ahmadiyya.

4621	**477**	800l. multicoloured	90	65
4622	**477**	1000l. multicoloured	1·00	75
4623	**477**	2000l. multicoloured	1·90	2·00
4624	**477**	3000l. multicoloured	2·50	3·00

478 Elvis Presley

2008. Elvis Presley. Multicoloured.

4625	1500l. Type **478**	1·50	1·60
4626	1500l. Facing to left	1·50	1·60
4627	1500l. Facing towards left, holding microphone	1·50	1·60
4628	1500l. As No. 4626, but signature at top left and country inscr at bottom right	1·50	1·60
4629	1500l. Wearing mauve shirt (37×50 mm)	1·50	1·60
4630	1500l. In full-face close-up (37×50 mm)	1·50	1·60
4631	1500l. Wearing white jacket and red shirt (37×50 mm)	1·50	1·60
4632	1500l. Wearing green jacket, seen from back (37×50 mm)	1·50	1·60
4633	1500l. Seen in black/white, hands raised (37×50 mm)	1·50	1·60
4634	1500l. In close-up, wearing glasses (37×50 mm)	1·50	1·60

Nos. 4625/8 commemorate the 35th anniversary of Elvis Presley's Aloha from Hawaii Concert.

479 Mother Penguin and Two Chicks

2008. Penguins. Designs showing cartoon penguins. Multicoloured.

4635	3000l. Type **479**	2·50	3·00
4636	3000l. Penguin karaoke	2·50	3·00
4637	3000l. Four penguin chicks		
4638	3000l. Mother penguin with hat, spade and red patterned skirt and two young penguins	2·50	3·00
MS4639	100×70 mm. 7000l. Penguin couple on iceberg	7·00	7·00

480 Nativity Scene

2008. Christmas. Multicoloured.

4640	1000l. Type **480**	1·00	75
4641	1500l. Mary and baby Jesus in manger	1·50	1·60
4642	2000l. Joseph and baby Jesus in manger	1·90	2·00
4643	3000l. Angels and baby Jesus in manger	2·50	3·00

No. 4640 shows the complete scene and Nos. 4641/3 details from it.

481 Pres. Barack Obama

2009. Inauguration of Pres. Barack Obama. Sheet 133×94 mm.

MS4644	3000l. Type **481**×4	10·00	10·00

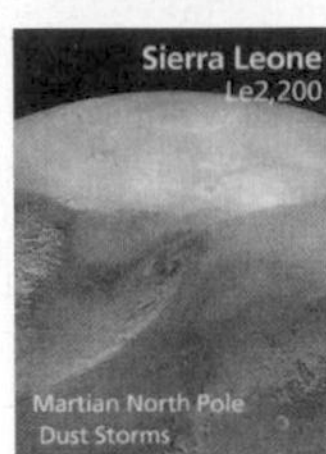

482 Dust Storms at Martian North Pole

2009. 50 Years of Space Exploration. Multicoloured.

MS4645	150×100 mm. 2200le.×6 Type **482**; Saturn; Jupiter's atmosphere; Craters on Mercury's surface; Venus; Mercury	13·00	13·00
MS4646	150×100 mm. 2200le.×6 Spitzer Space Telescope; Galaxy M81; Hubble Space Telescope; Galaxy M64; The Cat's Eye Nebula; Hoag's Object (all horiz)	13·00	13·00
MS4647	130×100 mm. 3000le.×4 Astronaut and sun shining in a dark sky in low earth orbit; South Pole of the Sun; Solar eruption; Solar eclipse (all horiz)	10·00	10·00
MS4648	100×130 mm. 3000le.×4 Apollo 11 Lunar Module *Eagle*; Mercury-Redstone rocket; Space shuttle *Atlantis* on Launch Pad; Space shuttle *Endeavour*	10·00	10·00

483 Pope John Paul II

2009. Pope John Paul II Commemoration. Sheet 127×194 mm containing T 483 and similar vert designs.

MS4649	3000l.×4 Type **483**; Wearing white; Wearing mitre and green robes; Wearing mitre and gold robes	10·00	10·00

484 Yi Jianlian

2009. National Basketball Association. Yi Jianlian (New Jersey Nets). Sheet 139×202 mm containing T 484 and similar vert designs. Multicoloured.

MS4650	1500le. Type **484**×2; 1500le. Wearing dark blue×2; 1500le. Facing left×2	3·00	3·00

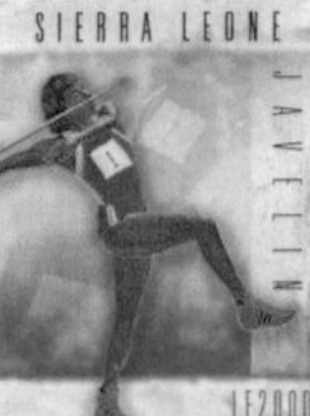

485 Javelin

2009. Olympic Games, Beijing (2008). Sheet 157×79 mm containing T 485 and similar vert designs. Multicoloured.

MS4651	2000l.×4 Type **485**; Fencing; Football; Weightlifting	7·50	7·50

The stamps and margins of No. **MS**4651 form a composite design.

486 *Landscape of Yangshuo*

2009. China 2009 World Stamp Exhibition, Luoyang (1st issue). Paintings by Chang Dai-shien. Multicoloured.

MS4652	120×150 mm. 1500l.×4 Type **486**; *Scholar admiring Plum Blossoms; The Golden Summit ofMount Emei; Lotuses after the Rain*	5·00	5·00

487 Temple of Heaven, Beijing

2009. China 2009 World Stamp Exhibition (2nd issue). Sites and Scenes of China. Multicoloured.

MS4653	100×130 mm. 1500l.×4 Type **487**; Dalian Exhibition Centre; Xian South Gate, Shaanxi Province; National Grand Theatre, Beijing	5·00	5·00

488 Pink and Red Peonies

2009. China 2009 International Stamp Exhibition and Peony Festival, Luoyang

4654	**488**	1500l. multicoloured	1·60	1·75

489 Elvis Presley

2009. Elvis Presley Commemoration. Sheet 154×124 mm containing T 489 and similar vert designs. Multicoloured.

MS4655	3000l.×4 Type **489**; Singing (gold borders); In close-up (yellow-green borders); In profile (dull violet borders)	10·00	10·00

490 Abraham Lincoln taking the Oath at his Second Inauguration

2009. Birth Bicentenary of Abraham Lincoln (US President 1861–5) and Inauguration of President Barack Obama. Sheet 100×130 mm containing T 490 and similar horiz designs. Multicoloured.

MS4656	3000l.×4 Type **490**; Barack Obama sworn in as 44th President; Barack Obama places his hand on the Lincoln bible; Abraham Lincoln's Inauguration Bible	10·00	10·00

The stamps within **MS**4656 each contain a portion of the US President's seal, so that the four stamps show the whole seal.

491 Handel's Birthplace, Halle

2009. 250th Death Anniv of George Frideric Handel (composer). Sheet 164×94 mm containing T 491 and similar vert designs. Multicoloured.

MS4657 2500l.×6 Type **491**; Handel concert at The Foundling Hospital, London; Portrait by Thomas Hudson; Handel music at Ranelagh Gardens, London; Marble statue of Handel by Louis-Francois Roubiliac; Singers Farinelli and Senesino in Handel's opera *Flavio* 11·00 11·00

492 Chauncey Billups

2009. National Basketball Association All-Star Tournament, Phoenix. Two sheets, each 150×200 mm, containing T 492 and similar vert designs. Multicoloured.

MS4658 1250l.×12 West: Type **492**; Kobe Bryant; Tim Duncan; Pau Gasol; Yao Ming; Dirk Nowitzki; Shaquille O'Neal; Tony Parker; Chris Paul; Brandon Roy; Amare Stoudemire; David West 18·00 18·00

MS4659 1250l.×12 East: Ray Allen; Kevin Garnett; Danny Granger; Devin Harris; Dwight Howard; Allen Iverson; LeBron James; Joe Johnson; Rashard Lewis; Paul Pierce; Dwyane Wade; Mo Williams 18·00 18·00

493 Ferrari 312 T2, 1977

2009. Ferrari Race Cars. Sheet 120×100 mm containing T 493 and similar horiz designs. Multicoloured.

MS4660 3000l.×4 Type **493**; 126 C2, 1982; 126 C3, 1983; F2007, 2007 3·00 3·00

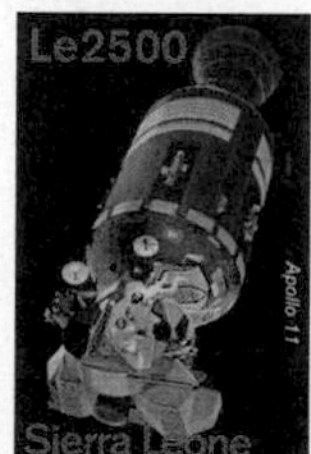

494 Apollo 11

2009. 40th Anniv of First Manned Moon Landing. Sheet 150×100 mm containing T 494 and similar vert designs. Multicoloured.

MS4661 2500l.×6 Type **494**; Astronaut Neil Armstrong; Apollo 11 plaque; Apollo 11 Command Module; Apollo 11 Lunar Module; Apollo 11 crew in quarantine 11·00 11·00

495 Cavalier King Charles Spaniel

2009. 125th Anniv of American Kennel Club. Two sheets, each 100×120 mm, containing T 495 and similar horiz designs showing Cavalier King Charles spaniels (MS4662) or English springer spaniels (MS4663). Multicoloured.

MS4662 3000l.×4 Type **495**; Laying on grass in front of hat; In close-up, laying with head on paw; Close-up, in garden 5·00 5·00

MS4663 3000l.×4 Springer spaniel sat on decking; Close-up of head; Standing; Sat in front of overturned tub 10·00 10·00

496 Pres. Barack Obama and Italian Prime Minister Silvio Berlusconi

2009. Meeting of Pres. Barack Obama with Italian Prime Minister Silvio Berlusconi at G8 Summit, L'Aquila, Italy.

MS4664 **496** 8000l. multicoloured 7·25 5·25

497 Fringed Panaeolus (*Panaeolus papilionaceus*)

2009. Fungi of the World. Multicoloured.

4665	1000l. Type **497**	1·00	75
4666	1500l. Orange latex lactarius (*Lactarius deliciosus*)	1·50	1·60
4667	2000l. Purple laccaria (*Laccaria amethystina*)	1·90	2·00
4668	3000l. Liver lactarius (*Lactarius hepaticus*)	2·50	2·75

MS4669 1700l.×6 Death cap amanita (*Amanita phalloides*); Cinnabar polypore (*Pycnoporus cinnabarinus*); King bolete (*Boletus edulis*); Panther amanita (*Amanita pantherina*); Fly amanita (*Amanita muscaria*); Mica inky cap (*Coprinus micaceus*) (all horiz) 9·50 9·50

498 Birman–lilac point

2009. Cats of the World. Multicoloured.

4670	1000l. Type **498**	1·00	75
4671	1500l. Singapura–sepia agouti	1·50	1·60
4672	2000l. Scottish fold–blue tortie tabby and white	1·90	2·00
4673	3000l. Asian shaded–lilac shaded silver	2·50	2·75

MS4674 130×100 mm. 2000l.×4 Somali–lilac; British Angora–red shaded silver; Maine coon–Maine wave; Turkish van–tortie and white 10·00 10·00

499 Giraffe

2009. Sierra Leone Wildlife. Multicoloured.

4675	1000l. Type **499**	1·00	75
4676	1500l. Bonobo	1·50	1·60
4677	2000l. African bush elephant	1·90	2·00
4678	3000l. Zebra	2·75	2·50

MS4679 185×88 mm. 2000l.×4 Cheetah; Red colobus monkey; Hippopotamus; Lion 7·50 7·50

500 *Penthea filicornis*

2009. Orchids of Africa. Multicoloured.

4680	1000l. Type **500**	1·00	75
4681	1500l. *Herchelia graminfolia*	1·50	1·60
4682	2000l. *Satyrium princeps*	1·90	2·00
4683	3000l. *Herschelia charpentieriana*	2·75	2·50

MS4684 150×100 mm. 1500l.×6 *Eulophia quartiniana; Ansellia gigantea* var. *azanica; Angraecum infundibulare; Disperis capensis; Bartholina burmanniana; Disa uniflora* (all horiz) 8·75 8·75

501 Pied Kingfisher (*Ceryle rudis*)

2009. Birds of Africa. Multicoloured.

4685	1000l. Type **501**	1·00	75
4686	1500l. House sparrow (*Passer domesticus*)	1·10	1·60
4687	2000l. Skylark (*Alauda arvensis*)	1·90	2·00
4688	3000l. Black-chested snake-eagle (*Circaetus pectoralis*)	2·75	2·50

MS4689 151×109 mm. 2000l.×4 Greenfinch (*Carduelis chloris*); Pangani longclaw (*Macronyx aurantiigula*); Barn swallow (*Hirundo rustica*); Namaqua sandgrouse (*Pterocles namaqua*) (all vert) 7·50 7·50

502 Pope Benedict XVI giving Blessing

2009. Visit of Pope Benedict XVI to Israel. Sheet 150×100 mm containing T 502 and similar vert designs showing Pope at Latin Patriarch Church, Jerusalem. Multicoloured.

MS4690 2600l. Type **502**; 2600l. Benedict XVI (different); 2800l. As Type **502**; 2800l. As 2600l. 8·75 8·75

503 Feng Ru (first Chinese aircraft designer and aviator) and Newspaper Article, 1909

2009. Centenary of Chinese Aviation and Aeropex 2009 Exhibition, Beijing. Multicoloured.

MS4691 145×95 mm. 2700l.×4 Type **503**; Feng Ru with early aircraft, Auckland; Feng Ru in aircraft, 1912; *Feng Ru II* in flight 9·25 9·25

MS4692 120×80 mm. 7500l. Feng Ru and his assistants with early aircraft and statue of Feng Ru (51×38 mm) 5·75 5·75

504 The Three Stooges

2009. The Three Stooges. Sheet 104×130 mm containing T 504 and similar horiz designs. Multicoloured. Litho.

MS4693 2700l.×4 Type **504**; With bottles of liquor; Curly with hands in mangle and Larry turning handle; With glasses of beer 9·25 9·25

505 Tower Bridge, London

2009. Bridges of the World. T 505 and similar horiz designs. Multicoloured.

MS4694 140×110 mm. 2000l.×6 Type **505**; Hangzhou Bay Bridge, Zhejiang, China; Juscelino Kubitschek Bridge, Brasilia, Brazil; Sydney Harbour Bridge; Ponte Vecchio, Florence, Italy; Bosphorus Bridge, Istanbul, Turkey 11·00 11·00

MS4695 110×80 mm. 7000l. Golden Gate Bridge, San Francisco 6·25 6·25

505a Rat

2010. Chinese Lunar Calendar. 30th Anniv of Chinese Zodiac Stamps. Multicoloured.

MS4695a 800l.×12 Type **505a**; Ox; Tiger; Rabbit; Dragon; Snake; Horse; Ram; Monkey; Cock; Dog; Pig 9·00 9·00

505b Tiger

2010. Chinese New Year. Year of the Tiger. Multicoloured.

MS4695b 8000l.×2 Type **505b**; Tiger (walking to left) 1·50 1·50

The stamps and margins of **MS**4696 form a composite background design showing a tiger's head.

506 Abraham Lincoln

2010. Birth Bicentenary (2009) of Abraham Lincoln. Multicoloured.

MS4696 2700l. Type **506**×4 9·25 9·25

507 Elvis Presley

2010. 75th Birth Anniv of Elvis Presley. Multicoloured.

MS4697 2700l.×4 Type **507**; Playing guitar; With hand resting on guitar; Wearing white, hand raised to face 9·25 9·25

508 Darwin's Frog

2010. Birth Bicentenary (2009) of Charles Darwin (biologist and evolutionary theorist). Multicoloured.

MS4698 2500l.×4 Type **508**; Darwin's fox; Galapagos tortoise; Galapagos marine iguana 9·25 9·25

509 Pres. John F. Kennedy

2010. 50th Anniv of Election of President John F. Kennedy. Multicoloured.

MS4699 4000l.×4 Type **509**; Pres. Kennedy with arm raised; Seated, smiling; Profile and 'KENNEDY FOR PRESIDENT' 3·50 3·50

510 Elvis Presley as Walter Hale in *The Trouble with Girls*, 1969

2010. Elvis Presley in *The Trouble with Girls*. Multioloured.

MS4700 90×125 mm. 8000l. Type **510** 7·50 7·50

MS4701 125×90 mm. 8000l. Poster for *The Trouble with Girls* 7·50 7·50

MS4702 90×125 mm. 8000l. Wearing black jacket, smiling 7·50 7·50

MS4703 125×90 mm. 8000l. Standing beside train 7·50 7·50

511 Mexico

2010. World Cup Football Championship, South Africa. Multicoloured.

4704	1900l. Type **511**	1·75	1·75
4705	1900l. Switzerland	1·75	1·75
4706	1900l. Honduras	1·75	1·75
4707	1900l. Greece	1·75	1·75
4708	1900l. Nigeria	1·75	1·75
4709	1900l. Germay	1·75	1·75
4710	1900l. New Zealand	1·75	1·75
4711	1900l. Chile	1·75	1·75
4712	1900l. North Korea	1·75	1·75
4713	1900l. Cameroon	1·75	1·75
4714	1900l. South Korea	1·75	1·75
4715	1900l. Algeria	1·75	1·75
4716	1900l. Argentina	1·75	1·75
4717	1900l. Slovakia	1·75	1·75
4718	1900l. France	1·75	1·75
4719	1900l. South Africa	1·75	1·75
4720	1900l. Japan	1·75	1·75
4721	1900l. Netherlands	1·75	1·75
4722	1900l. Spain	1·75	1·75
4723	1900l. United States	1·75	1·75
4724	1900l. Paraguay	1·75	1·75
4725	1900l. Brazil	1·75	1·75
4726	1900l. Serbia	1·75	1·75
4727	1900l. Slovenia	1·75	1·75
4728	1900l. Ghana	1·75	1·75
4729	1900l. England	1·75	1·75
4730	1900l. Italy	1·75	1·75
4731	1900l. Uruguay	1·75	1·75
4732	1900l. Denmark	1·75	1·75
4733	1900l. Côte d'Ivoire	1·75	1·75
4734	1900l. Australia	1·75	1·75
4735	1900l. Portugal	1·75	1·75

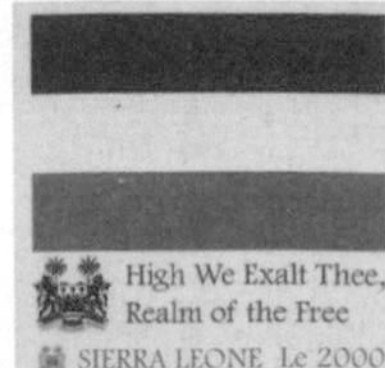

512 National Flag and Arms

2010. National Stamp.

4736	**512**	2000l. multicoloured	1·80	1·90

SIERRA LEONE Le 2000

513

2010. Personalised Stamp. Multicoloured.

4737	**513**	2000l. multicoloured	1·80	1·90

514 Michael Jackson

2010. Michael Jackson (singer) Commemoration. Multicoloured.

MS4738 4000l.×4 Type **514**; Wearing cream jacket with black lapel; In profile, facing right, head tilted back; Wearing black and gold jacket, holding microphone close to mouth 12·00 12·00

MS4739 4000l.×4 Wearing black, facing to right; Wearing white collared shirt; Wearing white T shirt and shirt; Wearing black and red roll-neck 12·00 12·00

515 Scout holding Badge and Olive Branch

2010. Centenary of Boy Scouts of America. Multicoloured.

MS4740 182×134 mm. 4000l. ×4 Type **515**×2; Eagle scout medal and merit badges for dog care, small-boat sailing, law and plant science; Scout medal and merit badges for astronomy, energy, theatre and home repairs 12·00 12·00

MS4741 150×154 mm. 4000l.×4 Two eagle scout badges and 'Be prepared' badge; Scout holding badge and olive branch×2; Eagle scout badge and eagle badges with star and heart backgrounds (all horiz) 12·00 12·00

516 Pope John Paul II

2010. Fifth Death Anniv of Pope John Paul II. Multicoloured.

MS4742 4000l.×4 Type **516**; Wearing red cassock and gold robes; With hands raised in blessing; Wearing mitre 14·00 14·00

MS4743 4000l.×4 With hand raised; With mitre and staff (at right of stamp); With mitre and staff (at left of stamp); Wearing white zucchetto (skullcap) (candlestick at right) 14·00 14·00

The stamps and margins of **MS**4742 form a composite design.

517 *Protogoniomorpha parhassus*

2010. Butterflies of Sierra Leone. Multicoloured.

MS4744 170×100 mm. 4000l.×4 Type **517**; *Kallimoides rumia rumia; Précis pelarga; Salamis cacta cacta* 12·00 12·00

MS4745 100×70 mm. 6000l. *Junonia sophia sophia*; 6000l. *Junonia oenone* 12·00 12·00

MS4746 100×70 mm. 6000l. *Hypolimnas misippus*; 6000l. *Hypolimnas salmacis salmacis* 12·00 12·00

The stamps and margins of Nos. **MS**4744 and **MS**4746 form composite background designs of a poppy field (**MS**4744) or silhouettes of white flowers (**MS**4746).

518 Three Modern Guides and Four Early Guides

2010. Centenary of Girlguiding. Multicoloured.

MS4747 150×100 mm. 2700l.×4 Type **518**; Three modern guides blowing bubbles and troop of early guides; Four modern guides and five early guides; Group of modern guides, some with arms raised in triumph and early guides 9·25 9·25

MS4748 70×100 mm. 8000l. Brownie saluting 9·25 9·25

519 Princess Diana

2010. Princess Diana Commemoration. Multicoloured.

MS4749 150×110 mm. 4000l.×4 Type **519**; Wearing blue jacket and white blouse; Wearing white sleeveless dress; Wearing pearl necklace and earrings 19·00 19·00

MS4750 99×71 mm. 10000l. Wearing grey and black jacket 8·50 8·50

MS4751 99×71 mm. 10000l. Wearing white hat 8·50 8·50

Pt. 1

SINGAPORE

An island to the south of the Malay peninsula, formerly part of the Straits Settlement but became a separate Crown Colony on 1 April 1946. From 1 August 1958 an internally self-governing territory designated the State of Singapore. From 16 September 1963 part of the Malaysian Federation until 9 August 1965, when it became an independent republic within the Commonwealth.

100 cents = 1 dollar.

1948. As T 58 of Straits Settlements, but inscr "MALAYA SINGAPORE".

1	1c. black	15	1·50
2	2c. orange	15	1·00
3	3c. green	50	2·25
19	4c. brown	2·25	10
19a	5c. mauve	3·50	2·00
5	6c. grey	40	1·00
6	8c. red	50	1·00
21a	8c. green	9·00	4·75
7	10c. purple	30	10
22a	12c. red	14·00	16·00
8	15c. blue	11·00	10
9	20c. black and green	5·50	1·25
24a	20c. blue	10·00	10
25	25c. purple and orange	3·50	10
25a	35c. red and purple	10·00	1·00
11	40c. red and purple	9·50	5·50
12	50c. black and blue	3·25	10
13	$1 blue and purple	10·00	4·25
14	$2 green and red	48·00	6·00
15	$5 green and brown	£110	7·50

1948. Silver Wedding. As T 32a of St. Helena.

31	10c. violet	75	1·00
32	$5 brown	£110	50·00

1949. 75th Anniv of U.P.U. As T 33d/g of St Helena.

33	10c. purple	75	70
34	15c. blue	6·00	4·25
35	25c. orange	6·00	3·00
36	50c. black	6·00	3·25

1953. Coronation. As T 33h of St. Helena.

37	10c. black and purple	2·25	30

1 Chinese Sampan

4 CENTS SINGAPORE MALAYA

3 Singapore River

1955

38	**1**	1c. black	10	1·00
39	-	2c. orange	2·50	1·50
40	-	4c. brown	1·00	15
41	-	5c. purple	65	50
42	-	6c. blue	65	70
43	-	8c. turquoise	1·25	1·50
44	-	10c. lilac	3·00	10
45	-	12c. red	5·00	3·00
46	-	20c. blue	2·25	10
47	-	25c. orange and violet	7·00	1·50
48	-	30c. violet and lake	3·75	10
49	-	50c. blue and black	2·25	10
50	-	$1 blue and purple	35·00	30
51	**3**	$2 green and red	42·00	1·75
52	-	$5 multicoloured	42·00	5·00

DESIGNS—HORIZ (as Type **1**) (2c. to 20c. are sailing craft): 2c. Malay kolek; 4c. Twa-kow lighter; 5c. Lombok sloop; 6c. Trengganu pinas; 8c. Palari schooner; 10c. Timber tongkong; 12c. Hainan junk; 20c. Cocos-Keeling schooner; 25c. Douglas DC-4M2 "Argonaut" aircraft; 30c. Oil tanker; 50c. "Chusan III" (liner). VERT (as Type **3**): $1 Raffles statue; $5 Arms of Singapore.

16 The Singapore Lion

1959. New Constitution. Lion in yellow and sepia.

53	**16**	4c. red	65	75
54	**16**	10c. purple	1·00	40
55	**16**	20c. blue	2·25	3·00
56	**16**	25c. green	2·50	2·25
57	**16**	30c. violet	2·50	3·25
58	**16**	50c. slate	3·25	3·25

17 State Flag

1960. National Day.

59	**17**	4c. red, yellow and blue	1·50	1·50
60	**17**	10c. red, yellow and grey	2·75	30

18 Clasped Hands

1961. National Day.

61	**18**	4c. black, brown and yellow	1·00	1·75
62	**18**	10c. black, green and yellow	1·25	10

19 "Arachnis" "Maggie Oei" (orchid)

20 Yellow Seahorse

1962. Orchids, Fishes and Birds.

63	**19**	1c. multicoloured	30	1·00
64	**20**	2c. brown and green	30	2·00
65	-	4c. black and red	30	1·25
66	-	5c. red and black	20	10
67	-	6c. black and yellow	55	1·25
68	-	8c. multicoloured	1·25	3·50
69	-	10c. orange and black	40	10
70	-	12c. multicoloured	1·25	3·50
70a	-	15c. multicoloured	4·50	10
71	-	20c. orange and blue	1·00	10
72	-	25c. black and orange	75	10
73	-	30c. multicoloured	1·25	40
74	-	50c. multicoloured	1·25	10
75	-	$1 multicoloured	21·00	60
76	-	$2 multicoloured	9·00	1·00
77	-	$5 multicoloured	18·00	8·50

DESIGNS—HORIZ (as Type **20**): 4c. Six-banded Tiger barb; 5c. Orange clownfish; 10c. Harlequinfish; 25c. Three-spotted gourami. (As Type **19**): 50c. White-rumped shama; $1 White-throated kingfisher.VERT (as Type **20**): 6c. Archer-fish; 20c. Copper-banded butterflyfish. (As Type **19**): 8c. "Vanda" "Tan Chay Yan" (orchid); 12c. "Grammatophyllum speciosum" (orchid); 15c. Black-naped tern; 30c. "Vanda" "Miss Joaquim" (orchid); $2 Yellow-bellied sunbird; $5 White-bellied sea eagle.

34 "The Role of Labour in Nation-Building"

1962. National Day.

78	**34**	4c. yellow, red and black	1·25	2·25
79	**34**	10c. yellow, blue and black	1·50	75

35 Blocks of Flats, Singapore

1963. National Day.

80	**35**	4c. multicoloured	50	80
81	**35**	10c. multicoloured	1·75	20

36 Dancers in National Costume

1963. South East Asia Cultural Festival.

82	**36**	5c. multicoloured	50	50

37 Workers

1966. 1st Anniv of Republic.

89	**37**	15c. multicoloured	75	30
90	**37**	20c. multicoloured	1·00	1·25
91	**37**	30c. multicoloured	1·25	2·00

38 Flag Procession

1967. National Day.

92	**38**	6c. red, brown and slate	50	90
93	**38**	15c. purple, brown and slate	80	10
94	**38**	50c. blue, brown and slate	1·50	1·60

Nos. 92/4 are respectively inscr "Build a Vigorous Singapore" in Chinese, Malay and Tamil, in additon to the English inscr.

39 Skyscrapers and Afro-Asian Map

1967. 2nd Afro-Asian Housing Congress.

95	**39**	10c. multicoloured	30	10
96	**39**	25c. multicoloured	75	1·00
97	**39**	50c. multicoloured	1·40	1·60

40 Symbolical Figure wielding Hammer and Industrial Outline of Singapore

1968. National Day. Inscription at top in Chinese (6c.), Malay (15c.) or Tamil (50c.).

98	**40**	6c. red, black and gold	35	65
99	**40**	15c. green, black and gold	45	15
100	**40**	50c. blue, black and gold	1·00	1·25

43 Mirudhangam

45 Sword Dance

1968

101	**43**	1c. multicoloured	15	2·25
102	-	4c. multicoloured	60	3·50
103	**45**	5c. multicoloured	60	1·75
104	-	6c. black, lemon and orange	1·75	2·25
105	-	10c. multicoloured	20	10
106	-	15c. multicoloured	60	10
107	-	20c. multicoloured	1·00	1·75
108	-	25c. multicoloured	1·25	1·75
109	-	30c. multicoloured	40	1·50
110	-	50c. black, red and brown	50	1·00
111	-	75c. multicoloured	3·00	4·25
112	-	$1 multicoloured	4·50	1·25
113	-	$2 multicoloured	3·50	1·00
114	-	$5 multicoloured	14·00	1·50
115	-	$10 multicoloured	38·00	15·00

DESIGNS—VERT (as Type **43**): 4c. Pi Pa; $2 Rebab; $10 Ta Ku. (As Type **45**): 6c. Lion Dance; 10c. Bharatha Natyam; 15c. Tari Payong; 20c. Kathak Kali; 25c. Lu Chih Shen and Lin Chung; 50c. Tari Lilin; 75c. Tarian Kuda Kepang; $1 Yao Chi. HORIZ (as Type **43**): $5 Vine. (As Type **45**): 30c. Dragon dance.

58 E.C.A.F.E. Emblem

1969. Plenary Session of Economic Commission for Asia and the Far East.

116	**58**	15c. black, silver and blue	35	20
117	**58**	30c. black, silver and red	65	1·25
118	**58**	75c. black, silver and violet	1·00	2·50

59 "100000" and Slogan as Block of Flats

1969. Completion of "100000 Homes for the People" Project.

119	**59**	25c. black and green	1·00	50
120	**59**	50c. black and blue	1·25	1·25

60 Aircraft over Silhouette of Singapore Docks

1969. 150th Anniv of Founding of Singapore.

121	**60**	15c. black, red and yellow	2·50	70
122	-	30c. black and blue	2·50	1·00
123	-	75c. multicoloured	4·50	1·00
124	-	$1 black and red	9·00	10·00
125	-	$5 red and black	18·00	45·00
126	-	$10 black and green	27·00	45·00
MS127		120×120 mm. Nos. 121/6	£375	£400

DESIGNS: 30c. U.N. emblem and outline of Singapore; 75c. Flags and outline of Malaysian Federation; $1 Uplifted hands holding crescent and stars; $5 Tail of Japanese aircraft and searchlight beams; $10 Bust from statue of Sir Stamford Raffles.

61 Sea Shells

1970. World Fair, Osaka. Multicoloured.

128	15c. Type **61**	1·25	15
129	30c. Veil-tailed guppys	1·75	70
130	75c. Greater flamingo and helmeted hornbill	5·00	2·75
131	$1 Orchid	5·00	5·50
MS132	94×154 mm. Nos. 128×31	24·00	24·00

62 "Kindergarten"

1970. 10th Anniv of People's Association.

133	**62**	15c. brown and orange	85	20
134	-	50c. blue and orange	2·25	2·75
135	-	75c. purple and black	3·50	4·50

DESIGNS: 50c. "Sport"; 75c. "Culture".

63 Soldier charging

1970. National Day. Multicoloured.

136	15c. Type **63**	1·25	20
137	50c. Soldier on assault course	3·75	3·50
138	$1 Soldier jumping	5·00	11·00

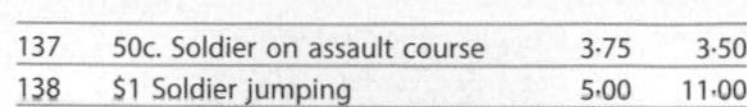

64 Sprinters

1970. Festival of Sports.

139	**64**	10c. mauve, black and blue	2·00	3·25
140	-	15c. black and orange	2·50	3·50
141	-	25c. black, orange and green	2·75	3·75
142	-	50c. black, green and mauve	3·00	3·75

DESIGNS: 15c. Swimmers; 25c. Tennis players; 50c. Racing cars.

65 "Neptune Aquamarine" (freighter)

1970. Singapore Shipping.

143	**65**	15c. multicoloured	2·75	65
144	-	30c. yellow and blue	6·00	5·50
145	-	75c. yellow and red	10·00	10·00

DESIGNS: 30c. Container berth; 75c. Shipbuilding.

66 Country Names in Circle

1971. Commonwealth Heads of Government Meeting, Singapore. Multicoloured.

146	15c. Type **66**	90	20
147	30c. Flags in circle	1·25	80
148	75c. Commonwealth flags	2·25	4·00
149	$1 Commonwealth flags linked to Singapore (63×61 mm)	3·00	7·00

67 Bicycle Rickshaws

1971. Tourism. ASEAN Year. (ASEAN = Association of South East Asian Nations).

150	**67**	15c. black, violet and orange	80	25
151	-	20c. indigo, orange & blue	1·10	1·00
152	-	30c. red and purple	1·40	1·75
153	-	50c. multicoloured	3·75	7·00
154	-	75c. multicoloured	5·00	9·00

DESIGNS—SQUARE: 20c. Houseboat "village" and boats; 30c. Bazaar. HORIZ (68×18 mm): 50c. Modern harbour skyline; 75c. Religious buildings.

68 Chinese New Year

1971. Singapore Festivals. Multicoloured.

155	15c. Type **68**	1·25	15
156	30c. Hari Raya	2·50	2·50
157	50c. Deepavali	3·50	6·50
158	75c. Christmas	4·00	7·50
MS159	150×125 mm. Nos. 155/8	75·00	48·00

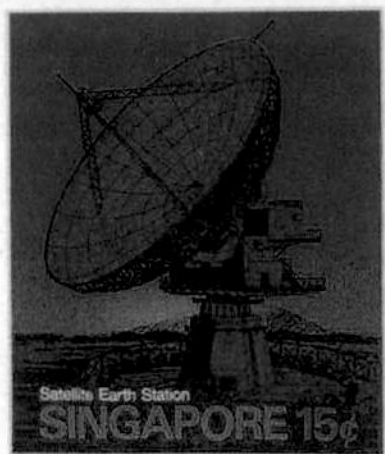

69 "Dish" Aerial

1971. Opening of Satellite Earth Station.

160	**69**	15c. multicoloured	3·00	1·50
161	-	30c. multicoloured	7·50	9·00
162	-	30c. multicoloured	7·50	9·00
163	-	30c. multicoloured	7·50	9·00
164	-	30c. multicoloured	7·50	9·00

DESIGNS: Nos. 161/4 were printed in se-tenant blocks of four throughout the sheet, the four stamps forming a composite design similar to Type **69**. They can be identified by the colour of the face values which are: yellow (No. 161), green (No. 162), red (No. 163) or orange (No. 164).

70 "Singapore River and Fort Canning, 1843–7" (Lieut. E. A. Porcher)

1971. Art. Multicoloured.

165	10c. Type **70**	2·00	2·00
166	15c. "The Padang, 1851" (J. T. Thomson)	2·50	3·00
167	20c. "Singapore Waterfront, 1848–9"	3·00	3·75
168	35c. "View from Fort Canning 1846" (J. T. Thomson)	6·50	8·00
169	50c. "View from Mt. Wallich, 1857" (P. Carpenter)	9·00	13·00
170	$1 "Singapore Waterfront, 1861" (W. Gray)	11·00	17·00

The 50c. and $1 are larger, 69×47 mm.

71 One Dollar of 1969

1972. Coins.

171	-	15c. orange, black and green	1·25	35
172	**71**	35c. black and red	2·25	3·25
173	-	$1 yellow, black and blue	4·00	8·50

DESIGNS: 15c. One-cent coin of George V; $1 One hundred and fifty dollar gold coin of 1969.

72 "Moon Festival" (Seah Kim Joo)

1972. Contemporary Art. Multicoloured.

174	15c. Type **72**	70	30
175	35c. "Complimentary Forces" (Thomas Yeo) (36×54 mm)	1·25	2·00
176	50c. "Rhythm in Blue" (Yusman Aman) (36×54 mm)	1·50	3·50
177	$1 "Gibbons" (Chen Wen Hsi)	3·25	6·50

73 Lanterns and Fish

1972. National Day. Designs symbolizing Festivals. Multicoloured.

178	15c. Type **73**	75	20
179	35c. Altar and candles	1·00	2·00
180	50c. Jug, bowl and gifts	1·25	3·00
181	75c. Candle	2·00	4·50

74 Student Welding

1972. Youth.

182	**74**	15c. multicoloured	80	30
183	-	35c. multicoloured	1·50	3·00
184	-	$1 orange, violet and green	3·25	7·50

DESIGNS: 35c. Sport; $1 Dancing.

75 "Maria Rickmers" (barque)

1972. Shipping. Multicoloured.

185	15c. "Neptune Ruby" (container ship) (42×29 mm)	2·00	80
186	75c. Type **75**	6·00	8·00
187	$1 Chinese junk	6·50	9·00
MS188	152×84 mm. Nos. 185/7	45·00	45·00

76 P.Q.R. Slogan

1973. "Prosperity Through Quality and Reliability" Campaign. Multicoloured.

189	15c. Type **76**	50	15
190	25c. Badge	1·25	2·75
191	75c. Text (different)	1·40	3·25
192	$1 Seal	1·40	4·50

77 Jurong Bird Park

1973. Singapore Landmarks.

193	**77**	15c. black and orange	80	15
194	-	35c. black and green	1·50	2·50
195	-	50c. black and brown	2·25	3·25
196	-	$1 black and purple	3·00	5·00

DESIGNS: 35c. National Theatre; 50c. City Hall; $1 Fullerton Building and Singapore River.

78 Aircraft Tail-fins

1973. Aviation. Multicoloured.

197	10c. Type **78**	50	10
198	35c. Emblems of Singapore Airlines and destinations	1·50	2·00
199	75c. Emblem on tail-fin	1·75	2·50
200	$1 Emblems encircling the globe	2·25	3·50

79 "Culture"

1973. National Day.

201	**79**	10c. orange and black	1·00	2·00
202	-	35c. orange and black	1·00	2·25
203	-	50c. orange and black	1·25	2·50
204	-	75c. orange and black	1·40	2·75

Nos. 201/4 were printed in se-tenant blocks of four within the sheet, and form a composite design representing Singapore's culture.

80 Athletics, Judo and Boxing

1973. 7th S.E.A.P.* Games.

205	**80**	10c. gold, silver and blue	55	20
206	-	15c. gold and black	1·75	1·50
207	-	25c. gold, silver and black	1·25	1·50
208	-	35c. gold, silver and blue	2·75	3·00
209	-	50c. multicoloured	1·50	3·75
210	-	$1 silver, blue and green	2·75	6·50
MS211		130×111 mm. Nos. 205/10	32·00	35·00

DESIGNS—SQUARE (as Type **80**): 15c. Cycling, weightlifting, pistol-shooting and sailing; 25c. Footballs; 35c. Table-tennis bat, shuttlecock, tennis ball and hockey stick. HORIZ (41×25 mm): 50c. Swimmers; $1 Stadium.

*S.E.A.P. = South East Asian Peninsula.

81 Agave　**82** Mangosteen

1973. Multicoloured. (a) Flowers and plants as T 81.

212	1c. Type **81**	1·00	1·50
213	5c. "Coleus blumei"	10	50
214	10c. "Vinca rosea"	15	10
215	15c. "Helianthus angustifolius"	1·50	10
216	20c. "Licuala grandis"	45	60
217	25c. "Wedelia trilobata"	3·75	55
218	35c. "Chrysanthemum frutescens"	1·00	1·00
219	50c. "Costus malorticanus"	1·00	55
220	75c. "Gerbera jamesonii"	2·50	1·00

(b) Fruits as T 82.

221	$1 Type **82**	1·50	40
222	$2 Jackfruit	1·75	1·25
223	$5 Coconut	1·75	4·50
224	$10 Pineapple	3·00	7·00

83 Tiger and Orang-Utans

1973. Singapore Zoo. Multicoloured.

225	5c. Type **83**	85	85
226	10c. Leopard and waterbuck	90	45
227	35c. Leopard and thamin	3·00	5·00
228	75c. Horse and lion	4·50	7·50

84 Delta Guppy

1974. Tropical Fish. Multicoloured.

229	5c. Type **84**	70	60
230	10c. Half-black delta guppy	70	15
231	35c. Delta guppy (different)	2·25	3·50
232	$1 Black delta guppy	3·00	8·50

85 Scout Badge within "9"

1974. 9th Asian-Pacific Scout Conference.

233	**85**	10c. multicoloured	30	10
234	**85**	75c. multicoloured	1·00	2·00

86 U.P.U. Emblem and Multiple "Centenary"

1974. Centenary of U.P.U.

235	**86**	10c. brown, purple and gold	15	10
236	-	35c. blue, deep blue & gold	40	1·60
237	-	75c. multicoloured	80	2·75

DESIGNS: 35c. U.P.U. emblem and multiple U.N. symbols; 75c. U.P.U. emblem and multiple peace doves.

87 Family Emblem

1974. World Population Year. Multicoloured.

238	10c. Type **87**	30	10
239	35c. Male and female symbols	80	1·40
240	75c. World population map	1·25	2·75

88 "Tree and Sun" (Chia Keng San)

1974. Universal Children's Day. Mult.

241	5c. Type **88**	40	65
242	10c. "My Daddy and Mummy" (Angeline Ang)	40	20
243	35c. "A Dump Truck" (Si-Hoe Yeen Joong)	1·25	2·75
244	50c. "My Aunt" (Raymond Teo)	1·40	3·50
MS245	138×100 mm. Nos. 241/4	23·00	28·00

89 Street Scene

1975. Singapore Views. Multicoloured.

246	15c. Type **89**	80	20
247	20c. Singapore River	1·50	1·25
248	$1 "Kelong" (fish-trap)	3·00	7·00

90 Emblem and Lighters' Prows

1975. 9th Biennial Conference of Int Association of Ports and Harbours, Singapore. Multicoloured.

249	5c. Type **90**	30	15
250	25c. Freighter and ship's wheel	1·75	1·50
251	50c. Oil-tanker and flags	2·25	3·00
252	$1 Container-ship and propellers	3·50	6·50

91 Satellite Earth Station, Sentosa

1975. "Science and Industry". Mult.

253	10c. Type **91**	35	10
254	35c. Oil refineries (vert)	2·25	3·00
255	75c. "Medical Sciences"	2·50	4·25

92 "Homes and Gardens"

1975. 10th National Day. Multicoloured.

256	10c. Type **92**	20	10
257	35c. "Shipping and Shipbuilding"	1·25	1·75
258	75c. "Communications and Technology"	1·40	2·75
259	$1 "Trade, Commerce and Industry"	1·40	2·75

93 South African Crowned Cranes

1975. Birds. Multicoloured.

260	5c. Type **93**	1·75	80
261	10c. Great Indian hornbill	1·75	30
262	35c. White-throated kingfishers and white-collared kingfisher	7·00	7·00
263	$1 Sulphur-crested cockatoo and blue and yellow macaw	10·00	14·00

94 "Equality"

1975. International Women's Year. Mult.

264	10c. Type **94**	25	10
265	35c. "Development"	1·40	2·50
266	75c. "Peace"	1·60	5·00
MS267	128×100 mm. Nos. 264/6	15·00	20·00

95 Yellow Flame

1976. Wayside Trees. Multicoloured.

268	10c. Type **95**	60	10
269	35c. Cabbage tree	1·50	2·50
270	50c. Rose of India	1·75	2·50
271	75c. Variegated coral tree	2·25	4·75

96 "Arachnis hookeriana x Vanda" Hilo Blue

1976. Singapore Orchids. Multicoloured.

272	10c. Type **96**	1·25	10
273	35c. "Arachnis Maggie Oei x Vanda insignis"	3·00	3·50
274	50c. "Arachnis Maggie Oei x Vanda" Rodman	3·50	4·00
275	75c. "Arachnis hookeriana x Vanda" Dawn Nishimura	4·50	7·00

97 Festival Symbol and Band

1976. 10th Anniv of Singapore Youth Festival. Multicoloured.

276	10c. Type **97**	20	10
277	35c. Athletes	1·25	1·75
278	75c. Dancers	1·40	2·75

98 "Queen Elizabeth Walk"

1976. Paintings of Old Singapore. Mult.

279	10c. Type **98**	50	20
280	50c. "The Padang"	2·00	4·00
281	$1 "Raffles Place"	3·75	6·00
MS282	164×91 mm. Nos. 279/81	15·00	23·00

99 Chinese Costume

1976. Bridal Costumes. Multicoloured.

283	10c. Type **99**	65	10
284	35c. Indian costume	1·25	2·00
285	75c. Malay costume	2·25	4·75

100 Radar, Missile and Soldiers

1977. 10th Anniv of National Service. Multicoloured.

286	10c. Type **100**	65	10
287	50c. Tank and soldiers	2·50	2·50
288	75c. Soldiers, wireless operators, pilot and Douglas A-4 Skyhawk aircraft	3·50	4·50

101 Lyrate Cockle

102 Spotted Hermit Crab

1977. Multicoloured. (a) Shells as T 101.

289	1c. Type **101**	1·00	2·00
290	5c. Folded or plicate scallop	20	10
291	10c. Marble cone	20	10
292	15c. Scorpion conch	1·00	40
293	20c. Amplustre or royal paper bubble	1·00	10
294	25c. Spiral babylon	1·25	2·50
295	35c. Royal thorny or spiny oyster	1·50	1·50
296	50c. Maple-leaf triton or winged frog shell	2·00	10
297	75c. Troschel's murex	3·00	20

(b) Fish and Crustaceans as T 102.

298	$1 Type **102**	2·00	15
299	$2 Zuge's stingray	2·00	75
300	$5 Cuttlefish	2·00	3·00
301	$10 Lionfish	3·00	5·50

103 Shipbuidling

1977. Labour Day. Multicoloured.

302	10c. Type **103**	30	10
303	50c. Building construction	1·25	2·00
304	75c. Road construction	1·75	2·50

104 Keyhole and Banknotes

1977. Cent of Post Office Savings Bank. Mult.

305	10c. Type **104**	30	10
306	35c. On-line banking service	75	50
307	75c. GIRO service	1·75	1·50

105 Flags of Member Nations

1977. 10th Anniv of ASEAN (Association of South-East Asian Nations). Multicoloured.

308	10c. Type **105**	30	10
309	35c. "Agriculture"	75	75
310	75c. "Industry"	1·75	1·75

106 "Chingay Procession" (Liang Yik Yin)

1977. Children's Art. Multicoloured.

311	10c. Type **106**	30	10
312	35c. "At the Bus Stop" (Chong Khing Ann) (horiz)	1·00	50
313	75c. "Playground" (Yap Li Hwa) (horiz)	2·25	2·75
MS314	160×97 mm. Nos. 311/13	11·00	18·00

107 "Life Sciences"

1977. Singapore Science Centre. Mult.

315	10c. Type **107**	20	10
316	35c. "Physical sciences"	45	30
317	75c. "Science and technology"	1·25	1·75
318	$1 Singapore Science Centre	1·50	1·75

108 Botanical Gardens and Esplanade, Jurong Bird Park

1978. Parks and Gardens. Multicoloured.

319	10c. Type **108**	20	10
320	35c. Lagoon, East Coast Park (vert)	80	80
321	75c. Botanical Gardens (vert)	1·50	2·25

109 Red-whiskered Bulbul

1978. Singing Birds. Multicoloured.

322	10c. Type **109**	60	20
323	35c. Oriental white-eye ("White eye")	1·75	1·50
324	50c. White-rumped shama	2·00	2·50
325	75c. White-crested laughing thrush and melodious laughing thrush ("China Thrush")	2·25	3·50

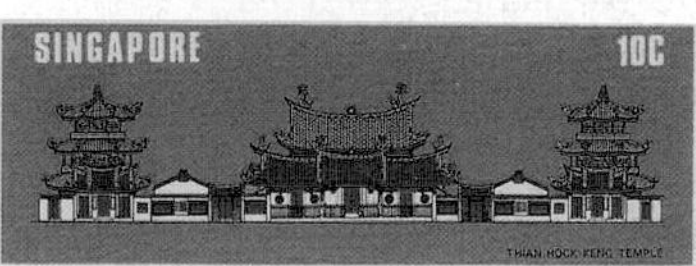

110 Thian Hock Keng Temple

1978. National Monuments. Multicoloured.

326	10c. Type **110**	55	80
327	10c. Hajjah Fatimah Mosque	55	80
328	10c. Armenian Church	55	80
329	10c. Sri Mariamman Temple	55	80
MS330	173×86 mm. 35c.×4, as Nos. 326/9	3·50	3·75

Stamps from No. **MS**330 are similar in design to Nos. 326/9 but have no borders and the inscriptions are slightly larger.

111 Map of South East Asia showing Cable Network

1978. A.S.E.A.N. Submarine Cable (1st issue). Philippines–Singapore Section.

331	**111**	10c. multicoloured	15	10
332	**111**	35c. multicoloured	60	85
333	**111**	50c. multicoloured	80	1·50
334	**111**	75c. multicoloured	90	2·00

See also Nos. 385/8 and 458/61.

112 "Neptune Spinel" (bulk carrier)

1978. 10th Anniv of Neptune Orient Shipping Lines. Multicoloured.

335	10c. Type **112**	70	20
336	35c. "Neptune Aries" (tanker)	1·75	1·75
337	50c. "Anro Temasek" (container ship)	2·00	2·75
338	75c. "Neptune Pearl" (container ship)	2·50	4·25

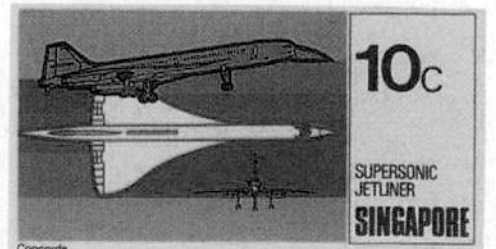

113 Concorde

1978. Aviation. Multicoloured.

339	10c. Type **113**	1·00	30
340	35c. Boeing 747-200	1·00	1·25
341	50c. Vickers Vimy	1·25	2·50
342	75c. Wright Brothers' Flyer I	1·50	4·00

114 10-Kilometre Marker

1979. Metrication. Multicoloured.

343	10c. Type **114**	15	10
344	35c. Tape measure	30	50
345	75c. Weighing scales	65	1·25

115 Vanda Hybrid

1979. Orchids.

346	**115**	10c. multicoloured	30	10
347	-	35c. multicoloured	60	75
348	-	50c. multicoloured	70	1·00
349	-	75c. multicoloured	80	1·40

DESIGNS—HORIZ: 35c. VERT: 50, 75c. Different varieties of vanda hybrid.

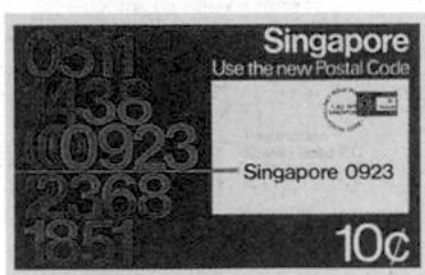

116 Envelope with new Singapore Postcode

1979. Postal Code Publicity.

350	**116**	10c. multicoloured	10	10
351	-	50c. multicoloured	60	90

The 50c. design is as Type **116**, but the envelope is addressed to the Philatelic Bureau, General Post Office and has the postcode "Singapore 0104".

117 Early Telephone and Overhead Cables

1979. Centenary of Telephone Service.

352	**117**	10c. brown and blue	15	10
353	-	35c. orange and violet	30	40
354	-	50c. blue, turquoise & grn	45	70
355	-	75c. green and orange	65	1·25

DESIGNS: 35c. Telephone dial and world map; 50c. Modern telephone and city scene; 75c. Latest computerized telephone and circuit diagram.

118 "Lantern Festival" (Eng Chun-Ngan)

1979. International Year of the Child. Children's Drawings. Multicoloured.

356	10c. Type **118**	10	10
357	35c. "Singapore Harbour" (Wong Chien Chien)	30	40
358	50c. "Use Your Hands" (Leong Choy Yeen)	40	70
359	75c. "Soccer" (Tan Cheong Hin)	60	1·25
MS360	154×98 mm. Nos. 356/9	3·75	4·25

119 View of Gardens

1979. 120th Anniv of Botanic Gardens.

361	**119**	10c. multicoloured	30	10
362	-	50c. multicoloured	1·00	1·50
363	-	$1 multicoloured	1·50	2·50

DESIGNS: 50c., $1 Different views of Botanic Gardens.

120 Hainan Junk

1980. Ships. Multicoloured.

364	1c. Type **120**	1·00	2·00
365	5c. Full-rigged clipper	30	55
366	10c. Fujian junk	30	10
367	15c. Golekkan (sailing craft)	40	15
368	20c. Palari (sailing craft)	70	40
369	25c. East Indiaman	80	50
370	35c. Galleon	90	50
371	50c. Caravel	60	70
372	75c. Jiangsu trading junk	1·00	1·50
373	$1 "Kedah" (coaster)	70	1·00
374	$2 "Murex" (tanker)	1·00	1·60
375	$5 "Chusan" (screw steamer)	1·50	2·75
376	$10 "Braganza" (paddle-steamer)	2·50	5·00

Nos. 373/6 are 42×25 mm.

121 Straits Settlements 1867 1½c. Stamp and Map of Singapore, 1843

1980. "London 1980" International Stamp Exn. Mult.

377	10c. Type **121**	20	10
378	35c. Straits Settlements 1906 $500 stamp and treaty between Johore and British Colony of Singapore	35	25
379	$1 1948 $2 stamp and map of Malaysia	60	1·10
380	$2 1969 150th Anniv of Singapore $10 commemorative and letter to Col. Addenbrooke from Sir Stamford Raffles	1·00	2·25
MS381	148×104 mm. Nos. 377/80	2·00	4·50

122 C.P.F. Emblem and "Keys to Retirement Benefits"

1980. 25th Anniv of Central Provident Fund Board. Multicoloured.

382	10c. Type **122**	10	10
383	50c. "C.P.F. savings for home ownership"	40	40
384	$1 "C.P.F. savings for old-age"	75	1·25

123 Map of South East Asia showing Cable Network

1980. A.S.E.A.N. (Association of South-East Asian Nations) Submarine Cable Network (2nd issue). Completion of Indonesia–Singapore Section.

385	**123**	10c. multicoloured	10	10
386	**123**	35c. multicoloured	50	50
387	**123**	50c. multicoloured	60	1·10
388	**123**	75c. multicoloured	75	2·00

124 A.S.E.A.N. Trade Fair Emblem

1980. A.S.E.A.N. (Association of South-East Asian Nations) Trade Fair.

389	**124**	10c. multicoloured	15	10
390	**124**	35c. multicoloured	35	30
391	**124**	75c. multicoloured	60	1·00

125 Ixora

1980. National Tree Planting Day. Flowers. Multicoloured.

392	10c. Type **125**	10	10
393	35c. Allamanda	40	45
394	50c. Sky vine	50	70
395	75c. Bougainvillea	60	1·10

126 International Currency Symbols

1981. 10th Anniv of Singapore Monetary Authority.

396	**126**	10c. black, red and yellow	10	10
397	**126**	35c. multicoloured	30	30
398	**126**	75c. multicoloured	55	1·25

1981. No. 65 surch 10 CENTS.

399	10c. on 4c. black and red	30	40

128 Woodwork

1981. Technical Training. Multicoloured.

400	10c. Type **128**	10	10
401	35c. Building construction	25	25
402	50c. Electronics	40	60
403	75c. Precision machining	50	1·10

129 Figures representing various Sports

1981. "Sports for All".

404	**129**	10c. multicoloured	30	10
405	-	75c. multicoloured	2·00	2·50
406	-	$1 multicoloured	2·50	3·50

DESIGNS: 75c. and $1 Figures representing different sports.

130 "The Right to Environmental Aids"

1981. International Year for Disabled Persons. Multicoloured.

407	10c. Type **130**	10	10
408	35c. "The right to social integration"	30	25
409	50c. "The right to education"	45	50
410	75c. "The right to work"	60	90

131 Control Tower and Passenger Terminal Building, Changi Airport

1981. Opening of Changi Airport.

411	**131**	10c. multicoloured	10	10
412	**131**	35c. multicoloured	20	30
413	**131**	50c. multicoloured	30	75
414	**131**	75c. multicoloured	40	1·50
415	**131**	$1 multicoloured	45	1·60
MS416		154×105 mm. Nos. 411/15	2·25	4·50

The background emblem differs for each value.

132 "Parthenos sylvia"

1982. Butterflies. Multicoloured.

417	10c. Type **132**	40	15
418	50c. "Danaus vulgaris"	1·00	75
419	$1 "Trogonoptera brookiana"	1·40	1·75

133 A.S.E.A.N. Emblem

1982. 15th Anniv of A.S.E.A.N. (Association of South-East Asian Nations).

420	**133**	10c. multicoloured	10	10
421	**133**	35c. multicoloured	30	35
422	-	50c. multicoloured	40	65
423	-	75c. multicoloured	60	1·00

The 50 and 75c. values are as Type **133** but are inscribed "15th ASEAN Ministerial Meeting".

134 Football and Stylized Player

1982. World Cup Football Championship, Spain.

424	**134**	10c. black, light blue & bl	20	10
425	-	75c. multicoloured	75	1·50
426	-	$1 multicoloured	95	1·50

DESIGNS: 75c. Football and World Cup, Asian Four emblem; $1 Football and globe.

135 Sultan Shoal Lighthouse, 1896

1982. Lighthouses of Singapore. Mult.

427	10c. Type **135**	50	15
428	75c. Horsburgh Lighthouse, 1855	1·40	1·75
429	$1 Raffles Lighthouse, 1855	1·50	2·00
MS430	148×104 mm. Nos. 427/9	5·50	5·50

136 Yard Gantry Cranes

1982. 10th Anniv of Container Terminal. Multicoloured.

431	10c. Type **136**	10	10
432	35c. Computer	25	40
433	50c. Freightlifter	35	85
434	75c. Straddle carrier	65	1·75

137 Scouts on Parade

1982. 75th Anniv of Boy Scout Movement. Multicoloured.

435	10c. Type **137**	15	10
436	35c. Scouts hiking	30	25
437	50c. Scouts building tower	50	35
438	75c. Scouts canoeing	60	80

138 Productivity Movement Slogans

1983. Productivity Movement.

439	**138**	10c. orange and green	10	10
440	-	35c. brown and blue	25	50
441	-	50c. red, yellow and grey	40	90
442	-	75c. red and yellow	55	1·25

DESIGNS: 35c. Family and housing ("Benefits of Productivity"); 50c. Works meeting ("Quality Control Circles"); 75c. Aspects of Singapore business ("Everybody's Business").

139 Commonwealth Logo and Country Names

1983. Commonwealth Day.

443	**139**	10c. multicoloured	10	10
444	**139**	35c. multicoloured	20	35
445	**139**	75c. multicoloured	45	1·10
446	**139**	$1 multicoloured	65	1·40

140 Soccer

1983. 12th South-East Asia Games. Mult.

447	10c. Type **140**	10	10
448	35c. Racket games	20	25
449	75c. Athletics	45	50
450	$1 Swimming	65	70

141 Policeman and Family

1983. Neighbourhood Watch Scheme. Mult.

451	10c. Type **141**	15	10
452	35c. Policeman and children	55	55
453	75c. Policeman and inhabitants with linked arms	1·00	2·00

142 1977 A.S.E.A.N. Stamps and Statue of King Chulalongkorn

1983. Bangkok Int Stamp Exhibition. Mult.

454	10c. Type **142**	20	10
455	35c. 1980 A.S.E.A.N. stamps and map of South-east Asia	55	50
456	$1 1982 A.S.E.A.N. stamps and signatures of Heads of State	1·25	1·60
MS457	147×104 mm. Nos. 454/6	4·25	6·50

143 Map of South-East Asia showing Cable Network

1983. A.S.E.A.N. (Association of South-East Asian Nations) Submarine Cable Network (3rd issue). Completion of Malaysia–Singapore–Thailand section.

458	**143**	10c. multicoloured	15	10
459	**143**	35c. multicoloured	55	75
460	**143**	50c. multicoloured	80	1·25
461	**143**	75c. multicoloured	1·25	2·00
MS462		146×100 mm. Nos. 331, 388, 458/61	4·75	6·00

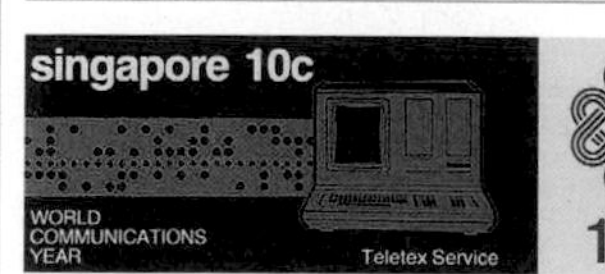

144 Teletex Service (image scaled to 66% of original size)

1983. World Communications Year.

463	**144**	10c. yellow, green & black	20	15
464	-	35c. yellow, red and brown	55	75
465	-	75c. green, blue & dp blue	1·10	1·75
466	-	$1 yellow, brown and black	1·50	2·75

DESIGNS: 35c. World telephone numbering plan; 75c. Satellite transmission; $1 Sea communications.

145 Blue-breasted Banded Rail ("Slaty-breasted Rail")

1984. Coastal Birds. Multicoloured.

467	10c. Type **145**	60	15
468	35c. Black bittern	1·50	1·50
469	50c. Brahminy kite	1·75	2·25
470	75c. Moorhen ("Common Moorhen")	2·00	3·25

146 House of Tan Yeok Nee

1984. National Monuments. Multicoloured.

471	10c. Type **146**	15	10
472	35c. Thong Chai building	40	65
473	50c. Telok Ayer market	55	1·10
474	$1 Nagore Durgha shrine	80	2·50

147 1970 $1 National Day Stamp

1984. "25 Years of Nation Building". Multicoloured.

475	10c. Type **147**	15	10
476	35c. 1981 $1 "Sports for All" stamp	50	70
477	50c. 1969 25c. "100, 000 Homes for the People" stamp	60	1·00
478	75c. 1976 10c. Wayside Trees stamp	70	1·25
479	$1 1981 $1 Opening of Changi Airport stamp	80	1·75
480	$2 1981 10c. Monetary Authority stamp	1·40	4·00
MS481	132×106 mm. Nos. 475/80	6·00	7·50

148 Schoolchildren

1984. "Total Defence".

482	**148**	10c. brown and red	15	40
483	-	10c. brown, olive and blue	15	40
484	-	10c. brown, violet and salmon	15	40
485	-	10c. brown, light brown and mauve	15	40
486	-	10c. brown, yellow & olive	15	40

DESIGNS: No. 483, People of Singapore; 484, Industrial workers; 485, Civil Defence first aid worker; 486, Anti-aircraft gun crew.

149 Coleman Bridge

1985. Bridges of Singapore.

487	10c. black (Type **149**)	15	10
488	35c. black (Cavenagh Bridge)	30	40
489	75c. black (Elgin Bridge)	55	70
490	$1 black (Benjamin Sheares Bridge)	70	90

150 "Ceriagrion cerinorubellum" (damselfly)

1985. Insects. Multicoloured.

491	5c. Type **150**	1·25	50
492	10c. "Apis javana" (bee)	1·25	65
493	15c. "Delta arcuata" (wasp)	1·50	1·50
494	20c. "Xylocopa caerulea" (bee)	1·00	1·75
495	25c. "Donacia javana" (water beetle)	1·00	1·50
496	35c. "Heteroneda reticulata" (ladybird)	1·50	30
497	50c. "Catacanthus nigripes" (bug)	1·50	1·25
498	75c. "Chremistica pontianaka" (cicada)	1·50	2·50
499	$1 "Homoexipha lycoides" (cricket) (35×30 mm)	2·75	60
500	$2 "Traulia azureipennis" (grasshopper) (35×30 mm)	1·50	1·50
501	$5 "Trithemis aurora" (dragonfly) (35×30 mm)	2·00	3·50
502	$10 "Scambophyllum sanguinolentum" (grasshopper) (35×30 mm)	3·50	7·00

151 Tennis, Canoeing, Judo and Children Playing

1985. 25th Anniv of People's Assn. Mult.

503	10c. Type **151**	25	10
504	35c. Lion dance, martial arts and athletes with flags	30	35
505	50c. Tae-kwon-do, Indian dance and Dragon dance	40	50
506	75c. Boxing, table tennis, basketball and dancing	75	1·00

152 Modern Housing Estate and Squatter Settlement

1985. 25th Anniv of Housing and Development Board. Designs show different aspects of housing at left. Multicoloured.

507	10c. Type **152**	15	10
508	35c. Singapore family (home-ownership)	30	45
509	50c. Group of residents (community development)	40	1·00
510	75c. Construction workers (building technology)	55	1·75
MS511	126×105 mm. Nos. 507/10	3·25	5·00

153 Brownies

1985. 75th Anniv of Girl Guide Movement. Multicoloured.

512	10c. Type **153**	15	10
513	35c. Guides practising first aid	35	40
514	50c. Senior Branch	45	60
515	75c. Adult leaders and guides	65	90

154 Badges and Emblems of Singapore Youth Organizations

1985. International Youth Year. Multicoloured.

516	10c. Type **154**	15	10
517	75c. Hand protecting sapling	80	65
518	$1 Stylized figures and dove	1·00	85

155 Guava

1986. Singapore Fruits. Multicoloured.

519	10c. Type **155**	30	10
520	35c. Jambu air	85	65
521	50c. Rambutan	1·10	1·25
522	75c. Ciku	1·40	2·00

156 Laboratory Technician and Salesmen with Bar Graph

1986. 25th Anniv of National Trades Union Congress. Multicoloured.

523	10c. Type **156**	30	50
524	10c. Computer operator and welder	30	50
525	10c. Draughtsmen and surveyors	30	50
526	10c. Group of workers	30	50
MS527	148×100 mm. As Nos. 523/6, but each stamp with a face value of 35c.	4·00	6·00

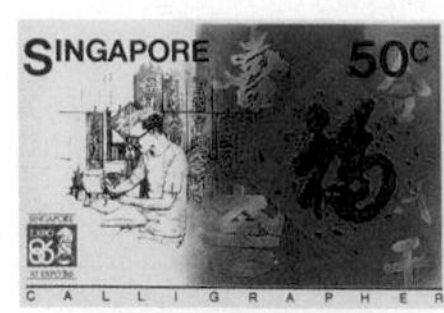

157 Calligraphy

1986. "Expo '86" World Fair, Vancouver. Multicoloured.

528	50c. Type **157**	55	75
529	75c. Garland maker	70	95
530	$1 Batik printer	85	1·25

158 Industrial Automation

1986. 25th Anniv of Economic Development Board. Multicoloured.

531	10c. Type **158**	10	10
532	35c. Manufacture of aircraft components	25	30
533	50c. Electronics industry	30	50
534	75c. Biotechnology industry	50	90

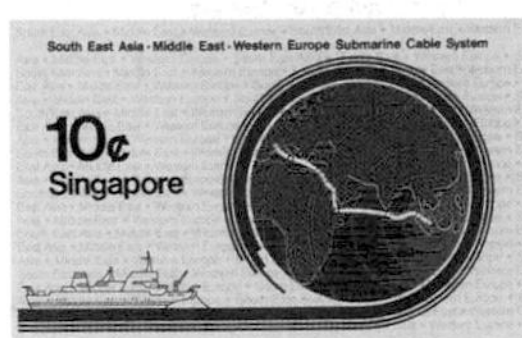

159 Map showing Route of Cable and "Vercors" (cable ship)

1986. SEA-ME-WE Submarine Cable Project.

535	**159**	10c. multicoloured	40	10
536	**159**	35c. multicoloured	85	55
537	**159**	50c. multicoloured	1·10	90
538	**159**	75c. multicoloured	1·40	2·00

160 Stylized Citizens

1986. 21st Anniv of Citizens' Consultative Committees.

539	**160**	10c. multicoloured	30	45
540	-	35c. multicoloured	45	60
541	-	50c. multicoloured	55	70
542	-	75c. multicoloured	75	85

DESIGN: 35c. to 75c. Citizens.

Nos. 539/42 were printed together, se-tenant, forming a composite design.

161 Peace Doves and People of Different Races

1986. International Peace Year. Multicoloured.

543	10c. Type **161**	15	10
544	35c. Doves and map of A.S.E.A.N. countries	50	70
545	$1 Doves and globe	1·25	3·00

162 Orchard Road

1987. Singapore Skyline. Multicoloured.

546	10c. Type **162**	15	10
547	50c. Central Business District	50	65
548	75c. Marina Centre and Raffles City	75	1·50

163 Flags of Members Nations and Logo

1987. 20th Anniv of Association of South-east Asian Nations.

549	**163**	10c. multicoloured	15	10
550	**163**	35c. multicoloured	35	40
551	**163**	50c. multicoloured	55	65
552	**163**	75c. multicoloured	65	90

164 Soldier with Rocket Launcher and Tank

1987. 20th Anniv of National Service. Multicoloured (except No. MS557).

553	10c. Type **164**	55	70
554	10c. Radar operator and patrol boat	55	70
555	10c. Fighter pilot and General Dynamics Fighting Falcon and Douglas A-4 Skyhawk aircraft	55	70
556	10c. Servicemen pledging allegiance	55	70
MS557	148×100 mm. 35c.×5. As Nos. 553/6 and Singapore lion symbol (red and black)	4·75	6·00

165 Singapore River and Dragon Boats

1987. River Conservation. Multicoloured.

558	10c. Type **165**	30	10
559	50c. Kallang Basin, canoe and fishing punt	80	1·25
560	$1 Kranji Reservoir, athletes and cyclist	2·25	4·25

166 Majapahit Gold Bracelet and Museum

1987. Centenary of National Museum. Each showing different drawings of Museum. Multicoloured.

561	10c. Type **166**	30	10
562	75c. Ming fluted kendi (water vessel)	1·25	1·75
563	$1 Patani hulu pekakak keris (sword)	1·40	3·00

167 Omni-theatre

1987. 10th Anniv of Singapore Science Centre. Multicoloured.

564	10c. Type **167**	15	10
565	35c. Omni planetarium	1·50	1·25
566	75c. Model of body cell	1·50	2·75
567	$1 Physical sciences exhibits	1·50	3·25

168 Modern Anti-aircraft Gun

1988. Centenary of Singapore Artillery. Mult.

568	10c. Type **168**	55	15
569	35c. 25-pounder field gun firing salute	1·40	1·25
570	50c. Gunner and 12-pounder gun, c. 1920	1·50	2·00
571	$1 Gunner and Maxim gun, 1889	2·25	4·50

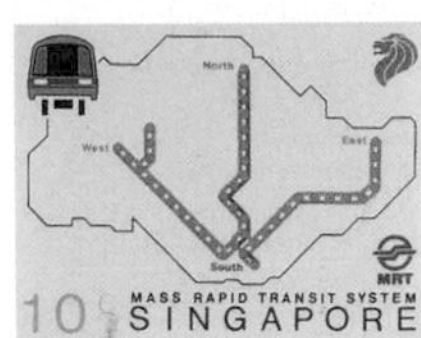

169 Route Map

1988. Singapore Mass Rapid Transit System. Multicoloured.

572	10c. Type **169**	1·25	15
573	50c. Train on elevated section	2·50	2·25
574	$1 Train in tunnel	4·00	5·00

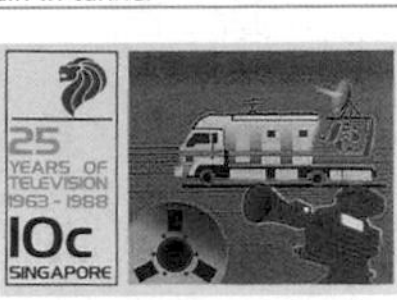

170 Camera, Film and Outside Broadcast Van

1988. 25th Anniv of Television in Singapore. Multicoloured.

575	10c. Type **170**	40	10
576	35c. Camera, studio lights and microphone	80	75
577	75c. Television set and transmitter	1·25	1·50
578	$1 Globe on TV screen and dish aerial	1·75	2·25

171 Water Droplet and Blocks of Flats

1988. 25th Anniv of Public Utilities Board. Multicoloured.

579	10c. Type **171**	20	10
580	50c. Electric light bulb and city centre	1·10	1·00
581	$1 Gas flame and factories	2·00	2·50
MS582	116×75 mm. Nos. 579/81	4·75	6·50

172 Greeting Neighbours

1988. 10th Anniv of National Courtesy Campaign. Each showing campaign mascot "Singa". Multicoloured.

583	10c. Type **172**	20	10
584	30c. Queueing at checkout	50	55
585	$1 Helping the elderly	1·50	2·75

173 Modern 30 Metre Turntable Fire Appliance

1988. Centenary of Fire Service. Multicoloured.

586	10c. Type **173**	1·00	25
587	$1 Steam fire engine, c. 1890	3·25	3·25

174 Container Ships and Warehouses

1989. 25th Anniv of Singapore Port Authority. Multicoloured.

588	10c. Type **174**	55	10
589	30c. Shipping and oil storage depot	1·00	50
590	75c. Container ships and Singapore skyline	1·50	1·50
591	$1 Container port at night	1·60	1·60

175 "Sago Street"

1989. Paintings of Chinatown by Choo Keng Kwang. Multicoloured.

592	10c. Type **175**	40	15
593	35c. "Pagoda Street"	1·25	1·00
594	75c. "Trengganu Street"	2·00	2·75
595	$1 "Temple Street"	2·25	3·25

176 North-west Singapore City, 1920

1989. Maps of Singapore. Multicoloured.

596	15c. Type **176** (top left)	1·50	1·75
597	15c. North-east Singapore (top right)	1·50	1·75
598	15c. South-west Singapore (bottom left)	1·50	1·75
599	15c. South-east Singapore (bottom right)	1·50	1·75
600	50c. Singapore Island and Dependencies, 1860s	2·25	2·00
601	$1 British Settlement of Singapore, 1820s	3·00	3·50

Nos. 596/9 were printed together, se-tenant, forming a composite design.

Individual stamps can be identifed by the position of the lion emblem which is quoted in brackets.

177 Clown Triggerfish

1989. Fishes. Multicoloured.

602	15c. Type **177**	1·75	20
603	30c. Blue-girdled angelfish	2·75	1·50
604	75c. Emperor angelfish	4·25	5·00
605	$1 Regal angelfish	4·75	6·50

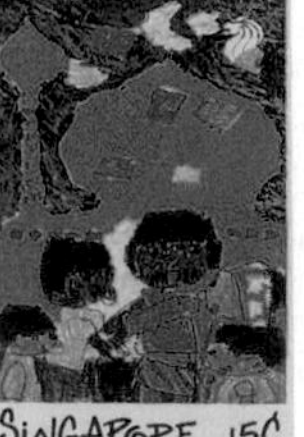

178 "Hari Raya Puasa" (Loke Yoke Yum)

1989. Festivals of Singapore Children's Drawings. Multicoloured.

606	15c. Type **178**	40	10
607	35c. "Chinese New Year" (Simon Koh)	70	65
608	75c. "Thaipusam" (Henry Setiono)	1·40	1·40
609	$1 "Christmas" (Wendy Ang Lin Min)	1·75	1·75
MS610	126×75 mm. Nos. 606/9	4·00	4·00

179 North Entrance of Stadium

1989. Opening of Singapore Indoor Stadium. Multicoloured.

611	30c. Type **179**	85	30
612	75c. Arena	1·75	1·50
613	$1 East entrance	2·00	1·75
MS614	104×104 mm. Nos. 611/13	4·50	4·50

180 "Singapore River, 1839" (Louis le Breton)

1990. Lithographs of 19th-century Singapore. Multicoloured.

615	15c. Type **180**	70	15
616	30c. "Chinatown, 1837" (Barthelemy Lauvergne)	1·25	70
617	75c. "Singapore Harbour, 1837" (Barthelemy Lauvergne)	2·25	2·25
618	$1 "View from the French Resident's House, 1824" (Deroy)	2·50	2·75

181 1969 150th Anniv of Singapore Stamp Issue

1990. 150th Anniv of the Penny Black. Mult.

619	50c. Type **181**	1·00	60
620	75c. Indian stamps, including bisect, used from Singapore in 1859	1·25	1·50
621	$1 Indian stamps used from Singapore in 1854	1·90	1·90
622	$2 Penny Black and Two Pence Blue	3·00	5·00
MS623	134×90 mm. Nos. 619/22	8·50	7·50

No. **MS**623 also commemorates the "Stamp World London 90" international stamp exhibition.

5c SINGAPORE

182 Zoological Gardens

183 Chinese Opera Singer and Siong Lim Temple

1990. Tourism. Multicoloured. (a) As T 182.

624	5c. Type **182**	30	40
625	15c. Sentosa Island	30	10
626	20c. Singapore River	30	20
627	25c. Dragon Boat Festival	55	75
628	30c. Raffles Hotel	70	30
629	35c. Coffee shop bird singing contest	1·25	75
630	40c. Jurong Bird Park	2·00	1·00
631	50c. Chinese New Year boat float	1·25	45
632	75c. Peranakan Place	1·75	70

(b) As T 183.

633	$1 Type **183**	4·50	1·25
634	$2 Malay dancer and Sultan Mosque	6·00	2·25
635	$5 Indian dancer and Sri Mariamman Temple	8·00	7·00
636	$10 Ballet dancer and Victoria Memorial Hall	12·00	11·00

184 Armed Forces Personnel

1990. 25th Anniv of Independence. Mult.

637	15c. Type **184**	1·25	20
638	35c. Inhabitants of Singapore	1·75	1·00
639	75c. Workers and technological achievements	2·50	2·75
640	$1 Cultural activities	3·25	5·00

185 Stag's Horn Fern

1990. Ferns. Multicoloured.

641	15c. Type **185**	25	10
642	35c. Maiden hair fern	60	75
643	75c. Bird's nest fern	1·25	2·00
644	$1 Rabbit's foot fern	1·60	2·50

186 Carved Dragon Pillar, Hong San See Temple

1991. National Monuments. Multicoloured.

645	20c. Type **186**	50	80
646	20c. Hong San See Temple (40×25 mm)	50	80
647	50c. Interior of dome, Abdul Gaffoor Mosque	80	1·10
648	50c. Abdul Gaffoor Mosque (40×25 mm)	80	1·10
649	75c. Statue of Vishnu, Sri Perumal Hindu Temple	1·10	1·50
650	75c. Sri Perumal Temple (40×25 mm)	1·10	1·50
651	$1 Stained glass window, St. Andrew's Cathedral	1·25	1·75
652	$1 St. Andrew's Cathedral (40×25 mm)	1·25	1·75

187 "Vanda Miss Joaquim"

1991. "Singapore '95" International Stamp Exhibition. Orchids (1st issue). Mult.

653	$2 Type **187**	4·00	5·00
654	$2 "Dendrobium anocha"	4·00	5·00
MS655	123×80 mm. Nos. 653/4	11·00	12·00

See also Nos. 674/5, 725/6, 755/6, 795/6 and **MS**817.

188 Changi Airport Terminal II, 1991, and Boeing 747-400

1991. Singapore Civil Aviation. Mult.

656	20c. Type **188**	1·25	25
657	75c. Changi Airport Terminal I, 1981, and Boeing 747-200	2·50	2·00
658	$1 Paya Lebar Airport, 1955–1981, and Concorde	2·50	2·25
659	$2 Kallang Airport, 1937–1955, and Douglas DC-2	3·75	6·00

189 "Arachnopsis Eric Holttum"

1991. Orchid Dress Motifs. Multicoloured.

660	20c. Type **189**	1·00	25
661	30c. "Cattleya meadii"	1·25	1·50
662	$1 "Calanthe vestita"	3·00	5·00

190 Long-tailed Tailor Bird ("Common Tailorbird")

1991. Garden Birds. Multicoloured.

663	20c. Type **190**	45	25
664	35c. Scarlet-backed flower-pecker	1·50	1·50
665	75c. Black-naped oriole	2·25	3·25
666	$1 Common iora	2·50	3·75

191 Productivity Discussion

1991. 10th Anniv of Productivity Movement. Multicoloured.

667	20c. Type **191**	40	30
668	$1 Construction workers	1·10	2·50

192 Railway Creeper

1992. "Phila Nippon '91" International Stamp Exhibition, Tokyo. Wild Flowers. Mult.

669	30c. Type **192**	75	25
670	75c. Asystasia	1·25	1·25
671	$1 Singapore rhododendron	1·50	2·00
672	$2 Coat buttons	2·50	5·25
MS673	132×90 mm. Nos. 669/72	7·50	8·50

1992. "Singapore '95" International Stamp Exn. Orchids (2nd issue). As T 187. Mult.

674	$2 "Dendrobium Sharifah Fatimah"	2·75	4·25
675	$2 "Phalaenopsis Shim Beauty"	2·75	4·25
MS676	123×80 mm. Nos. 674/5	11·00	12·00

193 "Singapore Waterfront" (Georgette Chen Liying)

1992. Local Artists (1st series). Multicoloured.

677	20c. Type **193**	40	20
678	75c. "Kampung Hut" (Lim Cheng Hoe)	85	1·25
679	$1 "The Bridge" (Poh Siew Wah)	1·10	1·40
680	$2 "Singapore River" (Lee Boon Wang)	2·25	4·50

See also Nos. 818/21.

194 Football

1992. Olympic Games, Barcelona. Mult.

681	20c. Type **194**	25	20
682	35c. Athletics	35	30
683	50c. Swimming	55	65
684	75c. Basketball	1·25	1·25
685	$1 Tennis	1·50	1·50
686	$2 Sailing	2·00	2·75
MS687	132×90 mm. Nos. 681/6	9·50	11·00

195 Chinese Family and Samfu Pattern

1992. Singapore Costumes of 1910. Mult.

688	20c. Type **195**	40	20
689	35c. Malay family and sarong pattern	50	45
690	75c. Indian family and sari pattern	1·00	1·25
691	$2 Straits Chinese family and belt pattern	2·00	3·50

196 Infantryman, Air Force Pilot and Navy Gunner

1992. 25th Anniv of National Service. Mult.

692	20c. Type **196**	60	30
693	35c. Navy diver, General Dynamics F-16 Fighting Falcon and FH-88 155 mm howitzer	85	75
694	$1 General Dynamics F-16 Fighting Falcon in flight, corvette and AMX-13SM1 tank	2·50	4·00

197 Crafts from A.S.E.A.N. Countries

1992. 25th Anniv of A.S.E.A.N. (Association of South-East Asian Nations). Multicoloured.

695	20c. Type **197**	40	20
696	35c. National dances	90	1·00
697	$1 National landmarks	2·00	3·75

198 Mosaic Crab

1992. Crabs. Multicoloured.

698	20c. Type **198**	55	25
699	50c. Johnson's freshwater crab	1·00	1·25
700	75c. Singapore freshwater crab	1·50	2·25
701	$1 Swamp forest crab	1·75	3·00

199 Coins

1992. 25th Anniv of Singapore Currency. Mult.

702	20c. Type **199**	1·00	1·75
703	75c. Currency note from "orchid" series	1·75	2·75
704	$1 Currency note from "ship" series	2·25	3·00
705	$2 Currency note from "bird" series	2·75	3·25

Nos. 702/5 were printed together, se-tenant, forming a composite design.

200 Sun Bear

1993. South-East Asian Mammals. Mult.

706	20c. Type **200**	30	20
707	30c. Orang-utan	60	65
708	75c. Slow loris	1·10	1·40
709	$2 Greater Malay chevrotain ("Large Mouse Deer")	2·25	3·75

201 "Thank You"

1993. Greetings Stamps. Multicoloured.

710	20c. Type **201**	60	90
711	20c. "Congratulations"	60	90
712	20c. "Best Wishes"	60	90
713	20c. "Happy Birthday"	60	90
714	20c. "Get Well Soon"	60	90

202 Shophouses

1993. Conservation of Tanjong Pagar District. Multicoloured.

715	20c. Type **202**	50	20
716	30c. Jinrikisha Station	2·50	70
717	$2 View of Tanjong Pagar	3·75	4·00

203 "Cranes" (painting) (Chen Wen Hsi)

1993. "Indopex '93" International Stamp Exhibition, Surabaya.

718	**203**	$2 multicoloured	2·75	4·25

204 Football

1993. 17th South-East Asian Games, Singapore. Mult.

719	20c. Type **204**	30	20
720	35c. Basketball	70	60
721	50c. Badminton	90	1·25
722	75c. Athletics	1·00	1·50
723	$1 Water polo	1·40	2·00
724	$2 Yachting	2·25	4·00

1993. "Singapore '95" International Stamp Exhibition. Orchids (3rd issue). As T 187 but 25×35 mm. Multicoloured.

725	$2 "Phalaenopsis amabilis"	3·00	4·00
726	$2 "Vanda sumatrana"	3·00	4·00
MS727	123×80 mm. Nos. 725/6	7·50	8·00

No. **MS**727 also commemorates "Taipei '93" Asian International Stamp Exhibition, Taiwan.

205 "Danaus chrysippus"

1993. Butterflies. Multicoloured.

728	20c. Type **205**	30	30
729	50c. "Cethosia hypsea"	65	65
730	75c. "Amathusia phidippus"	90	1·50
731	$1 "Papilio demolion"	1·25	2·00

206 Papaya

1993. "Bangkok '93" International Stamp Exhibition. Local Fruits. Multicoloured.

732	20c. Type **206**	40	20
733	35c. Pomegranate	60	50
734	75c. Starfruit	1·25	1·50
735	$2 Durian	2·25	4·00
MS736	120×89 mm. Nos. 732/5	4·00	5·50

207 Egrets drinking

1993. Endangered Species. Swinhoe's Egret ("Chinese Egret"). Multicoloured.

737	20c. Type **207**	50	95
738	25c. Egrets eating	55	1·00
739	30c. Egrets searching for fish	65	1·10
740	35c. Egrets in flight	70	1·10

Nos. 737/40 were printed together, se-tenant, with the background forming a composite design.

208 Palm Tree

1993. Self-adhesive. Imperf.

741	**208**	(20c.) multicoloured	30	50

No. 741 was only valid for use on mail to local addresses and was initially sold at 20c.

209 Tiger Cowrie

1994. Reef Life (1st series). Multicoloured.

742	5c. Type **209**	30	30
743	20c. Sea-fan	60	75
744	25c. Tunicate	65	25
745	30c. Clown anemonefish	70	50
746	35c. Ruppell's nudibranch	75	75
747	40c. Sea-urchin	1·00	1·50
748	50c. Soft coral	1·00	50
749	75c. Pin cushion star	1·50	70
750	$1 Knob coral (31×27 mm)	4·50	1·75
751	$2 Mushroom coral (31×27 mm)	7·00	3·50
752	$5 Bubble coral (31×27 mm)	10·00	7·50
753	$10 Octopus coral (31×27 mm)	15·00	12·00

See also No. 784.

1994. "Singapore '95" International Stamp Exhibition. Orchids (4th issue). As T 187 but each 25×35 mm. Multicoloured.

755	$2 "Paphiopedilum victori-aregina"	4·00	4·50
756	$2 "Dendrobium smillieae"	4·00	4·50
MS757	123×80 mm. Nos. 755/6	7·50	8·00

No. **MS**757 also commemorates "Hong Kong'94" International Stamp Exhibition.

210 Dancers

1994. Singapore Festival of Arts. Mult.

758	20c. Type **210**	45	20
759	30c. Actors and puppet	65	55
760	50c. Musicians	1·00	1·00
761	$1 Artists	1·75	3·00

211 Civilian taking Pledge, National Day Parade and Soldier with Anti-tank Missile

1994. 25th Anniv of Operationally-ready National Servicemen. Multicoloured.

762	20c. Type **211**	90	30
763	30c. Serviceman on beach with family and on jungle patrol	1·10	1·25
764	35c. Serviceman relaxing at home and with machine gun	1·25	1·25
765	75c. National Service officer at work and commanding patrol	2·00	3·00

212 Black-crowned Night Heron

1994. Care for Nature. Herons. Multicoloured.

766	20c. Type **212**	50	60
767	50c. Green-heron ("Little Heron")	70	85
768	75c. Purple heron	85	1·00
769	$1 Grey heron	95	1·25

Nos. 766/9 were printed together, se-tenant, forming a composite design.

213 Traditional and Modern Education

1994. 175th Anniv of Modern Singapore. Mult.

770	20c. Type **213**	25	25
771	50c. Rickshaws and Mass Rapid Transit train	70	75
772	75c. Sampans and modern container port	1·00	1·40
773	$1 Victorian buildings and modern skyline	1·25	2·00
MS774	135×95 mm. Nos. 770/3	3·50	4·00

214 Balloons

1994. Self-adhesive Greetings Stamps. Multicoloured.

775	(20c.) Type **214**	55	80
776	(20c.) Fireworks	55	80
777	(20c.) Gift-wrapped parcel	55	80
778	(20c.) Bouquet of flowers	55	80
779	(20c.) Birthday cake	55	80

215 Logo and Globe

1994. 50th Anniv of I.C.A.O. Multicoloured.

780	20c. Type **215**	20	20
781	35c. Boeing 747 and Changi Airport control tower	60	60
782	75c. Projected hypersonic aircraft over airport	85	1·25
783	$2 Control tower, satellite and Boeing 747	2·00	3·25

1994. Reef Life (2nd series). Multicoloured design as T 209, but inscr "FOR LOCAL ADDRESSES ONLY".

784	(20c.) Blue-spotted stingray	25	30

No. 784 exists with either ordinary or self-adhesive gum.

216 Singapore International Convention and Exhibition Centre, Suntec City

1995. Opening of Singapore International Convention and Exhibition Centre. Multicoloured.

786	(20c.) Type **216**	20	20
787	75c. Suntec City skyline	85	85
788	$1 Temasek Boulevard	1·10	1·40
789	$2 Fountain Terrace	1·75	2·75

No. 786 is inscr "FOR LOCAL ADDRESSES ONLY".

217 "Love, LOVE, Love"

1995. Self-adhesive Greetings Stamps.

790	**217**	(20c.) multicoloured	90	1·00
791	-	(20c.) red and black	90	1·00
792	-	(20c.) multicoloured	90	1·00
793	-	(20c.) multicoloured	90	1·00
794	-	(20c.) multicoloured	90	1·00

DESIGNS: No. 791, "LOVE" forming spiral around heart; No. 792, "LOVE, LOVE"; No. 793, "Love" in four different languages; No. 794, Geometric symbols.

1995. "Singapore '95" International Stamp Exhibition. Orchids (5th issue). As T 187. Multicoloured.

795	$2 Vanda "Marlie Dolera"	2·00	3·00
796	$2 "Vanda limbata"	2·00	3·00
MS797	123×80 mm. Nos. 795/6 with sheet margins showing animals from Singapore Zoo	10·00	10·00

See also No. **MS**817.

218 Ribbons and "My Singapore, My Country, Happy Birthday"

1995. 30th Anniv of Independence. Multicoloured.

798	(22c.) Type **218**	20	20
799	50c. Chinese inscr and 1985 Housing and Development 50c. stamp (horiz)	65	80
800	75c. National anthem, Civil Aviation 20c. and inscr in Malay (horiz)	90	1·50
801	$1 National flag, 1986 Economic Development Board and inscr in Tamil	1·25	2·25
MS802	120×78 mm. Nos. 798/801	5·50	6·50

No. 798 is inscribed "For Local Addresses Only".

219 Rejoicing Crowd and 1945 B.M.A. $5 Stamp

1995. 50th Anniv of End of Second World War. Multicoloured.
803 (22c.) Type **219** 30 20
804 60c. Lord Mountbatten accepting Japanese surrender at Singapore and 1945 B.M.A. 15c. stamp 1·00 1·00
805 70c. Emergency food kitchen (horiz) 80 1·25
806 $2 Police road block during State of Emergency (horiz) 2·75 4·00
No. 803 is inscribed "For Local Addresses Only".

220 Yellow-faced Angelfish

1995. Marine Fishes. Multicoloured.
807 (22c.) Type **220** 35 25
808 60c. Harlequin sweetlips 80 1·00
809 70c. Lionfish 90 1·50
810 $1 Pennant coralfish ("Longfin bannerfish") 1·25 2·25
No. 807 is inscribed "For Local Addresses Only".

221 Envelope, Stamps and Museum

1995. Opening of Singapore Philatelic Museum. Each showing Museum. Multicoloured.
811 (22c.) Type **221** 50 25
812 50c. Stamps and stamp booklet 1·10 65
813 60c. Stamps and philatelic equipment 1·25 1·25
814 $2 Museum displays 3·25 5·50
No. 811 is inscribed "FOR LOCAL ADDRESSES ONLY".

222 Two, Four and Six Digit Post Codes

1995. Introduction of Six Digit Postal Codes. Mult.
815 (22c.) Type **222** 30 25
816 $2 Six empty post code boxes 2·25 3·50
No. 815 is inscribed "For local addresses only".

1995. "Singapore '95" International Stamp Exhibition. Orchids (6th issue). Sheet 123×80 mm, containing Nos. 795/6 with sheet margins showing Sentosa Gardens.
MS817 $2×2 multicoloured 8·00 9·00

223 "Tropical Fruits" (Georgette Chen Liying)

1995. Local Artists (2nd series). Multicoloured.
818 (22c.) Type **223** 30 25
819 30c. "Bali Beach" (Cheong Soo Pieng) 40 40
820 70c. "Gibbons" (Chen Wen Hsi) 80 1·25
821 $2 "Shi (Lion)" (Pan Shou) (22½×38½ mm) 2·25 3·75
No. 818 is inscribed "FOR LOCAL ADDRESSES ONLY".

224 Bukit Pasoh, Chinatown

1996. Architectural Conservation. Multicoloured.
822 (22c.) Type **224** 35 25
823 35c. Jalan Sultan, Kampong Glam 50 50
824 70c. Dalhousie Lane, Little India 80 1·25
825 $1 Supreme Court, Civic District 1·10 2·25
No. 822 is inscribed "FOR LOCAL ADDRESSES ONLY".

225 Pair of Rats

1996. Chinese New Year ("Year of the Rat"). Multicoloured.
826 (22c.) Type **225** 30 25
827 $2 Rat holding orange 3·00 4·00
No. 826 is inscribed "FOR LOCAL ADDRESSES ONLY".
See also Nos. **MS**832/3 and **MS**838.

226 The Straits of Singapore, 1794 (Thomas Jefferys)

1996. Old Maps. Multicoloured.
828 (22c.) Type **226** 35 25
829 60c. Singapore (19th-century) 65 75
830 $1 Singapore by James Duncan, 1835 1·00 1·50
831 $2 Singapore by J. B. Tassin, 1839 2·00 3·25
No. 828 is inscribed "FOR LOCAL ADDRESSES ONLY".

1996. "Indonesia 96" International Youth Stamp Exhibition, Bandung. Sheet 123×80 mm.
MS832 22c. As Type **225**; $2 No. 827 11·00 12·00

1996. "CHINA '96" 9th Asian International Stamp Exhibition, Peking. Sheet 123×80 mm.
MS833 22c. As Type **225**; $2 No. 827 11·00 12·00

227 17th-century Chinese Calligraphy by Zhang Ruitu and Museum Building

1996. Inauguration of Asian Civilizations Museum. Each including museum building. Multicoloured.
834 (22c.) Type **227** 35 25
835 60c. Javanese divination manuscript, 1842 70 70
836 70c. 19th-century temple hanging, South India 80 1·00
837 $2 17th to 19th-century calligraphic implements, Iran and Turkey 2·00 3·50
No. 834 is inscribed "FOR LOCAL ADDRESSES ONLY".

1996. "CAPEX '96" International Stamp Exhibition, Toronto. Sheet 123×80 mm.
MS838 22c. As Type **225**; $2 No. 827 13·00 14·00

228 "Children in Library" (Ivan Chang)

1996. Self-adhesive Greetings Stamps. "Courtesy". Children's Drawings. Multicoloured.
839 (22c.) Type **228** 30 30
840 35c. "Children crossing Road" (Cheong Kah Yin) 50 60
841 50c. "Waiting for Bus" (Jeannie Fong) 65 80
842 60c. "In the Rain" (Liew Cai Yun) 75 95
843 $1 "On the Train" (Yong Wan Quan) 1·25 1·60
MS844 200×130 mm. 22c. As Type **228** and Nos. 840/3 4·75 5·50
No. 839 is inscribed "For Local Addresses Only".

229 Wind Surfing and Dinghy Sailing

1996. Olympic Games, Atlanta. Multicoloured.
845 (22c.) Type **229** 35 25
846 60c. Tennis and football 90 80
847 70c. Pole vaulting and hurdling 90 1·10
848 $2 Diving and swimming 2·25 4·00
MS849 120×70 mm. 22c. As Type **229** and Nos. 846/8 4·00 5·50
No. 845 is inscribed "For Local Addresses Only".

230 "Cinnamomum iners"

1996. Singapore Trees. Multicoloured.
850 (22c.) Type **230** 30 25
851 60c. "Hibiscus tiliaceus" 70 90
852 70c. "Parkia speciosa" 80 1·25
853 $1 "Terminalia catappa" 1·25 1·75
No. 850 is inscribed "FOR LOCAL ADDRESSES ONLY".

231 Panmen Gate, Suzhou, China

1996. Singapore–China Joint Issue. Multicoloured.
854 (22c.) Type **231** 30 25
855 60c. Singapore waterfront 80 1·25
MS856 120×78 mm. 22c. As Type **231** and No. 855 1·40 2·00
No. 854 is inscribed "FOR LOCAL ADDRESSES ONLY".

232 Conference Logo

1996. Inaugural Ministerial Conference of World Trade Organization.
857 **232** (22c.) multicoloured 30 30
858 **232** 60c. multicoloured 70 1·25
859 **232** $1 multicoloured 1·25 1·90
860 **232** $2 multicoloured 2·25 3·75
No. 857 is inscribed "For local addresses Only".

233 Ox

1997. Chinese New Year ("Year of the Ox").
861 **233** (22c.) multicoloured 15 20
862 - $2 multicoloured 1·75 2·50
DESIGN: $2 Stylized ox.
No. 861 is inscribed "FOR LOCAL ADDRESSES ONLY".

1997. "HONG KONG '97" International Stamp Exhibition. Chinese New Year ("Year of the Ox"). sheet 123×80 mm.
MS863 22c. As Type **233**; $2 No. 862 6·00 7·00

234 Shuttlecock

1997. "SINGPEX '97" International Stamp Exhibition. Traditional Games. Multicoloured.
864 (22c.) Type **234** 20 20
865 35c. Marbles 40 40
866 60c. Tops 55 75
867 $1 Fivestones 80 1·50
MS868 140×75 mm. 22c. As Type **234** and Nos. 865/7 1·75 2·50
No. 864 is inscribed "For Local Addresses Only".

235 Bullock Cart **236** Taxi

1997. Transportation. Multicoloured. Ordinary or self-adhesive gum (No. 871), ordinary gum (others). (a) As T 235.
869 5c. Type **235** 15 50
870 20c. Bicycle (vert) 1·00 60
871 (22c.) Jinrickshaw (vert) 40 20
872 30c. Electric tram 1·00 30
873 35c. Trolley bus 1·25 30
874 40c. Trishaw (vert) 70 50
875 50c. Vintage car (vert) 1·00 45
876 60c. Horse-drawn carriage 1·50 50
877 70c. Fire engine 2·00 60
MS878 132×76 mm. 22c. As No. 871 and Nos. 869/70, 872/7 8·00 8·00

(b) As T 236.
879 $1 Type **236** 1·50 80
880 $2 Bus (43×24 mm) 3·50 1·60
881 $5 Mass Rapid Transit train 6·00 4·50
882 $10 Light Rapid Transit carriages (43×24 mm) 8·50 9·50
MS883 119×71 mm. Nos. 879/82 17·00 20·00
No. 871 is inscribed "For Local Addresses Only".

237 Man's Head

1997. Self-adhesive Greeting Stamps. "Friends". Multicoloured.
885 (22c.) Type **237** 45 60
886 (22c.) Hands holding umbrella 45 60
887 (22c.) Two emperor penguins 45 60
888 (22c.) Two butterflies 45 60
889 (22c.) Cup and saucer 45 60
890 (22c.) Large flower 45 60
891 (22c.) Candle 45 60
892 (22c.) Tree 45 60
893 (22c.) Jar with stars 45 60
894 (22c.) Simple telephone 45 60

Nos. 885/94 are inscribed "FOR LOCAL ADDRESSES ONLY".

1997. "Pacific '97" International Stamp Exhibition, San Francisco. sheet 123×80 mm, containing designs as Nos. 861/2.

MS895	22c. As Type **233**; $2 No. 862	8·00	9·00

238 Family with Car

1997. Renovation of Housing and Development Board Estates. Multicoloured.

896	(22c.) Type **238**	20	20
897	30c. Family at playground	30	35
898	70c. Couple walking through garden	60	80
899	$1 Family on balcony	80	1·50

No. 896 is inscribed "FOR LOCAL ADDRESSES ONLY".

239 Globe and Hand Clasp

1997. 30th Anniv of A.S.E.A.N. (Association of Southeast Asian Nations). Multicoloured.

900	(22c.) Type **239**	20	20
901	35c. Dancers, kite flying and decorated truck	35	40
902	60c. Dish aerial and map	55	70
903	$1 National landmarks	80	2·00

No. 900 is inscribed "FOR LOCAL ADDRESSES ONLY".

240 Flower and Tree ("Clean Environment")

1997. 25th Anniv of the Ministry of the Environment. Multicoloured.

904	(22c.) Type **240**	20	20
905	60c. Fish and river ("Clean Waters")	55	60
906	70c. Bird and sky ("Clean Air")	60	70
907	$1 Dustbin and block of flats ("Clean Homes")	80	1·25

No. 904 is inscribed "FOR LOCAL ADDRESSES ONLY".

241 "Drupa morum"

1997. Singapore—Thailand Joint Issue. Sea Shells. Multicoloured.

908	(22c.) Type **241**	20	20
909	35c. "Nerita chamaeleon"	30	40
910	60c. "Littoraria melanostoma"	45	60
911	$1 "Cryptospira elegans"	1·50	2·00
MS912	125×80 mm. 22c. As Type **241** and Nos. 909/11	1·75	2·50

No. 908 is inscribed "FOR LOCAL ADDRESSES ONLY".

1997. "Shanghai '97" International Stamp and Coin Exhibition. Sheet 123×80 mm.

MS913	22c. As Type **233**; $2 No. 862	4·25	5·50

242 Tiger

1998. Chinese New Year ("Year of the Tiger").

914	**242**	(22c.) multicoloured	15	20
915	-	$2 multicoloured	1·50	2·00

DESIGN: $2 Stylized tigers.

No. 914 is inscribed "FOR LOCAL ADDRESSES ONLY".

243 Pentaceratops

1998. Dinosaurs. Multicoloured. Self-adhesive. Imperf.

916	(22c.) Type **243**	35	45
917	(22c.) Apatosaurus	35	45
918	(22c.) Albertosaurus	35	45

Nos. 916/18 are inscribed "For Local Addresses Only".

244 Lesser Green Leafbird

1998. Songbirds. Multicoloured.

919	(22c.) Type **244**	35	20
920	60c. Magpie robin	70	65
921	70c. Straw-crowned bulbul ("Straw-headed bulbul")	80	80
922	$2 Yellow-bellied prinia	1·60	2·25

No. 919 is inscribed "For Local Addresses Only".

1998. "Israel 98" International Stamp Exhibition. Sheet 122×80 mm.

MS923	22c. As Type **242**; $2 No. 915	2·25	3·25

245 "Hello" in Yellow and Orange Bubble

1998. Self-adhesive Greetings Stamps. Multicoloured.

924	(22c.) Type **245**	50	65
925	(22c.) "hello" in red and yellow bubble	50	65
926	(22c.) "hello" in yellow and green bubble	50	65
927	(22c.) "Hello" in violet and blue bubble	50	65
928	(22c.) "Hello" in black, red and yellow bubble	50	65

Nos. 924/8 are inscribed "FOR LOCAL ADDRESSES ONLY".

246 Rhino Beetle

1998. 25th Anniv of Singapore Zoological Gardens and Launch of New "Fragile Forest" Display. Multicoloured. Self-adhesive.

929	(22c.) Type **246**	50	65
930	(22c.) Surinam horned frog	50	65
931	(22c.) Green iguana	50	65
932	(22c.) Atlas moth	50	65
933	(22c.) Giant scorpion	50	65
934	(22c.) Hissing cockroach	50	65
935	(22c.) Two-toed sloth	50	65
936	(22c.) Cobalt blue tarantula	50	65
937	(22c.) Archer fish	50	65
938	(22c.) Greater mousedeer	50	65

Nos. 929/38 are inscribed "FOR LOCAL ADDRESSES ONLY".

247 Students and Workers Demonstrating, 1955–59

1998. "The Singapore Story" Exhibition. Mult.

939	(22c.) Type **247**	25	20
940	60c. Self-government, 1959–63	55	55
941	$1 Creation of Malaysian Federation, 1961–65	80	90
942	$2 Celebrating Independence, 1965	1·60	2·25
MS943	214×105 mm. 22c. As Type **247** and Nos. 940/2 (sold at $7)	9·00	10·00

No. **MS**943, which also commemorates "SINGPEX '98" National Stamp Exhibition, was only available in a special folder.

No. 939 is inscribed "FOR LOCAL ADDRESSES ONLY".

248 "Phalaenopsis rosenstromii"

1998. Singapore–Australia Joint Issue. Orchids. Multicoloured.

944	(22c.) Type **248**	35	20
945	70c. "Arundina graminifolia"	80	65
946	$1 "Grammatophyllum speciosum"	85	90
947	$2 "Dendrobium phalaenopsis"	1·60	2·25
MS948	134×73 mm. 22c. As Type **248** and Nos. 945/7	3·75	4·50

No. 944 is inscribed "For Local Addresses Only".

249 "Canna" Hybrid

1998. Flowers of Singapore. Multicoloured.

949	(22c.) Type **249**	30	30
950	(22c.) "Caesalpinia pulcherrima"	30	30
951	(22c.) "Wedilia trilobata"	30	30
952	(22c.) "Dillenia suffruticosa"	30	30
953	35c. "Zephyranthes rosea"	45	50
954	35c. "Cassia alata"	45	50
955	60c. "Heliconia rostrata"	60	70
956	60c. "Allamanda cathartica"	60	70
MS957	206×82 mm. Nos. 949/56	2·25	2·75

Nos. 949/52 are inscribed "FOR LOCAL ADDRESSES ONLY".

250 Hari Raya Aidilfitri (Muslim)

1998. Festivals. Multicoloured.

958	(22c.) Type **250**	35	35
959	(22c.) Christmas	35	35
960	(22c.) Chinese New Year	35	35
961	(22c.) Deepavali (Hindu)	35	35
962	30c. Boy and decorations (Hari Raya Aidilfitri) (20×39 mm)	45	50
963	30c. Girl with holly (Christmas) (20×39 mm)	45	50
964	30c. Boy with lanterns (Chinese New Year) (20×39 mm)	45	50
965	30c. Girl with oil lamps (Deepavali) (20×39 mm)	45	50

Nos. 958/61 are inscribed "For Local Addresses Only" and come with either ordinary or self-adhesive gum.

Nos. 958/61 were printed together, se-tenant, forming a composite design.

1998. "Italia 98" International Stamp Exhibition, Milan. Sheet 123×80 mm.

MS970	22c. As Type **242**; $2 No. 915	2·50	3·50

251 Parliament House, 1827

1998. Historical Buildings. Multicoloured.

971	(22c.) Type **251**	30	20
972	70c. Chapel of former Convent of the Holy Infant Jesus, 1903	70	65
973	$1 Hill Street Building, 1934	85	95
974	$2 Sun Yat Sen Nanyang Memorial Hall, 1900	1·60	2·25

No. 971 is inscribed "For Local Addresses Only".

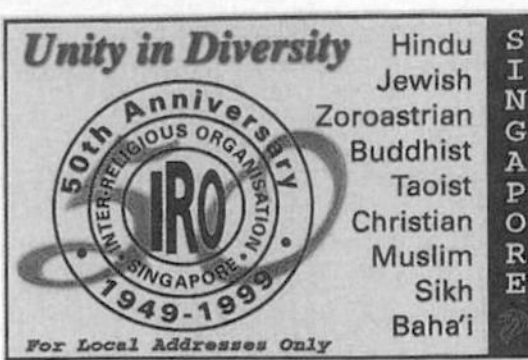

252 Anniversary Logo and List of Religions

1999. 50th Anniv of Inter-Religious Organization.

975	**252**	(22c.) multicoloured	30	20
976	**252**	60c. multicoloured	55	55
977	**252**	$1 multicoloured	85	1·10

No. 975 is inscribed "For Local Addresses Only".

253 Rabbit

1999. Chinese New Year ("Year of the Rabbit").

978	**253**	(22c.) multicoloured	25	20
979	-	$2 multicoloured	1·50	2·00

DESIGN: $2 Stylized rabbits.

No. 978 is inscribed "FOR LOCAL ADDRESSES ONLY".

254 Clipper, Tank Locomotive and Tongkang Junk

1999. Maritime Heritage. Multicoloured.

980	(22c.) Type **254**	40	20
981	70c. Twakow (barge) and Sampan Kotek (vert)	85	65
982	$1 Fujian junk (vert)	1·25	1·10
983	$2 Maduran golekkan (sailing vessel)	1·75	2·25
MS984	200×67 mm. 22c. As Type **254** and Nos. 981/3	3·50	4·00

No. **MS**984 also includes the "Australia '99" World Stamp Exhibition, Melbourne, emblem on the sheet margin.

No. 980 is inscribed "For Local Addresses Only".

1999. "iBRA '99" International Stamp Exhibtion, nuremberg. Sheet 123×80 mm.

MS985	22c. As Type **253**; $2 No. 979	2·00	2·75

255 Washing Lines ("Think of others")

1999. Self-adhesive Greeting Stamps. "Try a Little Kindness". Multicoloured.

986	(22c.) Type **255**	35	55
987	(22c.) Man throwing litter ("Do not litter")	35	55
988	(22c.) Girl feeding cat and dog ("Be kind to animals")	35	55
989	(22c.) Man watching television ("Be considerate")	35	55
990	(22c.) Boy putting money in collection tin ("Be generous")	35	55

Nos. 986/90 are inscribed "FOR LOCAL ADDRESSES ONLY".

256 Hong Kong Harbour

1999. Singapore–Hong Kong, China Joint Issue. Multicoloured.

991	(22c.) Type **256**	25	20
992	35c. Singapore skyline	45	40
993	50c. Giant Buddha, Lantau Island, Hong Kong	60	55
994	60c. Merlion statue, Sentosa Island, Singapore	70	75

995 70c. Street scene, Hong Kong 75 80
996 $1 Bugis Junction, Singapore 1·00 1·10
MS997 125×93 mm. 22c. As Type **256** and Nos. 992/6 3·25 4·00
No. 991 is inscribed "FOR LOCAL ADDRESSES ONLY".

1999. "PhilexFrance '99" International Stamp Exhibtion, Paris. Sheet 123×80 mm.
MS998 22c. As Type **253**; $2 No. 979 2·00 2·50

257 Peacock Butterfly

1999. Singapore–Sweden Joint Issue. Butterflies. Multicoloured.
999 (22c.) Type **257** 55 20
1000 70c. Blue pansy 1·00 65
1001 $1 Great egg-fly 1·25 95
1002 $2 Red admiral 2·00 2·50
MS1003 129×75 mm. 22c. As Type **257** and Nos. 1000/2 4·25 4·50
No. 999 is inscribed "FOR LOCAL ADDRESSES ONLY".

1999. "China '99" International Stamp Exhibition, Peking. sheet 123×80 mm.
MS1004 22c. As Type **253**; $2 As No. 979 2·25 2·75

258 Pres. Yusof bin Ishak

1999. Yusof bin Ishak (first President of Singapore) Commemoration.
1005 **258** $2 multicoloured 2·50 2·00

259 Green Turtle

1999. Amphibians and Reptiles. Multicoloured.
1006 (22c.) Type **259** 30 20
1007 60c. Green crested lizard 60 60
1008 70c. Copper-cheeked frog 70 70
1009 $1 Water monitor 90 1·25
No. 1006 is inscribed "For Local Addresses Only".

260 New Parliament House from North

1999. Opening of New Parliament House. Mult.
1010 (22c.) Type **260** 30 20
1011 60c. North-east view 60 60
1012 $1 South-east view 90 1·00
1013 $2 West view 1·60 2·25
No. 1010 is inscribed "For Local Addresses Only".
The lion's head emblem on these stamps is printed in optically variable ink which changes colour when viewed from different angles.

261 Sir Stamford Raffles and Sir Frank Swettenham (British Governers) and Raffles Museum

1999. New Millennium (1st issue). 20th Century Singapore. Multicoloured.
1014 (22c.) Type **261** 30 35
1015 (22c.) Past and present schooling 30 35
1016 35c. Street scene, 1900, and Samsui woman 45 55
1017 35c. Parliament (Government) 45 55
1018 60c. British surrender, 1942, and Lord Mountbatten celebrating Japanese surrender, 1945 60 70
1019 60c. Soldiers firing missile and fighter aircraft 60 70
1020 70c. Singapore River, 1902, and modern forms of transportation 70 80
1021 70c. Festival scenes 70 80
1022 $1 Housing, past and present 95 1·10
1023 $1 Skyscrapers 95 1·10
Nos. 1014/15 are inscribed "for Local addresses only".
See also Nos. 1027/30.

262 Dragon

2000. Chinese New Year ("Year of the Dragon"). Multicoloured.
1024 (22c.) Type **262** 25 20
1025 $2 Dragon curled around spheres 1·75 2·25
MS1026 105×65 mm. $10 As No. 1025 8·00 9·50
No. 1024 is inscribed "FOR LOCAL ADDRESSES ONLY".
No. **MS**1026 was only sold in a decorative hongbao (envelope).

263 Information Technology Equipment

2000. New Millennium (2nd issue). Singapore in 2000. Multicoloured.
1027 (22c.) Type **263** 20 20
1028 60c. Symbols of Arts and Culture 60 60
1029 $1 Heritage artifacts 95 1·10
1030 $2 Modern global communications 1·60 2·25
MS1031 140×75 mm. 22c. As Type **263** and Nos. 1028/30 2·75 3·75
No. 1027 is inscribed "For local addresses only".

264 Post Office from across Singapore River, 1854

2000. Opening of Singapore Post Centre. Postal Landmarks. Multicoloured.
1032 (22c.) Type **264** 25 20
1033 60c. General Post Office, c. 1873 60 60
1034 $1 G.P.O. Fullerton Building, 1928 95 1·00
1035 $2 Singapore Post Centre, 2000 1·90 2·25
MS1036 110×94 mm. 22c. As Type **264** and Nos. 1033/5 2·75 3·50
No. 1032 is inscribed "FOR LOCAL ADDRESSES ONLY".

2000. "Bangkok 2000" International Stamp Exhibition. Sheet 123×75 mm. Multicoloured.
MS1037 22c. As Type **262**; $2 No. 1025 1·75 2·25

265 "yipee"

2000. Self-adhesive Greetings Stamps. Multicoloured.
1038 (22c.) Type **265** 45 60
1039 (22c.) "yeah" 45 60
1040 (22c.) "hurray" 45 60
1041 (22c.) "yes" 45 60
1042 (22c.) "happy" 45 60
Nos. 1038/42 are inscribed "For Local Addresses Only".

2000. "The Stamp Show 2000" International Stamp Exhibition, London. Sheet, 123×75 mm, containing Nos. 1024/5. Multicoloured.
MS1043 22c. As Type **262**; $2 No. 1025 1·90 2·40

2000. "naba 2000" National Stamp Exhibition, St. Gallen, Switzerland. Sheet, 123×75 mm, containing Nos. 1024/5. Multicoloured.
MS1044 22c. As Type **262**; $2 No. 1025 1·90 2·40

266 Singapore River, 1920s

2000. "A Century on Singapore River". Showing scenes and common map section. Multicoloured.
1045 (22c.) Type **266** 35 40
1046 (22c.) South Boat Quay, 1930s 35 40
1047 (22c.) Social gathering, 1950s 35 40
1048 (22c.) Skyscrapers, 1980s 35 40
1049 (22c.) River Regatta, 1900s 35 40
1050 60c. Sampans at river mouth, 1990s 50 60
1051 60c. Stevedores, 1910s 50 60
1052 60c. Lighters, 1940s 50 60
1053 60c. Men at work on junk, 1960s 50 60
1054 60c. Unloading with crane, 1970s 50 60
Nos. 1045/9 are inscribed "For local addresses only".
Nos. 1045/54 were printed together, se-tenant, with the backgrounds forming a composite design.

267 "Future Lifestyle" (Liu Jiang Wen)

2000. "Stampin' the Future" (children's stamp design competition). Multicoloured.
1055 (22c.) Type **267** 25 20
1056 60c. "Future Homes" (Shaun Yew Chuan Bin) 60 60
1057 $1 "Home Automation" (Gwendolyn Soh) 90 1·00
1058 $2 "Floating City" (Dawn Koh) 1·60 2·25
MS1059 125×80 mm. Nos. 1055/8 3·00 3·50
No. 1055 is inscribed "FOR LOCAL ADDRESSES ONLY".

268 Archer Fish

2000. Wetland Wildlife. Multicoloured.
1060 (22c.) Type **268** 35 30
1061 (22c.) Smooth otter and cubs 35 30
1062 $1 White-collared kingfisher ("Collared Kingfisher") 1·40 1·50
1063 $1 Orange fiddler crab 1·40 1·50
MS1064 294×210 mm. Nos. 1060/3, both perf and imperf in se-tenant blocks of 4 5·50 6·50
Nos. 1060/1 are inscribed "For Local Addresses Only".
Nos. 1060/3 were printed together, se-tenant, with the backgrounds forming composite designs.

269 High Jump and Swimming

2000. Olympic Games, Sydney. Designs showing a sport within the outline of another. Multicoloured.
1065 (22c.) Type **269** 25 20
1066 60c. Discus and badminton 60 60
1067 $1 Hurdles and football 90 1·00
1068 $2 Gymnastics and table tennis 1·75 2·25
No. 1065 is inscribed "For local addresses only".

270 Chinese New Year

2000. Festivals. Multicoloured. (a) Normal gum.
1069 (22c.) Type **270** 55 55
1070 (22c.) Hari Raya Aidilfitri 55 55
1071 (22c.) Deepavali 55 55
1072 (22c.) Christmas 55 55
1073 30c. Chinese New Year (different) (diamond, 36×23 mm) 65 70
1074 30c. Hari Raya Aidilfitri (different) (diamond, 36×23 mm) 65 70
1075 30c. Deepavali (different) (diamond, 36×23 mm) 65 70
1076 30c. Christmas (different) (diamond, 36×23 mm) 65 70

(b) Self-adhesive.
1077 (22c.) Type **270** 75 85
1078 (22c.) As No. 1070 75 85
1079 (22c.) As No. 1071 75 85
1080 (22c.) As No. 1072 75 85
Nos. 1069/72 and 1077/80 are inscribed "FOR LOCAL ADDRESSES ONLY".

2000. "Guangzhou 2000" International Stamp and Coin Exhibition, China. Sheet 123×75 mm. Multicoloured.
MS1081 (22c.) As Type **262**; $2 No. 1025 2·25 2·75

271 Snake

2001. Chinese New Year ("Year of the Snake"). Mult.
1082 (22c.) Type **271** 30 20
1083 $2 Two snakes 2·00 2·50
No. 1082 is inscribed "FOR LOCAL ADDRESSES ONLY".

2001. "Hong Kong 2001" Stamp Exhibition. Sheet 123×75 mm. Multicoloured.
MS1084 22c. As Type **271**; $2 No. 1083 3·25 3·50

272 Tan Tock Seng

2001. Famous Citizens of Singapore. Multicoloured.
1085 $1 Type **272** 1·00 1·10
1086 $1 Eunos bin Abdullah 1·00 1·10
1087 $1 P. Govindasamy Pillai 1·00 1·10
1088 $1 Edwin John Tessensohn 1·00 1·10

273 People holding Hands ("Co-operation")

2001. 25th Anniv of Commonwealth Day. Mult.
1089 (22c.) Type **273** 25 20
1090 60c. People using computers ("Education") 60 60
1091 $1 Sporting activities ("Sports") 1·25 1·00
1092 $2 Dancers and musicians ("Arts and Culture") 1·75 2·25
No. 1089 is inscribed "FOR LOCAL ADDRESSES ONLY".

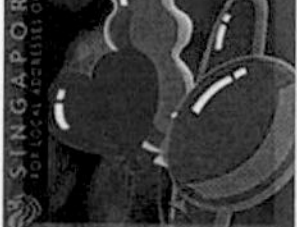

274 Balloons

2001. Self-adhesive Greetings Stamps. "Occasions". Multicoloured.
1093 (22c.) Type **274** 40 50
1094 (22c.) Stars 40 50
1095 (22c.) Tulips 40 50
1096 (22c.) Parcels 40 50
1097 (22c.) Musical instruments 40 50
Nos. 1093/7 are inscribed "FOR LOCAL ADDRESSES ONLY".

275 "Music" ("a")

2001. Arts Festival. Multicoloured.

1098	(22c.) Type **275**	25	20
1099	60c. "Painting" ("r")	55	45
1100	$1 "Dance" ("t")	90	1·00
1101	$2 "Theatre" ("s")	1·75	2·00

No. 1098 is inscribed "For Local Addresses Only".

2001. "BELGICA 2001" International Stamp Exhibtion, Brussels. Sheet 123×75 mm. Multicoloured.

MS1102	(22c) Type **271**; $2 No. 1083	3·25	3·50

276 Cockatiels **277**

2001. "Singpex '01" National Stamp Exhibition. Pets. (a) Multicoloured.

1103	(22c.) Type **276**	25	35
1104	(22c.) Fish in tank	25	35
1105	(22c.) Tortoise	25	35
1106	(22c.) Ducklings	25	35
1107	(22c.) Cat looking at mouse (24×34 mm)	25	35
1108	(22c.) Dog looking at fish in bowl (24×34 mm)	25	35
1109	50c. West Highland white terrier and bird (24×41 mm)	55	65
1110	50c. Two cats (24×41 mm)	55	65
1111	$1 Green-winged macaw and Senegal parrot (24×41 mm)	85	90
1112	$1 Cat in basket and rabbit (24×41 mm)	85	90

(b) T 277 and similar multicoloured frame. Self-adhesive.

1113	(22c.) Type **277** (24×24 mm)	30	30
1114	(22c.) As Type **277**, but 24×34 mm	30	30

Nos. 1103/8 and 1113/14 are inscribed "For local addresses only".

Nos. 1103/12 were printed together, se-tenant, forming a composite picture of household pets.

2001. "Philanippon '01" International Stamp Exhibition, Tokyo. Sheet 123×75 mm. Multicoloured.

MS1115	(22c.) Type **271**; $2 No. 1083	2·00	2·75

278 Young Ah Meng

2001. Orang Utan Conservation. Designs showing Ah Meng. Multicoloured. (a) Ordinary gum.

1116	(22c.) Type **278**	25	35
1117	60c. Ah Meng with mate	55	60
1118	$1 Ah Meng with offspring	85	95
1119	$1 Three generations of Ah Meng's family	85	95
MS1120	190×180 mm. Nos. 1116/19 (sold for $3.90)	4·75	5·00

(b) Self-adhesive.

1121	(22c.) Type **278**	50	50

Nos. 1116 and 1121 are inscribed "For Local Addresses Only".

No. **MS**1120 is in the shape of a seated orang utan.

279 *Melastoma malabathricum*

2001. Singapore–Switzerland Joint Issue. Flowers. Multicoloured.

1122	(22c.) Type **279**	25	20
1123	60c. *Leontopodium alpinum*	60	60
1124	$1 *Saraca cauliflora*	90	1·10
1125	$2 *Gentiana clusii*	1·75	2·50
MS1126	98×68 mm. Nos. 1122/5	3·25	4·00

No. 1122 is inscribed "FOR LOCAL ADDRESSES ONLY".

Two types of 50c.:

I. Inscribed "xanthometopon" in error.

II. Correctly inscribed "xanthometapon".

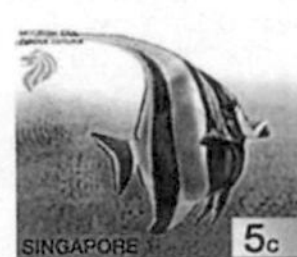

280 Moorish Idol

2001. Tropical Marine Fish. Multicoloured. Size 26×19 mm. (a) Ordinary gum.

1127	5c. Type **280**	15	30
1128	20c. Thread-finned butterflyfish	45	20
1129	(22c.) Copper-banded butterflyfish	45	20
1130	30c. Pearl-scaled butterflyfish	50	25
1130a	31c. Eight-banded butterflyfish	60	25
1130b	(31c.) Eight-banded butterflyfish	60	25
1131	40c. Melon butterflyfish ("Rainbow Butterflyfish")	85	30
1132	50c. Yellow-faced angelfish	1·00	35
1133	60c. Emperor angelfish	1·25	45
1134	70c. Sail-finned tang	1·50	50
1135	80c. Palette surgeonfish ("Palette Tang")	1·60	55
MS1136	149×90 mm. Nos. 1127/35	7·00	8·00

(b) Size 29×24½ mm.

1137	$1 Blue turquoise	2·00	70
1138	$2 Brown discus	3·00	1·40
1139	$5 Red alenguer	6·00	3·50
1140	$10 Red turquoise	11·00	8·00
MS1141	128×75 mm. Nos. 1137/40	22·00	24·00

(c) Self-adhesive.

1142	(22c.) As No. 1129	30	35
1142c	(23c.) As No. 1129	30	35

Nos. 1129 and 1142 are inscribed "FOR LOCAL ADDRESSES ONLY". No. 1130b is inscribed "2nd Local". No. 1142c is inscribed "1st Local".

281 Horse

2002. Chinese New Year ("Year of the Horse"). Multicoloured.

1143	(22c.) Type **281**	25	20
1144	(22c.) As Type 290 but horse embossed in silver	1·00	1·50
1145	$2 Two horses rearing	1·40	1·60
1146	$2 As No. 1145, but horses embossed in gold	3·00	4·00

Nos. 1143/4 are inscribed "FOR LOCAL ADDRESSES ONLY" and were sold for 22c. each.

282 Long-tailed Porcupine

2002. Natural History Drawings from The William Farquhar Collection (1st series). Animals, Reptiles, Fruits and Plants. Multicoloured. Ordinary or self-adhesive gum.

1147	(22c.) Type **282**	35	40
1148	(22c.) Tapir	35	40
1149	(22c.) "Landak Kelubu"	35	40
1150	(22c.) Slow loris	35	40
1151	(22c.) "Biawak Tanah" (lizard)	35	40
1152	(22c.) Flying fox	35	40
1153	(22c.) Small-clawed otter	35	40
1154	(22c.) "Biawak Pasir" (lizard)	35	40
1155	(22c.) "Tupai Kerawak" (mouse) (vert)	35	40
1156	(22c.) Mouse deer (vert)	35	40
1157	(22c.) "Buah rumenia"	35	40
1158	(22c.) "Manggis Hutan"	35	40
1159	(22c.) "Cempedak"	35	40
1160	(22c.) "Bunga Dedap"	35	40
1161	(22c.) "Jeringau" (vert)	35	40
1162	(22c.) "Rotang" (vert)	35	40
1163	(22c.) "Tuba" (vert)	35	40
1164	(22c.) "Tebu Gagak" (vert)	35	40
1165	(22c.) "Temu Kunci" (vert)	35	40
1166	(22c.) "Rambutan" (vert)	35	40

Nos. 1147/56 (animals and reptiles), 1157/66 (fruits and plants), and are inscribed "For Local Addresses Only". Each stamp was sold for 22c.

2002. Natural History Drawings from The William Farquhar Collection (2nd series). Birds and Fish. As T 282. Multicoloured. Ordinary or self-adhesive gum.

1187	(22c.) "Burung Gaji-gaji"	35	40
1188	(22c.) "Kuau Cermin"	35	40
1189	(22c.) "Ayam Kolam"	35	40
1190	(22c.) "Kelengking"	35	40
1191	(22c.) "Burung Kuang"	35	40
1192	(22c.) "Puhung"	35	40
1193	(22c.) "Burung Kunyit" (vert)	35	40
1194	(22c.) "Burung Pacap Sayat Biru" (vert)	35	40
1195	(22c.) "Burung Murai" (vert)	35	40
1196	(22c.) "Burung Berek-Berek" (vert)	35	40
1197	(22c.) "Ikan Tenggiri Papan"	35	40
1198	(22c.) "Ikan Kertang"	35	40
1199	(22c.) "Ikan Kakatua"	35	40
1200	(22c.) "Ikan Bambangan"	35	40
1201	(22c.) "Ikan Parang"	35	40
1202	(22c.) "Ikan Buntal Pisang"	35	40
1203	(22c.) "Ikan Ketang"	35	40
1204	(22c.) "Pari Hitam"	35	40
1205	(22c.) "Telinga Gajah"	35	40
1206	(22c.) "Ikan Babi"	35	40

Nos. 1187/96 (birds), 1197/206 (fish), and are inscribed "For Local Addresses Only". Each stamp was sold for 22c.

283 Lego Town

2002. Toys. Multicoloured.

1227	(22c.) Type **283**	35	20
1228	60c. Cowboy, Indian, soldier and robot	75	55
1229	70c. Dolls	80	95
1230	$1 Racing cars and bike	1·10	1·25

No. 1227 is inscribed "For local addresses only" and was sold for 22c.

284 Red-throated Sunbird

2002. Singapore – Malaysia Joint Issue. Birds. Multicoloured.

1231	(22c.) Type **284**	40	20
1232	40c. Asian fairy bluebird	75	50
1233	$1 Black-naped oriole	1·00	1·00
1234	$2 White-bellied woodpecker	1·75	2·50
MS1235	135×94 mm Nos. 1231/4	4·25	4·50

2002. "Philakorea 2002" International Stamp Exhibition, Seoul.

MS1236	123×75 mm. Nos. 1143 and 1145	2·50	3·00

285 Kolam (doorstep decoration), Deepavali

286 Kolam (doorstep decoration), Deepavali

2002. Festivals. Multicoloured. (a) T 285. Ordinary or self-adhesive gum.

1237	(22c.) Type **285**	70	70
1238	(22c.) Ketupat (rice cake) wrapper, Hari Raya Aidilfitri	70	70
1239	(22c.) Snowflake in bauble, Christmas	70	70
1240	(22c.) Fish paper decoration, Chinese New Year	70	70

(b) T 286.

1245	50c. Type **286**	90	1·00
1246	50c. Ketupat (rice cake) wrapper, Hari Raya Aidilfitri	90	1·00
1247	50c. Snowflake in bauble, Christmas	90	1·00
1248	50c. Fish paper decoration, Chinese New Year	90	1·00

Nos. 1237/44 are inscribed "For Local Addresses Only" and each stamp was sold for 22c.

The central designs on Nos. 1237/48 are foil holograms.

287 Flame of the Forest

2002. Heritage Trees Scheme. Multicoloured.

1249	(22c.) Type **287**	30	20
1250	60c. Rain Tree	70	50
1251	$1 Kapok Tree	1·00	1·40
1252	$1 Tembusu	1·00	1·40

No. 1249 also comes self-adhesive.

Nos. 1249 and 1253 are inscribed "FOR LOCAL ADDRESSES ONLY" and were sold for 22c.

288 Esplanade, Performing Arts Centre, Marina Bay

2002. Esplanade, Theatres on the Bay. Esplanade from different angles. Multicoloured.

1254	(22c.) Type **288**	30	20
1255	60c. With brown background	70	50
1256	$1 Single shell of Esplanade	1·00	1·00
1257	$2 Aerial view of both shells	2·00	2·50
MS1258	104×80 mm. Nos. 1254/7	3·50	4·00

289 Two Yachts

2002. Singapore-A Global City. (1st series). Leisure and Lifestyle. Multicoloured.

1259	$2 Type **289**	2·00	2·25
1260	$2 Conductor's hands and baton	2·00	2·25
MS1261	135×95 mm. Nos. 1259/60	5·00	6·00

See also Nos. 1277/**MS**1279 and 1405/**MS**1407.

290 Goat

2003. Chinese New Year ("Year of the Goat"). Multicoloured.

1262	(22c.) Type **290**	30	20
1263	$2 Goat butting tree	2·00	2·50

No. 1262 is inscribed "FOR LOCAL ADDRESSES ONLY" and was sold for 22c.

291 Empress Place Building as Government Offices

2003. Opening of Asian Civilizations Museum in Empress Place Building. Multicoloured.

1264	(22c.) Type **291**	35	20
1265	60c. Empress Place Building as Registrar's Office	80	50
1266	$1 Empress Place Museum	1·25	1·25

1267 $2 Empress Place Building, as Asian Civilizations Museum 2·50 3·00

No. 1264 is inscribed "For local addresses only" and was sold for 22c.

292 Tarsier

2003. Creatures of the Night. Multicoloured.

1268 (22c.) Type **292** 35 20
1269 40c. Barn owl 85 50
1270 $1 Bablrusa 1·10 1·25
1271 $2 Clouded leopard 2·25 2·75
MS1272 136×94 mm. Nos. 1268/71 4·00 4·50

No. 1268 is inscribed "FOR LOCAL ADDRESSES ONLY" and was sold for 22c.

293 Community Policewomen and Block of Flats

2003. Singapore Police Force. Multicoloured No. 1273 is inscribed "For Local Addresses Only" and was sold at 22c.

1273 (22c.) Type **293** 45 20
1274 40c. Traffic policeman with motor-cycle 80 50
1275 $1 Maritime policeman and launch 1·75 1·50
1276 $2 Singapore police on U.N. peacekeeping duties 2·75 2·75

294 Satellite

2003. Singapore–A Global City (2nd series). Communications and Technology. Multicoloured.

1277 $2 Type **294** 2·00 2·25
1278 $2 Robot 2·00 2·25
MS1279 135×95 mm. Nos. 1277/8 4·00 4·50

295 Cheshire Cat ("Joy!")

2003. Greetings Stamps. "Joy and Caring". Multicoloured. Ordinary or self-adhesive gum.

1280 (22c.) Type **295** 30 40
1281 (22c.) Heart with smiling face ("joy!") 30 40
1282 (22c.) Teddy bear ("joy!") 30 40
1283 (22c.) Woman laughing ("joy") 30 40
1284 (22c.) Ostrich ("joy!") 30 40
1285 (22c.) Apple ("caring") 30 40
1286 (22c.) Hand with painted heart ("Helping Hands") 30 40
1287 (22c.) Multicoloured hearts ("To-getherness") 30 40
1288 (22c.) Daisy ("Beauty of a caring heart") 30 40
1289 (22c.) Night sky ("KEEPING IN TOUCH KEEPS US GOING") 30 40

Nos. 1280/9 are inscribed "For local addresses only", and were sold for 22c. each.

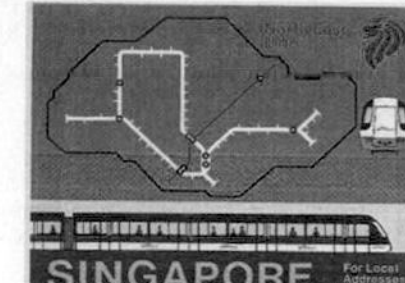

296 Map of Singapore Mass Rapid Transit System

2003. Opening of North East Line of Singapore Mass Rapid Transit System. Multicoloured.

1300 (22c.) Type **296** 40 20
1301 60c. Passengers 80 45
1302 $2 Control centre 2·50 3·00
MS1303 135×93 mm. 10c. Type **169**; 60c. As No. 573; $2 As No. 574 and Nos. 1300/2 5·50 6·00

No. 1300 is inscribed "For Local Addresses Only" and were sold at 22c. each.

297 National Flag

2003. National Day. Multicoloured.

1304 (22c.) Type **297** 30 20
1305 60c. *Vanda* "Miss Joaquim" 75 45
1306 $1 "Merlion" statue and Singapore skyline 1·10 1·00
1307 $2 Children 2·00 2·50
MS1308 140×75 mm. Nos. 1304/7 3·75 4·00

No. 1305 is inscribed "For local addresses only" and were sold for 22c. each.

298 Alouette III (helicopter)

2003. Centenary of Powered Flight. Multicoloured. Ordinary or self-adhesive gum.

1309 (22c.) Type **298** 40 40
1310 (22c.) E-2C Hawkeye 40 40
1311 (22c.) Hawker Hunter 40 40
1312 (22c.) Super Puma AS-332M (helicopter) 40 40
1313 (22c.) Hercules C-130H 40 40
1314 (22c.) F-16 C/D Fighting Falcon 40 40
1315 (22c.) AH-64D Apache (helicopter) 40 40
1316 (22c.) KC-135R Stratotanker 40 40
1317 (22c.) Cessna 172 40 40
1318 (22c.) F-5E Tiger II 40 40
1319 (22c.) A340-500 40 40
1320 (22c.) B747-400 40 40
1321 (22c.) B777-200 40 40
1322 (22c.) B747-400 Freighter 40 40
1323 (22c.) A320 40 40
1324 (22c.) Concorde 40 40
1325 (22c.) B737-100 40 40
1326 (22c.) Comet IV 40 40
1327 (22c.) Viscount 40 40
1328 (22c.) Airspeed Consul 40 40
MS1329 282×188 mm. Nos. 1309/28 7·00 7·00

Nos. 1309/28, and are inscribed "For local addresses only" and were sold at 22c. each.

2003. "Bangkok 2003" World Stamp Exhibition, Thailand. Sheet 123×75 mm. Multicoloured.

MS1350 (22c.) Type **290**; $2 No. 1263 2·75 3·50

299 Singapore Botanic Gardens

2003. Parks and Gardens. Multicoloured. (a) Ordinary gum.

1351 (22c.) Type **299** 40 20
1352 60c. Fort Canning Park 75 50
1353 $1 Marina City Park 1·40 1·60
1354 $1 Stork's nest, Sungei Buloh Wetland Reserve 1·40 1·60

(b) Self-adhesive gum.

1355 (22c.) Type **299** 40 45

Nos. 1351 and 1355 are inscribed "FOR LOCAL ADDRESSES ONLY" and were sold for 22c.

2003. "China 2003" International Stamp Exhibition, Mianyang. Sheet 122×75 mm.

MS1356 (22c.) Type **290**; $2 No. 1263 2·75 3·50

300 Monkey with Heart

2004. Chinese New Year ("Year of the Monkey"). Multicoloured.

1357 (23c.) Type **300** 40 30
1358 $2 Two monkeys 2·25 2·50

No. 1357 is inscribed "FOR LOCAL ADDRESSES ONLY" and was sold for 22c.

2004. Hong Kong 2004 International Stamp Exhibition. Sheet 123×75 mm.

MS1359 (23c.) Type **300**; $2 No. 1358 3·00 3·50

301 "Farmer's House" (Liu Kang)

2004. Paintings by Liu Kang and Ong Kim Seng. Multicoloured. Ordinary or self-adhesive gum.

1360 (23c.) Type **301** 40 40
1361 (23c.) "Artist and Model" (Liu Kang) 40 40
1362 (23c.) "Lanterns Galore" (Liu Kang) 40 40
1363 (23c.) "Enjoying a Smoke, Kashmir" (Liu Kang) 40 40
1364 (23c.) "Life by the River" (Liu Kang) 40 40
1365 (23c.) "Tenth Trip up to Huang-shan" (Liu Kang) 40 40
1366 (23c.) "My Young Wife" (Liu Kang) (vert) 40 40
1367 (23c.) "Kek Lok Si, Penang" (Liu Kang) (vert) 40 40
1368 (23c.) "Souri" (Liu Kang) (vert) 40 40
1369 (23c.) "Siesta in Bali" (Liu Kang) (vert) 40 40
1370 (23c.) "Kampong Tengah, Singapore" (Ong Kim Seng) 40 40
1371 (23c.) "Gyantse Market" (Ong Kim Seng) 40 40
1372 (23c.) "Sebatu Spring, Bali" (Ong Kim Seng) 40 40
1373 (23c.) "Jetty, Bangkok" (Ong Kim Seng) 40 40
1374 (23c.) "Resort, Bali" (Ong Kim Seng) 40 40
1375 (23c.) "Dance Studio, Bali" (Ong Kim Seng) 40 40
1376 (23c.) "Telok Ayer Market" (Ong Kim Seng) 40 40
1377 (23c.) "Kathmandu, Nepal" (Ong Kim Seng) 40 40
1378 (23c.) "Portofino, Italy" (Ong Kim Seng) (vert) 40 40
1379 (23c.) "Boats at Rest" (Ong Kim Seng) (vert) 7·00 7·00

Nos. 1360/79 are inscribed "For local addresses only" and were sold for 23c. each.

302 "Harmony" Sculpture and Suzhou Industrial Park

2004. 10th Anniv of Suzhou Industrial Park.

1400 **302** 60c. multicoloured 1·25 1·00

303 Colonial and Modern Buildings

2004. Singapore Skyline. Multicoloured.

1401 (23c.) Type **303** 40 20
1402 60c. Merlion statue and waterfront 1·00 60
1403 70c. Singapore skyline 1·10 1·40
MS1404 Two sheets, each 113×80 mm. (a) $1 Singapore from the Roads, c. 1900 (95×35 mm). (b) $5 Singapore skyline, 2004 (95×35 mm) Set of 2 sheets 7·50 8·50

No. 1401 is inscribed "1st Local" and was sold for 23c.

304 Containers

2004. Singapore—A Global City (3rd series). Trade and Industry. Multicoloured.

1405 $2 Type **304** 2·50 2·75
1406 $2 Oil refinery 2·50 2·75
MS1407 135×95 mm. Nos. 1405/6 and double stamp-size label 5·00 5·50

305 Football Field

2004. Centenary of FIFA (Federation Internationale de Football Association). Multicoloured.

1408 30c. Type **305** 40 25
1409 60c. Football 80 50
1410 $1 Football shirt 1·25 1·00
1411 $2 World map 3·00 3·25

306 Three Candles (Deepavali)

2004. Festivals. Multicoloured. Ordinary or self-adhesive gum (23c).

1412 (23c.) Type **306** 35 35
1413 (23c.) One candle (Hari Raya Aidilfitri) 35 35
1414 (23c.) Toy Father Christmas and Rudolph (Christmas) 35 35
1415 (23c.) Plum blossom and oranges (Chinese New Year) 35 35
1416 50c. Woman and oil lamp (Deepavali) 65 75
1417 50c. Girl holding sparkler (Hari Raya Aidilfitri) 65 75
1418 50c. Carol singers (Christmas) 65 75
1419 50c. Woman wearing orange kimono 65 75

Nos. 1412/19 are inscribed "1st LOCAL" and were sold at 23c. each.

307 Column, City Hall

2004. National Day. Monuments. Multicoloured.

1424 (23c.) Type **307** 40 50
1425 (23c.) City Hall (41×27 mm) 40 50
1426 30c. Concert Hall bell tower 50 60
1427 30c. Victoria Theatre and Concert Hall (41×27 mm) 50 60
1428 60c. Dome of courthouse 90 1·25
1429 60c. Supreme Court (41×27 mm) 90 1·25
1430 $1 Detail of gate, the Istana 1·40 1·75
1431 $1 The Istana (41×27 mm) 1·40 1·75
MS1432 140×70 mm. Nos. 1425, 1427, 1429 and 1431 2·75 3·50

Nos. 1424/5 are inscribed "1st Local" and were sold for 23c. each.

308 Running

2004. Olympic Games, Athens, Greece. Designs showing Olympic sports depicted on pebbles. Multicoloured.

1433	(23c.) Type **308**	40	20
1434	30c. Swimming	55	25
1435	$1 Weight-lifting	1·40	1·10
1436	$2 Sailing	2·75	3·25

2004. World Stamp Championship, Singapore. Sheet 161×85 mm containing Nos. 1259/60, 1277/8 and 1405/6. Multicoloured.

MS1437	$2 Containers; $2 Oil refinery; $2 Two yachts; $2 Conductor's hands and baton; $2 Satellite; $2 Robot	14·00	16·00

309 Linked Wrists and Singapore Post Centre

2004. 150th Anniv of Introduction of Stamps. Designs showing early Singapore stamps and postmarks. Multicoloured.

1438	(23c.) Type **309**	40	20
1439	60c. King George VI and General Post Office, Fullerton Building	90	55
1440	$1 King Edward VII and General Post Office	1·40	1·10
1441	$2 Queen Victoria and the Post Office, Singapore River	2·25	2·75
MS1442	135×94 mm. Nos. 1438/41	4·50	4·75

No. 1438 is inscribed "1st Local" and was sold for 23c.

310 Seashore Nutmeg

2004. Wildlife of Chek Jawa. Multicoloured. Ordinary gum.

1443	(23c.) Type **310**	65	65
1444	(23c.) Oriental pied hornbill	65	65
1445	$1 Knobbly Sea stars	1·50	1·50
1446	$1 Common seahorses	1·50	1·50

311 Rooster

2004. Self-adhesive.

1447	(23c.) Type **310**	40	50
1448	(23c.) Oriental pied hornbill	40	50

Nos. 1443/6 were printed together, se-tenant, the backgrounds forming a composite design.

Nos. 1443/4 and 1447/8 were each inscribed "1st Local" and sold for 23c. each.

312 Balloon Dog

2005. Chinese New Year ("Year of the Rooster"). Multicoloured.

1449	(23c.) Type **311**	40	20
1450	$2 Rooster and hen	2·75	3·25

No. 1449 is inscribed "1st Local" and was sold for 23c.

2005. Greetings. Multicoloured. (a) Ordinary gum.

1451	(23c.) Type **312**	40	45
1452	(23c.) Lily	40	45
1453	(23c.) Gift box	40	45
1454	(23c.) Love heart and bears flower arrangement	40	45
1455	(23c.) Candle	40	45

(b) Size 30×25 mm. Self-adhesive.

1456	(23c.) Candle	35	45
1457	(23c.) Love heart and bears flower arrangement	35	45
1458	(23c.) Gift box	35	45
1459	(23c.) Lily	35	45
1460	(23c.) Balloon dog	35	45

Nos. 1451/60 were each inscribed "1st Local" and sold for 23c.

313 *Thumbelina*

2005. Birth Bicentenary of Hans Christian Andersen (artist and children's writer). Multicoloured.

1461	(23c.) Type **313**	40	20
1462	60c. *The Ugly Duckling*	70	55
1463	$1 *The Emperor's New Clothes*	1·25	1·25
1464	$2 *The Little Mermaid*	2·25	2·75
MS1465	200×67 mm. Nos. 1461/4	4·25	4·50

No. 1461 was inscribed "1st Local" and initially sold for 23c.

314 National University of Singapore Monument and Globe

2005. Centenary of National University of Singapore. Multicoloured.

1466	(23c.) Type **314**	40	20
1467	60c. Students	70	55
1468	70c. Dancers and sculpture outside building	80	90
1469	$1 Science student and equipment	1·25	1·40

2005. Pacific Explorer 2005 World Stamp Expo, Sydney. Sheet 123×75 mm. Multicoloured.

MS1469a	(23c) Type **311**; $2 Rooster and hen	4·50	4·75

315 Istana Kampong Gelam (Malay Heritage Centre)

2005. Malay Heritage Centre. Multicoloured.

1470	(2nd.) Type **315**	40	20
1471	60c. Fountain pen and seal	70	55
1472	$1 Mandolin	1·25	1·25
1473	$2 Sail boat	2·25	2·75

No. 1470 was inscribed "2nd Local" and initially sold for 31c.

316 Admiral Zheng He

2005. 600th Anniv of the Voyages of Admiral Zheng He. Multicoloured.

1474	(23c.) Type **316**	40	35
1475	(23c.) Three sailing ships	40	35
1476	60c. Four sailing ships	80	70
1477	$1 Sailing ships near port	1·40	1·60

Nos. 1474/5 were inscribed "1st Local" and initially sold for 23c.

317 Football, Table Tennis and Cycling

2005. 117th International Olympic Committee Session. Each showing the five competing cities and flight paths to Singapore. Multicoloured.

1478	(23c.) Type **317**	50	25
1479	50c. Athletics, tennis and basketball	70	50
1480	60c. Football, tennis and javelin throwing	75	65
1481	$1 Gymnastics and athletics	1·10	1·40

No. 1478 was inscribed "1st Local" and initially sold for 23c.

318 Smiling Stickmen (needlework)

2005. National Day. "Fabric of the Nation". Showing needlework by Singaporeans. Multicoloured. Ordinary or self-adhesive gum.

1482	(23c.) Type **318**	30	40
1483	(23c.) Hearts on patches	30	40
1484	(23c.) Smiling yellow flower	30	40
1485	(23c.) Round Tower	30	40
1486	(23c.) Red orchid	30	40
1487	(23c.) Sun, rainbow and cloud	30	40
1488	(23c.) "Peace"	30	40
1489	(23c.) Outline of Singapore with red heart inside	30	40
1490	(23c.) White orchid	30	40
1491	(23c.) Red heart with orange flowers inside	30	40
1492	(23c.) "Happy Birthday"	30	40
1493	(23c.) Two hands	30	40
1494	(23c.) Cats and dogs	30	40
1495	(23c.) Stars	30	40
1496	(23c.) Washing on lines	30	40
1497	(23c.) Plane and patchwork clouds	30	40
1498	(23c.) Patchwork quarters	30	40
1499	(23c.) Plate with food	30	40
1500	(23c.) Hearts	30	40
1501	(23c.) Skyline	30	40
1502	(23c.) "1" and flowers	30	40
1503	(23c.) Four children and jigsaw pieces	30	40
1504	(23c.) Four heads around flag	30	40
1505	(23c.) Rainbow and clouds	30	40
1506	(23c.) Face upturned amongst bowed heads	30	40
1507	(23c.) Four butterflies	30	40
1508	(23c.) Cross-stitch	30	40
1509	(23c.) Heart-shaped fruit	30	40
1510	(23c.) Frog	30	40
1511	(23c.) Bird kites	30	40
1512	(23c.) Four hands around yellow heart	30	40
1513	(23c.) Skyline and "Singapore My Home"	30	40
1514	(23c.) Green orchid	30	40
1515	(23c.) Patchwork hearts as tree	30	40
1516	(23c.) "I", heart and outline of Singapore	30	40
1517	(23c.) Hand and buttons	30	40
1518	(23c.) "Singapore", hills and heart	30	40
1519	(23c.) Four hearts in quarters	30	40
1520	(23c.) Hearts, stars and people in quarters	30	40
1521	(23c.) "The Pledge"	30	40
MS1522	62×90 mm. $1 Needlework designs (39×60 mm)	1·40	1·60

All were inscribed "1st Local" and initially sold for 23c.

2005. TAIPEI 2005 International Stamp Exhibition. Sheet 123×75 mm. Multicoloured.

MS1562a	(23c.) Type **311**; $2 Rooster and hen	4·50	4·75

319 Belgian Centre for Comic Strip Art, Brussels

2005. Architecture. Multicoloured.

1563	(23c.) Type **319**	40	20
1564	60c. Kandahar Street	70	55
1565	$1 Bukit Pasoh Road	1·25	1·25
1566	$2 Museum of Musical Instruments, Belgium	2·25	2·75
MS1567	170×95 mm. Nos. 1563/6	4·25	4·50

No. 1563 was inscribed "1st Local" and initially sold for 23c.

Stamps of the same design were issued by Belgium.

320 Colugo

2005. HSBC Tree Top Walk, Central Catchment Nature Reserve. Multicoloured. Ordinary gum.

1568	(23c.) Type **320**	50	50
1569	60c. Fruits of Singapore adenia (climbing vine)	90	90
1570	$1 Red-crowned barbet (bird)	1·50	1·75
1571	$1 Common tree nymph (butterfly)	1·50	1·75

No. 1568 also come self-adhesive.

Nos. 1568/71 were printed together, se-tenant, forming a composite background design showing rainforest and tree top walk.

321 Dog chasing ball

2006. Chinese New Year ("Year of the Dog"). Multicoloured.

1573	(23c.) Type **321**	45	20
1574	$2 Two dogs	2·25	2·75

322 "White Cloud"

2006. Art by Tan Swie Hian. Multicoloured.

1575	(23c.) Type **322**	40	45
1576	(23c.) "Ganges"	40	45
1577	(23c.) "Soaring over the Flower Field"	40	45
1578	(23c.) "Kuta is a Song"	40	45
1579	(23c.) "The Winged Steed" (sculpture)	40	45
1580	50c. "Black Panther (pine)" (29×59 mm)	55	65
1581	50c. "Gingko (Male)" (29×59 mm)	55	65
1582	50c. "White Elephant" (29×59 mm)	55	65
1583	50c. "Summer Lotus" (29×59 mm)	55	65
1584	50c. "Water Dhyana" (29×59 mm)	55	65
MS1585	62×90 mm. $2 Calligraphy (40×59 mm)	2·75	3·00

Nos. 1575/9 were inscribed "1st LOCAL" and initially sold for 23c.

323 Indo-Pacific Bottlenose Dolphin

2006. Undersea World. Sea Mammals. Multicoloured.

1586	(23c.) Type **323**	40	20
1587	(31c.) Indo-Pacific hump-backed dolphin	50	30
1588	$1 Finless porpoise	1·25	1·25
1589	$2 Dugong	2·50	3·00
MS1590	140×74 mm. Nos. 1586/9	4·25	4·50

(b) Self-adhesive.

1591	(23c.) As No. 1586	35	35

No. 1586/7 are inscribed "1ST LOCAL" and "2ND LOCAL" and were initially sold for 23c. and 31c. respectively.

324 Chinese New Year **325** Chinese New Year

2006. Festivals. Multicoloured. (a) Ordinary gum. (i) As T 324.

1592	(23c.) Type **324**	35	35
1593	(23c.) Christmas	35	35
1594	(23c.) Deepavali	35	35
1595	(23c.) Hari Raya Aidilfitri	35	35

(ii) As T 325.

1596	50c. Type **325**	60	70
1597	50c. Christmas	60	70
1598	50c. Deepavali	60	70
1599	50c. Hari Raya Aidilfitri	60	70

(b) Self-adhesive. As T 324.

1600	(23c.) Type **324**	35	40
1601	(23c.) Christmas	35	40
1602	(23c.) Deepavali	35	40
1603	(23c.) Hari Raya Aidilfitri	35	40

326 Clog Maker

2006. Vanishing Trades. Multicoloured. (a) Ordinary gum.

1604	(23c.) Type **326**	40	40
1605	(23c.) Wooden bucket maker	40	40
1606	(23c.) Spice grinder	40	40
1607	(23c.) Snake charmer	40	40
1608	(23c.) Satay man	40	40
1609	80c. Mama store	95	1·10
1610	80c. Roti man	95	1·10
1611	80c. Backlane barber	95	1·10
1612	80c. Chinese medicinal tea shop	95	1·10
1613	80c. Tin bucker maker	95	1·10

Nos. 1604/8 and 1614/18 are inscribed "1st Local" and were initially sold for 23c.

(b) Self-adhesive.

1614	(23c.) Type **326**	30	40
1615	(23c.) As No. 1605	30	40
1616	(23c.) As No. 1606	30	40
1617	(23c.) As No. 1607	30	40
1618	(23c.) As No. 1608	30	40

2006. Washington 2006 International Stamp Exhibition. Sheet 123×75 mm. Multicoloured.

MS1619	(23c.) Type **321**; $2 No. 1574	3·75	4·00

327 Keyboard (Government)

2006. 25th Anniv of Infocomm. Multicoloured.

1620	(23c.) Type **327**	30	30
1621	60c. Trade	75	55
1622	80c. Boy using computer (Education)	1·00	1·00
1623	$1 Satellite dish (Telecommunications)	1·25	1·40

328 SCCCI Building

2006. Centenary of Singapore Chinese Chamber of Commerce and Industry. Multicoloured.

1624	(23c.) Type **328**	40	30
1625	(31c.) *Dendrobium* "Singapore Chinese Chamber of Commerce and Industry"	1·50	80
1626	80c. Logo of World Chinese Entrepreneurs Convention	1·40	1·40
1627	$1 Administration building, Nanyang University	1·40	1·40
1628	$2 War Memorial and Sun Yat Sen Nanyang Memorial Hall	2·25	2·75
MS1629	140×75 mm. Nos. 1624/8	6·00	6·50

No. 1624 is inscribed "1ST LOCAL" and No. 1625 "2ND LOCAL". They were initially sold for 23c. and 31c. respectively.

329 City of Singapore

2006. National Day. Multicoloured.

1630	(23c.) Type **329**	30	30
1631	60c. People of Singapore	75	55
1632	80c. Containers	1·00	1·00
1633	$1 Entertainers	1·25	1·40
MS1634	113×80 mm. $2 City of Singapore reflected in glass globe (48×48 mm)	2·25	2·50

No. 1630 Is Inscribed "1st Local" and was initially sold for 23c.

2005. TAIPEI 2005 International Stamp Exhibition. Sheet 123×75 mm. Multicoloured.

MS1562a	(23c.) Type **311**; $2 Rooster and hen	2·75	2·00

330 Orchids

331 £1 Coin

2006. International Monetary Fund and World Bank Group Boards of Governors Annual Meetings. (a) Horiz designs as T 330. Multicoloured.

1635	50c. Type **330**	70	40
1636	80c. Esplanade–Theatres on the Bay	1·00	80
1637	$1 Singapore skyline	1·25	1·10

(b) Square designs as T 331. Gold and black ($1) or silver and black ($5).

1638	$1 £1 coin	1·50	1·50
1639	$5 £5 coin	6·50	7·50

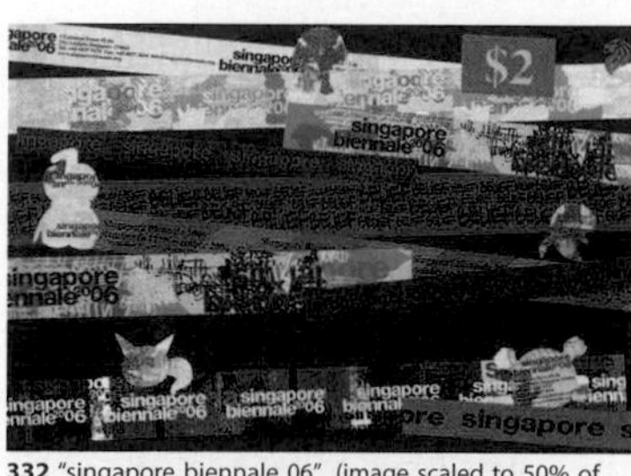

332 "singapore biennale 06" (image scaled to 50% of original size)

2006. Singapore Biennale (2006).

1640	**332** $2 multicoloured	2·25	2·50

333 Vanda "Mimi Palmer"

2006. Flowers. Multicoloured.

1641	(23c.) Type **333**	40	30
1642	(23c.) Renanthera "Singaporeans"	40	30
1643	70c. Vanda "Miss Joaquim"	90	90
1644	70c. Mokara "Lion's Gold"	90	90
1645	$1 Heron and hollyhocks (48×35 mm)	1·25	1·25
1646	$2 Moorhen and irises (48×35 mm)	2·25	2·75

Nos. 1641/2 are inscribed "1st Local" and were initially sold for 23c. each.

Nos. 1641/commemorate the 40th Anniversary of Diplomatic Relations between Singapore and Japan. Stamps in similar designs were issued by Japan.

Nos. 1645/6 depict details from two different screen paintings by Houitsu Sakai both with the title "Flowers and Birds of the Four Seasons".

334 Singapore Merlion and St. Peter's Basilica, Rome

2006. 25th Anniv of Diplomatic Relations between Singapore and Vatican City. Multicoloured.

1647	50c. Type **334**	1·00	45
1648	$2 Flags of Singapore and Vatican City	3·00	3·25
MS1649	123×75 mm. Nos. 1648/9	4·00	4·00

335 Common Palm Civet

2006. "Fun with Nature" (children's nature education programme). Multicoloured. (a) Ordinary gum.

1650	(23c.) Type **335**	50	50
1651	(23c.) Common flying dragon	50	50
1652	$1 Black-spotted sticky frog	1·75	2·00
1653	$1 Common tiger butterfly	1·75	2·00

Nos. 1650/1 and 1654/5 were inscribed "1st Local" and initially sold for 23c. each. Nos. 1650/3 were printed together, se-tenant, forming a composite background design.

(b) Self-adhesive.

1654	(23c.) Type **335**	40	40
1655	(23c.) As No. 1652	40	40

2006. Belgica 2006 International Stamp Exhibition, Brussels. Sheet 123×75 mm. Multicoloured.

MS1656	(23c.) Type **321**; $2 Two dogs	2·50	2·75

336 Pig

2007. Chinese New Year ("Year of the Boar"). Multicoloured.

1657	(25c.) Type **336**	25	20
1658	$2 Two pigs	2·25	2·50

No. 1657 is inscribed "1st LOCAL" and was sold for 25c.

337 Family with Bicycle and Children holding Hands

2007. 10th Anniv of Singapore Kindness Movement. Designs showing winning Singapore entries for ASEAN–Japan children's competition. Multicoloured. Ordinary or Self-adhesive gum.

1659	(25c.) Type **337**	30	30
1660	(25c.) Girl catching falling girl (horiz)	30	30
1661	(25c.) Distribution of Red Cross parcels (horiz)	30	30
1662	(25c.) Four people sharing umbrella (horiz)	30	30
1663	(25c.) Children visiting the elderly (horiz)	30	30
1664	(25c.) Boy opening door for woman	30	30
1665	(25c.) People on bus (horiz)	30	30
1666	(25c.) Woman and boy (horiz)	30	30
1667	(25c.) Sighted person helping blind man (horiz)	30	30
1668	(25c.) Zebra crossing (horiz)	30	30

Nos. 1659/68 are all inscribed "1st LOCAL" and were initially sold for 25c. each.

338 Korean Wedding Costumes

2007. Traditional Wedding Costumes. Mult.

1679	(25c.) Type **338**	45	50
1680	(25c.) Korean (man in dark grey)	45	50
1681	65c. Chinese	80	90
1682	65c. Indian	80	90
1683	65c. Malay	80	90
1684	65c. Eurasian	80	90
1685	$1.10 Korean (man in dark blue)	1·25	1·50
1686	$1.10 Korean (man in white)	1·25	1·50
MS1687	170×95 mm. Nos. 1679/86	5·50	5·75

Stamps in similar designs were issued by Korea.

339 Chinese Dances

2007. Cultural Dances. Multicoloured.

1688	(25c.) Type **339**	40	30
1689	(31c.) Indian classical dancer	50	40
1690	$1.10 Eurasian and Western dances	1·25	1·25
1691	$2 Malay dances	2·25	2·50

No. 1688 is inscribed "1ST LOCAL" and was initially sold for 25c.

No. 1689 is inscribed "2ND LOCAL" and was initially sold for 31c.

340 Crimson Sunbird

2007. Flora and Fauna . Multicoloured.

(a) Ordinary gum

1692	5c. Type **340**	10	10
1693	20c. Yellow-rumped flycatcher	25	15
1694	(25c.) Frangipani (30×27 mm)	25	20
1694a	(26c.) Blue pea vine (30x27 mm) (6.5.09)	25	20
1694b	(26c.) Pigeon orchid (30x27 mm) (6.5.09)	25	20

1694c	(26c.) *Dillenia suffruticosa* (23.6.2010)	20	25
1695	30c. Blue-throated bee-eater	35	25
1696	(31c.) Torch ginger (30×27 mm)	35	25
1696a	(32c.)	35	25
1697	45c. Yellow wagtail	55	40
1698	50c. Stork-billed kingfisher	65	45
1699	55c. Blue-crowned hanging parrot	70	45
1700	65c. Common goldenback (woodpecker)	90	60
1701	80c. Jambu fruit dove	1·00	70
1702	$1.10 Large Indian civet (49×29 mm)	1·25	1·25
1703	$2 Banded leaf monkey (49×29 mm)	2·50	2·50
1704	$5 Malayan pangolin (49×29 mm)	4·75	4·75
1705	$10 Cream-coloured giant squirrel (49×29 mm)	8·75	8·75

(b) Self-adhesive

	(26c.) As No. 1694c (23.6.2010)	20	25
1706	(25c.) As No. 1694	20	25
1706b	(26c.) As No. 1694a (6.5.09)	20	25
1706c	(26c.) As No. 1694b (6.5.09)	20	25

Nos. 1694/c and 1706/d were all inscr '1ST LOCAL'. Nos. 1694 and 1706 were initially sold for 25c. and Nos. 1694*a*/*c* and 1706*b*/*d* for 26c.

Nos. 1696/a were both inscr '2ND LOCAL' and originally sold for 31c. (1696) or 32c. (1696a).

341 Singapore Men taking Oath of Allegiance

2007. 40 Years of National Service. Multicoloured.

1707	(26c.) Type **341**	30	20
1708	(32c.) Basic military training exercises	35	25
1709	$1.10 Drill and regimentation	1·40	1·25
1710	$2 Operational training with rifles	2·75	3·00

Nos. 1707 is inscr '1st local' and was initially sold for 26c.

No. 1708 is inscr '2nd local' and was initially sold for 32c.

2007. Bangkok 2007 20th Asian International Stamp Exhibition. Sheet 123×75 mm. Multicoloured.

MS1711	(26c.) Type **336**; $2 Two pigs	2·75	2·75

342 Secretariat Building, Brunei

2007. 40th Anniv of ASEAN (Association of South-east Asian Nations). Ancient and Modern Architecture. Multicoloured.

1712	(26c.) Type **342**	45	45
1713	(26c.) National Museum of Cambodia	45	45
1714	(26c.) Fatahillah Museum, Jakarta, Indonesia	45	45
1715	(26c.) Lao Typical House	45	45
1716	(26c.) Malayan Railway Headquarters Building, Kuala Lumpur, Malaysia	45	45
1717	(26c.) Yangon Post Office, Myanmar	45	45
1718	(26c.) Malacañang Palace, Philippines	45	45
1719	(26c.) National Museum of Singapore	45	45
1720	(26c.) Vimanmek Mansion, Bangkok, Thailand	45	45
1721	(26c.) Presidential Palace, Hanoi, Vietnam	45	45

Nos. 1712/21 are all inscribed '1st Local'. Similar designs were issued on the same day by the ten member countries, Indonesia, Malaysia, Philippines, Thailand, Brunei, Vietnam, Laos, Myanmar and Cambodia.

343 Chinatown

2007. National Day. Tourist Landmarks. Mult.

1722	(26c.) Type **343**	35	25
1723	65c. Kampong glam	80	70
1724	80c. Little India	90	90
1725	$1.10 Orchard Road	1·40	1·60
MS1726	122×80 mm. $5 Merlion statue at Marina Bay (vert)	5·50	6·00

No. 1722 is inscr '1st local' and was sold for 26c.

344 National Cadet Corps

2007. Uniformed Groups in Schools. Multicoloured.

1727	(32c.) Type **344**	45	45
1728	(32c.) The Singapore Scout Association	45	45
1729	(32c.) Girl Guides Singapore	45	45
1730	(32c.) The Girls' Brigade Singapore	45	45
1731	(32c.) The Boys' Brigade in Singapore	45	45
1732	(32c.) St. John Ambulance Brigade Singapore	45	45
1733	(32c.) Red Cross Youth	45	45
1734	(32c.) National Police Cadet Corps	45	45
1735	(32c.) National Civil Defence Cadet Corps	45	45

Nos. 1727/35 were inscr '2nd Local' and sold for 32c. each.

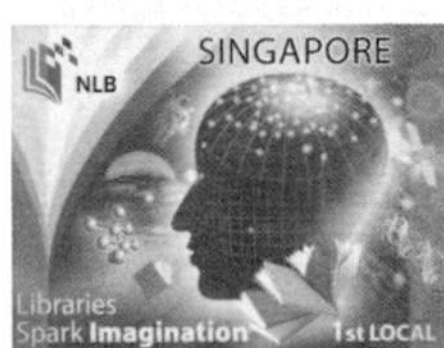

345 False Clown Anemone Fish and Sea Anemone (*Stichodactyla* sp.)

2007. Shores and Reefs. Multicoloured. Ordinary gum.

1736	(26c.) Type **345**	50	50
1737	(26c.) Singapore goby and blind shrimp (*Alpheus* sp.)	50	50
1738	$1.10 Hawksbill turtle and remora (*Echeneis naucrates*)	1·90	2·25
1739	$1.10 Razorfish (*Aeoliscus strigatus*) and sea urchin (*Diadema* sp.)	1·90	2·25

(b) Self-adhesive.

1740	(26c.) As Type **345**	50	50
1741	(26c.) As No. 1737	50	50

Nos. 1736/9 were printed together, se-tenant, forming a composite background design.

Nos. 1736/7 and 1740/1 were inscr '1st Local' and initially sold for 26c. each.

346 Profile ('Libraries Spark Imagination')

2007. National Library Board 'L2010' Five Year Plan. Multicoloured.

1742	(26c.) Type **346**	40	30
1743	80c. Couple dancing ('Libraries Bring Knowledge Alive')	1·10	85
1744	$1.10 Students using computer ('Libraries Create Possibility')	1·60	1·25
1745	$2 Montage of profiles ('Libraries for Life Knowledge for Success')	3·00	3·50

No. 1742 is inscribed '1st LOCAL' and was sold for 26c.

347 Roof of Terminal 3 with Skylights and Reflector Panels

2008. Opening of Terminal 3 at Singapore Changi Airport. Multicoloured.

1746	(26c.) Type **347**	45	30
1747	65c. Singapore Airlines Airbus A380	1·00	70
1748	$1.10 Palm trees and 'Green Wall' vertical garden inside Terminal 3	1·60	1·40
1749	$2 Terminal 3 and Control Tower	3·00	3·50

No. 1746 was inscr '1st Local' and sold for 26c.

348 Rat

2008. Chinese New Year ('Year of the Rat'). Multicoloured. (a) Ordinary gum.

1750	(26c.) Type **348**	40	30
1751	65c. Rat and orange	75	60
1752	$1.10 Two rats (44×34 mm)	1·50	1·75

(b) Self-adhesive.

1753	(26c.) As Type **348**	30	30

Nos. 1750 and 1753 were inscr '1st Local' and sold for 26c. each.

349 Chinese New Year

2008. Festivals. Multicoloured. (a) Ordinary gum.

1754	(26c.) Type **349**	40	40
1755	(26c.) Christmas (Mary, shepherds and sheep)	40	40
1756	(26c.) Deepavali (people celebrating, fireworks and elephants)	40	40
1757	(26c.) Hari Raya Aidilfitri (women carrying food and lighted lamp)	40	40
1758	(32c.) Easter	45	45
1759	(32c.) Hari Raya Haji	45	45
1760	(32c.) Chinese Mid-Autumn Festival	45	45
1761	(32c.) Pongal	45	45
1762	55c. Chinese New Year (children carrying hong baos)	65	65
1763	55c. Christmas (flying Santas and reindeer)	65	65
1764	55c. Deepavali (people carrying oil lamps and peacocks)	65	65
1765	55c. Hari Raya Aidilfitri (couple, girl kneeling and boy receiving gift)	65	65

(b) Self-adhesive.

1766	(26c.) As Type **349**	45	50
1767	(26c.) As No. 1755	45	50
1768	(26c.) As No. 1756	45	50
1769	(26c.) As No. 1757	45	50

Nos. 1754/7 and 1766/9 are inscr '1st LOCAL' and sold for 26c. each.

Nos. 1758/61 are inscr '2nd LOCAL' and sold for 32c. each.

2008. Taipei 2008 21st Asian International Stamp Exhibition. Sheet 160×80 mm containing Nos. 1750/2.

MS1770	(26c.) Type **348**; 65c. Rat and orange; $1.10 Two rats (44×24 mm)	2·40	2·75

350 Porcelain Plate

2008. Peranakan Museum Collection. Showing Peranakan embroidery, beadwork and porcelain. Multicoloured.

1771	(26c.) Type **350**	40	40
1772	(26c.) Bird design	40	40
1773	(32c.) Dragon embroidery	50	50
1774	(32c.) Peony embroidery	50	50
1775	65c. Phoenix and flowers design from vase	90	1·00
1776	65c. Flying phoenix design from vase	90	1·00
1777	$1.10 Crane design from plate	1·40	1·75
1778	$1.10 Poppy design porcelain	1·40	1·75

Nos. 1771/2 are inscr '1st Local' and sold for 26c. each.

Nos. 1773/4 are inscr '2nd Local' and sold for 32c. each.

351 Crowd celebrating

2008. Youth Olympic Games, Singapore, 2010. Multicoloured.

1779	(26c.) Type **351**	40	40
1780	$2 Crowd with flag, schoolchildren and Supreme Court building	2·40	2·75

Nos. 1779/80 were printed together, se-tenant, forming a composite design showing a crowd celebrating the announcement that Singapore had been selected as host city.

No. 1779 is inscr '1st local' and sold for 26c.

352 Carne de porco à Alentejana (pork and clams)

2008. Local Delights

1781	(26c.) Type **352**	45	45
1782	(26c.) Lombo de bacalhau braseado em lascas (grilled codfish slices)	45	45
1783	(26c.) Yangzhou fried rice	45	45
1784	(26c.) Crispy fried chicken	45	45
1785	65c. Roti Prata	80	80
1786	65c. Hainanese chicken rice	80	80
1787	65c. Laksa	80	80
1788	65c. Satay	80	80
MS1789	140×90 mm. $2×2 Clay pot rice (vert); Chilli crab (vert)	5·00	5·00

Nos. 1781/4 and 1785/8 were each printed together, se-tenant, as blocks of four stamps forming a composite design of a dish.

Nos. 1781/4 are inscr '1ST LOCAL' and sold for 26c. each.

Stamps in similar designs were issued by Macau.

353 Table Tennis

2008. Olympic Games, Beijing. Multicoloured.

1790	(26c.) Type **253**	35	35
1791	(32c.) Sailing	40	40
1792	$1.10 Shooting	1·50	1·50
1793	$1.10 Badminton	1·50	1·50

No. 1790 is inscr '1ST LOCAL' and sold for 26c.

No. 1791 is inscr '2ND LOCAL' and sold for 32c.

2008. Olympex Olympic Stamp Expo, Beijing. Sheet 160×80 mm containing Nos. 1750/2.

MS1794	(26c.) Type **348**; 65c. Rat and orange; $1.10 Two rats (44×24 mm)	2·75	2·75

354 Parliament House (David Tay Poey Cher)

2008. National Day. 'Singapore Today'. Ddesigns showing photographs by Cultural Medallion winning photographers. Multicoloured.

1795	(26c.) Type **354**	50	50
1796	(26c.) Tampines North Community Centre (Foo Tee Jun)	50	50
1797	(26c.) Metal sculptures and high-rise buildings of financial sector (Chua Soo Bin)	50	50
1798	(26c.) North Bridge and financial sector (Teo Bee Yen)	50	50
1799	(26c.) People in Temple Street (Si Ma Lu Guanyin) (Tan Lip Seng)	50	50
1800	50c. People at Orchard MRT Station (David Tay Poey Cher)	75	75
1801	50c. Train at Orchard MRT Station (Foo Tee Jun)	75	75
1802	50c. Glass-fronted and other high-rise buildings (Chua Soo Bin)	75	75
1803	50c. Temple within Central Business District (Teo Bee Yen)	75	75
1804	50c. Fish stall at Tekka Market (Tan Lip Seng)	75	75
MS1805	75×75 mm. $2 Montage of photographs of Singapore buildings (60×60 mm)	2·75	2·75

Nos. 1795/9 were all inscr '1ST LOCAL' and sold for 26c. each.

355 Pilots, Fighter Plane and Helicopter

2008. 40th Anniv of the Republic of Singapore Air Force (RSAF). Multicoloured.

1806	(26c.) Type **355**	60	35
1807	(32c.) Weapon Systems Officers monitoring aircraft in Singapore airspace	70	60
1808	65c. Unmanned Aerial Vehicle and pilot (on ground)	1·00	75
1809	80c. Senior Technicians and helicopter	1·50	1·40
1810	$1.10 Weapon Systems Officers and Air Defence Artillery	1·75	2·00

No. 1806 is inscr '1st Local' and sold for 26c.
No. 1807 is inscr '2nd Local' and sold for 32c.

356 Racing Car and City of Singapore

2008. First Formula 1 Singapore Grand Prix. Multicoloured.

1811	$2 Type **356**	2·00	2·25
1812	$2 Racing car and chequered flag	2·00	2·25

Nos. 1811/12 were each printed together, se-tenant, forming a composite background design.

2008. Jakarta 2008 International Stamp Exhibition, Jakarta, Indonesia. Sheet 160×80 mm containing Nos. 1750/2.

MS1813	(26c.) Type **348**; 65c. Rat and orange; $1.10 Two rats (44×24 mm)	3·00	3·25

357 Postman, 2008

2008. Postal Services through the Years. Multicoloured.

1814	(26c.) Type **357**	40	25
1815	(32c.) Postman with motor scooter, c. 1980	55	35
1816	50c. Postman with bicycle, c. 1970	1·25	90
1817	80c. Postman and pillar box, c. 1950	1·40	1·25
1818	$1.10 Postman, c. 1910	1·50	1·75

No. 1814 is inscr '1ST LOCAL' and sold for 26c.
No. 1815 is inscr '2ND LOCAL' and sold for 32c.

358 Pepper (*Piper nigrum*)

2008. Cash Crops of Early Singapore. T 358 and similar vert designs. Multicoloured. (a) Ordinary gum.

1819	(26c.) Type **358**	55	30
1820	65c. Tapioca (*Manihot esculenta*)	1·25	95
1821	$1.10 Rubber (*Hevea brasiliensis*)	1·75	1·75
1822	$2 Nutmeg (*Myristica fragrans*)	2·75	3·50

(b) Self-adhesive.

1823	(26c.) As Type **358**	40	40

359 Dragon Fruit

2008. Fruits. Multicoloured.

1824	65c. Type **359**	1·25	1·25
1825	$1.10 Durian	1·75	1·75
MS1826	135×94 mm. Nos. 1824/5	3·00	3·25

Stamps in similar designs were issued by Vietnam.

360 Ox

2009. Chinese New Year. Year of the Ox. Multicoloured. (a) Ordinary gum.

1827	(26c.) Type **360**	55	35
1828	65c. Ox (facing left)	1·25	1·10
1829	$1.10 Two oxen (34×44 mm)	1·75	2·25

(b) Self-adhesive.

1830	(26c.) Type **360**	45	45

Nos. 1827 and 1830 were inscr '1st Local' and initially sold for 26c. each.

361 Couple's Faces in Champagne Glass

2009. Greetings Stamps. 'Let's Celebrate'. Multicoloured. Ordinary or self-adhesive gum.

1831	(26c.) Type **361**	45	50
1832	(26c.) Girl and birthday candles	45	50
1833	(26c.) Couple	45	50
1834	(26c.) Girl with teddy bear and wrapped presents	45	50
1835	(26c.) Boy holding red balloons	45	50

362 Cathay, 1939

2009. Cinema Theatres of Yesteryear. Multicoloured.

1841	(26c.) Type **362**	45	25
1842	50c. The Majestic, 1928	75	60
1843	80c. Capitol Building, 1933	1·25	85
1844	$1.10 Queens, c.1920	1·75	2·00
1845	$1.10 Rex, 1946	1·75	2·00

No. 1840 was inscribed '1st Local' and originally sold for 26c.

2009. China 2009 World Stamp Exhibition, Luoyang, China. Sheet 120×75 mm containing Nos. 1827/9.

MS1846	(26c.) Type **360**; 65c. Ox (facing left); $1.10 Two oxen (34×44 mm)	3·00	3·25

2009. Hong Kong 2009 International Stamp Exhibition. Sheet 120×75 mm containing Nos. 1827/9.

MS1847	(26c.) Type **360**; 65c. Ox (facing left); $1.10 Two oxen (34×44 mm)	3·00	3·25

363 Map of Circle Line System on Singapore Map

2009. Launch of SMRT Circle Line. Multicoloured.

1848	(26c.) Type **363**	60	30
1849	80c. New Circle Line station	1·40	1·10
1850	$1.10 Circle Line train	1·75	1·60
1851	$2 Circle Line Operation Control Centre	3·50	4·00

364 Visitor Centre

2009. 150th Anniv of Singapore Botanic Gardens. Multicoloured.

1852	(26c.) Type **364**	50	50
1853	(26c.) Rain tree and Band Stand	50	50
1854	$1.10 Orchids, girl on a swing (sculpture) and pavilion	1·70	2·00
1855	$1.10 Flying swans and helico-nias at Swan Lake	1·70	2·00
MS1856	113×80 mm. $2 Black swans (47×47 mm)	3·50	3·50

Nos. 1852/5 were printed together, se-tenant, forming a composite design.

365 Ice Kacang (shaved ice with red beans)

2009. Local Desserts. Multicoloured.

1857	(26c.) Type **365**	35	35
1858	(32c.) Ondeh-ondeh (dough filled with palm sugar)	45	45
1859	65c. Ang ku kueh (rice flour cake with bean paste or peanut paste filling)	90	90
1860	80c. Lapis sagu (tapioca layer cake)	1·10	1·10
1861	$1.10 Mithai (assorted Indian sweets)	1·50	1·50

No. 1857 was inscr '1ST LOCAL' and originally sold for 26c.
No. 1858 was inscr '2ND LOCAL' and originally sold for 32c.

366 *Standing Figure* (Wee Beng Chong)

2009. National Day. Sculptures. Multicoloured.

1862	50c. Type **366**	75	75
1863	50c. *We're Happy. Are You Happy?* (Teo Eng Seng)	75	75
1864	50c. *Art Trees* (Han Sai Por)	75	75
1865	50c. *Aspirations* (Anthony Poon)	75	75
1866	50c. *Nude 2* (Tay Chee Toh) (horiz)	75	75
1867	50c. *Signature* (Brother Joseph McNally) (horiz)	75	75
1868	50c. *Wealth* (Ng Eng Teng) (horiz)	75	75
MS1869	113×80 mm. $2 Sculptures (as shown on Nos. 1862/8) (95×37 mm)	2·75	2·75

367 Gymnast ('Excellence')

2009. Youth Olympic Games, Singapore, 2010 (2nd issue). Multicoloured.

1870	(26c.) Type **367**	35	35
1871	65c. Athlete greeting tennis player ('Hello')	90	90
1872	$1.10 Three athletes ('Friend-ship')	1·50	1·50
1873	$2 Hurdler ('Respect')	2·75	2·75

No. 1870 was inscr '1st Local' and originally sold for 26c.

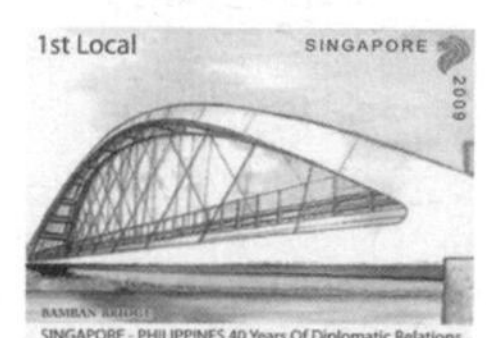
368 Bamban Bridge, Philippines

2009. 40th Anniv of Diplomatic Relations between Singapore and the Philippines. Bridges. Multicoloured.

1874	(26c.) Type **368**	35	35
1875	65c. Cavenagh Bridge, Singapore	95	95
1876	80c. Henderson Waves and Alexandra Arch, Singapore	1·10	1·10
1877	$1.10 Marcelo B. Fernan Bridge, Cebu, Philippines	1·60	1·60
MS1878	120×75 mm. Nos. 1874/7	4·00	4·00

No. 1874 was inscr '1st Local' and originally sold for 26c.
Stamps in similar designs were issued on the same date by the Phillippines.

369 Singaraja Statue, Bali

2009. Tourist Attractions. Multicoloured.

1879	(26c.) Type **369**	35	35
1880	65c. Merlion and Sentosa Island resort	90	90
1881	80c. Taman Mini Indonesia Park, Jakarta	1·10	1·10
1882	$1.10 Sentosa Island resort	1·50	1·50
MS1883	120×75 mm. Nos. 1879/82	2·75	2·75

No. 1879 was inscr '1ST LOCAL' and originally sold for 26c.
Stamps in similar designs were issued by Indonesia.

370 Park and City Skyline, Singapore

2009. Asia-Pacific Economic Co-operation (APEC) Meetings, Singapore. Multicoloured.

1884	(26c.) Type **370**	35	35
1885	80c. Singapore at night	1·10	1·10
1886	$1.10 Airliner and cargo	1·50	1·50
1887	$2 Harbour and city skyline, Singapore	2·75	2·75

No. 1884 was inscr '1st LOCAL' and originally sold for 26c.

371 Tiger

2010. Chinese New Year. Year of the Tiger. Multicoloured. (a) Ordinary gum.

1888	(26c.) Type **371**	35	35
1889	65c. Pink and black tiger	90	90
1890	$1.10 Two tigers (35×45 mm)	1·50	1·50

(b) Self-adhesive.

1891	(26c.) Type **371**	35	35

Nos. 1888 and 1891 were inscr '1st Local' and originally sold for 26c.

372 Modern Flats

2010. Anniversaries. Multicoloured.

1892	50c. Type **372** (50th anniv of Housing and Development Board)	75	75
1893	50c. Citizens (50th anniv of People's Association)	75	75
1894	$1 Customs Officers (Centenary of Singapore Customs) (horiz)	1·40	1·40
1895	$1 Scouts (Centenary of scout-ing in Singapore) (horiz)	1·40	1·40

373 Children in Playground

2010. Playgrounds. Multicoloured.
1896 (26c.) Type **373** 35 35
1897 50c. Playground with 'dragon's head' tubular apparatus 75 75
1898 65c. Slide, treetop boardwalk and path with steps through trees 90 90
1899 80c. Roundabout, rings and climbing frame 1·10 1·10
1900 $1.10 Tubular apparatus and seesaw 1·50 1·50
1901 $2 Rope climbing frames and slides 2·75 2·75

No. 1896 was inscr '1st Local' and originally sold for 26c.

374 Common Birdwing

2010. Butterflies. Multicoloured.

(a) Phosphorised paper.
1902 (26c.) Type **374** 45 45
1903 80c. Tailed jay 1·10 1·10
1904 $1.10 Common posy 1·90 1·90
1905 $2 Blue glassy tiger 3·25 3·25

(b) Self-adhesive
1906 (26c.) As Type **374** 45 45

2010. London 2010 Festival of Stamps. Sheet 120×75 mm containing Nos. 1888/90
MS1907 (26c.) Type **371**; 65c. Pink and black tiger; $1.10 Two tigers (35×45 mm) 3·25 3·25

375 Saga (*Adenanthera pavonina*)

2010. 'know 10 trees'

(a) Ordinary gum
1908 (26c.) Type **375** 45 45
1909 (26c.) Rain tree (*Samanea saman*) 45 45
1910 (26c.) Yellow flame (*Peltophorum pterocarpum*) 45 45
1911 (26c.) Tembusu (*Fagraea fragrans*) 45 45
1912 (26c.) Angsana (*Pterocarpus indicus*) (vert) 45 45
1913 (26c.) Sea almond (*Terminalia catappa*) (vert) 45 45
1914 (26c.) Broad-leafed mahogany (*Swietenia macrophylla*) (vert) 45 45
1915 (26c.) Sea apple (*Syzygium grande*) (vert) 45 45
1916 (26c.) Senegal mahogany (*Khaya senegalensis*) (vert) 45 45
1917 (26c.) Trumpet tree (*Tabebuia rosea*) (vert) 45 45

(b) Self-adhesive
1918 (26c.) As Type **375** 45 45
1919 (26c.) As No. 1909 45 45
1920 (26c.) As No. 1910 45 45
1921 (26c.) As No. 1911 45 45
1922 (26c.) As No. 1912 (vert) 45 45
1923 (26c.) As No. 1913 (vert) 45 45
1924 (26c.) As No. 1914 (vert) 45 45
1925 (26c.) As No. 1915 (vert) 45 45
1926 (26c.) As No. 1916 (vert) 45 45
1927 (26c.) As No. 1917 (vert) 45 45

Nos. 1908/27 were all inscr '1st Local' and originally sold for 26c. each.

2010. Bangkok 2010 International Stamp Exhibition, Thailand. Sheet 120×75 mm containing Nos. 1888/90
MS1928 (26c.) Type **371**; 65c. Pink and black tiger; $1.10 Two tigers (35×45 mm) 3·25 3·25

376 Bowyer Block

2010. National Day. Multicoloured.
1929 (26c.) Type **376** 35 35
1930 (32c.) College of Medicine Building 45 45
1931 55c. Command House 80 80
1932 65c. Hwa Chong Institution Clock Tower 1·10 1·10
1933 80c. Former Raffles College 1·40 1·40
1934 $1.10 Tan Teck Guan Building 1·90 1·90
MS1935 113×80 mm. $2 Hwa Chong Institution clock tower, Tan Teck Guan Building entrance, stone carving from College of Medicine Building, grille from Command House, pillar and urn from former Raffles College and Bowyer Block clock tower (100×40 mm). P 14×13½ 3·25 3·25

No. 1929 was inscr '1st Local' and originally sold for 26c.

No. 1930 was inscr '2nd Local' and originally sold for 32c.

377 Mascots Lyo and Merly on Globe

2010. Youth Olympic Games, Singapore (3rd issue). Multicoloured.
1936 (26c.) Type **377** 35 35
1937 65c. Lyo and Merly on desert island 1·10 1·10
1938 $1.10 Merly on surfboard 1·75 1·75
1939 $2 Lyo playing basketball 3·50 3·50

No. 1936 was inscr '1st Local' and originally sold for 26c.

378 Second World War Soldiers (Battle for Pasir Panjang)

2010. Kent Ridge Park Heritage Trail. Multicoloured.
1940 (32c.) Type **378** 55 55
1941 65c. Straw-headed bulbul, white lilies and canopy walk 90 90
1942 80c. White lilies, eagle and canopy walk 1·10 1·10
1943 $1.10 *Dillenia suffruticosa*, other trees and pavilion 1·50 1·50

Nos. 1940/3 were printed together, *se-tenant*, forming a composite design showing plants and trees.

No. 1940 was inscr '2nd LOCAL' and originally sold for 32c.

379 Lion Dance (Chinese New Year)

2010. Festivals in Singapore. Multicoloured.

(a) Ordinary gum
1944 (26c.) Type **379** 45 45
1945 (26c.) Candles, greenery and star (Christmas) 45 45
1946 (26c.) Candles in holders (Hari Raya Aidilfitri) 45 45
1947 (26c.) Peacocks (Deepavali) 45 45
1948 55c. Fruit and wreath (Chinese New Year) 85 85
1949 55c. Baubles (Christmas) 85 85
1950 55c. Mosaic pattern with streamers and star and crescent within star (Hari Raya Aidilfitri) 85 85
1951 55c. Lamp (Deepavali) 85 85

(b) Self-adhesive
1952 (26c.) As Type **379** 45 45
1953 (26c.) As No. 1945 45 45
1954 (26c.) As No. 1946 45 45
1955 (26c.) As No. 1947 45 45

Nos. 1944/7 and 1952/5 were all inscr '1st LOCAL' and originally sold for 26c. each.

380 Rabbit

2011. Chinese New Year. Year of the Rabbit

(a) Ordinary gum
1956 (26c.) Type **380** 40 40
1957 65c. Rabbit (facing left) 1·10 1·10
1958 $1.10 Two rabbits (35×45 mm) 2·00 2·00

(b) Self-adhesive
1959 (26c.) As Type **380** 1·00 1·00

Nos. 1956 and 1959 were inscr '1st Local' and originally sold for 26c.

T **380** and similar multicoloured designs.

381 Children's Drawings and Paintings (image scaled to 68% of original size)

2011. 'Spirit of Giving'. Multicoloured.
1960 $1.10 Type **381** 1·75 1·75
1961 $2 Children's drawings and paintings including helping hands and children packing parcel and giving gift to woman in wheelchair 3·50 3·50

2011. Indipex 2011 International Stamp Exhibition, New Delhi. Sheet 120×75 mm containing Nos. 1956/8
MS1962 (26c.) As Type **380**; 65c. Rabbit (facing left); $1.10 Two rabbits (35×45 mm) 3·50 3·50

382 Common Tilapia (*Oreochromis mossambicus*)

2011. Pond Life. Multicoloured.

(a) Ordinary gum
1963 5c. White-colllared kingfisher (*Todiramphus chloris*) (40×30 mm) (13 Apr) 10 10
1964 20c. Diving beetle (*Cybister rugosus*) (40×30 mm) (13 Apr) 25 25
1965 (26c.) Water lily (*Nymphaea odorata*) (30×27 mm) (13 Apr) 35 35
1966 30c. Common redbolt dragonfly (*Rhodothemis rufa*) (13 Apr) 40 40
1967 (32c.) Water hyacinth (*Eichhornia crassipes*) (30×27 mm) (13 Apr) 40 40
1968 45c. Ornate coraltail damselflies (*Ceriagrion cerinorubellum*) (40×30 mm) (13 Apr) 50 50
1969 50c. Black marsh terrapin (*Siebenrockiella crassicollis*) (40×30 mm) (13 Apr) 50 50
1970 55c. White-breasted waterhen (*Amaurornis phoenicurus*) (40×30 mm) (13 Apr) 80 80
1971 65c. Common greenback frog (*Rana erythraea*) (40×30 mm) (13 Apr) 1·00 1·00
1972 80c. Common toad (*Bufo melanostictus*) (40×30 mm) (13 Apr) 1·30 1·30
1973 $1.10 Type **382** 2·25 2·25
1974 $2 Pond wolf spider (*Pardosa pseudoannulata*) 5·50 5·50
1975 $5 Water strider (*Neogerris parvulus*) 9·00 9·00
1976 $10 Water scorpion (*Laccotrephes simclatus*) 12·00 12·00

(b) Self-adhesive
1977 (26c.) As No. 1965 (13 Apr)

No. 1965 was inscr '1st Local' and was originally valid for 26c.

No. 1967 was inscr '2nd Local' and orignally sold for 32c.

No. 1977 was issued in booklets of ten originally sold for $2.55, a discount of 5c. off the face value of the stamps.

Nos. 1978/9 have been left for additions to this definitive series.

383 Bristol Box Kite taking off from Farrer Park, 16 March 1911

2011. Centenary of Aviation in Singapore. Multicoloured.
1980 (26c.) Type **383** 40 40
1981 45c. Fokker F-7A, Seletar Airport, c. 1930 60 60
1982 65c. Airspeed Consul, Kallang Airport 1·10 1·10
1983 80c. F-15SG, Paya Lebar Air Base 1·40 1·40
1984 $1.10 Airbus A380, Singapore Changi Airport 2·00 2·00

No. 1980 was inscr '1st LOCAL' and originally sold for 26c

POSTAGE DUE STAMPS

The postage due stamps of Malayan Postal Union were in use in Singapore from 1948 until replaced by the following issue.

D1

1968
D1 **D1** 1c. green 60 2·00
D2 **D1** 2c. red 1·60 2·50
D3 **D1** 4c. orange 2·00 5·50
D4 **D1** 8c. brown 1·00 2·00
D5 **D1** 10c. mauve 1·00 90
D6 **D1** 12c. violet 2·75 3·25
D7 **D1** 20c. blue 2·00 3·50
D8 **D1** 50c. green 11·00 5·50

D2

1978
D16a **D2** 1c. green 15 4·50
D17a **D2** 4c. orange 20 7·50
D18a **D2** 10c. blue 50 2·50
D19a **D2** 20c. blue 65 2·75
D20a **D2** 50c. green 90 4·00

D3

1989
D21 **D3** 1c. green 25·00 25·00
D22 **D3** 4c. brown 35·00 35·00
D23 **D3** 5c. mauve 20 50
D24 **D3** 10c. red 20 40
D25 **D3** 20c. blue 30 60
D26 **D3** 50c. green 60 1·00
D27 **D3** $1 brown 4·25 5·00

Index